THE COLUMBIA
GRANGER'S®
INDEX TO POETRY
IN ANTHOLOGIES

OTHER COLUMBIA UNIVERSITY PRESS PUBLICATIONS

The Columbia Granger's® World of Poetry Online at www.columbiagrangers.org

The Columbia Granger's® Index to African-American Poetry (1999)

THE COLUMBIA GRANGER'S® INDEX TO POETRY IN ANTHOLOGIES

TWELFTH EDITION, COMPLETELY REVISED
INDEXING ANTHOLOGIES
PUBLISHED THROUGH DECEMBER 31, 2001

EDITED BY

TESSA KALE

COLUMBIA UNIVERSITY PRESS

NEW YORK

THE COLUMBIA GRANGER'S® INDEX TO POETRY
IN ANTHOLOGIES

COPYRIGHT © 1904, 1918, 1929, 1940, 1945, 1953, 1957, 1962,
1973, 1978, 1982, 1986, 1990, 1994, 1996, 1997, 2002

BY COLUMBIA UNIVERSITY PRESS

TWELFTH EDITION COMPLETELY REVISED

LIBRARY OF CONGRESS CATALOGING-IN-PUBLICATION DATA

Kale, Tessa.
    The Columbia Granger's index to poetry in Anthologies. 12th ed.,
completely rev., indexing anthologies published through December 31,
2001 / edited by Tessa Kale.
    p.   cm.
ISBN 0–231–12448–1
    1. Poetry—Indexes. 2. English poetry—Indexes.
I. Granger, Edith. Index to poetry. II. Title.
    PN 1022.H39   2002
    16.80881—dc21   2002017459
                                                             CIP

COLUMBIA UNIVERSITY PRESS BOOKS ARE PRINTED ON
PERMANENT AND DURABLE ACID-FREE PAPER.

PRINTED IN THE UNITED STATES OF AMERICA

c 10 9 8 7 6 5 4 3 2

CONTENTS

PREFACE   ix

HOW TO USE THE INDEXES   xi

LIST OF ANTHOLOGIES   xv

ABBREVIATIONS   xxix

TITLE, FIRST LINE, AND LAST LINE INDEX   1

AUTHOR INDEX   1511

SUBJECT INDEX   1871

The Columbia Granger's® Index to Poetry in Anthologies

TWELFTH EDITION

PUBLISHER
WILLIAM STRACHAN

DIRECTOR OF DESIGN AND PRODUCTION
LINDA SECONDARI

EDITOR
TESSA KALE

TECHNICAL EDITOR
STEPHEN STERNS

ASSISTANT EDITOR
KEITH NEWTON

STAFF

AMY CAROTHERS   STEPHEN HOBAN
HAESUN KIM   CAROLYN FARGNOLI
COLIN ENRIQUEZ   KIVA OFFENHOLLEY

PREFACE

Granger's is one of the oldest continuously published reference works in the United States. Since the fourth edition in 1953, the book has been in fact, if not in name, The Columbia Granger's® Index to Poetry in Anthologies.

The words "in Anthologies" are new since the eleventh edition. They distinguish this volume from its companion, *The Columbia Granger's® Index to Poetry in Collected and Selected Works*, which was first published in 1996. With the publication of that volume, Granger's effectively became a two-volume work, indexing the two types of poetry book most frequently shelved by libraries—anthologies and collections of the work of individual authors.

In this volume we return to anthologies. The twelfth edition locates 81,000 poems. It locates by title, first line, author, and subject all the poetry in anthologies that the Press, together with our consultants, identified as those whose high editorial and design standards make them likely to be found on library shelves. Of these anthologies, 149 are new.

This edition indexes 12,735 authors writing from all parts of the world, and from remotest antiquity to present. They write on more than 4,000 subjects, ranging from Aardvarks to Zulus.

We have continued the practice, inaugurated in the seventh edition, of singling out 40 anthologies—30 of which we recommend, and 10 of which we recommend highly.

We provide last-line indexing for 10,000 of the most frequently anthologized poems.

In the Subject Index we have arranged citations alphabetically by authors' names, enabling users to focus their searches.

HOW TO USE THE INDEXES

This volume is divided into three sections:
- —Title, First Line, and Last Line Index
- —Author Index
- —Subject Index

Each section is arranged alphabetically.

Every poem covered here is cited at least once in each of the three sections (except for those not in the Subject Index because they are too abstract to be assigned to any heading there). Every poem cited here appears in at least one anthology listed on pages 15–27.

See also the explanatory notes at the beginning of each of the three sections, pages 1, 1511, and 1871.

Title, First Line, and Last Line Index

The clearest way to explain the Title, First Line, and Last Line Index is to begin by showing how it answers specific questions brought to it.

Where can I find a poem called "The Thought-Fox"*?* Go to the Title, First Line, and Last Line Index. The citation for "The Thought-Fox" is followed by the name of the poem's author, Ted Hughes, and by the letter code MakPoe. Look up MakPoe in the List of Anthologies, where the codes, not the titles of anthologies, are arranged alphabetically. There you learn that you can read "The Thought-Fox" in *The Making of a Poem*, edited by Mark Strand and Eavan Boland and published by W. W. Norton in 2000.

What is the title of the poem that begins "I met a traveler from an antique land"*?* The first-line citation is followed by the title, "Ozymandias," and then by the author, Percy Bysshe Shelley, and 70 letter codes, including MakPoe and CenSon, which stand for anthologies. The List of Anthologies shows that they are *The Making of a Poem* (W. W. Norton, 2000) and *A Century of Sonnets* (Oxford, 1999).

What poem ends with the line "You have stolen their souls with your eyes"*?* The last-line citation is followed by the title, "Seizing the Day," and then by the author, Judith Ortiz Cofer, and two letter codes, PueRic and SwNoth. The List of Anthologies indicates that the title of the anthology coded PueRic is *Puerto Rican Writers at Home in the USA* (Open Hand Publishing, Seattle, 1991) and *Sweet Nothings: An Anthology of Rock and Roll in American Poetry* (Indiana University Press, Bloomington, 1994).

First Lines and Last Lines. First-line and last-line citations are followed by the title (except where the poem has no title). The sign (LL) following last-line citations distinguishes them from first lines.

You know, for example, that "They also serve who only stand and wait" is not a title because the title, "On His Blindness," follows it, and because the initial letters of all the words (except the first one) are lowercase. You know that the citation is a last line and not a first line because it is followed by (LL).

When the first line or the last line of a poem is the same as or slightly longer than the title, only one of them is listed. The poem with the first line "And did those feet in ancient time" has no listing for title because the title is the same.

Brackets. Brackets usually show variant spellings. For example, see the first-line citation "Whan that Aprille [*or* April *or* Aprill] with his[e] shoures [*or* showres] sote [*or* soote]." In the several anthologies in which that first line appears, the spelling may vary as indicated in brackets.

Capitalization. The first letter of the first word in every citation is capitalized, even when in its published form it appears as lowercase.

Initial Articles. An article—"a," "an," or "the"—that begins a title or a line is transposed to the end of the citation. "The Seder" by Enid Dame, for example, is listed as "Seder, The."

Titles. Initial capitals in the important words usually indicate that the citation is the title of the poem. "After Getting Drunk, Becoming Sober in the Night," for example, by Po Chu-i, is a title.

Parentheses. When an entire citation is enclosed by parentheses, it usually means that it is a variant title, variant first line, or variant last line. Parentheses are used instead of brackets when it is necessary to indicate a version that varies widely from the standard version, with the result that, in this alphabetized index, it can also be found in a place far from where the standard version is listed.

See, for example, "Virtue" by Nicholas Grimald.

> Virtue. Nicholas Grimald.   SCGP
>   (Description of Virtue.)   NoSiC

In the anthology indicated by the code NoSiC, the poem can be found under the title, "Description of Virtue." This information is especially useful when looking for a poem in the table of contents or the title index of the anthology indicated.

Indentation. Indentation of a citation indicates that it is a selection. See, for example, "Canterbury Tales, The."

> Canterbury Tales, The. Geoffrey Chaucer, Middle English.
>   Canon Assistant's Tale, The. OxBoV, tr. by David Wright

"Canon Assistant's Tale, The" is indented because it is a selection from *The Canterbury Tales.*

Author Index

Under each author's name, poems are listed alphabetically by title or, where the poem has no title, by first line.

What poems can I find by Louise Bogan? The Author Index lists 51 poems.

Subject Index

Under each subject heading, poems are listed alphabetically by author's name.

What poems can I find about marriage? The subject index shows that there are 590 poems about marriage, by 410 different poets, including Gwendolyn Brooks and John Donne. Citations for all these poems can be found in the Title, First Line, and Last Line Index, where the letter codes, which refer to the List of Anthologies, indicate in which books the poems have been published.

Did Chaucer write poems about religion? Go to the heading for "Religion" and locate "Chaucer" in the list of poems alphabetized by author.

LIST OF ANTHOLOGIES

Anthologies marked with two asterisks (**) are recommended for priority acquisition by small libraries, one asterisk (*) for further acquisition. See PREFACE for fuller explanation.

AEP   An Anthology of Elizabethan Poetry. *Sukanta Chaudhuri, ed.* (1992)   Oxford University Press. 170p.

AF   *Against Forgetting; Twentieth—Century Poetry of Witness. *Carolyn Forché, ed.* (1993)   W. W. Norton & Company. 81p.

AfrBLW   Afrekete; an Anthology of Black Lesbian Writing. *L. Joyce DeLaney and Catherine E. McKinley, eds.* (1995)   Anchor Books. 317p.

AH   *American Hymns Old and New. Vols. 1–2. *Albert Christ-Janer, Charles W. Hughes, and Carleton Sprague Smith, eds.* (1980)   Columbia University Press. 1,459p.

AiP   America in Poetry. *Charles Sullivan, ed.* (1988)   Harry N. Abrams. 207p.

AllShUp   All Shook Up; Collected Poems about Elvis. *Will Clemens, ed.* (1st ed., 2001)   University of Arkansas Press. 131p.

AmFaPo   *Americans' Favorite Poems; The Favorite Poem Project Anthology. *Robert Pinsky and Maggie Dietz, eds.* (1st ed., 2000)   W. W. Norton. 327p.

AmPoNex   American Poetry; The Next Generation. *Gerald Costanzo and Jim Daniels, eds.* (1st ed., 2000)   Carnegie Mellon Univ. Press. 480p.

AngWePo   Anglo-Welsh Poetry, 1480–1990. *Raymond Garlick and Roland Mathias, eds.* (1993)   Poetry Wales Press. 377p., pap.

AnOE   An Anthology of Old English Poetry. *Charles W. Kennedy, ed.* (1960)   Oxford University Press. 174p.

APN-1   *American Poetry; The Nineteenth Century. Vol. 1. *John Hollander, ed.* (1993)   The Library of America. 1,099p.

APN-2   *American Poetry; The Nineteenth Century. Vol. 2. (1993)   The Library of America. 1,050p.

APSN   American Poetry since 1950; Innovators and Outsiders. *Eliot Weinberger, ed.* (1993)   Marsilio. 433p.

APT-1   **American Poetry; The Twentieth Century, Vol. 1. *Robert Hass, John Hollander, Carolyn Kizer, Nathaniel Mackey, and Marjorie Perloff, eds.* (2000)   The Library of America. 986p.

APT-2   **American Poetry; The Twentieth Century. Vol. 2. *Robert Hass, John Hollander, Carolyn Kizer, Nathaniel Mackey, and Marjorie Perloff, eds.* (2000)   The Library of America. 1,009p.

ArkPo   Ariake; Poems of Love and Longing by the Women Courtiers of Ancient Japan. *Liza Dalby and Rae Grant, eds.* (2000)   Chronicle Books. 79p.

ArPe   Arabic & Persian Poems. *Omar S. Pound, ed.* (1970)   New Directions Books. 80p.

ARWW   An Anthology of Russian Women's Writing, 1777–1992. *Catriona Kelly, ed.* (1994)   Oxford University Press. 535p.

ASW   The Anglo-Saxon World; an Anthology. *Kevin Crossley-Holland, ed.* (1982)   Oxford University Press. 308p.

AuPH   Austria in Poetry and History. *Frederick Ungar, ed.* (1984)   Frederick Ungar Publishing Co. 345p.

AWP   An Anthology of World Poetry. *Mark Van Doren, ed.* (Rev. and Enl. ed., 1936)   Reynal & Hitchcock. 1,468p.

AWTN   Acquainted with the Night; Insomnia Poems. *Lisa Russ Spaar, ed.* (1999)   Columbia University Press. 183p.

BAP-01   The Best American Poetry, 2001. *Robert Hass, ed.* (2001)   Simon & Schuster. 287p.

BAP-97   The Best American Poetry, 1997. *James Tate, ed.* (1997)   Scribner. 269p.

BASC   **The Broadview Anthology of Seventeenth Century Verse and Prose. *Alan Rudrum, Joseph Black, and Holly Faith Nelson, eds.* (1st ed., 2000)   Broadview Press. 1303p.

BB   The Beat Book; Poems and Fiction of the Beat Generation. *Anne Waldman, ed.* (1996) Sham-
              bhala. 351p., pap.

BBASP   Burning Bright; an Anthology of Sacred Poetry. *Patricia Hampl, ed.* (1995) Ballantine Books.
              178p.

BeJo   Ben Jonson and the Cavalier Poets. *Hugh MacLaen, ed.* (1974) W. W. Norton & Company.
              591p.

BiHa   Bitter Harvest; an Anthology of Contemporary Irish Verse. *John Montague, ed.* (1989) Scrib-
              ner's. 211p.

BIrV   The Book of Irish Verse; an Anthology of Irish Poetry from the Sixth Century to the Present. *John
              Montague, ed.* (1974) Macmillan.

BloBone   Blood and Bone; Poems by Physicians. *Angela Belli and Jack Coulehan, eds.* (1st ed., 1998)
              University of Iowa Press. 160p.

BLPSL   The Best 100 Love Poems of the Spanish Language. *Rigas Kappatos and Pedro Lastra, eds.*
              (1998) Seaburn Publishing. 275p.

BlSi   Black Sister; Poetry by Black American Women, 1746–1980. *Erlene Stetson, ed.* (1981) Indiana
              University Press. 312p.

BLT   A Book of Luminous Things; an International Anthology of Poetry. *Czeslaw Milosz, ed.* (1996)
              Harcourt Brace and Company. 320p.

BMAP   The Bloodaxe Book of Modern Australian Poetry. *John Tranter and Philip Mead, eds.* (1991,
              1994) Bloodaxe Books. 474p., pap.

BodElec   **The Body Electric; America's Best Poetry from The American Poetry Review. *Stephen Berg,
              David Bonanno, and Arthur Vogelsang, eds.* (1st ed., 2000) W.W. Norton. 820p.

BoLoP   A Book of Love Poetry. *Jon Stallworthy, ed.* (1974) Oxford University Press; also published
              in Great Britain as The Penguin Book of Love Poetry. 393p.

BoWoP   A Book of Women Poets from Antiquity to Now. *Aliki Barnstone, ed.* (1980) Schocken Books.
              613p.

BPo   The Black Poets. *Dudley Randall, ed.* (1971) Bantam Books. 355p., pap.

BRP   Best Remembered Poems. *Martin Gardner, ed.* (1992) Dover Publications. 210p.

BrRo   Bread and Roses; an Anthology of Nineteenth- and Twentieth-Century Poetry by Women Writers.
              Diana Scott, ed. (1982) Virago Press. 282p., pap., o.p.

BWW   British Women Writers. *Dale Spender and Janet Todd, eds.* (1989) Peter Bedrick Books. 921p.,
              pap.

CA   Celebrating America; a Collection of Poems and Images of the American Spirit. *Laura Whipple,
              ed.* (1994) Philomel Books. 79p.

CABP   The Columbia Anthology of British Poetry. *Carl Woodring and James Shapiro, eds.* (1995)
              Columbia University Press. 891p.

CaDao   Ca Dao Vietnam; a Bilingual Anthology of Vietnamese Folk Poetry. *John Balaban, ed.* (3rd ed.,
              1980) Mosaic Press. 87p.

CAGL   *The Columbia Anthology of Gay Literature. *Byrne R. S. Fone, ed.* (1998) Columbia University
              Press. 829p.

CaPo   Cavalier Poets; Selected Poems. *Thomas Clayton, ed.* (1978) Oxford University Press. 364p.

CarOv   Carrying Over; Poems from the Chinese, Urdu, Macedonian, Yiddish, and French African. *Carolyn
              Kizer, ed.* (1988) Copper Canyon Press. 122p.

CavPo   The Cavalier Poets; an Anthology. *Thomas Crofts, ed.* (1995) Dover Publications, Inc. 92p.

CBAP   The Collins Book of Australian Poetry. *Rodney Hall, ed.* (1981, 1984) Fontana/Collins. 460p.,
              o.p.

CBCWP   The Columbia Book of Civil War Poetry. *Richard Marius, ed.* (1994) Columbia University
              Press. 543p.

CBWP-1   Collected Black Women's Poetry. Vol. I. *Joan R. Sherman, ed.* (1988) Oxford University Press.

CBWP-2   Collected Black Women's Poetry. Vol. II. (1988) Oxford University Press.

CBWP-3   Collected Black Women's Poetry. Vol. III. (1988) Oxford University Press.

CBWP-4   Collected Black Women's Poetry. Vol. IV. (1988) Oxford University Press.

CDa   Carrying the Darkness; the Poetry of the Vietnam War. *W. D. Ehrhart, ed.* (1989) Texas Tech
              University Press. 288p.

CDW — Carriers of the Dream Wheel: Contemporary Native American Poetry. *Duane Niatum, ed.* (1975) Harper & Row. 300p.

CenSon — A Century of Sonnets; The Romantic-Era Revival, 1750–1850. *Paula R. Feldman and Daniel Robinson, eds.* (1st ed., 1999) Oxford University Press. 279p.

ChAP — A Child's Anthology of Poetry. *Elizabeth Hauge Sword and Victoria Flournoy McCarthy, eds.* (1995) Ecco Press. 323p.

ChinPo — Chinese Poetry; an Anthology of Major Modes and Genres. *Wai-Lim Yip, ed.* (3rd ed., 2000) Duke University Press. 357p.

ChiP — Chinese Poems. *Arthur Waley, ed.* (1946) Unwin Paperbacks. 181p., pap.

ChIV-1 — Chapters into Verse. Vol. I: Genesis to Malachi. *Robert Atwan and Laurance Wieder, eds.* (1993) Oxford University Press. 481p.

ChIV-2 — Chapters into Verse. Vol. II: Gospels to Revelation. *Robert Atwan and Laurance Wieder, eds.* (1993) Oxford University Press. 391p.

ChrPo — Christmas Poems. *John Hollander and J. D. McClatchy, eds.* (1999) Alfred A. Knopf. 254p.

CIP-2 — Contemporary Irish Poetry; an Anthology. *Anthony Bradley, ed.* (New and rev. ed., 1988) University of California Press.

CItWP — Contemporary Italian Women Poets; a Bilingual Anthology. *Cinzia Sartini Blum and Lara Trubowitz, eds.* (1st ed., 2001) Italica Press. 308p.

ClHu — *The Classic Hundred; All-Time Favorite Poems. *William Harmon, ed.* (1990) Columbia University Press. 250p.

CLPP — City Lights Pocket Poets Anthology. *Lawrence Ferlinghetti, ed.* (1995) City Lights Books

CoAmPo — Contemporary American Poetry. *Donald Hall, ed.* (2d ed., 1972) Penguin Books. 280p., pap.

CoAP — The Contemporary American Poets; American Poetry since 1940. *Mark Strand, ed.* (1969) World. 390p., pap.

CoBCP — The Columbia Book of Chinese Poetry; from Early Times to the Thirteenth Century. *Burton Watson, ed.* (1984) Columbia University Press. 385p.

CoBLCP — The Columbia Book of Later Chinese Poetry. *Jonathan Chaves, ed.* (1986) Columbia University Press. 490p.

ColAnChi — *The Columbia Anthology of Traditional Chinese Literature. *Victor Mair, ed.* (1st ed., 1994) Columbia University Press. 1,335p.

ColAP — The Columbia Anthology of American Poetry. *Jay Parini, ed.* (1995) Columbia University Press. 757p.

CRP — Contemporary Religious Poetry. *Paul Ramsey, ed.* (1987) Paulist Press. 227p., pap.

CrYelRi — Crossing the Yellow River; Three Hundred Poems from the Chinese. *Sam Hamill, ed.* (1st ed., 2000) Boa Editions. 280p.

CTC — Confucius to Cummings; an Anthology of Poetry. *Ezra Pound and Marcella Spann, eds.* (1964) New Directions. 353p., pap.

CuPo — The Cubist Poets in Paris. *L. C. Breunig, ed.* (1st ed., 1995) University of Nebraska Press. 326p.

DiPo — The Direction of Poetry; an Anthology of Rhymed and Metered Verse Written in the English Language since 1975. *Robert Richman, ed.* (1988) Houghton Mifflin. 168p.

DTA — Dreaming the Actual; Contemporary Fiction and Poetry by Israeli Women Writers. *Miriyam Glazer, ed.* (2000) State University of New York. 396p.

EaItPo — The Early Italian Poets. *Sally Purcell, ed.* (1st ed., 1981) Anvil Press Poetry. 320p.

EaWin — East Window; The Asian Translations. *W. S. Merwin, ed.* (1st ed., 1998) Copper Canyon Press. 337p.

EBEV — Everyman's Book of English Verse. *John Wain, ed.* (1981) J. M. Dent. 672p.

EBNV — The Everyman Book of Narrative Verse. *David Herbert, ed.* (1990) J. M. Dent. 315p.

EBVV — Everyman's Book of Victorian Verse. *J. R. Watson, ed.* (1982) J. M. Dent. 373p.

ECEV — Eighteenth-Century English Verse. *Dennis Davison, ed.* (1988) Penguin Books. 321p., pap., o.p.

ECWP — Eighteenth Century Women Poets; an Oxford Anthology. *Roger Lonsdale, ed.* (1989) Oxford University Press. 555p.

EH — *The Essential Haiku; Versions of Bashō, Buson, and Issa. *Robert Hass, ed.* (1994) Ecco Press. 329p.

LIST OF ANTHOLOGIES

EmeKit   Emergency Kit; Poems for Strange Times. *Jo Shapcott and Matthew Sweeney, eds.* (1st ed., 1996) Faber and Faber. 306p.

EMWP   **Early Modern Women Poets (1520–1700). *Jane Stevenson and Peter Davidson, eds.* (2001) Oxford University Press. 585p.

EnlH   The Enlightened Heart; an Anthology of Sacred Poetry. *Stephen Mitchell, ed.* (1989) Harper & Row. 171p.

EnLoPo   English Love Poems. *John Betjeman and Geoffrey Taylor, eds.* (1957; paperback ed., 1964) Faber and Faber. 220p.

EroLit   Erotic Literature; Twenty-four Centuries of Sensual Writing. *Jane Mills, ed.* (1st ed., 1993) HarperCollins. 375p.

ErotSp   The Erotic Spirit. *Sam Hamill, ed.* (1st ed., 1996) Shambhala Press. 200p.

ESCV   English Seventeenth-Century Verse; Vol. 1. *Louis L. Martz, ed.* (1963, 1969) W. W. Norton. 525p., pap.

ESEAA   *Every Shut Eye Ain't Asleep; an Anthology of Poetry by African Americans since 1945. *Michael S. Harper and Anthony Walton, eds.* (1994) Little, Brown. 327p.

ESPB   English and Scottish Popular Ballads. *Helen Child Sargent and George Lyman Kittredge, eds.* (1904, 1932; reissued 1947) Houghton Mifflin. 730p.

ExTi   *The Extraordinary Tide; New Poetry by American Women. *Susan Aizenberg and Erin Belieu, eds.* (1st ed., 2001) Columbia University Press. 464p.

FaBoA   The Faber Book of America. *Christopher Ricks and William L. Vance, eds.* (1992) Faber and Faber. 467p.

FaBoCh   The Faber Book of Children's Verse. *Janet Adam Smith, ed.* (1953) Faber and Faber. 412p., pap.

FaBoEE   The Faber Book of Epigrams and Epitaphs. *Geoffrey Grigson, ed.* (1977) Faber and Faber. 291p., o.p.

FaBoMo   The Faber Book of Modern Verse. *Michael Roberts, ed.* (4th ed., revised by Peter Porter, 1982) Faber and Faber. 416p., pap.

FaBoTC   Faber Book of Twentieth-Century Scottish Poetry. *Douglas Dunn, ed.* (1992) Faber and Faber. 424p.

FaBoTw   The Faber Book of Twentieth Century Verse. *John Heath-Stubbs and David Wright, eds.* (3d ed., 1975) Faber and Faber. 348p.

FaBoVe   The Faber Book of Vernacular Verse. *Tom Paulin, ed.* (1990) Faber and Faber. 407p.

FaBoWar   The Faber Book of War Poetry. *Kenneth Baker, ed.* (1996) Faber and Faber. 598p.

FaBoWP   The Faber Book of 20th Century Women's Poetry. *Fleur Adcock, ed.* (1987) Faber and Faber. 330p.

FFC   A Formal Feeling Comes; Poems in Form by Contemporary Women. *Annie Finch, ed.* (1994) Story Line Press. 308p., pap.

FHYEP   Five Hundred Years of English Poetry; Chaucer to Arnold. *Barbara Lloyd-Evans, ed.* (1989) Peter Bedrick Books. 1,200p., p.

FIT   Found in Translation; a Hundred Years of Modern Hebrew Poetry. *Gabriel Levin, ed.* (1999) Menard Press. 126p.

FSCP   Five Seventeenth-Century Poets; Donne, Herbert, Crashaw, Marvell, Vaughan. *Brijraj Singh, ed.* (1992) Oxford University Press. 297p.

FSt   The Forbidden Stitch; an Asian American Women's Anthology. *Shirley Geok-lin Lim and Mayumi Tsutakawa, eds.* (1989) Calyx Books. 290p.

FTOS   From the Other Side of the Century; a New American Poetry 1960–1990. *Douglas Messerli, ed.* (1994) Sun & Moon Press. 1,136p.

FuPo   The Fugitive Poets: Modern Southern Poetry in Perspective. *William Pratt, ed.* (1991) J. S. Sanders & Company. 159p., pap.

GeHe   George Herbert and the Seventeenth-Century Religious Poets. *Marie Di Ceare, ed.* (1978) W. W. Norton. 401p., pap.

GeoH   The Geography of Hope; Poets of Colorado's Western Slope. *David J. Rothman, ed.* (2nd ed., 2000) Conundrum Press. 146p.

GeoHom   The Geography of Home; California's Poetry of Place. *Christopher Buckley and Gary Young, eds.* (1st ed., 1999) Heyday Books. 444p.

GePo   German Poetry; from the Beginnings to 1750. *Ingrid Walsøe–Engel, ed.* (1992) Continuum. 338p., pap.

GI   The Gospels in Our Image; an Anthology of Twentieth-Century Poetry Based on Biblical Texts. *David Curzon, ed.* (1995) Harcourt Brace. 279p.

GifTon   The Gift of Tongues; Twenty-five Years of Poetry from Copper Canyon Press. *Sam Hamill, ed.* (1st ed., 1996) Copper Canyon Press. 356p.

GLP   Gay & Lesbian Poetry in Our Time; an Anthology. *Carl Morse and Joan Larkin, eds.* (1988) St. Martin's Press. 463p.

GM   The Great Machines; Poems and Songs of the American Railroad. *Robert Hedin, ed.* (1996) University of Iowa Press. 251p.

GotH   Ghosts of the Holocaust; an Anthology of Poetry by the Second Generation. *Stewart J. Florsheim, ed.* (1989) Wayne State University Press. 190p.

GraLe   Grape Leaves; a Century of Arab American Poetry. *Gregory Orfalea and Sharif Elumusa, eds.* (1st ed., 1988) University of Utah Press. 300p.

GrAn   The Greek Anthology and Other Ancient Epigrams. *Peter Jay, ed.* (1981) Penguin Books. 447p., pap.

GS   The Gazer's Spirit: Poems Speaking to Silent Works of Art. *John Hollander, ed.* (1995) The University of Chicago Press. 380p.

GSo   Great Sonnets. *Paul Negri, ed.* (1994) Dover. 96p., pap.

GT   The Garden Thrives; Twentieth-Century African-American Poetry. *Clarence Major, ed.* (1996) HarperCollins. 470p., pap.

GTBS-P   Golden Treasury of the Best Songs & Lyrical Poems in the English Language. *Francis Turner Palgrave and John Press, eds.* (5th ed., 1964)) Oxford University Press. 526p.

HA   The Haiku Anthology. *Cor Van Den Heuvel, ed.* (1986) Simon and Schuster. 367p., pap.

HAP   The Harper Anthology of Poetry. *John Frederick Nims, ed.* (1981) Harper & Row. 842p.

HarvBoo   The Harvill Book of Twentieth-Century Poetry in English. *Michael Schmidt, ed.* (1st ed., 1999) The Harvill Press. 728p.

HATNAP   Harper's Anthology of 20th Century Native American Poetry. *Duane Niatum, ed.* (1988) Harper & Row. 396p., o.p.

HAWP   The Heinemann Book of African Women's Poetry. *Frank Chipasula, ed.* (1995) Heinemann Publishers. 227p.

HBAPE   The Heinemann Book of African Poetry in English. *Adewale Maja-Pearce, ed.* (1990) Heinemann. 224p., pap.

HCAP   The Harvard Book of Contemporary American Poetry. *Helen Vendler, ed.* (1985) Belknap Press. 440p.

HeIP-4   The Heath Introduction to Poetry. *Joseph DeRoche, ed.* (4th ed., 1992) D. C. Heath. 561p., pap.

HeMarv   Heights of the Marvelous; a New York Anthology. *Todd Colby, ed.* (1st ed., 2000) St. Martin's Griffin. 224p.

HePo   Hellenistic Poetry; an Anthology. *Barbara Hughes Fowler, ed.* (1990) University of Wisconsin Press. 357p.

HHAm   Hand in Hand; an American History through Poetry. *Lee Bennett Hopkins, ed.* (1994) Simon and Schuster. 144p.

HP   Holocaust Poetry. *Hilda Schiff, ed.* (1995) HarperCollins. 234p.

HW   Her Words; an Anthology of Poetry about the Great Goddess. *Burleigh Mutén, ed.* (1999) Shambhala. 249p.

IBA   Inside Black Australia; an Anthology of Aboriginal Poetry. *Kevin Gilbert, ed.* (1988) Penguin. 213p.

IBB   The Illustrated Border Ballads. *John Marden, ed.* (1990) University of Texas Press. 192p.

IllVoic   Illinois Voices. *Kevin Stein and G. E. Murray, eds.* (1st ed., 2001) University of Illinois Press. 366p.

InPK-6   An Introduction to Poetry. *X. J. Kennedy, ed.* (6th ed., 1986) Little, Brown. 480p., pap.

INSAB   **I never saw another butterfly; Children's Drawings and Poems from Terezin Concentration Camp, 1942–1944. *Hana Volavková, ed.* (2nd ed., 1993) Schocken Books. 106p.

InTrad   In the Tradition; an Anthology of Young Black Writers. *Kevin Powell and Ras Baraka, eds.* (1st ed., 1992) Harlem River Press. 398p.

InvLad   The Invisible Ladder; an Anthology of Contemporary American Poems for Young Readers. *Liz Rosenberg, ed.* (1st ed., 1996) Henry Holt and Co. 209p.

InvLi   Invisible Light; Poems about God. *Diana Culbertson, ed.* (2000) Columbia University Press. 174p.

IQMS   *In Quest of the Miracle Stag; The Poetry of Hungary. *Adam Makkai, ed.* (1996) Atlantic-Centaur, Inc; Corvina Publishers; and M. Szivárvány. 964p.

ISC   In Search of Color Everywhere: A Collection of African–American Poetry. *E. Ethelbert Miller, ed.* (1994) Stewart, Tabori & Chang. 256p., pap.

ITBLP   The Ideals Treasury of Best Loved Poems. *Patricia A. Pingry, ed.* (1997) Ideals Publications. 160p.

ItGoST   In the Grip of Strange Thoughts; Russian Poetry in a New Era. *J. Kates, ed.* (1999) Zephyr Press. 444p.

ItPo   Italian Poetry, 1950–1990. *Gian Paulo Renello and Gayle Ridinger, eds.* (1996) Dante University of America. 407p.

ItWoWo   It's a Woman's World; a Century of Women's Voices in Poetry. *Neil Philip, ed.* (1st ed., 2000) Dutton Children's Books. 93p.

JDP   Japanese Death Poems; Written by Zen Monks and Haiku Poets on the Verge of Death. *Yoel Hoffmann, ed.* (1986) Charles E. Tuttle. 366p.

KaS   Knock at a Star: A Child's Introduction to Poetry. *X. J. Kennedy, ed.* (1982) Little, Brown and Company. 148p.

KGB   The KGB Bar Book of Poems. *Star Black and David Lehman, eds.* (2000) HarperCollins. 256p.

LB   Lavender's Blue. *Kathleen Lines, ed.* (1989) Oxford University Press. 180p.

LCAP-2   The Longman Anthology of Contemporary American Poetry. *Stuart Friebert and David Young, eds.* (2d ed., 1989) Longman. 629p., pap.

LoL   The Language of Life; a Festival of Poets. *Bill Moyers, ed.* (1995) Doubleday. 450p., pap.

LTA   Letters to America: Contemporary American Poetry on Race. *Jim Daniels, ed.* (1995) Wayne State University Press. 230p., pap.

LW   Love's Witness; Five Centuries of Love Poetry by Women. *Jill Hollis, ed.* (1993) Carroll and Graf Publishers, 334p., pap.

MakPoe   **The Making of a Poem; a Norton Anthology of Poetic Forms. *Mark Strand and Eavan Boland, eds.* (1st ed., 2000) W. W. Norton. 366p.

MAP   Modern Arabic Poetry; an Anthology. *Salma Khadra Jayyusi, ed.* (1987) Columbia University Press. 498p.

MeLP   Metaphysical Lyrics & Poems of the Seventeenth Century; Donne to Butler. *Herbert J. Grierson, ed.* (1921) Oxford University Press. 302p.

MFP   Modern French Poetry. *Martin Sorrell, ed.* (1992) Forest Books. 242p., pap.

MFPA   Making for Planet Alice; New Women Poets. *Maura Dooley, ed.* (1997) Bloodaxe Books. 173p.

MHP   Modern Hebrew Poetry; a Bilingual Anthology. *Ruth Finer Mintz, ed.* (1966) University of California Press. 371p.

MiEL   Middle English Lyrics, Authoritative Texts, Critical and Historical Backgrounds, Perspectives on Six Poems. *Maxwell S. Luria, ed.* (1974) W. W. Norton. 360p., pap.

MirDau   Miriam's Daughters; Jewish Latin American Women Poets. *Marjorie Agosin, ed.* (1st ed., 2001) Sherman Asher Publishing. 240p.

MiVo   Mixed Voices; Contemporary Poems about Music. *Emilie Buchwald and Ruth Roston, eds.* (1st ed., 1991) Milkweed Editions. 185p.

MLL   More Latin Lyrics; from Virgil to Milton. *Dame Felicitas Corrigan, ed.* (1977) W. W. Norton. 392p.

MoAmPo   Modern American Poetry. *Louis Untermeyer, ed.* (8th rev. ed., 1962) Harcourt, Brace. 701p., o.p.

MoASP   Motion; American Sports Poems. *Noah Blaustein, ed.* (2001) University of Iowa Press. 250p.

MoBrPo   Modern British Poetry. (7th rev. ed., 1962) Harcourt, Brace. 500p., o.p.

MoCV   Modern Canadian Verse. *A. J. M. Smith, ed.* (1967) Oxford University Press. 426p.

ModIr   Modern Irish Poetry. *Patrick Crotty, ed.* (1st ed., 1995) The Blackstaff Press. 436p.

MPUn   A More Perfect Union; Poems and Stories About the Modern Wedding. *Virginia Hartman and Barbara Esstman, eds.* (1st ed., 1998) St. Martin's Press. 295p.

NAAL-2v1   The Norton Anthology of American Literature. Vol. 1.   *Nina Baym, ed.*   (2nd ed., 1985)   W. W. Norton. 2,535p., pap.

NAAL-2v2   The Norton Anthology of American Literature. Vol. 2.   (2nd ed., 1985)   W. W. Norton. 2,652p., pap.

NAAL-3   *The Norton Anthology of American Literature.   (3rd ed., 1989)   W. W. Norton. 2,459p., pap.

NAAL-5   **The Norton Anthology of American Literature. Shorter.   (5th ed., 1999)   W. W. Norton. 2,879p., pap.

NAEL-5v1   The Norton Anthology of English Literature. Vol. 1.   *M. H. Abrams, ed.*   (5th ed., 1986)   W. W. Norton. 2,616p.

NAEL-5v2   The Norton Anthology of English Literature. Vol. 2.   (5th ed., 1986)   W. W. Norton.

NAEL-6v1   *The Norton Anthology of English Literature. Vol.1.   (6th ed., 1993)   W. W. Norton. 2,543p.

NAEL-6v2   *The Norton Anthology of English Literature. Vol. 2.   (6th ed., 1993)   W. W. Norton. 2,543p.

NAEL-7v1   *The Norton Anthology of English Literature. Vol. 1.   *Stephen Greenblatt, ed.*   (7th ed. 2000)   W. W. Norton. 2,974p.

NAfrP   The New African Poetry; an Anthology.   *Tanure Ojaide and Tijan M. Sallah, eds.*   (1999)   Lynne Rienner Publishers. 233p.

NALW   **The Norton Anthology of Literature by Women; the Tradition in English.   *Sandra M. Gilbert and Susan Guber, eds.*   (1985)   W. W. Norton. 2,457p.

NAPBL   The New American Poets; a Bread Loaf Anthology.   *Michael Collier, ed.*   (2000)   Univ. Press of New England. 280p.

NAWM-5v1   The Norton Anthology of World Masterpieces. Vol. 1.   *Maynard Mack, ed.*   (5th ed., 1985)   W. W. Norton. 2,052p.

NAWM-7v1   *The Norton Anthology of World Masterpieces. Vol. 1.   *Sarah Lawall and Maynard Mack, eds.*   (7th ed., 1999)   W. W. Norton. 2,270p.

NAWM-7v2   *The Norton Anthology of World Masterpieces. Vol. 2.   *Sarah Lawall and Maynard Mack, eds.*   (7th ed., 1999)   W. W. Norton. 2,194p.

NBLV   *The Norton Book of Light Verse.   *Russell Baker, ed.*   (1986)   W. W. Norton. 447p.

NBV   New Black Voices; an Anthology of Contemporary Afro-American Literature.   *Abraham Chapman, ed.*   (1972)   Mentor. 606p., pap.

NCAP   Nineteenth Century American Poetry.   *William C. Spengemann and Jessica F. Roberts, eds.*   (1996)   Penguin Books. 447p., pap.

NeAmPo   The New Young American Poets.   *Kevin Prufer, ed.*   (1st ed., 2000)   Southern Illinois University Press. 243p.

NeAP   The New American Poetry, 1945–1960.   *Donald M. Allen, ed.*   (1960)   Grove Press. 454p., o.p.

NeBl   New Blood.   *Neil Astley, ed.*   (1st ed., 1999)   Bloodaxe Books. 240p.

NegPo   The Negritude Poets; an Anthology of Translations from the French.   *Ellen Conroy Kennedy, ed.*   (1989)   Thunder's Mouth Press. 284p.

NeIt   New Italian Poets.   *Dana Gioia and Michael Palma, eds.*   (1991)   Story Line Press. 385p., pap.

NePenScot   The New Penguin Book of Scottish Verse.   *Robert Crawford and Mick Imlah, eds.*   (1st ed., 2000)   Penguin Press. 554p.

NewEx   The New Exeter Book of Riddles.   *Kevin Crossley-Holland and Lawrence Sail, eds.*   (1st ed., 1999)   Enitharmon Press. 66p.

NIL-7   *The Norton Introduction to Literature. *Jerome Beaty and J. Paul Hunter, eds.*   (7th ed., 1998)   W. W. Norton, 2,278p., cloth

NIP-4   *The Norton Introduction to Poetry.   (4th ed., 1991)   W. W. Norton. 578p.

NLP   The New Lake Poets.   *William Scammell, ed.*   (1991)   Bloodaxe Books. 160p.

NNaP   The New Naked Poetry; Recent American Poetry in Open Forms.   *Stephen Berg and Robert Mesey, eds.*   (1976)   Bobbs-Merrill. 478p., o.p.

NoAM   *The Norton Anthology of Modern Poetry. *Richard Ellmann and Robert O'Clair, eds.*   (2nd ed., 1988)   W. W. Norton. 1,863p.

NOBA   The New Oxford Book of American Verse.   *Richard Ellmann, ed.*   (1976)   Oxford University Press. 1,076p.

NOBAu The New Oxford Book of Australian Verse. *Les A. Murray, ed.* (Enl. ed., 1991) Oxford University Press. 399p.

NOBC The New Oxford Book of Canadian Verse in English. *Margaret Atwood, ed.* (1982) Oxford University Press. 477p.

NOBE The New Oxford Book of English Verse, 1250–1950. *Helen Gardner, ed.* (1972) Oxford University Press. 974p.

NOBL The New Oxford Book of English Light Verse. *Kingsley Amis, ed.* (1978) Oxford University Press. 347p.

NOBRP The New Oxford Book of Romantic Period Verse. *Jerome J. McGann, ed.* (1993) Oxford University Press. 832p.

NOBVV The New Oxford Book of Victorian Verse. *Christopher Ricks, ed.* (1987) Oxford University Press. 654p.

NOCV The New Oxford Book of Christian Verse. *Donald Davie, ed.* (1981) Oxford University Press. 320p.

NOEC The New Oxford Book of Eighteenth Century Verse. *Roger Lonsdale, ed.* (1984) Oxford University Press. 870p.

NOIV The New Oxford Book of Irish Verse. *Thomas Kinsella, ed.* (1986) Oxford University Press. 422p.

NoP-4 **The Norton Anthology of Poetry. *Margaret Ferguson, Mary Jo Salter, and Jon Stallworthy, eds.* (4th ed., 1996) W. W. Norton. 1,998p., pap.

NOSC The New Oxford Book of Seventeenth Century Verse. *Alistair Fowler, ed.* (1991) Oxford University Press. 831p.

NoSic The New Oxford Book of Sixteenth Century Verse. *Emrys Jones, ed.* (1991) Oxford University Press. 769p.

NOxBChV The New Oxford Book of Children's Verse. *Neil Philip, ed.* (1996) Oxford University Press. 371p.

NPeEn *The New Penguin Book of English Verse. *Paul Keegan, ed.* (1st ed., 2000) Penguin Press. 1,139p.

NTCP A New Treasury of Children's Poetry; Old Favorites and New Discoveries. *Joanna Cole, ed.* (1984) Doubleday. 224p., pap.

OBAL Oxford Book of American Light Verse, The. *William Harmon, ed.* (1979) Oxford University Press. 540p.

OBCA The Oxford Book of Children's Verse in America. *Donald Hall, ed.* (1985) Oxford University Press. 319p.

OBCoV The Oxford Book of Comic Verse. *John Gross, ed.* (1994) Oxford University Press. 512p.

OBCP The Oxford Book of Christmas Poems. *Michael Harrison and Christopher Stuart-Clark, eds.* (1983) Oxford University Press. 160p.

OBEV The Oxford Book of English Verse, 1250–1918. *Sir Arthur Quiller-Couch, ed.* (New ed., rev. and enl., 1939) Oxford University Press. 1,083p.

OBGa The Oxford Book of Garden Verse. *John Dixon Hunt, ed.* (1993) Oxford University Press. 341p.

OBMV The Oxford Book of Modern Verse, 1892–1935. *William Butler Yeats, ed.* (1936) Oxford University Press. 454p.

OBNV The Oxford Book of Narrative Verse. *Iona Opie, ed.* (1983) Oxford University Press. 407p.

OBSP The Oxford Book of Story Poems. *Michael Harrison and Christopher Stuart-Clark, eds.* (1990) Oxford University Press. 175p.

OBSV The Oxford Book of Satirical Verse. *Geoffrey Grigson, ed.* (1980) Oxford University Press. 454p.

OBVE The Oxford Book of Verse in English Translation. *Charles Tomlinson, ed.* (1980) Oxford University Press. 608p.

OBWP The Oxford Book of War Poetry. *Jon Stallworthy, ed.* (1984) Oxford University Press. 358p.

OBWVE The Oxford Book of Welsh Verse in English. *Gwyn Jones, ed.* (1977) Oxford University Press, 313p.

OHMEL One Hundred Middle English Lyrics. *Robert D. Stevick, ed.* (2nd ed., 1994) University of Illinois Press. 194p.

OHMPC   One Hundred More Poems from the Chinese; Love and the Turning Year. *Kenneth Rexroth, ed.* (1970) New Directions. 140p.

OHMPJ   One Hundred More Poems from the Japanese. (1974) New Directions. 120p., pap.

OHPC   One Hundred Poems from the Chinese. (1971) New Directions. 148p., pap.

OHPJ   One Hundred Poems from the Japanese. (1964) New Directions. 140p.

OMIP   The Oxford Anthology of Modern Indian Poetry. *Vinay Dharwadker and A. K. Ramanujan, eds.* (1994) Oxford University Press. 265p.

OpBo   The Open Boat; Poems from Asian America. *Garrett Hongo, ed.* (1993) Doubleday. 303p.

OPOU   100 Poems on the Underground. *Gerald Benson, Judith Cherniak, and Cicely Herbert, eds.* (1991) Cassell Publishers. 144p., pap.

OPRER   Outsiders; Poems about Rebels, Exiles, and Renegades. *Laure-Anne Bosselaar, ed.* (1999) Milkweed Editions. 323p.

OTCP   The Oxford Treasury of Children's Poems. *Michael Harrison and Christopher Stuart-Clark, eds.* (1988) Oxford University Press. 174p.

Oth   Other; British and Irish Poetry since 1970. *Richard Caddel and Peter Quartermain, eds.* (1st ed., 1999) Wesleyan University Press. 280p.

OWoS   On Wings of Song; Poems about Birds. *J. D. McClatchy, ed.* (2000) Alfred A. Knopf. 256p.

OxAEP-1   The Oxford Anthology of English Poetry. Vol. I: Spenser to Crabbe. *John Wain, ed.* (1990) Oxford University Press. 659p.

OxAEP-2   The Oxford Anthology of English Poetry. Vol. II: Blake to Heaney. (1990) Oxford University Press. 770p.

OxBA   The Oxford Book of American Verse. *F. O. Matthiessen, ed.* (1950) Oxford University Press. 1,130p.

OxBB   The Oxford Book of Ballads. *James Kinsley, ed.* (1969) Oxford University Press. 711p.

OxBC   The Oxford Book of Contemporary Verse, 1945–1980. *D. J. Enright, ed.* (1980) Oxford University Press. 299p.

OxBEV   *The Oxford Book of English Verse. *Christopher Ricks, ed.* (1999) Oxford University Press. 690p.

OxBoLi   *The Oxford Book of Light Verse. *W. H. Auden, ed.* (1938) Oxford University Press. 552p.

OxBS   The Oxford Book of Scottish Verse. *John MacQueen and Tom Scott, eds.* (1966) Oxford University Press. 633p.

OxBSo   *The Oxford Book of Sonnets. *John Fuller, ed.* (2000) Oxford University Press. 362p.

OxBSP   The Oxford Book of Short Poems. *P. J. Kavanagh and James Michie, eds.* (1985) Oxford University Press. 307p.

OxBTC   *The Oxford Book of Twentieth-Century English Verse. *Philip Larkin, ed.* (1973) Oxford University Press. 641p.

OxIBACP   The Oxford Illustrated Book of American Children's Poems. *Donald Hall, ed.* (1999) Oxford University Press. 96p.

OxNR   *The Oxford Nursery Rhyme Book. *Iona Opie, ed.* (1955) Oxford University Press. 224p.

OxWW   The Oxford Book of Women's Writing in the United States. *Linda Wagner-Martin and Cathy N. Davidson, eds.* (1995) Oxford University Press. 596p.

PAI   Poetry; an Introduction. *Ruth Miller and Robert A. Greenberg, eds.* (1981) St. Martin's Press. 589p.

PasH   Passionate Hearts; the Poetry of Sexual Love. *Wendy Maltz, ed.* (1996) New World Library. 209p.

PBA   Poems from Black Africa. *Langston Hughes, ed.* (1963) Indiana University Press. 160p.

PBCAP   The Pittsburgh Book of Contemporary American Poetry. *Ed Ochester and Peter Oresick, eds.* (1993) University of Pittsburgh Press. 397p.

PBCIP   The Penguin Book of Contemporary Irish Poetry. *Peter Fallon and Derek Mahon, eds.* (1990) Penguin Books. 462p., pap.

PBMAP   The Penguin Book of Modern African Poetry. *Gerald Moore and Ulli Beier, eds.* (1984) Penguin Books. 315p., pap.

PBRV   *The Penguin Book of Renaissance Verse 1509-1659. *David Norbrook, ed.* (1992) Penguin Books. 920p., pap.

PeECV   The Penguin Book of English Christian Verse. *Peter Levi, ed.* (1984) Penguin Books. 379p.

PeFWW   The Penguin Book of First World War Poetry.   *Jon Silkin, ed.*   (1979)   Penguin Books. 258p.,
             pap.
PeLi   The Penguin Book of Limericks.   *E. O. Parrott, ed.*   (1983)   Penguin Books. 304p., pap.
PeLV   The Penguin Book of Light Verse.   *Gavin Ewart, ed.*   (1980)   Penguin Books. 639p., pap., o.p.
PeNZ   The Penguin Book of New Zealand Verse.   *Ian Wedde and Harvey McQueen, eds.*   (1985)   Pen-
             guin Books. 575p., pap., o.p.
PeSAV   The Penguin Book of Southern African Verse.   *Stephen Gray, ed.*   (1989)   Penguin Books. 402p.,
             o.p.
PeVV   Victorian Verse.   *George MacBeth, ed.*   (1986)   Penguin Books. 441p.
PEW   Poetry by English Women; Elizabethan to Victorian.   *R. E. Pritchard, ed.*   (1990)   Continuum.
             272p., pap.
PFTM-1   Poems for the Millennium; the University of California Book of Modern & Postmodern Poetry.
             Vol. 1.   *Jerome Rothenberg and Pierre Joris, eds.*   (1995)   University of California Press.
             811p.
PFTM-2   Poems for the Millennium; the University of California Book of Modern & Postmodern Poetry.
             Vol. 2.   *Jerome Rothenberg, ed.*   (1998)   University of California Press. 871p.
PGA   Poems from the Greek Anthology.   *Kenneth Rexroth, ed.*   (1962)   University of Michigan Press.
             111p.
PmAP   Postmodern American Poetry; a Norton Anthology.   *Paul Hoover, ed.*   (1994)   W. W. Norton &
             Company. 701p.
PNI   Poets from the North of Ireland.   *Frank Ormsby, ed.*   (New ed., 1990)   The Blackstaff Press. 336p.
PoArWo   The Poetry of Arab Women; a Contemporary Anthology.   *Nathalie Handal, ed.*   (1st ed., 2001)
             Interlink Books. 355p.
PoBW   Poems Between Women; Four Centuries of Love, Romantic Friendship, and Desire.   *Emma Don-
             oghue, ed.*   (1997)   Columbia University Press. 209p.
PoCoUp   Poetry Comes Up Where It Can; an Anthology: Poems from the Amicus Journal, 1990–2000.   *Brian
             Swann, ed.*   (1st ed., 2000)   University of Utah Press. 168p.
PoE   Poetry in English; an Anthology.   *M. L. Rosenthal, ed.*   (1987)   Oxford University Press. 1,196p.
PoetW   *The Poetry of Our World; an International Anthology of Contemporary Poetry.   *Jeffrey Paine, ed.*
             (2000)   HarperCollins. 511p., cloth.
PoM   The Postmoderns; the New American Poetry Revised.   *Donald Allen and George F. Butterick, eds.*
             (1982)   Grove Press. 436p., pap.
PoPoPo   Poems, Poets, Poetry; an Introduction and Anthology.   *Helen Vendler, ed.*   (1996)   Bedford Books.
             656p., pap.
PoRA   Poems to Read Aloud.   *Edward Hodnett, ed.*   (Rev. ed., 1967)   W. W. Norton. 390p., o.p.
PoSol   The Poetry of Solitude; a Tribute to Edward Hopper.   *Levin Gail, ed.*   (1995)   Universe Publishing.
             80p.
PoSu   The Poetry of Survival; Post-War Poets of Central and Eastern Europe.   *Daniel Weissbort, ed.*
             (1991)   Anvil Press Poetry. 384p.
PoToHe   Poems that Touch the Heart.   *A. L. Alexander, ed.*   (1956)   Doubleday. 403p.
PoWW   Poetry of the World Wars.   *Michael Foss, ed.*   (1990)   Peter Bedrick Books. 192p.
PriapPo   The Priapus Poems; Erotic Epigrams from Ancient Rome.   *Richard W. Hooper, ed.*   (1st ed., 1999)
             University of Illinois Press. 147p.
Prnts   Parents; an Anthology of Poems by Women Writers.   *Myra Schneider and Dilys Wood, eds.*   (2000)
             Enitharmon Press. 218p.
PueRic   Puerto Rican Writers at Home.   *Faythe Turner, ed.*   (1991)   Open Hand Publishing. 349p.
PuP-23   The Pushcart Prize XXIII; Best of the Small Presses.   *Bill Henderson, ed.*   (1st ed., 1999)   Pushcart
             Press. 606p.
PWR   Poetry Worth Remembering; an Anthology of Poetry.   *Roy W. Watson, ed.*   (1986)   Brunswick.
             274p., o.p.
RA   Rebel Angels: 25 Poets of the New Formalism.   *Mark Jarman and David Mason, eds.*   (1996)
             Story Line Press. 259p., pap.
RaBo   The Rag and Bone Shop of the Heart: Poems for Men.   *Robert Bly, James Hillman, and Michael
             Meade, eds.*   (1992)   Harper Collins. 536p.
RACG   The Routledge Anthology of Cross-Gendered Verse.   *Alan Michael Parker and Mark Willhardt,
             eds.*   (1996)   Routledge. 216p., pap.

RB   The Rattle Bag; an Anthology of Poetry. *Seamus Heaney and Ted Hughes, eds.* (1982) Faber and Faber. 498p., pap.

ReBoTo   Returning a Borrowed Tongue; an Anthology of Filipino and Filipino American Poetry. *Nick Carbo, ed.* (1st ed., 1995) Coffee House Press. 238p.

ReEnLa   Reinventing the Enemy's Language; Contemporary Native Women's Writings of North America. *Joy Harjo and Gloria Bird, eds.* (1st ed., 1997) W.W. Norton. 573p.

ReLy   Reading Lyrics. *Robert Gottlieb and Robert Kimball, eds.* (1st ed., 2000) Pantheon Books. 705p.

ReMoGo   The Real Mother Goose. *Blanche Fisher Wright, ed.* (1944) Checkerboard Press. 128p.

ReTh   Real Things; an Anthology of Popular Culture in American Poetry. *Jim Elledge and Susan Swartwout, eds.* (1st ed., 1999) Indiana University Press. 336p.

RomPo   Roman Poets of the Early Empire. *A. J. Boyle and J. P. Sullivan, eds.* (1st ed., 1991) Penguin Books. 450p.

RusPo   Russian Poetry. *R. A. D. Ford, ed.* (3rd ed., 2000) Mosaic Press. 93p.

RWP   Romantic Women Poets; an Anthology. *Duncan Wu, ed.* (1997) Blackwell Publishers. 629p.

SacPr   A Sacrifice of Praise; an Anthology of Christian Poetry in English from Caedmon to the Mid-Twentieth Century. *James H. Trott, ed.* (1999) Cumberland House Publishing. 797p.

SaLy   Sappho's Lyre; Archaic Lyric and Women Poets of Ancient Greece. *Diane J. Rayor, ed.* (1991) University of California Press. 207p.

SAmP   Six American Poets; an Anthology. *Joel Conarroe, ed.* (1991) Random House. 281p.

SCAP   Seventeenth-Century American Poetry. *Harrison T. Meserole, ed.* (1968) Doubleday. 540p., o.p.

SCGP   Six Centuries of Great Poetry. *Robert Penn Warren and Albert Erskine, eds.* (1955) Dell. 544p., pap., o.p.

SCV   Six Centuries of Verse. *Anthony Thwaite, ed.* (1984) Thames Methuen. 290p., pap.

SeSe   The Second Set; the Jazz Poetry Anthology; Volume 2. *Sascha Feinstein and Yusef Komunyakaa, eds.* (1996) Indiana University Press. 250p.

SinGod   *Singing to the Goddess; Poems to Kālī and Umā from Bengal. *Rachel Fell McDermott, ed.* (1st ed., 2001) Oxford University Press. 189p.

Son   The Sonnet; an Anthology. *Robert M. Bender and Charles L. Squier, eds.* (1987) Washington Square Press. 428p.

SoOfWa   The Sound of Water; Haiku by Bashō, Buson, Issa, and Other Poets. *Sam Hamill, ed.* (1st ed., 2000) Shambala. 125p.

SoSe-8   Sound and Sense; an Introduction to Poetry. *Laurence Perrine and Thomas R. Arp, eds.* (8th ed., 1992) Harcourt Brace Jovanovich. 342p.

SpanPo   Spanish Poetry; a Dual-Language Anthology. *Angel Flores, ed.* (1st ed., 1998) Dover Publications. 401p.

SPE   Surrealist Poetry in English. *Edward B. Germain, ed.* (1978) Penguin Books. 348p., pap.

SpirFl   Spirit and Flame; an Anthology of Contemporary African American Poetry. *Keith Gilyard, ed.* (1st ed., 1997) Syracuse University Press. 304p.

Spl   Splinters; a Book of Very Short Poems. *Michael Harrison, ed.* (1989) Oxford University Press. 121 p.

SPl   Secret Places. *Charlotte Huck, ed.* (1993) Greenwillow Books. 32p.

SpudSo   Spud Songs; an Anthology of Potato Poems to Benefit Hunger Relief. *Gloria Vando and Robert Stewart, eds.* (1st ed., 1999) Helicon Nine Editions. 200p.

SSCS   Sky Scrape / City Scape. *Jane Yolen, ed.* (1996) Boyds Mills Press. 32p.

SSLK   Shimmy Shimmy Shimmy like My Sister Kate. *Nikki Giovanni, ed.* (1996) Henry Holt and Company. 188p.

STP   Shaking the Pumpkin; Traditional Poetry of the Indian North Americans. *Jerome Rothenberg, ed.* (Rev. ed., 1986) Alfred van der Marck Editions.

StPo   Story Poems, New and Old. *William Cole, ed.* (1957) World. 255p., o.p.

STV   Sappho to Valéry; Poems in Translation. *John Frederick Nims, ed.* (Rev. and enl., 1990) University of Arkansas Press. 415p.

SurPaPo   Surrealist Painters and Poets. *Mary Ann Caws, ed.* (1st ed., 2001) MIT Press. 525p.

SurWo   Surrealist Women; an International Anthology. *Penelope Rosemont, ed.* (1998) University of Texas Press. 516p.

SuSp   Sunflower Splendor; Three Thousand Years of Chinese Poetry. *Wu-chi Liu and Irving Yucheng Lo, eds.* (1975) (1975) Indiana University Press. 635p., pap.

SWaP   She Wields a Pen; American Women Poets of the Nineteenth Century. *Janet Gray, ed.* (1997) University of Iowa Press. 374p.

SwNoth   Sweet Nothings; an Anthology of Rock and Roll in American Poetry. *Jim Elledge, ed.* (1st ed., 1994) Indiana University Press. 283p.

SxFrPo   Six French Poets of the Nineteenth Century; Lamartine, Hugo, Baudelaire, Verlaine, Rimbaud, Mallarmé. *A. M. Blackmore, ed.* (2000) Oxford University Press. 334p.

TAL   A Treasury of Asian Literature. *John D. Yohannon, ed.* (1984) Mentor Books. 432p., pap.

TANSG   These Are Not Sweet Girls; Poetry by Latin American Women. *Marjorie Agosin, ed.* (1994) White Pine Press. 368p., pap.

TAP   The Treasury of American Poetry. *Nancy Sullivan, ed.* (1978) Doubleday. 838p.

TaR   Telling and Remembering; a Century of American Jewish Poetry. *Steven J. Rubin, ed.* (1997) Beacon Press. 499p.

TCAPo   **Three Centuries of American Poetry. *Allen Mandelbaum and Robert D. Richardson, Jr., eds.* (1st ed., 1999) Bantam Books. 733p.

TCAWP   Twentieth Century Anglo-Welsh Poetry. *Dannie Abse, ed.* (1997) Seren Books / Dufour Editions. 273p.

TCLAP   Twentieth-Century Latin American Poetry. *Stephen Tapscott, ed.* (1996) University of Texas Press. 418p.

TCRusP   Twentieth-Century Russian Poetry. *John Glad and Daniel Weissbort, eds.* (1992) University of Iowa Press. 384p.

TFi   **The Top 500 Poems. *William Harmon, ed.* (1992) Columbia University Press. 113p.

TLR   Talking like the Rain; a First Book of Poems. *X. J. Kennedy, ed.* (1992) Little Brown and Company. 96p.

TOF   Tongues of Fire; an Anthology of Religious and Poetic Experience. *Karen Armstrong, ed.* (1987) Penguin Books. 352p., pap., o.p.

TouFir   Touching the Fire; Fifteen Poets of Today's Latino Renaissance. *Ray González, ed.* (1st ed., 1998) Anchor Books. 304p.

TrCP   The Treasury of Christian Poetry. *Lorraine Eitel, ed.* (1982) Fleming H. Revell. 182p., o.p.

TreFP   Treasury of Favorite Poems. *Joseph H. Head, ed.* (3rd ed., 2000) Gramercy Books. 336p.

TriCat   The Triumphant Cat. *Walter Payne, ed.* (1993) Carrol and Graf Publishers. 160p.

TrJP   A Treasury of Jewish Poetry. *Nathan Ausubel, ed.* (1957) Crown. 471p., o.p.

TRP   To Read a Poem. *Donald Hall, ed.* (2d ed, 1992) Harcourt, Brace, Jovanovich. 411p.

TTTS   Talking to the Sun; an Illustrated Anthology of Poems for YoungPeople. *Kenneth Koch and Kate Farrell, eds.* (1985) Metropolitan Museum of Art/Henry Holt. 112p.

TTY   3000 Years of Black Poetry. *Alan Lomax and Raoul Abdul, eds.* (1970) Dodd, Mead. 263p., pap., o.p.

TuT   Turning Tides; Modern Dutch and Flemish Verse in English Versions by Irish Poets. *Peter van de Kamp, ed.* (1994) Story Line Press. 432p.

TwCP   Twentieth-Century Poetry; American and British (1900–1970). *John Malcolm Brinnin and Bill Read, eds.* (Rev. ed., 1970) McGraw Hill 515p. (*Text ed entitled* The Modern Poets)

TWW   Two Worlds Walking; Short Stories, Essays, and Poetry by Writers with Mixed Heritages. *Diane Glancy and C. W. Truesdale, eds.* (1st ed., 1994) New Rivers Press. 308p.

Unle   Unleashed; Poems by Writers' Dogs. *Amy Hempel and Jim Shepard, eds.* (1st ed., 1995) Three Rivers Press. 175p.

UnPo   *Understanding Poetry. *Cleanth Brooks and Robert Penn Warren, eds.* (4th ed., 1976) Holt, Rinehart and Winston. 602p.

UnSA   Unsettling America; an Anthology of Contemporary Multicultural Poetry. *Maria Mazziotti Gillan, ed.* (1994) Penguin Books. 406p., pap.

UrbNat   Urban Nature; Poems about Wildlife in the City. *Laure-Anne Bosselaar, ed.* (1st ed., 2000) Milkweed Editions. 265p.

UV   Unauthorized Versions; Poems and Their Parodies. *Kenneth Baker, ed.* (1990) Faber and Faber. 446p.

VCAP   The Vintage Book of Contemporary American Poetry. *J. D. McClatchy, ed.* (1990) Vintage Books. 560p.

VCWP   The Vintage Book of Contemporary World Poetry. (1996) Vintage Books. 655p., pap.

VerBaPo   Very Bad Poetry. *Kathryn Petras, ed.* (1st ed., 1997) Vintage Books. 126p.

VGW   The Voice That Is Great Within Us; American Poetry of theTwentieth Century. *Hayden Carruth, ed.* (1970) Bantam Books. 722p., pap.

ViWPN   Victorian Women Poets; a New Annotated Anthology. *Virginia Blain, ed.* (2001) Longman. 382p.

VoR   Voices of the Rainbow; Contemporary Poetry by American Indians. *Kenneth Rosen, ed.* (1975) Viking Press. 232p., pap.

VWP   Victorian Women Poets; an Anthology. *Angela Leighton and Margaret Reynolds, eds.* (1991) Blackwell. 691p., pap.

WaCA   Wheel and Come Again; an Anthology of Reggae Poetry. *Kwame Dawes, ed.* (1st ed., 1998) Goose Lane Editions. 218p.

WeW-3   Western Wind; an Introduction to Poetry. *John Frederick Nims, ed.* (3rd ed., 1992) Random House. 639p., pap.

WHSW   Who Has Seen the Wind? an Illustrated Collection of Poetry for Young People. *Kathryn Sky-Peck, ed.* (1991) Museum of Fine Arts, Boston. 63p.

WiU   The World in Us; Lesbian and Gay Poetry of the Next Wave. *Elena Georgiou and Michael Lassell, eds.* (2000) St. Martin's Press. 392p.

WoPoe   World Poetry; an Anthology of Verse from Antiquity to Our Time. *Katharine Washburn and John S. Major, eds.* (1998) 1338p.

WoRP   Women Romantic Poets, 1785-1832; an Anthology. *Jennifer Breen, ed.* (1992) J. M. Dent & Sons. 182p.

WPE   The Women Poets in English; an Anthology. *Ann Stanford, ed.* (1972) McGraw-Hill. 374p., o.p.

WPoS   Women in Praise of the Sacred: 43 Centuries of Spiritual Poetry by Women. *Jane Hirshfield, ed.* (1994) HarperCollins Publishers. 259p.

WPOW   Women Poets of the World. *Joanna Bankier and Deirdre Lashgari, eds.* (1983) Macmillan. 442p., o.p.

WWork   Women Working; an Anthology of Stories and Poems. *Nancy Hoffman and Florence Howe, eds.* (1979) The Feminist Press. 269p.

YaYoPo   The Yale Younger Poets Anthology. *George Bradley, ed.* (1st ed., 1998) Yale University Press. 306 pp.

ZenPo   Zen Poetry. *Lucien Stryk and Takashi Ikemoto, eds.* (1st ed., 1995) Grove Press. 124p.

ABBREVIATIONS

abr.	abridged		*mod.*	modernized or modern
ad.	adapted		*N.T.*	New Testament
add.	additional		*O.T.*	Old Testament
arr.	arranged		*orig.*	original
at.	attributed		*par.*	paraphrase or paraphrased
Bk.	book		*pr.*	prose
br.	brief		*Pt.*	part
ch.	chapter		*rev.*	revised
comp.	compiled or compiler		*sc.*	scene
comps.	compilers		*Sec.*	section
cond.	condensed		*sel.*	selection
diff.	different		*sels.*	selections
fr.	from		*sl.*	slightly
frag.	fragment		*st.*	stanza
incl.	included or including		*sts.*	stanzas
introd.	introduction or introductory		*tr.*	translator, translation, or translated
ll.	lines		*trs.*	translators or translations
LL.	last line		*var.*	various
med.	medieval		*vers.*	version or versions
misc.	miscellaneous		*wr.*	wrong or wrongly

TITLE, FIRST LINE, AND LAST LINE INDEX

Titles, first lines, and last lines are arranged in one alphabetical listing in the Title, First Line, and Last Line Index. Titles are distinguished by initial capital letters on the important words. All first-line entries are followed by the title of the poem, if there is a title. When the title and the first line of a poem are identical, or nearly so, only one of them is listed, although occasionally, for purposes of clarity, the first line has been added in quotation marks and in parentheses to the title entry.

Anthology codes are listed after titles, first lines, and last lines. Last lines are distinguished from first lines by the symbol (LL). However, more complete information as to translators, acts and scenes, abridgments, and various titles is given in the title entry.

An indented citation indicates that the poem is a selection from the work listed one level above. A citation indented and inside parentheses indicates a variant title, variant first line, or variant last line as used in the anthologies that follow.

Generic title entries, such as Ode, Song, Sonnet, are followed by the first line in quotation marks for easy identification. Such entries, of course, may also be located by first-line listing.

Numerals in citations of poems by Horace refer to the Odes; *in citations of poems by Ovid, to the* Elegies; *and in citations of poems by Tennyson, to* In Memoriam A.H.H.

Titles and first lines beginning with "O" and "Oh" are filed separately, with cross-references where necessary. Names beginning "Mac," "Mc," and "M'" are filed in alphabetical order.

A

A.   Louis Zukofsky.
  "A" 4.   VGW
    "Giant sparkler, / Lights of the river."   VGW
  "A" 11.   APSN; APT-2; ColAP; VGW
  "A" 12.
    "In peace."   APT-2
    "Like Grandpa Paul / The water is all of my mind."   ChIV-1
    "Red horse, A."   PFTM-2
  "A" 15.
    "Hinny / by / stallion, An."   APSN
  "A" 18.
    "*He* has become as / talkative as Bottom a weaver and says for."   APSN
    "Unearthing / my valentine, An."   APSN
    "Weeping: the food he eats."   APSN
    "When they use elbow or arm boards to."   APSN
A, a, a, a / Yet I love whereso I go.   *Unknown.*   MiEL
A, a, a, Domine Deus.   David Jones.   FaBoTw; HarvBoo; NOCV
A B C.   Charles Stuart Calverley.   OBCoV
A, B, C, and D / Pray, playmates, agree.   Alphabet, The.   *Unknown.*   ReMoGo
A B C D.   *Unknown.*   OxNR
A B C D E F G H.   I've Got a Gal in Kalamazoo.   Harry Warren.   ReLy
A, B, C, D, E, F, G, Little Robin Redbreast.   *Unknown.*   OxNR
A—B—on the Learned Bartholo Sylva.   Anne Cooke Bacon.   EMWP
A Bas la Gloire!   Edward Wyndham Tennant.   FaBoWar
A-bide a- a.   Monk.   John Taggart.   FTOS; PFTM-2
A black, E white, I red, U green, O blue, vowels.   Voyelles.   Arthur Rimbaud.   WoPoe, *tr. by* F. Scott Fitzgerald
A black, E white, I red, U green, O blue: vowels.   Vowels.   Arthur Rimbaud.   SxFrPo, *tr. by* Martin Sorrell
A-clank to my stride. (LL)   Angry Samson.   Robert Graves.   ChIV-1; OxBEV
A. D. Blood.   Edgar Lee Masters.   APT-1   *Fr.* Spoon River Anthology.

A' day aboot the hoose I work.   Nocht o' Mortal Sicht.   Bessie J. B. Macarthur.   OxBS
A, dere God, what I am fayn.   *Unknown.*   MiEL
A. E. F.   Carl Sandburg.   MoAmPo
A. E. Housman.   W. H. Auden.   OxAEP-2
A. E. Housman and a Few Friends.   Humbert Wolfe.   UV
A-eee! Shee-yew! Sheeeeee! So dangerous! So high!   Road to Shu Is Hard, The.   Li Po.   WoPoe, *tr. by* Elling O. Eide
À fin all was strange.   Gravity and Grace.   Claudia Keelan.   BodElec
. . . a flight of fancy and breath of fresh air.   I Applied for the Board.   Jimmy Santiago Baca.   LoL
"A huge brightly lit ship emerges from the harbor," says K.   Brief History of the City.   Robert Peterson.   GeoHom
A.   "I was a Have." B.   "I was a 'Have-not.'"   Rudyard Kipling.   FaBoTw   *Fr.* Epitaphs of the War [1914–1918].
A is an Apple, as everyone knows.   Abecedary.   Thomas M. [*or* "Tom"] Disch.   OBCoV
A is for apron in plastic or cloth.   Edna's Alphabet.   Barry Humphries.   OBCoV
À l'Ange Avantgardien.   Francis Reginald.   MoCV
Á La Recherche.   Miklós Radnóti.   IQMS, *tr. by* Peter Zollman
A! Mercy, Fortune; have pitee on me.   *Unknown.*   MiEL
A mezzo-litro. Grazie, professore. (LL)   Richard Wilbur.   LCAP-2; NAAL-2v2; NoAM
A, my dere, a, my dere Son.   Mary Weeps for Her Child.   *Unknown.*   OxBoLi
A Nos Glorieux Morts.   Jan Eijkelboom.   TuT, *tr. by* Michael O'Loughlin
A peels an apple, while B kneels to God.   Primer of the Daily Round, A.   Howard Nemerov.   WeW-3
A Perigord pres del muralh.   Bertrans [*or* Bertran *or* Bertrand] de Born.   CTC, *tr. by* Ezra Pound
À Quoi Bon Dire.   Charlotte Mew.   MakPoe; NPeEn; OxBEV; OxBTC; VWP
A Says "You're right. He's brilliant but not sound."   In the Bistro.   Gwen Harwood.   FaBoWP
A-sitting on a gate. (LL)   Lewis Carroll.   FaBoCh; NAEL-5v2; NAEL-6v2; NOBE; NOBL; NoAM; NoP-4; PeLV; TFi; UV   *Fr.* Through the Looking-Glass.
A-Sitting on a Gate.   Lewis Carroll.   *See* Through the Looking-Glass

A. Smith, I. Brown and my own self. Dear Stars, Rock Me to Sleep. István Sinka. IQMS, *tr.* by Adam Makkai

A! Sone, tak hede to me whos sone thou wast. *Unknown.* OHMEL

A. Stands for Absolutely Anything. Noël Coward. NBLV *Fr.* Little Ones' A. B. C., The.

A stands for Archibald who told no lies. Joseph Hilaire Pierre Belloc. NoAM *Fr.* Moral Alphabet, A.

A-swell within her billowed skirts. Mad Woman of Punnet's Town, The. Leonard Alfred George Strong. MoBrPo

A Terre. Wilfred Owen. FaBoWar; OxBTC; PAI; PeFWW; PoWW

A. To start with, grapple your opponent 'round. Strato [*or* Straton]. CAGL, *tr.* by Daryl Hine

A-traipsin' from a shindig, I unsaddles. Agamemnon before Troy. John Frederick Nims. Son

A un Desconocido. Lorna Dee Cervantes. TouFir

A was an archer, who [*or* and] shot at a frog. *Unknown.* LB; OxNR

A-zellen meat-weare I shall get noo meat. Shop o' Meat-Weare. William Barnes. NOBVV

Aa's a broken-hairted keelman and Aa's ower heid in love. Cushie Butterfield. George Ridley. FaBoVe

Aa the skippers of bonny Lothen. Young Allan. *Unknown.* ESPB

Aa this while, Peter wis doun ablò i the yaird. Bible, *N.T.*. FaBoVe *Fr.* St. Mark.

Aaron. George Herbert. BASC; ChIV-1; FSCP; GeHe; MeLP; NOSC; PeECV; SacPr

Aaron Nicholas, Almost Ten. Janet Campbell Hale. VoR

Aaron Stark. Edwin Arlington Robinson. APN-2; MoAmPo; Son
  (Withal a meagre man was Aaron Stark.) NCAP

Aasvogel brolga colibri dickcissel. Bird Bee. Bob Cobbing. Oth

Abalone, like inkfish. Relaxed Abalone, The. Rosmarie Waldrop. InPK-6

Abandoing All Pretense, the Vandals. Alan Michael Parker. NAPBL

Abandon'd Day, why dost thou now appear? On My Wedding Day. Sarah Fyge Egerton. EMWP

Abandoned, The. Nathan [*or* Natan] Alterman. MHP, *tr.* by Ruth Finer Mintz

Abandoned, The. Zbigniew Herbert. PoSu, *tr.* by Michael March

Abandoned by my words I'm left alone. Jonah's Prayer. Mihály Babits. IQMS, *tr.* by Peter Zollman

Abandoned camps / pineapple breasts untouched. Rake, The. Abu Nuwas. ArPe, *tr.* by Omar S. Pound

Abandoned earthworks nobody tends. Su Tung-p'o (Su Shih). CoBCP *Fr.* Eastern Slope.

Abandoned Farmhouse. Ted Kooser. WeW-3

Abandoned in the grass. Southwest. Viktor Krivulin. TCRusP, *tr.* by Anna Barker and Daniel Weissbort

Abandoning the Plans of Visiting West Lake. Hsü Wei. SuSp, *tr.* by Irving Y. Lo

Abandoning Your Car in a Snowstorm: Rosslyn, Virginia. Michael C. Blumenthal. NoAM

Abandonment. Al-Zahra Al-Mansouri. PoArWo, *tr.* by Richard McKane and Tahia Abdel Nasser

Abandonment of Autos. Bruce Dawe. CBAP

Abate, fair fugitive, abate thy speed. Ovid. NOEC, *tr.* by Matthew Prior *Fr.* Metamorphoses.

Abattoir, The. Ania Walwicz. BMAP

Abbé rambles—Marquis, I think you'll find, The. On the Grass. Paul Verlaine. SxFrPo, *tr.* by Martin Sorrell

Abbey Church at Bath, The. Henry Harington. FaBoEE

Abbey Cwmhir. Harri Webb. AngWePo

Abbienti. Steven C. Levi. GotH

Abbot John. Fulbert of Chartres. MLL, *tr.* by Helen Waddell

Abbot John, in stature small, The. Abbot John. Fulbert of Chartres. MLL, *tr.* by Helen Waddell

Abt Vogler. Robert Browning. FHYEP; NAEL-5v2; NAEL-6v2; TOF

Abbott's Lagoon. Dennis Schmitz. GeoHom

Abbreviated serpent among crystal rocks. Capture of Larache, The. Luis de Góngora y Argote. SpanPo, *tr.* by Frances Fletcher

ABC, An. *Unknown.* OBCA *Fr.* New England Primer, The.

Abdelazer. Aphra Behn.
  "Love in fantastic [*or* fantastique] triumph sat [*or* sate *or* satt]." BASC; NALW; NOBE; NOSC; NPeEn; NoP-4; OBEV; OxAEP-1; OxBEV; PEW; WPE; WeW-3
  Song: Love Armed [*or* Arm'd]. BASC; NALW; NOBE; NOSC; NPeEn; NoP-4; OBEV; OxAEP-1; OxBEV; PEW; WPE; WeW-3

Abduction, The. Stanley Kunitz. WeW-3

Abecedary. Thomas M. [*or* "Tom"] Disch. OBCoV

Abecedary of slaughter. Europa. Anatol Stern. PFTM-1

Abel. Demetrios Capetanakis. GTBS-P

Abel. John Wheelwright. ChIV-1

Abel and Abel. Silvio Giussani. ItPo, *tr.* by Gayle Ridinger

Abel's Blood. Henry Vaughan. OBWVE

Abel's Bride. Denise Levertov. FaBoWP; NALW; VGW

Abelard to Eloisa. Judith Madan. RACG

Abelard was: God is. Sic et Non. Sir Herbert Read. FaBoTw

Abenamar, Abenamar. *Unknown.* AWP, *tr.* by Robert Southey

Aberdarcy: The Chaucer Road. Kingsley Amis. NOBL *Fr.* Evans Country, The.

Aberdarcy: The Main Square. Kingsley Amis. NOBL; NoAM; OxBTC *Fr.* Evans Country, The.

Aberdare, Llanwynno through. Glyn Cynon Wood. *Unknown.* OBWVE, *tr.* by Gwyn Williams

Aberdeen. Robin Robertson. NePenScot

Abeulo, why are there flies? Abuelo, Answers and Questions. Maurice Kilwein Guevara. TouFir

Abhorring a Vacuum. Chris Wallace-Crabbe. BMAP

Abide, gud men, and hald your pays. *Unknown.* MiEL

Abide in Me, O Lord, and I in Thee. Harriet Beecher Stowe. AH

Abide Not in the Realm of Dreams. William Henry Burleigh. AH

Abide With Me. Henry Francis Lyte. EBVV; InvLi; NOCV; PWR

Abiding Mountain. Muso Soseki. EaWin, *tr.* by W. S. Merwin

Abiku. J. P. Clark Bekedermo. HBAPE; PBMAP *Fr.* Reed in the Tide, A.

Abiku. Wole Soyinka. PBA; PBMAP; PoetW

Ability to Make a Face Like a Spider While Singing Blues: Junior Wells, The. Sandra McPherson. SeSe

Abiquiu. Luis Lopez. GeoH

Abishag. Jacob [*or* Jakov] Fichman. TrJP, *tr.* by Sholom J. Kahn

Abishag. Rainer Maria Rilke. AWP, *tr.* by Jethro Bithell

Abishag. André Spire. TrJP, *tr.* by Emanuel Eisenberg

Abla. *Var.* authors. AWP, *tr.* by E. Powys Mathers *Fr.* Mu'allaqat, The.

Ablaze in reddened clouds there stood the morning. Day of the Landscape, The. Alfred Margul-Sperber. AuPH, *tr.* by Lowell A. Bangerter

Ablution. Angelina Muñiz Huberman. MirDau, *tr.* by Aurora Camacho

Abnegation. Adrienne Rich. WPE

Abner Silver's "Pu-leeze! Mr. Hemingway!" Ring Lardner. OBAL

Abnormal Is Not Courage, The. Jack Gilbert. CoAP; YaYoPo

Aboard a Boat at Night, Drinking with My Wife. Harry Mathews. CoBCP, *tr.* by Burton Watson

Aboard a Boat at Night, Drinking with My Wife. Mei Yao Ch'en. CoBCP, *tr.* by Burton Watson

Aboard at a Ship's Helm. Walt Whitman. APN-1; NOBA; OxBA

Abode of Arrival. Ahmed Taha. NAfrP, *tr.* by Clarissa C. Burt

Abode of the nightingale is bare, The. Alone. Walter De la Mare. EnLoPo

Abolished, and its weeks spent walking aimlessly. Where When Was. Reginald Shepherd. GT

Abomination. Mary Crockett Hill. AmPoNex

Abomination of Evil, The. "Angelus Silesius." GePo, *tr.* by George C. Schoolfield *Fr.* Cherubical Wanderer, The.

Aboriginal achievement. Ernie Dingo. IBA

Aboriginal Australia. Jack Davis. IBA

Aboriginal Reserve. Jack Davis. IBA

Aborigine Sound Poem. *Unknown.* PFTM-1

Abortion. Ai. BoWoP

Abortion. Iman Mirsal. NAfrP, *tr.* by Clarissa C. Burt

Abortion, An. Frank O'Hara. TAP

Abortion, The. Anne Sexton. LCAP-2; VGW

Abortions will not let you forget. Gwendolyn Brooks. ESEAA; ISC; IllVoic; NAAAL; NAAL-5; NALW; PoPoPo *Fr.* Street in Bronzeville, A.

Abou Ben Adhem. Leigh Hunt. BRP; ChAP; ITBLP; NOBE; OBEV; OxAEP-2; PWR; TFi
  (Abou Ben Adhem and the Angel.) TreFP

Abou Ben Adhem and the Angel. Leigh Hunt. *See* Abou Ben Adhem

About a fly. Story, The. Charles Simic. NNaP

About a Hat. Alexander Ilyich Bezymensky [*or* Bezymenskii]. TCRP, *tr.* by Daniel Weissbort

About a Transdanurban Almond Tree. Janus Pannonius. IQMS, *tr.* by Adam Makkai

About a year has passed. I've returned to the place of battle. Elegy. Joseph Brodsky. AF, *tr.* by Joseph Brodsky

About all these I write freely. Other Life, The. Nina Cassian. PoSu, *tr.* by Cristian Andrei and Daniel Weissbort

About an Excavation. Charles Reznikoff. NTCP; VGW

About Atlanta. Ntozake Shange. ISC

About beef, for instance? Christmas. Leigh Hunt. OBCP

About Children. Phyllis McGinley. OBAL

About cruelty yet. (LL) W.C.W. Watching Presley's Second Appearance on The Ed Sullivan Show: Mercy Hospital, Newark, 1956. David Wojahn. AllShUp; SwNoth

About eight of us were nailing up forts. Words for My Daughter. John Balaban. RaBo

About Face. Alice Fulton. AllShUp

About Geese. Li Shang-yin. SuSp, *tr. by* Eugene Eoyang

About him, and lies down to pleasant dreams. (LL) William Cullen Bryant. APN-1; AWP; BRP; ColAP; NAAL-2v1; NAAL-3; NAAL-5; NCAP; NOBA; OBEV; OxBA; PoToHe; PWR; TAP; TreFP; TCAPo; TFi *Fr.* Thanatopsis.

About Horse. Li Ho.

"Last month of the year, grass roots taste sweet." SuSp

"Master dragon-tamer has fled the world, The." SuSp

About Ice. Malcolm Lowry. OxBSo

About love it has no right. (LL) I Am with Those. Ingrid Jonker. BoWoP; HAWP, *tr. by* Jack Cope and William Plomer

About Marriage. Denise Levertov. NALW

About Menophila's morals there are strange rumours. Argentarius. GrAn

About Mount Uludağ. Nazim Hikmet. WoPoe, *tr. by* Randy Blasing and Mutlu Konuk

About my crevice and burrow. (LL) Drumlin Woodchuck, A. Robert Frost. APT-1; NOBA; NoAM

About My Grandfather. József Kiss.

"Make haste slowly, my friend, make haste slowly." IQMS, *tr. by* Anthony Edkins

About our hips. Harriet Jacobs. SpirFl

About suffering they were never wrong. Musée des Beaux Arts. W. H. Auden. CABP; ClHu; GS; GTBS-P; HAP; HeIP-4; InPK-6; NAEL-5v2; NAEL-6v2; NIL-7; NOBE; NPeEn; NoAM; NoP-4; OxAEP-2; OxBEV; PAI; PoE; PoPoPo; PoRA; RaBo; SCV; SoSe-8; TFi; TRP; TrCP; TwCP

About ten days or so. Reassurance, The. Thom Gunn. NPeEn

About ten million years ago. Speck Speaks, A. Adrian Mitchell. OBSP

About the bush, Willie. *Unknown.* ReMoGo

About the Cool Water. Sappho. OBVE; PGA, *tr. by* Kenneth Rexroth

About the field / Crow moves. Issa. ZenPo, *tr. by* Takashi Ikemoto and Lucien Stryk

About the glimmering weirs. (LL) A. E. Housman. AWP; NPeEn

About the grave / Waves of spring mist. Naito Joso. ZenPo, *tr. by* Takashi Ikemoto and Lucien Stryk

About the house a multitude of moths. Sunflower. Leonid Nikolaevich Martynov. TCRP, *tr. by* J. R. Rowland

About the little chambers of my heart. Gone. Mary Elizabeth Coleridge. OBEV; PoBW; VWP

About the Men. Adele Ne Jame. PoArWo

About the pain the folk. Your Name is Gift. Stella P. Chipasula. HAWP

About the Phoenix. James Merrill. NoAM

About the Princes. András Szkhárosi Horvát.

"You live in dishonor grave, Dukes and Mighty Princes." IQMS, *tr. by* Adam Makkai

About the Shark, phlegmatical one. Maldive Shark, The. Herman Melville. APN-2; ColAP; NAAL-2v1; NAAL-3; NCAP; NOBA; NoP-4; OxBA; PAI; PoE; RB; TAP; TCAPo

About the Shipwrecked Frandus. Janus Pannonius. IQMS, *tr. by* Iain MacLeod

About the size of an old-style dollar bill. Poem: "About the size of an old-style dollar bill." Elizabeth Bishop. HCAP; NoAM; PoPoPo; PoetW; VCAP

About the Teeth of Sharks. John Ciardi. OBCA; OxIBACP

About the tow'r an' churchyard wall. Echo, The. William Barnes. SCGP

About the worth of happiness. Valentin's Song. Ferdinand Raimund. AuPH, *tr. by* Lowell A. Bangerter

About this lady many fruitful trees. Lady with the Unicorn, The. Vernon Watkins. TwCP

About this time streetlamps flicker up like. Ken Edwards. Oth *Fr.* Five Nocturnes, after Derek Jarman.

About this unimportant Peer. (LL) Lord Heygate. Joseph Hilaire Pierre Belloc. OBCoV; OxBoLi

About this Woman. Judith Rodriguez. BMAP

About Time. Laurens Vancrevel. TuT, *tr. by* Greg Delanty

About Time. Laurens Vancrevel. TuT, *tr. by* Anne Kennedy

About to leave, yet by the lamplight she lingers. Chou Pang-yen. SuSp *Fr.* Tune: "Beautiful Lady Yü, The."

About Tu Fu. Li Po. CrYelRi, *tr. by* Sam Hamill

About twilight we came to the whitewashed pub. East Coast Journey. James Keir Baxter. NoP-4; PeNZ

About Two Kinds of Faith: That of Christ and That of the Pope's Ragged Patchwork. András Szkhárosi Horvát.

"Hurry up, Christendom, think about salvation." IQMS, *tr. by* Adam Makkai

About two miles east of here. King Cobra as Political Assassin, The. Ray A. Young Bear. HATNAP

About us. Rest shall we. (LL) Impercipient, The. Thomas Hardy. EBVV; NAEL-5v2; NAEL-6v2

About women no one can know. There are some. Mary Magdalene. Saunders Lewis. OBWVE, *tr. by* Gwyn Morgan

About Yule, when [*or* quhen] the wind blew cule. Young Waters. *Unknown.* ESPB; OxBB

Above a ceiling of emerald junipers. Dry Spell of Faith, A. Timothy Geiger. AmPoNex

Above, a mountain ten thousand feet high. Alarm at First Entering the Yangtze Gorges. Po Chü-i. ChiP, *tr. by* Arthur Waley

Above a stretch of still unravaged weald. Garden Party, The. Donald Davie. OxBEV

Above, above. Behold. *Unknown.* WoPoe, *tr. by* Alfons L. Korn, Mary Kawena Pukui and M. K. Pukui

Above all, define standards. Neocolonialism. Felix Mnthali. PeSAV

Above all gifts we most should prize. Walter Savage Landor. FaBoEE

Above all guard yourself against bitterness, black child. Black City, The. Breyten Breytenbach. PoetW, *tr. by* Sonia Van Schalwyk and Leon de Kock

Above all rivers thy river hath renown. William Dunbar. *See* London, thou art of townes

Above an empty heart. (LL) He Resigns. John Berryman. HarvBoo; OxBSP; WeW-3

Above, below, in sky and sod. Over-Heart, The. John Greenleaf Whittier. ChIV-2; NOCV

Above everything, I make a jagged, blue edge. Easter Revolt Painted on a Tablespoon, The. Maurice Kilwein Guevara. TouFir

Above her face. 1815. Jeffrey Wainwright. NPeEn

Above high-tide mark on the long beach. Half Measures. Thomas McGrath. BodElec

Above his dreamy abstract stare. (LL) Ex-Queen Among the Astronomers, The. Fleur Adcock. FaBoWP; NAEL-6v2; NALW; NoP-4

Above It All. Philip Levine. NOBA

Above, it's spring, I think. Poem for R. Kim Ly Bui-Burton. PasH

Above me no seraphim or nymphs. On Being Kicked Out of the Harold Washington Library Center for Napping on the Floor. Thom Ward. OPRER

Above me the abbey, grey arches on the cliff. Caedmon. Norman Nicholson. FaBoTw

Above my desk / the Rabbi of Auschwitz. On a Drawing by Flavio. Philip Levine. BodElec

Above my head, as I sleep, are. Limpopo. Walter Battiss. PeSAV

Above Pate Valley. Gary Snyder. CoAP; CoAmPo; GeoHom; LCAP-2; NoP-4; TRP

Above the baby powder clouds. Spring Evening. Frederick Turner. RA

Above the boat. Kikaku. BLT; ZenPo, *tr. by* Takashi Ikemoto and Lucien Stryk

Above the Boca del Arno the sky. Outside Pisa. Chitra Divakaruni. OpBo

Above the brink. Lethe. Mary Barnard. APT-2

Above the Circus of the World she sat. Rome. Madison Cawein. APN-2

Above the city of White Emperor the clouds leave by the city gate. City of White Emperor, The. Tu Fu. SuSp, *tr. by* Wu-Chi Liu

Above the corner of Water and Seventeenth, when pigeons. Rooftop. James Kimbrell. AmPoNex

Above the Crags that fade and gloom. From a Window in Princes Street. William Ernest Henley. EBVV

Above the creek dallies a bright moon. Quatrain: "Above the creek dallies a bright moon." Yüan Hao-wen. SuSp, *tr. by* Irving Y. Lo

Above the Dock. Thomas Ernest Hulme. FaBoMo; GTBS-P

Above the fence. Shukyo. JDP, *tr. by* Yoel Hoffmann

Above the field drowses the kite. Kite, The. Aleksandr Aleksandrovich Blok. PeFWW, *tr. by* David McDuff

Above the Fray Is Only Thin Air. A. R. Ammons. BodElec

Above the freeway, over the music. Jazz Station. Michael S. Harper. NoAM

Above the fresh ruffles of the surf. Hart Crane. APT-2; CAGL; ColAP; NAAL-2v1; NAAL-5; NOBA; NoAM; OxBA; PoE; TAP; VGW; WoPoe *Fr.* Voyages.

Above the High. Geoffrey Grigson. EnLoPo

Above the hood of an illegally parked red Toyota Corolla. I Found Orpheus Levitating. Nick Carbó. NAPBL; ReBoTo

Above the Lake. Aleksandr Aleksandrovich Blok. TCRP, *tr. by* Geoffrey Thurley

Above the lake the sun is high. On The Reedy Lake. János Vajda. IQMS, *tr. by* Jean Overton Fuller

Above the Pool. John Montague. NOIV

Above the pools, above the valley of fears. Élévation. Charles Baudelaire. AWP, *tr. by* Arthur Symons

Above the quiet dock in midnight. Above the Dock. Thomas Ernest Hulme. FaBoMo; GTBS-P

Above the spleen of the landscape. July. Julio Herrera y Reissig. TCLAP, *tr. by* Andrew Rosing

Above the Timberline. Alan Michael Parker. AmPoNex

Above the Tree. Elizabeth Stoddard. SWaP

Above the twelve mountains autumn grasses fade. Bamboo Branch Song. Ho Ching-ming. CoBLCP, *tr. by* Jonathan Chaves

Above the voiceful windings of a river. At the Grave of Henry Vaughan. Siegfried Sassoon. GTBS-P

Above the walls the west light hangs, until. Walled Garden. Dorothy Wellesley, Duchess of Wellington. OBGa

Above the waste allotments the dawn halts. (LL) Light Breaks Where No Sun Shines. Dylan Thomas. FaBoMo; MoBrPo; OxAEP-2; OxBEV; OxBTC

Above the whispering sea. Air Raid Across the Bay at Plymouth. Stephen Spender. AF

Above the white pond. Decline. Georg Trakl. WoPoe, *tr. by* Robert Firmage

Above the white pond. Downfall. Georg Trakl. AF, *tr. by* Daniel Simko

Above the window a gray obelisk hangs. Sterile Dish, The. Lenka Valachová. SurWo, *tr. by* Katerina Pinosová

Above the yellow Offices of State. Petersburg Strophes. Osip Emilevich Mandelstam [*or* Mandelshtam]. TCRP, *tr. by* Bernard Meares

Above them spread a stranger sky. Indian's Welcome to the Pilgrim Fathers, The. Lydia Huntley Sigourney. TCAPo

Above, through lunar woods a goddess flees. Lovers, The. William Jay Smith. MoAmPo

Above Us. Julia Hartwig. BLT, *tr. by* Stanislaw Baranczak

Above us, stars. Beneath us, constellations. Flying at Night. Ted Kooser. InPK-6; PBCAP

Above Vitebsk. Shirley Kaufman. TaR

Above yon sombre swell of land. Plough, The. Richard Henry [*or* Hengist] Horne. OBEV

Above, you paint the sky. How to Paint a Perfect Christmas. Miroslav Holub. OBCP, *tr. by* Ian Milner and George Theiner

Abraham. Edwin Muir. ChIV-1

Abraham. Delmore Schwartz. ChIV-1; TaR

Abraham and Isaac. Else Lasker-Schüler. BoWoP

Abraham built a town of sod. Abraham and Isaac. Else Lasker-Schüler. BoWoP

Abraham Davenport. John Greenleaf Whittier. NoP-4; TCAPo

Abraham Got All the Stars N the Sand. Ruth Forman. AmPoNex

Abraham Lincoln. William Cullen Bryant. *See* Death of Lincoln, The

Abraham Lincoln. Mildred Plew Meigs. CA

Abraham Lincoln Walks at Midnight. Nicholas Vachel Lindsay. APT-1; CBCWP; IllVoic; MoAmPo; NOBA; OxBA; TAP; TCAPo; TFi; VGW

Abraham's children played with shells. Hagar and Ishmael. Else Lasker-Schüler. BoWoP

Abraham's Madness. Bink Noll. ChIV-1

Abraham's Sacrifice of Isaac. Sir John Stradling. NOSC

Abraham to kill him. Emily Dickinson. ChIV-1; SoSe-8

Abram Brown. *Unknown*. OxNR

Abroad in the meadows to see the young lambs. Innocent Play. Isaac Watts. NOEC

Abroad Thoughts. Edward Blishen. NOBL

Abrupt and charming mover. Stephen Spender. CAGL

Absalom and Achitophel. Dryden. BASC; FHYEP; HAP; NAEL-5v1; NAEL-6v1; NAEL-7v1; NOSC; PoE

 (Achitophel.) AWP

 Achitophel: The Earl of Shaftsbury. NOBE

 "In pious times ere [*or* e'r] priest-craft did begin." FHYEP; HAP; MakPoe; NOSC; PoE

 (Monmouth.) NPeEn

 "Numerous host of dreaming saints succeed, A." NOBE; OBSV

 "Of these the false Achitophel was first." HAP; NOBE; OxBEV

 (Shaft[e]sbury.) NOSC

 Shaftesbury. NPeEn

 "So several factions from this first ferment." NOBE

 "Some by their friends, more by themselves thought wise." ChIV-1; OBSV

 "Some of their chiefs were princes of the land." EBEV; OxBEV; SCV

 "This Plot, which fail'd for want of common Sense." NPeEn

 "With all these loads of injuries opprest." EBEV

 Zimri: "In the first rank of These did Zimri stand" HAP

 (Zimri: "Numerous host of dreaming saints succeed") AWP

 (Zimri: "Some of their chiefs were princes of the land") AWP

 Zimri: The Duke of Buckingham. NOBE; OBSV

Absalom and Achitophel, Part 2. Dryden.

 "Doeg, though without knowing how or why." FHYEP

 "Now stop you noses, Readers, all and come." AWP

 Og [and Doeg]. AWP

 "To make quick way I'll leap o'er heavy blocks." OBSV

Absence. Elizabeth Cobbold. CenSon *Fr.* Sonnets of Laura.

Absence. John Hoskyns [*or* Hoskins]. MeLP

 (Ode.) SCGP

(Present in Abscence.) GTBS-P

Absence. Jaime Jacinto. ReBoTo

Absence. Richard Jago. OBEV

Absence. Frances Anne [*or* "Fanny"] Kemble.

 "What shall I do with all the days and hours." PoToHe

 What Shall I Do? PoToHe

Absence. Charlotte Mew. MoBrPo

Absence. Gabriela Mistral. SpanPo, *tr. by* Kate Flores

Absence. William Shakespeare. *See* Sonnets

Absence. Shinkichi Takahashi. ZenPo, *tr. by* Takashi Ikemoto and Lucien Stryk

Absence, The. Sylvia Townsend Warner. MoBrPo

Absence / Can you imagine. Can You Imagine. Artur Miedzyrzecki. PoSu, *tr. by* Stanislaw Baranczak

Absence, hear[e] [thou] my protestation. Absence. John Hoskyns [*or* Hoskins]. MeLP

Absence, Luminescent. Valerie Martínez. TouFir

Absence of the Soul. Federico García Lorca. WoPoe, *tr. by* Alan S. Trueblood *Fr.* Lament for Ignacio Sanchez Mejias.

Absences. Philip Larkin. OxBEV

Absent, The. Edwin Muir. NoAM

Absent, The. May Muzaffar. PoArWo, *tr. by* Tahia Abdel Nasser

Absent from Dances 1925. Stephanie Strickland. ExTi

Absent from thee, I languish still. Song: "Absent from thee, I languish still." John Wilmot, 2d Earl of Rochester. BoLoP; EnLoPo; NPeEn; OxBEV

Absent Lover. *Unknown*. PBA, *tr. by* A. C. Jordan

Absent-Minded Beggar, The. Rudyard Kipling. FaBoWar

Absent Ones, The. Maxine W. Kumin. PAI

Absent ones whisper and the night is dense, The. Night is the. Deaf Lantern. Alejandra Piznarnick. MirDau, *tr. by* Celeste Kostopulos-Cooperman

Absentia Animi. Gunnar Ekelof. PFTM-1

Absentmindedly. 529 1983. Gerda Mayer. Spl

Absinthe-Drinker, The. Arthur Symons. FaBoTw; NOBVV

Absinthe, green, bewitching moon. Good Friday. João da Cruz e Sousa. TCLAP, *tr. by* Flavia Vidal

Absolute dark; and if you say, A cloud, The. Mutations. Robert Fitzgerald. APT-2

Absolute September. Mary Jo Salter. ExTi

Absolute zero: the locust sings. Summer. Conrad Potter Aiken. NoAM

Absolutely Abstemious Ass, The. Twenty-Six Nonsense Rhymes. Edward Lear. RB

Absolutely Ordinary Rainbow, An. Les A. Murray. CBAP; HarvBoo

Absolution. Diane Ward. FTOS

Absorption of Rock. Maxine Hong Kingston. OpBo

Abstaining from the congregation. Yom Kippur, 5726. Cynthia Ozick. TaR

Abstinence Sows Sand All Over. William Blake. EBEV; FaBoEE; OxBEV *Fr.* Gnomic Verses.

Abstract. Sam Hamill. BodElec

Abstracted by silence from the age of seven. On Himself. David Wright. OPOU

Abstracted, sour, as he reaches across a dish. Scylla and Charybdis. Thomas Kinsella. OxBTC

Abstraction. Eleanor Wilner. ExTi

Abstracts hover like dull angels, The. Magi. Sylvia Plath. GI

Abstruse Buddhahood and Taoist immortality are both unattainable. Mixed Emotions. Huang Ching-jen. SuSp, *tr. by* Chang Yin-nan

Abu. Dudley Randall. BPo

Abu Nowas for the Barmacides. *Unknown*. AWP *Fr.* Thousand and One Nights, The.

Abu Salim, Healer. Rachel Tzvia Back. DTA

Abuelo, Answers and Questions. Maurice Kilwein Guevara. TouFir

Abundance. John Cage. APSN *Fr.* Diary: How to Improve the World (You Will Only Make Matters Worse).

Abundance. Carl Phillips. PuP-23

Abundant Catch (Luke 5:4–10). Czeslaw Milosz. GI

Abundantly. In His Name / Phillis. (LL) Letter from Phillis Wheatley, A. Robert Earl Hayden. ESEAA; NAAAL; NoAM

Abuse Poems: For Kodzo and Others. Komi Ekpe. PFTM-2, *tr. by* Kofi Awoonor

Abused Child. Michael O'Reilly. BloBone

Abysmal circle is in the sky, An. At the moment we are an infinite line, Sabah Al-Kharrat Zwein. PoArWo, *tr. by* Kaissar Afif *Fr.* As If in Flaw, or in the Flaw of Space.

Abysmal corners will dis (be) located. Vitality. Maria Amalia Fonte Boa. BoWoP, *tr. by* Willis Barnstone and Nelson Cerqueira

Abyss. Diane Di Prima. BB

Abyss of Death, The. Ma'ruf Al-Rasafi. MAP, *tr. by* Issa Boullata and Christopher Middleton

AC. Geraldine Monk. Oth

Acacia is drooping, The. Girl from Rafah. Samih Al-Qasim. MAP, *tr. by* Charles Doria and Sharif Elmusa

Academia; or The Humours of the University of Oxford. Alicia D'Anvers.
"Hail peaceful Shade, whose sacred verdant side." NOSC
To the University. NOSC

Academic. Theodore Roethke. FaBoEE; OBAL

Academic Graffiti. W. H. Auden.
"Henry Adams / Was mortally afraid of Madams." OBAL

Academies like structures in a mist, The. (LL) Wallace Stevens. ColAP; NOBA *Fr.* Notes toward a Supreme Fiction.

Academy of the future is opening its doors, The. Ted Berrigan. PFTM-2 *Fr.* Sonnets, The.

Accelerated leaf fall October looks like. It Is Difficult to Exaggerate the Importance of Mushrooms as Food. Chris Torrance. Oth

Accentuate the Positive. Johnny Mercer. ReLy

Accept, Boscawen, these unpolished lays. Sacred Dramas. Hannah More. RWP

Accept from me not silence. Edouard J. Maunick. NegPo *Fr.* As Far as Yoruba Land.

Accept, much honoured shade! the artless lays. On the Death of Mrs. Rowe. Elizabeth Carter. ECWP

Accept My Full Heart's Thanks. Ella Wheeler Wilcox. PoToHe

Accept, my God, the praises which I bring. Offering: Part One, The. Mary Lee, Lady Chudleigh. WPE

Accept, my love, as true a heart. Les Estreines. Matthew Prior. OxBSP

Accept, O Priapus, the moister. Catullus. PriapPo, *tr. by* Richard W. Hooper

Accept the university of death. (LL) Gwendolyn Brooks. NAAAL; WPE *Fr.* Womanhood, The.

Accept thou Shrine of my Dead Saint! Henry King, Bishop of Chichester. HAP; MeLP; NAEL-6v1; SCGP

Acceptance. Robert Frost. GSo; OxBA

Acceptance. John Wieners. FTOS

Accepting. Motion of the Cypher. Ray DiPalma. FTOS

Accessories shop, The. Pierre McOrlan. MFP, *tr. by* Martin Sorrell

Accident, An. Frank A. Cross. CDa

Accident, The. Liz Rosenberg. PBCAP

Accident in Art. Richard Hovey. APN-2

Accidental Meeting with an Old Friend While Traveling at Night, An. Tai Shu-lun. SuSp, *tr. by* William H. Nienhauser

Accidents will happen by land and by sea. William McGonagall. VerBaPo *Fr.* Clepington Catastrophe, The.

Acclaim the dawn of Mother's Day! Mother's Day. Edwin Becker. PWR

Acclamation, An. John Davies. SacPr

Accommodating Lion, An. Tudor Jenks. OBCA

Accompani'd with thine. (LL) Soldier Going to the Field, The. Sir William Davenant [*or* D'Avenant]. FaBoWar; NOBE; OBWP

Accompanying a Gift. Lizelia Augusta Jenkins Moorer. CBWP-3

Accomplices. Bei Dao. AF, *tr. by* Bonnie S. McDougall

Accomplices. Zhao Zhenkai. VCWP

Accomplices, The. Conrad Potter Aiken. NOBA

According to Brueghel. William Carlos Williams. LCAP-2; NAAL-2v2; NAAL-5; NoAM *Fr.* Pictures from Brueghel.

According to *Culture Shock.* Yes. Denise Duhamel. AmPoNex

According to Dineen, a Gael unsurpassed. From the Irish. Ian Duhig. NeBl

According to metaphysical creed. Thomas Hood. EBVV *Fr.* Miss Kilmansegg and Her Precious Leg.

According to my Mood. Benjamin Zephaniah. NOxBChV

According to my Teachers. Gwendolyn Brooks. ESEAA *Fr.* Children Going Home.

According to old Sigmund Freud. Limerick: "According to old Sigmund Freud." *Unknown.* PeLi

According to our Code of Honor. From a Revolutionary to J. L. Borges. Roque Dalton. TCLAP, *tr. by* Julie Schumacher

According to some learn'd opinions. Irish Antiquities. Thomas Moore. FaBoEE

According to the classification born a woman. Femmemasochism. Alicia Galaz Vivar. TANSG, *tr. by* Dave Oliphant

According to the director. Happy and Unhappy Families 2. Lisel Mueller. ExTi

Accordionist, The. Vasily [*or* Vasilii] Vasilevich Kazin. TCRP, *tr. by* Daniel Weissbort

Account, An. Mick North. NLP

Account of the Cruelty of the Papists, An. Benjamin Harris. SCAP

Accountability. Paul Laurence Dunbar. APN-2

Accountability. William Stafford. LCAP-2

ACCOUNTED our commodities. Quiet Neighbour, A. John Heywood. NoSic

Accounting. Claribel Alegría. TANSG, *tr. by* Darwin Flakoll

Accounting Cat, The. John Clarke. UV

Accoutrement. "Marnia." LW

Accretion / dispossession. Object of Burial Is Intent, The. Rebecca Reynolds. AmPoNex

Accross the fallow clods at early morn. Pewits Nest. John Clare. FaBoVe

Accursed power which stands on Privilege, The. On a General Election. Joseph Hilaire Pierre Belloc. FaBoEE; NOBE; NOBL; NPeEn; OBSV; OxBEV; OxBTC

Accursed. The curse which with its curving unsheathed letter will never. Nigger in a Photograph, The. Ece Ayhan. PFTM-2, *tr. by* Murat Nemet-Nejat

Accurst [*or* accursed], and in a cursed [*or* cursed] hour he hies. (LL) John Milton. FHYEP; NAEL-5v1; NAEL-6v1; OxAEP-1 *Fr.* Paradise Lost.

Accuse me not, beseech thee, that I wear. Elizabeth Barrett Browning. CenSon *Fr.* Sonnets from the Portuguese.

Accuser, The. Shirley Kaufman. GifTon

Ace of spades. Poem. "Paul Dermée." CuPo

Acer. Peter Finch. AngWePo

Achaian Invasion of Sparta, The. *Unknown.* GrAn, *tr. by* Peter Jay

Ache of it, The. (LL) Ache of Marriage, The. Denise Levertov. ColAP; InPK-6; NALW; NOBA; NoAM; PmAP; PoM; PoPoPo; TAP; VCAP

Ache of love! (LL) On the Beach at Fontana. James Joyce. MoBrPo; OBMV; RB; RaBo

Ache of Marriage, The. Denise Levertov. ColAP; InPK-6; NALW; NOBA; NoAM; PmAP; PoM; PoPoPo; TAP; VCAP

Achill. Derek Mahon. BiHa; PBCIP; PNI

Achill Woman, The. Eavan Boland. BiHa; HarvBoo

Achilles. John Gay.
"Soldier, think before you marry." PeLV
Song: "Think of dress in every light." OxBSP

Achilles and Priam. Homer. NAWM-7v1, *tr. by* Robert Fagles *Fr.* Iliad, The.

Achilles and the Tortoise. Miroslav Holub. PoSu, *tr. by* Stuart Friebert

Achilles' baneful wrath resound, O goddess, that imposed. Homer. NOSC, *tr. by* George Chapman *Fr.* Iliad, The.

Achilles' Dream. Homer. CAGL, *tr. by* Emile Victor Rieu *Fr.* Iliad, The.

Achilles' Lament and the Funeral of Patroclus. Homer. CAGL, *tr. by* Emile Victor Rieu *Fr.* Iliad, The.

Achilles Over the Trench. Homer. OBVE, *tr. by* Alfred Tennyson, 1st Baron Tennyson *Fr.* Iliad, The.

Achilles' Song. Robert Duncan. FTOS

Achilles with wild fury in his heart. Homer. OBWP *Fr.* Iliad, The.

Aching nostalgia. *Unknown.* OHMPJ

Aching. Speech / is a mouth. (LL) Language, The. Robert Creeley. PmAP; TAP

Achitophel. Dryden. AWP *Fr.* Absalom and Achitophel.

Achitophel: The Earl of Shaftsbury. Dryden. NOBE *Fr.* Absalom and Achitophel.

Achtung. Thomas Hardy. *See* Sapphic Fragment

Acid for the whorls of the fingertips; for the face, a surgeon's knife; oblivion to the name. Escape. Kenneth Fearing. APT-2

Acid today / is trendy entertainment. Why I Choose Black Men for My Lovers. La Loca. CLPP

Acis and Galatea. John Gay.
Air: "O ruddier than the cherry!" NAEL-5v1; NAEL-6v1; NOEC
"I rage, I melt, I burn." NAEL-5v1; NAEL-6v1
(Song: "O ruddier than the cherry") NOBE

Ackermann Steppe, The. Adam Mickiewicz. WoPoe, *tr. by* Vyt Bakaitis

Acknowledgement. Keorapetse Kgositsile. SeSe

Acme and Septimius. Catullus. *See* Carmina

Acne blossoms scarlet on their cheeks. Porirua Friday Night. Sam Hunt. PeNZ

Acoma. William Oandasan. HATNAP

Acon. "H. D.". VGW

Acorn, The. Gail Mazur. ExTi

Acorn Song, The. *Unknown.* APN-2, *tr. by* Stephen Powers *Fr.* Sacred Songs of the Konkau.

Acorn Speaks, The. Theo Sontrop. TuT, *tr. by* Theo Dorgan

Acorns come down from heaven, the. *Unknown.* APN-2, *tr. by* Stephen Powers *Fr.* Sacred Songs of the Konkau.

Acquaintance with Time in Early Autumn. Robert Penn Warren. NAAL-5

Acquainted with the Night. Robert Frost. APT-1; AWTN; AmFaPo; GSo; HAP; HarvBoo; MoAmPo; NOBA; NoAM; NoP-4; PoE; SAmP; Son; TAP; TFi; TRP; TwCP; VGW; WeW-3

Acre of Grass, An. W. B. Yeats. HarvBoo; NoAM

Acrimony hangs at the curtain. Conclusion Is Not Drawn, The. Nicole Espagnol. SurWo, *tr. by* Myrna Bell Rochester

Acrobat of Pain. João da Cruz e Sousa. TCLAP, *tr. by* Flavia Vidal

Acropolis. Lawrence Durrell. OxAEP-2

Acrospirical Meanderings in a Tongue of the Time. Chris Torrance. Oth

Across a limpid stream white birds aslant. On the River. Ku K'uang. SuSp, tr. by Irving Y. Lo

Across a purple west the ship is swimming. Death of Pan, The. Gyula Reviczky. IQMS, tr. by Watson Kirkconnell

Across a red west of great mesas. Desert Wisdom. Reg Saner. PoCoUp

Across a room. Blood or Color. Marjorie Welish. FTOS

Across a windowsill a smell of toasted bread. Ah, Nadya, Nadyenka. Bulat Shalvovich Okudzhava. ItGoST, tr. by Ronnie Apter and Mark Herman

Across America in tears to the door of my cottage in the Western night. (LL) Allen Ginsberg. HarvBoo; LCAP-2; NAAL-5; PoM

Across daubed rock evacuates its dead. (LL) Requiem for the Plantagenet Kings. Geoffrey Hill. CABP; NAEL-5v2; NAEL-6v2; NoAM

Across from glorious Erytheia. Stesichoros. SaLy, tr. by Diane Rayor

Across from the tract of cinderblock houses. By All Lights: 1959. B. H. Boston. GeoHom

Across muscles and through seizure. Newton's Descent. Irene Plazewska. SurWo

Across My Face the Nights Fall. Patrizia Cavalli. CItWP, tr. by Cinzia Sartini Blum and Lara Trubowitz

Across new thresholds. (LL) Future and the Ancestor, The. Andrée Chedid. HAWP; WPOW, tr. by Mirène Ghossein and Samuel Hazo

Across North Wales. Dafydd ap Gwilym Resents the Winter. Rolfe Humphries. WoPoe

Across old peach cans and old jelly jars. (LL) Birth in a Narrow Room, The. Gwendolyn Brooks. BlSi; NoP-4

Across Roblin Lake, two shores away. Wilderness Gothic. Alfred Wellington Purdy. HeIP-4; MoCV; NOBC; NoP-4

Across Space and Time. Charles Olson. PoM

Across the Bay. Donald Davie. CABP; NoAM

Across the Bay. Naomi Shihab Nye. ExTi

Across the bridge, where in the morning blow. Sunday Chimes in the City. Louise Imogen Guiney. APN-2

Across the brook of Time man leaping goes. Laus Mariae. Sidney Lanier. Son

Across the channel, Mare Island welders cut. Bird-Watching. Dennis Schmitz. LCAP-2

Across the correct perspective to the painted sky. Landscape. David Gascoyne. FaBoMo

Across the dark fields the family is spread. Wild Radishes. John Kinsella. NeBl

Across the dim frozen fields of night. Night Train. Robert Francis. GM

Across the Duchy shire wherever I turn. (LL) Thermal Stair, The. William Sydney Graham. FaBoMo; HarvBoo

Across the Eastern sky has glowed. Crowing of the Red Cock, The. Emma Lazarus. TaR

Across the expedient and wicked stones. (LL) Auto Wreck. Karl Shapiro. APT-2; NIL-7; NIP-4; RB; VGW

Across the Field of the Old Corporal. Vietnamese Oral Tradition. CaDao, tr. by John Balaban

Across the field the great willow rocking its head. Chosen to Be Water. Christopher Gilbert. SwNoth

Across the flesh and feeling of soledad. Orisha. Jayne Cortez. BlSi

Across the footpath (tidy. Mercy. Andrew Lansdown. NOBAu

Across the huddled lamplight window glass. Sunt Lacrimae Rerum et Mentem Mortalia Tangunt. R. P. Blackmur. APT-2

Across the Jarbok. Gerrit Achterberg. TuT, tr. by Dennis O'Driscoll

Across the lake the small houses appear. For Two Children. David Malouf. BMAP

Across the meadow, sea smoke. Seal Island. Tom Sexton. PoCoUp

Across the millstream below the bridge. Blue Swallows, The. Howard Nemerov. MakPoe; NoP-4; OWoS

Across the mist flowers and grass appear far and hazy. Gathering Lotus. Chu Ch'ing-yü. SuSp, tr. by Irving Y. Lo

Across the narrow beach we flit. Sandpiper, The. Celia Laighton Thaxter. OBCA; PWR

Across the narrow street from the old hotel that now. Affect of Elms, The. Reginald Gibbons. UrbNat

Across the night. From Creature to Ghost. Pauline Hanson. TAP

Across the night a crimson comet lies. Comet, The. János Vajda. IQMS, tr. by Watson Kirkconnell

Across the Place du Marché Ste-Catherine. Squares and Courtyards. Marilyn Hacker. WiU

Across the Prairie's silent waste I stray. Richard Henry Wilde. APN-1 Fr. Hesperia.

Across the red cliff, dotted in, stand the apparent colonnades. Apparent Colonnades, The. Jeffrey Wainwright. HarvBoo

Across the road. Flock. Lance Henson. VoR

Across the sands. Michael McClintock. HA

Across the Sands of Dee. (LL) Charles Kingsley. EBVV; OxAEP-2; TreFP Fr. Alton Locke.

Across the sandy dry plains. Apocalypse. Charlie R. Braxton. InTrad

Across the Sea. William Allingham. EnLoPo

Across the Sea, Along the Shore. Arthur Hugh Clough. ChIV-2

Across the sea will come Adze-head. Adze-Head. Unknown. BIrV, tr. by James Carney

Across the sky run streaks of white light, aching. Before Olympus. John Gould Fletcher. MoAmPo

Across the snout. Ars Poetica. Robert Desnos. AF, tr. by Carolyn Forché

Across the snowy pastures of the estate. Fox Who Watched for the Midnight Sun, The. Norman Dubie. LCAP-2

Across the still lake. O. Mabson Southard. HA

Across the street: closed shops. Sunday A.M. Not in Manhattan. John Hollander. PoSol

Across the street—the freeway. Beneath the Shadow of the Freeway. Lorna Dee Cervantes. PBCAP

Across the Swamp. Olav H. Hauge. RaBo; WoPoe, tr. by Robert Bly

Across the tracks in Cheyenne, behind the biggest billboard. Long Way Outside Yellowstone, A. Thomas McGrath. VGW

Across the ward green biros of monitors. Monitors. Geoffrey Holloway. NLP

Across the waves that vague, moss-covered knell. Surf Motel, The. Stephen Knight. NeBl

Across those plains where once there roamed the Indian and the Scout. Mid-West, The. Unknown. OBCoV

Across to the Peloponnese. James Welch. CDW

Across upon this undulated board of verdure chequered bright. David Jones. NoAM Fr. In Parenthesis.

Acrostic on Wharton, An. Unknown. OBSV

Acrostick Eligie on the Death of the No Less Prudent than Victorious Prince Oliver Lord Protector, An. Elianour Havey. EMWP

Acrostick on Mrs. Elizabeth Hull, An. John Saffin. SCAP

Acrostick on Mrs. Winifret Griffin, An. John Saffin. SCAP

Acrostiteliostichon. Joshua Sylvester. OxBSo Fr. Du Bartas: His Divine Weeks and Works.

Act, The. William Carlos Williams. SAmP; VGW

Act II - Crossing At the Tracks. Fiona Templeton. FTOS Fr. You: The City.

Act I, Scene ix, Air XI—"A Soldier and a Sailor." John Gay. See Begger's Opera

Act like a crazy dog. Wear sashes & other fine clothes, carry a. Crazy Dog Events. Jerome Rothenberg. RaBo

Act #2. John Weiners. BB

Act of Love, The. Robert Creeley. HAP

Act One. Chana Bloch. ExTi

Act I / Orlando hails. Five-Minute Orlando Macbeth, The. George MacBeth [or Macbeth]. NOBL; PeLV

Act Six. Peter Goldsworthy. NOBAu

Actaeon. Rayner Heppenstall. FaBoTw

Acteon. Ovid. CTC, tr. by Arthur Golding Fr. Metamorphoses.

Acting, dear Thornton, its perfection draws. Robert Lloyd. ECEV Fr. Actor, The.

Action. James Oppenheim. TrJP

Action-Packed Sonnet. Prageeta Sharma. HeMarv

Action Would Kill It / A Gamble. Robert Adamson. BMAP; CBAP

Actions. Marcel Schwob. TrJP, tr. by William Brown Meloney

Actions in my brain: these verbs, whose celerity. Amelia Rosselli. ItPo, tr. by Gayle Ridinger

Actions to save the world. For Sho the New Head Priest of Erin-ji. Muso Soseki. EaWin, tr. by W. S. Merwin

Actis and Deidis of the Illustere and Vailyeand Campioun Schir William Wallace, Knicht of Ellerslie, The. Blind Harry.
    "In Abyrdeyn he gert a consaill cry." NePenScot
    Sevint Buik, Lines 1029–92, The. NePenScot

"Active balls?" said an old man of Stoneham. Limerick: "'Active balls?' said an old man of Stoneham." C. D. Cudmore. PeLi

Actor, The. Robert Lloyd.
    "Acting, dear Thornton, its perfection draws." ECEV

Actor Speaks, An. Ben Scammell. NLP

Actors, The. Nizar Qabbani. MAP, tr. by Diana Der Hovanessian and Lena Jayyusi

Actors in the theatre. Written at Hsiang-kuo Temple on the Occasion of Watching Actors in the Hsing-hsiang Garden of the T'ung-t'ien-chieh Tao-ch'ang. Wang An-shih. SuSp, tr. by Jan W. Walls

Acts 8; On the Baptized Æthiopian. Richard Crashaw. See On the Baptized Ethiopian

Acts of Love. Edgar Silex. NAPBL

Acts of my life swarm down the street like Puerto Rican kids, The. William Meredith. VCAP Fr. Consequences.

Acts of Power. Sharan Strange. InTrad

Acts of Youth, The. John Weiners. BB

Acts passed beyond the boundary of mere wishing. Stephen Spender. OxBTC

Actual Vision of Morning's Extrusion. Alan Dugan. YaYoPo

Actually: it's the balls I look for, always. Balls. Anne McNaughton. RaBo

Actually Swallowed. Douglas Messerli. FTOS

Acum / minature minat minet. Acer. Peter Finch. AngWePo

Acupuncture and Cleansing at 48. Len Roberts. BodElec

Ad Amicam. Francis Thompson. Son

Ad Coelum. William Pattison. OxBSP

Ad Finem. Heinrich Heine. AWP, tr. by Elizabeth Barrett Browning

Ad Henricum Wottonem. Thomas Bastard. FaBoEE

Ad Infinitum. Joan Aronsten. NOBAu

Ad Leuconoen. Horace. AWP, tr. by F. P. Adams Fr. Odes.

Ad Librum. Samuel, Jr. Danforth. SCAP

Ad Limina. Joseph Campbell. BIrV

Ad-men bandy slogans, like Pupils Guaranteed. Eyeball Works, The. Stephen Knight. NeBl

Ad Miró. Pierre Alechinsky. PFTM-2, tr. by Michael Fineberg

Ad Quintilianum. Martial. RomPo, tr. by Robert Louis Stevenson

Adage: "Gardener's rule applies to youth and age, The." Henry James Byron. NBLV

Adagio. Gerald William Barrax. GT

Adagio at Twilight. John Carter. PasH

Adam. Anthony Hecht. TaR

Adam. Yevgeny [or Evgenii] Mikhailovich Vinokurov. TCRusP, tr. by Daniel Weissbort

Adam, a brown old vulture in the rain. Ancient History. Siegfried Sassoon. ChIV-1

Adam and Eve. Itsik [or Itzik or Itzig] Manger. TrJP, tr. by Jacob Sonntag

Adam and Eve. John Milton. PeECV Fr. Paradise Lost.

Adam and Eve. Karl Shapiro.
    Exile. CRP
    "In the beginning, at every step, he turned." CRP
    "One who gave the warning with his wings, The." CRP
    Recognition of Eve, The. ChIV-1
    Sickness of Adam, The. CRP
    "Whatever it was she had so fiercely fought." ChIV-1

Adam and Eve. Charles Hubert Sisson. FaBoTw

Adam and Eve led out of Paradise. John Milton. NPeEn Fr. Paradise Lost.

Adam and God. Anne Wilkinson. MoCV

Adam Bell, Clim of the Clough, and William of Cloudesly. Unknown. ESPB
    (Adam Bel, Clym of the Cloughe, and Wyllyam of Cloudesle.) OxBB

Adam Describes His Own Creation and That of Eve; Having Repeated His Warning, the Angel Departs. John Milton. NAWM-7v1 Fr. Paradise Lost.

Adam Fallen. John Milton. NAWM-5v1; NAWM-7v1; NOCV Fr. Paradise Lost.

Adam / Had 'em. On the Antiquity of Microbes. Strickland W. Gillilan. NBLV

Adam / Had 'em. Poem to Answer the Question: How Old Are Fleas? Unknown. Spl

Adam, I think I'm going to be a mother. Imre Madách. IQMS, tr. by Iain MacLeod Fr. Tragedy of Man.

Adam, indignant, would not eat with Eve. Paradise Saved. Alec Derwent Hope. OxBC; OxBSo

Adam Lay Ybounden [or I-bounden]. Unknown. CTC; ChIV-2; HAP; MiEL; NOBE; NOCV; OxBoLi; PoE; TFi; TOF; TRP; WeW-3
    (Adam Lay Bound.) NAEL-5v1; NAEL-6v1; NAEL-7v1
    (Adam lay i-bounde.) OHMEL
    (Adam lay ibowndyn, bowndyn in a bond.) OxBEV
    (Adam Lay Y-Bounden.) PeLV
    (Adam lay y-bownden bownden in a bond.) NPeEn

Adam lay ybounden [or i-bounden], bounded in a bond. Adam Lay Ybounden [or I-bounden]. Unknown. CTC; ChIV-2; HAP; MiEL; NOBE; NOCV; OxBoLi; PoE; TFi; TOF; TRP; WeW-3

Adam, my child, my son. Adam. Anthony Hecht. TaR

Adam Posed. Anne Finch, Countess of Winchilsea. ChIV-1; ECWP
    (Adam Pos'd.) NPeEn
    (Cou'd our first father, at his toilsome plough.) NPeEn
    (Could our first father, at his toilsome plow.) NoP-4

Adam, quoth He, the beauties manifold. Guillaume de Salluste Du Bartas. InvLi, tr. by Joshua Sylvester Fr. Divine Weeks and Works, The.

Adam's Complaint. Denise Levertov. BoWoP; NNaP

Adam's Curse. W. B. Yeats. BIrV; NAEL-5v2; NAEL-6v2; NoAM; NoP-4; WeW-3

Adam's Dream. Edwin Muir. NoP-4

Adam's Song to Heaven. Edgar Bowers. CoAmPo

Adam's Task. John Hollander. NIL-7; NIP-4; NoP-4; WoPoe

Adam scriveyn [or scrivain or scrivein], if ever it thee bifalle. Chaucer's Wordes unto Adam, his Owne Scriveyn. Geoffrey Chaucer. NAEL-6v1; NAEL-7v1

Adam Sign, The. Salah 'Abd al-Sabur. MAP, tr. by Alistair Elliot and Matthew Sorenson Fr. Ode of Signs.

Adam Unfallen. John Milton. NOCV Fr. Paradise Lost.

Adam was my grandfather. For All Blasphemers. Stephen Vincent Benét. OxBA

Adam, Where Art Thou? Endre Ady. IQMS, tr. by Anton N. Nyerges

Adam will never change. I. Eve. Julio Marzán. PueRic

Adam, your namesake lives. Namesake. Imtiaz Dharker. NeBl

Adapt Thyself. Shem-Tob ben Joseph Palquera. TrJP, tr. by Rabbi Ettelson

Add up without me. (LL) Roll-Call in the Concentration Camp. Dan Pagis. FIT; PoSu, tr. by Robert Friend

Adde Merum Vinoque. Tibullus.
    "Fill up my glass again! The anodyne." WoPoe, tr. by Rachel Hadas

Added to a Letter Sent to a Traveler. Pao Ling-hui. ColAnChi, tr. by Anne Birrell and Jeanne Larsen

Added to / making a Republic. Charles Olson. PFTM-2 Fr. Maximus Poems, The.

Adder's Epigrams. Colin Ellis. FaBoEE

Adder, whose art condenses and refines. Adder's Epigrams. Colin Ellis. FaBoEE

Addiction. Sheryl St. Germain. IllVoic

Addiction to the exceptional event. Barbarossa. Hubert Witheford. PeNZ

Adding father's name. Nicholas Virgilio. HA

Addition to Kipling's "The Dead King (Edward VII), 1910" Max Beerbohm. FaBoEE; OBCoV

Addition to the Opposition. Aleksandr Yeryomenko [or Eremenko]. TCRP, tr. by Albert C. Todd

Additional Poem, An. John Ashbery. FaBoMo

Address. Alurista. PAI

Address. Andrew Geddes Bain. PeSAV

Address. Leonard Nolens. TuT, tr. by Michael O'Loughlin

Address. Bruce Smith. Son Fr. In My Father's House.

Address. Adrienne Su. AmPoNex

Address by an Ex-Confederate Soldier to the Grand Army of the Republic, An. Maurice Thompson. CBCWP

Address / occupation / age. Address. Alurista. PAI

Address of my house has changed, The. Prison. Mahmoud Darwish. AF, tr. by Denys Johnson-Davies

Address to a Bachelor on a Delicate Occasion. Priscilla Pointon. ECWP

Address to a Child during a Boisterous Winter Evening. Dorothy Wordsworth. WoRP

Address to a Haggis. Robert Burns. See To a Haggis

Address to Ethiopia. Priscilla Jane Thompson. CBWP-2

Address to Her Husband. Mehetabel Wright. ECWP
    (Disappointed Wife, The.) LW

Address to Lady———, Who Asked What the Passion of Love Was? Charles Morris. NOEC

Address to My Soul. Elinor Wylie. AWP; OxBA

Address to Nature on its Cruelty, An. Ellen Johnston. VWP

Address to Poetry, An. Helen Maria Williams.
    "Blest Poesy! Oh sent to calm." NOBRP

Address to Poets. John Keble. SacPr

Address to the Deil. Robert Burns. NOEC; NePenScot; OxBS

Address to the King, An. John Gower.
    "For vein honour or for the worldes good." SacPr
    Peace. SacPr

Address to the Muses, An. Joanna Baillie.
    "Ye are the spirits who preside." ECWP

Address to the New Tay Bridge, An. William McGonagall.
    "Beautiful new railway bridge of the Silvery Tay." VerBaPo

Address to the Ocean. Byron. ITBLP Fr. Childe Harold's Pilgrimage.

Address to the Ocean. "Barry Cornwall." TreFP

Address to the Plebeians, An. John Learmont.
    "Poor crawlin' bodies, sair neglectit." NOEC

Address to the Soul Occasioned by a Rain, An. Edward Taylor. NAAL-2v1; NOBA; OxBA
    (Let by Rain.) ColAP; NAAL-3; OxBEV

Address to the Unco Guid, or the Rigidly Righteous. Robert Burns. ChIV-1; NOBE; NOCV; OxBEV; OxBS

Address to the Woodlark. Robert Burns. OWoS

Address to Venus. Lucretius. AWP; OBVE Fr. De Rerum Natura (On the Nature of Things).

Address to Venus. Edmund Spenser. AWP Fr. Faerie Queene, The.

Addressed to ———. Lady Mary Wortley Montagu. ECWP

Addressed to a Beech Tree. Christian Carstairs. ECWP

Addressed to a Koto-player. Su Man-shu. SuSp, *tr.* by Wu-Chi Liu

Addressed to Haydon. John Keats. CenSon

Addressed to Sensibility. Ann Yearsley. RWP

Addressing the readers of a well-run newspaper, that is, one abounding. Silent World Is Our Only Homeland, The. Francis Ponge. AF, *tr.* by Beth Archer

Adds the cool head, and the unblemish'd [*or* unblemished] heart! (LL) To the Naiad of the Arun. Charlotte Smith. CenSon; RWP

Adela, Adela, Adela Chart. To Henry James. Robert Louis Stevenson. OBCoV

Adelaide Crapsey. Carl Sandburg. APT-1

Adelaide's Dream. Christopher Middleton. PeLV

Adelaide's Lament. Frank Loesser. ReLy

Adelina Patti. Adah Isaacs Menken. CBWP-1

Adequate of Hell, The. (LL) Emily Dickinson. NAAL-2v1; NAAL-3; NOBA; NOCV; NoP-4; SAmP

Adew, my King, court, cuntrey, and my kin. To Henry Constable and Henry Keir. Alexander Montgomerie. OxBS

Adhesion to this body. Squeeze. Abigail Child. FTOS

Adhesive Autopsy of Walt Whitman, The. Jonathan Williams. PoM

Adhiambo. Gabriel Okara. *See* To Adhiambo

Adieu. Pierre Reverdy. CuPo

Adieu. Mary E. Tucker. CBWP-1

Adieu, Adieu, Forever. Priscilla Jane Thompson. CBWP-2

"Adieu, adieu," forevermore. (LL) Tennyson. EBVV; FHYEP; NAEL-6v2 *Fr.* In Memoriam A. H. H.

Adieu and Recall to Love, The. Robert Merry. NOBRP

Adieu, blind fortune, with thy miserable purse. Adieu, to Fortune. Henry Francis Fynn. PeSAV

Adieu, dear life! here am I left alone. On My Late Dear Wife. Jonathan Richardson. NOEC

Adieu, dear name which birth and nature gave. Elegy on a Maiden Name, An. Jane Cave. CABP; ECWP

Adieu, dear object of my love's excess. Orinda to Lucasia Parting, October, 1661, at London. Katherine Philips. BASC

Adieu, Farewell, Earth's Bliss[e]. Thomas Nashe [*or* Nash]. EBEV; HAP; HeIP-4; NPeEn; NoP-4; NoSic; OxBEV; TFi; TRP *Fr.* Summer's Last Will and Testament.

Adieu, New-England's smiling meads. Farewell to America. To Mrs. S. W, A. Phillis Wheatley. NoP-4

"Adieu!" she cries; and waved [*or* waves] her lily hand. (LL) Sweet William's Farewell to Black-Eyed [*or* Black-Ey'd] Susan. John Gay. BoLoP; NOEC

Adieu, sweet Angus, Maeve and Fand. Passing of the Shee, The. John Millington Synge. BIrV; FaBoEE

Adieu, the years are a broken song. *Unknown.* NOBAu

Adieu, to Fortune. Henry Francis Fynn. PeSAV

Adieu to My Landlady, An. George Farewell. NOEC

Adieu, you haughty maiden! Adieu, Adieu, Forever. Priscilla Jane Thompson. CBWP-2

"Adiew, madam my mother dear." Lord Maxwell's Last Goodnight. *Unknown.* ESPB

Adina. Harold Milton Telemaque. TTY

Adios, Carenage. Derek Walcott. PoetW *Fr.* Schooner Flight, The.

Adjectives. Moishe Nadir. TrJP, *tr.* by Joseph Leftwich

Adlatts parke is wyde and broad. Will Stewart and John. *Unknown.* ESPB

Adler. Gerald Stern. TaR

Adlestrop. Edward Thomas. HAP; HarvBoo; NAAL-5v2; NAEL-6v2; NOBE; NoP-4; OBEV; OxBTC; UV

Administrator, An. Geoffrey Grigson. FaBoEE

Admiral Hosier's Ghost. Richard Glover. NOEC

Admiral's Caravan, The. Charles Edward Carryl.
(Camel's Complaint, The.) NOxBChV; OBCA; OxIBACP
"Canary-birds feed on sugar and seed." OTCP
Song of the Camel, The. OTCP

Admiralls Being Slaine, They Likewise, The. Anne Dowriche. EMWP

Admirals (Columbus). Suzanne Gardinier. NeAmPo

Admiration. Josephine D. Henderson Heard. CBWP-4

Admirations—and Contempts—of time, The. Emily Dickinson. APN-2

Admire Cranmer! Stevie Smith. NoAM

Admire the face of plastered stone. Quebec Farmhouse. John Glassco. NOBC

Admire the old man, admire him, admire him. Admire Cranmer! Stevie Smith. NoAM

Admire thy wreath? And wherefore should I not. To a Plagiarist. Moses Ibn Ezra. TrJP, *tr.* by Solomon Solis-Cohen

Admire, when you come here, the glimmering hair. Vuillard: "The Mother and Sister of the Artist." W. D. Snodgrass. CoAP

Admiring it and adding noughts in vain. (LL) Star-Gazer. Louis MacNeice. ModIr; NAEL-5v2; NAEL-6v2; NoP-4

Admiring stranger, that with ling'ring feet. Written in Tintern Abbey, Monmouthshire. Edward Gardner. CenSon

Admission. Henry Vaughan. ESCV

Admit them, admit them. (LL) Song of a Man Who Has Come Through. D. H. Lawrence. FaBoMo; GTBS-P; HarvBoo; OxBTC; PeFWW; PoE; RaBo; TRP

Admit them, admit them. (LL) D. H. Lawrence. FaBoMo; GTBS-P; OxBTC; PeFWW; PoE; RaBo; TRP *Fr.* Song of a Man Who Has Come Through.

Admit then and be glad. Poem for an Anniversary. Cecil Day Lewis. CABP

Admonition. Tzu Yeh. CrYelRi, *tr.* by Sam Hamill

Admonition by the Auctor to all yong Gentilwomen: And to al other Maids being in Love, The. Isabella Whitney.
"Ye virgins that from Cupid's tents." PEW

Admonition to a Traveller. William Wordsworth. GTBS-P

Admonition to Montgomerie. James I, King of England. GTBS-P; OxBS

Admonition to Myself, An. Chao Meng-fu. CoBLCP; WoPoe, *tr.* by Jonathan Chaves

Admonition to the Muse. Geoffrey Taylor. FaBoEE

Admonitions. Lucille Clifton. BPo; NALW

Adolescence. W. H. Auden. OxBEV
(Adolescence.) NoAM

Adolescence. W. H. Auden. *See* Adolescence

Adolescence. Allison Joseph. AmPoNex

Adolescence—I. Rita Dove. ISC; NAAL-5; NoAM

Adolescence—II. Rita Dove. AWTN; HCAP; ISC; NAAL-5; NoAM; PoPoPo; VCAP

Adolescence—III. Rita Dove. ISC; NAAL-5; NoAM

Adolf Hitler ———1 April, 1945. W. D. Snodgrass. BodElec *Fr.* Führer Bunker, The.

Adolf Hitler ———20 April, 1934; 1900 hours. W. D. Snodgrass. BodElec *Fr.* Führer Bunker, The.

Adolicus; that's a creeper rug, its small. "Robin Hyde." PeNZ *Fr.* Houses, The.

Adonais; An Elegy on the Death of John Keats. Shelley. CABP; EBEV; FHYEP; NAEL-6v2; NOBRP; OxAEP-2; TFi
(Adonais.) CABP
("I weep for Adonais—he is dead!") CABP
(Mourn Not for Adonais.) NOBE
"One remains, the many change and pass, The." NPeEn; SCV

Adonis. "H. D.". AWP

Adonis. *Unknown.* NPeEn; NoSic, *tr.* by Theocritus

Adonis, Dying. Praxilla. WPOW, *tr.* by Richard Lattimore

Adoramus Te, Christe. David [*or* Daibhi][*or* Daithi] O'Bruadair [*or* Ó Bruadair]. NOIV, *tr.* by Thomas Kinsella

Adoration of the Anchor. Laura Jensen. LCAP-2

Adoration of the Disk by King Akhnaten and Princess Nefer Neferiu Aten. *Unknown.* AWP *Fr.* Book of the Dead.

Adoration of the Kings, The. William Carlos Williams. ChrPo

Adoration of the Magi, The. Christopher Pilling. OBCP

Adore November's sacred seventeenth day. Morris Kyffin. AngWePo *Fr.* Blessednes of Brytaine, The.

Adore the lifted standard of the Cross. On the Cross. Alcuin. MLL, *tr.* by Helen Waddell

Adore the Roses; nor delay. Rosary Beads. Herman Melville. NCAP

Adore we the Lord. *Unknown.* NOIV

Adown the Heights of Ages. Priscilla Jane Thompson. CBWP-2

Adreint al with shennesse, y-drawe down with shame. (LL) Who is This that Cometh from Edom? William Herebert. ChIV-1; MiEL; SacPr

Adrian Henri's Talking after Christmas Blues. Adrian Henri. PeLV

Adriani Morientis ad Animam Suam. Emperor Hadrian. OBVE; OxBSP, *tr.* by Matthew Prior

Adriano; or, The First of June. James Hurdis. ECEV

Adrift between the earth and sky. Shun 'Oku Soen. JDP, *tr.* by Yoel Hoffmann

Adult. Linda Gregg. BLT

Adulterers and customers of whores. Womanisers. John Press. BoLoP

Adulterers and whoremongers / were there, with all unchaste. Michael Wigglesworth. ColAP *Fr.* Day of Doom, The.

Adulteries, murthers, robberies, thefts. Roger Williams. SCAP

Adultery. James Dickey. TAP

Adultery. Carol Ann Duffy. EmeKit

Adupe. Jayne Cortez. ESEAA

Advance of Education, The. Josephine D. Henderson Heard. CBWP-4

Advance of the Grizzly, The. Barbara Guest. BodElec

Advance to Hamburg broke with all the plans, The. England Nil. Anne Rouse. MFPA; NeBl

Advanced out toward the external from. Charles Olson. NAAL-5; PoM *Fr.* Maximus Poems, The.

Advantages of Being a World Class Athlete, The. Anthony Lacavaro. MoASP

Advent. Brian Coffey.
  "Awakening like return to Earth from Moon." CIP-2
  "'My son my son' the Blakean figure mourns and affirms." BiHa
  "What have they done to Klio what have they done to our Muse." BiHa

Advent. William Everson. NeAP; TrCP

Advent. Anne Hartigan. CIP-2

Advent. Christina Georgina Rossetti. ChrPo; TrCP

Advent; a Carol. Patric Dickinson. OBCP

Advent Calendar. Gjertrud Schnackenberg. ChrPo

Advent Lyrics. *Unknown.* ASW, *tr. by* Kevin Crossley-Holland *Fr.* Christ 1.

Advent 1955. Sir John Betjeman. OBCP

Advent 1966. Denise Levertov. APSN; NNaP

Advent of our God With eager hearts we greet, The. C. Coffin. SacPr

Advent of the new habit, The. Breakfast with Cats. Molly Peacock. KGB

Advent wind begins to stir, The. Advent 1955. Sir John Betjeman. OBCP

Adventure. Bill Griffiths. Oth *Fr.* Building: The New London Hospital.

Adventure. Jule Styne. ReLy

Adventure is all in a three-wheel pushchair. It lives in, The. Produce from the colonies. Pierre McOrlan. MFP, *tr. by* Martin Sorrell

Adventure of the Quartz Pebble, The. Vasco [*or* Vasko] Popa. PoSu, *tr. by* Anne Pennington *Fr.* Quartz Pebble, The.

Adventures of Huckleberry Finn, The. "Mark Twain."
  "And did young Stephen sicken." NBLV; OBAL
  Emmeline Grangerford's "Ode to Stephen Dowling Bots, Dec'd." NBLV; OBAL
  (Ode to Stephen Dowling Bots, Dec'd.) APN-2; TCAPo

Adventures of Id, The. Morris Gilbert Bishop. OBCoV

Adventures of Isabel. Ogden Nash. ChAP; MoAmPo; NOxBChV; NTCP; OBAL; OBCA; OxIBACP

Adventures of Master F. I, The. George Gascoigne.
  (And If I Did What Then?) NoP-4
  Farewell, A. EBEV; HAP; NOBE; SCGP

Adventurous baron the bright locks admired, The. Pope. EroLit *Fr.* Rape of the Lock, The.

Adventurous mariner! in whose gray skiff. Sonnet 18: "Adventurous mariner! in whose gray skiff." Amos Bronson Alcott. APN-1

Adventurous Muse, The. Isaac Watts. NOEC

Adversary, The. Phyllis McGinley. FaBoEE; OBCA; OxBSP; SoSe-8

Advertisement of a Lost Day. Lydia Huntley Sigourney. TreFP

Advertisements. Thomas McGrath. BodElec

Advertising Agency Song, The. *Unknown.* NBLV

Advertising Rhymes. *Unknown.*
  Burma-Shave Roadside Signs. OBCoV
  Force. OBCoV
  "Jim Dumps was a most unfriendly man." OBCoV
  "There was a little man." OBCoV
  "They come as a boon and a blessing to men." OBCoV
  Waverly Pen, The. OBCoV
  "WITHIN THIS VALE." OBCoV

Advice. Gwendolyn B. Bennett. BlSi

Advice. Lee Cataldi. BMAP

Advice. Bill Holm. RaBo

Advice. Langston Hughes. NBLV; SAmP

Advice for a Journey. Sidney Keyes. PoWW

Advice from Euterpe. Carter Revard. VoR

Advice from Poor Robin's Almanack. *Unknown.* OBCP

Advice Gratis to Certain Women. Phoebe Cary. APN-2

Advice of an Efficiency Expert, The. Augustus Young. CIP-2

Advice of Housewives. Thomas Tusser. NoSic *Fr.* Five Hundred Points of Good Husbandry.

Advice on Adultery. Gwyneth Lewis. MFPA *Fr.* Welsh Espionage.

Advice to a Child. Eleanor Farjeon. OTCP

Advice to a Clam-Digger. Wilbert Snow. APT-1

Advice to a Discarded Lover. Fleur Adcock. PeNZ

Advice to a First Cousin. Alberto Rios. NAAL-5; NIL-7

Advice to a Forest. Maxwell Bodenheim. TrJP

Advice to a Lover. Thomas Yalden. ECEV

Advice to a Man Who Lost a Dog. Howard Baker. APT-2

Advice to a Prophet. Richard Wilbur. HarvBoo; MoAmPo; NoP-4; OBWP; OxBC; PoE; TwCP; VCAP

Advice to a Raven in Russia [December, 1812]. Joel Barlow. APN-1; NAAL-2v1; NAAL-3; NOBA; OBWP; OxBA

(Advice to a Raven in Russia.) ColAP

Advice to a Reckless Youth. Ben Johnson. TreFP

Advice to a Young Lady Lately Married. Esther Lewis. ECWP

Advice to a Young Man. *Unknown.* CAGL, *tr. by* James J. Wilhelm

Advice to a Young Philosopher. Anselm Berrigan. HeMarv

"Advice" to a Young Poet. Raymond Mazisi Kunene. PeSAV, *tr. by* the author

Advice to Bores. Abraham Ibn-Chasdai. TrJP, *tr. by* J. Chotzner

Advice to His Grace. "Ephelia." EMWP

Advice to Hotheads. Samuel ben Elhanan Isaac, of Padua Archevolti. TrJP, *tr. by* A. B. Rhine

Advice to Lovers. John Armstrong. NOEC *Fr.* Oeconomy of Love; a Poetical Essay, The.

Advice to My Best Brother, Colonel Francis Lovelace. Richard Lovelace. BeJo

Advice to My Son. Peter Meinke. PAI

Advice to Paulinus. Pacifico Massimi. CAGL, *tr. by* James J. Wilhelm *Fr.* Hecateleguim.

Advice to Pilgrims. Robinson Jeffers. APT-1

Advice to Sophronia. Mary Leapor. ECWP

Advice to the Orchestra. David Wagoner. NoAM

Advice to the Young. Miriam Waddington. NIP-4; NOBC

Advice to Travelers. Walker Gibson. NBLV
  (Before Starting.) KaS

Advice to Virgins. Katherine Philips. EMWP

Advice to Young Ladies. Alec Derwent Hope. NoAM; NoP-4

Advice to Young Ladies. Ann Plato. SWaP

Adviser to the Court. Tu Fu.
  "By the water-clock it's past dawn as the day watch sounds." CarOv, *tr. by* Carolyn Kizer
  East of the Palace Gates: Working Late. CarOv, *tr. by* Carolyn Kizer
  End of an Audience. CarOv, *tr. by* Carolyn Kizer
  "Last year I rejoined the Emperor by this road." CarOv, *tr. by* Carolyn Kizer
  "Leaving the audience by the quiet corridors." CarOv, *tr. by* Carolyn Kizer
  On the Way Out. CarOv, *tr. by* Carolyn Kizer
  Reply to a Friend's Advice. CarOv, *tr. by* Carolyn Kizer
  "Sound of the fifth watch! Dawn hastens to obey." CarOv, *tr. by* Carolyn Kizer
  "Their sleeves like purple orchids." CarOv, *tr. by* Carolyn Kizer
  To a Brother Official. CarOv, *tr. by* Carolyn Kizer
  "When day begins to darken." CarOv, *tr. by* Carolyn Kizer
  Working All Night in Springtime. CarOv, *tr. by* Carolyn Kizer

Adze-Head. *Unknown.* BlrV, *tr. by* James Carney

Ae Fond Kiss. Robert Burns. NAEL-5v2; NAEL-6v2; NePenScot; OBEV
  (Song.) BoLoP; NOBRP; NOEC; NPeEn

Ae fond kiss, and then we sever. Ae Fond Kiss. Robert Burns. NAEL-5v2; NAEL-6v2; NePenScot; OBEV

Ae weet forenicht i' the yow-trummle. Watergaw, The. Hugh MacDiarmid. FaBoVe; HarvBoo; NAEL-5v2; NAEL-6v2; NPeEn; NePenScot

Aedh Tells of the Rose in His Heart. W. B. Yeats. MoBrPo
  (Aedh Tells of the Rose in His Heart.) MoBrPo

Aegean, The. Maria Luisa Spaziani. NeIt, *tr. by* Beverly Allen

Aegean Melancholy. Odysseus Elytis. VCWP

Aelf-Scin, The. Michael McClure. PoM

Aella; a Tragycal Enterlude. Thomas Chatterton.
  "Budding floweret blushes at the light, The." OxAEP-1
  Minstrel's Song. HAP; NOBE; SCGP
  (Mynstrelle's Songe ("O! synge untoe mie roundelaie").) EnLoPo; NOEC; OxAEP-1
  (Mynstrelles Songe.) CABP
  Mynstrelles Songe: "Angelles bee wrogte to bee of neidher kynde" EnLoPo
  ("O! synge untoe mie roundelaie.") CABP
  "Oh! sing unto my roundelay [*or* O! Synge untoe mie roundelaie]." HAP; NOBE; SCGP
  (Song: "O sing into my roundelay.") OBEV
  There Lackethe Somethynge Stylle. OxAEP-1

Aeneas Arrives in Carthage. Virgil [*or* Vergil]. NAWM-5v1; NAWM-7v1, *tr. by* Robert Fitzgerald *Fr.* Aeneid [*or* Eneados, *Aeneis*], The.

Aeneas at Washington. Allen Tate. APT-2; FuPo; NOBA; NoAM; OxBA

Aeneas' Image of War. Virgil [*or* Vergil]. OBVE, *tr. by* Gawin [*or* Gavin] Douglas *Fr.* Aeneid [*or* Eneados, *Aeneis*], The.

Aeneas in the Underworld. Virgil [*or* Vergil]. NAWM-5v1; NAWM-7v1, *tr. by* Robert Fitzgerald *Fr.* Aeneid [*or* Eneados, *Aeneis*], The.

Aeneas Searches for his Wife. Virgil [*or* Vergil]. NPeEn, *tr. by* Henry Howard, Earl of Surrey *Fr.* Aeneid [*or* Eneados, *Aeneis*], The.

Aeneas (with Achates) Meets His Mother, Venus. Virgil [*or* Vergil]. OBVE, *tr. by* Gawin [*or* Gavin] Douglas *Fr.* Aeneid [*or* Eneados, *Aeneis*], The.

Aeneid (Dryden translation).   Virgil [*or* Vergil].
   Book 2.
     "By destiny compell'd, and in despair."   FaBoWar, *tr. by* John Dryden
   Book 3.
     "At length I land upon the Strophades."   OWoS, *tr. by* John Dryden
     Harpies, The.   OWoS, *tr. by* John Dryden
Aeneid [*or* Eneados, *Aeneis*], The.   Virgil [*or* Vergil].
   Aeneas Arrives in Carthage.   NAWM-5v1; NAWM-7v1, *tr. by* Robert Fitzgerald
   Aeneas' Image of War.   OBVE, *tr. by* Gawin [*or* Gavin] Douglas
   Aeneas in the Underworld.   NAWM-5v1; NAWM-7v1, *tr. by* Robert Fitzgerald
   Aeneas Searches for his Wife.   NPeEn, *tr. by* Henry Howard, Earl of Surrey
   Aeneas (with Achates) Meets His Mother, Venus.   OBVE, *tr. by* Gawin [*or* Gavin] Douglas
   Aeolus Looses the Winds.   NPeEn, *tr. by* Gawin [*or* Gavin] Douglas
   "Affrayit, I glistnyt of sleip, and stert on feit."   OBVE, *tr. by* Gawin [*or* Gavin] Douglas
   "Amyd the wod his modir met thame tway."   OBVE, *tr. by* Gawin [*or* Gavin] Douglas
   "And first the walles and dark entrie I sought."   NPeEn, *tr. by* Henry Howard, Earl of Surrey
   "And now Aeneas charges straight at Turnus."   OBWP
   "And now the dewy night had nearly come to its halfway."   WoPoe, *tr. by* Cecil Day Lewis
   "And now we gan draw near unto the gate."   NoSic, *tr. by* Henry Howard, Earl of Surrey
   "And oft the owle with rufull song complaind."   OBVE, *tr. by* Henry Howard, Earl of Surrey
   "And Turnus than, quhar he at erth dyd ly."   OBVE, *tr. by* Gawin [*or* Gavin] Douglas
   "Arms, and the Man I sing, who, forc'd by Fate."   FaBoWar; OBVE; OxBEV; WoPoe, *tr. by* John Dryden
   "As bryght Phebus, scheyn soverane hevynnys e."   NPeEn; OxBS, *tr. by* Gawin [*or* Gavin] Douglas
   "As, sum tyme, dois the curser stert and ryn."   OBVE, *tr. by* Gawin [*or* Gavin] Douglas
   "As this convine and ordinance was mayd."   OBVE, *tr. by* Gawin [*or* Gavin] Douglas
   "As when a Fragment, from a Mountain torn."   OBVE, *tr. by* John Dryden
   "Attentively he heard us, while we spoke."   OBVE, *tr. by* John Dryden
   (Batalis and the Man, The.)   CTC
   "Batellis [*or* Batalis] and the man I will descrive."   OBVE, *tr. by* Gawin [*or* Gavin] Douglas
   "Be this was said a grondyn dart leit he glide."   NPeEn, *tr. by* Gawin [*or* Gavin] Douglas
   "It was the time when, granted from the gods."   NAEL-5v1
   Laocoön.   OBVE, *tr. by* Henry Howard, Earl of Surrey
   "Loe! formest of a rout that followd him."   OBVE, *tr. by* Henry Howard, Earl of Surrey
   "Then indeed into all our fluttering hearts."   FaBoWar, *tr. by* Charles Hubert Sisson
   "Whom when I saw assembled in such wise."   PoE
   "Bot now the haisty, egir, and wild Dido."   OBVE, *tr. by* Gawin [*or* Gavin] Douglas
   Building of Carthage, The.   OBVE, *tr. by* Gawin [*or* Gavin] Douglas
   Building of Carthage, The.   OBVE, *tr. by* John Dryden
   "By a bold people's stubborn arms oppressed."   BASC, *tr. by* Abraham Cowley
   Charon.   OBVE, *tr. by* John Dryden
   (Charon.)   OBVE
   Charon.   NPeEn, *tr. by* John Dryden
   "Come is the ending day, Troy's hour is come."   MLL
   Creusa.   NoSic, *tr. by* Henry Howard, Earl of Surrey
   "Dawn at that hour."   WoPoe, *tr. by* Robert Fitzgerald
   "Dawn leaves the bed of Dark and climbs the sky."   EroLit, *tr. by* Kenneth McLeish
   "Dear Sister, my resentment had not been."   OBVE
   Death of Priam, The.   OBVE, *tr. by* Sir John Denham
   Death of Priam, The.   NPeEn, *tr. by* John Dryden
   Death of Turnus, The.   NAWM-5v1; NAWM-7v1, *tr. by* Robert Fitzgerald
   Defeat of Turnus, The.   OBVE, *tr. by* Gawin [*or* Gavin] Douglas
   Dido by Night.   OBVE, *tr. by* Henry Howard, Earl of Surrey
   Dido's Suicide.   OBVE, *tr. by* Gawin [*or* Gavin] Douglas
   Dido to Her Sister Anna.   OBVE, *tr. by* Henry Howard, Earl of Surrey
   Diomede Mourns His Fate and That of His Friends to the Latian Ambassador Who Seeks His Alliance against Aeneas.   OBVE, *tr. by* John Dryden

"Eneas wonderit the greitnes of Cartaige."   OBVE, *tr. by* Gawin [*or* Gavin] Douglas
Euryalus and Nisus Meet Their Deaths.   NoSic, *tr. by* Thomas Phaer \VP/[*or* Phayer]
"Exulting in his Strength, he seems to dare."   OBVE, *tr. by* John Dryden
Fame.   NPeEn; OBVE, *tr. by* John Dryden
"Gods who rule the ghosts; all silent shades."   NAWM-5v1; NAWM-7v1, *tr. by* Robert Fitzgerald
"Heaven, the earth, and all the liquid main [*or* mayne], The."   OBVE
"Heere we doe not lynger; thee vowd sollemnitye finnisht."   NoSic, *tr. by* Richard Stanyhurst
"Hence to deep Acheron they take their way."   NPeEn, *tr. by* John Dryden
"How hard a fate enthrals the wretched maid."   ECWP
How They Took the City.   NAWM-5v1; NAWM-7v1, *tr. by* Robert Fitzgerald
"I sing of warfare and a man at war."   NAWM-5v1; NAWM-7v1, *tr. by* Robert Fitzgerald
"In Heaven, Queen Juno saw. She's trapped."   EroLit, *tr. by* Kenneth McLeish
"It was then night: the sound[e] and quiet sleep [*or* slepe]."   MakPoe, *tr. by* Henry Howard, Earl of Surrey
Jilted Queen, The.   NAEL-7v1, *tr. by* Henry Howard, Earl of Surrey
"Loud Report through Lybian Cities goes, The."   NPeEn; OBVE, *tr. by* John Dryden
"Meanwhile the two men pressed on where the pathway led."   NAWM-5v1; NAWM-7v1, *tr. by* Robert Fitzgerald
Night-Piece, The.   MakPoe, *tr. by* Henry Howard, Earl of Surrey
"Now manhood and garbroyls I chaunt, and martial horror."   BIrV; OBVE
"O boys, O strong of heart in vain."   MLL
"Omnipotent Olympus' king meanwhile."   NAWM-5v1; NAWM-7v1, *tr. by* Robert Fitzgerald
"Onto the hallowit steid bryng in, thai cry."   OBVE, *tr. by* Gawin [*or* Gavin] Douglas
Passion of the Queen, The.   NAWM-5v1; NAWM-7v1, *tr. by* Robert Fitzgerald
"Perhaps you may of Priam's Fate enquire."   NPeEn, *tr. by* John Dryden
Polyphemus.   NoSic, *tr. by* Richard Stanyhurst
"Priests, prophets, helpless. She's beside herself."   EroLit, *tr. by* Kenneth McLeish
"Prince, with Wonder, sees the stately Tow'rs, The."   OBVE, *tr. by* John Dryden
Prologue.   NAWM-5v1; NAWM-7v1, *tr. by* Robert Fitzgerald
Prologue to Book Seven.   NPeEn; OxBS, *tr. by* Gawin [*or* Gavin] Douglas
Pyres, The.   WoPoe, *tr. by* Robert Fitzgerald
"Queen, for her part, all that evening ached, The."   NAWM-5v1; NAWM-7v1, *tr. by* Robert Fitzgerald
"Quhen thou art careit to that cuntree."   OBVE, *tr. by* Gawin [*or* Gavin] Douglas
"Room fell silent, and all eyes were on him, The."   NAWM-5v1; NAWM-7v1, *tr. by* Robert Fitzgerald
Rubric, The.   OBVE, *tr. by* Gawin [*or* Gavin] Douglas
Shield of Aeneas, The.   NAWM-5v1; NAWM-7v1, *tr. by* Robert Fitzgerald
"Sky rumbles. Gathers. Rain."   EroLit, *tr. by* Kenneth McLeish
Sleep of Palinurus, The.   WoPoe, *tr. by* Cecil Day Lewis
Sybil, The.   OBVE, *tr. by* Gawin [*or* Gavin] Douglas
"There Charon stands, who rules the dreary Coast."   OBVE, *tr. by* John Dryden
"Thir riveris and thir watteris kepit war."   OxBEV, *tr. by* Gawin [*or* Gavin] Douglas
"Thus fell the King, who yet surviv'd the state."   OBVE, *tr. by* Sir John Denham
"To my prowd foe thus, sister, humblie saye."   OBVE, *tr. by* Henry Howard, Earl of Surrey
Turnus and the Courser.   OBVE, *tr. by* Gawin [*or* Gavin] Douglas
Turnus and the Stone.   OBVE, *tr. by* John Dryden
Turnus and the Wanton Courser.   OBVE, *tr. by* John Dryden
Turnus Summons His Allies, Aeneas Is "Perturbit wyth Gret Thochtis"   OBVE, *tr. by* Gawin [*or* Gavin] Douglas
"Unhappy Dido burns, and in her rage."   NAEL-7v1, *tr. by* Henry Howard, Earl of Surrey
"Venus the gleaming goddess."   NAWM-5v1; NAWM-7v1, *tr. by* Robert Fitzgerald
"Wee leave Creete Country; and our sayls unwrapped uphoysing."   BIrV; OBVE
"Wood with bushes broad there was, begrown with bigtree boughs, A."   NoSic, *tr. by* Thomas Phaer \VP/[*or* Phayer]
Wooden Horse Is Brought into Troy, The.   OBVE, *tr. by* Gawin [*or* Gavin] Douglas
Aeolian Harp, The.   Samuel Taylor Coleridge.   *See* Effusions
Aeolian Harp, The.   Herman Melville.   NCAP

Aeolus Looses the Winds.   Virgil [*or* Vergil].   NPeEn, *tr.* by Gawin [*or* Gavin] Douglas   *Fr.* Aeneid [*or* Eneados, *Aeneis*], The.

Aerial, The.   Reiner Kunze.   PoSu, *tr.* by Ewald Osers

Aerial, The.   Robert Minhinnick.   TCAWP

Aerial / born in the heights.   Banyan.   Elsa Cross.   TANSG, *tr.* by Patricia Dubrava

Aerogrammes.   Russell Leong.   OpBo

Aerolingual Poet of Prey.   Eugene B. Redmond.   SpirFl

Aerophorion.   Henry James Pye.

   Air Balloon, The.   NOEC

   "Hail then ye daring few! who proudly soar."   NOEC

Aeroplane.   Pudjipangu.   NOBAu, *tr.* by George von Brandenstein

Aeschyleans, The.   Bernadette Mayer.   FTOS

Aesop at Play.   Phaedrus.   AWP, *tr.* by Christopher Smart

Aesop, mine author, makis mention.   Tale of the Upland Mouse and the Burgess Mouse, The.   Robert Henryson.   OBNV

Aesop Revised by Archy.   Don Marquis.   APT-1

Aesop's Fable of the Frogs.   Jean de La Fontaine.   OBVE, *tr.* by John Hookham Frere

Aestas.   Joshua Sylvester.   NOSC

Aesthete, The.   Sir William Schwenck Gilbert.   *See* Patience

Aesthetic Point of View, The.   W. H. Auden.   *See* Limerick: "As the poets have mournfully sung."

Aesthetic Point of View, The.   W. H. Auden.   *See* Shorts [1948–1957]

Aesthetics of the Bases Loaded Walk.   Joe Wenderoth.   AmPoNex

Aestivation [an Unpublished Poem, by My Late Latin Tutor].   Oliver Wendell Holmes.   NOBL; OBAL; TCAPo   *Fr.* Autocrat of the Breakfast Table, The.

Aestuary, An.   George Croly.   NOBRP

Aeterna Poetae Memoria.   Archibald MacLeish.   Son

Æthelstan King, lord of eorls.   Battle of Brunanburh.   *Unknown.*   AnOE, *tr.* by Charles Kennedy

Æthelstan the King, ruler of earls.   Battle of Brunanburh.   *Unknown.*   ASW, *tr.* by Kevin Crossley-Holland

Afakem! Afakem! Lalla Taouchamt!   Praise to the Tattoo Mistress.   Mririda n'Ait Attik.   WoPoe, *tr.* by Daniel Halpern and Paula Paley

Afar in the desert I love to ride.   War (?) in the Desert, A.   *Unknown.*   PeSAV

Afar though near the silence waxes.   Cloak, The.   Norman Henry Pritchard, II.   GT

Afay in de ewigkeit! (LL)   Hans Breitmann's Party [*or* Barty].   Charles Godfrey Leland.   NOBL; OBAL; OBCoV

Afetr a pretty amorous discourse.   Imperfect Enjoyment, The.   William Walsh.   NOSC

Affable Irregular, An.   W. B. Yeats.   BIrV; NOBE; NPeEn; PoE   *Fr.* Meditations in Time of Civil War.

Affair of Honour.   George Whalley.   MoCV

Affair of the Heart.   Peter Porter.   BMAP

Affair With a Chair, An.   Christopher Pilling.   NLP

Affairs of Memory.   Teresa Calderón.   TANSG, *tr.* by Celeste Kostopulos-Cooperman

Affairs of the world, The.   To the Emperor's Messenger.   Muso Soseki.   EaWin, *tr.* by W. S. Merwin

Affect of Elms, The.   Reginald Gibbons.   UrbNat

Affectionate.   Else Von Freytag-Loringhoven.   PFTM-1

Affectionate Shepherd [*or* Shephearde], The.   Richard Barnfield [*or* Barnefield].   (Affectionate Shepherd, The.)   OBGa

   "But if thou wilt not pittie my complaint."   CAGL; NoSic

   Daphnis to Ganymede.   CAGL

   "If thou wilt come and dwell with me at home."   CAGL

   "Oh would to God he would but pitty mee."   CAGL

   ("Or if thou dar'st to climb the highest trees.")   OBGa

   "Scarce had the morning starre hid from the light."   CAGL

   ("To play withall, new weaned from her dam.") (LL)   OBGa

   (Tears of an Affectionate Shepherd Sick for Love, The.)   CABP

   "When will my May come, that I may embrace thee?"   CAGL

Affections, instincts, principles, and powers.   Written in Butler's Sermons.   Matthew Arnold.   OxBSo

Affinity, The.   Anna Wickham.   NALW

Affirmative Action Blues (1993).   Elizabeth Alexander.   ExTi

Affirming it a Soul. (LL)   Emily Dickinson.   APN-2; WPoS

Affliction.   Bible, O.T.   TrJP   *Fr.* Lamentations.

Affliction.   Sir John Davies.   NOBE; WoPoe   *Fr.* Nosce Teipsum.

Affliction (1).   George Herbert.   BASC; ESCV; FHYEP; FSCP; GeHe; MeLP; NAEL-5v1; NAEL-6v1; NAEL-7v1; NOBE; NOSC; NoP-4

Affliction (3).   George Herbert.   NOSC

Affliction (4).   George Herbert.   ESCV; GeHe; NOSC

   (Affliction (IV).)   CABP

Affliction (IV).   George Herbert.   *See* Affliction (4)

Affliction: "Kill me not every [*or* ev'ry] day."   George Herbert.   NOSC

Affliction of Margaret—The The.   William Wordsworth.   GTBS-P; RACG

Affliction shall advance the flight in me. (LL)   Easter Wings.   George Herbert.   AngWePo; BASC; CABP; ChIV-1; ESCV; FHYEP; FSCP; GeHe; HAP; HeIP-4; InPK-6; MakPoe; MeLP; NAEL-5v1; NAEL-6v1; NAEL-7v1; NIL-7; NIP-4; NOSC; NoP-4; PAI; PBRV; PoE; PoPoPo; SacPr; TFi; TOF; TRP; TrCP; WeW-3; WoPoe

Afloat between lives and stale truths.   Guardian Angel, The.   Stephen Dunn.   OPRER

Afoot and light-hearted I take to the open road.   Walt Whitman.   NOBA

Afraid! Of whom am I afraid?   Emily Dickinson.   PoE

Afreeka Brass.   Mwatabu Okantah.   SeSe

Afresh'd with paint the shop had glare.   New Storefront.   Russell Atkins.   GT

Africa.   Maya Angelou.   NIL-7; NIP-4

Africa.   David Diop.   NegPo; PBA; PBMAP; TTY

Africa.   Change Is Not Always Progress.   Haki R. Madhubuti.   TAP

Africa.   Claude McKay.   APT-1; NAAAL; NAAL-5; Son

Africa.   Joaquin Miller.   APN-2

Africa.   Lizelia Augusta Jenkins Moorer.   CBWP-3

Africa.   Rosario Morales.   PueRic

Africa cannot be wounded.   Angel in the Temple of Luxor, An.   Rodney M. McNeil.   InTrad

Africa of the Statue, The.   Amina Said.   HAWP; NAfrP, *tr.* by Eric Sellin

Africa's Plea.   Roland Tombekai Dempster.   TTY

Africa Says.   Carl Phillips.   PoPoPo

Africa Sky.   Kojo Laing.   HBAPE

Africa Thing, The.   Adam David Miller.   NBV

Africa waters the roots of my tree.   Africa.   Rosario Morales.   PueRic

Africa, you were once just a name to me.   Meaning of Africa, The.   Abioseh Nicol.   PBA

African Boog.   Allen Fisher.   Oth

African Chief, The.   William Cullen Bryant.   ColAP

African China.   Melvin B. Tolson.   ColAP

African Christmas.   John Press.   OBCP

African Desert.   Samuel Greenberg.   APT-1

African Dream.   Bob Kaufman.   GT

African Easter.   Abioseh Nicol.   PBA

African Elegy, An.   Robert Duncan.   NoAM

African image is not an image by equation but an image by *analogy*, The.   "African Image Is Not An Image by Equation. . . , The."   Léopold Sédar Senghor.   PFTM-1

African in Louisiana.   Kojo Gyinaye Kyei.   PBA

African Lion, The.   A. E. Housman.   NOxBChV

African of the statue, the.   Africa of the Statue, The.   Amina Said.   HAWP; NAfrP, *tr.* by Eric Sellin

African Poem.   Agostinho Neto.   PBMAP; PoetW, *tr.* by W. S. Merwin

African Queen.   Willem M. Roggeman.   TuT, *tr.* by Gabriel Rosenstock

African Sculpture.   Christopher Gilbert.   ESEAA

African sister, standing there in her radiant beauty.   Poetry for the Goddess.   William T. Crawley III.   InTrad

African Sleeping Sickness.   Wanda Coleman.   PmAP

African Student.   Noel H. Brettell.   PeSAV

African Sunday.   Maureen Owen.   PmAP

African Thunderstorm, An.   James David Rubadiri.   PBMAP

African Trader's Complaint, The.   Dennis C. Osadebay.   PBA

Afro-American Beats III: An American Memory of Africa.   Kofi Awoonor.   *See* American Memory of Africa, An

Aft' them white trash any mo' (LL)   Mrs. Johnson Objects.   Clara Ann Thompson.   BlSi; CBWP-2

Aften hae I played at the cards and the dice.   Rantin Laddie, The.   Robert Burns.   ESPB

After.   Ralph Hodgson.   MoBrPo

After.   Philip Bourke Marston.   NOBVV

After.   May Probyn.   VWP

After a Bath.   Aileen Fisher.   OTCP

After a black day, I play Haydn.   Allegro.   Tomas Tranströmer.   SPE, *tr.* by Robert Bly

After a Death.   Roo Borson.   NIL-7

After a Death.   Charles Tomlinson.   HarvBoo

After a Death.   Tomas Tranströmer.   VCWP, *tr.* by Robert Bly

After a fearful maze where doubt.   Chimera.   Barbara Howes.   TwCP

After a Friendship.   Robert Minhinnick.   AngWePo

After a hundred years.   Emily Dickinson.   APN-2; AWP; OxBA

After a Journey.   Thomas Hardy.   EBEV; EnLoPo; GTBS-P; HarvBoo; NPeEn; OxAEP-2; OxBEV; OxBTC; PoE

After a little I could not have told. Song of the Tortured Girl, The. John Berryman. CoAP

After a Long Illness. Robert Duncan. PFTM-2

After a long nap. Issa. SoOfWa, *tr.* by Sam Hamill

After a long night of love. (LL) Kenneth Rexroth. APSN; APT-2 *Fr.* Love Poems of Marichiko, The.

After a long winter, giving / each other nothing. Chiyojo [*or* Chiyo *or* Chiyo-Ni *or* Kaga no Chiyo *or* Fukuda Chiyo-Ni]. BoWoP

After a month and a half without rain. August Rain. Robert Bly. LCAP-2

After a night of languour without rest. Sea-Breeze at Matanzas, The. Epes Sargent. APN-1

After a night of rage. Love Poem for a Wife, 2. A. K. Ramanujan. OMIP; WoPoe

After a night of rain. In a Japanese Moss Garden. Brad Leithauser. OBGa

After a Parting. Alice Thompson Meynell. NOBVV

After a Passage in Baudelaire. Robert Duncan. PoE

After a ship had been wrecked. Parrot at Sea, A. Yelena [*or* Elena] Shwarts [*or* Shvarts]. ItGoST, *tr.* by Catriona Kelly

After a slow day of repose. Old Dog. Michael L. Johnson. UrbNat

After a Spring meeting in their nineteenth-century fastness at. Irish Hierarchy Bans Colour Photography. Paul Durcan. BiHa; PBCIP

After a Storm, Going a Hawking. George Daniel. NOSC

After a supper of roasted lamb and eggplant. World Is a Wedding, The. Adele Ne Jame. PoArWo

After a Tempest. William Cullen Bryant. APN-1

After a throbbing night, the house still dark, pull. Those of Pure Origin. Roy Fuller. FaBoMo

After a Time. Elizabeth Jennings. HarvBoo

After a time the grave got up and went away. (LL) As He Came near Death. Roy Fisher. FaBoMo; HarvBoo; NPeEn

After a Train Journey. May Sarton. GM

After a week of physical anguish. Evening Lull, An. Walt Whitman. NAAL-2v1; NAAL-3

After all, Charlie, we shall see them go. Longshore Intellectual. Sean Lucy. CIP-2

After all, I still have each other. (LL) *Unknown.* OBCoV; PeLi

After all the drive-in theaters have closed. Translated from the American. Sherman Alexie. UnSA

After All These Years. May Sarton. PoBW

After all this time without you. I Wish I Didn't Love You So. Frank Loesser. ReLy

After all those years. Accomplices. Zhao Zhenkai. VCWP

After all, you are my rather tedious hero;. To Myself. Kenneth Slessor. BMAP

After an age when thunderbolts and hail. Sonnet XVI: "After an age when thunderbolts and hail." Louise Labé. BoWoP, *tr.* by Willis Barnstone

After an hundred and thirty years' nap. On the Erection of Shakespeare's Statue in Westminster Abbey. Pope. FaBoEE

After Anacreon. Lew Welch. NeAP; PoM *Fr.* Taxi Suite.

After Annunciation. Anna Wickham. MoBrPo

After Apple-Picking. Robert Frost. APT-1; MoAmPo; NAAL-2v2; NAAL-5; NOBA; NoAM; OxBA; PAI; PoE; SAmP; SoSe-8; TAP; TCAPo; TFi; TRP; UnPo

After Arguing against the Contention That Art Must Come from Discontent. William Stafford. NoAM

After Asia. Michael Stephens. CDa

After Aughrim. Emily Lawless. OBEV

After autumn's fever and its vivid trees. Six Poems on Nothing. Gwyneth Lewis. HarvBoo

After Babel. Peter Goldsworthy. NOBAu

After Beethoven. Raymond Roseliep. HA

After Blenheim. Robert Southey. *See* Battle of Blenheim, The

After Burying Her Son, A Mother Speaks. Mark Pawlak. GifTon

After Carnival. Peter Rafferty. NLP

After Christmas. W. H. Auden. ChrPo; MoBrPo; OBCP *Fr.* For the Time Being; a Christmas Oratorio.

After Christmas. Michael Richards. OBCP

After church meeting. Tanka. Lenard D. Moore. SpirFl

After church spires and city chimneys have sunk below the horizon. In England. Duo Duo (Li Shizheng). PoetW, *tr.* by Maghiel Van Crevel

After Collecting the Autumn Taxes. Po Chü-i. BLT; ChiP, *tr.* by Arthur Waley

After Communion. Christina Georgina Rossetti. SacPr; WPoS

After Dark. Adrienne Rich. LCAP-2; VGW

After dark / Near the South Dakota border. Having Lost My Sons, I Confront the Wreckage of the Moon: Christmas, 1960. James Wright. CoAP; HCAP; NAAL-2v2

After Dark Vapours Have Oppressed Our Plains. John Keats. CenSon; NPeEn

After Death. Christina Georgina Rossetti. NAEL-5v2; NAEL-6v2; NALW

After Death. Algernon Charles Swinburne. NOBVV; PeVV

After death, and clean as a finishing line. (LL) Crafty Butcher, The. Susan Hampton. BMAP; NOBAu

After Death Nothing Is. Seneca. EBEV; OBVE, *tr.* by John Wilmot, 2d Earl of Rochester *Fr.* Troades.

After death, suppose we were judged by animals:. Tribunal, The. Chris Wallace-Crabbe. ChIV-2

After Delivering Your Lunch. Lynne Yamaguchi Fletcher. FSt

After Dinner. Robert Burns. *Fr.* Graces————at the Globe Tavern.

After dinner Erasmus. Edmund Clerihew Bentley. OBCoV *Fr.* Clerihews.

After-Dinner Poem (Terpsichore), An. Oliver Wendell Holmes. TCAPo

After dream / How real. Ome Shushiki. ZenPo, *tr.* by Takashi Ikemoto and Lucien Stryk

After dreaming some hours of the land of Cockaigne. Thomas Moore. BIrV *Fr.* Fudge Family in Paris, The.

After Eden. Rachel Tzvia Back. DTA

After Eden. James Simmons. PNI

After Edward Hopper. Lawrence Raab. PoSol

After Eight Years of Marriage. Mamta Kalia. ItWoWo

After eight years of marriage. After Eight Years of Marriage. Mamta Kalia. ItWoWo

After Elegies. Jean Valentine. LCAP-2

After 11 years. Most Beautiful Woman at My Highschool Reunion, The. Ellen Marie Bissert. GLP

After Estrangement. Molly Bendall. AmPoNex

After Ever Happily [*or,* The Princess and the Woodcutter]. Ian Serraillier. OBSP

After every war. End and the Beginning, The. Wislawa Szymborska. VCWP, *tr.* by Stanislaw Baranczak

After Experience Taught Me. W. D. Snodgrass. CoAP; OBWP

After explanations and regulations, he. WASP Woman Visits a Black Junkie in Prison, A. Etheridge Knight. NBV

After Fall, 1956. Devorah Amir. DTA, *tr.* by Miriyam Glazer

After father's wake. Nicholas Virgilio. HA

After fifteen months you fly in. Visitation Rights. Heather Wishik. GLP

After Fighting for Hours. Kate Gleason. BAP-97

After Five Years. Augustus Young. BIrV

After five years maternity leave. Gap, The. Annie Foster. NLP

After Friedan and the flare. Wildsisters Bar. Judith Vollmer. SwNoth

After Frost. Brian Patten. EBEV

After Galen. Oliver St. John Gogarty. FaBoEE; OBMV; PoRA

After gazing at stars. Tom Tico. HA

After Getting Drunk, Becoming Sober in the Night. Po Chü-i. BLT; ChiP, *tr.* by Arthur Waley

After Getting Drunk, I Scribble Songs and Poems in Grass Script—Written as a Joke. Lu Yu. CoBCP, *tr.* by Burton Watson

After-Glow of Pain, The. Clara Ann Thompson. CBWP-2

After Goliath. Kingsley Amis. NOBL; OxBTC

After Grave Deliberation. Elizabeth Flynn. NBLV

After Greece. James Merrill. CoAmPo; ColAP; NOBA; TRP

After Grief. Stanley Plumly. LCAP-2

After hangin' Danny Deever in the mornin'! (LL) Danny Deever. Rudyard Kipling. BRP; EBVV; FaBoWar; GTBS-P; MoBrPo; NAEL-5v2; NAEL-6v2; NOBE; NOBVV; NPeEn; NoAM; OxBEV; OxBTC; OxBoLi; PeVV; SCGP; SCV; TFi; UnPo

After having loved we lie close together. Sailing. Henrik Nordbrandt. VCWP, *tr.* by Henrik Norbrandt and Alexander Taylor

After having slain very many beasts. Sonnet XIX: "After having slain very many beasts." Louise Labé. BoWoP, *tr.* by Willis Barnstone

After he died. She Lived. Lucille Clifton. LoL

After He Had Gone. Sylvia Townsend Warner. MoBrPo

After he leaves. Alexis Rotella. HA

After he stripped off my clothes. Villana [*or* Vallana]. BoWoP

After hearing about the death of Melvin. Return to Temptation. Mary Weems. SpirFl

After Hearing Heterosexual Poets in October 1974: What It Seems Like To Write a Male Homosexual Love Poem Now. Joseph Cady. CAGL

After Her Man Had Left Her for the Sixth Time That Year (An Uncommon Occurrence). Haki R. Madhubuti. GT

After her pills the girl slept and counted. Tally. Josephine Miles. NoAM

After her wedding-night, the nymph. Martial. RomPo, *tr.* by Peter Whigham

After high school Latin class. Preparing the Dead. Paulette Roeske. IllVoic

After Hilaire Belloc. Max Beerbohm. OBCoV; UV

After his ham & cheese in the drape factory cafeteria. Torque. David Rivard. PBCAP

After his shower he reaches for. Robe, The. Martha Rhodes. ExTi

After his talking destroyed her. Antarctica. Ronald Albert Simpson. CBAP

After his tryst. Fujiwara no Teika. WoPoe, *tr.* by Steven D. Carter

After Horace. Alfred Denis Godley. NOBL

After hot loveless nights, when cold winds stream. Sisters, The. Roy Campbell. BoLoP; FaBoTw; NoP-4; OBMV

After I got religion and steadied down. Edgar Lee Masters. APT-1 *Fr.* Spoon River Anthology.

After I had cut off my hands. Intrusion. Denise Levertov. VCAP

After I Had Worked All Day. Charles Reznikoff. VGW *Fr.* Five Groups of Verse.

After I had worked all day at what I earn my living. Charles Reznikoff. APT-2

After I Seized the Pentagon. Robert Hass. YaYoPo

After I step. George Swede. HA

After I Was Dead. Laura Mullen. ExTi

After I write *My face burned and I wanted to cry.* Courage, or One of Gene Horner's Fiddles. Lisa Coffman. AmPoNex

After-Image. Linda Bierds. ExTi

After it rains you should sigh a little for the spongy world. Sounds, The. Gerald Stern. BodElec

After Jericho. Ronald Stuart Thomas. OxBC

After Jesus raised him from the dead. Lazarus. Ron Koertge. OPRER

After Jill died they remembered how she liked this chair. Jill's Death. George Buchanan. PNI

After kicking on the swing. To the Tune "I Paint My Lips Red." Li Ch'ing-chao. BoWoP, *tr. by* Chung Ling and Kenneth Rexroth

After Lalon. Allen Ginsberg. BB

After late evenings. After Touch. Jan Clausen. GLP

After Liberation. J. C. Bloem. TuT, *tr. by* Seamus Heaney

After Life. Anna Hajnal. IQMS, *tr. by* Jeannette Nichols

After Listening to Jack Teagarden. . . . James McKean. SeSe

After Long Rain. Wang Wei. TAL

After Long Silence. W. B. Yeats. BoLoP; EnLoPo; HeIP-4; NAEL-5v2; NAEL-6v2; OBMV; UnPo

After long wars when comes release. Herba Santa. Herman Melville. NCAP

After Longfellow. *Unknown.* NOBL

After Lorca. Robert Creeley. CoAmPo; LCAP-2; PmAP

After Love. Maxine W. Kumin. TAP

After Love. Sara Teasdale. APT-1

After Lunch. Po Chü-i. ChiP, *tr. by* Arthur Waley

  (Accepts the life given him, long or short.) (LL) CoBCP, *tr. by* Burton Watson

  (After lunch—one short nap.) ChiP, *tr. by* Arthur Waley

After lunch the old Duchess of Teck. Limerick: "After lunch the old Duchess of Teck." *Unknown.* PeLi

After making love. Midnight. Alison Kolodinsky. PasH

After Making Love We Hear Footsteps. Galway Kinnell. ColAP; NAAL-5; NIL-7; NIP-4; NoAM; NoP-4; PasH; RaBo; VCAP

After many scorns [*or* scornes] like these. Ben Jonson. NAEL-6v1; NAEL-7v1 *Fr.* Celebration of Charis in Ten Lyric[k] Pieces [*or* Peeces], A.

After Margrave died, nothing. History of a Literary Movement. Howard Nemerov. PoE

After Mass. "Michael Field." WPE

After mass, became drunk, fell down, and made violent love to nobody. My Life in Yonago. Sharon Mesmer. HeMarv

After Midnight. Louis Simpson. BLT; NoAM

After Midnight. Charles Vildrac. AWP, *tr. by* Jethro Bithell

After midnight I heard a scream. By Night. Robert Francis. APT-2; VGW

After midnight the blizzard howls itself out. Blizzard. Bill Holm. MiVo

After midnight they load up. Boat People. Yusef Komunyakaa. AF; CDa; PoPoPo

After Midsummer. Edith Jay Scovell. OxBTC

After much biologic research. Original Summer Girl, The. Carolyn Wells. SWaP

After much driving. 1974—The Sounds. Christina Beer. PeNZ

After Music. Josephine Preston Peabody. TCAPo

After my bath. After a Bath. Aileen Fisher. OTCP

After my determined calendar of checkups. Emergency. Julio Marzán. PueRic

After my illness, so hard to be a traveler. Yang Chi. CoBLCP *Fr.* From Sand River to Ts'ai Rock.

After my reading. Exile. Danton R. Remoto. ReBoTo

After Night Flight Son Reaches Bedside of Already Unconscious Father, Whose Right Hand Lifts in a Spasmodic Gesture, as Though Trying to Make Contact: 1955. Robert Penn Warren. NOBA *Fr.* Mortmain.

After night in. Lucien Stryk. IllVoic *Fr.* Issa: A Suite of Haiku.

After night's thunder far away had rolled. Haymaking. Edward Thomas. MoBrPo

After Nightfall. William Renton. NOBVV

After noon I lie down. Josephine Miles. APT-2

After one moment when I bowed my head. Convert, The. Gilbert Keith Chesterton. ChIV-2; SacPr

After one whole quart of brandy. Bewitched, Bothered and Bewildered. Lorenz Hart. APT-2

After our fierce loving. Profile on the Pillow, The. Dudley Randall. BPo; TAP

After Our War. John Balaban. CDa; GifTon

After Ovid, Tristia. Peter Scupham. HarvBoo

After Parade the little American girl left the theater. Fairy Scene. Jean Cocteau. CuPo

After Passing the Examination. Meng Chiao. SuSp, *tr. by* Irving Y. Lo

After Passing the Examination. Po Chü-i. ChiP, *tr. by* Arthur Waley

After Paul Durcan left his wife. Levite and His Concubine at Gibeah, The. Paul Durcan. ModIr

After Picasso. Franz Wright.

  Depiction of Childhood. BLT

  "It is the little girl." BLT

After practice: right foot. Boy Juggling a Soccer Ball, A. Christopher Merrill. MoASP

After Prayers, Lie Cold. Clive Staples Lewis. SacPr

After Publication of Under the Volcano. Malcolm Lowry. FaBoTw

After Rain. Patricia K. Page. NOBC; PoE

After Rain. Tu Fu. CrYelRi, *tr. by* Sam Hamill

After rain. Mountain Study. Peter Van Toorn. NOBC

After rain a bright moon appears. Written beneath Hui Mountain, When Tsou Liu-yi Comes by for a Visit. Wang Shih-chieng. SuSp, *tr. by* Richard John Lynn

After rain, in the darkened room, the body. Body in Youth, The. Ellen Hinsey. YaYoPo

After rain, mushrooms. Washington Etude. Elizabeth Alexander. NAPBL

After rain, through afterglow, the unfolding fan. Train Ride. John Wheelwright. VGW

After Rain, Visiting the Temple of Heavenly Peace. Wang Shih-chieng. CoBLCP, *tr. by* Jonathan Chaves

After Reading in a Letter Proposals for Building a Cottage. John Clare. OxAEP-2

After Reading Lao Tzu. Po Chü-i. CrYelRi, *tr. by* Sam Hamill

After Reading *Mickey in the Night Kitchen* for the Third Time Before Bed. Rita Dove. LoL; ReTh

After Reading *Poems to Einhir*. Gwyn Williams. TCAWP

After Reading Reznikoff. Kate Daniels. ExTi

After Reading Shakspere. Edwin Markham. APN-2

After Reading St. John the Divine. Gene Derwood. WPE

After Reading the Book of Splendor. Emily Warn. GifTon

After Reading "The Country of the Pointed Firs." Jean Garrigue. VCAP

After Reading the Life of Mrs. Catherine Stubbs in Isaac Ambrose's "War with the Devils." Isaac Hann. NOCV

After Reading the Poems of Master Han Shan. Wang Chiu-ssu. CoBLCP, *tr. by* Jonathan Chaves

  "Floating, floating, the river waters." WoPoe, *tr. by* Jonathan Chaves

  "This crazy man has escaped the world." WoPoe, *tr. by* Jonathan Chaves

After scanning its face again and again. Gary Snyder. NOBA *Fr.* Myths and Texts.

After school he lured Ceolred, who was sniggering with fright, down to the old quarries, and flayed him. Then, leaving Ceolred, he journeyed for hours, calm and alone, in his private derelict sandlorry named *Albion*. (LL) Geoffrey Hill. HAP; NPeEn; NoAM; NoP-4 *Fr.* Mercian Hymns.

After School, Street Football, Eighth Grade. Dennis Cooper. WiU

After Seeing Paintings in a Small Book by T. C. Cannon (1946–1978). Alice Sadongei. HATNAP

After seven years and as the wine. Ourselves or Nothing. Carolyn Forché. BodElec; GifTon

After shaking paws with his dog. W. H. Auden. GI; PoE *Fr.* Horae Canonicae.

After sharp words from the fine mind. Flowering Bars, The. Charles Donnelly. CIP-2

After she rose from the dark throat. Undine. Nicole Cooley. AmPoNex

After six little spaces of chill, and six of burning. (LL) John Crowe Ransom. APT-1; AWP; HAP; MoAmPo; NAAL-2v2; NoAM; PoRA; RB; TAP; VGW *Fr.* Sixteen Poems in Eight Pairings.

After 65. Richard Howard. BAP-01

After Snow—Impromptu. Yü Chi. CoBLCP, *tr. by* Jonathan Chaves

After Snow, Longing for Elder Brother Hsi-ch'iao. Wang Shih-chieng. ColAnChi

After so long. Diaspora. S. V. Atalla. PoArWo

After so long a race as I have run. Edmund Spenser. CABP *Fr.* Amoretti.

After so many years. Hand Mirror. Daisy Zamora. LoL, *tr. by* Barbara Paschke

After so much battering of fire and steel. Butchers and Tombs. Ivor Gurney. PeFWW

After Solstice. Tu Fu. CrYelRi, *tr.* by Sam Hamill

After solstice, the sunlight slowly lengthens. From. After Solstice. Tu Fu. CrYelRi, *tr.* by Sam Hamill

After some years Bohemian came to this. Epigram: "After some years Bohemian came to this." James Vincent Cunningham. VGW

After Soufrière. "Michael Field." VWP

After Source of the Peach Blossom Stream. Wang Wei. ChinPo, *tr.* by Yip Wai-lim

After spring has come. *Unknown.* ArkPo, *tr.* by Edwin A. Cranston

After spring snow, the capital's a city of mud. Working for the Government. Wang An-shih. CrYelRi, *tr.* by Sam Hamill

After-State. Frederick William Faber. CenSon

After such years of dissension and strife. Dust to Dust. Thomas Hood. NBLV

After sundown the clouds start to burn. Thunderstorm. Sam Mitchell. NOBAu, *tr.* by George von Brandenstein

After Supper. David Keller. SwNoth

After supper in the big room. Broken Sonnets. Kim Addonizio. OPRER

After ten days I come here again. On the Sixteenth Day I Visit the Temple Again. Pien Kung. CoBLCP, *tr.* by Jonathan Chaves

After ten thousand years I will repeat my claim. Back to the First Bar. Emmy Bridgwater. SurWo

After ten years in the red-light district. Ikkyu Sojun. ZenPo, *tr.* by Takashi Ikemoto and Lucien Stryk

After that war, when death had gone away. Joan Miró. Ruthven Todd. SPE

After the abduction by the eagle, after the lovely indiscretion with the boy. Hebe and Ganymede. *Unknown.* CAGL, *tr.* by John Boswell

After the act of stabbing and. Stone Wall and Celebration. János Pilinszky. PoSu, *tr.* by Peter Jay

After the air of summer. (LL) Roman Fountain. Louise Bogan. APT-2; NoP-4; WPOW

After the all been done and i. Island Mary. Lucille Clifton. NALW

After the Anti-Semitic Calls on a Local Talk Station. Lyn Lifshin. UnSA

After the Apocalypse. Samih Al-Qasim.
  "I feel my limbs." MAP

After the Ball. Imamu Amiri Baraka. NAAL-2v2

After the baths and bowel-work, he was dead. Gwendolyn Brooks. ColAP *Fr.* Notes from the Childhood and the Girlhood.

After the Battle. Victor Hugo. SxFrPo, *tr.* by E. H. Blackmore and A. M. Blackmore

After the Battle. Anton Malczewski. WoPoe, *tr.* by Jerzy Peterkiewicz and Burns Singer

After the Big Flood, we elected. Transposition of Clermont, The. Les A. Murray. EmeKit

After the bird has flown. (LL) Refusal to Mourn, A. Derek Mahon. ModIr; PNI

After the blast of lightning from the east. End, The. Wilfred Owen. ChIV-1

After the Bomb Tests. Jane Cooper.
  "Atom bellies like a cauliflower, The." MakPoe

After the border, it was trees all the way to. British Columbia. William Stafford. GifTon

After the boy threw the pregnant turtle. Turtle Blessing. Penny Harter. TWW

After the break-in. Unnatural Light. Peter Meinke. UrbNat

After the brief bivouac of Sunday. Stenographers, The. Patricia K. Page. HeIP-4; NALW; NoAM

After the Broken Arm. Ron Padgett. CoAmPo; SPE

After the Burial. James Russell Lowell. UnPo

After the burial-parties leave. Hyænas [or Hyenas], The. Rudyard Kipling. NAEL-5v2; NAEL-6v2; OBSV

After the Children Have Gone to Bed. Nicholas Samaras. TWW

After the cloud came to a dead stop. Genoa. Dino Campana. PFTM-1

After the cloud embankments. Reconnaissance. Arna Bontemps. APT-2; BPo

After the Colombian Earthquake. Maurice Kilwein Guevara. NAPBL

After the Convention. Robert Lowell. NoAM

After the Dance. Reuben Jackson. GT

After the Dance for the Dead. Sogetsuni. SoOfWa, *tr.* by Sam Hamill

After the dancing ended, and the Russians. Slow Night on Texas Street, A. James Kimbrell. NAPBL

After the Death of an Elder Klallam. Duane Niatum. CDW

After the Defeat. Yannis Ritsos. AF, *tr.* by Edmund Keeley

After the Deluge. Wole Soyinka. HBAPE

After the Dinner Party. Robert Penn Warren. NAAL-5

After the door shuts and the footsteps die. Hunt in the Black Forest, A. Randall Jarrell. CoAP; LCAP-2

After the dread tales and red yarns of the Line. First Time In. Ivor Gurney. FaBoVe

After the eating, the drinking, the singing. Song: "After the eating, the drinking, the singing." Liu Yung. CrYelRi, *tr.* by Sam Hamill

After the End. Ann Townsend. AmPoNex

After the End of the World. David Jauss. SeSe

After the event the rockslide. Clarity. A. R. Ammons. HCAP; TAP

After the explosion or cataclysm, that big. Eternal City, The. A. R. Ammons. HCAP

After the eyes that looked, the lips that spake. Bayard Taylor. CBCWP

After the Fair. Thomas Hardy. HAP *Fr.* At Casterbridge Fair.

After the Fall of Saigon. Yusef Komunyakaa. AF; CDa

After the fallen sun the wind was sad. Moonrise Over Battlefield. Edgell Rickword. PoWW

After the feast, my Shapcott, see. Oberon's Palace. Robert Herrick. CaPo

After the fierce midsummer all ablaze. Friendship After Love. Ella Wheeler Wilcox. APN-2; LW

After the fiercest pangs of hot desire. Song, A. Richard Duke. BoLoP; ECEV

After the Fifth of June. Yusuf Al-Khal. MAP, *tr.* by May Jayyusi and Naomi Shihab Nye

After the final heave, house collapsing. Gaza, Undated. Rachel Tzvia Back. DTA

After the First Communion. Sunday Afternoon. Denise Levertov. CoAmPo; PAI

After the first death, there is no other. (LL) Refusal to Mourn the Death, by Fire, of a Child in London, A. Dylan Thomas. AF; EBEV; FaBoMo; FaBoWar; GTBS-P; HarvBoo; HeIP-4; MoBrPo; NOBE; NoAM; NoP-4; OBWVE; OxAEP-2; OxBTC; PAI; PoE; PoWW; TFi; TwCP; UnPo

After the First Frost. Lew Blockcolski. VoR

After the first powerful plain manifesto. Express, The. Stephen Spender. HeIP-4; MoBrPo; NIL-7; NoAM; TwCP

After the first shallows have dropped away. Daily the Ocean between Us. Patricia Goedicke. TAP

After the first terror. Nuclear Winter. Thomas McGrath. GifTon

After the Flight of the Earls. Fearflatha O'Gnive [or O'Gnimh]. NOIV

After the Flood. John Foulcher. NOBAu

After the Flood. Maurice Kilwein Guevara. NAPBL

After the Flood. Sir David Lindsay [or Lyndsay]. ChIV-1; OxBS *Fr.* Monarche, The.

After the Flood. Arthur Rimbaud. SxFrPo, *tr.* by Martin Sorrell

After the full moon. Alexis Rotella. HA

After the Funeral. Dylan Thomas. AngWePo; FaBoMo; NAEL-5v2; NAEL-6v2; NoP-4; OBWVE; OxAEP-2; TCAWP

After the Funeral of Assam Hamady. Sam Hamod. GraLe; UnSA

After the general had broken the blockade at Hsüan-chou. Ballad of the Maiden of Lan-ling. Chin Ho. ColAnChi, *tr.* by Victor H. Mair

After the gods left, the trucks of evening. Atlantis. Joanna Fuhrman. AmPoNex

After the Golden Wedding. James Kenneth Stephen.
  "She's not a faultless woman; no!" EBVV; NOBVV

After the green storm / True color. Mukai Kyorai. ZenPo, *tr.* by Takashi Ikemoto and Lucien Stryk

After the Harvest. Tu Fu. CrYelRi, *tr.* by Sam Hamill

After the heavy losses that the Athenians suffered at Aegospotami / and a little later. After the Defeat. Yannis Ritsos. AF, *tr.* by Edmund Keeley

After the horrors of Heathrow. 747 (London–Chicago). Robert Conquest. OxBC

After the hours that Sarajevans pass. Bright Lights of Sarajevo, The. Tony Harrison. EmeKit

After the Hunt. Detlev, Freiherr von Liliencron. AWP, *tr.* by Ludwig Lewisohn

After the Hurricane. Sinéad Morrissey. MFPA

After the Industrial Revolution, All Things Happen at Once. Robert Bly. CoAP; CoAmPo

After the Inscription on a Greek Stele of a Woman Holding Her Grandchild on Her Knees. *Unknown.* GrAn, *tr.* by Stephen Spender

After the Irish of Egan O'Rahilly. Egan [or Aodhagán] O'Rahilly [or O'Reilly or Ó Rathaille]. *See* Time of Change, A

After the Last Bulletins. Richard Wilbur. CoAP; CoAmPo; MoAmPo

After the Last Dynasty. Stanley Kunitz. InvLad; TAP

After the last exhausted horse. Pat Taffe and Arkle. Tracey Herd. MFPA

After the leaves have fallen, we return. Plain Sense of Things, The. Wallace Stevens. APT-1; EmeKit; HCAP; NAAL-5; NoAM; PAI

After the legshows and the brandies. Louis MacNeice. OxBSP *Fr.* Entered in the Minutes.

After *The Little Mariner*. Olga Broumas. BodElec

After the long and portentous eclipse of the patient sun. Green Song. Dame Edith Sitwell. BWW

After the Massacre. Musaemura Bonus Zimunya. PeSAV

After the midnight unfolding of the White Rose. Feast of Stephen, The. Kevin Nichols. OBCP

After the midwinter marriages—the bride of snow. John Hollander. VCAP *Fr.* Powers of Thirteen.

After the milk-white hounds of the moon. (LL) Madman's Song. Elinor Wylie. MoAmPo; PoRA

After / the Moratorium Reading. Nigel Roberts. NOBAu

After the murder. Last Quatrain of the Ballad of Emmett Till, The. Gwendolyn Brooks. ESEAA; LCAP-2; NAAL-5; WPE

After the night's black veil. Separation from Clorila, The. José Manuel Martínez de Navarrete. BLPSL, *tr.* by Rene de Costa, Rigas Kappatos and Eleni Paidoussi

After the Noise of Saigon. Walter McDonald. OPRER

After the noose, and the black diary deeds. Richard Murphy. ModIr; NOIV; PBCIP *Fr.* Battle of Aughrim, The.

After the nuclear strike. War Games. Connie Bensley. FaBoWar

After the Pangs of a Desperate Lover. Dryden. PeLV *Fr.* Evening's Love, An.

After the paradiso and the milky way and the kosmos, seeming. Yolanda Meets the White Boys. Jessica Tarahata Hagedorn. OpBo

After the Party. Luigi Fontanella. NeIt, *tr.* by W. S. Di Piero

After the planes unloaded, we fell down. Dead in Europe, The. Robert Lowell. OxBA; OxBC; WoPoe

After the Pleasure Party. Herman Melville. APN-2; NAAL-2v1; NAAL-3 (Fear me, virgin whosoever.) NCAP

After the ploughshare and the stumbling team. (LL) As the Team's Head-Brass. Edward Thomas. CABP; GTBS-P; HarvBoo; NAEL-5v2; NAEL-6v2; NoP-4; OBWP; OxAEP-2; OxBTC; PeFWW; PoE; RB

After the Poem. Sydney Clouts. PeSAV

After the poem the coastline took. After the Poem. Sydney Clouts. PeSAV

After the Poem Who Knows. Alan Michael Parker. NAPBL

After the police left, having told me of your death. Amor Diving. Marion Lomax. NeBl

After the Prom. Lisa D. Chavez. AmPoNex

After the promise has been kept, or. Afterward. Robert Penn Warren. BodElec

After the Quarrel. Priscilla Jane Thompson. CBWP-2

After the Rain. Kristina Rungano. HAWP

After the rain of stars. At the Gate of the Valley. Zbigniew Herbert. PoSu, *tr.* by Czeslaw Milosz

After the rain, the vegetables from your garden. Yang Shih-ch'i. CoBLCP *Fr.* Libationer Hu Became Ill from Eating Sunflowers. These Poems Are Playfully Presented to Him and Are Also Intended to Thank Him for the Vegetables He Sent Me.

After the rain, when the earth releases. Eating Wild Mushrooms. Gary Young. GeoHom

After the ranks of stubble have lain bare. Autumn Ploughing. John Masefield. OxBEV

After the rapture comes, and everyone goes away. March Journal. Charles Wright. LCAP-2

After the rare arch-poet Jonson died. Upon M. Ben Jo[h]nson: Epigram. Robert Herrick. BeJo; CaPo

After the red-rose-bordered hem. (LL) To Ireland in the Coming Times. W. B. Yeats. NOIV; NoAM

After the revolution came the Fuehrer. Traditional Tune. Muriel Rukeyser. TaR

After the rushing waters had subsided the Lenape of the turtle were close together, in hollow houses, living together there. *Unknown.* APN-2 *Fr.* Walam Olum; or, Red Score [of the Lenâpé], The [*or* The Wallam Olum; The Red Score or Painted History of the Lenni Lenape].

After the Sea-Ship. Walt Whitman. APN-1

After the search for meaning bills in the mail. George Swede. HA

After the second book. Poet at Work. Richard Tipping. BMAP

After the Second Operation. Patricia Goedicke. TAP

After the Seizer there were ten chiefs, and there was much warfare south and east. *Unknown.* OBVE *Fr.* Walam Olum; or, Red Score [of the Lenâpé], The [*or* The Wallam Olum; The Red Score or Painted History of the Lenni Lenape].

After the sentence. Letters to Martha. Dennis Brutus. PeSAV

After the shower. Cor Van den Heuvel. HA

After the silence of the centuries? (LL) Man with the Hoe, The. Edwin Markham. APN-2; BRP; GS; MoAmPo; TCAPo; TFi

After the Small Pox. Mary Jones. PEW

After the snowfall. Lorraine Ellis Harr. HA

After the spring song, "Vast emptiness, no holiness," Shunoku. ZenPo, *tr.* by Takashi Ikemoto and Lucien Stryk

After the stars were all hung separately. Book of How, The. Merrill Moore. MoAmPo

After the stars were all hung separately out. Merrill Moore. *See* After the stars were all hung separately

After the Storm. Edmond Yi-teh Chang. OpBo

After the Storm. Henri Faust. YaYoPo

After the Storm. Henrietta Cordelia Ray. CBWP-3

After the storm, after the rain stopped pounding. Song of Napalm. Bruce Weigl. CDa

After the Storm, August. Gail Mazur. ExTi

After the storm / On Mount Mimuro. Noin. OHPJ

After the streets fall silent. To Those Who Have Gone Home Tired. William Daniel Ehrhart. CDa

After the sudden rain. Old Currawong. Jennifer Rankin. BMAP

After the sun's eclipse. Teresa. Richard Wilbur. NoAM

After the Supper and Talk. Walt Whitman. MoAmPo; NAAL-2v1; NAAL-3

After the Surprising Conversions. Robert Lowell. CoAmPo; HAP; NAAL-2v2; NoAM; PAI; TRP

After the sweat of swathes and the sinking madder sun. Drink of Spring, A. John Ennis. CIP-2; PBCIP

After the test they sent an expert. School Days. William Stafford. LCAP-2

After the third evening roud. Vasco [*or* Vasko] Popa. PoSu, *tr.* by Anne Pennington *Fr.* Raw Flesh.

After the third evening round. Vasco [*or* Vasko] Popa. *See* After the third evening roud

After the tiff there was stiff silence, till. Lovers, The. William Robert Rodgers. BIrV; OxBSP; PNI

After the Trial. Weldon Kees. MakPoe

After the tumult and the blood. At Vshchizh. Fyodor [*or* Feodor] Ivanovich Tyutchev. OBWP; OxBEV; WoPoe, *tr.* by Henry Gifford and Charles Tomlinson

After the uprising of the 17th June. Solution, The. Bertolt Brecht. PoSu, *tr.* by Dereck Bowman

After the Verdict. Tony Medina. SpirFl

After the Vietnam War. Steven Ford Brown. CDa

After the Visit. Thomas Hardy. NOBE

After the Voices. Victor Hugo. SxFrPo, *tr.* by E. H. Blackmore and A. M. Blackmore

After the wailing had already begun. On Reading a Recent Greek Poet. Bertolt Brecht. WoPoe, *tr.* by John Peck

After the wake and speeches, when the guests in black. Lazarus. James Keir Baxter. HarvBoo

After the War. Douglas Dunn. OxBC

After the war, the terror people underwent produced profound if not irrevocable. Hazardous Waste. James Sherry. FTOS

After the War; When Coltrane Only Wanted to Play Dance Tunes. Matthew Graham. SeSe

After the Wedding. David Biespiel. NAPBL

After the Wedding Party. Matthew Rohrer. ReTh

After the whey-faced anonymity. South Country. Kenneth Slessor. BMAP; CBAP

After the whoosh of doors slid shut. At Lansdowne Bridge. Arthur Nortje. HBAPE

After the Wilderness. Andrew Hudgins. CBCWP

After the words of the magnificence and doom. Country Burial. Janet Lewis. CRP

After the worst part of four years. Sick Man, The. E. du Perron. TuT, *tr.* by Pat Boran

After the Zhivago of it all, the terrible sleeve. Housekeeping. Lucie Brock-Broido. ExTi

After Theresienstadt. Myra Sklarew. TaR

After these things should be. (LL) New House, The. Edward Thomas. EBEV; MoBrPo; NOBE; OBEV; OBWVE

After these years of lectures heard. To a Friend, on Her Examination for the Doctorate in English. James Vincent Cunningham. VGW

After they all leave. Surely You Remember. Dahlia Ravikovitch [*or* Ravikovich]. VCWP

After they had not made love. Happy Ending. Fleur Adcock. LW

After They Have Tired of the Brilliance of Cities. Stephen Spender. FaBoMo

After they passed I climbed. Story, A. William Stafford. NNaP

After They Put Down Their Overalls. Lenrie Peters. TTY

After they sawed through the bone. Daughter, That Picture of You. Keith Gilyard. SpirFl

After thinking this fortnight of Whig and of Tory. My Opinion. Charles Sackville, 6th Earl of Dorset. BASC

After this day's hope—see how the Somme, the Seine, and the wild Slav. Léopold Sédar Senghor. NegPo *Fr.* Ode for Three Koras and Balaphong.

After this life here, we're to be awakened one day. Vladimir Holan. *See* Is it true that after this life of ours we shall one day be awakened

After this much time, it's still impossible. The SS man with his stiff hair and his uniform. Spit. C. K. Williams. GotH; TaR

After this oracle there will be no more oracles. Last Statement for a Last Oracle. Alan Dugan. NoAM

After-Thought. William Wordsworth. CenSon *Fr.* River Duddon [A Series of Sonnets], The.

After-Thought, The. Stevie Smith. OxBC

After thy labour take thine ease. Mount of the Muses, The. Robert Herrick. CaPo

After Tonight. Gary Soto. NoAM

After Tosca. Raymond Roseliep. HA

After Touch. Jan Clausen. GLP

After Treblinka. How We See. Edward Bond. HP

After Trinity. John Meade Falkner. OxBTC

After Twenty Years. Adrienne Rich. TRP

After Twenty Years. Fadwa Tuqan [or Tuquan]. AF, *tr. by Unknown*

After twenty years I want to call it that, but was it? Rape. Joan Larkin. GLP

After two sittings, now our Lady State. Andrew Marvell. OBSV *Fr.* Last Instructions to a Painter, The.

After Two Years. Richard Aldington. MoBrPo

After us there will be. Scrap. Tomasz Jastrun. AF, *tr. by Daniel Bourne*

After W. B. Yeats. Gilbert Keith Chesterton. NOBL

After wandering for so many hours up and down. Reminiscence. Vladimir Holan. PoSu, *tr. by George Theiner*

After War. Ivor Gurney. HarvBoo; OxBSP

After watching your appeal from ev'ry angle. All of You. Cole Porter. ReLy

After we had loved each other intently. Listening to the Köln Concert. Robert Bly. RaBo

After we knew that we were dead we sat down and cried a little. Dead, The. Louis Dudek. NOBC

After we make love, I teach you. In Language. Eugene Gloria. OpBo

After weeks of watching the roof leak. Gary Snyder. InPK-6; KaS *Fr.* Hitch Haiku.

After what felt like a lifetime of rent. Writing. Andrew Motion. DiPo

After what had / to be said. Drunk. Carroll Arnett. VoR

After Whistler. Stanley Plumly. LCAP-2

After Winter. Sterling Allen Brown. GT

After Wiriyamu Village Massacre by Protuguese. Jack A. Mapanje. AF; PeSAV

After-Word. Ras Baraka. InTrad

After Work. Gary Snyder. NNaP

After working the midtown ambulance night slot. One Too Many Mornings. David Rivard. PBCAP

After Years of Feasting and No Sacrifice. Linda Zisquit. DTA

After years of relative clumsiness. Arachne. Judith Kazantzis. BrRo

After years the reunion. Brushed the dogs. Party. Eddy Van Vliet. VCWP, *tr. by John Van Tiel*

After Yeats. Allen Ginsberg. FTOS

After Yes. James Harms. AmPoNex

After you brought her home with your first child. Richard Murphy. BiHa; ModIr *Fr.* Price of Stone, The.

After you finish your work. Ballad of Orange and Grape. Muriel Rukeyser. ChAP; NoAM; NoP-4

After you have enriched your soul. Edgar Lee Masters. OBAL *Fr.* Spoon River Anthology.

After you have gone. Song of Parting. Wang Po-ch'eng. CrYelRi, *tr. by Sam Hamill*

After You Left. Heather McHugh. BodElec

After you left me forever. Semele Recycled. Carolyn Kizer. NALW

After you've been to bed together for the first time. Life Story. Tennessee Williams. GLP

After You've Gone. J. Turner Layton. ReLy

After you've shown me the bedraggled cockatoo. Cockatoo. Pam Bridgeman. Prnts

After your death. Poem: "After your death." Bill Knott. SPE

After your death, the fortune teller. Dad-Baby, The. Amanda Dalton. NeBl

After your visit. Marlene Mountain. HA

Aftereffects of a mother's neglects, The. Mother, Mother, Are You All There? Felicia Lamport. NBLV

Afterglow, The. Henrietta Cordelia Ray. CBWP-3

Afterglow goldens the. Mountain Afterglow, The. James Laughlin. VGW

Aftergrowth. "Rachel" [or "Rahel"]. MHP, *tr. by Ruth Finer Mintz*

Afterimages. Audre Lorde. LTA; VCAP

Afterimages. Shinkichi Takahashi. ZenPo, *tr. by Takashi Ikemoto and Lucien Stryk*

Afterlives. Derek Mahon. CIP-2

Aftermath. Henry Wadsworth Longfellow. APN-1; NAAL-2v1; NAAL-3; NOBA; PoPoPo; TAP

Aftermath. Siegfried Sassoon. MoBrPo; PoWW; TrJP

Afternoon. Louisa Sarah Bevington. PEW

Afternoon. Louisa S. Guggenberger. NOBVV

Afternoon. Yannis Ritsos. AF, *tr. by Edmund Keeley*

Afternoon. Shinkichi Takahashi. ZenPo, *tr. by Takashi Ikemoto and Lucien Stryk*

Afternoon 3. Saburoh Kuroda. SPE

Afternoon. Across the garden, in Green Hall. Love in the Classroom. Al Zolynas. BLT; LTA

Afternoon—Amagansett Beach. John Hall Wheelock. APT-1; PoRA

Afternoon and two men. In the Woods. Heinz Piontek. CLPP, *tr. by Jerome Rothenberg*

Afternoon at the Beach, An. Edgar Bowers. VCAP

Afternoon cooking in the fall sun. Song: "Afternoon cooking in the fall sun." Robert Hass. LoL

Afternoon falls, The. Water Wheel, The. Antonio Machado Ruiz. SpanPo, *tr. by James Duffy*

Afternoon Gossip, An. Priscilla Jane Thompson. CBWP-2

Afternoon Happiness. Carolyn Kizer. GeoHom

Afternoon Hours. Rossana Ombres. PeFWW *Fr.* Excursion to Ravenna of A Young Girl with Her Parents.

Afternoon I was killed, The. Close. Andrew Motion. HarvBoo

Afternoon in February. Henry Wadsworth Longfellow. APN-1; ColAP

Afternoon in Pangasinan with No Electricity, An. Regie Cabico. ReBoTo

Afternoon in the Garden. Ethel Louisa Mason Anderson. NOBAu

Afternoon is all fallen plaster, black stones, dry thorns, The. Afternoon. Yannis Ritsos. AF, *tr. by Edmund Keeley*

Afternoon is invading my eyes. Drunken Poem. David Helwig. NOBC

Afternoon is offered to us, The. Love: "Afternoon is offered to us, The." Oscar Cerruto. BLPSL, *tr. by Rene de Costa, Rigas Kappatos and Eleni Paidoussi*

Afternoon is sad and gray, The. Tropical Afternoon. "Rubén Dario." TCLAP, *tr. by Lysander Kemp*

Afternoon it changes. Place, The. Robert Creeley. BodElec

Afternoon, its lazy ways, The. Girl. Octavio Paz. STV, *tr. by John Frederick Nims*

Afternoon Light. Jacob [or Jakov] Fichman. MHP, *tr. by Ruth Finer Mintz*

Afternoon of a Faun, The. Stéphane Mallarmé. NAWM-7v2, *tr. by Henry Weinfield*

Afternoon of a Faun, The. Stéphane Mallarmé. WoPoe, *tr. by Louis Simpson*

Afternoon on a Hill. Edna St. Vincent Millay. APT-1; ChAP; NTCP; OBCA; OxBA; TTTS

Afternoon Service at Mellstock. Thomas Hardy. PeECV

Afternoon Sleep. Robert Bly. WoPoe

Afternoon storm has hit, An. After the Fall of Saigon. Yusef Komunyakaa. AF; CDa

Afternoon sun is on their faces, The. Women in Dutch Painting. Eunice De Souza. OMIP

Afternoon sun / somewhere in the South, The. Landscapes. Duriel Harris. SpirFl

Afternoon the neighborhood boys tied me and Mary Lou Mahar, The. Sixth Grade. Marie Howe. KGB

Afternoon with a light brush stroke, The. Slow Delight. Leopoldo Lugones. BLPSL, *tr. by Rene de Costa, Rigas Kappatos and Eleni Paidoussi*

Afternoon, with light strokes, The. Indulgence. Leopoldo Lugones. TCLAP, *tr. by Julie Schumacher*

Afternoons. Philip Larkin. NPEEn; OxBEV; PoetW

Afternoons of dove-slurred languor. Ford Castle: The Borders. Geoffrey Holloway. NLP

Afternoons with Baedeker. Osbert Lancaster.
   "Distant Seychelles are not so remote, The." NOBL; PeLV
   Eireann. NOBL; PeLV
   English. NOBL; PeLV
   French. NOBL; PeLV
   "Here those of us who really understand." NOBL; PeLV
   "I shall not linger in that draughty square." NOBL; PeLV
   "In 1910 a royal princess." NOBL; PeLV
   Manhattan. NOBL; PeLV

Afterthought. Elizabeth Jennings. NOxBChV; OBCP

Afterwake, The. Adrienne Rich. NOBA

Afterward. Herman Melville. APN-2 *Fr.* Clarel: A Poem and Pilgrimage in the Holy Land.

Afterward. Robert Penn Warren. BodElec

Afterwards. Tristan Corbière.
   "It's getting dark, little thief of starlight!" WoPoe, *tr. by Randall Jarrell*

Afterwards. Thomas Hardy. EBEV; GTBS-P; HarvBoo; MoBrPo; NOBE; NoP-4; OxAEP-2; OxBEV; PoPoPo; TFi; TOF; WoPoe

Afterwards. Frances Ridley Havergal. SacPr

Afterwards: Caliban. Talvikki Ansel. AmPoNex

Afterwards, in the shower. Dolce. Kennette Wilkes. PasH

Afterwards she blamed it on the wind, cold. Meteorology. Linda France. MFPA

Afterwards, the compromise. After Love. Maxine W. Kumin. TAP

Afterwards, They Shall Dance. Bob Kaufman. TwCP; VGW

Afterwards, when we have slept, paradise. Knowing, The. Sharon Olds. PasH

Aftir that harvest inned had hise sheves. Thomas Hoccleve [or Occleve]. NPeEn Fr. Complaint, The.

Afton Water. Robert Burns. See Flow Gently, Sweet Afton

Again. Thomas Brush. CDa

Again. Robert Creeley. VCAP

Again. Glyn Jones. OBWVE; TCAWP

Again. Charlotte Mew. MoBrPo

Again. Lenard D. Moore. GT

Again. Jon Stallworthy. OxBC

Again! Ferdinand von Saar. AuPH, tr. by Lowell A. Bangerter

Again and again I kiss thy gates at departing. Roma. Rutilius. CTC, tr. by Ezra Pound

Again and again it sounds, / Thonah! Thonah! (LL) Unknown. APN-2; TCAPo, tr. by Washington Matthews Fr. Mountain Chant, The.

Again and again that scene, enthralling in ordinariness. Swept Away. László Kálnoky. IQMS, tr. by Kenneth McRobbie and Zita McRobbie

Again and again / While History is unforgiven. (LL) In the Naked Bed, in Plato's Cave. Delmore Schwartz. APT-2; MoAmPo; NOBA; NoAM; VGW

Again and then again. . . the year is born. New Year's Day. Robert Lowell. ChrPo; CoAmPo; TRP

Again as Evening's Shadow Falls. Samuel Longfellow. AH

Again at Christmas did we weave. Tennyson. EBVV; NAEL-6v2; NAWM-7v2; PeECV Fr. In Memoriam A. H. H.

Again for Hephaistos, the Last Time. Richard Howard. GLP

Again he made his way through bloody hell. Non Piu Leggevano. Árpád Tóth. IQMS, tr. by Jess Perlman

Again, here it comes, the nothing. Salamanders. A. K. Ramanujan. PoetW

Again, his friend's death made the man sit still. John Berryman. NOBA

Again I am summoned to the eternal field. First Love. Edwin Rolfe. APT-2

"Again I find myself alone." Charlotte Brontë. PEW (My Dreams.) VWP

Again I'm caught staring. Pleasures of the Imagination. Peter McDonald. PNI

Again I'm on the Tisza's banks as the sun climbs. Morning Splendour of the Tisza, The. György Bessenyei. IQMS, tr. by Gavin Ewart

Again I reply to the triple winds. January. William Carlos Williams. MoAmPo

Again I see you, ah my queen. Juana. Alfred de Musset. AWP, tr. by Andrew Lang

Again, in the Book of Books, to-day. Prodigals. Phoebe Cary. SacPr

Again in the mirrored dusk the paddles sank. Thomas Kinsella. PBCIP Fr. Downstream.

Again last night I dreamed the dream called Laundry. Mad Scene, The. James Merrill. CoAP; NOBA; PoE; TAP

Again let me do a lot of extraordinary talking. Song of the Militant Romance, The. Percy Wyndham Lewis. FaBoTw; OxBTC

Again Love, glancing meltingly. Ibycus. SaLy, tr. by Diane Rayor

Again Love struck me like a smith with a giant. Anacreon. SaLy, tr. by Diane Rayor

Again retreated—and a second time faced the screen. (LL) Ivor Gurney. HarvBoo; NAEL-5v2; NAEL-6v2; NPeEn; NoP-4; OBWP; PeFWW; PoWW Fr. Silent One, The.

Again September, like the swarm of seasons past. Bella [or Izabella] Akhatovna Akhmadulina. TCRP

Again stands superb as a temple. (LL) Incident, An. Douglas Le Pan. MoCV; NoP-4

Again the cab slips west down 14th almost. Overheard in the Love Hotel. Robert Polito. KGB

Again the call of the winter birds. Poem for Carroll, Descendant of Chiefs. Lance Henson. VoR

Again the Cousin's whistle! Go, my Love. (LL) Andrea del Sarto. Robert Browning. CTC; NAEL-5v2; NAEL-6v2; NOBVV; NoP-4; PoE

Again the flutter of desert. Negev. David Rokeah [or Rokeakh]. MHP, tr. by Ruth Finer Mintz

Again the glory of the days! Battle Summers, The. Herman Melville. APN-2

Again the golden month, still. In September. John Ormond. TCAWP

Again the lake is a pretty catchphrase. Skater, The. Hester Knibbe. TuT, tr. by Micheal O'Siadhail

Again the last ebb. Dieppe. Samuel Beckett. NOIV

Again the light of. Epitaph: Snake River. Lance Henson. VoR

Again the morning is wet. On High Street. Andrea Hollander Budy. UrbNat

Again, the same dream. Nightmare. Matilde Salganicoff. MirDau, tr. by Celeste Kostopulos-Cooperman

Again the shells were falling. Fresco Come to Life. Boris Leonidovich Pasternak. AF

Again the snow-clogged pillars. On the Islands. Aleksandr Aleksandrovich Blok. TCRP, tr. by Geoffrey Thurley

Again the veld revives. Namaqualand after Rain. William Plomer. PeSAV

Again the violet of our early days. Spring. Ebenezer Elliott. OxAEP-2

Again the wood, and long-withdrawing vale. To Spring. Charlotte Smith. BWW; RWP; WPE

Again the world opens up like a girl's room. February Sun. Paul Rodenko. TuT, tr. by Mary E. O'Donnell

"Again they come," and muttered [or mutter'd] as he died. (LL) George Crabbe. EBNV; ECEV; FHYEP; OBNV Fr. Borough, The.

Again this procession of the speechless. Daybreak. W. S. Merwin. NAAL-2v2

Again thou reignest in thy golden hall. To the Harvest Moon. William Stanley Roscoe. CenSon

Again to your Naucratis and the Nile. (LL) Doricha. Poseidippus. AWP; FaBoEE; OBVE, tr. by E. A. Robinson

Again to your Naucratis and the Nile. (LL) Var. authors. AWP; FaBoEE; OBVE; WoPoe, tr. by Edwin Arlington Robinson Fr. Variations of Greek Themes.

Again today it is. Self-Portrait Approaching Promontory, Utah. Michael Pettit. GM

Again, traveller, you have come a long way led by that star. Epitaph: "Again, traveller, you have come a long way led by that star." Thomas McGrath. RaBo

Again very queer but I'll go on looking. (LL) Wodwo. Ted Hughes. HarvBoo; NoAM; WoPoe

Again we have lasted till the snowtime. Snow. Vladimir Nikolaevich Kornilov. TCRP, tr. by Daniel Weissbort

Again when all the radiant sons of light. George Sandys. NOSC Fr. Paraphrase Upon Job, A.

Again your kindly, smiling face I see. Mother. Max Ehrmann. PoToHe

Against a backdrop of Pennsylvania hills. Such a Boat of Land. Lamont B. Steptoe. UnSA

Against a feathery sky. (LL) Adolescence—I. Rita Dove. ISC; NAAL-5; NoAM

Against a Rich Man Despising Poverty. Phineas Fletcher. NOSC (To a Rich Man.) SacPr

Against a Sickness: To the Female Double Principle God. Alan Dugan. NoAM

Against a Wen. Unknown. ASW, tr. by Kevin Crossley-Holland

Against Absence. Sir John Suckling. CaPo; CavPo

Against an elm a sheep was tied [or ty'd]. John Gay. NOEC; NPeEn Fr. Fables.

Against an Old Lecher. Sir John Harington [or Harrington]. FaBoEE

Against Blame of Woman. Gerald Fitzgerald, 4th Earl of Desmond. BIrV, tr. by The Earl of Longford

Against both bar and tower the black sea runs. (LL) Point Shirley. Sylvia Plath. NIL-7; NIP-4

Against Broccoli. Roy Blount, Jr. NBLV; OBAL

Against compulsory military service: a "deferment" of each limb. Deferment. Marcel Duchamp. PFTM-1

Against Conscription. Wei Chuang. CrYelRi, tr. by Sam Hamill

Against Constancy. John Wilmot, 2d Earl of Rochester. NOSC; OxAEP-1

Against Coupling. Fleur Adcock. EmeKit; NALW

Against downed trees. Festal Song. Unknown. CrYelRi, tr. by Sam Hamill

Against Extremity. Charles Tomlinson. HarvBoo

Against far off snow mountains. Murakami Kijo. OHMPJ

Against Fruition. Abraham Cowley. BeJo; NOSC Fr. Mistress, The.

Against Fruition. Sir John Suckling. BeJo; CaPo; CavPo; NOSC

Against Gaudy-Bragging-Undoughty Daccus. John Davies of Hereford. FaBoEE

Against him, die, and find death good. (LL) Love On the Farm. D. H. Lawrence. CABP; MoBrPo; NAEL-5v2; NAEL-6v2; NoAM; NoP-4; SCGP

Against his coat. Alexis Rotella. HA

Against his forearm, leaning up against the barn. (LL) Land of Little Sticks, 1945. James Tate. BodElec; LCAP-2

Against Homosexuality. Thomas Gilbert. NOEC Fr. View of the Town, A. In an Epistle to a Friend.

Against Hope. Abraham Cowley. MeLP; NOSC Fr. Mistress, The.

Against Horace. Mihály Babits. IQMS, tr. by Adam Makkai and John Gordon Nichols

Against Idleness and Mischief. Isaac Watts. See How Doth the Little Busy Bee

Against Indifference. Charles Webbe. OBEV

Against its own best time. (LL)　Sex without Love.　Sharon Olds.　HeIP-4; NIL-7; NIP-4; TRP

Against Love.　Katherine Philips.　BoWoP; WPE

Against Meaning.　Andrei Codrescu.　PmAP

Against Minoan sunlight.　Wishes for Her.　Denis Devlin.　CIP-2; NOIV

Against my will.　Footprints.　Dan Pagis.　VCWP, tr. by Stephen Mitchell

Against Numerology.　Richard Caddel.　Oth

Against Parting.　Natan Zach.　HP; PoSu

Against Proud Poor Phryna.　John Davies of Hereford.　FaBoEE

Against Romanticism.　Kingsley Amis.　NoAM

Against Silence.　Pamela Stewart.　ExTi

Against Slavery.　William Cowper.　NOEC　Fr. Task, The.

Against Sodomy.　Charles Churchill.　ECEV　Fr. Times, The.

Against Still Life.　Margaret Atwood.　MoCV

Against Te Rauparaha.　Alistair Campbell.　PeNZ　Fr. Sanctuary of Spirits.

Against that time, if ever that time come.　William Shakespeare.　OxAEP-1　Fr. Sonnets.

Against the burly air I strode.　Genesis.　Geoffrey Hill.　ChIV-1; HAP; HarvBoo; OxBC; PeECV; TOF

Against the Current.　Luciana Frezza.　CItWP, tr. by Cinzia Sartini Blum and Lara Trubowitz

Against the Evidence.　David Ignatow.　NNaP

Against the Fear of Death.　Lucretius.
　What has this Bugbear death to frighten Man.
　"What has this Bugbear death to frighten Man."　NPeEn, tr. by John Dryden

Against the invisible antagonist.　Celestial Emperor, The.　Howard Nemerov.　BodElec

Against the iron fence surrounding pools.　Uncle Harry at the La Brea Tar Pits.　Ruth Whitman.　TaR

Against the King.　William Drummond, of Hawthornden.　NOSC

Against the king, sir, now why would ye fight?　Against the King.　William Drummond, of Hawthornden.　NOSC

Against the lamp I sit by the south window.　Sitting at Night.　Po Chü-i.　TAL

Against the Laws.　Friedrich Wilhelm Nietzsche.　WoPoe, tr. by W. S. Merwin

Against the poet and the legislator. (LL)　W. H. Auden.　ChIV-1; Son　Fr. Sonnets from China.

Against the potent poison of your hate. (LL)　White House, The.　Claude McKay.　ISC; NAAAL; NIP-4

Against the rubber tongues of cows and the hoeing hands of men.　Thistles.　Ted Hughes.　FaBoCv; NPeEn; NoAM; OxBSP; OxBTC; SoSe-8

Against the Silences to Come.　Ron Loewinsohn.　PoM

Against the snow a tall Being of Beauty.　Being Beauteous.　Arthur Rimbaud.　SxFrPo, tr. by Martin Sorrell

Against the stranger. (LL)　Sand Nigger.　Lawrence Joseph.　GraLe; OPRER

Against the Wind.　Amir Gilbo'a.　MHP

Against Them Who Lay Unchastity to the Sex of Women.　William Habington.　BeJo　Fr. Castara.

Against these turbid turquoise skies.　Les Ballons.　Oscar Wilde.　NOBVV

Against time and the damages of the brain.　To Walker Evans.　James Agee.　APT-2

Against what light.　Black Dada Nihilismus.　Imamu Amiri Baraka.　PFTM-2; PoM

Against Whatever It Is That's Encroaching.　Charles Simic.　ColAP

Against Women.　Unknown.
　"Woman is by aptitude."　OBWVE

Against your black I set the dainty deer.　Contrasts.　Iain Crichton Smith.　NePenScot

Against your ear. (LL)　Distant Drum, The.　Calvin C. Hernton.　GT; TTY

Agamemnon.　Aeschylus.　NAWM-5v1
　Chorus: "Great Fortune is an hungry thing.".　AWP, tr. by Gilbert Murray
　"Fo' a yeah or mo' on this roof I'se layed."　CTC, tr. by Dallam Simpson
　"For Ares, gold-exchanger for the dead."　FaBoWar, tr. by Robert Browning
　"Great Fortune is an hungry thing."　AWP, tr. by Gilbert Murray
　"If I were to tell of our labours, our hard lodging."　FaBoWar, tr. by Louis MacNeice
　Signal Fire, The.　CTC, tr. by Dallam Simpson

Agamemnon before Troy.　John Frederick Nims.　Son

Agamemnon's Tomb.　Sacheverell Sitwell.　OBMV
　"One by one, as harvesters, all heavy laden."　MoBrPo

Agape.　César Vallejo.　TCLAP, tr. by Gordon Brotherston and Edward Dorn

Agape the sooty collier stands.　John Dalton.　NOEC　Fr. Descriptive Poem, Addressed to Two Ladies at Their Return from Viewing the Mines, near Whitehaven, A.

Agatha Christie to.　Said.　George Starbuck.　OBAL

Agbor Dancer.　J. P. Clark Bekedermo.　PBA

Age.　Abraham Cowley.　AWP

Age.　Robert Creeley.　PmAP

Age.　Rae Desmond Jones.　CBAP

Age.　Walter Savage Landor.　FaBoEE; NOBVV; OxBEV

Age.　Philip Larkin.　OxBEV

Age.　Ferdinand von Saar.　AuPH, tr. by Lowell A. Bangerter

Age, An.　Laura Jensen.　LCAP-2

Age after age, the uninstructing dead. (LL)　Gulf, The.　Derek Walcott.　NoP-4; PoPoPo; PoetW

Age, and the deaths, and the ghosts.　He Resigns.　John Berryman.　HarvBoo; OxBSP; WeW-3

Age Demanded, The.　Ernest Hemingway.　IllVoic

Age Demanded, The.　Ezra Pound.　TCAPo　Fr. Hugh Selwyn Mauberley (Life and Contacts).

Age demanded an image, The.　Ezra Pound.　HAP; HarvBoo; MoAmPo; NPeEn; VGW　Fr. Hugh Selwyn Mauberley (Life and Contacts).

Age in her embraces passed [or pass'd, or past], An.　Mistress, The: A Song.　John Wilmot, 2d Earl of Rochester.　EBEV; NOBE; NOSC; NPeEn

Age in Prospect.　Robinson Jeffers.　MoAmPo

Age in Youth.　Trumbull Stickney.　ColAP

Age is a quality of mind.　How Old Are You?　H. S. Fritsch.　PoToHe

Age / is a way of feeling cold that takes me by surprise.　Easter.　Adelia Prado.　TANSG, tr. by Ellen Watson

Age is wheat chaff.　Boat on the Pacific, A.　Najaat Al-Udwany.　PoArWo, tr. by Moulouk Berry and Ali Farghaly

Age is when to a man.　Samuel Beckett.　BIrV; ModIr　Fr. Words and Music.

Age Looks Back at Youth.　Thomas Vaux, 2d Baron Vaux of Harrowden.　NoSic

(Age Looks Back at Youth.)　NoSic

Age of a Dream, The.　Lionel Pigot Johnson.　OBMV

Age of Benevolence, The.　Carlos Wilcox.
　"Sultry noon, not in the summer's prime, A."　APN-1

Age of Bronze, The.　Byron.
　"Alas, the country! how shall tongue or pen."　OBSV

Age of Correggio and the Carracci, The.　Charles Bernstein.　BodElec

Age of Cruelty, The.　Gregory Orfalea.　GraLe

Age of earth and us all chattering.　Susan Howe.　PFTM-2　Fr. Pythagorean Silence.

Age of Gold.　Pietro Metastasio.　CTC, tr. by Ezra Pound

Age of Innocence.　Graham Hough.　PoRA

Age of Plastic, The.　John Forbes.　BMAP

Age of Reason, The.　William Langland.　NOCV　Fr. Vision of Piers Plowman, The.

Age of seventy is gone, The.　I Know Inside.　Yüan Mei.　CoBLCP, tr. by Jonathan Chaves

Age of Terror.　Denise Levertov.　PFTM-2

Age of the Rubber Seals.　Buland Al-Haidari [or Al-Haydari].　MAP, tr. by Patricia Alanah Byrne and Salma Khadra Jayyusi

Age of unhappiness has arrived, or is it, The.　Antonio Porta.　CLPP

Age of War, The.　Unknown.　NOBRP

Age / requires this task, The.　Different Image, A.　Dudley Randall.　BPo; TAP

Age three.　Growth.　Shuntaro Tanikawa.　PoetW, tr. by Harold Wright

Aged Bard's Wish (Translation of a Gaelic Poem Composed in the Isle of Skye), The.　Anne Grant.　RWP

Aged, bittersweet, in salt crusted, the pink meat.　Smithfield Ham.　Dave Jeddie Smith.　HCAP

Aged Lover Discourses in the Flat Style, The.　James Vincent Cunningham.　NoAM

Aged Lover Renounceth Love, The.　Thomas Vaux, 2d Baron Vaux of Harrowden.　NoSic; SCGP

Aged man, that mowes [or mows] these fields.　Dialogue betwixt Time and a Pilgrim[e], A.　Aurelian Townshend [or Townsend].　NOBE; NPeEn; OxBEV

Aged nightingale / How sweet.　Masaoka Shiki.　ZenPo, tr. by Takashi Ikemoto and Lucien Stryk

Aged Pilot Man, The.　"Mark Twain."　OBAL

Aged Sophocles, the light of life has dimmed.　Sophocles.　Unknown.　GrAn, tr. by Lee T. Pearcy

Agelaus was kind to Acestorides.　Nicarchus of Alexandria.　GrAn

Agent of Love.　A. K. Redwing.　VoR

Agents, The.　Robert Conquest.　SPE

Ages, The.　William Cullen Bryant.　APN-1

Ages have passed since the stately Odes flourished.　Li Po.　ColAnChi, tr. by Victor H. Mair　Fr. Poems in an Old Style.

Ages like wine.　My Loneliness.　Thérèse 'Awwad.　PoArWo, tr. by Kamal Boullata

Ages of Man, The.　Abraham Ibn Ezra.　TrJP, tr. by Nina Davis Salaman

Ages of the world will not turn back, The.   Fourth Ecologue: Pollio, The.   Virgil [*or* Vergil].   WoPoe, *tr.* by David R. Slavitt

Agincourt.   Michael Drayton.   *See* Battle of Agincourt, The

Agincourt, Agincourt!   Song of the English Bowmen.   *Unknown.*   FaBoWar

Agincourt Carol, The.   *Unknown.*   EBEV; NoP-4

Aging.   Richard Beer-Hofmann.   AuPH, *tr.* by Naemah Beer-Hofmann

Aging.   *Unknown.*   WoPoe, *tr.* by Graeme Wilson

Aging is an agony.   Aging.   *Unknown.*   WoPoe, *tr.* by Graeme Wilson

Aging pilgrim on a, An.   Kenneth Rexroth.   APT-2; BodElec

Agitante calescimus illo &c. (LL)   Edmund Spenser.   NAEL-5v1; NAEL-6v1; NAEL-7v1   *Fr.* Shepheardes [*or* Shepeards *or* Shepherd's] Calender, The.

Agitation of the air, An.   End of Summer.   Stanley Kunitz.   LoL; MoAmPo; VGW

Agitato Ma Non Troppo.   John Crowe Ransom.   OxBA   *Fr.* Sixteen Poems in Eight Pairings.

Aglaura.   Sir John Suckling.
   Song: "No, no, fair heretic[k], it needs must be.".   BeJo; CaPo; CavPo
   Song: "Why so pale and wan, fond lover?".   AWP; BASC; BeJo; BoLoP; CaPo; CavPo; ClHu; EnLoPo; GTBS-P; HAP; HeIP-4; ITBLP; NAEL-5v1; NAEL-6v1; NAEL-7v1; NBLV; NIL-7; NIP-4; NOBE; NPeEn; NoP-4; OBEV; OxAEP-1; OxBEV; PAI; PoE; PoRA; TFi; UnPo

Agnes Moorehead, Hedy Lamarr.   Think Back.   Gerry Gomez Pearlberg.   WiU

Agnosco Veteris Vestigia Flammae.   James Vincent Cunningham.   VGW

Agnosto Theo [To an Unknown God].   Thomas Hardy.   InvLi

Agon.   Branko Miljkovic.   WoPoe, *tr.* by Charles Simic

Agonia Christiana.   János Pilinszky.   IQMS, *tr.* by Adam Makkai

Agonie, The.   George Herbert.   *See* Agony [*or* Agonie], The

Agonising pincer-jaws of Heaven, The. (LL)   Sanctity.   Patrick Kavanagh.   BIrV; NOIV; NoP-4

Agony.   Giuseppe Ungaretti.   PeFWW, *tr.* by Charles Tomlinson

Agony . . . A Resurrection, An.   Assumpta Acam-Oturu.   HAWP; NAfrP

Agony, An. As Now.   Imamu Amiri Baraka.   BPo; NAAL-2v2; PoE   (Agony. As Now, An.)   NoP-4; UnSA

Agony: I say their agony, The.   Peasants.   Syl Cheney-Coker.   NAfrP

Agony in the Garden, The.   Felicia Dorothea Hemans.   TrCP

Agony [*or* Agonie], The.   George Herbert.   CABP; ESCV; FSCP; GeHe   (Philosophers have measur'd mountains.)   CABP; FSCP

Agoraphobia.   Linda Pastan.   ExTi

Agosu if you go tell them.   Kofi Awoonor.   HBAPE

Agreed that all these birds.   All These Birds.   Richard Wilbur.   NOBA

Agreeing with that Latin writer, Great is Truth and will prevail in a bit. (LL)   Magna Est Veritas.   Stevie Smith.   NPeEn; OxBC; OxBEV

Agreement of Predicate Pronouns, The.   Thomas M. [*or* "Tom"] Disch.   KGB

Agricultural labourer, who has, An.   Alan Brownjohn.   NOxBChV   *Fr.* Pitman's Common Sense Arithmetic, 1917.

Agricultural Show, Flemington, Victoria, The.   Suzanne Gardinier.   CBAP

Agriculture.   Robert Dodsley.
   Rustic Courtship.   ECEV
   "When Patty, lovely Patty, graced the crowd."   ECEV

Agriculture.   Martial.   WoPoe, *tr.* by Fred Chappell

Agrippina, well aware of Claudius' greed.   Of Moulds and Mushrooms.   Ruthven Todd.   NePenScot

Ah.   Robin Blaser.   FTOS

Ah.   Robert Greene.   HAP; NoSic; RACG   *Fr.* Greene's Mourning Garment.

Ah. (LL)   Dialogue, A.   George Herbert.   FSCP; GeHe; NOSC; OBEV

Ah.   Felix White Sr.'s Introduction to Wakjankaga.   *Winnebago Oral Tradition.*   NAAL-5

Ah, ah, ah.   Moses and the Princess.   Peter Dickinson.   NOxBChV

Ah, all the sands of the earth lead unto heaven.   Persian Miniature.   William Jay Smith.   CoAP

Ah and woe!   Hell.   Andreas Gryphius.   WoPoe, *tr.* by Michael Hamburger

Ah, Are You Digging on My Grave?   Thomas Hardy.   MoBrPo; NAEL-5v2; NAEL-6v2; PAI

Ah bed, the field where joy's peace some do see.   Sir Philip Sidney.   EnLoPo   *Fr.* Astrophil and Stella.

Ah Ben! / Say how, or when.   Ode for Him [*or* Ben Jonson], An.   Robert Herrick.   AWP; BASC; BeJo; CaPo; NOSC; SCGP

Ah blackbird, giving thanks.   *Unknown.*   NOIV

Ah blessed absence of God.   God's Absence.   Mechthild von Magdeburg.   WPoS, *tr.* by Oliver Davies

Ah blow! thou art the last, the last!   Broken Heart.   Henrietta Cordelia Ray.   CBWP-3

Ah, breathe on it softly—it dies in an hour. (LL)   Riddle, A: "'Twas in heaven pronounced, and 'twas muttered in hell."   Catherine Maria Fanshawe.   NOBRP; OxBEV

Ah, broken is the golden bowl!—the spirit flown forever!   Lenore.   Edgar Allan Poe.   APN-1; TCAPo

[Ah certainty of love in the hand].   Janine Pommy-Vega.   CLPP

Ah! changed and cold, how changed and very cold!   Dead before Death.   Christina Georgina Rossetti.   NAEL-5v2; NAEL-6v2; NALW

Ah, Chloris! could I now but sit.   Sir Charles Sedley.   GTBS-P   *Fr.* Mulberry Garden, The.

Ah, Christ, I love you rings to the wild sky.   Allen Tate.   ChrPo; Son   *Fr.* Sonnets at Christmas.

Ah! could I read Schemhammphorasch.   Schemhammphorasch.   Rose Terry Cooke.   SWaP

Ah, could you now with thinking tongue.   Yvor Winters.   IllVoic

Ah! County Guy, the hour is nigh.   Sir Walter Scott.   GTBS-P   *Fr.* Quentin Durward.

Ah! curst Ambition, to thy lures we owe.   Thomas Tickell.   ECEV   *Fr.* On the Prospect of Peace.

Ah Dalmatia, if only I could send word of your dear sons.   Ante Kosovic.   PeNZ

Ah, Dangerous Swain, tell me no more.   Song: "Ah, Dangerous Swain, tell me no more."   Mary De La Rivíere Manley.   LW

Ah dear associate of youth's tender days.   To Love.   Edward Gardner.   CenSon

Ah Dearest, let us haste us.   Martin Opitz.   GePo

Ah dearest limbs, my life's best joy and stay.   Robert Sidney.   NoSic

Ah, Death is Like the Long Cool Night.   Heinrich Heine.   NAWM-7v2, *tr.* by Hal Draper

Ah dextrous Chirurgeons, mitigate your plan.   On Having Piles.   Sir Walter Scott.   FaBoEE

Ah, did you once see Shelley plain.   Memorabilia.   Robert Browning.   FHYEP; NAEL-5v2; NAEL-6v2; NOBVV; NPeEn; NoP-4; OxBEV; PoE; PoPoPo; RB

Ah, Douglass, we have fall'n on evil days.   Douglass.   Paul Laurence Dunbar.   CBCWP; GSo; NAAAL; Son

Ah, Eros doth not always smite.   "Michael Field."   VWP

Ah face, young face, sweet with unpassionate joy.   Faded.   Augusta Davies Webster.   VWP

Ah! fair and lovely bloom the flowers of youth.   Youth and Age.   Mimnermus.   AWP, *tr.* by John Addington Symonds

Ah, fair Zenocrate, divine Zenocrate.   Christopher Marlowe.   EBEV   *Fr.* Tamburlaine the Great.

Ah false Amyntas, can that hour.   Aphra Behn.   WPE   *Fr.* Dutch Lover, The.

Ah, Faustus, / Now hast thou but one bare hour[e] [*or* hower] to live.   Christopher Marlowe.   FaBoVe; HeIP-4; PeECV   *Fr.* Doctor Faustus.

Ah, flow on, flow on.   Sail Peacefully Home.   Simeon Grigoryevich Frug.   TrJP

Ah, flowers that we wear!   And Yet the Earth Remains Unchanged.   *Unknown.*   CA

Ah for the throes of a heart sorely wounded!   Damsel, The.   Omar ben Abi Rabi'a.   AWP, *tr.* by W. G. Palgrave

A[h]! fredome [*or* freedom] is a noble thing!   John Barbour.   FaBoCh; NePenScot; OBEV; OxBS; TreFP   *Fr.* Bruce, The.

Ah, friend you have changed; neckless.   Friend, Ah You Have Changed!   Frank Mkalawile Chipasula.   HBAPE

Ah, gaze not on those eyes! forbear.   Vain Advice, The.   Catherine Cockburn.   LW

Ah, God, the way your little finger moved.   Stephen Crane.   APN-2   *Fr.* War Is Kind.

Ah, good-evening. It's the two of them again.   His Lamp Near Daybreak.   Yannis Ritsos.   AWTN, *tr.* by Martin McKinsey

Ah, good morning, *'Pare. Kumusta naman?*   Manong Chito Tells Manong Ben about His Dream over Breakfast at the Manilatown Cafe.   Vince Gotera.   ReBoTo

Ah! Grandmother weaves!   Grandmother Sleeps.   Liz Sohappy Bahe.   CDW

Ah! habit, how unmusical and shy.   Habit.   Natalie Clifford Barney.   PoBW

Ah! Hannah, why should'st thou despair.   Christopher Smart.   ChIV-1   *Fr.* Hymns for the Amusement of Children.

Ah! he is fled!   British [*or* Brittish] Church, The.   Henry Vaughan.   ESCV; PeECV

Ah, he was a grand man.   Tullynoe: Tête-à-Tête in the Parish Priest's Parlour.   Paul Durcan.   ModIr; NPeEn; OBCoV

Ah heart, heart, look! I throw myself at your feet. (LL)   Stormy Night.   William Robert Rodgers.   ModIr; PNI

Ah heaven!—what *truth* to him. (LL)   College Colonel, The.   Herman Melville.   CBCWP; FaBoWar; NCAP; OBWP

Ah! hills belov'd!—where once a happy child.   To the South Downs.   Charlotte Smith.   CBWP-3

Ah, holy Jesus, how hast thou offended.   F. Heermann.   SacPr, *tr.* by Robert Bridges

Ah! I could curse them in my woe.   Revenge.   Mary E. Tucker.   CBWP-1

Ah If at Least I Could.   Alda Merini.   CItWP, *tr.* by Cinzia Sartini Blum and Lara Trubowitz

Ah, if only the village were so small. Poem of the Girl from Velázquez. Ricardo Molinari. TCLAP, *tr.* by Inés Probert

Ah in the thunder air. Trees in the Garden. D. H. Lawrence. MoBrPo

Ah, is there no, no place on earth. Weariness. Mary E. Tucker. CBWP-1

Ah, it is so! Women's Rondo. *Unknown.* NOBAu

Ah—it's the skeleton of a lady's sunshade. Sunshade, The. Thomas Hardy. OxBTC

Ah, Jesu Kri. María Sabina. STP *Fr.* Chants, The.

Ah, Jesu Kri. María Sabina. PFTM-2, *tr.* by Henry Munn *Fr.* Midnight Velada, The.

Ah Julia! ask a Christmas rhyme. Irregular Verses. Dorothy Wordsworth. PoBW

Ah! knew he but his happiness, of men. Country Pastor, The. Timothy Dwight. SacPr

Ah! let not hope fallacious, airy, wild. Mary Hays. CenSon

Ah! light lovely lady with delicate lips aglow. At Mass. *Unknown.* BIrV, *tr.* by Robin Flower

Ah! little cause has Petrarch to complain. Elizabeth Cobbold. CenSon *Fr.* Sonnets of Laura.

Ah! little fly, alighting fitfully. Calvus to a Fly. Charles Tennyson Turner. NOBVV

Ah, little road, all whirry in the breeze. Road, The. Helene Johnson. BlSi

Ah, look, / How sucking their last sweetness from the air. Divers, The. Peter Quennell. MoBrPo

Ah! Love, my Master, hear me swear. Of His Death. Meleager. AWP, *tr.* by Andrew Lang

Ah, love, the teacher we decried. Pure Hypothesis, A. May Kendall. VWP

Ah, Love, You Smell of Petroleum. Judy Grahn. PoBW

Ah! Lovely Appearance of Death! Charles Wesley. AH

Ah, Lucasta, why so bright. To Lucasta. Richard Lovelace. CaPo

Ah, lute, how well I know each tone of thee. George Henry Boker. APN-2 *Fr.* Sonnets: A Sequence on Profane Love.

Ah Mater, quo te deplorem fonte? Dolores. George Herbert. PBRV *Fr.* Memoriae Matris Sacrum.

Ah me, if I grew sweet to man. Tragic Mary Queen of Scots, The. Michael "Field." EnLoPo; LW; OBMV

Ah me! it is the loon alone—the loon upon the lake. (LL) Loon upon the Lake, The. *Ojibwa Oral Tradition.* APN-2; OWoS, *tr.* by Charles Fenno Hoffman

Ah me, my friend! it will not, will not last! Elegy 11: "Ah me, my friend! it will not, will not last!" William Shenstone. NOEC

Ah me, the aspidistra grows dusty behind the window pane. In North Great George's Street. "Seumas O'Sullivan." BIrV

Ah my Anthea! must my heart still break? To Anthea. Robert Herrick. CaPo

Ah my daughter, my grandchild! All You Others, Eat. Djurberaui. NOBAu, *tr.* by Catherine H. Berndt

Ah! my Dear. Full and True Account of a Dreaded Fire, that Lately Broke out in the Pope's Breeches, A. *Unknown.* EroLit

Ah, my dear friend and brother. John Keats. FHYEP *Fr.* Epistle to George Keats.

Ah my dear[e] angry [or angrie] Lord. Bitter-Sweet. George Herbert. FHYEP; GeHe; NOBE; OxBSP; PAI

Ah my Perilla! do'st thou grieve to see. To Perilla. Robert Herrick. BeJo; CaPo; NOSC; SCGP

Ah, my subject, the rose, I know. In a Queen's Domain. Sarah Morgan Bryan Piatt. NCAP

Ah, Nadya, Nadyenka. Bulat Shalvovich Okudzhava. ItGoST, *tr.* by Ronnie Apter and Mark Herman

Ah, Necromancy Sweet! Emily Dickinson. NOBA

Ah no, ah no, they weren't all gross and slow. Michael Foley. PNI *Fr.* True Life Love Stories.

Ah! no, not these! Parentage. Alice Thompson Meynell. NALW; NPeEn; PeVV; VWP

Ah! no! / You are not a soldierly upright row! Upon a Row of Old Books and Shoes in a Pawnbroker's Window. Suzanne Gardinier. CBAP

Ah, nobody knows. Frost. Stella Benson. OxBTC

Ah, not to be cut off. Rainer Maria Rilke. EnlH

Ah, now the puszta is indeed a waste! Puszta in Winter, The. Sándor Petőfi. IQMS, *tr.* by Watson Kirkconnell

Ah nuts! It's boring reading French newspapers. Les Luths. Frank O'Hara. NOBA; NoAM

Ah, old lady, are you still alive? Letter to My Mother. Sergey [or Sergei] Aleksandrovich Yesenin [or Essenin]. TCRP, *tr.* by Geoffrey Thurley

Ah, pirates, pirates, pirates! Fernando Pessoa. PFTM-1 *Fr.* Maritime Ode.

Ah, pity love where'er it grows! Old Man's Complaint, The. *Unknown.* OxBSP

Ah! poor intoxicated little knave. To a Fly, Taken out of a Bowl of Punch. "Peter Pindar." NOEC

Ah, poor negro Sadi, what sorrows, what anguish. Poor Negro Sadi, The. Charlotte Dacre. RWP

Ah poor repair for th'loss of such a Friend. (LL) On the Death of My Dear Friend and Play-Fellow Mrs. E. D. Having Dream'd the Night Before I Heard Thereof that I Had Lost a Pearl. Jane Barker. EMWP; PoBW

Ah Posthumus! our year[e]s hence fly[e]. His Age, Dedicated to His Peculiar Friend, Master John Wickes, under the Name of Posthumus. Robert Herrick. CaPo

Ah Poverties, Wincings, and Sulky Retreats. Walt Whitman. OxBSP

Ah, ra, chickera. *Unknown.* OxNR

Ah rosie. H. C. Artmann. PFTM-2, *tr.* by Jerome Rothenberg

Ah! sad wer we as we did peace. Turnstile, The. William Barnes. NOBVV; NPeEn; OxBEV

Ah secret voice of dark love! Ah bleating without wool! Ah wound! Ah prick of gall, sunken camellia! Federico García Lorca. CAGL, *tr.* by David William Foster *Fr.* Sonetos del Amor Oscuro [Sonnets of Dark Love].

Ah, see the fair chivalry come, the companions of Christ! Te Martyrum Candidatus. Lionel Pigot Johnson. OBMV

Aн, silly pug, wert thou so sore afraid? *Unknown.* NoSic

Ah silly pugg wert thou so sore afraid. Queen of England Elizabeth I. NoP-4

Ah! silly soul, what wilt thou say. Madrigal: "Ah! silly soul, what wilt thou say." William Drummond, of Hawthornden. SacPr

Ah, Sleep, to me thou com'st not in the guise. To Sleep. Lord Alfred Bruce Douglas. GSo

Ah, so, yes. Ah, so, yes. Larry Eigner. PFTM-2

Ah! Sorrows known too soon! and felt too long! (LL) Reaches Sicily. Mary Robinson. CenSon; RWP

Ah, Spain, already your tragic landscapes. Spanish War, The. Hugh MacDiarmid. NOBC

Ah, stay thy treacherous hand, forbear to trace. Verses on Sir Joshua Reynolds's Painted Window at New College, Oxford. Thomas Warton, the Younger. NOEC

Ah, Sun-Flower [or Ah! Sun-Flower]. William Blake. AWP; EBEV; FHYEP; HAP; NAEL-6v2; NIP-4; NOBRP; NOEC; NPeEn; NoP-4; PoE; PoPoPo; RB; SCGP; TFi; TOF; UnPo; WeW-3 *Fr.* Songs of Experience.

Ah, take these lips away; no more. Deadly Kisses. Pierre de Ronsard. AWP, *tr.* by Andrew Lang

Ah! tell me why, deluded Sex, thus we. Emulation, The: A Pindarick Ode. *Unknown.* EMWP

Ah, thankless! canst thou envy him who gains. To a Friend, Who Thinks Sensibility a Misfortune. Anna Seward. CenSon

Ah! that I were once more a careless Child! (LL) Sonnet to the River Otter. Samuel Taylor Coleridge. CenSon; OxBSo

Ah that the Tiger. Cristina Campo. CItWP, *tr.* by Cinzia Sartini Blum and Lara Trubowitz *Fr.* Tiger's Absence.

Ah, that you escape in the flash. Ah, That You Escape. José Lezama Lima. TCLAP, *tr.* by Willis Barnstone

Ah, the blowfly is whining there, its maggots are eating the flesh. Blowflies Buzz, The. *Unknown.* NOBAu, *tr.* by Catherine H. Berndt

Ah, the cold, cold days. Grandmother Remembers, A. Janet Lewis. IllVoic

Ah, the woods, the woods. Indians in the Woods, The. Janet Lewis. IllVoic

Ah! the year is slowly dying. Passing of the Old Year. Mary Weston Fordham. CBWP-2

Ah! there's a house that I do know. Slow to Come, Quick a-Gone. William Barnes. NOBVV

Ah! / These under-formings in the mind. Herman Melville. TCAPo *Fr.* Clarel: A Poem and Pilgrimage in the Holy Land.

Ah! think'st thou, Laura, then, that wealth. Stanzas: "Ah! think'st thou, Laura, then, that wealth." Charlotte Smith. NoP-4

Ah! Thomas, wherefore wouldst thou doubt. Christopher Smart. ChIV-2 *Fr.* Hymns and Spiritual Songs for the Fasts and Festivals of the Church of England.

Ah, those lips, kissed by so many. Mikhail Alekseievich Kuzmin. CAGL, *tr.* by Simon Karlinsky

Ah, through the open door. Spring Morning. D. H. Lawrence. MoBrPo

Ah! thus man spoils Heaven's glorious works with Blood! (LL) Sea View, The. Charlotte Smith. CenSon; ECWP

Ah tink it's time. New Dub, A. "Mbala." WaCA

Ah, 'twas a glorious autumn night. Two Meetings, The. Eugene Field. PWR

Ah, vale of woe, of gloom and darkness moulded. Song: "Ah, vale of woe, of gloom and darkness moulded." Rachel [or Rahel] Morpurgo. TrJP, *tr.* by Nina Davis Salaman

Ah, what a redoubtable god! (LL) Stephen Crane. OxBSP; TAP *Fr.* Black Riders [and Other Lines], The.

Ah! what a weary race my feet have run. Sonnet: To the River Lodon. Thomas Warton, the Younger. CenSon; NOEC; OxBSo

Ah what avails the sceptered race. Walter Savage Landor. *See* Ah what avails the sceptred race

Ah what avails the sceptred race. Rose Aylmer. Walter Savage Landor. AWP; BoLoP; EnLoPo; HAP; NAEL-5v2; NAEL-6v2; NOBE; NOBRP; OBEV; OxAEP-2; SCGP; TFi; UnPo; WeW-3

Ah what avails the sceptred race! Walter Savage Landor. *See* Ah what avails the sceptred race

Ah! what avails, when sinking down to sleep. Written in Ill Health. Anna Maria Smallpiece. CenSon

Ah, what of life! Does no one answer me? Ah, What of Life! Does No One Answer Me? Francisco de Quevedo y Villegas. SpanPo, *tr. by* William M. Davis

Ah! what pleasant visions haunt me. Galley of Count Arnaldos, The. Henry Wadsworth Longfellow. OBEV

Ah, what shall I be at fifty. Tennyson. NAEL-5v2; NAEL-6v2 *Fr.* Maud [A Monodrama].

Ah! what time wilt thou come? when shall that cry. Dawning, The. Henry Vaughan. GeHe; NOCV

Ah! where the hedge athirt the hill. When We That Now Ha' Childern Wer Childern. William Barnes. NOBVV

Ah, wherefore, lonely, to and fro. To. Herman Melville. NCAP

Ah! wherefore with infection should he live. William Shakespeare. SCGP *Fr.* Sonnets.

Ah, who can look on that celestial face. On the Statue of an Angel, by Bienaimé, in the Possession of J.S. Copley Greene, Esq. Washington Allston. APN-1

Ah! who would wish to feel, or learn to love? (LL) Sappho's Address to the Stars. Mary Robinson. CenSon; RWP

Ah! Why, Because the Dazzling Sun. Emily Jane Brontë. *See* Stars

Ah! why from me art thou for ever flown. Jane Cave. ECWP *Fr.* Head-Ache, The; An Ode to Health.

Ah! why has happiness—no second Spring? (LL) Sonnet Written at the Close of Spring [*or* Elegiac Sonnet]. Charlotte Smith. CenSon; ECWP; RWP

Ah! why is rapture so allied to pain? (LL) To Phaon. Mary Robinson. CenSon; RWP

Ah! why will Mem'ry with officious care. To Mrs. G. Charlotte Smith. RWP

Ah, wicked King! Accursed Gaveston! Christopher Marlowe. CAGL *Fr.* Edward the Second.

Ah, will no soul give ear unto my moan? Echo, An. Sir William Alexander, Earl of Stirling. NOSC

Ah! with no careless pen would I report. Bessie Rayner Parkes. VWP *Fr.* Summer Sketches.

Ah, with the grape my fading life provide. Omar Khayyám. EBEV; GTBS-P, *tr. by* Edward Fitzgerald *Fr.* Rubáiyát of Omar Khayyám [of Naishápúr], The.

Ah Woe Is Me. Propertius. AWP, *tr. by* F. A. Wright *Fr.* Elegies.

Ah woe is me, of passion naught I knew. Propertius. AWP, *tr. by* F. A. Wright *Fr.* Elegies.

Ah! Woman Still. Frances Sargent Osgood. ColAP

Ah, yes, I wrote the "Purple Cow." Cinq Ans Après. Frank Gelett Burgess. OBAL; OBCoV; TFi

Ah, yes, to your misfortune. Patrizia Cavalli. NeIt; VCWP, *tr. by* Judith Baumel

Ah! yesterday, d'ye know, I voun' Polly Be-en Upzides wi' Tom. William Barnes. NOBVV

Ah, you beast of love. Hayden Carruth. VGW

Ah (you say), this is Holy Wisdom. "H. D." NALW; NoAM *Fr.* Tribute to the Angels.

Ah, you should see Cynddylan on a tractor. Cynddylan on a Tractor. Ronald Stuart Thomas. AngWePo; TCAWP

Ah, your dewy pinions swinging. To the West Wind. Marianne von Willemer. AuPH, *tr. by* Aurelia G. Scott

Ahead I bear; the Eagle of Gál. *Unknown.* OBMV, *tr. by* Ernest Rhys *Fr.* Red Book of Hergest, The.

Ahead, the sun's face in a flaring hood. First Walk on the Moon. May Swenson. RACG

Ahem! Application. Paul Gallico. TriCat

A[h]kond of Swat, The. Edward Lear. FaBoCh; PeLi

Aholibah. Algernon Charles Swinburne. ChIV-1

Ahora. Sandra Maria Esteves. PueRic

Ahv drank. Jist Ti Let Yi No. Tom Leonard. NePenScot

Aid me Bellona, while the dreadful fight. Edmund Waller. BeJo *Fr.* Battle [*or* Battel] of the Summer-Islands, The.

Aideen's Grave. Sir Samuel Ferguson. NOIV

AIDS, Among Other Things. Peter Kocan. ChIV-2

AIDS Education, Seventh Grade. Ruth L. Schwartz. NeAmPo

Aiken Drum. *Unknown.* FaBoCh; OxNR

Ailing bird over the desert made its agony, An. Our Life. Mbella Sonne Dipoko. PBMAP

Ailing Japanese Monk, The. Hsiang Ssu. CoBCP, *tr. by* Burton Watson

Ailing mallard, An. Hakuro. JDP, *tr. by* Yoel Hoffmann

Ailing Woman Felt Her Forces Ebb, The. Rosalía de Castro. NAWM-7v2, *tr. by* S. Griswold Morley

Ailing woman felt her forces ebb, The. Ailing Woman Felt Her Forces Ebb, The. Rosalía de Castro. NAWM-7v2, *tr. by* S. Griswold Morley

Aim Was Song, The. Robert Frost. SoSe-8

Aimless. Louis Palagyi. TrJP, *tr. by* Watson Kirkconnell

Aimless caress slips through my fingers, The. Lost Caress, The. Alfonsina Storni. BLPSL, *tr. by* Rene de Costa, Rigas Kappatos and Eleni Paidoussi

Ain' committed no federal crime. Ezra Pound. FaBoTw *Fr.* Cantos.

Ain't been on Market Street for nothing. Ballad of the Hoppy-Toad. Margaret Abigail Walker. BlSi; NBV

Ain't got the change of a nickel. I Ain't Got Nothin' But the Blues. Duke Ellington. ReLy

Ain't I a Woman? Sojourner Truth. BlSi

Ain't It a Shame About Mame. Johnny Burke. ReLy

Ain't Misbehavin' Harry Brooks. ReLy

Ain't She Sweet? Milton Ager. ReLy

Ain't That the Way It Goes? Fred E. Ahlert. ReLy

Ain't We Got Fun. Richard A. Whiting. ReLy

Ainadamar. Nigel Jenkins. TCAWP

Air. Charlotte Gardelle. CuPo

Air. John Godfrey. FTOS

Air. Jennifer Maiden. BMAP

Air. Kathleen Jessie Raine. MoBrPo

Air. Ann Taylor. NOxBChV

Air, The. Andrew Hudgins. InvLad

Air a-gittin' cool an' coolah. Signs of the Times. Paul Laurence Dunbar. APN-2

Air and Angels. Charles North. FTOS

Air Balloon, The. Henry James Pye. NOEC *Fr.* Aerophorion.

Air-borne ants attacked softer parts of the cyclist, measuring. Race on Gathering Bites. Kojo Laing. HBAPE

Air commented in a whisper, The. (LL) Gallantry. Keith Douglas. NAEL-5v2; NAEL-6v2; NoAM; OBWP

Air Dagger. Jack Marshall. GeoHom

Air, earth and water meet at the sea's edge. Naked Girl Swimming, A. Arthur Rex Dugard Fairburn. PeNZ

Air: "Flaxen-headed cow-boy, as simple as may be, A." John O'Keefe [*or* O'Keeffe]. NOEC

Air Force called it Quadrant Bombing, The. Intersection in the Sky. Mcavoy Layne. CDa

Air force jet set down like a god, The. Jackie in Cambodia. Catherine Bowman. ReTh

Air: "Forgetting." Pierre Reverdy. CuPo

Air: "Fox may steal your hens, sir, A." John Gay. NOEC *Fr.* Begger's Opera.

Air grows calm and clear, The. Ode to Francisco Salinas. Luís De León. SpanPo, *tr. by* Edwin Morgan

Air hazed by seed and bug, arms heavy. Eye Blade. George Evans. AF

Air I Hear, The. Keorapetse Kgositsile. PBMAP

Air: "I ne'er could any lustre see." Richard Brinsley Sheridan. NOEC *Fr.* Duenna, The.

Air in Newfound-land [*or* Aire in Newfoundland-land] is wholesome, good, The. Pleasant Life in Newfoundland, The. Robert Hayman. NOBC

Air in the room is dark and greasy, The. Concise History of the Vietnam War: 1965–1968, A. Ron Weber. CDa

Air is a smoke-tree, the wind, The. Reviewing Past Lives while Leaf-Burning. Anita Endrezze. HATNAP

Air is mild and winter at an end, The. To the Stork. Mihály Tompa. IQMS, *tr. by* Yakov Hornstein

Air Is Motionless with Heat, The. Maria Petrovykh. TCRusP, *tr. by* Sharon Leiter

Air is motionless with heat, The. Air Is Motionless with Heat, The. Maria Petrovykh. TCRusP, *tr. by* Sharon Leiter

Air is quiet, The. Coming of Teddy Bears, The. Dennis Lee. TLR

Air is / Sucked clear of dross, The. January. Hoffman Reynolds Hays. SPE

Air is suffocating, The. Ironing Goatskin. Víctor Hernández Cruz. PueRic

Air is swimming with the bugs' forlorn Morse code on a hellish mid-morning, The. Divorced. Don Share. OPRER

Air is thick with nerves and smoke, The. University Examinations in Egypt. Dennis Joseph Enright. OxBTC; TwCP

Air New Zealand. Christian Karlson Stead. PeNZ *Fr.* Clodian Songbook.

Air: "O ruddier than the cherry!" John Gay. NAEL-5v1; NAEL-6v1; NOEC *Fr.* Acis and Galatea.

Air of June Sings, The. Edward Dorn. NeAP; PoM

Air Plant, The. Hart Crane. MoAmPo; PAI

Air Raid. Sachiko Yoshihara. GifTon, *tr. by* Naoshi Koriyama and Edward Lueders

Air Raid Across the Bay at Plymouth. Stephen Spender. AF

Air's enveloping capacious sleeves, The. Between. Ágnes Nemes Nagy. IQMS, *tr. by* Alan Dixon

Air's heaviness in the dark room, as if a vague bloodlike, The. Dark Room, The. Enrique Lihn. TCLAP; VCWP, *tr. by* David Unger

Air: Sentir avec Ardeur. Marie-Françoise-Catherine de, Marquise de Boufflers Beauveau. CTC; WPOW, *tr. by* Ezra Pound

Air shrill with life. Below White Cliffs. Abigail Albrecht. GeoHom

Air: "Since laws were made for ev'ry degree." John Gay. NAEL-6v1; NOEC *Fr.* Begger's Opera.

Air: "So full of courtly reverence." Dudley North, 3d Baron North. OxBSP

Air: "Sportsmen keep hawks, and their quarry they gain, The." John Gay. NOEC *Fr.* Polly; an Opera.

Air stiffens to a crust, The. Wound, The. Louise Glück. NoAM

Air Street. David Morley. NLP

Air, the dream-inspiring air, The. Idyl of Spring, An. Henrietta Cordelia Ray. CBWP-3

Air: "The Love of a Woman." Robert Creeley. VCAP; VGW

Air was full of Gitane Filtre, her reflection, The. My Mother's Clothes. Pascale Petit. Prnts

Air was soft, the ground still cold, The. April 5, 1974. Richard Wilbur. HCAP

Air which thy smooth voice doth break, The. Speaking and Kissing. Thomas Stanley. BeJo

Air without has taken fever, The. July. Alexander L. Posey. APN-2

Airborne. Elizabeth Garrett. MFPA

Air[e] and Angels. John Donne. BASC; ESCV; MeLP; NAEL-5v1; NAEL-6v1; NAEL-7v1

Aire for the sweet cad. Joy Island. Marianne Vitale. HeMarv

Airey Force. Letitia [*or* Laetitia] Elizabeth Landon. RWP

Airing clothes and belongings in the courtyard. Sentimental Poem. Po Chü-i. CoBCP, *tr. by* Burton Watson

Airing out the robe. Basho. JDP, *tr. by* Yoel Hoffmann

Airing Painful Memories. Yüan Chên. CoBCP, *tr. by* Burton Watson

Airing the Chapel. Sylvia Kantaris. LW

Airlift. Karen Chamberlain. GeoH

Airliner. Francis Webb. CBAP; NOBAu

Airly Beacon. Charles Kingsley. EBVV; OBEV

Airman. Stephen Spender. UV

(Airman.) UV

(Discovered in Mid-Ocean.) MoBrPo

Airman, The. Aleksandr Semionovich Kushner. TCRusP, *tr. by* Daniel Weissbort

Airman Who Flew over Shakespeare's England, The. Hyam Plutzik. APT-2

Airport. Martin Johnston. CBAP

Airport coffee tastes less of America, The. Gulf, The. Derek Walcott. NoP-4; PoPoPo; PoetW

Airports of the World. Eugene Richie. KGB

Airs and Graces. Peter Fallon. PBCIP

Airs of Palestine. John Pierpont.

"Here let us pause:—the opening prospect view." APN-1

"In what rich harmony, what polished lays." APN-1; TreFP

"Now, he recalls the lamentable wail." APN-1

"On Arno's bosom, as he calmly flows." APN-1

Airs of Pei. Confucius.

Efficient Wife's Complaint, The. CTC, *tr. by* Ezra Pound

"Wind o' the East dark with rain." CTC, *tr. by* Ezra Pound

Airs! that wander and murmur round. Siesta, The. *Unknown.* AWP, *tr. by* William Cullen Bryant

Airstrip in Essex, 1960, An. Donald Hall. LCAP-2

Airstrip is soggy with humidity, The. Aubade: Macedonia. Nicholas Samaras. YaYoPo

Airy Christ, The. Stevie Smith. ChIV-2; NOCV

Airy Hall Iconography. Frederick D'Aguiar. Oth

Airy spirits, you who love. Inscription in a Beautiful Retreat Called Fairy Bower. Hannah More. ECWP; NoP-4

Aisle of a Temple, The. William Congreve. OxAEP-1

Aisle of Dogs. Chase Twichell. EmeKit

Aisles and abysses; leagues no man explores. Caverns. Madison Cawein. APN-2

Aisling. Paul Muldoon. PNI

Aja, I am joyful; this is good! Utitia' q's Song. *Unknown.* APN-2, *tr. by* Franz Boas

Ajanta. Muriel Rukeyser. APT-2; MoAmPo; NNaP

Ajax. David Osborne Hamilton. YaYoPo

Ajax. Sophocles.

Chorus: "Fair Salamis, the billow's roar.". AWP, *tr. by* Winthrop Mackworth Praed

Ajax and his Brother. Homer. OBVE, *tr. by* Alexander Pope *Fr.* Iliad, The.

Ajax, / lion-coloured stallion from Sealey's stable. Derek Walcott. PoetW *Fr.* Divided Child, The.

Ajax Samples, The. Laura Jensen. LCAP-2

Ajax, the bull-dog, on his cushioned place. Ajax. David Osborne Hamilton. YaYoPo

Ajax the swift swerv'd never from the side. Homer. OBVE *Fr.* Iliad, The.

Ajo Lily. Peggy Shumaker. PoCoUp

AKA. Bruce Andrews. PFTM-2

Akat'ani / x'aax' Tlingit Concrete Poem. Nora Dauenhauer. NIP-4

Akhmatova. Deborah Digges. ExTi

Akiba. Muriel Rukeyser. TaR

Al Aaraaf. Edgar Allan Poe. APN-1

Song: "Young flowers were whispering in melody.". NOBA

"Neath blue-bell or streamer." OxBA

Al dar / At three. Viernes Santo / Good Friday. Francisco Alarcon. GeoHom

Al it is fantam that we mid fare. All Is Phantom. *Unknown.* SacPr

Al nyght by the rose, rose. *Unknown. See* All night by the rose, rose

Al that I may swynke or swete. *Unknown. See* All that I may swynk or swet

Al Wat Kind Is. Ingrid De Kok. HAWP

Al were he mytre, crowne [*or* croune], or diademe. (LL) Gentilesse. Geoffrey Chaucer. AWP; MiEL; NAEL-5v1

Al worldly welthe passed me fro. *Unknown.* OHMEL

Ala, mala, mink, monk. *Unknown.* OxNR

Alabama Centennial. Naomi Long Madgett. BPo

Alabama Song. Bertolt Brecht. PFTM-1

Alabaster legs of the lonely woman, The. Merry Window, The. Francis Scarfe. SPE

Alabushevo. Viktor Aleksandrovich Nekipelov. TCRP, *tr. by* Albert C. Todd

Aladdin. James Russell Lowell. TCAPo

Alakanak Break-Up. Mei-Mei Berssenbrugge. PmAP

Alan Turing's Imitation Game. Intimations. Howard Nemerov. BodElec

Alarm, The. Hildebrand Jacob. NOEC

Alarm at First Entering the Yang-tze Gorges. Po Chü-i. ChiP, *tr. by* Arthur Waley

Alarmclock is ringing. (LL) My Alba. Allen Ginsberg. CLPP; NOBA

Alarmed Skipper, The. James Thomas Fields. NBLV

Alarming New Development, An. Ron Schreiber. GLP

Alarum. Urszula Koziol. WPOW, *tr. by* Czeslaw Milosz

Alarum, The. Sylvia Townsend Warner. MoBrPo

Alas! Sadi [*or* Saadi *or* Sa'di]. AWP, *tr. by* L. Cranmer-Byng *Fr.* Gulistan, The.

Alas, Alack! Walter De la Mare. OPOU

Alas! Alas! the father said. Cornelius Whur. VerBaPo *Fr.* Armless Artist, The.

Alas! alas! the while. *Unknown.* MiEL

Alas! alas! thou turn'st in vain. Claim to Love. Giovanni Battista Guarini. AWP, *tr. by* Thomas Stanley

Alas, alas, well evil I sped! Undo! *Unknown.* NOCV

Alas, all my years, where have they disappeared? Walther [*or* Walter] von der Vogelweide. GePo

Alas! and am I born for this. On Liberty and Slavery. George Moses Horton. APN-1

Alas! behold! how steep! how high! Road to Shu Is Hard, The. Li Po. SuSp, *tr. by* Irving Y. Lo

Alas! Carolina! J. Gordon Coogler. OBAL; VerBaPo

Alas, dear Clio, every day. To Clio, from Rome. John Dyer. NOEC

Alas, dear mother, fairest queen and best. Anne Bradstreet. BASC; EMWP

Alas, departing is ground of wo! *Unknown.* MiEL

Alas! for all the pretty women who marry dull men. Meditation at Kew. Anna Wickham. FaBoTw; MoBrPo; NALW

Alas for Juan and Haidee! They were. Byron. NePenScot *Fr.* Don Juan.

Alas for me, who loved a falcon well! Lady Laments for Her Lost Lover, by Similitude of a Falcon, A. *Unknown.* AWP; EaltPo, *tr. by* Dante Gabriel Rossetti

Alas! for Peter not an helping Hand. George Crabbe. NPeEn; NoP-4; OxBEV *Fr.* Borough, The.

Alas, for the blight of my fancies! Love Versus Learning. Constance Naden. VWP; ViWPN

Alas! for the South. J. Gordon Coogler. OBAL

Alas for the voyage, O High King of Heaven. Farewell to Ireland. Saint Columcille [*or* Columba]. AWP, *tr. by* Douglas Hyde

Alas for this unhappy night! Song of Instruction, A. Te Kooti Rikirangi. PeNZ, *tr. by* Margaret Orbell

Alas, for us, who need beware. On Worldly Prelates. Charles Wesley. ChIV-2

Alas for Youth. Firdowsi. AWP, *tr. by* R. A. Nicholson

Alas, good friend, what profit you can see. Lines to a Reviewer. Shelley. OxBSP

Alas, have I not pain enough, my friend. Sir Philip Sidney. NoP-4; NoSic *Fr.* Astrophil and Stella.

Alas, his mind is sunk. Boethius. MLL, *tr.* by Helen Waddell *Fr.* Consolation of Philosophy, The ("De Consolacione Philosophie").

Alas how barbarous are we. Upon the graving of her Name upon a Tree in Barnelmes Walks. Katherine Philips. PBRV

Alas, how easily things go wrong! Sweet Peril. George Macdonald. ITBLP

Alas! How should I sing? *Unknown.* NOIV

Alas, how soon the hours are over. Plays. Walter Savage Landor. NBLV; OxBSP; OxBoLi; PeLV

Alas! I draw breath heavily. Old Woman's Song, An. Akjartoq. WPOW, *tr.* by Tom Lowenstein and Knud Rasmussen

Alas! I have lost my God. Rejected. Lord Alfred Bruce Douglas. PeVV

Alas! in every aspiration bold. Richard Polwhele. NOBRP *Fr.* Unsex'd Females, The.

Alas, is wiser far [*or* farre] than I. (LL) Bait[e], The. John Donne. InPK-6; NAEL-5v1; NAEL-6v1; NAEL-7v1; NOSC; PoRA; RB

Alas! Lord and Lady Dalhousie are dead, and buried at last. William McGonagall. VerBaPo *Fr.* Death of Lord and Lady Dalhousie, The.

Alas, madam[e], for stealing [*or* stelying] of a kiss [*or* kysse]. Sir Thomas Wyatt. BoLoP

Alas, my brothers. "H. D." NOBA *Fr.* Helen in Egypt.

Alas, my God, I know not what. (LL) Thanksgiving, The. George Herbert. ESCV; GeHe

Alas, my love they knocked you down. Breach in the Wall, The. *Unknown.* EMWP

Alas, my Purse! how can lean and low! Soliloquy on an Empty Purse. Mary Jones. ECWP

Alas our good kaspar is dead. Kaspar Is Dead. Hans [*or* Jean] Arp. PFTM-1

Alas! our pleasant moments fly. On Parting. Edward Coote [*or* Coate] Pinkney. APN-1; TCAPo

Alas poor Death, where does thy great strength lye? Meditations for July 25, 1666. Philip Pain. SCAP

Alas! poor Fanny! wretched girl, alas! Fanny's Removal in 1714. John Winstanley. NOEC

Alas! Poor Queen. Marion Angus. NPeEn; NePenScot

Alas poore Scholler, whither wilt thou goe. Robert Wild. "In a melancholly studdy." PBRV

Alas, shall I not see again. Heinrich von Morungen. GePo

Alas! Sir John Ogilvy is dead, aged eighty-seven. Late Sir John Ogilvy, The. William McGonagall. VerBaPo

Alas, so all thing[e]s now[e] do[e] hold[e] their peace. Complaint by Night, A. Henry Howard, Earl of Surrey. SCGP

Alas! so all thing[e]s now[e] do[e] hold[e] their peace. Henry Howard, Earl of Surrey. *See* Complaint by Night, A

Alas, successive sorrows crowd the space! (LL) To the Strawberry. Helen Maria Williams. CenSon; OxBSo; RWP

Alas, that ever that speche was spoken. *Unknown.* EnLoPo

Alas, that I should be. To My Infant Daughter. Yvor Winters. VGW; WoPoe

Alas, that I should die. Song of a Woman Abandoned by the Tribe. *Unknown.* WPE, *tr.* by Mary Austin

Alas, That Is the Name of Our Town; I Have Been Concealing It All This Time. Joshua Clover. NeAmPo

Alas! that such a soul should taste of death. In Memory of Arthur Clement Williams. Eloise Bibb. CBWP-4

Alas, that wisdom, and youth. Walther [*or* Walter] von der Vogelweide. GePo

Alas, the country! how shall tongue or pen. Byron. OBSV *Fr.* Age of Bronze, The.

Alas, the ignorance of unhappy men. Boethius. MLL *Fr.* Consolation of Philosophy, The ("De Consolacione Philosophie").

Alas! the state of things tonight. Conversation with Death, A. Sileas Na Ceapaich. EMWP

Alas! the time has come, old dress. Lines to an Old Dress. Mary E. Tucker. CBWP-1

Alas, then, for the homeless beggar old! (LL) Summer and Winter. Shelley. OxAEP-2; SCGP

Alas! they were so young, so beautiful. Byron. EroLit; OxBEV *Fr.* Don Juan.

Alas, 'tis true I have gone here and there. William Shakespeare. EBEV; NAEL-6v1; NAEL-7v1; NoSic; OxAEP-1 *Fr.* Sonnets.

Alas! 'Tis Very Sad to Hear. Walter Savage Landor. GTBS-P; WeW-3

Alas, to be / Mortal, and know our sad mortality! Echo. George Santayana. APN-2

Alas, what is the world? a sea of glass. Meditation 10. Philip Pain. NOBA

Alas! When the instinct rules. Wrestling. "Rachel" [*or* "Rahel"]. FIT, *tr.* by Robert Friend

Alas! Where Have They Vanished, All Those Years of Mine! Walther [*or* Walter] von der Vogelweide. AuPH, *tr.* by Lowell A. Bangerter

Alas, why say you I am rich? when I. Robert Sidney. NoSic

Alas! young men, come, make lament. Dirge of St. Malo, The. George Washington Cable. APN-2

Alasdair, O calf of my senses. Song to Alasdair Mac Colla, A. Dorothy Brown (Diorbhail nic a Bhriuthainn). EMWP

Alasdair of Glengarry. Sileas Na Ceapaich. "Alasdair of Glengarry." NePenScot, *tr.* by Derick Thomson

Alaska. Mary Weston Fordham. CBWP-2

Alaskan Fragments June 1981—Summer Solstice. Wendy Rose. HATNAP

Alaskan Mountain Poem #1. Leslie Marmon Silko. VoR

Alastor; or, The Spirit of Solitude. Shelley. NAEL-6v2
  Invocation: "Earth, ocean, air, belovèd brotherhood!". NAEL-5v2
  "There was a poet whose untimely tomb." FHYEP; TOF
  "Wildly he wandered on." TOF

Alba. Imamu Amiri Baraka. FTOS

Alba. Samuel Beckett. BIrV

Alba. Confucius. CTC, *tr.* by Ezra Pound *Fr.* Songs of T'ang.

Alba. Ezra Pound. HAP; TCAPo; WeW-3

Alba Innominata. *Unknown.* AWP, *tr.* by Ezra Pound

Alba ("When the nightingale to his mate"). Ezra Pound. APT-1; OBVE; VGW; WeW-3 *Fr.* Langue d'Oc.

Alba, With a Refrain from the Provençal. *Unknown.* WoPoe, *tr.* by Tim Reynolds

Albacete knives, magnificent, The. Quarrel, The. Federico García Lorca. AF, *tr.* by Robert Bly

Albania and the Death of Enver Hoxha. Will Alexander. PFTM-2

Albany in a time of khaki. Gathering Place, The. Alan Alexander. NOBAu

Albatross, The. Charles Baudelaire. SxFrPo, *tr.* by James McGowan

Albatross, The. Charles Baudelaire. OWoS, *tr.* by Richard Wilbur

Albeit my prayers have not so long delay'd. Cino da Pistoia. EaItPo, *tr.* by Dante Gabriel Rossetti

Albeit the Venice girls get praise. Ballad of the Women of Paris. François Villon. AWP, *tr.* by Algernon Charles Swinburne

Albert Einstein's the man we must credit. Limerick: "Albert Einstein's the man we must credit." Stanley J. Sharpless. PeLi

Albert is haranguing his mother about his name. In the Heat of the Morning. Anne Szumigalski. FaBoWP

Albert james was black long before me. Albert James. Reuben Jackson. UnSA

Albert Sidney Johnston. Kate Brownlee Sherwood. CBCWP

Albert Speer. W. D. Snodgrass. NoAM

Albert Victor loved his mother. Joseph Gwyer. VerBaPo *Fr.* On the Death of the Duke of Clarence.

Alberta. Priscilla Jane Thompson. CBWP-2

Albion's England. William Warner.
  "Merry mate amongst the rest, of cloisterers thus told, A." NoSic
  Tale of the Beginning of Friars and Cloisterers, A. NoSic

Albion's most lovely daughter sat on the banks of the. Mrs. Albion You've Got a Lovely Daughter. Adrian Henri. OxBTC

Albion's Triumph. Aurelian Townshend [*or* Townsend].
  Song: "What mak's me so unnimbly ryse.". OxBEV

Albion, teach me (and not with loud, unsubtle). László Arany. IQMS, *tr.* by John Gordon Nichols *Fr.* Hero of the Mirages, The.

Albuera. Thomas Hardy. FaBoWar *Fr.* Dynasts, The.

Album. Josephine Miles. APT-2; ColAP; FaBoWP

Album, The. Cecil Day Lewis. EnLoPo; OxBTC

Album—A Runthru. Clark Coolidge. FTOS

Album is a banquet: from the store, An. To Dora W[ordsworth]. Charles Lamb. OxBSo

Album Leaf. Stéphane Mallarmé. OBVE, *tr.* by Keith Bosley

Album Leaves. Arthur Rex Dugard Fairburn.
  Back Street. PeNZ
  Conversation in the Bush. PeNZ
  "Girl comes out of a doorway in the morning, A." PeNZ
  "Observe the young and tender frond." PeNZ
  "On my land grew a green tree." PeNZ
  Possessor, The. PeNZ

Albuquerque Graveyard, The. Jay Wright. ESEAA

Alcaics; to H. F. B. Robert Louis Stevenson. OBEV

Alcander's Flower Garden. William Mason. OBGa *Fr.* English Garden, The.

Alceste in the Wilderness. Anthony Hecht. CoAmPo

Alceste is here, that al may desteyne. (LL) Geoffrey Chaucer. AWP; EBEV; HAP; NOBE; OBEV; SCGP *Fr.* Legend of Good Women, The.

Alcestis. Euripides.
  "In heaven-high musings and many." AWP, *tr.* by A. E. Housman
  Strength of Fate, The. AWP, *tr.* by A. E. Housman

Alcestis on the Poetry Circuit. Erica Jong. NALW

Alcestis to Admetus. Mary Elizabeth Coleridge. ViWPN

Alchemical. Paul Celan. VCWP, *tr.* by Michael Hamburger

Alchemist, The. Louise Bogan. APT-2; AWP; MoAmPo

Alchemist, The. Richard Church. OxBTC

Alchemist, The. Ben Jonson.
  "I will have all my beds blown[e] up, not stuft." EBEV; OxBEV

Alchemists say the Stone turns lead to gold. David Foster. NOBAu *Fr.*
  Fleeing Atalanta, The.

Alchemy. Alan Michael Parker. AmPoNex

Alchemy of Day, The. Anne Hébert. BoWoP, *tr. by* A. Poulin, Jr.

Alcheringa [Arunta of Australia, *alcheringa*], *n.* 1. The Eternal Dream Time.
  Alcheringa Definitions. Orpingalik. PFTM-1

Alcheringa Definitions. Orpingalik. PFTM-1

Alciphron and Leucippe. Walter Savage Landor. OBEV

Alcohol. Franz Wright. LCAP-2

Alcoholic. John Berryman. BodElec; NOCV

Alcoholic in the 3rd Week of the 3rd Treatment, The.   John Berryman.
  BodElec

Alcoholic's Son at Ten, The. Kathleen Peirce. PBCAP

Alcott. James Russell Lowell. TCAPo *Fr.* Fable for Critics, A.

Alcyna met them at the outer gate. Ludovico Ariosto. OBVE *Fr.* Orlando
  Furioso.

Aldebaran at Dusk. George Sterling. TCAPo

Alderman. Marilyn Nelson Waniek. LTA

Aldport (Mystery Tour). Kingsley Amis. NOBL *Fr.* Evans Country, The.

Ale they drink in Giggleswick, The. Dominic Bevan Wyndham Lewis. UV
  Fr. Downland Crisis, A.

Aleatory. Mary Zeppa. MiVo

Aleng Maria. Eugene Gloria. ReBoTo

Aleph Poem. Jerome Rothenberg. FTOS

Alert to the providing water. (LL) Predictor of Famine, The. William Carlos
  Williams. APT-1; VGW

Aleutian Islands. Blaise Cendrars. BLT, *tr. by* Monique Chefdor

Alex at the Barber's. John Fuller. PeLV

Alex, perhaps a colour of which neither of us had dreamt. Letter to Alex
  Comfort. Dannie Abse. FaBoTw; TwCP

Alexander and Campaspe. John Lyly.
  (Cards and Kisses.) NOBE; OBEV
  (Cupid and Campaspe.) GTBS-P; OxAEP-1; SCGP
  (Cupid and My Campaspe.) NoP-4
  ("Cupid and my Campaspe played.") NoP-4
  Cupid and My Campaspe Played. NoSic; PoRA
  "O! [*or* Oh] for a bowl of fat canary." NOBE; NoSic
  (Oh, For a Bowl of Fat Canary.) NoP-4
  Serving Men's Song, A. NOBE; NoSic
  (Spring's Welcome.) OBEV
  Trico's Song. NoSic
  (Welcome to Spring.) NOBE
  (What Bird So Sings.) SCGP
  "What bird so sings, yet so does wail?" NoSic

Alexander at Thebes. Anna Andreyevna Akhmatova. FaBoWar, *tr. by* Max
  Hayward and Stanley Kunitz

Alexander Jannai. Constantine P. Cavafy. TrJP, *tr. by* Simon Chasen

Alexander's Feast; or, The Power of Music [*or* Musique]. Dryden. GTBS-P;
  NAEL-5v1; NAEL-6v1; NAEL-7v1; NOBE; PeECV; TFi

Alexander's Ragtime Band. Irving Berlin. ReLy; TCAPo

Alexander's Song. *Unknown.* LB
  (Man of Thessaly, [The].) OxNR

Alexandre Dumas and His Son. Dorothy Parker. APT-1 *Fr.* Pig's-Eye View
  of Literature, A.

Alexandreis. Anne Killigrew. NoP-4

Alexandria. Mongane Wally Serote. NAfrP

Alexis. Plato. GrAn
  (Alexis.) GrAn

Alexis, here she stayed; among these pines. Sonnet: "Alexis, here she stayed;
  among these pines." William Drummond, of Hawthornden. NOSC

Alfonso was his name; his sad cantina. Skin Diving in the Virgins. John
  Malcolm Brinnin. TAP

Alfonzo Prepares to Go Over the Top. Rita Dove. LoL

Alfred: A Masque. James Thomson.
  (Ode: Rule, Brittania!) NAEL-5v1; NAEL-6v1; NAEL-7v1
  Rule, Britannia! GTBS-P; NOEC; OBWP; TreFP
  "When Britain first, at heaven's command." GTBS-P; NOEC; OBWP; TreFP

Alfred Corning Clark. Robert Lowell. RB

Alfred de Musset. Maurice Evan Hare. OBCoV

Alfred, Lord Tennyson. Dorothy Parker. APT-1; NALW *Fr.* Pig's-Eye View
  of Literature, A.

Algy. *Unknown.* KaS

Algy met a bear. Algy. *Unknown.* KaS

Ali Ben Shufti. Anthony Thwaite. OxBTC

Alibazan. Laura Elizabeth Richards. OBCA

Alibi of a Dead Man. Giovanni Raboni. ItPo, *tr. by* Gayle Ridinger

Alicante. Jacques Prévert. BoLoP, *tr. by* Lawrence Ferlinghetti

Alice. Isa Blagden. PoBW

Alice. Michael S. Harper. ISC

Alice. Noy Holland. Unle

Alice. Gale Jackson. SpirFl

Alice Blue Gown. Harry Tierney. ReLy

Alice, dear, what ails you. Frosty Night, A. Robert Graves. MoBrPo;
  OxBTC

Alice Fell; or, Poverty. William Wordsworth. OBNV

Alice grown lazy, mammoth but not fat. Last Days of Alice. Allen Tate.
  APT-2; FuPo; NAAL-2v2; NOBA; OxBA; UnPo

Alice is tall and upright as a pine. Charles Cotton. BoLoP; EnLoPo; OxBSo;
  Son *Fr.* Resolution to Four Sonnets, of a Poetical Question Put to Me by a
  Friend, Concerning Four Rural Sisters.

Alice of Daphne, 1799. John Ennis. PBCIP

Alice Potato. Thomas Zvi Wilson. SpudSo

Alice's Adventures in Wonderland. Lewis Carroll.
  Alice's Recitation. NOBL; OBCoV; PeLV; UV
  "Beautiful Soup, so rich and green." UV
  Crocodile, The. ChAP; FaBoCh; FaBoEE; NBLV; NOBL; NOBVV; OxBEV;
    RB; TFi; TTTS; UV
  Duchess's Lullaby, The. FaBoCh; NBLV; UV
  Evidence Read at the Trial of the Knave of Hearts. GTBS-P; NOBVV;
    NPeEn; OxBoLi; PeLV
  Father William. ChAP; NOBL; NOBVV; NPeEn; OBCoV; OxBEV; PoRA;
    TFi; UnPo
  ("Fury said to.") KaS
  ("Fury said to / a mouse.") NOxBChV
  (Fury said to a mouse.) KaS
  "Fury said to a / mouse, That he." NoAM; OBCoV
  Lobster Quadrille, A. NoAM; OxAEP-2; UV
  Long Tale, A. NoAM; OBCoV
  (Lullaby, A.) NOxBChV
  Mad Hatter's Song, The. NOBL; UV
  (Mouse's Tale, The.) NOxBChV
  Song of the Mock Turtle, The. UV
  "Speak roughly to your little boy." FaBoCh; NBLV; UV
  "They told me you had been to her." GTBS-P; NOBVV; NPeEn; OxBoLi;
    PeLV
  "'Tis the voice of the Lobster: I heard him /declare declare." NOBL;
    OBCoV; PeLV; UV
  "Will you walk a little faster?" said a [*or* the] whiting to a [*or* the] snail."
    NoAM; OxAEP-2; UV

Alice's Recitation. Lewis Carroll. NOBL; OBCoV; PeLV; UV *Fr.* Alice's
  Adventures in Wonderland.

Alice's Cat, New Year's Eve 1990. Anne Grimes. Prnts

Alien. William Price Turner. OxBS

Alienation. Howard Phillips Lovecraft. APT-1

Alison. *Unknown.* HAP

Alison and Willie. *Unknown.* ESPB

Alison [*or* Allison] Gross. *Unknown.* ESPB; FaBoCh; OxBB

Alive for an Instant. Kenneth Koch. PmAP

Alive, I flourish. Edna Eglinton. NewEx

Alive, in a slippery grave. (LL) Weed Puller. Theodore Roethke. HCAP;
  NAAL-2v2

Alive, ne'er parted be. (LL) Song: "Sweetest love, I do not go[e]." John
  Donne. AWP; BoLoP; ESCV; FHYEP; HeIP-4; MeLP; NAEL-7v1;
  NOBE; NoSic; PAI; TFi

Alive or Not. Alfred Wellington Purdy. NOBC

Alive, ridiculous, and dead, forgot! (LL) Pope. NPeEn; OBSV; OxBEV *Fr.*
  Epistle [II,] to a Lady[: Of the Characters of Women].

Alive, this man was Manes, a common slave. Anyte [*or* Anytes]. BoWoP

Alive Together. Lisel Mueller. IllVoic

Alive with expectation. (LL) Soul Music: The Derry Air. Eamon Grennan.
  BiHa; PBCIP

All. Antoni Slonimski. TrJP, *tr. by* Wanda Dynowska

All a January day, in the house above the cliff. Winter at Gurnard's Head.
  David Wright. NLP

All a-tremble she awoke. Annunciation, The. Amrita Pritam. WPOW, *tr. by*
  Krishna Gorowara and Khushwant Singh

All Abdéra mourned at the funeral pyre. Anacreon. GrAn

All about. All about all with a word seeming across the world. Time Travel.
  Nick Piombino. FTOS

All about Boys and Girls. John Ciardi. NOxBChV

All about Carrowmore the lambs. Carrowmore. Lucie Brock-Broido.
  PoPoPo

All adult dogs I have known embrace Buddhism to some degree. Max's Lecture on Canine Buddhism. Amy Gerstler. Unle

All after pleasures as I rid one day. Christmas. George Herbert. ChrPo; GeHe; NOSC; PeECV; TOF; TrCP

All afternoon I hope. Gillian Clarke. NewEx

All afternoon I thought the decision must fall. Sleeping Man Must Be Awakened to Be Killed, A. Erin Belieu. NeAmPo

All afternoon my brothers and I have worked in the orchard. Planting a Sequoia. Dana Gioia. GeoHom

All afternoon the town readied for storm. Letter from the Coast, A. Mark Doty. HarvBoo

All, All a-Lonely. *Unknown.* OxBoLi

All, all are gone, the old familiar faces. (LL) Old Familiar Faces, The. Charles Lamb. AWP; GTBS-P; NOBE; NOBRP; OBEV; OxAEP-2; OxBEV; RB

All, All of a Piece Throughout. Dryden. HAP *Fr.* Secular Masque, The.

All Alone. Mary E. Tucker. CBWP-1

All alone in my little cell. *Unknown.* NOIV

All along the backwater. Kenneth Grahame. NOxBChV; NTCP; OTCP; WHSW *Fr.* Wind in the Willows, The.

All along the valley, stream that flashest white. In the Valley of Cauteretz. Tennyson. BoLoP; NAEL-5v2; NAEL-6v2; NOBE

All along this road. Basho. SoOfWa, *tr. by* Sam Hamill

All Arcadia hath not seen. (LL) John Milton. OBEV; OxBSP *Fr.* Arcades.

All are architects of fate. Builders, The. Henry Wadsworth Longfellow. PWR

All are but parts of one stupendous whole. Pope. FHYEP *Fr.* Essay on Man, An.

All are ghosts beside. (LL) Ralph Waldo Emerson. APN-1; CBCWP

All are not born to soar—and ah! how few. On Imitation. Samuel Taylor Coleridge. OxBSP

All arms combined magnificently together. (LL) Persian Version, The. Robert Graves. NOBL; NoAM; NoP-4; OBWP; WeW-3

All around my house at midnight: rain. Dawn: Clear Skies. Yang Shih-ch'i. CoBLCP, *tr. by* Jonathan Chaves

All around old Chattanooga. Freedom at McNealy's. Priscilla Jane Thompson. CBWP-2; SWaP

All around, shards of a lost tradition. Lost Tradition, A. John Montague. CIP-2; PBCIP

All around the altar, huge lianas. Reading the Bible Backwards. Eleanor Wilner. NoP-4

All around the Town. Phyllis McGinley.
J's the Jumping Jay-Walker. SSCS

All Around the Town. Genevieve Taggard. APT-2

All Around Us. Constance Urdang. PBCAP

All ashes, all ashes again. (LL) On Neal's Ashes. Allen Ginsberg. PmAP; PoM

All asleep: mountain peaks and chasms. Alcman. SaLy, *tr. by* Diane Rayor

All at once something. Before Summer Rain. Rainer Maria Rilke. WoPoe, *tr. by* Mark Rudman

All attempts to remove. Mr. Cogito Meditates on Suffering. Zbigniew Herbert. VCWP, *tr. by* John Carpenter

All beauty, resonance, integrity. Le Livre Est sur la Table. John Ashbery. SPE

All Being Well. Wilfrid Wilson Gibson. OxBTC

All beneath the white-rose tree. Three Captains, The. *Unknown.* AWP, *tr. by* Andrew Lang

All birds love to babble where a man wants quiet. In the Mountains. Ssu-k'ung Shu. SuSp, *tr. by* Edward H. Schafer

All birds that swim are mine. My Birds. Solomon Mutswairo. PeSAV, *tr. by* Donald E. Herdeck and Solomon Mutswairo

All blessings ask a blessed mood. Rods and Kisses. Coventry Patmore. SacPr

"All-bounteous Heaven," Castalio cries. Unanswerable Apology for the Rich, An. Mary Barber. ECWP

All Britain knows of this noble city. Durham. *Unknown.* ASW, *tr. by* Kevin Crossley-Holland

All busy punching tickets. Crickets. David McCord. NTCP

All but Blind. Walter De la Mare. MoBrPo; WeW-3

All but the blithe / Hexameters. (LL) Verse: "What should we know." Oliver St. John Gogarty. FaBoCh; OBMV; PoRA

All but unutterable Name! Divine Presence, The. Adelaide Anne Procter. SacPr

All by itself. Ransetsu. SoOfWa, *tr. by* Sam Hamill

All Changeth. William Drummond, of Hawthornden. NePenScot

All Christian men in my behalf. On Sir John Calf. *Unknown.* FaBoEE

All Circumstances are the Frame. Emily Dickinson. InvLi

All Clear. Roger Woddis. PeLV

All Clowns Are Masked. Delmore Schwartz. OxBA *Fr.* Repetitive Heart, The.

All colors come from the sun. And it does not have. Sun, The. Czeslaw Milosz. ChAP

All craftsmen share a knowledge. They have held. Craftsmen. Victoria Mary Sackville-West. OxBTC

All creation and say, You can have it. (LL) You Can Have It. Philip Levine. AmFaPo; NoP-4; VCAP

All creatures, each has a home. In Praise of Poor Scholars. T'ao Ch'ien [*or* T'ao Yuan-ming]. SuSp, *tr. by* Eugene Eoyang

All dat English you used to know. Don't Know No English. Nicolás Guillén. PFTM-1

All day. James Tipton. HA

All day, a small mild Negro man with a broom. Sweeper of Ways, The. Howard Nemerov. HCAP

All day a strong wind blew. Strong Wind, A. Austin Clarke. RB

All day, all night, I worry. Tu Fu. CrYelRi, *tr. by* Sam Hamill *Fr.* Random Pleasures.

All day and every day the sea shone, steeped in its blueness. When I Was Young. Alun Llywelyn-Williams. OBWVE, *tr. by* Gwyn Williams

All day and night, music. Jelaluddin [*or* Jalal al-Din] Rumi. EnlH

All day and night, save winter, every weather. Aspens. Edward Thomas. FaBoVe; NPeEn; OxBEV

All Day at Work. Deborah Abbott. PasH

All day beside the shattered tank he'd lain. Reconciliation. Cecil Day Lewis. PoWW; TwCP

All-Day Bird, the artist, The. Claritas. Denise Levertov. VGW

All day, day after day, they're bringing them home. Homecoming. Bruce Dawe. BMAP; CBAP; EmeKit

All day he roams the garden. Lessons. Graham Thomas. AngWePo

All day he slept, his mouth on pennyroyal. Soldier in the Park, The. Elizabeth Riddell. CBAP

All day I always want to know. When I Am 19 I Was a Medic. D. F. Brown. CDa

All day I have been closed up. Of Rain and Air. Wayne Dodd. BLT

All day i have wandered in these southern reaches. B. P. Nichol. PFTM-2 *Fr.* Martyrology 7, The.

All Day I Hear the Noise of Waters. James Joyce. SCGP

All day I heard a humming in my ears. Awaking of the Poetic Faculty, The. George Henry Boker. Son

All day I hoe weeds. *Unknown.* OHMPJ

All day I search for you without success. To Peace. Suzanne Gardinier. AmPoNex

All day I think about it, then at night I say it. Who Says Words With My Mouth. Jelaluddin [*or* Jalal al-Din] Rumi. AmFaPo, *tr. by* Coleman Barks and John Moyne

All day I tried to distinguish. Elms. Louise Glück. NoAM

All day I've been searching for omens, flimsy as they are, and the cat. Aubade. Mark Wunderlich. WiU

All day, I wear a grey disguise that buttons. Downtown Seattle in the Fog. Tina Koyama. FSt

All Day It Has Rained. Alun Lewis. AngWePo; GTBS-P; NAEL-5v2; NAEL-6v2; NOBE; NoP-4; OBWP; OBWVE; OxBTC; TCAWP

All day, knowing you dead. Hours, The. John Peale Bishop. OxBA

All day long. (LL) Counting the Mad. Donald Justice. CoAmPo; NIP-4; NoP-4; PAI; TRP; UnPo

All Day Long. Léopold Sédar Senghor. PoetW, *tr. by* Melvin Dixon

All day long, at Scott's or Menzies', I await the gorging crowd. Wail of the Waiter, The. Marcus Clarke. NOBAu

All day long I have been working. Madonna of the Evening Flowers. Amy Lowell. NAAL-5; NALW

All day long on the long and narrow rails. All Day Long. Léopold Sédar Senghor. PoetW, *tr. by* Melvin Dixon

All day long, prismatic dazzle. Midnight. Mary Ursula Bethell. PeNZ

All day long she works to not feel fat. She culls. Weight. Jay Schneiders. OPRER

All day long to the judgement-seat. Gallio's Song. Rudyard Kipling. ChIV-2

All day long you're asking me. I Don't Know Why (I Just Do). Fred E. Ahlert. ReLy

All day my sheep have mingled with yours. Norman Cameron. OxBS *Fr.* Three Love Poems.

All day pinecones drop like shot birds. Late November. Sherod Santos. Son

All day she studies her new. Bihari. ErotSp, *tr. by* Sam Hamill

All day subdued, polite. Negro Servant. Langston Hughes. VGW

All day the bicycles come and go. Nicholas Hasluck. NOBAu *Fr.* Rottnest Island.

All day the fever tells lies. Allegory: Attic and Fever. David Wojahn. YaYoPo

All day the fitful rain. Vermont Ballad: Change of Season. Robert Penn Warren. ColAP

All day the great guns barked and roared. Molly Pitcher. Laura Elizabeth Richards. HHAm

All day the jets have rifled through the air. Jets. Christopher Meredith. AngWePo

All day the red spit of the chain-shot tore. Arthur Rimbaud. OBWP *Fr.* Eighteen-Seventy.

All day the sound of chopping axes. Campfireburners. Anatoly [*or* Anatolii] Zhigulin. TCRP, *tr.* by Vladimir Lunis and Albert C. Todd

All day the unnatural barking of dogs. Dog, The. Valentin Iremonger. BIrV

All day the wood is open, with the maples. Hemlocks in Autumn. Edward Weismiller. YaYoPo

All day to the loose tile behind the parapet. Wasps' Nest, The. George MacBeth [*or* Macbeth]. OxBTC

All day we had ridden through scarred, tawny hills. Spain, 1809. Frank Lawrence Lucas. EBNV

All Day We've Longed for Night. Sarah Webster Fabio. BlSi

All doctrines split asunder. Giun. JDP, *tr.* by Yoel Hoffmann

All dogs prefer prose, especially this one; I died in the summer. Untitled. John Irving. Unle

All dripping in tangles green. Tuft of Kelp, The. Herman Melville. APN-2; FaBoEE

All Dull, my Lord, my Spirits flat, and dead. Edward Taylor. NOSC; TCAPo *Fr.* Preparatory Meditations Before My Approach to the Lord's Supper.

All during a night. Shune. OHPJ

All early, when the day. Spouse of Jesus Laments Her Heart's Flame, The. Friedrich Spee. GePo, *tr.* by George C. Schoolfield

All ears, nose, tongue and gut. Ellen Bryant Voigt. ExTi *Fr.* Kyrie.

All earthly pomp or beauty to express. Old Song Ended, An. J. D. McClatchy. ChrPo

All else for use, One only for desire. Deo Optimo Maximo. Louise Imogen Guiney. SacPr

All endeavor to be beautiful. Primer of Plato. Jean Garrigue. NOBA

All er Nothin' Richard Rodgers. ReLy

All Erdly Joy Returns in Pane. William Dunbar. SacPr

All evening, below a sprig of yarrow. Heading Out West. John Balaban. OPRER

All evening I have watched the lightning. Lightning. Haniel Long. APT-1

All Except Hannibal. Robert Graves. EmeKit

All eyesthemselves it vexes not, nor harms. (LL) On a Vase of Gold-Fish. Charles Tennyson Turner. NOBVV; NPeEn

All fathers in Western civilization must have. Father of My Country, The. Diane Wakoski. NoAM; TAP

All feeling hearts must feel for him. Coming Storm, The. Herman Melville. APN-2

All filthy facts, and secret acts. Michael Wigglesworth. NAAL-3 *Fr.* Day of Doom, The.

All fixed: early arrival at the flat. Nothing to Fear. Kingsley Amis. OxBC

All Flesh Is Grass. Bible, *O.T.* TrJP *Fr.* Isaiah.

All flesh is grass, and so are feathers too. Horace Walpole, 4th Earl of Orford. FaBoEE; NOEC

All flesh waxeth old as a garment. Bible, Apocrypha. OBVE *Fr.* Ecclesiasticus.

All folks who pretend to religion and grace. Place of the Damned [*or* Damn'd], The. Jonathan Swift. ChIV-2; FaBoEE; OBSV

All for her sake must the maiden die! (LL) Marriage. Mary Elizabeth Coleridge. LW; NALW; PEW; PoBW; VWP; ViWPN

All for Love. Byron. *See* Stanzas Written on the Road between Florence and Pisa

All for Nothing. Lőrinc Szabó. IQMS, *tr.* by Edwin Morgan

All four pillars of enlightenment. Toyo Eicho. JDP, *tr.* by Yoel Hoffmann

All freezes again. Riei. JDP, *tr.* by Yoel Hoffmann

All freight, the sudden trains that uncouple my passage home. Freight Train, Freight Train. Alvin Greenberg. GM

All Friends Together. Ronald Albert Simpson. NOBAu

All gentlemen and yeomen good. Robin Hood and the Shepherd. *Unknown.* ESPB

All glory cannot vanish from the hills. Passing of the Forest, The. William Pember Reeves. PeNZ

All God's Chillun Got Rhythm. Walter Jurmann. ReLy

All good to kindred natures cleaveth soon. (LL) Sonnet: He Compares All Things with His Lady, and Finds Them Wanting. Guido Cavalcanti. AWP; EaItPo, *tr.* by Dante Gabriel Rossetti

All grave old men, and souldiers they had bene, but for age. Homer. OBVE *Fr.* Iliad, The.

All great events have harbingers. Nicarchus of Alexandria. GrAn

All great things crush themselves; such end the gods. Lucan. NoSic *Fr.* Pharsalia.

All Greece hates. Helen. "H. D." APT-1; BoWoP; ColAP; FaBoWP; MoAmPo; NAAL-2v2; NAAL-5; NALW; NIL-7; NOBA; NoAM; NoP-4; PAI; TAP

All Grows Old. Yevgeny [*or* Evgenii] Mikhailovich Vinokurov. TCRusP, *tr.* by Daniel Weissbort

All grows old. And what has aged. All Grows Old. Yevgeny [*or* Evgenii] Mikhailovich Vinokurov. TCRusP, *tr.* by Daniel Weissbort

All hail, once pleasing, once inspiring shade. Lines Written in Windsor Forest. Pope. EBEV

All Hail the Power of Jesus' Name. Edward Perronet. NOCV; SacPr

All hail! thou gorgeous sunset. Sunset. Mary Weston Fordham. CBWP-2

All hail! thou noble Land. America to Great Britain. Washington Allston. APN-1

All hail to the Empress of India, Great Britain's Queen. William McGonagall. VerBaPo *Fr.* Royal Review, The.

All hallelujahs, Oh ye heav'nly quires. Poem upon the Triumphant Translation of. . . Mrs. Anne Eliot, A. John Danforth. SCAP

All Hallow. Josephine Miles. APT-2

All Hallows. Louise Glück. HCAP; PoPoPo

All hazards of the field. Militaris Cantio. *Unknown.* IQMS, *tr.* by Matthew Mead

All he owns is. Squirrel near Library. Genevieve Taggard. WPE

All Hellas is his monument, though his bones. Euripides. Thucydides. GrAn, *tr.* by Peter Jay

All his children in the same house. Job the Father. Richard Shelton. PBCAP

All his hopes were hands, his ventures hands. Hands, The. Tony Harrison. FaBoTw

All his life, Mr. George Bernard Shaw. Limerick: "All his life, Mr. George Bernard Shaw." Audrey Herbert. PeLi

All holy influences dwell within. Children Band, The. Sir Aubrey De Vere. OBEV

"All honor to him, who shall win the fight." For Those Who Fail. Joaquin Miller. PoToHe

All honour to the persevering toil. Press, The. Thomas Phipson. PeSAV

All houses wherein men have lived and died. Henry Wadsworth Longfellow. PWR; TCAPo

All how silent and how still. Noon. John Clare. OxAEP-2

All human kind on earth. Boethius. NoSic *Fr.* Consolation of Philosophy, The ("De Consolacione Philosophie").

All human race would fain be wits. Jonathan Swift. OBSV

All human things are subject to decay. Dryden. BASC; CABP; FHYEP; HAP; NAEL-5v1; NAEL-6v1; NAEL-7v1; NoP-4; OBSV; OxAEP-1; OxBoLi; PeLV; PoE; TFi

All human things are subject to decay. Approaching a Significant Birthday, He Peruses The Norton Anthology of Poetry. R. S. Gwynn. RA

All human[e] things are subject to decay. Dryden. NOBE; OBCoV; OxBEV; SCV *Fr.* Mac Flecknoe [or, A Satire upon the True-Blue Protestant Poet T. S.].

(All hung with stars!), there still would be no bear. (LL) Great Bear, The. John Hollander. ColAP; NoAM; TwCP

All hushed and still within the house. Emily Jane Brontë. FaBoCh; NOBVV; NPeEn

All I can do is curse, complain. Cassandra's Answer. John Montague. BiHa

All I can do is to offer my testimony. (LL) Rattlesnake Country. Robert Penn Warren. NAAL-2v2; VCAP

All I can give you is broken-face gargoyles. Broken-Face Gargoyles. Carl Sandburg. MoAmPo; OxBA

All I could see from where I stood. Edna St. Vincent Millay. BRP; ColAP; MoAmPo; TCAPo *Fr.* Renascence.

All I Do Is Dream of You. Arthur Freed. ReLy

All I know is a door into the dark. Forge, The. Seamus Heaney. NAEL-5v2; NAEL-6v2; NoP-4; OxAEP-2

All I Need Is the Girl. Stephen Sondheim. ReLy

All I possess on the waves and I depart. (LL) Quatrains for Joy. Muhammad Al-Ghuzzi. MAP; NAfrP, *tr.* by John Heath-Stubbs and May Jayyusi

All I Want. Luci Tapahonso. ItWoWo; UnSA

All I want from this life. Necessities. Mei Yao Ch'en. CrYelRi, *tr.* by Sam Hamill

All I want is a room somewhere. Wouldn't It Be Luverly? Alan Jay Lerner. ReLy

All I want is the bread to turn out like hers just once. All I Want. Luci Tapahonso. ItWoWo; UnSA

All I want now is a small dirt patio beneath two or three pines. 20 Years of Grant Applications and State College Jobs. Christopher Buckley. GeoHom

All I want to say is that I do not know. Valediction—To My Father. Eddy Van Vliet. VCWP, *tr.* by John Van Tiel

All I wanted was to brew him rhubarb wine. My First Forty Years. Kevin Ireland. PeNZ

All I wanted / was your / love. To Mother and Steve. Mari E. Evans. BPo

All I Was Doing Was Breathing.   Mirabai [or Mira Bai].   WoPoe, tr. by Robert Bly

All ignorance toboggans into know.   E. E. Cummings.   NAAL-2v2; NOBA; OxBA

All Illusion Is a Form of Hope.   Aida Gelbtrunk.   MirDau, tr. by Roberta Gordenstein

All Impelled Onward Alike.   Robert Blair.   OxAEP-1   Fr. Grave, The.

All in a Garden Green.   William Ernest Henley.   OBMV

All in a moment, through the gloom were seen.   John Milton.   TreFP   Fr. Paradise Lost.

All-in-All seems here a Greek, The. (LL)   Attic Landscape, The.   Herman Melville.   NCAP; NOBA; OBAL

All in Due Time.   James Vincent Cunningham.   NIP-4

All in green went my love riding.   E. E. Cummings.   HeIP-4; NoAM; NoP-4; OxBA; PAI; PoRA

All in June.   William Henry Davies.   OxBSP

All in the April evening [morning].   Sheep and Lambs.   Katharine Tynan.   OBEV; SacPr

All in the diffidence that faltered. (LL)   Ezra Pound.   APT-1; FaBoMo; FaBoTw; HarvBoo; NAAL-2v2; NOBA; NOBE; NoAM; OxBA; RaBo; VGW   Fr. Cantos.

All in the diffidence that faltered. (LL)   Ezra Pound.   FaBoTw; NOBE; OxBA; RaBo; WoPoe   Fr. Cantos.

All in the Downs the fleet was moored [or moor'd].   Sweet William's Farewell to Black-Eyed [or Black-Ey'd] Susan.   John Gay.   BoLoP; NOEC

All Intents.   Larry Eigner.   VGW

All Ireland's now one vessel's company.   Fearghal Og MacWard.   BIrV   Fr. Flight of the Earls, The, 1607.

All is best, though we oft doubt.   John Milton.   NOBE; NOSC; OBEV; OxBEV   Fr. Samson Agonistes.

ALL IS COOL AND BOUNDLESS AS A ROLLING.   For Monk.   Michael McClure.   SeSe

All is Emptiness, and I Must Spin.   Thomas Kinsella.   PBCIP

All is lithogenesis – or lochia.   Hugh MacDiarmid.   NPeEn   Fr. On a Raised Beach.

All Is Not So Simple.   Shin Shalom.   MHP, tr. by Ruth Finer Mintz

All is nothing, nothing all.   Robert Penn Warren.   NOBA   Fr. Tiberius on Capri.

All is One for Monk.   Imamu Amiri Baraka.   ISC

All is passed—all that loomed ahead as evil.   Reaching Forty.   'Abd al-Razzaq 'Abd al-Wahid.   MAP, tr. by Diana Der Hovanessian and Lena Jayyusi

All Is Phantom.   Unknown.   SacPr

All is the same still. Earth and heaven locked in.   Emily Brontë.   Cecil Day Lewis.   GTBS-P

All is transformed and is sacred.   Octavio Paz.   BLPSL, tr. by Rene de Costa, Rigas Kappatos and Eleni Paidoussi   Fr. Sunstone.

All Is Vanity.   Andreas Gryphius.   GePo, tr. by George C. Schoolfield

All Is Vanity.   Anne Finch, Countess of Winchilsea.
   "Bolder Youth, grown of capable arms, A."   FaBoWar

"All Is Vanity, Saith the Preacher."   Byron.   ChIV-1; TrCP

All Is Well.   Arthur Hugh Clough.   PAI

All joy to mortals, joy and mirth.   Aphra Behn.   WPE   Fr. Emperor of the Moon.

All kinds of lines can be traced on a map.   Requiem for the Left Hand.   Nancy Morejón.   TANSG, tr. by Joy Renjilian-Burgy

All kings, and all their favourites [or favorites].   Anniversary [or Anniversarie], The.   John Donne.   BASC; BoLoP; ESCV; FHYEP; FSCP; HAP; MeLP; NOBE; NoP-4; NoSic; SCGP; TFi; WeW-3

All-Knowing God, 'Tis Thine to Know.   Unknown.   AH

All Last Night.   Lascelles Abercrombie.   FaBoTw

All Legendary Obstacles.   John Montague.   BIrV; CIP-2; NOIV; PBCIP; PNI
   (All legendary obstacles lay between.)   NoP-4

All light has left the yard.   My Brothers Make a Lantern.   David Scott Ward.   AmPoNex

All look or [or and] likeness caught from earth.   Phantom.   Samuel Taylor Coleridge.   NAEL-5v2; NAEL-6v2; OxBSP

All losses are restored [or restor'd] and sorrows end. (LL)   William Shakespeare.   AWP; CTC; ClHu; EBEV; HAP; HeIP-4; NAEL-5v1; NAEL-6v1; NAEL-7v1; NOBE; NoSic; OBEV; OxAEP-1; PAI; PoE; PoRA; SCGP; TFi   Fr. Sonnets.

All love, all beauty. (LL)   Dublinesque.   Philip Larkin.   NoAM; OxBC

All Lovely Things.   Conrad Potter Aiken.   PoRA

All married men desire to have good wives.   Lady Anne Harris Southwell.   EMWP

All-meaning circle, The.   Shoichi.   ZenPo, tr. by Takashi Ikemoto and Lucien Stryk

All meet here with us, finally.   Ostriches and Grandmothers!   Imamu Amiri Baraka.   NeAP

All men are bad and in their badness reign. (LL)   William Shakespeare.   CAGL; NoSic; OxAEP-1; SCGP   Fr. Sonnets.

All men are brothers and each people is my own.   My Song to the Jewish People.   Leib Olitski.   TrJP, tr. by Jacob Sonntag

All men from all lands.   Inscription for a Wayside Spring.   Frances Darwin Cornford.   BrRo

All Men have Follies, which they blindly trace.   Cameleon's Defence, The.   Unknown.   TCAPo

All men may hasty-gone happiness find.   Shepherd-Song.   Sigmund von Birken.   GePo, tr. by George C. Schoolfield

All men wait for battle and when it comes.   Apple Tree and a Pig, An.   Emyr Humphreys.   OBWVE

All month a smell of burning, of dry peat.   July 1914.   Anna Andreyevna Akhmatova.   PeFWW; WPOW

All Morning.   Gregory Orr.   TRP

All morning, I watch him.   Sunday.   Carl Phillips.   GT

All morning the dream lingers.   All Morning.   Gregory Orr.   TRP

All morning we saw flames in the distance.   Last Still Days in a Bunker, The.   Walter McDonald.   AF

All moves within the visual frame.   Monument, A.   Charles Madge.   FaBoMo

All moving things.   Enshi.   JDP, tr. by Yoel Hoffmann

All music, sauces, feasts, delights and pleasures.   Thomas Traherne.   OxBSP   Fr. Christian Ethics.

All must be used.   Barracks Apt. 14.   Theodore Weiss.   CoAP; TAP

All my dead people.   Over the Edge.   Fleur Adcock.   PeNZ

All my favourite characters have been.   Mythology.   Lawrence Durrell.   OxBTC

All my future plans, dear.   Blue Room, The.   Richard Rodgers.   OBAL; ReLy

All my life I have struggled from gentleness.   Finale.   Sue Lenier.   LW

All my life I taught Zen to the people.   Enni Ben'en.   JDP, tr. by Yoel Hoffmann

All my life, I've dreamed of lakes and rivers.   Broken Boat, A.   Tu Fu.   CrYelRi, tr. by Sam Hamill

All my life I waited for an angel.   I'll String Along with You.   Harry Warren.   ReLy

All my life / they have told me.   Frank Horne.   BPo   Fr. Letters [or Notes] Found near a Suicide.

All my life through.   Retrospective.   Ogata Kenzon.   WoPoe, tr. by Richard L. Wilson

All my neckties.   Sooner or Later.   John Digby.   SPE

All my other lives. (LL)   Waxwings.   Robert Francis.   APT-2; BLT; LCAP-2; RaBo

All my past life is mine no more.   Love And Life.   John Wilmot, 2d Earl of Rochester.   BoLoP; EnLoPo; HAP; NOBE; NPeEn; OBEV; OxBEV

All my past life is mine no more.   Love and Life.   Grace Buchanan Sherwood.   NoP-4

All my people who are still at home.   Home on Palm.   Selwyn Hughes.   IBA

All My Pretty Ones.   Anne Sexton.   NAAL-2v2; NoAM

All my senses, like beacon's flame.   Fulke Greville, 1st Baron Brooke.   CABP; NOSC; NoSic   Fr. Caelica.

All my sheep / Gather in a heap.   Last Words before Winter.   Louis Untermeyer.   MoAmPo

All my shortcomings, in this year of grace.   Dear Uncle Stranger.   Conrad Potter Aiken.   ColAP; NOBA; NoAM

All my thoughts always speak to me of love.   Dante Alighieri.   AWP; EaItPo, tr. by Dante Gabriel Rossetti   Fr. La Vita Nuova.

All my thoughts of you are good ones.   Holy Ghost.   Larissa Szporluk.   NeAmPo

All Nature is a temple where the alive.   Correspondences.   Charles Baudelaire.   AWP, tr. by Allen Tate

All Nature is but art, unknown to thee.   Pope.   ECEV   Fr. Essay on Man, An.

All nature ministers to Hope. The snow.   Hartley Coleridge.   CenSon

All Nature mourn, and share my misery. (LL)   Sonnet: "I hate the Spring in parti-coloured vest."   Mary Locke.   CenSon; ECWP

All Nature seems at work. Slugs leave their lair.   Work without Hope.   Samuel Taylor Coleridge.   CenSon; GSo; NAEL-5v2; NAEL-6v2; NOBE; OBEV; OxAEP-2; OxBSo; PAI; Son; WoPoe

All nearness pauses, while a star can grow.   E. E. Cummings.   NoAM

All Night.   Tzu Yeh.   CrYelRi, tr. by Sam Hamill

All night a noise of leaping fish.   Fisher, The.   Roderic Quinn.   CBAP

All night, all day, in dizzy, downward flight.   Winter Landscape, A.   Mathilde Blind.   ViWPN

All night, all night.   Interrogations of the Sparrow.   Elizabeth Spires.   FFC

All night and all day the wind roared in the trees.   Mid-Country Blow.   Theodore Roethke.   HarvBoo

All night, and as the wind lieth among.   Speech for Psyche in the Golden Book of Apuleius.   Ezra Pound.   HarvBoo

All night Brazil approached you through the dark.   Brazil.   Bill Manhire.   HarvBoo

All Night by the Rose. *Unknown.* HeIP-4; MiEL, *tr. by* Michael Rosen
(Al nyght by the rose, rose.) OHMEL
(Alnight by the rose, rose.) NPeEn

All night by the rose, rose. All Night by the Rose. *Unknown.* HeIP-4; MiEL, *tr. by* Michael Rosen

All-Night Diner, The. Markham Johnson. ReTh

All night eerily! (LL) Voices from Things Growing in a Churchyard. Thomas Hardy. FaBoVe; OxBTC

All night fell hammers, shock on shock. London Fete, A. Coventry Patmore. EBVV; HAP; PeVV

All night had shout of men and cry. Easter Night. Alice Thompson Meynell. BrRo; ChIV-2; SacPr

All night he craned with an unbending neck. Bateleur. Douglas Livingstone. PeSAV

All night I am the doe, breathing. Strange People, The. Louise Erdrich. PoPoPo

All night I could not sleep. *Unknown.* BoWoP *Fr.* Tzu Yeh Songs.

All night I could not sleep. Zi Ye. WPoS

All night / I float / in the shallow ponds. White Night. Mary Oliver. AWTN

All night I sat reading a book. Reader, The. Wallace Stevens. SAmP

All night I walked among your spirits, Richard. Mourning Letter from Paris, A. Conrad Kent Rivers. BPo

All night I weep[e], all day I cry, Ay me[e]. Mary Sidney Wroth, Countess of Montgomery. NOSC *Fr.* Pamphilia to Amphilanthus.

All-Night Issue, The. Jackie Warren-Moore. SpirFl

All night it humps the air. Cannery Town in August. Lorna Dee Cervantes. NoAM

All night long. Wake. Giuseppe Ungaretti. WoPoe, *tr. by* George Garrett

All night long, and every night. Young Night Thought. Robert Louis Stevenson. OTCP; PWR

All night long, I couldn't fall asleep. Listening to the Rain. K'ang Hai. CoBLCP, *tr. by* Jonathan Chaves

All night long I think of life's labyrinth. Betsugen. ZenPo, *tr. by* Takashi Ikemoto and Lucien Stryk

All night long into my sleeping bag's head pad the blood. Far Side of Introspection, The. Alfred M. [or "Al"] Lee. CoAP

All night long the hockey pictures. To a Sad Daughter. Michael Ondaatje. NoAM

All Night She Dreams. Cheryl Savageau. TWW

All-night stations—Tremayne pictures them, The. Insomnia of Tremayne, The. Donald Justice. AWTN

All-night Taxi Stand, The. Kenneth Slessor. BMAP

All night the booming minute gun. Wreck, The. Felicia Dorothea Hemans. TreFP

All night, the camel-back saddle-cloth was invisible. Next Day the Fog Was Even Worse, The. Yüan Mei. CoBLCP, *tr. by* Jonathan Chaves

All night the cocks crew, under a moon like day. Tears in Sleep. Louise Bogan. MakPoe

All night the expensive Sthenelais I laid. Sthenelais. *Unknown.* GrAn, *tr. by* Guy Davenport

All night the pimp's cars slide past the burning mill. Homage to Elvis, Homage to the Fathers. Bruce Weigl. ReTh

All night the snowstorm raged, by morning it had cleared. Music. Vladislav Felitsianovich Khodasevich. TCRusP, *tr. by* Daniel Weissbort

All night the sound had. Rain, The. Robert Creeley. AmFaPo; CoAP; CoAmPo; ColAP; ErotSp; InvLad; PmAP; PoE; RaBo; TRP; VGW

All night the tall young man. Merlin and the Snake's Egg. Leslie Norris. OBSP

All night, the west wind blows over the capital. Snowstorm: At a Gathering at Chang Chu-fu's House, with Tzu-yeh Attending, We All Wrote Poems on This Subject—I Got the Rhyme-Word, "Hu." Tsung Ch'en. CoBLCP, *tr. by* Jonathan Chaves

All night the west wind cuts the banana leaves. Tune: "Remembering the Prince." Na-lan Hsing-te. SuSp, *tr. by* William Golightly

All night they marched, the infantrymen under pack. 1935. Stephen Vincent Benét. MoAmPo

All night they whine upon their ropes and boom. Nocturne of the Wharves. Arna Bontemps. BPo; ColAP; GT

All night, this headland. Sleepless at Crown Point. Richard Wilbur. InPK-6; WeW-3

All night vigil. Always Running. Luis J. Rodriguez. UnSA

All Nite Long. Kalamu ya Salaam. SpirFl *Fr.* New Orleans Haiku.

All no's become yes's under the law. Commandments, The. Lamea Abbas Amara. PoArWo, *tr. by* Mike Maggio

All of a Sudden. Teresa de Jesús. WPOW, *tr. by* Maria A. Proser, James Scully and Arlene Scully

All of a sudden my delight in sightseeing wanes. Tune: "Pure Serene Music." Chang Yen. ColAnChi, *tr. by* Jiaosheng Wang

(All of a Sudden) My Heart Sings. Henri Herpin. ReLy

All of a Summer. Jakov [or Jacob] Steinberg. FIT, *tr. by* Robert Friend

All of a summer's day. (LL) Milton by Firelight. Gary Snyder. CoAP; NAAL-2v2

All of Me. Seymour Simons. ReLy

All of My Life. Betty Comden. ReLy

All of my life. All of My Life. Betty Comden. ReLy

All of our lives. (LL) Phantasia for Elvira Shatayev. Adrienne Rich. NALW; WWork

All of the pens leaked. Assignment, The. Len Roberts. OPRER

All of Them. Qasim Haddad. MAP, *tr. by* Charles Doria and Sharif Elmusa

All of them the wind took, all of them the light lured. Alone. Hayyim Nahman [or Khayim Nakhman or Chaim Nachman] Bialik. TrJP, *tr. by* Jessie Sampter

All of These. Denis Glover. PeNZ

All of those sensuous bodies. Landscape with Nymphs and Satyrs. Norman Henry Pritchard, II. PoPoPo

All of us always turning away for solace. Delmore Schwartz. OxBA

All of us are sick, Sir. Nissim Ezekiel. OBCoV *Fr.* Songs for Nandu Bhende.

All of Us Here. Irving Feldman.
  Of Course, We Would Wish. VCAP
  "Of course, we would wish them angelic lookouts." VCAP
  Simple Outlines, Human Shapes. VCAP
  "Simple outlines, human shapes, daily acts, plain poses." VCAP
  Surely They're Just So Large. VCAP
  "Surely they're just so large as their burdens allow." VCAP

All of us on the sofa in a line, kneeling. Sofa in the Forties, A. Seamus Heaney. EmeKit

All of us were there. Kaleidoscope. Maria Elena Cruz Varela. VCWP, *tr. by* Mairym Cruz-Bernal

All of You. Cole Porter. ReLy

All of you are seeing me off, east of the Emperor's city. Wen Cheng-ming. CoBLCP *Fr.* Improvised on Horseback to Say Good-bye to Those Who Are Seeing Me Off.

All of you that desire to hear a jest. *Unknown.* *See* All you that desire to here of a jest

All of you that pour the bath for Pallas. Callimachus. HePo, *tr. by* Barbara Hughes Fowler *Fr.* Hymns.

All old women sometimes come to this. Old Women of Toronto. Miriam Waddington. NOBC

All on my own I'm happy. Muso Soseki. EaWin, *tr. by* W. S. Merwin

All on the road to Alibazan. Alibazan. Laura Elizabeth Richards. OBCA

All on the threshold, yet all short of life. (LL) Triad, A. Christina Georgina Rossetti. NAEL-5v2; NAEL-6v2; NALW

All One in Christ. John Oxenham. SacPr

All or Nothing at All. Arthur Altman. ReLy

All other fair, like flowers, untimely fade. (LL) Edmund Spenser. AWP; NAEL-5v1; Son *Fr.* Amoretti.

All Other Love Is Like the Moon. *Unknown.* MiEL; SacPr

All others talked as if. Caedmon. Denise Levertov. NoAM; NoP-4

All our dreams are possible. Illicit Passion. Abena Busia. NAfrP

"All our French poets can turn an inspired line." Nihilist as Hero, The. Robert Lowell. OMIP

All our friends keep knocking at the door. I Don't Want to Walk Without You. Jule Styne. ReLy

All Our Joy Is Enough. Geoffrey Scott. OBMV

All our lives. Tall Buildings. Munib-ur-Rahman. OMIP, *tr. by* Kathleen Grant Jaeger

All our lives we've been told how things work. Paso Robles, San Luis Obispo, San Luis Obispo. David Oliveira. GeoHom

All our roads go nowhere. On Inhabiting an Orange. Josephine Miles. NoAM

All our stones like as much sun as possible. Forecast. Josephine Miles. NoAM

All out of doors [or out-of-doors] looked darkly in at him. Old Man's Winter Night, An. Robert Frost. APT-1; AWP; HAP; MoAmPo; NAAL-2v2; NoAM; OxBA; VGW

All over America women are burning dinners. What's That Smell in the Kitchen? Marge Piercy. NBLV; NIL-7; NIP-4

All over Chicago, Jim, the angels are making love. Ode to the Angels Who Move Perpetually toward the Dayspring of Their Youth. Paul Carroll. IllVoic

All over Ireland, survivors held wakes. Famine. David Citino. SpudSo

All over the plain of the world lovers are being hurt. Christian Karlson Stead. PeNZ *Fr.* Quesada.

All passes. Art alone. Austin Dobson. CTC *Fr.* Ars Victrix.

All paths lead. Winter. John Davies. AngWePo

All perished—brides and infants. Song of a Jewish Boy. "M. J." TrJP, *tr. by* A. Glanz-Leyeles

All Possession Is Theft. Lauris Edmond. PeNZ

All Praise to Thee. F. Bland Tucker. AH

All praise your face, your verses none abuse. Horace Walpole, 4th Earl of Orford. FaBoEE

All projects failed, in the August afternoon. Henry's Fate. John Berryman. ColAP

All quail to the wallowing. Lynne McMahon. ExTi

All Quiet. David Ignatow. CoAmPo

All Quiet along the Potomac Tonight. Ethel Lynn Beers. CBCWP

"All ready?" cried the captain. Slave-Ships, The. John Greenleaf Whittier. TCAPo

All Religions Are One. William Blake. NAEL-6v2

All Revelation. Robert Frost. APT-1

All right, gentlemen who cry blue murder as always. Draft of a Reparations Agreement. Dan Pagis. HP; PoSu; WoPoe, tr. by Stephen Mitchell

All right, I may have lied to you, and about you. Love, 20c the First Quarter Mile. Kenneth Fearing. HAP; WoPoe

All right, I was Welsh. Does it matter? Welsh Testament, A. Ronald Stuart Thomas. TCAWP

All right. Try this. Northern Pike. James Wright (1927–80). NAAL-2v2

All rites pertaining to his maried state. (LL) Christopher Marlowe. NoSic; PBRV Fr. Hero and Leander.

All roocoogirls. Song: "All roocoogirls." Hans Andreus. TuT, tr. by Peter Van de Kamp

All round the Browns stretched forty acres of potatoes. Brown Family, The. Colleen Thibaudeau. NOBC

All round the horizon black clouds appear. On a Sea-Storm nigh the Coast. Richard Steere. SCAP

All ruins, the empire; mountains and rivers in view. Spring Scene. Tu Fu. ChinPo, tr. by Yip Wai-lim

All's over, then: does truth sound bitter. Lost Mistress, The. Robert Browning. BoLoP; NOBE; OBEV

All's Right with the World. Gerald Massey. EBVV

All's right with the world! (LL) Robert Browning. BRP; ITBLP; NTCP; OBEV; PAI; PoToHe; TrCP; UnPo Fr. Pippa Passes.

All's Vast. Francis Thompson. MoBrPo; OBMV; Son Fr. Heart, The.

All's Well. John Greenleaf Whittier. OxBSP

All's well—a crush of stars. December Pastures. Andrey [or Andrei] Andreievich Voznesensky [or Voznesenskii]. RusPo, tr. by Robert Arthur Douglas Ford

All's Well That Ends Well. William Shakespeare.
    "O Lord, sir, let me live, or let me see my death!" OxAEP-1

All Saints' Day. John Keble. SacPr

All Saints' Day, Nov. 1. Christopher Wordsworth. SacPr

All saints revile her, and all sober men. White Goddess, The. Robert Graves. HarvBoo; MoBrPo; NAEL-5v2; NAEL-6v2; NoP-4

All say my husband looks superior. (LL) Mulberry by the Path. Unknown. SuSp; WoPoe, tr. by Hans H. Frankel

All sea is sea. How mad it is to blame. Antipater of Thessalonica. GrAn

All Seasons in One. Unknown. HeIP-4

All seem to know what is for heaven alone. (LL) Love in the Valley. George Meredith. EBVV; NOBE; OBEV

All shiny in your mind! (LL) Some People. Rachel Lyman Field. ChAP; NTCP

All Shook Up. Don Bogen. AllShUp

All Shook Up. Dan Sicoli. AllShUp; SwNoth

All, shut up. Give him your love. (LL) Beast in the Space, The. William Sydney Graham. EmeKit; FaBoTw; OxAEP-2

All silence keep, both goats and sheep. Michael Wigglesworth. NAAL-3 Fr. Day of Doom, The.

All silence says music will follow. Onion Bucket. Lorenzo Thomas. GT

All silent stood; at last stood forth one dolon, that did dare. Homer. FaBoWar, tr. by George Chapman Fr. Iliad, The.

All songs / are tattoos. Singer, The. Diane Wakoski. HeIP-4

All sorts of men through various labours press[e]. Verses Written by Mrs. Hutchinson. Lucy Hutchinson. BASC; NOSC

All sorts of plants are beautiful. Quick Sell the Pig. Matthew Rohrer. AmPoNex

All Soul's Day. Willem Jan Otten. TuT, tr. by Micheal O'Siadhail

All Soul's Day. Maurya Simon. ExTi

All Souls' Ruth Bidgood. AngWePo

All Souls' Day. Herman von Gilm zu Rosenegg. AuPH, tr. by Lowell A. Bangerter

All Souls' Night. Frances Darwin Cornford. EnLoPo; OxBSP; OxBTC

All Souls' Night. W. B. Yeats. OxAEP-2 Fr. Vision, A.

All Souls' over, the roast seeds eaten, I set. Totem. Eamon Grennan. ModIr

All Splendor on Earth. Karin Kiwus. BoWoP, tr. by Almut McAuley

All spring, my sorrows grew like lotus leaves. Alone by the Autumn River. Li Shang-yin. ColAnChi, tr. by Sam Hamill

All Still. William Barnes. NOBVV

All such proclivities are tabulated. Quiet Glades of Eden, The. Robert Graves. BoLoP

All sullen and obscene, they toiled in pain. Epitaphs. Edmund Wilson. APT-2

All summer I heard them. Snakes of September, The. Stanley Kunitz. ColAP

All summer long hurricanes. Tourist Weather. Silvia Curbelo. TouFir

All summer the sheep were strewn like crumbs. Flanking Sheep in Mosedale. David Scott. NLP

All swoln with chasing, down Adonis sits. William Shakespeare. EroLit Fr. Venus and Adonis.

All tempest. Witter Bynner. APT-1

All Ten Commandments I Have Broken. Unknown. SacPr

All that autumn of austerity. Rose Furuya Hawkins. FSt Fr. Proud Upon an Alien Shore.

All that blazing day, swift-breasted swallows, envious crows, grackles in trees. Thunderstorm in South Dakota. Kay Boyle. WPE

All that blesses the step of the antelope. Else a great Prince in prison lies. Denise Levertov. VGW

All that ever was dismembered. Lay of the Rover. Aimé Césaire. WoPoe, tr. by Gregson Davis

All that Friday. Ulster Unionist Walks the Streets of London, An. Tom Paulin. PNI

All That Glisters Is Not Gold. William Shakespeare. CTC Fr. Merchant of Venice, The.

All That Glitters. Maureen Owen. PmAP

All that he is . . . does . . . is attractive. Meleager. GrAn

All That I Am. Verna Arvey. AH

All that I am hangs by a thread tonight. Muse, The. Anna Andreyevna Akhmatova. PoetW; TCRP, tr. by Max Hayward, Max Hayward and Stanley Kunitz

All that I had I brought. Exchanges. Ernest Christopher Dowson. OBMV

All that I have. Handfuls of Wind. Yekhi'el [or Yehiel] Mar. MHP, tr. by Ruth Finer Mintz

All that I may swynk or swet. Care Away. Unknown. OxBoLi

All that I've never thought of—think of me! (LL) Sick Child, A. Randall Jarrell. InPK-6; NoP-4; OxBC; VGW

All that I was, became really—my past. Home. Ivan Zhdanov. TCRP, tr. by John High

All that I wrote in love, for love of art. (LL) Plea to Boys and Girls, A. Robert Graves. GTBS-P; NAEL-5v2; NAEL-6v2

All That Is Left. Basho. AWP, tr. by Curtis Hidden Page

All That Is Left. Michael Hartnett. NOIV

All That Is Lovely in Men. Robert Creeley. RaBo

All that is moulded of iron. Woodworker's Ballad. Herbert Edward Palmer. OBEV

All that is past of us. Goethe. WoPoe, tr. by Louis MacNeice Fr. Faust.

All that juniper west of. Priorities at Friday Ranch. William Stafford. BodElec

All that matters is to be at one with the living God. Pax. D. H. Lawrence. EnlH; PeECV; TrCP

All That My Soul Possessed. Nikolai Alekseievich Zabolotsky [or Zabolotskii]. TCRusP, tr. by Kathy Lewis and Bob Perelman

All That Really Happens. Joe Wenderoth. BodElec

All that running water outside. Marshes, The. Jane Mayhall. TAP

All That's Past. Walter De la Mare. NOBE; OBMV; OxBTC

All that the night. Nocturne. Xavier Villaurrutia. TCLAP, tr. by Xavier Leroux

All that was evil—to thy mother. (LL) Byron. J. Gordon Coogler. OBAL; VerBaPo

All that winter you were gone. Solitaire. George Hitchcock. GifTon

All that year, the fronts of houses. 1919. Donald Revell. BodElec

All that you have lost, they told me, is yours. Boundaries. José Emilio Pacheco. PoetW; STV; TCLAP, tr. by John Frederick Nims

All that you send: the unexpected disaster. My Country. Olga Fiodorovna Berggolts [or Bergholts]. TCRP, tr. by Daniel Weissbort

All that you've danced they take from you. Last Waltz in Santiago. Ariel Dorfman. AF, tr. by Ariel Dorfman

All the afternoon there has been a chirping of birds. Free Fantasia on Japanese Themes. Amy Lowell. MoAmPo

All the air quivers, and the east sky glows. (LL) Front, A. Randall Jarrell. NoP-4; OBWP; OxBC; PoWW; VGW

All the black same I dance my blue head off! (LL) King David Dances. John Berryman. ChIV-1; OxBC; OxBSP

All the boys always wanted her, so. Leda's Sister and the Geese. Katharyn Machan Aal. SoSe-8

All the bright day I rode my bike along the river. River, The. Patti Tana. PasH

All the cattle are resting in the fields. Poem to the Sun. *Ancient Egyptian Oral Tradition*. TTTS, *tr. by* Christopher Wertz

All the children on this ward are dying of AIDS. Sacrament of Poverty, The. Marilyn Nelson. ExTi; GT

All the Cilicians are bad. Demodocus. GrAn

All the day I worked and played. John Davidson. EBVV *Fr.* To the Street Piano.

All the Death-Room Needs. Michael Hartnett. CIP-2

All the dreary Sunday morning. Ted Hughes. HAP *Fr.* Skylarks.

All the Earth, All the Air. Theodore Roethke. HarvBoo

All the earth where she could open at it. XX. P. Inman. FTOS

All the field hands. Basho. SoOfWa, *tr. by* Sam Hamill

All the flies are reading microscopic books. Serious Readers. Peter Redgrove. OxBC

All the flowers by the lake. Day and Night. Haniel Long. APT-1

All the flowers of the spring. John Webster. NOSC; PoRA; SCGP *Fr.* Devil's Law Case, The.

All the fruit is ripe, plunged in fire, cooked. Friedrich Hölderlin. WoPoe, *tr. by* Robert Bly

All the full-moon night in the coomb. In the Night of the Full Moon. Carl Busse. AWP, *tr. by* Jethro Bithell

All the Generations Before Me. Yehuda Amichai [*or* Amikhai]. FIT, *tr. by* Robert Friend

All the Generations Before Me. Yehuda Amichai [*or* Amikhai]. PoSu, *tr. by* Harold Schimmel

All the great jockeys were born premature. To the Man Saying "Come on Seis" at Hollywood Park. David Hayward. MoASP

All the here and all the there. Our Two Worthies. John Crowe Ransom. OBAL

All the Hills and Vales Along. Charles Hamilton Sorley. EBEV; FaBoCh; MoBrPo; OBWP; OxAEP-2; PeFWW; PoWW

All the Hosts of Heaven. Simeon ben, of Mainz Isaac ben Abun. TrJP, *tr. by* Nina Davis Salaman

All the hot night. Masaoka Shiki. OHMPJ

All the ladies feeling lucky at love. Autobiography of a Black Man. G. E. Patterson. AmPoNex

All the laughing girls wait for the hands. Your Face Here. Robin S. Chapman. PoCoUp

All the lizards are asleep. Nature Study. Craig Raine. NoAM

All the mill-horses of Europe. Discovery of America, The. James Logie Robertson. NOBVV; NePenScot

All the morning I have lain snugly in bed. Rising Late, and Playing with A-ts'ui, Aged Two. Po Chü-i. ChiP, *tr. by* Arthur Waley

All the new thinking is about loss. Meditation at Lagunitas. Robert Hass. AmFaPo; ColAP; GeoHom; MakPoe; NoP-4; VCAP

All the night in woe. William Blake. FHYEP; NOBRP *Fr.* Songs of Experience.

All the night sleep came not upon my eyelids. Algernon Charles Swinburne. NPeEn

All, the Nothing, The. Yves Bonnefoy. VCWP, *tr. by* Lisa Sapinkopf

All the opportunities we miss by being born too soon! Born Too Soon. John Fuller. OBCoV

All the Past We Leave Behind. Walt Whitman. AH

All the People Who Are Now Red Trees. Martín Espada. TouFir

All the perversions of the soul. Small Farm, A. Michael Hartnett. CIP-2; PBCIP

All the preachers claimed it was Satan. TV. Rodney Jones. IllVoic; ReTh

All the Pretty Little Horses. *Unknown*. OxBoLi; TTTS

All the sailors on deck have been blind for many years. (LL) Snowfall in the Afternoon. Robert Bly. NOBA; SPE

All the Same. Clarence Major. BodElec

All the Same, It Would Make You Laugh. Michael Hartnett. CIP-2, *tr. by* Michael Hartnett

All the sexually active people in Westport. Chaste Stranger, The. James Tate. NoAM

All the Sioux were defeated. Our clan. Report to Crazy Horse. William Stafford. NoAM

All the sisters of mercy. Canto Llano. Anita Endrezze. CDW

All the skippers o Scarsburgh. Young Allan. *Unknown*. ESPB

All the sleepless night. All Night. Tzu Yeh. CrYelRi, *tr. by* Sam Hamill

All the Soups. Martha Rhodes. ExTi

All the soups I've made in my life. All the Soups. Martha Rhodes. ExTi

All the Spirit Powers Went to Their Dancing Place. Gary Snyder. UnPo

All the Stars Are Foxfire. Van K. Brock. AllShUp

All the teeth ever I had are worn down and fallen out. Rudaki. WoPoe, *tr. by* Basil Bunting

All the things. The objects. Cold Term. Imamu Amiri Baraka. BPo

All the Things You Are. Jerome Kern. ReLy

All the time I pray to Buddha. Issa. EH, *tr. by* Robert Hass

All the time I was talking as if you listened. Words. Carlos A. Angeles. ReBoTo

All the time the teacher. Fights After School. Norman J. Loftis. SpirFl

All the time they were praying. Death Bed, The. Waring Cuney. APT-2

All the time we knew his corpse was rotting. Bones of Lazarus. John Bensko. YaYoPo

All the toys of the world would break. (LL) Love Poem: "My clumsiest dear, whose hands shipwreck vases." John Frederick Nims. IllVoic; InPK-6

All the trees they are so high. Trees So High, The. *Unknown*. OxBoLi

All the voices of the wood called "Muriel!" Then I Saw What the Calling Was. Muriel Rukeyser. ColAP; FaBoWP

All the Way. Sammy Cahn. ReLy

All the way clear to Aliquippa. Mac Wellman. HeMarv *Fr.* Rat Minaret: Miniaturist-Divan, The.

All the way driving in. End of the Row. Anne Born. Prnts

All the way home. (LL) This Little Pig Went to Market. Mother Goose. LB; OxBEV; OxNR; ReMoGo

All the way to the hospital. Almond Tree, The. Jon Stallworthy. NoAM

All the while among. Fragrance of Life, Odor of Death. Denise Levertov. AF

All the while, believe me, I prayed. Sappho. BoWoP

All the while I was quite happy. (LL) Nikki-Rosa. Nikki Giovanni. BlSi; HeIP-4; PAI; TAP

All the while they were talking the new morality. Encounter, The. Ezra Pound. PAI

All the whole world is living without war. Canzone: He Speaks of His Condition through Love. Folcachiero de' Folcachieri. AWP; EaItPo, *tr. by* Dante Gabriel Rossetti

All the Wide Grin of Him. Eleanor Wilner. ExTi

All the wives of my father. Song of the Initiate. Patrice Kayo. PBMAP

All the women who leave tell me they're happy. Streamers. Sandra McPherson. VCAP

All the words that I utter. Where My Books Go. W. B. Yeats. OBEV

All the World. *Unknown*. TrJP, *tr. by* Israel Zangwill

All the world for love may die. (LL) Ben Jonson. NAEL-6v1; NAEL-7v1; NOSC *Fr.* Celebration of Charis in Ten Lyric[k] Pieces [*or* Peeces], A.

All the world's a school. Schoolmaster. George Rostrevor Hamilton. FaBoEE

"All the World's a Stage." Victor Gray. NBLV; PeLi

All the World's a Stage. Sir Walter Ralegh. *See* What Is Our Life?

All the world's a stage. William Shakespeare. ITBLP; RB; UV *Fr.* As You Like It.

All the world shall come to serve Thee. All the World. *Unknown*. TrJP, *tr. by* Israel Zangwill

All the year where cherries grow. (LL) Cherry-ripe [*or* Cherrie-ripe]. Robert Herrick. BASC; BeJo; CaPo; OBEV; PAI; PeLV

All the years waiting, the whole, barren, young. Sex. Jean Valentine. FaBoWP

All their lights went out. In the Dark Word, Khurbn. Jerome Rothenberg. TaR

All their lives in a box! What generations. Silkworms, The. Douglas Stewart. CBAP

All their pipes were still. Praise of Spenser. William Browne (1591–1643). OxAEP-1

All There Is to Know about Adolph Eichmann. Leonard Cohen. InPK-6

All These Are Vile. John Keats. OBCoV

All These Birds. Richard Wilbur. NOBA

All these dormant fields are held beneath the fog. Muscat Pruning. William Everson. APT-2

All these fair sounds and sights I made my own. (LL) Long Island Sound. Emma Lazarus. APN-2; SWaP

All these girls licking & sucking. Leaving Syracuse. Al Young. ESEAA

All these hang-ups, all this time wasted when. Manic: A Conversation with Jimi Hendrix. Tim Seibles. OPRER

All these illegitimate babies. Valuable. Stevie Smith. OxBTC

All these journeys. Ferry Me Across. B. P. Nichol. FTOS

All these [*or* those] heads these ears these eyes. Song of the Old Woman. *Unknown*. BoWoP, *tr. by* Armand Schwerner and Paul-Emile Victor

All these undertakings! Xenophon's Song. István Vas. IQMS, *tr. by* George Gömöri and Clive Wilmer

All these years behind windows. Animals, The. W. S. Merwin. VCAP

All they said was true. Edgar Lee Masters. APT-1 *Fr.* Spoon River Anthology.

All things. Hadewijch II. WPoS

All Things. Laura Riding Jackson. ColAP

All Things Are Current Found. Henry David Thoreau. TCAPo

All things are doubly fair. Art. Théophile Gautier. AWP, *tr. by* George Santayana

All things are real. Letter to a Friend: Who Is Nancy Daum? James Schuyler. PmAP

All things are words of some strange tongue, in thrall. Compass. Jorge Luis Borges. PoetW, *tr. by* Richard Wilbur

"All things become thee, being thine," I think sometimes. Woman. Randall Jarrell. NOBA

All Things Bright and Beautiful. Cecil Frances Alexander. SacPr; UV
(All things bright and beauteous.) VWP
(Creation, The.) ChAP

All things brown and beautiful. Flea's Hymn. Oodgeroo of the tribe Noonuccal (Kath Walker). Unle

All Things Can Tempt Me. W. B. Yeats. OxBSP

All things come apart. Daisen. ZenPo, *tr. by* Takashi Ikemoto and Lucien Stryk

All things come to one hideous Charybdis. Simonides. SaLy, *tr. by* Diane Rayor

All Things Decay and Die. Robert Herrick. CaPo

All things decay with Time: The Forrest sees. All Things Decay and Die. Robert Herrick. CaPo

All Things Drink. Thomas Stanley. AWP

All Things dull and Ugly. "Monty Python." UV

All things felt sweet were felt sweet overmuch. Two Dreams, The. Giovanni Boccaccio. OBGa, *tr. by* Algernon Charles Swinburne

All things I can endure, save one. Magdalen. Amy Levy. VWP; ViWPN

All things in nature are beautiful types to the soul that can read them. Correspondences. Christopher Pearse Cranch. APN-1

All things in this life that he could. (LL) Performance, The. James Dickey. CoAP; CoAmPo; FaBoWar; PoE

All things innocent, hapless, forsaken. (LL) Meadow Mouse, The. Theodore Roethke. ChAP; HeIP-4; PAI; RB; TRP

All things must have an end; the world itself. Henry Wadsworth Longfellow. TCAPo *Fr.* Michael Angelo: A Fragment.

All things remain in God. (LL) Crazy Jane on God. W. B. Yeats. EBEV; OxBTC; RACG

All things save Beauty alone. (LL) Ezra Pound. HAP; TCAPo; UnPo; VGW *Fr.* Hugh Selwyn Mauberley (Life and Contacts).

All things that live. Writing What I've Seen. Yuan Mei. GifTon, *tr. by* Jerome P. Seaton

All things within this fading world hath [*or* have] end. Before the Birth of One of Her Children. Anne Bradstreet. AmFaPo; BoWoP; EMWP; NAAL-2v1; NAAL-3; NAAL-5; NOBA; PAI; PeECV; SacPr; WPE; WPOW

All this dead wood. Advertisements. Thomas McGrath. BodElec

All this did not happen in Budapest. Cart With Four Oxen, The. Sándor Petőfi. IQMS, *tr. by* Ila Egon

All this fall. Baudelaire's Spleen. Jaime Manrique. WiU

All this foolishness. Basho. EH, *tr. by* Robert Hass

All this is true without deceit. (LL) Mother Goose. OxNR; ReMoGo

All this time I had forgotten. Girl at the Chu Lai Laundry. Bruce Weigl. CDa

All those buffalos have green horns. Song of the Red & Green Buffalo, A. *Unknown.* STP, *tr. by* William Whitman

All those seen from behind who were moving away singing. Endless Journeys. Pierre Reverdy. WoPoe, *tr. by* John Ashbery

All those ships that never sailed. Bob Kaufman. PFTM-2

All those sleep shapes. Paul Celan. VCWP, *tr. by* Michael Hamburger

All those summers, waiting. Waiting for You to Come By. Simon J. Ortiz. CDW

All those who, over the sorrows of strangers, led their spirits to dance and to delight. From All Sides Laughter Shall Strike Them. Amir Gilbo'a. MHP, *tr. by* Ruth Finer Mintz

All those women working. Working. Maxine Scates. PBCAP

All thoughts, all passions, all delights. Love. Samuel Taylor Coleridge. GTBS-P; OBEV

All thro' the breathing night there seemed to flow. Venetian Night, A. Hugo von Hofmannsthal. AWP, *tr. by* Ludwig Lewisohn

All through spring, nothing but wind and rain. Tune: "Bean Leaves Yellow." Lu Yu. SuSp, *tr. by* James J. Y. Liu

All through the day, little peach blossoms in the garden. Little Peach Blossoms in the Garden. Li Shang-yin. SuSp, *tr. by* Eugene Eoyang

All through the march, besides bag and blanket. Crazed Man in Concentration Camp. Agnes Gergely. BoWoP, *tr. by* Edwin Morgan

All Through the Night. *Unknown.* ITBLP

All through the Rains. Gary Snyder. CoAmPo

All through the Stranger's Wood. Isaac Leibush [*or* Yitskhok Leybush] Peretz [*or* Perets]. TrJP, *tr. by* Joseph Leftwich

All through the valley, the people are whispering. Return of the Wolves. Anita Endrezze. HATNAP

All through those final, fitful weeks we walked off the restlessness. Spring Comes to Chicago. Campbell McGrath. NeAmPo

All to be said goes on every morning in this yard. In the Backyard. Julio Marzán. PueRic

All today I lie in the bottom of the wardrobe. Yoko. Thom Gunn. NoAM

All tongues tell their monsters, shapes. Gypsy Teaches Her Grandchild Wolfen Ways, The. Susan Swartwout. ReTh

All too late. *Unknown.* EBEV

All Too Soon. Sergey [*or* Sergei] Aleksandrovich Yesenin [*or* Essenin]. RusPo, *tr. by* Robert Arthur Douglas Ford

All too soon, I fear. *Unknown.* ArkPo, *tr. by* Helen Craig McCullough

All too soon we will depart. All Too Soon. Sergey [*or* Sergei] Aleksandrovich Yesenin [*or* Essenin]. RusPo, *tr. by* Robert Arthur Douglas Ford

All travellers [*or* travelers] at first incline. Stella's Birthday [1721]. Jonathan Swift. NAEL-5v1; NAEL-6v1; OxAEP-1

All trembling in my arms Aminta lay. Aphra Behn. RACG *Fr.* Voyage to the Isle of Love, A.

All Tropic Places Smell of Mold. Karl Shapiro. VGW

All trucks were from Hell and deserved my bite. Coach. Wyatt Prunty. Unle

All truths wait in all things. Walt Whitman. ColAP *Fr.* Song of Myself.

All under the leaves, the leaves of life. Seven Virgins, The. *Unknown.* OBEV

All veiled in black, with faces hid from sight. Mourning Women. Mathilde Blind. ViWPN

All walking leans to the left. Pencilled by the Rain. Peter Hooper. PeNZ

All was as it is, before the beginning began, before. Jacob. Delmore Schwartz. ChIV-1; TaR

All was in flight. Wind Was There, The. Bravig Imbs. SPE

All was quiet in this park. Pain. Mbella Sonne Dipoko. PBMAP

All was taken away from you: white dresses. On Angels. Czeslaw Milosz. AF; BBASP *tr. by* Czeslaw Milosz

All was winter and chill. Christmas Star. Boris Leonidovich Pasternak. TCRP

All waters as the shore. (LL) Ave atque Vale. Algernon Charles Swinburne. NAEL-5v2; NAEL-6v2; NOBE; OBEV

All We Ask Is Justice. Mrs. Henry Linden. CBWP-4

All we can expect are. Sartor Resartus. Art Goodtimes. GeoH

All we can hope to leave them now is money. (LL) Homage to a Government. Philip Larkin. EBEV; NoAM; OxBEV

All we have willed or hoped or dreamed of good shall exist. Eternity Affirms the Hour. Robert Browning. SacPr

All we make is enough. All Our Joy Is Enough. Geoffrey Scott. OBMV

All we were going strong last night this time. John Berryman. FaBoMo *Fr.* Sonnets to Chris.

All week she's cleaned. Domestic Work, 1937. Natasha Trethewey. SpirFl

All week, the explosions have increased. Feast of San Silvestro, The. V. Penelope Pelizzon. AmPoNex

All were to[o] little for the merchant's [*or* merchauntes] hand[e]. George Gascoigne. Son *Fr.* Gascoigne's Memories.

All what I am, it is you. (LL) When, to my deadly [*or* deadlie] pleasure. Sir Philip Sidney. EnLoPo; NPeEn

All which isn't singing is mere talking. E. E. Cummings. VGW

All who are sick at heart and cry in bitterness. Garden of Song, The. Moses Ibn Ezra. TOF, *tr. by* David Goldstein

All who come into being as flesh. Harper's Song for Inherkhawy, The. *Unknown.* WoPoe, *tr. by* John L. Foster

All wilie sleights, that subtile women know. Torquato Tasso. OxBEV, *tr. by* Edward Fairfax *Fr.* Godfrey of Bulloigne; or, The Recoverie of Jerusalem [Gerusalemme Liberata].

All winter long you listened for the boom. Stoic: for Laura von Courten, The. Edgar Bowers. CoAP

All winter through I bow my head. Scarecrow, The. Walter De la Mare. MoBrPo; OxBTC

All winter your brute shoulders strained against collars, padding. Names of Horses. Donald Hall. AmFaPo; HAP; InPK-6; SoSe-8; TRP

All women are beautiful as they rise. Poem for Easter. Robert Kelly. ErotSp; VGW

All words forgotten / Thou, Lord, and I. (LL) Scribe, The. Walter De la Mare. FaBoCh; OBMV; TrCP

All work and no play makes Jack a dull boy. *Unknown.* OxNR

All worldly shapes shall melt in gloom. Last Man, The. Thomas Campbell. NOBRP

All worries and troubles. Muso Soseki. EaWin, *tr. by* W. S. Merwin

All Writing Is Garbage. Antonin Artaud. PFTM-1

All / wrong. Charles Olson. NoAM *Fr.* Maximus Poems, The.

All ye nations, pause a moment! listen to the Negro's voice. Voice of the Negro, The. Lizelia Augusta Jenkins Moorer. CBWP-3

All ye poets of the age. Namby-Pamby. A Panegyric on the New Versification, Address'd to A——— P———, Esq. Henry Carey. NOEC; NPeEn; OBSV; UV

All ye that handle harp and viol. Moses Hayyim, of Padua Luzzatto. TrJP, *tr. by* Nina Davis Salaman *Fr.* Unto the Upright Praise.

All ye that pass along Love's trodden way. Dante Alighieri. AWP; EaItPo, *tr. by* Dante Gabriel Rossetti *Fr.* La Vita Nuova.

All ye that passe be [*or* by] this holy place. Second Epitaph, A. *Unknown.* MiEL

All ye who, far from town, in rural hall. On a Wet Summer. John Codrington Bampfylde. NOEC; OxBSo

All ye woods, and trees, and bowers. John Fletcher. FaBoCh *Fr.* Faithful Shepherdess, The.

All Year Long. *Unknown.* OHMPC, *tr. by* Kenneth Rexroth

All year long, he never visits his home town. Merchant's Joy, The. Chang Yü. CoBLCP; ColAnChi, *tr. by* Jonathan Chaves

All year, Mozart went under. To a Daughter at Fourteen Forsaking the Violin. Carole Oles. WeW-3

All year the flax-dam festered in the heart. Death of a Naturalist. Seamus Heaney. HAP; NoAM; OxBC; OxBEV; WeW-3

All you are doing and saying is to America dangled mirages. To a President. Walt Whitman. NAAL-2v1; NAAL-3

All you can about animals as persons. What You Should Know to Be a Poet. Gary Snyder. APSN; NNaP; PFTM-2; PoM

ALL-YOU-CAN-EAT / catfish houses. Keith Cartwright. AmPoNex

All you lords of Scottland ffaire. Tom Potts. *Unknown.* ESPB

All You Others, Eat. Djurberaui. NOBAu, *tr. by* Catherine H. Berndt

All you preachers. Stairway to Paradise. B. G. DeSylva. TCAPo

All you that are to mirth Inclin'd. Anna Alcox. EMWP

All you that delight to spend some time. Little John a Begging. *Unknown.* ESPB

All you that desire to here of a jest. Unfortunate Miller; or, The Country Lasses Witty Invention, The. *Unknown.* OxBB

All you that have indulgent Parents been. Upon the Death of My Deare and Lovely Daughter J. P. Jane Pulter, Baptized May 1 1625 and Died Oct 8 1646 Aet. 20. Hester Lee Pulter. EMWP

All you violated ones with gentle hearts. For Malcolm X. Margaret Abigail Walker. BPo; NAAAL; Son

All your days are holy days. Lullaby for Rachael. James Simmons. PNI

Allace depairting, grund of wo. Fairweill. *Unknown.* OxBS

Allace! So Sobir Is the Micht. Mersar. OxBS

Allah. Siegfried August Mahlmann. AWP, *tr. by* Henry Wadsworth Longfellow

Allansford Pursuit, The. *Unknown.* RB; WoPoe, *tr. by* Robert Graves

Allas, allas the while! *Unknown.* *See* Alas! alas! the while

Allas, departyng is ground of wo. *Unknown.* *See* Alas, departing is ground of wo!

"Allas," sche seide, "how that this manis mynde." Boethius. OBMV, *tr. by* John Walton *Fr.* Consolation of Philosophy, The ("De Consolacione Philosophie").

Allegiance. Forrest Hamer. MoASP

Allegiance. Sheenagh Pugh. TCAWP

Allegiance is assigned. Choice. James Vincent Cunningham. VGW

Allegorical Matters. Stephen Dobyns. BodElec

Allegory. Rafael Campo. RA

Allegory. Carla Harryman. FTOS

Allegory, An. Barcroft Henry Boake. CBAP

Allegory, An. David Ignatow. VGW

Allegory: Attic and Fever. David Wojahn. YaYoPo

Allegory of the Brevity of Things Human. Luis de Góngora y Argote. SpanPo; WoPoe, *tr. by* Roy Campbell *Fr.* Spectre of the Rose, The.

Allegory of the Wolf Boy, The. Thom Gunn. HarvBoo; OxBC

Allegro. Tomas Tranströmer. SPE, *tr. by* Robert Bly

Alleluia, alleluia, / Alleluia, now sing we. *Unknown.* MiEL

Alleluia! Christ Is Risen Today. John Henry, Jr. Hopkins. AH

Alleluia! light. Alleluia-verse for the Virgin. Hildegard von Bingen. WPoS, *tr. by* Barbara Newman

Alleluya. "Rubén Dario." TTY, *tr. by* Lysander Kemp

Allen. Joe Lothamer. GeoH

Allen Ginsberg. Toi Derricotte. PBCAP

Allen Ginsberg. Howl. Beau Sia. HeMarv

Alley, The. Lola Ridge.
   "Because you are four years old." TCAPo

Alley; an Imitation of Spenser, The. Pope. NOEC

Alley Cat. Esther Valck Georges. OTCP; Spl

Allf por la Calle San Luis. Carmen Tafolla. WWork

Allie. Robert Graves. PeLV

Allie, call the birds in. Allie. Robert Graves. PeLV

Alligator, The. Beatrice Witte Ravenel. WPE

Alligator Bride, The. Donald Hall. CoAmPo; SPE

Alligator, hippopotamus, fox, rhinoceros. Ruler, The. Robin Blaser. FTOS

All–intellectual eye, our solar round. James Thomson. NOEC *Fr.* To the Memory of Sir Isaac Newton.

Allow that the sea is pink, rich lobster pink. You and You, In the Pink. Christopher Pilling. NLP

Alloy. Muriel Rukeyser. NoAM

Alma. Tom Lehrer. NBLV

Alma; or, The Progress of the Mind. Matthew Prior.
   "In Britain's isles, as Heylyn notes." NOEC

Almagest, Last Letter to Zakarias. Siv Cedering Fox. PBCAP

Almanac. May Swenson. APT-2

Almanac, 1939, An. Kevin Young. AmPoNex

Almanac Verse. Samuel Danforth. SCAP

Almanac Verse. *Unknown.* SCAP

Almanack for the Year of Our Lord, 1657, An. Samuel Bradstreet. SCAP

Almendares. Sandra M. Castillo. TouFir

Almería. Pablo Neruda. FaBoWar, *tr. by* Donald D. Walsh

Almighty and everlasting God, we thank Thee. Prayer for Every Day. *Unknown.* PBA, *tr. by* Kweku Martin

Almighty creator and ruler as well. Hymn to the Creator. John Clare. NOBVV

Almighty God in Being Was. Silas Ballou. AH

Almighty God, Thy Constant Care. Henry Stevenson Washburn. AH

Almighty God, who fillest the recesses of the heavens. Invocation: "Almighty God, who fillest the recesses of the heavens." Bishop Patrick. NOIV

Almighty God, Whose Justice Like a Sun. Joseph Hilaire Pierre Belloc. SacPr

Almighty Lord, with One Accord. Melancthon Woolsey Stryker. AH

Almighty [*or* Almightie] Judge, how shall poor[e] wretches brook. Judgement. George Herbert. ESCV; GeHe

Almighty Power, who rul'st this world of storms. Ode, An: "Almighty Power, who rul'st this world of storms." Anne Batten Cristall. RWP

Almighty Sovereign of the Skies! Nathan Strong. AH

Almighty Spake, and Gabriel Sped, Th' George Richards. AH

Almighty! What Is Man? Solomon ibn Gabirol. TrJP, *tr. by* Emma Lazarus

Almond flourisheth, the birch trees flow, The. Signs of Spring. Sir Thomas Browne. NOSC

Almond Tree, The. Jon Stallworthy. NoAM

Almoner, An. "Michael Field." VWP

Almora Spring. Sumitranandan Pant. OMIP, *tr. by* David Rubin

Almost a child again. In the Formal Garden. Peter Jones. OBGa

Almost a God. Emanuel Carnevali. APT-2

Almost a Love Poem. Yehuda Amichai [*or* Amikhai]. HP, *tr. by* Glenda Abramson

Almost at the end of the century. Feast Day. W. S. Merwin. BodElec

Almost Aubade. Marilyn Hacker. NoAM

Almost before the princess had grown cold. True Story of Snow White, The. Bruce Bennett. ReTh

Almost Bird. Amanda Dalton. NeBl *Fr.* Room of Leaves.

Almost Blue. Mark Doty. SeSe

Almost Casanova despite the phlebitis with everything else. Almost Casanova Electricity. Jackson Mac Low. FTOS

Almost everything I know is glad. Opus from Space. Pattiann Rogers. PoCoUp

Almost Going. David Huddle. PBCAP

Almost Human. Cecil Day Lewis. NoAM

Almost Like Being in Love. Frederick Loewe. ReLy

Almost naked like the children of the sea. (LL) Portrait. Antonio Machado Ruiz. RaBo; STV; WoPoe, *tr. by* Robert Bly

Almost none. Ghazal 15. Mirza Asadullah Khan Ghalib. EaWin, *tr. by* Aijaz Ahmad and W. S. Merwin

Almost Persuaded. Philip Paul Bliss. AH

Almost sheer fatigue. Early Pregnancy. Penelope Shuttle. BrRo

Almost singing, she stares past the crowd and flies. Old Woman Awaiting the Greyhound Bus. Duane Niatum. CDW

Almost Spring, Driving Home, Reciting Hopkins. Maxine W. Kumin. ExTi

Almost twenty years. Drinking Cold Water. Peter Everwine. NNaP

Almost two years now I've been sleeping. After Elegies. Jean Valentine. LCAP-2

Almost Winter, snow in the air. Cold Landscape. Augusta Peaux. TuT, *tr. by* Tony Curtis

Alms. Stanley Plumly. BodElec

Almswomen. Edmund Charles Blunden. OBMV; OxBTC

Almyghty god, fadir of heuene. Petition to Father and Son and Holy Ghost, A. *Unknown.* SacPr

Alnight by the rose, rose. *Unknown.* *See* All night by the rose, rose

Alnwick Castle. Fitz-Greene Halleck. APN-1

Aloe, agave, portulaca, prickly pear. Life of Ideas, The. Chris Wallace-Crabbe. OBGa

Aloft in Heavenly Mansions, Doubleyou One.   Playboy of the Demi-World[: 1938], The.   William Plomer.   OxBTC; UV

Aloha Oe.   Don Blanding.   PoToHe

Aloha'oe.   Queen Lili'u-o-ka-lani.   SWaP

Alone.   Anna Andreyevna Akhmatova.   BoWoP; GifTon, *tr.* by Stephen Berg

Alone.   Hayyim Nahman [*or* Khayim Nakhman *or* Chaim Nachman] Bialik.   TrJP, *tr.* by Jessie Sampter

Alone.   Ambrose Bierce.   APN-2   *Fr.* Devil's Dictionary, The.

Alone.   Chu Shu-chen.   BoWoP; OHPC, *tr.* by Kenneth Rexroth

Alone.   Walter De la Mare.   EnLoPo

Alone.   Michael S. Harper.   ISC

"Alone."   Edgar Allan Poe.   APN-1; NAAL-2v1; NAAL-3

Alone.   Sappho.   AWP, *tr.* by William Ellery Leonard

Alone.   Celia Laighton Thaxter.   TCAPo

Alone.   Tomas Tranströmer.   WoPoe, *tr.* by Robin Fulton

Alone.   Carolyn Wells.   PoToHe

Alone a lady was standing.   Lady Stood Alone, A.   Dietmar von Aist [*or* Eist].   AuPH, *tr.* by Lowell A. Bangerter

Alone am I, and alone I wish to be.   Christine de Pisan.   BoWoP

Alone and Godless, stopped by the sudden edge.   Patrick MacDonogh.   BIrV   *Fr.* Escape to Love.

Alone at home one afternoon.   Love Letters.   Lotte Kramer.   Prnts

Alone at last in my room.   By the Looking-Glass.   Augusta Davies Webster.   VWP

Alone at Night.   Kwon P'il.   GifTon, *tr.* by Sung-Il Lee

Alone at night.   1951.   Frank O'Hara.   LCAP-2

Alone, at night, with all the world.   Evil Nigger Waits for Lightnin'   Imamu Amiri Baraka.   NOBA

Alone at the end of green *allées* alone.   Statues in the Public Gardens, The.   Howard Nemerov.   CoAmPo

Alone by the Autumn River.   Li Shang-yin.   ColAnChi, *tr.* by Sam Hamill   (Alone Beside the Autumn River.)   CrYelRi

Alone far in the wilds and mountains I hunt.   Walt Whitman.   SAmP   *Fr.* Song of Myself.

Alone for a Week.   Dolores Kendrick.   FFC

Alone, I live alone.   *Unknown*.   MiEL

Alone I sat; the summer day.   Emily Jane Brontë.   NALW

Alone I Stand.   Ho Ching-ming.   CoBLCP, *tr.* by Jonathan Chaves

Alone I stand in autumn cold.   "Spring in Ch'in's Garden."   Mao Tse-tung [*or* Mao Zedong].   SuSp, *tr.* by Eugene Eoyang

Alone I tiptoe through the stars.   Star Journey.   Naomi Long Madgett.   BPo

Alone I tow my death along. (LL)   Hidesong.   Aig Higo.   PBMAP; TTY

Alone in a cold autumn I stood.   Midstream.   Mao Tse-tung [*or* Mao Zedong].   MoCV, *tr.* by Earle Birney

Alone in a room Pope Gregory whispered his name.   W. H. Auden.   SacPr   *Fr.* Memorial for the City.

Alone in an Inn at Southampton, April the 25th, 1737.   Aaron Hill.   NOEC

Alone in Martyrdom.   Christine de Pisan.   NAWM-7v1, *tr.* by Muriel Kittel

Alone in martyrdom I have been left.   Alone in Martyrdom.   Christine de Pisan.   NAWM-7v1, *tr.* by Muriel Kittel

Alone, in mourning, wearing an archaic black gown.   Sonnet: "Alone, in mourning, wearing an archaic black gown."   J. V. Foix.   WoPoe, *tr.* by M. L. Rosenthal

Alone in my secluded hut.   To Li Po on a Winter Day.   Tu Fu.   CrYelRi, *tr.* by Sam Hamill

Alone in my sorrow, where do my thoughts go?   Thinking of My Wife.   P'an Yüeh.   CoBCP, *tr.* by Burton Watson

Alone in the field, I touch.   Against Silence.   Pamela Stewart.   ExTi

Alone in the great storm. (LL)   Presaging.   Rainer Maria Rilke.   AWP; TrJP, *tr.* by Jessie Lemont

Alone in the Night.   Li Ch'ing-chao.   OHPC, *tr.* by Kenneth Rexroth

Alone in the quiet night.   Gunnar Ekelof.   WoPoe, *tr.* by Rika Lesser   *Fr.* Guide to the Underworld.

Alone in this desert under the cold moon.   If I Forget Thee.   Emanuel Litvinoff.   TrJP

Alone in Your House.   Kim Addonizio.   PasH

Alone Is the Hunter.   Harold Littlebird.   VoR

Alone it stands in Poesy's fair land.   Sonnet, The.   Ella Wheeler Wilcox.   APN-2

Alone, lonely, working at my loom. (LL)   Busy in the Spring.   Tzu Yeh.   CrYelRi; ErotSp, *tr.* by Sam Hamill

Alone on Lykaion since man hath been.   Trumbull Stickney.   OxBA; Son   *Fr.* Sonnets from Greece.

Alone on the hill of storms.   Battle of the Stars.   Adah Isaacs Menken.   CBWP-1

Alone on the lawn.   Dancing Cabman, The.   John Bingham Morton.   NOBL

Alone on the road.   Nicholas Virgilio.   HA

Alone on the tower.   Diver.   Ronald Albert Simpson.   CBAP

Alone, quite alone now.   Missing — Believed Drowned.   Michael Greening.   FaBoWar

Alone retired in my native cell.   *Unknown*.   EMWP

Alone she feeds the white swans.   Swans of Vadstena, The.   Ralph Gustafson.   MoCV

Alone the pallid cuckoo now.   Pallid Cuckoo.   David Campbell.   CBAP

Alone, the wild goose refuses food and drink.   Lone Wild Goose.   Tu Fu.   CrYelRi, *tr.* by Sam Hamill

Alone Together.   Arthur Schwartz.   ReLy

Alone tonight one fish ripples the lake.   Matsuo Allard.   HA

Alone, unfriended, on a foreign shore.   Indian, The.   Eliza Kirkham Mathews.   CenSon

Alone up here on the mountain.   *Unknown*.   NOIV

Alone, with harsh marine aloneness.   Elegy: "Alone, with harsh marine aloneness."   José Gorostiza.   TCLAP, *tr.* by Rachel Benson

Along a tarn a delator entangled a dragline.   Antic Quatrains.   Jackson Mac Low.   PmAP

Along Fall River, gibbons cry all night.   Fall River Song.   Li Po.   CrYelRi, *tr.* by Sam Hamill

Along Galeana Street.   Octavio Paz.   VCWP, *tr.* by Elizabeth Bishop

Along History.   Muriel Rukeyser.   NALW; NNaP

Along how many Main Streets have I walked.   Eternal Return, The.   Robert Silliman Hillyer.   AiP

Along Lenox Avenue folk said.   Old Pettigrew.   Melvin B. Tolson.   GT

Along my journey.   Basho.   SoOfWa, *tr.* by Sam Hamill

Along Overgrown Paths.   James Schuyler.   BAP-01

Along railroad tracks.   Temple City Blvd. and Ellis Ln.   Carol Lem.   GeoHom

Along that footpath, shepherd, past the oaks.   Theocritus.   GrAn

Along the amazing road drawn from the throat of recent dates.   Path of Affection, The.   Laila 'Allush.   PoArWo, *tr.* by Abdelwahab M. Elmessiri

Along the avenue of cypresses.   Giorno dei Morti.   D. H. Lawrence.   NOBE

Along the Banks.   Joel Barlow.   AH; ChIV-1

Along the Banks of the Charles.   Adelina da Silva.   NAfrP, *tr.* by Don Burness

Along the banks where Babel's current flows.   Along the Banks.   Joel Barlow.   AH; ChIV-1

Along the blushing borders bright with dew.   James Thomson.   NOBE   *Fr.* Seasons, The.

Along the bridge Lord Marmion rode.   Sir Walter Scott.   FaBoWar   *Fr.* Marmion.

Along the Charles.   Kenneth Rosen.   UrbNat

Along the dark, and silent night.   Bell-Man, The.   Robert Herrick.   BeJo

Along the field as we came by.   A. E. Housman.   HAP; MoBrPo; WeW-3

Along the garden terrace, under which.   George Meredith.   NOBVV   *Fr.* Modern Love.

Along the Grand Canal.   Ch'in Kuan.   BLT, *tr.* by Kenneth Rexroth

Along the great coast south of Bordeaux.   Michael O'Loughlin.   PBCIP   *Fr.* Shards, The.

Along the lake the bugle rings.   Echo Reverie.   Henrietta Cordelia Ray.   CBWP-3

Along the line of smoky hills.   Indian Summer.   Wilfred Campbell.   NOBC

Along the Mekong.   John Balaban.   CDa

Along the narrow street with a hero's name.   Outing, The.   Marina Kudimova.   TCRP, *tr.* by Albert C. Todd

Along the north-south street, glass birds.   Tsuneko—Psychiatric Medications Clinic.   Susan Kolodny.   OPRER

Along the path of ghosts, the ashen path.   Package for Another World.   Jemal Sharah.   NOBAu

Along the path that skirts the wood.   Three Musicians, The.   Aubrey Beardsley.   NOBVV; PeVV

Along the precipice, above the chasm, on the very brink.   Unruly Horses.   Vladimir Semionovich Vysotsky [*or* Vysotskii].   TCRP, *tr.* by Albert C. Todd

Along the promenade? (LL)   To Evoke Posterity.   Robert Graves.   HarvBoo; NPeEn

Along the ramparts which surround the town.   In the Defences.   Elizabeth Akers Allen.   SWaP

Along the river most homes here.   Quatrain at Chen-chou.   Wang Shih-chieng.   CoBLCP, *tr.* by Jonathan Chaves

Along the River, Seeing the Home of Absconded Farmers.   Kao Ch'i.   CoBLCP, *tr.* by Jonathan Chaves

Along the river where fish with redpetal gills.   End of Civilization as We Know It, The.   Colleen J. McElroy.   UrbNat

Along the road all shapes must travel by.   Prolonged Sonnet: In the Last Days of the Emperor Henry VII.   Simone dall' Antela.   AWP; EaltPo, *tr.* by Dante Gabriel Rossetti

Along the road, the bright painted crosses.   Talvikki Ansel.   YaYoPo   *Fr.* In Fragments, In Streams.

Along the Road to Stone Lake.   Su Tung-p'o (Su Shih).

Tune: Sand of Silk-washing Stream ("Flutter, flutter, on clothes and cap, jujube flowers fall"). CoBCP, *tr.* by Burton Watson

Tune: Sand of Silk-washing Stream ("Layer on layer of hemp leaves, jute leaves shining"). CoBCP, *tr.* by Burton Watson

Tune: Sand of Silk-washing Stream ("Soft grasses, a plain of sedge fresh with passing rain"). CoBCP, *tr.* by Burton Watson

Tune: Sand of Silk-washing Stream ("Throw on rouge and powder, watch the governor pass!"). CoBCP

Along the roadside. Buson. SoOfWa, *tr.* by Sam Hamill

Along the roadside, like the flowers of gold. John Greenleaf Whittier. APN-1; NAAL-2v1; OxBA *Fr.* Among the Hills.

Along the row of small white houses. Lovely Leda. Yaroslav [*or* Iaroslav] Vasilevich Smelyakov [*or* Smeliakov]. TCRP, *tr.* by Simon Franklin and Albert C. Todd

Along the shore. Basho. EH, *tr.* by Robert Hass

Along the side. Another Day. Belinda Zubicueta Carmona. TANSG, *tr.* by Celeste Kostopulos-Cooperman

Along the sprawled body of the derailed. Outside Fargo, North Dakota. James Wright (1927–80). LCAP-2; NNaP

Along the starlit Seine went music swelling. Pauline. Felicia Dorothea Hemans. RWP

Along the Strand. Alfred Mombert. TrJP, *tr.* by Jethro Bithell

Along the street noon, flying unchecked. Betrothed, The. Aleksandr Andreievich Prokofiev. TCRP, *tr.* by Lubov Yakovleva

Along the Tölös River. Song of the Tölös. Hulü Chin. ColAnChi, *tr.* by Victor H. Mair

Along this road where tiny frost-crabs edged. Vermont: Spring Rains. Edward Weismiller. YaYoPo

Along those roads we cannot hear him bark. (LL) Tymnes. FaBoCh; FaBoEE; Spl| WoPoe, *tr.* by Edmund Charles Blunden *Fr.* Epigrams.

Along thy dead indifference of walls. (LL) Berg, The. Herman Melville. ColAP; NCAP; NOBA; NoP-4; PoPoPo; TAP; TCAPo

Along Without: A Fiction in Film for Poetry. Douglas Messerli.

"NARRATOR: Suddenly someone wakes me. Still half-asleep, I see standing in front." FTOS

Alons au bois le may cueillir. Charles, Duc d' Orléans. AWP, *tr.* by W. E. Henley

Alonzo the Brave and the Fair Imogine. Matthew Gregory Lewis. NOBRP

Aloof. Christina Georgina Rossetti. NOBE; OBEV *Fr.* Thread of Life, The.

Aloof upon the day's immeasured dome. Black Vulture, The. George Sterling. APT-1

Aloof within the day's enormous dome. George Sterling. *See* Aloof upon the day's immeasured dome

Aloofe, aloofe, and come no neare. Sea Marke. John Smith. SCAP; TCAPo

Alpha. Melvin B. Tolson. APT-2 *Fr.* Harlem Gallery.

Alpha and Omega, God alone. Father, The. Joshua Sylvester. InvLi; SacPr

Alpha and Omega, God, my God! Prayer to God the Father. Hildebert. MLL, *tr.* by Helen Waddell

αα, ay, ay! . . stutterer Demosthenes. Them and [uz]. Tony Harrison. NoP-4

Alphabet. *Unknown.* OxNR

Alphabet. *Unknown. See* New England Primer, The

Alphabet, The. Jejuri Arun Kolatkar. OMIP, *tr.* by Vinay Dharwadker

Alphabet, The. Karl Shapiro. APT-2; NoAM; TaR

Alphabet, The. *Unknown.* ReMoGo

Alphabet Calendar of Amergin, The. *Unknown.* BIrV, *tr.* by Robert Graves

Alphabet Murders, The. John Tranter.

Alphabet Murders, The. BMAP

"We could point to the poem and say 'that map.'" BMAP

Alphabet Murders, The. John Tranter. BMAP *Fr.* Alphabet Murders, The.

Alphabet 9, 10. Inger Christensen. PFTM-2, *tr.* by Pierre Joris

Alphabet of Ahtt. Nathaniel Mackey. FTOS

Alphabet Soup. Fatima Lim-Wilson. ReBoTo

Alphabet war-makers. Zangezi: R, K, L, G. Velemir [*or* Viktor Vladimirovich] Khlebnikov. PFTM-1

Alphabet wonders, The. Out of a Sudden. Tom Raworth. Oth

Alphabetical Song on the Corn Law Bill. *Unknown.* OxBoLi

Alphabets. Seamus Heaney. NoAM

Alphonso of Castile. Ralph Waldo Emerson. NOBA

Already at a thousand feet. Blackberries. Maurina Sherman. GeoHom

Already Autumn, and from the belt of Boötes. To Epicles. Antipater of Thessalonica. GrAn, *tr.* by Tony Harrison

Already autumn begins here in the mossy rocks. Thinking of "The Autumn Fields." Robert Bly. NNaP

Already blushes on thy cheek. Nemesis. Ralph Waldo Emerson. NOBA

Already Embraced by the Arm of Heavenly Solace. Nelly Sachs. HP; PoSu, *tr.* by Michael Roloff

Already fallen plum-bloom stars the green. Poor Man's Pig, The. Edmund Charles Blunden. MoBrPo

Already I am no longer looked at with lechery or love. Sunset of the City, A. Gwendolyn Brooks. FaBoWP; LCAP-2

Already my temples are grey. Anacreon. SaLy, *tr.* by Diane Rayor

Already Night, Already Day. Hedva Harechavi. DTA, *tr.* by Miriyam Glazer

Already, no more dreams of going to the capital. Living in Retirement at Te-ch'ing. Chao Meng-fu. CoBLCP, *tr.* by Jonathan Chaves

Already old, and still without a name. Song of T'ung-ku. Tu Fu. CrYelRi, *tr.* by Sam Hamill

Already past mid-June. Out of Work, Out of Touch, Out of Sorts. Catherine Davis. FFC

Already prepared in the golden chamber. Antipater of Sidon. GrAn

Already she seems bone thin. Poem about Breasts, A. James Wright (1927–80). TAP

Already something of a stranger now. Epil y Filiast. Harri Webb. AngWePo; TCAWP

Already subject to rebuke, instead. Sonnet 20: Remembering, from a Nazi Prison, a Teacher Years Before. William Pitt Root. MiVo

Already swallows build their homes of mud. Thyillos. GrAn

Already the creamy Volkswagen rocks back. American Roadside Elegy, An. Dave Jeddie Smith. EmeKit

Already the field, fair with leaves, in her fruitful bringing to birth. Theaitetus. GrAn

Already this tremor in my hands. Black Irish Blues. Joe-Anne McLaughlin. OPRER

Already to mine eyelids' shore. "Michael Field." VWP

Already waiting. (LL) Hadewijch II. HW; WPoS

Already your flowering youth is gently evaporating. To Il y a. Hélène d'Oettingen. CuPo

Also an old image has a moment's birth. Moon. Nathan [*or* Natan] Alterman. MHP, *tr.* by Ruth Finer Mintz

Also for little ones, just like me. Leah Goldberg. MHP, *tr.* by Ruth Finer Mintz *Fr.* Songs of the Stream.

Also I love him: me he's done no wrong. John Berryman. NoP-4

Also in sleep I see you, comprehend. Fire in the Stone, The. Tuvia Rivner. MHP, *tr.* by Ruth Finer Mintz

Also survive its meanings, and my own. (LL) After Greece. James Merrill. CoAmPo; ColAP; NOBA; TRP

Also ther was a disciple of Plato. Geoffrey Chaucer. SacPr *Fr.* Canterbury Tales, The.

Also Ulysses once—that other war. Kilroy. Peter Viereck. MoAmPo

Alstonefield V. Peter Riley.

"Another damp Sunday morning up and walk over." Oth

Altar. Marilyn Chin. PoPoPo

Altar, The. George Herbert. AngWePo; BASC; CABP; ChIV-1; ESCV; GeHe; NAEL-5v1; NAEL-6v1; NAEL-7v1; NOSC; NoP-4; TrCP

Altar boy marches up the altar steps, The. Soldiers. Padraic Fiacc. PNI

Altar of glasses behind the bar, The. Drinking Art, The. Robert Minhinnick. AngWePo; TCAWP

Altar, 'tis of death! for there are laid, The. Marriage Vow, The. Letitia [*or* Laetitia] Elizabeth Landon. VWP

Altarwise by Owl-Light. Dylan Thomas.

"Altarwise by owl-light in the half-way house." FaBoMo; Son

"Death is all metaphors, shape in one history." Son

"Let the tale's sailor from a Christian voyage." FaBoMo

"Now stamp the Lord's Prayer on a grain of rice." FaBoMo

"What is the metre of the dictionary?" FaBoMo

Altazor. Vincente Huidobro.

"Altazor how did you lose your first serenity?" PFTM-1

Canto 2 (excerpts). BLPSL, *tr.* by Rene de Costa, Rigas Kappatos and Eleni Paidoussi

Canto I (excerpt). PFTM-1

"Here and now I have to dilute myself into many things." TCLAP, *tr.* by Stephen Fredman

"I am king." TCLAP, *tr.* by Stephen Fredman

"So you're a windmill." TCLAP, *tr.* by Stephen Fredman

"Woman the world is furnished by your eyes." BLPSL, *tr.* by Rene de Costa, Rigas Kappatos and Eleni Paidoussi

Altazor how did you lose your first serenity? Vincente Huidobro. PFTM-1 *Fr.* Altazor.

Alter or mend eternal Fact. (LL) Past, The. Ralph Waldo Emerson. FaBoCh; TAP; WoPoe

Alter! When the Hills do. Emily Dickinson. SoSe-8; TCAPo

Altered look about the hills, An. Emily Dickinson. OxBA; SoSe-8

Altermann, sipping wine, reads with a look. Dom Moraes. NoP-4 *Fr.* Two from Israel.

Alternately in Anecdotes go on. "Peter Pindar." OBCoV *Fr.* Bozzy and Piozzi.

Alternative Endings to an Unwritten Ballad. Paul Dehn. OBCoV

Alternatives. Kingsley Amis. OxBC

Altho' we mourn for one now gone. Edward Edwin Foot. VerBaPo

Although a poor blind boy[!]. (LL) Blind Boy, The. Colley Cibber. GTBS-P; NOEC

Although a temple. Underneath Our Skirts. Katie Donovan. NeBl

Although art is autonomous. On This Day I Complete My Fortieth Year. Peter Porter. BMAP

Although art is, in the end, anonymous. Having Completed My Fortieth Year. John Tranter. BMAP

Although, great Queen, thou now in silence lie. Anne Bradstreet. NAAL-5; NALW

Although he can not admit it even to himself. Long Woman Bathing, The. Maurice Kilwein Guevara. TouFir

Although he has no form. Mukta Bai. BoWoP

Although hindsight accords a degree of humored. Battle of Valcour Island, The. Richard Kenney. YaYoPo

Although I can see him still. Fisherman, The. W. B. Yeats. HAP; NoAM

Although I Conquer All the Earth. *Unknown.* TTTS

Although I cry and though my eyes still shed. Sonnet XIV. Louise Labé. BoWoP, *tr. by* Willis Barnstone

Although I do not know. Saigyo. AWP

Although I hide it. Kanemori. OHPJ

Although I put away his life. Emily Dickinson. MoAmPo

Although I shelter from the rain. Lamentation of the Old Pensioner, The. W. B. Yeats. HAP; PeVV; TRP; WeW-3

Although I try. In the Autumn, on Retreat at a Mountain Temple. Lady Izumi. WPoS

Although I was her pupil, / even I reproach Myrtis. Korinna [*or* Corinna]. BoWoP

Although I work, and seldom cease. Dorothy Parker. APT-1 *Fr.* Pig's-Eye View of Literature, A.

Although it is a cold evening. At the Fishhouses. Elizabeth Bishop. APT-2; AmFaPo; CoAP; FaBoWP; HAP; HCAP; LCAP-2; NAAL-2v2; NAAL-5; NALW; PoPoPo; PoRA; PoetW; VCAP

Although it is night, I sit in the bathroom, waiting. Adolescence—II. Rita Dove. AWTN; HCAP; ISC; NAAL-5; NoAM; PoPoPo; VCAP

Although it is not plainly visible to the eye. *Var. authors.* AWP *Fr.* Kokin Shu.

Although it is not yet evening. Persistence of Song, The. Howard Moss. NoP-4

Although it never rivaled wheat, soybean. Commercial Leech Farming Today. Thomas Lux. BodElec

Although lamps burn along the silent streets. James Thomson. EBVV *Fr.* City of Dreadful Night, The.

Although my claws weaken. Sweetness. *Unknown.* BIrV, *tr. by* John Montague

Although my feet. Ono no Komachi. ArkPo, *tr. by* Robert H. Brower and Earl Miner

Although my life, which thou hast scarred and shaken. I Shall Forget. "Laurence Hope." OxBSo

Although only a fool would mock. Queen Mother to New Queen. Robert Graves. OBSV

Although [*or* Altho'] I be the basest of mankind. St. Simeon Stylites. Tennyson. NOBVV

Although propriety be crossed. New Year's Gift, A. William Cartwright. BeJo

Although she feeds me bread of bitterness. America. Claude McKay. NAAAL; NAAL-5; NIL-7; NIP-4; NoAM; TAP; TTY

Although she had lain. (LL) Africa. Maya Angelou. NIL-7; NIP-4

Although she's a girl, Dorkion. Asclepiades. GrAn; PGA

Although some are afraid that to speak of a spade as a spade is a social mistake. Rigoletto. Newman Levy. OBAL

Although the aepyornis. He "Digesteth Harde Yron." Marianne Craig Moore. APT-1; NoAM; OWoS

Although the autumn moon. Kanshu. JDP, *tr. by* Yoel Hoffmann

Although the field lay cut in swaths. Timothy. Timothy Steele. InPK-6; RA

Although the lamp was out, above its darkness. Wedding Ring, The. Zinaida Nikolayevna [*or* Nikolaevna] Gippius. ARWW, *tr. by* Catriona Kelly

Although the lime's long faded, wan. End of the Year. Paula Ludwig. AuPH, *tr. by* Lowell A. Bangerter

Although the Sky. Elmaz Abinader. PoArWo

Although the snow still lingers. Last Snow. Andrew Young. OxBTC

Although the trumpet blew so loud. (LL) Tennyson. NAEL-6v2; NOCV *Fr.* In Memoriam A. H. H.

Although the wind. Lady Izumi. WPoS; WoPoe, *tr. by* Mariko Aratani and Jane Hirshfield

Although their hair is turning gray. Meeting of Friends, A. Phillis Levin. RA

Although, those years, we squandered. Plaint of Flowers, A. Ernest Sandeen. CRP

Although thy blood be frozen, and thy scalp. To a Covetous Churl. Edward May. FaBoEE

Although thy hand and faith, and good work[e]s too. John Donne. EBEV *Fr.* Elegies.

Although Tormented. Kalonymos ben Judah. TrJP

Although we do not all the good we love. John Davies of Hereford. Son *Fr.* Holy Rood, The.

Although you be, as I am, one of those. For Christopher Isherwood and Chester Kallman. W. H. Auden. SacPr

Although you have given me a stomach upset. Symptoms. Sophie Hannah. MFPA

Although you never asked to come with me. Peter Scupham. NewEx

Although you're far away. We'll Gather Lilacs. Ivor Novello. ReLy

Although your ears must be plentifully occupied. Julius Polyaenus. GrAn

Although your white bones waste in. On a Hound. Simonides. PGA, *tr. by* Kenneth Rexroth

Altocumulus. AC. Geraldine Monk. Oth

Alton Locke. Charles Kingsley.

   "O [*or* Oh] Mary, go and call the cattle home." EBVV; OxAEP-2; TreFP

   Sands of Dee, The. EBVV; OxAEP-2; TreFP

Altruism. Dionisio D. Martinez. TouFir

Aluqa, the demon who swims underwater in streams. Meadow Bug. Rossana Ombres. NeIt, *tr. by* Ruth Feldman

Alvargonzález, being single. Antonio Machado Ruiz. SpanPo, *tr. by* Denise Levertov

Alvin Cash/Keep on Dancin' David Henderson. GT

Always. Irving Berlin. ReLy

Always. Mark Strand. EmeKit; NoP-4; TRP

Always a third one's there. Uninvited, The. Dorothy Livesay. NOBC; NoP-4

Always afraid to say more than it meant. (LL) Letter, The. W. H. Auden. FaBoTw; NoAM

Always an angel rises from the figure. Masseuse, The. Olga Broumas. WiU

Always at night I found them. Children of Saigon, The. Walter McDonald. AF

Always before your voice my soul. E. E. Cummings. MoAmPo

Always Begin Where You Are. Thomas Hornsby Ferril. VGW

Always boys in my poems! Sandro Penna. CAGL, *tr. by* John McRae

Always driven, always in the bite of the blast. And Yet We Are Here! Karl Wolfskehl. TrJP, *tr. by* Ernst Morowitz and Carol North Valhope

Always / Etheridge Knight. (LL) Poem to Galway Kinnell, A. Etheridge Knight. BodElec; NNaP

Always expecting the winter. In Dream: The Privacy of Sequence. Ray A. Young Bear. CDW

Always first to rise. In My Father's House. George Barlow. ESEAA

Always for thirty years now. Fish Peddler and Cobbler. Kenneth Rexroth. NNaP

Always for your never named sake. (LL) Lost Baby Poem, The. Lucille Clifton. AmFaPo; BlSi; ESEAA; ISC; WPE

Always, from My First Boyhood. John Peale Bishop. VGW

Always Homing Now Soul Toward Light. Lorna Goodison. VCWP

Always homing now soul toward light. Always Homing Now Soul Toward Light. Lorna Goodison. VCWP

Always I am enjoying your company. (LL) Patriot, The. Nissim Ezekiel. EmeKit; FaBoVe

Always I have meant to write of Apollo Café. Apollo Café. Stephen Gray. PeSAV

Always I have searched for the mislaid tin spoon. One Fine Day. János Pilinszky. PoSu, *tr. by* Peter Jay

Always I lay upon the brink of love. Judas. Vassar Miller. ChIV-2; MoAmPo

Always I recall the river arbor at twilight. As in a Dream. Li Ch'ing-chao. CoBCP, *tr. by* Burton Watson

Always—I tell you this they learned. Robert Frost. VGW *Fr.* Hill Wife, The.

Always I thought they suffered, the way they huffed. On the Bearing of Waitresses. Rodney Jones. ReTh

Always in the Parting Year. Else Lasker-Schüler. TrJP, *tr. by* Ralph Manheim

Always, it shall be this way. Look to the Mountain. Simon J. Ortiz. PoCoUp

Always it was a summer afternoon. House of Broughton Street, The. Mary Ann Larkin. AiP

Always it was going on. Today Is Friday. Ramon Guthrie. PoE

Always Know. Kalamu ya Salaam. SpirFl

Always on Monday, God's name is in the morning papers. Day after Sunday, The. Phyllis McGinley. MoAmPo; OBSV; UnPo

Always on time, like the waves. (LL) Impossible Pictures, The. Tom Paulin. CABP; CIP-2

Always passing bars has dulled. Panther, The. Rainer Maria Rilke. WoPoe, *tr. by* William DeWitt Snodgrass

Always pruning, always cropping? Matthew 9.12. Francis Quarles. ChIV-2

Always Returning: Holidays and Burials. Not Every Week. D. A. Powell. WiU

Always Running. Luis J. Rodriguez. UnSA

Always She Moves from Me. Shirley Kaufman. WPE

Always so late in the day. Always. Mark Strand. EmeKit; NoP-4; TRP

Always the arriving winds of words. Words. William Robert Rodgers. OxBSP; PNI

Always the children are included. Mourning the Death, by Hemorrhage, of a Child from Honai. Basil T. Paquet. CDa

Always the Following Wind. W. H. Auden. MoBrPo

Always the same fine snow. Visitor, The. Anna Andreyevna Akhmatova. TCRusP, *tr. by* Daniel Weissbort

Always the same hills. Pietà. Ronald Stuart Thomas. NPeEn

Always the same, sweet hurt. Why Do So Few Blacks Study Creative Writing? Cornelius Eady. GT; LTA

Always the same, when on a fated night. Onset, The. Robert Frost. APT-1; MoAmPo; OxBA

Always the setting forth was the same. Odysseus. W. S. Merwin. NOBA; NoP-4

Always these gallows. Mirrors. Fu'ad [*or* Fuad] Rifqa [*or* Rifka]. MAP, *tr. by* Sargon Boulus and Samuel Hazo

Always this waking dream of palmtrees. Islands, The. Robert Earl Hayden. ESEAA

Always Throw the First Punch. Miguel Algarin. PueRic

Always to be shrieked at people's estimation of undisturbed extinction. Loop, Fleck, Sound *and So On*. Marianne Vitale. HeMarv

Always to stand here by the old windows where she lay. Autumn Wind. Adriann Roland Holst. TuT, *tr. by* Desmond Egan

Always to want to. Tortoise, The. Cid Corman. InPK-6; VGW

Always too eager for the future, we. Next, Please. Philip Larkin. CABP; HarvBoo; MoBrPo

Always True to You in My Fashion. Cole Porter. ReLy

"If a custom-tailored vet." NBLV

Always, / We hear at night approaching steps. Steps in the Night. Mahmoud Darwish. VCWP, *tr. by* Denys Johnson-Davies

Always with love, with love. (LL) Letter, The. Elizabeth Riddell. LW; NOBAu

Always you are there—standing. Michael Harlow. PeNZ *Fr.* Poem Then, for Love.

Alysoun. Geoffrey Chaucer. NPeEn *Fr.* Canterbury Tales, The.

Alzheimer's. Bob Hicok. AmPoNex

Alzheimer's: The Wife. C. K. Williams. VCAP

Am, by being dead, immortal; Can ghosts die? (LL) Computation, The. John Donne. NoSic; OxBSP; SoSe-8

Am I. Message Clear. Edwin Morgan. NePenScot

Am I a dead man? Am I a dead man? John Berryman Listening to Robert Johnson's "King of the Delta Blues," January 1972. David Wojahn. SeSe

Am I a stone and not a sheep. Good Friday. Christina Georgina Rossetti. ChIV-2

Am I afraid of the tenth day? Kalyānkumār Mukhopādhyāy. SinGod, *tr. by* Rachel Fell McDermott

Am I alone. Sir William Schwenck Gilbert. NAEL-5v2; NAEL-6v2; NBLV *Fr.* Patience.

Am I Blue? Grant Clarke. ReLy

Am I despised because you say. To a Gentlewoman Objecting to Him His Grey Hairs. Robert Herrick. BeJo; CaPo

Am I dreaming? Unreceived Messages. Robert Walker. IBA

Am I failing? For no longer can I cast. George Meredith. SCGP *Fr.* Modern Love.

Am I mad, O noble Festus. Distracted Puritan, The. Richard Corbet [*or* Corbett]. BASC; BeJo; OBCoV; OxBoLi

Am I really a sports fan, I ask myself. Boxing Match, The. David Ignatow. MoASP

Am I right to see myself introduced. Hand Further, The. Clark Coolidge. PmAP

Am I thirty two? That's nice. For My Birthday. Attila József. IQMS, *tr. by* Earl M. Herrick

Am I thus conquered [*or* conquer'd]? have I lost the powers. Mary Sidney Wroth, Countess of Montgomery. BASC; CABP; NAEL-5v1; NAEL-6v1; NAEL-7v1; NOSC *Fr.* Pamphilia to Amphilanthus.

Am I thy gold? Or purse, Lord, for thy wealth. Edward Taylor. NOSC; OxBA; TAP; TCAPo *Fr.* Preparatory Meditations Before My Approach to the Lord's Supper.

Am I to become profligate as if I were a blonde? Meditations in an Emergency. Frank O'Hara. PmAP; TAP; VCAP

Am I to blame the drink or the downpour? Antipater of Thessalonica. GrAn

Am I to go on. *Unknown.* ArkPo, *tr. by* Helen Craig McCullough

"Am I to lose you now?" The words were light. Am I to Lose You? Louisa Sarah Bevington. NOBVV; OxBSo

Am I your only love—in the whole world—now? Tell Me Again. Nigâr Hanim. ItWoWo, *tr. by* Talat Sait Halman and Tâlat S. Halman

Am quite myself again. (LL) Oh, When I Was In Love. A. E. Housman. BoLoP; MoBrPo; TTTS

Am, the world's my smilebutton. (LL) What the Motorcycle Said. Mona Van Duyn. NIL-7; NIP-4

Am/Trak. Imamu Amiri Baraka. PmAP

Amadu I live alone inside four walls of books. Letter to a Tormented Playwright. Syl Cheney-Coker. HBAPE; PBMAP

Amalkanti. Nirendranath Chakrabarti. OMIP, *tr. by* Sujit Mukherjee

Amalkanti is a friend of mine. Amalkanti. Nirendranath Chakrabarti. OMIP, *tr. by* Sujit Mukherjee

Amanda. Lisa Glatt. AmPoNex

Amanda! Robin Klein. OTCP

Amanda Barker. Edgar Lee Masters. APT-1; NoAM *Fr.* Spoon River Anthology.

Amang the holtis hair. (LL) Robin [*or* Robene] and Makyne. Robert Henryson. OBEV; PeLV

Amantes, Los. Richard Garcia. TouFir

Amantium Irae. Richard Edwards [*or* Edwardes]. OBEV; SCGP

(Amantium Irae.) OBEV; SCGP

(Amantium irae amoris redintigratia est.) OxBEV

(Fallyng out of faithfull frends, is the renewing of love, The.) (LL) OxBEV

(In goyng to my naked bedde, as one that would have slept.) OxBEV

Amarantha sweet and fair[e]. To Amarantha, That She Would Dishevel[l] Her Hair[e]. Richard Lovelace. BeJo; NIL-7; OBEV

Amaryllis Belladonna. Patricia Pogson. NLP

Amateur, The. Russell Edson. LCAP-2

Amateur Drummer. Roberta Gould. MiVo

Amateurs of Heaven, The. Howard Nemerov. SoSe-8

Amaze. Adelaide Crapsey. APT-1

Amazed, amazed, amazed, amazed. (LL) Rhyme for a Child Viewing a Naked Venus in a Painting [of "The Judgement of Paris"]. Robert Browning. NPeEn; OBCoV

Amazed we read of Nature's early throes. Man the Monarch. Mary Leapor. ECWP

Amazing Grace. Anselm Hollo. PoM

Amazing Grace. John Newton. SacPr

Amazing Grace in the Back Country. Robert Penn Warren. ColAP

Amazing, how the young man who empties. Wing Road. Eamon Grennan. PBCIP

Amazing monster! that, for aught I know. Leigh Hunt. NBLV; NPeEn; SCGP *Fr.* Fish, the Man, and the Spirit, The.

Amazing Sight! The Saviour Stands. Henry Alline. AH *Fr.* Christ Inviting Sinners to His Grace.

Amazon Club. Kenward Elmslie. PmAP

Amazone. Mary Jo Bona. UnSA

Ambassador, The. Bruce Weigl. CDa

Ambassador Puser the ambassador. Memorial Rain. Archibald MacLeish. MoAmPo; OBWP

Amber Bead, The. Robert Herrick. BeJo; CaPo

Amber husk / fluted with gold. Sea Poppies. "H. D." APT-1; NALW

Ambition. Bruce Berger. GeoH

Ambition. William Henry Davies. MoBrPo

Ambition. Robert Herrick. CaPo

Ambition. Maggie Pogue Johnson. CBWP-4

Ambition. Henrietta Cordelia Ray. CBWP-3

Ambition. Nathaniel Parker Willis. OBCA

Ambition, The. Robert Harris. BMAP

Ambition—following down this far famed slope. William Wordsworth. OxBSo *Fr.* Memorials of a Tour of the Continent; 1820.

Ambitious Ant, The. Amos Russel Wells. OBCA; OBSP

Ambitious ant would a-travelling go, The. Ambitious Ant, The. Amos Russel Wells. OBCA; OBSP

Amble. Maxine Chernoff. PmAP *Fr.* Japan.

Amboyna; or, The Cruelties of the Dutch to the English Merchants. Dryden. Prologue: "As needy gallants in the scriv'ners' hands." OBSV

Ambrose is an Old Etonian and he. Fiction: The House Party. Gavin Ewart. PeLV

Ambrosia, brought safe. Leonidas of Tarentum. GrAn

Ambulance men touched her cold, The. Death of Marilyn Monroe, The. Sharon Olds. HeIP-4; ReTh

Ambulances. Philip Larkin. FaBoTw; NAEL-5v2; NAEL-6v2; NoP-4; OxBC

Ambulando. Charles Brasch. PeNZ

Ambush of the Fourth Platoon, The. David Hall.

"There is no place to hide." CDa

Ambushed myself discovered. Humility. Marie Luise Kaschnitz. WPOW, *tr.* by Michael Hamburger

Amelia was just fourteen and out of the orphan asylum. Charles Reznikoff. ColAP; WWork *Fr.* Testimony.

Amen. "H. D." WPoS *Fr.* Walls Do Not Fall, The.

Amen. Alvaro Mutis. TCLAP, *tr.* by Sophie Cabot Black and Maria Negroni

Amen. Christina Georgina Rossetti. WPoS

Amen, Amen, Amen. (LL) "H. D." APT-1; NAAL-5 *Fr.* Walls Do Not Fall, The.

Amen. The casket like a spaceship bears her. Annie Hill's Grave. James Merrill. WeW-3

Amen, who scared off my girl. (LL) Rattle Bag, The. Dafydd [*or* David] ap Gwilym. NBLV; RB; WoPoe, *tr.* by Joseph P. Clancy

Amendis to the Telyouris and Sowtaris for the Turnament Maid on Thame, The. William Dunbar. OBSV

Amendment. Thomas Traherne. InvLi

Amends. Adrienne Rich. HarvBoo *Fr.* Not Somewhere Else, But Here.

Amergin's Songs. Amergin. NOIV

America. Kofi Awoonor. HBAPE

America. Robert Creeley. MakPoe

America. Henry Dumas. ChAP

America. Allen Ginsberg. CoAP; HCAP; MakPoe; NoAM; PFTM-2; PmAP; PoE; PoM; PoPoPo; TRP

America. Claude McKay. NAAAL; NAAL-5; NIL-7; NIP-4; NoAM; TAP; TTY

America. Herman Melville. APN-2

America. John Newlove. NOBC

America. Wendy Rose. CDW

America. Samuel Francis Smith. AiP; TCAPo

America. Samuel Francis Smith.
"My country, 'tis of thee." HHAm

America. Stephen Sondheim. ReLy

America. Phillis Wheatley. TCAPo

America. James M. Whitfield. APN-2; NAAAL

America. Walt Whitman. FaBoA

America, America. K. Nisar Ahmad. OMIP, *tr.* by A. K. Ramanujan

America calling. Haki R. Madhubuti. NAAAL

America for Me. Henry Van Dyke. ChAP

America, I Do Not Call Your Name Without Hope. Pablo Neruda. AF; TCLAP, *tr.* by Robert Bly

America I'm putting my queer shoulder to the wheel. (LL) America. Allen Ginsberg. CoAP; HCAP; MakPoe; NoAM; PFTM-2; PmAP; PoE; PoM; PoPoPo; TRP

America I've given you all and now I'm nothing. America. Allen Ginsberg. CoAP; HCAP; MakPoe; NoAM; PFTM-2; PmAP; PoE; PoM; PoPoPo; TRP

America in 1918. John Reed.
"I have watched the summer day come up from the top of a pier of the Williamsburgh Bridge." APT-1

America Is Hard to See. Robert Frost. AiP; FaBoA

America, it is to thee. From America. James M. Whitfield. APN-2; BPo

America's Welcome Home. Henry Van Dyke. AiP

America's Wounded Knee. Phillip [*or* "Phil"] William George. VoR

America that was supposed to be, The. (LL) Indian Movie, New Jersey. Chitra Divakaruni. NIL-7; UnSA

America the Beautiful. Katharine Lee Bates. APN-2; FaBoA; HHAm; TAP

America / The tongues of your rivers burn with thirst. Lackawanna Elegy. Iwan [*or* Yvan] Goll. AF, *tr.* by Galway Kinnell

America to Great Britain. Washington Allston. APN-1

America, you are luckier. United States, The. Goethe. AiP; FaBoA, *tr.* by Robert Bly

America, you ode for reality! America. Robert Creeley. MakPoe

American, An. Rudyard Kipling. FaBoA
(American, An.) FaBoA
(American Spirit speaks, The.) FaBoA
(I—I shall save him at the last!) (LL) FaBoA

American Airlines to Chicago. Funeral. Clarence Major. BodElec

American Apocalypse. Edward Hirsch. IllVoic

American Avalon. Connie Deanovich. AmPoNex

American Bandstand. Michael Waters. SwNoth

American Beauty, An. Carolyn Kizer. GeoHom

American Change. Allen Ginsberg. HCAP

American Cheese. G. E. Murray. IllVoic

American Dream: First Report. Joseph Papaleo. UnSA

American Dreams. "Sapphire." AfrBLW

American Farm, 1934. Genevieve Taggard. VGW

American Flag, The. Joseph Rodman Drake. APN-1; BRP

American Forest Girl, The. Felicia Dorothea Hemans. RWP

American girl in Versailles, An. "C. K. B." PeLi

American Heartbreak. Langston Hughes. APT-2; BPo

American Heritage. Robert Sward. OBAL

American Heritage Potato, The. Jim Barnes. SpudSo

American History. Michael S. Harper. BPo; ESEAA; HCAP; NAAL-5; NoAM; PoPoPo

American Indian, The. *Unknown.* NBLV

American Indian Art: Form and Tradition. Diane Di Prima. BB

[American Journal]. Robert Earl Hayden. ESEAA; ISC

American jump, American jump. *Unknown.* OxNR

American Letter. Archibald MacLeish. OxBA

American Lights, Seen from Off Abroad. John Berryman. LCAP-2; OBAL; OBCoV

American Literature. Lisel Mueller. PoSol

American Living-room: A Tract, The. William Meredith. BodElec

American Memory of Africa, An. Kofi Awoonor. HBAPE
(Afro-American Beats III: An American Memory of Africa.) PBMAP

American muse, whose strong and diverse heart. Stephen Vincent Benét. APT-2 *Fr.* John Brown's Body.

American Names. Stephen Vincent Benét. APT-2; FaBoA; OBAL; OxBA

American Odalisque. Jane Miller. GifTon

American Poem, An. Eileen Myles. WiU

American Poetry. James Bertolino. SpudSo

American Poetry. Louis Simpson. FaBoA; NOBA; NoAM; TAP

American Pragmatist Fell in Love, The. Tom Devaney. AmPoNex

American Primitive. William Jay Smith. InPK-6; MoAmPo; OxBSP; PAI; RaBo; TwCP

American Rain. Marilyn Chin. OpBo

American Rhapsody. Kenneth Fearing. APT-2; MoAmPo

American River Sky Alcohol Father. Jean Valentine. ExTi

American Roadside Elegy, An. Dave Jeddie Smith. EmeKit

American's a hustler, for he says so, The. Ballad of Abbreviations, A. Gilbert Keith Chesterton. NOBL

American's Apostrophe to Boz, The. William Edmonstoune [*or* Edmondstoune] Aytoun.
"We received thee warmly—kindly—though we knew thou wert a quiz." OBCoV

American Soldier, The. Philip Freneau. TAP

American Solitude. Grace Schulman. PoSol

American Son. Mitsuye Yamada. UnSA

American Sonnet (10). Wanda Coleman. NAAAL

American Sonnets for My Father. Daniela Gioseffi. UnSA

American Spring Song. Sherwood Anderson. APT-1

American Standard. David Baratier. AmPoNex

American Sublime, The. Wallace Stevens. FaBoA

American Tourist. B. C. Ramachandra Sharma. OMIP, *tr.* by A. K. Ramanujan

American Tradition. William Wordsworth. CenSon *Fr.* River Duddon [A Series of Sonnets], The.

American Tragedy. Joe Bolton. AmPoNex

American Trains. Reginald Gibbons. GM

American Traveller, The. "Orpheus C. Kerr." OBAL

American Twilights, 1957. James Wright (1927–80). CoAP

American Variation on How Rilke Loved a Princess and Got to Stay in Her Castle. Alan Dugan. BodElec

American who would have preferred / to be merely an Indian. (LL) Mr. Brodsky. Charles Tomlinson. NoAM; OxBC

Americana. Sam Witt. NeAmPo

Americana 3. Carl Rakosi. APT-2

Americanized. Bruce Dawe. CBAP

Americans in 1933–4–5–6–7–8–, Etc. Merrill Moore. FaBoA

Amerigo has his finger on the pulse of China. Composed Near the Bay Bridge (after a wild party). Marilyn Chin. ExTi

Amhrán na mBréag. Pearse Hutchinson. PBCIP

Amid dancing and. Kalamu ya Salaam. SpirFl *Fr.* New Orleans Haiku.

Amid the cares of married strife. Tell Her So. *Unknown.* PoToHe

Amid the holy weather of winter, one speaks. Snow. George Dillon. IllVoic

Amid the hush of the distant hills which house. Gettysburg. Edgar Lee Masters. CBCWP

Amid the medley of ironic things. Cage, The. Rosamund Marriott Watson. VWP

Amid the turbulent waters. Turbulent Water, The. *Unknown.* TAL

Amid these clear and windy hills. In Praise of California Wines. Yvor Winters. APT-2

Amid these fragments of heroic days. Sonnet. James Russell Lowell. NCAP

Amid this fearful trance, a thundering sound. William Falconer. ECEV *Fr.* Shipwreck, The.

Amid this hot green glowing gloom. Interlude. Dame Edith Sitwell. MoBrPo

Amidst a smoking desolation. Vladislav Felitsianovich Khodasevich. TCRP

Amidst bamboo, gate pulled shut. Nodding Off. Kao Ch'i. CoBLCP, *tr. by* Jonathan Chaves

Amidst high weeds that in rank plenty grew. (LL) Philip Freneau. NAAL-3; TCAPo *Fr.* House of Night, The.

Amidst our troubles, a sudden blessing. Ghazal: Comet. Jacqueline Osherow. ExTi

Amidst the notes. Akiko Yosano. OHMPJ

Amiens's Song. William Shakespeare. AWP; GTBS-P; NAEL-5v1; NOBE; NoSic; OBEV; SCGP *Fr.* As You Like It.

Amiens's Song. William Shakespeare. AWP; GTBS-P; NAEL-5v1; NoSic; OBEV; SCGP; TTTS; UnPo *Fr.* As You Like It.

Amin, you came to Iraq, wanting to see. Poem to al-Raihani. Ma'ruf Al-Rasafi. MAP, *tr. by* Issa Boullata and Christopher Middleton

Aminta. Torquato Tasso.
    "Blest age! when ev'ry purling stream." BASC, *tr. by* Aphra Behn
    Golden Age, The. AWP; OBVE, *tr. by* Leigh Hunt
    Golden Age, The. A Paraphrase on a Translation out of French. BASC, *tr. by* Aphra Behn
    "O lovely age of gold!" AWP; OBVE, *tr. by* Leigh Hunt

Amish, The. John Updike. OBAL

Amish Rug, An. Michael Longley. CIP-2; PNI

Amití Amoureuse. Gregorio Scalise. ItPo, *tr. by* Gayle Ridinger

Amnesia. Bruce Weigl. CDa

Amnesiac. Mark Osaki. CDa

Amnesty. "Ivan Venediktovich Elagin." TCRP; TCRusP, *tr. by* Bertram D. Wolfe

Amoeba named Sam, and his brother, An. Limerick: "Amoeba named Sam, and his brother, An." *Unknown.* PeLi

Among. William Carlos Williams. *See* Among / of / green

Among a race high-handed, strong of heart. Non-Combatant, The. Sir Henry John Newbolt. FaBoWar

Among black trees. Olga Popova. ItGoST, *tr. by* J. Kates

Among branches. Gray Glove. Roo Borson. NOBC

Among green shades and flowering ghosts, the remembrances of love. Two Fires, The. Judith Wright. MoBrPo

Among Hawks. Lance Henson. VoR

Among His Books. Edith Nesbit. NOBVV

    (Silent room—grey with a dusty blight, A.) PEW

Among His Books. Robert Southey. *See* Scholar, The

Among men who do not love her, linger here. (LL) Composed by the Sea-Side, near Calais, August, 1802. William Wordsworth. CenSon; Son

Among moon gazers. Basho. SoOfWa, *tr. by* Sam Hamill

Among mortal petals-and-leaves / light. (LL) Iris. Muriel Rukeyser. APSN; ColAP

Among mosquitoes. Mary Kinzie. FFC

Among My Friends. Robert Duncan. CLPP; HarvBoo

Among my friends love is a great sorrow. Among My Friends. Robert Duncan. CLPP; HarvBoo

Among my people. (LL) Prologue: "I have come down." Odia Ofeimun. HBAPE; NAfrP

Among My Souvenirs. Edgar Leslie. ReLy

Among my thoughts I count it wonderful. Guido Guinicelli. EaItPo, *tr. by* Dante Gabriel Rossetti

Among Myths and Specters of the Future. Gabriella Leto. CItWP, *tr. by* Cinzia Sartini Blum and Lara Trubowitz

Among / of / green. Locust Tree in Flower, The. William Carlos Williams. Spl; TTTS

Among pelagian travellers. On the Circuit. W. H. Auden. NOBL; OxBTC

Among Philistines. R. S. Gwynn. RA

Among rocks and valleys. Muso Soseki. EaWin, *tr. by* W. S. Merwin

Among Saga's / Tall weeds. Masaoka Shiki. ZenPo, *tr. by* Takashi Ikemoto and Lucien Stryk

Among School Children. W. B. Yeats. CABP; GTBS-P; HAP; HarvBoo; MoBrPo; NAEL-5v2; NAEL-6v2; NAWM-7v2; NIL-7; NIP-4; NOBE; NPeEn; NoAM; NoP-4; OxBEV; OxBTC; PoE; PoPoPo; SCGP; TFi; TRP

Among snake-patterned swords Weland tasted sorrow. Deor. *Unknown.* EBEV

Among snake-patterned swords Weland tasted sorrow. *Unknown. See* Weland, that dauntless man, well learned to bear [*or* well knew about exile]

Among some hills there dwelt in parody. Song of Absinthe Granny, The. Ruth Stone. NALW

Among Strangers. Silvia Curbelo. OPRER

Among Strangers. William Stafford. NNaP

Among the ancient tombs both high and low. On an Ancient Tomb East of the Village. Po Chü-i. TAL

Among the barley stalks. Tesshi. JDP, *tr. by* Yoel Hoffmann

Among the Berkshire Hills. Henrietta Cordelia Ray. CBWP-3

Among the blest [*or* blessed] in endless joys remain. (LL) On My Dear Grandchild Simon Bradstreet, [Who Died on 16TH November, 1669, Being But A Month And One Day Old]. Anne Bradstreet. NAAL-2v1; NAAL-3; SCAP

Among the bumblebees in red-top hay, a freckled field of brown-eyed. Adelaide Crapsey. Carl Sandburg. APT-1

Among the clamor the single shout. Song. Blanca Wiethüchter. TANSG, *tr. by* Shaun Griffin and Emma Sepúlveda-Pulvirenti

Among the crevices of the rocks. (LL) Mid-day. "H. D." APT-1; NAAL-5

Among the crooked lanes, on every hedge. James Thomson. NPeEn *Fr.* Seasons, The.

Among the dancers I beheld her dance. Albertuccio della Viola. EaItPo, *tr. by* Dante Gabriel Rossetti

Among the dead we come. *Unknown.* PGA

Among the deepening shades. (LL) W. B. Yeats. NoAM; PoE; SCGP

Among the drinking doves, Galla Placidia. Rossana Ombres. PeFWW *Fr.* Excursion to Ravenna of A Young Girl with Her Parents.

Among the faults we in that book descry. Cino da Pistoia. EaItPo, *tr. by* Dante Gabriel Rossetti

Among the favorites whom it pleased me well. William Wordsworth. NAEL-6v2 *Fr.* Prelude, The; Growth of a Poet's Mind [1850 vers.].

Among the Firs. Eugene Lee-Hamilton. NOBVV

Among the first to wake. What wakes with me? Study, A. Alice Thompson Meynell. VWP

Among the glittering stars your voices named. (LL) Post-Script: for Gweno. Alun Lewis. AngWePo; BoLoP; GTBS-P

Among the grains how small you were. Anasphere: Le torse antique. Christopher Middleton. HarvBoo

Among the greatest plagues, one is the third day ague. Of Scolding Wives and the Third Day Ague. Henricus Selyns. AiP; SCAP

Among the green slim reeds. (LL) Snake Trying, The. W. W. Eustace Ross. MoCV; NOBC

Among the heaps of brick and plaster lies. Charles Reznikoff. APT-2

Among the Hebrides. Emily Jane Pfeiffer. ViWPN

Among the high-branching, leafless boughs. View from an Attic Window, The. Howard Nemerov. CoAP; CoAmPo

Among the Hills. John Greenleaf Whittier.
    Prelude: "Along the roadside, like the flowers of gold." APN-1; NAAL-2v1; OxBA
    (Prelude to *Among the Hills*.) NAAL-3

Among the iodoform, in twilight-sleep. Leg, The. Karl Shapiro. HAP; MoAmPo; UnPo; WeW-3

Among the later dinosaurs. Pachycephalosaurus. Richard Armour. ChAP

Among the leaves the small birds sing. W. H. Auden. BBASP; TrCP *Fr.* Horae Canonicae.

Among the lilies, and forgetting them. (LL) Obscure Night of the Soul, The. Saint John of the Cross. AWP; OBMV, *tr. by* Arthur Symons

Among the Luminals. Walter Lowenfels. APT-2 *Fr.* Elegy in the Manner of a Requiem in Memory of D.H. Lawrence.

Among the men and women the multitude. Among the Multitude. Walt Whitman. APN-1; CAGL

Among the Multitude. Walt Whitman. APN-1; CAGL

Among the Narcissi. Sylvia Plath. FaBoMo; RB; SCV

Among the orchard weeds, from every search. Hen's Nest. John Clare. Son

Among the other children playing. Ugly Girl, The. Nikolai Alekseievich Zabolotsky [*or* Zabolotskii]. TCRP, *tr. by* Daniel Weissbort

Among the oxen (like an ox I'm slow). Nativity, The. Clive Staples Lewis. ChIV-2; TrCP

Among the pickled foetuses and bottled bones. Ezra Pound. MoAmPo *Fr.* Hugh Selwyn Mauberley (Life and Contacts).

Among the pines—White Stone Slope. Yang Shih-ch'i. CoBLCP, *tr. by* Jonathan Chaves *Fr.* Intendant Yao Shan Has Requested Six Poems on Living in the Mountains, The.

Among the pitiful dicotyledons. Ants, The. Svetlana Kekova. ItGoST, *tr. by* Judith Hemschemeyer

Among the plovers and the stonechats. Of Difference Does It Make. Tom Paulin. BiHa

Among the primary rocks. Forest, The. Miroslav Holub. PoSu, *tr. by* George Theiner

Among the rain. Great Figure, The. William Carlos Williams. AiP; HeIP-4; InPK-6; NoAM; SAmP; TTTS

Among the red words that drink his voice. (LL) Yuba City School. Chitra Divakaruni. GeoHom; LTA; OpBo

Among the Rocks. Robert Browning. OxBSP *Fr.* James Lee's Wife.

Among the rocks. At the Cemetery, Walnut Grove Plantation, South Carolina, 1989. Lucille Clifton. LoL

Among the Roman love-poets, possession. Note on Propertius I.5. Fleur Adcock. BoLoP; PeNZ

Among the shades I heard my father's father. Horace Gregory. APT-2 *Fr.* Chorus for Survival.

Among the smoke and fog of a December afternoon. Portrait of a Lady. T. S. Eliot. APT-1; TwCP

Among the smooth hills of Manika. Magwere, Who Waits Wondering. Kingsley Fairbridge. PeSAV

Among the splendour of torches of darkness, shedding darkness on the lost bride and her groom. (LL) Bavarian Gentians. D. H. Lawrence. CABP; FaBoCh; FaBoMo; GTBS-P; HAP; HarvBoo; InPK-6; NAEL-5v2; NAEL-6v2; NOBE; NPeEn; NoAM; NoP-4; OxBEV; PAI; PoE; PoPoPo; TFi; TRP; TTTS

Among the springs which flow from Ida's head. *Unknown, formerly at. to* Homer. OBVE *Fr.* Hymn to Venus, The.

Among the swells, the storm past, surfers sit. At Will Robers Beach. Timothy Steele. WeW-3

Among the taller wood with ivy hung. Vixen, The. John Clare. RB

Among the things mother told me. Two Angels, The. Sharif Elmusa. GraLe

Among the Vertues Intellectual. Lady Diana Primrose. EMWP *Fr.* Chain of Pearl, A.

Among the yeomen's sons on my estate. *Unknown.* CAGL *Fr.* Don Leon.

Among them marble where the man may lie. Thurn, A. John Berryman. NOBA

Among them too are the Muses. Pindar. WoPoe, *tr. by* Padraic Fallon *Fr.* Pythian Odes.

Among these arthritic contours. Cae Iago: May Day. Roland Mathias. TCAWP

Among these tempests great and manifold. His Hope or Sheet-Anchor. Robert Herrick. CaPo

Among These Trooper of Christs Souldiers, Came. . . Mr. Roger Harlackenden. Edward Johnson. SCAP

Among Those Killed in the Dawn Raid Was a Man Aged a Hundred. Dylan Thomas. OxBSo; Son

Among tired men. Urban. Oliver Davies. AngWePo

Among trees / my father was a spruce. Family Photograph. Gerald Vizenor. VoR

Among twenty snowy mountains. Thirteen Ways of Looking at a Blackbird. Wallace Stevens. APT-1; HCAP; HeIP-4; InPK-6; NAAL-2v2; NOBA; NoAM; OWoS; PAI; PoE; RB; SAmP; TAP; TCAPo; TFi

Among us are those who apply. Kiss Tomorrow Goodbye. Marjorie Welish. FTOS

Among us here in this place. (LL) Lady Ise. BoWoP; WoPoe, *tr. by* Irma Brandeis and Etsuko Terasaki

Amongest many kings. Desire of Dominion. Timothy Kendall. NoSic

Amongst the Cliffs. Han Yü. OHMPC, *tr. by* Kenneth Rexroth

Amongst the highly placed. From a German War Primer. Bertolt Brecht. AF

Amongst the leaves so green. (LL) Robin Hood and Allen [*or* Allin] -a-Dale. *Unknown.* ESPB; OxAEP-1

Amongst the poets Dacus numbered is. Sir John Davies. NoSic *Fr.* Epigrams.

Amongst these graves where good men lie. In an Irish Churchyard. "Violet Fane." VWP

Amor America (1400). Pablo Neruda. PoetW, *tr. by* Jack Schmitt

Amor Diving. Marion Lomax. NeBl

Amor Loci. W. H. Auden. NOCV

Amor Mysticus. Sister Marcela de Carpio de San Felix. AWP, *tr. by* John Hay

Amor Vincit Omnia. Edgar Bowers. VCAP

Amores. Ovid.
  Complaisant Swain, The. AWP, *tr. by* F. A. Wright
  "I do not ask—for you are fair." AWP, *tr. by* F. A. Wright
  Ovid in Love.
    "Day being humid and my head, The." WoPoe, *tr. by* Derek Mahon
  Ovid in Love: 2. WoPoe, *tr. by* Derek Mahon
    "This strange sea-going craze began." WoPoe, *tr. by* Derek Mahon
  "She'd looks, she'd style." EroLit, *tr. by* Kenneth McLeish

Amoret. Mark Akenside. OBEV

Amoretti. Edmund Spenser.
  "After so long a race as I have run." CABP
  ("As she doth laugh at me and makes my pain her sport.") (LL) NoP-4
  "Coming [*or* Comming] to kiss[e] her lips [*or* lyps], such grace I found." EBEV; NAEL-5v1; NAEL-6v1; OxBSo; Son
  ("Comming to kisse her lyps, (such grace I found).") NAEL-7v1; PBRV
  ("Doubt which ye misdeem, fair love, is vain, The.") AEP
  "Doubt which ye misdeeme, fayre love, is vaine, The." NAEL-5v1; NAEL-6v1; NAEL-7v1
  (Easter.) NOBE; OBEV; PeECV
  "Fair bosom! fraught with virtue's richest treasure." NIP-4
  ("Fair is my love, when her fair golden hairs.") GSo

"Fair [*or* Fayre] is my love, when her fair [*or* fayre] golden heares." Son
"Fair proud, now tell me, why should fair be proud." Son
"Fair ye be sure, but cruel and unkind." Son
("Fayre is my love, when her fayre golden heares.") NoP-4
(54.) CABP
"Fresh Spring the herald of love's mighty king." AWP; HAP; OBEV; PoE; Son
"Glorious image of the Maker's beauty, The." SacPr; Son
("Happy ye leaves when as those lilly hands.") NAEL-6v1; NAEL-7v1; NoP-4
("Happy ye leaves! whenas those lily hands.") GSo
"I joy to see how in your drawen work." NoP-4; PBRV; PoE
("Like as a huntsman after weary chase.") CABP
("Lyke as a huntsman after weary chace.") NAEL-6v1; NAEL-7v1; NPeEn; NoP-4; PBRV
("Lyke as a ship that through the ocean wyde.") NAEL-6v1; NAEL-7v1
("Men call you fayre, and you doe credit it.") NoP-4
("More then most faire, full of the living fire.") NoP-4
("Most glorious Lord of life, that on this day.") GSo
("Most Glorious Lord of lyfe that on this day.") NAEL-6v1; NAEL-7v1; NPeEn; NoP-4; PeECV
("Most happy letters fram'd by skilfull trade.") NAEL-7v1
("Of this worlds Theatre in which we stay.") NAEL-7v1
("One Day I Wrote Her Name Upon the Strand.") GSo
(75.) CABP
(67.) CABP
Sonnet 1: "Happy ye leaves! whenas those lily hands." EBEV; NAEL-5v1; PoE; Son
(Sonnet 3: 'The sovereign beauty.') AEP
Sonnet 4: "New year, forth looking out of Janus' gate." NoSic
Sonnet 8: "More than most fair [*or* fayre], full of the living fire [*or* fyre]." OxBSo; PoE; Son
(Sonnet 10: 'Unrighteous Lord of Love.') AEP
Sonnet 13: "In That proud port, which her so goodly graceth." Son
Sonnet 15: "Ye tradeful merchants that, with weary toil." HeIP-4; NIP-4; Son
Sonnet 22: "This holy season, fit to fast and pray." PoE
Sonnet 27: "Fair proud, now tell me, why should fair be proud." Son
Sonnet 30: "My love is like to ice, and I to fire." PAI
Sonnet 34: "Like as a ship, that through the ocean wide." NAEL-5v1; PoE
Sonnet 37: "What guile [*or* guyle] is this, that those her golden tresses." NAEL-5v1; NAEL-6v1; PAI; Son
Sonnet 44: "When those renowned noble peers of Greece." PoE
Sonnet 54: "Of this world's Theatre in which we stay." NAEL-5v1; NoP-4
Sonnet 55: "So oft as I her beauty do behold." Son
Sonnet 56: "Fair ye be sure, but cruel and unkind." Son
Sonnet 57. OxBSo
Sonnet 61: "Glorious image of the Maker's beauty, The." SacPr; Son
Sonnet 64: "Coming [*or* Comming] to kiss[e] her lips [*or* lyps], such grace I found." EBEV; NAEL-5v1; NAEL-6v1; OxBSo; Son
Sonnet 65: "Doubt which ye misdeeme, fayre love, is vaine, The." NAEL-5v1; NAEL-6v1; NAEL-7v1
(Sonnet 65: 'The doubt which ye misdeem.') AEP
Sonnet 67: "Like a huntsman after weary chase." HeIP-4; NAEL-5v1; PoE; Son
(Sonnet 68: 'Most glorious Lord of Life.') AEP
Sonnet 68: "Most glorious Lord of Life that on this day." ChIV-2; HAP; NAEL-5v1; NOCV; NoSic; PoE; SacPr; Son
Sonnet 70: "Fresh Spring the herald of love's mighty king." AWP; HAP; OBEV; PoE; Son
Sonnet 71: "I joy to see how in your drawen work." NoP-4; PBRV; PoE
Sonnet 72: "Oft when my spirit doth spread her bolder wings." Son
Sonnet 74: "Most happy letters framed by skilfull trade." NAEL-5v1
Sonnet 75: "One day I wrote her name upon the strand." AWP; BoLoP; EBEV; HAP; HeIP-4; NAEL-5v1; NAEL-6v1; NAEL-7v1; NoP-4; NoSic; OxBSo; PAI; PoE; PoPoPo; Son; TFi; WeW-3
Sonnet 76: "Fair bosom! fraught with virtue's richest treasure." NIP-4
Sonnet 77: "Was it a dream, or did I see it plain." NIP-4; OxBSo
Sonnet 78: "Lacking my love, I go from place to place." NoSic
Sonnet 79: "Men call you fair [*or* fayre], and you do[e] credit it." AWP; NAEL-5v1; Son
Sonnet 80. CABP
Sonnet 81: "Fair [*or* Fayre] is my love, when her fair [*or* fayre] golden heares." Son
Sonnet 82: "Joy of my life, full oft for loving you." HeIP-4
Sonnet 89: "Like as the culver on the bared bough." PoE
(Sovereign beauty which I do admire, The.') AEP
"Sweet warrio[u]r, when shall I have peace with you?" OxBSo

("What guyle is this, that those her golden tresses.") NoP-4

("Ye tradefull Merchants that with weary toyle.") NoP-4

Amoris Victima. Arthur Symons.

"And yet, there was a hunger in your eyes." PeVV

Amorous Leander, beautiful and young. Christopher Marlowe. CAGL *Fr.* Hero and Leander.

Amorous maiden antique, An. Limerick: "Amorous maiden antique, An." *Unknown.* PeLi

Amorous Neptune. Christopher Marlowe. NOBE *Fr.* Hero and Leander.

Amorous Sonnet Defining Love. Francisco de Quevedo y Villegas. BLPSL, *tr.* by Rene de Costa, Rigas Kappatos and Eleni Paidoussi

Amos. Bible, *O.T.*

O Ye That Would Swallow the Needy. TrJP

Amours de Voyage. Arthur Hugh Clough. NOBVV

Claude to Eustace. PeLV

Claude to Eustace—*from Bellagio.* FaBoVe

Claude to Eustace: "I am in love, meantime, you think; no doubt you would think so." FaBoVe; NPeEn

Claude to Eustace: "These are the facts. The uncle, the elder brother, the squire." FaBoVe

Claude to Eustace: "Yes, we are fighting at last, it appears. This morning, as usual." EBVV; NPeEn; OxAEP-2; PeVV

"Dear Eustatio, I write that you may write me an answer." EBVV; FaBoVe; OxAEP-2

"Dear Miss Roper, It seems, George Vernon, before we left Rome, said." FaBoVe

"Dulce it is, and *decorum*, no doubt, for the country to fall, to." EBVV; FaBoWar; OxAEP-2

Georgina Trevellyn to Luisa: "Dearest Louisa, Enquire if you please about Mr. Claude." FaBoVe

"I have but one chance left,—and that is going to Florence." FaBoVe

"Is it illusion? or does there a spirit from perfecter ages." EBEV; OxAEP-2

"It is most curious to see what a power a few calm words." NPeEn

"Luther, they say, was unwise; he didn't see how things were going." FaBoVe

Mary Trevellyn to Miss Roper. FaBoVe

"Now supposing the French or the Neopolitan soldier." PeLV

"Only think, dearest Louisa, what fearful scenes we have witnessed!" EBVV; NPeEn

Rome. EBVV; OxAEP-2

"Rome disappoints me still; but I shrink and adapt myself to it." EBVV; OxAEP-2

"So, I have seen a man killed!" EBVV; NPeEn; PeVV

Spirit from Perfecter Ages. EBEV; OxAEP-2

"When God makes a great Man he intends all others to crush him." OBSV

Amparo. Federico García Lorca. SpanPo, *tr.* by Rachel Benson and Robert O'Brien

Amparo. Amparo. Federico García Lorca. SpanPo, *tr.* by Rachel Benson and Robert O'Brien

Amphibious Crocodile. John Crowe Ransom. FuPo; OBAL

Amphitryon. Dryden.

(Mercury's Song [to Phaedra].) NOSC; OxBSP

Song: "Fair Iris I love, and hourly I die." AWP

Amphora, The. Fyodor [*or* Fiodor] Kuz'mich Sologub. AWP, *tr.* by Babette Deutsch and Avrahm Yarmolinsky

Ample make this Bed. Emily Dickinson. MoAmPo; NAAL-2v1; NAAL-3; OxBA; WoPoe

Ample the air above the western peaks. After Nightfall. William Renton. NOBVV

Amputated husband, The. Downtown Sunday. Robert Crawford. OPRER

Amsterdam. Jean Garrigue. TAP

Amsterdam. Francis Jammes. AWP, *tr.* by Jethro Bithell

Amsterdam Chronicle. Rein Bloem. TuT, *tr.* by John Hughes

Amsterdam Letter. Jean Garrigue. VCAP

Amulet. Ted Hughes. NOxBChV

Amulet. Carl Rakosi. APT-2

Amulet, The. Isaac Rosenberg.

"Slime clung, The." PeFWW

Amusedly, among the ancient Dead. (LL) Sonnet: "Oh! Death will find me, long before I tire." Rupert Brooke. NoP-4; PoRA

Amusing myself with rocks, I sit peering into the valley. Temple of Bequeathed Love, The. Po Chü-i. CoBCP, *tr.* by Burton Watson

Amusing Our Daughters. Carolyn Kizer. VCAP; VGW

Amyd the wod his modir met thame tway. Virgil [*or* Vergil]. OBVE, *tr.* by Gawin [*or* Gavin] Douglas *Fr.* Aeneid [*or* Eneados, *Aeneis*], The.

Amymone. Rufinus. GrAn, *tr.* by Alan Marshfield

An' a rogue is married to, etc. (LL) Sergeant's Weddin', The. Rudyard Kipling. OBCoV; OxBTC

An' de walls come tumblin' down. (LL) Joshua Fit de Battle of Jericho [*or ob* Jerico]. *Unknown.* APN-2; BPo; NOBA; TAP

An' get hame my rantin laddie. (LL) Baron o [*or of*] Leys, The. *Unknown.* ESPB; OxBB

An heavenly music, furred with praise. (LL) Upon a Wasp Chilled [*or* Child] with Cold. Edward Taylor. NAAL-2v1; NAAL-3; NAAL-5; NOBA; NOCV; OxBEV

An' him chucks on some riddim. Riddim an' Hardtimes. Lillian Allen. WaCA

Historic Moment, An. William J. Harris. KaS

An noo he's king ower a' his ain. (LL) King Orfeo. *Unknown.* ESPB; OxBB; OxBoLi

An' raise dat rucus to-night. (LL) Raise a "Rucus" To-Night. *Unknown.* BPo; TAP

An' so it seems it is reported. Young Lass's Soliloquy, A. Rebekah Carmichael. ECWP

An' so ole Tho'nton bounced you. Turncoat, The. Priscilla Jane Thompson. CBWP-2

An' thank en, I do veel a little shy. (LL) False Friends-like. William Barnes. NOBVV; NPeEn; OxBSo

An' the Crucified maun bleed. (LL) Innumerable Christ, The. Hugh MacDiarmid. EBEV; HarvBoo; OxAEP-2; OxBS

An' the dawn comes up like thunder outer China 'crost the Bay! (LL) Mandalay. Rudyard Kipling. BRP; HarvBoo; MoBrPo; NOBE; NPeEn; OxAEP-2

An' then she made the lasses, O. (LL) Green Grow the Rashes [A Fragment]. Robert Burns. CTC; NAEL-5v2; NAEL-6v2; NoP-4; OxAEP-2; PeLV; SCGP

An' there's no discharge in the war! (LL) Boots. Rudyard Kipling. BRP; MoBrPo

An' Tommy ain't a bloomin' fool—you bet that Tommy sees! (LL) Tommy. Rudyard Kipling. CABP; EBEV; FaBoWar; MoBrPo; NoP-4; OBWP; OxAEP-2; OxBTC; PeVV; UV

An' tryin' to be good. (LL) Favorite Slave's Story, The. Priscilla Jane Thompson. CBWP-2; RACG

Anabaptist, The. Rowland Watkyns. BASC

Anabasis. "St.-John Perse."

Anabasis. OBVE

"Such is the way of the world." OBVE

("Such is the way of the world and I have nothing but good to say of it.") PFTM-1

Anabasis. "St.-John Perse." OBVE *Fr.* Anabasis.

Anacapa. Abigail Albrecht. GeoHom

Anacreon. Johann Wilhelm Ludwig Gleim. GePo, *tr.* by George C. Schoolfield

Anacreon. Friedrich von Hagedorn. GePo, *tr.* by George C. Schoolfield

Anacreon's Dove. Samuel Johnson. AWP

Anacreon's Grave. Goethe. STV, *tr.* by John Frederick Nims

Anacreontic. Austin Clarke. NOIV

Anacreontic. R. S. Gwynn. RA

Anacreontic. Robert Herrick. CaPo; OxBoLi

Anacreontic. Robert Herrick. CaPo

Anacreontic. Robert Herrick. CavPo

(Anacreontic.) CavPo

(We may / See erected.) (LL) CavPo

Anacreontic. John Thelwall. NOBRP

Anacreontic, on Parting with a Little Child. Samuel Wesley. NOEC

Anacreontic to Flip. Royall Tyler. OBAL

Anacreontic[k] Verse. Robert Herrick. PeLV

Anactoria. Algernon Charles Swinburne. RACG

Anadarko John. Carroll Arnett. VoR

Anaesthesia. Jean Valentine. TAP

Anagram. George Herbert. ChIV-2; GeHe

Anagram, An. *Unknown.* TCAPo

Anagram Born of Madness at Czernowitz, 12 November 1920. Norman Dubie. BodElec

Anagrammic scramble. Scourge / of sound. Alphabet of Ahtt. Nathaniel Mackey. FTOS

Anahorish. Seamus Heaney. HarvBoo; PBCIP

Anaktoria. Sappho. WoPoe, *tr.* by Guy Davenport

Analogue. Marie Ponsot. CLPP

Analogy. Brian Higgins. FaBoTw

Analogy. János Székely. IQMS, *tr.* by George Gömöri

Analysands. Dudley Randall. BPo

Analysis. Syl Cheney-Coker. NAfrP

Anamorphosis Eisenhower. Sam Truitt.

"But her favorite poems take place underwater." AmPoNex

"In Geneva I pawned my pocket watch and passport." AmPoNex

Kerf, The. AmPoNex

Old World Monkeys. AmPoNex

Anarchy and grow your own. Durham. Tony Harrison. NoAM

Anasazi drink from underground rivers, The. David Ferry. FaBoA

Anasphere: Le torse antique. Christopher Middleton. HarvBoo

Anastasia and Sandman. Larry Levis. BAP-97

Anastasia McLaughlin. Tom Paulin. PBCIP

Anastasia, the Graces blossom and you were their flower. Julianus of Egypt. GrAn

Anathema. Maranatha! John Wheelwright. APT-2

Anathemata, The. David Jones.

    Angle-Land. HarvBoo

    "Did he meet Lud at the Fleet Gate? did count the top." EBEV

    "Did he strike soundings off Vecta Insula?" HarvBoo; NoAM

    "Ship's master:/ before him, in the waist and before it." FaBoTw; WoPoe

    "We already and first of all discern him making this thing other." PeECV

Anatomy Lesson. Jack Coulehan. BloBone

Anatomy of Departure. Elizabeth Garrett. NeBl

Anatomy of Happiness, The. Ogden Nash. TAP

Anatomy of Humor, The. Morris Gilbert Bishop. NBLV

Anatomy of Melancholy, The. Robert Burton.

    Authors [or Author's] Abstract of Melancholy, The. NOSC

    "When I go[e] musing all alone." NOSC

Anatomy [or Anatomie] of the World, An[: The First Anniversary]. John Donne.

    First Anniversary [or Anniversarie], The.

    "And new philosophy calls all in doubt." NOSC

    ("World's infection, to be none of it, The.") (LL) NAEL-5v1; NAEL-6v1; NAEL-7v1

Ancapagari. Carolyn Forché. YaYoPo

Ancestor. Thomas Kinsella. BIrV; ModIr; NOIV; NPeEn; OxBEV; PBCIP; PoE

    (I was going up to say something.) NoP-4

Ancestor Worship. Emyr Humphreys. AngWePo

Ancestors. Raymond Garlick. AngWePo

Ancestors. Rowley Habib. PeNZ

Ancestors. Dudley Randall. BPo

Ancestral Burden. Alfonsina Storni. TCLAP, tr. by Andrew Rosing

Ancestral Echoes/Rap Music. Charles Lynch. SwNoth

Ancestral Faces. Kwesi Brew. PBA

Ancestral Houses. W. B. Yeats. OBGa Fr. Meditations in Time of Civil War.

Ancestral Messengers/Composition 13. Ntozake Shange. GT

Ancestral Weight. Alfonsina Storni. WPOW, tr. by Marti Moody and Kate Flores

Anchises, Paris, and Adonis too. Spoken by Venus on Seeing Her Statue Done by Praxiteles. Unknown. FaBoEE

Anchor, The. John Blight. BMAP

Anchor at Hampton Roads we lay, An. Cumberland, The. Henry Wadsworth Longfellow. CBCWP

Anchor: I must fight with the waves whipped up by the wind. Cynewulf. ASW Fr. Riddles (Exeter Book).

Anchor: "Oft I must strive with wind and wave." Cynewulf. AnOE, tr. by Charles W. Kennedy Fr. Riddles (Exeter Book).

Anchorage. Joy Harjo. HATNAP; LTA; OPRER

Anchorage, The. Mark Wunderlich. NeAmPo

Anchored now to Neptune's temple floor, this. Dedication, A. Macedonius. GrAn, tr. by Adrian Wright

Anchored on the Chin-huai River, the rain has vanished. Tune: "Magnolia Blossoms, Slow"—Traveling on the Yangtze. Chiang Ch'un-lin. SuSp, tr. by Bruce Carpenter

Anchorsmiths, The. Charles Dibdin. NOEC

Ancient Airs. Li Po. CrYelRi, tr. by Sam Hamill

Ancient Airs. Li Po. SuSp, tr. by Joseph J. Lee

    (Ancient Air.) BLT

    (Westward over Lotus Mountain.) BLT

Ancient annals strewn left and right. Occasional Poem. Han Yü. SuSp, tr. by Charles Hartman

Ancient Autumn. Charles Simic. ColAP

Ancient Barbarossa, the Kaiser Frederick old, The. Barbarossa. Friedrich Rückert. AWP, tr. by Elizabeth Craigmyle

Ancient biologist, Heine, An. Limerick: "Ancient biologist, Heine, An." Carol Rumens. PeLi

Ancient borassus palms, masculine and feminine. Two Trees. Grace Schulman. ExTi

Ancient chestnut's blossoms threw, An. Alciphron and Leucippe. Walter Savage Landor. OBEV

Ancient Couple on Lu Mountain, The. Mark Van Doren. VGW

Ancient Custom, An. Anatoly Steiger. TCRusP, tr. by John Glad

Ancient Evenings. Michael Hofmann. EmeKit

Ancient exalted seed-scatterer whom time gave no progenitor. Maker on High, The. Columba, Saint. NePenScot, tr. by Edwin Morgan

Ancient Feeling. Wu Wei-yeh. CoBLCP, tr. by Jonathan Chaves

Ancient Gesture, An. Edna St. Vincent Millay. NALW; NIL-7

Ancient Greek Song of Exile. Felicia Dorothea Hemans. RWP

Ancient Gypsy, The. Mihály Vörösmarty. IQMS, tr. by Peter Zollman

Ancient History. Arthur Guiterman. KaS; OBCA

Ancient History. Siegfried Sassoon. ChIV-1

Ancient "Kayán," The. Endre Ady. IQMS, tr. by Watson Kirkconnell

Ancient Lights. Austin Clarke. BIrV

Ancient Masters were profound and subtle, The. Lao Tzu. EnlH Fr. Tao Te Ching.

Ancient Monuments. John Ormond. AngWePo; OBWVE

Ancient Music. Ezra Pound. HeIP-4; NBLV; OBAL; OBCoV; OxBA; PeLV; TCAPo; UV

Ancient nomadic snowman has rolled around. Snowman, The. Patricia K. Page. NOBC

Ancient of Days. William Croswell Doane. AH

Ancient of Days, old friend, no one believes you'll come back. Stone Canyon Nocturne. Charles Wright. ColAP; GeoHom; HCAP; LCAP-2; VCAP

Ancient One, Wise One, Old Mother. Cicada. Eclipse. HW

Ancient Ones, The. Patricia Reis. HW

Ancient Ones, The: Betátakin. Janet Lewis. APT-2

Ancient Origin. Muso Soseki. EaWin, tr. by W. S. Merwin

Ancient pages of the Talmud. Talmud, The. Simeon Grigoryevich Frug. TrJP, tr. by Alice Stone Blackwell

Ancient person, for whom I. Song of a Young Lady to Her Ancient Lover, A. John Wilmot, 2d Earl of Rochester. BASC; BoLoP; EBEV; NOSC; NPeEn; NoP-4; OxAEP-1; OxBEV

Ancient person of my heart. (LL) Song of a Young Lady to Her Ancient Lover, A. John Wilmot, 2d Earl of Rochester. BASC; BoLoP; EBEV; NOSC; NPeEn; NoP-4; OxAEP-1; OxBEV

Ancient Pistol, peacock Payne. Tennyson. FaBoEE

Ancient poets ne'er did dream, The. James McIntyre. VerBaPo Fr. Oxford Cheese Ode.

Ancient pool. Sound. Basho. KaS

Ancient Revisits, An. Laura Riding Jackson. APT-2

Ancient Rites of the Condoling Council. Unknown.

    "Tehkarihhoken! / Continue to listen!" APN-2

Ancient saga tells us how, An. Dead Cow Farm. Robert Graves. FaBoWar; PoWW

Ancient Sage, The. Tennyson. SacPr

Ancient Signs. Edward Hirsch. TaR

Ancient silent pond. Basho. WoPoe, tr. by John S. Major

Ancient Song, An. Marina Ivanovna Tsvetayeva [or Tsvetaeva]. TCRusP, tr. by John Glad

Ancient Song of a Woman of Fez, An. Unknown. BoWoP, tr. by Willis Barnstone

Ancient spring year after year abides. Temple of the Orchid Fragrance Goddess. Li Ho. SuSp, tr. by Michael Fish

Ancient terror burns in things, a deep and secret sigh, An. As the Great Days Flow. Enrique Molina. TCLAP, tr. by Naomi Lindstrom

Ancient to Ancients, An. Thomas Hardy. GTBS-P; OxBTC; SCGP

Ancient Wisdom, Rather Cosmic. Ezra Pound. NOBA

Ancientest of cats, truest. Hoppy. Reginald Gibbons. DiPo

Ancientness surrounds me. Death. Patty L. Harjo. VoR

Ancients happily could sing, The. Our Naughty Time. Friedrich von Logau. GePo, tr. by George C. Schoolfield

Ancients lie buried under barren hills, The. Occasional Poem, A. Lu Yu. SuSp, tr. by Chiang Yee

Ancients of the World, The. Ronald Stuart Thomas. OPOU; RB

Ancre at Hamel: Afterwards, The. Edmund Charles Blunden. PeFWW

And. Robert Creeley. LCAP-2

And. Desire. Kurt Schwitters. PFTM-1

And a certaine Priest comming that way. Luke 10. Richard Crashaw. SacPr

And a child I slept. (LL) View from an Attic Window, The. Howard Nemerov. CoAP; CoAmPo

And a cruel wind blows. (LL) End of Summer. Stanley Kunitz. LoL; MoAmPo; VGW

And a faggot of useless memories. (LL) Louis MacNeice. BIrV; CIP-2; ModIr; PNI Fr. Autumn Journal.

And a father's love add up to silence. (LL) Story, A. Li-Young Lee. LoL; RaBo

And a fool, and a smart one, a miser. Bakhyt Kenjeev. ItGoST, tr. by Nina Kossman

And a glass of brandy neat. (LL) Sweeney Erect. T. S. Eliot. OxBTC; VGW

And a green coat covers me all. (LL) Walnut, A. Mother Goose. LB; OxNR; ReMoGo

And a green gown. (LL) Daffadowndilly. Mother Goose. NTCP; OxNR

And a hundred storks perch on the sun's right hand. (LL) Among Those Killed in the Dawn Raid Was a Man Aged a Hundred. Dylan Thomas. OxBSo; Son

And a man with his back to the East. (LL) Unwelcome. Mary Elizabeth Coleridge. OBEV; VWP; WPE

And a pond edged with grayish leaves. (LL) Neutral Tones. Thomas Hardy. CABP; EBVV; HAP; HeIP-4; InPK-6; MoBrPo; NAEL-5v2; NAEL-6v2; NOBVV; NPeEn; NoAM; TFi; UnPo

And a singe runs through lace and feather. (LL) Utilitarian View of the Monitor's Fight, A. Herman Melville. APN-2; ColAP; NAAL-2v1; NAAL-3; NCAP; UnPo

And a single fishing boat. (LL) Seeking a Mooring. Wang Wei. BoWoP; WPOW

And a smile on the face of the tiger. (LL) Limerick: "There was a young lady of Riga." Cosmo Monkhouse. NIL-7; PeLi

And a stray face spins me back to the black-haired girl. Rain. Jeff Gundy. IllVoic

And a tall tree sprouted from his father's grave. (LL) Truisms, The. Louis MacNeice. NOBE; OBSV; PNI

And a tenth part of Okeanos is given to dark night. Styx. Robert Duncan. VCAP

And a' the glory shall be thine, / Amen! Amen! (LL) Holy Willie's Prayer. Robert Burns. EBEV; NAEL-6v2; NOBRP; NOEC; OBCoV; OBSV; OxBS; PoE; TFi

And a thread of anger snaking from their eyes. (LL) Poem of Return. Jofre Rocha. NAfrP; PBMAP, tr. by Don Burness

And a thread too bright for the eye. (LL) Shroud. George Mackay Brown. NoP-4; RB

And a wasted town. (LL) War Poet. Sidney Keyes. FaBoWar; NoP-4; PoWW

And a whore and a rogue may part when they please. (LL) Oaths. Thomas [or "Tom"] Brown. FaBoEE; OBCoV

And a wig-wag. (LL) Unknown. LB; OxNR

And abortions are hidden. (LL) Edgar Lee Masters. APT-1; FaBoEE; NOBA; OBSV; OxBA; PoE Fr. Spoon River Anthology.

And above all to gaze with innocence. As if nothing would happen. Paths of the Mirror. Alejandra Pizarnik. PFTM-2, tr. by Jason Weiss

And adjust, no one to drive the car. (LL) To Elsie. William Carlos Williams. APT-1; AmFaPo; NAAL-2v2; NAAL-5; NOBA; OxBA; PoE; PoPoPo

And after all a slave sits out the centuries. Ghosts II. Lauris Edmond. PeNZ

And, after all, it is to them we return. Geoffrey Hill. NoAM Fr. Apology for the Revival of Christian Architecture in England, An.

And after all your trapesings, child, lie still! (LL) St. Helena Lullaby, A. Rudyard Kipling. EBEV; FaBoCh; FaBoWar; OBMV

And after singing Psalm the Twelfth. Rochester Extempore. John Wilmot, 2d Earl of Rochester. ChIV-1

And after this it is hard to keep chewing away at our truth. (LL) Ox Looks at Man, An. Carlos Drummond de Andrade. PoetW; TCLAP, tr. by Mark Strand

And after this quick bash in the dark. Portrait of a Young Girl Raped at a Suburban Party. Brian Patten. OxBTC

And afterwards, after the shedding of mucus. Talk with My Cousin Alone, A. Hone Tuwhare. PeNZ

And afterwards, here, in the dark bosom of the darkest river. Men of Dawn, The. Efraín Huerta. TCLAP, tr. by Todd Dampier

And Again. Alison Fell. LW

And again I see the long pouring headland. Return, The. Alistair Campbell. PeNZ

And again Jesus spoke to them in parables, saying. Edwin Arlington Robinson. GI Fr. St. Matthew.

And ages drop in it like rain. (LL) Two Rivers. Ralph Waldo Emerson. APN-1; NCAP; NOBA; OxBA; PoE

And al is thorugh [or thrugh] thy negligence and rape. (LL) Chaucer's Wordes unto Adam, his Owne Scriveyn. Geoffrey Chaucer. NAEL-6v1; NAEL-7v1

And all beset with flowers. (LL) To the Western Wind. Robert Herrick. CaPo; OBEV

And all deceive. (LL) Tomorrow. Anna Laetitia Barbauld. ECWP; PEW

And all dishevelled wandering stars. (LL) Who Goes with Fergus? W. B. Yeats. FaBoCh; InPK-6; NAEL-5v2; NAEL-6v2; NOBE; NOBVV; NoAM; PeVV; PoE; PoRA; TRP

And all her silken flanks with garlands drest. Vlamertinghe. Edmund Charles Blunden. NoP-4; OBWP; PeFWW

And all his fondest wishes, blend with mine. (LL) Previous to her Interview with Phaon. Mary Robinson. CenSon; RWP

And all his island shivered into flowers. (LL) Live Blindly and upon the Hour. Trumbull Stickney. APN-2; TCAPo; WoPoe

And all his Pictures Faded. (LL) Sir Joshua Reynolds. William Blake. FaBoEE; OxBoLi; PeLV

And all is done as I have told. (LL) Mental Traveller, The. William Blake. ChIV-2; NAEL-5v2; NAEL-6v2; PoE; WoPoe

And all is hushed at Shiloh. (LL) Shiloh [A Requiem]. Herman Melville. APN-2; CBCWP; ColAP; NOBA; NoP-4; OBWP; OxBA; SCV; TCAPo

And all is rolled back in the book of days. (LL) Alphabet, The. Karl Shapiro. APT-2; NoAM; TaR

And all is well, though [or tho'] faith and form. Tennyson. NAEL-6v2 Fr. In Memoriam A. H. H.

And all men are at home. (LL) House of Christmas, The. Gilbert Keith Chesterton. ChrPo; MoBrPo; SacPr

And all my hearts in unison strike twelve. (LL) Science of the Night, The. Stanley Kunitz. APT-2; ColAP; MoAmPo; TwCP

And all my pulses beat at once and stop. (LL) Dante Alighieri. AWP; EaItPo, tr. by Dante Gabriel Rossetti Fr. La Vita Nuova.

And all my woe. (LL) Fantasy, A. Mathilde Blind. PoBW; VWP; ViWPN

And all night long we lie in sleep. Boyish sleep. Hamlin Garland. APN-2

And all of wood. Watch it closely. (LL) Monument, The. Elizabeth Bishop. HCAP; NOBA; NoAM; TRP

And all our dead princes. (LL) Epil y Filiast. Harri Webb. AngWePo; TCAWP

And All That Jazz. John Kander. ReLy

And all that mighty heart is lying still! (LL) Composed upon Westminster Bridge, September 3, 1802. William Wordsworth. AWP; CABP; CenSon; ClHu; FaBoCh; GTBS-P; HAP; HeIP-4; ITBLP; InPK-6; MakPoe; NAEL-5v2; NAEL-6v2; NAWM-7v2; NOBRP; NPeEn; NoP-4; OPOU; OxBEV; OxBSo; PoE; SCGP; Son; TFi; UnPo

And all that was taken away! (LL) How I Got That Name. Marilyn Chin. GeoHom; LoL

And all the birds fly out of my scene. (LL) Meeting, The. Muriel Rukeyser. MoAmPo; TrJP

And all the birds in the air couldn't catch me. (LL) Nut Tree, A. Mother Goose. OxBoLi; OxNR; TTTS

And all the comely dress without the paint of art. (LL) Abraham Cowley. BASC; BeJo

And all the great conclusions coming near. (LL) Answers. Elizabeth Jennings. OxBSP; OxBTC

And all the hills echoed [or ecchoed]. (LL) William Blake. AWP; FHYEP; NAEL-5v2; NAEL-6v2; PeLV; RACG; SCGP Fr. Songs of Innocence.

And all the little schoolchildren sat down. (LL) E. E. Cummings. FaBoEE; OBAL

And all the old songs. And nothing to lose. (LL) Emigrant Irish, The. Eavan Boland. AmFaPo; EmeKit

And all the rest but vanity we find. (LL) Vanity of All Worldly Things, The. Anne Bradstreet. ChIV-1; SCAP

And all the summer through the water saunter. (LL) On This Island. W. H. Auden. HarvBoo; NAEL-5v2; NAEL-6v2; OxBEV; PoE

And all the while Duessa wept full bitterly. (LL) Edmund Spenser. FHYEP; NoSic Fr. Faerie Queene, The.

And all the while, he knew there was no river. (LL) Eli, Eli. Judith Wright. BMAP; CBAP; GI

And all the wickedness in this world that man might work or think. William Langland. NOCV Fr. Vision of Piers Plowman, The.

And all the year have some grean Ears. (LL) Love and Discipline. Henry Vaughan. GeHe; SacPr

And all these through her eyes, have stopped [or stopt] her ears [or eares]. (LL) My Picture Left in Scotland. Ben Jonson. BeJo; NAEL-5v1; NAEL-6v1; NAEL-7v1; NPeEn

And all this is folly to the world. (LL) Girl, A. Ezra Pound. MoAmPo; NOxBChV

And all thy sons, O Nature, learn my tale. (LL) Ode to Simplicity. William Collins. NOBE; OBEV; OxAEP-1

And all we flow from, soul in soul. (LL) Tennyson. EBVV; NAEL-6v2 Fr. In Memoriam A. H. H.

And all we need of hell. (LL) My Life Closed Twice. Emily Dickinson. APN-2; BoLoP; BoWoP; HeIP-4; LW; MoAmPo; NAAL-2v1; NAAL-3; NIP-4; NOBA; NoAM; OxBA; OxBSP; SAmP; SCV; SacPr; TCAPo; TFi

And almost gently asks: Are you a Jew?. (LL) First Time, The. Karl Shapiro. APT-2; VGW

And already they are beginning to witness that Armageddon. Armageddon. István Vas. IQMS, tr. by William Jay Smith

And alter with age. (LL) Lockless Door, The. Robert Frost. NOBA; TCAPo

And always take the garbage out! (LL) Sarah Cynthia Sylvia Stout Would Not Take the Garbage Out. Shel [or Shelley] Silverstein. OBCA; OxIBACP

And, always, there is desire. Beyond Having. Ray Gonzalez. TouFir

And anger moment by moment balanced. (LL) To Have without Holding. Marge Piercy. NIL-7; NIP-4

And another child. (LL) Once in a Lifetime, Snow. Les A. Murray. CBAP; NoP-4

And answer, echoes, answer, dying, dying, dying. (LL) Tennyson. AWP; ClHu; EBVV; FHYEP; FaBoCh; GTBS-P; HeIP-4; InPK-6; NAEL-5v2; NoP-4; PeVV; TFi *Fr.* Princess, The.

And answer made King Arthur, breathing hard. Tennyson. PeECV *Fr.* Idylls of the King.

And are gone. (LL) Emplumada. Lorna Dee Cervantes. NoAM; PBCAP

And are they dancing: or gazing at the earth. (LL) Are They Dancing. Edward Dorn. NeAP; PoM

And are ye sure the news is true? There's Nae Luck about the House. Jean Adams. NePenScot

And are ye sure the news is true? Sailor's Wife, The. William Julius Mickle. GTBS-P

And art thou grieved, sweet and sacred Dove. Grieve Not the Holy Spirit, etc. George Herbert. ESCV

And, as a boiling vessel cools once more. West, The. Alphonse Marie Louis de Lamartine. SxFrPo, *tr.* by E. H. Blackmore and A. M. Blackmore

And as at first still lodge him in the manger. (LL) Guest, The. *Unknown.* FaBoCh; PoRA; SacPr; TrCP

And as for Man. Loren C. Eiseley. GM

And as for me, though that I konne [*or* can] but [*or* my wit be] lyte. Geoffrey Chaucer. HeIP-4 *Fr.* Legend of Good Women, The.

And, as he goes, the transient vision mourns. (LL) Winter-Piece, A. Ambrose Philips. NOEC; NPeEn

And as he laboured, his mind ran o'er. Henry Wadsworth Longfellow. FaBoWar *Fr.* Building of the Ship, The.

And as her silver body downeward went. Christopher Marlowe. OxBEV *Fr.* Hero and Leander.

And As I Came Out from the Temples. Joan Murray. YaYoPo

And as I rise slapping my feet. I Wake Thinking of Myself as a Man. Susan Griffin. GLP

And as I walk along, thinking of this. Pleasure Dome, The. Shrikant Verma. OMIP, *tr.* by Vinay Dahrwadker

And, as in well-growne woods, on trees, cold spinie grashoppers. Homer. NPeEn, *tr.* by George Chapman *Fr.* Iliad, The.

And as in winter time when Jove his cold-sharpe javelines throwes. Homer. NPeEn; OBVE *Fr.* Iliad, The.

And as life is to the living, so death is to the dead. (LL) Two Mysteries, The. Mary Mapes Dodge. PWR; TrCP

And as silently steal away. (LL) Day Is Done, The. Henry Wadsworth Longfellow. APN-1; BRP; ChAP; ITBLP; NCAP; NOBA; OxBA; PWR; PoRA; TreFP

And as the world turns, so turns the light. Bryan Ferry. B.D. Love. SwNoth

And as to the meaning, it's what you please. (LL) Ballad: "Auld wife sat at her ivied door, The." Charles Stuart Calverley. CABP; NBLV; OBCoV; OxAEP-2; UV

And as to you Death, and you bitter hug of mortality, it is idle to try to alarm. Walt Whitman. ColAP *Fr.* Song of Myself.

And as we came down the staircase. Valse Oubliée. John Heath-Stubbs. OxBTC

And as we love ourselves we hate our foe. (LL) This Is No Case of Petty Right or Wrong. Edward Thomas. PeFWW; PoWW

And as when with the West-wind's flawes the sea thrusts up her waves. Homer. OBVE *Fr.* Iliad, The.

And ash (not unlike flour) for one small loaf. (LL) Tony Harrison. NAEL-5v2; NAEL-6v2 *Fr.* School of Eloquence, The.

And ask the gods to pardon this clear flame. (LL) Henry David Thoreau. APN-1; ColAP; NOBA; TAP; TCAPo *Fr.* Walden.

And ask them for your name again. (LL) 'Mystery Boy' Looks for Kin in Nashville. Robert Earl Hayden. LCAP-2; NoAM; NoP-4; PoE

And Assemble the engine again' (LL) Dying Airman, The. *Unknown.* OxBoLi; PeLV; RB

And at night light upon his back. (LL) For Freckle-Faced Gerald. Etheridge Knight. BPo; ESEAA

And at the door of the eye. Keorapetse Kgositsile. PBMAP *Fr.* Present is a Dangerous Place to Live, The.

And, at the end, need no Paradise. (LL) Tell Me Now. Wang Chi. ChiP; FaBoCh, *tr.* by Arthur Waley

And at the last I cast my mine eye aside. The Lady of the Arbour. WPE *Fr.* Flower and the Leaf, The.

And at the upper end of that faire rowme. Edmund Spenser. NPeEn *Fr.* Faerie Queene, The.

And at this I was mildly abashed. (LL) Study in Aesthetics, The. Ezra Pound. APT-1; NOBA

And auld Robin Forbes hes gien tem a dance. Auld Robin Forbes. Susanna Blamire. ECWP

And awake, my heart, to be loved; awake, awake! (LL) Awake, My Heart, to Be Loved. Robert Bridges. GTBS-P; MoBrPo; NOBE; OBEV

And away goes the mare. (LL) Start, The. *Unknown.* LB; OxNR

And B, A. Charles Hubert Sisson. OxBC

And bad the world adieu. (LL) Edom o' Gordon. *Unknown.* NePenScot; OxBB

And bake up a few hundred more. (LL) Pancake Collector, The. Jack Prelutsky. OBCA; OxIBACP

And be a friend to man. (LL) House by the Side of the Road, The. Sam Walter Foss. BRP; ITBLP

And be among her cloudy trophies hung. (LL) Ode on Melancholy. John Keats. CABP; FHYEP; HAP; InPK-6; NAEL-5v2; NAEL-6v2; NAWM-7v2; NIL-7; NOBE; NPeEn; NoP-4; OBEV; OxAEP-2; OxBEV; PoE; PoRA; SCGP; TFi

And be anonymous? (LL) Our Hunting Fathers. W. H. Auden. FaBoMo; HarvBoo; NoAM

And be buried in the dust of marching feet. (LL) For Black Poets Who Think of Suicide. Etheridge Knight. HeIP-4; InPK-6; LTA; NAAAL

And be like him and he will then love me. (LL) William Blake. AWP; AmFaPo; CABP; ChAP; FHYEP; HeIP-4; NAEL-5v2; NAEL-6v2; NAWM-7v2; NOBRP; NOEC; NoP-4; OBEV; PeECV; PoE; PoPoPo; SCGP; TFi *Fr.* Songs of Innocence.

And be the mistress of Mankind! (LL) Upon [His] Leaving His Mistress. John Wilmot, 2d Earl of Rochester. BASC; EnLoPo; NBLV; NOSC

And bear awhile—what Death alone can cure! (LL) By the Same. To Solitude. Charlotte Smith. CenSon; RWP

And bearing brilliant and nobel human beings. (LL) To the Tune "The River Is Red." Ch'iu Chin. AiP; BoWoP; ItWoWo, *tr.* by Chung Ling and Kenneth Rexroth

And beat him today. (LL) Jack. Charles Henry Ross. NOxBChV; Spl

And Beaumonts and Bens be his Kellys above. (LL) Oliver Goldsmith. NOEC; NPeEn; OxBEV *Fr.* Retaliation.

"AND BECAUSE IT IS MY HEART." (LL) Stephen Crane. APN-2; MoAmPo; NoP-4; TCAPo *Fr.* Black Riders [and Other Lines], The.

And before existing fade. (LL) Post Card. Guillaume Apollinaire. AF; FaBoWar, *tr.* by Oliver Bernard

And before him you may all rejoyce. Epistle of Love and of Consolation unto Israel, An. Dorothy White. EMWP

And being good for nothing else, be wise. (LL) Disabled Debauchee, The. John Wilmot, 2d Earl of Rochester. BASC; BoLoP; HAP; NAEL-5v1; NAEL-6v1; NAEL-7v1; NOBL; NPeEn; NoP-4; OBSV

And believing she was a maid. Faithless Wife, The. Federico García Lorca. BoLoP, *tr.* by A. L. Lloyd

And beside the moon, a single star. (LL) Jaan Kaplinski. BLT; GifTon; WoPoe, *tr.* by Sam Hamill and Rina Tamm

And Betty's praised for labours not her own. (LL) Pope. EBNV; NOEC *Fr.* Rape of the Lock, The; an Heroi-Comical Poem.

And bid them seek the morn the hills and fields once more. (LL) New Man, The. Jones Very. APN-1; NOBA; TCAPo

And bide with her thou luvis best. (LL) Alexander Scott. NePenScot; OBEV

And bided my time. (LL) Ballad of Nat Turner, The. Robert Earl Hayden. BPo; VGW

And Bidpai said: / the thieves have stormed. Story, The. Muhammad Al-Faituri [*or* Al-Fituri *or* Al-Fayturi]. MAP, *tr.* by Sargon Boulus and Peter Porter

And Bidpai said: / while the clowns laugh. Incident. Muhammad Al-Faituri [*or* Al-Fituri *or* Al-Fayturi]. MAP, *tr.* by Sargon Boulus and Peter Porter

And bids my hair stand up? (LL) Mother of God, The. W. B. Yeats. BBASP; ChIV-2; ChrPo

And binding with briars my joys and desires. (LL) William Blake. AWP; EnLoPo; FHYEP; HAP; NAEL-5v2; NAEL-6v2; NPeEn; NoP-4; OBGa; OxAEP-2; OxBEV; PoE; PoPoPo; RB; SCGP; TFi; TOF; TRP *Fr.* Songs of Experience.

And black Fate took these stubborn spearmen. On the Thessalians Who Fought at Marathon. Aeschylus. GrAn, *tr.* by Edwin Morgan

And blessed be the women who get you through. Robin Morgan. GLP *Fr.* Hallowing of Hell, The.

And blesses all creation with the sun. God Looks on Nature With a Glorious Eye. John Clare. BBASP

And blew. "*Childe Roland to the Dark Tower came.*" (LL) Childe Roland to the Dark Tower Came. Robert Browning. NAEL-5v2; NAEL-6v2; NAWM-7v2; NOBVV; NoP-4; OBNV; PeVV; PoE; PoPoPo

And blights with plagues the Marriage hearse. (LL) William Blake. AWP; CABP; ClHu; FHYEP; HAP; HeIP-4; InPK-6; NAEL-5v2; NAEL-6v2; NAWM-7v2; NIL-7; NIP-4; NOBE; NOBRP; NOEC; NPeEn; NoP-4; OxAEP-2; OxBEV; PoE; PoPoPo; RB; SCGP; SCV; TFi; TRP; UnPo; WeW-3 *Fr.* Songs of Experience.

And blood hangs in the pine-soaked air. (LL) Adolescence—III. Rita Dove. ISC; NAAL-5; NoAM

And bloody Faith the foulest birth of Time. (LL) Feelings of a Republican on the Fall of Bonaparte. Shelley. CenSon; Son

And blossom in purple and red. (LL) Tennyson. EBVV; FHYEP; NOBE; NOBVV; OxAEP-2; OxBEV; PoE; UV; WoPoe *Fr.* Maud [A Monodrama].

And blow the candle out. (LL)   Prophecy. Elinor Wylie.   BoWoP; FaBoWP; ItWoWo; VGW

And blow you all a kiss from the tomb. (LL)   New England Bachelor, A. Richard Eberhart.   MoAmPo; NoAM

And boars root safely along our circumference. (LL)   Sulpicia. Michael Longley.   OxBSo; RACG

And both thy servants be. (LL)   Man. George Herbert.   BASC; ESCV; FSCP; GeHe; NAEL-5v1; NAEL-6v1; NAEL-7v1; NoP-4

And bowing not knowing to what. (LL)   For the Anniversary of My Death. W. S. Merwin.   CoAP; ColAP; HCAP; InPK-6; NAAL-2v2; NOBA; PAI; PoPoPo; VCAP

And braves as he may the night of darkness and tears. (LL)   Winter Nightfall. Robert Bridges.   MoBrPo; OBEV; SCGP

And brick upon grey brick. (LL)   Louis MacNeice.   CIP-2; OxBTC   Fr. Closing Album, The.

And brighter bliss of heaven. (LL)   I Love Thy Kingdom, Lord. Timothy Dwight.   AH; TCAPo

And bring about the collapse of the whole empire. (LL)   Shame. Richard Wilbur.   CoAmPo; EmeKit; FaBoMo; OBCoV; OxBC

And bring them home. (LL)   T'ang Hsien-tsu. CoBLCP; ColAnChi, tr. by Jonathan Chaves   Fr. Twenty-two Quatrains on Receiving the Obituary Notice for my Son Shih-Chü.

And bring to my baby a fresh penny roll. (LL)   Mouse's Lullaby, The. Palmer Cox.   NOxBChV; OBCA; OxIBACP; TLR

And bringe [or brynge] us to his heighe [or hye, or highe] blisse [or blisss]! Amen. (LL)   Geoffrey Chaucer.   FHYEP; NAEL-6v1; NAWM-5v1   Fr. Canterbury Tales, The.

And broad old cesspools glittered in the sun. (LL)   Mouse's Nest. John Clare. InPK-6; NAEL-5v2; NAEL-6v2; NPeEn; PAI; RB

And broken hedge-flowers sweet, mark his impetuous way. (LL)   Reverie, A. Joanna Baillie.   ECWP; WoRP

And brothers give you back the sword. (LL)   Message to Siberia. Alexander Sergeyevich Pushkin.   AWP; TTY, tr. by Max Eastman

And buds and blossoms like the rest. (LL)   Tennyson.   EBVV; FHYEP; GTBS-P; NAEL-6v2; NOBE; NPeEn   Fr. In Memoriam A. H. H.

And builds a Hell in Heaven's despite. (LL)   William Blake.   EnLoPo; FHYEP; NAEL-5v2; NAEL-6v1; NOBE; NPeEn; NoP-4; OxAEP-2; OxBEV; OxBSP; PoE; RB; SCGP; SCV; TFi   Fr. Songs of Experience.

And built a braver Palace than before. (LL)   World, The. George Herbert. GeHe; NOSC

And Burgh under Stanemuir there dwels Dickie. (LL)   Dick o' the Cow. Unknown.   ESPB; IBB; OxBB

And buried him where he fell. (LL)   Vigil Strange I Kept on the Field One Night. Walt Whitman.   APN-1; CAGL; CBCWP; ColAP; HeIP-4; MoAmPo; NAAL-2v1; NAAL-3; NOBA; NoP-4; OBWP; PoE; PoPoPo; TAP; TCAPo

And burn[e], yet[t] burning you will love the smart.   Mary Sidney Wroth, Countess of Montgomery.   BASC   Fr. Pamphilia to Amphilanthus.

And but a chair. (LL)   Pilgrimage, The. George Herbert.   BASC; ESCV; GeHe; NAEL-5v1; NAEL-6v1; NAEL-7v1; NOSC; PAI; PoE

And but in darkness is she visible. (LL)   To an Old Lady. William Empson. FaBoTw; GTBS-P; NOBE; NoAM; OxAEP-2; OxBEV

And buzzings of the honied hours. (LL)   Tennyson.   EBVV; NAEL-6v2; OBGa   Fr. In Memoriam A. H. H.

And by a river forth I gan costey.   John Lydgate.   OBGa   Fr. Complaint of the Black Knight, The.

And, by one o'clock, is gone. (LL)   V. B. Nimble, V. B. Quick. John Updike. NoP-4; OBCoV

And by that light around the dome appear'd.   Philip Freneau.   NAAL-3; TCAPo   Fr. House of Night, The.

And call ye[e] this to utter what is just.   Bible, O.T.   BASC; NPeEn; NoP-4; PEW, tr. by Mary Sidney Herbert, Countess of Pembroke   Fr. Psalms.

And called their friend, my Father, God. (LL)   Cottage, The. Jones Very. APN-1; OxBA

And calling Justice, all things burn. (LL)   Decay. George Herbert.   ESCV; SCGP

And calm of mind all passion spent. (LL)   John Milton.   BASC; FHYEP; NAEL-6v1; NOBE; NOCV; NOSC; OBEV; OxBEV

And calmly waits for more. (LL)   History Goes to Work. Elizabeth Garrett. MFPA; NeBl

And Camelot, and starlit Stonehenge. (LL)   Channel Firing. Thomas Hardy. CABP; EBEV; HAP; HarvBoo; HeIP-4; NAEL-5v2; NAEL-6v2; NIL-7; NIP-4; NoAM; NoP-4; OxAEP-2; OxBEV; OxBTC; PAI; PeECV; PeFWW; PoE; PoPoPo; PoRA; PoWW; RB; SoSe-8; TFi; UnPo

And can I ever bid these joys farewell?   John Keats.   TOF   Fr. Sleep and Poetry.

And can it be, that I should gain.   Free Grace. Charles Wesley.   NOCV; SacPr

And can return no more. (LL)   First Love. John Clare.   BoLoP; EnLoPo; HAP; NOBVV; NoP-4; PoPoPo

And can't explode? (LL)   Sherbet. Cornelius Eady.   GT; LTA

And cannot change to grey. (LL)   Christina Georgina Rossetti.   FaBoVe; NPeEn

And cannot come again. (LL)   Yon Far Country. A. E. Housman.   EBEV; HarvBoo; MoBrPo; NOBE; NOBVV; NPeEn; NoAM; OPOU; OxAEP-2; OxBEV; OxBTC; TFi

And cannot say it. (LL)   George Oppen.   APSN; NNaP   Fr. Some San Francisco Poems.

And cannot understand the Han man's song. (LL)   Song of the Breaking of the Willow.   Unknown.   CoBCP; ColAnChi, tr. by Burton Watson

And Canst Thou, Sinner, Slight.   Abby Bradley Hyde.   AH

And carry you away. (LL)   For the Courtesan Ch'ing Lin. Wu Tsao.   BoWoP; WPOW; WoPoe, tr. by Chung Ling and Kenneth Rexroth

And, cast by conscience out, spendsavour salt? (LL)   Candle Indoors, The. Gerard Manley Hopkins.   ChIV-2; OxAEP-2

And certainly they say, for fine behaving.   John Hookham Frere.   OBCoV   Fr. Whistlecraft.

And change[,] with hurried hand, has swept these scenes.   Frederick Goddard Tuckerman.   APN-2; HAP; NOBA; TAP; TCAPo   Fr. Sonnets.

And charms the most concealed, are doubly graced. (LL)   She Endeavors to Fascinate Him. Mary Robinson.   CenSon; RWP

And cheat the cruel day! (LL)   And on My Eyes Dark Sleep by Night. "Michael Field."   LW; OBMV

And cheroots upon the floor. (LL)   On Seeing an Old Poet in the Café Royal. Sir John Betjeman.   OxBEV; UV

And children still grow up with longing eyes.   Twilight of the Outward Life. Hugo von Hofmannsthal.   WoPoe, tr. by Peter Viereck

And children swarmed to him like settlers. He became a land. (LL)   Edward Lear. W. H. Auden.   OxAEP-2; OxBSo

And choose it for my own. (LL)   Yellow Flower, The. William Carlos Williams.   HAP; HarvBoo

And Christe receive thy saule. (LL)   Lyke-Wake Dirge, The [or A].   Unknown. EMWP; FaBoCh; HAP; NOBE; NPeEn; OBEV; OxBEV; PeECV; TFi; WeW-3; WoPoe

And claim the crown, through Christ, my own. (LL)   Free Grace. Charles Wesley.   NOCV; SacPr

And clamour and the night. We are in Ghent. (LL)   Dante Gabriel Rossetti. NPeEn; PeVV   Fr. Trip to Paris and Belgium, A.

And classic bronze of Benin. (LL)   Different Image, A. Dudley Randall. BPo; TAP

And clearly I recall the second day's end.   Perfect Disc of the Moon, The. Richard Kenney.   Son

And closed her up, as in a tomb[e]. (LL)   Funeral[l] Rites of the Rose, The. Robert Herrick.   CaPo; NOSC; OBEV

And cluck your children in about your knee? (LL)   Sonnet to Gath. Edna St. Vincent Millay.   BoWoP; MoAmPo

And Coffers heaped with Tears! (LL)   Emily Dickinson.   NAAL-2v1; NAAL-3

And cold as any icicle. (LL)   Parting, without a Sequel. John Crowe Ransom. MoAmPo; NoP-4; OxBA; SoSe-8

And collars of his keen-nosed pups. (LL)   Leonidas.   GrAn; PGA

And combining Stern Duty with pleasure. (LL)   Smile of the Goat, The. Oliver Herford.   OBCoV; PeLV

And comes from a country far away as health. (LL)   Tulips. Sylvia Plath. HAP; NoP-4; PAI; WPE; WeW-3

And coming the proud over all o' the birds o' the sea.' (LL)   Sea Change. John Masefield.   FaBoTw; OBMV; RB

And confident Thou'lt raise me with the just. (LL)   On Himself, upon Hearing What Was His Sentence. James Graham, Marquess of Montrose.   NOSC; NPeEn; NePenScot

And confirmation of the old despair. (LL)   James Thomson.   GTBS-P; NOBE; NePenScot   Fr. City of Dreadful Night, The.

And Consciousness—is Noon. (LL)   Emily Dickinson.   APN-2; NCAP

And consummation comes, and jars two hemispheres. (LL)   Convergence of the Twain, The. Thomas Hardy.   CABP; FaBoTw; HarvBoo; HeIP-4; InPK-6; MakPoe; MoBrPo; NAEL-5v2; NAEL-6v2; NIL-7; NIP-4; NPeEn; NoAM; NoP-4; OxBEV; OxBTC; PAI; PeVV; PoPoPo; SCGP; TFi

And continue special friends. (LL)   Twelve Articles. Jonathan Swift.   NBLV; OBCoV

And continued to knock him about. (LL)   Limerick: "There was an old man who screamed out." Edward Lear.   EBEV; NOBVV; NPeEn; OxAEP-2; OxBEV

And copper and worn my farthing.   Elizaveta Kuzmina-Karavayeva.   TCRP

And could no longer recollect my name. (LL)   Epigram: "Good Fortune, when I hailed her recently." James Vincent Cunningham.   APT-2; VCAP

And couldn't write. (LL)   Bookshop Idyll, A. Kingsley Amis.   OxBTC; PeLV

And courts the fatal fire by which it dies! (LL)   Supposed To Be Written by Werter. Charlotte Smith.   CenSon; RWP

And covered up—our names. (LL)   Emily Dickinson.   APN-2; AWP; BoWoP; MakPoe; MoAmPo; NAAL-2v2; NAAL-3; NAAL-5; NAWM-7v2; NOBA; PAI; SAmP

And crash a grunting cheat that's young. (LL)   Maunder's Praise of His Strowling Mort, The.   Unknown.   OxBoLi; PeLV

And creates a mighty traffic problem. (LL)   Guilt, Desire and Love.   James Baldwin.   CAGL; GLP

And cries of love are cries of fear. (LL)   Song for a Birth or a Death.   Elizabeth Jennings.   EBEV; HarvBoo

And crowd to Stella's at four score. (LL)   Stella's Birthday [1721].   Jonathan Swift.   NAEL-5v1; NAEL-6v1; OxAEP-1

And crown Him Lord of all! (LL)   All Hail the Power of Jesus' Name.   Edward Perronet.   NOCV; SacPr

And crown with love my ever-during night. (LL)   My Sweetest Lesbia.   Catullus.   NAEL-6v1; NAEL-7v1; NPeEn; NoP-4, tr. by Thomas Campion

And cruell maid, because I see.   Cruell Maid, The.   Robert Herrick.   CaPo

And curl forever in some far-off farmyard flower. (LL)   Beehive.   Jean Toomer.   GT; TTY

And cursed th' access[e] of that celestial[l] thief. (LL)   Sir Walter Ralegh.   NAEL-5v1; NoSic; SCGP; Son   Fr. Commendatory Verses to Edmund Spenser's Fairy Queen.

And custom for the spreading laurel tree. (LL)   Prayer for My Daughter, A.   W. B. Yeats.   HAP; NAEL-5v2; NAEL-6v2; NoAM; NoP-4; OxBTC; PoRA; RaBo; TFi

And cut them and gave them to me / in my hand. (LL)   Act, The.   William Carlos Williams.   SAmP; VGW

And dance. (LL)   Lal Ded [or Lalla].   WPoS; WoPoe, tr. by Coleman Barks

And dance like a wave of the sea. (LL)   Fiddler of Dooney, The.   W. B. Yeats.   EBVV; FaBoCh; NBLV; OxAEP-2

And dances with the Daffodils. (LL)   Daffodils, The.   William Wordsworth.   BRP; ClHu; InPK-6; NAEL-5v2; NAEL-6v2; NOBRP; PoRA; SCGP; SoSe-8; TFi; TTTS; UnPo

And dandelion-seed under the ground. (LL)   "H. D."   APT-1; BoWoP; FaBoWP   Fr. Sigil.

And da[u]nce to th' music[k] of your chain[e]s. (LL)   Vintage to the Dungeon, The.   Richard Lovelace.   BeJo; CaPo

And day and night yield one delight once more? (LL)   Sudden Light.   Dante Gabriel Rossetti.   BoLoP; CABP; CTC; NOBE; NOBVV; NPeEn; NoP-4; OxBEV

And day not long enough. (LL)   Basho.   WoPoe; ZenPo, tr. by Takashi Ikemoto and Lucien Stryk

And dead. (LL)   Palladas [or Pallades].   GrAn; WoPoe, tr. by Tony Harrison

And death, after all, was only "another room" (LL)   Resurrection of Arp.   Arthur James Marshall Smith.   MoCV; NOBC

And death be strong, yet love is strong as death. (LL)   Christina Georgina Rossetti.   OxBSo; Son   Fr. Monna Innominata.

And death brooded over the pride of the Plain! (LL)   Cities of the Plain, The.   John Greenleaf Whittier.   chIV-1; NCAP

And death i think is no parenthesis. (LL)   Since feeling is first.   E. E. Cummings.   MoAmPo; NoP-4

And death is no evil. (LL)   Night.   Robinson Jeffers.   AWP; ColAP; MoAmPo; NOBA; OxBA

And Death must dig the level where these agree. (LL)   Elizabeth Barrett Browning.   BWW; CABP; CenSon; OBEV; OxAEP-2   Fr. Sonnets from the Portuguese.

And Death once dead, there's no more dying then. (LL)   William Shakespeare.   AWP; HAP; HeIP-4; NAEL-5v1; NAEL-6v1; NAEL-7v1; NOBE; NOCV; OBEV; OxAEP-1; PoE; SCGP; SacPr; Son; TFi   Fr. Sonnets.

And death shall be no more: Death, thou shalt die. (LL)   John Donne.   BASC; FHYEP; HAP; HeIP-4; ITBLP; InPK-6; MeLP; NAEL-5v1; NAEL-6v1; NAEL-7v1; NAWM-5v1; NIL-7; NIP-4; NOBE; NOSC; NPeEn; OPOU; OxAEP-1; OxBEV; OxBSo; PAI; PoE; PoRA; SCGP; SCV; SacPr; SoSe-8; TRP; TrCP; WeW-3   Fr. Holy Sonnets.

And Death Shall Have No Dominion.   Dylan Thomas.   chIV-2; MoBrPo; NoAM; RB

And deck the broken stones like saxifrage. (LL)   She.   Richard Wilbur.   CoAmPo; NIL-7

And deep-eyed children cannot long be children.   Ballad of the Outer Life.   Hugo von Hofmannsthal.   AWP; TrJP, tr. by Jethro Bithell

And defecar on those goddam guidebook. (LL)   Sinalóa.   Earle Birney.   MoCV; OxBC; PeLV

And despairs day, but for thy volume's light. (LL)   Ben Jonson.   BASC; BeJo; HAP; HeIP-4; NAEL-6v1; NAEL-7v1; NOSC; NoP-4; OxAEP-1; PoPoPo

And did ever a man go black with sun in a Belgian swamp.   Nigger.   Karl Shapiro.   OxBA

And Did the Animals?   Mark Van Doren.   VGW

And did these feet, in pre-war days.   New Jerusalem, The.   Allan M. Laing.   UV

And Did Those Feet in Ancient Time.   William Blake.   AWP; ClHu; FaBoCh; HAP; HeIP-4; NAEL-5v2; NAWM-7v2; NOBRP; NPeEn; OxBEV; PAI; PeECV; PoE; PoRA; SCGP; TFi; WoPoe   Fr. Milton.

And did we come into our own.   Letter to Derek Mahon.   Michael Longley.   CIP-2

And did you know.   Snowflakes.   Clive Sansom.   OBCP

And did you not hear of a jolly young waterman.   Jolly Young Waterman, The.   Charles Dibdin.   NOEC; OxAEP-1

And did young Stephen sicken.   "Mark Twain."   NBLV; OBAL   Fr. Adventures of Huckleberry Finn, The.

And didst thou love the race that loved not thee?   Jean Ingelow.   SacPr

And died, content. (LL)   Stephen Crane.   APN-2; NAAL-2v2   Fr. Black Riders [and Other Lines], The.

And dies! (LL)   Already Embraced by the Arm of Heavenly Solace.   Nelly Sachs.   HP; PoSu, tr. by Michael Roloff

And dies between three cannibals. (LL)   Fly, The.   Karl Shapiro.   NoAM; SoSe-8

And dinner waiting, and the sun not yet gone down. (LL)   Phyllis McGinley.   APT-2; WPE   Fr. I Know a Village.

And dinner will be cold. (LL)   A. E. Housman.   HarvBoo; MoBrPo; UnPo

And disembodied bones. (LL)   Eagle and the Mole, The.   Elinor Wylie.   AWP; BoWoP; MoAmPo; NALW; UnPo

And dish water gives back no images. (LL)   No Images.   Waring Cuney.   APT-2; NIP-4; SSLK; TTY

And dive off in my grave like the old swimmin'-hole. (LL)   Old Swimmin'-Hole, The.   James Whitcomb Riley.   APN-2; BRP

And do not even own clothing. (LL)   Salutation.   Ezra Pound.   HeIP-4; MoAmPo; NOBA; OxBA; TAP; VGW

And do not flow over like you or like me. (LL)   Jugs, The.   Paul Celan.   HP; OBVE, tr. by Christopher Middleton

And do they so? have they a Sense.   And do they so?   Henry Vaughan.   BASC; ESCV; GeHe; MeLP; SacPr

And do they wear that lubricating lie.   Alfred Austin.   VerBaPo   Fr. Human Tragedy, The.

And does another thousand start again? (LL)   Mahratta Ghats, The.   Alun Lewis.   AngWePo; OBWVE; PoWW; TCAWP

And does not drift away. (LL)   Medusa.   Louise Bogan.   APT-2; AWP; BoWoP; MoAmPo; NALW; NoAM; NoP-4; PAI; WPE

And does the heart grow old? You know.   To My Wife.   James Vincent Cunningham.   VCAP

And Don't Be Deaf to the Singing Beyond.   Carter Revard.   HATNAP

And don't blubber like lubbers when I turn up my keel. (LL)   Tom Deadlight.   Herman Melville.   APN-2; NCAP

"And don't bother telling me anything."   César Vallejo.   SPE, tr. by Robert Bly

And don't have any kids yourself. (LL)   This Be The Verse.   Philip Larkin.   NPeEn; NoAM; PoPoPo; PoetW

And dost thou faithlessly abandon me?   Unrealities, The.   Johann Christoph Friedrich von Schiller.   AWP, tr. by James Clarence Mangan

And dost thou still, thou mass of breathing stone.   To the Fragment of a Statue of Hercules, Commonly Called the Torso.   Samuel Rogers.   CenSon; GS

And doublecrossed my mother's womb. (LL)   Before I Knocked.   Dylan Thomas.   FaBoTw; RB

And down again, to thank the young man. (LL)   Ballad of the Orioles in the Fields.   Ts'ao Chih.   ColAnChi; SuSp, tr. by Hans H. Frankel

And draw me to her in the blessed place! (LL)   Petrarch.   NAWM-5v1; NAWM-7v1, tr. by Morris Gilbert Bishop   Fr. Sonnets to Laura.

And dream my time away. (LL)   Expostulation and Reply.   William Wordsworth.   FHYEP; NAEL-5v2; NAEL-6v2; NOBRP

And drew her backward home. (LL)   Subverted Flower, The.   Robert Frost.   APT-1; ColAP; HAP; NOBA; NoAM; OxBA; PoE

And drink my cup of jade-white wine. (LL)   Reading the Poetry of Meng Chiao: Two Poems.   Su Tung-p'o (Su Shih).   ColAnChi; WoPoe, tr. by Burton Watson

And drink them both into the grave. (LL)   Twins.   Robert Graves.   FaBoEE; OBCoV

And drinks, and stares, diversified with boggles? (LL)   Leigh Hunt.   NBLV; NPeEn; PeLV; SCGP   Fr. Fish, the Man, and the Spirit, The.

And Dromio's denouement of tragic mirth. (LL)   Twins, The.   Karl Shapiro.   MoAmPo; TrJP

And drops all the spoons. (LL)   Round the World with the Rumpus God.   Meret Oppenheim.   SurPaPo; SurWo, tr. by Catherine Schelbert

And drums for the king. (LL)   Rock-a-bye, baby, thy cradle is green.   Mother Goose.   OxNR; ReMoGo

And drunk the milk of Paradise. (LL)   Kubla Khan: or, A Vision in a Dream.   Samuel Taylor Coleridge.   AWP; BRP; CABP; FHYEP; FaBoCh; HAP; HeIP-4; InPK-6; NAEL-5v2; NAEL-6v2; NAWM-7v2; NIL-7; NIP-4; NOBE; NOBRP; NPeEn; NoP-4; OBEV; OBGa; OxAEP-2; OxBEV; PAI; PoE; PoPoPo; PoRA; SCGP; SCV; SoSe-8; TFi; TOF; TRP; WeW-3; WoPoe

And dulls to distance all we are. (LL)   Ambulances.   Philip Larkin.   FaBoTw; NAEL-5v2; NAEL-6v2; NoP-4; OxBC

And dust is for a time. (LL)   In Distrust of Merits.   Marianne Craig Moore.   APT-1; ColAP; MoAmPo; NAAL-2v2; NAAL-5; OBWP; OxBA

And Duty in the lofty ends of life. (LL)   Sonnet: Of Beauty and Duty.   Dante Alighieri.   AWP; EaltPo, tr. by Dante Gabriel Rossetti

And dying in black and white we fight for what we love, not are. (LL)   Ode: Salute to the French Negro Poets.   Frank O'Hara.   GLP; NNaP; NeAP; PFTM-2; PoM

And e'en for change of scene would seek the shades below. (LL) Byron. NAEL-5v2; NAEL-6v2 *Fr.* Childe Harold's Pilgrimage.

And each anointed sense will see. (LL) Extreme Unction. Ernest Christopher Dowson. MoBrPo; OBMV; PeECV; PeVV

And each as silent as a man being shaved. (LL) Prolonged Sonnet: When the Troops Were Returning from Milan. Niccolò degli Albizzi. AWP; EaItPo; OBVE, *tr. by* Dante Gabriel Rossetti

And each slow dusk a drawing-down of blinds. (LL) Anthem for Doomed Youth. Wilfred Owen. AF; CABP; CAGL; ClHu; EBEV; FaBoMo; FaBoWar; GSo; GTBS-P; HAP; HarvBoo; HeIP-4; InPK-6; MoBrPo; NAEL-5v2; NAEL-6v2; NOBE; NPeEn; NoAM; NoP-4; OBEV; OBWP; OxBEV; OxBTC; PoE; PoPoPo; SCV; SoSe-8; Son; TCAWP; TFi; WeW-3

And Earth is but a star, that once had shone. (LL) James Elroy Flecker. OBMV; OxBTC; UV *Fr.* Golden Journey to Samarkand, The.

And earth, sea, man, are all in each. (LL) Dante Gabriel Rossetti. NAEL-5v2; NAEL-6v2 *Fr.* House of Life, The.

And eats its dead-dog off a golden dish. (LL) Coventry Patmore. OxBEV; PeVV *Fr.* Unknown Eros, The.

And eats the meadow flowers. (LL) Cow, The. Robert Louis Stevenson. NTCP; PWR; TLR; WHSW

And eke men shal nat [*or* nought] make[n] ernest of game. (LL) Geoffrey Chaucer. NAEL-6v1; NAEL-7v1; NAWM-5v1 *Fr.* Canterbury Tales, The.

And eluding the dead hands, begging him to play. (LL) Foal. Vernon Watkins. AngWePo; OxBTC

And empty grows every bed. (LL) John Berryman. ColAP; HCAP; NAAL-2v2; NoP-4; PoE; VCAP *Fr.* Dream Songs.

And engines / that devour America. (LL) Lawrence Ferlinghetti. HeIP-4; NeAP; NoAM; PmAP; PoM; TAP

And Error loves and nourishes thy soul. (LL) Be Still. The Hanging Gardens Were a Dream. Trumbull Stickney. APN-2; WoPoe

And escaped from the people of Basing. (LL) Limerick: "There was an old person of Basing." Edward Lear. EBEV; NPeEn; OxAEP-2; PAI; PeLi

And Eternity in an hour. (LL) William Blake. EnlH; InPK-6 *Fr.* Auguries of Innocence.

And Ettrick mourns with her their Poet dead. (LL) William Wordsworth. EBEV; NAEL-6v2; NOBE; SCV

And ev'n Devotion! (LL) To a Louse [On Seeing One on a Lady's Bonnet at Church]. Robert Burns. FaBoVe; NAEL-5v2; NAEL-6v2; NOBRP; NOEC; NePenScot; OxBS

And even the English—maybe they might die. (LL) Epigram: "World laid low, and the wind blew like a dust, The." *Unknown.* FaBoWar; NOIV, *tr. by* Thomas Kinsella

And every sheave a golden tree. (LL) George Peele. FaBoCh; NOBE; OxBoLi *Fr.* Old Wives' [*or* Wife's] Tale, The.

And every Space that a Man views around his dwelling-place. William Blake. BLT *Fr.* "Milton."

And every wave is charmed. (LL) Terminus. Ralph Waldo Emerson. APN-1; AWP; NCAP; NOBA; OxBA; TAP; TCAPo

And every Wednesday, as the swift days move. Folgore da San Geminiano [*or* Gimignano]. EaItPo, *tr. by* Dante Gabriel Rossetti

And every year a world my will did deem. George Gascoigne. Son *Fr.* Gascoigne's Memories.

And everyone, everyone pointing up and shouting! (LL) Child on Top of a Greenhouse. Theodore Roethke. KaS; LCAP-2; NOxBChV; NoP-4; VGW

And exchange names and addresses. (LL) Truce. Paul Muldoon. FaBoWar; PBCIP; PNI

And excited the heart of Argive. Alcaeus [*or* Alkaios]. SaLy, *tr. by* Diane Rayor

And faded on the blowing of the horn. (LL) T. S. Eliot. FaBoTw; NPeEn; OxBEV *Fr.* Four Quartets.

And faintly trust the larger hope. (LL) Tennyson. EBVV; FHYEP; HAP; NAEL-6v2; NAWM-7v2; SacPr; TOF *Fr.* In Memoriam A. H. H.

And faith knows nothing of reasons. All Illusion Is a Form of Hope. Aida Gelbtrunk. MirDau, *tr. by* Roberta Gordenstein

And faith to Love—to our dead at rest. (LL) Augusta Davies Webster. VWP; ViWPN *Fr.* Mother and Daughter.

And fall. (LL) November Night. Adelaide Crapsey. APT-1; PAI; Spl; TCAPo

And fall in blood: we bring him even now. (LL) Six o'Clock. Trumbull Stickney. APN-2; OxBA

And fame of his descendants. (LL) Virgil [*or* Vergil]. NAWM-5v1; NAWM-7v1, *tr. by* Robert Fitzgerald *Fr.* Aeneid [*or* Eneados, *Aeneis*], The.

And fate change me to worms. (LL) Against Constancy. John Wilmot, 2d Earl of Rochester. NOSC; OxAEP-1

And fear lit by the breadth of such calmly turns to praise. (LL) City Limits, The. A. R. Ammons. HCAP; NAAL-2v2; NOBA; NoAM; NoP-4; PoPoPo; VCAP

And fears not portly Azcan nor his hoos. (LL) Bantams in Pine-Woods. Wallace Stevens. NOBA; NoAM; OxBA; SAmP; UnPo

And feed my soul, with luxury of woe! (LL) Sappho Rejects Hope. Mary Robinson. CenSon; RWP

And feel like flowers that fade. (LL) Sir Henry Taylor. OBEV; RACG *Fr.* Philip van Artevelde.

And fell it on the start. (LL) John Berryman. HCAP; PoPoPo; VCAP *Fr.* Dream Songs.

And fiery tempered steel. (LL) Fragment 113: "Not honey, / not the plunder of the bee." "H. D." APT-1; NAAL-2v2

And fill your heads with crotchets. (LL) Distracted Puritan, The. Richard Corbet [*or* Corbett]. BASC; BeJo; OBCoV; OxBoLi

And find, in your wife, a Companion and Friend. (LL) Conclusion of a Letter to the Rev. Mr. C——, The. Mary Barber. CABP; ECWP

And find your way to the parlour of Government House. (LL) Invitation to Hsiao Ch'u-shih. Po Chü-i. ChiP; OBVE, *tr. by* Arthur Waley

And Finished knowing—then. (LL) I Felt a Funeral in My Brain. Emily Dickinson. APN-2; BoWoP; HeIP-4; NAAL-2v1; NAAL-3; NALW; NOBA; NoP-4; OxBA; PoE; PoRA; RaBo; SCV; SoSe-8; TAP; TCAPo; TFi

And fire their only future. (LL) Asians Dying, The. W. S. Merwin. CoAP; HCAP; NOBA; PoPoPo; VCAP

And firesides buried under fallen thatch. (LL) William Allingham. BIrV; NOIV *Fr.* Laurence Bloomfield in Ireland.

And firmly stands when Crowns and Scepters fall. (LL) On the 3 of September, 1651. Katherine Philips. BASC; EMWP; PBRV

And first the walles and dark entrie I sought. Virgil [*or* Vergil]. NPeEn, *tr. by* Henry Howard, Earl of Surrey *Fr.* Aeneid [*or* Eneados, *Aeneis*], The.

And flew far out of sight. (LL) Catch a Little Rhyme. Eve Merriam. OBCA; OxIBACP

And flies with the cloud. (LL) Chimes. Alice Thompson Meynell. MoBrPo; WPE

And float with them about the summer waters. (LL) Happy Is England! I Could Be Content. John Keats. CenSon; OxAEP-2

And flood a fresher throat with song. (LL) Tennyson. EBVV; NAEL-6v2 *Fr.* In Memoriam A. H. H.

And flourished in the open field. (LL) Timothy. Timothy Steele. InPK-6; RA

And fly to the Jasper Capital! (LL) Song of the Man of Green Hill, The. Kao Ch'i. CoBLCP; ColAnChi, *tr. by* Jonathan Chaves

And fold within the wet wings of thy dove. (LL) Elizabeth Barrett Browning. CenSon; Son *Fr.* Sonnets from the Portuguese.

And for Alice, his wife, pray too. (LL) Shameful Death. William Morris. GTBS-P; PeVV

And for breakfast she said we have strawberries. (LL) Strawberries. W. S. Merwin. AmFaPo; NoP-4

And for her sake trip up Death. (LL) Little Elegy. X. J. Kennedy. CoAP; CoAmPo

And, for our tongue, that still is so empayr'd. George Chapman. PBRV *Fr.* Homer's Iliad, To the Reader.

And for short time an endless[e] monument [*or* moniment]. (LL) Edmund Spenser. BoLoP; FHYEP; NAEL-6v1; NAEL-7v1; NOBE; NoSic; OBEV; OxAEP-1

And for special things. Grim Sisters, The. Liz Lochhead. CABP

And for the soul. Argonautica. George Seferis. PoetW, *tr. by* Rex Warner

And for what, except for you, do I feel love? Wallace Stevens. APT-1

And for what purpose? Why go to the cross? For the Last Time on My Native Estate. Ilya Iankelevich Gabai. TCRP, *tr. by* Albert C. Todd

And forced the underbrush—and that was all. (LL) Most of It, The. Robert Frost. APT-1; BLT; HAP; NAAL-2v2; NoP-4; TOF; TRP; WeW-3

And forget it, long before it is worn out. (LL) Present from the Emperor's New Concubine, A. Pan Chieh-yü. BoWoP; OHMPC; WoPoe, *tr. by* Kenneth Rexroth

And Forgive Us Our Trespasses. Aphra Behn. EBEV

And found it of some interest. (LL) Le Jazz Hot. Anselm Hollo. PoM; SeSe

And found Life stepping on my feet! (LL) Esthete in Harlem. Langston Hughes. BPo; ColAP

And foxes stunk and littered in St. Paul's. (LL) On Lord Holland's Seat near Margate, Kent. Thomas Gray. NOEC; NPeEn

And frame from thinking and is realized. (LL) To an Old Philosopher in Rome. Wallace Stevens. APT-1; ColAP; EnlH; NOBA; NoAM

And free land of the grave. (LL) Crossing Alone the Nighted Ferry. A. E. Housman. GTBS-P; HarvBoo; NOBE; NPeEn; NoP-4; OxBEV; OxBSP

And freed [*or* free'd] his soul the nearest way. (LL) On the Death of Dr [*or* Mr] Robert Levet [a Practiser in Physic]. Samuel Johnson. ChIV-2; EBEV; NAEL-5v1; NAEL-6v1; NAEL-7v1; NOBE; NOEC; NPeEn; NoP-4; OBEV; OxAEP-1; OxBEV; PeECV; PoE; SCGP; SCV; TFi

And Freedom's banner streaming o'er us. (LL) American Flag, The. Joseph Rodman Drake. APN-1; BRP

And frightened Miss Muffet away. (LL) Miss Muffet. Mother Goose. LB; OxNR; ReMoGo

And from louts to run away. (LL) Sir Philip Sidney. NAEL-6v1; NAEL-7v1; NoSic; OxAEP-1 *Fr.* Astrophil and Stella.

And from my bosom find a surer rest. (LL)   Earth, The.   Jones Very.   APN-1; OxBA

And from the Citie Tegea there came the Paragone.   Ovid.   OBVE   *Fr.* Metamorphoses.

And from the house his mother called his name. (LL)   Childhood.   Edwin Muir.   HeIP-4; NPeEn; NePenScot; NoP-4

And from the red grating in the distance.   Natural History.   Giampiero Neri.   ItPo, *tr. by* Gayle Ridinger

And from the woods the late resounding note.   Philip Freneau.   TCAPo   *Fr.* House of Night, The.

And from within the howls of Death I heard.   Philip Freneau.   TCAPo   *Fr.* House of Night, The.

And frowzy pores that taint the ambient air. (LL)   On Jacob Tonson, His Publisher.   FaBoEE; OBSV

And futile as regret. (LL)   Bewick Finzer.   Edwin Arlington Robinson.   MoAmPo; NAAL-2v2

And gained her maidenhead. (LL)   Twa Magicians, The.   *Unknown.*   ESPB; OxBB

And gained in service of our fair / And universal Queen. (LL)   Pangloss's Song: A Comic-Opera Lyric.   Richard Wilbur.   NBLV; NoAM

And gallop terribly against each other's bodies. (LL)   Autumn Begins in Martins Ferry, Ohio.   James Wright (1927–80).   ColAP; HCAP; HeIP-4; InPK-6; MoASP; NAAL-5; NoAM; VCAP; WeW-3

And gather roses, while 'tis called to-day. (LL)   Of His Lady's Old Age.   Pierre de Ronsard.   AWP; CTC, *tr. by* Andrew Lang

And gathering swallows twitter in the skies. (LL)   To Autumn.   John Keats.   AWP; ClHu; EBVV; FHYEP; HAP; HeIP-4; ITBLP; InPK-6; MakPoe; NAEL-5v2; NAEL-6v2; NAWM-7v2; NIL-7; NIP-4; NOBE; NOBRP; NPeEn; OBEV; OxAEP-2; OxBEV; PAI; PoE; RB; RaBo; SCGP; SCV; SoSe-8; TFi; TRP; UnPo; WeW-3

And gave away her heart. (LL)   Ballad of Aunt Geneva, The.   Marilyn Nelson Waniek.   FFC; GT

And gave me back my beauty. (LL)   Fired Pot, The.   Anna Wickham.   FaBoTw; FaBoWP; LW; NPeEn; OxBTC

And gave the discourse a definitive blow. (LL)   Poem on the Supposition of the Book Having Been Published and Read, A.   Elizabeth Hands.   ECWP; WoRP

And gazing, died. (LL)   White Women, The.   Mary Elizabeth Coleridge.   BrRo; NALW; ViWPN

And ghosts then keep their distance; and I know some liberty. (LL)   Wessex Heights.   Thomas Hardy.   EBVV; SCGP

And gibbets me. (LL)   Zone of Death.   William Everson.   SacPr; VGW

And give her no scouts doing their one good deed.   Elderly Lady Crossing on Green.   Wyatt Prunty.   RA

And give thanks it was not I, nor yet one close to I. (LL)   Open Sea, The.   William Meredith.   CoAP; TAP; UnPo

And give to February twenty-nine. (LL)   Mother Goose.   OxNR; ReMoGo

And glittering eyelids of my soul's desire. (LL)   Love And Sleep.   Algernon Charles Swinburne.   BoLoP; GSo; OxBSo

& go to the moon. (LL)   Bean Spasms.   Ted Berrigan.   PmAP; SPE

And God—at every Gate. (LL)   Emily Dickinson.   APN-2; NOCV; SoSe-8

And God bless me. (LL)   I See the Moon.   *Unknown.*   NTCP; OxNR

And God said, I will build a church here.   Island, The.   Ronald Stuart Thomas.   InvLi

And God said, "Let the waters generate."   John Milton.   NOSC   *Fr.* Paradise Lost.

And God said to the soul.   God Speaks to the Soul.   Mechthild von Magdeburg.   WPoS, *tr. by* Oliver Davies

And God saw that the wickedness of man was great.   Bible, *O.T.*   NAWM-5v1   *Fr.* Genesis.

And God shall bless you from above. (LL)   To My Dear Children.   Anne Bradstreet.   BASC; NAAL-3

And God stepped out on space.   James Weldon Johnson.   APT-1; AmFaPo; ChIV-1; ISC; MoAmPo; NAAAL; PoRA; SSLK; SacPr; TrCP

And God will save the Queen. (LL)   1887.   A. E. Housman.   NIP-4; NOBVV; SCGP; UnPo

And gods disgusting.—You and I, Cassandra. (LL)   Cassandra.   Robinson Jeffers.   APT-1; HeIP-4

And going to the office in the train. (LL)   Dreamers.   Siegfried Sassoon.   MoBrPo; NoAM; Son

And gold on my neck the sun. (LL)   Collier, The.   Vernon Watkins.   FaBoTw; OBWVE; TCAWP

And gone all trace of me! (LL)   Tess's Lament.   Thomas Hardy.   FaBoTw; FaBoVe

And good-bye to the bar and its moaning. (LL)   Three Fishers [Went Sailing], The.   Charles Kingsley.   EBVV; PWR

And grant his reign over the entire building. (LL)   Homage to the British Museum.   William Empson.   FaBoMo; MoBrPo; NPeEn; OxBEV; PoE

And grave by grave we civilize the ground. (LL)   To the Western World.   Louis Simpson.   CoAP; CoAmPo; NOBA; TAP; TRP

And great souls, at one stroke, may do and dote. (LL)   Elizabeth Barrett Browning.   CenSon; NAEL-5v2; NAEL-6v2; WPE   *Fr.* Sonnets from the Portuguese.

And great thy wisdom, Vander Brüin. (LL)   Dutch Proverb, A.   Matthew Prior.   FaBoEE; NOEC; OBCoV

And green plaid shorts goes strolling.   Eros in His Striped Blue Shirt.   Reginald Shepherd.   WiU

And grey hairs were on my head. (LL)   William Blake.   FHYEP; RACG   *Fr.* Songs of Experience.

And grow incorporate into thee. (LL)   Tennyson.   EBVV; GTBS-P; NAEL-6v2; NAWM-7v2; NOBE; NPeEn; PAI; UnPo   *Fr.* In Memoriam A. H. H.

And guiltlessly watch the wrist-ropes fall? (LL)   True Descenders.   James Kimbrell.   AmPoNex; NAPBL

And gulp from them the dailiness of life. (LL)   Well Water.   Randall Jarrell.   InPK-6; NAAL-2v2; NAAL-5; NOBA; OxBSP; VCAP; VGW

And Gwydion said to Math, when it was Spring.   Wife of Llew, The.   Francis Ledwidge.   MakPoe

And habit builds the bridge at last! (LL)   Builder's Lesson, A.   John Boyle O'Reilly.   PWR; PoToHe

And half the heaven of the blest! (LL)   Aphra Behn.   WPE; WPOW   *Fr.* Lucky Chance, The.

And half the seed of Europe, one by one. (LL)   Parable of the Old Men and the Young, The.   Wilfred Owen.   ChIV-1; HarvBoo; PAI

And handled with a Chain. (LL)   Much Madness Is Divinest Sense.   Emily Dickinson.   APN-2; BoWoP; HeIP-4; NAAL-2v1; NAAL-3; NALW; NAWM-7v2; NCAP; NOBA; NoAM; NoP-4; OPOU; OxBA; RaBo; SAmP; SoSe-8; TCAPo; TFi; TRP; WPE

And hang from implacable boughs. (LL)   Chagrin.   Isaac Rosenberg.   HarvBoo; MoBrPo

And Hannah prayed, and said.   Bible, *O.T.*   BoWoP   *Fr.* First Samuel.

And haply may forget. (LL)   Song: "When I am dead, my dearest."   Christina Georgina Rossetti.   AWP; BoLoP; CABP; EBEV; NAEL-5v2; NAEL-6v2; NOBE; NOBVV; NPeEn; NoP-4; OBEV; OxAEP-2; PoRA; SCV; VWP; ViWPN; WPE

And hardly safe from brother traitors there. (LL)   To Sir Toby.   Philip Freneau.   NAAL-2v1; NAAL-3; NoP-4; TAP

And has the nature of infinity. (LL)   Instructions to the Player.   Carl Rakosi.   APT-2; MiVo

And has the remnant of my life.   Thoughts on my sick-bed.   Dorothy Wordsworth.   PEW

And have forgotten since their beauty passed. (LL)   Tears.   Edward Thomas.   GTBS-P; NAEL-5v2; NAEL-6v2

And have I strove in vain to move.   To Anna Matilda.   Robert Merry.   NOBRP

And have one Titan at a time. (LL)   Master, The.   Edwin Arlington Robinson.   CBCWP; MoAmPo

And Have the Bright Immensities.   Howard Chandler Robbins.   AH

And having nothing, yet hath all. (LL)   Character of a Happy Life, The.   Sir Henry Wotton.   BASC; GTBS-P; NOBE; NOSC; OBEV; OxBEV; SacPr

And haze and vista, and the far horizon fading away. (LL)   Farm Picture, A.   Walt Whitman.   BLT; TRP

And He Answered Them Nothing.   Richard Crashaw.   ChIV-2; SacPr

And he called to him his twelve disciples.   Philip Larkin.   GI   *Fr.* St. Matthew.

And he cast it down, down, on the green grass.   New Ghost, The.   Fredegond Maitland Shove.   SacPr

And he did—nine soliloquies later. (LL)   Hamlet.   Stanley J. Sharpless.   NBLV; PeLi

And he drops, and turns, and goes. (LL)   In the Servants' Quarters.   Thomas Hardy.   FaBoSc; MoBrPo

And He hath not forgotten my age. (LL)   Old Man's Comforts and How He Gained Them, The.   Robert Southey.   UV; UnPo

And he held me fast, and he said, At last.   Ella Wheeler Wilcox.   VerBaPo   *Fr.* Drops of Water.

And he is the one who has made it all. (LL)   Simple Purification, The.   Kabir.   EnlH; WoPoe, *tr. by* Robert Bly

And he picked up a baseball. (LL)   Origin of Baseball, The.   Kenneth Patchen.   APT-2; CLPP

And he pronounced it firm. (LL)   Emily Dickinson.   NCAP; SacPr

And he said, So is the kingdome of God.   Bible, *N.T.*   OBVE   *Fr.* St. Mark.

And he said, So soule doth magnifie the Lord.   Bible, *N.T.*   OBVE   *Fr.* St. Mark.

And he sees them, sees their faces.   Remembering.   László Kálnoky.   IQMS, *tr. by* Kenneth McRobbie and Zita McRobbie

And he, "To begin with a swelled head and end with swelled feet." (LL)   Ezra Pound.   Robert Lowell.   NAAL-2v2; NOBA; NoAM

And he took a little weeping to my eyes. (LL)   Heroes.   Sorley MacLean (Somhairle MacGill-Eain).   FaBoTC; FaBoWar

And he trembled like a heatwave and faded. (LL)   Seamus Heaney.   NPeEn; PBCIP   *Fr.* Station Island.

And he was left lamenting. (LL) Lord Ullin's Daughter. Thomas Campbell. GTBS-P; NOBRP

And he went unto Ramah. There he met. Dance of Saul with the Prophets, The. Saul [or Shaul] Tchernichowsky [or Tchernichovsky]. TrJP, tr. by I. M. Lask

And he will make it plain. (LL) William Cowper. CABP; EBEV; ECEV; FHYEP; FaBoCh; NOBE; NOCV; NOEC; NPeEn; OxBEV; PWR; SCGP; SacPr; TFi; TOF   Fr. Olney Hymns.

And heal my troubled breast which cries [or cryes], / Which dies [or dyes]. (LL) Longing. George Herbert. ESCV; UV

And hear my senses clamor in their rout. (LL) Dante Alighieri. AWP; EaItPo, tr. by Dante Gabriel Rossetti   Fr. La Vita Nuova.

And hear no more at all. (LL) Blows the Wind Today. Robert Louis Stevenson. NPeEn; SCGP

And heard the sound of rushing wind. (LL) Coming of the Plague, The. Weldon Kees. ChIV-1; VGW

And hears an unintelligible prayer. (LL) Feast of Stephen, The. Anthony Hecht. HAP; NoAM; VCAP

And hears, far off, her muted children cry. (LL) Milkmaid. Laurie Lee. BoLoP; FaBoTw

And heartier loves; that lamp is from the tomb. (LL) Leaders of the Crowd, The. W. B. Yeats. EBEV; MoBrPo; OxAEP-2

And Heaven reflected in her face. (LL) To a Young Lady. William Cowper. GTBS-P; SacPr

And held her in my arms! (LL) Politics. W. B. Yeats. AmFaPo; HeIP-4; OxBTC; PoE; SCV

And Henry, a stock-broker, doing well. (LL) Sonnet Reversed. Rupert Brooke. NOBL; OxBSo; PeLV

And her eyes lightnings and her shoulders wings. (LL) In Progress. Christina Georgina Rossetti. BoWoP; NAEL-5v2; NAEL-6v2; WPE

And Her Mother Came Too. Ivor Novello. OBCoV; ReLy

And her quietus is to render thee. (LL) William Shakespeare. HeIP-4; NAEL-5v1; NAEL-6v1; NAEL-7v1   Fr. Sonnets.

And her thorns were my only delight. (LL) William Blake. BoLoP; FHYEP; NAEL-5v2; NAEL-6v2; NOBRP   Fr. Songs of Experience.

And here a line in memory of his name and death. (LL) Osceola. Walt Whitman. NAAL-2v1; NAAL-3

And here and there, on trees by lightning scathed. James Thomson. NePenScot   Fr. Castle of Indolence, The.

And here and there with laurel shrubs between. Philip Freneau. NAAL-3   Fr. House of Night, The.

And Here are the Poets in Their Sad Portraits. Belkis Cuza Malé. TANSG, tr. by Pamela Carmell

And here are the poets in their sad portraits. And Here are the Poets in Their Sad Portraits. Belkis Cuza Malé. TANSG, tr. by Pamela Carmell

And here face down beneath the sun. You, Andrew Marvell. Archibald MacLeish. APT-1; AWP; ColAP; HAP; HeIP-4; MoAmPo; NAAL-2v2; NOBA; NoAM; NoP-4; OxBA; PoRA; SoSe-8; TFi; TRP; TwCP

And here, forgetting human wisdom. At the Fishmonger's. Nikolai Alekseievich Zabolotsky [or Zabolotskii]. TCRusP, tr. by Alec Merivale

And here I wish my soul died with my breath. Ovid. OBVE   Fr. Tristium.

And here's the child's Dad. Unknown. OxNR

And here the cross on the window means myself. Louis MacNeice. ModIr   Fr. Hand of Snapshots, A.

And here the precious dust is laid;. Thomas Carew. See And here the precious dust is laid [or layd]

And here the precious dust is laid [or layd]. Maria Wentworth. Thomas Carew. CaPo; MeLP; NPeEn; PeECV

And here we are back. Going Back Patiently. Frank Mkalawile Chipasula. HBAPE

And hid his face amid a crowd of stars. (LL) When You Are Old. W. B. Yeats. AWP; AmFaPo; BoLoP; CTC; ClHu; EBVV; HeIP-4; MoBrPo; NAEL-5v2; NAEL-6v2; NAWM-7v2; NOBVV; NoAM; NoP-4; OBEV; OxBEV; OxBTC; TFi; WoPoe

And hide its face / for shame. (LL) Death. William Carlos Williams. NAAL-2v2; OxBA; VGW

And hide the shame! (LL) Ichabod[!]. John Greenleaf Whittier. APN-1; NAAL-2v1; NAAL-3; NAAL-5; NOBA; OxBA; TAP; TCAPo

And hide thy shame beneath the ground. (LL) Tennyson. NAEL-6v2; PeECV   Fr. In Memoriam A. H. H.

And Him. (LL) Emily Dickinson. APN-2; NAAL-2v1; NAAL-3; NAAL-5; TCAPo

And, Hinges. Ted Greenwald. FTOS

And his arm lay lightly around my breast—and that night I was happy. (LL) When I Heard At The Close Of The Day. Walt Whitman. APN-1; NAAL-2v1; NAAL-3; NoAM; OxBA; PoE

And his black whiskers and his little dancing feet. (LL) Behaving Like a Jew. Gerald Stern. BodElec; InvLad; LoL; TaR

And his first minute, after noon[e], is night. (LL) Lecture upon the Shadow, A. John Donne. AWP; ESCV; NAEL-5v1; NAEL-6v1; NAEL-7v1; NoSic; SCGP; UnPo

And His graver of frost. (LL) To a Snowflake. Francis Thompson. MoBrPo; SacPr

And his late kingdom, only from the road. (LL) Robert Louis Stevenson. NOBVV; NPeEn; OxBEV

And his name was Willy Wood. (LL) Aiken Drum. Unknown. FaBoCh; OxNR

And his overthrow, our chorus. (LL) Thomas Love Peacock. AWP; CABP; FaBoCh; FaBoWar; HAP; NAEL-5v2; NAEL-6v2; NOBE; NOBRP; NPeEn; OxAEP-2   Fr. Misfortunes of Elphin, The.

And His own face to see. (LL) Mystery, The. Ralph Hodgson. InvLi; MoBrPo

And his sepulchre shall not be whicted. (LL) Ambrose Bierce. APN-2; OBAL; PeLi   Fr. Devil's Dictionary, The.

And his son Judas, who was called Maccabeus. Bible, Apocrypha. TrJP   Fr. First Maccabees.

And home shall never come. (LL) Twa Brothers, The. Unknown. EBEV; ESPB; OxBB

And hope felt strong and life itself not weak. (LL) Christina Georgina Rossetti. NOBE; OBEV   Fr. Thread of Life, The.

And hope to see you soon Yrs Cal. (LL) Dream, The. Robert Earl Hayden. ESEAA; NBV

And Hope without an object cannot live. (LL) Work without Hope. Samuel Taylor Coleridge. CenSon; GSo; NAEL-5v2; NAEL-6v2; NOBE; OBEV; OxAEP-2; OxBSo; PAI; Son; WoPoe

And hoping a little, a little, that either may be. (LL) Blackberry Winter. John Crowe Ransom. APT-1; OxBA; PoRA

And how beguile you? Death has no repose. James Elroy Flecker. OxBTC   Fr. Golden Journey to Samarkand, The.

And how do you do again? (LL) Mother Goose. LB; OxNR; ReMoGo

And how do you react to exile? Politely. Mr Jones as the Transported Poet. T. Harri Jones. TCAWP

And how were we able to sing. From the Willow Branches. Salvatore Quasimodo. WoPoe, tr. by Michael Egan

And how young they were, how innocent. (LL) Taking of the Koppie, The. Uys Krige. FaBoWar; PeSAV

And humbly, or most royally, adds her own. (LL) Kiltartan Legend. Padraic Fallon. ModIr; NOIV

And hundreds of miles of water. (LL) Bodies of Water. Greg Williamson. NAPBL; NeAmPo

And hurl me to the shark, I shall not die! (LL) Leg, The. Karl Shapiro. HAP; MoAmPo; UnPo; WeW-3

And hurls for him, O half hurls earth for him off under his feet. (LL) Hurrahing in Harvest. Gerard Manley Hopkins. MoBrPo; NAEL-5v2; NAEL-6v2; OxBSo; PeECV; PoE; SacPr; TOF

And hymn thy favourite name! (LL) Ode to Evening. William Collins. AWP; CABP; HAP; NAEL-5v1; NAEL-6v1; NAEL-7v1; NOBE; NOEC; OBEV; OxAEP-1; PoE; SCGP; TFi

And I a beginner. Answer to Yo / Question. Sonia Sanchez. BPo

And I am an unhappy stranger. Mexican Loneliness. Jack Kerouac. CLPP

And I am in the wilderness alone. (LL) William Cullen Bryant. APN-1; ColAP; NAAL-2v1; NAAL-3; NAAL-5; NCAP; NOBA; OxBA; TAP; TCAPo

And I am lost in the beautiful white ruins / of America. (LL) Having Lost My Sons, I Confront the Wreckage of the Moon: Christmas, 1960. James Wright. CoAP; HCAP; NAAL-2v2

And I am Marie of Roumania. (LL) Dorothy Parker. NBLV; NIP-4; OBAL; OBCoV   Fr. Some Beautiful Letters.

And I Am Old to Know. Pauline Hanson. TAP

And I am proud of my young beauty. (LL) Tzu Yeh. WPOW; WoPoe, tr. by Chung Ling and Kenneth Rexroth

And I am safe and always have been. (LL) Kaddish. David Ignatow. RaBo; TaR

And I asked for directions from a bird who is myself. Paavo Haavikko. PFTM-2, tr. by Anselm Hollo   Fr. Winter Palace, The.

And I became alone. (LL) Emily Dickinson. FaBoVe; MoAmPo; TOF

And I can speak a little then. (LL) Tennyson. EBVV; GTBS-P; NAEL-6v2; NAWM-7v2   Fr. In Memoriam A. H. H.

And I captive am again[e]. (LL) Mary Sidney Wroth, Countess of Montgomery. LW; PEW   Fr. Urania.

And I choose—just a Crown. (LL) Emily Dickinson. APN-2; NALW; SacPr; TRP; WPOW; WPoS

And i could do for many days / Without eggs. (LL) Egg Thoughts. Russell Hoban. NTCP; OTCP

And I dance submerged. Dance, The. Marjorie Agosin. TCLAP, tr. by Cola Franzen

And I don't feel so well myself. (LL) On the Vanity of Earthly Greatness. Arthur Guiterman. APT-1; HeIP-4; OBCA; PAI; TrJP

And I don't want no Bail. (LL) Girl Held without Bail. Margaret Abigail Walker. BPo; WWork

And I eat men like air. (LL) Lady Lazarus. Sylvia Plath. AmFaPo; ChIV-2; CoAmPo; FaBoWP; HCAP; HarvBoo; NAAL-2v2; NAAL-5; NALW; NIL-

7; NIP-4; NOBA; NoAM; NoP-4; OxWW; PoPoPo; PoetW; TAP; TRP; VCAP; VGW

And I envied her the baby within. Man Impregnated. Moniza Alvi. NeBl

"And I fare you well, Lady Ouncebell." Lord Lovel. *Unknown.* ESPB

And I fell in love with a woman so tall that. From the Travels of Gulliver. Suniti Namjoshi. GLP

And I forget to age, through her sweet will. (LL) Augusta Davies Webster. OxBSo; ViWPN *Fr.* Mother and Daughter.

And I hadn't been. (LL) Come In. Robert Frost. APT-1; MoAmPo; NOBA; NoP-4; RaBo; TRP

And I hated myself. (LL) I, the Survivor. Bertolt Brecht. HP; PoSu

And I have broken down before the wind. (LL) Nocturne of the Wharves. Arna Bontemps. BPo; ColAP; GT

And I have chosen the sea as no man's land. Edouard J. Maunick. NegPo *Fr.* As Far as Yoruba Land.

And I have come upon this place. L'An Trentiesme de Mon Eage. Archibald MacLeish. NOBA

And I have learned how diving's done. Fantasia. Dorothy Livesay. MoCV

And I have murdered it in my early manhood. (LL) Dirty Word, The. Karl Shapiro. CoAP; InPK-6

And I have never gone back. (LL) Night Thoughts. Lu Yu. OHPC; WoPoe, *tr.* by Kenneth Rexroth

And I have stepped into the iceworld—at the snout. 66°7' N/22°17' W. Peter Rafferty. NLP

And I have tried to keep them from falling. (LL) Ezra Pound. APT-1; FaBoMo; PoE *Fr.* Cantos.

And I hear the pad of feet to the union hall. Thomas McGrath. NNaP *Fr.* Letter to an Imaginary Friend.

And I, I was a good child on the whole. Elizabeth Barrett Browning. BrRo *Fr.* Aurora Leigh.

And I implode from sheer emptiness. (LL) Houdini. Moniza Alvi. EmeKit; MFPA

And I in my bed again! (LL) Western Wind. *Unknown.* BoLoP; CTC; ClHu; EBEV; EnLoPo; FaBoCh; HAP; HeIP-4; InPK-6; NAEL-6v1; NAEL-7v1; NIL-7; NOBE; NoSic; OPOU; OxBSP; SCGP; SoSe-8; TFi; UnPo; WeW-3; WoPoe

And I killed the Molione boys. Ibycus. SaLy, *tr.* by Diane Rayor

And I know the amplitude of time. (LL) Walt Whitman. CAGL; ColAP *Fr.* Song of Myself.

And I know where sleeps Holofernes. (LL) Judith. Adah Isaacs Menken. APN-2; CBWP-1; SWaP; ViWPN

And I lean toward mine. (LL) Beginning. James Wright (1927–80). ColAP; VCAP

And I let the fish go. (LL) Fish, The. Elizabeth Bishop. APT-2; ChAP; FaBoWP; HAP; HarvBoo; HeIP-4; InPK-6; MoASP; MoAmPo; NAAL-2v2; NAAL-5; NALW; NOBA; NoAM; NoP-4; PAI; PoE; PoPoPo; PoetW; RB; TFi; TRP

And I lie listening awake? (LL) Fragment 36 [or Thirty-Six]: "I know not what to do." "H. D." NALW; OxBA; PoBW; VGW

And I live at the back of beyond. (LL) Overheard in County Sligo. Gillian Clarke. HarvBoo; TCAWP

And I'll never come back any more. (LL) Didn't My Lord Deliver Daniel? *Unknown.* AH; APN-2

And I looked back very hard at him. (LL) Rabbit, The. Elizabeth Madox Roberts. OBCA; OxIBACP

And I love my Daddy like he loves his Dollar. (LL) American Primitive. William Jay Smith. InPK-6; MoAmPo; OxBSP; PAI; RaBo; TwCP

And I love the rain. (LL) April Rain Song. Langston Hughes. NOxBChV; NTCP; OBCA; OxIBACP

And I'm here, sizing the dark, saving my mother's seat. (LL) Sitting at Night on the Front Porch. Charles Wright. ColAP; GeoHom; LCAP-2

And I made myself a surrogate wedding-day. Sisters, The. Nicki Jackowska. BrRo

And I may laugh at them because I knew them. (LL) Isaac and Archibald. Edwin Arlington Robinson. APT-1; OxBA

And I mine own and yours no more. (LL) Madam, Withouten Many Words. Sir Thomas Wyatt. NAEL-6v1; NAEL-7v1; NoP-4

And I more pleasure in your praise. (LL) To E. Fitzgerald. Tennyson. NOBVV; NPeEn

And I myself—am murmuring. Rustle of Birches. Gennady Aygi. TCRusP, *tr.* by Peter France

And I nae mair maun toddle about the tree. (LL) Alison [or Allison] Gross. *Unknown.* ESPB; FaBoCh; OxBB

And I no more shall be. (LL) Fire in My Meditation Burned. Henry Ainsworth. AH; ChIV-1

And I, O Fear, will dwell with thee! (LL) Ode to Fear. William Collins. NOEC; SCGP

And I [or ich] bowed[e] my body and beheld all about [or bihelde al aboute]. William Langland. CTC *Fr.* Vision of Piers Plowman, The.

And I remain despairing of the port. (LL) Petrarch. HAP; OBVE; OxBEV; SCGP; Son; WeW-3, *tr.* by Sir Thomas Wyatt *Fr.* Sonnets to Laura.

And I remember Spain. Louis MacNeice. OBWP; OxAEP-2 *Fr.* Autumn Journal.

And I remembered the cry of the peacocks. (LL) Domination of Black. Wallace Stevens. APT-1; MoAmPo; OWoS; OxBA; TCAPo

And I replied [or reply'd], *My Lord.* (LL) Collar, The. George Herbert. AWP; BASC; CABP; ClHu; EBEV; FSCP; FaBoVe; GeHe; HAP; HeIP-4; InvLi; MeLP; NAEL-5v2; NAEL-6v1; NAEL-7v1; NIL-7; NIP-4; NOBE; NOCV; NOSC; NPeEn; NoP-4; OBWVE; PBRV; PoE; PoPoPo; PoRA; SCGP; SCV; SacPr; TFi; TOF; WeW-3

And I rode the Greyhound down to Brooklyn. Wild Strawberry. Maurice Kenny. HATNAP

And I sailing, sailing swiftly from the county of Mayo. (LL) County of Mayo, The. Thomas Flavell [or Lavell]. BIrV; OBEV, *tr.* by George Fox

And I saw a crowd of Hungarians under the trees with their women and children and a keg of beer and an accordion. (LL) Happiness. Carl Sandburg. IllVoic; OxBA

And I saw askant the armies. Walt Whitman. FaBoWar *Fr.* Memories of President Lincoln.

And I saw the midnight sun. (LL) Midnight Sun. Johnny Mercer. APT-2; ReLy

And I say, "Cousin Harriet, here is the *Boston Evening Transcript.*" (LL) *Boston Evening Transcript,* The. T. S. Eliot. APT-1; InPK-6; TCAPo

And I Shall Be the Mouth of Copper. Marianne van Hirtum. SurWo, *tr.* by Guy Flandre and Peter Wood

And I shall depart. And the birds will remain singing. Definitve Journey, The. Juan Ramón Jiménez. SpanPo, *tr.* by Angel Flores

And I shall not be here when you are gone. (LL) Why He Was There. Edwin Arlington Robinson. APT-1; NOBA; OxBSo

And I shall traverse old love's domain / Never again. (LL) At Castle Boterel. Thomas Hardy. EBEV; GTBS-P; NOBE; NPeEn; OxAEP-2; OxBEV; PeVV; PoE; SCV

And I shall walk on down the street, down the street. (LL) Bella [or Izabella] Akhatovna Akhmadulina. TCRusP; WPOW, *tr.* by Daniel Weissbort

And I shan't be home no more. (LL) Song of the Dying Gunner A.A.1. Charles Causley. FaBoWar; PoWW

And I shout at Iva, whine at you. Easily. Marilyn Hacker. VCAP *Fr.* Taking Notice.

And I Speak of Cosmic Things. Vsevolod Nekrasov. TCRusP, *tr.* by Daniel Weissbort

And I standing in the shade. Petition. Ronald Stuart Thomas. FaBoMo

And i' th' morning steal all to bed. (LL) John Lyly. NoSic; OBCoV *Fr.* Endimion.

And I to my wife or mistress flee. (LL) Poet's Shuffle, The. Calvin Forbes. GT; LTA

And I took her down by the river. Faithless Wife, The. Federico García Lorca. SpanPo, *tr.* by Robert O'Brien and Robert O'Brien

And I took her to the river. Unfaithful Wife, The. Federico García Lorca. WoPoe, *tr.* by Michael Hartnett

And I took myself for a walk in the woods that day. Family Outing—a Celebration. Nicki Jackowska. BrRo

And I've always admired fiction but I've never admired the fiction. Various Multitudes Contained by the Loves of My Love, The. Anselm Berrigan. HeMarv

And I was born with you, wasn't I, Blues? Blues Don't Change, The. Al Young. ESEAA; GT

And I was there, waving, and I would be there at the other end. (LL) Whole Self, The. Naomi Shihab Nye. GraLe; PoArWo

And I was unaware. (LL) Darkling Thrush, The. Thomas Hardy. AmFaPo; CABP; ClHu; EBVV; HAP; HarvBoo; MoBrPo; NAEL-5v2; NAEL-6v2; NIL-7; NIP-4; NOBE; NOBVV; NPeEn; NoAM; NoP-4; OBEV; OWoS; OxBEV; PAI; PoE; PoPoPo; RB; SoSe-8; TFi; TOF; UnPo; WoPoe

And I went up to that chandeliered place. Poem. Calvin C. Hernton. GT

And I when I meet you mean to discover you by the like in you. (LL) Among the Multitude. Walt Whitman. APN-1; CAGL

"And I will come after, on little Jack Nag." (LL) Robin and Richard. Mother Goose. OxBoLi; OxNR; ReMoGo

And I will [or shall] dwell in the house of the Lord for ever [or forever]. (LL) Bible, *O.T.* AWP; NAWM-5v1; NIL-7; NIP-4; TFi; TrJP *Fr.* Psalms.

And I will venture, though I fall or tire. (LL) Francis Quarles. BASC; NOSC *Fr.* Emblems.

And I with only a reed in my hands. Memory 1. George Seferis. PoetW, *tr.* by Edmund Keeley and Philip Sherrard

And I with thee will choose to live. (LL) John Milton. AWP; BASC; FHYEP; GTBS-P; HAP; NAEL-6v1; NAEL-7v1; NOSC; NoP-4; OBEV; TFi

And I, woman, cloaked in blues. I, Woman. Irma McClaurin. BlSi

And I would be for ever where they were. (LL) Ballata: His Talk with Certain Peasant Girls. Franco Sacchetti. AWP; EaltPo, *tr.* by Dante Gabriel Rossetti

And ice below, and above—I toil somewhere in between. Vladimir Semionovich Vysotsky [or Vysotskii]. TCRP

And if a juggler arrives in town. When Tomorrow Is Too Long. Tanure Ojaide. HBAPE

And if any man should ask me. Deliverance. Frances Ellen Watkins Harper. WPOW

And if he ever should come back. Last Words, The. Maurice Maeterlinck. AWP, tr. by Frederick York Powell

And If He Had Been Wrong for Me. Robert Duncan. RaBo

And If I Did What Then? George Gascoigne. See Adventures of Master F. I, The

And if I do. Koju. JDP, tr. by Yoel Hoffmann

And if I dye, who will saye: This was Immerito? (LL) Iambicum Trimetrum. Edmund Spenser. BoLoP; EBEV; NPeEn; OBEV

And if I lived in those olden times. Anonymous. Víctor Hernández Cruz. PueRic

And if it's not askin' too much, pleeease. B.B. Blues. Mary Weems. SpirFl

And if it snowed and snow covered the drive. Poem. Simon Armitage. HarvBoo

And if men ask you why you fled, and what. Refugees. Donald Davidson. FuPo

And if my light should. Elaine Randell. Oth Fr. Snoad Hill Poems, The.

And, if not shot or hang'd [or hanged], you'll get knighted. (LL) Stanzas: "When a man hath no freedom to fight for at home." Byron. FaBoEE; NBLV; NoP-4; OxAEP-2; PAI; TRP

And If the Angel Should Ask. Hayyim Nahman [or Khayim Nakhman or Chaim Nachman] Bialik. MHP, tr. by Ruth Finer Mintz

And if tonight my soul may find her peace. Shadows. D. H. Lawrence. OxBTC

And if ye stand in doubt. John Skelton. NAEL-5v1; NAEL-6v1 Fr. Colin Clout.

And if you sleep, and if the sheets are clean. Aleksandr Semionovich Kushner. TCRP

And I'm your servant, J. M. Synge. (LL) Curse, The. John Millington Synge. FaBoEE; NOIV; OBCoV

And imagined her. She Had Known Brothers. Sherley Anne Williams. GT

And in a while you'll tell another tale. (LL) Anne Bradstreet. BASC; EMWP

And, in Africa, a carcass quick with flies. (LL) Black Tambourine. Hart Crane. InPK-6; NoAM; OxBA; OxBSP; TAP

And in August the barley grew up out of the grave. (LL) Requiem for the Croppies. Seamus Heaney. BIrV; CIP-2; FaBoMo; OBWP

And in blue skies the Orb is manifest to sight. (LL) Epi-strauss-ium. Arthur Hugh Clough. NAEL-5v2; NAEL-6v2

And in conclusion I'll say. Goodbye. Bella [or Izabella] Akhatovna Akhmadulina. BoWoP, tr. by Barbara Einzig

And in God's house are many scansions. (LL) Poetry. Mary Elizabeth Fullerton. GI; NOBAu

And in immense perdition sinks the soul. (LL) To the University of Cambridge, in New-England. Phillis Wheatley. NAAAL; NAAL-2v1; NAAL-3; NAAL-5; TAP; TCAPo

And in its ashes plant the tree of peace! (LL) Worship. John Greenleaf Whittier. ChIV-2; NOCV

And, in its marriage robe, the heavy body wound. (LL) John Keats. FHYEP; NAEL-6v2

And in my joys for thee my only annoy. (LL) Sir Philip Sidney. NAEL-6v1; NAEL-7v1 Fr. Astrophil and Stella.

And in one another's blameless eyes go blind. (LL) Tally Stick, The. Jarold Ramsey. NIL-7; NIP-4

And in our faults by lies we flatter'd be. (LL) William Shakespeare. AWP; AmFaPo; EBEV; HeIP-4; NAEL-5v1; NAEL-7v1; NPeEn; NoSic; OxAEP-1; OxBEV; PAI; SoSe-8 Fr. Sonnets.

And in September, O what keen delight. Folgore da San Geminiano [or Gimignano]. EaItPo, tr. by Dante Gabriel Rossetti Fr. Sonnets of the Months.

And in September, O what keen delight! Sonnets of the Months: September. Folgore da San Geminiano [or Gimignano]. AWP, tr. by Dante Gabriel Rossetti

And in that land dwells a king. Sir Cawline. Unknown. ESPB

And in that region there were shepherds out in the field. Bertolt Brecht. GI Fr. St. Luke.

And in the ear[e], not conscience ring. (LL) Windows, The. George Herbert. BASC; ESCV; GeHe; MeLP; NAEL-5v1; NAEL-6v1; NAEL-7v1; NOCV; NoP-4; PeECV; PoE; TrCP

And in the end, the entire earth may answer to a single name. Franco Buffoni. ItPo, tr. by Gayle Ridinger

And in the evening the black river. Shadow Valley. Robert Morgan. AngWePo

And in the evening there was light. (LL) What the Birds Said. John Greenleaf Whittier. APN-1; NOBA

And in the 51st Year of That Century, While My Brother Cried in the Trench, While My Enemy Glared from the Cave. Hyam Plutzik. RB

And in the frosty season, when the sun. William Wordsworth. FaBoCh; WoPoe Fr. Prelude; Growth of a Poet's Mind [1805 vers.], The.

And in the Hanging Gardens. Conrad Potter Aiken. APT-1; MoAmPo

And in the Human Heart. Conrad Potter Aiken. Son

And in the Item loved the Whole. (LL) Herman Melville. Conrad Potter Aiken. NoAM; TAP

And in the light of truth thy Bondman let me live! (LL) Ode to Duty. William Wordsworth. AWP; FHYEP; GTBS-P; NAEL-5v2; NAEL-6v2; NOBRP; OBEV

And in the midst of all, a fountaine stood. Edmund Spenser. EroLit Fr. Faerie Queene, The.

And in the morning the king loved you most. Arcanum One. Gwendolyn MacEwen. MoCV

And in the mountains of Kiev, Sviatoslav. Unknown. WoPoe, tr. by Harry Strickhausen Fr. Song of Igor's Campaign, The.

And in the river the nameless body sifts. Solitaire. Conrad Potter Aiken. ColAP

And in their holiness made power. Winkte. Maurice Kenny. GLP

And in this faith I choose to live and die. (LL) His Mother's Service to Our Lady. François Villon. AWP; CTC, tr. by Dante Gabriel Rossetti

And in this way we'll singe his skin for him. (LL) Sonnet: He Rails against Dante, Who Had Censured His Homage to Becchina. Cecco Angiolieri, da Siena. AWP; EaItPo, tr. by Dante Gabriel Rossetti

And in thy wisdom, make me wise. (LL) Tennyson. EBVV; HAP; NAEL-6v2; NAWM-7v2; SacPr; TrCP Fr. In Memoriam A. H. H.

And in your fragrant bosom[e] dies [or dyes]. (LL) Song, [A.]: "Ask[e] me no more where Jove bestow[e]s." Thomas Carew. AWP; BASC; BeJo; CaPo; CavPo; ClHu; EnLoPo; HAP; MeLP; NAEL-5v1; NAEL-6v1; NAEL-7v1; NOBE; NOSC; NoP-4; OBEV; OxBEV; PAI; PoE; PoRA; SCGP; TFi

And indeed I shall anchor, one day—some summer morning. Landfall. Randolph Stow. BMAP

And insults. (LL) Yury [or Iurii] Ivask. TCRP; TCRusP, tr. by John Glad

And into his dead mouth slip the set of teeth. (LL) Michael Longley. BiHa; CIP-2; ModIr; NPeEn Fr. Wreaths.

And invite the wind inside. (LL) Exaggeration of Despair, The. Sherman Alexie. BAP-97; NeAmPo

And I—Oh the hopelessness!—cannot write! (LL) Letter from a Contract Worker. Antonio Jacinto. PBMAP; PoetW, tr. by Margaret Dickinson and Michael Wolfers

And is it possible?—and must it be. Hic Jacet. Rosamund Marriott Watson. ViWPN

And is it true that I must go from Troy? William Shakespeare. OxAEP-1 Fr. Troilus and Cressida.

And is our life, a life wherein we borrow. Matthew X. 28. Roger Wolcott. SCAP

And is the best known, not defining Him. (LL) What God Is. Robert Herrick. BeJo; NOSC

And is the water come? Sure't cannot be. Upon Sir John Lawrence's Bringing Water over the Hills [to My L. Middlesex His House at Witten]. Sir John Suckling. CaPo

And is there care in heauen [or heaven]? and is there loue [or love]. Edmund Spenser. NOCV; NoSic Fr. Faerie Queene, The.

And is there glory from the heavens departed? Lost Pleiad, The. Felicia Dorothea Hemans. NOBRP

And is there honey still for tea? (LL) Old Vicarage, Grantchester, The. Rupert Brooke. MoBrPo; NoP-4; OxBTC; PoRA

And is there sadness in thy dreams, my boy? Dreaming Child, The. Felicia Dorothea Hemans. NOBRP

And is there then no earthly place. Thomas Moore. OBSV Fr. Rhymes on the Road.

And is thine everlasting Store. (LL) Dialogue between the Resolved Soul and Created Pleasure, A. Andrew Marvell. ESCV; FSCP; GeHe; MeLP

And is this—Yarrow?—This the Stream. Yarrow Visited [September, 1814]. William Wordsworth. GTBS-P

And is thy glass run out? Is that oil spent. Upon the Poet of His Time, Ben Jonson: His Honoured Friend and Father. James Howell. NOSC

And Isabel calmly cured the doctor. (LL) Adventures of Isabel. Ogden Nash. ChAP; MoAmPo; NOxBChV; NTCP; OBAL; OBCA; OxIBACP

And Ishmael crouch'd beside a crackling briar. Ishmael. Herbert Edward Palmer. OBEV

And Israel's body as smoke through the air! (LL) O the Chimneys. Nelly Sachs. AF; PoetW; PoetW, tr. by Michael Roloff

And it all died down. From My Lai the Thunder Went West. Richard Ryan. CIP-2

And It Came to Pass at Midnight. Yannai. TrJP

And it came to pass in those days, that there went out a decree from Caesar Augustus. Bible, N.T. NAWM-5v1 Fr. St. Luke.

And it came to pass just as they had foretold. Adam Cornford. CLPP *Fr.* Rapture, The.

And it is hard to tell one. To a Friend Who Wouldn't Bother to Strain His Noodleboard Because Even So It Is Hard to Go Hunting When Your Rifle Is Blunt and Love Is Soft as an Old Blanket. Jacob Glatshteyn. PFTM-1

And It Is Still That Way. Hedva Harechavi. DTA, *tr. by* Miriyam Glazer

And it isn't for you. (LL) Several Voices Out of a Cloud. Louise Bogan. APT-2; NALW

And it's hard to see the mountains. Can I Say. Dolly Bird. WPOW

And it's the summer civil war. "Eduard Veniaminovich Limonov." TCRusP, *tr. by* William Tjalsma *Fr.* Secret Notebook.

And it seemed, while we waited, he began to walk towards us. Geoffrey Hill. NoAM; NoP-4 *Fr.* Mercian Hymns.

And it shall come to pass in that day, that the Lord shall set his hand again the second time to recover the remnant of his people, which shall be left, from Assyria, and from Egypt, and from Path'ros, and from Cush, and from E'lam, and fro. (LL) Bible, *O.T.* AWP; OBVE; TrJP *Fr.* Isaiah.

And it shall come to pass in the end of days. Bible, *O.T.* TrJP *Fr.* Isaiah.

And it shall come to pass when the days shall grow long. When the Days Shall Grow Long. Hayyim Nahman [*or* Khayim Nakhman *or* Chaim Nachman] Bialik. TrJP, *tr. by* A. M. Klein

And it was at that age. . . Poetry arrived. Poetry. Pablo Neruda. PoetW; VCWP, *tr. by* Alastair Reid

And it was then. Poem for the Father. Alejandra Pizarnik. TCLAP, *tr. by* Frank Graziano and María Rosa Fort

And it will be life to separate us, not death. Fragment. Alessandro Ceni. ItPo, *tr. by* Gayle Ridinger

And it will not affect your nostrils long. Odor of a Metal Is Not Strong, The. Merrill Moore. OxBSo

And its bleak sacrifice? (LL) Islands, The. "H. D." MoAmPo; TCAPo

And its hero the Conqueror Worm. (LL) Conqueror Worm, The. Edgar Allan Poe. APN-1; AWP; NCAP; NOBA; TCAPo

And its wavering image here. (LL) Bridge, The. Henry Wadsworth Longfellow. APN-1; ITBLP

And Jack from Joan, and they shall never marry. (LL) Another Song. Donald Justice. CoAmPo; VGW

And Jesus said to him, "Foxes have holes." Karl Kirchwey. GI *Fr.* St. Matthew.

And Joseph was brought down to Egypt. Bible, O.T. NAWM-5v1 *Fr.* Genesis.

And Jude, now you're married, will stretch on the floor. (LL) On an Island. John Millington Synge. BIrV; FaBoVe; MoBrPo; NPeEn; OxBEV; OxBSP; PeVV

And just by crossing the short sea. Channel Crossing. George Barker. GTBS-P

And just what the fuck else were we supposed to do. (LL) Rape. Jayne Cortez. GT; PmAP

And keep his ears glued to the big clock they keep winding. (LL) If Someone Tells You It's Not for Sure. Jaime Sabines. PoetW; TCLAP, *tr. by* Philip Levine

And keep on safely sleeping. (LL) Summary for Alastor. Laura Riding Jackson. FuPo; WoPoe

And keep them all like gentlemen! (LL) Dove and the Wren, The. Mother Goose. OxNR; ReMoGo

And kept my spirit with the free. (LL) Vision, A. John Clare. EBVV; GTBS-P; NAEL-5v2; NAEL-6v2; NOBVV; OxBEV; PoE

And kept on drinking. (LL) Miniver Cheevy. Edwin Arlington Robinson. APT-1; AWP; ChAP; ClHu; FaBoCh; HeIP-4; MoAmPo; NAAL-2v2; NAAL-5; NBLV; NoAM; NOBA; NoP-4; OBSV; OxBA; PAI; PeLV; PoRA; RaBo; SCV; SoSe-8; TAP; TCAPo; TFi

And killed the mice in his father's barn. (LL) Mother Goose. OxBEV; OxNR; ReMoGo

And kiss him into slumbers like a bride. (LL) John Fletcher. OxBSP; SCGP *Fr.* Tragedy of Valentinian, The.

And kissed my sister instead of me. (LL) Mother Goose. NOBL; OxNR; ReMoGo

And kneeling one day at the sea's edge God. Making of Eve, The. Julia Copus. NeBl

And knit again the knot that should not slide. (LL) Sir Thomas Wyatt. CTC; EnLoPo

And knows herself in death. (LL) Great Breath, The. "Æ." MoBrPo; OBEV; OBMV

And knows not whether he be first or last. (LL) Time, Real and Imaginary. Samuel Taylor Coleridge. NOBE; OBEV; OxBSP

And landing upon their heads. (LL) Between Ourselves. Audre Lorde. ISC; WPOW

And Langland told how heaven could not keep love. Beach, The. Peter Scupham. HarvBoo

And last but not least, my own brother. My Lost Brother. Ben Scammell. NLP

And last night a man came in. Spring Street Bar. Mei-Mei Berssenbrugge. WPOW

And last, when Words are into Clouds devolv'd. (LL) Love's Witness. Aphra Behn. BoWoP; LW

And later try hard to make them seem light. (LL) Under a Certain Little Star. Wislawa Szymborska. PoetW; VCWP, *tr. by* Magnus J. Krynski and Robert A. Maguire

And, laterally / to Adam's pulsing eye. Cloud, The. Derek Walcott. ChIV-1

And laugh—but smile no more. (LL) Haunted Palace, The. Edgar Allan Poe. APN-1; NAAL-3; NOBA; OxBA; TAP; TCAPo; TFi

And laugh—No more have I. (LL) Emily Dickinson. APN-2; FaBoVe; NALW; NCAP; NOBA; NoP-4

And laughing Ceres reassume the land. (LL) Pope. NOEC; NPeEn; OxBEV *Fr.* Epistle IV, to Richard Boyle, Earl of Burlington.

And leaf-shadow are lost. (LL) Evening. "H. D." APT-1; FaBoMo; HarvBoo; VGW; WPE

And leaps from dreams to hail the coming day. (LL) South, The. Emma Lazarus. APN-2; ColAP

And learn a style from a despair. (LL) This Last Pain. William Empson. EBEV; FaBoMo; GTBS-P; HarvBoo; MoBrPo; NoAM; NPeEn

And learn their languages. (LL) Kshemendra. EaWin; WoPoe, *tr. by* J. Moussaieff Masson and W. S. Merwin *Fr.* Kavikanthabharana.

And leave dull verse to the dull peaceful time. (LL) Soldier Addresses His Body, The. Edgell Rickword. PeFWW; PoWW

And leave her dreaming in the silent land. (LL) Old House, The. Amy Levy. PEW; VWP; ViWPN

And leave him then, being made a ready horse? (LL) John Donne. BASC; NoP-4; OxAEP-1; PeLV *Fr.* Elegies.

And leave our desert to its peace! (LL) Matthew Arnold. EBVV; NAEL-5v2; PoE

And leave th' earth to their food. (LL) H[oly] Communion, The. George Herbert. ChIV-1; ESCV

And leave the house. (LL) Childhood Is the Kingdom Where Nobody Dies. Edna St. Vincent Millay. FaBoWP; NALW

And leave to these thy true integrity. (LL) To Dante [*or* Sonnet: Guido Cavalcanti to Dante Alighieri]. Guido Cavalcanti. AWP; OBVE, *tr. by* Percy Bysshe Shelley

And leave you with them empty bed blues. (LL) Empty Bed Blues. Bessie Smith. APT-2; OBAL; UnPo

And leaves his hold and cackles, groans, and dies. (LL) Badger. John Clare. FHYEP; HAP; NPeEn; PAI; SCGP

And leaves thrust violently upon the pane. (LL) Autumn Chapter in a Novel. Thom Gunn. FaBoMo; OxBTC

And led the flock away. (LL) Emily Dickinson. APN-2; ITBLP; TAP

And left it to us! (LL) Ancient History. Arthur Guiterman. KaS; OBCA

And left me old, and cold, and grey. (LL) May. Christina Georgina Rossetti. NOBVV; NPeEn; OxBEV

And left the vivid air signed with their honour. (LL) I Think Continually of Those Who Were Truly Great. Stephen Spender. HAP; HarvBoo; HeIP-4; MoBrPo; NOBE; NoP-4; OxBTC; PAI; PoRA; RaBo; TFi

And left with a debt to another white man. (LL) St. Peter Claver. Toi Derricotte. LTA; PBCAP

And let him hate you through the glass. (LL) Midnight Skaters, The. Edmund Charles Blunden. FaBoTw; GTBS-P; MoBrPo; NOBE; NPeEn; PeFWW; WoPoe

And let me die [or dye] before my death! (LL) Regeneration. Henry Vaughan. BASC; ChIV-1; ESCV; FSCP; GeHe; MeLP; NAEL-5v1; NAEL-6v1; NAEL-7v1; NoP-4; PoE

And let my heart within travail and moan. (LL) Dante Alighieri. AWP; EaltPo, *tr. by* Dante Gabriel Rossetti *Fr.* La Vita Nuova.

And let the ape and tiger die. (LL) Tennyson. EBVV; NAEL-6v2; NAWM-7v2 *Fr.* In Memoriam A. H. H.

And let us have a lark instead. (LL) To Minerva. Thomas Hood. NBLV; NOBL; OxBoLi; PeLV

And let your full lips laugh at Fate! (LL) To a Dark Girl. Gwendolyn B. Bennett. BlSi; ColAP; NAAAL

And letting them out again. (LL) Gwendolyn Brooks. NAAAL; NAAL-2v2; NoAM; NOBA *Fr.* Street in Bronzeville, A.

And Libye land likewise wyth warlick victorye conquoure. (LL) Virgil [*or* Vergil]. BIrV; OBVE *Fr.* Aeneid [*or* Eneados, *Aeneis*], The.

And lies down, who was my moon or more. (LL) Complaint. James Wright (1927–80). NOBA; TAP; VGW

And life be nothing, it shall not stop kissing. (LL) E. E. Cummings. MoAmPo; NAAL-2v2

And life for me ain't been no crystal stair. (LL) Mother to Son. Langston Hughes. AmFaP; ChAP; ISC; NAAAL; NAAL-2v2; NAAL-5; NTCP; OBCA; OxIBACP; SAmP; TTY; WoPoe

And lifts them back in with warm spoons. (LL) Lady Lowbodice. *Unknown.* PeLi; PeLV

And light enough, to read it. (LL) Image from Beckett, An. Derek Mahon. ModIr; NPeEn

And Lightly, like the Flowers. Pierre de Ronsard. AWP, *tr.* by W. E. Henley

And lightly weight the air. (LL) Three Modes of History and Culture. Imamu Amiri Baraka. ESEAA; PmAP

And like a dying lady, lean and pale. Waning Moon, The. Shelley. FHYEP; OxBSP

And like a finer light in light. (LL) Tennyson. FHYEP; NAEL-6v2 *Fr.* In Memoriam A. H. H.

And like a thunderbolt he falls. (LL) Eagle, The. Tennyson. ChAP; ClHu; FaBoCh; FHYEP; GTBS-P; HeIP-4; InPK-6; ITBLP; NAEL-5v2; NAEL-6v2; NOBVV; NoP-4; NTCP; OWoS; OxBSP; PAI; SCGP; TFi; TRP; UnPo

And like thy father sing in tunefulness. Joseph Ezobi. TrJP, *tr.* by D. I. Friedmann *Fr.* Silver Bowl, The.

And, like thy shadow, follow thee. (LL) Compensation. Ralph Waldo Emerson. APN-1; NOBA

And listen to his great sigh. (LL) Anne Sexton. BodElec; BoWoP *Fr.* Furies, The.

And little hunted hares. (LL) Bells of Heaven, The. Ralph Hodgson. MoBrPo; NOBE; OBEV; OxBSP

And live forever, like the dust. (LL) Poem in Three Parts. Robert Bly. CoAmPo; NOBA; PAI

And lived with her. (LL) Marriage, A. Robert Creeley. NeAP; RaBo

And lives to-day in Bread and Wine. (LL) Christmas. Sir John Betjeman. ChrPo; OBCP; OxBTC

And lo! Ben Adhem's name led all the rest! (LL) Abou Ben Adhem. Leigh Hunt. BRP; ChAP; ITBLP; NOBE; OBEV; OxAEP-2; PWR; TFi

And lo, there is descending, yea, a narrow footpath. I Chant of the Miracle Stag (Christian Version). *Hungarian Oral Tradition.* IQMS, *tr.* by Adam Makkai

And loftier passions, prompt the loftier theme! (LL) Her Reflections on the Leucadian Rock Before She Perishes. Mary Robinson. CenSon; RWP

And lonesome, very lonesome, is my strand. (LL) Autumn. Christina Georgina Rossetti. BrRo; VWP

And Look for God. Else Lasker-Schüler. BBASP, *tr.* by Robert P. Newton

—And looked and looked our infant sight away. (LL) Over 2000 Illustrations and a Complete Concordance. Elizabeth Bishop. APT-2; HCAP; HarvBoo; LCAP-2; NAAL-2v2; NoAM; PoetW; VCAP

And looked, and said, "It is a dream." (LL) Arthur Hugh Clough. NAEL-5v2; NAEL-6v2 *Fr.* Dipsychus [and the Spirit].

And, looking out, she might. Mariana. R. F. Langley. HarvBoo

And Loplop, Bird-Superior, has transformed himself into flesh. Max Ernst. PFTM-1 *Fr.* Hundred Headless Woman, The.

And Lords whose parents were the Lord knows who. (LL) Daniel Defoe. NOBL; OBSV *Fr.* True-born Englishman, The.

And lose my everlasting rest. (LL) Song: "Absent from thee, I languish still." John Wilmot, 2d Earl of Rochester. BoLoP; EnLoPo; NPeEn; OxBEV

And love, and man's unconquerable mind. (LL) To Toussaint L'Ouverture. William Wordsworth. CenSon; InPK-6; NOBE; PoRA

And love arrived may find us somewhere else. (LL) Delay. Elizabeth Jennings. NIL-7; NIP-4; OPOU; OxBTC

And Love doth hold my hand, and makes me write. (LL) Sir Philip Sidney. NoP-4; NoSic *Fr.* Astrophil and Stella.

And love her as hard as you can. (LL) Way, The. Robert Creeley. BoLoP; NeAP

And Love Hung Still. Louis MacNeice. CIP-2; MoBrPo *Fr.* Trilogy for X.

And Love hung still as crystal over the bed. Louis MacNeice. CIP-2; MoBrPo *Fr.* Trilogy for X.

And love is where yesterday is at. (LL) That Day. Anne Sexton. BoWoP; CoAmPo

And love thee evermore. (LL) James Graham, Marquess of Montrose. BeJo; OxBEV

And love with old familiar love. (LL) Christina Georgina Rossetti. NALW; NoP-4; VWP

And love you so much. (LL) Steps. Frank O'Hara. CoAmPo; PmAP

And lovers float down from the cliffs like rain. (LL) Salvador Dali. David Gascoyne. OxBTC; SPE

And Lowells speak only to God. (LL) Boston. John Collins Bossidy. FaBoEE; NBLV; OBAL; OBCoV; OxBoLi; PeLV

And lust is there, and nights not spent alone. (LL) Edna St. Vincent Millay. APT-1; NAAL-2v2; NAAL-5; NALW

And made the kites to whet their beaks clack clack. (LL) Captain Carpenter. John Crowe Ransom. APT-1; FaBoMo; FuPo; MoAmPo; NOBA; NoAM; OxBA; TRP; TwCP; WoPoe

And made ye white. (LL) How Lillies Came White. Robert Herrick. BeJo; CaPo

And magic wills that are more strong than ours. (LL) Anna Hempstead Branch. APT-1; NALW *Fr.* Sonnets from a Lock Box.

And make a dust of their seraphic song. (LL) On Some Shells Found Inland. Trumbull Stickney. APN-2; Son

And make America again! (LL) Let America Be America Again. Langston Hughes. AF; AiP

And make us blest at last. (LL) Mistress: A Song, The. John Wilmot, 2d Earl of Rochester. EBEV; NOBE; NOSC; NPeEn

And makes a constant sacrament of praise. (LL) Peter Quince at the Clavier. Wallace Stevens. APT-1; HeIP-4; InPK-6; MoAmPo; NAAL-5; NAWM-7v2; NOBA; NoAM; NoP-4; OxBA; PAI; PoE; SAmP; TAP; TCAPo; TFi; TwCP

And makes him bring back one leg. (LL) Riddle: "Two legs sat upon three legs." Mother Goose. LB; NTCP; OxNR

And makes me end where I begun[ne]. (LL) Valediction: Forbidding Mourning, A. John Donne. AmFaPo; BASC; ESCV; FHYEP; HAP; HeIP-4; MeLP; NAEL-5v1; NAEL-6v1; NAEL-7v1; NIL-7; NOBE; NOSC; NPeEn; OxBEV; PAI; PoE; SCGP; SoSe-8; TFi; UnPo; WeW-3

And makes the Happiness she does not find. (LL) Samuel Johnson. CABP; EBEV; ECEV; NAEL-6v1; NAEL-7v1; NOEC; NoP-4; OxAEP-1; TFi

And making Death a Victory. (LL) Prometheus. Byron. NOBE; OxAEP-2

And mama complains. Muddy Kid Comes Home. Sandra Cisneros. FFC

And man's religion be complete. (LL) On the Religion of Nature. Philip Freneau. NAAL-2v1; NAAL-3; NAAL-5

And many are amazed and many doubt. (LL) Henry Wadsworth Longfellow. APN-1; OxBA; TAP; TCAPo

And many voices marshalled in one hymn. Hymn. Thomas Lovell Beddoes. NOBVV

And marching Time drew on, and wore me numb. Thomas Hardy. *See* You did not come

And Marie Carmichael, and me. (LL) Mary Hamilton. *Unknown.* ESPB; NePenScot; NoP-4; SCGP

And Marie said, My soule doth magnifie the Lord. Bible, *N.T. See* My soul magnifies the Lord

And mark it with his name forevermore? (LL) Sonnet: "Oh for a poet—for a beacon bright." Edwin Arlington Robinson. APN-2; NCAP; OxBA

And marries either's Dust. (LL) La Belle Confidente. Thomas Stanley. BeJo; MeLP

And me happiest when I compose poems. Birth of Tragedy, The. Irving Layton. MoCV; NoAM; NoP-4

And me swinging my legs. (LL) Good Hot Dogs. Sandra Cisneros. NOxBChV; OxIBACP

And mechanical America Montezuma still. (LL) Cypresses. D. H. Lawrence. NAEL-5v2; NAEL-6v2

And melt to pity the annalist's iron tongue. (LL) Scotland 1941. Edwin Muir. CABP; NePenScot; OxBS

And men, coming and going on the earth. (LL) Clouds. Rupert Brooke. OBEV; OBMV; OxBTC

And mend my rhyme [*or* ryme]. (LL) Denial[l]. George Herbert. BASC; ESCV; FSCP; GeHe; NAEL-5v1; NAEL-6v1; NAEL-7v1; NOBE; NPeEn; NoP-4; PBRV; TOF

And 'midst the stars inscribe Belinda's name. (LL) Pope. CABP; FHYEP; HAP; NAEL-6v1; NAEL-7v1; NAWM-7v2; NoP-4; OBNV; PeLV

And miles to go before I sleep. (LL) Stopping by Woods on a Snowy Evening. Robert Frost. APT-1; BRP; ChAP; ClHu; ColAP; FaBoCh; HAP; HarvBoo; HeIP-4; ITBLP; InPK-6; MoAmPo; NAAL-2v2; NAAL-5; NIL-7; NIP-4; NOBA; NTCP; NoAM; NoP-4; OBCA; OxBA; PAI; PoE; PoPoPo; PoRA; RB; SAmP; SCV; SoSe-8; TAP; TFi; TOF; TRP; TTTS

And mingle all the world with thee. (LL) Tennyson. CAGL; FHYEP; NAEL-6v2 *Fr.* In Memoriam A. H. H.

And mingles all without a plan? (LL) Tennyson. EBEV; NAWM-7v2 *Fr.* In Memoriam A. H. H.

And mirth was bounty with a humbler name. (LL) Prologue to Hugh Kelly's *A Word to the Wise.* Samuel Johnson. EBEV; NPeEn; OxAEP-1

And mock you with me after I am gone. (LL) William Shakespeare. AWP; EBEV; HAP; HeIP-4; NAEL-5v1; NAEL-6v1; NAEL-7v1; NoSic; OxAEP-1; PAI; PoRA; SCGP; Son *Fr.* Sonnets.

And mocks my loss of liberty. (LL) How Sweet I Roamed [*or* Roam'd] from Field to Field. William Blake. EnLoPo; NAEL-5v2; NOEC; TFi

And Modred thought, "The time is hard at hand." (LL) Tennyson. NAEL-5v2; NAEL-6v2 *Fr.* Idylls of the King.

And Monelle said: I will speak to you of actions. Actions. Marcel Schwob. TrJP, *tr.* by William Brown Meloney

And Monelle said: I will speak to you of moments. Moments. Marcel Schwob. TrJP, *tr.* by William Brown Meloney

And Monelle said: I will speak to you of things dead. Things Dead. Marcel Schwob. TrJP, *tr.* by William Brown Meloney

And—more—is Nature's Roman, never to be scourged. (LL) House-Top, The. Herman Melville. APN-2; CBCWP; NAAL-2v1; NAAL-3; NCAP; NOBA; TCAPo

And more—O transport!—reach its home and you. (LL) Passage of the Mountain of St. Gothard, The. Georgiana Cavendish, Duchess of Devonshire. ECWP; RWP

And moulder in dust away! (LL) Children's Hour, The. Henry Wadsworth

Longfellow. APN-1; BRP; ChAP; ITBLP; OBAL; OBCA; TCAPo; WHSW

And move to space beneath our sky. (LL) M., Singing. Louise Bogan. ColAP; NoAM

And moved again and flashed again, time flashed again. (LL) Martial Cadenza. Wallace Stevens. OxBA; VGW

And moved his brush to write a new song. (LL) Sailing Homeward. Chan Fang-sheng. AWP; ChiP; FaBoCh, tr. by Arthur Waley

And Mr. Ferritt. Judith Wright. MoBrPo

And murmuring of innumerable bees. (LL) Tennyson. EBVV; GTBS-P; NAEL-5v2; NAEL-6v2; NOBVV; NPeEn; OBEV; OxBEV; SCGP Fr. Princess, The.

And must be done better. (LL) For Sheridan. Robert Lowell. HCAP; PoetW

And must I lose a soul's inheritance? (LL) Hélas! Oscar Wilde. CAGL; MoBrPo; NAEL-5v2; NAEL-6v2; Son

And Must I Sing? What Subject Shall I Choose? Ben Jonson. BeJo

And my buffalo have found me. (LL) Ballad of William Sycamore, The. Stephen Vincent Benét. MoAmPo; PoRA

And my delight is causer of this strife. (LL) Petrarch. OBVE; Son, tr. by Sir Thomas Wyatt Fr. Sonnets to Laura.

And my discordant nerves peace in your limbs. (LL) Watching Tennis. John Heath-Stubbs. OxBSo; Son

And my father saying things. (LL) My Father's Song. Simon J. Ortiz. HATNAP; NIL-7

And my Love loves me! (LL) Answer to a Child's Question. Samuel Taylor Coleridge. ITBLP; NOxBChV

And my lung full of budgerigars. (LL) Pneumoconiosis. Duncan Bush. AngWePo; TCAWP

And my neck from the gallows-tree. (LL) Maid Freed from the Gallows, The. Unknown. AWP; ESPB

And my nineteen years weigh heavily on my feet. (LL) October. Patrick Kavanagh. CIP-2; GTBS-P

And my opinion is that God sent the whale in time of need. William McGonagall. VerBaPo Fr. Famous Tay Whale, The.

And my Pyramides. (LL) His Poetry His Pillar. Robert Herrick. BeJo; CaPo; NOSC

And my whole heart will rise. (LL) Canzonetta: Of His Lady in Absence. Giacomino Pugliesi. AWP; EaItPo, tr. by Dante Gabriel Rossetti

And my young sweetheart sat at board with me. Idyl. Alfred Mombert. AWP, tr. by Ludwig Lewisohn

And myself. (LL) Lights Out. Edward Thomas. HarvBoo; NOBE; OxAEP-2; PoWW; WoPoe

And nailed a small wing over the corn. (LL) Hawk, The. George Mackay Brown. NoP-4; RB

And naked seemed, to stand each lifeless tree. (LL) Philip Freneau. NAAL-2v1; NAAL-3 Fr. House of Night, The.

And naked was my pastime in between. (LL) James Vincent Cunningham. APT-2; OBAL; TRP; WoPoe Fr. Five Epigrams.

And Naomi said/ Unto her two daughters-in-law. Bible, O.T. TrJP Fr. Ruth.

And ne'er the first assault to proffer. (LL) Of Scolding Wives and the Third Day Ague. Henricus Selyns. AiP; SCAP

And never come back again. (LL) Mother Goose. FaBoVe; ReMoGo

And never could understand! (LL) Vampire, The. Rudyard Kipling. NOBVV; OxBEV

And never for a moment suppose that they understand. (LL) Ram's Horn, The. John Hewitt. BIrV; ModIr; PNI

And never get up at all? (LL) Skyscrapers. Rachel Lyman Field. ChAP; NOxBChV; SSCS

And never look inside. (LL) Parting Gift. Elinor Wylie. APT-1; OxBA

And never more will be. (LL) William Wordsworth. GTBS-P; HAP; NAEL-6v2 Fr. Lucy.

And never scent the ground where they must lie. (LL) Simple Autumnal. Louise Bogan. MoAmPo; Son

And never stain a cheek for it. (LL) To His Book[e]. Martial. AWP; OBVE, tr. by Robert Herrick

And never wake to feel the day's disdain. (LL) Samuel Daniel. CTC; GTBS-P; NAEL-5v1; NAEL-7v1; NIP-4; NOBE; NPeEn; NoSic; OxAEP-1; OxBEV; OxBSo; SCGP; Son; TFi Fr. To Delia.

And never went there again. (LL) Mother Goose. LB; OxBoLi; OxNR; ReMoGo

And new philosophy calls all in doubt. John Donne. NOSC Fr. Anatomy [or Anatomie] of the World, An[: The First Anniversary].

And night and distant travel; for the train. Last Evening. Rainer Maria Rilke. OBWP

And night came down over the solemn waste. Matthew Arnold. OxBEV Fr. Sohrab and Rustum.

And night for night snow fell before my window. Seasons. Christine Busta. AuPH, tr. by Lowell A. Bangerter

And night's trees stood up. (LL) Lawrence Ferlinghetti. NeAP; PoM

And Night shall fold him in soft wings. (LL) Into Battle. Julian Grenfell. FaBoWar; OBEV; OBMV; OBWP; OxBTC; PeFWW

And no birds sing. (LL) La Belle Dame sans Merci [A Ballad]. John Keats. AWP; BRP; CABP; ClHu; FHYEP; FaBoCh; GTBS-P; HAP; HeIP-4; NAEL-5v2; NAEL-6v2; NAWM-7v2; NOBE; NOBRP; NPeEn; NoP-4; OBEV; OBSP; OxAEP-2; OxBEV; PAI; PoE; PoPoPo; PoRA; RB; SCGP; SCV; SoSe-8; TFi; TRP; UV; UnPo; WoPoe

And No Help Came. Peter Porter. BMAP

And no one has warned me that freedom. February 8, 1980: And No One Has Warned Me. Stanislaw Baranczak. AF, tr. by Magnus J. Krynski

And no one will worry a bit. (LL) Does It Matter? Siegfried Sassoon. MoBrPo; PAI; PeFWW; PoWW

And No Regrets. Lex Banning. NOBAu

And no verse illegitimate. (LL) Upon His Verses. Robert Herrick. NAEL-5v1; NAEL-6v1; NAEL-7v1

And Noah was six hundred years old when the flood of waters. Bible, O.T. NAWM-5v1 Fr. Genesis.

And noble patriot! guard with love thy name. (LL) Toussaint L'Ouverture. Henrietta Cordelia Ray. CBWP-3; SWaP

And nobody cares for me. (LL) Isaac Bickerstaffe. LB; OxNR Fr. Love in a Village.

And nobody shouts halt. Auschwitz, 1987. Adam Zych. HP, tr. by Hilda Schiff

And none but thee. (LL) British Church, The. George Herbert. AngWePo; ESCV; PeECV

And none has quite escaped my smile. (LL) Let No Charitable Hope. Elinor Wylie. APT-1; ColAP; MoAmPo; NAAL-2v2; NALW; OxBA; OxBSP; VGW

And none remain'd to give the rest. (LL) Cornelian, The. Byron. CAGL; TreFP

And none shall speak his name. (LL) Poet. Karl Shapiro. MoAmPo; NoAM

And nor knows nor cares for Beeny, and will laugh there nevermore. (LL) Beeny Cliff. Thomas Hardy. CABP; OxAEP-2; RB

And not a single regret. (LL) Edgar Lee Masters. IllVoic; NoAM; OxBA; TAP Fr. Spoon River Anthology.

And not be afraid. (LL) To Turn Back. John Haines. CoAmPo; TRP

And not be / one. (LL) From the House of Yemanjá. Audre Lorde. NALW; NoAM; NoP-4

And, not crying in vain. And, Not Crying in Vain. Marina Ivanovna Tsvetayeva [or Tsvetaeva]. GI, tr. by Nancy Pollak

And not even when we ran over the badger. Between Hovers. Michael Longley. ModIr

And not kill you. (LL) Try Tropic. Genevieve Taggard. APT-2; MoAmPo

And not restore my life, but close my eyes. (LL) Orinda to Lucasia. Katherine Philips. BASC; NOSC

And not silence but to our grieving. Poppies of This Year. Gennady Aygi. TCRusP, tr. by Peter France

And not simply by the fact that this shading of. That the Science of Cartography Is Limited. Eavan Boland. HarvBoo; NoP-4; SpudSo

And not waving but drowning. (LL) Not Waving But Drowning. Stevie Smith. AmFaPo; CABP; EmeKit; FaBoWP; GTBS-P; HAP; HarvBoo; HeIP-4; MakPoe; NAEL-5v2; NAEL-6v2; NALW; NOBE; NPeEn; NoAM; NoP-4; OxAEP-2; OxBEV; OxBTC; PoE; PoPoPo; TFi; UV; WeW-3

And not your yellow hair. (LL) For Anne Gregory. W. B. Yeats. NAEL-5v2; NAEL-6v2; OxAEP-2

And nothing I can keep from him. (LL) Guest, The. Anna Andreyevna Akhmatova. RaBo; WoPoe, tr. by Vera Dunham and Jane Kenyon

And nothing permanent on earth. (LL) William Habington. BASC; BeJo; MeLP; NOBE; NPeEn; OBEV; OxBEV; SCGP Fr. Castara.

And nothing to say or do? (LL) William Vaughn Moody. APN-2; NOBA; OxBA; TCAPo

And nought beyond, oh, earth! (LL) Graves of a Household, The. Felicia Dorothea Hemans. NOBRP; RWP; TreFP; WPE

And now a few questions to end with. Edoardo Sanguineti. ItPo, tr. by Gayle Ridinger Fr. Scartabello.

And now a fig for the lower house. Fig for the Lower House, A. Patrick Carey [or Cary]. NOSC

And now a garden pland with nicest care. John Clare. OBGa Fr. Wish, The.

And now Aeneas charges straight at Turnus. Virgil [or Vergil]. OBWP Fr. Aeneid [or Eneados, Aeneis], The.

And now all Nature seemed [or seem'd] in love. On a Bank [or Banck] as I Sat[e] [a-]Fishing; a Description of the Spring. Sir Henry Wotton. AmFaPo; BASC; NOSC

And now. An attempt. Behold the Lilies of the Field. Anthony Hecht. EmeKit

And now: And now: here begins Our Voyage, hunters and naturalists of indefatigable enthusiasm. Adolf Wolfli. PFTM-1 Fr. From The Cradle to the Graave, or, through working and sweating, suffering and hardship, even through prayyer into damnation.

And now, at last, all proud deeds done. Old Mythologies. John Montague. NoP-4

And now behold your tender Nurse the *Ayre.*   Sir John Davies.   NPeEn   *Fr.* Orchestra; or, A Poem[e] of Da[u]ncing.

And now Eurynome had bath'd the king.   Homer.   NOSC; OBVE, *tr.* by George Chapman   *Fr.* Odyssey.

And now gentlemen.   Base of All Metaphysics, The.   Walt Whitman.   APN-1

And now his well-known bow the Master bore.   Homer.   OBVE, *tr.* by Alexander Pope   *Fr.* Odyssey.

And now I appear on the doorstep.   Prophet, The.   Yevgeny [*or* Evgenii] Mikhailovich Vinokurov.   TCRP, *tr.* by Daniel Weissbort

And now I know.   Always Know.   Kalamu ya Salaam.   SpirFl

And now I live, and now my life is done. (LL)   Tichborne's Elegy.   Chidiock Tichborne [*or* Tichbourne].   AmFaPo; HAP; HeIP-4; NoP-4; NoSic; PoPoPo; TFi

And now I'm engaged to Miss Joan Hunter Dunn. (LL)   Subaltern's Love-Song, A.   Sir John Betjeman.   BoLoP; HAP; NOBL; NoAM; OxAEP-2; OxBTC; TwCP

And now I, Meleager, am among them.   Epigram.   Meleager.   GrAn, *tr.* by Peter Whigham

And now I too must wrestle with a brother.   On the Pains of Translating Miklós Radnóti.   Frederick Turner.   RA

And now I will convey thee to thy world.   Byron.   NOBRP   *Fr.* Cain: A Mystery.

And now, in accents deep and low.   Washington Allston.   APN-1   *Fr.* Sylphs of the Seasons, The.

And now, it seems, you are fearful.   Dark, The.   Richard Poole.   AngWePo

And now, kind friends, what I have wrote.   Julia A. Moore.   VerBaPo   *Fr.* Author's Early Life, The.

And now, lash'd on by destiny severe.   William Falconer.   OxAEP-1   *Fr.* Shipwreck, The.

And now let mee dispose such things.   Isabella Whitney.   BWW   *Fr.* Manner of Her Will and What She Left to London and to All Those in It, at Her Departing, The.

And now, like a posy, a pretty one plump in his hands. (LL)   Catch.   Robert Francis.   InPK-6; RaBo

And now love sang: but his was such a song.   Dante Gabriel Rossetti.   NAEL-5v2; NAEL-6v2; OxBSo   *Fr.* House of Life, The.

And now man-slaughtering Pallas took in hand.   Homer.   OBVE, *tr.* by George Chapman   *Fr.* Odyssey.

And now, Mistress Mummy, since thus you've been found.   Child's Address to the Kentucky Mummy, The.   Hannah Flagg Gould.   SWaP

And now my pampered beast.   Epitaph for My Cat.   Jean Garrigue.   TAP

And now my story's [*or* is] done. (LL)   Mother Goose.   LB; OxNR; ReMoGo

And now one prayer.   *Unknown.*   OBVE   *Fr.* Elder Edda, The.

And now she cleans her teeth into the lake.   Camping Out.   William Empson.   FaBoMo; OxBTC

And now she knows: The big fist shattering her face.   Female and the Silence of a Man, The.   June Jordan.   NAAAL

And now take thought, my sonnet, who is he.   Sonnets of the Months: Conclusion.   Folgore da San Geminiano [*or* Gimignano].   AWP; EaItPo, *tr.* by Dante Gabriel Rossetti

And now th'art set wide ope, the Speare's sad art.   I Am the Door [*or* Doore].   Richard Crashaw.   GeHe; NAEL-5v1; NAEL-6v1; NAEL-7v1

& Now the book is closed.   Ted Berrigan.   SPE   *Fr.* Merorial Day: a collaboration.

And now the dark comes on, all full of chitter noise.   Sound of Night, The.   Maxine W. Kumin.   SoSe-8; WPE

And now the dewy night had nearly come to its halfway.   Virgil [*or* Vergil].   WoPoe, *tr.* by Cecil Day Lewis   *Fr.* Aeneid [*or* Eneados, *Aeneis*], The.

And now the purple dusk of twilight time.   Star Dust.   Mitchell Parish.   ReLy

And now the Queene of women had intent.   Homer.   OBVE   *Fr.* Odyssey.

And now the Reich's last hour is coming round.   Report from Germany, 1944.   Ernst Waldinger.   AuPH, *tr.* by Lowell A. Bangerter

And now the Storm-blast came, and he.   Samuel Taylor Coleridge.   OWoS   *Fr.* Rime of the Ancient Mariner, The.

And now the words.   Mourning Song.   Robert Pearl.   STP, *tr.* by Armand Schwerner

And now their hour is come. (LL)   Compensation.   Ralph Waldo Emerson.   APN-1; TAP

And now there rolls in, as on casters, a character.   Fame.   Vladimir Vladimirovich Nabokov.   TCRP, *tr.* by Vladimir Nabokov

"And now to God the Father," he ends.   Thomas Hardy.   InPK-6; MoBrPo; SCV   *Fr.* Satires of Circumstance in Fifteen Glimpses.

And now to the ab[b]yss I pass.   Andrew Marvell.   PBRV   *Fr.* Upon Appleton House [To My Lord Fairfax].

And now, unveiled, the toilet stands displayed.   Pope.   ECEV; NOBE; OxAEP-1; OxBEV   *Fr.* Rape of the Lock; an Heroi-Comical Poem, The.

And now was Paris come / From his high towres.   Homer.   OBVE   *Fr.* Iliad, The.

And now we gan draw near unto the gate.   Virgil [*or* Vergil].   NoSic, *tr.* by Henry Howard, Earl of Surrey   *Fr.* Aeneid [*or* Eneados, *Aeneis*], The.

And now we three in Euston waiting-room. (LL)   Parting in Wartime.   Frances Darwin Cornford.   FaBoWP; NIP-4

And now we walked along the solid mire.   Dante Alighieri.   OBVE   *Fr.* Divina Commedia.

And now we watch you crawl, you crawl.   Archie Weller.   IBA

And now what monarch would not gardener be.   To Amanda Walking in the Garden.   N. Hookes.   NOSC; OBGa

And now with him she sleeps in Yarrow. (LL)   Braes of Yarrow, The.   John Logan.   GTBS-P; SCGP

And now, with the reflected lights that glow.   Dante Alighieri.   NAWM-7v1, *tr.* by Allen Mandelbaum   *Fr.* Divine Comedy, The (Mandelbaum Translation).

And now you ask.   My Message.   Cecil Rajendra.   PoetW

And Now You're Ready Who While She Was Here.   James Vincent Cunningham.   GrAn; OBVE, *tr.* by James Vincent Cunningham   *Fr.* Five Epigrams.

And Now Yu.   David S. Mills.   InTrad

And nuzzling each other in the smelly fold. (LL)   Magnificat.   Michele Roberts.   BrRo; PoBW

And, O, pray too for me! (LL)   Walter Savage Landor.   OBEV; TreFP   *Fr.* Citation and Examination of William Shakespeare, The.

And obedient mind. (LL)   William Carlos Williams.   APT-1; OxBA   *Fr.* Paterson.

And occaisional herring and mouse. (LL)   Old Cat's Confessions, An.   Christopher Pearse Cranch.   APN-1; OBCA

And of new love that they would learn. (LL)   Wife in London, A.   Thomas Hardy.   NOBVV; OBWP

And of the curveship lend a myth to God. (LL)   Hart Crane.   AiP; AmFaPo; ChIV-1; ClHu; ColAP; FaBoA; HarvBoo; MakPoe; MoAmPo; NAAL-5; NOBA; NoP-4; OxBA; PoE; PoPoPo; TFi; TRP   *Fr.* Bridge, The.

And of thir [*or* their] vain contest appeer'd [*or* appeared] no end. (LL)   John Milton.   FHYEP; NAEL-5v1; NAEL-6v1; NAWM-5v1; NAWM-7v1   *Fr.* Paradise Lost.

And oft the owle with rufull song complaind.   Virgil [*or* Vergil].   OBVE, *tr.* by Henry Howard, Earl of Surrey   *Fr.* Aeneid [*or* Eneados, *Aeneis*], The.

And often swore my lips were sweet. (LL)   Mother, I Cannot Mind My Wheel.   Walter Savage Landor.   AWP; BoLoP; NAEL-5v2; NAEL-6v2; NOBE; OBEV; OBVE

And—oh, heaven! 'twas her sister! (LL)   Masquerading.   May Probyn.   NPeEn; VWP

And, oh, may no other maiden know such reproach as I! (LL)   Cashel of Munster.   William English.   BIrV; OBEV, *tr.* by Sir Samuel Ferguson

And, oh! 'tis delicious to hate you! (LL)   Thomas Moore.   EnLoPo; OxBSP

And oh, 'tis true, 'tis true. (LL)   A. E. Housman.   ChAP; HeIP-4; ITBLP; InPK-6; MoBrPo; NAEL-5v2; NAEL-6v2; NoAM; PoE; TFi

And old men shall drop by the wayside. (LL)   *Unknown.*   PBA; TTY, *tr.* by A. C. Jordan

And on hers / Though she doesn't know it.   Poem with Light on Its Shoulder.   Mary Ann Samyn.   AmPoNex

And on My Eyes Dark Sleep by Night.   "Michael Field."   LW; OBMV

And on the beach undid his corded bales. (LL)   Matthew Arnold.   EBEV; EBVV; FHYEP; HAP; NAEL-5v2; NAEL-6v2; NOBE; NOBVV; NoP-4; OBEV; OxAEP-1; PoE; SCGP; TFi

And on the mere the wailing died away. (LL)   Tennyson.   EBNV; NIP-4; NOBVV; OBNV; OxAEP-2   *Fr.* Morte d'Arthur.

And on the morrow, at first peep o' the day.   Folgore da San Geminiano [*or* Gimignano].   EaItPo, *tr.* by Dante Gabriel Rossetti

And on the porch, across the upturned chair.   Poet at Seven, The.   Donald Justice.   WeW-3

And on the right the slogan Born To Lose. (LL)   Black Jackets.   Thom Gunn.   HeIP-4; NAEL-5v2; NAEL-6v2; NoP-4; TwCP

And on the seventh slept a deep Negro sleep. (LL)   To New York.   Léopold Sédar Senghor.   PoetW; WoPoe, *tr.* by Melvin Dixon

And on the wall was limned a mouldering corse.   On the Wall.   Immanuel di Roma.   TrJP, *tr.* by Solomon Solis-Cohen

And on this day, which poets unto thee.   Ovid.   OBVE   *Fr.* Tristium.

And once again Good Friday comes.   From My Diary, 3.   Vera Bulich.   ARWW, *tr.* by Catriona Kelly

And once again the angel of Death came.   George MacBeth [*or* Macbeth].   HP   *Fr.* Rumanian of Maria Banus, The.

And One for My Dame.   Anne Sexton.   NoP-4

And one for the little boy that [*or* who] lives in the lane. (LL)   Mother Goose.   LB; OxBEV; OxNR; ReMoGo

And one in a velvet gown. (LL)   "Hark, Hark, the Dogs Do Bark."   Mother Goose.   OxNR; ReMoGo

And one is One, free in the tearing wind. (LL)   In a Dark Time.   Theodore Roethke.   APT-2; HAP; HeIP-4; MoAmPo; NAAL-2v2; NAAL-5; NOBA; NoAM; NoP-4; PeECV; PoE; RaBo; TAP; TFi; VCAP

And one morning while in the woods I stumbled suddenly upon the /thing thing.   Between the World and Me.   Richard Wright.   ISC; PAI

And one sweet smile o'erpaid an age of fears! (LL) Describes the Fascinations of Love. Mary Robinson. CenSon; RWP

And one there was, a dreamer born. John Greenleaf Whittier. NCAP *Fr.* Tent on the Beach: [The Dreamer].

And one wants to know everything about everything. Limited Liability. John Ashbery. BodElec

And only bitter land was washed away. (LL) Childhood. Margaret Abigail Walker. NoP-4; Son; WPOW

And only: money. My One. Heather McHugh. BAP-01

And only slightly shrunken. (LL) Fumi Saito. BoWoP; WoPoe, *tr. by* Edith Marcombe Shiffert and Yuki Sawa

And only there, please highly for their sake. (LL) William Cowper. NAEL-5v1; NAEL-6v1; NAEL-7v1 *Fr.* Task, The.

And only wake with you! (LL) Stars. Emily Jane Brontë. AWTN; BrRo; NAEL-5v2; NAEL-6v2; NALW

And ony sma'er thocht's impossible. (LL) At My Father's Grave. Hugh MacDiarmid. GTBS-P; HarvBoo; NePenScot

And open unseen gates with key of gold? (LL) City Visions. Emma Lazarus. APN-2; SWaP

And Opposition of the Stars. (LL) Definition of Love, The. Andrew Marvell. BASC; BoLoP; EBEV; ESCV; FHYEP; FSCP; GeHe; ITBLP; MeLP; NAEL-5v1; NAEL-6v1; NAEL-7v1; NOBE; NOSC; NPeEn; NoP-4; OBEV; OxBEV; PBRV; SCGP; TFi; UnPo

And Ops, ere yet Dictaean Jove was born. (LL) John Milton. NAEL-5v1; NAEL-6v1 *Fr.* Paradise Lost.

And other folk should get the ugly ones. (LL) Sonnet: Of All He Would Do. Cecco Angiolieri, da Siena. AWP; EaItPo, *tr. by* Dante Gabriel Rossetti

And other hippopotamusses. (LL) Habits of the Hippopotamus. Arthur Guiterman. OBCA; OxIBACP

And other wond'rous works were done. Christopher Smart. NOCV *Fr.* Hymns and Spiritual Songs for the Fasts and Festivals of the Church of England.

And others doth offend when 'tis let loose. (LL) Love's Offence. Sir John Suckling. CaPo; NOSC

And others to shriek and collapse. (LL) Limerick: "As tourists inspected the apse." Edward Gorey. PeLV; PeLi

And our eternal home. (LL) Man Frail, and God Eternal. Isaac Watts. ECEV; InvLi; NPeEn; OBVE; OxBEV; PWR; SacPr; TOF

And our hearts, like thy waters, be mingled in peace. (LL) Meeting of the Waters, The. Thomas Moore. NOIV; OxBoLi

And our ordinary garments decent in the dead one's eyes. (LL) Journey to the Place of Ghosts. Jay Wright. GT; VCAP

And our wheels grazed his dead face. (LL) Isaac Rosenberg. FaBoMo; GTBS-P; NAEL-5v2; NAEL-6v2; NoAM; OBWP; PeFWW; PoWW; TrJP

And out into the winds her life withdrew. (LL) Virgil [or Vergil]. NAWM-5v1; NAWM-7v1, *tr. by* Robert Fitzgerald *Fr.* Aeneid [or Eneados, Aeneis], The.

And out of his eyes two great tears rolled, like stones, and he died. (LL) Death of a Son. Jon Silkin. GTBS-P; OxBTC

And out of the swing of the sea. (LL) Heaven-Haven. Gerard Manley Hopkins. HeIP-4; MoBrPo; NOBE; NOCV; NoAM; OBEV; OxAEP-2; OxBSP; PAI; PeECV; RB; SoSe-8; TFi; TOF

And over all the sky—the sky! far, far out of reach, studded, breaking out, the eternal stars. (LL) Bivouac on a Mountain Side. Walt Whitman. AiP; CBCWP; OxBA

And over-read what I have writ. (LL) Departure of the Good Daemon, The. Robert Herrick. BASC; NPeEn

And over their city stands the pinnacled corn. (LL) Merlin. Geoffrey Hill. InPK-6; TRP

And Pablo Neruda / that Chilean omnivore of poetry. Lawrence Ferlinghetti. BB *Fr.* Work-in-Progress.

And palms before my feet! (LL) Donkey, The. Gilbert Keith Chesterton. ChIV-2; GI; InPK-6; MoBrPo; OBEV; RB

And Paphos' son was Cinyras, a man. Ovid. NAWM-7v1, *tr. by* Allen Mandelbaum *Fr.* Metamorphoses.

And Paradise does come. Joy. Gavin Bantock. OxBTC

And Paris be it or Helen dying. Fragment on Death, A. François Villon. CTC; PeVV, *tr. by* Algernon Charles Swinburne

And part it, giving half to him. (LL) Tennyson. CAGL; NAEL-6v2 *Fr.* In Memoriam A. H. H.

And passes into gloom again. (LL) Tennyson. NAEL-6v2; PeECV *Fr.* In Memoriam A. H. H.

And passing away. (LL) Kenneth Rexroth. APSN; APT-2 *Fr.* Love Poems of Marichiko, The.

And passionate as the dawn. (LL) Fisherman, The. W. B. Yeats. HAP; NoAM

And Peace, and Art, and Labour joined her train. (LL) Visit of Hope to Sydney Cove, near Botany-Bay. Erasmus Darwin. ECEV; NOEC

And peace on earth for men. (LL) Afterthought. Elizabeth Jennings. NOxBChV; OBCP

And people will think this like. Anna Andreyevna Akhmatova. TCRP

And Pergamos, / City of the Phrygians. Euripides. AWP; OBVE *Fr.* Iphigenia [or Iphigeneia] in Aulis.

And perish at the last. (LL) Upon the Troublesome Times. Robert Herrick. CaPo; CavPo

And perish in our own. (LL) Daisy. Francis Thompson. AWP; MoBrPo; OBEV

And personal. (LL) Cordon Negro. Essex Hemphill. CAGL; GLP

And pierced with a bewilderment of birds. (LL) Learning by Doing. Howard Nemerov. HAP; TwCP; WeW-3

And Pilate Said. Joy Davidman. YaYoPo

And Pity pour her healing tear. (LL) Lines, / Written on Seeing My Husband's Picture, painted when he was young: "Those are the features, those the smiles." Anna Sawyer. ECWP; LW

And plain old Margaret Fuller died as well. (LL) Ballad of Ladies Lost and Found. Marilyn Hacker. FFC; VCAP

And please do not presume it was the way we planned it. And Please Do Not Presume. Deryn Rees-Jones. MFPA

And ploughs down palaces, and thrones, and towers. (LL) Serf, The. Roy Campbell. GTBS-P; MoBrPo; OBMV

And pneumonia finished me. (LL) Edgar Lee Masters. APT-1; IllVoic *Fr.* Spoon River Anthology.

And point with taper spire to Heaven. (LL) Wish, A. Samuel Rogers. GTBS-P; NOBE; OBEV; OxAEP-2

And points us to a better time than ours. (LL) West London. Matthew Arnold. SCGP; Son

And polished by the Master's hand. (LL) Christopher Smart. ChIV-1; NOCV *Fr.* Hymns for the Amusement of Children.

And poplars stand there still as death. (LL) Southern Mansion. Arna Bontemps. APT-2; AiP; GT; NAAAL; TTY

And powerful passion bears him to your feet. (LL) Charlotte Lennox. ECWP; LW *Fr.* Art of Coquetry, The.

And praise him who did make and mend our eyes. (LL) Love (2). George Herbert. GeHe; Son

And praise his name on every chord. (LL) Let Tyrants Shake Their Iron Rod. William Billings. AH; TCAPo

And pray for Kharma under the holy mountain. (LL) Chard Whitlow. Henry Reed. MoBrPo; NBLV; NOBL; NoP-4; OBCoV; OxBTC; PeLV; UV; UnPo

And pretty maids all in [or of] a row. (LL) Mother Goose. LB; OxNR; ReMoGo

And prove that death but routs life into victory. (LL) Herman Melville. APN-2; NCAP; TCAPo *Fr.* Clarel: A Poem and Pilgrimage in the Holy Land.

And pull him close, stoned out of my gourd. (LL) David Cassidy Then. Dennis Cooper. ReTh; WiU

And pulled my voice / into the ring of the dance. (LL) Caedmon. Denise Levertov. NoAM; NoP-4

And purpose of our being here? (LL) Arthur Hugh Clough. NOBVV; OxBSP

And put him into bed? Why don't they pose? (LL) Disabled. Wilfred Owen. FaBoWar; NAEL-5v2; NAEL-6v2; NIL-7; NoAM; OBWVE; OxBTC; PeFWW; PoPoPo; SCGP

And put his gun to the back of her head. (LL) Praise of a Collie. Norman MacCaig. NePenScot; RB

And put in twa een o' tree. (LL) Tam Lin. *Unknown.* ESPB; NOBE; OBEV; OBNV; OxBB; OxBS

And Pykes, the Tyrants of the watry Plains. (LL) Pope. ECEV; FHYEP *Fr.* Windsor-Forest [or Windsor Forest].

And quiet Pilgrimage. (LL) Man of Life Upright, The. Thomas Campion. NoSic; PoRA

And quiet sleep and a sweet dream when the long trick's over. (LL) Sea Fever. John Masefield. BRP; CABP; ChAP; ITBLP; MoBrPo; OxAEP-2; OxBTC; UV

And quite invisible but for the end of his nose. (LL) Amphibious Crocodile. John Crowe Ransom. FuPo; OBAL

And rain bear shame! (LL) Tune: "Rapt with Wine, Loudly Singing; Joy in Spring's Coming." Kuan Yün-shih. ColAnChi; SuSp, *tr. by* Richard John Lynn

And rain still falling. (LL) Nisei: Second Generation Japanese-American. James Masao Mitsui. GifTon; OpBo

And raise her children to eternal day. (LL) Along the Banks. Joel Barlow. AH; ChIV-1

And ran on. (LL) Stephen Crane. APN-2; ChAP; MoAmPo; NOBA; NoP-4; TCAPo *Fr.* Black Riders [and Other Lines], The.

And rattles her crutch, which may put forth a small bloom, / perhaps white. (LL) Pursuit. Robert Penn Warren. FuPo; HAP; MoAmPo; TwCP

And read that moderate man Voltaire. (LL) Respectable Burgher, The. Thomas Hardy. ChIV-2; NoAM

And read your Bible, sir, and mind your purse. (LL) Byron. NOBE; SCV *Fr.* Don Juan.

And removed the black keys from his piano. (LL) Michael Longley. BiHa; ModIr *Fr.* Wreaths.

And renownèd be thy grave! (LL) William Shakespeare. AWP; ClHu; EBEV;

GTBS-P; HAP; NAEL-5v1; NOBE; NoSic; OxAEP-1; PAI; PoRA; RB; SCGP; SCV; SoSe-8; TFi   *Fr.* Cymbeline.

And rested on a drying hill. (LL)   Sir Gawaine and the Green Knight.   Yvor Winters.   NoAM; PoRA; VGW

And retreating, always retreating, behind it. (LL)   Brazil, January 1, 1502.   Elizabeth Bishop.   BLT; FaBoWP; NoAM; PoPoPo; PoetW; VCAP

And returned on the previous night. (LL)   Limerick: "There was a young lady named [*or* called] Bright."   Arthur Buller.   NOBL; OxBoLi; PeLV; PeLi

And returned to their homes by another way. (LL)   Three Kings, The.   Henry Wadsworth Longfellow.   ChIV-2; ChrPo

And ride in triumph through Persepolis?   Christopher Marlowe.   FaBoWar   *Fr.* Tamburlaine the Great.

And right before daybreak the little owl returned.   Every Life.   Brenda Hillman.   BodElec

And ringeth faintly in the grassy stones. (LL)   Frederick Goddard Tuckerman.   APN-2; HAP; TAP   *Fr.* Sonnets.

And rise, O moon, from yonder down.   Tennyson.   NAEL-6v2   *Fr.* In Memoriam A. H. H.

And roaring then the ashen skies resound.   On the Third Day.   János Pilinszky.   IQMS, *tr. by* Adam Makkai

And rode away horseless to the King's white hall. (LL)   Riddle: "White bird featherless."   *Unknown.*   FaBoVe; OxBEV; OxNR

And roll head over heels and tangle my hair full of wisps. (LL)   Walt Whitman.   ColAP; ITBLP   *Fr.* Song of Myself.

And ruin is the lot of all. (LL)   Hurricane, The.   Philip Freneau.   TAP; TCAPo

And rural mirth and manners are no more. (LL)   Oliver Goldsmith.   OBSV; UV   *Fr.* Deserted Village, The.

And sae this ends my sang. (LL)   Lord Livingston.   *Unknown.*   ESPB; OxBB

And safe in heaven dead. (LL)   Jack Kerouac.   NeAP; PFTM-2; PmAP; PoM   *Fr.* Mexico City Blues.

And said: "He had n't very far to fall." (LL)   Ambrose Bierce.   APN-2; OBAL   *Fr.* Devil's Dictionary, The.

And said I that my limbs were old.   Sir Walter Scott.   OxAEP-2   *Fr.* Lay of the Last Minstrel, The.

And said, "Nay, we are seven!" (LL)   William Wordsworth.   NAEL-5v2; NAEL-6v2; NOBRP

And said, "Not yet! in quiet lie." (LL)   Daybreak.   Henry Wadsworth Longfellow.   ITBLP; PWR

And said, What a good boy am I! (LL)   Mother Goose.   LB; OxNR; ReMoGo; SoSe-8

And said: "Why don't you get out of the rain?" (LL)   Anna Andreyevna Akhmatova.   BoLoP; PoetW; RaBo, *tr. by* Max Hayward and Stanley Kunitz

And sanctify this ALTAR to be thine. (LL)   Altar, The.   George Herbert.   AngWePo; BASC; CABP; ChIV-1; ESCV; GeHe; NAEL-5v1; NAEL-6v1; NAEL-7v1; NOSC; NoP-4; TrCP

And sank beneath thy chain to a lamented grave. (LL)   Spleen, The.   Anne Finch, Countess of Winchilsea.   NALW; NOSC

And sank her in the sea. (LL)   Demon Lover, The.   *Unknown.*   HAP; SCGP; TFi; UnPo; WeW-3

And Satan's self had thoughts of taking orders. (LL)   Tophet.   Thomas Gray.   ChIV-1; FaBoEE; NOEC; OxBSP

And save ourselves unaided. (LL)   Storm Fear.   Robert Frost.   APT-1; ColAP; OxBA; TCAPo

And save the serpent in their midst. (LL)   In Memory of My Feelings.   Frank O'Hara.   APSN; ColAP; HarvBoo; NAAL-2v2; NeAP; PoM

And saved the sum of things for pay. (LL)   Epitaph on an Army of Mercenaries.   A. E. Housman.   FaBoWar; NAEL-6v2; NPeEn; NoP-4; OxBEV; SCGP; SoSe-8

And say dat's good enough for nigger. (LL)   Song: "We raise de wheat."   *Unknown.*   BPo; NAAAL; PAI; TAP

And say His name. (LL)   Canticle to the Waterbirds, A.   William Everson.   APSN; APT-2; GeoHom; NeAP; PoM

And say I made you for Becchina's sake. (LL)   Sonnet: Of Love, in Honor of His Mistress Becchina.   Cecco Angiolieri, da Siena.   AWP; EaItPo, *tr. by* Dante Gabriel Rossetti

And say my glory was I had such friends. (LL)   Municipal Gallery Revisited, The.   W. B. Yeats.   GTBS-P; OxBTC

And scholars, soldiers, kings unhonoured die. (LL)   Oliver Goldsmith.   NOEC; NPeEn   *Fr.* Travel[l]er; or, A Prospect of Society, The.

And schoolboys lag with satchels in their hands. (LL)   Description of the Morning, A.   Jonathan Swift.   EBEV; ECEV; HAP; HeIP-4; NIL-7; NOBE; NOEC; NoP-4; OxAEP-1; OxBEV; PAI; PoPoPo; SoSe-8; TFi

And scorning say, "See what it is to love." (LL)   Sir Philip Sidney.   NoP-4; OxAEP-1   *Fr.* Astrophil and Stella.

And seal the hushèd casket of my soul. (LL)   To Sleep.   John Keats.   NIP-4; OBEV; OxBSo; Son

And seasons, changeless since the day she died. (LL)   Cross of Snow, The.   Henry Wadsworth Longfellow.   APN-1; AWTN; ColAP; GSo; HeIP-4; NOBA; NoP-4; OxBA; TAP; TCAPo

And see the men at play. (LL)   Golf Links, The.   Sarah Norcliffe Cleghorn.   InPK-6; PAI

And see thy blood warm when thou feel'st it cold. (LL)   William Shakespeare.   HeIP-4; NoSic; SCGP; Son   *Fr.* Sonnets.

And see what kind of world comes out. (LL)   Dead Water.   Wen Yi-tuo *or* Wen I-to.   PFTM-1; WoPoe, *tr. by* Arthur Sze

And see you safely through diminished fields. (LL)   Riding a One-eyed Horse.   Henry Taylor.   HeIP-4; InPK-6

And seeing the multitudes, he went up.   Bible, *N.T.*   NAWM-5v1   *Fr.* St. Matthew.

And seem the symbol of my present woe. (LL)   To the Curlew.   Helen Maria Williams.   CenSon; WoRP

And sees within my eyes the tears of two. (LL)   Elizabeth Barrett Browning.   BWW; CenSon; LW; OBEV; OxAEP-2   *Fr.* Sonnets from the Portuguese.

And send it a thousand miles, thinking. (LL)   Exile's Letter.   Li Po.   CTC; FaBoMo; OxBA, *tr. by* Ezra Pound

And send it from above! (LL)   My Spirit Longeth for Thee.   John Byrom.   NOBE; SacPr

And sent him to take a ground sweat. (LL)   Night before Larry Was Stretched, The.   *Unknown.*   BIrV; NOBL; NOIV; OxBoLi

And serve but Him alone. (LL)   Nut-brown Maid, The.   *Unknown.*   NoSic; OBEV

And settled upon his eyes in a black soot. (LL)   'More Light! More Light!'   Anthony Hecht.   AF; CoAP; CoAmPo; EmeKit; HAP; HP; NOBA; NoAM; NoP-4; OBWP; RB; TaR; TwCP; UnPo; VCAP; VGW

And several strengths from drowsiness campaigned.   Sermon on the Warpland, The.   Gwendolyn Brooks.   BPo; NOBA

And shadows end. (LL)   Day Is Dying in the West.   Mary Artemisia Lathbury.   AH; SacPr

And shakes against the sea. (LL)   Tiles.   Witter Bynner.   APT-1; TCAPo

And shall be evermore. (LL)   Now Thank We All Our God.   Martin Rinckhart [*or* Rinkhart].   GePo; SacPr, *tr. by* Catherine Winkworth

And shall do so, until the world's last day. (LL)   Her Descending Down.   Margaret Lucas Cavendish, Duchess of Newcastle.   BASC; NOSC

And shall forever span them and compactly hold and enclose them. (LL)   On the Beach at Night Alone.   Walt Whitman.   APN-1; TAP

And shall it ever be again—the joy.   Late.   Benjamin Paul Blood.   APN-2

And shall sing forth thy praise over this meat. (LL)   Edward Taylor.   ColAP; SCAP   *Fr.* Preparatory Meditations Before My Approach to the Lord's Supper.

And Shall Trelawny Die?   Robert Stephen Hawker.   OxAEP-2

And shall we ever seek in vain.   All Alone.   Mary E. Tucker.   CBWP-1

And shall we view these miracles and more.   John Rollin Ridge.   APN-2   *Fr.* California.

And share my bed with Capricorn and Cancer. (LL)   Dylan Thomas.   FaBoMo; Son   *Fr.* Altarwise by Owl-Light.

And sharp-broken / Dinner plates. (LL)   Tinker's Wife.   Patrick Kavanagh.   CIP-2; NoAM

And shatter your virginity. (LL)   Corinna in Vendome.   Pierre de Ronsard.   BoLoP; WoPoe, *tr. by* Robert Mezey

And she, being old, fed from a mashed plate.   Old Woman.   Iain Crichton Smith.   FaBoTw; HarvBoo; NePenScot; OxBEV; OxBTC

And she beside another lad. (LL)   A. E. Housman.   HAP; MoBrPo; WeW-3

And she can't see me. (LL)   Pancake Day.   Mother Goose.   LB; OxNR; ReMoGo

And she compliant to his every wish. (LL)   Note on Propertius I.5.   Fleur Adcock.   BoLoP; PeNZ

And she dropt me a curtesy. (LL)   Mother Goose.   OxNR; ReMoGo

And she [has] crept under / [T]he warming pan [*or* frying pan]. (LL)   Mother Goose.   FaBoVe; LB; OxNR; ReMoGo

And she is beautiful, our daughter.   To Our Daughter.   Jennifer Armitage.   BrRo

And she is gone. (LL)   Only a little shall we speak of thee.   Mary Elizabeth Coleridge.   PoBW; VWP

And she said I was quite fortunate.   My Mother and I Had a Discussion One Day.   Denise Sweet.   ReEnLa

And she saying, I cannot quite.   Heartland.   Trent Busch.   BAP-01

And She Washed His Feet with Her Tear[e]s, and Wiped Them with the Hairs of Her Head.   Sir Edward Sherburne.   MeLP; NOSC

(Proud Egyptian Queen, The.)   OxBSP

And she who flies the lover,—chains the soul! (LL)   To a Sigh.   Mary Robinson.   CenSon; RWP

And she who slays is she who bears, who bears. (LL)   Parentage.   Alice Thompson Meynell.   NALW; NPeEn; PeVV; VWP

And she will not cast me away. (LL)   Makeda (Queen of Sheba).   HW; WPoS

And shone that smile on us and sang. (LL)   Homage to the Empress of the Blues.   Robert Earl Hayden.   APT-2; ESEAA; HCAP; LCAP-2; NAAAL; NAAL-5

And shook my head. (LL)   Moment Please, A.   Samuel Allen.   PAI; SSLK

And should I have the right to smile? (LL)   Portrait of a Lady.   T. S. Eliot. APT-1; TwCP

And shouts Munjoie! Munjoie! to hold the field. (LL)   *Unknown.*   NAWM-5v1; NAWM-7v1, *tr. by* Frederick Goldin   *Fr.* Song of Roland, The.

And show his fainting soul,—a glimpse of Heaven. (LL)   Sonnet Introductory. Mary Robinson.   CenSon; RWP

And show the world what women ought to do. (LL)   Cloe to Artimesa. *Unknown.*   ECWP; PoBW

And shuts his eyes. (LL)   Darwin in 1881.   Gjertrud Schnackenberg.   NoAM; NoP-4

And sick for home. (LL)   Outside Fargo, North Dakota.   James Wright (1927–80).   LCAP-2; NNaP

And sighs of rapture, fan the blush of shame! (LL)   Her Passion Increases. Mary Robinson.   CenSon; RWP

And signifies the same with none. (LL)   Samuel Butler (1612–80).   NOBL; OBSV   *Fr.* Hudibras.

And silence matched the silence under snow. (LL)   In the Theatre.   Dannie Abse.   BloBone; NoAM; TCAWP

And silently cut and run. (LL)   Day Is Done, The.   Phoebe Cary.   APN-2; OBAL

And simplify me when I'm dead. (LL)   Simplify Me When I'm Dead.   Keith Douglas.   FaBoWar; NoAM; OxBTC

And since thou own'st that praise, I spare thee mine. (LL)   To Mary Unwin. William Cowper.   CenSon; GTBS-P; OBEV

And sing the songs he loved to hear. (LL)   Tennyson.   EBVV; FHYEP; NAEL-6v2   *Fr.* In Memoriam A. H. H.

And sing / with you. (LL)   Where are those Songs?   Micere Githae Mugo. HAWP; PoetW

And singleness: we salute you / season of no bungling. (LL)   Variations Done for Gerald Van De Wiele.   Charles Olson.   APT-2; NOBA; NeAP; NoAM

And sink into the marsh near them. (LL)   Widow's Lament in Springtime, The. William Carlos Williams.   APT-1; HAP; NAAL-2v2; NAAL-5; NOBA; NoAM; PoE; SAmP; SoSe-8; TAP; TCAPo

And sits by your bed, and brings her knitting. (LL)   Good Luck and Bad. John Milton Hay.   FaBoEE; NBLV

And six I'll gie to thee. (LL)   Fair Annie.   *Unknown.*   ESPB; OxBB

And slander everywhere attended me.   Slander.   Anna Andreyevna Akhmatova.   TCRP, *tr. by* Daniel Weissbort

And sleep. (LL)   Knoxville, Tennessee.   Nikki Giovanni.   BPo; BlSi; OxIBACP

And sleepy winter, like the sleep of death. (LL)   Elinor Wylie.   BoWoP; MoAmPo   *Fr.* Wild Peaches.

And smelled the clinging blood upon the stones. (LL)   Visit to Castletown House, A.   Michael Hartnett.   BiHa; PBCIP

And smoke and spit, no matter where.   Amanda Ros.   VerBaPo

And so an easier life our Cyclops drew.   Theocritus.   OBVE   *Fr.* Idylls.

And so, as in the opening of a *quasida.*   Desert Song.   John Ash.   HarvBoo

And so, as this great sphere (now turning slow).   Sonnet.   Frederick Goddard Tuckerman.   ColAP

And so cold. (LL)   This Is Just to Say.   William Carlos Williams.   APT-1; ChAP; HarvBoo; HeIP-4; InPK-6; KaS; NAAL-2v2; NAAL-5; NIL-7; NIP-4; NOBA; NoAM; NoP-4; OPOU; PAI; PoPoPo; TAP; TRP

And so do I. (LL)   Weathers [*or* Weather].   Thomas Hardy.   FaBoCh; MoBrPo; OBMV; RB

And so, Ernie, your laughing head floats.   Late Author: Snapshot in the Rain, The.   Dan Pagis.   FIT, *tr. by* Robert Friend

And so—for God's sake—hock and soda-water! (LL)   Byron.   CTC; NAEL-5v2; NAEL-6v2; NOBL; OxBEV; OxBSP   *Fr.* Don Juan.

And so for nights.   Night-Blooming Cereus, The.   Robert Earl Hayden.   APT-2; ESEAA

And so from bridge to bridge we went, talking.   Dante Alighieri.   WoPoe, *tr. by* Susan Mitchell   *Fr.* Divina Commedia.

And so he will! And so he will! (LL)   Wind, The.   James Stephens.   InPK-6; KaS; NoAM; PAI

And so I eat from a brown pot.   Brown Pot.   Ray Gonzalez.   TouFir

And so I led her down to the river.   Unfaithful Wife, The.   Federico García Lorca.   ErotSp, *tr. by* Sam Hamill

And so I remain in a civil way, your servant to command, Mary. (LL)   Mary the Cook-Maid's Letter to Dr. Sheridan.   Jonathan Swift.   NPeEn; OxBoLi; PeLV

And so I rest your constant friend. (LL)   Letter to the Honourable Lady Miss Margaret Cavendish Holles-Harley, A.   Matthew Prior.   NOEC; NoAM; OxBC; OxBSP

And so I went forth, exhilarated.   Robyn Selman.   WiU

And so I went, hands thrust in torn pockets.   My Bohemia.   Arthur Rimbaud. SxFrPo, *tr. by* Martin Sorrell

And so I went singing along. (LL)   Mother Goose.   OxNR; ReMoGo

And so it came about that there was no way.   Late Show, The.   Rachel Wetzsteon.   NeAmPo

And so it comes.   Train in the Desert—1916.   Christopher Buckley.   GM

And so it happens that late at night we come home after standing the livelong day.   Animal Has Drawn a Human, The.   Bert Schierbeek.   PFTM-2, *tr. by* Charles McGeehan

And so, Jesus, I see your feet again.   Pietà.   Rainer Maria Rilke.   GI

And so live ever—or else swoon to death. (LL)   Bright Star.   John Keats. AWTN; CABP; CenSon; EnLoPo; GSo; GTBS-P; HAP; InPK-6; MakPoe; NAEL-5v2; NAEL-6v2; NIL-7; NIP-4; NPeEn; OxBSo; PoE; SCV; Son; TFi

And so make a *city* here. (LL)   Abraham Cowley.   BASC; NOBE; NOSC; NoP-4; OBEV; OxAEP-1; PBRV   *Fr.* Mistress, The.

And so, making clear in advance.   Praise to the Rich.   Marina Ivanovna Tsvetayeva [*or* Tsvetaeva].   TCRP, *tr. by* Elaine Feinstein and Angela Livingstone

And so must I lose her whose mind.   Prothalamium.   Donagh MacDonagh. BIrV

And so, my dear, unheard, a single Santa Barbara sparrow.   Another Lo-Cal Elegy.   Stephen Yenser.   UrbNat

And so night after night, God, you come to me.   Israel.   Yitzhak Lamdan. MHP, *tr. by* Ruth Finer Mintz

And so, on my return, the terrapins.   Mercy.   Roddy Lumsden.   NeBl

And so, one gives voice to the empty page. (LL)   Call to Arms.   "Lu Hsün." SuSp; WoPoe, *tr. by* William R. Schultz

And so Rome's soldier settles down.   Horace.   MLL, *tr. by* Helen Waddell   *Fr.* Odes.

And so she makes music wherever she goes. (LL)   Mother Goose.   OxBoLi; OxNR

And so stand stricken, so remembering him! (LL)   Edna St. Vincent Millay. HarvBoo; HeIP-4; LW; OxBSo

And so that all these ages, these years.   From the Domain of Arnheim.   Edwin Morgan.   EmeKit

And so the castles of world trade.   Velemir [*or* Viktor Vladimirovich] Khlebnikov.   TCRP   *Fr.* Good World.

And so the others were the first to leave.   After the Party.   Luigi Fontanella. NeIt, *tr. by* W. S. Di Piero

And so their spirits soared.   Homer.   NAWM-7v1, *tr. by* Robert Fagles   *Fr.* Iliad, The.

And so they all went home again. (LL)   Three Young Rats.   *Unknown.* OxBoLi; OxNR

And so they found that the gold of the olive root had dripped in the / recesses of his heart.   Autopsy, The.   Odysseus Elytis.   AF

And so they kissed, and rode along their way. (LL)   Geoffrey Chaucer. NAWM-5v1; NAWM-7v1, *tr. by* Theodore Morrison   *Fr.* Canterbury Tales, The.

And so they lived; and so they died. (LL)   Epitaph, An: "Interred [*or* Interr'd] beneath this marble stone."   Matthew Prior.   FaBoEE; NAEL-5v1; NAEL-6v1; NAEL-7v1; OBCoV; OBSV

And so through the Jaffa Gate, the street.   Western Wall, The.   Shirley Kaufman.   TaR

And so to bed. My heart is full of poems.   Back Trouble.   Emily Grosholz. RA

And so we too [*or* two] came where the rest have come.   Question, The.   Frank Templeton Prince.   BoLoP; GTBS-P

And so you found that poor room dull.   Appearances.   Robert Browning. OxBSP

And Socks of sullennes exce[e]ding[e] sweet[e]. (LL)   Sir John Davies. NoSic; OxBSo; PBRV   *Fr.* Gulling[e] Sonnets, The.

And some beneath the waggon shun the shower. (LL)   John Clare.   NOBVV; NPeEn

And some chose trade they fared the better.   William Langland.   NOCV   *Fr.* Vision of Piers Plowman, The.

And some there be which have no memorial.   In Memoriam.   M. R. Peacocke. NLP

And something that . . . that is theirs—no longer ours.   Dispossessed, The. John Berryman.   VGW

And sometimes I bring her a bottle of *Nuit d'Amour*. (LL)   Dover Bitch, The. Anthony Hecht.   NBLV; NIL-7; NIP-4; NOBA; NOBL; OBAL; PeLV; UnPo; VGW

And sometimes I hear this song in my head.   Harriet Jacobs.   SpirFl

And sometimes in the cool night I see you are an animal.   Ode for Soft Voice. Michael McClure.   NeAP

And songs of love, the lover soothe to sleep! (LL)   Describes Her Bark.   Mary Robinson.   CenSon; RWP

And songs that sing forever. (LL)   Recollections of "Lalla Rookh."   John Townsend Trowbridge.   APN-2; OBAL

And soon I shall know I was talking to my own soul. (LL)   Adrienne Rich. BoWoP; NoAM   *Fr.* Twenty-one Love Poems.

And soothe the pensive visionary mind! (LL)   To Melancholy. Written on the Banks of the Arun, October 1785.   Charlotte Smith.   CenSon; RWP

And sorrow's cankering worm her heart devours! (LL)   Suspects His Constancy.   Mary Robinson.   CenSon; RWP

And sped along without shadows. (LL)　Iron Spike.　Seamus Heaney. BodElec; TRP

And spin that chicken over my head, sprayin' blood like rain. (LL)　Nobody Here But Us.　Richard Garcia.　OPRER; TouFir

And spit out the teeth. (LL)　Watermelons.　Charles Simic.　OBAL; VCAP

And spit whenever we wanted to. (LL)　Mrs. Trollope in America.　Helen Smith Bevington.　NBLV; OBAL

And split the tomb. (LL)　Advent.　William Everson.　NeAP; TrCP

And spoke the feeling for them, which was what they had lacked. (LL)　Large Red Man Reading.　Wallace Stevens.　APT-1; HAP; LCAP-2

And spotless Pleasure builds her sacred bower. (LL)　Edmund Spenser. NAEL-5v1; NAEL-6v1; NAEL-7v1　*Fr.* Amoretti.

And squeezes through the blinds of the open window.　Heat Sours, The. David Biespiel.　AmPoNex

And 'squires resort—to guzzle Beer. (LL)　To a New England Poet.　Philip Freneau.　NAAL-2v1; NAAL-3

And Stalin lay down in the earth.　Poet and Tsar.　Grigory [*or* Grigorii] Mikhailovich Pozhenyan [*or* Pozhenian].　TCRP, *tr. by* John Glad

And stand like stone and cannot turn away. (LL)　Bay, The.　James Keir Baxter.　HarvBoo; PeNZ

And Stands There Sighing.　Elizabeth Jane Coatsworth.　KaS

And start to die together. (LL)　My Son, My Executioner.　Donald Hall.　LoL; TRP

And started a worm farm. (LL)　E. E. Cummings.　NAAL-2v2; NBLV; NOBA; RB; TwCP

And started away in surprise. (LL)　Limerick: "There was a young lady whose eyes."　Edward Lear.　EBEV; NOBVV

And stayed His hand! (LL)　What Thomas an Buile Said in a Pub.　James Stephens.　MoBrPo; PoRA

And steal the bags to hold the crumbs. (LL)　Common Cormorant [*or* Shag], The.　Christopher Isherwood.　FaBoCh; NBLV

And Steinberg, who is off the wagon, by the way, and that insane woman who lives upstairs, and a few reporters, if anything should break. (LL)　Love, 20c the First Quarter Mile.　Kenneth Fearing.　HAP; WoPoe

And stiffen, and remain. (LL)　Winter Holding off the Coast of North America. N. Scott Momaday.　CDW; ColAP

And still, at sea all night, we had a sense.　James Merrill.　HCAP　*Fr.* Scripts for the Pageant.

And still be dear to sorrow and to love! (LL)　On the Departure of the Nightingale.　Charlotte Smith.　RWP; WoRP

And still Love sang, and what he sang was this. (LL)　Dante Gabriel Rossetti. NAEL-5v2; NAEL-6v2; OxBSo　*Fr.* House of Life, The.

And still my feelings sprout richest.　Uphold Me.　Karen Gershon.　LW

And still no stronger. Swathed in rugs he lingered.　Day in August, A.　Frank Ormsby.　PBCIP; PNI

And still our horses rustle like the rain. (LL)　Youth Dreams, The.　Rainer Maria Rilke.　AWP; TrJP, *tr. by* Ludwig Lewisohn

And still the sun rosies the fronts of houses.　Evening of the Whirlwind.　Amir Gilbo'a.　MHP, *tr. by* Ruth Finer Mintz

And still, this is the God Hermes, sitting by my hearth. (LL)　Maximus.　D. H. Lawrence.　BLT; TOF

And straight I called unto mind [*or* mynde] that it was Christmas Day[e]. (LL)　Burning Babe, The.　Robert Southwell.　ChRPo; ESCV; FaBoCh; HAP; HeIP-4; NAEL-5v1; NAEL-6v1; NAEL-7v1; NOBE; NOCV; NoSic; OBCP; OBEV; OxAEP-1; OxBEV; PAI; RB; SCGP; SacPr; TFi; TOF; TRP; TrCP; WoPoe

And strangely happy with myself. (LL)　Bagel, The.　David Ignatow.　CoAmPo; TwCP

And strangle it, and with it, rhetoric. (LL)　Conrad Potter Aiken.　FaBoMo; NoAM; TwCP　*Fr.* Preludes for Memnon; or, Preludes to Attitude.

And strives to utter what it feels, in vain. (LL)　To Dr. Moore, in Anser to a Poetical Epistle Written by Him in Wales.　Helen Maria Williams. ECWP; WoRP

And strut down the streets with paint on my face. (LL)　Gwendolyn Brooks. ESEAA; NAAAL; NAAL-2v2; NOBA; NOxBChV; NoAM　*Fr.* Street in Bronzeville, A.

And such as it is to be of these more or less I am. (LL)　Walt Whitman. FaBoA; TTTS　*Fr.* Song of Myself.

And such beginnings touch their END. (LL)　Paradise.　George Herbert. AngWePo; BASC; GeHe; NOSC

And such exactly she would be: whatever is superfluous.　Nike.　Ernest Bryll. FaBoWar, *tr. by* Czeslaw Milosz

And suddenly, again.　Of Gravity and Angels.　Jane Hirshfield.　PasH

And suddenly, and all at once, the rain! (LL)　Memorial Rain.　Archibald MacLeish.　MoAmPo; OBWP

And Suddenly It Is Evening.　Salvatore Quasimodo.　WoPoe, *tr. by* J. Ruth Gendler

And Summer mornings the mute child, rebellious.　Eleven.　Archibald MacLeish.　HAP; WeW-3

And summer turns her head with its dark tangle.　Ralegh's Prizes.　Robert Pinsky.　DiPo; VCAP

And summons read, the great consult began. (LL)　John Milton.　FHYEP; NAEL-5v1; NAEL-6v1; OxAEP-1　*Fr.* Paradise Lost.

And sup with thee in glory by and by. (LL)　St. Peter.　Christina Georgina Rossetti.　ChIV-2; NOCV

And swinges the scaly horror of his folded tail. (LL)　Lizards and Snakes. Anthony Hecht.　FaBoMo; TwCP

And sword upon parched veldt and fields of rain-swept gorse. (LL)　Courtyards in Delft.　Derek Mahon.　CIP-2; ModIr; NPeEn; PBCIP; PNI

And Syllables Grow Wings There.　Quincy Troupe.　SpirFl

And take a lesson from this tale of the Spider and the Fly. (LL)　Spider and the Fly, The.　Mary Howitt.　ITBLP; OTCP; PWR; UV

And take my flight / For Heaven. (LL)　Robert Herrick.　BeJo; CaPo; OBEV

And take short views. (LL)　Under Which Lyre, a Reactionary Tract for the Times.　W. H. Auden.　MoBrPo; NOBL; PeLV

And take their walks across the ceiling. (LL)　Folk Who Live in Backward Town, The.　Mary Ann Hoberman.　OBCA; OxIBACP

And take thy rest. (LL)　On This Day I Complete My Thirty-sixth Year. Byron.　CAGL; FHYEP; NAEL-6v2; NPeEn; NoP-4; OBWP; PoE

And take up his cold hands. (LL)　Legend, The.　Garrett Kaoru Hongo.　LoL; MakPoe; OpBo; TRP

And take your wounds from it gladly. (LL)　Ité.　Ezra Pound.　HAP; MoAmPo

And taking stock of this and that. (LL)　Brock.　Paul Muldoon.　NoAM; NoP-4

And taking the moon and leaving the paper dark. (LL)　Prediction, The.　Mark Strand.　LCAP-2; NoP-4; SPE; VCAP

And tangled dry.　It Sounded.　Larry Eigner.　FTOS

And taught his gorgon destinies to sing. (LL)　Luis de Camões.　Roy Campbell.　FaBoTw; OxAEP-2

And tell it as I saw it on the spot. (LL)　My Dream.　Christina Georgina Rossetti.　BrRo; VWP; ViWPN

And tell the ages what we are! (LL)　Children of the Night, The.　Edwin Arlington Robinson.　APN-2; OxBA

And tell thy soul their roots are left in mine. (LL)　Elizabeth Barrett Browning. CenSon; EBVV; LW; OxBSo; WPE　*Fr.* Sonnets from the Portuguese.

And tells the jest without the smile. (LL)　Youth and Age.　Samuel Taylor Coleridge.　GTBS-P; OBEV

And thank you for the evening of the night on which I fell off my horse in the shadows. That was really useful. (LL)　Thank You.　Kenneth Koch. NeAP; PoM

And that allows the poem to come. (LL)　Jerome Rothenberg.　FTOS; PFTM-2 *Fr.* Khurbn.

And that drums had to be rolling, rolling, rolling. (LL)　Dry Loaf.　Wallace Stevens.　NOBA; OxBA; PoRA; RaBo

And that has made all the difference. (LL)　Road Not Taken, The.　Robert Frost.　APT-1; AiP; ChAP; FaBoCh; HAP; HarvBoo; HeIP-4; ITBLP; MoAmPo; NAAL-2v2; NAAL-5; NIL-7; NIP-4; NoAM; NoP-4; OxBA; PoPoPo; SAmP; SoSe-8; TAP; TCAPo; TFi; TRP; TwCP

And that inverted Bowl they call the Sky.　72.　Edward Fitzgerald.　CABP

And that is how I came to know. (LL)　Duel, The.　Eugene Field.　APN-2; ITBLP; NOxBChV; OBAL; OBCA; PoRA; TFi

And that is how it is. (LL)　Philanthropist and the Jelly-fish, The.　May Kendall.　VWP; ViWPN

And that is how we had an accident. (LL)　Murderer, The.　Stevie Smith. FaBoWP; OxBSP

And that is how you die. And that is how you die. (LL)　Protocols.　Randall Jarrell.　LCAP-2; OxBC; VGW

And that is this, and this with thee remains. (LL)　William Shakespeare. NAEL-5v1; NAEL-6v1; NAEL-7v1; OxAEP-1; Son　*Fr.* Sonnets.

And That Is Your Glory.　Yehuda Amichai [*or* Amikhai].　BBASP, *tr. by* Stephen Mitchell

And that my mother, who is dead, was by. (LL)　Sonnet: He Craves Interpreting of a Dream of His.　Dante da Maiano.　AWP; EaItPo, *tr. by* Dante Gabriel Rossetti

(And that quickly) speak your man. (LL)　Ben Jonson.　NAEL-6v1; NAEL-7v1　*Fr.* Celebration of Charis in Ten Lyric[k] Pieces [*or* Peeces], A.

And that's a silly solution for sure! (LL)　Sharing Lodging with Hsieh Shih-hou.　Mei Yao Ch'en.　CoBCP; ColAnChi, *tr. by* Burton Watson

And that's all that you'll be underground. (LL)　God, A Poem.　James Fenton. DiPo; NoAM; NoP-4; OBCoV

And that's my situation, Folks— (LL)　This Form of Life Needs Sex.　Allen Ginsberg.　CLPP; NNaP

And that's to keep thy Lent. (LL)　To Keep a True Lent.　Robert Herrick. SacPr; TrCP

And that's why He made you a cripple. (LL)　Limerick: "To his club-footed child said Lord Stipple."　Edward Gorey.　OBCoV; PeLi

And that's why I'm going to Tilbury Town. (LL)　John Evereldown.　Edwin Arlington Robinson.　APN-2; NCAP; OxBA

And that stands all awry. (LL)　Mother Goose.　OxBoLi; OxNR

And that the same last eddy swallows up. (LL)   Orchard-Pit, The.   Dante Gabriel Rossetti.   EnLoPo; NAEL-5v2; NAEL-6v2; PeVV; SCV

And that was all his travel's story. (LL)   Idiot Boy, The.   William Wordsworth.   NOBRP; OBNV

And that was how it died. (LL)   Nose, The.   Iain Crichton Smith.   OBSP; RB

And that water these words what can they do what can they do prince. (LL)   Elegy of Fortinbras.   Zbigniew Herbert.   PoSu; VCWP; WoPoe, tr. by Czeslaw Milosz

And that what is less than they must sooner or later lift off from these States. (LL)   To a President.   Walt Whitman.   NAAL-2v1; NAAL-3

And that which fleeteth doth outrun swift time. (LL)   Rome.   Joachim Du Bellay.   AWP; FaBoWar, tr. by Ezra Pound

And that which never is to die, for ever must be young. (LL)   To Mr. Hobbes [or Hobs].   Abraham Cowley.   BASC; BeJo

And that will be the best. (LL)   A. E. Housman.   MoBrPo; SCGP

And that words are the nets to capture it. (LL)   Pen, The.   Muhammad Al-Ghuzzi.   MAP; NAfrP, tr. by John Heath-Stubbs and May Jayyusi

And the age ended, and the last deliverer died.   W. H. Auden.   See So an age ended, and its last deliverer died

And the ancestor dead long ago in Domingo or Guadaloupe. (LL)   To Francis Jammes.   Robert Bridges.   NPeEn; OxBSo

And the angel, taking some pains, told.   Joseph's Suspicion.   Rainer Maria Rilke.   TrCP

And the apple-blossom is allowed to wither on the bough. (LL)   Swineherd.   Eiléan Ní Chuilleanáin.   BIrV; CIP-2; FaBoWP; NPeEn; WPOW

And the banquet, the exile, the first crime.   Octavio Paz.   PoetW, tr. by Eliot Weinberger   Fr. Sunstone.

And the Beatles' first LP. (LL)   Annus Mirabilis.   Philip Larkin.   NBLV; NIP-4; NOBL; OBAL

And the bells dream. (LL)   Poem: "Frail sound of a tunic trailing, A."   Antonio Machado Ruiz.   AWP; WoPoe, tr. by John Dos Passos

And the best will come back to you. (LL)   Life's Mirror.   "Madeline Bridges."   PWR; PoToHe

And the bewildered [or bewilder'd] chimes. (LL)   Fountain, The.   William Wordsworth.   GTBS-P; OxAEP-2

And the Bishop said: "The ways of God are strange!" (LL)   "They."   Siegfried Sassoon.   NAEL-5v2; NAEL-6v2; OBSV; OBWP

And the bitter storm augments; the wild winds wage.   John Josselyn.   SCAP

And the blackberries a-growing. (LL)   What's the Railroad to Me?   Henry David Thoreau.   GM; HHAm; TAP

And the blind goddess, when we touched her.   Blind Goddess, The.   Fadhila Chabbi.   PoArWo, tr. by Yaseen Noorani

And the blood was coming down all over her face and waist. (LL)   Charles Reznikoff.   ColAP; WWork   Fr. Testimony.

And the body underneath it says: I am. (LL)   Knight, Death, and the Devil, The.   Randall Jarrell.   GS; WeW-3

And the buffaloes are gone. (LL)   Buffalo Dusk.   Carl Sandburg.   ChAP; OBCA

And the child draws another inscrutable house. (LL)   Sestina: "September rain falls on the house."   Elizabeth Bishop.   APT-2; InPK-6; LCAP-2; NAAL-5; NIL-7; NoP-4; PoE; PoPoPo; PoetW

And the Cock Begins to Crow.   Richard K. Avery.   AH

And the colours have all passed [or pass'd] away from her eyes! (LL)   Reverie of Poor Susan, The.   William Wordsworth.   GTBS-P; OxBoLi

And the Communists have nothing to offer but fat cheeks and eyeglasses and lying policemen.   Kral Majales.   Allen Ginsberg.   PFTM-2; PoM

And the condemned man ate a hearty meal.   Runner, The.   Louis Simpson.   AF

And the congregation telleth out their praise. (LL)   Bible, Apocrypha.   OBVE; TrJP   Fr. Ecclesiasticus.

And the Cow's dead, the old Cow's dead.   Dead Cow Farm.   Robert Graves.   FaBoWar; PoWW

And the crew of the captain's gig! (LL)   Yarn of the Nancy Bell, The.   Sir William Schwenck Gilbert.   EBNV; FaBoCh; NOBL; TFi; UV

And the Cycles wheel! (LL)   Called Back.   Emily Dickinson.   MoAmPo; NOBA; NOCV

And the daughter of my father.   Dissidents, The.   Catherine Obianuju Acholonu.   HAWP

And the day it's well return'd again. (LL)   Fire of Frendraught, The.   Unknown.   ESPB; OxBB

And the Days Are Not Full Enough.   Ezra Pound.   RB; Spl

And the dead begin from their dark to sing in my sleep. (LL)   Journey to the Interior.   Theodore Roethke.   LCAP-2; TRP; VGW

And the dead nations never rise again. (LL)   Jewish Cemetery at Newport, The.   Henry Wadsworth Longfellow.   APN-1; ChIV-1; ColAP; FaBoA; HAP; HeIP-4; NAAL-5; NCAP; NOBA; NoP-4; OxBA; PoPoPo; TAP; TCAPo

And the deep river ran on. (LL)   As I Walked Out One Evening.   W. H. Auden.   HeIP-4; InPK-6; NIL-7; NOBE; NoAM; NoP-4; OxAEP-2; PoPoPo; RB; TwCP; UnPo

And the deepened stillness as a calm, cast over us.   David Jones.   NPeEn   Fr. In Parenthesis.

And the Dervish spat.   Dervish, The.   Muhammad Al-Faituri [or Al-Fituri or Al-Fayturi].   MAP, tr. by Sargon Boulus and Peter Porter

And the disconnected number I still call. (LL)   Tony Harrison.   NAEL-5v2; NAEL-6v2   Fr. School of Eloquence, The.

And the dish ran away with the spoon. (LL)   High Diddle Diddle.   Mother Goose.   OxBoLi; OxNR; ReMoGo

And the dish ran away with the spoon. (LL)   Unknown.   LB; OxBEV; OxNR

And the Earth Rebelled.   Yuri Suhl.   TrJP, tr. by Max Rosenfeld

And "the earth under our feet."   At Kenneth Burke's Place.   William Carlos Williams.   NOBA

And the faint but perceptible scent of sweet clear water. (LL)   Rosemary Dobson.   ItWoWo; NOBAu   Fr. Daily Living.

And the fire and the rose are one. (LL)   T. S. Eliot.   CABP; FaBoMo; FaBoTw; GTBS-P; NAEL-5v2; NAEL-6v2; NAWM-7v2; NOBA; NOBE; NoAM; OxAEP-2; OxBTC; PeECV; TAP; TFi   Fr. Four Quartets.

And the first grey of morning filled the east.   Matthew Arnold.   EBNV; OBNV

And the first murderer lay upon the earth. (LL)   Imperial Adam.   Alec Derwent Hope.   BMAP; CBAP; ChIV-1; HAP; HarvBoo; NIP-4; NoAM; NoP-4

And the flower weeps.   Christopher Okigbo.   PBMAP   Fr. Heavensgate (1961).

And the fresh-severed head of it, my head. (LL)   Show, The.   Wilfred Owen.   MoBrPo; OBWVE; OxBEV; OxBTC; PeFWW

And the fret lies on me. (LL)   Lamentation of the Old Pensioner, The.   W. B. Yeats.   HAP; InPK-6; NoAM; TRP; WeW-3

And the fumbling. Oh blessèd Lord the fumbling.   Betty.   Paul Mariani.   SwNoth

And the gears notch and the engines wheel. (LL)   Clear Night.   Charles Wright.   GeoHom; VCAP

And the general view. (LL)   Lady "Rogue" Singleton.   Stevie Smith.   FaBoWP; OPOU; OxBSP

And the glitter of jewels? (LL)   On Her Decision to Stop Wearing Clothes.   Mahadevi.   ErotSp; WPoS, tr. by Jane Hirshfield

And the gods shook, they knew not why. (LL)   Uriel.   Ralph Waldo Emerson.   APN-1; NAAL-2v1; NAAL-3; NOBA; OxBA

And the graduates can't stand the college-trained staff.   Lucky Eugene.   Michael Foley.   PNI

And the grass on the mountains. (LL)   Grass on the Mountain, The.   Unknown.   APT-1; AWP, tr. by Mary Austin

And the grave's the place to seek them. (LL)   Robert Louis Stevenson.   NOBVV; OxBEV

And the Great Mother said.   Linda Reuther.   HW   Fr. Homecoming.

And the green grass growing over us. (LL)   Basil Bunting.   NPeEn; OxBEV   Fr. Villon.

And the green leaves they grow rarely. (LL)   Cruel Mother, The.   Unknown.   ESPB; InPK-6; OxBB

And the ground spinning beneath us / goes on talking. (LL)   For Alva Benson, and for Those Who Have Learned to Speak.   Joy Harjo.   HATNAP; UnSA

And the ground spoke when she was born.   For Alva Benson, and for Those Who Have Learned to Speak.   Joy Harjo.   HATNAP; UnSA

And the Haggards Ride no more. (LL)   To R. K.   James Kenneth Stephen.   FaBoEE; NBLV; NOBL; PeLV; UV

And the heart.   Rose of Silence.   Gennady Aygi.   ItGoST, tr. by Peter France

And the heat weighs a dreamy load. (LL)   Half-Way Pause, A.   Dante Gabriel Rossetti.   NOBVV; OxBEV

And the hills of Ise. (LL)   Snow Party, The.   Derek Mahon.   CIP-2; HarvBoo; ModIr; NPeEn; OxBC; PBCIP; PNI

AND THE HORN may now paw the air howling goodbye.   Elegy for Alto.   Christopher Okigbo.   HBAPE; VCWP

And the Hotel Room Held Only Him.   Mari E. Evans.   PAI

And the hunter home from the hill. (LL)   Requiem: "Under the wide and starry sky."   Robert Louis Stevenson.   BRP; EBVV; MoBrPo; NBLV; NOBE; NOBVV; NePenScot; OBEV; OxBEV; PoRA; SCGP; TFi

And the immodest thigh. (LL)   Man Who Married Magdalene, The.   Louis Simpson.   NoAM; TAP

And the knob turns. (LL)   Meditations in an Emergency.   Frank O'Hara.   PmAP; TAP; VCAP

And the lake is crystal-clear. (LL)   Lal Ded [or Lalla].   AWTN; WPoS, tr. by Coleman Barks

And the lake was a dark spot.   Night Without Stars, A.   Nancy Eimers.   ExTi

And the last beam of hope was almost gone. (LL)   On Hearing of the Intention of a Gentleman to Purchase the Poet's Freedom.   George Moses Horton.   APN-1; NAAAL

And the last day being come, Man stood alone.   Trumbull Stickney.   APN-2; NoP-4

And the leaves of the Judgement / Book unfold! (LL)   Bedouin Song.   Bayard Taylor.   APN-2; TCAPo

And the light, a wakened heyday of air.　November Sunday Morning.　Alvin Feinman.　CoAP

And the lightning laughs at the clouds.　Lightning, The.　Judah Al-Harizi.　BLT, *tr. by* T. Carmi

And the Lord God planted a garden eastward in Eden.　Bible, *O.T.*　OBGa　*Fr.* Genesis.

And the lost delicate suitors who could sing. (LL)　Geoffrey Hill.　NPeEn; OxBEV　*Fr.* Apology for the Revival of Christian Architecture in England, An.

And the love, whatever it was, an infection. (LL)　Wanting to Die.　Anne Sexton.　CoAmPo; ColAP; NoAM; TAP; TRP; VCAP

And the luck of our husbands and lovers, who keep free women. (LL)　Carolyn Kizer.　FFC; VCAP　*Fr.* Pro Femina.

And the luckier lot betide you. (LL)　Ben Jonson.　BeJo; EBEV　*Fr.* Gypsies Metamorphosed, The.

And the message of the yew tree is blackness—blackness and silence. (LL)　Moon and the Yew Tree, The.　Sylvia Plath.　BBASP; CoAP; FaBoMo; FaBoWP; VGW; WPE; WPOW

And the midnight message of Paul Revere. (LL)　Henry Wadsworth Longfellow.　AiP; BRP; EBNV; FaBoTw; HHAm; ITBLP; OBAL; OBCA; OBNV; PWR; TCAPo; TFi　*Fr.* Tales of a Wayside Inn.

And the mighty Twins? (LL)　Leda and the Swan.　Oliver St. John Gogarty.　EBNV; HAP

And the minutes, the hours, the days. (LL)　Bloody Men.　Wendy Cope.　HarvBoo; NoP-4

And the mist rising from the water has hidden the hills. (LL)　Fisherman.　Ou-yang Hsiu.　BLT; OHPC, *tr. by* Kenneth Rexroth

And the mome raths outgrabe. (LL)　Lewis Carroll.　AmFaPo; BRP; CABP; ChAP; ClHu; EBEV; EBVV; HeIP-4; ITBLP; InPK-6; NAEL-5v2; NAEL-6v2; NBLV; NOBE; NOBL; NOBVV; NOxBChV; NTCP; NoAM; NoP-4; OBSP; OxAEP-2; OxBEV; PeLV; PeVV; PoRA; RB; TFi; TRP; TTTS; UV　*Fr.* Through the Looking-Glass.

And the morning green, and the build-up of weather, and my brows.　Morning, Noon and Night.　Mark Strand.　BAP-97

And the moss on the shore burning red. (LL)　In the Home of the Scholar Wu Su-chiang.　Wu Tsao.　BoWoP; WPOW

And the need of a world of men for me. (LL)　Parting at Morning.　Robert Browning.　AWP; CABP; FHYEP; HeIP-4; NAEL-5v2; NAEL-6v2; NOBE; OBEV; OxBSP; PAI; SCGP; SoSe-8; TFi; UnPo

And the new sun rose bringing the new year. (LL)　Tennyson.　FHYEP; NAEL-5v2; NAEL-6v2　*Fr.* Idylls of the King.

And the notion I cannot endure! (LL)　Lewis Carroll.　EBEV; NAEL-5v2; NAEL-6v2; OxAEP-2　*Fr.* Hunting of the Snark, The.

And the old men, supervising grown grandsons, nephews.　Charlene-N-Booker 4Ever.　Forrest Hamer.　GeoHom

And the Old Women Gathered.　Mari E. Evans.　BlSi

And the ones that got tough.　Inheritors, The.　William Peskett.　PNI

And the only windows were the windows they drew. (LL)　Ghetto.　Michael Longley.　EmeKit; NoP-4; PNI

And the others went back. (LL)　Moon Eclipse Exorcism.　*Unknown.*　STP; WoPoe, *tr. by* Armand Schwerner

And the past. (LL)　"H. D."　NALW; VGW　*Fr.* Eurydice.

And the path is born behind him. (LL)　Vasco [*or* Vasko] Popa.　PoSu; WoPoe, *tr. by* Anne Pennington　*Fr.* St Sava's Spring.

And the picture carried with singing into the temple. (LL)　Because I Paced My Thought.　John Hewitt.　CIP-2; PNI

And the pig got up and slowly walked away. (LL)　Pig, The.　*Unknown.*　FaBoEE; OBCoV

And the pink's in us. (LL)　After Reading *Mickey in the Night Kitchen* for the Third Time Before Bed.　Rita Dove.　LoL; ReTh

And the place of their waiting a long burrow.　David Jones.　FaBoMo　*Fr.* In Parenthesis.

And the place was water.　Paean to Place.　Lorine Niedecker.　APSN; APT-2

And the point in the spectrum.　"H. D."　APT-1; NALW　*Fr.* Tribute to the Angels.

And the poor stars.　At the Poorhouse.　Federico García Lorca.　PFTM-1

And the poor, when they're old, have little of peace! (LL)　To the Four Courts, Please.　James Stephens.　BIrV; MoBrPo; UnPo

And the pump has frozen tonight. (LL)　Star-Talk.　Robert Graves.　MoBrPo; OxBTC

And the Queen Anne's lace! (LL)　Portrait by a Neighbour.　Edna St. Vincent Millay.　ItWoWo; OBCA

And the quiet of love in her feet. (LL)　Cap and Bells, The.　W. B. Yeats.　MoBrPo; NoAM; RB

And the rain will continue. (LL)　Monsoon Girl.　Harry Clifton.　BiHa; PBCIP

And the reconstruction of the mind. (LL)　Planetarium.　Adrienne Rich.　FaBoWP; HCAP; NAAL-2v2; NALW; NIL-7; NIP-4; NOBA; NoAM; VCAP

"And the rich He hath sent empty away." (LL)　Our Lady.　Mary Elizabeth Coleridge.　OBEV; OBMV; ViWPN; WPE

And the right one with its white foot. (LL)　Truth Is, The.　Linda Hogan.　HATNAP; ItWoWo; LTA

And the roads deep in snow? (LL)　First Death in Nova Scotia.　Elizabeth Bishop.　CoAP; FaBoWP; HarvBoo; LCAP-2; NOBA

And the Same Words.　David Ignatow.　NNaP

And the sea, the moving sea, the sea. / God is cold. (LL)　Man Adrift on a Slim Spar, A.　Stephen Crane.　APN-2; NAAL-2v2

And the sea where it goes. (LL)　Buried Life, The.　Matthew Arnold.　FHYEP; NAEL-5v2; NAEL-6v2

And the Seventh Dream Is the Dream of Isis.　David Gascoyne.　SPE

And the silence off on the hills might be an echo.　W. S. Merwin.　GI　*Fr.* "Prodigal Son, The."

And the silver age, unattainable.　Viktor Krivulin.　TCRusP, *tr. by* Anna Barker and Daniel Weissbort

And the single straight cord of the trumpets marine.　Cantor.　Guillaume Apollinaire.　CuPo

And the skies are blear and grey. (LL)　Ballad of the Bird-Bride.　Rosamund Marriott Watson.　VWP; ViWPN

And the smile on the face of the Tiger. (LL)　There Was a Young Lady of Niger.　Cosmo Monkhouse.　NBLV; TLR

And the snake says to the toad.　Niyi Osundare.　NAfrP　*Fr.* Waiting Laughters.

And the soldiers with their guns. (LL)　Carrickfergus.　Louis MacNeice.　NAEL-5v2; NAEL-6v2; NOIV; NoAM; PNI

And the soul creeps out of the tree. (LL)　All Hallows.　Louise Glück.　HCAP; PoPoPo

And the Squire, and Lady Susan, murmur mildly to me now. (LL)　Friends Beyond.　Thomas Hardy.　EBVV; FaBoVe; GTBS-P; NOBVV; OBEV

And the stone fell.　Sentence, The.　Anna Andreyevna Akhmatova.　AmFaPo, *tr. by* Judith Hemschemeyer

And the storm has ceased to blow. (LL)　Thomas Campbell.　GTBS-P; NOBE; OBEV; OBWP; OxAEP-2

And the storm reestablished itself.　Morning Jitters.　John Ashbery.　FTOS

And the strutting fern lay seeds on the black sill. (LL)　After the Funeral.　Dylan Thomas.　AngWePo; FaBoMo; NAEL-5v2; NAEL-6v2; NoP-4; OBWVE; OxAEP-2; TCAWP

And the style of your prose growing limper and limper. (LL)　Academic.　Theodore Roethke.　FaBoEE; OBAL

And the sun was born.　Heart of Time.　Fanny Carrión de Fierro.　TANSG, *tr. by* Sally Cheney Bell

And the sweet name to my mouth. (LL)　Italia, Io Ti Saluto!　Christina Georgina Rossetti.　VWP; WPE

And the telephone comes to mean.　Lollies Noir.　Dorothy Porter.　BMAP

And the things we have seen and have known and have heard of fail us. (LL)　On a Dead Child.　Robert Bridges.　EBEV; NOBE; NOBVV; NoAM; OBMV; OxAEP-2; SCGP

And the thoughts of youth are long, long thoughts. (LL)　My Lost Youth.　Henry Wadsworth Longfellow.　APN-1; AWP; ITBLP; NAAL-2v1; NAAL-3; NOBA; OBEV; OxBA; PoRA; TAP; TCAPo; TFi

And the tide rises, the tide falls. (LL)　Tide Rises, the Tide Falls, The.　Henry Wadsworth Longfellow.　APN-1; ITBLP; NOBA; OxBA; PAI; PoE; PoPoPo; PoRA; TAP

And the tither a bonny brier. (LL)　Fair Janet.　*Unknown.*　ESPB; OxBB

And the tooth that bruises. (LL)　Pisces.　Ronald Stuart Thomas.　CABP; OxBC

And the Trains Go On.　Philip Levine.　GM

And the trains that go from Rouen at the ending of the day. (LL)　Rouen.　May Wedderburn Cannan.　NAEL-5v2; NAEL-6v2; OBWP; OxBTC

And the Vietnamese boat-people of Portadown. (LL)　Home.　Frank Ormsby.　ModIr; PBCIP; PNI

And the voice in my dreaming ear melted away. (LL)　Soldier's Dream, The.　Thomas Campbell.　GTBS-P; OxAEP-2

And the voice said: Walk.　Little Falls.　Robert Hogg.　MoCV

And the warm weather is holding.　Flame Ode.　Barry MacSweeney.　Oth

And the way goes on in the worn earth.　Archibald MacLeish.　NoAM　*Fr.* Conquistador.

And the Whiskey Boys are drunk outside Philadelphia. (LL)　After the Industrial Revolution, All Things Happen at Once.　Robert Bly.　CoAP; CoAmPo

And the whole deck put on its leaves again. (LL)　Old Ships, The.　James Elroy Flecker.　MoBrPo; OBMV; PoRA

And the whole earth was of one language, and of one speech.　Bible, *O.T.*　NAWM-5v1　*Fr.* Genesis.

& the whole garden will bow. (LL)　E. E. Cummings.　MoAmPo; NAAL-2v2

And the wild seed of Abraham is cold.　Nicodemus.　Howard Nemerov.　GI; TaR

And the wind drove a cloud to seaward, and the sun began to /shine shine. (LL)　Revenge of Hamish, The.　Sidney Lanier.　APN-2; EBNV; NCAP

And the woman calling. (LL)　Voice, The.　Thomas Hardy.　BoLoP; EnLoPo;

GTBS-P; HAP; HarvBoo; NAEL-5v2; NAEL-6v2; NPeEn; NoAM; NoP-4; OxAEP-2; OxBEV; PAI; PoE; TFi

And the women warbled: Nothing like us ever was. (LL) Four Preludes on Playthings of the Wind. Carl Sandburg. MoAmPo; NOBA

And the Word became flesh and dwelt among us. Jorge Luis Borges. GI *Fr.* St. John.

And the word came—was it a god. Calling, The. Ronald Stuart Thomas. PoetW

And the world changed. Survival: Infantry. George Oppen. FTOS

And the world's danger. (LL) I Saw a Stable. Mary Elizabeth Coleridge. ChIV-2; OBCP; OxBSP; SacPr

And the World was Calm. Chris Wallace-Crabbe. BMAP

And the worst friend and enemy is but Death. (LL) Rupert Brooke. NPeEn; OBWP *Fr.* 1914.

And thee returning on thy silver wheels. (LL) Tithonus. Tennyson. CABP; HAP; NAEL-5v2; NAEL-6v2; NAWM-7v2; NOBE; NOBVV; NPeEn; NoP-4; OxBEV; PAI; PoE; SCGP

And theekit it o'er wi' rashes. (LL) Bessy [*or* Bessie] Bell and Mary Gray. *Unknown.* ESPB; OxBB

And their brief multitude. (LL) Roads. Edward Thomas. HarvBoo; PeFWW

And their experience count as mine. (LL) On an Invitation to the United States. Thomas Hardy. AWP; AiP; FaBoA

And their eyes are burning. (LL) O What Is That Sound [Which So Thrills the Ear]. W. H. Auden. FaBoWar; PoE

And their hands, the way. Song 9. Harry Gilonis. Oth

And their snuff-laden breath blowing lightly over me in my first sleep. (LL) Frau Bauman, Frau Schmidt, and Frau Schwartze. Theodore Roethke. APT-2; CoAP; NAAL-2v2; NOBA; NoAM; TAP

And their terrible eyes are watching you. (LL) Kenneth Patchen. APT-2; VGW

And their tongues are teasing oil from whales. (LL) Lady in Kicking Horse Reservoir, The. Richard Hugo. CoAP; LCAP-2; NAAL-2v2; NoAM; NoP-4; VCAP

And Their Winter and Night in Disguise. George Oppen. APSN; NNaP *Fr.* Some San Francisco Poems.

And then (and only then) did Aaron laugh. (LL) Aaron Stark. Edwin Arlington Robinson. APN-2; MoAmPo; Son

And then as regards the great wave. System. Tiziano Rossi. ItPo, *tr. by* Gayle Ridinger

And then down into the black soul. Helmut Heissenbüttel. PFTM-2, *tr. by* Pierre Joris *Fr.* Textbook 10.

And then find out the rest. (LL) King Billy. Edwin Morgan. NePenScot; NoP-4

And then forever to be gone. (LL) Falling Star, The. Sara Teasdale. ChAP; OBCA

And then he loved her very well. (LL) Pumpkin-Eater, The. Mother Goose. OxNR; ReMoGo

And then he would lift this finest. Out-of-the-Body Travel. Stanley Plumly. LCAP-2

And then I arrived at the powerful green hill. (LL) Then I Saw What the Calling Was. Muriel Rukeyser. ColAP; FaBoWP

And then I feel quite sure she'd answer Yes. (LL) Sonnet: Of Becchina, the Shoemaker's Daughter. Cecco Angiolieri, da Siena. AWP; EaItPo, *tr. by* Dante Gabriel Rossetti

And then I pressed the shell. Shell, The. James Stephens. MoBrPo

And then I sat me down, and gave the rein. Sonnet: "And then I sat me down, and gave the rein." Gustav Rosenhane. AWP, *tr. by* Sir Edmund William Gosse

And then I see the cattle of my own town. My Dream about the Cows. Lucille Clifton. TRP

And then I smile and title it. If I Write a Poem. A. Van Jordan. SpirFl

And then I start getting this feeling of exaltation. (LL) Blessing in Disguise, A. John Ashbery. ColAP; PoM

And then in mid-May the first morning of steady heat. Late Spring. Robert Hass. BLT

And then it was. Poem for My Father. Alejandra Piznarnick. TANSG, *tr. by* Susan Bassnett

And then meet here. (LL) His Winding-Sheet. Robert Herrick. BASC; CaPo; OBEV

And then moves on. (LL) Fog. Carl Sandburg. APT-1; BRP; ChAP; HeIP-4; ITBLP; InPK-6; MoAmPo; NAAL-2v2; NAAL-5; OBCA; OxIBACP; PAI; Spl; TAP; TCAPo; TFi; TTTS

And then my country spoke to me. Osip Emilevich Mandelstam [*or* Mandelshtam]. TCRP *Fr.* Stanzas.

And Then No More. Friedrich Rückert. BIrV, *tr. by* James Clarence Mangan

And then of course we argued about teachers. Tsitsa. Kofi Anyidoho. NAfrP

And then one day Hershey played by the door. Delmore Schwartz. TrJP *Fr.* Genesis.

And then rides back to shave again. (LL) Commuter. Elwyn Brooks White. HHAm; NBLV

And then she shall be a true lover of mine. (LL) Scarborough Fair. *Unknown.* OxBoLi; PeLV

And then start down! (LL) Afternoon on a Hill. Edna St. Vincent Millay. APT-1; ChAP; NTCP; OBCA; OxBA; TTTS

And then the blue world daring onward. Handball Players at Brighton Beach, The. Irving Feldman. TaR

And then the dark fell and "there has never." Journey, The. Eavan Boland. BiHa

And then the lighting of the lamps. (LL) T. S. Eliot. OPOU; TCAPo *Fr.* Preludes (I–IV).

And Then the Water. Milo De Angelis. NeIt, *tr. by* Lawrence Venuti

And then they have their answer home. (LL) Quip, The. George Herbert. BASC; GeHe; NOSC; OxAEP-1; OxBEV

And then went down to the ship. Ezra Pound. MoAmPo; NAAL-5; NoAM; OBVE; PoE; VGW *Fr.* Cantos.

And thEn with bronZe lance heads beaRing yet Arms. Writing through the Cantos. John Cage. PmAP

And then with patience bid me bear my fire. (LL) Sir Philip Sidney. NAEL-5v1; NAEL-6v1; NAEL-7v1 *Fr.* Astrophil and Stella.

And then, without his knowing, sweet sleep descended down. William Williams. OBWVE, *tr. by* Gwyn Jones and Lewis Saunders *Fr.* View of Christ's Kingdom, A.

And then you suddenly cried, and turned away. (LL) Hill, The. Rupert Brooke. MoBrPo; OxBSo; OxBTC; Son

And there a clump of houses with a church. (LL) Onset, The. Robert Frost. APT-1; MoAmPo; OxBA

And there are times truly. Underdeveloped Country, An. Dennis Joseph Enright. NOBL

And there, beyond the barbed wire, the view. Natzweiler. Rutger Kopland. VCWP, *tr. by* James Brockway

And there goes Miss Bell with her fusty old Nut. (LL) Long John Brown & Little Mary Bell. William Blake. ECEV; RB

"And there goes the bell for the third month." Fight of the Year, The. Robert McGough. OBCP

And there I found a gray and ancient ass. Pegasus Lost. Elinor Wylie. MoAmPo

And there I found myself more truly and more strange. (LL) Tea at the Palaz of Hoon. Wallace Stevens. APT-1; AmFaPo; FaBoMo; WoPoe

And there is dying in an hospital. (LL) Old Man Travelling [Animal Tranquillity and Decay, a Sketch]. William Wordsworth. FaBoCh; NPeEn; OBWP

And there is no bottom to evil. (LL) Aleksander Wat. AF; WoPoe, *tr. by* Czeslaw Milosz *Fr.* Persian Parables.

And there is no sign of the wind. (LL) Fear. Charles Simic. HCAP; WeW-3

And there is nothing at all—neither fear. Natalya [*or* Natal'ia] Gorbanevskaya [*or* Gorbanyevskaya *or*Gorbanevskaia]. BoWoP

And there lay the lovers, lip-locked. Paulus [*or* Paulos] Silentiarius. ErotSp, *tr. by* Sam Hamill

And there shall come forth a rod out of the stem of Jesse. Bible, *O.T.* AWP; OBVE; TrJP *Fr.* Isaiah.

And there she's leand her back to a thorn. Cruel Mother, The. *Unknown.* ESPB

And there the island lay, the waves around. Enchanted Island, The. Letitia [*or* Laetitia] Elizabeth Landon. CABP; NOBRP

And there the mountains began to move. March of the Cordilleras, The. Raúl Zurita. TCLAP, *tr. by* Jack Schmitt

And there was great mourning in Israel in every place. Bible, Apocrypha. TrJP *Fr.* First Maccabees.

And thereafter come . . . tears. Tears. Alena Synková. INSAB

And therefore if to love can be desert. Elizabeth Barrett Browning. CenSon *Fr.* Sonnets from the Portuguese.

And there is his evyn on Crystes owyn day. (LL) St. Stephen and King Herod. *Unknown.* ESPB; OxBoLi

And these about me die. Sandalphon. Ezra Pound. TCAPo

And these mountains which my eyes have seen. Bible, Pseudepigrapha. TrJP *Fr.* Enoch.

And these prounounced *POOH!* (LL) Pooh! Walter De la Mare. HAP; OBCoV; PeLV

And these the last verses that I write for her. (LL) Tonight I Can Write the Saddest Lines. Pablo Neruda. BoLoP; PoetW; TCLAP, *tr. by* W. S. Merwin

And these / these are scavengers birds. In the Zoo. A. K. Ramanujan. VCWP

And they all lived together in a little crooked house. (LL) There Was a Crooked Man. Mother Goose. LB; OxBoLi; OxNR; PeLV

And they always aske me "who do you." In the Tradition Too. Ras Baraka. InTrad

And they are rich and ransom all ill deeds. (LL) William Shakespeare. HeIP-4; OxAEP-1 *Fr.* Sonnets.

And they are too many to bury. (LL)   We Were Three.   Claribel Alegría.   AF; TCLAP, *tr.* by Carolyn Forché

And they both lived happily ever after.   After Ever Happily [*or*, The Princess and the Woodcutter].   Ian Serraillier.   OBSP

And they come in a smaller size. (LL)   Fifteen Million Plastic Bags.   Adrian Mitchell.   EmeKit; OBSV; OxBTC

And they gave me this jolly red nose. (LL)   Francis Beaumont.   FaBoCh; OxNR   *Fr.* Knight of the Burning Pestle, The.

And they have to get it right. We just need.   Love Poem, A.   John Ashbery.   HCAP

And they'll all kowtow. (LL)   Brush Up Your Shakespeare.   Cole Porter.   OBAL; OBCoV; ReLy

And they stopped before that bad sculpture of a fisherman.   Charles Olson.   NAAL-2v2; TRP   *Fr.* Maximus Poems, The.

And they went to sea in a sieve. (LL)   Jumblies, The.   Edward Lear.   CABP; EBEV; NAEL-5v2; NAEL-6v2; NOxBChV; OxBoLi; PeLV; PeVV; PoRA; TFi; UV

And They were there in the City of Fire, enflamed.   JuJu.   Askia Muhammad Touré.   SeSe

And they will likewise all have places. (LL)   Oh No.   Robert Creeley.   HeIP-4; InPK-6

And Thine Elect, rejectest never. (LL)   Father, The.   Joshua Sylvester.   InvLi; SacPr

And thine immortal wine! (LL)   Indian Summer.   Emily Dickinson.   APN-2; MoAmPo; NAAL-2v1; NAAL-3; NAAL-5; TCAPo

And things that are yet to be done. Open the door! (LL)   On a Night of Snow.   Elizabeth Jane Coatsworth.   MoAmPo; OBCA

And think it's crazy. (LL)   After Lorca.   Robert Creeley.   CoAmPo; LCAP-2; PmAP

And thinks it unlikely. Though people have been shot for sprawl. (LL)   Quality of Sprawl, The.   Les A. Murray.   EmeKit; HarvBoo; NoP-4

And thinning sheaf of days. (LL)   Bridge.   A. R. Ammons.   CoAP; NAAL-2v2

And this bright moon—whose house is it setting on? (LL)   Thinking of East Mountain.   Li Po.   CoBCP; TTTS, *tr.* by Burton Watson

And this goes down for union. (LL)   Frederick Douglass.   NAAL-2v1; NAAL-3; NAWM-7v2   *Fr.* Narrative of the Life of Frederick Douglass, an American Slave.

And This is a Beautiful Night That in the Heart.   Patrizia Valduga.   CItWP, *tr.* by Cinzia Sartini Blum and Lara Trubowitz

And this is how you live: a woman, children.   Primary Ground, A.   Adrienne Rich.   NNaP

And This Is My Beloved.   Alexander Borodin.   ReLy

And This Is So.   Joseph H. Ball.   PasH

And this is the oppressor's language. (LL)   Burning of Paper instead of Children, The.   Adrienne Rich.   HarvBoo; LCAP-2; NAAL-2v2; VCAP

And this is the way they ring.   Ringing the Bells.   Anne Sexton.   HCAP; PoE; TAP; VGW

And this is where.   Ian Wedde.   PeNZ   *Fr.* Angel.

And this, ladies and gentlemen, whom I am not in fact.   Suicide, The.   Louis MacNeice.   ModIr

And this our life, exempt from public haunt.   William Shakespeare.   PoToHe   *Fr.* As You Like It.

And this reft house is that the which he built.   On a Ruined House in a Romantic Country.   Samuel Taylor Coleridge.   CenSon

And this should be the wise man's pattern. (LL)   Scholar in the Narrow Street, The.   Tso Ssu.   AWP; ChiP, *tr.* by Arthur Waley

And this, too, is love.   Gwyneth Lewis.   NeBl   *Fr.* Parables & Faxes.

And "thole a litel" a long weye is. (LL)   *Unknown.*   OHMEL; OxBSP

And those black rocks which overhung the stream.   Black Rocks.   Charles Hubert Sisson.   DiPo

And those level fingernails of theirs.   Franco Buffoni.   ItPo, *tr.* by Gayle Ridinger

And those of sorrows yet to come. (LL)   Shrubbery, The.   William Cowper.   NOBE; OBGa

And those roads in South Dakota that feel around in the darkness. (LL)   Come with Me.   NOBA; NoAM

And thou, all they, hast all the all of me. (LL)   William Shakespeare.   NOBE; OBEV   *Fr.* Sonnets.

And thou art now no longer near!   To the Parted One.   Goethe.   AWP, *tr.* by Christopher Pearse Cranch

And thou hast stolen a jewel, Death.   Gerald Massey.   TreFP   *Fr.* Babe Christabel.

And thou like Adamant draw mine iron heart. (LL)   John Donne.   EBEV; GSo; InvLi; MeLP; NAEL-5v1; NAEL-6v1; NAEL-7v1; NOBE; NOCV; NOSC; NoP-4; OxAEP-1; SCGP; Son   *Fr.* Holy Sonnets.

And thou, remembered Sagamore.   Sagamore, The.   B. P. Shillaber.   TreFP

And thou thy joys with me. (LL)   We Have Lived and Loved Together.   Charles Jefferys [*or* Jeffries].   ITBLP; PoToHe

And thou to be alone. (LL)   Night Wind, The.   Emily Jane Brontë.   EBVV; NAEL-5v2; NAEL-6v2; NALW; NIL-7

And thou wert sad—yet I was not with thee.   Lines on Hearing That Lady Byron Was Ill.   Byron.   EBEV; NPeEn; OxAEP-2

And thou, who never yet of human wrong.   Byron.   NAEL-5v2; NAEL-6v2   *Fr.* Childe Harold's Pilgrimage.

And thou! whose sense, whose humour, and whose rage.   Inscriptio.   Pope.   OxBSP

And (though I am perswade) that I.   Isabella Whitney.   BWW   *Fr.* Manner of Her Will and What She Left to London and to All Those in It, at Her Departing, The.

And though you have everything, you are lacking one thing: God! (LL)   To Roosevelt.   "Rubén Dario."   PFTM-1; TCLAP, *tr.* by Lysander Kemp

And thought on the Lamb of God. (LL)   Sheep and Lambs.   Katharine Tynan.   OBEV; SacPr

And threw him down the stairs. (LL)   Mother Goose.   LB; OxNR; ReMoGo

And through the Caribbean Sea.   Margaret Danner.   BPo

And thus declared that Arab lady.   Solomon and the Witch.   W. B. Yeats.   ChIV-1; NoAM; WoPoe

And thus, forever driven towards new shores.   Lake, The.   Alphonse Marie Louis de Lamartine.   NAWM-7v2, *tr.* by Andrea Moorhead

And thus, I bid you, live again! (LL)   On Observing a Large Red-Streak Apple.   Philip Freneau.   NAAL-2v1; NAAL-3

And thus I die. (LL)   Four Ways of Dying.   Steve Chimombo.   HBAPE; NAfrP

And Thus in Nineveh.   Ezra Pound.   VGW

And thus like slaves we sell our soules to sinne.   Michael Drayton.   CAGL   *Fr.* Piers Gaveston.

And thus the people every year.   Attack of the Squash People.   Marge Piercy.   NBLV

And thus they grew like giggling fir trees. (LL)   Blocks.   Frank O'Hara.   HCAP; LCAP-2; SPE

And thus went out this lamp of light.   Account of the Cruelty of the Papists, An.   Benjamin Harris.   SCAP

And Thymodês also, lamenting a death unforeseen.   Epitaph of a Sailor.   Damagetus.   GrAn, *tr.* by Dudley Fitts

& tie strings together.   Ode Long Kesh.   Barry MacSweeney.   Oth

And Time locked in his tower? (LL)   Merlin.   Edwin Muir.   FaBoTw; NePenScot; OxBS; RB

And time to begin a new. (LL)   Dryden.   BASC; NAEL-5v1; NAEL-6v1; NPeEn; OxAEP-1; OxBEV; PoE; SCGP

And tint her life on Yarrow. (LL)   Braes of Yarrow, The.   *Unknown.*   ESPB; OxBB

And to Be Born Is Here an Unnameable Feast.   Gonzalo Rojas.   TCLAP, *tr.* by Christopher Maurer

And to die is different from what any one supposed, and luckier. (LL)   Walt Whitman.   ColAP; NoP-4; SAmP   *Fr.* Song of Myself.

And to do that to birds was why she came. (LL)   Never Again Would Birds' Song Be the Same.   Robert Frost.   APT-1; HAP; InPK-6; NIP-4; NoAM; NoP-4; OWoS; SoSe-8; Son; VGW

And to Her-Without-Bounds I send.   Robert Duncan.   APSN; NOBA   *Fr.* Passages.

And to my dead heart run them in! (LL)   Celestial Surgeon, The.   Robert Louis Stevenson.   EBVV; MoBrPo; PoToHe

And to possess them, Honour[']d *Margaret*. (LL)   To the Lady Margaret Ley.   John Milton.   GTBS-P; OBEV

And to Private Ball it came as if a rigid beam of great weight.   David Jones.   OBWVE   *Fr.* In Parenthesis.

And to see the city again and to see it again.   Patrizia Cavalli.   NeIt

And to the Ile the name of him then buried in it gave. (LL)   Ovid.   CTC; OBVE, *tr.* by Arthur Golding   *Fr.* Metamorphoses.

And to the Young Men.   Merrill Moore.   MoAmPo

And toll your voyage out again again. (LL)   Frontispiece.   May Swenson.   CoAP; WPE

And Tom went roaring down the street. (LL)   Tom, Tom, the piper's son.   Mother Goose.   LB; OxNR

And tomb time, death, and substance in thy maw. (LL)   To Night.   Thomas Lovell Beddoes.   CenSon; Son

And tombstones rewrite names on dead men's graves. (LL)   Culbin Sands.   Andrew Young.   GTBS-P; OxBS; OxBTC

And tomorrow.   Exile.   Teresa Calderón.   TANSG, *tr.* by Celeste Kostopulos-Cooperman

And tonight's headline news.   Lydia's Phantasmagoria.   Gloria Vando.   TouFir

And took the other to remind me of him. (LL)   Heraclitus of Halicarnassus.   GrAn; WoPoe, *tr.* by Edwin Morgan

And toss it in the oven for baby and me. (LL)   Mother Goose.   LB; OxNR; ReMoGo

And, touched with love like mine, preserve my absent friend. (LL)   William Collins.   NOEC; OxAEP-1

And tribal, intimate revenge. (LL)   Punishment.   Seamus Heaney.   EmeKit; NAEL-5v2; NAEL-6v2; NoAM; NoP-4; OxAEP-2; PBCIP; PoPoPo

And trodden out the Mills. (LL)   Emily Dickinson.   NCAP; NOBA; NoAM; SAmP

And trotted home behind the lad. (LL)   Recreation.   Jane Taylor.   OBCoV; OxBoLi; PEW; WoRP

And trouble him; then Death's his Epilogue. (LL)   De Morte.   Sir Henry Wotton.   BASC; NOSC; OxBSP

And true savant of this dark nature be. (LL)   Sun This March, The.   Wallace Stevens.   APT-1; HarvBoo

And Truly It Is a Most Glorious Thing.   William Bradford.   AH

And trumpet of your resurrection. (LL)   Black Rock of Kiltearn.   Andrew Young.   FaBoTw; RB

And trust the unknown for the known. (LL)   Over-Heart, The.   John Greenleaf Whittier.   ChIV-2; NOCV

And Truth diffuse her Radiance from the Stage. (LL)   Samuel Johnson.   EBEV; NAEL-5v1; NAEL-6v1; NAEL-7v1; NOEC; OxAEP-1

And Truth reveal herself to you! (LL)   Insincere Wish Addressed to a Beggar, An.   Mary Elizabeth Coleridge.   NOBVV; NPeEn; PEW; VWP

And *try* if we cannot feel forsaken. (LL)   In Neglect.   Robert Frost.   OxBSP; VGW

And turn once more our *Water* into *Wine*! (LL)   Religion.   Henry Vaughan.   ESCV; NOCV; OxAEP-1; PeECV; TOF

And turned into a cluster of frogs. (LL)   Gu Cheng.   PFTM-2; VCWP, tr. by Eva Hung   Fr. Bulin File, The.

And turned my face toward the mountain range. (LL)   Virgil [or Vergil]. NAWM-5v1; NAWM-7v1, tr. by Robert Fitzgerald   Fr. Aeneid [or Eneados, Aeneis], The.

And Turnus than, quhar he at erth dyd ly.   Virgil [or Vergil].   OBVE, tr. by Gawin [or Gavin] Douglas   Fr. Aeneid [or Eneados, Aeneis], The.

And two blankets embroidered with smallpox. (LL)   Meeting the British.   Paul Muldoon.   BiHa; CIP-2; EmeKit; NoAM; NoP-4; PNI

And two I knew, an old man and a boy.   Frederick Goddard Tuckerman.   APN-2   Fr. Sonnets.

And two to bear my soul away. (LL)   Before Sleeping.   Unknown.   FaBoCh; OxNR

And understand our wistful speech! (LL)   Caged Bird, A.   Sarah Orne Jewett.   APN-2; ColAP

And universals / are not that world.   Ron Welburn.   NBV

And unsuckled. (LL)   Coca-Cola and Coco Frío.   Martín Espada.   ReTh; UnSA

And unto miserly merchant hulks converted. (LL)   Good Ships.   John Crowe Ransom.   OxBSo; WeW-3

And "Ut Pictura Poesis" Is Her Name.   John Ashbery.   VCAP

And vanishes along the level of the roofs. (LL)   Morning at the Window.   T. S. Eliot.   AWP; OxBEV; TCAPo

And verse is one of them—this most of all. (LL)   Washing-Day.   Anna Laetitia Barbauld.   ECWP; PEW; WoRP

And vindicates its cause. (LL)   In Love for Long.   Edwin Muir.   BoLoP; MoBrPo

And vowed he'd steal no more. (LL)   Tarts, The.   Mother Goose.   LB; OxNR; ReMoGo

And wait, and tend our agonizing seeds. (LL)   From the Dark Tower.   Countee Cullen.   APT-2; BPo; ColAP; MakPoe; NAAL-2v2; Son

And waken unavailing tears. (LL)   Emily Jane Brontë.   NOBVV; OxBEV

And walk the rest of the way. (LL)   Draft Horse, The.   Robert Frost.   APT-1; EmeKit; HeIP-4; PAI; PoE; SAmP; TRP; WoPoe

And walks on earth unseen forevermore. (LL)   Henry Wadsworth Longfellow.   NCAP; TCAPo   Fr. Tales of a Wayside Inn.

And warmth and chill of wedded life and death. (LL)   Pontoosuce.   Herman Melville.   APN-2; NCAP; NOBA; TCAPo

And was a povre Persoun of a Toun.   Geoffrey Chaucer.   SacPr   Fr. Canterbury Tales, The.

And was helped to a hansom outside. (LL)   Arrest of Oscar Wilde at the Cadogan Hotel, The.   Sir John Betjeman.   EBEV; MoBrPo; NPeEn; NoAM; NoP-4; OxBTC

And was it along this torpid muddy river.   Mythical Founding of Buenos Aires, The.   Jorge Luis Borges.   TCLAP, tr. by Alastair Reid

And was it not a worthy sight.   John Pickering [or Pikerying].   NoSic   Fr. Horestes.

And was not afraid / Mister? (LL)   Music Swims Back to Me.   Anne Sexton.   ColAP; MiVo; VCAP

And was the day of my delight.   Tennyson.   NAEL-6v2   Fr. In Memoriam A. H. H.

And wasna he a roguey.   Piper o' Dundee, The.   Unknown.   OxBS

And wasnt there ever a time when flies.   Flies.   Jack Kerouac.   CLPP

And watch the moon through the clear autumn. (LL)   Jewel Stairs' Grievance, The.   Li Po.   NOBA; OBVE, tr. by Ezra Pound

And watch the product coming up. (LL)   Garden Song, A.   George R. Sims.   NOBVV; OBCoV; OBGa

And watches for the trout in the holy well. (LL)   Gateposts.   Medbh McGuckian.   BiHa; MakPoe; ModIr; PBCIP

And waters wide and fleet. (LL)   Song: "If thou art sleeping, maiden."   Gil Vicente.   AWP; CTC, tr. by Henry Wadsworth Longfellow

And Wayland's work / Is worn away. (LL)   Junk.   Richard Wilbur.   HAP; WeW-3

And we all sing. (LL)   Summer Words of [or for] a Sistuh [or Sister] Addict.   Sonia Sanchez.   BPo; BlSi; UnPo

And we are all.   Herostratos and Herostratos.   Sergey Stratanovsky.   ItGoST, tr. by J. Kates

And we, are birds beak to beak.   Wishful Thinking Is the Master of Reality.   Duo Duo (Li Shizheng).   AF, tr. by Gregory Lee

And we call it wisdom. It is pain. (LL)   90 North.   Randall Jarrell.   CoAP; HarvBoo; NAAL-2v2; NOBA; NoAM; TAP; VCAP

And we clap hands together. (LL)   Green Grass.   Unknown.   OxBoLi; OxNR

And we fall, face forward, fighting, on the deck. (LL)   Thirty Bob a Week.   John Davidson.   CABP; EBEV; EBVV; FaBoTw; NOBE; NOBVV; NPeEn; NePenScot; OxBEV; OxBS; OxBTC

And we gave her all our money but our subway fares. (LL)   Recuerdo.   Edna St. Vincent Millay.   APT-1; ChAP; NAAL-2v2; NAAL-5; NoAM; OxBA; TAP

And we guardsmen fed to the tigers. (LL)   Lament of the Frontier Guard.   Li Po.   OBVE; OBWP; VGW, tr. by Ezra Pound

And we guardsmen fed to the tigers. (LL)   Lament of the Frontier Guard.   Rihaku.   APT-1; NPeEn, tr. by Ezra Pound

And we had focused back on the furniture of the air. (LL)   Melodic Trains.   John Ashbery.   GM; NoP-4

And we join the line—back to back.   Dream: Queue for Paraffin.   Gennady Aygi.   ItGoST, tr. by Peter France

And we kill blood.   Aleksandr Trubin.   TCRP

And we'll have a pudding in half an hour! (LL)   Girls and Boys Come out to Play.   Unknown.   LB; ReMoGo

And we'll strive to please you every day. (LL)   William Shakespeare.   EBEV; FaBoCh; NOBE; NoSic; OxAEP-1; PoRA; SCGP; TFi   Fr. Twelfth Night.

And we love Art for Art's sake.   Marc Blitzstein.   TrJP   Fr. Cradle Will Rock, The.

And we missed it, lost it for ever. (LL)   Youth and Art.   Robert Browning.   CTC; NAEL-5v2; NAEL-6v2; NOBVV; NPeEn

And we, of the damned poor, trot our frost-furred horses.   Thomas McGrath.   GifTon   Fr. Letter to an Imaginary Friend.

And we rebuild our cities, not dream of islands. (LL)   Paysage Moralisé.   W. H. Auden.   HarvBoo; MoBrPo; UnPo

And we shall remember 1926 until our blood is dry. (LL)   Do You Remember 1926?   Idris Davies.   AngWePo; OBWVE

And we take him in. (LL)   Snow in the Suburbs.   Thomas Hardy.   MoBrPo; OBMV; OxBTC

And we thought of wilderness.   African Desert.   Samuel Greenberg.   APT-1

And We Were Born.   Amina Said.   HAWP, tr. by Eric Sellin

And we were speaking easily and all the light stayed low.   In Judgment of the Leaf.   Kenneth Patchen.   VGW

And weariness follows, and the infinite ache. (LL)   Body of a Woman.   Pablo Neruda.   ErotSp; TCLAP, tr. by W. S. Merwin

And weave but nets to catch the wind. (LL)   John Webster.   NOSC; PoRA; SCGP   Fr. Devil's Law Case, The.

And wed thy folk agein to stedfastnesse. (LL)   Lak of Stedfastnesse.   Geoffrey Chaucer.   AWP; MiEL

And weel paid shall thy cowte foal be. (LL)   Lochmaben Harper, The.   Unknown.   ESPB; OxBB

And weep the more, because I weep in vain. (LL)   Sonnet [on the Death of Mr. Richard West].   Thomas Gray.   CenSon; NOEC; OxBSo; PoE

And weeping anarchic Aphrodite. (LL)   In Memory of Sigmund Freud.   W. H. Auden.   HAP; NoAM; OxBA

And went to bed at noon. (LL)   Last War, The.   Kingsley Amis.   OBSV; OxBC

And wept. (I heard her tears). (LL)   Blessed Damozel, The.   Dante Gabriel Rossetti.   AWP; CABP; EBVV; NAEL-5v2; NAEL-6v2; NOBE; NOBVV; NoP-4; OBEV; OxAEP-2; PoE; TFi

And were I not, as a man may say, cautious.   Robert Browning.   OBCoV   Fr. Flight of the Duchess, The.

And were it for thy profit, to obtain.   On Change of Weathers.   Francis Quarles.   OxBSP

And whan this werk al brought was to an ende.   Geoffrey Chaucer.   OWoS   Fr. Parlement of Foules, The.

And what a charm is in the rich hot scent.   Among the Firs.   Eugene Lee-Hamilton.   NOBVV

And what a jaded tide will find for us / to play with when this game begins to pall. (LL)   Epiderm.   Michael Dransfield.   BMAP; CBAP

And what a time a reel of tape can play! (LL)   I Was Fair Beat.   Robert Garioch.   OBCoV; OxBTC

And what did she get, the soldier's wife. What Did the Nazi Send His Wife? Bertolt Brecht. FaBoWar, *tr.* by *Unknown*

And what did the rubies say. Pablo Neruda. GifTon, *tr.* by William O'Daly *Fr.* Book of Questions, The.

And What Do I Owe You, God. Jack Kerouac. InvLi

And what I was is no affair of yours. (LL) In Peterborough Churchyard. Paulus [*or* Paulos] Silentiarius. FaBoEE; NOBL

And What If after So Many Words. César Vallejo. RaBo, *tr.* by Robert Bly and Douglas Lawder

And what if now I told you this, let's say. At a Reading. J. D. McClatchy. DiPo

And what is a Ceiling when the Ceiling has flown? (LL) Floor and the Ceiling, The. William Jay Smith. OBCA; OxIBACP

And what is life? Primer for Schoolchildren, A. Richard Weber. CIP-2

And what is love? Misunderstanding, pain. Epigram. James Vincent Cunningham. CRP; HAP

And what more do we know of it. Light Falls Obliquely. Eric Gamalinda. ReBoTo

And what, my thoughtless sons, should fire you more. James Thomson. ECEV *Fr.* Seasons, The.

And What of Me? Liz Sohappy Bahe. CDW

And what of those. And What of Those Arbors of Vines. Vidya. WoPoe, *tr.* by Andrew Schelling

And what's your tune? Thomas Lovell Beddoes. NPeEn *Fr.* Death's Jest Book.

And what thou art may never be destroyed. (LL) No Coward Soul Is Mine. Emily Jane Brontë. BWW; BrRo; EBVV; InvLi; NAEL-6v2; NALW; OxAEP-2; TRP; TrCP; WPoS   -

And what was the big room he walked in? Before a Fall. Geoffrey Grigson. SPE

And what were you searching for, in that dream? Gloria Gervitz. MirDau, *tr.* by Stephen Tapscott *Fr.* Yiskor.

And what you best like. (LL) Love's Clock. Sir John Suckling. CaPo; NOSC

And whelm'd in deeper gulphs than he. (LL) Castaway, The. William Cowper. NAEL-5v1; NOBE; NOBRP; NOEC; NPeEn; OxBEV; PoE; TRP

And when God sends a cheerful[l] hour, refrains. (LL) To Cyriack Skinner. John Milton. GTBS-P; OBEV; Son

And when he cried the little children died in the streets. (LL) Epitaph on a Tyrant. W. H. Auden. AF; HeIP-4; NoAM; OxBEV; OxBSP; RB

And when he returned to his birthplace he found sea. Odysseus. Haim [*or* Chaim *or* Khayim] Guri [*or* Gouri]. MHP, *tr.* by Ruth Finer Mintz

And when he was awakened by the cold, she was washing her hair. Dream Recalling a Temptation, A. Maysoun Saqr Al-Qasimi. PoArWo, *tr.* by Subhi Hadidi and Nathalie Handal

And when he was in heaven once again. Ovid. NAWM-7v1, *tr.* by Allen Mandelbaum *Fr.* Metamorphoses.

And when I die. Last Instructions. Garth Tate. ISC

And when I go up as a pilgrim in winter, to recover. Abraham Sutskever [*or* Sutzkever]. HP, *tr.* by Cynthia Ozick *Fr.* Poems from a Diary.

And When I Lamented. Heinrich Heine. TrJP, *tr.* by Emma Lazarus *Fr.* Homeward Bound.

And when I pay death's duty. Poem. Robin Blaser. NeAP

And when I rose, I found myself in prayer. (LL) To William Wordsworth. Samuel Taylor Coleridge. FHYEP; NAEL-5v2; NAEL-6v2

And when I say eyes right I want to hear. Weapons Training. Bruce Dawe. OBCoV

And when I went to the woods. King Solomon's Magnetic Quiz. John Wieners. FTOS

And when, in the city in which I love you. City in Which I Love You, The. Li-Young Lee. ChIV-1

And when it does, we lie back in our watery hair and rock. (LL) Spider Crystal Ascension. Charles Wright. HCAP; LCAP-2; VCAP

And when like her, oh Sákí, you shall pass. Omar Khayyám. TRP, *tr.* by Edward Fitzgerald *Fr.* Rubáiyát of Omar Khayyám [of Naishápúr], The.

And when Lincoln came here. Bath. John Knoepfle. IllVoic

And when my legs had already grown numb. Yevgeny [*or* Evgenii] Mikhailovich Vinokurov. TCRP

And when she came back she found 'em all a-loffing. (LL) There Was an Old Woman Who Lived in a Shoe. Mother Goose. OxNR; ReMoGo

And when she'd finished—having smoothed out. Bishop Reading. J. D. McClatchy. KGB

And when she wakes she will not think it long. (LL) Rest. Christina Georgina Rossetti. GSo; NOBE; OBEV

And when she was bad, she was horrid. (LL) There Was a Little Girl. Mother Goose. OxNR; ReMoGo

And when that ballad lady went. Road in Kentucky, A. Robert Earl Hayden. ColAP

And when the Assyrians stopped waging war against the Chaldeans, they buried the dead. Stranger, Stranger. Jorge de Lima. TCLAP, *tr.* by Luiz Fernández García

And when the center opened. Ahora. Sandra Maria Esteves. PueRic

And when the moment. Kiss. Susan Aizenberg. ExTi

And when the star that comes at the set of the sun. Mousetrap, The. Callimachus. HePo, *tr.* by Barbara Hughes Fowler

And when they asked her what she wanted to be. Vocation. Judith Herzberg. WPOW, *tr.* by Manfred Wolf

And when they came together in one place. Homer. OBVE, *tr.* by Tennyson *Fr.* Iliad, The.

And when they drew near to Jerusalem. Boris Leonidovich Pasternak. GI *Fr.* St. Matthew.

And when they had sung a hymn, they went out to the Mount of Olives. Boris Leonidovich Pasternak. GI *Fr.* St. Mark.

And when they sat down in the morning. Sunday. Timothy Liu. NeAmPo

And when they would ask. Grocer's Dream, The. Giovanna Pollarolo. TANSG, *tr.* by Marjorie Agosin

And when thus the night availed. *Unknown.* IQMS, *tr.* by René Bonnerjea *Fr.* Betrothal of Saint Catherine, The.

And when we die at last. Heaven and Hell. Nalungiaq. STP, *tr.* by Edward Field

And when we were in love there was grace and good temper. (LL) Oh send to me an apple that hasn't any kernel. *Unknown.* FaBoCh; WoPoe, *tr.* by Gwyn Williams

And when you have forgotten the bright bedclothes. When You Have Forgotten Sunday: The Love Story. Gwendolyn Brooks. BPo; WPOW

And when you showed me Brooklyn Bridge. Hymn. Jack Kerouac. CLPP

And where. Sunday Brunch. Reuben Jackson. ISC

And where am I from? From an anecdote. Natalya [*or* Natal'ia] Gorbanevskaya [*or* Gorbanyevskaya *or*Gorbanevskaia]. TCRP

And Where Are the Graves. Moses Ibn Ezra. WoPoe, *tr.* by Robert Mezey

And Where Do You Stand on the National Question. Tom Paulin. CIP-2

And where is sleep? (LL) Hafiz [*or* Hafez]. AWP; TAL *Fr.* Odes.

And where no snow had. Brian Coffey. ModIr *Fr.* For What for Whom Unwanted.

And where thou mad'st an end, there I'le begin. (LL) Lamp[e], The. Henry Vaughan. ChIV-2; ESCV

And Where Were You. Len Roberts. BodElec

And while above Tsarskoye Selo. Lone Performer, The. Velemir [*or* Viktor Vladimirovich] Khlebnikov. TCRP, *tr.* by Gary Kern

And while stirring I saw. Year Passes in My Morning Teacup, The. Marilyn Chin. GeoHom

And while the song and tears of Ahkmatova. Lonely Masquerader. Velemir [*or* Viktor Vladimirovich] Khlebnikov. TCRusP, *tr.* by Kathy Lewis and Bob Perelman

And whistle and I'll come soon. (LL) Eppie Morrie. *Unknown.* ESPB; OxBB

And white owl's feather! (LL) Fairies, The. William Allingham. FaBoCh; NOBE; NOBVV; NOxBChV; OBEV; OTCP; TFi

And who is He that, sculptured in huge stone. "Moses" of Michael Angelo, The. Robert Browning. GS

And who shall separate the dust. Common Dust. Georgia Douglas Johnson. TTY

And whoever forces himself to love anybody. Retort to Jesus. D. H. Lawrence. PeECV

And whom I love, I love indeed. (LL) Pains of Sleep, The. Samuel Taylor Coleridge. AWTN; FHYEP; NAEL-5v2; NAEL-6v2

And why an honoured [*or* honour'd] ragged shirt, that shows. To a Lady with Child that Asked [*or* Ask'd] an Old Shirt. Richard Lovelace. BASC; NOSC

And why does Gratt teach English? Why, because. Professor Gratt. Donald Hall. OBAL

And why is it yet unfound? (LL) Facing West from California's Shores. Walt Whitman. MoAmPo; NAAL-2v1; NAAL-3; NAAL-5; NIL-7; TAP

And why so coffin'd in this vile disguise. John Cleveland. BASC

And why this vault and tomb? Alike we must. Wiston Vault. Katherine Philips. BASC; NOSC

And why to me this, thou lame lord of fire. Execration upon Vulcan, An. Ben Jonson. BeJo

And wild for to hold though I seem tame. (LL) Whoso List to Hunt. Sir Thomas Wyatt. BoLoP; CABP; EBEV; HAP; NAEL-5v1; NAEL-6v1; NAEL-7v1; NoSic; OBVE; OxBSo; PoE; SCGP; TFi; WoPoe

And will be our bliss with saints above. (LL) Loving and Liking [Irregular Verses Addressed to a Child]. Dorothy Wordsworth. SacPr; WoRP

And will he [*or* a'] not come again? William Shakespeare. NoSic *Fr.* Hamlet.

And will not open again. (LL) Like the Touch of Rain. Edward Thomas. BoLoP; EnLoPo

And will not scare. (LL) Skunk Hour. Robert Lowell. CoAP; CoAmPo; ColAP; EmeKit; FaBoMo; HAP; HCAP; HarvBoo; HeIP-4; InPK-6; LCAP-

2; MoAmPo; NAAL-2v2; NAAL-5; NIL-7; NIP-4; NOBA; NoAM; NoP-4; OxBC; PAI; PoE; PoPoPo; PoetW; SCV; TAP; TFi; TRP; VCAP

And will not stop. (LL)   Kenneth Rexroth.   APSN; APT-2   *Fr.* Love Poems of Marichiko, The.

And will they always be so tender, her.   Swift Love, Sweet Motor.   Hildegarde Flanner.   WPE

And will they cast the altars down.   In Portugal, 1912.   Alice Thompson Meynell.   NOCV

"And will you cut a stone for him."   Stone, The.   Wilfrid Wilson Gibson.   MoBrPo

And willing nations knew their lawful lord. (LL)   Dryden.   BASC; FHYEP; HAP; NAEL-5v1; NAEL-6v1; NAEL-7v1; NOSC; PoE

And willows could not hold more steady sound. (LL)   Repose of Rivers.   Hart Crane.   APT-2; AWP; ColAP; MoAmPo; NOBA; OxBA; PoE

And wilt thou have me fashion into speech.   Elizabeth Barrett Browning.   BWW; BrRo; CABP; CenSon; VWP   *Fr.* Sonnets from the Portuguese.

And wilt [*or* wylt] thou le[a]ve me thus?   Lover's Appeal, The.   Sir Thomas Wyatt.   EnLoPo; GTBS-P; NAEL-5v1; NoSic; SCGP

And wilt thou, love, my soul display.   Lover's Farewell, The.   George Moses Horton.   NAAAL

And win us both to May. (LL)   Gardens of the Villa D'Este, The.   Anthony Hecht.   ColAP; OBGa

And winter pulled a sheet over his head. (LL)   Sleeping Giant, The.   Donald Hall.   PAI; TwCP

And with each motion she ensnared a heart. (LL)   On Lydia Distracted.   Philip Ayres.   EnLoPo; Son

And with God be the rest! (LL)   Prospice.   Robert Browning.   FHYEP; ITBLP; NAEL-5v2; NAEL-6v2; PoRA; TrCP

And with great fear I inhabit the middle of the night.   Acts of Youth, The.   John Weiners.   BB

And with him.   Time Signature.   Linda Andrews.   MiVo

And with March a Decade in Bolinas.   Joanne Kyger.   BLT

And with my hunger what hast thou to do? (LL)   John Milton.   EBEV; PeECV   *Fr.* Paradise Regained [*or* Regain'd].

And with new light salute our longing eyes. (LL)   Sir Richard Fanshawe.   NOSC; OBVE   *Fr.* Il Pastor Fido.

And with no language but a cry. (LL)   Tennyson.   CABP; EBVV; FHYEP; NAEL-6v2; PeECV   *Fr.* In Memoriam A. H. H.

And with red molecular eyes.   Crow.   Viktor Aleksandrovich Sosnora.   ItGoST, *tr. by* Dinara Georgeoliani and Mark Halperin

And with that worde he said in this manere. (LL)   Geoffrey Chaucer.   NAEL-5v1; NAEL-6v1   *Fr.* Canterbury Tales, The.

And within that time / develop. (LL)   I Have Tried Hard.   Zindzi Mandela.   HAWP; NAfrP

And within the indestructable night I am alone. (LL)   Passage Over Water.   Robert Duncan.   NOBA; NoAM

And women feel the same for worthy men. (LL)   Dante Alighieri.   AWP; EaItPo, *tr. by* Dante Gabriel Rossetti   *Fr.* La Vita Nuova.

And won't be there.   Shiyo.   JDP, *tr. by* Yoel Hoffmann

And wonders what's to pay. (LL)   Fairies Break Their Dances, The.   A. E. Housman.   OxBSP; PeVV

And work to do that never ends. (LL)   Han Yü.   CoBCP; WoPoe, *tr. by* Burton Watson   *Fr.* Autumn Thoughts.

And workmen whistling. (LL)   Image.   Thomas Ernest Hulme.   InPK-6; NPeEn; OxBTC

And would love more, could I but love thee less. (LL)   Sir John Suckling.   BeJo; CaPo   *Fr.* Aglaura.

And would suffice. (LL)   Fire and Ice.   Robert Frost.   APT-1; BRP; ColAP; FaBoEE; HeIP-4; InPK-6; MoAmPo; NAAL-2v2; NAAL-5; NOBA; NoAM; OxBA; PAI; RaBo; SoSe-2; TAP; TFi

And would you gather turds.   History of Love, A.   William Carlos Williams.   VGW

And wring his bosom—is—to die. (LL)   Oliver Goldsmith.   CABP; GTBS-P; HAP; NPeEn; NoP-4; OxBEV; SCGP; TFi; UnPo   *Fr.* Vicar of Wakefield, The.

And write this poem for money, rage, and love. (LL)   Thief, The.   Stanley Kunitz.   MoAmPo; VGW

And writing novels with her broom. (LL)   On the Same.   Roy Campbell.   OBCoV; OxBTC

And ye can't catch a bowl full.   Riddle: "House full, [a] yard full, [A]."   *Unknown.*   LB; NTCP

And ye shall walk in silk attire.   Siller Croun, The.   Susanna Blamire.   ECWP; LW

And, yeah, brothers.   Dark Prophecy: I Sing of Shine.   Etheridge Knight.   BPo; ESEAA; LTA; PBCAP

And, Yes, Those Spiritual Matters.   Christopher Gilbert.   ESEAA

And Yet.   Patricia Goedicke.   ExTi

And yet abide the World! (LL)   Emily Dickinson.   APN-2; NAAL-2v1; NAAL-3; NAWM-7v2; NOBA; OxBA; RB; SAmP

And yet, and yet, these days are incomplete. (LL)   Friendship After Love.   Ella Wheeler Wilcox.   APN-2; LW

And yet, because thou overcomest so.   Elizabeth Barrett Browning.   CenSon   *Fr.* Sonnets from the Portuguese.

And yet God has not said a word! (LL)   Porphyria's Lover.   Robert Browning.   AWP; FHYEP; HAP; NAEL-5v2; NAEL-6v2; OBEV; PAI

And yet hath prayer, the heav'n-breathing foliage of faith.   Robert Bridges.   OxBTC   *Fr.* Testament of Beauty, The.

And yet I cannot reprehend the flight.   Samuel Daniel.   OBEV   *Fr.* To Delia.

And yet I have hated her all my life. (LL)   William Langland.   NAEL-6v1; NAEL-7v1   *Fr.* Vision of Piers Plowman, The.

And Yet I Know.   James Wright (1927–80).   BodElec

And yet I[ich] bare the flower[flour] away. (LL)   All Night by the Rose.   *Unknown.*   HeIP-4; MiELL, *tr. by* Michael Rosen

And yet in some very subtle way,   "H. D."   NALW   *Fr.* Tribute to the Angels.

And yet in washing one, she washèd both. (LL)   Mary [*or* Marie] Magdalene.   George Herbert.   ESCV; SacPr

And yet she loves my master. (LL)   My Mistress.   *Unknown.*   NOSC; OBCoV

And Yet the Books.   Czeslaw Milosz.   OPOU

And Yet the Earth Remains Unchanged.   *Unknown.*   CA

And yet the southern whale does some time come.   Whales, The.   Marguerite Young.   WPE

And yet, there was a hunger in your eyes.   Arthur Symons.   PeVV   *Fr.* Amoris Victima.

And yet they expose me more than all my other poems. (LL)   Here the Frailest Leaves of Me.   Walt Whitman.   APN-1; CAGL; NAAL-2v1; NAAL-3; NAAL-5

And yet this great wink of eternity.   Hart Crane.   ColAP; HAP; MoAmPo; OxBA; PoE; RaBo; TRP; UnPo; VGW; WoPoe   *Fr.* Voyages.

And Yet We Are Here!   Karl Wolfskehl.   TrJP, *tr. by* Ernst Morowitz and Carol North Valhope

And yet, we have need as we tremble.   Say—So I'll Say.   Giancarlo Majorino.   ItPo, *tr. by* Gayle Ridinger

And yet we should consider how we go forward.   Old Man on the River Bank, An.   George Seferis.   AmFaPo

And yet, where would we be without the American culture.   Goodbye Nkrumah.   Diane Di Prima.   PoM

And yet who—did not! (LL)   Did Not.   Thomas Moore.   BoLoP; PeLV

And yet (woe's me!) is pity absent thence? (LL)   Canzone: His Portrait of His Lady, Angiola of Verona.   Fazio degli Uberti.   AWP; EaItPo, *tr. by* Dante Gabriel Rossetti

And yet you experienced the flames of Hell.   Proof.   Czeslaw Milosz.   TOF, *tr. by* the author

And you above them, wounded and dominant. (LL)   Messengers.   Louise Glück.   ColAP; HCAP; VCAP

And you as well must die, belovèd dust.   Edna St. Vincent Millay.   PoRA; TAP

And you can hide it behind your crocodile tie pin. (LL)   Neckties.   Liz Lochhead.   NePenScot; OBCoV

And you could leave me now.   At Parting.   Edith Nesbit.   OBGa

And you, Dìka, put lovely garlands round your hair.   Sappho.   SaLy, *tr. by* Diane Rayor

And you for ever clay. Have done! (LL)   Reader over My Shoulder, The.   Robert Graves.   NAEL-5v2; NAEL-6v2

And you have failed, O Poet? Sad!   Failures.   May Kendall.   VWP; ViWPN

And You, Helen.   Edward Thomas.   BoLoP; OBWVE; TCAWP

And you just *know* he knows he knows. (LL)   Sloth, The.   Theodore Roethke.   ChAP; OBAL; OBCA; OxIBACP; TRP

And you, kind and innocent accomplice, didn't give it to me. (LL)   To simulate the burning of the heart.   Patrizia Cavalli.   NeIt; VCWP, *tr. by* Judith Baumel

And you know, I believe him. (LL)   Creation.   Simon J. Ortiz.   CDW; ColAP; HATNAP

And you'll have the strength again.   Ordeal, The.   Olga Fiodorovna Berggolts [*or* Bergholts].   TCRP, *tr. by* Daniel Weissbort

And you'll say a nation totters.   George Douglas Howard Cole.   OxBTC   *Fr.* Civil Riot.

And you look like hell when they're through with you. (LL)   Hearse Song, The.   *Unknown.*   OxBoLi; RB

And you, Lucifer, standing there aloof.   Imre Madách.   IQMS, *tr. by* Iain MacLeod   *Fr.* Tragedy of Man.

And you, my sister Moscow, are at ease.   Osip Emilevich Mandelstam [*or* Mandelshtam].   TCRP   *Fr.* Stanzas.

And you my spent heart's treasure.   Félix Lope de Vega Carpio.   HAP; OxBEV; WoPoe, *tr. by* Geoffrey Hill   *Fr.* Pentecost Castle, The.

And "you're hurt" exclaim! (LL)   Wounded Deer Leaps Highest, A.   Emily Dickinson.   APN-2; AWP; TAP

And you remain. (LL)   Iris.   David St. John.   LCAP-2; MakPoe

And you sang eloquently.   For Sappho/After Sappho.   Carolyn Kizer.   GifTon

And you shan't wake up till you're clean plum dead! (LL) Nine Little Goblins, The. James Whitcomb Riley. NOxBChV; OBCA

And you smile up at us—eternally. (LL) In Memory of My Mother. Patrick Kavanagh. BIrV; CIP-2; NoAM; RaBo

And you, smoke, dissonance, a psalm, a stairwell. (LL) Elegy. Carolyn Forché. ExTi; LoL

And you stalwart loins. (LL) From Pent-up Aching Rivers. Walt Whitman. APN-1; BoLoP; NAAL-2v1; NAAL-3; NOBA

And you too perished long ago, by a bush with matted roots. Anyte [or Anytes]. GrAn

And you, Vanya. Yury [or Iurii] Pavlovich Odarchenko. TCRP

And you will hear in every passing century. Words of Departure. Jorge de Lima. TCLAP, tr. by Luiz Fernández García

And you will understand / My hatred. (LL) Hatred. Gwendolyn B. Bennett. BlSi; RaBo

And you, you . . . you, you utter / You wait! (LL) Beyond Words. Robert Frost. Spl; WeW-3

And your dreams, my Telemachus, are blameless. (LL) Odysseus to Telemachus. Joseph Brodsky. BLT; PAI, tr. by George L. Kline

And your eyes peel to red mud. (LL) Babylon Revisited. Imamu Amiri Baraka. BPo; NoAM

And your little job is done. (LL) Madam Life's a Piece in Bloom. William Ernest Henley. EBVV; NAEL-5v2; NAEL-6v2; OxBEV; PeVV

And your money, too. (LL) 50–50. Langston Hughes. NOBA; NoAM; PoE

And your true name is Mistress Betty. (LL) On a Romantic Lady. Mary Monck. ECWP; NOEC; RACG

And Zero at the Bone. (LL) Snake, The. Emily Dickinson. BoWoP; ClHu; HAP; HeIP-4; NAAL-2v1; NAAL-3; NALW; NIP-4; NOBA; NoAM; NoP-4; OBCA; OxBA; PAI; PoE; RB; SAmP; SoSe-8; TAP; TFi; TRP; WeW-3; WoPoe

Andalusia—in the rolling of its saying. Man Who Loved Flamenco, The. Joseph Awad. GraLe

Andalusian Exile, An. Ahmad Shauqi. BBASP; MAP, tr. by M. Mustafa Badawi and John Heath-Stubbs

Andalusian merchant, that returns, The. Unknown. FaBoCh Fr. Wonders.

Andante. Gwen Harwood. HarvBoo

Andirons were the dragons, The. Castle in the Fire, The. Mary Jane Carr. ChAP

Andonis, My Daughter. Thomas Love Peacock. VoR

Andraitx—Pomegranate Flowers. D. H. Lawrence. NoP-4

André who was killed in Riga. Constellation of Dead Brothers. Victor Serge. AF, tr. by James Brook

Andrea del Sarto. Robert Browning. CTC; NAEL-5v2; NAEL-6v2; NOBVV; NoP-4; PoE

Andreas. Unknown.
   St. Andrew's Voyage to Mermedonia. AnOE, tr. by Charles W. Kennedy

Andrée Rexroth. Kenneth Rexroth. APSN; APT-2; VGW

Andrew Jackson & Martin Van Buren. Jackson Mac Low. APSN Fr. Presidents of the United States of America, The.

Andrew Jackson's last name's the same as my first. Jackson Mac Low. APSN Fr. Presidents of the United States of America, The.

Andrew Jackson's Speech. Robert Bly. CoAmPo

Andrew Lammie. Unknown. See Trumpeter of Fyvie, The

Andrew Rykman's Prayer. John Greenleaf Whittier.
   "Pardon, Lord, the lips that dare." SacPr

Andreyevsky Church, The. "Nikolai Nikolaevich Morshen." TCRusP, tr. by John Glad

Androgyny. Steve [or Stephen] Orlen. OPRER

Andromache, I think of you. The Simois. Swan, The. Charles Baudelaire. WoPoe, tr. by Louis Simpson

Andromache, I think of you—this meagre stream. Swan, The. Charles Baudelaire. SxFrPo, tr. by James McGowan

Andromache's lament is still in our ears. Alpheios. GrAn

Andromache's Lamentation. Homer. OBVE, tr. by William Congreve Fr. Iliad, The.

Andromache's Wedding. Sappho. BoWoP, tr. by Willis Barnstone

Andromeda. Gerard Manley Hopkins. EBEV; FaBoMo; OxAEP-2; SCGP

Andromeda. Charles Kingsley.
   "Whelming the dwellings of men, and the toils of the slow-/ footed oxen." PeVV

Andromeda, by Perseus saved and wed. Aspecta Medusa. Dante Gabriel Rossetti. OxBSP

Andromeda / forgot. Sappho. BoWoP

And—which is more—you'll be a Man, my son! (LL) If. Rudyard Kipling. BRP; ChAP; ITBLP; OxBTC; PWR; UV

Andy-Diana DNA Letter. Andrew Weiman. HAP

Andy Hasselgard. Dave Etter. IllVoic

Andy Warhol Speaks to His Two Filipino Maids. Alfred A. Yuson. ReBoTo

Ane Ballat of Our Lady. William Dunbar. See Ballad of Our Lady

Ane Godly Dream. Elizabeth Melville, Lady Culross.
   "I luikit up unto that Castell fair." EMWP
   "Upon one day as I did mourn full sore." ChIV-1

Ane Satire [or Satyre] of the Three [or Thrie] Estaitis. Sir David Lindsay [or Lyndsay].
   "My patent pardouns ye may see." OBSV

Anear the centre of that northern crest. James Thomson. GTBS-P; NOBE; NePenScot Fr. City of Dreadful Night, The.

Anear the centre of that northern crest. James Thomson. GS Fr. City of Dreadful Night, The.

Anecdote from William IV Street. Dennis Joseph Enright. OxBC

Anecdote of Love, An. John Clare. NOBVV

Anecdote of the Jar. Wallace Stevens. ColAP; FaBoA; HCAP; HeIP-4; InPK-6; MoAmPo; NAAL-2v2; NAAL-5; NAWM-7v2; NIL-7; NOBA; NoAM; NoP-4; OxBA; OxBSP; PAI; PoPoPo; SAmP; TAP; TCAPo; TFi; UnPo

Anecdote of the Prince of Peacocks. Wallace Stevens. AWTN

Anecdotes of the Late War. Charles Olson. CBCWP

Anesthetist is singing, The. In the Operating Room. Alden Nowlan. NOBC

Angel. Andrew Elliott. PNI

Angel. John Forbes. NOBAu

Angel. Brad Leithauser. DiPo

Angel. John Henry, Cardinal Newman. SacPr

Angel. Marisela Norte. GeoHom

Angel. Ruth Padel. MFPA

Angel. Maxine Scates. PBCAP

Angel. Ian Wedde.
   "And this is where." PeNZ

Angel, The. William Blake. NAEL-5v2; PoE
   (I Askéd a Thief.) NoP-4

Angel, The. William Blake. FHYEP; RACG Fr. Songs of Experience.

Angel, The. Alfred Hayes. TrJP

Angel, The. Galway Kinnell. LCAP-2; NoAM

Angel, The. James Wright. YaYoPo

Angel and the girl are met, The. Annunciation, The. Edwin Muir. CRP; ChIV-2; NOCV; PAI

Angel Atrapado 7. John Yau. BodElec

Angel Boley. Stevie Smith. EBNV

Angel came to me, An. Madeleine L'Engle. OBCP Fr. Three Songs of Mary.

Angel Eyes. Matt Dennis. ReLy

Angel Finally Admits What She Knows to Lou Binkler of Bethany, Missouri, An. Catie Rosemurgy. AmPoNex

Angel in Blythburgh Church, An. Peter Porter. NoP-4

Angel in the Deluge. Rosario Murillo. CLPP, tr. by Alejandro Murguía

Angel in the House, The. Coventry Patmore.
   Attainment, The. FaBoEE
   Constancy Rewarded. NOBVV; OxBSP
   County Ball, The. EBVV
   Going to Church. PeVV
   Kiss, The. BoLoP; EnLoPo; NOBVV
   Love at Large. EBVV; NOBVV
   Love Serviceable. EnLoPo
   Lover, The. OxAEP-2
   Married Lover, The. OBEV; OxAEP-2; SacPr
   Paragon, The. NAEL-6v2
   Perspective. FaBoEE
   Rainbow, The. GTBS-P
   Revelation, The. EnLoPo; GTBS-P; HAP; OxBSP
   Sahara. EBVV
   (Salisbury; the Cathedral Close.) EBVV
   Spirit's Epochs, The. EBEV; OxBSP
   Tribute, The. EBEV
   "'Twas when the spousal time of May." OxAEP-2

Angel in the Temple of Luxor, An. Rodney M. McNeil. InTrad

Angel, king of streaming morn. Sun. Henry Rowe. OBEV

Angel of Death, The. Unknown. SacPr

Angel of Dread, The. Miklós Radnóti. PFTM-1

Angel of letters, feed me. Alphabet Soup. Fatima Lim-Wilson. ReBoTo

Angel of moment is dust, The. Gavin Selerie. Oth Fr. Roxy.

Angel of Peace, Thou Hast Wandered Too Long. Oliver Wendell Holmes. AH

Angel of simple human affairs, The. Mother Sabbath. Nikolai Alekseievich Klyuyev [or Kliuev or Klyuev]. TCRusP, tr. by John Glad

Angel of the Rain. Harriet McEwen Kimball. TreFP

Angel on the Beach, An. Hamutal Bar Yosef. DTA, tr. by Shirley Kaufman

Angel [or Angell] saith to Joseph mild, The. For Innocents' Day. Luke Wadding [or Waddinge]. NOIV

Angel's Flight. Maxine Scates. PBCAP

Angel's Message, The.　Clara Ann Thompson.　CBWP-2

Angel's Song.　Charles Causley.　OBCP

Angel's Visit, The.　Eugene Field.　PWR

Angel said to me: Why are you laughing?, The.　Sarah.　Delmore Schwartz.　ChIV-1; TaR

Angel slide your hand.　Poem in Yellow after Tristan Tzara, A.　Jerome Rothenberg.　PoM

Angel Surrounded by Paysans.　Wallace Stevens.　HCAP; LCAP-2

Angel Syphilis in the circle of Signators, The.　Robert Duncan.　PFTM-2　*Fr.* Passages.

Angel that presided o'er my birth, The.　William Blake.　InPK-6; OxBSP; RB　*Fr.* Gnomic Verses.

Angel was tired of heaven, as he lounged in the golden street.　Woman and the Angel, The.　Robert W. Service.　ChIV-1

Angel who divided us in remote times, The.　Angel Who Separated Us with the Flame, The.　Rossana Ombres.　CItWP, *tr.* by Cinzia Sartini Blum and Lara Trubowitz

Angel with a voice like summer show'rs, An.　Repose.　Henrietta Cordelia Ray.　CBWP-3

Angela Davis.　Alice S. Cobb.　BlSi

Angela Dominguez, Ever Present.　Nancy Morejón.　TANSG, *tr.* by Joy Renjilian-Burgy

Angelica Rescued from the Sea-Monster, by Ingres; in the Luxembourg.　Dante Gabriel Rossetti.　CenSon

Angelica the Doorkeeper.　*Unknown.*　RB, *tr.* by Anne Pennington

Angelical whites of your eyes, The.　Susan.　Robin Magowan.　SPE

Angelitos Negros: A Salsa Ballet.　Miguel Algarin.　Prologue.　PueRic

Angelles bee wrogte to bee of neidher kynde.　Thomas Chatterton.　EnLoPo　*Fr.* Aella; a Tragycal Enterlude.

Angellica's Lament.　Aphra Behn.　LW

Angells' eyes, whome veyles cannot deceive, The.　Robert Southwell.　*See* Angels' eyes, whom veils cannot deceive, The

Angels.　Anne Szumigalski.　NOBC

Angels, The.　Cleopatra Mathis.　ExTi

Angels, The.　Paul Ramsey.　CRP

Angels, The.　Marguerite Young.　WPE

Angels and ministers of grace defend us!　William Shakespeare.　EBEV; OxAEP-1　*Fr.* Hamlet.

Angels are bending, The.　Cradle Song.　W. B. Yeats.　NOBVV

Angels are stooping, The.　Cradle Song, A.　W. B. Yeats.　NOxBChV

Angels, as well as birds, on silent wing.　On Angels.　W. W. Eustace Ross.　MoCV

Angels Came a-Mustering, The.　*Unknown.*　TrJP, *tr.* by Israel Zangwill

Angels' eyes, whom veils cannot deceive, The.　Of the Blessed Sacrament of the Altar.　Robert Southwell.　OBEV

Angels, from the realms of glory.　Nativity.　James Montgomery.　NOCV

Angels in Heav'n, as we may say.　Poem upon the Caelestial Embassy, A.　Richard Steere.　SCAP

Angels in the House, The.　*Unknown.*　TreFP

Angels in Winter.　Nancy Willard.　ColAP; LCAP-2

Angels of Juárez, Mexico, The.　Ray Gonzalez.　TouFir

Angels of the Ruins, The.　Rafael Alberti.　AF, *tr.* by Geoffrey Connell

Angels rejoice in, The.　Their Rectitude Their Beauty.　Donald Davie.　HarvBoo

Angels' Song, The.　Edmund Hamilton Sears.　*See* It Came upon the Midnight Clear

Angels, sound upon your trumpets! Seraph-armies, sing and ring!　Concerning the Joyous and Splendid Resurrection of Christ.　Catharina Regina von Greiffenberg.　AuPH, *tr.* by Lowell A. Bangerter and George C. Schoolfield

Angels Sung a Carol, The.　Edward Taylor.　AH

Angels take approaches, The. Some enter by root.　Angels, The.　Paul Ramsey.　CRP

Angels' voices lost to air.　Fugue.　Shara McCallum.　NAPBL

Angels walking under the palm trees.　Little Carol of the Virgin, A.　Félix Lope de Vega Carpio.　SpanPo, *tr.* by Denise Levertov

Angels' Weather.　Bruce Beaver.　BMAP

Angelus.　Kathleen Jessie Raine.　BBASP

Anger.　Robert Creeley.　PFTM-2

Anger.　Mary Lamb.　NOxBChV

Anger.　César Vallejo.　TCLAP, *tr.* by Thomas Merton

Anger Against Children.　Robert Bly.　"Parents take their children into the deepest Oregon forests."　LoL

Anger, and the vow are the same. (LL)　Bad Old Days, The.　Kenneth Rexroth.　NNaP; NoAM; PAI

Anger in its time and place.　Anger.　Mary Lamb.　NOxBChV

Anger Lay by Me All Night Long.　Elizabeth Daryush.　RB

Anger's Freeing Power.　Stevie Smith.　OxBC

Anger Sweetened.　Molly Peacock.　FFC

Anger that breaks a man down into boys, The.　Anger that Breaks the Man into Chidren, The.　César Vallejo.　RaBo, *tr.* by Robert Bly

Anger which breaks a man into children.　Anger.　César Vallejo.　TCLAP, *tr.* by Thomas Merton

Anghiari is medieval, a sleeve sloping down.　Journey, The.　James Wright (1927–80).　NAAL-5; NoAM; PoE

Angilbert's Prayer.　Angilbert.　MLL, *tr.* by Helen Waddell

Angina Pectoris.　Nazim Hikmet.　VCWP

Anglais Mort à Florence.　Wallace Stevens.　SAmP

Angle-Land.　David Jones.　HarvBoo; NoAM　*Fr.* Anathemata, The.

Angle of Geese.　N. Scott Momaday.　CDW; HATNAP

Angle of Vision.　Robert Rendall.　OxBTC

Angler rose, he took his rod, The.　Epitaph.　Robert Louis Stevenson.　OBCoV

Angler's Calendar, The.　Yun Sŏndo.　"Is it a cuckoo that cries?"　WoPoe, *tr.* by Peter H. Lee　"Sun's fair rays are shining, The."　WoPoe, *tr.* by Peter H. Lee

Anglers Song, The.　William Basse [*or* Bas].　"As inward love breeds outward talk."　NOSC

Anglican curate in want, An.　Ronald Arbuthnott Knox.　OBCoV

Anglican firelight.　Other Voice, The.　Tom Paulin.　PNI

Angling.　*Unknown.*　WoPoe, *tr.* by Nguyen Ngoc Bich

Angling, a Day.　Galway Kinnell.　MoASP

Anglo-American Chainpoem.　*Unknown.*　SPE

Anglo-Saxon Comedy.　Peter Rose.　BMAP

Anglo Saxon Street.　Earle Birney.　HeIP-4; NIL-7; NOBC

Anglorum Feriae.　George Peele.　"Write write yow Croniclers of Tyme and Fame."　PBRV

Angola.　Amélia Veiga.　HAWP, *tr.* by Julia Kirst

Angola Question Mark.　Langston Hughes.　BPo; TTY

Angrier than my now occasional.　Preface to the Memoirs, A.　James Merrill.　NOBA

Angry boy takes out his realistic gun, The.　Need for Attention, The.　William Wadsworth.　KGB

Angry Bride, The.　*Unknown.*　WoPoe, *tr.* by Kevin O'Rourke

Angry Dusk.　Jack Lindsay.　NOBAu

Angry Poet, The.　Frank O'Connor.　CIP-2

Angry Samson.　Robert Graves.　ChIV-1; OxBEV

Angry Summer, The.　Idris Davies.　AngWePo　(Mrs. Evans Fach, You Want Butter Again.)　OBWVE

Angry Summer 20, The.　Idris Davies.　TCAWP

Angry Summer 28, The.　Idris Davies.　TCAWP

Angry with China.　Douglas Messerli.　FTOS

Angry word is like a boomerang, An.　Angry Word, An.　Margaret E. Bruner.　PoToHe

Angry young husband called Bicket, An.　Limerick.　John Galsworthy.　PeLi

Angrye winds not ay, The.　All Changeth.　William Drummond, of Hawthornden.　NePenScot

Angst, poetry, urbanized fret.　Limerick.　Sydney Bernard Smith.　PeLi

Angst-ridden amorist, Fred, An.　Love Song of J. Alfred Prufrock, The.　J. Walker.　PeLi

Anguish.　Adelaide Crapsey.　APT-1

Anguish.　Stéphane Mallarmé.　AWP, *tr.* by Arthur Symons

Anguish.　Henry Vaughan.　OxAEP-1

Anguish.　Andrey [*or* Andrei] Andreievich Voznesensky [*or* Voznesenskii].　RusPo, *tr.* by Robert Arthur Douglas Ford

Anguish, a door, Le Portel, body bent over jagged rock.　Placements I.　Clayton Eshleman.　PFTM-1

Anguish exists.　Ars Poetica.　Roque Dalton.　TCLAP, *tr.* by Richard Schaaf

Anguish of a naked body is more terrible, The.　Prayer to the Lord Ramakrishna, A.　James Wright (1927–80).　NNaP

Anguish of Ants, The.　David Campbell.　BMAP

Ani Maamin, A Song Lost and Found Again.　Elie Wiesel.　"Behold, God of Abraham, God of mercy."　HP

Anima Has a Predilection, The.　Michael Harlow.　PeNZ　*Fr.* Poem Then, for Love.

Anima quodammodo omnia.　Translation.　Howard Nemerov.　CRP

Animal Acts.　Charles Simic.　LCAP-2

Animal bones and some mossy tent rings.　Lament for the Dorsets.　Alfred Wellington Purdy.　NoAM

Animal Crackers in My Soup.　Ted Koehler.　ReLy

Animal Fair.　*Unknown.*　NTCP

Animal Has Drawn a Human, The.　Bert Schierbeek.　PFTM-2, *tr.* by Charles McGeehan

Animal Howl, The.　"M. J."　TrJP, *tr.* by A. Glanz-Leyeles

Animal I wanted, The.   Kenneth Patchen.   VGW

Animal Magnetism; the Pseudo-Philosopher Baffled.   Laurence Hynes Halloran.   NOEC

Animal runs, it passes, it dies, The. And it is the great cold.   Death Rites II.   *Unknown.*   TTY, *tr. by* C. M. Bowra

Animal Spirits.   John E. Smelcer.   PoCoUp

Animal That Drank Up Sound, The.   William Stafford.   VGW

Animal Tranquillity and Decay.   William Wordsworth.   OxBEV

Animal understands itself, The.   Fable.   Luiza Neto Jorge.   SurWo, *tr. by* Jean R. Longland

Animal Weather-Forecasting.   Thomas Lodge.   NoSic

Animal willows of November.   Willows of Massachusetts, The.   Denise Levertov.   NAAL-2v2

Animals.   Robinson Jeffers.   APT-1

Animals.   Frank O'Hara.   HarvBoo

Animals, The.   W. S. Merwin.   VCAP

Animals, The.   Edwin Muir.   CRP; ChIV-1; EBEV; HeIP-4; MoBrPo

Animals are coming, The.   Songs to Welcome the Society of the Mystic Animals.   *Unknown.*   STP, *tr. by* Richard Johnny John and Jerome Rothenberg

Animals Are Entering Our Lives.   Lisel Mueller.   ExTi

Animals Are Passing from Our Lives.   Philip Levine.   CoAP; ColAP; NOBA; RaBo; TAP

Animals are the latest decorating craze.   Some Cool.   Alice Fulton.   AllShUp

Animals do not sleep. At night.   Face of the Horse, The.   Nikolai Alekseievich Zabolotsky [*or* Zabolotskii].   RB; TCRP, *tr. by* Daniel Weissbort

Animals have no names.   Walk, A.   Nikolai Alekseievich Zabolotsky [*or* Zabolotskii].   RB, *tr. by* Daniel Weissbort

Animals' Houses.   James Reeves.   OTCP

Animals in That Country, The.   Margaret Atwood.   NALW; NoAM

Animals in the pastures.   Landscape.   Hendrik Marsman.   TuT, *tr. by* Michael Longley

Animals never sleep. At night when it's dark.   Face of a Horse, The.   Nikolai Alekseievich Zabolotsky [*or* Zabolotskii].   TCRusP, *tr. by* Kathy Lewis and Bob Perelman

Animals we have seen, all marvelous creatures, The.   Park in Milan, The.   William Jay Smith.   CoAP

Animals were, The.   Ode to the Cat.   Pablo Neruda.   VCWP, *tr. by* John Hollander

Animism.   Birago Diop.   NegPo, *tr. by* Ellen Conroy Kennedy

Animula.   T. S. Eliot.   CRP

Animula.   George Oppen.   FTOS

Animula vagula blandula.   Conrad Potter Aiken.   OBAL; OBCoV

Animula, Vagula, Blandula.   Stevie Smith.   OBVE

Aniseed has a sinful taste.   Egypt.   Keith Douglas.   HarvBoo

Anishinabe children sing songs of sleep.   For the Children.   Thomas Love Peacock.   VoR

Anishinabe Grandmothers.   Gerald Vizenor.   VoR

Anita and Giovanni.   Henrietta Cordelia Ray.   CBWP-3

Ank'hor Vat.   Denis Devlin.   BIrV; CIP-2; ModIr; NOIV

Ankle's chief end is exposiery, The.   Limerick.   Anthony Euwer.   PeLi

Ankotarinya.   *Unknown.*   CBAP, *tr. by* T. G. H. Strehlow

Ann, Ann! / Come! quick as you can!   Alas, Alack!   Walter De la Mare.   OPOU

Ann Griffith.   Ronald Stuart Thomas.   PeECV

Ann Griffiths.   Sally Roberts Jones.   AngWePo

Anna Akhmatova's Funeral.   Martin Mooney.   ModIr

Anna Akhmatova Spends the Night on Miami Beach.   John Balaban.   GifTon

Anna Blossom Has Wheels.   Kurt Schwitters.   PFTM-1

Anna Blume.   Kurt Schwitters.   NAWM-7v2, *tr. by* David Britt

Anna Dering on Bartolomeo Silva, Doctor of Turin.   Anne Lok [*or* Locke].   EMWP

Anna Elise.   *Unknown.*   OxNR

Anna Grasa.   Bruce Weigl.   CDa

Anna had been singing there since early morning.   Pestel, the Poet, and Anna.   "David Samuilovich Samoylov" [*or* "Samoilov"].   TCRP, *tr. by* Lubov Yakovleva

Anna Liffey.   Eavan Boland.   BodElec; ModIr

Anna Playing in a Graveyard.   Caroline Gilman.   OBCA

Anna's Dream.   Nancy Shiffrin.   GotH

Anna Speaks of the Childhood of Mary Her Daughter.   Lucille Clifton.   NALW

Annabel Lee.   Edgar Allan Poe.   AWP; AiP; BRP; ChAP; HeIP-4; ITBLP; NAAL-2v1; NAAL-3; NAAL-5; NCAP; OBSP; TCAPo; TFi

Annabell and the Witches.   Mick Gowar.   OBSP

Annals say: when the monks of Clonmacnoise, The.   Seamus Heaney.   EmeKit; ModIr   *Fr.* Lightenings.

And, the last day being come, Man stood alone.   Trumbull Stickney.   APN-2; NoP-4

Anne and the Field-Mouse.   Ian Serraillier.   NOxBChV

Anne Boleyn.   Eloise Bibb.   CBWP-4

Anne Bradstreate.   Another.   Anne Bradstreet.   TCAPo

Anne Frank Huis.   Andrew Motion.   HarvBoo

Anne Hathaway Composes Her 18th Sonnet.   Neil Curry.   NLP

Anne Rutledge.   Edgar Lee Masters.   CBCWP; HAP; MoAmPo; NOBA; NoAM; OxBA; PAI; TFi   *Fr.* Spoon River Anthology.

Anne Steele.   Jean Balderston.   MPUn

Anne, who are dead—and whom I loved in a rather asinine fashion.   Wonderful Things.   Ron Padgett.   PmAP

Annette came through the meadows.   Pastoral.   Henrietta Cordelia Ray.   CBWP-3

Annette has MS, she needs Mickey's help.   Funicello at 50.   Klipschutz.   ReTh

Annette Myers.   *Unknown.*   OxBoLi

Anniad, The.   Gwendolyn Brooks.   BlSi

Annie and Rhoda, sisters twain.   Sisters, The.   John Greenleaf Whittier.   AWP

Annie Hill's Grave.   James Merrill.   WeW-3

Annie, my first-born, gentle child.   To Annie.   Mary E. Tucker.   CBWP-1

Annie of Tharaw, my true love of old.   Annie of Tharaw.   *Unknown.*   GePo, *tr. by* Henry Wadsworth Longfellow

Annie Pearl Smith Discovers Moonlight.   Patricia Smith.   GT

Annihilation.   Conrad Potter Aiken.   MoAmPo

Annihilation.   Elizabeth Oakes-Smith.   TCAPo   *Fr.* Atheism.

Anniversaries.   Thomas Kinsella.

1956.   ModIr

Anniversaries.   May Probyn.   VWP

Anniversaries of War.   Yehuda Amichai [*or* Amikhai].   VCWP, *tr. by* Benjamin Harshav

Anniversary.   Judith Ortiz Cofer.   PueRic; TouFir

Anniversary.   Odysseus Elytis.   AF

Anniversary.   Dorothy Hewett.   BMAP

Anniversary.   Gary Metras.   PasH

Anniversary.   John Wain.   TwCP

Anniversary.   Davi Walders.   MPUn

Anniversary, An.   Thomas Hardy.   OxBTC

Anniversary, The.   Ai.   BodElec

Anniversary [*or* Anniversarie], The.   John Donne.   BASC; BoLoP; ESCV; FHYEP; FSCP; HAP; MeLP; NOBE; NoP-4; NoSic; SCGP; TFi; WeW-3

Anniversary of Death, An.   John Wieners.   PoM

Anniversary on the Hymeneals of My Noble Kinsman, Thomas Stanley, Esquire, An.   Richard Lovelace.   CaPo

Anniversary Poem.   George Oppen.   APSN; NNaP   *Fr.* Some San Francisco Poems.

Anniversary Poem for the Cheyennes Who Fell at Sand Creek.   Lance Henson.   VoR

Anniversary Soak.   Paul Groves.   TCAWP

Anniversary with Agave Plants.   Margherita Guidacci.   CItWP, *tr. by* Cinzia Sartini Blum and Lara Trubowitz

Anno Domini MCMXLVII.   Salvatore Quasimodo.   GI, *tr. by* Jack Bevan

Anno 1829.   Heinrich Heine.   AWP; OBVE, *tr. by* Charles Stuart Calverley

Annotation in Her Last Court Diary.   Kimiko Hahn.   ExTi

Annotations of Auschwitz.   Peter Porter.   HP

"London is full of chickens, on electric spits."   OxBTC

Annotations Tropes and Lacunae of the Itoku Master.   Ray DiPalma.   FTOS

Annotators agree Composer X.   St Cecilia's Day Epigram.   Peter Porter.   PeLV

Announced by all the trumpets of the sky.   Snow-Storm [*or* Snowstorm], The.   Ralph Waldo Emerson.   APN-1; ITBLP; NAAL-2v1; NAAL-3; NCAP; NOBA; NoP-4; OxBA; PoE; PoPoPo; TAP; TCAPo; TFi; TreFP; UnPo

Announcement of a New Grand Acceleration Company for the Promotion of the Speed of Literature.   Thomas Moore.   OBCoV

Announcer, The.   Vladimir Nikolaevich Kornilov.   TCRP, *tr. by* Daniel Weissbort

Annual Gaiety.   Wallace Stevens.   MoAmPo

Annual Legend.   Winfield Townley Scott.   CoAP

Annual of the Dark Physics, An.   Norman Dubie.   BodElec

Annual Returns.   Greg Williamson.   RA

Annuciation, The.   Elizabeth Jennings.   ChrPo

Annuity, The.   George Outram.   PeVV

Annul Wars.   Rabbi Nahman [*or* Nachman] of Bratzlav.   TrJP, *tr. by* Jacob Sloan

Annunciation.   John Donne.   TrCP   *Fr.* Holy Sonnets.

Annunciation.   Ken Etheridge.   AngWePo

Annunciation.   Anna Kamienska.   GI, *tr. by* David Curzon and Grażyna Drabik

Annunciation.   Primo Levi.   AF; GI

Annunciation. Rainer Maria Rilke. OBVE, *tr. by* James Blair Leishman

Annunciation. Kay Smith. NIL-7; NIP-4

Annunciation, The. Samuel Menashe. GI

Annunciation, The. Douglas Messerli. FTOS

Annunciation, The. Stephen Mitchell. GI

Annunciation, The. Edwin Muir. CRP; ChIV-2; NOCV; PAI

Annunciation, The. Amrita Pritam. WPOW, *tr. by* Krishna Gorowara and Khushwant Singh

Annunciation in an Initial R. Angie Estes. ExTi

Annunciations. Nuala Ni Dhomhnaill. ModIr, *tr. by* Michael Hartnett

Annus Mirabilis. Dryden.
  "By viewing nature, nature's handmaid, art." BASC
  (London after the Great Fire, 1666.) NOBE
  New London, The. FaBoCh
  "Now on their coasts our conquering navy rides." OxAEP-1
  "Now van to van the foremost squadrons meet." OBWP
  "Our fleet divides, and straight the Dutch appear." BASC; FaBoWar
  "Swell'd with our late successes on the foe." EBEV
  "Yet London, empress of the northern clime." NAEL-5v1; NAEL-6v1; NAEL-7v1; PeECV

Annus Mirabilis. Philip Larkin. NBLV; NIP-4; NOBL; OBAL

Annus Mirabilis 1989. Elaine Feinstein. HP

Anoint the Ariston. Odysseus Elytis.
  "I was late in understanding the meaning of humility." GifTon, *tr. by* Olga Broumas
  "Whatever I was able to acquire in my life by way of acts visible to all." GifTon, *tr. by* Olga Broumas

Anointed stone, the coruscated crown, The. Circumstance, The. Hart Crane. PFTM-1

Anointing, An. Thylias Moss. GT; ReTh

Anon out of the earth a fabric huge. John Milton. MakPoe *Fr.* Paradise Lost.

Anonymous. Víctor Hernández Cruz. PueRic

Anonymous Drawing. Donald Justice. CoAP; HeIP-4

Anonymous handsome, The. Rejoicing That Attend the Murder of Famous Men, The. Robley, Jr. Wilson. PBCAP

Anonymous Wedding Photo. Jennifer O'Grady. AmPoNex

An[o]on they kiste, and riden [*or* ryden] forth hir weye [*or* waye). (LL) Geoffrey Chaucer. FHYEP; NAEL-6v1; NAEL-7v1; NAWM-5v1; PoE *Fr.* Canterbury Tales, The.

Anorexia. Peter Hollenbeck. CDa

Anorexia. Alice Jones. BloBone

Anorexia. Jennifer Maiden. BMAP

Anorexic, The. Ruth Anderson Barnett. OPRER

Another. Thomas Lovell Beddoes. Son

Another. Anne Bradstreet. BASC; EMWP; LW; NAAL-3; OxBA; SCAP; TCAPo; WPE

Another. Robert Herrick. BeJo

Another. Richard Lovelace. CaPo; OxBEV

Another [Epigram]. Pope. FaBoEE
  (To a Blockhead.) NBLV

Another [Epitaph]: "Here lies John Trot, the Friend of all mankind." William Blake. FaBoEE

Another [Epitaph on Lady Mary Villiers]. Thomas Carew. BeJo; CaPo
  (Another.) CavPo
  (Epitaph, An.) OBEV

Another [On the Duke of Buckingham]. Thomas Carew. NOSC

Another [Madrigal]. Edward Herbert, 1st Baron Herbert of Cherbury. NOSC

Another [To His Booke]. Robert Herrick. NOSC

Another Alexandra. Mongane Wally Serote. PeSAV

Another and Another and. Theodore Weiss. DiPo

Another and another and another. James Henry. NOBVV; NPeEn; OxBEV

Another armored animal—scale. Pangolin, The. Marianne Craig Moore. APT-1; HAP; NOBA; NoAM

Another autumn. Nicholas Virgilio. HA

Another bend. John Wills. HA

Another buddy dead. Still Later There Are War Stories. D. F. Brown. CDa

Another Canto. John Bingham Morton. UV

Another Century. David Keplinger. AmPoNex

Another Charme for Stables. Robert Herrick. BeJo

Another conference year has passed. To the Conference. Mrs. Henry Linden. CBWP-4

Another cove of shale. On the Marginal Way. Richard Wilbur. CoAP; NOBA

Another damp Sunday morning up and walk over. Peter Riley. Oth *Fr.* Alstonefield V.

Another Day. Belinda Zubicueta Carmona. TANSG, *tr. by* Celeste Kostopulos-Cooperman

Another day. Morning Becomes Electric. Bruce Dawe. BMAP

Another day has gone for keeps. Night in the Ghetto. *Unknown, fr. Terezin Concentration Camp.* INSAB

Another day let slip! Its hours have run. Wasted Day, The. Robert Fuller Murray. EBVV

Another doctor story. Our G.P., Marcus. Nicarchus of Alexandria. GrAn

Another dreadful tale of woe as I will here unfold. Annette Myers. *Unknown.* OxBoLi

Another Duffer. Sam Hamill. BodElec

Another Epitaph on an Army of Mercenaries. Hugh MacDiarmid. FaBoWar; InPK-6; NAEL-5v2; NAEL-6v2; NoAM; NoP-4; OBWP; RB

Another evening we sprawled about discussing. Charles on Fire. James Merrill. HeIP-4

Another Face. Ray A. Young Bear. CDW

Another fire dying down, the view from here. Kindertotenlieder. Timothy Liu. NeAmPo

Another Fools' Day touches down, another homecoming. Another Fools' Day Touches Down: Shush. Jack A. Mapanje. HBAPE

Another for Miss Pardo's Album. Mihály Vörösmarty. IQMS, *tr. by* Paul Tabori

Another for the Briar Rose. William Morris. NOBVV; OxBEV

Another four I've left yet to bring on. Four Seasons of the Year, The. Anne Bradstreet. SCAP

Another Full Moon. Ruth Fainlight. BrRo

Another Genealogy. Luiza Neto Jorge. SurWo, *tr. by* Jean R. Longland

Another Grace for a Child. Robert Herrick. *See* Grace for a Child

Another gray morning. Gray Poem. Peter Everwine. GeoHom

Another hill town. Hotel Paradiso e Commerciale. John Malcolm Brinnin. TwCP

Another holiday. Letter to Breyten Breytenbach from Hong Kong. C. J. Driver. PeSAV

Another hot afternoon upstairs after school. Killarney Clary. GeoHom

Another Hundred People. Stephen Sondheim. ReLy

Another hundred people just got off of the train. Another Hundred People. Stephen Sondheim. ReLy

Another Impostor. Bruce Jackson. AmPoNex

Another. In Defense of Their Inconstancy [*or* Inconstancie]. A Song. Ben Jonson. BeJo
  (In the Person of Womankind (In Defense of Their Inconstancy).) NAEL-5v1; NAEL-6v1

Another Kind of Skin. Frances Sackett. Prnts

Another Lady's [*or* Ladyes] Exception, Present at the Hearing. Ben Jonson. NAEL-6v1; NAEL-7v1 *Fr.* Celebration of Charis in Ten Lyric[k] Pieces [*or* Peeces], A.

Another land, another age, another self. Covered Bridge. Robert Penn Warren. AiP

Another Lazarus. Sally Roberts Jones. TCAWP

Another Letter to a Friend. Mary Mollineux. PoBW

Another Life. Frank Bidart. HCAP; VCAP

Another Life. Taslima Nasrin. VCWP, *tr. by* Carolyne Wright

Another Little Boy. *Unknown.* NOxBChV

Another Lo-Cal Elegy. Stephen Yenser. UrbNat

Another Love Affair / Another Poem. E. Ethelbert Miller. ISC

Another Man Done Gone. *Unknown.* NAAAL

Another Me. Api. OMIP, *tr. by* A. K. Ramanujan

Another Meditation at the same Time. Edward Taylor. NOSC; OxBA; TAP; TCAPo *Fr.* Preparatory Meditations Before My Approach to the Lord's Supper.

Another Merchant of Death. Merchant of Death. Ramabai Espinet. WaCA

Another Moment. Sim Kombem. NAfrP

Another morn than ours. (LL) Death-Bed, The. Thomas Hood. GTBS-P; NOBE; OBEV; TreFP

Another mule kicking. Another Mule. Sterling Plumpp. GT

Another nickel in the slot. Hero in the Land of Dough, A. Robert Clairmont. KaS

Another night coats the nose and ears. Night Patrol. William Daniel Ehrhart. CDa

Another Night in the Ruins. Galway Kinnell. CoAP; InvLad
  (In the evening / haze darkening on the hills.) AF

Another of the placid beauties! Natalya Nikolayevna Goncharov. Don Coles. NOBC

Another on the Sun Shine. Lucy Hutchinson. EMWP

Another one, half-cracked: John Heydon. Ezra Pound. TCAPo *Fr.* Quia Pauper Amavi.

Another one was coming toward me. So I Lost My Temper. Rose Romano. UnSA

Another Planet. Boris Iulianovich Poplavsky [*or* Poplavskii]. TCRP; TCRusP, *tr. by* Emmet Jarrett, Dick Lourie and Richard Lourie

Another Poem about the Madness of Women. Tom Wayman. NOBC

Another Poem about the Vandals. Alan Michael Parker. NeAmPo

Another Poem for Me (after Recovering from an O.D.). Etheridge Knight. NNaP

Another Poem to My Mother. Clementina Suárez. TANSG, *tr. by* Janet N. Gold

Another Poetics. Octavio Armand. TCLAP, *tr. by* Carol Maier

Another Race. Delmira Agustini. TCLAP, *tr. by* Karl Kirchwey

Another Rhythm. Akasha (Gloria) Hull. ISC

Another's gone, and who comes next. Pass of Death, The. George Darley. NOBRP

Another Sarah. Anne Porter. TTTS

Another season centers on this place. Gourd Dancer, The. N. Scott Momaday. CDW

Another September. Thomas Kinsella. BIrV; CABP; CIP-2; HarvBoo; NoP-4

Another service, roses strewn and acrid. Rose of Brooklyn, The. Gregory Orfalea. GraLe

Another shout from the wharves. "H. D." NOBA *Fr.* Helen in Egypt.

Another Song. Donald Justice. CoAmPo; VGW

Another Song. William [*or* Villeam] Ross [*or* Ros]. NePenScot, *tr. by* Derick Thomson

Another Song about Paris. Dave Frishberg. ReLy

Another Song about That Same Dead Person or Mole—Whichever it Was. *Unknown.* STP, *tr. by* Richard Johnny John and Jerome Rothenberg

Another Song of the Same Woman, to Some Partridges, Sent to Her Alive. Florencia del Pinar. BoWoP, *tr. by* Julie Allen

Another Spirit Advances. Jules Romains. AWP, *tr. by* Joseph T. Shipley

Another Spring. Tu Fu. CrYelRi, *tr. by* Sam Hamill

Another Spring. Tu Fu. BLT; OHPC, *tr. by* Kenneth Rexroth

Another Spring on Olmstead Street. Len Roberts. UrbNat

Another summer we must have blinked and missed. Back End. Peter Rafferty. NLP

Another Summit. Muso Soseki. EaWin, *tr. by* W. S. Merwin

Another Sunday Morning. Derek Mahon. CIP-2

Another Sunday Morning. Carter Revard. VoR

Another sunset of scrambled eggs. Ménage à Trois. Howard Moss. VCAP

Another Time. W. H. Auden. OxBA

Another to Bring in the Witch. Robert Herrick. BeJo

Another to the River Ankor. Michael Drayton. NOSC *Fr.* Idea.

Another to Urania. Benjamin Colman. ChIV-1; SCAP

Another True Maid. Matthew Prior. FaBoEE

Another Version. Lisel Mueller. IllVoic

Another Version of an Ocean. Reginald Shepherd. NeAmPo

Another Voice. Victor Hugo. SxFrPo, *tr. by* E. H. Blackmore and A. M. Blackmore

Another warning sound! The funeral bell. Stanzas to the Memory of the Late King. Felicia Dorothea Hemans. RWP

Another way—to see. (LL) Emily Dickinson. APN-2; MoAmPo

Another wedding & Aunt Cherry. Cherry. Stuart Dybek. PBCAP

Another While. Morris Jacob Rosenfeld. TrJP

Another Woman. Imtiaz Dharker. EmeKit

Another World. Sándor Weöres. IQMS, *tr. by* Adam Makkai and Donald E. Morse

Another year! Anita Virgil. HA

Another year! another deadly blow! November, 1806. William Wordsworth. OBWP

Another Year Come. W. S. Merwin. PAI

Another year gone. Basho. EH; NIL-7, *tr. by* Robert Hass

Another year it may betide. *Unknown.* HAP

Another year like a frail flower is bound. Written in Autumn. Thomas Cole. AiP

Another youthful advocate of truth and right has gone. To the Memory of J. Horace Kimball. "Ada" (Sarah Louisa Forten). BlSi

Anseo. Paul Muldoon. CIP-2; ModIr; NPeEn; PNI

Anster Fair. William Tennant.
  "My pulse beats fire—my pericranium glows." NePenScot
  "Upon a little dappled nag, whose mane." NOBRP

Answeare to my Lady Alice Edgertons Songe, Of I prethy send mee back my Hart, An. Lady Jane Cavendish. EMWP

Answer. Mildred Bowers. YaYoPo

Answer. Bei Dao. PoetW; VCWP, *tr. by* Donald Finkel

Answer, An. Ahmad al-Mushari Al-'Udwani. MAP, *tr. by* Charles Doria and Hilary Kilpatrick

Answer, An. Robert Frost. OBCoV

Answer, An. Perceval Gibbon. PeSAV

Answer, The. Sir Robert Aytoun [*or* Ayton]. NOSC

Answer, The. Bei Dao. AF; PFTM-2, *tr. by* Bonnie S. McDougall

Answer, The. Anne Finch, Countess of Winchilsea. NAEL-7v1; NALW; NoP-4

Answer, The. George Herbert. FaBoVe; NPeEn

Answer, The. John Montague. CIP-2

Answer for Hope. Richard Crashaw. MeLP
  (M. [*or* Mr.] Crashaw's Answer for Hope.) NOSC
  (On Hope.) NOBE

Answer Me. Adah Isaacs Menken. CBWP-1; PoBW; ViWPN

Answer Song. David Trinidad. WiU

Answer to a Child's Question. Samuel Taylor Coleridge. ITBLP; NOxBChV

Answer to a Kind Enquiry. Mary Holtby. UV

Answer to a Love-Letter in Verse, An. Lady Mary Wortley Montagu. ECWP
  (Answer to a Love-Letter, An.) LW

Answer to a Man's Question, "What Can I Do About Women's Liberation?", An. Susan Griffin. GLP

Answer to Another Persuading a Lady to Marriage, An. Katherine Philips. HAP; WeW-3
  (Answer to another perswading a Lady to Marriage, An.) NPeEn; PBRV
  (To One Persuading a Lady to Marriage.) LW; OBEV

Answer to Cloe [*or* Chloe] Jealous. Matthew Prior. NOBE; OxBEV
  (Better Answer, A.) NAEL-6v1; NAEL-7v1; OxAEP-1
  (Better Answer to Cloe [*or* Chloe] Jealous, A.) AWP; NAEL-5v1; NOEC; NPeEn

Answer to Herrick, An. Harry Gilonis. Oth

Answer to Master [*or* Mr.] Ben Jonson's Ode, to Persuade Him Not to Leave the Stage, An. Thomas Randolph. BASC; BeJo

Answer to ——'s Professions of Affection. Byron. OxBSP

Answer to the Parson, An. William Blake. FaBoEE; NBLV; OxBoLi; WoPoe

Answer to Ting Yuan Ch'en, An. Ou-yang Hsiu. OHPC, *tr. by* Kenneth Rexroth

Answer to Vice-Prefect Chang. Wang Wei. ChinPo, *tr. by* Yip Wai-lim

Answer to Voznesensky and Evtushenko. Frank O'Hara. LCAP-2; NNaP; PoM

Answer to Yo / Question. Sonia Sanchez. BPo

Answered Prayers. Ella Wheeler Wilcox. PWR

Answering a Child. Sarah Morgan Bryan Piatt. NCAP

Answering Li Ying Who Showed Me His Poems about Summer Fishing. Yü Hsüan-chi. BoWoP, *tr. by* Geoffrey Waters

Answering Machine Message. Sari Friedman. GotH

Answers. Elizabeth Jennings. OxBSP; OxBTC

Answers, The. Robert Clairmont. OTCP

Answers from the Elements. Jelaluddin [*or* Jalal al-Din] Rumi. BBASP, *tr. by* Coleman Barks and John Moyne

Answers on a Postcard. David Morley. NLP

Ant, The. Richard Flecknoe. NOSC

Ant, The. Richard Lovelace. BASC; CaPo

Ant, The. Ogden Nash. OBAL

Ant climbs up a trunk, The. Short Story, A. David Escobar Galindo. ChAP, *tr. by* Jorge Piche

Ant Dodger. Bill Knott. PBCAP

Ant-Heap, The. Arthur Christopher Benson. EBVV

Ant Hill, The. Cynthia Zarin. NoP-4

Ant-Hills. "Marian Douglas." OBCA

Ant on the tablecloth, An. Departmental. Robert Frost. HeIP-4; MoAmPo; NAAL-2v2; NAAL-5; NOBA; NOBL; OBAL; PeLV; SoSe-8

Ant-seething city, city full of dreams. Seven Old Men, The. Charles Baudelaire. OBVE, *tr. by* Roy Campbell

Ant Trap, The. Joe Rosenblatt. NOBC

Ant wyht in wode be fleme. (LL) Lenten Is [*or* Ys] Come [with Love to Toune]. *Unknown.* HAP; MiEL

Antarctica. Derek Mahon. NPeEn; PBCIP

Antarctica. Ronald Albert Simpson. CBAP

Ante-bellum Negro prayed, The. Must Be Freed. Lizelia Augusta Jenkins Moorer. CBWP-3

Ante-Bellum Sermon, An. Paul Laurence Dunbar. APN-2; BPo; NAAAL

Ante Mortem. Robinson Jeffers. MoAmPo

Antelope white against the charred hills, The. Field. Dana Levin. AmPoNex

Anteroom: Geneva. Denis Devlin. CIP-2

Anthea bade me tie [*or* tye] her sho[o]e. Sho[o]e Tying, The. Robert Herrick. CaPo

Anthem: "Let us praise our Maker, with true passion extol Him." W. H. Auden. NOCV

Anthem, An. Sonia Sanchez. UnSA

Anthem for Doomed Youth. Raymond Garlick. AngWePo

Anthem for Doomed Youth. Wilfred Owen. AF; CABP; CAGL; ClHu; EBEV; FaBoMo; FaBoWar; GSo; GTBS-P; HAP; HarvBoo; HeIP-4; InPK-6; MoBrPo; NAEL-5v2; NAEL-6v2; NOBE; NPeEn; NoAM; NoP-4;

OBEV; OBWP; OxBEV; OxBTC; PoE; PoPoPo; SCV; SoSe-8; Son; TCAWP; TFi; WeW-3

Anthem for St. Cecilia's Day.   W. H. Auden.
"In a garden shady this holy lady."   FaBoTw; TwCP

Anthem for the Cathedral of Exeter.   Joseph Hall.   SacPr

Anthologistics.   Arthur Guiterman.   NBLV

Anthology Poem.   Petra von Morstein.   BoWoP, *tr. by* Rosmarie Waldrop

Anthropophagites See a Sign on NC Highway 177 That Looks like Heaven, The. Jonathan Williams.   OBAL

Anthuriums, Pahoa.   Joan Swift.   PoCoUp

Anti-aircraft seen from a certain distance.   Dam Neck, Virginia.   Richard Eberhart.   PoWW

Anti-dithyrambics.   John Peck.   HarvBoo

Anti-Lazarus, The.   Nicanor Parra.   GI, *tr. by* Edith Grossman

Anti-Love Poems.   Elizabeth Brewster.   NOBC

Anti-master-man, floribund ascetic, An.   Landscape with Boat.   Wallace Stevens.   APT-1

Anti-mnemonic self-vaccination.   Joyce Mansour.   MFP, *tr. by* Martin Sorrell

Anti-Semanticist, The.   Everett Hoagland.   BPo; NBV

Anti-Semitic Demonstration, An.   Gail Newman.   GotH

Anti-Suffragists, The.   Charlotte Perkins Stetson Gilman.   SWaP

Antic Hay.   Aldous Leonard Huxley.
"Christlike is my behaviour."   OBCoV

Antic Quatrains.   Jackson Mac Low.   PmAP

Antichrist, The.   Stefan George.   WoPoe, *tr. by* Peter Viereck

Antichrist, or the Reunion of Christendom; an Ode.   Gilbert Keith Chesterton. NOBE; NOBL; OBSV; OxAEP-2

Antichrist, playing his lissome flute and merry.   Armageddon.   John Crowe Ransom.   ChIV-2

Anticipation, The.   Thomas Traherne.   BASC

Antidepressant.   Adrienne Su.   AmPoNex

Antiginides' two daughters, Melo.   Leonidas of Tarentum.   GrAn

Antigone.   Lajos Áprily.   IQMS, *tr. by* Watson Kirkconnell

Antigone.   Sophocles.   NAWM-5v1

Antigone and Oedipus.   Henrietta Cordelia Ray.   BlSi; CBWP-3

Antigonish.   Hughes Mearns.   BRP; NBLV
(Little Man, The.)   NOxBChV

Antikrates knew the stars.   Philodemus.   PGA

Antinous.   Mikhail Alekseievich Kuzmin.   CAGL, *tr. by* Michael Green

Antiodemis, Aphrodite's pet cherub, from a baby.   Antipater of Sidon.   GrAn

Antipathy.   Rowland Watkyns.   FaBoEE

Antiphanes, son of the same, to Hermes.   Dedication of a Torch.   Crinagoras. GrAn, *tr. by* Alistair Elliot

Antiphon: "Let all the world in ev'ry corner sing / *My God and King*."   George Herbert.   PeECV

Antiphon for Divine Wisdom.   Hildegard von Bingen.   WPoS, *tr. by* Barbara Newman

Antiphon for the Angels.   Hildegard von Bingen.   WPoS, *tr. by* Barbara Newman

Antiphon for the Holy Spirit.   Hildegard von Bingen.   WPoS, *tr. by* Barbara Newman

Antiphonal Hymn in Praise of Inanna.   Enheduanna.   BoWoP

Antiphony.   João da Cruz e Sousa.   TCLAP, *tr. by* Nancy Vieira Couto

Antiplatonic[k], The.   John Cleveland.   NOSC; NPeEn; PBRV

Antipsalm.   Novica Tadic.   VCWP, *tr. by* Charles Simic

Antiquary.   John Donne.   EBEV; NOSC

Antiquary, The.   Joseph Campbell.   OxBTC

Antiquary, The.   Sir Walter Scott.
Oyster, The.   FaBoCh
Red Harlaw.   OxBB

Antique Harvesters.   John Crowe Ransom.   MoAmPo; OxBA

Antiquitez de Rome.   Joachim Du Bellay.   OBVE, *tr. by* Edmund Spenser   *Fr.* Ruins of Rome.

Antiseptic Baby and the Prophylactic Pup, The.   Strictly Germ-proof.   Arthur Guiterman.   TrJP

Antistrophe.   Giacomo Leopardi.   WoPoe, *tr. by* Robert Bringhurst

Antlered forests, The.   Ank'hor Vat.   Denis Devlin.   BIrV; CIP-2; ModIr; NOIV

Antlered scarab rolled a dungball, The.   Near Damascus.   W. S. Di Piero. ChIV-2

Anton Mikhailovich spat, said "Ugh," spat again, said "Ugh" again, spat. Symphony No. 2.   Daniil Kharms.   AF, *tr. by* George Gibian

Anton Steiner sits behind a rosewood desk.   Chief of Medicine, The.   Arthur Ginsberg.   BloBone

Antonette's Boogie.   Kendel Hippolyte.   WaCA

Antonio.   Laura Elizabeth Richards.   OBCA
(Antonio, Antonio.)   OxIBACP

Antonio Banderas in His Underwear.   Regie Cabico.   WiU

Antonio Ce De Baca.   Mi Tío Baca el Poeta de Socorro.   Jimmy Santiago Baca.   PmAP

Antonio Torres Heredia.   Arrest of Antoñito el Camborio.   Federico García Lorca.   SpanPo, *tr. by* Robert O'Brien

Antony and Cleopatra.   William Shakespeare.
"Barge she sat in, like a burnish'd throne, The."   SCV
Cleopatra.   SCV
Cleopatra's Lament.   UnPo
Death of Cleopatra.   OxAEP-1
Drinking Song, A.   NoSic
"Enobarbus, Antony."   OxAEP-1
"Eros, thou yet behold'st me?"   EBEV; OxAEP-1
"How now! is he dead?"   OxAEP-1
"I will tell you, / The barge she sat in, like a burnisht throne."   OxBEV
"Miserable change now at my end, The."   EBEV
"Most noble empress, you have heard of me?"   OxAEP-1
"Noblest of men, woo't die?"   OxAEP-1
"O! bear me witness, night."   OxAEP-1
"Thou hast a sister by the mother's side."   OxAEP-1

Antony's Oration [over Caesar's Body].   William Shakespeare.   MakPoe; OxAEP-1; OxBEV   *Fr.* Julius Caesar.

Antrim.   Robinson Jeffers.   BIrV; NOBA; VGW

Ants.   Yusuf Al-Sa'igh.   MAP, *tr. by* Diana Der Hovanessian and Salma Khadra Jayyusi

Ants.   Alfred Kreymborg.   APT-1

Ants.   Ramón López Velarde.   TCLAP, *tr. by* Samuel Beckett

Ants, The.   John Clare.   OxBSo

Ants, The.   William Empson.   OxBSo

Ants, The.   Svetlana Kekova.   ItGoST, *tr. by* Judith Hemschemeyer

Ants and the Sun.   Khalil Khouri.   MAP, *tr. by* Sharif Elmusa and Christopher Middleton

Ants are walking under the ground, The.   People, The.   Elizabeth Madox Roberts.   NOxBChV

Ants ate half its left wing.   Crane in Reeds.   William Heyen.   PoCoUp

Ants look up as I trot by.   Dog's Song.   Robert Wallace.   TLR

Antwerp.   Ford Madox Ford.
"For the white-limbed heroes of Hellas ride by upon their horses."   FaBoWar
"This is Charing Cross."   FaBoWar; PeFWW

Antwerp to Ghent.   Dante Gabriel Rossetti.   NPeEn; PeVV   *Fr.* Trip to Paris and Belgium, A.

Anvil, The.   Alfred Noyes.   SacPr

Anvil arrow bow box and brahmin.   Alphabet, The.   Jejuri Arun Kolatkar. OMIP, *tr. by* Vinay Dharwadker

Anvil—God's Word, The.   John Clifford.   PoToHe

Anxiety.   Mary Julia Young.   CenSon

Anxiety for the Future.   Christian Morgenstern.   WoPoe, *tr. by* William DeWitt Snodgrass

Anxious and trembling for the birth of Fate. (LL)   Pope.   EBEV; EBNV; ECEV; NOBE; NOEC; OxAEP-1   *Fr.* Rape of the Lock, The; an Heroi-Comical Poem.

Any Chippewa.   Song of the Captive Sioux Woman.   *Chippewa Oral Tradition.*   NAAL-5

Any clear thing that blinds us with surprise.   Fishnet.   Robert Lowell.   HCAP; PoetW; VCAP

Any color, so long as it's red.   Red.   Eugene Field.   CA

Any Complaints?   Vernon Scannell.   OxBTC

Any country is only a way of failing.   Considerations.   David Helwig.   NOBC

Any dogsbody can sit up all night.   Power Cut.   Seamus Deane.   PBCIP

Any Fool Can Make a Rule.   Henry David Thoreau.   TCAPo

Any fool knows a Br'er in a rocker.   Br'er Sterling and the Rocker.   Michael S. Harper.   NAAAL

Any girl who's reached the age.   Boy Friend, The.   Sandy Wilson.   ReLy

Any Husband or Wife.   Carol Haynes.   *See* Any Wife or Husband

Any Husband to Many a Wife.   Emily Jane Pfeiffer.   VWP; ViWPN

Any Lover to Any Beloved.   Faiz Ahmad Faiz.   WoPoe, *tr. by* Naomi Lazard

Any Man's Advice to His Son.   Kenneth Fearing.   IllVoic

Any movement kills something.   Roberto Juarroz.   VCWP

Any Nest I Can't Sleep in Should Be Burned.   Christopher Davis.   AmPoNex

Any niche is my college.   Hedge Schoolmaster, A.   Padraic Fallon.   CIP-2

Any other time would have done.   Witter Bynner.   APT-1

Any Part of Piggy.   Noël Coward.   NBLV; PeLV

Any Saint.   Francis Thompson.   MoBrPo

Any Soul to Any Body.   Cosmo Monkhouse.   NOBVV; OxBEV

Any strong sensation is a welcome break.   Radiator.   Kimiko Hahn.   ExTi

Any thing to me. Hark[e], Despair away. (LL)   Bag, The.   George Herbert. ESCV; GeHe

Any Two Wheels.   Jane Miller.   BodElec

Any Wife or Husband. Carol Haynes. ITBLP
  (Any Husband or Wife.) PoToHe
Any Wife to Any Husband. Robert Browning. RACG
Any woman's death diminishes me. (LL) From an Old House in America.
  Adrienne Rich. NNaP; TRP
Any woman who can give birth to God deserves, I think, a pretty lively. So
  Let's Look at It Another Way. John Godfrey. PmAP
Anyemiyoo / do you remember *oshimashi*? Messages. Naana Banyiwa Horne.
  NAfrP
Anyone can get it wrong, laying low. Lies. Martha Collins. ExTi; PuP-23
Anyone here ever seen a white beetle? Dung-beetle. Breyten Breytenbach.
  PoetW, *tr. by* André Brink
Anyone Lived in a Pretty How Town. E. E. Cummings. ChAP; ColAP; HAP;
  InPK-6; MoAmPo; NAAL-2v2; NAAL-5; NOBA; NoP-4; PoPoPo; RB;
  TAP; TFi; TwCP; VGW
Anyone who has ever been hit. Sting, The. Tom Paulin. EmeKit
Anyone who has waded. Love's Constancy. Hadewijch. WPoS, *tr. by* Oliver
  Davies
Anyone with quiet pace who. Walking West. William Stafford. RB
Anys for my saik. (LL) Ballad of Kynd Kittok, The. William Dunbar.
  OxBoLi; PeLV
Anything. Brenda Brooks. PoBW
Anything but the space between. (LL) Annunciation. Kay Smith. NIL-7;
  NIP-4
Anything Goes. Cole Porter. APT-1; OBAL; ReLy
Anytime the thunder starts to rumble down. Sunny Disposish. Philip Charig.
  ReLy
Anyway. Barbara Jagger. Prnts
Anyway the time has come to explain. Poem. Jack Kerouac. CLPP
Anywhere, anywhere, out of this room! (LL) Scherzo, A. Dora Greenwell.
  NOBVV; NPeEn
Aodh Ruadh O'Domhnaill. Thomas MacGreevy [*or* McGreevy]. CIP-2;
  OBMV
Aoibhinn, A Leabhráin, Do Thriall. *Unknown.* BIrV, *tr. by* Flann O'Brien
Apache, Omaha, Osage, Choctaw, Comanche, Cherokee, Oglala, Micmac.
  Parading with the Veterans of Foreign Wars. Carter Revard. OPRER
El Apagón. Sandra M. Castillo. TouFir
Apart from my sisters, estranged. Cinderella. Olga Broumas. InPK-6
Apart from You. Daryl Hine. CAGL
Apart possibly from waving hello to the cliff-divers. Johnny Weissmuller Dead
  in Acapulco. Clive James. NOBAu
Apart, thank Heaven, from all to do. Owl, The. Walter De la Mare. OxBSP
Apartment, The. Brady Street, San Francisco. Michael Lassell. WiU
Apartment is empty, The. My wife's slip hangs weightlessly, twisted over a
  chair. Farewell to Russia. Lev Mak. TCRusP, *tr. by* Daniel Weissbort
Apathy Is Ascribed to the Modest Man. Bhartrihari. WoPoe, *tr. by* Barbara
  Stoler Miller
Ape. Russell Edson. PmAP; RaBo
Apeherd. "Mang Ke."
  "It's a good harvest this year." PFTM-2, *tr. by* Nicholas Jose and Wu Baohe
  Section II. PFTM-2, *tr. by* Nicholas Jose and Wu Baohe
Apeneck Sweeney spreads his knees. Sweeney Among the Nightingales. T. S.
  Eliot. APT-1; FaBoMo; HAP; HarvBoo; HeIP-4; NAAL-2v2; NAEL-5v2;
  NAEL-6v2; NOBA; NOBE; NPeEn; NoAM; NoP-4; OBMV; OxBA;
  OxBEV; PoPoPo; TFi; WeW-3
Apex. Nate Salsbury. NBLV
Aphorisms. Francis Picabia. SurPaPo, *tr. by* Marcel Jean
Aphrodisiac, The. Medbh McGuckian. PBCIP
Aphrodite Vrania. Charles Reznikoff. APT-2
Apiary. B. H. Boston. GeoHom
Apis Mellifica. Roger McDonald. NOBAu
APO 96225. Larry Rottman. CDa
Apocalypse. Charlie R. Braxton. InTrad
Apocalypse. Dennis Joseph Enright. OBSV
Apocalypse. Francis Ernest Kobina Parkes. PBA
Apocalypse and Resurrection. John Clifford Bayliss. SPE
Apocalypse Dub. Dennis Scott. WaCA
Apocolocyntosis. Seneca.
  "This said, she twirled the thread on an ugly spool." RomPo, *tr. by* J. P.
  Sullivan
Apocrypha. János Pilinszky. PoSu, *tr. by* Ted Hughes
Apocryphal Gospel, An. Jorge Luis Borges.
  "Wretched are the poor in spirit: for what they were on earth." GI, *tr. by*
  Norman Thomas Di Giovanni
Apolitical Intellectuals. Otto René Castillo. AF, *tr. by* Margaret Randall
Apollinaire. Unhistorical Events. Bob Kaufman. CLPP
Apollo. Elizabeth Alexander. ExTi
Apollo. Thomas Holley Chivers. APN-1

Apollo and Daphne. Ovid. NAWM-7v1, *tr. by* Allen Mandelbaum *Fr.*
  Metamorphoses.
Apollo and Daphne. Paul Whitehead.
  Hunting Song. OxBoLi
Apollo and Daphne. Yvor Winters. APT-2; Son
Apollo and Hyacinthus. Ovid. CAGL, *tr. by* Rolfe Humphries *Fr.*
  Metamorphoses.
Apollo and Marsyas. Zbigniew Herbert. PoSu; WoPoe, *tr. by* Czeslaw Milosz
  and Peter Dale Scott
Apollo as lately a circuit he made. Circuit of Apollo, The. Anne Finch,
  Countess of Winchilsea. NALW
Apollo Café. Stephen Gray. PeSAV
Apollo Defeats Patroclus. Homer. OBVE, *tr. by* Christopher Logue *Fr.* Iliad,
  The.
Apollo, having been given my desire. Lament for Evolution. Joy Davidman.
  YaYoPo
Apollo, if the sweet desire is still alive that inflamed you beside. Petrarch.
  NAWM-7v1, *tr. by* Robert M. Durling *Fr.* Sonnets to Laura.
Apollo kept my father's sheep. Daughter of Admetus, A. Thomas Sturge
  Moore. FaBoTw
Apollo's first, at last, the true God's priest. (LL) Thomas Carew. BASC;
  CABP; CaPo; CavPo; NAEL-6v1; NAEL-7v1; NoP-4
Apollo Strikes Patroclus. Homer. *See* Iliad, The
Apollophanes married for an alibi. Lucilius. GrAn
Apologia (Nkomati). Wole Soyinka. HBAPE
Apologia Pro Poemate Meo. Wilfred Owen. MoBrPo; NAEL-5v2; NAEL-
  6v2; PeFWW
Apologia pro Vita Sua. A. R. Ammons. HCAP; NOBA
Apologia pro Vita Sua. Samuel Taylor Coleridge. OxBSP
Apologia pro Vita Sua. Pope. NOBE *Fr.* Epistle to Dr. Arbuthnot.
Apologia pro Vita Sua. Sedulius Scottus. BIrV, *tr. by* Helen Waddell
Apologie for the Precedent Hymnes on Tereas, An. Richard Crashaw. ESCV
Apologist's Evening Prayer, The. Clive Staples Lewis. SacPr; TrCP
Apologue. Tony Connor. BoLoP
Apology. Richard Cecil. BodElec
Apology. Anthony Cronin. CIP-2
Apology. Duane Niatum. HATNAP
Apology. Elizabeth Spires. FFC
Apology. William Carlos Williams. OxBA; SAmP
Apology, An. William Morris. AWP; EBVV; NAEL-5v2; NAEL-6v2 *Fr.*
  Earthly Paradise, The.
Apology, An. Diane Wakoski. TAP
Apology and Explanation. John Sparrow. OBCoV
Apology arouses father's curiosity, An. At the same time, it can also seem.
  Delaying Relevance. Ben Marcus. HeMarv
Apology for Actors, An. Thomas Heywood.
  Author to His Book[e], The. NOSC
Apology for Bad Dreams. Robinson Jeffers. APT-1; MoAmPo; NOBA;
  OxBA
Apology for Domitian. Robert Penn Warren. NOBA; PAI
Apology for the Revival of Christian Architecture in England, An. Geoffrey
  Hill.
  Eve of St Mark, The. NPeEn; OxBEV
  Idylls of the King. NoAM; PoE
  Laurel Axe, The. NAEL-5v2; NAEL-6v2; NPeEn; NoAM; PoE
  Quaint Mazes. NoAM
Apology for Understatement. John Wain. OxBTC
Apology of Genius. Mina Loy. APT-1
Apology to Andrew. Richard Jones. AWTN
Apon the midsummer evin, mirriest of Michtis. William Dunbar. OxBS
Apostacy, The. Thomas Traherne. OxBEV; SacPr
Apostasy. Aus of Kuraiza. TrJP, *tr. by* Hartwig Hirschfeld
Apostasy of One and But One Lady, The. Richard Lovelace. CaPo
Apostate, The. Alfred Edgar Coppard. OBMV
Apostates and run-aways. Michael Wigglesworth. ColAP *Fr.* Day of Doom,
  The.
Apostrophe to Man. Edna St. Vincent Millay. NAAL-5; NALW
Apostrophe to the Ocean. Byron. OxAEP-2 *Fr.* Childe Harold's Pilgrimage.
Apotheosis. Wu Yun. ColAnChi, *tr. by* Edward H. Schafer
Apotheosis of Medusa. Pat Parnell. HW
Apotheosis of the Kitchen Goddess II. Teresa Noelle Roberts. HW
Appalachian Book of the Dead III, The. Charles Wright. AWTN
Appalachian Convalescence. Robert Conquest. OxBC
Appalachian Trees Encircled by Police Tape. Greg Williamson. NeAmPo
Appaloosa, The. Michael S. Weaver. GT
Appaloosa Hail Storm. Gerald Hausman. GifTon

Apparatus is right, The. Note to the Ophthalmologist. Dolores Kendrick.
  FFC

Apparel of green woods and meadows gay. On Revisiting Cintra after the
  Death of Catarina. Luis de Camões [or Camõens]. AWP, tr. by Richard
  Garnett

Apparent Colonnades, The. Jeffrey Wainwright. HarvBoo

Apparent Failure. Robert Browning. NAEL-5v2; NAEL-6v2; NOBE

Apparent gale, vaned in winding storms, The. Secrecy. Samuel Greenberg.
  APT-1

Apparently, my people begin and end in Iowa. Belladonna. Dennis Finnell.
  SpudSo

Apparently with no surprise. Emily Dickinson. NAAL-2v1; NAAL-3;
  NAAL-5; SAmP; SoSe-8; TCAPo

Apparition, The. John Donne. BASC; ESCV; EnLoPo; FSCP; HeIP-4;
  NAEL-5v1; NAEL-6v1; NAEL-7v1; NAWM-5v1; NOBE; NOBL; NoSic;
  OBEV; PoE; SCGP; SCV; SoSe-8; TFi

Apparition, The. Bernard O'Donoghue. NoP-4

Apparition, The. Stephen Phillips. OBEV

Apparition, The. Carol J. Pierman. ReTh

Apparition of a salsa band, The. Latin Night at the Pawnshop. Martín Espada.
  TRP

Apparition of His Mistress[e] Calling Him to Elizium [or Elysium], The.
  Robert Herrick. CaPo

Apparition of these faces in the crowd, The. In a Station of the Metro. Ezra
  Pound. APT-1; ChAP; ColAP; HAP; HeIP-4; InPK-6; MoAmPo; NAAL-
  2v2; NAAL-5; NIL-7; NIP-4; NOBA; NPeEn; NoAM; NoP-4; OxBA; PAI;
  PoE; PoPoPo; TAP; TCAPo; TFi; UnPo; VGW; WeW-3

Apparition, The—A Retrospect. Herman Melville. APN-2; NCAP; TCAPo

Apparitions, The. W. B. Yeats. TRP

Appeal. Edith Nesbit. LW

Appeal. Noémia da Sousa. PBMAP; TTY; WPOW

Appeal. Mihály Vörösmarty. IQMS, tr. by Watson Kirkconnell

Appeal to Cats in the Business of Love, An. Thomas Flatman. EnLoPo;
  HAP; OBCoV

Appeal to My Countrywomen, An. Frances Ellen Watkins Harper. BlSi
  (Appeal to My Country Women, An.) NAAAL

Appeal to the Moongod Nanna-Suen to Throw Out Lugalanne. Enheduanna.
  BoWoP, tr. by Aliki and Willis Barnstone

Appeal to Women, An. "Ada" (Sarah Louisa Forten). SWaP

Appear, O Mother, was the perpetual cry. Invocation. Wilfred Watson.
  MoCV

Appearance and Reality. John Hollander. OBAL

Appearances. Robert Browning. OxBSP

Appellants, The. Alice Rahon. SurWo, tr. by Myrna Bell Rochester

Appendix to the Vision of Peace, An. Yehuda Amichai [or Amikhai]. PoSu,
  tr. by Glenda Abramson and Tudor Parfitt

Appetizers' Bruce Andrews. FTOS Fr. Tizzy Boost.

Applauding youths laughed with young prostitutes. Harlem Dancer, The.
  Claude McKay. APT-1; BPo; ISC; NAAL-5; NIL-7; NIP-4; NoAM; Son;
  TAP; TCAPo

Apple. Susan Stewart. BAP-01

Apple, The. Bruce Guernsey. IllVoic

Apple, The. Plato. WeW-3

Apple, The. Ray Smith. TrCP

Apple, The. Vladimir Alekseievich Soloukhin. TCRusP, tr. by Daniel
  Weissbort

Apple-Barrel of Johnny Appleseed, The. Nicholas Vachel Lindsay. OxBA

Apple Blight. Paul Zimmer. VGW

Apple Blossom. Louis MacNeice. PeECV; RB

Apple-blossom, a great spread of it. And Where Do You Stand on the National
  Question. Tom Paulin. CIP-2

Apple blossoms look like snow. Comparison, A. John Chipman Farrar.
  WHSW

Apple Core. Clarence Major. GT

Apple-Culture. John Philips. OxAEP-1 Fr. Cyder.

Apple Dumplings. Mary E. Tucker. CBWP-1

Apple Dumplings and a King, The. "Peter Pindar." OBSV

Apple falls, falling in the quiet night, The. (LL) Robert Penn Warren.
  CBCWP; MoAmPo Fr. Kentucky Mountain Farm.

Apple for the sea, marble narcissus flower, An. Mahmoud Darwish. MAP
  Fr. Beirut.

Apple Gathering, An. Christina Georgina Rossetti. NAEL-5v2; NAEL-6v2

Apple-green west and an orange bar. Frost To-night. Edith Matilda Thomas.
  TCAPo

Apple Island. Robert Graves. EmeKit

Apple of islands, Sirmio, & bright peninsulas, set. 31. Catullus. AmFaPo, tr.
  by Peter Whigam Fr. Carmina.

Apple on its bough is her desire, The. Garden Abstract. Hart Crane. OBGa

Apple Orchard in the Spring, An. William Martin. PWR

Apple Peeler. Robert Francis. LCAP-2

Apple-pie, apple-pie. Unknown. OxNR

Apple-raid, The. Vernon Scannell. NOxBChV

Apple Tree, The. James Keir Baxter. OxBC

Apple Tree and a Pig, An. Emyr Humphreys. OBWVE

Apple-Tree Man, The. Charles Causley. OBSP

Apple Trees, The. Louise Glück. HCAP

Apple unbitten in the palm, The. (LL) As Bad as a Mile. Philip Larkin.
  InPK-6; OxBC; OxBEV; OxBSP

Apple Valley School has closed its books, The. Country School. Ted Kooser.
  KaS

Apples. Donald Hall. LCAP-2

Apples. Patricia Pogson. NLP

Apples, Normandy, 1944. Frank Ormsby. PNI Fr. Northern Spring, A.

Apples of gold, in silver pictures shrined. Edward Taylor. NAAL-2v1;
  NAAL-3; NAAL-5 Fr. Preparatory Meditations Before My Approach to
  the Lord's Supper.

Apples on Champlain. Richard Kenney. NoP-4

Applicant, The. Sylvia Plath. EmeKit; NAAL-2v2; NOBA; PoPoPo; TwCP

Application. Paul Gallico. TriCat

Apply to Master Janus last of all. (LL) Sonnet: To Brunetto Latini. Dante
  Alighieri. AWP; EaItPo, tr. by Dante Gabriel Rossetti

Appointed Rounds. Louis Jenkins. RaBo

Appointment, The. Louis Simpson. BodElec

Appointment, The. Leonard Alfred George Strong. OxBTC

Appointment on a rainy afternoon. Buttons. Tessa Rose Chester. MFPA

Appointments you did not make. Night Words. Isabel Meyrelles. SurWo, tr.
  by Jean R. Longland

Appomattox. Terese Svoboda. ExTi

Appraisal. Sara Teasdale. MoAmPo

Apprehension. Hannah Flagg Gould. SWaP

Apprehension. Jeremy Ingalls. YaYoPo

Apprehension this spring . . . the leaves, the leaves. Homage and Lament for
  Ezra Pound in Captivity. Robert Duncan. NOBA

Apprentice's day off. Buson. EH, tr. by Robert Hass

Approach of the Storm, The. Chippewa Oral Tradition. NAAL-5; OBVE;
  TTTS, tr. by Frances Densmore

Approach of War, The. Ellen Hinsey. AmPoNex

Approach to a City. William Carlos Williams. PoRA

Approach to the bar, The. Pole Vaulter. David Allan Evans. MoASP

Approaches, The. W. S. Merwin. NOBA

Approaching a Significant Birthday, He Peruses The Norton Anthology of
  Poetry. R. S. Gwynn. RA

Approaching Dance, The. Unknown. APN-2 Fr. War Dance.

Approaching death. William Carlos Williams. FaBoMo Fr. Asphodel, That
  Greeny Flower.

Approaching Winter, The. Dániel Berzsenyi. IQMS, tr. by Peter Zollman

Approximate and unfulfilled, a devilish nymph. Personals. Star Black. KGB

Approximate Man, The. Tristan Tzara.
  [Part One] PFTM-1
  "Sunday heavy potlid on the boiling blood." PFTM-1

Approximately. Diane Ward. FTOS

Après le Bain. William Carlos Williams. OBAL

L'Après-midi d'un Faune. Stéphane Mallarmé. AWP, tr. by Aldous Huxley

Apricot about to fade, raindrops quiet now. Things Seen. Yüan Mei.
  CoBLCP, tr. by Jonathan Chaves

Apricot Garden. Yüan Chên. SuSp, tr. by Angela Jung Palandri

Apricot Tree. Magda Isanos. BoWoP

Apricot Tree, The. Gyula Illyés. IQMS, tr. by Christine Brooke-Rose

Apricots Die Young. Meng Chiao.
  "Don't let freezing hands play with these pearls." SuSp
  "In vain I gather up these stars from the ground." SuSp
  "It must have been a single thread of tears." SuSp
  "Nipping chill, the frost killed spring." SuSp
  "When I tread the earth, I fear to hurt the ground." SuSp
  "When my son was born, the moon was not bright." SuSp

April. Remy [or Remi] Belleau. AWP, tr. by Andrew Lang

April. Vidame de Chartres. AWP, tr. by Algernon Charles Swinburne

April. Cornelius Eady. ESEAA

April. Amy Lowell. PoBW

April. Henrietta Cordelia Ray. CBWP-3

April. Charles Reznikoff. APT-2

April. Folgore da San Geminiano [or Gimignano]. EaItPo, tr. by Dante
  Gabriel Rossetti Fr. Sonnets of the Months.

April. Angela Shaw. NeAmPo

April. Samuel Thompson. BIrV

April. Jean Valentine. TAP

April. Charles Wright. GeoHom
April 5, 1974. Richard Wilbur. HCAP
April 5th. Vera Gherarducci. CItWP, *tr.* by Cinzia Sartini Blum and Lara Trubowitz
April 30, 1975. John Balaban. CDa
April, 1885. Robert Bridges. OxBSP; OxBTC
April again, and it is a year again. Elegy. Sidney Keyes. NoP-4
April, and a fool's good day. April Notebook. Christian Karlson Stead. PeNZ
April, and the last of the plum blossoms. Sleepless Night, A. Philip Levine. BLT
April, April, / Laugh thy girlish laughter. Song. Sir William Watson. OBEV
April. Bad month. Visit spa. Limerick. Stanley J. Sharpless. PeLi
April Fool, The. Eugene Field. PWR
April Fool Birthday Poem for Grandpa. Diane Di Prima. CLPP
April Fool's Day, or St. Mary Egypt. John Berryman. ChIV-2 *Fr.* Dream Songs.
April Fools' Day. Yusef Komunyakaa. GT
April Gale. Ivor Gurney. Spl
April Hill, The. Janet Lewis. CRP
April in Hollywood. Wanda Coleman. GeoHom
April in Houston. Dolores de Iruretagoyena de Humphrey. ReBoTo
April in Paris. Vernon Duke. ReLy
April in the Old Park. Anna Hajnal. IQMS, *tr.* by Daniel Gerard Hoffman
April in Town. Lizette Woodworth Reese. APN-2
April in Town. Yury [*or* Iurii] Ryashentsev [*or* Riashentsev]. TCRP, *tr.* by Daniel Weissbort
April Inventory. W. D. Snodgrass. CoAP; ColAP; HAP; NoAM; NoP-4; PAI; TAP; TRP; TwCP; VCAP
April is in my mistress' face. All Seasons in One. *Unknown.* HeIP-4
April Is on the Way. Alice Moore Dunbar-Nelson. NAAAL
April is the cruellest month, breeding. T. S. Eliot. APT-1; CABP; FaBoMo; HAP; MoAmPo; NAAL-2v2; NAAL-5; NAEL-5v2; NAEL-6v2; NAWM-7v2; NOBA; NOBE; NoAM; NoP-4; NPeEn; OxAEP-2; OxBA; OxBTC; PoE; TAP; TCAPo; TFi; UnPo *Fr.* Waste Land, The.
April Mortality. Léonie Adams. APT-2; MoAmPo
April, New Hampshire. Sharon Olds. BodElec
April 1962. Paul Goodman. VGW
April Notebook. Christian Karlson Stead. PeNZ
April plunges the classroom into light. Remembering the Ardèche. Emily Grosholz. RA
April, pride of woodland ways. April. Remy [*or* Remi] Belleau. AWP, *tr.* by Andrew Lang
April Rain. Robert Loveman. TrJP
  (It isn't raining for me.) ITBLP
  (Rain Song.) ITBLP
April Rain Song. Langston Hughes. NOxBChV; NTCP; OBCA; OxIBACP
April's in the air. April in Paris. Vernon Duke. ReLy
April Showers. Louis Silvers. ReLy
April sun burned through the dirty glass, The. Sorrow and Rapture. Maura Stanton. IllVoic
April this year, not otherwise. Song of a Second April. Edna St. Vincent Millay. OxBA
April Wind. Frederick Turner. RA
April winds rise, and the willow whips, The. Spring Shade. Robert Fitzgerald. APT-2
April Woman. Salma Khadra Jayyusi. MAP, *tr.* by Charles Doria and the author
April. You hearken, my fellow. Earth's Lyric. Bliss Carman. APN-2
Aprill. Edmund Spenser. NAEL-5v1; NAEL-6v1; OBEV *Fr.* Shepheardes [*or* Shepeards *or* Shepherd's] Calender, The.
Aprilly. Bert Leston Taylor. OBAL
Apron of Flowers, The. Robert Herrick. CaPo
Apron Strings. Marge Piercy. TAP
Aprons of Silence. Carl Sandburg. NOBA
Apropos of Garden Statuary: A Disquisition upon a Minor Genre. Robert Druce. OBGa
Aquarium, The. Thom Gunn. NOxBChV *Fr.* Three for Children.
Aquarium du Trocadéro. Duncan Bush. AngWePo; TCAWP
Arab and His Donkey, An. *Unknown.* NBLV
Arab came to the river side, An. Arab and His Donkey, An. *Unknown.* NBLV
Arab Chieftain to His Young Wife, An. Abid ibn al-Abras. ArPe, *tr.* by Omar S. Pound
Arab in a bloodied turban on a tall mangy camel, An. War. "Georgy [*or* Georgii] Avdeievich Rayevsky [*or.*" Raevskii]. TCRP, *tr.* by Albert C. Todd
Arab Love-Song, An. Francis Thompson. AWP; MoBrPo

Arab Traveler in a Space Ship, An. Muhammad Al-Maghut. MAP
Arab woman is wailing in the parlor, The. Eugene Paul Nasser. GraLe *Fr.* Disputation with Kahlil Gibran, A.
Arabella Stuart. Felicia Dorothea Hemans. RWP
Arabesque. Ahmed Taha. NAfrP, *tr.* by Clarissa C. Burt
Arabia. John Meade Falkner. OxBTC
Arabic. Naomi Shihab Nye. PoArWo
Arabic tapestry embroidered. Embroidered Memory. Lorene Zarou-Zouzounis. PoArWo
ArabInnocents. Joanna Kadi. PoArWo
Arachne. Rose Terry Cooke. APN-2
Arachne. William Empson. OBMV
Arachne. Judith Kazantzis. BrRo
Aragon Ballroom, The. John Dickson. IllVoic
Aranda Song. *Unknown.* CBAP, *tr.* by T. G. H. Strehlow
Ararat. Charles Tomlinson. NoP-4
Arawata Bill. Denis Glover.
  Camp Site. PeNZ
  River Crossing, The. PeNZ
  "With his weapon a shovel." PeNZ
Arbor, The. Sappho. WoPoe, *tr.* by Guy Davenport
Arbor Amoris. François Villon. AWP, *tr.* by Andrew Lang
Arbor 1937, The. Susan Stewart. ExTi
Arbor Vitae. Coventry Patmore. OxBEV; PeVV *Fr.* Unknown Eros, The.
Arbour, The. Anne Brontë. EBVV
Arbutus. Adelaide Crapsey. APT-1
Arc Inside and Out, The. A. R. Ammons. NoAM; NoP-4
Arc of the pitching arm, The. Pitching Coups. Ron Wellburn. MoASP
Arcades. John Milton.
  "O're [*or* O'er] the smooth enamel'd [*or* enameled *or* enamelled] green." OBEV; OxBSP
  Song: "Nymphs and Shepherds dance no more." OxBEV
Arcadia. Sir Philip Sidney.
  (Bargain, The.) NOBE; OBEV; OxAEP-1
  Delight of Solitariness, The. NoSic
  (Ditty, A.) AWP; GTBS-P
  Epithalamium: "Let mother Earth." OxAEP-1, *tr.* by Robert Hass
  Fortune, Nature, Love. PoE
  Hark, plaintful ghosts! Infernal furies, hark.
    Like Those Sick Folks. OxBSP
  Madrigal: "Why dost thou haste away." NoSic
  My Muse what ails this ardour.
  My Sheep Are Thoughts. NoSic
  "My true love hath my heart [*or* hart], and I have his." BoLoP; NPeEn; NoSic; OxBEV; PoE; SCGP; TFi; UV
  "Since wailing is a bud of causeful sorrow." MakPoe
  (Solitariness.) SCGP
  What Length of Verse? NoP-4; PoE
  Ye Goat-herd Gods. HAP; NAEL-5v1; NAEL-6v1; NOBE; NoSic
  ("Yee Gote-heard Gods, that love the grassie mountaines.") NPeEn; OxBEV; PBRV
  "Ye [*or* you] goat-herd gods, that love the grassy mountains." HAP; NAEL-5v1; NAEL-6v1; NOBE; NoSic
  (Ye Goatherd Gods.) NoP-4
Arcanum One. Gwendolyn MacEwen. MoCV
Arch, The. Herman Melville. NCAP
Arch inverted: white peony. Absence, Luminescent. Valerie Martínez. TouFir
Archaeological Find. Willem M. Roggeman. TuT, *tr.* by Gabriel Rosenstock
Archaeological Picnic, The. Sir John Betjeman. EnLoPo
Archæologist, The. James Simmons. PBCIP
Archaeologist recently, An. Archaeological Find. Willem M. Roggeman. TuT, *tr.* by Gabriel Rosenstock
Archaeology of Divorce, The. Patricia Storace. FFC
Archaeology of Love, The. Richard Murphy. EnLoPo
Archaic Song of Dr. Tom the Shaman. *Unknown.* STP, *tr.* by Jerome Rothenberg
Archaic Torso of Apollo. Rainer Maria Rilke. WoPoe, *tr.* by Edward Snow
Archaic Torso of Apollo. Rainer Maria Rilke. NAWM-7v2; RaBo, *tr.* by Stephen Mitchell
Archaic Torsos. David Shapiro. BodElec
Archangel. Ai. SeSe
Archangel bears down from his pinnacle, The. Pearls. Janet Fisher. MFPA
Archbishop is away, The. The church is gray. Gray Stones and Gray Pigeons. Wallace Stevens. SAmP
Archeology. Lorna Dee Cervantes. TouFir
Archer with time, The. Evening. Ronald Stuart Thomas. HarvBoo

Archetypal Chillies. John Kinsella. NeBl

Archeus Terrae. John Peck. HarvBoo

Archibald Higbie. Edgar Lee Masters. APT-1 *Fr.* Spoon River Anthology.

Archibald MacLeish Suspends the Five Little Pigs. Louis Untermeyer. MoAmPo *Fr.* Mother Goose Up-to-Date.

Archie o [*or* of] Cawfield. *Unknown.* ESPB; OxBS

Archimedes, the early truth-seeker. Limerick. Stanley J. Sharpless. PeLi

Archinos, this retsina bottle contains. Rhianus. GrAn

Archipelago, The. John Ashbery. BodElec

Archipelago, The. Herman Melville. APN-2

Architect. Adrienne Rich. BAP-01

Architect Monk, The. Laurence Lieberman. BodElec

Architecture is when the sun shines on a facade daily. Frank Kuppner. NePenScot *Fr.* Old Guidebook to Prague, An.

Archive Film Material. Ruth Fainlight. HP

Archive of Confessions, a Genealogy of Confessions, An. Joshua Clover. NeAmPo

Archives. Michael S. Harper. MoASP

Archivist in us shudders at such cold, The. Love-Letter-Burning. Daniel Hall. NoP-4

Archpoet's Confession, The. *Unknown.* WoPoe, *tr. by* Phillip Holland

Archy and Mehitabel. Don Marquis.
  Archy at the Zoo. NBLV; OBAL
  Archy Confesses. APT-1
  Archy Interviews a Pharoah. OBCoV
  Song of Mehitabel, The. APT-1; OBCoV

Arctic Convoy. James King Annand. OxBS

Arctic honey blabbed over the report causing darkness, The. Leaving the Atocha Station. John Ashbery. PmAP

"Arcturus" is his other name. Emily Dickinson. NOBA

Arcturus, the bear driver. Night Sky. Louise Erdrich. HATNAP

Ardan Mór. Francis Ledwidge. AWP

Ardelia to Flavia, an Epistle. Charlotte Lennox. PoBW

Arden is not Eden, but Eden's rhyme. In Arden. Charles Tomlinson. OxBC

Ardent in love and cold in charity. Man's [a] Sliding Mood, A. Mary Elizabeth Fullerton. CBAP; NOBAu

Ardent lover cannot find, The. Address to Her Husband. Mehetabel Wright. ECWP

Are a firm and lacquered black. (LL) 11 rue Daguerre. John Montague. ModIr; NPeEn

Are added unto them that have plenty of water. (LL) Green, Green Is El Aghir. Norman Cameron. NPeEn; NePenScot; OBWP; OxBTC

Are all such off'rings, as are crusht, and bruis'd. Francis Quarles. FaBoEE

Are *all* the dragons fled? Concerning Dragons. H. D. C. Pepler. NOxBChV

Are all with thee,—are all with thee! (LL) Henry Wadsworth Longfellow. NAAL-2v1; NAAL-3 *Fr.* Building of the Ship, The.

Are always at home. (LL) Baby-Sermon, A. George Macdonald. NOxBChV; Spl

Are ashes under Uricon. (LL) On Wenlock Edge. A. E. Housman. GTBS-P; HarvBoo; MoBrPo; NAEL-5v2; NAEL-6v2; NOBE; NoP-4; OxAEP-2; OxBTC; PoRA; RB; SCGP; TFi

Are blue. The top of the sky / is too. (LL) Vaquero. Edward Dorn. NeAP; PoM

Are blurred into one face: a child's set face. (LL) Hunt in the Black Forest, A. Randall Jarrell. CoAP; LCAP-2

Are born of like / elements. (LL) Ring of, The. Charles Olson. NOBA; VGW

Are by the sunbeams tickled by degrees. (LL) Coming of Good Luck, The. Robert Herrick. FaBoEE; NPeEn; OxBEV; OxBSP; Spl

Are casually sitting down to eat. (LL) Divine Love. Michael Benedikt. CoAP; CoAmPo

Are cat and dog, and rogue and whore. (LL) Phyllis [*or* Phillis] [*or* Progress of Love, The]. Jonathan Swift. EBNV; OBCoV; OBSV; PoE

Are dark windows? (LL) World Outside, The. Denise Levertov. CoAmPo; TRP

Are etched deep within. Archetypal Chillies. John Kinsella. NeBl

Are ever different. (LL) Ode to Language. Robert Kelly. PFTM-2; SeSe

Are frosted like a wedding-cake. (LL) Winter Time [*or* Winter-Time]. Robert Louis Stevenson. EBVV; MoBrPo

Are high-propped on a pillow of blue cloud. (LL) To Tan-Ch'iu. Li Po. AWP; ChiP, *tr. by* Arthur Waley

Are his company. (LL) Ballad of John Cable and Three Gentlemen. W. S. Merwin. CoAP; MakPoe; NOBA; YaYoPo

Are Holy-Land! (LL) To Helen. Edgar Allan Poe. APN-1; AWP; BRP; BoLoP; ClHu; ColAP; HAP; HeIP-4; NAAL-2v1; NAAL-3; NAAL-5; NIP-4; NOBA; NOBE; NoP-4; OBEV; OxBA; PoE; PoPoPo; PoRA; TAP; TCAPo; TFi; WeW-3

Are hot as any hottentot and not the goods for me! (LL) Dame Edith Sitwell. FaBoMo; GTBS-P *Fr.* Façade.

Are ligneous, muscular, chemical. Lives of the Heart, The. Jane Hirshfield. ExTi

Are melodiously mingled in my warm New England breast. (LL) Longfellow's Visit to Venice. Sir John Betjeman. NOBL; OBCoV

Are naked as a line of poetry in a war. (LL) Song of the Borderguard, The. Robert Duncan. NeAP; PoM

Are not more far apart. (LL) We Never Said Farewell. Mary Elizabeth Coleridge. OxBSP; WPE

Are of bones. Pause of Joe, The. Imamu Amiri Baraka. FTOS

Are of the dying on the dead. (LL) Walter Savage Landor. FaBoEE; NPeEn

Are on your face. (LL) Troop Ship, The. Isaac Rosenberg. OxBEV; PoWW

ARE quiet unquiet between cap and nose. Murderers, The. Paul Van Ostaijen. PFTM-1

Are shaken with earth's old and weary cry. (LL) Sorrow of Love, The. W. B. Yeats. MoBrPo; NOBVV; NPeEn; NoAM; OxBEV

Are sisters under their skins! (LL) Ladies, The. Rudyard Kipling. FaBoWar; MoBrPo; NAEL-5v2; NAEL-6v2

Are so needy. (LL) Return, The. Rosario Castellanos. TANSG; TCLAP, *tr. by* Magda Bogin

Are sorrows hard to bear,—the ruin. Burdens. Edward Dowden. NOBVV

Are still allow'd to fiddle with the case. (LL) Elinda's [*or* Ellinda's] Glove. Richard Lovelace. CaPo; NOSC

Are such things done on Albion's shore? (LL) William Blake. FHYEP; PeECV *Fr.* Songs of Experience.

Are sweet like wanton loves because I hate. (LL) White City, The. Claude McKay. APT-1; BPo; NoAM; RaBo; TAP

Are taking me. (LL) Kenneth Rexroth. APSN; APT-2 *Fr.* Love Poems of Marichiko, The.

Are the cliffs of your dream the colour of dawn? Buried Birds, The. Ida G. M. Gerhardt. TuT, *tr. by* Medbh McGuckian

Are the dark seeds, and they end. (LL) It Is This Way with Men. C. K. Williams. RaBo; VCAP

Are the desolate, dark weeks. These. William Carlos Williams. APT-1; MoAmPo; NOBA; OxBA

Are the horns of the hall on fire? Battle of Finnsburg, The. *Unknown.* AnOE, *tr. by* Charles W. Kennedy

Are the natural prey of the incarnate Christ. (LL) Letter to John Donne, A. Charles Hubert Sisson. HarvBoo; NOCV

Are the sure signs of a fine day. (LL) *Unknown.* FaBoVe; OxNR

Are there not twelve whole hours in every day. Day of Denial, The. Jones Very. NOBA

Are there / Short-cuts in the sky. Den Sute-Jo, Lady. ZenPo, *tr. by* Takashi Ikemoto and Lucien Stryk

Are these ashes in my hand. "H. D." APT-1 *Fr.* Sigil.

Are they blind, the lords of Gaza. Angry Samson. Robert Graves. ChIV-1

Are they clinging to their crosses. Antichrist, or the Reunion of Christendom; an Ode. Gilbert Keith Chesterton. NOBE; NOBL; OBSV; OxAEP-2

Are They Dancing. Edward Dorn. NeAP; PoM

Are they exiles here from the rest of the world? What Do the Birds Think? Alfred Wellington Purdy. MoCV

Are They Not All Ministering Spirits? Robert Stephen Hawker. OxAEP-2

Are They Shadows [That We See]? Samuel Daniel. NOSC *Fr.* Tethy's Festival.

Are they there in the daytime. Marfa Lights, The. W. S. Merwin. BodElec

Are those fingers, the ones playing Bach just now. Porno-Bach. Shuntaro Tanikawa. PoetW, *tr. by* Harold Wright

Are those two stars, her eyes, my life's light gone. Giles Fletcher, the Elder. Son *Fr.* Licia.

Are too long, too many; and not enough. (LL) Elegy for David Beynon. Leslie Norris. AngWePo; TCAWP

Are we not still young and easy / Don't shout. (LL) Underwear. Lawrence Ferlinghetti. EmeKit; OBAL

Are We Not the People. Al-Samau'al ibn Adiya.
  "Now listen to boasting which leaves the heart dazed." TrJP

Are We the Same. Charmaine Papertalk-Green. IBA

Are we to keep Christ writhing on the cross! (LL) Calvary. Edwin Arlington Robinson. GI; MoAmPo; Son

Are you a glass of milk, rich and cold? Song for the Moon. Nazik Al-Mala'ika. BBASP; MAP, *tr. by* Christopher Middleton and Matthew Sorenson

Are you a trailor, or are you a trolley? Are You You? Edmund Vance Cooke. PWR

Are you alive? Pool, The. "H. D." APT-1; HarvBoo

Are you an ethnic poet? After the Dance. Reuben Jackson. GT

"Are you awake, Gemelli." Star-Talk. Robert Graves. MoBrPo; OxBTC

Are you bound for Boulder? the lady asked. If a Fish Fell in a Forest. John Nelson. GeoH

Are you dead, Pyrrho? Epitaph in Dialogue on the Sceptic Philosopher Pyrrho. Julianus of Egypt. GrAn, *tr. by* Lee T. Pearcy

Are you grown up now, John, now that it's over? John and Anne. William Meredith. BodElec

Are you, happy man, grandson of Kronos. Korinna [or Corinna]. SaLy, tr. by Diane Rayor

Are You Havin' Any Fun? Sammy Fain. ReLy

Are you healed or do you only think you're healed? Mutable Earth. Louise Glück. BodElec

Are You Lonesome Tonight? Lou Handman. ReLy

Are you looking for me? Mathenge. Marjorie Oludhe Macgoye. HBAPE

Are you looking for me? I am in the next seat! Robert Bly. WoPoe Fr. Two Translations from Kabir.

Are you looking for us? We are here. 151st Psalm, The. Karl Shapiro. TaR

Are You Makin' Any Money? Herman Hupfeld. ReLy

Are you out, woman of the lean pelt. Ire. Ronald Stuart Thomas. OxBSP

Are you ready? soul said again. Two Trinities. Kenneth Mackenzie. CBAP

Are you self of my self. Alice Fulton. AllShUp Fr. Wonder Stings Me More than the Bee.

Are you sleeping endlessly? You never did before, Korinna. Korinna [or Corinna]. SaLy, tr. by Diane Rayor

Are you still living, my darling? Letter to My Mother. Sergey [or Sergei] Aleksandrovich Yesenin [or Essenin]. RusPo, tr. by Robert Arthur Douglas Ford

Are you still longing. Yosano Akiko. ErotSp, tr. by Sam Hamill

Are You the New Person Drawn toward Me? Walt Whitman. APN-1; OxBSP

Are you the sole owner of a seedy night club? Club Midnight. Charles Simic. BodElec

"Are You There?" Strickland W. Gillilan. PoToHe

Are you very weary? Rest a little bit. Rest. Unknown. PoToHe

Are you washed in the blood of the Lamb? (LL) General William Booth Enters into Heaven. Nicholas Vachel Lindsay. APT-1; ChIV-2; ColAP; MoAmPo; NOBA; OxBA; PoE; TAP; TCAPo

Are you You or Me or It? Hello Up There. Marge Piercy. NBLV

Are You You? Edmund Vance Cooke. PWR

Are you? (LL) "Forever." Charles Stuart Calverley. NOBL; NOBVV

Are your rocks shelter for ships. Shrine, The. "H. D." ColAP

Are your sorrows hard to bear? Length of Life, The. Amos Russel Wells. PWR

Aren't lightning flashes the same shape in other countries too? 1914. Max Jacob. PFTM-1

Ares. Albert Ehrenstein. TrJP, tr. by Babette Deutsch and Avrahm Yarmolinsky

Ares at last has quit the field. Under Which Lyre, a Reactionary Tract for the Times. W. H. Auden. MoBrPo; NOBL; PeLV

Arethusa Saved. Ovid. WoPoe, tr. by Thom Gunn Fr. Metamorphoses.

Areyto. Víctor Hernández Cruz. PmAP

Argalus and Parthenia. Francis Quarles.

Hos Ego Versiculos. NOSC

"Like to the damaske rose you see." NOSC

Argenteuil County. Peter Dale Scott. MoCV

Argentina in one swing of the bell skirt. Beautiful Train, The. William Empson. OxAEP-2

Argentine gaucho named Bruno, An. Limerick. Unknown. NOBL

Argoed. T. Gwynn Jones. OBWVE, tr. by Anthony Conran

Argonautica. George Seferis. PoetW, tr. by Rex Warner

Argonautica, The. Apollonius Rhodius. HePo, tr. by Barbara Hughes Fowler

Argonautica, The. Gaius Valerius Flaccus.

Book 7. RomPo, tr. by Kenneth McLeish and Frederic Raphael

"Dust takes you from the stranger's company." RomPo, tr. by Kenneth McLeish and Frederic Raphael

Argonauts, The. D. H. Lawrence. NoAM

Argos. Homer. ModIr, tr. by Michael Longley Fr. Odyssey.

Arguing liberation theology. My Dada. Judith Kazantzis. Prnts

Argument. René Char. AF

Argument. Jonathan Galassi. KGB

Argument, An. Thomas Moore. BoLoP; EnLoPo; OxBSP

Argument, The. All Religions Are One. William Blake. NAEL-6v2

Argument, The. Samuel Butler (1612–80). BASC; EBEV; NAEL-5v1; NAEL-6v1; NAEL-7v1 Fr. Hudibras.

Argument, The. Christiane Jacox Kyle. YaYoPo

Argument, The. Sir Thomas Wyatt. SacPr

Argument ended. Hal Roth. HA

Argument. Man has no notion of moral fitness but from Education, The. There Is No Natural Religion. William Blake. NAEL-6v2

Argument of His Book, The. Robert Herrick. AWP; BASC; BeJo; CaPo; CavPo; EBEV; HAP; NAEL-5v1; NAEL-6v1; NAEL-7v1; NOSC; NPeEn; NoP-4; OxAEP-1; PeECV; PoE; PoPoPo; PoRA; SacPr; TFi; TTTS; WoPoe

Argument of the Third Booke, The. Lucy Hutchinson. EMWP

Argument: On 1942, An. David Mura. LoL; PoPoPo

Arguments. Lisa Suhair Majaj. PoArWo

Aria. Irène Hamoir. SurWo, tr. by Myrna Bell Rochester

Aria 1. Ingeborg Bachmann. See In the Storm of Roses

Aria Senza da Capo. Robert Finch. MoCV

Ariadne Lay, Theseus' Ship Sailing Away. Propertius. WoPoe, tr. by Vincent Katz

Arid fields / The only life. Kagami Shiko. ZenPo, tr. by Takashi Ikemoto and Lucien Stryk

Arid Husband, The. E. L. T. Mesens. SPE

Arid that country and high, anger of sun on the mountains, but. Rattlesnake Country. Robert Penn Warren. NAAL-2v2; VCAP

Aridity. "Michael Field." OBMV

Aridness of Air, The. Silvio Giussani. ItPo, tr. by Gayle Ridinger

Ariel. David Campbell. CBAP

Ariel. Sylvia Plath. HCAP; HeIP-4; LCAP-2; NAAL-2v2; NALW; NOBA; NoAM; NoP-4; PoE; VCAP

Ariel's Song: "Come unto these yellow sands." William Shakespeare. CTC; FaBoCh; NOBE; NOSC; NPeEn; NoSic; OBEV; SCGP; SoSe-8; TFi; TTTS Fr. Tempest, The.

Ariel's Song: "Where the bee sucks, there suck I." William Shakespeare. See Tempest, The

Ariel Singing. Timothy Liu. NeAmPo

Ariel to Miranda:—Take. With a Guitar, to Jane. Shelley. FHYEP

Ariel was glad he had written his poems. Planet on the Table, The. Wallace Stevens. APT-1; HAP; HCAP; PoPoPo; SAmP

Arioso Dolente. Anne Stevenson. Prnts

Ariosto. Osip Emilevich Mandelstam [or Mandelshtam]. OBVE

Ariosto's Orlando Furioso Book 34. Sir John Harington [or Harrington]. "Thus all that day, they spent in divers talke." PBRV

Arise and go now to the city of slaughter. City of Slaughter, The. Hayyim Nahman [or Khayim Nakhman or Chaim Nachman] Bialik. TrJP, tr. by A. M. Klein

Arise and See the Glorious Sun. Francis Hopkinson. AH

Arise, arise! (LL) William Shakespeare. AWP; FaBoCh; ITBLP; NIL-7; NIP-4; NoSic; TFi; UV Fr. Cymbeline.

Arise, arise, / Dull fancy, from the bed of earth. My Carol. Mildmay Fane, 2d Earl of Westmorland. BeJo

Arise earelie. Katherine Dowe. EMWP

Arise faint Muse bring one heart-melting verse. Elegie on the Deploreable Departure of the Honored and Truely Religious Chieftain John Hull, An. John Saffin. SCAP

Arise my body, my small body, we have striven. After Prayers, Lie Cold. Clive Staples Lewis. SacPr

Arise, my soul, arise, Shake off thy guilty fears. Charles Wesley. SacPr

Arise, my soul, on wings enraptured [or enraptur'd], rise. Thoughts on the Works of Providence. Phillis Wheatley. InvLi; NAAL-2v1; NAAL-3; NAAL-5

Arise, My Soul! With Rapture Rise! Samuel J. Smith. AH

Arise, O Glorious Zion. William G. Mills. AH

Arise!—the Sea-god's groaning shell. Rebellion of the Waters, The. George Darley. NOBRP

"Arise! thrust in Thy sickle." (LL) Corruption. Henry Vaughan. ESCV; GeHe; NAEL-5v1; NAEL-6v1; NAEL-7v1; NOCV; NOSC

Arise to the Day's Toil. Assumpta Acam-Oturu. HAWP

Arise up on thy feet, O Quiet Heart! Unknown. AWP Fr. Book of the Dead.

Arise ye daughters of a land. Women's Marseillaise, The. F. E. M. Macaulay. BrRo

Arise, Ye Saints of Latter Days. Unknown. AH

Aristeides. Antipater of Sidon. AWP, tr. by Charles Whibley

Aristocrat, The. Gilbert Keith Chesterton. OBCoV

Aristocrateia, / You've crossed the dark stream. Mnasalcas. GrAn

Aristocrats. Keith Douglas. FaBoMo; FaBoWar; NAEL-5v2; NAEL-6v2; NoAM; NoP-4; OBWP

(Sportsmen.) OxBEV

Aristomache loved a drink: / The old chatterbox was fonder. Argentarius. GrAn

Aristomenes. Byron. NPeEn

Aristophanes. Plato. GrAn, tr. by Peter Jay

Aristotle's Story. Mother Goose. OxNR; ReMoGo

Aristotle said. Greek History. Olga Nolla. TANSG, tr. by Paula Vega

Aristotle was a little man with / eyes like a lizard. Humanities Lecture. William Stafford. NNaP; NoAM

Arithmetic. Unknown. ReMoGo

Arithmetic of the Lips. Unknown. EroLit

Arithmetic on the Frontier. Rudyard Kipling. OBWP

Arithmetical Progression of the Verb "To Be." Walter Conrad Arensberg. APT-1

Arithmetique [or Arithmetic] nine digits, and no more. Upon the Loss[e] of His Little Finger. Thomas Randolph. BeJo; NOSC

Arizona Highways. James Welch. CDW; NoAM
Arizona Midnight. Robert Penn Warren. AmFaPo
Arizona Nature Myth. James Michie. FaBoA; NOBL
Arizona Nocturne. Carlos Reyes. UrbNat
Arjuna, his war flag a rampant monkey. *Unknown.* WoPoe, *tr. by* Barbara Stoler Miller *Fr.* Bhagavad-Gita, The.
Arjuna sat dejected. *Unknown.* WoPoe, *tr. by* Barbara Stoler Miller *Fr.* Bhagavad-Gita, The.
Ark. Gu Cheng. VCWP
Ark. Ronald Johnson.
Ark 34, Spire on the Death of L. Z. FTOS
Ark 37, Prospero's Songs to Ariel (constructed in the form of a quilt snipped from Roger Tory Peterson's *A Field Guide to Western Birds*). APSN
Ark 44, The Rod of Aaron. FTOS
Beam 4. APSN
Beam 7. APSN
Beam 25, A Bicentennial Hymn. APSN
Beam 30, The Garden. FTOS
"Prosper / O / cell." APSN
"Sound is sea: pattern lapping pattern. If we erase the air and slow the." APSN
"To do as Adam did." FTOS
Ark, The. Jay Macpherson.
Ark Anatomical. NOBC
Ark Apprehensive. NOBC
Ark Artefact. NOBC
Ark Articulate. NOBC
Ark Astonished. NOBC
Ark Overwhelmed. NOBC
Ark Parting. NOBC
Ark to Noah. NOBC
Ark 34, Spire on the Death of L. Z. Ronald Johnson. FTOS *Fr.* Ark.
Ark 37, Prospero's Songs to Ariel (constructed in the form of a quilt snipped from Roger Tory Peterson's *A Field Guide to Western Birds*). Ronald Johnson. APSN *Fr.* Ark.
Ark 44, The Rod of Aaron. Ronald Johnson. FTOS *Fr.* Ark.
Ark Anatomical. Jay Macpherson. NOBC *Fr.* Ark, The.
Ark Apprehensive. Jay Macpherson. NOBC *Fr.* Ark, The.
Ark Artefact. Jay Macpherson. NOBC *Fr.* Ark, The.
Ark Articulate. Jay Macpherson. NOBC *Fr.* Ark, The.
Ark Astonished. Jay Macpherson. NOBC *Fr.* Ark, The.
Ark for Lawrence Durrell, An. Robert Duncan. RaBo
Ark Overwhelmed. Jay Macpherson. NOBC *Fr.* Ark, The.
Ark Parting. Jay Macpherson. NOBC *Fr.* Ark, The.
Ark to Noah. Jay Macpherson. NOBC *Fr.* Ark, The.
Arkansas Testament, The. Derek Walcott. CBCWP
Arkestra glitters in their Saturn gowns, The. After the End of the World. David Jauss. SeSe
Arkheanassa. Asclepiades. GrAn, *tr. by* Peter Jay
Arm around the plexi with your head to the side. Zoo, The. Jordan Davis. HeMarv
Arm for a pillow, my happiness overflows. (LL) White Crane Hill. Su Tung-p'o (Su Shih). CoBCP; ColAnChi; GifTon, *tr. by* Burton Watson
Arm of bronze outstretched against all evil!, The. (LL) Dance of the Macabre Mice. Wallace Stevens. NOBA; OxBA; PFTM-1
Arm thee with thunder, heavenly muse. Law Given at Sinai, The. Isaac Watts. ChIV-1
Armada, The. Thomas Babington Macaulay, 1st Baron Macaulay. FaBoCh
"Night sank upon the dusky beach, and on the purple sea." PeVV
Armada of Thirty Whales, An. Daniel Gerard Hoffman. YaYoPo
Armadillo, The. Elizabeth Bishop. APT-2; ColAP; HCAP; NAAL-2v2; NAAL-5; NIL-7; NOBA; NoAM; NoP-4; TAP; VCAP; VGW
Armadillo Charm. Carlos Cumpian. IllVoic
Armadillos are flattened on roads every week. Armadillo Charm. Carlos Cumpian. IllVoic
Armageddon. John Crowe Ransom. ChIV-2
Armageddon. István Vas. IQMS, *tr. by* William Jay Smith
Armageddon in Albyn. Sydney Goodsir Smith.
War in Fife, The. NePenScot
Arme, Arme, Arme, Arme, great Neptune rowze, awake. John Smith of His Friend Master John Taylor. John Smith. SCAP
Armed Forces. Lucy Lakides. CDa
Armed Forces Day. Steve Hassett. CDa
Armed with his crutches, the thief, wolf-like. Outsider, The. Syl Cheney-Coker. HBAPE
Armenian Language Is the Home of the Armenian, The. Moushegh Ishkhan. BLT; WoPoe, *tr. by* Diana Der Hovanessian

Armenonville. Edna St. Vincent Millay. NoP-4
Armful, The. Robert Frost. OxBSP
Armgart. "George Eliot."
"Armgart, to many minds the first success." VWP
Armies and lemmings do not go. New from Ethiopia and the Sudan, The. John Pepper Clark Bekedermo. HBAPE
Armies in the Fire. Robert Louis Stevenson. EBVV
armillaria mellea. Tony Baker. Oth
Arminius. Daniel Casper von Lohenstein.
"Here lies the noble flesh of Spartacus the knave." GePo
"Light-spring, oh sun, in light our wedding joys immure." GePo
Sonnet: "Here lies the noble flesh of Spartacus the knave.". GePo
Sonnet: "Light-spring, oh sun, in light our wedding joys immure.". GePo
Sonnet: "Wisest of all men lies buried on this spot, The.". GePo
"Wisest of all men lies buried on this spot, The." GePo
Armistice. Paul Dehn. OxBTC
Armistice Day. Charles Causley. NAEL-5v2; NAEL-6v2; NoP-4; OBWP
Armistice Day '77, Honiton. John Tripp. TCAWP
Armitage Street. David Hernandez. UnSA
Armless Artist, The. Cornelius Whur.
"Alas! Alas! the father said." VerBaPo
Armor. James Dickey. CoAP
Armor, dogs and horses. Sea Breeze. Mitch Highfill. HeMarv
Armor of the Petrograd oak is rusty, but, The. Yury [*or* Iurii] Mikhailovich Kublanovsky [*or* Kublanovskii]. TCRusP *Fr.* In Petrograd.
Armored for battle. (LL) Sappho. NAWM-7v1; WPOW, *tr. by* Richmond Lattimore
Armored in oxygen. Astronauts. Robert Earl Hayden. ESEAA
Armorial. Ralph Gustafson. MoCV
Armour. Aldous Leonard Huxley. OxBSo
Armour has foregathered, snuffling. Opening of an Offensive. Hamish Henderson. FaBoWar
Arms and the Boy. Wilfred Owen. HAP; MoBrPo; OxBEV; OxBSP; PoE; WeW-3
Arms and the girl I sing—O rare. Fearful Women. Carolyn Kizer. ExTi
Arms and the Man. Samuel Butler (1612–80). NOSC *Fr.* Hudibras.
Arms, and the Man I sing, who, forc'd by Fate. Virgil [*or* Vergil]. FaBoWar; OBVE; OxBEV; WoPoe, *tr. by* John Dryden *Fr.* Aeneid [*or* Eneados, *Aeneis*], The.
Arms and the Woman. Dorothy Livesay. PoBW
Arms and the Woman. Dorothea MacKellar. NOBAu
Arms at my side like some inadequate sign. Mountain Town—Mexico. Eldon Grier. NOBC
Arms folded. Jack Kerouac. HA
Arms reversed and banners craped. Dirge for McPherson, A. Herman Melville. CBCWP
Army. Ciaran Carson. BiHa; PBCIP
Army Ballad. Wang Wei. ColAnChi, *tr. by* Stephen Owen
Army Beach with Trumpets. Jack Spicer. APSN
Army Corps on the March, An. Walt Whitman. AiP; CBCWP
Army Dance, The. *Unknown.* FaBoWar
Army horses, gangs and droves. Meeting the Herdsmen. Mei Yao Ch'en. SuSp, *tr. by* Jonathan Chaves
Army, Navy. *Unknown.* OxNR
Army of Occupation. Sarah Morgan Bryan Piatt. NCAP
Army of unalterable law, The. (LL) Cousin Nancy. T. S. Eliot. OBAL; OxBSP
Army of unalterable law, The. (LL) Lucifer in Starlight. George Meredith. AWP; CABP; ChIV-1; EBVV; GSo; HAP; InPK-6; NAEL-5v2; NAEL-6v2; NOBE; NOBVV; NoP-4; OBEV; OxBEV; OxBSo; PoE; SCGP; Son; TFi; UnPo
Army returned home wet with sunlight, The. One Night Away from Day. John Digby. SPE
Arnolfinis both sat to Van Eyck. Limerick. Sir Robert Witt. PeLi
Aroma of fresh bread, The. Thing or Two about Childhood, A. Yury Iofe. TCRusP, *tr. by* John Glad
Around, around the sun we go. Mother Goose's Garland. Archibald MacLeish. OBAL
Around Costessey. Francis Webb.
Art. BMAP
Around existence twine. Basho. TAL
Around five in the next garden, a rooster. Likelihood of Snow, The/ The Danger of Fire. Gerald Dawe. PNI
Around flowers. Fear of the Future. Gillian Ferguson. NeBl
Around her leg she wore a purple garter. Far Away. *Unknown.* FaBoWar
Around her shrine no earthly blossoms blow. La Madonna dell' Acqua. John Ruskin. NOBVV

Around me roar and crash the pagan isms. Pagan Isms, The. Claude McKay. BPo

Around me the images of thirty years. Municipal Gallery Revisited, The. W. B. Yeats. GTBS-P; OxBTC

Around my garden the little wall is low. Losing a Slave-Girl. Po Chü-i. AWP, tr. by Arthur Waley

Around my porch and lowly casement spread. Written at a Farm. John Codrington Bampfylde. CenSon

Around My Room. William Jay Smith. TLR

Around stones called precious. Black Meat. Jean Follain. BLT

Around the battlements go by. War on the Periphery. George Johnston. NOBC

Around the Campfire. Andrew Hudgins. CBCWP

Around the cold pool in the metal light. Hotel Normandie Pool, The. Derek Walcott. VCWP

Around the Corner. Charles Hanson Towne. PoToHe

Around the Corner from Francis Bacon. Paul Durcan. BiHa; ModIr

Around the corner I have a friend. Around the Corner. Charles Hanson Towne. PoToHe

Around the dried-up bay the road. Irish Sheep, The. Job Degenaar. TuT, tr. by Aidan Sharkey

Around the fireplace, pointing at the fire. On Falling Asleep by Firelight. William Meredith. ChIV-1; NoAM

Around the gleaming map of Europe. Autobahnmotorwayautoroute. Adrian Mitchell. RB

Around the Green Gravel. Unknown. ReMoGo

Around the house stood an. Grandmothers Land. William Oandasan. HATNAP

Around the house the flakes fly faster. Birds at Winter Nightfall. Thomas Hardy. MoBrPo

Around the quays, kicked off in twos. Fishing Boats in Martigues. Roy Campbell. FaBoEE; OxBSP

Around the rick, around the rick. Unknown. OxNR

Around the small house. Buson. EH, tr. by Robert Hass

Around the temple, pines and cedars. Wen Cheng-ming. CoBLCP Fr. Chung-i Temple, The.

Around This Body of Mine. Amelia Rosselli. CItWP, tr. by Cinzia Sartini Blum and Lara Trubowitz

Around this rod my writhing self might twist. Anna Hempstead Branch. APT-1 Fr. Sonnets from a Lock Box.

Around were all the roses red. Spleen. Paul Verlaine. AWP, tr. by Ernest Dowson

Arous'd and angry, I'd thought to beat the alarum, and urge relentless war. Epigraph to "Drum-Taps." Walt Whitman. PAI

Arousing the lands where dwell the five peoples. Unknown. WoPoe, tr. by Raimundo Panikkar Fr. Vedic Hymns.

Arp and the barbered arbor. Maison Aragon. Tristan Tzara. PFTM-1

Arp might have done a version in white marble. Walrus Tusk from Alaska, A. Alfred Corn. MakPoe

Arraigned by silence, I recall. Brethren, The. Seamus Deane. PNI

Arraignment of Paris, The. George Peele.
   Fair and Fair. OBEV
   (Oenone and Paris.) NOBE

Arran. Unknown. FaBoCh, tr. by Kuno Meyer

Arran. Unknown. NePenScot, tr. by Thomas Owen Clancy

Arran of the many deer. Arran. Unknown. NePenScot, tr. by Thomas Owen Clancy

Arran of the many stags. Arran. Unknown. FaBoCh, tr. by Kuno Meyer

Arrange the scene with only a shade of difference. Incident, An. Douglas Le Pan. MoCV; NoP-4

Arranged Marriage, The. Vietnamese Oral Tradition. CaDao, tr. by John Balaban

Arrangement. Glenna Luschei. GeoHom

Arrangements with Earth for Three Dead Friends. James Wright (1927–80). NIL-7; NIP-4

Arras. Patricia K. Page. MoCV

Arrest of Antoñito el Camborio. Federico García Lorca. SpanPo, tr. by Robert O'Brien

Arrest of Oscar Wilde at the Cadogan Hotel, The. Sir John Betjeman. EBEV; MoBrPo; NPeEn; NoAM; NoP-4; OxBTC

Arria to Poetus. Mary E. Tucker. CBWP-1

Arrival. Debra Kang Dean. UrbNat

Arrival. Gerald McCarthy. CDa

Arrival. John Wain. EBEV

Arrival, The. Alexander McLachlan. NOBC Fr. Emigrant, The.

Arrival at Santos. Elizabeth Bishop. FaBoWP; OxBC

Arrival at the Waldorf. Wallace Stevens. HCAP

Arrival in Hades. Edith Södergran. WoPoe, tr. by David McDuff

Arrival of the Bee Box, The. Sylvia Plath. FaBoMo; FaBoWP; HCAP; NALW; NPeEn

Arrival of the Mail. William Cowper. ECEV Fr. Task, The.

Arrivals at a Watering-Place. Winthrop Mackworth Praed. NOBL; NOBRP; NPeEn; PeLV

Arrivals, Departures. Philip Larkin. MoBrPo

Arrivants. Musaemura Bonus Zimunya. HBAPE; NAfrP

Arrivants: A New World Trilogy, The. Edward Kamau Brathwaite.
   New World a-Comin' NoP-4

Arrive. The Ladies from the Ladies' Betterment League. Lovers of the Poor, The. Gwendolyn Brooks. ESEAA; IllVoic; LCAP-2; LTA; NAAL-2v2; NOBA; NoAM

Arrived from scattered cities, several lands. Shipment to Maidanek. Ephraim G. Fogel. HP; OBWP; TrJP

Arrived now at our ship, we launched and set. Homer. NOSC, tr. by George Chapman Fr. Odyssey.

Arrived upon the downs of asphodel. Classic Encounter. "Christopher Caudwell." OxBTC

Arrives like a jinn, instantly. Resuscitation Team. U. A. Fanthorpe. FaBoWP

Arriving after Rain at the Temple of Heavenly Peace. Wang Shih-chieng. SuSp, tr. by Richard John Lynn

Arriving at Ba Gorge in the Morning. Wang Wei. WoPoe, tr. by Willis Barnstone, Tony Barnstone and Xu Haixin

Arriving at Hangchou. Yüan Mei. CoBLCP, tr. by Jonathan Chaves

Arriving at Hsün-yang. Po Chü-i. ChiP, tr. by Arthur Waley

Arriving at North Pond by Stupid Brook on a Morning Walk after the Rain. Liu Tsung-yüan. SuSp, tr. by Jan W. Walls

Arriving in Lo-yang Again. Shao Yung. CoBCP, tr. by Burton Watson

Arrogance. Walter De la Mare. OxBSP

Arrow and the Song, The. Henry Wadsworth Longfellow. BRP; ColAP; PWR; PoToHe; TCAPo; UV

Arrow Flying Past, An. Gustavo Adolfo Bécquer. SpanPo, tr. by J.M. Cohen

Arrow in the Wall. Andrey [or Andrei] Andreievich Voznesensky [or Voznesenskii]. RusPo, tr. by Robert Arthur Douglas Ford

Arrow Song. Unknown. TCAPo

Arrowhead Christian Center and No-Smoking Luncheonette. Janet Sylvester. ReTh

Arrowhead from the Ancient Battlefield of Ch'ang-p'ing, An. Li Ho. FaBoWar, tr. by A. C. Graham

Arrows of the narrow moon flock down direct, The. Communion of Saints: The Poor Bastard under the Bridge. Marie Ponsot. VGW

Arrows striking all sides of the body and St. Sebastian smiling. Consent. Carol Frost. OPRER

Arroyo, The. Brenda Hillman. ExTi

Ars. Marina Ivanovna Tsvetayeva [or Tsvetaeva]. BoWoP, tr. by Willis Barnstone and Edward Brown

Ars Poetica. Claribel Alegría. LoL; TANSG, tr. by Darwin Flakoll

Ars Poetica. Jorge Luis Borges. TCLAP, tr. by W. S. Merwin

Ars Poetica. Roque Dalton. TCLAP, tr. by Richard Schaaf

Ars Poetica. Robert Desnos. AF, tr. by Carolyn Forché

Ars Poetica. Jane Hirshfield. BodElec

Ars Poetica. Vincente Huidobro. PFTM-1; TCLAP, tr. by David Guss

Ars Poetica. Attila József. IQMS, tr. by Michael Beevor

Ars Poetica. Archibald MacLeish. APT-1; AWP; ColAP; HAP; HeIP-4; IllVoic; InPK-6; MoAmPo; NAAL-2v2; NIP-4; NOBA; OxBA; PoRA; TAP; TFi; WeW-3

Ars Poetica. Linda Pastan. NIP-4

Ars Poetica. Victor Van Vriesland. TrJP, tr. by Adriaan J. Barnouw

Ars Poetica. Sándor Weöres. IQMS, tr. by Edwin Morgan

Ars Poetica about Ultimates. Tram Combs. TwCP

Ars Victrix. Austin Dobson.
   "All passes. Art alone." CTC

Arsenic. Howard Moss. CoAP

"Arsenio" (she writes to me), "I, breathing gently here." Thrust and Riposte. Eugenio Montale. PeFWW, tr. by Gavin Ewart

Arsh Potatoes. Robert Phillips. SpudSo

Arson. Charles Harper Webb. GeoHom

Arsonist Tells His Story to the Attorney, The. Charles Rafferty. AmPoNex

Art. Susan Aizenberg. ExTi

Art. Washington Allston. APN-1

Art. Denise Duhamel. AmPoNex

Art. Ralph Waldo Emerson. APN-1

Art. Théophile Gautier. AWP, tr. by George Santayana

Art. Théophile Gautier. WoPoe, tr. by Louis Simpson

Art. Herman Melville. AmFaPo; NAAL-2v1; NAAL-3; NOBA

Art. Herman Melville. APN-2; ColAP; NCAP

Art. James Thomson.

"Singing is sweet; but be sure of this." NOBVV

Art. *Unknown.* NBLV

Art. Francis Webb. BMAP *Fr.* Around Costessey.

Art, I. Alfred Noyes. OBEV

Art, II. Alfred Noyes. OBEV

Art above Nature, to Julia. Robert Herrick. BeJo; NOSC
  (When I behold a forest spread.) CABP

Art and Extinction. Tony Harrison. HarvBoo

Art and Life. Agnes Mary Frances Robinson. OxBSo; VWP

Art for Art's Sake. Marc Blitzstein. TrJP *Fr.* Cradle Will Rock, The.

Art goes to sleep for the birth of a new world. Proclamation without
  Pretention. Tristan Tzara. NAWM-7v2, *tr. by* Mary Ann Caws

Art History (Sandro Botticelli). Alena N´dvorníková. SurWo

Art in Architecture. Regie Cabico. WiU

Art is the true and happy science of the soul. Robert Bridges. GS *Fr.*
  Testament of Beauty, Book III, The.

Art McCooey. Patrick Kavanagh. CIP-2

Art, my dears, is not cleaning up. Andy Warhol Speaks to His Two Filipino
  Maids. Alfred A. Yuson. ReBoTo

Art of a Cold Sun. G. E. Murray. IllVoic

Art of Biography, The. Edmund Clerihew Bentley. NOBL; PeLV *Fr.*
  Clerihews.

Art of Clay, The. Duane Niatum. HATNAP

Art of Cookery, The. William King.
  "Far from the parlour have your kitchen placed." ECEV

Art of Coquetry, The. Charlotte Lennox.
  "First form your artful looks with studious care." ECWP; LW

Art of Dancing, The. Soame Jenyns.
  "But let me now my lovely charge remind." ECEV
  "Dare I in such momentous points advise." ECEV
  "Let each fair maid, who fears to be disgraced." ECEV
  "Now haste, my Muse, pursue thy destined way." ECEV

Art of definition—is this, An. Ken Edwards. Oth *Fr.* Five Nocturnes, after
  Derek Jarman.

Art of Disappearing, The. Naomi Shihab Nye. LoL

Art of Getting Lost, The. Art Goodtimes. GeoH

Art of Hurricanes, The. Víctor Hernández Cruz. TouFir

Art of Interpretation, The. Julia Copus. NeBl

Art of joining, union, The. Five Notebooks for Exit Art. Cecilia Vicuña.
  PFTM-2

Art of Kissing, The. Mary Ann Samyn. AmPoNex

Art of losing isn't hard to master, The. One Art. Elizabeth Bishop. APT-2;
  AmFaPo; DiPo; HAP; HarvBoo; MakPoe; NAAL-2v2; NAAL-5; NALW;
  NoAM; NoP-4; PoE; PoPoPo; PoetW; SoSe-8; VCAP

Art of Love, The. Arnaut Daniel. NAWM-7v1, *tr. by* Frederick Goldin

Art of Love, The. Kenneth Koch.

Art of Measuring Light, The. Ellen Hinsey. AmPoNex; YaYoPo

Art of Picasso, The. Salvador Dali. SPE, *tr. by* David Gascoyne

Art of Poetry, An. James Philip McAuley. NOCV

Art of Poetry, The. Horace.
  "As woods whose change appears." OBVE
  "Should some ill Painter in a wild design." OBVE

Art of Poetry, The. Pope. ECEV *Fr.* Essay on Criticism, An.

Art of Poetry, The. Paul Verlaine. NAWM-7v2, *tr. by* Carlyle Ferren
  MacIntyre

Art of Poetry, The. Paul Verlaine. SxFrPo, *tr. by* Martin Sorrell

Art of Politics, The. James Bramston.
  Time's Changes. NOEC

Art of Preserving Health, The. John Armstrong.
  Causes of Old Age. ECEV
  Diet. VerBaPo
  Madness. NOEC
  Transience. NOEC
  Urban Pollution. ECEV; NOEC

Art of Preserving Health, The. John Armstrong.
  "But if through genuine tenderness of heart." OBGa

Art of Satire, The. Pope. ECEV; OBSV *Fr.* Epilogue to the Satires, in Two
  Dialogues.

Art of the Fugue: A Prayer, The. James Wright (1927–80). BBASP

Art of the Nickname, The. Dominique Parker. SpirFl

Art of the Snake Story, The. Amy England. BAP-01

Art of Translation, The. Adrienne Rich. BodElec

Art of War, The. Joseph Fawcett.
  Feast of Blood, The. NOEC

Art of Wenching, The. *Unknown.*
  "Be punctual then to know." NOEC

Art of Writing, The. Lu Chi.

Music of Words, The. WoPoe, *tr. by* Tony Barnstone and Chou Ping

Riding Crop, The. WoPoe, *tr. by* Tony Barnstone and Chou Ping

Satisfaction, The. WoPoe, *tr. by* Sam Hamill

Art Pepper. Edward Hirsch. SeSe

Art photographer alone, The. Quantum. Martin Johnston. CBAP

Art Poétique. Paul Verlaine. AWP, *tr. by* Arthur Symons

Art Review. Kenneth Fearing. APT-2

Art thou. To a Hermit Thrush. Adelaide Crapsey. APT-1

Art thou beguild now? tut, a Lady can. Cyril Tourneur. OxBEV *Fr.*
  Revenger's Tragedy, The.

Art Thou Gone in Haste? John Webster. OxBoLi *Fr.* Thracian Wonder, The.

Art thou lonely, O my brother? Art Thou Lonely? John Oxenham. PoToHe

Art Thou Lonely? John Oxenham. PoToHe

Art thou not hungry for thy children, Zion. To Zion. Judah Halevi. AWP, *tr.*
  by Maurice Samuel

Art thou pale for weariness. To the Moon. Shelley. GTBS-P; OxAEP-2;
  TTTS

Art thou poor, yet hast thou golden slumbers? Thomas Dekker. GTBS-P;
  HAP; NoSic; RB; SCGP; UnPo *Fr.* Pleasant Comedy of Patient Grissell
  [*or* Grissel *or* Grissill], The.

Art thou poore yet hast thou golden Slumbers. Thomas Dekker. PBRV

Art Thou That She. *Unknown.* OxBSP

Art Thou, Time, Way, and Wayfarer. (LL) "I Am the Way." Alice Thompson
  Meynell. NOBVV; OBMV; OxBSP

Art thou weary, art thou languid. Guide from St. Stephen the Sabaite, The.
  John Mason Neale. SacPr

Art was our bones. Emmett Williams. PFTM-2 *Fr.* Ultimate Poem, The.

Artemeias, surely when you from the nether world's bark. Antipater of Sidon.
  HePo *Fr.* Epigrams.

Artemidorus sold his land to buy a boy. Martial. CAGL, *tr. by* Richard
  O'Connell *Fr.* Epigrams.

Artemis. Olga Broumas. YaYoPo

Artemis. Perses. GrAn, *tr. by* Peter Whigham

Artemis in Echo Park. Eloise Klein Healy. GeoHom

Arthur. Geoffrey Adkins. FaBoWar

Arthur. Ogden Nash. NoP-4; PeLi

Arthur Murray Taught Me Dancing in a Hurry. Johnny Mercer. ReLy

Arthur O'Bower has broken his bands [*or* band]. Wind, The. *Unknown.*
  FaBoCh; OxNR

Arthur Ridgewood, M.D. Frank Marshall Davis. BPo

Arthur's Anthology of English Poetry. Laurence David Lerner. PeLV

Arthur's Dream. Layamon. NAEL-7v1 *Fr.* Brut, The.

Arthur's Fight with Orgoglio and Duessa. Edmund Spenser. EBNV *Fr.*
  Faerie Queene, The.

Arthur's Seat. Thomas Mercer.
  "Where is the gallant race that rose." OxBS

Arthur Thinks on Kennedy. Myra Cohn Livingston. HHAm

Arthur was mortally wounded, grievously badly. Layamon. NAEL-7v1 *Fr.*
  Brut, The.

Arthur wes forwunded, wunder ane swithe. Layamon. PoE *Fr.* Brut, The.

Arthur! whose path is in the quiet shade. To Arthur de Noé Walker. Walter
  Savage Landor. OxBSo

Artichokes. Georges Ribemont-Dessaignes. PFTM-1

Artifice of Absorption. Charles Bernstein.
  "By absorption I mean engrossing, engulfing." PFTM-2
  "Intersection, The." PFTM-2

Artificer. X. J. Kennedy. TwCP

Artificial Beauty. Lucianus [*or* Lucian]. AWP, *tr. by* William Cowper

Artillery [*or* Artillerie]. George Herbert. GeHe; NoP-4
  (As I one evening sat before my cell.) NoP-4

Artillery was burying us. Konstantin Levin. TCRP

Artilleryman's Vision, The. Walt Whitman. CBCWP

Artist, An. Seamus Heaney. PoetW *Fr.* Sweeney Redivivus.

Artist, An. Robinson Jeffers. HarvBoo; VGW

Artist, The. Han Yongwun. WoPoe, *tr. by* Bruce Taylor

Artist, The. *Unknown.* STP; WoPoe, *tr. by* Elvira Abascal and Denise
  Levertov

Artist, The. William Carlos Williams. LCAP-2; PAI; RB; SAmP

Artist and a Wailing Mother, An. Freddy Macha. NAfrP

Artist: disciple, abundant, multiple, restless, The. Artist, The. *Unknown.*
  STP; WoPoe, *tr. by* Elvira Abascal and Denise Levertov

Artist has to be enslaved, An. Vladimir Nikolaevich Sokolov. TCRP

Artist in our midst, An. Fool, I tell myself, why risk. Faraway Landscape.
  Richard Michelson. GotH

Artist is the creator of beautiful things, The. Oscar Wilde. NAEL-5v2 *Fr.*
  Picture of Dorian Gray, The.

Artist must leave these woods now, The. Departure, The. Reed Whittemore.
  TAP

Artist, that underneath my table. Spider, The. Edward Littleton. NOEC

Artist who lived in St. Ives, An. Limerick. A. G. Prys-Jones. PeLi

Artist who lived near Montmartre, An. Limerick. Sir John Waller. PeLi

Artists' Letters. Thomas Kinsella. BiHa

Artorius. John Heath-Stubbs. EBEV
"Raft drifted, The." PeECV

Arts Are Black, The. Charlie R. Braxton. InTrad

Arts are old, old as the stones, The. Nicholas Vachel Lindsay. APT-1 *Fr.* Mae Marsh, Motion Picture Actress.

Arturo. Maria Gillan. UnSA

Arundel Tomb, An. Philip Larkin. NoP-4; OxAEP-2

ARVN colonel smokes a cigarette, An. (LL) Assassination of Robert Goulet as Performed by Elvis Presley: Memphis, 1968, The. David Wojahn. AllShUp; IllVoic

As a bathtub lined with white porcelain. Bathtub [*or* Bath Tub], The. Ezra Pound. NIP-4; TRP; WeW-3

As a boy, I'd still have asked. Barbie Says Math is Hard. Kyoko Mori. InvLad; ReTh

As a Boy With a Richness of Needs I Wandered. Clifford Dyment. OxBTC; TCAWP

As a brave man faces the foe. At Sea. Richard Hovey. APN-2

As a carp ascends to heaven. Carp, The. Michael Stevens. CDa

As a Child. Robert Bly. InvLad

As a child before she knew. Experiments with God. Karen Gershon. HP

As a child holds a pet. Port Bou. Stephen Spender. TwCP

As a child / I bought a red scarf. Four Sheets to the Wind and a One-Way Ticket to France. Conrad Kent Rivers. BPo

As a child I came upon a grasshopper. Bulat Shalvovich Okudzhava. TCRP

As a child, I could never sleep. For Karen. Elizabeth Robinson. AmPoNex

As a child I got up. Lost Songs. Vladimir Alekseievich Soloukhin. TCRP, *tr. by* Daniel Weissbort

As a child I learned from the twisted necks. Airlift. Karen Chamberlain. GeoH

As a child I loved. Childhood. Nikolai Stepanovich Gumilyov [*or* Gumiliov *or* Gumilev]. TCRusP, *tr. by* Joseph Kiegel

As a child, I was a fussy eater. Notes for a Poem on Being Asian American. Dwight Okita. NIL-7; UnSA

As a child, I would awaken dark mornings. Cameo. Natasha Trethewey. NeAmPo

As a child (in Australia). Strange Adventure. Rossana Ombres. NeIt, *tr. by* Ruth Feldman

As a child of cedar, hemlock, and the sea. No One Remembers [Abandoning] the Village of White Fir. Duane Niatum. CDW

As a child running loose. Learning to Speak. Peter Everwine. NNaP

As a child, they could not keep me from wells. Personal Helicon. Seamus Heaney. NPeEn

As a critic the poet Buchanan. On Robert Buchanan, Who Attacked Him under the Pseudonym of "Thomas Maitland." Dante Gabriel Rossetti. FaBoEE

As a dare-gale skylark scanted in a dull cage. Caged Skylark, The. Gerard Manley Hopkins. MoBrPo; OBMV; OWoS; SoSe-8; Son

As a devout Christian, my father. Perhaps No Poem at All But All I Can Say and I Cannot Be Silent. Denise Levertov. SacPr

As a fond mother, when the day is o'er. Nature. Henry Wadsworth Longfellow. ITBLP; TAP

As a friend to the children commend me the Yak. Yak, The. Joseph Hilaire Pierre Belloc. MoBrPo; NBLV; NOBL; NoAM

As a full fruit, ripe. Grenade. Francis Scarfe. FaBoWar

As a girl she body surfed on the tidal sandbars. Swimming with Seiger. Rick Agran. AmPoNex

As a hungry fledgling, who sees and hears. Vittoria da Colonna, Marchesa di Pescara. WPOW

As a lad I never had any idea of the taste of sorrow. Tune: "Picking Mulberry Seeds" Written on a Wall en route to Po-shan. Hsin Ch'i-chi. ColAnChi, *tr. by* Jiaosheng Wang

As a landscape in the far distance. Fumi Saito. WoPoe, *tr. by* Edith Marcombe Shiffert and Yuki Sawa

As a man and woman make. White Lilies, The. Louise Glück. PoPoPo

As a man is able. (LL) Man's Requirements, A. Elizabeth Barrett Browning. RACG; ViWPN

As a man turns to face on-coming snow. (LL) Decision, The. Theodore Roethke. CRP; VGW

As a man who soon must be without. Hunger. Gaspara Stampa. WPOW, *tr. by* Brenda Webster

As a naked man I go. In Waste Places. James Stephens. MoBrPo; SCGP

As a people favoured by the Almighty. Eden Says No. Robert Johnstone. PNI

As a Plane Tree by the Water. Robert Lowell. CoAP; MoAmPo; NOBA; OxBA

As a poet put it once, an ant / may seem 'a monstrous elephant.' Lucilius. GrAn

As a prodigal daughter I have gone back to my memories. Prodigal Daughter. Angelina Muñiz Huberman. MirDau, *tr. by* Aurora Camacho

As a queen sits down, knowing that a chair will be there. Walking to Sleep. Richard Wilbur. VCAP

As a reed with the reeds in the river. (LL) Musical Instrument, A. Elizabeth Barrett Browning. CABP; EBVV; NAEL-5v2; NAEL-6v2; NPeEn; NoP-4; OBEV; PEW; PoE; PoPoPo; VWP; ViWPN; WPE

As a rule all servants dress in their masters' livery. French Dress. Friedrich von Logau. GePo, *tr. by* George C. Schoolfield

As a rule, the patients I know do not pace. Robert Pinsky. NoAM *Fr.* Essay on Psychiatrists.

As a Sad Man, When Evenings Grayer Grow. Trumbull Stickney. APN-2

As a Seal upon Thy Heart. Bible, *O.T.* BoWoP; TrJP, *tr. by* Willis Barnstone *Fr.* Song of Solomon, The [*or* The Song of Songs].

As a servant earnestly desireth the shadow, and as an hireling looketh for the reward of his work. Bible, *O.T.* AWTN, *tr. by* King James Version *Fr.* Job.

As a short before the main feature. Experiment. Wislawa Szymborska. PoSu, *tr. by* Magnus F. Krynski

As a signet of carbuncle in a setting of gold. Bible, Apocrypha. TrJP *Fr.* Ecclesiasticus.

As a soul from whom companionships subside. Edgar Lee Masters. GeoHom *Fr.* Spoon River Anthology.

As a starved little bird, who sees and hears. Vittoria da Colonna, Marchesa di Pescara. *See* As a hungry fledgling, who sees and hears

As a symbol. Sabina Lampadius. WPoS

As a teen-ager I was very shy. Norma. Sonia Sanchez. UnSA

As a teenager I would drive Father's. Running on Empty. Robert Phillips. InPK-6

As a torn paper might seal up its side. Pruned Tree, The. Howard Moss. VCAP

As a tot. How Long Has This Been Going On? George Gershwin. ReLy

As a voice in a vision that's vanished. From Lines of Swinburne. Charles Bernstein. FTOS

As a warm gust strokes young poplars. Requiescat. Leo Ross. TuT, *tr. by* Sean Dunne

As a whip maps the countries of the air. (LL) Transit. Richard Wilbur. DiPo; LCAP-2; NIL-7

As a white candle. Old Woman, The. Joseph Campbell. AWP; MoBrPo; OxBTC; PoToHe

As a white stone draws down the fish. Behaviour of Fish in an Egyptian Tea Garden. Keith Douglas. FaBoMo; RB

As a young girl. Changeling, The. Judith Ortiz Cofer. NIL-7; TouFir

As a young girl attending Sunday mass. Purpose of Nuns, The. Judith Ortiz Cofer. TouFir

As a young man I loved my beloved. Love. Otto Stoessl. AuPH, *tr. by* Lowell A. Bangerter

As Adam Early in the Morning. Walt Whitman. APN-1; ChIV-1; ColAP; OxBA; PAI; SAmP

As Aesop was with boys at play. Aesop at Play. Phaedrus. AWP, *tr. by* Christopher Smart

As all the world may see. (LL) Lazy Pussy, The. Palmer Cox. OBCA; OxIBACP

As Always. James Harms. NAPBL

As an American traveler I have. Internal Migration: On Being on Tour. Alan Dugan. NoAM

As an intruder I trudged with careful innocence. Old Mansion. John Crowe Ransom. FuPo; HeIP-4; NOBA; OxBA

As an unperfect actor on the stage. William Shakespeare. NoSic; Son *Fr.* Sonnets.

As Ann came in one summer's day. Sleeper, The. Walter De la Mare. MoBrPo

As Anne, long barren, mother did become. To St John Baptist. Henry Constable. ChIV-2; NoSic

As any of these, with as much or as little reason. (LL) Barnsley and District. Donald Davie. NoAM; OxBC

As any she belied with false compare. (LL) William Shakespeare. AWP; BoLoP; CABP; EBEV; HAP; HeIP-4; InPK-6; NAEL-5v1; NAEL-6v1; NAEL-7v1; NIL-7; NIP-4; NoSic; OxAEP-1; OxBEV; PAI; PoE; PoPoPo; SoSe-8; Son; TFi; WeW-3 *Fr.* Sonnets.

As any words, or wagon, / can be made. (LL) In Cold Hell, in Thicket. Charles Olson. APT-2; PmAP; PoM

As anything else, to ease your pain! (LL) Thomas Hardy. InPK-6; Son *Fr.* Satires of Circumstance in Fifteen Glimpses.

As apple tree among the trees of wood. Bible, *O.T.* EMWP, *tr. by* Barbara, Lady Scourie Mackay *Fr.* Song of Solomon, The.

As, at a railway junction, men. Sic Itur. Arthur Hugh Clough. EBVV

As autumn marched, the pond was drained.   From the Outland.   Peter Davison. UrbNat

As Bad as a Mile.   Philip Larkin.   InPK-6; OxBC; OxBEV; OxBSP

As Birds Are Fitted to the Boughs.   Louis Simpson.   BoLoP

As black as ink and isn't ink.   *Unknown.*   OxNR

As black in the hollows of white.   Instructing Clarity in a Confusion.   Arkadii Dragomoschenko.   ItGoST, *tr.* by Elena Balashova and Lyn Hejinian

As bold Mirmillo the grey dawn descries.   Sir Samuel Garth.   ECEV   *Fr.* Dispensary, The.

As boy, I thought myself a clever fellow.   Byron.   NAEL-6v2   *Fr.* Don Juan.

As bright will shine, etc. (LL)   Sir William Schwenck Gilbert.   NAEL-5v2; NAEL-6v2   *Fr.* Iolanthe.

As brycht Phebus, shene souerane, hevynnis e.   Gawin [*or* Gavin] Douglas. NePenScot   *Fr.* Eneados.

As bryght Phebus, scheyn soverane hevynnys e.   Virgil [*or* Vergil].   NPeEn; OxBS, *tr.* by Gawin [*or* Gavin] Douglas   *Fr.* Aeneid [*or* Eneados, *Aeneis*], The.

As by the stream[e]s of Babylon [*or* Babilon].   Thomas Campion.   BASC

As by the wood drifts thistle-down.   Herman Melville.   APN-2   *Fr.* Clarel: A Poem and Pilgrimage in the Holy Land.

As Cabeza de Vaca was.   Charles Olson.   BodElec

As campfire embers gleam.   Peace and the Desert.   Kevin Gilbert.   IBA

As careful mothers do to sleeping lay.   On the Deputy of Ireland's Child.   Sir John Davies.   FaBoEE

As carefully as your honor. (LL)   Meeting a Bear.   David Wagoner.   HAP; WeW-3

As Catullus wrote, a man's voice deserts him.   Aleksandr Semionovich Kushner.   ItGoST, *tr.* by Paul Graves and Carol Ueland

As certain as color.   Ono no Komachi.   OHPJ

As Children Together.   Carolyn Forché.   NoAM; OxWW

As children we dashed.   Pig Melons.   John Kinsella.   NeBl

As Christ intact before the infidel. (LL)   Constancy.   "Michael Field."   VWP; ViWPN

As Christ the Lord was passing by.   He Came Unto His Own, and His Own Received Him Not.   Mary Elizabeth Coleridge.   ViWPN

As clever Tom Clinch, while the rabble was bawling.   Clever Tom Clinch Going to Be Hanged.   Jonathan Swift.   NOIV

As close as you your weding kept.   I. W. To her unconstant Lover.   Isabella Whitney.   EMWP; PBRV

As clouds think of her clothing, as blossoms think of her face.   Suite in the Ch'ing-p'ing Mode, A.   Li Po.   ColAnChi, *tr.* by Elling O. Eide

As Concerning Man.   Alexander Radcliffe.   NOSC; OBSV

As cool as the pale wet leaves.   Alba.   Ezra Pound.   HAP; TCAPo; WeW-3

As Cortez on the Aztecs made. (LL)   America Is Hard to See.   Robert Frost. AiP; FaBoA

As Corydon went shiv'ring by.   Fire Us with Ice, Burn Us with Snow.   Mary Monk.   LW

As cruel as a Turk: Whence came.   Herman Melville.   OxBA   *Fr.* Clarel: A Poem and Pilgrimage in the Holy Land.

As Cynddylan passes proudly up the lane. (LL)   Cynddylan on a Tractor. Ronald Stuart Thomas.   AngWePo; TCAWP

As day did darken on the dewless grass.   Wind at the Door, The.   William Barnes.   GTBS-P; OxAEP-2

As day new opening fills the hemisphere.   Sir William Davenant [*or* D'Avenant].   NOSC   *Fr.* Gondibert.

As Dick and I.   Lines Left at Mr Theodore Hook's House in June, 1834. "Thomas Ingoldsby."   OBCoV

As did the Outlaw Murray of the forest frie? (LL)   Outlaw Murray, The. *Unknown.*   ESPB; OxBB

As Difference Blends into Identity.   Josephine Miles.   NoAM

As doctors give physic by way of prevention.   For My Own Monument. Matthew Prior.   OBEV

As Dorothy Parker once said to her boyfriend.   Just One of Those Things. Cole Porter.   APT-1; ReLy

As Down a Lone Valley.   Timothy Dwight.   AH

As dull as the life of the cloister.   Limerick.   *Unknown.*   PeLi

As dusk fell, nurse went in to stoke up the fire and heat the children's formulae. Nature Study.   Trevor Winkfield.   KGB

As each year might assign. (LL)   He Never Expected Much.   Thomas Hardy. NAEL-5v2; NAEL-6v2; NoAM; OxBTC; SCV

As earthquakes happened far too frequently.   Inquisition, The.   Victor Hugo. SxFrPo, *tr.* by E. H. Blackmore and A. M. Blackmore

As Easily as Trees.   Robert Francis.   APT-2

As Eileen unchains her bicycle.   Moonstones.   David Trinidad.   WiU

As Endymion.   Odysseus Elytis.   GifTon, *tr.* by Olga Broumas

As, even today, the airman, feeling the plane sweat.   Icarus.   Valentin Iremonger.   BIrV; CIP-2; ModIr

As evening splendors fade.   Nightfall.   Alexander L. Posey.   APN-2

As ever in my great task-ma[i]ster's eye. (LL)   Sonnet 7.   John Milton.   HeIP-4; NAEL-5v1; NAEL-6v1; NOSC; NoP-4; PAI; PoE; SCGP; Son

As Expected.   Thom Gunn.   GLP

As F——at her Toilet sat.   Song.   Margaret, Lady Godolphin.   EMWP

As far as Cho-fu-Sa. (LL)   River Merchant's Wife; a Letter, The.   Li Po. AWP; BoLoP; ClHu; HAP; InPK-6; MoAmPo; NAAL-2v2; NIP-4; NOBA; NOBE; NoAM; OBMV; OBVE; OxBA; RB; RaBo; TAP; TFi; TRP; TTTS; TwCP; UnPo; WeW-3, *tr.* by Ezra Pound

As far as Chō-fū-Sa. (LL)   River-Merchant's Wife: A Letter, The.   Ezra Pound. AmFaPo; HarvBoo; NAAL-5; NIL-7; NoP-4; PoPoPo; RACG; TCAPo

As far as Cho-fu-Sa. (LL)   River-Merchant's Wife: A Letter, The.   Rihaku. APT-1; NPeEn, *tr.* by Ezra Pound

As far as statues go, so far there's not.   From Trollope's Journal.   Elizabeth Bishop.   CBCWP

As Far as Yoruba Land.   Edouard J. Maunick.

"Accept from me not silence."   NegPo

"And I have chosen the sea as no man's land."   NegPo

"Enter in the circle."   NegPo

"For there is an African virtue of the tree."   NegPo

"I am from everywhere."   NegPo

"I have mentioned it by name."   NegPo

"I have understood nothing."   NegPo

"I made the motions of the sacred place."   NegPo

"Ofatedo / seek it out upon the skin of Africa."   NegPo

"Point no scornful finger at Yoruba Land."   NegPo

"Speaking of Gethsemane in Yoruba Land."   NegPo

"This is where the warrior from Ibokun came."   NegPo

"Trees were forbidden me, The."   NegPo

"Where does this poem come from?"   NegPo

As Firerorefiddle, the Fiend of the Fell. (LL)   Gus: The Theatre Cat.   T. S. Eliot.   OBCA; OxBTC

As Firmly Cemented Clam-Shells.   Basho.   PAI, *tr.* by Nobuyuki Yuasa

As, first, your pains in bearing me was such.   To the Right Worshipful Lady Her Most Dear Mother, the Lady Prudentia Munda, the True Pattern of Piety and Virtue, C. M. Wisheth Increase of Happiness.   "Constantia Munda."   EMWP

As flowers fall at the river city, memories come to me.   Wen Cheng-ming. CoBLCP

As Flows the Rapid River.   Samuel Francis Smith.   AH

As for Granata, the Siberian gulag, Ostia.   Mario Luzi.   ItPo, *tr.* by Gayle Ridinger   *Fr.* Pieces from a Mortal Duet.

As for him who.   Fragment.   William Carlos Williams.   Spl

As for me I am a child of the god of the mountains.   Gary Snyder.   NOBA; PFTM-2   *Fr.* Myths and Texts.

As for me, I delight in the everyday Way.   *Unknown.*   CoBCP

As for me / I have seen Llywelyn.   Day Which Endures Not, A.   A. G. Prys-Jones.   OBWVE, *tr.* by Anthony Conran

As for me, my Nanna ignores me.   Condemning the Moongod Nanna. Enheduanna.   BoWoP

As for my life, I've led it.   Placid Man's Epitaph, A.   Thomas Hardy. MoBrPo

As for Poets.   Gary Snyder.   BB; PmAP

As for the hibiscus.   Basho.   EH, *tr.* by Robert Hass

As for the Quince.   Nuala Ni Dhomhnaill.   BiHa; CIP-2; PBCIP, *tr.* by Paul Muldoon

As Fowlers Lie in Wait.   Bible, *O.T.*   TrJP   *Fr.* Jeremiah.

As Frazier one night at her Post in the Drawing Room stood.   Katherine Colyear, Countess of Dorchester.   EMWP

As freedom is a breakfastfood.   E. E. Cummings.   NOBA; OxBA; TAP; VGW

As From a Quiver of Arrows.   Carl Phillips.   WiU

As from a shell, a husk, I stripped you bare.   Lőrinc Szabó.   IQMS, *tr.* by Watson Kirkconnell   *Fr.* Cricket Music.

As from an ancestral oak.   Similes for Two Political Characters of 1819. Shelley.   RB

As from each fragrant sweet the honny Bee.   Upon the Necessity and Benefite of Learning Written in the Beginning of a Common Place Booke Belonging to W. B. a Young Scholler.   Anna Norman Ley.   EMWP

As from my own he swept you far away. (LL)   Do This Favour For Me.   Luis de Camões [*or* Camões].   BoLoP; WoPoe, *tr.* by Roy Campbell

As from the Dorset shore I travell'd home.   White Horse of Westbury, The. Charles Tennyson Turner.   EBEV; PeVV

As from the house your mother sees.   Robert Louis Stevenson.   NePenScot *Fr.* To Any Reader.

As from their ancestral oak.   Shelley.   *See* As from an ancestral oak

As funny as I can. (LL)   Height of the Ridiculous, The.   Oliver Wendell Holmes.   OBAL; OBCA

As G-5 put it, Bac Ha hamlet was a good.   Bac Ha.   David Huddle.   CDa

As Gentle Dews Distill.   George Rogers.   AH

As glad to have my body[,] as my mind. (LL)   Blossom [*or* Blossome], The.

John Donne. AWP; ESCV; MeLP; NAEL-5v1; NAEL-6v1; NAEL-7v1; SCGP; UnPo

As Gold is better that's in fire tride. John Taylor. PBRV *Fr.* Sculler, The.

As gold nuggets contained in crystal. Sanctuary. Angelina Muñiz Huberman. MirDau, *tr.* by Aurora Camacho

As goldsmiths gold, which we may wear like hope. (LL) Epigram: "Time heals not: it extends a sorrow's scope." James Vincent Cunningham. VGW; WoPoe

As good there, as he[e]re to burn[e]. (LL) Mary Sidney Wroth, Countess of Montgomery. NAEL-6v1; NAEL-7v1 *Fr.* Pamphilia to Amphilanthus.

As good to write as for to lie and groan. Sir Philip Sidney. NoSic *Fr.* Astrophil and Stella.

As graceful as the Babylonian willow. To Isa Sleeping. Thomas Holley Chivers. APN-1

As grit swirls in the wind the word spreads. Center of Attention, The. Daniel Gerard Hoffman. UnPo

As guns pounded on the shore. (LL) Europe and America. David Ignatow. NNaP; UnPo

As happy as Cliff Klingenhagen is. (LL) Cliff Klingenhagen. Edwin Arlington Robinson. APN-2; MoAmPo; NCAP; Son

As He Came near Death. Roy Fisher. FaBoMo; HarvBoo; NPeEn

As he climbs down our hill, my kestrel rises. Esyllt. Glyn Jones. AngWePo; OBWVE

As he filled up his order book pp. Limerick. *Unknown.* PeLi

As he knelt by the grave of his mother and father. Milkweed and Monarch. Paul Muldoon. NoP-4; PoetW

As he lay dead. Dilemma. Phoebe Hesketh. Prnts

As he left the ship he saw this, only this. Descent of the Vulture, The. Marya Alexandrovna Zaturenska. WPE

As he left them there, as he left them there. (LL) W. H. Auden. FaBoCh; NOBE; NoAM; OxBEV; UV *Fr.* Five Songs.

As he moves the mine-detector. Hunting Civil War Relics at Nimblewill Creek. James Dickey. CoAmPo

As he passed us and vanished. (LL) Tao and Unfitness at Inistiogue on the River Nore. Thomas Kinsella. NPeEn; PBCIP

As he rode back Yesugei came on a camp of the Tatar. *Unknown.* WoPoe, *tr.* by Paul Kahn *Fr.* Secret History of the Mongols, The.

As he said vanity, so vain say I. Vanity of All Worldly Things, The. Anne Bradstreet. ChIV-1; SCAP

As he sang upon a tree! (LL) Rivals, The. James Stephens. OBEV; OBMV

As he sinks two into the chains. (LL) Makin' Jump Shots. Michael S. Harper. ISC; MoASP; PoE

As he stood against the fretted hedge, which was like white lace. (LL) To a Conscript of 1940. Sir Herbert Read. OBWP; PoWW

As he stood in their shop, Mr. Boosey. Jimmy Pearse. PeLi

As he takes from you, I engraft you new. (LL) William Shakespeare. AWP; NAEL-5v1; NAEL-6v1; NAEL-7v1; NoSic; SCGP; Son *Fr.* Sonnets.

As he that sees a dark and shady grove. Holy Baptism (1). George Herbert. GeHe

As He, the maker of this Song. (LL) Meditation for His Mistress[e], A. Robert Herrick. CaPo; NOBE; NOSC; OBEV

As he was a poet sublimer than me. (LL) Answer to Cloe [*or* Chloe] Jealous. Matthew Prior. NOBE; OxBEV

As he went on fishing his way. (LL) Lady and the Bear, The. Theodore Roethke. ChAP; NBLV

As he would burn or better far his book. (LL) To Elizabeth, Countess of Rutland. Ben Jonson. BeJo; NoP-4

As Hector turned for home his helmet flashed. Homer. NAWM-7v1, *tr.* by Robert Fagles *Fr.* Iliad, The.

As here on earth's soil God's Son Eternal. Cynewulf. SacPr, *tr.* by Charles William Kennedy *Fr.* Ascension, The.

As his hideous body grabs them. (LL) Bride of Frankenstein, The. Edward Field. CoAP; HeIP-4; ReTh

As his lithe, fathoming heart absorbed and buried. (LL) Turtle Dove, The. Geoffrey Hill. FaBoTw; OxBEV

As honest Jacob on a night. Patriarch, The. Robert Burns. ChIV-1

As honey in wine / wine, honey. Epigram. Meleager. GrAn, *tr.* by Peter Whigham

As Hour and Year Collapsed. Joe Wenderoth. NAPBL

As I am mine, their sweating selves; but worse. (LL) I Wake and Feel the Fell of Dark, Not Day. Gerard Manley Hopkins. AWTN; CABP; FaBoVe; NAEL-6v2; NPeEn; NoP-4; OxAEP-2; OxBSo; PeVV; TRP

As I Am My Father's. Rose Drachler. TaR

As I am unhappy. Akiko Yosano. WPOW

As I approach / The mountain village. Noin. OHPJ

As I beheld a winters evening air. Another. Richard Lovelace. OxBEV

As I believe the three of us would be. (LL) Sonnet: "Guido, I wish that you and Lapo and I." Dante Alighieri. RB; TTTS, *tr.* by Kenneth Koch

"As I cam in by boney Glasgow town." Glasgow Peggie. *Unknown.* ESPB

As I cam in by Dunidier. Battle of Harlaw, The. *Unknown.* ESPB

As I cam thro the Garrioch land. Battle of Harlaw, The. *Unknown.* ESPB

As I Came Down from Lebanon. Clinton Scollard. APN-2

As I came from the. Kenneth Rexroth. APSN *Fr.* Love Poems of Marichiko, The.

As I came home through Drury's woods. Cold Fear. Elizabeth Madox Roberts. WPE

As I Came in by Fiddich-Side. *Unknown.* RB (Willie Macintosh). ESPB

As I came out of the New York Public Library. Nuns in the Wind. Muriel Rukeyser. NNaP

As I came over Windy Gap. Running to Paradise. W. B. Yeats. OxBoLi

As I came round the harbor buoy. Long White Seam, The. Jean Ingelow. NOBVV; OxBEV

As I came to the edge of the woods. Come In. Robert Frost. APT-1; MoAmPo; NOBA; NoP-4; RaBo; TRP

As I Composed This Little Book. Rosalía de Castro. NAWM-7v2, *tr.* by S. Griswold Morley

As I descended black, impassive Rivers. Arthur Rimbaud. NAWM-7v2, *tr.* by Stephen Stepanchev

As I did the washing one day. Shirt of a Lad, The. *Unknown.* OBWVE, *tr.* by Anthony Conran

As I did walke my selfe alone. King James and Brown. *Unknown.* ESPB

As I do now, before the advancing day. (LL) Edna St. Vincent Millay. HeIP-4; VGW

As I do zew, wi' nimble hand. Lwonesomeness. William Barnes. NOBVV; OxBEV

As I drive to the junction of lane and highway. At Castle Boterel. Thomas Hardy. EBEV; GTBS-P; NOBE; NPeEn; OxAEP-2; OxBEV; PeVV; PoE; SCV

As I Ebb'd with the Ocean of Life. Walt Whitman. APN-1; NAAL-2v1; NAAL-3; NAAL-5; NOBA; TAP; TCAPo

As I fear the friends below. (LL) Dirge: "From a friend's friend I taste friendship." Stevie Smith. HarvBoo; NPeEn

As I gaed down to Collistown. Cunning Clerk, The. *Unknown.* OxBB

As I gaed in by the Duke o' Athole's gates. Duke o' Athole's Nurse, The. *Unknown.* OxBB

As I get older, I like quiet sitting. Quiet Sitting. Wang Chiu-ssu. CoBLCP, *tr.* by Jonathan Chaves

As I glance through a few thin pages and switch off the light. (LL) Achill. Derek Mahon. BiHa; PBCIP; PNI

As I go up to Heaven. (LL) Woman. Valente Goenha Malangatana. PBA; PBMAP, *tr.* by Dorothy Guedes and Philippa Rumsey

As I grow older. Issa. NIL-7, *tr.* by Daniel C. Buchanan

As I guard o'er the fold. (LL) William Blake. FHYEP; ITBLP; OBEV *Fr.* Songs of Innocence.

As I have often said—If art is infancy and criticism the day of atonement. Roget, Papier, Schism! Michael Portnoy. HeMarv

As I have said, I floated to the earth. Shelley. FHYEP *Fr.* Prometheus Unbound [A Lyrical Drama in Four Acts].

As I have seen a child. High Adventure. A. W. Spalding. ITBLP

As I in hoary [*or* hoarie] Winter's night stood[e] shivering[e] in the snow[e]. Burning Babe, The. Robert Southwell. ChrPo; ESCV; FaBoCh; HAP; HeIP-4; NAEL-5v1; NAEL-6v1; NAEL-7v1; NOBE; NOCV; NoSic; OBCP; OBEV; OxAEP-2; OxBEV; PAI; RB; SCGP; SacPr; TFi; TOF; TRP; TrCP; WoPoe

As I lay asleep in Italy. Shelley. FHYEP; NPeEn; OBSV; OxAEP-2; RB; SCV; WoPoe *Fr.* Mask [*or* Masque] of Anarchy, The.

As I lay at your feet the other day. At Her Feet. "Violet Fane." PoBW

As I lay, fullness of praise. Rattle Bag, The. Dafydd [*or* David] ap Gwilym. NBLV; RB; WoPoe, *tr.* by Joseph P. Clancy

As I lay here alone. It Just Doesn't Matter. Rodney M. McNeil. InTrad

As I lay upon a night. My Thought Was on a Maid So Bright. *Unknown.* MiEL

As I Lay with My Head in Your Lap Camerado. Walt Whitman. CAGL; CBCWP; NAAL-2v1; NAAL-3; OxBA

As I leaned at my window. Song of Samuel Sweet, The. Charles Causley. OBNV

As I Leave You. Chrystos. ReEnLa

As I lie here in the sun. Jonah. Randall Jarrell. ChIV-1

As I lie next to you. Music. Natasha Josefowitz. PasH

As I life abroad endured. February. Berthold Viertel. AuPH, *tr.* by Lowell A. Bangerter

As I listened from a beach-chair in the shade. Their Lonely Betters. W. H. Auden. NAEL-5v2; NAEL-6v2; NoAM; OBGa

As I Looked at a Lake, and Traveled to a Certain Friend. Chu Yün-ming. CoBLCP, *tr.* by Jonathan Chaves

As I me rod this endre day. *Unknown.* OHMEL

As I, my Harriet, bless thy friendship's cheering light. (LL) Captive Escaped in the Wilds of America, The. Addressed to the Hon. Mrs. O'Neill. Charlotte Smith. CenSon; Son

As I one evening [or ev'ning] sat before my cell. Artillery [or Artillerie]. George Herbert. GeHe

As I pass'd [or passed] by a river side [or riverside]. Carnal and the Crane, The. *Unknown.* ESPB

As I pass through my incarnations in every age and race. Gods of the Copybook Headings, The. Rudyard Kipling. NoAM; OBSV; OxBTC

As I reach to close each book. Against the Evidence. David Ignatow. NNaP

As I remember, barracks still stand. Aleksandr Lavrin. TCRP

As I ride, as I ride. Through the Metidja to Abd-el-Kadr. Robert Browning. WoPoe

As I rode in to Burrumbeet. Traveller, The. C. J. Dennis. NOBAu

As I roved out impatiently. In the Ringwood. Thomas Kinsella. PBCIP

As I roved out on a May morning. Johnny's the Lad I Love. *Unknown.* OxBoLi

As I roved out one summer's morning, speculating most curiously. Colleen Rue. *Unknown.* BIrV

As I row over the plain. Tadamichi. OHPJ

As I Sat at the Café. Arthur Hugh Clough. GTBS-P; NBLV; OBCoV; OxBoLi *Fr.* Spectator ab Extra.

As I sat at the café, I said to myself. Arthur Hugh Clough. NOBE; NOBVV; OxBoLi *Fr.* Dipsychus [and the Spirit].

As I sat by my window last evening. Miss Foggerty's Cake. *Unknown.* NBLV

As I sat down by the bus window in the gate of Verona. Silent Angel, The. James Wright (1927–80). BodElec

As I sat down one evening. Frozen Logger, The. *Unknown.* OBAL

As I sat down to breakfast in state. Country Clergyman's Trip to Cambridge, The. Thomas Babington Macaulay, 1st Baron Macaulay. OBSV; OxBoLi; PeLV

As I Sat in the Armchair of the Tsar. Bulat Shalvovich Okudzhava. TCRP, *tr. by* Deming Brown

As I Sat on a Sunny Bank. *Unknown.* OxBoLi; OxNR

As I sate *Musing,* by my selfe alone. Margaret Lucas Cavendish, Duchess of Newcastle. BWW

As I sd to my / friend, because I am. I Know a Man. Robert Creeley. AmFaPo; NIP-4; NOBA; OxBSP; PoM; VCAP

As I see it, T'ao Yüan-ming. Supervisor, Han Chün-mei, Has Shown Me Five Poems. Tai Piao-yüan. CoBLCP, *tr. by* Jonathan Chaves

As I should lay alone. (LL) Whistle, Daughter, Whistle. *Unknown.* OxNR; ReMoGo

As I sit alone at present, dreaming darkly of a Dun. (LL) In the Gloaming. Charles Stuart Calverley. NOBL; OBCoV; PeLV

As I sit by the ruddy oak fire. Nestle-down Cottage. Mary Weston Fordham. CBWP-2

As I sit looking out of a window of the building. Instruction Manual, The. John Ashbery. HAP; NOBA; NeAP; NoAM; PoM; YaYoPo

As I Sit Writing Here. Walt Whitman. NAAL-2v1; NAAL-3

As I stepped out the doorway it was ten o'clock. Peace, Horror. Miklós Radnóti. AF, *tr. by* Emery E. George

As I stood / Ling'ring upon the threshold, half-concealed. Xantippe. Amy Levy. BrRo

As I strole the city, oft I. Jonathan Swift. BIrV *Fr.* Legion Club, The.

As I talked, I kept thinking. Murderer, The. Christopher Davis. OPRER

As I travel the Strath of Drumochter. Lament for the State of the Country, A. Iain Lom. NePenScot, *tr. by* Meg Bateman

As I travel, there are no flowers. No Flowers. Ch'ien Ch'ien-i [or Ch'ien Ch'ien-yi]. CoBLCP, *tr. by* Jonathan Chaves

As I traveled from the city. Poem. Salah Fa'iq. MAP, *tr. by* Patricia Alanah Byrne and Salma Khadra Jayyusi

As I walk'd thinking through a little grove. Catch: On a Wet Day. Franco Sacchetti. AWP; EaItPo, *tr. by* Dante Gabriel Rossetti

As I walked down by the river. Ballad for Katharine of Aragon, A. Charles Causley. FaBoTw

As I walked fforth one morninge. Christopher White. *Unknown.* ESPB

As I Walked [or Walk'd] by Myself. *Unknown.* FaBoEE; OxBSP; OxNR; ReMoGo

As I walked out early. Thomas A. Clark. Oth *Fr.* Sixteen Sonnets.

As I walked out in the streets of Laredo. Cowboy's Lament, The. *Unknown.* APN-2; ChAP; FaBoA

As I Walked Out One Evening. W. H. Auden. HeIP-4; InPK-6; NIL-7; NOBE; NoAM; NoP-4; OxAEP-2; PoPoPo; RB; TwCP; UnPo

  (Song: "As I walked out one evening") MoBrPo

As I walked out one evening down by the Strawberry Lane. Captain Wedderburn's Courtship. *Unknown.* ESPB

As I walked out that sultry night. Full Moon. Robert Graves. NOBE

As I walked over the western plain. Legend. Charles Causley. TOF

As I wandered on the beach. Great Blue Heron, The. Carolyn Kizer. CoAP; InvLad; WPE

As I wandrede her by weste. *Unknown.* MiEL

As I was a-gwine down the road. Turkey in the Straw. *Unknown.* TCAPo

As I Was a-Walking by Yon Green Garden. *Unknown.* NePenScot

As I was a-walking on Westminster Bridge. *Unknown.* OxNR

As I was by one brought forth, I would bring forth another. (LL) Fain Would I Wed. Thomas Campion. NAEL-5v1; NAEL-6v1; NAEL-7v1

As I was cast in my ffirst sleepe. Young [or Younge] Andrew. *Unknown.* ESPB; OxBB

As I was fishing off Pondy Point. Jim Desterland. Hyam Plutzik. RB; VGW

As I was going along, long, long. Mother Goose. OxNR; ReMoGo

As I was going by Charing Cross. King Charles the First. *Unknown.* FaBoCh; OxNR

As I was going o'er Tipple Tine. *Unknown.* OxNR

As I was going to Banbury. *Unknown.* OxNR

As I was going to Derby. Derby Ram, The. *Unknown.* OxNR; ReMoGo

As I was going to sell my eggs. Bandy Legs. Mother Goose. OxNR; ReMoGo

As I was going to St. Ives. Mother Goose. LB; NTCP; OxNR; ReMoGo

As I was going up Pippen Hill. Mother Goose. OxNR; ReMoGo

As I was going up the hill. Jack the Piper. *Unknown.* OxNR

As I was helplessly young. (LL) Childhood. Frances Darwin Cornford. FaBoWP; KaS; OxBEV; OxBSP; OxBTC

As I was in my hut. Gray She-Wolf, The. *Unknown.* WoPoe, *tr. by* W. S. Merwin

As I was lodged at Shih-hao one night. Draft Board at Shih-hao, The. Tu Fu. CrYelRi, *tr. by* Sam Hamill

As I was lumb'ring down de street. Buffalo Gals. *Unknown.* APN-2

As I was musing by myself alone. Mirth and Melancholy. Margaret Lucas Cavendish, Duchess of Newcastle. WPE

As I was putting away the groceries. Bali Hai Calls Mama. Marilyn Nelson Waniek. ISC

As I was sitting in my chair. Perfect Reactionary, The. Hughes Mearns. NTCP

As I Was Standing in the Street. *Unknown.* NTCP

As I was strolling lonely in the Backs. In the Backs. James Kenneth Stephen. NOBVV

As I was waiting for the bus. Sight Unseen. Kingsley Amis. NoAM

As I was walkin' the jungle round, a-killin' of tigers an' time. Ballad. Guy Wetmore Carryl. NBLV

As I was walking. Kore. Robert Creeley. NAAL-5; RaBo

As I was walking all alane [or alone]. Twa Corbies, The. *Unknown.* AWP; ESPB; FaBoCh; GTBS-P; HAP; InPK-6; NPeEn; NePenScot; OBEV; OWoS; OxBEV; OxBS; PAI; RB; SCGP; UnPo

As I was walking forth one day. Royal health to the Rising Sun, The. *Unknown.* BASC

As I was walking in a field of wheat. *Unknown.* OxNR

As I was walking in the fields last Tuesday of all days. Slender Lad, The. *Unknown.* OBWVE, *tr. by* Kenneth Hurlstone Jackson

As I was walking in the Mall of late. Horace. BASC; NPeEn, *tr. by* John Oldham *Fr.* Imitation of Horace, An. Book 1, Satire 9.

As I was walking mine alane. Archie o [or of] Cawfield. *Unknown.* ESPB; OxBS

As I was walking [or wa'king] all alone [or alane]. Wee Wee Man, The. *Unknown.* EBEV; ESPB; FaBoCh; OxBB

As I watch the moon. Ōe no Chisato. OHPJ

As I went by a dyer's door. Dyer, The. *Unknown.* OxNR

As I went down that yella bank. Riddle. *Unknown.* FaBoVe

As I went down the hill along the wall. Meeting and Passing. Robert Frost. OxBA; OxBSo

As I Went Down to David's Town. George Craig Stewart. AH

As I went down to Dymchurch Wall. In Romney Marsh. John Davidson. EBVV; OxBTC

As I went out a Crow. Last Word of a Bluebird, The. Robert Frost. NOxBChV; OxIBACP

As I went out one frosty morning. Frozen Stiff. Sean O Riordain. ModIr, *tr. by* Patrick Crotty

As I went over the water. *Unknown.* OxNR

As I went through a guttery gap / I met a wee man with a red cap. Riddle. *Unknown.* FaBoVe

As I went through the garden gap. Cherry, A. *Unknown.* ReMoGo

As I went through yon guttery gap / I met my Uncle Davy. Riddle. *Unknown.* FaBoVe

As I Went to Bonner. *Unknown.* OxBoLi; OxNR; ReMoGo

As I went up by Ovillers. Ballad of the Three Spectres. Ivor Gurney. OBWP

As I went up the Brandy hill. *Unknown.* OxNR

As I would free the white almond from the green husk. Aubade. Amy Lowell. NIL-7

As ice on Mont Blanc's frozen crest. Twenty Years After. János Vajda. IQMS, *tr. by* Neville Masterman

As if a nest of hornets rose to sting. János Arany. IQMS, *tr. by* Watson Kirkconnell *Fr.* Toldi.

As if a one-room schoolhouse were all we knew. Michael Longley. CIP-2; PNI

As If a Phantom Caress'd Me. Walt Whitman. SAmP

As if a quiet branch drew a line. " Eduard Veniaminovich Limonov." TCRusP, *tr. by* Mary Jane White

As if as if as if a hiss a swish of. Golden Bough: The Feather Palm. Susan Mitchell. ExTi

As if dead the buried text. III. Danielle Collobert. MFP, *tr. by* Martin Sorrell

As if God were an old man. Task, The. Denise Levertov. InvLi

As if having a thought makes anything, and assuming. Four Minute History of Getting It Together in Order to Be Fabulous, Briefly, A. Anselm Berrigan. HeMarv

As if he had been poured. Grauballe Man, The. Seamus Heaney. OxBEV; PoetW

As if I craved error, as if love were ahistorical. Testimonial. Claudia Rankine. ExTi; NeAmPo

As if I didn't have enough. Small Aircraft. Bella [*or* Izabella] Akhatovna Akhmadulina. BoWoP, *tr. by* Daniel Halpern

As if I had committed, against the whole scheme of life, a /desecration desecration. (LL) Moss-Gathering. Theodore Roethke. BLT; VGW

As if in a presence of an intelligence. Cold, The. Charles Simic. HCAP

As If in Flaw, or in the Flaw of Space. Sabah Al-Kharrat Zwein. "Abysmal circle is in the sky, An. At the moment we are an infinite line." PoArWo, *tr. by* Kaissar Afif

As if in snow you walked. And you walked in snow. Song of Blue and Red, A. Amir Gilbo'a. MHP, *tr. by* Ruth Finer Mintz

As if it had forgotten everything—hatred, vindictiveness, the meaning of pain. Custom. Carol Frost. MoASP

As if it had not been. (LL) Moment, A. Mary Elizabeth Coleridge. LW; PEW

As if it's as if it's part of the whole endeavor to get back the finger beclouding what's. Methodology. Bruce Andrews. FTOS

As if it were a scene made-up by the mind. Often I Am Permitted to Return to a Meadow. Robert Duncan. ColAP; HarvBoo; NOBA; PFTM-2; PmAP

As if it were / forever that they move, that we. Merritt Parkway. Denise Levertov. NeAP; PoM

As if it were his own! (LL) Emily Dickinson. AmFaPo; TAP; TCAPo

As if our sneakers froze to the ground. Call of the Lake, The. Andrey [*or* Andrei] Andreievich Voznesensky [*or* Voznesenskii]. TCRP; VCWP

As if some irremediable poison. London. J. R. Rowland. CBAP

As if some little Arctic flower. Emily Dickinson. APN-2

As if somebody ordered it. Tashkent Breaks into Bloom. Anna Andreyevna Akhmatova. BoWoP, *tr. by* Richard McKane

As if the Checks were given. (LL) Emily Dickinson. AmFaPo; HeIP-4; ITBLP; MoAmPo; SAmP; TAP; TFi; WPoS

As if the flow of the waters. Ka Waiapo Lani. Queen Lili'u-o-ka-lani. SWaP

As if the sky broke up. On the Origin of the Contrary. Miroslav Holub. VCWP, *tr. by* Stuart Friebert

As if the snow itself were a country. White, White. David Morley. NLP

As if they don't always remember that twining. Steelhead in the Whitehorse Rearing Pond. Joan Swift. PoCoUp

As if they might start speaking. (LL) Breasts. Maxine Chernoff. PmAP; ReTh; SpudSo

As if they were his ripe prize vegetables. (LL) My Father's Garden. David Wagoner. DiPo; NIL-7; NIP-4

As if thou hadst sealed my pardon, with thy blood. (LL) John Donne. BASC; ChIV-2; ClHu; EBEV; FHYEP; HAP; HeIP-4; MakPoe; MeLP; NAEL-5v1; NAEL-6v1; NAEL-7v1; NAWM-5v1; NOBE; NOSC; OxAEP-1; OxBEV; OxBSo; PAI; PeECV; PoE; SCGP; Son; TFi; TOF; WoPoe *Fr.* Holy Sonnets.

As if to draw the light to the body. There Were No Deer in the Thicket. David Biespiel. AmPoNex

As if to lift my babe-in-arms. Bihari. ErotSp, *tr. by* Sam Hamill

As if words could shed their skin. Morning. Pauline Kaldas. PoArWo

As imperceptibly as grief. Emily Dickinson. APN-2; NAAL-2v1; NOBA; NoP-4; PoE; SoSe-8

As in a Dream. Li Ch'ing-chao. CoBCP, *tr. by* Burton Watson

As in a duskie [*or* dusky] and tempestuous night. Sonnet. William Drummond, of Hawthornden. NOSC; OxAEP-1

As in a film by Godard: alone. Pier Paolo Pasolini. PFTM-2, *tr. by* Pasquale Verdicchio *Fr.* Desperate Vitality, A.

As in a parable the truant father. Pealing, The. Olga Broumas. BodElec

As in a Watteau fete of rose and silver blue. Tempest, The. Marya Alexandrovna Zaturenska. MoAmPo

As in Frege's luminous counter-example. Counter-Example, The. David Shapiro. PmAP

As in his burning throne he sits emparadised. (LL) Giles Fletcher, the Younger. ChIV-2; NOSC; SacPr *Fr.* Christ's Victory and Triumph.

As in Sodom one day, our day. "Porfirio Barba-Jacob." CAGL, *tr. by* Jeff Bingham and Juan Antonio Serna Servin *Fr.* Song of an Impossible Blue.

As in that trance of wondrous thought I lay. Shelley. NPeEn *Fr.* Triumph of Life, The.

As in that twilight, superstitious age. On Rembrant; Occasioned by His Picture of Jacob's Dream. Washington Allston. APN-1

As in the age of shepherd king and queen. Dans l'Allée. Paul Verlaine. AWP, *tr. by* Arthur Symons

As in the gardens, all through May, the rose. His Lady's Tomb. Pierre de Ronsard. AWP, *tr. by* Andrew Lang

As in the house I sate [*or* sat]. Poverty. Thomas Traherne. TrCP

As in the midst of battle there is room. George Santayana. APN-2; AWP *Fr.* Sonnets.

As in thee resteth my joye and confort. *Unknown.* OHMEL

As incense smoke thins, a stupendous. God's Measurements. Laurence Lieberman. IllVoic

As innocent as now thou art. (LL) To His Son [*or* Sonne], Vincent Corbet[t]. Richard Corbet [*or* Corbett]. BeJo; FaBoCh; NOSC; OxAEP-1

As into the Garden Elizabeth Ran. A. E. Housman. NBLV

As inward love breeds outward talk. William Basse [*or* Bas]. NOSC *Fr.* Anglers Song, The.

As is a wanton woman in the spring. (LL) Sonnet: Of Love in Men and Devils. Cecco Angiolieri, da Siena. AWP; EaItPo, *tr. by* Dante Gabriel Rossetti

As is the sand upon the ocean's shore. One Generation Passeth Away. Jones Very. ChIV-1

As Israel's king lost his in shepherd's weed. (LL) To St John Baptist. Henry Constable. ChIV-2; NoSic

As it befell on a bright holiday. Bitter Withy, The. *Unknown.* NOCV

As it befell upon one time. Hughie Grame. *Unknown.* ESPB

As it blossoms Aaron's rod. Rod, The. Georgy [*or* Georgii] Nikolaevich Obolduyev [*or* Oboldúev]. TCRP, *tr. by* Vera Dunham

As it comes back, brick by smoky brick. In the Lost Province. Tom Paulin. PBCIP

As it fell on a holy day. John Dory. *Unknown.* ESPB

As it fell one holy-day [*or* on a light holyday *or* high holyday]. Little Musgrave and Lady Barnard. *Unknown.* ESPB; OxBB

As it fell out in a long summer's day. Fair Margaret and Sweet William. *Unknown.* ESPB; OxBB

As it fell out on a holy day [*or* upon a bright holiday *or* upon one day]. Bitter Withy, The. *Unknown.* NOCV

As it fell out one May morning. Holy Well, The. *Unknown.* FaBoCh; NOCV

As it fell out upon a day [*or* one day]. Dives and Lazarus. *Unknown.* ESPB; OxBB

As it fell upon a day. Vision of Truth, A. Sir John Collings Squire. NOBL

As it fell upon a day. *Var. authors.* NOBE; OBEV *Fr.* Passionate Pilgrim, The.

As it has for so long. Morning in Norfolk. George Barker. HarvBoo

As it leaves the bell. (LL) Buson. EH; NIL-7, *tr. by* Robert Hass

As It Should Be. Derek Mahon. EmeKit

As it was doomed to be. (LL) Ticonderoga: A Legend of the West Highlands. Robert Louis Stevenson. EBNV; OBNV

As it was in the beginning. Robin Morgan. HW *Fr.* Network of the Imaginary Mother, The.

As it[t] befel[l] in midsum[m]ertime [*or* midsumer-time]. Sir Andrew Bart[t]on. *Unknown.* ESPB; OxBB

As Jock the Leg and the merry merchant. Jock the Leg and the Merry Merchant. *Unknown.* ESPB

As Julia once a-slumbering lay. Captived Bee; or, The Little Filcher, The. Robert Herrick. CaPo

As kerosene climbs through a wick. Transmigration. Bruce Berger. GeoH

As Kingfishers Catch Fire. Gerard Manley Hopkins. EBEV; EBVV; EnlH; FaBoMo; MoBrPo; NAEL-5v2; NAEL-6v2; NOBVV; NOCV; NPeEn; NoP-4; OxAEP-2; PoE; RB

As kythed in that wild auld carline that day! (LL) Old Wife in High Spirits. Hugh MacDiarmid. OxBTC; PoE

As Lady Wei's star pupil, your calligraphy. Homage to the Painter General Ts'ao. Tu Fu. CrYelRi, *tr. by* Sam Hamill

As Lambs into the Pen. Dorothy Wellesley, Duchess of Wellington. FaBoTw

As lamps burn silent, with unconscious light. Modesty. Aaron Hill. OxBSP

As landscapes richen after rain, the eye. Foliage of Vision. James Merrill. VGW

As lark ascending. Praying. P. J. Kavanagh. OxBSP

As late I lay in slumber's shadowy vale. Samuel Taylor Coleridge. CenSon *Fr.* Effusions.

As late I rambled in the happy fields. To a Friend Who Sent Me Some Roses. John Keats. CenSon

As late we lived upon the gentle stream. Lines Written in Boston on a Beautiful Autumnal Day. Margaret Fuller. SWaP

As life improved, their poems. Postscript. Ronald Stuart Thomas. FaBoMo; OxBC

As life runs on, the road grows strange. Sixty-Eighth Birthday. James Russell Lowell. OxBSP

As Life What Is So Sweet? *Unknown.* OxBSP

As light-shy owls stare into the sun. Old Houses on the Quays. Augusta Peaux. TuT, *tr. by* Tony Curtis

As little Jenny Wren / Was sitting by the shed. Jenny Wren. Mother Goose. OxNR; ReMoGo

As Lob among his cows one day. Lob's Courtship. Elizabeth Hands. ECWP

As long ago, my love, how long ago! (LL) Echo. Christina Georgina Rossetti. BoLoP; EBVV; LW; NOBE; NoP-4; PEW; PoBW; PoE; VWP

As long ago they raced. Dream of Trains, A. Mark Van Doren. GM

As long ago we carried to your knees. Mother. *Unknown.* PoToHe

As long as Fame's imperious music rings. Three Quatrains. Edwin Arlington Robinson. NCAP

As Long As He Needs Me. Lionel Bart. ReLy

As Long As I Live. Ted Koehler. ReLy

As long as I was living in the village. *Unknown.* CoBCP

As long as it was still noon and the earth. Callimachus. HePo *Fr.* Hecale.

As long as the corpses aren't carried off. (LL) Torture Chamber. Enrique Lihn. PoetW; VCWP, *tr. by* Mary Crow

As long as we feel another's pain. Andrey Dmitrievich Dementyev [*or* Dement'ev]. TCRP

As long as we look forward, all seems free. Western Approaches, The. Howard Nemerov. ColAP; HCAP; TAP

As Love And I. Michael Drayton. NoSic *Fr.* Idea.

As loving Hind that (Hartless) wants her Deer. Another. Anne Bradstreet. EMWP; LW; NAAL-3; OxBA; SCAP; WPE

As Lucy Went a-Walking. Walter De la Mare. OBSP

As mad sexton's bell, tolling. Thomas Lovell Beddoes. FaBoCh; WoPoe *Fr.* Death's Jest Book.

As many red herrings as grow [*or* grew] in the wood. (LL) Man in the wilderness asked [of] me [*or* said to me], The [*or* A]. Mother Goose. FaBoCh; LB; OxNR; ReMoGo; Spl

As maples turn the size. Hearing of Reagan's Trip to Bitburg. Lyn Lifshin. GotH

As martyrs gridirons, when God calls the roll. (LL) Rolling the Lawn. William Empson. HarvBoo; MoBrPo; OBGa

As May was opening the rosebuds. Birth of the Foal. Ferenc Juhász. RB; WoPoe, *tr. by* David Wevill

As men, for fear the stars should sleep and nod. Divinity. George Herbert. NOSC

As men that are with visions grac'd. To Rosania (now Mrs Montague) Being With Her, 25th September 1652. Katherine Philips. PoBW

As 'mid moonbeams shifted through a cloud! (LL) Palimpsest, A. "Michael Field." VWP; ViWPN

As 'mid these moldering walls I pensive stray. Written in a Ruinous Abbey. Susan Evance. CenSon

As Mozart composed a sonata. Limerick. *Unknown.* PeLi

As much as pilots are happy when they are traversing the sea. Angelo [*or* Andrea] Poliziano. CAGL, *tr. by* James J. Wilhelm *Fr.* Greek Epigrams.

As much as the image of you, I have seen. Astropastoral. Douglas Crase. KGB

As Much As You Can. Constantine P. Cavafy. RB

As musing pensive in my silent home. Written at Scarborough. August, 1799. Mary Tighe. CenSon

As my black hair. (LL) Lady Horikawa. BoWoP; OHPJ

As My Cat Eats the Head of a Field Mouse He Has Caught. M. Loncar. NAPBL

As my eyes. Frances Densmore. APT-1 *Fr.* Chippewa Music.

As my eyes search the prairie. Spring Song. *Unknown.* OBVE, *tr. by* Frances Densmore

As my father's breathing. Stone at the Bottom, The. Manuel Ulacia. VCWP, *tr. by* Reginald Gibbons

As my imagination rises. Beyond Imagination. David Rokeah [*or* Rokeakh]. MHP, *tr. by* Ruth Finer Mintz

As my master doth set by me. (LL) Jolly Pinder of Wakefield, The. *Unknown.* ESPB; PBRV

As my mind in fancy wanders. Negro Has a Chance, The. Maggie Pogue Johnson. CBWP-4

As my mother ages and becomes. My Mother in Old Age. Eric Ormsby. NIP-4

As my new life begins, I start smiling at the people around me. Farewell to Kurdistan. Rosemary Tonks. OxBTC

As my shadow touches them. Crab. Angela Dove. Prnts

As My Way Passed Through T'ung-ch'uan, I Wished to Visit the Policy Critic of the Right, Mei, but Did Not Know Where to Find Him. Tai Piao-yüan. CoBLCP, *tr. by* Jonathan Chaves

As "Name of individual, partnership, or corporation to whom paid." Royalties. Dennis Joseph Enright. NOBL; PeLV

As Nature H——'s clay was blending. On a Certain Effeminate Peer. John Winstanley. FaBoEE

As near Portobello lying. Admiral Hosier's Ghost. Richard Glover. NOEC

As needy gallants in the scriv'ners' hands. Dryden. OBSV *Fr.* Amboyna; or, The Cruelties of the Dutch to the English Merchants.

As night follows night. *Unknown.* ErotSp, *tr. by* Sam Hamill

As night succeeds night. *Unknown.* ArkPo, *tr. by* Helen Craig McCullough

As night was falling slowly on city, town and bush. Bastard from the Bush, The. *Unknown.* NOBAu

As Nilus' sudden ebbing here. Dream Broke, A. William Cartwright. NOSC

As not yet come to our impiety. (LL) Fulke Greville, 1st Baron Brooke. NoSic; SacPr *Fr.* Caelica.

As o'er my latest book I pored. Printer's Error. P. G. Wodehouse. OBCoV

As o'er thy loved one now in grief ye bendeth. Solace. Josephine D. Henderson Heard. CBWP-4

As Ocean's Stream. Fyodor [*or* Feodor] Ivanovich Tyutchev. AWP, *tr. by* Babette Deutsch and Avrahm Yarmolinsky

As oft I do record. Jinny. *Unknown.* NOSC

As often as some where before my feet. Francis Daniel Pastorius. SCAP

As old age approaches. Yün Shou-p'ing. CoBLCP *Fr.* Lament for Myself, A.

As old age weakens me, I grow lazy and foolish. Departing from Ch'in-chou. Tu Fu. CrYelRi, *tr. by* Sam Hamill

As Old As Then. Jan Eijkelboom. TuT, *tr. by* Michael O'Loughlin

As on all its sides a kitchen-match darts white. Spanish Dancer. Rainer Maria Rilke. NAWM-7v2, *tr. by* Stephen Mitchell

As on an autumn night a herdman's fire. János Arany. IQMS, *tr. by* Watson Kirkconnell *Fr.* Toldi.

As on that noble sorrow we attend. (LL) Lovers. "Michael Field." PoBW; ViWPN

As on the Cross, the Saviour hung. Deep Spring. *Unknown.* SacPr

As on the Heather. Reinmar von Hagenau. AWP, *tr. by* Jethro Bithell

As on the highway's quiet edge. Coast, The: Norfolk. Frances Darwin Cornford. OxBTC

As once grave Pluto drove his royal wheels. Proserpine's Ragout. Mary Leapor. ECWP

As once, if not with light regard. Ode on the Poetical Character. William Collins. NAEL-5v1; NOEC; PoE

As once in heaven Dante looked back down. Backward Look, The. Howard Nemerov. OxBC

As once the winged energy of delight. Rainer Maria Rilke. EnlH *Fr.* Sonnets to Orpheus.

As one, at midnight, wakened by the call. Prelude. Wilfrid Wilson Gibson. MoBrPo

As one grows older and Caesar, Hitler. Walk Home, The. Reed Whittemore. CoAmPo

As one hears the cry. Kasa no Iratsume. ArkPo, *tr. by* Edwin A. Cranston

As One Non-Combatant to Another. George Orwell. OxBTC

As One Put Drunk into the Packet-Boat. John Ashbery. HAP; HCAP; VCAP

As one sees on the branch in the month of May the rose. Roses. Pierre de Ronsard. WoPoe, *tr. by* Vernon Watkins

As one that for a weary space has lain. Odyssey, The. Andrew Lang. OBEV; PoRA

As one that strives, being sick, and sick to death. To Celia, upon Love's Ubiquity. Thomas Carew. CavPo

As One Who Bears beneath His Neighbor's Roof. Robert Silliman Hillyer. MoAmPo

As one who cons at evening o'er an album, all alone. James Whitcomb Riley. ITBLP *Fr.* Old Sweetheart of Mine, An.

As one who destined from his friends to part. On Being Forced to Part with his Library for the Benefit of his Creditors. William Stanley Roscoe. CenSon

As one who goes between high garden walls. Personality. Agnes Mary Frances Robinson. VWP

As one who goes from holding converse sweet. Lowlands. William Reed Huntington. APN-2

As one who hangs down-bending from the side. William Wordsworth. NAEL-6v2 *Fr.* Prelude, The; Growth of a Poet's Mind [1850 vers.].

As one who has sailed across an unknown sea. Solitary, The. Rainer Maria Rilke. TrJP, *tr. by* C. F. MacIntyre

As one, who, journeying westward with the sun. Uncalled. Madison Cawein. TCAPo

As one who late hath lost a friend adored. Mary Tighe. CenSon

As One Who Wanders into Old Workings. Cecil Day Lewis. FaBoMo

As one young guy screwed another young guy. David Trinidad. WiU *Fr.* Eighteen to Twenty-One.

As other men, so I myself do muse. Michael Drayton. NOSC; NoSic; Son *Fr.* Idea.

As our good manners required. (LL) Manners. Elizabeth Bishop. NOxBChV; OxBC; RB

As our king lay musing on his bed. King Henry Fifth's Conquest of France. *Unknown.* ESPB

As over muddy shores a dragon flock. Fear, The. Lascelles Abercrombie. OBMV

As Parmigianino did it, the right hand. Self-Portrait in a Convex Mirror. John Ashbery. HCAP; NAAL-2v2

As phoebus in his spheris hicht. Marie Maitland Lauder. EMWP

As Phyllis the gay, at the break of the day. Song 3. Edward Moore. ECEV

As played by the phantoms of Shrule. Limerick. Tony Butler. PeLi

As Porcelain. (LL) Emily Dickinson. NALW; NCAP

As praiseworthy / the power of breathing. Lorine Niedecker. VGW

As proper mode of quenching legal lust. Gerald Massey. NOBVV

As puffed up. First Robin. Jane Yolen. NOxBChV

As real as melancholy, baldness, headache. Lovesickness: A Medieval Text. Jack Coulehan. BloBone

As realpeople. (LL) We Walk the Way of the New World. Haki R. Madhubuti. BPo; ESEAA

As reason's pow'rs by day our God disclose. Phillis Wheatley. SacPr *Fr.* Thoughts on the Works of Providence.

As red as her lips were she wasn't there. La Milagrosa. Víctor Hernández Cruz. TouFir

As riper years approach us. Glimpses of Infancy. Priscilla Jane Thompson. CBWP-2

As Rochefoucauld his maxims drew. Verses on the Death of Dr. Swift, D.S.P.D., Occasioned by Reading a Maxim in Rochefoucauld. Jonathan Swift. NAEL-6v1; NAEL-7v1; NOEC

As round as an apple, as deep as a cup. Well, The. Mother Goose. OxNR; ReMoGo

As round as an apple, as deep as a pail. *Unknown.* OxNR

As round the rose's heart the golden threads. Soul Incense. Henrietta Cordelia Ray. CBWP-3

As Sam crumbles lumps of tofu on her tray. Gardens We Have Left. David Mura. OpBo

As sea-foam blown of the winds, as blossom of brine that is drifted. Henry Cuyler Bunner. OBAL *Fr.* Home.

As sea. rain. Takings. Gael Turnbull. Oth

As second wife, I never liked the first. Concubine, The. *Vietnamese Oral Tradition.* CaDao, *tr. by* John Balaban

As seventh sign, the antique heavens show. Feast of the Ram's Horn. Harvey Shapiro. VGW

As Shadows Cast by Cloud and Sun. William Cullen Bryant. AH

As shakes the canvass of a thousand ships. Cornelius Mathews. APN-1 *Fr.* Poems on Man in His Various Aspects under the American Republic.

As she beats her ordinary bread. (LL) In Salem. Lucille Clifton. ESEAA; PAI

As she had sowed them with her odoruos foot. (LL) Ben Jonson. BeJo; OxBSP *Fr.* Sad Shepherd, The.

As she is showering, I wake to see. Aubade, An. Timothy Steele. PasH; RA

As she laughed I was aware of becoming involved in her laughter. Hysteria. T. S. Eliot. OxBEV

As she liv'd peerless. William Shakespeare. OxAEP-1 *Fr.* Winter's Tale, The.

As she passes over them. (LL) Wind and Silver. Amy Lowell. BoWoP; HeIP-4; KaS; MoAmPo; PAI; Spl; TCAPo

As shepherds in the red dusk went to hurry. Watteau, a Dream. Emile Nelligan. WoPoe, *tr. by* David Rattray

As shines the sunbeam through dark clouds. Hope. Mary E. Tucker. CBWP-1

As ships, becalmed at eve, that lay. Qua Cursum Ventus. Arthur Hugh Clough. OBEV

As shows [*or* shews] the air[e], when with a rainbow graced. Upon Julia's Ribband. Robert Herrick. CaPo

As silent as a mirror is believed. Legend. Hart Crane. OxBA

As simple an act. Way Out West. Imamu Amiri Baraka. NeAP

As since he dares not come within my sight. (LL) Dream[e], The. Ben Jonson. BeJo; NOBE; NOSC

As sincerely as possible. Steve Benson. FTOS *Fr.* Reverse Order.

As Sisyphus against the infernal steep. Byron. OBSV *Fr.* English Bards and Scotch Reviewers.

As slow I climb the cliff's ascending side. At Tynemouth Priory, after a Tempestuous Voyage. William Lisle Bowles. Son

As slow our ship her foamy track. Journey Onwards, The. Thomas Moore. GTBS-P; OxAEP-2

As slowly he sat up, near his left shoulder. Lazarus. Ágnes Nemes Nagy. IQMS, *tr. by* Adam Makkai

As slowly wanders thy sequestered stream. To the River Wensbeck. William Lisle Bowles. CenSon

As small-arms fire explodes outside the walls. (LL) Little Brown Brother. Nick Carbó. AmPoNex; ReBoTo

As soft as silk, as white as milk. Walnut, A. Mother Goose. LB; OxNR; ReMoGo

As some brave Admiral in former War. Disabled Debauchee, The. John Wilmot, 2d Earl of Rochester. BASC; BoLoP; HAP; NAEL-5v1; NAEL-6v1; NAEL-7v1; NOBL; NPeEn; NoP-4; OBSV

As some fond virgin, whom her mother's care. Epistle to Miss [*or* Miss Teresa] Blount, on Her Leaving the Town after the Coronation. Pope. BoLoP; EBEV; FHYEP; NAEL-5v1; NAEL-6v1; NAEL-7v1; NOBE; NOEC

As someone on his back for months of illness. Ausiàs March. STV

As Sometimes in a Grove. Frederick Goddard Tuckerman. NCAP

As soon as April pierces to the root. Geoffrey Chaucer. NAWM-5v1; NAWM-7v1, *tr. by* Theodore Morrison *Fr.* Canterbury Tales, The.

As soon as he realized he was lost, that. Lifeline. Vijay Seshadri. BAP-97

As soon as I knew all the verses of the Shema. Samuel. Judith Baumel. TaR

As soon as I left. Mammals. Lesley Dauer. NAPBL

As soon as I lie down in my soft bed. Sonnet 9. Louise Labé. BoWoP, *tr. by* Willis Barnstone

As Soon As It's Here It's Gone But So What. Emilie Buchwald. MiVo

As soon as my sister and I got out of our. Sisters of Sexual Treasure, The. Sharon Olds. PBCAP

As soon as night descends, we meet. Mary Magdalène (I). Boris Leonidovich Pasternak. AF, *tr. by* Lydia Pasternak Slater

As soon as the idea of the Flood had subsided. After the Flood. Arthur Rimbaud. SxFrPo, *tr. by* Martin Sorrell

As soon as the night turns into dawn. In Re Conferences. Vladimir Vladimirovich Mayakovsky [*or* Maiakovskii]. TCRP, *tr. by* Albert C. Todd

As soon as thou wast skilled in falconry. (LL) Lady Laments for Her Lost Lover, by Similitude of a Falcon, A. *Unknown.* AWP; EaItPo, *tr. by* Dante Gabriel Rossetti

As Spring the Winter Doth Succeed. Anne Bradstreet. AH

As stands a statue on its pedestal. George Henry Boker. APN-2 *Fr.* Sonnets: A Sequence on Profane Love.

As still he envied me, so fair she was! (LL) Bishop Orders His Tomb at Saint Praxed's Church, The. Robert Browning. CABP; EBVV; FHYEP; HAP; HeIP-4; NAEL-5v2; NAEL-6v2; NAWM-7v2; NOBVV; NPeEn; NoP-4; OBAL; PoE; SCGP; TFi

As structures go, it wasn't such a bad one. Old Complex, The. John Ashbery. FTOS

As sultry as the cruising hum. Muted Music. Robert Penn Warren. APT-2

As, sum tyme, dois the curser stert and ryn. Virgil [*or* Vergil]. OBVE, *tr. by* Gawin [*or* Gavin] Douglas *Fr.* Aeneid [*or* Eneados, *Aeneis*], The.

As sunbeams stream through liberal space. Ralph Waldo Emerson. NOBA

As sweet Polly Oliver lay musing in bed. Sweet Polly Oliver. *Unknown.* FaBoWar

As Syllable from Sound. (LL) Emily Dickinson. APN-2; EnlH; MoAmPo; NAAL-2v1; NAAL-3; NAAL-5; NAWM-7v2; NCAP; NIL-7; OxBA; PoPoPo

As the Allied tanks trod Germany to shard. May, 1945. Peter Porter. HP; OxBC

As the army corps advances. (LL) Army Corps on the March, An. Walt Whitman. AiP; CBCWP

As the basket comes in procession, greet it, women. Callimachus. HePo, *tr. by* Barbara Hughes Fowler *Fr.* Hymns.

As the Beer Trucks Eclipse the Light of Morning. Anthony R. Vigil. AmPoNex

As the black curtain of the night. Reveille Matin, or Good Morrow to a Friend. Mildmay Fane, 2d Earl of Westmorland. NOSC

As the black storm upon the mountain top. William Wordsworth. NAEL-6v2 *Fr.* Prelude, The; Growth of a Poet's Mind [1850 vers.].

As the blind Milton's memory of light. City Visions. Emma Lazarus. APN-2; SWaP

As the boat glides slowly. Pall Hanging over Manila. Mila D. Aguilar. ReBoTo

As the Breeze that Cools the Blood. Gustavo Adolfo Bécquer. SpanPo, *tr. by* Edward F. Gahan

As the broad mountain where the shadows flit. Thomas Cole. APN-1 *Fr.* Voyage of Life, The.

As the Buck Lay Dead. Marsden Hartley. APT-1

As the cat. Poem. William Carlos Williams. ChAP; HarvBoo; KaS; NoP-4; PAI; PoPoPo; SoSe-8; TTTS

As the chameleon, who is known. Chameleon, The. Matthew Prior. OBSV

As the choir of stars begins. Dream of the Condor, The. José Santos Chocano. TCLAP, *tr. by* Andrew Rosing

As the clouds that are so light. Clouds That Are So Light, The. Edward Thomas. FaBoTw

As the companion is dead. Vigil. Cecília Meireles. TCLAP, *tr.* by James Merrill

As the crescent moon is born from the Western Sea. Ch'en Tzu-ang. SuSp *Fr.* Impressions of Things Encountered.

As the Crow Flies, Let Him Fly. Samuel Hoffenstein. "Early bird may catch the worm, The." NBLV

As the day stands when the Sun begins to glow. Dante Alighieri. NAWM-5v1 *Fr.* Divina Commedia.

As the days grow longer. Lengthening Days. *Unknown*. ReMoGo

As the Dead Prey upon Us. Charles Olson. APT-2; NeAP

As the despair of warmth in January. Conjunction. Semyon [*or* Semion] Izrailevich Lipkin. TCRP, *tr.* by Albert C. Todd

As the divorced [*or* divorc'd] soul from her body parts. (LL) Surrender, The. Henry King, Bishop of Chichester. BoLoP; EBEV; NOSC

As the dust from the wet dream of a nation. Written in Unbridled Repugnance near Sioux Falls, Alabama—April 30, 1974. A. K. Redwing. VoR

As the elevator car left our floor. Limerick. *Unknown*. PeLi

As the Flower of the Grass. May Probyn. VWP

As the full moon rises. Poem. Kenneth Rexroth. GifTon

As the gook woman howls. In the Mourning Time. Robert Earl Hayden. BPo

As the great bhikshu descends into the West. Bodhidharma Crossing the Graywolf River on a Ry-Krisp. Tim McNulty. GifTon

As the Great Days Flow. Enrique Molina. TCLAP, *tr.* by Naomi Lindstrom

As the Great Horse Rots on the Hill. Hyam Plutzik. APT-2

As the great old trees. Issa. SoOfWa, *tr.* by Sam Hamill

As the hart panteth after the water brooks. Bible, *O.T.* AWP; TrJP *Fr.* Psalms.

As the heroes of Marathon their renown we know. (LL) Towards Lillers. Ivor Gurney. NAEL-5v2; NAEL-6v2; NoP-4

As the Human Village Prepares for Its Fate. Tom Clark. BodElec

As the immense dew of Florida. Nomad Exquisite. Wallace Stevens. APT-1; ColAP

As the late night passes. Hirose Izen. OHMPJ

As the lean tree burst into grief. (LL) Mad Scene, The. James Merrill. CoAP; NOBA; PoE; TAP

As the man next door on his porch. Nothing but Bad News. Jennifer Richter. MoASP

As the mists rise in the dawn. Fujiwara no Sadayori. OHPJ

As the natives got ready to serve. Limerick. Ed Cunningham. PeLi

As the ninth wave of the sea. (LL) Song of Blodeuwedd, The. *Unknown*. NoP-4; WoPoe, *tr.* by Robert Graves

As the observer wills. (LL) Study of Two Pears. Wallace Stevens. APT-1; BLT; NAAL-2v2; NoAM; OxBA

As the phobic said: it is torture. Suspension: Junior Wells on a Small Stage in a Converted Barn. Sandra McPherson. SeSe

As the poets have mournfully sung. Limerick. W. H. Auden. PeLi *Fr.* Shorts [1948–1957].

As the poor end of each dead day drew near. He Liked the Dead. Malcolm Lowry. OxBTC

As the prey-freighted eagle cleaves the storm. Free-booter, The. George Darley. OxBSo

As the primal spunk of the cosmos bellowed Out! (LL) Spunk Talking. Anne Rouse. MFPA; NeBl

As the primrose spreads so sweetly. (LL) Cruel Brother, The. *Unknown*. ESPB; OxBB

As the procession passes the palace the blinds are drawn. William McGonagall. VerBaPo *Fr.* Funeral of the German Emperor, The.

As the queen upon her throne. (LL) Learning to Read. Frances Ellen Watkins Harper. BlSi; NAAAL; NALW

As the rain is lagging, wayward, in the river. On the Fragile Labyrinth. José Emilio Pacheco. STV, *tr.* by John Frederick Nims

As the rock and ocean that we were made from. (LL) Carmel Point. Robinson Jeffers. APT-1; BLT; NAAL-2v2; NAAL-5; NoAM; NoP-4

As the seed of a mole for. Perpetua. Olga Broumas. ErotSp

As the seed waits eagerly watching for its flower and fruit. William Blake. PoE *Fr.* Vala; or The Four Zoas.

As the sound fades. Basho. EH, *tr.* by Robert Hass

As the stars hide in the light before daybreak. Avoiding News by the River. W. S. Merwin. GifTon

As the stores close, a winter light. February Evening in New York. Denise Levertov. NoAM

As the suffering hart confounded. Sándor Kisfaludy. IQMS, *tr.* by Watson Kirkconnell *Fr.* Unhappy Love.

As the sun declined the snow at our feet. Prose Poem. Humphrey Jennings. SPE

As the sun sets, the mountain air becomes cool. Sailing along the Tai Stream from Stone Bridge to the Foot of Mo-ho Peak. Wang Shih-chieng. SuSp, *tr.* by Chang Yin-nan

As the sun that lights creation. Africa. Lizelia Augusta Jenkins Moorer. CBWP-3

As the sweet sweat of roses in a still. John Donne. BASC; PeLV *Fr.* Elegies.

As the Team's Head-Brass. Edward Thomas. CABP; GTBS-P; HarvBoo; NAEL-5v2; NAEL-6v2; NoP-4; OBWP; OxAEP-2; OxBTC; PeFWW; PoE; RB

As the thread of my breath. *Unknown*. ArkPoo, *tr.* by Edwin A. Cranston

As the thrushes do. (LL) I So Liked Spring. Charlotte Mew. OxAEP-2; OxBEV; OxBTC

As the train approaches the tunnel, the kids. Children's Train, The. Dorianne Laux. GM

As the true stars at daybreak. (LL) Daybreak. Galway Kinnell. BLT; ChAP

"As the twig is bent, the tree's inclined." Thomas Hood. NOBVV *Fr.* Miss Kilmansegg and Her Precious Leg.

As the two ripe halves. Anatomy of Departure. Elizabeth Garrett. NeBl

As the war-trumpet drowns the rustic flute. Pindar. Antipater of Sidon. AWP, *tr.* by John Addington Symonds

As the wheel follows the hoof. Kenneth Rexroth. APSN *Fr.* Love Poems of Marichiko, The.

As the Window Darkens. Laura Jensen. LCAP-2

As the wise men of old brought gifts. Gift, The. William Carlos Williams. ChIV-2

As the Word came to prophets of old. Prophets for a New Day. Margaret Abigail Walker. BPo; NAAAL

As the young phoenix, duteous to his sire. Renewal. "Michael Field." ViWPN

As the youthful morning's light, On S. John the Baptist. Thomas Stanley. ChIV-2

As their names occurred. (LL) Anseo. Paul Muldoon. CIP-2; ModIr; NPeEn; PNI

As theirs, I lay, like them, my best gifts on thy shrine! (LL) Proem: "I love the old melodious lays." John Greenleaf Whittier. APN-1; OxBA; TAP

As then I had mine, in the place that was happy and poor. (LL) Time's Fool. Ruth Pitter. MoBrPo; OxBTC; PoRA; WPE

As then in death, so now in love. (LL) C[h]aritas Nimia; or, The Dear[e] Bargain. Richard Crashaw. ESCV; NOCV; NOSC

As there, along the elmy hedge, I go. Troubles of the Day. William Barnes. GTBS-P

As These Letters—humid, sunless. The writing occurs on their walls. (LL) Sun. Michael Palmer. APSN; PFTM-2

As they came from the East. Kings and Stars. John Erskine. TrCP

As they came in by the Eden side. Slaughter of the Laird of Mellerstain, The. *Unknown*. ESPB

As they do now at me. (LL) George Gascoigne. EBEV; HAP; NOBE; SCGP *Fr.* Adventures of Master F. I, The.

As they sat and talked beneath the boundary trees. Married Love. Sherod Santos. Son

As they sat sipping their glasses in the courtyard. Dinner at the Hotel de la Tigresse Verte. Donald Evans. TCAPo

As they to glory ride therein. (LL) Edward Taylor. NAAL-2v1; NAAL-3; OxBA; SCAP *Fr.* God's Determinations [touching his Elect].

As they were saying this. Alec Derwent Hope. GI *Fr.* St. Luke.

As thin little Proclus was fanning the fire. Lucilius. GrAn

As this convine and ordinance was mayd. Virgil [*or* Vergil]. OBVE, *tr.* by Gawin [*or* Gavin] Douglas *Fr.* Aeneid [*or* Eneados, *Aeneis*], The.

As this in Kew thirst for the Red Dawn. (LL) Note on Local Flora. William Empson. EBEV; FaBoMo; OxAEP-2; OxBEV

As Thomas was cudgelled [*or* cudgell'd *or* cudgel'd] one day by his wife. Three Epigrams. Jonathan Swift. FaBoEE

As Thoreau might say. Three Poems 1989. Larry Eigner. PFTM-2

As those we love decay, we die in part. James Thomson. OBEV; SCGP *Fr.* On the Death of Mr. William Aikman the Painter.

As those who are not athletic at breakfast day by day. Nature Morte. Louis MacNeice. NoAM

As thou wert loth to see, before thy feet. Guido Cavalcanti. EaItPo, *tr.* by Dante Gabriel Rossetti

As though. Chopin Preludes, Opus 28. J. R. Solonche. MiVo

As though a bare bulb hung. Billy. Linda McCarriston. LoL

As though an aged person were to wear. Elegy for the Monastery Barn. Thomas Merton. VGW

As though his subject had decided to remain a prayer. (LL) Painter, The. John Ashbery. EmeKit; HCAP; NOBA; NoP-4; PoE; PoPoPo; YaYoPo

As though I walked the wood with sagamore George. (LL) Frederick Goddard Tuckerman. NOBA; TAP *Fr.* Sonnets.

As though it soared suchwise through heaven too. (LL) Royal Palm. Hart Crane. MoAmPo; NoAM

As though it was meant to happen. (LL) Jack Johnson Does the Eagle Rock. Cornelius Eady. ESEAA; MoASP

As though recalling a moment in Creation. Palace of Fine Arts in San Francisco, The. Fidelito Cortes. ReBoTo

As though something knew Bly was coming. Despair. Tom Wayman. CDa

As though squeaks in the piano were not enough, a mouse. Summerhouse Piano. Sascha Feinstein. AmPoNex

As three blind mice? [*or* Three blind mice]. (LL) Mother Goose. LB; OxBEV; OxNR; ReMoGo

As through a mist, the pious prosperous ghosts. (LL) Indian Reservation: Caughnawaga. Abraham Moses Klein. NOBC; NoP-4

As through a neighb'ring grove, where ancient beech. William Mason. OBGa *Fr.* English Garden, The.

As through earth's garden once I strayed. Crushed Flower, The. Mary E. Tucker. CBWP-1

As through the land at eve we went. Tennyson. SCGP *Fr.* Princess, The.

As through the trellis peers the sudden Bridegroom. (LL) At the Indian Killer's Grave. Robert Lowell. NOBA; VGW

As thumb is genius of the hand. Objects in Mirror are Closer Than They Appear. Jeffrey Skinner. PBCAP

As thus the snows arise, and foul and fierce. James Thomson. ECEV *Fr.* Seasons, The.

As Time Goes By. Herman Hupfeld. ReLy

As Time One Day by Me Did Pass. Henry Vaughan. ESCV; GeHe; MeLP

As time will turn our bodies straight. Religion Is That I Love You. Kenneth Patchen. APT-2

As to an unknown lover I returned. Touro Synagogue. Ruth Whitman. TaR

As to Being Alone. James Oppenheim. TrJP

As to Himself at last eternity changes him. Tomb of Edgar Poe, The. Stéphane Mallarmé. NAWM-7v2, *tr. by* Henry Weinfield

As to His Choice of Her. Wilfrid Scawen Blunt. GSo; Son *Fr.* Love Sonnets of Proteus, The.

As to How Much. Louis Zukofsky. APT-2

As to my own concerns, it seems odd, given. Robert Pinsky. NoAM *Fr.* Essay on Psychiatrists.

As to th'Eternall often in anguishes. Bible, *O.T.* BASC; OxBEV, *tr. by* Mary Sidney Herbert, Countess of Pembroke *Fr.* Psalms.

As to the blooming prime. To Favonius. Edmund Bolton. NoSic

As to thy greater light a sacrifice. (LL) Glowworm, The. Thomas Stanley. BeJo; NOSC

As Toilsome I Wander'd Virginia's Woods. Walt Whitman. APN-1; BLT; NAAL-2v1; NAAL-3

As Tom the porter went up Ludgate Hill. Tom the Porter. John Byrom. NOEC

As Tommy Snooks and Bessy Brooks. Mother Goose. LB; OxNR; ReMoGo

As tongueless Echo in the pastoral vale. To the Greek Anthologists. George Rostrevor Hamilton. FaBoEE

As tourists inspected the apse. Limerick. Edward Gorey. PeLV; PeLi

As Tranquil Streams. Marion Franklin Ham. AH

As travellours [*or* travellers] when the twilight's come. Pilgrimage, The. Henry Vaughan. ChIV-2; ESCV

As tree and wheat rise green. Nile the Hermit. *Unknown.* GrAn, *tr. by* Guy Davenport

As twilight softly turns to sombre brown. Question at Night. Mihály Babits. IQMS, *tr. by* Peter Zollman

As two fair vessels side by side. "Michael Field." VWP

As unpredictable as picnic weather, blue. Guide to the Perplexed. David Malouf. NOBAu

As unto the bow the cord is. Henry Wadsworth Longfellow. EBNV *Fr.* Song of Hiawatha, The.

As usual, the clock in The Clock Bar was a good few minutes. Hamlet. Ciaran Carson. FaBoVe; ModIr; PNI

As usual, the first gate was modest. It is dilapidated. She can't tell. Tan Tien. Mei-Mei Berssenbrugge. OpBo

As usual, the guard who worked. On the Last Day of the World. Sherod Santos. GeoHom

As usual, the seasons change too fast. To Eva. Jacqueline Osherow. TaR

As Venus one day, at her toilet affairs. Venus Attiring the Graces. William Whitehead. ECEV

As Venus wandered 'midst the Idalian bower. Camellia, The. William Stanley Roscoe. CenSon

As virtuous men pass[e] mildly away. Valediction: Forbidding Mourning, A. John Donne. AmFaPo; BASC; ESCV; FHYEP; HAP; HeIP-4; MeLP; NAEL-5v1; NAEL-6v1; NAEL-7v1; NIL-7; NOBE; NOSC; NPeEn; OxBEV; PAI; PoE; SCGP; SoSe-8; TFi; UnPo; WeW-3

As warm as bread or as a homecoming. (LL) Upstate. Derek Walcott. GT; OPRER

As was my duty, I oversaw the carting in of birds. Monologue of the Falconer's Wife. Colette Inez. PuP-23

As water Rarified doth make *Winds* blow. Of Cold Winds. Margaret Lucas Cavendish, Duchess of Newcastle. EMWP

As water, silk. On Sitting Down to Write, I Decide Instead to Go to Fred Herko's Concert. Diane Di Prima. PmAP

As we babble about the sky and the weather and the forests of change. (LL) Mixed Feelings. John Ashbery. HAP; WeW-3

As we crossed the field, I told her. (LL) Centaur, The. May Swenson. APT-2; FaBoWP; TwCP

As we drove back, crossing the hill. Locked House, A. W. D. Snodgrass. VCAP

As we eye the blue horizon's bend. I Can Dream, Can't I? Irving Kahal. ReLy

As We Forgive Those. Eric Pankey. GI

As we get older we do not get any younger. Chard Whitlow. Henry Reed. MoBrPo; NBLV; NOBL; NoP-4; OBCoV; OxBTC; PeLV; UV; UnPo

As we go about the toils of life. As We Sow We Shall Reap. Maggie Pogue Johnson. CBWP-4

As we grow old / What triumph. Issa. ZenPo, *tr. by* Takashi Ikemoto and Lucien Stryk

As We Grow Older. Rollin J. Wells. PoToHe

As we have to be. (LL) Hymn to Priapus. D. H. Lawrence. OBMV; PoE; SCGP

As we left the garden-party. Leaving. Richard Wilbur. HarvBoo

As we live, we are transmitters of life. We Are Transmitters. D. H. Lawrence. OxBTC

As we made love for the third day. Ecstasy. Sharon Olds. EmeKit

As we say farewell to autumn. Yün Shou-p'ing. CoBLCP *Fr.* Chrysanthemums.

As We Sow We Shall Reap. Maggie Pogue Johnson. CBWP-4

As we speed out of youth's sunny station. Life's Journey. Ella Wheeler Wilcox. PWR

As we stood on the [edge of the crag] *or* cliff's edge. Against the Wind. Amir Gilbo'a. MHP

As wearied pilgrims, once possessed. His Own Epitaph. Robert Herrick. CaPo

As weary-hearted as that hollow moon. (LL) Adam's Curse. W. B. Yeats. BIrV; NAEL-5v2; NAEL-6v2; NoAM; NoP-4; WeW-3

As Weary Pilgrim, Now at Rest. Anne Bradstreet. ColAP; NAAL-2v1; NAAL-3; SCAP

As Well As Any Other. Laura Riding Jackson. APT-2

As well as these poor poems. Black Box, The. Gavin Ewart. OBCoV

As well as things. (LL) Riprap. Gary Snyder. HCAP; NAAL-2v2; NAAL-5; NOBA; NeAP; NoAM; PmAP; PoM; PoPoPo; VCAP

As well, maybe, that you cannot read our minds. Enemy, The. Randolph Stow. NOBAu

As what he loves may never like too much. (LL) On My First Son[ne]. Ben Jonson. AWP; AmFaPo; BASC; BeJo; CABP; ClHu; EBEV; FaBoEE; HAP; InPK-6; MakPoe; NAEL-5v1; NAEL-6v1; NAEL-7v1; NIL-7; NIP-4; NOSC; NPeEn; NoP-4; OxBEV; OxBSP; PBRV; PoE; PoPoPo; RB; RaBo; SCGP; TFi; TRP; WeW-3; WoPoe

As, when a beauteous nymph decays. Stella's Birthday, 1725. Jonathan Swift. CABP; NOEC

As When a Child. Charles Lamb. Son

As when a Conqu'rour does in Triumph come. To My Lady Morland at Tunbridge. Aphra Behn. PoBW

As when a Fragment, from a Mountain torn. Virgil [*or* Vergil]. OBVE, *tr. by* John Dryden *Fr.* Aeneid [*or* Eneados, *Aeneis*], The.

As when a ship, that flyes faire under saile. Edmund Spenser. FHYEP *Fr.* Faerie Queene, The.

As when a traveller, forced to journey back. Parting. William Johnson Cory. CAGL

As when an architect some palace wall. Homer. OBVE *Fr.* Iliad, The.

As when at first primitive men were dwelling on the fruitful earth. Mildred Cecil, Lady Burleigh. EMWP

As when desire, long darkling, dawns, and first. Dante Gabriel Rossetti. Son *Fr.* House of Life, The.

As when devouring flames some forest seize. Homer. OBVE *Fr.* Iliad, The.

As when, down some broad River dropping,we. Frederick Goddard Tuckerman. APN-2 *Fr.* Sonnets.

As when far off the warbled strains are heard. Samuel Taylor Coleridge. CenSon *Fr.* Effusions.

As when I fell a-sleeping. (LL) Anthony Munday. NOBE; OBEV *Fr.* Primaleon of Greece.

As when into the garden paths by night. Old Age. Frederick Tennyson. NOBVV

As when it hapneth that some lovely Towne. Content and Resolute. William Drummond, of Hawthornden. NPeEn; PBRV

As when of frequent bees. Homer. OBVE *Fr.* Iliad, The.

As when of old some orator renowned. John Milton. ChIV-1 *Fr.* Paradise Lost.

As when rooting in a bin. Dick, a Maggot. Jonathan Swift. NBLV

As When Some Hungry Fledgling Hears and Sees. Vittoria da Colonna, Marchesa di Pescara. BoWoP

As when some mighty Hero first appears. To Mrs. Manley, upon Her Tragedy Call'd The Royal Mischief. Mary Pix. EMWP

As, when some treasurer lays down the stick. Dryden. NOSC *Fr.* Love Triumphant.

As when the bright[e] Crulean firmament. Sir John Davies. NoSic *Fr.* Gulling[e] Sonnets, The.

As when the cheerfull Sunne, elamping wide. Giles Fletcher, the Younger. PBRV *Fr.* Christs Victorie, and Triumph in Heaven, and Earth, over, and after death.

As when the glorious Magazine of Light. On the 3 of September, 1651. Katherine Philips. BASC; EMWP; PBRV

As when the winds, ascending by degrees. Homer. OBVE *Fr.* Iliad, The.

As when, to one who long hath watched, the morn. John Codrington Bampfylde. CenSon; NOEC

As when two men have loved a woman well. Dante Gabriel Rossetti. NoP-4 *Fr.* House of Life, The.

As when two monarchs of the brindled breed. Paul Whitehead. NOEC *Fr.* Gymnasiad, or Boxing Match, The.

As when we grope amid the gloom of night. (LL) Clouded Morning, The. Jones Very. GSo; NOBA

As when with downcast eyes we muse and brood. Tennyson. CenSon

As whenever. Simonides. SaLy, *tr. by* Diane Rayor

As where a wind blows. Guardian Angel of Not Feeling, The. Jorie Graham. ExTi

As white their bark, so white this lady's hours. (LL) Virginal, A. Ezra Pound. ColAP; MoAmPo; NAAL-2v2; NIL-7; NIP-4; NOBA; OxBA; Son; TAP; TCAPo

As who by being poisoned doth poison know. (LL) Sir Philip Sidney. NAEL-5v1; NAEL-6v1; NAEL-7v1 *Fr.* Astrophil and Stella.

As who was not, in laughter, pain, and love. (LL) Days of 1964. James Merrill. CoAP; HCAP; NAAL-2v2; PoE; VCAP

As with any child, you find your own more beautiful. Failure. Dana Gioia. KGB

As with heaped bees at hiving time. Robert Louis Stevenson. NOBVV *Fr.* Rivers and winds among the twisted hills.

As with tending a newborn, the days pass slowly, the months. Sewing Without Mother: A Zuihitsu. Kimiko Hahn. PuP-23

As With Them. Boris Leonidovich Pasternak. TCRusP, *tr. by* Bogdan Boychuk and Mark Rudman

As with your shadow I with these did play. (LL) William Shakespeare. AWP; EBEV; NAEL-5v1; NAEL-6v1; NAEL-7v1; NOBE; NoSic; OBEV; OxAEP-1 *Fr.* Sonnets.

As withereth the primrose by the river. Palinode, A. Edmund Bolton. NoSic

As women do. (LL) Snow White and the Seven Dwarfs. Anne Sexton. HCAP; PoPoPo

As Women of Our Race. Mrs. Henry Linden. CBWP-4

As woods whose change appeares. Horace. OBVE *Fr.* Art of Poetry, The.

As ye go through these palm-trees. Song of the Virgin Mother, A. Félix Lope de Vega Carpio. AWP, *tr. by* Ezra Pound

As yonder lamp in my vacated room. Lamp, The. Charles Whitehead. OBEV

As you advance in years you long. Of Change of Opinions. Victor Gustave Plarr. NOBVV

As you all know, tonight is the night of the full. 12 O'Clock News. Elizabeth Bishop. OxBC

As you are big for you! (LL) Little Elf, The. John Kendrick Bangs. NTCP; OBCA

As You Came from the Holy Land [of Walsingham]. *Unknown, sometimes at. to* Sir Walter Ralegh. EnLoPo; HAP; NPeEn; NoSic; OBEV; OxAEP-2; OxBEV; PBRV; RB; TFi

(Walsingham[e].) BoLoP; FaBoCh; NOBE; SCGP

As You Come In. Anne Marriott. NOBC

As you described your mastectomy in calm detail. American Beauty, An. Carolyn Kizer. GeoHom

As you drank deep as Thor, did you think of milk or wine? Fish Food. John Wheelwright. APT-2

As you haven't asked me for advice. Plug. Edmund Vance Cooke. PWR

As you lay in sleep. Cartography. Louise Bogan. TRP

As You Leave Me. Etheridge Knight. NNaP

As You Like It. William Shakespeare.
  Amien's Song. AWP; GTBS-P; NAEL-5v1; NOBE; NoSic; OBEV; SCGP; TTTS; UnPo
  (Blow, Blow, Thou Winter Wind.) NAEL-6v1
  Good in Everything. PoToHe
  "It was a lover and his lass." AWP; GTBS-P; NAEL-5v1; NAEL-6v1; NOBE; NoSic; OBEV; RB; SCGP; TFi; TTTS
  Motley's the Only Wear. OBCoV
  Orlando's Rhymes. CTC

Seven Ages of Man, The. ITBLP; RB; UV

Song: "If the scorn of your bright eyne.". CTC

(Song: "What shall he have that kill'd the dear?") CTC

"Thou seest, we are not all alone unhappie." OxBEV

(Under the Greenwood Tree.) NoP-4

"What would you have? Your gentleness shall force." OxAEP-1

As You Like It. Theodore Weiss. TAP

As you plaited the harvest bow. Harvest Bow, The. Seamus Heaney. BiHa; HarvBoo; ModIr; PBCIP; PNI

As you read, a white bear leisurely. To the Reader. Denise Levertov. PoM; VGW

As you see each of the stars has a voice. Glassy Sea. W. S. Merwin. BodElec

As you sip your brand of scotch. Bosnia Tune. Joseph Brodsky. FaBoWar

As you stand still in the hall thinking what. Purr, The. Molly Peacock. ExTi; PasH

As you walk on your way thinking of other things. Epitaph from Athens. *Unknown.* GrAn, *tr. by* Peter Jay

As you would a faithful horse. (LL) Freedom at McNealy's. Priscilla Jane Thompson. CBWP-2; SWaP

As your bright leaf? (LL) Sea Poppies. "H. D." APT-1; NALW

As your mind dissolves in God. (LL) Lal Ded [*or* Lalla]. WPoS; WoPoe, *tr. by* Coleman Barks

Asagumori. Kenneth Rexroth. GifTon

Asante. Leticia R. Benson. InTrad

Asante Sana, Te Te. Thadious M. Davis. BlSi

Ascend Lu-Shan. Pao Chao. ChinPo, *tr. by* Yip Wai-lim

Ascend my shoulders, firmly keep thy seat. Homer. OBVE *Fr.* Battle of the Frogs and Mice, The.

Ascend the Heron Tower. Wang Chih-huan. ChinPo, *tr. by* Yip Wai-lim

Ascend the Phoenix Terrace. Li Po. ChinPo, *tr. by* Yip Wai-lim

Ascend the Three Mountains Toward the Evening: Looking Back at the Capital. Hsieh T'iao. ChinPo, *tr. by* Yip Wai-lim

Ascending pile, The. John Milton. NOSC *Fr.* Paradise Lost.

Ascending Red Cedar Moon. Duane Niatum. CDW

Ascends the sky. (LL) Morning. William Blake. FaBoCh; WoPoe

Ascension. Denis Devlin. BIrV; ChIV-2

Ascension, The. Cynewulf.
  Redeemer, The.
    "As here on earth's soil God's Son Eternal." SacPr, *tr. by* Charles William Kennedy

Ascension-Day. Henry Vaughan. ESCV

Ascension Hymn. Henry Vaughan. ESCV; GeHe; NOSC; TrCP

Ascension Hymn. Henry Vaughan. *See* They Are All Gone into the World of Light!

Ascension: 1925, The. John Malcolm Brinnin. InPK-6

Ascension of Our Lord Jesus Christ, The. Christopher Smart. NOCV *Fr.* Hymns and Spiritual Songs for the Fasts and Festivals of the Church of England.

Ascension Thursday. Saunders Lewis. OBWVE, *tr. by* Gwyn Morgan

Ascensions, The. William Pillen [*or* Pillin]. RaBo

Ascent of Man, The. Mathilde Blind.
  Chaunts of Life. VWP
  Motherhood. ViWPN

Ascent of Species. John Milton. NOSC *Fr.* Paradise Lost.

Ascent of Vasco da Gama, The. Fernando Pessoa. PeSAV, *tr. by* F.E.G. Quintanilha

Ascent to the Sierras. Robinson Jeffers. OxBA

Ascetic art student named Josh, An. Limerick. D. H. Cudmore. PeLi

Ascetic Dyes His Robes, The. Kabir. WoPoe, *tr. by* Pritish Nandy

Ascetic / He emerges from its belly into the grave. Chaldean Ruins, The. Dunya Mikhail. PoArWo, *tr. by* Samira Kawar

Asclepiades the Miser was horrified. Miser and the Mouse, The. Lucilius. GrAn

Asclepias who loves to love. Meleager. GrAn

Asclepius cured the body: to make men whole. On Plato's Grave. *Unknown.* GrAn, *tr. by* William J. Philbin

Ascot Waistcoat. David McCord. NBLV

Asdrubral Jiménez. Charles McDonald. NLP

Asenath. Diana Hume George. ChIV-1

Ash. Jayanta Mahapatra. VCWP

Ash and the Oak, The. Louis Simpson. CoAmPo

Ash I leave behind, The. Kasei. JDP, *tr. by* Yoel Hoffmann

Ash Keys. Michael Longley. PBCIP

Ash on an old man's sleeve. T. S. Eliot. FaBoTw; NPeEn; OxBEV *Fr.* Four Quartets.

Ash Plant, The. Seamus Heaney. BiHa

Ash Range, The. Laurie Duggan.

One. One. BMAP

Ash Range, The. Laurie Duggan.

Five. One. BMAP

Ash Wednesday. Christina Georgina Rossetti. TrCP

Ash Wednesday [or Ash-Wednesday]. T. S. Eliot. APT-1; MoAmPo; OxBA; VGW

"At the first turning of the second stair." NOBA

"Because I do not hope to turn again." SacPr

"If the lost word is lost, if the spent word is spent." UV

Ashen feelers of the frigid morrow, The. Specter, The. Ernst Hardt. AWP, tr. by Jethro Bithell

Ashes. Annie Foster. NLP

Ashes. Alejandra Pizarnik. TCLAP, tr. by Frank Graziano and María Rosa Fort

Ashes, The. Carolyn Kizer. BAP-01

Ashes of me. Witch! Leonora Speyer. APT-1

Ashes of Soldiers. Walt Whitman. FaBoWar

Ashikaga Tadayoshi's Palace. Muso Soseki. EaWin, tr. by W. S. Merwin

Ashkelon is not cut off with the remnant of a valley. Judith. Adah Isaacs Menken. APN-2; CBWP-1; SWaP; ViWPN

Ashleaves froze without an ashleaf sound, The. (LL) Michael Hartnett. BIrV; PBCIP Fr. Thirteen Sonnets.

Ashtabula Disaster, The. Julia A. Moore. OBAL; VerBaPo

Asian American. Making It Stick. Lawson Fusao Inada. BAP-97

Asian Desert. Dorothy Wellesley, Duchess of Wellington. OBMV

Asians Dying, The. W. S. Merwin. CoAP; HCAP; NOBA; PoPoPo; VCAP

Aside. Ronald Stuart Thomas. OxBC

Aside from rain, the weather stays the same. Letter from Home. G. E. Patterson. AmPoNex

Aside from stormy weather, what problems does he have? (LL) Merchant's Joy, The. Chang Yü. CoBLCP; ColAnChi, tr. by Jonathan Chaves

Asides on the Oboe. Wallace Stevens. FaBoMo; MoAmPo

Ask, and let your words diminish your asking. Waiting. Jean Valentine. YaYoPo

Ask anyone up Harlem way. Bojangles of Harlem. Dorothy Fields. ReLy

Ask in one life no more. Word by Night. Charles Brasch. PeNZ

Ask, is it well, O thou consumed of fire. Burning of the Law, The. Meïr of Rothenburg. TrJP, tr. by Nina Davis Salaman

Ask many women and they'll claim no knowledge, but some. Jennie Fontana. NewEx

Ask Me. William Stafford. LoL

Ask me how do I feel. If I Were a Bell. Frank Loesser. ReLy

Ask me no more, my truth to prove. Winter Song. Elizabeth Tollet. ECWP; NOEC

Ask me no more: the moon may draw the sea. Tennyson. NAEL-5v2; NAEL-6v2 Fr. Princess, The.

Ask Mummy Ask Daddy. John Agard. OTCP

Ask No Return. Horace Gregory. MoAmPo; VGW Fr. Chorus for Survival.

Ask no return for love that's given. Horace Gregory. MoAmPo; VGW Fr. Chorus for Survival.

Ask not overmuch for fair. He That Loves a Rosy Cheek. Heinrich von Rugge. AWP, tr. by Jethro Bithell

Ask not the cause why sullen Spring. Song to a Fair Young Lady, Going Out of the Town in the Spring. Dryden. OBEV

Ask not why hearts turn magazines of passions. Funeral Elegy Upon that Pattern and Patron of Virtue, A. John Norton. SCAP

Ask not why sorrow shades my brow. Song: Montrose. Charles Cotton. NOSC

Ask the Empresse of the night. Magnet, The. Thomas Stanley. NOBE

Ask the Lord of the East, "Where lie the ends of the earth?" Tune: "Song of the Lunar Palace"—Sending Off Spring. Kuan Yün-shih. SuSp, tr. by Richard John Lynn

Ask the old men in Chinatown. Not Translation, Not Poetry. Daryl Ngee Chinn. LTA

Ask you what provocation I have had? Pope. ECEV; OBSV Fr. Epilogue to the Satires, in Two Dialogues.

Ask[e] me why I send you here. Primrose, The. Robert Herrick. OBEV

Asked, Don't you dream, do you ever. Erolog. Michael Palmer. FTOS

Asked how old he was. Issa. EH, tr. by Robert Hass

Asked me for a kiss. (LL) Suicide's Note. Langston Hughes. APT-2; PoPoPo; SAmP

Askest, 'How long thou shalt stay.' Visit, The. Ralph Waldo Emerson. APN-1; NOBA

Asking Favors. Wilma Elizabeth McDaniel. GeoHom

Asking what, asking what?—all a boy's afternoon. Debate: Question, Quarry, Dream. Robert Penn Warren. VGW

Asleap / sleap. Susan Howe. FTOS Fr. Defenestration of Prague.

Asleep beneath the cold and virgin stars. Village Night. Gyula Juhász. IQMS, tr. by Anthony Edkins

Asleep he wheezes at his ease. Roger the Dog. Ted Hughes. ChAP

Asleep in spring unaware of dawn. Spring Dawn. Meng Hao Jan. ColAnChi, tr. by Elling O. Eide

Asleep in the City. Michael Smith. PBCIP

Asleep in the Valley. Paul Verlaine. SxFrPo, tr. by Martin Sorrell

Asleep, My Love? William Shakespeare. CTC Fr. Midsummer Night's Dream, A.

Asleep on the sand, dozing on the water, they form a flock. About Geese. Li Shang-yin. SuSp, tr. by Eugene Eoyang

Asleep upon a chair. (LL) Ballad of Father Gilligan, The. W. B. Yeats. EBVV; MoBrPo; PoRA

Asleep while the children howl and the house burns. Goddess. Judith Johnson Sherwin. BoWoP

Asmodeus. Geoffrey Hill. FaBoTw

(Asmodeus.) FaBoTw

Asoka's Love Song. Alexander Lernet-Holenia. AuPH, tr. by Lowell A. Bangerter

Asparagus bed. Robert Spiess. HA

Asparagus I bite off their heads. Alexis Rotella. HA

Aspatia's Song. Francis Beaumont. AWP; HAP; NOBE; OBEV; SCGP Fr. Maid's Tragedy, The.

Aspect of Love, Alive in the Ice and Fire, An. Gwendolyn Brooks. BPo; PAI; TAP

Aspecta Medusa. Dante Gabriel Rossetti. OxBSP

Aspects. Norman MacCaig. OxBS

Aspects of Eve. Linda Pastan. CRP

Aspects of Love. Ruth Miller.

"Love? We should smother it." LW

Aspects of Now. Gwyn Williams.

"Today has it all, sunshine." OBWVE

Aspects of Robinson. Weldon Kees. CoAP

Aspects of the World like Coral Reefs. William Bronk. VGW

Aspen Tree. Paul Celan. PoetW, tr. by John Felstiner

Aspen Tree. Paul Celan. PoSu, tr. by Michael Hamburger

Aspen tree, your leaves glance white into the dark. Aspen Tree. Paul Celan. PoetW, tr. by John Felstiner

Aspen tree, your leaves glance white into the dark. Aspen Tree. Paul Celan. PoSu, tr. by Michael Hamburger

Aspens. Edward Thomas. FaBoVe; NPeEn; OxBEV

Asphalt. Chimalum Nwankwo. NAfrP

Asphalt memory of blood and pain. (LL) Harlem Gallery: From the Inside. Larry Neal. BPo; NBV

Asphalt Musings. Carl Hancock Rux. HeMarv

Asphodel. David Malouf. CBAP

Asphodel, That Greeny Flower. William Carlos Williams.

"Approaching death." FaBoMo

Paterson, Book 5: The River of Heaven. HarvBoo

Asphyxiated Man, The. Victor Serge. AF, tr. by James Brook

Aspiration. Mário de Andrade. TTY, tr. by John Nist

Aspiration. Adah Isaacs Menken. CBWP-1; ViWPN

Aspiration. Emily Jane Pfeiffer. ViWPN

Aspiration. Henrietta Cordelia Ray. CBWP-3

Aspiration. Edward William Thomson. SacPr

Aspirin. Elizabeth Alexander. AmPoNex

Aspiring Man, by learned pens. Brief Essay on Man. Arthur Guiterman. OBAL

Ass-Face. Dame Edith Sitwell. OBMV

Ass in the Lion's Skin, The. Aesop. AWP, tr. by William Ellery Leonard

Ass passed like an ass, The. Entry into Jerusalem. Dmitry [or Dmitrii] Aleksandrovich Prigov. ItGoST, tr. by Robert Reid

Ass put on a lion's skin and went, An. Ass in the Lion's Skin, The. Aesop. AWP, tr. by William Ellery Leonard

Ass, that for her slowness, was forbid, The. On Balaam's Ass. Francis Quarles. ChIV-1

Ass will with his long ears fray, An. Samuel Butler (1612–80). FaBoEE

Assail the breast, when passion rages there! (LL) Phaon Forsakes Her. Mary Robinson. CenSon; RWP

Assailant. John Raven. BPo

Assassination. Haki R. Madhubuti. GT

Assassination, The. Robert Silliman Hillyer. MoAmPo

Assassination, The. Donald Justice. VCAP

Assassination of Charlie Parker, The. Arthur Brown. SeSe

Assassination of John Lennon as Depicted by the Madame Tussaud Wax Museum, Niagara Falls, Ontario, 1987, The. David Wojahn. PBCAP Fr. Mystery Train: A Sequence.

Assassination of Robert Goulet as Performed by Elvis Presley: Memphis, 1968, The. David Wojahn. AllShUp; IllVoic

Ass[e], The. Robert Herrick. ChIV-1

Assemble, all ye maidens, at the door. Elegy on a Lady, Whom Grief for the Death of Her Betrothed Killed. Robert Bridges. OBEV

Assembler. Debra Allbery. PBCAP

Assembling the Dead at Dachau. Barbara Helfgott Hyett. GotH

Assembly Line. "Shu Ting." VCWP

Assembly of Ladies, The. The Lady of the Assembly.
Palace of Pleasant Regard, The. WPE
"In September, at falling of the leaf." OBGa

Assembly Point D. Tony Lopez.
"Dauntless the slug-horn to my lips I set." Oth

Assembly tree and bowl of thorns. Blouse of Felt. Amina Calil. BAP-01

Assents by eternally voting 'I.' (LL) Ambrose Bierce. APN-2; OBAL Fr. Devil's Dictionary, The.

Asserted our one night's identity. (LL) Louis MacNeice. CIP-2; MoBrPo Fr. Trilogy for X.

Asseverations. Arthur Nortje. HBAPE

Assignation with a Somnambulist. John Streeter Manifold. CBAP

Assignment, The. Len Roberts. OPRER

Assimilation. Eugene Gloria. ReBoTo

Assist me while I wander here. Caroline Codling. FaBoVe

Assistance, The. Paul Blackburn. NeAP; PoM

Assorted needles and coloured threads. Sewing Lesson, The. Kate Lilley. BMAP

Assuming rain, the exotic. "Night in the Tropics" (1858–59?). Michael Waters. MiVo

Assumption. Padraic Fallon. BIrV; NOIV

Assumption about the Harlem Brown Baby. Salih Michael Fisher. GLP

Assumption of Miriam from the Street in the Winter of 1942, The. Jerzy Ficowski.
"Snowflakes were teeming down." HP, tr. by Keith Bosley

Assurance. Josephine D. Henderson Heard. CBWP-4

Assurance, An. Nicholas Breton. SCGP

Assurbanipal loved me. Birth of Aisha and Her Death, The. Abdul Wahab [or 'Abd al-Wahhab] Al-Bayati [or Al-Bayyati]. MAP, tr. by Sargon Boulus and Christopher Middleton

Assuredly, a lively scene! Arthur Hugh Clough. PeLV Fr. Dipsychus [and the Spirit].

Assuredly, that fissured face. Eulogy to W.H. Auden. Derek Walcott. ESEAA

Assyrian came down like the wolf on the fold, The. Destruction of Sennacherib, The. Byron. BRP; CABP; ChAP; ChIV-1; FHYEP; FaBoCh; FaBoWar; HAP; HeIP-4; NoP-4; OBWP; OxAEP-2; PAI; RB; SCGP; TFi; TrCP; WeW-3; WoPoe

Assyrian [or Assyrians'] King in peace, with foul desire, The [or Th']. Sardanapalus. Henry Howard, Earl of Surrey. NAEL-6v1; NAEL-7v1; NoSic

Aster. Plato. GrAn; WoPoe, tr. by Peter Jay

Astig. Eric Fructuoso. ReBoTo

Astolfo flies by Chariot to the Moon, where he collects Orlando's lost wits. Ludovico Ariosto. NPeEn Fr. Orlando Furioso.

Astonish me beyond words. (LL) Pastoral: "Little sparrows, The." William Carlos Williams. SAmP; TwCP

Astonished Muse finds thousands at her side, The. (LL) Ode, Inscribed to W. H. Channing. Ralph Waldo Emerson. APN-1; HAP; NAAL-2v1; NAAL-3; NOBA; OxBA; TAP; TCAPo

Astonished stood Lucrece and Nara. Lucrece and Nara. Laura Riding Jackson. APT-2

Astonishing love, The. Oh, Astonishing Love. Javier Sologuren. BLPSL, tr. by Rene de Costa, Rigas Kappatos and Eleni Paidoussi

Astræa. Ralph Waldo Emerson. APN-1

Astræa. John Greenleaf Whittier. APN-1

Astrea in this time. William Drummond, of Hawthornden. NOSC Fr. Urania, or Spiritual Poems.

Astrid brought an oxhorn. Show and Tell. Roddy Lumsden. NeBl

Astrid comes from upstate New York. Feminine Intuition. Stephanie Brown. AmPoNex; BAP-97

Astride a mount pawing misty sedge grass. Spring Day in the Countryside, A. Wen T'ing-yün. SuSp, tr. by William R. Schultz

Astride an ox, you pass the village far in the distance. Buffalo Boy. Huang T'ing-chien. SuSp, tr. by William R. Schultz

Astrologer, The. Agathias. GrAn, tr. by Guy Davenport

Astrologer, The. Sir Thomas More. WoPoe, tr. by James Vincent Cunningham

Astrologer Predicts at Mary's Birth, The. Lucille Clifton. NALW

Astrologer's Song, An. Rudyard Kipling. MoBrPo

Astronauts. Robert Earl Hayden. ESEAA

Astronomer, / I strike my gong for you. Mirror of a Day Chiming Marigold, The. Diane Wakoski. NALW

Astronomer with patient, searching gaze, The. Slowness of Belief in a Spiritual World, The. Jones Very. NCAP

Astronomer Works Nights: A Parable of Science, The. Bin Ramke. YaYoPo

Astronomica, The. Marcus Manilius.
"Why do we in worries waste our lives, and torture." RomPo, tr. by Eugene O'Connor

Astronomies and slangs to find you, dear. John Berryman. AWTN Fr. Sonnets to Chris.

Astronomy. A. E. Housman. NoP-4; OBWP

Astronomy. M. L. Williams. GeoHom

Astropastoral. Douglas Crase. KGB

Astrophel. Edmund Spenser.
"Such skill, matcht with such courage as he had." OBWP

Astrophil and Stella. Sir Philip Sidney.
"Ah bed, the field where joy's peace some do see." EnLoPo
"Alas, have I not pain enough, my friend." NoP-4; NoSic
"As good to write as for to lie and groan." NoSic
"Be your words made (good sir) of Indian ware." NoSic
("Because I breathe not love to ev'ry one.") CABP
"Because I breathe not love to every one." NoSic
"Because I oft, in dark abstracted guise." NoSic
("Come sleep, Oh sleep, the certain knot of peace.") AWTN; NoP-4
("Come sleepe, o sleepe, the certaine knot of peace.") OxBEV
"Desire, though thou my old companion art." NAEL-5v1; NAEL-6v1; NAEL-7v1
"Envious wits, what hath been mine offence." PoE; Son
"Fie, school of Patience, fie; your lesson is." NAEL-5v1; NAEL-6v1; NAEL-7v1
"Fly, fly, my friends." NAEL-7v1; NoSic
"Go, my flock, go get you hence." NoSic
"Have I caught my heav'nly jewel." NoSic
"Having this day my horse, my hand, my lance." HAP; NAEL-5v1; NAEL-6v1; NAEL-7v1; PoE; Son
"Highway, since you my chief Parnassus be." SCGP
(Highway, The.) OBEV; OxAEP-1
(His Lady's Cruelty.) OBEV
"I might, unhappy word, O me, I might." NPeEn
"I never drank of Aganippe well." NAEL-5v1; NAEL-6v1; NAEL-7v1; NoSic; Son
"I on my horse, and Love on me doth try." NAEL-5v1; NAEL-6v1; NAEL-7v1; NoP-4; PoE
"In a grove most rich of shade." NoSic; PBRV
"In highest way of heav'n the sun did ride." Son
"In martial sports I had my cunning tried." NAEL-5v1; NAEL-6v1; NAEL-7v1; NoSic
"In nature apt to like when I did see." NAEL-5v1; NAEL-6v1; NAEL-7v1
"In truth, O Love, with what a boyish kind." OxBSo; PoE
"It is most true that eyes are formed to serve." NAEL-5v1; NAEL-6v1; NAEL-7v1; NoSic; Son
("Leave that sir Phip, least off your necke be wroong.") (LL) PBRV
"Let dainty wits cry on the sisters nine." NoSic; Son
"Love, by sure proof I may call thee unkind." Son
"Love still a boy, and oft a wanton is." Son
(Loving in truth, and fain in verse my love to show.) GSo
"Loving in truth, and fain[e] in verse my love to show." AWP; CABP; EBEV; HAP; NAEL-5v1; NAEL-6v1; NAEL-7v1; NPeEn; NoP-4; NoSic; OxAEP-1; OxBSo; PoE; SCGP; Son; TFi
"My mouth doth water, and my breast doth swell." NAEL-5v1; NAEL-6v1; NAEL-7v1; Son
"No more, my dear, no more these counsels try." SCGP
("Not at first sight, nor with a dribbed shot.") PBRV
"Not at [the] first sight, nor with a dribbed shot." NAEL-5v1; NAEL-6v1; NAEL-7v1
"Now that of absence the most irksome night." NAEL-5v1; NAEL-6v1; NAEL-7v1
"Nymph of the garden where all beauties be." PoE
("O Grammer rules, ô now your virtues show.") NoP-4
"O happy Thames, that didst my Stella bear." OxAEP-1
"O joy, too high for my low style to show." NAEL-5v1; NAEL-6v1; NAEL-7v1; OxAEP-1
"O kiss, which dost those ruddy gems impart." NAEL-5v1; NAEL-6v1; NAEL-7v1; OxBSo; Son
("O kisse, which doest those ruddie gemmes impart.") PBRV
"O tears, no tears, but rain from beauty's skies." Son
(O the Sad Moon.) NOBE
"Of all the kings that ever here did reign." NoSic
"Oft with true sighs, oft with uncalled tears." NAEL-5v1; NAEL-6v1; NAEL-7v1
"On Cupid's bow how are my heart-strings bent." NoSic

"Only joy, now here you are." HAP; NAEL-5v1; NAEL-6v1; NAEL-7v1; NoP-4; NoSic

"Queen Virtue's court, which some call Stella's face." NAEL-5v1; NAEL-6v1; NAEL-7v1

("Queene *Vertues* court, which some call *Stellas* face.") PBRV

"Reason, in faith thou art well served, that still." NAEL-5v1; NAEL-6v1; NAEL-7v1

(Sleep.) OBEV

"Some lovers speak, when they their Muses entertain." NAEL-5v1; NAEL-6v1; NAEL-7v1; NoSic; Son

First Song. OxAEP-1

Second Song. NoSic

Fourth Song. HAP; NAEL-5v1; NAEL-6v1; NAEL-7v1; NoP-4; NoSic

Eleventh Song. NAEL-6v1; NAEL-7v1; NoSic; OxAEP-1

Eighth Song. NoSic; PBRV

Ninth Song. NoSic

Sonnet 1: "Loving in truth, and fain[e] in verse my love to show.". AWP; CABP; EBEV; HAP; NAEL-5v1; NAEL-6v1; NAEL-7v1; NPeEn; NoP-4; NoSic; OxAEP-1; OxBSo; PoE; SCGP; Son; TFi

Sonnet 2: "Not at [the] first sight, nor with a dribbed shot.". NAEL-5v1; NAEL-6v1; NAEL-7v1

Sonnet 3: "Let dainty wits cry on the sisters nine." NoSic; Son

Sonnet 5: "It is most true that eyes are formed to serve." NAEL-5v1; NAEL-6v1; NAEL-7v1; NoSic; Son

Sonnet 6: "Some lovers speak, when they their Muses entertain." AEP; NAEL-5v1; NAEL-6v1; NAEL-7v1; NoSic; Son

Sonnet 7: "When Nature made her chief work, Stella's eyes." NAEL-5v1; NAEL-6v1; NAEL-7v1; NIL-7; NIP-4; Son

Sonnet 9: "Queen Virtue's court, which some call Stella's face." NAEL-5v1; NAEL-6v1; NAEL-7v1

Sonnet 10: "Reason, in faith thou art well served, that still." NAEL-5v1; NAEL-6v1; NAEL-7v1

Sonnet 11: "In truth, O Love, with what a boyish kind." OxBSo; PoE

Sonnet 14: "Alas, have I not pain enough, my friend." NoP-4; NoSic

Sonnet 15: "You that do search for every purling spring." NAEL-5v1; NoSic; OxAEP-1; Son

Sonnet 16: "In nature apt to like when I did see." NAEL-5v1; NAEL-6v1; NAEL-7v1

Sonnet 18: "With what sharp checks I in myself am shent." NAEL-5v1; NAEL-6v1; NAEL-7v1; NoSic

Sonnet 19: "On Cupid's bow how are my heart-strings bent." NoSic

Sonnet 20: "Fly, fly, my friends." AEP; NAEL-7v1; NoSic

Sonnet 21: "Your words my friend (right healthful caustics) blame." NAEL-5v1; NAEL-7v1; NoSic; PoE

Sonnet 22: "In highest way of heav'n the sun did ride." Son

Sonnet 25: "Wisest scholar of the wight most wise, The." NoP-4

Sonnet 26: "Though dusty wits dare scorn astrology." Son

Sonnet 27: "Because I oft, in dark abstracted guise." NoSic

Sonnet 28: "You that with allegory's curious frame." NAEL-7v1; NoSic

Sonnet 30: "Whether the Turkish new moon minded be." NoSic; PoE

Sonnet 31: "With how sad steps, O Moon[e], thou climb'st the skies." AEP; AWP; BoLoP; CABP; EnLoPo; GSo; HAP; HeIP-4; NAEL-5v1; NAEL-6v1; NAEL-7v1; NPeEn; NoSic; OxAEP-1; OxBSo; PoE; PoRA; SCGP; Son; TFi; TRP

Sonnet 33: "I might, unhappy word, O me, I might." NPeEn

Sonnet 37: "My mouth doth water, and my breast doth swell." NAEL-5v1; NAEL-6v1; NAEL-7v1; Son

Sonnet 39: "Come Sleep! O sleep the certain knot of peace." GSo; NAEL-5v1; NAEL-6v1; NAEL-7v1; NoSic; OxAEP-1; OxBSo; PoE; PoRA; SCGP; SCV; Son; TFi

Sonnet 40: "As good to write as for to lie and groan." NoSic

Sonnet 41: "Having this day my horse, my hand, my lance." AEP; HAP; NAEL-5v1; NAEL-6v1; NAEL-7v1; PoE; Son

Sonnet 45: "Stella oft sees the very face of woe." NAEL-5v1; NAEL-6v1; NAEL-7v1; NoSic; PoE

Sonnet 47: "What, have I thus betrayed my liberty?" NAEL-5v1; NAEL-6v1; NAEL-7v1; NoP-4

Sonnet 48: "Soul's joy, bend not those morning stars from me." NoP-4

Sonnet 49: "I on my horse, and Love on me doth try." NAEL-5v1; NAEL-6v1; NAEL-7v1; NoP-4; PoE

Sonnet 52: "Strife is grown between Virtue and Love, A." NAEL-5v1; NAEL-6v1; NAEL-7v1; NoP-4

Sonnet 53: "In martial sports I had my cunning tried." NAEL-5v1; NAEL-6v1; NAEL-7v1; NoSic

Sonnet 54: "Because I breathe not love to every one." NoSic

Sonnet 56: "Fie, school of Patience, fie; your lesson is." NAEL-5v1; NAEL-6v1; NAEL-7v1

Sonnet 61: "Oft with true sighs, oft with uncalled tears." NAEL-5v1; NAEL-6v1; NAEL-7v1

Sonnet 64: "No more, my dear, no more these counsels try." SCGP

Sonnet 65: "Love, by sure proof I may call thee unkind." Son

Sonnet 69: "O joy, too high for my low style to show." NAEL-5v1; NAEL-6v1; NAEL-7v1; OxAEP-1

Sonnet 71: "Who will in fairest book of Nature know." NAEL-5v1; NAEL-6v1; NAEL-7v1; NoP-4; NoSic; PoE

Sonnet 72: "Desire, though thou my old companion art." AEP; NAEL-5v1; NAEL-6v1; NAEL-7v1

Sonnet 74: "I never drank of Aganippe well." NAEL-5v1; NAEL-6v1; NAEL-7v1; NoSic; Son

Sonnet 74: "Love still a boy, and oft a wanton is." Son

Sonnet 75: "Of all the kings that ever here did reign." NoSic

Sonnet 81: "O kiss, which dost those ruddy gems impart." NAEL-5v1; NAEL-6v1; NAEL-7v1; OxBSo; Son

Sonnet 82: "Nymph of the garden where all beauties be." PoE

Sonnet 84: "Highway, since you my chief Parnassus be." SCGP

Sonnet 87: "When I was forced from Stella ever dear." NAEL-5v1; NAEL-6v1; NAEL-7v1

Sonnet 89: "Now that of absence the most irksome night." NAEL-5v1; NAEL-6v1; NAEL-7v1

Sonnet 90: "Stella, think not that I by verse seek fame." NoP-4; NoSic

Sonnet 91: "Stella, while now by honour's cruel might." NAEL-5v1; NAEL-6v1; NAEL-7v1; PoE

Sonnet 92: "Be your words made (good sir) of Indian ware." NoSic

Sonnet 98: "Ah bed, the field where joy's peace some do see." EnLoPo

Sonnet 99: "When far-spent night persuades each mortal eye." NoSic; PoE; Son

Sonnet 100: "O tears, no tears, but rain from beauty's skies." Son

Sonnet 103: "O happy Thames, that didst my Stella bear." OxAEP-1

Sonnet 104: "Envious wits, what hath been mine offence." PoE; Son

Sonnet 107: "Stella, since thou so right a Princess art." NoP-4; OxAEP-1

Sonnet 108: "When sorrow (using mine own fire's might)." NAEL-6v1; NAEL-7v1

"Soul's joy, bend not those morning stars from me." NoP-4

"Stella oft sees the very face of woe." NAEL-5v1; NAEL-6v1; NAEL-7v1; NoSic; PoE

(Stella's Kiss.) NoSic

"Stella, since thou so right a Princess art." NoP-4; OxAEP-1

"Stella, think not that I by verse seek fame." NoP-4; NoSic

"Stella, while now by honour's cruel might." NAEL-5v1; NAEL-6v1; NAEL-7v1; PoE

"Strife is grown between Virtue and Love, A." NAEL-5v1; NAEL-6v1; NAEL-7v1; NoP-4

"Though dusty wits dare scorn astrology." Son

(To Sleep.) NOBE

(Voices at the Window.) NOBE; OBEV

"What, have I thus betrayed my liberty?" NAEL-5v1; NAEL-6v1; NAEL-7v1; NoP-4

"When far-spent night persuades each mortal eye." NoSic; PoE; Son

"When I was forced from Stella ever dear." NAEL-5v1; NAEL-6v1; NAEL-7v1

"When Nature made her chief work, Stella's eyes." NAEL-5v1; NAEL-6v1; NAEL-7v1; NIL-7; NIP-4; Son

"When sorrow (using mine own fire's might)." NAEL-6v1; NAEL-7v1

"Whether the Turkish new moon minded be." NoSic; PoE

(Who Is It That This Dark Night.) NAEL-5v1; PoE; SCGP

"Who is it that this dark[e] night." NAEL-6v1; NAEL-7v1; NoSic; OxAEP-1; PBRV

"Who will in fairest book of Nature know." NAEL-5v1; NAEL-6v1; NAEL-7v1; NoP-4; NoSic; OxBEV; PoE

("Whose senses in so evil consort, their stepdame Nature lays.") NoP-4

"Wisest scholar of the wight most wise, The." NoP-4

("With how sad steps, Oh Moon, thou climb'st the skies.") NoP-4

"With what sharp checks I in myself am shent." NAEL-5v1; NAEL-6v1; NAEL-7v1; NoSic

"You that do search for every purling spring." NAEL-5v1; NoSic; OxAEP-1; Son

"You that with allegory's curious frame." NAEL-7v1; NoSic

"Your words my friend (right healthful caustics) blame." NAEL-5v1; NAEL-7v1; NoSic; PoE

Astrophysics. Sylvia Townsend Warner.
"To no believable blue I turn my eyes." OxBSo

Astute Melanesians on Munda. Limerick. *Unknown.* PeLi

Asylum. Breyten Breytenbach. VCWP, *tr. by* Stephen Gray

Asylum. Rafael Campo. NeAmPo

Asylum. Ciaran Carson. PNI

Asylum. Herman Fong. BAP-97

Asylum. John Freeman. OBMV

Asylum of Gestures. Carl Hancock Rux. HeMarv

Asymmetry 205. Jackson Mac Low. PFTM-2

Asymmetry of the Universe. Fabio Doplicher. NeIt, *tr.* by Stephen Sartarelli

At a Bach Concert. Adrienne Rich. NIL-7; NIP-4; YaYoPo

At a Calvary near the Ancre. Wilfred Owen. ChIV-2; GI

At a Concert of Music. Conrad Potter Aiken. MoAmPo

At a Country Hotel. Howard Nemerov. PoRA

At a Danse Macabre. Charles Spear. PeNZ

At a Dinner Party. Amy Levy. PoBW

At a Friends' Meeting. Mary Elizabeth Coleridge. WPE

At a Funeral. Dennis Brutus. PBMAP

At a Grave. Martinus Nijhoff. TuT, *tr.* by Desmond Egan

At a House in the Bamboo Grove. Wang Wei. CrYelRi, *tr.* by Sam Hamill

At a March against the Vietnam War. Robert Bly. SPE

At a party I spy a handsome psychiatrist. Afternoon Happiness. Carolyn Kizer. GeoHom

At a place in the mountains. Savior Is Abducted in Puerto Rico, The. Martín Espada. TRP

At a pleasant evening party I had taken down to supper. Ferdinando and Elvira; or, The Gentle Pieman. Sir William Schwenck Gilbert. OBCoV

At a Potato Digging. Seamus Heaney. CIP-2

At a quarter to seven we sat down to dine. Shall We Join the Ladies? David Ross. ReLy

At a Reading. Thomas Bailey Aldrich. OBAL

At a Reading. J. D. McClatchy. DiPo

At a Reception. Karen Gershon. LW

At a roadside shrine. Buson. SoOfWa, *tr.* by Sam Hamill

At a sale of Cupids. A hawk looks at them. (LL) Token, The. Frank Templeton Prince. FaBoTw; OxBTC

At a shout to a disco drum, the women dance. Uni-Gym, The. Anne Rouse. NeBl

At a Solemn Music[k]. John Milton. GTBS-P; HeIP-4; NOBE; OBEV; SCGP; SacPr

At a springe-well [*or* springe wel] under a thorn. Spring under a Thorn, The. *Unknown.* MiEL

At a summer home in Ningpo, near Shanghai. Picture of my Mother's Family, A. Wing Tek Lum. OpBo

At a Sunlit Window. Ondra Lysohorsky. AF, *tr.* by Ewald Osers

At a Symphony. Louise Imogen Guiney. APN-2

At a Welsh Waterfall. Gerard Manley Hopkins. NOBVV

At a Window. Carl Sandburg. PoToHe

At Aberdeen. George Macdonald. FaBoEE

At alarming bell daybreak, before. Eiléan Ní Chuilleanáin. CIP-2 *Fr.* Site of Ambush.

At all times I see them. Harbach 1944. János Pilinszky. AF; HP; PoSu; WoPoe, *tr.* by Janos Csokits and Ted Hughes

At an acute. Thunderstorm. Pavel Davydovich Kogan. TCRP, *tr.* by Daniel Weissbort

At an English conference presentation. Dancing in the Dark. Demetrice A. Worley. SpirFl

At an Exhibition of Historical Paintings, Hobart. Vivian Smith. CBAP; NOBAu

At an Inn. Thomas Hardy. NOBVV

At an Inn in Yü-kan. Liu Ch'ang-ch'ing. SuSp, *tr.* by William H. Nienhauser

At an open window sitting. Written on Whitsun-Monday, 1795. Matilda Barbara Betham-Edwards. ECWP

At Annika's Place. Siv Widerberg. NTCP, *tr.* by Verne Moberg

At any turn. East Song. Alvaro Mutis. TCLAP, *tr.* by Sophie Cabot Black and Maria Negroni

At Apollinaire's Grave. Allen Ginsberg. BB

At April. Angelina Weld Grimké. BlSi; GT

At Arrow Rapids, the water splashes foam. Wang T'ing-hsiang. CoBLCP *Fr.* Traveling by Boat.

At Asuka, the river of birds in flight. Mourning Princess Asuka. Kakinomoto no Hitomaro. WoPoe, *tr.* by Helen Craig McCullough

At Auke Bay the whales dance. Sheila Nickerson. GifTon

At Autumn Cove, so many white monkeys. Autumn Cove. Li Po. CoBCP; ColAnChi; TTTS, *tr.* by Burton Watson

At Baia. "H. D." APT-1; ColAP; NAAL-2v2; NOBA; PoBW

At Ballyshannon, Co. Donegal. William Allingham. NOBVV

At Barstow. Charles Tomlinson. NoAM; TwCP

At behest of usura. (LL) Ezra Pound. APT-1; HarvBoo; NAAL-2v2; NAAL-5; NOBA; PoE *Fr.* Cantos.

At bend of bay. Old Sailor Looking at a Container Ship. Robert Carson. AiP

At Betharram. Robert Hedin. GifTon

At birth. I was not born. Only you were. (LL) Helen Todd: My Birthname. Sandra McPherson. LCAP-2; LoL

At Bon Odori. James Masao Mitsui. OpBo

At Branwen's Grave. Dudley G. Davies. AngWePo

At break of dawn. W. H. Auden. CAGL *Fr.* Three Posthumous Poems.

At break of day from frightful dreams. Ellenore. William Taylor. NOBRP

At break of day we leave the western gate. After Rain, Visiting the Temple of Heavenly Peace. Wang Shih-chieng. CoBLCP, *tr.* by Jonathan Chaves

At Breakfast. Giovanna Pollarolo. TANSG, *tr.* by Marjorie Agosin

At breakfast, my mother has a list of things. Her List. Sharon Olds. BodElec

At breakfast they are sober, subdued. Grenoble Café. Jean Garrigue. APT-2

At Brill on the hill. *Unknown.* OxNR

At Candlemas. Charles Causley. OBCP

At Casa Grande, only the names. Dry Rivers—Arizona. Ramona Wilson. ReEnLa

At Casterbridge Fair. Thomas Hardy.
   After the Fair. HAP
   Ballad-Singer, The. BoLoP
   Former Beauties. NoAM; OBMV

At Castle Boterel. Thomas Hardy. EBEV; GTBS-P; NOBE; NPeEn; OxAEP-2; OxBEV; PeVV; PoE; SCV

At Castor Bay. Sam Hunt. PeNZ

At certain times, this could be the Twelve Nights of Haydn, our husbands. Pandora's Box. Sarah Kirsch. PFTM-2, *tr.* by Wayne Kvam

At Ch'ang-an—a full foot of snow. Early Levée, An. Po Chü-i. ChiP, *tr.* by Arthur Waley

At Ch'ang-ku, Reading: To Show to My Man Pa. Li Ho. CoBCP; ColAnChi, *tr.* by Burton Watson

At Ch'ang-men Palace. Li Po. CrYelRi, *tr.* by Sam Hamill

At Ch'ang-men, the grass is green. To the Tune: In the Hills. Hsueh Chao-yun. CrYelRi, *tr.* by Sam Hamill

At Ch'en Ch'u. Wang Shih-chieng. OHMPC, *tr.* by Kenneth Rexroth

At Chadwicks Bar and Grill. Lance Henson. HATNAP

At Chancellorsville. Andrew Hudgins. CBCWP

At Chien-nan, sudden news of retaking Chi-pei. Hearing of Imperial Forces Retaking Ho-Nan and Ho-Pei. Tu Fu. ChinPo, *tr.* by Yip Wai-lim

At Christmas-Tide. Henrietta Cordelia Ray. CBWP-3

At Christmas, when old friends are meeting. Good Will to Men—Christmas Greetings in Six Languages. Dorothy Brown Thompson. OBCP

At Cock-crow. Prudentius. MLL, *tr.* by Helen Waddell

At Cockcrow. Lizette Woodworth Reese. SacPr

At Communion. Madeleine L'Engle. TrCP

At Cooloolah. Judith Wright. BMAP; HarvBoo

At counters where I eat my lunch. Marble-Top. Elwyn Brooks White. OBAL

At court I met it, in clothes brave enough. On Something, that Walk[e]s Somewhere. Ben Jonson. BASC; BeJo; NAEL-5v1; NAEL-6v1; NAEL-7v1; OxBSP; PAI; PoE; SCGP

At Cove at our camp in the open canyon. At Cove on the Crooked River. William Stafford. CoAmPo

At Cove on the Crooked River. William Stafford. CoAmPo

At dangerous places. Three-Step Waterfall. Muso Soseki. EaWin, *tr.* by W. S. Merwin

At Dawn. Michael Patrick Hearn. CA

At dawn a knot of sea-lions lies off the shore. Animals. Robinson Jeffers. APT-1

At Dawn, Climbing the Heavenly Pillar Peak of Mysterious Mountain. Hsü Chung-hsing.

"I shake my robe—and mists disperse, leaving clear autumn sky." CoBLCP

At dawn, falling asleep on the freeway. Fault, The. Carol Muske. GeoHom

At dawn four-footed, at midday erect. Oedipus and the Riddle. Jorge Luis Borges. WoPoe, *tr.* by John Hollander

At dawn I hasten toward the Purple Hall. Thoughts While Studying at Hanlin Academy Sent to My Colleagues at the Chi-hsien Academy. Li Po. SuSp, *tr.* by Joseph J. Lee

At dawn I plucked orchids in the park. Spending the Night on Stone Gate Mountain. Hsieh Ling-yün. SuSp, *tr.* by Francis Westbrook

At dawn I rode to escort the Doctors of Art. Escorting Candidates to the Examination Hall. Po Chü-i. ChiP, *tr.* by Arthur Waley

At dawn I set out from the sunlit cliffs. On My Way from South Mountain to North Mountain, I Glance at the Scenery from the Lake. Hsieh Ling-yün. ColAnChi, *tr.* by Kang-i Sun Chang

At dawn I sighed to see my hairs fall. On his Baldness. Po Chü-i. ChiP, *tr.* by Arthur Waley

At dawn I squat on the garage. Sound. James [*or* Jim] Harrison. VGW

At dawn of the day the Creator. Gaspara Stampa. BoWoP

At dawn remembering her bad grammar. George Swede. HA

At dawn setting out from a cassia and orchid shore. Picking Rushes. *Unknown.* CoBCP, *tr.* by Burton Watson

At dawn she lay with her profile at that angle. Daybreak. Stephen Spender.
     BoLoP
At dawn she unmasked. Masquerading. May Probyn. NPeEn; VWP
At dawn the dove croons. California Spring. Charles Wright. ColAP
At dawn the ridge emerges massed and dun. Attack. Siegfried Sassoon.
     MoBrPo; NOBE; OxBTC
At Dawn the Virgin Is Born. Félix Lope de Vega Carpio. SpanPo, tr. by W. S.
     Merwin
At dawn they came for you. Requiem. Anna Andreyevna Akhmatova.
     TCRusP, tr. by Daniel Weissbort
At dawn to-morrow. After Hilaire Belloc. Max Beerbohm. OBCoV
At dawn we buried Melanippus. At sunset. Callimachus. HePo Fr.
     Epigrams.
At Day's End. Hayyim Nahman [or Khayim Nakhman or Chaim Nachman]
     Bialik. MHP, tr. by Ruth Finer Mintz
At Daybreak. Adam Zagajewski. VCWP, tr. by Renata Gorcyznski
At daybreak, when the falcon claps his wings. Ballad Written for a
     Bridegroom. François Villon. AWP
At daylight on St. John's, the day after Epiphany, we got our orders. March
     toward the Front, The. Odysseus Elytis. AF
At dead of night, the sailors sprawled on deck. Nearing La Guaira. Derek
     Walcott. TTY
At Delphos shrine one did a doubt propound. Upon Master Edmund Spenser.
     Francis Beaumont. FaBoEE
At Devlin's Siding. Barcroft Henry Boake. CBAP
At Dieppe. Arthur Symons.
     Grey and Green. NOBVV; PeVV
     "Grey-green stretch of sandy grass, The." NOBVV; PeVV
At dinner, she is hostess, I am host. George Meredith. NAEL-6v2; NOBVV;
     NPeEn; PoE; Son Fr. Modern Love.
At dinner we discuss marriage. Good Company. William Matthews.
     BodElec
At Dirty Dick's and Sloppy Joe's. W. H. Auden. BoLoP; FaBoTw Fr. Sea
     and the Mirror, The.
At distance far approaching to the tomb. Philip Freneau. NAAL-2v1; NAAL-
     3; TCAPo Fr. House of Night, The.
At Dryhope lived a lady fair. Dowie Dens of Yarrow, The. Unknown. IBB
At Dunbar, Castle or Arcade. Double Feature. Robert Earl Hayden. NoAM
At dusk, everything blurs and softens. Riding Out at Evening. Linda
     McCarriston. BBASP
At dusk / from the island in the river. If the Owl Calls Again. John Haines.
     CoAP; GifTon; HeIP-4
At dusk heavy clouds grieve the long day. Poem to the Tune of "Tsui hua yin."
     Li Ch'ing-chao. WPOW, tr. by Marsha Wagner
At dusk hot water from the hose. Marlene Mountain. HA
At dusk I sought lodging at Shih-hao village. Recruiting Officer of Shih-hao.
     Tu Fu. ColAnChi; SuSp, tr. by Irving Y. Lo
At dusk the silence by the sea. About Time. Laurens Vancrevel. TuT, tr. by
     Greg Delanty
At dusk, the sun-bleached fence. Winter Fruit. Juan Delgado. TouFir
At dusk you appear, a school-girl still. Boris Leonidovich Pasternak. WoPoe,
     tr. by Theodore Weiss Fr. Illness.
At Eagle Farm I stand at the passenger gate. Flights. Roger McDonald.
     CBAP
At early morning, clear and cold. Troopship, The. Lionel Pigot Johnson.
     EBVV
At Ease. Walter De la Mare. GTBS-P
At Egypt. Clark Coolidge.
     "I came here. I don't know you here." PmAP
     "Morning muezzin in orange and a mosquito." FTOS
     "New hunt / the morning bent, A." APSN
At eight I was brilliant with my body. Black Hair. Gary Soto. MoASP;
     UnSA
At eight stealing a mirror glance. Li Shang-yin. CoBCP
At 8 / The magnets of my fickle thoughts. Acts of Power. Sharan Strange.
     InTrad
At eight years old, his cancer running rampage. Candor. John Graham-Pole.
     BloBone
At End. Louise Chandler Moulton. PWR
At end of day. (LL) Roundelay: "On all that strand." Samuel Beckett.
     ModIr; OxBEV
At Eton with Orwell, at Oxford with Waugh. On Himself. Cyril Connolly.
     OBCoV
At Eutaw springs the valiant died. To the Memory of the Brave Americans.
     Philip Freneau. AiP
At Evening. Anthony Thwaite. OxBEV
At evening, sitting on this terrace. Bat. D. H. Lawrence. GTBS-P; HAP
At evening the horse comes down unled. Shadow of Himself, The. William
     Renton. NOBVV

At evening too the dazzled light. Joseph Gwyer. VerBaPo Fr. On a
     Procession with the Prince of Wales.
At Evening when Flicker. Shin Shalom. MHP, tr. by Ruth Finer Mintz
At evening when the lamp is lit. Land of Story-Books, The. Robert Louis
     Stevenson. ChAP; ITBLP; NePenScot; PWR
At fifteen I'd buy bottles. White Port and Lemon Juice. Yusef Komunyakaa.
     ISC
At fifteen I joined the army. Home. Unknown. OHMPC, tr. by Kenneth
     Rexroth
At Fifteen I Went Off to the Army. Unknown. CoBCP, tr. by Burton Watson
At Fifteen I Went to War. Unknown. ChinPo, tr. by Yip Wai-lim
At fifteen, shaving by then, I passed. At the Rainbow. Robert Vasquez.
     GeoHom
At Fifty. Vivian Shipley. ExTi
At fingertip control. Kites at the Washington Monument. Greg Williamson.
     NAPBL
At First. Charles Hubert Sisson. OxBC
At first a childhood, limitless and free. Imaginary Career. Rainer Maria Rilke.
     BBASP, tr. by Stephen Mitchell
At first, come back, I'd nothing else to do. Another Lazarus. Sally Roberts
     Jones. TCAWP
At first from your verse. To Dennis Brutus. Kofi Awoonor. HBAPE
At first he had felt the scrape of a little murmur, his own throat struggling.
     Motion Pictures: 4. Barbara Guest. BodElec
At first he refused to deliver junk mail because it was stupid, all. Appointed
     Rounds. Louis Jenkins. RaBo
At first, I had no time for their half-built temples. Manora. Pimone Triplett.
     NAPBL
At first I laughed to hide my nervousness. Learning to Laugh. Allison Joseph.
     PasH
At first I lost it in your beard. Poem for the Man Who Said Shit. David
     Clewell. OPRER
At first I thought I would feel. Nothing Could Take Away the Bear-King's
     Image. Ray A. Young Bear. HATNAP
At first I thought there was a superfine. Fleming Helphenstine. Edwin
     Arlington Robinson. OxBSo
At first I was given centuries. Margaret Atwood. HAP; WPOW
At first in that place, at all times, above the earth. Unknown. APN-2 Fr.
     Walam Olum; or, Red Score [of the Lenâpé], The [or The Wallam Olum;
     The Red Score or Painted History of the Lenni Lenape].
At first it seemed a swaying field of flowers. Archive Film Material. Ruth
     Fainlight. HP
At first it was a small cold palmful. Feeding the Bat. Hilary Llewellyn-
     Williams. TCAWP
At first it was an imperceptible tremor of the skin. Divorce, The. Hans
     Magnus Enzensberger. WoPoe, tr. by Herbert Graf
At first it was as though you had passed. Many Wagons Ago. John Ashbery.
     HCAP
At first my mother balked I already had. Sea Monkeys, The. Barbara J.
     Orton. NeAmPo
At first nobody could bear the heat, like. In Andrea's Garden. Susan
     Hampton. BMAP
At first she led them out onto the floor. Dance, The. Irene McKinney.
     PBCAP
At first she thought the lump in the road. Red String. Minnie Bruce Pratt.
     WiU
At first she turned the whole thing to a joke. Aleksandr Aleksandrovich Blok.
     TCRP
At First Sight. Robert Graves. FaBoEE; OxBSP
At first the angel was pefectly wingless. That Cold Summer. Nin Andrews.
     BAP-97
At first the dead. Elegy. Henriqueta Lisboa. TCLAP, tr. by Hélcio Veiga
     Costa
At first the pains crawl cautious in me. Pain, The. Jeni Couzyn. HAWP
At first the surprise. Dancing with God. Stephen Dunn. NIP-4
At first, there's a thin, bright Rider. Apocalypse Dub. Dennis Scott. WaCA
At first there was nothing. Then a closed space. Endymion. Thomas Kinsella.
     PBCIP
At first they look like any other birds. Cardinals in a Shower at Union Square.
     Stanley Plumly. BodElec
At first those closest to you shot holes in you. Asylum. Breyten Breytenbach.
     VCWP, tr. by Stephen Gray
At first we heard the jingling of her ornaments. Egyptian Dancer at Shubra.
     Bernard Spencer. NoAM
At first we look like nomads plodding. Curlers at Dusk. David Roderick.
     MoASP
At first we see the tiny leaves. Strawberry, The. Maggie Pogue Johnson.
     CBWP-4
At five in the afternoon. Lament for Ignacio Sánchez Mejías. Federico García
     Lorca. NAWM-7v2, tr. by J. L. Gili and Stephen Spender

At five in the afternoon. Lament for Ignacio Sánchez Mejías. Federico García Lorca. OBVE, *tr.* by Arthur Lloyd

At five in the afternoon. Federico García Lorca. WoPoe, *tr.* by Alan S. Trueblood *Fr.* Lament for Ignacio Sanchez Mejias.

At five in the morning. Conversation Through the Door, A. Anna Swirszczynska. AF, *tr.* by Czeslaw Milosz

At five this morn, when Phoebus raised his head. Tunbridge Wells. John Wilmot, 2d Earl of Rochester. OBSV

At Flores in the Azores Sir Richard Grenville lay. Tennyson. EBNV; OBWP *Fr. Revenge,* The.

At fortune's spite. (LL) Lament for Five Sons Lost in a Plague. Abu Dhu'ayb al-Hudhali. ArPe; WoPoe, *tr.* by Omar Pound and Omar S. Pound

At Forty. A. K. Ramanujan. VCWP

At Forty. Yevgeny Aleksandrovich Yevtushenko [*or* Evtushenko]. RusPo, *tr.* by Robert Arthur Douglas Ford

At forty, a man's not yet old. Inscribed on the Arbor of the Old Drunkard (Tsui-weng-t'ing) at Ch'u-chou. Ou-yang Hsiu. SuSp, *tr.* by Irving Y. Lo

At forty-six I am still the baby. Late Arrivals. Sybil Kollar. FFC

At four in the morning he wakes. More a Man Has the More a Man Wants, The. Paul Muldoon. ModIr

At four in the morning the smoke of the forded river. While We Slept. David Wolff. TrJP

At four o'clock. Roosters. Elizabeth Bishop. APT-2; ChIV-2; NALW

At 4:30 A.M. / she rose. Ntozake Shange. BoWoP *Fr.* For Colored Girls Who Have Considered Suicide When the Rainbow Is Enuf.

At 14th Street and First Avenue. Strawberries in Mexico. Ron Padgett. SPE

At Francis Allen's on the Christmas Eve. Tennyson. NAEL-5v2; NAEL-6v2 *Fr.* Morte d'Arthur.

At Frank 'n' Helen's. Constance Urdang. PBCAP

At Fyvie's yetts there grows a flower. Trumpeter of Fyvie, The. *Unknown.* OxBB

At Galway Races. W. B. Yeats. WoPoe

At Gen's Embarkation for Yuan China. Muso Soseki. EaWin, *tr.* by W. S. Merwin

At general Electric, where they eat their/young. Robert Farr. SpirFl

At Gettysburg full anonymity. Yugoslav Cemetery. Celeste Turner Wright. WPE

At girls who wear glasses. (LL) Dorothy Parker. APT-1; NALW; OBAL *Fr.* Some Beautiful Letters.

At Glastonbury. Henry Kingsley. PoRA

At Gold Hill Monastery. Su Tung-p'o (Su Shih). OHPC, *tr.* by Kenneth Rexroth

At Golgotha I stood alone. Edwin John Ellis. OBMV *Fr.* Himself.

At Graceland with a Six Year Old, 1985. David Wojahn. AllShUp; PBCAP *Fr.* Mystery Train: A Sequence.

At Grandfather's. Clara Doty Bates. OBCA

At Grass. Philip Larkin. HAP; HarvBoo; NPeEn; OxBEV; OxBTC; RB; WeW-3

At Great Torrington, Devon. *Unknown.* FaBoEE

At Guaracara Park. Eric Roach. WoPoe

At Gull Lake; August, 1810. Duncan Campbell Scott. NOBC

At half-past eight o'clock, booms, hencoops, spars. Byron. NPeEn *Fr.* Don Juan.

At half-past five—the earth cooling. Bachelor Farmer. Roger McDonald. CBAP

At Half past Three, a single Bird. Emily Dickinson. APN-2; MoAmPo; NAWM-7v2; OxBA

At Hallowmas, whan nights grow lang. Hallow-Fair. Robert Fergusson. OxBS

At hame it's hard to feel. (LL) Parley of Beasts. Hugh MacDiarmid. ChIV-1; MoBrPo; NoAM; OBMV

At Harper's Ferry Just before the Attack. Edward W. Williams. CBCWP

At Harvard a randy old Dean. Limerick. *Unknown.* PeLi

At Heaven's Border, the autumn clouds are thin. After Rain. Tu Fu. CrYelRi, *tr.* by Sam Hamill

At Henry's bier let some thing fall out well. John Berryman. NoP-4 *Fr.* Dream Songs.

At her body floating in the water. (LL) Grain-Barge Wife, The. Wu Chia-chi. CoBLCP; ColAnChi, *tr.* by Jonathan Chaves

At her departure his disdain return'd. Homer. OBVE *Fr.* Iliad, The.

At Her Feet. "Violet Fane." PoBW

At Her Grave. Kuthaiyir. ArPe, *tr.* by Omar S. Pound

At his cramped desk. Star-Fix. Marilyn Nelson Waniek. ESEAA; LTA

At His Execution. Rudyard Kipling. ChIV-2

At His Father's Grave. John Ormond. FaBoTw; OBWVE

At Home. John Quarles. SacPr

At Home. Christina Georgina Rossetti. VWP

At Home. Wang An-shih. CrYelRi, *tr.* by Sam Hamill

At home, abroad, and everywhere. (LL) Another. Anne Bradstreet. EMWP; LW; NAAL-3; OxBA; SCAP; WPE

At home alone, O Nomades. Home, Sweet Home, with Variations, III. Henry Cuyler Bunner. OBAL

At home at Annika's place. At Annika's Place. Siv Widerberg. NTCP, *tr.* by Verne Moberg

At Home from Church. Sarah Orne Jewett. APN-2

At home I have had to live as an alien. Wales Re-visited. Harry Guest. TCAWP

At home I loved to wear old clothes. Wang Chien. SuSp *Fr.* Palace Poems.

At Home in Dakar. Margaret Danner. BlSi

At Home in Heaven. Robert Southwell. ESCV

At home, in my flannel gown, like a bear to its floe. 90 North. Randall Jarrell. CoAP; HarvBoo; NAAL-2v2; NOBA; NoAM; TAP; VCAP

At home in the damp hills of Champagne. M. François le Vaillant Recalls His Travels to the Interior Parts of Africa. Patrick Cullinan. PeSAV

At Home in the Summer Mountains. Yu Xuanji. WPoS, *tr.* by Jane Hirshfield

At home the sea is in the town. Sea Eats the Land at Home, The. Kofi Awoonor. EmeKit; PBMAP

At home we pray every morning, we. Gwendolyn Brooks. OxWW *Fr.* Ulysses.

At Honey Street in Ostrova. Jerome Rothenberg. PFTM-2 *Fr.* Khurbn.

At Horizon's End, Thinking of Li Po. Tu Fu. SuSp, *tr.* by Eugene Eoyang

At Hsin-fêng an old man—four-score and eight;. Old Man with the Broken Arm, The. Po Chü-i. ChiP, *tr.* by Arthur Waley

At Hung-tung Mountain, the war-drums sounded. To the Filial Son, Ts'ui. Hsü Pen. CoBLCP, *tr.* by Jonathan Chaves

At Iku's Embarkation for Yuan China. Muso Soseki. EaWin, *tr.* by W. S. Merwin

At It. Ronald Stuart Thomas. OxBC

At Ithaca. "H. D." ColAP; VGW

At its own stable door. (LL) I Like to See It Lap the Miles. Emily Dickinson. APN-2; BoWoP; InPK-6; MoAmPo; NAAL-2v1; NAAL-3; NAWM-7v2; NOBA; NoAM; NoP-4; OBAL; OBCA; OxBA; SoSe-8; TFi

At Jad Gate Pass mountain ridges several thousand-fold. Wang Ch'ang-ling. SuSp *Fr.* Following the Army on Campaign.

At Jonestown. Lucille Clifton. NAAAL

At Kan's Embarkation for Yuan China. Muso Soseki. EaWin, *tr.* by W. S. Merwin

At Kenneth Burke's Place. William Carlos Williams. NOBA

At Kfar Kana. Charles Causley. TOF

At Kino Viejo, Mexico. Alberto A. Ríos. NoAM

At Kisheneff two wicked men. Russia's Resentment. Lizelia Augusta Jenkins Moorer. CBWP-3

At Lai Family Village, the spring is beautiful. Walking Outside the City Walls on the Day of the Cold Food Festival. Pien Kung. CoBLCP, *tr.* by Jonathan Chaves

At Lake Yi. Wang Wei. CrYelRi, *tr.* by Sam Hamill

At Lansdowne Bridge. Arthur Nortje. HBAPE

At Last. John Montague. PBCIP

At Last. Elizabeth Siddal. VWP

At last a juggler is led out under the stars. Initiate, The. W. S. Merwin. NNaP

At last, at last the night. Soft Time of the Year, The. Hayden Carruth. PoCoUp

At last, by chance and guardian fancy led. Philip Freneau. NAAL-2v1; NAAL-3; TCAPo *Fr.* House of Night, The.

At last earnest sternness is transformed to sweet. Hatred Surely Does Not Kiss. Kaspar Stieler. GePo, *tr.* by George C. Schoolfield

At last free. Sumangalamata. WPoS

At last he is quiet; his harsh words. Smile for Daddy. Elizabeth Bartlett. Prnts

At last here is freedom for my poor, bedazzled head. In Which He Rejoices Over Having Discarded Love. Bálint Balassi. IQMS, *tr.* by Joseph Leftwich

At last I can figure out the nature of that whisking sound. Fate in Incognito. Michael Benedikt. OBAL

At last I have a way to understand. Rāmprasād Sen. SinGod, *tr.* by Rachel Fell McDermott

At last I've broken Unmon's barrier! Daito. ZenPo, *tr.* by Takashi Ikemoto and Lucien Stryk

At last I've seduced the *au pair.* Limerick. Cyril Ray. PeLi

At last it came into her mind, the answer. Precipice, The. Judith Wright. BMAP

At last love has come. I would be more ashamed. Sulpicia. BoWoP

At last, my old, inveterate foe. To Melancholy. Anne Finch, Countess of Winchilsea. WPE

At last, O thou serene retreat. To Retirement. Luís De León. TrJP, *tr.* by Thomas Walsh

At last; so this is you, my dear! Christopher Found. Amy Levy. ViWPN

At last the beef appears in sight. Edward Chicken. NOEC *Fr.* Collier's Wedding, The.

At last the cure, I bid farewell to pain. Oblivion. Ibrahim Naji. MAP, *tr. by* Issa Boullata and John Heath-Stubbs

At last, the senses sharpen. All around. Postscript. R. L. Barth. CDa

At last there came. Indian Summer. Hamlin Garland. APN-2

At last these two stout erles did meet. *Unknown.* FaBoWar *Fr.* Battle of Otterbourne, The.

At last Wayman gets the girl into bed. Wayman in Love. Tom Wayman. NIL-7; NIP-4; NOBC

At last you'll know why you came. See Willow. James Bertolino. PoCoUp

At last you yielded up the album, which. Lines on a Young Lady's Photograph Album. Philip Larkin. EnLoPo; HAP

At least a hundred times. For Edward Hicks. David Helwig. NOBC

At least I broke and stole that branch with love. (LL) For C. Philip Whalen. NeAP; VGW

At least I can offer that. / Com'mere, boy! (LL) Brass Spittoons. Langston Hughes. MoAmPo; NoAM

At least I'll keep. (LL) Hiding Place. Richard Armour. NIL-7; NIP-4

At least 100 seabirds attended my grandmother's funeral. My Grandmother's Funeral. Thomas Lux. WeW-3

At least that's. Vermont Has a High Suicide Rate. Richard Donze. BloBone

At least the mechanics are honest. Ode to My Car. Gig Ryan. BMAP

At least—to pray—is left—is left. Emily Dickinson. APN-2; NCAP; TCAPo

At least we can meet at the Indian Market. Promise! Mafika Pascal Gwala. NAfrP

At least we shall have descendants. (LL) To Pi Ssu Yao. Tu Fu. BLT; OHPC, *tr. by* Kenneth Rexroth

At least we shall have roses, laughed my companion. Fortune. Mary Ursula Bethell. PoBW

At least you left me the green. Burden Lifters, The. Michael Waters. SwNoth

At length, by flight, I over-went the Pack. Francis Quarles. ESCV *Fr.* Emblems.

At length by so much importunity pressed [*or* press'd]. Lover, The; a Ballad. Lady Mary Wortley Montagu. ECWP; NAEL-5v1; NAEL-6v1; NAEL-7v1; NoP-4; OxBEV; PEW

At length I land upon the Strophades. Virgil [*or* Vergil]. OWoS, *tr. by* John Dryden *Fr.* Aeneid (Dryden translation).

At length, my Lord, I have the bliss. Thomas Moore. OBSV *Fr.* Fudge Family in Paris, The.

At length my soul the fatal union finds. Octavia Walsh. ECWP

At Length the Busy Day Is Done. Francis Hopkinson. AH

At length the soft nocturnal minutes fly. Bricklayer's Labours, The. Robert Tatersal. NOEC

At length their long kiss severed, with sweet smart. Dante Gabriel Rossetti. EBVV; NAEL-5v2; NAEL-6v2; NOBVV *Fr.* House of Life, The.

At Length There Dawns the Glorious Day. Ozora Stearns Davis. AH

At length with jostling, elbowing, and the aid. Byron. OBSV *Fr.* Vision of Judgment, The.

At Les Deux Magots. Maura Dooley. LW

At Li's Mountain Hermitage. Wang Wei. CrYelRi, *tr. by* Sam Hamill

At Lindos. May Sarton. WPE

At London, Thames is a broad stream. Disaster to Steamer Victoria at London. James McIntyre. VerBaPo

At long last I am leaving. Senseki. JDP, *tr. by* Yoel Hoffmann

At Long Last Love. Cole Porter. ReLy

At Lord's. Francis Thompson. EBVV; OPOU; OxBSP; PeLV

At Loschwitz above the city. Birch-Tree at Loschwitz, The. Amy Levy. TrJP

At low tide like this how sheer the water is. Bight, The. Elizabeth Bishop. APT-2; EmeKit; FaBoWP; HCAP; NAAL-2v2; PoetW; RB; VCAP

At Luca Signorelli's Resurrection of the Body. Jorie Graham. HCAP

At Ma-re Mount shall be kept holiday. (LL) Poem, The: "Rise Oedipus, and if thou canst unfold." Thomas Morton. NAAL-3; SCAP

At Maiden Castle in Dorset. Maiden Castle. Dorothy Wellesley, Duchess of Wellington. PoBW

At Maruža's. Imants Ziedonis. WoPoe, *tr. by* Barry Callaghan

At Mass. Nicholas Vachel Lindsay. VGW

At Mass. *Unknown.* BIrV, *tr. by* Robin Flower

At Matyne houre in midis of the nicht. Honour with Age. Walter Kennedy. OxBS

At me—The Sea withdrew. (LL) By the Sea. Emily Dickinson. APN-2; HAP; InPK-6; NAAL-2v1; NAAL-3; WeW-3

At Melville's Tomb. Hart Crane. APT-2; HAP; HarvBoo; MoAmPo; NAAL-2v2; NAAL-5; NoAM; NoP-4; TAP; UnPo; VGW

At Memphis the horn'd bull told our friend. Tauromancy at Memphis. Diogenes Laertius. GrAn, *tr. by* Dudley Fitts

At midnight, coming home, I passed a tiger. Coming Home Late at Night. Tu Fu. BLT

At midnight I noticed on my sheet a. Aleksei Eliseievich Kruchyonykh [*or* Kruchionykh *or* Kruchenykh]. TCRP

At midnight, I wake to a breeze. Armed Forces. Lucy Lakides. CDa

At midnight I walk over the bailey-bridge. Catching My Breath. Robert Minhinnick. TCAWP

At midnight I would hear my father rise. Lament at Night. H. Leivick [*or* Leyvick]. AWTN, *tr. by* Marie Syrkin

At midnight, in a cold bed, I cannot sleep. Cold Night. Po Chü-i. CrYelRi, *tr. by* Sam Hamill

At midnight, in his guarded tent. Fitz-Greene Halleck. APN-1 *Fr.* Marco Bozzaris.

At midnight in the alley. Tom-Cat, The. Don Marquis. PoRA

At midnight, in the month of June. Sleeper, The. Edgar Allan Poe. NAAL-2v1; NAAL-3; NCAP; NOBA; OxBA; TAP

At midnight the teacher lectures on his throne. Reflections at Lake Louise. Allen Ginsberg. BBASP

At midnight, your face in a dream brings a sigh. My Love's Dark Place Is Fragrant like Narcissus. Ikkyu Sojun. ErotSp, *tr. by* Sam Hamill

At Midsummer. Norman Dubie. NoAM

At Monday dawn, I climbed into my skin. Diary. David Wagoner. CoAP

At morning light the ark lay grounded fast. Problem in History, A. Robert Wallace. CRP

At morning we all look out. Hedge Life. James Dickey. LCAP-2

At Moss Beach. Kim Addonizio. GeoHom

At Mother Teresa's. Naomi Shihab Nye. OPRER

At Mount Rushmore I look up into one. Loneliness of Lincoln, The. X. J. Kennedy. HHAm

At Muktinath. Chitra Divakaruni. FSt

At my age to go ten thousand miles. Old and Traveling. Yuan Mei. GifTon, *tr. by* Jerome P. Seaton

At My Country Home in Chung-nan. Wang Wei. CoBCP, *tr. by* Burton Watson

At my dear Land of Story-Books. (LL) Land of Story-Books, The. Robert Louis Stevenson. ChAP; ITBLP; NePenScot; PWR

At my father's. George Swede. HA

At My Father's Grave. Hugh MacDiarmid. GTBS-P; HarvBoo; NePenScot

At My Father's House. Nancy Travis. ISC

At my father's wake. Desmet, Idaho, March 1969. Janet Campbell Hale. VoR

At my memory's uncertain dawn. Turkey, The. Nikolai Stepanovich Gumilyov [*or* Gumiliov *or* Gumilev]. TCRP, *tr. by* Simon Franklin

At My Mother's Bedside. Marcia Lee Masters. WPE

At my wedding he came over the grass. Yew Berries. Ruth Padel. MFPA

At my windowpane a bird. That Is All I Heard. "Yehoash." TrJP, *tr. by* Isidore Goldstick

At Nature's Shrine. Henrietta Cordelia Ray. CBWP-3

At new moon on the crater / This summer. (LL) Burning Island. Gary Snyder. APSN; VCAP

At Night. Bella [*or* Izabella] Akhatovna Akhmadulina. BoWoP, *tr. by* Daniel Halpern and Albert Todd

At Night. Dennis Brutus. VCWP

At Night. Frances Darwin Cornford. MoBrPo

At Night. Margherita Guidacci. WPOW, *tr. by* Marina La Palma

At Night. Jane Hirshfield. BodElec

At Night. Elizabeth Jennings. OTCP

At Night. Alice Thompson Meynell. OxAEP-2

At Night. Sara Teasdale. APT-1

At night along this coast. At Moss Beach. Kim Addonizio. GeoHom

At night and in the wind and the rain. Refugees. Chaim Grade. HP, *tr. by* Marc Kaminsky

At Night atop Shou-hsiang Citadel, Hearing Tartar Flutes. Li Yi. SuSp, *tr. by* Paul Kroll

At night, by the fire. Domination of Black. Wallace Stevens. APT-1; MoAmPo; OWoS; OxBA; TCAPo

At night Chinamen jump. Poem. Frank O'Hara. NoAM; NOBA; PmAP

At night, circling weightless, we dreamed of roses. Geoffrey Lehmann. BMAP *Fr.* Roses.

At night, coolness like water lapping. Talvikki Ansel. YaYoPo *Fr.* In Fragments, In Streams.

At night / he'd lie in bed. Louis B. Russell. Bruce Guernsey. InPK-6

At Night, Hearing Someone Singing in the House Next Door. Mei Yao Ch'en. CoBCP, *tr. by* Burton Watson

At night I dreamt I was back in Ch'ang-an. Dreaming that I Went with Li and Yü to Visit Yüan Chên. Po Chü-i. ChiP, *tr. by* Arthur Waley

At night I follow bell and chant. Staying Overnight at Spirit-Source Temple. Wen Cheng-ming. CoBLCP, *tr. by* Jonathan Chaves

At night I sit, uneasy and unhappy. To Yung-erh—Imitating a Work by Master Jade Stream. Li Tung-yang. CoBLCP, *tr. by* Jonathan Chaves

At night, in my dream, I stoutly climbed a mountain. Dream of Mountaineering, A. Po Chü-i. BLT; ChiP, *tr. by* Arthur Waley

At night, in New York's Central Park. New York Elegy. Yevgeny Aleksandrovich Yevtushenko [*or* Evtushenko]. TCRP, *tr. by* Albert C. Todd and John Updike

At night in Vinton County a Satanic cult. Offering. Debra Allbery. PBCAP

At night / my mother opened a chest and took out. White Wedding Slippers. Anna Swirszczynska. AF, *tr. by* Czeslaw Milosz

At night my sleep. Oto. JDP, *tr. by* Yoel Hoffmann

At night on my bed I longed for. Bible, *O.T.* WPoS *Fr.* Song of Solomon.

At night on the radiant Rialto. Lilatu Laili. Amin Al-Rihani. GraLe

At night packed in darkness and down. Winter Mirror II. Judith Mok. TuT, *tr. by* Michael O'Loughlin

At night, sometimes, when I cannot sleep. 11 rue Daguerre. John Montague. ModIr; NPeEn

At night the child takes down. Smoke. Susan Mitchell. EmeKit

At night the day is constantly woken up. Work. Andrei Codrescu. PmAP; SPE

At night the suburban boulevards are full of snow; the bandits are. War. Max Jacob. AF, *tr. by* Michael Brownstein

At night the wallpaper shakes. At Night. Margherita Guidacci. WPOW, *tr. by* Marina La Palma

At night they pound the vermilion newt. Painting Her Nails. Yang Wei-chen. CoBLCP, *tr. by* Jonathan Chaves

At night-time, ere I go to sleep. Soldier's Betrothed, The. Richard Billinger. AuPH, *tr. by* Lowell A. Bangerter

At night to the blind man. Eyes. Vladimir Dmitrievich Tsybin. TCRP, *tr. by* Lubov Yakovleva

At night what things will stalk abroad. Lux in Tenebris. Katharine Tynan. SacPr

At night when ale is in. Of Drunkenness. George Turberville. NBLV

At night, when Beacon Hill. Green and Red, Verde y Rojo. Martín Espada. PueRic

At night / yes night. Loneliness. Amjad Nasir. BBASP; MAP, *tr. by* Charles Doria and May Jayyusi

At nightfall the autumn woods cry out. Grodek. Georg Trakl. PeFWW

At nightfall the sky was various. Two Lines from Paul Celan. Mark Halperin. GifTon

At nightfall, when the inquisitive elves in elf-pants. Lunatic of Lindley Meadow, The. August Kleinzahler. PmAP

At nine I knew what Jesus would do. Uncle. Julia Kasdorf. PBCAP

At nine in the morning there passed a church. Faintheart in a Railway Train. Thomas Hardy. CTC; EnLoPo

At Nine Rivers, in the tenth year, in winter—heavy snow. Releasing a Migrant 'Yen' (Wild Goose). Po Chü-i. ChiP, *tr. by* Arthur Waley

At nine year he is full bad. (LL) Properties of a Good Greyhound, The. Dame Juliana Berners. RB; WoPoe, *tr. by* Seamus Heaney

At noon, I leave my clothes out to dry. Drying Clothes. Yang Wan-li. SuSp, *tr. by* Jonathan Chaves

At noon I must have been conceived. Mikhail Alekseievich Kuzmin. CAGL, *tr. by* Michael Green

At noon, in the dead centre of a faith. Desertmartin. Tom Paulin. CIP-2; ModIr; NPeEn; PBCIP; PNI

At noon in the desert a panting lizard. At the Bomb Testing Site. William Stafford. CoAP; NIL-7; NIP-4; NoAM; OBWP; RB

At noon sneaky. Cold Lunch. William Corbett. PmAP

At noon they talk of evening and at evening. Cypresses. Robert Francis. APT-2; LCAP-2

At noon, Tithonus, withered by his singing. Wedding, The. Conrad Potter Aiken. TAP

At noon today, I woke from a nightmare. Mexico, 1940. Ai. NoAM

At North Farm. John Ashbery. ColAP; HarvBoo; HCAP; PoE

At on of Apollonaire's Wednesdays I saw, sitting on the big divan. Greetings, Blaise Cendrars. Sonia Delaunay. CuPo

At once, and he died looking towards my face. (LL) Dream. Richard Watson Dixon. EBEV; NOBVV; OxBEV; PeVV; SCGP

At once on th' Eastern cliff of Paradise. John Milton. PeECV *Fr.* Paradise Lost.

At once whatever happened starts receding. Whatever Happened? Philip Larkin. OxBSo; Son

At 100 Mile House the cowboys ride in rolling. Cariboo Horses, The. Alfred Wellington Purdy. HeIP-4; NOBC

At one point, you have to sift the sand to even glimpse. Minor Figure. Mary Ruefle. ExTi

At one time I lived. Visiting My Old Hut in Late Spring. Muso Soseki. EaWin, *tr. by* W. S. Merwin

At our ease. Pagan Fires. Tawfiq Zayyad. MAP, *tr. by* Charles Doria and Sharif Elmusa

At our gate he groaneth, groaneth. At Our Golden Gate. Joaquin Miller. APN-2

At Our Golden Gate. Joaquin Miller. APN-2

At our hearts? (LL) At April. Angelina Weld Grimké. BlSi; GT

At Pakiri Beach. David Mitchell. PeNZ

At Parting. Duo Duo (Li Shizheng). AF, *tr. by* Gregory Lee

At Parting. Ho Sun. CoBCP, *tr. by* Burton Watson

At Parting. Edith Nesbit. OBGa

At Parting. Anne Ridler. FaBoWar; LW

At peace. Hakusetsu. JDP, *tr. by* Yoel Hoffmann

At Peach Blossom Bank is Peach Blossom Retreat. Song of Peach Blossom Retreat. T'ang Yin. CoBLCP, *tr. by* Jonathan Chaves

At Pegasus. Terrance Hayes. AmPoNex

At Pei-mang how they rise to Heaven. Desecration of the Han Tombs, The. Chang Tsai. ChiP, *tr. by* Arthur Waley

At Pens-hurst. Edmund Waller. *See* At Penshurst [Another]

At Penshurst [Another]. Edmund Waller. BeJo
 (At Pens-hurst.) PBRV
 (Had *Dorothea* liv'd when mortals made.) PBRV

At Perigord near to the wall. Perigord pres del muralh, A. Bertrans [*or* Bertran *or* Bertrand] de Born. CTC, *tr. by* Ezra Pound

At Piccadilly Circus. Vivian de Sola Pinto. OBMV

At Pleasure Bay. Robert Pinsky. NAAL-5

At Polwart on the Green. Polwart on the Green. Allan Ramsay. NOEC; NPeEn; OxBEV

At prayer / Bead-swinging. Issa. ZenPo, *tr. by* Takashi Ikemoto and Lucien Stryk

At Present I Am Working as a Security Guard. Edison Dupree. OPRER

At present / soup dishes serve us as mess tins. From the War. Aleksandr Petrovich Mezhirov. TCRP, *tr. by* Deming Brown

At Provincetown. Daniel Gerard Hoffman. YaYoPo

At Puri, the crows. Taste for Tomorrow. Jayanta Mahapatra. VCWP

At Queensferry. William Ernest Henley. OxBSo

At Quincey's moat the squandering village ends. Almswomen. Edmund Charles Blunden. OBMV; OxBTC

At Rest from the Grim Place. Arthur Nortje. PBMAP

At Rest in the Blast. Marianne Craig Moore. MoAmPo

At River's Head, birds swarm through willow flowers. Drinking with Elder Cheng the Eighth at Crooked River. Tu Fu. CrYelRi, *tr. by* Sam Hamill

At Robert Fergusson's Grave, October 1962. Robert Garioch. OxBS

At Rochecoart / Where the hills part. Provincia Deserta. Ezra Pound. OxBA

At Sainte-Marguerite. Trumbull Stickney. APN-2; OxBA; TCAPo

At Saxman, the totems slash down. Circle of Totems, The. Peggy Shumaker. PBCAP

At Sea. Richard Hovey. APN-2

At Seascale our shoes were full of sand. My Father's Shadow. Dorothy Nimmo. Prnts

At see-saw across the gate. (LL) Jack and Gill. Mother Goose. OxBoLi; OxNR; PeLV

At Set of Sun. "George Eliot." PoToHe

At Seven a Son. Elaine Feinstein. HarvBoo

At seven I dreamed again and again. On Alabama Ave., Paterson, NJ, 1954. Rachel De Vries. UnSA

At seven you just nick it. Public Dinner, A. Thomas Hood. OBCoV

At Seventeen. Arthur Symons. OxBSo *Fr.* Violet.

At seventeen I've come to read a poem. Twelve O'Clock. Carolyn Kizer. ExTi

At seventy miles an hour. Bull and Egret. Chinua Achebe. PFTM-2

At Shagger's Funeral. Bruce Dawe. NOBAu

At Shagger's funeral there wasn't much to say. At Shagger's Funeral. Bruce Dawe. NOBAu

At sight of sparkling Bowls or beauteous Dames. Verses in Baretti's Commonplace Book. Samuel Johnson. OxAEP-1

At silo filling time the air was similarly wet. Silo Treading. Bruce Beaver. BMAP

At six A.M. the log cabins. Moose in the Morning, Northern Maine. Mona Van Duyn. ColAP

At six years old I had before mine eyes. Old Man. James Henry. NOBVV

At Sixteen. Ann Darr. LW

At sixteen, I worked after high school hours. Who Burns for the Perfection of Paper. Martín Espada. InvLad

At sixteen my mother had been a swimmer. Back to Back. Debra Kang Dean. NAPBL

At sixty Grandfather. Phone Booth at the Corner, The. Juan Delgado. TouFir

At sixty I, Dionysios of Tarsos, lie here. *Unknown.* GrAn

At sixty, it might be well to start. Collector, The. Desiré Flynn. BrRo

At slammed door and smoker's cough in the hall. (LL) Docker. Seamus Heaney. HeIP-4; NOIV

At spirit séances in Queen's. Limerick. Morris Gilbert Bishop. PeLi

At spring's end, I long for home. End to Spring, An. Li Ch'ing-chao. CrYelRi, *tr. by* Sam Hamill

At St. Sulpice. Erin Belieu. NAPBL

At stated .ic times. Composed in the Composing Room. Franklin Pierce Adams. NIL-7; NIP-4; OBAL

At stroke of midnight God shall win. (LL) Four Ages of Man, The. W. B. Yeats. PAI; TrCP

At Su Terrace Viewing the Past. Li Po. CoBCP, *tr. by* Burton Watson

At such a time, of year and day. Hill-Shade, The. William Barnes. OxBEV

At summer eve, when Heaven's ethereal bow. Thomas Campbell. EnRP *Fr.* Pleasures of Hope, The.

At Summer's End. Jean Janzen. GeoHom

At Summer's End. Charles Harper Webb. GeoHom

At sun-up, inside. Snakeroot. J. L. Jacobs. AmPoNex

At Sunrise. Rosa Zagnoni Marinoni. PoToHe

At Sunset. Henrietta Cordelia Ray. CBWP-3

At Sunset. Margaret Elizabeth Munson Sangster. PWR (Sin of Omission, The.) ITBLP; PoToHe

At sunset from the top of the stair watching. Otranto. Barbara Guest. FTOS

At sunset I come out of the door. *Unknown.* ChinPo, *tr. by* Yip Wai-lim

At Ta-an I Got Sick from Wine and Had to Lay Over for Half a Day. Governor Wang Invited Me to His Place Again. Lu Yu. ColAnChi, *tr. by* Burton Watson

At Tauba's death I swore. Lamenting Tauba. Laila Akhyaliyya. BoWoP, *tr. by* Willis Barnstone

At tea in cocktail weather. Publisher's Party. Phyllis McGinley. OBAL

At ten a clock, when I the fire rake. Epigram. Francis Daniel Pastorius. SCAP

At ten A.M. the young housewife. Young Housewife, The. William Carlos Williams. APT-1; ColAP; HeIP-4; NAAL-2v2; NAAL-5; TAP

At ten I wanted fame. I had a comb. Behind Grandma's House. Gary Soto. UnSA

At Terezin. Teddy. INSAB

At that time. David Diop. *See* In those days / When civilization kicked us in the face

At that time I read a book about a girl prone. Seeing a Basket of Lobelia the Color of a Bathrobe. Molly Peacock. SpudSo

At the Abbey Theatre. W. B. Yeats. Son

At the age of empty spaces. How Do Your Eggs Want You (?). Pedro Juan Pietri. PueRic

At the airport hotel. Business in Germany. Stewart Florsheim. GotH

At the alder-darkened brink. Hamlen Brook. Richard Wilbur. HarvBoo; VCAP; WeW-3

At the Altar. Robert Lowell. InPK-6 *Fr.* Between the Porch and the Altar.

At the Altar-Rail. Thomas Hardy. MoBrPo *Fr.* Satires of Circumstance in Fifteen Glimpses.

At the ancient pond. Basho. SoOfWa, *tr. by* Sam Hamill

At the ancient well. Buson. SoOfWa, *tr. by* Sam Hamill

At the antipodes of poetry, dark winter. Discovery of Thought, A. Wallace Stevens. APT-1

At the Ascension. Luís De León. SpanPo, *tr. by* James Edward Tobin

At the "Atlantic" Dinner, December 15, 1874. Oliver Wendell Holmes. OBCoV

At the Back of Progress. Taslima Nasrin. VCWP

At the back of the bookshop a Karate expert. Enzensberger at 'Exiles.' John Tranter. BMAP

At the back of the houses there is the wood. House in the Wood, The. Randall Jarrell. LCAP-2

At the Back of the North Wind. George Macdonald. "Where did you come from, baby dear?" ITBLP; WHSW

At the backyard fence. Michael Dudley. HA

At the Badr Trench. Safiya bint Musafir. WPOW, *tr. by* Bridget Connelly and Deirdre Lashgari

At the Ball! Charles Henry Webb. OBAL

At the Ball Game. William Carlos Williams. MoASP; NoAM; NOBA; OxBA; PoE

At the beginning. Akiko Yosano. OHMPJ

At the beginning I noticed. Stone Diary, A. Pat Lowther. NOBC

At the beginning of winter a cold spirit comes. *Unknown.* BoWoP; ChiP

At the black canvas of estrangement. Jewish Bride, The. Paul Durcan. BiHa

At the Black Edge. Ger Killeen. AmPoNex

At the blackboard I had missed. Zimmer's Head Thudding against the Blackboard. Paul Zimmer. PBCAP

At the Bomb Testing Site. William Stafford. CoAP; NIL-7; NIP-4; NoAM; OBWP; RB

At the bottom. David Lloyd. HA

At the bottom of the sea. Me at the Bottom of the Sea. Alfonsina Storni. TCLAP, *tr. by* Andrew Rosing

At the bramble-end of the car lot, five wild turkeys. Turkeys in August. Gray Jacobik. UrbNat

At the break of dawn. Kakei. SoOfWa, *tr. by* Sam Hamill

At the break of day I come to an old temple. Visit to the Broken Hill Temple, A. Ch'ang Chien. SuSp, *tr. by* Joseph J. Lee

At the bridal bed of star-crossed Petalê. Lost Bride, The. Antiphanes. GrAn, *tr. by* Dudley Fitts

At the brim, at the lip. Close. Robert Duncan. PmAP

At the British Museum. Richard Aldington. MoBrPo

At the British War Cemetery, Bayeux. Charles Causley. NAEL-5v2; NAEL-6v2; NoP-4; OBWP; OxBC; PoWW

At the brookside I stroll. Tune: "The Dark Clouds of Ch'u" Visiting the Rainy Crag Alone. Hsin Ch'i-chi. ColAnChi, *tr. by* Jiaosheng Wang

At the brow of a hill a fair shepherdess dwelt. Lass of the Hill, The. Mary Jones. ECWP

At the burial of an epoch. Anna Andreyevna Akhmatova. FaBoWar; PoetW, *tr. by* Max Hayward *Fr.* In 1940.

At the bus stop on the first frigid. Nobody's Hell. Douglas Goetsch. AmPoNex

At the Cafe Door. Constantine P. Cavafy. CAGL, *tr. by* Edmund Keeley and Philip Sherrard

At the Carnival. Anne Spencer. APT-1; BlSi

At the Cascade. Henrietta Cordelia Ray. CBWP-3

At the Castle. Jerome Rothenberg. FTOS

At the Cave. Artur Miedzyrzecki. PoSu, *tr. by* Stanislaw Baranczak

At the Cavour. Arthur Symons. NOBVV; NPeEn; OxBSP

At the Cedars. Duncan Campbell Scott. NOBC

At the Cemetery, Walnut Grove Plantation, South Carolina, 1989. Lucille Clifton. LoL

At the Center of Injustice. Violeta Parra. TANSG, *tr. by* Karen Kerschen

At the center of the earth. Song. *Unknown.* STP, *tr. by* Jerome Rothenberg

At the center of the earth there is a mother. Our Mother. Susan Griffin. HW

At the ceremony of *Emobo*. Ceremony. Kattie M. Cumbo. BlSi

At the Chiang-ning River Mouth. Wang An-shih. SuSp, *tr. by* Jan W. Walls

At the church they killed a pig once. Pogrom. Phyllis Kahaney. GotH

At the city's heart stood the shrine to Dido's ghost. Catius As Conius Silius Italicus. RomPo, *tr. by* Marcus Wilson *Fr.* Punica, The.

At the Closed Gate of Justice. James David Corrothers. NAAAL

At the closing, he cut the final check. Conifer King, The. Michael Bugeja. UrbNat

At the Convent Gate. Charlotte Mew. VWP

At the corner of Wood Street, when daylight appears. Reverie of Poor Susan, The. William Wordsworth. GTBS-P; OxBoLi

At the country inn, thousands of peach trees. Inscribed on a Painting. T'ang Yin. CoBLCP, *tr. by* Jonathan Chaves

At the crack of dawn, Monday stands beside you. Monday. Vijaya Mukhopadhyay. OMIP, *tr. by* Vijaya Mukhopadhyay, Sunil B. Ray and Carolyne Wright

At the crossroad. Nakamichi. JDP, *tr. by* Yoel Hoffmann

At the Crossroads. Thomas Kinsella. NoAM

At the Crossroads. Bill Knott. PBCAP

At the Dark Hour. Paul Dehn. BoLoP

At the dark street corner. Guilt, Desire and Love. James Baldwin. CAGL; GLP

At the dawn I seek Thee. Morning Song. Solomon ibn Gabirol. TrJP, *tr. by* Nina Davis Salaman

At the dawning of our youth. Poetograd. Nikolai Ivanovich Glazkov. TCRP, *tr. by* Daniel Weissbort

At the day camp years ago where we drove. Dawn. Betsy Sholl. LTA

At the dead of night by the side of the Sea. Sea-Side Cave, The. Alice Cary. APN-2; ColAP

At the death and neglect of my dark proud race. (LL) First-born, The. Jack Davis. BMAP; IBA

At the demolishing, this seat. Andrew Marvell. NOSC *Fr.* Upon Appleton House [To My Lord Fairfax].

At the Desk. Theodor Storm. WoPoe, *tr. by* Robert Bly

At the Discharge of Cannon Rise the Drowned. Hubert Witheford. PeNZ

At the documentary level, a voice on tape. Topos. Jane Miller. GifTon

At the Door. Lillie Fuller Merriam. PoToHe

At the Door of Anticipation. Hala Mohammad. PoArWo, *tr. by* Cornelia Al-Khaled

At the Door of Mercy Sighing. Thomas Mackellar. AH

At the Door of the Native Studies Director. Robert H. Davis. HATNAP

At the Doors. "Der Nistor." TrJP, *tr. by* Joseph Leftwich

At the Draper's. Thomas Hardy. MoBrPo *Fr.* Satires of Circumstance in Fifteen Glimpses.

At the earliest ending of winter. Not Ideas about the Thing but the Thing Itself. Wallace Stevens. APT-1; HAP; HCAP; LCAP-2; PFTM-2; SAmP; TAP

At the east where the black water lies stands the large corn. Corn Ceremony. *Apache Oral Tradition.* TCAPo

At the edge. Denise Levertov. NAAL-2v2

At the edge. Alexis Rotella. HA

At the edge of all the ages. Song of Finis, The. Walter De la Mare. MoBrPo

At the Edge of the Jungle. Patrick Lane. NOBC

At the edge of the precipice I become logical. George Swede. HA

At the edge of the world, a traveler long used to grief. My Boat Moored on a River. Yen Yü. SuSp, *tr. by* Irving Y. Lo

At the Edge of Town. William Stafford. NNaP

At the Egyptian Exhibit. Daniel Tobin. NAPBL

At the Electronic Frontier. Miguel Algarin. UnSA

At the End. Richard Ryan. PBCIP

At the end a / "The Prisoner of Zenda." Prisoner of Zenda, The. Richard Wilbur. NBLV; OBCoV

At the end of a crazy-moon night. Lal Ded [*or* Lalla]. AWTN; WPoS, *tr. by* Coleman Barks

At the end of a freight train rolling away. Late Lights in Minnesota. Ted Kooser. BLT

At the end of a melancholy world. End of the World, The. João Cabral de Melo Neto. VCWP

At the end of a path, I built a thatch-roofed shack. Fire, Sixth Month, 408. T'ao Ch'ien [*or* T'ao Yuan-ming]. CrYelRi, *tr. by* Sam Hamill

At the end of delight, one. Limit. Diane Ward. FTOS

At the end of emotion and description there is a village. Which Religion Vouchsafes. Jane Miller. GifTon

At the end of his act. Road Show. Geoff Page. BMAP

At the end of January you will see again. Starting 1973: What to Do Now that Peace Has Been Announced. Joseph Cady. CDa

At the end of life paralysis or those creeping teeth. Bog and Candle. Robert David Fitzgerald. CBAP

At the end of my suffering. Wild Iris, The. Louise Glück. ColAP

At the end of myself pencil tip. George Swede. HA

At the End of September. Sándor Petőfi. IQMS, *tr. by* Adam Makkai and Valerie Becker Makkai

At the End of Spring. Po Chü-i. ChiP, *tr. by* Arthur Waley

At the End of Spring. Yü Hsüan-chi. BoWoP, *tr. by* Geoffrey Waters

At the end of Tarriers' Lane, which was the street. Wm. Brazier. Robert Graves. NOBL

At the end of the Affair. Maxine W. Kumin. TAP

At the end of the battle. César Vallejo. TCLAP, *tr. by* Clayton Eshleman *Fr.* Spain, Take This Cup from Me.

At the end of the garden walk. Cold Green Element, The. Irving Layton. NOBC; NoP-4

At the end of the journey we built. Journeys. Meg Campbell. PeNZ

At the end of the rainbow there's happiness. I'm Always Chasing Rainbows. Joseph McCarthy. ReLy

At the end of the road, in a drab chapel. Mother Tongue. Jon Stallworthy. NoAM

At the end of the row. Objection to Being Stepped On, The. Robert Frost. NBLV; OBCoV

At the end of the war I arose. Driver, The. James Dickey. VGW

At the End of the Weekend. Ted Kooser. PBCAP

At the Entrance. M. R. Peacocke. NLP

At the Entrance. Douglas Stewart. CBAP

At the equinox when the earth was veiled in a late rain, wreathed with wet poppies, waiting spring. Continent's End. Robinson Jeffers. AWP

At the Executed Murderer's Grave. James Wright (1927–80). HCAP; VCAP

At the exhausted lovers where they sleep. (LL) But That Is Another Story. Donald Justice. CoAP; NoP-4

At the Exhibition of Parables. Donald Revell. BodElec

At the Exiled King's River Pavilion. U'ng Binh. CaDao, *tr. by* John Balaban

At the factory I worked. Mexicans Begin Jogging. Gary Soto. LTA

At the Faucet of June. William Carlos Williams. APT-1

At the feet o' Jesus. Feet o' Jesus. Langston Hughes. ISC

At the ferro-concrete bike sheds. Tattoo, The. Peter Finch. TCAWP

At the Ferry. U. A. Fanthorpe. FaBoWP

At the field's edge. White Hare, The. Lilian Bowes-Lyon. OxBTC

At the Fillmore. Philip Levine. NNaP

At the first peep of dawn she roused me. William Carlos Williams. TCAPo *Fr.* Wanderer, The: A Rococo Study.

At the first turning of the second stair. T. S. Eliot. NOBA *Fr.* Ash Wednesday [*or* Ash-Wednesday].

At the Fishhouses. Elizabeth Bishop. APT-2; AmFaPo; CoAP; FaBoWP; HAP; HCAP; LCAP-2; NAAL-2v2; NAAL-5; NALW; PoPoPo; PoRA; PoetW; VCAP

At the Fishmonger's. Nikolai Alekseievich Zabolotsky [*or* Zabolotskii]. TCRusP, *tr. by* Alec Merivale

At the flea market across from the Commerce Speedway. Talismans. Maudelle Driskell. AllShUp

At the Flyfisher's Shack. Sydney Lea. RA

At the font the black marble. Baroque. Marie-Claire Bancquart. MFP, *tr. by* Martin Sorrell

At the Foot of Mount Zion. Endre Ady. IQMS, *tr. by* Leslie A. Kery

At the Fountain. Marcabrun. AWP, *tr. by* Harriet Waters Preston

At the Freud Hilton. Campbell McGrath. AmPoNex

At the Frick. Anthony Hecht. GS

At the frontier the long train slows to a stop. Frontier, The. John Hewitt. BIrV

At the full face of the forest lies our little town. To the Red Lory. John Shaw Neilson. NOBAu

At the gate of old Granada, when all its bolts are barred. Lamentation for Celin, The. *Unknown.* AWP, *tr. by* John Gibson Lockhart

At the Gate of the Valley. Zbigniew Herbert. PoSu, *tr. by* Czeslaw Milosz

At the Gates. Kofi Awoonor. PBMAP; VCWP *Fr.* Night of My Blood (1971).

At the gates of Zion, over Kedron. Ivan Alekseievich Bunin. TCRP

At the Government Office Building. Taking Leave of Two Officials. Tu Fu. CrYelRi, *tr. by* Sam Hamill

At the Grave of Henry Vaughan. Siegfried Sassoon. GTBS-P

At the Great Wall of China. Edmund Charles Blunden. GTBS-P

At the Grey Round of the Hill. W. B. Yeats. RB

At the Gwen John Exhibition. Charles McDonald. NLP

At the Hammersmith Palais. Alan Riddell. NOBAu

At the Havana Hilton. Sandra M. Castillo. TouFir

At the hayfield's edge, a few stalks. Quick and the Dead, The. Galway Kinnell. BAP-01

At the head of a march to the last new Jerusalem. (LL) James Russell Lowell. NOBA; OxBA; TAP; TCAPo *Fr.* Fable for Critics, A.

At the heart of the ridiculous, the sublime. (LL) Antarctica. Derek Mahon. NPeEn; PBCIP

At the Heng-ts'ui Pavilion of Fa-hui Monastery. Su Tung-p'o (Su Shih). SuSp, *tr. by* Irving Y. Lo

At the Hermitage of Master Fu. Wang Wei. CrYelRi, *tr. by* Sam Hamill

At the high school football game, the boys. Homecoming. Dorianne Laux. ExTi

At the Holi festival of color. Mirabai [*or* Mira Bai]. BoWoP

At the hour when the heat of the day is overcome. Dante Alighieri. NAWM-5v1 *Fr.* Divina Commedia.

At the House of Ghosts. Adrian C. Louis. MoASP

At the Indian Killer's Grave. Robert Lowell. NOBA; VGW

At the instant of drowning he invoked the three sisters. Three Fates, The. Rosemary Dobson. BMAP; BoWoP

At the Jaffé Memorial Fountain, Botanic Gardens. Frank Ormsby. CIP-2

At the Jewish Museum. Linda Pastan. TaR

At the Jewish New Year. Adrienne Rich. TaR

At the Keyhole. Walter De la Mare. MoBrPo

At the Klamath Berry Festival. William Stafford. InPK-6

At the lacquered table—my recent calligraphy. Wen Cheng-ming. CoBLCP *Fr.* Chung-i Temple, The.

At the Lake—Remembering My Dead Son, Yü. Pien Kung. CoBLCP, *tr. by* Jonathan Chaves

At the large foot of a fair hollow tree. Country-Mouse, The. Abraham Cowley. NPeEn; OBVE

At the last moment, they said, my cousin held. Matter of Division, A. Frankie Paino. AmPoNex

At the last, tenderly. Last Invocation, The. Walt Whitman. MoAmPo; OxBA

At the last will join you in dust. (LL) Sad Remembrance. Mei Yao Ch'en. CoBCP; ColAnChi, *tr. by* Burton Watson

At the last, your hand feels steady. (LL) After Dark. Adrienne Rich. LCAP-2; VGW

At the Lesbian and Gay Pride March we. Some of Us Wear Pink Triangles. Walta Borawski. CAGL

At the Lighthouse. "Nikolai Nikolaevich Morshen." TCRusP, *tr. by* John Glad

At the lip of a big black vagina. Where I Live. Wanda Coleman. GeoHom

At the long tables of time. Jugs, The. Paul Celan. HP; OBVE, *tr. by* Christopher Middleton

At the Loom. Robert Duncan. VGW *Fr.* Passages.

At the Lord's Table waiting, robed and stoled. Incident, An. Frederick Tennyson. SacPr

At the melting of snow, February. On the Hoping Life. Hans Leifhelm. AuPH, *tr. by* Lowell A. Bangerter

At the mental ward I chew. Recommitted. Juan Delgado. TouFir

At the Metro: Old Irrelevant Images. Jack A. Mapanje. PBMAP

At the mid hour of night, when stars are weeping, I fly. Echo. Thomas Moore. GTBS-P; NOBE; OBEV

At the midnight in the silence of the sleep-time. Epilogue. Robert Browning. NAEL-5v2; NAEL-6v2; NOBE

At the Monument to Pierre Louÿs. Richard Howard. VCAP

At the Mosque. Chairil Anwar. PoetW, *tr. by* Burton Raffel

At the Mountain of the Mysterious Tomb Visiting Master P'ou. Wu Wei-yeh. CoBLCP, *tr. by* Jonathan Chaves

At the mouth of Wu-ling Stream. Riding a Boat on Wu-ling Stream. Tao-chi. CoBLCP, *tr. by* Jonathan Chaves

At the Movie: Virginia, 1956. Ellen Bryant Voigt. LTA; NoAM

At the movies I always love the look. Sunday Matinee. Sybil Kollar. FFC

At the Nachi Kannon Hall. Muso Soseki. EaWin, *tr. by* W. S. Merwin

At the Nature-Strip. Judith Rodriguez. CBAP

At the New Moon: Rosh Hodesh. Marge Piercy. TaR

At the New Year. John Hollander. TaR

At the news from Fal's high plain I cannot sleep. Geoffrey Keating. NOIV

At the news of your death. Lament for the Death of a Bullfighter. Joshua Beckman. AmPoNex

At the ninth month, our imperial soldiers ford distant waters. Song of Distant Waters, A. Wen T'ing-yün. SuSp, *tr. by* William R. Schultz

At the northe ende of Selver White. *Unknown.* MiEL

At the Nuclear Rally. Laura Boss. UnSA

At the Office Early. Ted Kooser. PBCAP

At the officers' table, for half an hour afterwards, port. Class Incident from Graves. Alan Brownjohn. OxBTC

At the offset it was calculated. Edoardo Sanguineti. ItPo, *tr. by* Gayle Ridinger *Fr.* Scartabello.

At the old pond. Buson. WoPoe, *tr. by* Tony Barnstone

At the Olive Grove of the Resistance. Robert Hedin. GifTon

At the onset of its sprint, the blazing circle climbs straight ahead. Brush Fire. Fily-Dabo Sissoko. NegPo, *tr. by* Ellen Conroy Kennedy

At the open grave. Nicholas Virgilio. HA

At the orgy I humped twenty-two. Limerick. *Unknown.* PeLi

At the outpost three years. Body Is Pain, The. *Vietnamese Oral Tradition.* CaDao, *tr. by* John Balaban

At the outset she still carried it quite well. Mary's Visitation. Rainer Maria Rilke. GI

At the palace of rocks, spring clouds white. Palace of Rocks, The. Yüan Chieh. SuSp, *tr. by* William H. Nienhauser

At the park. Returned from California. Simon J. Ortiz. HATNAP

At the Party. W. H. Auden. OxBSP

At the Party. Mikhail Alekseievich Kuzmin. CAGL, *tr. by* Simon Karlinsky

At the party she said. What's So Funny 'bout Peace, Love and Understanding. Robert Long. SwNoth

At the Pauwels. Diane Glancy. CRP

At the place of light. Prophetic Powers. *Unknown.* APN-2, *tr. by* Henry Rowe Schoolcraft

At the Playground. William Stafford. TLR

At the Poem Society a black-haired man stands up to say. Kenneth Koch. NNaP; NeAP

At the Point. Robert Mezey. GeoHom

At the point of shining feathers. Night a Sailor Came to Me in a Dream, The. Diane Wakoski. TAP; VGW

At the Polo-Ground. Sir Samuel Ferguson. NOIV

At the Poorhouse. Federico García Lorca. PFTM-1

At the Portals of the Future. Lines. Frances Ellen Watkins Harper. APN-2

At the post house lodge, plum flowers scattering. Tune: Treading on Grass. Ou-yang Hsiu. CoBCP, *tr. by* Burton Watson

At the Powwow. Cheryl Savageau. TWW

At the Protestant Museum. Hugh Maxton. CIP-2

At the quarry's edge. King Lear. Peter Huchel. PoSu, *tr. by* Michael Hamburger

At the Rainbow. Robert Vasquez. GeoHom

At the rapids father and boy pitch in a young birch. Woods Burial. John Peck. PoCoUp

At the Record Hop. Wanda Coleman. NAAAL

At the retreat, Lee wasn't allowed. Nirvana. James Tate. BodElec

At the Rio Grande near the End of the Century. Ray Gonzalez. TouFir

At the rise of summer a hundred beasts and trees. Beginning of Summer, The. Po Chü-i. ChiP, *tr. by* Arthur Waley

At the river-bend. Larry Gates. HA

At the River Tower Parting from My Younger Brother, Fu-ling. Wu Wei-yeh. CoBLCP, *tr. by* Jonathan Chaves

At the roots of clouds a cutworm hollowing. Five Dawn Skies in November. David Wagoner. VCAP

At the round earth's imagined corners, blow. John Donne. BASC; ChIV-2; ClHu; EBEV; FHYEP; HAP; HeIP-4; MakPoe; MeLP; NAEL-5v1; NAEL-6v1; NAEL-7v1; NAWM-5v1; NOBE; NOSC; OxAEP-1; OxBEV; OxBSo; PAI; PeECV; PoE; SCGP; Son; TFi; TOF; WoPoe *Fr.* Holy Sonnets.

At the Salvation Army. Simon J. Ortiz. NAAL-5 *Fr.* From Sand Creek.

At the San Francisco Airport. Yvor Winters. AiP; HeIP-4; InPK-6; NIL-7; NIP-4; NOBA

At the School for the Gifted. Carol Muske. ExTi

At the Sea's Edge. Gwen Harwood. CBAP

At the seashore I came upon a golden shell. Seashell. "Rubén Dario." SpanPo, *tr. by* Anita Volland

At the Seaside [*or* Sea-Side]. Robert Louis Stevenson. NTCP; TLR; WHSW

At the Shore. Mary Oliver. PoCoUp

At the side. Woman Washing. Patricia Bishop. Prnts

At the siege of Belle Isle. Mother Goose. OxNR; ReMoGo

At the sight of the beauty that greets them, for the charm they have broken. (LL) London Snow. Robert Bridges. EBEV; EBVV; GTBS-P; MoBrPo; NOBE; NOBVV; NoAM; OxAEP-2; OxBTC; TFi

At the Sky's End, Thinking of Li Po. Li Po. ColAnChi, *tr. by* David Lattimore

At the Slackening of the Tide. James Wright (1927–80). UnPo; VGW

At the slick edges of the mirror, without a trace. (LL) Shaving. Richard Blanco. AmPoNex; NAPBL

At the small end of an illness. World Contracted to a Recognizable Image, The. William Carlos Williams. APT-1

At the sorrow of my sweet pipings. (LL) Hymn of Pan. Shelley. FaBoCh; OBEV

At the South Pole. Jean Earle. Prnts

At the spring. To Light. Linda Hogan. HATNAP

At the Stanley Spencer Exhibition. John Riley. Oth

At the Stop Light, the Braided Blond Man. Anthony R. Vigil. AmPoNex

At the stormy moment of dawn. Swifts. Philippe Jaccottet. VCWP, *tr. by* Derek Mahon

At the street bookstall in Karlsruhe, my father. Homage to Ferd. Holthausen. Gwen Harwood. NOBAu

At the Swings. Henry Taylor. MPUn

At the Tavern. *Unknown.* MiEL

At the Telephone Club. Henri Coulette. CoAP

At the Temple of Kuan Yin in the Rain. Su Tung-p'o (Su Shih). CrYelRi, *tr. by* Sam Hamill

At the Thatched Hall of the Ts'ui Family. Tu Fu. CrYelRi, *tr. by* Sam Hamill

At the third hour always. Rain. Paul Murray. BIrV

At the time it seemed unimportant: he was lying. Day, The. Roy Fuller. OxBTC

At the time of Matines, Lord, thu were itake. Hours of the Passion, The. *Unknown.* MiEL

At the time of night-prayer, as the sun slides down. Night and Sleep. Jelaluddin [*or* Jalal al-Din] Rumi. WoPoe, *tr. by* Robert Bly

At the time of the White Dawn. Song of the Fallen Deer. *Unknown.* OBVE, *tr. by* Frank Russell

At the time when blossoms. *Unknown.* BoWoP *Fr.* Tzu Yeh Songs.

At the time when blossoms fall from the cherry-tree. Summer Song. Emperor Wu of Han [*or* Wu Ti *or* Ou-ty *or* Liu Ch'e *or* Liu Ch'u]. ChiP, *tr. by* Arthur Waley

At the Tomb of Rachel. "Yehoash." TrJP, *tr. by* Isidore Goldstick

At the Tomb of Sophokles. Simmias [*or* Simias] of Rhodes. GrAn, *tr. by* Dudley Fitts

At the Top of My Voice. Vladimir Vladimirovich Mayakovsky [*or* Maiakovskii]. TCRP, *tr. by* Max Hayward and George Reavey

"My most respected / comrades of posterity!" AF

At the top of the hill you were Muriel. My Mother in Three Acts. Jane Cooper. ExTi

At the top of the house the apples are laid in rows. Moonlit Apples. John Drinkwater. OBMV; OxBTC; PoRA

At the top of this ridge I could whistle happily. Descending the Ridge of Flying Clouds. T'ang Hsien-tsu. CoBLCP, *tr. by* Jonathan Chaves

At the topmost peak, one thatch hut. Visiting a Recluse on West Mountain and Not Finding Him In. Ch'iu Wei. CoBCP, *tr. by* Burton Watson

At the Tourist Center in Boston. Margaret Atwood. NoP-4

At the Train Museum. Linda Pastan. GM

At the Un-National Monument along the Canadian Border. William Stafford. HAP; HeIP-4

At the undulating head he aims. Emu Shot. Tjinapirrgarri. NOBAu, *tr. by* George von Brandenstein

At the Vietnam War Memorial, Washington, D.C. Robert Dana. CDa

At the Wailing Wall. Aidan Carl Mathews. BiHa; CIP-2

At the Washing of My Son. David Ray. RaBo

At the Washing of My Son. Su Tung-p'o (Su Shih). OHPC, *tr. by* Kenneth Rexroth

At the Well. Paul Blackburn. APSN; PFTM-2

At the Well. Leonard Nathan. PBCAP

At the western window I paused from writing rescripts. Being on Duty All Night in the Palace and Dreaming of the Hsien-yu Temple. Po Chü-i. ChiP, *tr. by* Arthur Waley

At the Window. "Rachel" [*or* "Rahel"]. FIT, *tr. by* Robert Friend

At the window frame concealing. Saint. Stéphane Mallarmé. NAWM-7v2, *tr. by* Henry Weinfield

At the Window in the Dark. Victor Hugo. SxFrPo, *tr. by* E. H. Blackmore and A. M. Blackmore

At the window, sleet. O. Mabson Southard. HA

At the window that veils her old. Saint. Stéphane Mallarmé. SxFrPo, *tr. by* E. H. Blackmore and A. M. Blackmore

At the "Ye That Do Truly." Charles Williams. NOCV

At the Zoo. John Davies. AngWePo

At the Zoo. William Makepeace Thackeray. NTCP

At the Zoo. Israel Zangwill. TrJP

At thee the Mocker sneers in cold derision. Maid of Orleans, The. Johann Christoph Friedrich von Schiller. AWP, *tr. by* James Clarence Mangan

At thieves I bark; at lovers wag my tail. *Unknown, after the Latin of* Joachim du Bellay. FaBoEE

At Thirty-three. Hans Magnus Enzensberger. VCWP, *tr. by* Hans Magnus Enzensberger and Michael Hamburger

At this Adonis smiles as in disdain. William Shakespeare. EBEV *Fr.* Venus and Adonis.

At this hour exiles look for sleep in pills. An ambulance. Body Politic. Silvio Giussani. ItPo, *tr. by* Gayle Ridinger

At This Juncture. Blanca Wiethüchter. TANSG, *tr. by* Shaun Griffin and Emma Sepúlveda-Pulvirenti

At this moment in time. They Flee from Me That Sometime Did Me Seek. Gavin Ewart. OxBC

At this remote village, I have no neighbors. Quatrain. Chang Yü. CoBLCP, *tr. by* Jonathan Chaves

At this speed, my friend, our origins are groundless. Transcanadian. Robert Hedin. GifTon

At this th' Impatient Hero sowrly smil'd. Homer. OBVE, *tr. by* John Dryden *Fr.* Iliad, The.

At this time I find the bed very arid. Reason for Poetry, The. Nancy Morejón. WPOW, *tr. by* Anita Whitney

At this time there are few. Baby Is Born out of a White Owl's Forehead—1972, A. Alice Notley. ExTi

At Thomas Hardy's Birthplace, 1953. James Wright (1927–80). CoAmPo

At 3 A.M. Wendy Cope. LW

At three A.M., alone, not sleepy. Richard's Blues. Richard Cecil. SeSe

At 3 a.m. I run my tongue. Death's Head. Phyllis Gotlieb. NOBC

At three in the afternoon. Meditation on Yellow. Olive Senior. WaCA

At three-thirty in the morning in America. Myra Sklarew. TaR *Fr.* Lithuania.

At thy approach, my cheek with blushes glows. Elizabeth Singer Rowe. PEW *Fr.* Paraphrase on the Canticles, A.

At Tikal. William Bronk. APSN

At times I fear. Portugal Laurel, The. John Wright. BloBone

At times I resort, beyond man's discerning. Cynewulf. AnOE *Fr.* Riddles (Exeter Book).

At Times I Say: Let's Try to Be Joyous. Cristina Campo. CItWP, *tr. by* Cinzia Sartini Blum and Lara Trubowitz

At times I see it, present. Bright Day, A. John Montague. CIP-2

At times it seemed the country itself was a cloud. England. Mary Jo Salter. DiPo

At Times Spirit Surges. David Shimoni. MHP, *tr. by* Ruth Finer Mintz

At times spirit surges up from bodies' prison. At Times Spirit Surges. David Shimoni. MHP, *tr. by* Ruth Finer Mintz

At times the heart looks toward open fields. Near Twelve Mile Point. Lance Henson. HATNAP

At Timon's Villa. Pope. *See* Epistle IV, to Richard Boyle, Earl of Burlington

At Tripod Lake on that day His Majesty quit this world. Ballad of Yüan-yüan. Wu Wei-yeh. CoBLCP, *tr. by* Jonathan Chaves

At Tripolis. Constance Carrier. WPE

At twelve, I quit reciting. Year I Was Diagnosed with a Sacrilegious Heart, The. Martín Espada. TouFir

At 12 o'clock in the afternoon. Epigram. Meleager. GrAn; WoPoe, *tr. by* Peter Whigham

At twelve o'clock midnight, the lines are cut. Midnight Vigil. Fran Haraway. HHAm

At 28 I was still faithless. 28. Philip Levine. GeoHom

At 29. Speculations on the Present through the Prism of the Past. June Jordan. GT

At twenty, I loved Lise. She was frail and white. Oswald Durand. *See* Like Lise, moreover, my mother was white

At Twilight. Hayyim Nahman [*or* Khayim Nakhman *or* Chaim Nachman] Bialik. FIT, *tr. by* Robert Friend

At twilight. Virginia Brady Young. HA

At twilight I went into the street. Descending Figure. Louise Glück. FaBoWP

At two A.M. a thing, jumping out of a manhole. News Report. David Ignatow. TwCP

At Tynemouth Priory, after a Tempestuous Voyage. William Lisle Bowles. Son (Written at Tinemouth, Northumberland, after a Tempestuous Voyage.) CenSon

At Upton-on-Severn. *Unknown*. FaBoEE

At various times, I have asked myself what reasons. Poem Written in a Copy of Beowulf. Jorge Luis Borges. PoetW, *tr. by* Alastair Reid

At Villequier. Victor Hugo. SxFrPo, *tr. by* E. H. Blackmore and A. M. Blackmore

At Viscount Nelson's lavish funeral. 1805. Robert Graves. FaBoCh; FaBoWar; OBCoV; OBSV; PeLV

At Vshchizh. Fyodor [*or* Feodor] Ivanovich Tyutchev. OBWP; OxBEV; WoPoe, *tr. by* Henry Gifford and Charles Tomlinson

At War. Charles Mungoshi. FaBoMo

At water's edge, clouds float up. Night of the Fourteenth. Ho Ching-ming. CoBLCP, *tr. by* Jonathan Chaves

At Waterfall Temple. Chang K'o-chiu. CrYelRi, *tr. by* Sam Hamill

At wawking [*or* wauking] of the fauld. (LL) Allan Ramsay. OxBS; SCGP *Fr.* Gentle Shepherd, The.

At wells and dunghills. (LL) Anahorish. Seamus Heaney. HarvBoo; PBCIP

At westward window of a palace gray. My Lighthouses. Helen Hunt Jackson. APN-2; ColAP

At whatever age he was, he was apt with that. Won't It Be Fine? Robert Creeley. BAP-97

At whiles (yea oftentimes) I muse over. Dante Alighieri. AWP; EaItPo, *tr. by* Dante Gabriel Rossetti *Fr.* La Vita Nuova.

At Whole-World-In-View-Hut. Muso Soseki. EaWin, *tr. by* W. S. Merwin

At Will Robers Beach. Timothy Steele. WeW-3

At Wilshire and Santa Monica I saw an opossum. Oldest Living Thing in L.A., The. Larry Levis. UrbNat

At winter's end. Snowman Sniffles. N. M. Bodecker. TLR

At Woodlawn I heard the dead cry. Theodore Roethke. APT-2; HAP; HCAP; NAAL-2v2; NoP-4; TRP; VGW

At words poetic, I'm so pathetic. Cole Porter. OBAL; ReLy; UnPo

At Work. Suzanne Gardinier. AmPoNex

At Work. Artur Miedzyrzecki. PoSu, *tr. by* John Batki and Artur Miedzyrzecki

At work his arms wave like a windmill. Secretary, The. Peter Redgrove. OxBTC

At Worthing, an exile from Geraldine G———. My Life Is a———. Frederick Locker-Lampson. OBCoV

At year's end is there anything one can depend on? Harmonizing with a Poem by Left Assistant Yu Kao-chih Requesting Sick Leave. Shen Yüeh. ColAnChi, *tr. by* Richard Mather

At Yellow Crane Tower Taking Leave of Meng Hao-jan. Li Po. CoBCP, *tr. by* Burton Watson

At Ynysddu. Graham Thomas. AngWePo

At yonder meadow's rand. Cavalry Song. Hugo Zuckermann. AuPH, *tr. by* Lowell A. Bangerter

At Yorktown. Charles Olson. HarvBoo

At your door. Weariness in the Evening of January Thirty-Second. 'Isam Mahfouz. MAP, *tr. by* Sargon Boulus and Samuel Hazo

At your entreaty [*or* Intreaty], I at last have writ. Maidenhead. "Ephelia." WPE

At Your Feet, Jerusalem. Uri Zvi Greenberg. MHP, *tr. by* Ruth Finer Mintz

At your light side trees shy. Poem. Bill Knott. SPE

At your silver wedding in '64 we gave. Psycho. Peter Olds. PeNZ

At Yuen Yang Lake. Wu Wei-yeh. OHMPC, *tr. by* Kenneth Rexroth

Atalanta in Calydon. Algernon Charles Swinburne.
  Before the Beginning of Years. NAEL-5v2; NAEL-6v2
  (Chorus.) EBVV; GTBS-P; OBEV
  (Chorus from Atalanta in Calydon.) NoP-4
  When the Hounds of Spring AWP; CTC; EBVV; HAP; NAEL-5v2; NAEL-6v2; NOBE; OBEV; OxBEV; PoE; SCGP; TFi; WeW-3

Atameros. John Beevers. SPE

Atavism. Elinor Wylie. NALW

Atavistic: Traces after the Rain. Juan Felipe Herrera. TouFir

Atheism. Elizabeth Oakes-Smith.
  Annihilation. TCAPo
  "Doubt, cypress crowned, upon a ruined arch." TCAPo

Atheling Grange; or, The Apotheosis of Lotte Nussbaum. William Plomer. OBNV

Athelstan King / Lord among Earls. Battle of Brunanburh. *Unknown.* FaBoWar; OBVE; OBWP; PeVV, *tr. by* Alfred Tennyson, 1st Baron Tennyson

Athelstan the king, captain of earls. Brunanburg. *Unknown.* PoE, *tr. by* Kemp Malone

Athelstane. Priscilla Jane Thompson. CBWP-2

Athenagoras begot Eubulus—. Epitaph. Chairemon. GrAn, *tr. by* Richard Evans

Athenian Garden, An. Trumbull Stickney. APN-2; NoP-4

Athenians' Answer, The. Elizabeth Singer Rowe. BASC

Athens. John Milton. NOSC; PeECV *Fr.* Paradise Regained [*or* Regain'd].

Athens and Jerusalem. Rose Drachler. TaR

Athirst in spirit, through the gloom. Prophet, The. Alexander Sergeyevich Pushkin. AWP, *tr. by* Babette Deutsch and Avrahm Yarmolinsky

Athlete, one vacation, An. Accommodating Lion, An. Tudor Jenks. OBCA

Athwart the sky a lowly sigh. London. John Davidson. NOBE

Atieno washes dishes. Freedom Song, A. Marjorie Oludhe Macgoye. HAWP; ItWoWo; WoPoe

Atieno yo. (LL) Freedom Song, A. Marjorie Oludhe Macgoye. HAWP; ItWoWo; WoPoe

Atlanta Exposition Ode. Mary Weston Fordham. CBWP-2; SWaP

Atlantic City Waiter. Countee Cullen. APT-2

Atlantic is a sea of bones. Lucille Clifton. ESEAA

Atlantic is a stormy moat; and the Mediterranean, The. Eye, The. Robinson Jeffers. NOBA; NoAM; OxBA

Atlantis. W. H. Auden. OxAEP-2

Atlantis. Hart Crane. NAAL-5 *Fr.* Bridge, The.

Atlantis. Mark Doty.
  "Jimi and Tony." WiU
  Michael's Dream. WiU
  "Michael writes to tell me his dream." WiU
  New Dog. WiU

Atlantis. Louis Dudek.
  "I have been in a marine aquarium and I have seen." MoCV
  Marine Aquarium, The. MoCV

Atlantis. Joanna Fuhrman. AmPoNex

Atlantis. Slavko Mihalic. PoSu, *tr. by* Charles Simic

Atlas of the Difficult World, An. Adrienne Rich.
  "Catch if you can your country's moment, begin." NAAL-5
  "Dark woman, head bent, listening for something, A." GeoHom
  "Here is a map of our country." NAAL-5
  "I know you are reading this poem." NAAL-5
  "Late summers, early autumns, you can see something that binds." NAAL-5
  "On this earth, in this life, as I read your story, you're lonely." NAAL-5
  "One night on Monterey Bay the death-freeze of the century." GeoHom
  "*Soledad.* = f.*Solitude, loneliness, homesickness; lonely retreat.*" GeoHom
  "What homage will be paid to a beauty built to last." NAAL-5

Atmosphere Is Incandescent, The. Rosalía de Castro. SpanPo, *tr. by* Edwin Morgan

Atom bellies like a cauliflower, The. Jane Cooper. MakPoe *Fr.* After the Bomb Tests.

Atomic Bride. Thomas Sayers Ellis. BAP-97; NeAmPo

Atomic Fairy Tale. Yury [*or* Iurii] Kuznetsov. TCRP, *tr. by* Anatoly Liberman

Atomic Pantoum. Peter Meinke. WeW-3

Atomic Psalm. Maurya Simon. GifTon

Atonement. Margaret E. Bruner. PoToHe

Atoning Yesterday, The. Louise Imogen Guiney. SWaP

Atop the bamboo grove slants sunset's glow. After Snow, Longing for Elder Brother Hsi-ch'iao. Wang Shih-chieng. ColAnChi

Atossa. Matthew Arnold. TriCat

Atrides summon'd all to arms, to arms himself dispos'd. Homer. FaBoWar, *tr. by* George Chapman *Fr.* Iliad, The.

Atrium. Alessandro Ceni. ItPo, *tr. by* Gayle Ridinger

Atta boy! Atta boy! (LL) To Greet a Letter-Carrier. William Carlos Williams. OBAL; SAmP

Attack. Siegfried Sassoon. MoBrPo; NOBE; OxBTC

Attack of the Squash People. Marge Piercy. NBLV

Attainment, The. Coventry Patmore. FaBoEE *Fr.* Angel in the House, The.

Attempt at Jealousy, An. Craig Raine. NoAM

Attempt at Jealousy, An. Marina Ivanovna Tsvetayeva [*or* Tsvetaeva]. TCRusP; WPOW, *tr. by* Bob Perelman, Aleksandar Petrov and Shirley Rihner

Attempt at Jealousy, An. Marina Ivanovna Tsvetayeva [*or* Tsvetaeva]. OxBEV; TCRP; WoPoe, *tr. by* Elaine Feinstein

Attend, all ye who list to hear our noble England's praise. Thomas Babington Macaulay, 1st Baron Macaulay. FaBoCh

Attend my fable if your ears be clean. Roy Campbell. OBSV; PeSAV *Fr.* Wayzgoose, The.

Attend my lays, ye ever honour'd nine. Hymn to the Morning, An. Phillis Wheatley. TAP

Attend us, but old age and poverty. (LL) Mary Collier. ECWP; NOEC *Fr.* Woman's Labour; an Epistle to Mr. Stephen Duck, The.

Attend, ye mournful Parents, while. Another to Urania. Benjamin Colman. ChIV-1; SCAP

Attended only by the loveless moon. (LL) Stars and Planets. Norman MacCaig. OPOU; OxBSP

Attention. Rae Armantrout. PmAP

Attention. Adrienne Rich. TAP

Attention was commanded through a simple, unadorned, unexplained, often decentered presence. Jealousy. Mei-Mei Berssenbrugge. OpBo; PmAP

Attention Young Bachelors. Violeta Parra. TANSG, *tr. by* Shaun Griffin and Emma Sepúlveda-Pulvirenti

Attentive eyes, fantastic heed. Poet, A. Thomas Hardy. NoAM

Attentively he heard us, while we spoke. Virgil [*or* Vergil]. OBVE, *tr. by* John Dryden *Fr.* Aeneid [*or* Eneados, *Aeneis*], The.

Atthis, for you the thought of me has become hateful. Sappho. SaLy, *tr. by* Diane Rayor

Atthis hung up the belt with the pompoms. Leonidas of Tarentum. GrAn

Atthis, my darling, thou did'st stray. "Michael Field." PoBW; ViWPN

Atthis, the immanence of death. (LL) "Michael Field." PoBW; ViWPN

Attibon Legba. René Depestre. NegPo, *tr. by* Ellen Conroy Kennedy *Fr.* Epiphanies of the Voodoo Gods.

Attic, The. Henri Coulette. PoRA

Attic, The. Marie Howe. ExTi

Attic Landscape, The. Herman Melville. NCAP; NOBA; OBAL

Attic maid! with honey fed. To the Swallow. Euenus. OBVE, *tr. by* William Cowper

Attic room and window my ice skates on the wall. My Legs Señor. William S. Burroughs. BB

Atticus ("Peace to all such! but were there one whose fires"). Pope. AWP; InPK-6; NOBE; OxBEV; TRP *Fr.* Epistle to Dr. Arbuthnot.

Attila József. Attila József. AF, *tr. by* John Batki

Attis. Catullus. WoPoe, *tr. by* Reynolds Price

Attis. Catullus. OBVE; STV, *tr. by* Peter Whigham *Fr.* Carmina.

Attitude. Magda Portal. TANSG, *tr. by* Shaun Griffin and Emma Sepúlveda-Pulvirenti

Attraction. Ella Wheeler Wilcox. LW

Attractive at that distance, hair fanning out. Double, The. Joan Aleshire. OPRER

Attribute all to the gods: often they raise. Archilochus. SaLy, *tr. by* Diane Rayor

Attributes assumed, retribution entertained. What is borne amongst them? Too much or too little. Indulgences of bartered acclaim; an expenditure, a hissing. Wine, urine and ashes. (LL) Geoffrey Hill. NoAM; NoP-4 *Fr.* Mercian Hymns.

Attributes of a Gentleman, The. Ronald of Orkney, Saint. NePenScot, *tr. by* Paul Bibire

Atween the world o' licht. Scotland. William Soutar. OxBS

Au Jardin des Plantes. John Wain. OxBTC

Au Tombeau de Mon Père. Ronald McCuaig. NOBAu

Aubade. Amy Lowell. NIL-7

Aubade. *Unknown.* NAWM-7v1, *tr. by* Peter Dronke

Aubade. *Unknown, at. to* John Donne. BoLoP; NOBE
  (Daybreak.) OBEV

Aubade. Mark Wunderlich. WiU

Aubade, An. Irving Layton. WoPoe

Aubade, An: "As she is showering, I wake to see." Timothy Steele. PasH; RA

Aubade: "At break of dawn." W. H. Auden. CAGL *Fr.* Three Posthumous Poems.

Aubade: "Cold snap. Five o'clock." Richard Kenney. NoP-4

Aubade for Hope. Robert Penn Warren. MoAmPo
  (Dawn: and foot on the cold stair treading or.) FuPo

Aubade: "Geese flew by as you entered me, The." Kate C. Richardson. PasH

Aubade: "Hark! hark! the lark at heaven's gate sings." William Shakespeare. OBEV *Fr.* Cymbeline.

Aubade: "Hours before dawn we were woken by the quake." William Empson. FaBoMo; FaBoTw; OxAEP-2; OxBEV; OxBTC

Aubade: "I work all day, and get half-drunk at night." Philip Larkin. AWTN; BodElec; CABP; NAEL-6v2; NoP-4; PoetW; SoSe-8; TRP

Aubade: "It's all the same to morning what it dawns on." Nuala Ni Dhomhnaill. BiHa; PBCIP, *tr. by* Michael Longley

Aubade: "Jane, Jane, / Tall as a crane." Dame Edith Sitwell. BWW; MoBrPo; NALW; NoAM; PoRA

Aubade: "Lark now leaves his watery [*or* wat'ry] nest, The." Sir William Davenant [*or* D'Avenant]. *See* Lark Now Leaves His Watery [*or* Wat'ry] Nest

Aubade: "Lights are out in the street, and a cool wind swings, The." Rosamund Marriott Watson. ViWPN

Aubade: Macedonia. Nicholas Samaras. YaYoPo

Aubade: Opal and Silver. Mark Doty. HarvBoo

Aubade Triste. Agnes Mary Frances Robinson. NOBVV

Aubade: "Waking is this easy." Marilyn Chin. NIP-4

Aubade: "What dawn is it?" Karl Shapiro. VGW

Aubade: "World was very large, The. Then." Louise Glück. BodElec

A.U.C. 334: about this date. Advice to Young Ladies. Alec Derwent Hope. NoAM; NoP-4

Aucassin and Nicolette. *Unknown*.
   Who Would List. CTC, tr. by Andrew Lang

Auchanachie Gordon is bonny and braw. Lord Saltoun and Auchanachie. *Unknown*. ESPB

Aucthour Maketh Her Wyll and Testament, The. Isabella Whitney. BWW; EMWP; NoP-4
   (Will and Testament.) NAEL-7v1
   (Wyll and Testament.) PEW

Auction Sale, The. Henry Reed. MoBrPo

Auction Sale—Household Furnishings. Adele DeLeeuw. PoToHe

Auctioneer. Carl Sandburg. NOxBChV

Auden at Milwaukee. Stephen Spender. AiP

Auden, MacNeice, Day Lewis, I have read them all. British Leftish Poetry, 1930–40. Hugh MacDiarmid. FaBoTw; NoAM

Audible and Inaudible. Yannis Ritsos. AF, tr. by Minas Savas

Audible Still. J. Adwaita Dèr Mouw. TuT, tr. by Peter Van de Kamp

Audible still, very very distant, is the night train. Audible Still. J. Adwaita Dèr Mouw. TuT, tr. by Peter Van de Kamp

Audience with the emperor, Hall of Inherited Brilliance. Presented to Piao, the Prince of Pai-ma. Ts'ao Chih. CoBCP, tr. by Burton Watson

Auditor Thinks about Female Nature, An. Jamie Grant. NOBAu

Auditory Hallucinations. Joyce Mansour. HAWP, tr. by Carol Cosman

Audley Court. Tennyson. NOBVV; PeVV

Audrey Causey. Pavane on Mr Wray's Locations, A. Tony Baker. Oth

Audrey Hepburn moons big-eyed on the cover. Guide to Holland, A. Peter Sirr. PBCIP

Audubon: A Vision. Robert Penn Warren. APT-2
   Love and Knowledge. NAAL-5
   Tell Me a Story. FuPo; NAAL-5
   Was Not the Lost Dauphin. NAAL-5

Audubon, Drafted. Imamu Amiri Baraka. TTY

Audubon Drive, Memphis. James Seay. AllShUp; SwNoth

Auf dem Wasser zu Singen. Stephen Spender. EnLoPo

Auf meiner Herzliebsten Äugelein. Heinrich Heine. AWP, tr. by Richard Garnett

Augher Clogher Fivemiletown. Omagh Post Office Rhyme. *Unknown*. FaBoVe

Auguries of Innocence. William Blake. EBEV; FaBoCh; OxAEP-2; OxBoLi; PeECV; TFi
   "Bat that flits at close of eve, The." UV
   "Robin Redbreast in a cage, A." OWoS; OxBoLi
   Three Things to Remember. OWoS; OxBoLi
   "To see a World in a Grain of Sand." EnlH; InPK-6; KaS; NPeEn; OxBEV

Augury. W. H. Oliver. PeNZ

August. Katharine Pyle. OBCA

August. Henrietta Cordelia Ray. CBWP-3

August. Adrienne Rich. NNaP
   (August 1972.) BodElec
   (Two horses stand in a yellow light.) BodElec

August. Folgore da San Geminiano [or Gimignano]. CTC; EaItPo, tr. by Dante Gabriel Rossetti Fr. Sonnets of the Months.

August. Edmund Spenser. Fr. Shepheardes [or Shepeards or Shepherd's] Calender, The.

August. William Stafford. BodElec

August. Pamela Stewart. ExTi

August. John Updike. OBCA Fr. Child's Calendar, A.

August. Elinor Wylie. APT-1; MoAmPo

August 17, 1970. Don Receveur. CDa

August 18. Joanne Kyger. PoM

August 29: Charlie "Yardbird" Parker's birthday. Bird Lives. Faye Moskowitz. MiVo

August 1914. Isaac Rosenberg. EBEV; HarvBoo; NOBE; NPeEn; OBWP; OxBEV; OxBTC; PeFWW

August 1968. W. H. Auden. OxBSP

August 1972. Adrienne Rich. *See* August

August 1990. C. Mikal Oness. GeoHom

August a haze amniotic our dream aether and lens of distance. Tree sentinels in.

Christopher Dewdney. FTOS Fr. Spring Trances in the Control Emerald Night.

August and the drive-in picture is packed. Dear John Wayne. Louise Erdrich. UnSA

August Bank Holiday. Jacques Prévert. MFP, tr. by Martin Sorrell

August day, An. Times Square. Alter Brody. TaR

August Fires. Glover Davis. GeoHom

August heat. Emily Romano. HA

August heat. Haiku. Gerald Vizenor. VoR

August Heaven has failed in its divine ministration. Lament for Ying, A. Ch'u Yüan. SuSp, tr. by Wu-Chi Liu

August, Los Angeles, Lullaby. Carol Muske. PBCAP

August Midnight, An. Thomas Hardy. NOBVV

August Moon. Cesare Pavese. AF, tr. by William Arrowsmith

August Night. Sara Teasdale. MoAmPo

August Nights. Jean Janzen. GeoHom

August on Sourdough, a Visit from Dick Brewer. Gary Snyder. LoL; NAAL-5

August, on the Rented Farm. Dave Jeddie Smith. ColAP

August Rain. Robert Bly. LCAP-2

August Rain, after Haying. Jane Kenyon. ExTi

August sky, The. George Swede. HA

August Sleepwalker, The. Bei Dao. PFTM-2, tr. by Bonnie S. McDougall

August Sleepwalker, The. Zhao Zhenkai. VCWP

August stretches into fall. Clouds spread. Near the Mississippi. Steve Gehrke. AmPoNex

August the First; Court Martial. The Mother Speaks. Marjorie Oludhe Macgoye. HBAPE

August the First: The Shadow. Patel Speaks. Marjorie Oludhe Macgoye. HBAPE

August the First: The Watchman Speaks. Marjorie Oludhe Macgoye. HBAPE

August. The mums nod past, each a prickly heart on a sleeve. (LL) Teach Us to Number Our Days. Rita Dove. ESEAA; NoAM

August Town. Bob Stewart. WaCA

August 'twas the twenty-fifth. Bar[']s Fight[, August 28, 1746]. Lucy Terry. BPo; BlSi

August Was Foggy. Gary Snyder. NNaP

August Zero. Jane Miller. BodElec

Augustus was a chubby lad. Story of Augustus Who Would Not Have Any Soup, The. Heinrich Hoffmann. NBLV

Auld Deil cam to the man at the pleugh, The. Farmer's Curst Wife, The. *Unknown*. ESPB

Auld freen and helper up the hill. Poetical Epistle tae Cullybackey Auld Nummer. Thomas Given. FaBoVe

Auld House, The. William Soutar. OxBS

Auld Lang Syne. Robert Burns. AWP; NAEL-5v2; NAEL-6v2; NOBE; NOSC; NePenScot; OBEV; OxAEP-2; OxBEV; OxBS; SCGP

Auld Matrons. *Unknown*. ESPB

Auld mune on her back, The. Leander Stormbound. Sydney Goodsir Smith. OxBS

AULD NIBOR I'm three times, doubly, o'er your debtor. Second Epistle to Davie. Robert Burns. NePenScot

Auld Noah was at hame wi' them a' Parley of Beasts. Hugh MacDiarmid. ChIV-1; MoBrPo; NoAM; OBMV

Auld Reikie, a Poem. Robert Fergusson.
   "Auld Reikie! wale o' ilka town." NePenScot

Auld Robin Forbes. Susanna Blamire. ECWP

Auld Robin Gray. Lady Anne Lindsay. ECWP; GTBS-P; LW; NOEC; OBEV; OxBEV; PeSAV; WPE

Auld Sang. William Soutar. OxBS

Auld Seceder Cat, The. *Unknown*. FaBoCh

Auld wife sat at her ivied door, The. Ballad. Charles Stuart Calverley. CABP; NBLV; OBCoV; OxAEP-2; UV

Auld wumman cam' in, a mere rickle o' banes, in a faded black dress, An. Old Wife in High Spirits. Hugh MacDiarmid. OxBTC; PoE

Aulus / is childless. Lucilius. GrAn

Aulus, my girlfriend's in a dreadful plight. Martial. RomPo, tr. by Anthony Reid

Aum Mani. Mani-Mani Gatha. Jackson Mac Low. PFTM-1

Aunt Annie said, When I turned seventeen. Legacies. Emily Grosholz. FFC

Aunt Chloe. Frances Ellen Watkins Harper.
   Deliverance, The. SWaP
   "Master only left old Mistus." SWaP

Aunt Chloe's Politics. Frances Ellen Watkins Harper. NAAAL; NALW

Aunt Hannah Jackson. Fenton Johnson. APT-1

Aunt Helen. T. S. Eliot. NPeEn; OBAL

Aunt Jemima of the Ocean Waves. Robert Earl Hayden. LCAP-2

Aunt Jennifer's Tigers. Adrienne Rich. ColAP; FaBoWP; HeIP-4; InPK-6; NALW; NIL-7; NIP-4; NoAM; NoP-4; OPOU; TRP

Aunt Jessie. Wanda Coleman. GT

Aunt Julia. Norman MacCaig. RB

Aunt Laura Moves toward the Open Grave of Her Father. Joseph De Roche. HeIP-4

Aunt Lil. Paul Zweig. BodElec

Aunt Lily stood / behind her candy counter / passing out Mary Janes, Hersheys, and advice. Candy Lady, The. Laura Boss. UnSA

Aunt Liza / Yes? Peter Abrahams. PBA Fr. Tell Freedom.

Aunt Martha. Wil'um Lee. InTrad

Aunt Martha bustles. Old Houses. Melvin B. Tolson. GT

Aunt Rose—now—might I see you. To Aunt Rose. Allen Ginsberg. CLPP; ColAP; NAAL-2v2; NoAM; PAI; PmAP; PoE; TaR; VGW

Aunt Sue has a head full of stories. Aunt Sue's Stories. Langston Hughes. APT-2; SAmP

Aunt Sue's Stories. Langston Hughes. APT-2; SAmP

Aunt Toni's Heart. Rafael Campo. RA

Aunt Zillah Speaks. Herbert Edward Palmer. FaBoTw

Auntie's Skirts. Robert Louis Stevenson. WHSW

L'Aura Amara. Arnaut Daniel. CTC, tr. by Ezra Pound

Aurelia. Robert Malise Bowyer Nichols. OBMV

Aurelia, when your zeal makes known. Headache, The. Mary Leapor. ECWP; PEW

Aurelius & Furius, true comrades. 11. Catullus. NAWM-7v1, tr. by Charles Martin

Aurelius! patron of starvelings. To Aurelius. Catullus. CAGL, tr. by Eugene O'Connor

Aureng-Zebe. Dryden.
  Prologue: "Our author by experience finds it true." OxBoLi

Aurora. Sir William Alexander, Earl of Stirling.
  I Envy Not Endymion. Son
  I Hope, I Fear. Son
  "O happy Tithon! if thou know'st thy harp." OBEV
  Oh, If Thou Knew'st How Thou Thyself Dost Harm. Son
  Sonnet: "Cleare moving cristall, pure as the Sunne beames." OxBS
  Sonnet: "I dreamed the nymph that o'er my fancy reigns." NOSC
  Sonnet: "Ile give thee leave my love, in beauties field." OxBS
  (To Aurora.) GTBS-P

Aurora. Emily Dickinson. APN-2; NCAP

Aurora. Timothy Steele. DiPo

Aurora Borealis. Edouard Roditi. SPE
  (Crystallization of color, A.) SPE

Aurora, lady grey. Simple Pastoral, A. George Alexander Stevens. NOEC

Aurora Leigh. Elizabeth Barrett Browning. VWP
  "And I, I was a good child on the whole." BrRo
  "Books, books, books!" WPOW
  "Critics say that epics have died out, The." FaBoWar; NAEL-5v2; NAEL-6v2; NALW; NoP-4; PeVV
  First Book: Young Aurora's Fostermother. NALW
  "I just knew it when we swept above the old roofs of Dijon." PeVV
  "I think I see my father's sister stand." NALW
  "My mother was a Florentine." NALW
  "Of writing many books there is no end!" NOBVV
  Sweetness of England, The. OxAEP-2
  "Then, land!—then, England! oh, the frosty cliffs." NAEL-5v2; NAEL-6v2
  "Then, must it be." NALW
  "There he glowed on me." NAEL-6v2
  "There it is! / You play beside a death-bed like a child." BrRo
  "Times followed one another. Came a morn." NAEL-6v2
  "Whoever lives true life, will love true love." OxAEP-2

Auroras of Autumn, The. Wallace Stevens. APT-1
  "Farewell to an idea. . .A cabin stands." HCAP; PoE
  "Farewell to an idea. . .The mother's face." HCAP; PoE
  "Is there an imagination that sits enthroned." HCAP
  "It is a theatre floating through the clouds." HCAP
  "This is where the serpent lives, the bodiless." PoE
  "Unhappy people in a happy world, An." PoE

Aus Einem April. Frank O'Hara. HarvBoo

Auschwitz. János Pilinszky. IQMS, tr. by Peter Jay

Auschwitz. Salvatore Quasimodo. AF, tr. by Jack Bevan

Auschwitz, 1987. Adam Zych. HP, tr. by Hilda Schiff

Auschwitz from Colombo. Anne Ranasinghe. GotH

Auspex. James Russell Lowell. TAP

Austere the Music of My Songs. Fyodor [or Fiodor] Kuz'mich Sologub. AWP, tr. by Babette Deutsch and Avrahm Yarmolinsky

Austerities. Charles Simic. EmeKit

Australia. Gary Catalano. NOBAu

Australia. Alec Derwent Hope. NoAM
  (Nation of trees, drab green and desolate grey, A.) BMAP; NoP-4

Australia 1970. Judith Wright. CBAP; HarvBoo; MakPoe; NoAM

Australian Dream, The. David Campbell. CBAP

Australian Emigrant, The. Francis Fisher Browne.
  Australian Emigrant, The. VWP
  "Bark went forth, with the morning's smile, A." VWP

Australian Garden, An. Peter Porter. OBGa

Australorp. Edith Speers. NOBAu

Austrian Army, An. Alaric Alexander Watts. NOBL; PeLV

Austrian Song. Anton Wildgans. AuPH, tr. by Lowell A. Bangerter

Autet e bas. Arnaut Daniel. CTC, tr. by Ezra Pound

Authentic! Shadows of it, The. Matins. Denise Levertov. FaBoWP; NOBA; NoAM

Author, The. Charles Churchill.
  "Gods! with what pride I see the titled slave." OBSV
  "When with much pains this boasted learning's got." OBSV

Author Apologizes to a Lady, for His Being a Little Man, The. Christopher Smart. BoLoP

Author Consults a Critic and Sells His Manuscript, The. Francis Hawling. NOEC Fr. Signal; or, A Satire against Modesty, The.

Author Loving These Homely Meats, The. John Davies of Hereford. NPeEn; OBCoV; Son Fr. Scourge of Folly, The.

Author of American Ornithology Sketches a Bird, Now Extinct, The. David Wagoner. BLT

Author of Christine, The. Richard Howard. CoAP

Author, of His Own Fortune, The. Sir John Harington [or Harrington]. FaBoEE

Author of light, revive my dying spright. Thomas Campion. InvLi

Author of the Jesus Papers Speaks, The. Anne Sexton. PFTM-2

Author of this is Ossian, The. Unknown. NePenScot, tr. by Derick Thomson

Author's Apology for His Book, The. John Bunyan.
  "When at the first I took my pen in hand." FaBoVe

Author's Dream to the Lady Mary, the Countess Dowager of Pembroke, The. Aemilia Bassano Lanyer. BASC

Author's Early Life, The. Julia A. Moore.
  "And now, kind friends, what I have wrote." VerBaPo

Author's Epitaph, Made by Himself, The. Sir Walter Ralegh. See Even Such Is Time

Author's Epitaph, Written by Himself, An. Abel Evans. FaBoEE

Author's Prologue. Dylan Thomas. ChIV-1
  (Prologue to the Collected Poems.) AngWePo

Author's Quietus, The. Henry Carey. FaBoVe

Author's Resolution, The. George Wither. See Fair Virtue, the Mistress of Philarete

Author to Her Book, The. Anne Bradstreet. BASC; ColAP; EMWP; InPK-6; MakPoe; NAAL-2v1; NAAL-3; NAAL-5; NALW; NOBA; NoP-4; OxBA; PoE; SCAP; TAP; TCAPo

Author to His Body on Their Fifteenth Birthday, 29.ii.80, The. Howard Nemerov. NoAM

Author to His Book, The. George Alsop. SCAP

Author to His Book[e], The. Thomas Heywood. NOSC Fr. Apology for Actors, An.

Author to His Wife, of a Woman's Eloquence, The. Sir John Harington [or Harrington]. BoLoP

Author to the Reader, The. Randall Jarrell. OxBC

Author Unknown. William Montgomerie. OxBS

Authoress, armed with a skewer, An. Limerick. Unknown. PeLi

Authorities do not permit us, The. Joy. Susan Wicks. MFPA

Authority is a disease, and cure. Samuel Butler (1612–80). FaBoEE

Authors and actors and artists and such. Bohemia. Dorothy Parker. APT-1; NBLV

Authors and poets in prose and in rhyme. Night We Called It a Day, The. Tom Adair. ReLy

Authors of the Town, The. Richard Savage.
  "First, let me view what noxious nonsense reigns." OBSV

Authors [or Author's] Abstract of Melancholy, The. Robert Burton. NOSC Fr. Anatomy of Melancholy, The.

Authorship. James Ball Naylor. NBLV

Authours Epitaph, Made by Himself, The. Sir Walter Ralegh. NIL-7
  (Verses Found in His Bible in the Gatehouse at Westminster.) SacPr
  (Verses Made the Night before His Beheading.) CABP

Auto-erotic. Unknown. PeLi

Auto Mirror. Adam Zagajewski. BLT

Auto Mobile. A. R. Ammons. OBAL

Auto Wreck. Karl Shapiro. APT-2; NIL-7; NIP-4; RB; VGW

Autobahnmotorwayautoroute. Adrian Mitchell. RB

Autobiographia Literaria. Frank O'Hara. NNaP; NOBA; TTTS

Autobiographical. Abraham Moses Klein. MoCV; NoAM

Autobiographical Fragment. Kingsley Amis. OBCoV

Autobiographical Poem. Elaine Equi. KGB

Autobiographical Response from a Provincial Wasteland (in Reply to a New Year's Greeting Sent with a Bouquet). Elizaveta Shakhova. ARWW, tr. by Catriona Kelly

Autobiography. John Burnside. NePenScot

Autobiography. Charles Causley. Son

Autobiography. Mbella Sonne Dipoko. TTY

Autobiography. Janet Dubé. BrRo

Autobiography. Thom Gunn. NoAM

Autobiography. Joy Harjo. LTA

Autobiography. Sonja Åkesson. BoWoP, tr. by Ingrid Claréus

Autobiography. Louis MacNeice. ModIr; NOIV; NPeEn; PNI; RB

Autobiography. Dan Pagis. FIT, tr. by Robert Friend; PoSu
(I died with the first blow and was buried.) AF; VCWP

Autobiography. Robert Viscusi. UnSA

Autobiography. Tom Weatherly. NBV

Autobiography, An. Ernest Rhys. OBEV; OBWVE
(I am content to have from Death.) (LL) AngWePo

Autobiography 2 (hellogoodby). Michael Palmer. HarvBoo

Autobiography, Chapter XVII: Floating the Big Piney. Jim Barnes. HATNAP

Autobiography, Chapter XLII: Three Days in Louisville. Jim Barnes. HATNAP

Autobiography: Last Chapter. Jim Barnes. CDW

Autobiography of a Black Man. G. E. Patterson. AmPoNex

Autobiography of a Lungworm. Roy Fuller. NoAM; OxBC

Autobiography of John Doe, The. Jon Lavieri. OPRER

Autocrat of the Breakfast Table, The. Oliver Wendell Holmes.
Aestivation [an Unpublished Poem, by My Late Latin Tutor]. NOBL; OBAL; TCAPo
Chambered Nautilus, The. APN-1; ColAP; ITBLP; NAAL-3; NCAP; NOBA; NoP-4; TCAPo; TFi
Contentment. APN-1; OxBA; PWR
Deacon's Masterpiece; or, The Wonderful "One-Hoss Shay", The. APN-1; BRP; ITBLP; NAAL-3; NOBA; OBAL; OBCA; OxBA; PoRA; TAP; TCAPo; TFi
Living Temple, The. APN-1
Voiceless, The. APN-1

Autograph on the Soul, The. Adah Isaacs Menken. CBWP-1

Autolycus as Peddler. William Shakespeare. NPeEn; NoSic Fr. Winter's Tale, The.

Autolycus Sings. William Shakespeare. See Winter's Tale, The

Autolycus's Song ("Jog on, jog on, the footpath way"). William Shakespeare. FaBoCh; NoSic Fr. Winter's Tale, The

Autolycus's Song ("When daffodils begin to peer"). William Shakespeare. See Winter's Tale, The

Automat. David Ray. PoSol

Automatic Crystal, The. Aimé Césaire. SurPaPo, tr. by Clayton Eshleman and Annette Smith

Automatic Text for Anne Ethuin. Elisabeth Lenk. SurWo, tr. by Gisela Baumhauer and Greta Wenziger

Automobile, The. Russell Edson. LCAP-2; RaBo

Automobile, The. Vladislav Felitsianovich Khodasevich. TCRusP, tr. by Daniel Weissbort

Automobiles of the Asylum. Philip Hammial. BMAP

Automotrici stutter along the branch lines. Off the Beaten Track. Peter Rafferty. NLP

Autopsy. James L. Foy. BloBone

Autopsy. Arthur Nortje. HBAPE

Autopsy, The. Odysseus Elytis. AF

Autopsychography. Fernando Pessoa. WoPoe, tr. by Keith Bosley

Autumn. Bella [or Izabela] Akhatovna Akhmadulina. BoWoP, tr. by Barbara Einzig

Autumn. Roy Campbell. GTBS-P; MoBrPo; OBMV; OxBTC

Autumn. Alice Cary. APN-2

Autumn. John Clare. BBASP; HAP; WeW-3

Autumn. Walter De la Mare. NPeEn; OxBTC

Autumn. Fan Ch'eng-ta. SuSp, tr. by Irving Y. Lo Fr. Seasonal Poems on Fields and Gardens.

Autumn. Maurice Gilliams. TuT, tr. by Sean Dunne

Autumn. Friedrich Hölderlin. WoPoe, tr. by David Rattray Fr. Seasons, The.

Autumn. Thomas Hood. OBEV; OxAEP-2
(Ode: Autumn.) UnPo

Autumn. Thomas Ernest Hulme. FaBoMo; NPeEn

Autumn. Alphonse Marie Louis de Lamartine. SxFrPo, tr. by E. H. Blackmore and A. M. Blackmore

Autumn. Walter Savage Landor. EnLoPo Fr. Ianthe.

Autumn. Philip Levine. NNaP

Autumn. Detlev, Freiherr von Liliencron. AWP, tr. by Ludwig Lewisohn

Autumn. Henry Wadsworth Longfellow. APN-1

Autumn. Archibald MacLeish. IllVoic

Autumn. Itsik [or Itzik or Itzig] Manger. TrJP

Autumn. Gabriela Mistral. SpanPo, tr. by Muriel Kittel

Autumn. Yunna Petrovna [or Iunna Pinkhusovna] Moritz [or Morits]. TCRP, tr. by J. R. Rowl and Odile Taliani

Autumn. Thomas Nashe [or Nash]. NoSic; SCGP Fr. Summer's Last Will and Testament.

Autumn. Ngo Chi Lan. EaWin, tr. by Nguyen Ngoh Bich and W. S. Merwin

Autumn. Boris Leonidovich Pasternak. TCRP, tr. by Henry Kamen

Autumn. Robert Peterson. GeoHom

Autumn. Alexander L. Posey. APN-2

Autumn. Alexander Sergeyevich Pushkin. AWP, tr. by Max Eastman

Autumn. Rainer Maria Rilke. TrJP, tr. by C. F. MacIntyre

Autumn. Christina Georgina Rossetti. BrRo; VWP

Autumn. Vernon Scannell. OxBTC

Autumn. Thomas William Shapcott. CBAP

Autumn. Stevie Smith. See He Told His Life Story to Mrs. Courtly

Autumn. Su Tung-p'o (Su Shih). OHPC, tr. by Kenneth Rexroth

Autumn. Priscilla Jane Thompson. CBWP-2

Autumn. James Thomson. Fr. Seasons, The.

Autumn. Mihály Tompa. IQMS, tr. by Watson Kirkconnell

Autumn. Unknown. NOEC

Autumn. Unknown. OBMV

Autumn. Jean Starr Untermeyer. MoAmPo

Autumn. Vietnamese Oral Tradition. CaDao, tr. by John Balaban

Autumn. Andrey [or Andrei] Andreievich Voznesensky [or Voznesenskii]. TCRP

Autumn. Wang Wei. OHMPC, tr. by Kenneth Rexroth

Autumn. Charles Wright. GeoHom

Autumn: A Dirge. Shelley. TreFP

Autumn (A Fragment). Alexander Sergeyevich Pushkin. WoPoe, tr. by Edwin Morgan

Autumn Again. Sándor Petőfi. IQMS, tr. by Lydia Pasternak-Slater

Autumn, and we're still like the will-o'-the wisp. To Li Po. 'Aisha bint Ahmad al-Qurtubiyya. SuSp, tr. by Eugene Eoyang

Autumn approaches. Basho. SoOfWa, tr. by Sam Hamill

Autumn Aspens: Cumbres Pass. Reg Saner. PoCoUp

Autumn Begins in Martins Ferry, Ohio. James Wright (1927–80). ColAP; HCAP; HeIP-4; InPK-6; MoASP; NAAL-5; NoAM; VCAP; WeW-3

Autumn blast—wild boar. Urn. Shinkichi Takahashi. ZenPo, tr. by Takashi Ikemoto and Lucien Stryk

Autumn breeze. Kanna. JDP, tr. by Yoel Hoffmann

Autumn breezes. Buson. SoOfWa, tr. by Sam Hamill

Autumn burgeons, sounds rise everywhere. Autumn Night—Sleepless. Wu Wei-yeh. CoBLCP, tr. by Jonathan Chaves

Autumn Call. Hans Leifhelm. AuPH, tr. by Lowell A. Bangerter

Autumn Chapter in a Novel. Thom Gunn. FaBoMo; OxBTC

Autumn chrysanthemums have beautiful color. T'ao Ch'ien [or T'ao Yuan-ming]. SuSp Fr. Drinking Wine.

Autumn cicada, The. Naito Joso. OHMPJ

Autumn, cloud blades on the horizon. Clear after Rain. Tu Fu. BLT; OHPC, tr. by Kenneth Rexroth

Autumn colors / on the leaves. Autumn Plants, Flowers, Bamboo, Rocks. Yün Shou-p'ing. CoBLCP, tr. by Jonathan Chaves

Autumn colors trickle through the gauze curtains. Woman's Room in Autumn, A. Yüan Hung-tao. CoBLCP, tr. by Jonathan Chaves

Autumn come / Cicada husk. Masaoka Shiki. ZenPo, tr. by Takashi Ikemoto and Lucien Stryk

Autumn constellations, The. Moon Festival. Tu Fu. OHPC, tr. by Kenneth Rexroth

Autumn Cove. Li Po. CoBCP; ColAnChi; TTTS, tr. by Burton Watson

Autumn, Crystal Eye. Margot Ruddock. OBMV

Autumn Day. Rainer Maria Rilke. WoPoe, tr. by John Felsteiner

Autumn Day. Rainer Maria Rilke. TrJP

Autumn Day. Rainer Maria Rilke. AuPH, tr. by Lowell A. Bangerter

Autumn Day, An. Clara Ann Thompson. CBWP-2

Autumn Day, An—Leisurely Boating on West Lake. Lin Pu. SuSp, tr. by Jonathan Chaves

Autumn day its course has run—The Autumn evening falls, The. Charlotte Brontë. NOBVV

Autumn Dusk at a Mountain Lodge. Wang Wei. ChinPo, tr. by Yip Wai-lim

Autumn eats its leaf out of my hand: we are friends. Corona. Paul Celan. PoSu, tr. by Michael Hamburger

Autumn ends. Kosai. JDP, tr. by Yoel Hoffmann

Autumn ends. Shogetsu. JDP, *tr.* by Yoel Hoffmann
Autumn / Even the birds. Basho. ZenPo, *tr.* by Takashi Ikemoto and Lucien Stryk
Autumn Evening. George Anthony. SPE
Autumn evening. (LL) Basho. EH; NIL-7, *tr.* by Robert Hass
Autumn evening. Basho. OHPJ
Autumn evening. Buson. EH, *tr.* by Yoel Hoffmann
Autumn evening. Rosamond Haas. HA
Autumn evening. Issa. EH, *tr.* by Robert Hass
Autumn Evening. Robinson Jeffers. ChAP
Autumn Evening. Adalbert Stifter. AuPH, *tr.* by Lowell A. Bangerter
Autumn Evening beside the Lake. Li Ch'ing-chao. OHPC, *tr.* by Kenneth Rexroth
Autumn evening / Knees in arms. Issa. ZenPo, *tr.* by Takashi Ikemoto and Lucien Stryk
Autumn feels slowed down, The. Paula Becker to Clara Westhoff. Adrienne Rich. NAAL-2v2; VCAP
Autumn finds me old and poorer. Meng Chiao. SuSp *Fr.* Autumn Meditations.
Autumn Fires. Robert Louis Stevenson. NOxBChV
Autumn flowers. War Lament. *Unknown.* CrYelRi, *tr.* by Sam Hamill
Autumn Flowers. Jones Very. APN-1
Autumn flowers, The. Kin'ei. JDP, *tr.* by Yoel Hoffmann
Autumn frost, The. (LL) Basho. ChAP; EH, *tr.* by Robert Hass
Autumn Fullness. Ernst Goll. AuPH, *tr.* by Lowell A. Bangerter
Autumn Garden. Dino Campana. STV, *tr.* by John Frederick Nims
Autumn gust. Ensetsu. JDP, *tr.* by Yoel Hoffmann
Autumn has come invisibly. Toshiyuki. OHPJ
Autumn has come / To the lonely cottage. Eikei. OHPJ
Autumn has turned the dark trees toward the hill. Quail in Autumn. William Jay Smith. OWoS
Autumn hath all the summer's fruitful treasure. Thomas Nashe [*or* Nash]. NoSic; SCGP *Fr.* Summer's Last Will and Testament.
Autumn hues, The. Isan. JDP, *tr.* by Yoel Hoffmann
Autumn in New York. Vernon Duke. ReLy
Autumn in Sigulda. Andrey [*or* Andrei] Andreievich Voznesensky [*or* Voznesenskii]. TCRP, *tr.* by W. H. Auden
Autumn is finished—yesterday a flash. First Morning. George Keithley. PoCoUp
Autumn is here and darkness comes earlier now; the rain is falling. Death of Sagittarius. Milán Füst. IQMS, *tr.* by Jess Perlman
Autumn is unquiet everywhere. Green Side, The. Jennifer Maiden. BMAP
Autumn is weary, halt, and old. October Redbreast, The. Alice Thompson Meynell. MoBrPo
Autumn Journal. Louis MacNeice.
  "And I remember Spain." OBWP; OxAEP-2
  "Close and slow, summer is ending in Hampshire." NPeEn
  "Conferences, adjournments, ultimatums." OxBTC
  "Nightmare leaves fatigue." BIrV; CIP-2; ModIr; PNI
  "Now we are back to normal, now the mind is." OxAEP-2
  "September has come and I wake." NoP-4
  "Shelley and jazz and lieder and love and hymn-tunes." NOBL; NPeEn
  Which things being so, as we said when we studied
  "I ought to be glad." OBCoV
Autumn Leaves. Marilyn Chin. ExTi; PoPoPo
Autumn Leaves. James Cushing. SeSe
Autumn Leaves. Mikhail Naimy. GraLe, *tr.* by Sharif Elmusa and Gregory Orfalea
Autumn Leaves. Clara Ann Thompson. CBWP-2
Autumn Leaves. Jones Very. APN-1
Autumn Leaves. Charles Henry Webb. OBAL
Autumn Leaves Are Virgin Mary. Unsi Al-Haj [*or* Hajj]. MAP, *tr.* by Patricia Alanah Bryne and Salma Khadra Jayyusi
Autumn leaves that strew the brooks, The. Remembrance Sunday. Dennis Joseph Enright. NPeEn
Autumn light. Tadashi Kondo. HA
Autumn made colors burn, The. Venus Khoury-Gata. BoWoP
Autumn Meditations. Meng Chiao.
  "Autumn finds me old and poorer." SuSp
  "Bones of the lonely-wretched spend no quiet nights." SuSp
  "In autumn moonlight the face turns icy." SuSp
  "Old and sick, many strange broodings." SuSp
Autumn met me today as I walked over Castle Hill. Stand-To, The. Cecil Day Lewis. NoP-4; OBWP
Autumn moon. Issa. EH, *tr.* by Robert Hass
Autumn moon / Tide foams. Basho. ZenPo, *tr.* by Takashi Ikemoto and Lucien Stryk

Autumn moonlight. Basho. EH, *tr.* by Robert Hass
Autumn Morning at Cambridge. Frances Darwin Cornford. PoRA
Autumn Morning in Shokoku-ji, An. Gary Snyder. HAP; VGW; WeW-3 *Fr.* Four Poems for Robin.
Autumn Mushrooms. Kenneth Mackenzie. CBAP
Autumn nears. The branches yellow. Aleksey [*or* Aleksei] Eisner. TCRP
Autumn nibbles its leaf right from my hand: We're friends. Corona. Paul Celan. PoetW, *tr.* by John Felstiner
Autumn Night. Tu Fu. EaWin, *tr.* by W. S. Merwin
Autumn Night: A Letter Sent to Ch'iu. Wei Ying-wu. ChinPo, *tr.* by Yip Wai-lim
Autumn night, in a hotel, the two, An. Georgy [*or* Georgii Viktorovich] Adamovich. TCRP
Autumn Night—Sleepless. Wu Wei-yeh. CoBLCP, *tr.* by Jonathan Chaves
Autumn nights, it seems. Ono no Komachi. WoPoe, *tr.* by Helen Craig McCullough
Autumn 1942. Roy Fuller. PoWW
Autumn, 1939. Alun Lewis. PoWW
Autumn of the Lonely. Georg Trakl. AuPH, *tr.* by Lowell A. Bangerter
Autumn, on Retreat at a Mountain Temple. Lady Izumi. *See* In the Autumn, on Retreat at a Mountain Temple
Autumn on the Riverbank. Chao Shan-ch'ing. CrYelRi, *tr.* by Sam Hamill
Autumn, once again enchanting. Autumn Again. Sándor Petőfi. IQMS, *tr.* by Lydia Pasternak-Slater
Autumn Plants, Flowers, Bamboo, Rocks. Yün Shou-p'ing. CoBLCP, *tr.* by Jonathan Chaves
Autumn Ploughing. John Masefield. OxBEV
Autumn Prelude. Andrey [*or* Andrei] Andreievich Voznesensky [*or* Voznesenskii]. RusPo, *tr.* by Robert Arthur Douglas Ford
Autumn rain. Chuck Brickley. HA
Autumn Rain, The. Christopher Pearse Cranch. TCAPo
Autumn rains blow. Autumn. *Vietnamese Oral Tradition.* CaDao, *tr.* by John Balaban
Autumn Refrain. Wallace Stevens. APT-1
Autumn resumes the land, ruffles the woods. Geoffrey Hill. NAEL-5v2; NAEL-6v2; NPeEn; NoAM; PoE *Fr.* Apology for the Revival of Christian Architecture in England, An.
Autumn River. T'ang Hsien-tsu. CoBLCP, *tr.* by Jonathan Chaves
Autumn Rose. Amal Moussa. PoArWo, *tr.* by Khaled Mattawa
Autumn's done; they have the golden corn in, The. Trumbull Stickney. APN-2
Autumn's end: frost and dew become heavy. Morning Walk in Autumn to South Valley Passing an Abandoned Village. Liu Tsung-yüan. ChinPo, *tr.* by Yip Wai-lim
Autumn's onset means cooling breezes. Juan Chi. SuSp *Fr.* Poems Expressing My Feelings.
Autumn Sentiments. Yüan Hao-wen. SuSp, *tr.* by Irving Y. Lo
Autumn Sequel. Louis MacNeice.
  Canto XX: "To Wales once more, though not on holiday now." ModIr
  Fanfare for the Makers, A. NOBE
Autumn Sequence. Jan Freeman.
  Fifteen. OxWW
Autumn Sequence. Adrienne Rich. VGW
Autumn 1710. *Unknown.* IQMS, *tr.* by Watson Kirkconnell
Autumn Shade. Edgar Bowers.
  "Awakened by some fear, I watch the sky." VCAP
  "I drive home with the books that I will read." VCAP
  "In nameless warmth, sun light in every corner." VCAP
  "Snow and then rain. The roads are wet. A car." VCAP
Autumn slipped into Paris yesterday. Endre Ady. IQMS, *tr.* by Anton N. Nyerges
Autumn Song. József Bajza. IQMS, *tr.* by Watson Kirkconnell
Autumn Song. Charles Baudelaire. SxFrPo, *tr.* by James McGowan
Autumn Song. Johann Ludwig Tieck. AWP, *tr.* by James Clarence Mangan
Autumn Song. Paul Verlaine. NAWM-7v2, *tr.* by Carlyle Ferren MacIntyre
Autumn Song. Paul Verlaine. WoPoe, *tr.* by Louis Simpson
Autumn Song. Paul Verlaine. SxFrPo, *tr.* by Martin Sorrell
Autumn Sonnets, The. May Sarton.
  "If I can let you go as trees let go." PoBW
  ("Love will endure—if I can let you go.") (LL) PoSu
Autumn Spring. Hsüeh T'ao. SuSp, *tr.* by Eric W. Johnson
Autumn Sun over the *T'ung* Tree. Wang An-shih. SuSp, *tr.* by Jan W. Walls
Autumn Sunset, An. Edith Wharton. APN-2
Autumn Supper. Dimitris Tsaloumas. BMAP
Autumn Testament. James Keir Baxter.
  "Rata blooms explode, the bow-legged tomcat, The." PeNZ
  "Spider crouching on the ledge above the sink, The." PeNZ
  "To wish to climb a ladder to the loft." PeNZ

Autumn: the ninth year of Yüan Ho. Temple, The. Po Chü-i. ChiP; OBMV, *tr. by* Arthur Waley

Autumn this soon! Farewell. Arthur Rimbaud. SxFrPo, *tr. by* Martin Sorrell

Autumn Thoughts. Han Yü. CoBCP, *tr. by* Burton Watson

"Leaves fall turning turning to the ground." CoBCP; WoPoe, *tr. by* Burton Watson

"This morning I can't seem to get out of bed." CoBCP

"When white dew descends on the hundred grasses." CoBCP

Autumn Thoughts. Ma Chih-yüan. CoBLCP, *tr. by* Jonathan Chaves *Fr.* To the Tune "T'ien ching sha."

Autumn Thoughts. Ts'en Shen. SuSp, *tr. by* C. H. Wang

Autumn Thoughts. Tu Fu.

"I have heard the affairs in Ch'ang-an are like a game of chess." SuSp

"Jade dews deeply wilt and wound the maple woods." SuSp

"Waters of K'un-ming Pool recalled the achievements of Han times, The." SuSp

Autumn Thoughts. Mary E. Tucker. CBWP-1

Autumn-time has come, The. My Triumph. John Greenleaf Whittier. APN-1; NOBA

Autumn twilight. Cor Van den Heuvel. HA

Autumn twilight. Nicholas Virgilio. HA

Autumn Twilight in the Mountains. Wang Wei. OHMPC, *tr. by* Kenneth Rexroth

Autumn Verses. "Rubén Dario." BLPSL, *tr. by* Rene de Costa, Rigas Kappatos and Eleni Paidoussi

Autumn Verses. "Rubén Dario." SpanPo, *tr. by* Kate Flores

Autumn Violets. Christina Georgina Rossetti. ViWPN

Autumn Vista. Li Meng-yang. CoBLCP, *tr. by* Jonathan Chaves

Autumn Warrior. Barney Bush. HATNAP

Autumn waters. Enryo. JDP, *tr. by* Yoel Hoffmann

Autumn wheat turns green and lush as spring wheat yellows. Fan Ch'eng-ta. SuSp, *tr. by* Wu-Chi Liu *Fr.* Four Songs in Imitation of Wang Chien.

Autumn Wind. Ruth Dallas. PeNZ *Fr.* Letter to a Chinese Poet.

Autumn Wind. Adriann Roland Holst. TuT, *tr. by* Desmond Egan

Autumn Wind. Emperor Wu of Han [*or* Wu Ti *or* Ou-ty *or* Liu Ch'e *or* Liu Ch'u]. OHMPC, *tr. by* Kenneth Rexroth

Autumn wind, The. Nicholas Virgilio. HA

Autumn Wind, The. Emperor Wu of Han [*or* Wu Ti *or* Ou-ty *or* Liu Ch'e *or* Liu Ch'u]. ChiP; FaBoCh, *tr. by* Arthur Waley

Autumn Wind, The. Emperor Wu of Han [*or* Wu Ti *or* Ou-ty *or* Liu Ch'e *or* Liu Ch'u]. SuSp, *tr. by* Ronald C. Miao

Autumn wind / Across the fields. Onitsura. ZenPo, *tr. by* Takashi Ikemoto and Lucien Stryk

Autumn wind / Blasting the stones. Basho. ZenPo, *tr. by* Takashi Ikemoto and Lucien Stryk

Autumn wind blows across the sea in the deepening twilight, An. Inscribed on Byron's Poetic Works. Su Man-shu. SuSp, *tr. by* Wu-Chi Liu

Autumn wind blows white clouds, The. Autumn Wind. Emperor Wu of Han [*or* Wu Ti *or* Ou-ty *or* Liu Ch'e *or* Liu Ch'u]. OHMPC, *tr. by* Kenneth Rexroth

Autumn wind / Gods, Buddha. Masaoka Shiki. ZenPo, *tr. by* Takashi Ikemoto and Lucien Stryk

Autumn wind / Mountain's shadow. Issa. ZenPo, *tr. by* Takashi Ikemoto and Lucien Stryk

Autumn wind rises. Song of the Autumn Wind. Emperor Wu of Han [*or* Wu Ti *or* Ou-ty *or* Liu Ch'e *or* Liu Ch'u]. CoBCP, *tr. by* Burton Watson

Autumn wind rises; white clouds fly. Autumn Wind, The. Emperor Wu of Han [*or* Wu Ti *or* Ou-ty *or* Liu Ch'e *or* Liu Ch'u]. ChiP; FaBoCh, *tr. by* Arthur Waley

Autumn wind soughs and sighs, the setting sun is red. Tune: "Song of River Goddess"—Moorinig My Boat at Fen-shui at Night. Huang Shu. SuSp, *tr. by* James J. Y. Liu

Autumn wind: ten thousand trees wither. Stone on the Hilltop, The. Lu Yu. CoBCP; ColAnChi, *tr. by* Burton Watson

Autumn wind / The beggar looks. Issa. ZenPo, *tr. by* Takashi Ikemoto and Lucien Stryk

Autumn winds. Soryu. JDP, *tr. by* Yoel Hoffmann

Autumn winds blow along the river. Grain-Barge Wife, The. Wu Chia-chi. CoBLCP; ColAnChi, *tr. by* Jonathan Chaves

Autumn winds blow in from Chieh-shih Mountain. Sadness in the Autumn Chambers. Yün Shou-p'ing. CoBLCP, *tr. by* Jonathan Chaves

Autumn winds descend and sweep. Autumn 1710. *Unknown.* IQMS, *tr. by* Watson Kirkconnell

Autumn winds rise. Autumn Wind, The. Emperor Wu of Han [*or* Wu Ti *or* Ou-ty *or* Liu Ch'e *or* Liu Ch'u]. SuSp, *tr. by* Ronald C. Miao

Autumn winds, swish-swish, sorrow killing men. Old Song. *Unknown.* ChinPo, *tr. by* Yip Wai-lim

Autumn winds whistle sadly, the air grows chill. Song of Yen. Ts'ao P'i. SuSp, *tr. by* Ronald C. Miao

Autumn Woods. William Cullen Bryant. APN-1

Autumnal. Joseph Awad. GraLe

Autumnal. "Rubén Dario." SpanPo, *tr. by* Anita Volland

Autumnal. Ernest Christopher Dowson. EBVV

Autumnal. Mark Irwin. PuP-23

Autumnal full moon. Basho. SoOfWa, *tr. by* Sam Hamill

Autumnal Sketch, An. August Kleinzahler. PmAP

Autumnal skies. Vespers. Emile Ologoudou. PBMAP

Autumnal[l], The. John Donne. BASC; FSCP; NOSC *Fr.* Elegies.

Avalanche. Quincy Troupe. PFTM-2; SpirFl

Avalon. Thomas Holley Chivers. APN-1

Avant-garde snippet banal regarded both elements. 34th Merzgedicht in Memoriam Kurt Schwitters. Jackson Mac Low. PFTM-2

Avarice. Anthony Hecht. OxBSP

Avatars. V. Indira Bhavani. OMIP, *tr. by* Martha Ann Selby

Ave atque Vale. Algernon Charles Swinburne. NAEL-5v2; NAEL-6v2; NOBE; OBEV

Ave atque Vale. Rosamund Marriott Watson. NOBE; OBEV

Ave Caesar. Robinson Jeffers. NOBA; NoAM; OxBA; OxBSP

Ave Imperatrix! Oscar Wilde. PeVV

Ave Maria. Hart Crane. NOBA; NoAM *Fr.* Bridge, The.

Ave Maria. Frank O'Hara. CLPP; HCAP; HarvBoo; MakPoe; NAAL-2v2; NNaP; NoP-4; PmAP; PoM; PoPoPo; VCAP

Ave Maria, Gratia Plena. Oscar Wilde. ChIV-2

Ave Maris Stella. *Unknown.* CTC

Ave, Virgo! Gr-r-r—you swine! (LL) Soliloquy of the Spanish Cloister. Robert Browning. FHYEP; FaBoVe; InPK-6; NAEL-5v2; NAEL-6v2; NIL-7; NIP-4; NOBL; NOBVV; NoP-4; OxBEV; PAI; PeVV; TOF; UV

'Ave you 'eard o' the Widow at Windsor. Widow at Windsor, The. Rudyard Kipling. NAEL-5v2; NAEL-6v2; NoAM

Avenge O Lord thy slaughtered [*or* slaughter'd] Saints, whose bones. On the Late Massacre [*or* Massacher] in Piedmont [*or* Piemont]. John Milton. AWP; CABP; GSo; GTBS-P; HAP; HeIP-4; NAEL-5v1; NAEL-6v1; NIL-7; NOBE; NOCV; NPeEn; NoP-4; OBWP; OxBEV; OxBSo; PoPoPo; SCGP; Son; TFi; TRP; UnPo; WeW-3

Avengers, The. Edwin Markham. MoAmPo

Avenue. Robert Pinsky. TaR

Avenue, The. Frances Darwin Cornford. LW

Avenue, The. Paul Muldoon. PBCIP

Avenue Bearing the Initial of Christ into the New World, The. Galway Kinnell. "Fishmarket closed, the fishes gone into flesh, The." CoAmPo

Avenue of tombs! I stand before, An. In Père La Chaise. Joaquin Miller. APN-2

Avenue was green and long, and green, The. Visit to Castletown House, A. Michael Hartnett. BiHa; PBCIP

Average joe comes in, An. Short-Order Cook. Jim Daniels. ReTh

Aviary. Mark DeFoe. UrbNat

Avid of life and love, insatiate vagabond. Verlaine. Richard Hovey. APN-2

Avignon. Remco Campert. PoetW, *tr. by* Jeffery Paine

Avila. John Yau. BodElec

Avocado. Gary Snyder. PmAP

Avocado Pit, The. Carl Rakosi. APT-2

Avoid extremes; and shun the fault of such. Pope. FHYEP *Fr.* Essay on Criticism, An.

Avoid the reeking herd. Eagle and the Mole, The. Elinor Wylie. AWP; BoWoP; MoAmPo; NALW; UnPo

Avoiding fishnet. Buson. WoPoe, *tr. by* Tony Barnstone

Avoiding News by the River. W. S. Merwin. GifTon

Aw wish my lover she was a cherry. Pitman's Lovesong, A. *Unknown.* FaBoVe

Await us, weighing the unstripped bough. (LL) Farewell to Van Gogh. Charles Tomlinson. GTBS-P; NoP-4; PoE

Awaji Island. Kanemasa. OHMPJ

Awake. Mary Elizabeth Coleridge. ViWPN

Awake! Walther [*or* Walter] von der Vogelweide. AWP, *tr. by* Jethro Bithell

Awake, Aeolian lyre, awake. Progress of Poesy, The. Thomas Gray. AWP; GTBS-P; NOEC; OBEV

Awake all night till the. *Unknown.* PGA

Awake, alone, aware. Insomniac Poem. Ron Loewinsohn. NeAP

Awake, and with attention hear. 34. Chapter of the Prophet Isaiah, The. Abraham Cowley. ChIV-1

Awake, arise, / Pull out your eyes. Mother Goose. OxNR

Awake, arise, the hour is come. Radical War Song, A. Thomas Babington Macaulay, 1st Baron Macaulay. OBSV

Awake at night. Basho. EH, *tr. by* Robert Hass

Awake, awake, my Lyre! Abraham Cowley. GTBS-P *Fr.* Davideis.

Awake, Awake! [Thou Heavy Sprite]. Thomas Campion. ChIV-1

Awake! for morning in the bowl of night. Omar Khayyám. NOBVV; NPeEn;

OxAEP-2; OxBEV; PeVV; TAL; UV, *tr. by* Edward Fitzgerald   *Fr.* Rubáiyát of Omar Khayyám [of Naishápúr], The.

Awake! for Morning on the Pitch of Night.   Strugnell's Rubáiyát.   Wendy Cope.   UV

Awake, glad heart! get up, and sing.   Christ's Nativity.   Henry Vaughan.   ESCV

Awake I steal what they dream.   Sleepers.   Branko Miljkovic.   WoPoe, *tr. by* Charles Simic

Awake, My Fair.   Judah Halevi.   TrJP, *tr. by* Alice Lucas

Awake my Fanny! leave all meaner things.   John Wilkes.   EroLit   *Fr.* Essay on Woman.

Awake, my heart's delight, awake.   Fair Melody: To Be Sung by Good Christians, A.   Hans Sachs.   GePo, *tr. by* Catherine Winkworth

Awake, My Heart, to Be Loved.   Robert Bridges.   GTBS-P; MoBrPo; NOBE; OBEV

Awake, my love, who sleep in the dawn!   Lady's Farewell, The.   Nuño Fernández Torneol.   WoPoe, *tr. by* Robert Bridges

Awake, my soul, and with the sun.   Morning Hymn.   Thomas Ken.   NOSC; SacPr

Awake My Soul, Betimes Awake.   Isaac Chanler.   AH

Awake, My Soul! In Grateful Songs.   Andrew Fowler.   AH

Awake, my soul! lift up thine eyes.   Call, The.   Anna Laetitia Barbauld.   SacPr

Awake, my St. John! leave all meaner things.   Pope.   NAEL-5v1; NAEL-6v1; NAWM-7v2   *Fr.* Essay on Man, An.

Awake, O Lord, Awake Thy Saints.   Morgan Llwyd.   AngWePo

Awake, O Magyar nation, and open wide your eyes.   Verses of a True Hungarian Patriot, The.   *Unknown.*   IQMS, *tr. by* René Bonnerjea and Earl M. Herrick

Awake, [*or* Awake!] ye forms of verse divine!   Fitz-Greene Halleck.   APN-1   *Fr.* Croaker Papers, The.

Awake or sleeping (for I know not which).   Old-World Thicket, An.   Christina Georgina Rossetti.   VWP

Awake sad heart, whom sorrow ever drowns.   Dawning, The.   George Herbert.   ESCV; NOSC

Awake sound sleeper! hark, what dismal knells.   Upon the Death of His Much Esteemed Friend Mr. Jno Saffin Junr.   Grindall Rawson.   SCAP

Awake!   The day is coming now.   Awake!   Walther [*or* Walter] von der Vogelweide.   AWP, *tr. by* Jethro Bithell

Awake, thou best of sense.   Upon the Times.   Mildmay Fane, 2d Earl of Westmorland.   BeJo

Awake thy cloud-harp, angel of the rain!   Angel of the Rain.   Harriet McEwen Kimball.   TreFP

Awake, vain Man; 'tis time th'Abuse to see.   Advice to His Grace.   "Ephelia."   EMWP

Awake, ye forms of verse divine!   National Painting, The.   Joseph Rodman Drake.   GS

Awake yee westerne nymphs, arise and sing.   Samuel Danforth.   SCAP

Awaken Hungarian youth! See how your national language.   To Hungarian Youth.   Dávid Baróti Szabó.   IQMS, *tr. by* Matthew Mead

Awaken / Oh, boughs of passion.   Awakening.   Fawziyya Al-Sindi.   PoArWo, *tr. by* Joseph T. Zeidan

Awaken soldiers and be prepared, be mindful of your first oath.   Soldier's Song.   Helene Kafka.   AuPH, *tr. by* Lowell A. Bangerter

Awaken them; they are knobs of sound.   Sanskrit.   Jayanta Mahapatra.   VCWP

Awakened at midnight.   Basho.   SoOfWa, *tr. by* Sam Hamill

Awakened by love, your body's animals want to get out.   René Daumal.   PFTM-1   *Fr.* Clavicles for a Great Poetic Game.

Awakened by some fear, I watch the sky.   Edgar Bowers.   VCAP   *Fr.* Autumn Shade.

Awakened by the radiant beams of morn.   Anxiety.   Mary Julia Young.   CenSon

Awakened in a Field.   Juan Delgado.   GeoHom

Awakened to this other bleakness.   Falcon Drinking.   Dimitris Tsaloumas.   BMAP

Awakening.   Fawziyya Al-Sindi.   PoArWo, *tr. by* Joseph T. Zeidan

Awakening.   Robert Bly.   CoAmPo

Awakening.   John Haines.   SPE

Awakening.   Henrietta Cordelia Ray.   CBWP-3

Awakening.   Lucien Stryk.   BodElec

Awakening.   Anita Virgil.   HA

Awakening, The.   Robert Creeley.   NeAP

Awakening, The.   Alejandra Piznarnick.   TCLAP, *tr. by* Frank Graziano and María Rosa Fort

Awakening from Drunkenness on a Spring Day.   Li Po.   TAL

Awakening like return to Earth from Moon.   Brian Coffey.   CIP-2   *Fr.* Advent.

Awakening spring: how many leaves!   Willow.   Li Shang-yin.   SuSp, *tr. by* Eugene Eoyang

Awakening transports of an inner view of things. (LL)   Roots and Branches.   Robert Duncan.   FTOS; VGW

Awaking from a dream, you look for.   Shadow, The.   Luis Cernuda.   CAGL, *tr. by* Rick Lipinski

Awaking of the Poetic Faculty, The.   George Henry Boker.   Son

Awaking on grass, sheep, goat.   Sheep.   Shinkichi Takahashi.   ZenPo, *tr. by* Takashi Ikemoto and Lucien Stryk

Award.   Ray Durem.   BPo; TTY

Aware.   D. H. Lawrence.   MoBrPo; NoAM

Aware at first only of the dust of sound.   Wild Geese Flying.   Barbara Howes.   OWoS

Aware Aware.   Tram Combs.   TwCP

Aware to the dry throat of the wide hell in the world.   King David Dances.   John Berryman.   ChIV-1; OxBC; OxBSP

Away. (LL)   Move.   Lucille Clifton.   MakPoe; NAAAL

Away.   Max Ehrmann.   PoToHe

Away!   Robert Frost.   NOBA

Away above a harborful.   Lawrence Ferlinghetti.   BoLoP; PoM   *Fr.* Pictures of a Gone World.

Away and away I sail in my light boat.   Boating in Autumn.   Lu Yu.   ChiP, *tr. by* Arthur Waley

Away, away. (LL)   This Is the Key.   *Unknown.*   FaBoCh; OxBoLi

Away, away in the Northland.   Legend of the Northland, A.   Phoebe Cary.   OBCA; OBSP

Away! away! / Tempt me no more, insidious Love.   Complaint, The.   Mark Akenside.   OBEV

Away, away! You are safer in the tomb. (LL)   To a Shade.   W. B. Yeats.   NAEL-5v2; NAEL-6v2

Away, birds, away!   Bird Scarer, The.   *Unknown.*   ReMoGo

Away, Delights.   Francis Beaumont.   NOBE; OBEV   *Fr.* Captain, The.

Away despair; my gracious Lord doth hear[e].   Bag, The.   George Herbert.   ESCV; GeHe

Away down deep and away up high.   At the Playground.   William Stafford.   TLR

Away down East, away down West.   *Unknown.*   TLR

Away down into the shadowy depths of the Real I once lived.   Myself.   Adah Isaacs Menken.   CBWP-1; ViWPN

Away, fear, with thy projects, no false fire.   Of His Conversion.   William Alabaster.   NoSic

Away, for we are ready to a man!   James Elroy Flecker.   NOBE   *Fr.* Golden Journey to Samarkand, The.

Away from earth and its cares set free.   Eternity.   Josephine D. Henderson Heard.   CBWP-4

Away from eyes.   Rod Willmot.   HA

Away from Home.   *Unknown.*   PWR

Away from the city that hurts and mocks.   I Cover the Waterfront.   Edward Heyman.   ReLy

Away from you.   Roger McGough.   OBCoV   *Fr.* Summer with Monika.

Away from you three or four years.   Back from Green Dragon.   Mei Yao Ch'en.   CoBCP, *tr. by* Burton Watson

Away in a Manger.   Martin Luther.   AH

Away in this chambered secret, I'll draw sound.   In the Bathtub, to Mnemosyne.   John Wheelwright.   APT-2

Away; let nought to Love displeasing.   Winifreda.   *Unknown.*   OBEV

Away loose-reined careers of poetry!   Urian Oakes.   NOCV   *Fr.* Elegie upon the Death of the Reverend. . .Mr. Thomas Shepard, An.

Away, Melancholy.   Stevie Smith.   CABP; OxBTC

Away mine ashes, then thy fire doth glow. (LL)   Ebb and Flow, The.   Edward Taylor.   InvLi; SCAP

Away the horde rode, in a storm of hail.   Uncertain Battle, The.   David Gascoyne.   PoWW

Away! the moor is dark beneath the moon.   Stanzas—April, 1814.   Shelley.   SCGP

Away thou fondling motley humourist.   John Donne.   NoSic   *Fr.* Satires.

Away to Canada.   Joshua McCarter Simpson.
   "Grieve not, my wife—grieve not for me."   TCAPo

Away Vane World.   Alexander Montgomerie.   NOCV

Away with all whimsical bubbles of air.   Botany Bay.   John Freeth.   NOEC

Away with silks, away with lawn.   Clothes Do but Cheat and Cozen [*or* Cousen] Us.   Robert Herrick.   CaPo; ErotSp

Away with the curly, golden hair.   To a Lady.   Francisco de Terrazas.   BLPSL, *tr. by* Rene de Costa, Rigas Kappatos and Eleni Paidoussi

Away with you, away with you, James de Grant!   James Grant.   *Unknown.*   ESPB

Away, ye gay landscapes, ye gardens of roses!   Lachin y Gair.   Byron.   NePenScot; OxBS

Aweary Am I.   Abu 'l-Ala al-Ma'Arri.   AWP, *tr. by* R. A. Nicholson

Awed I Behold Once More.   Ralph Waldo Emerson.   APN-1; ColAP

Awesome are the works of God. Works of God, The. Moses Ibn Ezra. TrJP, *tr. by* Solomon Solis-Cohen

Awful. September 22nd. Vera Gherarducci. CItWP, *tr. by* Cinzia Sartini Blum and Lara Trubowitz

Awful but cheerful. (LL) Bight, The. Elizabeth Bishop. APT-2; EmeKit; FaBoWP; HCAP; NAAL-2v2; PoetW; RB; VCAP

Awful shadow of some unseen Power, The. Hymn to Intellectual Beauty. Shelley. FHYEP; HAP; HeIP-4; NAEL-5v2; NAEL-6v2; NOBRP; NoP-4; PoE; TOF

Awhile in the dead of the winter. Seasons and Times. William Barnes. NOBVV

Awhile meet Doubt and Faith. Burden of Easter Vigil, A. Lionel Pigot Johnson. SacPr

Awkward on a hillock of grass. Forever the Snake. Jennifer Rankin. BMAP

Awkward was she yesterday. Maiden, The. Peter Hille. AWP, *tr. by* Jethro Bithell

Awoke in this. Perugia. Art Lange. PmAP

Awoken: two eyes home. Proposal. Maggie Nelson. HeMarv

Axe angles, An. Junk. Richard Wilbur. HAP; WeW-3

Axe-fall, echo and silence. Noonday silence. Noonday Axeman. Les A. Murray. NoP-4

Axe Handles. Gary Snyder. ColAP; LoL; NoAM; PmAP; PoPoPo; VCAP

Axe-Helve, The. Robert Frost. OxBA

Axe rang sharply 'mid those forest shades, An. Western Emigrant, The. Lydia Huntley Sigourney. SWaP

Axe rings in the wood, The. Remembered Morning. Janet Lewis. MakPoe; SoSe-8; WPE

Axes / After whose stroke the wood rings. Words. Sylvia Plath. CoAmPo; HCAP; NAAL-2v2; NALW; PoE; VCAP

Axiom. Walter Conrad Arensberg. APT-1

Axiom of Maria. Larissa Szporluk. NeAmPo

Axion Esti. Odysseus Elytis.
("Praised be the wooden table.") VCWP, *tr. by* Edmund Keeley and Philip Sherrard

Axis around which the many-centered spiral unwinds is only the, The. Big L, The. Vera Hérold. SurWo, *tr. by* Guy Ducornet

Axle Song. Mairtin O Direain. BiHa

Axle Song. Mark Van Doren. APT-2

Axolotl, The. David McCord. OBAL

Ay! / Ay! Las calles lloran / Streets Are Crying. Francisco Alarcon. GeoHom

Ay, Ay, Ay of the Kinky-Haired Negress. Julia de Burgos. AmFaPo, *tr. by* Jack Agüeros

Ay, ay, ay, that am kinky-haired and pure black. Ay, Ay, Ay of the Kinky-Haired Negress. Julia de Burgos. AmFaPo, *tr. by* Jack Agüeros

Ay, Bashful Thou! Mor Nighean Uisdein. EMWP

Ay, beshrew you! by my fay. John Skelton. *See* Ay [*or* Aye], besherewe yow [*or* beshrew you!] be [*or* by] my fay

Ay, buzz and buzz away. Dost thou suppose. Eugene Lee-Hamilton. Son *Fr.* Imaginary Sonnets.

Ay, Democracy / Lops, lops; but where's her planted bed? Herman Melville. TCAPo *Fr.* Clarel: A Poem and Pilgrimage in the Holy Land.

Ay, gaze upon her rose-wreath'd hair. Revenge. Letitia [*or* Laetitia] Elizabeth Landon. NOBRP; NPeEn

Ay, his mother was a mad one. Sad Boy, The. Laura Riding Jackson. RB

Ay me, alas, heigh ho, heigh ho! Madrigal. Thomas Weelkes. FaBoCh; NPeEn; OxBoLi

Ay me, alas! the beautiful bright hair. Canzone: His Lament for Selvaggia. Cino da Pistoia. AWP; EaltPo, *tr. by* Dante Gabriel Rossetti

Ay me, how many perils doe unfold [*or* enfold]. Edmund Spenser. FHYEP *Fr.* Faerie Queene, The.

Ay, Oliver! I was but seven, and he was eleven. Echo and the Ferry. Jean Ingelow. EBVV

Ay [*or* Aye], besherewe yow [*or* beshrew you!] be [*or* by] my fay. Mannerly Margery Mylk and Ale. John Skelton. NAEL-5v1

Ay, screen thy favourite dove, fair child. Child Screening a Dove from a Hawk, A. Letitia [*or* Laetitia] Elizabeth Landon. NOBRP

Ay, so, God be wi' ye! Now I am alone. William Shakespeare. OxAEP-1 *Fr.* Hamlet.

Ay, tear her tattered ensign down! Old Ironsides. Oliver Wendell Holmes. APN-1; AiP; BRP; NAAL-2v1; NAAL-3; NCAP; PWR; TAP; TCAPo; TFi

Ay, 'Tis Thus. *Unknown.* TrJP, *tr. by* Israel Zangwill

Ay Waukin O. Robert Burns. NOEC

Ay, whaur's the snaws o langsyne? (LL) Ballat o the Leddies o Langsyne. François Villon. OBVE; OxBEV, *tr. by* Tom Scott

Aya! / Ayaya, it is beautiful, beautiful it is out-doors when the summer comes at last. Summer Song. *Unknown.* APN-2, *tr. by* Franz Boas

Aye, at that time our days wer but vew. Childhood. William Barnes. NOBVV

Ay[e], but to die, and go we know not where. William Shakespeare. RB *Fr.* Measure for Measure.

"Aye! I am a poet and upon my tomb." And Thus in Nineveh. Ezra Pound. VGW

"Aye, squire," said Stevens, "they back him at evens." How We Beat the Favourite. Adam Lindsay Gordon. CBAP; PeVV

Aye there it is! It wakes tonight. Emily Jane Brontë. NALW

Aye, thou art welcome, heaven's delicious breath! October. William Cullen Bryant. APN-1

Aye, underneath yon shadowy side. Airey Force. Letitia [*or* Laetitia] Elizabeth Landon. RWP

Aye, well I know 'tis ghastly to descend that valley. On the Same Picture. Walt Whitman. GS

Aye! What a thing is the passing of Cronos, the angular-minded. John Cowper Powys. OBWVE *Fr.* Ridge, The.

Ayee! Ai! This is heavy earth on our shoulders. Burying Ground by the Ties. Archibald MacLeish. GM

Ayíasma. Gunnar Ekelof. WoPoe, *tr. by* Wystan Hugh Auden and Leif Sjöberg

Ayres that Were Sung and Played, at *Brougham Castle* in *Westmerland*, in the Kings Entertainment, The. Thomas Campion.
Dance, The. FaBoCh

Azalea Poem, The. Jack Coulehan. BloBone

Aziola, The. Shelley. EBEV

Azouou. Mririda n'Ait Attik. WPOW, *tr. by* René Euloge, Daniel Halpern and Paula Paley

Azra, The. Heinrich Heine. AWP, *tr. by* John Hay

Azure Because of You. Eduardo Carranza. BLPSL, *tr. by* Rene de Costa, Rigas Kappatos and Eleni Paidoussi

Azure, essence of change and horizons. Azuri. Askia M. Toure. SpirFl

Azure, I come! from the caves of death withdrawn. Helen, the Sad Queen. Paul Valéry. AWP, *tr. by* Joseph T. Shipley

Azure, or green, or purple when the sun. Azure, or Green, or Purple. William Plomer. PeSAV

Azure striation swirls beyond the stones. Marilyn Hacker. Son *Fr.* La Fontaine de Vaucluse.

B

b. Charles Bukowski. BodElec

B. Larry Eigner. NeAP

B: Amazing! I did not think that they could speak this tongue. (LL) Black Boys Play the Classics. Toi Derricotte. ExTi; SpirFl

B. B. Blues. Mary Weems. SpirFl

B C D Goldfish, A. *Unknown.* NTCP

B kw rm. Euenus. GrAn, *tr. by* Alistair Elliot

B Negative. X. J. Kennedy. CoAmPo

B Network, The. Haki R. Madhubuti. IllVoic

B stands for Bear. When bears are seen. Joseph Hilaire Pierre Belloc. NoAM *Fr.* Moral Alphabet, A.

B, taught by Pope to do his good by stealth. Misconception, A. James Russell Lowell. OBAL

Ba Cottage. Andrew Young. OxBSP

Baa, baa, black sheep, have you any wool? Mother Goose. LB; OxBEV; OxNR; ReMoGo

Baal Shem Tov. Abraham Moses Klein. TrJP

Baalbeck. Nadia Tuéni. PoArWo

Baap-Nemesthe Reggae Song. Dorothy Wong Loi Sing. WaCA

Baba Mostafa. Mimi Khalvati. Prnts

Babbitt and the Bromide, The. George Gershwin. OBCoV; ReLy

Babbitt met a Bromide on the avenue one day, A. Babbitt and the Bromide, The. George Gershwin. OBCoV; ReLy

Babbling. Oswald de Andrade. TCLAP, *tr. by* Flavia Vidal

Babe Christabel. Gerald Massey.
"And thou hast stolen a jewel, Death." TreFP

Babe Jesus lay in Mary's lap. Christmas Carol, A. George Macdonald. SacPr

Babe was born in the reign of George, A. Mervyn Laurence Peake. FaBoWar *Fr.* Rhyme of the Flying Bomb, The.

Babe was laid in the Manger, The. Nativity, A. Rudyard Kipling. ChrPo; GI

Babe, we are well met. Thou Swell. Richard Rodgers. ReLy

Babe, with a cry brief and dismal, The. Limerick. Edward Gorey. OBAL; PeLi

Babel. Giuseppe Ungaretti. PFTM-1

Babes in the Wood, The. *Unknown.* OBNV; OxAEP-1

Babes on Broadway. Ralph Freed. ReLy

Babiaantje, The. Frank Templeton Prince. MoBrPo

Babies Haven't Any Hair. Samuel Hoffenstein. NBLV

Babies twist in their mothers' arms. The men.   When a Beautiful Woman Gets on the Jutiapa Bus.   Belle Waring.   EmeKit; PBCAP

Babii Yar.   Yevgeny Aleksandrovich Yevtushenko [*or* Evtushenko].   HP; TCRP; VCWP, *tr.* by George Reavey

Babits.   Lőrinc Szabó.   IQMS, *tr.* by John Gordon Nichols   *Fr.* Cricket Music.

Baboon, The.   Rhydwen Williams.   OBWVE, *tr.* by R. Gerallt Jones

Babur.   Dom Moraes.   OMIP

Baby and I.   *Unknown.*   OxNR

Baby at the Bottom of the River.   W. S. Rendra.   WoPoe, *tr.* by Harry Aveling

Baby, Baby All the Time.   Bobby Troup.   ReLy

Baby, baby, naughty baby.   Mother Goose.   NOBL; OxNR

Baby bird has fallen from its tree and lies feebly peeping dead center of the bright circle under our streetlight, A.   More Trouble with the Obvious.   Michael Van Walleghen.   IllVoic

Baby brother can't wait.   Barbershop Ritual.   Sharan Strange.   ISC; InTrad

Baby carriage abandoned, A.   Empress of Imagined Fertility, The.   Leah Aini.   DTA, *tr.* by Miriyam Glazer

Baby coughed and coughed, clearing its lungs, The.   Christmas at Bristol.   William Scammell.   NLP

Baby Dolly.   *Unknown.*   ReMoGo

Baby Elephant, A.   Nikolai Stepanovich Gumilyov [*or* Gumiliov *or* Gumilev].   TCRusP, *tr.* by Carl R. Proffer

Baby Hilary, Sir Edmund, The.   Kathleen Leland Baker.   NBLV

Baby, / I just want you to.   Shades of Pharoah Sanders Blues for My Baby.   John O'Neal.   NBV

Baby I'm sick. I need.   Night Thoughts: Baby & Demon.   Gwen Harwood.   CBAP

Baby, if you love me.   Down and Out.   Langston Hughes.   PoE

Baby in the House, A.   Patrick Williams.   PNI

Baby is born [*or* borne], us bliss [*or* blis] to bring, A.   Dear Son, Leave Thy Weeping.   *Unknown.*   CTC

Baby Is Born Out of a White Owl's Forehead—1972, A.   Alice Notley.   ExTi

Baby, It's Cold Outside.   Frank Loesser.   ReLy

Baby Poem Industry Poem, The.   W. N. Herbert.   NeBl

Baby Random.   Belle Waring.   PBCAP

Baby's Dance, The.   Mother Goose.   *See* Dance, Little Baby

Baby's Drinking Song.   James Kirkup.   NTCP; OTCP

Baby's feet, like sea-shells pink, A.   Algernon Charles Swinburne.   WeW-3   *Fr.* Étude Réaliste.

Baby's Pantoum.   Anne Waldman.   FFC

Baby's pee, The.   Ruth Yarrow.   HA

Baby-Sermon, A.   George Macdonald.   NOxBChV; Spl
   (Lightning and thunder, The.)   KaS

Baby-Sitting.   Gillian Clarke.   FaBoWP; TCAWP

Baby Song.   Thom Gunn.   AmFaPo; RB   *Fr.* Three Songs.

Baby, the newborn, is the oldest, The.   Name the Oldest Member of Your Family.   Kalamu ya Salaam.   OPRER

Baby Vallejo.   David Rivard.   SeSe

Baby Verse, A.   *Unknown.*   OxNR

Baby Villon.   Philip Levine.   CoAP

Baby watched a ford, whereto, A.   Wagtail and Baby.   Thomas Hardy.   PeLV

Baby, / You shall be free.   Kadia the Young Mother Speaks.   Jessie E. Sampter.   TrJP

Babylon.   Siegfried Sassoon.   ChIV-1

Babylon.   Tennyson.   ChIV-1

Babylon and Sion (Goa and Lisbon).   Luis de Camões [*or* Camões].   AWP, *tr.* by Richard Garnett

Babylon: 539 B.C.E.   Charles Reznikoff.   ChIV-1

Babylon, I did not come to you for the sake of coming.   Matsemela Manaka.   PeSAV   *Fr.* Pula.

Babylon; or, The Bonnie Banks o' Fordie.   *Unknown.*   ESPB; OxBB

Babylon Revisited.   Imamu Amiri Baraka.   BPo; NoAM

Babylon that was beautiful is Nothing now.   Babylon.   Siegfried Sassoon.   ChIV-1

Babysitter's Devotion, The.   Kevin Prufer.   AmPoNex

Bac Ha.   David Huddle.   CDa

Baccalaureate.   David McCord.   NBLV; OBAL

Bacchae.   Euripides.
   Home of Aphrodite, The.   AWP, *tr.* by Gilbert Murray

Bacchanal.   Peter De Vries.   NBLV; NOBL; OBAL

Bacchanal.   Barbara J. Orton.   NeAmPo

Bacchus.   Ralph Waldo Emerson.   APN-1; AWP; NOBA; OBEV; OxBA; TCAPo

Bacchus.   William Empson.   NoAM

Bacchus in Tuscany.   Francesco Redi.
   Bacchus's Opinion of Wine, and Other Beverages.   AWP; OBVE

Bacchus must now his power resign.   Drinking-Song, A.   Henry Carey.   OBEV

Bacchus, receive my offering, not.   Eratosthenes.   GrAn

Bach and the Sentry.   Ivor Gurney.   HarvBoo

Bachelor.   William Meredith.   NoAM

Bachelor, The.   William Barnes.   PeVV

Bachelor Farmer.   Roger McDonald.   CBAP

Bachelor's-Buttons.   William Jay Smith.   DiPo

Bachelor's Song, The.   Thomas Flatman.   *See* On Marriage

Bachelors, The.   Edward Cortez Garrett.   ReBoTo

Back again. Day one. Fingers blue with cold. I joined the lengthening queue.   Slate Street School.   Ciaran Carson.   CABP

Back Again, Home.   Haki R. Madhubuti.   BPo; NAAAL

Back and forth, back and forth.   Fall 1961.   Robert Lowell.   OBWP; VGW

Back and Side Go Bare, Go Bare.   William Stevenson.   HeIP-4; NAEL-5v1; NAEL-6v1, *tr.* by John Still   *Fr.* Gammer Gurton's Needle.

Back away from that, (she said).   Fireworks on the Grass.   Archilochus.   WoPoe, *tr.* by Guy Davenport

Back before we all become "multicultural."   Reading Room.   Allison Joseph.   NAPBL

Back End.   Peter Rafferty.   NLP

Back End of the Horse, The.   Paul Groves.   TCAWP

Back Far Enough, Down Deep Enough.   Constance Urdang.   PBCAP

Back from Green Dragon.   Mei Yao Ch'en.   CoBCP, *tr.* by Burton Watson

Back from the line one night in June.   Corporal Stare.   Robert Graves.   FaBoWar

Back from the palace of a famous king.   Larkin Automatic Car Wash, The.   Gavin Ewart.   NoAM

Back from the sea now, back to their sources shall return deep rivers.   Ovid.   RomPo, *tr.* by Peter Green   *Fr.* Tristia.

Back from the spring in the green draw.   Living in at Least Two Worlds.   C. L. Rawlins.   OPRER

Back from the west, back from the war, Marcellus.   Crinagoras.   GrAn

Back from the Word-Processing Course, I Say to My Old Typewriter.   Michael C. Blumenthal.   NoAM

Back home again on one of those bright mornings.   Los Angeles after the Rain.   Dana Gioia.   UrbNat

Back home the black women are all beautiful.   W. W.   Imamu Amiri Baraka.   HeIP-4; NOBA; PAI

Back in Black Mountain / a child will smack your face.   Black Mountain Blues.   Bessie Smith.   PFTM-1

Back in 55, when I was just a lad.   Good Old Days, The.   Stephen Clayton.   IBA

Back in 1935.   Bud.   William T. Crawley III.   InTrad

Back in 1962 the world was.   North and South.   Linda France.   NeBl

Back in nineteen twenty-seven.   Talking Dust Bowl.   Woody Guthrie.   APT-2

Back in our young days whenever.   Farewell to Fan Yun at An Ch'eng.   Shen Yüeh.   OHMPC, *tr.* by Kenneth Rexroth

Back in *tachanka* days, when Red and Green.   Makhno's Philosophers.   John Streeter Manifold.   CBAP; NOBAu

Back in the caveman days business was fair.   Oxford Hysteria of English Poetry, The.   Adrian Mitchell.   PeLV

Back in the dear old thirties' days.   Poet of Bray, The.   John Heath-Stubbs.   NOBL

Back in the painted pavilion, again in late spring.   Tune: "Butterflies Lingering over Flowers."   Ou-yang Hsiu.   SuSp, *tr.* by Eugene Eoyang

Back in the Return.   Huw Menai.
   "Pieces of coal, hewn from the deeps of earth."   AngWePo
   "Where shall the eyes a darkness find."   OBWVE

Back in the same room that an hour ago.   Private Bottling, A.   Don Paterson.   EmeKit; NePenScot

Back in the World.   Ai.   BAP-97

Back into the Garden.   Sarah Webster Fabio.   BlSi

Back is the question.   Back?   T. Harri Jones.   AngWePo; TCAWP

Back of Chicago the open fields—were you ever there?   Evening Song.   Sherwood Anderson.   GM

Back of the dam, under.   Town of Hill, The.   Donald Hall.   TAP

Back on Times Square, Dreaming of Times Square.   Allen Ginsberg.   CLPP; PoE

Back out of all this now too much for us.   Directive.   Robert Frost.   APT-1; ColAP; HAP; MakPoe; MoAmPo; NAAL-2v2; NOBA; NoAM; NoP-4; PoE; SAmP; TFi

Back path, steeped in musk and mint, A.   Flower-Patterned Snake.   So Chong-Ju.   VCWP, *tr.* by David R. McCann

Back Seat of My Mother's Car, The.   Julia Copus.   MFPA; NeBl

Back Steps Lookout.   Rhyll McMaster.   BMAP

Back Street.   Arthur Rex Dugard Fairburn.   PeNZ   *Fr.* Album Leaves.

Back, the yoke, the yardage, The. Lapped seams.   Shirt.   Robert Pinsky.   ColAP; HarvBoo; NAAL-5

Back Then.   Yusef Komunyakaa.   GT

Back then even the good girls got dizzy. Dizzy Girls in the Sixties. Gary Soto. ReTh

Back then I cut off a lock. Semyon [*or* Semion] Isaakovich Kirsanov. TCRP *Fr.* Your Poem.

Back then I was still young. Blaise Cendrars. PFTM-1 *Fr.* Prose of the Trans-Siberian and of Little Jeanne of France, The.

Back then it seemed that wherever a girl took off her clothes. Skin. Lucia Maria Perillo. IllVoic

Back then when so much was clear. Tenderness. Stephen Dunn. NIP-4

Back there where fishermen can't swim. Where Fishermen Can't Swim. Matthew Sweeney. BiHa

Back through clouds. Train Tune. Louise Bogan. GM

Back through the Looking Glass to This Side. John Ciardi. NBLV

Back to Back. Debra Kang Dean. NAPBL

Back to Base. Jenny Joseph. BrRo

Back to Dublin. Robert Arthur Douglas Ford. MoCV

Back to him. Tune: "Partridge Sky"—Parting Sorrows. Na-lan Hsing-te. SuSp, *tr. by* William Golightly

Back to it. Larry Eigner. FTOS

Back to silent big soap flakes. Don't Hope to Gain by What Has Preceded. Joanne Kyger. PoM

Back to the cold transparent ham again! (LL) Sonnet to Vauxhall. Thomas Hood. NPeEn; OBCoV; OxBSo

Back to the First Bar. Emmy Bridgwater. SurWo

Back to the Ghetto. Jacob Glatstein [*or* Glatsteyn]. TrJP, *tr. by* Joseph Leftwich

Back to the green deeps of the outer bay. Sir Charles G. D. Roberts. NOBC *Fr.* Songs of the Common Day.

Back to the instruction manual which has made me dream of Guadalajara. (LL) Instruction Manual, The. John Ashbery. HAP; NOBA; NeAP; NoAM; PoM; YaYoPo

Back to the Land. On the Line. Emmy Bridgwater. SurWo

Back to the mystery of the Primal One. (LL) Pavilion for Listening to Fragrance, The. Chang Yü. CoBLCP; WoPoe, *tr. by* Jonathan Chaves

Back to the ordinary. (LL) Roe-Deer. Ted Hughes. NOxBChV; NoAM; OxAEP-2

Back to the play of constant give and change. (LL) Missing, The. Thom Gunn. CAGL; NoP-4

Back to Town. John Hollander. NoAM

Back to work happy at the thought possibly so. (LL) Personal Poem. Frank O'Hara. CLPP; PmAP

Back Trouble. Emily Grosholz. RA

Back-Up Singer, The. Dorothy Barresi. SwNoth

Back water done rose around Sumner, now, The. High Water Everywhere. Charlie Patton. APT-1

Back when it took all day to come up. Hearing. W. S. Merwin. NoAM

Back will go the head with the dark curls. Castanets. Bernard Spencer. WeW-3

Back wings, The. Between Walls. William Carlos Williams. APT-1; TAP; VGW

Back-yard chrysanthemum, A. Kaen. JDP, *tr. by* Yoel Hoffmann

Back Yard, July Night. William Cole. KaS

Back? T. Harri Jones. AngWePo; TCAWP

Backdrop: The dining room at Stonington. James Merrill. NoAM *Fr.* Book of Ephraim, The.

Background, dark vine at the edge of the porch, The. (LL) Forties Flick. John Ashbery. FTOS; NoAM

Background is instrumental. Eating the Forest. D. F. Brown. CDa

Backgrounds. Moniza Alvi. NeBl

Backgrounds Observed. Jean Earle. TCAWP

Backgrounds to Italian Paintings: Fifteenth Century. Anne Ridler. WPE

Backing into the Future. Dick Gallup. BAP-97

Backing to breaking down. What Has Yet to Be Sung. Malkia Amala Cyril. AfrBLW

Backlash Blues, The. Langston Hughes. BPo

Backroad leafmold stonewall chipmunk. Silent Poem. Robert Francis. CRP; LCAP-2

Backside to the Wind. Paul Durcan. PBCIP

Backward & down into inbetween as Vicki says. Mean Drunk Poem. Sharon Thesen. NOBC

Backward—as if retentive. Company, The. Robert Creeley. FTOS

Backward Look, The. Howard Nemerov. OxBC

Backward, turn backward, O time, in your flight. Rock Me to Sleep[, Mother]. Elizabeth Akers Allen. APN-2; BRP; ITBLP; OBCA; SWaP

Backwater Blues. Bessie Smith. NAAAL

Backwoodsman, The. James Kirke Paulding.
"Here lay dark Pittsburgh, from whose site there broke." APN-1
"In truth it was a landscape wildly gay." APN-1
"Neglected Muse! of this our western clime." APN-1

"'Tis true—yet 'tis no pity that 'tis true." APN-1

"'Twas sunset's hallow'd time—and such an eve." APN-1

Backyard. Diane Di Prima. PmAP

Backyard. John Tranter. BMAP

Backyard, dry flower half-border, unpeopled landscape. Disjecta Membra. Charles Wright. BAP-97

Backyards and barnlots. Book of Galahad, The. Jack Spicer. FTOS

Bacon's Epitaph, Made by His Man. John Cotton. SCAP; TCAPo

Bacon-smell. Geranium-smell. Hangman's Room, The. János Pilinszky. PoSu, *tr. by* Peter Jay

Bad actors love to play great villains. Lucilius. GrAn

Bad and Good. Alexander Resnikoff. NTCP

Bad Birds. William Trowbridge. UrbNat

Bad Blood. U Tam'si Tchicaya. NegPo, *tr. by* Ellen Conroy Kennedy

Bad Break, A! W. T. Goodge. NOBAu

Bad company is a disease. Rowland Watkyns. FaBoEE

Bad day at the market for Canobie Dick, A. Story of Canobie Dick, The. Libby Houston. OBSP

Bad Days Will End, The. Penelope Rosemont. SurWo

Bad Dream. Louis MacNeice. NoAM

Bad Government. Kuan Hsiu. WoPoe, *tr. by* Jerome P. Seaton

Bad Habit, The. Charles Henri Ford. SPE

Bad Karma. Mary Crockett Hill. AmPoNex

Bad Kittens, The. Elizabeth Jane Coatsworth. OBCA

Bad Landlord, The. William Chamberlayne. NOSC *Fr.* Pharonnida.

Bad Luck Card. Langston Hughes. NoP-4; SAmP; TRP

Bad Luck to This Marching. Benjamin Hall Kennedy. OBCoV

Bad Man. Langston Hughes. NAAAL

Bad money drives out good. What Do You Want: A Meaningful Dialogue, or a Satisfactory Talk? Ogden Nash. OBCoV

Bad monkeys to the windows. (LL) My Husband, before Leaving. *Unknown.* EaWin; WoPoe, *tr. by* J. Moussaieff Masson and W. S. Merwin

Bad Morning. Langston Hughes. OBAL

Bad Old Days, The. Kenneth Rexroth. NNaP; NoAM; PAI

Bad quartos were my first love. Bibliographer. Josephine Miles. FaBoWP

Bad Report—Good Manners. Spike Milligan. NOxBChV

Bad Run at King's Rest. Douglas Livingstone. PeSAV

Bad Season Makes the Poet Sad, The. Robert Herrick. BASC; BeJo; CaPo; CavPo; NAEL-5v1; NAEL-6v1; NAEL-7v1; SCGP

Bad (she said) was. Hymn to a Woman under Interrogation. Reiner Kunze. PoSu, *tr. by* Ewald Osers

Bad Sir Brian Botany. Alan Alexander Milne. NOxBChV

Bad Taste. Going Baroque. Jean V. Gier. ReBoTo

Bad Time for Poetry. Bertolt Brecht. PoSu, *tr. by* Ralph Manheim and John Willett

Bad Truth. Jane Rohrer. BodElec

Badger. John Clare. FHYEP; HAP; NPeEn; PAI; SCGP

Badger, The. John Clare. FaBoVe

Badger and the hare, The. (LL) Passing of the Shee, The. John Millington Synge. BIrV; FaBoEE

Badger grunting on his woodland track, The. John Clare. FaBoVe

Badger is the thirteenth astrological sign, The. Disasterology. Jeffrey McDaniel. NeAmPo

Badgers, The. Seamus Heaney. ModIr

Badly-Chosen Lover. Rosemary Tonks. EmeKit

Badman of the Guest Professor. Ishmael Reed. BPo; SSLK

Badminton. Sir Alfred Comyn Lyall. PeVV *Fr.* Studies at Delhi, 1876.

Baedeker for Metaphysicians. Brian Higgins. FaBoTw

Baffled for just a day or two. Emily Dickinson. PAI; PoBW

Baffled Knight, The. *Unknown.* ESPB
(Courteous Knight, The.) OxBB

Baffling Picture. Lajos Kassák. IQMS, *tr. by* Edwin Morgan

Bag, The. George Herbert. ESCV; GeHe
(Away despair! my gracious Lord doth heare.) FSCP

Bag of Mice. Nick Flynn. AmPoNex; NAPBL

Bag of Tools, A. R. L. Sharpe. PoToHe

Bag which was left and not only taken but turned away was not found, A. Gertrude Stein. TCAPo *Fr.* Tender Buttons.

Bag Woman. Dudley Randall. NoAM

Bagel, The. David Ignatow. CoAmPo; TwCP

Baggot Street Deserta. Thomas Kinsella. CIP-2; NoAM

Bagpipe Music. Ciaran Carson. ModIr

Bagpipe Music. Louis MacNeice. CABP; GTBS-P; HarvBoo; MakPoe; NAEL-5v2; NAEL-6v2; NBLV; NOBE; NOBL; NoAM; NoP-4; OBSV; OxBEV; OxBTC; PeLV; RB; TFi; UV

Bagpipes at the Biltmore. Robert Conquest. OBCoV

Bags of Meat. Thomas Hardy. RB

Bags Packed and We Expected This. Ramona Wilson. VoR

Bah! I have sung women in three cities. Cino. Ezra Pound. VGW

Bahnhofstrasse. James Joyce. NPeEn

Bailey Gatzert: The First Grade, 1945. Lonny Kaneko. LTA

Bailiff of a fertile garden plot, The. *Unknown.* PriapPo, tr. by Richard W. Hooper *Fr.* Priapus Poems, The.

Bailiff's Daughter of Islington, The. *Unknown.* ESPB; OxBB; OxBoLi

Bailiff, why your useless plaints about. *Unknown.* RomPo, tr. by Eugene O'Connor *Fr.* Priapean Corpus, The.

Bait, The. Eric Chock. OpBo

Bait[e], The. John Donne. InPK-6; NAEL-5v1; NAEL-6v1; NAEL-7v1; NOSC; PoRA; RB

Baith Gud[e] and Fair and Womanlie [*or* Womanly]. *Unknown.* OxBS

Bajji. Rashidah Ismaili. HAWP

Bakchos the wine-god / dissolver of limbs. *Unknown.* GrAn

Baked and cleaned. Grandmother. Siv Cedering Fox. PBCAP

Baked Oysters Rockefeller. Marjorie M. Evasco. ReBoTo

Baked the day she suddenly dropped dead. Tony Harrison. DiPo; NAEL-5v2; NAEL-6v2 *Fr.* School of Eloquence, The.

Baker hadn't yet unfastened the iron shutters of his shop when the, The. Leaves of Hypnos No. 128. René Char. AF, tr. by Cid Corman

Baker's Dozen of Wild Beasts, A. Carolyn Wells. OBCA

Baker's Tale, The. Lewis Carroll. EBEV; NAEL-5v2; NAEL-6v2; OxAEP-2 *Fr.* Hunting of the Snark, The.

Balaam. Charles Causley. EBNV

Balaam's Blessing. Bible, *O.T.* OBVE, tr. by William Tyndale *Fr.* Numbers.

Balade. Charles, Duc d' Orléans. NAWM-7v1, tr. by Sarah Spence

Balade: "Hide [*or* Hyd], Absalon, thy gilte tresses clere." Geoffrey Chaucer. AWP; EBEV; HAP; NOBE; OBEV; SCGP *Fr.* Legend of Good Women, The.

Balade whych Anne Askewe made and sange whan she was in Newgate, The. Anne Askew. *See* Ballad Which Anne Askew Made and Sang When She Was in Newgate, The

Balalaïka. Pierre Albert-Birot. CuPo

Balance. James Harris. PasH

Balance. Marilyn Nelson Waniek. FFC; RA

Balance and Beauty. Clarence Major. FTOS

Balancing. Austere. Life. Keith Waldrop. PmAP *Fr.* Shipwreck in Haven, A.

Balancing / its weight on the horizon's balustrade. Knot, The. Vinda Karandikar. OMIP, tr. by Vinay Dharwadker

Balancing on Oriental spike heels. Three Gypsies. Shalin Hai-Jew. UnSA

Balanide 2. Paul Verlaine. CAGL, tr. by Alan Stone

Balankin was as gude a mason. Lamkin. *Unknown.* ESPB

Balboa, the Entertainer. Imamu Amiri Baraka. NoAM

    (It cannot come / except you make it.) AF

Bald-bare, bone-bare, and ivory yellow: skull. U.S. Sailor with the Japanese Skull, The. Winfield Townley Scott. APT-2

Bald head with the fringe, The. Jane Beeson. NewEx

Bald-headed man, his pate, A. Bald-Headed Man, A. Bhartrihari. WoPoe, tr. by Barbara Stoler Miller

Bald heads forgetful of their sins. Scholars, The. W. B. Yeats. NoP-4

Bald Mountain. Wang An-shih. ColAnChi, tr. by Victor H. Mair

Bald Mountain Zaum-Poems. *Unknown.* PFTM-1

Baldanders. Christopher Reid. NPeEn

Balder. Sydney Thompson Dobell.

    Chanted Calendar, A. OBEV

Balder Dead. Matthew Arnold.

    "But when the Gods and Heroes heard, they brought." PeVV

    "Forth from the east, up the ascent of Heaven." PeVV

Balding, already quite round. Saturday with Dad. Liz Houghton. Prnts

Baleful phantoms underground, The. (LL) Low Barometer. Robert Bridges. CABP; NOCV; NoAM; SCGP

Baleful Return. Ramón López Velarde. TCLAP, tr. by Victor Tulli

Balgu Song. *Unknown.* CBAP, tr. by Clancy McKenna

Bali Hai Calls Mama. Marilyn Nelson Waniek. ISC

Balitaw. Bataan Faigao. ReBoTo

Balkis was in her marble town. Lascelles Abercrombie. MoBrPo *Fr.* Judith.

Ball. Birago Diop. PBMAP

Ball, almost, The. Basketball. Ronald Wallace. PBCAP

Ball no question makes of Ayes and Noes, The. 70. Edward Fitzgerald. CABP

Ball Poem, The. John Berryman. ChAP; CoAP; MoAmPo; NOBA; NoAM

Ball's Bluff. Herman Melville. CBCWP; FaBoWar; OBWP

Ball will bounce, but less and less, A. It's not. . Juggler. Richard Wilbur. TAP

Ballad. W. H. Auden. *See* O What Is That Sound [Which So Thrills the Ear]

Ballad about a Smoke-Filled Railway Carriage. Aleksandr Kochetkov. TCRP, tr. by Lubov Yakovleva

Ballad about Friendship, A. Semyon [*or* Semion] Petrovich Gudzenko. TCRP, tr. by Gordon McVay

Ballad about the Circus. Aleksandr Petrovich Mezhirov. TCRP, tr. by Deming Brown

Ballad about the German Censor, The. "David Samuilovich Samoylov [*or* Samoilov]. TCRP, tr. by Lubov Yakovleva

Ballad against the Enemies of France. François Villon. AWP, tr. by Algernon Charles Swinburne

Ballad: Alice Brand. Sir Walter Scott. OxAEP-2 *Fr.* Lady of the Lake, The.

Ballad: "As I was walkin' the jungle round, a-killin' of tigers an' time." Guy Wetmore Carryl. NBLV

Ballad: "Auld wife sat at her ivied door, The." Charles Stuart Calverley. CABP; NBLV; OBCoV; OxAEP-2; UV

Ballad: Between the Boxcars. Robert Penn Warren. GM

    I Can't Even Remember the Name. CRP

    ("I can't even remember the name of the one who fell.") GM

Ballad by Hans Breitmann. Charles Godfrey Leland. APN-2; NOBL; TCAPo

Ballad for Gloom. Ezra Pound. MoAmPo

Ballad for Katharine of Aragon, A. Charles Causley. FaBoTw

Ballad: "He was strolling with another woman." Gabriela Mistral. BLPSL, tr. by Rene de Costa, Rigas Kappatos and Eleni Paidoussi

Ballad: "He went by with another." Gabriela Mistral. SpanPo, tr. by Muriel Kittel

Ballad: "I'll tell you a story / concerning John and Joan." Peter Reading. PeLV

Ballad: "I put my hat upon my head." Samuel Johnson. NOBL; OxAEP-1; UV

Ballad: "If the man who turnips cries." Samuel Johnson. OxAEP-1

Ballad: "Knight went down to the river's rim, A." Gerda Mayer. OBSP

Ballad of a Barber, The. Aubrey Beardsley. NOBVV; PAI

Ballad of a Bun, A. Sir Owen Seaman. UV

Ballad of a Ferocious Tiger. Kao Ch'i. SuSp, tr. by Irving Y. Lo

Ballad of a Little Lamp, A. René Depestre. NegPo, tr. by Ellen Conroy Kennedy

Ballad of a Nun, A. John Davidson. MoBrPo; UV

Ballad of a Shadow. Alice Oswald. MFPA

Ballad of a Strange Thing. Howard Phelps Putnam. OxBA

Ballad of Abbreviations, A. Gilbert Keith Chesterton. NOBL

Ballad of Agincourt, The. Michael Drayton. *See* Battle of Agincourt, The

Ballad of an Old Woman. Frank A. Collymore. NOxBChV

Ballad of Aunt Geneva, The. Marilyn Nelson Waniek. FFC; GT; RA

Ballad of Barnaby, The. W. H. Auden. OBNV *Fr.* Six Commissioned Texts.

Ballad of 'Beau Brocade,' The. Austin Dobson. OxAEP-2

Ballad of Biddy Early, The. Nancy Willard. FFC

Ballad of Billie Potts, The. Robert Penn Warren. FuPo; NOBA; OxBA

Ballad of Billy Rose, The. Leslie Norris. AngWePo

Ballad of Birmingham. Dudley Randall. BPo; HeIP-4; ISC; InPK-6; NIL-7; NIP-4; NoAM; NoP-4; SoSe-8

Ballad of Black Grief. Federico García Lorca. STV, tr. by John Frederick Nims

Ballad of Bouillabaisse, The. William Makepeace Thackeray. OBEV; OxAEP-2

Ballad of Ching Mountain. Meng Chiao. SuSp, tr. by Stephen Owen

Ballad of Christmas, A. Walter De la Mare. OBCP

Ballad of Don and Dave and Di, The. John Heath-Stubbs. EBNV

Ballad of East and West, The. Rudyard Kipling. EBNV; OBNV

Ballad of Faith. William Carlos Williams. OBAL

Ballad of Fat Margot. Augustus Young. CIP-2

Ballad of Fate. Vadim Nikolaevich Delone. TCRP, tr. by Nina Kossman

Ballad of Father Gilligan, The. W. B. Yeats. EBVV; MoBrPo; PoRA

Ballad of Fisher's Boardinghouse, The. Rudyard Kipling. PoRA

Ballad of François Villon, A. Algernon Charles Swinburne. PoRA

Ballad of George R. Sims, The. Sir John Betjeman. OBCoV; UV

Ballad of Going Down to the Store, A. Miron Bialoszewski. BLT, tr. by Czeslaw Milosz

Ballad of Hampstead Heath, The. James Elroy Flecker. MoBrPo

Ballad of Hector in Hades. Edwin Muir. HarvBoo; NOBE; NoAM

Ballad of Hell, A. John Davidson. MoBrPo

    (Christmas Eve.) EBVV

Ballad of Hiram Hover, The. Bayard Taylor. OBAL

Ballad of Hunters, A. C. J. Driver. PeSAV

Ballad of Indolence. Herman De Coninck. TuT, tr. by Eamon Grennan

Ballad of Jan Palach, Student and Heretic. Ondra Lysohorsky. AF, tr. by Ewald Osers

Ballad of John Cable and Three Gentlemen. W. S. Merwin. CoAP; MakPoe; NOBA; YaYoPo

Ballad of Joking Jesus, The. James Joyce. ChIV-2

Ballad of Keith of Ravelston, The.   Sydney Thompson Dobell.   OBEV   *Fr.* Nuptial Eve, A.

Ballad of Kynd Kittok, The.   William Dunbar.   OxBoLi; PeLV

Ballad of Ladies Lost and Found.   Marilyn Hacker.   FFC; VCAP

Ballad of Lager Bier, The.   Edmund Clarence Stedman.   OBAL

Ballad of Late Annie, The.   Gwendolyn Brooks.   ColAP   *Fr.* Notes from the Childhood and the Girlhood.

Ballad of Long Bank, The.   Li Po.   WoPoe, *tr. by* Elling O. Eide

Ballad of Mrs. Noah, The.   Robert Duncan.   NOBA; NoAM

Ballad(:) Of Motion.   Billy Mills.   NOBA; Oth

Ballad of Mulan, The.   *Unknown.*   SuSp, *tr. by* William H. Nienhauser

Ballad of Mulan, The.   *Unknown.*   ColAnChi, *tr. by* Arthur Waley

Ballad of Nat Turner, The.   Robert Earl Hayden.   BPo; VGW

Ballad of Noah's Daughter.   Rossana Ombres.   NeIt, *tr. by* Ruth Feldman

Ballad of O'Bruadir, The.   Frederick Robert Higgins.   OBMV

Ballad of Old Women & of How They Are Constrained to Simulate Youth in Order to Avoid Shocking the Young.   Norman Talbot.   NOBAu

Ballad of One Doomed to Die.   Federico García Lorca.   AWTN, *tr. by* Langston Hughes

Ballad of Orange and Grape.   Muriel Rukeyser.   ChAP; NoAM; NoP-4

Ballad of Our Lady.   William Dunbar.
  "Empryce of prys, imperatrice."   EBEV

Ballad of Passive Paederasty, A.   Aleister Crowley.   CAGL

Ballad of Past Meridian, A.   George Meredith.   PeVV

Ballad of Peach Blossom Spring.   Yüan Mei.   CoBLCP, *tr. by* Jonathan Chaves

Ballad of Persse O'Reilly, The.   James Joyce.   PeLV   *Fr.* Finnegans Wake.

Ballad of Reading Gaol, The.   Oscar Wilde.   OBNV; OxAEP-2
  "For oak and elm have pleasant leaves."   MakPoe; NoAM
  "He did not wear his scarlet coat."   CABP; EBNV; MoBrPo; NOBE; NOBVV; NPeEn; NoAM; OBMV; OxBEV; TFi; UV
  "He does not sit with silent men."   NPeEn; OxBEV
  "In Debtor's Yard the stones are hard."   NOBVV
  "There is no chapel on the day."   EBVV; NoAM
  "Yet each man kills the thing he loves."   OxBEV

Ballad of Religion and Marriage, A.   Amy Levy.   NPeEn; VWP; ViWPN

Ballad of Remembrance, A.   Robert Earl Hayden.   BPo; ESEAA

Ballad of Rudolph Reed, The.   Gwendolyn Brooks.   RB

Ballad of Sally in Our Alley, The.   Henry Carey.   *See* Sally in Our Alley

Ballad of Selling a Child.   Wang Chiu-ssu.   CoBLCP; ColAnChi, *tr. by* Jonathan Chaves

Ballad of Sue Ellen Westerfield, The.   Robert Earl Hayden.   ESEAA; NoAM

Ballad of the Army Carts.   Tu Fu.   WoPoe, *tr. by* David Lattimore

Ballad of the Bayonet, A.   Ernest Bryll.   FaBoWar, *tr. by* Czeslaw Milosz

Ballad of the Bird-Bride.   Rosamund Marriott Watson.   VWP; ViWPN

Ballad of the Blue Envelope, The.   Nikolai Semionovich Tikhonov.   TCRP, *tr. by* Michael Frayn

Ballad of the Bread Man.   Charles Causley.   RB

Ballad of the Bright Angel.   Bruce Berger.   GeoH

Ballad of the Bushman.   Eileen Duggan.   PeNZ

Ballad of the Cadger.   May Kendall.   ViWPN

Ballad of the Cool Fountain.   *Unknown.*   BoWoP, *tr. by* Edwin Honig

Ballad of the Days of the Messiah.   Abraham Moses Klein.   TrJP

Ballad of the Deserted Mansion.   Kao Ch'i.   CoBLCP, *tr. by* Jonathan Chaves

Ballad of the Despairing Husband.   Robert Creeley.   NeAP; OBAL; RaBo

Ballad of the Dogs.   Lars Gustafsson.   WoPoe, *tr. by* Philip Martin

Ballad of the Emeu, The.   Bret Harte.   NBLV

Ballad of the Fatherless Boy.   Wang Chiu-ssu.   CoBLCP, *tr. by* Jonathan Chaves

Ballad of the Ferocious Tiger.   Hsü Pen.   CoBLCP, *tr. by* Jonathan Chaves

Ballad of the Gibbet.   François Villon.   AWP, *tr. by* Andrew Lang

Ballad of the Girl Whose Name Is Mud.   Langston Hughes.   SAmP

Ballad of the Good Lord Nelson, A.   Lawrence Durrell.   PeLV

Ballad of the Goodly Fere.   Ezra Pound.   ChIV-2; MoAmPo; PoRA; TrCP

Ballad of the Government Granary Clerk.   Ho Ching-ming.   CoBLCP; ColAnChi, *tr. by* Jonathan Chaves

Ballad of the Homing Man, The.   Ernest Rhys.   AngWePo

Ballad of the Hoppy-Toad.   Margaret Abigail Walker.   BlSi; NBV

Ballad of the Ichthyosaurus.   May Kendall.   ViWPN

Ballad of the Icondic.   John Ciardi.   OBAL

Ballad of the Landlord.   Langston Hughes.   HCAP; NAAAL; NOBA

Ballad of the Little Cart, A.   Ch'en Tzu-lung.   SuSp, *tr. by* Wu-Chi Liu

Ballad of the Londoner.   James Elroy Flecker.   EnLoPo

Ballad of the Lords of Old Time.   François Villon.   AWP; PeVV, *tr. by* Algernon Charles Swinburne

Ballad of the Magic Glasses.   Maura Stanton.   FFC

Ballad of the Maiden of Lan-ling.   Chin Ho.   ColAnChi, *tr. by* Victor H. Mair

Ballad of the Man Who's Gone.   Langston Hughes.   SAmP

Ballad of the Merchant.   Hsü Pen.   CoBLCP, *tr. by* Jonathan Chaves

Ballad of the Morning Streets.   Imamu Amiri Baraka.   TTTS

Ballad of the Mulberry Road.   *Unknown.*   ChinPo, *tr. by* Yip Wai-lim

Ballad of the Nails, The.   Nikolai Semionovich Tikhonov.   TCRP, *tr. by* Michael Frayn

Ballad of the Neighborhood Shaman.   Kao Ch'i.   CoBLCP, *tr. by* Jonathan Chaves

Ballad of the Oedipus Complex.   Lawrence Durrell.   OBCoV

Ballad of the Orioles in the Fields.   Ts'ao Chih.   ColAnChi; SuSp, *tr. by* Hans H. Frankel

Ballad of the Outer Life.   Hugo von Hofmannsthal.   AWP; TrJP, *tr. by* Jethro Bithell

Ballad of the Oysterman, The.   Oliver Wendell Holmes.   TCAPo

Ballad of the Sad Young Men, The.   Tommy Wolf.   ReLy

Ballad of the Scarecrow Christ.   Elder Olson.   ChIV-2

Ballad of the Shape of Things, The.   Sheldon Harnick.   ReLy

Ballad of the Shot Heart.   Nikolai Vasil'evich Panchenko.   TCRP, *tr. by* Daniel Weissbort

Ballad of the Shrieking Man, The.   James Fenton.   EmeKit

Ballad of the Stonegut Sugar Works.   James Keir Baxter.   PeNZ

Ballad of the Tempest.   James Thomas Fields.   TreFP

Ballad of the Ten Casino Dancers.   Cecília Meireles.   BoWoP; TCLAP, *tr. by* James Merrill

Ballad of the Three Spectres.   Ivor Gurney.   OBWP

Ballad of the Underpass.   Patricia Beer.   HarvBoo

Ballad of the Were-Wolf, A.   Rosamund Marriott Watson.   VWP; ViWPN

Ballad of the Western Island in the North Country.   *Unknown.*   ChiP, *tr. by* Arthur Waley

Ballad of the Women of Paris.   François Villon.   AWP, *tr. by* Algernon Charles Swinburne

Ballad of the Wondrous Moment.   Pavel Grigoryevich Antokolsky.   TCRP, *tr. by* Bernard Meares

Ballad of the Yorkshire Ripper, The.   Blake Morrison.
  "Ower t'ills o Bingley."   FaBoVe

Ballad of Trees and the Master, A.   Sidney Lanier.   APN-2; ChIV-2; ColAP; ITBLP; NOBA; OxBA; TCAPo

Ballad of Villon and Fat Madge, The.   François Villon.   OBVE

Ballad of William Bloat, The.   *Unknown.*   NOBL; PeLV

Ballad of William Sycamore, The.   Stephen Vincent Benét.   MoAmPo; PoRA

Ballad of Winky.   Merrill Markoe.   Unle

Ballad of Yi River.   Ho Ching-ming.   CoBLCP, *tr. by* Jonathan Chaves

Ballad of Yüan-yüan.   Wu Wei-yeh.   CoBLCP, *tr. by* Jonathan Chaves

Ballad of Yukon Jake, The.   Edward E., Jr. Paramore.   TCAPo

Ballad: "Oh, quietly mad I'd like to be."   Vladislav Felitsianovich Khodasevich.   TCRP, *tr. by* Michael Frayn

Ballad on the Investigation of a Disaster.   Yao Chen.   ColAnChi, *tr. by* Victor H. Mair

Ballad on the Marriage of Philip and Mary, A.   John Heywood.
  "Egles byrde hath spred his wings, The."   PBRV

Ballad on the Taxes, A.   Edward Ward.   OxBoLi

Ballad, since Love himself hath fashioned thee.   Lapo Gianni.   EaItPo, *tr. by* Dante Gabriel Rossetti

Ballad-Singer, The.   Thomas Hardy.   BoLoP   *Fr.* At Casterbridge Fair.

Ballad: "Tender infant, meek and mild, The."   Samuel Johnson.   OxAEP-1

Ballad: Time of Roses.   Thomas Hood.   OBEV; OxAEP-2

Ballad to a Traditional Refrain.   Maurice James Craig.   BIrV

Ballad to Mrs. Catherine Fleming in London from Malshanger Farm in Hampshire, A.   Anne Finch, Countess of Winchilsea.   ECWP

Ballad: "What's that approaching like dust like poverty."   Charles Simic.   LCAP-2

Ballad Which Anne Askew Made and Sang When She Was in Newgate, The.   Anne Askew.   CABP; EMWP; NoSic; WPE
  (Balade whych Anne Askewe made and sange whan she was in newgate, The.)   NPeEn; PBRV
  (Ballad Which Anne Askewe Made and Sang When She Was in Newgate, The.)   NoP-4
  (Like as the armed knight.)   SacPr
  (Lines In Prison.)   SacPr
  (Lyke as the armed knyght.)   NPeEn; PBRV

Ballad Written for a Bridegroom.   François Villon.   AWP

Ballade 1.   Eustache Deschamps.   WoPoe, *tr. by* David Curzon and Jeffrey Fiskin

Ballade 2.   Eustache Deschamps.   WoPoe, *tr. by* David Curzon and Jeffrey Fiskin

Ballade at Thirty-Five.   Dorothy Parker.   APT-1

Ballade d'une Grande Dame.   Gilbert Keith Chesterton.   OxBoLi

Ballade de Marguerite.   *Unknown.*   AWP, *tr. by* Oscar Wilde

Ballade des Belles Milatraisses.   Rosalie Jonas.   BlSi

Ballade for the Duke of Orléans.   Richard Wilbur.   WoPoe

Ballade: "Hide, Absalom, thy gilte tresses clear."   Geoffrey Chaucer.   WoPoe, *tr. by* Burton Raffel and Selden Rodman   *Fr.* Legend of Good Women, The.

Ballade: "I was in blossom when I was a child."   Charles, Duc d' Orléans.   WoPoe, *tr. by* Willis Barnstone and Tony Barnstone

Ballade Made in the Hot Weather.   William Ernest Henley.   MoBrPo

Ballade of an Omnibus.   Amy Levy.   ViWPN

Ballade of Broken Flutes.   Edwin Arlington Robinson.   APN-2

Ballade of Dead Actors.   William Ernest Henley.   EBVV; OBMV

Ballade of Dead Gentlemen.   Clive Staples Lewis.   OBCoV

Ballad[e] of Dead Ladies.   François Villon.   AWP; CTC; OBVE; PoRA, *tr. by* Dante Gabriel Rossetti

Ballade of Evolution, A.   Grant Allen.   EBVV

Ballade of Hell and of Mrs. Roebeck.   Joseph Hilaire Pierre Belloc.   NPeEn

Ballade of Lost Objects.   Phyllis McGinley.   CRP; NBLV; PoRA

Ballade of Lovers.   May Probyn.   VWP

Ballade of Sayings.   W. S. Merwin.   NNaP

Ballade of Suicide, A.   Gilbert Keith Chesterton.   NBLV; OBCoV

Ballade of the Chinese Lover.   Stuart Merrill.   APN-2

Ballade of the Ladies of Time Past.   François Villon.   WoPoe, *tr. by* Richard Wilbur

Ballade of the Men Who Were Hanged.   François Villon.   WoPoe, *tr. by* Fred Chappell

Ballade of the Moment After.   Paul Goodman.   BodElec

Ballade of the New God.   Thomas M. [*or* "Tom"] Disch.   RA

Ballade of the Outcasts.   Stuart Merrill.   APN-2

Ballade of the Poetic Life.   Sir John Collings Squire.   OBMV

Ballade: "Pretty maid she died, she died, in love-bed as she lay, The."   Paul Fort.   AWP, *tr. by* Frederick York Powell   (Pretty Maid, The.)   OBMV

Ballade: "Tell me where, in what country, where."   François Villon.   STV, *tr. by* John Frederick Nims

Ballade to End With, A.   François Villon.   WoPoe, *tr. by* Richard Wilbur

Ballade to His Mistress.   François Villon.   WeW-3, *tr. by* Norman Cameron

Ballade Tragique à Double Refrain.   Max Beerbohm.   OBSV

Ballade un Peu Banale.   Arthur James Marshall Smith.   MoCV

Ballad[e] [upon a Wedding], A.   Sir John Suckling.   BASC; BeJo; CaPo; EBEV; EBNV; NAEL-7v1; NoP-4

Ballat o the Hingit.   François Villon.   OBVE, *tr. by* Tom Scott

Ballat o the Leddies o Langsyne.   François Villon.   OBVE; OxBEV, *tr. by* Tom Scott

Ballata.   Guido Cavalcanti.   EaItPo, *tr. by* Dante Gabriel Rossetti

"Being in thought of love, I chanced to see."   AWP, *tr. by* Dante Gabriel Rossetti

Ballata II: Last Song: from Exile.   Guido Cavalcanti.   WoPoe, *tr. by* George Sutherland Fraser and G. S. Fraser

Ballata 5: "Light do I see within my Lady's eyes."   Guido Cavalcanti.   CTC, *tr. by* Ezra Pound

Ballata: Concerning a Shepherd-Maid.   Guido Cavalcanti.   AWP; EaItPo, *tr. by* Dante Gabriel Rossetti

Ballata: He Will Gaze upon Beatrice.   Dante Alighieri.   AWP; EaItPo, *tr. by* Dante Gabriel Rossetti

Ballata: His Talk with Certain Peasant Girls.   Franco Sacchetti.   AWP; EaItPo, *tr. by* Dante Gabriel Rossetti

Ballata: In Exile at Sarzana.   Guido Cavalcanti.   AWP; EaItPo, *tr. by* Dante Gabriel Rossetti

Ballata: Of a Continual Death in Love.   Guido Cavalcanti.   AWP; EaItPo, *tr. by* Dante Gabriel Rossetti

Ballata: Of His Lady among Other Ladies.   Guido Cavalcanti.   AWP; EaItPo, *tr. by* Dante Gabriel Rossetti

Ballata: Of True and False Singing.   *Unknown.*   AWP; EaItPo, *tr. by* Dante Gabriel Rossetti

Ballata: One Speaks of the Beginning of His Love.   *Unknown.*   AWP; EaItPo, *tr. by* Dante Gabriel Rossetti

Ballatetta.   Ezra Pound.   VGW

Ballerina.   Rosario Ferré.   TANSG, *tr. by* Nancy Diaz

Ballerina.   Carl Sigman.   ReLy

Ballet of the Fifth Year, The.   Delmore Schwartz.   APT-2; OxBA; TwCP

Ballet [*or* Ballit] of de Boll Weevil, De.   *Unknown.*   NOBA

Ballin' the Jack.   Christopher Smith.   ReLy

Balliol Rhymes.   *Var. authors.*

"First come I. My name is Jowett."   FaBoEE; NOBL; PeLV

"I am Branson; Nature's laws."   FaBoEE

"I am featly-tripping Lee."   FaBoEE

"I am rather tall and stately."   FaBoEE; NOBL

"I am the Dean, and this is Mrs. Liddell."   FaBoEE

"I am the Dean of Christ Church, Sir."   FaBoEE; NOBL

"I'm the great Sir William Anson."   FaBoEE

On the Hon. George Nathaniel Curzon, Commoner of Balliol.   FaBoEE; NOBL; OBCoV; PeLV

"Positivists ever talk in s-/Uch an epic style as Dawkins."   FaBoEE

Ballistical student named Raffity, A.   Limerick.   D. H. Cudmore.   PeLi

[De] Ballit of de Boll weevil.   *Unknown.*   NOBA

Balloon, The.   Mother Goose.   OxNR; ReMoGo

Balloon Faces.   Carl Sandburg.   PoE

Balloon Heart.   Beth Gylys.   AmPoNex

Balloons.   Dan Pagis.   FIT, *tr. by* Robert Friend

Balloons.   Sylvia Plath.   FaBoWP; PoE

Balloons hang on wires in the Marigold Gardens, The.   Balloon Faces.   Carl Sandburg.   PoE

Ballot, The.   John Pierpont.   APN-1   *Fr.* Word from a Petitioner.

Ballot and the Bullet, The.   Chris Van Wyk.   PeSAV

Ballot / This means voting, The.   Ballot and the Bullet, The.   Chris Van Wyk.   PeSAV

Ballroom was filled with fashion's throng, The.   Bird in a Gilded Cage, A.   Arthur J. Lamb.   TCAPo

Balls.   Anne McNaughton.   RaBo

Ballydavid Pier.   Thomas Kinsella.   BIrV

Ballygrand Widow.   Deborah Randall.   NeBl

Ballymurphy painted white, inside and out.   Jerusalem.   David Morley.   NLP

Ballyshannon foundered off the coast of Cariboo, The.   Etiquette.   Sir William Schwenck Gilbert.   FaBoCh

Balmy as summer. It won't last.   Sunday Morning through Binoculars.   Eamon Grennan.   PBCIP

Balmy comforts that are fled, The.   Song.   Anne Batten Cristall.   RWP

Balsham Bells.   Kenrick Prescot.   NOEC

Baltazar Beats His Tutor at Scrabble.   Belle Waring.   ExTi

Balthasar's Song.   William Shakespeare.   AWP; CTC; NoSic; PAI; UV   *Fr.* Much Ado about Nothing.

Baltic Sea froze in 1307, The. Birds flew north.   Annual of the Dark Physics, An.   Norman Dubie.   BodElec

Baltic Summer.   Yunna Petrovna [*or* Iunna Pinkhusovna] Moritz [*or* Morits].   TCRP, *tr. by* Bernard Meares

Baltimore Buzz.   Eubie Blake.   ReLy

Baltimore evening I saw, The.   Soul Music.   Baron Wormser.   LTA; SwNoth

Baltimore Oriole.   Hoagy Carmichael.   ReLy

Balulalow.   John James.   OBEV

Bamboo.   Eric Rolls.   NOBAu

Bamboo Branch Song.   Ho Ching-ming.   CoBLCP, *tr. by* Jonathan Chaves

Bamboo Branch Song.   Liu Yu Hsi.   CoBCP, *tr. by* Burton Watsonp

"Gorges of Wu are hoary and im in the season of mist and rain, The."   SuSp

"Up in the hills are bank on bank of blossoming peach and plum trees."   SuSp

Bamboo Branch Song of Han-chia.   Wang Shih-chieng.   CoBLCP, *tr. by* Jonathan Chaves

Bamboo Branch Song of the Seacoast.   Yang Wei-chen.   CoBLCP, *tr. by* Jonathan Chaves

Bamboo Branch Song of West Lake.   Yang Wei-chen.   CoBLCP, *tr. by* Jonathan Chaves

Bamboo by Li Ch'e Yun's Window, The.   Po Chü-i.   OHMPC, *tr. by* Kenneth Rexroth

Bamboo cold creeps into my room, The.   Sleepless Nights.   Tu Fu.   CrYelRi, *tr. by* Sam Hamill

Bamboo Elegy: Two.   Edmond Yi-teh Chang.   OpBo

Bamboo Garden.   Muso Soseki.   EaWin, *tr. by* W. S. Merwin

Bamboo Grove.   Wang Wei.   ChinPo, *tr. by* Yip Wai-lim

Bamboo hat, straw coat.   Buson.   SoOfWa, *tr. by* Sam Hamill

Bamboo hut and a plum tree bower, A.   Bamboo Hut, The.   Nguyễn Trãi.   WoPoe, *tr. by* Nguyen Ngoc Bich

Bamboo Mat.   Yuan Chen.   CrYelRi; ErotSp, *tr. by* Sam Hamill

Bamboo path leads through the First Stage, A.   Climbing Pien-chueh Temple.   Wang Wei.   ColAnChi, *tr. by* Stephen Owen

Bamboo's chill creeps into the chamber.   Tired Night, A.   Tu Fu.   SuSp, *tr. by* Jan W. Walls

Bamboo Villa, The.   Shen Chou.   CoBLCP, *tr. by* Jonathan Chaves

Bamboos Grow Well under Good Rule, The.   *Unknown.*   WoPoe, *tr. by* Ezra Pound

Bamboos rustle, the wind in battle array.   Written While Lying on My Pillow in the Morning on the Twelfth Day of the Eleventh Month.   Fan Ch'eng-ta.   SuSp, *tr. by* Wu-Chi Liu

Banana tree, The.   Basho.   SoOfWa, *tr. by* Sam Hamill

Bananas down at the Safeway, The.   High-Class Bananas, The.   Gary Gildner.   PBCAP

Bananas ripe and green, and ginger-root.   Tropics in New York, The.   Claude McKay.   APT-1; GT; MakPoe; NoAM; TTY

Band of the bold were gathered together, The. *Unknown.* AnOE, *tr. by* Charles W. Kennedy *Fr.* Exodus.

Band Played On, The. John F. Palmer. OBAL

Band plays an intro. Lady's Way. Reuben Jackson. GT

Bandit, The. Vladimir Aleksandrovich Lugovskoy [*or* Lugovskoi]. TCRP, *tr. by* Gordon McVay

Bandstand. Michael S. Harper. SeSe

Bandy Legs. Mother Goose. OxNR; ReMoGo

Bang Bang Bang. History of the Flood, The. John Heath-Stubbs. NOxBChV; OxBTC

Bang bang you're dead fifty bullets in you head. Children's Games. Malkia Amala Cyril. InTrad

Bang! the starter's gun. Dorthi Charles. KaS

Bangkok. Francis Reginald Scott. MoCV

Bangla Desh: 1. Faiz Ahmad Faiz. CarOv, *tr. by* Carolyn Kizer

Bangla Desh: 2. Faiz Ahmad Faiz. CarOv, *tr. by* Carolyn Kizer

Bangla Desh: 3. Faiz Ahmad Faiz. CarOv, *tr. by* Carolyn Kizer

Baning Summer. Thomas Nashe [*or* Nash]. *See* Summer's Last Will and Testament

Banished, dispossessed dead, The. Litany of the Rooms of the Dead. Franz Werfel. TrJP, *tr. by* Edith Abercrombie Snow

Banished Gods, The. Derek Mahon. OxBC

Banishment. Tu Fu.
  "It's the fourteenth of August, and I'm too hot." CarOv, *tr. by* Carolyn Kizer
  "Joy in this meeting grieves our two white heads." CarOv, *tr. by* Carolyn Kizer
  Reunion. CarOv, *tr. by* Carolyn Kizer
  Too Much Heat, Too Much Work. CarOv, *tr. by* Carolyn Kizer

Banishment from Ur. Enheduanna. BoWoP, *tr. by* J. J. A. van Dijk and W. W. Hallo

Banishment of Poverty by His Royal Highness James Duke of Albany, The. Francis Sempill.
  "Pox fa that pultron Povertie." NePenScot

Bank of fine grass and light breeze, A. Night Thoughts aboard a Boat. Tu Fu. SuSp, *tr. by* James J. Y. Liu and Irving Y. Lo

Bank of spring clouds, rain swelling the stream, A. Going Out to the Country on a Boat Trip, Sheltering from Rain Beneath a Tree. Kao Ch'i. CoBLCP, *tr. by* Jonathan Chaves

Bánk the Palatine. József Katona.
  "Speak out, speak, well." IQMS, *tr. by* Gavin Ewart and Paul Tabori

Bank to bank, the stream is wide. T'ao Ch'ien [*or* T'ao Yuan-ming]. SuSp *Fr.* Seasons Come and Go, The.

Banker, The. Raymond Roseliep. HA

Banking Potatoes. Herbert Asquith. NAAAL

Banking Potatoes. Yusef Komunyakaa. NoP-4

Bankis of Helicon, The. *Unknown.*
  "Declair, ye bankis of Helicon." OxBS

Bankrupt. Cortlandt W. Sayres. PoToHe

Banks are steep, The. Drought. Water too low. Wye Below Bredwardine, The. John Powell Ward. TCAWP

Banks o' Doon, The. Robert Burns. BoLoP; NOBE; NOEC; OBEV; TFi
  (And left the thorn wi' me.) (LL) OBEV
  (And sae was pu'd ere noon.) (LL) NAEL-5v2; NAEL-6v2
  (But left the thorn wi' me.) (LL) AWP; TFi; UnPo

Banks of reed. Christopher Okigbo. PBMAP *Fr.* Limits (1962).

Banks of the Condamine, The. *Unknown.* NOBAu

Banneker. Rita Dove. ESEAA; LCAP-2; NAAL-5; NoAM

Banner of the Jew, The. Emma Lazarus. TrJP

Banners! Bunting! The engine throbs. Special Train, A. Daniel Gerard Hoffman. CDa

Banners of the Heart. Fawziyya Al-Sindi. PoArWo, *tr. by* Joseph T. Zeidan

Banquet. Ruth Bidgood. TCAWP

Banquet, The. George Herbert. ESCV; GeHe

Banquet, The. Letitia [*or* Laetitia] Elizabeth Landon. TreFP

Banquet, The. John Milton. NOSC *Fr.* Paradise Regained [*or* Regain'd].

Banquet at the Tso Family Manor. Tu Fu. OHPC, *tr. by* Kenneth Rexroth

Banquet: *Dissertation 2, Canzone 1,* The. Dante Alighieri. WoPoe

Banquet was a bonza, a rare recherché feed, The. Thank you, Mr Rason, for the Apples. E. G. Murphy. OBCoV

Bantam rooster, A. Kikaku. KaS

Bantams in Pine-Woods. Wallace Stevens. NOBA; NoAM; OxBA; SAmP; UnPo

Banyan. Elsa Cross. TANSG, *tr. by* Patricia Dubrava

Banyan roots almost reach. Singapore, July 4th. Sascha Feinstein. AmPoNex

Baobab Fruit Picking; or, Development in Monkey Bay. Jack A. Mapanje. PeSAV

Baptism. Dale Zieroth. NOBC

Bar. Langston Hughes. APSN

Bar, The. *Unknown.* PoToHe

Bar Kochba. Emma Lazarus. TrJP

Bar Mitzvah, The. Philip Schultz. TaR

Bar of Michael Angelo, The. (LL) Tennyson. EBVV; NAEL-6v2 *Fr.* In Memoriam A. H. H.

Bar of steel—it is only, A. Carl Sandburg. AiP *Fr.* Smoke and Steel.

Bar on the Piccola Marina, A. Noël Coward. NBLV
  (In a "bijou" abode.) ReLy

Bar Room Conversation. James Keir Baxter. PeLV *Fr.* Cressida.

Barabbas, Judas Iscariot. Morning After, The. Dorothy Wellesley, Duchess of Wellington. OBMV

Barb'd blossoms of the guarded gorse. Song of Winter, A. Emily Jane Pfeiffer. OBWVE

Barbara. Jacques Prévert. AF

Barbara. Jacques Prévert. MFP, *tr. by* Martin Sorrell

Barbara Allen. *Unknown.* EBNV
  (Barbara Allen's Cruelty.) OBEV

Barbara Frietchie. John Greenleaf Whittier. APN-1; AiP; CBCWP; CTC; ColAP; EBNV; HHAm; ITBLP; NCAP; NOBA; OBAL; OBCA; OxIBACP; TFi

Barbara remember. Barbara. Jacques Prévert. MFP, *tr. by* Martin Sorrell

Barbarian. Mohammed Khaïr-Eddine. PFTM-2, *tr. by* Pierre Joris

Barbarian pass is filled with windblown sand, The. Li Po. ChinPo, *tr. by* Yip Wai-lim

Barbarian Suite. Marilyn Chin. OpBo

Barbarians in a garden, softness does. In the Grounds. Douglas Dunn. NoP-4

Barbarossa. Friedrich Rückert. AWP, *tr. by* Elizabeth Craigmyle

Barbarossa. Hubert Witheford. PeNZ

Barbed Wire Fence Meditates upon the Goldfinch, A. Don McKay. NOBC

Barbed wire fences, harsh death bearing. Song of Dachau. Jura Soyfer. AuPH, *tr. by* Lowell A. Bangerter

Barbed-wire / is the cloak of saints. Our Ashes. Horst Bienek. AF

Barbells of the Gods, The. Mark Cox. OPRER

Barber, The. John Gray. NOBVV

Barber, barber, shave a pig. Mother Goose. LB; OxNR; ReMoGo

Barber is cutting the hair, A. Self-Portrait at Thirty-Nine. Ted Kooser. PBCAP

Barber shaved the mason, The. *Unknown.* OxNR

Barbershop Ritual. Sharan Strange. ISC; InTrad

Barbie at the end of the mind, The. Of Mere Plastic. David Trinidad. KGB

Barbie Doll. Marge Piercy. NIL-7; NIP-4

Barbie's Molester. Denise Duhamel. ReTh

Barbie Says Math Is Hard. Kyoko Mori. InvLad; ReTh

Barbizon, The. Nicole Brossard.
  Barbizon Hotel for Women, The. PFTM-2, *tr. by* Barbara Godard
  Temptation, The. PFTM-2, *tr. by* Barbara Godard

Barcarolle. May Probyn. VWP

Barcelona Days. Jaime Manrique. WiU, *tr. by* Edith Grossman

Bard. Gavin Bantock. FaBoTw

Bard is buried here, not strong, but sweet, A. Edward Cracroft Lefroy. AWP *Fr.* Echoes from Theocritus.

Bard, The [A Pindaric Ode]. Thomas Gray. GTBS-P; NOBE; NOEC; OxAEP-1

Bard whom pilf'red pastorals reknown, The. Pope. OBSV *Fr.* Epistle to Dr. Arbuthnot.

Bards, The. Walter De la Mare. NOBL

Bards of passion and of mirth. Ode. John Keats. FHYEP; OBEV; OxAEP-2

Bards of Wales, The. János Arany. IQMS, *tr. by* Peter Zollman

Bare Almond-Trees. D. H. Lawrence. FaBoVe

Bare branches tremble, The. Tzu Yeh. WPOW; WoPoe, *tr. by* Chung Ling and Kenneth Rexroth

Bare bulb, a scatter of nails, The. Ulster Twilight, An. Seamus Heaney. CIP-2; PBCIP

Bare Fig-trees. D. H. Lawrence. FaBoVe

Bare Floors. Melanie Hope. WiU

Bare-handed, I hand the combs. Stings. Sylvia Plath. NALW

Bare hands wash. Tonight I Thank the Potato. Robert Stewart. SpudSo

Bare oaks rock and snowcrust tumbles down, The. Thoughts Before Dawn. John Balaban. CDa

Bare Rocks and Stars. *Vietnamese Oral Tradition.* CaDao, *tr. by* John Balaban

Bare skin is my wrinkled sack. Shrouded Stranger, The. Allen Ginsberg. NeAP

Bare trees, The / alternate. Larry Eigner. PoM

Bare Windows. Martha Rhodes. ExTi

Barefaced baby with the three minute dream. Song: Miss Penelope Burgess, Balling the Jack. Thomas McGrath. MiVo

Barefoot and ragged, with neglected hair. On a Fair Beggar. Philip Ayres. EnLoPo

Barefoot Boy, The. John Greenleaf Whittier. APN-1; BRP; OBAL; OBCA
"Oh for boyhood's painless play." AiP

Barefoot Homiletics, after Wittgenstein and Boswell. Alan Dugan. BodElec

Barefoot I went and made no sound. Viper, The. Ruth Pitter. FaBoTw

Barefoot in the City. Lisa Buscani. AmPoNex

Barefoot through clover. Alexis Rotella. HA

Barefoot through the bazaar. Sindhi Woman. Jon Stallworthy. OxBC

Barefoot without a stitch she walks. Dance with Banderillas. Richard Duerden. NeAP

Barely a twelvemonth after. Horses, The. Edwin Muir. CABP; EmeKit; HAP; HeIP-4; MoBrPo; NOBE; NPeEn; NePenScot; NoAM; OxBTC; PoE; RB; TRP; WeW-3

Barely fifty, but already my face is old, hair white. Running from Trouble. Tu Fu. CrYelRi, tr. by Sam Hamill

Barely through. For Thurman Thomas. Reuben Jackson. ISC

Barely tolerated, living on the margin. Soonest Mended. John Ashbery. HCAP; NAAL-2v2; NAAL-5; PoetW; VCAP

Barely twelve years old. In Memory of My Arab Grandmother. Evelyn Arcad Zerbe. WPOW

Bargain, The. Sir Philip Sidney. NOBE; OBEV; OxAEP-1 Fr. Arcadia.

Bargain Sale, A. Samuel Ellsworth Kiser. PoToHe

Bargain with the Watchman. Eva Salzman. MFPA

Barge glided, The. Vision. Israel Zangwill. TrJP

Barge she sat in, like a burnish'd throne, The. William Shakespeare. SCV Fr. Antony and Cleopatra.

Barges on the Hudson. Babette Deutsch. WPE

Bark leaps love-fraught from the land, The. Charles Sangster. NOBC Fr. St. Lawrence and the Saguenay.

Bark of the rubgub [or rubagub] tree, The. (LL) Charles Edward Carryl. NBLV; OBCA Fr. Davy and the Goblin.

Bark-stripped and leafless. Disguised. Martha Rhodes. UrbNat

Bark went forth, with the morning's smile, A. Francis Fisher Browne. VWP Fr. Australian Emigrant, The.

Barks the melancholy dog. Wakeful in the Township. Elizabeth Riddell. NOBAu

Barley-Break, A. Sir John Suckling. BASC; CaPo; CavPo

Barley-Break; or, Last in Hell. Robert Herrick. CaPo

Barley-reaping song / Smith's hammer. Takai Kito. ZenPo, tr. by Takashi Ikemoto and Lucien Stryk

Barley's season / Dust mutes. Tan Taigi. ZenPo, tr. by Takashi Ikemoto and Lucien Stryk

Barman vaulted the counter, The. True Story Ending in False Hope, A. Pearse Hutchinson. PBCIP

Barn, The. Edmund Charles Blunden. MoBrPo

Barn, The. Elizabeth Jane Coatsworth. OBCP

Barn, The. Seamus Heaney. HAP

Barn, The. "Rachel" [or "Rahel"]. FIT, tr. by Robert Friend

Barn and the Down, The. Edward Thomas. OxBEV

Barn Fire. Thomas Lux. LCAP-2

Barn Owl. Leslie Norris. AngWePo

Barn's burnt down. Masahide. ZenPo, tr. by Takashi Ikemoto and Lucien Stryk

Barn-yard, The. Sheila Cussons. PeSAV, tr. by Johann de Lange

Barney Bigard. Suzanne Noguere. FFC

Barney Bodkin broke his nose. Unknown. OxNR

Barney Google. Billy Rose. OBAL

Barney McGee. Richard Hovey. OBAL

Barns huddle over the horns. November Harvest. Anita Endrezze. HATNAP

Barnsley and District. Donald Davie. NoAM; OxBC

Barnyard, The. Yvor Winters. APT-2

Barnyard Melodies. Fred Emerson Brooks. OBAL

Barometer of my moods today, mayfly. Mayfly. Louis MacNeice. ModIr

Baron has decided to mate the monster, The. Bride of Frankenstein, The. Edward Field. CoAP; HeIP-4; ReTh

Baron o [or of] Leys, The. Unknown. ESPB; OxBB

Baron of Brackley, The. Unknown. ESPB; OxBB

Baron of the sea, the great tropic, A. Marvel, The. Keith Douglas. RB

Baron-Samedi. René Depestre. PFTM-2, tr. by Joan Dayan Fr. Rainbow for the Christian West, A.

Barones and burgieses and bandemen als. William Langland. FaBoVe Fr. Vision of Piers Plowman, Prologue, The.

Baroque. Marie-Claire Bancquart. MFP, tr. by Martin Sorrell

Baroque Comment. Louise Bogan. APT-2

Baroque Exterior. "Ern Malley." BMAP

Baroque Sunburst, A. Amy Clampitt. ColAP

Baroque Wall-Fountain in the Villa Sciarra, A. Richard Wilbur. ColAP; GS; NAAL-2v2; NoP-4; OBGa; TwCP; VCAP

Barques we ride on over the sea. Trees, The. Bill Manhire. PeNZ

Barracks Apt. 14. Theodore Weiss. CoAP; TAP

Barracks-square, washed clean with rain, The. In Barracks. Siegfried Sassoon. FaBoTw

Bar[re] close as you can, and bolt fast too your door[e]. No Lock against Lechery. Robert Herrick. CaPo

Barred owls scream in the black pines, The. Owls. Louise Erdrich. TRP

Barrel Organ, The. Daniel Mark Epstein. DiPo Fr. Homage to Mallarmé.

Barrel-Organ, The. Alfred Noyes. BRP; MoBrPo; PoRA

Barrel-Organ, The. Arthur Symons. NOBVV

Barrelful of phlegm, A. Masaoka Shiki. JDP, tr. by Yoel Hoffmann

Barrels of blue potato-spray, The. Spraying the Potatoes. Patrick Kavanagh. BIrV; CABP

Barrels of the rifles turned, The. On Reconnaissance. Mikhail Arkadyevich [or Arkad'evich] Svetlov. TCRP, tr. by Daniel Weissbort

Barren. "Rachel" [or "Rahel"]. TrJP, tr. by L. V. Snowman

Barren branches. Kagai. JDP, tr. by Yoel Hoffmann

Barren Moors, The. William Ellery Channing. APN-1

Barren patch to the right of the cemetery, A. Reading Hamlet. Anna Andreyevna Akhmatova. PoetW, tr. by Max Hayward and Stanley Kunitz

Barren soil, the evil men, the slag and hideous rot, The. (LL) Rounded Catalogue Divine Complete, The. Walt Whitman. NAAL-2v1; NAAL-3

Barren Soul, A. Joseph Ezobi. TrJP, tr. by D. I. Friedmann Fr. Silver Bowl, The.

Barren Spring. Dante Gabriel Rossetti. EBVV; NoP-4 Fr. House of Life, The.

Barren Tree, The. Llewelyn Wyn Griffith.
"From his own solitude to the world unheeding." OBWVE

Barren Woman. Sylvia Plath. OxBSP

Barricade—a wall—a stronghold, A. Breech, The. Michael McClure. NeAP

Barrier, The. Louis Lavater. NOBAu

Barrio Beateo. Jesse F. García. UnSA

Bars. Nicolás Guillén. TCLAP, tr. by Eric Orozco

Bar[']s Fight[, August 28, 1746]. Lucy Terry. BPo; BlSi; NAAAL

Bars on Eighth Avenue in Harlem, The. Harlem Gallery: From the Inside. Larry Neal. BPo; NBV

Bartender, make it straight and make it two. Ex-Judge at the Bar, An. Melvin B. Tolson. NAAAL

Barter. Marie Blake. PoToHe

Barter. Sara Teasdale. ITBLP; SoSe-8

Bartleme Fair. George Alexander Stevens. NOEC

Bartley Costello, eighty years old. Gaeltacht. Pearse Hutchinson. BIrV; ModIr; PBCIP

Bartók. Gyula Illyés. IQMS, tr. by Robert C. Kenedy

Bartók. László Nagy. IQMS, tr. by Adam Makkai

Barton in the Beans. Joanne Limburg. NeBl

Baruch. Bible, Apocrypha.
Path of Wisdom, The. TrJP

Baruch Spinoza. Jorge Luis Borges. WoPoe, tr. by Willis Barnstone

Baruch Spinoza of Amsterdam / was seized by a desire to reach God. Mr. Cogito Tells about the Temptation of Spinoza. Zbigniew Herbert. GI, tr. by John Carpenter

Bas Bleu; or, Conversation, The. Hannah More.
Cold Ceremony. ECWP
"Long was Society o'er-run." PEW

Bas-Relief. Carl Sandburg. ColAP

Base Details. Siegfried Sassoon. FaBoWar; MoBrPo; NPeEn; OxBEV; OxBSP; PeFWW

Base metal hanger by your master's thigh! One Writing against His Prick. Unknown. NOSC

Base of All Metaphysics, The. Walt Whitman. APN-1

Base Stealer, The. Robert Francis. NTCP

Base words are uttered only by the base. W. H. Auden. OxBSP; PeLV Fr. Shorts [1939–1947].

Baseball. Paul Hoover. MoASP

Baseball. Linda Pastan. MoASP

Baseball. Frank Dempster Sherman. OBCA

Baseball. Christopher Stanard. SpirFl

Baseball and Classicism. Tom Clark. PmAP

Baseball and Writing. Marianne Craig Moore. BoWoP; FaBoA; MoASP

Baseball Canto. Lawrence Ferlinghetti. MoASP

Based on a volume of / Japanese prints. (LL) From the Grove Press. Anthony Hecht. OBAL; OBCoV

Baseline pressure. Ulli Freer. Oth Fr. Dents.

Basement, The. Alan Shapiro. TaR

Bash on Basho: Six of the Best. Geoffrey Holloway. NLP

Bashert. Irena Klepfisz. AF
  "These words are dedicated to those who died." TaR
Bashful young fellow of Brighton, A. Limerick. E. O. Parrott. PeLi
Basho 1. Cees Nooteboom. TuT, *tr. by* Michael O'Loughlin
Basho 2. Cees Nooteboom. TuT, *tr. by* Michael O'Loughlin
Basho 3. Cees Nooteboom. TuT, *tr. by* Michael O'Loughlin
Basho 4. Cees Nooteboom. TuT, *tr. by* Michael O'Loughlin
Bashō, a Departure. Robert Hass. LoL
Bashō, coming. Snow Party, The. Derek Mahon. CIP-2; HarvBoo; ModIr; NPeEn; OxBC; PBCIP; PNI
Bashō says the body is composed of one hundred bones and nine openings. Midsummer. Nicholas Christopher. UrbNat
Basia. "Johannes Secundus."
  Kisses, The. EroLit, *tr. by* Wayland Young
  "Not alwayes give a melting kiss." OBVE
Basic Science. Fanny Howe. ExTi
Basics. James Dickey. BodElec
Basis then, of belief: base 10? base alphabet? base, The. St. Anzas IX. B. P. Nichol. FTOS
Basket Case. Basil T. Paquet. CDa; FaBoWar
Basket of dirty clothes, A. Repetition of Words and Weather. Ruth Stone. BoWoP
Basket of Summer Fruit, A. Charles Harpur. NOBAu
Basketball. Nikki Giovanni. NOxBChV
Basketball. Louis Jenkins. MoASP
Basketball. Ronald Wallace. PBCAP
Basketball is like this for young Indian boys, all arms and legs. Defending Walt Whitman. Sherman Alexie. AmPoNex
Baskets of ripe fruit in air. Gardener Janus Catches a Naiad. Dame Edith Sitwell. MoBrPo; OBGa
Basking close to the sun as they are able. Goldfish in the Garden Pond. Valerie Worth. NOxBChV
Basking Shark. Norman MacCaig. NePenScot
Bass, The. John A. Stone. BloBone
Bast Shoe, The. Nikolai Ivanovich Glazkov. TCRP, *tr. by* Daniel Weissbort
Bastard, The. Richard Savage.
  "In gayer hours, when high my fancy ran." NOEC; OBSV
Bastard from the Bush, The. *Unknown.* NOBAu
Bastard God, A! (LL) To the Christians. Francis Lauderdale Adams. ChIV-2; OxBS
Bastard Son is born with a tooth in his mouth and hair on his. Paavo Haavikko. WoPoe, *tr. by* Anselm Hollo *Fr.* Winter Palace, The.
Bastardly boy, sprung from some coward's loins. Christopher Marlowe. FaBoWar *Fr.* Tamburlaine the Great, Part 2.
Bastille, a Vision, The. Helen Maria Williams. RWP
Bat. D. H. Lawrence. GTBS-P; HAP
Bat, The. Emily Dickinson. NAAL-2v1; NAAL-3
Bat, The. Jane Kenyon. LoL
Bat, The. Theodore Roethke. APT-2; ChAP; OBCA; PAI
Bat, The. Dame Edith Sitwell. FaBoMo
Bat, bat, come under my hat. Mother Goose. OxNR; ReMoGo
Bat flits, A. Buson. EH, *tr. by* Robert Hass
Bat is born, A. Bats. Randall Jarrell. ChAP; NTCP; OBCA; PAI
Bat is dun with wrinkled Wings, The. Bat, The. Emily Dickinson. NAAL-2v1; NAAL-3
Bat on the Road, A. Seamus Heaney. PoE
Bat that blocks at close of play, The. Joyce Johnson. UV
Bat that flits at close of eve, The. William Blake. UV *Fr.* Auguries of Innocence.
Batalis and the Man, The. Virgil [*or* Vergil]. *See* Aeneid [*or* Eneados, *Aeneis*], The
Bateleur. Douglas Livingstone. PeSAV
Batellis [*or* Batalis] and the man I will descrive. Virgil [*or* Vergil]. OBVE, *tr. by* Gawin [*or* Gavin] Douglas *Fr.* Aeneid [*or* Eneados, *Aeneis*], The.
Bath. John Godfrey. FTOS
Bath. John Knoepfle. IllVoic
Bath, The. Robin Becker. PBCAP
Bath, The. Joel Oppenheimer. NeAP
Bath, The. Gary Snyder. NNaP; PmAP; TAP; VCAP
Bath-house bench pinched Graphicus' bottom, The. Strato [*or* Straton]. GrAn
Bath of Aphrodite. Brewster Ghiselin. APT-2
Bath; or, The Western Lass, The. Thomas D'Urfey [*or* Durfey].
  Dialogue, between Crab and Gillian. NOEC
Bath when you're born. Issa. EH, *tr. by* Robert Hass
Bathed by tree filtered sun. Zoo. Shuntaro Tanikawa. PoetW, *tr. by* Harold Wright
Bather whose clothing was strewed, A. Limerick. *Unknown.* PeLi

Bathers, The. W. S. Merwin. PoE
Bathhouse, The. Boris Abramovich Slutsky [*or* Slutskii]. TCRusP, *tr. by* Daniel Weissbort
Bathhouse, The. Boris Abramovich Slutsky [*or* Slutskii]. TCRP, *tr. by* J. R. Rowland
Bathing Girls, The. Tracey Herd. NeBl
Bathing My Mother. Frances Wilson. Prnts
Bathing the Infant. Su Tung-p'o (Su Shih). SuSp, *tr. by* Irving Y. Lo
Bathos, The. Richard Porson. FaBoEE
Bathroom. Elaine Feinstein. HarvBoo
Bathroom. Fanny Howe. ExTi
Bathroom, The. Group Therapy. Carolyn M. Rodgers. ISC
Bathsheba came out to the sun. Telling the Bees. Lizette Woodworth Reese. SWaP
Bathtub is white and full of strips, The. Kenneth Koch. NoAM *Fr.* Days and Nights.
Bathtub [*or* Bath Tub], The. Ezra Pound. NIP-4; TRP; WeW-3
Baton Rouge. Terre Haute. Boise. (LL) In the Elementary School Choir. Gregory Djanikian. OPRER; UnSA
Bats. Randall Jarrell. ChAP; NTCP; OBCA; PAI
Bats. Mary Oliver. HeIP-4
Bats. Dave Jeddie Smith. NoAM
Bats flitting here and there. Buson. EH, *tr. by* Robert Hass
Bats flying. Issa. EH, *tr. by* Robert Hass
Bats have no bankers and they do not drink. John Berryman. EmeKit *Fr.* Dream Songs.
Bats have not heard a word of their literary reputation. Enquiry Concerning the Bat, An. José Emilio Pacheco. TCLAP, *tr. by* Alastair Reid
Batt he gets children, not for love to reare 'em. Upon Batt. Robert Herrick. FaBoEE
Batter my heart, three-personed [*or* three person'd] God; for you. John Donne. BASC; CABP; ClHu; EBEV; FHYEP; FSCP; GSo; HAP; HeIP-4; InPK-5; InvLi; MeLP; NAEL-5v1; NAEL-6v1; NAEL-7v1; NIL-7; NIP-4; NOBE; NOSC; NPeEn; NoP-4; OxAEP-1; OxBSo; PAI; PBRV; PeECV; PoE; PoPoPo; SacPr; SoSe-8; Son; TFi; TOF; TrCP *Fr.* Holy Sonnets.
Battered and shiny like the moon. (LL) Shampoo, The. Elizabeth Bishop. APT-2; FaBoWP; HarvBoo; OxBC; VCAP
Battered Toddler, Page B6. Ellen Watson. OPRER
Batteries Out of Ammunition. Rudyard Kipling. WoPoe *Fr.* Epitaphs of the War [1914–1918].
Battery. Robin Morgan. GifTon
Battery woman. Pierre McOrlan. MFP, *tr. by* Martin Sorrell
Battle. John Davidson. CABP
Battle. Homer. OBVE, *tr. by* Tennyson *Fr.* Iliad, The.
Battle. Aleksandr Petrovich Tkachenko. ItGoST, *tr. by* Maia Tekses
Battle, A. Isabella Valancy Crawford. NOBC
Battle, The. Abraham Abulafia. WoPoe, *tr. by* Stanley Moss
Battle, The. Dan Pagis. FIT, *tr. by* Robert Friend
Battle, The. Louis Simpson. OBWP; PoWW
Battle at Horizon. Ben Marcus. HeMarv
Battle at the Edge of the Falls. César Moro. BLPSL, *tr. by* Rene de Costa, Rigas Kappatos and Eleni Paidoussi
Battle Autumn of 1862, The. John Greenleaf Whittier. CBCWP
Battle-Cry of Freedom, The. George Frederick Root. CBCWP
Battle Hymn of the Republic, The. Rafael Campo. NeAmPo
Battle Hymn [*or* Battle-Hymn] of the Republic, The. Julia Ward Howe. AH; APN-1; BRP; CBCWP; ColAP; FaBoA; HHAm; NOBA; NOCV; NoP-4; OBWP; PWR; SCV; SWaP; TAP; TCAPo; TFi; WPE
Battle is joined on the open plain. Sedulius Scottus. FaBoWar, *tr. by* James Carney *Fr.* Defeat of the Norsemen, The.
Battle Lines. John C. Schafer. CDa
Battle News. Samuel Hazo. CDa
Battle of Agincourt, The. Michael Drayton. EBNV; FaBoWar
  (Agincourt.) FaBoCh; OBEV; OxAEP-1
  (To the Cambro-Britons, and Their Harp, His Ballad of Agincourt.) BASC
Battle of Argoed Llwyfain, The. Taliesin. OBWVE, *tr. by* Anthony Conran
Battle of Aughrim, The. Richard Murphy.
  Casement's Funeral. ModIr; NOIV; PBCIP
  "Deep red bogs divided." CIP-2
  Green Martyrs. NOIV
  Luttrell. PBCIP
  Orange March. NOIV
  Planter. BIrV
  Rapparees. BIrV; NOIV; PBCIP
  Slate. PBCIP
  Wolfhound. NOIV
Battle of Blenheim, The. Robert Southey. BRP; FaBoWar; OBWP; TFi
  (After Blenheim.) GTBS-P; OxAEP-2; UV

(It was a summer evening.) CABP

('Twas a summer evening.) UV

Battle of Bothwell Bridge, The. *Unknown.* OxBB

(Bothwell Bridge.) ESPB

Battle of Brunanburh. *Unknown.* FaBoWar; OBVE; OBWP; PeVV, *tr. by* Tennyson

(Athelstan King.) CABP, *tr. by* Tennyson

Battle of Brunanburh. *Unknown.* AnOE, *tr. by* Charles Kennedy; ASW, *tr. by* Kevin Crossley-Holland

"Hēr Æoelstān cyning, eorla drihten." CABP

Battle of Finnsburg, The. *Unknown.* AnOE, *tr. by* Charles W. Kennedy

Battle of Flodden, The. *Unknown.* NoSic *Fr.* Scot[t]ish Field[e].

Battle of Gettysburg, The. Edgar Lee Masters. CBCWP

Battle of Harlaw, The. *Unknown.* ESPB

Battle of Inverlochy, The. *Unknown.* EMWP

Battle of Maldon, The. *Unknown.* AnOE; ASW; OBWP, *tr. by* Kevin Crossley-Holland0

(It was shattered.) OBWP, *tr. by* Kevin Crossley-Holland

"Courage shall grow keener, clearer the will." WoPoe, *tr. by* Michael Alexander

Battle of Murfreesboro. Allen Tate. FaBoA

Battle of Naseby, The. Thomas Babington Macaulay, 1st Baron Macaulay. FaBoWar; OxAEP-2

Battle of Niagara, The. John Neal.

"Fresher and fresher comes the air. The blue." APN-1

"It is that hour when listening ones will weep." APN-1

"O save thy children blue Ontario!" APN-1

"There's a fierce gray Bird, with a bending beak." APN-1

Battle of Otterburn [*or* Oterborne], The. *Unknown.* ESPB; IBB; OxBS

(It fell about the Lammas tide.) NePenScot

"At last these two stout erles did meet." FaBoWar

Battle of Philiphaugh, The. *Unknown.* ESPB

Battle of the Baltic. Thomas Campbell. GTBS-P; OBEV

Battle of the *Bonhomme Richard* and the *Serapis.* Walt Whitman. *See* Song of Myself

Battle of the Frogs and Mice, The. Homer.

"Ascend my shoulders, firmly keep thy seat." OBVE

Battle of the Kegs, The. Francis Hopkinson. OBAL

Battle of the Stars. Adah Isaacs Menken. CBWP-1

Battle of Valcour Island, The. Richard Kenney. YaYoPo

Battle of Waun Gaseg, The. Llywelyn ab y Moel. OBWVE, *tr. by* H. Idris Bell

Battle of Wills Disguised, A. Marge Piercy. HeIP-4

Battle on the Blackbird's Field, The. Vasco [*or* Vasko] Popa. PoSu; WoPoe, *tr. by* Anne Pennington *Fr.* Blackbird's Field, The.

Battle [*or* Battel] of the Summer-Islands, The. Edmund Waller.

"Aid me Bellona, while the dreadful fight." BeJo

Battle, Over and Over Again, The. Safiya Henderson-Holmes. UnSA

Battle rent a cobweb diamond-strung, The. Range-finding. Robert Frost. NIL-7; NIP-4; NoAM; OBWP; RB

Battle Report. Bob Kaufman. ISC; TTY

Battle-Retrospect. Amos Niven Wilder.

"Those sultry nights we used to pass outdoors." YaYoPo

Battle's uncertain work begins; and move. Luis de Camões [*or* Camões]. FaBoWar, *tr. by* Richard Burton *Fr.* Lusiads, The.

Battle Song. Ebenezer Elliott. OxAEP-2

Battle Song. Macuilxochitl. WPOW, *tr. by* Catherine Rodriguez-Nieto

Battle Song. Shaka, King of the Zulus. PeSAV, *tr. by* Henry Francis Fynn

Battle Summers, The. Herman Melville. APN-2

Battle swayed, The. Christopher Logue. FaBoWar *Fr.* War Music.

Battle waged strong, The. Release, The. Adah Isaacs Menken. CBWP-1

Battle Won Is Lost. Phillip [*or* "Phil"] William George. HHAm

Battledore. John Gray. NOBVV

Battlefield. Richard Aldington. OBWP

Battlefield. August Stramm. PeFWW

(Clods' friability lulls iron to sleep.) PFTM-1

Battles of Joshua. *Unknown.* VerBaPo

Battue of Berlin, The. Harry Graham.

"It was a winter's morning." UV

Batyushkov. Osip Emilevich Mandelstam [*or* Mandelshtam]. OBVE

Baubles, Bangles, and Beads. Alexander Borodin. ReLy

Baucis. Erinna. AWP, *tr. by* Richard Garnett

Baucis and Philemon. Ovid. NOSC, *tr. by* John Dryden *Fr.* Metamorphoses.

Baucis and Philemon. Jonathan Swift. NOEC

Baudelaire. Delmore Schwartz. TwCP; VGW

Baudelaire, dead broke, nonetheless allowed himself. Baudelaire's Ablutions. Roger Fanning. NAPBL

Baudelaire in Brussels. Anthony Cronin. BIrV

Baudelaire's Ablutions. Roger Fanning. NAPBL

Baudelaire's Spleen. Jaime Manrique. WiU

Baudelaire Series. Michael Palmer.

"Here the image of a child on a hill." APSN

Baudelaire took the train. Radiant Silhouette III. John Yau. OpBo

Bavarian Gentians. D. H. Lawrence. CABP; FaBoCh; FaBoMo; GTBS-P; HAP; HarvBoo; InPK-6; NAEL-5v2; NAEL-6v2; NOBE; NPeEn; NoAM; NoP-4; OxBEV; PAI; PoE; PoPoPo; TFi; TRP; TTTS

Baviad, The. William Gifford.

"Lo, Della Crusca! In his closet pent." NOBRP

Baxter Bickerton of Burlington. On Learning to Adjust to Things. John Ciardi. KaS; OBCA

Bay, The. James Keir Baxter. HarvBoo; PeNZ

Bay breeze, The. Salt. George Barlow. GT

Bay of Tsunu, The. Kakinomoto no Hitomaro. OHPJ

Bay Poem. Lance Henson. VoR

Bay Psalm Book, The. Bible, *O.T.*

Psalm 1: "O Blessed man, that in th'advice." SCAP

Psalm 19: "Heavens doe declare / The majest of God, The. SCAP

Psalm 23: "Lord to mee [*or* mee] a shepherd is, The." OBCA; TCAPo

Psalm 103: "O Thou my soule, Jehovah blesse." SCAP

Psalm 107: "O Give yee thanks unto the Lord." SCAP

Psalm 121: "I to the hills lift up mine eyes." OBCA

Bay's little waves licked the ankles, The. Grandmother. Eva Salzman. MFPA

Bay steed of your stable could not be caught in a portrait, The. Song of the Bay Steed of Governor Wei, A. Ts'en Shen. SuSp, *tr. by* Daniel Bryant

Bay the color of steel, of a warship, The. Rain. Roo Borson. NoP-4

Bay undz is es geven andersh. I knew nothing. My Mother's Sabbath Days. Irena Klepfisz. TaR

Bayer's children's aspirin is cheaper. Aspirin. Elizabeth Alexander. AmPoNex

Baying, The. James Bertolino. UrbNat

Bayonet Training. Vernon Scannell. FaBoWar

Bayonne Turnpike to Tuscarora. Allen Ginsberg. NNaP

BC : AD. U. A. Fanthorpe. OBCP; OxBEV

Be a Balm. Ilya Abu Madi. GraLe, *tr. by* George Dimitri Selim

Be a balm when time turns into a speckled snake. Be a Balm. Ilya Abu Madi. GraLe, *tr. by* George Dimitri Selim

Be a beggar, be a thief. Be Anything (But Be Mine). Irving Gordon. ReLy

Be a facilitator, not a roadblock, says the lady who runs the news stand. Spring Forward, Fall Back. Alpay Ulku. AmPoNex

Be a loafer / Wash off the dust of fame and gain in the vast waves. Lu Chih. SuSp *Fr.* Tune: "Pleasure in Front of the Hall."

Be a Painter. Joe Lothamer. GeoH

Be against all sorts of mortmain. (LL) Commission. Ezra Pound. BoLoP; TwCP

Be ahead of all parting, as though it already were. Rainer Maria Rilke. EnlH *Fr.* Sonnets to Orpheus.

Be all serene, thou dull inclement Sky. On a Friend's Taking a Journey. Elizabeth Teft. PoBW

Be always in time. *Unknown.* OxNR

Be an unlikely treasure hoard. (LL) Seafarer, The. Ezra Pound. APT-1; CTC; FaBoTw; HeIP-4; NoP-4; OxBA; TCAPo; WoPoe

Be Anything (But Be Mine). Irving Gordon. ReLy

Be assured, the Dragon is not dead. Vanity. Robert Graves. GTBS-P

Be attentive to this trembling shade. Be Attentive. Natan Zach. PoSu, *tr. by* Peter Everwine and Shulamit Yasny-Starkman

Be Bold! That's One Way. Archilochus. WoPoe, *tr. by* Guy Davenport

Be-Bop Boys. Langston Hughes. APSN; APT-2; OBAL

Be born a saint; or keep. Be Born a Saint. Pearse Hutchinson. PBCIP

Be Brothers. Ifi Amadiume. HAWP

Be Careful. *Unknown.* NBLV

Be careful. Open your life. Be Careful. Natan Zach. PoSu

"Be cheerful, sir:" William Shakespeare. EnlH *Fr.* Tempest, The.

Be composed—be at ease with me—I am Walt Whitman, liberal and lusty as Nature. To a Common Prostitute. Walt Whitman. MoAmPo

Be dark enough thy shades, and be thou more content. (LL) Introduction: "Did I, my lines intend for public[k] view, The." Anne Finch, Countess of Winchilsea. BWW; EMWP; NAEL-5v1; NAEL-6v1; NAEL-7v1; NALW; WPOW

Be dumb ye infant chimes, thump not the metal. Great Tom. Richard Corbet [*or* Corbett]. OxBoLi

Be ever meek and humble, nor essay. Meek and the Proud, The. Abraham Ibn-Chasdai. TrJP, *tr. by* J. Chotzner

Be extra careful by this door. Whisperer, The. Mark Van Doren. MoAmPo

Be faithful Go. (LL) Envoy of Mr. Cogito, The. Zbigniew Herbert. PoetW; WoPoe, *tr. by* Carpenter Bogdana, John Carpenter and Bogdana Carpenter

Be free of fruit to all. (LL) Of Caution. Francesco da Barberini. AWP; EaltPo, *tr. by* Dante Gabriel Rossetti

Be Frugal. Richard Church. OxBSP; OxBTC

Be gentle when the wind and dark waves come. When the Wind and Dark Waves Come. David J. Rothman. GeoH

Be glad, of all maidens floure. *Unknown.* MiEL

Be glaid, al ye that luvaris bene. Four May Poems. *Unknown.* OxBS

Be Glorified Eternally. Balthasar Hoffman. AH, *tr. by* Sheema Z. Buehne

Be gone, have done! Down, wanton, down! (LL) Down, Wanton, Down! Robert Graves. BoLoP; FaBoTw; HarvBoo; HeIP-4; InPK-6; NAEL-5v2; NAEL-6v2; NoAM; PoE

Be good. For Starters. Victoria McCabe. CRP

Be good, my Lord, since you can not be pretty. (LL) Lord Barrenstock. Stevie Smith. NALW; NBLV; OBSV

Be good to those who come after us. (LL) Eavesdropper. Breyten Breytenbach. PeSAV; PoetW, *tr. by* Ernst Van Heerden

Be governour baith guid and gratious. To the Queen. Henry Stuart [*or* Stewart], Lord Darnley. OxBS

Be happy, be happy again. Song of Delight. Shao Yung. CoBCP, *tr. by* Burton Watson

Be happy for me, girls, / my mother-in-law is dead! Traditional Women's Song of Algeria. *Unknown.* BoWoP, *tr. by* Willis Barnstone

Be He Ezra Pound, Kennedy, or King. Belle Randall. GifTon

Be his memory forever green and rich. Baal Shem Tov. Abraham Moses Klein. TrJP

Be hopeful, friend, when clouds are dark and days are. Be Hopeful. Strickland W. Gillilan. PoToHe

Be hushed, all voices and untimely laughter. Dead March, A. Mary C. Gillington. PeVV

Be in me as the eternal moods. Doria. Ezra Pound. MoAmPo

Be Indomitable, O My Heart. Nezahualcoyotl. WoPoe, *tr. by* Thelma D. Sullivan

Be it right or wrong, these men among. Nut-brown Maid, The. *Unknown.* NoSic; OBEV

Be it so, for I submit; his doom is fair. John Milton. NAWM-5v1 *Fr.* Paradise Lost.

Be just (domestics monarchs) unto them. George Alsop. SCAP

Be Kind. Margaret Courtney. PoToHe

Be kind and tender to the Frog. Frog, The. Joseph Hilaire Pierre Belloc. ChAP; NOxBChV; NTCP

Be kind / Be iron. Leonid Nikolaevich Martynov. TCRP

Be kind to her. To End Her Fear. John Freeman. OBMV

Be kind to thy father: for when thou were young. Be Kind. Margaret Courtney. PoToHe

Be kind to yourself, it is only one. Who Be Kind To. Allen Ginsberg. NNaP

Be land ready. Be Ready. Carl Sandburg. NOxBChV

Be lesse anothers Laurell, then thy praise. (LL) To His Honoured and Most Ingenious Friend Mr. Charles Cotton. Robert Herrick. CaPo; NOSC

Be life what it has been, and let us hold. To His Wife. Ausonius. AWP, *tr. by* Terrot Reaveley Glober

Be like God. (LL) Jack Spicer. NeAP; PmAP *Fr.* Imaginary Elegies.

Be Like the Bird. Victor Hugo. Spl

Be literal a moment. Recollect. Seamus Heaney. PoetW *Fr.* Squarings.

Be loved, my beloved. Spell for Jealousy. Jeni Couzyn. HAWP

Be many, and a blessing to mankind. (LL) William Wordsworth. FHYEP; NAEL-6v2 *Fr.* Prelude Growth of a Poet's Mind, The; [1850 vers.].

Be merciful to me, a fool! (LL) Edward Rowland Sill. APN-2; ITBLP

Be Merry. *Unknown.* RB

Be'mi'ster. William Barnes. EBVV

Be my stillborn son my son. Mulatto Lullaby. Ralph Dickey. ESEAA

Be near me when my light is low. Tennyson. CABP; EBVV; HAP; HeIP-4; NAEL-6v2; NAWM-7v2; NOCV; PeECV; SCGP; SCV *Fr.* In Memoriam A. H. H.

Be Never Discouraged. Daniel C. Colesworthy. PWR

Be not afeard: the isle is full of noises. William Shakespeare. OxAEP-1; RB *Fr.* Tempest, The.

Be not afraid of my body. (LL) As Adam Early in the Morning. Walt Whitman. APN-1; ChIV-1; ColAP; OxBA; PAI; SAmP

Be not amazed beloved, if sometimes my song grows dark. Be Not Amazed. Léopold Sédar Senghor. PBMAP

Be Not Silent. David ben Meshullam. TrJP

Be not thou so foolish nice. Invitation to Dalliance. *Unknown.* FaBoEE

Be not too wise, nor too foolish. Instructions of King Cormac. Cormac, King of Cashel. PoToHe

Be of Good Cheer. Robert Creeley. BodElec

Be Off! Stevie Smith. OxBC

Be off, or I'll kick you downstairs! (LL) Lewis Carroll. ChAP; NOBL; NOBVV; NPeEn; OBCoV; OxBEV; PoRA; TFi; UnPo *Fr.* Alice's Adventures in Wonderland.

Be one, and one another's all. (LL) Lovers' Infiniteness[e]. John Donne. ESCV; MeLP; NOSC

Be Patient. "George Klingle." PoToHe

Be patient, Morning Star, with Love; though close. Macedonius. GrAn

Be patient, solemn nose. Precious Five. W. H. Auden. PeECV

Be perpendicular to the basket. Foul Shots: A Clinic. William Matthews. MoASP

Be plain in dress and sober in your diet. Summary of Lord Lyttleton's Advice to a Lady, A. Lady Mary Wortley Montagu. FaBoEE; OxBEV

Be punctual then to know. *Unknown.* NOEC *Fr.* Art of Wenching, The.

Be quiet awful woman. Calming Kali. Lucille Clifton. HW

Be Quiet, Go Away. Wanda Coleman. NAAAL

Be, rather than be called, a child of God. On an Infant Which Died before Baptism. Samuel Taylor Coleridge. SacPr

Be Ready. Carl Sandburg. NOxBChV

Be reasonable, my pain, and think with more detachment. Inward Conversation. Charles Baudelaire. InPK-6, *tr. by* Robert Bly

Be reckoned [*or* reckon'd] but with herbs and flowers [*or* flow'rs]. (LL) Garden, The. Andrew Marvell. AWP; BASC; ClHu; ESCV; FSCP; GeHe; HAP; MakPoe; MeLP; NAEL-5v1; NAEL-6v1; NAEL-7v1; NIL-7; NIP-4; NOBE; NOSC; NPeEn; OBGa; OxBEV; PBRV; PoE; PoPoPo; PoRA; SCGP; TFi; TOF; TRP

Be respectful / Sparrows. Issa. ZenPo, *tr. by* Takashi Ikemoto and Lucien Stryk

Be rude to strangers. / *moral*: Behave. (LL) Rules and Regulations. Lewis Carroll. NOBVV; PeVV

Be sad, be cool, be kind. Long Shadow of Lincoln: A Litany, The. Carl Sandburg. CBCWP

Be Sad, My Heart. Francis Quarles. NIP-4

Be seated, pray. "A grave appeal?" Virtuoso, A. Austin Dobson. PeVV

Be Seeing You. Vasco [*or* Vasko] Popa. PoSu, *tr. by* Anne Pennington *Fr.* Raw Flesh.

Be silent, hide yourself. Silentium. Fyodor [*or* Feodor] Ivanovich Tyutchev. WoPoe, *tr. by* Charles Tomlinson

Be silent, you still music of the spheres. On a Gentlewoman that Sung and Played upon a Lute. William Strode. NOSC

Be so—ashamed of them. (LL) Emily Dickinson. APN-2; HAP; MoAmPo; NALW; TCAPo; WPE

Be still: be still: nor dare. Holy Hill, A. "Æ" AWP

Be still, my soul, be still; the arms you bear are brittle. A. E. Housman. MoBrPo; NOBVV; SCGP

Be still, my soul: the Lord is on thy side. Be Still, My Soul. Katharina von Schlegel. SacPr, *tr. by* Jane Borthwick and Jane L. Borthwick

Be still O green cliffs of the Dryads. Inscription for a Statue of Pan. *Unknown.* GrAn, *tr. by* Dudley Fitts

Be still, sweet babe, no harm shall reach thee. To an Unborn Infant. Isabella Kelly. ECWP

Be Still. The Hanging Gardens Were a Dream. Trumbull Stickney. APN-2; WoPoe

Be still. / Wait. (LL) Theodore Roethke. APT-2; HAP; HCAP; NAAL-2v2; NoP-4; TRP; VGW

Be still, while the music rises about us: the deep enchantment. At a Concert of Music. Conrad Potter Aiken. MoAmPo

Be stirring, girls! we ought to have a run. Franco Sacchetti. EaltPo, *tr. by* Dante Gabriel Rossetti

Be Strong. Maltbie Davenport Babcock. AH; ITBLP; PWR; SoSe-8

Be strong, brother! Imre Madách. IQMS, *tr. by* Iain MacLeod *Fr.* Tragedy of Man.

Be sure observe where brown Ostrea stands. John Gay. OxBEV *Fr.* Trivia; or, The Art of Walking the Streets of London.

Be sweetened by a strange tree. (LL) Magic Apple Tree, The. Elaine Feinstein. BrRo; HarvBoo

Be Swift O Sun. Ronald Allison Kells Mason. PeNZ

Be the mistress[e] of my choice. What Kind of Mistress[e] He Would Have. Robert Herrick. CaPo

Be the proud Thames of trade the busy mart! To the River Arun. Charlotte Smith. RWP

Be thine. Even so. (LL) Canzone: Of His Dead Lady. Giacomino Pugliesi. AWP; EaltPo, *tr. by* Dante Gabriel Rossetti

Be this was said a grondyn dart leit he glide. Virgil [*or* Vergil]. NPeEn, *tr. by* Gawin [*or* Gavin] Douglas *Fr.* Aeneid [*or* Eneados, Aeneis], The.

Be thorough in your scholarship. Tiruvalluvar. WoPoe, *tr. by* Emmons E. White *Fr.* Kural, The.

Be tied to the halberds, or grating, and whipped. Lay of the Lash, The. *Unknown.* FaBoWar

Be True [*or* Be True Thyself]. Horatius Bonar. PWR

BE2c is my 'bus; therefore I shall want, The. Pilot's Psalm, The. *Unknown.* PoWW

Be uncovered! / Hoe with look life! Sun rises. Wild Provoke of the Endurance Sky. Joseph Ceravolo. BodElec

Be unexpected Friends. (LL) Emily Dickinson. ChIV-2; SacPr

Be wise as thou art cruel; do not press. William Shakespeare. NoSic *Fr.* Sonnets.

Be with me, Beauty, for the fire is dying. On Growing Old. John Masefield. MoBrPo; PoRA

Be with me, Luis de San Angel, now. Hart Crane. NOBA; NoAM *Fr.* Bridge, The.

Be You. Norman Jordan. NBV

Be your words made (good sir) of Indian ware. Sir Philip Sidney. NoSic *Fr.* Astrophil and Stella.

Beacause God's gifts put man's best dreams to shame. (LL) Elizabeth Barrett Browning. BWW; CenSon *Fr.* Sonnets from the Portuguese.

Beach. Sophia De Mello Breyner. VCWP, *tr. by* Ruth Fainlight

Beach. Tiziano Rossi. ItPo, *tr. by* Gayle Ridinger

Beach. Shinkichi Takahashi. ZenPo, *tr. by* Takashi Ikemoto and Lucien Stryk

Beach, The. Douglas Goetsch. AmPoNex

Beach, The. Robert Graves. OxBSP

Beach, The. Peter Scupham. HarvBoo

Beach Burial. Kenneth Slessor. CBAP

Beach Glass. Amy Clampitt. FaBoWP; NoAM; NoP-4; VCAP

Beach in August, The. Weldon Kees. VGW

Beach, Later. Dennis Saleh. GeoHom

Beachcomber. George Mackay Brown. OxBC

Beaches. "Robin Hyde."
  "Close under here, I watched two lovers once." FaBoWP; PeNZ
  "Cool and certain, their oars will be lifted in dusk." PeNZ

Beaches of Chile were only a nickname, The. Sparkling Beaches, The. Raúl Zurita. TCLAP, *tr. by* Jack Schmitt

Beachy Head. Hilary Davies. Prnts

Beachy Head. Charlotte Smith. RWP
  "Early worshipper at Nature's shrine, An." MakPoe
  From Beachy Head. NOBRP; NoP-4
  "*I* once was happy, when while yet a child." PEW; WPE

Beacons from the abode where the Eternal are. (LL) Shelley. EBEV; FHYEP; NAEL-6v2; NOBRP; OxAEP-2; TFi

Beadle's Testimony, The. Jerome Rothenberg. NNaP

Beads of spring rain. Helen C. Acton. HA

Beagles. William Robert Rodgers. FaBoTw

Beaks evolved for gutter cracks, handouts. Pigeons. Daniel Tobin. UrbNat

Beaks of Eagles, The. Robinson Jeffers. NOBA

Beale Street Blues. William Christopher Handy. APT-1

Beam 4. Ronald Johnson. APSN *Fr.* Ark.

Beam 7. Ronald Johnson. APSN *Fr.* Ark.

Beam 25, a Bicentennial Hymn. Ronald Johnson. APSN *Fr.* Ark.

Beam 30, the Garden. Ronald Johnson. FTOS *Fr.* Ark.

Beam of light in the mouth of azure, A. Scene for the Mornings Preceding the Fire, A. Ghada El-Shafa'i. PoArWo, *tr. by* Atef Abu-Seif and Nathalie Handal

Beaming flowers in the thicket. Orchard Pavilion. Wang Pin-chih. ChinPo, *tr. by* Yip Wai-lim

Beams. Audre Lorde. ESEAA; NoAM

Beams. Paul Verlaine. SxFrPo, *tr. by* Martin Sorrell

Bean Eaters, The. Gwendolyn Brooks. AmFaPo; BlSi; ESEAA; HAP; HHAm; HeIP-4; LCAP-2; NALW; PoE; TAP; TRP; TTY; WeW-3

Bean Spasms. Ted Berrigan. PmAP; SPE
  (New York's lovely weather.) SPE

Bean-Stalk, The. Edna St. Vincent Millay. NOxBChV

Beans. Sean Dunne. ModIr *Fr.* Sydney Place.

Beans in blossom with their spots of jet, The. Field Path. John Clare. OxBSP

Beanstalk Country, The. Tennessee Williams. APT-2

Beanstalk, Meditated Later, The. Judith Wright. NoAM

Beanstalks, in any breeze, are a slack church parade. Broad Bean Sermon, The. Les A. Murray. BMAP; EmeKit; HarvBoo; MakPoe

Bear, The. Robert Frost. MoAmPo; NoAM

Bear, The. Ted Hughes. FaBoMo

Bear, The. Galway Kinnell. CoAP; MakPoe; NNaP; TAP; TRP; VCAP; VGW

Bear, The. Vladimir Aleksandrovich Lugovskoy [*or* Lugovskoi]. TCRP, *tr. by* Gordon McVay

Bear, The. N. Scott Momaday. CDW; HATNAP

Bear: A Totem Dance as Seen by Raven. Peter Blue Cloud. HATNAP

Bear and the Squirrels, The. Christopher Pearse Cranch. OBCA

Bear down / My Mother Country. Deliverance. Amelia Blossom Pegram. HAWP

Bear in mind. Drum. Langston Hughes. APT-2; MoAmPo

Bear me to Dictaeus. Acon. "H. D." VGW

Bear mother. Ursa Major. Federico García Lorca. PFTM-1

Bear my first thought, as waking, I hear. Night Walking. Robert Penn Warren. BodElec

Bear on the Delhi Road, The. Earle Birney. HeIP-4; MoCV; NOBC; NoAM; NoP-4

Bear [*or* Bare] that breath[e]s [*or* breaks] the northern blast the. Upon a Wasp Chilled [*or* Child] with Cold. Edward Taylor. NAAL-2v1; NAAL-3; NAAL-5; NOBA; NOCV; OxBEV

Bear puts both arms around the tree above her, The. Bear, The. Robert Frost. MoAmPo; NoAM

Bear's Blood. Ileana Malancioui. BoWoP, *tr. by* Stavros Deligiorgis

Bear's Song, The. *Unknown.* AWP, *tr. by* Constance Lindsay Skinner *Fr.* Three Songs from the Haida.

Bear sleeps in a cellarhole; pine needles, A. New Hampshire. Donald Hall. LCAP-2

Bear who eats with a silver spoon, A. Animal Acts. Charles Simic. LCAP-2

Bear with me. Elvis P. and Emma B. Elizabeth Ash Vélez. AllShUp

Beard-wagging stick-waving beggarman Cynic, A. Lucianus [*or* Lucian]. GrAn

Bearded Callistratus wedded rugged Afer. Martial. CAGL, *tr. by* Richard E. Prior *Fr.* Epigrams.

Bearded lady, The. Alan Pizzarelli. HA

Bearded Oaks. Robert Penn Warren. APT-2; ColAP; FuPo; MoAmPo; NAAL-2v2; NAAL-5; NOBA; NoAM; NoP-4; PAI; PoE; TAP; TwCP

Bearded Woman, by Ribera, The. Paul Muldoon. BiHa

Bearer of Evil Tidings, The. Robert Frost. NoAM; SAmP

Bearer's Song. Miu Hsi. ChiP, *tr. by* Arthur Waley

Bearers' Song. T'ao Ch'ien [*or* T'ao Yuan-ming]. ChinPo, *tr. by* Yip Wai-lim

Bearing no flowers. Chiyojo [*or* Chiyo *or* Chiyo-Ni *or* Kaga no Chiyo *or* Fukuda Chiyo-Ni]. NIL-7, *tr. by* Daniel C. Buchanan

Bearing so little ammunition. (LL) School Children, The. Louise Glück. ColAP; HCAP; PoPoPo; WeW-3

Bearing the bandages, water and sponge. Walt Whitman. FaBoWar *Fr.* Wound-Dresser, The.

Bearing the golden bough of Argicida. So that. (LL) Ezra Pound. MoAmPo; NAAL-5; NoAM; OBVE; PoE; VGW *Fr.* Cantos.

Bearing the lustre of a full moon. Bhartrihari. EroLit, *tr. by* Barbara Stoler Miller

Bearings III: Amber Wall. Wole Soyinka. PBMAP *Fr.* Shuttle in the Crypt, The.

Bears. Arthur Guiterman. PoRA

Bears. Adrienne Rich. PAI

Bears are kept by hundreds within fences, are fed cracked, The. Elizabeth's War with the Christmas Bear. Norman Dubie. LCAP-2; NoAM

Bears became cucumbers. Yury [*or* Iurii] Pavlovich Odarchenko. TCRP

Beast Flower. Yelena [*or* Elena] Shwarts [*or* Shvarts]. TCRP, *tr. by* Nina Kossman

Beast in Man, The. George Clutesi. HATNAP

Beast in the Space, The. William Sydney Graham. EmeKit; FaBoTw; OxAEP-2

Beast stands at my eye, A. Naked Land, The. Kenneth Patchen. SPE

Beast with Two Backs, The. Andrew Taylor. NOBAu

Beasts. Richard Wilbur. LCAP-2; TwCP

Beasts in the schoolroom, whose transparent faces, The. Blues for Warren. Thomas McGrath. AF

Beasts in their major freedom. Beasts. Richard Wilbur. LCAP-2; TwCP

Beat at the air till the light blows out. (LL) I Only Am Escaped Alone to Tell Thee. Howard Nemerov. CoAP; HeIP-4; NoAM

Beat! Beat! Drums! Walt Whitman. CBCWP; FaBoWar; HeIP-4; InPK-6; NAAL-2v1; NAAL-3; NAAL-5; NCAP; OBWP

Beat hell out of it. William Carlos Williams. APT-1; OxBA *Fr.* Paterson.

Beat It Night Dog. Aimé Césaire. NegPo, *tr. by* Clayton Eshleman and Denis Kelly

Beat out continuance in the choking veins. Blood Is Justified, The. Muriel Rukeyser. YaYoPo

Beat Poem by an Academic Poet. Vassar Miller. WPE

Beat the drums of skins. War Comes. Zalman Schneour. TrJP, *tr. by* Joseph Leftwich

Beat the knife on the plate and the fork on the can. Going In to Dinner. Edward Richard Burton Shanks. OBMV; OxBTC

Beata l'Alma. Sir Herbert Read. FaBoMo

Beaten Track, The. Steve Benson. FTOS

Beaten up. Justice Is Done. Oumar Ba. PBMAP

Beating, The. Ann Stanford. SoSe-8; WPE

Beating and beating at an intractable metal. (LL) Blackberrying. Sylvia Plath. HAP; HCAP; NAAL-2v2; NAAL-5; NOBA; NoAM; PoPoPo

Beating of a bloody fist upon / a splintered table. (LL) Ninth Symphony of

Beethoven Understood at Last as a Sexual Message, The. Adrienne Rich. PFTM-2; TAP

Beating the drum. Tattoo, The. Ania Walwicz. BMAP

Beatings. Joan Larkin. WiU

Beatings. Will Wells. GotH

Beatitudes. Bruce Dawe. GI

Beatitudes, The. Bible, *N.T.* OBVE *Fr.* St. Matthew.

Beatnik's Monologue, The. Andrey [*or* Andrei] Andreievich Voznesensky [*or* Voznesenskii]. TCRusP, *tr. by* Daniel Weissbort

Beatrice. J. Bernlef. TuT, *tr. by* Peter Van de Kamp

Beatrice lay naked on the narrow bed. Plot, The. William Dickey. YaYoPo

Beats the golden bird no more. (LL) Edna St. Vincent Millay. APT-1; MoAmPo; OxBA; PoRA *Fr.* Memorial to D. C.

Beau: Golden Retrievals. Mark Doty. Unle

Beau Ideal, The. Jessie Pope. FaBoWar

Beau's Reply. William Cowper. FaBoCh

Beaufort, fair Beaufort, thou art a favored spot. General Robert Smalls. Josephine D. Henderson Heard. CBWP-4

Beauharnois (1). Margaret Atwood. PoetW *Fr.* Four Small Elegies.

Beauharnois (3). Margaret Atwood. PoetW *Fr.* Four Small Elegies.

Beauharnois, Glengarry (2). Margaret Atwood. PoetW *Fr.* Four Small Elegies.

Beauing, belling, dancing, drinking. Rakes of Mallow, The. *Unknown.* OBCoV

Beaulieu. Clarence Major. FTOS

Beaumaris Bay. Richard Llwyd.
   "Here, still sequestered, Penmon's sacred dome." AngWePo

Beauté, La. Charles Baudelaire. AWP, *tr. by* Lord Alfred Bruce Douglas

Beauteous Ethel's father has a, The. Piazza Tragedy, A. Eugene Field. NBLV

Beauteous thou art, the spirit knows not how. Elsewhere. "Michael Field." VWP

Beauties of Nature, The. Robert Burns. TreFP

Beautiful. Diminutive. Carlos Drummond de Andrade. TCLAP, *tr. by* Virginia de Araújo

Beautiful, The. E. H. Burrington. TreFP

Beautiful, The. Mary E. Tucker. CBWP-1

Beautiful, accomplished, splendid—if he can be had—and brave. Verses Written by Alis Daughter of Gryffydd Son of Iefan When Her Father Asked Her What Sort of Husband She Would Like. Alis Ferch Gruffyd ab Ieuan ap Lleywelyn Fychan. EMWP

Beautiful, also, are the souls of my people. (LL) My People. Langston Hughes. APT-2; NOxBChV

Beautiful American Word, Sure, The. Delmore Schwartz. APT-2; VGW

Beautiful and dangerous. (LL) Slam, Dunk, and Hook. Yusef Komunyakaa. ISC; MoASP

Beautiful are the fingers of the loved one. When She Plays upon the Harp or Lute. Moses Ibn Ezra. TrJP, *tr. by* Solomon Solis-Cohen

Beautiful As. Lucie Thésée. SurWo, *tr. by* Myrna Bell Rochester

Beautiful as a high foamy wave spurting in a crystal ball. Beautiful As. Lucie Thésée. SurWo, *tr. by* Myrna Bell Rochester

Beautiful as a tiered cloud, skysails set and shrouds twanging. Clipper-Ships. John Gould Fletcher. TCAPo

Beautiful as the flying legend of some leopard. Judith of Bethulia. John Crowe Ransom. APT-1; FaBoMo; NOBA; NoAM

Beautiful as the pomegranate is the white face of Ophrah. Hot Flame of My Grief, The. Moses Ibn Ezra. TrJP, *tr. by* Solomon Solis-Cohen

Beautiful Beeshareen Boy, The. Mathilde Blind. VWP

Beautiful, black-eyed boy. Beautiful Beeshareen Boy, The. Mathilde Blind. VWP

Beautiful Black Men. Nikki Giovanni. BPo; NAAAL

Beautiful Black Women. Imamu Amiri Baraka. BPo; PoM

Beautiful boy, flower fair. To an English Boy. Hilary. EroLit, *tr. by* John Boswell

Beautiful cashier's white face has risen once more, The. Before the [*or* a] Cashier's Window in a Department Store. James Wright (1927–80). CoAP

Beautiful Changes, The. Richard Wilbur. CoAP; HCAP; NAAL-5; NIL-7; PoE

Beautiful, clear, July light. Dante Park. Miguel Algarin. PueRic

Beautiful Creatures Brief as These. Douglas G. Jones. MoCV

Beautiful Days. Mary Kinzie. ExTi

Beautiful, delicate bright gazelle, The. Love-song. Walter James Turner. OBMV

Beautiful element of unreason under it? (LL) Black Earth. Marianne Craig Moore. APT-1; FaBoMo

Beautiful Evelyn Hope is dead! Evelyn Hope. Robert Browning. TreFP

Beautiful excess of Jesus on the waters, The. To Swim, to Believe. Maxine W. Kumin. MoASP

Beautiful eyes of the dead, The. Carried Away. Anne Elder. CBAP

Beautiful faces are those that wear. Beautiful Things. Ellen Palmer Allerton. PWR

Beautiful from his tail-tip. Fox, The. Mary Oliver. PoCoUp

Beautiful girl is very young, The. In the Looking Glass. Anna Andreyevna Akhmatova. TCRP, *tr. by* Daniel Weissbort

Beautiful heights, joy of the world, city of a great king. Jerusalem. Judah Halevi. TOF, *tr. by* David Goldstein

Beautiful his peacock crown. In Praise of Krishna. Ruskhan. WoPoe, *tr. by* Stephen Schaffer and Allen Shapiro

Beautiful Imogene is finally alone, The. Harold and Imogene. Paul Violi. ReTh

Beautiful in the foregone drawing-room and the dance. Jane Austen. Patricia Beer. CABP

Beautiful IRELAND! Who will preach to thee? Who Will Show Us Any Good? Lady Jane Francesca Wilde. VWP

Beautiful is fair, the just is fair, The. Fair and Unfair. Robert Francis. VGW

Beautiful is she, this woman. *Unknown.* AWP, *tr. by* Constance Lindsay Skinner *Fr.* Three Songs from the Haida.

Beautiful Is the Loved One. Moses Ibn Ezra. TrJP, *tr. by* Solomon Solis-Cohen

Beautiful Ladies. Mcavoy Layne. CDa

Beautiful ladies through the orchard pass. Les Demoiselles de Sauve. John Gray. NOBVV; PeVV

Beautiful Land of Nod, The. Ella Wheeler Wilcox. PWR

Beautiful landscape, The. Garden at the General's Residence, The. Muso Soseki. EaWin, *tr. by* W. S. Merwin

Beautiful light down there. Evening Change. John Haines. GifTon

Beautiful Lunacy! that shapest flight. Thomas Tod Stoddart. NOBRP *Fr.* Death-Wake; or, Lunacy, The.

Beautiful maid of Delgo, I liked your face so black. Shu' Shu' of Delgo. Albert Brodrick. PeSAV

Beautiful Maid of the Mill, The. Wilhelm Müller.
   Whither? AWP, *tr. by* Henry Wadsworth Longfellow

Beautiful man and his wife, The. Window Dressing. William Peskett. PNI

Beautiful man is sleeping under a pine tree, A. Monk's Dream. Dave Etter. SeSe

Beautiful Melite, in the throes of middle age. Agathias. ErotSp, *tr. by* Sam Hamill

Beautiful miracle. Love Is Just around the Corner. Leo Robin. ReLy

Beautiful Mistress, A. Thomas Carew. CavPo

Beautiful music! / Dangerous rhythm! Continental (You Kiss While You're Dancing), The. Herb Magidson. ReLy

Beautiful must be the mountains whence ye come. Nightingales. Robert Bridges. MoBrPo; NOBE; OBEV; OBMV; SCGP; TFi; UnPo

Beautiful, my delight. To Be Sung on the Water. Louise Bogan. VGW

Beautiful natural blossoms. To a Beautiful Pear Tree. James Wright (1927–80). HAP

Beautiful new railway bridge of the Silvery Tay. William McGonagall. VerBaPo *Fr.* Address to the New Tay Bridge, An.

Beautiful, O so beautiful. Voice from the Bush—Through Me. Graham Brady. IBA

Beautiful Ones, The. Gonzalo Rojas. BLPSL, *tr. by* Rene de Costa, Rigas Kappatos and Eleni Paidoussi

Beautiful or Ugly It Doesn't Matter. Valentine Penrose. SurWo, *tr. by* Roy Edwards

Beautiful place is the town of Lo-yang, A. Lo-yang. Emperor Ch'ien Wen-Ti. AWP; ChiP, *tr. by* Arthur Waley

Beautiful railway bridge of the silv'ry Tay. Tay Bridge Disaster, The. William McGonagall. UV; VerBaPo

Beautiful Railway Bridge of the Silvery Tay! William McGonagall. NePenScot; VerBaPo *Fr.* Railway Bridge of the Silvery Tay, The.

Beautiful rain falls, the unheeded angel, The. In Time. Kathleen Jessie Raine. WPE

Beautiful River. Robert Lowry. APN-2

Beautiful Sea, The. Mary E. Tucker. CBWP-1

Beautiful Signor. Cyrus Cassells. WiU

Beautiful solution, The. When Torrid Rhymes with Forehead. Ray DiPalma. FTOS

Beautiful Soup, so rich and green. Lewis Carroll. UV *Fr.* Alice's Adventures in Wonderland.

Beautiful star in heav'n so bright. Star of the Evening. James M. Sayles. UV

Beautiful summer night, A. Summer Night. Antonio Machado. BLT, *tr. by* Willis Barnstone

Beautiful, The! what is not perfect here below. Beautiful, The. Mary E. Tucker. CBWP-1

Beautiful Things. Ellen Palmer Allerton. PWR

Beautiful Toilet, The. Ezra Pound. OBVE

Beautiful Train, The.　William Empson.　OxAEP-2

Beautiful trees make paths beneath themselves.　Juan Chi.　CoBCP, tr. by Burton Watson　Fr. Singing of Thoughts.

Beautiful, visitors used to say.　Dusting.　Daniel Hall.　YaYoPo

Beautiful was the appearance of Cormac in that assembly.　Cormac Mac Airt Presiding at Tara.　Unknown.　BIrV, tr. by Douglas Hyde

Beautiful Woman.　Dale Zieroth.　NOBC

Beautiful woman, a cup of wine, and a garden, A.　Moses Ibn Ezra.　TrJP, tr. by Solomon Solis-Cohen　Fr. Book of Tarshish, The.

Beautiful woman, you crown the hours.　Beautiful Woman.　Dale Zieroth.　NOBC

Beautiful World, The.　Albert Verwey.　TuT, tr. by Tony Curtis

Beautiful yellow cassia, so tender.　To the Tune: Partridge Sky.　Li Ch'ing-chao.　CrYelRi, tr. by Sam Hamill

Beautiful you rise upon the horizon of heaven.　Hymn to the Sun, The.　Akhenaton [or Akhnaton].　TTY, tr. by J. E. Manchip White

Beautiful Young Nymph Going to Bed, A.　Jonathan Swift.　ECEV; EroLit; NOEC; NPeEn; OxBEV

Beautifully Janet slept.　Janet Waking.　John Crowe Ransom.　APT-1; ColAP; FuPo; InPK-6; MoAmPo; NAAL-2v2; NoAM; PoE; RB; TAP

Beauty.　"Badawi al-Jabal."　MAP, tr. by John Heath-Stubbs and Matthew Sorenson

Beauty.　Laurence Binyon.　MoBrPo

Beauty.　Madison Cawein.　APN-2

Beauty.　Peter Hille.　AWP, tr. by Jethro Bithell

Beauty.　Isaac Rosenberg.　TrJP

Beauty.　Christopher Smart.　SacPr　Fr. Hymns for the Amusement of Children.

Beauty.　Thomas Stanley.　AWP; OBVE

Beauty.　Jones Very.　SacPr

Beauty.　Walt Whitman.　WeW-3

Beauty.　Elinor Wylie.　APT-1; NAAL-2v2; OxBA

Beauty—a beam, nay, flame.　Fading Beauty.　Giambattista [or Giovanni Battista] Marino.　AWP, tr. by Samuel Daniel

Beauty Accurst.　Richard Le Gallienne.　RACG

Beauty and Denial.　William Cartwright.　BeJo

Beauty and Her Visitors.　Winthrop Mackworth Praed.　NOBRP

Beauty and majesty are fallen at odds.　Richard Barnfield [or Barnefield].　OxBSo　Fr. Cynthia, with Certain[e] Sonnets.

Beauty and Sadness.　Cathy Song.　NoAM

Beauty and Terror.　Lesbia Harford.　CBAP

Beauty and the Beast.　Olga Broumas.　YaYoPo

Beauty and the Beast.　Gillian Conoley.　BodElec

Beauty and the Beast.　Rita Dove.　ESEAA; NoAM

Beauty and the Beast.　George R. Sims.

　"He gazed on the face of the high-born maid."　VerBaPo

Beauty and the Prince Formerly Known as Beast.　Eleanor Brown.　NeBl

Beauty as a Shield.　Elsie Robinson.　PoToHe

Beauty Bathing.　Anthony Munday.　NOBE; OBEV　Fr. Primaleon of Greece.

Beauty be not caused—It Is.　Emily Dickinson.　TAP

Beauty clear and fair.　John Fletcher.　NOSC; OBEV　Fr. Elder Brother, The.

Beauty does not come cheap.　Cocksucker's Blues.　Justin Chin.　WiU

Beauty does not walk through lovely days.　Beauty and Terror.　Lesbia Harford.　CBAP

Beauty his transient eyes descried. (LL)　Image-Maker, The.　Oliver St. John Gogarty.　OBEV; OBMV; PoRA

Beauty I love, yet more than this I love.　Faint Love.　Arthur Symons.　CABP

Beauty in Trouble.　Robert Graves.　OBCoV

Beauty in woman; the high will's decree.　Sonnet: He Compares All Things with His Lady, and Finds Them Wanting.　Guido Cavalcanti.　AWP; EaItPo, tr. by Dante Gabriel Rossetti

Beauty is not enough; who wishes to be fair.　Petronius Arbiter.　RomPo, tr. by J. P. Sullivan

Beauty is the straw I clutch at, but to say straw.　Beauty Is the Straw.　Amy Witting.　NOBAu

Beauty itself lies here, in whom alone.　Epitaph.　Thomas Randolph.　BASC

Beauty kissed your mouth, and gave the petals.　Macedonius.　GrAn

Beauty no more the subject be.　Song, The.　Thomas Nabbes.　NOSC

Beauty, no other thing is, than a beam[e].　Definition of Beauty, The.　Robert Herrick.　BeJo; CaPo

Beauty of Ilona Zrínyi, The.　István Gyöngyösi.　IQMS, tr. by Watson Kirkconnell

Beauty of Israel is slain[e] upon thy high places, The.　Bible, O.T.　NPeEn; OBVE; OBWP; TrJP　Fr. Second Samuel.

Beauty of Job's Daughters, The.　Jay Macpherson.　ChIV-1; MoCV; NOBC

Beauty of manhole covers—what of that? The.　Manhole Covers.　Karl Shapiro.　NoAM

Beauty of red bark, The.　Ruispiri—A Comic Ballad.　Bulat Shalvovich Okudzhava.　RusPo, tr. by Robert Arthur Douglas Ford

Beauty of songs your absence I should not show.　Sonnet.　Bernadette Mayer.　PmAP

Beauty of the Friend it was that taught me, The.　Makhfi.　WPOW

Beauty of the South, The!　Tune: "Memories of the South."　Po Chü-i.　ColAnChi, tr. by Jiaosheng Wang

Beauty of the Stars, The.　Moses Ibn Ezra.　TrJP, tr. by Solomon Solis-Cohen

Beauty of the unused, The.　Unspeakable.　Margaret Avison.　NOBC

Beauty of Things, The.　Robinson Jeffers.　APT-1

Beauty of women, their weakness, those pale hands.　Paul Verlaine.　SxFrPo, tr. by Martin Sorrell

Beauty renders Hermes pleasing.　Unknown.　PriapPo, tr. by Richard W. Hooper　Fr. Priapus Poems, The.

Beauty Rohtraut.　Eduard Friedrich Mörike [or Möricke].　AWP; OBVE, tr. by George Meredith

Beauty runs a pawnshop.　Pawnshop, The.　Chu Hsiang.　WoPoe, tr. by Kai-yu Hsu

Beauty's Transitoriness.　Christian Hofmann von Hofmannswaldau.　GePo, tr. by George C. Schoolfield

Beauty sat bathing by a spring.　Anthony Munday.　NOBE; OBEV　Fr. Primaleon of Greece.

Beauty so sudden for that time of year. (LL)　November Cotton Flower.　Jean Toomer.　ColAP; NoAM; UnPo

Beauty, sweet love, is like the morning dew.　Samuel Daniel.　NOBE; NoSic; OBEV　Fr. To Delia.

Beauty That All Night Long, A.　Jelaluddin [or Jalal al-Din] Rumi.　AWP, tr. by Edward Fitzgerald

Beauty, That Lying Bitch.　Paula McLain.　AmPoNex

Beauty! thou art a wanderer on the earth.　Walter Savage Landor.　SCGP　Fr. Pericles and Aspasia.

Beauty, Time and Love.　Samuel Daniel.　NOBE; OBEV　Fr. To Delia.

Beaver Pond.　Anne Marriott.　NOBC

Because.　Kate Light.　AmPoNex

Because.　James McAuley.　BMAP; CBAP; NOBAu

Because.　Emperor Tenji.　OHMPJ

Because a thermal motif heard.　Dennis Phillips.　FTOS　Fr. Etudes.

Because all this food is grown in the store.　Picketing Supermarkets.　Tom Wayman.　NIP-4

Because among them all thou art the best. (LL)　Sonnet: To His Lady Joan, of Florence.　Guido Cavalcanti.　AWP; EaItPo, tr. by Dante Gabriel Rossetti

Because as they cut it was that special green, they decided.　Two Brothers in a Field of Absence.　Cynthia MacDonald.　NIP-4

Because beer tingles.　Beer Drops.　Melba Joyce Boyd.　BlSi

Because Charles couldn't.　Jeanne Duval's Confession.　Yusef Komunyakaa.　BAP-97

Because, dear Lord, Their way is rough and steep.　Prayer for Shut-Ins.　Ruth Winant Wheeler.　PoToHe

Because Duke's voice.　Twilight Seduction.　Yusef Komunyakaa.　SeSe

Because each part of our face carries its own kind of information, takes its.　Plagiarism.　Ben Marcus.　HeMarv

Because / Each species is specialized.　Why There Are No Unicorns.　Judith Ortiz Cofer.　PueRic

Because he can't work any faster. (LL)　Unknown.　LB; OxBEV

Because he dies; he only wishes they would hear him sing. (LL)　Airy Christ, The.　Stevie Smith.　ChIV-2; NOCV

Because he had spoken harshly to his mother.　Revelation.　Robert Penn Warren.　NoAM

Because he is young.　Var. authors.　AWP　Fr. Manyo Shu, Part 1 of 4.

Because he loved his rooster, and his wife.　Grandfather's Mint.　Edward Cortez Garrett.　ReBoTo

Because he played games seriously.　Competition.　Stephen Dunn.　MoASP

Because he puts the compromising chart.　Zola.　Edwin Arlington Robinson.　OxBA

Because he's lost the way.　Case in Point, A.　August Kleinzahler.　PmAP

Because he seemed to walk with an intent.　James Thomson.　NePenScot　Fr. City of Dreadful Night, The.

Because he sent a head of cattle on.　Island and the Cattle, The.　Nicholas Moore.　SPE

Because he took a stand for peace.　Martin Luther King.　Aileen Fisher.　HHAm

Because he was a butcher and thereby.　Reuben Bright.　Edwin Arlington Robinson.　APN-2; MoAmPo; NOBA; Son; TAP

Because her brood is stolen away. (LL)　Tennyson.　NAEL-6v2; NAWM-7v2　Fr. In Memoriam A. H. H.

Because his heart went with you in your hand. (LL)　Sonnets of the Months: Conclusion.　Folgore da San Geminiano [or Gimignano].　AWP; EaItPo, tr. by Dante Gabriel Rossetti

Because his nose and face were one festering sore. Orf. Ted Hughes. NoAM

Because his soul was great. (LL) Private of the Buffs; or, The British Soldier in China. Sir Francis Hastings Doyle. FaBoWar; OBEV

Because his soup was cold, he needs must sulk. House-Mates. Leon Gellert. CBAP; NOBAu

Because I Am. (LL) Curing Homosexuality. Jim Everhard. CAGL; GLP

Because I am done with this thing called work. Robinson's Resignation. Simon Armitage. HarvBoo

Because I am idolatrous and have besought. Epigram. Ernest Christopher Dowson. OxBSP

"Because I am mad about women." Wild Old Wicked Man, The. W. B. Yeats. RaBo

Because I breathe not love to every one. Sir Philip Sidney. NoSic Fr. Astrophil and Stella.

Because I brought him here. By Accident. Jane O. Wayne. InvLad

Because I come from the West Indies. Palm Tree King. John Agard. EmeKit; Oth

Because I could sing to High Heaven. Caedmon. Aidan Carl Mathews. PBCIP

Because I'd seen a man. Air, The. Andrew Hudgins. InvLad

Because I do not hope to turn again. T. S. Eliot. SacPr Fr. Ash Wednesday [or Ash-Wednesday].

Because I don't want you to shear my fleece. (LL) Answer to the Parson, An. William Blake. FaBoEE; NBLV; OxBoLi; WoPoe

Because I feel that, in the Heavens above. To My Mother. Edgar Allan Poe. OxBA

Because I find not whom to speak withal. Dante Alighieri. EaItPo, tr. by Dante Gabriel Rossetti

Because I grew up vaguely Methodist. I Can't Become a Buddhist. Adrienne Su. NAPBL

Because I had loved so deeply. Compensation. Paul Laurence Dunbar. APN-2; BPo

Because I have a luncheon date. (LL) In Westminster Abbey. Sir John Betjeman. FaBoWar; HarvBoo; InPK-6; NBLV; NIL-7; NIP-4; NOBL; NoAM; OBSV; OxAEP-2; TOF

Because I have had occasion to remember, quote, paraphrase, I. Louis Zukofsky. APT-2

Because I have turned my head for years. Bittern, The. Sandra McPherson. LCAP-2

Because I know deep in my own heart. Song. Pauli Murray. BlSi

Because I know this man, let him be clear. (LL) Meaning of the Look, The. Elizabeth Barrett Browning. SacPr; TrCP

Because I lay my. Why Is God Love, Jack? Allen Ginsberg. FTOS

Because I left him there so you could see. After the End. Ann Townsend. AmPoNex

Because I Let Go Your Hands. Osip Emilevich Mandelstam [or Mandelshtam]. TCRusP, tr. by John Glad

Because I liked you better. A. E. Housman. CAGL; NOBVV; NPeEn; OxBEV; OxBTC; PeVV

Because I love my father. Portrait of My Father and His Grandson. Richard Jones. IllVoic

Because I'm tall my legs are long my left leg's lame. Paper Memorial Stone. Sang Yi. PFTM-1

Because I'm writing about the snow not the sentence. Fifth Prose. Michael Palmer. NoP-4; PmAP

Because I oft, in dark abstracted guise. Sir Philip Sidney. NoSic Fr. Astrophil and Stella.

Because I once beat you up. For a Far-out Friend. Gary Snyder. BB; NeAP; PoM

Because I Paced My Thought. John Hewitt. CIP-2; PNI

Because I send Thee all. (LL) To His Savior [or Saviour]. The New Years [or yeers] Gift. Robert Herrick. ChIV-2; NAEL-6v1

Because I think not ever to return. Ballata: In Exile at Sarzana. Guido Cavalcanti. AWP; EaItPo, tr. by Dante Gabriel Rossetti

Because I used to shun. Spark, The. Joseph Mary Plunkett. AWP

Because I've seen their musculature joined. Why I Believe in Angels. Rick Mulkey. AmPoNex

Because I was brought up in a working class family. Art. Denise Duhamel. AmPoNex

Because I was content with these poor fields. Musketaquid. Ralph Waldo Emerson. APN-1

Because I was 37 and he was 10. Bass, The. John A. Stone. BloBone

Because I was too much with myself. Secret, The. Peter Cooley. PoCoUp

Because I would not dull you with my song. (LL) William Shakespeare. AWP; OBEV Fr. Sonnets.

Because if you existed. Poetry Is Not You. Rosario Castellanos. TANSG, tr. by Magda Bogin

Because if you existed. You Are Not Poetry. Rosario Castellanos. TCLAP, tr. by Maureen Ahern

Because, in the road, I met her foster-nurse. (LL) Remembering Golden Bells. Po Chü-i. AWP; ChiP, tr. by Arthur Waley

Because in Vietnam the vision of a Burning Babe. Advent 1966. Denise Levertov. APSN; NNaP

Because it has no pure products. Learning to Love America. Shirley Lim. GeoHom

Because it is the day of Palms. Palm Sunday: Naples. Arthur Symons. PeVV

Because it isn't harmonious. Reasons for Loving the Harmonica. Julie Kane. MiVo

Because it might hurt, and because looseness. Red. Lance Larsen. AmPoNex

Because life's too short to blush. About Face. Alice Fulton. AllShUp

Because mine eyes can never have their fill. Ballata: He Will Gaze upon Beatrice. Dante Alighieri. AWP; EaItPo, tr. by Dante Gabriel Rossetti

Because My Baby Don't Mean Maybe Now. Walter Donaldson. ReLy

Because my faltering feet may fail to dare. Her Faith. Joseph Hilaire Pierre Belloc. SacPr

Because my grief seems quiet and apart. Sonnet. Robert Nathan. TrJP

Because my Lord was born to suffer. Sister Juana Inés de la Cruz. WPoS; WoPoe, tr. by Alan S. Trueblood Fr. Fifth Villancico, in Alternating Voices, Written for the Feast of the Nativity in Puebla, 1689, The.

Because my mother was too beautiful. Pall. Laura Kasischke. AmPoNex

Because my mouth. Minstrel Man. Langston Hughes. AmFaPo

Because my name is Lazarus and I live. (LL) Convert, The. Gilbert Keith Chesterton. ChIV-2; SacPr

Because my song was bold. Summary for Alastor. Laura Riding Jackson. FuPo; WoPoe

Because nothing else can be done. Midnight Supper. Ruth L. Schwartz. NeAmPo

Because of body's hunger are we born. Sehnsucht. Anna Wickham. MoBrPo

Because of Clothes. Laura Riding Jackson. APT-2

Because of its erotic and cool underparts and the sunset emblazoned on its. Grid Erectile. Christopher Dewdney. FTOS

Because of lake-water damage and otter dung. (LL) Margin Prayer from an Ancient Psalter. Ian Duhig. EmeKit; NeBl

Because of love and because of making love. My Son. Yehuda Amichai [or Amikhai]. WoPoe, tr. by Benjamin Harshav and Barbara Harshav

Because of My Father's Job. James Masao Mitsui. NIL-7; OpBo; UnSA

Because of the change of key midway in "Come Back to Sorrento." Song of Reasons. Robert Pinsky. HCAP

Because of the steelworks. On the Buses with Dostoyevsky. Geoff Hattersley. NeBl

Because of these men's courage, no smoke rose. Simonides. GrAn; WoPoe, tr. by Peter Jay

Because of thieves, a dog barked all night through. Master and the Dog, The. Ignacy Krasicki. WoPoe, tr. by Jerzy Peterkiewicz and Burns Singer

Because of this love. Unknown. ArkPo, tr. by Helen Craig McCullough

Because of your nose, like a leaf blade. Wheel, The. Molly Peacock. RA

Because our being grows in mind. For the Opening of the William Dinsmore Briggs Room. Yvor Winters. CRP

Because our world has music, and we dance. World Well Lost 4, The. Marc André Raffalovich. CAGL

Because passion is the absence we speak. Linda Zisquit. DTA Fr. Unopened Letters.

Because passion is the silence we share. Linda Zisquit. DTA Fr. Unopened Letters.

Because river-fog. River-Fog. Kiyowara Fukuyabu. AWP, tr. by Arthur Waley

Because river-fog. Var. authors. AWP Fr. Shui Shu.

Because, separated from us by a language. Landlady in Bangkok, The. Karen Swenson. GifTon

Because she desired him. Red Trousseau. Carol Muske. BodElec

Because she is the most popular doll. Bicentennial Barbie. Denise Duhamel. AmPoNex

Because she wants to touch him. Parable of the Four-Poster. Erica Jong. LW

Because she was a white girl. Death of Janis Joplin, The. Robert Phillips. SwNoth

Because She Would Ask Me Why I Loved Her. Christopher John Brennan. CBAP

Because spring brings miserable green and painful red. Song to the Tune "Ting Feng Po." Liu Yung. WoPoe, tr. by Sam Hamill

Because spring brings miserable green and painful red. Song. Liu Yung. CrYelRi, tr. by Sam Hamill

Because still on the youthful wing. Nameless Love, The. John Henry Mackay. CAGL, tr. by Hubert Kennedy

Because they are shame, and cannot flee from it. Wild Turkeys; The Dignity of the Damned. Brigit Pegeen Kelly. IllVoic

Because the film is running backwards. Woman in the Film, The. Lesley Dauer. NAPBL

Because the geeks and jocks were set in stone. Why I Skip My High School Reunions. Craig Arnold. AmPoNex

Because the girl Nastasia. God. Bella [or Izabella] Akhatovna Akhmadulina. RusPo, tr. by Robert Arthur Douglas Ford

Because the languages are enclosed and heated. Cliff Notes. Bob Perelman. PmAP

Because the male will be. Leviticus (Chapter 7, Verse 2–5). Manuela Fingueret. MirDau, tr. by Roberta Gordenstein

Because the mind is forever building its model airplane. At St. Sulpice. Erin Belieu. NAPBL

Because the mind's eye lit the sun. (LL) Blue Swallows, The. Howard Nemerov. MakPoe; NoP-4; OWoS

Because the Pleasure-Bird Whistles. Dylan Thomas. SPE
   (January 1939.) SPE

Because the Poor Have Nothing. Violeta Parra. TANSG, tr. by Karen Kerschen

Because the question was, "Where am I?" Sailor, The. Safaa Fathy. PoArWo, tr. by S. V. Atalla

Because the rosy condition. I'm Gonna Slap Those Doctors. Jack Coulehan BloBone

Because the shells were screeching overhead. (LL) Breakfast. Wilfrid Wilson Gibson. FaBoWar; OBMV; OxBTC

Because the smoke. For Paul Celan and Primo Levi. Harvey Shapiro. TaR

Because the stake was driven. Rocks. Shinkichi Takahashi. ZenPo, tr. by Takashi Ikemoto and Lucien Stryk

Because the warm honey. Sanctuary. Bruce Boyd. NeAP

Because the wind has changed, because I guess. Clearing the Title. James Merrill. HarvBoo

Because the Wind Remembers. Frank Mkalawile Chipasula. HBAPE

Because their fathers had been drilled. Last Republicans, The. Austin Clarke. CIP-2

Because there are avenues. After Tonight. Gary Soto. NoAM

Because there is safety in derision. Apparitions, The. W. B. Yeats. TRP

Because there was a man somewhere in a candystripe silk shirt. Homage to the Empress of the Blues. Robert Earl Hayden. APT-2; ESEAA; HCAP; LCAP-2; NAAAL; NAAL-5

Because there was disquiet in the wind. This Poor Man. W. J. Gruffydd. OBWVE, tr. by Gwyn Jones

Because they are secretly Jewish and eat matzoh on Saturday. Why We Fear the Amish. Robin Becker. BodElec

Because they *are* shame, and cannot flee from it. Wild Turkeys: The Dignity of the Damned. Brigit Pegeen Kelly. ExTi

Because They Hesitated between Roses and Darkness. Venus Khoury-Gata. PoArWo, tr. by Lucy McNair

Because they loaded their rifles with rain. Because They Hesitated between Roses and Darkness. Venus Khoury-Gata. PoArWo, tr. by Lucy McNair

Because they're both Italian, and I prefer sneakers to boots, sneakers to wing tips. 14 Reasons Why I Mention Mario Lanza to the Man I Love Every Chance I Get Tonight. Jim Elledge. IllVoic

Because they're living; so I leave 'em. (LL) Free Thoughts on Several Eminent Composers. Charles Lamb. OxBoLi; PeLV

Because this evening Miss Hoang Yen. Her Life Runs Like a Red Silk Flag. Bruce Weigl. AF

Because this graveyard is a hill. Visions and Interpetations. Li-Young Lee. NIP-4

Because this is the moment. Inside, The. David Wojahn. YaYoPo

Because, this month, when napkins, pretty spoons. Roman Presents. Martial. OBCP, tr. by James Michie

Because Thou Did'st Give. Harry Morris. CRP

Because thou hast the power and own'st the grace. Elizabeth Barrett Browning. CenSon Fr. Sonnets from the Portuguese.

Because thy name moves right in what they say. (LL) Elizabeth Barrett Browning. CTC; CenSon Fr. Sonnets from the Portuguese.

Because time subdues sharp angles and closes wounds. Burial. Paulin Joachim. TTY, tr. by Oliver Bernard

Because we are doing better. Letters from the Front. Michael Klein. WiU

Because we are strangers. (LL) Gaeltacht. Pearse Hutchinson. BIrV; ModIr; PBCIP

Because we hooked up most days courtesy. Long-Distance Call to Gregg, Who Lived with AIDS as Long as He Could. Alfred Corn. WiU

Because we live in the browning season. Kopis'taya. Paula Gunn Allen. HATNAP

Because we love, this day, this age, more times than once. Because. Kate Light. AmPoNex

Because We're Here. *Unknown.* FaBoWar

Because we're running out of time. By Heart. Ruth Sharman. Prnts

Because we suspected / the pillow would say "I know." Lady Ise. BoWoP; WoPoe, tr. by Irma Brandeis and Etsuko Terasaki

Because we've had more than our share. Oldies But Goodies. Grace Bauer. MiVo

Because we were baffled. White Bird, The. Wilfred Watson. MoCV

Because when they die. On the Suicide of Young Writers. Wilma Stockenström. PeSAV, tr. by Stephen Gray

Because, without these, I would be a stranger here. (LL) Studying the Language. Eiléan Ní Chuilleanáin. EmeKit; NPeEn

Because women are expected to keep silent about. On Stripping Bark from Myself. Alice Walker. NAAAL

Because ye made your backs your shields, it came. Folgore da San Geminiano [or Gimignano]. EaItPo, tr. by Dante Gabriel Rossetti

Because you are beautiful I will have to tell you a number / of my secrets. Open Secrets. Gwendolyn MacEwen. LW

Because you are four years old. Lola Ridge. TCAPo Fr. Alley, The.

Because you are old and departing I have wetted my handkerchief. Seeing Hsia Chan off by River. Po Chü-i. TAL

Because You Asked about the Line between Prose and Poetry. Howard Nemerov. VCAP; WeW-3

Because you care, each task will be much lighter. Because You Care. Frank Crane. PoToHe

Because you have thrown of[f] your Prelate Lord. On the New Forcers of Conscience under the Long Parliament. John Milton. BASC; NAEL-5v1; NAEL-6v1; NOSC; PBRV; Son

Because You love cremation grounds. Rāmlāl Dāsdatta. SinGod, tr. by Rachel Fell McDermott

Because You Mentioned the Spiritual Life. Stephen Dunn. BodElec

Because You're American. Kevin Stein. ReTh

Because you will suffer soon and die, your choices. Ghetto. Michael Longley. EmeKit; NoP-4; PNI

Because your eyes are slant and slow. Prophetic Soul. Dorothy Parker. LW

Bechuanas—Matclapees. Speech. Chief Mothibi. PeSAV

Beckie, my luve!—What is't, ye twa-faced tod? Sonnet. George Campbell Hay. OxBS

Beckon. Gillian Conoley. BodElec

Become as little children. Sylvia Townsend Warner. FaBoWar

Become at last a bee. Bee, A. Peter Didsbury. EmeKit

Become essential, man, for if the world should flee. "Angelus Silesius." GePo, tr. by George C. Schoolfield Fr. Cherubical Wanderer, The.

Become the prey of the world. (LL) Vultures Grow Impatient, The. Amina Said. HAWP; NAfrP, tr. by Eric Sellin

Become Your Face. Marianne Vitale. HeMarv

Becoming a Farmer. Tu Fu. CrYelRi, tr. by Sam Hamill

Becoming a hare terrified me. Dialogue with Herz. Antonio Porta. ItPo, tr. by Gayle Ridinger

Becoming a Redwood. Dana Gioia. GeoHom

Becoming an Eskimo isn't hard once you must. Bum's Rush. Michael Dransfield. CBAP

Becoming an osprey frozen skyhigh / to challenge me. (LL) Michael McClure. BB; NeAP Fr. Peyote Poem.

Becoming dusk. Robert Spiess. HA

Becoming Milton. Coleman Barks. RaBo

Becoming of Age. Simon Armitage. HarvBoo

Bed, The. Moniza Alvi. MFPA

Bed, The. Ray DiPalma. FTOS

Bed, The. Alec Derwent Hope. NoAM; OxBC; OxBSP

Bed! Bed! I couldn't go to bed! I Could Have Danced All Night. Frederick Loewe. ReLy

Bed Book, The. Sylvia Plath.
   "Most Beds are Beds." ChAP

Bed by the Window, The. Robinson Jeffers. APT-1

Bed calls. i sit in the dark in the living room. Bedtime Story. Wanda Coleman. NAAAL

Bed in Summer. Robert Louis Stevenson. BRP; NBLV; OTCP

Bed of Forget-Me-Nots, A. Christina Georgina Rossetti. VWP

Bed of the railway links me to these days of hell, The. Blues. Pierre Martory. KGB, tr. by John Ashbery

Bed shared, The. Life Sentence. János Pilinszky. IQMS, tr. by Peter Jay

Bed-Sitting Room, The. William Henry Davies. TCAWP

Bed Time. Peter Davison. UnPo

Bed with Mirrors. Gonzalo Rojas. TCLAP, tr. by Christopher Maurer

Bedbugs, The. Issa. EH, tr. by Robert Hass

Bede's Death Song. The Venerable Bede. ASW, tr. by Kevin Crossley-Holland

Bedlam; a Poem on His Majesty's Happy Escape from His German Dominions. *Unknown.*
   "What mean these loud aerial cracks I hear?" NOEC

Bedlamite, The. Thomas Mozeen. NOEC

Bedouin Eyes. Dima Hilal. PoArWo

Bedouin Song.   Bayard Taylor.   APN-2; TCAPo

Bedouin wind.   Song of the Andoumboulou: 15.   Nathaniel Mackey.   PFTM-2

Bedridden Peasant, The.   Thomas Hardy.   InvLi

Bedrock.   Gary Snyder.   PoE

Bedrooms.   Sandra McPherson.   ExTi

Beds.   Charlie Smith.   BAP-97

Beds are countries of delight.   Beds of Purification.   Jorge Debravo.   BLPSL, *tr.* by Rene de Costa, Rigas Kappatos and Eleni Paidoussi

Beds of Purification.   Jorge Debravo.   BLPSL, *tr.* by Rene de Costa, Rigas Kappatos and Eleni Paidoussi

Bedside.   Clive Matson.   PasH

Bedtime.   Eleanor Farjeon.   OTCP

Bedtime.   Denise Levertov.   TwCP

Bedtime.   *Unknown.*   ReMoGo

Bedtime Stories.   Silvia Curbelo.   TouFir

Bedtime Story.   Wanda Coleman.   NAAAL

Bedtime Story.   Gustav Hasford.   CDa

Bedtime Story.   Lou Lipsitz.   VGW

Bedtime Story.   George MacBeth [*or* Macbeth].   EmeKit; SoSe-8

Bedtime Story.   Lilian Moore.   NTCP

Bedtime Story.   Nayo-Barbara Watkins.   NBV

Bedtime tears / and evening sorrow.   Small Rains.   N. M. Bodecker.   Spl

Bee.   Philip Booth.   PoCoUp

Bee.   X. J. Kennedy.   OBCA; Spl

Bee.   Patricia Pogson.   NLP

Bee, A.   Basho.   EH, *tr.* by Robert Hass

Bee, A.   Peter Didsbury.   EmeKit

Bee, The.   James Dickey.   AmFaPo

Bee, The.   Emily Dickinson.   MoAmPo

Bee his burnished Carriage, A.   Emily Dickinson.   NOBA

Bee! I'm expecting you!   Letter to Bee.   Emily Dickinson.   SAmP; TLR; TTTS

Bee is not afraid of me, The.   Emily Dickinson.   APN-2

Bee-Keeper, The.   *Unknown.*   BoWoP

Bee-keeper kissed me, The.   Bee-Keeper, The.   *Unknown.*   BoWoP

Bee Meeting, The.   Sylvia Plath.   HCAP; HarvBoo; NALW; WPE

Bee of my mind, The.   Kamalākānta Bhattācārya.   SinGod, *tr.* by Rachel Fell McDermott

Bee's Last Journey to the Rose, The.   Brian Patten.   OTCP

Bee upon a briar-rose hung, a.   Flesh-Fly and the Bee, The.   Coventry Patmore.   FaBoEE

Be[e] ye my fictions; but her story. (LL)   Richard Crashaw.   BASC; BoLoP; EBEV; MeLP; NOSC; OBEV; OxAEP-1

Be[e] you all pleased [*or* pleas'd]? your pleasures grieve not[t] me[e].   Mary Sidney Wroth [*or* Wroath], Countess of Montgomery.   BWW; NOSC   *Fr.* Pamphilia to Amphilanthus.

Beech boles whiten in the swollen stream, The.   Autumn, 1939.   Alun Lewis.   PoWW

Beech leaves caught in a moment gust, The.   Departure.   Edmund Charles Blunden.   OxBSP

Beehive.   Jean Toomer.   GT; TTY

Beehive Cell.   Richard Murphy.   CIP-2; OxBSo

Beehive source.   Song, The.   Anne Baring.   HW

Beehould a cluster to itt selfe a vine.   William Alabaster.   ESCV   *Fr.* Divine Meditations.

Beekeeper.   Barbara J. Orton.   NeAmPo

Beekeepers' boxes.   Mount Bromley Hymn.   John Peck.   PoCoUp

Beeman Cliton hews / From the flower fed hive.   Apollonides.   GrAn

Been in the Storm So Long.   *Unknown.*   NAAAL

Beeny Cliff.   Thomas Hardy.   CABP; OxAEP-2; RB

Beer.   George Arnold.   OBAL

Beer.   Emperor Julian.   GrAn, *tr.* by Peter Jay

Beer Bottles.   Lindley Williams Hubbell.   APT-2

Beer Drops.   Melba Joyce Boyd.   BlSi

Beer, malt liquor talks.   Aunt Martha.   Wil'um Lee.   InTrad

Bees.   Emily Dickinson.   NAAL-2v1; NAAL-3

Bees and lilies there were.   Bring the Day!   Theodore Roethke.   CRP

Bees are Black, with Gilt Surcingles.   Bees.   Emily Dickinson.   NAAL-2v1; NAAL-3

Bees at my hive anticipate her hands.   Robert Sheppard.   Oth   *Fr.* Empty Diaries / Twentieth Century Blues 24.

Bees build around red liver.   Poor Christian Looks at the Ghetto, A.   Czeslaw Milosz.   HP; PoSu; VCWP

Bees build in the crevices, The.   W. B. Yeats.   BIrV; GTBS-P; NOBE   *Fr.* Meditations in Time of Civil War.

Bees that have been hiving above the church pond, The.   James Keir Baxter.   PeNZ   *Fr.* Jerusalem Sonnets.

Beeth hevy again, or elles moot I die. (LL)   Complaint of Chaucer to His Empty Purse, The.   Geoffrey Chaucer.   MiEL; NAEL-5v1; SCGP

Beethoven.   Henrietta Cordelia Ray.   CBWP-3

Beethoven, Opus 111.   Amy Clampitt.   NIP-4

(Beethoven, Opus III.)   NoP-4

Beethoven's Death Mask.   Stephen Spender.   OxBTC

Beethoven's Old Age.   István Vas.   IQMS, *tr.* by Daniel Gerard Hoffman

Beethoven's Sixth Symphony.   Steve Benson.   FTOS

Beethoven Sonata.   Ernst Waldinger.   AuPH, *tr.* by Lowell A. Bangerter

Beetle, The.   Nikolai Makarovich Oleynikov.   TCRP, *tr.* by Anatoly Liberman

Beetle Light.   Madeline DeFrees.   GifTon

Beetle on the Shasta Daylight.   Shirley Kaufman.   WPE

Beetles were blind in the ages of yore. (LL)   Song from the Coptic, A.   Goethe.   NOIV; WoPoe, *tr.* by James Clarence Mangan

Before.   William Ernest Henley.   MoBrPo   *Fr.* In Hospital.

Before.   Khaled Mattawa.   NeAmPo

Before.   Sean O'Brien.   EmeKit

Before.   May Probyn.   VWP

Before a bomb buried.   Salman.   Tawfiq Zayyad.   MAP, *tr.* by Charles Doria and Sharif Elmusa

Before a Cornfield.   Gottfried Benn.   WoPoe, *tr.* by Harvey Shapiro

Before a Fall.   Geoffrey Grigson.   SPE

Before a Fountain.   Karl Kraus.   AuPH, *tr.* by Lowell A. Bangerter

Before a going and coming that goes on forever. (LL)   Elegy for Alto.   Christopher Okigbo.   HBAPE; VCWP

Before a grotto of blue-tinted rock.   At the Frick.   Anthony Hecht.   GS

Before a January dawn, under a moondog sky.   Emma Lee Warrior.   *See* It's a good thing Dad deserted Mom

Before a man goes to sleep a man takes off.   Six Local Poems.   David Avidan.   FIT, *tr.* by Robert Friend

Before a Pack of deep-mouth'd Lusts I flee.   Francis Quarles.   ESCV   *Fr.* Emblems.

Before a Painting.   James Weldon Johnson.   GT

Before a Statue of Achilles.   George Santayana.   APN-2

Before Action.   Leon Gellert.   CBAP

Before an audible sound, an almost recognizable.   Prelude to Memorial Song: 100 Years Later.   Phillip [*or* "Phil"] William George.   VoR

Before and after Marriage.   Anne Campbell.   PoToHe

Before Bannockburn.   John Barbour.   OxBS   *Fr.* Bruce, The.

Before Bannockburn.   Robert Burns.   FaBoCh

(Robert Bruce's Address to His Army.)   FaBoWar

(Robert Bruce's March to Bannockburn.)   NePenScot

Before bulging eyes.   Celebration, The.   Felix Mnthali.   PBMAP

Before Chilembwe Tree.   Jack A. Mapanje.   PBMAP

Before Dawn.   Tom Clark.   BodElec

Before dawn i rose thirsty.   Other.   Lance Henson.   VoR

Before dawn, on the street again.   It's Not Me Shouting at No One.   Lawrence Joseph.   GraLe

Before dusk on the lake, the moon just full.   Chang Chih-ho.   SuSp   *Fr.* Fisherman's Songs.

Before Easter.   Mihály Babits.   IQMS, *tr.* by Peter Zollman

Before ever I knew men were hunting me.   Black Huntsmen, The.   Irving Layton.   WoPoe

Before first light, we would open the nets.   Talvikki Ansel.   YaYoPo   *Fr.* In Fragments, in Streams.

Before Gereint, foe's affliction.   Gereint ab Erbin.   *Unknown.*   OBWVE, *tr.* by Joseph P. Clancy

Before Gereint, the enemy's punisher.   *Unknown.*   WoPoe, *tr.* by Gwyn Williams   *Fr.* Black Book of Carmarthen, The.

Before God's footstool to confess.   Thy Best.   Henry Cole.   PWR; PoToHe

Before God's last *Put out the Light* was spoken. (LL)   Once by the Pacific.   Robert Frost.   APT-1; GSo; HAP; HeIP-4; MoAmPo; NAAL-2v2; NIL-7; NOBA; Son; TRP; VGW; WeW-3

Before he collapsed. (LL)   Passion of Ravensbrück.   János Pilinszky.   AF; GI; HP; PoSu, *tr.* by Ted Hughes

Before he died.   Conversions.   Neal Bowers.   AllShUp

Before he died.   Equena.   STP

Before he leaves on his fated journey.   Bede's Death Song.   The Venerable Bede.   ASW, *tr.* by Kevin Crossley-Holland

Before he went to feed with owls and bats.   Nebuchadnezzar's Dream.   John Keats.   ChIV-1

Before her mirror Rebecca combs out her dark hair.   Rebecca.   Vadim Leonidovich Andreyev [*or* Andreiev].   TCRP, *tr.* by Olga Carlisle

Before her wandering feet. (LL)   Rose of the World, The.   W. B. Yeats.   MoBrPo; NAEL-5v2; NAEL-6v2

Before his butchered legions in the snow. (LL)   Russia 1812.   Victor Hugo.   FaBoWar; OBWP, *tr.* by Robert Lowell

Before his immense window high as a cathedral window, the great unre-. Great Unrestrained Sadist, The. Hans [or Jean] Arp. PFTM-1

Before Hui-le Peak, sands like snow. At Night atop Shou-hsiang Citadel, Hearing Tartar Flutes. Li Yi. SuSp, tr. by Paul Kroll

Before I arrived. Issa. SoOfWa, tr. by Sam Hamill

Before I Could Call Myself Ángel González. Angel González. VCWP, tr. by Steven Ford Brown

Before I die I must just find this rhyme. Leaving for the Front. Alfred Lichtenstein. PeFWW, tr. by Patrick Bridgwater

Before I got my eye put out. Emily Dickinson. APN-2; PoE

Before I have begun to live. (LL) Matthew Arnold. FHYEP; NAEL-6v2

Before I knew there were men. My Life with Horses. Polly Clark. NeBl

Before I Knocked. Dylan Thomas. FaBoTw; RB

Before I know it, winter and spring depart. Lamenting the Dead. P'an Yüeh. CoBCP, tr. by Burton Watson

Before I laughed with him. What She Said. Maturai Eruttalan Centamputan. BoLoP; WoPoe, tr. by A. K. Ramanujan

Before I met you no one attracted me. Let's Begin. Otto Harbach. ReLy

Before / I opened my mouth. On Reading Poems to a Senior Class at South High. David Chapman Berry. SoSe-8

Before I regained them. (LL) Legs, The. Robert Graves. PeLV; RB

Before I set sail, I will not fail. Skin the Goat's Curse on Carey. Unknown. BIrV

Before I sigh my last gasp, let me breathe. Will, The. John Donne. EBEV; NoSic

Before I Was Born. Solomon ibn Gabirol. TOF, tr. by David Goldstein

Before I woke I knew her gone. Robert Malise Bowyer Nichols. OBMV Fr. Flower of Flame, The.

Before in the old time. (LL) Song: "Oh roses for the flush of youth." Christina Georgina Rossetti. GTBS-P; NOBVV

Before it came inside. What's That. Anne Sexton. LCAP-2

Before It Is Too Late. Frank Herbert Sweet. PoToHe

Before, it was a fascinating game. Day of the Dead. Rigoberto González. AmPoNex

Before it was quite unsheathed from reality. (LL) Hurt Hawks. Robinson Jeffers. APT-1; ChAP; ColAP; HarvBoo; MoAmPo; NAAL-2v2; NOBA; NoAM; NoP-4; OWoS; OxBA; RB; TAP; TFi; TRP; UnPo

Before jade pavilions the new moon dims. Unknown. SuSp Fr. Tzu-yeh Songs of the Four Seasons.

Before John and Maria's Wedding. Hilda Raz. ExTi

Before journeying to the vast sea, I already knew his name. On a Crab. P'i Jih-hsiu. SuSp, tr. by William H. Nienhauser

Before light became time. Unknown. WoPoe, tr. by Christopher Drake Fr. Omoro Sōshi, The.

Before Lord God made the sea and the land. Lost in the Stars. Kurt Weill. ReLy

Before lowering the perfumed curtain to express her love. Tune: "Chrysanthemums Fresh." Liu Yung. SuSp, tr. by James J. Y. Liu

Before man came to blow it right. Aim Was Song, The. Robert Frost. SoSe-8

Before men walked. Taliesin and the Mockers. Vernon Watkins. AngWePo

Before mine eye to feed my greedy will. George Gascoigne. Son Fr. Gascoigne's Memories.

Before morning you shall be here. Alba. Samuel Beckett. BIrV

Before my back was bent I was eloquent. Unknown. OBWVE Fr. Hateful Old Age.

Before my brother-in-law lost his telephone job. World without End. Kevin Stein. SwNoth

Before my cheeks were fairly dry. Child's Party, A. Sarah Morgan Bryan Piatt. SWaP

Before my drift-wood fire I sit. Burning Drift-Wood. John Greenleaf Whittier. APN-1

Before my face the picture hangs. Robert Southwell. NoSic Fr. Upon the Image of Death.

Before my fourth birthday my father. Hula Skirt, 1959, The. Kimiko Hahn. UnSA

Before my mother left she lost both rings. Joan Michelson. Prnts Fr. Departures.

Before my train comes round. (LL) Underground. May Kendall. VWP; ViWPN

Before myne eye to feede my greedy will. (LL) George Gascoigne. NoSic; Son Fr. Gascoigne's Memories.

Before night comes I think of you and for you before I fall. Before Night Comes. Léopold Sédar Senghor. VCWP, tr. by Melvin Dixon

Before Olympus. John Gould Fletcher. MoAmPo

Before Our Encounter. Margherita Guidacci. CItWP, tr. by Cinzia Sartini Blum and Lara Trubowitz

Before our headlights the coyote. Arizona Nocturne. Carlos Reyes. UrbNat

Before our human dream (or terror) wove. Sea, The. Jorge Luis Borges. TCLAP, tr. by John Updike

Before Parting. Algernon Charles Swinburne. NOBVV

Before Passover. Seymour Mayne. NOBC

Before Sedan. Austin Dobson. PeVV

Before she has her floor swept. Portrait by a Neighbour. Edna St. Vincent Millay. ItWoWo; OBCA

Before she let me love her. Brief Encounter. Norman J. Loftis. SpirFl

Before, she used to need a translator. Body Language. Linda France. NeBl

Before she walked into the river. Lorna Crozier. LW Fr. Last Testaments.

Before Sleep. Fleur Adcock. PeNZ Fr. Night-Piece.

Before Sleep. Anne Ridler. SacPr

Before Sleeping. Unknown. FaBoCh; OxNR (Prayer: "Matthew, Mark, Luke, and John.") OxBoLi

Before-snow sky lasted like the perpetual twilight, The. Annotation in Her Last Court Diary. Kimiko Hahn. ExTi

Before Starting. Walker Gibson. See Advice to Travelers

Before Summer Rain. Rainer Maria Rilke. WoPoe, tr. by Mark Rudman

Before sunrise the stork was there. Lake Morning in Autumn. Douglas Livingstone. NoP-4

Before the Actual Cold. Ray A. Young Bear. VoR

Before the Anæsthetic; or, A Real Fright. Sir John Betjeman. HarvBoo

Before the Attack. Semyon [or Semion] Petrovich Gudzenko. TCRusP, tr. by Denis Johnson and Shirley Rihner

Before the Attack. Semyon [or Semion] Petrovich Gudzenko. TCRP, tr. by Gordon McVay

Before the barn-door crowing. John Gay. OxBSP Fr. Begger's Opera.

Before the Beginning. Christina Georgina Rossetti. InvLi; SacPr

Before the Beginning: Maybe God and a Silk Flower Concubine Perhaps. Pattiann Rogers. PuP-23

Before the Beginning of Years. Algernon Charles Swinburne. NAEL-5v2; NAEL-6v2 Fr. Atalanta in Calydon.

Before the beginning Thou hast foreknown the end. Before the Beginning. Christina Georgina Rossetti. InvLi; SacPr

Before the Birth of One of Her Children. Anne Bradstreet. AmFaPo; BoWoP; EMWP; NAAL-2v1; NAAL-3; NAAL-5; NOBA; PAI; PeECV; SacPr; WPE; WPOW

(All things within this fading world hath end.) ColAP; NoP-4; PEW

Before the blond horsemen rode into our village. Event, An. Edward Field. CoAP

Before the Brain Surgery. Paula Tatarunis. BloBone

Before the Court. Aleksandr Aleksandrovich Blok. TCRP, tr. by Geoffrey Thurley

Before the day is everywhere. Martha Blake. Austin Clarke. ModIr; OxBEV

Before the days of self service. Fast Gas. Dorianne Laux. GeoHom

Before the descent. William J. Higginson. HA

Before the dream is gone. For Emma. Luigi Fontanella. NeIt, tr. by Michael Palma

Before the dumb hoof. In the blood, Winnowing. Carl Phillips. WiU

Before the Eiffel was complete. Song of the Eiffel Tower. David Shapiro. BodElec

Before the 1820 rising in the West of Scotland a network of. Untitled. Tom Leonard. Oth

Before the falling summer sun. Musings. William Barnes. HAP; NOBE

Before the Feast of Shushan. Anne Spencer. BlSi; NAAAL

Before the firmament was ever formed. Singing of the Source of Holy Church. Wu Li. ColAnChi, tr. by Jonathan Chaves

Before the frisk of snow. Potato, The. Roderick Townley. SpudSo

Before the gate of Little Su. Bamboo Branch Song of West Lake. Yang Wei-chen. CoBLCP, tr. by Jonathan Chaves

Before the glare o' dawn I rise. Shearer's Wife, The. Louis Esson. NOBAu

Before the Great Void, we burn the fragrant incense. To Purity and Truth. Unknown. TrJP, tr. by William C. White

Before the hearse Death's chaplain seem'd to go. Philip Freneau. TCAPo Fr. House of Night, The.

Before the Hunger: Megan's Blessing. Margaret Blanchard. SpudSo

Before the indifferent beak could let her drop? (LL) Leda and the Swan. W. B. Yeats. CABP; ClHu; EBEV; EroLit; GSo; GTBS-P; HAP; HarvBoo; HeIP-4; InPK-6; MoBrPo; NAEL-5v2; NAEL-6v2; NAWM-7v2; NIL-7; NIP-4; NOBE; NPeEn; NoAM; NoP-4; OWoS; OxAEP-2; OxBEV; OxBSo; PAI; PoE; PoPoPo; SCV; SoSe-8; Son; TFi; TRP; WeW-3

Before the last curve of the day. Valerio Magrelli. ItPo, tr. by Gayle Ridinger

Before the Law stands a doorkeeper. Before the Law. Franz Kafka. PFTM-1

Before the light went out. (LL) Reading by Mechanic Light. Thomas McGrath. BodElec; GifTon

Before the Map of Russia. "Teffi". TCRP, tr. by Albert C. Todd

Before the Mirror. Elizabeth Stoddard. SWaP

Before the Mirror. Algernon Charles Swinburne. OBEV ("White rose in red rose-garden.") GS

Before the mists descended on your body. Epitaph for a Poet. Homero [or Umberto] Aridjis. PoetW; STV; TCLAP, tr. by John Frederick Nims

Before the Moone should cirlcewise close both hir hornes in one. Ovid. NPeEn, *tr.* by Arthur Golding   *Fr.* Metamorphoses.

Before the mountains were brought forth, before. Christina Georgina Rossetti. Son   *Fr.* Later Life: A Double Sonnet of Sonnets.

Before the [*or a*] Cashier's Window in a Department Store. James Wright (1927–80). CoAP

Before the Pacific. Blanca Varela. BoWoP, *tr.* by Willis Barnstone

Before the Paling of the Stars. Christina Georgina Rossetti. TrCP

Before the Parade Passes By. Jerry Herman. ReLy

Before the Peak of Returning Joy the sand was like snow. Song of War, A. Li Po. TAL

Before the plums fell asleep. On the Way to Mind. Milo De Angelis. NeIt, *tr.* by Lawrence Venuti

Before the plums slept. Towards the Mind. Milo De Angelis. ItPo, *tr.* by Gayle Ridinger

Before the Poetry Reading. Louis Simpson. OxBC

Before the prayer begun. (LL) Lady Maisry. *Unknown.* ESPB; OxBB

Before the Press scarce one co'd see. To His Book. Robert Herrick. OxBSP

Before the Rape. William Shakespeare. *Fr.* Rape of Lucrece, The.

Before the revival of quartz pinks and icy blues. Silver Sands, The. Richard Blanco. AmPoNex; NAPBL

Before the Roman came to Rye or Caesar conquered Gaul. Rolling Chinese Wall, The. Roger Woddis. UV

Before the Roman came to Rye or out to Severn strode. Rolling English Road, The. Gilbert Keith Chesterton. FaBoCh; NOBE; NOBL; OBEV; OBMV; OxAEP-2; OxBTC; UV

Before the Scales, Tomorrow. Otto René Castillo. AF, *tr.* by Barbara Paschke

Before the Shrine of the Filial Marquis. Inscribed on a Painting. Ni Tsan. CoBLCP, *tr.* by Jonathan Chaves

Before the sirens started, he was late. Tube Ride to Martha's. Matthew Sweeney. ModIr

Before the six[t]h day of the next new year. On the Card[e]s, and Dice. Sir Walter Ralegh. ChIV-2; RB

Before the solemn bronze Saint Gaudens made. William Vaughn Moody. APN-2; CBCWP; OxBA

Before the spectacled professor snipped. Richard Murphy. ModIr   *Fr.* Price of Stone, The.

Before the starry threshold of *Jove*[']*s* court. John Milton. FHYEP

Before the Statue of Apollo. Saul [*or Shaul*] Tchernichowsky [*or* Tchernichovsky]. TrJP, *tr.* by L. V. Snowman

Before the Storm. Richard Dehmel. AWP, *tr.* by Ludwig Lewisohn

Before the Storm. Kenneth O. Hanson. CoAP

Before the stout harvesters falleth the grain. Summer Shower, The. Thomas Buchanan Read. TreFP

Before the Stuff Comes Down. Gary Snyder. HeIP-4

Before the sun goes down. Astrid Hjertenaes Andersen. BoWoP

Before the thing begins we have. Poetry Reading. Vernon Scannell. NOBL

Before the white chrysanthemum. Buson. EH, *tr.* by Robert Hass

Before the Wholesale Produce Market. Roasting Potatoes. Denise Levertov. SpudSo

Before the wig and the dress coat. Amor America (1400). Pablo Neruda. PoetW, *tr.* by Jack Schmitt

Before the World Was Made. W. B. Yeats. GTBS-P

Before Their Tanks. Tawfiq Zayyad. MAP, *tr.* by Charles Doria and Sharif Elmusa

Before their time? They too will die. (LL) Tennyson. EBVV; NAEL-6v2   *Fr.* In Memoriam A. H. H.

Before there is a breeze again. Judith Ortiz Cofer. ExTi   *Fr.* Three Poems in Memory of Mamá (Grandmother).

Before there was a trace of this world of men. Bibi Hayati. EnlH; WPoS

Before These Wars. Carol Rumens. Prnts

Before They Made Things Be Alive They Spoke. Lucario Cuevish. STP, *tr.* by Jerome Rothenberg

Before this autumn wind. Issa. SoOfWa, *tr.* by Sam Hamill

Before this grief, mountains must bend down. Dedication. Anna Andreyevna Akhmatova. PFTM-1

Before this longing. Her Longing. Theodore Roethke. NAAL-2v2

Before this, when I was stationed at Hsün-yang. On Being Removed from Hsün-yang and Sent to Chung-chou. Po Chü-i. ChiP, *tr.* by Arthur Waley

Before this world's great frame, in which all things. Hymn of Heavenly Love, An. Edmund Spenser. SacPr

Before thy door too long of late. Horace. AWP, *tr.* by Austin Dobson   *Fr.* Odes.

Before Twilight. Eyezion. Anne Batten Cristall. RWP

Before we go to Paradise by way of Kensal Green. (LL) Rolling English Road, The. Gilbert Keith Chesterton. FaBoCh; NOBE; NOBL; OBEV; OBMV; OxAEP-2; OxBTC; UV

Before we got you off to school. Starting School. Annie Foster. NLP

Before we met and you what I had passed. (LL) Meeting and Passing. Robert Frost. OxBA; OxBSo

Before we pushed off for Moon in Mañana land. For Dear Life. Alane Rollings. OPRER

Before we shall again behold. Endimion Porter and Olivia. Sir William Davenant [*or* D'Avenant]. NOBE

Before when you left you would always forget. Patrizia Cavalli. NeIt

Before, whenever I talked to myself, I used to say. Parable of the Unfaithful Wife. Rosario Castellanos. TANSG, *tr.* by Magda Bogin

Before you arrive, forget. Africa Says. Carl Phillips. PoPoPo

Before you ask for justice. Make sure. Paavo Haavikko. WoPoe, *tr.* by Anselm Hollo   *Fr.* Fifteen Epigrams in Praise of the Tyrant.

Before You Came. Faiz Ahmad Faiz. PoetW, *tr.* by Agha Shahid Ali

Before you came things were just what they were. Before You Came. Faiz Ahmad Faiz. WoPoe, *tr.* by Naomi Lazard

Before you can learn the trees, you have to learn. Learning the Trees. Howard Nemerov. VCAP

Before You Cut Loose. Simon Armitage. EmeKit

Before You Leave. Ai. GT

Before you left for the Lucky Strike. Waitress's Kid, The. Peggy Shumaker. PBCAP

Before you, mother Idoto. Christopher Okigbo. PBMAP   *Fr.* Heavensgate (1961).

Before you praise Spring's advent note. Quatrain. Tu Fu. TAL

Before you run out into the street and they shoot. (LL) Margaret Atwood. HAP; WPOW

Before you start an argument. Good Time Charlie. Jimmy Van Heusen. ReLy

Before you thought of Spring. Emily Dickinson. SAmP

Before you up the mountain go. William Wordsworth. VerBaPo   *Fr.* Thorn, The.

Before your face in the moonlight my face. Soyŏng Problems. Sang Yi. PFTM-1

Before your hair was ever cut. *Unknown.* GrAn

Before your waking I only knew. Before Your Waking. Anna Gréki. HAWP; WPOW, *tr.* by Anita Barrows

Before Your Wonders I Stand, My World. Shimon Halkin. MHP, *tr.* by Ruth Finer Mintz

Beg-Innish. John Millington Synge. MoBrPo

Beg your pardon, Lord Priapus. *Unknown.* PriapPo, *tr.* by Richard W. Hooper   *Fr.* Priapus Poems, The.

Began the year by seeing the rat uncheesed. Bio-Rodent-Oriole. Edwin Torres. HeMarv

Began to tell his tale, as you shall hear. (LL) Geoffrey Chaucer. NAWM-5v1; NAWM-7v1, *tr.* by Theodore Morrison   *Fr.* Canterbury Tales, The.

Beggar, The. Muhammad Al-Ghuzzi. MAP, *tr.* by John Heath-Stubbs and May Jayyusi

Beggar, The. Margaret E. Bruner. PoToHe

Beggar, The. Adrian Mitchell. FaBoTw

Beggar, The. Thomas Moss. NOEC

Beggar at the Gate, The. Ian Wedde. PeNZ

"Beggar," he says. Little John a Begging. *Unknown.* ESPB

Beggar in patched robe stands in my doorway, A. Liu K'o-chuang. CoBCP   *Fr.* Ten Poems Recording Things that Happened at the Ye.

Beggar-Laddie, The. *Unknown.* ESPB

Beggar Love. Adriann Roland Holst. TuT, *tr.* by Desmond Egan

Beggar Maid, The. Sydney E. Jerrold. SacPr

Beggar outside Cape Town Station, A. Sarah Ruden. AmPoNex

Beggar prove thy equal there, The! (LL) Birth-Day, The. Mary Robinson. ECWP; WoRP

Beggar's Bush. John Fletcher.

Beggar's Holiday, The. NOSC

Beggar's Serenade. John Heath-Stubbs. BoLoP

Beggar shouts his martial wares, The. Beggar, The. Adrian Mitchell. FaBoTw

Beggar to Beggar Cried. W. B. Yeats. NoAM; OxAEP-2

Beggar to Burgher. Arthur Rex Dugard Fairburn. PeNZ

Beggar to Mab, the Fairy [*or* Fairie] Queen, The. Robert Herrick. CaPo

Beggar Woman, The. William King. ECEV; NOEC

Beggars have changed places, but the lash goes on, The. (LL) Great Day, The. W. B. Yeats. BIrV; OxBSP

Begger's Opera. John Gay.
   Air: "Fox may steal your hens, sir, A." NOEC
   (Act I, Scene ix, Air XI—"A Soldier and a Sailor.") NoP-4
   Air: "Since laws were made for ev'ry degree." NAEL-6v1; NOEC
   Employments of Life, The. PeLV
   "Through all the employments of life." PeLV
   "'Tis woman that seduces all mankind!" PeLV

"Thus I stand like the Turk, with his doxies around." PeLV

Song: "Before the barn-door crowing." OxBSP

Song: "Can love be controlled by advice?" OxBSP

Song: "If any wench Venus's girdle wear." PeLV

Song: "Were I laid on Greenland's coast." EnLoPo; NAEL-5v1; NAEL-6v1; NPeEn; OxBEV; OxBoLi; PeLV

(Macheath and Polly.) NOEC

"O Polly, you might have toy'd and kist." EnLoPo

(Over the Hills and Far Away.) NOBE

"Virgins are like the fair flower in its lustre." NIL-7

Would You Have a Young Virgin? EnLoPo; NAEL-5v1; NAEL-6v1

(Youth and Love.) NOBE

Begging. Henry Vaughan. ESCV

Begging Another, on Colour of Mending the Former. Ben Jonson. NAEL-6v1; NAEL-7v1 Fr. Celebration of Charis in Ten Lyric[k] Pieces [or Peeces], A.

Begging at the door of a Master. (LL) Plea for Mercy, A. Kwesi Brew. PBA; PBMAP; WoPoe

Begging for Food. T'ao Ch'ien [or T'ao Yuan-ming]. SuSp, tr. by Wu-Chi Liu

Begging silently with a paper cup under the viaduct. Old Indian Granny, The. Chrystos. ReEnLa

Begin afresh, afresh, afresh. (LL) Trees, The. Philip Larkin. HarvBoo; NoAM; NoP-4; OPOU

Begin Again. "Susan Coolidge." ITBLP

Begin and never cease! (LL) While Shepherds Watched [Their Flocks by Night]. Nahum Tate. ChrPo; NOCV; NOSC; SacPr; UV

Begin, ephebe, by perceiving the idea. Wallace Stevens. ColAP; NOBA Fr. Notes toward a Supreme Fiction.

Begin the Beguine. Cole Porter. ReLy

Begin to charm, and as thou strok'st mine ears. To Music. Robert Herrick. CaPo

Begin to gleam across the mournful plain? (LL) Raven Days, The. Sidney Lanier. APN-2; OxBA; TCAPo

Begin unto my God with timbrels. Bible, Apocrypha. TrJP Fr. Judith.

Begin with a kiss[e]. Up Tail[e]s All. Robert Herrick. BeJo

"Begin with Zeus," Aratus said; but, Muse. Strato [or Straton]. CAGL, tr. by Daryl Hine

Begin[ne] with Jove; then is the work[e] half[e] done. Evensong. Robert Herrick. BASC

Beginner, The. Rudyard Kipling. FaBoTw Fr. Epitaphs of the War [1914–1918].

Beginner, / Perpetual beginner. Theodore Roethke. NOBA Fr. Meditations of an Old Woman.

Beginning. Alden Nowlan. NOBC

Beginning. James Wright (1927–80). ColAP; VCAP

Beginning, A. Richard Jones. IllVoic

Beginning, The. Vladimir Nikolaevich Sokolov. TCRP, tr. by Simon Franklin

Beginning, The. Wallace Stevens. VGW

Beginning at my car's left headlight. Spider. Joan Swift. UrbNat

Beginning by Value. Christopher Gilbert. GT

Beginning from you, Phoebus, I shall tell the glory. Argonautica, The. Apollonius Rhodius. HePo, tr. by Barbara Hughes Fowler

Beginning My Studies. Walt Whitman. NAAL-2v1; NAAL-3; OxBA

Beginning of a Beautiful Day (A Symphony), The. Daniil Kharms. AF, tr. by George Gibian

Beginning of a Long Poem on Why I Burned the City, The. Lawrence Benford. TTY

Beginning of art, The. Basho. EH, tr. by Robert Hass

Beginning of Autumn: A Poem to Send to Tzu-yu. Su Tung-p'o (Su Shih). CoBCP, tr. by Burton Watson

Beginning of Spring—A Stroll with My Wife. Hsü Chün-ch'ien. CoBCP, tr. by Burton Watson

Beginning of Summer, The. Po Chü-i. ChiP, tr. by Arthur Waley

Beginning of the Book, The. Edmond Jabès. AF, tr. by Rosmarie Waldrop

Beginning of the End, The. Roddy Lumsden. NeBl

Beginning of the End, The. Jon Stallworthy. OxBC

Beginning of Things, The. Fatima Lim-Wilson. ReBoTo

Beginning Speech. "Adonis" [or "Adunis"]. MAP, tr. by John Heath-Stubbs and Lena Jayyusi

Beginning: Some landscape & words about nature, The. Kirk Lonegren's Home Movie Taking Place Just North of Prince George, with Sound. Sharon Thesen. NOBC

Beginning the Year at Rosebud, S. D. Roberta Hill Whiteman. CDW

Beginning to dangle beneath. In the Marble Quarry. James Dickey. NoP-4

Beginning to fear his own unworthiness. Soldier of Urbina, A. Jorge Luis Borges. PoetW, tr. by Alastair Reid

Beginning when I was six I became my father's accomplice. Robert Malise Bowyer Nichols. CLPP Fr. Get-Away.

Beginning with a Stain. Alice Notley. PmAP

Beginnings. Robert Earl Hayden. NAAL-5

Beginnings. Peter Sirr. PBCIP

Beginnings. Michael S. Weaver. PBCAP

Begins another. (LL) Arrivants. Musaemura Bonus Zimunya. HBAPE; NAfrP

Begins here, the ciphered forest. Raul Bopp. TCLAP, tr. by Renato Rezende Fr. Black Snake.

Begins the crying. Guitar. Federico García Lorca. InPK-6, tr. by Keith Waldrop

Begins to live / That day. (LL) Word is dead, A. Emily Dickinson. SAmP; TCAPo

Begins with the saxophone's chromatic weather. Getting Even. Mark Fleckenstein. MiVo

Begone, calm. Spell of Weather, A. Eve Merriam. CA

Begonia's soil is rich and wet, The. Collusion. Medbh McGuckian. BiHa

Begonias. Su Tung-p'o (Su Shih). OHPC, tr. by Kenneth Rexroth

Begotten by the meeting of rock with rock. Sea Holly. Conrad Potter Aiken. APT-1

Begotten of the Spleen. Charles Simic. LCAP-2

Beguines who hear these words. Unknown. WPoS Fr. Soul Speaks, The.

Begun before Easter. Thomas McGrath. NNaP Fr. Letter to an Imaginary Friend.

Behaving Like a Jew. Gerald Stern. BodElec; InvLad; LoL; TaR

Behavior of Mirrors on Easter Island, The. Julio Cortázar. TCLAP, tr. by Paul Blackburn

Behavior of the pigeon, The. Buson. EH, tr. by Robert Hass

Behaviour of Fish in an Egyptian Tea Garden. Keith Douglas. FaBoMo; RB

Behind a duck, how many ducks? Five? No. Three. This is not the end. (LL) Army. Ciaran Carson. BiHa; PBCIP

Behind a vermilion gate, on the eve of the Skills Festival. Fan Ch'eng-ta. SuSp, tr. by Irving Y. Lo Fr. Seasonal Poems on Fields and Gardens.

Behind a web of bottles, bales. Gombeen, The. Joseph Campbell. BIrV

Behind Bars, Sel. Fadwa Tuqan [or Tuquan]. AF, tr. by Hatem Hussaini

Behind Calyx Hall's towers the sun has just set. On a Painting of the Radiant Emperor's Night Revels by Candlelight. Kao Ch'i. SuSp, tr. by Irving Y. Lo

Behind every arras. Polonius. Miroslav Holub. WoPoe, tr. by Ian Milner

Behind glass, my room is neat. Out of Chaos Out of Order Out. Michele Roberts. BrRo

Behind Grandma's House. Gary Soto. UnSA

Behind her big fan. Tête-à-Tête. May Probyn. NPeEn; VWP

Behind him lay the gray Azores. Columbus. Joaquin Miller. APN-2; BRP

Behind his wife stood, ever fixed alone. Abraham Cowley. NPeEn Fr. Davideis.

Behind Ise Shrine. Basho. SoOfWa, tr. by Sam Hamill

Behind King's Chapel what the earth has kept. At the Indian Killer's Grave. Robert Lowell. NOBA; VGW

Behind Me. Martha Rhodes. ExTi

Behind me, and will not go away. (LL) Follower. Seamus Heaney. CABP; PNI

Behind Me—dips Eternity. Emily Dickinson. APN-2

Behind me I do not see the ancient men. Song on Climbing Yu-chou Gate Tower. Ch'en Tzu-ang. CoBCP, tr. by Burton Watson

Behind me, Ovranopolis softens in the distance. Crossing the Strait. Nicholas Samaras. TWW

Behind: me, wag. (LL) John Berryman. ColAP; HAP; HCAP; HarvBoo; HeIP-4; NAAL-2v2; NOBA; NoAM; NoP-4; PoetW; TAP; TRP; TwCP; VCAP Fr. Dream Songs.

Behind my side of the headboard. Lobengula: Having a son at 38. Nikky Finney. SpirFl

Behind our shield of health, each. Onlookers. Luci Shaw. SacPr

Behind secluded screens the hush of daytime scenes. Summertime. Su Shun-ch'in. SuSp, tr. by Michael E. Workman

Behind shut doors, in shadowy quarantine. First Time, The. Karl Shapiro. APT-2; VGW

Behind Sokolnik station, where there's a butcher's shop. Monastery. Yevgeny [or Evgenii] Borisovich Rein. TCRusP, tr. by Daniel Weissbort

Behind sunglasses. Anita Virgil. HA

Behind the calm famous faces knowledge of what crimes? Collapsible. Tom Raworth. SPE

Behind the counter at the dry cleaner's. Journal. Amy Fusselman. HeMarv

Behind the gate of light. Season of Beginning and End. Zuhur Dixon. MAP, tr. by Patricia Alanah Byrne and Salma Khadra Jayyusi

Behind the gates of sunset. (LL) Eden. Emily Grosholz. FFC; RA

Behind the glass door. Long Afternoon, The. Louis Simpson. BodElec

Behind the Headlines. Raymond Garlick. TCAWP

Behind the house the upland falls. After the Pleasure Party. Herman Melville. APN-2; NAAL-2v1; NAAL-3

Behind the Line. Edmund Charles Blunden. OxBEV

Behind the Line. Ivor Gurney. HarvBoo

Behind the Log. Edwin John Pratt.
   "There is a language in a naval log." MoCV

Behind the moth-eaten curtain, 'stead of press. Mary Davys. ECWP *Fr.*
   Modern Poet, The.

Behind the screen door. My Father Breaks the Neighbor's Nose. Hayan
   Charara. AmPoNex

Behind the small, fixed windows of the album. Life of a Salesman. Emily
   Grosholz. RA

Behind the smooth texture. Like an Animal. Jimmy Santiago Baca. AF

Behind the tiller the sea runs thick. High Seas on the Caspian. Boris
   Petrovich Kornilov. TCRP, *tr. by* Bernard Meares

Behind the Veil. Andrew Lansdown. NOBAu

Behind the veil, behind the veil. (LL) Tennyson. EBVV; FHYEP; HAP;
   NAEL-6v2; NAWM-7v2; NPeEn; TOF *Fr.* In Memoriam A. H. H.

Behind their mortgaged houses. (LL) Men at Forty. Donald Justice. NoAM;
   VCAP

Behind you / a riot of pallid orphans. Small Country. Claribel Alegría.
   BoWoP, *tr. by* Aliki and Willis Barnstone

Behind you, now. Schwerner, Chaney, Goodman. Raymond R. Patterson.
   NBV

Behind you: the owl, whose eyes. Robert Bringhurst. PoCoUp *Fr.*
   Conversations with a Toad.

Behold. *Unknown.* WoPoe, *tr. by* Alfons L. Korn, Mary Kawena Pukui and
   M. K. Pukui

Behold a Shaking. Christina Georgina Rossetti.
   "Blessed that flock safe penned in Paradise." WPoS

Behold, a virgin shall conceive. Bible, *O.T.* AWP *Fr.* Isaiah.

Behold, behold, the day shall come when as. Lybica. Jane Seager. EMWP

Behold from sluggish winter's arm. Primo Vere. Giosuè Carducci. AWP, *tr.*
   by John Bailey

Behold, God of Abraham, God of mercy. Elie Wiesel. HP *Fr.* Ani Maamin,
   A Song Lost and Found Again.

Behold her lip, how thin it is; her nose. Shrew, The. Rowland Watkyns.
   AngWePo

Behold her, single in the field. Solitary Reaper, The. William Wordsworth.
   AWP; CABP; ClHu; FHYEP; FaBoCh; HAP; HeIP-4; NAEL-5v2; NAEL-
   6v2; NOBE; NOBRP; NoP-4; OBEV; OxAEP-2; OxBEV; PAI; PoPoPo;
   PoRA; SCGP; SCV; SoSe-8; TFi; UnPo; WeW-3

Behold how every man, drawn with delight. Samuel Daniel. NoSic *Fr.*
   Musophilus; or, Defence of All Learning.

Behold, how good and how pleasant it is. Bible, *O.T.* AWP *Fr.* Psalms.

Behold, how Sodom swaggers in its Pride. George Lestey. CAGL *Fr.* Fire
   and Brimstone; or, The Destruction of Sodom.

Behold I see the haven nigh at hand. Edmund Spenser. FHYEP *Fr.* Faerie
   Queene, The.

Behold, I send thee to the heights of song. To W. S. M. Arthur W. Monroe.
   APN-2

Behold me waiting—waiting for the knife. William Ernest Henley. MoBrPo
   Fr. In Hospital.

Behold, my dearest, how the fragrant rose. To Her Love. Edward May.
   FaBoEE

Behold My Mother! Abu Dulama. ArPe, *tr. by* Omar S. Pound

Behold, my servant shall deal prudently. Bible, *O.T.* NAWM-5v1 *Fr.* Isaiah.

Behold My Treasures, Darling. Endre Ady. IQMS, *tr. by* Adam Makkai

Behold, O Aspasia! I Send You Verses. Walter Savage Landor. SCGP *Fr.*
   Pericles and Aspasia.

Behold Pelides with his yellow hair. Before a Statue of Achilles. George
   Santayana. APN-2

Behold, she said, a falling star! Ephemeron. Annie Fields. PoBW

Behold that tree, in Autumn's dim decay. Anna Seward. WoRP *Fr.* Sonnets.

Behold the brave fellow who sits in his Yellow. All-night Taxi Stand, The.
   Kenneth Slessor. BMAP

Behold the child, by Nature's kindly law. Pope. ECEV *Fr.* Essay on Man,
   An.

Behold the critic, pitched like the *castrati*. Theodore Roethke. OBCoV *Fr.*
   Three Epigrams.

Behold the Deeds! Henry Cuyler Bunner. NBLV

Behold the dread Mt. Shasta, where it stands. Mount Shasta. John Rollin
   Ridge. APN-2

Behold the duck. / It does not cluck. Duck, The. Ogden Nash. RB

Behold the ever-tim'rous hare. April. Samuel Thompson. BIrV

Behold the fatal day arrive! Jonathan Swift. PeLV; SCV *Fr.* Verses on the
   Death of Dr. Swift, D.S.P.D.

Behold the gloomy tyrant's awful form. Winter. Anne Hunter. CenSon

Behold, The Grave of a Wicked Man. Stephen Crane. APN-2; NoP-4; TAP
   Fr. Black Riders [and Other Lines], The.

Behold the great Creator makes. Psalm for Christmas Day. Thomas Pestel [*or*
   Pestell]. SacPr

Behold the horned goat of Bacchos, how lordly. Anyte [*or* Anytes]. SaLy, *tr.*
   by Diane Rayor

Behold, the King of glory now is come. Laurence Clarkson. PBRV *Fr.*
   Single Eye All Light, no Darkness, A.

Behold the Lilies of the Field. Anthony Hecht. EmeKit

Behold the manly mesomorph. W. H. Auden. OxBSP *Fr.* Shorts [1948–
   1957].

Behold, the Meads. Guillaume de Poitiers. AWP, *tr. by* Harriet Waters Preston

Behold, the old earth is young again! Sibyl, The. Agnes Mary Frances
   Robinson. VWP

Behold the rocky wall. Two Streams, The. Oliver Wendell Holmes. APN-1

Behold, the Shade of Night Is Now Receding. Saint Gregory the Great. AH,
   tr. by Ray Palmer

Behold the Thin Green. Andrea Zanzotto. VCWP, *tr. by* Ruth Feldman

Behold the way our fine-feathered friend. My Funny Valentine. Richard
   Rodgers. ReLy

Behold the wreckage. Make the Bed. Stephen Cushman. AWTN

Behold these woods, and mark, my sweet. Thomas Randolph. BASC

Behold This and Always Love It. Meridel Le Sueur. HW

Behold this fleeting world, how all things fade. Epitaph of the Death of
   Nicholas Grimald, An. Barnabe Googe. SCGP

Behold this little volume here enrolled. On the Bible. *Unknown.* NOSC

Behold This Swarthy Face. Walt Whitman. APN-1

Behold those wingèd images. Legend of the Hive, A. Robert Stephen
   Hawker. EBVV

Behold, thou art fair. Bible, *O.T.* TrJP *Fr.* Song of Solomon, The [*or* The
   Song of Songs].

Behold through the veil of distance a pleasing image. Jonathan. "Rachel" [*or*
   "Rahel"]. TrJP, *tr. by* L. V. Snowman

Behold thy darling, which thy lustfull care. Francis Quarles. ESCV *Fr.*
   Emblems.

Behold what blessings Wealth to life can lend! Pope. OxBEV *Fr.* Epistle III,
   to Allen Lord Bathurst.

Behold what hap *Pigmalion* had to frame. Samuel Daniel. PBRV *Fr.* Delia.

Behold, whatever wind prevail. Mid-Day Moon, The. John Banister Tabb.
   APN-2

Behold with Joy. Elhanan Winchester. AH

Behold! wood into bird and bird to wood again. Boomerang. William Hart-
   Smith. NOBAu

Behold yon breathing prospect bids the Muse. James Thomson. PoE *Fr.*
   Seasons, The.

Behold yon hill, how it is swell'd with pride. Describes the Place Where
   Cynthia Is Sporting Herself. Philip Ayres. EnLoPo

Behold young Raphael coming back. Raphael. Priscilla Jane Thompson.
   CBWP-2

Beholde, how good and joyfull a thinge it is, brethren to dwell to gether in
   unitye. Bible, *O.T.* See Behold, how good and how pleasant it is

Beholde this fle. Barnabe Googe. See Behold this fleeting world, how all
   things fade

Beho[u]ld, a silly [*or* sely *or* little] tender babe. New Prince, New Pomp[e].
   Robert Southwell. ChrPo; ESCV; NOBE; NOCV; NoSic; SacPr; TrCP

Beho[u]ld the father is His daughter's son[ne]. Nativity of Christ[e], The.
   Robert Southwell. OxBEV

Beija-Flor. Diane Ackerman. NIP-4

Beijing Spring. Marilyn Chin. ExTi

Being. Adriann Roland Holst. TuT, *tr. by* Paula Meehan

Being a boy from the hills, brought up. Welshman in Exile Speaks, The.
   T. Harri Jones. AngWePo; OBWVE

Being a colored poet. Jacket Notes. Ishmael Reed. UnSA

Being a Good *Americani*. Fawaz Turki. GraLe

Being a Monster. Lawrence Raab. OPRER

Being a person. Lady Izumi. WoPoe, *tr. by* Steven D. Carter

Being a Wife. Selima Hill. EmeKit

Being a woman, I am. Wife Speaks, The. Mary Stanley. PeNZ

Being alone is the next best thing. Evensong. Marc Cohen. KGB

Being always / Poor. (LL) Ennui. Langston Hughes. OBAL; OBCA

Being an Immigrant. Matilde Salganicoff. MirDau, *tr. by* Celeste Kostopulos-
   Cooperman

Being Aware. Dennis Cooper. GLP; PmAP

Being Beauteous. Arthur Rimbaud. SxFrPo, *tr. by* Martin Sorrell

Being black in America. Lonely Eagles. Marilyn Nelson Waniek. ESEAA

Being Called For. Rosemary Dobson. BMAP; CBAP

Being double dead: going, and bidding go[e]. (LL) Expiration, The. John
   Donne. MeLP; OxBSP

Being drunk upstairs and listening. Green Revolutions. Barbara Guest.
   FaBoWP

Being finer than my soul, I fear, A. (LL) Palace-Burner, The. Sarah Morgan Bryan Piatt. NCAP; SWaP

Being given a lover's key is an intimate gesture. Vicki and Daphne. Cheryl Clarke. WiU

Being helpless. *Unknown.* ArkPo, *tr. by* Edwin A. Cranston

Being his resting place. Dog Sleeping on My Feet, A. James Dickey. NAAL-2v2

Being human, don't ever say what happens tomorrow. Simonides. SaLy, *tr. by* Diane Rayor

Being in earnest. Allen Fisher. Oth *Fr.* Stepping Out.

Being in Love. Marvin Bell. InvLad

Being in thought of love, I chanced to see. Guido Cavalcanti. AWP; EaItPo, *tr. by* Dante Gabriel Rossetti *Fr.* Ballata.

Being Jewish in a Small Town. Lyn Lifshin. UnSA

Being just your sort of con. (LL) Sacrificial Wolf. Anne Rouse. MFPA; NeBl

Being mighty a master, being a father and fond. (LL) In the Valley of the Elwy. Gerard Manley Hopkins. NOBVV; NOCV; OxAEP-2; TOF

Being Modern in Jerusalem. Evelyn Posamentier. GotH

Being my self captived here in care. Sonnet 73. Edmund Spenser. AEP

Being neither white nor black? (LL) Cross. Langston Hughes. ColAP; GT; HarvBoo; NoP-4; SAmP; SoSe-8; TAP

Being old is not so bad. You wake up. Nobody Here but Us. Richard Garcia. OPRER; TouFir

Being on Duty All Night in the Palace and Dreaming of the Hsien-yu Temple. Po Chü-i. ChiP, *tr. by* Arthur Waley

Being one day at my window all alone. Petrarch. AWP *Fr.* Sonnets to Laura.

Being polite to your official guests. (LL) Easter Hymn. Alec Derwent Hope. ChIV-2; GI

Being set on the idea. Atlantis. W. H. Auden. OxAEP-2

Being Sick Together. Elaine Equi. IllVoic

Being Somebody. Edwin Honig. TAP

Being the child of a Mad Mother. Dīnrām. SinGod, *tr. by* Rachel Fell McDermott

Being There. Thomas Sayers Ellis. AmPoNex

Being to timelessness as it's to time. E. E. Cummings. HAP

Being tongue tied is what. Tongue Tied. Jaime Jacinto. ReBoTo

Being Visited by a Friend during Illness. Po Chü-i. ChiP, *tr. by* Arthur Waley

Being witless it said no prayer. Death of an Angel, The. Russell Edson. LCAP-2

Being your slave, what should I do[e] but tend. William Shakespeare. CAGL; HAP; NoSic; OBEV *Fr.* Sonnets.

Beings' lives gel in my womb. (LL) Pregnancy. Sandra McPherson. BoWoP; LoL

Beings of the Mind, The. Felicia Dorothea Hemans. RWP

Beinn Naomh. Kathleen Jessie Raine.

Summit, The. OxBS

Beirut. Mahmoud Darwish.

"Apple for the sea, marble narcissus flower, An." MAP

Beirut. Claire Gebeyli. PoArWo, *tr. by* Mona Takyeddine Amyuni

Beirut. Nadia Tuéni. PoArWo

Beirut-Hell Express, The. Etel Adnan. GraLe

"Human race is going to the cemetery, The." WPOW

Bejeweled makeup, cloud-coiffure, training golden garments. Palace Poem. Ts'ao Ching-chu. WoPoe, *tr. by* Nancy Hodes and Tung Yuan-fang

Bel m'es quan lo vens m'alena. Arnaut Daniel. AWP, *tr. by* Harriet Waters Preston

Bela. Gerald Stern. BodElec

Belated Lament. Attila József. IQMS, *tr. by* John P. Sadler

Belex his flint adjusts and rights. By the Jordan. Herman Melville. NCAP

Belfast. Louis MacNeice. PeECV

Belfast Confetti. Ciaran Carson. BiHa; CIP-2; NPeEn; PNI

Belfast Lough. *Unknown.* BIrV, *tr. by* John Montague

Belfast Tune. Joseph Brodsky. VCWP

Belgian, with cumbrous tread and iron boots. Malines. James Kenneth Stephen. OBCoV

Belief. "Angelus Silesius." GePo, *tr. by* George C. Schoolfield *Fr.* Cherubical Wanderer, The.

Belief. Philip Levine. ColAP

Belief. Josephine Miles. FaBoWP; NoAM; TAP

Belief. Ella Wheeler Wilcox. PWR

Belief, and the love, and the truth, The. (LL) Mein Kind, wir waren Kinder. Heinrich Heine. AWP; OBVE; TrJP, *tr. by* Elizabeth Barrett Browning

Belief, great mustard seed, sends mountains to the sea. "Angelus Silesius." GePo, *tr. by* George C. Schoolfield *Fr.* Cherubical Wanderer, The.

Belief to regulate. (LL) Last Night that She Lived, The. Emily Dickinson. BoWoP; HeIP-4; NAAL-2v1; NAAL-3; OxBA

Believe and leave to wonder. (LL) God and Yet a Man, A? *Unknown.* HAP; MiEL

Believe Me. Esther Ettinger. DTA, *tr. by* Mariana Barr

Believe me, I knew you, though faintly, and I loved, I loved you / All. (LL) Gwendolyn Brooks. ESEAA; ISC; IllVoic; NAAAL; NAAL-5; NALW; PoPoPo *Fr.* Street in Bronzeville, A.

Believe Me, If All Those Endearing Young Charms. Thomas Moore. NAEL-5v2; NAEL-6v2

Believe me, Love, this vagrant life. To Cordelia. Joseph Stansbury. NOBC

Believe me, she grew more beautiful from moment to moment. Believe Me. Esther Ettinger. DTA, *tr. by* Mariana Barr

Believe me, sir, I'd like to spend whole days. Martial. OBVE; RomPo, *tr. by* James Vincent Cunningham

Believe not that the world is for naught, made. Believe Not. Isaac Leibush [*or* Yitskhok Leybush] Peretz [*or* Perets]. TrJP, *tr. by* Solomon Liptzin

Believe that we bloom upon this stalk of time. Muriel Rukeyser. YaYoPo *Fr.* Night Flight: New York.

Believer's Riddle, The. Ralph Erskine.

  "I though from condemnation free." SacPr

  "Mine arms embrace my God, yet I." SacPr

  "My life's a maze of seeming traps." SacPr

  "My life's a pleasure and a pain." SacPr

  "To tell the world my proper name." SacPr

Believers' Best Buy. Roger Woddis. UV

Believing in the Absurd. Harold Norse. CLPP

Believing in Those Inexorable Laws. Muriel Rukeyser. Son

Belinda frown'd, Thalestris call'd her Prude. (LL) Pope. NPeEn; OxBEV *Fr.* Rape of the Lock, The; an Heroi-Comical Poem.

Belinda lived in a little white house. Tale of Custard the Dragon, The. Ogden Nash. ITBLP; MakPoe; OBCA; OTCP; PoRA

Belisarius. Henry Wadsworth Longfellow. APN-1

Bell-Birds. Henry Clarence Kendall. NOBAu

Bell horses, bell horses, what time of day? Mother Goose. OxNR; ReMoGo

Bell-Man, The. Robert Herrick. BeJo

Bell of Linh Mu Pagoda tolls, The. Ship of Redemption. *Vietnamese Oral Tradition.* CaDao, *tr. by* John Balaban

Bell-rope that gathers God at dawn, The. Broken Tower, The. Hart Crane. APT-2; ColAP; MoAmPo; NOBA; NoAM; NoP-4; OxBA; PoPoPo

Bell Speech. Richard Wilbur. MoAmPo

Bell strikes *one*: we take no note of time. Edward Young. ECEV *Fr.* Night Thoughts.

Bell—that swings slowly and slowly over. (LL) Still and All. Burns Singer. HarvBoo; OxBS

Bell Tower. Léonie Adams. MoAmPo

Bell wakes me at 6 in the pale spring dawn, The. Letter from Pretoria Central Prison. Arthur Nortje. HBAPE

Bell was not a jar, when, The. Suicide Rates, The. Lewis Warsh. FTOS

Bella and the Golem. Rossana Ombres. CItWP, *tr. by* Cinzia Sartini Blum and Lara Trubowitz

Belladonna. Dennis Finnell. SpudSo

Belle Isle Men, The. Anthony Butts. AmPoNex

Belle Isle, 1949. Philip Levine. ColAP; VCAP

Belle Layotte. George Washington Cable. APN-2

Belle of the Ball-Room, The. Winthrop Mackworth Praed. NOBRP *Fr.* Every-Day Characters.

Bellman, The. Robert Herrick. CaPo

Bellman himself they all praised to the skies The. Lewis Carroll. OBCoV *Fr.* Hunting of the Snark, The.

Bellman's Song, The. *Unknown.* EBEV; SCGP

Bellocq's Ophelia. Natasha Trethewey. NeAmPo

Bellona the fierce, who held man in disdain. On a Lady, Preached into the Colic, by One of Her Lovers. Aaron Hill. ECEV

Bellow of good Master Bull, The. Ballade un Peu Banale. Arthur James Marshall Smith. MoCV

Bellower with the antlers. Suibne Geilt. NOIV

Bellows Maker of Oxford, The. John Hoskyns [*or* Hoskins]. FaBoEE

Bellows: O wise man, weigh your words. Cynewulf. ASW *Fr.* Riddles (Exeter Book).

Bellringing was another. To My Father. Tony Curtis. AngWePo; TCAWP

Bellrope. Robert Morgan. BLT

Bells, The. Rosalía de Castro. SpanPo, *tr. by* Edwin Morgan

Bells, The. Edgar Allan Poe. APN-1; BRP; ChAP; ITBLP; OBAL; OBCA; TAP; TCAPo; TFi; TreFP

Bells, The. Saul [*or* Shaul] Tchernichowsky [*or* Tchernichovsky]. MHP, *tr. by* Ruth Finer Mintz

Bells, The. *Unknown.* ReMoGo

Bells are booming down the bohreens. Ireland with Emily. Sir John Betjeman. GTBS-P; OxBTC

Bells. Bells. Bells. Earth Mother. Sonia Sanchez. ItWoWo

Bells for John Whiteside's Daughter. John Crowe Ransom. APT-1; ColAP; FuPo; HAP; HarvBoo; HeIP-4; InPK-6; MakPoe; MoAmPo; NAAL-2v2; NIL-7; NIP-4; NOBA; NoAM; NoP-4; OxBA; PAI; PoE; RB; TAP; TFi; UnPo; VGW; WeW-3

Bells from the steeple resound, The. Limerick. John Stanley. PeLi

Bells of Grey Crystal. Dame Edith Sitwell. OxBSP

Bells of Heaven, The. Ralph Hodgson. MoBrPo; NOBE; OBEV; OxBSP

Bells of hell go ting-a-ling-a-ling, The. Unknown. OBCoV Fr. Soldiers' Songs of the First World War.

Bells of San Blas, The. Henry Wadsworth Longfellow. APN-1; OxBA

Bells of Shandon, The. Francis Sylvester Mahony. OBEV
  (Shandon Bells, The.) OxAEP-2

Bells of St. Michael. Mary Weston Fordham. CBWP-2

Bells of the Armistice wake his family, The. Last Look in the Sambre Canal, A. John Bensko. YaYoPo

Bells of waiting Advent ring, The. Christmas. Sir John Betjeman. ChrPo; OBCP; OxBTC

Bells ov Alderburnham, The. William Barnes. EBVV

Belly Dancer. Diane Wakoski. NALW; NoAM

Belmans Song, A. Thomas Ravenscroft. NPeEn; PBRV

Belong to the life of a railroad man. (LL) Casey Jones. T. Lawrence Seibert. GM; ITBLP

Belonging. Rafael Campo. AmPoNex; WiU

Belonging. Leslie Norris. TCAWP

Belonging to a New Family. Mohammad Bennis. MAP; NAfrP, tr. by Charles Doria and Sharif Elmusa

Belongings. A. V. Christie. AmPoNex

Belongings. Catherine Davis. FFC

Beloved. Iyamide Hazeley. NAfrP

Beloved, The. David Roberts. OBWVE, tr. by H. Idris Bell

Beloved! amid the earnest woes. To F——. Edgar Allan Poe. APN-1

Beloved friends! more glorious times than ours. To My Friends. Johann Christoph Friedrich von Schiller. AWP, tr. by James Clarence Mangan

Beloved husband, greatest part of our soul. Elizabeth Hoby, Wife, to Thomas Hoby, Knight, Her Husband. Elizabeth Cooke Hoby. EMWP

Beloved, I only love thee! let it pass. (LL) Elizabeth Barrett Browning. CTC; CenSon; Son Fr. Sonnets from the Portuguese.

Beloved, it is good. Dream Song. Unknown. OBVE, tr. by Francis Densmore

Beloved, it is morn! Song. Emily Hickey. SacPr

Beloved, let us once more praise the rain. Conrad Potter Aiken. UnPo Fr. Preludes for Memnon; or, Preludes to Attitude.

Beloved, may your sleep be sound. Lullaby. W. B. Yeats. BoLoP; FaBoTw; OBMV

Beloved, my Beloved, when I think. Elizabeth Barrett Browning. CenSon; Son; WPE Fr. Sonnets from the Portuguese.

Beloved, My Glory in Thee Is Not Ceased. "Michael Field." VWP

Beloved, Now I Love God First. "Michael Field." PoBW

Beloved person must I think, The. Var. authors. AWP; TAL Fr. Kokin Shu.

Beloved Spic. Martín Espada. OPRER

Beloved, thou hast brought me many flowers. Elizabeth Barrett Browning. CenSon; EBVV; LW; OxBSo; WPE Fr. Sonnets from the Portuguese.

Beloved, what do you want of me? Marguerite Porete. WPoS

Beloved, / What does it take to put a house in order? Don Mager. GLP Fr. Letters from a Married Man.

Belovëd, when I saw thee sleeping there. To———, Sleeping. Adah Isaacs Menken. PoBW

Beloved, you are like thread in the loom. Ancient Feeling. Wu Wei-yeh. CoBLCP, tr. by Jonathan Chaves

Below. Federico García Lorca. PFTM-1

Below deck. Galley Oars. Ali ibn Hariq. WoPoe, tr. by Christopher Middleton

Below fair Peebles, on the river's side. Alexander Pennecuik. NOEC Fr. Marriage betwixt Scrape, Monarch of the Maunders, and Blobberlips, Queen of the Gypsies, A.

Below Freezing. Tomas Tranströmer. VCWP, tr. by Robert Bly

Below Hekla. Selima Hill. FaBoWP

Below Incense Burner Peak I built a new mountain dwelling. New Thatched Hall, A. Po Chü-i. CoBCP, tr. by Burton Watson

Below its floor, mint. Fountain. Elizabeth Robinson. AmPoNex

Below lies one whose name was traced in sand. My Epitaph. David Gray. EBVV

Below Loughrigg. Fleur Adcock. PeNZ

Below me the city was in flames. Improved Binoculars, The. Irving Layton. NOBC

Below the dam. John Wills. HA

Below the Great Wall—the watering hole. Horse-Watering Hole, The. Yang Wei-chen. CoBLCP, tr. by Jonathan Chaves

Below the Hall what meets my eyes? Pine-trees in the Courtyard, The. Po Chü-i. ChiP, tr. by Arthur Waley

Below the Ruweisat Ridge. (LL) Death Valley. Sorley MacLean (Somhairle MacGill-Eain). FaBoWar; NePenScot

Below the Surface-Stream. Matthew Arnold. NOBVV; NPeEn; OxBSP

Below the thunders of the upper deep. Kraken, The. Tennyson. NAEL-5v2; NAEL-6v2; NoP-4; PeECV; TOF

Below thir stanes lie Jamie's banes. On a Noisy Polemic. Robert Burns. FaBoEE

Below us, as far on as eye could see. (LL) Tennyson. GSo; OxBSo; Son

Below White Cliffs. Abigail Albrecht. GeoHom

Belphoebe and Timias. Edmund Spenser. NAEL-6v1; NAEL-7v1 Fr. Faerie Queene, The.

Belshazzar! from the banquet turn. To Belshazzar. Byron. ChIV-1

Belshazzar had a Letter. Emily Dickinson. ChIV-1

Belshazzar saw this blue. Up There. Ruth Stone. ExTi

Belshazzer's Feast. Eloise Bibb. CBWP-4

Belvedere Marittimo. Greg Williamson. AmPoNex; NeAmPo

Ben Barley was a barman stout. Ben Barley. Gerard Benson. UV

Ben Battle was a soldier bold. Faithless Nelly Gray. Thomas Hood. NOBL; NOBRP; UV

Ben Bolt. Thomas Dunn English. APN-1

Ben, do not leave the stage. Answer to Master [or Mr.] Ben Jonson's Ode, to Persuade Him Not to Leave the Stage, An. Thomas Randolph. BASC; BeJo

Ben Jonson Entertains a Man from Stratford. Edwin Arlington Robinson. MoAmPo

Ben Webster: "Did You Call Her Today?" Ron Welburn. SeSe

Bench of Boors, The. Herman Melville. APN-2; AWTN; NAAL-2v1; NAAL-3; OBAL; SoSe-8
  (In bed I muse on Tenier's boors.) NoP-4

Benches are broken, the grassplots brown and bare, The. South End. Conrad Potter Aiken. OxBA

Bend after bend, the long embankment. Tao-chi. CoBLCP

Bend and touch lightly with my lips the white face in the coffin. (LL) Reconciliation. Walt Whitman. APN-1; FaBoWar; HAP; MoAmPo; NAAL-2v1; NAAL-3; NAAL-5; NoP-4; OBWP; OxBA; OxBSP; PAI; WeW-3; WoPoe

Bend down my strange face to yours and forgive you. (LL) All My Pretty Ones. Anne Sexton. NAAL-2v2; NoAM

Bend in the River. Simon J. Ortiz. HATNAP; PoPoPo

Bend in the river followed us for days, The. Twenty-four Logics in Memory of Lee Hickman. Michael Palmer. BodElec

Bend of the gulf. Elena Clementelli. CItWP, tr. by Cinzia Sartini Blum and Lara Trubowitz Fr. Etruscan Notebook.

BEND of the river brings into view two triumphal arches, A. Arriving at Hsün-yang. Po Chü-i. ChiP, tr. by Arthur Waley

Bend thy bow, Dian! shoot thy silver shaft. New Moon, The. William Gilmore Simms. APN-1

Bending above the spicy woods which blaze. October. Helen Hunt Jackson. APN-2

Bending back. Alan Pizzarelli. HA

Bending, I bow my head. Combing. Gladys Cardiff. CDW; GifTon

Bending the Bow. Robert Duncan. HarvBoo

Beneath a gas-mantle that the moths bombard. West, The. Michael Longley. BiHa; PBCIP

Beneath a holm repaired two jolly swains. Virgil [or Vergil]. AWP, tr. by John Dryden Fr. Eclogues.

Beneath a sable vaile, and Shadowes deepe. Mans Knowledge, Ignorance in the Misteries of God. William Drummond, of Hawthornden. SacPr

Beneath a shaggy tire tree. Devil's Swing, The. Fyodor [or Fiodor] Kuz'mich Sologub. TCRP, tr. by April FitzLyon

Beneath all the statistics. New York. Federico García Lorca. RaBo, tr. by Robert Bly

Beneath Aphrodite's golden portico you now lie. Moiro. SaLy, tr. by Diane Rayor

Beneath both the feet of Boötes you may see. Aratus. HePo Fr. Phaenomena.

Beneath Cold Mountain. Michael Hannon. GeoHom

Beneath his brush, gods and spirits must appear! (LL) Song of Cursive Calligraphy. Hsieh Chin. CoBLCP; ColAnChi, tr. by Jonathan Chaves

Beneath its canopy of poisoned air. (LL) On a Line from Valéry. Carolyn Kizer. FFC; GifTon

Beneath its wings. Sappho. SaLy, tr. by Diane Rayor

Beneath / leaf mold. Marlene Mountain. HA

Beneath me this dark garden plunges, buoyant. Villa d'Este. Edwin Denby. OBGa

Beneath my feet when Flora cast. Rose, The. Elizabeth Tollet. ECWP

Beneath My Hand and Eye the Distant Hills, Your Body. Gary Snyder. NAAL-5

Beneath my palm-trees, by the riverside. John Keats. NOBE *Fr.* Endymion: A Poetic Romance.

Beneath my weight, the duckboards bow. Mermaid Tank, The. Stephen Knight. NeBl

Beneath our eaves the moonbeams play. Moon and Candle-light. William Renton. NOBVV

Beneath our feet and o'er our head. Holy Field, The. Henry Hart Milman. SacPr

Beneath our windows. (LL) It Being Forbidden. Martha Rhodes. KGB; NAPBL

Beneath the blossoms with a pot of wine. Drinking Alone in the Moonlight. Li Po. ColAnChi; WoPoe, *tr. by* Elling O. Eide

Beneath the brushed wing of the mallard. Lint. Rita Dove. TRP

Beneath the cross of Jesus. Elizabeth Cecilia Clephane. SacPr

Beneath the Good how far—but far above the Great. (LL) Progress of Poesy, The. Thomas Gray. AWP; GTBS-P; NOEC; OBEV

Beneath the Malebolge lies Hastings street. Christ Walks in This Infernal District Too. Malcolm Lowry. MoCV; NOBC

Beneath the myrtle's secret shade. Progress of Love, The. Robert Dodsley. ECEV

Beneath the sagging roof. Ezra Pound. MoAmPo *Fr.* Hugh Selwyn Mauberley (Life and Contacts).

Beneath the Shadow of the Freeway. Lorna Dee Cervantes. PBCAP

Beneath the shadow of Tongariro mountain. Song of Yearning, A. Kohine Whakarua Ponika. PeNZ, *tr. by* the author

Beneath the Shrine of the Three Loyal Ones. Wen Cheng-ming. CoBLCP *Fr.* Improvised on Horseback to Say Good-bye to Those Who Are Seeing Me Off.

Beneath the silent eaves, a tinkling as of jade. Studio for Listening to the Snow, The. Yang Chi. CoBLCP, *tr. by* Jonathan Chaves

Beneath the sky, the cone-shaped drum is rumbling. Léon Laleau. NegPo, *tr. by* Ellen Conroy Kennedy *Fr.* Black Music.

Beneath the small peach branches. Tune: "Telling of Innermost Feelings"—Wandering in Spring. Ch'en Tzu-lung. SuSp, *tr. by* Bruce Carpenter

Beneath the suffocating night. (LL) A. E. Housman. MoBrPo; NOBVV; OxBTC; PoE

Beneath the trees. Memoriae Positum R. G. Shaw. James Russell Lowell. CBCWP

Beneath the umbrageous shadow of a shade. Pastoral; in the Modern Style, A. "Worcester." NOEC

Beneath the walnut tree. (LL) White Lady, The. Rosamund Marriott Watson. VWP; ViWPN

Beneath the willow wound round with ivy. Hops. Boris Leonidovich Pasternak. BoLoP; TTTS

Beneath their flames, cities of candelabra. Chestnut Avenue: at Alton House, The. Charles Tomlinson. FaBoTw

Beneath these alien stars. Pioneer Woman. Vesta Pierce Crawford. AiP

Beneath these fruit-tree boughs that shed. Green Linnet, The. William Wordsworth. GTBS-P

Beneath these poppies buried deep. Epitaph on Robert Southey. Thomas Moore. FaBoEE

Beneath these shades, beside yon winding steam. On Visiting the Graves of Hawthorne and Thoreau. Jones Very. TAP

Beneath this smooth stone by the bone of his bone. *Unknown.* FaBoEE

Beneath this sod lie the remains. Epitaph on a Young Poet Who Died before Having Achieved Success. Amy Lowell. OBAL

Beneath this stone a Poet Laureate lies. Epitaph on William Whitehead. *Unknown.* FaBoEE

Beneath this stone does William Hazlitt lie. W. H. *Eheu!* Samuel Taylor Coleridge. FaBoEE

Beneath this stone in hopes of Zion. At Upton-on-Severn. *Unknown.* FaBoEE

Beneath this stone lies Cath'rine Gray. On an Old Woman Who Sold Pots. *Unknown.* PAI

Beneath this stone lies William Burke. Epitaph. R. P. Weston. OBCoV

Beneath this world of stars and flowers. Idea, The. Agnes Mary Frances Robinson. VWP

Beneath those parts, where stretching to its bound. Claude Quillet. ECEV *Fr.* Callipaedia; or, The Art of Getting Beautiful Children.

Beneath Thy Wing. Hayyim Nahman [*or* Khayim Nakhman *or* Chaim Nachman] Bialik. TrJP, *tr. by* Helena Frank

Beneath yon larkspur's azure bells. Blue-Bird, The. Herman Melville. NOBA

Beneath yon ruin'd abbey's moss-grown piles. Thomas Warton, the Younger. NOEC; OxAEP-1 *Fr.* Pleasures of Melancholy, The.

Beneath your cooling coverlet you lie. Radiation Victim. Colin Thiele. NOBAu

Benedicite, What Dreamed I This Night? *Unknown.* HAP

Benediction. James Berry. OPOU

Benediction. Stuart Dybek. UrbNat

Benediction. Stanley Kunitz. VGW

Benediction. David Lee. GifTon

Benediction of the air, The. (LL) John Greenleaf Whittier. APN-1; NAAL-3; NAAL-5; NOBA; OxBA; TAP; TFi

Beneficent, believe me, / His Eccentricities. (LL) Bat, The. Emily Dickinson. NAAL-2v1; NAAL-3

Benefits and Abuse of Alcohol, The. Eubulus. NBLV, *tr. by* Richard Cumberland

Benefits of Sorrow. Lizelia Augusta Jenkins Moorer. CBWP-3

Benicasim. Sylvia Townsend Warner. OBWP

Benjamin. Ogden Nash. PeLi

Benjamin Banneker Sends His *Almanac* to Thomas Jefferson. Jay Wright. VCAP

Benjamin Pantier. Edgar Lee Masters. APT-1 *Fr.* Spoon River Anthology.

Bent, all sleepin, you laugh off. West West. Bruce Andrews. FTOS

Bent Branches. Amjad Nasir. MAP, *tr. by* Charles Doria and May Jayyusi

Bent double, like old beggars under sacks. Dulce et Decorum Est. Wilfred Owen. AmFaPo; CABP; FaBoTw; FaBoWar; HarvBoo; HeIP-4; InPK-6; MoBrPo; NAEL-5v2; NAEL-6v2; NIL-7; NIP-4; NoAM; NoP-4; OBWP; OxBEV; PeFWW; PoE; PoPoPo; PoWW; RaBo; TCAWP; TFi; TRP; UnPo

Bent old men and women and dirty children scavenging. Environment. Lionel Kearns. NOBC

Bent over, staggering in panic or despair. Tableau. Judith Wright. CBAP

Bent Sae Brown, The. *Unknown.* ESPB

Bent we cannot re-bend. (LL) Summer Is Ended. Christina Georgina Rossetti. NOBVV; NPeEn; OxBEV

Bents and Broom, The. *Unknown.* OxBB

Beoleopard; or, The Witan's Whail. *Unknown.* OBCoV

Beowulf. Kingsley Amis. OxBC

Beowulf. *Unknown.* ASW; NAEL-7v1

Beowulf and Wiglaf Slay the Dragon. AnOE, *tr. by* Charles W. Kennedy

Beowulf's Death. AnOE, *tr. by* Charles W. Kennedy

Coming of Grendel, The. OPOU, *tr. by* Gerald Benson

Fire-Dragon and the Treasure, The. AnOE, *tr. by* Charles W. Kennedy

Funeral Pyre, The. AnOE, *tr. by* Charles W. Kennedy

Hrothgar Answered. WoPoe, *tr. by* Frederick Rebsamen

"Hwæt, wē gār-dena in gēardagum." CABP

Last Survivor's Speech, The. NAEL-5v1

("Hold thou now, Earth, now hand of man cannot.") NAEL-6v1

Lay of Finn, The. AnOE, *tr. by* Charles W. Kennedy

"Oft in the hall I have heard my people." HeIP-4

"So Hrothgar's men lived happy in his hall." PoE

Such Is the Grief of the Grey-Haired Man. WoPoe, *tr. by* Michael O'Brien

Tale of Sigemund, The. AnOE, *tr. by* Charles W. Kennedy

Beppo; a Venetian Story. Byron. NOBL; OBNV; OBSV

"England! with all thy faults I love thee still." UnPo

(Italy versus England.) NOBE

"'Tis know, at least it should be, that throughout." NOBRP

Bequests. *Unknown.* OxNR

Bereave me not of these delightful dreams. To a Friend. William Lisle Bowles. CenSon

Bereaved Swan, The. Stevie Smith. FaBoTw

Bereavement. Elizabeth Barrett Browning. SacPr; WPE

Bereavement in their death to feel. Emily Dickinson. SWaP

Bereft. Robert Frost. APT-1; MoAmPo; OxBA; SoSe-8

Bereft. Thomas Hardy. BoLoP; NoAM

Bereft. Josephine D. Henderson Heard. CBWP-4

Berg, The. Herman Melville. ColAP; NCAP; NOBA; NoP-4; PoPoPo; TAP; TCAPo

Bergamot. Justin Chin. AmPoNex

Bergen-Belsen 1945. Lyn Lifshin. GotH

Berkeley. Mairtin O Direain. BiHa

Berkeley, Late Spring. Forrest Hamer. GeoHom

Berlin Metro. Desmond O'Grady. BiHa

Berlin Wall Tune, The. Joseph Brodsky. AF, *tr. by* Joseph Brodsky

Berlioz in the Madhouse. Halvard Johnson. MiVo

Bermuda Triangle. Joel Long. AmPoNex

Bermudas. Andrew Marvell. AWP; BASC; ESCV; FHYEP; FaBoCh; GeHe; NAEL-5v1; NAEL-6v1; NAEL-7v1; NOBE; NOCV; NPeEn; NoP-4; OBEV; PBRV; PeECV; PoE; RB; SCGP; TFi; WoPoe

(Song of the Emigrants in Bermuda.) GTBS-P

Bernald, who the rural affairs was placed o'er. Fall of Zolnok, The. Sebestyén Tinódi. IQMS, *tr. by* George Borrow

Bernard Peyton is dead. Young Men Dead. John Peale Bishop. APT-1

Bernice Got Next to Isis.   Leslie Simon.   FFC

Berries.   Walter De la Mare.   MoBrPo

Berry Picking.   Irving Layton.   HeIP-4; MoCV; NIP-4; NoP-4

Berryman.   W. S. Merwin.   GifTon

Bertha in the Lane.   Elizabeth Barrett Browning.   ViWPN

Berthe Morisot.   Anne Waldman.   PmAP

Bertolt Brecht lamented that he lived in an age when it was almost a crime to talk about trees.   Triage.   Lisel Mueller.   IllVoic

Berzsenyi.   Árpád Tóth.   IQMS, tr. by Watson Kirkconnell

Beshrew that heart that makes my heart to groan.   William Shakespeare.   OxAEP-1   Fr. Sonnets.

Beside a chapel I'd a room looked down.   Dread.   John Millington Synge.   BoLoP; MoBrPo; OxBSP

Beside a Chrysanthemum.   So Chong-Ju.   VCWP, tr. by David R. McCann

Beside a runnel build my shed.   After Reading in a Letter Proposals for Building a Cottage.   John Clare.   OxAEP-2

Beside a spreading elm, from whose high boughs.   Reverie, A.   Joanna Baillie.   ECWP; WoRP

Beside his heavy-shouldered team.   Bullocky.   Judith Wright.   CBAP

Beside me a memory of every detail and.   And It Is Still That Way.   Hedva Harechavi.   DTA, tr. by Miriyam Glazer

Beside me,—in the car,—she sat.   Natura Naturans.   Arthur Hugh Clough.   HAP; NOBVV

Beside me in this garden.   Korean Mums.   James Schuyler.   PmAP; VCAP

Beside me she sat, hand hooked and hovering.   Egyptian Passage, An.   Theodore Weiss.   TAP

Beside one loch, a hind's neat skeleton.   So Many Summers.   Norman MacCaig.   HarvBoo

Beside the Bed.   Charlotte Mew.   BWW; MoBrPo; OxBSP; WPE

Beside the boisterous brook of Green-head Ghyll [or Gill].   (LL)   Michael [A Pastoral Poem].   William Wordsworth.   FHYEP; NAEL-5v2; NAEL-6v2; NOBRP; OxAEP-2

Beside the Brokenstraw or Licking Creek.   John Chapman.   Richard Wilbur.   OxBC

Beside the gravel pile, the lizard.   Of His Life.   Wayne Dodd.   BLT

Beside the green water.   Tune: "Four Pieces of Jade"—Retirement.   Ma Chih-yüan.   SuSP, tr. by Sherwin S. S. Fu

Beside the haystack in the floods, The.   (LL)   Haystack in the Floods, The.   William Morris.   CABP; EBEV; EBNV; EBVV; HAP; NAEL-5v2; NAEL-6v2; NoP-4; OBNV; OxAEP-2; PeVV; PoRA

Beside the highway.   Eve.   Dorothy Livesay.   ItWoWo; NALW

Beside the pounding cataracts.   City of the End of Things, The.   Archibald Lampman.   NOBC

Beside the road.   Basho.   TTTS

Beside the Seaside.   Sir John Betjeman.
   "Green shutters, shut your shutters! Windyridge."   OxBTC

Beside the sewing-table chained and bent.   Leaf from the Devil's Jest-Book, A.   Edwin Markham.   APN-2

Beside the ungathered rice he lay.   Slave's Dream, The.   Henry Wadsworth Longfellow.   NAAL-2v1; NAAL-3; NAAL-5

Beside the wine.   Claustrophobia.   Sean O Riordain.   NOIV, tr. by Thomas Kinsella

Beside this dike, I shake off the world's dust.   Visiting Pai-an Pavilion.   Hsieh Ling-yün.   CrYelRi, tr. by Sam Hamill

Besides it sound more exotic.   (LL)   Palm Tree King.   John Agard.   EmeKit; Oth

Besides the autumn poets sing.   Emily Dickinson.   OxBA

Besides the grave.   (LL)   Robert Frost.   HAP; NoP-4; RACG

Besieged.   Zalman Schneour.   TrJP, tr. by Joseph Leftwich

Besieged Serenity.   Vasco [or Vasko] Popa.
   Echo.   PoSu
   Journey.   PoSu

Bess.   William Stafford.   NNaP

Bessie.   Alvin Aubert.   SeSe

Bessie Smith's Funeral.   Alvin Aubert.   SeSe

Bessy Bell and Mary Gray.   Mother Goose.   OxNR; ReMoGo

Bessy [or Bessie] Bell and Mary Gray.   Unknown.   ESPB; OxBB

Best, The.   Elizabeth Barrett Browning.   OxBEV; OxBSP; VWP
   (Best Thing in the World, The.)   EBVV; NOBVV

Best and brightest, come away.   To Jane: The Invitation.   Shelley.   GTBS-P; NAEL-5v2; NAEL-6v2; NPeEn

Best be done before the last degree.   Lao Tzu.   WoPoe, tr. by Moss Roberts   Fr. Tao Te Ching.

Best clock. Best carpet. Best three chairs.   Study.   Tony Harrison.   CABP

Best Cowboy Movie, The.   Elizabeth Smither.   PeNZ

Best Friend, The.   William Henry Davies.   OBMV

Best Is Yet to Come, The.   Cy Coleman.   ReLy

Best-loved Night!, The.   (LL)   Hymn to the Night.   Henry Wadsworth Longfellow.   APN-1; NOBA; OxBA; PWR; TAP; TCAPo

Best Man in the Vield, The.   William Barnes.
   Sam and Bob.   PeVV, tr. by Hualing Nieh

Best Meals of My Life, The.   Joseph Duemer.   SpudSo

Best of all is to be idle.   Against Whatever It Is That's Encroaching.   Charles Simic.   ColAP

Best of both worlds being got, The.   Poets' Corner.   Robert Graves.   FaBoEE

Best of thy sex! if sacred friendship can.   To Phylocles, Inviting Him to Friendship.   "Ephelia."   NOSC; WPE

Best of Tuscan cheer to feed your youth, The.   (LL)   Folgore da San Geminiano [or Gimignano].   CTC; EaItPo, tr. by Dante Gabriel Rossetti   Fr. Sonnets of the Months.

Best Religion, The.   Heinrich Heine.   TrJP, tr. by Emma Lazarus   Fr. Tannhäuser.

Best slave, The.   Alcestis on the Poetry Circuit.   Erica Jong.   NALW

Best Slow Dancer, The.   David Wagoner.   NoAM; VCAP

Best Thing in the World, The.   Elizabeth Barrett Browning.   See Best, The

Best thing in the world, The.   Tune: "A Thousand Autumns."   Huang T'ing-chien.   ColAnChi, tr. by J. R. Hightower

Best Things in Life Are Free, The.   Ray Henderson.   ReLy

Best way to insult God, The.   Anne Carson.   BodElec   Fr. Truth about God, The.

Best?   Siv Widerberg.   NTCP, tr. by Verne Moberg

Bestiary.   Oliver Reynolds.   TCAWP   Fr. Tone Poem.

Bestiary, A.   Kenneth Rexroth.   OBAL
   Fox.   NNaP
   Horse.   NNaP
   Raccoon.   KaS; NNaP
   Vulture.   NNaP
   Wolf.   NNaP

Bestiary, The.   Unknown.
   Whale, The.   CRP, tr. by Richard Wilbur

Bestiary for the Fingers of My Right Hand.   Charles Simic.   LCAP-2

Bestrew the benches: for my bride and me.   Unknown.   WoPoe, tr. by Wystan Hugh Auden and Paul B. Taylor   Fr. Elder Edda, The.

Beth Gêlert; or, The Grave of the Greyhound.   William Robert Spencer.   EBNV; OBNV

Bethel, Horeb, Engedi, Soar.   Exile: Welsh Service from Daventry.   Llewelyn Wyn Griffith.   AngWoPo

Bethlehem.   Marina Ivanovna Tsvetayeva [or Tsvetaeva].   GI, tr. by Nina Kossman

Bethlehem in Germany.   Advent Calendar.   Gjertrud Schnackenberg.   ChrPo

Bethsabe's Song.   George Peele.   ChiV-1; NOBE; NPeEn; NoSic; OxBEV; OxBSP; OxBoLi; RB   Fr. David and [Fair] Bethsabe.

Betjeman, 1984.   Charles Causley.   NOBL; OxBTC; PeLV; UV

Betrayal.   Léon Laleau.   NegPo, tr. by Ellen Conroy Kennedy   Fr. Black Music.

Betrayal.   Adam Zagajewski.   VCWP, tr. by Renata Gorczynski

Betrayal, The.   "Nirala."   OMIP, tr. by Arvind Krishna Mehrotra

Betrayed by friend dragged from the garden hailed.   Ecce Homunculus.   Ronald Allison Kells Mason.   PeNZ

Betrothal of Saint Catherine, The.   Unknown.
   "And when thus the night availed."   IQMS, tr. by René Bonnerjea

Betrothed, The.   Aleksandr Andreievich Prokofiev.   TCRP, tr. by Lubov Yakovleva

Betsy Baker.   Unknown.   OxNR

Better Answer, A.   Matthew Prior.   See Answer to Cloe [or Chloe] Jealous

Better Answer to Cloe [or Chloe] Jealous, A.   Matthew Prior.   See Answer to Cloe [or Chloe] Jealous

Better Come Drink Wine with Me.   Po Chü-i.   CoBCP, tr. by Burton Watson

Better Days.   Essex Hemphill.   CAGL

Better disguised than the leaf-insect.   Lake, The.   Ted Hughes.   FaBoTw

Better get drunk and cry.   Otomo no Tabito.   OHMPJ

Better hurry along.   (LL)   Alexander's Ragtime Band.   Irving Berlin.   ReLy; TCAPo

Better never to have met you.   Yakamochi (Otomo no Yakamochi).   OHMPJ

Better not go to these deep woods.   Great Fountains, The.   Anne Hébert.   BoWoP, tr. by Willis Barnstone

Better not to go back to the village.   Malefic Return, The.   Ramón López Velarde.   OBVE, tr. by Samuel Beckett

Better one thin frail line of friendship in a letter.   Letter, The.   John Blight.   CBAP

Better Resurrection, A.   Christina Georgina Rossetti.   NOBVV; VWP; ViWPN

Better stuffed in a bag; drowned.   W. D. Snodgrass.   BodElec   Fr. Führer Bunker, The.

Better than a closet martinet.   What Happened?   John Wieners.   FTOS; PoM

Better than a dream, it left gargantuan. My Bomb. Beckian Fritz Goldberg. ExTi

Better than Gold. Abram Joseph Ryan. PoToHe

Better than grandeur, better than gold. Better than Gold. Abram Joseph Ryan. PoToHe

Better—than Music! For I—who heard it. Emily Dickinson. APN-2

Better the book against the rock. Three Poems about Children. Austin Clarke. CIP-2

Better the crime. Octavio Paz. PoetW, *tr. by* Eliot Weinberger *Fr.* Sunstone.

Better Things. George Macdonald. PWR

Better to be the rock above the river. La Crosse at Ninety Miles an Hour. Richard Eberhart. APT-2

Better to close the book and say good-night. Double Autumn, The. James Reeves. OxBSP

Better to dream away this profound June dusk. Returning a Lawn to the Field It Was. Brendan Galvin. PoCoUp

Better to live as a rogue and a bum. Mahsati. WPOW

Better to see your cheek grown hollow. Madman's Song. Elinor Wylie. MoAmPo; PoRA

Better to smell the violet cool than sip. Better Things. George Macdonald. PWR

Better trust all and be deceived. Faith. Frances Anne [*or* "Fanny"] Kemble. SWaP

Betty. Paul Mariani. SwNoth

Betty Barnes, the Book-Burner. Rosamund Marriott Watson. ViWPN

Betty Blue. Mother Goose. OxNR; ReMoGo

Betty Botter bought some butter. *Unknown.* OTCP; OxNR

Betty by the Sea. Ronald McCuaig. NOBAu

Betty Pringle's Pig. Mother Goose. OxNR

Betuix twell houris and ellevin. Amendis to the Telyouris and Sowtaris for the Turnament Maid on Thame, The. William Dunbar. OBSV

Between. Vladimir Holan. PoSu, *tr. by* Ian Milner and Jarmila Milner

Between. Ágnes Nemes Nagy. IQMS, *tr. by* Alan Dixon

Between. Ágnes Nemes Nagy. VCWP, *tr. by* Hugh Maxton

Between. Christian Karlson Stead. PoetW

Between a centipede and a flamingo. Difference. János Pilinszky. IQMS, *tr. by* Peter Jay

Between a Contractor and His Wife. *Unknown.* NOEC

Between a sleep and a sleep. (LL) Algernon Charles Swinburne. NAEL-5v2; NAEL-6v2 *Fr.* Atalanta in Calydon.

Between a sunny bank and the sun. Two Houses. Edward Thomas. FaBoCh

Between a Tyrant and a King. Difference between a King and a Tyrant, The. Timothy Kendall. NoSic

Between a winter's day and night. Blue Hour, The. Margarita Iosifovna Aliger. TCRP, *tr. by* Albert C. Todd

Between Acts. Janice Lowe. InTrad

Between an Unemployed Artist and His Wife. *Unknown.* NOEC

Between Aphorisms. Dorothy E. Reid. YaYoPo

Between arid mountains. Lake. Octavio Paz. TCLAP, *tr. by* Rachel Benson

Between Bombardments: A Journal. Karen Alkalay-Gut.
   "Instead of his leash." DTA
   "So we begin to plan." DTA
   "Some people terrified for their lives cut." DTA
   "Think of the children in Baghdad." DTA
   "Tonight we wait for the alarm." DTA
   "Unable to move." DTA

Between Days. Yusef Komunyakaa. ESEAA

Between dreams and day an immense distance. First Light. Lisa Suhair Majaj. PoArWo

Between each layer of tattered, broken flesh. Burial Detail. Andrew Hudgins. CBCWP

Between extremities. W. B. Yeats. NoAM

Between five and fifty. Praise. Jane Cooper. TAP

Between flocculent elbows, the soft peony wings. (LL) One of the Strangest. May Swenson. APT-2; OWoS

Between Gaeta and Capua. Franz Grillparzer. AuPH, *tr. by* Lowell A. Bangerter

Between going and staying the day wavers. Between Going and Staying. Octavio Paz. TCLAP, *tr. by* Eliot Weinberger

Between great coloured vanes the butterflies. Wings. Judith Wright. CBAP; NOBAu

Between grief on my knees and death on my feet. Choice. Abd al-Aziz Al-Maqalih. MAP, *tr. by* Lena Jayyusi and Christopher Middleton

Between his hands. *Unknown.* EaWin, *tr. by* J. Moussaieff Masson and W. S. Merwin

Between Hovers. Michael Longley. ModIr

Between hunger and love? (LL) Mundus et Infans. W. H. Auden. MoBrPo; NoAM

Between Language and Desire. Silvia Curbelo. TouFir

Between living and dreaming. Antonio Machado Ruiz. EnlH

Between me and the sunset, like a dome. Man against the Sky, The. Edwin Arlington Robinson. OxBA; TCAPo

Between me and the sunset, the whole of life. Present Evening, The. Eugenio Florit. TCLAP, *tr. by* Hoffman Reynolds Hays

Between me and the wood. Jay Macpherson. NOBC *Fr.* Ark, The.

Between my finger and my thumb. Digging. Seamus Heaney. BIrV; CIP-2; NAEL-5v2; NAEL-6v2; NoP-4; SpudSo; TwCP

Between my thighs like a valentine before. (LL) Tom Clark. PmAP; SPE *Fr.* You.

Between myself and thee! (LL) My Playmate. John Greenleaf Whittier. APN-1; NOBA

Between old battles and the ones I should. Pittsburgh in Passing. Samuel Hazo. GraLe

Between Our Folding Lips. Thomas Edward Brown. VerBaPo

Between Ourselves. Audre Lorde. ISC; WPOW

Between Ourselves and the Dead! (LL) Emily Dickinson. FaBoVe; NCAP

Between pale office workers. Looking Out to Sea Again on the Uptown Express. Sanford Fraser. UrbNat

Between pond and sheepbarn, by maples and watery birches. Sister on the Tracks, A. Donald Hall. GM

Between present and future happiness the abyss gapes. Tuti's Ice Cream. Chairil Anwar. PoetW, *tr. by* Burton Raffel

Between rebellion as a private study and the public. Last Poem. Charles Donnelly. BIrV

Between Rivers and Seas. Lance Henson. VoR

Between sandbanks marsh reflecting twilight clouds. Birthday Party. Kusano Shimpei. PFTM-1

Between Scylla and Charybdis. Yunna Petrovna [*or* Iunna Pinkhusovna] Moritz [*or* Morits]. ItGoST, *tr. by* Daniel Weissbort

Between Seasons. Li-Young Lee. TRP

Between the Acts. Elise Paschen. IllVoic

Between the boughs of a tall tree the sun rises like a persimmon in the gray sky. One Wintry Day. Pyong-hwa Cho. PoetW, *tr. by* Peter H. Lee

Between the brown hands of a server-lad. Maundy Thursday. Wilfred Owen. NPeEn; OxBSo

Between the conscious and the unconscious, the mind has put up a swing. Kabir. EnlH

Between the dark and the daylight. If. Franklin Pierce Adams. OBAL

Between the dark and the daylight. Children's Hour, The. Henry Wadsworth Longfellow. APN-1; BRP; ChAP; ITBLP; OBAL; OBCA; TCAPo; WHSW

Between the Devil and the Deep Blue Sea. Ted Koehler. ReLy

Between the earth and the sky. Inheritance, The. Sami Mahdi. MAP, *tr. by* May Jayyusi

Between the fear. Age of Terror. Denise Levertov. PFTM-2

Between the foam and the tide. To a Boy. Nancy Morejón. TANSG, *tr. by* Joy Renjilian-Burgy

Between the form of Life and Life. Emily Dickinson. APN-2

Between the Gardening and the Cookery. Bookshop Idyll, A. Kingsley Amis. OxBTC; PeLV

Between the ghetto's slumber. Casbah, The. Mamdouh 'Udwan. MAP, *tr. by* May Jayyusi and Naomi Shihab Nye

Between the idea and the word. Between. Vladimir Holan. PoSu, *tr. by* Ian Milner and Jarmila Milner

Between the lines. Between the Lines. Belinda Zubicueta Carmona. TANSG, *tr. by* Celeste Kostopulos-Cooperman

Between the Lines. Michael Hamburger. HP

Between the Moon and the Sun. Dave Jeddie Smith. BodElec

Between the pale blue of the morning sky. Dawn on the Willamette. Ella Higginson. SWaP

Between the Porch and the Altar. Robert Lowell.
   At the Altar. InPK-6

Between the railway and the mine. Blackberry, The. Norman Nicholson. MoBrPo

Between the stone huts of the vineyard hill. Deaf Mute Girl, The. István Vas. IQMS, *tr. by* Charles Abraham Wagner

Between the Wars. Robert Hass. VCAP

Between the wet trees and the sorry steeple. W. H. Louise Imogen Guiney. APN-2

Between the World and Me. Richard Wright. ISC; PAI
   (And one morning while in the woods I stumbled suddenly.) SSLK

Between them is the land of broken colors. Black Horse Rider, The. Pierre Loving. SPE

Between thirty and forty one is distracted by the Five Lusts. On Being Sixty. Po Chü-i. AWP; ChiP, *tr. by* Arthur Waley

Between to live and to think. Cloister. Gabriel Zaid. TCLAP, *tr. by* Mónica Hernández-Cancio

Between town and the. Quarry Pool, The. Denise Levertov. VGW

Between two fears, that is, between two loves. Poetic License. Leonard Nolens. TuT, tr. by Michael O'Loughlin

Between two fires. (LL) Conflict, The. Cecil Day Lewis. MoBrPo; NoP-4

Between two golden tufts of summer grass. Lying in the Grass. Sir Edmund William Gosse. EBVV

Between two rivers. Island. Langston Hughes. HCAP

Between two rivers, / North of the park. Langston Hughes. APT-2; HCAP Fr. Lenox Avenue Mural.

Between Us. James Merrill. PoE

Between us. Nizar Qabbani. MAP

Between Walls. William Carlos Williams. APT-1; TAP; VGW

Between What I See and What I Say. Octavio Paz. TCLAP, tr. by Eliot Weinberger

Between Worlds. Jacqueline Berger. AmPoNex

Between your sheets you soundly sleep. Between Your Sheets. Lady Mary Wortley Montagu. LW; PEW

Betweene the Spyder and the gentle Bee. (LL) Edmund Spenser. NoP-4; PBRV; PoE Fr. Amoretti.

Betweenpie mountains—lights a lovely mile. (LL) My Own Heart Let Me More Have Pity On. Gerard Manley Hopkins. FaBoMo; MoBrPo; NOBVV; NoP-4; TOF

Betweens. Norman McCaig. SPE

Betwixt two ridges of plow[e]d [or ploughed] land sat [or lay] Wat. Hunting of the Hare, The. Margaret Lucas Cavendish, Duchess of Newcastle. BASC; BWW; FaBoVe; NAEL-7v1; NOSC

Beulah Railway, The. Unknown. GM

Beverley's Saga. Grace Nichols. WaCA

Beverly Hills, Chicago. Gwendolyn Brooks. ESEAA; VGW Fr. Womanhood, The.

Beware. Kenneth Fearing. APT-2

Beware. Marina Ivanovna Tsvetaeva [or Tsvetaeva]. WoPoe, tr. by David McDuff

Beware: Do Not Read This Poem. Ishmael Reed. BPo; NIP-4; PAI (Tonite, thriller was / abt an ol woman, so vain she.) GT

Beware of Dogmas. Ebenezer Elliott. FaBoEE

Beware of gnawing the ideogram of nothingness. Karasumaru-Mitsuhiro. ZenPo, tr. by Takashi Ikemoto and Lucien Stryk

Beware of Ruins. Alec Derwent Hope. NoAM

Beware of the month Lenaion, bad days. Hesiod. WoPoe, tr. by Richmond Lattimore Fr. Works and Days.

Beware of thinking nothing's there. Virtual Particles. Frank Wilczek. NBLV

Beware the cuckoo, though she bring. Beware the Cuckoo. Ernest G. Moll. NOBAu

Beware! The Israelite of old, who tore. Warning, The. Henry Wadsworth Longfellow. APN-1; ChIV-1; NCAP; TCAPo

Beware the Kleptomaniac. Kleptomaniac, The. Roger McGough. NOxBChV

Beware. There are fawns. Kydios. WoPoe, tr. by Sam Hamill

Bewick and Graham. Unknown. ESPB

Bewick and the Graeme, The. Unknown. OxBB

Bewick Finzer. Edwin Arlington Robinson. MoAmPo; NAAL-2v2

Bewildered with the broken tongue. Words in Time. Archibald MacLeish. PoRA

Bewilderment at the Entrance of the Fat Boy into Eden, A. Daryl Hine. NOBC

Bewitched, Bothered and Bewildered. Lorenz Hart. APT-2 (He's a fool, and don't I know it.) ReLy

Bewley's Oriental Café, Westmoreland Street. Paul Durcan. CIP-2

Bewteis of the Fute-Ball, The. Unknown. OxBS

Bewty of hir amorus ene, The. Off Womanheid Ane Flour Delice. Unknown. OxBS

Bewwitching the blossoms of the spring grove. Unknown. SuSp Fr. Tzu-yeh Songs of the Four Seasons.

Beyond. Unknown. PWR

Beyond all this, the wish to be alone. Wants. Philip Larkin. GTBS-P

Beyond any. No Precedent. Muso Soseki. EaWin, tr. by W. S. Merwin

Beyond barred windows. Washing Stream, The. Li Ch'ing-chao. ErotSp, tr. by Sam Hamill

Beyond, beneath, within, wherever blood. Quintina of Crosses, A. Chad Walsh. TrCP

Beyond, beyond the mountain line. Dreams. Cecil Frances Alexander. NOxBChV

Beyond Compare. David Ross. ReLy

Beyond empty pews. Nicholas Virgilio. HA

Beyond Fear. Odia Ofeimun. HBAPE

Beyond Freedom. Michael Hannon. GeoHom

Beyond Gethsemane! (LL) Gethsemane. Rudyard Kipling. FaBoTw; NPeEn; PeFWW

Beyond Having. Ray Gonzalez. TouFir

Beyond Imagination. David Rokeah [or Rokeakh]. MHP, tr. by Ruth Finer Mintz

Beyond Kerguelen. Henry Clarence Kendall. NOBAu

Beyond Knowledge. Alice Thompson Meynell. ChIV-1

Beyond Light. Muso Soseki. EaWin, tr. by W. S. Merwin

Beyond Melody. Nathan [or Natan] Alterman. MHP, tr. by Ruth Finer Mintz

Beyond Nagel's Funeral Parlor. Elizabethans Called It Dying, The. James Schuyler. NeAP; PoM

Beyond Phigalia. Alec Derwent Hope. BMAP

Beyond Poetry. Shakuntala Hawoldar. HAWP

Beyond Religion. Lucretius. AWP, tr. by William Ellery Leonard

Beyond serenity / Gray kites. Tan Taigi. ZenPo, tr. by Takashi Ikemoto and Lucien Stryk

Beyond stars. L. A. Davidson. HA

Beyond that first domestic kiss. Epithalamion. Terese Svoboda. ExTi

Beyond that shadowy nest of red madrones. (LL) What Could Happen. Dorianne Laux. BodElec; GeoHom

Beyond the Alps. Robert Lowell. LCAP-2; NOBA

Beyond the bamboo fence, cooking fire and smoke. Liu Tsung-yüan. SuSp Fr. Farmers.

Beyond the Beaten Way. George Sands Johnson. PWR

Beyond the blind, the rain rattles down. Tune: Ripples Sifting Sand. Li Yü. CoBCP, tr. by Burton Watson

Beyond the Blue Horizon. Leo Robin. ReLy

Beyond the breakers. Joyce Mansour. MFP, tr. by Martin Sorrell

Beyond the Chiltern coast, this church. Edlesborough. Anne Ridler. SacPr

Beyond the Dip of Bell. (LL) Emily Dickinson. BoWoP; TCAPo

Beyond the East Gate. Unknown. TAL

Beyond the edge of the sepia. Lament for a Cricket Eleven. Kenneth Allott. OxBTC

Beyond the End. Denise Levertov. NeAP; VGW

Beyond the foot of the bed: a seascape whose ocean. On Motel Walls. David Wagoner. DiPo

Beyond the gate the cormorant had gone and not returned. Quatrain. Tu Fu. SuSp, tr. by Jerome P. Seaton

Beyond the Grave. Margaret E. Bruner. PoToHe

Beyond the great valley an odd instinctive rising. Ascent to the Sierras. Robinson Jeffers. OxBA

Beyond the hour we counted rain that fell. Old Countryside. Louise Bogan. HAP; WPE

Beyond the Hunting Woods. Donald Justice. CoAmPo

Beyond the Image: plot of what is unutterable. Beyond the Image. Henriqueta Lisboa. TCLAP, tr. by Hélcio Veiga Costa

Beyond the Last Lamp. Thomas Hardy. NOBE

Beyond the last window. Blind. Vincente Huidobro. CuPo

Beyond the laughing billboard girl. Leroy Gorman. HA

Beyond the low marsh-meadows and the beach. Pines and the Sea, The. Christopher Pearse Cranch. ColAP

Beyond the mountain passes. Crossing Han River. Li P'in. OHMPC, tr. by Kenneth Rexroth

Beyond the night. Night. Marjorie Agosin. ExTi

Beyond the park, at River's Head. Drinking at Crooked River. Tu Fu. CrYelRi, tr. by Sam Hamill

Beyond the people. Kevin Young. AmPoNex Fr. Escape Artist, The.

Beyond the point where the rivers. Old Man Advancing. Muso Soseki. EaWin, tr. by W. S. Merwin

Beyond the porch. John Wills. HA

Beyond the Profit of Today. Unknown. PoToHe

Beyond the red traffic light, young chestnut leaves. Czeslaw Milosz. BodElec Fr. Lithuania, after Fifty-Two Years.

Beyond the snatch of time, my daily life. Juo. ZenPo, tr. by Takashi Ikemoto and Lucien Stryk

Beyond the sphere which spreads to widest space. Dante Alighieri. AWP; CTC; EaItPo, tr. by Dante Gabriel Rossetti Fr. La Vita Nuova.

Beyond the steady rock the steady sea. Fable, The. Yvor Winters. APT-2

Beyond the stream at Seta stretches an endless view. Liu Ya-tzu. SuSp Fr. Miscellaneous Poems on Lake Biwa.

Beyond the temple, a hidden cliff. Yang Shih-ch'i. CoBLCP Fr. Group of Officials, A.

Beyond the town a sterile quarter grew. Poets, The. Aleksandr Aleksandrovich Blok. TCRP, tr. by Geoffrey Thurley

Beyond the view of crossroads ringed with breath. Rubaiyat. Mimi Khalvati. MFPA

Beyond the wall I hear the cry of someone selling clams. (LL) Impromptu on a Hangover. P'i Jih-hsiu. CoBCP; ColAnChi, tr. by Burton Watson

Beyond the waste of commerce there are hills. Office Window. Llewelyn Wyn Griffith. AngWePo

Beyond the World. Muso Soseki. EaWin, tr. by W. S. Merwin

Beyond time and space. Declaration. Nikolai Ivanovich Glazkov. TCRP, *tr. by Daniel Weissbort*

Beyond Vermont's green hills, against the skies. Richard Henry Wilde. APN-1 *Fr. Hesperia.*

Beyond Words. Robert Frost. Spl; WeW-3

Bhagavad-Gita, The. *Unknown.*
    "Arjuna, his war flag a rampant monkey." WoPoe, *tr. by Barbara Stoler Miller*
    "Arjuna sat dejected." WoPoe, *tr. by Barbara Stoler Miller*
    "Hear father yet thou Long-Armed Lord! these latest words I say." TAL
    "Learn from me, Son of Kunti! also this." TOF
    "Learn now, dear Prince! how, if thy soul be set." TAL
    "Nay, but of such an one." TOF
    "Now will I open unto thee—whose heart." TAL
    "Sovereign soul, The / Of him who lives self-governed and at peace." TOF
    "Steadfast a lamp burns sheltered from the wind." TOF
    "Tell me." WoPoe, *tr. by Barbara Stoler Miller*
    "Therefore, who doeth work rightful to do." TAL
    "This, for my soul's peace, have I heard from Thee." TAL
    "Those who realize true wisdom." EnIH
    "Who is that BRAHMA? What that Soul of Souls." TAL
    "Yet hard / The travail is for such as bend their minds." TOF

Bi-Focal. William Stafford. RB

Bialik tradition back home was, A. Earrings. Annette Bialik Harchik. GotH

Bianca. Arthur Symons. PeVV

Bianca among the Nightingales. Elizabeth Barrett Browning. BrRo; GTBS-P

Bias of the will betray, The. (LL). Ralph Waldo Emerson. APN-1; TCAPo *Fr. Quatrains.*

Bible, The. David Levi.
    "Thou, Zion, old and suffering." TrJP

Bible, The. Lizelia Augusta Jenkins Moorer. CBWP-3

Bible, The. Thomas Traherne. PeECV

Bible Defence of Slavery. Frances Ellen Watkins Harper. APN-2

Bible is an antique Volume, The. Emily Dickinson. APN-2; ChIV-1; NAAL-2v1; NAAL-3; NoP-4

Bible Lesson. Harvey Shapiro. TaR

Bible. Poland. Lodz Ghetto. Nineteen hundred forty one. Micrographic Manuscript, Miniature (2). Esther Ettinger. DTA, *tr. by Mariana Barr*

Bible says Sennacherib's campaign was spoiled, The. Sonnet. Clive Staples Lewis. TrCP

Bible. Spain. Saragossa. Fourteen hundred and something. Micrographic Manuscript, Miniature (1). Esther Ettinger. DTA, *tr. by Mariana Barr*

Bible Story. Charles Causley. TOF

Bible Study. Gloria C. Oden. ESEAA; GT

Biblical Meditations. Yehuda Amichai [*or* Amikhai]. WoPoe, *tr. by Benjamin Harshav and Barbara Harshav*

Bibliographer. Josephine Miles. FaBoWP

Bibliolaters. James Russell Lowell.
    God Is Not Dumb. ChIV-1

Bibulous eagle behind me at the ball game, The. One to Nothing. Carolyn Kizer. OBAL

"Biby's" Epitaph. *Unknown. See Dahn the Plug'ole*

Bic lighter, A. Tee. Reuben Jackson. UnSA

Bicause I have the still kept fro lyes and blame. Petrarch. OBVE

Bicentennial Anti-Poem for Italian-American Women. Daniela Gioseffi. UnSA

Bicentennial Barbie. Denise Duhamel. AmPoNex

Bickering of vowels on the buses, The. Irish Childhood in England: 1951, An. Eavan Boland. CIP-2

Bicycle. David Malouf. BMAP

Bicycle Racers, The. Ann Townsend. AmPoNex; NeAmPo

Bicycle Rider, The. Thomas William Shapcott. CBAP

Bicycle rolls on the road, A. Malcolm de Chazal. SurPaPo, *tr. by Patricia Terry Fr. Sens Plastique.*

Bicycles go by in twos and threes, The. Inniskeen Road: July Evening. Patrick Kavanagh. CIP-2; NPeEn; NoAM; OxBSo

Bicycles! Tricycles! John Banister Tabb. OBAL

Bid a strong ghost stand at the head. Prayer for My Son, A. W. B. Yeats. EBEV; OxAEP-2; RaBo

Bid for a new majority, The. No Transport. Tony Lopez. Oth

Bid me Good Morning. (LL) Life. Anna Laetitia Barbauld. GTBS-P; NAEL-6v2; NoP-4; OBEV; OxAEP-1; PWR

Bid me no more good-night; because. Good-night. James Shirley. BeJo

Bid me not go where neither suns nor showers [show'rs]. Valediction. William Cartwright. BeJo

Bid me remember, O my gracious Lord. Mary Elizabeth Coleridge. SacPr *Fr. Death.*

Bid me strike a match and blow. (LL) In Memory of Eva Gore-Booth and Con Markievicz. W. B. Yeats. NPeEn; NoAM; OBMV; OxBTC

Bid me to live, and I will live. To Anthea, Who May Command Him Anything. Robert Herrick. BASC; CaPo; GTBS-P; NOBE; NOSC; OBEV; OxBEV

Bid the fond mother spill her infant's blood. To One Who Said I Must Not Love. Sarah Fyge Egerton. ECWP

Bid you be merry and remember death. (LL) De Cœnatione Micae. Martial. FaBoCH; RomPo, *tr. by Robert Louis Stevenson*

Bid your Papa Goodnight. Sweet exhibition! Mrs. Hopley, on Seeing Her Children Say Goodnight to Their Father. Gerard Manley Hopkins. FaBoEE

Bidding Farewell to Secretary Chou. Yu Hsin. CrYelRi, *tr. by Sam Hamill*

Bidin' My Time. George Gershwin. ReLy

Bids Farewell to Lesbos. Mary Robinson. CenSon; RWP

Bids spheres and atoms in just order move. (LL) Hand and Foot, The [*or* Hand and the Foot, The]. Jones Very. APN-1; OxBA; SacPr; TAP

Big animals: despondent / at table: unsated, The. Poem. Paul Klee. PFTM-1

Big as a down duvet the night. Lullaby. Molly Peacock. PasH

Big Baboon, The. Joseph Hilaire Pierre Belloc. MoBrPo

Big Bad Art Thing, The. Carter Ratcliff. KGB

Big Bar. Kenward Elmslie. PmAP

Big Ben is cracked, we needs must own. To Disraeli. Shirley Brooks. NOBL

Big Bessie Throws Her Son into the Street. Gwendolyn Brooks. VGW *Fr. Catch of Shy Fish, A.*

Big Billie Potts was big and stout. Ballad of Billie Potts, The. Robert Penn Warren. FuPo; NOBA; OxBA

Big Bluejay Composition. Ron Padgett. PmAP

Big box, / Little box. *Unknown.* OxNR

Big Boy came. Catch. Langston Hughes. NoAM

Big brown eyes, little dark Australian boy. Slum Dwelling. Jack Davis. IBA

Big Cars. Jane Flanders. PBCAP

Big Chariot, The. *Unknown.* ChiP, *tr. by Arthur Waley*

Big Chill Variations. Reuben Jackson. UnSA

Big cities are reeking with grief. Limerick. *Unknown.* PeLi

Big core into the spreading nettles, The. (LL) My Grandfather and His Apple-Tree. John Ormond. AngWePo; TCAWP

Big Daddy Lipscomb, who used to help them up. Say Good-bye to Big Daddy. Randall Jarrell. MoASP

Big doors of the country stand open and ready, The. Walt Whitman. ColAP; ITBLP *Fr. Song of Myself.*

Big Engines, The. Jack Kerouac. NeAP *Fr. Mexico City Blues.*

Big enough for an ox, the cauldron. Anyte [*or* Anytes]. GrAn

Big farm girl with the dumb prophetic body, The. Bitter Harvest. Alistair Campbell. PeNZ

Big Fire at the Architectural College, The. Andrey [*or* Andrei] Andreievich Voznesensky [*or* Voznesenskii]. CLPP, *tr. by Anselm Hollo*

Big Girls. Tracey Herd. MFPA

Big guns again. / No speakee well. Imperator Victus. Hart Crane. OxBA

Big house, / Little house. *Unknown.* OxNR

Big House Revisited, The. Tony Medina. SpirFl

Big Island whispered to little island. In the Sea. Brendan Kennelly. BiHa

Big Jigsaw. Chris Forhan. NAPBL

Big John. Norman J. Loftis. SpirFl

Big John's Tears Fall to the River. Siobhan Campbell. MFPA

Big L, The. Vera Hérold. SurWo, *tr. by Guy Ducornet*

Big living room is crowded, The. Fifties Rock Party, 1985. Judith Berke. SwNoth

Big man in batakari, The. Steps. Kojo Laing. NAfrP

Big Momma. Haki R. Madhubuti. AmFaPo; BPo

Big Muddy daddy my daddys gris-gris to the world, A. Mud Water Shango. Tom Weatherly. GT; NBV; SeSe

Big No-No, The. Chris Greenhalgh. NeBl

Big-nose looks best in mountain-coarse clothes. My Man Pa Replies. Li Ho. CoBCP; ColAnChi, *tr. by Burton Watson*

Big Parade, The. Stephen Knight. NeBl; TCAWP

Big Rabbit goes to see his baby. *Unknown.* STP

Big rats! Big rats! *Unknown.* ColAnChi *Fr. Classic of Odes.*

Big river goes east, The. Lyrics to the Tune "The Charms of Niennu:" At the Red Cliff I Ponder Over Antiquity. Su Tung-p'o (Su Shih). WoPoe, *tr. by David Lattimore*

Big Rock-Candy Mountain, The. Louis Edward Sissman. GM

Big Rock Candy Mountains, The. *Unknown.* FaBoA; NOBA; OBAL; TTTS

Big rocks into pebbles. Rocks. Florence Parry Heide. NTCP

Big ship sails on the alley alley oh, The. Big Ship Sails, The. *Unknown.* FaBoVe

Big sleep, the high window, The. John Whitworth. NewEx

Big sound on the ground. (LL)   E. E. Cummings.   OxBA; VGW

Big steel tourist shield says maybe, The.   On a Field Trip at Fredericksburg. Dave Jeddie Smith.   HCAP; PoPoPo

Big stones of the cistern behind the barn, The.   Twilights.   James Wright (1927–80).   LCAP-2

Big sweet muscles of an athlete's dream, The.   Massacre of the Innocents. Alec Derwent Hope.   GI

Big Swimming.   Edwin Ford Piper.   APT-1

Big Tease.   Ania Walwicz.   BMAP

Big tom was a black nigga man.   River Town Packin House Blues.   Quincy Troupe.   LoL

Big-uddered piebald cattle low.   Christmas Holiday.   Alun Lewis.   PoWW

Big Wind.   Theodore Roethke.   ColAP; HarvBoo; TRP; VGW

Big with great purposes and proud, they sat.   Homer.   OBVE   Fr. Iliad, The.

Big Words, The.   Brendan Kennelly.   EmeKit

Big yellow woman.   Laurel Street, 1950.   Dorothy Perry Thompson.   SpirFl

Big young bareheaded woman, A.   Proletarian Portrait.   William Carlos Williams.   BLT; OBAL; SAmP; TAP

Big Zeb Johnson.   Everett Hoagland.   GT

Bigamy.   Roy McFadden.   PNI   Fr. Memories of Chinatown.

Bigger fish have country cousins here, The.   Frank Ormsby.   PNI   Fr. Northern Spring, A.

Bigger thomas.   Big House Revisited, The.   Tony Medina.   SpirFl

Biggest Killing, The.   Edward Dorn.   VGW

Bight, The.   Elizabeth Bishop.   APT-2; EmeKit; FaBoWP; HCAP; NAAL-2v2; PoetW; RB; VCAP

Biglow Papers, The.   James Russell Lowell.

　Courtin', The.   NOBA; OBAL

　('Cruetin Sarjunt, The.)   TCAPo

　("Gineral B. is a sensible man.")   OBCoV

　Introduction.   TCAPo

　Letter, A ("This kind o' sogerin' ain't a mite like our October trainin'"). OxBA

　Letter, A ("Thrash away, you'll hev to rattle.")   OxBA

　Letter Six—The Pious Editors' Creed.   APN-1; NCAP

　Rev. Homer Wilbur's "Festina Lente."   OBAL

Bigness of cannon, The.   E. E. Cummings.   MoAmPo

Bignonia blossoms on both shores, a streamful of water.   In a Boat on the Cha River.   Chang Yü.   CoBLCP, tr. by Jonathan Chaves

Bilbea, I was in Babylon on Saturday night.   Bilbea.   Carl Sandburg.   APT-1

Bilberries.   Gerda Mayer.   SpI

Bilingual Sestina.   Julia Alvarez.   ExTi; FFC

Bill.   Peter Kocan.   CBAP

Bill.   P. G. Wodehouse.   ReLy

Bill Bailey, Won't You Please Come Home.   Hughie Cannon.   OBAL

Bill collectors gather.   Ain't We Got Fun.   Richard A. Whiting.   ReLy

Bill Gets Burned.   Howard Phelps Putnam.   APT-2

Bill hated the separation implied by the term.   Nature Poetry.   Meg Kearney. UrbNat

Bill (Original Version).   P. G. Wodehouse.   ReLy

Bill, Posted, A.   Philip Kobylarz.   BAP-97

Bill / Was ill.   Careless Talk.   Mark Hollis.   NBLV

Bill Williams was in Hell without a guide.   Bill Gets Burned.   Howard Phelps Putnam.   APT-2

Billboard girl.   Leroy Gorman.   HA

Billboards.   Eric Amann.   HA

Billie Holiday.   Sterling Plumpp.   IllVoic

Billie Holiday Chronicles, The.   Patricia Jones.

　Birth of Rhythm and Blues, The.   ReTh

Billie Holiday's burned voice.   Canary.   Rita Dove.   ESEAA; LoL; SeSe; VCAP

Billie in Silk.   Angela Jackson.   ReTh; SeSe

Billie's Blues.   Alfred Corn.   CAGL

Billowing clouds surging across the heavens.   Tune: "Fisherman's Pride." Li Ch'ing-chao.   ColAnChi, tr. by Jiaosheng Wang

Billy.   Linda McCarriston.   LoL

Billy Batter.   Dennis Lee.   TLR

Billy, Billy.   Unknown.   ReMoGo

Billy Budd, Foretopman.   Herman Melville.

　Billy in the Darbies.   APN-2; HAP; NAAL-2v1; NCAP; NOBA; OxBoLi; WoPoe

Billy Goat Gruff.   Troll to her Children, The.   Jane Yolen.   OTCP

Billy in one of his nice new sashes.   Harry Graham.   NBLV; NOxBChV; PeLV   Fr. Some Ruthless Rhymes.

Billy in the Darbies.   Herman Melville.   APN-2; HAP; NAAL-2v1; NCAP; NOBA; OxBoLi; WoPoe   Fr. Billy Budd, Foretopman.

Billy's Famous Lounge.   Joe Wenderoth.   NAPBL

Binary.   Chris Wallace-Crabbe.   OBCoV

Binary mathematician, A.   Limerick.   Unknown.   PeLi

Binds us together with you. (LL)   Chorus of the Rescued.   Nelly Sachs. PoSu; WPOW

Bing Crosby was singing "White Christmas."   When I First Saw Snow. Gregory Djanikian.   UnSA

Bingen on the Rhine.   Caroline Elizabeth Norton.   TreFP

Bingo.   Unknown.   TTTS

Binnorie; or, The Two Sisters.   Unknown.   OBEV; PoE

Binsey Poplars (Felled 1879).   Gerard Manley Hopkins.   EBVV; NAEL-5v2; NAEL-6v2; NoAM; PAI; RB

Bio 7.   David Moolten.   BloBone

Bio-Rodent-Oriole.   Edwin Torres.   HeMarv

Biographia Literaria.   Joan Retallack.   FTOS

Biographical News.   Daria Menicanti.   CItWP, tr. by Cinzia Sartini Blum and Lara Trubowitz

Biography.   Imamu Amiri Baraka.   TAP

Biography.   Mariella Bettarini.   CItWP, tr. by Cinzia Sartini Blum and Lara Trubowitz

Biography.   Abraham Moses Klein.   TrJP

Biography.   John Masefield.

　"Other bright days of action have seemed great."   OxBTC

Biography.   Michael Ondaatje.   NoAM

Biography of an Agnostic.   Louis Ginsberg.   TrJP

Biography of Southern Rain.   Kenneth Patchen.   VGW

Biological / and dynastic phenomenon, The.   Art of Picasso, The.   Salvador Dali.   SPE, tr. by David Gascoyne

Biological Light.   Primus St. John.   GifTon

Biology Teacher.   Zbigniew Herbert.   PoSu, tr. by John Carpenter

Biplane shuttles through the telegraph wires, The.   Sunday.   Philippe Soupault. PFTM-1

Birch.   Karen Shepard.   Unle

Birch bark, soundings in the linden wood.   Standing at Pasternak's Table, Peredelkino.   James Ragan.   TWW

Birch begins to crack its outer sheath, The.   Young Birch, A.   Robert Frost. SAmP

Birch Canoe.   Carter Revard.   NoP-4

Birch-Tree at Loschwitz, The.   Amy Levy.   TrJP

Birches.   Robert Frost.   APT-1; AmFaPo; FaBoVe; HarvBoo; HeIP-4; ITBLP; MoAmPo; NAAL-2v2; NAAL-5; NoAM; NoP-4; OxBA; PAI; PoPoPo; PoRA; RB; SAmP; SoSe-8; TAP; TCAPo; TFi; TRP

Birches falling down the hillside. (LL)   For My Grandmother, Bridget Halpin. Michael Hartnett.   BIrV; ModIr; PBCIP

Birches stand in their beggar's row, The.   February; the Boy Breughel. Norman Dubie.   LCAP-2

Bird.   Kim Addonizio.   UrbNat

Bird.   Joy Harjo.   SeSe

Bird.   Frieda Hughes.   NeBl

Bird.   Ágnes Nemes Nagy.   BoWoP; PoSu, tr. by Bruce Berlind

Bird.   Yona Volach.   DTA, tr. by Miriyam Glazer

Bird, The.   Robert Greacen.   PNI

Bird, The.   Max Michelson.   TrJP

Bird, The.   "St.-John Perse."   OWoS, tr. by Robert Fitzgerald

Bird, The.   Henry Vaughan.   ESCV; GeHe; OBEV; PoE

Bird, The.   Susan M. Whitmore.   AmPoNex

Bird and the Bell, The.   Christopher Pearse Cranch.   APN-1

Bird and Waterfall Music.   Wang Wei.   OHMPC

Bird at Dawn, The.   Harold Monro.   MoBrPo

Bird Bee.   Bob Cobbing.   Oth

Bird came down the Walk, A.   Emily Dickinson.   APN-2; AmFaPo; ColAP; HeIP-4; ITBLP; MoAmPo; NAAL-2v1; NAAL-3; NAAL-5; NAWM-7v2; NCAP; NOBA; NTCP; NoAM; NoP-4; OBAL; OBCA; OxBA; PoRA; SAmP; TFi

Bird Catcher, The.   Unknown.   TTY, tr. by Ulli Beier

Bird chase bird.   Bush Telegram.   Tom Pickard.   Oth

Bird-cherry was my wife, The.   Yury [or Iurii] Timofeievich Galanskov. TCRusP, tr. by Olive Dehn

Bird chirped at my window this morning, A.   April.   Amy Lowell.   PoBW

Bird comes, A / delicately as a little girl.   Akiko Yosano.   WPOW

Bird-creole or the billowing froth of bride song.   Iain Sinclair.   Oth   Fr. Ebbing of Kraft, The.

Bird does not live / charles christopher parker is dead.   Assassination of Charlie Parker, The.   Arthur Brown.   SeSe

Bird Dressed as Solitude and Tears.   Jeannette Miller.   TANSG, tr. by Paula Vega

Bird flew tangent-wise to the open window, A.   Bird, The.   Robert Greacen. PNI

Bird flies and I gum it to a concept, A. Letter to Anne Ridler. George Sutherland Fraser. OxBS

Bird half wakened in the lunar moon, A. On a Bird Singing in its Sleep. Robert Frost. APT-1

Bird I cannot name crows, A. (LL) New Poem, A. Robert Duncan. NNaP; PoM

Bird in a Gilded Cage, A. Arthur J. Lamb. TCAPo

Bird in the Hand, A. Vassar Miller. CRP

Bird is calling from the willow, A. Unknown. NOIV Fr. Four Glosses.

Bird is lost, The. Yardbird's Skull. Owen Dodson. VGW

Bird is meditation, The. Bird Is Meditation, The. Amina Said. HAWP, tr. by Eric Sellin

Bird is my neighbor, a whimsical fellow and dim, The. Crane Is My Neighbor, The. John Shaw Neilson. CBAP

Bird-Language. W. H. Auden. OWoS

Bird Language. Christopher Pearse Cranch. APN-1

Bird Lives. Faye Moskowitz. MiVo

Bird, most ardent for life of all our blood kin, The. Bird, The. "St.-John Perse." OWoS, tr. by Robert Fitzgerald

Bird Named Isidore, The. Evelyn Posamentier. GotH

Bird Nests. Angela Shaw. NeAmPo

Bird of Death. Sharon Olinka. TWW

Bird of Endless Time, The. James Laughlin. WeW-3

Bird of Fire, The. Alda Merini. CItWP, tr. by Cinzia Sartini Blum and Lara Trubowitz

Bird of Night, The. Randall Jarrell. KaS

Bird of Power. Jim Tollerud. VoR

Bird of the bitter bright grey golden morn. Ballad of François Villon, A. Algernon Charles Swinburne. PoRA

Bird of the moths! that radiant wing. Butterfly, The. Robert Stephen Hawker. EBVV

Bird of the tropic! thou, who lov'st to stray. To the White Bird of the Tropic. Helen Maria Williams. CenSon

Bird of the woodland, sing me a song. To the Mock-Bird. Mary Weston Fordham. CBWP-2

Bird on a Jaunt. T. Harri Jones. TCAWP

Bird on Briar. Unknown. MiEL

Bird rests in the air, the stone rests on the land, The. "Angelus Silesius." GePo, tr. by George C. Schoolfield Fr. Cherubical Wanderer, The.

Bird's fire-fangled feathers dangle down, The. (LL) Of Mere Being. Wallace Stevens. APT-1; HCAP; NoP-4; WoPoe

Bird's Song, A. Dame Edith Sitwell. NALW

Bird saw the young Burara girls, twisting their strings, making string figures, The. Unknown. NOBAu Fr. Goulburn Island Song Cycle.

Bird Scarer, The. Unknown. ReMoGo

Bird-shaped island, with secretive bird-voices. New Guinea. James Philip McAuley. NOCV

Bird-Shooting. Eugenio Montale. ItPo, tr. by Gayle Ridinger

Bird-Singing Stream. Wang Wei. ChinPo, tr. by Yip Wai-lim

Bird sings from the tree, A. Heartsong. Khaled Mattawa. BAP-97; NAPBL; NeAmPo

Bird Sips Water. Keith Bosley. Spl

Bird Song. William Carlos Williams. SAmP

Bird Song, The. Mrs. Henry Linden. CBWP-4

Bird Starver's Cry. Unknown. FaBoVe

Bird swerved dapple-white in the blue sky, The. Winged in Gold. Euros Bowen. OBWVE, tr. by the author

Bird that I don't know, A. Country Life, A. Randall Jarrell. MoAmPo

Bird, the long throat bent back, and the eyes in hiding. (LL) Winter Swan. Louise Bogan. APT-2; ColAP; OWoS

Bird, to Its Young, The. Mihály Tompa. IQMS, tr. by Watson Kirkconnell

Bird Was Singing, A. Dietmar, von Aist [or Eist]. AWP, tr. by Jethro Bithell

Bird watchers top my honors list. Up from the Egg; the Confessions of a Nuthatch Avoider. Ogden Nash. PoRA

Bird-Watching. Dennis Schmitz. LCAP-2

Bird-witted. Marianne Craig Moore. APT-1; NAAL-2v2

Bird-Woman. Rachel McAlpine. PeNZ

Bird, you sing and sing. Kukutis in the Reich's Guard House. Marcelijus Martinaitis. TWW, tr. by Laima Sruoginis

Birdcatcher, The. Ralph Hodgson. MoBrPo

Birdfoot's Grampa. Joseph Bruchac. UnSA

Birdie McReynolds. Samuel Hoffenstein. NBLV

Birdland. Allen Fisher. Oth

Birdless heaven, seadusk, one lone star, A. Tutto è Sciolto. James Joyce. OBMV

Birds. Frieda Hughes. NeBl

Birds. Robinson Jeffers. APT-1; VGW

Birds. Unknown. AWP Fr. Thousand and One Nights, The.

Birds. Judith Wright. NoP-4

Birds. Subnarcosis. Andrea Zanzotto. ItPo, tr. by Gayle Ridinger

Birds, The. Aristophanes.
  Chorus of Birds. AWP

Birds against the April wind, The. What the Birds Said. John Greenleaf Whittier. APN-1; NOBA

Birds and Fishes. Robinson Jeffers. NAAL-2v2; NAAL-5; NoP-4

Birds and leaves disconnect in Fall. Zimmer in Fall. Paul Zimmer. CA

Birds and periodic blood. 5:30 A.M. Adrienne Rich. NOBA

Birds and their chatter overwhelm me with feeling, The. Unknown. CoBCP

Birds are gone to bed the cows are still, The. Hares at Play. John Clare. RB; WoPoe

Birds Are in the Air at Ease. Francisco de Quevedo y Villegas. SpanPo, tr. by William M. Davis

Birds are in the bushes and the wolf is at the door, The. (LL) Everything in Its Place. Arthur Guiterman. NBLV; OBAL; OBCoV

Birds at dawn fly around in confusion now you are gone, The. Lament for Te Heuheu Herea. Te Heuheu Tukino. PeNZ, tr. by Margaret Orbell

Birds at Winter Nightfall. Thomas Hardy. MoBrPo

Birds become frightened when the mountain moon sets. Majestic Valley. Chu Yi-tsun. SuSp, tr. by Chang Yin-nan

Birds, birds, birds. Beat Poem by an Academic Poet. Vassar Miller. WPE

Birds come like fishes out of the air, The. Prey to Prey. David Rowbotham. CBAP

Birds drip from the trees. Daybreak. Bert Meyers. SPE

Birds even in the city. New York. Steven Blevins. PoCoUp

Birds / Fly into the depths of our existence. Seed, The. Tomasz Jastrun. AF, tr. by Michael March

Birds fly under the bridge, The. Dar a Luz. Elmaz Abinader. GraLe

Birds follow the sun / rain coming on / we drive South. Lady's Days. Larry Neal. NBV

Birds from the Mountains, The. Chang Chi. OHMPC, tr. by Kenneth Rexroth

Birds go to sleep by the sweet, wild twist of her song, The. (LL) Outlaw of Loch Lene, The. Unknown. BIrV; OBEV, tr. by Jeremiah Joseph Callanan

Birds have long been silent, The. Cult of Love, The. Hadewijch. NAWM-7v1, tr. by Peter Dronke

Birds have Vanished, The. Li Po. BLT; EnlH, tr. by Sam Hamill

Birds have vanished, The. Snowy River. Liu Tsung-yüan. CrYelRi, tr. by Sam Hamill

Birds have vanished down the sky, The. Zazen on Ching-t'ing Mountain. Li Po. CrYelRi, tr. by Sam Hamill

Birds have vanished into the sky, The. Birds Have Vanished, The. Li Po. BLT; EnlH, tr. by Sam Hamill

Birds in Snow. "H. D." APT-1

Birds in the high Hall-garden. Tennyson. NAEL-5v2; NAEL-6v2; PeVV Fr. Maud [A Monodrama].

Birds Leaving. Johanna Kruit. TuT, tr. by Medbh McGuckian

Birds' Nest. John Clare. OWoS; OxBSP

Birds Nest. Gloria Fuertes. RaBo

Birds' Nests. Edward Thomas. OWoS

Birds of a feather flock together. Birds of a Feather. Unknown. ReMoGo

Birds of Detroit. Greg Pape. PBCAP

Birds of Killingworth (The Poet's Tale), The. Henry Wadsworth Longfellow. OxBA Fr. Tales of a Wayside Inn.

Birds of Passage, The. Jones Very. NCAP

Birds of Prey. Claude McKay. APT-1

Birds of Tin, The. Charles Madge. SPE

Birds on a Powerline. Herbert Asquith. NAAAL

Birds' Refuge, The. Sojourner Kincaid Rolle. GeoHom

Birds sang in the wet trees, The. Wet Evening in April. Patrick Kavanagh. OPOU

Birds sang sweet as ony bell, The. Sir Aldingar. Unknown. ESPB

Birds singing. Jack Kerouac. HA

Birds suddenly dropped dead. Fata Morgana in Flanders. Willem M. Roggeman. TuT, tr. by Gabriel Rosenstock

Birds That Woke Us: An Urban Pastoral, The. Jeffrey Harrison. UrbNat

Birds the more white, against green stream. Quatrain. Tu Fu. SuSp, tr. by Jerome P. Seaton

Birds Waking. W. S. Merwin. NOBA

Birdsong. Burns Singer. FaBoTw

Birdsong. Unknown, fr. Terezin Concentration Camp. INSAB

Birdsong 2. Unknown, fr. Terezin Concentration Camp. INSAB

Birdsong Brook. Wang Wei. SuSp, tr. by Irving Y. Lo

Birdsong Valley. Wang Wei. CrYelRi, tr. by Sam Hamill

Birdsville Track, The. Douglas Stewart.
  "Oh the corrugated-iron town." CBAP

Birdwatchers of America. Anthony Hecht. NOBA; NoAM

Birdwatching at Fan Lake.   Anita Endrezze.   HATNAP

Birks of Aberfeldy [Composed on the Spot], The.   Robert Burns.   CTC

Birmingham.   Louis MacNeice.   MoBrPo; OxAEP-2

Birth.   Gioconda Belli.   TANSG, *tr.* by Steven F. White

Birth.   Edith Bruck.   BoWoP, *tr.* by Ruth Feldman

Birth.   Louise Erdrich.   NoP-4

Birth.   Amir Gilbo'a.   MHP

Birth.   Gabriela Melinescu.   BoWoP

Birth, A.   James Dickey.   NOBA

Birth, The.   Paul Muldoon.   EmeKit

Birth (al-Maulid).   Muhammad al-Mahdi Al-Majdhoub.   MAP, *tr.* by Charles Doria and Salma Khadra Jayyusi

Birth-Bond, The.   Dante Gabriel Rossetti.   Son   *Fr.* House of Life, The.

Birth-Day, The.   Mary Robinson.   ECWP; WoRP

Birth days: as of the spirit.   Birthday Triptych.   Peter Scupham.   HarvBoo

Birth-Dues.   Robinson Jeffers.   MoAmPo

Birth-Hour.   Lindley Williams Hubbell.   YaYoPo

Birth in a Narrow Room, The.   Gwendolyn Brooks.   BlSi; NoP-4

Birth Is Death, Death Is Birth.   Friedrich von Logau.   GePo, *tr.* by George C. Schoolfield

Birth, 1975.   Cheryl Van Dyke.   GifTon

Birth of a Coachman.   Paul Durcan.   PBCIP

Birth of a Shark, The.   David Wevill.   TwCP

Birth of a Son.   Sam Hunt.   PeNZ

Birth of Aisha and Her Death, The.   Abdul Wahab [*or* 'Abd al-Wahhab] Al-Bayati [*or* Al-Bayyati].   MAP, *tr.* by Sargon Boulus and Christopher Middleton

Birth of Jesus, The.   Josephine D. Henderson Heard.   CBWP-4

Birth of John Henry, The.   Melvin B. Tolson.   BPo; NAAAL; TTY   *Fr.* Harlem Gallery.

Birth of Love.   Robert Penn Warren.   APT-2; UnPo; VCAP

Birth of Moshesh, The.   David Granmer T. Bereng.   TTY, *tr.* by Jack Cope and Dan Kunene

Birth of Rhythm and Blues, The.   Patricia Jones.   ReTh   *Fr.* Billie Holiday Chronicles, The.

Birth of Robin Hood, The.   *Unknown.*   OxBB
   (Willie and Earl Richard's Daughter.)

Birth of Shaka, The.   Mbuyiseni Oswald Mtshali.   PBMAP

Birth of Sohráb, The.   Firdowsi.   TAL   *Fr.* Shahnamah, The.

Birth of the Blues, The.   Ray Henderson.   ReLy

Birth of the Foal.   Ferenc Juhász.   RB; WoPoe, *tr.* by David Wevill

Birth of the Smile, The.   Rainer Maria Rilke.   EroLit, *tr.* by J. B. Leishman

Birth of the Squire; an Eclogue, The.   John Gay.   NAEL-5v1; NAEL-6v1; NOEC

Birth of the Sun, The.   Pablo Antonio Cuadra.   TCLAP, *tr.* by Thomas Merton

Birth of Time, The.   Josephine D. Henderson Heard.   CBWP-4

Birth of Tragedy, The.   Irving Layton.   MoCV; NoAM; NoP-4

Birth of Venus, The.   Muriel Rukeyser.   NALW

Birth, old age.   Ly Ngoc Kieu.   WPoS

Birth Stone.   Lorna Goodison.   VCWP

Birth Wail, The.   Henrietta Tindal.   VWP

Birthcry!   Raymond Roseliep.   HA

Birthday.   Christine Hume.   AmPoNex

Birthday, A.   Christina Georgina Rossetti.   AWP; CABP; LW; NAEL-5v2; NAEL-6v2; NALW; NOBE; NOBVV; OBEV; PEW; PeVV; PoE; TFi; TTTS; UV; VWP; ViWPN; WPE

Birthday, A.   Anne Rouse.   MFPA

Birthday Cake.   Paul Goodman.   BodElec

Birthday Crown, The.   William Alexander, Archbishop of Armagh.   SacPr

Birthday greetings / From a friend.   Birthday Wishes to a Physician.   Lizelia Augusta Jenkins Moorer.   CBWP-3

Birthday Ode to Mr. Alfred Austin, A.   Sir Owen Seaman.   NOBL

Birthday Party.   Kusano Shimpei.   PFTM-1

Birthday Poem, A.   James Simmons.   OxBSP; PNI

Birthday Poem from Venice.   Patricia Beer.   OxBC

Birthday Sonnet.   Elinor Wylie.   MoAmPo

Birthday Sonnet for Grace.   Bernadette Mayer.   PmAP

Birthday Triptych.   Peter Scupham.   HarvBoo

Birthday Wish, A.   Dorothy Nell McDonald.   PoToHe

Birthday Wishes to a Husband.   Lizelia Augusta Jenkins Moorer.   CBWP-3

Birthday Wishes to a Minister of the Gospel.   Lizelia Augusta Jenkins Moorer.   CBWP-3

Birthday Wishes to a Physician.   Lizelia Augusta Jenkins Moorer.   CBWP-3

Birthdays.   Hilde Domin.   BoWoP, *tr.* by Tudor Morris

Birthdays.   Mother Goose.   FaBoCh; LB; NBLV; OTCP; OxNR
   (Week of Birthdays, A.)   ReMoGo

Birthdays from the ocean one desert april noon.   That "Craning of the Neck."   Isabella Gardner.   WPE

Birthdays? yes, in a general way.   Sincere Flattery of R. B.   James Kenneth Stephen.   NOBL

Birthmarks.   Rajani Parulekar.   OMIP, *tr.* by Vinay Dharwadker

Birthnight: To F, The.   Walter De la Mare.   NPeEn

Birthplace.   Tahereh Saffarzadeh.   WPOW, *tr.* by Deirdre Lashgari

Birthplace, The.   Seamus Heaney.   ModIr

Birthplace Revisited.   Gregory Corso.   NeAP; PoM; VGW

Birthright.   John Drinkwater.   OxBTC

Birthright, The.   Peter Davison.   YaYoPo   *Fr.* Breaking of the Day, The.

Biscuit, a basket. Hattie went to Market, A.   Hattie Went to Market.   Leslie Simon.   FFC

Biseth you in this ilke lif.   William Herebert.   MiEL

Bishop Blomfield's First Charge to His Clergy.   Sydney Goodsir Smith.   FaBoEE

Bishop Hatto.   Robert Southey.   OBNV; OBSP
   (Bishop Hatto and the Rats.)   OxAEP-2

Bishop James A. Shorter.   Josephine D. Henderson Heard.   CBWP-4

Bishop of Chester, The.   On Dr. Keene, Bishop of Chester.   Thomas Gray.   FaBoEE

Bishop Orders His Tomb at Saint Praxed's Church, The.   Robert Browning.   CABP; EBVV; FHYEP; HAP; HeIP-4; NAEL-5v2; NAEL-6v2; NAWM-7v2; NOBVV; NPeEn; NoP-4; OBAL; PoE; SCGP; TFi

Bishop Orders His Tomb in St. Praxed's.   Morris Gilbert Bishop.   OBAL

Bishop Reading.   J. D. McClatchy.   KGB

Bishop tells us: "When the boys come back," The.   They.   Siegfried Sassoon.   NAEL-5v2; NAEL-6v2; OBSV; OBWP

Bismark.   John Jay Chapman.   APN-2

Bison, The.   Joseph Hilaire Pierre Belloc.   NoAM

Bison *in the bath, the image noted,* A.   James Fenton.   PeLV   *Fr.* Wild Life Studies.

Bistro Styx, The.   Rita Dove.   NoP-4

Bit an apple on its red.   Green Red Brown and White.   May Swenson.   VGW

Bit by bit; thus.   Bit by Bit.   Hans Faverey.   TuT, *tr.* by Peter Van de Kamp

Bit o' Sly Coorten, A.   William Barnes.   PeLV

Bit of Brass, A.   Padraic Fallon.   ModIr; NPeEn

Bit of jungle in the street, A.   Alley Cat.   Esther Valck Georges.   OTCP; Spl

Bit of Marble, A.   Clinton Scollard.   APN-2

Bit of talcum, A.   Reflection on Babies.   Ogden Nash.   NBLV

Bitch.   Carolyn Kizer.   GifTon

Bitch, A.   Anna Swir.   GifTon, *tr.* by Czeslaw Milosz and Leonard Nathan

Bitch, The.   Sergey [*or* Sergei] Aleksandrovich Yesenin [*or* Essenin].   TCRP, *tr.* by Daniel Weissbort

Bitch-Kitty, The.   Jonathan Williams.   PoM

Bitcherel.   Eleanor Brown.   MFPA; NeBl

Bite, and the taste of tongues.   Empty Pain-Killer Bottles, The.   Tom Raworth.   SPE

Bite back passion. Spring now sets.   Li Shang-yin.   WoPoe, *tr.* by A. C. Graham

Bite. The tug of fate, The. (LL)   Pier: Under Pisces, The.   James Merrill.   LCAP-2; NoAM

Biting air.   Winter Days.   Gareth Owen.   OBCP

Biting Back.   Patricia Smith.   GT

Biting winds, dark clouds, monkeys howling in the trees.   Summit, A.   Tu Fu.   CrYelRi, *tr.* by Sam Hamill

Bits and Pieces, The.   Chris Wallace-Crabbe.
   Opener.   BMAP

Bits of a photograph lie on the dresser, The. (LL)   Lamentations.   Alter Brody.   APT-2; TrJP

Bits of Reminiscence.   "Shu Ting."   CarOv; VCWP, *tr.* by Carolyn Kizer and Y. H. Zhao

Bitsy cotton bathing-costume, A.   Lake Balaton.   Ágnes Nemes Nagy.   IQMS, *tr.* by Hugh Maxton

Bitter.   Ifi Amadiume.   HAWP; NAfrP

Bitter aftertaste of spring sky, The.   Ballad of Fate.   Vadim Nikolaevich Delone.   TCRP, *tr.* by Nina Kossman

Bitter air, The.   L'Aura Amara.   Arnaut Daniel.   CTC, *tr.* by Ezra Pound

Bitter Angel.   Amy Gerstler.   PmAP

Bitter bamboo sound for a stranger their sighing flutes. (LL)   Ravine on a Cold Evening.   Li Ho.   ColAnChi; SuSp, *tr.* by Maureen Robertson

Bitter batter boop!   Last Cry of the Damp Fly, The.   Dennis Lee.   NTCP

Bitter, bitter jewel.   "H. D."   NALW   *Fr.* Tribute to the Angels.

Bitter bullshit rotten white parts, The / alone (LL)   Leroy.   Imamu Amiri Baraka.   BPo; PmAP

Bitter Cold.   *Unknown.*   OHMPC, *tr.* by Kenneth Rexroth

Bitter Cold: A Song.   Ts'ao Ts'ao.   ChinPo, *tr.* by Yip Wai-lim

Bitter cold, but don't complain when Heaven sends down snow.   It Has Snowed

Repeatedly and We Can Count On a Good Crop of Wheat and Barley. Lu Yu. SuSp, *tr. by* Burton Watson

Bitter Cold, Living in the Village. Po Chü-i. SuSp

Bitter cold. No one is abroad. Bitter Cold. *Unknown.* OHMPC, *tr. by* Kenneth Rexroth

Bitter Cup, A. Mihály Vörösmarty. IQMS, *tr. by* Watson Kirkconnell

Bitter for remembrance of the healing which has passed. (LL) Lincoln. John Gould Fletcher. CBCWP; MoAmPo

Bitter Fruit of the Tree. Sterling Allen Brown. NoP-4

Bitter Harvest. Alistair Campbell. PeNZ

Bitter Harvest. Tzu Yeh. CrYelRi, *tr. by* Sam Hamill

Bitter Mangoes, The. George Scurfield. FaBoWar

Bitter morning, A. Haiku. J. W. Hackett. HA

Bitter night. The westwind. Winter Storm. Lucien Stryk. UrbNat

Bitter pinecone may be eaten, The. Empty Purse, The. Tu Fu. TAL

Bitter rain in my courtyard. To the Tune "The Joy of Peace and Brightness." Wu Tsao. BoWoP

Bitter Sanctuary. Harold Monro. FaBoMo; OBMV

Bitter-Sweet. George Herbert. FHYEP; GeHe; NOBE; OxBSP; PAI
   (Ah my dear angry Lord.) NoP-4

Bitter taste of liberty, The. (LL) Africa. David Diop. NegPo; PBA; PBMAP; TTY

Bitter tea. Penny Harter. HA

Bitter the wind tonight. Vikings, The. *Unknown.* BIrV, *tr. by* John Montague

Bitter winds of winter. Senryu. JDP, *tr. by* Yoel Hoffmann

Bitter Withy, The. *Unknown.* NOCV
   (As it fell out on a holy day.) NoP-4

Bitter Wood. Martin Carter. WoPoe

Bitter year it was. What woman ever, A. Wreath, The. Robert Graves. BoLoP

Bitterberry Daybreak. Ingrid Jonker. PeSAV, *tr. by* Cherry Clayton

Bitterer, too, are ye? (LL) Tuft of Kelp, The. Herman Melville. APN-2; FaBoEE

Bittern, The. Sandra McPherson. LCAP-2

Bittern booms, A. John Wills. HA

Bittern, I'm sorry to see you stretched. Yellow Bittern, The. Cathal Buidhe Mac Giolla Ghunna. NOIV, *tr. by* Thomas Kinsella

Bitterness. Anita Virgil. HA

Bitterness of death is on me now, The. Cup, The. Jones Very. APN-1

Bittersweet Growing Up the Red Wall. Robert Kelly. PmAP

Bitto and Nannion do not. Asclepiades. GrAn

Bitto gives to Athena. Antipater of Sidon. GrAn; PGA

Bivouac on a Mountain Side. Walt Whitman. AiP; CBCWP; OxBA

Bix to Buxtehude to Boulez. Victor Dog, The. James Merrill. NoAM; NoP-4

Bizarre? / mysterioso? Thelonious. Reuben Jackson. ESEAA

Bizerta. George Campbell Hay. NePenScot

Black. Maxine Chernoff. PmAP *Fr.* Japan.

Black. Grace Nichols. Oth

Black A, white E, red I, green U, blue O—vowels. Vowels. Arthur Rimbaud. TTTS, *tr. by* Kenneth Koch

Black absence hides upon the past. Stanzas. John Clare. EnLoPo; NOBVV

Black and Blue (What Did I Do to Be So Black and Blue?). Andy Razaf. *See* (What Did I Do to Be So) Black and Blue?

Black and Divided or Chittlins and Caviar. Nicole Breedlove. InTrad

Black and glossy as a bee and curled was my hair. Ambapali. WPOW

Black and White. Shirley Lim. UnSA

Black and white, The. Eugenio Montale. WoPoe, *tr. by* Dana Gioia *Fr.* Motets, The.

Black and White Galaxie, The. Michael S. Weaver. UnSA

Black Angel, The. Henri Coulette. CoAP

Black Angel / Doing what she's gotta do. Singer, The. Gerald William Barrax. CoAP

Black Art. Imamu Amiri Baraka. BPo; ESEAA; NAAAL

Black Artist's role in America is to aid in the destruction / of America as he knows it, The. State/meant. Imamu Amiri Baraka. BB

Black as my fate, or cold as my despair. (LL) Charlotte Smith. BoWoP; WPE *Fr.* Montalbert.

Black as my night, anonymous here. American Memory of Africa, An. Kofi Awoonor. HBAPE

Black as snow and ice as cool / Miles stood horn-handed while. Boxcar. Terrance Hayes. AmPoNex

Black Autumn. Aida Cartagena de Portalatin. TANSG, *tr. by* Daisy Cocco De Filippis

Black Back-Ups, The. Kate Rushin. ReTh

Black Bagatelles. Rodney Hall. CBAP

Black Banana House. Gavin Moses. InTrad

Black Bean Soup. Lucien Stryk. BodElec

Black bear does a strange and shuffling dance, The. Bear: A Totem Dance as Seen by Raven. Peter Blue Cloud. HATNAP

Black Bear sang, drumming on a log. Moon of Huckleberries. Phillip [*or* "Phil"] William George. VoR

Black bear sits alone, A. Galway Kinnell. RaBo *Fr.* Lastness.

Black beauty, which above that common light. Sonnet of Black Beauty. Edward Herbert, 1st Baron Herbert of Cherbury. NOSC

Black beds gain the most potent. Shadow Beds. Delmira Agustini. TANSG, *tr. by* Mark McCaffrey

Black bird, black voice. In the Orchard. Anne Stevenson. ColAP

Black bird on a black and snowy branch, A. Igor Vladimirovich Chinnov. TCRusP, *tr. by* John Glad

Black bitch cat scratched the rat's jelly-brain clean, The. Dreaming of French Fries behind the Projects in Far Rockaway. Dennis Bernstein. SpudSo

Black black black black black. Photoheliograph (For Lady A.). Harry Crosby. APT-2

Black Blues. Bloke Modisane. PBA

Black Book, The. John Berryman.
   "Grandfather, sleepless in a room upstairs." VGW

Black Book of Carmarthen, The. *Unknown.*
   Gereint Son of Erbin. WoPoe, *tr. by* Gwyn Williams
   Song of the Graves, The. OBMV, *tr. by* Ernest Rhys

Black Bourgeoisie. Imamu Amiri Baraka. BPo; ESEAA

Black Box, The. Gavin Ewart. OBCoV

Black boy, the night hides you. Black Boy. Norman Rosten. TrJP

Black Boys Play the Classics. Toi Derricotte. ExTi; SpirFl

Black bread. (LL) Naturally. Audre Lorde. BlSi; ISC

Black Bread. Tom Paulin. CIP-2

Black bread and a faithful wife. "Eduard Georgievich Bagritzky" [*or* "Bagritsky"]. TCRP

Black Buoy. Robert H. Davis. HATNAP

Black, Byzantine eyes. Absent from Dances 1925. Stephanie Strickland. ExTi

Black cat yawns, The. Cat. Mary Britton Miller. TLR; WHSW

Black cats creep across my path. Everything Happens to Me. Matt Dennis. ReLy

Black Child. Maureen Watson. IBA

Black child's soft mouth atremble. Black Child. Maureen Watson. IBA

Black City, The. Breyten Breytenbach. PoetW, *tr. by* Sonia Van Schalwyk and Leon de Kock

Black clad and mithered he harries his weight. Lamper, The. Maggie Hannan. NLP

Black Cloud, The. William Henry Davies. RB

Black clouds have risen in my sky. Rāmprasād Sen. SinGod, *tr. by* Rachel Fell McDermott

Black Clouds—Spilled Ink. Su Tung-p'o (Su Shih). ColAnChi, *tr. by* Burton Watson

Black clouds spread over the sky. Looking from the Pavilion over the Lake. Su Tung-p'o (Su Shih). OHPC, *tr. by* Kenneth Rexroth

Black Cock, The. Ishmael Reed. ISC

Black Cockatoos. Judith Wright. OWoS

Black Coffee. Paul Francis Webster. ReLy

Black Cottage, The. Robert Frost. CBCWP; VGW

Black Crispus Attucks taught. Dark Symphony. Melvin B. Tolson. ColAP; NAAAL; SSLK

Black Cup, The. César Vallejo. WoPoe, *tr. by* Willis Barnstone and Tony Barnstone

Black Dada Nihilismus. Imamu Amiri Baraka. PFTM-2; PoM

Black Dog. Ray A. Young Bear. CDW

Black Draftee from Dixie, The. Carrie Williams Clifford. BlSi

Black Dream, you come. Sappho. SaLy, *tr. by* Diane Rayor

Black Earth. Marianne Craig Moore. APT-1; FaBoMo

Black English. Richard Katrovas. LTA

Black-Eyed Susan. John Gay. *See* Sweet William's Farewell to Black-Eyed [*or* Black-Ey'd] Susan

Black-faced [*or* fac'd] house will love, A. (LL) On the Baptized Ethiopian. Richard Crashaw. ChIV-2; FaBoEE, *tr. by* Richard Crashaw

Black Faced Sheep, The. Donald Hall. LCAP-2

Black flies kept nagging in the heat, The. Tao and Unfitness at Inistiogue on the River Nore. Thomas Kinsella. NPeEn; PBCIP

Black Flower. Walter Pavlich. TWW

Black fool, why winter here? These frozen skies. Advice to a Raven in Russia [December, 1812]. Joel Barlow. APN-1; NAAL-2v1; NAAL-3; NOBA; OBWP; OxBA

Black fox loped out of the hills, The. Dream of a Black Fox. Brendan Kennelly. PBCIP

Black girl black girl. Blackberry Sweet. Dudley Randall. HAP; ISC; KaS; SoSe-8; WeW-3

Black Girl Goes By, A. Emile Roumer. TTY, *tr. by* Edna Worthley Underwood

Black glassmaker, The. Jean-Joseph Rabéarivelo [*or* Rebéarivelo]. PBMAP *Fr.* Traduits de la Nuit.

Black Gold, blackgold. . .aint no oil. Blackgoldblueswoman. Kirk Hall. NBV

Black grayed into white a nightmare of bicycling. Michael Dransfield. *See* Black greyed into white a nightmare of bicycling

Black, green and gold at sunset: pageantry. At a Funeral. Dennis Brutus. PBMAP

Black greyed into white a nightmare of bicycling. That Which We Call a Rose. Michael Dransfield. CBAP; NOBAu

Black grows the sudden sky, betokening rain. Sudden Shower. John Clare. OxAEP-2

Black Hair. Gary Soto. MoASP; UnSA

Black Hair. *Unknown.* EroLit

Black hair and red cheeks: for how long? Cui Shaoxuan. WPoS

Black Hairs, The. Heinz Pasman. RaBo, *tr. by* Robert Bly

Black Hat, The. Clayton Eshleman. VGW

Black Heart. Kwame Dawes. WaCA

Black Heart as Ever Green, The. Carolyn M. Rodgers. IllVoic

Black heart is pulsing to its ant-egg dole. (LL) Mad Negro Soldier Confined at Munich, A. Robert Lowell. FaBoMo; OxBC

Black Hen, The. Mother Goose. LB; ReMoGo

Black hen, The. Raymond Roseliep. HA

Black Henry. Tejumola Ologboni. NBV

Black Horse Rider, The. Pierre Loving. SPE

Black Huntsmen, The. Irving Layton. WoPoe

Black I am and much admired. Mother Goose. OxNR

Black in a tentlike cloak, at rest. Incident in Transylvania. Roger McDonald. BMAP

Black Irish Blues. Joe-Anne McLaughlin. OPRER

Black iron fence closes the graves in, A. Visiting Emily Dickinson's Grave with Robert Francis. Robert Bly. LCAP-2

Black is beautiful. Ron Welburn. NBV

Black is not. Poem Looking for a Reader, A. Haki R. Madhubuti. ISC

Black is; slavery was; I am. This Child Is the Mother. Gloria C. Oden. BlSi

Black is the first nail I ever stepped on. Negritude. James A. Emanuel. BPo

Black is the night. What Is Black? Mary O'Neill. NTCP

Black Island. Charles Pressoir. NegPo, *tr. by* Ellen Conroy Kennedy

Black Jackets. Thom Gunn. HeIP-4; NAEL-5v2; NAEL-6v2; NoP-4; TwCP

Black Jam for Dr. Negro. Mari E. Evans. BPo

Black Java Pepper. Arthur Sze. OpBo

Black Jewel, The. W. S. Merwin. LCAP-2

Black jewel like, The. Akahito. OHMPJ

Black key. White key. No. Unrelenting Flood. William Matthews. BodElec

Black king dance out front of the crowd. Four Poems. Velemir [*or* Viktor Vladimirovich] Khlebnikov. PFTM-1

Black knight. To Josh Gibson (Legendary Slugger of the Old Negro Baseball League). George, Jr. Mosby. ISC

Black Kőrös. József Erdélyi. IQMS, *tr. by* Alan Dixon

Black Lace Fan My Mother Gave Me, The. Eavan Boland. BiHa; HarvBoo; ModIr; NPeEn

Black lake, black boat, two black, cut-paper people. Crossing the Water. Sylvia Plath. HCAP; RB

Black Light. Peter Markus. AmPoNex

Black like me. (LL) Dream Variation[s]. Langston Hughes. APT-2; HAP; ISC; ITBLP; NAAAL; NAAL-2v2; NOBA; NoP-4; SAmP; SSLK

Black, long-tailed, The. Yellow Season, The. William Carlos Williams. MoAmPo

Black Love Black Hope. Doughtry Long. SeSe

Black'm saut'm rough'm glower'm saw. Riddle. *Unknown.* FaBoVe

Black Magic. Sonia Sanchez. BPo

Black Magicians / Come home: the pink meat image. Change: *Kyoto-Tokyo Express*, The. Allen Ginsberg. APSN

Black Maid to the Fair Boy, The. Henry Reynolds. NOSC

Black Majesty. Countee Cullen. VGW

Black Man, The. Sergey [*or* Sergei] Aleksandrovich Yesenin [*or* Essenin]. TCRP, *tr. by* Geoffrey Thurley

Black Man Go Back to the Old Country. High Modes: Vision as Ritual: Confirmation. Michael S. Harper. NBV

Black Man's Lament, The. Léon Damas. NegPo, *tr. by* Ellen Conroy Kennedy

Black Man's Son, The. Oswald Durand. TTY

(At twenty, I loved Lise. She was frail and white.) NegPo, *tr. by* Ellen Conroy Kennedy

Black Man's Sonata, A. Michael S. Weaver. UnSA

Black Man Talks of Reaping, A. Arna Bontemps. APT-2; BPo; ColAP; NAAAL; SSLK

Black Man, 13th Floor. James A. Emanuel. NBV

Black March. Stevie Smith. EmeKit

Black Marigolds. Bilhana. AWP, *tr. by* E. Powys Mathers

Black Mary Janes, white-ruffled sox. Yesterday. Mary Weems. SpirFl

Black Meat. Jean Follain. BLT

Black men with outasight afros. (LL) Beautiful Black Men. Nikki Giovanni. BPo; NAAAL

Black men? (LL) Black Woman. Naomi Long Madgett. BlSi; GT; ISC

Black Messengers, The. César Vallejo. PoetW; TCLAP, *tr. by* Rachel Benson

Black milk of dawn [*or* daybreak] we drink it at dusk [*or* nightfall]. Death Fugue, A. Paul Celan. HP; PoSu; TrJP; VCWP

Black milk of daybreak we drink it at nightfall. Fugue of Death. Paul Celan. PoetW, *tr. by* Christopher Middleton

Black milk of daybreak we drink it at sundown. Death Fugue. Paul Celan. AuPH; HP; VCWP; WoPoe, *tr. by* Michael Hamburger

Black milk of morning we drink you at dusktime. Death Fugue, A. Paul Celan. CLPP; GifTon; PFTM-2, *tr. by* Jerome Rothenberg

Black Mood. Rosalía de Castro. STV, *tr. by* John Frederick Nims; WeW-3

Black Mother Praying. Owen Dodson. ISC

Black Mountain Blues. Bessie Smith. PFTM-1

Black mountains pricked with pointed pine. Watershed, The. Alice Thompson Meynell. VWP

Black Music. Léon Laleau.

Betrayal. NegPo, *tr. by* Ellen Conroy Kennedy

Cannibal. NegPo, *tr. by* Ellen Conroy Kennedy

Legacies. NegPo, *tr. by* Ellen Conroy Kennedy

Sacrifice. NegPo, *tr. by* Ellen Conroy Kennedy

Voodoo. NegPo, *tr. by* Ellen Conroy Kennedy

Black Music. Yevgeny [*or* Evgenii] Borisovich Rein. TCRP, *tr. by* Lubov Yakovleva

Black Muzzle. Su Tung-p'o (Su Shih). CoBCP, *tr. by* Burton Watson

Black my beginning. Elizabeth Bewick. NewEx

Black- / ness. Combination II. Helmut Heissenbüttel. PFTM-2, *tr. by* Jerome Rothenberg

Black Night, The. Antar [*or* Antara]. WoPoe, *tr. by* Desmond O'Grady

Black night spies upon my window, The. Gestures from My Window. Yolanda Bedregal. TANSG, *tr. by* Carolyne Wright

Black Night. / White snow. Aleksandr Aleksandrovich Blok. AWP *Fr.* Twelve, The.

Black November Turkey, A. Richard Wilbur. LCAP-2; NAAL-2v2; OWoS

Black, numb fingernails, The. (LL) On a Field Trip at Fredericksburg. Dave Jeddie Smith. HCAP; PoPoPo

Black of brow, with cheeks aglow. Glance, A. *Unknown.* NOIV, *tr. by* Thomas Kinsella

Black one, last as usual, swings her head, The. Fetching Cows. Norman MacCaig. NoP-4; OxBC

Black Orchid. David Jauss. SeSe

Black Ore. René Depestre. NegPo, *tr. by* Ellen Conroy Kennedy

Black panther is sleeping on the crags, The. Black Panther, The. Sarveshwar Dayal Saxena. OMIP, *tr. by* Vinay Dharwadker

Black Patch on Lucasta's Face, A. Richard Lovelace. BeJo; CaPo

Black peak at Xuan Loc, The. It Is Monsoon at Last. Basil T. Paquet. CDa

Black Pebble, The. James Reeves. OTCP

Black People! Imamu Amiri Baraka. BPo

Black people are born singers. On Judgement Day. Sipho Sepamla. PBMAP

Black People Cry. Steve Barney. IBA

Black Piano, The. Endre Ady. IQMS, *tr. by* Adam Makkai

Black Pine Tree in an Orange Light. Sylvia Plath. BodElec

Black Plateau, The. W. S. Merwin. NNaP

Black Poet Leaps to His Death, A. Etheridge Knight. BodElec

Black Poet, White Critic. Dudley Randall. BPo; CoAmPo

Black Poets, The. Charles Bukowski. LTA

Black Poets should live—not leap. For Black Poets Who Think of Suicide. Etheridge Knight. HeIP-4; InPK-6; LTA; NAAAL

Black poets, The / young. Black Poets, The. Charles Bukowski. LTA

Black Poppy (At the Temple). David St. John. BodElec

Black Postcards. Tomas Tranströmer. WoPoe, *tr. by* Joanna Bankier

Black Power. Raymond R. Patterson. NBV

Black Power Poem. Ishmael Reed. BPo

Black Pride. Margaret Goss Burroughs. BlSi

Black Rape. Michelle T. Clinton. InTrad

Black Rat, The. Iris Clayton. IBA

Black raven in the snowy dusk. Aleksandr Aleksandrovich Blok. TCRP *Fr.* Three Messages.

Black reapers with the sound of steel on stones. Reapers. Jean Toomer.

APT-2; BPo; ColAP; GT; HAP; NIL-7; NoAM; NoP-4; SoSe-8; TRP; WeW-3

Black Riders, The.   César Vallejo.   RaBo, *tr. by* Robert Bly
  (There are blows in life so violent—I can't answer!)   AF, *tr. by* Robert Bly
Black Riders [and Other Lines], The.   Stephen Crane.
  "Behold, the Grave of a Wicked Man."   APN-2; NoP-4; TAP
  Black Riders, The.   APN-2; NAAL-2v2; NoP-4; TAP
  Blades of Grass, The.   MoAmPo
  Book of Wisdom, The.   MoAmPo
  God in Wrath, A.   OxBSP; TAP
  "God lay dead in Heaven."   APN-2
  Heart, The.   APN-2; MoAmPo; NoP-4; TCAPo
  "I saw a man pursuing the horizon."   APN-2; ChAP; MoAmPo; NOBA; NoP-4; TCAPo
  "I stood upon a high place."   APN-2
  I Walked in a Desert.   NAAL-2v2
  "If I should cast off this tattered coat."   APN-2
  "It Was Wrong to Do This" Said the Angel.   PAI
  Learned Man [Came to Me Once], A.   MoAmPo
  "Livid lightnings flashed in the clouds, The."   InvLi
  "Man Feared That He Might Find an Assassin, A."   APN-2; NAAL-2v2; NoP-4
  "Many red devils ran from my heart."   TAP
  Many Workmen.   TAP
  Scaped.   APN-2
  "Should the wide world roll away."   APN-2
  "There was set before me a mighty hill."   APN-2
  Think As I Think.   WeW-3
  (Youth, A.)   MoAmPo
  "Youth in apparel that glittered, A."   APN-2; NAAL-2v2
Black Riders Came from the Sea.   Stephen Crane.   APN-2; NAAL-2v2; NoP-4; TAP   *Fr.* Black Riders [and Other Lines], The.
Black Riviera, The.   Mark Jarman.   GeoHom
Black rock, cross (how the north wind has rolled), The.   Tomb.   Stéphane Mallarmé.   SxFrPo, *tr. by* E. H. Blackmore and A. M. Blackmore
Black Rock of Kiltearn.   Andrew Young.   FaBoTw; RB
Black Rocks.   Charles Hubert Sisson.   DiPo
Black Rook in Rainy Weather.   Sylvia Plath.   NAAL-2v2; NIL-7; NoP-4
Black Sampson, The.   Josephine D. Henderson Heard.   CBWP-4; SWaP
Black Series.   Brenda Hillman.   BodElec
Black Sheep, The.   Gojko Djogo.   AF, *tr. by* Michael March
Black Silk.   Tess Gallagher.   EmeKit; FaBoWP
Black Silk Pajamas.   Danton R. Remoto.   ReBoTo
Black Sister.   Kattie M. Cumbo.   BlSi
Black skin against bright green.   Black Sister.   Kattie M. Cumbo.   BlSi
Black Slip.   Terry Wolverton.   WiU
Black Snake.   Raul Bopp.
  "Begins here, the ciphered forest."   TCLAP, *tr. by* Renato Rezende
  "I pass the swamp borders."   TCLAP, *tr. by* Renato Rezende
  "I wake up."   TCLAP, *tr. by* Renato Rezende
  "Sky very blue."   TCLAP, *tr. by* Renato Rezende
  "This is the rotten-breathed forest."   TCLAP, *tr. by* Renato Rezende
Black Soap.   Sandra McPherson.   VCAP
Black Soldier Remembers, A.   Horace Coleman.   CDa
Black Soldier's Civil War Chant.   *Unknown.*   *See* Negro Soldier's Civil War Chant
Black Song.   Amin Nakhla.   MAP, *tr. by* Matthew Sorenson
Black spaces, The.   Anita Virgil.   HA
Black Stone Lying on a White Stone.   César Vallejo.   TCLAP, *tr. by* Robert Bly and John Knoepfle
Black Stone on a White Stone.   César Vallejo.   WoPoe, *tr. by* Willis Barnstone
Black swallows swooping or gliding.   Skaters, The.   John Gould Fletcher.   KaS; MoAmPo
Black Swallows Will Return, The.   Gustavo Adolfo Bécquer.   BLPSL, *tr. by* Rene de Costa, Rigas Kappatos and Eleni Paidoussi
Black Swan, The.   Randall Jarrell.   PoE
Black swans with wings over their eyes.   For Martin Luther King.   Charles Fort.   LTA
Black Tambourine.   Hart Crane.   InPK-6; NoAM; OxBA; OxBSP; TAP
Black Train, The.   Thomas McGrath.   GM
Black Tulips.   Martha Vertreace.   IllVoic
Black Vahine.   To Vahine (Painted by Gaugin).   Enrique Molina.   BLPSL, *tr. by* Rene de Costa, Rigas Kappatos and Eleni Paidoussi
Black village of gravestones.   Heptonstall.   Ted Hughes.   OxAEP-2
Black Vulture, The.   George Sterling.   APT-1
  (Aloof within the day's enormous dome.)   TCAPo
Black Walnut Tree, The.   Mary Oliver.   MakPoe

Black water. White waves. Furrows snowcapped.   Seamus Heaney.   NoAM   *Fr.* Station Island.
Black Wet, The.   W. N. Herbert.   NeBl
Black, white, and red, O red like the soil of Africa. (LL)   We Delighted, My Friend.   Léopold Sédar Senghor.   PBA; TTY, *tr. by* Miriam Koshl
Black Winds, The.   William Carlos Williams.   APT-1
Black Winter.   Frank Stewart.   CDa
Black within, and red without.   Chimney, A.   Mother Goose.   OxNR; ReMoGo
Black Woman.   Naomi Long Madgett.   BlSi; GT; ISC
Black Woman.   Léopold Sédar Senghor.   TTY, *tr. by* Anne Atik
Black woman comes up to me at break in the writing, A.   For Black Women Who Are Afraid.   Toi Derricotte.   ExTi
Black Woman Throws a Tantrum.   Nayo-Barbara Watkins.   NBV
Blackamoors, The.   Rowland Watkyns.   AngWePo
Blackberries.   Maurina Sherman.   GeoHom
Blackberry, The.   Norman Nicholson.   MoBrPo
Blackberry Eating.   Galway Kinnell.   InPK-6; InvLad; NIL-7; NIP-4; SoSe-8
Blackberry-Picking.   Seamus Heaney.   ChAP
Blackberry Sweet.   Dudley Randall.   HAP; ISC; KaS; SoSe-8; WeW-3
Blackberry Winter.   John Crowe Ransom.   APT-1; OxBA; PoRA
Blackberrying.   Sylvia Plath.   HAP; HCAP; NAAL-2v2; NAAL-5; NOBA; NoAM; PoPoPo
Blackbird, The.   William Ernest Henley.   MoBrPo   *Fr.* Echoes.
Blackbird, The.   *Unknown.*   NOIV
Blackbird, The.   Humbert Wolfe.   NOxBChV
Blackbird, blackbird.   Bye Bye Blackbird.   Ray Henderson.   ReLy
Blackbird, blackbird, where's.   Killer Blues.   Calvin Forbes.   IllVoic
Blackbird calls in grief, The.   *Unknown.*   NOIV
Blackbird feeds his fire. Outside, a quick 30 below. (LL)   Christmas Comes to Moccasin Flat.   James Welch.   CDW; NoAM
Blackbird of Derrycairn, The.   *Unknown.*   BIrV, *tr. by* Austin Clarke
Blackbird's farewell song, The. (LL)   Vasco [*or* Vasko] Popa.   PoSu; WoPoe, *tr. by* Anne Pennington   *Fr.* Blackbird's Field, The.
Blackbird's Field, The.   Vasco [*or* Vasko] Popa.
  Battle on the Blackbird's Field.   PoSu; WoPoe, *tr. by* Anne Pennington
Blackbird sang, the skies were clear and clean, The.   At Queensferry.   William Ernest Henley.   OxBSo
Blackbird sat / In the cedar-limbs, The. (LL)   Thirteen Ways of Looking at a Blackbird.   Wallace Stevens.   APT-1; HCAP; HeIP-4; InPK-6; NAAL-2v2; NOBA; NoAM; OWoS; PAI; PoE; RB; SAmP; TAP; TCAPo; TFi
Blackbird Singing, A.   Ronald Stuart Thomas.   OBWVE
Blackbird, singing on the highest branch / Of the oak.   Argentarius.   GrAn
Blackbird swooped, The.   Snowy Sky.   Shinkichi Takahashi.   ZenPo, *tr. by* Takashi Ikemoto and Lucien Stryk
Blackbirds to a swan.   In Praise of a Sword Given Him by His Prince.   Colman mac Lenini.   WoPoe, *tr. by* Richard O'Connell
Blackboard in my mind holds words eye dream, A.   And Syllables Grow Wings There.   Quincy Troupe.   SpirFl
Blackboard is erased in the attic, The.   Rain Moving In.   John Ashbery.   NoP-4
Blackboard's white turned dark, The; I.   Relief of Myopia, The.   U. A. Fanthorpe.   Spl
Blackbottom.   Toi Derricotte.   GT; LTA; PBCAP
Blackcock, The [*or* The Black Cock].   Joanna Baillie.   WoRP
Blackcurrant River.   Arthur Rimbaud.   SxFrPo, *tr. by* Martin Sorrell
Blacke is the beauty of the brightest day.   Christopher Marlowe.   OxBEV   *Fr.* Tamburlaine the Great, Part 2.
Blacken thy heavens, Jove.   Prometheus.   Goethe.   AWP, *tr. by* John S. Dwight
Blackened and bleeding, helpless, panting, prone.   Chicago.   Bret Harte.   APN-2; AiP
Blackened iron, The.   Rain in May.   Jane Hirshfield.   GeoHom
Blackgoldblueswoman.   Kirk Hall.   NBV
Blackie Thinks of His Brothers.   Stanley Crouch.   GT
Blackman came walking I.   Dreadwalk.   Dennis Scott.   WaCA
Blackness.   Primer for Blacks.   Gwendolyn Brooks.   ISC
Blackness of one quarter lights up the mauve of three, The.   Northland in Cold, The.   Li Ho.   CoBCP, *tr. by* Burton Watson
Blacks in frame houses.   Song: I Want a Witness.   Michael S. Harper.   LTA
Blacksmith Pain.   Otto Julius Bierbaum.   AWP, *tr. by* Jethro Bithell
Blacksmith's boy went out with a rifle, The.   Legend.   Judith Wright.   NOBAu; RB
Blacksmith's quite a logical man, The.   Palladas [*or* Pallades].   GrAn
Blacksmiths, The.   *Unknown.*   RB; WoPoe, *tr. by* Wesli Court   *See also* Smoke-Blackened Smiths
  (Swarte-smeked Smithes.)   HAP
  (Swarte smeked smethes smatered with smoke.)   FaBoVe; MiEL

Blackstone Rangers, The. Gwendolyn Brooks. ESEAA; NoAM Gang Girls. IllVoic

Blacktail Row. Liu Yu Hsi. CrYelRi, *tr. by* Sam Hamill

Blackthorn. Euros Bowen. OBWVE, *tr. by* the author

Bladder Song. Leonard Nathan. BLT

Blade better, A. Waldere 2. *Unknown.* ASW, *tr. by* Kevin Crossley-Holland

Blade days, The. Invisible Autumn. Joseph Ceravolo. FTOS

Blade licks out and acts, A. Thomas Kinsella. BiHa *Fr.* Technical Supplement, A.

Blade of Grass Sings to the River, The. Leah Goldberg. TrJP, *tr. by* Robert Friend *Fr.* Songs of the Stream.

Blade of Grass Sings to the Stream, The. Leah Goldberg. MHP, *tr. by* Ruth Finer Mintz *Fr.* Songs of the Stream.

Blade touches the fish heart, over, The. Gutting the Salmon. Robert Adamson. BMAP

Blades and slime, the limits, The. Dario Villa. ItPo, *tr. by* Gayle Ridinger

Blades of Grass, The. Stephen Crane. MoAmPo *Fr.* Black Riders [and Other Lines], The.

Blaen Cwrt. Gillian Clarke. AngWePo

Blah, Blah, Blah. George Gershwin. OBAL; ReLy

Blake. Lucille Clifton. ExTi

Blake Leads a Walk on the Milky Way. Nancy Willard. OBCA

Blake shuts his eyes. Life Mask. Charles Brasch. PeNZ

Blam! Blam! Blam! Pow! Blam! Pow! For a Black Poet. Gerald William Barrax. NBV

Blame It on My Youth. Edward Heyman. ReLy

Blame it on the weather, the news. Blues, The. Mark Vinz. MiVo

Blame Not My Cheekes. Thomas Campion. SCGP; UnPo

Blame not my lute, for he must sound [*or* sssnd *or* Sownde]. Blame Not My Lute. Sir Thomas Wyatt. EBEV; NAEL-5v1; NAEL-7v1; PoE; SCGP

Blame not thyself too much, I said, nor blame. Tennyson. NAEL-5v2; NAEL-6v2 *Fr.* Princess, The.

Blame the spring wind. (LL) Tzu Yeh. EroLit; WPOW; WoPoe, *tr. by* Chung Ling and Kenneth Rexroth

Blame the Vicar. Sir John Betjeman. SacPr

Blames, for Rane and Diane. Glenn Sheldon. MiVo

Blaming Sons. Ch'ien T'ao. ChiP, *tr. by* Arthur Waley

Blaming Sons. T'ao Ch'ien [*or* T'ao Yuan-ming]. CoBCP; ColAnChi, *tr. by* Burton Watson

Blanca's Red Lips. Gloria Vando. TouFir

Blanchefleur and Jellyflorice. *Unknown.* ESPB

Blanco. Octavio Paz.
   "Stirring, A." PFTM-2, *tr. by* Eliot Weinberger

Blanco. Gary Soto. GeoHom

Blank Abandon of Beds, The. Star Black. KGB

Blank Misgivings of a Creature Moving About in Worlds Not Realized. Arthur Hugh Clough.
   "Here am I yet, another twelvemonth spent." CenSon
   "Though to the vilest things beneath the moon." OxBSo
   "Yes, I have lied, and so must walk my way." CenSon

Blank to Fill In on the Visa of Pollen. Aimé Césaire. WoPoe, *tr. by* Gregson Davis

Blank Verse Written on the Sea Shore. Hannah Cowley. ECWP

Blanket Hog. Paul B. Janeczko. TLR

Blanket, its weight, while we were growing, The. In the Lungs. Milo De Angelis. NeIt, *tr. by* Lawrence Venuti

Blason, A. Alec Derwent Hope. NOBAu

Blasphemers lewd, and swearers shrewd. Michael Wigglesworth. ColAP *Fr.* Day of Doom, The.

Blasphemous wretch! How canst thou think or say. Sarah Fyge Egerton. PEW *Fr.* Female Advocate or, An Answer to a Late Satyr, The.

Blasphemy, A. Rodney Jones. IllVoic; WeW-3

Blast of anniversary excitement, true. Edoardo Cacciatore. ItPo, *tr. by* Gayle Ridinger *Fr.* Full Powers: Five Warning Signs.

Blast of wind, a momentary breath, A. Barnabe Barnes. EBEV *Fr.* Divine Century of Spiritual Sonnets, A.

Blasted horn, do do di do, A. Courtyard Noises from the North, Twenty-fourth Precinct. Colette Inez. UrbNat

Blasted / I was a 15 / yr old junkie. 1980–1990: A Poet's Personal Review. Asha Bandele. InTrad

Blasted with sighs, and surrounded with tears. Twicknam [*or* Twickenham] Garden. John Donne. BASC; EBEV; ESCV; EnLoPo; MeLP; OBGa; PoE; SCGP

Blasting from Heaven. Philip Levine. CoAP

Blasts of Autumn as they scatter round, The. Written in October. Charlotte Smith. NoP-4

Blasts of wind amidst autumn rains. Rill of the House of the Luans. Wang Wei. ChinPo, *tr. by* Yip Wai-lim

Blasts rip Newspaper Gray [*or* grey] Mannahatta's mid day Air Spires. Friday the Thirteenth. Allen Ginsberg. NNaP

Blaze awake in the night and detest. Sleep's Underside. Melissa Kirsch. AWTN

Blaze of promise everywhere, The. (LL) Always. Mark Strand. EmeKit; NoP-4; TRP

Blazing fire and Christmas treat. (LL) Garden Year, The. Sara Coleridge. ChAP; OTCP

Blazing in darkness, all they wish to see. (LL) Magi, The. Louise Glück. GI; HarvBoo

Blazing stanchions and the corporate lights, The. Euclid Avenue. Harry Clifton. PBCIP

Bleach in the foot-bathtub. Sunday Morning, 1950. Irene McKinney. PBCAP

Bleached wood massed in bone piles, The. Kalaloch. Carolyn Forché. NoAM; YaYoPo

Bleak the February light. Kingdom of Heaven. Léonie Adams. MoAmPo

Bleaklow. Pauline Stainer. NeBl

Bleat. Barbara Guest. FTOS

Bled / holding on / to details. Monogram 23. Martina Werner. BoWoP, *tr. by* Rosmarie Waldrop

Bleecker Street. Jean Garrigue. TAP

Bleecker Street. Hugh Seidman. BodElec

Bleeding. May Swenson. NALW

Bleeding hearts talk of happy days. Today Is Not like They Said. Kirk Hall. NBV

Bleeding Nun, The. *Unknown.* NOBRP

Bleeding to death. The counter-attack had failed. (LL) Counter-Attack. Siegfried Sassoon. MoBrPo; OxAEP-2; PeFWW; PoWW

Blend of joy and of hopeless surrender, A. (LL) Last Love. Fyodor [*or* Feodor] Ivanovich Tyutchev. BoLoP; WoPoe, *tr. by* Vladimir Vladimirovich Nabokov

Blenheim. John Philips.
   War Poetry. NOEC

Blenheim Oranges. Edward Thomas. *See* Gone, Gone Again

Bless'd art Thou, O Lord of all. Prayer before Sleep. Alice Lucas. TrJP

Bless Him, O constant companions. Bless Him. *Unknown.* TrJP, *tr. by* Israel Abrahams

Bless me with forgiveness, Lord, for all my sins of youth. He Pleads for Forgiveness Before His Intended Marriage. Bálint Balassi. IQMS, *tr. by* Joseph Leftwich

Bless the Lord, O my soul: and all that is within me. Bible, *O.T.* AWP *Fr.* Psalms.

Bless the Lord, O my soul. O Lord my God. Bible, *O.T.* NAWM-5v1; TrJP *Fr.* Psalms.

Bless thou the Lord, O my soul. Praise ye the Lord. (LL) Bible, *O.T.* NAWM-5v1; TrJP *Fr.* Psalms.

Bless you, bless you, burnie-bee [*or* bonnie-bee]. Mother Goose. OxNR

Bless you, Mother. On the Appeal from the Race of Sheba: II. Léopold Sédar Senghor. TTY

Blesse me! what damps are here? how stiffe an aire? Charnel-house, The. Henry Vaughan. FSCP

Blesse thee, Lord, because I Grow. Paradise. George Herbert. SacPr

Blessed. Soné. TrJP, *tr. by* David Kuselewitz

Blessed above women / shall Jael the wife of Heber the Kenite be. Bible, *O.T.* WPOW *Fr.* Judges.

Blessed angell not a word replies, The. Ludovico Ariosto. OBVE *Fr.* Orlando Furioso.

Blessed are the files marked action in the inward tray. Beatitudes. Bruce Dawe. GI

Blessed are the lovers. Most Ancient Names of Fire, The. Roberto Sosa. ErotSp, *tr. by* Jo Anne Engelbert

Blessed are the man and the woman. Bible, *O.T. See* Blessed is the man that walketh not in the counsel of the ungodly [*or* wicked]

Blessed are the poor[e] in spirit for theirs is the kingdom[e] of heaven. Bible, *N.T.* OBVE *Fr.* St. Matthew.

Blessed Are They. Wilhelmina Stitch. PoToHe

Blessed are they that sow and shall not reap. Blessed Are They That Sow. Avraham ben- Yitzhak. WoPoe, *tr. by* Robert Mezey

Blessed are they who are pleasant to live with—. Blessed Are They. Wilhelmina Stitch. PoToHe

Blessed are they who meet her on the earth. (LL) Sonnet: Of Beatrice de' Portinari, on All Saints' Day. Dante Alighieri. AWP; EaItPo, *tr. by* Dante Gabriel Rossetti

Blessed are they who sow but do not reap. Blessed. Soné. TrJP, *tr. by* David Kuselewitz

Blessed Art Thou, O Lord. *Unknown.* TrJP, *tr. by* Theodor H. Gaster *Fr.* Dead Sea Scrolls, The.

Blessed as the Gods! Sicilian Maid is he. Dreams of a Rival. Mary Robinson. CenSon; RWP

Blessed Assurance. Fanny Crosby. AH; SWaP

Blessed be he who has breathed it. (LL) Woman from the Book of Genesis, A. "Dovid Knut." TCRP; TCRusP, *tr.* by John Glad

Blessed be the Paps which Thou hast Sucked. Bible, *N.T.* ChIV-2; NOSC, *tr.* by Richard Crashaw *Fr.* St. Luke.

Blessed be thou, levedy. *Unknown.* MiEL

Blessed be you beautiful. Quarter-Hour Between God and the Office. Lőrinc Szabó. IQMS, *tr.* by Egon F. Kunz

Blessed by the day which bids my grief subside. To Mr. William Long, On His Recovery from a Dangerous Illness, 1785. William Hayley. Son

Blessed Comforter Divine. Lydia Huntley Sigourney. AH

Blessed conversion, and a strange, A. Conversion of S. Paul, The. George Wither. ChIV-2

Blessed damozel leaned out, The. Blessed Damozel, The. Dante Gabriel Rossetti. AWP; CABP; EBVV; NAEL-5v2; NAEL-6v2; NOBE; NOBVV; NoP-4; OBEV; OxAEP-2; PoE; TFi

Blessed Is Everyone. *Unknown.* AH

Blessed Is God. Bible, Apocrypha. TrJP, *tr.* by D. C. Simpson *Fr.* Tobit.

Blessed Is the Man. Marianne Craig Moore. ChIV-1

Blessed is the man that walketh not in the assembly of the wicked. Psalm 1. Genrik Veniaminovich Sapgir. ItGoST, *tr.* by J. Kates

Blessed is the man that walketh not in the counsel of the ungodly [*or* wicked]. Bible, *O.T.* AWP *Fr.* Psalms.

Blessed is yon shepherd on the turf reclined. Charlotte Smith. RWP

Blessed Lord, What It Is to Be Young. David McCord. KaS; NTCP

Blessed Mary. *Unknown.* OxBSP

Blessed Match, The. Hannah Senesh. TrJP

Blessed offender [*or* offendour], who thyself hast [*or* haist] tried [*or* try'd]. To Saint Mary Magdalen. Henry Constable. NoSic

Blessed Pentecost is here again that comes up new each year. Blessed Pentecost. *Hungarian Oral Tradition.* IQMS, *tr.* by Dermot Spence

Blessed sweet Pentecost's weather brightly glowing. For Wine Drinkers. Bálint Balassi. IQMS, *tr.* by René Bonnerjea

Blessed that flock safe penned in Paradise. Christina Georgina Rossetti. WPoS *Fr.* Behold a Shaking.

Blessed the match that was burned. Blessed Match, The. Hannah Senesh. TrJP

Blessed Trinity have pity! Childless. Giolla Brighde MacNamee. BIrV, *tr.* by Frank O'Connor

Blessed Virgin Compared to the Air We Breathe, The. Gerard Manley Hopkins. NOBVV; PeVV

Blessed with a joy that only she. Gift of God, The. Edwin Arlington Robinson. MoAmPo; OxBA

Blessednes of Brytaine, The. Morris Kyffin. "Adore November's sacred seventeenth day." AngWePo

Blessednesse of Faithfull Soules by Death, The. William Drummond, of Hawthornden. SacPr

Blessing, A. James Wright (1927–80). AmFaPo; InPK-6; NAAL-2v2; NoAM; NOBA; PoE; RaBo; TRP; TwCP; VCAP

Blessing Attributed to Saint Clare, The. Clare of Assisi. BBASP, *tr.* by Regis J. Armstrong

Blessing his handiwork, his drawbridge closed. Artificer. X. J. Kennedy. TwCP

Blessing in Disguise, A. John Ashbery. ColAP; PoM

Blessing of the Priests. Bible, *O.T.* TrJP *Fr.* Numbers.

Blessing of your voice, your chaste touch, The. (LL) What I Learned from My Mother. Julia Kasdorf. AmPoNex; PBCAP

Blessing on the house, A. Thomas A. Clark. Oth

Blessing on the printer's art, A! Sarah Josepha Buell Hale. SWaP *Fr.* Three Hours; or, The Vigil of Love.

Blessing Without Company. *Unknown.* BPo

Blessings as rich and fragrant crown your heads. To the Best, and Most Accomplished Couple. Henry Vaughan. PeECV

Blessings in abundance come. Good-Night, or Blessing, The. Robert Herrick. CaPo

Blessings on thee, little man. John Greenleaf Whittier. APN-1; BRP; OBAL; OBCA

Blessings [*or* Blessing] on the hand of women! Hand That Rocks the Cradle Is the Hand That Rules the World, The. William Ross Wallace. ITBLP

Blest age! when ev'ry purling stream. Torquato Tasso. BASC, *tr.* by Aphra Behn *Fr.* Aminta.

Blest are the moments, doubly blest. Hymn. William Wordsworth. SacPr

Blest be the God of love. Evensong [*or* Even-Song]. George Herbert. ESCV

Blest be the man, who first the method found. To My Brother at St. John's College in Cambridge. Elizabeth Tollet. ECWP

Blest be the thing that brought the shadow hither. (LL) I Heard a Noise and Wishèd for a Sight. Thomas Bateson. EBEV; HAP

Blest Be the Wondrous Grace. George Barrell Cheever. AH

Blest Is the Man Whose Tender Breast. Abijah Davis. AH

Blest is the tarn which towering cliffs o'ershade. Blest is the tarn which towering cliffs o'ershade. Sara Coleridge. VWP

Blest leaf! whose aromatic gales dispense. Isaac Hawkins Browne. UV *Fr.* Pipe of Tobacco, A.

Blest Order, which in power dost so excel[l]. Priesthood, The. George Herbert. ESCV

Blest pair of *Sirens*, pledges of Heav'ns [*or* Heaven's] joy. John Milton. GTBS-P; HeIP-4; NOBE; OBEV; SacPr; SCGP

Blest Poesy! Oh sent to calm. Helen Maria Williams. NOBRP *Fr.* Address to Poetry, An.

Blest privacy! Happy retreat, wherein. My Country Audit. Mildmay Fane, 2d Earl of Westmorland. BeJo; NOSC

Blest solitude, in me; even now, take me. To Solitude. Mihály Csokonai Vitéz. IQMS, *tr.* by Edmund Charles Blunden

Blest the infant Babe. William Wordsworth. TOF *Fr.* Prelude, The; Growth of a Poet's Mind [1850 vers.].

Blew It. Michael Castro. SeSe

Blight. Arna Bontemps. ColAP

Blight. Ralph Waldo Emerson. APN-1; NCAP; NOBA; TCAPo

Blight of Love, The. Mary E. Tucker. CBWP-1

Blight rests in your face, The. To a Publisher. . . Cut-out. Imamu Amiri Baraka. NeAP

Blighted apples will not shine. Apple Blight. Paul Zimmer. VGW

Blighted laurel, and a moldering tomb, A! (LL) To Phaon. Mary Robinson. CenSon; RWP

Blighter that is at the end of the sea, The. Blighter, The. Fernando Pessoa. PeSAV, *tr.* by Charles Eglington

Blighters. Siegfried Sassoon. FaBoTw; NoAM; OxBEV; OxBSP; PoWW

Blind. John Kendrick Bangs. PoToHe

Blind. Vincente Huidobro. CuPo

Blind. Norman V. Pearce. PoToHe

Blind, The. Charles Baudelaire. SxFrPo, *tr.* by James McGowan

Blind Bartimæus. Henry Wadsworth Longfellow. ChIV-2

Blind Boy, The. Colley Cibber. GTBS-P; NOEC

Blind Boy's Pranks, The. William Thom. OBEV

Blind child / Guided by his mother, A. Takarai [*or* Enomoto] Kikaku. OHPJ

Blind City. Mona Saudi. PoArWo, *tr.* by Kamal Boullata

Blind clouds, poisonous vapors hang over this mountain city. Overjoyed at Soviet Russia's Entry Into the War. Liu Ya-tzu. SuSp, *tr.* by Wu-Chi Liu

Blind fortune, if thou wants a guide. Fortune's Legacy. *Unknown.* NOSC

Blind Goddess, The. Fadhila Chabbi. PoArWo, *tr.* by Yaseen Noorani

Blind horse trotting up an icy ledge, A. Kosen. ZenPo, *tr.* by Takashi Ikemoto and Lucien Stryk

Blind Love. William Shakespeare. GTBS-P *Fr.* Sonnets.

Blind loving wrestling touch! Sheathed hooded sharptoothed touch! Walt Whitman. CAGL *Fr.* Song of Myself.

Blind Man, The. Anne Batten Cristall. ECWP
  (Fragment, A: The Blind Man.) RWP

Blind Man, The. Fazil Abdulovich Iskander. ItGoST, *tr.* by Avril Pyman

Blind Man, The. Ksenya [*or* Kseniia] Nekrasova. TCRP, *tr.* by Vera Rich

Blind Man, The. Margaret Elizabeth Sangster. PoToHe

Blind Man, The. Konstantin Mikhailovich Simonov. TCRP, *tr.* by Lubov Yakovleva

Blind Man, The. Yaroslav [*or* Iaroslav] Vasilevich Smelyakov [*or* Smeliakov]. TCRP, *tr.* by Simon Franklin

Blind Man, The. Judith Wright.
  Country Dance. BMAP; CBAP

Blind Man at the Fair, The. Joseph Campbell. AWP

Blind man, blind man. Mother Goose. OxNR

Blind man's, The. Raymond Roseliep. HA

Blind Men and the Elephant, The. John Godfrey Saxe. ITBLP; OBCA; OTCP; PoToHe
  (It was six men of Indostan.) BRP; OxIBACP

Blind Musician, The. 'Ali Mahmud Taha. MAP, *tr.* by Issa Boullata and Thomas G. Ezzy

Blind Musicians, The. *Unknown.* TAL

Blind musicians, the blind musicians, The. *Unknown.* ColAnChi, *tr.* by Jeffrey Riegel *Fr.* Classic of Odes.

Blind poet, fiddler, Raftery. For Raftery. Alan Alexander. NOBAu

Blind Sheep, The. Randall Jarrell. OBAL

Blind-Sided. Rick Mulkey. AmPoNex

Blind Solo. Michael S. Weaver. UnSA

Blind Steersmen. Francis Ernest Kobina Parkes. PBA

Blind Thamyris, and blind Maeonides. Ode to the Human Heart. Edward Laman Blanchard. NOBL

Blind woman was more intimate with it, The. Blaga Dimitrova. BBASP, *tr. by* Heather McHugh

Blindest buzzard that I know, The. Sketch, A. Christina Georgina Rossetti. GTBS-P; VWP

Blindfold I should to Myra run. Lady Sophia Burrell. LW *Fr.* Chloe and Myra.

Blindman's Buff. Peter Viereck. MoAmPo

Blindman's Cries, The. Tristan Corbière. WoPoe, *tr. by* Martin James

Blindness we may forgive, but baseness we will smite. (LL) William Vaughn Moody. APN-2; CBCWP; OxBA

Blinkered Mind, The. Amy Witting. NOBAu

Bliss. George Johnston. NOBC

Bliss of Heaven, Maria, shall be thine, The. Charles Tennyson Turner. CenSon

Bliss of Man, The (could pride that blessing find). Pope. NOEC *Fr.* Essay on Man, An.

Blisses about my pilgrimage as pain. (LL) Hap. Thomas Hardy. AWP; CABP; EBVV; GSo; MoBrPo; NAEL-5v2; NAEL-6v2; NoAM; NoP-4; OxBSo; Son

Blistered and dry was the desert I trod. Palm, The. Roy Campbell. MoBrPo

Blithe Fancy lightly builds with airy hands. After Reading Shakspere. Edwin Markham. APN-2

Blizzard. Bella [*or* Izabella] Akhatovna Akhmadulina. TCRP, *tr. by* Albert C. Todd

Blizzard. Bill Holm. MiVo

Blizzard, The. Roger McDonald. NOBAu

Blizzard of Sixty-Six, The. William Daniel Ehrhart. CDa

Blizzard sweeps the streets, A. Aleksandr Aleksandrovich Blok. TCRP

Blizzard wrapped the earth in gloom, The. Winter Night. Boris Leonidovich Pasternak. TCRP, *tr. by* Yakov Hornstein

Blizzards blow and blow, The. To Make Birds Sing. Vladimir Alekseievich Soloukhin. TCRP, *tr. by* Daniel Weissbort

Blkfern-jungal. Aileen Corpus. BMAP

Block City. Robert Louis Stevenson. AmFaPo; NTCP

Block of flats, somewhere in Turin. One Man. William Scammell. NLP

Blockade Swallow, The. Olga Fiodorovna Berggolts [*or* Bergholts]. TCRusP, *tr. by* Daniel Weissbort

Blocking the Pass. Charles Madge. FaBoMo

Blocks. Frank O'Hara. HCAP; LCAP-2; SPE

Blocks rowdy with jays and strumpet sparrows. Aviary. Mark DeFoe. UrbNat

Blocks, The / which are the buildings and walls. Edward Dorn. NOBA *Fr.* Oxford.

Blodwen / Her name like the hours. Gloria Evans Davies. OBWVE

Bloke I know came rolling home as shickered as he could be, A. Shickered as He Could Be. *Unknown.* NOBAu

Blond. Joseph De Roche. HeIP-4

Blond-haired, green-eyed, Italian girl. Amazone. Mary Jo Bona. UnSA

Blond light blew away grayness, shadows, mists. Facing Bonnard. Aleksander Wat. BLT

Blond stones all round-sided. Morning at Point Dume. May Swenson. DiPo

Blond whose skin was translucent as a glass slipper, The. Blue Suede Shoes. Diane Wakoski. AllShUp

Blonde Ambition. Maureen Seaton. ReTh

Blonde hair at the edge of the pavement. Mitching. Michael Smith. CIP-2

Blonde neighbor lady tells my wife, The. Opposite of Green, The. Alvin Aubert. ISC

Blonde White Women. Patricia Smith. GT; UnSA

Blondie. Jean Earle. TCAWP

Blood. Ray Bremser. NeAP

Blood. Naomi Shihab Nye. GraLe
   ("True Arab knows how to catch a fly in his hands, A.") UnSA

Blood. Lucien Stryk. BodElec

Blood. Franz Wright. LCAP-2

Blood, The. Nina Cassian. WPOW

Blood and Gold. Endre Ady. IQMS, *tr. by* Watson Kirkconnell

Blood, blood! The lines of every printed sheet. George Henry Boker. APN-2

Blood Donor. Robert Morgan. AngWePo; TCAWP

Blood falling in drops to the earth. Where Are the Men Seized in this Wind of Madness? Alda do Espirito Santo. PBMAP; TTY; WPOW, *tr. by* Alan Ryder

Blood flows in me, but what does it have to do. Living by the Red River. James Wright (1927–80). NNaP

Blood from our fingertips comes welling. Song of a Hungarian Jacobin. Endre Ady. IQMS, *tr. by* Sir Maurice Bowra

Blood from the shoulder drips from couch to floor. Judith. Félix Lope de Vega Carpio. WoPoe, *tr. by* Brian Soper

Blood Heifer. Dahlia Ravikovitch [*or* Ravikovich]. DTA, *tr. by* Chana Bloch and Ariel Bloch

Blood in the Desert's Eyes, The. Syl Cheney-Coker.
   "Philosopher, The." PBMAP

Blood is Justified, The. Muriel Rukeyser. YaYoPo

Blood of Ishtar, The. Qadesha (Sacred Whore). Cosi Fabian. HW

Blood of Others, The. Gioconda Belli. TANSG, *tr. by* Steven F. White

Blood only blood is able to beat to strike the right note. Whispered. Jiri Orten. AF, *tr. by* Lyn Coffin

Blood or Color. Marjorie Welish. FTOS

Blood puddles on the Spanish white floor. Almendares. Sandra M. Castillo. TouFir

Blood-red flower of revolution, The. (LL) Roses and Revolutions. Dudley Randall. BPo; CoAmPo; TAP

Blood searching in his head without metaphor, The. (LL) Letters and Other Worlds. Michael Ondaatje. NoAM; NOBC; NoP-4

Blood-shotten through the bleak gigantic trees. Winter Twilight, A. John Banister Tabb. APN-2

Blood-Sister. Adrienne Rich. NAAL-2v2

Blood splatters itself on snow. Imprint of Microscopic Life Found in Arctic Stones. Patricia Goedicke. GifTon

Blood sprouts like early spring. Sunday Morning. Anne Rouse. NeBl

Blood-stained, continue cutting weeds and shade. (LL) Reapers. Jean Toomer. APT-2; BPo; ColAP; GT; HAP; NoAM; NIL-7; NoP-4; SoSe-8; TRP; WeW-3

Blood-stained fruit of labor, sweated out of Black slaves. On Sweet Coffee. Ábrahám Barcsay. IQMS, *tr. by* Thomas Kabdebo

Blood surges in my temples. Wet Bodies. Franz Douskey. PasH

Blood thudded in my ears. I scuffed. First Confession. X. J. Kennedy. CoAmPo

Blood Ties. Thelma Seto. TWW

Blood was her dress and her embassy. Self-portraits by Frida Kahlo. Joanna Rawson. BodElec

Bloodletting. Anselm Berrigan. HeMarv

Bloods and bucks of this lewd town, The. Horace. *See* Ribald Romeos less and less berattle

Bloody and a sudden end, A. John Kinsella's Lament for Mrs. Mary Moore. W. B. Yeats. RB

Bloody Hand. Ciaran Carson. PBCIP

Bloody knife blade, A. Richard Wright. APT-2

Bloody Masculinity. Ifi Amadiume. HAWP

Bloody men are like bloody buses. Bloody Men. Wendy Cope. HarvBoo; NoP-4

Bloody Pause. "Astra." BrRo

Bloody trunk [*or* Bloudy trunck] of him who did possess[e], The. Sir Richard Fanshawe. NOSC, *tr. by* Sir Richard Fanshawe *Fr.* Il Pastor Fido.

Bloom of youth had faded from her face, The. Forsaken, The. Agnes Strickland. CenSon

Bloom on the fruit is perfect, The. At Les Deux Magots. Maura Dooley. LW

Blooms such as wither at finger-touch. Brian Coffey. BIrV *Fr.* Muse, June, Related.

Bloomsbury Snapshot. Connie Bensley. OBCoV

Blossom. May Probyn. VWP

Blossom, The. William Blake. FHYEP *Fr.* Songs of Innocence.

Blossom, The. William Shakespeare. OBEV *Fr.* Love's Labour's Lost.

Blossom [*or* Blossome], The. John Donne. AWP; ESCV; MeLP; NAEL-5v1; NAEL-6v1; NAEL-7v1; SCGP; UnPo

Blossom that lov'st on shadowy banks to lie. Forget-Me-Not, The. Mary Russell Mitford. CenSon

Blossoming bulbs, pots swathed in pink and green. Easter Afternoon. Rachel Hadas. UrbNat

Blossoming myrtle tree. Woman's Ritornelle. Theodor Storm. WoPoe, *tr. by* James Wright

Blossoming plum! Issa. SoOfWa, *tr. by* Sam Hamill

Blossoming white in the rose garden. Blue Rose. Carol Muske. ExTi

Blossoms. Ernst Goll. AuPH, *tr. by* Lowell A. Bangerter

Blossoms. Frank Dempster Sherman. OBCA

Blossoms at night. Issa. EH, *tr. by* Robert Hass

Blossoms bright, the moon dark, shadowed in thin mist. Tune: Deva-like Barbarian. Li Yü. CoBCP, *tr. by* Burton Watson

Blossoms crowd the branches: too beautiful to endure. Spring-gazing Song. Hsüeh T'ao. BoWoP, *tr. by* Carolyn Kizer

Blossoms have fallen, The. Princess Shikishi. BoWoP

Blossoms in the Wind. Takajiro Ohnishi. FaBoWar

Blossoms lift the branches. Beautiful Days. Mary Kinzie. ExTi

Blossoms of the wood have scattered their spring crimson. Tune: Crows Crying at Night. Li Yü. CoBCP, *tr. by* Burton Watson

Blossoms on the pear. Buson. TAL

Blossoms scent the air. Gozan. JDP, *tr. by* Yoel Hoffmann

Blot in the 'Scutcheon, A. Robert Browning.

Earl Mertoun's Song. OBEV

Blouse of Felt. Amina Calil. BAP-01

Blow, blow, thou winter wind. William Shakespeare. AWP; GTBS-P; NAEL-5v1; NOBE; NoSic; OBEV; SCGP *Fr.* As You Like It.

Blow, blow, ye spicy breezes. Ambrose Bierce. APN-2; OBAL *Fr.* Devil's Dictionary, The.

Blow, Boys, Blow [*or* Blow, Bullies, Blow]. *Unknown.* FaBoVe

Blow, Bugle, Blow. Tennyson. *See* Princess, The

Blow if you will. Gansan. JDP, *tr. by* Yoel Hoffmann

Blow / Ill wind. Ill Wind. Ted Koehler. ReLy

Blow, Northern Wind. *Unknown.* MiEL; OBEV

Blow of an ax. Buson. EH, *tr. by* Robert Hass

Blow softly down the valley. King of Ireland's Cairn, The. "Ethna Carbery." WPE

Blow the fire, blacksmith. Mother Goose. OxNR

Blow the rest away. (LL) Friendship. Dinah Maria Mulock Craik. ITBLP; PoToHe

Blow the Winds, I-Ho. *Unknown.* OxBoLi

Blow them back on the branches. (LL) Our Little Sister is Worried. *Unknown.* OHMPC; WoPoe, *tr. by* Kenneth Rexroth

Blow, West Wind. Robert Penn Warren. ColAP

Blow, whistle / Blow away. Beyond the Blue Horizon. Leo Robin. ReLy

Blow, wind, blow! and go, mill, go! Mother Goose. OxNR

Blow, Winds. William Shakespeare. OxAEP-1 *Fr.* King Lear.

Blow, winds, and crack your cheek! rage! blow! William Shakespeare. OxAEP-1 *Fr.* King Lear.

Blow Your Trumpet, Gabriel. *Unknown.* APN-2

Blowflies Buzz, The. *Unknown.* NOBAu, *tr. by* Catherine H. Berndt (Djalbarmiwi's Song.) CBAP

Blowing Eggs. Anne Caston. NAPBL

Blowing hard at the bus stop. Transit. Margaret Avison. FaBoWP

Blowing softly over his eyelashes. Kettle Rooted to the Void. Anabel Torres. TANSG, *tr. by* Celeste Kostopulos-Cooperman

Blowing stones. Basho. EH, *tr. by* Robert Hass

Blowing ten thousand years ago. (LL) Languages. Carl Sandburg. APT-1; ColAP

Blown apart by loss, she let herself go. Rita Dove. FFC

Blown away, flying and flying and flying. (LL) Venice Beach: Brief Song. Dorothy Barresi. SeSe; SwNoth

Blown by winds, the thistledown. Tu Fu. CrYelRi, *tr. by* Sam Hamill *Fr.* Random Pleasures.

Blown from Sleep's trumpet. (LL) Louse Hunting. Isaac Rosenberg. EBEV; FaBoWar; NAEL-5v2; NAEL-6v2; NoAM; NoP-4; OxAEP-2; OxBEV; OxBTC; PeFWW

Blown from the west. Buson. EH, *tr. by* Robert Hass

Blown[e] in the morning, thou shalt fade ere noon. Sir Richard Fanshawe. OBEV *Fr.* Il Pastor Fido.

Blown in the wind / the silver river. Inscribed on a Snowscape. Yün Shou-p'ing. CoBLCP, *tr. by* Jonathan Chaves

Blown sand heaps on me, that none may learn, The. Rudyard Kipling. PeFWW *Fr.* Epitaphs of the War [1914–1918].

Blows birthday candles for the world. (LL) Birth of Tragedy, The. Irving Layton. MoCV; NoAM; NoP-4

Blows the Wind Today. Robert Louis Stevenson. NPeEn; SCGP (To S. R. Crockett.) EBVV; NOBE; NePenScot

Blowzy dove, A. Beak wide open, on a khamsin day. Reflections on a Dove. Hamutal Bar Yosef. DTA, *tr. by* Shirley Kaufman

Blp. (LL) Loch Ness Monster's Song, The. Edwin Morgan. NePenScot; OPOU

Bludging off the old man. Got No Shame. Selwyn Hughes. IBA

Blue. Rafael Alberti. PoetW, *tr. by* Mark Strand

Blue. William Heyen. GotH

Blue Again. Dorothy Fields. ReLy

Blue and the Gray, The. Francis Miles Finch. APN-2; CBCWP

Blue and White. Mary Elizabeth Coleridge. OBEV

Blue and white. Poems at the Porthole. Lorine Niedecker. FTOS

Blue and white tie arrived at the man's neck through, The. Tell Us, Josephine. Ron Padgett. FTOS

Blue Angel, The. Allen Ginsberg. BB

Blue Arm. Bernard Spencer. NoAM

Blue arm stuck out of the train's window, A. Watching Trains. Joanna Fuhrman. AmPoNex

Blue arrived. And its time was painted. Blue. Rafael Alberti. PoetW, *tr. by* Mark Strand

Blue as a new moon midnight. Fresh Mussels. Charles McDonald. NLP

Blue Bell Boy. *Unknown.* ReMoGo

Blue-Bird, The. Herman Melville. NOBA

Blue Black. Bloke Modisane. PBA

Blue-black of a winter morning. Waking Up Twice. Jack Anderson. PasH

Blue Blood. James Stephens. MoBrPo; OBCoV; OBMV

Blue, blue is the grass about the river. Beautiful Toilet, The. Ezra Pound. OBVE

Blue blue the summit. Heaven Peak. Muso Soseki. EaWin, *tr. by* W. S. Merwin

Blue Blue Your Collar. *Unknown.* CoBCP, *tr. by* Burton Watson

Blue boat of morning and already. Tourism in the Late 20th Century. Silvia Curbelo. BodElec

Blue Bonnets over the Border. Sir Walter Scott. OxBS

Blue Booby, The. James Tate. NoAM; SPE (Blue booby lives, The.) SPE

Blue Book 18 Pages 1–4. Steve Benson. FTOS

Blue boughs, green fruit. Furnished Room, The. James Merrill. NOBA

Blue City, The. Alfred Wellington Purdy. NoP-4

Blue Clay. Ellease Southerland. GT

Blue cloud sky. Tune: "Sumuche Dancers." Fan Chung-yen. ColAnChi, *tr. by* J. R. Hightower

Blue crane fishing in Cooloolah's twilight, The. At Cooloolah. Judith Wright. BMAP; HarvBoo

Blue Crest of Fondness. Unsi Al-Haj [*or* Hajj]. MAP, *tr. by* Sargon Boulus and Alistair Elliot

Blue cyanus growing. In the Grass. Josef Weinheber. AuPH, *tr. by* Lowell A. Bangerter

Blue day / a blue jay, A. March. Elizabeth Jane Coatsworth. Spl

Blue Day Journey, The. Gwyn Jones. OBWVE

Blue Days. Rita Dove. ExTi

Blue, dew-drenched. Gardens for the Fire and the Rain. Muhammad Al-As'ad. MAP, *tr. by* Charles Doria and Lena Jayyusi

Blue Diamond. Claudia Keelan. BodElec

Blue Dome, The. Deborah Randall. NeBl

Blue duiker, left hindleg, The. Piece of Earth, A. Douglas Livingstone. PeSAV

Blue eagle and the demon of the steppes, The. Staircase with a Hundred Steps, The. Benjamin Péret. SPE, *tr. by* David Gascoyne

Blue eye-pupil in my park, A. Swan, The. Delmira Agustini. TANSG, *tr. by* Mark McCaffrey

Blue-eyed Mary. Mary Eleanor Wilkins Freeman. OBCA

Blue Fly. Joaquim Maria Machado de Assis. TTY, *tr. by* Frances Ellen Buckland

Blue-Fly, The. Robert Graves. NAEL-5v2; NAEL-6v2; NoAM

Blue Funk. Joel Oppenheimer. NeAP

Blue-geese, white-geese, you may say. "H. D." APT-1; NOBA *Fr.* Flowering of the Rod, The.

Blue Girls. John Crowe Ransom. APT-1; ColAP; MoAmPo; NoAM; NoP-4; RB; TAP; WeW-3 (Twirling your blue skirts, traveling the sward.) FuPo (Vanity of the Blue Girls, The.) FuPo

Blue Glass. Fleur Adcock. FaBoWP

Blue go up & blue go down. American Lights, Seen from off Abroad. John Berryman. LCAP-2; OBAL; OBCoV

Blue Grass. Arthur Schwartz. ReLy

Blue-green bamboo, white sand, village on the river. Trip to the Village of the River of White Sand, A. Tao-chi. CoBLCP, *tr. by* Jonathan Chaves

Blue-green greyish gum leaves, The. Celebrators '88. Kevin Gilbert. IBA

Blue-handed, with difficult string. Winter Rose, The. Gillian Ferguson. NeBl

Blue Heron, The. Theodore Goodridge Roberts. NOBC

Blue Horses. Ed Roberson. GT

Blue Horses, The. James McAuley. BMAP

Blue Hour, The. Margarita Iosifovna Aliger. TCRP, *tr. by* Albert T. Todd

Blue ice curdling on the stream, The. (LL) Emily Jane Brontë. BWW; NOBVV; SCGP

Blue in the west the mountain stands. Vickery's Mountain. Edwin Arlington Robinson. MoAmPo

Blue is for the troublemakers. Letters from School, The. Juan Delgado. TouFir

Blue is Our Lady's colour. Blue and White. Mary Elizabeth Coleridge. OBEV

Blue is this night of stars. Inquietude. Pauli Murray. BlSi

Blue Island Intersection. Carl Sandburg. MoAmPo

Blue Jacket, The. Marion Angus. NePenScot

Blue Jay. Paul Lake. RA

Blue Jay, The. D. H. Lawrence. NPeEn

Blue Jay [*or* Bluejay]. Robert Francis. LCAP-2

Blue jay scuffling in the bushes follows, The. On the Move. Thom Gunn. HAP; NoP-4; OxAEP-2; OxBTC; PoE; TRP; TwCP

Blue jays in the pines. Robert Spiess. HA

Blue Jeaned Rock Queen in Search of Happiness on a Blind Thursday at 1/3 Speed and Crying, A.   A. K. Redwing.   VoR

Blue Kashmir, '74.   Carol Muske.   PuP-23

Blue kingfisher dives on you in fire, The. (LL)   Colloquy in Black Rock.   Robert Lowell.   MoAmPo; NAAL-2v2

Blue laguna rocks and quivers, The.   Port of Holy Peter.   John Masefield.   OBMV

Blue leather harness slips off glistening shoulders.   Radiant Silhouette I.   John Yau.   OpBo

Blue light is the night harbor-slip.   Louis Zukofsky.   PoE   *Fr.* 29 Poems.

Blue light, morning.   This Decoration.   Hayden Carruth.   NNaP

Blue like Death.   James Welch.   CDW

Blue Mist.   Sergey [*or* Sergei] Aleksandrovich Yesenin [*or* Essenin].   RusPo, *tr. by* Robert Arthur Douglas Ford

Blue mist rises from fragrant herbs in the bronze plate.   Yang Yi.   SuSp

Blue mist. Snow plenitude.   Sergey [*or* Sergei] Aleksandrovich Yesenin [*or* Essenin].   RusPo, *tr. by* Robert Arthur Douglas Ford

Blue mists surround the mountains now.   Lines Written on a Farewell View of the Franconia Mountains at Twilight.   Henrietta Cordelia Ray.   CBWP-3

Blue Monday.   Calvin Forbes.   ESEAA

Blue Monday.   Langston Hughes.   SAmP

Blue Monday.   Diane Wakoski.   NALW; PmAP

Blue Monday.   Al Young.   SpirFl

Blue Moon.   Mimi Khalvati.   MFPA

Blue Moon.   Richard Rodgers.   ReLy

Blue Mountain.   Roberta Hill Whiteman.   VoR

Blue mountains to the north of the walls.   Taking Leave of a Friend.   Li Po.   RB, *tr. by* Ezra Pound

Blue mouth of the shark, The.   Coming.   Robert Kelly.   PmAP

Blue Movies.   Maurya Simon.   GifTon

Blue of the heaps of beads poured into her breasts.   Blue Monday.   Diane Wakoski.   NALW; PmAP

Blue Paisley Shirt, The.   Thomas William Shapcott.   BMAP

Blue Rapids.   Lu Yu.   CoBCP; ColAnChi; SuSp, *tr. by* Burton Watson

Blue Ridge.   Ellen Bryant Voigt.   NoAM

Blue River.   Muhammad ibn Ghalib al-Rusafi.   WoPoe, *tr. by* Cola Franzen

Blue robe on their shoulder[s], A.   Seven Fiddlers, The.   Sebastian Evans.   EBVV

Blue Rock, The.   Sojourner Kincaid Rolle.   GeoHom

Blue Room, The.   Richard Edwards [*or* Edwardes].   Spl

Blue Room, The.   Richard Rodgers.   OBAL; ReLy

Blue Rose.   Carol Muske.   ExTi

Blue seagulls yell insults.   Seagulls.   Daria Menicanti.   CItWP, *tr. by* Cinzia Sartini Blum and Lara Trubowitz

Blue Shade.   Aaron Shurin.   FTOS

Blue Skies.   Irving Berlin.   ReLy

Blue Skies, White Breasts, Green Trees.   Gerald Stern.   BodElec

Blue sky blue water.   Home.   Calvin Forbes.   GT

Blue sky in a human face.   Mac Wellman.   HeMarv   *Fr.* Rat Minaret: Miniaturist-Divan, The.

Blue Sky in Morning.   Rob MacKenzie.   Oth

Blue snow is turning black, The.   Poem.   Aleksandr Trifonovich Tvardovsky [*or* Tvardovskii].   RusPo, *tr. by* Robert Arthur Douglas Ford

Blue, so blue that eye of sky.   Lament.   Jacques Rabémanganjara.   NegPo, *tr. by* Ellen Conroy Kennedy

Blue Song.   Mary Macleod (Màiri Nighean Alasdair Ruaidh).   NePenScot, *tr. by* Robert Crawford

Blue spaces do not see themselves, The.   Stepan Petrovich Shchipachov [*or* Shchipachiov].   TCRP

Blue Suburban.   Howard Nemerov.   ColAP

Blue Suede Shoes.   Ai.   ReTh

Blue Suede Shoes.   Diane Wakoski.   AllShUp

Blue Swallows, The.   Howard Nemerov.   MakPoe; NoP-4; OWoS

Blue Symphony.   John Gould Fletcher.   APT-1

Blue Tail Fly or Jimmy Cracked Corn, The.   Daniel Decatur Emmett.   TCAPo

Blue That Isn't Even Blue or in Any Case, A.   Amelia Rosselli.   CItWP, *tr. by* Cinzia Sartini Blum and Lara Trubowitz

Blue. The green. The river-bed, The.   Scene, The.   Ágnes Nemes Nagy.   PoSu, *tr. by* Bruce Berlind

Blue thigh of daybreak, sweetened, fall apart—.   Michael Masse.   Sam Witt.   NeAmPo

Blue! 'Tis the Life of Heaven, the Domain.   John Keats.   OxBSo

Blue Tit on a String of Peanuts.   Norman MacCaig.   CABP

Blue unsolid tongue, if you could talk.   Overturned Lake, The.   Charles Henri Ford.   SPE

Blue vein, bright on her temple, pitifully beating, The. (LL)   Boy with His Hair Cut Short.   Muriel Rukeyser.   NALW; NoAM; TwCP; VGW; WPE

Blue Water.   Li Po.   CrYelRi; ErotSp, *tr. by* Sam Hamill

Blue water ripples the well at the corner of the mossy rock.   Evening on the Mountain: Song to the Moon in the Well.   Yi Kyubo.   WoPoe, *tr. by* Kevin O'Rourke

Blue whale swam through blue air in the basement, The.   Ghost Shirt, The.   Lucia Maria Perillo.   BAP-01

Blue Wind, The.   Nadja.   SurWo, *tr. by* Richard Howard

Blue Winter.   Robert Francis.   LCAP-2

Bluebeard.   Mark Bibbins.   WiU

Bluebeard.   Edna St. Vincent Millay.   APT-1

Bluebeard's Closet.   Rose Terry Cooke.   APN-2; TCAPo

Blueberry Man.   David Bergman.   GLP

Bluebird alights, The.   Michael McClintock.   HA

Bluebird & / honeymoon over.   Spring.   Reed Bye.   TTTS

Bluebird in Cutleaf Beech.   Wendy Wilder Larsen.   KGB

Bluefish boil the water silver; they tangle in the chase.   Blues: Late August.   Cleopatra Mathis.   ExTi

Bluegill rises, A.   John Wills.   HA

Bluejay and the Mockingbird, The.   Howard Nemerov.   BodElec

Bluejay sails, A.   John Wills.   HA

Bluejay screeches from a pine. (LL)   What Happened Here Before.   Gary Snyder.   APSN; NNaP; PoM

Blueness of the Day, The.   David Mura.   OPRER

Blueprint for Disaster.   Christian Morgenstern.   WoPoe, *tr. by* David R. Slavitt

Blueprints.   Madeline DeFrees.   ExTi

Blues.   Edward Kamau Brathwaite.   GT

Blues.   Léon Damas.   NegPo, *tr. by* Ellen Conroy Kennedy

Blues.   John Fuller.   NOBL

Blues.   Suzanne Gardinier.   AmPoNex

Blues.   Pierre Martory.   KGB, *tr. by* John Ashbery

Blues.   Sonia Sanchez.   GT

Blues.   Léopold Sédar Senghor.   PBMAP

Blues, The.   Langston Hughes.   TLR

Blues, The.   Mark Vinz.   MiVo

Blues 1.   Barry Wallenstein.   SeSe

Blues 2.   Barry Wallenstein.   SeSe

Blues ain't culture.   Liberation / Poem.   Sonia Sanchez.   NBV

Blues and blues.   Remembered.   Sterling Plumpp.   GT

Blues are the big thing.   Raymond Roseliep.   HA

Blues at Dawn.   Langston Hughes.   SAmP

Blues at Lord's, The.   Siegfried Sassoon.   PeLV

Blues at 1.   Dorothy Perry Thompson.   SpirFl

Blues begins to moan in her stomach never quite full, A.   Drummond's Lover Sings the Blues.   Norman Weinstein.   WaCA

Blues blow in their purity, The.   Blue Monday.   Al Young.   SpirFl

Blues del SIDA / AIDS Blues.   Francisco Alarcon.   GeoHom

Blues Don't Change, The.   Al Young.   ESEAA; GT

Blues for Aunt Ruth.   Norita Dittberner-Jax.   MiVo

Blues for Bird.   Linda France.   NeBl

Blues for Franks Wooten.   Tom Weatherly.   NBV

(Blues for Franks Wooten / House of the Lifting of the Head.)   GT

Blues for the Lonely.   Jeremy Robson.   SeSe

Blues for the Nightowl.   Elton Glaser.   PBCAP

Blues for Warren.   Thomas McGrath.   AF

Blues for Zoot.   Sascha Feinstein.   AmPoNex

Blues in "C."   Ron Overton.   SeSe

Blues in the Night.   Johnny Mercer.   APT-2; ReLy

Blues (in Two Parts), The.   Val Ferdinand.   NBV

Blues is the black o' the face, The.   Black Blues.   Bloke Modisane.   PBA

Blues lady / with the beaded face.   Grinding Vibrato.   Jayne Cortez.   BlSi

Blues: Late August.   Cleopatra Mathis.   ExTi

Blues meant Swiss-Up, The.   Riding Across John Lee's Finger.   Stanley Crouch.   GT

Blues Villanelle for Sonny Criss.   Sascha Feinstein.   AmPoNex

Bluesky.   Pierre Albert-Birot.   CuPo

Bluesman in pungent mood, The.   Tobacco Warehouse Blues.   Houston A. Baker, Jr.   SeSe

Bluesman's Blues, A.   Lenard D. Moore.   ISC

Bluetits.   Ruth Smith.   Prnts

Blunting, The.   Richard Eberhart.   BodElec

Blunts.   Major L. Jackson.   SpirFl

Blurb for *Anna Livia Plurabelle*, A.   James Joyce.   OBCoV

Blurb for *Haveth Childers Everywhere*, A.   James Joyce.   OBCoV

Blurred in a whirlwind, a mighty cloud of dust.   Indignation.   José Santos Chocano.   TCLAP, *tr. by* Andrew Rosing

Blurring a definition. Quick! you are old. (LL)   Realization, The.   Yvor Winters.   APT-2; HarvBoo

Blush and blow, blush and blow. Sad Spring-Song. Sarah Morgan Bryan Piatt. NCAP

Blustery wind is terrible with song, The. October. Vladimir Ivanovich Narbut. TCRP, *tr. by* Lubov Yakovleva

Bo-be-o-bee sang the mouth. Velemir [*or* Viktor Vladimirovich] Khlebnikov. TCRP

Bo-peep / Little Bo-peep. *Unknown.* OxNR

Bo peeper. *Unknown.* OxNR

Bo Tree. Patricia Pogson. Prnts

Boädicea. Tennyson.

"Hear Icenian, Catieuchlanian, hear Coritanian, Trinobant!" FaBoWar

Boadicea often would goad. Limerick. Douglas Catley. PeLi

Boar's Head Carol, The. *Unknown.* MiEL

Board of War has quelled the mutiny, The. To the Minister Liu. Yü Hsüan-chi. BoWoP, *tr. by* Geoffrey Waters

Boarded the train there's no getting off. (LL) Metaphors. Sylvia Plath. HeIP-4; InPK-6; SoSe-8

Boarder, The. Louis Simpson. InPK-6

Boarders look so good and new, The. Legend of the Crossing-Sweeper. May Kendall. VWP

Boarding the boat. Seira. JDP, *tr. by* Yoel Hoffmann

Boast not proud English, of thy birth and blood. Roger Williams. SCAP

Boastful young fellow of Neath, A. Limerick. Frank Richards. PeLi

Boasting of My Son. Li Shang-yin. ColAnChi, *tr. by* James J. Y. Liu

Boat, A. Richard Brautigan. KaS

Boat, A. Jordan Davis. HeMarv

Boat, The. Caroline Gilman. OBCA

Boat, The. Ferenc Kazinczy. IQMS, *tr. by* Watson Kirkconnell

Boat, The. Robert Pack. CoAP

Boat, The. Anne Sexton. NAAL-5 *Fr.* Death of the Fathers, The.

Boat Down the River of Yellow Silt, A. Kimiko Hahn. ExTi

Boat gathers you in, A. One Reason I Went to Prison. James Moore. CDa

Boat is chafing at our long delay, The. Song. John Davidson. OBEV

Boat-load of emigrant Huns, A. Wreck of the Deutschland, The. David Annett. PeLi

Boat moored, lunch in a lonely village, The. Dappled Horse, The. Mei Yao Ch'en. CoBCP; ColAnChi, *tr. by* Burton Watson

Boat of sandalwood and oars of magnolia, A. Boating Song. Li Po. TAL

Boat of Stars. Li Ch'ing-chao. ErotSp, *tr. by* Sam Hamill

(To the Tune: Boat of Stars.) CrYelRi

Boat on the Pacific, A. Najaat Al-Udwany. PoArWo, *tr. by* Moulouk Berry and Ali Farghaly

Boat on the River of Heaven. (LL) Kenneth Rexroth. APSN; APT-2 *Fr.* Love Poems of Marichiko, The.

Boat on the Shore. Andrey [*or* Andrei] Andreievich Voznesensky [*or* Voznesenskij]. RusPo, *tr. by* Robert Arthur Douglas Ford

Boat People. Yusef Komunyakaa. AF; CDa; PoPoPo

Boat Poem. Bernard Spencer. EmeKit; FaBoTw; OxBTC

Boat-pullers, The. Mei Yao Ch'en. SuSp, *tr. by* Jonathan Chaves

Boat's Blueprint, The. Ian Hamilton Finlay. NePenScot

Boat slows, moors by beach-run in smoke, A. Stayover at Chien-Teh River. Meng Hao Jan. ChinPo, *tr. by* Yip Wai-lim

Boat Song. Henrietta Cordelia Ray. CBWP-3

Boat Song. Sir Walter Scott. OxAEP-2 *Fr.* Lady of the Lake, The.

Boat Song, A. Saint Columba. NOIV

Boat Stealing. William Wordsworth. RB *Fr.* Prelude, The; Growth of a Poet's Mind [1805 vers.].

Boat that did not rock or wobble once, A. Seamus Heaney. ModIr *Fr.* Lightenings.

Boat tilts on your image on the waves, The. Romantic Movement, The. Philip Lamantia. CLPP

Boathouse, The. Robert Minhinnick. AngWePo

Boating in Autumn. Lu Yu. ChiP, *tr. by* Arthur Waley

Boating Song. Li Po. TAL

Boatman, The. Jay Macpherson. MoCV

Boatman, have they crossed? "Not all." Doom Ferry. Sir Arthur Thomas Quiller-Couch. EBVV

Boatman he can dance and sing, The. Dance the Boatman. *Unknown.* AiP

Boatman of Ts'ang-lang is quite old, The. Fisherman. Ts'en Shen. SuSp, *tr. by* C. H. Wang

Boatman's Dance. Daniel Decatur Emmett. APN-1

Boatman's Song, A. Wang Chien. SuSp, *tr. by* William H. Nienhauser

Boatmen / how late you've come! Song of the Transport Workers—Seeing Off Fang Wen-yü on His Way to His Post as Inspector of Transportation. Pien Kung. CoBLCP, *tr. by* Jonathan Chaves

Boatpond, broken off, looks back at the sky, The. X. Jean Valentine. ExTi

Boats. Bernadette Mayer. FTOS

Boats Are Afloat, The. Chu Hsi. OHPC, *tr. by* Kenneth Rexroth

Boats are careened in the harbour. Here is a bed. (LL) Sailing to an Island. Richard Murphy. ModIr; PBCIP

Boats in a Fog. Robinson Jeffers. NAAL-2v2; NoP-4; OxBA

Boats' lights in the dawn going so swiftly the, The. Charles Olson. BodElec *Fr.* Maximus Poems, The.

Boats of orchid-wood float on the river. Gathering Lotus with Singing Girls. Mo Shih-lung. CoBLCP, *tr. by* Jonathan Chaves

Boats sail upstream and downstream alike, The. Poem to the Sun. *Ancient Egyptian Oral Tradition.* TTTS, *tr. by* Christopher Wertz

Boaz Asleep. Victor Hugo. SxFrPo

Bob Marley New King of the Music. Anthony McNeill. WaCA

Bob marley new king of the music. Bob Marley New King of the Music. Anthony McNeill. WaCA

Bob Marley's Dead. Rachel Manley. WaCA

Bob Robin. Mother Goose. OxNR

Bob's Lane. Edward Thomas. PoE

(Women He Liked.) TCAWP

Bob Southey! You're a poet—poet-laureate. Byron. CTC; OBSV *Fr.* Don Juan.

Bob / You make me move in an ancient way. Stepping to da Muse/Sic. Afua Cooper. WaCA

Bobbin Stops, The. István Sinka. IQMS, *tr. by* Adam Makkai

Bobbing on the breeze blown waves. Way of the Water-Hyacinth. Zawgee. AmFaPo, *tr. by* Lyn Aye

Bobbing with the crowds. Urban Experience: Part One, The. Lew Blockcolski. VoR

Bobby Shaftoe's [*or* Shafto's] gone to sea. Bobby Shaftoe. Mother Goose. OxNR; ReMoGo

Bobby Snooks. *Unknown.* ReMoGo

Bobby-soxers exchange clandestine feels. At the Record Hop. Wanda Coleman. NAAAL

Bobs on the water. Boat-like can cleave it. In Praise of the Body. Anna Hajnal. IQMS, *tr. by* Kenneth McRobbie

Bocas: A Daughter's Geography. Ntozake Shange. NAAAL

Boddhisattva Doctrine: Enter / Nirvana only when all beings, sentient. John Cage. APSN *Fr.* Diary: How to Improve the World (You Will Only Make Matters Worse).

Bodega, Goodbye. Edwin Honig. NoAM

Bodhidharma Crossing the Graywolf River on a Ry-Krisp. Tim McNulty. GifTon

Bodies, The. Elizabeth Spires. NIL-7

Bodies broken on, The. Lucille Clifton. NAAAL

Bodies like driftwood, The. Seeing the Documentary by the British Liberating Bergen-Belsen. Lyn Lifshin. GotH

Bodies of men and women engirth me, and I engirth them, The. Walt Whitman. *See* I sing the body electric

Bodies of Water. Greg Williamson. NAPBL; NeAmPo

Bodies / tidal waves. Ana Istarú. TANSG, *tr. by* Mary Jane Treacy

Bodo. Thomas Lux. OPRER

Body. Robert Creeley. FTOS

Body, The. William Bronk. VGW

Body, The. Robert Herrick. CaPo

Body and mind, we used to think, were two. Body and Mind. Conrad Hilberry. GM

Body and Soul. B. H. Fairchild. MoASP

Body and Soul. Edward Heyman. ReLy

Body and Soul. Luciana Notari. CItWP, *tr. by* Cinzia Sartini Blum and Lara Trubowitz

Body and Soul: Poem for Two Readers. John Taggart. FTOS

Body Bags. R. S. Gwynn. RA

Body beside the Ties, The. Kenneth Patchen. CLPP

Body beside your body sleeps like death, The. Sleep of the Insomniac, The. William Virgil Davis. YaYoPo

Body Count. Leonard Nathan. PBCAP

Body has its own story, The. She. Lynn Emanuel. BodElec

Body held in front of me. (LL) Elder Sister, The. Sharon Olds. NIL-7; NIP-4

Body in Youth, The. Ellen Hinsey. YaYoPo

Body Inside the Soul, The. Bell Hooks. ISC

Body is immobile, left behind, The. Octet Before Winter. Claire Malroux. VCWP, *tr. by* Marilyn Hacker

Body is like a November birch facing the full moon, The. Solitude Late at Night in the Woods. Robert Bly. VGW

Body Is Pain, The. *Vietnamese Oral Tradition.* CaDao, *tr. by* John Balaban

Body is the body of the Buddha, The. Ten Thousand Sutras. Sam Hamill. ErotSp

Body is the Soul's [*or* Soules] poor[e] house, or home, The. Body, The. Robert Herrick. CaPo

Body Is the Victory and the Defeat of Dreams, The.   Katerina Anghelaki-Rooke.   WPOW, *tr. by* Philip Ram

Body Language.   Linda France.   NeBl

Body Language.   Sylvia Kantaris.   LW

Body leaning slightly back, the arms held firm and straight, The.   Sonata.   John Fuller.   DiPo

Body lies under the ground.   Dirge.   Gavin Bantock.   OxBTC

Body, long oppressed, The.   This Corruptible.   Elinor Wylie.   MoAmPo

Body Mutinies, The.   Lucia Maria Perillo.   IllVoic

Body my house.   Question.   May Swenson.   APT-2; VGW

Body of a Rook.   David Wevill.   MoCV

Body of a woman, white hills, white thighs.   Pablo Neruda.   ErotSp; TCLAP, *tr. by* W. S. Merwin

Body of a woman, white hills, white thighs.   Pablo Neruda.   RaBo, *tr. by* Robert Bly

Body / of / Benjamin Franklin, The.   Epitaph.   Benjamin Franklin.   TCAPo

Body of God, The.   D. H. Lawrence.   ChIV-2

Body of John.   Ronald Allison Kells Mason.   PeNZ

Body of man is evolved to a brain, The.   For Maulana Karenga & Pharoah Sanders.   Imamu Amiri Baraka.   APSN

Body of man is like a flicker of lightning, The.   Van Hanh.   EaWin; WoPoe, *tr. by* Nguyen Ngoc Bich and W. S. Merwin

Body of my love is a familiar country, The.   Sestina.   Mary Stanley.   PeNZ

Body of the Beloved, The.   Jorge Carrera Andrade. *tr. by* Rene de Costa, Rigas Kappatos and Eleni Paidoussi

"Your body is bathed eternally."   BLPSL.

Body Politic.   Silvio Giussani.   ItPo, *tr. by* Gayle Ridinger

Body's Beauty.   Dante Gabriel Rossetti   Son   *Fr.* House of Life, The.

Body's products become, The.   Two Sonnets.   John Ashbery.   VGW

Body sinks and rises, A.   Deer, The.   Shara McCallum.   NAPBL

Body-Snatcher.   Ambrose Bierce.   APN-2   *Fr.* Devil's Dictionary, The.

Body, Soul, and Godhead.   "Angelus Silesius."   GePo, *tr. by* George C. Schoolfield   *Fr.* Cherubical Wanderer, The.

Body was given to me—what to do with it, A.   Osip Emilevich Mandelstam [*or* Mandelshtam].   TCRP

Body: What bodies else but Man's did Nature make.   Dialogue betwixt the Body and the Mind, A.   Margaret Lucas Cavendish, Duchess of Newcastle.   PEW

Boers have poked another, The.   Steve Biko is Dead.   Jack A. Mapanje.   PeSAV

Boethius at Cavalzero.   John Macoubrie.   CRP

Bofors A. A. Gun, The.   Gavin Ewart.   PoWW

Bog and Candle.   Robert David Fitzgerald.   CBAP

Bog-Face.   Stevie Smith.   NPeEn; RB

Bog Queen.   Seamus Heaney.   NoAM; PAI; RACG

Boggy wood as full of springs as trees, A.   Idea of Entropy at Maenporth Beach, The.   Peter Redgrove.   FaBoMo

Bogland.   Seamus Heaney.   HeIP-4; NoAM; NOIV; PBCIP; PNI; PoetW; PoPoPo

Bogs, purgatory, wolves and ease, by fame.   Barten Holyday.   FaBoEE

Bohemia.   Dorothy Parker.   APT-1; NBLV

Bohemians, The.   Ivor Gurney.   FaBoWar; PeFWW

Bohol's Tarsier Population.   Clovis L. Nazareno.   ReBoTo

Boiling an Egg.   Stanley Cook.   OTCP

Boiling Falls.   Liu E.   CoBLCP, *tr. by* Jonathan Chaves

Boiling over inwardly.   Archpoet's Confession, The.   *Unknown.*   WoPoe, *tr. by* Phillip Holland

Boiling up over the years.   Georgy [*or* Georgii] Vladimirovich Ivanov.   TCRP

Bois de Boulogne.   Ahmad Shauqi.   MAP, *tr. by* M. Mustafa Badawi and John Heath-Stubbs

Bojangles of Harlem.   Dorothy Fields.   ReLy

Bold Benbow rubs his jovial eyes.   Chancery Morals.   Winthrop Mackworth Praed.   NOBRP

Bold, cautious, true, and my loving comrade.. (LL)   As Toilsome I Wander'd Virginia's Woods.   Walt Whitman.   APN-1; BLT; NAAL-2v1

Bold Pedlar and Robin Hood, The.   *Unknown.*   ESPB

Bold Robin has robed him in ghostly attire.   Thomas Love Peacock.   OxAEP-2   *Fr.* Maid Marian.

Bold Troubleshooters.   Peter Veale.   NOBL

Bolder Youth, grown of capable arms, A.   Anne Finch, Countess of Winchilsea.   FaBoWar   *Fr.* All Is Vanity.

Bolding Vedas! Shanks New Nisa!   Place-Names of China.   Alan Bennett.   NOBL; UV

Boldness[e] in Love.   Thomas Carew.   CaPo; CavPo

Bolivia: Another End of Ace.   Tom Raworth.   PFTM-2

Boll-weevil's coming, and the winter's cold.   November Cotton Flower.   Jean Toomer.   ColAP; NoAM; UnPo

Bolt, The.   Mary Kinzie.   ExTi

Bolt and bar the shutter.   Mad as the Mist and Snow.   W. B. Yeats.   RaBo

Bolt-hole of brigandage, old keep.   Old Roscoff.   Tristan Corbière.   WoPoe, *tr. by* Derek Mahon

Bolt upright, reading her Bible for hours.   Great-great-grandmother.   Guy Butler.   PeSAV

Bolted space.   Martin Shea.   HA

Bomb Disposal, The.   Ciaran Carson.   CIP-2

Bomb Is Made, The.   Keith Sinclair.   PeNZ

Bomb of Annihilation, The.   Ilya Abu Madi.   GraLe, *tr. by* George Dimitri Selim

Bomb That Fell on Abdu's Farm, The.   Gregory Orfalea.   GraLe

Bomb Then, Bomb Now.   Bruce Andrews.   PmAP

Bomb will explode in the bar at twenty past one, The.   Terrorist, He Watches, The.   Wislawa Szymborska.   PoSu

Bomb will go off in the bar at one-twenty, The.   Terrorist Is Watching, A.   Wislawa Szymborska.   WoPoe, *tr. by* Austin Flint

Bomb will go off in the bar at one twenty p.m., The.   Wislawa Szymborska.   *See* Bomb will explode in the bar at twenty past one, The

Bombardment.   D. H. Lawrence.   FaBoWar

Bombax Tree, The.   Fily-Dabo Sissoko.   NegPo, *tr. by* Ellen Conroy Kennedy

Bombed in London.   Rudyard Kipling.   WoPoe   *Fr.* Epitaphs of the War [1914–1918].

Bomber, The.   "Brian Vrepont."   NOBAu

Bombing.   Paul Rodenko.   TuT, *tr. by* Mary E. O'Donnell

Bombing at about ninety miles an hour with the exhaust skittering.   Cocktails.   Ciaran Carson.   BiHa; ModIr; PBCIP

Bombshell.   Tracey Herd.   NeBl

Bon jour, bon jour a vous!   *Unknown.*   MiEL

Bonanza Creek.   John E. Smelcer.   PoCoUp

Bond, The.   Nuala Ni Dhomhnaill.   PBCIP, *tr. by* Medbh McGuckian

Bond and Free.   Robert Frost.   APT-1

Bondage.   Gyula Illyés.   IQMS, *tr. by* Doreen Bell

Bondmen, and helots, and serfs were we.   Cry of the Oppressed, The.   Henrietta Tindal.   VWP

Bonds.   Guillaume Apollinaire.   CuPo

Bonds of Affection.   Letitia [*or* Laetitia] Elizabeth Landon.   TreFP

Bonds of Friendship, The.   Simon Dach.   GePo, *tr. by* Ingrid Waløe-Engel

Bone.   C. K. Williams.   UrbNat

Bone and Skin, two millers thin.   On Two Monopolists.   John Byrom.   FaBoEE

Bone Die, The.   Maggie Hannan.   NLP

Bone driller of every abscess.   Humbly, He Speaks to His Tools.   Venus Khoury-Gata.   PoArWo, *tr. by* Lucy McNair

Bone-Flower Elegy.   Robert Earl Hayden.   APT-2; NoAM

Bone-idle, I lie listening to the rain.   Dejection.   Derek Mahon.   PBCIP; WoPoe

Bone Prison, The.   E. Howard Harries.   AngWePo

Bone Scan.   Gwen Harwood.   HarvBoo

Bone that has no Marrow, The.   Emily Dickinson.   SacPr; TAP

Bone Thoughts on a Dry Day: Chicago.   George Starbuck.   TwCP

Bone Yard.   Jim Barnes.   CDW

Boneless tongue, so small and weak, The.   Tongue, The.   Phillips Burrows Strong.   PoToHe

Bones.   Ted Hughes.   HarvBoo

Bones.   Carl Sandburg.   TCAPo

Bones, The.   W.S. Merwin.   CoAmPo

Bones and Drums.   Ron Welburn.   SeSe

Bones float in raised stone.   Kalamu ya Salaam.   SpirFl   *Fr.* New Orleans Haiku.

Bones: I must wear mine. (LL)   Deer Lay down Their Bones, The.   Robinson Jeffers.   APT-1; NoAM

Bones in a sand cliff. So I could say frigidity prevails.   Salisbury Plain.   Elizabeth Robinson.   AmPoNex

Bones is a crazy pony.   Bones.   Ted Hughes.   HarvBoo

Bones of birds are full of air, The.   End of a Season.   Thomas McGrath.   BodElec

Bones of Chuang Tzu, The.   Chang Heng.   AWP, *tr. by* Arthur Waley

Bones of Lazarus.   John Bensko.   YaYoPo

Bones of My Father, The.   Etheridge Knight.   BodElec

Bones of the lonely-wretched spend no quiet nights.   Meng Chiao.   SuSp   *Fr.* Autumn Meditations.

Bones show through images.   Dark Senses.   Tom Raworth.   Oth

Bones that cannot bear the light, The. (LL)   Genesis.   Geoffrey Hill.   ChIV-1; HAP; HarvBoo; OxBC; PeECV; TOF

Bones tuned, the body sings.   He Hola.   Keri Hulme.   PeNZ

Boney.   *Unknown.*   FaBoVe

Bonfires, The.   Rudyard Kipling.   NPeEn

Bong, Mr., bong, Mr., bong, Mr., bong. (LL)   Dirge: "1-2-3 was the number he played but today the number came 3-2-1." Kenneth Fearing. APT-2; NIL-7; NIP-4; PoRA; RB; TrJP

Bonguemba. Antoine-Roger Bolamba. NegPo, *tr.* by Ellen Conroy Kennedy

Bonhoeffer in his skylit cell. Christmas Trees. Geoffrey Hill. ChrPo; NOCV

Bonie Doon. Robert Burns. GTBS-P; NoP-4

Bonnard; a Novel. Richard Howard. CoAP

Bonnie Annie. *Unknown.* ESPB

Bonnie Annie Livieston. *Unknown.* OxBB

Bonnie, bonnie bairn who sits poking in the ase, The. Castles in the Air. James Ballantine. TreFP

Bonnie Broukit Bairn, The. Hugh MacDiarmid. FaBoCh; FaBoVe; HAP; HarvBoo; NePenScot

Bonnie Charlie's now awa. Will Ye No Come Back Again? Carolina Oliphant, Baroness Nairne. NePenScot

Bonnie House o' Airlie, The. *Unknown.* ESPB; OBEV; OxBB; OxBS

Bonnie James Campbell. *Unknown.* ESPB

Bonnie Laddie's Lang a-Grouwin', The. *Unknown.* OxBS

Bonnie lassie, will ye go, will ye go, will ye go. Birks of Aberfeldy, The [Composed on the Spot]. Robert Burns. CTC

Bonnie Lesley. Robert Burns. CTC; GTBS-P; NOBE; OBEV (Saw Ye Bonny Lesley.) OxBS

Bonnie [*or* Bonny] George [*or* James] Campbell. *Unknown.* OxBB; OxBoLi; SCGP
(O it's up in the Highlands.) ESPB

Bonnie [*or* Bonny] Kilmeny gaed up the glen. James Hogg. OBEV; OxAEP-2 *Fr.* Queen's Wake, The.

Bonny Baby Livingston. *Unknown.* ESPB

Bonny Barbara Allan. *Unknown.* NoP-4
(It was in and about the Martinmas time.) NoP-4

Bonny Barbara Allan ("In Scarlet Town where I was born"). *Unknown.* AWP; BoLoP; ESPB; HeIP-4; InPK-6; NAEL-5v1; NAEL-6v1; NAEL-7v1; NePenScot; OxBB; PAI

Bonny Bee Hom. *Unknown.* ESPB

Bonny Birdy, The. *Unknown.* ESPB

Bonny Bobby Shaftoe [*or* Shafto]. (LL) Bobby Shaftoe. Mother Goose. OxNR; ReMoGo

Bonny Brown Girl, The. *Unknown. See* Brown Girl, The

Bonny Bunch of Roses O, The. *Unknown.* OxBoLi

Bonny Cravet, The. Mother Goose. OxNR

Bonny [*or* Bonnie] Dundee. Sir Walter Scott. FaBoCh; OxBoLi; OxBS; UV *Fr.* Doom of Devorgoil, The.

Bonny Earl of Livingston, The. *Unknown. See* Fair Mary of Wallington

Bonny Earl of Murray, The. *Unknown.* ESPB; NOSC; OBEV; OxBB; OxBS; SCGP

Bonny fine maid of a noble degree, A. Robin Hood and Maid Marian. *Unknown.* ESPB

"Bonny heir, and the well-faird heir, The." Heir of Linne, The. *Unknown.* ESPB

Bonny Hind, The. *Unknown.* ESPB
(Bonny Heyn, The.) OxBB

Bonny holms of Yarrow, The! (LL) Yarrow Unvisited [1803]. William Wordsworth. GTBS-P; PoRA

Bonny John Seton. *Unknown.* ESPB

Bonny Kilmeny gaed up the glen. James Hogg. NePenScot *Fr.* Queen's Wake, The.

Bonny Lass of Anglesey, The. *Unknown.* ESPB

Bonny Lizie Baillie. *Unknown.* ESPB

Bonus. A. R. Ammons. HCAP

Bony. Simon J. Ortiz. CDW

Bony cow of youth walked by, The. Queen candidates trod through the mud and straw. Third Farming Poem. Brenda Coultas. HeMarv

Bony, pubescent, boys body pulled. Black Banana House. Gavin Moses. InTrad

Bood is beabig brighdly, love, The. To Bary Jade. Charles Follen Adams. OBAL

Boogie: 1 A.M. Langston Hughes. APSN; APT-2

Boogie Woogie Bugle Boy. Hughie Prince. ReLy

Book, The. William Drummond, of Hawthornden. ChIV-1
(Booke of the World, The.) SacPr
(Lessons of Nature, The.) GTBS-P
(Of this faire Volumne which wee World doe name.) SacPr

Book, The. Edmond Jabès. AF, *tr.* by Rosmarie Waldrop

Book, The. Henry Vaughan. AngWePo; BASC; GeHe; InvLi; PBRV

Book, a friend, a song, a glass, A. Happy Life, The. William Thompson. ECEV

Book and a jug and a dame, A. Limerick. *Unknown.* PeLi

Book-burning Pit, The. Lo Yin. SuSp, *tr.* by Edward H. Schafer

Book does not begin, he replied, The. Beginning of the Book, The. Edmond Jabès. AF, *tr.* by Rosmarie Waldrop

Book Ends. Tony Harrison. DiPo; NAEL-5v2; NAEL-6v2 *Fr.* School of Eloquence, The.

Book: Enemey ended my life, deprived me, An. Cynewulf. ASW *Fr.* Riddles (Exeter Book).

Book, for Growing Old, the. Yves Bonnefoy. PoetW, *tr.* by Emily Grosholz

Book Full of Pictures, A. Charles Simic. NoP-4

Book I Held Grew Cold, The. Ernst Toller. TrJP, *tr.* by Ashley Dukes

Book Moth: "Moth ate a word. To me it seemed, A." Cynewulf. AnOE *Fr.* Riddles (Exeter Book).

Book of Books, The. Sir Walter Scott. ChIV-1

Book of Company which, The. Autobiography 2 (hellogoodbye). Michael Palmer. HarvBoo

Book of Dreams, The. Richard Garcia. TouFir

Book of Ephraim, The. James Merrill.
"Backdrop: The dining room at Stonington." NoAM
"Correct but cautious, that first night, we asked." NoP-4
"Life like the periodical not yet." HCAP
Lost in Translation. HCAP; LCAP-2; NAAL-2v2; NoAM; NoP-4; VCAP
"Zero hour. Waiting yet again." HCAP

Book of Exits, miraculously copied, The. Real Thing, The. Eiléan Ní Chuilleanáin. ModIr

Book of Galahad, The. Jack Spicer. FTOS

Book of Gawain, The. Jack Spicer. PoM *Fr.* Holy Grail, The.

Book of Glass, A. David Shapiro. PmAP

Book of hours, The. Hours, The. Paul Ramsey. CRP

Book of How, The. Merrill Moore. MoAmPo
(After the stars were all hung separately out.) FuPo

Book of Human Anomalies, The. Albert Goldbarth. OPRER

Book of Hunting. Julians Barnes. WPE

Book of Job and a Draft of a Poem to Praise the Paths of the Living, The. George Oppen. NNaP

Book of Jonah, The. Mihály Babits. IQMS, *tr.* by István Tótfalusi

Book of Kells, The. Padraic Colum. BIrV

Book of Lies, The. James Tate. YaYoPo

Book of Music, A. Jack Spicer. APSN; PoM

Book of My Enemy Has Been Remaindered, The. Clive James. OBCoV

Book of Persephone, The. Robert Kelly. PoM

Book of Questions, The. Edmond Jabès.
Book of the Living, The. PFTM-2, *tr.* by Rosmarie Waldrop
Jew answers every question with another question, The. PFTM-2, *tr.* by Rosmarie Waldrop
"To be in the book. To figure in the book of questions, to be part of it." PFTM-1, *tr.* by Rosmarie Waldrop

Book of Questions, The. Pablo Neruda.
"And what did the rubies say." GifTon, *tr.* by William O'Daly
"How did the grapes come to know." GifTon, *tr.* by William O'Daly
"Tell me, is the rose naked." GifTon, *tr.* by William O'Daly
"Who works harder on earth." GifTon, *tr.* by William O'Daly

Book of Roses, The. Sa'id 'Aql.
"My ecstasy is that I have met you." MAP

Book of Routh. Carolyn Beard Whitlow. FFC

Book of Sharp Silhouettes, The. Molly Bendall. NAPBL

Book of summer is the butterfly, A. Butterfly, The. John Fuller. Spl

Book of Tarshish, The. Moses Ibn Ezra.
"Beautiful woman, a cup of wine, and a garden, A." TrJP, *tr.* by Solomon Solis-Cohen
Joy of Life. TrJP, *tr.* by Solomon Solis-Cohen

Book of the Dead, The. Muriel Rukeyser. APT-2

Book of the Dead. *Unknown.*
Adoration of the Disk by King Akhnaten and Princess Nefer Neferiu Aten. AWP
Dead Man Ariseth and Singeth a Hymn to the Sun, The. AWP
(Death as a Lotus Flower.) TTY, *tr.* by Ulli Beier
He Approacheth the Hall of Judgment. AWP
He Asketh Absolution of God. AWP
He Biddeth Osiris to Arise from the Dead. AWP
He Cometh Forth into the Day. AWP
He Commandeth a Fair Wind. AWP
He Defendeth His Heart against the Destroyer. AWP
He Embarketh in the Boat of Ra. AWP
He Entereth the House of the Goddess Hathor. AWP
He Establisheth His Triumph. AWP
He Holdeth Fast to the Memory of His Identity. AWP
He Is Declared True of Word. AWP
He Is like the Lotus. AWP, *tr.* by Ulli Beier

He Is like the Serpent Saka. AWP

He Kindleth a Fire. AWP

He Knoweth the Souls of the East. AWP

He Knoweth the Souls of the West. AWP

He Maketh Himself One with Osiris. AWP

He Maketh Himself One with the God Ra. AWP, *tr. by* Robert Hillyer

He Maketh Himself One with the Only God, Whose Limbs Are the Many Gods. AWP

He Overcometh the Serpent of Evil in the Name of Ra. AWP

He Prayeth for Ink and Palette That He May Write. AWP

He Singeth a Hymn to Osiris, the Lord of Eternity. AWP

He Singeth in the Underworld. AWP

He Walketh by Day. AWP

Other World, The. AWP, *tr. by* Robert Silliman Hillyer

Book of the Dead Man #1, The. Marvin Bell. GifTon

Book of the Dead Man #43, The. Marvin Bell. GifTon

Book of the Dead Man (#58), The. Marvin Bell. OPRER; TaR

Book of the Dead Man #87, The. Marvin Bell. PuP-23

Book of the defeated man. Qasim Haddad. MAP *Fr.* Standing While We Die.

Book of the Living, The. Edmond Jabès. PFTM-2, *tr. by* Rosmarie Waldrop *Fr.* Book of Questions, The.

Book of the Sabbath is sealed like an unwritten dream, The. Excerpts from the Sabbath Dream Book. Esther Ettinger. DTA, *tr. by* Mariana Barr

Book of Thel, The. William Blake. NAEL-5v2; NAEL-6v2; PoE

"Eternal gates' terrific porter lifted the northern bar, The." OxBEV (Secrets of the Earth, The.) NOBE

Book of Urizen [*or* First Book of Urizen], The. William Blake. NOBRP

Book of verses underneath the bough, A. Omar Khayyám. CABP; NOBE; OBEV; TRP; WoPoe, *tr. by* Edward Fitzgerald *Fr.* Rubáiyát of Omar Khayyám [*of* Naishápúr], The.

Book of Wisdom, The. Stephen Crane. MoAmPo *Fr.* Black Riders [and Other Lines], The.

Book of Wisdom, The. Robert Lowell. ChIV-1

Book of Yolek, The. Anthony Hecht. HP; MakPoe; NoP-4; TaR; WeW-3

Book remained at the edge of his dead waist, A. César Vallejo. TCLAP, *tr. by* Clayton Eshleman *Fr.* Spain, Take This Cup from Me.

Book Review. Russell Davies. FaBoEE

Book reviews. Waking Up. Yolanda Palis. ReBoTo

Book to read, A. (LL) Books Fall Open. David McCord. OBCA; OxIBACP

Book was writ[t] of late called [*or* call'd] *Tetrachordon*, A. On the Detraction Which Followed upon My Writing Certain Treatises. John Milton. OxBSo; PoE; Son

Book-Worms, The. Robert Burns. FaBoEE

Bookbuying in the Tenderloin. Robert Hass. YaYoPo

Booke of *Common Pray'r* excels the rest, The. Francis Quarles. PBRV *Fr.* Divine Fancies.

Booke of the World, The. William Drummond, of Hawthornden. *See* Book, The

Booker T. and W. E. B. Dudley Randall. NoAM

Booker Washington Trilogy, The. Nicholas Vachel Lindsay.

John Brown. MoAmPo

(Negro Sermon—Simon Legree, A.) MoAmPo

Simon Legree—A Negro Sermon. TAP

Bookful Blockhead, The. Pope. OBSV *Fr.* Essay on Criticism, An.

Bookishness. Sharif Elmusa. GraLe

Bookmark. Saint Theresa [*or* Teresa] of Avila. *See* Lines Written in Her Breviary

Bookmark, A. Thomas M. [*or* "Tom"] Disch. RA

Bookmoth: A moth devoured words. When I heard. Cynewulf. *See* Moth ate a word. To me it seemed, A

Books. William Wordsworth. *Fr.* Prelude; Growth of a Poet's Mind [1850 vers.], The.

Books, The. (LL) He Was Lucky. Anna Swirszczynska. HP; PoSu

Books are a load of crap. (LL) Study of Reading Habits, A. Philip Larkin. InPK-6; NOBL; OBCoV

Books, books, books! Elizabeth Barrett Browning. WPOW *Fr.* Aurora Leigh.

Books; china; a life / Reprehensibly perfect. (LL) Philip Larkin. HeIP-4; OxBC; PoE; TwCP

Books Fall Open. David McCord. OBCA; OxIBACP

Books of Ovid's changed shapes, The. In the Praise of Music. Humphrey [*or* Humfrey] Gifford. NoSic

Books of the Dead, The. Marta Kornblith. MirDau, *tr. by* Roberta Gordenstein

Books of the Old Testament, The. Thomas Russell. ChIV-1

Bookshop Idyll, A. Kingsley Amis. OxBTC; PeLV

Bookstore. Toi Derricotte. ExTi

Bookworm. Cynewulf. WoPoe, *tr. by* Edwin Morgan *Fr.* Riddles (Exeter Book).

Boom! Howard Nemerov. NBLV; NIL-7; NIP-4

Boom above my knees lifts, and the boat, The. Sailing to an Island. Richard Murphy. ModIr; PBCIP

Boom / The shrill whistle of the wolf. Bird of Power. Jim Tollerud. VoR

Boom Time. Stephen Clayton. IBA

Boomerang. William Hart-Smith. NOBAu

Boomerang. John Perreault. SPE

Boomerang, The. Carrie May Nichols. PoToHe

Boomerang: A Blatantly Political Poem. Quincy Troupe. AF

Boon nature scattered, free and wild. Sir Walter Scott. OxAEP-2 *Fr.* Lady of the Lake, The.

Boon Nature to the woman bows. Coventry Patmore. EBEV *Fr.* Angel in the House, The.

Boone understands. Potatoes of the Field, The. Thomas Michael McDade. SpudSo

Booth led boldly with his big bass drum. General William Booth Enters into Heaven. Nicholas Vachel Lindsay. APT-1; ChIV-2; ColAP; MoAmPo; NOBA; OxBA; PoE; TAP; TCAPo

Boots. Rudyard Kipling. BRP; MoBrPo

Boots and Saddles. Louis Simpson. BodElec

Boots are being polished. Where Will You Be? Patricia Parker. AfrBLW; GLP

Boots, / Shoes. *Unknown.* OxNR

Booty from the German War. Friedrich von Logau. GePo, *tr. by* George C. Schoolfield

Booze and the blowens cop the lot. (LL) Villon's Straight Tip to All Cross Coves. William Ernest Henley. AWP; OxAEP-2

Bop Lyrics. Allen Ginsberg. OBAL

Boppin' is Safer than Grindin' Thulani Davis. GT

Bora Ring. Judith Wright. NoAM

Border. Gillian Clarke. HarvBoo

Border. Taslima Nasrin. VCWP

Border, The. Martha Collins. ExTi

Border, The. Joanna Rawson. AmPoNex; BodElec

Border Affair, A. Charles Badger, Jr. Clark. APT-1

Border clashes flare northeast of the Empire. Song of Yen. Kao Shih. SuSp, *tr. by* Joseph J. Lee

Border collie has been bred to keep, A. Our Dog Chasing Swifts. U. A. Fanthorpe. Spl

Border Mountain Moon. Lu Yu. CoBCP, *tr. by* Burton Watson

Border of the realm. Keizan. JDP, *tr. by* Yoel Hoffmann

Borderland—that's where, if one knew how, The. Life of Art, The. Denise Levertov. BodElec

Borderlands. Louise Imogen Guiney. TCAPo

Borders. Michael S. Weaver. GT

Borders, Cages and Walls. Homero [*or* Umberto] Aridjis. PoCoUp, *tr. by* George McWhirter

Boreas. Samuel Rowlands. NoSic

Bored by Ascham and Zeno. Glad Eye, The. Paul Muldoon. NoAM

Bored, confused actually. have started several letters. Four Lines of a Black Love Letter Between Teachers. Ed Roberson. NBV

Boredom, and the horror, and the glory, The. (LL) In Memory of the Unknown Poet, Robert Boardman Vaughn. Donald Justice. DiPo; NoAM

Borges and Myself. Jorge Luis Borges. PoetW, *tr. by* Norman Thomas Di Giovanni

Borgia, thou once wert [*or* were] almost too august. On Seeing a Hair of Lucretia Borgia. Walter Savage Landor. HAP; NPeEn; WeW-3

Boricua: you. Boricua. Jose Angel Figueroa. PueRic

Boring and boring for food. (LL) Legend of the Northland, A. Phoebe Cary. OBCA; OBSP

Boring executors approach their locks, The. Poem against Catholics. John Fuller. OBSV; PeLV

Borinkins in Hawaii. Víctor Hernández Cruz. PueRic

Boris Pasternak. Anna Andreyevna Akhmatova. TCRP, *tr. by* Max Hayward and Stanley Kunitz

Born, born, we know how it goes. (LL) Holy Family. Muriel Rukeyser. ChIV-2; MoAmPo

Born by river. Remember? Eva Johnson. IBA

Born by the mediterranean. Ghaflah—the sin of forgetfulness. Dima Hilal. PoArWo

Born crying, and after crying, die. Palladas [*or* Pallades]. GrAn

Born I was to be old. Anacreontic. Robert Herrick. CaPo; OxBoLi

Born in another country, under a different flag. Irish Requiem, An. Michael O'Loughlin. PBCIP

Born in the quarter-night, brash. Delta Traveller. Charles Wright. LCAP-2

Born in wealth and wealthily nursed. Thomas Hood. EBVV *Fr.* Miss Kilmansegg and Her Precious Leg.

Born in Winter. Francis Quarles. NOSC

Born naked. Buried naked. So why fuss? Palladas [*or* Pallades]. GrAn

Born, nurtured, wedded, prized, within the pale. Lafayette. Dolley Madison. AiP

Born of rejection, of the boundless snow. (LL) From the Highest Camp. Thom Gunn. Son; TwCP

Born of the sorrowful of heart. Countee Cullen. SSLK *Fr.* Four Epitaphs.

Born of Woman. Wislawa Szymborska. GI

Born on a sunday. Mama Dot. Frederick D'Aguiar. Oth

Born on a tabletop in Joe's cafeé. Davy Crockett. *Unknown.* FaBoVe

Born on the run, ambushed by sword and flame. Epitaph for Mariana Gryphius, His Brother Paul's Little Daughter. Andreas Gryphius. WoPoe, *tr. by* Christopher Benfey

Born salesman, A. And One for My Dame. Anne Sexton. NoP-4

Born to these gentle stones and grass. Urn Burial. Ted Hughes. EBEV

Born Too Soon. John Fuller. OBCoV

Born Tying Knots. Samuel Makidemewabe. STP, *tr. by* Howard Norman

Born with a monocle he stares at life. En Monocle. Donald Evans. APT-1

Born with all arms, he sought a separate peace. Deserter, The. John Streeter Manifold. CBAP

Borne over deep seas in swift ship. Attis. Catullus. WoPoe, *tr. by* Reynolds Price

Borodino. Mikhail Yuryevich Lermontov. FaBoWar, *tr. by* Frances Darwin Cornford and Esther Polinowsky Salaman

Borough, The. George Crabbe.
  Condemned Man, The. NPeEn
  (Evening Sail, The.) TreFP
  Letter 1. CABP
  Peter Grimes. EBNV; ECEV; FHYEP; OBNV
    "Priest attending, found he spoke at times, The." PoE
    "Thus by himself compelled to live each day." NOBE
  Schools. CTC
  Vicar, The. OBSV
  Winter Views Serene. WoPoe
  "Yes! e'en in Sleep th'impressions all remain." NPeEn

Borrow me borrow my life. Procedure. Ann Lauterbach. BodElec

Borrow to your heart's content. *Unknown.* GrAn

Borrowed this dust. (LL) Passing Through. Stanley Kunitz. BodElec; LoL

Borrowing my house / From insects. Issa. ZenPo, *tr. by* Takashi Ikemoto and Lucien Stryk

Borrowing Rice from Ju-hui. Mei Yao Ch'en. SuSp, *tr. by* Jonathan Chaves

Bosch. Rafael Alberti. WoPoe, *tr. by* Carolyn Tipton

Bosnia. November. And the mountain roads. Sarajevo. Lawrence Durrell. GTBS-P

Bosnia Tune. Joseph Brodsky. FaBoWar

Bosom of / green buds, A. Mare Nostrum. Joel Oppenheimer. NeAP

Bosom of his Father and his God, The. (LL) Thomas Gray. AWP; BRP; CABP; ClHu; EBEV; FHYEP; GTBS-P; HAP; HeIP-4; InPK-6; MakPoe; NAEL-6v1; NAEL-7v1; NIL-7; NOBE; NOEC; NoP-4; NPeEn; OBEV; OxAEP-1; OxBEV; PoPoPo; SCGP; SCV; TFi; TreFP; UnPo; UV; WeW-3 *Fr.* Elegy Written in a Country Churchyard.

Bosporus laps on Europe's shores, The. Constantinople. Mihály Csokonai Vitéz. IQMS, *tr. by* Kenneth White

Boss, The. James Russell Lowell. NCAP; OBAL

Boss, The. Boris Abramovich Slutsky [*or* Slutskii]. TCRP, *tr. by* J. R. Rowland

Boss Communication. Mari E. Evans. SeSe

Boss gets on my nerves, The. Gentleman Is a Dope, The. Richard Rodgers. ReLy

Boss I went. Don Marquis. OBCoV *Fr.* Archy and Mehitabel.

Boss knows what shape I'm in, The. He tells me. Drunk Last Night with Friends, I Go to Work Anyway. Philip Dow. InPK-6

Boss rat, boss rat. Boss Rat. *Unknown.* WoPoe, *tr. by* John S. Major

Boss's Wife, The. *Unknown.* CBAP

Bossed around in the sack but honey don't you be tellin me what to do. You Know I Like to Be. Chrystos. WiU

Boston. John Collins Bossidy. FaBoEE; NBLV; OBAL; OBCoV; OxBoLi; PeLV

Boston. Edwin Arlington Robinson. APN-2

Boston Ballad [1854], A. Walt Whitman. OBAL
  (Clear the way there Jonathan!) APN-1
  (Leaves of Grass (1855).) APN-1

Boston Beguine, The. Sheldon Harnick. ReLy

Boston Common. John Berryman. CBCWP

Boston Evening Transcript, The. T. S. Eliot. APT-1; InPK-6; TCAPo

Boston has a festival. In the Public Garden. Marianne Craig Moore. NOBA

Boston Hymn. Ralph Waldo Emerson. CBCWP; InvLi; TCAPo

Boston in Distress. *Unknown.* NOEC

Boston Year. Elizabeth Alexander. GT; OPRER

Bot now the haisty, egir, and wild Dido. Virgil [*or* Vergil]. OBVE, *tr. by* Gawin [*or* Gavin] Douglas *Fr.* Aeneid [*or* Eneados, *Aeneis*], The.

Bot of ane bowrd in to bed I sall yow breif yit. William Dunbar. EBEV *Fr.* Tretis of the Tua Mariit Wemen and the Wedo, The.

Botanic Garden, The. Erasmus Darwin.
  "Descend, ye hovering sylphs! aerial choirs." ECEV
  Economy of Vegetation, The.
  Kew. OBGa
  Loves of the Plants, The.
    "CARYO's sweet smile DIANTHUS proud admires." NOBRP
    "Fair Chunda smiles amid the burning waste." NOBRP
    Nightmare. NOEC
    "On DOVE's green brink the fair TREMELLA stood." NOBRP
    "So on his Nightmare through the evening fog." NOEC
    "Weak with nice sense, the chaste MIMOSA stands." NOBRP
    "Where cool'd by rills and curtain'd round by woods." NOBRP

Botanical Fanaticism. Thylias Moss. TRP

Botany Bay. John Freeth. NOEC

Both Earth and Heaven. Huda Na'mani. MAP, *tr. by* John Heath-Stubbs and Lena Jayyusi

Both gentlemen, or yoemen bould. True Tale of Robin Hood, A. *Unknown.* ESPB

Both gloomy and dark was the shadowy night. Song. Anne Batten Cristall. RWP

Both grandfather and father worked. Tale of Red-Haired Motele, Mister Inspector, Rabbi Isaiah and Commissar Blokh, The. Iosif Pavlovich Utkin. TCRusP, *tr. by* Denis Johnson and Kathy Lewis

Both her mourner and her tomb. (LL) On the Countess Dowager of Pembroke. William Browne (1591–1643). AWP; BASC; HAP; PoRA; TFi

Both Keats and Boccaccio tell a. Limerick. Joyce Johnson. PeLi

Both Less and More. Richard Watson Dixon. SCGP

Both my grandmas came from far away. Both My Grandmothers. Edward Field. CA

Both of us are getting worse. Dance of the Cherry Blossom. Jackie Kay. EmeKit

Both of us wordless against the dawn and death. (LL) My Grandmother Died in the Early Hours of the Morning. T. Harri Jones. AngWePo; TCAWP

Both robbed of air, we both lie in one ground. Hero and Leander. John Donne. NoSic; SoSe-8

Both sacred wisdom. Withered Zen. Muso Soseki. EaWin, *tr. by* W. S. Merwin

Both Schubert on the waters and Mozart in the din of birds. Osip Emilevich Mandelstam [*or* Mandelshtam]. TCRP *Fr.* Ottave.

Both skyed. Japanese Print. Austin Clarke. NOIV

Both Strangers. Jamil Sidqi Al-Zahawi. MAP, *tr. by* Issa Boullata and Christopher Middleton

Both the year's, and the day's deep midnight is. (LL) Nocturnal[l] upon Saint Lucy's [*or* S. Lucy's *or* S. Lucies] Day, Being the Shortest Day, A. John Donne. BASC; CABP; EBEV; ESCV; FHYEP; MeLP; NAEL-5v1; NAEL-6v1; NAEL-7v1; NOBE; NoP-4; NOSC; OxAEP-1; PoE; SCGP; TFi

Both were dwellers. Reluctant prophet. Luci Shaw. SacPr

Both whom one fire had burnt, one water drowned. (LL) Hero and Leander. John Donne. NoSic; SoSe-8

Both Your Mothers. Jerzy Ficowski. HP; PoSu, *tr. by* Keith Bosley

Bothie of Tober-na-Vuolich, The [A Long-Vacation Pastoral]. Arthur Hugh Clough.
  Highland Glen near Loch Ericht, A. FaBoVe
  "Then was the dinner served, and the Minister prayed for a blessing." PeLV

Bothwell Bridge. *Unknown.* *See* Battle of Bothwell Bridge, The

Botticelli's St. Sebastian. Brigit Pegeen Kelly. ExTi

Bottle, The. Ralph Knevet. ChIV-2

Bottle contained a little amber and a little, The. Some Glow on the Sill. Clark Coolidge. FTOS

Bottle Creek Blues. Sam Hunt. PeNZ

Bottle in the Sea. George Seferis. WoPoe, *tr. by* Edmund Keeley and Philip Sherrard *Fr.* Mythistorima.

Bottle of perfume that Willie sent, The [*or* A]. Limerick. *Unknown.* PeLi

Bottle of Suze, A. Pablo Picasso. PFTM-1

Bottled [New York]. Helene Johnson. APT-2; BlSi

Bottles are for sleeping in. Bottles in the Zoological Museum. William Peskett. PNI

Bottom of the sea is cruel, The. (LL) Hart Crane. ColAP; NAAL-2v2; NAAL-5; OxBA; PoE; VGW; WoPoe *Fr.* Voyages.

Bottom of things is neither life nor death, The. Roberto Juarroz. VCWP *Fr.* Vertical Poetry.

Bottom's Song. William Shakespeare. CTC *Fr.* Midsummer Night's Dream, A.

Bottomed by tugging combs of water. Swan, The. William Robert Rodgers. PNI

Bottomless pits. There's one in Castleton. Tony Harrison. HarvBoo; NAEL-5v2; NAEL-6v2 *Fr.* School of Eloquence, The.

Boudoir Feelings. Li Shang-yin. SuSp, *tr. by* Eugene Eoyang

Boudoir Lament. Yü Hsüan-chi. BoWoP, *tr. by* Geoffrey Waters

Boudoir Thoughts. Hsü Kan.
  "Deepening shadows bring on sorrow, The." SuSp
  "Drifting clouds, distant and vast, The." SuSp
  "Sadly, sadly the season draws to an end." SuSp
  "Steep, steep the lofty mountain peak." SuSp

Bouge of Court, The. John Skelton.
  "Sail is up, Fortune ruleth our helm, The." NoSic

Bough, cradle and all. (LL) Mother Goose. OxBEV; OxNR; ReMoGo

Boughs do shake and the bells do ring, The. Harvest Song. *Unknown.* OxNR

Boughs, the boughs are bare enough, The. Winter with the Gulf Stream. Gerard Manley Hopkins. NoAM

Bought at the drug store, very cheap; and later pawned. Green Light. Kenneth Fearing. PoE; VGW

Bought Locks. Martial. AWP, *tr. by* Sir John Harington \VP/[*or* Harrington]

Boulders. John Wills. HA

Boulogne to Amiens and Paris. Dante Gabriel Rossetti. PeVV *Fr.* Trip to Paris and Belgium, A.

Boult to Marina. "Ern Malley." BMAP

Bounce, buckram, velvet's dear. *Unknown.* OxNR

Bound each to each by natural piety. (LL) Rainbow, The. William Wordsworth. FHYEP; GTBS-P; InPK-6; ITBLP; NAEL-5v2; NAEL-6v2; NOBE; NOBRP; NoP-4; OxBSP; PAI; PoPoPo; SacPr; TFi

Bound homeward under. Keido. JDP, *tr. by* Yoel Hoffmann

Bound, hungry to pluck again from the thousand. For the Twentieth Century. Frank Bidart. KGB

Bound in a moonlight circle. 49 Stomp, The. Lew Blockcolski. VoR

Bound in the women who chain by. For Grizzel McNaught (1709–1792). Anne Finch (b. 1908). FFC

Bound to my heart as Ixion to the wheel. Dame Edith Sitwell. MoBrPo *Fr.* Three Poems of the Atomic Bomb.

Bound up it always. Mikata Shami [*or* Mikata no Sami]. OHMPJ

Bound upon the accursed tree. Crucifixion, The. Henry Hart Milman. SacPr

Bound with the entrails of thy foe. (LL) Fly Caught in a Cobweb, A. Richard Lovelace. BeJo; CaPo

Boundaries. José Emilio Pacheco. PoetW; STV; TCLAP, *tr. by* John Frederick Nims

Bounding Billow, cease thy motion. Stanzas Written between Dover and Calais, in July, 1792. Martha Robinson. ECWP

Bounding Line. Genevieve Taggard. APT-2

Boundless, bitter is her sorrow. Tune: "Dreaming of the South." Wen T'ing-yün. SuSp, *tr. by* William R. Schultz

Boundless Moment, A. Robert Frost. NAAL-2v2

Boundless shaping Power, A. Lao Tzu. WoPoe, *tr. by* Moss Roberts *Fr.* Tao Te Ching.

Boundless will to ease us, A. (LL) To Cloe. George Lansdowne Granville [*or* Grenville], Baron. FaBoEE; NBLV; OxBEV

Bounds of this court's jurisdiction, The. (LL) Ambrose Bierce. APN-2; OBAL *Fr.* Devil's Dictionary, The.

Bounty. Josephine Miles. NoAM

Bounty of Jehovah Praise, The. George Sandys. AH

Bounty of Our Age, The. Henry Farley. FaBoCh; FaBoEE; NOSC

Bouquet of Belle Scavoir. Wallace Stevens. MoAmPo

Bouquet of Objects, A. Elaine Equi. PmAP

Bouquet of zephyr-flowers hitched to a hitching, A. You at the Pump. Frank O'Hara. FTOS

Bouquets. Robert Francis. ChAP

Bourbons. Walter Savage Landor. OBSV

Bourgeois Poet, The. Karl Shapiro. BodElec; IllVoic
  "Bourgeois poet closes the door of his study and lights his pipe, The." BodElec; IllVoic
  "Each in her well-lighted picture window, reading a book or magazine." BodElec
  "I drove three thousand miles to ask a question. No answer, naturally." BodElec
  "Look of shock on an old friend's face after years of not meeting, The." BodElec
  "Of love and death in the Garrison State I sing." BodElec
  "Oriental, you give and give. No Christian ever gave like you." BodElec
  "Prophets say to Know Thyself: I say it can't be done, The." BodElec

"Quintana lay in the shallow grave of coral." BodElec

"Rice around the lingam stone will be distributed in the dying sun, The." BodElec

"Teachers of culture hate science but the teachers of science do not hate culture, The." BodElec

"To make the child in your own image is a capital crime." BodElec

"World is my dream, says the wise child, ever so wise, The." BodElec

Bourgeoisie. Maksimilian Aleksandrovich Voloshin. TCRP, *tr. by* Albert C. Todd

'Bout th' husband oak [*or* oke], the vine. William Habington. BeJo; NPeEn *Fr.* Castara.

Bout with Burning. Vassar Miller. MoAmPo

Bow, daughter of Babylon, bow thee to dust! Babylon. Tennyson. ChIV-1

Bow Down, Mountain. Norma Farber. AH

Bow down my soul in worship very low. St. Isaac's Church, Petrograd. Claude McKay. NAAAL

Bow hither out of heaven and see and save. (LL) Easter Hymn. A. E. Housman. EBEV; GI

Bow to Allah. Brian G. Gilmore. ISC

Bow-wow, says the dog. Mother Goose. OxNR

Bow, wow, wow, / Whose dog art thou? Caesar's Song. Mother Goose. OxNR; ReMoGo

Bowed by the weight of centuries he leans. Man with the Hoe, The. Edwin Markham. APN-2; BRP; GS; MoAmPo; TCAPo; TFi

Bowells of the Earth my bowells hide, The. Lucy Hastings, Countess of Huntingdon. EMWP

Bower among the Beans. Emily Jane Pfeiffer. ViWPN

Bower of Bliss, The. Edmund Spenser. NAEL-6v1; NAEL-7v1; OBGa *Fr.* Faerie Queene, The.

Bower of Blisse Destroyed, The. Edmund Spenser. NPeEn *Fr.* Faerie Queene, The.

Bower of Pleasure, The. Mary Robinson. CenSon; RWP

Bowge of Courte, The. John Skelton.
  "Ye remembre the gentylman ryghte nowe." OxBEV

Bowing "New Sabbath" or "Mount Ephraim" (LL) Church Romance, A. Thomas Hardy. FaBoTw; NOBE; OxAEP-2; OxBSo; OxBTC; PeECV

Bowl. Wallace Stevens. PAI

Bowl, The. John Wilmot, 2d Earl of Rochester. *See* Upon Drinking in a Bowl

Bowl, The. Barbara Smith. WWork

Bowl bowl bowl bowl bowl. Harold's Bowl and Food. Denis Johnson. Unle

Bowl for the bishop, a crushed and bitter bowl, A. Almería. Pablo Neruda. FaBoWar, *tr. by* Donald D. Walsh

Bowl he starts with, The. Man. His Bowl. His Raspberries, The. Claudia Rankine. GT

Bowl of Roses, A. William Ernest Henley. MoBrPo

Bowlegged lady crawled across the river on cables. Brooklyn Bridge. Matthew Rohrer. NeAmPo

Bowlegged, pinchered sand-digger. Statilius Flaccus. GrAn

Bowling-Green, The. William Somervile [*or* Somerville].
  "Where fair Sabrina's wand'ring currents flow." NOEC

Bowls. Marianne Craig Moore. APT-1

Bowmen, The. Paavo Haavikko. WoPoe, *tr. by* Anselm Hollo

Box is only temporary, The. (LL) Arrival of the Bee Box, The. Sylvia Plath. FaBoMo; FaBoWP; HCAP; NALW; NPeEn

Box of nails, A. John Wills. HA

Boxcar. Terrance Hayes. AmPoNex

Boxers, The. Paul Whitehead. ECEV *Fr.* Gymnasiad, The, or Boxing Match.

Boxes, The. Solitude. 'Enayat Jaber. PoArWo, *tr. by* Wen Chin Ouyang

Boxing Day. Yusef Komunyakaa. ISC

Boxing Match, The. David Ignatow. MoASP

Boxing the Fox. Pearse Hutchinson. CIP-2

Boy. Mary Kinzie. FFC

Boy, A. John Ashbery. NeAP

Boy, The. Marilyn Hacker. ExTi; WiU

Boy, about eleven or twelve, The. Testimony: The United States (1901–10) Recitative/The South. Charles Reznikoff. FTOS

Boy accepted them, The. Daedalus: The Dirge. George Oppen. FTOS

Boy Actor, The. Noël Coward. OxBTC

Boy and Girl. Mother Goose. OxNR; ReMoGo

Boy and horse, a similar brain: the horse doesn't cry when its rider lies in the dust. Theognis. CAGL, *tr. by* Peter Bing and Rip Cohen *Fr.* Second Book of Theognis, The.

Boy and the Deer, The. Andrew Peynetsa. STP, *tr. by* Dennis Tedlock

Boy and the Flute, The. Bjørnstjerne Bjørnson. AWP, *tr. by* Sir Edmund William Gosse

Boy and the girl loved each other very much, The. They saw the world. Boy and the Girl, The. Todd Colby. HeMarv

Boy and the Mantle, The. *Unknown.* ESPB; OxBB

Boy and the Sparrow. Mother Goose. OxNR; ReMoGo

Boy at the Paterson Falls. Toi Derricotte. PBCAP

Boy at the Window. Richard Wilbur. RaBo

Boy Breaking Glass. Gwendolyn Brooks. AiP; ESEAA; NAAL-2v2; NoAM; NoP-4

Boy, bring me candles on a silver salver. Candles. Hélène Swarth. WPOW, *tr. by* Jonathan Crewe

Boy Changed into a Stag Clamours at the Gate of Secrets, The. Ferenc Juhász. IQMS, *tr. by* David Wevill

Boy Crazy. Maurya Simon. GeoHom

Boy Died in My Alley, The. Gwendolyn Brooks. NoAM

Boy Fishing, The. Edith Jay Scovell. FaBoWP

Boy Friend, The. Sandy Wilson. ReLy

Boy from his bedroom-window, The. At Ballyshannon, Co. Donegal. William Allingham. NOBVV

Boy hammers a piece of lead pipe, A. Streak, The. Julia Kasdorf. AmPoNex

Boy, hold my wreath for me. Serenader, The. *Unknown.* GrAn, *tr. by* Dudley Fitts

Boy I can remember when February. New Constructions. John Ashbery. KGB

Boy, if your ass / is as hard as your head, / you'll go far in this world. (LL) Tuskegee Airfield. Marilyn Nelson Waniek. ESEAA; GT

Boy in a Hospital. Diana Helen Melhem. PoArWo

Boy in the Barn, The. *Unknown.* ReMoGo

Boy is as old as the stars, A. To My God in His Sickness. Philip Levine. NNaP

Boy Juggling a Soccer Ball, A. Christopher Merrill. MoASP

Boy just like you took me out to see them, A. What the End Is For. Jorie Graham. NoP-4; PoPoPo

Boy-mad no longer. Leaving the Boys Behind. Rufinus. GrAn, *tr. by* Alan Marshfield

Boy of Egremond, The. Samuel Rogers. NOBRP

Boy of twelve, shaping a fuselage, The. Models. Howard Nemerov. AF

Boy of Winander, The. William Wordsworth. PoE *Fr.* Prelude, The; Growth of a Poet's Mind [1850 vers.].

Boy on a Swing. Mbuyiseni Oswald Mtshali. NIL-7

Boy rehearsing the Continental Stroll, The. American Bandstand. Michael Waters. SwNoth

Boy Remembers in the Field. Raymond Knister. NOBC

Boy Riding Forward Backward. Robert Francis. LCAP-2

Boy's Afraid of the Live Tiger, The. Cesare Greppi. ItPo, *tr. by* Gayle Ridinger

Boy's cocks, Diodore. Epigram. Strato [*or* Straton]. GrAn, *tr. by* Thomas Meyer

Boy's father dies, This. Shadow-Casting. James Galvin. MoASP

Boy's Poem, A. Alexander Smith.
   "Steamer left the black and oozy wharves, The." PeVV

Boy's Song, A. James Hogg. NOxBChV; OBEV; OTCP; OxAEP-2

Boy's Summer, A. Paul Laurence Dunbar. CA

Boy sits in the classroom, The. Learning Experience. Marge Piercy. NoAM

Boy skips flat stones out to sea—each does fine, A. Notations of Ten Summer Minutes. Norman MacCaig. EmeKit; NPeEn

Boy Sleeping. Ann Lauterbach. PmAP

Boy stood on the burning deck, The. Casabianca. Felicia Dorothea Hemans. BRP; NAEL-6v2; NOBRP; NPeEn; RWP; ViWPN; VWP

Boy stoops, picking greens with his mother, A. Greens. David Ray. VGW

Boy that is good, The [*or* A]. Description of a Good Boy, The. Henry Dixon. OxNR

Boy, the way Glenn Miller played. Those Were the Days. Charles Strouse. ReLy

Boy was bright, like the retarded girl, The. Leonard. Jeffrey McDaniel. AmPoNex

Boy was going take the bus out, The. Elvis Lives. Charles Bukowski. AllShUp

Boy was shot in Irkutsk, The. Komsomol Song. Iosif Pavlovich Utkin. TCRP, *tr. by* Lubov Yakovleva

Boy who Dreamed the Country Night, The. Christopher Koch. NOBAu

Boy who played and talked and read with me, A. Exile. Donald Hall. NoP-4

Boy who throws the ball, The. Beadle's Testimony, The. Jerome Rothenberg. NNaP

Boy with a fair-curled head, The. Henry Cuyler Bunner. VerBaPo *Fr.* In School House.

Boy with Book of Knowledge. Howard Nemerov. NoP-4

Boy with His Hair Cut Short. Muriel Rukeyser. NALW; NoAM; TwCP; VGW; WPE

Boy with yellow hair, his clothes in place, A. War Memento (Somewhere in France 1915). Roger Hecht. CRP

Boy yell, bull elephant charge. Inmates. Maggie Hannan. NLP

Boy, yes, you with the teasing glances. Fragment 360. Anacreon. CAGL, *tr. by* Alfred Corn

Boyarina Morozova, The. Nikolai Ivanovich Glazkov. TCRP, *tr. by* Daniel Weissbort

Boycott. Khalil Mutran. MAP, *tr. by* Issa Boullata and Thomas G. Ezzy

Boyhood of Christ, The. Columba, Saint. NOIV

Boyish sleep. Hamlin Garland. APN-2

Boyne Water, The. *Unknown.* NOIV

Boys and girls come out to play. Mother Goose. OxBEV; OxNR

Boys and girls crying with hunger, all over the village. Painting of Peach Blossom Spring, A. Shen Chou. CoBLCP, *tr. by* Jonathan Chaves

Boys are an inextricable maze. To Theodorus et al. Rhianos. CAGL, *tr. by* Daryl Hine

Boys forget about women. Excuse, The. Carl H. Greene. NBV

Boys have to slash their fingers to become brothers. Girls trade. Anointing, An. Thylias Moss. GT; ReTh

Boys / I don't promise you nothing. Admonitions. Lucille Clifton. BPo; NALW

Boys in sporadic but tenacious droves. Horse Chestnut Tree, The. Richard Eberhart. MoAmPo

Boys in the Backroom, The. Frederick Hollander. ReLy

Boys kicking a ball on a vast square beneath an obelisk. Above Us. Julia Hartwig. BLT, *tr. by* Stanislaw Baranczak

Boys Make Men. *Unknown.* PWR

Boys' members, Diodorus, come in three. Strato [*or* Straton]. CAGL, *tr. by* Daryl Hine

Boys of Ch'ien-t'ang practice riding the bore, The. Song of Surfing on the Bore. Cheng Hsieh. CoBLCP; ColAnChi, *tr. by* Jonathan Chaves

Boys of Mullabaun [*or* Mullaghbawn], The. *Unknown.* BIrV

Boys of Summer, The. E. Ethelbert Miller. SpirFl

Boys of These Men Full Speed. Muriel Rukeyser. NNaP

Boys' Own. Brendan Cleary. NeBl

Boys, the Broom Handle, the Retarded Girl, The. Alicia Ostriker. ExTi

Boysick (by gadzooks thunderstruck), The. Honey Lamb, The. Jonathan Williams. PoM

Bozzy and Piozzi. "Peter Pindar."
   Town Eclogue, A. OBCoV

Br'er Sterling and the Rocker. Michael S. Harper. NAAAL

Br-r-r-am-m-m, rackety-am-m, OM, *Am.* What the Motorcycle Said. Mona Van Duyn. NIL-7; NIP-4

Braced in the sinewy vigour of thy breed. Horse and His Rider, The. Joanna Baillie. ECWP; NOEC

Bracelet, The. John Donne. NoSic

Bracelet, The. Thomas Stanley. BeJo

Bracelet of Grass, The. William Vaughn Moody. APN-2; TCAPo

Bracelet to Julia, The. Robert Herrick. BASC; OBEV

Bracelets. William Strode. NOSC

Bracelets jingle every time. Love Poem, A. Vagura. WoPoe, *tr. by* Peter Dent and Edwin Gerow

Bracketed by a diesel switcher and five. Note on the L and N. Richmond Lattimore. GM

Brackish reach of shoal off Madaket—, A. Quaker Graveyard in Nantucket, The. Robert Lowell. ColAP; HAP; MakPoe; NAAL-2v2; NAAL-5; NoAM; NOBA; OxBA; PeECV; TAP; UnPo; VCAP

Brady Street, San Francisco. Michael Lassell. WiU

Braes o' Yarrow, The. *Unknown. See* Dowie Houms o' Yarrow, The

Braes of Yarrow, The. John Logan. GTBS-P; SCGP

Braes of Yarrow, The. *Unknown.* ESPB; OxBB

Brag, sweet tenor bull. Basil Bunting. HarvBoo; NoAM; NoP-4; NPeEn; PoE *Fr.* Briggflatts [An Autobiography].

Braggart Duck. Shinkichi Takahashi. ZenPo, *tr. by* Takashi Ikemoto and Lucien Stryk

Brahma. Ralph Waldo Emerson. APN-1; AWP; ColAP; HAP; NOBA; NoP-4; OBEV; OxBA; PAI; PoE; PoRA; TAP; TCAPo; TFi; UnPo; UV

Brahma. Andrew Lang. NOBL; PeLV; UV

Brahmin, The. James Montgomery.
   "Once on the mountain's balmy lap reclined." NOBRP

Braid Claith. Robert Fergusson. NOEC; OxBEV; OxBS

Braille for Left Hand. Octavio Armand. TCLAP, *tr. by* Carol Maier

Brain Cells, The. Donald Hall. TAP

Brain forgets, but the blood will remember, The. Dark Chamber, The. Louis Untermeyer. MoAmPo

Brain itself in its skull, The. Harsh Climate. Charles Simic. LCAP-2

Brain on Ice. Michael Warr. UnSA

Brain, within its Groove, The.	Emily Dickinson.	NCAP; NoAM; NOBA; SAmP

Brainless creatures simply fuck.	Vive La Différence.	Strato [or Straton].	GrAn, tr. by Teddy Hogge

Brainsick race that wanton youth ensues, The.	Unknown.	NoSic

Brainstorm.	Howard Nemerov.	HAP; TRP

Braly Street.	Gary Soto.	GeoHom; UnSA

Brambleberry, The.	Sándor Weöres.	IQMS, tr. by Adam Makkai and Valerie Becker Makkai

Bran, a chaff, a very barley [y]awn, A.	Edward Taylor.	ChIV-2; NOSC; TCAPo	Fr. Preparatory Meditations before My Approach to the Lord's Supper.

Bran you're flabbergast.	Bran at the Island of Women.	Unknown.	WoPoe, tr. by Greg Delanty

Branch, A.	Cor Van den Heuvel.	HA

Branches of grape-vine thick as ankles.	Elm Tree in Paddington, An.	Robert Adamson.	BMAP

Branches' snow is like the cotton fluff, The.	Element Mother, The.	Lorine Niedecker.	FTOS

Branches, you, The / And you. (LL)	Mysteries Remain, The.	"H. D."	NOBA; TAP; VGW; WPOW

Brancusi's Golden Bird.	Mina Loy.	APT-1; HarvBoo

Brandy Station, Virginia.	David Moolten.	BloBone

Brandy, who got it from a blood transfusion.	Twelfth Floor West.	Marilyn Hacker.	ExTi

Branwell's Sestina.	James Reaney.	MoCV	Fr. Suit of Nettles, A.

Branwen's Starling.	R. Williams Parry.	OBWVE, tr. by Gwyn Jones

Branwen was buried here, so long ago.	At Branwen's Grave.	Dudley G. Davies.	AngWePo

Brass and parrots' feathers.	Oshun, the River Goddess.	Unknown.	WoPoe, tr. by Ulli Beier

Brass band plays in a brass oven, A.	Moscow: Summer '86.	Yevgeny [or Evgenii] Bunimovich.	TCRP, tr. by Bradley Jordan and Albert C. Todd

Brass-green bird with grass, A.	Smooth Gnarled Crape Myrtle.	Marianne Craig Moore.	APT-1

Brass Horse, The.	Drummond Allison.	FaBoTw

Brass Knuckles.	Stuart Dybek.	PBCAP

Brass Spittoons.	Langston Hughes.	MoAmPo; NoAM

Brassica (oleracea) is a cabbage.	Cabbage.	Rosemary Norman.	BrRo

Brats.	X. J. Kennedy.	NBLV

Bratzlav Rabbi to His Scribe, The.	Jacob Glatstein [or Glatsteyn].	TrJP, tr. by Jacob Sloan

Brave as a postage stamp.	Sporting Goods.	Philippe Soupault.	TTTS, tr. by Rosmarie Waldrop

Brave as a postage stamp, he went his way.	Philippe Soupault.	See Brave as a postage stamp

Brave comrade, answer! When you joined the war.	George Henry Boker.	APN-2

Brave flowers, that I could gallant it like you.	Contemplation upon Flowers, A.	Henry King, Bishop of Chichester.	MeLP; OBEV; SCGP

Brave Grant, thou hero of the war.	General Grant—the Hero of the War.	George Moses Horton.	CBCWP

Brave infant of Saguntum, clear[e].	Ben Jonson.	BASC; BeJo; CABP; NAEL-5v1; NAEL-6v1; NAEL-7v1; NOBE; NoP-4; NOSC; PBRV

Brave lads in olden musical centuries.	Alcaics; to H. F. B.	Robert Louis Stevenson.	OBEV

Brave Man, The.	Wallace Stevens.	SAmP

Brave Man and Brave Woman.	Mrs. Henry Linden.	CBWP-4

Brave man with a sword!, The. (LL)	Oscar Wilde.	EBVV; NoAM; OBNV; OxAEP-2	Fr. Ballad of Reading Gaol, The.

Brave New World.	Archibald MacLeish.	NOBA; OxBA

Brave news is come to town.	Unknown.	OxNR

Brave Old Duke of York, The.	Unknown.	OxNR

Brave Page Boys, The.	Julia A. Moore.
"Enos Page the youngest brother."	VerBaPo

Brave Rover.	Max Beerbohm.	NBLV

Brave Sparrow.	Michael Collier.	UrbNat

Brave Teuton, though thy awful name.	Schemmelfennig.	Bret Harte.	OBAL

Brave, wise, and Venus' son. (LL)	In a Bye-Canal.	Herman Melville.	APN-2; NCAP

Brave youth, to whom Fate in one hour.	For a Picture Where a Queen Laments over the Tomb of a Slain Knight.	Thomas Carew.	CaPo

Bravely from Fairyland he rode, on furlough.	Broken Girth, The.	Robert Graves.	BIrV

Braver Deeds.	Gary Young.
"It's Sunday, October ninth, and the earth here is barren after harvest."	GeoHom

Braveries.	Robert Pinsky.	HarvBoo

Bravery runs in my family.	Coward.	A. R. Ammons.	OBAL

Bravest battle that ever was fought, The.	Joaquin Miller.	ITBLP	Fr. Bravest Battle, The.

Braving the Wilds All Unexplored with music.	Robert Freeman.	AH

Braw, snortin', roarin', fearsome beastie.	To a Bull Moose.	Eugene O'Neill.	UV

Brawling of a sparrow in the eaves, The.	Sorrow of Love, The.	W. B. Yeats.	NAEL-5v2; NAEL-6v2; OxBEV; PeVV

Brazen Image.	Anne Hartigan.	CIP-2

Brazen Tongue.	William Rose Benét.	MoAmPo

Brazil.	Bill Manhire.	HarvBoo

Brazil, January 1, 1502.	Elizabeth Bishop.	BLT; FaBoWP; NoAM; PoetW; PoPoPo; VCAP

Brazilian Fazenda.	Patricia K. Page.	FaBoWP

Breach in the Wall, The.	Unknown.	EMWP

Breach of clear heaven opens, A.	Enlightment.	Ch'en Yü-i.	OHMPC, tr. by Kenneth Rexroth

Bread.	Stanley Burnshaw.	APT-2; TrJP

Bread.	Mahmoud Darwish.	MAP, tr. by Lena Jayyusi and Christopher Middleton

Bread.	James Dickey.	LCAP-2

Bread.	Michael Hartnett.	See Domestic Scene

Bread.	Brendan Kennelly.	PBCIP

Bread.	W. S. Merwin.	SPE; VCAP

Bread.	Gabriela Mistral.	WPOW, tr. by Allan Francovich and Kathleen Weaver

Bread and a Pension.	Louis Johnson.	PeNZ

Bread and Music.	Conrad Potter Aiken.	See Discordants

Bread and Wine.	Nina Cassian.	AWTN, tr. by Andrea Deletant and Brenda Walker

Bread and Wine.	Friedrich Hölderlin.
"Oh friend, we arrived too late."	RaBo

Bread goes up so bread goes up again.	Inflation.	Nicanor Parra.	AF, tr. by Miller Williams

Bread Hot from the Oven, The.	John Thompson.	NOBC

Bread: I'm told a certain object grows.	Cynewulf.	ASW	Fr. Riddles (Exeter Book).

Bread Is Born.	Anne Hébert.	BoWoP, tr. by Maxine W. Kumin

Bread is poisoned and the air's drunk dry, The.	Osip Emilevich Mandelstam [or Mandelshtam].	TCRP

Bread Man, The.	Lucinda Roy.	GT

Bread of Heaven, on Thee we Feed.	Josiah Conder.	TrCP

Bread of this World; Praises III, The.	Thomas McGrath.	RaBo

Bread-oh, bread-oh, ten-cent bread. . . .	Bread Man, The.	Lucinda Roy.	GT

Bread-Word Giver.	John Wheelwright.	ChIV-2

Breaded Fish.	A. K. Ramanujan.	NoP-4

Breaded Meat, Breaded Hands.	Michael S. Harper.	ISC

Break.	Ben Howard.	UrbNat

Break, The.	Delmira Agustini.	TANSG, tr. by Mark McCaffrey

Break, Break, Break.	Tennyson.	AWP; BRP; CIHu; FHYEP; GTBS-P; HAP; HeIP-4; NAEL-5v2; NAEL-6v2; NIL-7; NIP-4; NOBE; NOBVV; NoP-4; PoRA; PWR; RB; SoSe-8; TFi; TreFP; WeW-3

Break from the Bush, A.	Yusef Komunyakaa.	CDa

Break not the slumbers of the bride.	Hymeneal Song on the Nuptials of the Lady Anne Wentworth and the Lord Lovelace, An.	Thomas Carew.	CaPo

Break of Dawn, The.	Thomas Sayers Ellis.	InTrad

Break of Day in the Trenches.	Isaac Rosenberg.	CABP; FaBoMo; GTBS-P; HarvBoo; MoBrPo; NAEL-5v2; NAEL-6v2; NIL-7; NoAM; NOBE; NoP-4; NPeEn; OBWP; OxAEP-2; OxBEV; PeFWW; PoWW; TFi

Break off the yoke and set me free. (LL)	Who Shall Deliver Me?	Christina Georgina Rossetti.	SacPr; TOF

Break Thou the Bread of Life.	Mary Artemisia Lathbury.	AH

Break through and stare. (LL)	Madrigal: "Your love is dead, lady, your love is dead."	Ronald Stuart Thomas.	BoLoP; EnLoPo

Break-up, The.	Abraham Moses Klein.	NOBC

Breakdancing.	Jorie Graham.	BodElec

Break[e] of Day.	John Donne.	NAEL-5v1; NAEL-6v1; NAEL-7v1; SoSe-8

Breakers' jumbled yard: valley, The.	Port Talbot.	John Davies.	AngWePo

Breakfast.	Wilfrid Wilson Gibson.	FaBoWar; OBMV; OxBTC

Breakfast.	Harry Graham.	EBNV

Breakfast.	Thom Gunn.	OxBC

Breakfast.	William Carlos Williams.	SAmP

Breakfast alone.	Alexis Rotella.	HA

Breakfast enjoyed.	Basho.	SoOfWa, tr. by Sam Hamill

Breakfast for Barbarians, A.	Gwendolyn MacEwen.	NOBC

Breakfast is drunk down . . . Damp earth.	Our Daily Bread.	César Vallejo.	TCLAP, tr. by James Wright

Breakfast on the Balcony. Yevgeny [*or* Evgenii] Borisovich Rein. TCRusP, *tr. by* Daniel Weissbort

Breakfast over, islanded by noise. Woman in Kitchen. Eavan Boland. BiHa

Breakfast Poem. Clare Pollard. NeBl

Breakfast Song in Time of Diet. Stoddard King. OBAL

Breakfast with Cats. Molly Peacock. KGB

Breakfast with Gerard Manley Hopkins. Anthony Brode. NOBL

Breaking from under that thy cloudy veil. Edward Herbert, 1st Baron of Cherbury. OxAEP-1

Breaking Green. Michael Ondaatje. NOBC

Breaking Ground. Thom Gunn. OBGa

Breaking in song. (LL) Returning to Goleufryn. Vernon Watkins. AngWePo; OBWVE

Breaking of the Day, The. Peter Davison.
  Birthright, The. YaYoPo
  Dead Sea, The. YaYoPo
  Delphi. YaYoPo
  Gift of Tongues, The. YaYoPo

Breaking of the Glass, The. 'Abdallah Al-Tayyib. MAP, *tr. by* Salma Khadra Jayyusi and Christopher Middleton

Breaking Points. Eamon Grennan. ModIr

Breaking the Chain. Tony Harrison. UV

Breaking the morning ice on the well's bucket was no great hardship. On the Pilgrim's Way in Kent, as It Leads to the Coldrum Stones. "Asphodel." BrRo

Breaking the Precepts. Yasin Taha Hafiz. MAP, *tr. by* Sharif Elmusa and Christopher Middleton

Breaking the Rock Down. Ralph Angel. BodElec

Breaking through the first door, he found. Seven Dreams. John Clifford Bayliss. SPE

Breaking up the clouds. (LL) Pushing. Christopher Gilbert. LTA; SoSe-8

Breaking waves dashed high, The. Landing of the Pilgrim Fathers [in New England], The. Felicia Dorothea Hemans. BRP; HHAm; ITBLP; NAEL-6v2; NoP-4; WPE

Breaking with honey buds, shall ever equal. (LL) Express, The. Stephen Spender. HeIP-4; MoBrPo; NIL-7; NoAM; TwCP

Breaks like the Atlantic Ocean on my head. (LL) Man And Wife. Robert Lowell. BoLoP; CoAmPo; ColAP; NAAL-2v2; VCAP

Breakthrough. Carolyn M. Rodgers. BPo

Bream swam by the tramcar window, A. Near Shinobazu Pond. Shinkichi Takahashi. ZenPo, *tr. by* Takashi Ikemoto and Lucien Stryk

Breast Examination. Wanda Coleman. GT

Breastès round, and long small armès twain, The. (LL) Smiling Mouth and Laughing Eyen Grey, The. Charles, Duc d' Orléans. HAP; MiEL

Breasting the thick brushwood that hid my track. Wet Day, A. Andrew Young. NePenScot

Breasts. Maxine Chernoff. PmAP; ReTh; SpudSo

Breasts. Donald Hall. OBAL

Breasts. Charles Simic. NNaP; RaBo

Breasts of a barmaid of Crale, The. Limerick. *Unknown*. NOBL

Breasts of all the women crumpled like gas bags when, The. State Will Be Served Even by Poets, The. Julian Beck. PFTM-2

Breath. Reginald Gibbons. BodElec

Breath. Deema K. Shehabi. PoArWo

Breath. Mark Strand. HCAP

Breath, The. Robert Bly. WoPoe *Fr.* Two Translations from Kabir.

Breath'd in their distant homes by wife or child! (LL) Buoy-Bell, The. Charles Tennyson Turner. GSo; PeVV; Son

Breath He Holds, The. Rick Noguchi. NeAmPo

Breath is warm. Dirty Dreams and God Smiling. Alane Rollings. IllVoic

Breath leaves the sentences and does not come back, A. Losing a Language. W. S. Merwin. NoP-4

Breath of Air, A. James Wright (1927–80). NOBA

Breath of balm from foreign branches pressed, The. Martial. RomPo, *tr. by* Anthony Reid

Breath of God sank down on fallow land, The. March Night. Herbert Strutz. AuPH, *tr. by* Lowell A. Bangerter

Breath of my life—no less, The. Epigram. Meleager. GrAn, *tr. by* Peter Whigham

Breath of Nature, The. Chuang Tzu. BBASP, *tr. by* Thomas Merton

Breath of the sun, crowned. Wole Soyinka. PBMAP *Fr.* Shuttle in the Crypt, The.

Breath's slow, The. Changing Room. John A. Scott. BMAP

Breathcrystal. Paul Celan. PFTM-2, *tr. by* Pierre Joris

Breathe Dust. Fred Wah. NOBC

Breathe in and out, legs in stirrups, bottom up, eyes focused on a faded happy face tacked to the ceiling. Clog of Her Body, The. Diana García. TouFir

"Breathe light into the page," he said. Lesson in Anatomy, A. Liz Rosenberg. NIL-7

Breathe my breath also through these songs. (LL) Chanting the Square Deific. Walt Whitman. APN-1; NAAL-2v1; NAAL-3

Breathe not, hid Heart: cease silently. To an Unborn Pauper Child. Thomas Hardy. GTBS-P

Breathes there the [*or* a] Man with soul so dead. Sir Walter Scott. ITBLP; NePenScot; OxBEV; OxBS; SoSe-8; TFi *Fr.* Lay of the Last Minstrel, The.

Breathing. (LL) Orchids. Theodore Roethke. ColAP; HarvBoo; TRP

Breathing. James Tate. LCAP-2

Breathing. Rod Willmot. HA

Breathing air with snow falling through it. Thoughts Breathing in a Blizzard. "Antler." PoCoUp

Breathing do I draw that air to me. Song of Breath. Peire Vidal. AWP, *tr. by* Ezra Pound

Breathing Exercises. Leonard Nathan. PBCAP

Breathing something German at the end. Gift to Be Simple, The. Howard Moss. TwCP

Breathing Space July. Tomas Tranströmer. RB, *tr. by* Robert Bly

Breathless she stood, her graceful head bent low. Listening Nydia. Henrietta Cordelia Ray. CBWP-3

Breathless Storm. Michael Burkard. BodElec

Breathless swimmer in that cold green element, A. (LL) Cold Green Element, The. Irving Layton. NOBC; NoP-4

Breathless, we flung us on the windy hill. Hill, The. Rupert Brooke. MoBrPo; OxBSo; OxBTC; Son

Breaths. Birago Diop. TTY, *tr. by* Anne Atik

Brébeuf and His Brethren. Edwin John Pratt.
  Martyrdom of Brébeuf and Lalemant, 16 March 1649, The. NOBC

Brébeuf and His Brethren. Francis Reginald Scott. NOBC

Brechfa Chapel. Roland Mathias. AngWePo

Bredon Hill. A. E. Housman. EBVV; MoBrPo; NAEL-5v2; NAEL-6v2; OxAEP-2; SoSe-8; UV

Breech, The. Michael McClure. NeAP

Breed in a lively animal. (LL) Adrienne Rich. NIP-4; NOBA; TAP *Fr.* Two Songs.

Breed's described, The: Now, Satire, if you can. Daniel Defoe. OBSV *Fr.* True-born Englishman, The.

Breeze blew fair, the waving sea, The. Charnel Ship, The. Lucretia Davidson. TreFP

Breeze has passed, The. Spring at Wu Ling. Li Ch'ing-chao. ErotSp, *tr. by* Sam Hamill

Breeze in Translation. Belle Waring. PBCAP

Breeze is springing up, A. Mark yon grey cloud. Sea-View, A. Ann Radcliffe. RWP

Breeze sent a wrinkling darkness. Waiting for the Storm. Timothy Steele. MakPoe

Breeze stirs banana leaves behind the house, A. Complaining about the Second Wife. *Vietnamese Oral Tradition*. CaDao, *tr. by* John Balaban

Breeze strokes the water of the spring, A. Takushitsu. EaWin, *tr. by* W. S. Merwin

Breeze Tells Me, Loved One, The. Antonio Machado Ruiz. SpanPo, *tr. by* James Duffy

Breezes sigh, rising over bright tiled steps. Evening near Serpent River. Tu Fu. CrYelRi, *tr. by* Sam Hamill

Breezes taste, The. September. John Updike. KaS

Breezeways in the tropics winnow the air. Letter from the Caribbean, A. Barbara Howes. CoAP; UnPo

Breezin' along with the Breeze. Haven Gillespie. ReLy

Breezing Dawn of the New Day, The. Mongane Wally Serote. PeSAV

Breezy Delicious Day. Edwin Torres. HeMarv

Breitmann in Paris. Charles Godfrey Leland. APN-2

Breitmann in Politics. Charles Godgrey Leland.
  "Dere's a liddle fact in hishdory vitch few hafe onnershtand." OBAL

Brennbaum. Ezra Pound. MoAmPo *Fr.* Hugh Selwyn Mauberley (Life and Contacts).

Brent; a Poem to Thomas Palmer Esq. William Diaper.
  "Had mournful Ovid been to Brent condemned." OBSV
  "Happy are you, whom Quantock overlooks." NOEC; OBSV

Brer Rabbit, You's de Cutes' of 'Em All. James Weldon Johnson. APT-1

Brereton Omen, The. Felicia Dorothea Hemans.
  "Yes! I have seen the ancient oak." CTC

Bresson's Movies. Robert Creeley. NoP-4; PmAP

Brethren, The. Seamus Deane. PNI

Brethren, behold, how suddenly he died. Funeral Oration. Dezső Kosztolányi. IQMS, *tr. by* George Gömöri and Clive Wilmer

Brethren, I know that many of you have come here today. Fundamentals. Ian Duhig. NeBl

Breughel's Winter. Rutger Kopland. VCWP, *tr. by* James Brockway

Brevity. Friedrich Hölderlin. NAWM-7v2, *tr. by* Christopher Middleton

Brevity. Judith Wright. HarvBoo *Fr.* Notes at Edge.

Brevity of Embraces. Armanda Guiducci. CItWP, *tr. by* Cinzia Sartini Blum and Lara Trubowitz

Brewed *tacita* of espresso, A. Donatilia's Unrequited Love Remedy. Virgil Suárez. AmPoNex

Brewer's Man, The. Leonard Alfred George Strong. OBCoV; PeLV

Brewing of Soma, The. John Greenleaf Whittier.
  "Dear Lord and Father of mankind." AH; NOCV; SacPr

Breyten Prays for Himself. Breyten Breytenbach. PoetW; VCWP, *tr. by* Denis Hirson

Brian O'Linn. *Unknown.* NBLV; RB
  (Brian O Linn.) OBCoV
  (Brian O Linn had no breeches to wear.) OBCoV
  (Bryan O'Lynn.) FaBoVe

Bric-à-Brac. Dorothy Parker. APT-1

Brick distinguishes this country. Amsterdam Letter. Jean Garrigue. VCAP

Brick-dust in sunlight. Roy Fisher. NPeEn *Fr.* City.

Brickie who had a fine tool, A. Limerick: "Brickie who had a fine tool, A." E. O. Parrott. PeLi

Bricklay'r throws his trowel by, The. Evan Lloyd. NOEC
  Fr. Methodist, The.

Bricklayer's Labours, The. Robert Tatersal. NOEC

Bricklayer tells the busdriver, The. Continuity, The. Paul Blackburn. NeAP

Brid one brere, brid, brid one brere. Bird on Briar. *Unknown.* MiEL

Bridal Birth. Dante Gabriel Rossetti. Son *Fr.* House of Life, The.

Bridal Morn, The. *Unknown.* WoPoe

Bridal Rites. Rebecca McClanahan. MPUn

Bridal Song, A: "Roses, their sharp spines being gone." John Fletcher. NOBE; NOSC; NoSic *Fr.* Two Noble Kinsmen, The.

Bridal Song: "Cynthia, to thy power." Francis Beaumont. OBEV *Fr.* Maid's Tragedy, The.

Bridal Song: "Now sleep, bind fast the flood of air." George Chapman. OxBSP *Fr.* Masque of the Middle Temple and Lincoln's Inn, The.

Bridal Song: "O come, soft rest of cares, come Night." Christopher Marlowe. NOBE; OBEV *Fr.* Hero and Leander.

Bridal Veil, The. Alice Cary. TCAPo

Bride, A. Harry Fainlight. BoLoP

Bride, The. Bella [*or* Izabella] Akhatovna Akhmadulina. BoWoP; MPUn

Bride, The. Vladislav Felitsievich Khodasevich. TCRusP, *tr. by* Daniel Weissbort

Bride, The. D. H. Lawrence. NoAM; OxBTC

Bride, The. Alicia Ostriker. TaR

Bride cam' out o' the byre, The. Wooed and Married and A' Alexander Ross. OxBS

Bride loved old words, and found her pleasure marred. James Vincent Cunningham. OBAL *Fr.* Five Epigrams.

Bride-Night Fire, The. Thomas Hardy.
  "O Tim, my own Tim I must call 'ee—I will!" FaBoVe

Bride of Frankenstein, The. Edward Field. CoAP; HeIP-4; ReTh

Bride of Lammermoor, The. Sir Walter Scott.
  (Look Not Thou.) OxBSP
  Lucy Ashton's Song. NAEL-6v2; NOBE; NPeEn; OBEV; OxAEP-2; OxBS; WoPoe

Bride of Quietness, The. Kelly Cherry. FFC

Bride of the Greek Isle, The. Felicia Dorothea Hemans. RWP

Bride of the Iconoclasts, The. Benjamin Paul Blood.
  "Stop!—Gaze thro' this hushed gallery! The air." APN-2

Bride's Day. Susan Howe. FTOS *Fr.* Defenestration of Prague.

Bride's Farewell, The. Felicia Dorothea Hemans. TreFP

Bride's Hours, A. Jean Valentine. FaBoWP; MPUn

Bride she is winsome and bonny, The. Song: Woo'd and married and a' Joanna Baillie. NAEL-6v2; NoP-4

Bride Song. Christina Georgina Rossetti. OBEV; WPE *Fr.* Prince's Progress, The.

Bride: Virginity, virginity, where have you gone leaving me behind? Sappho. SaLy, *tr. by* Diane Rayor

Bride wore a gown, The. Catherine Bowman. ExTi *Fr.* El Paso Times "World of Women," The.

Bridegroom, The. Rudyard Kipling. FaBoEE *Fr.* Epitaphs of the War [1914–1918].

Bridegroom, beloved of my heart. *Unknown.* WPoS

Bridegroom, dear to my heart. *Ancient Sumerian Oral Tradition.* EroLit, *tr. by* Diane Noah Kramer

Bridegroom of Cana, The. Marjorie Lowry Christie Pickthall. TrCP

Bridegroom of forty-one, / who tomorrow goes off to war, The. Siberian

Wooing. Yevgeny Aleksandrovich Yevtushenko [*or* Evtushenko]. VCWP, *tr. by* Albert C. Todd

Bridegroom with his bride, The! (LL) St. Agnes' Eve. Tennyson. OBEV; SacPr

Brides, The. Alec Derwent Hope. HAP; PAI

Brides Come to Yuba City, The. Chitra Divakaruni. OpBo; UnSA

Brides of Elvis, The. David Ray. AllShUp

Bridge. A. R. Ammons. CoAP; NAAL-2v2

Bridge. Christopher Okigbo. PBMAP *Fr.* Heavensgate (1961).

Bridge, The. Hart Crane. APT-2; NAAL-2v2
  Atlantis. NAAL-5
  Ave Maria. NOBA; NoAM
  Cape Hatteras. MoAmPo
    Power. MoAmPo
  Cutty Sark. FaBoMo
  Powhatan's Daughter.
    Dance, The. MoAmPo; NAAL-5; OxBA
    Harbor Dawn, The. MoAmPo; NOBA; NoAM; OxBA
    River, The. GM; MoAmPo; NAAL-5; NOBA; OxBA
    "Stick your patent name on a signboard." GM; MoAmPo; NAAL-5; NOBA; OxBA
    Van Winkle. MoAmPo
  (Proem: To Brooklyn Bridge.) HAP; HeIP-4; NoAM; TAP; WeW-3
  Three Songs. NAAL-2v2
    National Winter Garden. NAAL-2v2; OxBA
  To Brooklyn Bridge. AiP; AmFaPo; ChIV-1; ClHu; ColAP; FaBoA; HarvBoo; MakPoe; MoAmPo; NAAL-5; NOBA; NoP-4; OxBA; PoE; PoPoPo; TFi; TRP
  Tunnel, The. MoAmPo; NAAL-5; OxBA

Bridge, The. Khalil Hawi. MAP, *tr. by* Diana Der Hovanessian and Lena Jayyusi

Bridge, The. Victor Hugo. SxFrPo, *tr. by* A. M. and E. H. Blackmore

Bridge, The. Henry Wadsworth Longfellow. APN-1; ITBLP

Bridge, The. O. V. de L. Milosz. BLT

Bridge, The. Alicia Ostriker. ExTi *Fr.* Mastectomy Poems, The.

Bridge, The. John Banister Tabb. APN-2

Bridge, The. Charlotte Zolotow. CA

Bridge, and a hot concrete road, A. Desert of Love, The. János Pilinszky. IQMS; OBVE, *tr. by* Ted Hughes

Bridge-Builder, The. Will Allen Dromgoole. *See* Building the Bridge

Bridge engineer, Mister Crumpett, A. *Unknown.* KaS

Bridge, fallen, A. And so. Through Clouds, Their Whispers. Martha Rhodes. NAPBL

Bridge-Guard in the Karroo. Rudyard Kipling. OBWP

Bridge in the South. Jorge Teillier. TCLAP, *tr. by* Carolyne Wright

Bridge instead of a Wall, A. *Unknown.* PoToHe

Bridge is certainly the simplest answer, The. Manly Ferry. John Philip. NOBAu

Bridge of Death, The. *Unknown.* AWP, *tr. by* Andrew Lang

Bridge of Heraclitus, The. George Reavey. BIrV

Bridge of Sighs, The. Thomas Hood. BRP; EBEV; GTBS-P; OBEV; OxAEP-2; TreFP

Bridge of volumes, The. World in Yellow, A. Marcel Duchamp. PFTM-1

Bridge on the Sangarios, A. Agathias. GrAn, *tr. by* Guy Davenport

Bridge Poem, The. Kate Rushin. GLP

Bridge toll-booth—, The. David E. Lecount. HA

Bridge under our wheels moaned, some said, because it was built in a time, The. Cricket Mountain. Khaled Mattawa. NAPBL

Bridge Where the Moon Crosses, The. Muso Soseki. EaWin, *tr. by* W. S. Merwin

Bridges. Leslie Norris. TCAWP

Brief Autumnal. *Unknown.* GrAn; PAI; WeW-3, *tr. by* Dudley Fitts

Brief Curriculum. Reiner Kunze. PoSu, *tr. by* Michael Hamburger

Brief day ending. Frank K. Robinson. HA

Brief Ectasy. Luciana Notari. CItWP, *tr. by* Cinzia Sartini Blum and Lara Trubowitz

Brief Elegie on My Dear Son John, A. John Saffin. SCAP

Brief Encounter. Norman J. Loftis. SpirFl

Brief Entanglements. Richard Garcia. TouFir

Brief Essay on Man. Arthur Guiterman. OBAL

Brief History of the City. Robert Peterson. GeoHom

Brief is our life, now in the midst of the years. To Adelhard, Archbishop of Canterbury. Alcuin. MLL, *tr. by* Helen Waddell

Brief Journey West, The. Howard Nemerov. NoAM

Brief Lessons in Eroticism 1. Gioconda Belli. ErotSp; TANSG, *tr. by* Steven F. White

Brief Letter to Donald Walsh (in memoriam). Angel Cuadra. AF, *tr. by* Katherine Rodriguez Nieto

Brief Lives. Olive Senior. EmeKit

Brief meeting today, A. For Ko Who Has Come Back from China. Muso Soseki. EaWin, *tr. by* W. S. Merwin

Brief Note from Jerusalem, A. Gabriel Preil. FIT, *tr. by* Robert Friend

Brief, on a flying night. Chimes. Alice Thompson Meynell. MoBrPo; WPE

Brief procession, The. Bessie Smith's Funeral. Alvin Aubert. SeSe

Brief Thoughts on Cats Growing on Trees. Miroslav Holub. PoSu, *tr. by* Ian Milner and Jarmila Milner

Brief Thoughts on Cracks. Miroslav Holub. PoSu, *tr. by* Ian Milner and Jarmila Milner

Brief Thoughts on Floods. Miroslav Holub. PoSu, *tr. by* Ian Milner and Jarmila Milner

Brief was the meeting,—tear-stained, full of fears. To A.H.B. Margaret Witter Fuller. PoBW

Brief Wyoming Meditation. Diane Di Prima. BB

Briefcase, The. Paul Muldoon. CABP

Briefly It Enters, and Briefly Speaks. Jane Kenyon. HW

Brigadier. Arthur James Marshall Smith. MoCV

Briggflatts [An Autobiography]. Basil Bunting.
  "Brag, sweet tenor bull." HarvBoo; NoAM; NoP-4; NPeeEn; PoE
  "Grass caught in willow tells the flood's height that has subsided." FaBoMo
  Poet appointed dare not decline.
  "Loaded with mail of linked lies." FaBoWar
  "Riding silk, adrift at noon." WoPoe

BRight. No Thanks, No. 70. E. E. Cummings. PFTM-1

Bright. Water Maid. Christopher Okigbo. PBMAP

Bright. (LL) End of a War, The. Sir Herbert Read. OBMV; PeFWW

Bright after Dark. Pearse Hutchinson. PBCIP

Bright, all white and blue. Andreyevsky Church, The. "Nikolai Nikolaevich Morshen." TCRusP, *tr. by* John Glad

Bright and beautiful art thou. October. Mary Weston Fordham. CBWP-2

Bright and early we went down to the fishmarket. Words from Confinement. Cesare Pavese. AF, *tr. by* William Arrowsmith

Bright and pleasant, A. Fukyu. JDP, *tr. by* Yoel Hoffmann

Bright are the days which the Fates hold in store for us. To William (Whom We Have Missed). P. G. Wodehouse. NOBL

Bright as a single poppy in a field. Alfred Raymond Bellinger. YaYoPo

Bright as the day, and like the morning fair. Cloe. George Lansdowne Granville [*or* Grenville], Baron. FaBoEE; NIP-4; OxBEV

Bright as the light that burns at night. Venetia. Adah Isaacs Menken. CBWP-1

Bright autumn moon. Six Ways, The. Issa. EH, *tr. by* Robert Hass

Bright awning is cranked, A. Alan Pizzarelli. HA

Bright blossoms seldom last long. T'ao Ch'ien [*or* T'ao Yuan-ming]. SuSp

Bright books! the perspectives to our weak sights. To His Books. Henry Vaughan. BASC

Bright burnished day, they are laying fresh roof down. Men Roofing. Eamon Grennan. PBCIP

Bright cards above the fire bring no friends near. Christmas 1944. Denise Levertov. AF

Bright Cigar-Shaped Object Hovers over Mount Pleasant, A. John Kinsella. NeBl

Bright-coloured, mirror-plated, strung with lights. Merry-go-round. James Philip McAuley. CBAP

Bright, consuming Spirit. No power on earth so great as Thee. Song of Hungarrda, The. Ngunaitponi. NOBAu

Bright Day, A. William Henry Davies. OBWVE

Bright Day, A. John Montague. CIP-2

Bright drips the morning from its trophied nets. Sonnet of Fishes. George Barker. FaBoMo; Son

Bright enamoured youth above, The. Love's Mystery. Joseph Beaumont. NOSC

Bright eyes, sweet lips, with many fevers fill. Desire. Ada Cambridge. OxBSo

Bright Field, The. Ronald Stuart Thomas. AngWePo; TCAWP

Bright flowers and dim moon, enmeshed in thin drifting mist. Tune: "Deva-like Barbarian." Li Yü. SuSp, *tr. by* Daniel Bryant

Bright-footed Thetis did the sphere aspire. Homer. NoSic *Fr.* Iliad, The.

Bright, glowing Sappho! child of love and song. Ode to Sappho. Elizabeth Oakes-Smith. ColAP

Bright green young grass comes up in the garden. Life Is Long. *Unknown.* OHMPC, *tr. by* Kenneth Rexroth

Bright-haired am I, my face and body white. T. Carmi. MHP, *tr. by* Ruth Finer Mintz *Fr.* René's Songs.

Bright hard day over harbour where sea, A. Winter Lanscape—Halifax. Douglas Lochhead. NIP-4

Bright-harnest [*or* Bright-harnessed] Angels sit in order serviceable. (LL) John

Milton. BASC; ChrPo; MeLP; NAEL-5v1; NAEL-6v1; NAEL-7v1; NOBE; NOCV; NoP-4; OBEV; PBRV; SCGP *Fr.* On the Morning of Christ's Nativity

Bright leaps a living brook! (LL) From the Flats. Sidney Lanier. APN-2; NOBA; NoP-4; OxBA

Bright Light of Responsibility, The. Jennifer L. Knox. BAP-97

Bright Lights of Sarajevo, The. Tony Harrison. EmeKit

Bright lure seized, the old hook bitten, The. (LL) Next Poem, The. Dana Gioia. DiPo; NoP-4

Bright mirror I braved: The devil in it, The. Cleopatra to the Asp. Ted Hughes. EBEV; RACG

Bright moon appears from the east ridge, The. Moonlit Night at Fragrant Mountain Temple. Wang Shih-chieng. SuSp, *tr. by* Richard John Lynn

Bright moon born of the sea. Watching the Moon with Thoughts of Far Away. Chang Chiu-ling. CoBCP, *tr. by* Burton Watson

BRIGHT moon illumines the night-prospect. *Unknown.* BoWoP; ChiP

Bright moon like frost, The. Tune: "Always Having Fun." Su Tung-p'o (Su Shih). ColAnChi, *tr. by* J. R. Hightower

Bright moon, oh how white it shines, The. *Unknown.* ChiP *Fr.* Seventeen Old Poems.

Bright moon rising above T'ien Shan, A. Moon over Mountain Pass. Li Po. SuSp, *tr. by* Joseph J. Lee

Bright moon shines upon the pavilion, A. Seven Poems of Lament. Ts'ao Chih. SuSp, *tr. by* Ronald C. Miao

Bright moon slowly, slowly rises, The. Slowly, Slowly Poem, The. Yüan Hung-tao. CoBLCP; ColAnChi, *tr. by* Jonathan Chaves

Bright moon soars over the Mountain of Heaven, The. Moon over the Mountain Pass, The. Li Po. TAL

Bright moon, when did you appear? Tune: Prelude to Water Music. Su Tung-p'o (Su Shih). CoBCP, *tr. by* Burton Watson

Bright moon, when will she appear?, The. Tune: "Prelude to Water Music." Su Tung-p'o (Su Shih). SuSp, *tr. by* Eugene Eoyang

Bright moon white and silver, The. *Unknown.* SuSp

Bright moonlight shines through the trees. Busy in the Spring. Tzu Yeh. CrYelRi; ErotSp, *tr. by* Sam Hamill

Bright over Europe fell her golden hair. (LL) Letty's Globe. Charles Tennyson Turner. NOBVV; NPeeEn; OBEV; OxBEV; OxBSo; PeVV

Bright Queen of Heaven, God's Virgin Spouse. Knot, The. Henry Vaughan. BASC

Bright ran thy line, O Galloway. Robert Burns. OxBoLi *Fr.* Epigrams on Lord Galloway.

Bright Receding. Heather Ramsdell. AmPoNex

Bright sea, The. From the Seashore. Anna Petrovna Bunina. NAWM-7v2, *tr. by* Pamela Perkins

Bright shadows of true Rest! some shoots of bliss[e]. Son-Days [dayes]. Henry Vaughan. AngWePo; GeHe; NOSC

Bright silver penny, A. (LL) Walter De la Mare. NOxBChV; OBMV

Bright spark, shot from a brighter place. Star[re], The. George Herbert. ESCV; PeECV

Bright Star. John Keats. AWTN; CABP; CenSon; EnLoPo; GSo; GTBS-P; HAP; InPK-6; MakPoe; NAEL-5v2; NAEL-6v2; NIL-7; NIP-4; NPeeEn; OxBSo; PoE; SCV; Son; TFi
  (Bright star, would I were steadfast as thou art.) NAWM-7v2; NoP-4

Bright sun lights out over the western bank. T'ao Ch'ien [*or* T'ao Yuan-ming]. SuSp

Bright Sunlight. Amy Lowell. APT-1

Bright, thin, new moon appears, The. New Moon. Tu Fu. OHPC, *tr. by* Kenneth Rexroth

Bright town, tossed by waves of time to a hill. Ode to Swansea. Vernon Watkins. OBWVE

Bright Tulips, we do know. To a Bed of Tulips. Robert Herrick. CaPo

Bright Venus, Who across the Heavens Stray. Louise Labé. AWTN, *tr. by* Graham Martin

Bright vocabularies are transient as rainbows. Precious Moments. Carl Sandburg. MoAmPo

Bright wanderer, fair coquette of heaven. Shelley. *See* She left me at the silent time

"Brighter than a thousand suns"—that blinding glare. Judith Wright. HarvBoo *Fr.* Shadow of Fire: Ghazals, The.

Brightest and Best of the Sons of the Morning. Reginald Heber. SacPr

Brightest of the Bright, The. Egan [*or* Aodhagán] O'Rahilly [*or* O'Reilly *or* Ó Rathaille]. BIrV, *tr. by* James Clarence Mangan

Brightest planet of the ETERNAL SPHERE, The! (LL) [Sonnet] Conclusive. Mary Robinson. CenSon; RWP

Brightest threads on life's pathway, The. Home and Mother. Hettye Rayburn Ramsey. PWR

Brightly shone the sun in my hut. Those Who Lost Everything. David Diop. PBA, *tr. by* Langston Hughes

Brightly the sun of summer shone. Memory. Anne Brontë. EBVV

Brightness. Denis Glover. PeNZ

Brightness. Maggie Nelson. HeMarv

Brightness most bright I beheld on the way, forlorn. Egan [*or* Aodhagán] O'Rahilly [*or* O'Reilly *or* Ó Rathaille]. NOIV

Brightness of rain wavering. Polderland. Hendrik Marsman. TuT, *tr.* by Seamus Deane

"Brigid is a caution, sure!"—What's that ye say? Her Sister. "Moira O'Neill." OxBTC

Brigitte Bardot in Grangetown. Tony Curtis. TCAWP

Brihadaranyaka Upanishad. *Unknown.* *Fr.* Upanishads, The.

Brill. Clark Coolidge. PmAP

Brilliant— / A day that is less than zero. Alicia Ostriker. ExTi *Fr.* Mastectomy Poems, The.

Brilliant-bellied newt flashes, The. Summer Matures. Helene Johnson. BlSi

Brilliant, bright—the flowers of the cold season! Pavilion for Listening to Fragrance, The. Chang Yü. CoBLCP; WoPoe, *tr.* by Jonathan Chaves

Brilliant Day, A. Charles Tennyson Turner. NOBVV

Brilliant fierce eagles. Lancet, The. Denis Devlin. NOIV

Brilliant kernel of the night, The. Robert Louis Stevenson. EBVV *Fr.* Light-Keeper, The.

Brilliant moon. Issa. SoOfWa, *tr.* by Sam Hamill

Brilliant now, they seem to tremble and ring out. (LL) Window at Key West, A. Honor Moore. KGB; WiU

Brilliant Sad Sun. William Carlos Williams. HarvBoo

Brilliant Sky. Jean Joubert. GifTon, *tr.* by Denise Levertov

Brilliant stills of food, the cozy, The. Ladies' Home Journal, The. Sandra M. Gilbert. NIP-4

Brilliant Windows. Larry Kramer. GeoHom

Brilliantly Philosophising. Hanny Michaelis. TuT, *tr.* by Peter Van de Kamp

Brim-shadow, The. Alan Pizzarelli. HA

Brimming Water. Tu Fu. OHPC, *tr.* by Kenneth Rexroth

Bring a leaf to me. Invitation Standing. Paul Blackburn. VGW

Bring back the life. Give me the Red on the Black of the Bullet (for Claude Reece Jr.). Jayne Cortez. LTA

Bring, bring to deck my brow, ye Sylvan girls. She Endeavors to Fascinate Him. Mary Robinson. CenSon; RWP

Bring Daddy home. *Unknown.* OxNR

Bring dreams of Christ to dusky cane-lipped throngs. (LL) Georgia Dusk. Jean Toomer. APT-2; BPo; NAAL-2v2; NAAL-5; NoAM; NoP-4

Bring Flowers. Felicia Dorothea Hemans. TreFP

Bring flowers to crown the cup and lute. Letitia [*or* Laetitia] Elizabeth Landon. VWP *Fr.* New Monthly Magazine, 44 286–8.

Bring flowers, young flowers, for the festal board. Felicia Dorothea Hemans. TreFP

Bring forth May flowers. (LL) *Unknown.* FaBoVe; OxNR; ReMoGo

"Bring forth the horse!" The horse was brought. Byron. TreFP *Fr.* Mazeppa.

Bring forth the prisoner. Dialogue, A. Elizabeth Newell. EMWP

Bring her down. Song to the Alpaca. Denise Y. Arnold. PoCoUp

Bring Kateen-beug and Maurya Jude. Beg-Innish. John Millington Synge. MoBrPo

"Bring little children unto me." Sunday Schools. Anna Sawyer. ECWP

Bring me my garland, bring me a wreath. Maniac's Song, The. Ann Taylor. NOBRP

Bring me my rose-buds, drawer, come. Frolic[k], A. Robert Herrick. FaBoEE

Bring me the sunflower, I'll plant it here. Eugenio Montale. PoetW, *tr.* by William Arrowsmith

Bring me the sunset in a cup. Emily Dickinson. APN-2; MoAmPo; NOCV

Bring me wine, but wine which never grew. Bacchus. Ralph Waldo Emerson. APN-1; AWP; NOBA; OBEV; OxBA; TCAPo

Bring now the last flower in to warm this room. At My Mother's Bedside. Marcia Lee Masters. WPE

Bring on the Clowns. Jack Prelutsky. OTCP

Bring out the tall tales now that we told. Ghost Story. Dylan Thomas. OBCP

Bring rain. Santo Domingo Corn Dance. Lynn Riggs. APT-2

Bring snow-white lilies, pallid heart-flushed roses. Pantheist's Song of Immortality, The. Constance Naden. ViWPN; VWP

Bring Tara quickly, Mountain. Andha Candī. SinGod, *tr.* by Rachel Fell McDermott

Bring the Day! Theodore Roethke. CRP

Bring the good old bugle, boys, we'll sing another song. Marching through Georgia. Henry Clay Work. APN-2; CBCWP

Bring the holy crust of Bread. Charmes. Robert Herrick. BeJo

Bring the North. William Stafford. LCAP-2

Bring the Wine! Li Po. CoBCP, *tr.* by Burton Watson

Bring them to me. Bring them to me. Bring them to me. *Unknown.* APN-2 *Fr.* Minnetare Songs.

Bring Us In Good Ale. *Unknown.* EBEV; MiEL; OBCoV

(Bryng us in good ale, and bryng us in good ale!) OHMEL

Bring visions when you ring my bell. To a Guest. Vladislav Felitsinovich Khodasevich. TCRP, *tr.* by Michael Frayn

Bringers of Beethoven, The. Reiner Kunze. PoSu, *tr.* by Gisela and Gordon Brotherston

Bringing a Dead Man Back into Life. Russell Edson. TRP

Bringing its belly home, slung from a pole. (LL) Fetching Cows. Norman MacCaig. NoP-4; OxBC

Bringing on tears shed only for myself. (LL) Cruising with the Beach Boys. Dana Gioia. GeoHom; SwNoth

Bringing Our Sheaves with Us. Elizabeth Akers. TreFP

Bringing the plants inside that flourished. Wintering over at the End of the Century. Alvin Greenberg. UrbNat

Brings him with gold to the shrine, brings he in arms to the gate? (LL) Arthur Hugh Clough. EBEV; OxAEP-2 *Fr.* Amours de Voyage.

Brisk Chaunticleer his matins had begun. Morning-Piece; or, An Hymn for the Hay-Makers, A. Christopher Smart. NOEC

Brisk methinks I am, and fine. Anacreontic[k] Verse. Robert Herrick. PeLV

Brisk Wind, A. William Barnes. SCGP

Brissit brawnis and broken banis. Bewteis of the Fute-Ball, The. *Unknown.* OxBS

Bristol Channel, The. Thomas Edward Brown. NOBVV

Bristol, thine heart hath throbbed to glory: slaves. To the Right Hon. and Right Revd. Fredrick, Earl of Bristol, Bishop of Derry, Etc., Etc. Ann Yearsley. RWP

Bristowe Tragedie: or, The Dethe of Syr Charles Bawdin. Thomas Chatterton. OxBB

Britain. Oliver Goldsmith. NOEC; NPeEn *Fr.* Travel[l]er; or, A Prospect of Society, The.

Britain's Remembrancer Canto 4. George Wither.
  "If by mischance the people in the street." PBRV

Britannia, free from foes and foreign kings. Seneca. RomPo, *tr.* by Anthony James Boyle

Britannia rules the waves. James Kenneth Stephen. NOBL *Fr.* England and America.

Britannia's daughters, much more fair than nice. Edward Young. ECEV *Fr.* Satires.

Britannia's isles proclaim. To the First of August. Ann Plato. BlSi

Britannia's Pastorals. William Browne (1591–1643).
  Golden Age: Flower-weaving, The. NPeEn
  Golden Age, The. NOSC
  (Hail, Thou my Native Soil.) OxAEP-1
  Memory. OBEV
  Morning. NOSC

Brither-men wha eftir us live on. Ballat o the Hingit. François Villon. OBVE, *tr.* by Tom Scott

British Army now carries two rifles, The. Identification in Belfast (I.R.A. Bombing). Robert Lowell. OxBC

British Church, The. George Herbert. AngWePo; ESCV; PeECV

British Columbia. William Stafford. GifTon

British Connection, The. Padraic Fiacc. PNI

British Garden, A. Wes Magee. OBGa

British Grenadiers, The. *Unknown.* FaBoWar; OxBoLi

British Journalist, The. Humbert Wolfe. FaBoEE; OBCoV; OxBEV; OxBTC

British Leftish Poetry, 1930–40. Hugh MacDiarmid. FaBoTw; NoAM

British Museum Reading Room, The. Louis MacNeice. MoBrPo; NOBE

British [*or* Brittish] Church, The. Henry Vaughan. ESCV; PeECV

British Prison Ship, The. Philip Freneau.
  "Two hulks on Hudson's stormy bosom lie." TCAPo

Britomart at Isis' Church. Edmund Spenser. PoE *Fr.* Faerie Queene, The.

Britomart chaseth Ollyphant. Edmund Spenser. NAEL-6v1; NAEL-7v1 *Fr.* Faerie Queene, The.

Britomart in the House of the Enchanter Busyrane. Edmund Spenser. NPeEn *Fr.* Faerie Queene, The.

Brittania's Pastorals Book 2. William Browne (1591–1643).
  "Happyer those times were, when the Flaxen clew." PBRV

Brittle autumn leaves. Takao. JDP, *tr.* by Yoel Hoffmann

Brittle beauty [*or* beautie], that nature made so frail[e]. Frailty and Hurtfulness of Beauty, The. Henry Howard, Earl of Surrey. EnLoPo

Brittle pampas grass. Ryusai. JDP, *tr.* by Yoel Hoffmann

Brixton groans. Intercity Dub. Jane King. WaCA

Brken Promises. Sibby Anderson-Thompkins. InTrad

Bro Duncanson. C. S. Giscombe. GT *Fr.* "In" Sequence, The.

Bro, they been callin[g] that sister by the wrong name. (LL) Gwendolyn Brooks. Haki R. Madhubuti. ESEAA; OPRER

Broad-acred Ascra bore me. Mnasalcas. GrAn

Broad and ample he warms himself. Epigram. *Unknown.* NOIV, *tr.* by Thomas Kinsella

Broad and far-reaching, the level plain. Rhyme-Prose on the Desolate City. Pao Chao. CoBCP, *tr. by* Burton Watson

Broad and flat. Flat Mountain. Muso Soseki. EaWin, *tr. by* W. S. Merwin

Broad August burns in milky skies. Day-Dreams. William Canton. NOBVV

Broad-Ax, The. Walt Whitman. MoAmPo *Fr.* Song of the Broad-Axe.

Broad-backed hippopotamus, The. Hippopotamus, The. T. S. Eliot. AWP; NAEL-5v2; NAEL-6v2; OBMV; PAI; SacPr; TCAPo; VGW

Broad beach / Sea wind and the sea's irregular rhythm, The. Afternoon: Amagansett Beach. John Hall Wheelock. APT-1; PoRA

Broad Bean Sermon, The. Les A. Murray. BMAP; EmeKit; HarvBoo; MakPoe

Broad Is the Road. Isaac Watts. AH

Broad sun-stoned beaches. Midsummer, Tobago. Derek Walcott. MakPoe; OPOU; VCWP

Broader leaves collect, The. Dew at the Edge of a Leaf. Marvin Bell. InvLad

Broadway. Carl Sandburg. AiP

Broadway. Walt Whitman. NAAL-2v1; NAAL-3

Broadway Idyl, A. Mary E. Tucker. *See* Loew's Bridge: A Broadway Idyl

Broadway Melody. Arthur Freed. ReLy

Broadway Opening. Miguel Algarin. PueRic

Broagh. Seamus Heaney. FaBoVe; ModIr; NPeEn

Brocade City lies in dust and smoke. Becoming a Farmer. Tu Fu. CrYelRi, *tr. by* Sam Hamill

Brocade threads and summer reeds. Song for a Young General. Tu Fu. CrYelRi, *tr. by* Sam Hamill

Broceliande. Marilyn Hacker. ExTi

Brock. Paul Muldoon. NoAM; NoP-4

Broken, The. W. S. Merwin. LCAP-2

Broken ALTAR, Lord, thy servant rear[e]s, A. Altar, The. George Herbert. AngWePo; BASC; CABP; ChIV-1; ESCV; GeHe; NAEL-5v1; NAEL-6v1; NAEL-7v1; NoP-4; NOSC; TrCP

Broken and Beirut. Suheir Hammad. PoArWo

Broken Appointment, A. Thomas Hardy. HarvBoo; NAEL-5v2; NAEL-6v2; NoAM; NOBVV

(And marching Time drew on, and wore me numb.) NoP-4

Broken Boat, A. Tu Fu. CrYelRi, *tr. by* Sam Hamill

Broken bowl. Penny Harter. HA

Broken bundle of mirrors. . .!, A. (LL) Near Perigord. Ezra Pound. APT-1; FaBoMo

Broken Chain, The. Dora Greenwell. VWP

Broken Dark, The. Robert Earl Hayden. AWTN; GT

Broken Doll, The. Nuala Ni Dhomhnaill. BiHa; ModIr, *tr. by* John Montague

Broken-down hotel on an inhospitable sea, A. Far from Home. Nicholas Christopher. NoP-4

Broken down, somewhere near Bakersfield. To an Exeter City Cocktail Waitress. Jon Veinberg. GeoHom

Broken dream, A. Ichimu. JDP, *tr. by* Yoel Hoffmann

Broken-Face Gargoyles. Carl Sandburg. MoAmPo; OxBA

Broken Field, The. Sara Teasdale. APT-1

Broken Friendship. Mary Elizabeth Coleridge. VWP

Broken from the bursting bough. Apple, The. Ray Smith. TrCP

Broken Girth, The. Robert Graves. BIrV

Broken Heart, The. John Donne. EBEV; FSCP

Broken Heart, The. John Ford.

  Love's Martyrs. NOBE; NOSC

  "Oh [*or* O], no more, no more, too late." NOBE; NOSC

  (Song: "Oh no more, no more, too late") OxBSP

Broken Heart. Henrietta Cordelia Ray. CBWP-3

Broken Helix. Dina Ben-Lev. AmPoNex

Broken Home. William Stafford. NNaP

Broken Home, The. James Merrill. ColAP; HAP; HCAP; NAAL-2v2; NAAL-5; NoAM; NOBA; NoP-4; PoPoPo

Broken in pieces all asunder. Affliction (4). George Herbert. ESCV; GeHe; NOSC

Broken kite, sprawled. Elizabeth Searle Lamb. HA

Broken Lampstand, The. Wu Wei-yeh. CoBLCP; ColAnChi, *tr. by* Jonathan Chaves

Broken Men, The. Rudyard Kipling. HarvBoo

Broken Mirror, The. Bob Perelman. FTOS

Broken Necklace. Jill Bamber. Prnts

Broken Oar, The. Henry Wadsworth Longfellow. OxBSo

Broken or sold. Or given away. Or used and forgotten. Or lost. (LL) Green Light. Kenneth Fearing. PoE; VGW

Broken pillar of the wing jags from the clotted shoulder, The. Hurt Hawks. Robinson Jeffers. APT-1; ChAP; ColAP; HarvBoo; MoAmPo; NAAL-2v2; NOBA; NoAM; NoP-4; OWoS; OxBA; RB; TAP; TFi; TRP; UnPo

Broken Silence. Louis M. Abbey. BloBone

Broken sods, a whipped flag, The. Burial, A. Seamus Deane. CIP-2; PNI

Broken Sonnets. Kim Addonizio. OPRER

Broken Sword, The. Edward Rowland Sill. *See* Opportunity

Broken Tower, The. Hart Crane. APT-2; ColAP; MoAmPo; NOBA; NoAM; NoP-4; OxBA; PoPoPo

Broken Vase, The. Victor Hugo. SxFrPo, *tr. by* E. H. Blackmore and A. M. Blackmore

Broken View, A. Robert Francis. APT-2

Broken window, A. Michael McClintock. HA

Bronco Busting, Event #1. May Swenson. APT-2

Brontë Sisters, The. Anna Semionovna Prismanova. ARWW, *tr. by* Catriona Kelly

Bronx. Joseph Rodman Drake. APN-1

Bronx Park. Richard Foerster. UrbNat

Bronze by gold heard the hoofirons, steelyringing. James Joyce. PFTM-1 *Fr.* Ulysses.

Bronze clock brought, The. Margaret Atwood. PoetW *Fr.* Four Small Elegies.

Bronze god running, The. At Guaracara Park. Eric Roach. WoPo

Bronze Horseman, The. Alexander Sergeyevich Pushkin.

  "On a shore washed by desolate waves, *he* stood." WoPoe, *tr. by* D. M. Thomas

  Tale of St. Petersburg, A. WoPoe, *tr. by* D. M. Thomas

Bronze soldier hitches a bronze cape, The. In Memoriam Francis Ledwidge. Seamus Heaney. CIP-2; NoAM

Bronze warship-beaks, old voyage-avid weapons. Philip of Thessalonica. GrAn

Bronzeville Mother Loiters in Mississippi, A. Meanwhile, a Mississippi Mother Burns Bacon. Gwendolyn Brooks. ESEAA; IllVoic

Bronzeville Woman in a Red Hat. Gwendolyn Brooks. NALW

  (Bronzeville Woman in a Red Hat / Hires Out to Mrs. Miles.) GT

Brooding Grief. D. H. Lawrence. PoE

Brooding on the eightieth letter of *Fors Clavigera*. Geoffrey Hill. HAP; PoE *Fr.* Mercian Hymns.

Brooding upon its unexerted power. Gas and Hot Air. Morris Gilbert Bishop. OBAL

Brook, The. Tennyson. FHYEP *Fr.* Brook; An Idyl, The.

Brook; An Idyl, The. Tennyson. OxAEP-2

  Brook, The. FHYEP

Brook and road. Simplon Pass, The. William Wordsworth. NPeEn

Brook and road, The. William Wordsworth. CABP *Fr.* Prelude, The; Growth of a Poet's Mind [1805 vers.].

Brook glides on to the river, The. Reverie. Henrietta Cordelia Ray. CBWP-3

Brook in the City, A. Robert Frost. OxBA

Brook speaks with an eloquent tongue, The. Sent to Chief Abbot of Tung-lin Monastery. Su Tung-p'o (Su Shih). SuSp, *tr. by* Chiang Yee

Brooklyn. Michael S. Weaver. SpirFl

Brooklyn Botanic Garden, The. Timothy Liu. UrbNat

Brooklyn Bridge. Matthew Rohrer. NeAmPo

Brooklyn Bridge. William Jay Smith. CA

Brooklyn Bridge, Brooklyn Bridge. William Jay Smith. CA

Brooklyn Heights. John Wain. OxBTC

Brooklyn Narcissus. Paul Blackburn. PmAP

Broom, Green Broom. *Unknown.* OxBoLi; PoRA

Broom of Cowdenknows, The. *Unknown.* ESPB

Broom out the floor now, lay the fender by. June. Francis Ledwidge. BIrV; NOIV

Broom Squire's Song, The. *Unknown.* OxNR

Broom, The; or, The Flower of the Desert. Giacomo Leopardi.

  "Upon the arid shoulder." WoPoe, *tr. by* John Heath-Stubbs

Broomfield Hill, The. *Unknown.* ESPB; OxBB

Brooms. Charles Simic. NNaP

Brother, The. Peter Everwine. NNaP

Brother, The. Semion Yakovlevich Nadson. TrJP, *tr. by* H. Badanes

Brother and Sister. Lewis Carroll. NOxBChV

Brother and Sister. "George Eliot." NALW

  "But sudden came the barge's pitch-black prow." NOBVV

  I Cannot Choose but Think upon the Time. Son

  "Our brown canal was endless to my thought." NOBVV

  School Parted Us. Son

  "Those long days measured by my little feet." NOBVV

Brother and Sisters. Judith Wright. BMAP; FaBoWP

Brother, are you startled too at night from troubled dreaming. To My Brothers. Käthe Leichter. AuPH, *tr. by* Lowell A. Bangerter

Brother Ass, Brother Ass, you are full of fancies. James Keir Baxter. HarvBoo *Fr.* Jerusalem Sonnets.

Brother Baptis' on Woman Suffrage. Rosalie Jonas. BlSi

Brother Ben.   John Rybicki.   AmPoNex

Brother Body.   Peter Cooley.   OPRER

Brother, Can You Spare a Dime?   Jay Gorney.   APT-2; ReLy

Brother Fire.   Louis MacNeice.   AF; NOBE; NoAM

Brother, Hast Thou Wandered Far.   James Freeman Clarke.   AH

Brother, I Am Here.   "Shu Ting."   CarOv; GifTon, tr. by Carolyn Kizer and Y. H. Zhao

Brother, I am here. (LL)   "Shu Ting."   CarOv; GifTon, tr. by Carolyn Kizer and Y. H. Zhao

Brother, I pardon thee. (LL)   Sidney Lanier.   NOBA; TCAPo   Fr. Hymns of the Marshes.

Brother, I will not howl challenges.   We Are Equals.   Gwendoline C. Konie.   HAWP

Brother, if on the heels of war Western man.   My Brother.   Mikhail Naimy.   GraLe, tr. by Sharif Elmusa and Gregory Orfalea

Brother, it seems, you have been beaten.   Struggle for Life.   Frigyes Karinthy.   IQMS, tr. by Peter Zollman

Brother Jonathan, Brother Kafka.   Vincent O'Sullivan.
   "Figure who stands on the beach, A."   PeNZ
   "Last things/ the turning leaves slip in the wind."   PeNZ
   "To be in a place for spring and not have lived its winter."   PeNZ

Brother men who come along now, we.   Ballade of the Men Who Were Hanged.   François Villon.   WoPoe, tr. by Fred Chappell

Brother, my brother, whither do you pass?   To a Face in a Crowd.   Robert Penn Warren.   FuPo

Brother nightwatchman I have shared your way.   Nightwatchman.   Deborah Randall.   NeBl

Brother Number Three comes strolling along.   Tune: "Song of the Lunar Palace."   Lu Chih.   SuSp, tr. by Hellmut Wilhelm

Brother of the Streets.   Sam Cornish.   TRP

Brother soldiers—With them in battle I reached the waters of the Sava.   By the Waters of the Sava.   Uri Zvi Greenberg.   MHP, tr. by Ruth Finer Mintz

Brother Symmes conversed with her on the ship.   Ann Stanford.   CRP   Fr. Covenant of Grace, The.

Brother / This world.   Rāmprasād Sen.   SinGod, tr. by Rachel Fell McDermott

Brother, thou art gone before us: and thy saintly soul is flown.   Where the Wicked Cease from Troubling, and the Weary Are at Rest.   Henry Hart Milman.   SacPr

Brother, Though from Yonder Sky.   James Henry Bancroft.   AH

Brother, today I sit on the brick bench outside the house.   To My Brother Miguel.   César Vallejo.   PoetW; TCLAP, tr. by John Knoepfle and James Wright

Brother Where Dost Thou Dwell.   Henry David Thoreau.   NCAP

Brother, you who have the light, tell me where mine is.   Melancholy.   "Rubén Darío."   SpanPo, tr. by Anita Volland

Brotherhood.   Thomas Kinsella.   HarvBoo

Brotherhood.   Octavio Paz.   LoL, tr. by Eliot Weinberger

Brotherhood is not by the blood certainly, The.   Speech to Those Who Say Comrade.   Archibald MacLeish.   OxBA

Brotherhood of Men.   Richard Eberhart.   PoWW

Brotherless Sisters.   Unknown.   WoPoe, tr. by Charles Simic

Brothers.   James Weldon Johnson.   NAAAL

Brothers.   Heinrich Lersch.   FaBoWar, tr. by Christopher Middleton

Brothers.   Giuseppe Ungaretti.   PeFWW, tr. by Jonathan Griffin

Brothers, The.   Edwin Muir.   GTBS-P; HeIP-4

Brothers and men that shall after us be.   Ballad of the Gibbet.   François Villon.   AWP, tr. by Andrew Lang

Brothers and Sisters.   Michael Foley.   PNI

Brothers at the Bar.   Naomi Long Madgett.   NBV

Brothers bop & pop and be-bop in cities locked up.   B Network, The.   Haki R. Madhubuti.   IllVoic

Brothers / brothers / everywhere.   Utopia.   Jewel C. Latimore.   BPo

Brothers Grimm grew weaker and flickered, blue light, The.   California Girlhood, A.   Alice Notley.   PmAP

Brothers Loving Brothers.   Vega.   ISC

Brothers, my teeth hurt.   Strictly for Posterity.   Charles Simic.   NNaP

Brothers rolling around in the big back seat.   Vacation, 1969.   Dorothy Barresi.   SwNoth

Brothers / this big woman.   Song at midnight.   Lucille Clifton.   ErotSp; UnSA

Brought back from the tedium of dying.   Return of a Popular Statesman.   Vincent Buckley.   CBAP

Brought by the breeze.   "Shunzei's daughter."   ArkPo, tr. by Robert H. Brower and Earl Miner

Brought gifts / home for me.   My Daddy, Whenever He Went Some Place.   David Huddle.   PBCAP

Brought here in slave ships and pitched overboard.   Love Your Enemy.   Yusef Iman.   BPo; GI; TTY

Brought to bed by sickness, cut off from men.   Replying to a Poem from My Cousin Hui-lien.   Hsieh Ling-yün.   CoBCP, tr. by Burton Watson

Brought to burning eyelids sleep. (LL)   La Nuit Blanche.   Rudyard Kipling.   MoBrPo; UV

Brought up as I was to ask of the weather.   Point Grey.   Daryl Hine.   NOBC

Broughty Wa's.   Unknown.   ESPB

Brow, brow, brenty.   Unknown.   OxNR

Brow of a horse in that moment when, The.   Anastasia and Sandman.   Larry Levis.   BAP-97

Brown Adam.   Unknown.   ESPB; OxBB

Brown and furry / Caterpillar in a hurry.   Caterpillar, The.   Christina Georgina Rossetti.   FaBoVe

Brown berry of a man, bald head, A.   My Father's Dreams.   Cynthia Fuller.   Prnts

Brown Bess.   Rudyard Kipling.   FaBoWar

Brown, brittle, wait-a-bit weeds.   Indian Cave Jerry Ramsey Found, The.   William Stafford.   NoAM

Brown-coloured Trotter!   Praises of the Canna, The.   Unknown.   PeSAV, tr. by John Croumbie Brown

Brown Curtain, The.   Alberto Giacometti.   SurPaPo, tr. by Mary Ann Caws

Brown-dappled fawn, The.   Fawn in the Snow, The.   William Rose Benét.   MoAmPo

Brown enormous odor he lived by, The.   Prodigal, The.   Elizabeth Bishop.   APT-2; ChIV-2; CoAP; LCAP-2; TwCP

Brown-faced nurse has murmured something unintelligible, The.   Microcosmos.   Susan Miles.   OxBTC

Brown Family, The.   Colleen Thibaudeau.   NOBC

Brown gingham, pink, and skirts of Alice blue. (LL)   In an Iridescent Time.   Ruth Stone.   MoAmPo; NALW; OxWW

Brown Girl, The.   Unknown.   ESPB
   (Bonny Brown Girl, The.)   OxBB

Brown Girl, Blonde Okie.   Gary Soto.   NOxBChV

Brown Girl Dead, A.   Countee Cullen.   GT; TAP

Brown harbour of our land.   Far from the Beach.   Alda do Espírito Santo.   HAWP, tr. by Jacques-Noël Gouat

Brown in the snow, a car with a heater.   Strangers.   William Stafford.   NNaP

Brown lilac, roses filled with rain;.   World on Sunday.   James McAuley.   BMAP

Brown lived at such a lofty farm.   Brown's Descent; or, The Willy-Nilly.   Robert Frost.   MoAmPo; PoRA

Brown Lullaby.   Adam Small.   PeSAV

Brown men mesh the brown pools with nets.   Dragonfish, The.   John Balaban.   CDa

Brown o' San Juan.   Henry Cuyler Bunner.   OBAL   Fr. Home.

Brown of her—her eyes, her hair, her hair, The[!] (LL)   Farmer's Bride, The.   Charlotte Mew.   BWW; BoLoP; EBNV; FaBoWP; MoBrPo; NALW; OxBTC; WPE

Brown of Ossawatomie.   John Greenleaf Whittier.   NCAP

Brown Owls come here in the blue evening.   Healing Songs.   Tohono O'odham (Owl Woman) (Juana Manwell).   SWaP, tr. by Frances Densmore

Brown Penny.   W. B. Yeats.   BoLoP; FaBoCh

Brown Pot.   Ray Gonzalez.   TouFir

Brown rat has taken up residence with me, A.   Little Citizen, Little Survivor.   Hayden Carruth.   OPRER

Brown Robyn's [or Robin's] Confession.   Unknown.   ESPB; OxBB

Brown semicolons move doggedly.   Ant Trap, The.   Joe Rosenblatt.   NOBC

Brown Skin Girl.   Tommy McClennan.   FaBoVe

Brown-skinned boy asleep beneath a clump, A.   Mind Pictures.   Beatrice Hastings.   PeSAV

Brown Thrush, The.   Lucy Larcom.   OBCA
   (There's a merry brown thrush sitting up in the tree.)   NOxBChV

Brownies' Celebration, The.   Palmer Cox.   OBCA

Browning.   Robert Louis Stevenson.   NOBVV

Browning makes the verses.   Browning.   Robert Louis Stevenson.   NOBVV

Browning of leaves, The.   Querida, La.   Bino A. Realuyo.   ReBoTo

Brown's Descent; or, The Willy-Nilly.   Robert Frost.   MoAmPo; PoRA

Bruadar and Smith and Glinn.   Curse, A.   Unknown.   BIrV, tr. by Douglas Hyde

Bruce, The.   John Barbour.
   Before Bannockburn.   OxBS
   Book 16: Bruce in Ireland halts his army at Limerick so that a laundrywoman may give birth.
   "Syne went thai southwart in the land."   NePenScot
   Freedom [or Fredome].   FaBoCh; NePenScot; OBEV; OxBS; TreFP

Bruce and Nina.   Clarence Major.   BodElec

Bruce did-in 24 bluegills with a big spoon.   Bruce and the Bluegills.   David Marlatt.   AmPoNex

Bruce Ismay's Soliloquy.   Derek Mahon.   PNI

Brueghel in Naples.   Dannie Abse.   NIP-4

Brueghel's Winter.   Walter De la Mare.   GS

Bruise of This, The. Mark Wunderlich. NeAmPo

Bruised Reed Shall He Not Break, A. Christina Georgina Rossetti. OxAEP-2

Bruisingly cradled in a Harvard chair. Louis Edward Sissman. NoP-4 *Fr.* Dying: An Introduction.

Brummell at Calais. John Glassco. MoCV

Brunanburg. *Unknown.* PoE, *tr. by* Kemp Malone

Bruno, our father, joyous, gentle, old. Epitaph for Bruno of Angers. Marbod of Rennes. MLL, *tr. by* Helen Waddell

Brush Fire. Fily-Dabo Sissoko. NegPo, *tr. by* Ellen Conroy Kennedy

Brush-Fire. U Tam'si Tchicaya. NegPo, *tr. by* Sangodare Akanji (Fire the river that's to say, The.) PBMAP

Brush in rocks, draw a stream. Yün Shou-p'ing. CoBLCP *Fr.* Landscape.

Brush of evening clouds, A. To the Tune "Intoxicated with Shadows of Flowers." Yü Ch'ing-tsêng. EroLit, *tr. by* Chung Ling and Kenneth Rexroth

Brush up Your Shakespeare. Cole Porter. OBAL; OBCoV; ReLy

Brushing away the dust, I opened the broken box. In a Book-Box I Found the Lost Manuscript of a Poem Sent to Me by the Late Kao [Ch'i]. Chang Yü. CoBLCP, *tr. by* Jonathan Chaves

Brushing flies. Buson. EH, *tr. by* Robert Hass

Brushing my clothes, I followed the sandy dikes. Passing White Banks Pavilion. Hsieh Ling-yün. SuSp, *tr. by* Francis Westbrook

Brushing my sins. Raymond Roseliep. HA

Brussels and Oxford. William Hurrell Mallock. EBVV

Brussels in Winter. W. H. Auden. OxBTC

Brussels: Simple Frescos 1. Paul Verlaine. SxFrPo, *tr. by* Martin Sorrell

Brussels: Simple Frescos 2. Paul Verlaine. SxFrPo, *tr. by* Martin Sorrell

Brut, The. Layamon.
  Arthur's Dream. NAEL-7v1
  Passing of Arthur, The. PoE

Brutal shuddering machines, yellow, bite into given earth. Landscape Gardeners, The. Geoffrey Grigson. OBGa

Brutal to Love. Queen of Carthage, The. Louise Glück. AmFaPo

Brute Image. John Ashbery. NoP-4

Brute Strength. Wanda Coleman. PmAP

Brutish recall. Echo. Robert Creeley. BodElec

Brutus. Abraham Cowley. BASC

Brutus' Last Song. Christiania Whitehead. NeBl

Bryan and Pereene. James Grainger. ECEV
  "North-east wind did briskly blow, The." VerBaPo

Bryan, Bryan, Bryan, Bryan. Nicholas Vachel Lindsay. APT-1; OxBA; OxBoLi

Bryan Ferry. B.D. Love. SwNoth

Bryan O'Lynn was a Dutchman born. Brian O'Linn. *Unknown.* NBLV; RB

Bryant. James Russell Lowell. NOBA; TAP *Fr.* Fable for Critics, A.

Bryce & Tomlins. Kenneth Fearing. APT-2

Brynbwrla. Kingsley Amis. NOBL *Fr.* Evans Country, The.

Bryng us all to his blisse! (LL) Robin Hood and the Monk. *Unknown.* ESPB; OBNV

Bubba Esther, 1888. Ruth Whitman. TaR

Bubble, The. Richard Crashaw. PBRV *Fr.* Bulla.

Bubble; a Song, The. Robert Herrick. CaPo

Bubble of Air. Muriel Rukeyser. TaR

Bubbled baby gave an abrupt burp, The. Edmund Wilson. OBCoV *Fr.* Easy Exercises in the Use of Difficult Words.

Bubbled with brimming kisses at my mouth. (LL) Dante Gabriel Rossetti. CABP; NAEL-5v2; NAEL-6v2; OxBSo *Fr.* House of Life, The.

Bubbles on the Water. Yang Wan-li. SuSp, *tr. by* Jonathan Chaves

Bubbling brook doth leap when I come by, The. Nature. Jones Very. ColAP

Bubbling Wine. Abu Zakariya. TTY, *tr. by* A. J. Arberry

Buck in the Snow, The. Edna St. Vincent Millay. ColAP; NALW; NoP-4

Buckdancer's Choice. James Dickey. HeIP-4; NOBA; NoAM; NoP-4

Bucket, The. Rose Romano. UnSA

Bucket, The. Samuel Woodworth. *See* Old Oaken Bucket, The

Bucket of azaleas, A. Basho. EH, *tr. by* Robert Hass

Buckets in my head stand open, The. Buckets in My Head, The. Lucie Thésée. SurWo, *tr. by* Myrna Bell Rochester

Buckles glitter, billies lean, The. American Twilights, 1957. James Wright (1927–80). CoAP

Buckroe, after the Season, 1942. Virginia Hamilton Adair. APT-2

Bucolic. Aimé Césaire. VCWP

Bucolic Eclogues. Ethel Louisa Mason Anderson.
  Waking, Child, While You Slept. WPE

Bud. William T. Crawley III. InTrad

Bud, The. Saint Francis and the Sow. Galway Kinnell. AmFaPo; ChAP; InPK-6; NAAL-5; RB

Bud fantasies, dreams of an ear of corn. Paean to Eve's Apple. James Liddy. CIP-2

Budd, The. Edmund Waller. PBRV

Buddgelin Bey. Rex Marshall. IBA

Buddha. Arno Holz. AWP, *tr. by* William Ellery Leonard

Buddha. Jack Kerouac. BB

Buddha, The. Daya Pawar. OMIP, *tr. by* Eleanor Zelliot

Buddha and Brahma. Henry Adams. APN-2

Buddha / Cherry flowers. Hoitsu. ZenPo, *tr. by* Takashi Ikemoto and Lucien Stryk

Buddha in Glory. Rainer Maria Rilke. EnlH, *tr. by* Stephen Mitchell

Buddha is not once strange. In a Warm Bath. Carl Rakosi. TAP

Buddha, known to men by many names, The. Buddha and Brahma. Henry Adams. APN-2

Buddha Law / Shining. Issa. ZenPo, *tr. by* Takashi Ikemoto and Lucien Stryk

Buddha of Sōkkuram, The. Shirley Kaufman. GifTon

Buddha's death-day / Old hands. Basho. ZenPo, *tr. by* Takashi Ikemoto and Lucien Stryk

Buddha's Nirvana / Beyond flowers. Issa. ZenPo, *tr. by* Takashi Ikemoto and Lucien Stryk

Buddha's Satori. Muso Soseki. EaWin, *tr. by* W. S. Merwin

Buddha took some Autumn leaves. Kenneth Rexroth. BLT *Fr.* City of the Moon, The.

Buddhist monastery across a stone bridge, A. I Went to Gold Mountain to Visit a Ch'an Master But He Was Not at Home. Mo Shih-lung. CoBLCP, *tr. by* Jonathan Chaves

Buddhist Monk Cut and Burned His Own Flesh to Make The Rains Stop—A Man from His Native Place Asked Me to Write a Poem to Send to Him, A. Hsü Wei. CoBLCP; ColAnChi, *tr. by* Jonathan Chaves

Budding floweret blushes at the light, The. Thomas Chatterton. OxAEP-1 *Fr.* Aella; a Tragycal Enterlude.

Budding young playwright named Coward, A. Limerick: "Budding young playwright named Coward, A." Doris Pulsford. PeLi

Buddy. Andrew Hudgins. Unle

Buddy Bolden Cylinder, The. William Matthews. SeSe

Buddy, can you spare a dime? (LL) Brother, Can You Spare a Dime? Jay Gorney. APT-2; ReLy

Buddy, have you heard? (LL) Deferred. Langston Hughes. APSN; APT-2

Buddy Holly. David Wojahn. SwNoth

Buddy Holly Poem, The. Maurice Kilwein Guevara. TouFir

Buddy Holly Watching *Rebel Without a Cause*, Lubbock, Texas, 1956. David Wojahn. PBCAP *Fr.* Mystery Train: A Sequence.

Budgie Finds His Voice. Wendy Cope. UV

Budging the sluggard ripples of the Somme. Hospital Barge at Cérisy. Wilfred Owen. HarvBoo; RB; TCAWP

Buds from winter's frost-work lift, The. Coming of Spring, The. Henrietta Cordelia Ray. CBWP-3

Buffalo are coming. We will feed and feast. We wish to be fortunate and we expect it, The. *Unknown.* APN-2 *Fr.* Minnetare Songs.

Buffalo Bill opens a pawn shop on the reservation. Evolution. Sherman Alexie. NeAmPo; PoPoPo

Buffalo Bill's. Portrait. E. E. Cummings. HeIP-4; InPK-6; NAAL-2v2; NIP-4; NOBA; OxBSP; PoE; RB; TAP; VGW

Buffalo Blood. Lance Henson. STP

Buffalo Boy. Huang T'ing-chien. SuSp, *tr. by* Michael E. Workman

Buffalo breathed quietly inside, The. Crow-Children Walk My Circles in the Snow, The. Ray A. Young Bear. CDW

Buffalo, buffalo, buffalo, buffalo. Death Chant. Peter Blue Cloud. VoR

Buffalo burned sage. Kin. Ruth Forman. AmPoNex

Buffalo Dusk. Carl Sandburg. ChAP; OBCA

Buffalo Evening. Robert Creeley. BodElec

Buffalo Gals. *Unknown.* APN-2

Buffalo—Isle of Wight Power Cable. Anselm Hollo. PoM

Buffalo Poem #1. Geary Hobson. UrbNat

Buffalo Skinners, The. *Unknown.* RB

Buffaloes are gone, The. Buffalo Dusk. Carl Sandburg. ChAP; OBCA

Buffeted by the waves. Archilochus. SaLy, *tr. by* Diane Rayor

Bufo. Pope. OBSV *Fr.* Epistle to Dr. Arbuthnot.

Bug, flower, bird on slipware fired and fluted. Syrinx. James Merrill. HCAP

Bugle blows, setting the marchers moving, The. Army Ballad. Wang Wei. ColAnChi, *tr. by* Stephen Owen

Bugler boy from barrack (it is over the hill), A. Bugler's First Communion, The. Gerard Manley Hopkins. NoAM

Bugler's First Communion, The. Gerard Manley Hopkins. NoAM

Bugs. Mary Ann Hoberman. OBCA
  Combinations. OBSP

Bugs. *Unknown.* HHAm

Buik of Alexander, The. John Barbour.

Prologue to the Avowis of Alexander. OxBS

Build cities. Turn. Andrée Chedid. PoArWo, *tr. by* Lucy McNair

Build for yourself a strong-box. Then Laugh. Bertha Adams Backus. PWR; PoToHe

"Build me a nation," said the Lord. Then and Now. Frances Ellen Watkins Harper. PWR

"Build me straight, O worthy Master!" Building of the Ship, The. Henry Wadsworth Longfellow. CBCWP

Build over me no marble monument. Alcestis to Admetus. Mary Elizabeth Coleridge. ViWPN

Builder demolishes houses, The. Dialectics. Edvard Kocbek. PoSu

Builder's Lesson, A. John Boyle O'Reilly. PWR; PoToHe

Builders. Dmitry [*or* Dmitrii] Borisovich Kedrin. TCRP, *tr. by* Albert C. Todd

Builders, The. Henry Wadsworth Longfellow. PWR

Building. I. E. Dickenga. PWR

Building. Gary Snyder. BB

Building, The. As You Come In. Anne Marriott. NOBC

Building an Outhouse. Ronald Wallace. PBCAP

Building in Stone. Sylvia Townsend Warner. MoBrPo

Building Nicole's Mama. Patricia Smith. SpirFl

Building of a New Church, The. *Unknown.* FaBoEE; HHAm

Building of Carthage, The. Virgil [*or* Vergil]. OBVE, *tr. by* Gawin [*or* Gavin] Douglas   *Fr.* Aeneid [*or* Eneados, *Aeneis*], The.

Building of Carthage, The. Virgil [*or* Vergil]. OBVE, *tr. by* John Dryden *Fr.* Aeneid [*or* Eneados, *Aeneis*], The.

Building of the Ship, The. Henry Wadsworth Longfellow. CBCWP

   "And as he laboured, his mind ran o'er." FaBoWar

   Ship of State, The. PWR

   "Then the Master." NAAL-2v1; NAAL-3

Building Society Blues. Roger Roughton. SPE

Building the Bridge. Will Allen Dromgoole. WeW-3

   (Bridge-Builder, The.) PoToHe

Building the cart again. (LL) Ox Cart Man. Donald Hall. LCAP-2; LoL

Building the Dam. Reuel Denney. YaYoPo

Building the dollhouse. Rosamond Haas. HA

Building: The New London Hospital. Bill Griffiths.

   Fragment 1. Oth

   Fragment 4. Oth

   Fragment 9. Oth

   Fragment 11. Oth

   Fragment 12. Oth

   Fragment 13. Oth

   Fragment 18. Oth

   Shepherd's Calendar. Oth

   Shepherd's Calendar cont'd. Oth

   Ship, The. Oth

   South Song. Oth

Building upon the Sand. Eliza Cook. TreFP

Buildings are at their stations, untimely, The. Elegy for New York, The. Douglas Crase. MakPoe

Buildings of the, The. Sherley Anne Williams. GeoHom *Fr.* Iconography of Childhood, The.

Built by Hank Wurlitzer, 7 ft. 8 inches, to house the first petrocommunications system. Big Bar. Kenward Elmslie. PmAP

Built for a cotton king, who loved the view. Richard Murphy. ModIr *Fr.* Price of Stone, The.

Buke of the Howlat, The. Sir Richard Holland.

   Douglas and the Bruce's Heart. OxBS

Bulahdelah—Taree Holiday Song Cycle, The. Les A. Murray.

   "People are eating dinner in that country north of Legge's Lake, The." BMAP

Bulbs do not winter well, The. January Ovaries. Susan Hahn. ExTi

Bulge, The. George Johnston. MoCV

Bulging rampart streaked with pink and jade, The. Watchers, The. Charles Spear. PeNZ

Bulging yellow clouds. Richard Wright. APT-2

Bulin File, The. Gu Cheng.

   Bulin is Dead, It Seems. PFTM-2, *tr. by* Eva Hung

   Bulin Met Bandit. PFTM-2, *tr. by* Eva Hung

   Discovery. PFTM-2; VCWP, *tr. by* Eva Hung

Bulin is Dead, It Seems. Gu Cheng. PFTM-2, *tr. by* Eva Hung *Fr.* Bulin File, The.

Bulin Met Bandit. Gu Cheng. PFTM-2, *tr. by* Eva Hung *Fr.* Bulin File, The.

Bulk of these years is already gone out of mind, The. Orientius. WoPoe, *tr. by* John Peck *Fr.* Poem on Divine Providence.

Bulkeley, Hunt, Willard, Hosmer, Meriam, Flint. Hamatreya. Ralph Waldo Emerson. TCAPo

Bulkhead sweating, and under naked bulbs, The. Mess Deck. Alan Ross. FaBoWar; PoWW

Bull, The. Ralph Hodgson. MoBrPo; OBMV; OxBTC

Bull, The. Victoria Mary Sackville-West. WPE

Bull, The. William Carlos Williams. TwCP

Bull and Egret. Chinua Achebe. PFTM-2

Bull Calf, The. Irving Layton. InPK-6

Bull does not know you, nor the fig tree, The. Federico García Lorca. WoPoe, *tr. by* Alan S. Trueblood *Fr.* Lament for Ignacio Sanchez Mejias.

Bull's eyes and targets. *Unknown.* OxNR

Bull, the Fleece are crammed [*or* cramm'd], and not a room, The. Tennyson. NOBVV; PeVV

Bulla. Richard Crashaw.

   Bubble, The. PBRV

Bulldozers come, they rip, The. Marge Piercy. NBLV *Fr.* Sand Roads.

Bullet passed, The. In a Plantation. Basil T. Paquet. CDa

Bullets whip the air this last afternoon. Conjectural Poem. Jorge Luis Borges. TCLAP, *tr. by* Norman Thomas Di Giovanni

Bullfight. Miroslav Holub. RB, *tr. by* Ian Milner and Jarmila Milner

Bullfinch in Town, The. Henrietta, Lady Luxborough Knight. ECWP

Bullfrog. Brendan Galvin. PoCoUp

Bullhead. John Engels. MoASP

Bullock, The. Prelude. Federico García Lorca. PFTM-1

Bullocky. Judith Wright. CBAP

Bully. Martín Espada. LTA

Bully night / I do not like. Bully Night. Roger McGough. OTCP

Bulosan Listens to a Recording of Robert Johson. Alfred Encarnacion. OpBo

   (Bulosan Listens to a Recording of Robert Johnson.) LTA; UnSA

Bum's Rush. Michael Dransfield. CBAP

Bumblebee, You Saw Big Mama. Jayne Cortez. SurWo

Bumbler for sure, A. Bee. Philip Booth. PoCoUp

Buna. Primo Levi. AF, *tr. by* Ruth Feldman

Bunch of Blue Ribbons, The. *Unknown.* ReMoGo

Bunch of Drifter Sons Hollered, A. Gottfried Benn. PFTM-1

Bunch of frightened rookies, A. This Is the Army, Mr. Jones. Irving Berlin. ReLy

Bunch of Grapes, The. George Herbert. ChIV-1; ESCV; GeHe; NAEL-5v1; NAEL-6v1; NAEL-7v1; NOSC; TOF

Bunch of grapes leaves Bacchus satisfied, A. *Unknown.* PriapPo, *tr. by* Richard W. Hooper *Fr.* Priapus Poems, The.

Bunch of Larks, The. Robert Leighton. EBVV

Bunch of orange buds by mail from Florida, A. (LL) Orange Buds by Mail from Florida. Walt Whitman. NAAL-2v1; NAAL-3

Bunch of the boys were whooping it up in the Malamute saloon, A. Shooting of Dan McGrew, The. Robert W. Service. BRP; EBNV; PoRA; RB; UV

Bunches of carnations in a tin pitcher. Joke, A. Aleksander Wat. BLT

Bundaberg Rum. W. N. Scott. NOBAu

Bundled by Tuc's tight jagged. Notes on a Visit to Le Tuc d'Audoubert. Clayton Eshleman. PmAP

Bundles. Carl Sandburg. MoAmPo

Bundles for Them. Gertrude Stein. PFTM-1

Bungaloid Growth. Colin Ellis. FaBoEE

Bungalow in Quogue. P. G. Wodehouse. ReLy

Bungalows, The. John Ashbery. CoAP

Bungler, The. Amy Lowell. LW

Bunk Johnson Blowing. Muriel Rukeyser. SeSe

Bunker's Hill, or the Soldier's Lamentation. John Freeth. NOEC

Bunker the ambassador. Does Bunker have a bunker? Ambassador, The. Bruce Weigl. CDa

Bunkers, The. Michael O'Loughlin. PBCIP *Fr.* Shards, The.

Bunnies are a feeble folk, The. Bunny Romance, A. Oliver Herford. OBCA

Bunnies Romance, A. Oliver Herford. OBCA

Bunthorne's Song. Sir William Schwenck Gilbert. CABP *Fr.* Patience.

Buonaparte. Tennyson. Son

Buoy-Bell, The. Charles Tennyson Turner. GSo; PeVV; Son

Burd Ellen and Young Tamlane. *Unknown.* ESPB

Burd Helen was her mother's dear. Broughty Wa's. *Unknown.* ESPB

Burd Isabel and Earl Patrick. *Unknown.* ESPB

Burden. Peter Kane Dufault. NoP-4

Burden, The. Anne Caston. NAPBL

Burden, The. Francesca Yetunde Pereira. PBA

Burden Lifters, The. Michael Waters. SwNoth

Burden of Decision, The. Peter Everwine. NNaP

Burden of Easter Vigil, A. Lionel Pigot Johnson. SacPr

Burdened. Ella Wheeler Wilcox. SWaP

Burdened with family feelings, I went. Burnt. Boris Abramovich Slutsky [*or* Slutskii]. HP, *tr. by* Daniel Weissbort

Burdens. Edward Dowden. NOBVV

Burdens. Laura Riesco. TANSG, *tr. by* Shaun Griffin and Emma Sepúlveda-Pulvirenti

Burdens of All, The. Frances Ellen Watkins Harper. PWR

Burdock leaves beside the ledge, The. Brisk Wind, A. William Barnes. SCGP

Bureau 2. Josephine Miles. NALW

Bureau of Labor Statistics, The. Bureaucratic Limerick. William Harmon. OBAL

Bureaucratic Limerick. William Harmon. OBAL

Burgeoning trees are thick with leaves, The. East Wind. Ou-yang Hsiu. OHPC, *tr. by* Kenneth Rexroth

Burgess was drunk when he was admitted. Hospital—Retrospections, The. Kenneth Mackenzie. CBAP

Burghers, The. Thomas Hardy. EBNV

Burglar of Babylon, The. Elizabeth Bishop. RB

Burial. Paulin Joachim. TTY, *tr. by* Oliver Bernard

Burial. Henry Vaughan. GeHe

Burial, A. Seamus Deane. CIP-2; PNI

Burial, The. John Webster. NOSC; PoRA; SCGP   *Fr.* Devil's Law Case, The.

Burial Detail. Andrew Hudgins. CBCWP

Burial Flags. Ralph Nixon Currey. PoWW

Burial in the East. Pablo Neruda. TRP, *tr. by* Ben Belitt

Burial of a Fairy Queen. Mary E. Tucker. CBWP-1

Burial of a Fisherman in Hydra. Grace Schulman. BoWoP

Burial of An Irish President. Austin Clarke. BIrV

Burial of King Cormac, The. Sir Samuel Ferguson. NOIV

Burial of Latané, The. John Reuben Thompson. CBCWP

Burial of Sir John Moore [after [*or* at] Corunna], The. Charles Wolfe. FaBoWar; GTBS-P; NOBE; NOBRP; OBEV; OBWP; OxAEP-2; OxBEV; PWR; PoRA; TFi; TreFP; UV

Burial of the Dead, The. T. S. Eliot. NPeEn   *Fr.* Waste Land, The.

Burial of the Dog. Susan Musgrave. NoAM

Burial of the Spirit of a Young Poet. Richard Hughes. MoBrPo

Burial Path. Ruth Bidgood. AngWePo

Burial Songs. *Unknown.* ChiP, *tr. by* Arthur Waley

Burials. George Crabbe.   *Fr.* Parish Register, The.

Burials. Amelia Blossom Pegram. HAWP

Buried above ground. (LL) Lines Written during a Period of Insanity. William Cowper. EBEV; HAP; NOEC; NPeEn; NoP-4

Buried alive. Labyrinth. Jaime Torres Bodet. TCLAP, *tr. by* Sonja Karsen

Buried at Springs. James Schuyler. CoAP; PoM

Buried Birds, The. Ida G. M. Gerhardt. TuT, *tr. by* Medbh McGuckian

Buried Graves, The. Brad Leithauser. NoP-4

Buried in this low grave his pale limbs lie. Epitaph for One Killed at Roncesvalles. *Unknown.* MLL, *tr. by* Helen Waddell

Buried Life, The. Matthew Arnold. FHYEP; NAEL-5v2; NAEL-6v2

Buried shrine disgorges through its foul, The. Tomb of Charles Baudelaire, The. Stéphane Mallarmé. SxFrPo, *tr. by* E. H. Blackmore and A. M. Blackmore

Buried Stream, The. James Keir Baxter. HarvBoo; OxBC

Buried in the blue vault of the air? (LL) Dead Mole, A. Andrew Young. GTBS-P; NePenScot; OxBSP

Burke. Samuel Taylor Coleridge. CenSon   *Fr.* Effusions.

Burlesque dancer, The. Striptease. Andrey [*or* Andrei] Andreievich Voznesensky [*or* Voznesenskii]. TCRusP, *tr. by* Daniel Weissbort

Burlesque Ode, on the Author's Clearing a New House of Some Workmen, A. George Keate.
"Midst the fair range of buildings which, new-reared." NOEC

Burlesque upon the Great Frost. Charles Cotton.
"But, to leave fooling, I assure ye." OBCoV

Burlington Bertie from Bow. William Hargreaves. OBCoV

Burly, dozing, humble-bee. Humble-Bee, The. Ralph Waldo Emerson. APN-1; NCAP; NOBA; OxBA

Burma-Shave Roadside Signs. *Unknown.* OBCoV   *Fr.* Advertising Rhymes.

Burmese Figures. *Unknown.* EaWin, *tr. by* W. S. Merwin

Burn drowns steadily in its own downpour, The. Waterfall. Seamus Heaney. HeIP-4

Burn generations. People of Fire. Nidaa Khoury. DTA, *tr. by* Karen Alkalay-Gut

Burn not too oft who flutters at thy flame. Meleager. GrAn

Burn Out Burn Quick. Abraham Reisen. TrJP, *tr. by* Joseph Leftwich

Burn Ovid with the rest. Lovers will find. Penal Law. Austin Clarke. BoLoP; GTBS-P; ModIr; NOIV; OxBEV; PAI

Burn the generations. People of Fire. Nidaa Khoury. PoArWo, *tr. by* Linda Zisquit

Burn this Sari. A. Jayaprabha. OMIP

Burned and dusty garden said, The. Athenian Garden, An. Trumbull Stickney. APN-2; NoP-4

Burned Bridge, The. Ruth Stone. WPE

Burnie bee, burnie bee. *Unknown.* ReMoGo

Burning. Galway Kinnell. CoAP

Burning. Gary Snyder. NeAP; PoM   *Fr.* Myths and Texts.

Burning, The. N. Scott Momaday. HATNAP

Burning Babe, The. Robert Southwell. ChrPo; ESCV; FaBoCh; HAP; HeIP-4; NAEL-5v1; NAEL-6v1; NAEL-7v1; NOBE; NOCV; NoSic; OBCP; OBEV; OxAEP-1; OxBEV; PAI; RB; SCGP; SacPr; TFi; TOF; TRP; TrCP; WoPoe
(As I in hoarie Winters night stoode shivering in the snow.) AEP; PBRV; PoPoPo

Burning / burning / burning / there was finally something. Crow's Last Stand. Ted Hughes. HarvBoo

Burning Bush. Alison Apotheker. PoCoUp

Burning Bush. Martin Feinstein. TrJP

Burning dinner is not incompetence but war. (LL) What's That Smell in the Kitchen? Marge Piercy. NBLV; NIL-7; NIP-4

Burning Drift-Wood. John Greenleaf Whittier. APN-1

Burning Field, The. Velemir [*or* Viktor Vladimirovich] Khlebnikov. TCRusP, *tr. by* Kathy Lewis and Bob Perelman   *Fr.* Laundress, The.

Burning Graves at Netherton, The. Roy Fisher. Oth

Burning Hills. Michael Ondaatje. NOBC; NoAM

Burning in Secret. "Shunzei's daughter." WoPoe, *tr. by* Steven D. Carter

Burning Island. Gary Snyder. APSN; VCAP

Burning my h[e]art who had him kindly warm[e]d. (LL) Mary Sidney Wroth, Countess of Montgomery. NPeEn; OxBSo; PBRV   *Fr.* Pamphilia to Amphilanthus.

Burning of Auchindown. *Unknown.* *See* Willie Macintosh

Burning of Paper instead of Children, The. Adrienne Rich. HarvBoo; LCAP-2; NAAL-2v2; VCAP

Burning of the Books, The. Bertolt Brecht. PoSu, *tr. by* John Willeh

Burning of the Law, The. Meïr of Rothenburg. TrJP, *tr. by* Nina Davis Salaman

Burning of the Leaves, The. Laurence Binyon.
"Now is the time for the burning of the leaves." GTBS-P; NOBE; NPeEn; OxBTC

Burning of the Temple, The. Isaac Rosenberg. FaBoMo; PeFWW; TrJP

Burning Off. Geoffrey Dutton. NOBAu

Burning Oneself Out. Adrienne Rich. BodElec

Burning Oneself to Death. Shinkichi Takahashi. ZenPo, *tr. by* Takashi Ikemoto and Lucien Stryk

Burning Shewolf. Vasco [*or* Vasko] Popa. PFTM-2; VCWP, *tr. by* Charles Simic

Burning Shit at An Khe. Bruce Weigl. CDa
(Into that pit / I had to climb down.) AF

Burning Spear wails with a hole, a hollow, in his voice. Music. Rohan B. Preston. WaCA

Burning the Cat. W. S. Merwin. NIP-4

Burning the Christmas Greens. William Carlos Williams. APT-1; ChrPo; NAAL-2v2; NAAL-5; NOBA; NoAM

Burning the Dreams. Muriel Rukeyser. AF

Burning the Letters. Randall Jarrell. MoAmPo

Burning the Small Dead. Gary Snyder. NNaP

Burning under the bleached scalp; behind dry lips / a loaded gun. (LL) Face to Face. Adrienne Rich. NAAL-2v2; NoAM

Burning Want. Les A. Murray. HarvBoo

Burning Wheel, The. Aldous Leonard Huxley. ChIV-1

Burnished, burned-out, still burning as the year. Public Garden, The. Robert Lowell. OBGa; PoRA; TAP

Burns up the building: Lord forbid the same. (LL) Address to the Soul Occasioned by a Rain, An. Edward Taylor. NAAL-2v1; NOBA; OxBA

Burnt. Boris Abramovich Slutsky [*or* Slutskii]. HP, *tr. by* Daniel Weissbort

Burnt Bush, The. Jack R. Clemo. FaBoTw

Burnt Child, The. W. S. Merwin. NoAM

Burnt Lands. G. D. Roberts. GSo

Burnt Norton. T. S. Eliot. APT-1; HarvBoo; MoAmPo; NAAL-2v2; NAAL-5; PoE   *Fr.* Four Quartets.

Burnt out year, The. New Year Letter. Edward Kamau Brathwaite. GT

Burnt Ship, A. John Donne. EBEV; FaBoWar; InPK-6; OBWP

Burnt Sienna. Norman Henry Pritchard, II. GT

Burnt sienna and sun they lie. Monarchs Steering. Shirley Lim. GeoHom

Burragorang. Nan McDonald. NOBAu

Burrel Bullai. Rex Marshall. IBA

Burro once, sent by express, A. Advice to Travelers. Walker Gibson. NBLV

Burroughs. Robert Glück. WiU

Burrowing deep into earth until the grave is complete. Wolf. Peter Blue Cloud. HATNAP; VoR

Burrowing into the grass. Last Farewell to Kukutis. Marcelijus Martinaitis. TWW, tr. by Laima Sruoginis.

Burrowing with his teeth. History of the Caesars, A. Isidor Schneider. APT-2

Burst agonized and clear! (LL) Emily Dickinson. APN-2; AWP; ColAP; HeIP-4; MoAmPo; NAAL-2v1; NAAL-3; NAAL-5; NOBA; NoP-4; OxBA; PoPoPo; PoRA; SAmP; TAP; TCAPo; TFi; WPE

Burst of iris so that, A. Iris. William Carlos Williams. LCAP-2; WeW-3

Burst, to illumine our tempestuous day. (LL) England in 1819. Shelley. CenSon; NAEL-5v2; NAEL-6v2; NAWM-7v2; NOBE; OxAEP-2; OxBEV; OxBSo; Son; TFi; UnPo

Bursting ripe plum, A. Richard Wright. APT-2

Burthen of my anger on my soul. Wheat-miners. "Michael Field." ViWPN

Bury and Dig. Minnie Bruce Pratt. PoBW

Bury Her at Even. "Michael Field." OBMV

Bury Me in a Free Land. Frances Ellen Watkins Harper. BPo; ColAP; ISC; NAAAL; TCAPo

Bury me in my pink pantsuit, you said—and I did. Fare, The. Molly Peacock. ExTi

Bury Me with a Band. Ofelia Zepeda. ReEnLa

Bury my heart at Wounded Knee. (LL) American Names. Stephen Vincent Benét. APT-2; FaBoA; OBAL; OxBA

Bury the Great Horse. Douglas Garman. UV Fr. Ode on the Death of Haig's Horse.

Bury this old Illinois farmer with respect. Illinois Farmer. Carl Sandburg. HHAm

Bury your heart in some deep green hollow. Charlotte Mew. WPE

Burying Ground by the Ties. Archibald MacLeish. GM

Bus, The. Leonard Cohen. HeIP-4

Bus driver from Delhi to Agra, A. Mud. George Kalamaras. BAP-97

Bus Driver Poem, The. Khaled Mattawa. AmPoNex

Bus driver tore my ticket, The. Fidel in Ohio. Martín Espada. TouFir

Bus halts its long brawl, The. At Kfar Kana. Charles Causley. TOF

Bus Ride. Kate Daniels. PBCAP

Bus Station, The. Sean Dunne. ModIr Fr. Sydney Place.

Bus Stop. Donald Justice. LCAP-2

Bus-stop on the Somme, The. David Rowbotham. NOBAu

Bus Trip, The. Joel Oppenheimer. NeAP

Bus was taking me, The. To S.V. György Petri. VCWP, tr. by George Gömöri and Clive Wilmer

Buses came late, each driver sullen. Christmas Bells, Saigon. Walter McDonald. AF

Bush. Josephine Jacobsen. NoP-4

Bush, The. Bernard O'Dowd. "To other eyes and ears you are a great." CBAP

Bush, a gathering smoke, The. Blackthorn. Euros Bowen. OBWVE, tr. by the author

Bush-bristling juniper and you the thorn. Génèvres Hérissez, et Vous, Houx Espineux. Pierre de Ronsard. WoPoe, tr. by Donald Davie

Bush Justice. Charles Harpur. CBAP

Bush land scrub land. Country North of Belleville, The. Alfred Wellington Purdy. NOBC

Bush Navigator: The Last Morning of Hands. Peggy Shumaker. PBCAP

Bush of loo brush, A. Curly Kale. David Lindley. NLP

Bush Section, A. Blanche Edith Baughan. "Logs, at the door, by the fence; broadcast over the paddock." PeNZ

Bush Speaks, The. Ernest G. Moll. NOBAu

Bush Telegram. Tom Pickard. Oth

Bush, The. Yes. It burned like they say it did. Deuteronomy. Robert Bringhurst. NOBC

Bush warbler. Basho. EH, tr. by Robert Hass

Bush was on that dump, A. Burnt Bush, The. Jack R. Clemo. FaBoTw

Bushed. Earle Birney. MoCV; NOBC; NoAM; NoP-4

Bushed. Charles Lillard. NOBC

Bushed. Barry McKinnon. NOBC

Bushranger, A. Kenneth Slessor. CBAP; NOBAu

Busie old foole, unruly Sunne. John Donne. See Busy old fool, unruly sun

Business Girls. Sir John Betjeman. UV

Business in Germany. Stewart Florsheim. GotH

Business Life, The. David Ignatow. NNaP

Business-like harlot named Draper, A. Limerick. Unknown. PeLi

Business men boast of their skill and cunning. Business Men. Ch'en Tzu-ang. ChiP, tr. by Arthur Waley

Business of Poetry, The. Harold Norse. CLPP

Business Personals. John Ashbery. BodElec

Business Reverses. Edgar Lee Masters. ChIV-2

Buster's Last Hand. Jennifer O'Grady. AmPoNex

Buster's Visitation. Stephen Dunn. Unle

Bustle in a House, The. Emily Dickinson. HAP; HeIP-4; NAAL-2v1; NAAL-3; NAAL-5; NoP-4; OxBA; SAmP; SacPr

Bustopher Jones: The Cat about Town. T. S. Eliot. OBCoV; TriCat

Busts of the great composers glimmered in niches. Mrs. Snow. Donald Justice. NoP-4

Busy. Yüan Mei. CoBLCP, tr. by Jonathan Chaves

Busy, curious, thirsty fly. On a Fly Drinking Out of [or from] His Cup. William Oldys. OBEV; OxAEP-1; OxBEV

Busy Heart, The. Rupert Brooke. MoBrPo

Busy in the Spring. Tzu Yeh. CrYelRi; ErotSp, tr. by Sam Hamill

Busy is the life of the weaving woman! Song of the Weaving Woman. Yüan Chên. SuSp, tr. by Wu-Chi Liu

Busy old fool, unruly sun. Sun Rising, The. John Donne. BASC; BoLoP; CABP; ClHu; ESCV; FHYEP; FSCP; HAP; HeIP-4; MeLP; NAEL-5v1; NAEL-6v1; NAEL-7v1; NIL-7; NIP-4; NOBE; NOSC; NoP-4; PAI; PoE; PoPoPo; SCV; TFi; WeW-3

Busy old lady, charitable tray. Reason for Refusal. Martin Bell. FaBoWar

Busy with love, the bumble bee. Meleager. BoLoP; GrAn

Busy with Many Jobs. Tadeusz Rózewicz. PoSu, tr. by Adam Czerniawski

Busy with very urgent jobs. Busy with Many Jobs. Tadeusz Rózewicz. PoSu, tr. by Adam Czerniawski

Busy yellow bee, after his mighty quest, A. Unknown. NOIV

But. Vladimir Holan. PoSu, tr. by Ian Milner and Jarmila Milner

But a dream within a dream? (LL) Edgar Allan Poe. NCAP; NOBA; OxBA; TAP; TCAPo

But a large quantity of brandy. Small Faculty Stag for the Visiting Poet, A. Earle Birney. OxBC; PeLV

But a smile could make it sweet. (LL) Tennyson. NAEL-5v2; NAEL-6v2 Fr. Maud [A Monodrama].

But accept it for friendship's sake. (LL) Cave of Making, The. W. H. Auden. FaBoVe; OxAEP-2

But ae braithless note. Sydney Goodsir Smith. OBVE Fr. Gangrel Rymour and the Pairdon of Sanct Anne, The.

But after one such love, can love no more. (LL) Broken Heart, The. John Donne. EBEV; FSCP

But ah, Desire still cries, give me some food. (LL) Sir Philip Sidney. NAEL-5v1; NAEL-6v1; NAEL-7v1; NoP-4; NoSic; PoE Fr. Astrophil and Stella.

But ah, how few the God that loves! (LL) Heaven and Hell. Francis Thompson. OxBSP; SacPr

But ah! what glories yon blue vault emblaze? Hymn to Indra, A. Sir William Jones. NOBRP

But ah! when first to breathe man does begin. On Time, Death, and Eternity. Robert Peter. VerBaPo

But, ah! ye maids, beware the gipsy's lures! John Langhorne. ECEV Fr. Country Justice, The.

But ain't it long, and ain't it good and thick. Unknown. PriapPo, tr. by Richard W. Hooper Fr. Priapus Poems, The.

But, alas, who less[e] could do[e] that found so good occasion? (LL) Think'st thou to seduce me then. Thomas Campion. NAEL-5v1; NAEL-7v1; OxAEP-1; OxBSP

But Alive. Charles Strouse. ReLy

But all he was is overworn. (LL) Tennyson. CAGL; EBVV; HeIP-4; NAEL-6v2; NAWM-7v2 Fr. In Memoriam A. H. H.

But all is new unhallowed ground. (LL) Tennyson. ChrPo; EBVV; NAEL-6v2 Fr. In Memoriam A. H. H.

But all time roars outside this room. (LL) Thom Gunn. AmFaPo; RB Fr. Three Songs.

But all too late, grief's out of date. Michael Wigglesworth. NAAL-3 Fr. Day of Doom, The.

But always, without fail THE NECK. (LL) Travel[l]er's Curse after Misdirection[, The]. Robert Graves. MoBrPo; NBLV; OBCoV

But anxious cares the pensive nymph oppressed. Pope. EBNV; OxAEP-1 Fr. Rape of the Lock, The; an Heroi-Comical Poem.

But are not of? (LL) Midnight on the Great Western. Thomas Hardy. NOBE; OxAEP-2; WoPoe

But Artemis, my girls. Telesilla. SaLy, tr. by Diane Rayor

But as for me, I never could. (LL) Dorothy Parker. APT-1; NALW Fr. Pig's-Eye View of Literature, A.

But as long-liv'd as present love. (LL) Of English Verse. Edmund Waller. BeJo; CABP; NAEL-5v1; NOSC; PoE

But as my friend, take to a younger bed. Sappho. SaLy, tr. by Diane Rayor

But ask whatever else, and we will dare! (LL) James Russell Lowell. APN-1; CBCWP; NOBA; OBWP

But at a distance, in another tree. (LL) No Possum, No Sop, No Taters. Wallace Stevens. HCAP; OxBA; TAP; VGW

But at last there came the day, the hour of shovels and buckets. Angels of the Ruins, The. Rafael Alberti. AF, tr. by Geoffrey Connell

But at night, when there is most need. Atrium. Alessandro Ceni. ItPo, tr. by Gayle Ridinger

But at the common table. (LL) Te Deum. Charles Reznikoff. ChIV-1; TrJP

But at the immolation of a race who cries? (LL)   Death of a Whale.   John Blight.   BMAP; CBAP

But aye her whistle would fetch him back. (LL)   Allansford Pursuit, The.   *Unknown.*   RB; WoPoe, *tr. by* Robert Graves

But, baby, where are you? (LL)   Ballad of Birmingham.   Dudley Randall.   BPo; HeIP-4; ISC; InPK-5; NIL-7; NIP-4; NoAM; NoP-4; SoSe-8

But Bacchus was not so content: he quyght forsooke their land.   Ovid.   CTC, *tr. by* Arthur Golding   *Fr.* Metamorphoses.

But bargains: those he will not strike. (LL)   Age.   Walter Savage Landor.   FaBoEE; NOBVV; OxBEV

But be. (LL)   Ars Poetica.   Archibald MacLeish.   APT-1; AWP; ColAP; HAP; HeIP-4; IllVoic; InPK-6; MoAmPo; NAAL-2v2; NIP-4; NOBA; OxBA; PoRA; TAP; TFi; WeW-3

But be contented: when that fell arrest.   William Shakespeare.   NAEL-5v1; NAEL-6v1; NAEL-7v1; OxAEP-1; Son   *Fr.* Sonnets.

But Beautiful.   Jimmy Van Heusen.   ReLy

But Bird.   Paul Zimmer.   SeSe

But break, my heart, for I must hold my tongue! (LL)   William Shakespeare.   OxAEP-1; SCV   *Fr.* Hamlet.

But bright—as if the soul had come for the night.   Dream: Flight of a Dragonfly.   Gennady Aygi.   ItGoST, *tr. by* Peter France

But brims the poisoned well. (LL)   Fragments of a Lost Gnostic Poem of the Twelfth [*or* 12th] Century.   Herman Melville.   APN-2; NOBA; NoP-4; OxBSP; PoPoPo; TCAPo

But bring us in good ale! (LL)   *Unknown.*   EBEV; MiEL; OBCoV

But buy Your spirit, Lord. (LL)   Charles Reznikoff.   TaR; VGW

But can see better there, and laughing there.   Gwendolyn Brooks.   ColAP   *Fr.* Notes from the Childhood and the Girlhood.

But chief of all.   John Milton.   *See* Chief of all

But clasp'd to his bosom, the infant was dead. (LL)   Erl-King, The.   Goethe.   AWP; OBVE; STV

But colorless. Colorless. (LL)   Poppies in July.   Sylvia Plath.   FaBoWP; LCAP-2; RB

But come, come in till then! Come in till then! (LL)   Cinderella.   Randall Jarrell.   LCAP-2; NAAL-2v2; VCAP

But copying is, what in her Nature writes. (LL)   Sir Philip Sidney.   NoSic; Son   *Fr.* Astrophil and Stella.

But Could You?   Vladimir Vladimirovich Mayakovsky [*or* Maiakovskii].   TCRP, *tr. by* Bernard Meares

But Custard keeps crying for a nice safe cage. (LL)   Tale of Custard the Dragon, The.   Ogden Nash.   ITBLP; MakPoe; OBCA; OTCP; PoRA

But Death intenser—Death is Life's high mead. (LL)   Why Did I Laugh Tonight?   John Keats.   CenSon; NAEL-6v2

But declared she would never leave Portugal. (LL)   Limericks, II (iv).   Edward Lear.   OBCoV; OxBoLi; PeLV; PeLi

But did not paradise itself contain.   Age of Innocence.   Graham Hough.   PoRA

But dilute the lonely self-watchful passion. (LL)   Place for No Story, The.   Robinson Jeffers.   APT-1; AiP

But Dionysos had no healing physic for his comrade fallen, of dancing he thought no more.   Nonnus.   CAGL, *tr. by* W. H. D. Rouse   *Fr.* Dionysiaca.

But discover it no more. (LL)   Eden is that Old-Fashioned House.   Emily Dickinson.   ChIV-1; NALW

But do not let us quarrel any more.   Andrea del Sarto.   Robert Browning.   CTC; NAEL-5v2; NAEL-6v2; NOBVV; NoP-4; PoE

But does every man feel like this at forty.   Second Life, The.   Edwin Morgan.   OxBS

But Don John of Austria rides home from the Crusade. (LL)   Lepanto.   Gilbert Keith Chesterton.   EBNV; FaBoWar; MoBrPo; OBMV; OBNV; RB

But don't tell the neighbours, you bastard. (LL)   *Unknown.*   OBCoV; PeLi

But don't want to; I still don't want to know. (LL)   X-Ray.   Dannie Abse.   AngWePo; BloBone

But, down on down, the uninhabitable sorrow. (LL)   Kingfisher, The.   Amy Clampitt.   HCAP; OWoS

But drives a blue car through the / stars. (LL)   Two Years Later.   John Wieners.   PmAP; PoM; RaBo

But dropped like Adamant. (LL)   Emily Dickinson.   APN-2; NAWM-7v2; NCAP; SoSe-8

But dwell in darkness, for your god is blind.   George Chapman.   OxBSo; Son   *Fr.* Coronet for His Mistress Philosophy, A.

But dwell in darkness, for your God is blind. (LL)   George Chapman.   OxBSo; SCGP; Son   *Fr.* Coronet for His Mistress Philosophy, A.

But—'e'll never be the man 'is Father woz. (LL)   Chorus of a Song That Might Have Been Written by Albert Chevalier.   Max Beerbohm.   OBCoV; UV

But end at where we came.   Floating Epitaphs, Their Possible Explanations in Poro Point.   Alejandrino Hufana.   ReBoTo

But equally a want of books and men! (LL)   England, 1802, III.   William Wordsworth.   OBEV; Son

But ere I could fly thence', it pierced my heart. (LL)   Sir Philip Sidney.   NAEL-7v1; NoSic   *Fr.* Astrophil and Stella.

But ere sterne conflict mixt both strengths, faire Paris stept before.   Homer.   OBVE   *Fr.* Iliad, The.

But even leaving, longing to be back.   Escaping from Autopia.   Chryss Yost.   GeoHom

But, fair Iëmpsar (wife of Potiphar).   Joshua Sylvester.   ChIV-1   *Fr.* Maidens Blush, The.

But farre away from these, another sort.   Edmund Spenser.   CAGL   *Fr.* Faerie Queene, The.

But Fate and gloomy Night encompass thee around. (LL)   To the Memory of Mr Oldham.   Dryden.   AWP; BASC; EBEV; HAP; InPK-6; NAEL-6v1; NAEL-7v1; NIL-7; NIP-4; NOBE; NOSC; NPeEn; NoP-4; OxAEP-1; OxBEV; PAI; PoE; PoPoPo; SCGP; TFi; TRP

But fear, thirst, hunger, and this huddled chill. (LL)   Montana Pastoral.   James Vincent Cunningham.   APT-2; MoAmPo; VGW

But Fear Thou Not, O Jacob.   Bible, *O.T.*   TrJP   *Fr.* Jeremiah.

But finding nothing, sullenly withdrew. (LL)   Range-finding.   Robert Frost.   NIL-7; NIP-4; NoAM; OBWP; RB

But first one must free oneself.   Patrizia Cavalli.   NeIt; VCWP, *tr. by* Patrizia Cavalli and Robert McCraken

But, fool, seek'st not to get into her heart. (LL)   Sir Philip Sidney.   OxBSo; PoE   *Fr.* Astrophil and Stella.

But for a brief / Moment, a poised minute.   Grasshopper, A.   Richard Wilbur.   HAP

But for a woodpecker.   Basho.   SoOfWa, *tr. by* Sam Hamill

But for His bride. (LL)   World, The (1).   Henry Vaughan.   AWP; ChIV-2; EBEV; ESCV; FSCP; HAP; NAEL-5v1; NAEL-6v1; NAEL-7v1; NOBE; NOCV; NOSC; NPeEn; OxAEP-1; OxBEV; PBRV; PeECV; SCGP; SacPr; TFi; TrCP

But for Lust.   Ruth Pitter.   FaBoTw; NPeEn; OxBTC

But, for such as our earth is now, it lasted long. (LL)   Season of Phantasmal Peace, The.   Derek Walcott.   EmeKit; PoPoPo; PoetW; VCWP

But for their powers, accept my piety [*or* pietie]. (LL)   To William Camden.   Ben Jonson.   AWP; BASC; BeJo; NAEL-5v1; NAEL-6v1; NAEL-7v1; NOSC; NPeEn

But for them the bombers answer everything. (LL)   Second Air Force.   Randall Jarrell.   NAAL-2v2; NAAL-5

But for these apertures.   Witter Bynner.   APT-1

But for to make it spring again. (LL)   Hock-Cart, or Harvest Home, The.   Robert Herrick.   BASC; BeJo; CaPo; EBEV; NAEL-5v1; NAEL-6v1; NAEL-7v1; NOSC; OxAEP-1

But for two, even mornings' Beware.   Marina Ivanovna Tsvetayeva [*or* Tsvetaeva].   WoPoe, *tr. by* David McDuff

But for your terror.   To Death.   Oliver St. John Gogarty.   FaBoEE; OBMV

But frankly, gayly shall we get the gods. (LL)   Meditation at Kew.   Anna Wickham.   FaBoTw; MoBrPo; NALW

But from it fly. (LL)   John Fletcher.   NOBE; NOSC; NoSic   *Fr.* Two Noble Kinsmen, The.

But get some color and music out of life? (LL)   Investment, The.   Robert Frost.   APT-1; OxBA

But give me for my soul, those beauteous maids.   Those Beauteous Maids.   Moses Ibn Ezra.   TrJP, *tr. by* Solomon Solis-Cohen

But God is Silent / Psalm 114.   Daniel Berrigan.   InvLi

But God was seen no longer any more. (LL)   He Said: "If in His Image I Was Made."   Trumbull Stickney.   APN-2; TCAPo

"But good Sir, look here"—said he.   Mihály Fazekas.   IQMS, *tr. by* Thomas Kabdebo   *Fr.* Matt the Gooseherd.

But gripped, gripped and is now a cenotaph. (LL)   Relic.   Ted Hughes.   NAEL-5v2; NAEL-6v2; NoP-4

But hark! the cry is Astur.   Thomas Babington Macaulay, 1st Baron Macaulay.   OBWP   *Fr.* Lays of Ancient Rome.

But he did for them both by his plan of attack. (LL)   General, The.   Siegfried Sassoon.   FaBoWar; NAEL-5v2; NAEL-6v2; NPeEn; NoAM; NoP-4; OBWP; OxBEV; OxBSP; OxBTC; OxBoLi; PoE

But he didn't catch me. (LL)   Little Turtle, The.   Nicholas Vachel Lindsay.   NOxBChV; NTCP; OBAL; OBCA; OBSP; OxIBACP

But he never would tell us of whom. (LL)   Limerick: "There was an old man of Khartoum."   William Ralph Inge.   NOBL; PeLi

But / He said.   For Kinna 2.   Christine Ama Ata Aidoo.   HAWP

But He Was Cool; or, He Even Stopped for Green Lights.   Haki R. Madhubuti.   BPo

But hear. If you stay, and the child be born.   Thomas Hardy.   MoBrPo   *Fr.* Satires of Circumstance in Fifteen Glimpses.

But helpless Pieces of the Game He plays. 69.   Edward Fitzgerald.   CABP

But her arm—damp, small.   Mary Kinzie.   FFC

But her favorite poems take place underwater.   Sam Truitt.   AmPoNex   *Fr.* Anamorphosis Eisenhower.

But her sweet odour did them all excel[l]. (LL)   Edmund Spenser.   EBEV; NAEL-5v1; NAEL-6v1; OxBSo; Son   *Fr.* Amoretti.

But here no cannon thunders to the gale. William Wordsworth. CenSon *Fr.* River Duddon [A Series of Sonnets], The.

But here's the piece, made up to sell. Landscape, The. George Daniel. NOSC

But high up—my river of spirits. Going to Sleep in Childhood. Gennady Aygi. ItGoST, *tr. by* Peter France

But his actual candle blazed with artifice. (LL) Quiet Normal Life, A. Wallace Stevens. NAAL-2v2; NAAL-5; NoAM

But his shoes were far too tight. (LL) Incidents in the Life of My Uncle Arly. Edward Lear. OBCoV; OxBoLi

But hit's mighty ha'd to giggle w'en dey's nuffin' in de pot. (LL) Philosophy. Paul Laurence Dunbar. BPo; NAAAL

"But hold y. . . hold y. . ." says Robin. Jolly Pinder of Wakefield, The. *Unknown.* ESPB

But how can I tell their story / if I was not there? Vocabulary. Ariel Dorfman. AF, *tr. by* Ariel Dorfman

But How It Came from Earth. Conrad Potter Aiken. MoAmPo

But how many merry monthes be in the yeere? Robin Hood and the Curtal Friar. *Unknown.* ESPB

But how much more unfortunate are those. Joseph Hilaire Pierre Belloc. UV

But how thoroughly departmental. (LL) Departmental. Robert Frost. HeIP-4; MoAmPo; NAAL-2v2; NAAL-5; NOBA; NOBL; OBAL; PeLV; SoSe-8

But I am completely nourished. (LL) Decade, [A]. Amy Lowell. MoAmPo; NALW; PasH; PoBW

But I Am Growing Old and Indolent. Robinson Jeffers. APT-1; ColAP; NOBA; TAP

But I / am not an isolated god. Wall of Dreams (2). Ahmed Taha. NAfrP, *tr. by* Clarissa C. Burt

But I am not someone of spiteful. Sappho. SaLy, *tr. by* Diane Rayor

But I am—other than me—I am the gentle cricket. Chameleon. Daria Menicanti. CItWP, *tr. by* Cinzia Sartini Blum and Lara Trubowitz

But I can't squeeze more love into their stone. (LL) Tony Harrison. DiPo; NAEL-5v2; NAEL-6v2 *Fr.* School of Eloquence, The.

But I could not both live and utter it. (LL) My Life Has Been the Poem I Would Have Writ. Henry David Thoreau. APN-1; NCAP; TCAPo

But I Do Not Need Kindness. Gregory Corso. NeAP

But I don't care where the water goes if it doesn't get into the wine. (LL) Gilbert Keith Chesterton. ChIV-1; MoBrPo *Fr.* Flying Inn, The.

But I forget.—My pilgrim's shrine is won. Byron. NAEL-5v2; NAEL-6v2 *Fr.* Childe Harold's Pilgrimage.

But I haven't come to that—and I hope I never shall—and that's the Village Poor House! (LL) Our Village—by a Villager. Thomas Hood. FaBoVe; OBSV

But I'm driving. Your Character is Your Destiny. Erin Belieu. ExTi

But I'm minded on it againe. Ye haue heard this yarn afore. Peter Reading. EmeKit

But I'm talking about / Harlem to you! (LL) Langston Hughes. APSN; APT-2 *Fr.* Lenox Avenue Mural.

But I remember his hands. (LL) Fifth Grade Autobiography. Rita Dove. ISC; NIL-7; NIP-4

But I shall be gone. (LL) Sound of Trees, The. Robert Frost. APT-1; NoAM

But I shall stay at home. (LL) Country Boy in Winter, A. Sarah Orne Jewett. APN-2; ColAP; OBCA

But I sing the excellence of heroes. Korinna [*or* Corinna]. SaLy, *tr. by* Diane Rayor

But I still don't know what the joke is, to tell them. (LL) Toyland. Roy Fisher. HarvBoo; NPeEn

But I was afraid my heart would break. (LL) Mid-Autumn Moon. Su Tung-p'o (Su Shih). CoBCP; GifTon, *tr. by* Burton Watson

But I was *born* to other things. (LL) Tennyson. FHYEP; NAEL-6v2 *Fr.* In Memoriam A. H. H.

But I was dead, an hour or more. Escape. Robert Graves. MoBrPo

But I was young and foolish, and now am full of tears. (LL) Down by the Salley Gardens. W. B. Yeats. CTC; EBVV; EnLoPo; NAEL-5v2; NAEL-6v2; NPeEn; NoAM; OBEV; PoPoPo; SoSe-8

But I will not say so. (LL) Women. Heath. CTC; NoSic

But if he came straight for me. Pernette De [*or* Du] Guillet. EroLit, *tr. by* T. Anthony Perry *Fr.* Élégie.

But if I look the ice is gone from the lake. Spring of the Thief. John Logan. NNaP

But if I should ask the king? Answering a Child. Sarah Morgan Bryan Piatt. NCAP

But if I tell you how my heart swings wide. Sunflower Sonnet Number One. June Jordan. Son

But if one of those children came near that we have set / on fire. Robert Bly. CDa *Fr.* Teeth Mother Naked at Last, The.

But if there be a power too just and strong. Dryden. NOCV *Fr.* Religio Laici.

But if they'd give us toys and twice the stuff. Christmas at the Orphanage. Bill Knott. OPRER

But if thou wilt not pittie my complaint. Richard Barnfield [*or* Barnefield]. CAGL *Fr.* Affectionate Shepherd [*or* Shephearde], The.

But if through genuine tenderness of heart. John Armstrong. OBGa *Fr.* Art of Preserving Health, The.

But if we could see and hear, this Vision—were it not He? (LL) Higher Pantheism, The. Tennyson. CABP; InvLi

But if you break the bloody glass you won't hold up the weather. (LL) Bagpipe Music. Louis MacNeice. CABP; GTBS-P; HarvBoo; MakPoe; NAEL-5v2; NAEL-6v2; NBLV; NOBE; NOBL; NoAM; NoP-4; OBSV; OxBEV; OxBTC; PeLV; RB; TFi; UV

But if you [*or* yow] list, my tale shul ye he[e]re. (LL) Geoffrey Chaucer. NAEL-5v1; NAEL-6v1 *Fr.* Canterbury Tales, The.

'But in that Sleep of Death what Dreams may Come?' Mary Elizabeth Coleridge. VWP

But in the dome of mighty Mars the red. Geoffrey Chaucer. OBWP *Fr.* Canterbury Tales, The.

But in the end one tires of the high-flown. About the Phoenix. James Merrill. NoAM

But in the last days it shall come to pass. Bible, *O.T.* FaBoWar, *tr. by* King James Version *Fr.* Micah.

But in the locked ghettos. Not Only in the Six-Day War. Charles Fishman. GotH

But in the virtues of the feeling mind' (LL) Evening, Gertrude. Anne Batten Cristall. ECWP; RWP

But is for others undiminished somewhere. (LL) Sad Steps. Philip Larkin. NAEL-6v2; NoAM; NoP-4

But Islands of the Blessed, bless you, son. Answer, An. Robert Frost. OBCoV

But it could be worse. (LL) Sonnet for Minimalists. Mona Van Duyn. FFC; WeW-3

But it is given in friendship. (LL) Visitors. Tu Fu. BLT; OHPC, *tr. by* Kenneth Rexroth

But it was just one of those things. (LL) Just One of Those Things. Cole Porter. APT-1; ReLy

But it was right that she. His Wife. Shirley Kaufman. LCAP-2

But its radiocarbon ticks. Hardy's "Shelley's Skylark." Daniel Hall. YaYoPo

But, John, have you seen the world, said he. Angle of Vision. Robert Rendall. OxBTC

But Jove against the Greeks sent forth his son. Homer. FaBoWar, *tr. by* Edward Earl of Derby *Fr.* Iliad, The.

But just to see a chapel like this room. But Just to See. Cyprian Norwid. WoPoe, *tr. by* Jerzy Peterkiewicz, Burns Singer and Jon Stallworthy

But keep that earlier, wilder image bright. (LL) To Cole, the Painter, Departing for Europe. William Cullen Bryant. AiP; ColAP; TAP; TCAPo

But kiss him & give him both drink and apparel. (LL) William Blake. FHYEP; NBLV; OBSV *Fr.* Songs of Experience.

But know not how, for still I think of you. (LL) Sir Philip Sidney. NoSic; PoE *Fr.* Astrophil and Stella.

But know not what's *resisted.* (LL) Address to the Unco Guid, or the Rigidly Righteous. Robert Burns. ChIV-1; NOBE; NOCV; OxBEV; OxBS

But, knowing now that they would have her speak. Defense of Guenevere, The. William Morris. NAEL-5v2; NAEL-6v2

But known of what he died. (LL) Workbox, The. Thomas Hardy. InPK-6; NAEL-5v2; NAEL-6v2; UnPo

But leave, because I cannot as I should! (LL) To John Donne. Ben Jonson. BeJo; NAEL-5v1; NAEL-6v1; NAEL-7v1

But leave the Wise to wrangle, and with me. Omar Khayyám. OxBEV *Fr.* Rubáiyát of Omar Khayyám [*of* Naishápúr], The.

But left the thorn wi' me. (LL) Bonie Doon. Robert Burns. GTBS-P; NoP-4

But let me now my lovely charge remind. Soame Jenyns. ECEV *Fr.* Art of Dancing, The.

But let one of you hear this. Korinna [*or* Corinna]. SaLy, *tr. by* Diane Rayor

But lets the poet see how heav'n can shine. (LL) Coleridge. Theodore Watts-Dunton. GSo; Son

But lif' up yo' haid w'en de King go by! (LL) Spiritual, A. Paul Laurence Dunbar. BPo; SacPr

But listen. Go on, tell me the season is over. Alan Wearne. BMAP

But Littleman he can't dance alone. (LL) Mother Goose. LB; OxNR; ReMoGo

But lo! at length the day is lingered out. Francis Thompson. OBMV *Fr.* Sister Songs.

But look a trial down from some far height. Full Vision. Henrietta Cordelia Ray. CBWP-3

But look in your mirror for the other one. Antonio Machado Ruiz. RaBo *Fr.* Moral Proverbs and Folk Songs.

But love survives the venom of the snake. (LL) In Hospital: Poona (1). Alun Lewis. AngWePo; OBWVE; TCAWP

But love whilst that thou mayst be loved again. (LL)   Samuel Daniel.   NoP-4; NoSic; SCGP   *Fr.* To Delia.

But lovers are like umbrellas arnt they?   Accoutrement.   'Marnia.   LW

But may be ravenously unripped in hell? (LL)   Algernon Charles Swinburne.   OxBSo; UV   *Fr.* Heptalogia, The.

But Men loved Darkness[e] Rather Than [*or* Then] Light.   Richard Crashaw.   ChIV-2

But minds me o' my Jean. (LL)   Of a' the Airts [the Wind Can Blaw].   Robert Burns.   AWP; OxBS

But Money gives me pleasure all the time. (LL)   Fatigue.   Joseph Hilaire Pierre Belloc.   NBLV; NOBL; OxBTC; UV

But most beautiful of all is the Un-found Island.   Most Beautiful, The.   Guido Gozzano.   TTTS, *tr.* by Victoria Pesce

But most by numbers judge a poet's song.   Pope.   ECEV; FHYEP; HAP; NIL-7; NIP-4   *Fr.* Essay on Criticism, An.

But Mozart did.   Aleatory.   Mary Zeppa.   MiVo

But My Blood.   Rose Romano.   UnSA

But my good little man, you have made a mistake.   To a Boy-Poet of the Decadence.   Sir Owen Seaman.   PeLV

But *Nancy* still with me. (LL)   In a Letter to A.R.C. on Her Wishing to Be Called Anna.   Matilda Barbara Betham-Edwards.   ECWP; PoBW; WoRP

But nane but thee for me. (LL)   False Lover Won Back, The.   *Unknown.*   ESPB; OxBB

But nearer than Guardian Angel.   "H. D."   NALW   *Fr.* Tribute to the Angels.

But neither stops her song. (LL)   I Ask My Mother to Sing.   Li-Young Lee.   IllVoic; InvLad; LoL; OpBo; UnSA

But night, the reserved, the reticent, gives more than it takes. (LL)   As One Put Drunk into the Packet-Boat.   John Ashbery.   HAP; HCAP; VCAP

But no point explaining to those who abstain. (LL)   Drinking Alone in the Moonlight.   Li Po.   ColAnChi; WoPoe, *tr.* by Elling O. Eide

But nobody seems to know whose. (LL)   Edward Gorey.   OBCoV; PeLi

But none shall thus lament for me! (LL)   Lament of the Captive, The.   Richard Henry Wilde.   APN-1; ColAP; TCAPo

But not because we were girls. (LL)   Barbie Says Math is Hard.   Kyoko Mori.   InvLad; ReTh

But Not for Me.   George Gershwin.   ReLy

But not from her protecting care. (LL)   Lullaby: "Beloved, may your sleep be sound."   W. B. Yeats.   BoLoP; FaBoTw; OBMV

But not here. (LL)   Where Knock Is Open Wide.   Theodore Roethke.   HAP; VGW

But not in our alley! (LL)   Sally in Our Alley.   Henry Carey.   AWP; BoLoP; GTBS-P; NOBE; OBEV; OxAEP-1

But not on a shell, she starts.   Paltry Nude Starts on a Spring Voyage, The.   Wallace Stevens.   HCAP

But Not That One.   John Ashbery.   LCAP-2

But nothing happens. (LL)   Exposure.   Wilfred Owen.   FaBoMo; NoAM; OBWP; PeFWW; PoWW; RB; TCAWP

But nothing promised that is not performed. (LL)   To Juan at the Winter Solstice.   Robert Graves.   EBEV; FaBoMo; HarvBoo; MoBrPo; NAEL-5v2; NAEL-6v2; NPeEn; NoAM; NoP-4; PoE; RaBo; TwCP

But now. (LL)   What She Said.   Maturai Eruttalan Centamputan.   BoLoP; WoPoe, *tr.* by A. K. Ramanujan

But now at thirty years my hair is grey.   Byron.   NOBE; SCV   *Fr.* Don Juan.

But now had Hesper from the Hero's sight.   Joel Barlow.   APN-1   *Fr.* Columbiad, The.

But now hear what meat there needs eat thou must.   Alexander Barclay.   NoSic   *Fr.* Eclogues.

But now I am home again there is nobody I know. (LL)   Fairy Story.   Stevie Smith.   NOxBChV; OBSP

But now I call him dirty louse. (LL)   Immortals, The.   Isaac Rosenberg.   FaBoTw; TrJP

But now I feel hunger, which declares.   John Milton.   InvLi   *Fr.* Paradise Regained [*or* Regain'd].

But now I have a will, yet want a wit.   Intellectual Powers of the Soul, The.   John Davies.   SacPr

But now I only know I am,—that's all. (LL)   I Feel I Am.   John Clare.   FHYEP; OxBSo

But now in death your evening lights the dead. (LL)   Aster.   Plato.   GrAn; WoPoe, *tr.* by Peter Jay

But now it's the Yiddish itself I'm forgetting.   Shoyn Fergéssin: "I've Forgotten" in Yiddish.   Albert Goldbarth.   TaR

But now lead on.   John Milton.   NPeEn   *Fr.* Paradise Lost.

But now Mr. Ferritt.   And Mr. Ferritt.   Judith Wright.   MoBrPo

But now my boys, leave off, and list to me.   Christopher Marlowe.   FaBoWar   *Fr.* Tamburlaine the Great, Part 2.

But now, no longer deaf to honour's call.   Homer.   OBVE   *Fr.* Iliad, The.

But now Sarpedon watching his comrades drop and die.   Homer.   NAWM-7v1, *tr.* by Robert Fagles   *Fr.* Iliad, The.

But now this man of hell toward me turned.   Philip Freneau.   NAAL-2v1; NAAL-3   *Fr.* House of Night, The.

But now you come at noon. (LL)   Ten O'Clock Scholar, [The].   Mother Goose.   LB; OxNR; ReMoGo

But O! delighting me. (LL)   Reason Has Moons.   Ralph Hodgson.   FaBoCh; OxBSP

But, O immortals! What had I to plead.   Christopher Smart.   NOEC   *Fr.* Hymn to the Supreme Being.

But O, my Muse, what numbers wilt thou find.   Joseph Addison.   OBWP   *Fr.* Campaign, The.

But O! the freedom, pleasure and the ease.   Lawrence Spooner.   NOEC   *Fr.* Looking-Glass for Smokers, A.

But oblivion, not thy forgiveness, FRANCE. (LL)   Ezra Pound.   FaBoTw; WoPoe   *Fr.* Cantos.

But of all plagues, the greatest is untold.   Juvenal.   BASC; OBSV, *tr.* by John Dryden   *Fr.* Satires.

But often on the mountain peaks when.   Alcman.   SaLy, *tr.* by Diane Rayor

But oh, that we could sleep up there. (LL)   Sleeping on the Ceiling.   Elizabeth Bishop.   APT-2; OBGa; TTTS

But ole Mosser hain't cotch me, an' he never will! (LL)   Wild Negro Bill.   *Unknown.*   BPo; NAAAL

But on the third day Christ arose.   Herman Melville.   APN-2   *Fr.* Clarel: A Poem and Pilgrimage in the Holy Land.

But once upon a time.   Cranach.   Sir Herbert Read.   FaBoMo

But one and all if they would dusk the day. (LL)   Death Song, A.   William Morris.   NAEL-5v2; NAEL-6v2

But one felt it was doing them good. (LL)   *Unknown.*   OBCoV; PeLi

But one half glaunce, most gladly dye [*or* die]. (LL)   Vanity of Spirit.   Henry Vaughan.   ESCV; GeHe; NOSC; TOF

But only God can make a tree. (LL)   Trees.   Joyce Kilmer.   APT-1; BRP; ChAP; ITBLP; TCAPo; UV

But only not to think about the journey.   But Only Not to think.   Irina Ratushinskaya [*or* Ratushinskaia].   AF

But only three in all God's universe.   Elizabeth Barrett Browning.   CenSon   *Fr.* Sonnets from the Portuguese.

But Oothoon is not so; a virgin filled with virgin fancies.   William Blake.   ECEV   *Fr.* Visions of the Daughters of Albion.

But peaceful was the night.   John Milton.   FaBoCh   *Fr.* On the Morning of Christ's Nativity.

But perfectly random and coastal.   Dennis Phillips.   FTOS   *Fr.* Exile.

But Perhaps [God Needs the Longing].   Nelly Sachs.   BoWoP; WPoS, *tr.* by Ruth Mead

But pinned to the heart of darkness a tattered fire-flag flies. (LL)   Stand-To, The.   Cecil Day Lewis.   NoP-4; OBWP

But pity for the grief they cannot feel. (LL)   Prisoners, The.   Stephen Spender.   FaBoMo; MoBrPo

"But plett a wand o bonnie birk."   Sweet William's Ghost.   *Unknown.*   ESPB

But pretty though as / roses is.   Three Sayings from Highlands, North Carolina.   Jonathan Williams.   OBAL

But proves at night a bed of down. (LL)   Upon the Sudden Restraint of the Earl[e] of Somerset, Then Falling from Favor [*or* Favour].   Sir Henry Wotton.   NOBE; NOSC; NPeEn; OxBEV

But Roaring Bill (who killed him) thought it right. (LL)   Pacifist, The.   Joseph Hilaire Pierre Belloc.   FaBoWar; OBCoV

But Robin he walkes in the greene fforest.   Robin Hood and the Butcher.   *Unknown.*   ESPB

But see here comes thy reverend Sire.   John Milton.   EBEV   *Fr.* Samson Agonistes.

But see! the well-plumed hearse comes nodding on.   Robert Blair.   ECEV   *Fr.* Grave, The.

But shall not question much. (LL)   Twice.   Christina Georgina Rossetti.   NOBE; OBEV; TOF; TrCP; VWP

But she didn't do it. And now it's too late. (LL)   Too Many Daves.   "Dr. Seuss."   OBCA; OxIBACP

But she is not kind. (LL)   In Mind.   Denise Levertov.   NAAL-5; NALW

But she thought she should go back to Sweden. (LL)   Limerick: "There was a young lady of Sweden."   Edward Lear.   EBEV; PeVV

But should some snarling critic chance to view.   Jane Brereton.   ECWP   *Fr.* Epistle to Mrs Anne Griffiths.

But sickness is catching; lovers, permit me entrance. (LL)   Urban Gallery.   Rachel Wetzsteon.   AmPoNex; NeAmPo

But silence, burnt dust on the valves, and whisky. (LL)   Private Bottling, A.   Don Paterson.   EmeKit; NePenScot

But silence, nought can praise her. (LL)   Dialogue between two shepherds, Thenot and Piers, in praise of ASTRÆA.   Mary Sidney Herbert, Countess of Pembroke.   EMWP; NAEL-6v1

But, sires, o word forgat I in my tale.   Geoffrey Chaucer.   EBEV   *Fr.* Canterbury Tales, The.

But So As by Fire.   George Oppen.   APT-2; NNaP   *Fr.* Some San Francisco Poems.

But some do say, We marvel much, that you can sit Silent.   Something about Silence.   Elizabeth Hincks.   EMWP

But soon th'endearments of a husband cloy. Soame Jenyns. ECEV *Fr.* Modern Fine Lady, The.

But speech. Friedrich Hölderlin. WoPoe, *tr. by* Richard Sieburth *Fr.* Hymns and Fragments.

"But Still in Israel's Paths They Shine." Carter Revard. VoR

But still regard the destitute. (LL) Lord, Hear My Prayer. John Clare. BBASP; ChIV-1; NOCV; TrCP

But stop and loiter all the time to sing it in ecstatic songs. (LL) Beginning My Studies. Walt Whitman. NAAL-2v1; NAAL-3; OxBA

But stories somehow lengthen when begun. (LL) Byron. NOBL; OBNV; OBSV

But sudden came the barge's pitch-black prow. "George Eliot." NOBVV *Fr.* Brother and Sister.

But suffer it so. (LL) I Need Not Go. Thomas Hardy. NOBE; OBEV; OxBTC

But suh, you've made a mistake. Oh, yes suh! I can't be. Sidney, Looking for her Mother. Dolores Kendrick. ISC

But sun me in the Capitol. (LL) Mithridates. Ralph Waldo Emerson. APN-1; NCAP

But sweet sister death has gone debauched today and stalks. David Jones. NPeEn; OBWP; OxAEP-2; PeFWW *Fr.* In Parenthesis.

But tarries yet the Cause for which He died. (LL) Christmas Ghost-Story, A. Thomas Hardy. ChrPo; OBWP

But tell me, child, your choice; what shall I buy You? Handsome Heart, The. Gerard Manley Hopkins. FaBoVe

But tell me if the man whom I see here. Dante Alighieri. NAWM-7v1, *tr. by* Allen Mandelbaum *Fr.* Divine Comedy, The (Mandelbaum Translation).

But that from slow dissolving pomps of dawn. Darkness. Arthur Hugh Clough. OxBSP

But That Is Another Story. Donald Justice. CoAP; NoP-4

But that's because back in the time of Plato. Comment on an Observation by One of My Masters. John Hollander. SpudSo

But that's how it is in this world. One minute battling traffic. Next, head. Such a Way to Go. Martha Silano. AmPoNex

But that was nothing to what things came out. Welsh Incident. Robert Graves. NOBE; OBSP; OxBEV; OxBTC

But that which most I wonder at, which most. Innocence. Thomas Traherne. BASC; CABP; ChIV-2; ESCV; MiEL; NOSC

But the breeze has dropped, and silence is the last word. (LL) Fear of Death. John Ashbery. FaBoMo; TAP

But the brief pleasures of life! but the. Lyf So Short, The. Palladas [*or* Pallades]. GrAn, *tr. by* Dudley Fitts

But the child keeps on playing, so I play. (LL) Lost Children, The. Randall Jarrell. CoAP; TAP

But the choir-boy is happy and gay. (LL) Low Church. Stanley J. Sharpless. NBLV; OBCoV; PeLV

But the clerk just curses at him. (LL) Ballad of the Government Granary Clerk. Ho Ching-ming. CoBLCP; ColAnChi, *tr. by* Jonathan Chaves

But the clover is honey and sun and the smell of sleep. (LL) Nebuchadnezzar. Elinor Wylie. ChIV-1; MoAmPo

But the Copperbelt night is a snake. Leader, The. Dorothy Livesay. MoCV

But the darkness has passed, and it's daylight at last, and the night has been long—ditto ditto my song—and thank goodness they're both of them over! (LL) Sir William Schwenck Gilbert. NOBL; OBCoV; OxBoLi; PeLV; PoRA *Fr.* Iolanthe.

But the fleet hours pass pitilessly fleeter. Alfred Austin. VerBaPo *Fr.* Human Tragedy, The.

But the future is different. Future, The. Angel González. VCWP, *tr. by* Steven Ford Brown

But the glory of the Lord is all in all. (LL) Dominus Illuminatio Mea. Richard Doddridge Blackmore. OBEV; SacPr

But the lady's longing would not allow her to sleep. *Unknown.* EroLit *Fr.* Sir Gawain and the Green Knight.

But the last black horse of all. Last Ones, The. "Robin Hyde." PeNZ

But the multitude saw why she wore the bandage." (LL) Edgar Lee Masters. OBSV; PAI *Fr.* Spoon River Anthology.

But the rushing wind killed the budding words. (LL) One Night at Victoria Beach. Gabriel Okara. PBMAP; PoetW

But the sheet was Belfast linen. (LL) Ballad of William Bloat, The. *Unknown.* NOBL; PeLV

But the show was over. (LL) Artist, The. William Carlos Williams. LCAP-2; PAI; RB; SAmP

But the sweet little Bees large Monument. (LL) Black Patch on Lucasta's Face, A. Richard Lovelace. BeJo; CaPo

But the Wine-press of Los is eastward of Golgonooza, before the Seat. William Blake. NOBRP *Fr.* Milton.

But the world shall end when I forget. (LL) Itylus. Algernon Charles Swinburne. NPeEn; UV

But then an even greater sense of the inexpressible. Mario Luzi. ItPo, *tr. by* Gayle Ridinger *Fr.* In the Dark Body of Metamorphosis.

But Then and There the Sun Bore Down. N. Scott Momaday. CDW

But then, flaking off bit by bit, it dissolves--this. Requiem in C. Biagio Cepollaro. ItPo, *tr. by* Gayle Ridinger

But then, how it was sweet! (LL) Confessions. Robert Browning. GTBS-P; NOBE; NOBVV

But there ain't no eagle / On a dime. (LL) Fact. Langston Hughes. APSN; PFTM-1

But there are. John Keats. NPeEn *Fr.* Endymion: A Poetic Romance.

But there is no joy in Mudville—mighty Casey has struck out. (LL) Casey at the Bat. Ernest Lawrence Thayer. APN-2; AiP; AmFaPo; BRP; ChAP; FaBoA; ITBLP; OBAL; OBCA; OBCoV; OxIBACP; PoRA; TCAPo

But there is no road through the woods. (LL) Way through The Woods, The. Rudyard Kipling. ChAP; FaBoCh; HarvBoo; NOBE; NOxBChV; NoAM; OBEV; OxAEP-2; OxBTC; SCGP; WHSW; WoPoe

But there was / once / a time. Eléni Vakaló. WPOW

But there will be life. Death to the Gold Mine! Lindiwe Mabuza. HAWP

But there—something rests on your hand and even. Sapphics for Patience. Anne Finch (b. 1908). FFC

But they come by tens. (LL) Old Lem. Sterling Allen Brown. APT-2; BPo; TTY

But they did not speak; it was not worth while. (LL) Toys Talk of the World, The. Katharine Pyle. NOxBChV; OBCA

But they have been dreamed too, in quiet rooms. Other Places, The. Charles E. Butler. YaYoPo

But they knew they were on duty, replacing. Pope's Carnations Knew Him. Thom Gunn. OBGa

But they know that my country. They Know. Tawfiq Zayyad. MAP, *tr. by* Charles Doria and Sharif Elmusa

But they're salesmen. (LL) Moroccans with the carpets, The. Patrizia Cavalli. NeIt; VCWP, *tr. by* Kenneth Koch

But thine arithmetic is quite correct. (LL) Fragment of a Greek Tragedy. A. E. Housman. NOBL; PeLV; WoPoe

But this fruit-dish (I suppose it is for fruit). Good Thing, A. Ray Mathew. CBAP

But this is our desire, and of its worth. Gyroscope, The. Muriel Rukeyser. YaYoPo

But this security in Jove the great sea-rector spied. Homer. NOSC, *tr. by* George Chapman *Fr.* Iliad, The.

But this, so feminine? Donald Davie. OxBTC *Fr.* Forests of Lithuania, The.

But thou, Israel, My servant. Bible, O.T. TrJP *Fr.* Isaiah.

But though it scar'd, it did not bite. (LL) Silken Snake, The. Robert Herrick. OxBSP; PBRV

But till that day, plase God, I'll stick to wearin' o' the Green. (LL) Wearing of [*or* Wearin' o'] the Green, The. *Unknown.* AWP; OxBoLi

But 'tis to love, as I love you. (LL) Friendship between Ephelia and Ardelia. Anne Finch, Countess of Winchilsea. BWW; ECWP; NALW; NoP-4; PoBW

But, to leave fooling, I assure ye. Charles Cotton. OBCoV *Fr.* Burlesque upon the Great Frost.

But to live in the tragic world forever. (LL) Story about Chicken Soup, A. Louis Simpson. NNaP; PoE; PoWW; TAP; UnSA

But to our tale: the Donna Inez sent. Byron. NAEL-6v2 *Fr.* Don Juan.

But to the bad children, Christmas does not come. (LL) Curse on Herod, A. Amy Witting. ChIV-2; NOBAu

But true expression, like th' unchanging sun. Pope. FHYEP *Fr.* Essay on Criticism, An.

But turning toward Ololon in terrible majesty Milton. William Blake. OxAEP-2 *Fr.* Milton.

But 'twas a famous victory. (LL) Battle of Blenheim, The. Robert Southey. BRP; FaBoWar; OBWP; TFi

But twelve short years you lived, my son. His Son. Callimachus. AWP, *tr. by* G. B. Grundy

But Venus first. Sister Juana Inés de la Cruz. BoWoP *Fr.* First Dream.

But war his overturning trumpet blew. Frederick Goddard Tuckerman. APN-2 *Fr.* Sonnets.

But was I the first martyr, who. Stephen to Lazarus. Clive Staples Lewis. ChIV-2; SacPr

But was there ever dog that praised his fleas? (LL) To a Poet, Who Would Have Me Praise Certain Bad Poets, Imitators of His and Mine. W. B. Yeats. CTC; FaBoEE

But we are exiles from our fathers' land. (LL) Canadian Boat Song. John Galt. FaBoCh; OBEV

But we are set to strive to make our mark. Frederick Goddard Tuckerman. TrCP *Fr.* Sonnets.

But we have none! but we have none! (LL) George Darley. NAEL-5v2; NAEL-6v2; NPeEn *Fr.* Syren Songs.

But we have to see behind all them, there is something. They Receive Instructions against Chile. Pablo Neruda. AF

But we left him alone with his glory. (LL) Burial of Sir John Moore [*after [or* at] Corunna], The. Charles Wolfe. FaBoWar; GTBS-P; NOBE; NOBRP; OBEV; OBWP; OxAEP-2; OxBEV; PWR; PoRA; TFi; TreFP; UV

But we never give Pain or complain. (LL) Breyten Prays for Himself. Breyten Breytenbach. PoetW; VCWP, *tr.* by Denis Hirson

But we're going West tomorrow, with our fortune in our hands. (LL) Western Wagons. Rosemary Benét. AiP; HHAm

But We Shall Bloom. Haim [*or* Chaim *or* Khayim] Guri [*or* Gouri]. TrJP, *tr.* by David Kuselewitz

But we, whose sands run low. Helen Waddell. MLL

But weep to have that which it fears to lose. (LL) William Shakespeare. AWP; EnLoPo; HAP; HeIP-4; NOBE; NoSic; OxAEP-1; PoE; PoRA; SCGP; Son; TreFP *Fr.* Sonnets.

But were always a rose. (LL) Rose Family, The. Robert Frost. NIL-7; OBAL; OBCA

But westward, look, the land is bright. (LL) Say Not the Struggle Nought Availeth. Arthur Hugh Clough. AWP; EBVV; GTBS-P; ITBLP; NAEL-5v2; NAEL-6v2; NOBE; NOBVV; NoP-4; OBEV; OxBEV; SCGP; SacPr; TFi

But what an idea she'd gotten into her head. Silvana Colonna. ItPo, *tr.* by Gayle Ridinger

But what flowers is not his face. My Love is Like a Lily. Kim Ly Bui-Burton. PasH

But what is more thought than a dark over the sun? What is Thought but Won't Hold Still. Clark Coolidge. FTOS

But what is strength without a double share. John Milton. ChIV-1 *Fr.* Samson Agonistes.

But, what of that? (LL) Emily Dickinson. APN-2; NCAP; TAP; TCAPo

But what underneath him lies. (LL) Fulke Greville, 1st Baron Brooke. CABP; NOSC; NoSic *Fr.* Caelica.

But whaur's the Minister? (LL) Last Lauch. Douglas Young. NBLV; OxBS

But when Demophilus begins to sing, / The raven dies. (LL) *Var. authors.* AWP; FaBoEE; OBAL *Fr.* Variations of Greek Themes.

But when I waked, I saw that I saw not. John Donne. NOBE *Fr.* Storm[e], The.

But when the Gods and Heroes heard, they brought. Matthew Arnold. PeVV *Fr.* Balder Dead.

But when the golden-thron'd Aurora made. *Unknown, formerly at. to* Homer. OBVE *Fr.* Hymn to Venus, The.

But when the misbegotten child had grown. Ovid. NAWM-7v1, *tr.* by Allen Mandelbaum *Fr.* Metamorphoses.

But when to mischief mortals bend their will. Pope. OxAEP-1 *Fr.* Rape of the Lock, The; an Heroi-Comical Poem.

But when you are sad, think, Heaven could give no more. (LL) At Parting. Anne Ridler. FaBoWar; LW

But where are the snows of yester-year? (LL) Ballad[e] of Dead Ladies. François Villon. AWP; CTC; OBVE; PoRA, *tr.* by Dante Gabriel Rossetti

But where, O where the skillful healer of the soul? (LL) Andalusian Exile, An. Ahmad Shauqi. BBASP; MAP, *tr.* by M. Mustafa Badawi and John Heath-Stubbs

But where's the bloody horse? (LL) On Some South African Novelists. Roy Campbell. FaBoEE; GTBS-P; InPK-6; MoBrP; NOBL; OBCoV; OxAEP-2; OxBEV; OxBTC; PeLV

But where's the man who counsel can bestow. Pope. OxAEP-1 *Fr.* Essay on Criticism, An.

But wherefore did he take away the crown? William Shakespeare. OxAEP-1 *Fr.* King Henry IV, Pt. II.

But which it only needs that we fulfil. (LL) Prayer in Spring, A. Robert Frost. AH; TrCP

"But who are [*or* art] thou, with curious beauty graced." Opportunity. Niccolò Machiavelli. AWP, *tr.* by James Elroy Flecker

But who is she that walks from yonder hill. Mary Leapor. ECWP *Fr.* Mira's Picture, a Pastoral.

But who killed Johannes, mama . . . ? Lullaby. Jeremy Cronin. PeSAV

But who killed the Jews? (LL) Riddle: "From Belsen a crate of gold teeth." William Heyen. HP; SoSe-8

But who shall parcel out. William Wordsworth. TOF *Fr.* Prelude, The; Growth of a Poet's Mind [1850 vers.].

But whose initial? Left here, illuminated. Annunciation in an Initial R. Angie Estes. ExTi

"But why did he do it, Grandpa?" I said. Confederate Veteran Tries to Explain the Event, A. Robert Penn Warren. CBCWP

"But why do you go?" said the lady, while both sat[e] under the yew. Lord Walter's Wife. Elizabeth Barrett Browning. HAP; NPeEn

But why is Father Larkin talking to the dead? David Jones. PoE *Fr.* In Parenthesis.

But will disclose it in the end. (LL) Lord of Lorn and the False [*or* Fals] Steward, The. *Unknown.* ESPB; OxBB

But winter and rough weather. (LL) William Shakespeare. AWP; GTBS-P; NAEL-5v1; NoSic; OBEV; SCGP; TTTS; UnPo *Fr.* As You Like It.

But with a sure sense of its intrinsic nature. (LL) Garage in Cork, A. Derek Mahon. DiPo; PBCIP

But with long use her tears are dry. (LL) Tennyson. EBVV; NAEL-6v2; NAWM-7v2; PeECV *Fr.* In Memoriam A. H. H.

But with regard to me, I'll satisfy. Dante Alighieri. NAWM-7v1, *tr.* by Allen Mandelbaum *Fr.* Divine Comedy, The (Mandelbaum Translation).

But Woe is mee! who have so quick a Sent. Edward Taylor. TCAPo *Fr.* Preparatory Meditations before My Approach to the Lord's Supper.

But word is come to Warrington. Sir John Butler. *Unknown.* ESPB

But would not bend to shame. (LL) Vashti. Frances Ellen Watkins Harper. BlSi; NALW

But yesterday the earth drank like a child. Letter to His Friend Isaac, A. Judah Halevi. TrJP, *tr.* by Emma Lazarus

But yet, alas, the scar shall still remain. (LL) Sir Thomas Wyatt. NoSic; OxBSP

But you are mine. (LL) Lullaby: "Someone would like to have you for her child." *Unknown.* TTTS; WoPoe, *tr.* by Kwabenia Nketia

But you are not all the avenger. Gunnar Ekelof. PFTM-2, *tr.* by Muriel Rukeyser and Leif Sjöberg *Fr.* Mölna Elegy.

But you know what's. Epilogue (At the Proper Distance). Mariella Bettarini. CItWP, *tr.* by Cinzia Sartini Blum and Lara Trubowitz

But you like none, none you, for constant heart. (LL) William Shakespeare. CTC; EBEV; NoSic; OBEV; OxAEP-1; OxBEV; SCGP *Fr.* Sonnets.

But you, Thomas Jefferson. Brave New World. Archibald MacLeish. NOBA; OxBA

"But you who are so happy here, tell me." Dante Alighieri. EnlH *Fr.* Divina Commedia.

But you will die to-day. (LL) Her Strong Enchantments Failing. A. E. Housman. FaBoTw; NOBE; NOBVV; OxBEV; PeVV; WoPoe

But you will last very long. (LL) Scented Herbage of My Breast. Walt Whitman. APN-1; NAAL-2v1; NAAL-3

But you ye untold latencies will thrill to every page. (LL) Shut Not Your Doors. Walt Whitman. NOBA; OxBA

But young men think it is, and we were young. (LL) Epitaph. A. E. Housman. FaBoEE; HarvBoo; NOBVV; OxBEV; Spl

But your imagining was wrong. Silvana Colonna. ItPo, *tr.* by Gayle Ridinger

Butane, Kerosene, Gasoline. Ann Townsend. NAPBL

Butch once remarked to me how sinister it was. That Pull from the Left. Louise Erdrich. NoAM

"Butch" Weldy. Edgar Lee Masters. APT-1 *Fr.* Spoon River Anthology.

Butcher, A. Thomas Hood. PeLV

Butcher, The. Hugo Williams. OxBTC

Butcher carves veal for two, The. Butcher, The. Hugo Williams. OxBTC

Butcher had prepared the leg of the lamb, The. Robert Duncan. APSN *Fr.* Passages.

Butcher of Abbeville, The. *Unknown.* NAWM-7v1, *tr.* by Ned Dubin

Butcher's Wife, The. Louise Erdrich. HATNAP; NoP-4

Butcher Shop. Charles Simic. AF; InPK-6; LCAP-2; NNaP

Butcher, the baker, the grocer, the clerk, The. There's No Business Like Show Business. Irving Berlin. ReLy

Butchering must be wholesale and the smell, The. Poem to Gentiles. Maxwell Bodenheim. TaR

Butchers, The. Homer. ModIr; NPeEn *Fr.* Odyssey.

Butchers and Tombs. Ivor Gurney. PeFWW

Butt stay my thoughts, make end, geve fortune way. Sir Walter Ralegh. NPeEn *Fr.* Ocean's Love to Cynthia, The.

Butter Charm. *Unknown.* FaBoVe

Butterflies. Angelina Weld Grimké. GT

Butterflies, butterflies. Corn-grinding Song. *Unknown.* AWP, *tr.* by Natalie Curtis

Butterflies in flight. Chikuro. JDP, *tr.* by Yoel Hoffmann

Butterflies in love with evening flowers will not leave until the very end. Walk in the Country, A. T'ang Yen-ch'ien. SuSp, *tr.* by Edward H. Schafer

Butterflies Love Flowers. Li Ch'ing-chao. ErotSp, *tr.* by Sam Hamill
(To the Tune: Butterflies Love Flowers.) CrYelRi

Butterflies might all land on me!, The. (LL) Five-Color. Yang Chi. CoBLCP; WoPoe, *tr.* by Jonathan Chaves

Butterflies of Anxiety. Najaat Al-Udwany. PoArWo, *tr.* by Moulouk Berry and Ali Farghaly

Butterflies paired in ecstatic flight. On a Painting of Ants and Butterflies. Huang T'ing-chien. SuSp, *tr.* by Michael E. Workman

Butterflies, white butterflies, in the sunshine. Butterflies. Angelina Weld Grimké. GT

Butterfly. Buson. EH, *tr.* by Robert Hass

Butterfly. D. H. Lawrence. BLT; NoAM; TTTS

Butterfly, The. Pavel Friedmann. HP, *tr.* by Dennis Silk

Butterfly, The. Pavel Friedmann. INSAB

Butterfly, The. John Fuller. Spl

Butterfly, The. Robert Stephen Hawker. EBVV

Butterfly, a cabbage-white, The. Flying Crooked. Robert Graves. FaBoMo; OxBSP; PeLV; RB; TwCP

Butterfly attending the embroidered flowers, A. (LL)　Linen Industry, The. Michael Longley.　CIP-2; ModIr; NoP-4; PBCIP; PNI

Butterfly, butterfly, butterfly, butterfly.　Butterfly Song.　*Unknown.*　OBVE; TLR, *tr. by* Frances Densmore

Butterfly came to die, A.　Etel Adnan.　PoArWo　*Fr.* Spring Flowers Own, The.

Butterfly Effect, The.　Harry Humes.　BAP-97

Butterfly Garden, The.　Alfred Noyes.　OBGa

Butterfly is the eye, The.　Camouflage.　Marianne Boruch.　BAP-97

Butterfly lands on Park Place, A.　Alexis Rotella.　HA

Butterfly Net, The.　John Bensko.　YaYoPo

Butterfly on Rock.　Irving Layton.　NOBC; NoAM

Butterfly's Ball [and the Grasshopper's Feast], The.　William Roscoe.　NOBRP; OxBEV

Butterfly's Dream, The.　Hannah Flagg Gould.　SWaP

Butterfly Song.　*Unknown.*　OBVE; TLR, *tr. by* Frances Densmore

Butterfly, the wind blows sea-ward, strong beyond the garden wall!　Butterfly. D. H. Lawrence.　BLT; NoAM; TTTS

Butterfly to His Love, The.　Ann Radcliffe.　RWP　*Fr.* Mysteries of Udolpho, The.

Butterfly Upon the Sky, The.　Emily Dickinson.　NOxBChV

Button, A.　Sensation Type and His Friends, The.　Michael Davidson.　FTOS

Button-grass flats, pale through the drizzle: My eyes.　High Country.　Tim Thorne.　BMAP

Button to chin.　*Unknown.*　OxNR

Button up Your Overcoat.　Ray Henderson.　ReLy

Buttoning his fly.　Raymond Roseliep.　HA

Buttons.　Tessa Rose Chester.　MFPA

Buttons.　Walter De la Mare.　PeLi

Buttons.　Mother Goose.　OxNR; ReMoGo

Buttons, a farthing a pair.　Buttons.　Mother Goose.　OxNR; ReMoGo

Buttons and Bows.　Ray Evans.　ReLy

Buwayb.　River and Death, The.　Badr Shakir Al-Sayyab.　PFTM-2, *tr. by* Pierre Joris

Buwayb / Buwayb.　Death and the River.　Badr Shakir Al-Sayyab.　MAP, *tr. by* Lena Jayyusi and Christopher Middleton

Buxom young fellow from London came down, A.　Nine Times a Night.　*Unknown.*　EroLit

Buy a book in brown paper.　Blurb for *Anna Livia Plurabelle*, A.　James Joyce.　OBCoV

Buy a love potion, a gin, a double. (LL)　Gone Are the Days.　Norman MacCaig.　CABP; OxBC

Buy me an ounce and I'll sell you a pound.　E. E. Cummings.　OxBA

Buy One Now.　Dennis Joseph Enright.　NOBL

Buy our little magazine.　Do It Yourself.　Joan Aiken.　KaS; NOxBChV

Buy the paper, take it home.　Coming and Going.　Mitchell Goodman.　VGW

Buy Us a Little Grain.　Christine Lavant.　WPOW, *tr. by* Michael Hamburger

Buying.　Jean Follain.　BLT, *tr. by* Heather McHugh

Buying Fish.　Susan Wicks.　MFPA

Buying Flowers.　Po Chü-i.　TAL

Buying leeks.　Buson.　EH, *tr. by* Robert Hass

Buying new shoes / takes so long.　John Agard.　OTCP

Buzz.　Jim Tollerud.　VoR

Buzz and Hum.　Ben Jonson.　OxNR

Buzz Buzz, the Blue Flies.　*Unknown.*　CoBCP, *tr. by* Burton Watson

Buzz frantic.　Ted Hughes.　NoAM　*Fr.* Orts.

Buzz in the Window.　Ted Hughes.　NoAM　*Fr.* Orts.

Buzz-saw snarled and rattled in the yard, The.　"Out, Out—"　Robert Frost.　APT-1; AmFaPo; ColAP; HAP; HarvBoo; HeIP-4; NAAL-2v2; NAAL-5; OxBA; PAI; RB; SoSe-8; TCAPo; TRP; UnPo; VGW

Buzz subsides. I have come on stage, The.　Boris Leonidovich Pasternak.　*See* Noise dies down. I have appeared, The

Buzz you into unisex twilight.　Amazon Club.　Kenward Elmslie.　PmAP

Buzzard has nothing to fault himself with, The.　In Praise of Self-Deprecation. Wislawa Szymborska.　BLT

Buzzards of my boyhood days are back again, The.　Pembrokeshire Buzzards. Tony Curtis.　TCAWP

Buzzards over Pondy Woods, The.　Robert Penn Warren.　Pondy Woods. MoAmPo

Buzzing darkly almost like thunder.　Mosquitoes.　P'i Jih-hsiu.　SuSp, *tr. by* William H. Nienhauser

BuzzZ.　Alan Pizzarelli.　HA

By a bank as I lay.　Dawn.　*Unknown.*　NoSic

By a bold people's stubborn arms oppressed.　Virgil [*or* Vergil].　BASC, *tr. by* Abraham Cowley　*Fr.* Aeneid [*or* Eneados, Aeneis], The.

By a broken bridge outside the courier station.　Tune: "Song of Divination"— On the Plum Tree.　Lu Yu.　SuSp, *tr. by* James J. Y. Liu

By a clear well, within a little field.　Giovanni Boccaccio.　AWP; EaItPo, *tr. by* Dante Gabriel Rossetti　*Fr.* Sonnets.

By a departing light.　Emily Dickinson.　APN-2

By a forest as I gan fare.　*Unknown.*　MiEL

By a freak of the lustful that spreads like a disease.　Old Home, The.　Amanda Ros.　VerBaPo

By a great, swift water.　Aleksander Wat.　AF; WoPoe, *tr. by* Czeslaw Milosz　*Fr.* Persian Parables.

By a lake below the mountain.　Lady of Trees, The.　Mary Elizabeth Coleridge.　VWP

By a mad miracle I go intact.　Street Song.　Sylvia Plath.　MiVo

By a route obscure and lonely.　Dream-Land [*or* Dreamland].　Edgar Allan Poe.　APN-1; NAAL-2v1; NAAL-3; NOBA; OxBA; TAP

By a Stream on Mount T'ien-t'ung.　Wang An-shih.　SuSp, *tr. by* Jan W. Walls

By a way wandering as I went.　Thank God for All.　John Lydgate.　SacPr　Marc Matthews.　WaCA

By a ways through mento prayers.　By a Ways.　Marc Matthews.　WaCA

By absence, and unkind neglect.　Visit, The.　*Unknown.*　ECWP

By absence from the heart. (LL)　To the Evening Star.　Thomas Campbell.　GTBS-P; NePenScot

By absorption I mean engrossing, engulfing.　Charles Bernstein.　PFTM-2　*Fr.* Artifice of Absorption.

By Accident.　Jane O. Wayne.　InvLad

By accident, I gaze at.　View from the Roof, Waverly Place.　Cornelius Eady.　InvLad

By Achmelvich Bridge.　Norman MacCaig.　OxBS

By admonitions taught. (LL)　Answer, The.　Anne Finch, Countess of Winchilsea.　NAEL-7v1; NALW; NoP-4

By All Lights: 1959.　B. H. Boston.　GeoHom

By all love's soft, yet mighty powers.　Song.　John Wilmot, 2d Earl of Rochester.　BASC

By all the published facts in the case.　About Children.　Phyllis McGinley.　OBAL

By an ancient road, abundant thistle plants.　Liu Tsung-yüan.　SuSp　*Fr.* Farmers.

By an Unknown Poet from Eastern Europe, 1955.　György Petri.　VCWP, *tr. by* George Gömöri and Clive Wilmer

By and by. (LL)　Hope.　Langston Hughes.　OBAL; OBCA; OxIBACP; TRP

By and by.　Epitaph on a Waiter.　David McCord.　APT-2; NBLV; NIP-4; OBAL; OBCoV

By and by, the seasons come and go.　T'ao Ch'ien [*or* T'ao Yuan-ming].　SuSp　*Fr.* Seasons Come and Go, The.

By art a poet is not made;.　For a Poet.　George Wither.　ChIV-2

By Arthur's Dale as late I went.　Bonny Bee Hom.　*Unknown.*　ESPB

By Babel's Streams *with music.*　Philip Freneau.　AH

By becoming a Cabinet Minister. (LL)　On the Birth of His Son.　Su Tung-p'o (Su Shih).　AWP; OBVE; WoPoe, *tr. by* Arthur Waley

By Birth I'm a Slave, yet can give you a Crown.　Enigma.　Matthew Prior.　PeLV

By Blue Ontario's Shore.　Walt Whitman.　APN-1　Poet, The.　MoAmPo

By broken fence is proved a common field. (LL)　Fulke Greville, 1st Baron Brooke.　NAEL-6v1; Son　*Fr.* Caelica.

By candlelight, I read your poems.　Reading Yuan Chen on a Boat.　Po Chü-i.　CrYelRi, *tr. by* Sam Hamill

By channels of coolness the echoes are calling.　Bell-Birds.　Henry Clarence Kendall.　NOBAu

By chapel bare, with walls sea-beat.　Haglets, The.　Herman Melville.　APN-2

By Chreist and St. Patrick, the nation's our own! (LL)　Lilli Burlero [A New Song].　Thomas Wharton, 1st Marquess.　BASC; NOIV; OxBoLi

By Cool Siloam's Shady Rill.　Reginald Heber.　NOCV

By custom doomed to folly, sloth and ease.　Anne Ingram, Viscountess Irwin.　NAEL-7v1

By Cypris, Cupid!　Meleager.　GrAn

By dark severance the apparition head.　Painted Head.　John Crowe Ransom.　APT-1; FuPo; NOBA; NoAM; OxBA

By day and also by night and you are.　Ian Wedde.　PeNZ　*Fr.* Earthly: Sonnets for Carlos.

By day his world extends, far, knotted, hot.　Boy.　Mary Kinzie.　FFC

By day she woo[e]s me, soft, exceeding fair.　World, The.　Christina Georgina Rossetti.　BoWoP; NALW; PEW; ViWPN

By day the bat is cousin to the mouse.　Bat, The.　Theodore Roethke.　APT-2; ChAP; OBCA; PAI

By day the skyscraper looms in the smoke and sun and has a soul.　Skyscraper. Carl Sandburg.　HHAm

By day these men ask nothing, and obey.　Infantry.　Alun Lewis.　PoWW

By denying me the seas, the right to run and fly.　Osip Emilevich Mandelstam [*or* Mandelshtam].　TCRP

By Derwent's rapid stream as oft I strayed. Anna Seward. CenSon *Fr.* Sonnets.

By destiny compell'd, and in despair. Virgil [*or* Vergil]. FaBoWar, *tr. by* John Dryden *Fr.* Aeneid (Dryden translation).

By dint of color. Dab of Color, A. Theodore Weiss. VGW

By divination came the Dorians. In Arcadia. Lawrence Durrell. MoBrPo

By dream[e]s, each one into a several [*or* sev'rall] world. (LL) Dream[e]s. Robert Herrick. BeJo; CaPo; HAP; NAEL-5v1; NAEL-6v1; NAEL-7v1; OPOU; OxBSP; Spl

By duty bound, and not by custom led. To the Memory of My Dear and Ever Honored Father Thomas Dudley Esq. Who Deceased July 31, 1653, and of His Age 77. Anne Bradstreet. NAAL-2v1; NAAL-3

By ear, she sd. Charles Olson. NeAP *Fr.* Maximus Poems, The.

By easy slope to west as if it had. Cheyenne Mountain. Helen Hunt Jackson. APN-2

By famine when he died. (LL) Leonidas. GrAn; PGA

By far the greater half have I seen through. Half-and-Half Song, The. Li Mi-an. ColAnChi, *tr. by* Lin Yutang

By fate, not option, frugal Nature gave. Xenophanes. Ralph Waldo Emerson. APN-1; NOBA

By favorable breezes fanned. Cythère. Paul Verlaine. AWP, *tr. by* Arthur Symons

By feathers green, across Casbeen. Phoenix, The. Arthur Christopher Benson. OBEV

By fifty, you know who you are and, more. Fifty-Fifty. Al Young. SpirFl

By Fire or Flood. David Lindley. NLP

By Flower-and-Moon Pavilion, I stay my carriage. Liu Ya-tzu. SuSp *Fr.* Miscellaneous Poems on Lake Biwa.

By flowering pear. Buson. SoOfWa, *tr. by* Sam Hamill

By Forced Marches. Michael Hofmann. HarvBoo

By Forty-Sixth. Fernando D'Almeida. NAfrP, *tr. by* Faustine Boateng Gyima

By God. Anne Carson. BodElec *Fr.* Truth about God, The.

By God penis, you must be guarded. Penis, The. Dafydd [*or* David] ap Gwilym. EroLit; WoPoe, *tr. by* Dafydd Johnston

By Hallucination Visited. Robert Horan. SPE

By hand-drawn cart, an excursion at evening. Lotus Lake. Ts'ao P'i. CoBCP, *tr. by* Burton Watson

By Hatred out of Envy by Despair. (LL) Epigram: "I had gone broke, and got set to come back." James Vincent Cunningham. MoAmPo; OxBSP; VCAP

By he comes *back* at the *ga*llop again. (LL) Windy Nights. Robert Louis Stevenson. KaS; OTCP; PoRA

By Heart. Ruth Sharman. Prnts

By Heaven! *Unknown.* CoBCP, *tr. by* Burton Watson

By Heaven 'tis false, I am not vain. Defiance, The. Aphra Behn. EnLoPo

By Her Aunt's Grave. Thomas Hardy. MoBrPo *Fr.* Satires of Circumstance in Fifteen Glimpses.

By her the heaven is in his course contained. Edmund Spenser. PoE *Fr.* Faerie Queene, The.

By Heraclides. *Unknown.* OBVE, *tr. by* William Cowper

By his commandment hee maketh the snow to fall apace. Bible, Apocrypha. OBVE *Fr.* Ecclesiasticus.

By his left shoulder, as he sat up again. Lazarus. Ágnes Nemes Nagy. IQMS, *tr. by* Ila Egon

By holding my mirror out of the window I see. Motho Ke Motho Ka Batho Babang (A Person Is a Person because of Other People). Jeremy Cronin. AF

By homely Anguish strung. (LL) Emily Dickinson. APN-2; HeIP-4; NAAL-2v1; NAAL-3; NoP-4; OxBSP; PoE; PoPoPo; TAP; TCAPo

By impetuous gods. (LL) Lady Izumi. BoWoP; WoPoe, *tr. by* Willis Barnstone

By its own nature. Magnificent Peak. Muso Soseki. EaWin, *tr. by* W. S. Merwin

By its shape, like thrushes in clear evenings. (LL) Bride, The. D. H. Lawrence. NoAM; OxBTC

By June our brook's run out of song and speed. Hyla Brook. Robert Frost. APT-1; TCAPo

By landscape reminded once of his mother's figure. Adolescence. W. H. Auden. OxBEV

By Loch Ness they can toss, like confetti. Limerick. Bill Greenwell. PeLi

By Logan's streams that rin sae deep. Logan Braes. John Mayne. OxBS

By looking too long on your perfect face. Pierre de Ronsard. EroLit *Fr.* Sonnets to Helen.

By mirrors, horoscopes / and blood. (LL) Family Jewels. Essex Hemphill. GLP; GT

By mist. O. Mabson Southard. HA

By Monday morning it seems certain. Missing. Tracey Herd. MFPA

By moonlight. Buson. EH, *tr. by* Robert Hass

By mourning beauty crowned[!] (LL) Ode: "Sleep sweetly in your humble graves." Henry Timrod. CBCWP; MakPoe; NOBA; OxBA; TAP

By moving a single board. (LL) Gary Snyder. InPK-6; KaS *Fr.* Hitch Haiku.

By my cold, clean, whispering spring. (LL) Anyte [*or* Anytes]. GrAn; OBVE; PGA; WoPoe, *tr. by* Kenneth Rexroth

By my father. (LL) Self-Portrait. A. K. Ramanujan. NoP-4; PoetW

By my further doing. (LL) Wind Suffers of Blowing, The. Laura Riding Jackson. NPeEn; RB

By natural instinct they change their Lord. (LL) Dryden. ChIV-1; OBSV *Fr.* Absalom and Achitophel.

By naughty boys. (LL) Pigtail. Tadeusz Rózewicz. HP; PoSu

By Night. Philip Jerome Cleveland. SacPr

By Night. Robert Francis. APT-2; VGW

By night around my temple grove. Buddha. Arno Holz. AWP, *tr. by* William Ellery Leonard

By night I saw the *Hunter's moon.* Indian Gone, The! Josiah D. Canning. APN-1

By night on my bed I sought him whom my soul loveth. Bible, *O.T.* TrJP, *tr. by* Willis Barnstone *Fr.* Song of Solomon, The [*or* The Song of Songs].

By night they haunted a thicket of April mist. Spectral Lovers. John Crowe Ransom. APT-1; HeIP-4

By night, Tingribirdi, the hills burned. Babur. Dom Moraes. OMIP

By night we lingered [*or* linger'd] on the lawn. Tennyson. EBVV; FHYEP; HAP; NAEL-6v2; NAWM-7v2; PeECV; TOF *Fr.* In Memoriam A. H. H.

By night within my bed, I roamed here and there. Michael Drayton. ChIV-1 *Fr.* Most Excellent Song Which Was Solomon's, The.

By none but me can the tale be told. White Ship, The. Dante Gabriel Rossetti. OBNV

By noon, as I recall, the sky was clear. Rural Colloquy with a Painter. Timothy Steele. CRP

By noon, the bestial roar of surplus-driven labor. Silence, 2. Stefan Brecht. CLPP

By noon the heat became unbearable. Tea. Ch'u Ch'uang I. OHMPC, *tr. by* Kenneth Rexroth

By noon we'll be deep into it—. Conjugal Visits. Al Young. NAAAL

By now I should be entering on the supreme stage. Pilgrim's Problem. Clive Staples Lewis. TrCP

By now it's like returning to a foreign town, especially. In Port Talbot. John Davies. TCAWP

By now, the satchel's leather has reclaimed its living redolence. Steerage. Albert Goldbarth. TaR

By now you will have met. Voice. W. S. Merwin. NNaP

By numbers here from shame or censure free. Samuel Johnson. NOEC; NPeEn; OBSV; OxAEP-1 *Fr.* London: A Poem in Imitation of the Third Satire of Juvenal.

By ones, by twos. (LL) Issa. EH; ZenPo, *tr. by* Takashi Ikemoto and Lucien Stryk

By our first strange and fatal[l] interview. John Donne. BoLoP; CABP; EBVV; ESCV; FSCP; MeLP; NAEL-5v1; NAEL-6v1; NAEL-7v1; NPeEn; NoSic; OxAEP-1; SCGP *Fr.* Elegies.

By-Products. Baron Wormser. ReTh

By proxy his bomb exploded, his valour shone. (LL) From the Irish. James Simmons. ModIr; PBCIP; PNI

By Rail through the Earthly Paradise, Perhaps Bedfordshire. Denise Levertov. NNaP

By reason good, good reason her to love. (LL) Sir Philip Sidney. NAEL-5v1; NAEL-6v1; NAEL-7v1 *Fr.* Astrophil and Stella.

By reason of two and poore of one. God and Man Set as One. *Unknown.* SacPr

By rights one should experience holy dread. Eros. Timothy Steele. RA

By road, a matter of several miles. (LL) Brown's Descent; or, The Willy-Nilly. Robert Frost. MoAmPo; PoRA

By's beard the Goat, by his bush-tail the Fox. Of Kate's Baldness. John Davies of Hereford. FaBoEE

By Saint [*or* Saynt] Mary, my lady. John Skelton. NOBE; NPeEn; NoSic; OBEV; OxBoLi; SCGP; TTTS *Fr.* Garland [*or* Garlande *or* Garlands] of Laurel[l], The.

By scribbled names on walls, by telephone number. Village Spa. Phyllis McGinley. OBCoV

By sea, by land, harass us. Boycott. Khalil Mutran. MAP, *tr. by* Issa Boullata and Thomas G. Ezzy

By silver reeds in a silver stream. (LL) Silver. Walter De la Mare. MoBrPo; PoRA; TTTS

By six he's started. I wake to a wince and arrh. Demolisher. Alan Gould. BMAP

By sloth on sorrow fathered. Lollocks. Robert Graves. RB

By some derision of wild circumstance. Reunion. Edwin Arlington Robinson. NOBA

By some sad means, when reason holds no sway. Philip Freneau. TCAPo *Fr.* House of Night, The.

By sparrows drawn, there's now no chance. Disaster, The. Mary Savage. ECWP

By spring banks waterplants are green. Painting "Solitary Fisherman by a Spring River" The. Ni Tsan. CoBLCP, *tr.* by Jonathan Chaves

By St. Thomas Water. Charles Causley. OBSP

By steps we may ascend to God. (LL) John Milton. NAEL-5v1; NAEL-6v1 *Fr.* Paradise Lost.

By strangers' coasts and waters, many days at sea. Catullus 101. Catullus. WoPoe, *tr.* by Robert Fitzgerald

By-street was bathed in sun, The. Andrey [*or* Andrei] Bely [*or* Belyi]. PFTM-1 *Fr.* Dramatic Symphony, The.

By Stubborn Stars. Kenneth Leslie.
    "Silver herring throbbed thick in my seine, The." NOBC; OxBSo

By sundown we came to a hidden village. Conquerors. Henry Treece. OBWVE; TCAWP

By T'ing Yang Waterfall. Hsieh Ling-yün. OHMPC, *tr.* by Kenneth Rexroth

By taking the impressions of watch-cases he discovered, one day. William McGonagall. VerBaPo *Fr.* Sprig of Moss, The.

By Talland Church as I did go. Planted Heel, The. Sir Arthur Thomas Quiller-Couch. EBVV

By That Long Scan of Waves. Walt Whitman. NAAL-2v1; NAAL-3 *Fr.* Fancies at Navesink.

By that summer snapshot on someone else's porch. I Swear. Bella [*or* Izabella] Akhatovna Akhmadulina. TCRP, *tr.* by Albert C. Todd

By that the Manciple hadde his tale ended. Geoffrey Chaucer. NAEL-5v1; NAEL-6v1 *Fr.* Canterbury Tales, The.

By the Arno. Oscar Wilde. EBVV

By the ascension [*or* Assention] of thy Lawn, see All. (LL) To Dianeme. Robert Herrick. CaPo; NOSC

By the Babylonish waters. Heinrich Heine. TrJP, *tr.* by Charles Godfrey Leland *Fr.* Hebrew Melodies.

By the Bivouac's Fitful Flame. Walt Whitman. BLT; NoAM; NoP-4; OxBA; PoE

By the blue taper's trembling light. Thomas Parnell. NOEC

By the Boat House, Oxford. Anne Stevenson. FaBoWP

By the bonnie milldams o' Binnorie. (LL) Binnorie; or, The Two Sisters. *Unknown.* OBEV; PoE

By the Campfire. Konstantin Mikhailovich Simonov. TCRP, *tr.* by Lubov Yakovleva

By the child dying at his mother's side. Five Sorrowful Mysteries, The. Francis Jammes. GI, *tr.* by Jeffrey Fiskin

By the City Gate. Ts'ui Hao. OHMPC, *tr.* by Kenneth Rexroth

By the crumbling fire we talked. Witness. John Montague. CIP-2

By the Danube. Attila József. IQMS, *tr.* by Peter Zollman

By the dry road the fathers cough and spit. Brief Journey West, The. Howard Nemerov. NoAM

By the fierce flames of love I'm in a sad taking. Love Song. Royall Tyler. TAP

By the fifth month. Suikoku. JDP, *tr.* by Yoel Hoffmann

By the Fire. Mother Goose. OxNR
    (Pussy-cat by [*or* beside] the fire.) ReMoGo

By the Fire-Side. Robert Browning. EBVV

By the first of August. I Remember. Anne Sexton. LW

By the flat cup and the splash of new vontage. Horace. CTC, *tr.* by Ezra Pound *Fr.* Odes.

By the flow of the inland river. Blue and the Gray, The. Francis Miles Finch. APN-2; CBCWP

By the Ford. Edward Thomas. OxBSP

By the gas-fire, kneeling. Olga Poems. Denise Levertov. LCAP-2; NNaP

By the gate with star and moon. Medallion. Sylvia Plath. HeIP-4

By the Gold River, in mid-autumn, the bows of our enemy are drawn. Early Geese. Tu Mu. SuSp

By the hearth a holier Lar! (LL) Celia's Home-Coming. Agnes Mary Frances Robinson. OBEV; VWP

By the images of things. Epoch. Vladimir Holan. PoSu, *tr.* by Ian and Jarmila Milner

By the injustice of the skies for punishment? (LL) Cold Heaven, The. W. B. Yeats. AWP; CTC; GTBS-P; HAP; NPeEn; NoAM; OxBSP; RB

By the Jordan. Herman Melville. NCAP

By the lake at Armenonville in the Bois de Boulogne. Armenonville. Edna St. Vincent Millay. NoP-4

By the lamplit stall I loitered, feasting my eyes. Sight. Wilfrid Wilson Gibson. MoBrPo

By the light of the harvest moon. Moons. Peter Fallon. BiHa

By the light of the moon. (LL) So We'll Go No More A-Roving. Byron. AWP; BoLoP; CABP; ChAP; ClHu; FHYEP; HAP; HeIP-4; MakPoe; NAEL-5v2; NAEL-6v2; NOBE; NPeEn; NePenScot; NoP-4; OPOU; OxBS; OxBSP; PAI; PoE; PoRA; SCGP; TFi; TTTS; WoPoe

By the light of the night. Journey of the Shadow, The. Nada El-Hage. PoArWo, *tr.* by Nathalie El-Hani

By the Light of the Silvery Moon. Edward Madden. ReLy

By the long sojourning. Meo Abbracciavacca. EaItPo, *tr.* by Dante Gabriel Rossetti

By the Looking-Glass. Augusta Davies Webster. VWP

By the lyre I rose, fell with the flute. Thebes. Honestus. GrAn, *tr.* by Peter Jay

By the Margin of the Great Deep. "Æ." OBEV

By the margin of the ocean, one morning [*or* one pleasant evening] in the month of June. Bonny Bunch of Roses O, The. *Unknown.* OxBoLi

By the Nape. Sandra Alcosser. ExTi

By the new Boot's, a tool-chest with flagpoles. Kingsley Amis. NOBL; NoAM; OxBTC *Fr.* Evans Country, The.

By the North Gate, the wind blows full of sand. Lament of the Frontier Guard. Li Po. APT-1; NPeEn; OBVE; OBWP; VGW, *tr.* by Ezra Pound

By the North Sea. Aleksandr Aleksandrovich Blok. TCRP, *tr.* by Geoffrey Thurley

By the old Moulmein Pagoda, lookin' lazy at [*or* eastward to] the sea. Mandalay. Rudyard Kipling. BRP; HarvBoo; MoBrPo; NOBE; NPeEn; OxAEP-2

By the old temple. Basho. EH, *tr.* by Robert Hass

By the older flood of the ocean, to swallow it. (LL) Haunted Country. Robinson Jeffers. APT-1; OxBA

By the Pasture Bars. George Sands Johnson. PWR

By the Pond. Roy Fisher. *Fr.* City.

By the Potomac. Thomas Bailey Aldrich. Son

By the River. Wang An-shih. CoBCP, *tr.* by Burton Watson

By the River Ashley. Mary Ursula Bethell.
    "Hour is dark. The river comes to its end, The." PeNZ
    "Sauntering home from church we lingered." PeNZ
    "That bridge from the city, that was Waimakariri." PeNZ

By the riverbank idly I pick white-budded reeds. Thoughts South of the Yangtze. Yü Hu. CoBCP, *tr.* by Burton Watson

By the Rivers. Shirley Kaufman. GifTon

"By the Rivers of Babylon." Mary Weston Fordham. CBWP-2

By the rivers of Babylon there we sat down and wept. Psalm 137. Genrik Veniaminovich Sapgir. ItGoST, *tr.* by J. Kates

By the rivers of Babylon, there we sat down, yea, we wept, when [*or* then] we remembered Zion. Bible, O.T. AWP; NAWM-5v1; TrJP *Fr.* Psalms.

By the Rivers of Babylon We Sat Down and Wept. Byron. ChIV-1

By the Road. Geoffrey Grigson. OxBTC

By the road in spring, rain has added flowers. Tune: "Happy Events Approaching." Ch'in Kuan. SuSp, *tr.* by James J. Y. Liu

By the road to the contagious hospital. Spring and All. William Carlos Williams. APT-1; ChAP; ColAP; HAP; InPK-6; MakPoe; NAAL-2v2; NAAL-5; NOBA; NoAM; OxBA; PoE; PoPoPo; TAP; TCAPo; TFi; TRP

By The Road to the Sunnyvale Air-Base. Yvor Winters. APT-2

By the roots of my hair some god got hold of me. Hanging Man, The. Sylvia Plath. HCAP; VCAP

By the rude bridge that arched the flood. Concord Hymn. Ralph Waldo Emerson. AWP; AiP; BRP; ClHu; ColAP; FaBoA; HAP; HeIP-4; NOBA; NoP-4; OBWP; OxBA; PeECV; PoPoPo; TAP; TCAPo; TFi

By the rushy-fringèd bank. John Milton. OxBEV *Fr.* Comus; a Masque Presented at Ludlow Castle.

By the sad waters of separation. Exile. Ernest Christopher Dowson. BoLoP

By the Same. To Solitude. Charlotte Smith. CenSon; RWP

By the Sea. Emily Dickinson. APN-2; HAP; InPK-6; NAAL-2v1; NAAL-3; WeW-3
    (I Started Early, Took My Dog.) ColAP

By the sea. Muso Soseki. EaWin, *tr.* by W. S. Merwin

By the Sea. Christina Georgina Rossetti. NOBVV; NPeEn

By the sea's side hear the dark-vowelled birds. (LL) Especially When the October Wind. Dylan Thomas. AngWePo; MoBrPo; OBWVE; OxAEP-2; OxBTC

By the second / night of the storm, the ground had grown. Currents. Rose Solari. AmPoNex

By the sewage puddles of Sabra and Shatila. You Can't Kill a Baby Twice. Dahlia Ravikovitch [*or* Ravikovich]. VCWP

By the solemn proceeds of thy innocent rum. (LL) Alas! Carolina! J. Gordon Coogler. OBAL; VerBaPo

By the Sound. John Hollander. MakPoe

By the spring pond, deep and wide. Duckweed Pond. Wang Wei. CoBCP, *tr.* by Burton Watson

By the Statue of King Charles [*or* I] at Charing Cross. Lionel Pigot Johnson. MoBrPo; NOBE; OBEV; OBMV; PeVV

By the Swanannoa. William Gilmore Simms. APN-1

By the third day, the rain. Thanksgiving. Steve Hassett. CDa

By the time I got to them, the woman was stoned. Burden, The. Anne Caston. NAPBL

By the time the priest started into his sermon. Divorce Referendum, Ireland, 1986, The. Paul Durcan. BiHa; PBCIP

By the time they are finished. Oya Now. Ifi Amadiume. NAfrP

By the time you read this. Letter. W. S. Merwin. HAP

By the time you swear you're his. Unfortunate Coincidence. Dorothy Parker. LW; NoP-4

By the water-clock it's past dawn as the day watch sounds. Tu Fu. CarOv, *tr. by* Carolyn Kizer *Fr.* Adviser to the Court.

By the Waterfall. Friedrich Adler. TrJP, *tr. by* Jethro Bithell

By the Waters of Babylon. Heinrich Heine. TrJP, *tr. by* Charles Godfrey Leland *Fr.* Hebrew Melodies.

By the Waters of Babylon. Emma Lazarus. WPE

By the waters of Babylon we sat down and wept. Psalm 137. *Unknown.* WoPoe, *tr. by* Miles Coverdale

By the Waters of the Sava. Uri Zvi Greenberg. MHP, *tr. by* Ruth Finer Mintz

By the way we met. William Shakespeare. OBCoV *Fr.* Comedy of Errors, The.

By the Well of Living and Seeing. Charles Reznikoff. "Highway I was walking on, The." FTOS

By the whole heave and settle of the sea. (LL) Frederick Goddard Tuckerman. APN-2; TCAPo *Fr.* Sonnets.

By the Winding River I. Tu Fu. OHPC, *tr. by* Kenneth Rexroth

By the Winding River II. Tu Fu. OHPC, *tr. by* Kenneth Rexroth

By the women of Marblehead! (LL) Skipper Ireson's Ride. John Greenleaf Whittier. APN-1; NCAP; NOBA; OBAL; OBCA; OxBA

By their impressive long run back. (LL) Unfinished Race, The. Norman Cameron. OxBS; OxBSo

By their nephews and their nieces. (LL) Good and Bad Children. Robert Louis Stevenson. ChAP; EBVV; FaBoCh; OBCoV

By Themis & the wine that made me tipsy. Phanias. GrAn

By themselves in the twilight. Leonidas. PGA

By then, by the time my brother. Not Knowing. Gary Soto. NoP-4

By these, by these same chains, O Rome. Alcuin. MLL

By thine own named town made famous in thy fall. Michael Drayton. NOSC *Fr.* Polyolbion.

By this fire I still can feel the wind. Blues. Suzanne Gardinier. AmPoNex

By this good wicked spirit, sweet angel devil. (LL) Michael Drayton. NOBE; NoSic *Fr.* Idea.

By this Leander being near the land. Christopher Marlowe. EBEV; NPeEn *Fr.* Hero and Leander.

By this mighty arm his rights shall be obtained! (LL) Black Sampson, The. Josephine D. Henderson Heard. CBWP-4; SWaP

By this [*or* thys] fire [*or* fyre] I warm[e] my handes [*or* handys]. Months, The. *Unknown.* MiEL

By this the Northerne wagoner had set. Edmund Spenser. FHYEP; NoSic *Fr.* Faerie Queene, The.

By this the sun had sucked up the vast deep. Michael Drayton. NOSC *Fr.* Noah's Flood.

By this time. Mid-Year Report: For Haruko. June Jordan. ReTh

By this time had they reached the Stygian pool. Ben Jonson. NOSC *Fr.* On the Famous Voyage.

By this time long-gowned Lumen walked abroad. William Rankins. OBSV *Fr.* Satyrus Peregrinans.

By this title, the book declares itself, and the amount of riches that it conceals. A—B—on the Learned Bartholo Sylva. Anne Cooke Bacon. EMWP

By Those Eyes Where Sweet Expression. Lady Caroline Lamb. RWP

By those true tears y' are weeping. (LL) To a Gentlewoman Objecting to Him His Grey Hairs. Robert Herrick. BeJo; CaPo

By Three Kinds of Flowers I'm Challenged. *Hungarian Oral Tradition.* IQMS, *tr. by* Adam Makkai

By thunders of white silence, overthrown. (LL) Hiram Powers' "Greek Slave." Elizabeth Barrett Browning. GS; NALW; ViWPN

By Timo's locks. Meleager. GrAn

By unnumbered ways of dream to death. (LL) Immortality. "Æ." AWP; OBMV

By vew of her he ginneth to revive. Edmund Spenser. CAGL *Fr.* Faerie Queene, The.

By viewing nature, nature's handmaid, art. Dryden. BASC *Fr.* Annus Mirabilis.

By Vows of Love Together Bound. Eleazar Thompson Fitch. AH

By vulgar Eros long misled. Song. Sarah Ponsonby. PoBW

By warm blood of bird. Spell to Protect Our Love. Jeni Couzyn. HAWP

By Water Divined. Kathleene West. GifTon

By Wauchopeside. Hugh MacDiarmid. EBEV; OxAEP-2

By way of a leak. Times Square Water Music. Amy Clampitt. UrbNat

By way of a vanished bridge we cross this river. Garden Shukkei-en, The. Carolyn Forché. ExTi

By Way of Preface. Edward Lear. *See* How Pleasant to Know Mr. Lear

By way of pretext. *Var. authors.* AWP *Fr.* Manyo Shu, Part 1 of 4.

By west, under a wilde wode-side. *Unknown.* MiEL

By what appalling dim upheaval. Simon Gerty. Elinor Wylie. OBAL

By what eternal streams. (LL) To One in Paradise. Edgar Allan Poe. BoLoP; OBEV; OxBA; TAP

By what sends. Children's Rhymes. Langston Hughes. BPo; NOxBChV

By woods and water, whose houses are these. Grand Houses at Lo-yang, The. Po Chü-i. ChiP, *tr. by* Arthur Waley

By Yangtze and Han. Tu Fu. CrYelRi, *tr. by* Sam Hamill

By your breasts. Conversation between the Chevalier de Chamilly and Mariana Alcoforado in the Manner of a Song of Regret. *Unknown.* BoWoP, *tr. by* Helen R. Lane

By your unnumbered charities. Hospital for Defectives. Thomas Blackburn. GTBS-P; OxBTC

Bye and bye. (LL) Chillen Get Shoes. Sterling Allen Brown. APT-2; NoP-4

Bye, baby bunting. Mother Goose. OxBEV; OxNR; ReMoGo

Bye, bye, baby bunting / Daddy's gone a-hunting. *Unknown.* OxNR

Bye Bye Blackbird. Ray Henderson. ReLy

Bye Bye Blackbird. John James. Oth

Bypassing Rue Descartes. Czeslaw Milosz. VCWP, *tr. by* Renata Gorczynski and Robert Hass

Byrnies, The. Thom Gunn. NoAM; OxBTC

Byron. J. Gordon Coogler. OBAL; VerBaPo

Byron and Shelley and Keats. Dorothy Parker. APT-1; NALW *Fr.* Pig's-Eye View of Literature, A.

Bystander, The. Rosemary Dobson. CBAP

Byzantium. W. B. Yeats. EBEV; FaBoMo; HAP; HarvBoo; MoBrPo; NAEL-5v2; NAEL-6v2; NAWM-7v2; NIL-7; NIP-4; NOBE; NoAM; NoP-4; OxBEV; OxBTC; PoE

Byzantium I Come Not From. Ray Bradbury. IllVoic

BZZZZZZZ. Amy Gerstler. PmAP

C

C. C. Rider. Lucille Clifton. GT

C. calls to tell me Mercury is in retrograde, so watch out. Just last night, walking. Chapel of the Miraculous Medal. Mark Wunderlich. NAPBL

C——e, whom providence hath placed. To the Hon. Mrs. C——e. Jane West. ECWP

"C" ing in Colors: Blue. Safiya Henderson-Holmes. SpirFl

"C" ing in Colors: Red. Safiya Henderson-Holmes. SpirFl

C. L. M. John Masefield. MoBrPo; OxBTC

C Major of this life: so, now I will try to sleep, The. (LL) Abt Vogler. Robert Browning. FHYEP; NAEL-5v2; NAEL-6v2; TOF

C o y O t e. Marlene Mountain. HA

C / olumbus from his after-. Colombe. Edward Kamau Brathwaite. VCWP

C Stands for Civilization. Kenneth Fearing. TrJP

C. T. at the Five Spot. Thulani Davis. SeSe

C33. Hart Crane. CAGL

Ca' the Yowes to the Knowes. *Unknown.* OxBS

Cabal at Nickey Nackey's, The. Aphra Behn. NOSC

Cabalistic Rabbis, The. Rosita Kalina. MirDau, *tr. by* Roberta Gordenstein

Cabalists, The. Angelina Muñiz Huberman. MirDau, *tr. by* Aurora Camacho

Cabaret. Sterling Allen Brown. APT-2; NAAAL

Cabaret. Fred Ebb. ReLy

Cabaret McGonagall. W. N. Herbert. NeBl

Cabato. Ray Gonzalez. TouFir

Cabbage. Rosemary Norman. BrRo

Cabbage Butterfly, The. Henri Cole. UrbNat

Cabin-Boy, The. George Villiers, 2d Duke of Buckingham. NOSC

Cabin in the Clearing, A. Robert Frost. APT-1

Cabin in the Sky. John Latouche. ReLy

Cabin Tale, A. Paul Laurence Dunbar. NAAAL

Cabinet of Seeds Displayed, A. Howard Nemerov. CRP

Cable Ship, The. Harry Edmund Martinson. RB, *tr. by* Robert Bly

Cabralism. The civilization of the donées. The willing and the exportation. Babbling. Oswald de Andrade. TCLAP, *tr. by* Flavia Vidal

Cachalot, The. Edwin John Pratt. "Thousand years now had his breed, A." MoCV "Where Cape Delgado strikes the sea." MoCV

Cackle, cackle, Mother Goose. *Unknown.* OxNR

Cacoëthes Scribendi. Oliver Wendell Holmes. NBLV; OBCoV

"Cacophony?!"—Let it be that! If in. Bartók. Gyula Illyés. IQMS, *tr. by* Robert C. Kenedy

Cactus. Jean-Joseph Rabéarivelo [*or* Rebéarivelo]. NegPo, *tr. by* Ellen Conroy Kennedy

(That multitude of moulded hands.) PBMAP

Cada Puerco Tiene Su Sábado. Martín Espada. TouFir

Cadaver Politic. Tom Paulin. PNI

Cadgwith. Lionel Pigot Johnson. SacPr

Cae Iago: May Day. Roland Mathias. TCAWP

Caedmon. Denise Levertov. NoAM; NoP-4

Caedmon. Aidan Carl Mathews. PBCIP

Caedmon. Norman Nicholson. FaBoTw

Caedmon's Hymn. Caedmon. EBEV

Cædmon's Hymn. Caedmon. ASW, *tr. by* Kevin Crossley-Holland

Caelia. William Browne (1591–1643). Son

Caelica. Fulke Greville, 1st Baron Brooke.

"*Cupid,* in *Myra's* faire bewitching eyes." PBRV

("Farewell sweet Boy, complaine not of my truth.") NPeEn

Farewell to Cupid. Son

("I with whose colors *Myra* drest her head.") OxBEV; PBRV

"In night, when colors [*or* colours] all to black[e] are cast." NAEL-7v1; NPeEn; Son

"In those years when our sense, desire and wit." NOCV

Love's Glory. Son

Myra. HAP; NOBE; NoSic; OBEV

"Nurse-life wheat within his green husk growing, The." NoP-4

Sion Lies Waste. ChIV-1; NoSic; PeECV

Sonnet "All my senses, like beacon's flame". CABP; NOSC; NoSic

Sonnet: "Caelica, I overnight was finely used" NAEL-6v1; Son

Sonnet: "Down[e] in the depth of mine iniquity." CABP; NOSC; NoSic; NPeEn; PBRV; SacPr

Sonnet: "Earth with thunder torn, with fire blasted, The" NoSic

Sonnet: "Eternall Truth, almighty, infinite" NoSic; SacPr

Sonnet: "Little Hearts, where light-wing'd Passion raignes, The." PBRV

Sonnet: "Love is the peace, whereto all thoughts do strive" NPeEn; NoSic

Sonnet: "Man, dream[e] no more of curious mysteries" NOSC; NoSic

Sonnet: "O false and treacherous Probability." SacPr

Sonnet: "Three things there be in mans opinion dear[e]" NOCV; NOSC; NoSic

Sonnet: "Whenas [*or* When as] man's life, the light of human lust" CABP; NOSC; NoSic

"When all this All doth pass from age to age." EBEV; NoSic

"World, that all contains, is ever moving, The." NoSic

Caernarfon, 2 July 1969. T. Glynne Davies. OBWVE, *tr. by* Joseph P. Clancy

Caesar. W. S. Merwin. LCAP-2

Caesar and Brutus. Anne Finch, Countess of Winchilsea. EMWP

Caesar! renowned in silence as in war. On the Prospect from Westminster Bridge. Elizabeth Tollet. ECWP

Caesar's back, and they've built him a throne to sit on. Brutus' Last Song. Christiana Whitehead. NeBl

Caesar's Palace. Moorer Denies Holyfield in Twelve. Olena Kalytiak Davis. AmPoNex; MoASP

Caesar's Song. Mother Goose. OxNR; ReMoGo

Cæsura. John Ashbery. ChIV-1

Caesura. Kenneth Mackenzie. CBAP; NOBAu

Cafe. Czeslaw Milosz. PoSu, *tr. by* Jan Darowski

Café du Dôme. Else Von Freytag-Loringhoven. APT-1; SurPaPo

Café in Warsaw. Allen Ginsberg. HAP

Café of Situations, The. Martin Johnston. BMAP *Fr.* In Transit: A Sonnet Square.

Café: 3 A.M. Langston Hughes. GLP; HCAP

Caffer Commando, The. Thomas Pringle. PeSAV

Cage, The. Geoffrey Chaucer. OWoS *Fr.* Canterbury Tales, The.

Cage, The. David Gascoyne. SPE

Cage, The. John Montague. CIP-2; PNI

Cage, The. James Stephens. OxBEV; OxBTC

Cage, The. Rosamund Marriott Watson. VWP

Cage Bird swung. Cage Bird and Sky Bird. Leslie Norris. OTCP

Cage of Voices, The. Horace Gregory. APT-2

Cage wrote 4'33." Pedagogy. Lin Max. MiVo

Caged Bird. Maya Angelou. WeW-3

Caged Bird, A. Sarah Orne Jewett. APN-2; ColAP

Caged Birds. Ignacy Krasicki. WoPoe, *tr. by* Jerzy Peterkiewicz and Burns Singer

Caged Goldfinch, The. Thomas Hardy. OWoS

Caged Rats. Ebenezer Elliott. EBEV

Caged Skylark, The. Gerard Manley Hopkins. MoBrPo; OBMV; OWoS; SoSe-8; Son

Caged Stone. Martha Vertreace. IllVoic

Cages, The. James Tate. YaYoPo

Cahoots. Carl Sandburg. APT-1

Cain. Irving Layton. MoCV

Cain: A Mystery. Byron.

"And now I will convey thee to thy world." NOBRP

"Hear, Jehovah! / May the eternal serpent's curse be on him!" NOBRP

"Oh! thou dead / And everlasting witness! whose unsinking." ChIV-1

Cain cannot die. (LL) Cain the Immortal. Yusuf Al-Khal. MAP; PFTM-2, *tr. by* Sargon Boulus and Samuel Hazo

Can't nobody tell me any different. Song No. 3. Sonia Sanchez. FFC; NOxBChV

Cain the Immortal. Yusuf Al-Khal. MAP; PFTM-2, *tr. by* Sargon Boulus and Samuel Hazo

Caint call your name. Hermit Cackleberry Brown, on Human Vanity, The. Jonathan Williams. OBAL; PoM

Cairo Jag. Keith Douglas. HarvBoo; PoWW

Cajun. Sheryl St. Germain. OPRER

Cake in the oven, clothes out on the line. Rockin' a Man, Stone Blind. Carolyn Beard Whitlow. FFC

Cakes Continue to Rise. Rick Agran. AmPoNex

Cala-Achí! Ha! Aha! Yeha! Ahau! Wow! Achí! *Unknown.* STP *Fr.* Rabinal-Achí.

Calamiterror. George Barker.

Section VI. SPE

Calamity and conflagration! Strife! Scythinus. CAGL, *tr. by* Daryl Hine

Calamity in London; Family of Ten Burned to Death. William McGonagall. VerBaPo

Calamity of seals begins with jaws, The. Seals at High Island. Richard Murphy. BiHa; CIP-2; ModIr; PBCIP

Calcined stones come back, The. Homecoming of Love Amongst Illustrious Ruins. Rafael Alberti. CLPP, *tr. by* Kenneth Rexroth

Calculated figures, estimated lives. Boom Time. Stephen Clayton. IBA

Calculating Clara. Harry Graham. PeLV *Fr.* Some Ruthless Rhymes.

Calculus fit to compute on, A. Limerick. Gina Berkeley. PeLi

Calcutta sits like a stone on my chest. Calcutta and I. Sunil Gangopadhyay. OMIP, *tr. by* Sujit Mukherjee

Caleb Barnes. David Wright. NLP

Caledonia. Colleen J. McElroy. BlSi; NAAAL

Caledonia. Anthony Powell. NOBL

Caledonian Antisyzygy, The. Hugh MacDiarmid. OxBEV

Calendar. Cecil Bodker. BoWoP, *tr. by* Nadia Christensen and Alexander Taylor

Calendar full, future unknown, The. Black Postcards. Tomas Tranströmer. WoPoe, *tr. by* Joanna Bankier

Calendar is ironic, The. The stripper dances. Dancing Sunshine Lounge, The. Thomas Rabbitt. ReTh

Calendar of Oengus, The. *Unknown.*

"This sad world we inhabit." NOIV

Calendar of the Air. Yevgeny [*or* Evgenii] Borisovich Rein. TCRP, *tr. by* Lubov Yakovleva

Calenture, The. Randolph Stow. BMAP

Calf. Katrina Porteous. NeBl

Calf and the Ox, The. Avianus. WoPoe, *tr. by* David R. Slavitt

Caliban. Edward Kamau Brathwaite. HarvBoo

Caliban in Blue. Walter McDonald. CDa

Caliban in the Coal Mines. Louis Untermeyer. MoAmPo; TrJP

Caliban's Books. Michael Donaghy. EmeKit

Caliban's Journal. Suniti Namjoshi. RACG

Caliban upon Setebos; or, Natural Theology in the Island. Robert Browning. AWP; EBEV; FHYEP; NAEL-5v2; NAEL-6v2; NOBVV; OxAEP-2; PeVV

Calico-pale paddocks through the window, The. Song for Past Midnight. Geoffrey Lehmann. CBAP

Calico Pie. Edward Lear. FaBoCh; NOxBChV

Calico summer, The. Moon/light quarter/back sack. Samuel F. Reynolds. SpirFl

California. Paul Hoover. BAP-97

California. John Rollin Ridge.

"And shall we view these miracles and more." APN-2

California. David St. John. SwNoth

California Coast. Jean V. Gier. ReBoTo

California Dreaming. Carol Lem. GeoHom

California Dreaming. Rochelle Nameroff. SwNoth

California, 1852. Sharyn Jeanne Skeeter. ISC

California Entertainment, 1936. Wilma Elizabeth McDaniel. GeoHom

California Girlhood, A. Alice Notley. PmAP

California, Here I Come. Joseph Meyer. ReLy

California Hills in August. Dana Gioia. DiPo; InPK-6

California Light. Sherley Anne Williams. GeoHom

California Madrigal. Bret Harte. APN-2

California night. The Devil's wind. In Chandler Country. Dana Gioia. GeoHom

California Peninsula: El Camino Real. Al Young. GT; GeoHom

California Poem. Chryss Yost. GeoHom

California Potatoes. Denise Low. SpudSo

California, *She Replied*. Kathy Fagan. GeoHom

California Spring. Charles Wright. ColAP

California Twilight. Charles Wright. GeoHom

California Winter. Karl Shapiro. AiP

California Winter. Edward Rowland Sill. APN-2

Caliph shot a gazelle, The. Humorous Verse. Abu Dulama. TTY, *tr. by* Raoul Abdul

Calisto. John Crowne.
   Song: "Kind lovers, love on." OxBSP

Call. Sarah Kirsch. PFTM-2, *tr. by* Wayne Kvam *Fr.* Kite-Flying.

Call. Noémia da Sousa. HAWP, *tr. by* Jacques-Noël Gouat

Call, The. Anna Laetitia Barbauld. SacPr

Call, The. John Hall. MeLP; NOSC

Call, The. Robert Harris. BMAP

Call, The. Dennis Haskell. NOBAu

Call, The. Thomas Osbert Mordaunt. *See* Verses Written during the War, 1756–1763

Call, The. Sir Walter Scott. *See* Old Mortality

Call, The. *Unknown.* OBEV

Call and assemble together Aotearoa. Call Together. Kohine Whakarua Ponika. PeNZ, *tr. by* Sam Karetu

Call Awe, then, what you will, long long ago. Freight. John Frederick Nims. GM

Call back your odours, lonely flowers. Night-Blooming Flowers. Felicia Dorothea Hemans. NOBRP

Call Boy. Sterling Allen Brown. GM

Call, by all means, but just once. Voice. Ann Sansom. NeBl

Call—call—and bruise the air. Expression. Isaac Rosenberg. MoBrPo

Call for more pens, more paper, and more ink. (LL) Cacoëthes Scribendi. Oliver Wendell Holmes. NBLV; OBCoV

Call for the Robin-Redbreast and the Wren. John Webster. EBEV; FaBoCh; HAP; NOSC; NPeEn; OxAEP-1; OxBEV; PoRA; RB; SCGP; TFi *Fr.* White Devil, The.

Call her, call her for me, that girl. Kofi Awoonor. PBMAP *Fr.* Three poems from Rediscovery (1964).

Call her walking-mort; say where she goes. Walking-Mort, The. Djuna Barnes. APT-1

Call in the Midst of the Crowd, A. Alfred Corn.
   Fire: The People. NAAL-2v2; VCAP

Call in the midst of the crowd, A. Walt Whitman. *See* On my Northwest coast in the midst of the night a fisherman's group stands watching

Call in your reporters. Guess Who's in Town? (Nobody but That Gal of Mine). J. C. Johnson. ReLy

Call It a Good Marriage. Robert Graves. BoLoP

Call it a louse—I'm. Cid Corman. VGW

Call It Fear. Joy Harjo. NAAL-5

Call it the refrigerator's hum at night. Villanelle for the Middle of the Night. Jacqueline Osherow. MakPoe

Call it treason, but I'm eating my way. Peach. Lance Larsen. AmPoNex

Call Me Irresponsible. Jimmy Van Heusen. ReLy

Call Me Mister. Harold Rome. ReLy

Call me not false, beloved. Rudyard Kipling. FaBoEE *Fr.* Epitaphs of the War [1914–1918].

Call me old-fashioned, but I'm never mean. Eater of Wives, The. Linda France. MFPA

Call me Polyxena, the wife of Archelaus. Dioscorides. HePo *Fr.* Epigrams.

Call me to the one among your moments. Rainer Maria Rilke. EnlH *Fr.* Sonnets to Orpheus.

Call not thy wanderer home as yet. Germinal. "Æ." BIrV; MoBrPo; OBEV; OBMV

Call of Aristippus, The. John Gilbert Cooper.
   Elves and Fairies. ECEV

Call of Nature, The. Tony Harrison. NoAM

Call of the Christian, The. John Greenleaf Whittier. NOCV

Call of the Desirous. José Lezama Lima. TCLAP, *tr. by* Willis Barnstone

Call of the Lake, The. Andrey [*or* Andrei] Andreievich Voznesensky [*or* Voznesenskii]. TCRP; VCWP

Call of the River Nun, The. Gabriel Okara. PBA

Call of the Soul, The. *Unknown.* WoPoe, *tr. by* Ronald Perry

Call out. Call loud: 'I'm ready! Come and find me!' Hide and Seek. Vernon Scannell. NOxBChV

Call out the colored girls. For the Record. Audre Lorde. ESEAA

Call the roller of big cigars. Emperor of Ice-Cream, The. Wallace Stevens.

APT-1; FaBoMo; HAP; HCAP; HeIP-4; InPK-6; NAAL-2v2; NAAL-5; NAWM-7v2; NIL-7; NIP-4; NOBA; NoAM; NoP-4; OxBA; PoE; PoPoPo; TAP; TCAPo; TFi; TRP; WeW-3

Call to Arms. "Lu Hsün." SuSp; WoPoe, *tr. by* William R. Schultz

Call to Arms. Tso Yen-nien. CoBCP, *tr. by* Burton Watson

Call to Lieutenants. Sebestyén Tinódi.
   "You, who are lieutenants in the army." IQMS, *tr. by* Joseph Leftwich

Call Together. Kohine Whakarua Ponika. PeNZ, *tr. by* Sam Karetu

Call yourself alive? Look, I promise you. Temptation. Nina Cassian. AF, *tr. by* Brenda Walker

Callas. Edward Field. BodElec

Called Back. Emily Dickinson. MoAmPo; NOBA; NOCV

Called dog men. Royals. James Schuyler. FTOS

Called him "Big Joe" yes and Joe Turner it was his name. Hayden Carruth. GifTon *Fr.* Sleeping Beauty, The.

Called on Hermes. Still Waiting for My Winter Coat: A Sequence of Fragments. Hipponax. WoPoe, *tr. by* Anselm Hollo

Called [*or* Cal'd] out by the clap of the thunder. (LL) Hag, The. Robert Herrick. BeJo; CaPo; FaBoCh

Called out on Christmas Eve for a working-party. Devil on Ice. Donald Davie. NoAM

Called up: Tinker to Evers to Chance. Dorothy Barresi. MoASP

Caller Herrin' Carolina Oliphant, Baroness Nairne. OxBS; WoRP

Caller Oysters. Robert Fergusson. NePenScot

Caller rain frae abune. Douglas Young. OBVE

Callers. Christine Evans. TCAWP

Calligram, 15 May 1915. Guillaume Apollinaire. OBWP, *tr. by* O. Bernard

Calligraphy of geese. Buson. EH, *tr. by* Robert Hass

Calligraphy Practice. Ou-yang Hsiu. CoBCP, *tr. by* Burton Watson

Callin Buddy / Bolden. Callin Buddy. SeSe

Calling, A. W. S. Merwin. BodElec

Calling, The. Luis Palés Matos. BLPSL, *tr. by* Rene de Costa, Rigas Kappatos and Eleni Paidoussi

Calling, The. Ronald Stuart Thomas. PoetW

Calling all black people, come in, black people, come / on in. (LL) SOS. Imamu Amiri Baraka. BPo; NAAAL

Calling, and Correcting. Robert Herrick. BeJo

Calling black people. SOS. Imamu Amiri Baraka. BPo; NAAAL

Calling on a Taoist Priest in Tai-t'ien Mountain but Failing to See Him. Li Po. SuSp, *tr. by* Joseph J. Lee

Calling on Peadar O'Donnell at Dungloe. John Hewitt. CIP-2

Calling the Doctor (1000 A.D.). Nizami Arudi. ArPe; WoPoe, *tr. by* Omar Pound

Calling the Roll. Nathaniel Graham Shepherd. OBCA

Calling the White Donkey. Ray Gonzalez. TouFir

Calling to [my] mind[e] since first my love begun. Michael Drayton. NOBE; SCGP *Fr.* Idea.

Calling up the Spirit of the Lost Child. Maggie Penn. TWW

Calling you home, little Jewboy in alarm. (LL) Getting Lost in Nazi Germany. Marvin Bell. GotH; TaR

Calliope. John Skelton. OxBEV

Calliope. Calliope. John Skelton. OxBEV

Calliope in the Labour Ward. Elaine Feinstein. BrRo

Callipaedia; or, The Art of Getting Beautiful Children. Claude Quillet.
   Process of Conception, The. ECEV

Callow eagle in its downy nest, The. Aspiration. Emily Jane Pfeiffer. ViWPN

Calls through the valleys of Hall. (LL) Song of the Chattahoochee. Sidney Lanier. APN-2; ColAP; TCAPo

Calm, The. Suicide's Note. Langston Hughes. APT-2; PoPoPo; SAmP

Calm, The. Dulce Maria Loynaz. TANSG, *tr. by* Alan West

Calm, activity—each has its use. At times. Soen. ZenPo, *tr. by* Takashi Ikemoto and Lucien Stryk

Calm and lovely paradise, A. Nathaniel Parker Willis. APN-1 *Fr.* Melanie.

Calm as that second summer which precedes. Charleston. Henry Timrod. APN-2; CBCWP; ColAP; NOBA; OxBA; TAP; TCAPo

Calm comes from burning. Etymological Dirge. Heather McHugh. ExTi

Calm down, my sorrow, we must move with care. Meditation. Charles Baudelaire. InPK-6, *tr. by* Robert Lowell

Calm garden. French Garden. Léopold Sédar Senghor. NegPo, *tr. by* Ellen Conroy Kennedy

Calm hair, meandering in pellucid gold. (LL) On Seeing a Hair of Lucretia Borgia. Walter Savage Landor. HAP; NPeEn; WeW-3

Calm in the half-light. Muted Tones. Paul Verlaine. SxFrPo, *tr. by* Martin Sorrell

Calm is the landscape when the storm has passed. Peace in the Welsh Hills. Vernon Watkins. GTBS-P; OxBTC

Calm is the morn without a sound. Tennyson. EBEV; EBVV; FHYEP; HeIP-

4; NAEL-6v2; NAWM-7v2; NOBE; NPeEn; OxBEV; PeECV   *Fr.* In Memoriam A. H. H.

Calm moon, A.   Basho.   EH, *tr. by* Robert Hass

Calm on the bosom of thy God.   Felicia Dorothea Hemans.   OBEV   *Fr.* Siege of Valencia, The.

Calm, on the Listening Ear of Night.   Edmund Hamilton Sears.   AH

Calm thou mayst smile, when all around thee weep. (LL)   Epigram: "On parent knees, a naked new-born child."   Sir William Jones.   FaBoEE; OBEV

Calm was the sea to which your course you kept.   George Santayana.   TCAPo

Calm[e], The.   John Donne.   NoSic
   (Our storme is past, and that storms tyrannous rage.)   PBRV

Calm[e] was the day, and through the trembling air [*or* ayre].   Edmund Spenser.   AWP; EBEV; GTBS-P; HAP; NPeEn; NoSic; OBEV; OxAEP-1; OxBEV; SCGP; TFi; WoPoe

Calming Kali.   Lucille Clifton.   HW

Calmly he smoked till he'd finished his pipe.   Ballad of the Nails, The.   Nikolai Semionovich Tikhonov.   TCRP, *tr. by* Michael Frayn

Calmly sleeping, not a thing to worry about. (LL)   Night Rain: A Wall Collapses—Sent To My Neighbors.   Yang Shih-ch'i.   CoBLCP; ColAnChi, *tr. by* Jonathan Chaves

Caltrop leaves tug on the waves, the lotus quivers in the wind.   Lotus-gatherer's Song.   Po Chü-i.   SuSp, *tr. by* Irving Y. Lo

Calv'ry's tragedy is ended.   Empty Tomb, The.   Clara Ann Thompson.   CBWP-2

Calvary.   Sorley MacLean (Somhairle MacGill-Eain).   NePenScot

Calvary.   Edwin Arlington Robinson.   GI; MoAmPo; Son

Calvary.   *Unknown.*   AH

Calvary.   *Unknown.   See* Now Goeth [*or* goth *or* goothe] Sun [*or* Sonne *or* Sunne] under Wood

"Calvary."   W. B. Yeats.   PeECV
   "I am Judas."   GI

Calverly's.   Edwin Arlington Robinson.   APT-1; NoAM

Calvin Klein's Obsession.   Ciaran Carson.   EmeKit

Calvinist Sang.   Alexander Scott.   OxBS

Calvus to a Fly.   Charles Tennyson Turner.   NOBVV

Calypso.   W. H. Auden.   PeLV

Calypso.   Edward Kamau Brathwaite.   HarvBoo

Calypso.   Ernst Jandl.   PFTM-2

Calypso.   Shara McCallum.   AmPoNex

Calypso / Is a bit of a dipso.   Forever Ambrosia.   Christopher Darlington Morley.   OBAL

Calypsomania.   Anthony Brode.   PeLV

Camarada arrived at his village.   Homecoming.   Joao Pedro.   NAfrP, *tr. by* Don Burness

Cambodia.   James Fenton.   AF

Cambodian kids speak English faster, The.   Conspiracy, The.   Robert Hill Long.   OPRER

Cambria.   John Davies of Hereford.
   "Great Grandame Wales, from whom those ancestors."   AngWePo

Cambridge and the Alps.   William Wordsworth.   *Fr.* Prelude, The; Growth of a Poet's Mind [1850 vers.].

Cambridge in the Long.   Amy Levy.   ViWPN

Cambridge ladies who live in furnished souls, The.   E. E. Cummings.   HeIP-4; MakPoe; NAAL-2v2; NOBA; NoAM; NoP-4; OBAL; OxBA; PAI; TAP; TCAPo

Cambridge Songs.   *Unknown.*
   Heriger and the False Prophet.   WoPoe, *tr. by* Fred Chappell
   Levis Exsurgit Zephirus.   WoPoe, *tr. by* David Ferry
   "Wind is thin."   BoWoP

Cambridge Street, summer.   Days of 1981.   Mark Doty.   ReTh

Camden, most reverend head, to whom I owe.   To William Camden.   Ben Jonson.   AWP; BASC; BeJo; NAEL-5v1; NAEL-6v1; NAEL-7v1; NOSC; NPeEn

Came a stranger late among us.   In Memory of James M. Rathel.   Josephine D. Henderson Heard.   CBWP-4

Came buffalo heads.   Dirty Money.   Christine Hume.   AmPoNex

Came by sporting a nowhere hat.   At the Entrance.   M. R. Peacocke.   NLP

Came fresh transfigurings of freshest blue. (LL)   Sea Surface Full of Clouds.   Wallace Stevens.   APT-1; MoAmPo; VGW

Came in my full youth to the midnight cave.   Ajanta.   Muriel Rukeyser.   APT-2; MoAmPo; NNaP

Came Neptunus / his mind leaping / like dolphins.   Ezra Pound.   APSN; APT-1; PFTM-2   *Fr.* Cantos.

Came the hammer, so to speak.   How Came What Came Alas.   HeidiLynn Nilsson.   NeAmPo

Came to lakes; came to dead water.   Field of Light, A.   Theodore Roethke.   TwCP

Came to me— / Who?   Rudaki.   BoLoP; OBVE; OxBEV; WoPoe, *tr. by* Basil Bunting

Came to my side, and put down his head in love. (LL)   Dream, The.   Louise Bogan.   InPK-6; MoAmPo; NALW; NoAM

Camel.   Boris Alekseievich Chichibabin.   TCRP, *tr. by* Albert C. Todd

Camel.   Laila Akhyaliyya.   BoWoP, *tr. by* Willis Barnstone

Camel.   Shinkichi Takahashi.   ZenPo, *tr. by* Takashi Ikemoto and Lucien Stryk

Camel, The.   Al-Munsif Al-Wahaybi.   MAP, *tr. by* Salma Khadra Jayyusi and Naomi Shihab Nye

Camel and plow. The sharp blade.   Tiller of the Soil.   Avraham Shlonsky.   MHP, *tr. by* Ruth Finer Mintz

Camel-Rider, The.   *Unknown.*   AWP, *tr. by* Wilfrid Scawen Blunt

Camel's Bite.   Ben Bennani.   GraLe

Camel's Complaint, The.   Charles Edward Carryl.   *See* Admiral's Caravan, The

Camel's hump is an ugly lump, The.   Rudyard Kipling.   NOxBChV   *Fr.* Just-So Stories.

Camel's humps, The.   Camel.   Shinkichi Takahashi.   ZenPo, *tr. by* Takashi Ikemoto and Lucien Stryk

Cameleon Lover, The.   *Unknown.*   TCAPo

Cameleon's Defence, The.   *Unknown.*   TCAPo

Camelia.   Igor Moiseievich Irtenev.   TCRP, *tr. by* Bradley Jordan

Camellia.   Henriqueta Lisboa.   TCLAP, *tr. by* Hélcio Veiga Costa

Camellia, The.   Buson.   EH, *tr. by* Robert Hass

Camellia, The.   William Stanley Roscoe.   CenSon

Camellia tips, The.   Buson.   SoOfWa, *tr. by* Sam Hamill

Camelot.   Frederick Loewe.   ReLy

Camels of the Kings.   Leslie Norris.   OBCP

Camelus Saltat.   George Meredith.   OxBSo

Camelus Saltat: Continued.   George Meredith.   OxBSo

Cameo.   Natasha Trethewey.   NeAmPo

Cameo, The.   Edna St. Vincent Millay.   MoAmPo; UnPo; WPE

Cameo in Sudden Light.   Lorenzo Thomas.   FTOS

Cameo No. II.   June Jordan.   BPo

Camera at the crossing sees the city.   Gauley Bridge.   Muriel Rukeyser.   NNaP

Camera Obscura.   Valerie Martínez.   NAPBL

Camera Obscura, The.   John Addington Symonds.   NOBVV

Camerados.   Bayard Taylor.   UnPo

Caminando.   Víctor Hernández Cruz.   PFTM-2

Camino Real.   Adrienne Rich.   BodElec

Camme and I listened to Nat King Cole and she sweetly lay her head.   We Encounter Nat King Cole as We Invent the Future.   Joy Harjo.   ReTh

Camões, alone, of all the lyric race.   Luis de Camões.   Roy Campbell.   FaBoTw; OxAEP-2

Camoes and the Debt.   Sophia de Mello Breyner Andresen.   BoWoP, *tr. by* Willis Barnstone and Nelson Cerqueira

Camouflage.   Marianne Boruch.   BAP-97

Camouflaged, they detach lengths of sea and sky.   Destroyers in the Arctic.   Alan Ross.   PoWW

Camouflaged Troop-Ship.   Amy Lowell.   AiP

Camp.   Janet Fisher.   MFPA

Camp, The.   Mary Robinson.   NOBRP

Camp Fire.   Alfonsina Storni.   TANSG, *tr. by* Mark McCaffrey

Camp in the Prussian Forest, A.   Randall Jarrell.   FaBoWar; MoAmPo; OBWP; OxBC; PoWW
   (I walk beside the prisoners to the road.)   HP

Camp 1940.   Léopold Sédar Senghor.   PoetW, *tr. by* Melvin Dixon

Camp Notes.   Mitsuye Yamada.   WPOW

Camp of Souls, The.   Isabella Valancy Crawford.   NOBC

Camp Site.   Denis Glover.   PeNZ   *Fr.* Arawata Bill.

Campagna.   John Peck.   HarvBoo

Campaign.   Ciaran Carson.   BiHa; CIP-2; PNI

Campaign, The.   Joseph Addison.
   Poem to His Grace the Duke of Marlborough, A.   OBWP

Campaign, The.   Josephine Miles.   WPE

Campbell's Black Bean Soup.   Kevin Young.   NeAmPo

Campèa.   Andrea Zanzotto.   VCWP, *tr. by* Ruth Feldman

Campesino looked at the air, A.   Problems With Hurricanes.   Víctor Hernández Cruz.   PmAP

Campesino's Lament, The.   Judith Ortiz Cofer.   PueRic; TouFir

Campesinos.   Juan Delgado.   GeoHom

Campfire.   Anna Lindtová.   INSAB

Campfire emits an embered glow, A.   Night Marauders.   Gerry Bostock.   IBA

Campfire Extinguished.   Raymond Roseliep.   HA; InPK-6

Campfireburners.   Anatoly [*or* Anatolii] Zhigulin.   TCRP, *tr. by* Vladimir Lunis and Albert C. Todd

Camphor Laurel.   Judith Wright.   BMAP

Campidoglio.   Robert Garioch.   OBVE

Camping Clean. Reg Saner. PoCoUp

Camping Out. William Empson. FaBoMo; OxBTC

Camping Out on Rainy Mountain. Jim Barnes. CDW

Camping Provencial. Notices: (1). Peter Reading. PeLV *Fr.* Travelogue.

Campo dei Fiori. Czeslaw Milosz. HP

Camps, The. Hayden Carruth. GifTon

Camps hold [*or* held] their distance—[of] brown chestnuts and grey smoke, The. Derek Walcott. PoetW *Fr.* Midsummer.

Camptown Races. Stephen Collins Foster. TCAPo
   (Gwine to Run All Night; or, De Camptown Races.) OBAL

Campus on the Hill, The. W. D. Snodgrass. AiP; NoAM; TAP; TwCP

Can a mote of sunlight defeat its purpose. Louis Zukofsky. APT-2

Can a sad song take the place of crying? Sad Song. *Unknown.* CoBCP, *tr.* by Burton Watson

Can America be reckoned as the country of the free? Negro Ballot, The. Lizelia Augusta Jenkins Moorer. CBWP-3

Can blot the star that shines on Paris now. (LL) Verlaine. Edwin Arlington Robinson. APN-2; NAAL-2v2; NCAP

Can-Can. John Fuller. PeLV *Fr.* Fox-Trot.

Can centre both the worlds of Heaven and Hell. (LL) Stanzas: "Often rebuked, yet always back returning." Emily Jane Brontë. NALW; NOBVV; OBEV; OxBEV; PEW; SCGP; VWP

Can come as often as he wants. (LL) Ono no Komachi. BoWoP; WPOW; WoPoe, *tr.* by Ikuko Atsumi and Kenneth Rexroth

Can death be faithful or the grave be just. Resurrection, The. Nathaniel Wanley. NPeEn

Can even winter's crystal gems be spared. (LL) December. Christopher Pearse Cranch. APN-1; TCAPo

Can get across it if I try. (LL) I May, I Might, I Must. Marianne Craig Moore. AmFaPo; ChAP; FaBoWP; OBAL; OxBSP

Can God delight in such a sight. Michael Wigglesworth. NAAL-3 *Fr.* Day of Doom, The.

Can he be fair that withers at a blast. Francis Quarles. PeECV *Fr.* Pentelogia.

Can. Hist. Earle Birney. OxBC

Can I explain this to you? Your eyes. Knife, The. Keith Douglas. NoAM

Can I forget the sweet days that have been. William Henry Davies. AngWePo

Can I forget thee? No, while mem'ry lasts. On Parting with a Friend. Mary Weston Fordham. CBWP-2

Can I go on loving anyone at fifty. Book of Wisdom, The. Robert Lowell. ChIV-1

Can I look back, and view with tranquil eye. Mary Tighe. CenSon

Can I not come to Thee, my God, for these. To His Ever-Loving God. Robert Herrick. OxBEV

Can I not sin, but thou wilt be. To His Conscience. Robert Herrick. BeJo; ChIV-1; NAEL-5v1

Can I not sing but "hoy." Jolly Shepherd, The. *Unknown.* NOBE

Can I Say. Dolly Bird. WPOW

Can I see another's woe. William Blake. AWP; FHYEP; InvLi; OxAEP-2 *Fr.* Songs of Innocence.

Can I Tell You My Love with a Portrait. Nikolai Alekseievich Klyuyev [*or* Kliuev *or* Klyuev]. TCRusP, *tr.* by John Glad

Can I, who have for others oft compil'd. Of My Dear Son [*or* Deare Sonne], Gervase Beaumont. Sir John Beaumont. NOBE

Can it be. Living Alone with Jesus—. Maxine W. Kumin. UnSA

Can it be growing colder when I begin. Adrienne Rich. NAAL-2v2 *Fr.* Twenty-one Love Poems.

Can it be right to give what I can give? Elizabeth Barrett Browning. CTC; CenSon; Son *Fr.* Sonnets from the Portuguese.

Can It Be True That One Lives on Earth? Nezahualcoyotl. WoPoe, *tr.* by Thelma D. Sullivan

Can it be true, that we can meet. Slumbering Passion. Josephine D. Henderson Heard. CBWP-4

Can jamrock. Is Culcha Weapon? Brian Meeks. WaCA

Can life's best consciousness of joy. Questioning. Henrietta Cordelia Ray. CBWP-3

Can. Lit. Earle Birney. NOBC

Can love be controlled by advice? John Gay. OxBSP *Fr.* Begger's Opera.

Can man forget this story? (LL) Hymn[e] on the Nativity [*or* Nativitie] of My Saviour, A. Ben Jonson. BeJo; ChIV-2; SacPr; TrCP

Can never fail cuckolding two or three spouses. (LL) Two or Three; a Recipe [*or* Receipt] to Make a Cuckold. Pope. BoLoP; FaBoEE

Can nothing serve thy turne but summum ius. Upon a Booke Written at the Beginning of the Parliament 1640. Anna Norman Ley. EMWP

Can nothing settle my uncertain breast. Galatians 6.14. Francis Quarles. ChIV-2

Can one make works which are not works of "art"? Speculations. Marcel Duchamp. PFTM-1

Can one take captives by writing. Lyn Hejinian. FTOS *Fr.* Guard, The.

Can Pigeons Be Heroes? Ruth L. Schwartz. WiU

Can redwhite & blue I enter. Self World. Clarence Major. NBV

Can someone / called Daughter of a Stone. Rāmprasād Sen. SinGod, *tr.* by Rachel Fell McDermott

Can someone make my simple wish come true? Lonely Hearts. Wendy Cope. OBCoV

Can'st thou forget, O! Idol of my soul! To Phaon. Mary Robinson. CenSon; RWP

Can still propose the old labors. (LL) Heroes. Robert Creeley. NOBA; NoP-4

Can't be a model, there'd be times I. Alan Wearne. BMAP *Fr.* Nightmarkets, The.

Can't find what you can't see / can you? (LL) American History. Michael S. Harper. BPo; ESEAA; HCAP; NAAL-5; NoAM; PoPoPo

Can't Help Lovin' Dat Man. Jerome Kern. ReLy

Can't make excuses for you, Cinque. Janet Campbell Hale. VoR

"Can't see out of my left eye." Spinning. Alfred Wellington Purdy. NOBC; NoAM

Can't seem to wake you, kid, guess it. Body beside the Ties, The. Kenneth Patchen. CLPP

Can't Stand It. Vladimir Vladimirovich Mayakovsky [*or* Maiakovskii]. TCRP, *tr.* by Bernard Meares

Can't swim; uses credit cards and pills to combat. Difference between Pepsi and Coke, The. David Lehman. PmAP; ReTh

Can't Tell. Nellie Wong. ItWoWo; LTA; OpBo

Can't We Be Friends? Paul James. ReLy

Can't we find some way / to meet again. To Ibn Zaidun. Wallāda. WPOW, *tr.* by Deirdre Lashgari and James Monroe

Can't we two go walkin' together. Heather on the Hill, The. Frederick Loewe. ReLy

Can't wring blood from. Lepidoptery. James Sherry. FTOS

Can't You Line It? *Unknown.* NAAL

Can the German language crack and snore and rumble, thunder. German Language, The. Friedrich von Logau. GePo, *tr.* by George C. Schoolfield

Can the lover share his soul. Epithalamium. Walter James Turner. OBMV

Can the Mole Take. Cecil Day Lewis. OBMV

Can the single cup of wine. To his Brother Hsing-chien. Po Chü-i. ChiP, *tr.* by Arthur Waley

Can there be a collision between picture and application? Steve McCaffery. FTOS *Fr.* Evoba.

Can these movements which move themselves. Belly Dancer. Diane Wakoski. NALW; NoAM

Can think of all this with nostalgia. (LL) Christmas Family Reunion. Peter De Vries. NBLV; NOBL

Can This Be Love? Paul James. ReLy

Can this decay, but is beginning ever. (LL) Fragment of Petronius Arbiter, A. Petronius Arbiter. ErotSp; OxBEV; WoPoe, *tr.* by Ben Jonson

Can Tho, *favela* of crowing cocks. Can Tho. Herbert Krohn. CDa

Can turn a heart to dust. (LL) Longing for Someone. Li Po. CrYelRi; ErotSp, *tr.* by Sam Hamill

Can Vei La Lauzeta Mover. Bernard [*or* Bernart] de Ventadour [*or* Ventadorn]. APSN, *tr.* by Paul Blackburn

Can we imagine our rewards. (LL) Picture of Little J. A. in a Prospect of Flowers, The. CoAmPo; PmAP

Can we not force from wid[d]owed poetry. Thomas Carew. BASC; CABP; CaPo; CavPo; NAEL-6v1; NAEL-7v1; NoP-4

Can Ye Sew Cushions? *Unknown.* FaBoCh

Can You Change a Shilling? Toni Del Renzio. SPE

Can you claim to win. Nabíncandra Cakrabartī. SinGod, *tr.* by Rachel Fell McDermott

Can you feel the swell—. Early Triangles. Ron Padgett. FTOS

Can you hear it. Cricket at Central California Women's Facility. Dixie Salazar. GeoHom

Can you hear it/ a *faint echo/ vespers from the book of ancestry/ once bound.* What we have lost. Duriel Harris. SpirFl

Can you hear it? Somebody's reading a poem to me over the telephone. Somebody Consoles Me with a Poem. Sandor Csoori. GifTon, *tr.* by Len Roberts and László Vértes

Can you hear me? Under my name I am. Gloria Gervitz. MirDau, *tr.* by Stephen Tapscott *Fr.* Yiskor.

Can You Imagine. Artur Miedzyrzecki. PoSu, *tr.* by Stanislaw Baranczak

Can you imagine the air filled with smoke? Smoke. Philip Levine. MakPoe

Can you keep a secret? *Unknown.* LB

Can you make me a cambric [*or* cambriek] shirt. *Unknown.* OxNR

Can you read and write English? Yes ___. No___. Into Such Assembly. Myung Mi Kim. FSt

Can you really tell the difference between / a Chinese and a Japanese? (LL) Notes for a Poem on Being Asian American. Dwight Okita. NIL-7; UnSA

Can you recall the playful brushwood fire. Fires. József Kiss. IQMS, *tr.* by Peter Zollman

Can you tell me where my car is. How Fast. Martha Rhodes. NAPBL

Can you tell that I'm unhappy. Ain't It a Shame about Mame. Johnny Burke. ReLy

Cana. Thomas Merton. ChIV-2; TrCP
   (Once when our eyes were clean as noon.) GI

Cana. Peter Steele. GI

Cana Revisited. Seamus Heaney. FaBoMo
   (No round-shouldered pitchers here.) GI

Canaan. Benyamin [*or* Benjamin] Galai. MHP, *tr.* by Ruth Finer Mintz

Canada: Case History: 1973. Earle Birney. PeLV

Canadian Authors Meet, The. Francis Reginald Scott. NOBC

Canadian Boat Song. John Galt. FaBoCh; OBEV; OxBS

Canadian Boat Song, A. Thomas Moore. TreFP

Canadian Prairie's View of Literature, The. David Donnell. NOBC

Canadians. Ivor Gurney. FaBoTw

Canal Bank Walk. Patrick Kavanagh. CIP-2; FaBoTw; MoBrPo; NoAM; NoP-4

Canal flows quietly, The. Soliloquy. Eugenio Montale. ItPo, *tr.* by Gayle Ridinger

Canal Street. Bernard Heidsieck.
   Canal Street 33/14. PFTM-2, *tr.* by Nicholas Zürbrugg
   Canal Street 39/27. PFTM-2, *tr.* by Nicholas Zürbrugg

Canaries were his hobby. Glass Blower, The. James Scully. TwCP

Canary. Rita Dove. ESEAA; LoL; SeSe; VCAP

Canary, The. Ogden Nash. PeLV

Canary-birds feed on sugar and seed. Charles Edward Carryl. OTCP *Fr.* Admiral's Caravan, The.

Canary Man and You, The. Rick Alley. AmPoNex

Canberra in April. J. R. Rowland. NOBAu

Cancer and Nova. Hyam Plutzik. AmFaPo

Cancer Cells, The. Richard Eberhart. HAP

Cancer Hospital, The. Roy Fuller.
   Your Absence. OxBSo

Cancer's a Funny Thing. John Burdon Sanderson Haldane. OxBTC

Cancer Winter. Marilyn Hacker. RA

Cancion: "O love, I never, never thought." Juan II, of Castile. AWP, *tr.* by George Ticknor

Cancion: "When I am the sky." Denise Levertov. NALW; PoM

Canciones. Kenneth Zamora Damacion. OPRER

Candaules, King of Lydia. Queen of Lydia, The. Charles Hubert Sisson. OxBC

Candelaria and the Sea Turtle. Gladys Cardiff. HATNAP

Candescent lies the air. Rosalía de Castro. NAWM-7v2, *tr.* by S. Griswold Morley

Candid Camera. Angelo Lumelli. ItPo, *tr.* by Gayle Ridinger

Candid Man, The. Stephen Crane. MoAmPo *Fr.* War Is Kind.

Candid Professor confesses, A. Limerick. Thomas Thorneley. PeLi

Candid, Warhol. Campbell's Black Bean Soup. Kevin Young. NeAmPo

Candidi lectores, callide callete; vestrum fovet Psittacum, etc. (LL) John Skelton. NoSic; OxBoLi *Fr.* Speak [*or* Speke], Parrot.

Candish deriv'd from Noble Parentage. Epitaph for Richard Cavendish, Engraved on his Monument in Hornsey Church. Margaret Russell Clifford, Countess of Cumberland. EMWP

Candle. Penelope Rosemont. SurWo

Candle, A. Mother Goose. ReMoGo

Candle, A. Sir John Suckling. BASC

Candle a Saint, The. Wallace Stevens. PoRA

Candle at Canterbury, A. Tessa Rose Chester. MFPA

Candle burned out, my boat is windblown, The. Dreaming of My Wife. Yuan Chen. CrYelRi, *tr.* by Sam Hamill

Candle Casts Dark Shadows, The. Li Shang-yin. OHMPC, *tr.* by Kenneth Rexroth

Candle, climb upward. Just for Today. Ervin Drake. ReLy

Candle in a Glass, A. Marge Piercy. TaR

Candle in a long street, A. Hamra Night. Sa'di Yusuf. FaBoWar, *tr.* by Abdullah Al-Udhari

Candle Indoors, The. Gerard Manley Hopkins. ChIV-2; OxAEP-2

Candle light blue banners incense. Land O'Lakes, Wisconsin: Vajrayana Seminary. Allen Ginsberg. BBASP

Candle light shines low on the dark window, The. For My Brother Hagok. Ho Nansorhon. WoPoe, *tr.* by Kichung Kim

Candle lit in darkness of black waters, A. On the Lake. Victoria Mary Sackville-West. OBMV

Candle takes the first desperate, The. Homage to Chagall. Duane Niatum. CDW

Candlemas Day. Sister Mary Madeleva. CRP

Candles. Hélène Swarth. WPOW, *tr.* by Jonathan Crewe

Candles are burning, The. Poet's Resurrection, The. Jenő Dsida. IQMS, *tr.* by Peter Zollman

Candles Draw Well after All, The. Laura Jensen. LCAP-2

Candles of my father, protect the page. My Father Writing Joe Hamrah in a Blackout. Gregory Orfalea. GraLe

Candles. Red tulips, ninety cents the bunch. Evening Musicale. Phyllis McGinley. OBAL; OBCoV; Son

Candlestick, The. Jaroslav Seifert. AF, *tr.* by Ewald Osers

Candor. John Graham-Pole. BloBone

Candour of the gods is in thy gaze, The. George Santayana. APN-2 *Fr.* Sonnets.

Candour spurned, and art rewarded. (LL) January, 1795. Mary Robinson. ECWP; OxBEV; WoRP

Candy. Alex Kramer. ReLy

Candy. Ogden Nash. *See* Candy / Is dandy

Candy / Is dandy. Reflections on Ice-breaking. Ogden Nash. APT-2; AiP; NBLV; OBAL; PeLV

Candy Lady, The. Laura Boss. UnSA

Candy Man, The. Leslie Bricusse. ReLy

Candy Man, The. *Unknown.* FaBoVe

Candy man was guid tae me, The. Candy Man, The. *Unknown.* FaBoVe

Cane of Ch'iung Bamboo, The. Hsü Chung-hsing. CoBLCP, *tr.* by Jonathan Chaves

Canefield and the Sea, The. Joao Cabral de Melo Neto. TCLAP, *tr.* by Louis Simpson

Canicula. Mary Kinzie. FFC

Canis Major. Robert Frost. KaS; MoAmPo

Canker'd, cursed creature, crabbed, corbit kittle, Sir Thomas Maitland's Satyr upon Sir Niel Laing. Sir Thomas Maitland. NePenScot

Canna. Shinkichi Takahashi. ZenPo, *tr.* by Takashi Ikemoto and Lucien Stryk

Canna turn Arthur O'Bower. (LL) Wind, The. *Unknown.* FaBoCh; OxNR

Canned in manuscripts, newspapers, books. (LL) Belonging to a New Family. Mohammad Bennis. MAP; NAfrP, *tr.* by Charles Doria and Sharif Elmusa

Canner, Exceedingly Canny, A. Limerick. Carolyn Wells. PeLi

Cannery Town in August. Lorna Dee Cervantes. NoAM

Cannibal. Thom Gunn. NOxBChV *Fr.* Three for Children.

Cannibal. Léon Laleau. NegPo, *tr.* by Ellen Conroy Kennedy *Fr.* Black Music.

Cannibal Hymn, The. *Unknown.* TTY, *tr.* by Samuel A. B. Mercer

Cannibal Hymn, The. *Unknown.*
   "Sky is a dark bowl, the stars die and fall, The." WoPoe, *tr.* by Willis and Tony Barnstone

Cannibal Women in the Avocado Jungle of Death. Maureen Seaton. ExTi

Cannibalism. Diana Chang. WPOW

Cannon Hill. Sandra Hochman. YaYoPo

Cannot for less be told. (LL) Elixir [*or* Elixer], The. George Herbert. BASC; ESCV; EnlH; FaBoCh; GeHe; NOSC; NoP-4; SacPr

Cannot pull it up. (LL) Well, The. Mother Goose. OxNR; ReMoGo

"Cannot quite expect that. You ain't ruined," said she. (LL) Ruined Maid, The. Thomas Hardy. BoLoP; FaBoVe; HeIP-4; NAEL-5v2; NAEL-6v2; NBLV; NIL-7; NOBL; OxBTC; PAI; PeLV; PeVV; SCV; TFi; TRP

Cannot, the tempest tells me, disappoint. (LL) Rain. Edward Thomas. FaBoWar; HarvBoo; MakPoe; NAEL-5v2; NAEL-6v2; NPeEn; NoP-4; OBWP; OxBEV; OxBTC; PeFWW; PoWW

Canny bord ower there. Rape. Tom Pickard. FaBoTw

Canny moment, lucky fit. Sir Walter Scott. FaBoCh *Fr.* Guy Mannering.

Canoer, The. Diane Wakoski. HeIP-4

Canogait kirkyaird in the failing year. At Robert Fergusson's Grave, October 1962. Robert Garioch. OxBS

Canon 4. Cristina Campo. CItWP, *tr.* by Cinzia Sartini Blum and Lara Trubowitz *Fr.* Tiger's Absence.

Canon's Yeoman's Tale, The. Geoffrey Chaucer. *Fr.* Canterbury Tales, The.

Canonical Hours. William Dickey. CoAP

Canonization, The. John Donne. BASC; CABP; ESCV; EnLoPo; FHYEP; FSCP; FaBoVe; HAP; NAEL-5v1; NAEL-6v1; NAEL-7v1; NAWM-5v1; NIL-7; NIP-4; NOBE; NOSC; NPeEn; NoP-4; PBRV; PoE; PoPoPo; SCGP; SoSe-8; TFi; TRP; UnPo; WoPoe

Canopic old Egyptian jugs. Instructions for Your New Osiris. Lorenzo Thomas. PmAP

Canopus. Bert Leston Taylor. NOBL

Canopy of nerve ends. Epiderm. Michael Dransfield. BMAP; CBAP

Canst thinke the cargoe wherewith ship is fraught. Upon the Decease of Mrs. Anne Griffin. John Fiske. SCAP

Canst Thou Draw out Leviathan with an Hook. Allen Curnow. PeNZ

Canst thou draw out leviathan with an hook[e]? Bible, *O.T.* OBVE *Fr.* Job.

Canst thou indeed be he that still would sing. Dante Alighieri. AWP; EaItPo, *tr.* by Dante Gabriel Rossetti *Fr.* La Vita Nuova.

Cant. Imamu Amiri Baraka. NAAL-2v2

Cant. 5.6 & c. Elizabeth Singer. ChIV-1

Cantares Mexicanos. *Unknown.*

  Chalcan Female Song. PFTM-1

Cantata. Jack Spicer. APSN

Cante Jondo. Yusef Komunyakaa. BodElec

Canterbury Tales, The. Geoffrey Chaucer.

  Canon's Yeoman's Tale, The.

    "Also ther was a disciple of Plato." SacPr

  Clerk's Tale, The.

    "Griselda's dead, and so's her patience." PoRA

  (Cock and the Hen, The.) OBNV

  Franklin's Prologue, The. NAEL-5v1; NAEL-6v1

  Franklin's Tale, The. NAEL-5v1; NAEL-6v1

  Friar's Prologue, The. PoE

  Friar's Tale, The. PoE

  General Prologue, The. FHYEP; NAEL-6v1; NAEL-7v1; NAWM-5v1; PoE

    Good Parson, The. NOCV

    Knighthood, The. UV

    (Madame Eglantine.) NOBE

    "Marchant was ther with a forked berd, A." CTC

    Parson and the Plowman Described, The. SacPr

    "Sergeant of the Lawe, war and wys, A." CTC

    Seven Pilgrims: A Monk. OBCoV

    Seven Pilgrims: A Prioress[e]. CTC; NPeEn

    Seven Pilgrims: A Wyf of Bathe. EBEV

    "Somonour was ther with us in that place, A." OBCoV

    "This Pardoner had hair as yellow as wax." SCV

    ("Whan that April with his showres soote.") NoP-4

    ("When April with its sweet showers.") TFi

    ("When the sweet showers of April fall and shoot.") SCV

  General Prologue. NAWM-5v1; NAWM-7v1, *tr. by* Theodore Morrison

  Introduction to the Franklin's Prologue and Tale. NAEL-5v1; NAEL-6v1

  (Introduction to the Pardoner's Prologue and Tale.) FHYEP; NAEL-5v1; PoE

  Introduction to the Pardoner's Tale. NAEL-6v1; NAEL-7v1

  Introduction to the Pardoner's Tale. NAWM-7v1, *tr. by* Theodore Morrison

  Introduction to the Parson's Tale, The. NAEL-5v1; NAEL-6v1

  Knight's Interruption of the Monk's Tale, The. NAWM-5v1, *tr. by* Theodore Morrison

  Knight's Tale, The.

    "But in the dome of mighty Mars the red." OBWP

    "On t'other side there stood destruction bare." FaBoWar, *tr. by* John Dryden

    Saturn. NPeEn

    Temple of Mars, The. NPeEn

  ("Lordinges—quod he—in chirches whan I preche.") NAEL-7v1

  Man of Law's Epilogue, The. NAEL-7v1

  Manciple's Tale, The.

    Cage, The. OWoS

    "Lat take a cat, and fostre him wel[l] with milk." TriCat

  Miller's Prologue, The. NAEL-6v1; NAEL-7v1; NAWM-5v1

  Miller's [*or* Milleres] Tale, The. NAEL-6v1; NAEL-7v1; NAWM-5v1; OxBoLi; PeLV

    Alysoun. NPeEn

    "Fair was this yonge wyf, and therwithal." EBEV

  Miller's Tale, The. NAWM-5v1; NAWM-7v1, *tr. by* Theodore Morrison

  Nun's Priest's Prologue, The. FHYEP

  Nun's Priest's Tale, The. FHYEP; NAEL-6v1; NAWM-5v1

    "There liv'd, as Authors tell, in Days of Yore." OBVE

    "Yeerd she hadde, enclosed al aboute, A." OWoS

  Nun's Priest's Tale, The. NAWM-5v1, *tr. by* Theodore Morrison

  Pardoner's Prologue, The. FHYEP; NAEL-6v1; NAWM-5v1; PoE

  Pardoner's Tale, The. FHYEP; NAEL-6v1; NAEL-7v1; NAWM-5v1; PoE

    "But, sires, o word forgat I in my tale." EBEV

    Death and the Three Revellers. OBNV

    "It's of three rioters I have to tell." SCV

    ("Thise riotoures thre of whiche I telle.") NPeEn

    Three Rioters, The. EBNV

    "Whan they han goon nat fully half a mile." OxBEV

  Pardoner's Tale, The. NAWM-5v1; NAWM-7v1, *tr. by* Theodore Morrison

  Parson's Introduction, The. NAEL-7v1

  ("Poore widwe [*or* widow], somdeel [*or* somedeal] stape in age, A.") NAEL-5v1; NAEL-7v1

  Prologue to the Miller's Tale. NAWM-5v1; NAWM-7v1, *tr. by* Theodore Morrison

  Prologue to the Pardoner's Tale. NAWM-5v1; NAWM-7v1, *tr. by* Theodore Morrison

  Prologue to Sir Thopas. NAEL-5v1

  Tale of Sir Thopas, The. NAEL-5v1

  Wife of Bath's Prologue, The. FHYEP; NAEL-5v1; NAEL-6v1; NAEL-7v1

    "Experience, though noon auctoritee." OxBEV; OxBoLi; PeLV

    "If poor (you say) she drains her husband's purse." OBSV

    "My fourthe housbonde was a revelour." NPeEn

  Wife of Bath: Prologue, The. NAWM-7v1, *tr. by* Theodore Morrison

  Wife of Bath's Tale, The. FHYEP; NAEL-5v1; NAEL-6v1; NAEL-7v1

  Wife of Bath, The. NAWM-7v1, *tr. by* Theodore Morrison

Cantica: Our Lord Christ: Of Order. Saint Francis of Assisi. AWP; EaItPo; OBVE, *tr. by* Dante Gabriel Rossetti

Canticle. Michael McClure. NeAP; PoM

Canticle. David Shapiro. TTTS

Canticle for Abba Jacob, A. Marilyn Nelson Waniek. FFC

Canticle for Good Friday. Geoffrey Hill. ChIV-2

Canticle of Darkness. Wilfred Watson. MoCV

Canticle of the Brother Sun, The. Saint Francis of Assisi. BBASP, *tr. by* Regis J. Armstrong and Ignatius C. Brady

Canticle of the Creatures. Saint Francis of Assisi. WoPoe, *tr. by* James Schuyler

Canticle of the Sun. Saint Francis of Assisi. EnlH, *tr. by* Stephen Mitchell

Canticle of the Void, The. Paul Murray. InvLi

Canticle to Apollo, A. Robert Herrick. CaPo

Canticle to the Waterbirds, A. William Everson. APSN; APT-2; GeoHom; NeAP; PoM

Cantico del Sole. Saint Francis of Assisi. CTC; OBAL, *tr. by* Ezra Pound

Cantiga de Amigo. Pero Meogo. WoPoe, *tr. by* Keith Bosley

Cantinas, The. Malcolm Lowry.

  Delirium in Vera Cruz. FaBoTw; NoP-4; OxBTC

Canto 1. János Arany. *Fr.* Toldi.

Canto the First. Byron. CABP; FHYEP; NAEL-5v2; NAEL-6v2; PoE *Fr.* Don Juan.

Canto 1. Ezra Pound. MoAmPo; NAAL-5; NoAM; OBVE; PoE; VGW *Fr.* Cantos.

Canto the Second. Byron. *Fr.* Don Juan.

Canto 2. Ezra Pound. APT-1; HAP; MoAmPo; NOBA; NoAM; OxBA *Fr.* Cantos.

Canto 2 (excerpts). Vincente Huidobro. BLPSL, *tr. by* Rene de Costa, Rigas Kappatos and Eleni Paidoussi *Fr.* Altazor.

Canto the Third. Byron. *Fr.* Don Juan.

Canto 3. Ezra Pound. TAP *Fr.* Cantos.

Canto 4. Byron. *Fr.* Childe Harold's Pilgrimage.

Canto the Fourth. Byron. *Fr.* Don Juan.

Canto 4. Ezra Pound. APT-1 *Fr.* Cantos.

Canto 5. János Arany. *Fr.* Toldi.

Canto 6. János Arany. *Fr.* Toldi.

Canto the Seventh. Byron. *Fr.* Don Juan.

Canto 7. Ezra Pound. NOBA; NoAM *Fr.* Cantos.

Canto 8. János Arany. *Fr.* Toldi.

Canto the Ninth. Byron. *Fr.* Don Juan.

Canto 11. János Arany. *Fr.* Toldi.

Canto the Eleventh. Byron. NOBRP *Fr.* Don Juan.

Canto 12. János Arany. *Fr.* Toldi.

Canto the Twelfth. Byron. *Fr.* Don Juan.

Canto 13. Ezra Pound. APT-1; FaBoMo; PoE *Fr.* Cantos.

Canto the Fourteenth. Byron. *Fr.* Don Juan.

Canto 17. Ezra Pound. APT-1; NAAL-2v2; OBMV *Fr.* Cantos.

Canto XX: "To Wales once more, though not on holiday now." Louis MacNeice. ModIr *Fr.* Autumn Sequel.

Canto 30. Ezra Pound. HarvBoo *Fr.* Cantos.

Canto 32. Ezra Pound. PFTM-1

Canto 36. Ezra Pound. APT-1 *Fr.* Cantos.

Canto XLV. Ezra Pound. ColAP

Canto 45. Ezra Pound. APT-1; HarvBoo; NAAL-2v2; NAAL-5; NOBA; PoE *Fr.* Cantos.

Canto 47. Ezra Pound. APT-1; PoE; VGW *Fr.* Cantos.

Canto 49. Ezra Pound. PFTM-1

Canto 49. Ezra Pound. APT-1 *Fr.* Cantos.

Canto 51. Ezra Pound. PFTM-1

Canto 80. Ezra Pound. FaBoTw *Fr.* Cantos.

Canto 81. Ezra Pound. APT-1; FaBoMo; FaBoTw; HarvBoo; NAAL-2v2; NOBA; NOBE; NoAM; OxBA; RaBo; VGW *Fr.* Cantos.

Canto 90. Ezra Pound. APSN; APT-1; VGW *Fr.* Cantos.

Canto 116. Ezra Pound. APSN; APT-1; PFTM-2 *Fr.* Cantos.

Canto 117 et seq., Notes for. Ezra Pound. *Fr.* Cantos.

Canto Amor. John Berryman. CoAP; MoAmPo; VGW

Canto de li Augei di Frunda in Frunda, Il. Matteo Maria Boiardo. WoPoe, *tr. by Peter Russell*

Canto Eleven. Tomas Venclova. WoPoe, *tr. by Vyt Bakaitis*

Canto I (excerpt). Vincente Huidobro. PFTM-1 *Fr. Altazor.*

Canto Llano. Anita Endrezze. CDW

Canto the Tenth. Byron. *Fr. Don Juan.*

Cantonese Love-Songs. Chiu Tsz-Yung and Cecil Clement.
   Lament for Fortune's Frailty, A. ColAnChi, *tr. by Cecil Clementi*

Cantor. Guillaume Apollinaire. CuPo

Cantos. Ezra Pound.
   Canto 1. ColAP; MoAmPo; NAAL-5; NoAM; OBVE; PFTM-1; PoE; VGW
   Canto 2. APT-1; HAP; MoAmPo; NOBA; NoAM; OxBA
   Canto 3. TAP
   Canto 4. APT-1
   Canto 7. NOBA; NoAM
   Canto 13. APT-1; FaBoMo; PoE
   Canto 17. APT-1; NAAL-2v2; OBMV
   Canto 30. HarvBoo
   Canto 36. APT-1
   (Canzone: Donna Mi Priegha.) CTC
   (Donna Mi Priegha.) OBVE
   Canto 45. APT-1; HarvBoo; NAAL-2v2; NAAL-5; NOBA; PoE
   Canto 47. APT-1; PoE; VGW
   Canto 49. APT-1
   Canto 80. FaBoTw
     "Tudor indeed is gone and every rose." WoPoe
   Canto 81. APT-1; FaBoMo; FaBoTw; HarvBoo; NAAL-2v2; NOBA; NOBE; NoAM; OxBA; RaBo; VGW
     "What thou lovest well remains." FaBoTw; NOBE; OxBA; RaBo; WoPoe
   Canto 90. APSN; APT-1; VGW
   Canto 116. APSN; APT-1; PFTM-2
   Canto 117 et seq., Notes for.
     "For the blue flash and the moments." APT-1
     ("Ed ascoltando al leggier mormorio.") PoE
     ("Has he tempered the viol's wood.") HAP
     ("Serenely in the crystal jet.") PoE

Cantus Amoris 2. Richard Rolle of Hampole. SacPr

Canute at Ely. *Unknown.*
   Cnut's Song. PoE

Canvas square, The. At the Gwen John Exhibition. Charles McDonald. NLP

Canzone: "Consider the three functions of the tongue." Marilyn Hacker. NoAM

Canzone: Donna Mi Priegha. Ezra Pound. *See Cantos*

Canzone: He Beseeches Death for the Life of Beatrice. Dante Alighieri. AWP; EaItPo, *tr. by Dante Gabriel Rossetti*

Canzone: He Speaks of His Condition through Love. Folcachiero de' Folcachiero. AWP; EaItPo, *tr. by Dante Gabriel Rossetti*

Canzone: His Lament for Selvaggia. Cino da Pistoia. AWP; EaItPo, *tr. by Dante Gabriel Rossetti*

Canzone: His Portrait of His Lady, Angiola of Verona. Fazio degli Uberti. AWP; EaItPo, *tr. by Dante Gabriel Rossetti*

Canzone: "No better lost than any other woman." Marilyn Hacker. NoAM

Canzone: Of His Dead Lady. Giacomino Pugliesi. AWP; EaItPo, *tr. by Dante Gabriel Rossetti*

Canzone: Of His Love, with the Figure of a Sudden Storm. Prinzivalle Doria. AWP; EaItPo, *tr. by Dante Gabriel Rossetti*

Canzone: To Love and to His Lady. Guido Delle Colonne. AWP; EaItPo, *tr. by Dante Gabriel Rossetti*

Canzonet. Mary Robinson. NOBRP

Canzonetta: A Bitter Song to His Lady. Pier Moronelli da Fiorenza. AWP; EaItPo; OBVE, *tr. by Dante Gabriel Rossetti*

Canzonetta: He Will Neither Boast nor Lament to His Lady. Jacopo da Lentino. AWP, *tr. by Dante Gabriel Rossetti*

Canzonetta: Of His Lady, and of His Making Her Likeness. Jacopo da Lentino. AWP; EaItPo, *tr. by Dante Gabriel Rossetti*

Canzonetta: Of His Lady in Absence. Giacomino Pugliesi. AWP; EaItPo, *tr. by Dante Gabriel Rossetti*

Cap, a sword, flowers, A. Yury [*or Iurii*] Pavlovich Odarchenko. TCRP

Cap and Bells, The. W. B. Yeats. MoBrPo; NoAM; RB

Cap'tain Zombi. René Depestre. PFTM-2, *tr. by Joan Dayan Fr. Rainbow for the Christian West, A.*

Cap tipped back, propped by a window, still can't settle down. Sitting Outdoors. Lu Yu. CoBCP, *tr. by Burton Watson*

Cape Ann. T. S. Eliot. NAEL-5v2; NAEL-6v2; NoAM *Fr. Landscapes.*

Cape Coast Castle Revisited. Jo Ann Hall-Evans. BlSi

Cape Cod. George Santayana. APN-2

Cape Hatteras. Hart Crane. MoAmPo *Fr. Bridge, The.*

Cape of Good Hope, The. Jean Cocteau. CuPo

Cape of Storms, The. John Wheatley. PeSAV

Cape show a glimpse of her bare butt. (LL) Asclepiades. GrAn; PGA

Capel Calvin. Idris Davies. AngWePo

Capework of the wind. (LL) Sleepless at Crown Point. Richard Wilbur. InPK-6; WeW-3

Capital. John Tripp. AngWePo

Capital is fast asleep at dawn, The. Menshikov. Yaroslav [*or Iaroslav*] Vasilevich Smelyakov [*orSmeliakov*]. TCRP, *tr. by Lubov Yakovleva*

Capital Punishment. Nina Cassian. PoSu, *tr. by Nina Cassian*

Capital ship for an ocean trip, A. Charles Edward Carryl. NBLV; OBCA *Fr. Davy and the Goblin.*

Capitalist Poem #36. Campbell McGrath. NAPBL

Capitalist Projections. Brenda Coultas. HeMarv

Capitals. Raymond Garlick. AngWePo

Capitals Are Rocked, The. Nikolai Alekseyevich Nekrasov. AWP, *tr. by Babette Deutsch and Avrahm Yarmolinsky*

Capitol, The. Innokenty Fiodorovich Annensky. WoPoe, *tr. by Stephen Berg*

Capped arbiter of beauty in this street. Hart Crane. FaBoMo *Fr. For the Marriage of Faustus and Helen.*

Capper Kaplinski at the North Side Cue Club. Hayden Carruth. MoASP

Capriccio of Roman Ruins and Sculpture with Figures, A. J. D. McClatchy. GS

Capriccios. Jaime Sabines. TCLAP, *tr. by Claudine-Marie D'Angelo*

Caprichosa. Angelina Weld Grimké. PoBW

Capricious, avaricious kind—, A. Russian Mind, The. Vyacheslav Ivanovich Ivanov. TCRP, *tr. by Albert C. Todd*

Capt. Smith and Pocahontas. Eloise Bibb. CBWP-4

Captain, The. Francis Beaumont.
   Away, Delights. NOBE; OBEV

Captain, The. Blanca Varela. WPOW, *tr. by Lynne Alvarez*

Captain Amasa Delano's Dilemma. Yusef Komunyakaa. BodElec

Captain calls his crew to the deck, The. Landing of Rochambeau, The. Michael Davidson. FTOS

Captain Car. *Unknown. See Edom o' Gordon*

Captain Car; or, Edom o Gordon. *Unknown.* ESPB

Captain Carpenter. John Crowe Ransom. APT-1; FaBoMo; FuPo; MoAmPo; NOBA; NoAM; OxBA; TRP; TwCP; WoPoe

Captain Cook. *Aborigine Oral Tradition.* NOBAu, *tr. by Percy Mumbulla*

Captain Fox sits reading metaphysics. Captain Fox. Robert Greacen. PNI

Captain Gungho, my men. Dead at Quang Tri, The. Yusef Komunyakaa. CDa

Captain James Leson, U. S. M. C. Bryan Alec Floyd. CDa

Captain of a Seventy-three, The. (LL) Little Billee. William Makepeace Thackeray. FaBoCh; NOBL; OxAEP-2

Captain or Colonel, or Knight in Arms. When the Assault Was Intended to the City. John Milton. GTBS-P; OxBSo; SCGP; Son

Captain Quiros and Mr William Lane. Terra Australis. Douglas Stewart. NOBAu

Captain Reece. Sir William Schwenck Gilbert. OBCoV

Captain's Log. Todd Colby. HeMarv

Captain said, Quack! Quack!, The. (LL) Mother Goose. LB; NTCP; OxNR; ReMoGo

Captain scans the ruffled zone, The. Edward Edwin Foot. VerBaPo *Fr. Homeward-Bound Passenger Ship, The.*

Captain Spud and His First Mate, Spade. John Ciardi. OBCA

Captain Stratton's Fancy. John Masefield. MoBrPo; OBEV

Captain, the drumhead court bring nigh! Dying Soldier, The. Karl Kraus. AuPH, *tr. by Lowell A. Bangerter*

Captain Ward and the *Rainbow*. *Unknown.* ESPB

Captain Wattle and Miss Roe. Charles Dibdin. OxBoLi

Captain Wedderburn's Courtship. *Unknown.* ESPB

Captain, what do you think, I asked. Military Creed, The. Ernest Crosby. FaBoWar

Captains. Nikolai Stepanovich Gumilyov [*or Gumiliov or Gumilev*].
   "On polar and on southern seas." TCRP

Captains among the ghosts, heroes among the Dead! (LL) Hymn to the Fallen. *Unknown.* ChiP; FaBoWar; OBWP, *tr. by Arthur Waley*

Captains Courageous. Frank O'Hara. FTOS

Caption for a Miniature. Joanne Kyger. BB

Captive. Peretz Hirshbein. TrJP, *tr. by Joseph Leftwich*

Captive. Theognis. WoPoe, *tr. by Richmond Lattimore*

Captive Dove, The. Anne Brontë. EBVV; VWP

Captive Escaped in the Wilds of America, The. Addressed to the Hon. Mrs. O'Neill. Charlotte Smith. CenSon; Son

Captive mahogany of a private Roman, The. Roman Elegies. Joseph Brodsky. VCWP, *tr. by Joseph Brodsky*

Captive or king, it's all a matter of chance. Temple of Hsiang Yü, The. Li Shan-fu. SuSp, *tr.* by Irving Y. Lo

Captive's Song. *Unknown.* APN-2, *tr.* by Fannie Reed Giffen

Captive Stone, The. Jim Barnes. CDW

Captived Bee; or, The Little Filcher, The. Robert Herrick. CaPo

Captives, bound in iron bands. Broken Chain, The. Dora Greenwell. VWP

Captivity. Louise Erdrich. HATNAP; NoAM

Captivity. Amy Levy. ViWPN

Captivity, The. Oliver Goldsmith.
  (Memory.) OBEV
  O Memory, Thou Fond Deceiver. OxBSP

Capture of Edwin Alonzo Boyd, The. Peter Miller. MoCV

Capture of Larache, The. Luis de Góngora y Argote. SpanPo, *tr.* by Frances Fletcher

Captured Goddess, The. Amy Lowell. NAAL-5

Caput apri refero. Boar's Head Carol, The. *Unknown.* MiEL

Car Cemetery, The. Ciaran Carson. CIP-2

Car / I give you over to. Car Wash. Myra Cohn Livingston. NTCP

Car is also / a high-speed hermitage, A. Portrait of the Autist as a New World Driver. Les A. Murray. CBAP

Car je suis La Belle France. (LL) Deodand, The. Anthony Hecht. DiPo; NoAM

Car locked, I started home across the grass. Crossing Lincoln Park. Karl Shapiro. IllVoic

Car shuddered and stopped, The. Last Love. Nikolai Alekseievich Zabolotsky [*or* Zabolotskii]. TCRP, *tr.* by Daniel Weissbort

Car, then he moves, opening door suddenly, The. Edward. Honor Moore. WiU

Car Wash. Myra Cohn Livingston. NTCP

Caravaggio. Michelangelo Coviello.
  Self-Portrait. ItPo, *tr.* by Gayle Ridinger

Caravaggio: Swirl and Vortex. Larry Levis. GeoHom

Caravan. Michael Longley. CIP-2; ModIr; PNI

Caravan, The. Gwendolyn MacEwen. MoCV

Caravan heading east on Highway 6, A. Highway 6. Timothy Liu. AmPoNex

Carbon Dioxide. Ágnes Nemes Nagy. IQMS, *tr.* by Adam Makkai

Carcass, A. Charles Baudelaire. NAWM-7v2; SxFrPo, *tr.* by James McGowan

Card comes to tell you, A. Non Piangere, Liù. Peter Porter. OxBC

Card-Players, The. Philip Larkin. BLT; OxBC

Card-Players, The. David Ray. VGW

Card table in the library stands ready, A. James Merrill. HCAP; LCAP-2; NAAL-2v2; NoAM; NoP-4; VCAP *Fr.* Book of Ephraim, The.

Cardboard box of sugared orange—, A. From Superstition. Boris Leonidovich Pasternak. TCRP, *tr.* by Yakov Hornstein

Cardiff Castle. Taliesin Williams.
  "Tourist, as he views the place, The." AngWePo

Cardinal Bembo's Epitaph on Raphael. Thomas Hardy. FaBoEE

Cardinal Ideograms. May Swenson. NoP-4; OBCA; OxIBACP

Cardinal Newman. Christina Georgina Rossetti. NAEL-5v2; NAEL-6v2

Cardinal's Dog, The. John Glassco. MoCV

Cardinals in a Shower at Union Square. Stanley Plumly. BodElec

Cardplayer's glaze is on Gulliver's eyes, The. Gulliver Plays Cards. Nikolai Semionovich Tikhonov. TCRP, *tr.* by Michael Frayn

Cardplayers, The. Jack Spicer. APSN

Cards and Kisses. John Lyly. *See* Alexander and Campaspe

Cards are shuffled and the deck, The. Patrick Kavanagh. NPeEn *Fr.* Great Hunger, The.

Care Away. *Unknown.* OxBoLi
  (Al that I may swynke or swete.) OHMEL

Care away, away, away, / Care away for evermore! *Unknown.* MiEL; OxBoLi

Care-Charmer Sleep. Samuel Daniel. GTBS-P; NAEL-5v1; NAEL-7v1; NIP-4; NOBE; NPeEn; NoSic; OxAEP-1; OxBEV; OxBSo; SCGP; Son; TFi *Fr.* To Delia.

Care-Charmer Sleep. Bartholomew Griffin. NoSic; SCGP *Fr.* Fidessa, More Chaste than Kind[e].

Care-charmer Sleep[e], son[ne] of the sable night. Samuel Daniel. GTBS-P; NAEL-5v1; NAEL-7v1; NIP-4; NOBE; NPeEn; NoSic; OxAEP-1; OxBEV; OxBSo; SCGP; Son; TFi *Fr.* To Delia.

Care-charmer sleepe, sweet ease in restles miserie. Bartholomew Griffin. NoSic; SCGP *Fr.* Fidessa, More Chaste than Kind[e].

Care-charming Sleep [Thou Easer of All Woes]. John Fletcher. OxBSP; SCGP *Fr.* Tragedy of Valentinian, The.

Care thy father once bestowed on me, The. To My Nephew, J. B. Clement Barksdale. OxBSP

Careers. Imamu Amiri Baraka. TRP

Careful is my hart therfore. (LL) *Unknown.* MiEL; OxBoLi

Careful man I ought to be, A. Little Chap Who Follows Me, The. *Unknown.* PoToHe

Careful: my knife drills your soul. Killer, The. A'yunini. STP, *tr.* by Jerome Rothenberg

Careful observers may foretell the hour. Description of a City Shower, A. Jonathan Swift. NAEL-6v1; NAEL-7v1; NIL-7; NPeEn; NoP-4

Careful suburban dead turn their backs, The. Sacrificial Wolf. Anne Rouse. MFPA; NeBl

Careful that these *Frisbees.* Giulia Niccolai. ItPo, *tr.* by Gayle Ridinger *Fr.* Frisbees.

Careful[l] observers may foretell the hour. Description of a City Shower, A. Jonathan Swift. HeIP-4; NAEL-5v1; NOEC; OBSV; PoE; UnPo

Carefully dissected her knee. (LL) Miss Gee. W. H. Auden. EBNV; OxBTC; UV

Carefully section by section. Project. Piera Oppezzo. CItWP, *tr.* by Cinzia Sartini Blum and Lara Trubowitz

Careless Content. John Byrom. NOEC; OBCoV

Careless explorer named Blake, A. Limerick. Ogden Nash. PeLi

Careless Gallant, The. Thomas Jordan. HAP; OxBoLi
  (Coronemus Nos Rosis Antequam Marcescant.) OBEV
  (Epicure, The, Sung by One in the Habit of a Town Gallant.) NOBE; PeLV

Careless hunter, breaking camp, A. Forest Fire. Vadim Sergeievich Shefner. TCRP, *tr.* by Daniel Weissbort

Careless Love. Stanley Kunitz. FaBoWar

Careless Love. *Unknown.* UnPo

Careless old cook of Salt Ash, A. Limerick. *Unknown.* PeLi

Careless Talk. Mark Hollis. NBLV

Carentan O Carentan. Louis Simpson. CoAP; NOBA; OBWP; PoE; RB; WoPoe

Cargoes. John Masefield. BRP; CABP; InPK-6; MoBrPo; NOBE; OBEV; OBMV; PAI; PoRA; TFi

Cargoes of the Radanites. Harry Alan Potamkin. TrJP

Cargoless. Dohaku. JDP, *tr.* by Yoel Hoffmann

Caria and Philistia considered. Cry Faugh! Robert Graves. MoBrPo

Caribbean Sea. Gabriela Mistral. TANSG, *tr.* by Maria Jacketti

Cariboo Horses, The. Alfred Wellington Purdy. HeIP-4; NOBC

Carillonneur. Ricardo M. de Ungria. ReBoTo

Caring for My Lover. Jelaluddin [*or* Jalal al-Din] Rumi. WoPoe, *tr.* by Willis Barnstone

Carious Exposure. Gladys Cardiff. CDW

Caritas. Olga Broumas.
  "Erik Satie, accused." WiU
  "With the clear." WiU

Carl Hamblin. Edgar Lee Masters. OBSV; PAI *Fr.* Spoon River Anthology.

Carle He Came o'er the Croft, The. Allan Ramsay. OxBS

Carlos, calm down, love. Don't Kill Yourself. Carlos Drummond de Andrade. WoPoe, *tr.* by Mark Strand

Carlos, keep calm, love. Don't Kill Yourself. Carlos Drummond de Andrade. TCLAP, *tr.* by Elizabeth Bishop

Carlton, Patrick and I. Boys of Summer, The. E. Ethelbert Miller. SpirFl

Carlyle combined the lit'ry life. Dorothy Parker. APT-1; NALW *Fr.* Pig's-Eye View of Literature, A.

Carlyle on Burns. William Jeffrey. OxBS *Fr.* On Glaister's Hill.

Carmarthen hills are green and low. Carmarthenshire. Dudley G. Davies. AngWePo

Carmarthenshire. Dudley G. Davies. AngWePo

Carmel. Dennis Schmitz. GeoHom

Carmel Point. Robinson Jeffers. APT-1; BLT; NAAL-2v2; NAAL-5; NoAM; NoP-4

Carmelita. D. A. Feinfeld. BloBone

Carmen. Théophile Gautier. WoPoe, *tr.* by John Theobald

Carmen Ancillae. John Hollander. YaYoPo

Carmen Elegiacum. Thomas Morton. SCAP

Carmen is thin—a touch of bister. Carmen. Théophile Gautier. WoPoe, *tr.* by John Theobald

Carmen Possum. *Unknown.* NBLV

Carmen Saeculare. Charles Hubert Sisson. OBVE, *tr.* by Christopher Smart

Carmencita loves Patrick. Little Song. Langston Hughes. TLR

Carmencita said I had a small ibon. In Tagalog Ibon Means Bird. Nick Carbó. AmPoNex

Carmina. Catullus.
  Carmen 3.
  (Death of Lesbia's Bird, The.) AWP, *tr.* by Samuel Taylor Coleridge
  ("Pity! mourn in plaintive tone.") AWP, *tr.* by Samuel Taylor Coleridge
  Carmen 4.
  ("Stranger, the bark you see before you says.") AWP; OBVE, *tr.* by John Hookham Frere
  (Yacht, The.) AWP; OBVE, *tr.* by John Hookham Frere

Carmen 5.
("Come and let us live my Deare.")   OBVE, *tr. by* Richard Crashaw
("Lesbia / live with me.")   EroLit, *tr. by* Peter Whigham
("My sweetest Lesbia, let us live and love.")   AWP; EBEV; HAP; HeIP-4; NAEL-5v1; NoSic; OBVE; PoE; PoRA; SCGP; TFi; WeW-3, *tr. by* Thomas Campion
("So let's live—really live!—for love and loving.")   STV, *tr. by* John Frederick Nims
  "Sunne may set and rise, The."   FaBoEE; NoSic; OBVE, *tr. by* Sir Walter Alexander Raleigh
("Yes! my Lesbia! let us prove.")   OBVE, *tr. by* Walter Savage Landor
Carmen 8.
("Harden now thy tyred hart, with more than flinty rage.")   OBVE, *tr. by* Thomas Campion
("O poor Catullus, stupid long enough!")   STV, *tr. by* John Frederick Nims
Carmen 10.
(Fib Detected, A.)   AWP, *tr. by* John Hookham Frere
("Varus, whom I chanced to meet.")   AWP; OBVE, *tr. by* John Hookham Frere
Carmen 11.   WoPoe, *tr. by* Frederick Morgan
Carmen 13.
("Fabullus I will treat you handsomely.")   OBVE, *tr. by* Richard Lovelace
Carmen 22.
("Suffenus, whom so well you know.")   AWP, *tr. by* Walter Savage Landor
("Suffenus whom you know, the Witty.")   OBVE, *tr. by* Matthew Prior
(To Varus.)   AWP, *tr. by* Walter Savage Landor
Carmen 31.
"Apple of islands, Sirmio, & bright peninsulas, set."   AmFaPo, *tr. by* Peter Whigham
("Gem of all isthmuses and isles that lie.")   AWP, *tr. by* Charles Stuart Calverley
("Jewel of the almost islands and the isles.")   STV, *tr. by* John Frederick Nims
(Sirmio.)   AWP, *tr. by* Charles Stuart Calverley
Carmen 32.
"My lovely, sweet Ipsithilla."
Carmen 34.
("Diana guardeth our estate.")   AWP, *tr. by* Richard Claverhouse Jebb
(Hymn to Diana.)   AWP, *tr. by* Richard Claverhouse Jebb
Carmen 39.
("Egnatius has fine teeth, and those.")   OBVE, *tr. by* Walter Savage Landor
Carmen 45.
(Acme and Septimius.)   AWP; OBVE, *tr. by* Abraham Cowley
"Phyllis Corydon clutched to him."   BoLoP
("Whilst on Septimius' panting Breast.")   AWP; OBVE, *tr. by* Abraham Cowley
Carmen 51.
("Like to a god he seems to me.")   AWP, *tr. by* William Ellery Leonard
Carmen 55.
("Now if thou hast one dram of Grace.")   OBVE, *tr. by* Nahum Tate
Carmen 63.
(Attis.)   OBVE, *tr. by* Peter Whigham
("Over oceans sped he, Attis, in the speediest of ships.")   STV, *tr. by* John Frederick Nims
Carmen 65.
(Grief.)   RaBo, *tr. by* Jacob Rabinowitz
("Grief reached across the world to get me.")   RaBo, *tr. by* Jacob Rabinowitz
Carmen 69.
("That no fair woman will, wonder not why.")   OBVE, *tr. by* Richard Lovelace
Carmen 70.
("My girl says she'll take no one else as a lover.")   STV, *tr. by* John Frederick Nims
("My Mistresse sayes she'll marry none but me.")   OBVE, *tr. by* Richard Lovelace
Carmen 72.
("That me alone you lov'd, you once did say.")   OBVE, *tr. by* Richard Lovelace
("Thou saidst that I alone thy heart could move.")   OxBSP, *tr. by* William Walsh
(To His False Mistress.)   OxBSP, *tr. by* William Walsh
Carmen 75.
("None could ever say that she.")   AWP; OBVE, *tr. by* Walter Savage Landor
("Now my mind's been brought to such a state—and it's your fault.")   STV, *tr. by* John Frederick Nims
(True or False.)   AWP, *tr. by* Walter Savage Landor
Carmen 85.

("Her that I love, I hate! 'How's that, do you know?' they wonder.")   STV, *tr. by* John Frederick Nims
("I love and hate. Ah! never asky why so!")   OBVE, *tr. by* Walter Savage Landor
(Odi et Amo.)   CTC, *tr. by* Ezra Pound
Carmen 92.
("Each Moment of the long-liv'd Day.")   OBVE, *tr. by* Tom Brown
("Lesbia forever on me rails.")   AWP; OBVE, *tr. by* Jonathan Swift
("Lesbia loads me night and day with her curses.")   BoLoP, *tr. by* Peter Whigham
(Lesbia Railing.)   AWP, *tr. by* Jonathan Swift
Carmen 96.
("Friend, if the mute and shrouded dead.")   AWP, *tr. by* H.W. Garrod
(Love and Death.)   AWP, *tr. by* H.W. Garrod
Carmen 101.
("By ways remote and distant waters sped.")   AWP, *tr. by* Aubrey Beardsley
(On the Burial of His Brother.)   AWP, *tr. by* Aubrey Beardsley
Carmina Burana.   *Unknown.*
"Come, come, my companion."   GePo
"Crown of all travailing."   MLL
Dum Diana Vitrea.   WoPoe, *tr. by* Richmond Lattimore
"I am constantly wounded."   PGA; WoPoe, *tr. by* Kenneth Rexroth
"I loved / secretly."   BoWoP
"Ich was ein chint so wolgetan."   EroLit, *tr. by* David Parlett
"O Fortune."   MLL
"O happy hour."   MLL
"She stood in her scarlet gown."   MLL
"They have crucified their Lord afresh."   MLL
Under the Linden Tree.   EroLit, *tr. by* David Parlett
"What profit to Darius of his reign?"   MLL
Carnage, could you do better? (LL)   Vultures.   Margaret Atwood.   LCAP-2; OWoS
Carnal and the Crane, The.   *Unknown.*   ESPB
Carnal Knowledge.   Dannie Abse.   BloBone
Carnal Knowledge.   Thom Gunn.   BoLoP
Carnal Knowledge.   Gwen Harwood.   BMAP; CBAP
Carnal Knowledge 2.   Gwen Harwood.   HarvBoo
Carnation Milk.   *Unknown.*   InPK-6
  (Virtues of Carnation Milk, The.)   OBAL
Carnation milk is the best in the land.   Carnation Milk.   *Unknown.*   InPK-6
Carnations.   Theodore Roethke.   BLT
Carnies.   Debra Allbery.   PBCAP
Carnival.   Primus St. John.   GT
Carnival at the River.   Robert Greacen.   PNI
Carnival Songs.   Lorenzo de' Medici.
  Triumph of Bacchus and Ariadne.   CTC, *tr. by* Richard Aldington
Caro mio, Pulcinello, kindly hear my wail of woe.   Nocturne at Danieli's, A.   Sir Owen Seaman.   UV
Caro ragazzo, yes, sure, let's meet.   Part of a Letter to the Codignola Boy.   Pier Paolo Pasolini.   VCWP, *tr. by* David Stivender
Carol.   Ben Jonson.   ChrPo
Carol, A.   Cecil Day Lewis.   ChrPo
Carol, A.   Donald Hall.   ChrPo
Carol: "Deep in the fading leaves of night."   William Robert Rodgers.   OBCP
Carol, every violet has.   Alfred Noyes.   MoBrPo   *Fr.* Flower of Old Japan, The.
Carol for Advent.   John Heath-Stubbs.   OxBC
Carol, for Candlemas Day.   *Unknown.*   NOSC
Carol for the Last Christmas Eve.   Norman Nicholson.   NOxBChV; OBCP
Carol, in the Park, Chewing on Straws.   Judy Grahn.   WPOW   *Fr.* Common Woman, The.
Carol: "Mary laid her Child among."   Norman Nicholson.   OBCP
Carol: "Now is the world withdrawn all."   Howard Nemerov.   TrCP
Carol of Death, The.   Walt Whitman.   SCV   *Fr.* Memories of President Lincoln.
Carol of Patience.   Robert Graves.   OBCP
Carol of the Poor Children, The.   Richard Middleton.   OBCP
Carol of the Three Kings.   W. S. Merwin.   ChrPo
Carol: "On vague hills the prophet bird."   W. S. Merwin.   YaYoPo
Carol: "There was a boy bedded in bracken."   John Short.   FaBoCh; FaBoTw
Carol: "While shepherds watched their flocks by night."   "Saki."   UV
Carolina.   Henry Timrod.   APN-2; CBCWP
Carolina, Carolina / At last they've got you on the map.   Charleston.   Cecil Mack.   ReLy
Carolina gave me Dinah.   Dinah.   Joe Young.   ReLy
Carolina in the Morning.   Walter Donaldson.   ReLy

Carolina, in which he was killed. (LL) Robert G. Shaw. Henrietta Cordelia Ray. BiSi; CBWP-3; Son

Carolina mourns to-day. For he, the gifted. Tribute to Capt. F. W. Dawson. Mary Weston Fordham. CBWP-2

Caroline Street, Cardiff. John Tripp. TCAWP

Caroline von Günderode. Alejandra Pizarnik. SurWo, *tr. by* Natalie Kenvin

Caroling softly souls of slavery. (LL) Song of the Son. Jean Toomer. ISC; MakPoe; NIL-7; NIP-4

Carouse on the affluent kisses of the tide. (LL) Tide Turning. John Frederick Nims. DiPo; IllVoic

Carp. Dionisio D. Martinez. TouFir

Carp, The. Michael Stevens. CDa

Carp, The. *Vietnamese Oral Tradition.* CaDao, *tr. by* John Balaban

Carp and sturgeon dazzle the silver. Along the Charles. Kenneth Rosen. UrbNat

Carp are secrets, The. Lifting Illegal Nets by Flashlight. James Wright (1927–80). NNaP

Carpe Diem. William Shakespeare. *See* Twelfth Night

Carpe Diem: Time Piece. Marilyn Krysl. PuP-23

Carpenter. George Mackay Brown. OxBC

Carpenter, The. Mary Brent Whiteside. TrCP

Carpenter is intent on the pressure of his hand, The. El Greco: Espolio. Earle Birney. MoCV

Carpenter living in Crewe, A. Limerick. E. O. Parrott. PeLi

Carpenter's Complaint, The. Edward Baugh. OBCoV

Carpenter's made a hole, The. Hole in the Floor, A. Richard Wilbur. NOBA

Carpenter's Son, The. John Berryman. ChIV-2

Carpenter's Son, The. A. E. Housman. ChIV-2; MoBrPo; OxAEP-2; UV

Carpenter's son, carpenter's son. Craftsman. Luci Shaw. TrCP

Carpenter's Wife, The. *Unknown.* OxBB
    (Demon [*or* Daemon] Lover.) HAP; UnPo; WeW-3
    (James Harris.) ESPB

Carpet. Nancy Morejón. TANSG, *tr. by* Joy Renjilian-Burgy

Carpos and Calamos. Nonnus. *Fr.* Dionysiaca.

Carrefour. Amy Lowell. BoWoP; LW

Carriage brushes through the bright, The. Solo for Ear-Trumpet. Dame Edith Sitwell. MoBrPo

Carriage from Sweden, A. Marianne Craig Moore. HAP; TwCP

Carriage tops flapping in spring wind by the waters of the Ju. Following the Rhymes of Fellow Graduate P'ei Chung-mou. Huang T'ing-chien. SuSp, *tr. by* Michael E. Workman

Carriages and horses stir up Ch'ang-an's thick dust. Apricot Garden. Yüan Chên. SuSp, *tr. by* Angela Jung Palandri

Carrickfergus. Louis MacNeice. NAEL-5v2; NAEL-6v2; NOIV; NoAM; PNI

Carried Away. Anne Elder. CBAP

Carried her unprotesting out the door. Gwendolyn Brooks. BPo; HAP; NAAAL; NoP-4; WPE; WeW-3 *Fr.* Womanhood, The.

Carrier Indians. Ken Belford. NOBC

Carrier Letter. Hart Crane. BoLoP
    (Exile.) NIL-7

Carriers of the Dream Wheel. N. Scott Momaday. CDW; ColAP

Carrion. Harold Monro. PeFWW *Fr.* Youth in Arms.

Carrion, A. Charles Baudelaire. AWP, *tr. by* Allen Tate

Carrion Comfort. Gerard Manley Hopkins. BBASP; GSo; HeIP-4; MakPoe; NAEL-5v2; NAEL-6v2; NoAM; NoP-4; PoE; Son; TFi; TOF

Carrion Crow, The. Eliza Cook.
    "I plunged my beak in the marbling cheek." VerBaPo

Carrion crow sat upon [*or* on] an oak, The [*or* A]. Mother Goose. LB; OxNR; ReMoGo

Carrion-eater's nobility calls back from God, The. Dreamed Realization, A. Gregory Corso. NeAP; PoM; VGW

Carrousel Tune. Tennessee Williams. NBLV; OBAL

Carrowmore. Lucie Brock-Broido. PoPoPo

Carry her over the water. W. H. Auden. FaBoTw; RB *Fr.* Ten Songs.

Carry Me. Flavien Ranaivo. NegPo, *tr. by* Ellen Conroy Kennedy

Carry me ackee go a Linstead market. Linstead Market. *Unknown.* FaBoVe

Carry Me Back to Old Virginny. James A. Bland. APN-2; TCAPo

Carry me back to old Virginny. Notes for a Southern Road Map. Phyllis McGinley. NBLV

Carry me down into that liquid place again. Late Afternoon. Molly Fisk. PasH

Carry pride in your fist. When You Leave. Juan Delgado. TouFir

Carrying a bunch of marigolds. Negro Woman, A. William Carlos Williams. SAmP

Carrying generations of lust on his tiny feet. Agent of Love. A. K. Redwing. VoR

Carrying her full cargo of roses. (LL) Big Wind. Theodore Roethke. ColAP; HarvBoo; TRP; VGW

Carrying My Mind Around. *Tlingit Oral Tradition.* TCAPo

Carrying My Wife. Moniza Alvi. NeBl

Carrying my world. Father. Myra Cohn Livingston. NTCP

Carrying their packages of groceries in particular. Old Men and Old Women Going Home on the Street Car. Merrill Moore. MoAmPo

Cars Once Steel and Green, Now Old. Louis Zukofsky. VGW *Fr.* 29 Poems.

Cart With Four Oxen, The. Sándor Petőfi. IQMS, *tr. by* Ila Egon

Cartagena. Gary Snyder. BB

Cartagena de Indias. Earle Birney. MoCV

Carthage. Najaat Al-Udwany. PoArWo, *tr. by* Moulouk Berry and Ali Farghaly

Carthusians. Ernest Christopher Dowson. NAEL-5v2; NAEL-6v2

Cartload of Shoes, A. Abraham Sutskever [*or* Sutzkever]. HP, *tr. by* David G. Roskies

Cartography. Louise Bogan. TRP

Cartoon Physics, Part 1. Nick Flynn. NAPBL

Cartoon Physics, Part 2. Nick Flynn. NAPBL

Carts clang and clatter. Ballad of the Army Carts. Tu Fu. WoPoe, *tr. by* David Lattimore

Caruso: A voice. Sleeping with Women. Kenneth Koch. PoM

Carving on the jamb of an embrasure, A. Priory of St Saviour, Glendalough, The. Donald Davie. OxBC

Cary Grant was dying all that time. What It Was Like the Night Cary Grant Died. Eloise Klein Healy. WiU

CARYO's sweet smile DIANTHUS proud admires. Erasmus Darwin. NOBRP *Fr.* Botanic Garden, The.

Caryophyllaceae / like a scroungy, The. Spring Coming. A. R. Ammons. HeIP-4; InPK-6

Casa Guidi Windows. Elizabeth Barrett Browning.
    "I heard last night a little child go singing." PEW; VWP

Casabianca. Elizabeth Bishop. FaBoWP; NIL-7; OxBSP; WoPoe

Casabianca. Felicia Dorothea Hemans. BRP; NAEL-6v2; NOBRP; NPeEn; RWP; VWP; ViWPN

Casanova on His Deathbed. Philip Casey. BiHa

Casanova's Ankle. Elizabeth Smither. PeNZ

Casanova was turned by an ankle. Casanova's Ankle. Elizabeth Smither. PeNZ

Casbah, The. Mamdouh 'Udwan. MAP, *tr. by* May Jayyusi and Naomi Shihab Nye

Cascade, The. Edgell Rickword. FaBoTw

Cascades of Death. Angelina Muñiz Huberman. MirDau, *tr. by* Aurora Camacho

Cascadilla Falls. A. R. Ammons. NOBA

Cascando. Samuel Beckett. ModIr; NOIV

Case, The. Hoffman Reynolds Hays. SPE

Case at Sessions, A. Walter Savage Landor. OBSV

Case History. Dannie Abse. TCAWP

Case in Point, A. August Kleinzahler. PmAP

"Case of Assault", A. Lydia Stephanou. BoWoP, *tr. by* Kimon Friar

Case of the Same Name, A. Giampiero Neri. ItPo, *tr. by* Gayle Ridinger

Case to the Civilians, A. *Unknown.* FaBoEE

Cased in your bone and plaster. Succubus, The. Harriet Rose. BrRo

Casement's Funeral. Richard Murphy. ModIr; NOIV; PBCIP *Fr.* Battle of Aughrim, The.

Caserta Garden. Richard Wilbur. OBGa

Casey at the Bat. Ernest Lawrence Thayer. APN-2; AiP; AmFaPo; BRP; ChAP; FaBoA; ITBLP; OBAL; OBCA; OBCoV; OxIBACP; PoRA; TCAPo

Casey Jones. T. Lawrence Seibert. GM; ITBLP

Casey Jones. *Unknown.* OxBoLi; PeLV

Cash Positive. Peter McDonald. PNI

Cashel of Munster. William English. BIrV; OBEV, *tr. by* Sir Samuel Ferguson

Cashier, The. Andrey [*or* Andrei] Andreievich Voznesensky [*or* Voznesenskii]. TCRP, *tr. by* W. H. Auden

Casi todos / Almost all. Blues del SIDA / AIDS Blues. Francisco Alarcon. GeoHom

Casida of Sobbing. Federico García Lorca. AF, *tr. by* Robert Bly

Casida of the Dark Doves. Federico García Lorca. WoPoe, *tr. by* Edwin Honig

Casino. Richard Tipping. BMAP

Casket Song, A. William Shakespeare. NAEL-5v1; NoSic; SCGP; TFi *Fr.* Merchant of Venice, The.

Cass Romanski, 23, and his fiancée made dinner at his family. 10 Dead Friends. Dennis Cooper. WiU

Cassandra. Louise Bogan. APT-2; HAP; MoAmPo; NALW; VGW

Cassandra. Elena Chizhova. ARWW, *tr. by* Catriona Kelly

Cassandra. William Dickey. YaYoPo

Cassandra. Robinson Jeffers. APT-1; HeIP-4

Cassandra. Edwin Arlington Robinson. APT-1; NoAM; OxBA

Cassandra and Friend. Norman Henry Pritchard, II. GT

Cassandra declining to follow. Limerick. Basil Ransome-Davies. PeLi

Cassandra's Answer. John Montague. BiHa

Cassandra's kind. Three To's and an Oi. Heather McHugh. ExTi

Cassette tape, The. T.A.P.O.A.F.O.M. Thomas Sayers Ellis. BAP-01

Cassia hall has collapsed, The. Deserted Estate at South Garden, The. Hsü Pen. CoBLCP, tr. by Jonathan Chaves

Cassiopeia at Noon. Michelle Boisseau. ExTi

Cassius Hueffer. Edgar Lee Masters. OxBA Fr. Spoon River Anthology.

Cassock, bands and hymn-book too. (LL) Impromptu. Samuel Wilberforce. NBLV; OWoS

Cast. After the Funeral of Assam Hamady. Sam Hamod. UnSA

Cast a cold eye. W. B. Yeats. FaBoEE Fr. Under Ben Bulben.

Cast Away. Christopher Pilling. NLP

"Cast down your bucket where you are." Atlanta Exposition Ode. Mary Weston Fordham. CBWP-2; SWaP

Cast Off, The. Marge Piercy. NoAM

Cast off all shame. Jana Bai. WPoS

Cast on 120 stitches / Rep. to the end of the row. On a Grey-haired Old Lady Knitting at an Orchestral Concert. Suzanne Gardinier. CBAP

Cast on the turbid current of the street. Julia Ward Howe. SWaP Fr. Lyrics of the Street.

Cast on this shore at end of year. Indian Summer. Lizette Woodworth Reese. SWaP

Cast our caps and cares away. John Fletcher. NOSC Fr. Beggar's Bush.

Cast Shadows. Marcel Duchamp. PFTM-1

Cast thy bread upon the waters. Bible, O.T. AWP; OBVE Fr. Ecclesiastes.

Cast Thy Bread upon the Waters. Phoebe A. Hanaford. AH

Cast your eyes and look over to the ocean and see ships. Desert Conflict. Calvin Makabo. PeSAV, tr. by Alexander Qoboshane

Castalian Scots, nou may ye cry, Allace! Fair Cop, A. Robert Garioch. OBCoV

Castanet Clicks. Pat Mora. OxIBACP

Castanets. Bernard Spencer. WeW-3

Castara. William Habington.
    Against Them Who Lay Unchastity to the Sex of Women. BeJo
    Dialogue between Araphil and Castara, A. BeJo
    Nox Nocti Indicat Scientiam. BASC; BeJo; MeLP; NOBE; NPeEn; OBEV; OxBEV; SCGP
    To a Friend, Inviting Him to a Meeting upon Promise. BeJo
    To Castara ("Do[e] not Their profane orgies hear[e]."). BeJo
    To Castara ("Give me a heart where no impure"). BeJo
    To Castara, upon an Embrace. BeJo; NPeEn
    To Castara, upon Beautie. BeJo
    To Roses in the Bosom[e] of Castara. BeJo; EnLoPo; MeLP; NOSC; OBEV; SCGP
    To the World: the Perfection of Love. BeJo
    Upon Castara's Absence. BeJo

Castara, see that dust, the sportive wind. William Habington. BeJo Fr. Castara.

Castaway, A. Augusta Davies Webster.
    "Poor little diary, with its simple thoughts." NPeEn; ViWPN
    "Well, well, I know the wise ones talk and talk." BrRo

Castaway, The. William Cowper. NAEL-5v1; NOBE; NOBRP; NOEC; NPeEn; OxBEV; PoE; TRP
    (Obscurest night involved the sky.) NoP-4; PoPoPo

Castaways, The. Claude McKay. APT-1

Castellated, tall. Bat, The. Dame Edith Sitwell. FaBoMo

Castilian. Elinor Wylie. ColAP

Casting. Howard Nemerov. OxBSP

Casting. Kevin Young. GT

Casting All Your Care Upon God, for He Careth for You. Thomas Washbourne. SacPr

Casting and Gathering. Seamus Heaney. NoP-4

Casting Sequences. Marjorie Welish. FTOS

Casting, up a salt creek in the sea-rank air. San Pedro Road. Robert Hass. GeoHom

Castle by the Sea, The. Ludwig Uhland. AWP, tr. by Henry Wadsworth Longfellow

Castle Howard, the Seat of the Rt. Hon. Charles, Earl of Carlisle. Anne Ingram, Viscountess Irwin.
    "From every place you cast your wandering eyes." OBGa

Castle in Lynn, A. Linda McCarriston. LoL

Castle in the Fire, The. Mary Jane Carr. ChAP

Castle of Chillon, The. Letitia [or Laetitia] Elizabeth Landon. CenSon

Castle of Indolence, The. James Thomson.
    Land of Indolence, The. NOEC

Leper-House and the Impenitents, The. NePenScot

Castle to castle. Caernarfon, 2 July 1969. T. Glynne Davies. OBWVE, tr. by Joseph P. Clancy

Castle was nigh, with its towers so high, The. Pathetic Lament, A. Eliza Cook. VerBaPo

Castles. A. Leyeles. TrJP

Castles in the Air. James Ballantine. TreFP

Castles of crystal. Trams. Dame Edith Sitwell. NOxBChV

Castles with lofty. Goethe. AWP, tr. by Bayard Taylor Fr. Faust.

Castleside Song. Wang Ch'ang-ling. CoBCP, tr. by Burton Watson

Castoff Skin. Ruth Whitman. InPK-6

Castration. Nigel Jenkins. AngWePo; TCAWP

Castration of the Pen. Erica Jong. NALW

Casts light for a shadow. (LL) Song: "You are as gold." "H. D." APT-1; MoAmPo; TCAPo

Casual Meeting. Margaret E. Bruner. PoToHe

Casual Wear. James Merrill. NIP-4 Fr. Topics.

Casually. (LL) Issa. ChAP; EH, tr. by Robert Hass

Casualties. Robert Herrick. BASC

Casualties, The. John Pepper Clark Bekedermo. HBAPE

Casualties are not only those who are dead. Casualties, The. John Pepper Clark Bekedermo. HBAPE

Casualties (1970). J. P. Clark Bekedermo.
    Season of Omens. PBMAP

Casualty. Seamus Heaney. ModIr; NAEL-5v2; NAEL-6v2; PBCIP; PoE

Casualty. Langston Hughes. APT-2

Casualty. Edwin Rolfe. APT-2

Cat. Emily Dickinson. SAmP

Cat. Mary Britton Miller. TLR; WHSW

Cat. Joe Rosenblatt. NOBC

Cat, The. William Henry Davies. NOBE

Cat, The. Rose Fyleman. NOxBChV

Cat, The. Ogden Nash. WHSW

Cat, The. Raymond Roseliep. HA

Cat, The. Vietnamese Oral Tradition. CaDao, tr. by John Balaban

Cat and Mouse. Ted Hughes. OxBSP

Cat and the Moon, The. W. B. Yeats. FaBoCh; HarvBoo; TTTS; WHSW

Cat and the Pig, The. Gerard Benson. NOxBChV

Cat and the Weather. May Swenson. HAP; WeW-3

Cat as Cat, The. Denise Levertov. NOBA

Cat came, A. James McMichael. GeoHom Fr. Four Good Things.

Cat composed as an uncut pie, A. In the Barn. Roger Fanning. OPRER

Cat Goddesses. Robert Graves. OxBSP

Cat has bitten it quite in two, The. (LL) Mother Goose. LB; ReMoGo

Cat has his sport, The. Innocent, The. Denise Levertov. KaS

Cat, if you go outdoors you must walk in the snow. On a Night of Snow. Elizabeth Jane Coatsworth. MoAmPo; OBCA

Cat in the Dovecote. Avner Trainin. MHP, tr. by Ruth Finer Mintz

Cat in the Snow. Aileen Fisher. NTCP

Cat May Look at a King, A. Unknown. OxBoLi

Cat Morgan Introduces Himself. T. S. Eliot. NOBL; PeLV

Cat-naps take in pipe-bowl light. (LL) Bench of Boors, The. Herman Melville. APN-2; AWTN; NAAL-2v1; NAAL-3; OBAL; SoSe-8

Cat of Carlyshe Kynde, A. John Skelton. TriCat Fr. Phyllyp Sparowe [or Philip Sparrow].

Cat of Cats, The. William Brighty Rands. NOxBChV

Cat on my bosom, The. Cat as Cat, The. Denise Levertov. NOBA

Cat rubs his body, The. December Nap. Dennis Saleh. GeoHom

Cat runs the dripping fence. Drizzle. Shinkichi Takahashi. ZenPo, tr. by Takashi Ikemoto and Lucien Stryk

Cat's Cradle. Lynne Wycherley. Prnts

Cat's Meat. Harold Monro. OBMV

Cat's purr, A. Robert Duncan. VGW Fr. Passages.

Cat's Second Song, The. Nancy Willard. FFC

Cat's whiskers, The. Penny Harter. HA

Cat said / on the corner, A. Vietnam #4. Clarence Major. NBV

Cat sat asleep by the side of the fire, The. Unknown. OxNR

Cat shattered the casserole, The. Cat, The. Vietnamese Oral Tradition. CaDao, tr. by John Balaban

Cat sits on the pavement by the house, A. Lonely Man, The. Randall Jarrell. OxBC

Cat takes a look at the weather. Cat and the Weather. May Swenson. HAP; WeW-3

Cat Washing. Linda Molony. NOBAu

Cat went here and there, The. Cat and the Moon, The. W. B. Yeats. FaBoCh; HarvBoo; TTTS; WHSW

Cat! who hast passed [*or* pass'd] thy grand climacteric. To a Cat. John Keats. CenSon; FaBoCh; OxBSo; TriCat

Catacombs in San Callisto, The. Rolf Jacobsen. BLT, *tr.* by Roger Greenwald

Catalog [*or* Catalogue]. Rosalie Moore. ITBLP; NTCP *Fr.* Catalogue.

Catalogue Army. Naomi Shihab Nye. ReTh

Catalogue of the Birds. Geoffrey Chaucer. NPeEn *Fr.* Parlement of Foules, The.

Catalpa Tree. Miriam Waddington. MoCV

Cataract Isle, The. Christopher Pearse Cranch. APN-1

Cataract of Death far thundering from the heights, The. (LL) Mezzo Cammin. Henry Wadsworth Longfellow. APN-1; NAAL-2v1; NAAL-3; NCAP; PoE; TAP; TCAPo

Cataract of Lodore, The. Robert Southey. "How does the water / Come down at Lodore?" NOxBChV

Cataracts flying down a thousand fathoms roll up a raging billow. Liu Ya-tzu. SuSp *Fr.* Miscellaneous Poems on Lake Biwa.

Catch. Robert Francis. InPK-6; RaBo

Catch. Langston Hughes. NoAM

Catch. Mother Goose. LB; OxNR

Catch, A. Henry Aldrich. FaBoEE; NOSC; OxBSP

Catch, The. Raymond Carver. MoASP

Catch, The. Brewster Ghiselin. HAP

Catch, The. Stanley Kunitz. APT-2

Catch, The. Rebecca Seiferle. ExTi

Catch, The. Richard Wilbur. DiPo; WeW-3

Catch a Little Rhyme. Eve Merriam. OBCA; OxIBACP

Catch a moth in the Amazon; pin it under glass. Every Where and Every When. Arthur Sze. OpBo

Catch him, crow! Carry him, kite! *Unknown.* OxNR

Catch if you can your country's moment, begin. Adrienne Rich. NAAL-5 *Fr.* Atlas of the Difficult World, An.

Catch me glassy vapid. Downtime. Lisa Buscani. AmPoNex

Catch, my Uncle Jack said. Elizabeth. Michael Ondaatje. NoAM

Catch not my breath, O clamorous heart. Tennyson. NAEL-5v2; NAEL-6v2 *Fr.* Maud [A Monodrama].

Catch of Shy Fish, A. Gwendolyn Brooks. Big Bessie Throws Her Son into the Street. VGW

Catch: On a Wet Day. Franco Sacchetti. AWP; EaItPo, *tr.* by Dante Gabriel Rossetti

Catch What You Can. Jean Garrigue. VGW

Catches her into its way. (LL) Remembered Morning. Janet Lewis. MakPoe; SoSe-8; WPE

Catches tigers / In red weather. (LL) Disillusionment of Ten O'Clock. Wallace Stevens. APT-1; NAAL-2v2; NoAM; OxBA; PAI; RB; SAmP; SoSe-8; TCAPo; TRP; TTTS

Catching My Breath. Robert Minhinnick. TCAWP

Catching One Clear Thought Alive. Paula Gunn Allen. WPOW

Catching Webs. Judith Beveridge. NOBAu

Catechism, 1958. W. M. Ransom. CDW

Catechism of d Neoamerican Hoodoo Church. Ishmael Reed. NBV

Category Mistakes in Biochemistry. Rob MacKenzie. Oth

Caterpillar. Emily Dickinson. SAmP; TAP

Caterpillar. Annie Foster. NLP

Caterpillar, A. Basho. EH, *tr.* by Robert Hass

Caterpillar, The. Christina Georgina Rossetti. FaBoVe *Fr.* Sing-Song.

Caterpillar. "I'm learning / To crawl." (LL) Tickle Rhyme, The. Ian Serraillier. NTCP; Spl

Caterpillar's Lullaby. Jane Yolen. Spl

Caterpillars. Aileen Fisher. TLR

Catharine of Arragon. Eloise Bibb. CBWP-4

Cathedral bell, The. Nicholas Virgilio. HA

Cathedral bells were tolling. I'll Be Seeing You. Sammy Fain. ReLy

Cathedral Builders. John Ormond. NoP-4; PeECV; TCAWP

Cathedral. Full of awe and reverence. To Liberty. Ágnes Nemes Nagy. IQMS, *tr.* by Ila Egon

Cathedral Is, The. John Ashbery. InPK-6

Cathedrals sway in the blue face of the steel. Citizen. Julia Fields. GT

Catherine. Karla Kuskin. NTCP

Catherine, describing a perfect circle. Virgin Martyrs. John Heath-Stubbs. OxBC

Catherine said "I think I'll bake." Catherine. Karla Kuskin. NTCP

Catherine, though not from fortune's glittering stores. On Some Violets Planted in My Garden by a Friend. Elizabeth Cobbold. CenSon

Cathexis. Frederick, Jr. Bryant. NBV

Cathleen. Nuala Ni Dhomhnaill. ModIr, *tr.* by Paul Muldoon

Cathleen. *Unknown.* BIrV, *tr.* by Thomas MacIntyre

Cathleen Sweeping. George Johnston. NOBC

Catholic Bells, The. William Carlos Williams. NOBA; OxBA; SAmP

Catholic Love. Charles Wesley. SacPr

Cathy. Beatrix Gates. WiU *Fr.* Triptych.

Catkins, like caterpillars slung arow. Lost Lane. Dorothy Wellesley, Duchess of Wellington. WPE

Catnip from the other side. (LL) King of Cats Sends a Postcard to His Wife, The. Nancy Willard. OBCA; OxIBACP

Cato. Joseph Addison. Cato's Soliloquy. "Soul, secure in her existence, smiles, The." TreFP

Cato. Charles Hubert Sisson. NOCV

Cats. Charles Baudelaire. TriCat, *tr.* by Dugald Sutherland MacColl

Cats. Eleanor Farjeon. OTCP; WHSW

Cats and Dogs. N. M. Bodecker. TLR

Cats and Dogs. Howard Moss. OBAL

Cats hurry to cross our path. Explanation of a Sign. Pyotr Vegin. TCRusP, *tr.* by Daniel Weissbort

Cats making love. Basho. EH, *tr.* by Robert Hass

Cats of Kilkenny, The. *Unknown.* ChAP; PeLi; ReMoGo

Cats sleep / Anywhere. Cats. Eleanor Farjeon. OTCP; WHSW

Cats sleep fat and walk thin. Rosalie Moore. ITBLP; NTCP *Fr.* Catalogue.

Cattle. Peter Skrzynecki. CBAP

Cattle in the common field, The. On the Heights. Walter Savage Landor. FaBoEE

Cattle Loading. Gordon Mackay-Warna. NOBAu, *tr.* by George von Brandenstein

Cattle out of their byres are dungy still, lambs. Gorse Fires. Michael Longley. NoP-4

Cattle Show. Hugh MacDiarmid. FaBoMo; HAP; MoBrPo; OBMV; OxBEV; OxBTC

Cattle then are sick, The. (LL) Summer Time on Bredon. Hugh Kingsmill. NOBL; UV

Cattle Thief, The. Emily Pauline Johnson. WPOW

Cattle-trains edge along the river, bringing morning on a white vibration. Ceiling Unlimited. Muriel Rukeyser. MoAmPo

Catullus, what keeps you from killing yourself? No good reason. What for? Catullus. WoPoe, *tr.* by Charles Martin

Caught. Carole Bernstein. AmPoNex

Caught between catastrophe and habit. Shoreline after Storm. Eamon Grennan. PoCoUp

Caught between two streams of traffic, in the gloom. T. S. Eliot. Robert Lowell. NOBA; NoAM

Caught caterpillar. Landscapes. Pauline Kaldas. PoArWo

Caught in a cloud this morning, this barn. For the Barn at Bread Loaf. William Stafford. BodElec

Caught in an anger exact as a machine! (LL) Tired and Unhappy, You Think of Houses. Delmore Schwartz. APT-2; MoAmPo

Caught in my mittens' mohair barbs. Microscope in Winter, The. Sandra McPherson. LCAP-2; VCAP

Caught in the centre of a soundless field. Myxomatosis. Philip Larkin. NoAM

Caught in the Swamp. Joseph Ceravolo. BodElec

Caught me sittin. All is One for Monk. Imamu Amiri Baraka. ISC

Caught shoplifting. Martin Shea. HA

Caught still as Absalom. Chagrin. Isaac Rosenberg. HarvBoo; MoBrPo

Caught—the bubble. Sonnet. Elizabeth Bishop. APT-2

Cauld blaws the wind frae east to west. Up in the Morning Early. Robert Burns. OPOU

Cauld, grey waater heaves on the neap tide. Itherness. Ellie McDonald. CABP

Cauld Lad of Hilton, The *or* The Wandering Spectre. *Unknown.* OxBoLi (Ghost's Song, The.) FaBoCh

Cauliflowers. Paul Muldoon. ModIr

Cause and Effect. Matthew Prior. *See* Reasonable Affliction, A

Cause nobody deals with Aretha—a mother with four children. Poem for Aretha. Nikki Giovanni. BPo; WWork

Cause of this stab in my side. Tryst, The. *Unknown.* OBWVE, *tr.* by Joseph P. Clancy

Cause you don't love me. Bad Luck Card. Langston Hughes. NoP-4; SAmP; TRP

Causes are in Time; only their issue, The. Allegory of the Wolf Boy, The. Thom Gunn. HarvBoo; OxBC

Causes of Old Age. John Armstrong. ECEV *Fr.* Art of Preserving Health, The.

Caustic Soda. Liz Houghton. Prnts

Caution, The. Catherine Cockburn. LW

Cautionary Limerick. *Unknown.* NBLV

Cautious and Incantatory. Gwensways. Eugene B. Redmond. SpirFl

Cautious Gunslinger, The.   Edward Dorn.   NOBA; PmAP   *Fr.* Gunslinger.

Cautiously bubbles that spring water.   *Unknown.*   ColAnChi, *tr.* by Jeffrey Riegel   *Fr.* Classic of Odes.

Cavafy in Redondo.   Mark Jarman.   GeoHom

Cavalier Lyric.   James Simmons.   UV

Cavalier's Farewell, The.   Guillaume Apollinaire.   WoPoe, *tr.* by Anne Greet

Cavalry Crossing a Ford.   Walt Whitman.   AiP; CBCWP; HeIP-4; InPK-6; NAAL-2v1; NAAL-3; NAAL-5; NoAM; OxBA; PAI; SAmP; TAP; TCAPo; TFi; TRP; UnPo

Cavalry Song.   Hugo Zuckermann.   AuPH, *tr.* by Lowell A. Bangerter

Cave.   John Montague.   CIP-2; ModIr   *Fr.* Cave of Night, The.

Cave, The.   Arthur Rex Dugard Fairburn.   PeNZ

Cave of bronze amplifier of the storms.   Alice Rahon.   SurWo, *tr.* by Nancy Deffebach and Vanina Deler

Cave of Despair, The.   Edmund Spenser.   OBNV   *Fr.* Faerie Queene, The.

Cave of Gold Essence—in Ning-tu, The.   T'ang Hsien-tsu.   CoBLCP, *tr.* by Jonathan Chaves

Cave of Making, The.   W. H. Auden.   FaBoVe; OxAEP-2

Cave of Night, The.   John Montague.
    Cave.   CIP-2; ModIr

Cave of the Thousand Pines.   Muso Soseki.   EaWin, *tr.* by W. S. Merwin

Cave we found, but vacant all within, The.   Homer.   OBVE   *Fr.* Odyssey.

Caverns.   Madison Cawein.   APN-2

Caverns of the Grave I've seen, The.   William Blake.   SCGP

Caviar of death between bread, The.   Christmas Fare.   Dilys Wood.   Prnts

Cavour.   Menella Bute Smedley.   VWP

Caw caw caw crows shriek in the white sun over grave stones.   Allen Ginsberg.   BB

Caw Caw Caw / on a far shingle long ago.   Sea and Ourselves at Cape Ann, The.   Lawrence Ferlinghetti.   PoM

Caw Caw the Crows Caw Caw.   *Unknown.*   STP, *tr.* by Richard Johnny John and Jerome Rothenberg

Caxtons are mechanical birds with many wings.   Martian Sends a Postcard Home, A.   Craig Raine.   NAEL-5v2; NAEL-6v2; NPeEn; NoAM; NoP-4

Cayenne in our blood.   Kalamu ya Salaam.   SpirFl   *Fr.* New Orleans Haiku.

Ce Dur Appel de l'Espoir (1960).   Joseph Miezan Bognini.
    My Days Overgrown.   PBMAP

Cease murdering the dead.   No More Crying Out.   Giuseppe Ungaretti.   PeFWW, *tr.* by Jon Silkin

Cease then, my song, cease the unequal lay. (LL)   On Imagination.   Phillis Wheatley.   BlSi; NAAAL; OxWW; RWP

Cease then my tongue, and lend unto my mind.   Edmund Spenser.   InvLi   *Fr.* Hymn[e] of Heavenly Beauty [*or* Beautie], An.

Ceaseless snow.   Mitsune.   OHMPJ

Ceaseless weaving of the uneven water, The.   Aphrodite Vrania.   Charles Reznikoff.   APT-2

Cecil B. De Mille.   Nicolas Bentley.   OBCoV

Cedar, The.   Han G. Hoekstra.   TuT, *tr.* by Peter Van de Kamp

Cedar and jagged fir.   Lonely Land, The.   Arthur James Marshall Smith.   NOBC

Cedar umbrella / Off to Mount Yoshino.   Basho.   ZenPo, *tr.* by Takashi Ikemoto and Lucien Stryk

Cedars.   Nadia Tuéni.   PoArWo

Cedars of Lebanon, The.   Alphonse Marie Louis de Lamartine.   AWP, *tr.* by Toru Dutt

Céilí.   Ciaran Carson.   PBCIP
    (It Used to Be.)   CIP-2

Ceiling, The.   Theodore Roethke.   KaS

Ceiling Unlimited.   Muriel Rukeyser.   MoAmPo

Ceiling wihtout a star. (LL)   Child.   Sylvia Plath.   HCAP; NAAL-5

Celandine.   Edward Thomas.   OxBTC; TCAWP

Celebrants chanted, The.   Four Ways of Dying.   Steve Chimombo.   HBAPE; NAfrP

Celebrants, The, came chanting, "God is dead!"   Death of God, The.   Howard Nemerov.   OxBC; OxBSP

Celebration.   Joseph Ceravolo.   FTOS

Celebration.   Thomas McGrath.   GifTon

Celebration.   Ray A. Young Bear.   CDW

Celebration, The.   Felix Mnthali.   PBMAP

Celebration: Birth of a Colt.   Linda Hogan.   HATNAP

Celebration for My Mother.   Wendy Rose.   CDW

Celebration of Charis in Ten Lyric[k] Pieces [*or* Peeces], A.   Ben Jonson.   BeJo; OxAEP-1
    Another Lady's [*or* Ladyes] Exception, Present at the Hearing.   NAEL-6v1; NAEL-7v1
    Begging Another, on Colour of Mending the Former.   NAEL-6v1; NAEL-7v1
    Claiming [*or* Clayming] a Second Kiss[e] by Desert.   NAEL-6v1

Her Man Described by Her Own[e] Dictamen.   NAEL-6v1; NAEL-7v1

Her Triumph.   BASC; CTC; EBEV; NAEL-6v1; NAEL-7v1; NOSC; NPeEn; NoP-4

His Discourse with Cupid.   NAEL-6v1

His Excuse for Loving.   NAEL-6v1; NAEL-7v1; NOSC

How He Saw Her.   NAEL-6v1; NAEL-7v1

(Triumph of Charis, The.)   NOBE; TFi

(Triumph, The.)   OBEV

Urging Her of a Promise.   NAEL-6v1; NAEL-7v1

What He[e] Suffered.   NAEL-6v1; NAEL-7v1

Celebration of Home Birth: November 15th, 1981, A.   Sandra Maria Esteves.   PueRic

Celebration of the Body.   Daisy Zamora.   LoL, *tr.* by Dinah Livingston

Celebrators '88.   Kevin Gilbert.   IBA

Celestial Alphabet Event.   Jacques Gaffarel.   PFTM-1

Celestial choir! enthroned in realms of light.   To His Excellency General Washington.   Phillis Wheatley.   NAAAL; NAAL-2v1; NAAL-3; NAAL-5; WPE

Celestial City, The.   Giles Fletcher, the Younger.   ChIV-2; NOSC; SacPr   *Fr.* Christ's Victory and Triumph.

Celestial Emperor, The.   Howard Nemerov.   BodElec

Celestial Evening, October 1967.   Charles Olson.   NAAL-5; PoM   *Fr.* Maximus Poems, The.

Celestial Love.   Michelangelo Buonarroti.   AWP, *tr.* by John Addington Symonds

Celestial Music.   Louise Glück.   BBASP

Celestial Surgeon, The.   Robert Louis Stevenson.   EBVV; MoBrPo; PoToHe

Celestial Wisdom.   Juvenal.   AWP, *tr.* by Samuel Johnson   *Fr.* Satires.

Celia Celia.   Adrian Mitchell.   FaBoEE; OPOU

Celia's Home-Coming.   Agnes Mary Frances Robinson.   OBEV; VWP

Celia Singing.   Thomas Stanley.   BeJo; NOSC

Celibacy.   Austin Clarke.   ModIr

Cell, The.   Lyn Hejinian.
    "In the dark sky there."   FTOS

Cell, The.   John Thelwall.   NOEC

Cell by cell the baby made herself, the cells.   Sara in Her Father's Arms.   George Oppen.   NNaP

Cell is but two metres long, A.   Eighteen Dead, The.   Jan Campert.   TuT, *tr.* by Mary E. O'Donnell

Cell of Himself, The.   Arthur Freeman.   TwCP

Cell Song.   Etheridge Knight.   NNaP
    (Night.)   GT
    (Upon Your Leaving.)   GT

Cellar, The.   Laure-Anne Bosselaar.   SpudSo

Cellist.   Instructions to the Player.   Carl Rakosi.   APT-2; MiVo

Cells.   Rudyard Kipling.   FaBoWar

Cells Breathe in the Emptiness.   Galway Kinnell.   VGW

Celluloid of a photograph holds them well, The.   Six Young Men.   Ted Hughes.   OBWP; PoWW

Celtic Cross.   Norman MacCaig.   OxBS

Celts, The.   Stevie Smith.   NoP-4

Cement-grey floors and walls.   On the Island.   Dennis Brutus.   AF

Cemetery, A.   Emily Dickinson.   MoAmPo; OxBA

Cemetery at Petit Saconnex, The.   Deema K. Shehabi.   PoArWo

Cemetery in Pernambuco.   João Cabral de Melo Neto.   TCLAP, *tr.* by Jane Cooper

Cemetery in Punta Arenas.   Enrique Lihn.   TCLAP; VCWP, *tr.* by David Unger

Cemetery in the Mind, The.   Dambudzo Marechera.   NAfrP

Cemetery of the Whales, The.   Yevgeny Aleksandrovich Yevtushenko [*or* Evtushenko].   RusPo, *tr.* by Robert Arthur Douglas Ford

Cenotaph.   John Yau.   PmAP

Cenotaph, The.   Charlotte Mew.   OxAEP-2; WPE

Cenotaph at the Isthmos.   Simonides.   GrAn, *tr.* by Peter Jay

Cenotaph stands in the Park, The.   Greenwood's.   Michael Sharkey.   NOBAu

Censorship.   John Ciardi.   NBLV

Censorship.   Arthur Waley.   OxBTC

Census man, The.   Madam and the Census Man.   Langston Hughes.   SAmP

Census of Animal Bodies: Driving Home.   Madeline DeFrees.   UrbNat

Centaur, The.   May Swenson.   APT-2; FaBoWP; TwCP
    (Summer that I was ten, The.)   NOxBChV

Centaur Overheard, The.   Edgar Bowers.   CoAmPo

Centaur, siren [*or* syren], I forgo[e], The.   Another.   Richard Lovelace.   CaPo

Centaur Song.   "H. D."   VGW

Centaurs, The.   Paul Muldoon.   BiHa

Centenarian's Story, The.   Walt Whitman.   CTC

Centennial of Melville's birth this morning. Japanese City. Kenward Elmslie. PmAP

Center of all centers, core of cores. Buddha in Glory. Rainer Maria Rilke. EnlH, *tr. by* Stephen Mitchell

Center of Attention, The. Daniel Gerard Hoffman. UnPo

Center of lake of light. (LL) Jack Kerouac. NeAP; PmAP *Fr.* Mexico City Blues.

Centered. P. Inman. FTOS

Centipede. Rita Dove. InvLad

Centipede, The. *Unknown.* OBSP

Centipede adown the street, The. Don Marquis. NBLV; OBAL *Fr.* Archy and Mehitabel.

Central Park. Julian Symons. PeLV

Central Standard Time. Kevin Young. AmPoNex

Central stream of what we feel indeed, The. (LL) Below the Surface-Stream. Matthew Arnold. NOBVV; NPeEn; OxBSP

Centre of equal daughters, equal sons. America. Walt Whitman. FaBoA

Centuries. Ronald Stuart Thomas. CABP

Centuries of Meditations. Thomas Traherne.
  "Corn was Orient and Immortal Wheat, which never should, The." NPeEn

Centurion of the Thirtieth, A. Rudyard Kipling. *Fr.* Puck of Pook's Hill.

Century has gone by. And again, A. Variation on Nekrasov. "Naum Korzhavin." TCRP, *tr. by* Vladimir Lunis and Albert C. Todd

Century of Hands. Michael Davidson. FTOS

Century Piece for Poor Heine, A. John Logan. NNaP

Century's blind man!, The. (LL) Melting Pot. Michael Echeruo. PBMAP; TTY

Century's no longer new, The. Toast to 2000, A. Richard Percival Lister. OBCoV

Ceremonies for Candlemas[se] Eve. Robert Herrick. BeJo; CaPo; OBCP

Ceremoniously an egg. Egg Hatches Out a Flame, An. Drahomira Vandas. SurWo, *tr. by* Guy Ducornet

Ceremony. Al-Munsif Al-Wahaybi. MAP, *tr. by* Salma Khadra Jayyusi and Naomi Shihab Nye

Ceremony. Kattie M. Cumbo. BlSi

Ceremony. Jewel C. Latimore. BlSi

Ceremony. Richard M. Mishler. CDa

Ceremony. William Stafford. LCAP-2

Ceremony. Richard Wilbur. CoAP; NAAL-2v2; NAAL-5; NoAM

Ceremony after a Fire Raid. Dylan Thomas. AF

Ceremony must be found, The. Speaking of Poetry. John Peale Bishop. APT-1; OxBA

Ceremony of Sending. *Unknown.*
  Hidden People and the Star People, The. STP, *tr. by* Barbara Tedlock

Ceremony upon Candlemas Eve. Robert Herrick. OBCP

Ceres and Proserpina. Ovid. NAWM-7v1, *tr. by* Allen Mandelbaum *Fr.* Metamorphoses.

Ceriserie. Joshua Clover. BAP-01

Cernunnos. Hugh Maxton. CIP-2

Certain awe of profound marvelling, A. (LL) Dante Alighieri. AWP; EaItPo, *tr. by* Dante Gabriel Rossetti *Fr.* La Vita Nuova.

Certain branches cut. October. Denise Levertov. TRP

Certain dark underground eyes. Picture of Loot. Alan Sillitoe. OxBTC

Certain Evening, A. Gilbert Keith Chesterton. OxAEP-2

Certain Lady, A. Dorothy Parker. NIL-7; NIP-4

Certain Maxims of Archy. Don Marquis. OBAL

Certain Mercies. Robert Graves. GTBS-P

Certain overcoat lived at home for many years, A. Overcoat, The. Alda Merini. CItWP, *tr. by* Cinzia Sartini Blum and Lara Trubowitz

Certain painter, leaving in the morning, A. Saddled Ass, The. Jean de La Fontaine. NBLV, *tr. by* Deems Taylor

Certain people would not clean their buttons. Bohemians, The. Ivor Gurney. FaBoWar; PeFWW

Certain presuppositions are altered. Upland. A. R. Ammons. NOBA

Certain Questions for Monsieur Renoir. John Ormond. AngWePo

Certain scholar named Mr. Wang, A. *Unknown.* CoBCP

Certain sort of bravery, A. Thomas Hardy. FaBoWar *Fr.* Dynasts, The.

Certain things here are quietly American. Derek Walcott. NAEL-5v2; NAEL-6v2; NoP-4 *Fr.* Midsummer.

Certain Type of Scientist Speaks, A. Pope. ECEV *Fr.* Dunciad, The.

Certain words disappear from a language. Louisiana Perch. Ron Padgett. FTOS

Certain young chap named Bill Beebee, A. Limerick. *Unknown.* PeLi

Certain young gourmet of Crediton, A. Limerick. Charles Cuthbert Inge. PeLi

Certain young man of Hilgay, A. Limerick. Ida Thurtle. PeLi

Certain young pate who was addle, A. Limerick. Arthur Shaw. PeLi

Certain young sheik I'm not namin', A. Limerick. *Unknown.* PeLi

Certain youthful lady in Thoulouse, A. Sonnet: Of the Eyes of a Certain Mandetta. Guido Cavalcanti. AWP; EaItPo, *tr. by* Dante Gabriel Rossetti

Certaine verses written by the said ladie Jane with a pinne. Lady Jane Grey Dudley. EMWP

Certainly there was something to their stories. Childe Roland, etc. Elder Olson. OBAL

Certainly they are the same weathered trees. From the Field. Lenard D. Moore. GT

Certainly you've missed this on your reading list. Rilke's Letter from Rome. Star Black. KGB

Certainty. Octavio Paz. TCLAP, *tr. by* Charles Tomlinson

Certainty before Lunch. John Berryman. LCAP-2; OxBC

Certificate of Live Birth. Kimberly M. Blaeser. UnSA

'Cession's stahted on de gospel way, De. Spiritual, A. Paul Laurence Dunbar. BPo; SacPr

Ceyx and Alcyone. Ovid. NoSic, *tr. by* Arthur Golding *Fr.* Metamorphoses.

Cézanne. Gertrude Stein. TAP

Ch'ai-kuan Mountain Pass. Wang Shih-chieng. ColAnChi, *tr. by* Richard John Lynn

Ch'ang-an. Ho Ching-ming. CoBLCP, *tr. by* Jonathan Chaves

Ch'ang-an after snow resembles spring returning. Replying to "On the Occasion of Morning Audience after Snow" Poem by Assistant Secretary Wang of the Board of Sacrifices. Ts'en Shen. SuSp, *tr. by* Daniel Bryant

Ch'ang-an—one slip of moon. Tzu-yeh Song. Li Po. CoBCP, *tr. by* Burton Watson

Ch'ang-ku. Li Ho. SuSp, *tr. by* Maureen Robertson

Ch'ang-O. Li Shang-yin. ChinPo, *tr. by* Yip Wai-lim

Ch'en-hsi County. Ho Ching-ming. CoBLCP, *tr. by* Jonathan Chaves

Ch'i-yü-ko. *Unknown.* CoBCP, *tr. by* Burton Watson

Ch'iang Village. Tu Fu. CrYelRi, *tr. by* Sam Hamill
  "Flocks of chicken clucking from every corner." SuSp
  "From the jagged edges of purple clouds to the west." SuSp

Ch'in Chia's Wife's Reply. Ch'in Chia. BoWoP; ChiP, *tr. by* Arthur Waley

Ch'in emperor guarded the land against Tartar foes, The. Great Wall, The. Chu Ch'ing-yü. SuSp, *tr. by* Irving Y. Lo

Ch'ing Ming—Clear Bright. Oriole Song. Hsueh Chao-yun. CrYelRi, *tr. by* Sam Hamill

Ch'ing-yang Ford. *Unknown.* CoBCP, *tr. by* Burton Watson

Ch'iu-p-u teems with white gibbons. Li Po. SuSp *Fr.* Songs of Ch'iu-p'u.

Ch'ü Yüan's "sorrow." Chang Yang-hao. ColAnChi, *tr. by* Jerome P. Seaton

Cha Till Maccruimein (Departure of the 4th Camerons). Ewart Alan Mackintosh. FaBoWar

Chaadayev on Basmannaya. Oleg Grigorevich Chukhonstev. TCRP, *tr. by* Simon Franklin

Chaeronean Plutarch, to thy deathless praise. Plutarch. Agathias. AWP, *tr. by* John Dryden

Chagall's Cornflowers. Andrey [or Andrei] Andreievich Voznesensky [or Voznesenskii]. TCRP, *tr. by* Vera Dunham

Chagrin. Isaac Rosenberg. HarvBoo; MoBrPo

Chain. Audre Lorde. BlSi

Chain, The. Maxine W. Kumin. TaR

Chain of memory is resurrection I am a vain man, The. Charles Olson. APSN

Chain of Pearl, A. Lady Diana Primrose.
  Eight Pearle, The: Science. EMWP
  Fourth Pearl, The: Temperance. WPE

Chain saw stops, The. Robert Spiess. HA

Chain Store Daisy. Harold Rome. ReLy

Chained bodies. Middle Passage. Sonya Brooks. InTrad

Chained in the market-place he stood. African Chief, The. William Cullen Bryant. ColAP

Chains of hell that hold his friend, The. (LL) Horace. NAEL-5v1; NAEL-6v1; NAEL-7v1, *tr. by* Samuel Johnson *Fr.* Odes.

Chains that bind my thinking, The. Searching, The. Alice S. Cobb. BlSi

Chair. Hagiwara Sakutaro. PFTM-1

Chair and bed red. Reds in the Bed. Peter Finch. Oth

Chair in the Meadow, The. William Stafford. BodElec

Chair she sat in, like a burnished throne, The. T. S. Eliot. HarvBoo; SCV *Fr.* Waste Land, The.

Chair That Is Filled, The. Carrie Biggs. PWR

Chairmaker, The. Siobhan Campbell. MFPA

Chairs. Valerie Worth. NTCP

Chairs in Snow. Elwyn Brooks White. ChAP

Chairs move by themselves, and books. Alzheimer's. Bob Hicok. AmPoNex

Chairs to Mend. *Unknown.* LB
  (Old Chairs to Mend.) ReMoGo

Chalazion. Allison Joseph. NAPBL

Chalcan Female Song. *Unknown*. PFTM-1 *Fr.* Cantares Mexicanos.

Chaldean Ruins, The. Dunya Mikhail. PoArWo, *tr. by* Samira Kawar

Chalice: I heard a radiant ring, with no tongue. Cynewulf. ASW *Fr.* Riddles (Exeter Book).

Chalk and Soot. Wassily Kandinsky [*or* Kandinskii]. PFTM-1

Chalk mark sex of the nation, on walls we drummers know. Three Modes of History and Culture. Imamu Amiri Baraka. ESEAA; PmAP

Challenge. David Diop. NegPo, *tr. by* Ellen Conroy Kennedy

Challenge to the Reader, A. Tad Richards. SwNoth

Chamber is there, The! (LL) Bluebeard's Closet. Rose Terry Cooke. APN-2; TCAPo

Chamber maid. Christening Pot Boiler. Christopher Meredith. TCAWP

Chamber Music. Carl Phillips. NAPBL

Chambered Nautilus. Linda Hogan. BodElec

Chambered Nautilus, The. Oliver Wendell Holmes. APN-1; ColAP; ITBLP; NAAL-3; NCAP; NOBA; NoP-4; TCAPo; TFi *Fr.* Autocrat of the Breakfast Table, The.

Chameleon. Daria Menicanti. CItWP, *tr. by* Cinzia Sartini Blum and Lara Trubowitz

Chameleon, The. Matthew Prior. OBSV

Chameleon was wrong, The. Death Song, A. Steve Chimombo. HBAPE

Chamois Hunter's Love, The. Felicia Dorothea Hemans. RWP; VWP

Chamouni at Sunrise. Frederike Brün. SacPr, *tr. by* Timothy Dwight

Champagne goes straight to my head. Thinking of You, Hiroshima. Betsy Sholl. PBCAP

Champagne Rosée. John Kenyon. OBEV

Champion Chant. Rohan B. Preston. WaCA

Champs d'Honneur. Ernest Hemingway. AiP; IllVoic

"Champs Elysées of Broadway" says the awning. Elysian Fields. Marilyn Hacker. RA

Chance. Ai. ExTi

Chance and chance and thereby starlit. Animula. George Oppen. FTOS

Chance and Essence. "Angelus Silesius." GePo, *tr. by* George C. Schoolfield *Fr.* Cherubical Wanderer, The.

Chance led me once, when idling through the street. *Unknown*. CAGL *Fr.* Don Leon.

Chance Meetings. Conrad Potter Aiken. TCAPo

Chance to Meet Is Difficult, The. Li Shang-yin. WoPoe, *tr. by* Arthur Sze

Chancellor's Gravel-Drive, The. Po Chü-i. WoPoe, *tr. by* Arthur Waley

Chancery Morals. Winthrop Mackworth Praed. NOBRP

Chances, The. Wilfred Owen. OxBTC

Chances of Rhyme, The. Charles Tomlinson. FaBoMo

Chances "R." Allen Ginsberg. CAGL; HCAP

Chandeliers hemorrhage, Tritons, The. Figures in a Ruined Ballroom. George Hitchcock. VGW

Chang Liang's face was like a young woman's. Impromptu. Wu Wei-yeh. CoBLCP, *tr. by* Jonathan Chaves

Change. John Donne. EBEV *Fr.* Elegies.

Change. Robert Graves. OxBTC

Change, The. Samuel Chimsoro. NAfrP

Change, The. A. A. Hedge Coke. ReEnLa

Change, The. Abraham Cowley. MeLP *Fr.* Mistress, The.

Change, The. Henry King, Bishop of Chichester. NOSC

Change, The. Ellis Ayitey Komey. PBMAP

Change, The. Denise Levertov. BAP-97

Change, The. David [*or* Daibhi *or* Daithi] O'Bruadair [*or* Ó Bruadair]. BIrV, *tr. by* Austin Clarke

Change blots out change,—their very memory dies. Richard Henry Wilde. APN-1 *Fr.* Hesperia.

Change in Style, A. Eochadh [*or* Eochy] O'Hussey [*or* O'Heughusa]. NOIV

Change Is Not Always Progress. Haki R. Madhubuti. TAP

Change is the law. The new must oust the old. Last of His Tribe. Oodgeroo of the tribe Noonuccal (Kath Walker). BMAP

Change: *Kyoto-Tokyo Express*, The. Allen Ginsberg. APSN

Change. / life if u were a match i wd light u into something beautiful. change. Poem to Complement Other Poems, A. Haki R. Madhubuti. BPo; NAAAL; NBV

Change Me, Some God, Into That Breathing Rose! William Wordsworth. CenSon; Son *Fr.* River Duddon [A Series of Sonnets], The.

Change, move, dead clock, that this fresh day. Small Prayer. Weldon Kees. VGW

Change of tone, the human hope gone gray, The. (LL) Arrangements with Earth for Three Dead Friends. James Wright (1927–80). NIL-7; NIP-4

Change onward from ours to that of beings who walk other spheres, The. (LL) World below the Brine, The. Walt Whitman. APN-1; NoP-4

Change Partners. Irving Berlin. ReLy

Change / Polis / is this. (LL) Charles Olson. NOBA; PoE *Fr.* Maximus Poems, The.

Change Should Breed Change. William Drummond, of Hawthornden. OBEV

Change thy minde since she doth change. Robert Devereux, 2d Earl of Essex. PBRV

Changed. Charles Stuart Calverley. NOBVV

Changed and not changed. Three million years. Fossil, 1975. Janet Lewis. CRP

Changed Mind (or the Day I Woke Up). Tejumola Ologboni. NBV

Changed to Himself at last by eternity. Tomb of Edgar Allan Poe, The. Stéphane Mallarmé. SxFrPo, *tr. by* E. H. Blackmore and A. M. Blackmore

Changed, Yet Constant. Thomas Stanley. BeJo

Changeful Beauty. *Unknown*. EnLoPo, *tr. by* Andrew Lang

Changeling, The. Judith Ortiz Cofer. NIL-7; TouFir

Changeling, The. John Greenleaf Whittier. MakPoe

Changeling VIII. Kristjana Gunnars. NOBC

Changes. May Probyn. VWP

Changing. Daphne Rock. Prnts

Changing Address Books. Michael S. Glaser. UnSA

Changing clothes / But not. Issa. ZenPo, *tr. by* Takashi Ikemoto and Lucien Stryk

Changing Diapers. Gary Snyder. RaBo

Changing guests, each in a different mood, The. Dante Gabriel Rossetti. NAEL-5v2; NAEL-6v2 *Fr.* House of Life, The.

Changing Light at Sandover, The. James Merrill. NAAL-2v2

Changing Room. John A. Scott. BMAP

Changing the Oil. Eloise Klein Healy. WiU

Changing the Wheel. Bertolt Brecht. PoSu, *tr. by* Michael Hamburger

Changing What We Mean. Eloise Klein Healy. WiU

Chango. René Depestre. PFTM-2, *tr. by* Joan Dayan *Fr.* Rainbow for the Christian West, A.

Channel Boat, The. Akiko Yosano. "What shall I wear to sleep in alone?" WoPoe *tr. by* Janine Beichman

Channel Crossing. George Barker. GTBS-P

Channel Firing. Thomas Hardy. CABP; EBEV; HAP; HarvBoo; HeIP-4; NAEL-5v2; NAEL-6v2; NIL-7; NIP-4; NoAM; NoP-4; OxAEP-2; OxBEV; OxBTC; PAI; PeECV; PeFWW; PoE; PoPoPo; PoRA; PoWW; RB; SoSe-8; TFi; UnPo

Channing and Thoreau. James Russell Lowell. TCAPo *Fr.* Fable for Critics, A.

Chanson. Ernst Jandl. PFTM-2

Chanson d'Outre Tombe. Philip Whalen. BB

Chanson Dada. Tristan Tzara. PFTM-1

Chanson Delice. Beatrice E. Harmon. YaYoPo

Chansons d'Automne. Paul Verlaine. AWP, *tr. by* Arthur Symons

Chant. Roundness. Pierre Drieu la Rochelle. CuPo

Chant for Dark Hours. Dorothy Parker. ItWoWo

Chant for Reapers. Wilfrid Thorley. OBEV

Chant for Young/Brothas and Sistuhs, A. Sonia Sanchez. BPo

Chant from the Iroquois Book of Rites. *Unknown*. APN-2, *tr. by* Horatio Hale

Chant of Mystics, A. Amin Al-Rihani. "Hail, Sana'i, the Moon of the Soul." GraLe

Chant to the Fire-fly. William Ellery Channing. TCAPo

Chant to the Fire-Fly. *Unknown*. APN-2; OxIBACP, *tr. by* Henry Rowe Schoolcraft

Chantars No Pot Gaire Valer. Bernard [*or* Bernart] de Ventadour [*or* Ventadorn]. APSN, *tr. by* Paul Blackburn

Chanted Calendar, A. Sydney Thompson Dobell. OBEV *Fr.* Balder.

Chanticleer. Celia Laighton Thaxter. NOxBChV

Chanting Buddha's name. *Unknown*. SoOfWa, *tr. by* Sam Hamill

Chanting Cherubs, The [A Group by Greenough]. Richard Henry Dana. APN-1

Chanting in Tibet has not ceased, The. Moiré. Michael McClure. SPE

Chanting of banishment, / exhaling flame. Elegy for the Time at Hand. "Adonis" [*or* "Adunis"]. AF, *tr. by* Samuel Hazo

Chanting Poems. Wang Chiu-ssu. CoBLCP, *tr. by* Jonathan Chaves

Chanting the Square Deific. Walt Whitman. APN-1; NAAL-2v1; NAAL-3

Chanting These Verses on My Way to Yodoe. Su Man-shu. SuSp, *tr. by* Wu-Chi Liu

Chants, The. María Sabina. "Ah, Jesu Kri." STP

Chants Communal. Horace Logo Traubel. What Can I Do? TrJP

Chants Democratic and Native American: 5. Walt Whitman. *See* Respondez!

Chants to the Deity. *Unknown*. APN-2, *tr. by* Henry Rowe Schoolcraft

Chao-Mong-Mu freely laid his hands over the sky. Sermon. Emanuel Carnevali. APT-2

Chaos. Still Life: The Table. Theo Van Doesburg. PFTM-1

Chaos of mountains upon mountains, A. Tu Fu. ChinPo, *tr. by* Yip Wai-lim

Chaos rumoured. B. P. Nichol. PFTM-2 *Fr.* Martyrology 7, The.

Chaotic sun on asphalt camouflages. Argument. Jonathan Galassi. KGB

Chap was so pose that was adi, A. Limerick. Arthur Shaw. PeLi

Chapala still remembers the foreigner. Foreigner, A. Witter Bynner. APT-1

Chapel of the Miraculous Medal. Mark Wunderlich. NAPBL

Chapel's cowbell, The. Crusoe's Island. Derek Walcott. VCWP

Chaplet, The. Moses Mendes. TrJP

Chaplinesque. Hart Crane. APT-2; HeIP-4; NAAL-2v2; NAAL-5; NOBA; NoAM; OxBA; VGW

Chapmen. *Unknown.* FaBoVe; MiEL

Chappell—you who love to jest. How to Do It. Martial. WoPoe, *tr.* by Fred Chappell

Chapter XXIII: Of Marriage. Rosmarie Waldrop. PFTM-2 *Fr.* Key into the Language of America, A.

Chapter XXIV: Concerning Their Coyne. Rosmarie Waldrop. PFTM-2 *Fr.* Key into the Language of America, A.

Chapter and Verse. Gonzalo Rojas. TCLAP, *tr.* by Christopher Maurer

Chapter One. Stephanie Brown. BodElec

Chapter 2, Book 35. John Ashbery. BodElec

Character. Detonation. Francesco Cangiullo. PFTM-1

Character. Ralph Waldo Emerson. OxBSP

Character. Taslima Nasrin. VCWP

Character, A. William Blake. PeLV

Character, A. Clara Reeve. ECWP

Character, indistinct, entered, A. Thomas Kinsella. NoAM *Fr.* Songs of the Psyche.

Character of a Critic. Charles Churchill. NOEC *Fr.* Rosciad, The.

Character of a Good Parson, The. Dryden. NOCV

Character of a Happy Life, The. Sir Henry Wotton. BASC; GTBS-P; NOBE; NOSC; OBEV; OxBEV; SacPr

Character of a landscape stands always in a mysterious relation, The. Poem. Charles Madge. SPE

Character of a Roundhead, The. *Unknown.* NOSC

Character of Holland, The. Andrew Marvell. BASC; NOBL; PeLV

Character of Love Seen as a Search for the Lost, The. Kenneth Patchen. CLPP; VGW

Character of Sir Robert Walpole, The. Jonathan Swift. FaBoEE; PoE

Charade. *Unknown.* OxNR

Charcoal fire. Lucien Stryk. IllVoic *Fr.* Issa: A Suite of Haiku.

Chard Whitlow. Henry Reed. MoBrPo; NBLV; NOBL; NoP-4; OBCoV; OxBTC; PeLV; UV; UnPo

Charge, A. Herbert Trench. OBEV

Charge at Waterloo. Sir Walter Scott. FaBoWar

Charge of the Goddess, The. Doreen Valiente. HW, *tr.* by Starhawk

Charge of the Light Brigade, The. Tennyson. BRP; CABP; ChAP; FHYEP; FaBoWar; NAEL-5v2; NAEL-6v2; NOBVV; NoP-4; OBWP; OxAEP-2; OxBEV; PeVV; TFi; UV

Charge to the Poets, A. William Whitehead.
    "If nature prompts you, or if friends persuade." OBSV
    "Life of writing, unless wondrous short, A." ECEV

Charges the Indians five bucks a head to enter. (LL) Evolution. Sherman Alexie. NeAmPo; PoPoPo

Charioteer of Delphi, The. James Merrill. GS

Charis, guess[e], and do[e] not miss[e]. Ben Jonson. NAEL-6v1 *Fr.* Celebration of Charis in Ten Lyric[k] Pieces [or Peeces], A.

Charis one day in discourse. Ben Jonson. NAEL-6v1; NAEL-7v1 *Fr.* Celebration of Charis in Ten Lyric[k] Pieces [or Peeces], A.

Charisma. Ai. ExTi

C[h]aritas Nimia; or, The Dear[e] Bargain. Richard Crashaw. ESCV; NOCV; NOSC

Charité Espérance et Foi. Earle Birney. OxBC

Charity. Connie Bensley. FaBoWP

Charity. Henrietta Cordelia Ray. CBWP-3

Charity and Humility. Henry More. SacPr

Charity Overcoming Envy. Marianne Craig Moore. GS

Charlatan, The. Unsi Al-Haj [or Hajj]. PFTM-2, *tr.* by Pierre Joris

Charlene-N-Booker 4Ever. Forrest Hamer. GeoHom

Charles II. Andrew Marvell. OBSV *Fr.* Last Instructions to a Painter, The.

Charles II. *Unknown.* FaBoEE

Charles XII of Sweden. Samuel Johnson. NOBE *Fr.* Vanity of Human Wishes, The; The Tenth Satire of Juvenal Imitated.

Charles and Bruce, Geoff and Ron and Nancy. All Friends Together. Ronald Albert Simpson. NOBAu

Charles—and I say it wond'ring—thou must know. To Charles Diodati. John Milton. OxBSo, *tr.* by William Cowper

Charles Augustus Chaytor. You Can't Make Love by Wireless. P. G. Wodehouse. ReLy

Charles Augustus Fortescue. Joseph Hilaire Pierre Belloc. NoAM

Charles Carville's Eyes. Edwin Arlington Robinson. OxBA; TAP

Charles Dickens. Dorothy Parker. APT-1 *Fr.* Pig's-Eye View of Literature, A.

Charles Donnelly. Donagh MacDonagh.
    "Of what a quality is courage made." CIP-2

Charles! my slow heart was only sad, when first. Sonnet to a Friend Who Asked How I Felt When the Nurse First Presented My Infant to Me. Samuel Taylor Coleridge. CenSon

Charles on Fire. James Merrill. HeIP-4

Charles river reaps here like a sickle, The. Professor Kelleher and the Charles River. Desmond O'Grady. CIP-2; PBCIP

Charles Sumner. Henrietta Cordelia Ray. CBWP-3

Charles the First. Shelley.
    "Widow bird sate mourning for her love, A." GTBS-P; NOBE; OxBSP

Charles the King, our Emperor, the great. *Unknown.* NAWM-5v1; NAWM-7v1, *tr.* by Frederick Goldin *Fr.* Song of Roland, The.

Charles, the last king of Britain. Morgan Llwyd.
    "Law was ever above kings, The." AngWePo

Charles used to watch Naomi, taking heart. Laboratory Poem. James Merrill. InPK-6; TwCP

Charleston. Cecil Mack. ReLy

Charleston. Henry Timrod. APN-2; CBCWP; ColAP; NOBA; OxBA; TAP; TCAPo

Charleston in the Eighteen-Sixties. Adrienne Rich. CoAP; NAAL-2v2

Charley Barley, butter and eggs. *Unknown.* OxNR

Charley, Charley. *Unknown.* OxNR

Charley du Bignon. Mary E. Tucker. CBWP-1

Charley Warlie had a cow. *Unknown.* OxNR

Charlie Chaplin. Charlie Chaplin Poem, The. Osip Emilevich Mandelstam [or Mandelshtam]. PFTM-1

Charlie Douglas. Katrina Porteous. NeBl

Charlie is my Darling. James Hogg. NePenScot

Charlie MacPherson. *Unknown.* ESPB

Charlie, our one hope, called the chucos from Braly Street. Effects of Abstract Art, The. Gary Soto. GeoHom

Charlie Parker's on the off ramp. Valentine's Day. Kenneth May. SeSe

Charlie Piecan. L. Murray. OxBoLi

Charlie said he used to die. Beatrix Gates. WiU *Fr.* Triptych.

Charlie Wolf used to whittle skinning knives. Halcyon Days. Jim Barnes. CDW; VCAP

Charlot, who my controller is chief. Epistle from Fern Hill. Mary Jones. ECWP

Charlotte Brontë. "Susan Coolidge." OBCA

Charlotte Brontë. Paul Hamilton Hayne. APN-2

Charlotte Brontë said, "Wow, sister! *What* a man!" Limerick. Victor Gray. NOBL; PeLi

Charlotte Corday. Charles Tomlinson. OxBC

Charlotte, Her Book. Elizabeth Bartlett. FaBoWP

Charlotte was dug out of my body. Caterpillar. Annie Foster. NLP

Charm. *Unknown.* EMWP

Charm, A. *Unknown.* RB, *tr.* by Richard Hammer

Charm against the Toothache, A. John Heath-Stubbs. TwCP

Charm'd by thy suffrage, shall I yet aspire. To a Friend. Charlotte Smith. RWP

Charm for Lighting the Fire, A. *Unknown.* NOIV, *tr.* by Thomas Kinsella

Charm for Love and Lasting Affection, A. *Unknown.* NOIV, *tr.* by Thomas Kinsella

Charm Mary put on the butter, The. Charm for Love and Lasting Affection, A. *Unknown.* NOIV, *tr.* by Thomas Kinsella

Charm me asleep, and melt me so. Robert Herrick. BeJo; CaPo; OBEV

Charm of rouge on fragile cheeks, The. Maquillage. Arthur Symons. OxBSP

Charm of the Nine Healing Herbs. *Unknown.* WoPoe, *tr.* by David Cloutier

Charm Rhyme, A. *Unknown.* FaBoVe

Charm to Destroy the Male Child of the Laird of Parkis. Isabel Gowdie. EMWP

Charme, or an Allay for Love, A. Robert Herrick. FaBoCh

Charmed by a girl's soft ears. Downy Hair. Shinkichi Takahashi. ZenPo, *tr.* by Takashi Ikemoto and Lucien Stryk

Charmes. Robert Herrick. BeJo

Charming oysters I cry. Oysters. Jonathan Swift. ErotSp

Charming Woman, The. Helen Selina Blackwood, Countess of Dufferin. VWP; WPE

Charmion's Lament. Eloise Bibb. CBWP-4

Charms for a Sudden Stitch. *Unknown.* AnOE, *tr.* by Charles W. Kennedy

Charms for Unfruitful Land. *Unknown.* AnOE, *tr.* by Charles W. Kennedy

Charms of Small Women. Juan Ruiz, Archpriest of Hita. BLPSL, *tr.* by Rene de Costa, Rigas Kappatos and Eleni Paidoussi

Charms, that call down the moon from out her sphere. To Music, to Becalm a Sweet-sick Youth. Robert Herrick. CaPo

Charnel Ground, The. Allen Ginsberg. BB; BodElec

Charnel-house, The. Henry Vaughan. FSCP

Charnel Ship, The. Lucretia Davidson. TreFP

Charon. Louis MacNeice. FaBoTw; OxBEV; PNI

Charon. Virgil [*or* Vergil]. OBVE; NPeEn, *tr. by* John Dryden *Fr.* Aeneid [*or* Eneados, *Aeneis*], The.

Charon's Cosmology. Charles Simic. HCAP; PoPoPo

Charon! Thou slave! Thou fool! Thou Cavalier [*or* Cavaleer]! Mock Charon, A. Richard Lovelace. CaPo

Chart Indent. Richard Eberhart. BodElec

Chart Showing Rain, Winds, Isothermal Lines and Ocean Currents. Louise Owen. YaYoPo

Chartist Meeting. Mike Jenkins. AngWePo

Chartist's Complaint, The. Ralph Waldo Emerson. NCAP

Chartivel. Marie de France.
    Song from "Chartivel." AWP; EnLoPo; WPOW

Chartres. Edith Wharton. APN-2

Chartres of Gowrie, The. Don Paterson. NePenScot

Chase, The. Sir Walter Scott. NePenScot *Fr.* Lady of the Lake, The.

Chase, The. William Somervile [*or* Somerville].
    Hare-hunting. NOEC
    "See! there she goes." ECEV

Chase, The. Richard Tayson. AmPoNex

Chased from my calling to this hackneyed trade. James Kennedy. NOEC *Fr.* Exile's Reveries, The.

Chasing on the margins of pond-waters, the sun. J. D. McClatchy. WiU *Fr.* First Steps.

Chasm. A. R. Ammons. OBAL

Chaste Crocale by two boys, Astacus and Idas. Titus Calpurnius Siculus. RomPo, *tr. by* Guy Lee *Fr.* Eclogues.

Chaste Florimel. Matthew Prior. BoLoP

Chaste Maiden, shining scarlet, The. *Unknown.* ColAnChi, *tr. by* Jeffrey Riegel *Fr.* Classic of Odes.

Chaste Stranger, The. James Tate. NoAM

Chastity Belt. Yusef Komunyakaa. KGB

Chastity ("I Mean That Too, But Yet a Hidden Strength"). John Milton. NOSC *Fr.* Comus; a Masque Presented at Ludlow Castle.

Château, The. Henry Reed. NoP-4

Château Jackson. Louis MacNeice. OxBEV

Chateaux en Espagne. Henrietta Cordelia Ray. CBWP-3

Chatsworth. Charles Cotton. OBGa *Fr.* Wonders of the Peak, The.

Chattanooga. Ishmael Reed. NAAAL

Chattanooga Choo-Choo. Harry Warren. ReLy

Chatte-Show Host came with us, yclept Wogan, A. Chaucer: The Wogan's Tale. Stanley J. Sharpless. UV

Chatter of birds two by two raises a night song joining a litany of running water. Prairie Waters by Night. Carl Sandburg. NAAL-2v2

Chattering finch and water-fly. Skeleton, The. Gilbert Keith Chesterton. FaBoTw

Chattering swallow! what shall we. Swallow, The. Thomas Stanley. AWP

Chaucer. Henry Wadsworth Longfellow. APN-1; AWP; HeIP-4; NOBA; OBEV; OxBA; PoE; PoRA; Son; TAP; TCAPo; TFi; WoPoe

Chaucer's Wordes unto Adam, his Owne Scriveyn. Geoffrey Chaucer. CABP; NAEL-6v1; NAEL-7v1; OxBSP
    (To His Scribe Adam.) NAEL-5v1; NoP-4

Chaucer: The Wogan's Tale. Stanley J. Sharpless. UV

Chaunt of the Brazen Head, The. Winthrop Mackworth Praed.
    "I think the thing you call Renown." OBSV

Chauntecleer. Geoffrey Chaucer. OWoS *Fr.* Canterbury Tales, The.

Chaunts of Life. Mathilde Blind. VWP *Fr.* Ascent of Man, The.

Chaunts of the Brazen Head, The. Winthrop Mackworth Praed. NOBRP

Chauvinist. Norman MacCaig. NPeEn

Che is with-out longing. (LL) I Have a Young Sister. *Unknown.* FaBoVe; MiEL; NAEL-5v1; PeLV

Che Sara Sara. Rose Terry Cooke. SWaP

Cheap Replicas of the Eiffel Tower. Elton Glaser. PBCAP

Cheap Repository: The Story of Sinful Sally. Told by Herself. Hannah More. RWP

Cheap Seats, the Cincinnati Gardens, Professional Basketball, 1959. William Matthews. MoASP

Cheat, The. Joseph Beaumont. NOSC

Cheat of Cupid; or, The Ungentle Guest, The. Robert Herrick. AWP; OBVE

Cheated Heart. Arthur Rimbaud. SxFrPo, *tr. by* Martin Sorrell

Check every outflash, every ruder sally. Tennyson. CenSon

Check One. Regie Cabico. ReBoTo; WiU

Cheek by cheek on our pillow[s]. Lament. *Unknown.* ErotSp, *tr. by* Sam Hamill

Cheek of earth and say, There, there, child. (LL) Snow. Philip Levine. ColAP; UrbNat

Cheek to Cheek. Irving Berlin. ReLy

Cheekbone footprint husk if only they could write. Centered. P. Inman. FTOS

Cheer for the Consumer. Nixon Waterman. OBAL

Cheer up, my mates, the wind does fairly blow. Cheer Up, My Mates. Abraham Cowley. OxAEP-1

Cheerful Girls at Smiller's Bar, 1971, The. Jack A. Mapanje. HBAPE; NAfrP; PBMAP; PeSAV

Cheerleaders. Lisa Coffman. AmPoNex

Cheerly firme Vesta, clad in verdant Green. To Their Most Excellent Majesty of Great Brittaines Monarchy. Mary Fage. EMWP

Cheers. Charles McDonald. NLP

Cheers, Cheers for Old Cha Cha Ass. Walta Borawski. GLP

Cheese for the Archdeacon, A. Thomas Hughes. AngWePo

Cheeses, pâté. Rod Willmot. HA

Cheetie-Poussie-Cattie, O. *Unknown.* FaBoCh

Chef Yeats, that master of the use of herbs. Michael Hartnett. NOIV *Fr.* Farewell to English, A.

Chefs and saints may still appear to blithe it. (LL) Moon Landing. W. H. Auden. EmeKit; OxAEP-2

Chekhov, my country is Ward 6. Ward 6. Tanure Ojaide. HBAPE

Chelmsfords Fate. Benjamin Tompson. SCAP

Chembank Card. David S. Mills. InTrad

Chemical tapestry of your brain, The. In Ignorant Cadence. Maura Stanton. YaYoPo

Chemicals ripen the citrus. In California. Donald Davie. NoAM

Chen and Wei are brimming, The. *Unknown.* ChinPo, *tr. by* Yip Wai-lim

Cheng-tao Temple. Tai Piao-yüan. CoBLCP, *tr. by* Jonathan Chaves

Chengtu. Tu Fu. TAL

Chepstow: A Poem. Edward Davies. OBWVE
    "Will no young British bard, on rhyme intent." AngWePo

Chercheuses de Poux, Les. Arthur Rimbaud. AWP, *tr. by* T. Sturge Moore *Fr.* Illuminations.

Cherished Daughter, The. *Unknown.* WoPoe, *tr. by* Nguyen Ngoc Bich

Chernobyl. Mary Jo Salter. FFC

Chernobyl, / Eniwetok. Radioactive. Janine Canan. HW

Chernobyl Icon. Gwyneth Lewis. NeBl *Fr.* Parables & Faxes.

Cherokee, The. Mary Weston Fordham. CBWP-2

Cherokee Love Song, A. John Rollin Ridge. APN-2

Cherries. Joe Lamb. RaBo

Cherries. Zalman Schneour. TrJP, *tr. by* Joseph Leftwich

Cherries; a Parable, The. Thomas Moore. OBSV

Cherry. Stuart Dybek. PBCAP

Cherry, A. *Unknown.* ReMoGo

Cherry-Blossom Wand, The. Anna Wickham. MoBrPo

Cherry blossoms. Sobaku. ZenPo, *tr. by* Takashi Ikemoto and Lucien Stryk

Cherry blossoms. Lucien Stryk. IllVoic *Fr.* Issa: A Suite of Haiku.

Cherry blossoms, The. Onitsura. SoOfWa

Cherry blossoms / dizzying. Nishiyama Soin. ZenPo, *tr. by* Takashi Ikemoto and Lucien Stryk

Cherry blossoms fall. (LL) Basho. EH; SoOfWa, *tr. by* Sam Hamill

Cherry blossoms fall. Saruo. JDP, *tr. by* Yoel Hoffmann

Cherry blossoms fallen. Buson. EH, *tr. by* Robert Hass

Cherry-blossoms may be white, The. Cherry-Tree. József Erdélyi. IQMS, *tr. by* Watson Kirkconnell

Cherry blossoms? / In these parts. Issa. ZenPo, *tr. by* Takashi Ikemoto and Lucien Stryk

Cherry bowl with a blue revolver, A. Cherry Bowl with Blue Revolver: Neo-American Landscape. Juan Felipe Herrera. TouFir

Cherry-ripe [*or* Cherrie-ripe]. Robert Herrick. BASC; BeJo; CaPo; GTBS-P; OBEV; PAI; PeLV

Cherry Robbers. D. H. Lawrence. MoBrPo

Cherry-Tree. József Erdélyi. IQMS, *tr. by* Watson Kirkconnell

Cherry Tree, The. Thom Gunn. GLP

Cherry-Tree Carol, The. *Unknown.* ChrPo; EBEV; ESPB; HeIP-4; MakPoe; OxBB; OxBoLi; PeECV; SacPr; SCGP; TFi
    (Joseph Was an Old Man.) OBCP

Cherry Trees, The. Edward Thomas. NAEL-5v2; NAEL-6v2; OBWP; PeFWW; Spl

Cherry year, A. *Unknown.* OxNR

Cherrylog Road. James Dickey. CoAP; ColAP; HAP; HCAP; NAAL-2v2; NIL-7; NIP-4; TwCP; WeW-3

Cherubical Wanderer, The. "Angelus Silesius."
    Abomination Of Evil, The. GePo, *tr. by* George C. Schoolfield

Belief. GePo, *tr. by* George C. Schoolfield

Body, Soul, And Godhead. GePo, *tr. by* George C. Schoolfield

Chance And Essence. GePo, *tr. by* George C. Schoolfield

Each In His Own. GePo, *tr. by* George C. Schoolfield

God Is Nothing Physical. GePo, *tr. by* George C. Schoolfield

God Is To Me What I Desire. GePo, *tr. by* George C. Schoolfield

I Am As God And God As I. GePo, *tr. by* George C. Schoolfield

Light Exists In The Fire, The. GePo, *tr. by* George C. Schoolfield

Love. GePo, *tr. by* George C. Schoolfield

Man Is The Highest Thing. GePo, *tr. by* George C. Schoolfield

More Abandoned, The More Divine, The. GePo, *tr. by* George C. Schoolfield

One Knows Not What One Is. GePo, *tr. by* George C. Schoolfield

Only His Son Is With God. GePo, *tr. by* George C. Schoolfield

Rose, The. GePo, *tr. by* George C. Schoolfield

Secret Virginity, The. GePo, *tr. by* George C. Schoolfield

Sin. GePo, *tr. by* George C. Schoolfield

Spiritual Alchemy, The. GePo, *tr. by* George C. Schoolfield

Spiritual Ark And The Manna-Vessel, The. GePo, *tr. by* George C. Schoolfield

Spiritual Impregnation, The. GePo, *tr. by* George C. Schoolfield

Take Therefore That You May Have. GePo, *tr. by* George C. Schoolfield

To St. Augustine. GePo, *tr. by* George C. Schoolfield

Treasure Lies In the Cornerstone, The. GePo, *tr. by* George C. Schoolfield

Virtue's Goal Is God. GePo, *tr. by* George C. Schoolfield

Whoever Has Become All Divine. GePo, *tr. by* George C. Schoolfield

Cherwell, how pleased along thy willowed edge. To the River Cherwell. William Lisle Bowles. CenSon

Chess. Jorge Luis Borges. PoetW, *tr. by* Alastair Reid

Chess I'm eager to play. Attributes of a Gentleman, The. Saint Ronald of Orkney. NePenScot, *tr. by* Paul Bibire

Chess Piece Cornered. John Kinsella. BMAP

Chess Play, The. Nicholas Breton. NoSic

Chest X-Ray. Paula Tatarunis. BloBone

Chestnut Avenue: at Alton House, The. Charles Tomlinson. FaBoTw

Chestnut by the eaves. Basho. EH, *tr. by* Robert Hass

Chestnut Casts His Flambeaux, The. A. E. Housman. NAEL-6v2

Chestnut tree stands in the line of sight, A. St. Asaph's. Kingsley Amis. OxBTC

Chestnuts roasting on an open fire. Christmas Song, The. Robert Wells. ReLy

Chestnuts shine through the cloven rind, The. Song. Thomas Bailey Aldrich. TreFP

Chevrolet fires past two blond children, The. American Tragedy. Joe Bolton. AmPoNex

Chevy Chase. *Unknown.* OxBB

Chewing [of] the Cud, The. Robert Herrick. ChIV-1

Cheyenne Mountain. Helen Hunt Jackson. APN-2

Chez Jane. Frank O'Hara. CoAP; ColAP; NOBA; NeAP; NoAM; PoE

Chez toi, Mahmout. Satire. Ibn Sharaf. WoPoe, *tr. by* Letícia Garza-Falcón and Christopher Middleton

Chi River Gardens and Fields. Wang Wei. CrYelRi, *tr. by* Sam Hamill

Chiang Lin-chi Treats Me to Mudfish. Mei Yao Ch'en. SuSp, *tr. by* Jonathan Chaves

Chiang-nan is a glorious and beautiful land. Song of the Men of Chin-ling. Hsieh T'iao. ChiP, *tr. by* Arthur Waley

Chiapas. Gary Soto. NoAM

Chicago. Margaret Walker Alexander. GT

Chicago. Bret Harte. APN-2; AiP

Chicago. Edgar Lee Masters.
  "This is the city of great doges hidden." TCAPo

Chicago. Carl Sandburg. APT-1; AiP; AmFaPo; BRP; ColAP; IllVoic; MoAmPo; NAAL-2v2; NOBA; NoAM; OxBA; TAP; TFi; TRP; UnPo; VGW

Chicago Blues. Rohan B. Preston. AmPoNex

Chicago Charlie was a good time Romeo. Kansas City Kitty. Edgar Leslie. ReLy

Chicago *Defender* Sends a Man to Little Rock, The. Gwendolyn Brooks. NAAAL

Chicago Exposition Ode. Mary Weston Fordham. CBWP-2

Chicago "Manuel of Style" is really neat, The. John Tranter. NoAM *Fr.* Crying in Early Infancy.

Chicago Picasso, The. Gwendolyn Brooks. BPo *Fr.* Two Dedications.

Chicago Poem. Lew Welch. NeAP; PoM
  (I lived here nearly 5 years before I could / meet the middle western day.) BB

Chicago ran a fever of a hundred and one that groggy Sunday. Shooting of

John Dillinger outside the Biograph Theater July 22, 1934, The. David Wagoner. CoAP; RB

Chicago's avenues, as white as Poland. Derek Walcott. UrbNat *Fr.* Midsummer.

Chicago/3 Hours. Victor Hernández Cruz. PueRic

Chick feed is what I eat. Muso Soseki. EaWin, *tr. by* W. S. Merwin

Chick! my naggie. *Unknown.* OxNR

Chicken, The. Vladimir Holan. PoSu, *tr. by* Ian Milner and Jarmila Milner

Chicken & Sex. That's what I need constantly. I am quite insistent. Chicken & Sex. Brendan Cleary. NeBl

Chicken blessed and caressed. *Unknown.* NOEC *Fr.* Collection of Hymns . . . of the Moravian Brethren, A.

Chicken. How shall I tell you what it is. Presentation of Two Birds to My Son, A. James Wright (1927–80). YaYoPo

Chicken, she chided early, should not wait. Gwendolyn Brooks. ColAP *Fr.* Notes from the Childhood and the Girlhood.

Chicken thaws, blood, A. Eden. Claudia Rankine. GT

Chickens. (LL) Red Wheelbarrow, The. William Carlos Williams. APT-1; BLT; ChAP; ColAP; HarvBoo; HeIP-4; InPK-6; MoAmPo; NAAL-2v2; NAAL-5; NIL-7; NIP-4; NOBA; NoAM; NoP-4; PAI; PoE; SAmP; SoSe-8; TAP; TFi; TRP; TTTS; UnPo; WeW-3

Chickens, The. *Unknown.* TLR

Chickory. Zerubavel Gal'ed. TrJP

Chicory and Daisies. William Carlos Williams. APT-1

Chide, chide no more away. Expectation. Thomas Stanley. BeJo

Chief Defect of Henry King, The. Henry King, Who Chewed Bits of String, and Was Early Cut Off in Dreadful Agonies. Joseph Hilaire Pierre Belloc. NBLV; OBCoV; OxAEP-2; PeLV

Chief Leschi of the Nisqually. Duane Niatum. CDW

Chief of all. John Milton. NOSC *Fr.* Samson Agonistes.

Chief of Medicine, The. Arthur Ginsberg. BloBone

Chief of the West, Darkling, The. David Knight. MoCV

Chief Petty Officer. Charles Causley. OxBTC

Chief Stewardess on a Boeing, The. Limerick. Paul Alexander. PeLi

Chiefly to Mind Appears. Cecil Day Lewis. MoBrPo

Chieftain Iffucan of Azcan in caftan. Bantams in Pine-Woods. Wallace Stevens. NOBA; NoAM; OxBA; SAmP; UnPo

Chieftain to the Highlands bound, A. Lord Ullin's Daughter. Thomas Campbell. GTBS-P; NOBRP

Child. Sylvia Plath. HCAP; NAAL-5

Child. Raymond Roseliep. KaS

Child, A. Mary Lamb. *See* Parental Recollections

Child, The. Judith Wright. BMAP

Child (a boy) bouncing, A. To. William Carlos Williams. OBAL

Child, and all children. To a Christmas Two-Year-Old. Luci Shaw. TrCP

Child and Maiden. Sir Charles Sedley. GTBS-P *Fr.* Mulberry Garden, The.

Child Asleep, A. J. P. Clark Bekederemo. PBMAP *Fr.* Reed in the Tide, A.

Child awaits the angel, The. Angel, The. Alfred Hayes. TrJP

Child Bearers, The. Anne Sexton. BoWoP

Child Beater. Ai. BoWoP

Child Bride. Garnett Kilberg Cohen. MPUn

Child brought blue clay from the creek, The. Image, The. Robert Hass. BLT

Child Burial. Paula Meehan. EmeKit; MakPoe; ModIr

Child calling and calling, The. Evening. Karen Volkman. NIL-7

Child came to the dark library, The. Saturday in the '20s, A. Jean Earle. AngWePo

Child Christ at the Top of the Stairs. James Ragan. TWW

Child climbs to the island's highest point, The. Edouard Glissant. NegPo *Fr.* Indies, The.

Child Compassion, The. Margot Ruddock. OBMV

Child / Curious and innocent, A. To Robert Louis Stevenson. William Ernest Henley. MoBrPo

Child, Do Not Throw This Book About. Joseph Hilaire Pierre Belloc. NoAM (Dedication on the Gift of a Book to a Child.) EBEV

Child, dream of a pomegranate tree. Winter Garden. Janet Lewis. APT-2

Child Dying, The. Edwin Muir. FaBoTw; GTBS-P; PoWW; RB; WoPoe

Child Frightened by a Thunderstorm. Ted Kooser. KaS

Child gives her mother a drawing of Heaven, The. Making Babies. Hilary Llewellyn-Williams. TCAWP

Child had got two bullets in the head, The. Night of the Fourth: A Recollection, The. Victor Hugo. SxFrPo, *tr. by* E. H. Blackmore and A. M. Blackmore

Child had longings all unspoken, The. In the Toy Shop. May Kendall. ViWPN

Child, in love with prints and maps, The. Voyage, The. Charles Baudelaire. NAWM-7v2, *tr. by* Charles Henri Ford

Child in Prison, A. Gofraidh Fionn O'Dalaigh. NOIV

Child in the City, A. Lucien Stryk. UrbNat

Child is Born, A. Elina Wechsler. MirDau, *tr.* by Darrell Lockhart

Child is born amonges man, A. Hand by Hand We Shall Us Take. *Unknown.* OHMEL

Child is born in blood, O child of blood, The. (LL) New Year's Day. Robert Lowell. ChrPo; CoAmPo; TRP

Child is born, they cry, a child, A. Christmas. Stevie Smith. ChrPo

Child is Father to the Man, The. Gerard Manley Hopkins. NOBL; NOBVV *Fr.* Trio of Triolets, A.

Child is Not a Knife, A. Göran Sonnevi. PFTM-2, *tr.* by Rika Lesser

Child is not dead, The. Child Who Was Shot Dead by Soldiers at Nyanga, The. Ingrid Jonker. HAWP; PeSAV; WoPoe, *tr.* by Jack Cope, Uys Krige and William Plomer

Child is Revenant to the Man, The. Vincent Buckley. BMAP

Child, Is Thy Father Dead? Ebenezer Elliott. NOBRP

Child-King, The. Morris Wintchevsky. TrJP, *tr.* by Alter Brody

Child, leave the tape recorder. Jennie Hargraves Nampijinpa. IBA

Child Life. Mary E. Tucker. CBWP-1

Child listen / I am singing. White-arm. STP

Child Maurice. *Unknown.* ESPB

Child Maximilian in a White Frock, The. Shortened History in Pictures, A. Jamie McKendrick. OxBSo

Child midst ancient mountains I have stood, A. Mountain Sanctuaries. Felicia Dorothea Hemans. CenSon

Child My Choice, A. Robert Southwell. SacPr

Child my mother, A. Hair. Breda Sullivan. Prnts

Child Myro made this tomb, The. Anyte [*or* Anytes]. GrAn

Child need not be very clever, A. Grandpa Is Ashamed. Ogden Nash. OBCoV

Child Noryce is a clever young man. Child Maurice. *Unknown.* ESPB

Child not yet is lulled to rest, The. Cradle-Song at Twilight. Alice Thompson Meynell. NOBVV; NPeEn; VWP

Child of Adam. Viola C. White. YaYoPo

Child of distress, who meet'st the bitter scorn. To the Poor. Anna Laetitia Barbauld. ECWP; NoP-4

Child of Europe. Czeslaw Milosz. AF, *tr.* by Jan Darowski

Child of my heart! My sweet, beloved first-born! To My Child. "Barry Cornwall." CenSon

Child of my love! though thou be bright as day. Shadow. Mary Elizabeth Coleridge. VWP

Child of My Winter Born. W. D. Snodgrass. MoAmPo *Fr.* Heart's Needle.

Child of Our Bodies. Samuel Hazo. GraLe

Child of Our Time. Eavan Boland. CIP-2

Child of silence and shadow. Yvonne Caroutch. BoWoP

Child of that hour when rock and ocean meet. (LL) Hatteras Calling. Conrad Potter Aiken. ColAP; NOBA; TAP

Child of the clouds! remote from every taint. William Wordsworth. CenSon *Fr.* River Duddon [A Series of Sonnets], The.

Child of the potent spell and nimble eye. Henry Headly. ECEV *Fr.* Invocation to Melancholy, An.

Child of the Romans. Carl Sandburg. NAAL-2v2

Child of the Sun. Lillian M. Fisher. HHAm

Child of the sun, in whom his rays appear. La Gialletta Gallante, or the Sunburned Exotic Beauty. Edward Herbert, 1st Baron Herbert of Cherbury. NOSC

Child of the way. Benseki. JDP, *tr.* by Yoel Hoffmann

Child on the Shore, The. Ursula K. Le Guin. KaS

Child on Top of a Greenhouse. Theodore Roethke. KaS; LCAP-2; NOxBChV; NoP-4; VGW

Child Owlet. *Unknown.* ESPB

Child Reads an Almanac, The. Francis Jammes. AWP, *tr.* by Ludwig Lewisohn

Child's a plaything for an hour, A. Parental Recollections. Mary Lamb. OxBAV; OxBSP

Child's Address to the Kentucky Mummy, The. Hannah Flagg Gould. SWaP

Child's Birthday, A. Henry Rago. IllVoic

Child's Calendar, A. John Updike.

  August. OBCA

  May. OBCA

Child's castle crumbles; hot air shimmers, The. Mercury Bay Eclogue. M. K. Joseph. PeNZ

Child's Christmas Day, A. *Unknown.* OBCP

Child's Christmas in Puerto Rico, A. Aurora Levins Morales. PueRic

Child's Dream, A. Frances Darwin Cornford. NOxBChV

Child's dream sluggish in me wakes, A. Saint Stephen's. Martina Wied. AuPH, *tr.* by Lowell A. Bangerter

Child's foot is not yet aware it's a foot, The. To the Foot from Its Child. Pablo Neruda. RB, *tr.* by Alastair Reid

Child's Grace, A. *Unknown.* FaBoCh *Fr.* Two Graces.

Child's Grave, Hale County, Alabama. Jim Simmerman. WeW-3

Child's Parliment. Chenjerai Hove. HBAPE

Child's Party, A. Sarah Morgan Bryan Piatt. SWaP

Child's Pet, A. William Henry Davies. RB

Child's Sight, The. Hy Sobiloff. VGW

Child's Song. Robert Lowell. RB

Child's Song. Sir Thomas More. ChAP

Child's Song in Spring. Edith Nesbit. NOxBChV

Child's Story, The. Elizabeth Jennings. HarvBoo

Child's teeth click against the marble, The. Tale of Me, The. Eiléan Ní Chuilleanáin. Prnts

Child's Thought, A. Bertha Moore. VerBaPo

Child's Thought of God, A. Elizabeth Barrett Browning. InvLi

Child's wisdom is in saying, The. Child's Sight, The. Hy Sobiloff. VGW

Child said *What is the grass?* fetching it to me with full hands, A. Walt Whitman. ColAP; ITBLP; NoP-4; SAmP *Fr.* Song of Myself.

Child saw the bombers skate like stones across the fields, The. Come to the Stone. Randall Jarrell. VGW

Child screams in his room, Rage, The. Unjustly Punished Child. Sharon Olds. PBCAP

Child Screening a Dove from a Hawk, A. Letitia [*or* Laetitia] Elizabeth Landon. NOBRP

Child Scribbles, The. Nizar Qabbani. MAP, *tr.* by Diana Der Hovanessian and Lena Jayyusi

Child should always say what's true, A. Whole Duty of Children. Robert Louis Stevenson. NBLV

Child stood in the shed, The. The child went mad. Carpenter's Son, The. John Berryman. ChIV-2

Child Taken from the Mother, The. Minnie Bruce Pratt. GLP

Child that his strength upbore. St Christopher. Austin Clarke. ModIr

Child, the current of your breath is six days long. Unknown Girl in the Maternity Ward. Anne Sexton. NoAM

Child this Day is Born, A. *Unknown.* ChrPo

Child to His Sick Grandfather, A. Joanna Baillie. CABP; ECWP; NOEC; RACG; WoRP

Child Waters. *Unknown.* ESPB; OxBB

Child! we must quit these visionary scenes. Hannah More. ECWP *Fr.* Search after Happiness, The.

Child went out one day, A. I Eat Kids Yum Yum! Dennis Lee. TLR

Child Who Was Shot Dead by Soldiers at Nyanga, The. Ingrid Jonker. HAWP; PeSAV; WoPoe, *tr.* by Jack Cope, Uys Krige and William Plomer

Child, who went gathering the flowers of death. *Unknown.* AWP *Fr.* Thousand and One Nights, The.

Child with a Cockatoo. Rosemary Dobson. CBAP

Child, with many a childish wile. To Cupid. Joanna Baillie. LW

Child, you were conceived in my upstairs room. To a Child Born in Time of Small War. Helen Sorrells. WPE

Childcity, Aprilcity. Paris. Gregory Corso. VGW

Childe Harold's Pilgrimage. Byron.

  Canto 3.

    "In my youth's summer I did sing of One." NOBRP

    "Is thy face like thy mother's, my fair child!" NAEL-5v2; NAEL-6v2

    "Lake Leman woos me with its crystal face." NAEL-5v2; NAEL-6v2; NOBRP

    "Sky is changed!—and such a change! Oh night, The." NOBRP

    "Stop!—for thy tread is on an Empire's dust!" NAEL-5v2; NAEL-6v2

    "There is a very life in our despair." NOBRP

    "There sunk the greatest, nor the worst of men." NOBRP

  Canto 4.

    "And thou, who never yet of human wrong." NAEL-5v2; NAEL-6v2

    "But I forget.—My pilgrim's shrine is won." NAEL-5v2; NAEL-6v2

    "Egeria! sweet creation of some heart." NOBRP

    "I stood in Venice, on the Bridge of Sighs." NAEL-5v2; NAEL-6v2

    "Or view the Lord of the unerring bow." GS

    "Roll on, thou deep and dark blue ocean—roll!" NOBRP

    "What from this barren being do we reap?" FHYEP; NOBRP

  Dying Gladiator, The. NOBE

  Ocean, The. ITBLP; OxAEP-2; TFi; UV

    (Solitude.) TreFP

    "There is a pleasure in the pathless woods." OxAEP-2

    "Oh, thou! in Hellas deemed of heavenly birth." NAEL-5v2; NAEL-6v2

  There Was a Sound of Revelry by Night. EBEV; FaBoWar; OBWP; OxAEP-2; TFI

    (Eve of Waterloo, The.) FaBoCh; NOBE

    Come, blue-eyed maid of heaven!—but thou, alas!" NOBRP

    "Once more upon the waters! yet once more!" FHYEP

Childe Maurice. *Unknown.* ESPB

(Childe Maurice hunted the Silver Wood.) OBSP

Childe Maurice hunted the Silver Wood. *Unknown. See* Gill Morice stood in stable-door

Child[e] My Choice [*or* Choyse], A. Robert Southwell. OxBEV; PeECV

Childe Roland, etc. Elder Olson. OBAL

Childe Roland to the Dark Tower Came. Robert Browning. NAEL-5v2; NAEL-6v2; NAWM-7v2; NOBVV; NoP-4; OBNV; PeVV; PoE; PoPoPo

Childe Rolandine. Stevie Smith. BrRo

Childe Watters in his stable stoode. Child Waters. *Unknown.* ESPB; OxBB

Childhood. Jens Baggesen. AWP, *tr. by* Henry Wadsworth Longfellow

Childhood. William Barnes. NOBVV

Childhood. Edith Bruck. AF

Childhood. Syl Cheney-Coker. NAfrP

Childhood. Frances Darwin Cornford. FaBoWP; KaS; OxBEV; OxBSP; OxBTC

Childhood. Chitra Divakaruni. OpBo

Childhood. Nikolai Stepanovich Gumilyov [*or* Gumiliov *or* Gumilev]. TCRusP, *tr. by* Joseph Kiegel

Childhood. Hoda Hussein. PoArWo, *tr. by* Cornelia Al-Khaled

Childhood. Donald Justice. LCAP-2

Childhood. Edwin Muir. HeIP-4; NPeEn; NePenScot; NoP-4

Childhood. Sharan Strange. GT

Childhood. Thomas Traherne. SacPr

Childhood. Henry Vaughan. NOSC

Childhood. Margaret Abigail Walker. NoP-4; Son; WPOW

Childhood and prime womanhood were spent in the nailer's darg. (LL) Geoffrey Hill. HAP; PoE *Fr.* Mercian Hymns.

Childhood, boyhood, young manhood. Robert Duncan. FTOS *Fr.* Poems from the Margins of Thom Gunn's Moly.

Childhood Fled. Charles Lamb. CenSon

Childhood in Jacksonville, Florida. Jane Cooper. ExTi; TAP

Childhood Is the Kingdom Where Nobody Dies. Edna St. Vincent Millay. FaBoWP; NALW

Childhood is the village of Rosycheekly. Metamorphoses. Yevgeny Aleksandrovich Yevtushenko [*or* Evtushenko]. TCRP, *tr. by* Arthur Boyars and Simon Franklin

Childhood memory: those pears, A. Sofiya Parnok. ARWW, *tr. by* Catriona Kelly

Childhood of a Spy. Dick Davis. DiPo

Childhood of the Ancients. Andrew Hudgins. InvLad

Childhood Painting Lesson. Henry Rago. WHSW

Childhood remembrances [*or* memories] are always a drag. Nikki-Rosa. Nikki Giovanni. BlSi; HeIP-4; PAI; TAP

Childhood Revisited. Gerry Bostock. IBA

Childhood's Retreat. Robert Duncan. NoAM

Childhood Stories. Matthew Rohrer. NAPBL

Childish Game, A. Reinmar von Hagenau. AWP, *tr. by* Jethro Bithell

Childish Prank, A. Ted Hughes. CABP; NPeEn; OxBC

Childless. Giolla Brighde MacNamee. BIrV, *tr. by* Frank O'Connor

Childless couple, The. Restoration. Jeffrey Skinner. PBCAP

Childlessness. James Merrill. CoAmPo; CoAP

Children. Bill Manhire. PeNZ

Children. Sandra McPherson. FaBoWP

Children. Po Chü-i. ChiP, *tr. by* Arthur Waley

Children. Charles Reznikoff. FTOS

Children. Su Tung-p'o (Su Shih). CoBCP, *tr. by* Burton Watson

Children. Teaching the Children. Myra Sklarew. CRP

Children, The. Qasim Haddad. MAP, *tr. by* Charles Doria and Sharif Elmusa

Children, The. Robert Minhinnick. AngWePo

Children, The. Constance Urdang. CoAP

Children, The. William Carlos Williams. SAmP

Children are at the door. At the Door. Lillie Fuller Merriam. PoToHe

Children are blooming like black flowers, The. AIDS Education, Seventh Grade. Ruth L. Schwartz. NeAmPo

Children are Colorblind. Genny Lim. FSt

Children are dumb to say how hot the day is. Cool Web, The. Robert Graves. AWP; GTBS-P; HarvBoo; NAEL-5v2; NAEL-6v2; NoAM; OxBEV; OxBTC; SCV; WoPoe

Children are dying, The. Final Count. Bobbi Sykes. IBA

Children aren't happy with nothing to ignore. Parent, The. Ogden Nash. Spl

Children at Christmas in 1945. Vladimir Holan. AF, *tr. by* C. G. Hanzlicek

Children ate, The. Bergen-Belsen 1945. Lyn Lifshin. GotH

Children Band, The. Sir Aubrey De Vere. OBEV

Children believe in clover, magic numbers. Sacred Children, The. Hoffman Reynolds Hays. SPE

Children, billy goat, have put crimson reins, The. Anyte [*or* Anytes]. HePo *Fr.* Epigrams.

Children born of fairy stock. I'd Love to Be a Fairy's Child. Robert Graves. ChAP

Children, brown as earth, continue to laugh away. Main Temple Street, Puri. Jayanta Mahapatra. VCWP

Children Disinterred. Marion Albina Bigelow.
"Come, lowly ones, and take your places now." VerBaPo

Children do not ask the proper questions. Leaping into the Gulf. Patricia Beer. OxBC

Children do not grow up. Biting Back. Patricia Smith. GT

Children / Don't harm the flea. Issa. ZenPo, *tr. by* Takashi Ikemoto and Lucien Stryk

Children don't know what worry means! Children. Su Tung-p'o (Su Shih). CoBCP, *tr. by* Burton Watson

Children enter, The. Sundown at Darlington 1878. Lance Henson. VoR

Children Go, The. Kenneth Mackenzie. BMAP

Children go forward with their little satchels, The. School Children, The. Louise Glück. ColAP; HCAP; PoPoPo; WeW-3

Children Going Home. Gwendolyn Brooks.
Jamal; Nineteen Cows In a Slow Line Walking. ESEAA
Kojo: I Am A Black. ESEAA
Merle; Uncle Seagram. ESEAA
Novelle; My Grandmother Is Waiting For Me To Come Home. ESEAA
Tinsel Marie; The Coora Flower. ESEAA
(Uncle Seagram.) IllVoic

The / children have a society of their own. John Cage. APSN *Fr.* Diary: How to Improve the World (You Will Only Make Matters Worse).

Children have brought their wood turtle, The. No. Mark Doty. EmeKit

Children have put purple, The. Anyte [*or* Anytes]. PGA

Children have tied you, billy-goat, with bright, The. Anyte [*or* Anytes]. GrAn

Children, if you dare to think. Warning to Children. Robert Graves. FaBoCh; NOxBChV; NPeEn; NoP-4; OxBEV

Children imitating cormorants. Issa. EH, *tr. by* Robert Hass

Children in Armour. Geoffrey Adkins. FaBoWar

Children in Slavery. Eliza Lee Cabot Follen. SWaP

Children in the Arbor. Glover Davis. GeoHom

Children March, The. Elizabeth Riddell. CBAP

Children of dreams are in terror, The. Text for These Distracted Times, A. Rodney Hall. CBAP

Children of Greenock, The. William Sydney Graham. FaBoTw

Children of Light. Robert Lowell. NAAL-2v2; OxBA

Children of Love. Harold Monro. MoBrPo

Children of my happier prime. Immolated. Herman Melville. NCAP

Children of Night. Amos Neufeld. GotH

Children of Saigon, The. Walter McDonald. AF

Children of the Atomic Age. Dominador I. Ilio. ReBoTo

Children of the Disappeared. Valerie Martínez. TouFir

Children of the early / Countryside. Penobscot. George Oppen. HarvBoo

Children of the Future. Jalauddin Mansur Nuriddin. SpirFl

Children of the future Age. William Blake. FHYEP *Fr.* Songs of Experience.

Children of the Mist. Rosamund Marriott Watson. VWP

Children of the Night, The. Edwin Arlington Robinson. APN-2; OxBA

Children of the Owl and the Pussy-Cat, The. Edward Lear. OBCoV

Children of the Poor, The. Gwendolyn Brooks. NAAAL; WPE *Fr.* Womanhood, The.

Children of the Sun. Fenton Johnson. TCAPo

Children of the Working Class. John Wieners. BB

Children of the world. César Vallejo. TCLAP, *tr. by* Clayton Eshleman *Fr.* Spain, Take This Cup from Me.

Children of the world are on the march, The. Children March, The. Elizabeth Riddell. CBAP

Children of wealth in your warm nursery. Elizabeth Daryush. NPeEn; OxBEV; OxBSo

Children of Zeus. Hesiod. WoPoe, *tr. by* Charles Doria *Fr.* Theogony.

Children on the lawn / joined hand to hand, The. Margaret Atwood. MoCV

Children—or. Or a Play. Leslie Scalapino. FTOS

Children picking up our bones. Postcard from the Volcano, A. Wallace Stevens. APT-1; HAP; HCAP; NoAM; SAmP; WeW-3

Children play like Yukana, The. Archie Weller. IBA

Children play with dolls and toys. Observations. Luvuyo Mkangelwa. NAfrP

Children Playing Checkers at the Edge of the Forest. Adrienne Rich. LCAP-2; WeW-3

Children run shouting, The. Glimpses. Philippe Jaccottet. VCWP, *tr. by* Derek Mahon

Children's Ball-Bouncing Song. *Unknown.* NOBAu

Children's Children. Sterling Allen Brown. APT-2

Children's Games. Malkia Amala Cyril. InTrad

Children's Hour, The. Henry Wadsworth Longfellow. APN-1; BRP; ChAP; ITBLP; OBAL; OBCA; TCAPo; WHSW

Children's Letters, The. Dorothy Livesay. NALW; NOBC

Children's Rhymes. Langston Hughes. BPo; NOxBChV

Children's Rhymes and Parodies. *Unknown.* NOBAu

Children's Train, The. Dorianne Laux. GM

Children's voices in the orchard. T. S. Eliot. FaBoCh; GTBS-P; NoAM; WeW-3 *Fr.* Landscapes.

Children, the Sandbar, That Summer. Muriel Rukeyser. LCAP-2

Children / this is the blood. Brother of the Streets. Sam Cornish. TRP

Children under, say, ten, shouldn't know. Cartoon Physics, Part 1. Nick Flynn. NAPBL

Children Walking Home from School through Good Neighborhood. Donald Justice. DiPo; NIL-7; NIP-4

Children wandered up and down, The. Cruise of the *Mystery*, The. Celia Laighton Thaxter. OBCA

Children were around my feet like dogs, The. Seventh Birthday of the First Child. Sharon Olds. PBCAP

Children were frightened by crescendoes, The. Fete, A. Larry Eigner. NeAP

Children were shouting together, The. Frolic. "Æ" MoBrPo

Children, when was. Napoleon. Miroslav Holub. ChAP; PoSu, *tr. by* Kaca Plakova

Children who love more than they hate. Families. Thomas Blackburn. OxBSP

Children, why do you fear, why turn away? For Miriam. Marjorie Oludhe Macgoye. HAWP; WPOW

Children, you are very little. Good and Bad Children. Robert Louis Stevenson. ChAP; EBVV; FaBoCh; OBCoV

Child's Grace, A. Robert Herrick. *See* Grace for a Child

Chile is bordered on the north by Peru. At the Center of Injustice. Violeta Parra. TANSG, *tr. by* Karen Kerschen

Chile's distant and it's a lie. 6. Raúl Zurita. TCLAP, *tr. by* Jack Schmitt

Chile's flag has three colors. Flag of Chile, The. Teresa de Jesús. AF, *tr. by* Maria Proser

Chilean Cigarette Pack, The. Ai Ch'ing. WoPoe, *tr. by* Hualing Nieh and Hualing Nieh

Chilean Elegies: 5, The. The Interior. Tom Wayman. NOBC

Chill, A. Bella [*or* Izabala] Akhatovna Akhmadulina. TCRusP, *tr. by* Kathy Lewis and Bob Perelman

Chill, A. Kanga. JDP, *tr. by* Yoel Hoffmann

Chill and harsh the year draws to its close. Ch'ien T'ao. ChiP

Chill autumn dusk, The. Richard Wright. APT-2

Chill leaves soughing / scatter sounds of rain. Autumn Sentiments. Yüan Hao-wen. SuSp, *tr. by* Irving Y. Lo

Chill of dawn grows on the tips of yellow chrysanthemum twigs, The. Tune: "Partridge Sky." Huang T'ing-chien. SuSp, *tr. by* James J. Y. Liu

Chill-rushing, / Hush-hushing, / Hush—hushing. (LL) Main-Deep, The. James Stephens. MoBrPo; OBMV; UnPo

Chill wind and dew repeat the autumn scene. Hibiscus Flowers. Li Shang-yin. SuSp, *tr. by* Eugene Eoyang

Chill wind stirs at horizon's end. At Horizon's End, Thinking of Li Po. Tu Fu. SuSp, *tr. by* Eugene Eoyang

Chilled by excess of passion. We Drink Farewell. Tu Mu. OHMPC, *tr. by* Kenneth Rexroth

Chilled by the Blasts of Adverse Fate. Jacob Duché. AH

Chilled in this Irish pub I wish my loves. John Berryman. FaBoMo; LCAP-2 *Fr.* Dream Songs.

Chilled through, I wake up. Kenneth Rexroth. APT-2 *Fr.* Love Poems of Marichiko, The.

Chilled with salt dew, tossed on dark waters deep. Mermaiden, A. Thomas Hennell. FaBoTw

Chillen Get Shoes. Sterling Allen Brown. APT-2; NoP-4

Chilling autumn rains. Basho. SoOfWa, *tr. by* Sam Hamill

Chilling breath of midwinter arrives, The. *Unknown.* SuSp

Chilling cold. Shoku'u. JDP, *tr. by* Yoel Hoffmann

Chills. Bella [*or* Izabala] Akhatovna Akhmadulina. ItGoST, *tr. by* F. D. Reeve

Chillun', listen here to me. All God's Chillun Got Rhythm. Walter Jurmann. ReLy

Chilly early Saturday, my study. Passion. Michael Ryan. BodElec

Chilly Night, A. Christina Georgina Rossetti. VWP

Chilterns, The. Rupert Brooke. MoBrPo

Chimera. Barbara Howes. TwCP

Chimes. Alice Thompson Meynell. MoBrPo; WPE

Chimes. Michael Smith. PBCIP

Chimney, A. Mother Goose. OxNR; ReMoGo

Chimney, breathing a little smoke, A. February. James Schuyler. NeAP

Chimney is a hole in the roof, The. White and Black Bones, The. Konrad Bayer. PFTM-2, *tr. by* Malcolm Green

Chimney of my neighbour's house. Soliloquy to Absent Friends. Douglas G. Jones. MoCV

Chimney Sweeper, The. William Blake. FHYEP; NAEL-5v2; NAEL-6v2; NAWM-7v2; NOEC; RB *Fr.* Songs of Experience.

Chimney Sweeper, The. William Blake. FHYEP; HeIP-4; InPK-6; NAEL-5v2; NAEL-6v2; NAWM-7v2; NOEC; OxAEP-2; PAI; PoE; SCGP; SoSe-8; TFi *Fr.* Songs of Innocence.

Chimney sweeper's boy am I, A. Chimney-Sweeper's Complaint, The. Mary Alcock. ECWP; NOEC

Chimneys. Ruth Bidgood. AngWePo

Chimneys: colder. Reindeer Report. U. A. Fanthorpe. OBCP

Chimneys, rank on rank, The. Evening. Richard Aldington. MoBrPo

Chin-ling. Liu Yu Hsi. SuSp, *tr. by* Paul Kroll

Chin-ling Post Station. Wen T'ien-hsiang. ColAnChi, *tr. by* Michael A. Fuller

Chin Music. Alan Soldofsky. MoASP

China. Dorianne Laux. LW

China. Bob Perelman. FTOS; PFTM-2

China Camp, California. Kim Addonizio. GeoHom

China island dream. Empire Smoke, Forgeries, Salient and The Ritz. Ray DiPalma. FTOS

China Maniacs. May Probyn. VWP

China Observed Through Greek Rain in Turkish Coffee. Henrik Nordbrandt. VCWP, *tr. by* Henrik Norbrandt and Alexander Taylor

Chinashop at seaborde. Civility a Bogey. Margaret Avison. NOBC

Chinchopper, chin. (LL) Forehead, Eyes, Cheeks, Nose, Mouth, and Chin. Mother Goose. FaBoVe; LB; OxNR; ReMoGo

Chinese Ballad. Mao Tse-tung [*or* Mao Zedong]. OxBEV, *tr. by* William Empson

Chinese Banquet, A. Kitty Tsui. GLP

Chinese Camp, Kamloops (circa 1883). Andrew Suknaski. NOBC

Chinese Dragons. David Bottoms. GifTon

Chinese Drawings. Witter Bynner.
"What though they conquer us?" NoP-4

Chinese Figures 1. *Unknown.* EaWin, *tr. by* W. S. Merwin

Chinese Figures 2. *Unknown.* EaWin, *tr. by* W. S. Merwin

Chinese Figures 3. *Unknown.* EaWin, *tr. by* W. S. Merwin

Chinese Garden, The. Horace Gregory. OBGa

Chinese Hot Pot. Wing Tek Lum. UnSA

Chinese Landscape Above Caracas. John Yau. BodElec

Chinese Laundry. Yury [*or* Iurii] Kazarnovsky [*or* Kazarnovskii]. TCRP, *tr. by* Bradley Jordan

Chinese magicians had conjured their chance. Tiles. Witter Bynner. APT-1; TCAPo

Chinese Nightingale, The. Nicholas Vachel Lindsay. MoAmPo

Chinese Villanelle. John Yau. PmAP

Chinese Winter. Frederick Robert Higgins. BIrV

Ching a Ring. James Robinson Planché. NOBL

Chingis Khan left his camp on Mount Chasutu. *Unknown.* WoPoe, *tr. by* Paul Kahn *Fr.* Secret History of the Mongols, The.

Chingwe's Hole, you devoured the Chief's prisoners. Glory Be to Chingwe's Hole. Jack A. Mapanje. HBAPE

Chinoiserie. Kay Sage. SurWo

Chinoiseries. Amy Lowell. PoRA

Chinook Songs. *Unknown.* APN-2, *tr. by* Franz Boas

Chip. George Starbuck. OBAL

Chip chip cherry. Riddle. *Unknown.* FaBoVe

Chip City. Linda France. MFPA

Chipmunk, The. Herman Melville. NCAP

Chipmunk can't drag it along. Alonzo Gonzales. STP

Chipmunk's Day, The. Randall Jarrell. OBCA

Chipmunk was standing. Alonzo Gonzales. STP

Chipmunks jump, and / Greensnakes slither. Valentine. Donald Hall. NTCP

Chippewa Love Song. *Unknown.* BoWoP, *tr. by* Frances Densmore

Chippewa Music. Frances Densmore.
I Am Walking. APT-1
I Have Found My Lover. APT-1
My Love Has Departed. APT-1
Sky Will Resound, The. APT-1
Song of Spring, A. APT-1
Song of the Butterfly, The. APT-1
Sound Is Fading Away, The. APT-1

Chirp Chirp the Katydids. *Unknown.* CoBCP, *tr. by* Burton Watson

Chirping / Grasshopper. Chigetsu, Lady. ZenPo, *tr. by* Takashi Ikemoto and Lucien Stryk

Chisel slid, I hit my little knuckle, The. Michael Haslam. Oth *Fr.* Continual Song.

Chiswick. Thomas Maurice. OBGa *Fr.* Richmond Hill.

Chivvy. Michael Rosen. OTCP

C[h]loe. Pope. AWP; NOBE; OBSV *Fr.* Epistle [II,] to a Lady[: Of the Characters of Women].

Chloe and Myra. Lady Sophia Burrell.
"Blindfold I should to Myra run." LW

Chloe, by your command, in verse I write. Letter from Artemisia in the Town, to Chloe [*or* Cloe], in the Country, A. John Wilmot, 2d Earl of Rochester. NPeEn; PoE

Chloe Divine. Thomas D'Urfey [*or* Durfey]. OBEV

Chloe or her modern sister, Lil. Chloe or . . . Laura Riding Jackson. APT-2

Chloe's a nymph in flowery groves. Chloe Divine. Thomas D'Urfey [*or* Durfey]. OBEV

Chloe's father is a professor of linguistics. Elegy for Chloe Nguyen. Marilyn Chin. UnSA

Chloe, why wish you that your years. To Chloe, Who Wished Herself Young Enough for Me. William Cartwright. BeJo; NOSC; OxAEP-1

Chloris, forbear a while. Song. Henry Bold. NOSC

Chloris in the Snow. William Strode. *See* On Chloris Walking in the Snow

Chloris, It Is Not Thy Disdain. Sidney Godolphin. BeJo

Chloris [*or* the Complaint of the Passionate Despised Shepheard]. William Smith.
"Feed, silly sheep, although your keeper pineth." Son
To the Most Excellent and Learned Shepherd, Colin Clout. Son

Chloris, since first our calm of peace. To Chloris, upon a Favour Received. Edmund Waller. OxBSP

Chocolate-coloured paint and the July sun. Dying Synagogue at South Terrace, The. Thomas McCarthy. BiHa

Chocolate Confessions. Magdalena Gomez. PueRic

Chocolate Milk. Ron Padgett. TTTS

Chocolates. Louis Simpson. OBCoV; OxBC

Choice. Abd al-Aziz Al-Maqalih. MAP, *tr. by* Lena Jayyusi and Christopher Middleton

Choice. A. R. Ammons. PAI

Choice. David Bromige. FTOS

Choice. James Vincent Cunningham. VGW

Choice. Emily Dickinson. NAAL-2v1; NAAL-3

Choice. Flavien Ranaivo. NegPo, *tr. by* Ellen Conroy Kennedy

Choice. Donna Trussell. SpudSo

Choice, The. Soame Jenyns. ECEV

Choice, The. John Masefield. MoBrPo *Fr.* Lollingdon Downs.

Choice, The. John Pomfret. NOEC

Choice, The. Dante Gabriel Rossetti. ChIV-2; GTBS-P; OBEV *Fr.* House of Life, The.

Choice, The. Nahum Tate. OxBSP

Choice, The. George Wither. OBEV

Choice, The. W. B. Yeats. NoAM; OxBSP; OxBTC

Choice, Inanna and the Galla. Pem Kremer. HW

Choice of the Cross, The. Dorothy Leigh Sayers. TrCP *Fr.* Devil to Pay, The.

Choice of Weapons, A. Stanley Kunitz. VGW

Choice soul, in whom, as in a glass, we see. Doom of Beauty, The. Michelangelo Buonarroti. AWP, *tr. by* John Addington Symonds

Choicer than all / flush of youth. Paulus [*or* Paulos] Silentiarius. GrAn

Choicer than the Mermaid Tavern? (LL) Lines on the Mermaid Tavern. John Keats. FHYEP; PoRA; SCGP

Choir Invisible, The. "George Eliot." EBVV

Choirmaster's Burial, The. Thomas Hardy. PeECV

Choise of valentines, The. Thomas Nashe [*or* Nash]. PBRV

Choke all week in the fumes and air stinking. Plainsong. Vladislav Felitsianovich Khodasevich. TCRP, *tr. by* Michael Frayn

Choked sunset. Roads. Peter Huchel. AF, *tr. by* Daniel S. Simko

Choked sunset glow. Roads. Peter Huchel. HP; PoSu, *tr. by* Michael Hamburger

Choker's Lane. Kenneth Slessor. BMAP

Chokes the garden. (LL) Idea of Trust, The. Thom Gunn. HarvBoo; NPeEn

Choking. Saniyya Salih. PoArWo, *tr. by* Kamal Boullata

Choking through the whole attack. (LL) Champs d'Honneur. Ernest Hemingway. AiP; IllVoic

Cholera. Nazik Al-Malaika. PoArWo, *tr. by* Husain Haddawy and Nathalie Handal

Cholera Camp. Rudyard Kipling. FaBoWar

Chomei at Toyama. Basil Bunting. OxBTC
"I have been noting events for forty years." NPeEn

Chook, chook, chook, chook, chook. *Unknown.* OxNR

Choose. Carl Sandburg. Spl

Choose Something like a Star. Robert Frost. APT-1; MoAmPo

Choose the colour that hits the mark. Ad Miró. Pierre Alechinsky. PFTM-2, *tr. by* Michael Fineberg

Choose Your Garden. Erin Belieu. ExTi

Choosing a Mast. Roy Campbell. FaBoTw; NoP-4

Choosing a Name. Anne Ridler. NOBE

Choosing Coffins. Raymond Souster. MoCV

Choosing Shoes. Ffrida Wolfe. ChAP

Choosing the Blues. Angela Jackson. ISC

Choosing Their Names. Thomas Hood. NOxBChV

Chop-Cherry. Robert Herrick. EnLoPo

Chopin. Marilyn Nelson. RA

Chopin Preludes, Opus 28. J. R. Solonche. MiVo

Chops Are Flyin. Stanley Crouch. GT

Chord. Langston Hughes. APSN

Chord. Anton Wildgans. AuPH, *tr. by* Lowell A. Bangerter

Chords. Eamer O'Keefe. Prnts

Chords knotted together like insane nouns. Tom Clark. SPE *Fr.* You.

Chords Passages 14. Robert Duncan. FTOS

Choric Song. Tennyson. HeIP-4 *Fr.* Lotus-Eaters, The.

Chortle, laugh, in a laughter of storm. Acrobat of Pain. João da Cruz e Sousa. TCLAP, *tr. by* Flavia Vidal

Chorus. W. H. Auden. *See* Wanderer, The

Chorus. Seneca. NPeEn, *tr. by* Jasper Heywood *Fr.* Hercules Furens.

Chorus: "All ye that handle harp and viol." Moses Hayyim, of Padua Luzzatto. TrJP, *tr. by* Nina Davis Salaman *Fr.* Unto the Upright Praise.

Chorus: "Babylon, I did not come to you for the sake of coming." Matsemela Manaka. PeSAV *Fr.* Pula.

Chorus: "Fair Salamis, the billow's roar." Sophocles. AWP, *tr. by* Winthrop Mackworth Praed *Fr.* Ajax.

Chorus for Survival. Horace Gregory.
"Among the shades I heard my father's father." APT-2
Ask No Return. MoAmPo; VGW
"Meek Shall Disinherit the Earth, The." APT-2

Chorus: "Great Fortune is an hungry thing." Aeschylus. AWP, *tr. by* Gilbert Murray *Fr.* Agamemnon.

Chorus: "If I drink water while this doth last." Thomas Love Peacock. NBLV *Fr.* Crotchet Castle.

Chorus: "In the name of the people." Matsemela Manaka. PeSAV *Fr.* Pula.

Chorus-leading, splashing out the wine. (LL) Postcard from North Antrim, A. Seamus Heaney. PBCIP; PNI

Chorus of a Song That Might Have Been Written by Albert Chevalier. Max Beerbohm. OBCoV; UV

Chorus of Angels. John Henry, Cardinal Newman. NOCV *Fr.* Dream of Gerontius, The.

Chorus of Birds. Aristophanes. AWP *Fr.* Birds, The.

Chorus of Nymphs, A. Andrey [*or* Andrei] Andreievich Voznesensky [*or* Voznesenskii]. VCWP, *tr. by* Vera Dunham

Chorus of Priests. Fulke Greville, 1st Baron Brooke. *See* Mustapha

Chorus of Satyrs, Driving Their Goats. Euripides. AWP *Fr.* Cyclops, The.

Chorus of the Archangels, The. Goethe. AWP; OBVE *Fr.* Faust.

Chorus of the Dead. Nelly Sachs. PFTM-1

Chorus of the Rescued. Nelly Sachs. PoSu; WPOW

Chorus of the Stars. Nelly Sachs. BBASP; PFTM-1, *tr. by* Michael Roloff

Chorus of the weeds, unnameably, The. Weeds as Partial Survivors. Alan Dugan. YaYoPo

Chorus Primus of Bashaws or Cadis. Fulke Greville, 1st Baron Brooke. NOSC *Fr.* Mustapha.

Chorus Sacerdotum. Fulke Greville, 1st Baron Brooke. HAP; NAEL-5v1; NAEL-6v1; NAEL-7v1; NOBE; OxBEV *Fr.* Mustapha.

Chorus: "Sweet are the ways of death to weary feet." Euripides. OBEV, *tr. by* John Byrne Leicester Warren, Lord de Tabley *Fr.* Medea.

Chorus: "That rain-strewn night in the woods, the chorus, chorus." David Wagoner. MiVo

Chorus: "Tis not enough for one that is a wife." Elizabeth Cary, Countess of Falkland. EMWP

Chorus to the Gods. Dryden. *See* Secular Masque, The

Chorus: "To throw away the key and walk away." W. H. Auden. MoBrPo

Chorus: "We do not wish anything to happen." T. S. Eliot. OxBTC *Fr.* Murder in the Cathedral.

Chorus: "We have not been happy, my Lord, we have not been too happy." T. S. Eliot. OxBTC *Fr.* Murder in the Cathedral.

Chorus: "What man is he that yearneth." Sophocles. AWP *Fr.* Oedipus at Colonus.

Chorus: "Worlds on worlds are rolling ever." Shelley. *See* Hellas

Choruses from "The Rock." T. S. Eliot.
"Eagle soars in the summit of heaven, The." OBMV
"I journeyed to the suburbs, and there I was told." UV

Chosen. Marilyn Nelson Waniek. ExTi; FFC

Chosen. W. B. Yeats. BoLoP

Chosen People, The. W. N. Ewer. OBCoV

(How Odd.) FaBoEE

Chosen Three, on Mountain Height, The. David H. Ela. AH

Chosen to Be Water. Christopher Gilbert. SwNoth

Chosen to walk in Heavenly places. Hope. Sydney E. Jerrold. SacPr

Chou and the South. *Unknown.* CTC, *tr. by* Ezra Pound *Fr.* Shi King.

Chough. Rex Warner. PoRA

Chough and crow to roost are gone, The. Outlaw's Song, The. Joanna Baillie. OBEV

Chrestus, your balls are depilated. Martial. CAGL, *tr. by* Joseph S. Salemi *Fr.* Epigrams.

ChrisEaster. Molly Peacock. FFC

Christ. *Unknown.* GrAn, *tr. by* Guy Davenport

Christ 1. *Unknown.* AnOE, *tr. by* Charles W. Kennedy

  Advent Lyrics. ASW, *tr. by* Kevin Crossley-Holland

    'O my Joseph, Jacob's son.' ASW

    "You govern the locks, You open life." ASW

Christ and Our Selves. Francis Quarles. SacPr

Christ and Satan. *Unknown.*

  Lamentations of the Fallen Angels. AnOE, *tr. by* Charles W. Kennedy

Christ and the Pagan. John Banister Tabb. TrCP

Christ and the Soldier. Siegfried Sassoon. NoP-4

Christ, as a light. James Clarence Mangan. SacPr *Fr.* St. Patrick's Hymn Before Tara.

Christ at the Apollo, 1962. Michael Waters. SwNoth

Christ Child, The. Mary Weston Fordham. CBWP-2

Christ child lay on Mary's lap, The. Christmas Carol. Gilbert Keith Chesterton. OBCP

Christ Climbed Down. Lawrence Ferlinghetti. VGW

Christ, / come down from your cross and wash your hands. Irreverent Epistle to Jesus Christ. Romelia Alarcón de Folgar. TANSG, *tr. by* Alison Ridley

Christ Crucified. Richard Crashaw. OBEV

Christ-cut: the cedar. Passion Week. William Everson. SacPr

Christ for the World! We Sing. Samuel Wolcott. AH

Christ has been done to death. Dutch Interiors. Jane Kenyon. ExTi

"Christ has risen." Whoever believes that / Should not behave as we do. Czeslaw Milosz. GI *Fr.* "Six Lectures in Verse."

Christ hath a garden walled around. Isaac Watts. FaBoCh

Christ home, Christ and his mother and all his hallows. (LL) Starlight Night, The. Gerard Manley Hopkins. GTBS-P; MoBrPo; NAEL-5v2; NAEL-6v2; PoE

Christ, I have read, did to His chaplains say. Salutation. Robert Herrick. CavPo; ChIV-2

Christ I Wudint Know Normal if I Saw It When. Bill Bissett. NOBC

Christ in the Clay-Pit. Jack R. Clemo. GTBS-P

Christ in the Universe. Alice Thompson Meynell. MoBrPo; NOBE; OxAEP-2; VWP

Christ Inviting Sinners to His Grace. Henry Alline.

  Amazing Sight! The Saviour Stands. AH

Christ is a Dixie Nigger. Frank Marshall Davis. APT-2

Christ Is Arisen. Goethe. TrCP, *tr. by* Bayard Taylor *Fr.* Faust.

Christ is now risen again. Of the Resurrection. Miles Coverdale. ChIV-2

Christ is our Rock, who in a rock is lain. Holy Sepulchre, The. Rowland Watkyns. BASC

Christ, keep me from the self-survey. Christopher Smart. SacPr *Fr.* Hymns for the Amusement of Children.

Christ, My Beloved. William Baldwin. NOCV

  (Spouse to the Younglings, The.) OxBSP

Christ, my Life, my Only Treasure. During His Courtship. Charles Wesley. NOCV

Christ of His gentleness. In the Wilderness. Robert Graves. ChIV-2; MoBrPo

Christ Our All in All. Christina Georgina Rossetti. SacPr

  "Thy lovely saints do bring Thee love." SacPr

Christ pleads with His Sweet Leman. *Unknown.* SacPr

Christ risen was rarely recognized by sight. For They Shall See God. Luci Shaw. TrCP

Christ's blessing on the newly born! (LL) My Sister's Sleep. Dante Gabriel Rossetti. NAEL-5v2; NAEL-6v2

Christ's cross across this face. Christ's Cross. Mugrón, Abbot of Iona. NePenScot, *tr. by* Thomas Owen Clancy

Christ's Flock of Lambs there also stands. Michael Wigglesworth. TCAPo *Fr.* Day of Doom, The.

Christ's Kirk on the Grene. *Unknown.* OxBS

Christ's Life Our Code. Benjamin Copeland. AH

Christ's Love-Song. *Unknown.* MiEL

Christ's Nativity. Henry Vaughan. ESCV

Christ's Passion. Abraham Cowley. ChIV-2; SacPr

Christ's Prayer in Gethsemane. *Unknown.* MiEL; SacPr

Christ's Reply. Edward Taylor. NAAL-2v1; NAAL-3 *Fr.* God's Determinations [touching his Elect].

Christ's Resurrection and Ascension. Philip Doddridge. NOCV

Christ's Sadness. Robert Herrick. CavPo

Christ's sake, look / out where yr going. (LL) I Know a Man. Robert Creeley. AmFaPo; NIP-4; NOBA; OxBSP; PoM; VCAP

Christ's teeth ascended with him into heaven. Michael Longley. BiHa; CIP-2; ModIr; NPeEn *Fr.* Wreaths.

Christ's Victory. Richard Crashaw. SacPr

Christ's Victory and Triumph. Giles Fletcher, the Younger.

  Celestial City, The. ChIV-2; NOSC; SacPr

  Christ's Triumph after Death, IV.

    Easter Morn. NOCV

    ("In midst of this city celestial.") NOBE

    "Say, earth, why hast thou got thee new attire." NOCV

  Christ's Victory on Earth.

    (Enchantress' Song, The.) NOSC

    "Love is the blossom where there blows." OBEV

    "Seemèd that Man had them devoured all." PeECV

    "Upon a grassie hillock He was laid." PeECV

    Wooing Song. OBEV

  Mercy Replies to Justice. SacPr

Christ Seen by Flemish Painters. Elizabeth Jennings. HarvBoo

Christ the Apple-Tree. *Unknown.* TCAPo

Christ 3. *Unknown.*

  Last Judgment, The. AnOE, *tr. by* Charles W. Kennedy

Christ to His Spouse [*or* The Beloved to the Spouse]. William Baldwin. NOCV

Christ to seek the lost was sent. Sympathy. Lizelia Augusta Jenkins Moorer. CBWP-3

Christ Triumphant. *Unknown.* MiEL; SacPr; WeW-3

  (I have laborede sore and suffered deyyth.) NPeEn

Christ 2. Cynewulf.

  Voyage of Life, The. AnOE

Christ Walks in This Infernal District Too. Malcolm Lowry. MoCV; NOBC

Christ was obedient unto his father. Katherine Parr, Lady Borough. EMWP *Fr.* In Contemplation of My Wretched Life.

Christ was the Word that spake it. *Unknown.* NoSic

Christ! What are patterns for? (LL) Patterns. Amy Lowell. APT-1; AWP; AmFaPo; BoWoP; MoAmPo; NoP-4; OxBA; WHSW

Christ, when he died. Christ's Victory. Richard Crashaw. SacPr

Christ who knows all His sheep. Good Shepherd, The. Richard Baxter. SacPr

Christ, whose glory fills the skies. Morning Hymn. Charles Wesley. NPeEn; TOF

Christ, you walked on the sea, In the Twentieth Century. James Philip McAuley. ChIV-2

Christabel. Samuel Taylor Coleridge. FHYEP; NAEL-5v2; NAEL-6v2; NOBRP

  Christabel and Geraldine.

    In the Touch of This Bosom There Worketh a Spell. RB

Christchurch, N. Z. Earle Birney. OxBC

Christ[e]'s Childhood[e]. Robert Southwell. ChIV-2

Christen Lyndesay to Ro. Hudsone. Christian Lindsay. EMWP

Christening, A. Donald Davie. OxBC

Christening Pot Boiler. Christopher Meredith. TCAWP

Christian, Be Up. Robert Nathan. AH

Christian constellations run, The. Circle, The. Lizelia Augusta Jenkins Moorer. CBWP-3

Christian Epigram. *Unknown.* WoPoe, *tr. by* John Peck

Christian Ethics. Thomas Traherne.

  "All music, sauces, feasts, delights and pleasures." OxBSP

  "Contentment is a sleepy thing." BBASP; NOCV

Christian Freedom. George Matheson. SacPr

Christian! going, gone!, A. Christian Slave, The. John Greenleaf Whittier. TCAPo

Christian Loses His Burden. John Bunyan. SacPr *Fr.* Pilgrim's Progress, The.

Christian Pilgrim's Hymn. William Williams. SacPr *Fr.* Guide me, O thou great Jehovah.

Christian Rome. Hildebert. MLL, *tr. by* Helen Waddell

Christian's Reply to the Philosopher, The. Sir William Davenant [*or* D'Avenant]. MeLP

Christian Slave, The. John Greenleaf Whittier. TCAPo

Christian Virtues. Charlotte Perkins Stetson Gilman. SWaP

Christiana. Peter Redgrove. OxBC

Christianite. William Stafford. NoAM

Christians awake, salute the happy morn. Hymn for Christmas Day, A. John Byrom. ECEV; NOCV; SacPr

Christina. Dora Greenwell. VWP

Christine to Her Son. Christine de Pisan. BoWoP, *tr. by* Barbara Howes

Christlike is my behaviour. Aldous Leonard Huxley. OBCoV *Fr.* Antic Hay.

Christmas. Sir John Betjeman. ChrPo; OBCP; OxBTC

Christmas. Steve Hassett. CDa

Christmas. George Herbert. ChrPo; GeHe; NOSC; PeECV; TOF; TrCP

Christmas. Leigh Hunt. OBCP

Christmas. Hans Just. AuPH, *tr. by* Lowell A. Bangerter

Christmas. Peter McDonald. PNI

Christmas. John Frederick Nims. ChrPo

Christmas. Stevie Smith. ChrPo

Christmas. Henry Timrod. APN-2

Christmas, The. Doll. Myra Cohn Livingston. TLR

Christmas and Common Birth. Anne Ridler. FaBoTw

Christmas and Death. Janet Frame. PeNZ

Christmas at Bristol. William Scammell. NLP

Christmas at Freelands. James Stephens. TrCP

Christmas at Sea. Robert Louis Stevenson. ChrPo; EBVV; NePenScot; PeVV

Christmas at the Orphanage. Bill Knott. OPRER

Christmas Ballad. Saint John of the Cross. STV, *tr. by* John Frederick Nims

Christmas, Belfast. Robert Coles. BloBone

Christmas Bells. Henry Wadsworth Longfellow. AH; ChrPo; OBCP

Christmas Bells, Saigon. Walter McDonald. AF

Christmas Bills. Joseph Hatton. OBCP

Christmas Card. Ted Hughes. OBCP

Christmas Card, After the Assassinations, A. Mona Van Duyn. ChrPo

Christmas Carol, A. George Macdonald. SacPr

Christmas Carol, A: "God rest you merry gentlemen." Gilbert Keith Chesterton. UV

Christmas Carol, A: "In the bleak mid-winter." Christina Georgina Rossetti. NOBVV; OxBEV; SacPr; VWP

Christmas Carol, A: "Shepherds went their hasty way, The." Samuel Taylor Coleridge. ChrPo

Christmas Carol, A: "There's a song in the air!" Josiah Gilbert Holland. SacPr

Christmas Carol: "Christ child lay on Mary's lap, The." Gilbert Keith Chesterton. OBCP

Christmas Carol: "Close to a quarter of a century since then." T. H. Parry-Williams. OBWVE, *tr. by* Joseph P. Clancy

Christmas Carol: "Three outas from the [High] bleak Karoo." D. J. Opperman. PeSAV, *tr. by* Anthony Delius

Christmas Carols. Patricia Beer. OxBC

Christmas Childhood, A. Patrick Kavanagh. ModIr

"My father played the melodion." RB

Christmas come tomorrow. Christmas with the Holy Family. Susan Cavin. GLP

Christmas comes but once a year. Mother Goose. OxNR; ReMoGo

Christmas comes like this: Wise men. Christmas Comes to Moccasin Flat. James Welch. CDW; NoAM

Christmas Creek. Henry Clarence Kendall. CBAP

Christmas Day. Roy Fuller. OBCP

Christmas Day. Christopher Smart. OBCP *Fr.* Hymns and Spiritual Songs for the Fasts and Festivals of the Church of England.

Christmas Day. Andrew Young. OBCP

Christmas Day in the Workhouse. George R. Sims. EBNV

(In the Workhouse.) OBCP

Christmas day is come; let all prepare for mirth. Christmas Day [Is Come]. Luke Wadding [*or* Waddinge]. NOSC

Christmas Day. 1696. Nicholas Hasluck. NOBAu *Fr.* Rottnest Island.

Christmas Day; the Family Sitting. John Meade Falkner. ChIV-2; NOCV; OxBTC

Christmas day was the least of it then, when I grew wild on the. Child's Christmas in Puerto Rico, A. Aurora Levins Morales. PueRic

Christmas declares the glory of the flesh. Christmas and Common Birth. Anne Ridler. FaBoTw

Christmas Dinner. Michael Rosen. OBCP

Christmas dinner was at two, The. Summer Christmas in Australia, A. Douglas Brook Wheelton Sladen. OBCP

Christmas Eve. Patricia Beer. OBCP

Christmas-Eve. Robert Browning.

Earth Breaks Up. TrCP

Christmas Eve. John Davidson. *See* Ballad of Hell, A

Christmas Eve. Walter De la Mare. ChrPo

Christmas Eve. Sascha Feinstein. SeSe

Christmas Eve. Lizelia Augusta Jenkins Moorer. CBWP-3

Christmas Eve. Christina Georgina Rossetti. ChrPo

Christmas Eve. George Swede. HA

Christmas Eve, and twelve of the clock. Oxen, The. Thomas Hardy. CABP; ChAP; ChrPo; EBEV; HAP; HarvBoo; InPK-6; MoBrPo; NOBE; NoAM; OBCP; OxAEP-2; OxBTC; PeECV; RB; SoSe-8; TFi; TOF; TRP; WeW-3

Christmas Eve in Whitneyville, 1955. Donald Hall. UnPo

Christmas Eve: Nuyorican Café. Miguel Algarin. PueRic

Christmas Eve Service at Midnight at St. Michael's. Robert Bly. NNaP

Christmas Eve, South, 1865. Mary E. Tucker. CBWP-1

Christmas Eve under Hooker's Statue. Robert Lowell. CoAmPo; OxBA

Christmas Everywhere. Phillips Brooks. PWR

Christmas Family Reunion. Peter De Vries. NBLV; NOBL

Christmas Fare. Dilys Wood. Prnts

Christmas Folk-Song, A. Lizette Woodworth Reese. OBCA; TrCP

Christmas future is far away. Have Yourself a Merry Little Christmas. Ralph Blane. ReLy

Christmas Ghost, A. Priscilla Jane Thompson. CBWP-2

Christmas Ghost-Story, A. Thomas Hardy. ChrPo; OBWP

Christmas hath a darkness. Christmas Eve. Christina Georgina Rossetti. ChrPo

Christmas hath made an end. Carol, for Candlemas Day. *Unknown.* NOSC

Christmas Holiday. Alun Lewis. PoWW

Christmas Hymn, A. Richard Wilbur. ChIV-2; ChrPo; OBCP; TrCP

Christmas in Biafra (1969). Chinua Achebe. ChrPo

Christmas in India. Rudyard Kipling. ChrPo

Christmas in the Wood. Frances Mary Frost. TrCP

Christmas Is Coming. Anthony Hecht. ChrPo

Christmas is coming [*or* a-coming], / And the geese are getting fat. *Unknown.* NTCP; OxNR; ReMoGo

Christmas is here. Mahogany Tree, The. William Makepeace Thackeray. ChrPo

Christmas is my name, far have I gone, have I gone, have I gone. Song Bewailing the Time of Christmas, So Much Decayed in England, A. *Unknown.* NoP-4; PBRV

Christmas Is Really for the Children. Steve Turner. OBCP

Christmas Landscape. Laurie Lee. OBCP

Christmas Letter Home. George Sutherland Fraser. OxBTC

Christmas Lullaby for a New-Born Child. Yvonne Gregory. NOxBChV

Christmas Mass for a Little Atheist Jesus. Claude Maillard. BoWoP, *tr. by* Maxine W. Kumin and Judith Kumin

Christmas Message, A. Gavin Ewart. FaBoMo

Christmas Morn. *Unknown.* OBCP

Christmas Morning. Elizabeth Madox Roberts. MoAmPo

(If Bethlehem were here to-day.) NOxBChV

Christmas Morning I. Carol [*or* Carole] Freeman. TTY

Christmas Mourning. Vassar Miller. ChIV-2; MoAmPo

Christmas Night. Lawrence Sail. OBCP

Christmas night: the solstice storm. Narrows of Birth, The. William Everson. PoM

Christmas night. The three of us. Foxes. Frieda Hughes. NeBl

Christmas, 1957. The Dell-Vikings and the Diamonds. Sound Systems. Ronald Wallace. SwNoth

Christmas 1956. György Petri. VCWP, *tr. by* George Gömöri and Clive Wilmer

Christmas 1944. Denise Levertov. AF

Christmas 1970. Spike Milligan. OBCP

Christmas 1962. Paul Mariah. GLP

Christmas: 1924. Thomas Hardy. FaBoEE; OBCP

Christmas Poem, A. Dick Davis. ChrPo

Christmas Prayer, A. Robert Louis Stevenson. TrCP

Christmas Present for My Mother. Sue MacIntyre. Prnts

Christmas Rede. Jane Barlow. SacPr

Christmas Revel, A. Dafydd [*or* David] Bach ap Madog Wladaidd. OBWVE

Christmas Rhyme, A. George Sands Johnson. PWR

Christmas Rhyme: North Tyrone. *Unknown.* FaBoVe

Christmas Robin, The. Robert Graves. ChrPo

Christmas Rush, The. Clara Ann Thompson. CBWP-2

Christmas, season of streamers, coloured lights. Christmas Story (1980). Pat Arrowsmith. BrRo

Christmas Shopping. Louis MacNeice. OBCP

Christmas Shopping. Carter Revard. UrbNat

Christmas Song. Joseph Mohr. AuPH, *tr. by* Lowell A. Bangerter

Christmas Song, The. Robert Wells. ReLy

Christmas Sonnet, A. Edwin Arlington Robinson. ChrPo

Christmas, South, 1866. Mary E. Tucker. CBWP-1

Christmas Spider, The. Michael Richards. Spl

Christmas Star. Boris Leonidovich Pasternak. TCRP

Christmas Star, The. Boris Leonidovich Pasternak. GI; WoPoe, *tr. by* Nina Kossman

Christmas Story, A. Alan Shapiro. TaR

Christmas Story (1980). Pat Arrowsmith. BrRo

Christmas Thank You's. Mick Gowar. OBCP

Christmas, the Year One, A.D. Sara Henderson Hay. PoRA

Christmas Thoughts, by a Modern Thinker. William Hurrell Mallock. NOBVV

Christmas Times. Maggie Pogue Johnson. CBWP-4

Christmas Tree. Stanley Cook. OBCP

Christmas Tree. Laurence Smith. OBCP

Christmas Tree, A. William Burford. SoSe-8

Christmas Tree, The. Patricia Beer. OBCP

Christmas Tree, The. Cecil Day Lewis. ChrPo

Christmas Tree, The. Lizelia Augusta Jenkins Moorer. CBWP-3

Christmas Trees. Geoffrey Hill. ChrPo; NOCV

Christmas twigs crispen and needles rattle, The. New Year's Poem. Margaret Avison. NOBC

Christmas was in the air and all was well. Karma. Edwin Arlington Robinson. APT-1; HeIP-4; MoAmPo; TrCP

Christmas with the Holy Family. Susan Cavin. GLP

Christo's. Paul Muldoon. CIP-2

Christopher. Sydney E. Jerrold. SacPr

Christopher Found. Amy Levy. ViWPN

Christopher Robin Changes Guard with Dylan Thomas. Bill Greenwell. UV

Christopher Robin goes / Hoppity, hoppity. Hoppity. Alan Alexander Milne. NTCP

Christopher Smart. Stanley Shaw. UV

Christopher Street 1979. Walter Holland. CAGL

Christopher White. *Unknown.* ESPB

Christs Sleeping Friends. Robert Southwell. ESCV

Christs Victorie, and Triumph in Heaven, and Earth, over, and after death. Giles Fletcher, the Younger.
   "As when the cheerfull Sunne, elamping wide." PBRV

Christus Natus Est. Countee Cullen. ChIV-2; ChrPo

Chromatin. J. H. Prynne. PFTM-2

Chrome Babies Eating Chocolate Snowmen in the Moonlight. A. K. Redwing. VoR

Chronic Meanings. Bob Perelman. PmAP

Chronica. Else Lasker-Schüler. PFTM-1

Chronicle. Mei-Mei Berssenbrugge. FSt; OpBo

Chronicle; a Ballad, The. Abraham Cowley. OxAEP-1

Chronicle in Verse, Vienna 1945. Paula von Preradovic. AuPH, *tr. by* Lowell A. Bangerter

Chronicle of Sigismund, The. Sebestyén Tinódi.
   "I've heard it sung—it may be true or no." IQMS, *tr. by* Michael Beevor

Chronicler, The. Alexander Bergman. TrJP

Chronos, Chronos, mend thy pace. Dryden. BASC; NAEL-5v1; NAEL-6v1; NPeEn; OxAEP-1; OxBEV; PoE; SCGP

Chrysalides. Thomas Kinsella. BIrV; ModIr

Chrysalis, A. Emily Jane Pfeiffer. ViWPN

Chrysanthemum growers. Buson. EH, *tr. by* Robert Hass

Chrysanthemums. Irene McKinney. PBCAP

Chrysanthemums in the Eastern Garden, The. Po Chü-i. ChiP, *tr. by* Arthur Waley

Chrysanthemums were yellow. Godo. JDP, *tr. by* Yoel Hoffmann

Chu Ch'ên Village. Po Chü-i. ChiP, *tr. by* Arthur Waley

Chuang Tzu and Hui Tzu were hundreds of years old. Chuang Tzu and Hui Tzu. Dick Barnes. GI

Chuang-tzu levels all things. Chuang Tzu, The Monist. Po Chü-i. ChiP, *tr. by* Arthur Waley

Chuck it, Smith ! (LL) Antichrist, or the Reunion of Christendom; an Ode. Gilbert Keith Chesterton. NOBE; NOBL; OBSV; OxAEP-2

Chuck Will's Widow Song. *Unknown.* BPo

Chüeh-chü. Tu Fu. CoBCP, *tr. by* Burton Watson

Chung-i Temple, The. Wen Cheng-ming.
   "Around the temple, pines and cedars." CoBLCP
   "At the lacquered table—my recent calligraphy." CoBLCP
   "Day drags on, as long as a year!, The." CoBLCP
   "Fine breeze blows through the temple halls, A." CoBLCP
   "Floating threads of spider webs hang." CoBLCP
   "In the sixth month, outside the gate." CoBLCP
   "Tea bowls, incense burning—a good feeling here!" CoBLCP
   "These long verandahs seem to be washed clean." CoBLCP
   "This little courtyard—the wind is pure." CoBLCP

Chung Tzu. *Unknown.* WoPoe, *tr. by* Arthur Waley

Chungnan ranges near the imperial capital. Mount Chung-Nan. Wang Wei. ChinPo, *tr. by* Yip Wai-lim

Chunks of night. Shadows. Patricia Hubbell. Spl

Chuparosa. Juan Delgado. AmPoNex

Church Bell in the Night, The. *Unknown.* NOIV, *tr. by* Kuno Meyer

Church Bells. Clara Ann Thompson. CBWP-2

Church Bells, The. Mrs. Henry Linden. CBWP-4

Church Bells, The. Bishop Richard Mant. SacPr

Church bells howitzers aloft to oust who suspect they've come as idea of beauty must. Impatient Heart, The. Bruce Andrews. FTOS

Church Boiler, The. David Scott. NLP

Church, / Chapel. *Unknown.* OxNR

Church Echoes. May Kendall. ViWPN

Church facing north, A. Stained Glass Window. Adelia Prado. TCLAP, *tr. by* Marcia Kirinus

Church Festivals. Christopher Harvey. NOSC

Church-Floor[e], The. George Herbert. EBEV; ESCV; MeLP; NOSC; PeECV

Church Going. Philip Larkin. CABP; GTBS-P; HarvBoo; HeIP-4; MoBrPo; NAEL-5v2; NAEL-6v2; NIL-7; NIP-4; NoAM; NoP-4; PAI; SCV; SoSe-8; TFi; TwCP; UnPo

Church in the Heart, The. Morris Abel Beer. PoToHe

Church is a business, and the rich, The. After Lorca. Robert Creeley. CoAmPo; LCAP-2; PmAP

Church is an iceberg, The. Winter Night. Charles Simic. HCAP

Church Ladies. Nancy Travis. ISC

Church-Lock and Key. George Herbert. ESCV; GeHe; OxBSP

Church Militant, The. George Herbert.
   "Religion stands on tip-toe in our land." PBRV

Church Monuments. George Herbert. BASC; ESCV; GeHe; HAP; NAEL-5v1; NAEL-6v1; NAEL-7v1; NOCV; NOSC; NPeEn; PoE; TRP

Church Mouse commends: tapeworms and slugs grow wings. Critics and Poets. Geoffrey Grigson. FaBoEE

Church-Music[k]. George Herbert. AmFaPo; ESCV; GeHe; OxBSP

Church of a Dream, The. Lionel Pigot Johnson. CABP; OBMV

Church of Heaven's triumphal Car, The. Live, Evil Veil. John Wheelwright. ChIV-1

Church-Porch, The. George Herbert. ESCV

Church Romance, A. Thomas Hardy. FaBoTw; NOBE; OxAEP-2; OxBSo; OxBTC; PeECV

Church's One Foundation, The. Samuel John Stone. SacPr; UV

Church's publication, The. Believers' Best Buy. Roger Woddis. UV

Church steeple fingers the sky, The. Asleep in the City. Michael Smith. PBCIP

Church the Garden of Christ, The. Isaac Watts. NOCV; PeECV

Churches, Chapels, Stores, and Houses. General Description of Men and Things in Cape Town, A. Frederic Brooks. PeSAV

Churches of Rome and of England, The. Dryden. UV *Fr.* Hind and the Panther, The.

Churchyard leans to the sea with its dead, The. Old Churchyard of Bonchurch, The. Philip Bourke Marston. EBVV

Churchyard under Snow. David Scott. NLP

Churl that wants another's fare, The. Dog in the River, The. Phaedrus. AWP, *tr. by* Christopher Smart

Churning Day. Seamus Heaney. ModIr

Churning (or lovemaking): Young man made for the corner, A. Cynewulf. *See* Young man made for the corner, A

Chyrsanthemums. Yün Shou-p'ing.
   "As we say farewell to autumn." CoBLCP

Cibber! write all thy verses upon glasses. Pope. FaBoEE

Cicada. Eclipse. HW

Cicada. Li Shang-yin. SuSp, *tr. by* Eugene Eoyang

Cicada, The. Ou-yang Hsiu. AWP, *tr. by* Arthur Waley

Cicada Blue. Charles Wright. KGB

Cicada chirp / Fan peddler. Kikaku. ZenPo, *tr. by* Takashi Ikemoto and Lucien Stryk

Cicada cries out, The. *Unknown.* OHMPJ

Cicada of the night. Kasenni. JDP, *tr. by* Yoel Hoffmann

Cicada's autumn song is lonely, The. Cicada Song. Liu Yung. CrYelRi, *tr. by* Sam Hamill

Cicada shell. Shuho. JDP, *tr. by* Yoel Hoffmann

Cicada shell, A. Basho. EH, *tr. by* R. H. Blyth and Robert Hass

Cicada sings, The. *Unknown.* OHPJ

Cicada Song. Liu Yung. CrYelRi, *tr. by* Sam Hamill

Cicadas. Richard Wilbur. NOBA

Cicala stoned with dew. Meleager. GrAn

Cid Calls His Vassals Together, The. They'll Go into Exile with Him. *Unknown.* WoPoe, *tr. by* Paul Blackburn *Fr.* Poem of the Cid, The.

Cid Enters Burgos, The. *Unknown.* WoPoe, *tr. by* Paul Blackburn *Fr.* Poem of the Cid, The.

Cid Ruy Díaz came into Burgos, The. *Unknown.* WoPoe, *tr. by* Paul Blackburn *Fr.* Poem of the Cid, The.

Cigar bands and glinting, dimestore lockets. (LL) Who I Think You Are. Elizabeth Alexander. FFC; RA

Cigarette Case. Stephen Kessler. GeoHom

Cigarette holder. Satin Doll. Johnny Mercer. ReLy

Cigarette smoke drifted, The. Bandit, The. Vladimir Aleksandrovich Lugovskoy [*or* Lugovskoi]. TCRP, *tr. by* Gordon McVay

Cigarette smoke floated. Milne's Bar. Norman MacCaig. FaBoTw

Cigarettes in my mouth. End of an Ethnic Dream, The. Jay Wright. SeSe

Cigarettes snuffed down a sleeve, a candy bar slid to the hip, bags of. Long Coats with Deep Pockets. Sean Thomas Dougherty. AmPoNex

Cill Chais. *Unknown.* NOIV, *tr. by* Thomas Kinsella

Cincinnati. Mitsuye Yamada. UnSA

Cinderella. Olga Broumas. InPK-6

Cinderella. Randall Jarrell. LCAP-2; NAAL-2v2; VCAP

Cinderella. Ruby C. Saunders. BISi

Cinderella. Anne Sexton. HeIP-4; NAAL-2v2

Cinderella boiled up borscht. Stepmother, The. Tatiana Shcherbina. ItGoST, *tr. by* J. Kates

Cinema—an asian girl with an african name. Rifacimento. Paul Violi. PmAP

Cinema is cruel, The. Image of Leda, An. Frank O'Hara. HCAP; LCAP-2

Cinema Point. Philip Mead. BMAP

Cineplex is showing a monster movie: our autobiography, The. Without Presumptions. Chris Forhan. NAPBL

Cinnabar cockerels sport resplendent hues. Cockfight. Liu Cheng. ColAnChi, *tr. by* Robert Joe Cutter

Cinnabar Well—I don't know where it is. Searching for Herb Brazier and Cinnabar Well, I Also Saw the Waterfall of Singing Strings. Alongside Was the Cliff of the Lord of the Mountain. Tao-chi. CoBLCP, *tr. by* Jonathan Chaves

Cinnamon Peeler, The. Michael Ondaatje. NOBC

Cino. Ezra Pound. VGW

Cinq Ans Après. Frank Gelett Burgess. OBAL; OBCoV; TFi
  (Confession.) NBLV
  (Purple Cow, The: Suite.) APN-2

Cinquain: A Warning. Adelaide Crapsey. *See* Warning, The

Cinque. Janet Campbell Hale. VoR

Cinquevalli. Edwin Morgan. HarvBoo; NePenScot

Circe. John Byrne Leicester Warren, 3d Baron De Tabley. NOBVV

Circe. "H. D." PoRA

Circe. Louis MacNeice. OBMV

Circe. Augusta Davies Webster.
  Circe. ("Sun drops luridly into the west, The.") PeVV; VWP

Circe. Gabriel Zaid. TCLAP, *tr. by* Andrew Rosing

Circe / Mud Poems. Margaret Atwood.
  "I made no choice / I decided nothing." NALW
  "It's the story that counts." NALW
  "Men with the heads of eagles." NoAM
  "People come from all over to consult me, bringing their limbs." NALW
  "This story was told to me by another traveller." NALW

Circle. 'Enayat Jaber. PoArWo, *tr. by* Wen Chin Ouyang

Circle, The. Lizelia Augusta Jenkins Moorer. CBWP-3

Circle, a Square, a Triangle and a Ripple of Water, A. Jane Cooper. TAP

Circle Game, The. Margaret Atwood. MoCV

Circle Jerk. Andrei Codrescu. PmAP

Circle of dancing gopis. (LL) Kenneth Rexroth. APT-2; BodElec

Circle of the Golem, The. Angelina Muñiz Huberman. MirDau, *tr. by* Aurora Camacho

Circle of Totems, The. Peggy Shumaker. PBCAP

Circle of Weeping, The. Amir Gilbo'a. MHP, *tr. by* Ruth Finer Mintz

Circles. Harry Behn. CA

Circles. Ralph Waldo Emerson. APN-1; TCAPo

Circles. Carl Sandburg. HHAm

Circling by the fire. Stories. J. Patrick Lewis. NOxBChV

Circuit Judge, The. Edgar Lee Masters. FaBoEE *Fr.* Spoon River Anthology.

Circuit of Apollo, The. Anne Finch, Countess of Winchilsea. NALW

Circular Fate. Askhari. InTrad

Circulation, The. Thomas Washbourne. NOCV

Circumambulating Arunachala. Gary Snyder. BB

Circumference between. (LL) Emily Dickinson. APN-2; MoAmPo; NAWM-7v2; OxBA

Circumstance. John Townsend Trowbridge. APN-2

Circumstance, The. Hart Crane. PFTM-1

Circus, The. Kenneth Koch. PmAP

Circus, The. Nikolai Alekseievich Zabolotsky [*or* Zabolotskii]. TCRP, *tr. by* Daniel Weissbort

Circus Animals' Desertion, The. W. B. Yeats. FaBoMo; FaBoTw; HarvBoo; MakPoe; NAEL-5v2; NAEL-6v2; NAWM-7v2; NIP-4; NOBE; NOIV; NoAM; NoP-4; OxBTC; PAI; TFi

Circus at the Barber's Shop. Kendrick Smithyman. PeNZ

Circus Circus swarms with us: floors strewn. Rumpelstiltskin Convention. Charles Webb. ReTh

Circus Garland, A. Rachel Lyman Field.
  Equestrienne. OBCA
  Gunga. OBCA
  Parade. OBCA
  Performing Seal, The. OBCA

Circus lions roared, The. In Tsvetnoy Boulevard. Pipe, The. German Borisovich Plisetsky [*or* Plisetskii]. TCRP, *tr. by* Keith Boseley

Circus Parade, The. Katharine Pyle. OBCA

Circus-Postered Barn, The. Elizabeth Jane Coatsworth. MoAmPo

Circus-Rider to Ringmaster. Thomas Hardy. RACG

Circus tent, The. Eric Amann. HA

Cirrostratus. CS. Geraldine Monk. Oth

Cit's Country Box, The. Robert Lloyd. NOEC
  (Some three or four mile out of town.) OBGa

Citadel. Edward Kamau Brathwaite. VCWP

Citation and Examination of William Shakespeare, The. Walter Savage Landor. Maid's Lament, The. OBEV; TreFP

Cities. Grigory [*or* Grigorii] Mikhailovich Pozhenyan [*or* Pozhenian]. TCRP, *tr. by* Lubov Yakovleva

Cities, The. "Æ." OBMV

Cities and Thrones and Powers. Rudyard Kipling. NOBE; NOxBChV; OxBTC *Fr.* Puck of Pook's Hill.

Cities and towns, ye haunts of wretchedness! Joseph Cottle. NOEC *Fr.* Malvern Hills.

Cities break up, The. "Adonis" [*or* "Adunis"]. PoetW *Fr.* Desert, The.

Cities of dream wander under the bark of a December forest, The. December Forest, A. Vesna Krmpotic. WPOW, *tr. by* Vasa D. Mihailovich

Cities of grass. Fort walls. The dumbstruck palace. His Dawn Vision. Seamus Heaney. PoetW

Cities of the Plain. Edgar Lee Masters. TCAPo

Cities of the Plain, The. John Greenleaf Whittier. ChIV-1; NCAP

Citizen. Julia Fields. GT

Citizen. Chris Wallace-Crabbe. CBAP

Citizen BOR Speaking. H. H. Tilley.
  "Democracy, my grannie's foot!" FaBoWar

Citizen's Way, The. Vladimir Burich. TCRP, *tr. by* Albert C. Todd

Citizens and Sky. Phillis Levin. FFC

Citizenship; Form 8889512, Sub-Section Q. Gilbert Keith Chesterton. OxBoLi

City. Sir John Betjeman. HarvBoo

City. Joseph Bruchac. CDW

City. Roy Fisher.
  By the Pond.
  "Brick-dust in sunlight." NPeEn

City. Angel González. VCWP, *tr. by* Steven Ford Brown

City. Langston Hughes. SSCS

City. Arthur Rimbaud. SxFrPo, *tr. by* Martin Sorrell

City. Michael Smith. PBCIP

City, A. (LL) State of Nature, A. John Hollander. AiP; NIL-7

City, The. Constantine P. Cavafy. WoPoe, *tr. by* Rae Dalven

City, The. Constantine P. Cavafy. AmFaPo, *tr. by* Edmund Keeley and Philip Sherrard

City, The. Robert Creeley. LCAP-2

City, The. Eddy Van Vliet. VCWP, *tr. by* John Van Tiel

City a Wrecked Ship, The. Amal Dunqul. MAP; NAfrP, *tr. by* Sharif Elmusa and Thomas G. Ezzy

City Afternoon. John Ashbery. HeIP-4; InPK-6; NIP-4

City Animals. Chase Twichell. UrbNat

City Baseball. Liz Rosenberg. CA

City Beneath the City, The. Eloise Klein Healy. GeoHom

City branching blindly through the clouds, The. Citizens and Sky. Phillis Levin. FFC

City bred. Moon. Frances Horovitz. BrRo

City built in darkness and cold air, A. Peter Levi. CRP *Fr.* Pancakes for the Queen of Babylon.

City by the Sea, The. Josephine D. Henderson Heard. CBWP-4

City cactus. Discovery. Zhao Zhenkai. VCWP, *tr. by* Chen Maiping and Bonnie S. McDougall

City Called Heaven. *Unknown.* NAAAL

City Child, The. Tennyson. NOxBChV

City Christmas. Phyllis McGinley. ChrPo; OBCoV

City Clerk, The. Thomas Ashe. EBVV

City Eclogue, A. "W. J." NOEC

City, Evening, and an Old Man: Me, The. "Dhoomil." OMIP; WoPoe, *tr. by* Vinay Dharwadker

City falls, The. (LL) Battle Report. Bob Kaufman. ISC; TTY

City Garden, A. William Stanley Braithwaite. GT

City Gent. Craig Raine. NoAM

City Girl in the Country. Elizabeth Smither. PeNZ

City Goddess. Leah Korican. HW

City Guard, The. (LL) Daft Days, The. Robert Fergusson. CABP; NOEC; NPeEn; OxAEP-1; OxBEV

City Hall. Belle Randall. CRP

City Hall of Maritzburg, one silver-misted dawn, The. Comrades Marathon, The. Chris Mann. PeSAV

City has spread quietly, suddenly, The. Everywhere. New Delhi, 1974. Vinay Dharwadker. OMIP

City has tits in rows, The. Grotesque. William Carlos Williams. TCAPo

City in death with the streets caved in and the traffic lights still, A. Catacombs in San Callisto, The. Rolf Jacobsen. BLT, *tr. by* Roger Greenwald

City in the Sea, The. Edgar Allan Poe. APN-1; NAAL-2v1; NAAL-3; NCAP; NOBA; NoP-4; OxBA; PoE; SCV; TAP; TCAPo; TFi; TRP

City in Which I Love You, The. Li-Young Lee. ChIV-1

City is beseiged, none may enter or leave, The. Nathan [*or* Natan] Alterman. MHP, *tr. by* Ruth Finer Mintz *Fr.* Joy of the Poor, The.

City is covered with places you, The. City, The. Eddy Van Vliet. VCWP, *tr. by* John Van Tiel

City is crossed by the river, The. Landscape of the Capibaribe River. João Cabral de Melo Neto. VCWP, *tr. by* Richard Zenith

City is free of sin, The. Pierre Albert-Birot. CuPo

City is of Night, The; perchance of Death. James Thomson. EBVV *Fr.* City of Dreadful Night, The.

City is silent, The. Dawn Over the Mountains. Tu Fu. OHPC, *tr. by* Kenneth Rexroth

City Johannesburg. Mongane Wally Serote. NAfrP

City Life. Alvin Greenberg. UrbNat

City Limits. Ted Kooser. GM

City Limits, The. A. R. Ammons. HCAP; NAAL-2v2; NOBA; NoAM; NoP-4; PoPoPo; VCAP

City Limits, The. Attila József. IQMS, *tr. by* Anton N. Nyerges

City, Lord, Where Thy Dear Life, The. William E. Dudley. AH

City Lyrics. Nathaniel Parker Willis. APN-1

City Morning, The. Sir William Davenant [*or* D'Avenant]. NOSC *Fr.* Gondibert.

City Mouse and the Garden Mouse, The. Christina Georgina Rossetti. NTCP

City mouse lives in a house, The. City Mouse and the Garden Mouse, The. Christina Georgina Rossetti. NTCP *Fr.* Sing-Song.

City of Beggars, The. Alfred Hayes. FaBoWar

City of Dreadful Night, The. James Thomson.
 "Although lamps burn along the silent streets." EBVV
 "Anear the centre of that northern crest." GTBS-P; NOBE; NePenScot
 "Because he seemed to walk with an intent." NePenScot
 "City is of Night, The; perchance of Death." EBVV
 City's Queen, The. GTBS-P; NOBE; NePenScot
 (City, The.) NOBE
 "He stood alone within the spacious square." NOBVV
 "How the moon triumphs through the endless nights!" NePenScot
 "I wandered in a suburb of the north." NOBVV
 "Large glooms were gathered in the mighty fane." EBEV
 "Lo, thus, as prostrate, 'In the dust I write.' " OxBS
 "Mighty river flowing dark and deep, The." EBVV
 "What men are they who haunt these fatal glooms." EBVV

City of Dreadful Night, The. James Thomson.
 "Anear the centre of that northern crest." GS

City of Esteli, The. June 10. Magdalena de Rodriguez. WPOW, *tr. by* Nina Serrano

City of Home is reached only in dreams, The. City of Home, The. Thomas William Shapcott. BMAP

City of Men. Aaron Shurin. FTOS

City of Orgies. Walt Whitman. APN-1; CAGL; ErotSp

City of Salt, The. Gregory Orr. BodElec

City of Slaughter, The. Hayyim Nahman [*or* Khayim Nakhman *or* Chaim Nachman] Bialik. TrJP, *tr. by* A. M. Klein

City of swarming, city full of dreams. Seven Old Men, The. Charles Baudelaire. SxFrPo, *tr. by* James McGowan

City of the End of Things, The. Archibald Lampman. NOBC

City of the Grail, The. Henry E. G. Rope. SacPr

City of the Moon, The. Kenneth Rexroth.
 "Buddha took some Autumn leaves." BLT

City of the Silent, The. William Gilmore Simms.
 "With ruder pomp, in more barbaric taste." APN-1

City of White Emperor, The. Tu Fu. SuSp, *tr. by* Wu-Chi Liu

City of Yes and the City of No, The. Yevgeny Aleksandrovich Yevtushenko [*or* Evtushenko]. TCRP, *tr. by* Geoffrey Dutton, Igor Mezhakoff-Koriakin and Tina Tupkina-Glaessner

City opens its streets, The. Transparent Life, The. Luigi Fontanella. NeIt, *tr. by* W. S. Di Piero

City Out of the Boy, The. Jeffrey Skinner. UrbNat

City Park. Christine Crow. SSCS

City Park. Erika Mitterer. AuPH, *tr. by* Lowell A. Bangerter

City Pigeons. Helen Chasin. WeW-3

City plum is not a plum, A. Christina Georgina Rossetti. NPeEn

City's Coat of Arms, The. László Nagy. IQMS, *tr. by* Adam Makkai

City's Queen, The. James Thomson. GS; GTBS-P; NOBE; NePenScot *Fr.* City of Dreadful Night, The.

City seems between us, A. It is only love. City Seems, A. Laura Riding Jackson. HarvBoo

City Shower, A. Jonathan Swift. *See* Description of a City Shower, A

City Sparrow. Jane Mayhall. TAP

City squats on my back, The. Route Six. Stanley Kunitz. APT-2

City stirred about me softly and distant, The. Hours of the Day, The. George Dillon. IllVoic

City-Storm. Harold Monro. MoBrPo

City streets and pavements receive me. In the Aging City. Fadwa Tuqan [*or* Tuquan]. MAP, *tr. by* Patricia Alanah Byrne, Salma Khadra Jayyusi and Naomi Shihab Nye

City streets coil around me, The. Jaikur and the City. Badr Shakir Al-Sayyab. MAP, *tr. by* Lena Jayyusi and Christopher Middleton

City Under Snow. Gwyn Williams. AngWePo

City Visions. Emma Lazarus. APN-2; SWaP

City With Towers. Vitězslav Nezval. PFTM-1

Civil Blood. Jill Breckenridge.
 General John Cabell Breckinridge. CBCWP

Civil Defense. Kenneth Burke. OBAL

Civil Elegies. Dennis Lee.
 "Often I sit in the sun and brooding over the city, always." NOBC

Civil Rights. Ira Sadoff. LTA

Civil Riot. George Douglas Howard Cole.
 "And you'll say a nation totters." OxBTC

Civil Servant, The. Michael Longley. BiHa; ModIr *Fr.* Wreaths.

Civil Service, The. William Langland. NOCV *Fr.* Vision of Piers Plowman, The.

Civil Song. Pier Paolo Pasolini. VCWP, *tr. by* Norman MacAfee

Civil War. Austin Clarke.
 "They are the spit of virtue now." NOIV

Civil War. Lucan.
 Book 5 ("Thus, by turns, the leaders suffered the wounds of war."). RomPo, *tr. by* Jane Wilson Joyce

Civil War. Maksimilian Aleksandrovich Voloshin. TCRP, *tr. by* Albert C. Todd

Civil War, The. Suzanne Rhodenbaugh. CBCWP

Civil war of that household, The. (LL) Small Farm, A. Michael Hartnett. CIP-2; PBCIP

Civil Wars, The. Samuel Daniel.
 "It was upon the twilight of that day." OBWP
 "Place there is, where proudly raised there stands, A." NoSic

Civilian. Josephine Miles. WPE

Civilian and Soldier. Wole Soyinka. AF; PBMAP; PoetW

Civilisation. János Arany. IQMS, *tr. by* Peter Zollman

Civilisation is hooped together, brought. Meru. W. B. Yeats. GSo; NoAM; OxBSo; PoPoPo

Civilities of Lamplight. Charles Tomlinson. OxBC

Civility a Bogey. Margaret Avison. NOBC

Civilization. Yüan Chieh. ChiP, *tr. by* Arthur Waley

Civilization Aha. Sipho Sepamla. PBMAP

Civilization and Its Discontents. John Ashbery. LCAP-2; TwCP

Civilization (Bongo, Bongo, Bongo). Bob Hilliard. ReLy

Civilization—spurns—the Leopard! Emily Dickinson. TCAPo

Civilizations are viscous. History shipwrecks, Gold slips from God no. Disdained Apparitions. René Char. AF, *tr. by* Paul Mann

Civilizing the Filipino. Nick Carbó. AmPoNex

Clack your beaks you cormorants and kittiwakes. Canticle to the Waterbirds, A. William Everson. APSN; APT-2; GeoHom; NeAP; PoM

Clacking and gouging when huddled. Snapshot of a Crab-Picker among Barrels Spilling Over, Apparently at the End of Her Shift. Dave Jeddie Smith. NoAM

Clad in the wealthy robes his genius wrought. On Shakespeare and Voltaire. Thomas Holcroft. NOEC

Claflin's Alumni. Lizelia Augusta Jenkins Moorer. CBWP-3

Claim, The. Edith Nesbit. NOBVV

Claim naught but th' honour of the victory. (LL) Masque of the Virtues against Love. Mary Monck. ECWP; NOEC

Claim to Fame. Beau Sia. HeMarv

Claim to Love. Giovanni Battista Guarini. AWP, *tr. by* Thomas Stanley

Claiming. Anita Virgil. HA

Claiming [*or* Clayming] a Second Kiss[e] by Desert. Ben Jonson. NAEL-6v1 *Fr.* Celebration of Charis in Ten Lyric[k] Pieces [*or* Peeces], A.

Claiming the Dust. Jean Janzen. GeoHom

Claims no particular status in space, or being of its own. (LL) Jealousy. Mei-Mei Berssenbrugge. OpBo; PmAP

Clair de Lune. Gwen Harwood. BMAP

Clair de Lune. Jules Laforgue. WoPoe, *tr. by* William Jay Smith

Clair de Lune. Paul Verlaine. AWP, *tr. by* Arthur Symons

Clairvoyant Journal. Hannah Weiner.
   "How can I describe anything when all these interruptions keep *arriving* and then." PmAP
   Mar 7 SIGNAL. PFTM-2

Clambering up the Cold Mountain path. Han-shan. EnlH

Clamming. Reed Whittemore. TAP

Clammy cement, The. Cold. Dennis Brutus. PeSAV

Clamor. Ann Lauterbach. PmAP

Clamour of the wind making music. Saint Columcille [*or* Columba]. BIrV

Clan Meeting: Births and Nations: A Blood Song. Michael S. Harper. NoAM

Clan of stony desert women, A. Velemir [*or* Viktor Vladimirovich] Khlebnikov. TCRP *Fr.* Night in the Trench, A.

Clang! Clang! Clang! Firemen, The. James Keir Baxter. NOxBChV

Clanking past the crest of a dune. Bad Run at King's Rest. Douglas Livingstone. PeSAV

Clanranald's Galley. Alexander MacDonald.
   Incitement for Rowing to Sailing-place. NePenScot, *tr. by* Hugh MacDiarmid

Clap, clap handies. Clap Handies. *Unknown.* ReMoGo

Clap, clap the double nightcap on! William Gifford. Walter Savage Landor. FaBoEE; GTBS-P

Clap Handies. *Unknown.* ReMoGo

Clap hands, clap hands / Hie, Tommy Randy. *Unknown.* OxNR

Clap hands, clap hands / Till father comes home. *Unknown.* OxNR

Clap hands, Daddy comes / With his pocket full of plums. *Unknown.* OxNR

Clap hands, Daddy's coming / Up the waggon way. *Unknown.* OxNR

Clap Your Hands for Herod. Josef Hanzlik. OBCP, *tr. by* Ian Milner

Clapping, The. Linda Gregg. BodElec

Clapping Chant, A. *Unknown.* FaBoVe

Clarel: A Poem and Pilgrimage in the Holy Land. Herman Melville.
   Afterward ("Seedsman of old Saturn's land."). APN-2; NCAP
   Concerning Hebrews. APN-2
   Cypriote, The. TCAPo
   Dirge: "Stay, Death. Not mine the Christus-wand." APN-1; NCAP
   Easter. APN-2
   Epilogue: "If Luther's day expand to Darwin's year." APN-2; NCAP; TCAPo
   Hostel, The. APN-2
   "Ah! / These under-formings in the mind." TCAPo
   ("'I pray,' said Rolfe, 'a word.'") OxBA
   Inscription, The: "While yet Rolfe's foot in stirrup stood.". APN-2
   "Emblazoned bleak in austral skies." TCAPo
   Southern Cross. TCAPo
   Medallion, The. APN-2
   New-Comer, A.
   "Ay, Democracy / Lops, lops; but where's her planted bed?" TCAPo
   Ungar's Harangue. TCAPo
   Of Mortmain. APN-2
   Of Rome. OxBA
   On Mammon. OxBA
   Pillow, The. APN-2
   Prelusive.
   "In Piranesi's rarer prints." TCAPo
   Recluse, The. APN-2
   (Shepherd's Dale, The.) TCAPo

   Symphonies. APN-2
   Ungar and Rolfe.
   "They felt how far beyond the scope." TCAPo
   Via Crucis. APN-2; NCAP

Clarence. Shel [*or* Shelley] Silverstein. OBCA

Clarence Mangan. Thomas Kinsella. CIP-2

Clarence Short Bull died. Sitting Bull's Will versus the Sioux Treaty of 1868 and Monty Hall. A. K. Redwing. VoR

Clari, the Maid of Milan. John Howard Payne.
   Home, Sweet Home! APN-1; BRP; TCAPo

Clarimonde. Théophile Gautier. AWP *Fr.* Taches Jaunes, Les.

Claritas. Denise Levertov. VGW

Claritas: / sun. Studies in Light. Diane Di Prima. PFTM-2

Claritas. The dry-eyed Latin word. Seamus Heaney. HarvBoo *Fr.* Seeing Things.

Clarity. A. R. Ammons. HCAP; TAP

Clarity. 'Enayat Jaber. PoArWo, *tr. by* Wen Chin Ouyang

(Clarity! clarity!) a semblance of motion, omniscience. Ted Berrigan. PFTM-2 *Fr.* Sonnets, The.

Clark Colven and his gay ladie. Clerk Colvill. *Unknown.* ESPB; OxBB

Clash of salutation. As keels thrust into shingle. Ambassadors, pilgrims. What is carried over? The Frankish gift, two-edged, regaled with slaughter. Geoffrey Hill. NoAM; NoP-4 *Fr.* Mercian Hymns.

Clasp, The. Sharon Olds. BodElec

Clasp you the God within yourself. Last Round, The. Anna Wickham. MoBrPo

Claspe, The. Margaret Lucas Cavendish, Duchess of Newcastle. BWW; PBRV

Clasped around warm weeks in tents. Actually Swallowed. Douglas Messerli. FTOS

Class. John Kander. ReLy

Class A, Salem, the Rookie League. Gary Fincke. MoASP

Class begins when I let go of the order of things. This is a class for anyone. Voucher. Michael Portnoy. HeMarv

Class Bully. Thomas Reiter. SwNoth

Class Incident from Graves. Alan Brownjohn. OxBTC

Class Song of '91. Eloise Bibb. CBWP-4

Classic. A. R. Ammons. NOBA

Classic Ballroom Dances. Charles Simic. LCAP-2; WeW-3

Classic Case, A. Gilbert Sorrentino. NeAP

Classic Encounter. "Christopher Caudwell." OxBTC

Classic landscapes of dreams are not, The. Snowfall, The. Donald Justice. CRP; VGW

Classic of Odes. *Unknown.*
   "Big rats! Big rats!" ColAnChi
   "Blind musicians, the blind musicians, The." ColAnChi, *tr. by* Jeffrey Riegel
   "Cautiously bubbles that spring water." ColAnChi, *tr. by* Jeffrey Riegel
   "Chaste Maiden, shining scarlet, The." ColAnChi, *tr. by* Jeffrey Riegel
   "Common people are very weary, The." ColAnChi, *tr. by* Jeffrey Riegel
   "Extensive the lands flanking that southern mountain." ColAnChi, *tr. by* Jeffrey Riegel
   "Foxes move in pairs." ColAnChi, *tr. by* Jeffrey Riegel
   "How do you cut an ax-handle?" ColAnChi, *tr. by* Jeffrey Riegel
   "In the seventh month, declining is the Fire Star." ColAnChi, *tr. by* Jeffrey Riegel
   "It takes a very stupid dolt." ColAnChi, *tr. by* Jeffrey Riegel
   "Kuan-kuan call the ospreys." ColAnChi, *tr. by* Jeffrey Riegel
   "Large-headed beauty, head so alluring, The." ColAnChi, *tr. by* Jeffrey Riegel
   "Lofty trees of the south, The." ColAnChi, *tr. by* Jeffrey Riegel
   "Make quiet, so quiet, your awesome bearing." ColAnChi, *tr. by* Jeffrey Riegel
   "On the offering mound, a dead roe." ColAnChi, *tr. by* Jeffrey Riegel
   "One who first gave birth to our people, The." ColAnChi, *tr. by* Jeffrey Riegel
   "Please, Sir Second-born." ColAnChi, *tr. by* Jeffrey Riegel
   "Restored Terrace is new and fresh, The." ColAnChi, *tr. by* Jeffrey Riegel
   "So plentiful, the babes-in-a-pot." ColAnChi, *tr. by* Jeffrey Riegel
   "Swallow flies away, The." ColAnChi, *tr. by* Jeffrey Riegel
   "That peachtree so frail." ColAnChi, *tr. by* Jeffrey Riegel
   "Throw me a quince." ColAnChi, *tr. by* Jeffrey Riegel
   "Towering is that southern mountain." ColAnChi, *tr. by* Jeffrey Riegel

Classic Scene. William Carlos Williams. NAAL-2v2; OxBA

Classical Head, The. John Forbes. *See* Four Heads & How to Do Them

Classical Quatrain, A. Paul Goodman. VGW

Classics Society. Tony Harrison. NoP-4 *Fr.* School of Eloquence, The.

Classroom at the Mall, The. R. S. Gwynn. RA

Clattering hoofs of horses, glitter of metal. Near the Mill. Hayim Lenski. FIT, *tr.* by Robert Friend

Claud Cockburn. Thomas McCarthy. PBCIP

Claude Allen. *Unknown.* APT-1

Claude to Eustace. Arthur Hugh Clough. PeLV *Fr.* Amours de Voyage.

Claude to Eustace: "I am in love, meantime, you think; no doubt you would think so." Arthur Hugh Clough. FaBoVe; NPeEn *Fr.* Amours de Voyage.

Claude to Eustace: "These are the facts. The uncle, the elder brother, the squire." Arthur Hugh Clough. FaBoVe *Fr.* Amours de Voyage.

Claude to Eustace: "Yes, we are fighting at last, it appears. This morning, as usual." Arthur Hugh Clough. EBVV; NPeEn; OxAEP-2; PeVV *Fr.* Amours de Voyage.

Claudia Petrovna. Yury [*or* Iurii] Pavlovich Odarchenko. TCRusP, *tr.* by Theodore Weiss

Claudius Gilbert. John Wilson. SCAP

Claudy. James Simmons. BiHa; CIP-2; PBCIP

Claus von Stauffenberg. Thom Gunn. OBWP

Clause for a Covenant. Constance Carrier. APT-2

Claustrophobia. Sean O Riordain. NOIV, *tr.* by Thomas Kinsella

Claustrophobia. Sean O Riordain. ModIr, *tr.* by Patrick Crotty

Clavering. Edwin Arlington Robinson. OxBA

Clavicles for a Great Poetic Game. René Daumal.
Clavicles for a Great Poetic Game ("Awakened by love, your body's animals want to get out."). PFTM-1

Clawed green-eyed. Song: "Clawed green-eyed." Lenrie Peters. PBMAP

Clay. Imamu Amiri Baraka. ESEAA

Clay. Charles Olson. APT-2 *Fr.* Maximus Poems, The.

Clay Image. Shinkichi Takahashi. ZenPo, *tr.* by Takashi Ikemoto and Lucien Stryk

Clay is the word and clay is the flesh. Patrick Kavanagh. ModIr; NPeEn; NoAM; NoP-4; OxBTC *Fr.* Great Hunger, The.

Clay Pipes, The. Cathal Ó Searcaigh. ModIr, *tr.* by Seamus Heaney

Clay, sand, and rock, seem of a diff'rent birth. Barten Holyday. FaBoEE

Clay trinkets that I knead here on the threshold. Old Dedication. Luciana Frezza. CItWP, *tr.* by Cinzia Sartini Blum and Lara Trubowitz

Clean. Ann Turner. SSCS

Clean as a lady. Tulip. Humbert Wolfe. MoBrPo

Clean bones crying in the flesh, The. (LL) Full Moon. Elinor Wylie. NALW; NoP-4

Clean in the light, with nothing to remember. Aspects. Norman MacCaig. OxBS

Clean is the autumn wind. Verses. Li Po. TAL

Clean otter, I have not seen other, The. Into the Ark. John Blight. BMAP

Clean people worry me, The. Clean People, The. Jim Heynen. GifTon

Clean Sheets. Lisa D. Chavez. AmPoNex

Clean slate, with your own face on, A. (LL) You're. Sylvia Plath. FaBoTw; FaBoWP; RB

Clean the spittoons, boy. Brass Spittoons. Langston Hughes. MoAmPo; NoAM

Clean up the mess, it is no mess of mine. (LL) Surgical Moves. Rachel Wetzsteon. AmPoNex; ExTi

Cleaning. Rick Alley. AmPoNex

Cleaning. Karel Soudijn. TuT, *tr.* by Peter Van de Kamp

Cleaning a Fish. Dave Jeddie Smith. NoAM

Cleaning Indian Dahl. Jane O. Wayne. InvLad

Cleanly rush of the mountain air, The. Dead Knight, The. John Masefield. GTBS-P

Cleanly, sir, you went to the core of the matter. Correct Compassion, A. James Kirkup. FaBoTw; OxBTC

Cleanness. *Unknown.*
"He who would acclaim Cleanness in becoming style." NOCV

Clear after Rain. Tu Fu. BLT; OHPC, *tr.* by Kenneth Rexroth

Clear after Rain. Tu Fu. CrYelRi, *tr.* by Sam Hamill

Clear air, the tree's shadow and your shadow, The. Order and the Days, The. Alicia Galaz Vivar. TANSG, *tr.* by Oliver Welden

Clear and bright is the splendor. Day of Cold Food, The. Li Ch'ing-chao. OHPC, *tr.* by Kenneth Rexroth

Clear and Colder. Robert Frost. OBCoV

Clear Ankor, on whose silver-sanded shore. Michael Drayton. NOSC *Fr.* Idea.

Clear Autumn. I gaze out into. Overlooking the Desert. Tu Fu. OHPC, *tr.* by Kenneth Rexroth

Clear Bright. Huang T'ing-chien. OHMPC, *tr.* by Kenneth Rexroth

Clear bright. Li Ch'ing-chao. BoWoP, *tr.* by Kenneth Rexroth

Clear bright morning, with its scented air, The. Fair Morning, The. Jones Very. GSo; NOBA

Clear brown eyes, kindly and alert, with 20-20 vision, The. Portrait. Kenneth Fearing. APT-2; MoAmPo

Clear Channel. Lorenzo Thomas. FTOS

Clear, clear—clearest! Moan. ZenPo, *tr.* by Takashi Ikemoto and Lucien Stryk

Clear cool note of the cuckoo which has ousted the legitimate nest-holder, The. Sincere Flattery of W. W. (Americanus). James Kenneth Stephen. NOBL

Clear dawn adorns the day of the Cold Food Festival, A. Tune: "Sand of Silk-washing Stream." Wei Chuang. SuSp, *tr.* by Lois Fusek

Clear Evening after Rain. Tu Fu. OHPC, *tr.* by Kenneth Rexroth

Clear fall afternoon beckons, A. Grigory [*or* Grigorii] Mikhailovich Pozhenyan [*or* Pozhenian]. TCRP

Clear Form Clashes, The. Giulia Niccolai. CItWP, *tr.* by Cinzia Sartini Blum and Lara Trubowitz

Clear form of your face, The. Scream is a Kind of Coffin, The. Paz Molina. TANSG, *tr.* by Steven F. White

Clear, fresh, sweet waters, where she who alone seems lady. Petrarch. NAWM-7v1, *tr.* by Robert M. Durling *Fr.* Sonnets to Laura.

Clear full moon. *Unknown.* OHMPJ

Clear in the blue, the moon! Ryuzan. ZenPo, *tr.* by Takashi Ikemoto and Lucien Stryk

Clear in the clearness of your eternal love. (LL) Prayer to Go to Paradise with the Donkeys, A. Francis Jammes. RB; WoPoe, *tr.* by Richard Wilbur

Clear Midnight, A. Walt Whitman. AWTN; HAP; OxBSP; SAmP; Spl

Clear mirage beyond the immaculate dune. Ablution. Angelina Muñiz Huberman. MirDau, *tr.* by Aurora Camacho

Clear mirror, The. Beyond Light. Muso Soseki. EaWin, *tr.* by W. S. Merwin

Clear moon arcs, The. Red Rock Ceremonies. Anita Endrezze. VoR

Clear moon brightly shining in the night. *Unknown.* CoBCP

Clear Night. Charles Wright. GeoHom; VCAP

Clear night in harvest time, A. I Pass the Night at General Headquarters. Tu Fu. OHPC, *tr.* by Kenneth Rexroth

Clear, noon sky at midsummer is God's eye, A. Cosmic Eye. A. K. Redwing. VoR

Clear ocean seems, The. Double Vision of Manannan, The. *Unknown.* BIrV, *tr.* by John Montague

Clear [*or* Cleere] are her eyes. Upon Her Eyes. Robert Herrick. BeJo

Clear river curves around our village, The. In a Village by the River. Tu Fu. CrYelRi, *tr.* by Sam Hamill

Clear Shell, A. Frances Bellerby. FaBoWP

Clear Skies, Still Sea. *Vietnamese Oral Tradition.* CaDao, *tr.* by John Balaban

Clear sky. Gitoku. JDP, *tr.* by Yoel Hoffmann

Clear stream girdles the long copse, The. On Returning to Sung Mountain. Wang Wei. SuSp, *tr.* by Paul W. Kroll

Clear the brown path, to meet his coulter's gleam! Ploughman, The. Oliver Wendell Holmes. CA

Clear the land, thatch the rush for roof. Meditation Hall. Liu Tsung-yüan. SuSp, *tr.* by Jan W. Walls

Clear—the senses bright—sitting in the black chair—Rocker. Michael McClure. BB; NeAP *Fr.* Peyote Poem.

Clear the Way. Charles MacKay. TreFP

Clear the way and build the road! Road, The. Zalman Schneour. TrJP, *tr.* by Joseph Leftwich

Clear the way there Jonathan! Walt Whitman. *See* To get betimes in Boston town I rose this morning early

Clear Valley. Muso Soseki. EaWin, *tr.* by W. S. Merwin

Clear View in Summer. Valentin Iremonger. ModIr

Clear vowels rise like balloons, The. (LL) Morning Song. Sylvia Plath. BoWoP; ColAP; HCAP; HarvBoo; HeIP-4; InPK-6; ItWoWo; LCAP-2; NAAL-2v2; NAAL-5; NIL-7; NIP-4; NOBA; NoP-4; PoPoPo; VCAP

Clear water. Basho. EH, *tr.* by Robert Hass

Clear water in a brilliant bowl. Poems of Our Climate, The. Wallace Stevens. APT-1; NoP-4; OxBA; SoSe-8; TwCP

Clear water of the imperial pond, The. Ise Tayu. BoWoP

Clear weather of juniper, The. Sloe Gin. Seamus Heaney. PNI

Clearances. Seamus Heaney. CIP-2; PBCIP
"In the last minutes he said more to her." PNI
"When all the others were away at Mass." BLT; PNI

Clearances, The. Iain Crichton Smith. NePenScot

Cleare moving cristall, pure as the Sunne beames. Sir William Alexander, Earl of Stirling. OxBS *Fr.* Aurora.

Clearing, The. Peter Everwine. NNaP

Clearing, The. Carl Phillips. BAP-01

Clearing at Dawn. Li Po. AWP, *tr.* by Arthur Waley

Clearing Away. Andrew Taylor. BMAP

Clearing for the Plough. Ernest G. Moll. NOBAu

Clearing-Station. Wilhelm Klemm. PeFWW, *tr.* by Patrick Bridgwater

Clearing the Title. James Merrill. HarvBoo

Clearly and without emotion / about the need for action, about killing people, / I wanted him. (LL)　Action Would Kill It / A Gamble.　Robert Adamson. BMAP; CBAP

Clearly your day has passed.　Boyarina Morozova, The.　Nikolai Ivanovich Glazkov.　TCRP, *tr.* by Daniel Weissbort

Clears the morning of doves.　Wind in the Trees, The.　Cathy Song.　OpBo

Cleator Moor.　Norman Nicholson.　FaBoTw

Cleavage.　A. R. Ammons.　OBAL

Cleaving, The.　Li-Young Lee.　OpBo
　"He gossips like my grandmother, this man."　IllVoic

Cleitagoras.　Leonidas of Tarentum.　AWP, *tr.* by William M. Hardinge

Clemena, if you are indeed.　To Clemena.　Elizabeth Thomas.　PoBW

Clementine.　Percy Montross.　OBAL
　(And so I lost my Clementine.) (LL)　APN-2
　(In a cabin, in a canon.)　APN-2

Clementine.　*Unknown.*　KaS

Clench thine eyes now,—'tis the last instant, girl.　Same, The.　Dante Gabriel Rossetti.　CenSon

Clenched ignorant against the sky! (LL)　Armadillo, The.　Elizabeth Bishop. APT-2; ColAP; HCAP; NAAL-2v2; NAAL-5; NIL-7; NOBA; NoAM; NoP-4; TAP; VCAP; VGW

Cleombrotus the bruiser.　Lucilius.　GrAn

Cleonicos.　Edward Cracroft Lefroy.　AWP　*Fr.* Echoes from Theocritus.

Cleopatra.　Anna Andreyevna Akhmatova.　FaBoWar; PoetW, *tr.* by Max Hayward and Stanley Kunitz

Cleopatra.　William Shakespeare.　SCV　*Fr.* Antony and Cleopatra.

Cleopatra.　William Wetmore Story.　APN-1

Cleopatra's Lament.　William Shakespeare.　UnPo　*Fr.* Antony and Cleopatra.

Cleopatra to the Asp.　Ted Hughes.　EBEV; RACG

Cleopatterer.　P. G. Wodehouse.　ReLy

Clepington Catastrophe, The.　William McGonagall.
　"Accidents will happen by land and by sea."　VerBaPo

Cleric, The.　Seamus Heaney.　ModIr　*Fr.* Sweeney Redivivus.

Cleric Courts His Lady, A.　*Unknown.*　MiEL

Cleric once heard with dismay, A.　Limerick.　Joan Dare.　PeLi

Clerical Oppressors.　John Greenleaf Whittier.　NAAL-2v1

Clerihew: "Spinoza / Collected curiosa."　*Unknown.*　NOBL

Clerihews.　Edmund Clerihew Bentley.
　"After dinner Erasmus."　OBCoV
　"Art of Biography, The."　NOBL; PeLV
　"'Dinner-time?' said Gilbert White."　OBCoV
　George III.　NOBL; NPeEn; OxBoLi; PeLV
　"How vigilant was Spenser."　OBCoV
　"I am not Mahomet."　NOBL
　"Intrepid Ricardo, The."　OBCoV
　J. S. Mill.　OxBoLi; PeLV
　Lord Clive.　NOBL; PeLV
　"'No,' said Charles Peace."　NOBL
　"'No, sir,' said General Sherman."　NOBL; OBCoV
　"Sir Christopher Wren."　NBLV; PeLV
　"Sir Humphry Davy."　OxBEV
　"'Susaddah!' exclaimed Ibsen."　OBCoV
　"There exists no proof as."　NOBL
　"When their lordships asked Bacon."　OBCoV
　"Wynkyn de Worde."　OBCoV

Clerk Colvill.　*Unknown.*　ESPB; OxBB

Clerk's Tale, The.　Geoffrey Chaucer.　*Fr.* Canterbury Tales, The.

Clerk's Twa Sons o Owsenford, The.　*Unknown.*　ESPB

Clerk Saunders.　*Unknown.*　ESPB; NePenScot; OBEV; OxBS
　(Clerk Saunders and May Margaret.)　EBNV
　(Clinking bell gaed thro' the toun, The.)　EBNV

Clerks.　Boris Abramovich Slutsky [*or* Slutskii].　TCRP, *tr.* by J. R. Rowland

Clerks, The.　Edwin Arlington Robinson.　APN-2; MoAmPo; NAAL-2v2

Clerks pretend to be shepherds, and under, The.　Peire Cardenal.　WoPoe, *tr.* by Paul Blackburn

Clever and Poor.　V. Penelope Pelizzon.　AmPoNex

Clever Daughter, The.　Susan Wicks.　MFPA

Clever Hen, The.　*Unknown.*　LB; ReMoGo

Clever man builds a city, A.　*Unknown.*　AWP, *tr.* by H. A. Giles　*Fr.* Shi King.

Clever Peter and the Ogress.　Katharine Pyle.　OBCA

Clever Tom Clinch Going to Be Hanged.　Jonathan Swift.　NOIV

Clever Woman, A.　Mary Elizabeth Coleridge.　BrRo; VWP; ViWPN

Cliché can be true: You hate to open the paper.　Insomnia: The Distances. Sydney Lea.　RA

Cliches with worn wit combined.　On a Lover of Books.　Geoffrey Grigson.

FaBoEE

Click, click, forever click, click.　Ballad of Mulan, The.　*Unknown.* ColAnChi, *tr.* by Arthur Waley

Click Go the Shears.　*Unknown.*　NOBAu

Clickety-clack.　Song of the Train.　David McCord.　NTCP

Cliff, The.　On the Wall of Cloud-Friend Hut.　Muso Soseki.　EaWin, *tr.* by W. S. Merwin

Cliff, The.　David Rowbotham.　NOBAu

Cliff dweller ruins.　Foster Jewell.　HA

Cliff Dwelling, A.　Robert Frost.　APT-1

Cliff Klingenhagen.　Edwin Arlington Robinson.　APN-2; MoAmPo; NCAP; Son

Cliff Notes.　Bob Perelman.　PmAP

Cliffs of scarlet cloud gleam in the west.　Return, The.　Tu Fu.　TAL

Cliffs that rise a thousand feet.　Sailing Homeward.　Chan Fang-sheng.　AWP; ChiP; FaBoCh, *tr.* by Arthur Waley

Clifton.　Joan Larkin.　GLP

Clifton Chapel.　Sir Henry John Newbolt.　OBEV

Climacteric.　Ralph Waldo Emerson.　TCAPo　*Fr.* Quatrains.

Climate and Lyre.　Radovan Pavlovski.　CarOv, *tr.* by Carolyn Kizer

Climate of Paradise, The.　Louis Simpson.　NOBA

Climate succumbing continuously as water gathered.　Nebraska.　Barbara Guest.　FTOS

Climate's very healthy once you're used to being dead, The. (LL)　On Learning to Adjust to Things.　John Ciardi.　KaS; OBCA

Climax of passion, the dancers are trembling, The.　Rumba.　José Zacarías Tallet.　TTY, *tr.* by Sangodare Akanji

Climb aboard a butterfly and take off on the breeze.　Dreamer's Holiday, A. Mabel Wayne.　ReLy

Climb at court for me that will.　Seneca.　OBVE, *tr.* by Andrew Marvell　*Fr.* Thyestes.

Climb Mount Fuji.　Issa.　EH, *tr.* by Robert Hass

Climb Mount Fuji.　Avedik Issahakian.　ChAP

Climb / through my hair, climb in.　Rapunzel.　Olga Broumas.　ReTh

Climbed high, to gaze upon the sea.　Ancient Air.　Li Po.　BLT

Climbing.　Lucille Clifton.　GT; LoL

Climbing.　Jennifer Maiden.　BMAP; CBAP

Climbing.　C. Mikal Oness.　GeoHom

Climbing a Solitary Islet in the River.　Hsieh Ling-yün.　SuSp, *tr.* by Francis Westbrook

Climbing, climbing, the path of stones.　Temple of the Ocean of Awakening. Shen Chou.　CoBLCP, *tr.* by Jonathan Chaves

Climbing Down the Snowy Mountain.　Muso Soseki.　EaWin, *tr.* by W. S. Merwin

Climbing from the Lethal dead.　Orpheus.　Yvor Winters.　NOBA; VGW

Climbing Gannett.　Roberta Hill Whiteman.　HATNAP

Climbing high, sadly I gaze at the Mountain of Eight Immortals.　Passing by Huai-yin I Have Feelings.　Wu Wei-yeh.　CoBLCP, *tr.* by Jonathan Chaves

Climbing K'uai Pavilion.　Huang T'ing-chien.　SuSp, *tr.* by Michael E. Workman

Climbing Mount Yang.　Yüan Hung-tao.　CoBLCP, *tr.* by Jonathan Chaves

Climbing on the Double Ninth Day.　Tu Fu.　ChinPo, *tr.* by Yip Wai-lim

Climbing P'iao-miao Peak.　Wu Wei-yeh.　CoBLCP, *tr.* by Jonathan Chaves

Climbing Phoenix Terrace at Chin-ling.　Li Po.　SuSp, *tr.* by Joseph J. Lee

Climbing Pien-chueh Temple.　Wang Wei.　ColAnChi, *tr.* by Stephen Owen

Climbing Sears Tower.　Dennis Schmitz.　IllVoic

Climbing Stone Drum Mountain.　Hsieh Ling-yün.　CrYelRi, *tr.* by Sam Hamill

Climbing Stone Drum Mountain Above the Shores of Shang-shu.　Hsieh Ling-yün.　SuSp, *tr.* by Francis Westbrook

Climbing Suilven.　Norman MacCaig.　HarvBoo

Climbing the Heights.　Tu Fu.　SuSp, *tr.* by Wu-Chi Liu

Climbing the hill a coil of snakes.　"Michael Field."　ViWPN

Climbing the Ling-Ying Terrace and Looking North.　Po Chü-i.　BLT; ChiP, *tr.* by Arthur Waley

Climbing the peak of Tamalpais the loose.　George Oppen.　NNaP　*Fr.* Some San Francisco Poems.

Climbing the Ridge.　Rosemerry Wahtola Trommer.　GeoH

Climbing the rutted path, the lights of the town.　Phases of Darkness, The. Paul Petrie.　TAP

Climbing the Stork Pavilion.　Wang Chih-huan.　ColAnChi, *tr.* by Richard W. Bodman

Climbing the Terrace of Kuan-yin and Looking at the City of Ch'ang-an.　Po Chü-i.　ChiP, *tr.* by Arthur Waley

Climbing the Tower by the Pond.　Hsieh Ling-yün.　SuSp, *tr.* by Francis Westbrook

Climbing the wax tree.　Sky.　Shinkichi Takahashi.　ZenPo, *tr.* by Takashi Ikemoto and Lucien Stryk

Climbing through the January snow, into the Lobo canyon. Mountain Lion. D. H. Lawrence. FaBoVe; OxBTC; RB

Climbing to a Mountain Monastery. Tu Hsün-ho. SuSp, *tr. by* Edward H. Schafer

Climbing to the Top of the City Walls at Kan-yü. Wang T'ing-hsiang. CoBLCP, *tr. by* Jonathan Chaves

Climbing Up to the Lo-yu Plain. Tu Mu. SuSp, *tr. by* Irving Y. Lo

Climbing Yun-lung Mountain. Su Tung-p'o (Su Shih). CrYelRi, *tr. by* Sam Hamill

Climbs back up to claim herself again. (LL) Woman Hanging from the Thirteenth Floor Window, The. Joy Harjo. GLP; HATNAP

Clinging to my breast, no stronger. Spinster's Lullaby. Vassar Miller. BoWoP

Clinging to the bell. Buson. SoOfWa, *tr. by* Sam Hamill

Clinic, The. Grace Herman. BloBone

Clinic Day. Jo Barnes. BrRo

Clio. Martha Sansom.
"Honour, that Guardian Angel, can alone." LW

Clio's Picture. *Unknown*.
"Here let the Muse perform the painter's art." ECWP

Clio's Protest. Richard Brinsley Sheridan. FaBoEE

Clip-clop go water-drops and bridles ring. Nude in a Fountain. Norman MacCaig. OxBS

Clipped / separated / piled up. Mulch. Adam David Miller. NBV

Clipper-Ships. John Gould Fletcher. TCAPo

Clippety cloppety, / Cesare Borgia. Chip. George Starbuck. OBAL

Clipping the same sad alnage of the years. (LL) Clerks, The. Edwin Arlington Robinson. APN-2; MoAmPo; NAAL-2v2

Clippings. Kimiko Hahn. ExTi

Cloak, The. Robert Graves. HarvBoo

Cloak, The. James McAuley. BMAP

Cloak, The. Norman Henry Pritchard, II. GT

Cloak of Dawn. Amadou Lamine Sall. NAfrP

Cloak of Laughter. Abigail Cresson. PoToHe

Clock. Valerie Worth. TLR

Clock, The. Charles Baudelaire. WoPoe, *tr. by* Roy Campbell

Clock, The. Jorge Carrera Andrade. TCLAP, *tr. by* Michael Surman

Clock, The. Mother Goose. ReMoGo

Clock-A-Clay. John Clare. EBEV; EBVV; NAEL-5v2; NAEL-6v2
(In the cowslips peeps I lye.) NOxBChV

Clock, calm, evil god that makes us shiver, The. Clock, The. Charles Baudelaire. WoPoe, *tr. by* Roy Campbell

Clock in the Square, A. Adrienne Rich. HeIP-4

Clock just now has nothing more to say, The. (LL) Campus on the Hill, The. W. D. Snodgrass. AiP; NoAM; TAP; TwCP

Clock of my days winds down, The. Alligator Bride, The. Donald Hall. CoAmPo; SPE

Clock on Hancock Street. June Jordan. FaBoWP

Clock Plods On, The. Valentine Ackland. PoBW

Clock's so huge you can watch the minute hand, The. Grand Central Station, 20 December 1987. Bruce Bawer. RA

Clock's untiring fingers wind the wool of darkness, The. Cradle Song. Louis MacNeice. MoBrPo

Clock stopped, A. Emily Dickinson. APN-2; NAAL-2v1; NAAL-3; NAAL-5; TCAPo

Clock strikes five—the watchman goes, The. Lady Sophia Burrell. ECWP
Fr. Verses to a Lady, on Her Saying She Preferred Commonaly to an Irish Peerage.

Clock strikes one that just struck two, The. Emily Dickinson. APN-2

Clock within us, speaking time, The. Making Love, Killing Time. Anne Ridler. SacPr

Clockface. Rhyll McMaster. BMAP

Clockface. Judith Thurman. Spl

Clocks. Louis Ginsberg. TrJP

Clocks are sorry, the clocks are very sad, The. Psalm and Lament. Donald Justice. DiPo

Clocks belled twelve. Main Street showed otherwise. Owl. Sylvia Plath. OWoS

Clocks blue seconds fold over me. Paregoric Babies. Jim Carroll. PmAP

Clocks out of order. Studies. Carlos Pellicer. TCLAP, *tr. by* Donald Justice

Clocks strike, The. Death of the Wild Warrior. Daniil Kharms. TCRusP, *tr. by* Robin Milner-Gulland

Clocks strike in the distance. On My Child's Death. Joseph, Freiherr von Eichendorff. WoPoe, *tr. by* William DeWitt Snodgrass

Clockwise and counter-clockwise turning. (LL) Poem Beginning with a Line by Pindar, A. Robert Duncan. NNaP; NeAP; PmAP; PoM; VCAP

Clockwork beings, winding out their lives. Insects. Isidor Schneider. APT-2; TrJP

Clockwork Doll. Dahlia Ravikovitch [*or* Ravikovich]. FIT, *tr. by* Robert Friend

Clockwork skating Wordsworth on the ice, A. Xmas for the Boys. Gavin Ewart. OBSV

Clod and the Pebble, The. William Blake. EnLoPo; FHYEP; NAEL-5v2; NAEL-6v1; NOBE; NPeEn; NoP-4; OxAEP-2; OxBEV; OxBSP; PoE; RB; SCGP; SCV; TFi *Fr.* Songs of Experience.

Clodian Songbook. Christian Karlson Stead.
"Air New Zealand." PeNZ
"Fucking, I feel at one with the world." PeNZ

Clods' friability lulls iron to sleep. August Stramm. *See* Yielding clod lulls iron off to sleep

Cloe. George Granville [*or* Grenville], Baron Lansdowne. FaBoEE; NIP-4; OxBEV

Cloe, blooming sweet as May. To Cloe. Hildebrand Jacob. NOEC

Cloe's the wonder of her sex. To Cloe. George Granville [*or* Grenville], Baron Lansdowne. FaBoEE; NBLV; OxBEV

Cloe to Artimesa. *Unknown*. ECWP; PoBW

Clog of Her Body, The. Diana García. TouFir

Clogged and soft and sloppy eyes. Gwendolyn Brooks. ColAP *Fr.* Notes from the Childhood and the Girlhood.

Cloister. Conrad Potter Aiken. MoAmPo *Fr.* Preludes for Memnon; or, Preludes to Attitude.

Cloister. Gabriel Zaid. TCLAP, *tr. by* Mónica Hernández-Cancio

Clonakilty. *Unknown*. FaBoEE

Clonfeacle. Paul Muldoon. CIP-2

Clonmel Jail. *Unknown*. BIrV, *tr. by* Valentin Iremonger

Cloodburst an' soarin' mune. Cloudburst and Soaring Moon. Hugh MacDiarmid. NoAM

Cloosmit the herring, hosts in the night. Ko-Ishin-Mit Goes Fishing. George Clutesi. HATNAP

Clora come view my Soul, and tell. Gallery, The. Andrew Marvell. BASC; ESCV; MeLP; NoP-4; PBRV; PoE

Clorinda and Damon. Andrew Marvell. ESCV

Cloris' Charms Dissolved by Eudora. Anne Killigrew. BASC

Cloris, I cannot say your eyes. To Cloris. Sir Charles Sedley. BoLoP

Close. Robert Duncan. PmAP

Close. Andrew Motion. HarvBoo

Close analysis revealed the existence of a key. Case of the Same Name, A. Giampiero Neri. ItPo, *tr. by* Gayle Ridinger

Close and slow, summer is ending in Hampshire. Louis MacNeice. NPeEn *Fr.* Autumn Journal.

Close by the basement door-step. Toad, A. Elizabeth Akers Allen. OBCA

Close by the shore, the shore. *Unknown*. WoPoe, *tr. by* Konstantinos Lardas *Fr.* Mourning Songs of Greece.

Close by those meads, for ever crowned with flow'rs. Pope. EBNV; OBSV; OxBoLi *Fr.* Rape of the Lock, The; an Heroi-Comical Poem.

Close by, to the north, there were two oranges. Jean-Joseph Rabéarivelo [*or* Rebéarivelo]. NegPo

Close cleaving unto Silence, into sound. Whisper. John Banister Tabb. APN-2

Close is lust's expectation. On a Bath-House in which Both Men and Women Bathe. Paulus [*or* Paulos] Silentiarius. GrAn, *tr. by* Andrew Miller

Close now the door; shut down the light. Supremer Sacrifice, The. Suzanne Gardinier. CBAP

Close Quarters. John Banister Tabb. OBAL

Close the dim eyes, for expression hath left them. Lines on a Dead Girl. Priscilla Jane Thompson. CBWP-2

Close to a house on a piece of ground. Garden, The. Bernadette Mayer. FTOS

Close to a quarter of a century since then. Christmas Carol. T. H. Parry-Williams. OBWVE, *tr. by* Joseph P. Clancy

Close to a tape shop. Sentiment. Sa'di Yusuf. MAP, *tr. by* Lena Jayyusi and Naomi Shihab Nye

Close to Aminta, on the Loss of Her Lover. Sarah Dixon. ECWP

Close to Me. Gabriela Mistral. TCLAP, *tr. by* Doris Dana

Close to Me. Gabriela Mistral. TANSG, *tr. by* Maria Jacketti

Close to nature my brother, your thoughts ring softly. To an Indian Poet. Patty L. Harjo. VoR

Close to the fireside confined. Invitation from a Country Cottage, The. Martha Sansom. ECWP

Close to the gates a spacious garden lies. Homer. OBGa; OBVE, *tr. by* Alexander Pope *Fr.* Odyssey.

Close to the gates of Paradise I flee. Eve. Ella Higginson. SWaP

Close under here, I watched two lovers once. "Robin Hyde." FaBoWP; PeNZ *Fr.* Beaches, The.

Close-up. Heather McPherson. PeNZ

Close up the casement, draw the blind. Shut Out That Moon. Thomas Hardy. NOBE; NoAM

Close up they're seen in fine detail. Painting of One Hundred Wild Geese, A. Tai Piao-yüan. CoBLCP, *tr. by* Jonathan Chaves

Close-ups of Summer. Norman MacCaig. OxBC

Close Your Eyes and See. Mikhail Naimy. GraLe, *tr. by* J.R. Perry

Close your eyes over my sins. Géza Páskándi. IQMS, *tr. by* Agnes Arany-Makkai *Fr.* Language Memory.

Closed Door, The. Muhammad Al-Faituri [*or* Al-Fituri *or* Al-Fayturi]. MAP, *tr. by* Sargon Boulus and Peter Porter

Closed Door, The. Theodosia Pickering Garrison. PoToHe

Closed Doors. Marie Thorson. PWR

Closed is that curious ear by Death's cold hand. William Mason. NOEC *Fr.* English Garden, The.

Closed like confessionals, they thread. Ambulances. Philip Larkin. FaBoTw; NAEL-5v2; NAEL-6v2; NoP-4; OxBC

Closed Mill. Maggie Anderson. PBCAP

Closed over wounds. (LL) Roads. Peter Huchel. HP; PoSu, *tr. by* Michael Hamburger

Closed Town, The. *Unknown, fr. Terezin Concentration Camp.* INSAB

Closed window looks down, A. Ka 'Ba. Imamu Amiri Baraka. BPo; ISC; NBV; PmAP; TAP

Closed World, The. Denise Levertov. NoP-4

Closely, like one creature, we. Marina Ivanovna Tsvetayeva [*or* Tsvetaeva]. *Fr.* Poem of the End.

Closer, closer / to paradise—. Issa. ZenPo, *tr. by* Takashi Ikemoto and Lucien Stryk

Closer in. C. S. Giscombe. GT *Fr.* "In" Sequence, The.

Closer to Home. Floyd Skloot. UrbNat

Closing, A. May Miller. ISC

Closing Album, The. Louis MacNeice. Dublin. CIP-2; OxBTC

Closing cycle rich in good, The. (LL) Tennyson. ChrPo; EBVV; FHYEP; NAEL-6v2 *Fr.* In Memoriam A. H. H.

Closing first the front door, and then the patio. Father's Belt. Shalin Hai-Jew. FSt

Closing of the Rodeo, The. William Jay Smith. AiP; TwCP

Closure. Douglas Messerli. FTOS

Closure Opening Its Trap. Suzanne Wise. AmPoNex

Clote (Water-Lily), The. William Barnes. FaBoVe; NPeEn

Cloth, A. Gertrude Stein. TCAPo *Fr.* Tender Buttons.

Cloth of Gold. Francis Reginald. MoCV

Cloth-plant grew till it covered the thorn bush, The. *Unknown.* BoWoP, *tr. by* Arthur Waley *Fr.* Shih Ching.

Cloth socks, straw sandals, robe of coarse cloth. Walking to the Temple of Precious Light. Wen Cheng-ming. CoBLCP, *tr. by* Jonathan Chaves

Clothed in buckskin, clothed in homespun. Pioneers. Aileen Fisher. CA

Clothed in yellow, red and green. *Unknown.* OxNR

Clothes. Wislawa Szymborska. PoSu, *tr. by* Grazyna Drabik

Clothes, The. Julia Copus. NeBl

Clothes Do But Cheat and Cozen [*or* Cousen] Us. Robert Herrick. CaPo; ErotSp

Clothes make no sound when I tread ground. Cynewulf. RB; WoPoe, *tr. by* Geoffrey Grigson *Fr.* Riddles (Exeter Book).

Clothes Make the Man. Jack Conway. NBLV

Clothes Maketh the Man. Theodore Weiss. NoAM

Clothes must play a part. Lovely to Look At. Dorothy Fields. ReLy

Clothes on the Washing Line. Frank Flynn. OTCP

Clothes Pit, The. Douglas Dunn. OxBTC

Clothes Without the Monk, The. Silvio Giussani. ItPo, *tr. by* Gayle Ridinger

Clothesline post is set, The. Lorine Niedecker. APT-2

Clothing us in a robe of more than glory. (LL) Coliseum, The. Edgar Allan Poe. APN-1; NOBA

Clotho, Lachesis, Atropos. Hilaire Kirkland. PeNZ

Cloud. Shinkichi Takahashi. ZenPo, *tr. by* Takashi Ikemoto and Lucien Stryk

Cloud, The. Dulce Maria Loynaz. TANSG, *tr. by* Alan West

Cloud, The. Shelley. CABP; FHYEP; NAEL-5v2; NAEL-6v2; NoP-4; PWR

Cloud, The. Derek Walcott. ChIV-1

Cloud above lotus / It too. Boryu. ZenPo, *tr. by* Takashi Ikemoto and Lucien Stryk

Cloud and water, lonely, desolate. Mooring at Night at the River Mouth, I Heard a Flute—Sent to My Elder Brother Hsi-ch'iao. Wang Shih-chieng. CoBLCP, *tr. by* Jonathan Chaves

Cloud-backed heron will not move, The. Heron, The. Vernon Watkins. AngWePo; GTBS-P; TCAWP; TwCP; UnPo

Cloud-capped peaks fill the eyes. On a Visit to Ch'ung Chen Taoist Temple. Yü Hsüan-chi. ColAnChi, *tr. by* Chung Ling and Kenneth Rexroth

Cloud—cloud—cloud— hurls. It. Gary Snyder. LCAP-2

Cloud doth gather, the green wood roar, The. Johann Christoph Friedrich von Schiller. AWP *Fr.* Piccolomini, The.

Cloud Factory, The. John Haines. SPE

Cloud Fantasy. Henrietta Cordelia Ray. CBWP-3

Cloud fields change into furniture. Emphasis Falls on Reality, An. Barbara Guest. FTOS; PmAP

Cloud Game, The. William Reichard. AmPoNex

Cloud hides the sun, A. A photograph. After Reading the Book of Splendor. Emily Warn. GifTon

Cloud in Trousers, A. Vladimir Vladimirovich Mayakovsky [*or* Maiakovskii]. TCRusP, *tr. by* Kathy Lewis and Bob Perelman

Cloud in Trousers, The. Vladimir Vladimirovich Mayakovsky [*or* Maiakovskii].

"Maria! Maria! Maria!" TCRP, *tr. by* Bernard Meares

Prologue: "I'll mock those thoughts of yours." TCRP, *tr. by* Bernard Meares

"You think this is some malarial dream?" TCRP, *tr. by* Bernard Meares

Cloud is the post office between continents, The. To Modigliani to Prove to Him That I Am a Poet. Max Jacob. TrJP, *tr. by* Wallace Fowlie

Cloud, journey of water through the sky. Cloud, The. Dulce Maria Loynaz. TANSG, *tr. by* Alan West

Cloud-maidens that float on forever. Aristophanes. AWP *Fr.* Clouds, The.

Cloud Messenger, The. Kalidasa.

"High on the Mount of Rama a yaksha dwelt, who for." WoPoe, *tr. by* Franklin Edgerton and Eleanor Edgerton

Cloud Mountain. Muso Soseki. EaWin, *tr. by* W. S. Merwin

Cloud moved close, A. The bulk of the wind shifted. Visitant, The. Theodore Roethke. PoE; RB; TRP; UnPo

Cloud no bigger than a button, A. Old Champagne Glass. Eddy Van Vliet. VCWP

Cloud of dust on the long white road, A. Teams, The. Henry Lawson. CBAP

Cloud of Unknowing, The. Christopher Edgar. BAP-01

Cloud Parade, The. Laura Jensen. LCAP-2

Cloud possessed the hollow field, A. High Tide at Gettysburg, The. Will Henry Thompson. CBCWP

Cloud-puffball, torn tufts, tossed pillows flaunt forth, then chevy on an air-. That Nature Is a Heraclitean Fire and of the Comfort of the Resurrection. Gerard Manley Hopkins. EnlH; FaBoMo; FaBoVe; GTBS-P; PFTM-1; PoE

Cloud Rains. Oumarou Watta. NAfrP

Cloud reflections float on flooded paddles. On the Way to Huang-ch'ang River. Wang Shih-chieng. SuSp, *tr. by* Richard John Lynn

Cloud's Anchor, The. Ian Hamilton Finlay. NePenScot

Cloud Song. Henrietta Cordelia Ray. CBWP-3

Cloud Unfolding, The. Ernesto Trejo. LTA

Cloudburst and Soaring Moon. Hugh MacDiarmid. NoAM

Clouded Evening, Late September. Sydney Lea. RA

Clouded Morning, The. Jones Very. GSo; NOBA

Clouded Sky. Miklós Radnóti. GifTon; HP, *tr. by* Stephen Berg, S. J. Marks, F. J. Marks and Steven Polgar

Clouded with snow / The cold winds blow. Winter. Walter De la Mare. OBMV

Cloudless summer day—. Haiku. Lenard D. Moore. SpirFl

Clouds. Complete Sound-Poems of Hugo Ball, The. Hugo Ball. PFTM-1

Clouds. Rupert Brooke. OBEV; OBMV; OxBTC

Clouds. Penny Harter. HA

Clouds. Denise Levertov. VCAP

Clouds. Philip Levine. LCAP-2

Clouds. Stanley Moss. BodElec

Clouds. Sándor Weöres. IQMS, *tr. by* Edwin Morgan

Clouds. Francis Webb. BMAP

Clouds, The. Aristophanes.

Song of the Clouds. AWP

Clouds, The. Basho. EH, *tr. by* Robert Hass

Clouds, The. Thomas M. [*or* "Tom"] Disch. RA

Clouds, The. Mirabai [*or* Mira Bai]. EnlH

Clouds, The. Sándor Petőfi.

"Farmer puts his field under the plow, The." IQMS, *tr. by* Peter Zollman

"Glorious night! / The giant moon, the tiny evening star." IQMS, *tr. by* Peter Zollman

"How many drops has the ocean sea?" IQMS, *tr. by* Peter Zollman

"How will the earth die? . . . will she freeze? will she burn?" IQMS, *tr. by* Peter Zollman

"Humankind has not declined!" IQMS, *tr. by* Peter Zollman

"I often wonder who will find." IQMS, *tr. by* Peter Zollman

"If all the hearts that shrivelled in their graves." IQMS, *tr. by* Peter Zollman

"Is the spirit the true lover of the flesh?" IQMS, *tr. by* Peter Zollman

"Sorrow? A Great Ocean." IQMS, *tr. by* Wystan Hugh Auden

"What happens to laughter." IQMS, *tr. by* Peter Zollman

"What's the merriest burial ground?" IQMS, *tr. by* Peter Zollman

Clouds, The. William Carlos Williams. VGW

Clouds and the stars didn't wage this war, The. For the Record. Adrienne Rich. NIL-7; NIP-4; VCAP

Clouds and water block the way home. Ailing Japanese Monk, The. Hsiang Ssu. CoBCP, *tr. by* Burton Watson

Clouds are marshalling across the sky, The. Meditations. Margaret Fuller. SWaP

Clouds are so deep, I don't know where. (LL) Looking for a Recluse but Failing to Find Him. Chia Tao. CoBCP; ColAnChi, *tr. by* Burton Watson

Clouds are swept into the sunset—a sky beyond the sky. Chu Yün-ming. CoBLCP *Fr.* Poem Inscribed on a Landscape Painting.

Clouds as I see them, rising, The. Clouds. Denise Levertov. VCAP

Clouds breaking up. Momen. JDP, *tr. by* Yoel Hoffmann

Clouds carry in another of June's remonstrances, The. Last week. Cloud Game, The. William Reichard. AmPoNex

Clouds circle the moon. Love Song. Ma Chih-yüan. CrYelRi, *tr. by* Sam Hamill

Clouds come and go, The. Basho. SoOfWa, *tr. by* Sam Hamill

Clouds darken the plain. Hand. Edouard Roditi. SPE

Clouds dream and disappear. Wistaria. Witter Bynner. APT-1

Clouds drifting off. Kizan. JDP, *tr. by* Yoel Hoffmann

Clouds fill the sky. Morning after. . . Love, The. Kattie M. Cumbo. BlSi

Clouds Gathering. Charles Simic. ColAP

Clouds grow thickest when the summit's nigh, The. (LL) Slow Through the Dark. Paul Laurence Dunbar. GSo; SacPr

Clouds had made a crimson crown, The. Moment, A. Mary Elizabeth Coleridge. LW; PEW

Clouds hover over the river's waves, the evening's in a haze. On a Painting by Hsia Kuei Entitled "Returning in Wind and Snow to a Village Home." Kao Ch'i. SuSp, *tr. by* Irving Y. Lo

Clouds now and then. Basho. OxBEV, *tr. by* Anthony Thwaite

Clouds of blossoms. Basho. EH, *tr. by* Robert Hass

Clouds of cherry blossoms! Basho. SoOfWa, *tr. by* Sam Hamill

Clouds of dust arise, rolling up from earth. *Unknown.* APN-2, *tr. by* Alice C. Fletcher *Fr.* Hako, The.

Clouds of Evening. Robinson Jeffers. MoAmPo

Clouds of flowers. Yaohiko. JDP, *tr. by* Yoel Hoffmann

Clouds of mosquitoes / It would be bare. Issa. ZenPo, *tr. by* Takashi Ikemoto and Lucien Stryk

Clouds of the heavens. Ephesos. Duris. GrAn, *tr. by* Peter Jay

Clouds on the Sea. Ruth Dallas. PeNZ *Fr.* Letter to a Chinese Poet.

Clouds out of darkness. Second Coming, The. Suzanne Benton. HW

Clouds pass over, endless. Passover: the Injections. William Heyen. HP

Clouds, piled in rows like merchandise, The. Millinery District. Charles Reznikoff. APT-2

Clouds scattered across the sky all so far away. Words, The. Lee Harwood. SPE

Clouds seen and unseen. Tune: "Traveler Welcoming the Immortal." Chang K'o-chiu. ChinPo, *tr. by* Yip Wai-lim

Clouds, shadows searching for what cast them. (LL) Tornados. Thylias Moss. GT; MakPoe

Clouds shouldered a path up the mountains, The. Drought, The. Gary Soto. NoAM

Clouds spout upon her. Rain on a Grave. Thomas Hardy. OxAEP-2

Clouds That Are So Light, The. Edward Thomas. FaBoTw

Clouds that drift so far and free. Wife's Thoughts, The. Hsü Kan. CoBCP, *tr. by* Burton Watson

Clouds, the source of rain, one stormy night, The. Lost in Heaven. Robert Frost. MoAmPo

Clouds were mountains, that day, behind the real mountains, The. View from Skates in Berkeley, The. Quincy Troupe. UnSA

Clouds, which rise with thunder, slake, The. All's Well. John Greenleaf Whittier. OxBSP

Cloudy Bay. Eileen Duggan. PeNZ

Cloudy Day. Jimmy Santiago Baca. LoL

Cloudy morning. *Unknown.* OHMPJ

Cloudy morning dark as night. Cloudy Morning. Joseph McCarthy, Jr. ReLy

Clover. Sidney Lanier. APN-2; ColAP

"Now comes the Course-of-things, shaped like an Ox." TCAPo

Clover fills the darkness quickly. Axiom of Maria. Larissa Szporluk. NeAmPo

Clover Flower, The. 'Ali 'Abdallah Khalifa. MAP, *tr. by* Alistair Elliot and Lena Jayyusi

Clover's simple Flame, The. Emily Dickinson. APN-2

Clown, The. Margaret E. Bruner. PoToHe

Clown, The. Janet Frame. PeNZ

Clown's Song, The. William Shakespeare. CTC; NOBE; NoSic; TFi *Fr.* Twelfth Night.

Clownlike, happiest on your hands. You're. Sylvia Plath. FaBoTw; FaBoWP; RB

Club, The. Mitsuye Yamada. FSt

Club House. Janice Lowe. InTrad

Club Midnight. Charles Simic. BodElec

Clues to what they remembered had been pasted into an album, The. Cenotaph. John Yau. PmAP

Clumped murmuring above a sump of loam. Woodlot, The. Amy Clampitt. HCAP

Clumsy clot of shadow in the fold, A. Moth, A. Henry Bellyse Baildon. NOBVV

Clustered trees filled with the sounds of autumn. Yüan Hao-wen. SuSp *Fr.* Random Verses on Mountain Life.

Clustering atop a leggy stem. Primula veris. Randolph Healy. Oth

Clusters in Thy vineyard turn to gold, O God, The. Grape-gathering. Avraham Shlonsky. TrJP, *tr. by* I. M. Lask

Clutching a fist of hair. Alexis Rotella. HA

Clutching the ward's wall rail. I'll See You Down the Lane. Alison Pryde. Prnts

Clyde Peeling's Reptiland in Allenwood, Pennsylvania. Kevin Young. NeAmPo

Clyde's Water. *Unknown.* ESPB

Clyde's Waters. *Unknown.* OxBB

Clymène, A. Paul Verlaine. AWP, *tr. by* Arthur Symons

Cnut's Song. *Unknown.* PoE *Fr.* Canute at Ely.

Coach. Wyatt Prunty. Unle

Coach, / Carriage. *Unknown.* OxNR

Coach waits, long, hot in the sun, The. Croeso i Gymru. Philip Owens. AngWePo

Coachman, The. Mother Goose. OxNR; ReMoGo

Coachman sits like a king, The. Movement. Nikolai Alekseievich Zabolotsky [*or* Zabolotskii]. TCRP, *tr. by* Daniel Weissbort

Coal. Audre Lorde. BlSi; ESEAA; NAAL-5; NALW; NBV; NoAM; VCAP

Coal-black raven, coal-black devil. Raven, The. Nikolai Ivanovich Glazkov. TCRP, *tr. by* Daniel Weissbort

Coal Fire in Winter, A. Thomas McGrath. ErotSp; GifTon; RaBo

Coal Miners, The. James Ballowe. IllVoic

Coal Train. Jay Parini. GM

Coal train, The. Anita Virgil. HA

Coal-white bird appears this spring, A. Almanac Verse. Samuel Danforth. SCAP

Coalmen, The. László Nagy. IQMS, *tr. by* Tony Connor

Coals go out, The. Galway Kinnell. RaBo *Fr.* Middle of the Way.

Coarse / jocosity / catches the crowd. Don Marquis. APT-1 *Fr.* Archy and Mehitabel.

Coast hills at Sovranes Creek, The. Place for No Story, The. Robinson Jeffers. APT-1; AiP

Coast, The: Norfolk. Frances Darwin Cornford. OxBTC

Coast View, A. Charles Harpur.

"Dead city walls may pen us in, but still." CBAP

Coastal. Valerie Martínez. AmPoNex

Coastline. Elaine Feinstein. BrRo

Coastline, The. Eddy Van Vliet. VCWP, *tr. by* Matthew Blake

Coastline never alters for the fisherman, The. Coastline, The. Eddy Van Vliet. VCWP, *tr. by* Matthew Blake

Coat. Vicki Feaver. LW

Coat, A. W. B. Yeats. NAEL-5v2; NAEL-6v2; NoAM; OxAEP-2; OxBSP

Coat, The. Dennis Lee. TLR

Coat-of-Mail: Dank earth, wondrously cold, The. Cynewulf. ASW *Fr.* Riddles (Exeter Book).

Cob, thou nor soldier, thief, nor fencer art. To Pertinax Cob. Ben Jonson. BeJo

Cobalt. Rolf Jacobsen. BLT, *tr. by* Roger Greenwald

Cobb's Barns. Anne Babson Carter. PoSol

Cobb Would Have Caught It. Robert Fitzgerald. HAP; TwCP

Cobble and Pebble in the teeth. Fang and Club upon. Narrative Charm for Ibbotroyd. Maggie O'Sullivan. Oth; PFTM-2

Cobble thrown a hundred years ago, A. Seamus Heaney. CIP-2; PBCIP; PNI

Cobbler, cobbler, mend my shoe. Mother Goose. OxNR

Cobbler in Jerusalem, A. Kahlil Gibran. GraLe

Coble o Cargill, The. *Unknown.* ESPB

Cobra is the night image of a chinese water-print. North Express. Joyce Mansour. WPOW, *tr. by* the author

Cobweb. Haniel Long. APT-1

Cobweb, The. Raymond Carver. BLT

Cobwebs. Melinda Goodman. WiU

Cobwebs. Christina Georgina Rossetti. CABP; NAEL-5v2; NAEL-6v2; NALW; VWP

Coca-Cola and Coco Frío.   Martín Espada.   ReTh; UnSA

Cocaine Lil [and Morphine Sue].   *Unknown.*   OxBoLi; RB

Cochineals and fig colours ripple.   Dining Out.   Judith Beveridge.   BMAP

Cock, A.   Anyte [*or* Anytes].   GrAn, *tr. by* Sally Purcell

Cock-a-Doo.   Stevie Smith.   OWoS

Cock-a-Doodle-Do.   *Unknown.*   ReMoGo

Cock-a-doodle-doo! / My dame has lost her shoe.   Mother Goose.   LB; OxNR; ReMoGo

Cock-a-doodle-doo the brass-lined rooster goes [*or* says].   Dog.   John Crowe Ransom.   OBAL

Cock-a-Hoop.   Isabella Gardner.   WPE

Cock and Bull Story, A.   *Unknown.*   ReMoGo

Cock and Hen: I watched a couple of curious creatures.   Cynewulf.   ASW   *Fr.* Riddles (Exeter Book).

Cock and the Fox, The.   Robert Henryson.   NAEL-7v1

Cock and the Fox, The.   Jean de La Fontaine.   AWP, *tr. by* Elizur Wright

Cock and the Hen, The.   Geoffrey Chaucer.   *See* Canterbury Tales, The

Cock and the Hen, The.   *Unknown.*   OxNR; ReMoGo

Cock and the Pearl, The.   Max Jacob.
"I thought he was bankrupt."   PFTM-1

Cock before Dawn.   Norman MacCaig.   OxBC

Cock, cock, cock, cock.   Cock and the Hen, The.   *Unknown.*   OxNR; ReMoGo

Cock-Crow.   Edward Thomas.   GTBS-P; MoBrPo; NPeEn; OxBSP; RB

Cock-Crow.   *Unknown.*   ReMoGo

Cock-crow and early-rise!   Dawn.   Joseph Kumbirai.   PeSAV, *tr. by* Douglas Livingstone

Cock-crow Song.   *Unknown.*   ChiP, *tr. by* Arthur Waley

Cock-crowing.   Henry Vaughan.   BASC; ESCV; GeHe; NAEL-7v1; NPeEn; PBRV

Cock crows / But no queen rises, The.   Depression before Spring.   Wallace Stevens.   OBAL

Cock crows—cock-a-doodle-doo!—the east grows bright, The.   On the Hall of Precious Virtue.   Yang Shih-ch'i.   CoBLCP; ColAnChi, *tr. by* Jonathan Chaves

Cock doth crow / To let you know, The.   Mother Goose.   OxNR

Cock-fight, The.   Ts'ao Chih.   ChiP, *tr. by* Arthur Waley

Cock has crow's an hour ago, The.   Morning Quatrains, The.   Charles Cotton.   NOSC; PeECV

Cock is crowing, The.   Written in March [While Resting on the Bridge at the Foot of Brother's Water].   William Wordsworth.   ChAP; NAEL-5v2; NAEL-6v2; NTCP; SCGP; UnPo

Cock of Glory is the *coq français*, The.   French, 1870–1871, The.   *Unknown.*   FaBoEE

Cock-phoenix, cock-phoenix goes back to his hometown.   Cock-Phoenix, Hen-Phoenix.   Ssu-ma Hsiang-ju.   ColAnChi, *tr. by* Anne Birrell

Cock Robin got up early.   *Unknown.*   OxNR

Cock's crow means profit, The.   Tseng Jui.   SuSp   *Fr.* Tune: "Sheep on Mountain Slope"—Lamenting the Times.

Cock's on the housetop blowing his horn, The.   Cock and Bull Story, A.   *Unknown.*   ReMoGo

Cock's on the wood pile, The.   *Unknown.*   OxNR

Cock that crowed this dawn up, heard, The.   Copernicus.   Robert David Fitzgerald.   NOBAu

Cock, warm roosting 'mid his feathers mates, The.   Winter's Day, A.   Joanna Baillie.   WoRP

Cock, warm roosting midst his feathered dames, The.   Joanna Baillie.   ECWP   *Fr.* Winter Day, A.

Cockaigne: A Dream.   Louis Edward Sissman.   DiPo

Cockatoo.   Pam Bridgeman.   Prnts

Cocked up a squint eye and said, "I bloody did that." (LL)   Cathedral Builders.   John Ormond.   NoP-4; PeECV; TCAWP

Cocker of Snooks, A.   Phyllis Gotlieb.   NOBC

Cockermouth.   David Wright.   NLP

Cockeyed Neruda dancing on a strobe.   In California with Neruda.   Shirley Lim.   GeoHom

Cockfight.   Liu Cheng.   ColAnChi, *tr. by* Robert Joe Cutter

Cockfights in the basements.   Side 26.   Víctor Hernández Cruz.   PueRic

Cocklorel would needs have the devil his guest.   Ben Jonson.   NOSC   *Fr.* Gypsies Metamorphosed, The.

Cockney of the North, The.   Harry Graham.   UV

Cockney's Garden, The.   Edgar Bateman.   OBGa

Cockroaches of Liberation.   Martín Espada.   TouFir

Cocks and Mares.   Ruth Stone.   RaBo

Cocks crow in the morn.   Cock-Crow.   *Unknown.*   ReMoGo

Cocksucker's Blues.   Justin Chin.   WiU

Cocktail is a pleasant drink, The.   R-E-M-O-R-S-E.   George Ade.   NBLV; OBAL; OBCoV; PeLV

Cocktails.   Ciaran Carson.   BiHa; ModIr; PBCIP

Cocktails / and signs of.   Louis Zukofsky.   APT-2   *Fr.* 29 Poems.

Cocktails for Two.   Sam Coslow.   ReLy

Coco-de-Mer.   W. N. Herbert.   NePenScot

Cocoa coursing through their veins. (LL)   In Praise of Cocoa, Cupid's Nightcap.   Stanley J. Sharpless.   NBLV; PeLV

Cocoa Morning.   Bob Kaufman.   NBV

Coconut for Katerina, A.   Sandra McPherson.   LCAP-2

Coconut / has the moon inside.   Philippine Figures.   *Unknown.*   EaWin, *tr. by* W. S. Merwin

Cocoon.   Rin Ishigaki.   WPOW, *tr. by* Ayusawa Takako

Cocoon.   David McCord.   OBCA

Cocoons.   Sean Thomas Dougherty.   AmPoNex

Cod inert as an old boot.   Mid-Channel.   Gwen Harwood.   BMAP

Coda.   Shafiq Al-Kamali.   MAP, *tr. by* Sargon Boulus and Christopher Middleton

Coda.   Marilyn Hacker.
"Did you love well what very soon you left?"   NoAM; RA

Coda.   "Ern Malley."   BMAP

Coda.   Ezra Pound.   NOBA

Coda.   William Carlos Williams.   NOBA

Coda: The Higher Keys.   James Merrill.
"Empty perfection, as I take you in."   NoAM

Coda: "There's little in leaving or giving."   Dorothy Parker.   APT-1

Code, The.   Robert Frost.   OBNV; UnPo

Code key.   John Cayley.   PFTM-2   *Fr.* Reveal Code: Indra's Net 8.

Codex.   Stephen Rodefer.   PmAP

Codicil.   Ruth Stone.   BoWoP

Codicil.   Derek Walcott.   NoAM

Coelia.   William Percy.
"Judged by my goddess' doom to endless pain."   Son
"Relent, my dear yet unkind Coelia."   Son

Coeur de Lion.   Richard I, Coeur de Lion.   *See* Ja Nul Homs Pris Ne Ira a Raison

Coffee.   Wanda Coleman.   ISC

Coffee.   James Vincent Cunningham.   MoAmPo; VGW

Coffee.   Gary Hotham.   HA

Coffee and jasmine on a tray.   Convalescence.   James Philip McAuley.   CBAP

Coffee and Tea.   *Unknown.*   ReMoGo

Coffee bowl called Part of Poland bursts, The.   Jack's Pigeon.   R. F. Langley.   HarvBoo

Coffee cups cool on the Vicar's harmonium.   Game of Consequences, A.   Paul Dehn.   NOBL

Coffee grinder.   "Paul Dermée."   CuPo

Coffee Imp, The.   Bella [*or* Izabella] Akhatovna Akhmadulina.   ItGoST, *tr. by* F. D. Reeve

Coffee Song (They've Got an Awful Lot of Coffee in Brazil), The.   Bob Hilliard.   ReLy

Coffee turned cold in the pot.   Quiet Evening, Home Away.   Joann Balingit.   ReBoTo

Coffin, The.   Heinrich Heine.   AWP, *tr. by* Louis Untermeyer

Coffin bearing the face of a boy, A.   Mirror for the Twentieth Century, A.   "Adonis" [*or* "Adunis"].   AF, *tr. by* Abdullah Al-Udhari

Coffin-Worm, The.   Ruth Pitter.   MoBrPo

Cogitabo Pro Peccato Meo.   William Habington.   ChIV-1

Cogito Ergo.   Jerzy Ficowski.   PoSu, *tr. by* Frank J. Corliss, Jr. and Grazyna Sandel

Cohorts of charabancs fanfared Offa's province and his concern, negotiating the by-ways from Teme to Trent.   Geoffrey Hill.   OxBEV   *Fr.* Mercian Hymns.

Coil there and squat, and pay your fee? (LL)   Interview with Doctor Drink.   James Vincent Cunningham.   OxBSP; VGW; WoPoe

Coiled like a lyncher's rope.   Portrait in Georgia.   Jean Toomer.   NAAL-2v2

Coilyear, gudlie in feir, tuke him be the hand, The.   *Unknown.*   OxBS   *Fr.* Rauf Coilyear.

Coin, The.   Edwin Morgan.   NePenScot   *Fr.* Sonnets from Scotland.

Coincidence.   Aida Gelbtrunk.   MirDau, *tr. by* Roberta Gordenstein

Coincidentally.   Frederic W. Platt.   BloBone

Coins for the ferry, The. (LL)   Being Called For.   Rosemary Dobson.   BMAP; CBAP

Coins handsome as Nero's; of good substance and.   Geoffrey Hill.   FaBoMo; HAP; NoAM   *Fr.* Mercian Hymns.

Coins in the hand.   On Her Decision to Stop Wearing Clothes.   Mahadevi.   ErotSp; WPoS, *tr. by* Jane Hirshfield

Coins of Van-Lich.   *Vietnamese Oral Tradition.*   CaDao, *tr. by* John Balaban

Coition's brief, a nasty cheat.   Petronius Arbiter.   RomPo, *tr. by* J. P. Sullivan

Cokboy.   Jerome Rothenberg.   PmAP

Cokkils. Sydney Goodsir Smith. OxBS

Cold. Dennis Brutus. PeSAV
  (Cold / the clammy cement.) AF

Cold. Poems About Prison. Dennis Brutus. PBMAP

Cold. Brian Coffey. CIP-2

Cold. Robert Francis. LCAP-2

Cold. Dorothy Roberts. NOBC

Cold, The. Lance Henson. CDW

Cold, The. Charles Simic. HCAP

Cold, The. Yvor Winters. APT-2

Cold air drains down from the peaks. In the Mountains as Autumn Begins. Wen T'ing-yün. OHMPC, *tr.* by Kenneth Rexroth

Cold airs from the river creep, The. Children of the Mist. Rosamund Marriott Watson. VWP

Cold and raw the north wind doth blow. Winter. Mother Goose. ReMoGo

Cold and single over the map of language. (LL) Illuminations. Louise Glück. HarvBoo; NALW

Cold and the colors of cold: mineral, shell. Cold. Robert Francis. LCAP-2

Cold Are the Crabs. Edward Lear. NAEL-5v2; NAEL-6v2

Cold as Heaven. Judith Ortiz Cofer. ExTi *Fr.* Three Poems in Memory of Mamá (Grandmother).

Cold as no love, and wild with all negation. Quand on n'a pas ce que l'on aime, il faut aimer ce que l'on a—. Stevie Smith. FaBoEE

Cold as No Plea. Death Sentence, The. Stevie Smith. NoP-4

Cold as the breath of winds that blow. Lucasta's World. Richard Lovelace. BeJo; CaPo

Cold-blooded Creatures. Elinor Wylie. OxBSP

Cold blows the blast--the night's obscure. George, the Younger Colman. NOEC *Fr.* Maid of the Moor, The; or, The Water-Fiends.

Cold blows the winter wind: 'tis Love. Love at the Door. Meleager. AWP, *tr.* by John Addington Symonds

Cold bugle calls, and the city moves on, A. (LL) Armistice Day. Charles Causley. NAEL-5v2; NAEL-6v2; NoP-4; OBWP

Cold Ceremony. Hannah More. ECWP *Fr.* Bas Bleu, The; or, Conversation.

Cold chain of life presseth heavily on me tonight, The. Fragment. Adah Isaacs Menken. CBWP-1

Cold chills invade my body. Happy New Year. Miguel Algarin. PueRic

Cold, cold room with cold, cold girls, A. Morse Lesson. Joy Corfield. FaBoWar

Cold, cold the year draws to its end. Old Poem. *Unknown.* AWP; BoWoP, *tr.* by Arthur Waley

Cold! cold! 'tis a chilly clime. Robert Southey. NOBRP *Fr.* Thalaba the Destroyer.

Cold! Cold! / Wide Lurg Plain is cold tonight. *Unknown.* NOIV

Cold Colloquy. Patrick Anderson. NOBC *Fr.* Poem on Canada.

Cold comes about, The. North Dakota, North Light. N. Scott Momaday. HATNAP

Cold coming we had of it, A. Journey of the Magi. T. S. Eliot. ChrPo; FaBoCh; FaBoMo; GI; HAP; HeIP-4; InPK-6; MoAmPo; NAAL-5; NAEL-5v2; NAEL-6v2; NOCV; NoP-4; OBCP; OBMV; OxBTC; PAI; PoE; TAP; TFi; TRP; TwCP

Cold-day cicada's cutting creak. Tune: "Bells in the Rain." Liu Yung. ChinPo, *tr.* by Yip Wai-lim

Cold days sit where it's warm. Written on the Wall of Pan-shan Temple. Wang An-shih. CoBCP, *tr.* by Burton Watson

Cold / December nights I'd go. Touched. Olga Broumas. GifTon

Cold Fear. Elizabeth Madox Roberts. WPE

Cold felt cold until our blood, The. Phantasia for Elvira Shatayev. Adrienne Rich. NALW; WWork

Cold floors. Endurance. Dennis Brutus. VCWP

Cold Fly. Yang Wan-li. CoBCP, *tr.* by Burton Watson

Cold Fly, The. Yang Wan-li. SuSp, *tr.* by Jonathan Chaves

Cold fountain, cold fountain, refreshing with love. Cold Fountain, Cold Fountain. *Unknown.* BLPSL, *tr.* by Rene de Costa, Rigas Kappatos and Eleni Paidoussi

Cold, gray dawn of the morning after, The. (LL) R-E-M-O-R-S-E. George Ade. NBLV; OBAL; OBCoV; PeLV

Cold Green Element, The. Irving Layton. NOBC; NoP-4

Cold has put blue horses where lambs were, The. Blue Horses. Ed Roberson. GT

Cold Heaven, The. W. B. Yeats. AWP; CTC; GTBS-P; HAP; NPeEn; NoAM; OxBSP; RB

Cold hue newly clears, a belt of haze, The. Autumn Spring. Hsüeh T'ao. SuSp, *tr.* by Eric W. Johnson

Cold hungry Seamen, tho' they oft endure. Meditations on Persecution. Mary Mollineux. EMWP

Cold in the earth—and the deep snow piled above thee! Remembrance. Emily Jane Brontë. BoLoP; BoWoP; CABP; EBEV; EnLoPo; HAP;

MakPoe; NAEL-5v2; NAEL-6v2; NOBE; NOBVV; NPeEn; NoP-4; OxAEP-2; OxBEV; PEW; PoE; PoPoPo; TFi; VWP; WPE; WeW-3

Cold in the North (After Yueh-Fu). Li Ho. ChinPo, *tr.* by Yip Wai-lim

Cold Irish Earth, The. Knute Skinner. InPK-6

Cold Is the North Wind. *Unknown.* CoBCP, *tr.* by Burton Watson

Cold is the winter. The wind is risen. *Unknown.* NOIV

Cold Landscape. Augusta Peaux. TuT, *tr.* by Tony Curtis

Cold Lantern, The. Yang Wan-li. SuSp, *tr.* by Jonathan Chaves

Cold limbs of the air, The. Mountain Wind, A. "Æ". AWP

Cold Lost Marbles. William S. Burroughs. BB

Cold Lunch. William Corbett. PmAP

Cold Meteorite, The. William Reed Huntington. APN-2

Cold mornings, he would warm his hands. Coroner. Elton Glaser. PBCAP

Cold Mountain is a house. Han-shan. WoPoe, *tr.* by Gary Snyder

Cold Mountain is full of weird sights. *Unknown.* CoBCP

Cold Mountain Poem No. 158. Han-shan. WoPoe, *tr.* by E. Bruce Brooks

Cold mountain turns dark green. Cold Mountain, The. Wang Wei. TAL

Cold Night. Ch'en Shih-tao. CoBCP, *tr.* by Burton Watson

Cold Night. Po Chü-i. CrYelRi, *tr.* by Sam Hamill

Cold night, the sidewalk we walk on icy, A. Christmas Eve Service at Midnight at St. Michael's. Robert Bly. NNaP

Cold night: the wild duck. Basho. EH, *tr.* by Robert Hass

Cold nights outside the taverns in Wyoming. Accountability. William Stafford. LCAP-2

Cold of autumn's frost penetrates the curtain, The. Tune: "Immortal's Auspicious Crane, An"—On Plum Blossoms. Hsin Ch'i-chi. SuSp, *tr.* by Irving Y. Lo

Cold Oxford unfamiliar now, around. Above the High. Geoffrey Grigson. EnLoPo

Cold Pastoral. Diotimus. GrAn, *tr.* by Dudley Fitts

Cold penetrates to the river's shore. To the Tune "Flowers in the Rain." Yang Shen. CoBLCP, *tr.* by Jonathan Chaves

Cold rain starting, A. Basho. EH, *tr.* by Robert Hass

Cold remote islands, The. Night. Louise Bogan. APT-2; NoP-4; UnPo

Cold River. Joan Larkin. WiU

Cold, Sharp Lamentation. Douglas Hyde. OBMV, *tr.* by Lady Augusta Gregory and Lady Gregory

Cold snap. Five o'clock. Aubade. Richard Kenney. NoP-4

Cold spot on the heart repeats, A. Deep. Timothy Holmes. PeSAV

Cold Spring. Kao Ch'i. SuSp, *tr.* by Irving Y. Lo

Cold Spring, A. Elizabeth Bishop. ColAP; TwCP

Cold stars and the whores. (LL) Street Corner College. Kenneth Patchen. APT-2; CLPP; MoAmPo

Cold steel may penetrate the flesh. Heart Wounds. Claire Richcreek Thomas. PoToHe

Cold Term. Imamu Amiri Baraka. BPo

Cold / the clammy cement. Dennis Brutus. *See* Clammy cement, The

Cold transparent ham is on my fork, The. Sonnet to Vauxhall. Thomas Hood. NPeEn; OBCoV; OxBSo

Cold was the night wind, drifting fast the snow[s] fell. Widow, The. Robert Southey. NOBRP; NOEC; UV

Cold water falling out of the split rock. Leonidas of Tarentum. GrAn

Cold, we sit in the warmth. Written on the Wall of Halfway Mountain Temple. Wang An-shih. SuSp, *tr.* by Jan W. Walls

Cold-Weather Love. Ronald G. Everson. MoCV

Cold wind at evening, A. Ballad of Yi River. Ho Ching-ming. CoBLCP, *tr.* by Jonathan Chaves

Cold wind hurls itself at, A. Paul Verlaine. SxFrPo, *tr.* by Martin Sorrell

Cold wind out of the wilderness, A. Thinking of Li Po. Tu Fu. CrYelRi, *tr.* by Sam Hamill

Cold wind stirs the blackthorn, A. Endure Hardness. Christina Georgina Rossetti. NOBVV

Cold winds rise from the edge of heaven. At the Sky's End, Thinking of Li Po. Tu Fu. ColAnChi, *tr.* by David Lattimore

Cold winter morning. Jim Handlin. HA

Cold winter sunlight stuns the window. To the Tune: Partridge Sky. Li Ch'ing-chao. CrYelRi, *tr.* by Sam Hamill

Cold world awakens. (LL) If the Owl Calls Again. John Haines. CoAP; GifTon; HeIP-4

Cold, yes / But don't test. Sokan. ZenPo, *tr.* by Takashi Ikemoto and Lucien Stryk

Colder. Erica Jong. LW

Coldest winter's day I remember, The. Leaving San Francisco. Marilyn Chin. GeoHom

Coldly, sadly descends. Rugby Chapel. Matthew Arnold. PeECV

Cole Porter. Dionisio D. Martinez. TouFir

Cole's Island. Charles Olson. PoM *Fr.* Maximus Poems, The.

Cole, that unwearied prince of Colchester. Gilbert Keith Chesterton. NOBL

Colebrook Dale.   Anna Seward.
  "While neighbouring cities waste the fleeting hours."   NOEC
Colebrook Dale.   Anna Seward.
  "Scene of superfluous grace, and wasted bloom."   PEW
Colenso Rhymes for Orthodox Children.   Bret Harte.   OBAL
Coleridge.   Washington Allston.   APN-1
Coleridge.   Medbh McGuckian.   CIP-2
Coleridge.   Ronald Stuart Thomas.   TOF
Coleridge.   Theodore Watts-Dunton.   GSo; Son
Coleridge received the Person from Porlock.   Thoughts about the Person from
  Porlock.   Stevie Smith.   NAEL-5v2; NAEL-6v2; NoAm; NoP-4
Colic Passion, The.   Jolanda Insana.
  "No fear of losing my sanity."   CItWP, *tr. by* Cinzia Sartini Blum and Lara
  Trubowitz
Colin.   Anthony Munday.   *See* Primaleon of Greece
Colin Clout.   John Skelton.
  "And if ye stand in doubt."   NAEL-5v1
  "Doctors that learned be."   OBSV
  "For though my rhyme be ragged."   OBCoV
  Spirituality vs. the Temporality, The.   NAEL-6v1
Colin, my dear and most entire beloved.   William Smith.   Son   *Fr.* Chloris [*or*
  the Complaint of the Passionate Despised Shepheard].
Colin, well fits thy sad cheer this sad stound.   Pastoral Eclogue upon the Death
  of Sir Philip Sidney Knight, A.   Lodowick [*or* Lewis] Bryskett.   NoSic
Colin, you can tell my words are crippled now.   James Keir Baxter.   HarvBoo;
  PeNZ   *Fr.* Jerusalem Sonnets.
Coliseum, The.   Edgar Allan Poe.   APN-1; NOBA
Colkelbie Sow.   *Unknown.*
  "Penny lost in the lak, The."   OxBS
Collaboration: Letter to Charlie Chaplin.   Peter Orlovsky.   CLPP
Collaborators / naked Vichy women.   Photo Taken in Winter, 1944.   Barbara
  Unger.   TWW
Collage.   Shara McCallum.   NAPBL
Collapsed addict mother, passed out, The.   Path Marked with Breadcrumbs, A.
  Tony Lopez.   Oth
Collapses by the water cooler. (LL)   Office Party.   Phyllis McGinley.   ChrPo;
  OBSV
Collapsible.   Tom Raworth.   SPE
Collapsing in the middle of the day.   Become Your Face.   Marianne Vitale.
  HeMarv
Collar, The.   George Herbert.   AWP; BASC; CABP; ClHu; EBEV; FSCP;
  FaBoVe; GeHe; HAP; HeIP-4; InvLi; MeLP; NAEL-5v2; NAEL-6v1;
  NAEL-7v1; NIL-7; NIP-4; NOBE; NOCV; NSCG; NPeEn; NoP-4;
  OBWVE; PBRV; PoE; PoPoPo; PoRA; SCGP; SCV; SacPr; TFi; TOF;
  WeW-3
Collarbone [*or* Collar-Bone] of a Hare, The.   W. B. Yeats.   OxAEP-2; OxBTC;
  RB
Collect Call.   Mcavoy Layne.   CDa
Collecting Antiques.   Cheng Hsieh.   CoBLCP, *tr. by* Jonathan Chaves
Collection, The.   Zhao Zhenkai.   VCWP, *tr. by* Chen Maiping and Bonnie S.
  McDougall
Collection Day.   Natasha Trethewey.   SpirFl
Collection of Emblemes, Ancient and Moderne, A.   George Wither.
  Husbandman, The.   NOSC
  Marigold, The.   NOSC; SacPr
  Planting.   NOSC
  Spade and the Wreath, The.   NOSC
  Spade, The.   NOSC
Collection of Hymns . . . of the Moravian Brethren, A.   *Unknown.*
  "Chicken blessed and caressed."   NOEC
  "What does a bird in Cross's air."   NOEC
Collective Invention, The.   Chris Wallace-Crabbe.   BMAP
Collective Portrait, The.   Robert Finch.   MoCV
Collective Search.   Patrick Sylvain.   InTrad
Collector, The.   Desiré Flynn.   BrRo
Collector's Marginalia, The.   Peter Sirr.   PBCIP
Collects her motions into shape. (LL)   Nude Descending a Staircase.   X. J.
  Kennedy.   NIP-4; OxBSP
Colleen Rue.   *Unknown.*   BIrV
College Colonel, The.   Herman Melville.   CBCWP; FaBoWar; NCAP; OBWP
College Formal: Renaissance Casino.   Langston Hughes.   APT-2
Collier, The.   Vernon Watkins.   FaBoTw; OBWVE; TCAWP
Collier Lass, The.   Frankie Armstrong.   BrRo
Collier's Wedding, The.   Edward Chicken.
  "At last the beef appears in sight."   NOEC
Collier's Wife, The.   D. H. Lawrence.   FaBoVe; OxBTC
Collins.   Lionel Pigot Johnson.   OxAEP-2

Colloam.   P. Inman.   FTOS
Colloquy in Black Rock.   Robert Lowell.   MoAmPo; NAAL-2v2
Colloquy with God, A.   Sir Thomas Browne.   SacPr   *Fr.* Religio Medici.
Colloquy with John Keats.   "Ern Malley."   BMAP
Collusion.   Medbh McGuckian.   BiHa
Collyn Clout.   John Skelton.
  "Over this the foresayd lay."   PBRV
Cologne.   Samuel Taylor Coleridge.   FaBoEE; NBLV
Colombe.   Edward Kamau Brathwaite.   VCWP
Colombine.   Paul Verlaine.   SxFrPo, *tr. by* Martin Sorrell
Colombo, March. The city white fire.   Auschwitz from Colombo.   Anne
  Ranasinghe.   GotH
Colon Bay.   *Unknown.*   FaBoVe
Colonel.   Kate Llewellyn.   NOBAu
Colonel, The.   Carolyn Forché.   MakPoe; OBWP; SoSe-8
Colonel Chartres.   John Arbuthnot.   *See* Epitaph on Colonel Francis Chartres
Colonel Cold strode up the Line.   Winter Warfare.   Edgell Rickword.
  FaBoWar; OBWP; OxBTC; PeFWW; PoWW
Colonel Fantock.   Dame Edith Sitwell.   MoBrPo; OBMV
Colonel Fazackerley.   Charles Causley.   OTCP
  (Colonel Fazackerley Butterworth-Toast.)   NOxBChV
Colonel in a casual voice, The.   Gallantry.   Keith Douglas.   NAEL-5v2;
  NAEL-6v2; NoAM; OBWP
Colonel's Soliloquy, The.   Thomas Hardy.   FaBoWP; OBWP
Colonels here in solemn manner meet, The.   Thomas [*or* "Tom"] Brown.
  FaBoEE
Colonial Nomenclature.   John Dunmore Lang.   NOBAu
Colonial Troops Transport, The.   *Vietnamese Oral Tradition.*   CaDao, *tr. by*
  John Balaban
Colonists / unearth their wealth.   Shaman Breaks.   Gerald Vizenor.   HATNAP
Colonization in Reverse.   Louise Bennett.   OBCoV
Colonus' Praise.   Sophocles.   OBVE   *Fr.* Oedipus at Colonus.
Colony, The.   John Hewitt.   ModIr
Colophon.   Oliver St. John Gogarty.   OBMV
Colophon to a Roll of Erinna's Poems.   Asclepiades.   GrAn, *tr. by* Lee T.
  Pearcy
Color ain't no faucet.   Within the Veil.   Michelle Cliff.   NAAAL
Color, Caste, Denomination.   Emily Dickinson.   TAP
Color of coral and of your lips, The.   From the French.   Charles North.
  FTOS
Color of ice and fire and solitude, The. (LL)   Wallace Stevens.   HCAP; PoE
  Fr. Auroras of Autumn, The.
Color of the flowers / has faded, The.   Ono no Komachi.   BoWoP
Color of the Grave is Green, The.   Emily Dickinson.   PoE
Color of violence is black, The.   Endangered Species.   Ai.   ESEAA
Color Sergeant, The.   James Weldon Johnson.   GT
Colored cowboy named Nat Love.   Deadwood Dick.   Elizabeth Alexander.
  RA
Colored Hats.   Gertrude Stein.   TTTS   *Fr.* Tender Buttons.
Colored leaves, The.   Kakinomoto no Hitomaro.   OHPJ
Colored pictures.   Charles Olson.   NoAM   *Fr.* Maximus Poems, The.
Colored pictures / of all things to eat: dirty.   Charles Olson.   NeAP; NoAM
  Fr. Maximus Poems, The.
Colored Soldiers, The.   Paul Laurence Dunbar.   APN-2; CBCWP; NAAAL
Colorful frames are erected beside the Yellow River, The.   Li K'ai-hsien.
  CoBLCP; ColAnChi, *tr. by* Jonathan Chaves   *Fr.* Watching the Swinging.
Coloring.   Mark DeCarteret.   AmPoNex
Coloring high means that the strange reason is in front.   Gertrude Stein.   TTTS
  Fr. Tender Buttons.
Colorizing: Turner Broadcasting Enterprises, Computer Graphics Division,
  Burbank, California, 1987.   David Wojahn.   PBCAP   *Fr.* Mystery Train:
  A Sequence.
Colorless dawns.   Dawn, The.   Ricardo Jaimes Freyre.   TCLAP, *tr. by* Victor
  Tulli
Colors.   Fortunato Depero.   PFTM-1
Colors are words' little sisters. They can't become soldiers.   Cobalt.   Rolf
  Jacobsen.   BLT, *tr. by* Roger Greenwald
Colors of Desire, The.   David Mura.   LoL
Colors of spring have returned to West Lake, A.   Song of Spring at West Lake,
  Sent to Circuit Officer Hsieh, A.   Ou-yang Hsiu.   SuSp, *tr. by* Irving Y. Lo
Colors of the country, powerful river.   At the River Tower Parting from My
  Younger Brother, Fu-ling.   Wu Wei-yeh.   CoBLCP, *tr. by* Jonathan Chaves
Colors of the Dark One have penetrated Mira's body; all the other colors washed
  out, The.   Why Mira Can't Go Back to Her Old House.   Mirabai [*or* Mira
  Bai].   EnlH, *tr. by* Robert Bly
Colors of tulips and roses are not the same, The.   Mirza Asadullah Khan
  Ghalib.   EnlH

Colors shifting. Time of Fish Dying. Gabriela Melinescu. BoWoP, *tr. by* Stavros Deligiorgis

Colors we depend on are, The. Love Bit, The. Joel Oppenheimer. PoM

Colors without objects—colors alone—. Colors Without Objects. May Swenson. APT-2

Colorstruck. Askhari. InTrad

Colossal: / Like towers and pavilions from the flat plain. Hsü Wei. SuSp

Colosseum. Harold Norse. TrJP

Colossians 3:3. George Herbert. ChIV-2

Colossus, The. Sylvia Plath. FaBoWP; HCAP; NALW; NOBA; NoAM; NoP-4; TAP; VCAP; WoPoe

Colour Bar. Oodgeroo of the tribe Noonuccal (Kath Walker). IBA

Colour of the Old Man's Eyes, The. Judy Gahagan. Prnts

Colour of the olives who shall say?, The. Tuscan Olives. Agnes Mary Frances Robinson. VWP

Coloured lanterns lit the trees, the grass, The. Arthur Symons. PeVV *Fr.* Scènes de la Vie de Bohème.

Coltish horseplay of the locker room, The. Feast of Stephen, The. Anthony Hecht. HAP; NoAM; VCAP

Coltrane and My Father. Ralph Sneeden. SeSe

Columba's Song. Edwin Morgan. HarvBoo

Columbia, all hail! Chicago Exposition Ode. Mary Weston Fordham. CBWP-2

Columbia, fairest nation of the world. Homes for All. Phoebe Cary. SWaP

Columbia's Agony. "Orpheus C. Kerr." OBAL

Columbia, Trust the Lord. *Unknown.* AH

Columbiad, The. Joel Barlow.
   "But now had Hesper from the Hero's sight." APN-1
   "From Mohawk's mouth, far westing with the sun." APN-1
   "From slavery then your rising realms to save." TCAPo
   "From sultry Mobile's gulf-indented shore." APN-1
   "He spoke; and silent tow'rd the northern sky." APN-1
   "My friends, I love your fame; I joy to raise." NCAP
   "Now graceful truce suspends the burning war." APN-1
   "Too much of Europe, here transplanted o'er." APN-1

Columbian poet, whom we've all respected. Letter to an American Visitor. Alex Comfort. FaBoWar; OxBTC

Columbine, The. Jones Very. ColAP; GSo; NOBA

Columbus. Joaquin Miller. APN-2; BRP

Columbus. Muriel Rukeyser. AF

Columbus. J. Slauerhoff. TuT, *tr. by* Desmond Egan

Columbus Day. Jimmie Durham. HATNAP; LTA

Columbus may have worked the wind. America Is Hard to See. Robert Frost. AiP; FaBoA

Columbus Reaches Juana, 1492. Ralph Gustafson. NOBC

Columbus to Ferdinand. Philip Freneau. OBCA

Column Intended for Buonaparte for a Triumphal Edifice in Milan, Now Lying by the Way-Side in the Simplon Pass, The. William Wordsworth. OxBSo *Fr.* Memorials of a Tour of the Continent; 1820.

Column of lemon sky lit one hill, A. Civil War, The. Suzanne Rhodenbaugh. CBCWP

Columns and Caryatids. Carolyn Kizer. WPE

Columns constructed from delirious dust. Lovely Stuff. Diane Ward. PmAP

Colville 1964. Kendrick Smithyman. PeNZ

Com all ye Nymphs and evrey Swaine. Off the Dutchesse. Elizabeth Taylor. EMWP

Com, Shuppere, Holy Gost, ofsech oure thoughtes. William Herebert. MiEL

Coma. Mimi Khalvati. Prnts

Comanche Ghost Dance: An Impression. Lance Henson. VoR

Comarnad it is a very bonny place. Richie Story. *Unknown.* ESPB

Comb and the Mirror, The. Elizabeth Spires. FFC

Combat, The. Edwin Muir. MoBrPo; NOBE

Combat, The. Thomas Stanley. AWP

Combat of Ferdia and Cúchulainn. *Unknown.* WoPoe, *tr. by* Thomas Kinsella *Fr.* Táin, The.

Combat raged not long, but ours the day, The. Burial of Latané, The. John Reuben Thompson. CBCWP

Combe, The. Edward Thomas. GTBS-P; RB

Combed thru the piers the wind. George Oppen. NNaP *Fr.* Some San Francisco Poems.

Combination II. Helmut Heissenbüttel. PFTM-2, *tr. by* Jerome Rothenberg

Combinations. Mary Ann Hoberman. OBSP *Fr.* Bugs.

Combines crossed the wheat field, The. Wheat. Diane Glancy. CRP

Combing. Gladys Cardiff. CDW; GifTon

Combing of my hair by grandma, The. Shower. Leah Aini. DTA, *tr. by* Linda Zisquit

Combing. The poem of the act of the mind. (LL) Of Modern Poetry. Wallace Stevens. ColAP; NAAL-2v2; NAAL-5; NoAM; OxBA; TAP

Combustion Engine. Katherine Pierpoint. MFPA

Come! (LL) Drum. Langston Hughes. APT-2; MoAmPo

Come a *brimmer* (my bullies) drink whole ones or nothing. Alexander Brome. PBRV *Fr.* Prisoners, The.

Come aa ye dottilt, brain-deid lunks. Cabaret McGonagall. W. N. Herbert. NeBl

Come again to the place. After the Visit. Thomas Hardy. NOBE

Come all gallant [*or you* gallant] seamen that unite a meeting. Death of Nelson, The. *Unknown.* OxBoLi

Come all ye jolly shepherds. When the Kye Comes Hame. James Hogg. OxBS

Come all ye Lewiston fac'try girls. Factory Girl's Come-All-Ye, The. *Unknown.* OBAL

Come, all ye men of England, and listen unto me. Verses. William Henry. PeSAV

Come All Ye Mourning Pilgrims. John A. Granade. AH

Come, All Ye People. George R. Seltzer. AH

Come all ye rounders, for I want you to hear. Casey Jones. T. Lawrence Seibert. GM; ITBLP

Come all ye wits, that with immortal rhymes. Invites Poets and Historians to Write in Cynthia's Praise. Philip Ayres. Son

Come, all you brave gallants, and listen a while. Robin Hood and the Butcher. *Unknown.* ESPB

Come all you gallant poachers, that ramble free from [*or void of*] care. Van Dieman's Land. *Unknown.* NOBAu; PeVV

Come all you jolly cowboys and listen to my song. Buffalo Skinners, The. *Unknown.* RB

Come all you Lachlan men, and a sorrowful tale I'll tell. Streets of Forbes, The. Jack McGuire. CBAP; NOBAu

Come all you rounders [*or muckers*] if you want [*or I want you*] to hear. Casey Jones. *Unknown.* OxBoLi; PeLV

Come all you sporty fellows. Stackalee. *Unknown.* APN-2

Come All You Tonguers. *Unknown.* PeNZ

Come all you very merry London girls that are disposed to travel. Maidens of London's Brave Adventures, Or, a Boon Voyage Intended for the Sea, The. Laurence Price. NOSC

Come all you young ladies and make no delay. *Unknown.* OxNR

Come all you young people who handle the gun. Shooting of His Dear. *Unknown.* OxBoLi

Come all young girls, both far and near, and listen unto me. Female Transport, The. *Unknown.* NOBAu

Come along in then, little girl! From a Very Little Sphinx. Edna St. Vincent Millay. OBAL; NOxBChV

Come along, 'tis the time, ten or more minutes past. Arthur Hugh Clough. OBCoV; OBSV *Fr.* Spectator ab Extra.

Come, And Be My Baby. Maya Angelou. OPOU

Come and let us live my Deare. Catullus. *See* Lesbia / live with me

Come and listen to the chiming. Bells of St. Michael. Mary Weston Fordham. CBWP-2

Come and see my shining palace built upon the sand! (LL) Second Fig. Edna St. Vincent Millay. APT-1; NALW; NoP-4

Come and see our French goods—you can try 'em. Limerick. *Unknown.* PeLi

Come at dawn, good friend. *Unknown.* BoWoP

Come at last to this point. Akiko Yosano. OHMPJ

Come Away, Come, Sweet Love. John Dowland. NAEL-5v1; NoSic

Come away! come, sweet love! To His Love. *Unknown.* NoP-4

Come Away, Death. William Shakespeare. *See* Twelfth Night

Come away, / Make no delay. Doomsday. George Herbert. GeHe

Come away to the skies. For His Wife, on Her Birthday. Charles Wesley. NOCV

Come away with me, Tom. Invitation, The. Charles Kingsley. NOBVV

Come Back, Alexander. Sati Kumar. OMIP, *tr. by* Manohar Bandopadhyay

Come Back Clean. Ella Wheeler Wilcox. VerBaPo

Come back early or never come. (LL) Autobiography. Louis MacNeice. ModLr; NOIV; NPeEn; PNI; RB

Come Back, Elvis, Come Back to Holyoke. Mary A. Koncel. ReTh

Come back Paul. (LL) *Unknown.* LB; OxNR

Come Back to Me. Burton Lane. ReLy

Come back to me! my life is young. Karazah to Karl. Adah Isaacs Menken. CBWP-1

Come back to me, O ye, my children. Mother's Recall. Mary Weston Fordham. CBWP-2

Come back to me, who wait and watch for you. Christina Georgina Rossetti. OxBSo *Fr.* Monna Innominata.

Come back to, this is your hand. (LL) You Begin. Margaret Atwood. NOBC; NoP-4

Come, balm of night, oh nightingale. Hans Jakob Christoffel von Grimmelshausen. GePo

Come, balmy sleep! tired Nature's soft resort! To Sleep. Charlotte Smith. CenSon; NAEL-6v2; RWP; Son; WPE

Come, be my camera. Documentary. Claribel Alegría. LoL; VCWP

Come, blessed ones, and sit on thrones. Michael Wigglesworth. NAAL-3 *Fr.* Day of Doom, The.

Come, blue-eyed maid of heaven!—but thou, alas! Byron. NOBRP *Fr.* Childe Harold's Pilgrimage.

Come, boy, bring us. Anacreon. SaLy, *tr. by* Diane Rayor

Come, Break with Time. Louise Bogan. MoAmPo

Come, bring with a noise. Robert Herrick. BeJo; OBCP

Come, brother, and tell me your life. Poem. Jorge Rebelo. PBMAP, *tr. by* Margaret Dickinson

Come, brother, come. Let's lift it. Cotton Song. Jean Toomer. APT-2; BPo

Come, brother, roll, roll! (LL) Cotton Song. Jean Toomer. APT-2; BPo

Come, brothers, everyone together. Mahendranāth Bhattācārya. SinGod, *tr. by* Rachel Fell McDermott

Come build in the empty house of the stare. (LL) W. B. Yeats. BIrV; GTBS-P; NOBE *Fr.* Meditations in Time of Civil War.

Come, butter, come. Mother Goose. OxNR

Come butter come! Butter Charm. *Unknown.* FaBoVe

Come carders an spinners an wavyers as weel. Factory Workers' Song. *Unknown.* FaBoVe

Come close or run away. Charlatan, The. Unsi Al-Haj [*or* Hajj]. PFTM-2, *tr. by* Pierre Joris

Come, come dear Night! Love's mart of kisses. Christopher Marlowe. NoSic *Fr.* Hero and Leander.

Come, come, for the rosebower has blossomed; come, come, for the beloved has arrived. Jelaluddin [*or* Jalal al-Din] Rumi. BBASP, *tr. by* A. J. Arberry

Come, come, my companion. *Unknown.* GePo *Fr.* Carmina Burana.

Come! Come! Though I call. Onitsura. NIL-7, *tr. by* Daniel C. Buchanan

Come, come, what doe I here? Henry Vaughan. ESCV

Come, cuddle your head on my shoulder, dear. Beautiful Land of Nod, The. Ella Wheeler Wilcox. PWR

Come dance a jig. Mother Goose. OxNR

Come Dance with Kitty Stobling. Patrick Kavanagh. HarvBoo; NPeEn; NoAM

Come, dark-eyed Sleep, thou child of Night. And on My Eyes Dark Sleep by Night. "Michael Field." LW; OBMV

Come darkest night, be[e]coming sorrow best. Mary Sidney Wroth, Countess of Montgomery. BASC; EMWP; NOSC *Fr.* Pamphilia to Amphilanthus.

Come, day, glad day, day running out of the night. Glad Day. Louis Untermeyer. TrJP

Come, dear children, let us away. Matthew Arnold. EBEV; FHYEP; FaBoCh; NAEL-5v2; NAEL-6v2; OBNV; OBSP

Come, Death, I'd have a word with thee. Motley. Walter De la Mare. PoWW

Come, divine lyre, speak to me. Sappho. SaLy, *tr. by* Diane Rayor

Come, don't let us be foolish. Sing, My Heart. Ted Koehler. ReLy

Come Dora, my darling, my angel, and help me to ask him to dine. (LL) Lord Walter's Wife. Elizabeth Barrett Browning. HAP; NPeEn

Come Down, Darkness. Muhammad Mahdi Al-Jawahiri. MAP, *tr. by* Christopher Middleton and Christopher Tingley

Come down from heaven to meet me when my breath. Invocation. Siegfried Sassoon. MoBrPo

Come down from the Cross, my soul, and save thyself. Descent from the Cross. "Michael Field." WPE

Come down, O Christ, and help me! reach thy hand. E Tenebris. Oscar Wilde. ChIV-2; MoBrPo; NAEL-5v2; NAEL-6v2; OxAEP-2; Son

Come down, O maid, from yonder mountain height. Tennyson. EBVV; GTBS-P; NAEL-5v2; NAEL-6v2; NOBVV; NPeEn; OBEV; OxBEV; SCGP *Fr.* Princess, The.

Come down to Kew in lilac-time (it isn't far from London!). (LL) Barrel-Organ, The. Alfred Noyes. BRP; MoBrPo; PoRA

Come down to you. (LL) To the Muse. James Wright (1927–80). NAAL-2v2; NNaP

Come dreadful child. Vampiro Nox. Marianne van Hirtum. SurWo, *tr. by* Guy Flandre and Peter Wood

Come, drunks and drug-takers; come, perverts unnerved! Several Voices Out of a Cloud. Louise Bogan. APT-2; NALW

Come each maiden lend an ear. Cheap Repository: The Story of Sinful Sally. Told by Herself. Hannah More. RWP

Come evening once again, season of peace. William Cowper. NAEL-6v1; NAEL-7v1 *Fr.* Task, The.

Come, Every Soul. John H. Stockton. AH

Come feed with me and be my love. Passionate Profiteer to His Love, The. "Sagittarius." OBCoV

Come! fill a fresh bumper, for why should we go. Ode for a Social Meeting. Oliver Wendell Holmes. OBAL

Come, fill the cup, and in the fire of spring. Omar Khayyám. TRP; UV, *tr. by* Edward Fitzgerald *Fr.* Rubáiyát of Omar Khayyám [*of* Naishápúr], The.

Come Fly with Me. Jimmy Van Heusen. ReLy

Come, follow me by the smell. Jonathan Swift. BIrV *Fr.* Verses Made for the Women Who Cry Apples, etc.

Come forth from thy oozy couch. Imitation of Julia A. Moore. "Mark Twain." OBAL

Come forth, old lion, from thy den. On Himself. Walter Savage Landor. FaBoEE

Come forth, you workers! Réveille. Lola Ridge. WPE

Come, friendly bombs, and fall on Slough. Slough. Sir John Betjeman. HarvBoo; MoBrPo; NoAM; OxAEP-2

Come, Friends and Neighbors, Come. Lewis Hartsough. AH

Come from China in a barrel of water, sell. Goldfish in the Charles River. Lewis Hyde. UrbNat

Come from the confines of the sunset world. Prudentius. MLL

Come from the woods with the citron-flowers. Bride of the Greek Isle, The. Felicia Dorothea Hemans. RWP

Come from Thy Palace. Thomas Randolph. OxBSP *Fr.* Conceited Pedlar, The.

Come, gaze with me upon this dome. E. E. Cummings. NoAM; OxBA

Come, gentle sleep, death's image though thou art. Thomas Warton, the Younger. OBVE

Come, gentlemen all, and listen a while. Robin Hood and the Bishop. *Unknown.* ESPB

Come gie's a sang, Montgomery cry'd. Tullochgorum. John Skinner. OxBS

Come girlies and fellas, as quick as you can. Mutton Bird Man. Rhyll McMaster. NOBAu

Come, give me kisses, Rhodope. Paulus [*or* Paulos] Silentiarius. ErotSp, *tr. by* Sam Hamill

Come give me needle stitchcloth silke and haire. Gentlewoman yt Married a Yonge Gent Who After Forsooke Whereuppon She Tooke Hir Needle in Which She Was Excelent and Worked upon Hir Sampler Thus, A. *Unknown.* EMWP

Come, Gobrys, there are other gods besides the Muses. Argentarius. GrAn

Come, Gorgo, put the rug in place. "Michael Field." VWP; ViWPN

Come, Happy Children. *Unknown.* AH

Come Harken unto Me. *Unknown.* AH

Come, heavy souls, oppressed that are. Casting All Your Care upon God, for He Careth for You. Thomas Washbourne. SacPr

Come here, closer, and fold. Remembering. Stephen J. Lyons. PasH

Come here, come here, you freely feed. Kemp Owyne. *Unknown.* ESPB

Come here, I want to show you something. Sightseeing. Rita Dove. GT

Come here, said my hostess, her face making room. Literary Dinner, A. Vladimir Vladimirovich Nabokov. OBAL; PeLV

Come here, said Turnbull, till you see the sadness. Switch. Sean O Riordain. ModIr, *tr. by* Patrick Crotty

Come here, thou proud pretender unto arts. There's Life in a Mussel; a Meditation. George Farewell. NOEC

Come hither my boy tell me what thou seest here. Lacedemonian Instruction. William Blake. WoPoe

Come hither to the hedge, and see. To the Muse. Jean Adams. ECWP

Come hither, womankind and all their worth. Kissing. Edward Herbert, 1st Baron Herbert of Cherbury. EnLoPo; NOSC

Come, hoist the sail, the fast let go! Pleasure Boat, The [*or* Pleasure-Boat, The]. Richard Henry Dana. APN-1

Come Holy Spirit, Dove Divine. Adoniram Judson. AH

Come, holy tortoise shell. Sappho. BoWoP

Come / Home. Shortest and Sweetest of Songs, The. George Macdonald. NOBVV

Come home, come home! and where an home hath he. Come Home, Come Home! Arthur Hugh Clough. HAP

Come Home, Father[!]. Henry Clay Work. APN-2

Come home with white gulls waving across gray. Winter Landscape. Stephen Spender. MoBrPo

Come, Hooker, come forth of thy native soile. Yee Shall Not Misse of a Few Lines in Remembrance of Thomas Hooker. Edward Johnson. SCAP

Come, human dogs, interfertilitate. Eugenist, The. Robert Graves. FaBoEE

Come Hymen come, for here to thee we bring. Luis de Góngora y Argote. SpanPo, *tr. by* Edward E. Wilson *Fr.* Solitudes, The.

Come, I will make the continent indissoluble. For You O Democracy. Walt Whitman. APN-1; CAGL; UV

Come In. Robert Frost. APT-1; MoAmPo; NOBA; NoP-4; RaBo; TRP

Come in at the low-silled window. Being Called For. Rosemary Dobson. BMAP; CBAP

Come in, Aunt Jemima. De Wintah Styles. Maggie Pogue Johnson. CBWP-4

Come in. I've just been dying for you. Song of Songs. Yelena [*or* Elena] Kryukova [*or* Kriukova]. TCRP, *tr. by* Albert C. Todd

Come in, Tom longtail, come short hose and round. *Unknown.* EBEV

Come inside the weather. By Hallucination Visited. Robert Horan. SPE

Come into Animal Presence. Denise Levertov. AmFaPo; HeIP-4

Come into dinner squalls the dame. Snaps for Dinner, Snaps for Breakfast, and Snaps for Supper. George Moses Horton. OBAL

Come into the Army, Maud. "Sagittarius." UV

Come into the Garden, Maud. Tennyson. EBVV; FHYEP; NOBE; NOBVV; OxAEP-2; OxBEV; PoE; UV; WoPoe *Fr.* Maud [A Monodrama].

Come into the orchard, Anne. Algernon Charles Swinburne. UV

Come into the Whenceness Which. Whenceness of the Which. *Unknown.* UV

Come is the ending day, Troy's hour is come. Virgil [*or* Vergil]. MLL *Fr.* Aeneid [*or* Eneados, *Aeneis*], The.

Come, Landlord, Fill the Flowing Bowl. *Unknown.* OxBoLi

Come lasses and lads, take leave of your dads. Rural Dance about the Maypole, The. *Unknown.* OxBoLi

Come leave the loathèd stage. Ode to Himself[e]. Ben Jonson. BeJo

Come, let me sound thy depths, unquiet sea. To My Own Heart. Maria Jane Jewsbury. VWP

Come, let's adore the King of Love. Love of Christ, The. John Austin. SacPr

Come, let's go / snow-viewing. Basho. ZenPo, *tr. by* Takashi Ikemoto and Lucien Stryk

Come, let's go climb on that jasmine-mantled rock. What Her Girlfriends Said to Her. Okkur Macatti. BoWoP, *tr. by* A. K. Ramanujan

Come, let's to bed. Mother Goose. LB; OxBoLi; OxNR

Come, Let's to Bed. *Unknown.* ReMoGo

Come, let us build a temple to oblivion. Tabernacle. D. H. Lawrence. ChIV-1

Come, let us dance and sing. Song. Anne Batten Cristall. RWP

Come, let us down. Ode: Hastening His Friend into the Country. Eldred Revett. NOSC

Come, let us join this festal lay. Rally Song. Mary Weston Fordham. CBWP-2

Come, let us now resolve at last. Reconcilement, The. John Sheffield, Duke of Buckingham and Normandy. OBEV

Come, let us tell the weeds in ditches. Last Hill in a Vista. Louise Bogan. FaBoWP

Come, Let Us Tune Our Loftiest Song. Robert A. West. AH

Come, let us walk. Spring in Virginia. Ramona Wilson. VoR

Come light and listen, you gentlemen all. Robin Hood and the Beggar, I. *Unknown.* ESPB

Come listen a while, you gentlemen all. Robin Hood Newly Revived. *Unknown.* ESPB

Come listen to me, you gallants so free. Robin Hood and Allen [*or* Allin] -a-Dale. *Unknown.* ESPB; OxAEP-1

Come, little babe. Cradle Song. Nicholas Breton. NOBE; OBEV

Come, little infant, love me now. Young Love. Andrew Marvell. OxAEP-1

Come, live with me and be my love. Cecil Day Lewis. BoLoP; NIP-4; OBMV *Fr.* Two Songs.

Come live with me and be my love. Bacchanal. Peter De Vries. NBLV; NOBL; OBAL

Come live with me and be my love. Further Proposal, A. Allen Ginsberg. NIL-7

Come, live with me and be my love. Samuel Hoffenstein. NBLV *Fr.* Invocation.

Come live with me and be my wife. Passionate Shepherd to His Love, The. Delmore Schwartz. SCGP

Come live with me[e] and be my Love. Passionate Shepherd To His Love, The. Christopher Marlowe. AWP; BoLoP; CTC; CiHu; GTBS-P; HAP; HeIP-4; ITBLP; InPK-6; MakPoe; NAEL-5v1; NAEL-6v1; NAEL-7v1; NBLV; NIL-7; NIP-4; NOBE; NoSic; OBEV; OxAEP-1; OxBEV; PAI; PoE; PoRA; RB; SCV; TFi; TRP; TTTS; WeW-3; WoPoe

Come live with me[e], and be[e] my love. Bait[e], The. John Donne. InPK-6; NAEL-5v1; NAEL-6v1; NAEL-7v1; NOSC; PoRA; RB

Come, love, hail the tombs. Rotating Tombs. Mikhail Naimy. GraLe, *tr. by* Sharif Elmusa and Gregory Orfalea

Come lovely and soothing Death. Walt Whitman. SCV *Fr.* Memories of President Lincoln.

Come, lowly ones, and take your places now. Marion Albina Bigelow. VerBaPo *Fr.* Children Disinterred.

Come, Madam, come, all rest my powers defy [*or* defie]. John Donne. BASC; BoLoP; FSCP; NAEL-6v1; NAEL-7v1; NoP-4; NoSic; PBRV; PoE *Fr.* Elegies.

Come, make an end of singing and of grieving. Come, Make an End. Alcuin. MLL, *tr. by* Helen Waddell

Come! Marget, come!—the team is at the gate! Country Lovers; or, Isaac and Marget Going to Town, on a Summer's Morning, The. George Smith. NOEC

Come May, the empire of the earth assume. To May. Jane West. CenSon

Come, memory, let us seek them there in the shadows. (LL) On the Death of

Friends in Childhood. Donald Justice. CoAmPo; ColAP; InPK-6; LCAP-2

Come, Muse, migrate from Greece and Ionia. Walt Whitman. MoAmPo *Fr.* Song of the Exposition.

Come, my Ardelia, to this bower. Retired Friendship, To Ardelia, A. Katherine Philips. BASC

Come, my beloved. Bible, *O.T.* WPoS *Fr.* Song of Solomon, The.

Come, my beloved. From the Garden. Anne Sexton. LW

Come, my brothers. Only Tourist in Havana Turns His Thoughts Homeward, The. Leonard Cohen. MoCV

Come my Celia, let us prove. Ben Jonson. BeJo; NPeEn; NoP-4; OxBEV, *Fr.* Volpone.

Come, my Corinna, come, let's go[e] a-Maying. (LL) Corinna's Going a-Maying. Robert Herrick. AEP; BASC; BeJo; CABP; CaPo; HAP; NAEL-5v1; NAEL-6v1; NAEL-7v1; NIP-4; NOBE; NOSC; NoP-4; OBEV; OxBEV; PBRV; PoE; PoPoPo; SCGP; TFi

Come (my dear) whilst youth conspires. Time Recover'd. Thomas Stanley. OBVE

Come, my Lucasia, since we see. Friendship's Mystery[s], to my dearest Lucasia. Katherine Philips. BASC; NAEL-7v1; PBRV; PEW

Come, my songs, let me express our baser passions. Ezra Pound. TwCP *Fr.* Lustra.

Come, mysterious night. Hymn to Night, A. Max Michelson. TrJP

Come, nationals in exile. Jihad. Thelma Seto. TWW

Come near come nearer. Out of the Depths I Cry unto You, O Death! Tawfiq [*or* Taufiq] Sayigh. MAP, *tr. by* Samuel Hazo and Anne Royal

Come, neighbour, take a walk with me. Hannah More. ECWP *Fr.* Gin-Shop, The; A Peep into Prison.

Come, neighbours, no longer be patient and quiet. Riot; or, Half a Loaf Is Better than No Bread, The. Hannah More. NOEC

Come Not Near My Songs. *Unknown.* AWP; WPE, *tr. by* Mary Austin

Come not the earliest petal here, but only. Quiet. Marjorie Lowry Christie Pickthall. NOBC; SacPr

Come Not the Seasons Here. Edwin John Pratt. NoP-4

Come not, when I am dead. Go By. Tennyson. PeVV

Come now, and let us wake them: time. Serenade. *Unknown.* AWP, *tr. by* Jethro Bithell

Come now, my friend, you must not say. "Ivan Venediktovich Elagin." TCRP

"Come now," said Bell, "this is choice." Limerick. Frank Richards. PeLi

Come now ye rural deities and show. Sir John, of Penicuik Clerk. OBGa *Fr.* Country Seat, The.

Come o'er the stream, Charlie. McLean's Welcome. James Hogg. OxBS

Come, O Friend, to Greet the Bride. Solomon Halevi Alkabez. TrJP, *tr. by* Heinrich Heine and Louis Untermeyer

Come, O Sabbath Day. Gustav Gottheil. AH

Come, O thou traveller unknown. Wrestling Jacob. Charles Wesley. NOBE; NOCV; NOEC; OBEV; OxAEP-1; PeECV; TOF

Come on along and listen to. Lullaby of Broadway. Harry Warren. ReLy

Come on, babe. And All That Jazz. John Kander. ReLy

Come on! Come on! This hillock hides the spire. Sunday Afternoon Service in St. Enodoc Church, Cornwall. Sir John Betjeman. NOCV

Come on, don't be afraid you'll spoil me. Serenade. Emanuel Carnevali. APT-2

Come On In, the Senility Is Fine. Ogden Nash. AiP

Come on, let threshing-floor and winepress stand! Autumn Call. Hans Leifhelm. AuPH, *tr. by* Lowell A. Bangerter

Come on, Mama, we'll slake the lime. Gennady Krasnikov. TCRP, *tr. by* Vladimir Lunis and Albert C. Todd

Come On, My Lucky Lads. Edmund Charles Blunden. PeFWW

Come on out, we are burning a fairy! (LL) Limerick: "Some Harvard men, stalwart and hairy." Edward Gorey. OBAL; OBCoV

Come on Percy, my pillion-proud, be. Cyril Connolly. OBCoV *Fr.* Where Engels Fears to Tread.

Come on, sir; he[e]re's the place: stand still. William Shakespeare. OxAEP-1; OxBEV *Fr.* King Lear.

Come on the wings of great desire. No Obligation. Victoria Mary Sackville-West. PoBW

Come on then, ye dwellers by nature in darkness. Aristophanes. AWP *Fr.* Birds, The.

Come on, ye critics! Find one fault who dare. On Mr. Edward Howard, upon His British Princes. Charles Sackville, 6th Earl of Dorset. OBSV

Come on, you . . . Do you want to live forever? (LL) Losers. Carl Sandburg. MoAmPo; NoAM

Come on, you too, whoo/do, we can do it. On the Removal of the Fascist American Right from Power. Etheridge Knight. BodElec

Come, Ophrah, fill my cup—but not with wine. Splendor of Thine Eyes, The. Moses Ibn Ezra. TrJP, *tr. by* Solomon Solis-Cohen

Come out come out come out. Moon Eclipse Exorcism. *Unknown*. STP; WoPoe, *tr.* by Armand Schwerner

Come out from the bath. (LL) Bath, The. Gary Snyder. NNaP; PmAP; TAP; VCAP

Come out, love—the night is enchanting! City Lyrics. Nathaniel Parker Willis. APN-1

Come out of Crete / and find me here. Horses in Flowers. Sappho. OBVE; WoPoe, *tr.* by Guy Davenport

Come out of your body among us & we're all one. How to Get Grizzly Spirit. *Unknown*. STP, *tr.* by James Koller

Come out to view. Basho. SoOfWa, *tr.* by Sam Hamill

Come Over and Help Us; a Rhapsody. John Wheelwright. APT-2

Come over here. Dance to the Amulets. U Tam'si Tchicaya. PBMAP

Come pass me the cup quickly and hand it on. Hafiz [*or* Hafez]. BBASP, *tr.* by R.M. Rehder

Come, passer-by, sit in this plane-tree's shade. Inscription on a Statue. Hermocreon. GrAn, *tr.* by Alistair Elliot

Come Peace, on snowy pinions. Ode to Peace. Mary Weston Fordham. CBWP-2

Come people; Aaron's drest [*or* dresst *or* dressed]. (LL) Aaron. George Herbert. BASC; ChIV-1; FSCP; GeHe; MeLP; NOSC; PeECV; SacPr

Come, Phoenix, come, if such a bird there be. On the Phoenix. Jean Adams. ECWP

Come pity [*or* pitie] us, all ye, who see. Widow's Tears [*or* Widdowes Teares]: or, Dirge of Dorcas, The. Robert Herrick. ChIV-2

Come play with me. To a Squirrel at Kyle-Na-No. W. B. Yeats. ChAP

Come play with me said the sun. Play. Frank Asch. NTCP

Come praise Colonus' horses and come praise. Sophocles. OBVE *Fr.* Oedipus at Colonus.

Come, Precious Soul. *Unknown*. AH

Come! Put by Pelops' Isle. Come! Put by Pelops' Isle. Alcaeus [*or* Alkaios]. WoPoe, *tr.* by Fred Beake

Come quick, come quick, come quick, come quick! (LL) Watch, The. Frances Darwin Cornford. InPK-6; MoBrPo; OxBTC

Come Rain or Come Shine. Johnny Mercer. ReLy

Come, Reason, come! each nerve rebellious bind. Invokes Reason. Mary Robinson. CenSon; RWP

Come right in this house, Will Johnson! Mrs. Johnson Objects. Clara Ann Thompson. BlSi; CBWP-2

Come saddle me my fastest steed. Geordie. *Unknown*. ESPB; OxBB

Come, said my soul. Walt Whitman. NOBA

Come, saints and sinners, hear me tell. Frederick Douglass. NAAL-2v1; NAAL-3; NAWM-7v2 *Fr.* Narrative of the Life of Frederick Douglass, an American Slave.

Come sapless blossom, creep not stil on earth. Sap, The. Henry Vaughan. ESCV

Come, see / real flowers. Basho. ZenPo, *tr.* by Takashi Ikemoto and Lucien Stryk

Come See the Place Where the Lord Lay. Richard Crashaw. ChIV-2

Come show thy Durham Breast. Emily Dickinson. NCAP

Come! show your jolly tricks, and be possessed. Francis Saltus Saltus. VerBaPo *Fr.* Masters, The.

Come sing with me in chorus: it's nothing, all we know. Antonio Machado Ruiz. STV

Come sit beneath my pine. On a Statue of Pan. *Unknown*. GrAn, *tr.* by W. G. Shepherd

Come sleep, come lightning, comes the dove at last. (LL) Usk, The. Charles Hubert Sisson. HarvBoo; NOCV

Come sleep, thou ease of sickness, want, and care. Of Sleep. Martha, Lady Giffard. EMWP

Come slowly—Eden! Emily Dickinson. FaBoVe; NALW; NCAP; TCAPo

Come, soft Eolian harp, while zephyr plays. To the Eolian Harp. Mary Robinson. CenSon; RWP

Come, sons of summer, by whose toil[e]. Hock-Cart, or Harvest Home, The. Robert Herrick. BASC; BeJo; CaPo; EBEV; NAEL-5v1; NAEL-6v1; NAEL-7v1; NOSC; OxAEP-1

Come soon, soon! (LL) To Night. Shelley. AWP; FHYEP; NAEL-5v2; NAEL-6v2; PoRA; TFi

Come, sound up your trumpets and beat up your drums. Young Earl of Essex's Victory over the Emperor of Germany, The. *Unknown*. ESPB

Come sounding thro' the town. (LL) Bonny Earl of Murray, The. *Unknown*. ESPB; NOSC; OBEV; OxBB; OxBS; SCGP

Come, sportive fancy, come with me and trace. Poet's Garret, The. Mary Robinson. RWP

Come, spread foam rubber on the floor. I Can't Have a Martini, Dear, but You Take One, or, Are You Going to Sit There Guzzling All Night? Ogden Nash. PoRA

Come spur[re] away. Ode to Master [*or* Mr.] Anthony Stafford to Hasten Him into the Country, An. Thomas Randolph. BASC; BeJo; NOBE; NOSC; OBEV

Come, stack arms, men! Pile on the rails. Stonewall Jackson's Way. John Williamson Palmer. CBCWP

Come, stir the fire. Safe. James Walker. OBCP

Come suddenly, O Lord, or slowly come. Take Ye Heed, Watch and Pray. Jones Very. ChIV-2

Come! supper is ready. Good Moolly Cow, The. Eliza Lee Cabot Follen. OBCA

Come, sweetheart mine. My Melancholy Baby. Ernie Burnett. ReLy

Come swiftly, soul. Call of the Soul, The. *Unknown*. WoPoe, *tr.* by Ronald Perry

Come take up your hats, and away let us haste. Butterfly's Ball [and the Grasshopper's Feast], The. William Roscoe. NOBRP; OxBEV

Come tawny bees. Diodorus Zonas. GrAn

Come tell me, was it all for nought. Borodino. Mikhail Yuryevich Lermontov. FaBoWar, *tr.* by Frances Darwin Cornford and Esther Polinowsky Salaman

Come the quick trumpet of the Judgement Day? (LL) Lament for a Leg. John Ormond. AngWePo; NoP-4; OBWVE

Come, the wind may never again. D.G.C. to J.A. Emily Jane Brontë. BrRo; EnLoPo

Come then, and like two doves with silvery [*or* silv'rie] wings. Apparition of His Mistress[e] Calling Him to Elizium [*or* Elysium], The. Robert Herrick. CaPo

Come, then, and mounted on the wings of Love. Thomas Carew. EroLit *Fr.* Rapture, A.

Come then, as ever, like the wind at morning! Invocation to Youth. Laurence Binyon. OBEV

Come then, my dear—although I warn you now. Between Aphorisms. Dorothy E. Reid. YaYoPo

Come then, my soule, approach this royall Burse. Francis Quarles. ESCV *Fr.* Emblems.

Come, Thou Almighty King. Charles Wesley. SacPr

Come, thou Fount of ev'ry blessing. Robert Robinson. SacPr

Come, thou monarch of the vine. William Shakespeare. NoSic *Fr.* Antony and Cleopatra.

Come thou, who art the wine and wit. His Winding-Sheet. Robert Herrick. BASC; CaPo; OBEV

Come Thunder. Christopher Okigbo. HBAPE

(Now that the triumphant march has entered the last street corners.) PBMAP; VCWP

Come tip a few with me. Alcaeus [*or* Alkaios]. WoPoe, *tr.* by Sam Hamill

Come to a sign. 4-Way Stop. Myra Cohn Livingston. KaS

Come to Agbarha. Where Everybody is King. Tanure Ojaide. NAfrP

Come to behold the death of the poor heart. (LL) Sonnet: To a Friend Who Does Not Pity His Love. Guido Cavalcanti. AWP; EaItPo, *tr.* by Dante Gabriel Rossetti

Come to Calvary's holy mountain. James Montgomery. SacPr

Come to guard us, come to bless us. Triple Benison, The. Henrietta Cordelia Ray. CBWP-3

Come to me. Tefillin. Yona Volach. DTA, *tr.* by Aryeh Cohen and Miriyam Glazer

Come to me, as you come. Kenneth Rexroth. APSN *Fr.* Love Poems of Marichiko, The.

Come to me, Eros, if you needs must come. To the God of Love. Edmund George Valpy Knox. NOBL

Come to me from Crete to this holy temple. Sappho. WPOW

Come to me from Krete to this holy. Sappho. SaLy, *tr.* by Diane Rayor

Come to me God; but do not come. To God. Robert Herrick. CavPo

Come to me in my dreams, and then. Longing. Matthew Arnold. SoSe-8

Come to me in the night—we shall sleep closely together [*or* Let us sleep entwined]. Love Song. Else Lasker-Schüler. BoWoP; TrJP

Come to me in the silence of the night. Echo. Christina Georgina Rossetti. BoLoP; EBVV; LW; NOBE; NoP-4; PEW; PoBW; PoE; VWP

Come to me, leaving the Peloponnesos. Alcaeus [*or* Alkaios]. SaLy, *tr.* by Diane Rayor

Come to me only with playthings now. Murmurings in a Field Hospital. Carl Sandburg. IllVoic

Come to me, Pan, with your wind-wild laughter. Song for a Forgotten Shrine to Pan. John Chipman Farrar. YaYoPo

Come to me quickly—Shadow of Darkness. (LL) Shadow of Darkness. Gladys May Casely Hayford. HAWP; PBA

Come to me when the swelling wind assails the wood with a sealike roar. Late Light. Edmund Charles Blunden. EnLoPo

Come to me with your triumphs and your woes. Beings of the Mind, The. Felicia Dorothea Hemans. RWP

Come to my window in the evening twilight. Sunset. Hayyim Nahman [*or* Khayim Nakhman *or* Chaim Nachman] Bialik. TrJP, *tr.* by Helena Frank

Come to Noah's for wine and strong waters. Limerick. *Unknown*. PeLi

Come to see the camellia. Camellia. Henriqueta Lisboa. TCLAP, *tr.* by Hélcio Veiga Costa

Come to Sunny Prestatyn. Sunny Prestatyn. Philip Larkin. NoAM; OBCoV

Come to term the started child shocks. Multipara: Gravida 5. Marie Ponsot. CLPP; VGW

Come to the Stone. Randall Jarrell. VGW

Come to the window. At Twilight. Hayyim Nahman [*or* Khayim Nakhman *or* Chaim Nachman] Bialik. FIT, *tr. by* Robert Friend

Come to the window! You're the painter used. Requiescam. Trumbull Stickney. ColAP

Come to these lonely woods to die alone? Dying Raven, The. Richard Henry Dana. APN-1

Come to weep out the night. (LL) To the Willow-Tree. Robert Herrick. CaPo; OBEV; SCGP

Come to your heaven, you [*or* yowe] heavenly choirs [*or* quires]. New Heaven, New War[re]. Robert Southwell. ChIV-2; ESCV; NOBE

Come too late to see. In the Room I. Jacqueline Brown. Prnts

Come towering, armed in adamant and gold. (LL) Thomas Warton, the Younger. NOEC; OxAEP-1 *Fr.* Pleasures of Melancholy, The.

Come, try this exercise. In the Dark. James Merrill. LCAP-2

Come, try your skill, kind gentlemen. Gipsy Girl, The. Ralph Hodgson. MoBrPo

Come unto Me, When Shadows Darkly Gather. Catharine H. Watterman. AH

Come unto these yellow sands. William Shakespeare. CTC; FaBoCh; NOBE; NOSC; NPeEn; NoSic; OBEV; SCGP; SoSe-8; TFi; TTTS *Fr.* Tempest, The.

Come up and see me sometime. Grace Nichols. EroLit *Fr.* Invitation.

Come up from the fields father, here's a letter from our Pete. Come Up from the Fields Father. Walt Whitman. APN-1; CBCWP; FaBoWar; HHAm; MoAmPo; OBWP; OxBA; SAmP; UnPo

Come Up, Methuselah. Cecil Day Lewis. OBMV

Come up, my horse, to Budleigh Fair. *Unknown.* OxNR

Come up to me at early dawn. Invitation. Solomon ibn Gabirol. TrJP, *tr. by* Israel Zangwill

Come up with me, American love. Pablo Neruda. PFTM-2, *tr. by* Nathaniel Tarn *Fr.* Heights of Macchu Picchu, The.

Come, virgin tapers of pure wax. Epithalamium. Richard Crashaw. NOCV

Come visit my pancake collection. Pancake Collector, The. Jack Prelutsky. OBCA; OxIBACP

Come, walk with me. Emily Jane Brontë. NOBVV

Come, warm your hands. Driftwood. Witter Bynner. APT-1

Come we shepheards whose blest Sight. Richard Crashaw. GeHe; NAEL-6v1; NAEL-7v1

Come, wed me, Lady Singleton. Lady "Rogue" Singleton. Stevie Smith. FaBoWP; OPOU; OxBSP

Come, weele associate this jolly Pilgrimage! [*or* jollie Pilgrimage!]. (LL) What Fair[e] Pomp[e]. Thomas Campion. NoSic; SCGP

Come, when no graver cares employ. Tennyson. GTBS-P; NOBVV; PeECV

Come when you're called. Good Advice. Mother Goose. OxNR; ReMoGo

Come, "Will," let's be good friends again. Sunshine after Cloud. Josephine D. Henderson Heard. CBWP-4

Come wisdome sweet, my spirit meet, for at thy feet I fall. Come Wisdome Sweet. Morgan Llwyd. AngWePo

Come with clean hands. *Unknown.* GrAn

Come with me. Parker's Mood. Clarence Beeks. NAAAL

Come with me and you may see. Christmas Rhyme, A. George Sands Johnson. PWR

Come with me into those things that have felt this despair for so long. Come with Me. Robert Bly. NOBA; NoAM

Come with our voices, let us war. Musical Strife; in a Pastoral Dialogue, The. Ben Jonson. BeJo

Come with rain, O loud Southwester! To the Thawing Wind. Robert Frost. OxBA

Come worthy Greek, Ulysses, come. Ulysses and the Siren [*or* Syren]. Samuel Daniel. HAP; NAEL-5v1; NAEL-6v1; NOBE; NoP-4; OBEV; OxAEP-1; PoE

Come ye hither all, whose taste. Invitation, The. George Herbert. ChIV-1; ESCV

Come, ye thankful people, come. Harvest Home. Henry Alford. SacPr

Come, ye thankful people, come. George J. Elvey. HHAm

Come, yellow broom. Glimpse, A. Robert Duncan. FTOS

Come you, ascend the ladder; all come in; all sit down. Invocation to the U' wannami. *Unknown.* APN-2, *tr. by* Matilda Coxe Stevenson

Come you, cartoonists. Halsted Street Car. Carl Sandburg. IllVoic; NAAL-2v2

Come you gallants all, to you I do call. Robin Hood's Chase. *Unknown.* ESPB

Comeahead then comeahead. Love Song of Tommo Frogley. Roger Crawford. UV

Comedian as the Letter C, The. Wallace Stevens. OxBA; TCAPo

Comedian, holding a chunk of flaming shale, The. Why That's Bob Hope. William Hathaway. ReTh

Comedy of Errors, The. William Shakespeare. "By the way we met." OBCoV

Comedy Tonight. Stephen Sondheim. ReLy

Comely young widow named Ransom, A. Limerick. *Unknown.* PeLi

Comes a brown. Corkby, Part Two. Jerome Rothenberg. NNaP

Comes a time. Poet in Old Age Fishing at Evening, The. Desmond O'Grady. CIP-2

Comes Death, and takes the table clean away. (LL) Comparison of the Life of Man, A. Richard Barnfield [*or* Barnefield]. NoSic; OxBSP

Comes down, white as an avalanche. Stroke. Arthur Ginsberg. BloBone

Comes easy as turning to look. Camping Clean. Reg Saner. PoCoUp

Comes home dumb with coal-dust deliberately. Her Husband. Ted Hughes. HarvBoo; OxBC

Comes like an idiot, babbling and strewing flowers. (LL) Spring. Edna St. Vincent Millay. APT-1; BoWoP; MoAmPo; NoP-4

Comes not the springtime here. Come Not the Seasons Here. Edwin John Pratt. NoP-4

Comes of his own accord to me. He That None Can Capture. May Swenson. LW

Comes out like a ribbon lies flat on the brush. (LL) Poem, or Beauty Hurts Mr. Vinal. E. E. Cummings. FaBoA; HarvBoo; MoAmPo; NAAL-2v2; NAAL-5; OBAL; OxBA; PFTM-1; PeLV; TRP

Comes the day, when he must die. Muspilli. *Unknown.* GePo, *tr. by* Carroll Hightower

Comes the deer to my singing. Hunting-Song. *Unknown.* AWP; PAI, *tr. by* Natalie Curtis

Comes the Gods to imitate! (LL) Grasshopper, The. Thomas Stanley. NOSC; OBVE

Comes the time when it's later. Wicker Basket, A. Robert Creeley. HAP; NoAM

Comes to Rest. Constantine P. Cavafy. CAGL, *tr. by* Edmund Keeley and Philip Sherrard

Comes to us from a distance. Music of the Altai Mountains. Kelvin Corcoran. Oth

Comet. Federico García Lorca. PFTM-1

Comet. Matthew Rohrer. NAPBL

Comet, The. Maria Luisa Spaziani. NeIt, *tr. by* Beverly Allen

Comet, The. János Vajda. IQMS, *tr. by* Watson Kirkconnell

Comet and Treefrog. Jarold Ramsey. PoCoUp

Comet Come. Norman Nicholson. NLP

Comets and Princes. Samuel Johnson. FaBoEE

Comets are like scythes, they do not hold. Now and Again: An Autobiography of Basket. Angie Estes. ExTi

Comfort. Elizabeth Barrett Browning. SacPr

Comfort. Maura Stanton. SoSe-8

Comfort in Puirtith. Helen B. Cruickshank. OxBS

Comfort-Maker. Jerry W., Jr. Ward. ISC

Comfort myself when that my hap is nought. (LL) Petrarch. AWP; HAP; NoSic; OxBSo, *tr. by* Henry Howard, Earl of Surrey *Fr.* Sonnets to Laura.

Comfort that does not comprehend. (LL) Return, The. Edna St. Vincent Millay. MoAmPo; NoAM; OxBA

Comfort to a Youth That Had Lost His Love. Robert Herrick. NOBE; OBEV

Comfort ye, comfort ye my people. Bible, *O.T.* OBVE; TrJP *Fr.* Isaiah.

Comfortably fixed for clothing and food, children married off. Half in the Family, Half Out. Po Chü-i. CoBCP, *tr. by* Burton Watson

Comforted by Limestone. Edward Dorn. NOBA *Fr.* Oxford.

Comforter, The. Thomas Moore. SacPr

Comic Adventures of Old Mother Hubbard and Her Dog, The. Sarah Catherine Martin. OxNR; ReMoGo

Comic Look at Damocles, A. Bill Knott. BodElec

Comical Revenge, The. Sir George Etherege. Song: "Ladies, though to your conquering eyes." OxBSP

Comin' thro' the Rye. Robert Burns. UV

Coming. Robert Kelly. PmAP

Coming. Philip Larkin. MoBrPo; OxBTC

Coming. Heather McHugh. EmeKit

Coming Across. Mehri. WPOW, *tr. by* Deirdre Lashgari

Coming Again to Heng-yang, I Mourn for Liu Tsung-yüan. Liu Yu Hsi. SuSp, *tr. by* Daniel Bryant

Coming, all is clear, no doubt about it. Hosshin. JDP, *tr. by* Yoel Hoffmann

Coming and Going. Robert Francis. TLR

Coming and Going. Mitchell Goodman. VGW

Coming and going like the dew. (LL) Body of Man, The. Van Hanh. EaWin; WoPoe, *tr. by* W. S. Merwin and Nguyen Ngoc Bich

Coming and going these several seasons. Abiku. John Pepper Clark Bekederemo. HBAPE; PBMAP

Coming around the corner of a dream. Cockaigne: A Dream. Louis Edward Sissman. DiPo

Coming around the corner of the dark trail . . . what was wrong with the. Inquisitors, The. Robinson Jeffers. MoAmPo

Coming at an end, the lovers. Book of Music, A. Jack Spicer. APSN; PoM

Coming at Night to a Fisherman's Hut. Chang Chi. BLT

Coming Back. Joseph Bruchac. CDW

Coming back. Buson. EH, *tr. by* Robert Hass

Coming Back Home. Ray A. Young Bear. CDW

Coming back one evening through deserted fields. Through All Your Abstract Reasoning. Brian Patten. FaBoTw

Coming back over the col between. Strength through Joy. Kenneth Rexroth. VGW

Coming back to the cave is when the hard part. Coming Back to the Cave. Rachel Wetzsteon. AmPoNex

Coming by evening through the wintry city. At a Bach Concert. Adrienne Rich. NIL-7; NIP-4; YaYoPo

Coming Down Cleveland Avenue. James Tate. YaYoPo

Coming Down from Derry Hill. Maggie Hannan. NLP

Coming down into an air brown as whiskey, the plane. Autobiography, Chapter XLII: Three Days in Louisville. Jim Barnes. HATNAP

Coming Downtown. Marilyn Hacker. PoBW

Coming from Kansas. Myra Cohn Livingston. NOxBChV

Coming from Montreal. Upstate. Simon J. Ortiz. LTA

Coming from the pool. Prey. Peter Makuck. UrbNat

Coming from the south. Six Ten Sixty-Nine. Conyus. GT

Coming from the woods. Haiku. Richard Wright. KaS

Coming, going, the waterbirds. On Non-dependence of Mind. Dogen. EnlH

Coming, going, the waterfowl. Dogen. ZenPo, *tr. by* Takashi Ikemoto and Lucien Stryk

Coming Home. D. F. Brown. CDa

Coming Home. Brian Turner. PeNZ

Coming Home, *Detroit*, 1968. Philip Levine. UrbNat

Coming home, I find you still in bed. Abortion. Ai. BoWoP

Coming Home in March. Harold Littlebird. VoR

Coming Home Late at Night. Tu Fu. BLT

Coming home late through the smoky. Coming Home. Brian Turner. PeNZ

Coming home with the last load I ride standing. Emergency Haying. Hayden Carruth. NNaP

Coming Homeward out of Spain. Barnabe Googe. NoSic
  (Commynge Home-warde out of Spayne.) NPeEn

Coming, I clench my hands. Dankyo-Myorin. ZenPo, *tr. by* Takashi Ikemoto and Lucien Stryk

Coming in again, you know the town by boards it makes eyes touch. Autobiography: Last Chapter. Jim Barnes. CDW

Coming in off the dock after writing. Station. Sharon Olds. PBCAP

Coming in to the store at first angry. Man Who Finds That His Son Has Become a Thief, The. Raymond Souster. NOBC

Coming into Their Own. Sheenagh Pugh. AngWePo

"Coming" is an empty word, "going" leaves no trace. Li Shang-yin. SuSp

Coming of Age. Michael Palma. UnSA

Coming of Age in the County Jail. Carter Revard. VoR

Coming of Archy, The. Don Marquis. TCAPo
  "Expression is the need of my soul." APT-1

Coming of Enkidu, The. *Unknown.* CAGL, *tr. by* N. K. Sandars *Fr.* Epic of Gilgamesh, The.

Coming of Good Luck, The. Robert Herrick. FaBoEE; NPeEn; OxBEV; OxBSP; Spl

Coming of Grendel, The. *Unknown.* OPOU, *tr. by* Gerald Benson *Fr.* Beowulf.

Coming of John, The. Amus Mor. SeSe

Coming of Light, The. Mark Strand. HCAP

Coming of Raka, The. N. P. van Wyk Louw. PeSAV, *tr. by* Guy Butler *Fr.* Raka.

Coming of Spring, The. Nora Perry. PWR

Coming of Spring, The. Henrietta Cordelia Ray. CBWP-3

Coming of Teddy Bears, The. Dennis Lee. TLR

Coming of that limpid star is twice, The. Sonnet 6. Louise Labé. BoWoP, *tr.* by Willis Barnstone

Coming of the Cold, The. Theodore Roethke. OBCP

Coming of the Plague, The. Weldon Kees. ChIV-1; VGW

Coming of the White Man, The. Patrick Anderson. MoCV *Fr.* Poem on Canada.

Coming of War, The; Actaeon. Ezra Pound. PoE

Coming of Wisdom with Time, The. W. B. Yeats. FaBoEE; HarvBoo; PAI; SoSe-8

Coming Off a Depression, She Prepares for Venice. A. V. Christie. NAPBL

Coming [*or* Comming] to kiss[e] her lips [*or* lyps], such grace I found. Edmund Spenser. EBEV; NAEL-5v1; NAEL-6v1; OxBSo; Son *Fr.* Amoretti.

Coming out. All right? Mama might worry. (LL) To My Brother Miguel. César Vallejo. PoetW; TCLAP, *tr. by* John Knoepfle and James Wright

Coming out of. Robert Duncan. SPE

Coming out of the mountains of a summer evening. St. Gervais. Michael Roberts. FaBoCh

Coming Out on Solid Ground After the Ice Age. Gary Paul Nabhan. PoCoUp

Coming Over Coldwater. Carol Muske. GeoHom

Coming Right Up. A. R. Ammons. OBCoV

Coming Storm, The. Herman Melville. APN-2

Coming Suddenly to the Sea. Louis Dudek. NOBC

Comin[g] thro' [*or* through] the Rye. Robert Burns. FaBoVe; OxAEP-2; OxBS

Coming through the rye. Rose Farmer, The. Herman Melville. APN-2

Coming to bed I come upon them lying. XX. Craig Arnold. NAPBL

Coming to cottonwoods, an. Prospecting. A. R. Ammons. CoAmPo

Coming to the farm that winter afternoon. Burragorang. Nan McDonald. NOBAu

Coming to the net. Brian G. Gilmore. SpirFl

Coming to This. Mark Strand. HCAP; VCAP

Coming to You. Daphne Marlatt. PoBW

Coming together. Recreation. Audre Lorde. NIL-7

Coming up England by a different line. I Remember, I Remember. Philip Larkin. HarvBoo; NOBL

Coming up the green lane from the sea. Tryst. John Hewitt. BiHa

Coming winter and a summoning / odour of balsam. (LL) Himalayan Balsam. Anne Stevenson. FaBoWP; OxAEP-2

Coming Woman, The. Mary Weston Fordham. CBWP-2; SWaP

Comings and Goings. Ann Townsend. NAPBL

Comings, goings, hard to settle down. Seeing Off Wang Yüan-chao—Reprise. Wu Wei-yeh. CoBLCP, *tr. by* Jonathan Chaves

Command, The. Avraham Huss. MHP, *tr. by* Ruth Finer Mintz

Commandeering the Wind. Su Shun-ch'in. SuSp, *tr. by* Irving Y. Lo

Commander Lowell. Robert Lowell. VGW

Commanding asker, if it be. Fair Beggar, The. Richard Lovelace. BeJo

Commanding pow'r, whose hand with plastic art. Statue of the Dying Gladiator, The. Felicia Dorothea Hemans. RWP

Commandments, The. Lamea Abbas Amara. PoArWo, *tr. by* Mike Maggio

Commemoration. Sir Henry John Newbolt. FaBoTw

Commemorative of a Naval Victory. Herman Melville. HAP; UnPo

Commencement. Constance Carrier. WPE

Commend thou me to each, as doth behove. (LL) Dante Alighieri. AWP; EaltPo, *tr. by* Dante Gabriel Rossetti *Fr.* La Vita Nuova.

Commendatory Sonnets. Edmund Spenser.
  To the Right Worshipfull, My Singular Good Frend, Master Gabriell Harvey, Doctor of the Lawes. NoSic

Commendatory Verses to Edmund Spenser's Fairy Queen. Sir Walter Ralegh.
  (Methought I Saw the Grave Where Laura Lay.) NAEL-6v1; NAEL-7v1
  (Vision upon the Fairy Queen, A.) NoP-4
  Vision upon This Concei[p]t of the Faerie [*or* Faery] Queen[e], A. NAEL-5v1; NoSic; SCGP; Son

Comment. Dorothy Parker. NBLV; NIP-4; OBAL; OBCoV *Fr.* Some Beautiful Letters.

Comment on an Observation by One of My Masters. John Hollander. SpudSo

Comment on Curb. Langston Hughes. APSN; APT-2 *Fr.* Lenox Avenue Mural.

Comment on My Host, A. Mark Solomon. OPRER

Commentary. Hyam Plutzik. TaR

Commentary Applied to Spiritual Things. Saint John of the Cross. TOF, *tr. by* K. Kavanaugh and O. Rodrigues

Commentary Text Commentary Text Commentary Text. David Shapiro. PmAP

Commerce and the Man. Ricardo M. de Ungria. ReBoTo

Commercial Leech Farming Today. Thomas Lux. BodElec

Commercials exaggerate. James McManus. IllVoic *Fr.* Who Needs Two.

Commination, A. Alec Derwent Hope. ChIV-2

Commingling sky, A. Freely Espousing. James Schuyler. FTOS; NeAP; NoP-4

Commiserating with the Poor. Li K'ai-hsien. CoBLCP, *tr. by* Jonathan Chaves

Commission. Ezra Pound. BoLoP; TwCP

Commissioner bet me a pony, The—I won. Songs of the Squatters. Robert Lowe, Viscount Sherbrooke. NOBAu

Commissioners believe that everything, The. Ordnance Survey in the Northern Counties. Mick North. NLP

Commit—flirtation with the muse of Moore. (LL) Byron. OxBoLi; PeLV *Fr.* Don Juan.

Commit thou all thy griefs and ways into his hands. Commit thy way unto the Lord. Paul Gerhardt. SacPr

Committee's fat, The. Un-American Investigators. Langston Hughes. BPo; HHAm

Common, The. Gail Mazur. UrbNat

Common Cormorant [*or* Shag], The. Christopher Isherwood. FaBoCh; NBLV; NOxBChV

Common Dust. Georgia Douglas Johnson. TTY

Common Fate of Books, The. Margaret Lucas Cavendish, Duchess of Newcastle. PBRV

Common feelings. Living. Jaime Torres Bodet. TCLAP, *tr. by* Sonja Karsen

Common Form. Rudyard Kipling. FaBoEE; FaBoTw; HarvBoo; NPeEn; PeFWW; WoPoe *Fr.* Epitaphs of the War [1914–1918].

Common Grave, The. James Dickey. CoAP

Common Ground, A. Denise Levertov. PoM

Common Lover's Song, The. Flavien Ranaivo. *See* Love Song: "Do not love me, my friend."

Common Man, The. Arthur James Marshall Smith. NOBC

Common man I might have been, The. In Brief. Angel Cuadra. AF, *tr. by* Katherine Rodriguez Nieto

Common miracle. Miracle Mart. Wislawa Szymborska. PoSu, *tr. by* Adam Czerniawski

Common Occurrence, A. Priscilla Jane Thompson. CBWP-2

Common Path, The. Glyn Jones. AngWePo

Common People, The. Rowland Watkyns. AngWePo; BASC

Common people are very weary, The. *Unknown.* ColAnChi, *tr. by* Jeffrey Riegel *Fr.* Classic of Odes.

Common Road, The. Silas H. Perkins. ITBLP

Common Sacrifice to Honour fall, A. (LL) Homer. NPeEn; OBVE, *tr. by* Sir John Denham *Fr.* Iliad, The.

Common Sense. Alan Brownjohn. NOxBChV *Fr.* Pitman's Common Sense Arithmetic, 1917.

Common speech is, spend and God will send, The. Magnum Vectigal Parsimonia. George Gascoigne. NoSic

Common tasks are beautiful if we. Common Tasks, The. Grace Noll Crowell. PoToHe

Common Things. Paul Laurence Dunbar. GT

Common Woman, The. Judy Grahn.
  Carol, in the Park, Chewing on Straws. WPOW
  Ella, in a Square Apron, Along Highway 80. NALW
  "She holds things together, collects bail." NALW

Commonplace, The. Walt Whitman. MoAmPo

Commonplace Day, A. Thomas Hardy. NOBVV

Commonwealth, Common Poverty. Gloria Vando. TouFir

Communal Krakovyak. Vladimir Druk. TCRP, *tr. by* Albert C. Todd

Communal Living. Alice Jones. BloBone

Commune above her in a drift of wings. (LL) Assumption. Padraic Fallon. BIrV; NOIV

Commune for Me, The. Viktor Fiodorovich Bokov. TCRP, *tr. by* Bernard Meares

Communication in Whi-te. Haki R. Madhubuti. BPo

Communication of His Thirtieth Birthday. Marvin Bell. CoAP

Communication to the City Fathers of Boston. George Starbuck. YaYoPo

Communion. Sarah Maguire. MFPA

Communion. P. M. Snider. PoToHe

Communion II. U Tam'si Tchicaya. NegPo, *tr. by* Ellen Conroy Kennedy

Communion of Saints: The Poor Bastard under the Bridge. Marie Ponsot. VGW

Communiqués from Yalta, The. R. P. Blackmur. APT-2

Communism. Ella Wheeler Wilcox. SWaP

Community. Sally Roberts Jones. AngWePo

Commuted Sentence, The. Stevie Smith. OxAEP-2

Commuter. Lisel Mueller. GM

Commuter. Elwyn Brooks White. HHAm; NBLV

Commuters. Betsy Hearne. SSCS

Commynge Home-warde out of Spayne. Barnabe Googe. *See* Coming Homeward out of Spain

Como lo Siento. Lorna Dee Cervantes. NoAM

Companion, The. Mary Low. SurWo

Companion, The. Edwin Arlington Robinson. NoAM

Companions. Charles Stuart Calverley. NOBL; PeLV

Companions of my favourite hours. Sappho Burns Her Books and Cultivates the Culinary Arts. Elizabeth Moody. ECWP

Companion's Progress, A. Paul Laurence Dunbar. GT

Company, The. Robert Creeley. FTOS

Company had advertised for men to unload a steamer across the river, The. Charles Reznikoff. ColAP *Fr.* Testimony.

Company in Loneliness. *Unknown.* NOIV

Company of mountains, an upthrust of mountains, A. Kinloch Ainort. Sorley MacLean (Somhairle MacGill-Eain). HarvBoo

Comparatives. *Unknown.* OxNR

Compare your body to a room. Five Weeks. Lee Ranaldo. HeMarv

Compared with loss of thee will not seem so. (LL) William Shakespeare. AWP; EBEV; NOBE; NoSic; OBEV; OxAEP-1 *Fr.* Sonnets.

Comparison, A. William Cowper. OxBSP

Comparison, A. John Chipman Farrar. WHSW

Comparison, A. Ágnes Nemes Nagy. IQMS, *tr. by* Alan Dixon

Comparison, The. Thomas Carew. BeJo

Comparison, The. John Donne. BASC; PeLV *Fr.* Elegies.

Comparison, The. *Unknown.*
  "Let dirty streets be paved with flow'ry green." NOEC

Comparison betwixt a Whore and a Booke, A. John Taylor.
  "Me thinks I heare some Cavillers object." PBRV

Comparison of Hands One Day Late Summer El Sobrante. Wendy Rose. HATNAP

Comparison of the Life of Man, A. Richard Barnfield [*or* Barnefield]. NoSic; OxBSP

Comparisons will be made. To the Writers' Worship in Zomba. Felix Mnthali. PeSAV

Compass. Elizabeth Alexander. NAPBL

Compass. Jorge Luis Borges. PoetW, *tr. by* Richard Wilbur

Compass of the Dying. Laurence Lieberman. IllVoic

Compassion for the Farmers. Li K'ai-hsien. CoBLCP, *tr. by* Jonathan Chaves

Compassion's Bird. Jay Wright. ESEAA

Compassionate Fool, The. Norman Cameron. GTBS-P; OxBSP; OxBTC; RB

Compelling a recognition. (LL) Paring the Apple. Charles Tomlinson. OxBTC; PoE; TRP

Compensation. E. M. Brainard. PoToHe

Compensation. Paul Laurence Dunbar. APN-2; BPo

Compensation. Ralph Waldo Emerson. APN-1; NOBA; TAP

Compensation. Harry Graham. PeLV *Fr.* Some Ruthless Rhymes.

Compensation. Robinson Jeffers. MoAmPo

Compensation. Henrietta Cordelia Ray. CBWP-3

Competition. Stephen Dunn. MoASP

Competitive product you said you'd send, The. (LL) Consumer's Report, A. Peter Porter. EmeKit; NOBL

Complacencies of the Fenced Yard. William Tester. Unle

Complacencies of the peignoir, and late. Sunday Morning. Wallace Stevens. APT-1; BBASP; ColAP; HAP; HCAP; HarvBoo; HeIP-4; MoAmPo; NAAL-2v2; NAAL-5; NAWM-7v2; NIL-7; NIP-4; NOBA; NoAM; NoP-4; OxBA; PoE; PoPoPo; SAmP; SoSe-8; TAP; TCAPo; TFi; TRP

Complacent old Don of Divinity, A. Limerick. *Unknown.* PeLi

Complacent they tell us, hard hearts and derisive. Woman's Future. May Kendall. VWP; ViWPN

Complacent Tortoise, The. Brian Patten. OBSP

Complaining. George Herbert. ChIV-1

Complaining about the Second Wife. *Vietnamese Oral Tradition.* CaDao, *tr. by* John Balaban

Complaint. William Carlos Williams. SAmP

Complaint. James Wright (1927–80). NOBA; TAP; VGW

Complaint, A. William Wordsworth. NOBE

Complaint, The. Mark Akenside. OBEV

Complaint, The. Thomas Hoccleve [*or* Occleve].
  Hoccleve Remembers His Madness. NPeEn

Complaint by Night, A. Henry Howard, Earl of Surrey. AEP; AWP; EBEV; OBVE; SCGP; Son
  (Alas! so all thing[e]s now[e] do[e] hold[e] their peace.) NAEL-5v1; NAEL-6v1; NAEL-7v1; NPeEn; NoSic; OxBEV

Complaint for a Sorcerer. Susy Hare. SurWo

Complaint for Mary and Marcel, A. Kay Boyle.
  Complaint for M and M, A. SurPaPo

Complaint from a Lady's Chamber. Wang Ch'ang-ling. ChinPo, *tr. by* Yip Wai-lim

Complaint Near the Jade Stairs. Hsieh T'iao. CrYelRi, *tr. by* Sam Hamill

Complaint Near the Jade Steps. Li Po. *See* Resentment Near the Jade Steps

Complaint of a Lover, The. Anne Killigrew. BASC

Complaint of a Lover Rebuked. Petrarch. HeIP-4; NAEL-5v1; OBVE, *tr. by* Henry Howard, Earl of Surrey *Fr.* Sonnets to Laura.

Complaint of Chaucer to His Empty Purse, The. Geoffrey Chaucer. MiEL; NAEL-5v1; NoP-4; SCGP
  (To you, my purs, and to noon other wight.) NAEL-6v1; NAEL-7v1; NoP-4

Complaint of Rosamond, The. Samuel Daniel.
  Lonely Beauty. CTC

Complaint of Thames 1647 When the Best of Kings Was Imprisoned by the Worst of Rebels at Holmbie, The. Hester Lee Pulter. EMWP

Complaint of the Absence of Her Lover Being upon the Sea. Henry Howard, Earl of Surrey. *See* Seafarer, The

Complaint of the Black Knight, The. John Lydgate.

"And by a river forth I gan costey." OBGa

Complaint of the Fair Armoress [*or* Armouress], The. François Villon. AWP; CTC; OBVE, *tr. by* Algernon Charles Swinburne

Complaint of the Morpethshire Farmer, The. Basil Bunting. CTC

Complaint of Troilus, The. Geoffrey Chaucer. NOBE; OBEV *Fr.* Troilus and Criseyde [*or* Criseide].

Complaint on the Oblivion of the Dead. Jules Laforgue. WoPoe, *tr. by* William Jay Smith

Complaint to a Court Poet. Rashidi Samarqandi. ArPe, *tr. by* Omar S. Pound

Complaint: To the Muse. Philip Whalen. BB

Complaint unto Pity, The. Geoffrey Chaucer. MiEL

Complaints of Poverty, The. Nicholas James.

"May poverty, without offence, approach." NOEC

Complaisant Swain, The. Ovid. AWP, *tr. by* F. A. Wright *Fr.* Amores.

Complaynt of the Comoun weill of Scotland, The. Sir David Lindsay [*or* Lyndsay]. PBRV *Fr.* Dreme, The.

Complements. Like figures in statuary. Sun and Moon. Mary Kinzie. FFC

Complete Birth of the Cool, The. C. D. Wright. LCAP-2

Complete Cynic, The. Keith Preston. NBLV

Complete Destruction. William Carlos Williams. SAmP

Complete earth, A. Avocado Pit, The. Carl Rakosi. APT-2

Complete in Thee, No Work of Mine. Aaron R. Wolfe. AH

Complete Semen Study. Michael Ryan. BodElec

Complete Sound-Poems of Hugo Ball, The. Hugo Ball. PFTM-1

Complete Thought I - XXV. Barrett Watten. PFTM-2

Complete with photomatic *stimmung*. Our Lady. John Godfrey. PmAP

Complete with Starry Night and Bourbon Shots. Albert Goldbarth. BAP-97

Completely. (LL) Apollo and Marsyas. Zbigniew Herbert. PoSu; WoPoe, *tr. by* Czeslaw Milosz and Peter Dale Scott

Completely round is the perfect pearl. Ballad of the Shape of Things, The. Sheldon Harnick. ReLy

Compleynt, compleynt I hearde upon a day. Ezra Pound. HarvBoo *Fr.* Cantos.

Compleynt of the Comoun Weill of Scotland, The. Sir David Lindsay [*or* Lyndsay]. OxBS *Fr.* Dreme, The.

Complicated Shadows. Stephen Corey. PasH

Components. Roger McDonald. CBAP

Compose compose beds. Sacred. Gertrude Stein. OBAL

Composed after a Journey across the Hamilton Hills, Yorkshire. William Wordsworth. CenSon

Composed as I am, like others. Elements of Composition. A. K. Ramanujan. VCWP

Composed at Neidpath Castle, the Property of Lord Queensberry, 1803. William Wordsworth. GTBS-P

Composed at Sunset at the Dunes of Ho-yen. Ts'en Shen. SuSp, *tr. by* Ronald C. Miao

Composed at the Request of a Lady, and Descriptive of Her Feelings. Maria Gowen Brooks. APN-1

Composed at the West Wall of Tsou-p'ing Three Days After the Festival of Pure Brightness. Wang Shih-chieng. ColAnChi, *tr. by* Richard John Lynn

Composed at thirty, my funeral oration: Here lies. Funeral Oration, A. David Wright. PeSAV

Composed by nature, time, human art. Reminder, The. Denise Levertov. PoCoUp

Composed by the Sea-Side, near Calais, August, 1802. William Wordsworth. CenSon; Son

Composed During a Walk on the Downs, in November 1787. Charlotte Smith. OxBSo

Composed in One of the Valleys of Westmoreland, on Easter Sunday. William Wordsworth. ChIV-2

Composed in the Composing Room. Franklin Pierce Adams. NIL-7; NIP-4; OBAL

Composed in the Tower before his execution. 'More Light! More Light!' Anthony Hecht. AF; CoAP; CoAmPo; EmeKit; HAP; HP; NOBA; NoAM; NoP-4; OBWP; RB; TaR; TwCP; UnPo; VCAP; VGW

Composed Near the Bay Bridge (after a wild party). Marilyn Chin. ExTi

Composed on Horseback, Returning from Lakeview Pavilion at Hangchow, Presented to Yü-ju and Lo-tao. Wang An-shih. SuSp, *tr. by* Jan W. Walls

Composed on the Theme "Willows by the Riverside." Yü Hsüan-chi. SuSp; WPOW, *tr. by* Jan W. Walls

Composed upon Westminster Bridge, September 3, 1802. William Wordsworth. AWP; CABP; CenSon; ChAP; ClHu; FaBoCh; GSo; GTBS-P; HAP; HeIP-4; ITBLP; InPK-6; MakPoe; NAEL-5v2; NAEL-6v2; NAWM-7v2; NOBRP; NPeEn; NoP-4; OPOU; OxBEV; OxBSo; PoE; PoPoPo; SCGP; Son; TFi; UnPo

Composed While under Arrest. Mikhail Yuryevich Lermontov. AWP, *tr. by* Max Eastman

Composing. "Anvari." WoPoe, *tr. by* Dick Davis

Composing mortals with immortal fire. (LL) W. H. Auden. FaBoTw; TwCP *Fr.* Anthem for St. Cecilia's Day.

Composition. Peter Blue Cloud. VoR

Composition. Hugh Seidman. BodElec

Composition in Retrospect. John Cage.

"You can't be serIous she said." APT-2

Composition of the Chalcans, A. *Unknown.* PFTM-1 *Fr.* Cantares Mexicanos.

Compositions in harmony. Big Bluejay Composition. Ron Padgett. PmAP

Compost. James Grainger. NOEC *Fr.* Sugar Cane, The.

Compromise. Akhtar-ul-Iman. OMIP; WoPoe, *tr. by* Vinay Dharwadker and C. M. Naim

Compromise, The. Ibn al-Rumi. ArPe, *tr. by* Omar S. Pound

Compromised by sorrow. Elegy for Chief Sealth. Duane Niatum. CDW

Computation, The. John Donne. NoSic; OxBSP; SoSe-8

Computer Aided Design: Creation. Jackie Hardy. NeBl

Computer's First Christmas Card, The. Edwin Morgan. NOxBChV; OxBEV

Comrade. Philippe Soupault. PFTM-1

Comrade Jesus. Sarah Norcliffe Cleghorn. APT-1

Comrade Stalin. Yuz [*or* Iosif Efimovich] Aleshkovsky. TCRP, *tr. by* Sarah W. Bliumis

Comrades, leave me here a little, while as yet 't is early morn. Granny's House. Phoebe Cary. APN-2

Comrades, leave me here a little, while as yet 'tis early morn. Tennyson. EBEV; NAEL-5v2; NAEL-6v2

Comrades Marathon, The. Chris Mann. PeSAV

Comrades, the morning breaks, the sun is up. Hafiz [*or* Hafez]. AWP *Fr.* Odes.

Comus; a Masque Presented at Ludlow Castle. John Milton. FHYEP

"By the rushy-fringèd bank." OxBEV

Chastity ("I Mean That Too, But Yet a Hidden Strength"). NOSC

(Comus Speaks.) NOBE

Echo. OBEV

Farewell of the Attendant Spirit. OBEV; OxAEP-1

(Lady Sings, The.) NOBE

(Comus' Summons.) NOSC

Mask, A. OxAEP-1

Sabrina Fair. EBEV; FaBoCh; NOBE; OBEV; OxAEP-1; OxBEV; WoPoe

Song: "By the rushy-fringèd bank.". OxBEV

(Spirit Epiloguizes, The.) NOBE

(Spirit's Epilogue, The.) NOSC

Star That Bids the Shepherd Fold, The. FaBoCh; NPeEn; OBEV

Comus's Song. Ben Jonson. OBCoV *Fr.* Pleasure Reconciled to Virtue.

Con Los Pájaros. Juan Delgado. AmPoNex

Conceit. Mervyn Laurence Peake. Spl

Conceit Begotten by the Eyes. Sir Walter Ralegh. NoSic

Conceited Pedlar, The. Thomas Randolph.

Come from Thy Palace. OxBSP

Conceived on a mattress of human hair. Innocence. Wislawa Szymborska. PoSu, *tr. by* Jan Darowski

Concentration Camp Blues. Henry Dumas. SeSe

Concentration Constellation. Lawson Fusao Inada. GeoHom

Concentric. Richard Kostelanetz. TAP

Concept like "I," which I am told by many, A. I Brood about Some Concepts, for Example. Alicia Ostriker. PBCAP

Conception. Joseph Ceravolo. FTOS

Conception. Waring Cuney. APT-2

Conception. Josephine Miles. ColAP; FaBoWP

Conception, an Archbishop said, The. Limerick. "L. E. J." PeLi

Conception is interesting: to see, as though reflected, The. Wet Casements. John Ashbery. NAAL-2v2; PoM

Concerning a Girl. Shuntaro Tanikawa. VCWP, *tr. by* Harold Wright

Concerning a nun, composer and herbalist. Short History of Illumination, A. Matthew Rohrer. AmPoNex

Concerning Death. Sister Mary Madeleva.

I Ask My Teachers. CRP

Concerning Dragons. H. D. C. Pepler. NOxBChV

Concerning Hebrews. Herman Melville. APN-2 *Fr.* Clarel: A Poem and Pilgrimage in the Holy Land.

Concerning Himself. Paul Fleming. GePo, *tr. by* George C. Schoolfield

Concerning My Neighbors, the Hittites. Charles Simic. VCAP

Concerning One Responsible Negro with Too Much Power. Nikki Giovanni. BPo

Concerning Paradise. Christopher Buckley. GeoHom

Concerning that exploit of yours. (LL) That Exploit of Yours. Ford Madox Ford. PeFWW; PoWW

Concerning the Afterlife, the Indians of Central California Had Only the Dimmest Notions. Robert Hass. LoL

Concerning the Awakening of My Soul. Henriëtte Roland-Holst. WPOW, *tr. by* Jonathan Crewe

Concerning the bees and the flowers. Limerick. *Unknown.* PeLi

Concerning the Fruit-bringing Autumn Season. Catharina Regina von Greiffenberg. GePo, *tr. by* George C. Schoolfield

Concerning the Infanticide, Marie Farrar. Bertolt Brecht. WoPoe, *tr. by* Hoffman Reynolds Hays

Concerning the Islands Newly Discovered. Joy Katz. NeAmPo

Concerning the Joyous and Splendid Resurrection of Christ. Catharina Regina von Greiffenberg. AuPH, *tr. by* Lowell A. Bangerter and George C. Schoolfield

Concerning the King of Sweden. Georg Rudolph Weckherlin. GePo, *tr. by* George C. Schoolfield

Concerning the Wolffsbrunnen near Heidelberg. Martin Opitz. GePo, *tr. by* George C. Schoolfield

Concerning your letter in which you ask. With Mercy for the Greedy. Anne Sexton. HCAP; NIL-7; TOF; VCAP

Concert. Josephine Miles. NALW

Concert. Robert Sward. VGW

Concert, The. Lisel Mueller. MiVo

Concert, The. *Unknown.* PeSAV, *tr. by* Stephen Gray

Concert Choir. Beth McGrath. MiVo

Concert conductor in Rio, A. Limerick. *Unknown.* PeLi

Concert-hall was crowded the night of the Crash, The. Paper Anniversary. Muriel Rukeyser. NoAM

Concert in the Old School Garret. *Unknown, fr. Terezin Concentration Camp.* INSAB

Concert Party: Busseboom. Edmund Charles Blunden. FaBoWar

Concert's what the English like, A. Concert, The. *Unknown.* PeSAV, *tr. by* Stephen Gray

Conchie, The. R. F. Palmer. FaBoWar

Conchita debemos to speak totalmente in English. Doña Josefina Counsels Doña Concepción Before Entering Sears. Maurice Kilwein Guevara. AmPoNex

Concierge at the front gate where relatives, The. Aeterna Poetae Memoria. Archibald MacLeish. Son

Conciousness. Ágnes Nemes Nagy. IQMS, *tr. by* Doreen Bell

Concise History of the Vietnam War: 1965–1968, A. Ron Weber. CDa

Concluding Aria. Gertrude Stein. PFTM-2 *Fr.* Mother of Us All, The.

Conclusion. Geoffrey Chaucer. WoPoe, *tr. by* Burton Raffel and Selden Rodman *Fr.* Troilus and Criseyde [*or* Criseide].

Conclusion. Ovid. CTC; OBVE, *tr. by* Arthur Golding *Fr.* Metamorphoses.

Conclusion. Shelley. NPeEn *Fr.* Sensitive Plant, The.

Conclusion, The. Dryden. BASC *Fr.* Religio Laici.

Conclusion, The. Sir Walter Ralegh. *See* Even Such Is Time

Conclusion: "But here no cannon thunders to the gale." William Wordsworth. CenSon *Fr.* River Duddon [A Series of Sonnets], The.

Conclusion: "Did you love well what very soon you left?" Marilyn Hacker. NoAM *Fr.* Coda.

Conclusion I reach at the Tate, The. Limerick. "Tallis." PeLi

Conclusion: "Image dance of change, An." Siegfried Sassoon. MoBrPo

Conclusion: "In one of those excursions (may they ne'er)." William Wordsworth. NAEL-6v2 *Fr.* Prelude, The; Growth of a Poet's Mind [1850 vers.].

Conclusion Is Not Drawn, The. Nicole Espagnol. SurWo, *tr. by* Myrna Bell Rochester

Conclusion of a Letter to the Rev. Mr. C——, The. Mary Barber. CABP; ECWP

Conclusion of the Matter, The. Christopher Smart. ChIV-1 *Fr.* Hymns for the Amusement of Children.

Concord Hymn. Ralph Waldo Emerson. AWP; AiP; BRP; ClHu; ColAP; FaBoA; HAP; HeIP-4; NOBA; NoP-4; OBWP; OxBA; PeECV; PoPoPo; TAP; TCAPo; TFi

(Hymn[:] Sung at the Completion of the Concord Monument, April 19, 1836.) APN-1; NAAL-2v1; NAAL-3

Concordat Proviso Ascendant. Christopher Dewdney.

"She is liquid darkness occult with desire." FTOS

Concrete Cat. Dorthi Charles. InPK-6

(EAr eAr stripestripestripestripe.) KaS

Concubine, The. *Vietnamese Oral Tradition.* CaDao, *tr. by* John Balaban

Condemn'd by Fate to way-ward Curse. Sot-Weed Factor, The. Ebenezer Cook. TCAPo

Condemned. Philippe Soupault. AF, *tr. by* Eden Paul

Condemned Man, The. George Crabbe. NPeEn *Fr.* Borough, The.

Condemned [*or* Condemn'd] to hope's delusive mine. On the Death of Dr [*or* Mr] Robert Levet [a Practiser in Physic]. Samuel Johnson. ChIV-2;

EBEV; NAEL-5v1; NAEL-6v1; NAEL-7v1; NOBE; NOEC; NPeEn; NoP-4; OBEV; OxAEP-1; OxBEV; PeECV; PoE; SCGP; SCV; TFi

Condemned Site. Mona Van Duyn. MakPoe

Condemning the Moongod Nanna. Enhedȗanna. BoWoP

Condition Blue/ Dress. Ron Welburn. NBV

Condition: hydroplane. Moon. Giovanni Raboni. ItPo, *tr. by* Gayle Ridinger

Conditions. Essex Hemphill.

XXII ("If there were seven blind men."). NAAAL

Conditions. Essex Hemphill.

XXIV ("In america."). NAAAL

Condo. Louise Glück. BodElec

CONDOLENCES . . . from our swollen lips laden with condolences. Elegy for Slit-Drum. Christopher Okigbo. HBAPE

Condom Tree, The. Chase Twichell. EmeKit

Conduct your blooming in the noise and whip of the whirlwind. (LL) Second Sermon on the Warpland, The. Gwendolyn Brooks. BPo; NOBA

Conductor, The. Dezső Kosztolányi. IQMS, *tr. by* Leslie A. Kery

Conductor's hands were black with money, The. Charon. Louis MacNeice. FaBoTw; OxBEV; PNI

Confabulation. John A. Stone. BloBone

Confederacy. Elise Paschen. FFC

Confederate Flags, The. Ambrose Bierce. CBCWP

Confederate Memorial Day. *Unknown.* CBCWP

Confederate Veteran Tries to Explain the Event, A. Robert Penn Warren. CBCWP

Conference, A. Renée Weiss. BodElec

Conference among ourselves we called, A. George Gascoigne. OBWP *Fr.* Fruits of War, The.

Conference of the Birds, The. Farid-uddin Attar. TOF, *tr. by* Afkham Darb and Dick Davis

"World's birds gathered for their conference, The." WoPoe, *tr. by* Afkham Darbandi and Dick Davis

Conferences, adjournments, ultimatums. Louis MacNeice. OxBTC *Fr.* Autumn Journal.

Confess We All, before the Lord. John Wilson. AH

Confessio Amantis. John Gower.

Pygmaleon. NPeEn; OxBEV

Rape of Lucrece, The. NPeEn, *tr. by* John Gower

Confessio Fidei. Dryden. NOBE *Fr.* Hind and the Panther, The.

Confession. Frank Gelett Burgess. *See* Cinq Ans Après

Confession. Pearl Cleage. ISC

Confession. Paul Gallico. TriCat

Confession. Susan Hahn. IllVoic

Confession. George Herbert. ESCV

Confession. Alice Lee. ReEnLa

Confession. George Oppen. HarvBoo

Confession, A. Jenő Dsida. IQMS, *tr. by* George Gömöri and Clive Wilmer

Confession, A. *Poets of the Tixall Circle.* EMWP

Confession, The. The "Archpoet."

"Never yet could I endure." EroLit, *tr. by* Helen Waddell

Confession of Cleopas, The. Eric Pankey. GI

Confession of Faith. Elinor Wylie. APT-1; MoAmPo

Confession of Gluttony. William Langland. NAEL-6v1; NAEL-7v1 *Fr.* Vision of Piers Plowman, The.

Confession of the Highway / The Hermit Speaks. Garrett Kaoru Hongo. GeoHom *Fr.* Cruising 99.

Confession Stone, The. Owen Dodson. TTY

Confession to J. Edgar Hoover. James Wright (1927–80). CoAmPo

Confession to Malcolm. Conyus. NBV

Confessional. Frank Bidart. GLP

Confessional. Tom Breidenbach. KGB

Confessional, The. Frederick William Faber. CenSon

Confessional, The. Nathaniel Parker Willis. APN-1

Confessional Poem. Louis Jenkins. RaBo

Confessional Poetry. Tony Harrison. DiPo

Confessions. Robert Browning. GTBS-P; NOBE; NOBVV

Confessions. Iman Mirsal. NAfrP, *tr. by* Clarissa C. Burt

Confessions from the Last Cloud. Jose Angel Figueroa. PueRic

Confide In a Friend. *Unknown.* PoToHe

Configurations. Grace Nichols. LW

Confined Love. John Donne. BASC

Confinement. Ann Sansom. NeBl

Confirmation, A. William Daniel Ehrhart. CDa

Confirmation, The. Edwin Muir. OxBS

Confirmation, The. Karl Shapiro. APT-2

Confirmers, The. A. R. Ammons. TAP

Confiscating Salt. Wang An-shih. CoBCP; ColAnChi, *tr. by* Burton Watson

Conflation of rapture and regret, The.　Asylum of Gestures.　Carl Hancock Rux.　HeMarv

Conflict, The.　Cecil Day Lewis.　MoBrPo; NoP-4

Conflict of Convictions, The.　Herman Melville.　APN-2; CBCWP; NOBA

Confluence.　John Knoepfle.　IllVoic

Confluences at San Francisco.　Elton Glaser.　PBCAP

Confluent water mirror red clouds.　Viewing the Three Lakes.　Hsieh T'iao.　ChinPo, tr. by Yip Wai-lim

Confounding deities, not men. (LL)　Nebuchadnezzar's Kingdom-Come.　David Rowbotham.　ChIV-1; NOBAu

Confront the darkness in another place. (LL)　Woods, The.　Derek Mahon.　NOIV; PBCIP

Confrontation with a Bouquet.　Maggie Bevan.　Prnts

Confrontation with an Artist.　Elisabeth Eybers.　PeSAV

Confronting a longing.　Poem to My Death.　Julia de Burgos.　BoWoP; TCLAP, tr. by Grace Schulman

Confronting each other the pictures stare.　Royal Portraits, The.　William Dean Howells.　APN-2

Confronting the solitude.　Song to Be Written on a Wave.　José Emilio Pacheco.　STV, tr. by John Frederick Nims

Confronting the wind, late autumn trees.　Drunk, Facing Crimson Leaves.　Po Chü-i.　CoBCP, tr. by Burton Watson

Confronting us again! (LL)　Emily Dickinson.　SacPr; TAP

Confucian scholars love strange antiquity.　Drinking Wine.　Lin Hung.　SuSp, tr. by Irving Y. Lo

Confucianist is versed in the Six Arts, The.　Juan Chi.　ColAnChi　Fr. Songs of My Soul.

Confused leaves fall, fluttering fragrant steps.　Tune: "Walk on the Imperial Street."　Fan Chung-yen.　ChinPo, tr. by Yip Wai-lim

Confused with my life, that is commonplace and solitary. (LL)　Next Day.　Randall Jarrell.　AmFaPo; HAP; HCAP; HarvBoo; NAAL-2v2; NoAM; NoP-4; VCAP; WeW-3

Confusion.　Christopher Hervey.　UV

Confusion of song. On the radio.　Clouded Evening, Late September.　Sydney Lea.　RA

Conga.　Leonard Bernstein.　ReLy

Conga.　Allen Fisher.　PFTM-2

Congealed vapors surge in vast space.　Seeing Off Editor Wang Chou-tz'u and Secretary Lin Shih-lai on Their Mission as Envoys to the Ryūkyū Islands.　Wang Shih-chieng.　CoBLCP, tr. by Jonathan Chaves

Congo, The.　Nicholas Vachel Lindsay.　APT-1; MoAmPo; NOBA; OxBA; PoRA; TAP

'Congo is myself' (Lumumba), The.　U Tam'si Tchicaya.　PBMAP　Fr. Le Ventre (1964).

Congratulatory Poem to Her Sacred Majesty Queen Mary, Upon Her Arrival in England, A.　Aphra Behn.　EMWP

Congregation was scandalised, The.　Robert Sat.　Tom Matthews.　PNI

Congress of the Insomniacs, The.　Charles Simic.　EmeKit

Congressmen Came Out to See Bull Run, The.　Stephen Vincent Benét.　CBCWP　Fr. John Brown's Body.

Congruence of the complement is vain, if it exists, The. (LL)　To a Steam Roller.　Marianne Craig Moore.　APT-1; BoWoP; FaBoMo; MoAmPo; OxBA; VGW

Coniagui Women.　Audre Lorde.　NAAL-2v2; NALW

Conies had their hiding-place, The.　He "Had Not Where to Lay His Head."　Frances Ellen Watkins Harper.　PWR

Conifer King, The.　Michael Bugeja.　UrbNat

Conjectural Poem.　Jorge Luis Borges.　TCLAP, tr. by Norman Thomas Di Giovanni

Conjecture. (LL)　Moon Is the Number 18, The.　Charles Olson.　APT-2; HarvBoo; PFTM-2; PoE

Conjergal Rights.　Thomas Edward Brown.　PeVV　Fr. In the Coach.

Conjugal.　Russell Edson.　PmAP

Conjugal Visits.　Al Young.　NAAAL

Conjunction.　Semyon [or Semion] Izrailevich Lipkin.　TCRP, tr. by Albert C. Todd

Conjunction of Jupiter and Venus, The.　William Cullen Bryant.　APN-1

Conjunctions.　Eamon Grennan.　PBCIP

Conjure with me: three letters.　Richard Skinner.　NewEx

Conjured.　Sterling Allen Brown.　NoP-4

Conjurer, The.　Maura Stanton.　YaYoPo

Conjurer. And of himself of God. (LL)　Witch Doctor.　Robert Earl Hayden.　NoAM; PAI

Conjuring Against Alien Spirits.　Quincy Troupe.　ISC

Conjuring Roethke.　James Tate.　OBAL

Connary, Blodgett, Day, Hapgood.　Paul Goodman.　BodElec

Connecticut.　Fitz-Greene Halleck.

Connecticut Road Song.　Anna Hempstead Branch.　TCAPo

Connecting Light.　Susan Michie.　Prnts

Connection in Bridgend.　John Tripp.　TCAWP

Connoisseur of Jews, The.　Jerome Rothenberg.　TaR

Connoisseur of pearl, A.　African China.　Melvin B. Tolson.　ColAP

Connoisseurs of coition aver.　Limerick.　Unknown.　PeLi

Connoisseuse of Slugs, The.　Sharon Olds.　LW

Connor is four and every day brings a clutch.　Connor in the Wind and Rain with His Coat on.　Paula McLain.　AmPoNex

Connuche.　Catron Grieves.　ReEnLa

Conquer the gloomy night of thy sorrow.　Defiance.　Solomon ibn Gabirol.　TrJP, tr. by Emma Lazarus

Conqueror Worm, The.　Edgar Allan Poe.　APN-1; AWP; NCAP; NOBA; TCAPo

Conquerors.　Henry Treece.　OBWVE; TCAWP

Conquest.　Pauli Murray.　GT

Conquest, The.　Oliver St. John Gogarty.　OBMV

Conquest of Granada, The.　Dryden.
"'Tis war again, and I am glad 'tis so."　FaBoWar

Conquest [or His Lady's Might].　Philippe Desportes.　AWP; NoSic

Conquistador.　Archibald MacLeish.
Prologue: "And the way goes on in the worn earth."　NoAM

Conrad in Twilight.　John Crowe Ransom.　FuPo; OxBA　Fr. Sixteen Poems in Eight Pairings.

Consanguinity of sound, The. (LL)　Matthew Green.　ECEV; NOEC　Fr. Spleen, The.

Conscience.　George Herbert.　ESCV

Conscience.　Victor Hugo.　SxFrPo, tr. by E. H. Blackmore and A. M. Blackmore

Conscientious Objector.　Edna St. Vincent Millay.　FaBoWar; WPOW

Conscientious Objector, The.　Karl Shapiro.　OxBA

Conscious.　Wilfred Owen.　PoWW

Conscript Goes, The.　William Sydney Graham.　FaBoWar

Consecration, A.　John Masefield.　MoBrPo

Consejos y Documentos al Rey Dom Pedro.　Santob de Carrion.
Jewish Poet Counsels a King, A.　TrJP

Consent.　Carol Frost.　OPRER

Consents to his inexorable will. (LL)　Playboy.　Richard Wilbur.　NOBA; NoAM

Consequences.　William Meredith.
My Acts.　VCAP
Of Choice.　VCAP
Of Love.　VCAP

Conservatory Pond, Central Park, New York, New York.　Joel Brouwer.　AmPoNex

Conserving the Magnitude of Uselessness.　A. R. Ammons.　NoAM

Consider.　W. H. Auden.　FaBoMo; OxAEP-2

Consider a coral or guano atoll.　Manichean Geography I.　Tom Paulin.　PNI

Consider a new habit—classical.　Arras.　Patricia K. Page.　MoCV

Consider abroad, how closely it brushes.　Foreign.　Kate Clanchy.　MFPA

Consider Famous Men, Dai Bach.　Idris Davies.　OBWVE

Consider for a moment how the body of a dancer.　Female Dancer.　James Camp.　Son

Consider his song.　Brian Coffey.　ModIr　Fr. For What For Whom Unwanted.

Consider honestly.　Jeepney.　Gemino H. Abad.　ReBoTo

Consider Icarus, pasting those sticky wings on.　To a Friend Whose Work Has Come to Triumph.　Anne Sexton.　InPK-6

Consider Kyffin, now—as Welsh.　Consider Kyffin.　Raymond Garlick.　TCAWP

Consider, my soul, this texture.　Two Meditations.　Rosario Castellanos.　PFTM-2, tr. by Julian Pulley

Consider, O my soul, what morn is this!　Meditation for Christmas, A.　Selwyn Image.　OBEV

Consider Phlebas, who was once handsome and tall as you. (LL)　T. S. Eliot.　NPeEn; OBVE; OxBEV　Fr. Waste Land, The.

Consider, praise, remember all of these.　All of These.　Denis Glover.　PeNZ

Consider, scholar, when you enter here.　Thoughts in the Library.　Mihály Vörösmarty.　IQMS, tr. by Hymen H. Hart

Consider the case of the many-minded men.　Friday Evening.　Sean Lucy.　CIP-2

Consider the egg. It's a miracle.　Eggomania.　Felicia Lamport.　NBLV

Consider the Emperor Nero.　Limerick.　Unknown.　PeLi

Consider the infinite fragility of an infant's skull.　Arguments.　Lisa Suhair Majaj.　PoArWo

Consider the Lillies of the Sea.　Anne Porter.　APT-2

Consider the lowering Lynx.　Limerick.　Langford Reed.　PeLi

Consider the sea's insatiate lust.　Island, The.　Brendan Kennelly.　PBCIP

Consider the sea's listless chime.　Dante Gabriel Rossetti.　NAEL-5v2; NAEL-6v2　Fr. House of Life, The.

Consider the significance.　Wire.　Rod Moran.　NOBAu

Consider the three functions of the tongue. Canzone. Marilyn Hacker. NoAM

Consider them, my soul, they are a fright! Blind, The. Charles Baudelaire. SxFrPo, *tr. by* James McGowan

Consider this and in our time. Consider. W. H. Auden. FaBoMo; OxAEP-2

Consider Well. Sir Thomas More. SacPr

Considerable Speck, A. Robert Frost. MoAmPo; OBAL; SAmP

Considerate Crocodile, The. Amos Russel Wells. OBCA; OxIBACP

Considerations. David Helwig. NOBC

Consideratus Considerandus. John Saffin. SCAP

Considered Reply to a Child, A. Jonathan Price. BoLoP

Considering How Exaggerated Music Is. Leslie Scalapino. FTOS

Considering Poverty and Homelessness. Robert Sund. GifTon

Considering the graveness. State of Seige. Teresa Calderón. TANSG, *tr. by* Celeste Kostopulos-Cooperman

Considering the Snail. Thom Gunn. NAEL-5v2; NAEL-6v2; OxBEV; TwCP

Considering Tulips. Mieke Tillema. TuT, *tr. by* Medbh McGuckian

Consistent disciples of Marx. Limerick. A. Cinna. PeLi

Consolation. Tanure Ojaide. EmeKit

Consolation. David Rivard. SwNoth

Consolation. Henry Howard, Earl of Surrey. *See* When Raging Love

Consolation. Dimitris Tsaloumas. BMAP

Consolation. W. B. Yeats. OxBSP

Consolation, A. William Shakespeare. *See* Sonnets

Consolation, The. Edward Young. NOEC *Fr.* Night Thoughts.

Consolation Aria. Johann Christian Günther. GePo, *tr. by* George C. Schoolfield

Consolation of Philosophy, The ("De Consolacione Philosophie"). Boethius.
"Alas, the ignorance of unhappy men." MLL *tr. by* Helen Waddell
"All human kind on earth." NoSic *tr. by* Queen of England Elizabeth I
"Happy he whose eyes have view'd." OBVE *tr. by* Samuel Johnson
"Happy, too happy was the world." MLL *tr. by* Helen Waddell
Happy Too Much. CTC, *tr. by* Queen of England Elizabeth I
"He that hath set his headlong heart." MLL *tr. by* Helen Waddell
"He who has made his reckoning with life." MLL *tr. by* Helen Waddell
"Heu Quam Praecipih Mersa Profundo" ("Alas, his mind is sunk") MLL, *tr. by* Helen Waddell
Heu Quam Precipiti ("'Allas,' sche seide, 'how that this manis mynde'"). OBMV, *tr. by* John Walton
"Hither, O captives, hither let you come." MLL *tr. by* Helen Waddell
Huc omnes pariter ("Now cometh alle ye that ben ibroght"). OBMV, *tr. by* John Walton
Lib. 2. Metrum 5 ("Happy that first white age! when wee"). NOSC; OBVE; PAI, *tr. by* Henry Vaughan
New Year's Eve ("Here, if the road shall bring thee back"). MLL, *tr. by* Helen Waddell
"O Father, give the spirit power to climb." MLL *tr. by* Helen Waddell
"O Maker of the starry world." MLL *tr. by* Helen Waddell
"O thou whose pow'r o'er moving worlds presides." OBVE *tr. by* Samuel Johnson
"O Thou whose reason guides the universe." MLL *tr. by* Helen Waddell
"Songs I wrote when I was young and ardent, The." MLL *tr. by* Helen Waddell
"Stars hidden by dark clouds." MLL *tr. by* Helen Waddell
"Then night was shaken from me." MLL *tr. by* Helen Waddell
"There is no race of men." MLL *tr. by* Helen Waddell
"This bird was happy once in the high trees." MLL *tr. by* Helen Waddell
"This concord tempers then the elements." MLL *tr. by* Helen Waddell
"Though countless as the Grains of Sand." OBVE *tr. by* Samuel Johnson
"What pleasure in such vehement commotion." MLL *tr. by* Helen Waddell
"Who thought in high midsummer." MLL *tr. by* Helen Waddell

Consolation to Empty Pitchers. K. S. Narasimhaswami. OMIP, *tr. by* A. K. Ramanujan

Consolations Before an Affair, Upper West Side. Noelle Kocot. BAP-01

Consolations of Art. Roy Fuller. OxBC

Consolations of Philosophy. Derek Mahon. BIrV; CIP-2; HarvBoo

Consolatory Poem Dedicated unto Mr. Cotton Mather, A. Nicholas Noyes. SCAP

Consoling the Yü Farmers. Fan Ch'eng-ta. SuSp, *tr. by* Wu-Chi Liu

Consoling Wu Te-cheng on the Death of His Son. Shen Chou. CoBLCP, *tr. by* Jonathan Chaves

Consorting with Angels. Anne Sexton. NALW

Conspiracy. Jack Spicer. APSN

Conspiracy, The. Robert Hill Long. OPRER

Constable Calls, A. Seamus Heaney. EmeKit; NOIV *Fr.* Singing School.

Constable's Clouds for Keats. Stanley Plumly. BodElec

Constance Hately. Edgar Lee Masters. APT-1 *Fr.* Spoon River Anthology.

Constancy. "Michael Field." VWP; ViWPN

Constancy. Elsa Gidlow. PoBW

Constancy. John Wilmot, 2d Earl of Rochester. OBEV

Constancy Rewarded. Coventry Patmore. NOBVV; OxBSP *Fr.* Angel in the House, The.

Constancy to an Ideal Object. Samuel Taylor Coleridge. NAEL-5v2; NAEL-6v2; NOBRP

Constancy[e]. Sidney Godolphin. BeJo; NOSC

Constant, The. A. R. Ammons. HAP; WeW-3

Constant Bride, The. Mary Jo Bang. NAPBL

Constant Cannibal Maiden, The. Wallace Irwin. OBAL

Constant keeping-past of shaken trees. Dante Gabriel Rossetti. NPeEn; PeVV *Fr.* Trip to Paris and Belgium, A.

Constant Labor, A. James W. Thompson. BPo

Constant Lover, A [*or* The]. Sir John Suckling. BASC; BeJo; CavPo; NAEL-6v1; NAEL-7v1; NBLV; NOSC; NPeEn; NoP-4; OxAEP-1; OxBEV; PBRV; PeLV; PoE *Fr.* Poem with the Answer, A.

Constant Memories. Patrick Sylvain. InTrad

Constant North, The. J. F. Hendry. OxBS

Constant Penelope sends to thee, careless Ulysses. Constant Penelope Sends to Thee. *Unknown*. EnLoPo; NAEL-5v1; NAEL-6v1; NPeEn; NoSic,

Constant welcome floors me, The. Constant Welcome, The. Siobhan Campbell. MFPA

Constantinople. Amin Al-Rihani. GraLe

Constantinople. Mihály Csokonai Vitéz. IQMS, *tr. by* Kenneth White

Constantinople (New Rome). *Unknown*. GrAn, *tr. by* Peter Jay

Constantly near you, I never in my entire. Horse Show, The. William Carlos Williams. NOBA; TAP; VGW

Constantly present and lovely. (LL) Bibi Hayati. EnlH; WPoS

Constantly Risking Absurdity. Lawrence Ferlinghetti. NeAP; PmAP; PoM; TAP

Constellation Frigidaire, The. Kim Roberts.
Darkness Was Upon the Face of the Deep. AmPoNex
Tilt, The. AmPoNex

Constellation like day; the horizon behind it by lights, A. Nocturnal Landscape. Anton Schnack. PeFWW, *tr. by* Christopher Middleton

Constellation of Dead Brothers. Victor Serge. AF, *tr. by* James Brook

Constellation Quilt, The. Mei-Mei Berssenbrugge. OpBo

Constellations, The. William Cullen Bryant. APN-1

Constellations of beauty. (LL) Ahmad al-Mushari Al-'Udwani. BBASP; MAP, *tr. by* Charles Doria and Hilary Kilpatrick *Fr.* Signs.

Constipation. Breyten Breytenbach. PoetW, *tr. by* A. J. Coetzee

Construction of the Museum. Michael Palmer. BodElec

Consultation. Jayne Cortez. SurWo

Consulting summer's clock. Emily Dickinson. SAmP

Consulting the omens. Kamalākānta Bhattācārya. SinGod, *tr. by* Rachel Fell McDermott

Consumer's Report, A. Peter Porter. EmeKit; NOBL
(Name of the product I tested is *Life*, The.) NoP-4

Consumptive, The. Priscilla Jane Thompson. CBWP-2

Consumptive man, The. Richard Wright. APT-2

Contact. Alison Chisholm. Prnts

Container, The. Cid Corman. VGW

Contemns its Power. Mary Robinson. CenSon

Contemns Philosophy. Mary Robinson. CenSon; RWP

Contemplate all this work of Time. Tennyson. EBVV; NAEL-6v2; NAWM-7v2 *Fr.* In Memoriam A. H. H.

Contemplating hell, as I once heard it. Contemplating Hell. Bertolt Brecht. WoPoe, *tr. by* Robert Firmage

Contemplating the sky. Tranquil Night. Luís De León. SpanPo, *tr. by* Edwin Morgan

Contemplation. John Frederick Nims. InPK-6

Contemplation of the Heavens. PeNZ

Contemplation on Bassets Down-Hill by the Most Sacred Adorer of the Muses Mrs. A. K., A. Anne Kemp. EMWP

Contemplation upon Flowers, A. Henry King, Bishop of Chichester. MeLP; OBEV; SCGP

Contemplations. Anne Bradstreet. ColAP; NAAL-3; NAAL-5; SCAP; TCAPo; WPE
"O Time the fatal wrack of mortal things." ColAP; WPOW
"Mariner that on smooth waves doth glide, The." WPOW
"Shall I then praise the heavens, the trees, the earth." NOSC
"So he that saileth in this world of pleasure." WPOW

Contemplations of Mary. Roy McFadden. PNI

Contemporary. Alejandrino Hufana. ReBoTo

Contemporary American Poetry. Alan Feldman. BAP-01

Contemporary Criticism, A. William Wetmore Story.
"He thanked me for my kindness, disagreed." APN-1

Contemporary Culture and the Letter "K." Alfred Corn. NoP-4

Contemporary Muse, The. Edgell Rickword. OBSV

Contemporary Poet, A. Steve Wilson. AmPoNex

Contemptuous of his home beyond. Frog's Fate, A. Christina Georgina Rossetti. NOBVV

Contend in a sea which the land partly encloses. Yachts, The. William Carlos Williams. APT-1; HeIP-4; MoAmPo; NOBA; NoAM; NoP-4; OxBA; PoE; SAmP; TFi

Contend to beare his bodie to his soule. (LL) Feltons Epitaph. *Unknown.* NPeEn; PBRV

Contending / Temple bell. Takai Kito. ZenPo, *tr. by* Takashi Ikemoto and Lucien Stryk

Content. Dora Greenwell. PoToHe

Content and Resolute. William Drummond, of Hawthornden. NPeEn; PBRV

Content and Ri[t]ch[e]. Robert Southwell. ChIV-2; NoSic

Content, content! within a quiet room. Content. Dora Greenwell. PoToHe

Content of History Will be Poetry, The. Edward Sanders. PFTM-2 *Fr.* Investigative Poetry.

Content thee, greedy heart. Size, The. George Herbert. GeHe

Content though blind, had I no better guide. (LL) To Mr. Cyriack Skinner upon His Blindness. John Milton. NOSC; NPeEn; PeECV; Son

Content with chipped bowl and tattered robe. Tosui Unkei. ZenPo, *tr. by* Takashi Ikemoto and Lucien Stryk

Contented, half to please. (LL) Fanny [*or* Frances] Macartney Greville. ECWP; NOEC; OxBEV

Contented that such hap[p]inesses move. (LL) Mary Sidney Wroth, Countess of Montgomery. BASC; NAEL-7v1; PEW *Fr.* Pamphilia to Amphilanthus.

Contenteder—to die. (LL) Emily Dickinson. APN-2; FaBoWar; OBWP

Contention of Ajax and Ulysses, The. James Shirley.

(Dirge.) AWP; NoP-4

Contentment. Charles Stuart Calverley. NOBVV

Contentment. William Cowper. ChIV-2 *Fr.* Olney Hymns.

Contentment. Oliver Wendell Holmes. APN-1; OxBA; PWR *Fr.* Autocrat of the Breakfast Table, The.

Contentment Is a Sleepy Thing. Thomas Traherne. *See* Christian Ethics

Contentment, to a Friend. Charlotte MacCarthy. PoBW

Contents of an Ink-bottle, The. Mary Elizabeth Coleridge. VWP

Contest Snake, The. Cheng Hsieh. CoBLCP, *tr. by* Jonathan Chaves

Continent's Edge. Mark Wunderlich. WiU

Continent's End. Robinson Jeffers. AWP

Continental Walk. Allen Fisher. PFTM-2

Continental (You Kiss While You're Dancing), The. Herb Magidson. ReLy

Continual Song. Michael Haslam.

84 01 ("Writing in a nearly lightless loft."). Oth

No Bloody Matter 43 42 ("Slightest vacuum when the concrete-mixer stops, The."). Oth

01 84 ("Wings."). Oth

30 55 ("Chisel slid, I hit my little knuckle, The."). Oth

Continually they cackle thus. Sir Osbert Sitwell. PoWW *Fr.* How Shall We Rise to Greet the Dawn?

Continuation of a Long Poem of These States. Allen Ginsberg.

S.F. Southward. NAAL-2v2

Continuation of Life. Boris Petrovich Kornilov. TCRP, *tr. by* Bernard Meares

Continue; I'll discover where you sweat (Kierkegaard). John Cage. PFTM-2 *Fr.* Diary: How to Improve the World (You Will Only Make Matters Worse).

Continued. Matthew Arnold. Son

Continues ceasing and ceasing. (LL) Extermination of the Jews, The. Marvin Bell. GotH; TaR

Continues in the Same State of Feeling. Francisco de Quevedo y Villegas. BLPSL, *tr. by* Rene de Costa, Rigas Kappatos and Eleni Paidoussi

Continuity. "Æ" MoBrPo

Continuity, The. Paul Blackburn. NeAP

Continuity of Life. William Bell Scott. OxBSo

Continuous. Tony Harrison. NPeEn

Continuous Time. Milo De Angelis. NeIt, *tr. by* Lawrence Venuti

Continuum. Allen Curnow. HarvBoo

Contours. Noël Coward. UV

Contra, The. Sandra M. Castillo. TouFir

Contraband. Denise Levertov. BLT

Contraception,—that's the bizarre, proper slang. Crystal Palace, The. John Davidson. PeVV

Contract. (For The Destruction and Rebuilding of Paterson), A. Imamu Amiri Baraka. FTOS

Contradictions: Tracking Poems. Adrienne Rich.

"My mouth hovers across your breasts." LW; NIL-7

Contraption,—that's the bizarre, proper slang. John Davidson. NePenScot *Fr.* Crystal Palace, The.

Contrary Motion. Elizabeth Garrett. NeBl

Contrary Theses (I). Wallace Stevens. OxBA; SAmP

Contrast, A. James Russell Lowell. NCAP

Contrast, A. Menella Bute Smedley. VWP

Contrast, The. Royall Tyler.

"Father and I went to camp." NAAL-3

"Marblehead's a rocky place." NAAL-3

Prologue: "Exult each patriot heart!—this night is shewn.". NAAL-3

Song: "Sun sets in night, and the stars shun the day, The.". NAAL-3

Contrasts. Blaise Cendrars. CuPo

Contrasts. Iain Crichton Smith. NePenScot

Contre Jour. Elizabeth Bartlett. FaBoWP

Contribution on Pornography, A. Wislawa Szymborska. PoSu, *tr. by* Adam Czerniawski

Contrite Heart, The. William Cowper. *See* Olney Hymns

Contrition. Ralph Knevet. ChIV-2

Contrition. Henry More. NOSC *Fr.* Psychozoia, or, the Life of the Soul.

Controlled woolgathering is my work too. (LL) Sheepdog Trials in Hyde Park. Cecil Day Lewis. NoAM; OxBTC

Controlling Factors. Mary Ruefle. ExTi

Conundrum of the Workshops, The. Rudyard Kipling. MoBrPo

Convalescence. Noël Coward. TTTS

Convalescence. James Philip McAuley. CBAP

Convalescing in London. Thomas M. [*or* "Tom"] Disch. RA

Convenience. Richard Murphy. ModIr *Fr.* Price of Stone, The.

Convent in '45, The. Maria Luisa Spaziani. NeIt, *tr. by* Beverly Allen

Convent Threshold, The. Christina Georgina Rossetti. NALW; NoP-4; VWP

"I tell you what I dreamed last night." PeVV

Convergence of the Twain, The. Thomas Hardy. CABP; FaBoTw; HarvBoo; HeIP-4; InPK-6; MakPoe; MoBrPo; NAEL-5v2; NAEL-6v2; NIL-7; NIP-4; NPeEn; NoAM; NoP-4; OxBEV; OxBTC; PAI; PeVV; PoPoPo; SCGP; TFi

Convergences / of the spirit! What. Pavane. Ronald Stuart Thomas. HarvBoo

Conversation. Buson. NTCP

Conversation. Ágnes Nemes Nagy. IQMS, *tr. by* Adam Makkai

Conversation. Dan Pagis. VCWP, *tr. by* Stephen Mitchell

Conversation, A. Gisèle Prassinos. PFTM-1

Conversation at Midnight. "Adelina Efimovna Adalis." TCRP, *tr. by* Bernard Meares

Conversation between Me and the Women. Anna Petrovna Bunina. ARWW, *tr. by* Sibelan Forrester

Conversation between the Chevalier de Chamilly and Mariana Alcoforado in the Manner of a Song of Regret. *Unknown.* BoWoP, *tr. by* Helen R. Lane

Conversation between Two Sisters, One Choosing an Aged Man, and the Other Choosing Youth, A. Angharad Pritchard. EMWP

Conversation brings us so close! Opening. Looking into a Face. Robert Bly. NOBA

Conversation Galante. T. S. Eliot. TCAPo

Conversation goodnightthankyou. (LL) Word in Edgeways, A. Charles Tomlinson. CABP; NOBL

Conversation in Front of a Helicopter. Rosario Murillo. CLPP, *tr. by* Alejandro Murguía

Conversation in Gibraltar 1943. Charles Causley. PoWW

Conversation in the Bush. Arthur Rex Dugard Fairburn. PeNZ *Fr.* Album Leaves.

Conversation in the Drawing Room, The. Weldon Kees. SPE

(That spot of blood on the drawingroom wall.) SPE

Conversation in Woodside. Kim Addonizio. GeoHom

Conversation of a Private and the Virgin. Nikolai Ivanovich Glazkov. TCRP, *tr. by* Daniel Weissbort

Conversation of Prayer, The. Dylan Thomas. EBEV; GTBS-P; NoP-4; OxAEP-2

Conversation Overheard. Quincy Troupe. NAAAL

Conversation Through the Door, A. Anna Swirszczynska. AF, *tr. by* Czeslaw Milosz

Conversation with a Japanese Student. Eleanor Wilner. GifTon

Conversation with a Neighbor. Olga Fiodorovna Berggolts [*or* Bergholts]. TCRP, *tr. by* Daniel Weissbort

Conversation with a New York Poet. Lev Vladimir Loseff [*or* Losev]. TCRusP, *tr. by* Henry Pickford

Conversation with cancer, The. Death Who. Philip Hodgins. BMAP

Conversation with Death, A. Sileas Na Ceapaich. EMWP

Conversation with Isadora Duncan. Molly Bendall. AmPoNex

Conversation with the Moon. Ludwig Goldscheider. AuPH, *tr. by* Lowell A. Bangerter

Conversational Melody, A Good Verse, A. Nikolai Alekseievich Klyuyev [*or* Kliuev *or* Klyuev]. TCRusP, *tr.* by John Glad

Conversations are simple: about food, The. Under the Window: Ouro Prêto. Elizabeth Bishop. VCAP

Conversations in Courtship. *Unknown.*

"Darling, you only, there is no duplicate." CTC

Pleasant Songs of the Sweetheart Who Meets You in the Fields. WoPoe, *tr.* by Ezra Pound and Noel Stock

Conversations in Mayan. Alonzo Gonzales Mó. STP, *tr.* by Allan F. Burns

Conversations in the Mountains. Li Po. RaBo; TAL, *tr.* by Robert Payne

Conversations with a Toad. Robert Bringhurst.

"Behind you: the owl, whose eyes." PoCoUp

Conversations with Dr. M. Rachel Loden. GotH

Conversations with Strangers. George Buchanan. PNI

Conversion. Thomas Ernest Hulme. FaBoMo; OxBSP

Conversion of S. Paul, The. George Wither. ChIV-2

Conversion of stones into bread would be a supernatural miracle, The. W. H. Auden. GI *Fr.* "Prolific and the Devourer," The.

Conversions. Neal Bowers. AllShUp

Convert, The. Gilbert Keith Chesterton. ChIV-2; SacPr

Convert, The. Margaret Danner. BPo

Convert Comes to the City, A. Nathan [*or* Natan] Alterman. MHP, *tr.* by Ruth Finer Mintz *Fr.* Joy of the Poor, The.

Convert's but a fly, that turns about, A. Samuel Butler (1612–80). FaBoEE

Conveying the effects of atmosphere. Appalachian Trees Encircled by Police Tape. Greg Williamson. NeAmPo

Convict. Edward Vincent Swart. PeSAV

Convict held his breath in the shadow of the doorway as the, The. Downward Mobility. Lewis Warsh. BAP-97

Convict's Tour to Hell, A. Francis MacNamara. NOBAu

Conviction fills the body. Radio. Barrett Watten. PmAP

Conviction IV. Stevie Smith. LW

Convicts' Rum Song. *Unknown.* FaBoVe; NOBAu

Convinced by Sorrow. Elizabeth Barrett Browning. SacPr *Fr.* Cry of the Human, The.

Convoy Escort. Rudyard Kipling. WoPoe *Fr.* Epitaphs of the War [1914–1918].

Convulsed, foaming immortal blood: farewell. (LL) Professor's Song, A. John Berryman. HeIP-4; NAAL-2v2; NOBA; NoAM; OxBC

Convulsions came; and, where the field. Apparition, The—A Retrospect. Herman Melville. APN-2; NCAP; TCAPo

Cooing pigeons, nursling swallows, all quiet without a sound. Spring Day. Su Tung-p'o (Su Shih). SuSp, *tr.* by Irving Y. Lo

Cook, The. Ray A. Young Bear. CDW

Cook admired the native courage, made. Rex Ingamells. NOBAu *Fr.* Great South Land, The.

Cook became the compote's bride, The. Procurers. Novella Nikolaevna Matveyeva [*or* Matveieva]. TCRP, *tr.* by Deming Brown

Cook called McMurray, A. Ogden Nash. PeLi

Cook County. Archibald MacLeish. IllVoic

(Weather.) MoAmPo

Cooking, it seems, is not your forte. Hungary. Sándor Petőfi. IQMS, *tr.* by Peter Zollman

Cooking to Music. Edward Kleinschmidt. MiVo

Cooky-Nut Trees, The. Albert Bigelow Paine. OBCA

Cool. Tamanari. JDP, *tr.* by Yoel Hoffmann

Cool and certain, their oars will be lifted in dusk. "Robin Hyde." PeNZ *Fr.* Beaches, The.

Cool as from underground springs and pure enough to drink. (LL) Man-Moth, The. Elizabeth Bishop. APT-2; MoAmPo; NALW; NOBA; NoAM

Cool black night thru the redwoods. First Party at Ken Kesey's with Hell's Angels. Allen Ginsberg. PmAP; TRP

Cool breezes—I sleep by the open window. *Unknown.* CoBCP *Fr.* Tzu Yeh Songs.

Cool brisk fingers in my hair. April in Hollywood. Wanda Coleman. GeoHom

Cool Cat. Michael Myer. TriCat

Cool, clear autumn morning, so still. Skywriting. Jamie Grant. EmeKit

Cool, damp forest shakes, The. Snakes. Nikolai Alekseievich Zabolotsky [*or* Zabolotskii]. TCRusP, *tr.* by Denis Johnson and Kathy Lewis

Cool fall night, A. Basho. EH, *tr.* by Robert Hass

Cool in its dream, I kissed the stone. Leah Goldberg. MHP, *tr.* by Ruth Finer Mintz *Fr.* Songs of the Stream.

Cool inaccessible air. Lola Ridge. APT-1 *Fr.* Ghetto, The.

Cool it is, and still. Basho. TAL

Cool it Mag. Margaret Are You Drug. George Starbuck. InPK-6

Cool of bamboo invades my room, The. Restless Night. Tu Fu. CoBCP, *tr.* by Burton Watson

Cool perfume of bamboo pervades my room. Summer Night. Tu Fu. TAL

Cool red rose and a pink cut pink, A. Gertrude Stein. TTTS *Fr.* Tender Buttons.

Cool reek of the field. Reek of companions. (LL) Cobb Would Have Caught It. Robert Fitzgerald. HAP; TwCP

Cool small evening shrunk to a dog bark and the clank of a bucket, A. Full Moon and Little Frieda. Ted Hughes. HarvBoo; NPeEn; OPOU; OxBC; OxBSP

Cool Tombs. Carl Sandburg. APT-1; ColAP; HAP; HeIP-4; MoAmPo; NAAL-2v2; NOBA; NoAM; OxBSP; TAP; TCAPo; TFi

Cool Web, The. Robert Graves. AWP; GTBS-P; HarvBoo; NAEL-5v2; NAEL-6v2; NoAM; OxBEV; OxBTC; SCV; WoPoe

Coole Park and Ballylee, 1931. W. B. Yeats. GTBS-P; NOIV; NoAM; OBGa; OBMV

Coole Park, 1929. W. B. Yeats. CABP; OBMV

Coolie cane chop. Coolie. Sándor Weöres. IQMS, *tr.* by Edwin Morgan

Coolie Chinee, The. Septimus Winner. OBAL

Coolness. Buson. EH; NIL-7, *tr.* by Robert Hass

Coolness. John Wills. HA

Coolness, like the evening tide. Brother, I Am Here. "Shu Ting." CarOv; GifTon, *tr.* by Carolyn Kizer and Y. H. Zhao

Coolness of melons. Basho. EH, *tr.* by Robert Hass

Coon Song. A. R. Ammons. NOBA

Cooper. James Russell Lowell. NOBA; OxBA; TAP; TCAPo *Fr.* Fable for Critics, A.

Cooper's Hill. Sir John Denham. BeJo; CABP; PBRV

"Here have I seen the king, when great affairs." PoE

"Here should my wonder dwell, and here my praise." NAEL-5v1; NAEL-6v1; NOSC; NPeEn

"My eye descending from the Hill, surveys." OxAEP-1; OxBEV

"O could I flow like thee, and make thy stream." NPeEn

Cooper, whose name is with his country's woven. Red Jacket. Fitz-Greene Halleck. APN-1

Coora Flower, The. Gwendolyn Brooks. IllVoic; NAAL-5; NIL-7; NoP-4

Coordinating cities gulls still gull, and, arms binged with wine, as wine. Ted Greenwald. FTOS *Fr.* Licorice Chronicles.

Cootchie, Miss Lula's servant, lies in marl. Cootchie. Elizabeth Bishop. FaBoWP

Cop's face for an odd second, The. Pharoah's Army Got Drowned. Lynn Domina. OPRER

Copernicus. Robert David Fitzgerald. NOBAu

Cophetua. Hugh MacDiarmid. OxBS

Coplas. Antonio Machado. AF, *tr.* by Robert Bly

Coplas about the Soul Which Suffers with Impatience to See God. Saint John of the Cross.

"I live without inhabiting / Myself." OBVE

Coppers. Boris Abramovich Slutsky [*or* Slutskii]. TCRusP, *tr.* by Daniel Weissbort

Copter lays flat the rice stalks, The. Ceremony. Richard M. Mishler. CDa

Coptic Socks. Roy Fuller. OBCoV

Copula. John Cope. GeoH

Copulate in the foam. (LL) News for the Delphic Oracle. W. B. Yeats. FaBoMo; NoAM

Copy of an Intercepted Despatch from His Excellency Don Strepitoso Diabolo. Thomas Moore. OBSV

Copy of Verses, A. John Wilson. SCAP

Copy [*or* copie] out on[e]ly that, and save expense. (LL) Jordan (2). George Herbert. BASC; CABP; ESCV; FSCP; GeHe; NAEL-5v1; NAEL-6v1; NAEL-7v1; NOSC; OBWVE; PBRV; SacPr

Copy-writer's Dream, The. Bruce Dawe. BMAP

Copycat, copycat / Shadow's a copycat! Copycat. Robert Heidbreder. OTCP

Coquettes with doctors; hoards her breath. Old Beauty, The. Phyllis McGinley. FaBoEE

Coral and emerald shade. Almora Spring. Sumitranandan Pant. OMIP, *tr.* by David Rubin

Coral and shells are heaped until it seems. Clouds, The. Thomas M. [*or* "Tom"] Disch. RA

Coral Grove, The. James Gates Percival. APN-1; ColAP

Coral Reef, The. John Blight. NOBAu

Coral Reef, The. Laurence Lieberman. CoAP

Coral toy, A. (LL) Emmett Till. James A. Emanuel. NIL-7; NIP-4

Coralie. Frederick Goddard Tuckerman. NCAP

Corals and Shells. William Bronk. APSN

Cord of Hope, The. Mikhail Naimy.

"Hope is agony." GraLe, *tr.* by Sharif Elmusa and Gregory Orfalea

Cordate head meanders through himself, The. Pit Viper. N. Scott Momaday. CDW; HATNAP

Cordelia's / In stony / Lonesome / Ground! (LL) Stony Lonesome. Langston Hughes. NOBA; SAmP

Cordon Negro. Essex Hemphill. CAGL; GLP

Cordova. Ibn Zaydun. AWP, *tr. by* H. A. R. Gibb

Cords made of cries. Bonds. Guillaume Apollinaire. CuPo

Core of masculinity does not derive from being male, The. Core of Masculinity, The. Jelaluddin [*or* Jalal al-Din] Rumi. RaBo, *tr. by* Coleman Barks

Corfu appears, and then the distant blue. On the Ferry, Toward Patras. Emily Grosholz. RA

Coridon's Song. John Chalkhill. NOSC

Corinna Bathes. George Chapman. OxAEP-1 *Fr.* Ovid's Banquet of Sense.

Corinna, from Athens, to Tanagra. Walter Savage Landor. OBEV *Fr.* Pericles and Aspasia.

Corinna In Vendome. Pierre de Ronsard. BoLoP; WoPoe, *tr. by* Robert Mezey

Corinna, pride of Drury Lane. Beautiful Young Nymph Going to Bed, A. Jonathan Swift. ECEV; EroLit; NOEC; NPeEn; OxBEV

Corinna's Going a-Maying. Robert Herrick. AEP; BASC; BeJo; CABP; CaPo; HAP; NAEL-5v1; NAEL-6v1; NAEL-7v1; NIP-4; NOBE; NOSC; NoP-4; OBEV; OxBEV; PBRV; PoE; PoPoPo; SCGP; TFi

Corinne at the Capitol. Felicia Dorothea Hemans. BrRo (Daughter of th' Italian heaven!) VWP

Corinne's Last Love-Song. Lady Jane Francesca Wilde. VWP

Coriolan. T. S. Eliot.
    Triumphal March. OBWP

Coriolanus. William Shakespeare.
    "Madam, the Lady Valeria is come to visit you." OxAEP-1
    "Read it not, noble lords." OxAEP-1
    "Why dost not speak?" OxAEP-1

Cork Examiner, December 4, 1846: More Starvation, The. Anna Mortál. SpudSo

Corkby, Part Two. Jerome Rothenberg. NNaP

Cormac Mac Airt Presiding at Tara. *Unknown.* BIrV, *tr. by* Douglas Hyde

Cormorant. Peter Preece. AngWePo

Cormorant. Lucien Stryk. IllVoic

Cormorant-boat, The. Shunzei. WoPoe, *tr. by* Valerie Durham

Cormorant fishing / How stirring. Basho. ZenPo, *tr. by* Takashi Ikemoto and Lucien Stryk

Cormorant has, The. Tails and Heads. Suzanne Knowles. RB

Cormorant in His [*or* Its] Element, The. Amy Clampitt. InPK-6; NoP-4

Cormorant still screams, The. Late. Louise Bogan. APT-2; VGW

Cormorants. John Blight. CBAP

Cormorants. John Kinsella. OWoS

Corn, The. Daniel David Moses. HATNAP

Corn Ceremony. *Apache Oral Tradition.* TCAPo

Corn Children. Carol Lee Sanchez. HW

Corn, corn, sweet Indian corn. William W. Cook. VerBaPo *Fr.* Indian Corn.

Corn-grinding Song. *Unknown.* AWP, *tr. by* Natalie Curtis

Corn grows large, the rushes tall, The. Autumn on the Riverbank. Chao Shan-ch'ing. CrYelRi, *tr. by* Sam Hamill

Corn has stood ripe on the stalks for months, The. Frost in the Corn, The. Robert McAlmon. AiP

Corn King beckoning to his Spring Queen, The. (LL) Girl in a Library, A. Randall Jarrell. NAAL-2v2; NOBA; NoAM

Corn Rigs Are Bonnie. Robert Burns. OxBS
    (Song.) BoLoP; NOBRP; PeLV

Corn Song. *Unknown.* APN-2, *tr. by* Henry Rowe Schoolcraft

Corn was Orient and Immortal Wheat, which never should, The. Thomas Traherne. NPeEn *Fr.* Centuries of Meditations.

Corneille's Pompey. Katherine Philips.
    Cornelia's Defiance. NOSC

Cornelian, The. Byron. CAGL; TreFP

Cornelius sighs... the lines I write. Martial. RomPo, *tr. by* Peter Whigham

Corner. Amal Dunqul. MAP, *tr. by* Sharif Elmusa and Thomas G. Ezzy

Corner *bodega* run by El Chino Chan, The. Rice Comes to El Volcán. Virgil Suárez. AmPoNex

Corner Boy's Farewell. Burns Singer. HarvBoo

Cornfields in Accra. Christine Ama Ata Aidoo. WPOW

Cornhusk bag. Talking Designs. Liz Sohappy Bahe. CDW

Cornish Emigrant's Song, The. Robert Stephen Hawker. EBVV

Cornkind. Frank O'Hara. CLPP

Cornucopia. Christopher Pearse Cranch. APN-1

Corona. Paul Celan. PoetW, *tr. by* John Felstiner

Corona. Paul Celan. PoSu, *tr. by* Michael Hamburger

Coronach. Tracey Herd. NeBl

Coronach. Alexander Scott. OxBS

Coronach. Sir Walter Scott. *Fr.* Lady of the Lake, The.

Coronal, A. William Carlos Williams. TCAPo

Coronary Thrombosis. William Price Turner. OxBS

Coronation ceremony was in Belize this time, The. Mosquito Kingdom. Ernesto Cardenal. VCWP, *tr. by* Donald D. Walsh

Coronemus Nos Rosis Antequam Marcescant. Thomas Jordan. *See* Careless Gallant, The

Coroner. Elton Glaser. PBCAP

Coroner's Inquest. W. D. Snodgrass. OxBEV

Coroner's Jury. Leonard Alfred George Strong. OxBTC

Coronet, The. Andrew Marvell. BASC; ESCV; FHYEP; FSCP; GeHe; MeLP; NAEL-5v1; NAEL-6v1; NAEL-7v1; NOCV; NOSC; NoP-4; PBRV; PoE; SCGP; SacPr; TOF

Coronet for His Mistress Philosophy, A. George Chapman.
    "But dwell in darkness, for your god is blind." OxBSo; Son
    "For words want art and art wants words to praise her." OxBSo
    "Her look doth promise and her life assure." OxBSo
    "Love flows not from my liver but her living." OxBSo; Son
    "Muses that fame's loose feathers beautify." OxBSo
    "Nor riches to the virtues of my love." OxBSo
    "Of her removed and soul-infused regard." OxBSo
    "So her close beauties further blaze her fame." OxBSo
    "To living virtues turns the deadly vices." OxBSo

Corporal. Ambrose Bierce. APN-2; OBAL *Fr.* Devil's Dictionary, The.

Corporal Charles Chungtu, U. S. M. C. Bryan Alec Floyd. CDa

Corporal Kevin Spina, U. S. M. C. Bryan Alec Floyd. CDa

Corporal Pym. Walter De la Mare. FaBoEE

Corporal Stare. Robert Graves. FaBoWar

Corporal Who Killed Archimedes, The. Miroslav Holub. PoSu, *tr. by* Ian Milner and Jarmila Milner

Corporate Entity. Archibald MacLeish. OBAL

Corporeal. Robert Ayres. OPRER

Corporeal summer, no marvel is lost. True Western Summer. Hildegarde Flanner. APT-2

Corposant. Peter Redgrove. OxBTC

Corpse, The. Jagannath Prasad Das. OMIP, *tr. by* Jayanta Mahapatra

Corpse and Mirror III. John Yau. ReTh

Corpse-bearing. Thomas Ashe. EBVV; NOBVV

Corpse-Keeper, The. *Unknown.* BoWoP

Corpse with streaming hair, A. (LL) Ballad of Hector in Hades. Edwin Muir. HarvBoo; NOBE; NoAM

Corpses, The. Lynn Emanuel. ExTi

Corpses in the Wood. Ernst Toller. TrJP, *tr. by* E. Ellis Roberts

Corpus Christi Carol, The. *Unknown.* MiEL; NAEL-5v1; NOBE; SCV
    (Knight of the Grail, The.) OBEV
    (Lully, lulley, lully, lulley.) EBEV; HAP; NPeEn; TFi

Corpus Christi wretyn theron. (LL) Corpus Christi Carol, The. *Unknown.* MiEL; NAEL-5v1; NOBE; SCV

Corpus Inscriptionum Latinarum 14.3565. *Unknown.* PriapPo, *tr. by* Richard W. Hooper

Correct but cautious, that first night, we asked. James Merrill. NoP-4 *Fr.* Book of Ephraim, The.

Correct Compassion, A. James Kirkup. FaBoTw; OxBTC

Correct my fault[e]s, protect my life, direct me when I die [*or* dye]! (LL) Child[e] My Choice [*or* Choyse], A. Robert Southwell. OxBEV; PeECV

Correction of proofs + desires in speed. Filippo Tommaso Marinetti. PFTM-1 *Fr.* Zang Tumb Tuuum.

Correggio's Cupolas at Parma. Aubrey Thomas De Vere. Son

Correlated Greatness. Francis Thompson. *See* Heart, The

Correlation which unites the human condition. Allen Fisher. Oth *Fr.* Emergent Manner.

Correspondence. Judith Ortiz Cofer. PueRic

Correspondence. Henri Coulette. DiPo

Correspondence. Peter Reading. PeLV

Correspondence between Mr. Harrison in Newcastle and Mr. Sholto Peach Harrison in Hull. Stevie Smith. NBLV; OxBC

Correspondence School Instructor Says Goodbye to His Poetry Students, The. Galway Kinnell. NOBA; NoAM; NoP-4; TAP

Correspondence: / when I have sad thoughts. Lady Ise. BoWoP

Correspondences. Charles Baudelaire. SxFrPo, *tr. by* James McGowan

Correspondences. Charles Baudelaire. AWP, *tr. by* Allen Tate

Correspondences. Charles Baudelaire. NAWM-7v2, *tr. by* Richard Wilbur

Correspondences. Christopher Pearse Cranch. APN-1

Correspondences. Robert Duncan. PoM

Corrugated iron shack, A. One room. Cradle, The. Roland Robinson. NOBAu

Corrupt Man in the French Pub, The. Brian Higgins. OxBTC

Corruption. Freddy Macha. NAfrP

Corruption. Henry Vaughan. ESCV; GeHe; NAEL-5v1; NAEL-6v1; NAEL-7v1; NOCV; NOSC

Corrymeela. "Moira O'Neill." AWP

Cors-y-Gwaed: Fenland of Blood. A. G. Prys-Jones. AngWePo

Corsair, The. Byron.

   O'er the glad waters of the dark blue sea.

   "Unlike the heroes of each ancient race." NOBRP

Corsica. Anna Laetitia Barbauld.

   On General Paoli and the Corsican Struggle for Liberty. ECWP

Corsons Inlet. A. R. Ammons. CoAP; ColAP; NAAL-2v2; NAAL-5; NOBA; NoAM; NoP-4; PoE; VCAP

Cortège. Paul Verlaine. AWP; OBVE, *tr. by* Arthur Symons

Cortes Swamp, The. Clovis L. Nazareno. ReBoTo

Cortez's Horse. Pat Mora. UnSA

Corydon and Thyrsis. Virgil [*or* Vergil]. AWP, *tr. by* John Dryden *Fr.* Eclogues.

Corydon's Farewell, on Sailing in the Late Expedition Fleet. *Unknown.* NOEC

Cosmetics Do No Good. Steve Kowit. BLT

Cosmic Eye. A. K. Redwing. VoR

Cosmic Leviathan, that monstrous fish. Cosmogony. Edgell Rickword. FaBoTw

Cosmo Dog. Terese Svoboda. Unle

Cosmogony. Edgell Rickword. FaBoTw

Cosmogony. *Unknown.* WoPoe, *tr. by* Richard Taylor

Cosmology. *Unknown.* WoPoe, *tr. by* J. Moussaieff Masson and W. S. Merwin

   (Goddess Lakshmi [*or* Laksmi], The.) EaWin; HW

Cosmopolitan Poetry. János Arany. IQMS, *tr. by* Madeline Mason

Cosmos in London. Arthur Nortje. HBAPE; PeSAV

Cosmos Shows His Power, The. Manuel González Prada. SpanPo, *tr. by* William M. Davis

Cosmus hath more discoursing in his head. Sir John Davies. NoSic *Fr.* Epigrams.

Cossacks snatched him from his mother, The. My Greatgreatuncle the Archbishop. Ruth Whitman. TaR

Cossante. Pero Meogo. WoPoe, *tr. by* Yvor Winters

Cost, The. Anthony Hecht. OxBC

Cost of Seriousness, The. Peter Porter. NoAM

Cost you your railway lines, washing lines, sex on billboards. To Look Out Once from High Windows. Sinéad Morrissey. MFPA

Costa Geriatrica. Stanley J. Sharpless. PeLV

Costanza. Felicia Dorothea Hemans. RWP

Costumes are a kind of late-colonial, The. Totalled. Peter McDonald. PNI

Côte de Liesse. Daryl Hine. NoP-4

Cotillion. John Gay. NoP-4

Cotillion. Carl Phillips. WiU

Cottage, The. Jones Very. APN-1; OxBA

Cottage for Sale, A. Larry Conley. ReLy

Cottage in the Wood, A. Russell Edson. LCAP-2

Cottage Pictures. Samuel Jackson Pratt.

   "No village dames and maidens now are seen." OBGa

Cottage Song. John Drinkwater. UV

Cottage Street, 1953. Richard Wilbur. BodElec; FaBoMo; HCAP; PoPoPo

Cottager's Complaint, on the Intended Bill for Enclosing Sutton-Coldfield, The. John Freeth. NOEC

Cottager to Her Infant, (By My Sister), The. Dorothy Wordsworth. TTTS

   (To My Niece Dorothy, a Sleepless Baby.) CABP

Cotter's Saturday Night, The. Robert Burns. NOBRP; TreFP

Cotton. Harry Edmund Martinson. RB, *tr. by* Robert Bly

Cotton Boll, The. Henry Timrod. APN-2

Cotton eyes soaking up blood. Blue Monday. Calvin Forbes. ESEAA

Cotton Flannelette. Les A. Murray. PoetW

Cotton Mather. Stephen Vincent Benét. APT-2

Cotton Song. Jean Toomer. APT-2; BPo

Cottonmouth Country. Louise Glück. CoAP

Cottonwood, willow, and briar. Leaves like Fish. Gladys Cardiff. CDW

Cou'd we stop the time that's flying. Unequal Fetters, The. Anne Finch, Countess of Winchilsea. OxBEV

Cougar. Brendan Galvin. UrbNat

Cough, a creaking stair, A. (LL) Still Life. Reed Whittemore. CoAP; CoAmPo

Cough twilight sheepskin coat, A. Guard. Viktor Krivulin. TCRusP, *tr. by* Daniel Weissbort

Could a man in your position. Where is Talcott Parsons Now? Sophie Hannah. MFPA

Could anyone among us. On a Clear Day You Can See Forever. Burton Lane. ReLy

Could Beatrice have written like Dante. Epigram. Anna Andreyevna Akhmatova. TCRP, *tr. by* Max Hayward and Stanley Kunitz

Could build so strong in a weak heart. (LL) Church-Floor[e], The. George Herbert. EBEV; ESCV; MeLP; NOSC; PeECV

Could but compose man's image and his cry. (LL) Sorrow of Love, The. W. B. Yeats. NAEL-5v2; NAEL-6v2; OxBEV; PeVV

Could have been. (LL) Middle Age. Patricia Beer. FaBoWP; HarvBoo

Could his career be as precarious as this? (LL) Li K'ai-hsien. CoBLCP; ColAnChi, *tr. by* Jonathan Chaves *Fr.* Watching the Swinging.

Could I but become a crimson rose. *Unknown.* GrAn

Could I but live again. Pisgah-Sights. II. Robert Browning. ChIV-1

Could I but ride indefinite. Emily Dickinson. SAmP

Could I have come back to you to wince. Visiting Zomba Plateau. Jack A. Mapanje. NAfrP

Could I leave her! I stayed behind. (LL) Second Thoughts. "Michael Field." LW; ViWPN

Could I Say I Touched You. Harold Littlebird. VoR

Could I take me to some cavern for mine hiding. Euripides. AWP, *tr. by* Gilbert Murray *Fr.* Hippolytus.

Could it be, Bud. For Bud. Michael S. Harper. ESEAA; PoE

Could it be Madness—this? (LL) Emily Dickinson. NCAP; OxBA; PoE; TRP; WPOW

Could man be drunk for ever. A. E. Housman. NAEL-5v2; NAEL-6v2; OBMV

Could mortal lip divine. Emily Dickinson. RB

Could not jar or spill. (LL) Bees. Emily Dickinson. NAAL-2v1; NAAL-3

Could not once blinding me, cruel[l], suffice? Samson to His Delilah. Richard Crashaw. ChIV-1

Could our first father, at his toilsome plough. Adam Posed. Anne Finch, Countess of Winchilsea. ChIV-1; ECWP

Could'st thou (O Earth) live thus obscure, and now. George Alsop. SCAP

Could to my sight that heavenly face restore. (LL) Sonnet on Catherine Wordsworth. William Wordsworth. CenSon; OxBSo; SCGP

Could we be so now! (LL) Even So. Dante Gabriel Rossetti. NOBE; NOBVV

Could ye come back to me, Douglas, Douglas. Douglas, Douglas, Tender and True. Dinah Maria Mulock Craik. TreFP

Could you bid an acorn. Lover's Reply to Good Advice. Richard Hughes. MoBrPo

Could you register birds. Holocaust. Myra Sklarew. CRP

Couldn't put Humpty Dumpty together again. (LL) Mother Goose. LB; OxBEV; OxBoLi; OxNR; ReMoGo

Council Pool's chockablock, The. Debbie and Co. John Tranter. BMAP

Counsel of Moderation, A. Francis Thompson. MoBrPo

Counsel to Girls. Robert Herrick. *See* To the Virgins, to Make Much of Time

Counsels of Sigrdrifa. *Unknown.* AWP *Fr.* Elder Edda, The.

Count Carrots. Gerda Mayer. OBSP

Count each affliction, whether light or grave. Sorrow. Aubrey Thomas De Vere. SacPr

Count, if you can, every leaf on every tree. Anacreon. WoPoe, *tr. by* Sam Hamill

Count of Senlis at His Toilet, The. John Byrne Leicester Warren, 3d Baron De Tabley. PeVV

Count on dead fingers of time the years that pass. Poem for Garcia Lorca. George Woodcock. NOBC

Count Ossie. Opal Palmer Adisa. WaCA

Count Ten. Bonaro W. Overstreet. PoToHe

Count the number of times boards crack. Insomnia. Wyatt Prunty. RA

Count the transmutations of solar years. Solar Years. David Rokeah [*or* Rokeakh]. MHP, *tr. by* Ruth Finer Mintz

Count up those books whose pages you have read. Indolence. Vernon Watkins. FaBoTw

Count Your Blessings. Mrs. Henry Linden. CBWP-4

Countdown takeoff. To the Moon and Back. William Plomer. OBCoV

Counter-Attack. Siegfried Sassoon. MoBrPo; OxAEP-2; PeFWW; PoWW

Counter-Example, The. David Shapiro. PmAP

Counter-Revolution. W. H. Oliver. PeNZ

Counter's crackle piles up the digits. Willowherb. Peter Rafferty. NLP

Counterblast against Garlic, A. Horace. NBLV, *tr. by* Roswell Martin Field *Fr.* Epodes.

Counterfable of Orpheus. Marie-Claire Bancquart. MFP, *tr. by* Martin Sorrell

Counterfeit Earth!, The. Albert Goldbarth. ReTh

Counterfeiter, The. Michael Davitt. PBCIP, *tr. by* Philip Casey

Counterfeiter, The. Greg Williamson. AmPoNex; RA

Counterlove, A. *Unknown.* NoSic

Counterpart, The. Elizabeth Jennings. TOF

Counterpoint, A. Robert Creeley. NeAP

Countess of Anglesey lead Captive by the Rebels, at the Disforresting of Pewsam, The. Sir William Davenant [*or* D'Avenant]. PBRV

Countess of Dufferin, The. Helen Selina Blackwood, Countess of Dufferin.
  OxAEP-2

Countesse of Douglas out of her boure she came, The. Knight of Liddesdale,
  The. *Unknown.* ESPB

Countesse of Pembrokes Arcadia, The. Sir Philip Sidney.
  "Such maner time there was (what time I n'ot)." PBRV
  "Then do I thinke in deed, that better it is to be private." PBRV

Counting. Mark Bibbins. WiU

Counting. Judith Ortiz Cofer. PueRic

Counting. Philip Larkin. PoetW

Counting Backwards. Evelyn Posamentier. GotH

Counting-out Rhyme. Eve Merriam. KaS

Counting-out Rhyme. Edna St. Vincent Millay. InPK-6; NOxBChV;
  OxIBACP; SoSe-8; TTTS

Counting-out Rhyme, A. *Unknown.* ReMoGo

Counting-out Rhymes. *Unknown.*
  "Eenie, meenie, minie, mo / Catch a thief by the toe." OxNR

Counting Sheep. Russell Edson. LCAP-2

Counting Small-Boned Bodies. Robert Bly. CDa; SPE

Counting the Beats. Robert Graves. GTBS-P; HAP; HarvBoo; OxAEP-2;
  OxBTC; WeW-3; WoPoe

Counting the Children. Dana Gioia. RA

Counting the eyes that see. (LL) Message on Cape Cod, The. Michael S.
  Weaver. GT; PBCAP

Counting the frequent drop from reeded eaves. (LL) On a Wet Summer. John
  Codrington Bampfylde. NOEC; OxBSo

Counting the Mad. Donald Justice. CoAmPo; NIP-4; NoP-4; PAI; TRP; UnPo

Counting the singles carefully. (LL) After Midnight. Louis Simpson. BLT;
  NoAM

Countless birds. Simonides. SaLy, *tr. by* Diane Rayor

Countless great lords and statesmen of past regimes, The. Thoughts on T'ien-
  chin Bridge. Shao Yung. CoBCP, *tr. by* Burton Watson

Countless things escape easily out of me. Afternoon 3. Saburoh Kuroda.
  SPE

Countries still trapped within the snare of servitude. On the Changes in France.
  János Batsányi. IQMS, *tr. by* Matthew Mead

Countries tears, be ye my spring; my hill, The. To the Memory of the Learned
  and Reverend, Mr. Jonathan Mitchell. Francis Drake. SCAP

Country. Diana Helen Melhem.
  "Person place thing tree." PoArWo
  "To write the country." PoArWo

Country, A. Fawziyya Abu Khalid. PoArWo, *tr. by* Farouk Mustafa

Country and Town. Charles Morris. NOEC

Country Bedroom, The. Frances Darwin Cornford. MoBrPo

Country beneath / the earth has a green sun, The. Procedures for Underground.
  Margaret Atwood. NALW

Country Boy in Winter, A. Sarah Orne Jewett. APN-2; ColAP; OBCA

Country Burial. Janet Lewis. CRP

Country Clergy, The. Ronald Stuart Thomas. GTBS-P; OxBTC; PeECV

Country Clergyman's Trip to Cambridge, The. Thomas Babington Macaulay,
  1st Baron Macaulay. OBSV; OxBoLi; PeLV

Country Club Romance, A. Derek Walcott. OxBC

Country Cottage. Tu Fu. OHPC, *tr. by* Kenneth Rexroth

Country Curate, The. Henry Taylor. NOEC

Country Dance. Dame Edith Sitwell. NoAM

Country Dance. Judith Wright. BMAP; CBAP *Fr.* Blind Man, The.

Country Dance, A. Charles Tennyson Turner. NOBVV; OxBEV

Country Dog in the City (On a Leash, Which Is Bizarre Enough) Comes Upon
  an Obedience Class, A. Roy Blount, Jr. Unle

Country Fair. Charles Simic. EmeKit

Country Faith, The. Norman Gale. OBEV

Country God, A. Edmund Charles Blunden. MoBrPo

Country Gods. Cometas. FaBoCh, *tr. by* T. F. Higham

Country Graveyard. Charles Pressoir. NegPo, *tr. by* Edna Worthley
  Underwood

Country here-abouts, The. Wire Song. Mark Todd. GeoH

Country House. Ch'u Ch'uang I. OHPMC, *tr. by* Kenneth Rexroth

Country House, The. Louis Simpson. NOBA

Country Justice, The. John Langhorne.
  Gypsies. NOEC
  Poor, The. NOEC
  Warning against the Gypsies, A. ECEV

Country kid in Mississippi I drew water, A. Little More Traveling Music, A.
  Al Young. NBV

Country Lassie, The. *Unknown.* TreFP

Country Life. Horace. AWP, *tr. by* John Dryden *Fr.* Epodes.

Country Life. Chenjerai Hove. HBAPE

Country Life, A. Randall Jarrell. MoAmPo

Country Life, A. Katherine Philips. BASC

Country Life: To His Brother, M. Tho: Herrick. Robert Herrick. CaPo

Country Life, to the Honored Mr. Endymion Porter[, Groome of the Bed-
  Chamber to His Maj.], The. Robert Herrick. BeJo

Country Lovers; or, Isaac and Marget Going to Town, on a Summer's Morning,
  The. George Smith. NOEC

Country Man, The. George Farewell.
  "Crunking crane heard high amongst the clouds, The." NOEC

Country Midwife: A Day, The. Ai. GT

Country-Mouse, The. Abraham Cowley. NPeEn; OBVE

Country North of Belleville, The. Alfred Wellington Purdy. NOBC

Country Nun. Geoff Page. CBAP

Country of a Thousand Years of Peace, The. James Merrill. NoP-4

Country of Dust, The. Vahan Tekeyan. AF, *tr. by* Diana Der Hovanessian and
  Marzbed Margossian

Country of early October had no fruit, The. Words of Evening, The. Yves
  Bonnefoy. VCWP, *tr. by* Richard Pevear

Country of hunchbacks!—where the strong, straight spine. Sonnet to Gath.
  Edna St. Vincent Millay. BoWoP; MoAmPo

Country of No Lack. Jean Starr Untermeyer. MoAmPo

Country of the Dead, The. Jared Angira. PBMAP

Country of Water. Bernice Ames. WPE

Country or Western Music. Gerald Early. BodElec

Country Pastor, The. Timothy Dwight. SacPr

Country Pathway, A. James Whitcomb Riley. CA

Country Pleasures. Martial. AWP, *tr. by* F. A. Wright

Country Press. Rosemary Dobson. FaBoWP; NOBAu

Country rings around with loud alarms, The. Dryden. OBSV *Fr.* Cymon and
  Iphigenia.

Country Road, A. Li Ho. CrYelRi, *tr. by* Sam Hamill

Country roads are yellow and brown. Street Lanterns. Mary Elizabeth
  Coleridge. PoRA

Country's Crisis, The. Brian [*or* Bryan] Merriman [*or* Merryman]. BIrV, *tr.
  by* David Marcus *Fr.* Midnight Court, The.

Country Scene. Wu Wei-yeh. CoBLCP, *tr. by* Jonathan Chaves

Country School. Allen Curnow. HarvBoo

Country School. Ted Kooser. KaS

Country School, The. *Unknown.* TCAPo

Country Seat, The. Sir John, of Penicuik Clerk.
  "Come now ye rural deities and show." OBGa

Country Song. William Shakespeare. AWP; GTBS-P; NAEL-5v1; NOBE;
  NoSic; OBEV; RB; SCGP; TFi; TTTS *Fr.* As You Like It.

Country Song, A. Douglas Stewart. NOBAu

Country Stars. William Meredith. VCAP

Country Summer. Léonie Adams. MoAmPo

Country Thought. Sylvia Townsend Warner. MoBrPo

Country Town, A. Philip James Bailey.
  (True Measure of Life, The.) TreFP
  "We live in deeds, not years; in thoughts, not breaths." PoToHe

Country Towns. Kenneth Slessor. CBAP

Country Villa. Jean Garrigue. TAP

Country Walk, A. Thomas Kinsella. CIP-2

Country Walk, The. John Dyer.
  "I am resolved, this charming day." ECEV

Country Wedding, The. Thomas Hardy. UnPo

Country Wife, The. Dana Gioia. RA

Country Wisdoms. Maggie Anderson. PBCAP

Country without a Mythology, A. Douglas Le Pan. MoCV; NOBC

Country? have lost our pride / as nationals no man can die for billboards / as
  have for freedom. Spring 61. Lenore Kandel. BB

Countryman's Return, The. Dylan Thomas. OxBTC

Countryside Sleeps, Trembling, The. Juan Ramón Jiménez. SpanPo, *tr. by*
  Eloise Roach

Counts itself lucky. Meleager. GrAn

County. Katayoon Zandvakili. AmPoNex

County Ball, The. Coventry Patmore. EBVV *Fr.* Angel in the House, The.

County of Mayo, The. Thomas Flavell [*or* Lavell]. BIrV; OBEV, *tr. by*
  George Fox

Coupl'a jiggers of moonlight and add a star. Moonlight Cocktail. Kim
  Gannon. ReLy

Couple, The. Ana Blandiana. WPOW, *tr. by* William M. Murray and the
  author

Couple from old Aberystwyth, A. Limerick. Stuart Woods. PeLi

Couple in the Next Room, The. John Ashbery. BodElec

Couple of Swells, A. Irving Berlin. OBCoV; ReLy

Couple painted on the Bridal Shop, The. Two Centuries in One Day. Eloise Klein Healy. GeoHom

Couple slumps on a veranda opening flat cokes, A. Personal Ad. Joanna Fuhrman. AmPoNex

Couple that walked, The. David Kherdian. UrbNat *Fr.* Taking the Soundings on Third Avenue.

Couple there was in Blefuscu, A. Limerick. W. F. N. Watson. PeLi

Couple Waiting, A. Matthew Sweeney. BiHa

Couples. Kate Jennings. BMAP

Couplet: February 24, 1847. Henry Wadsworth Longfellow. APN-1

Couplets. Yehuda Amichai [*or* Amikhai]. FIT, *tr. by* Robert Friend

Couplings buckled, cracked, collapsed. Wreck of the Circus Train, The. Hayden Carruth. GM

Courage. Anna Andreyevna Akhmatova. TCRP, *tr. by* Max Hayward and Stanley Kunitz

Courage. Boris Leonidovich Pasternak. FaBoWar

Courage. Sadi [*or* Saadi *or* Sa'di]. AWP, *tr. by* Sir Edwin Arnold *Fr.* Gulistan, The.

Courage, a Tale. Thom Gunn. GLP

"Courage!" he said, and pointed toward the land. Tennyson. SCGP

Courage my Soul, now learn to wield. Dialogue Between the Resolved Soul and Created Pleasure, A. Andrew Marvell. ESCV; FSCP; GeHe; MeLP

Courage, my Soul! now to the silent wood. Peace. Bhartrihari. AWP, *tr. by* Paul Elmer More

Courage, or One of Gene Horner's Fiddles. Lisa Coffman. AmPoNex

Courage shall grow keener, clearer the will. *Unknown.* WoPoe, *tr. by* Michael Alexander *Fr.* Battle of Maldon, The.

Courage that my mother had, The. Edna St. Vincent Millay. NALW

Courage to let go of the door, the handle, The. Maggid. Marge Piercy. TaR

Courage to Live. Grace Noll Crowell. PoToHe

Courage to wait, The. Greater Courage. Natan Zach. PoSu, *tr. by* Peter Everwine and Shulamit Yasny-Starkman

Coureurs de Bois. Douglas Le Pan. MoCV; NOBC

Couriers, The. Sylvia Plath. LCAP-2

Course, The. Robert Huff. CoAP

Course bread and water's most their fare. Observation Generall from Their Eating, Etc., The. Roger Williams. SCAP; SacPr

Course of a Life, The. Yehuda Amichai [*or* Amikhai]. BBASP, *tr. by* Chana Bloch

Course of a Particular, The. Wallace Stevens. APT-1; HCAP

Course of a Year, The. George Sands Johnson. PWR

Course of the sea over my entry, The. Sea and You, The. Julia de Burgos. TANSG, *tr. by* Heather Rosario Sievert

Courser and the Jennet, The. William Shakespeare. NOBE *Fr.* Venus and Adonis.

Coursing in emptiness. Lal Ded [*or* Lalla]. WPoS

Court considered the country's crisis, The. Brian [*or* Bryan] Merriman [*or* Merryman]. BIrV, *tr. by* David Marcus *Fr.* Midnight Court, The.

Court Historian, The. George Walter Thornbury. PeVV

Court is deep, deep, deep, how deep, The. Lyric to the Tune "Immortal by the River." Li Ch'ing-chao. WoPoe, *tr. by* Julie Landau

Court is kept att leeue London, The. Hugh Spencer's Feats in France. *Unknown.* ESPB

Court lady Addresses Her Lover, A. Edward de Vere, 17th Earl of Oxford. NoSic

Court of Divine Justice, The. Peter Klappert. YaYoPo *Fr.* Pieces of the One and a Half Legged Man.

Court of Love, The. *Unknown.*
  "On May-day, when the lark began to rise." NoSic

Courteous Indian, The. Roger Williams. NOSC; SCAP

Courteous Knight, The. *Unknown.* *See* Baffled Knight, The

Courteous pagan shall condemn[e], The. Courteous Indian, The. Roger Williams. NOSC; SCAP

Courteously self-assured, although alone. Charlotte Corday. Charles Tomlinson. OxBC

Courtesan to a Young Customer, A. Kshetrayya. WoPoe, *tr. by* V. Narayana Rao, A. K. Ramanujan and David Shulman

Courtesan to Her Lover, A. Kshetrayya. WoPoe, *tr. by* V. Narayana Rao, A. K. Ramanujan and David Shulman

Courtesies of good-morning and good-evening. On Dwelling. Robert Graves. FaBoMo; OxBSP

Courtesy, A Trenchant Grace, A. Cyrus Cassells. GT; WiU

Courthouse Graffiti for Two Voices. Martín Espada. InvLad

Courtier's Life, The. Sir Thomas Wyatt. FaBoEE; NoSic

Courtin', The. James Russell Lowell. NOBA; OBAL *Fr.* Biglow Papers, The.

Courting the Faerie Queen. Margaret Lucas Cavendish, Duchess of Newcastle. NOSC

Courtling, I rather thou shouldst utterly. To Censorious Courtling. Ben Jonson. NOSC

Courtship. Rita Dove. LCAP-2

Courtship. Mark Strand. HCAP; PoPoPo

Courtship, The. Ann Beresford. LW

Courtship of Inanna and Dumuzi, The. *Ancient Sumerian Oral Tradition.* "Word they had spoken, The." EroLit, *tr. by* Diane Wolkstein

Courtship of Miles Standish, The. Henry Wadsworth Longfellow. Miles Standish.
  In the Old Colony days, in Plymouth the land of the Pilgrims AiP

Courtship of the Yonghy-Bonghy-Bo, The. Edward Lear. EnLoPo

Courtyard, The. Eddy Van Vliet. VCWP, *tr. by* John Van Tiel

Courtyard is warmed by the coming of spring, The. Drumbeats. Yi Inbok. WoPoe, *tr. by* Kevin O'Rourke

Courtyard Noises from the North, Twenty-fourth Precinct. Colette Inez. UrbNat

Courtyard, quiet, The. Rainy Night. Ho Ching-ming. CoBLCP, *tr. by* Jonathan Chaves

Courtyard was hazy, The. Miraculous Marriage of Zarife Dominquez. Patricia Dubrava. MPUn

Courtyards in Delft. Derek Mahon. CIP-2; ModIr; NPeEn; PBCIP; PNI

Cousin. David Huddle. CDa

Cousin, I think the shape of a marriage. For a Wedding. Kate Clanchy. MFPA

Cousin, it's of you I always dream. Jane Cooper. FaBoWP *Fr.* March.

Cousin Kate. Christina Georgina Rossetti. VWP

Cousin Mary. Wanda Coleman. GT

Cousin Nancy. T. S. Eliot. OBAL; OxBSP

Cousin Sidney. Dannie Abse. AngWePo

Couturier from Haverford West, A. Limerick. E. O. Parrott. PeLi

Covenant of Grace, The. Ann Stanford.
  "Brother Symmes conversed with her on the ship." CRP

Coventry Cathedral. István Vas. IQMS, *tr. by* George Gömöri and Clive Wilmer

Cover Her Face. Thomas Kinsella. CIP-2

Cover me with your everlasting arms. Frances Anne [*or* "Fanny"] Kemble. CenSon; SWaP

Cover my head. Buson. EH, *tr. by* Robert Hass

Cover Photograph. Marilyn Nelson. InvLi

Cover up / Oh, quickly cover up. Mask, The. Laura Riding Jackson. HarvBoo

Cover us with your pools of fir. (LL) Oread. "H. D." APT-1; AWP; ColAP; HeIP-4; MoAmPo; NAAL-2v2; NAAL-5; NALW; NOBA; NPeEn; NoAM; OxBA; PoPoPo; TAP; TCAPo

Cover your arms. Elbows. Minnie Bruce Pratt. WiU

Cover your teeth. (LL) Kalaloch. Carolyn Forché. NoAM; YaYoPo

Covered Bridge. Robert Penn Warren. AiP

Covered with a glory that had lost its luster. Georgy [*or* Georgii] Vladimirovich Ivanov. TCRP

Covered with rags and cardboard and nothing. Women's Room in Pennsylvania Station, The. Kate Daniels. GM

Covered with snow, the herd, with none to guide. Without the Herdsman. Diotimus. AWP, *tr. by* John William Burgon

Covered with yellow leaves. Memory Gardens. Allen Ginsberg. NNaP

Covers it, like a stone covered in grass. (LL) Of the Lady Pietra degli Scrovigni. Dante Alighieri. AWP; EaItPo; MakPoe; NPeEn; OBVE, *tr. by* Dante Gabriel Rossetti

Covets nothing that it has let go. This then you may know / as the hero. (LL) Marianne Craig Moore. NOBA; OxBA *Fr.* Part of a Novel, Part of a Poem, Part of a Play.

Cow, The. Ogden Nash. NBLV; NoP-4; RB

Cow, The. Theodore Roethke. OBAL; OBCA

Cow, The. Robert Louis Stevenson. NTCP; PWR; TLR; WHSW

Cow and a calf, A. *Unknown.* OxNR

Cow Boy. Vincente Huidobro. PFTM-1

Cow-Boy's Song, The. Anna Maria Wells. OBCA; OxIBACP

Cow eats green grass, The. Response to Rimbaud's Later Manner. Thomas Sturge Moore. CABP; OBMV

Cow in Apple Time, The. Robert Frost. MoAmPo; OxBSP

Cow of morning spurted, The. Last Vision of Eoghan Rua Ó Súilleabháin, The. Michael Hartnett. PBCIP

Cow Worship. Gerald Stern. LoL

Coward. A. R. Ammons. OBAL

Coward. Maurya Simon. ExTi

Coward, The. Rudyard Kipling. FaBoEE; FaBoTw; HarvBoo; NPeEn; PeFWW; WoPoe *Fr.* Epitaphs of the War [1914–1918].

Coward, The. Eve Merriam. TrJP

Cowardice. Amado Nervo. BLPSL, *tr. by* Rene de Costa, Rigas Kappatos and Eleni Paidoussi

Cowards fear to die, but Courage stout. On the Snuff of a Candle. Sir Walter Ralegh. FaBoEE

Cowboy Film. Tom Matthews. PNI

Cowboy's Lament, The. *Unknown.* APN-2; ChAP; FaBoA
(Streets of Laredo, The.) RB

Cowboy Sayings. *Unknown.* CA

Cowboy Song. Charles Causley. PoRA

Cowboy stands beneath, The. Vaquero. Edward Dorn. NeAP; PoM

Cowboys, come and hear a story of Roy Bean in all his glory. Roy Bean. *Unknown.* OBAL

Cowherd, The; a Song. Ch'u Kuang-hsi. SuSp, *tr. by* Joseph J. Lee

Cowhorn-crowned, shockheaded, cornshuck-bearded. Knight, Death, and the Devil, The. Randall Jarrell. GS; WeW-3

Cowlady cowlady. Ladybird. *Unknown.* FaBoVe

Cowpasture and the ragged line. Abbey Cwmhir. Harri Webb. AngWePo

Cowper's Grave. Elizabeth Barrett Browning. OxAEP-2

Cowper's Tame Hare. Norman Nicholson. RB

Cows. Peter Kocan. NOBAu

Cows. James Reeves. NOxBChV; NTCP

Cows at Night, The. Hayden Carruth. GifTon

Cows bring in the last light, The. Black Plateau, The. W. S. Merwin. NNaP

Cows graze across the hill. Cows. Peter Kocan. NOBAu

Cows of Heaven, The. Saleem Barakat. MAP, *tr. by* Lena Jayyusi and Naomi Shihab Nye

Cows on a narrow fringe of marshland browsing. Magyar Scene Through Magyar Eyes, A. Gyula Juhász. IQMS, *tr. by* Godfrey Turton

Cows they had, many, like heavy clouds drifting in the meadow. Wheelbarrow, The. Russell Edson. LCAP-2

Cowslips for her covering. (LL) Epitaph upon a Virgin, An. Robert Herrick. CaPo; FaBoEE; OxBoLi

Coxcomb, The. Joseph Hall. OxAEP-1

Coy Nature (which remain'd, though aged grown). Abraham Cowley. NPeEn
Fr. Ode upon Doctor Harvey.

Coyne's. John Ennis. PBCIP

Coyote, The. Carter Revard. VoR

Coyote and the Locust, The. *Unknown.* AWP

Coyote Fragments. Lance Henson. HATNAP

Coyote / running. Sweat Song. Peter Blue Cloud. VoR

Coyote's song, A. New Realism. Joseph Ceravolo. PmAP

Coyote, Skunk, and the Prairie Dogs. *Navajo Oral Tradition.* NAAL-5

Coyotes. George John Whyte-Melville. NOxBChV

Coyotes are howling, The. Coyotes. George John Whyte-Melville. NOxBChV

Coyotismo. Janice Gould. ReEnLa

Crab. Angela Dove. Prnts

Crabapples. Michael Van Walleghen. IllVoic

Crabs. Marge Piercy. NBLV

Crabs. Dennis Saleh. GeoHom

Crabs in their shells, because they cannot play. Armour. Aldous Leonard Huxley. OxBSo

Crabs lie to themselves, The. Crabs. Dennis Saleh. GeoHom

Crack, The. Clark Coolidge. PmAP

Crack, The. Denise Levertov. NALW

Crack! crack! As the Flower of the Grass. May Probyn. VWP

Crack has overtaken your immune defenses. Sandra. Demetrice A. Worley. SpirFl

Crack ran through our hearthstone long ago, A. Refugees, The. Edwin Muir. NoAM

Crack—recall it vividly as first fabric. Light. Richard Kenney. Son

Cracked Bell, The. Charles Baudelaire. SxFrPo, *tr. by* James McGowan

Cracked Looking Glass. Jean Garrigue. VCAP

Cracked Portraits. Agha Shahid Ali. OpBo

Cracking Walnuts. Maria Jastrzebska. Prnts

Cracking whips, off to the wine shop. Streets of Ch'ang-an. Ch'u Kuang-hsi. CoBCP; ColAnChi, *tr. by* Burton Watson

Crackle of parched grass bent by wind, The. Peter Davison. YaYoPo *Fr.* Breaking of the Day, The.

Crackling embers on the hearth are dead, The. Night. Hartley Coleridge. OxBSo

Cracks on the walls, The. Star Blanket. Ray A. Young Bear. CDW

Crackup, last day of Carnival, first of Lint. Martin Johnston. BMAP *Fr.* In Transit: A Sonnet Square.

Cradle, The. Roland Robinson. NOBAu

Cradle Hymn, A. Isaac Watts. OBEV; SCGP

Cradle Song, A: "Angels are stooping, The." W. B. Yeats. NOxBChV

Cradle Song, A: "Golden slumbers kiss your eyes." Thomas Dekker. *See* Pleasant Comedy of Patient Grissell [*or* Grissel *or* Grissill], The

Cradle Song, A: "Sleep, sleep, beauty bright." William Blake. OBEV

Cradle Song, A: "Sweet dreams form a shade." William Blake. FHYEP; OBCP *Fr.* Songs of Innocence.

Cradle Song: "Angels are bending, The." W. B. Yeats. NOBVV

Cradle-Song at Twilight. Alice Thompson Meynell. NOBVV; NPeEn; VWP

Cradle Song: "Clock's untiring fingers wind the wool of darkness, The." Louis MacNeice. MoBrPo

Cradle Song: "Come, little babe." Nicholas Breton. NOBE; OBEV
(Sweet Lullaby, A.) RACG

Cradle Song: "Sleep, my child, my little daughter." *Unknown.* TrJP, *tr. by* Joseph Leftwich

Cradle Will Rock, The. Marc Blitzstein.
Art for Art's Sake. TrJP

Cradled and warm, fur-warm, in the she-wolf's lair. Wolf-Boy. David Malouf. CBAP

Craft of mine and delight. To My Craft. Ágnes Nemes Nagy. IQMS, *tr. by* Hugh Maxton

Craftsman. Luci Shaw. TrCP

Craftsmanship. Nikolai Nikolaevich Ushakov. TCRP, *tr. by* John Glad

Craftsmen. Victoria Mary Sackville-West. OxBTC

Crafty Butcher, The. Susan Hampton. BMAP; NOBAu

Crafty Farmer, The. *Unknown.* ESPB

Crafty Miss of London; or, The Fryar Well Fitted, The. *Unknown.* OxBB

Craggy rocks, crouching like elephants. Climbing Mount Yang. Yüan Hung-tao. CoBLCP, *tr. by* Jonathan Chaves

Cramped, and the bright sun shining on its tusks. (LL) Gratitude. Louise Glück. FaBoWP; TRP

Cramped like sardines on the Queens, and sedated. Tourists. Howard Moss. NoP-4; OBCoV; PeLV

Cranach. Sir Herbert Read. FaBoMo

Crane, The. Saleem Barakat.
Dilana and Diram. MAP, *tr. by* Lena Jayyusi and Naomi Shihab Nye

Crane, The. Charles Tomlinson. MoBrPo

Crane, The. Tu Mu. SuSp, *tr. by* John M. Ortinau

Crane calls in Nine Marshes. Crane Calls. *Unknown.* WoPoe, *tr. by* Constance A. Cook

Crane from the shore standing at the top of the steps, The. Going Alone to Spend a Night at the Hsien-Yu Temple. Po Chü-i. ChiP, *tr. by* Arthur Waley

Crane in Reeds. William Heyen. PoCoUp

Crane Is My Neighbor, The. John Shaw Neilson. CBAP

Crane's legs, The. Basho. EH, *tr. by* Robert Hass

Cranes, The. Po Chü-i. ChiP; OBVE; OWoS, *tr. by* Arthur Waley

Cranes of Ibycus, The. Emma Lazarus. APN-2

Crankadox leaned o'er the edge of the moon, The. Craqueodoom. James Whitcomb Riley. OBAL

Cranmer. Charles Hubert Sisson. FaBoTw

Cranmer and the Bread of Heaven. Anne Ridler. SacPr

Cranmer was person of this parish. Cranmer. Charles Hubert Sisson. FaBoTw

Crapshooters. Carl Sandburg. VGW

Craqueodoom. James Whitcomb Riley. OBAL

Crashing down mossy walls. Middle Age. Arlene L. Mandell. PasH

Craswall. Roland Mathias. OBWVE

Crateas the doctor and Damon the sexton. *Unknown.* GrAn

Crater. Lisa Williams. AmPoNex

Craving of Samuel Rouse for clearance to create, The. Slave and the Iron Lace, The. Margaret Danner. BPo

Crawled near my mind's poor birds. (LL) Trumbull Stickney. APN-2; InPK-6; OxBA; OxBSP *Fr.* Dramatic Fragments.

Crawlin' aboot like a snail in the mud. Image o' God, The. Joe Corrie. ChIV-1; OxBS

Crawling glaciers pierce me with the spears. Shelley. FHYEP *Fr.* Prometheus Unbound [A Lyrical Drama in Four Acts].

Crazed. Walter De la Mare. OxBSP

Crazed. Mary E. Tucker. CBWP-1; RACG

Crazed Girl, A. W. B. Yeats. None

Crazed Man in Concentration Camp. Agnes Gergely. BoWoP, *tr. by* Edwin Morgan

Crazed Woman, The. Jeannette Miller. TANSG, *tr. by* Paula Vega

Crazy as hell and typical of us. Making Contact. John Streeter Manifold. CBAP

Crazy as white shines in summer. City Baseball. Liz Rosenberg. CA

Crazy Boys. Beverly McLoughland. HHAm

Crazy Dog Events. Jerome Rothenberg. RaBo

Crazy Girl, The. Sharan Strange. InTrad

Crazy Horse Monument. Peter Blue Cloud. HATNAP; UnSA

Crazy Horse Speaks. Sherman Alexie. UnSA

Crazy Horse: The Last Morning. Lance Henson. VoR

Crazy in the Heart. Alec Wilder. ReLy

Crazy Jane Grown Old Looks at the Dancers. W. B. Yeats. EBEV

Crazy Jane on God. W. B. Yeats. EBEV; OxBTC; RACG

Crazy Jane Talks with the Bishop. W. B. Yeats. BoLoP; CABP; EBEV; InPK-6; NAEL-5v2; NAEL-6v2; NoAM; NoP-4; OxAEP-2; PAI; PoE; PoPoPo; TOF; TRP

Crazy Kate. William Cowper. NAEL-5v1; NAEL-6v1; NAEL-7v1 *Fr.* Task, The.

Crazy Mind. Kamalākānta Bhattācārya. SinGod, *tr. by* Rachel Fell McDermott

Crazy Mother, The. Margherita Guidacci. CItWP, *tr. by* Cinzia Sartini Blum and Lara Trubowitz

Crazy pigeon strutting outside my cell. Crazy Pigeon. Etheridge Knight. NBV

Crazy Rhythm. Irving Caesar. ReLy

Crazy She Calls Me. Bob Russell. ReLy

Crazy strings: they neigh, and boom and whine. Black Piano, The. Endre Ady. IQMS, *tr. by* Adam Makkai

Crazy Weather. John Ashbery. ColAP; PoE

Crazy Woman, The. Gwendolyn Brooks. ItWoWo; NALW

Creak, creak, loom and shuttle, hidden beyond the trees. Hearing Loom and Shuttle. Yü Chi. CoBLCP, *tr. by* Jonathan Chaves

Creaking of the universe must be, for those, The. Revealing Oneself to a Woman. Bin Ramke. YaYoPo

Cream Song, The. Apirana Ngata. PeNZ, *tr. by* Margaret Orbell

Creamcheese babies square and downy as bolsters. Peaceable Kingdom, The. Marge Piercy. TwCP

Creamy Breasts. Chao Luan-luan. EroLit, *tr. by* Chung Ling and Kenneth Rexroth

Create Desire. Karen Volkman. KGB; NAPBL

Created, The. Jones Very. APN-1; InvLi; NOCV

Created Clay. Maimee Lee Brown. PWR

Created purely from glass the saint stands. In Piam Memoriam. Geoffrey Hill. OxBC

Creation. Ifi Amadiume. HAWP

Creation. Sir Richard Blackmore.
  Digestive System, The. ECEV

Creation. Jeni Couzyn. HAWP

Creation. Mary Weston Fordham. CBWP-2

Creation. Robin Gurr. NOBAu

Creation. John Milton. NOSC *Fr.* Paradise Lost.

Creation. Eunice Odio. TCLAP, *tr. by* Martha Collins

Creation. Eunice Odio.
  "I'm at the point of hurting myself and listening to myself." TANSG, *tr. by* Arthur Natella

Creation. Simon J. Ortiz. CDW; ColAP; HATNAP

Creation, The. Cecil Frances Alexander. *See* All Things Bright and Beautiful

Creation, The. James Weldon Johnson. APT-1; AmFaPo; ChIV-1; ISC; MoAmPo; NAAAL; PoRA; SSLK; SacPr; TrCP

Creation: Enduring the Creator, He who now guides. Cynewulf. ASW *Fr.* Riddles (Exeter Book).

Creation Hymn. *Unknown.* WoPoe, *tr. by* Frederick Morgan *Fr.* Vedic Hymns.

Creation Myth on a Moebius Band. Howard Nemerov. OBCoV

Creation of Light, The. Sister Maura. CRP

Creation of My Lady, The. Francesco Redi. AWP, *tr. by* Sir Edmund Gosse

Creation of the Earth, The. *Navajo Oral Tradition.* TCAPo

Creation's and Creator's crowning good. Coventry Patmore. CABP *Fr.* Unknown Eros, The.

Creation's Lord, We Give Thee Thanks. William deWitt Hyde. AH

Creations mildest charms are there combined. Oliver Goldsmith. NOEC; NPeEn *Fr.* Travel[l]er; or, A Prospect of Society, The.

Creative Poverty. László Szabédi. IQMS, *tr. by* John Gordon Nichols

Creative Process, The. Mark Akenside. NOEC *Fr.* Pleasures of Imagination, The.

Creative Process, The. Amrita Pritam. OMIP, *tr. by* Amrita Pritam and Arlene Zide

Creator is to be remembred in due time, The. Bible, *O.T. See* Ecclesiastes

Creator of Infinities. Chadwick Hansen. AH

Creator Spirit, by whose aid. Veni Creator Spiritus. Charlemagne. AWP; SacPr, *tr. by* John Dryden

Creatrix. Anna Wickham. MoBrPo

Creature Has a Purpose, The. Thomas Lux. BodElec

Creature of charm is the gerbil, A. Limerick. *Unknown.* PeLi

Creatures all eyes and brows, and tresses streaming. Correggio's Cupolas at Parma. Aubrey Thomas De Vere. Son

Creatures in the Zoo. Babette Deutsch. APT-2

Creatures that live in a wave, glass-housed. Garfish. John Blight. BMAP

Creatures that we met this morning, The. Discovery of the New World. Carter Revard. SoSe-8; VoR

Creditor to His Proud Debtor, The. George Moses Horton. NAAAL

Credo. Robinson Jeffers. MoAmPo

Credo. Maxine W. Kumin. ExTi

Credo. Edwin Arlington Robinson. ITBLP; MoAmPo; NAAL-2v2; OxBA; TAP; TrCP

Creed. Belkis Cuza Malé. TANSG, *tr. by* Pamela Carmell

Creed for Free Women, A. Elsa Gidlow. HW

Creed of Mr. Nicholas Culpeper. Patricia Beer. OxBC

Creeds of the Bells. George W. Bungay. PWR

Creek, The. Roland Robinson. NOBAu

Creek of the Four Graves, The. Charles Harpur.
  "I verse a settler's tale of olden times." CBAP

Creek, shining, The. Creek, The. W. W. Eustace Ross. MoCV

Creep into thy narrow bed. Last Word, The. Matthew Arnold. NOBE; SCGP

Creeper grows over thorn. Confucius. CTC, *tr. by* Ezra Pound *Fr.* Songs of T'ang.

Creeping and healing. (LL) Minimal, The. Theodore Roethke. HCAP; NOBA; NoAM; RB

Creeping serrate line of dusty red, A. Fighting Fire. Hamlin Garland. APN-2

Creeps in half wanton, half asleep. Wagner. Rupert Brooke. FaBoTw; NOBL; PeLV

Creide's Lament for Cael. *Unknown.* NOIV

Créide's Lament for Dínertech. *Unknown.* NOIV

Cremation. Robinson Jeffers. BLT

Cremation of Sam McGee, The. Robert W. Service. BRP; NOBC; OBCoV; OBNV; TCAPo

Crepe paper Christmas. Teaching Poetry at Votech High, Santa Fe, the Week John Lennon Was Shot. Paula Gunn Allen. ReTh

Crept like a frightened girl. (LL) Harlot's House, The. Oscar Wilde. EBVV; MoBrPo; NAEL-5v2; NAEL-6v2; NoAM

Crepuscular. Richard Howard. TwCP

Crepuscule. Angela Shaw. NeAmPo

Crepuscule with Nellie. Charles Simic. SeSe

Crescendoes are indigo scarves. Gonsalves. Ron Welburn. SeSe

Crescent moon. Issa. EH, *tr. by* Robert Hass

Crescent moon, A. Ana Istarú. TANSG, *tr. by* Shaun Griffin and Emma Sepúlveda-Pulvirenti

Crescent Moon, The. Mei Yao Ch'en. OHPC, *tr. by* Kenneth Rexroth

Crescent moon hangs on the tip of the willows, A. Ch'ien Ch'ien-i [*or* Ch'ien Ch'ien-yi]. SuSp *Fr.* Willow Branch Songs.

Crescent moon shines, The. Crescent Moon, The. Mei Yao Ch'en. OHPC, *tr. by* Kenneth Rexroth

Crescent, tiny as the curtain hook, The. Moon, The. Hsüeh T'ao. SuSp, *tr. by* Eric W. Johnson

Cressida. James Keir Baxter.
  Bar Room Conversation. PeLV
  In the Lecture Room. PeLV

Crest Jewel, The. James Stephens. MoBrPo

Crests of foam where the milch-kine fed. Flood of Is in Brittany, The. Augusta Davies Webster. ViWPN

Crethis. Callimachus. AWP, *tr. by* Richard Garnett

Creusa. Virgil [*or* Vergil]. NoSic, *tr. by* Henry Howard, Earl of Surrey *Fr.* Aeneid [*or* Eneados, *Aeneis*], The.

Crib, The. Robert Finch. OBCP

Cricket. Issa. EH, *tr. by* Robert Hass

Cricket, The. Konstantin Mikhailovich Simonov. TCRP, *tr. by* Lubov Yakovleva

Cricket, The. Tu Fu. CrYelRi, *tr. by* Sam Hamill

Cricket, The. Frederick Goddard Tuckerman. APN-2; NCAP; NOBA; TCAPo

Cricket; an Heroic Poem. James Dance.
  "When the returning sun begins to smile." NOEC

Cricket and the greshope wenten hem to fight, The. Nonsense. *Unknown.* EBEV

Cricket at Central California Women's Facility. Dixie Salazar. GeoHom

Cricket at Oxford. Alan Ross. PeLV

Cricket cries, The. Fujiwara no Go-Kyōgoku. OHPJ

Cricket, crying, A. Shiko. JDP, *tr. by* Yoel Hoffmann

Cricket did not actually seek the hearth, The. Mary Oliver. PoCoUp *Fr.* West Wind.

Cricket is so small a thing, The. Cricket, The. Tu Fu. CrYelRi, *tr.* by Sam Hamill

Cricket Kept the House, The. Edith Matilda Thomas. OBCA

Cricket, lovely cricket. Victory Calypso, Lord's 1950. Egbert Moore. PeLV

Cricket Mountain. Khaled Mattawa. NAPBL

Cricket Music. Lőrinc Szabó.

  Babits. IQMS, *tr.* by John Gordon Nichols

  English Poetry. IQMS, *tr.* by John Gordon Nichols

  Moment, The. IQMS, *tr.* by Watson Kirkconnell

  On a Raft. IQMS, *tr.* by Watson Kirkconnell

  Shame. IQMS, *tr.* by John Gordon Nichols

  To Forget? IQMS, *tr.* by Watson Kirkconnell

  Tranquil Miracle, The. IQMS, *tr.* by Watson Kirkconnell

  With Flute, with Violin. IQMS, *tr.* by Watson Kirkconnell

Cricket on a rubbish-tip, A. Winter Cricket. John Heath-Stubbs. OBCP

Cricket, you'll sing no more. Aristodicus of Rhodes. GrAn

Cricketer's Retirement Day, The. Julia Copus. NeBl

Crickets. David McCord. NTCP

Crickets. Larry Wiggin. HA

Crickets' chirps become increasingly urgent. Upon Passing the Homestead. Huang T'ing-chien. SuSp, *tr.* by Michael E. Workman

Crickety Creek. Arkady Kutilov. TCRP, *tr.* by Bradley Jordan

Crickhowel. Richard Hall. AngWePo

Cried a man on the Salisbury Plain. Myra Cohn Livingston. KaS

Cried a scientist watching this creature dart by. Hummingbird. X. J. Kennedy. NOxBChV

Cried Innocence, "Mother, my thumbs, my thumbs!" Tortured, The. May Sarton. FFC

Cried the maid: "You must marry me, Hume!" Limerick. P. W. R. Foot. PeLi

Crier, The. Michael Drayton. NOSC

  (Cryer, The.) SCGP

Crier, The. Philip Kahclamet. STP, *tr.* by Dell Hymes

Cries of London, The. *Unknown.* OPOU

Cries of the Newsboy. Edith Matilda Thomas. SWaP

Cries of wild geese. Issa. ZenPo, *tr.* by Takashi Ikemoto and Lucien Stryk

Crime. Robert Penn Warren. FuPo

Crime Againts Nature. Minnie Bruce Pratt. WiU

Crime and Punishment. Kahlil Gibran. PoToHe *Fr.* Prophet, The.

Crime and Punishment. Paul Lake. RA

Crime and Punishment. János Pilinszky. IQMS, *tr.* by Adam Makkai

Crime at Its Best. Stoddard King. NBLV

Crime of the Ages, The. Augusta Cooper Bristol. APN-2

Crime Was in Granada, The. Antonio Machado Ruiz. SpanPo, *tr.* by Kate Flores

Crimea. Vladimir Vladimirovich Mayakovsky [or Maiakovskii]. RusPo, *tr.* by Robert Arthur Douglas Ford

Crimean Heroes, The. Walter Savage Landor. FaBoWar

Crimes of Lugalanne. Enheduanna. BoWoP

Criminal. Stephen Dunn. MoASP

Criminal, you took a great piece of my life. Badly-Chosen Lover. Rosemary Tonks. EmeKit

Crimson dragonfly, A. Kenneth Yasuda. HA

Crimson roses burn and glow, The. Vigil. Richard Dehmel. AWP, *tr.* by Ludwig Lewisohn

Criole Candjo. George Washington Cable. APN-2

Cripple, The. Khalil Khouri. MAP, *tr.* by Sharif Elmusa and Christopher Middleton

Cripple Creek. *Unknown.* APN-2

Cripple Dick upon a stick. *Unknown.* OxNR

Crippled beggar who lives, The. "Zelda." FIT, *tr.* by Robert Friend

Crisis is on me, A. My soul is mute. Ironical Elegy, Composed in Those Terribly Sad Moments When I Cannot Write. Andrey [or Andrei] Andreievich Voznesensky [or Voznesenskii]. RusPo, *tr.* by Robert Arthur Douglas Ford

Crisp / pale green, The. Salad La Raza. Janet Campbell Hale. VoR

Crispus Attucks. Robert Earl Hayden. ESEAA

Crispus Attucks McCoy. Sterling Allen Brown. BPo

Crist, buyere of alle icoren. William Herebert. MiEL

Critic. Elwyn Brooks White. NBLV *Fr.* Definitions.

Critic, A. Walter Savage Landor. FaBoEE

Critic, The. C. K. Williams. OPRER

Critic advises, A. Black Poet, White Critic. Dudley Randall. BPo; CoAmPo

Critic leaves at curtain fall, The. Elwyn Brooks White. NBLV *Fr.* Definitions.

Critic, must have a heart as well as a head. (LL) Thomas Edwards. CenSon; Son

Critical Condition. Sang Yi.

  Precipice. PFTM-1

Critical mass came over me, A. Depression, The. Ira Sadoff. BodElec

Critical Observations. Archibald MacLeish. OBAL

Criticism. Ebenezer Elliott. CenSon

Critics. Martial. AWP, *tr.* by Sir John Harington

Critics. Jonathan Swift. HAP; SCV *Fr.* On Poetry: a Rhapsody.

Critics and Connoisseurs. Marianne Craig Moore. APT-1; FaBoWP; NOBA; NoAM; OxBA

Critics and Poets. Geoffrey Grigson. FaBoEE

Critics cry unfair, The. In Defense of Black Poets. Conrad Kent Rivers. BPo

Critics say that epics have died out, The. Elizabeth Barrett Browning. FaBoWar; NAEL-5v2; NAEL-6v2; NALW; NoP-4; PeVV *Fr.* Aurora Leigh.

Critique. Anthony Barnett. Oth

Critter. W. M. Ransom. CDW

Crivens! This is jist typical. Maw Broon Visits a Therapist. Jackie Kay. MFPA

Cro-Kill. Anthony Lawrence. NOBAu

Cro-Magnons. Lawrence Ferlinghetti. BB

Croak of a raven hoar, The! Mammon Marriage. George Macdonald. BoLoP; EBVV; SacPr

Croaked the Eagle: "Nevermore." "Sagittarius." UV

Croaker Papers, The. Fitz-Greene Halleck.

  National Painting [or Paintings], The. APN-1

Croaking frog in a well sees the sky from end to end, A. Yüan Hao-wen. SuSp *Fr.* On Poetry.

Crocodile. William Jay Smith. OBCA

Crocodile, A. Thomas Lovell Beddoes. NOBVV; NPeEn; OxBEV; RB *Fr.* Last Man, The.

Crocodile, The. Lewis Carroll. ChAP; FaBoCh; FaBoEE; NBLV; NOBL; NOBVV; OxBEV; RB; TFi; TTTS; UV *Fr.* Alice's Adventures in Wonderland.

Crocodile, The. Oliver Herford. OBCA

Crocodile 1–15. Yang Lian. PFTM-2, *tr.* by Mabel Lee

Crocodile attacks with a glance, The. Crocodile 1–15. Yang Lian. PFTM-2, *tr.* by Mabel Lee

Crocodile once dropped a line, A. Crocodile, The. Oliver Herford. OBCA

Crocodile wept bitter tears, The. Crocodile. William Jay Smith. OBCA

Crocus Air. Winfield Townley Scott. APT-2

Crocus armies from the dead, The. Veni Coronaberis. Geoffrey Hill. DiPo; NoP-4

Crocus Night. James Schuyler. PoM

Crocuses, The. Frances Ellen Watkins Harper. BlSi

Croeso i Gymru. Philip Owens. AngWePo

Crofters few but crafty. Shore Tullye. Robert Rendall. OxBS

"Crom Cruach and his sub-gods twelve." Burial of King Cormac, The. Sir Samuel Ferguson. NOIV

Cromwell. Brendan Kennelly.

  Three Tides. ModIr

  Vintage. ModIr

Cromwell, our chief [or cheif] of men, who through a cloud. To the Lord General Cromwell. John Milton. NAEL-5v1; NAEL-6v1; NOSC; SCGP; Son

Cromwell: The Last Portrait. David Lindley. NLP

Crone, The. Karolina Pavlova. ARWW, *tr.* by Catriona Kelly

Crooked Afro. Frank X. Walker. SpirFl

Crooked bank still winds to something new, The. Sneyd Davies. NOEC *Fr.* Voyage to Tintern Abbey, A.

Crooked ear, crooked ear, / Walker at night. Corn Song. *Unknown.* APN-2, *tr.* by Henry Rowe Schoolcraft

Crooked in the skyward angle of a pyramid. Prey. Michael Dorris. PoCoUp

Crooked, like bough the march wind bends wallward across the sleet. Lavender Woman, The. Lizette Woodworth Reese. APN-2

Crooked paths go every way, The. Goat Paths, The. James Stephens. AWP; SCGP; UnPo

Crooked River Meditation. Tu Fu. CrYelRi, *tr.* by Sam Hamill

Crooked Sixpence, The. Mother Goose. *See* There Was a Crooked Man

Croon on Hennacliff, A. Robert Stephen Hawker. NOBVV

Crop of sweat and blood, of African slave labour. On Sweet Coffee. Ábrahám Barcsay. IQMS, *tr.* by Peter Zollman

Croppy Boy, The. *Unknown.* NOIV; OxBoLi

Crops are all gathered, The. Harvest Sacrifice. Su Tung-p'o (Su Shih). OHPC, *tr.* by Kenneth Rexroth

Crops like hedgehogs, high-crown'd hats. Modern Male Fashions. Mary Robinson. NOBRP

Croquet by Moonlight. Julia A. Moore.

"On a moonlight evening, in the month of May." VerBaPo

Cross. Langston Hughes. ColAP; GT; HarvBoo; NoP-4; SAmP; SoSe-8; TAP

Cross, The. Allen Tate. AWP; ChIV-2; MoAmPo; OxBA

Cross, The. Jones Very. NCAP

Cross at the morning. Once and Upon. Madeline Gleason. NeAP

Cross between a bakehouse and a bell tower, A. Elegy. Oleg Grigorevich Chukhonstev. TCRP, tr. by Simon Franklin

Cross Country. Rod Moran. NOBAu

Cross Country. Ann Sansom. MFPA

Cross Cut. Peter Davison. ColAP

Cross-framed square of kitchen light, A. Back Steps Lookout. Rhyll McMaster. BMAP

Cross leaves marks the tree we fancy, A. Owl Is an Only Bird of Poetry, An. Robert Duncan. NeAP; PoM

Cross of Snow, The. Henry Wadsworth Longfellow. APN-1; AWTN; ColAP; GSo; HeIP-4; NOBA; NoP-4; OxBA; TAP; TCAPo

Cross-Patch. Unknown. LB

Cross Patch / Draw the latch. Mother Goose. OxNR; ReMoGo

Cross Questions. John Wheelwright. APT-2

Cross-Road Epitaph, A. Amy Levy. VWP

Cross staggered him. At the cliff-top, The. Canticle for Good Friday. Geoffrey Hill. ChIV-2

Cross the Aegean Without Me, Then, Messalla. Tibullus. WoPoe, tr. by Humphrey Clucas

Cross the Aegean without me, then, Messalla. Cross the Aegean Without Me, Then, Messalla. Tibullus. WoPoe, tr. by Humphrey Clucas

Cross, the Cross, The. Tortoise-Shell. D. H. Lawrence. FaBoVe; NAEL-5v2; NAEL-6v2; OxAEP-2

'Cross the ford o' Kabul river in the dark! (LL) Ford o' Kabul River. Rudyard Kipling. FaBoTw; PeVV

Cross, the icon, The. Paradox, The. Francesca Yetunde Pereira. PBA

Cross-tree, The. Robert Herrick. CavPo; ChIV-2

Cross[e], The. George Herbert. ESCV

Crossed Apple, The. Louise Bogan. HeIP-4; NALW

(I've come to give you fruit from out of my orchard.) RACG

Crossed out delete and wrote his patient stet. (LL) Proof, The. Richard Wilbur. CRP; InvLi; OxBSP

Crossed-Over, Fiend-Snitched, X-ed Out. Mary Jo Bang. BAP-01

Crossed over on the other shore. Heartstopping. Nicole Espagnol. SurWo, tr. by Myrna Bell Rochester

Crossed Threads. Helen Hunt Jackson. APN-2

Crosses. Robert Herrick. CaPo

Crossing. Buson. EH, tr. by Robert Hass

Crossing. Diane Ward. FTOS

Crossing, The. Aleksandr Trifonovich Tvardovsky [or Tvardovskii]. TCRP, tr. by April FitzLyon Fr. Vasily Tyorkin.

Crossing Alone the Nighted Ferry. A. E. Housman. GTBS-P; HarvBoo; NOBE; NPeEn; NoP-4; OxBEV; OxBSP

Crossing Brooklyn Ferry. Walt Whitman. APN-1; ColAP; FaBoA; NAAL-2v1; NAAL-3; NAAL-5; NCAP; NOBA; NoAM; NoP-4; TAP

"Flood-tide below me! I see you face to face!" WoPoe

Crossing Brooklyn Ferry from Staten Island. New Boy, The. Peter E. Murphy. OPRER

Crossing Ching-Men to See a Friend Off. Li Po. ChinPo, tr. by Yip Wai-lim

Crossing Disappearing behind Them. Marjorie Welish. PmAP

Crossing half the sky. Basho. SoOfWa, tr. by Sam Hamill

Crossing Han River. Li P'in. OHMPC, tr. by Kenneth Rexroth

Crossing Kansas by Train. Donald Justice. AiP

Crossing Lincoln Park. Karl Shapiro. IllVoic

Crossing Nation. Allen Ginsberg. AiP

Crossing Over. William Meredith. NoAM

Crossing South of Li-chou, A. Wen T'ing-yün. SuSp, tr. by William R. Schultz

Crossing the Atlantic. Anne Sexton. NoAM

Crossing the autumn moor. Buson. EH, tr. by Robert Hass

Crossing the Bar. Tennyson. BRP; ChIV-2; ClHu; EBVV; HeIP-4; ITBLP; NAEL-5v2; NAEL-6v2; NOBE; NOBVV; NoP-4; OBEV; PWR; PeECV; PoRA; SacPr; SoSe-8; TFi; TrCP

Crossing the Border. Norman MacCaig. HarvBoo

Crossing the Border, First Series. Tu Fu.

"Drawing a bow you must draw a strong one." WoPoe, tr. by David Lattimore

Crossing the Frontier. Li Meng-yang. CoBLCP, tr. by Jonathan Chaves

Crossing the Hsiang River at Night. Meng Hao Jan. SuSp, tr. by Daniel Bryant

Crossing the keyboards of the palace. Viktor Krivulin. ItGoST, tr. by Michael Molnar

Crossing the Lang-yeh Mountain with a Friend. Wei Ying-wu. SuSp, tr. by Wu-Chi Liu

Crossing the Mountain, I Follow the Chin-chu River. Hsieh Ling-yün. CrYelRi, tr. by Sam Hamill

Crossing the ridge, the woodcutter loses his way. Li K'ai-hsien. CoBLCP Fr. Describing My Feelings upon Encountering Snow.

Crossing the River. Patrizia Vicinelli. ItPo, tr. by Gayle Ridinger Fr. Foundations of Being, The.

Crossing the River. Yang Shih-ch'i. CoBLCP, tr. by Jonathan Chaves

Crossing the river I pluck the lotus flowers. Unknown. ChiP Fr. Seventeen Old Poems.

Crossing the shallow holdings high above sea. Hungry Grass, The. Donagh MacDonagh. BIrV

Crossing the Square. Grace Schulman. ExTi

Crossing the Strait. Nicholas Samaras. TWW

Crossing the street. Broken Home, The. James Merrill. ColAP; HAP; HCAP; NAAL-2v2; NAAL-5; NOBA; NoAM; NoP-4; PoPoPo

Crossing the Water. Sylvia Plath. HCAP; RB

Crossing the Yangtze in a Strong Wind. Wang Shih-chieng. CoBLCP, tr. by Jonathan Chaves

Crossing the Yellow River. Wang Wei. CrYelRi, tr. by Sam Hamill

Crossing the Yellow River: June 12. Yüan Hao-wen. SuSp, tr. by Stephen West

Crossing there under the trees with leaden pace. False Enchantment. Jean Starr Untermeyer. MoAmPo

Crossing this lake at night in a shell canoe. Maine Lake at Night. Harry Morris. CRP

Crossing Ts'en River. Yang Wan-li. SuSp, tr. by Jonathan Chaves

Crossings. Linda Hogan. BodElec

Crossroads, The. Maria Luisa Spaziani. CItWP, tr. by Cinzia Sartini Blum and Lara Trubowitz

Crossroads in the Past. John Ashbery. BAP-01

Crotchet Castle. Thomas Love Peacock.

Chorus: "If I drink water while this doth last." NBLV

Priest and the Mulberry-Tree, The. OxAEP-2

Crouched in a sandbagged bunker. War Games. Walter McDonald. CDa

Crouched in its giant green the Indian hid. Vacant Lot. Dudley Randall. NoAM

Crouched on one knee one. Autumn Warrior. Barney Bush. HATNAP

Crouched on their women woven saddle rugs. Great Horse Fair, The. Desmond O'Grady. PBCIP

Crouched [or Crouch'd] on the pavement close by Belgrave Square. West London. Matthew Arnold. SCGP; Son

Crow. Robert Grenier. PmAP

Crow. Ted Hughes. PoE

That Moment. UV

Crow. Yunna Petrovna [or Iunna Pinkhusovna] Moritz [or Morits]. ItGoST, tr. by Daniel Weissbort

Crow. Viktor Aleksandrovich Sosnora. ItGoST, tr. by Dinara Georgeoliani and Mark Halperin

Crow, A. Basho. EH, tr. by Robert Hass

Crow, The. Issa. EH, tr. by Robert Hass

Crow after crow darts into the woods; the passers-by are few. Fan Ch'eng-ta. SuSp, tr. by Irving Y. Lo Fr. Seasonal Poems on Fields and Gardens.

Crow and Pie. Unknown. ESPB

Crow and the Birds. Ted Hughes. HarvBoo

Crow and the Fox, The. Jean de La Fontaine. AWP, tr. by Edward Marsh

Crow and the Fox, The. Reed Whittemore. BodElec

Crow came to our house one time, A. Crow. Yunna Petrovna [or Iunna Pinkhusovna] Moritz [or Morits]. ItGoST, tr. by Daniel Weissbort

Crow caws in the moonlight, A. Unknown. OHMPJ

Crow-Children Walk My Circles in the Snow, The. Ray A. Young Bear. CDW

Crow Cries at Night, The. Po Chü-i. SuSp, tr. by Irving Y. Lo

Crow flies off, The. Larry Gates. HA

Crow, in pulpit lone and tall. In the Pauper's Turnip-Field. Herman Melville. OxBSP

Crow in the snowy pine, A. Nicholas Virgilio. HA

Crow Jane. Imamu Amiri Baraka. PoM

(For dawn, wind / off the river.) BB

Crow or crowd with its detached features of twig bark and plunder walks to, The. Allegory. Carla Harryman. FTOS

Crow realized God loved him. Crow's Theology. Ted Hughes. GI

Crow's / Abandoned nest. Basho. ZenPo, tr. by Takashi Ikemoto and Lucien Stryk

Crow's-Eye View. Sang Yi.

Poem No. II. PFTM-1

Crow's First Lesson. Ted Hughes. NoAM

Crow's Last Stand. Ted Hughes. HarvBoo

Crow's Theology. Ted Hughes. GI

Crow's Way. Duane Niatum. CDW

Crow sat perched upon an oak, A. Crow and the Fox, The. Jean de La Fontaine. AWP, tr. by Edward Marsh

Crow sits on the prayerflagpole, A. Who Eats Who? Allen Ginsberg. BodElec

Crow went on laughing. (LL) Childish Prank, A. Ted Hughes. CABP; NPeEn; OxBC

Crowd, The. John Masefield. OxBTC

Crowd and Not Evening or Light. Leslie Scalapino. Series—3, The. PmAP

Crowd at the ball game, The. At the Ball Game. William Carlos Williams. MoASP; NOBA; NoAM; OxBA; PoE

Crowd was gathering beneath the tent, A. Clown, The. Margaret E. Bruner. PoToHe

Crowded Street, The. William Cullen Bryant. NCAP

Crowded Trolley Car, A. Elinor Wylie. SacPr

Crowded with beauties is thy lovely vale. Crickhowel. Richard Hall. AngWePo

Crowdieknowe. Hugh MacDiarmid. OxBS

Crowding this beach. Stone Speech. Charles Tomlinson. NPeEn

Crowding time back in a corner. (LL) Remembrance of Strange Hospitality. Yelena [or Elena] Shwarts [or Shvarts]. ItGoST; VCWP, tr. by Michael Molnar

Crowdoll. L. S. Asekoff. BodElec

Crowds amassed with sudden bursts of, The. Victoria Station. Luigi Fontanella. NeIt, tr. by Michael Palma

Crowds cheer silently for hours. Watching Ants Play Soccer in Central Park. Anthony Piccione. UrbNat

Crowds of shuffling feet pass over the bridge. Goddess Chiao, The. Unknown. CoBCP, tr. by Burton Watson

Crowds pour from the train. My, what a crew—like people possessed! Mother, The. Nikolai Ivanovich Dementyev [or Dement'ev]. TCRP, tr. by Max Hayward and Lubov Yakovleva

Crowing of the Red Cock, The. Emma Lazarus. TaR

Crown, The. John Donne. ChIV-2 Fr. Holy Sonnets.

Crown and Country. Jackie Kay. MFPA

Crown me with roses whilest I live. Abraham Cowley. OBVE Fr. Epicure, The.

Crown of all travailing. Unknown. MLL Fr. Carmina Burana.

Crown of Days. Unknown. TrJP, tr. by Herbert Loewe

Crown of glory unto woman's brow, The. (LL) Joan of Arc in Rheims. Felicia Dorothea Hemans. RWP; ViWPN

Crown of Happiness. Anne Hébert. BoWoP, tr. by Willis Barnstone

Crown of ivy! I submit my head, A. On Receiving a Crown of Ivy from the Same. Leigh Hunt. Son

Crown Prince of Dullness, The. Dryden. NOBE; OBCoV; OxBEV; SCV Fr. Mac Flecknoe [or, A Satire upon the True-Blue Protestant Poet T. S.].

Crown your Bacchus with lettuce leaves, not ivy. Lucilius. GrAn

Crown[e] of Sonnets [or Sonetts] Dedicated to Love, A. Mary Sidney Wroth, Countess of Montgomery. Fr. Pamphilia to Amphilanthus.

Crowned in hydrogen, it travels incognito. To the Sun. Tom Sleigh. UrbNat

Crowned with flowers, I saw fair Amarillis. Unknown. EnLoPo

Crowned with snows to catch the morning's fire. (LL) Snow. John Davidson. NPeEn; NePenScot

Crowning a bluff where gleams the lake below. Pontoosuce. Herman Melville. APN-2; NCAP; NOBA; TCAPo

Crowns all thy mean affairs. (LL) Waldeinsamkeit. Ralph Waldo Emerson. APN-1; NOBA

Crows. David McCord. MoAmPo

Crows. Lizette Woodworth Reese. APT-1; TCAPo

Crows. Mariana Romo-Carmona. WiU

Crows, The. Louise Bogan. FaBoWP; NALW

Crows, The. David McCord. MoAmPo

Crows, The. Maria Valli. CBAP

Crows are cawing, The. Coming and Going. Robert Francis. TLR

Crows are come again to pick my eyes, The. Soliloquy on Death. F. K. Fiawoo. PBA

Crows at Dusk. Li Po. CrYelRi, tr. by Sam Hamill

Crows came in, The. Caw Caw the Crows Caw Caw. Unknown. STP, tr. by Richard Johnny John and Jerome Rothenberg

Crows cawed, The. just before. dawn. Landscape Painting. Diane Glancy. TWW

Crows in a Strong Wind. Cornelius Eady. ESEAA; InvLad

Crows on City Walls. Unknown. ColAnChi, tr. by Anne Birrell

Crowther—Ours. Dyan Newson. IBA

Crucified. Francis Quarles. NOSC

Crucified Lord, you swim upon your cross. Geoffrey Hill. NAEL-5v2; NAEL-6v2; NoAM Fr. Lachrimae; or Seven Tears Figured in Seven Passionate Pavans.

Crucifix, The. Daniel Berrigan. CRP

Crucifix in a Deathhand. Charles Bukowski. PmAP

Crucifixion. Hayden Carruth. BodElec

Crucifixion. Unknown. BPo; TAP

Crucifixion, The. Mary Weston Fordham. CBWP-2

Crucifixion, The. Alice Thompson Meynell. SacPr

Crucifixion, The. Henry Hart Milman. SacPr

Crucifixion, The. Unknown. MiEL

Crucifixion of Our Blessed Lord. Christopher Smart. ChIV-2 Fr. Hymns and Spiritual Songs for the Fasts and Festivals of the Church of England.

Crucify Him! Giles Fletcher, the Elder. SacPr

'Crucify Him, Crucify Him!' Hark. Will You Crucify Your King? "Michael Field." ViWPN

Cruel arrows gone, The. Fleche. Larry Eigner. VGW

Cruel Brother, The. Unknown. ESPB; OxBB

Cruel, but composed and bland. Atossa. Matthew Arnold. TriCat

Cruel, Clever Cat. Geoffrey Taylor. FaBoEE

Cruel disease! Can there for beauty be. Verses Sent to Mr Bevil Higgons, on His Sickness and Recovery from the Small-pox, in the Year 1693. Catherine Cockburn. EMWP

Cruel girls we loved, The. Mothers and Daughters. David Campbell. BMAP

Cruel Mother, The. Unknown. ESPB; InPK-6; OxBB

Cruel Sister, The. Unknown. OxBB

Cruel the roar of the city ways. Cries of the Newsboy. Edith Matilda Thomas. SWaP

CRUEL, you pull away too soon your lips whenas you kiss me. Unknown. NoSic

Cruell Maid, The. Robert Herrick. CaPo

Crueller than owl or eagle. Ted Hughes. HAP Fr. Skylarks.

Cruellest thing they did, The. Finale. Judith Wright. EmeKit

Cruelties. Robert Herrick. CavPo

Cruelty. Don't talk to me about cruelty. Lucille Clifton. BodElec

Cruelty has a Human heart. William Blake. ChIV-1; NAEL-5v2; NAEL-6v2; NoP-4; RB Fr. Songs of Experience.

Cruelty, the Vandals Say. Alan Michael Parker. NeAmPo

'Cruetin Sarjunt, The. James Russell Lowell. See Biglow Papers, The

Cruise of the Mystery, The. Celia Laighton Thaxter. OBCA

Cruising. Gig Ryan. BMAP

Cruising 99. Garrett Kaoru Hongo. Confession of the Highway / The Hermit Speaks. GeoHom Porphyry of Elements, A. GeoHom

Cruising with the Beach Boys. Dana Gioia. GeoHom; SwNoth

Crum Appointment, The. Lizelia Augusta Jenkins Moorer. CBWP-3

Crumble Hall. Mary Leapor. In the Kitchen. ECWP

Crumbling is not an instant's Act. Emily Dickinson. NOBA; TCAPo

Crumpled like an embroidered pillowcase. Kinged. Shalin Hai-Jew. UnSA

Crunch, The. Gerda Mayer. OBSP

Crunking crane heard high amongst the clouds, The. George Farewell. NOEC Fr. Country Man, The.

Crusader's wife slipped from the garrison, A. Limerick. Ogden Nash. PeLi

Crusaders knew the Holy Places, The. Jenny Mastoraki. BoWoP

Cruse of Tears, The. A Russian Legend. Emily Jane Pfeiffer. ViWPN

Crush the manroot, swallow what you desire. Learning the Spells; a Diptych. Anita Endrezze. CDW

Crushed by the waves upon the crag was I. Sea Dirge. Archias of Byzantium. AWP, tr. by Andrew Lang

Crushed Flower, The. Mary E. Tucker. CBWP-1

Crusoe. Paul Valéry. PFTM-1

Crusoe had provided all the necessaries and was more or less at leisure in. Crusoe. Paul Valéry. PFTM-1

Crusoe in England. Elizabeth Bishop. APT-2; EmeKit; FaBoVe; HCAP; PoPoPo; RACG

Crusoe's Island. Derek Walcott. VCWP

Crust on Fresh Snow. Rolf Jacobsen. WoPoe, tr. by Olav Grinde

Crustaceans. Roy Fuller. NoAM

Crutch slipping towel over. Changing. Daphne Rock. Prnts

Crutches. Robert Herrick. CaPo

Cry, "All flesh is grass." (LL) On a Clergyman's Horse Biting Him. Unknown. FaBoEE; NBLV; OxBoLi

Cry, Baby. Unknown. ReMoGo

Cry, baby, cry, / Put your finger in your eye. Cry, Baby. Unknown. ReMoGo

Cry, crow. Sonnet. Hayden Carruth. NNaP; Son

Cry Faugh! Robert Graves. MoBrPo

Cry from the Ghetto, A. Morris Jacob Rosenfeld. TrJP, *tr.* by Charles Weber Linn

Cry is: "Back to God!" Without respite, The. Homeward Journey, The. Leonard [*or* Lazarus] Aaronson. TrJP

Cry of a People. Mary [*or* Mollie] Evelyn Moore Davis. SWaP

Cry of a Stone, A. Anna Trapnell.
　"Therefore John read how that thou wouldst." ChIV-2

Cry of a Stone, The. Anna Trapnell.
　"O he is a rest that requires." PBRV

Cry of Birth. J. P. Clark Bekederemo. PBMAP *Fr.* Reed in the Tide, A.

Cry of Blood, and of a Broken Covenant, The. Sir William Mure.
　"O Heavens! O Earth! heer I must pause a space." PBRV

Cry of South Africa, The. Olive Schreiner. PeSAV

Cry of the Animals, The. Mary Howitt. VWP

Cry of the Children, The. Elizabeth Barrett Browning. EBVV; OxAEP-2; VWP; ViWPN

Cry of the Daughter of My People, The. Bible, *O.T.* TrJP *Fr.* Jeremiah.

Cry of the deer / Where at its depths. Otsuyu. ZenPo, *tr.* by Takashi Ikemoto and Lucien Stryk

Cry of the guitar, The. Guitar, The. Federico García Lorca. SpanPo, *tr.* by Rachel Benson and Robert O'Brien

Cry of the Human, The. Elizabeth Barrett Browning.
　Convinced by Sorrow. SacPr
　" 'There is no God,' the foolish saith." SacPr

Cry of the Oppressed, The. Henrietta Tindal. VWP

Cry of the Peoples, The. Alter Brody. TrJP

Cry of the stag, The. Yakamochi (Otomo no Yakamochi). OHPJ

Cry of those being eaten by America, The. Those Being Eaten by America. Robert Bly. CoAP

Cry out for Sakhr when a dove with necklaces. Elegy for Her Brother Sakhr. Al-Khansa. BoWoP, *tr.* by Willis Barnstone

Cryer, The. Michael Drayton. *See* Crier, The

Crying. Galway Kinnell. ChAP; KaS; NTCP

Crying. Scott Montgomery. HA

Crying as you sleep. (LL) Nightsweats. Richard Tayson. AmPoNex; WiU

Crying Asia! that famous place. Marriage of Hector and Andromache, The. Sappho. OBVE, *tr.* by Guy Davenport

Crying in Early Infancy. John Tranter.
　"Chicago 'Manual of Style' is really neat, The." NoAM
　"Giving up women is worse than animal laxatives." NoAM
　"It's bad luck with a coughing baby." CBAP
　"Spy bears his bald intent like a maniac, The." CBAP
　"Sweat is a style of the body." NoAM
　"They burn the radio and listen to the blues." NoAM

Crying only a little bit. Crying. Galway Kinnell. ChAP; KaS; NTCP

Crying out for the help of me. (LL) Holy Well, The. *Unknown.* FaBoCh; NOCV

Crying plovers, The. Fujiwara No Sueyoshi. OHMPJ

Crying unseen, birds awaken me from my sleep. Impressions. Lu Yu. SuSp, *tr.* by Irving Y. Lo

Crying white candle, A. Haunted, The. Brad Leithauser. RA

Cryptic philosopher, Kant, The. Limerick. "E. F. C." PeLi

Crypto-Jews, The. Robin Becker. ExTi; OPRER; TaR

Cryptogram, The. David Lindley. NLP

Crystal, The. George Barker. OBMV

Crystal, The. Sidney Lanier. TCAPo

Crystal Cabinet, The. William Blake. FaBoCh; NPeEn; PAI

Crystal Chandeliers. David Ignatow. BodElec

Crystal, flawless beauty on the brows, A. Portrait, A. "Michael Field." VWP

Crystal Gazer, The. Sara Teasdale. MoAmPo

Crystal Lithium, The. James Schuyler. PmAP; PoM; VCAP

Crystal Moment. Edward Weismiller. YaYoPo

Crystal Night. Denise Levertov. TaR *Fr.* During the Eichmann Trial.

Crystal Night. Lyn Lifshin. GotH

Crystal Palace, The. John Davidson. PeVV
　"Contraption,—that's the bizarre, proper slang." NePenScot

Crystal parting the meads. River in the Meadows, The. Léonie Adams. MoAmPo

Crystal Text, The. Clark Coolidge.
　"Where is the wonder to not know?" PFTM-2

Crystal willow, a poplar of water, A. Octavio Paz. WoPoe, *tr.* by Eliot Weinberger *Fr.* Sunstone.

Crystallization of color spreads, A. Aurora Borealis. Edouard Roditi. SPE

Crystals like Blood. Hugh MacDiarmid. HAP; HarvBoo; RB

CS. Geraldine Monk. Oth

Csongor and Tünde. Mihály Vörösmarty.

Soliloquy of the Night, The. IQMS, *tr.* by Peter Zollman

Csontváry. László Nagy. IQMS, *tr.* by George Gömöri and Kenneth McRobbie

Cu Chuimne in his youth. Epitaph for Cu Chuimne. *Unknown.* NOIV; WoPoe, *tr.* by Thomas Kinsella

Cu Chuimne in youth. *Unknown.* BIrV

Cuando el tecolote canta, el Indio muere. Consuelo de Aerenlund. OPRER

Cuauhtemoc. Frank Lima. BodElec

Cuba. Sandra M. Castillo. TouFir

Cuba. Paul Muldoon. CIP-2; ModIr; PNI

Cuba, disheveled, naked to the waist. On a Monument to Martí. Walter Adolphe Roberts. TTY

Cuba Libre. Imamu Amiri Baraka. BB

Cuba, 1962. Ai. ESEAA

Cuban-American Gothic. Virgil Suárez. AmPoNex

Cubano / I was but a child when you marched. For Fidel Castro. Sandra Maria Esteves. PueRic

Cubes. Langston Hughes. APT-2

Cubic inch of some stars, A. Blue Tit on a String of Peanuts. Norman MacCaig. CABP

Cubical Domes, The. David Gascoyne. SPE

Cuchulain Comforted. W. B. Yeats. TOF

Cuchulainn. Michael O'Loughlin. BiHa; PBCIP

Cuckolded husbands have no certain sign. Pallados [*or* Pallades]. GrAn

Cuckoo. Robert Desnos. PFTM-1

Cuckoo. Jakua. JDP, *tr.* by Yoel Hoffmann

Cuckoo. Uko. JDP, *tr.* by Yoel Hoffmann

Cuckoo, The. Gerard Manley Hopkins. MoBrPo; OxBSP; RB; TTTS

Cuckoo, The. *Unknown.* OxNR

Cuckoo, The. *Unknown.* RB

Cuckoo, The. *Unknown.* FaBoVe

Cuckoo and the gowk, the. Riddle. *Unknown.* FaBoVe

Cuckoo-bird-castle-in-the-clouds. Twentieth Century Fresco. Sándor Weöres. IQMS, *tr.* by Adam Makkai

Cuckoo Calls from the Bamboo Grove, The. *Unknown.* OHMPC, *tr.* by Kenneth Rexroth

Cuckoo calls. / When I look there is only, A. Sanesada. OHPJ

Cuckoo, cherry tree. *Unknown.* FaBoVe

Cuckoo comes in April, The. *Unknown.* OxNR

Cuckoo cries, A. Basho. SoOfWa, *tr.* by Sam Hamill

Cuckoo cries, A. Goshuku. JDP, *tr.* by Yoel Hoffmann

Cuckoo cries / Go home, go home, The. Tune: "Song of Great Virtue"— Spring. Kuan Han-ch'ing. SuSp, *tr.* by Jerome P. Seaton

Cuckoo, cuckoo, cherry tree. *Unknown.* OxNR

Cuckoo, cuckoo / What do you do? *Unknown.* OxNR

Cuckoo, glad cuckoo, Oh! where wilt thou rest to-night? Cuckoo Song. Henrietta Cordelia Ray. CBWP-3

Cuckoo, I too. Bokukei. JDP, *tr.* by Yoel Hoffmann

Cuckoo: In former days my father and mother [*or* mother and father]. Cynewulf. ASW; AnOE *Fr.* Riddles (Exeter Book).

Cuckoo is a bonny [*or* fine *or* merry] bird, The. Cuckoo, The. *Unknown.* OxNR

Cuckoo, noisy among the Shenbaka flowers. Andal. BoWoP

Cuckoo's crying / Nothing special to do. Issa. ZenPo, *tr.* by Takashi Ikemoto and Lucien Stryk

Cuckoo's double note, The. Wiltshire Downs. Andrew Young. GTBS-P; OxBTC

Cuckoo's voice, The. Keido. JDP, *tr.* by Yoel Hoffmann

Cuckoo sings, The. Issa. EH, *tr.* by Robert Hass

Cuckoo sings / To me, to the mountain. Issa. ZenPo, *tr.* by Takashi Ikemoto and Lucien Stryk

Cuckoo snatches at the hairy worm, The. Food of Birds, The. Brewster Ghiselin. APT-2

Cuckoo Song. Henrietta Cordelia Ray. CBWP-3

Cuckoo Song, The. *Unknown.* OWoS

Cuckoo Song, The. *Unknown.* *See* Sumer Is Icumen [*or* Ycomen] In

Cucumber, The. Nazim Hikmet. VCWP

Cuddie [*or* Cuddy], for shame hold up thy heavy[e] head. Edmund Spenser. NAEL-5v1; NAEL-6v1; NAEL-7v1 *Fr.* Shepheardes [*or* Shepeards *or* Shepherd's] Calender, The.

Cuddled in the dark. 4½ Months: Halfway Song. George Barlow. ISC

Cudgeled Husband, The. Jonathan Swift. *See* Three Epigrams

Cui Bono? Horace Smith. NOBRP

Culbin Sands. Andrew Young. GTBS-P; OxBS; OxBTC

Culloden and After. Iain Crichton Smith. OxBS

Cult of Love, The. Hadewijch. NAWM-7v1, *tr.* by Peter Dronke

Cult of the Celtic, The. Anthony C. Deane. NOBL; PeLV

Cultivated Signals types. Footnote to Enright's "Apocalypse." Martin Bell. FaBoMo

Cultivation. Mrs. Henry Linden. CBWP-4

Cultivation of Orchids, The. Dionisio D. Martinez. TouFir

Cultural Exchange. Langston Hughes. BPo

Cultural Notes. Kenneth Fearing. PoE

Cultural Presupposition, The. W. H. Auden. PAI

Cultural Trip, A. Opal Palmer Adisa. GT

Culture. Alfred Kreymborg. APT-1

Culture and Anarchy. Adrienne Rich. NALW

Culture as Exhibit. "Ern Malley." BMAP

Culture Nervous. Ricardo M. de Ungria. ReBoTo

Culture's beginnings. Basho. SoOFWa; WoPoe, *tr. by* Sam Hamill

Cultured Girl Again, The. Ben King. OBAL

Cultures. Gloria Anzaldúa. UnSA

Cum here, Mandy, what's you chewin' When Daddy Cums from Wuk. Maggie Pogue Johnson. CBWP-4

Cumae. Merrill Moore. FuPo

Cumberland, The. Henry Wadsworth Longfellow. CBCWP

Cumberland Gap. *Unknown.* APN-2

Cumberland Station. Dave Jeddie Smith. HCAP

Cumnor Hall. William Julius Mickle. OxBB

Cuncta Semper. Rodolfo Di Biasio. NeIt, *tr. by* Stephen Sartarelli

Cunning and art he did not lack. Allansford Pursuit, The. *Unknown.* RB; WoPoe, *tr. by* Robert Graves

Cunning Clerk, The. *Unknown.* OxBB

Cunning Painter, that with curious care, The. Joshua Sylvester. PBRV *Fr.* Saluste du Bartas' Devine Weekes.

Cup, The. John Oldham. AWP

Cup, The. Jones Very. APN-1

Cup, The. Judith Wright. FaBoWP

Cup and Rose. Nizar Qabbani. MAP, *tr. by* Diana Der Hovanessian and Lena Jayyusi

Cup clinks out, my friend, The. Apollonides. GrAn

Cup of cocoa steams in the mirror, A. Mirror, The. Boris Leonidovich Pasternak. TCRusP, *tr. by* Bogdan Boychuk and Mark Rudman

Cup of Coffee, The. Carole Bernstein. AmPoNex

Cup of Coffee, a Sandwich, and You. Joseph Meyer. ReLy

Cup she carried in her hand, The. Two, The. Hugo von Hofmannsthal. AuPH, *tr. by* Lowell A. Bangerter

Cup takes its sweet joy and tells how it touches, The. Meleager. HePo *Fr.* Epigrams.

Cup, you come here! Tune: "Spring in the Ch'in Garden." Hsin Ch'i-chi. ColAnChi, *tr. by* J. R. Hightower

Cupbearer, O victorious Falcon, come! Qorratu'l-Ayn. WPOW *Fr.* He the Beloved.

Cupbearer, take your wine away. Abu al-Qasim Al-Shabbi. MAP *Fr.* Song of Ecstasy.

Cupboard, The. Walter De la Mare. NTCP

Cupid. Bernard O'Dowd. NOBAu

Cupid a Plowman. Moschus. *See* Cupid Turned Plowman

Cupid abroad was lated in the night. Night Visitor, A. Robert Greene. NoSic

Cupid and My Campaspe Played. John Lyly. NoSic; PoRA *Fr.* Alexander and Campaspe.

Cupid and Venus. Mark Alexander Boyd. *See* Fra Bank to Bank, Fra Wood to Wood I Rin

Cupid as he lay among. Wounded Cupid, The. Robert Herrick. AWP; OBVE

Cupid at Venus' breast. Meleager. GrAn

Cupid Far Gone. Richard Lovelace. CaPo

Cupid, I hate thee, which I'd have thee know. Cupid, I Hate Thee. Michael Drayton. SCGP

Cupid, in *Myra's* faire bewitching eyes. Fulke Greville, 1st Baron Brooke. PBRV *Fr.* Cælica.

Cupid Lost. Mary Sidney Wroth, Countess of Montgomery. *See* Pamphilia to Amphilanthus

Cupid's Call. James Shirley. BeJo; NOSC

Cupid's Wrongs Vindicated. Martin Parker. "Thou knowst I lov'd thee well." PBRV

Cupid, thou naughty boy, when thou wert loathed. Fulke Greville, 1st Baron Brooke. Son *Fr.* Caelica.

Cupid Turned Plowman. Moschus. AWP, *tr. by* Matthew Prior (Cupid a Plowman.) OBVE

Cupio Dissolvi. William Habington. ChIV-2

Cupolas flame, in Moscow where I live. Marina Ivanovna Tsvetayeva [*or* Tsvetaeva]. TCRusP, *tr. by* Bob Perelman, Aleksandar Petrov and Shirley Rihner *Fr.* Poems to Blok.

Cupping her chin and lying there, the Bren. Defensive Position. John Streeter Manifold. MoBrPo

Cups. Gwen Harwood. EmeKit; HarvBoo

Cur foretells the knell of parting day, The. Ambrose Bierce. APN-2; OBAL *Fr.* Devil's Dictionary, The.

Curandera, La. Diana García. TouFir

Cure, The. Eugene Wildman. OPRER

Cure at Porlock, A. Amy Clampitt. NoAM

Cure for Fault Finding, A. Strickland W. Gillilan. *See* Watch Yourself Go By

Cure for Poetry, A. Annabella Blount. ECWP

Cure for Poetry, A. *Unknown, after the Latin of* George Buchanan. FaBoEE

Cure of my unquietness. Martial. RomPo, *tr. by* Peter Whigham

Cured, I am frizzled, stale and small. (LL) Home After Three Months Away. Robert Lowell. HCAP; PoetW

Cures. David Rivard. AllShUp; SwNoth

Curfew. Teresa de Jesús. AF, *tr. by* Maria Proser

Curfew. Henry Wadsworth Longfellow. APN-1; OxBA

Curfew. Paul Éluard. BoLoP, *tr. by* Quentin Stevenson

Curfew Breakers, The. Samuel Chimsoro. NAfrP

Curfew Must Not Ring Tonight [*or* To-Night]. Rose Hartwick Thorpe. APN-2; BRP; SWaP

Curfew tolls the hour of locking up, The. Elegy in Newgate. William Cobbett. UV

Curfew tolls the knell of parting day, The. Thomas Gray. AWP; BRP; CABP; ClHu; EBEV; FHYEP; GTBS-P; HAP; HeIP-4; InPK-6; MakPoe; NAEL-6v1; NAEL-7v1; NIL-7; NOBE; NOEC; NPeEn; NoP-4; OBEV; OxAEP-1; OxBEV; PoPoPo; SCGP; SCV; TFi; TreFP; UV; UnPo; WeW-3

Curfew tolls the knell of parting day, The. Diversions of the Re-Echo Club. Carolyn Wells. OBAL

Curie. Gertrude Stein. Mina Loy. APT-1

Curing Homosexuality. Jim Everhard. CAGL; GLP

Curio's rich sideboard seldom sees the light. On a Stingy Beau. John Winstanley. FaBoEE

Curiosity. Alastair Reid. SoSe-8

Curiosity, it means. Woman peeking. Explaining the Origin of My Name. Fatima Lim-Wilson. AmPoNex

Curiosity-Shop, The. Peter Redgrove. OxBC

Curious. Langston Hughes. APT-2

Curious is this stonework! The Fates destroyed it. Ruin, The. *Unknown.* EBEV, *tr. by* Gavin Bone

Curious knot God made in paradise, A. Upon Wedlock and Death of Children. Edward Taylor. ColAP; NAAL-2v1; NAAL-3; NAAL-5; SacPr; TCAPo

Curious tale that threaded through the town, A. Le Loupgarou. Derek Walcott. OxBSo

Curious, the assembly that forms before a door, a large door always. Jews in Hell. Tom Mandel. PmAP

Curl-grass, curl-grass. Ezra Pound. APT-1

Curl Up and Diet. Ogden Nash. OBCoV

Curled like a foetus. On the Head of a Pin. Thomas McGrath. GifTon

Curlers at Dusk. David Roderick. MoASP

Curlews Lift. Ted Hughes. OWoS

Curling them around. Cutting Greens. Lucille Clifton. ESEAA; GT

Curly Kale. David Lindley. NLP

Curly Locks [!] Curly Locks [!] wilt thou be mine? Mother Goose. LB; OxNR; ReMoGo

Curr dhoo, curr dhoo. Mother Goose. OxNR

Currant bushes, the leaves of the currant, The. Indian Summer. Boris Leonidovich Pasternak. RusPo, *tr. by* Robert Arthur Douglas Ford

Currency Lads may fill their glasses, The. Lass in the Female Factory, The. *Unknown.* NOBAu

Current "Now, Voyager" Fantasy. Remy Holzer. OPRER

Currents. Tina Koyama. FSt

Currents. Rose Solari. AmPoNex

Curriculum Vitae. Ingeborg Bachmann. BoWoP; PFTM-2, *tr. by* Jerome Rothenberg

Curriculum vitae. Marie-Claire Bancquart. MFP, *tr. by* Martin Sorrell

Curriculum Vitae. Robert Gray. NOBAu

Curriculum Vitae. Lawrence Joseph. GraLe; PBCAP

Curriculum Vitae. Lisel Mueller. IllVoic

Curry spice in the air. Caroline Street, Cardiff. John Tripp. TCAWP

Curse, A. *Unknown.* BIrV, *tr. by* Douglas Hyde

Curse, The. Robert Francis. APT-2

Curse, The. John Hollander. UnPo

Curse, The. András Szkhárosi Horvát. "Dreadful are the happenings of our evil ages." IQMS, *tr. by* Adam Makkai

Curse, The. John Millington Synge. FaBoEE; NOIV; OBCoV

Curse. A Song, The. Robert Herrick. CaPo

Curse for a Nation, A. Elizabeth Barrett Browning. NALW; ViWPN; WPE; WPOW

Curse! Joy! Writing!, A. Natalya [or Natal'ia] Gorbanevskaya [or Gorbanyevskaya or Gorbanevskaia]. TCRusP, tr. by Daniel Weissbort

Curse of Cromwell, The. W. B. Yeats. BIrV

Curse of Kehama, The. Robert Southey.
Kehama's Curse. NOBRP

Curse of the Cat Woman. Edward Field. WeW-3

Curse on Herod, A. Amy Witting. ChIV-2; NOBAu

Curse on the star, dear Harry, that betrayed. Epistle from a Half-Pay Officer in the Country to His Friend in London, An. Richardson Pack. NOEC

Curse on Uruk, A. Enheduanna. BoWoP, tr. by Aliki Barnstone and Willis Barnstone

Curse the thorns of fate, and damn as well its roses. Curse the Thorns of Fate. Rûhî. WoPoe, tr. by Walter Andrews, Najaat Black and Mehmet Kalpakli

Curse the tongue in my head. Good Night! Good Night! John Holmes (1904–62). PoToHe

Curse upon Edward, The. Thomas Gray. OBEV

Curse upon that faithless maid, A. Aphra Behn. WPE Fr. Emperor of the Moon.

Cursed Be the Day. Bible, O.T. TrJP Fr. Jeremiah.

Cursed is a man in his forsaken years. Cursed is a Man. György Sárközi. IQMS, tr. by Roy Fuller

Cursive crawl, the squared-off characters, The. Writing. Howard Nemerov. VCAP

Curtain. Lance Henson. VoR

Curtain, The. Darl Macleod Boyle. YaYoPo

Curtain of cloud hangs, A. Muso Soseki. EaWin, tr. by W. S. Merwin

Curtain of daybreak is hanging, The. Unknown. APN-2, tr. by Washington Matthews Fr. Mountain Chant, The.

Curtain of the Wedding Bed, The. Liu Hsün's Wife. ChiP, tr. by Arthur Waley

Curtain rung down on his wise old age, The. Unknown. GrAn

Curtains drawn back, the door ajar. Robinson at Home. Weldon Kees. CoAP

Curtains of rock. Orpheus in the Underworld. David Gascoyne. FaBoTw

Curtains part to reveal the equal parts. Exquisite Alchemy. Debra Taub. SurWo

Curtains were half drawn, the floor was swept, The. After Death. Christina Georgina Rossetti. NAEL-5v2; NAEL-6v2; NALW

Curtis Fuller. Rick Madigan. SeSe

Curvd lines toe-drawn, round cornerd squares, The. Hop, Skip, and Jump. Gary Snyder. LCAP-2

Curve of the Water. Hilda Morley. PmAP

Curve of your lips, The. Olga Popova. ItGoST, tr. by J. Kates

Curved pelvic bone dug up, The. Children of the Disappeared. Valerie Martínez. TouFir

Curves of beauty are not softly wrought, The. Palaestral Study, A. Edward Cracroft Lefroy. CAGL

Curving, leaping line of light, A. Prairie Fires. Hamlin Garland. OBCA

Curzon! thou shouldst be living at this hour. Sonnet to the "Most Distinguished Chancellor" that Oxford Has Had. Max Beerbohm. UV

Cushie Butterfield. George Ridley. FaBoVe

Cushy cow bonny, let down thy milk. Mother Goose. OxNR; ReMoGo

Cusp of Desire, The. Maysoun Saqr Al-Qasimi. PoArWo, tr. by Subhi Hadidi and Nathalie Handal

Custer Lives in Humbolt County. Janet Campbell Hale. VoR

Custom. Carol Frost. MoASP

Custom, in this small article I find. On Snuff-Taking. Elizabeth Teft. ECWP

Custom Job: Hank Williams, Jr., and the Death Car, 1958. David Wojahn. PBCAP Fr. Mystery Train: A Sequence.

Custom of the World, The. Louis Simpson. BoLoP

Cut. Sylvia Plath. EmeKit; TAP

Cut brambles long enough. Sun Bu-er. WPoS

Cut branches back for a day. Trail Crew Camp at Bear Valley. 9000 Feet. Gary Snyder. HCAP

Cut Flower, A. Karl Shapiro. HAP; WeW-3

Cut Grass. Philip Larkin. NoAM; OxBC; RB

Cut Pages, The. Roy Fisher.
"He paints words with the past." Oth

Cut the Grass. A. R. Ammons. HAP; TAP; WeW-3

Cut the lemon and let two drops fall into the glass. Naked Face. Yannis Ritsos. PFTM-2, tr. by Kimon Friar

Cut the pear or I cut the pear. On Entries Emptiness. Dennis Phillips. FTOS

Cut the peony. Buson. EH, tr. by Robert Hass

Cut them on Monday, you cut them for health. Unknown. OxNR

Cut thistles in May. Unknown. OxNR

Cut yer name across me backbone. Convicts' Rum Song. Unknown. FaBoVe; NOBAu

Cut your price! Isso. JDP, tr. by Yoel Hoffmann

Cute secretary, none cuter, A. Limerick: "Cute secretary, none cuter, A." Ogden Nash. PeLi

Cutting, A. Ou-yang Hsiu. CrYelRi, tr. by Sam Hamill

Cutting a swath. Kifu. JDP, tr. by Yoel Hoffmann

Cutting Back the Ifugao Past. Al Robles. ReBoTo

Cutting back / wherever the weather. Pruning, The. Adam David Miller. NBV

Cutting Greens. Lucille Clifton. ESEAA; GT

Cutting Prow, The. Edward Sanders. PmAP

Cutting the Jewish Bride's Hair. Ruth Whitman. TaR

Cutting the throat of the sacrificial goat. What Her Girl-Friend Said. Peruñcattan. WoPoe, tr. by A. K. Ramanujan

Cutting, they called it. Castration. Nigel Jenkins. AngWePo; TCAWP

Cutting up an Ox. Chuang Tzu. EnlH, tr. by Thomas Merton

Cuttings. Theodore Roethke. APT-2; HCAP; LCAP-2; NAAL-2v2; NAAL-5; NOBA; NoAM; OBGa; TAP; UnPo; VCAP
(Cuttings (Sticks-in-a-drowse droop over sugary loam).) ColAP
(Cuttings (This urge, wrestle, resurrection of dry sticks).) ColAP

Cutty Sark. Hart Crane. FaBoMo Fr. Bridge, The.

Cutty Wren, The. Unknown. OxBoLi; UV

Cuz he's black and poor. About Atlanta. Ntozake Shange. ISC

Cuz' mama played jazz. Daniel Gray-Kontar. SpirFl

Cwmchwefri. T. Harri Jones. AngWePo

CXLII. Pita Amor. TANSG, tr. by Shaun Griffin and Emma Sepúlveda-Pulvirenti

CXXX. Pita Amor. TANSG, tr. by Shaun Griffin and Emma Sepúlveda-Pulvirenti

CXXXIV. Pita Amor. TANSG, tr. by Shaun Griffin and Emma Sepúlveda-Pulvirenti

CXXXIX. Pita Amor. TANSG, tr. by Shaun Griffin and Emma Sepúlveda-Pulvirenti

Cyclamens. "Michael Field." NOBVV; VWP; ViWPN

Cycle. Gottfried Benn. PFTM-1

Cycle. Bobbi Sykes. BMAP; IBA

Cycle Akhmatova, The. Marina Ivanovna Tsvetayeva [or Tsvetaeva].
"In my melodious city cupolas burn." AF

Cycle for Mother Cabrini, A. John Logan.
"Saint, who overlaps." CRP

Cycle of Inanna: The Courtship of Inanna and Dumazi, The. Unknown.
"Inanna spoke." WoPoe, tr. by Samuel Noah Kramer and Diane Wolkstein

Cycle of life is a worrisome thing, The. On Covering the Bones of Chang Chin, the Hired Man. Liu Tsung-yüan. SuSp; WoPoe, tr. by Jan W. Walls

Cycle of Months (Menstruation). Shuntaro Tanikawa. PFTM-2, tr. by Harold Wright

Cycles of Donji Vakuf. Tony Harrison. FaBoWar

Cyclist, The. Marge Piercy. NoAM

Cyclists, The. Amy Lowell. WPE

Cyclones. Anna Hajnal. IQMS, tr. by Laurence James

Cyclop! if any ask thee who imposed. Homer. NOSC, tr. by George Chapman Fr. Odyssey.

Cyclops. Ovid. CTC; OBVE, tr. by Arthur Golding Fr. Metamorphoses.

Cyclops, The. Euripides.
Chorus of Satyrs, Driving Their Goats. AWP
Love Song: "One with eyes the fairest.". AWP

Cyclops ("For love there is no other drug"). Theocritus. OBVE Fr. Idylls.

Cyclops, The ("And so an easier life"). Theocritus. See Idylls

Cyclus. Toeti Herarty. WoPoe, tr. by Harry Aveling

Cyder. John Philips.
Apple-Culture. OxAEP-1

Cymbeline. William Shakespeare.
(Aubade: "Hark! hark! the lark at heaven's gate sings.") OBEV
(Fidele.) GTBS-P; OBEV
Dirge for Fidele. AWP; ClHu; EBEV; GTBS-P; HAP; NAEL-5v1; NOBE; NoSic; OxAEP-1; PAI; PoRA; RB; SCGP; SCV; SoSe-8; TFi
("Fear no more the heat of the sun.") ITBLP; NAEL-6v1; NoP-4; OxBEV; PoPoPo; WoPoe
(Fidele's Dirge.) FaBoCh
"Hark, hark! the lark at heaven's gate sings." AWP; FaBoCh; ITBLP; NIL-7; NIP-4; NoSic; TFi; UV
"How found you him?" OxAEP-1
"Pray you fetch him hither." NPeEn
(Song.) CTC; NOSC; PoE
(Song: "Hark! hark! the lark at heaven's gate sings.") NOSC
"With fairest flowers, / Whilst summer lasts." EBEV; RB

Cymon and Iphigenia. Dryden. OBNV
Militia, The. OBSV

Cymru. David Gwenallt Jones. OBWVE, *tr. by* Gwyn Jones

Cynara. Ernest Christopher Dowson. *See* Non Sum Qualis Eram Bonae sub Regno Cynarae

Cynddylan on a Tractor. Ronald Stuart Thomas. AngWePo; TCAWP

Cynderaxa kind and good. Sir Richard Steele. OxBSP *Fr.* Funeral, The.

Cynic, The. St. George Tucker. OBAL

"Once at a merry wedding feast." NBLV

Cynic Satire, A. John Marston. NoSic *Fr.* Satires.

Cynic says: Now that we know, A. Limerick. Thomas Thorneley. PeLi

Cynical Portraits. Louis Paul. NBLV

Cynical sage with a kink, A. Limerick. Hassall Pitman. PeLi

Cynthia in the Snow. Gwendolyn Brooks. TLR

Cynthia Matz, with my finger in your cunt. Each Day. David Ignatow. BodElec; NNaP

Cynthia on Horseback. Philip Ayres. EnLoPo; OxBSo

Cynthia's Revels. Ben Jonson.

(Echo's Lament for Narcissus.) OxAEP-1

Echo's [*or* Eccho's] Song. NOSC

(Hymn to Cynthia.) NOSC; PoE; SCGP

(Hymn to Diana.) AWP; GTBS-P; HAP; NOBE; OBEV; PoRA; TFi

(Queen and Huntress.) NAEL-5v1; NAEL-6v1; NAEL-7v1; NoP-4

"Slow, slow, fresh fount, keep time with my salt tears." NAEL-6v1; NAEL-7v1; NoP-4; NOSC

(Song: "Slow, slow fresh fount, keep time with my salt tears.") OxBSP

Cynthia, to thy power. Francis Beaumont. OBEV *Fr.* Maid's Tragedy, The.

Cynthia, with Certain[e] Sonnets. Richard Barnfield [*or* Barnefield].

"Beauty and majesty are fallen at odds." OxBSo

("Cherry-lipped Adonis in his snowy shape.") Son

("Sighing, and sadly sitting by my Love." CAGL; PBRV

("Some talke of Ganimede th' Idalian Boy.") CAGL

"Sometimes I wish that I his pillow were." PBRV

"Sporting at fancie, setting light by love." CAGL

"Sweet Corrall lips, where Nature's treasure lies." CAGL

"Thus was my love, thus was my Ganymed." CAGL

Cypassis, that a thousand ways trim'st hair. Ovid. EBEV, *tr. by* Christopher Marlowe *Fr.* Elegies.

Cypress. Aleksandr Semionovich Kushner. ItGoST, *tr. by* Paul Graves and Carol Ueland

Cypress Boat. *Unknown.* WoPoe, *tr. by* Constance A. Cook

Cypress stood up like a church, The. Bianca Among the Nightingales. Elizabeth Barrett Browning. BrRo; GTBS-P

Cypresses. Robert Francis. APT-2; LCAP-2

Cypresses. D. H. Lawrence. NAEL-5v2; NAEL-6v2

Cypriote, The. Herman Melville. TCAPo *Fr.* Clarel: A Poem and Pilgrimage in the Holy Land.

Cypris who puts the sea to rest. Philodemus. GrAn

Cyriack, this three years['] day these eyes, though clear. To Mr. Cyriack Skinner upon His Blindness. John Milton. NOSC; NPeEn; PeECV; Son

Cyril Connolly. Enemies of Promise. Edmund Wilson. OBCoV

Cythera. David Ferry. DiPo; GS

Cythère. Paul Verlaine. AWP, *tr. by* Arthur Symons

Cytherea. Carlos Montemayor. BLPSL, *tr. by* Rene de Costa, Rigas Kappatos and Eleni Paidoussi

Cywdd to Morvydd, The. Dafydd [*or* David] ap Gwilym. NOEC

Cywydd o Fawl. Harri Webb. AngWePo; TCAWP

Czar's Last Christmas Letter: A Barn in the Urals, The. Norman Dubie. NoAM

D

D. Jeffrey McDaniel. NeAmPo

D-Day, 1994. Jack Coulehan. BloBone

D. . . dronken. *Unknown.* MiEL

D. G. C. to J. A. Emily Jane Brontë. BrRo; EnLoPo

D. G. Rossetti. Dorothy Parker. APT-1; NALW *Fr.* Pig's-Eye View of Literature, A.

D. H. Lawrence and James Joyce. Humbert Wolfe. FaBoEE

D Is for Dog. William Henry Davies. OxBSP

D-Y Bar. James Welch. CDW

D'ye ken John Peel with his coat so gay [*or* gray]? John Peel. John Woodcock Graves. OxBoLi

D-Zug. Julian Croft. NOBAu

Da da buy buy. (LL) Lilies of the Field. Anne Rouse. MFPA; NeBl

Da-di-da, da-di-da, da-da-dee. Call Me Mister. Harold Rome. ReLy

Da Silva Gives the Cue. Walter Hart Blumenthal. TrJP

Dab of Color, A. Theodore Weiss. VGW

Dacca Gauzes, The. Agha Shahid Ali. NIL-7; NoP-4

Daccus is all bedaub'd with golden lace. Against Gaudy-Bragging-Undoughty Daccus. John Davies of Hereford. FaBoEE

Dachshunds. William Jay Smith. OBAL

Dactyls. Vladislav Felitsianovich Khodasevich. TCRusP, *tr. by* Mary Jane White

Dad. Elaine Feinstein. Prnts

Dad, Return, The. Joanne Limburg. NeBl

Dad a da da. Aborigine Sound Poem. *Unknown.* PFTM-1

Dad and the Cat and the Tree. Kit Wright. OTCP

Dad-Baby, The. Amanda Dalton. NeBl

Dad pushed my mother down the cellar stairs. Those Paperweights with Snow Inside. Molly Peacock. RA

Dad waited while Mum bought the ham. Limerick. Coral E. Copping. PeLi

Dad was a nurseryman. 30 Miles from J-Town. Amy Uyematsu. GeoHom

Dada, having only a few years or months or days to live, looks for a law-. Artichokes. Georges Ribemont-Dessaignes. PFTM-1

Dada Manifesto on Feeble and Bitter Love. Tristan Tzara.

"Preamble = sardanapalus." PFTM-1

Dada would have liked a day like this. Lawrence Ferlinghetti. NeAP *Fr.* Pictures of a Gone World.

Daddy. Sylvia Plath. BoWoP; CoAP; ColAP; HCAP; HP; HeIP-4; InPK-6; MakPoe; NAAL-2v2; NAAL-5; NALW; NIL-7; NIP-4; NOBA; NoAM; NoP-4; PAI; PoE; PoPoPo; TFi; TwCP; UnPo; VCAP

Daddy. Bobby Troup. ReLy

Daddy, ain't you heard? (LL) Langston Hughes. APSN; APT-2 *Fr.* Lenox Avenue Mural.

Daddy and I are always here, you know. God Is Dead—Nietzsche. Elizabeth Bartlett. Prnts

Daddy and Mummy. Life Story. Taeko Tomioka. WPOW, *tr. by* Harry Guest, Lynn Guest and Kajima Shozo

Daddy, daddy, you bastard, I'm through. (LL) Daddy. Sylvia Plath. BoWoP; CoAP; ColAP; HCAP; HP; HeIP-4; InPK-6; MakPoe; NAAL-2v2; NAAL-5; NALW; NIL-7; NIP-4; NOBA; NoAM; NoP-4; PAI; PoE; PoPoPo; TFi; TwCP; UnPo; VCAP

Daddy don't smile. Crooked Afro. Frank X. Walker. SpirFl

Daddy drove with us kids in the back. October 27th. Vera Gherarducci. CltWP, *tr. by* Cinzia Sartini Blum and Lara Trubowitz

Daddy 43 but look 40. Abraham Got All the Stars n the Sand. Ruth Forman. AmPoNex

Daddy / is hot butter corn bread in the winter. Waitin on Summer. Ruth Forman. SpirFl

Daddy Poem, A. William J. Harris. NBV

(My father is a hand-.) ISC; UnSA

Daddy's Friends. Esther Iverem. GT

Daddy sits / in his brown. Sunflowers and Saturdays. Melba Joyce Boyd. BlSi

Daddy was a Belgian and so was Mammy too. Little Belgian Orphan, A. Amanda Ros. VerBaPo

Daddy would drop purple-veined vines. Banking Potatoes. Yusef Komunyakaa. NoP-4

Dae what ye wull ye canna parry. Hugh MacDiarmid. EBEV; OxAEP-2 *Fr.* Drunk Man Looks at the Thistle, A.

Daedal of my death, A. Madrigal. William Drummond, of Hawthornden. NOSC

Daedalus. Stephen Knight. TCAWP

Daedalus. Leonid Nikolaevich Martynov. TCRP, *tr. by* J. R. Rowland

Daedalus. Ovid. CTC; OBVE, *tr. by* Arthur Golding *Fr.* Metamorphoses.

Daedalus: The Dirge. George Oppen. FTOS

Daemon, The. Mikhail Yuryevich Lermontov.

"On the sightless seas of ether." AWP

Dæmonic and the Celestial Love, The. Ralph Waldo Emerson. APN-1 *Fr.* Initial, Dæmonic, and Celestial Love.

Daffadowndilly. Mother Goose. NTCP; OxNR

Daffodil. Waldo Williams. OBWVE, *tr. by* Gwyn Jones

Daffodil Song, The. Michael Drayton. AEP *Fr.* Shepherd's Garland, The.

Daffodils. Karen Volkman. NeAmPo

Daffodils. William Wordsworth. ChAP; ITBLP

(Daffodils, The.) GTBS-P; NOBE; OBEV; PWR; SCV; TreFP

Daffy-down-dilly is new come to town [*or* Daffadowndilly has come up to town]. Daffadowndilly. Mother Goose. NTCP; OxNR

Daft Days, The. Robert Fergusson. CABP; NOEC; NPeEn; OxAEP-1; OxBEV

Dafydd ap Gwilym Resents the Winter. Rolfe Humphries. WoPoe

Dafydd's Seagull and the West Wind. Glyn Jones. TCAWP

Dagger. Mikhail Yuryevich Lermontov. AWP, *tr. by* Max Eastman

Dago shovelman sits by the railroad track, The. Child of the Romans. Carl Sandburg. NAAL-2v2

Daguerreotype Taken in Old Age. Margaret Atwood. BoWoP; NoAM

Dahn the Plug'ole. *Unknown.* RB, *tr. by* Robert Bly
("Biby's" Epitaph.) NOxBChV
("Muvver was barfin' 'er biby one night, A.") NOxBChV

Dahomey. Audre Lorde. NAAL-2v2

Dai horse neighs against the bleak wind of Etsu, The. South-Folk in Cold Country. Ezra Pound. OBVE

Dai K lives at the end of a valley. One is not quite sure. Synopsis of the Great Welsh Novel. Harri Webb. AngWePo; TCAWP

Dai, Live. Jon Dressel. AngWePo

Daily Daily, The. Nicolás Guillén.
National Police Headquarters. PFTM-1

Daily Delights. Hameed Sa'id. MAP, *tr. by* Lena Jayyusi and Naomi Shihab Nye

Daily Habits. Heberto Padilla. VCWP

Daily Living. Rosemary Dobson.
Folding the Sheets. ItWoWo; NOBAu

Daily News. Tom Clark. SPE

Daily Space. João Cabral de Melo Neto. VCWP

Daily Task. Belinda Zubicueta Carmona. TANSG, *tr. by* Celeste Kostopulos-Cooperman

Daily the Drum. Anne Wilkinson. NOBC

Daily the Ocean between Us. Patricia Goedicke. TAP

Daily the wind-flowers age, and so do I. Weaving Love-Knots. Hsüeh T'ao. BoWoP, *tr. by* Carolyn Kizer

Daily to turn in Paul's, and help the trade. (LL) On English Monsieur. Ben Jonson. AEP; NBLV; NoP-4

Daily walked the fair and lovely. Azra, The. Heinrich Heine. AWP, *tr. by* John Hay

Daily warmth we, The. John Cage. APSN *Fr.* Diary: How to Improve the World (You Will Only Make Matters Worse).

Dainty Baby Austin! King of Oo-Rinktum-Jing, The. James Whitcomb Riley. NOxBChV

Dainty little maiden, whither would you wander? City Child, The. Tennyson. NOxBChV

Dainty Miss Apathy. Pooh! Walter De la Mare. HAP; OBCoV; PeLV

Daisies, The. James Stephens. AWP

Daisies, daisies, in a field of daisies? (LL) Hogwash. Robert Francis. LCAP-2; NIL-7; NIP-4; TRP

Daisy. Francis Thompson. AWP; MoBrPo; OBEV

Daisy. William Carlos Williams. MoAmPo

Daisy, The. Tennyson. EnLoPo; NOBVV

Daisy, The. Marya Alexandrovna Zaturenska. MoAmPo

Daisy and Lily. Waltz. Dame Edith Sitwell. BWW

Daisy, dead and dry. (LL) For the Candle Light. Angelina Weld Grimké. BlSi; NAAAL

Daisy, Five, Speaks to Sophia, Two. Ralph Lombreglia. Unle

Daisy Fraser. Edgar Lee Masters. HAP; PoE *Fr.* Spoon River Anthology.

Daisy: / garden aster of a shrubby habit. Michaelmas. Veronica Forrest-Thomson. HarvBoo

Dakota: October, 1822, Hunkpapa Warrior. Rod Taylor. WeW-3

Dakota Wheat-Field, A. Hamlin Garland. OBCA

Dalliance of the Eagles, The. Walt Whitman. HAP; HeIP-4; NAAL-2v1; NAAL-3; NoP-4; SAmP; TAP; TCAPo; TRP

Dam Bellona, The. Der Blinde Junge. Mina Loy. APT-1; HarvBoo

Dam Neck, Virginia. Richard Eberhart. PoWW

Damages, Two Hundred Pounds. William Makepeace Thackeray. OBSV

Damastes (Also Known as Procrustes) Speaks. Zbigniew Herbert. PoSu, *tr. by* John Carpenter

Dame, get up and bake your pies. *Unknown.* OxNR

Dame Lud dwelt deep in the haunted shade. Huntsman, The. Helen Adam. APT-2

Dame Nature, the goddess, one very bright day. On the Late Improvements at Nuneham, the Seat of the Earl of Harcourt. William Whitehead. OBGa

Dame Trot and her cat. Mother Goose. OxNR; ReMoGo

Dames. Harry Warren. ReLy

Damien. George Young. BloBone

Damis erected this mound for his dead steadfast. Anyte [*or* Anytes]. SaLy, *tr. by* Diane Rayor

Damis set this up, to commemorate. Anyte [*or* Anytes]. GrAn

Damit blackman. Domestics. Kattie M. Cumbo. BlSi

Damn'd for thy false Apostasy. (LL) To My Inconstant Mistress [*or* Mistris]. Thomas Carew. BeJo; EnLoPo; MeLP; NOBE; TFi

Damn it all! all this our South stinks peace. Sestina: Altaforte. Ezra Pound. APT-1; ColAP; FaBoTw; MakPoe; MoAmPo; NOBA; TCAPo

Damn it, honey, neither one of us. In the Twenty-Fifth Year of Marriage, It Goes On. Alicia Ostriker. PBCAP

Damn that celibate farm, that cracker-box house. Censorship. John Ciardi. NBLV

Damn the snow. Elegy for Thelonious. Yusef Komunyakaa. ESEAA

Damn Yankees. Jerry Ross.
Heart. ReLy

Damnation follows death in other men. On Poets. Pope. FaBoEE

Damned bird, why have you ruined my sleep. Argentarius. GrAn

Damned Minoan crevices, that I clog them up! Paranoia in Crete. Gregory Corso. NeAP

Damned Women. Charles Baudelaire. BoLoP, *tr. by* Roy Campbell

Damoetas and Daphnis. Theocritus. HePo, *tr. by* Barbara Hughes Fowler *Fr.* Idylls.

Damon and Cupid. John Gay. EnLoPo

DAMON and Phyllis squared. *Unknown.* NoSic

Damon & Pythias. Robert Creeley. LCAP-2

Damon, come drive thy flocks this way. Clorinda and Damon. Andrew Marvell. ESCV

Damon's Lament for His Clorenda, Yorkshire, 1654. Lupercio Leonardo de Argensola. WoPoe, *tr. by* Geoffrey Hill

Damon the Mower. Andrew Marvell. BASC; ESCV; GeHe; NAEL-5v1; NAEL-6v1; NAEL-7v1; NOSC

Damp night overwhelmed Phoebus at the western gates. Publius Papinius Statius. RomPo, *tr. by* Norman Austin and Ruth Morse *Fr.* Thebais [*or* Thebaid].

Damp[e], The. John Donne. NOSC

Dampness, and things drift out of focus. Viper Light. Barbara Leslie Jordan. ExTi

Damsel, The. Omar ben Abi Rabi'a. AWP, *tr. by* W. G. Palgrave

Damsel came in midnight rain, A. Thomas Love Peacock. OxAEP-2 *Fr.* Maid Marian.

Damsel of Peru, The. William Cullen Bryant. APN-1

Damside. Margaret Atwood. LCAP-2

Danaë. Barbara Howes. WPE

Danae and Perseus. Simonides. WoPoe, *tr. by* Richmond Lattimore

Danaïds, The. Mihály Babits. IQMS, *tr. by* Peter Zollman

Dança Mortal. H. C. ten Berge. TuT *Fr.* Lusitanian Variant, The.

Dance, The. Marjorie Agosin. TCLAP, *tr. by* Cola Franzen

Dance, The. Thomas Campion. FaBoCh *Fr.* Ayres that Were Sung and Played, at *Brougham Castle* in *Westmerland*, in the Kings Entertainment, The.

Dance, The. Hart Crane. MoAmPo; NAAL-5; OxBA *Fr.* Bridge, The.

Dance, The. Gareth Alban Davies. OBWVE, *tr. by* Gwyn Jones

Dance, The. Robert Duncan. NeAP

Dance, The. Cornelius Eady. GT

Dance, The. Daniel Halpern. ChAP

Dance, The. Irene McKinney. PBCAP

Dance, The. Siamanto. AF, *tr. by* Peter Balakian

Dance, The. Mark Strand. LCAP-2

Dance, The. William Carlos Williams. APT-1; HAP; HarvBoo; HeIP-4; InPK-6; NAAL-2v2; NAAL-5; NIL-7; NIP-4; NOBA; NoAM; OxBA; PAI; PoE; SAmP; SoSe-8; TAP; TFi
(In Breughel's great picture, The Kermess.) NoP-4; PoPoPo

Dance, The. William Carlos Williams. NAAL-2v2; NAAL-5

Dance a baby diddy. Mother Goose. OxNR

Dance, ballerina, dance. Ballerina. Carl Sigman. ReLy

Dance begins: to end about a form, The. Desert Music, The. William Carlos Williams. APSN

Dance Bodies #1. Eugene B. Redmond. ISC

Dance, dance in this museum case. Love Song to Eohippus. Peter Viereck. MoAmPo

Dance Figure. Ezra Pound. HeIP-4; MoAmPo

Dance Floor on the Mountain, The. Pentti Saarikoski.
"Winter solstice." VCWP

Dance for Ma Rainey, A. Al Young. NBV

Dance for Militant Dilettantes, A. Al Young. NBV

Dance Hall. Geoffrey Philp. WaCA

Dance Hall: Version. Geoffrey Philp. WaCA

Dance in the township hall is nearly over, The. Judith Wright. BMAP; CBAP *Fr.* Blind Man, The.

Dance is on the Bridge of Death, The. Bridge of Death, The. *Unknown.* AWP, *tr. by* Andrew Lang

Dance Lesson, A. A. Van Jordan. SpirFl

Dance, Little Baby. Mother Goose. ReMoGo
(Baby's Dance, The.) OxNR

Dance of Despair, The. Hayyim Nahman [*or* Khayim Nakhman *or* Chaim Nachman] Bialik. TrJP, *tr. by* A. M. Klein

Dance of Saul with the Prophets, The. Saul [*or* Shaul] Tchernichowsky [*or* Tchernichovsky]. TrJP, *tr. by* I. M. Lask

Dance of the Cherry Blossom. Jackie Kay. EmeKit

Dance of the Elephants, The. Michael S. Harper. LCAP-2

Dance of the Greased Women, The. Tristan Tzara. PFTM-1 *Fr.* Poemes Negres.

Dance of the Infidels. Al Young. ESEAA; NBV; SeSe

Dance of the Letters. Vince Gotera. OpBo

Dance of the Macabre Mice. Wallace Stevens. NOBA; OxBA; PFTM-1

Dance of the Magyars, The. Ádám Pálóczi Horváth. IQMS, *tr. by* John Gordon Nichols

Dance of the Rain Gods. Unknown. STP, *tr. by* Anselm Hollo

Dance of the Sevin Deidly Synnis, The. William Dunbar. MiEL; NePenScot; OxBS; PoE

Dance of the Soul. Vladimir Shchirovsky [*or* Shchirovskii]. TCRP, *tr. by* Bradley Jordan

Dance Pianist, The. Angela Ball. ExTi

Dance, room, quiet. My Flesh in Its Sweat. Giancarlo Majorino. ItPo, *tr. by* Gayle Ridinger

Dance She Does, The. Harryette Mullen. ISC

Dance Song. Unknown. ChiP; FaBoCh, *tr. by* Arthur Waley

Dance the Boatman. Unknown. AiP

Dance, Thumbkin, dance. Mother Goose. LB; OxNR; ReMoGo

Dance to the Amulets. U Tam'si Tchicaya. PBMAP

Dance to your [*or* thee] daddy. Mother Goose. FaBoVe; OxNR; ReMoGo

Dance with Banderillas. Richard Duerden. NeAP

Dance with me. . .dance with me. . .we are the song. . .we. Three / Quarters Time. Nikki Giovanni. CA

Dance with you, my sweet brown Harlem girl. (LL) Juke Box Love Song. Langston Hughes. NAAAL; SAmP; TTTS

Dance with your tongue, Poet, make an entrechat. Medrano Academy. Blaise Cendrars. CuPo

Danced in the evenin' Jenny in Love. Dolores Kendrick. ESEAA

Danced round the dreadful thing in fiendish glee. (LL) Lynching, The. Claude McKay. APT-1; ColAP; GT; NAAL-5

Dancer. Martinus Nijhoff. TuT, *tr. by* Desmond Egan

Dancer, The. Joseph Campbell. OBMV

Dancer, The. Maggie O'Sullivan. PFTM-2 *Fr.* Doubtless.

Dancer, The. Sadi [*or* Saadi *or* Sa'di]. AWP, *tr. by* Sir Edward Arnold *Fr.* Gulistan, The.

Dancer, The. Walter James Turner. NOBAu; OBMV

Dancer's Life, A. Donald Justice. LCAP-2

Dancer's world, A. Twist, The. Alfred B. Spellman. ISC

Dancers at the Moy. Paul Muldoon. BIrV

Dancers Exercising. Amy Clampitt. NoAM

Dancers of Colbek, The. Robert Mannyng [*or* Manning]. PoE *Fr.* Handling Sin.

Dances and Songs of the Winter Ceremonial. Unknown. APN-2, *tr. by* Franz Boas

Dances like Italy, imagining red. (LL) Walt Whitman at Bear Mountain. Louis Simpson. CoAmPo; TRP

Dances of Death. Aleksandr Aleksandrovich Blok.
"Night, street, a lamp, a chemist's window." OBVE
"Night, the street, the lamp, the drugstore, The." TCRP

Dancin' Our Lives Away. Lorena M. Craighead. InTrad

Dancing, The. Gerald Stern. LCAP-2; LoL; UnSA

Dancing a Spell. Marjorie M. Evasco. ReBoTo

Dancing at Oakmead Road. Maura Dooley. NeBl

Dancing Bear, The. Rachel Lyman Field. KaS; NTCP

Dancing Bear, The. Albert Bigelow Paine. OBCA

Dancing Cabman, The. John Bingham Morton. NOBL

Dancing Concerning a Form of Women, A. Robert Duncan. FTOS

Dancing, dancing as may be credible. (LL) Dance, The. William Carlos Williams. NAAL-2v2; NAAL-5

Dancing Girl. Walther [*or* Walter] von der Vogelweide. NAWM-7v1, *tr. by* Peter Dronke

Dancing Girl, The. Letitia [*or* Laetitia] Elizabeth Landon. CenSon

Dancing-Girl's Song. Kshetrayya. BoWoP, *tr. by* R. Appalaswamy and Tambimuttu

Dancing in Menopause. Dorothy Perry Thompson. SpirFl

Dancing in Paradise. Achy Obejas. WiU

Dancing in the dark. Dancing in the Dark. Arthur Schwartz. ReLy

Dancing in the Dark. Demetrice A. Worley. SpirFl

Dancing in Vacationland. Stephen Dobyns. EmeKit

Dancing Justified. Sir John Davies. NAEL-6v1 *Fr.* Orchestra; or, A Poem[e] of Da[u]ncing.

Dancing may do this and that. T'ain't No Sin to Dance around in Your Bones. Edgar Leslie. ReLy

Dancing on Beethoven's Birthday. Edith Rylander. MiVo

Dancing on the Ceiling. Richard Rodgers. ReLy

Dancing, phosphorescent drops. Yaroslav [*or* Iaroslav] Vasilevich Smelyakov [*or* Smeliakov]. TCRP

Dancing Pleiads and eternal men, The. (LL) Bacchus. Ralph Waldo Emerson. APN-1; AWP; NOBA; OBEV; OxBA; TCAPo

Dancing Sunshine Lounge, The. Thomas Rabbitt. ReTh

Dancing the Tarantella at the County Farm. Sandra Alcosser. ExTi

Dancing to the Track Singers at the Nightclub. Judith Berke. SwNoth

Dancing to vibrations of unheard melodies. Soul Music. Stephen Clayton. IBA

Dancing with God. Stephen Dunn. NIP-4

Dancing with Rex. Beth Cuthand. ReEnLa

Dandelion. Neil Curry. NLP

Dandelion. Juan Delgado. AmPoNex

Dandelion. Frigyes Karinthy. IQMS, *tr. by* Peter Zollman

Dandelions. Gerda Mayer. Spl

Dandelions. Craig Raine. NoAM

Dandelions. Will D. Stanton. SoSe-8

Dandelions for Chains. Sarah Kirsch. WPOW, *tr. by* Michael Hamburger

Dandelions purr in their sleep. Of Dandelions & Tourists. Joe Rosenblatt. NOBC

Dándole la mano a Mongo. Martín Espada. SeSe

Dane-Geld. Rudyard Kipling. OxBTC

Danger, Men in Trees. Doris Safie. GraLe; PoArWo

Dangerous Hats. Richard Garcia. TouFir

Dangerous Life. Lucia Maria Perillo. IllVoic

Dangerous to hear, is that melodious tongue. Describes Phaon. Mary Robinson. CenSon; RWP

Dangerous World, The. Naomi Replansky. PoBW

Daniel and Abigail. Epitaph. Miguel de Barrios. TrJP

Daniel at Breakfast. Phyllis McGinley. OBSV

Daniel Boone. Stephen Vincent Benét. APT-2; KaS

Daniel in the lion's den. Nebuchadnezzar's Kingdom-Come. David Rowbotham. ChIV-1; NOBAu

Daniel Jazz, The. Nicholas Vachel Lindsay. APT-1

Daniel Webster's Horses. Elizabeth Jane Coatsworth. MoAmPo; OBCA

Danish Wit. John Hollander. NBLV

Dank, dark basement entered cautiously from the rear, A. Practice: For Derek Walcott. Thomas Sayers Ellis. NAPBL; NeAmPo

Dannemora Contraband. Jackie Warren-Moore. SpirFl

Dannie Abse, Douglas Dunn. On Consulting "Contemporary Poets of the English Language." Anthony Thwaite. OxBEV; PeLV

Danny. John Millington Synge. PeVV

Danny Deever. Rudyard Kipling. BRP; EBVV; FaBoWar; GTBS-P; MoBrPo; NAEL-5v2; NAEL-6v2; NOBE; NOBVV; NPeEn; NoAM; OxBEV; OxBTC; OxBoLi; PeVV; SCGP; SCV; TFi; UnPo

Dans l'Allée. Paul Verlaine. AWP, *tr. by* Arthur Symons (L'Allée.) OBGa, *tr. by* Arthur Symons

Danse Africaine. Langston Hughes. NAAAL

Danse Russe. William Carlos Williams. AmFaPo; NoP-4
(If I when my wife is sleeping.) WoPoe
(If when my wife is sleeping.) NOBA; PoE; RaBo; SAmP; TAP

Dante. Anna Andreyevna Akhmatova. PoetW, *tr. by* Max Hayward and Stanley Kunitz

Dante. William Cullen Bryant. APN-1

Dante. Robert Duncan.
("I know a little language of my cat, though Dante says.") FTOS
Little Language, A. PoM

Dante. Henry Wadsworth Longfellow. NCAP

Dante. Michelangelo Buonarroti. AWP, *tr. by* Henry Wadsworth Longfellow

Dante. Henrietta Cordelia Ray. CBWP-3

Dante, a sigh that rose from the heart's core. To Dante Alighieri: He Reports, in a Feigned Vision, the Successful Issue of Lapo Gianni's Love. Guido Cavalcanti. AWP, *tr. by* Dante Gabriel Rossetti

Dante Alighieri, a dark oracle. Giovanni Boccaccio. AWP; EaItPo, *tr. by* Dante Gabriel Rossetti *Fr.* Sonnets.

Dante Alighieri, Cecco, your good friend. Sonnet: To Dante Alighieri on the Last Sonnet of the Vita Nuova. Cecco Angiolieri, da Siena. AWP; EaItPo, *tr. by* Dante Gabriel Rossetti

Dante Alighieri, if I jest and lie. Sonnet: To Dante Alighieri (He Writes to Dante, Then in Exile at Verona, Defying Him as No Better than Himself). Cecco Angiolieri, da Siena. AWP; EaItPo, *tr. by* Dante Gabriel Rossetti

Dante Alighieri in Becchina's praise. Sonnet: He Rails against Dante, Who Had Censured His Homage to Becchina. Cecco Angiolieri, da Siena. AWP; EaItPo, *tr. by* Dante Gabriel Rossetti

Dante Gabriel Rossetti. Dorothy Parker. APT-1; NALW *Fr.* Pig's-Eye View of Literature, A.

Dante, if thou within the sphere of Love. Giovanni Boccaccio. AWP; EaItPo, *tr. by* Dante Gabriel Rossetti *Fr.* Sonnets.

Dante Park. Miguel Algarin. PueRic

Dante, since I from my own native place. Cino da Pistoia. EaItPo, *tr.* by Dante Gabriel Rossetti

Dante, whenever this thing happeneth. To Dante Alighieri: He Conceives of Some Compensation in Death. Cino da Pistoia. AWP; EaItPo, *tr.* by Dante Gabriel Rossetti

Danube orchards, The. Denise Levertov. TaR *Fr.* During the Eichmann Trial.

Danube to the Severn gave, The. Tennyson. EBVV; GTBS-P; NAEL-6v2; NAWM-7v2 *Fr.* In Memoriam A. H. H.

Daphnaïda. Edmund Spenser.
  Elegy, An: "She fell away in her first ages spring." OBEV

Daphne. John Lyly. NoSic *Fr.* Midas.

Daphne. Jonathan Swift. NOBL

Daphne and Apollo. Ovid. NOEC, *tr.* by Matthew Prior *Fr.* Metamorphoses.

Daphne and Apollo. Ovid. OBVE, *tr.* by Arthur Golding *Fr.* Metamorphoses.

Daphne knows, with equal ease. Daphne. Jonathan Swift. NOBL

Daphne Stillorgan. Denis Devlin. CIP-2

Daphnis and Chloe. Haniel Long. APT-1

Daphnis dearest, wherefore weave me. Appeal. Edith Nesbit. LW

Daphnis the fair-skinned, who plays country songs. Theocritus. GrAn

Daphnis to Ganymede. Richard Barnfield [*or* Barnefield]. CAGL *Fr.* Affectionate Shepherd [*or* Shephearde], The.

Dapper Street. J. C. Bloem. TuT, *tr.* by Desmond Egan

Dapple-gray. Mother Goose. LB; OxNR; ReMoGo

Dapple-throned Aphrodite. Prayer to My Lady of Paphos. Sappho. HW, *tr.* by Mary Barnard

Dappled Horse, The. Mei Yao Ch'en. CoBCP; ColAnChi, *tr.* by Burton Watson

Dappled sky, a world of meadows, A. Jean Ingelow. PEW *Fr.* Divided.

Dar a Luz. Elmaz Abinader. GraLe

Dar es-Salaam: Harbour of Peace. Breyten Breytenbach. AF, *tr.* by Denis Hirson

Dar es-Salaam: it's when night is darkest. Dar es-Salaam: Harbour of Peace. Breyten Breytenbach. AF, *tr.* by Denis Hirson

Dar's a skool in West Virginny. To Professor Byrd Prillerman. Maggie Pogue Johnson. CBWP-4

Dar's plenty t'ings to write erbout. Dat Mule ob Brudder Wright's. Maggie Pogue Johnson. CBWP-4

Darby and Joan were dressed in black. *Unknown.* OxNR

Dardanelles 1916. Padraic Fallon. CIP-2

Dardanus. . .was son of Zeus the Lord of the clouds. Homer. CAGL, *tr.* by Emile Victor Rieu *Fr.* Iliad, The.

Dare frame thy fearful symmetry? (LL) William Blake. AWP; BBASP; BRP; ChAP; ClHu; FaBoCh; HAP; HeIP-4; ITBLP; InPK-6; MakPoe; NAEL-6v2; NAWM-7v2; NIL-7; NIP-4; NOBE; NOBRP; NOEC; NOxBChV; NPeEn; NoP-4; OBEV; OPOU; OxBEV; PeECV; PoE; PoPoPo; PoRA; RB; SCGP; SCV; SoSe-8; TFi; TTTS; UnPo; WHSW *Fr.* Songs of Experience.

Dare I in such momentous points advise. Soame Jenyns. ECEV *Fr.* Art of Dancing, The.

Dare to Do Right. George Lansing Taylor. PWR

Dare you see a Soul *at the White Heat?* Emily Dickinson. APN-2; NALW; TCAPo; WPoS

Daredevil. Ania Walwicz. BMAP

Daredevil riding on the concrete lip. Bicycle Racers, The. Ann Townsend. AmPoNex; NeAmPo

Darest thou my muse present thy Battlike winge. To the Kinges Most Excellent Majestye. Lady Anne Harris Southwell. EMWP

Daring to live for the impossible. (LL) Muriel Rukeyser. NALW; TaR; TrJP *Fr.* Letter to the Front.

Daring young lady of Guam, A. Limerick. *Unknown.* PeLi

Darius Green and His Flying-Machine. John Townsend Trowbridge. OBAL; OBCA

Dark, The. Myra Cohn Livingston. TLR

Dark, The. Richard Poole. AngWePo

Dark, The. Anita Virgil. HA

Dark accurate plunger down the successive knell. Subway, The. Allen Tate. NOBA

Dark against the sky yonder distant line. *Unknown.* APN-2, *tr.* by Alice C. Fletcher *Fr.* Hako, The.

Dark an' stormy may come de wedder. Slave Marriage Ceremony Supplement. *Unknown.* BPo; TAP

Dark and dim, the Bamboo Grove Monastery. Saying Goodby to the Monk Ling-ch'e. Liu Ch'ang-ch'ing. SuSp, *tr.* by Dell R. Hales

Dark and pillowy cloud, the sallow trees, The. Composed during a Walk on the Downs, in November 1787. Charlotte Smith. OxBSo

Dark Angel, The. Lionel Pigot Johnson. GTBS-P; MoBrPo; NOBE; NOBVV; OBMV; OxAEP-2

Dark angel who art clear and straight. Serenade: Any Man to Any Woman. Dame Edith Sitwell. NALW

Dark Angel, with thine aching lust. Dark Angel, The. Lionel Pigot Johnson. GTBS-P; MoBrPo; NOBE; NOBVV; OBMV; OxAEP-2

Dark Area. Russell Atkins. GT

Dark as the spring river, the earth. Farm Wife. Ellen Bryant Voigt. WWork

Dark as wells, his eyes. Long Person. Gladys Cardiff. CDW

Dark Beauty. Sa'id 'Aql. MAP, *tr.* by Naomi Shihab Nye and Matthew Sorenson

Dark Blood. Margaret Abigail Walker. NALW

Dark-blue clouds of night, in dusky lines, The. Summer's Day, A. Joanna Baillie. WoRP

Dark Blue Hussars. Nikolai Nikolaievich Aseyev [*or* Aseiev]. TCRP, *tr.* by Daniel Weissbort and Lubov Yakovleva

Dark branches. Alaskan Mountain Poem #1. Leslie Marmon Silko. VoR

Dark breast feathers of a future storm. (LL) Crazy Horse Monument. Peter Blue Cloud. HATNAP; UnSA

Dark brother touches me, The. Will Inman. GLP *Fr.* 108 Tales of a Po 'Buckra.

Dark Brown. Michael McClure.
  (Fuck Ode). BB

Dark brown, distant. Towers, The. José María Eguren. TCLAP, *tr.* by Iver Lofving

Dark brown is the river. Where Go the Boats? Robert Louis Stevenson. FaBoCh; NOxBChV; NTCP; TLR; WHSW

Dark cave, that ever dost cool shades retain. Ludovico Ariosto. NOBRP, *tr.* by William Parsons *Fr.* Orlando Furioso.

Dark Chamber, The. Louis Untermeyer. MoAmPo

Dark changes guard, The. Rounds, The. G. E. Murray. IllVoic

Dark chocolate fungus, A. Walking, when the Lake of the Air Is Blue with Spring. J. S. Harry. BMAP

Dark Christmas on Wildwood Road, The. Morris Gilbert Bishop. ChrPo

Dark clouds are gathering a way up in the sky. Buddgelin Bey. Rex Marshall. IBA

Dark clouds are gathering. The trick knee aches. Neighboring Storms. Greg Williamson. AmPoNex

Dark clouds have rolled clean away. Tune: "Rouged Lips" Rain Just Over on the Night of the Lantern Preview. Wu Wen-ying. ColAnChi, *tr.* by Jiaosheng Wang

Dark Conclusions. Ruth Stone. BoWoP

Dark Country, A. Derek Mahon. BIrV

Dark, dark, far mists rise. Things Seen. Wang Shih-chieng. CoBLCP, *tr.* by Jonathan Chaves

Dark Days, The. Greg Williamson. NeAmPo

Dark / days are past. Mysteries, The. "H. D." APT-1

Dark, deep, and cold the current flows. Plaint. Ebenezer Elliott. OBEV; SacPr

Dark Dialogues, The. William Sydney Graham. OxBS

Dark drum the vanishing horses' hooves. (LL) Closing of the Rodeo, The. William Jay Smith. AiP; TwCP

Dark Edge of Europe, The. Desmond O'Grady.
  "Twist of cloth on the flat stones, A." PBCIP

Dark Eleanor and Henry sat at meat. Rose of the World, The. John Masefield. PoRA

Dark Existence. Brenda Hillman. BodElec

Dark-Eyed Gentleman, The. Thomas Hardy. MoBrPo; NBLV; UnPo

Dark eyed, / O woman of my dreams. Dance Figure. Ezra Pound. HeIP-4; MoAmPo

Dark fall comes with fruit and fullness piled, The. Autumn of the Lonely. Georg Trakl. AuPH, *tr.* by Lowell A. Bangerter

Dark falls on this mid-western town. Love. Eavan Boland. HarvBoo

Dark Farmhouses. Charles Simic. LCAP-2

Dark Fates, The. Dezső Kosztolányi. IQMS, *tr.* by Lydia Pasternak-Slater

Dark fens of cedar; hemlock-branches gray. Frederick Goddard Tuckerman. APN-2 *Fr.* Sonnets.

Dark fragrance, sparse shadows. Night of the Fifteenth, Second Month. Yüan Mei. CoBLCP, *tr.* by Jonathan Chaves

Dark Girl. Arna Bontemps. APT-2

Dark gods if all our days. Idris Davies. TCAWP *Fr.* Gwalia Deserta.

Dark-haired girl, who holds my thoughts entirely, The. Peggy Browne. Turlough Carolan [*or* O'Carolan]. BIrV; OxBEV, *tr.* by Austin Clarke

Dark hall. Great green liquid windows, A. Thomas Kinsella. BiHa *Fr.* Technical Supplement, A.

Dark Harbor. Mark Strand.
  ("Is it you standing among the olive trees.") NoP-4
  "It is true, as someone has said, that in." NoP-4

Dark head sits brooding its, A. Song of the Andoumboulou: 7. Nathaniel Mackey. FTOS

Dark Hills, The. Edwin Arlington Robinson. AiP; HAP; MoAmPo; NoAM

Dark hills distant in the setting sun. Encountering a Snowstorm, I Stay with the Recluse of Mount Hibiscus. Liu Ch'ang-ch'ing. SuSp, *tr. by* Dell R. Hales

Dark Horse. Phillis Levin. FFC

Dark House, The. *Unknown.* NTCP

Dark house, by which once more I stand. Tennyson. EBEV; EBVV; FHYEP; GTBS-P; HAP; HeIP-4; NAEL-6v2; NAWM-7v2; NOBE; NPeEn; OxBEV; SCGP; SCV; SoSe-8; UnPo *Fr.* In Memoriam A. H. H.

Dark in a Corner of the Room. Gustavo Adolfo Bécquer. SpanPo, *tr. by* Kate Flores

Dark in the cubicle boxed from snow-darkness of night. History during Nocturnal Snowfall. Robert Penn Warren. DiPo

Dark is soft, like fur. Rhyme for Night. Joan Aiken. TLR

Dark is the hour, long the night. Christmas Eve. Walter De la Mare. ChrPo

Dark lintels, the blue and foreign stones, The. Adrienne Rich. NALW; NoAM *Fr.* Twenty-one Love Poems.

Dark Lord of Savaiki, The. Alistair Campbell. PeNZ

Dark Meadow Invites Me, A. José Lezama Lima. TCLAP, *tr. by* Willis Barnstone

Dark Mirage. "Badawi al-Jabal." MAP, *tr. by* Christopher Tingley and Richard Wilbur

Dark Mirror. Calvin Forbes. GT

Dark Mountains. Milton Lockyer. CBAP, *tr. by* Frank Wordick

Dark Night, The. Saint John of the Cross. BBASP; STV; WeW-3, *tr. by* Kieran Kavanaugh and Otilio Rodriquez; WoPoe, *tr. by* Frank Bidart (Obscure Night of the Soul, The.) AWP; OBMV, *tr. by* Arthur Symons

Dark o'clock. Bed, The. Ray DiPalma. FTOS

Dark One, / all I request is a portion of love. Mirabai [*or* Mira Bai]. ErotSp, *tr. by* Andrew Schelling

Dark one, / how can I sleep? Mirabai [*or* Mira Bai]. AWTN

Dark Phrases. Ntozake Shange. BlSi *Fr.* For Colored Girls Who Have Considered Suicide When the Rainbow Is Enuf.

Dark Pines under Water. Gwendolyn MacEwen. NOBC

Dark plume fetch me from yon blasted yew, A. William Wordsworth. CenSon; HAP *Fr.* River Duddon [A Series of Sonnets], The.

Dark Portrait, A. Lawrence Ferlinghetti. PmAP

Dark Prophecy: I Sing of Shine. Etheridge Knight. BPo; ESEAA; LTA; PBCAP

Dark Romance. Lucha Corpi. WPOW, *tr. by* Catherine Rodriguez-Nieto

Dark Room, The. Enrique Lihn. TCLAP; VCWP, *tr. by* David Unger

Dark Rosaleen. Owen Roe MacWard. AWP; BIrV; NOIV; OBEV; OxAEP-2, *tr. by* James Clarence Mangan

Dark scissors of his legs, The. Jogger on Riverside Drive, 5:00 A.M., The. Agha Shahid Ali. MoASP

Dark Senses. Tom Raworth. Oth

Dark shards from the grass, your voice in pieces, so far, belief. (LL) Los Angeles, the Angels. James Harms. NeAmPo; PuP-23

Dark Side, The. Adelaide Anne Procter. SacPr

Dark Song. Dame Edith Sitwell. FaBoTw

Dark Spaces: Thoughts on All Souls Day. John Knoepfle. IllVoic

Dark speckle, half with down, half feathered. Fledgling. Anthony Conran. AngWePo

Dark specks whirr like lint alive in the sunlight. Ephemeridae. Daniel Gerard Hoffman. YaYoPo

Dark Stag, The. Isabella Valancy Crawford. NOBC

Dark Star, Black Star. Rikki Ducornet. SurWo

Dark streets are deserted, The. After Midnight. Louis Simpson. BLT; NoAM

Dark Summer. Louise Bogan. APT-2

Dark swimmers, The. Larry Eigner. PoM

Dark Symphony. Melvin B. Tolson. ColAP; NAAAL; SSLK

Dark Testament. Pauli Murray. BlSi

Dark theme keeps me here, A. In Evening Air. Theodore Roethke. TAP

Dark Thing inside the Day, A. Linda Gregg. BLT

Dark, thinned, beside the wall of stone. In Time of Grief. Lizette Woodworth Reese. APN-2

Dark thoughts are my companions. I have wined. Epigram. James Vincent Cunningham. VGW

Dark to me is the earth. Dark to me are the heavens. Desolate City, The. *Unknown.* AWP; OBEV, *tr. by* Wilfrid Scawen Blunt

Dark Underfoot. Thom Ward. AmPoNex

Dark was before my eyes. There lay the abyss. Bridge, The. Victor Hugo. SxFrPo, *tr. by* E. H. Blackmore and A. M. Blackmore

Dark was the dawn, and o'er the deep. Negro Girl, The. Mary Robinson. RWP

Dark was the day for Childe Rolandine the artist. Childe Rolandine. Stevie Smith. BrRo

Dark was the sky, and not one friendly star. Philip Freneau. TCAPo *Fr.* House of Night, The.

Dark Welcome, The. James Keir Baxter. PeNZ *Fr.* Five Sestinas.

Dark which canopies the dawning skies, The. Light Invested. Carlos A. Angeles. ReBoTo

Dark whispers. Night Gives Old Woman the Word. Gail Tremblay. HATNAP; ItWoWo

Dark wind blows in the forest, crows and magpies mourn. Ballad of a Ferocious Tiger. Kao Ch'i. SuSp, *tr. by* Irving Y. Lo

Dark woman, head bent, listening for something, A. Adrienne Rich. GeoHom *Fr.* Atlas of the Difficult World, An.

Dark Wood, The. Dante Alighieri. BiHa, *tr. by* Seamus Heaney *Fr.* Divina Commedia.

Dark wrath of people, The. Georg Trakl. *See* Like the wild organs of the winter storm

Dark, wrinkled as a purple pink. Obscur et froncé. Arthur Rimbaud. EroLit, *tr. by* Kenneth McLeish

Dark young pine, at the center of the earth originating. Shootingway Ceremony Prayer. *Unknown.* WPoS; WoPoe, *tr. by* Gladys A. Reichard

Darkened bedroom, the double bed, The. Driving Wheel. Sherley Anne Williams. BlSi

Darkened copies of all trees, The. (LL) Emphasis Falls on Reality, An. Barbara Guest. FTOS; PmAP

Darkened farmhouse is asleep, The. Saving the Harvest. Geoffrey Lehmann. CBAP

Darkened Mind, The. James Russell Lowell. NCAP

Darkening. Anita Virgil. HA

Darkening Hotel Room. Alfred Corn. VCAP

Darkening was like riches in the room, The. Rainer Maria Rilke. *See* Darkness was a richness in the room, The

Darker by far than any coalpit stone. (LL) Edward Taylor. HAP; NAAL-2v1; NAAL-3; NOBA; NOSC; OxBA; OxBEV; SCAP; TCAPo *Fr.* God's Determinations [Touching His Elect].

Darkling Summer, Ominous Dusk, Rumorous Rain. Delmore Schwartz. APT-2

Darkling Swallows Will Come Again, The. Gustavo Adolfo Bécquer. SpanPo, *tr. by* Kate Flores

Darkling Thrush, The. Thomas Hardy. AmFaPo; CABP; ClHu; EBVV; HAP; HarvBoo; MoBrPo; NAEL-5v2; NAEL-6v2; NIL-7; NIP-4; NOBE; NOBVV; NPeEn; NoAM; NoP-4; OBEV; OWoS; OxBEV; PAI; PoE; PoPoPo; RB; SoSe-8; TFi; TOF; UnPo; WoPoe

Darkmotherscream. Andrey [*or* Andrei] Andreievich Voznesensky [*or* Voznesenskii]. RaBo; TCRP, *tr. by* Robert Bly and Vera Dunham

Darkness. Byron. CABP; NAEL-5v2; NAEL-6v2; PoE; TreFP

Darkness. Joseph Campbell. BIrV

Darkness. Arthur Hugh Clough. OxBSP

Darkness. Paavo Haavikko.
  "Days become years. Years." VCWP

Darkness, The. Charles E. Butler. YaYoPo

Darkness and rain and the wind. Loneliness. Ivan Alekseievich Bunin. TCRP, *tr. by* Yakov Hornstein

Darkness and stars i' the mid-day! they invite. Henry Vaughan. BeJo; NAEL-5v1; NAEL-6v1

Darkness and Void was all: myself alone. Mihály Vörösmarty. IQMS, *tr. by* Peter Zollman *Fr.* Csongor and Tünde.

Darkness—and white. Aleksandr Aleksandrovich Blok. TCRP

Darkness / as black as your eyelid. Anne Sexton. BodElec *Fr.* Furies, The.

Darkness begins a / retreat. After Christmas. Michael Richards. OBCP

Darkness broke into my life, and I knew. Delivery. Armanda Guiducci. CItWP, *tr. by* Cinzia Sartini Blum and Lara Trubowitz

Darkness, but. Recurrence. Michael White. GifTon

Darkness came early, though not yet cold. Apple-raid, The. Vernon Scannell. NOxBChV

Darkness comes out of the earth. Twilight. D. H. Lawrence. OBMV

Darkness crumbles away, The. Break of Day in the Trenches. Isaac Rosenberg. CABP; FaBoMo; GTBS-P; HarvBoo; MoBrPo; NAEL-5v2; NAEL-6v2; NIL-7; NOBE; NPeEn; NoAM; NoP-4; OBWP; OxAEP-2; OxBEV; PeFWW; PoWW; TFi

Darkness descends, do you see our hutment slowly dissolving? Seventh Eclogue. Miklós Radnóti. IQMS, *tr. by* Peter Zollman

Darkness falls like a wet sponge. Picture of Little J. A. in a Prospect of Flowers, The. John Ashbery. CoAmPo; PmAP

Darkness has called to darkness, and disgrace. As a Plane Tree by the Water. Robert Lowell. CoAP; MoAmPo; NOBA; OxBA

Darkness in the room was like enormous riches, The. Rainer Maria Rilke. *See* Darkness was a richness in the room, The

Darkness is for the poor, and thorough cold. Christmas Is Coming. Anthony Hecht. ChrPo

Darkness is not dark, nor sunlight the light of the sun. Foal. Vernon Watkins. AngWePo; OxBTC

Darkness lifts, imagine, in your lifetime, The. Undertaking, The. Louise Glück. FaBoWP

Darkness marks the distance where river meets ocean. Autumn River. T'ang Hsien-tsu. CoBLCP, *tr. by* Jonathan Chaves

Darkness Music. Muriel Rukeyser. BoWoP

Darkness of trees, The. George Oppen. APT-2; NNaP *Fr.* Some San Francisco Poems.

Darkness reigned. Sacrifice. Nana Issaia. BoWoP, *tr. by* Helle Tzalopoulou Barnstone

Darkness rolls upward, The. Blue Symphony. John Gould Fletcher. APT-1

Darkness slowly lifts. Morning. Sami Mahdi. MAP, *tr. by* May Jayyusi

Darkness stares from everywhere and no one's here. Last Poem, The. Jiri Orten. AF, *tr. by* Lyn Coffin

Darkness still shadows the mountain road. I Spend the Night in a Room by the River. Tu Fu. SuSp, *tr. by* Mark Perlberg

Darkness that man must dread at last. (LL) Tenebrae. Austin Clarke. BIrV; CIP-2; NOIV

Darkness was a richness in the room, The. From a Childhood. Rainer Maria Rilke. TrJP

Darkness Was upon the Face of the Deep. Kim Roberts. AmPoNex *Fr.* Constellation Frigidaire, The.

Darkness with white spots. Five-0. Ras Baraka. InTrad

Darktown Strutter's Ball, The. Shelton Brooks. ReLy

Darky Sunday School. *Unknown.* OxBoLi

Darling!because my blood can sing. E. E. Cummings. OxBA

Darling can you kill me: with your mickeymouse pillows. D. A. Powell. NeAmPo

Darling, dearest foal-hide flask. Love Song to the Foal-Hide Flask. Mihály Csokonai Vitéz. IQMS, *tr. by* Thomas Kabdebo and Valerie Becker Makkai

Darling, each morning a blooded rose. Corinna in Vendome. Pierre de Ronsard. BoLoP; WoPoe, *tr. by* Robert Mezey

"Darling," he said, "I never meant." Forgetfulness! Josephine D. Henderson Heard. CBWP-4

Darling, he said, I never meant. Two Truths. Helen Hunt Jackson. LW

Darling Henriette, if fate were symmetrical. Casanova on His Deathbed. Philip Casey. BiHa

Darling, how long before this breath will cease? Evanishings. Mary E. Tucker. CBWP-1

Darling, I won't be your hot love. Sulpicia. BoWoP

Darling of Gods and Men, beneath the gliding stars. Lucretius. WoPoe, *tr. by* Basil Bunting *Fr.* De Rerum Natura (On the Nature of Things).

Darling, on the moving stairs. And No Regrets. Lex Banning. NOBAu

Darling, pardon my confusion. What Is There to Say? Vernon Duke. ReLy

Darling, the plates have been cleared away. Beauty and the Beast. Rita Dove. ESEAA; NoAM

Darling, there is nothing between us that cannot be. Miss Havisham's Letter. Julia Copus. MFPA

Darling, there's the tree you run to. On the Street Where You Live. Frederick Loewe. ReLy

Darling, we'll both have equal shares in the sweet love you offer. 109. Catullus. NAWM-7v1, *tr. by* Charles Martin

Darling, you only, there is no duplicate. *Unknown.* CTC *Fr.* Conversations in Courtship.

Darn That Dream. Eddie DeLange. ReLy

Darned Mounseer, The. Sir William Schwenck Gilbert. NOBL *Fr.* Ruddigore.

Dart of Izdabel prevails! 'twas dipt, The. Dying Indian, The. Joseph Warton. NOEC; OxAEP-1

Darting here and there. Buson. SoOfWa, *tr. by* Sam Hamill

Dartmoor: Sunset at Chagford. Thomas Edward Brown. NOBVV

Darwin. Lorine Niedecker. APSN; APT-2

Darwin Descending. Russell Edson. LCAP-2

Darwin in 1881. Gjertrud Schnackenberg. NoAM; NoP-4

Darwinism. Agnes Mary Frances Robinson. VWP

Darwinism in the Kitchen. *Unknown.* NBLV

Darya Vlasyevna, my neigbor. Conversation with a Neighbor. Olga Fiodorovna Berggolts [*or* Bergholts]. TCRP, *tr. by* Daniel Weissbort

Das Kapital. Imamu Amiri Baraka. PFTM-2; PoM

Dash down yon cup of Samian wine! (LL) Byron. AWP; NOBE; OBEV; OxAEP-2 *Fr.* Don Juan.

Dash him to dust, and let the world repose. (LL) Advice to a Raven in Russia [December, 1812]. Joel Barlow. APN-1; NAAL-2v1; NAAL-3; NOBA; OBWP; OxBA

Dashing thro' the snow in a one-horse open sleigh. Jingle Bells. James S. Pierpont. TCAPo

Dashing White Sergeant, The. John Burgoyne. FaBoWar

Dasius, chucker-out / at the Turkish Baths. Martial. OBVE

Dass Cap'm Cayetano. Song of Cayetano's Circus, The. George Washington Cable. APN-2

Dat Mule ob Brudder Wright's. Maggie Pogue Johnson. CBWP-4

Dat's Love (Habanera). Georges Bizet. ReLy

Data. Joseph Ceravolo. BodElec

Data, data, data. Transfigured Night. Ralph Gustafson. MoCV

Data in the glass jar: some ten scorpions, The. In the Laboratory. Dan Pagis. PoSu, *tr. by* Robert Friend

Date palm and the cypress, The. Leaving Eden. Nadya Aisenberg. OPRER

Date with Robbe-Grillet, A. Elaine Equi. PeVV; PmAP

Dates. *Unknown.* AWP *Fr.* Thousand and One Nights, The.

Dates and chestnuts and tangerines. (LL) Michael Longley. BiHa; ModIr *Fr.* Wreaths.

Datur Hora Quieti. Sir Walter Scott. GTBS-P

Datura the Serpent, The. Valentine Penrose. SurWo, *tr. by* Myrna Bell Rochester

Dauber. John Masefield.
Rounding the Horn. MoBrPo

Daufuskie. Mari E. Evans. BlSi

Daughter. Olesya [*or* Olesia] Nikolayeva [*or* Nikolaeva]. ItGoST, *tr. by* Paul Graves and Carol Ueland

Daughter, how the door is creaking. Evening Prayer. Arthur Fitger. AWP, *tr. by* Jethro Bithell

Daughter, lying on a snow-white bed. To My Daughter. N. Balamani Amma. OMIP, *tr. by* N. Balamani Amma

Daughter-Mother-Maya-Seeta. Reetika Vazirani. NAPBL

Daughter of Admetus, A. Thomas Sturge Moore. FaBoTw

Daughter of earth and child of the wave be appeased. William Everson. NoAM *Fr.* Tendril in the Mesh.

Daughter of Genius! while thy tuneful lays. Occasioned by Reading Mrs. M. Robinson's Poems. Martha Hanson. CenSon

Daughter of gods and men, great ruling will. Klytemnestra. Emily Jane Pfeiffer. ViWPN

Daughter of Hyria, land of lovely dances. Korinna [*or* Corinna]. SaLy, *tr. by* Diane Rayor

Daughter of Jairus, The. Marina Ivanovna Tsvetayeva [*or* Tsvetaeva]. BoWoP, *tr. by* Paul Schmidt

Daughter of Jove, relentless Power. Hymn to Adversity. Thomas Gray. GTBS-P

Daughter of Liberty! whose knife. Hymn to the Guilotine. "Peter Pindar." NOBRP

Daughter of music. Song for the Year's End, A. Louis Zukofsky. TaR

Daughter of Night, chaotic Queen! Ode to the German Drama. *Unknown.* NOEC

Daughter of th'Italian heaven! Corinne at the Capitol. Felicia Dorothea Hemans. BrRo

Daughter of the Cavaliers, A. Old Belle, An. Lizette Woodworth Reese. SWaP

Daughter pail slipper sale underwail. Sand. Hannah Weiner. PFTM-2

Daughter's job: without a murmur, The. Household Fires. Indira Sant. OMIP, *tr. by* Vinay Dharwadker

Daughter, take this amulet. Mwana Kupona Msham. HAWP; WPOW *Fr.* Poem to Her Daughter.

Daughter, That Picture of You. Keith Gilyard. SpirFl

Daughter, this small stiletto which I found. Gift, The. Ann Darr. PAI

Daughter to that good Earl[e], once President. To the Lady Margaret Ley. John Milton. GTBS-P; OBEV

Daughters. "Astra." BrRo

Daughters, in the wind's boisterous roughing. Vernal Equinox. Ruth Stone. MoAmPo

Daughters, 1900. Marilyn Nelson Waniek. FFC

Daughters of Albion hear her woes, and ec[c]ho back her sighs, The. (LL) William Blake. CABP; NAEL-6v2

Daughters of Beulah! Muses who inspire the Poets Song. William Blake. PeECV *Fr.* Milton.

Daughters of Blum, The. Charles Wright. CoAP

Daughters of Jerusalem. Chapter V. Elizabeth Singer Rowe. PEW

Daughters of Jove, whose voice is melody. *Unknown.* AWP, *tr. by* Percy Bysshe Shelley *Fr.* Homeric Hymns.

Daughters of Time, the hypocritic Days. Days. Ralph Waldo Emerson. APN-1; ColAP; HAP; HeIP-4; NAAL-2v1; NAAL-3; NCAP; NOBA; NoP-4; OxBA; OxBSP; PoE; TAP; TCAPo; TFi

Daughters of War. Isaac Rosenberg. PeFWW

Daunce of Death, The. John Lydgate.
"O thow Minstral that cannest so note and pipe." OxBEV

Dauncing (bright Lady) then began to bee. Sir John Davies. NOBE *Fr.* Orchestra; or, A Poem[e] of Da[u]ncing.

Dauntless master, as he starts the human tale, The. (LL) Puella Parvula. Wallace Stevens. HCAP; LCAP-2

Dauntless the slug-horn to my lips I set. Tony Lopez. Oth *Fr.* Assembly Point D.

Dave Dirt's dog is a horrible hound. Heads or Tails? Kit Wright. OTCP

Dave rode across a bridge. *Unknown.* WoPoe, *tr. by* Siv Cedering Fox *Fr.* Three Swedish Spells.

Daventry Wonder, The. "Agricola." NOEC

David. Earle Birney. NOBC

David. Linda Pastan. CRP

David. Charles Reznikoff. ChIV-1

David and Bathsheba in the Public Garden. Robert Lowell. ChIV-1

David and [Fair] Bethsabe. George Peele.

  Bethsabe's Song. ChIV-1; NOBE; NPeEn; NoSic; OxBEV; OxBSP; OxBoLi; RB

  "Hot sun[ne], cool[e] fire, temper[e]d with sweet air[e]." ChIV-1; NOBE; NPeEn; NoP-4; NoSic; OxBEV; OxBSP; OxBoLi; RB

David and Goliath. Michael Drayton.

  "Our sacred Muse, of Israel's Singer sings." ChIV-1

David and Goliath. Priscilla Jane Thompson. CBWP-2

David and Goliath. P. Hately Waddell. ChIV-1

David and his three captains bold. David in the Cave of Adullam. Charles Lamb. ChIV-1

David and I that summer cut trails on the Survey. David. Earle Birney. NOBC

David Cassidy picks me on *The Dating Game.* David Cassidy Then. Dennis Cooper. ReTh; WiU

David Cassidy Then. Dennis Cooper. ReTh; WiU

David Drummond's destinie. Coble o Cargill, The. *Unknown.* ESPB

David Garrick. Oliver Goldsmith. NOEC; NPeEn; OxBEV *Fr.* Retaliation.

David in the Cave of Adullam. Charles Lamb. ChIV-1

David Leaves the Saints for Paterson. Martín Espada. PueRic

David Lowston. *Unknown.* PeNZ

David means beloved. Name, A. Linda Pastan. TaR

David ross called up from syracuse and wanted to know if. David Antin. PmAP

David's arm hung near-paralyzed. David Leaves the Saints for Paterson. Martín Espada. PueRic

David's Epitaph on Jonathan. Francis Quarles. ChIV-1

David's Lament. Bible, *O.T.* NPeEn; OBVE; OBWP; TrJP *Fr.* Second Samuel.

David's Lament for Jonathan. Peter Abelard. NAWM-5v1

David's Lament for Saul and Jonathan. Bible, *O.T. See* Second Samuel

David's Night in Veliès. James Merrill. HarvBoo

David's Peccavi. Robert Southwell. ChIV-1

David's Rumor. Liam Rector. OPRER

David sang to his hooknosed harp. King David. Stephen Vincent Benét. ChIV-1

David, we must have looked comic, sitting. Elegy for David Beynon. Leslie Norris. AngWePo; TCAWP

Davideis. Abraham Cowley.

  Gabriel's Appearance. NOSC

  Lot's Wife. NPeEn

  "Michal her modest flames sought to conceal." ChIV-1

  (Music.) OxAEP-1

  (Number, Weight, and Measure.) NOSC

  "So covetous Ballaam with fond intent." ChIV-1

  Supplication, A. GTBS-P

Davy and the Goblin. Charles Edward Carryl.

  (Nautical Ballad, A.) APN-2; OBAL

  (Robinson Crusoe's Story.) PoRA

  Walloping Window-Blind, The. NBLV; OBCA

Davy Crockett. *Unknown.* FaBoVe

Davy Davy Dumpling. *Unknown.* OxNR

Daw, The / The rook, and magpie, to the grey-grown oaks. James Thomson. NPeEn *Fr.* Seasons, The.

Dawdling with yellow tummy: I act on a mechanism outside in contrast to. Instant Control. Michael Portnoy. HeMarv

Dawlish Fair. John Keats. PeLV

Dawn. Nirmalprabha Bardoloi. OMIP, *tr. by* D. N. Bezbarua

Dawn. Gordon Bottomley. MoBrPo

Dawn. Buson. EH, *tr. by* Robert Hass

Dawn. Hopper: In the Cafe. W. R. Elton. PoSol

Dawn. John Ford. OBEV *Fr.* Lover's Melancholy, The.

Dawn. Angelina Weld Grimké. APT-1

Dawn. Ella Higginson. SWaP

Dawn. Philippe Jaccottet. VCWP

Dawn. Joseph Kumbirai. PeSAV, *tr. by* Douglas Livingstone

Dawn. Gabriela Mistral. TANSG, *tr. by* Maria Jacketti

Dawn. "Rachel" [*or* "Rahel"]. TrJP, *tr. by* A. M. Klein

Dawn. Arthur Rimbaud. SxFrPo, *tr. by* Martin Sorrell

Dawn. Arthur Rimbaud. TTTS, *tr. by* Enid Rhodes Peschal *Fr.* Illuminations.

Dawn. Arthur Rimbaud. TTTS *Fr.* Season in Hell, A.

Dawn. Betsy Sholl. LTA

Dawn. Lucien Stryk. InvLad

Dawn. George Swede. HA

Dawn. *Unknown.* NoSic

Dawn. Robert Penn Warren. BodElec

Dawn. Ella Wheeler Wilcox. PWR

Dawn. William Carlos Williams. APT-1; MoAmPo

Dawn, The. Ricardo Jaimes Freyre. TCLAP, *tr. by* Victor Tulli

Dawn, The. Tennyson. NAEL-5v2; NAEL-6v2

Dawn, The. *Unknown.* PoToHe

Dawn after dawn after dawn / then suddenly the Dark One. Ammianus. GrAn

Dawn after dawn comes on the wine. Ammianus. PGA

Dawn after mortal dawn, with vulgar joy / Acclaim the sun. (LL) Black November Turkey, A. Richard Wilbur. LCAP-2; NAAL-2v2; OWoS

Dawn and dusk. Man Who Reads Homer, A. Nishiwaki Junzaburo. WoPoe, *tr. by* Masaya Saito

Dawn: and foot on the cold stair treading. Aubade for Hope. Robert Penn Warren. MoAmPo

Dawn and night of fighting, lovers like actual wars. Sonnet: Kamikaze. Bernadette Mayer. FTOS

Dawn. . .and the city's lifeless dirt turns grey. Serenade at Dawn. Árpád Tóth. IQMS, *tr. by* Jess Perlman

Dawn; and the jew's-harp's sawing seesaw song. Pilots, Man Your Planes. Randall Jarrell. MoAmPo

Dawn at Chiao Mountain, Seeing Off K'un-lun on His Way Back to Ching-k'ou. Wang Shih-cheng. SuSp, *tr. by* Richard John Lynn

Dawn at that hour. Virgil [*or* Vergil]. WoPoe, *tr. by* Robert Fitzgerald *Fr.* Aeneid [*or* Eneados, Aeneis], The.

Dawn birds on Somerset, The. For Daniel Beels, Third Generation Bricklayer. John Rybicki. AmPoNex

Dawn. Birds sing in the courtyard. Spring Morning. Ch'en Yü-yi. OHMPC, *tr. by* Kenneth Rexroth

Dawn breaks. Saimu. JDP, *tr. by* Yoel Hoffmann

Dawn breaks, snow patches lie on the slopes. After Snow—Impromptu. Yü Chi. CoBLCP, *tr. by* Jonathan Chaves

Dawn brings with it, The. Juan Ramón Jiménez. SpanPo; WoPoe, *tr. by* James Wright *Fr.* Ten Short Poems.

Dawn broke. The pile of clouds kept growing softer. Stag of Irisoda, The. Lajos Áprily. IQMS, *tr. by* Adam Makkai

Dawn Chorus. Mary Holtby. UV

Dawn cicadas choke back sobs. Listening to a Monk Play the Reed Pipes. Hsüeh T'ao. ColAnChi, *tr. by* Jeanne Larsen

Dawn: Clear Skies. Yang Shih-ch'i. CoBLCP, *tr. by* Jonathan Chaves

Dawn comes and with it nostalgia. Along the Banks of the Charles. Adelina da Silva. NAfrP, *tr. by* Don Burness

Dawn comes out of its vast silence. I Am Consecrated to the Coming One. Wafaa' Lamrani. PoArWo, *tr. by* Richard McKane and Tahia Abdel Nasser

Dawn crack of sounds known, The. This Earth, My Brother. Kofi Awoonor. VCWP

Dawn departs, the morning is begun, The. My Mother. Claude McKay. NAAAL

Dawn Dissolves the Monsters. Paul Éluard. AF, *tr. by* Lloyd Alexander

Dawn drizzle [*or* Dawndrizzle] ended dampness steams from. Anglo Saxon Street. Earle Birney. HeIP-4; NIL-7; NOBC

Dawn edges its way through the crowd of huddled trees. October Morning, An. Jayanta Mahapatra. OMIP

Dawn enters; my Love wakens; here is day. (LL) Nuptial Song. John Byrne Leicester Warren, 3d Baron de Tabley. GTBS-P; PeVV

Dawn Fairy, The. Dunya Mikhail. PoArWo, *tr. by* Samira Kawar

Dawn. First light tearing. Clouds. Philip Levine. LCAP-2

Dawn had not streaked the spacious veil of night. Before Twilight. Eyezion. Anne Batten Cristall. RWP

Dawn Has Arisen, Our Welfare Is Assured. *Unknown.* WoPoe, *tr. by* Raimundo Panikkar *Fr.* Vedic Hymns.

Dawn Has Yet to Ripple In. Melville Cane. MoAmPo

Dawn in a tree of birds, A. Kenneth Rexroth. InPK-6

Dawn in Britain, The. Charles Montague Doughty.

  Gauls Sacrifice, The. FaBoTw

  Hymn to the Sun. FaBoTw

  Roman Officer Writes, A. FaBoTw

Dawn in January. Lance Henson. CDW

Dawn in New York. Claude McKay. APT-1

Dawn in the Heart of Africa. Patrice Emery Lumumba. PBA; TTY

Dawn in the Valley. Fily-Dabo Sissoko. NegPo, *tr. by* Ellen Conroy Kennedy

Dawn is, in essence, sinister as fire. Dew. Jennifer Maiden. CBAP

Dawn is smiling on the dew that covers, The.   Genesis of Butterflies, The. Victor Hugo.   AWP, *tr. by* Andrew Lang

Dawn leaves the bed of Dark and climbs the sky.   Virgil [*or* Vergil].   EroLit, *tr. by* Kenneth McLeish   *Fr.* Aeneid [*or* Eneados, *Aeneis*], The.

Dawn lightly laid her rosy hand. (LL)   Ballad of a Nun, A.   John Davidson. MoBrPo; UV

Dawn, / like petals of drenched roses.   Fish.   Bhanuji Rao.   OMIP, *tr. by* Jayanta Mahapatra

Dawn moon struggles to shine its light, The.   On Failing the Examination. Meng Chiao.   CoBCP; ColAnChi, *tr. by* Burton Watson

Dawn of a pleasant morning in May.   Lee to the Rear.   John Randolph Thompson.   CBCWP

Dawn of Love, The.   Henrietta Cordelia Ray.   BlSi; CBWP-3

Dawn of the Space Age.   John Ciardi.   OBAL

Dawn: off from the south cliff   Scene from South Hill to North Hill Passing the Lake.   Hsieh Ling-yün.   ChinPo, *tr. by* Yip Wai-lim

Dawn on the drab North Sea!   North Sea.   Jeffery Day.   PoWW

Dawn on the East Coast.   Alun Lewis.   OBWP

Dawn on the Willamette.   Ella Higginson.   SWaP

Dawn over the Mountains.   Tu Fu.   OHPC, *tr. by* Kenneth Rexroth

Dawn overtook Scheherazade and she fell silent.   Telling, The.   Andrew Hudgins.   RA

Dawn Presented Itself Bare-Armed and Immodest.   Amelia Rosselli.   CItWP, *tr. by* Cinzia Sartini Blum and Lara Trubowitz

Dawn Rhythms.   Margit Kaffka.   IQMS, *tr. by* Paul Tabori

Dawn rolled up slowly what the night unwound.   By the Sound.   John Hollander.   MakPoe

Dawn / rose like a hand at the edge of dark.   Crazy Horse: The Last Morning. Lance Henson.   VoR

Dawn's Carol.   Henrietta Cordelia Ray.   CBWP-3

Dawn's orb orange-raw shining over Palisades.   We Rise on Sun Beams and Fall in the Night.   Allen Ginsberg.   CLPP

Dawn's promising skies.   And This Is My Beloved.   Alexander Borodin. ReLy

"Dawn," said a stranger, "look, the cloud is tinted with blood."   Dawn Rhythms.   Margit Kaffka.   IQMS, *tr. by* Paul Tabori

Dawn shakes the candle, shoots a flame.   May It Be.   Boris Leonidovich Pasternak.   TrJP, *tr. by* C. M. Bowra

Dawn, streaks of rose-brown, dry.   Living Together.   Jean Valentine.   LCAP-2

Dawn that cares for nobody.   February.   W. S. Merwin.   NNaP

Dawn, The! The Dawn! The crimson-tinted, comes.   Dawn in New York. Claude McKay.   APT-1

Dawn to dusk, the weather constantly changed.   Written on the Lake while Returning to Stone Cliff Hermitage.   Hsieh Ling-yün.   CrYelRi, *tr. by* Sam Hamill

Dawn Wail for the Dead.   Oodgeroo of the tribe Noonuccal (Kath Walker). CBAPm ; BMAP

Dawn was apple-green, The.   Green.   D. H. Lawrence.   HarvBoo; MoBrPo

Dawning.   Richard Watson Dixon.   NOBVV

Dawning, The.   George Herbert.   ESCV; NOSC

Dawning, The.   Henry Vaughan.   GeHe; NOCV

Dawning Fair, Morning Wonderful.   *Unknown.*   AH

Dawning sun shines upon the royal wheat fields, The.   Pheasant on His Morning Flight, A.   Hsiao Kang.   ColAnChi, *tr. by* Victor H. Mair and Tsu-Lin Mei

Dawns with that unimaginable day. (LL)   On an Engraving by Casserius.   Alec Derwent Hope.   CBAP; HarvBoo

Dawnward I wake. In darkness wait.   Dawn.   Robert Penn Warren.   BodElec

Day.   Khairi Mansour.   MAP, *tr. by* Charles Doria and Lena Jayyusi

Day, A.   William Leroy Stidger.   PoToHe; SoSe-8

Day, The.   Roy Fuller.   OxBTC

Day, The.   John Glassco.   MoCV

Day 20.   Bruce Beaver.   BMAP   *Fr.* Odes and Days.

Day after Chasing Porcupines.   James Welch.   NoAM

Day after Conference, The.   Josephine D. Henderson Heard.   CBWP-4

Day after day.   Sister, You Cannot Think a Baby Out!   Irène Assiba d'Almeida.   HAWP

Day after Day.   Rabindranath Tagore.   OBMV   *Fr.* Gitanjali.

Day after day as the day sets.   Tirzah.   Jacob Cohen.   MHP, *tr. by* Ruth Finer Mintz

Day after day I sit and write.   Advice to Young Ladies.   Ann Plato.   SWaP

Day after day it goes on.   How Much Longer?   Robert Mezey.   OBWP

Day after day my silk dresses grow more loose.   New Wife, The.   Ng Shao. OHMPC, *tr. by* Kenneth Rexroth

Day after day, O lord of my life, shall I stand before thee face to face? Rabindranath Tagore.   OBMV   *Fr.* Gitanjali.

Day after decapitation, The.   Head, The.   Padraic Fallon.   CIP-2

Day after Sunday, The.   Phyllis McGinley.   MoAmPo; OBSV; UnPo

Day agone, as I rode sullenly, A.   Dante Alighieri.   AWP; EaItPo, *tr. by* Dante Gabriel Rossetti   *Fr.* La Vita Nuova.

Day and Night.   Aimé Césaire.   NAWM-7v2, *tr. by* Gregson Davis

Day and Night.   Haniel Long.   APT-1

Day and Night.   Eugenio Montale.   AF, *tr. by* William Arrowsmith

Day and night are never weary.   Greek Epigram.   Ezra Pound.   MoAmPo

Day and Night Handball.   Stephen Dunn.   MoASP

Day and night she dances.   Shulamit in Her Dreams.   Marcia Falk.   TaR

Day at a Time.   Michael Dransfield.   BMAP

Day at School, A.   Andrea M. Wren.   InTrad

Day Aviva Came to Paris, The.   Irving Layton.   MoCV

Day before Christmas.   Marchette Chute.   NTCP

Day before Spring, The.   Lizette Woodworth Reese.   SWaP

Day began with dismal dougt, The.   *Unknown.*   PoToHe

Day begins to droop, The.   Winter Nightfall.   Robert Bridges.   MoBrPo; OBEV; SCGP

Day being humid and my head, The.   Ovid.   WoPoe, *tr. by* Derek Mahon   *Fr.* Amores.

Day breaks—the first rays of the rising Sun, stretching her arms, The. *Unknown.*   NOBAu, *tr. by* Ronald M. Berndt   *Fr.* Dulngulg Song Cycle, The.

Day by Day.   Sir Richard of Chichester.   SacPr

Day by day I'm falling more in love with you.   Day by Day.   Paul Weston. ReLy

Day by day more brutal and more savage.   In the Bottomless Pit.   Maksimilian Aleksandrovich Voloshin.   TCRP, *tr. by* Yakov Hornstein

Day by Day the Manna Fell.   Josiah Conder.   TrCP

Day can become a Zen garden of raked sand, The.   Arthur Sze.   SpudSo

Day changed, The.   Page from the New Diary, A.   Nida Fazli.   OMIP, *tr. by* Baidar Bakht

Day concludes burning, The.   Desmond O'Grady.   CIP-2   *Fr.* Dying Gaul, The.

Day creeps down. The moon is creeping up.   Man on the Dump, The.   Wallace Stevens.   APT-1; HAP; NAWM-7v2; NoAM

Day darkens.   Bob Boldman.   HA

Day dawns with scent of must and rain, The.   Mirror in February.   Thomas Kinsella.   CIP-2; GTBS-P; MakPoe; NoAM

Day Death Comes, The.   Faiz Ahmad Faiz.   PoetW, *tr. by* Naomi Lazard

Day drags on, as long as a year!, The.   Wen Cheng-ming.   CoBLCP   *Fr.* Chung-i Temple, The.

Day Dream, A.   Emily Jane Brontë.   NALW

Day-dream, A.   Mary Elizabeth Coleridge.   VWP

Day-Dreams.   William Canton.   NOBVV

Day Dreams.   Tso Ssu.   ChiP, *tr. by* Arthur Waley

Day ends that way, with brilliant colors, so lovely, without, The.   Not Even Mythology.   Yannis Ritsos.   AF, *tr. by* Edmund Keeley

Day ends with the blur, The.   Pismo, 1959.   Robert Vasquez.   GeoHom

Day Flight.   Jack Davis.   CBAP

Day for Anne Frank, A.   C. K. Williams.   GotH; TaR

Day goes down red darkling, The.   Desolate.   Gerald Massey.   EBVV

Day grows old, the low-pitched lamp hath made, The.   Yet a Little While Is the Light with You.   Francis Quarles.   ChIV-2

Day had been a day of wind and storm, The.   After a Tempest.   William Cullen Bryant.   APN-1

Day has blinked, the streets are awash with blue, The.   Excitement.   Polly Clark.   NeBl

Day has her star, as well as Night.   Two Stars, The.   William Henry Davies. MoBrPo

Day has pleasures of its own, The.   I Love the Night.   Matilda Caroline Edwards.   PWR

Day! hast thou two faces.   Chartist's Complaint, The.   Ralph Waldo Emerson. NCAP

Day He Died, The.   Ted Hughes.   OxAEP-2

Day I met you I tore up, The.   Nizar Qabbani.   MAP

Day I watched them carry her, The.   Ballad of the Underpass.   Patricia Beer. HarvBoo

Day in an' day oot on his auld farrant loom.   Song for February, A.   Thomas Given.   FaBoVe

Day in August, A.   Frank Ormsby.   PBCIP; PNI

Day In—Day Out.   Johnny Mercer.   ReLy

Day in the Life, A.   Stef Pixner.   BrRo

Day in the Life of, A.   Conyus.   GT

Day in the Life of a Poet, A.   Quincy Troupe.   NBV

Day invited me to walk, The.   To Mrs.———, on the Death of Her Husband. Hannah Wallis.   ECWP

Day is a woman who loves you, The.   Open.   Driving Montana.   Richard Hugo. AmFaPo

Day is chilly, birds each lean upon another, The.   Returning from Kuang-ling.   Ch'in Kuan.   SuSp, *tr. by* Stephen West

Day is cold, and dark, and dreary, The.   Rainy Day, The.   Henry Wadsworth Longfellow.   AWP

Day is colorless like Swiss characters in a novel, The.   For Guillaume Apollinaire.   William Meredith.   CoAP

Day is curled [*or* curl'd] about again [*or* agen], The.   Anniversary on the Hymeneals of My Noble Kinsman, Thomas Stanley, Esquire, An.   Richard Lovelace.   CaPo

Day is dark and dreary, The.   If.   Franklin Pierce Adams.   APT-1; OBAL

Day Is Done, The.   Phoebe Cary.   APN-2; OBAL

Day is done, and the darkness, The.   Day Is Done, The.   Henry Wadsworth Longfellow.   APN-1; BRP; ChAP; ITBLP; NCAP; NOBA; OxBA; PWR; PoRA; TreFP

Day is done; the twilight grows more dark, The.   István Gyöngyösi.   IQMS, *tr. by* Watson Kirkconnell   *Fr.* János Kemény.

Day is drawing to its fall, A.   First Sight of Her and After.   Thomas Hardy.   FaBoVe

Day Is Dying in the West.   Mary Artemisia Lathbury.   AH; SacPr

Day is ending.   My Blue Heaven.   Walter Donaldson.   ReLy

Day is ending, The.   Afternoon in February.   Henry Wadsworth Longfellow.   APN-1; ColAP

Day Is Gone and All Its Sweets Are Gone, The.   John Keats.   CenSon

Day is great and strong, The.   World without Peculiarity.   Wallace Stevens.   HCAP

Day is long; the worn noon dreams, The.   Noon's Dream-Song.   Eugene Lee-Hamilton.   NOBVV

Day is mad, The. Mad is the house. Mad the bedsheets.   Erotica 12.   Yannis Ritsos.   PFTM-2, *tr. by* Kimon Friar

Day is o'er and twilight's shade, The.   Gerarda.   Eloise Bibb.   CBWP-4

Day is over and its cares and woes, The.   Good Night, Sweetheart.   Jimmy Campbell.   ReLy

Day Is Past and Gone, The.   John Leland.   AH

Day is past, the sun is set, The.   Evening.   Thomas Miller.   NOxBChV

Day is through, The.   Tomorrow Is Another Day.   Walter Jurmann.   ReLy

Day is turning ghost, The.   Commonplace Day, A.   Thomas Hardy.   NOBVV

Day Lady Died, The.   Frank O'Hara.   HCAP; LCAP-2; NAAL-2v2; NOBA; NeAP; NoAM; NoP-4; PAI; PFTM-2; PmAP; PoE; PoM; RaBo; SwNoth; TRP; VCAP

Day, like our souls, is fiercely dark.   Battle Song.   Ebenezer Elliott.   OxAEP-2

Day Lily and the Fox, The.   Emily Hiestand.   OPRER

Day-long bluster of the storm was o'er, The.   Drowned Spaniel, The.   Charles Tennyson Turner.   PeVV

Day-long cold hard rain drove, The.   Surviving.   James Welch.   CDW; HATNAP

Day must bring an ending of the self, A.   Raindrops.   György Sárközi.   IQMS, *tr. by* Roy Fuller

Day of anger after the holy night, The.   News from a Pacified Area.   James Keir Baxter.   OxBC

Day of Atonement.   Charles Reznikoff.   ChIV-1

Day of Cold Food, The.   Li Ch'ing-chao.   OHPC, *tr. by* Kenneth Rexroth

Day of Denial, The.   Jones Very.   NOBA

Day of Doom, The.   Michael Wigglesworth.   NAAL-2v1; SCAP

  "Adulterers and whoremongers / were there, with all unchaste."   ColAP

  "All filthy facts, and secret acts."   NAAL-3

  "All silence keep, both goats and sheep."   NAAL-3

  "Apostates and run-aways."   ColAP

  "Blasphemers lewd, and swearers shrewd."   ColAP

  "But all too late, grief's out of date."   NAAL-3

  "Can God delight in such a sight."   NAAL-3

  "Christ's Flock of Lambs there also stands."   TCAPo

  "Come, blessed ones, and sit on thrones."   NAAL-3

  "For at midnight brake forth a Light."   TCAPo

  "Glorious Judge will priviledge, The."   TCAPo

  "Had your intent been to repent."   NAAL-3

  ("Moreover, there with them appear.")   ColAP

  "Others argue, and not a few."   NAAL-3

  "Still was the night, serene and bright."   ColAP; NAAL-3

  "Still was the night, Serene and Bright."   ColAP; TCAPo

  "Then to the bar, all they drew near."   OBCA

  "There also stand a num'rous band."   ColAP

  "These words appall and daunt them all."   NAAL-3

  "They rush from Beds with giddy heads."   TCAPo

  "They wring their hands, their caitiff-hands."   NAAL-3

  "Thus all men's pleas the Judge with ease."   NAAL-3

  "Thus every one before the Throne."   TCAPo

  "Thus everyone before the throne."   NAAL-3

  "Thus he doth find of all mankind."   NAAL-3

  "Thus shall they lie, and wail, and cry."   NAAL-3

  "Unto the saints with sad complaints."   NAAL-3

  "Wallowing in all kind of sin."   ColAP

  "With cords of love God often strove."   NAAL-3

  "Wond'rous crowd then 'gan aloud, A."   NAAL-3

Day of fire is coming, the thrush, The.   Anne Sexton.   BodElec   *Fr.* Furies, The.

Day of God! Thou Blessed Day.   Hannah Flagg Gould.   AH

Day of heat, A. The woods burning. Time.   Monkey.   Vladislav Felitsianovich Khodasevich.   TCRP, *tr. by* Michael Frayn

Day of her wedding, she crouches in the kitchen, The.   Feast of St. Tortoise, The.   Nancy Willard.   LCAP-2

Day of Judgement.   Henry Vaughan.   ChIV-2

Day of Judgement, The.   Jonathan Swift.   BIrV; ChIV-1; NOBE; NOEC; NPeEn; OBSV; OxBEV; SCGP

Day of Judg[e]ment, The; an Ode.   Isaac Watts.   ECEV; HAP; NOBE; NOEC; OBEV; OxBEV

 (Day of Judgement, The.)   ChIV-2; SCGP

 (Day of Judgment, The.)   NoP-4

Day of Judgment, The.   Thomas of Celano.   *See* Dies Irae

Day of Judgment is here, The.   So Bring the Order for My Execution.   Faiz Ahmad Faiz.   VCWP, *tr. by* Agha Shahid Ali

Day of My Death, The.   Pier Paolo Pasolini.   VCWP

Day of my double birth, if such the year.   John Thelwall.   NOEC   *Fr.* Lines Written at Bridgewater, 27 July 1797.

Day of Resurrection, The.   Saint John of Damascus.   TrCP, *tr. by* John Mason Neale

Day of sea in the sky, made.   Day of Sea.   Sophia De Mello Breyner.   VCWP, *tr. by* Ruth Fainlight

Day of sunny face and temper, A.   Gwendolyn Brooks.   VGW   *Fr.* Catch of Shy Fish, A.

Day of the Dead.   Rigoberto González.   AmPoNex

Day of the fête—and what a day for it, The.   School Cadets.   Anne Elder.   CBAP

Day of the Landscape, The.   Alfred Margul-Sperber.   AuPH, *tr. by* Lowell A. Bangerter

Day on the Planet, A.   Brian Morse.   NOxBChV

Day on which you, The.   Enumeration.   Ilse Aichinger.   AF, *tr. by* Allen H. Chappel

Day One: Above the river I hear.   Hay.   Maxine W. Kumin.   BodElec

Day 1: Portrait of the Artist, Small-kid Time.   R. Zamora-Linmark.   ReBoTo

Day perched at ground-level.   More Rain.   Ben Scammell.   NLP

Day pounds hard against our temple doors, The.   Cooking to Music.   Edward Kleinschmidt.   MiVo

Day's exhaustion brings me to the valley of sleep, The.   I and I.   Khalil-ur-Rahman Azmi.   OMIP, *tr. by* C. M. Naim

Day's in dread of losing her bright features, The.   Ausiàs March.   STV

Day's noise was draining away in my mind, The.   Man in the Middle of the Street.   Petronius Arbiter.   WoPoe, *tr. by* Tim Reynolds

Day's Ration, The.   Ralph Waldo Emerson.   APN-1

Day's sweetest moments are at dawn.   Dawn.   Ella Wheeler Wilcox.   PWR

Day seawater swilled my lungs, The.   Does It Go Like this?   Maura Dooley.   NeBl

Day slow in going, A.   Buson.   EH, *tr. by* Robert Hass

Day Song.   Lance Henson.   HATNAP

Day that Eliot died I stood, The.   Thanks in Winter.   Harri Webb.   AngWePo

Day that I was christened, The.   Godmother.   Dorothy Parker.   PoRA

Day that I was crowned, The.   Emily Dickinson.   TCAPo

Day that they stole her tiger's-eye ring, The.   On Becoming a Tiger.   Lorna Goodison.   GT

Day the bombs hit Hellabrunn, The.   In the Menagerie.   Oleg Grigorevich Chukhonstev.   TCRP, *tr. by* Simon Franklin

Day the fat woman, The.   Beach in August, The.   Weldon Kees.   VGW

Day the gardeners planted, The.   For Beauty.   Susan Hahn.   ExTi

Day, The / is ready to close.   Saturday Night in the Village.   Giacomo Leopardi.   OBVE; WoPoe, *tr. by* Robert Lowell

Day the Tide, The.   Philip Booth.   CoAP

Day the two old women were dissecting two birds, The.   Richard Brought His Flute.   Nancy Morejón.   TCLAP, *tr. by* Kathleen Weaver

Day the wind was hardly, A.   Letter VI.   William Sydney Graham.   FaBoMo

Day the Winds, The.   Josephine Miles.   FaBoWP

Day They Came for Our House, The.   Don Mattera.   PeSAV

Day They Cleaned Up the Border El Salvador, February, 1981, The.   Wendy Rose.   HATNAP

Day They Eulogized Mahalia, The.   Audre Lorde.   ReTh

Day they strung the cable from America to Europe, The.   Cotton.   Harry Edmund Martinson.   RB, *tr. by* Robert Bly

Day Thou Gavest, Lord, Is Ended, The.   John Ellerton.   EBVV

Day time failed began as usual, The. Burial of a Fisherman in Hydra. Grace Schulman. BoWoP

Day to the reedy marsh had closed her eye. János Arany. IQMS, *tr. by* Watson Kirkconnell *Fr.* Toldi.

Day took such a time to pass, The. Note. Dimitris Tsaloumas. BMAP

Day Trip. Carole Satyamurti. OPOU

Day turns to evening on the lake. Hayim Lenski. FIT, *tr. by* Robert Friend

Day Twenty-three. Victor Coleman. NOBC

Day was clear as fire, The. Killer, The. Judith Wright. BMAP

Day was close, overcast like a grey belly, The. Winter. Philip Salom. NOBAu

Day was cloudy, The. No one could come to a decision. George Seferis. PoetW, *tr. by* Edmund Keeley and Philip Sherrard

Day was cloudy, The. No one could come to a decision. George Seferis. AF *Fr.* Last Day, The.

Day was here when it was his to know, The. New Tenants, The. Edwin Arlington Robinson. NoAM

Day was one of weariness, The. Beggar, The. Margaret E. Bruner. PoToHe

Day We Buried Our Bully, The. Mbuyiseni Oswald Mtshali. PeSAV

Day We Die, The. *Southern Bushmen Oral Tradition.* BLT; WoPoe, *tr. by* Arthur Markowitz

Day We Visited New Orleans, The. Robert Bly. KGB

Day wears on, The. John Wills. HA

Day when Charmus ran with five, The. Mighty Runner, A. Edwin Arlington Robinson. OBAL

Day when Charmus ran with five, The. *Var. authors.* OBAL *Fr.* Variations of Greek Themes.

Day when it will not matter, The. Day, The. John Glassco. MoCV

Day Which Endures Not, A. A. G. Prys-Jones. OBWVE, *tr. by* Anthony Conran

Day will come when I will, The. Farewell to a Southern Melody, A. Huang O [*or* Huang Ho]. BoWoP; WoPoe, *tr. by* Chung Ling and Kenneth Rexroth

Day will come, when't shall be said, The. Jonathan Swift. NOIV *Fr.* Life and Character of Dean Swift, The.

Day will dawn, when one of us shall harken, The. One of Us Two. Ella Wheeler Wilcox. PoToHe

Day will rise and the sun from eastward. Song. George Campbell Hay. OxBS

Day with the Foreign Legion, A. Reed Whittemore. CoAP; CoAmPo

Day without Night. Louise Glück. TaR

Day you appeared I began to speak, The. To Your Question. Duane Niatum. CDW

Day you came naked to Paris, The. Day Aviva Came to Paris, The. Irving Layton. MoCV

Day Zimmer Lost Religion, The. Paul Zimmer. InPK-6; PBCAP

Daybreak. Richard Henry Dana. APN-1

Daybreak. Philippe Jaccottet. MFP, *tr. by* Martin Sorrell

Daybreak. Galway Kinnell. BLT; ChAP

Daybreak. Henry Wadsworth Longfellow. ITBLP; PWR

Daybreak. W. S. Merwin. NAAL-2v2

Daybreak. Bert Meyers. SPE

Daybreak. Stephen Spender. BoLoP

Daybreak. *Unknown, at. to* John Donne. OBEV (Aubade.) BoLoP; NOBE

Daybreak. Christiania Whitehead. NeBl

Daybreak / Have you already seen the dawn. Three Dawns. Jean-Joseph Rabéarivelo [*or* Rebéarivelo]. NegPo, *tr. by* Ellen Conroy Kennedy

Daybreak in late spring, I embark at Ba Gorge. Arriving at Ba Gorge in the Morning. Wang Wei. WoPoe, *tr. by* Willis Barnstone, Tony Barnstone and Xu Haixin

Daybreak is still far away, The. Agonia Christiana. János Pilinszky. IQMS, *tr. by* Adam Makkai

Daybreak / mingles blood. Daybreak. Philippe Jaccottet. MFP, *tr. by* Martin Sorrell

Daybreak: the household slept. Father and Child. Gwen Harwood. CBAP; WPE

Daydream of Ants, The. Tanure Ojaide. NAfrP

Daydreaming on the Trail. Miyazawa Kenji. PFTM-1

Dayeinu—they said. Rosita Kalina. TANSG, *tr. by* Celeste Kostopulos-Cooperman

Daylight. Mariana Romo-Carmona. WiU

Daylight announces. Sunrise Comes to Second Avenue. Thylias Moss. TRP

Daylight changed without you. Daylight. Mariana Romo-Carmona. WiU

Daylight. For everyone but me. Nap. Dreams by No One's Daughter. Leslie Ullman. PBCAP

Daylight, full of small dancing particles. Jelaluddin [*or* Jalal al-Din] Rumi. LoL

Daylights. Rosanna Warren. NoAM

Daylong this tomcat lies stretched flat. Esther's Tomcat. Ted Hughes. OxBC; OxBEV

Days. Ralph Waldo Emerson. APN-1; ColAP; HAP; HeIP-4; NAAL-2v1; NAAL-3; NCAP; NOBA; NoP-4; OxBA; OxBSP; PoE; TAP; TCAPo; TFi

Days. Philip Larkin. EBEV; FaBoMo; NPeEn; OxAEP-2; OxBC; OxBEV; OxBSP; PeECV; PoetW; RB; TOF; WoPoe

Days. Gary Young. "I don't know where the owls go when they leave this place." GeoHom

Days and Nights. Kenneth Koch. "I certainly have lost something." NoAM Stones of Time, The. NoAM

Days and Nights. Kenneth Koch. *Fr.* Days and Nights.

Days are cold. Cottager to Her Infant, (By My Sister), The. Dorothy Wordsworth. TTTS

Days are sad, it is the holy tide, The. Holy Tide, The. Frederick Tennyson. OBEV; SacPr

Days become years. Years. Paavo Haavikko. VCWP *Fr.* Darkness.

Days can be sunny. I Got Rhythm. George Gershwin. ReLy

Days Drawing In. Edith Jay Scovell. FaBoWP *Fr.* First Year, The.

Days fail: night broods over afternoon, The. Edith Jay Scovell. FaBoWP *Fr.* First Year, The.

Days go I remain, The. (LL) Mirabeau Bridge, The. Guillaume Apollinaire. BoLoP; OBVE

Days Gone By, The. James Whitcomb Riley. APN-2; OBCA

Days grow and the stars cross over, The. Darkness Music. Muriel Rukeyser. BoWoP

Days grow long, the mountains, The. South Wind. Tu Fu. BLT; OHPC, *tr. by* Kenneth Rexroth

Days in White. Ingeborg Bachmann. BoWoP

Days Inn. Linda Smukler. WiU

Days like Prose. Alan Michael Parker. NeAmPo

Days of 1908. Constantine P. Cavafy. WoPoe, *tr. by* James Merrill

Days of 1908. Constantine P. Cavafy. PFTM-1

Days of 1941 and '44. James Merrill. GLP

Days of 1956. Robin Magowan. SPE

Days of 1964. James Merrill. CoAP; HCAP; NAAL-2v2; PoE; VCAP

Days of 1981. Mark Doty. ReTh

Days of Adam were 930 years, The. Dennis Joseph Enright. OBCoV *Fr.* Paradise Illustrated.

Days of April '43. George Seferis. PoetW, *tr. by* Edmund Keeley and Philip Sherrard

Days of my youth left me long ago, The. Chrysanthemums in the Eastern Garden, The. Po Chü-i. ChiP, *tr. by* Arthur Waley

Days of our ghosthood were these, The. Ghosts, The. Edith Jay Scovell. HarvBoo

Days of Our Youth, The. *Unknown.* AWP, *tr. by* Wilfrid Scawen Blunt

Days of Rain. Li Ho. CrYelRi, *tr. by* Sam Hamill

Days of Rain; the Rivers Have Overflowed. Su Tung-p'o (Su Shih). CoBCP, *tr. by* Burton Watson *Fr.* Days of Rain; the Rivers Have Overflowed: Two Poems.

Days of spring are here, The! the eglantine. Hafiz [*or* Hafez]. AWP *Fr.* Odes.

Days of the Unicorns, The. Phyllis Webb. NOBC

Days of Yore, The. Douglas Thompson. TreFP

Days pass easy over these ancient hills. We Are a People. Lance Henson. VoR

Days pass on that face, The. Gregorio Scalise. ItPo, *tr. by* Gayle Ridinger

Days shorten, the south blows wide for showers now, The. Salmon Fishing. Robinson Jeffers. APT-1

Days sparkling with ever new joys. (LL) Your Presence. David Diop. PBA; PBMAP, *tr. by* Ulli Beier

Days That Have Been. William Henry Davies. AngWePo

Days themselves, The. Position. Léon Damas. NegPo, *tr. by* Ellen Conroy Kennedy

Days Too Short. William Henry Davies. MoBrPo

Days wrap themselves around me, The. Ode to Your Back. Gloria Vando. TouFir

Dayseye hugging the earth, The. Daisy. William Carlos Williams. MoAmPo

Daystar. Rita Dove. AmFaPo; LCAP-2; NAAAL; NIL-7; NIP-4; OxWW

Daytime Dream. Tu Fu. WoPoe, *tr. by* Eva Shan Chou

Dazel'd thus, with height of place. Sir Henry Wotton. *See* Dazzled [*or* Dazel'd] thus with height of place

Dazzle. Dorothy Roberts. NOBC

Dazzle on the sea, my darling, The. Leaving Barra. Louis MacNeice. EBEV

Dazzled blood, The. Faustus Triumphant. Thom Gunn. FaBoMo

Dazzled [*or* Dazel'd] thus with height of place. Upon the Sudden Restraint of the Earl[e] of Somerset, Then Falling from Favor [*or* Favour]. Sir Henry Wotton. NOBE; NOSC; NPeEn; OxBEV

Dazzling and tremendous how quick the sun-rise would kill me.　Walt Whitman.　ColAP　*Fr.* Song of Myself.

DC Nocturne.　Kenneth Carroll.　AmPoNex

DDD.　Bruce Andrews.　FTOS

De.　Robert Alan Jamieson.　FaBoVe

De Aegypto.　Ezra Pound.　APT-1; VGW

De Ambiente.　Tatiana De la Tierra.　GLP

De Amore Suo.　Catullus.　OBVE, *tr.* by Richard Lovelace

De Ballit of de Boll Weevil.　*Unknown.*　NOBA

De Civitate Hominum.　Thomas MacGreevy [*or* McGreevy].　CIP-2

De Cœnatione Micae.　Martial.　FaBoCh; RompPo, *tr.* by Robert Louis Stevenson

De Day befo' Thanksgibin'.　Maggie Pogue Johnson.　CBWP-4

De Gustibus.　Robert Browning.　FHYEP; SCGP

De'il's [*or* Deil's] Awa wi' th' [*or* the] Exciseman, The.　Robert Burns.　OBCoV

De Imagine Mundi.　John Ashbery.　FaBoMo

De maiden mit nodings on. (LL)　Ballad by Hans Breitmann.　Charles Godfrey Leland.　APN-2; NOBL; TCAPo

De Morte.　Sir Henry Wotton.　BASC; NOSC; OxBSP

De Naevo in Facie Faustinae.　Thomas Bastard.　FaBoEE

De Natura Rerum.　Yves Bonnefoy.　VCWP, *tr.* by Lisa Sapinkopf

De nex' day de hide drap off'n yō' back. (LL)　Jack and Dinah Want Freedom.　*Unknown.*　BPo; NAAAL

De Pisis—Piacenza Papers.　Franco Buffoni.　ItPo, *tr.* by Gayle Ridinger

De Ponto.　Ovid.　OBVE, *tr.* by Henry Vaughan

De Principe Bono et Malo.　Sir Thomas More.　PBRV

De Profundis.　Thomas Campion.　InvLi

　(Their sin-sick souls by him shall be recured.) (LL)　InvLi; SacPr

De Profundis.　George Gascoigne.

　"From depth of dole wherein my soul doth dwell."　ChIV-1; SacPr

　"Skies gan scowl, o'ercast with misty clouds, The."　ChIV-1

De Profundis.　David Gascoyne.　PoWW

De Profundis.　László Kálnoky.　IQMS, *tr.* by Edwin Morgan

De Profundis.　Dorothy Parker.　NAAL-2v2

De Profundis.　Georg Trakl.　WoPoe, *tr.* by James Wright

De Puero Balbutiente.　Thomas Bastard.　NoSic; OxBEV; OxBSP

　(As when a man does walke upon the yce.) (LL)　OxBEV

　(De Puero Balbutiente.)　NoSic; OxBEV; OxBSP

　(Me thinkes tis pretie sport to heare a childe.)　OxBEV

De Puerorum osculis.　Giles de Gillies.　CAGL

De railroad bridge's.　Homesick Blues.　Langston Hughes.　GM; NAAAL

De Ramis Cadunt Folia (Love in Winter).　*Unknown.*　WoPoe, *tr.* by Phillip Holland

De Regimine Principum.　Thomas Hoccleve [*or* Occleve].

　Lament for Chaucer.　OBEV

　"O maister deere and fader reverent!"　EBEV

De Rerum Natura (On the Nature of Things).　Lucretius.

　Address to Venus.　AWP

　("Ah Wretch! thou cry'st, ah! miserable me.")　AWP; OBVE, *tr.* by John Dryden

　"Darling of Gods and Men, beneath the gliding stars."　WoPoe, *tr.* by Basil Bunting

　Fourth Book, Concerning the Nature of Love, The.

　　"When Love its utmost vigour does imploy."　NPeEn; OxBEV, *tr.* by John Dryden

　"Gods, by right of Nature, must possess, The."　NPeEn, *tr.* by John Wilmot, 2d Earl of Rochester

　"Great Venus, Queene [*or* Queen] of Beautie [*or* Beauty] and of grace."　AWP

　No Single Thing Abides.　AWP, *tr.* by W. H. Mallock

　"Now since the members of the world we view."　OBVE

　Suave Mari Magno.

　"Thus, therefore, he who feels the fiery dart."　EroLit, *tr.* by John Dryden

　What Has This Bugbear Death.　CTC, *tr.* by John Dryden

　"When storms blow loud, 'tis sweet to watch at ease."　AWP, *tr.* by W. H. Mallock

De Sade.　John Fuller.　NBLV; PeLV

De Se.　John Weever.　FaBoEE

De sol a sol.　Haroldo de Campos.　PFTM-2, *tr.* by Edwin Morgan　*Fr.* Transient Servitude.

De Souza Prabhu.　Eunice De Souza.　FaBoVe

De talles' tree in Paradise.　Blow Your Trumpet, Gabriel.　*Unknown.*　APN-2

De—um majorettes.　Ken Edwards.　Oth　*Fr.* Five Nocturnes, after Derek Jarman.

Dea ex Machina.　John Updike.　UV

Deacon Brown's Conclusion.　George Sands Johnson.　PWR

Deacon Morgan.　Naomi Long Madgett.　BlSi

Deacon's Masterpiece; or, The Wonderful "One-Hoss Shay," The.　Oliver Wendell Holmes.　APN-1; BRP; ITBLP; NAAL-3; NOBA; OBAL; OBCA; OxBA; PoRA; TAP; TCAPo; TFi　*Fr.* Autocrat of the Breakfast Table, The.

Deacon's wife was a bit desirish, The.　Pride of Ancestry.　Robert Frost.　OBAL

Dead, The.　René Arcos.　FaBoWar; PeFWW, *tr.* by Christopher Middleton

Dead, The.　Cecil Day Lewis.　TwCP

Dead, The.　Louis Dudek.　NOBC

Dead, The.　José María Eguren.　TCLAP, *tr.* by Iver Lofving

Dead, The.　Charles Heavysege.　NOBC

Dead, The.　Arthur James Marshall Smith.　NOBC

Dead, The.　Mark Strand.　HeIP-4

Dead, The.　Jones Very.　APN-1; HAP; NOBA; NoP-4; OxBA; SacPr; TAP; TCAPo

Dead and divine and brother of all, and here again he lies. (LL)　Sight in Camp [in the Daybreak Gray and Dim], A.　Walt Whitman.　CBCWP; NAAL-2v1; NAAL-3; NAAL-5; NoAM; OxBA; PAI; PoE; SAmP; TAP

Dead are a cadmium blue, The.　Charles Wright.　HCAP　*Fr.* Homage to Paul Cézanne.

Dead are always searched, The.　Enemy Dead, The.　Bernard Gutteridge.　FaBoWar; PoWW

Dead are gone and with them we cannot converse, The.　*Unknown.*　ChiP　*Fr.* Seventeen Old Poems.

Dead are horizontal and motionless, The.　Ancestor Worship.　Emyr Humphreys.　AngWePo

Dead Are My People.　Kahlil Gibran.　GraLe, *tr.* by Anthony Rizcallah Ferris

Dead are our mothers, whom we cherished.　Return Home 1918, The.　Franz Theodor Csokor.　AuPH, *tr.* by Lowell A. Bangerter

Dead are selfish, The.　Diatribe against the Dead.　Angel González.　VCWP, *tr.* by Steven Ford Brown

Dead Armadillos.　Gail White.　UrbNat

Dead at Clonmacnois [*or* Clonmacnoise], The.　Angus O'Gillan.　OBEV; OBMV, *tr.* by Thomas William Hazen Rolleston

Dead at Quang Tri, The.　Yusef Komunyakaa.　CDa

Dead at Villers-Bretonneux, The.　Inscription at Villers-Bretonneux.　Geoff Page.　NOBAu

Dead Baby, The.　William Carlos Williams.　NAAL-2v2

Dead beetle lies on a country road, A.　Seen from Above.　Wislawa Szymborska.　PoSu, *tr.* by Grazyna Drabik

Dead before Death.　Christina Georgina Rossetti.　NAEL-5v2; NAEL-6v2; NALW

Dead Beggar, an Elegy Addressed to a Lady, The.　Charlotte Smith.　BWW

Dead birds fell, but no one had seen them fly, The.　Some Dreams They Forgot.　Elizabeth Bishop.　NoAM

Dead Boy.　John Crowe Ransom.　FaBoMo; FuPo; HarvBoo; NoAM; NoP-4; OxBA; PoE; TwCP

Dead boy living among men as a man, A.　Head, A.　James Schuyler.　PoM

Dead Brother, The.　*Hungarian Oral Tradition.*　IQMS, *tr.* by Adam Makkai

Dead Butterfly, The.　Denise Levertov.　NoP-4

Dead by the Side of the Road, The.　Gary Snyder.　HAP

Dead Can Sing, The.　For the Dead Lecturer.　Diane Di Prima.　BB

Dead can sleep, The.　I Am Dead but I Know the Dead Are Not Like This.　Charles Bukowski.　PmAP

Dead cat.　Michael McClintock.　HA

Dead cats and turnip-tops come tumbling down the flood. (LL)　Description of a City Shower, A.　Jonathan Swift.　HeIP-4; NAEL-5v1; NAEL-6v1; NAEL-7v1; NIL-7; NOEC; NoP-4; NPeEn; OBSV; PoE; UnPo

Dead Center.　Alfred A. Yuson.　ReBoTo

Dead Child Speaks, A.　Nelly Sachs.　HP; PoSu

Dead Christ.　Andrew Hudgins.　RA

Dead Cities.　Madison Cawein.　APN-2

Dead city walls may pen us in, but still.　Charles Harpur.　CBAP　*Fr.* Coast View, A.

Dead cold spots in the air.　Beckon.　Gillian Conoley.　BodElec

Dead Color.　Charles Wright.　HCAP; LCAP-2

Dead cones upon the altar [*or* alder] shook. (LL)　In Memory of Jane Fraser [*or* Frazer].　Geoffrey Hill.　NAEL-5v2; NAEL-6v2; NIL-7; NoAM; OxBTC

Dead Cow Farm.　Robert Graves.　FaBoWar; PoWW

Dead Crab, The.　Andrew Young.　FaBoTw; RB

Dead dandelions, bald as drumsticks.　Dandelions.　Craig Raine.　NoAM

Dead! dead! the Child I lov'd so well!　On the Death of His Son.　Charles Wesley.　NOCV

Dead Dog.　Vernon Scannell.　OxBC

Dead Embryos.　Judit Tóth.　WPOW, *tr.* by Laura Schiff

Dead Erect, The.　Malika O'Lahsen.　HAWP

Dead Eyes.　Syl Cheney-Coker.　NAfrP

Dead Fiddle, The.　Humbert Wolfe.　TrJP

Dead Fly. Eiléan Ní Chuilleanáin. CIP-2

Dead for Two Years, Erhart Arranges to Meet Me in a Dream. John Balaban. CDa

Dead Friend, The. Agnes Mary Frances Robinson. VWP

Dead Gallop. Pablo Neruda. TCLAP, *tr.* by John Felstiner

Dead grow more intractable every day, The. Soldier's Rest. Roque Dalton. TCLAP, *tr.* by Richard Schaaf

Dead gull in the road, A. Charles Reznikoff. APT-2

Dead Hand. W. S. Merwin. InPK-6

Dead hangs the fruit on that tall tree. Burial of the Spirit of a Young Poet. Richard Hughes. MoBrPo

Dead have remembered, The. Posthumous Rehabilitation. Tadeusz Rózewicz. HP, *tr.* by Adam Czerniawski

Dead Heroes, The. Isaac Rosenberg. MoBrPo

Dead Horse, The. Cecília Meireles. TCLAP, *tr.* by James Merrill

Dead Horse Bay. Robert Adamson. NOBAu

Dead Horse in Field. Robert Penn Warren. BodElec

Dead Host's Welcome, The. John Fletcher. OxAEP-1 *Fr.* Lover's Progress, The.

Dead Idyll. César Vallejo. BLPSL, *tr.* by Rene de Costa, Rigas Kappatos and Eleni Paidoussi

Dead in Europe, The. Robert Lowell. OxBA; OxBC; WoPoe

Dead in Frock Coats. Carlos Drummond de Andrade. PFTM-1

Dead in other lands are settled, The. Order of the Dead, The. John Pepper Clark Bekederemo. HBAPE

Dead in the cold, a song-singing thrush. Last Rites. Christina Georgina Rossetti. FaBoVe; NPeEn

Dead in There. Langston Hughes. APSN

Dead in via, The. La Préface. Charles Olson. APT-2; PFTM-2; PoM

Dead is he? Yes, our stranger guest said dead. Augusta Davies Webster. ViWPN *Fr.* Medea in Athens.

Dead is now that blackguard and buried in earth. Translation by Mark Willhardt. William Dunbar. RACG

Dead is the root[e] whence all these fancies [*or* fancyes] grew[e]. (LL) Farewell to False Love, A. Sir Walter Ralegh. BoLoP; NAEL-5v1; NoSic

Dead Knight, The. John Masefield. GTBS-P

Dead Landscape. Attila József. WoPoe, *tr.* by Edwin Morgan

Dead Language. Johannes Bobrowski. WoPoe, *tr.* by Matthew Mead and Ruth Mead

Dead leaves are falling in the dormant air. Bridge, The. O. V. de L. Milosz. BLT

Dead leaves, one-time fair, The. Word to the West End, A. Thomas Ashe. EBVV

Dead lemon like a cowled old woman crouching in the cold, A. For *Under the Volcano*. Malcolm Lowry. NOBC

Dead Liebknecht, The. Hugh MacDiarmid. OBVE

Dead Love. Elizabeth Siddal. LW; NOBVV

Dead loves that were born for me. (LL) Stony Grey Soil. Patrick Kavanagh. CIP-2; HarvBoo; ModIr

Dead Man Ariseth and Singeth a Hymn to the Sun, The. *Unknown.* AWP *Fr.* Book of the Dead.

Dead Man Asks for a Song, The. *Unknown.* WoPoe, *tr.* by Willard Trask

Dead man is introduced back into life, The. They take him to a country fair, to a. Bringing a Dead Man Back into Life. Russell Edson. TRP

Dead man likes it when the soup simmers and the kettle hisses, The. Book of the Dead Man #87, The. Marvin Bell. PuP-23

Dead Man's Corner. Robert Silliman Hillyer. APT-2

Dead Man's Dump. Isaac Rosenberg. FaBoMo; GTBS-P; NAEL-5v2; NAEL-6v2; NoAM; OBWP; PeFWW; PoWW; TrJP

Dead man steps over sweaty sleepers. Let's Live Cheerfully. Shinkichi Takahashi. ZenPo, *tr.* by Takashi Ikemoto and Lucien Stryk

Dead man thinks he is alive when he sees blood in his stool, The. Book of the Dead Man #1, The. Marvin Bell. GifTon

Dead man touched me with his hand, A. Mariya [*or* Mariia] Avakkumova. TCRP

Dead March, A. Mary C. Gillington. PeVV

Dead Mole, A. Andrew Young. GTBS-P; NePenScot; OxBSP

Dead moths fell from the sky. Swirling swarms buried traffic lights. Cocoons. Sean Thomas Dougherty. AmPoNex

Dead of the Wilderness, The. Hayyim Nahman [*or* Khayim Nakhman *or* Chaim Nachman] Bialik. AWP, *tr.* by Maurice Samuel

Dead of Winter. Salvatore Quasimodo. WoPoe, *tr.* by George Garrett

Dead on the War Path. *Unknown.* FaBoWar, *tr.* by Herbert J. Spinden and H. J. Spinden

Dead! One of them shot by the sea in the east. Mother and Poet. Elizabeth Barrett Browning. NAEL-5v2; NAEL-6v2; NALW; VWP; ViWPN

Dead or living. Seed Is in Me, The. José Craveirinha. PBMAP

Dead person, I wander, A. Exile. Ingeborg Bachmann. PoSu, *tr.* by Daniel Huws

Dead Pianist, The. Sean Dunne. ModIr *Fr.* Sydney Place.

Dead piled up, thick, fragrant, on the fire escape, The. Autumn Leaves. Marilyn Chin. ExTi

Dead Poet, The. Lord Alfred Bruce Douglas. GSo

Dead Poet, The. Alfred Wellington Purdy. NOBC

Dead poets stalk the air. Rainy Night at the Writers' Colony. Josephine Jacobsen. TAP

Dead Ponies. Brenda Chamberlain. OBWVE; WPE

Dead's right grain, The. Future and the Ancestor, The. Andrée Chedid. HAWP; WPOW, *tr.* by Mirène Ghossein and Samuel Hazo

Dead Sea, The. Peter Davison. YaYoPo *Fr.* Breaking of the Day, The.

Dead Sea Scrolls, The. *Unknown.*

  Blessed Art Thou, O Lord. TrJP, *tr.* by Theodor H. Gaster

  Lo, I Am Stricken Dumb. TrJP, *tr.* by Theodor H. Gaster

  My Soul in the Bundle of Life. TrJP, *tr.* by E. Margaret Rowley

  Though Mine Eye Sleep Not. TrJP, *tr.* by Theodor H. Gaster

Dead Seal. Alfred Wellington Purdy. MoCV

Dead Seal [near McClure's Beach], The. Robert Bly. NNaP

Dead Shall Be Raised Incorruptible, The. Galway Kinnell. NOBA; PoE

Dead shall seem to live again!, The. (LL) Song: "What voice is this, thou evening gale!" Joanna Baillie. RWP; WoRP

Dead shalt thou lie; and nought. Sapphic Fragment. Thomas Hardy. OBVE

Dead sheep / beside the highway. Preparations. Leslie Marmon Silko. VoR

Dead Sister, The. Caroline Gilman. OBCA

Dead Soldier. Nicolás Guillén. TTY, *tr.* by Langston Hughes

Dead Soldiers. James Fenton. AF; FaBoWar; NoAM; NoP-4; OBWP

Dead Soldiers, The. Max Plowman. PoWW

Dead soul's epitaph in every face!, A. (LL) Street, The. James Russell Lowell. GSo; Son

Dead stare out of empty sockets, The. Dead, The. Arthur James Marshall Smith. NOBC

Dead Statesman, A. Rudyard Kipling. FaBoEE; FaBoWar; NBLV; OPOU; PoWW; WoPoe *Fr.* Epitaphs of the War [1914–1918].

Dead Stepfather, The. Terry Wolverton. WiU

Dead Still. Andrey [*or* Andrei] Andreievich Voznesensky [*or* Voznesenskii]. BoLoP; PasH, *tr.* by Richard Wilbur

Dead! the glorious Dead!—And shall they rise?, The. Magic Glass, The. Felicia Dorothea Hemans. NOBRP

Dead, The ("These hearts were woven"). Rupert Brooke. PeFWW; SoSe-8 *Fr.* 1914.

Dead, they'll burn you up with electricity. Argentarius. PGA

Dead time. Hollow depression interred invalid to resurgence, resistant. Theresa Hak Kyung Cha. PFTM-2 *Fr.* Dictée.

Dead to the Living, The. Edith Nesbit. VWP

Dead Turk, A. Li Kuang-t'ien. WoPoe, *tr.* by Kai-yu Hsu

'Dead,' was all he answered. (LL) Death of the Hired Man, The. Robert Frost. APT-1; HeIP-4; MoAmPo; NAAL-2v2; NAAL-5; NoP-4; OxBA; SAmP; TCAPo

Dead Water. Wen Yi-tuo *or* Wen I-to. PFTM-1; WoPoe, *tr.* by Arthur Sze

Dead Weasel, A. David Helwig. NOBC

Dead Wingman, The. Randall Jarrell. PoWW

Dead Witness, The. Buland Al-Haidari [*or* Al-Haydari]. MAP, *tr.* by Patricia Alanah Byrne and Salma Khadra Jayyusi

Dead, you will lie under a yard of earth. Argentarius. GrAn

Deadly Dance, The. *Unknown.* STP, *tr.* by Edward Kissam

Deadly Kisses. Pierre de Ronsard. AWP, *tr.* by Andrew Lang

Deadly Seven, The. Sydney Bernard Smith. PeLi

Deadly Weapon. Beatrix Gates. GLP

Deadman's Shoes. Kate Clanchy. MFPA

Deadsong. Don Domanski. NOBC

Deadwood Dick. Elizabeth Alexander. RA

Deaf and Blind, The. Paul Éluard. WoPoe, *tr.* by Paul Auster

Deaf Dancing to Rock, The. Lisel Mueller. SwNoth

Deaf Girl Playing. James Tate. LCAP-2

Deaf Lantern. Alejandra Piznarnick. MirDau, *tr.* by Celeste Kostopulos-Cooperman

Deaf Mute Girl, The. István Vas. IQMS, *tr.* by Charles Abraham Wagner

Deaf-Mute in the Pear Tree. Patricia K. Page. NoAM; NoP-4; PoE

Deaf-Mutes. Nikolai Ivanovich Glazkov. TCRP, *tr.* by Daniel Weissbort

Deaf to God, who calls and walks. Doomsday Morning. Genevieve Taggard. MoAmPo

Deafening peal, A. Yakusai, Layman. ZenPo, *tr.* by Takashi Ikemoto and Lucien Stryk

Deafness. Richard Ryan. BIrV; PBCIP

Deal table where he wrote, so small and plain, The. Birthplace, The. Seamus Heaney. ModIr

Dealer, bewitched by gain-promising dreams, A. Bush Justice. Charles Harpur. CBAP

Dealer in shirt-sleeves told his assistant Jenny, The. Newcombe at the Croydon Gallery. Arthur Nortje. HBAPE

Dealing Scraps. Ruth Garnett. ISC

Dean, adult education may seem silly. Lucretius versus the Lake Poets. Robert Frost. OBCoV

Dean Bourn, a Rude River in Devon, by Which Sometimes He Lived. Robert Herrick. *See* To Dean-bourn, a Rude River in Devon, by Which Sometimes He Lived

Dean-Bourn, farewell; I never look to see. To Dean-bourn, a Rude River in Devon, by Which Sometimes He Lived. Robert Herrick. BeJo; CaPo; PBRV

Dean Inge. Humbert Wolfe. FaBoEE

Dean of Paul's did search for his wife, The. Fragment of a Song on the Beautiful Wife of Dr. John Overall. *Unknown*. BoLoP

Dean of the University said, The. May 1968. Sharon Olds. NIP-4

Dear Albert, of Saxe-Coburg-Gotha. Limerick. W. F. N. Watson. PeLi

Dear Albert. This is a wholesome town. Really. Cherries grow. Letter to Goldbarth from Big Fork. Richard Hugo. BodElec

Dear Alice! you'll laugh when you know it. Talented Man, The. Winthrop Mackworth Praed. CABP; NOBL; PeLV

Dear and great Angel, wouldst thou only leave. Guardian-Angel, The. Robert Browning. PeECV

Dear, and so worthy both by your desert. William Alabaster. OxBSo

Dear Ann is gone unto her Rest. Short Testimony for Anne Whitehead, A. Jane Sowle. EMWP

Dear Ann, wherever you are. For Ann Scott-Moncrieff. Edwin Muir. GTBS-P

Dear Antigone, / after going over all the arguments. Letter. Leonard Nathan. PBCAP

Dear architect of fine *Chateaux en l'air*. To William Hayley, Esq.: In Reply to His Solicitation to Write with Him in a Literary Work. William Cowper. Son

Dear Arthur: In a country where a wealthy handful. Letter to Oberg from Pony. Richard Hugo. BodElec

Dear Auntie / Oh, what a nice jumper. Christmas Thank You's. Mick Gowar. OBCP

Dear Babe, whose meaning by fond looks expressed. Thomas Russell. CenSon

Dear, back my wounded heart restore. Divorce, The. Thomas Stanley. MeLP

Dear Bill, / When I search the past for you. Letter to William Carlos Williams, A. Kenneth Rexroth. NNaP

Dear Black Head. *Unknown*. BIrV, *tr. by* Sir Samuel Ferguson

Dear Bobbi: God, it's cold. Unpredicted, of course, by forecast. Letter to Hill from St. Ignatius. Richard Hugo. BodElec

Dear Boy, What a superlative day for a funeral. Micheál Mac Liammóir. Paul Durcan. PBCIP

Dear boy, you will not hear me speak. Pangloss's Song: A Comic-Opera Lyric. Richard Wilbur. NBLV; NoAM

Dear Brethren, Are Your Harps in Tune? Eunice Smith. AH

Dear brother, would you know the life. Letter, A. Ralph Waldo Emerson. APN-1

Dear child, first-born, what I could give outright. Hand-Shadows. Jarold Ramsey. NIP-4

Dear Child, My Darling Daughter. *Hungarian Oral Tradition*. IQMS, *tr. by* Anthony Edkins

"Dear children," they asked in every town. Wise Men Ask the Children the Way, The. Heinrich Heine. OBCP, *tr. by* Geoffrey Grigson

Dear Cleo, I can't complain about your absence. To the Muse. Philip Whalen. PoM

Dear Cloe [*or* Chloe], how blubbered is that pretty face! Answer to Cloe [*or* Chloe] Jealous. Matthew Prior. NOBE; OxBEV

Dear Col'nel, COBHAM's and your country's Friend! Pope. TOF

Dear Colonel, name the day. From a Young Woman to an Old Officer Who Courted Her. Elizabeth Frances Amherst. ECWP

Dear common flower, that grow'st beside the way. James Russell Lowell. NAAL-2v1; NAAL-3 *Fr.* To the Dandelion.

Dear Craoibhin Aoibhin, look into our case. At the Abbey Theatre. W. B. Yeats. Son

Dear critic, who my lightness so deplores. To a Captious Critic. Paul Laurence Dunbar. BPo

Dear D., I'm in a place where history. Out Here. Roger Mitchell. PoCoUp

Dear, damn'd, distracting Town, farewell! Farewell to London in the Year 1715, A. Pope. OBCoV

Dear Dave: Rain five days and I love it[. A relief]. Letter to Wagoner from Port Townsend. Richard Hugo. NNaP

Dear dear dear beat. To Allen Ginsberg & Co. Luciana Frezza. CItWP, *tr. by* Cinzia Sartini Blum and Lara Trubowitz

Dear, dear! what can the matter be? Oh, Dear! *Unknown*. ReMoGo

Dear Denise: Long way from, long time since Boulder[. I hope]. Letter to Levertov from Butte. Richard Hugo. NNaP

Dear Dennice: I'm this close but the pass is tough this year. Letter to Scanlon from Whitehall. Richard Hugo. NNaP

Dear Derrida. David Kirby. BAP-01

Dear / Diana. Andy-Diana DNA Letter. Andrew Weiman. HAP

Dear Dick: In order to xerox your book I had to break. Letter to Hugo from Later. Jane Hirshfield. GeoHom

Dear Dick: You know all that pissing and moaning around I've. Letter to Blessing from Missoula. Richard Hugo. BodElec

Dear Doctor Baron, Aberdeen. To Robert Baron. Arthur Johnston. NePenScot, *tr. by* Robert Crawford

Dear Doctor of St Mary's. Song upon Miss Harriet Hanbury, Addressed to the Revd Mr Birt. Sir Charles Hanbury Williams. OBCoV

Dear Doll, while the tails of our horses are plaiting. Thomas Moore. NOBRP *Fr.* Fudge Family in Paris, The.

Dear Dolly, stay thy scampering joints one minute. Ode to a Country Hoyden. "Peter Pindar." NOEC

Dear, doting Dick, for O! she saved my life. (LL) Privy-Love for My Landlady. George Farewell. NOEC; OBCoV

Dear Dove, that bear'st to my sole-laboring ark. Ad Amicam. Francis Thompson. Son

Dear earth, take old Amyntichus to your heart. *Unknown*. GrAn

Dear Echo, do me a favour; it's somewhat. . .*Some what?* Gauradas. GrAn

Dear Ellen, when you read these lines, O, throw them not aside! Lines to Ellen, the Factory Girl. Ellen Johnston. VWP

Dear Emily, my tears would burn your page. To Emily Dickinson. Yvor Winters. Son

Dear Eustatio, I write that you may write me an answer. Arthur Hugh Clough. EBVV; FaBoVe; OxAEP-2 *Fr.* Amours de Voyage.

Dear Ez. Christopher Pilling. NLP

Dear, farewell, a little while. Anacreontic, on Parting with a Little Child. Samuel Wesley. NOEC

Dear father and dear mother: Let me crave. Erotion. Martial. AWP, *tr. by* Kirby Flower Smith

Dear Father, Look Up. "Orpheus C. Kerr." OBAL

Dear fellow infidel, let's pray. Wing and Prayer. Jack Marshall. GeoHom

Dear Female Heart. Stevie Smith. FaBoEE; ItWoWo; NALW

Dear Fergusson—They've Ramsay's statue clean. Letter to Robert Fergusson. Alexander Scott. OxBS

Dear Folks. Patrick Kavanagh. FaBoTw

Dear Frank, Here is a poem. Josephine Miles. NALW

Dear Frank, with fancy, fire and style. Upon an Ingenious Friend, Over-Vain. Thomas Fitzgerald. OxBSP

Dear Frère Jacques. Letter to a Benedictine Monk. Marilyn Nelson Waniek. GT

Dear friend, be silent and with patience see. To My Noble Friend Master William Browne: Of the Evil Time. Michael Drayton. CABP

Dear friend! Believe me, Love's not always blind. Love Has Eyes. William Forster. CBAP

Dear friend, far off, my lost desire. Tennyson. CAGL; FHYEP; NAEL-6v2 *Fr.* In Memoriam A. H. H.

Dear friend, I fear my heart will break. Out of French. Sir Charles Sedley. FaBoEE

Dear friend, I pray thee, if thou wouldst be proving. Friendship. Ella Wheeler Wilcox. PoToHe

Dear Friend, since you have chosen to associate. Tennyson's Poems. Josephine D. Henderson Heard. CBWP-4; SWaP

Dear friend, the here-there emphasis is made. Letter. Janet Frame. PeNZ

Dear friend! whose holy, ever-living lines. Match, The. Henry Vaughan. ESCV

Dear Friend, Whose Presence in the House. James Freeman Clarke. AH

Dear friends. If we must lie, let's not lie around. (LL) Lies. Martha Collins. ExTi; PuP-23

Dear friends, if you'll be ruled by me. To My Friends against Poetry. Jane Barker. BASC

Dear friends, left darkling in the long eclipse. Prelude to a Volume Printed in Raised Letters for the Blind. Oliver Wendell Holmes. APN-1

Dear friends, there is no cause for so much sympathy. Illness. Po Chü-i. ChiP, *tr. by* Arthur Waley

Dear friends, we are gathered together. Tribute to the Bride and Groom, A. Priscilla Jane Thompson. CBWP-2

Dear Fronto, famed alike in peace and war. Country Pleasures. Martial. AWP, *tr. by* F. A. Wright

Dear galway / it is flooding here, in missouri. Poem to Galway Kinnell, A. Etheridge Knight. NNaP

Dear gentle hands have stroked my hair. Mother's Hands. W. Dayton Wedgefarth. PoToHe

Dear gentle soul, who went so soon away. Do This Favour for Me. Luis de Camões [*or* Camões]. BoLoP; WoPoe, *tr. by* Roy Campbell

Dear girl, you're growing very thin. To a Sick Friend. Hannah Wallis. ECWP

Dear God, allow me to recall my works. Sergey Gandlevsky. ItGoST, *tr. by* Philip Metres

Dear God / i didn't kill the butterfly. Burials. Amelia Blossom Pegram. HAWP

Dear God, I didn't know that Cytherea was bathing. Rufinus. HePo, *tr. by* Barbara Hughes Fowler

Dear God! there is no sadder fate in life. Burdened. Ella Wheeler Wilcox. SWaP

Dear gods, set me free from all the pain. Aeschylus. NAWM-5v1

Dear guests, you now have seen Love's corpse-light shine. (LL) George Meredith. NAEL-6v2; NOBVV; NPeEn; PoE; Son *Fr.* Modern Love.

Dear, had the world in its caprice. Respectability. Robert Browning. EnLoPo

Dear Happy Souls. Eunice Smith. AH

Dear Harp of My Country. Thomas Moore. NOIV

Dear head, four days ahead of love's day. For Tom. Richard Caddel. Oth

Dear Husband. Yambo Ouloguem. NegPo, *tr. by* Ellen Conroy Kennedy

Dear, I Love. Todd Colby. HeMarv

Dear, I must be gone. Parting. W. B. Yeats. FaBoTw

Dear, if unsocial privacies obsess me. Epigram. James Vincent Cunningham. VGW

Dear, if you change, I'll never choose again. Dear, If You Change. John Dowland. EnLoPo

Dear, in the terrible hour. More than They that Watch for the Morning. May Probyn. VWP

Dear J. D.: One should think of Chief Joseph here[, coming soft]. Letter to Reed from Lolo. Richard Hugo. NNaP

Dear Jack. William Makepeace Thackeray. OBCoV

Dear Jesse Helms. Lucille Clifton. GifTon

Dear Jim: This is as far as I ever chased a girl. Letter to Welch from Browning. Richard Hugo. NNaP

Dear John, Dear Coltrane. Michael S. Harper. ISC; NAAL-5; NIL-7; NIP-4; VCAP

Dear John: Great to see your long-coming, well-crafted book. Letter to Haislip from Hot Springs. Richard Hugo. BodElec

Dear John: This is a Dear John letter from booze. Letter to Logan from Milltown. Richard Hugo. NNaP

Dear John Wayne. Louise Erdrich. UnSA

Dear John, whoever now takes pen to write. James Philip McAuley. CBAP *Fr.* Letter to John Dryden, A.

Dear kindly Sergeant Krupke. Gee, Officer Krupke. Stephen Sondheim. OBAL; ReLy

Dear Knight, how great a drudge is he. Hudibras and Milton Reconciled. William Somervile [*or* Somerville]. NOEC

Dear Lamp, she swore by you. Asclepiades. GrAn

Dear Lela is my joy and crown. Lela's Charms. Lizelia Augusta Jenkins Moorer. CBWP-3

Dear letters, fond letters. Love Letters. Josephine D. Henderson Heard. CBWP-4; SWaP

Dear Literary Hero. Fan Letter, A. Amy Gerstler. BAP-97; BodElec

Dear little bird, the Graces' favourite. Tymnes. GrAn

Dear little Bog-Face. Bog-Face. Stevie Smith. NPeEn; RB

Dear Liz: Here's where I degraded myself for the last time. Letter to Libbey from St. Regis. Richard Hugo. BodElec

Dear Lizbie Browne. To Lizbie Browne. Thomas Hardy. FaBoVe; NOBVV; OxAEP-2

Dear lord, accept a sinful heart. William Cowper. NOCV *Fr.* Olney Hymns.

Dear Lord and Father of mankind. John Greenleaf Whittier. AH; NOCV; SacPr *Fr.* Brewing of Soma, The.

Dear Lord, Behold Thy Servants. Hosea, I Ballou. AH

Dear Lord, receive my son, whose winning love. Sir John Beaumont. OBEV *Fr.* Of My Dear Son, Gervase Beaumont.

Dear lords of life, stump-toothed, with ragged breath. Geoffrey Hill. DiPo *Fr.* Mystery of the Charity of Charles Péguy, The.

Dear love, dost thou sleep fairly? Parting at Morning. Dietmar von Aist [*or* Eist]. AWP, *tr. by* Frank C. Nicholson

Dear love, I am resolved with thee to live. Posy, A. Sir Robert Aytoun [*or* Ayton]. NOSC

Dear love / 'tis less than I have vowed. Love. Al-Abbas ibn al-Ahnaf. ArPe, *tr. by* Omar S. Pound

Dear Love you'd better know. Amymone. Rufinus. GrAn, *tr. by* Alan Marshfield

Dear Lyltsen, when I'm with thee. Lovelight. Gysbert Japicx. WoPoe, *tr. by* Rod Jellema

Dear Maiden. Heinrich Heine. AWP, *tr. by* John Todhunter

Dear Mama. Letter. Langston Hughes. PoE

Dear Mama, / Time I pay rent and get my food. Langston Hughes. APT-2; PoE *Fr.* Lenox Avenue Mural.

Dear Mamma, if you just could be. Lesson for Mamma, A. Sydney Dayre. OBCA

Dear Margie, hello. It is 5:15 A.M. Ted Berrigan. PmAP *Fr.* Sonnets, The.

Dear Martin, / Bumped into Arthur tonight. Correspondence. Peter Reading. PeLV

Dear Martin Folkes, dear scholar, brother, friend. John Byrom. NOBL *Fr.* Full and True Account of a Horrid and Barbarous Robbery, A.

Dear Marvin: Months since I left broke down and sobbing. Letter to Bell from Missoula. Richard Hugo. NNaP

Dear master, was it really for this you died? Cranmer and the Bread of Heaven. Anne Ridler. SacPr

Dear matted squirrel tongue. Radiant Silhouette V. John Yau. OpBo

Dear Michele: Once, according to a native, this town. Letter to Birch from Deer Lodge. Richard Hugo. BodElec

Dear Michiko, / Do songs sound different in prison? Letters from Poston Relocation Camp (1942–45). David Mura. LTA

Dear Mike: We didn't have a chance. Our starter had no change. Letter to Mantsch from Havre. Richard Hugo. MoASP

Dear Miss. Herman Gladwin. PeNZ

Dear Miss Roper, It seems, George Vernon, before we left Rome, said. Arthur Hugh Clough. FaBoVe *Fr.* Amours de Voyage.

Dear Mr Fisher I am writing. Paraphrases. Roy Fisher. PeLV

Dear Moly, why so oft in tears? Horace. OBVE, *tr. by* George Stepney *Fr.* Odes.

Dear Mother. Henry Cuyler Bunner. VerBaPo *Fr.* Their Wedding Journey.

Dear Mother. Ebba M. Leaf. PWR

Dear Mother, dear Mother, the Church is cold. William Blake. FHYEP; NBLV; OBSV *Fr.* Songs of Experience.

Dear Mother, Thank you for the egg cosy. Sister Agnes Writes to Her Beloved Mother. Paul Durcan. OBCoV

Dear Mr. Noman, does it ever strike you. On Noman, a Guest. Joseph Hilaire Pierre Belloc. FaBoEE

Dear Mr Pitt, I'm told. Church Boiler, The. David Scott. NLP

Dear mum's old picture. Dezső Kosztolányi. IQMS, *tr. by* Peter Zollman *Fr.* Laments of a Poor Little Child.

Dear native brook! wild streamlet of the west! Sonnet to the River Otter. Samuel Taylor Coleridge. CenSon; OxBSo

Dear, near and true—no truer Time himself. Dedication, A. Tennyson. OxBSP

Dear object of defeated care! Lines Written beneath a Picture. Byron. OxBSP

Dear object of my love, whose pow'rful charms. Sarah Hazard's Love Letter. John Ellis. NOEC

Dear Obour / Our crossing was without. Letter from Phillis Wheatley, A. Robert Earl Hayden. ESEAA; NAAAL; NoAM

Dear! of all happy in the hour, most blest. Rupert Brooke. EnLoPo *Fr.* 1914.

Dear old equivocal and closest friend. Author to His Body on Their Fifteenth Birthday, 29.ii.80, The. Howard Nemerov. NoAM

Dear one, forgive my appearing before you like this. Victorian Hangman Tells His Love, A. Bruce Dawe. NoAM

Dear [*or* Deare] love, for nothing less[e] than thee. Dream[e], The. John Donne. ESCV; MeLP; OBEV; TOF

Dear Parents. Letters in the Family. Adrienne Rich. NIL-7

Dear Paulus it's a busy trade of late. Lines Descriptive of Thomson's Island. Benjamin Lynde. SCAP

Dear Peggy, since the single state. Advice to a Young Lady Lately Married. Esther Lewis. ECWP

Dear Phoebus, hear my only vow. Poetess's Bouts-Rimés, The. *Unknown.* NOEC

Dear Pound, I am leaving England. (LL) Villanelle: The Psychological Hour. Ezra Pound. CTC; NAAL-2v2

Dear pursuing presence. Hindu to His Body, A. A. K. Ramanujan. PoetW

Dear Queenie, though it breaks my heart. Handmaid of Religion, The. Edgell Rickword. OBSV

Dear Reader. James Tate. SPE

Dear reader, though my uncombed verse be queer. *Unknown.* PriapPo, *tr. by* Richard W. Hooper *Fr.* Priapus Poems, The.

Dear Rosario. Maria Elena Caballero-Robb. ReBoTo

Dear Samson, / I put your hair. Love Letter. Carole C. Gregory Clemmons. BlSi

Dear San: Everybody doesn't write poetry. Feeling and Form. Marilyn Hacker. NoAM

Dear Saviour, If These Lambs Should Stray. Abby Bradley Hyde. AH

Dear school of my childhood. Lines to an Old School-House. Priscilla Jane Thompson. CBWP-2

Dear Serious Novel. Exchange of Letters. Wendy Cope. OBCoV

Dear Sir. Walter De la Mare. OBCoV

Dear Sir, You're quite wrong about me. Limerick. M. Trench. PeLi

Dear Sir, your astonishment's odd. Reply, A. *Unknown*. NBLV; NOBL; OxBEV; PeLi

Dear Sirs: Is it not time we formed a Boston. Communication to the City Fathers of Boston. George Starbuck. YaYoPo

Dear Sister, my resentment had not been. Virgil [*or* Vergil]. OBVE *Fr.* Aeneid [*or Eneados, Aeneis*], The.

Dear Son, Leave Thy Weeping. *Unknown*. CTC

Dear Spirit. Prayer to the Spirit of the New Year. Bobbi Sykes. IBA

Dear Stars, Rock Me to Sleep. István Sinka. IQMS, *tr. by* Adam Makkai

Dear Stella, midst the pious sorrow. Verses Inviting Stella to Tea on the Public Fast-Day. Anna Seward. ECWP

Dear steps may die away. Room. Robert Finch. MoCV

Dear Steward. Sleeper. Patricia Pogson. NLP

Dear these three who have come to see me. In Praise of Three Young Men. Lochlann Og O Dalaigh. NOIV

Dear things! we would not have you learn too much. Womankind. Gerald Massey. NOBVV

Dear Thomas, didst thou never pop. Simile, A. Matthew Prior. NOEC

Dear, Though the Night Is Gone. W. H. Auden. BoLoP

Dear Uncle Stranger. Conrad Potter Aiken. ColAP; NOBA; NoAM

Dear under-song in Clamor's hour. (LL) Recollections of Love. Samuel Taylor Coleridge. NAEL-5v2; NAEL-6v2

Dear uplands, Chester's favorable fields. Sidney Lanier. APN-2; ColAP

Dear Vi: You were great at the Roethke festival this summer. Letter to Gale from Ovando. Richard Hugo. BodElec

Dear waves, what will you do for me this year? Gerald Stern. InvLad *Fr.* Lucky Life.

Dear Webster. Connie Fife. ReEnLa

Dear, when we sit in that high, placid room. Touché. Jessie Redmond Fauset. BlSi

Dear Whoever-You-Are-That-You-Are. Letter from the Pygmies, A. Theodore Weiss. VGW

Dear, why do you say you love. Song, A: On His Mistress. Sir Robert Aytoun [*or* Ayton]. NOSC

Dear, why should you command me to my rest. Michael Drayton. *See* Idea

Dear, wild illusions of creative mind! To the Visions of Fancy. Ann Radcliffe. CenSon

Dear World. Paula Gunn Allen. HATNAP

Dear you: the lights here ask. Letters from the North Star. Kevin Young. NeAmPo

Dear youth, too early lost, who now art laid. On the Death of a Young and Favorite Slave. Martial. AWP, *tr. by* Goldwin Smith

Deare cherish this, and with it[t] my soules will. Mary Sidney Wroth, Countess of Montgomery. BWW *Fr.* Pamphilia to Amphilanthus.

Deare Cosen pardon me, if I mistowke. LD Ansure, The. Lady Dorothy Shirley. EMWP

Deare friend sit down, and bear awhile this shade. Palm-tree, The. Henry Vaughan. ESCV

Deare Infant, 'twas thy Mother's Fault. Mrs Thimelby, on the Death of Her Only Child. Gertrude Aston Thimelby. EMWP

Deare [*or* Dear], why should you command [*or* commaund] me to my rest. Michael Drayton. NOBE; Son *Fr.* Idea.

Dear[e], though to part it be a hell. To Dianeme. Robert Herrick. CaPo

Dearest Evelyn, I often think of you. Jungle Husband, The. Stevie Smith. FaBoWP; HarvBoo; NBLV; NIL-7; NIP-4; RB

Dearest Friend, Thou Art in Love. Heinrich Heine. TrJP, *tr. by* Emma Lazarus *Fr.* Homeward Bound.

Dearest, I did not think four years ago. To Helen. Winthrop Mackworth Praed. NOBVV

Dearest, if I almost cease to weep for you. Love's Guerdons. Edith Nesbit. NOBVV

Dearest, it was a night. Birthnight: To F, The. Walter De la Mare. NPeEn

Dearest Louisa, Enquire if you please about Mr. Claude. Arthur Hugh Clough. FaBoVe *Fr.* Amours de Voyage.

Dearest Love. Salma Khadra Jayyusi. PoArWo, *tr. by* Charles Doria

Dearest love, listen. Dearest Love. Salma Khadra Jayyusi. PoArWo, *tr. by* Charles Doria

Dearest [*or* Deerest] if I by my deserving. Mary Sidney Wroth, Countess of Montgomery. EMWP *Fr.* Pamphilia to Amphilanthus.

Dearest Reader. Michael Palmer. FTOS

Dearest, the cockroaches are having babies. Love from a Foreign City. Lavinia Greenlaw. EmeKit; MFPA

Dearest, thy tresses are not threads of gold. Comparison, The. Thomas Carew. BeJo

Dearest, when thou desirest to buy a ring. Ring Sonnet. Betty Scott Stam. SacPr

Dearest, you come suddenly, and suddenly, dearest, you depart. Dearest, You

Come Suddenly and Suddenly You Depart. Walafrid Strabo. CAGL, *tr. by* John Boswell

Dearly beloved Cousin, these. Epistle of Deborah Dough, The. Mary Leapor. ECWP

Dearly beloved gentle girl. Walther [*or* Walter] von der Vogelweide. GePo

Death. Maxwell Bodenheim. APT-1

Death. Maxwell Bodenheim. TrJP

Death. George Boleyn. *See* O Death, Rock Me Asleep

Death. Emily Jane Brontë. EBVV

Death. John Clare. GTBS-P

Death. Mary Elizabeth Coleridge. ViWPN

Death. Mary Elizabeth Coleridge.
"Bid me remember, O my gracious Lord." SacPr

Death. Peter France. TCRusP, *tr. by* Gennady Aygi

Death. Roy Fuller. NoAM

Death. Patty L. Harjo. VoR

Death. George Herbert. ESCV; FSCP; GeHe; NAEL-5v1; NAEL-6v1; NAEL-7v1; NoP-4

Death. Thomas Hood. GSo

Death. Bill Knott. PBCAP; SPE

Death. Sean O Riordain. NOIV, *tr. by* Thomas Kinsella

Death. Marilyn. Ōoka Mokoto. PFTM-2, *tr. by* Thomas Fitzimmons

Death. Rainer Maria Rilke. PFTM-1

Death. William Bell Scott. NOBVV

Death. *Unknown*. OBWVE; RB, *tr. by* Aneirin Talfan Davies

Death. *Unknown*. RaBo

Death. Henry Vaughan. AngWePo; ChIV-1

Death. Joe Wenderoth. AmPoNex

Death. William Carlos Williams. NAAL-2v2; OxBA; VGW

Death. W. B. Yeats. OxAEP-2; OxBSP

Death, alway cruel, Pity's foe in chief. Dante Alighieri. AWP; EaItPo, *tr. by* Dante Gabriel Rossetti *Fr.* La Vita Nuova.

Death, an Ode. John Forbes. BMAP

Death and Burial of Cock Robbin, The. *Unknown*. OWoS

Death and Co. Sylvia Plath. CoAmPo; EmeKit; LCAP-2

Death and darkness, get you packing. Easter Hymn. Henry Vaughan. ChIV-2; ESCV; SacPr

Death and Doctor Hornbook [A True Story]. Robert Burns. OxBS

Death and Love. Ben Jonson. NOBE *Fr.* Sad Shepherd, The.

Death and Morphine. Heinrich Heine. WoPoe, *tr. by* Robert Lowell *Fr.* Dying in Paris.

Death and Rebirth. Jean-Baptiste Tati-Loutard. PBMAP

Death and Resurrection. Priscilla Jane Thompson. CBWP-2

Death and the Bridge. Robert Lowell. HCAP

Death and the Dancer. Muriel Rukeyser. AF

Death and the Good Citizen. A. K. Ramanujan. PoetW

Death and the Lady. Léonie Adams. MoAmPo

Death and the Plowman. Sidney Keyes. OxBTC

Death and the River. Badr Shakir Al-Sayyab. MAP, *tr. by* Lena Jayyusi and Christopher Middleton

Death and the Sun. Derek Mahon. BiHa

Death and the Three Revellers. Geoffrey Chaucer. OBNV *Fr.* Canterbury Tales, The.

Death as a Lotus Flower. *Unknown*. *See* Book of the Dead

Death as History. Jay Wright. ESEAA

Death Asphodel. Jean Valentine. ExTi

Death at least gives separation repose. Dreaming of Li Po. Tu Fu. WoPoe, *tr. by* David Hinton

Death at Winson Green, A. Francis Webb. BMAP

Death be not proud, though some have called thee. John Donne. BASC; FHYEP; HAP; HeIP-4; ITBLP; InPK-6; MeLP; NAEL-5v1; NAEL-6v1; NAEL-7v1; NAWM-5v1; NIL-7; NIP-4; NOBE; NOSC; NPeEn; OPOU; OxAEP-1; OxBEV; OxBSo; PAI; PoE; PoRA; SCGP; SCV; SacPr; SoSe-8; TRP; TrCP; WeW-3 *Fr.* Holy Sonnets.

Death be not proud, thy hand gave not this blow. Elegy: "Death be not proud, thy hand gave not this blow." Lucy Harington, Countess of Bedford. EMWP; PeECV; WPE

Death, become a shewolf. Crown of Happiness. Anne Hébert. BoWoP, *tr. by* Willis Barnstone

Death Bed. Thomas Kinsella. CIP-2; PBCIP

Death-Bed, A. Rudyard Kipling. OxBEV; PoWW

Death Bed, The. Waring Cuney. APT-2

Death-Bed, The. Thomas Hood. GTBS-P; NOBE; OBEV; TreFP

Death-Bed, The. Siegfried Sassoon. AF; PeFWW

Death before forty's no bar. Lo! Obit on Parnassus. F. Scott Fitzgerald. NBLV

Death Bells. Lightnin' Hopkins. APT-2

Death by Drowning. Elizabeth Brewster. NOBC

Death by Heroin of Sid Vicious, The.　Paul Durcan.　NPeEn

Death by Water.　T. S. Eliot.　NPeEn; OBVE; OxBEV　*Fr.* Waste Land, The.

Death came before Marriage, Philaenion.　Perses.　GrAn

Death Camp.　Irena Klepfisz.　GLP; TaR

Death can be so lazy at times.　Death of a Lady.　John Pepper Clark Bekedermo.　HBAPE

Death, can you too be enamored?　To Death.　Johann Wilhelm Ludwig Gleim.　GePo, *tr. by* George C. Schoolfield

Death Certificate.　Rui Knopfli.　PeSAV, *tr. by* the author

Death Chant.　Peter Blue Cloud.　VoR

Death Circus, The.　John Tranter.　CBAP

Death comes in quantity from solved.　Tolerance of Crows, The.　Charles Donnelly.　CIP-2

Death comes in strange forms and contrasting images.　Catius As Conius Silius Italicus.　RomPo, *tr. by* Marcus Wilson　*Fr.* Punica, The.

Death, Dark Agent.　Jotie T'Hooft.　TuT, *tr. by* Seán Lysaght

Death, dark doer and soft hand.　Death, Dark Doer.　Jotie T'Hooft.　TuT, *tr. by* Peter Van de Kamp

Death Described by His True Effects.　George Chapman.　NOSC　*Fr.* Eugenia.

Death designs swirl high above faces that are of disbelief.　War Walking Near.　Ray A. Young Bear.　CDW

Death devours all lovely things.　Passer Mortuus Est.　Edna St. Vincent Millay.　FaBoWP; MoAmPo; OxBA

Death did not come to my mother.　Conception.　Josephine Miles.　ColAP; FaBoWP

Death feeds us up, keeps an eye on our weight.　Palladas [*or* Pallades].　GrAn

Death for the Dark Stranger.　Thomas McGrath.　VGW

Death fought; before giving in. (LL)　Sacrifice, The.　Frank Bidart.　GLP; VCAP

Death found strange beauty on the polished brow.　Death of an Infant.　Lydia Huntley Sigourney.　SWaP; TCAPo

Death from Cancer.　Robert Lowell.　TwCP　*Fr.* In Memory of Arthur Winslow.

Death Fugue.　Paul Celan.　AuPH; HP; VCWP; WoPoe, *tr. by* Michael Hamburger

Death Fugue, A.　Paul Celan.　CLPP; GifTon; PFTM-2, *tr. by* Jerome Rothenberg

Death Fugue, A.　Paul Celan.　HP; PoSu; TrJP; VCWP

Death gallops up the bridge of red railtie girders.　Death and the Bridge.　Robert Lowell.　HCAP

Death gapes to its hinges. (LL)　Harbach 1944.　János Pilinszky.　AF; HP; PoSu; WoPoe, *tr. by* Janos Csokits and Ted Hughes

Death, get out of here!　Rāmprasād Sen.　SinGod, *tr. by* Rachel Fell McDermott

Death has come near me. (LL)　Sappho.　NAWM-7v1; WPOW, *tr. by* Richmond Lattimore

Death has it in her hand, cut like a cross. (LL)　Sonnet: Of His Pain from a New Love.　Guido Cavalcanti.　AWP; EaItPo, *tr. by* Dante Gabriel Rossetti

Death Has No Features of His Own.　Gwen Harwood.　NOBAu

Death has torn ten years from us.　Philodemus.　PGA

Death hath deprived me of my dearest friend.　Remembrance of My Friend Mr. Thomas Morley, A.　John Davies of Hereford.　OxBSP

Death himself.　L M F B R.　Gary Snyder.　PoM

Death, I repent.　Kathleen Jessie Raine.　OxBTC　*Fr.* Two Invocations of Death.

Death in an ancient country was a simple passport.　Reuel Denney.　YaYoPo　*Fr.* Elegy on the Pilot.

Death in Larkspur Canyon, A.　Richard Garcia.　UrbNat

Death in Leamington.　Sir John Betjeman.　MakPoe; NoP-4; OxAEP-2; RB

Death in Life.　Thomas Vaux, 2d Baron Vaux of Harrowden.　NoSic (Death in Life.)　NoSic

Death in Mexico.　Denise Levertov.　NAAL-5

Death in the Dawn.　Wole Soyinka.　PBMAP　*Fr.* Idanre and Other Poems (1967).

Death in the Evening.　Miroslav Holub.　PoSu, *tr. by* George Theiner

Death in the Flower.　Letitia [*or* Laetitia] Elizabeth Landon.　RWP

Death in the Kitchen.　Thomas Hood.　NPeEn

Death Invited.　May Swenson.　WPE

Death is a Dialogue between.　Emily Dickinson.　WPoS

Death Is a Matter of Mathematics.　Barry Amiel.　FaBoWar; PoWW

Death is all metaphors, shape in one history.　Dylan Thomas.　Son　*Fr.* Altarwise by Owl-Light.

Death is another milestone on their way.　Funeral, The.　Stephen Spender.　MoBrPo; NoAM

Death Is Before Me Today.　*Unknown.*　WoPoe, *tr. by* W. S. Merwin

Death is in the air.　Anniversary.　Dorothy Hewett.　BMAP

Death is in your house, but I'm out here.　Heartless Art, The.　Tony Harrison.　NoP-4

Death is more than.　One X.　E. E. Cummings.　FaBoMo

Death is not death, for death is but the borning day.　Birth is Death, Death is Birth.　Friedrich von Logau.　GePo, *tr. by* George C. Schoolfield

Death is not harsh: Death is our lot: but harsh.　Epitaph from a Tomb in Asia Minor.　*Unknown.*　GrAn, *tr. by* Peter Whigham

Death is not the worst of it.　Worst of It, The.　Craig Reynolds.　CAGL

Death Is Sitting at the Foot of My Bed.　Oscar Hahn.　TCLAP, *tr. by* Sandy McKinney

Death is the *Cook* of *Nature*; and we find.　Nature's Cook.　Margaret Lucas Cavendish, Duchess of Newcastle.　BWW

Death is the strongest of all living things.　Warning to One.　Merrill Moore.　MoAmPo

Death is the supple Suitor.　Emily Dickinson.　NALW; NCAP

Death Is the Tranquil Night.　Heinrich Heine.　WoPoe

Death Is Your Salvation.　Nidaa Khoury.　DTA, *tr. by* Shirley Kaufman and Roger Tavor

Death, it is all about us lately.　Autumnal.　Joseph Awad.　GraLe

Death knocks all night at my door.　Journey to the Place of Ghosts.　Jay Wright.　GT; VCAP

Death lay in ambush.　Christopher Okigbo.　PBMAP; TTY　*Fr.* Distances.

Death, let me praise you now.　Laudare.　Constance Carrier.　APT-2

Death lies dead. (LL)　Forsaken Garden, A.　Algernon Charles Swinburne.　EBEV; GTBS-P; NOBE; NOBVV; NPeEn; NoP-4; OBGa; OxAEP-2; SCGP

Death loved him the best. (LL)　Envy.　Adelaide Anne Procter.　NOBVV; NPeEn; VWP

Death loves rich people.　Funny Poem.　Bill Knott.　PBCAP

Death March.　Charles Fishman.　CDa

Death May Be Very Gentle.　Oliver St. John Gogarty.　PoRA

Death, My Companion.　Alec Brock Stevenson.　FuPo

Death News.　Allen Ginsberg.　BB

Death. Nothing is simpler. One is dead.　Realization, The.　Yvor Winters.　APT-2; HarvBoo

Death of a Chief.　Khadambi Asalache.　PBMAP

Death of a Farmyard.　Geoffrey Grigson.　EmeKit

Death of a Fly.　Goethe.　STV, *tr. by* John Frederick Nims

Death of a Gardener.　Phoebe Hesketh.　OBGa

Death of a Grandmother.　Harvey Shapiro.　TaR

Death of a Grandparent.　Mrs. Jennette Bonneau.　Mary Weston Fordham.　CBWP-2

Death of a Lady.　John Pepper Clark Bekedermo.　HBAPE

Death of a Naturalist.　Seamus Heaney.　HAP; NoAM; OxBC; OxBEV; WeW-3

Death of a Negro Poet, The.　Conrad Kent Rivers.　BPo

Death of a Oaxaquenian.　Malcolm Lowry.　CLPP

Death of a Poet.　Charles Causley.　EmeKit; OxBTC

Death of a Ram.　Sedulius Scottus.　NOIV

Death of a Soldier, The.　Wallace Stevens.　APT-1; OBWP; OxBSP; SAmP; SoSe-8

Death of a Son.　Jon Silkin.　GTBS-P; OxBTC

Death of a Species.　Anthony Conran.　AngWePo

Death of a Toad, The.　Richard Wilbur.　NAAL-2v2; NAAL-5; NoAM

Death of a Vermont Farm Woman.　Barbara Howes.　MoAmPo

Death of a Warrior, The.　Jenny Mastoraki.　BoWoP, *tr. by* Kimon Friar

Death of a Whale.　John Blight.　BMAP; CBAP

Death of a Young Son by Drowning.　Margaret Atwood.　BoWoP; NIL-7; NOBC

Death of Abraham Lincoln, The.　William Cullen Bryant.　*See* Death of Lincoln, The

Death of Adonis, The.　William Shakespeare.　NoSic　*Fr.* Venus and Adonis.

Death of Adonis, The.　Theocritus.　NPeEn; OBVE, *tr. by* Philip Ayres

Death of Alexander, The.　*Unknown.*　OxBS (When Alysandyr Our King Was Dede.)　FaBoCh

Death of Allegory, The.　Billy Collins.　WeW-3

Death of an Angel, The.　Russell Edson.　LCAP-2

Death of an Infant.　Lydia Huntley Sigourney.　SWaP; TCAPo

Death of an Irishwoman.　Michael Hartnett.　CIP-2; EmeKit; PBCIP

Death of Antoñito el Camborio.　Federico García Lorca.　SpanPo, *tr. by* Robert O'Brien

Death of Art O'Leary, The.　Eibhlin Dubh O'Connell.　Your Grave Disfigures Me.　WoPoe, *tr. by* Patrick Galvin

Death of Chet Baker, The.　Miller Williams.　SeSe

Death of Cleopatra, The.　William Shakespeare.　OxAEP-1　*Fr.* Antony and Cleopatra.

Death of Crazy Horse, The.　Lucille Clifton.　ESEAA

Death of Daphnis, The.　Theocritus.　AWP　*Fr.* Idylls.

Death of David, The.　Hayyim Nahman [*or* Khayim Nakhman *or* Chaim Nachman] Bialik.　TrJP, *tr. by* Herbert Danby

Death of Don Pedro, The.   *Unknown.*   AWP, *tr. by* John Gibson Lockhart

Death of Enkidu, The.   *Unknown.*   CAGL, *tr. by* N. K. Sandars   *Fr.* Epic of Gilgamesh, The.

Death of Europe, The.   Charles Olson.   NeAP

Death of faithful Dobbin I deplore, The.   Elegy on the Death of Dobbin, the Butterwoman's Horse, An.   Francis Fawkes.   NOEC

Death of General Uncebunke; a Biography in Little, The.   Lawrence Durrell.   "My uncle sleeps in the image of death."   FaBoMo

Death of Gladys Presley, The.   Fleda Brown Jackson.   AllShUp

Death of God, The.   Howard Nemerov.   OxBC; OxBSP

Death of Grant, The.   Ambrose Bierce.   CBCWP

Death of Hector, The.   Homer.   NAWM-7v1, *tr. by* Robert Fagles   *Fr.* Iliad, The.

Death of Hektor, The.   Brian Coffey.   "Homer where born where buried of whom the son."   BiHa; ModIr

Death of Hoel, The.   Thomas Gray.   NOEC

Death of Irish, The.   Aidan Carl Mathews.   PBCIP

Death of Isadora Duncan, The.   Dionisio D. Martinez.   TouFir

Death of Ivan, The.   "David Samuilovich Samoylov" [*or* Samoilov].   TCRP, *tr. by* Lubov Yakovleva

Death of Janis Joplin, The.   Robert Phillips.   SwNoth

Death of John Berryman, The.   William Dickey.   BAP-97

Death of King Edward VII, The.   *Unknown.*   OxBoLi

Death of King George V.   Sir John Betjeman.   NOBE; OxBEV; OxBoLi

Death of Kings, The.   William Shakespeare.   TRP   *Fr.* King Richard II.

Death of Lesbia's Bird, The.   Catullus.   AWP, *tr. by* Samuel Taylor Coleridge   *Fr.* Carmina.

Death of Lincoln, The.   William Cullen Bryant.   NAAL-2v1; TAP
    (Abraham Lincoln.)   NAAL-3
    (Death of Abraham Lincoln, The.)   CBCWP
    (Oh, slow to smite and swift to spare.)   NCAP

Death of Lord and Lady Dalhousie, The.   William McGonagall.   "Alas! Lord and Lady Dalhousie are dead, and buried at last."   VerBaPo

Death of Lord Warriston, The.   *Unknown.*   OxBB

Death of Marilyn Monroe, The.   Sharon Olds.   HeIP-4; ReTh

Death of Moses, The.   "George Eliot."   ChIV-1

Death of Moses, The.   Frances Ellen Watkins Harper.   *Fr.* Moses: A Story of the Nile.

Death of Moses, The.   *Unknown.*   TrJP, *tr. by* Alice Lucas

Death of My Aunt.   *Unknown.*   OxBoLi

Death of My Father, The.   Yehuda Amichai [*or* Amikhai].   FIT, *tr. by* Robert Friend

Death of my poor father, The.   Lorine Niedecker.   APT-2

Death of Nelson, The.   *Unknown.*   OxBoLi

Death of nothing, funeral of Gaius!, The. (LL)   Lean Gaius, Who Was Thinner than a Straw.   Lucilius.   GrAn; OBVE; WoPoe, *tr. by* Peter Porter

Death of Orpheus, The.   Ovid.   WoPoe, *tr. by* Charles Boer   *Fr.* Metamorphoses.

Death of Othello.   William Shakespeare.   OxAEP-1   *Fr.* Othello.

Death of Pan, The.   Gyula Reviczky.   IQMS, *tr. by* Watson Kirkconnell

Death of Parcy Reed, The.   *Unknown.*   ESPB
    (God send the land deliverance.)   IBB

Death of Priam, The.   Virgil [*or* Vergil].   OBVE, *tr. by* Sir John Denham   *Fr.* Aeneid [*or* Eneados, *Aeneis*], The.

Death of Priam, The.   Virgil [*or* Vergil].   NPeEn, *tr. by* John Dryden   *Fr.* Aeneid [*or* Eneados, *Aeneis*], The.

Death of Robert, Earl of Huntingdon.   Anthony Munday.
    Dirge: "Weep, weep, ye woodmen, wail."   CTC

Death of Sagittarius.   Milán Füst.   IQMS, *tr. by* Jess Perlman

Death of Saul, The.   Philip Levine.   ChIV-1

Death of Shakespeare, The.   Gyula Juhász.   IQMS, *tr. by* John Gordon Nichols

Death of Sir Nihil, book the *n*th.   Tywater.   Richard Wilbur.   CoAmPo; TRP

Death of Slavery, The.   William Cullen Bryant.   CBCWP

Death of Sohráb, The.   Firdowsi.   TAL   *Fr.* Shahnamah, The.

Death of Sophocles, The.   Anna Andreyevna Akhmatova.   PoetW, *tr. by* Max Hayward and Stanley Kunitz

Death of Southwell, The.   John Logan.   "Topcliffe's horses shake."   CRP

Death of Tammuz, The.   Saul [*or* Shaul] Tchernichowsky [*or* Tchernichovsky].   TrJP, *tr. by* L. V. Snowman

Death of the Ball Turret Gunner, The.   Randall Jarrell.   ClHu; ColAP; HAP; HarvBoo; HeIP-4; InPK-6; LCAP-2; MoAmPo; NAAL-2v2; NAAL-5; NIL-7; NIP-4; NOBA; NoAM; NoP-4; OBWP; OxBA; PAI; PoE; PoPoPo; PoWW; RB; SoSe-8; TAP; TFi; UnPo; VCAP; VGW

Death of the Bird, The.   Alec Derwent Hope.   BMAP

Death of the Bosun's Mate.   Louis Johnson.   PeNZ

Death of the Day.   Walter Savage Landor.   NoP-4

Death of the Farm Workers' Cat.   Rigoberto González.   AmPoNex

Death of the Fathers, The.   Anne Sexton.
    Boat, The.   NAAL-5
    How We Danced.   NAAL-5

Death of the Flowers, The.   William Cullen Bryant.   OBCA; TreFP

Death of the Gods; an Ode Written in Imitation of Pindar, The.   L. Ker.   NOEC

Death of the Hired Man, The.   Robert Frost.   APT-1; HeIP-4; MoAmPo; NAAL-2v2; NAAL-5; NoP-4; OxBA; SAmP; TCAPo

Death of the Kapowsin Tavern.   Richard Hugo.   NAAL-2v2

Death of the King's Canary, The.   William Empson.
    "Not your winged lust but his must now change suit."   UV

Death of the Miners or, The Widows of the Earth.   Raymond Mazisi Kunene.   PeSAV, *tr. by* the author

Death of the Pilot Whales, The.   Peter Meinke.   PBCAP

Death of the Polar Explorers.   Gabriel Gbadamosi.   HBAPE

Death of the Race Car Driver, The.   Norman Dubie.   MoASP

Death of the Sheriff, The.   Robert Lowell.   MoAmPo

Death of the Shoemaker, The.   Ahmad Dahbur.   MAP, *tr. by* Charles Doria and Lena Jayyusi

Death of the Wild Warrior.   Daniil Kharms.   TCRusP, *tr. by* Robin Milner-Gulland

Death, of thee do I make my moan.   To Death, of His Lady.   François Villon.   AWP, *tr. by* Dante Gabriel Rossetti

Death of Thomas Merton.   Harry Clifton.   PBCIP

Death of Time.   Robert Penn Warren.   BodElec

Death of Turnus, The.   Virgil [*or* Vergil].   NAWM-5v1; NAWM-7v1, *tr. by* Robert Fitzgerald   *Fr.* Aeneid [*or* Eneados, *Aeneis*], The.

Death of Venus, The.   Robert Creeley.   NOBA

Death of Vitellozzo Vitelli, The.   Irving Feldman.   TwCP

Death of water is the birth of air, The. (LL)   Create Desire.   Karen Volkman.   KGB; NAPBL

Death of Will, The.   Charles Tomlinson.   OxBC

Death of Yesugei, The.   *Unknown.*   WoPoe, *tr. by* Paul Kahn   *Fr.* Secret History of the Mongols, The.

Death on Columbus Day.   James Tate.   YaYoPo

Death ("Once he will miss, twice he will miss").   *Unknown.*   AWP   *Fr.* Thousand and One Nights, The.

Death! / Plop.   Tragedy, A.   Théophile Julius Henry Marzials.   VerBaPo

Death plucks my ear and says.   Death Plucks My Ear.   Virgil [*or* Vergil].   WoPoe, *tr. by* Oliver Wendell Holmes

Death poems.   Toko.   JDP, *tr. by* Yoel Hoffmann

Death Poems in September.   Diane Di Prima.   BB

Death Rites II.   *Unknown.*   TTY, *tr. by* C. M. Bowra

Death roodly knocked him off his perch.   On a Government Surveyor.   Albert Brodrick.   PeSAV

Death's Boots.   Geoff Hattersley.   NeBl

Death's carnival was at its height, Amman.   Elegy of a Knight.   Fadwa Tuqan [*or* Tuqan].   PoArWo, *tr. by* Samira Kawar

Death's child and mine: My name will be poet. (LL)   Poem to My Death.   Julia de Burgos.   BoWoP; TCLAP, *tr. by* Grace Schulman

Death's Guerdon.   Lizette Woodworth Reese.   APN-2

Death's Head.   Phyllis Gotlieb.   NOBC

Death's head on your hand you neede not weare, A.   Thomas Dudley, Ah! Old Must Dye.   *Unknown.*   SCAP

Death's Jest Book.   Thomas Lovell Beddoes.
    "And what's your tune?"   NPeEn
    (Dirge.)   NOBVV; OxBEV
    "Fair and bright assembly: never strode, A."   CTC
    Old Adam, the Carrion Crow.   EBEV; NAEL-5v2; TFi
    (Sailors' Song.)   OxAEP-2
    (Sibilla's Dirge.)   NOBE
    (Song.)   NAEL-6v2
    Song by Isbrand.   NOBVV; OxBEV
    (Song from the Waters.)   NOBE
    Song on the Water.   FaBoCh; WoPoe
    (Song: "We have bathed, where none have seen us.")   NOBVV
    (Wolfram's Dirge.)   NOBE; OBEV; OxAEP-2

Death's memories are graves.   Death's Memories.   John Clare.   FHYEP

Death's pale cold orb has turned to an eclipse.   Avalon.   Thomas Holley Chivers.   APN-1

Death's Transfiguration.   Israel Zangwill.   TrJP

Death's Valley.   Walt Whitman.   GS

Death's Vision.   John Reynolds.
    Mysteries Revealed after Death.   NOEC

Death Scene, A.   Emily Jane Brontë.   OxAEP-2

Death Sentence, The.   Stevie Smith.   NoP-4

Death separation: sobs hard to swallow. Dreaming of Li Po. Tu Fu. ChinPo, *tr. by* Yip Wai-lim

Death shall be death forever unto thee. Forever Dead. Sappho. AWP, *tr. by* William Ellery Leonard

Death, since I find not one with whom to grieve. Canzone: He Beseeches Death for the Life of Beatrice. Dante Alighieri. AWP; EaItPo, *tr. by* Dante Gabriel Rossetti

Death slap, A. Terrorist, The. Sergey Stratanovsky. ItGoST, *tr. by* J. Kates

Death Song. *Unknown.* BoWoP, *tr. by* Reza Baraheni and Zahra-Soltan Shokoohtaezeh

Death Song. *Unknown.* APN-2, *tr. by* Henry Rowe Schoolcraft

Death Song, A. Steve Chimombo. HBAPE

Death Song, A. William Morris. NAEL-5v2; NAEL-6v2

Death Song for Aijuk, Dreamed by Paulinaq. Paulinaoq. WoPoe

Death Song for Owain ab Urien. Taliesin. OBWVE, *tr. by* Anthony Conran

Death Songs. *Unknown.* BoWoP, *tr. by* Reza Baraheni and Zahra-Soltan Shokoohtaezeh

Death Sonnet I. Gabriela Mistral. BoWoP, *tr. by* David Garrison

Death Stands above Me. Walter Savage Landor. NOBE; OxBSP

(Death Stands above Me, Whispering Low.) NoP-4

Death stepped out of the television. Gods Ash Their Cigarettes, The. S. K. Kelen. BMAP

Death struck him like a bullet, silent. Death Struck Him. Konstantin Mikhailovich Simonov. RusPo, *tr. by* Robert Arthur Douglas Ford

Death Sunyata Chant: A Rite for Passing Over. Diane Di Prima. BB

Death surrounds itself with the living. Mississippi. E. Ethelbert Miller. GT

Death Survey. Mongane Wally Serote. PeSAV

Death Sweet. Thomas Lovell Beddoes. NOBVV

Death takes our loved ones. Selfishness. Margaret E. Bruner. PoToHe

Death, that is small respecter of distinction. Trainwrecked Soldiers. John Frederick Nims. GM

Death, that struck when I was most confiding. Death. Emily Jane Brontë. EBVV

Death the dancer poked his skull. We Show You That Death as a Dancer. Hamish Henderson. PoWW

Death the Painter. Anthony Hecht. NoP-4

Death, Thou Hast Seized Me. Isaac Luzzatto. TrJP, *tr. by* Nina Davis Salaman

Death, thou wast once an uncouth hideous thing. Death. George Herbert. ESCV; FSCP; GeHe; NAEL-5v1; NAEL-6v1; NAEL-7v1; NoP-4

Death, though [*or* tho] I see him not, is near. Age. Walter Savage Landor. FaBoEE; NOBVV; OxBEV

Death to the first-born sons, always. Miriam's Song. Eleanor Wilner. TaR

Death to the Gold Mine! Lindiwe Mabuza. HAWP

Death to the killers, bringing light to life. (LL) Not Palaces. Stephen Spender. FaBoMo; MoBrPo; NoAM

Death to the Lady said. Death and the Lady. Léonie Adams. MoAmPo

Death to Van Gogh's Ear! Allen Ginsberg. VGW

Death took my father. Manos Karastefanís. James Merrill. TAP

Death took these early, to our land's great honour. On the Athenians Who Died at the Hellespont, 440–39 B.C. *Unknown.* GrAn, *tr. by* Peter Jay

Death Valley. Sorley MacLean (Somhairle MacGill-Eain). FaBoWar; NePenScot

Death-Wake; or, Lunacy, The. Thomas Tod Stoddart.

"Beautiful Lunacy! that shapest flight." NOBRP

"He sate like winter o'er the wasted year." NOBRP

Song: "'Tis light to love thee living, girl, when hope is full and fair." NOBRP

Death was at hand. Death. Sean O Riordain. NOIV, *tr. by* Thomas Kinsella

Death was hours ago but already words. Murder. Lucy Grealy. KGB

Death wasn't the only thing aboveboard in New Orleans. Summer the Beatles Went Over Seven Minutes on a Single, The. Doyle Wesley Walls. SwNoth

Death Who. Philip Hodgins. BMAP

Death, who'ld not change prerogatives with thee. Elegy upon the Lady Venetia Digby, An. Thomas Randolph. BASC

Death, why hast thou made life so hard to bear. Canzone: Of His Dead Lady. Giacomino Pugliesi. AWP; EaItPo, *tr. by* Dante Gabriel Rossetti

Death, why so cruel [*or* soe crewill]? What! no other way. Bacon's Epitaph, Made by His Man. John Cotton. SCAP; TCAPo

Death will not correct. Proofs. Tadeusz Różewicz. PoSu, *tr. by* Adam Czerniawski

Death without End. José Gorostiza.

"Filled with myself, walled up in my skin." TCLAP, *tr. by* Rachel Benson

Death, you have made it your pleasure. Las! Mort Qui T'a Fait Si Hardie. Charles, Duc d' Orléans. WoPoe, *tr. by* Fred Chappell

Death, you're more successful than America. Death, an Ode. John Forbes. BMAP

Deathbed, A. John Hawthorn. NOEC *Fr.* Journey and Observations of a Countryman, The.

Deathless Aphrodite, throned in flowers. Ode to Aphrodite. Sappho. AWP, *tr. by* William Ellery Leonard

Deathplace, A. Louis Edward Sissman. NoP-4

Deaths and Engines. Eiléan Ní Chuilleanáin. ModIr

Deaths of Orpheus and Hercules, The. Seneca. OBVE *Fr.* Medea.

Deathward. John Lyle Donaghy. BIrV

Deathwatch. Michael S. Harper. NAAAL; NAAL-5

Debasement is the password of the base. Answer, The. Bei Dao. AF; PFTM-2, *tr. by* Bonnie S. McDougall

Debate between Jane Vaughan of Caergai and Cadwaladr the Poet. Jane Vaughan. EMWP

Debate: Question, Quarry, Dream. Robert Penn Warren. VGW

Debate with the Rabbi. Howard Nemerov. TaR

Debbie and Co. John Tranter. BMAP

Debits and Credits. Rudyard Kipling.

We and They. NoAM

Debout. U Tam'si Tchicaya.

"Here is the stream again under the rainbow." PBA

Debridement. Michael S. Harper. NoAM

Debris of Life and Mind. Wallace Stevens. SAmP

Debt, The. Paul Laurence Dunbar. ColAP

Debt is paid, The. Past, The. Ralph Waldo Emerson. FaBoCh; TAP; WoPoe

Debts. Jessie Belle Rittenhouse. TCAPo

Decade, [A]. Amy Lowell. MoAmPo; NALW; OxWW; PasH; PoBW

Decades behind me. Right-of-Way: 1865, A. William Plomer. PeLV

Decalogue of the Artist. Gabriela Mistral. TCLAP, *tr. by* Doris Dana

Decampment. Ernst Stadler. PeFWW

Decay. George Herbert. ESCV; SCGP

Decay of Piety. William Wordsworth. TrCP

Decease, Release. Robert Southwell. NPeEn; NoSic

Deceased. Cid Corman. VGW

Deceased, The. Keith Douglas. FaBoTw

Deceav'd and undeceav'd to be. Self-Deceaver, The. Thomas Stanley. OBVE

Deceit in the Park. Patrick Hare. OBGa

Deceiver Time. Luis de Góngora y Argote. SpanPo, *tr. by* James Edward Tobin

Deceiving Words. Leonor Scliar-Cabral. MirDau, *tr. by* Regina Igel

Deceiving World. Robert Greene. NoSic

December. John Clare. OBCP

December. John Clare. ChrPo

"Glad Christmas comes, and every hearth." OBCP

December. Lucille Clifton. NOxBChV

December. Christopher Pearse Cranch. APN-1; TCAPo

December. Robert Francis. LCAP-2

December. Josephine D. Henderson Heard. CBWP-4

December. Maurice Kenny. HATNAP

December. Ron Padgett. SPE

December. Henrietta Cordelia Ray. CBWP-3

December. Folgore da San Geminiano [*or* Gimignano]. EaItPo, *tr. by* Dante Gabriel Rossetti *Fr.* Sonnets of the Months.

December. Miriam Van Hee. TuT, *tr. by* Joan McBreen

Dec. 5th 1644 Upon Robin Austins Recovery of the Smal Pox and General Popams Son John Diing of Them. Katherine Austen. EMWP

December 7 Always Brings Christmas Early. Amy Uyematsu. LTA

December 14, 1979: A Poetry Reading. Stanislaw Baranczak. AF, *tr. by* Magnus J. Krynski

December 15, 1811. Poem for My Family: Hazel Griffin and Victor Hernandez Cruz. June Jordan. BPo

December 15th. Vera Gherarducci. CItWP, *tr. by* Cinzia Sartini Blum and Lara Trubowitz

December 21st. Jean Valentine. LCAP-2

December 25, 1991. Rose Solari. AmPoNex

December 31. Ahmed Taha. NAfrP, *tr. by* Clarissa C. Burt

December. An arctic wind, new. Wall Calendar. Dan Pagis. VCWP, *tr. by* Tsipi Keller

December, and the closing of the year. Christmas Eve in Whitneyville, 1955. Donald Hall. UnPo

December at the feet of December. Key and the Tree, The. Alessandro Ceni. ItPo, *tr. by* Gayle Ridinger

December Day, Hoy Sound. George Mackay Brown. OxBS

December Forest, A. Vesna Krmpotic. WPOW, *tr. by* Vasa D. Mihailovich

December Morning. Anna Seward. ECWP

December Nap. Dennis Saleh. GeoHom

December nights are frosts and stars. Helen Waddell. MLL

December 9th.   Eileen Myles.   PmAP

December / no signs of a Chicago winter / no boulder-sized clumps of snow.   For My Father.   Duriel Harris.   SpirFl

December of My Springs, The.   Nikki Giovanni.   GT

December Offensive.   Anna Enquist.   TuT, *tr. by* Peter Van de Kamp

December Pastures.   Andrey [*or* Andrei] Andreievich Voznesensky [*or* Voznesenskii].   RusPo, *tr. by* Robert Arthur Douglas Ford

December: Prayer to St. Nicholas.   John Heath-Stubbs.   OBCP

December's Husbandry.   Thomas Tusser.   NoSic   *Fr.* Five Hundred Points of Good Husbandry.

December: the trees chafing.   Mile Hill.   Dennis Schmitz.   LCAP-2

December 30th.   Ivor Gurney.   NAEL-5v2; NAEL-6v2

December 27, 1966.   Louis Edward Sissman.   DiPo

Decent docent doesn't doze, The.   History of Education.   David McCord.   APT-2; OBAL

Deception.   Josephine D. Henderson Heard.   CBWP-4

Deception.   Kim Sujang.   WoPoe, *tr. by* Kevin O'Rourke

Deceptions.   Philip Larkin.   GTBS-P; HarvBoo; OxAEP-2

Deceptive Grin of the Gravel Porters, The.   Gavin Ewart.   FaBoMo

Decidedly we are out of the world. No longer any sound.   Arthur Rimbaud.   AWTN, *tr. by* Louise Varese   *Fr.* Night of Hell.

Decision.   *Unknown.*   PoToHe

Decision, The.   Theodore Roethke.   CRP; VGW

Decisions, The.   Rick Bursky.   ReTh

Deck thyself, maiden.   Esthonian Bridal Song.   Johann Gottfried von Herder.   AWP

Decked out in flannels and gripping my mitt.   4th Base.   Gary Gildner.   MoASP

Decked, stacked, pillaged from.   Middle Passage and After, The.   Larry Neal.   NBV

Decks awash, / Mast-top dipping.   Archilochus.   OBVE

Declaimer, The.   Henry Baker.   NOEC

Declair, ye bankis of Helicon.   *Unknown.*   OxBS   *Fr.* Bankis of Helicon, The.

Declaration.   Nikolai Ivanovich Glazkov.   TCRP, *tr. by* Daniel Weissbort

Declaration, The.   Nathaniel Parker Willis.   OBAL

Declaration of Hate.   Efraín Huerta.   TCLAP, *tr. by* Todd Dampier

Declaration of the Death of John Lewes, A.   Thomas Gilbart.   NoSic

Declaration of the Word as Such.   Aleksei Eliseievich Kruchyonykh [*or* Kruchionykh *or* Kruchenykh].   PFTM-1

Declare, O mind, from fond desires excluded.   Counterlove, A.   *Unknown.*   NoSic

Declare to man it was not sent in vain. (LL)   Latter Rain, The.   Jones Very.   APN-1; OxBA; TCAPo

Declaring war on Germany but not.   Some Words for President Wilson.   Samuel Hazo.   GraLe

Decline.   Georg Trakl.   WoPoe, *tr. by* Robert Firmage

Decommissioning.   Katrina Porteous.   NeBl

Decomposition with Laughter.   Homero [*or* Umberto] Aridjis.   TCLAP, *tr. by* Jerome Rothenberg

Decoration.   Mary Ursula Bethell.   PeNZ

Decoration.   Louise Bogan.   MoAmPo

Decoration Day.   Josephine D. Henderson Heard.   CBWP-4

Decorations climbing up the loft on a wobbly ladder.   My Christmas; Mum's Christmas.   Sarah Forsyth.   OBCP

Decorator is mixing his plaster, The.   Moon over Prague.   Vitězslau Nezval.   AF, *tr. by* Ewald Osers

Decoy.   John Ashbery.   PoM

Decoy Partridge, A.   Simmias [*or* Simias] of Rhodes.   GrAn, *tr. by* Peter Jay

Decoys, The.   W. H. Auden.   PoE

Decrees of God, The.   Chao Ying-tou.   TrJP, *tr. by* William C. White

Decrescendo.   Larry Levis.   SwNoth

Dedicace.   Aleister Crowley.   CAGL

Dedicated, The.   Philip Larkin.   OxBC

Dedicated Dancing Bull and the Water Maid, The.   Stevie Smith.   "Hop hop, thump thump."   WPE

Dedicated to Dr. W. H. Sheppard.   Maggie Pogue Johnson.   CBWP-4

Dedicated to the Right Rev'd D. A. Payne.   Mary Weston Fordham.   CBWP-2

Dedication.   Anna Andreyevna Akhmatova.   PFTM-1

Dedication.   Henry Wadsworth Longfellow.   TCAPo

Dedication.   N. P. van Wyk Louw.   PeSAV, *tr. by* Hugh Finn

Dedication.   Rochelle Owens.   PFTM-2

Dedication, A: "Anchored now to Neptune's temple floor, this."   Macedonius.   GrAn, *tr. by* Adrian Wright

Dedication, A: "Dear, near and true—no truer Time himself."   Tennyson.   OxBSP

Dedication: A Spear.   Anyte [*or* Anytes].   GrAn, *tr. by* John Heath-Stubbs and Carol A. Whiteside

Dedication, A: "They are rhymes rudely strung with intent less."   Adam Lindsay Gordon.   CBAP

Dedication: "Bob Southey! You're a poet—poet-laureate."   Byron.   CTC; OBSV   *Fr.* Don Juan.

Dedication Day.   Maggie Pogue Johnson.   CBWP-4

Dedication Day Poem.   Lizelia Augusta Jenkins Moorer.   CBWP-3

Dedication: "Had there been peace there never had been riven."   Drummond Allison.   FaBoTw

Dedication: "Health to great Gloucester—from a man unknown."   Charles Churchill.   OBSV

Dedication: "I would the gift I offer here."   John Greenleaf Whittier.   APN-1; OxBA

Dedication: "Let us honour if we can."   W. H. Auden.   PeLV   *Fr.* Shorts [1927–1932].

Dedication of a Torch.   Crinagoras.   GrAn, *tr. by* Alistair Elliot

Dedication of My First Son, A.   Mildmay Fane, 2d Earl of Westmorland.   BeJo

Dedication on the Cook.   Anna Wickham.   MoBrPo; NALW

Dedication on the Gift of a Book to a Child.   Joseph Hilaire Pierre Belloc.   *See* Child, Do Not Throw This Book About

Dedication: "Private faces in public places."   W. H. Auden.   FaBoEE; PeLV   *Fr.* Shorts [1927–1932].

Dedication: "Tall unpopular men."   Oliver St. John Gogarty.   OBMV

Dedication, The: "My God, thou that didst dye for me."   Henry Vaughan.   ESCV

Dedication to Aphrodite, A.   Hedylos.   GrAn, *tr. by* William Moebius

Dedication to G**** H******* Esq, A.   Robert Burns.   "Morality, thou deadly bane."   OBSV

Dedication to Hunger.   Louise Glück.   From the Suburbs.   FaBoWP; NALW

Dedication to My Wife, A.   T. S. Eliot.   BoLoP

Dedication to St. Michael.   Alcuin.   MLL, *tr. by* Helen Waddell

Dedication: to the Count of Niebla.   Luis de Góngora y Argote.   SpanPo, *tr. by* Frances Fletcher   *Fr.* Fable of Polyphemus and Galatea.

Dedication: "Unto the blithe and lordly fellowship."   Folgore da San Geminiano [*or* Gimignano].   EaItPo, *tr. by* Dante Gabriel Rossetti   *Fr.* Sonnets of the Months.

Dedication: "You whom I could not save."   Czeslaw Milosz.   WoPoe   (You whom I could not save / Listen to me.)   AF, *tr. by* Czeslaw Milosz

Dedicatory Epistle, with a Book of 1949.   Roy Fuller.   PeLV

Dedicatory Sonnet to S. T. Coleridge.   Hartley Coleridge.   CenSon; Son

Dee da dee D A A A A H. (LL)   Cabaret.   Sterling Allen Brown.   APT-2; NAAAL

Dee dee dee dee dee wee weee eeeeee wee we.   Communication in Whi-te.   Haki R. Madhubuti.   BPo

Deean Tractorman, Clear, The.   Edith Anne Robertson.   OxBS

Deean Tractorman, Deleerit, The.   Edith Anne Robertson.   OxBS

Deed / that was done in the Beginning, The.   Clerks.   Boris Abramovich Slutsky [*or* Slutskii].   TCRP, *tr. by* J. R. Rowland

Deeds Done and Suffered by Light.   Clayton Eshleman.   APSN

Deep.   Timothy Holmes.   PeSAV

Deep.   Patricia Pogson.   Prnts

Deep and boundless, the long autumn night.   Ts'ao P'i.   SuSp

Deep, and silent, and wide.   Louisa Sarah Bevington.   PEW   *Fr.* Two songs.

Deep and vast is parting sorrow as the vast slants.   Miscellanies of the Year Chi-hai.   Kung Tzu-chen.   SuSp, *tr. by* Irving Y. Lo

Deep Are the Wells.   Dezső Kosztolányi.   IQMS, *tr. by* Egon F. Kunz

Deep as this hour, ready again to sleep. (LL)   Night Feeding.   Muriel Rukeyser.   NoP-4; WPE

Deep autumn.   Basho.   EH, *tr. by* Robert Hass

Deep blue of the earth, The.   In the Arab House.   Al-Munsif Al-Wahaybi.   MAP, *tr. by* Salma Khadra Jayyusi and Naomi Shihab Nye

Deep blue sea baby.   Gaia.   Gary Snyder.   GifTon

Deep calleth unto deep.   Dial Call.   Christopher Darlington Morley.   NBLV

Deep, Deep in the Shade of the Court.   Ou-yang Hsiu.   ErotSp, *tr. by* Jerome P. Seaton

Deep for a deep winter. (LL)   Staying Alive.   David Wagoner.   CoAP; InPK-6

Deep grief wringing the heart.   At Gen's Embarkation for Yuan China.   Muso Soseki.   EaWin, *tr. by* W. S. Merwin

Deep in a distant bay, and deeply hidden.   Lonely Isle, The.   Claudian.   AWP, *tr. by* Howard Mumford Jones

Deep in a kingfisher hall, someone is heavy with wine.   Inscribed on the Fan of a Wealthy Old Man.   Shen Chou.   SuSp, *tr. by* Irving Y. Lo

Deep in a vale, a stranger now to arms.   American Soldier, The.   Philip Freneau.   TAP

Deep in a vale where rocks on every side.   Sonnet.   Gustav Rosenhane.   AWP, *tr. by* Sir Edmund William Gosse

Deep in an orchard, under hawthorn leaves.   Aubade.   *Unknown.*   NAWM-7v1, *tr. by* Peter Dronke

Deep in her seventh month, my sister dozes. Debra Bruce. FFC *Fr.* ("The Light They Make").

Deep in my heart I hear them, the gaunt hounds pacing. Hounds of the Soul, The. Louis Ginsberg. TrJP

Deep in my notebook a lily pad floats away. Matsuo Allard. HA

Deep in rank grass. Nicholas Virgilio. HA

Deep in the brain, far back. (LL) Night Crow. Theodore Roethke. InPK-6; NAAL-5; OxBSP; VGW

Deep in the brown bosom. Bangkok. Francis Reginald Scott. MoCV

Deep in the fading leaves of night. Carol. William Robert Rodgers. OBCP

Deep in the forest there is a pond. Deep in the Forest. *Unknown.* VGW; WoPoe, *tr. by* James [*or* Jim] Harrison

Deep in the grass there lies a dead gazelle. *Unknown.* AWP, *tr. by* L. Cranmer-Byng *Fr.* Shi King.

Deep in the leafy fierceness of the wood. Apollo and Daphne. Yvor Winters. APT-2; Son

Deep in the mountain. Sarumaru. OHPJ

Deep in the Mountain Wilderness. Wang Wei. OHMPC, *tr. by* Kenneth Rexroth

Deep in the night. Ransetsu. OHMPJ

Deep in the night and unable to sleep. Juan Chi. SuSp *Fr.* Poems Expressing My Feelings.

Deep in the night I woke: she, near me, held. Tennyson. EroLit *Fr.* Princess, The.

Deep in the pit where her bones lie. Deep in the Pit. Neeltje Maria Min. TuT, *tr. by* Peter Van de Kamp

Deep in the rippling spring. May Ushida. KaS

Deep in the roaring tide he plunged to endless night. (LL) Thomas Gray. GTBS-P; NOBE; NOEC; OxAEP-1

Deep in the shadows of his room. Lesson of Night, A. Charles Ghigna. MiVo

Deep in the Siberian mine. Message to Siberia. Alexander Sergeyevich Pushkin. AWP; TTY, *tr. by* Max Eastman

Deep in the underbrush. Sempo. JDP, *tr. by* Yoel Hoffmann

Deep in the wave is a coral grove. Coral Grove, The. James Gates Percival. APN-1; ColAP

Deep in the winter plain, two armies. Two Armies. Stephen Spender. OBWP; OxBTC

Deep in the wood I made a house. August. Katharine Pyle. OBCA

Deep in this grave her bones remain. Reflections, Written on Visiting the Grave of a Venerated Friend. Ann Plato. BlSi

Deep in thy tangled wood he sinks entwin'd. (LL) Prolonged Sonnet: In the Last Days of the Emperor Henry VII. Simone dall' Antela. AWP; EaItPo, *tr. by* Dante Gabriel Rossetti

Deep in your heart understand. Manly Love. Donald Malloch. CAGL

Deep inside me at my core is where my mother lives. Cassia Berman. "Deep inside me at my core." HW

Deep inside wood sleeps primal fire. Wood and Fire. Khuong Viet. WoPoe, *tr. by* Huynh Sanh Thong

Deep into autumn the acorns ripen. Lament of a Woman Acorn-gatherer. P'i Jih-hsiu. SuSp, *tr. by* William H. Nienhauser

Deep into patient Earth, from whose smooth breast it came! (LL) William Wordsworth. CenSon; HAP *Fr.* River Duddon [A Series of Sonnets], The.

Deep into the midst of a great, dark, wood. Snail's Lesson, The. Priscilla Jane Thompson. CBWP-2

Deep lane, poor families; I have few friends. At the End of Spring. Yü Hsüan-chi. BoWoP, *tr. by* Geoffrey Waters

Deep Mining. Irene McKinney. PBCAP

Deep night. I cannot sleep. Deep Night. Yuan Chi. OHMPC, *tr. by* Kenneth Rexroth

Deep on the convent-roof the snows. St. Agnes' Eve. Tennyson. OBEV; SacPr

Deep prolonged entry with the strong pink cock. She Loves. Olga Broumas. GLP

Deep Purple. Mitchell Parish. ReLy

Deep red bogs divided. Richard Murphy. CIP-2 *Fr.* Battle of Aughrim, The.

Deep River. Eugène Marais. PeSAV, *tr. by* Hugh Finn

Deep River. *Unknown.* BPo; SacPr; TAP
(There's nobody there for to turn me out.) (LL) APN-2

Deep scar engraved in the bark's dark silver, A. Vadim Leonidovich Andreyev [*or* Andreiev]. TCRP

Deep-Sea Bathing (Inna Reggae Dancehall). Rohan B. Preston. AmPoNex; WaCA

Deep-Sea Pearl, The. Edith Matilda Thomas. PoBW

Deep Shit. Daniel Tobin. NAPBL

Deep snow. Betty Drevniok. HA

Deep Song. Antonio Machado Ruiz. SpanPo, *tr. by* John Crow

Deep Spring. *Unknown.* SacPr

Deep-sworn Vow, A. W. B. Yeats. PoE; UnPo

Deep under the willows' shade the horse treads proudly. Passing by Kamata. Su Man-shu. SuSp, *tr. by* Wu-Chi Liu

Deep waters silent roul, so Grief like mine. Elegy on the Earl of Rochester. Anne Wharton. NOSC

Deep Well. Roland Robinson.
"I am at Deep Well where the spirit-trees." CBAP; NOBAu

Deep well knows it certainly, The. World-Secret. Hugo von Hofmannsthal. TrJP, *tr. by* Charles Wharton Stork

Deep within the shadows. Lament for a Courtesan. Li Ho. CrYelRi, *tr. by* Sam Hamill

Deep within the stream. J. W. Hackett. HA

Deep wooden note, A. Overheard. Denise Levertov. PoM

Deepening-Green Pavilion. Chu Yi-tsun. SuSp, *tr. by* Chang Yin-nan

Deepening shadows bring on sorrow, The. Hsü Kan. SuSp *Fr.* Boudoir Thoughts.

Deeper than sleep but not so deep as death. Night Feeding. Muriel Rukeyser. NoP-4; WPE

Deeper the drifts now, rain and sun won't ease. After Ovid, Tristia. Peter Scupham. HarvBoo

Deepest Well in Madras, The. N. V. M. Gonzalez. ReBoTo

Deeply repentant of my sinful ways. Gaspara Stampa. WPOW

Deepstep Come Shining. C. D. Wright.
"Meanwhile the cars continued in a persistent flow down." ExTi

Deer, The. Shara McCallum. NAPBL

Deer and the Snake, The. Kenneth Patchen. MoAmPo

Deer are just thankful it's over, The. Thanksgiving. Liz Rosenberg. PBCAP

Deer Cloud. Susan Clements. UnSA

Deer Enclosure. Wang Wei. ColAnChi, *tr. by* Richard W. Bodman and Victor H. Mair

Deer feed on. Upon Leaving the Parole Board Hearing. Conyus. GT

Deer gather in flocks by nature. Living in the Mountains. Tai Shu-lun. SuSp, *tr. by* William H. Nienhauser

Deer in rain / Three cries. Buson. ZenPo, *tr. by* Takashi Ikemoto and Lucien Stryk

Deer is humble, lovely as God made her, The. Deer and the Snake, The. Kenneth Patchen. MoAmPo

Deer Isle. Philip Booth. VGW

Deer Lay Down Their Bones, The. Robinson Jeffers. APT-1; NoAM

Deer licking. Issa. EH, *tr. by* Robert Hass

Deer looks through you to the other side, A. Iain Crichton Smith. HarvBoo *Fr.* Deer on the High Hills—a Meditation.

Deer-of-the-Waters: he laboured hard on his grammar. Red Indian Corpse. Peter Redgrove. OxBC

Deer on pine mountain, The. Onakatomi Yoshinobu. OHPJ

Deer on the High Hills—a Meditation. Iain Crichton Smith.

Deer Park. John Montague. PBCIP

Deer Park. Wang Wei. CrYelRi, *tr. by* Sam Hamill

Deer Sing. Confucius.
Fraternitas CTC; OBVE

Deer Song. Leslie Marmon Silko. VoR

Deer-tracks—I followed them: made. Air Street. David Morley. NLP

Deer walking quietly on the soft red earth. (LL) New Apartment. Linda Hogan. HATNAP; UnSA

Deer were bounding like blown leaves, The. Fire on the Hills. Robinson Jeffers. RaBo

Deevil's Waltz, The. Sydney Goodsir Smith. FaBoTw

Defeat. Witter Bynner. APT-1

Defeat. Kahlil Gibran. GraLe

Defeat, my Defeat, my solitude and my aloofness. Defeat. Kahlil Gibran. GraLe

Defeat of the Norsemen, The. Sedulius Scottus.
"Battle is joined on the open plain." FaBoWar, *tr. by* James Carney
"Heavens, ocean, and all earth, rejoice!" NOIV

Defeat of Turnus, The. Virgil [*or* Vergil]. OBVE, *tr. by* Gawin [*or* Gavin] Douglas *Fr.* Aeneid [*or* Eneados, Aeneis], The.

Defence of Fort McHenry. Francis Scott Key. *See* Star-Spangled Banner, The

Defence of Poetry, A. Giolla Brighde Mac Con Midhe. NOIV

Defence of Satire. Pope. *See* Epilogue to the Satires, in Two Dialogues

Defend it, call it a thing of worth. Defend It. Ágnes Nemes Nagy. IQMS, *tr. by* Alan Dixon

Defend the bad against the worse. (LL) Where Are the War Poets? Cecil Day Lewis. FaBoMo; NoP-4; OBWP; OxBSP; OxBTC

Defend Us, Lord, from Every Ill. John Hay. AH

Defending Walt Whitman. Sherman Alexie. AmPoNex

Defending you, my country, hurts. Battle Hymn of the Republic, The. Rafael Campo. NeAmPo

Defenestration of Prague. Susan Howe.

Bride's Day. FTOS

Defense of Fort McHenry. Francis Scott Key. *See* Star-Spangled Banner, The

Defense of Guenevere, The. William Morris. NAEL-5v2; NAEL-6v2

Defense Rests. Vassar Miller. MoAmPo

Defensive Position. John Streeter Manifold. MoBrPo

Defensive Rapture. Barbara Guest. FTOS

Deferment. Marcel Duchamp. PFTM-1

Deferred. Langston Hughes. APSN; APT-2

Defiance. Solomon ibn Gabirol. TrJP, *tr. by* Emma Lazarus

Defiance, The. Aphra Behn. EnLoPo

Defiant Farewell. Josef Luitpold. AuPH, *tr. by* Lowell A. Bangerter

Defiled Is My Name Full Sore. Anne Boleyn. WPE

Definition. Grace Noll Crowell. PoToHe

Definition of a Waterfall. John Ormond. AngWePo

Definition of Beauty, The. Robert Herrick. BeJo; CaPo

Definition of Blue. John Ashbery. NAAL-2v2

Definition of Love, The. Andrew Marvell. BASC; BoLoP; EBEV; ESCV; FHYEP; FSCP; GeHe; ITBLP; MeLP; NAEL-5v1; NAEL-6v1; NAEL-7v1; NOBE; NOSC; NPeEn; NoP-4; OBEV; OxBEV; PBRV; SCGP; TFi; UnPo

Definition of Nature. Eugene B. Redmond. NBV

Definition of the Soul. Boris Leonidovich Pasternak. TrJP, *tr. by* Babette Deutsch

Definitionless in this strict atmosphere. (LL) Lovely Love, A. Gwendolyn Brooks. BPo; NAAAL

Definitions. Joseph Joel Keith. PoToHe

Definitions. Elwyn Brooks White.
    Critic. NBLV

Definitions for Mendy. David Antin. APSN

Definitive Journey, The. Juan Ramón Jiménez. SpanPo, *tr. by* Angel Flores

Deflection toward the Relative Minor. Forrest Gander. OPRER

Deft, practised, eager. Usquebaugh. Wendy Cope. UV

Deftly, admiral, cast your fly. W. H. Auden. GTBS-P *Fr.* Five Songs.

Defying Gravity. Roger McGough. EmeKit

Defying the power of speech, the Law Commission on Mount Vulture! Myoyu. ZenPo, *tr. by* Takashi Ikemoto and Lucien Stryk

Degenerate Age, A. Solomon ibn Gabirol. TrJP, *tr. by* Emma Lazarus

Degenerate Douglas! O [*or* oh,] the unworthy lord! Composed at Neidpath Castle, the Property of Lord Queensberry, 1803. William Wordsworth. GTBS-P

Degree Four. Nathaniel Mackey. ESEAA

Degrees. Kevin Young. AmPoNex

Degrees of Gray in Philipsburg. Richard Hugo. CoAP; NAAL-2v2; NoAM; TRP; VCAP

Deid is now that dyvour and dollin in erd. William Dunbar. RACG *Fr.* Tua Mariit Wemen and the Wedo, The.

Deid sall ye ligg, and ne'er a memorie. Douglas Young. OBVE

Deign, Laura—now again the rainy season's here. Girl with Mind Wandering. Paul Valéry. STV, *tr. by* John Frederick Nims

Deign[e] at my hands this crown[e] of prayer and praise. John Donne. ChIV-2 *Fr.* Holy Sonnets.

Deil [*or* De'il] cam fiddling through the town, The. De'il's [*or* Deil's] Awa wi' th' [*or* the] Exciseman, The. Robert Burns. OBCoV

Deirdre. James Stephens. AWP; OBMV; PoRA

Deirdre's [*or* Deidre's] Lament for the Sons of Usnach. *Unknown.* NOIV, *tr. by* Sir Samuel Ferguson

Deity of Love Incorporate, A. Edward Taylor. TAP *Fr.* Preparatory Meditations before My Approach to the Lord's Supper.

Déjà Vu. Shirley Kaufman. DTA

Dejection. Derek Mahon. PBCIP; WoPoe

Dejection. Georg Trakl. PeFWW, *tr. by* Michael Hamburger

Dejection: An Ode. Samuel Taylor Coleridge. FHYEP; HeIP-4; NAEL-5v2; NAEL-6v2; NAWM-7v2; NOBE; NOBRP; NoP-4; OxAEP-2; PoE; PoPoPo; TFi; TOF
    (Dejection: An Ode, Written 4 April 1802.) NPeEn

Déjeuner sur l'Herbe. Bruce Beaver. BMAP

Déjeuner sur l'herbe. Tu Fu. BLT; CarOv, *tr. by* Carolyn Kizer

Delacroix pentit Chopin's heid. Ye Mongers Aye Need Masks for Cheatrie. Sydney Goodsir Smith. OxBS

Delay. Elizabeth Jennings. NIL-7; NIP-4; OPOU; OxBTC

Delay Has Danger. George Crabbe. NOBRP *Fr.* Tales of the Hall.

Delayed Action. Christian Morgenstern. RB, *tr. by* Lore Segal and W. D. Snodgrass

Delaying Relevance. Ben Marcus. HeMarv

Delia. Samuel Daniel.
    "Behold what hap *Pigmalion* had to frame." PBRV
    Sonnet 5: "Whilst Youth and Error" AEP

Delia. Henry Wadsworth Longfellow. TCAPo

Delia Very Angry. *Unknown.* NOEC

Deliberate as scrimshaw. Cat Washing. Linda Molony. NOBAu

Deliberately, long ago / the carcasses. From an Old House in America. Adrienne Rich. NNaP; TRP

Deliberation and flow bend. Allen Fisher. Oth *Fr.* Stepping Out.

Delicate Adonis is dying, Kytheria—what should we do? Sappho. SaLy, *tr. by* Diane Rayor

Delicate eyes that blinked blue Rockies all ash. On Neal's Ashes. Allen Ginsberg. PmAP; PoM

Delicate, firm, whole flesh of the still unburned, The. (LL) Advent 1966. Denise Levertov. APSN; NNaP

Delicate grasses, faint wind on the bank. Traveler at Night Writes His Thoughts, A. Tu Fu. CoBCP, *tr. by* Burton Watson

Delicate hands fashioned this portrait: good Prometheus. Erinna. SaLy, *tr. by* Diane Rayor

Delicate old injuries, the spines of names and leaves. (LL) Indian Boarding School: The Runaways. Louise Erdrich. HATNAP; NoAM; UnSA

Delicate sound of a moth; a page turning. Moths, The. Sean O Riordain. NOIV, *tr. by* Thomas Kinsella

Delicate young Negro stands, A. Anonymous Drawing. Donald Justice. CoAP; HeIP-4

Delicately bordered by poplars. (LL) In the Dordogne. John Peale Bishop. APT-1; OBWP; PeFWW; PoWW; VGW

Delicious, *fine* Sugar Hill. (LL) Harlem Sweeties. Langston Hughes. NoP-4; TTY

Delicious morning! how thy gentle beams. Blank Verse Written on the Sea Shore. Hannah Cowley. ECWP

Delight in books from evening. Francis Daniel Pastorius. NOSC; SCAP

Delight in Disorder. Robert Herrick. BASC; BeJo; CABP; CaPo; CavPo; ClHu; EBEV; EnLoPo; ErotSp; HAP; HeIP-4; InPK-6; NAEL-5v1; NAEL-6v1; NAEL-7v1; NIL-7; NIP-4; NOBE; NOSC; NPeEn; NoP-4; OBEV; OxAEP-1; OxBEV; PBRV; PeLV; PoE; PoRA; SCGP; TFi; TRP; WeW-3
    (Poetry of Dress, The.) GTBS-P
    (Sweet Disorder.) AWP

Delight of Humane kind, and Gods above. Lucretius. OBVE *Fr.* De Rerum Natura (On the Nature of Things).

Delight of Solitariness, The. Sir Philip Sidney. NoSic *Fr.* Arcadia.

Delight Song of Tsoai-Talee, The. N. Scott Momaday. CDW; InPK-6

Delight, then sorrow. Basho. SoOfWa, *tr. by* Sam Hamill

Delighted, incredulous bride, A. Maud Fitzgerald. *Unknown.* PeLi

Delightful, book, your trip. Aoibhinn, A Leabhráin, Do Thriall. *Unknown.* BIrV, *tr. by* Flann O'Brien

Delightful change from the town's abode. Barnyard Melodies. Fred Emerson Brooks. OBAL

Delightful mansion! blest retreat! Thought in a Garden, A. John Hughes. ECEV

Delights of the Door, The. Francis Ponge. RaBo, *tr. by* Robert Bly

Delineaments of the Giants, The. William Carlos Williams. NoAM; TAP *Fr.* Paterson.

Delirious the drought raved birds stretched on the fence. Remember. Ion Caraion. AF, *tr. by* Marguerite Dorian

Delirium. Norman J. Loftis. SpirFl

Delirium in Vera Cruz. Malcolm Lowry. FaBoTw; NoP-4; OxBTC *Fr.* Cantinas, The.

Deliverance. Frances Ellen Watkins Harper. WPOW

Deliverance. Amelia Blossom Pegram. HAWP

Deliverance, The. Frances Ellen Watkins Harper. SWaP *Fr.* Aunt Chloe.

Deliverance from a Fit of Fainting. Anne Bradstreet. TAP

Delivered at the Knighting of Lord Durgling by Great Bruce-Jean. Jean Toomer. GT

Delivered out of raw continual pain. St. Peter and the Angel. Denise Levertov. SacPr

Delivered / palpable / ours. (LL) Snapshots of a Daughter-in-Law. Adrienne Rich. FaBoWP; HCAP; NAAL-2v2; NALW; NIP-4; NoAM; NoP-4; VCAP

Deliverer, The. John Milton. NOBE; NOCV; OBEV; OxAEP-1 *Fr.* Samson Agonistes.

Delivering the Times, 1952–1944. David Huddle. PBCAP

Delivery. Armanda Guiducci. CItWP, *tr. by* Cinzia Sartini Blum and Lara Trubowitz

Delivery. Alicia Galaz Vivar. TANSG, *tr. by* Dave Oliphant

DeLiza Spend the Day in the City. June Jordan. NoAM

Dell, The. Gavin Ewart. OxBC

Delos. Lawrence Durrell. OxAEP-2

Delos. Bernard Spencer. NoAM

Delphi. Peter Davison. YaYoPo *Fr.* Breaking of the Day, The.

Delphi, coming around the corner of the house. Jane Mead. BodElec

Delphos, Ohio. Campbell McGrath. NeAmPo

Delta. Adrienne Rich. HarvBoo; LoL; NIL-7; NIP-4

Delta. Margaret Abigail Walker. YaYoPo

Delta, The / Itch of cayenne. Keith Cartwright. AmPoNex

Delta Traveller. Charles Wright. LCAP-2

Delug'd with tears, by what you heard before. To My Honoured Patron Humphery Davie. Benjamin Tompson. SCAP

Deluge 1939, The. Saunders Lewis. OBWVE, tr. by Gwyn Morgan

Delusive Hope! more transient than the ray. Sappho Rejects Hope. Mary Robinson. CenSon; RWP

Dem say him born. For Don Drummond. Lorna Goodison. WaCA

Dem say too many words mad him. Words Is Not Enough. Bob Stewart. WaCA

Demagogue, The. Phyllis McGinley. FaBoEE

Demand. Piera Oppezzo. CItWP, tr. by Cinzia Sartini Blum and Lara Trubowitz

Demanding that I explain / my treachery. (LL) Blonde White Women. Patricia Smith. GT; UnSA

Demands more Praise than Tongues can give. (LL) Church the Garden of Christ, The. Isaac Watts. NOCV; PeECV

Demands my soul, my life, my all. (LL) Hymn: "When I survey the wondrous cross." Isaac Watts. OxAEP-1; SacPr

DeMarco said the special bus. Knot Hole Gang, The. Brendan Galvin. MoASP

Demented underneath the moon, I watch. Asylum. Rafael Campo. NeAmPo

Dementia. John Cope. GeoH

Demeter. Genevieve Taggard. HW

Demeter and Cora. Dora Greenwell. VWP

Demeter Mourning. Rita Dove. NAAAL Fr. Mother Love.

Demeter's Blessing. Burleigh Mutén. HW

Demeter's Prayer to Hades. Rita Dove. NAAAL Fr. Mother Love.

Demeter's Song. Starhawk. HW

Demeter, Waiting. Rita Dove. BodElec

Demiurge's Laugh, The. Robert Frost. OxBA

Demo and Thermion Both Slay Me. Philodemus. WoPoe, tr. by George Economou

Democracy. Suzanne Gardinier. NeAmPo

Democracy. Langston Hughes. NAAL-5

Democracy, my grannie's foot! H. H. Tilley. FaBoWar Fr. Citizen BOR Speaking.

Democracy works (entre nous). Limerick. W. Stewart. PeLi

Democratic Barber; or, Country Gentleman's Surprise, The. John Parrish. NOEC

Democritus and Heraclitus. Matthew Prior. OxBSP

Democritus, dear droll, revisit Earth. Democritus and Heraclitus. Matthew Prior. OxBSP

Demographics. Catherine Bowman. ExTi

Demolisher. Alan Gould. BMAP

Demolition, The. Anne Stevenson. OxBSP

Demon Colors, Dark. Göran Sonnevi. PFTM-2, tr. by Rika Lesser

Demon in Paradise. Minuchihri. ArPe, tr. by Omar S. Pound

Demon in the morning, the. Epigram. Callimachus. WoPoe, tr. by Stanley Lombardo and Diane Rayor

Demon Lover, The. Unknown. HAP; SCGP; TFi; UnPo; WeW-3

(Carpenter's Wife, The.) OxBB

(James Harris.) ESPB

Demon [or Daemon] Lover. Unknown. See Carpenter's Wife, The

Demons. Diabolus in Musica. Lawrence F. O'Brien. MiVo

Demons. Alexander Sergeyevich Pushkin. WoPoe, tr. by D. M. Thomas

Demons of the Cities, The. Georg Heym. WoPoe, tr. by Peter Viereck

Demonstration, The. Thomas Traherne. BASC

Demoted I Arrive at Lan-t'ien Pass and Show This Poem to My Brother's Grandson Han Hsiang. Han Yü. SuSp, tr. by Charles Hartman

Demure you are over your left shoulder. Lines on a Boer War Pin-up Girl Seen in the Falcon Hotel, Bude. Christopher Hope. PeSAV

Den—for the beast, A. Marina Ivanovna Tsvetayeva [or Tsvetaeva]. TCRusP, tr. by Bob Perelman, Aleksandar Petrov and Shirley Rihner Fr. Poems to Blok.

Den of the bear. John Wills. HA

Denial[l]. George Herbert. BASC; ESCV; FSCP; GeHe; NAEL-5v1; NAEL-6v1; NAEL-7v1; NOBE; NPeEn; NoP-4; PBRV; TOF

Denials. Eric Gamalinda. ReBoTo

Denied, The. Lisa Sewell. AmPoNex

Denied, / Like Bessie. Of Walter White's Father in the Rain. Houston A. Baker, Jr. SeSe

Denmark sleeps soundly. Hamlet's Lost Monologue. László Kálnoky. IQMS, tr. by Kenneth McRobbie and Zita McRobbie

Denouement. Ruth Stone. BoWoP

Dense on the stream the vapours lay. Mowers: An Anticipation of the Cholera, 1848, The. Charles MacKay. EBVV

Dense white clouds embrace Thunder Peak. Written during My Stay at White Clouds Monastery on West Lake. Su Man-shu. SuSp, tr. by Wu-Chi Liu

Dented spider like a snowdrop white, A. In White. Robert Frost. TRP

Dentist, A. Unknown. FaBoEE

(Epitaph on a Dentist.) OxBoLi

Dentist's Window, A. James Keir Baxter. OxBC

Dentists continue to water their lawns even in the rain. Great Society, The. Robert Bly. NoAM; PAI

Dentologia; a Poem on the Diseases of the Teeth and Their Proper Remedies. Solyman Brown.

"Her lips disclosed to view." VerBaPo

Dents. Ulli Freer.

"Baseline pressure." Oth

Denuded Is the Earth. Antonio Machado Ruiz. SpanPo, tr. by Edward F. Gahan

Denunciation; or, Unfrock'd Again. Philip Whalen. NeAP

Denying they have been. (LL) Snow, The. Emily Dickinson. SoSe-8; WHSW

Denying what it means to doubt. Only the New Branches Bloom. Samuel Hazo. GraLe

Deo Gracias! (LL) Adam Lay Ybounden [or I-bounden]. Unknown. CTC; ChIV-2; HAP; MiEL; NOBE; NOCV; OxBoLi; PoE; TFi; TOF; TRP; WeW-3

Deo gracias Anglia. Agincourt Carol, The. Unknown. EBEV; NoP-4

Deo Gracias, Anglia. Unknown. EBEV

Deo Optimo Maximo. Louise Imogen Guiney. SacPr

Deodand, The. Anthony Hecht. DiPo; NoAM

Deor. Unknown. EBEV tr. by John Wain

Deor. Unknown. WoPoe, tr. by Peter Russell

Deor. Unknown. ASW

Deor's Lament. Unknown. AnOE, tr. by Charles W. Kennedy

Depart,—be off,—excede,—evade,—erump! (LL) Oliver Wendell Holmes. NOBL; OBAL; TCAPo Fr. Autocrat of the Breakfast Table, The.

Departed Youth. Hannah Cowley. CABP; ECWP

Departing at dawn, carriage bells ajingle. Early Walk on Shang Mountain, An. Wen T'ing-yün. SuSp, tr. by William R. Schultz

Departing from Ch'in-chou. Tu Fu. CrYelRi, tr. by Sam Hamill

Departing in Early Morning. Tu Mu. CrYelRi, tr. by Sam Hamill

Departmental. Robert Frost. HeIP-4; MoAmPo; NAAL-2v2; NAAL-5; NOBA; NOBL; OBAL; PeLV; SoSe-8

Departure. Gerrit Achterberg. TuT, tr. by Peter Van de Kamp

Departure. Edmund Charles Blunden. OxBSP

Departure. Louise Glück. GM

Departure. Thomas Hardy. Son

Departure. Edna St. Vincent Millay. MoAmPo

Departure. Bulat Shalvovich Okudzhava. ItGoST, tr. by Ronnie Apter and Mark Herman

Departure. Coventry Patmore. NOBE; OBEV Fr. Unknown Eros, The.

Departure. Pierre Reverdy. CuPo

Departure. Arthur Rimbaud. SxFrPo, tr. by Martin Sorrell

Departure. Mai Sayigh. PoArWo, tr. by Lena Jayyusi and Naomi Shihab Nye

Departure. Edgar Silex. NAPBL

Departure. Wang Wei. TAL

Departure. Mildred Weston. FFC

Departure, The. William Vaughn Moody. APN-2

Departure, The. Trumbull Stickney. ColAP

Departure, The. Reed Whittemore. TAP

Departure Aria. Johann Christian Günther. GePo, tr. by George C. Schoolfield

Departure in Middle Age. Roland Mathias. CRP; OBWVE

Departure in the Dark. Cecil Day Lewis. TwCP

Departure of '82. Sa'di Yusuf. MAP, tr. by Lena Jayyusi and Naomi Shihab Nye

Departure of the Good Daemon, The. Robert Herrick. BASC; NPeEn

Departure of the Prodigal Son, The. Rainer Maria Rilke. GI

Departure's Girl-friend. W. S. Merwin. CoAmPo

Departures. Joan Michelson.

Rings. Prnts

Dependence! heavy, heavy are thy chains. To Dependence. Charlotte Smith. CenSon

Dependencies, The. Howard Nemerov. VCAP

Dependency on and. Novelist Speaks, The. Ann Lauterbach. KGB

Depiction of Childhood. Franz Wright. BLT Fr. After Picasso.

Deportation. "M. B." TrJP, tr. by A. Glanz-Leyeles

Deposition from Love, A. Thomas Carew. BASC; BeJo; CaPo; CavPo; MeLP

Depot in Rapid City. Roberta Hill Whiteman. BoWoP

Depreciating Her Beauty. Wilfrid Scawen Blunt. OBMV Fr. Love Sonnets of Proteus, The.

Depressed by a Book of Bad Poetry, I Walk toward an Unused Pasture and Invite the Insects to Join Me. James Wright (1927–80). EmeKit

Depression. Wendy Cope. FaBoWP

Depression. Isabel Joshlin Glaser. HHAm

Depression. János Pilinszky. IQMS, *tr. by* Peter Jay

Depression. Sonia Sanchez. ESEAA

Depression, The. Ira Sadoff. BodElec

Depression before Spring. Wallace Stevens. OBAL

Depression Days. Pat Mora. UnSA

Depression in Winter. Jane Kenyon. LoL

Depressive Episode. Janet Holmes. ExTi

Deprived of his enemy, shrugged to a standstill. John Berryman. LCAP-2 *Fr.* Dream Songs.

Deprived of the green of that exclusive golf course, the scotch. Epistle to the Gentiles. Alfred Hayes. TrJP

Depth of Field. Linda Bierds. ExTi

Depth or the duration of his woe, The. (LL) On Being Cautioned against Walking on an Headland Overlooking the Sea, because It Was Frequented by a Lunatic. Charlotte Smith. CenSon; ECWP; NPeEn; WoRP

Depths of cold. Kasenjo. JDP, *tr. by* Yoel Hoffmann

Depths of Fields. Luis Cabalquinto. ReBoTo

Der Blinde Junge. Mina Loy. APT-1; HarvBoo

Der lived a king inta da aste. King Orfeo. *Unknown.* ESPB; OxBB; OxBoLi

Der teufel's los in Bal Mabille. Breitmann in Paris. Charles Godfrey Leland. APN-2

Derailment. William Heyen. PoCoUp

Derailment: A Delirium. Steve Chimombo. HBAPE

Derby Ram, The. *Unknown.* OxNR; ReMoGo

Derbyshire Born, Monmouth Is My Home. Clifford Dyment. AngWePo

Dere's a beeg jam up de reever, w'ere rapide is runnin' fas' Log Jam, The. William Henry Drummond. NOBC

Dere's a liddle fact in hishdory vitch few hafe onnershtand. Charles Godfrey Leland. OBAL *Fr.* Breitmann in Politics.

Dere's an ol' man called de Mississippi. Ol' Man River. Oscar Hammerstein, II. APT-2; ReLy

Dere's No Hidin' Place down Dere. *Unknown.* APN-2; BPo

Derelict, The. Rudyard Kipling. NoAM

Derry. Seamus Deane. CIP-2

Derry Morning. Derek Mahon. NOIV

Dervish, The. Muhammad Al-Faituri [*or* Al-Fituri *or* Al-Fayturi]. MAP, *tr. by* Sargon Boulus and Peter Porter

Dervorgilla's supremely lovely daughter. Portrait with Background. Oliver St. John Gogarty. OBMV

Derwent; an Ode. Sir John Carr.

Memories of Childhood. NOEC

Derzhavin. Georgy [*or* Georgii] Arkadevich Shengeli. TCRP, *tr. by* Daniel Weissbort

Désamère. Alice Notley.

"Overhead at night, above the planet." PFTM-2

Descano, California. Chryss Yost. GeoHom

Descant. Jane Mayes. PasH

Descartes and the Stove. Charles Tomlinson. FaBoMo

Descartes at Daybreak. Aidan Carl Mathews. CIP-2

Descend, embrace this daughter. Dialogue with the Dead. Amelia Rosselli. PFTM-2, *tr. by* Lawrence R. Smith

Descend, fair Truth, celestial maid, descend. Ode to Truth. Mary Whateley. ECWP

Descend from heaven O muse Melpomene. Epitaph of Our Late Queen Mary, An. George Cavendish. NoSic

Descend from Heaven [*or* Heav'n], Urania, by that name. John Milton. EBEV; NAEL-5v1; NAEL-6v1; NOSC; TOF *Fr.* Paradise Lost.

Descend, while three birds watch and the fourth flies. (LL) Winter Landscape. John Berryman. GS; HarvBoo; MoAmPo; TwCP

Descend, ye hovering sylphs! aerial choirs. Erasmus Darwin. ECEV *Fr.* Botanic Garden, The.

Descendant I am of Emperor Kao-yang, A. Ch'u Yüan. SuSp *Fr.* Li Sao.

Descendant of the ancestor Kao-yang. Encountering Sorrow. *Unknown.* CoBCP, *tr. by* Burton Watson

Descended, Adam to the bower where Eve. John Milton. NOCV *Fr.* Paradise Lost.

Descending. Valentin Iremonger. EnLoPo

Descending by the mountain-side. Guide and Guard. Herman Melville. NCAP

Descending Chestnut Ridge. Donald Davidson. FuPo *Fr.* Hermitage.

Descending Figure. Louise Glück. FaBoWP

Descending the Ridge of Flying Clouds. T'ang Hsien-tsu. CoBLCP, *tr. by* Jonathan Chaves

Descending through Dragon Gate. Tu Fu. CrYelRi, *tr. by* Sam Hamill

Descending to the cave where the Archangel / made his announcement. Nazareth. Rosario Castellanos. GI, *tr. by* Magda Bogin

Descent. Robyn Selman. TaR

Descent, The. James Tate. YaYoPo

Descent, The. William Carlos Williams. APT-1; HAP; SAmP; WeW-3

Descent beckons, The. Descent, The. William Carlos Williams. APT-1; HAP; SAmP; WeW-3

Descent from the Cross. "Michael Field." WPE

Descent of Abu Nuwas. Hasab al-Shaikh Ja'far. MAP, *tr. by* Diana Der Hovanessian and Salma Khadra Jayyusi

Descent of Odin, The. Thomas Gray. OxAEP-1

Descent of the Vulture, The. Marya Alexandrovna Zaturenska. WPE

Descent of Winter, The. William Carlos Williams.

"To freight cars in the air." InPK-6

Describe the Borough.—Though our idle tribe. George Crabbe. CABP *Fr.* Borough, The.

Describes Her Bark. Mary Robinson. CenSon; RWP

Describes Phaon. Mary Robinson. CenSon; RWP

Describes Rationally the Irrational Effects of Love. Sister Juana Inés de la Cruz. SpanPo, *tr. by* Samuel Beckett

Describes the Characteristics of Love. Mary Robinson. CenSon; RWP

Describes the Fascinations of Love. Mary Robinson. CenSon; RWP

Describes the Place Where Cynthia Is Sporting Herself. Philip Ayres. EnLoPo

Describing a Dream for Someone. Wang Seng-ju. ColAnChi, *tr. by* Anne Birrell

Describing a Suit. Hafiz Ibrahim. MAP, *tr. by* Christopher Middleton and Christopher Tingley

Describing My Feelings upon Encountering Snow. Li K'ai-hsien.

"Crossing the ridge, the woodcutter loses his way." CoBLCP

Describing My Feelings while Living in Retirement by the Riverside: Seven Poems to the Tune "Ch'ing-p'ing-yüeh." Yang Chi. CoBLCP, *tr. by* Jonathan Chaves

Describing My Feelings while Living in the Spring Quarters at Chiang-ning: Four Poems to the Tune "Ching-p'ing-yëh." Yang Chi. CoBLCP, *tr. by* Jonathan Chaves

Description of a City Shower, A. Jonathan Swift. HeIP-4; NAEL-5v1; NAEL-6v1; NAEL-7v1; NIL-7; NOEC; NoP-4; OBSV; PoE; UnPo (City Shower, A.) SCGP

Description of a Good Boy, The. Henry Dixon. OxNR

Description of a New England Spring. John Josselyn. SCAP

Description of an Author's Bedchamber, A. Oliver Goldsmith. BIrV

Description of an Irish Feast, The. Hugh MacGowran. NOIV; OBCoV, *tr. by* Jonathan Swift *See also* O'Rourke's Feast

Description of Cooke-ham [*or* Cookham], The. Emilia [*or* Aemelia] Lanier [*or* Lanyer]. BASC; CABP; NAEL-6v1; NAEL-7v1; NoP-4; PBRV

"Now let me come unto that stately tree." MakPoe

"Yet you (great lady) mistress of that place." OBGa

Description of Elysium. James Agee. YaYoPo

Description of London, A. John Bancks. NOEC; OBCoV

Description of Love, A. Sir John Beaumont. NOSC

Description of Maidenhead, A. John Wilmot, 2d Earl of Rochester. NOBL

Description of Perfect Beauty. Christian Hofmann von Hofmannswaldau. GePo, *tr. by* George C. Schoolfield

Description of Sir Geoffrey Chaucer, The. Robert Greene. CTC; NoSic; SCGP *Fr.* Greene's Vision.

Description of Some Confederate Soldiers, A. Randall Jarrell. CBCWP

Description of Spring. Henry Howard, Earl of Surrey. *See* Soote Season, The

Description of Spring in London, A. *Unknown.* NOEC

Description of Spring, Wherein Each Thing Renews Save Only the Lover. Henry Howard, Earl of Surrey. *See* Soote Season, The

Description of the Contrarious Passions in a Lover. Petrarch. OBVE; Son, *tr. by* Sir Thomas Wyatt *Fr.* Sonnets to Laura.

Description of the Morning, A. Jonathan Swift. EBEV; ECEV; HAP; HeIP-4; NIL-7; NOBE; NOEC; NoP-4; OxAEP-1; OxBEV; PAI; PoPoPo; SoSe-8; TFi

Description of the Shepherd and His Wife, The. Robert Greene. NoSic

Description of Tyme, A. Alexander Montgomerie. OxBEV; OxBS

Description of Virtue. Nicholas Grimald. *See* Virtue

Descriptive Passages. William Matthews. BodElec

Descriptive Poem, Addressed to Two Ladies at Their Return from Viewing the Mines, near Whitehaven, A. John Dalton.

Agape the sooty collier stands. NOEC

Descriptive Poetry. Friedrich Hölderlin. WoPoe, *tr. by* Vyt Bakaitis

Dese Bones Gwine to Rise Again. *Unknown.* OxBoLi

Dese days, I doh even bada combing out mi locks. Calypso. Shara McCallum. AmPoNex

Desecration of the Han Tombs, The. Chang Tsai. ChiP, *tr. by* Arthur Waley

Desert. Birago Diop. NegPo, *tr. by* Ellen Conroy Kennedy

Desert, The. "Adonis" [*or* "Adunis"].
   Diary of Beirut under Siege, 1982, The. PoetW

Desert, The. Al-Munsif Al-Wahaybi. MAP, *tr.* by Salma Khadra Jayyusi and Naomi Shihab Nye

Desert, The. Edmond Jabès. AF, *tr.* by Rosmarie Waldrop

Desert 1. Monica Mansour [*or* Mansur]. MirDau, *tr.* by Celeste Kostopulos-Cooperman

Desert caller, The. Eyeful Glances. Niyi Osundare. HBAPE

Desert Conflict. Calvin Makabo. PeSAV, *tr.* by Alexander Qoboshane

Desert Crossing. Dambudzo Marechera. NAfrP

Desert Cry, A. Magdalena Gomez. PueRic

Desert Flowers. Keith Douglas. FaBoTw; HarvBoo; NPeEn

Desert Has Many Teachings, The. Mechthild von Magdeburg. WPoS, *tr.* by Jane Hirshfield

Desert, II, The. Edmond Jabès. AF, *tr.* by Rosmarie Waldrop

Desert Landscape. Agha Shahid Ali. OMIP

Desert moves out on half the horizon, The. Supper after the Last, The. Galway Kinnell. NOBA

Desert Music, The. William Carlos Williams. APSN

Desert of Love, The. János Pilinszky. IQMS; OBVE, *tr.* by Ted Hughes

Desert Places. Robert Frost. APT-1; HarvBoo; InPK-6; MoAmPo; NAAL-2v2; NAAL-5; NOBA; NoAM; OxBA; PoE; RB; SoSe-8; TAP; TRP; UnPo

Desert Reservation. Barry Lopez. GifTon

Desert Song. John Ash. HarvBoo

Desert Warfare. Michael Longley. CIP-2

Desert Wisdom. Reg Saner. PoCoUp

Deserted. Madison Cawein. TCAPo

Deserted Angel, The. Anna Hajnal. IQMS, *tr.* by Jeannette Nichols

Deserted city, residence of Ch'en emperors. Residence of the Emperors of Ch'en, The. Yang Wei-chen. CoBLCP, *tr.* by Jonathan Chaves

Deserted Estate at South Garden, The. Hsü Pen. CoBLCP, *tr.* by Jonathan Chaves

Deserted harbour stillness. Every stone. Seamus Heaney. PoetW *Fr.* Squarings.

Deserted here, the old house. Old House, The. Franta Bass. INSAB

Deserted House. Dorothy Wellesley, Duchess of Wellington.
   Epilogue: "He is not dead nor liveth." OBMV

Deserted islands, broken sherds of land. Antipater of Thessalonica. GrAn

Deserted Mountain, The. *Unknown.* BIrV, *tr.* by John Montague

Deserted mountain, streams and stones, A. Searching for the Ruins of the Pavilion of the Drunken Old Man. Yang Shih-ch'i. CoBLCP, *tr.* by Jonathan Chaves

Deserted Orchard. Frances Mary Frost. YaYoPo

Deserted street, shadows of trees and houses, locked doors. Vista. Faiz Ahmad Faiz. VCWP, *tr.* by Agha Shahid Ali

Deserted Village, The. Oliver Goldsmith. NAEL-6v1; NOEC

Deserted Village, The. CABP; ECEV; FHYEP; MakPoe; NAEL-7v1; NOBE; NoP-4; OxAEP-1; TFi; TreFP

   "Even now the devastation is begun." EBEV

   "Ill fares the land, to hastening ills a prey." OBSV; UV

   "O luxury! Thou curst by Heaven's decree." BIrV

   "Sweet Auburn! parent of the blissful hour." EBEV

   "Sweet smiling village, loveliest of the lawn." NOIV

   Village Preacher, The.

      "Near yonder copse, where once the garden smiled." TreFP

   Village, The. NPeEn

   "Yes! let the rich deride, the proud disdain." OBSV

Deserted Village, The. "Robin Hyde." PeNZ; WPE

Deserted Well, The. Yusuf Al-Khal. MAP, *tr.* by Sargon Boulus and Naomi Shihab Nye

Deserted wharf. Chuck Brickley. HA

Deserter, A. Charles Reznikoff. TRP

Deserter, The. Ai. BodElec

Deserter, The. John Philpot Curran. OxAEP-1

Deserter, The. Gilbert Frankau. FaBoWar

Deserter, The. A. E. Housman. OBMV

Deserter, The. John Streeter Manifold. CBAP

Deserter, The. Stevie Smith. FaBoWP

Deserter, The. *Unknown.* FaBoWar

Desertion of the Women and Seals, The. George Mackay Brown. OxBC

Desertmartin. Tom Paulin. CIP-2; ModIr; NPeEn; PBCIP; PNI

Desiderato. William Johnson Cory. CAGL

Desideria. William Wordsworth. *See* Sonnet on Catherine Wordsworth

Desiderium. John Byrom. *See* My Spirit Longeth for Thee

Design. Robert Frost. APT-1; ColAP; HeIP-4; InPK-6; NAAL-2v2; NAAL-5; NIL-7; NOBA; NoAM; NoP-4; OxBSo; PAI; PoPoPo; RaBo; SAmP; SoSe-8; Son; TAP; TFi; TRP

Design. Mary Oliver. PoCoUp

Design. Peter Redgrove. OxBC

Design for a Quilt. John Ormond. AngWePo; TCAWP

Design for a Tomb. John Ormond. TCAWP

Design, or chance, makes others wive. Of the Marriage of the Dwarfs. Edmund Waller. NPeEn

Designer sits, head in hand, The. Design. Peter Redgrove. OxBC

Designs on your blouse are flickering wildly, The. One Second. Innokenty Fiodorovich Annensky. WoPoe, *tr.* by Stephen Berg

Désillusion. Lady Jane Francesca Wilde. VWP

Desire. "Æ." OBMV

Desire. Claribel Alegría. LoL

Desire. Ada Cambridge. OxBSo

Desire. Kathy Fagan. GeoHom

Desire. Paul Hoover. PmAP

Desire. Molly Peacock. RA

Desire. Kim Ports. PasH

Desire. Kurt Schwitters. PFTM-1

Desire. Sir Philip Sidney. *See* Thou Blind Man's Mark

Desire. Connemara Wadsworth. PasH

Desire 1. Thulani Davis. ISC

Desire and Jealousy. William Blake. ECEV *Fr.* Visions of the Daughters of Albion.

Desire as Light as a Shuttle. Joyce Mansour. HAWP, *tr.* by Mary Beach

Desire, get your bow ready / and go quietly after / another mark. Archias. GrAn

Desire has failed, desire has failed. Grasshopper Is a Burden. D. H. Lawrence. FaBoVe

Desire Is Dead. D. H. Lawrence. FaBoEE

Desire Loosening. Alcman. WoPoe, *tr.* by Rosanna Warren

Desire Moving through the Maps of the Material. "Adonis" [*or* "Adunis"].

   "Eiffel tower, The." PFTM-2, *tr.* by Allen Hibbard and Osama Isber

   "It came to pass." PFTM-2, *tr.* by Allen Hibbard and Osama Isber

   "It is my desire moving." PFTM-2, *tr.* by Allen Hibbard and Osama Isber

   "My passion is full of seeds issuing secretly from heraclitus and nietzsche." PFTM-2, *tr.* by Allen Hibbard and Osama Isber

   "No, my body is neither a pelican nor a water lily." PFTM-2, *tr.* by Allen Hibbard and Osama Isber

Desire of Dominion. Timothy Kendall. NoSic

Desire's destroyed my life; what gifts have I. Hafiz [*or* Hafez]. WoPoe, *tr.* by Dick Davis *Fr.* Three Poems on Friendship.

Desire's Persistence. Jay Wright. ESEAA

Desire, though thou my old companion art. Sir Philip Sidney. NAEL-5v1; NAEL-6v1; NAEL-7v1 *Fr.* Astrophil and Stella.

Desired, the snow falls upward. Michael Palmer. FTOS *Fr.* Letters to Zanzotto.

Desires. Connie Bensley. FaBoWP

Desiring his imprisoned Muse to enlarge. On the Doctors' Telling Him that till He Left Off Making Verses He Was Not Fit to be Discharged. James Carkesse. NOSC

Desiring nought but how to kill desire. (LL) Thou Blind Man's Mark. Sir Philip Sidney. HeIP-4; NAEL-5v1; NAEL-6v1; NAEL-7v1; SCGP; Son

Desirous is one who gets away from his mother. Call of the Desirous. José Lezama Lima. TCLAP, *tr.* by Willis Barnstone

Desk, The. David Bottoms. WeW-3

Desk, The. Cid Corman. VGW

Desks. Dave Jeddie Smith. HCAP

Desmet, Idaho, March 1969. Janet Campbell Hale. VoR

Desnos Reading the Palms of Men on Their Way to the Gas Chambers. Stephen Berg. GotH; TaR

Desolate. Gerald Massey. EBVV

Desolate City, The. *Unknown.* AWP; OBEV, *tr.* by Wilfrid Scawen Blunt

Desolate Field, The. William Carlos Williams. APT-1

Desolate rhythm of dying recurs, The. Fall. Michael Smith. CIP-2

Desolate that cry as though world were unworthy. Chough. Rex Warner. PoRA

Desolate, this rainy autumn evening. What Strikes My Eye. Wang Shih-chieng. SuSp, *tr.* by Richard John Lynn

Desolate wind from the city, A. Gunnar Ekelof. PFTM-2, *tr.* by Muriel Rukeyser and Leif Sjöberg *Fr.* Mölna Elegy.

Desolation. Jack Davis. BMAP

Desolation. John Henry, Cardinal Newman. SacPr

Desolation. *Unknown.* OBWVE, *tr.* by Aneirin Talfan Davies

Desolation in Zion. Bible, *O.T.* TrJP *Fr.* Lamentations.

Desolation Is a Delicate Thing. Elinor Wylie. MoAmPo

Despair. Andrey [*or* Andrei] Bely [*or* Belyi]. TCRP, *tr.* by Bernard Meares

Despair. (LL) Emily Dickinson. APN-2; MoAmPo; NAAL-2v1; NAAL-3; NAAL-5; NOBA; OxBA; TCAPo; TRP

Despair. Maxine W. Kumin. FFC

Despair. Denise Levertov. NNaP

Despair. Meng Chiao. CrYelRi, *tr.* by Sam Hamill

Despair. Tom Wayman. CDa

Despair and Hope. Israel Zangwill. TrJP

Despair, anger, grief. Black Java Pepper. Arthur Sze. OpBo

Despair before us, vanity behind. (LL) George Santayana. APN-2; AWP *Fr.* Sonnets.

Despair has prevented praise, but praise shall rise again. Venerating Senses Save Us. Jonathan Griffin. Oth

Despair is big with friends I love. William Meredith. VCAP *Fr.* Consequences.

Despair of all, and hope for none! Despair and Hope. Israel Zangwill. TrJP

Despairing Lover, The. William Walsh. FaBoCh; NBLV; NOBL; OxBoLi; PeLV

Desperate spinster of Clare, A. Limerick. *Unknown.* PeLi

Desperate Vitality, A. Pier Paolo Pasolini.
  "As in a film by Godard: alone." PFTM-2, *tr.* by Pasquale Verdicchio

Despise not any man that lives. Sam Walter Foss. PoToHe *Fr.* Work for Small Men.

Despise poetry, and you'll be named to office. Despair. Meng Chiao. CrYelRi, *tr.* by Sam Hamill

Despised and Rejected. Katharine Lee Bates. TrCP

Despised and Rejected. Christina Georgina Rossetti.
  "Then I cried out upon him: Cease." PeVV

Despite her sixty years Aunt Hannah Jackson rubs on other people's clothes. Aunt Hannah Jackson. Fenton Johnson. APT-1

Despite that I overslept. That's Not in My Job Description. Paul Beatty. NeAmPo

Despite the falling snow. (LL) She Tells Her Love while Half Asleep. Robert Graves. BoLoP; EBEV; FaBoTw; NOBE; OxBTC

Despite the grisly wounds portrayed in prints. Christ at the Apollo, 1962. Michael Waters. SwNoth

Despite the reigning darkness. Great Masturbator, The. Salvador Dali. PFTM-1

Despite the ruddy down upon your cheek. Strato [*or* Straton]. CAGL, *tr.* by Daryl Hine

Despite what Dorothea has said. New True Anthem, The. Kevin Gilbert. IBA

Despondency and Aspiration. Felicia Dorothea Hemans. RWP

Despondency Corrected. William Wordsworth. *Fr.* Excursion, The.

Desponding Phyllis was endued. Phyllis [*or* Phillis] [*or* Progress of Love, The]. Jonathan Swift. EBNV; OBCoV; OBSV; PoE

Desportes. Sir Arthur Gorges.
  "Tell me, my heart, how wilt thou do." NoSic

Despot's heel is on thy shore, The. My Maryland. James Ryder Randall. CBCWP

Despot treads thy sacred sands, The. Carolina. Henry Timrod. APN-2; CBCWP

Destination: Tule Lake Relocation Center, May 20, 1942. James Masao Mitsui. OpBo

Destinations. Josephine Jacobsen. WPE

Destined while living to sustain. Epitaph on Herself, An. Mehetabel Wright. ECWP

Destinie. Abraham Cowley. MeLP

Destiny. Sir Edwin Arnold. NOBVV; OxBSP

Destiny. Eloise Bibb. CBWP-4

Destiny. Rosario Castellanos. TANSG, *tr.* by George Bogin

Destiny. Maria Luisa Spaziani. NeIt, *tr.* by Beverly Allen

Destroy the heavy yoke beneath which you are bound! To Germany. Georg Rudolph Weckherlin. GePo, *tr.* by George C. Schoolfield

Destroyers in the Arctic. Alan Ross. PoWW

Destruction. Shakuntala Hawoldar. HAWP

Destruction. Joanne Kyger. BLT

Destruction. Shinkichi Takahashi. ZenPo, *tr.* by Takashi Ikemoto and Lucien Stryk

Destruction of Jerusalem, The. Thomas Deloney.
  "For true report rung in his royall eares." FaBoWar
  "Our Savior Christ tracing the bordering hills." ChIV-2

Destruction of Jerusalem by the Babylonian Hordes, The. Isaac Rosenberg. PeFWW

Destruction of Letters. Babette Deutsch. WPE

Destruction of Psara, The. Dionysios Solomos. WoPoe, *tr.* by Edmund Keeley and Philip Sherrard

Destruction of Sennacherib, The. Byron. BRP; CABP; ChAP; ChIV-1; FHYEP; FaBoCh; FaBoWar; HAP; HeIP-4; NoP-4; OBWP; OxAEP-2; PAI; RB; SCGP; TFi; TrCP; WeW-3; WoPoe

Destruction of Sodom, The. Daryl Hine. ChIV-1

Destruction of the beloved by the lover, The. With Passion without Compassion. Oscar Hahn. BLPSL, *tr.* by Rene de Costa, Rigas Kappatos and Eleni Paidoussi

Destruction of the Grecian Fort, The. Homer. OBVE, *tr.* by Alexander Pope *Fr.* Iliad, The.

Desultory Thoughts in London. Charles Lloyd.
  "Where have I wander'd, London, from thy haunts?" NOBRP

Desunt nonnulla. (LL) Christopher Marlowe. NoSic; PoE *Fr.* Hero and Leander.

Detach, Invading. Ron Padgett. FTOS

Detail. Mary Ursula Bethell. PeNZ

Detail, of course, The. Interstate 80. Michael Anania. IllVoic

Detailed History of the Western World. Joe Wenderoth. AmPoNex

Details of agony carefully into the Night Report. (LL) Malice of Innocence, The. Denise Levertov. BodElec; NNaP

Detected little things: a peach pit basket watch chain charm, an ivory cross wound. Father or Son. James Schuyler. FTOS

Detectives from the vice squad. Café: 3 A.M. Langston Hughes. GLP; HCAP

Deteriora. William Johnson Cory. CAGL

Determination of Time. Alena N´dvorníková. SurWo

Determined, Dared, and Done. (LL) Christopher Smart. NAEL-5v1; NAEL-6v1; NAEL-7v1; NOBE; OBWVE; PoE

Determined gait, A. Announcer, The. Vladimir Nikolaevich Kornilov. TCRP, *tr.* by Daniel Weissbort

Determines to Follow Phaon. Mary Robinson. CenSon; RWP

Determinism. Maurice Evan Hare. OBCoV

Detestable race, continue to expunge yourself, die out. Apostrophe to Man. Edna St. Vincent Millay. NAAL-5; NALW

Detonation. Francesco Cangiullo. PFTM-1

Detour. Michael Longley. CIP-2

Detouring through the rooms were men and fumes. Ivano Fermini. ItPo, *tr.* by Gayle Ridinger

Detroit 1958. Al Young. ESEAA

Detroit popped in the window. Entering Detroit. Víctor Hernández Cruz. PueRic

Detroit River. Constance Fenimore Woolson. APN-2

Deucalion and Pyrrha, sole survivors of the Flood, renew Creation by casting stones behind them. Ovid. NPeEn, *tr.* by John Dryden *Fr.* Metamorphoses.

Deuisioun of the Eirth, The. Sir David Lindsay [*or* Lyndsay]. NePenScot *Fr.* Dreme, The.

Deus "Sex" Machina. Harriet Mandelbaum. PeLi

Deuteronomy. Bible, *O.T.*
  "For the Lordes parte is his folke." OBVE
  Give Ear, Ye Heavens. TrJP

Deuteronomy. Robert Bringhurst. NOBC

Deuteronomy 30.19. Francis Quarles. ChIV-1

Deutschland. Hugh Maxton. PBCIP

Deutzia blossoms. Hakuto. JDP, *tr.* by Yoel Hoffmann

Deutzia has bloomed, The. Taikyo. JDP, *tr.* by Yoel Hoffmann

Deva-like Barbarian. Wen T'ing-yün. ColAnChi, *tr.* by Lois Fusek

Devastating flame of that fierce plague, The. Guido Cavalcanti. EaItPo, *tr.* by Dante Gabriel Rossetti

Developers, The. W. Les Russell. IBA

Developing a Wife. Andrew Taylor. CBAP
  (In the one cool room in the house.) BMAP

Development. Dennis Joseph Enright. OxBSP

Development, The. Marge Piercy. NBLV *Fr.* Sand Roads.

Development of Idiotcy, A. Ebenezer Jones. PeVV

Devil, A. Zbigniew Herbert. RB, *tr.* by Czeslaw Milosz

Devil, The. Bosch. Rafael Alberti. WoPoe, *tr.* by Carolyn Tipton

Devil, The. Robert Southey. NOxBChV

Devil and the Governor, The. William Forster.
  "In New South Wales, as I plainly see." CBAP

Devil and the Princess. *Unknown.* FaBoVe

Devil and the Shepherd, The. Fazil Abdulovich Iskander. TCRP, *tr.* by Daniel Weissbort

Devil below was ringing his knell, The. (LL) Inchcape Rock, The. Robert Southey. EBNV; OBNV; OBSP; OxAEP-2

Devil come and gets his own. (LL) Origin of the Snake, The. *Unknown.* NOxBChV; OxIBACP

Devil damn thee black, thou cream-faced loon, The. Paul Dehn. OBCoV *Fr.* Potted Swan.

Devil-Dancers, The. William Plomer. PeSAV

Devil, having nothing else to do, The. On Lady Poltagrue, a Public Peril. Joseph Hilaire Pierre Belloc. MoBrPo; OBCoV

Devil! I tell thee without nubbs or jubbs. After Reading the Life of Mrs.

Catherine Stubbs in Isaac Ambrose's "War with the Devils." Isaac Hann. NOCV

Devil in Texas, The. *Unknown.* NBLV; RB

Devil is a gentleman, and asks you down to stay, The. Aristocrat, The. Gilbert Keith Chesterton. OBCoV

Devil Is an Ass, The. Ben Jonson.
So White, So Soft, So Sweet. FaBoCh

Devil is dead, good people all, The. Devil's Funeral, The. Mary Elizabeth Coleridge. NALW

Devil now knew his proper cue, The. Shelley. OBSV *Fr.* Peter Bell the Third.

Devil on Ice. Donald Davie. NoAM

Devil's Advice to Story-Tellers, The. Robert Graves. NAEL-5v2; NAEL-6v2; NoAM

Devil's Destroying Angel Exploded, The. Tom Pickard. Oth

Devil's Dictionary, The. Ambrose Bierce.
Alone. APN-2
Body-Snatcher. APN-2
Corporal. APN-2; OBAL
Egotist. APN-2; OBAL
Elegy: "Cur foretells the knell of parting day, The." APN-2; OBAL
Freedom. APN-2
Gorgon. APN-2
Hypochondriasis. APN-2
Lead. APN-2; OBAL
Nose. APN-2; OBAL
Orthography. APN-2; OBAL; PeLi
Prospect. APN-2; OBAL
Rimer. APN-2
Safety-Clutch. APN-2; OBAL

Devil's Funeral, The. Mary Elizabeth Coleridge. NALW

Devil's Law Case, The. John Webster.
Burial, The. NOSC; PoRA; SCGP
(Vanitas Vanitatum.) NOBE; OBEV

Devil's no longer a myth, The. Limerick. "Little Billee." PeLi

Devil's Swing, The. Fyodor [*or* Fiodor] Kuz'mich Sologub. TCRP, *tr. by* April FitzLyon

Devil's Thoughts, The. Samuel Taylor Coleridge. OBSV; OxBoLi; PeLV

Devil take her, The. (LL) Sir John Suckling. AWP; BASC; BeJo; BoLoP; CaPo; CavPo; ClHu; EnLoPo; GTBS-P; HAP; HeIP-4; ITBLP; NAEL-5v1; NAEL-6v1; NAEL-7v1; NBLV; NIL-7; NIP-4; NOBE; NPeEn; NoP-4; OBEV; OxAEP-1; OxBEV; PAI; PoE; PoRA; TFi; UnPo *Fr.* Aglaura.

Devil take the human race!, The. Ill Humor. Goethe. STV, *tr. by* John Frederick Nims

Devil to Pay, The. Dorothy Leigh Sayers.
Choice of the Cross, The. TrCP

Devil was more generous than Adam, The. Samuel Butler (1612–80). FaBoEE

Devil, who plays a deep part, The. Limerick. "Little Billee." PeLi

Devilish and the dark, the dying and diseas'd, The. Rounded Catalogue Divine Complete, The. Walt Whitman. NAAL-2v1; NAAL-3

Devils. Norman Mailer. OBAL

Devils there many be, and Gods but one. (LL) Fulke Greville, 1st Baron Brooke. NOCV; NOSC; NoSic *Fr.* Caelica.

Devolution. Molly Peacock. FFC

Devonshire Street W.1. Sir John Betjeman. NPeEn

Devotion. Thomas Campion. NOBE; OBEV *See also* Follow Thy Fair Sun[ne] [Unhappy Shadow]

Devotion. Paul Fleming. GePo, *tr. by* F. Warnke

Devotion. Susan Minot. Unle

Devotional Sonnet, A. Timothy Steele. CRP

Devotions in Confidence. Margot Schilpp. AmPoNex

Devouring Time, blunt thou the lion's paws. William Shakespeare. AWP; EBEV; HeIP-4; NAEL-5v1; NAEL-6v1; NAEL-7v1; NoSic; OxAEP-1; PoE; SCGP *Fr.* Sonnets.

Devout but highly imaginative Jesuit, A. Almost Spring, Driving Home, Reciting Hopkins. Maxine W. Kumin. ExTi

Devout like a Branch. Cristina Campo. CItWP, *tr. by* Lara Trubowitz

Devout Lover, A. Thomas Randolph. OBEV

Devout Man Prays to His Relations, The. William Herebert. MiEL

Dew. Jennifer Maiden. CBAP

Dew. Charles Reznikoff. VGW

Dew and the clouds, The. (LL) I Found It. Fadwa Tuqan [*or* Tuquan]. BBASP; MAP, *tr. by* Patricia Alanah Byrne, Salma Khadra Jayyusi and Naomi Shihab Nye

Dew at the Edge of a Leaf. Marvin Bell. InvLad

Dew clear and bright. Tune: "Phoenix Hairpin"—Crab Apple. Ku T'ai-ch'ing. SuSp, *tr. by* Irving Y. Lo

Dew, clinging / To potato field. Masaoka Shiki. ZenPo, *tr. by* Takashi Ikemoto and Lucien Stryk

Dew falls, the sky is a long way up, the brimming waters are quiet, The. Autumn Night. Tu Fu. EaWin, *tr. by* W. S. Merwin

Dew in the morning, dust at noon. Barefoot Homiletics, after Wittgenstein and Boswell. Alan Dugan. BodElec

Dew is aflame on the flowers and trees, The. Having to Part from His Mistress at Dawn. Bálint Balassi. IQMS, *tr. by* Yakov Hornstein

Dew is on the grasses, dear, The. Youth. Georgia Douglas Johnson. NAAAL

Dew on a Dusty Heart. Jean Starr Untermeyer. MoAmPo

Dew on the bramble / Thorns. Buson. ZenPo, *tr. by* Takashi Ikemoto and Lucien Stryk

Dew on the garlic, The. Dew on the Young Garlic Leaves. T'ien Hung. OHMPC, *tr. by* Kenneth Rexroth

Dew on the Leek. *Unknown.* CoBCP, *tr. by* Burton Watson

Dew on the secret orchid. Grave of Little Su, The. Li Ho. WoPoe, *tr. by* A. C. Graham

Dew on the Young Garlic Leaves. T'ien Hung. OHMPC, *tr. by* Kenneth Rexroth

Dew spread / The seeds of hell. Issa. ZenPo, *tr. by* Takashi Ikemoto and Lucien Stryk

Dew whitens the jade steps. Resentment near the Jade Steps. Li Po. ErotSp, *tr. by* Sam Hamill

Dewdrops are the gems of morning. Old Man's Sigh, The. A Sonnet. Samuel Taylor Coleridge. CenSon

Dews of summer night[e] did fall[e], The. Cumnor Hall. William Julius Mickle. OxBB

Dewy morn / These saucepans. Buson. ZenPo, *tr. by* Takashi Ikemoto and Lucien Stryk

Dewy the earth with tears. Epitaph for His Niece, Sophia. Paul the Deacon. MLL, *tr. by* Helen Waddell

Dexter Gordon's tenor sax. February in Sydney. Yusef Komunyakaa. ESEAA; NAAAL

Dey's a so't o' threatenin' feelin' in de blowin' of de breeze. Soliloquy of a Turkey. Paul Laurence Dunbar. BPo

Dey want me to help score d ambush. (LL) Badman of the Guest Professor. Ishmael Reed. BPo; SSLK

Dey was hard times jes 'fo' Christmas round our neighborhood one year. Indignation Dinner, An. James David Corrothers. NAAAL

Dey was talkin' in de cabin, dey was talkin' in de hall. When Dey 'Listed Colored Soldiers. Paul Laurence Dunbar. BPo; CBCWP

Dharma is like an Avocado!, The. Avocado. Gary Snyder. PmAP

Dharma spring of the Sixth Patriarch, The. Hui-neng's Pond. Muso Soseki. EaWin, *tr. by* W. S. Merwin

Di sun si it all aready. History of Dub Poetry, The. "Mbala." WaCA

Diabolus in Musica. Lawrence F. O'Brien. MiVo

Diagnosis, The. James Tate. BAP-01

Diagnosis: My Mother's Breast. Lisa Fishman. AmPoNex

Diakka, The. Gerald Massey. NOBVV

Dial, The. Thomas Cole. APN-1

Dial Call. Christopher Darlington Morley. NBLV

Dial is dark, 'tis but half-past one, The. Rhyme of the Sun-Dial, A. William Bell Scott. NOBVV

Dialectic. Victor Serge. AF, *tr. by* James Brook

Dialectics. Edvard Kocbek. PoSu

Dialogue. Buland Al-Haidari [*or* Al-Haydari]. MAP, *tr. by* Patricia Alanah Byrne and Salma Khadra Jayyusi

Dialogue. Jared Angira. NAfrP

Dialogue. Leah Goldberg. MHP, *tr. by* Ruth Finer Mintz

Dialogue. Richard Lovelace. CavPo
(But time nor fate can part us joined thus.) (LL) CavPo

Dialogue. James McAuley. BMAP

Dialogue. Adrienne Rich. NIL-7; TAP

Dialogue, A. Elizabeth Carter. ECWP

Dialogue, A. George Herbert. FSCP; GeHe; NOSC; OBEV

Dialogue, A. David Ignatow. NNaP

Dialogue, A. Lizelia Augusta Jenkins Moorer. CBWP-3

Dialogue, A. Elizabeth Newell. EMWP

Dialogue, The. Funso Aiyejina. NAfrP

Dialogue, The. Vladimir Burich. TCRP, *tr. by* Katya Olmstead

Dialogue after Enjoyment. Abraham Cowley. BoLoP

Dialogue between a Squeamish Cotting Mechanic and His Sluttish Wife, in the Kitchen. Edward Ward. NOEC *Fr.* Nuptial Dialogues.

Dialogue between Araphil and Castara, A. William Habington. BeJo *Fr.* Castara.

Dialogue, between Crab and Gillian. Thomas D'Urfey [*or* Durfey]. NOEC *Fr.* Bath; or, The Western Lass, The.

Dialogue between Death and Youth, A. *Unknown.* NoSic

Dialogue between Father and Daughter. Robert Browning. OBCoV

Dialogue between Melancholy and Mirth, A. Margaret Lucas Cavendish, Duchess of Newcastle. BWW

Dialogue between Old England and New, A. Anne Bradstreet. BASC; EMWP

Dialogue between the Resolved Soul and Created Pleasure, A. Andrew Marvell. ESCV; FSCP; GeHe; MeLP

Dialogue between the Soul and [the] Body, A. Andrew Marvell. BASC; ESCV; FSCP; GeHe; HAP; MeLP; NAEL-5v1; NAEL-6v1; NAEL-7v1; NoP-4; OxAEP-1; OxBEV; SoSe-8; TFi

Dialogue between two shepherds, Thenot and Piers, in praise of Astræa. Mary Sidney Herbert, Countess of Pembroke. EMWP; NAEL-6v1

Dialogue betwixt God and the Soul, A. Sir Henry Wotton. MeLP; PeECV; SacPr

Dialogue betwixt Man, and Nature, A. Margaret Lucas Cavendish, Duchess of Newcastle. PBRV

Dialogue betwixt the Body and the Mind, A. Margaret Lucas Cavendish, Duchess of Newcastle. PEW

Dialogue betwixt Time and a Pilgrim[e], A. Aurelian Townshend [or Townsend]. NOBE; NPeEn; OxBEV

Dialogue: Lover and Lady. Ciullo d'Alcamo. AWP; EaItPo, tr. by Dante Gabriel Rossetti

Dialogue No. 5. Dmitry [or Dmitrii] Aleksandrovich Prigov. ItGoST, tr. by Robert Reid

Dialogue of Self and Soul, A. W. B. Yeats. FaBoMo; MoBrPo; NAEL-5v2; NAEL-6v2; NoAM; PoE

"Living man is blind and drinks his drop, A." RaBo

Dialogue of the Night of the Roses. Zuhur Dixon. MAP, tr. by Patricia Alanah Byrne and Salma Khadra Jayyusi

Dialogue of Thunder. Christine Hume. AmPoNex

Dialogue—2 Dollmakers. Gregory Corso. NeAP

Dialogue with Herz. Antonio Porta. ItPo, tr. by Gayle Ridinger

Dialogue with the Dead. Amelia Rosselli. PFTM-2, tr. by Lawrence R. Smith

Diameter of the Bomb Was Thirty Centimeters, The. Yehuda Amichai [or Amikhai]. PoSu

Diamond Cut Diamond. Ewart Milne. FaBoCh

Diamond of Character, The. Kabita Sinha. OMIP, tr. by Swapna Mitra

Diamonds Are a Girl's Best Friend. Leo Robin. ReLy

Diamonds are forever so I gave you quartz. Hardness Scale, The. Joyce Peseroff. TRP

Diamonds are mined. . .oil is discovered. Poem (for Langston Hughes), A. Nikki Giovanni. SSLK

Diana. Henry Constable.

("Deere to my soule, then leave me not forsaken.") NPeEn

"Hope, like the hyaena [or hyena], coming to be old." EnLoPo; SCGP; Son

"Miracle of the world, I never will deny." SCGP

"My lady's presence makes the roses red." NIL-7; NIP-4; OBGa

Of His Mistress, upon Occasion of Her Walking in a Garden. NIL-7; NIP-4; OBGa

"Resolved to love, unworthy to obtain." Son

"To live in hell, and heaven to behold." Son

"Uncivil sickness, hast thou no regard." OxBSo

Diana's Hunting-Song. Dryden. NOBE Fr. Secular Masque, The.

Diana was a white girl. What abou' de Law? Adam Small. PeSAV, tr. by Carrol Lasker

Dianae Sumus in Fide. Biancamaria Frabotta. CItWP, tr. by Cinzia Sartini Blum and Lara Trubowitz

Diane Arbus, New York. Nicole Cooley. AmPoNex

Diaphenia. Henry Constable. GTBS-P; NOBE

Diaries. Ben Scammell. NLP

Diary. Gerald Stern. OPRER

Diary. David Wagoner. CoAP

Diary. Mary Wilson. Spl

Diary, The. Goethe. STV, tr. by John Frederick Nims

Diary: How to Improve the World (You Will Only Make Matters Worse). John Cage.

Abundance. APSN

"Boddhisattva Doctrine: Enter / Nirvana only when all beings, sentient." APSN

"The / children have a society of their own." APSN

"Continue; I'll discover where you sweat (Kierkegaard)." PFTM-2

"Daily warmth we, The." APSN

"Get it, / she said, so it's unknown which parent." APSN

"Hearing of past actions." APSN

"Lazy dog (a bomb containing ten), The." APSN

"Let's Call It the / Collective Consciousness (We've Got)." APSN

"Mother wrote to say: 'Stay / in Europe. Soak up as much beauty as you.'" APSN

"Officials checked to make certain we'd." APSN

"Since the / Spirit's omnipresent, there's a difference." APSN

"They dance the world as." APSN

"To / know whether or not art is contemporary." APSN

"We've / poisoned our food, polluted our air." APSN

Diary of a Church Mouse. Sir John Betjeman. OxBTC

Diary of a Palestinian Wound. Mahmoud Darwish.

"We do not need to be reminded." MAP

Diary of an Old Soul. George Macdonald. TrCP

Diary of Beirut under Siege, 1982, The. "Adonis" [or "Adunis"]. PoetW Fr. Desert, The.

Diary Theme, The. Allen Fisher. Oth Fr. Emergent Manner.

Diaspora. S. V. Atalla. PoArWo

Diatribe against the Dead. Angel González. VCWP, tr. by Steven Ford Brown

Dibbukim (Dibbiks). Jerome Rothenberg. PFTM-2 Fr. Khurbn.

Dic Siôn Dayfydd. Thomas Jacob Thomas. OBWVE, tr. by H. Idris Bell

Dice of Love are, The. Anacreon. SaLy, tr. by Diane Rayor

Dick, a Maggot. Jonathan Swift. NBLV

Dick Briggs a wealthy farmer's son. Dick Briggs from Australia. Charles Robert Thatcher. NOBAu

Dick Briggs from Australia. Charles Robert Thatcher. NOBAu

Dick o' the Cow. Unknown. ESPB; IBB; OxBB

Dick Tracy's Yellow Hat. Peter Orlovsky. BB

Dickensian borough of Coketown, The. Limerick. Martin Fagg. PeLi

Dickery Dean. Dennis Lee. TLR

Dickery, dickery, dare. (LL) Mother Goose. OxNR; ReMoGo

Dickery [or dickory], dickery [or dickory], dare. Mother Goose. OxNR; ReMoGo

Dickinson. Anne Finch (b. 1908). FFC

Dictates of nature prove school-knowledge weak, The. Repentance. George Alexander Stevens. NOEC

Dictator, The. Lajos Kassák. IQMS, tr. by Paul Tabori

Dictators, The. Pablo Neruda. AF, tr. by Robert Bly

Dictée. Theresa Hak Kyung Cha.

Elitere Lyric Poetry. PFTM-2

Dictionary definition of change, The. Age of Plastic, The. John Forbes. BMAP

Dictum: For a Masque of Deluge. W. S. Merwin. YaYoPo

Did a wind come just as you got up or were. Dysraphism. Charles Bernstein. FTOS

Did all the lets and bars appear. March into Virginia, The. Herman Melville. HAP; NAAL-2v1; NCAP; PoE; TAP

Did but the law appoint us one. Popular Functionary, A. Charles Dibdin. NOEC

Did he have eyes and, if so, did he look. Martial. RomPo, tr. by Anthony Reid

Did he meet Lud at the Fleet Gate? did count the top. David Jones. EBEV Fr. Anathemata, The.

Did he strike soundings off Vecta Insula? David Jones. HarvBoo; NoAM Fr. Anathemata, The.

Did her skin smell. Of Woman Torn. Suheir Hammad. PoArWo

Did I boast of liberty? Mary Sidney Wroth, Countess of Montgomery. LW; PEW Fr. Urania.

Did I create that sky? Yes, for, if it was. Jack Kerouac. CLPP Fr. Scripture of the Golden Eternity, The.

Did I do it. Scrapping Limits. Salma Khadra Jayyusi. MAP, tr. by Charles Doria and the author

Did I evah tell you, Sonny. Uncle Jimmie's Yarn. Priscilla Jane Thompson. CBWP-2

Did I ever tell you that Mrs. McCave. Too Many Daves. "Dr. Seuss." OBCA; OxIBACP

Did I ever think. Var. authors. AWP Fr. Kokin Shu.

Did I follow Truth wherever she led. Edgar Lee Masters. OxBA Fr. Spoon River Anthology.

Did I go there enough? Was it enough when I tried. Clapping, The. Linda Gregg. BodElec

Did I, my lines intend for public[k] view. Introduction, The. Anne Finch, Countess of Winchilsea. BWW; EMWP; NAEL-5v1; NAEL-6v1; NAEL-7v1; NALW; WPOW

Did I not once have a pleasant childhood, heroic and fabulous, to be written on leaves of gold,—too much to ask! Morning. Arthur Rimbaud. SxFrPo, tr. by Martin Sorrell

Did I not say we grow old. Rufinus. GrAn

Did I not tell you, my soul, "By Cypris, you will be caught." Meleager. HePo Fr. Epigrams.

Did I step on your train? Before. May Probyn. VWP

Did it better: pathetic in bathtub, post-. Self-Portrait as Somebody Else. Laura Mullen. ExTi

Did it go wrong just about a hundred. Counter-Revolution. W. H. Oliver. PeNZ

Did it matter? They were only for me. (LL)   Kenneth Rexroth.   APSN; APT-2 *Fr.* Love Poems of Marichiko, The.

Did it once issue from the carver's hand.   W. H. Auden.   OxBSo   *Fr.* Voyage, A.

Did ivver ye see the like o' that?   Pride.   Violet Jacob.   OxBS

Did John's Music Kill Him?   Alfred B. Spellman.   NAAAL; SeSe

Did love him faithfully. (LL)   Uncle Ananias.   Edwin Arlington Robinson. MoAmPo; NIP-4

Did my father curse his father for his lust I wonder.   Young Man Thinks of Sons, The.   Ronald Allison Kells Mason.   PeNZ

Did Not.   Thomas Moore.   BoLoP; PeLV (Quantum Est Quod Desit.)   EnLoPo

Did not the heavenly rhetoric of thine eye.   William Shakespeare.   Son   *Fr.* Love's Labour's Lost.

Did Ophelia ask Hamlet to bed?   Limerick.   A. Cinna.   PeLi

Did Our Best Moment last.   Emily Dickinson.   NOBA

Did Shakespeare? If so, the less Shakespeare he! (LL)   House.   Robert Browning.   NAEL-5v2; NAEL-6v2

Did she drink tea? Yes, please. And after.   Star's Whole Secret, The.   Mary Jo Bang.   NAPBL

Did Shriner die or make it to New York?   Disappearance in West Cedar Street, A.   Louis Edward Sissman.   TwCP

Did / Somebody / Die? (LL)   World War II.   Langston Hughes.   APT-2; HCAP; PoPoPo

Did somebody give you a pat on the back?   Pass.   Edmund Vance Cooke. PWR

Did soon draw in again [or agen]. (LL)   Upon Her Feet.   Robert Herrick. BeJo; CaPo; OxBSP; PoE

Did the earth stretch out.   You, for My Meditation.   Sara de Ibáñez.   TCLAP, *tr. by* Andrew Rosing

Did the Harebell loose her girdle.   Emily Dickinson.   FaBoVe; NCAP

Did the people of Viet Nam.   What Were They Like?   Denise Levertov. HeIP-4; NIP-4; OBWP; PAI; VGW; WPE

Did the sun dip into the water this morning.   How the Tortoise Knew It Was Her Time.   Joan I. Siegel.   PoCoUp

Did the water splash me or did I dive in? I am dying to know. The truth.   Dive, The.   Mimi Goese.   HeMarv

Did then the bold slave rear at last the sword.   Robert Southey.   CenSon

Did they dare, did they dare, to slay Owen Roe O'Neil?   Lament for the Death of Eoghan Ruadh O'Neill.   Thomas Osborne Davis.   NOIV

Did they send me away from my cat and my wife.   Gunner.   Randall Jarrell. PAI

Did we not underwrite them when we were born? (LL)   Elegy for Minor Poets. Louis MacNeice.   CABP; PNI

Did ye ever hear o guid Earl o Bran.   Earl Brand.   *Unknown.*   ESPB

Did Ye See Me?   Robert Garioch.   OBCoV

Did yet inspire a cheer, which he forbore to check. (LL)   Byron.   NAEL-5v2; NAEL-6v2   *Fr.* Childe Harold's Pilgrimage.

Did you ask dulcet rhymes from me?   To a Certain Civilian.   Walt Whitman. CBCWP; FaBoWar

Did You Call Me, Father?   Mary E. Tucker.   CBWP-1

Did you eever iver ever.   Hand-clapping Rhyme.   *Unknown.*   NTCP

Did you eever, iver, over?   *Unknown.*   KaS

Did You Ever Cross Over to Sneden's.   Alec Wilder.   ReLy

Did you ever hear about Cocaine Lil?   Cocaine Lil [and Morphine Sue]. *Unknown.*   OxBoLi; RB

Did You Ever Hear an English Sparrow Sing?   Bertha Johnston.   ITBLP

Did you ever hear of Captain Wattle?   Captain Wattle and Miss Roe.   Charles Dibdin.   OxBoLi

Did you ever hear of Editor Whedon.   Edgar Lee Masters.   HAP; PoE   *Fr.* Spoon River Anthology.

Did you ever make some small success.   You Too.   Edmund Vance Cooke. PWR

Did you ever notice when a ride gets long.   Never Eat Oranges!   John Nelson. GeoH

Did you ever see someone cold-cock a blind nun?   Election Day, 1984. Carolyn Kizer.   ExTi; GifTon

Did you ever see the day.   On the Prince's Death, to the King.   Sir Robert Aytoun [or Ayton].   NOSC

Did you ever see two Yankees.   Give My Regards to Broadway.   George M. Cohan.   ReLy; TCAPo

Did you ever sit and ponder, sit and wonder, sit and think.   Life's a Funny Proposition after All.   George M. Cohan.   ReLy

Did you ever stop to figure that this very life we lead.   Nothing New Beneath the Sun.   George M. Cohan.   ReLy

Did you go at all to Chicago?   Stockyard, The.   Sir John Collings Squire. OxBTC

Did you go to the school by the river?   Did You Ever Cross Over to Sneden's. Alec Wilder.   ReLy

Did you hear of the curate who mounted his mare.   Thomas Love Peacock. OxAEP-2   *Fr.* Crotchet Castle.

Did you know it too all night long?   Expectation.   Ida G. M. Gerhardt.   TuT, *tr. by* Peter Van de Kamp

Did you like the city the water wrought drop by drop in the center of the pines? Federico García Lorca.   CAGL, *tr. by* David William Foster   *Fr.* Sonetos del Amor Oscuro [Sonnets of Dark Love].

Did you love well what very soon you left?   Marilyn Hacker.   NoAM   *Fr.* Coda.

Did you make your first journey? (LL)   Wild Goose, Wild Goose.   Issa. OHPJ; TTTS, *tr. by* Kenneth Rexroth

Did you run your fingers through your kids' hair? (LL)   For my Torturer, Lieutenant D.   Leila Djabali.   HAWP; WPOW, *tr. by* Anita Barrows

Did you say I've got a to learn?   Teach Me Tonight.   Sammy Cahn.   ReLy

Did you see him go by here tonight?   Stranger, The.   Aldo Palazzeschi. PFTM-1

Did you see me walking by the Buick Repairs?   Song.   Frank O'Hara.   TTTS

Did you see my wife, did you see, did you see.   *Unknown.*   OxNR

Did you tackle that trouble that came your way.   How Did You Die?   Edmund Vance Cooke.   PWR

Did you take me because you loved me?   Kenneth Rexroth.   APSN; APT-2 *Fr.* Love Poems of Marichiko, The.

Did you then celebrate.   Certain Questions for Monsieur Renoir.   John Ormond.   AngWePo

Did you wake me?   Encounter.   Rick Fournier.   PasH

Didactic Piece.   Louise Bogan.   NoAM

Didactic Poem on the Nature of History, A.D. 1954.   Helmut Heissenbüttel. PFTM-2, *tr. by* Jerome Rothenberg

Diddle, diddle, dumpling, my son John.   Mother Goose.   LB; OxNR; ReMoGo

Diddlety, diddlety, dumpty.   Mother Goose.   LB; OxNR

Didn't Chet Baker know.   Speed Ball.   Yusef Komunyakaa.   SeSe

Didn't He Ramble.   James Simmons.   PNI

Didn't like jazz, he once claimed.   William Carlos Williams.   Cornelius Eady. GT

Didn't My Lord Deliver Daniel?   *Unknown.*   AH; APN-2

Didn't think of the clasp.   Memory.   Robert Burns.   MoASP

Didn't we have a lovely evening?   Let's Put Out the Lights and Go to Sleep. Herman Hupfeld.   ReLy

Didn't you say we should trace.   Before Chilembwe Tree.   Jack A. Mapanje. PBMAP

Dido by Night.   Virgil [or Vergil].   OBVE, *tr. by* Henry Howard, Earl of Surrey   *Fr.* Aeneid [or Eneados, Aeneis], The.

Dido, Queen of Carthage.   Christopher Marlowe. "Grecian soldiers, tired with ten years' war."   FaBoWar

Dido's Suicide.   Virgil [or Vergil].   OBVE, *tr. by* Gawin [or Gavin] Douglas *Fr.* Aeneid [or Eneados, Aeneis], The.

Dido to Her Sister Anna.   Virgil [or Vergil].   OBVE, *tr. by* Henry Howard, Earl of Surrey   *Fr.* Aeneid [or Eneados, Aeneis], The.

Didst fettle for the great gray [or grey] drayhorse his bright and battering sandal! (LL)   Felix Randal.   Gerard Manley Hopkins.   EBEV; EBVV; FaBoMo; FaBoVe; GTBS-P; HAP; MoBrPo; NAEL-5v2; NAEL-6v2; NOBE; NoAM; NoP-4; OBEV; OxAEP-2; OxBSo; PeECV; PoE; PoRA; SCGP; Son; TFi; WeW-3; WoPoe

Didst thou not find the place inspired [or inspir'd].   Upon My Lady Carlisle's Walking in Hampton Court Garden.   Sir John Suckling.   BeJo; CaPo

Didyme waved an olive branch at me.   Asclepiades.   ErotSp, *tr. by* Sam Hamill

Didyme waved her wand at me.   Asclepiades.   GrAn; PGA, *tr. by* Kenneth Rexroth

Die blauen Veilchen der Äugelein.   Heinrich Heine.   AWP, *tr. by* James Thomson

Die, die my shriek, you will not be heard.   Die My Shriek.   Aaron Kushniroff. TrJP, *tr. by* Joseph Leftwich

Die Ego Self!   Drowning in the Last Days of Luxury.   Edwin Torres. HeMarv

Die is cast, and we must part, The.   Parting, The.   Josephine D. Henderson Heard.   CBWP-4

Die is cast, come weal, come woe, The.   Marriage.   Mary Weston Fordham. CBWP-2

Die Lotusblume ängstigt.   Heinrich Heine.   AWP, *tr. by* James Thomson

Die Musik, An.   David Malouf.   CBAP

Die My Shriek.   Aaron Kushniroff.   TrJP, *tr. by* Joseph Leftwich

DIE not before thy day, poor man condemned.   *Unknown.*   NoSic

Die oftener—Not so vitally. (LL)   Emily Dickinson.   NAAL-2v1; NAAL-3

Die, pussy, die.   *Unknown.*   OxNR

Die single, and thine image dies with thee. (LL)   William Shakespeare. NAEL-5v1; NAEL-6v1; NAEL-7v1; NoP-4; SCGP   *Fr.* Sonnets.

Die soon. (LL)   We Real Cool.   Gwendolyn Brooks.   AmFaPo; ESEAA; HAP; HHAm; HeIP-4; IllVoic; InPK-6; MakPoe; NAAAL; NAAL-5; NALW; PAI; PoE; RaBo; SoSe-8; TAP; TFi; TRP; TTY; WeW-3

Die while you're alive. Bunan. EnlH

Die, wild country, like the eaglehawk. Australia 1970. Judith Wright. CBAP; HarvBoo; MakPoe; NoAM

Die Zauberflöte. Rosamund Marriott Watson. ViWPN

Dieback. Elizabeth Dodd. UrbNat

Died. Elizabeth Barrett Browning. NOBVV

Died from fatigue, three laundresses together all. *Unknown.* FaBoEE

(Died once) must all be died again? (LL) Stephen to Lazarus. Clive Staples Lewis. ChIV-2; SacPr

Died, Sir Charles Wetherell's laundress, honest Sue. *Unknown.* FaBoEE

Diehards, The. Ruth Pitter. OBGa

Diella. Richard Lynche.
 Soon as the Azure-colored Gates. Son
 What Sugared Terms. Son

Dieppe. Samuel Beckett. NOIV

Dies IrÆ. Thomas Babington Macaulay, 1st Baron Macaulay. ChIV-2

Dies Irae. Thomas of Celano. AWP, *tr. by* Richard Crashaw
 (Day of Judgment, The.) OBVE

Dies Ire-Dies Pacis. John Oxenham. SacPr

Dies Merini. Alda Merini. CItWP, *tr. by* Cinzia Sartini Blum and Lara Trubowitz

Dies once for all; and sleep brings on eternal night. (LL) Torquato Tasso. AWP; OBVE, *tr. by* Leigh Hunt *Fr.* Aminta.

Diesel fumes rise. Dinner on the Miami River. Greg Pape. PBCAP

Diesel to Yesterday. John Tripp. AngWePo

Diesel trucks past the Scrovegni chapel. Ian Wedde. PeNZ *Fr.* Earthly: Sonnets for Carlos.

Diet. John Armstrong. VerBaPo *Fr.* Art of Preserving Health, The.

Diet, The. Maureen Burge. BrRo

Dieter bit his sealskin mitts, and pulled. Bush Navigator: The Last Morning of Hands. Peggy Shumaker. PBCAP

Dieu Qu'il la Fait. Charles, Duc d' Orléans. AWP, *tr. by* Ezra Pound

Difference. T. Harri Jones. OBWVE

Difference. János Pilinszky. IQMS, *tr. by* Peter Jay

Difference, The. Elizabeth Delmore. NLP

Difference, The. Jackie Hardy. NeBl

Difference, The. Stoddard King. OBAL

Difference, The. Tadhg Dall O'Huiginn. BIrV, *tr. by* Robin Flower

Difference between a King and a Tyrant, The. Timothy Kendall. NoSic

Difference between Despair, The. Emily Dickinson. NAAL-2v1; NAAL-3; TCAPo

Difference between Night and Day, The. Bin Ramke. YaYoPo

Difference between Pepsi and Coke, The. David Lehman. PmAP; ReTh

Difference between poetry and rhetoric, The. Power. Audre Lorde. GLP; NoAM

Difference between you and me, The. Half-Breed. Cherríe Moraga. UnSA

Difference betwixt King and Subjects, The. Robert Herrick. BASC

Difference of Zoos, A. Gregory Corso. VGW

Difference to me!, The. (LL) Jacob. Phoebe Cary. APN-2; OBAL

Difference to me, The. (LL) William Wordsworth. AWP; BoLoP; EnLoPo; GTBS-P; HAP; HeIP-4; NAEL-6v2; NIL-7; NIP-4; NPeEn; OxAEP-2; OxBSP; PAI; PWR; UV; UnPo; WeW-3 *Fr.* Lucy.

Differences between rich and poor, king and queen. Rank. Lincoln Kirstein. FaBoA; OBWP

Different. Marga Kool. TuT, *tr. by* Joan McBreen

Different. Clere Parsons. FaBoTw

Different History, A. Sujata Bhatt. HarvBoo

Different Horizon. Aimé Césaire. VCWP

Different Image, A. Dudley Randall. BPo; TAP

Different Love Poem, A / We Need a Change. Ntozake Shange. UnSA *Fr.* Okra to Greens.

Different Morning Altogether, A. Dima Hilal. PoArWo

Different Ones #6—Future Possibilities (An AIDS Soliloquy). Viki Akiwumi. InTrad

Different Poem, A. Onésima Silveira. PBMAP

Different Ship, A. Pablo Neruda. WoPoe, *tr. by* Ben Belitt

Different sky, A. Sail Away. Noël Coward. ReLy

Different Strokes Bar, San Francisco, The. Forrest Hamer. GeoHom

Different task remains; the secret paths, A. Mark Akenside. NOEC *Fr.* Pleasures of Imagination, The.

Different Voice, The. Frieda Hughes. NeBl

Difficult Adjustment, A. Lauris Edmond. FaBoWP

Difficult and Weighty Question, A. Janus Pannonius. IQMS, *tr. by* Adam Makkai

Difficult Body. Mark Wunderlich. NAPBL

Difficult Music, The. Reginald Shepherd. NeAmPo

Difficult Rhyme, A. Mother Goose. OxNR; ReMoGo

Difficult to manage. (LL) Broagh. Seamus Heaney. FaBoVe; ModIr; NPeEn

Difficult to say what all of this is all about. Poor Boy: Portrait of a Painting. John Ash. HarvBoo

Difficult verse I dislike that comes hard, and the easy writ easy. Hard and Easy. Ferenc Kazinczy. IQMS, *tr. by* Watson Kirkconnell

Difficult with You. Anna Cascella. CItWP, *tr. by* Cinzia Sartini Blum and Lara Trubowitz

Difficulties at Love. *Vietnamese Oral Tradition.* CaDao, *tr. by* John Balaban

Difficulties, the impossibilities, The. Robert Lowell. HCAP *Fr.* Mexico.

Difficulty to think at the end of day, The. Rabbit Is King of the Ghosts, A. Wallace Stevens. NoAM; TTTS

Diffugere Nives. Horace. *See* Odes

Diffugere Nives. A. E. Housman. AmFaPo

Digestive System, The. Sir Richard Blackmore. ECEV *Fr.* Creation.

Digger's Song, The. Barcroft Henry Boake. NOBAu

Digger's Song, The. Gerrard Winstanley. BASC; NOSC

Diggers, The. W. S. Merwin. SPE

Diggers' Song, The. *Unknown.* PBRV

Digging. Seamus Heaney. BIrV; CIP-2; NAEL-5v2; NAEL-6v2; NoP-4; SpudSo; TwCP

Digging. Edward Thomas. MoBrPo; OxBTC

Digging and building tire men out. Poem of the Western Fields. Wu Wei-yeh. CoBLCP, *tr. by* Jonathan Chaves

Digging deep in the garden. Planting Roses. Phillis Levin. FFC

Digging earth for puddles, she would wake stranded. Steps. Roberta Hill Whiteman. VoR

Digging for China. Richard Wilbur. TwCP

Digging for Indians. Gary Gildner. PBCAP

Digging in the Streets of Gold. Barry Seiler. UnSA

Digging Out the Buddha Relic. Muso Soseki. EaWin, *tr. by* W. S. Merwin

Digging Potatoes. Colette Inez. SpudSo

Digging Potatoes, 1950. Stanley Plumly. SpudSo

Digging Sing, A. *Unknown.* FaBoVe

Digging Soil. Peter Gruffydd. AngWePo

Digging / toward a Lenten extreme. Year. Milo De Angelis. NeIt, *tr. by* Lawrence Venuti

Digging up weeds by the little hedge. Elaine Randell. Oth

Digging was always my worst work. Grandfather in the Garden. Robert Minhinnick. OBGa

Diggins-Oh, The. *Unknown.* NOBAu

Dignity of Labor, The. Robert Bersohn. NBLV

Dignity of room, the value of rareness, The. (LL) November Surf. Robinson Jeffers. NAAL-2v2; OxBA

Dih dred ded. Mih Feel It. Ahdri Zhina Mandiela. WaCA

Dike, a flower bed, a bare linden tree, A. Igor Khomin. TCRusP, *tr. by* Daniel Weissbort

Dilana and Diram. Saleem Barakat. MAP, *tr. by* Lena Jayyusi and Naomi Shihab Nye *Fr.* Crane, The.

Dilemma. Patricia Beer. OxBC

Dilemma. Phoebe Hesketh. Prnts

Dilemma. David Ignatow. VGW

Dilemma, The. Sir John Collings Squire. OBCoV
 ('Good God!' said God, 'I've got my work cut out.') (LL) OBCoV

Dilemma of the Elm. Genevieve Taggard. MoAmPo

Diligent in the burnt fields above the sea. Find. Josephine Miles. WPE

Dillar, a dollar, A. Ten o'Clock Scholar, [The]. Mother Goose. LB; OxNR; ReMoGo

Dilly Dilly. *Unknown.* OxNR

Dilly Dilly Piccalilli. Clyde Watson. NTCP

Dim afternoon December afternoon. December. Robert Francis. LCAP-2

Dim apparition thou!—and bitter in my tear. (LL) Eyam. Anna Seward. ECWP; RWP

Dim, as the borrow'd beams of moon and stars. Dryden. BASC; NOSC *Fr.* Religio Laici.

Dim boy claps because the others clap, The. Freaks at Spurgin Road Field, The. Richard Hugo. LCAP-2; NoAM; SoSe-8

Dim burnt the lamp, and now the phantom Death. Philip Freneau. TCAPo *Fr.* House of Night, The.

Dim dawn behind the tamarisks—the sky is saffron-yellow. Christmas in India. Rudyard Kipling. ChrPo

Dim grey wastes of the silent hills. Helen Waddell. MLL

Dim light of daybreak now. Dawn Wail for the Dead. Oodgeroo of the tribe Noonuccal (Kath Walker). BMAP; CBAP

Dim Light Splits the Woods in Two Distinct Lines, The. Biancamaria Frabotta. CItWP, *tr. by* Cinzia Sartini Blum and Lara Trubowitz

Dim the light in your faces: be passionless in the room. Image, The. Richard Hughes. OBMV

Dim vales—and shadowy floods.   Fairyland [*or* Fairy-Land].   Edgar Allan Poe.   APN-1; NAAL-2v1; NAAL-3

Dim wind pillared the hills: stiller than mist it seemed.   Sunrise Trumpets.   Joseph Auslander.   TrJP

Dime after Dime.   Mary Weems.   SpirFl

Dime for Jesus who had died for men, A. (LL)   Karma.   Edwin Arlington Robinson.   APT-1; HeIP-4; MoAmPo; TrCP

Dime store. The goldfish swam in the murky.   Kite.   Laura Jensen.   LCAP-2

Dimensions.   Laura Riding Jackson.   FuPo

Diminutive.   Carlos Drummond de Andrade.   TCLAP, *tr. by* Virginia de Araújo

Diminutive.   Nancy Steele.   GifTon

Dimme eyes, deaf ears, cold stomach shew.   Verses Found in Thomas Dudley's Pocket after His Death.   Thomas Dudley.   SCAP

Dimming her lonely visions of despair. (LL)   Sonnet: "Now the bat circles on the breeze of eve."   Ann Radcliffe.   CenSon; WPE

Dimpling its tranquil surface. (LL)   Charlotte Smith.   NOBRP; NoP-4   *Fr.* Beachy Head.

Dimply damsel, sweetly smiling.   Ode: To Miss Margaret Pulteney.   Ambrose Philips.   OxAEP-1; UV

Din of work is subdued, The.   Lullaby.   W. H. Auden.   FaBoMo; GLP; NoAM

Din quiets, The. I step onto the boards.   Hamlet.   Boris Leonidovich Pasternak.   GI; WoPoe, *tr. by* Nina Kossman

Din / who am i floating.   Dedication.   Rochelle Owens.   PFTM-2

Dinah.   Joe Young.   ReLy

Dinah Kneading Dough.   Paul Laurence Dunbar.   NAAAL

Dinakdakan.   Maria Luisa B. Aguilar-Cariño.   ReBoTo

Dinas Emrys.   Brian Morris.   AngWePo

Dined with Auden. He'd been at Milwaukee.   Auden at Milwaukee.   Stephen Spender.   AiP

Diners in the Kitchen, The.   James Whitcomb Riley.   OBAL

Ding dang, bell rang.   *Unknown.*   OxNR

Ding ding ding!   Esanzo.   Antoine-Roger Bolamba.   NegPo, *tr. by* Ellen Conroy Kennedy

Ding, dong, bell. (LL)   William Shakespeare.   NAEL-5v1; NoSic; SCGP; TFi   *Fr.* Merchant of Venice, The.

Ding, dong, bell, / Pussy's in the well.   Mother Goose.   OxBEV; OxNR; ReMoGo

Ding-Donging.   Laura Riding Jackson.   NoP-4

Dingle dingle doosey.   *Unknown.*   OxNR

Dingty diddlety.   Mother Goose.   FaBoVe; OxNR

Dingy donkey, formal and unchanged, A.   Fable, A.   John Hookham Frere.   UV

Dining Out.   Judith Beveridge.   BMAP

Dining-Room Tea.   Rupert Brooke.   MoBrPo

Dink's Song.   *Unknown.*   OxBoLi

Dinky.   Theodore Roethke.   OBAL; OBCA; OxIBACP

Dinky Di.   *Unknown.*   NOBAu

Dinna bathir wi thi braiggil o wir lends.   Coco-de-Mer.   W. N. Herbert.   NePenScot

Dinner, The.   Rosario Morales.   PueRic

Dinner at Le Caprice.   Rachel Wetzsteon.   RA

Dinner at the Hotel de la Tigresse Verte.   Donald Evans.   TCAPo

Dinner for the Devil.   Ben Jonson.   NOSC   *Fr.* Gypsies Metamorphosed, The.

Dinner Guest: Me.   Langston Hughes.   BPo; LTA; SSLK

Dinner in the Sun.   Donald Berger.   NAPBL

Dinner on the Miami River.   Greg Pape.   PBCAP

"Dinner-time?" said Gilbert White.   Edmund Clerihew Bentley.   OBCoV   *Fr.* Clerihews.

Dinner Together.   Diana Rivera.   InvLad

Dinner was over, the tablecloth gone, The.   Poem on the Supposition of the Book Having Been Published and Read, A.   Elizabeth Hands.   ECWP; WoRP

Dino.   Michael Lassell.   GLP   *Fr.* Times Square Poems.

Dinogad's Petticoat.   *Unknown.*   OBWVE; RB, *tr. by* Gwyn Williams

Dinogad's smock is pied, pied.   Song to a Child.   *Unknown.*   WoPoe, *tr. by* Anthony Conran

Dinogon.   Michael Portnoy.   HeMarv

Dinosaurs.   Valerie Worth.   NTCP

Dinosaurs are not all dead, The.   Steam Shovel.   Charles Malam.   NTCP

Diodorus the hunchback / Went to Socles the quack.   Nicarchus of Alexandria.   GrAn

Diogenes.   Morris Gilbert Bishop.   NBLV

Diogenes.   Arthur Rex Dugard Fairburn.   PeNZ

Diogenes, that wise old bird.   Complete Cynic, The.   Keith Preston.   NBLV

Diomede Mourns His Fate and That of His Friends to the Latian Ambassador Who Seeks His Alliance against Aeneas.   Virgil [*or* Vergil].   OBVE, *tr. by* John Dryden   *Fr.* Aeneid [*or* Eneados, *Aeneis*], The.

Dion.   Plato.   GrAn, *tr. by* Peter Jay

Dion of Tarsus.   *Unknown.*   AWP, *tr. by* Alma Strettell

Dionysiaca.   Nonnus.

Carpos and Calamos.

"But Dionysos had no healing physic for his comrade fallen, of dancing he thought no more."   CAGL, *tr. by* W. H. D. Rouse

"Eros came near in the horned shape of a shaggy Silenos."   CAGL, *tr. by* W. H. D. Rouse

"Where Carpos wandered and died, I will fall headlong."   CAGL, *tr. by* W. H. D. Rouse

Dionysus and Ampelos.   CAGL, *tr. by* W. H. D. Rouse

Dionysus.   Genrik Veniaminovich Sapgir.   ItGoST, *tr. by* J. Kates

Dionysus as Psychiatrist.   Robert Pinsky.   HCAP   *Fr.* Essay on Psychiatrists.

Diophon, seeing / another man.   Lucilius.   GrAn

Dioramacist does not know, The.   Museum of the Second Creation, The.   Sandra McPherson.   LCAP-2

Dip down upon the northern shore.   Tennyson.   EBVV; NAEL-6v2   *Fr.* In Memoriam A. H. H.

Dip your head in the basin & go.   Shakin All Over.   John James.   Oth

Diphthongs are honey, the dentals are resin, The.   Learning the Language.   Brewster Ghiselin.   APT-2

Dipped now in Ocean, the She-Bear's stellar guardian.   Ovid.   RomPo, *tr. by* Peter Green   *Fr.* Tristia.

Dipping into Death like a soup. (LL)   Dreamed Realization, A.   Gregory Corso.   NeAP; PoM; VGW

Dipsychus [and the Spirit].   Arthur Hugh Clough.

How Pleasant It Is to Have Money.   NOBE; NOBVV; OxBoLi

I Dreamt a Dream.   NAEL-5v2; NAEL-6v2

Public Garden, The.   PeLV

"Scene is different, and the place, The."   PeVV

Temptation.   PeLV

There Is No God.   CABP; NAEL-5v2; NOBE; NOBVV; NPeEn; NoP-4; OxBEV; SacPr

Dipt by itself, and we were glad at heart. (LL)   Tennyson.   NOBVV; PeVV

Diptych.   Birago Diop.   NegPo, *tr. by* Ellen Conroy Kennedy

(Sun hung by a thread, The.)   PBMAP

Diptych: Jesus and the Stone.   Charles Baxter.   BBASP

Dirce.   Walter Savage Landor.   AWP; CTC; EBEV; FaBoEE; HAP; NAEL-6v2; NOBE; NPeEn; NoP-4; OBEV; OxAEP-2; OxBEV; OxBSP; PoRA; SCGP; TFi; WeW-3; WoPoe   *Fr.* Pericles and Aspasia.

Dire one and desired one.   Ode to Meaning.   Robert Pinsky.   MakPoe

Direct address to the swans: you, whose feet.   You, Failed Pronoun.   Eleanor Wilner.   ExTi

Direction.   Barbara Guest.   WPE

Direction.   Roberta Hill Whiteman.   CDW

Directions, The.   Christopher Gilbert.   GT

Directions for Dreamfishing.   Martin Johnston.   CBAP

Directions in Our Blood.   Barney Bush.   HATNAP

Directions that you took.   Old Haven.   Jean Garrigue.   WPE

Directions to the Nomad.   James Welch.   CDW

Directive.   Robert Frost.   APT-1; ColAP; HAP; MakPoe; MoAmPo; NAAL-2v2; NOBA; NoAM; NoP-4; PoE; SAmP; TFi

Director, The.   Edmund George Valpy Knox.   OBCoV

Dirge.   Thomas Lovell Beddoes.   NOBVV; OxBEV   *Fr.* Death's Jest Book.

Fidele.   William Shakespeare.   *See* Cymbeline

Dirge of Love.   William Shakespeare.   *See* Twelfth Night

Dirge.   William Shakespeare.   *See* Twelfth Night

Dirge.   James Shirley.   AWP; NoP-4   *Fr.* Contention of Ajax and Ulysses, The.

Dirge.   Sir Philip Sidney.   *See* Dirge: "Ring out your bells [*or* belles], let mourning shows [*or* shewes] be spread."

Dirge, A.   George Croly.   SacPr

Dirge, A.   John Webster.   *See* White Devil, The

Dirge, A: "Rough wind, that moanest loud."   Shelley.   NAEL-5v2; NOBE; PoRA; SCGP

Dirge, A: "Why were you born when the snow was falling?"   Christina Georgina Rossetti.   EBVV; NOBVV; OxBEV; SCGP

Dirge: "Body lies under the ground."   Gavin Bantock.   OxBTC

Dirge: "Calm on the bosom of thy God."   Felicia Dorothea Hemans.   OBEV   *Fr.* Siege of Valencia, The.

Dirge for a Hidden Art.   Mary Duroux.   IBA

Dirge for Fidele.   William Shakespeare.   AWP; ClHu; EBEV; GTBS-P; HAP; NAEL-5v1; NOBE; NoSic; OxAEP-1; PAI; PoRA; RB; SCGP; SCV; SoSe-8; TFi   *Fr.* Cymbeline.

Dirge for McPherson, A.   Herman Melville.   CBCWP

Dirge for the Living.   Rosalie Moore.   YaYoPo

Dirge for the New Sunrise.   Dame Edith Sitwell.   MoBrPo   *Fr.* Three Poems of the Atomic Bomb.

Dirge for the Ninth of Ab. *Unknown.* TrJP, *tr.* by Nina Davis Salaman

Dirge for Three Trumpets. *Unknown.* SPE

Dirge for Two Veterans. Walt Whitman. APN-1; BLT; CBCWP; MoAmPo

Dirge: "From a friend's friend I taste friendship." Stevie Smith. HarvBoo; NPeEn

Dirge: "Her house is become like a man dishonored." Bible, Apocrypha. TrJP *Fr.* First Maccabees.

Dirge: "I make this dirge for you Miss Mary Binning I miss you." *Unknown.* BoWoP, *tr.* by Armand Schwerner

Dirge: "I reached the middle of the mount." Ralph Waldo Emerson. TCAPo

Dirge in "Cymbeline." William Collins. *See* Fidele, A

Dirge in Jazz Time. Vassar Miller. FFC

Dirge in Woods. George Meredith. NAEL-5v2; NAEL-6v2; OBEV

Dirge: "It is harm to me and anguish." Mary Macleod (Màiri Nighean Alasdair Ruaidh). EMWP

Dirge of Jephthah's Daughter, The. Robert Herrick. ChIV-1

Dirge of St. Malo, The. George Washington Cable. APN-2

Dirge of the Three Queens. John Fletcher. OBEV *Fr.* Two Noble Kinsmen, The.

Dirge: "1-2-3 was the number he played but today the number came 3-2-1." Kenneth Fearing. APT-2; NIL-7; NIP-4; PoRA; RB; TrJP

Dirge: "Ring out your bells [*or* belles], let mourning shows [*or* shewes] be spread." Sir Philip Sidney. NoSic; OxAEP-1

  (Litany, A: "Ring out your bells") SCGP; UnPo

  (Ring Out Your Bells.) NoP-4

Dirge: "Stay, Death. Not mine the Christus-wand." Herman Melville. APN-1; NCAP *Fr.* Clarel: A Poem and Pilgrimage in the Holy Land.

Dirge: "Weep, weep, ye woodmen, wail." Anthony Munday. CTC *Fr.* Death of Robert, Earl of Huntingdon.

Dirge without Music. Edna St. Vincent Millay. AmFaPo

Dirigible, The. Chris Wallace-Crabbe. CBAP

Dirt and / clean them clean them clean them. Streetcleaner's Lament, The. Patricia Hubbell. SSCS

Dirt of my flesh, defeated, underground. (LL) At the Executed Murderer's Grave. James Wright (1927–80). HCAP; VCAP

Dirt road, A. Robert Spiess. HA

Dirt to Dirt. Hugh Seidman. BodElec

Dirtiest, downstream of Team, The. Grey Wagtail on the Tyne. Colin Simms. Oth

Dirtiest Man in the World, The. Shel [*or* Shelley] Silverstein. OBCA

Dirty Dreams and God Smiling. Alane Rollings. IllVoic

Dirty English Potatoes. X. J. Kennedy. SpudSo

Dirty Floor, The. Edward Field. *See* Floor Is Dirty, The

Dirty girl, / Thumb stump. (LL) Cut. Sylvia Plath. EmeKit; TAP

Dirty Little Accuser, The. Norman Cameron. OxBS

Dirty Money. Christine Hume. AmPoNex

Dirty money and the sleazy hearts, The. Matadors, The. Josephine Jacobsen. TAP

Dirty Niggers. Jacques Roumain. NegPo, *tr.* by Ellen Conroy Kennedy

Dirty tears are falling. (LL) Walking Around. Pablo Neruda. RaBo; SPE

Dirty word hops in the cage of the mind like the Pondicherry vulture, The. Dirty Word, The. Karl Shapiro. CoAP; inPK-6

Dîs Aliter Visum; or, Le Byron de Nos Jours. Robert Browning. NAEL-5v2; NAEL-6v2

Dis is gospel weathah sho' Song of Summer. Paul Laurence Dunbar. APN-2

Dis is one recitation. Language. Marc Matthews. WaCA

Dis sun are hot. This Sun Is Hot. *Unknown.* BPo

Disabled. Wilfred Owen. FaBoWar; NAEL-5v2; NAEL-6v2; NIL-7; NoAM; OBWVE; OxBTC; PeFWW; PoPoPo; SCGP

Disabled Debauchee, The. John Wilmot, 2d Earl of Rochester. BASC; BoLoP; HAP; NAEL-5v1; NAEL-6v1; NAEL-7v1; NOBL; NPeEn; NoP-4; OBSV

  (Maim[e]'d Debauchee, The.) SCGP

Disabled garment worker, The. In the Age of Postcapitalism. Lawrence Joseph. PBCAP

Disappearance in West Cedar Street, A. Louis Edward Sissman. TwCP

Disappeared Woman V. Marjorie Agosin. TANSG, *tr.* by Cola Franzen

Disappearing Island, The. Seamus Heaney. BodElec

Disappointed Wife, The. Mehetabel Wright. *See* Address to Her Husband

Disappointment. Mary E. Tucker. CBWP-1

Disappointment, A. Joanna Baillie. NOEC; WoRP

Disappointment, The. Aphra Behn. BASC; EMWP; EroLit; NAEL-7v1; NALW; NOSC; PEW

Disarmed with so genteel an air. Answer, The. Anne Finch, Countess of Winchilsea. NAEL-7v1; NALW; NoP-4

Disarticulated / arm torn out. Last Affair: Bessie's Blues Song. Michael S. Harper. ESEAA; HCAP; LCAP-2

Disaster. Charles Stuart Calverley. NBLV

Disaster, The. Mary Savage. ECWP

Disaster frowned. Martyr, The. Ibrahim Tuqan. MAP, *tr.* by John Heath-Stubbs and Lena Jayyusi

Disaster has struck the people. Tune: "Decorous and Pretty"—Respectfully Offered to Circuit Inspector Kao. Liu Chih. SuSp, *tr.* by Richard John Lynn

Disaster to Steamer Victoria at London. James McIntyre. VerBaPo

Disasterology. Jeffrey McDaniel. NeAmPo

Disasters. George Oppen. BodElec

Disasters come not singly. Disasters. Henry Wadsworth Longfellow. TreFP

Disasters numb within us, The. Life at War. Denise Levertov. VGW

Disbelief in Yourself Is Indispensable. Yevgeny Aleksandrovich Yevtushenko [*or* Evtushenko]. TCRP, *tr.* by Albert C. Todd

Discerns in speechless tears, both prayer and praise. (LL) Bereavement. Elizabeth Barrett Browning. SacPr; WPE

Discharge me? No! He knew I did just right. (LL) Code, The. Robert Frost. OBNV; UnPo

Disciples Asleep at Gethsemane. Paul Kane. GI

Discipline. Mary Ursula Bethell. PoBW

Discipline. George Herbert. FHYEP; FSCP; GeHe; MeLP; NAEL-5v1; NAEL-6v1; NAEL-7v1; NOBE; NOCV; NoP-4; OBEV; OxAEP-1; PAI

Disconcerting Object. J. Bernlef. TuT, *tr.* by Peter Van de Kamp

Disconnections. Silvana Colonna. ItPo, *tr.* by Gayle Ridinger

Disconsolate I / from the thinning line. Witness to Death. Richmond Lattimore. VGW

Disconsolate Morning. Elizabeth Madox Roberts. APT-1

Discontent, The. Anne Killigrew. BASC

Discontented Student, The. St. George Tucker. OBAL

Discontents in Devon. Robert Herrick. BeJo; CaPo; OxBSP

Discord in Childhood. D. H. Lawrence. HarvBoo

Discordants. Conrad Potter Aiken.

  (Bread and Music.) MoAmPo

  Music I Heard. AWP; NOBA; OxBA; PoRA

Discords. Fabio Doplicher. NeIt, *tr.* by Dana Gioia

Discourse of Beasts, A. Margaret Lucas Cavendish, Duchess of Newcastle. BASC; PEW

Discourse of Melancholy, A. Margaret Lucas Cavendish, Duchess of Newcastle. NOSC

Discourse of the Good Thief, The. Nicanor Parra. GI, *tr.* by Miller Williams

Discourse on Colonialism. Aime Cesaire.

  "How did you come to develop the concept of Negritude?" PFTM-1

Discourse on Method, The. Heberto Padilla. VCWP

Discourse on Peace, The. Jacques Prévert. CLPP, *tr.* by Lawrence Ferlinghetti

Discover Me. Opal Palmer Adisa. GT

Discover my home. (LL) Lal Ded [*or* Lalla]. BoWoP; WPoS

Discovered in Mid-Ocean. Stephen Spender. MoBrPo

  (Airman.) UV

Discoverer. James Michie. DiPo

Discoveries, Trade Names, Genitals, and Ancient Instruments. Carl Rakosi. APT-2

Discovering Lasseter. Conal Fitzpatrick. NOBAu

Discovery. Joseph Hilaire Pierre Belloc. OxBSP

Discovery. Gu Cheng. PFTM-2; VCWP, *tr.* by Eva Hung *Fr.* Bulin File, The.

Discovery. Brian Henry. AmPoNex

Discovery. Víctor Hernández Cruz. PueRic

Discovery. Benjamin Keech. PoToHe

Discovery. Hilda Schiff. HP

Discovery. Zhao Zhenkai. VCWP, *tr.* by Chen Maiping and Bonnie S. McDougall

Discovery, The. Gwendolyn MacEwen. NOBC

Discovery of America, The. James Logie Robertson. NOBVV; NePenScot

Discovery of LSD a True Story, The. Anselm Hollo. PoM

Discovery of the New World. Carter Revard. SoSe-8; VoR

Discovery of the Pacific, The. Thom Gunn. HeIP-4

Discovery of Thought, A. Wallace Stevens. APT-1

Discredited for some time to come. (LL) War Has Been Given a Bad Name. Bertolt Brecht. HP; PoSu

Discreet, not cryptic. I write to you from the garden. Message, A. Fleur Adcock. DiPo

Discreet Prayer, A. Dionisio D. Martinez. TouFir

Discrete Series. George Oppen. APT-2; PFTM-1

Discriminator, The. Vernon Scannell. OxBC

Discussing divorce. Alexis Rotella. HA

Disdain Punished. Dryden. EBNV; NOSC *Fr.* Theodore and Honoria, From [Fables Ancient and Modern from] Boccace.

Disdain Returned. Thomas Carew. BASC; BeJo; CavPo

True Beauty, The.   GTBS-P

Disdained Apparitions.   René Char.   AF, *tr.* by Paul Mann

Disdains to crop a weed, and will not come. (LL)   Madrigal: "My thoughts hold mortal[l] strife."   William Drummond, of Hawthornden.   GTBS-P; NOSC; OxBSP

Disease with floating moustaches, The.   Lovely Monster.   Joyce Mansour.   SurWo, *tr.* by Guy Flandre and Peter Wood

Diseases of Bath; a Satire, The.   *Unknown.*
   "If to the Pump Room in the morn we go."   NOEC

Disembarking at Quebec.   Margaret Atwood.   PoE

Disembodied Voices of Women, The.   Craig Arnold.   NAPBL

Disentangling our lives.   X-Ray, The.   Andrew Elliott.   PNI

Disfigure me, Lord. Take pity on me.   Antipsalm.   Novica Tadic.   VCWP, *tr.* by Charles Simic

Disfortune.   Joe Wenderoth.   AmPoNex

Disgrace.   David Hall.   CDa

Disguised.   Martha Rhodes.   UrbNat

Disguised as a mutant.   Stage and Screen, 1989.   Carol Muske.   BodElec

Disguised in my mouth as a swampland.   In the Morning.   Jayne Cortez.   BlSi

Disguises.   Thomas Edward Brown.   SacPr

Disgusted with.   Goshu.   JDP, *tr.* by Yoel Hoffmann

Disgusted with crimes that are piffling and messy.   Crime at Its Best.   Stoddard King.   NBLV

Dis[h], a dis[h], a green grass, A.   Green Grass.   *Unknown.*   OxBoLi; OxNR

Dish for a Poet, A.   *Unknown.*   OBCP

Disillusion.   Maureen Burge.   BrRo

Disillusion.   Bessie B. Decker.   PoToHe

Disillusion for Rubén Darío.   Nancy Morejón.   TCLAP, *tr.* by Kathleen Weaver

Disillusion with the French Revolution.   Charlotte Smith.   ECWP   *Fr.* Emigrants, The.

Disillusionment.   Virginia Graham.   NBLV

Disillusionment of Ten o'Clock.   Wallace Stevens.   APT-1; NAAL-2v2; NoAM; OxBA; PAI; RB; SAmP; SoSe-8; TCAPo; TRP; TTTS

Disinherited, The.   Charles Spear.   PeNZ

Disintegrate Me.   Denise Riley.   Oth   *Fr.* Seven Strangely Exciting Lies.

Disintegration.   Richard Kostelanetz.   InPK-6

Disjecta Membra.   Charles Wright.   BAP-97

Disloyal Lines to an Alumnus.   Edmund Wilson.   OBCoV

Dismantled Ship, The.   Walt Whitman.   OxBA; TCAPo

Dismissal of the Koyemshi.   *Zuni Oral Tradition.*   NAWM-7v2, *tr.* by Ruth L. Bunzel   *Fr.* Shalako.

Dismissed as plink plonk. I can't stand.   Webern.   Christopher Pilling.   NLP

Dismissing Progress and Its Progenitors.   George Reavey.   SPE

Dismissing reports and men, he put pressure on the.   Geoffrey Hill.   HAP   *Fr.* Mercian Hymns.

Dismount and drink this wine.   To See a Friend Off.   Wang Wei.   ChinPo, *tr.* by Yip Wai-lim

Dismounting, I offer you wine.   Seeing Someone Off.   Wang Wei.   SuSp, *tr.* by Irving Y. Lo

Disobedience.   Alan Alexander Milne.   NOxBChV; NTCP; OTCP; TLR; UV

Disorder, The.   Marilyn Chin.   LoL

Disorder and Frailty.   Henry Vaughan.   ChIV-1

Disown.   Rae Armantrout.   FTOS

Dispatch this note to our hero at once. (LL)   After the Broken Arm.   Ron Padgett.   CoAmPo; SPE

Dispensary, The.   Sir Samuel Garth.   OBSV
   "As bold Mirmillo the grey dawn descries."   ECEV

Display thy breasts, my Julia.   Upon Julia's Breasts.   Robert Herrick.   CaPo

Disposition No. 1.   Shafiq Al-Kamali.   MAP, *tr.* by Sargon Boulus and Christopher Middleton

Dispossessed, The.   John Berryman.   VGW

Dispossessed, The.   Thomas Kinsella.   NOCV

Dispossessions.   Jane Cooper.   FaBoWP

Dispraise of Absalom, The.   *Unknown.*   BIrV, *tr.* by Robin Flower

Disproportionate.   Timothy Geiger.   AmPoNex

Disputation with Kahlil Gibran, A.   Eugene Paul Nasser.
   "Arab woman is wailing in the parlor, The."   GraLe

Dispute between Women, A.   *Unknown.*   STP, *tr.* by Tom Lowenstein

Dispute of the Heart and Body of François Villon, The.   François Villon.   AWP; OBVE, *tr.* by Algernon Charles Swinburne

Dispute over Suicide, A.   *Unknown.*   TTY, *tr.* by T. Eric Peet

Disquieting Muses, The.   Sylvia Plath.   NALW

Disquieting muses again: what are "leftovers?", The.   Business Personals.   John Ashbery.   BodElec

Disregard.   Ai.   NoAM

Disrobe, my love.   Nizar Qabbani.   MAP

Dissecting Uncle Sorrow.   Rick Alley.   AmPoNex

Disseminating their / Circumference. (LL)   Emily Dickinson.   APN-2; HeIP-4; TCAPo

Dissert, A.   Margaret Lucas Cavendish, Duchess of Newcastle.   PEW

Dissidence.   Anthony Walton.   NAPBL

Dissidents, The.   Catherine Obianuju Acholonu.   HAWP

Dissolve us in pleasure, and soft repose. (LL)   John Gay.   EnLoPo; NAEL-5v1; NAEL-6v1   *Fr.* Begger's Opera.

Dissolving Presence, A.   Sándor Weöres.   IQMS, *tr.* by Adam Makkai and Donald E. Morse

Dissonance.   Amy Lowell.   APT-1

Dissonances.   Giusi Busceti.   ItPo, *tr.* by Gayle Ridinger

Disswasion hearing her assigne my helpe.   Rachel Speght.   PBRV   *Fr.* Dream[e], The [or A].

Distaff, The.   Erinna.   WPOW, *tr.* by Marylin Arthur

Distaff Side, The.   Harry Clifton.   PBCIP

Distance.   Peter Everwine.   GeoHom; NNaP

Distance.   Helen Hunt Jackson.   SWaP

Distance.   Evacuation.   Pol N Ndu.   PBMAP

Distance.   Luciana Notari.   CItWP, *tr.* by Cinzia Sartini Blum and Lara Trubowitz

Distance.   Eugene B. Redmond.   SeSe

Distance.   Mary Jo Salter.   ExTi

Distance.   David Wojahn.   YaYoPo

Distance.   Andrea Zanzotto.   VCWP, *tr.* by Ruth Feldman

Distance and a Certain Light.   May Swenson.   APT-2

Distance between Bodies, The.   Bill Manhire.   HarvBoo

Distance between Zero and One, The.   David Keplinger.   AmPoNex

Distance is at bay, and emptiness has gone.   Peaceable Kingdom.   Barbara Leslie Jordan.   ExTi

Distance, Overture.   Theatre.   Anne-Marie Albiach.   MFP, *tr.* by Martin Sorrell

Distance Spills Itself, The.   Yocheved Bat-Miriam.   MHP

Distance that lies from here, The.   Space Song.   Alfonso Cortes.   TCLAP, *tr.* by Thomas Merton

Distances.   Eavan Boland.   HarvBoo

Distances.   Otto René Castillo.   AF, *tr.* by Margaret Randall

Distances.   Katherine Gallagher.   Prnts

Distances.   Philippe Jaccottet.   VCWP, *tr.* by Derek Mahon

Distances.   Christopher Okigbo.
   "Death lay in ambush."   PBMAP; TTY

Distances, The.   W. S. Merwin.   NOBA

Distances, The.   Charles Olson.   NAAL-2v2; NeAP

Distances, The.   Henry Rago.   IllVoic

Distances (1964).   Christopher Okigbo.
   "From flesh into phantom."   PBMAP

Distances to the Friend, The.   Jonathan Williams.   NeAP

Distant, The.   Yannis Ritsos.   VCWP, *tr.* by Edmund Keeley

Distant and faint the Herd-Boy Star.   *Unknown.*   SuSp

Distant as the Duchess of Savoy.   *Unknown.*   MiEL

Distant balloon, A.   Nicholas Virgilio.   HA

Distant dove flutters, A.   Distant Dove.   Judah Halevi.   WoPoe, *tr.* by Gabriel Levin

Distant Drum, The.   Calvin C. Hernton.   GT; TTY

Distant Footsteps, The.   César Vallejo.   RaBo, *tr.* by John Knoepfle and James Wright

Distant Fury of Battle, The.   Geoffrey Hill.   FaBoWar; NoP-4

Distant Mountains.   Ou-yang Hsiu.   CoBCP, *tr.* by Burton Watson

Distant mountains, The.   Issa.   SoOfWa, *tr.* by Sam Hamill

Distant Roads.   Wu Wei-yeh.   CoBLCP, *tr.* by Jonathan Chaves

Distant rock, a far off land, A.   Spiritual Land.   Elizabeth Brown.   IBA

Distant Runners, The.   Mark Van Doren.   MoAmPo

Distant sea, memory.   Thirst for the Sea.   Magda Portal.   TANSG, *tr.* by Shaun Griffin and Emma Sepúlveda-Pulvirenti

Distant Seychelles are not so remote, The.   Osbert Lancaster.   NOBL; PeLV   *Fr.* Afternoons with Baedeker.

Distant soughing of pine forests caresses my ear, The.   Yitzhak Lamdan.   MHP   *Fr.* In the Khamsin.

Distant thunder.   Gary Hotham.   HA

Distant View from a Grass Hill.   Gensei.   WoPoe, *tr.* by Burton Watson

Distant Winter, The.   Philip Levine.   VGW

Distaste.   Ammianus.   GrAn, *tr.* by Peter Jay

Distich.   Shuraikh.   TrJP

Distil not poison in mine ears.   Song.   John Hall.   OxBSP

Distilled Water.   M. K. Joseph.   PeNZ

Distinct Call of the Alligator, The.   Betsy Sholl.   PBCAP

Distinction.   Paul Laurence Dunbar.   SacPr

Distinguish carefully between these two. Justice of the Peace, The. Joseph Hilaire Pierre Belloc. NOBVV; OBSV

Distinguished, and familiar, and aloof. (LL) Epigram: "And what is love? Misunderstanding, pain." James Vincent Cunningham. CRP; HAP

Distinguished the belt feed lever from the belt holding pawl. (LL) Fury of Aerial Bombardment, The. Richard Eberhart. APT-2; FaBoMo; HeIP-4; InPK-6; NIL-7; NIP-4; NoAM; NoP-4; OBWP; PAI; PoWW; RB; TAP; TwCP; UnPo; VGW

Distinguishes the fair and the shameful. Simonides. SaLy, tr. by Diane Rayor

Distracted Puritan, The. Richard Corbet [or Corbett]. BASC; BeJo; OBCoV; OxBoLi

Distracted with care. Despairing Lover, The. William Walsh. FaBoCh; NBLV; NOBL; OxBoLi; PeLV

Distraction. Henry Vaughan. GeHe

Distractions and the Human Crowd. Stevie Smith. OxBC

Distress. Flavien Ranaivo. NegPo, tr. by Ellen Conroy Kennedy

Distress upon the Farm. Laury Wells. IBA

Distressed: single cane, I return. Unknown. ChinPo, tr. by Yip Wai-lim

Distribution of Honours for Literature. Walter Savage Landor. FaBoEE

Distribution of Poetry. Jorge de Lima. PFTM-1

Distrust. Robert Herrick. CaPo

Distrust the pomp of Caesar. Valentin Petrovich Katayev [or Kataev]. TCRP

Disturbed by consciousness. Satori. Gayl Jones. BlSi

Disturbed by the chatter. Neighbour's Pear Tree. Tony Curtis. AngWePo

Disturbed, the kudu are running. On Clouds. Douglas Livingstone. PeSAV

Disturbing some brush. Foster Jewell. HA

Disturbing the Sallies Forth. Clark Coolidge. FTOS

Disturbing to have a person. Poem. Barbara Guest. FaBoWP

Disturbs me like a requiem. (LL) Old Tongue, The. Herbert Williams. AngWePo; TCAWP

Disused Shed in Co. Wexford, A. Derek Mahon. BiHa; CABP; CIP-2; EmeKit; ModIr; NOIV; NPeEn; NoP-4; OxBC; PBCIP; PNI

Disused Temple, The. Norman Cameron. OxBS; OxBTC

Ditchdigger, The. Igor Moiseievich Irtenev. TCRP, tr. by John High

Ditches. Karen Kipp. BodElec

Ditchley Portrait, The. Allen Fisher. Oth Fr. Emergent Manner.

Dittie to the Same Subject, A. Dame Gertrude More. EMWP

Ditties Lamentation for the cruelty of this age. Unknown. BASC

Ditty, A. Sir Philip Sidney. AWP; GTBS-P Fr. Arcadia.

Ditty, A: In Praise of Eliza, Queen of the Shepherds. Edmund Spenser. OBEV Fr. Shepheardes [or Shepeards or Shepherd's] Calender, The.

Ditty, A: "See where she sits upon the grassy green." Edmund Spenser. See Shepheardes [or Shepeards or Shepherd's] Calender, The

Ditty: "I went into my garden to gather some herbs." Sister Bertken [or Bertke]. WPOW, tr. by Jonathan Crewe

Ditty: "If you refuse me once, and think again." Edward Herbert, 1st Baron Herbert of Cherbury. NOSC

Ditty: "Why dost thou hate return instead of love." Edward Herbert, 1st Baron Herbert of Cherbury. NOSC

Dīvāni Shamsi Tabrīz. Jelaluddin [or Jalal al-Din] Rumi. "Man of God is drunken without wine, The." TAL

Dive. Langston Hughes. APT-2

Dive, The. Mimi Goese. HeMarv

Diver. Ronald Albert Simpson. CBAP

Diver, The. Robert Earl Hayden. BPo; MoASP

Diver, The. Felicia Dorothea Hemans. TreFP

Diver, The. Edward Leslie Mayo. CoAP

Diver, The. Christopher Merrill. MoASP

Diver, The. W. W. Eustace Ross. NOBC

Diver-Bird. Mike Jenkins. TCAWP

Diver does not abandon, A. Ono no Komachi. WoPoe, tr. by Mariko Aratani and Jane Hirshfield

Diver for the NYPD Talks to His Girlfriend, A. Richard Garcia. TouFir; UrbNat

Diverne's Waltz. Marilyn Nelson Waniek. FFC

Diverne stands in the kitchen as they dance. Diverne's Waltz. Marilyn Nelson Waniek. FFC

Diverne wanted to die, that August night. Chosen. Marilyn Nelson Waniek. ExTi; FFC

Divers, The. Peter Quennell. MoBrPo

Divers Doth Use. Sir Thomas Wyatt. NAEL-6v1; NAEL-7v1

Divers[e] [or Dyvers] doth[e] use, as I have heard and kno[w]. Divers Doth Use. Sir Thomas Wyatt. NAEL-5v1; OxBEV; Son

Diverse strangers flower and diverge. Crossing Disappearing behind Them. Marjorie Welish. PmAP

Diversions of the Re-Echo Club. Carolyn Wells. OBAL

Diverting History of John Gilpin, The. William Cowper. EBNV; OBNV

Dives and Lazarus. Unknown. ESPB; OxBB; TTY

Dives, when you and I go down to Hell. To Dives. Joseph Hilaire Pierre Belloc. ChIV-2; OBSV

Divestment of Beauty. Laura Riding Jackson. APT-2; HarvBoo

Divide your bread in two. Heavenly Jerusalem, Jerusalem of the Earth. Leah Goldberg. FIT, tr. by Robert Friend

Divided. Jean Ingelow. VWP "Dappled sky, a world of meadows, A." PEW

Divided Child, The. Derek Walcott. "Ajax, / lion-coloured stallion from Sealey's stable." PoetW

Divina Commedia. Dante Alighieri. Inferno. NAWM-5v1 "And now we walked along the solid mire." OBVE "And so from bridge to bridge we went, talking." WoPoe, tr. by Susan Mitchell Dark Wood, The. BiHa, tr. by Seamus Heaney "Middle of life's journey; I, The." STV "Through me come into the city full of pain." WoPoe, tr. by Armand Schwerner "Midway in our life's journey, I went astray." NAWM-5v1 Ugolino. OxBEV, tr. by Seamus Heaney Paradiso. "But you who are so happy here, tell me." EnlH "Glory of Him who moves all things rays forth, The." NAWM-5v1 "Piercing brightness of the living ray, The." TOF "That sun that breathed love's fire into my youth." NAWM-5v1 "Then, in the form of a white rose, the host." NAWM-5v1 Purgatorio. "As the day stands when the Sun begins to glow." NAWM-5v1 "At the hour when the heat of the day is overcome." NAWM-5v1 "Earnest to explore within and all around." OBVE "For better waters now the little bark." NAWM-5v1 "Love of God, unutterable and perfect, The." EnlH "This mountain of release is such that the." EnlH "When the Septentrion of the First Heaven." NAWM-5v1

Divina Commedia. Henry Wadsworth Longfellow. APN-1; OxBA; TAP; TCAPo

Divination by a Daffadill [or Daffodil]. Robert Herrick. CaPo

Divine approval is thy sweetest praise. (LL) To My Father. Henrietta Cordelia Ray. BlSi; CBWP-3; Son

Divine by the name of McWhinners, A. Limerick. Unknown. PeLi

Divine Century of Spiritual Sonnets, A. Barnabe Barnes. God's Virtue. NOCV Life of Man, The. EBEV No More Lewd Lays. Son

Divine Comedy, The (Mandelbaum Translation). Dante Alighieri. Inferno. NAWM-7v1, tr. by Allen Mandelbaum Paradiso. "Virgin Mary, daughter of your Son." NAWM-7v1, tr. by Allen Mandelbaum Purgatorio. "And now, with the reflected lights that glow." NAWM-7v1, tr. by Allen Mandelbaum "But tell me if the man whom I see here." NAWM-7v1, tr. by Allen Mandelbaum "But with regard to me, I'll satisfy." NAWM-7v1, tr. by Allen Mandelbaum "I have at times seen all the eastern sky." NAWM-7v1, tr. by Allen Mandelbaum "Natural thirst that never can be quenched." NAWM-7v1, tr. by Allen Mandelbaum "To course across more kindly waters now." NAWM-7v1, tr. by Allen Mandelbaum

Divine destroyer, pit[t]ly me no more. La Bourbon, A. Richard Lovelace. CaPo

Divine Fancies. Francis Quarles. "Booke of Common Pray'r excels the rest, The." PBRV "I saw him dead; I saw his Body fall." PBRV "I wish a greater knowledge, then t'attaine." PBRV On Death. PeECV On God's Favour. PeECV On Our Saviour's Passion. PeECV On the Life of Man. PeECV

Divine Image, A. William Blake. ChIV-1; NAEL-5v2; NAEL-6v2; NoP-4; RB Fr. Songs of Experience.

Divine Image, The. William Blake. BBASP; ChAP; FHYEP; InvLi; NAEL-5v2; NAEL-6v2; NOBE; NOBRP; NOEC; NoP-4; OxBEV; PeECV; PoE Fr. Songs of Innocence.

Divine Love. Michael Benedikt. CoAP; CoAmPo

Divine Meditations. William Alabaster. Son

"Beehould a cluster to itt selfe a vine." ESCV

(Ego Sum Vitis.) OxBEV

"Haile gracefull morning of eternall Daye." ESCV

"Jesu, thie love within mee is soe maine." ESCV

"My soule a world is by Contraccion." ESCV

Night, the Starless Night of Passion, The. ESCV

"Night, the starless[e] night of passion, The." ESCV

"Now I have found thee, I will ever more." ESCV

"Now that the midd day heate doth scorch my shame." ESCV

("Now that the midday heate doth scorch my shame.") OxBEV

"O starry Temple of unvalted space." ESCV

"O sweete and bitter monuments of paine." ESCV

"Sunne begins uppon my heart to shine, The." ESCV

"Three sortes of teares doe from myne eies distraine." ESCV

Upon the Ensignes of Christes Crucifyinge. ESCV

"Way feare with thy projectes, noe false fyre, A." ESCV

"What meaneth this, that Christ an hymne did singe." ESCV

"When without tears I looke on Christ, I see." ESCV

Divine Meditations. John Donne. *Fr.* Holy Sonnets.

Divine Mistress, A. Thomas Carew. BeJo; CavPo

Divine mystery. Sogetsuni. SoOfWa, *tr. by* Sam Hamill

Divine Oracles, tell me when. In Acknowledgment of the Praises of European Writers. Sister Juana Inés de la Cruz. SpanPo, *tr. by* Constance Urdang

Divine Presence, The. Adelaide Anne Procter. SacPr

Divine Rapture, A. Francis Quarles. *See* Emblems

Divine Revenge. Friedrich von Logau. GePo, *tr. by* George C. Schoolfield

Divine sea rocks its, The. Rocking. Gabriela Mistral. TANSG, *tr. by* Maria Jacketti

Divine Sonnet, A. William Alabaster. NoSic

Divine Thalia strike th' Harmonious Lute. On the Soft and Gentle Motions of Eudora. Anne Killigrew. PoBW

Divine, to the Divinitiy. (LL) Dark Angel, The. Lionel Pigot Johnson. GTBS-P; MoBrPo; NOBE; NOBVV; OBMV; OxAEP-2

Divine Weeks and Works, The. Guillaume de Salluste Du Bartas.

"Eden," the First Part of the First Day of the Second Week.

"Adam, quoth He, the beauties manifold." InvLi, *tr. by* Joshua Sylvester

Fourth Day of the First Week, The.

"He that to number all the stars would seek." NOSC, *tr. by* Joshua Sylvester

Zodiac, The. NOSC, *tr. by* Joshua Sylvester

Tower of Babel, The. NoSic, *tr. by* Joshua Sylvester

Divine Wooer, The. Phineas Fletcher. SacPr

"Me Lord? can'st Thou mis[s]pend." SacPr; TOF

Divinely Superfluous Beauty. Robinson Jeffers. HeIP-4; MoAmPo

Diviners, The. Mary Oliver. WPE

Diving. Charlotte Brontë. PEW

Diving into the Wreck. Adrienne Rich. ColAP; EmeKit; HCAP; HarvBoo; HeIP-4; InPK-6; MakPoe; NAAL-2v2; NAAL-5; NALW; NIL-7; NIP-4; NOBA; NoAM; NoP-4; OxWW; PoPoPo .

Divinity. George Herbert. NOSC

Division of an Estate. George Moses Horton. NAAAL

Division of Labor. Feyyaz Kayacan. WoPoe, *tr. by* Feyyaz Fergar

Division of O'Dowd, The. Alan Wearne. BMAP *Fr.* Nightmarkets, The.

Divorce. Adam Koehn. AiP

Divorce. Anna Wickham. MoBrPo; NALW

Divorce, The. Hans Magnus Enzensberger. WoPoe, *tr. by* Herbert Graf

Divorce, The. Thomas Stanley. MeLP

Divorce and Mr. Circe. David Gewanter. NAPBL

Divorce Referendum, The. Sarah Maguire. MFPA

Divorce Referendum, Ireland, 1986, The. Paul Durcan. BiHa; PBCIP

Divorce Song. *Unknown.* STP, *tr. by* Carl Cary

Divorced. Don Share. OPRER

Divorced, but friends again at last. Onion, Memory, The. Craig Raine. NAEL-5v2; NAEL-6v2; NoAM; NoP-4

Divorcee. C. Webster Wheelock. SoSe-8

Divorcing. Denise Levertov. NALW

Dixie [*or* Dixie's Land]. Daniel Decatur Emmett. APN-1; CBCWP; FaBoA; TCAPo

Dixie's Land. Daniel Decatur Emmett. *See* Dixie [*or* Dixie's Land]

Dizains, Les. Maurice Scève. WoPoe, *tr. by* Phillip Lopate

Dizzy Girls in the Sixties. Gary Soto. ReTh

Dizzy, lost, yet unbewailing! (LL) Shelley. NOBE; PoE *Fr.* Prometheus Unbound [A Lyrical Drama in Four Acts].

Djalbarmiwi's Song. *Unknown. See* Blowflies Buzz, The

Djanbun's the platypus. He was a man one time. Platypus, The. *Aborigine Oral Tradition.* NOBAu

Djinns, The. Victor Hugo. SxFrPo, *tr. by* E. H. Blackmore and A. M. Blackmore

Do as You Would Be Done By. Matilda Caroline Edwards. PWR

Do chóireoinn leaba duit. Leaba Shíoda. Nuala Ni Dhomhnaill. CABP

Do, Do, Do. George Gershwin. ReLy

Do gorillas have birthdays? Questions My Son Asked Me, Answers I Never Gave Him. Nancy Willard. LCAP-2

Do I begin at the here and now. From Rosary. Barbara Tran. PuP-23

Do I believe in Angels? Yes. Angel's Visit, The. Eugene Field. PWR

Do I look angry? He screamed. I Have to Go Now. Maggie Estep. HeMarv

Do I not know that groping for light in darkness. To a Friend. Boris Leonidovich Pasternak. TCRP, *tr. by* Yakov Hornstein

"Do I see a hat in the road?" I said. Old Sussex Road, The. Ian Serraillier. NTCP

Do I seem as cheerful. You Make Me Feel So Young. Mack Gordon. ReLy

Do I sleep? do I dream? Further Language from Truthful James. Bret Harte. NOBL

Do I still desire virginity? Sappho. SaLy, *tr. by* Diane Rayor

Do It Again. George Gershwin. ReLy

Do It Yourself. Joan Aiken. KaS; NOxBChV

Do Yrself. Larry Eigner. NeAP; PoM

Do leän down low in Linden Lea. (LL) My Orcha'd in Linden Lea. William Barnes. EBVV; FaBoVe; NOBVV; NPeEn; OxBEV

Do make thee blush at any time / Blame not my lute. (LL) Blame Not My Lute. Sir Thomas Wyatt. EBEV; NAEL-5v1; NAEL-7v1; PoE; SCGP

Do men suppose, when God's free-giving hand. George Wither. NOSC *Fr.* Collection of Emblemes, Ancient and Moderne, A.

Do nettles mar the month of May. Nettles in May. Euros Bowen. OBWVE, *tr. by the* author

Do not. Hayyim Nahman [*or* Khayim Nakhman *or* Chaim Nachman] Bialik. FIT, *tr. by* Robert Friend

Do not add a new one. (LL) Scaffold, The. Amal Dunqul. MAP; NAfrP, *tr. by* Sharif Elmusa and Thomas G. Ezzy

Do not allow the sun to dim. Sunbeams. Avner Trainin. MHP, *tr. by* Ruth Finer Mintz

Do Not Ask. Christine Lavant. WPOW, *tr. by* Michael Hamburger

Do not ask how, before cock-crow, my sister had departed. My Sister. Muhammad Al-Ghuzzi. MAP, *tr. by* John Heath-Stubbs and May Jayyusi

Do not ask me, dear friend, how I spent my leisure. Unfinished Letter to My Lady. Dániel Berzsenyi. IQMS, *tr. by* Peter Zollman

Do not ask: where? We Go. Karl Wolfskehl. TrJP, *tr. by* Ernst Morwitz, Carol North Valhope and Harry Zohn

Do not assume I came out on Christopher Street. Assumption about the Harlem Brown Baby. Salih Michael Fisher. GLP

Do not bathe her in blood. Abortion, An. Frank O'Hara. TAP

Do Not Be Afraid of No. Gwendolyn Brooks. ColAP *Fr.* Notes from the Childhood and the Girlhood.

Do not be always looking on the fire. Indian Counsel. Edwin Ford Piper. APT-1

Do not be angry if I tell you. Sofa, The. Medbh McGuckian. PBCIP; PNI

Do not be offended because. Excuse for Not Returning the Visit of a Friend, An. Mei Yao Ch'en. OHPC, *tr. by* Kenneth Rexroth

Do not beguile my heart. Complaining. George Herbert. ChIV-1

Do not call me with many words. Do not call me with desperate vows. First Smile. Nathan [*or* Natan] Alterman. FIT, *tr. by* Robert Friend

Do not complain of three-score, 'the time of obedient ears.' (LL) On Being Sixty. Po Chü-i. AWP; ChiP, *tr. by* Arthur Waley

Do not conceal[e] thy radiant eyes. To Cynthia, on Concealment of Her Beauty. Sir Francis Kynaston. MeLP; NOBE

Do not conceive that I shall here record. Virgin Declares Her Beauties, A. Francesco da Barberini. AWP; EaItPo, *tr. by* Dante Gabriel Rossetti

Do not crouch to-day and worship. Present, The. Adelaide Anne Procter. TreFP

Do not despair. For Johnny. John Pudney. OBWP

Do not enforce the tired wolf. John Crowe Ransom. MoAmPo; OxBA *Fr.* Sixteen Poems in Eight Pairings.

Do Not Expect Again a Phoenix Hour. Cecil Day Lewis. FaBoMo; MoBrPo; NoAM; OxBTC; PoRA

Do not fear to put thy feet. John Fletcher. NOSC *Fr.* Faithful Shepherdess, The.

Do not fill postcards with memories. Face Lost in the Wilderness. Fadwa Tuqan [*or* Tuquan]. MAP, *tr. by* Patricia Alanah Byrne, Salma Khadra Jayyusi and Naomi Shihab Nye

Do not fill postcards with memories. Face Lost in the Wilderness. Fadwa Tuqan [*or* Tuquan]. AF, *tr. by* Naomi Shihab Nye

Do not force me with present favor. Lady Hsi. Wang Wei. CoBCP, *tr. by* Burton Watson

Do Not Go Gentle into That Good Night. Dylan Thomas. AmFaPo; CABP; ChAP; ClHu; HAP; HarvBoo; HeIP-4; ITBLP; InPK-6; MakPoe; MoBrPo; NAEL-5v2; NAEL-6v2; NIL-7; NIP-4; NOBE; NPeEn; NoAM; NoP-4;

OxAEP-2; OxBTC; PAI; PeECV; PoE; PoPoPo; RB; SCV; SoSe-8; TCAWP; TFi; TOF; TRP; TwCP; UV; UnPo; WeW-3

Do not go sober into that dim light.   Do Not Go Sober.   Roger Woddis.   UV

Do Not Have Pity.   Aimé Césaire.   NAWM-7v2, *tr.* by Gregson Davis

Do not imagine that the exploration.   Discovery, The.   Gwendolyn MacEwen.   NOBC

Do not jeer at the child, when with a whip and spur.   To the German People.   Friedrich Hölderlin.   WoPoe, *tr.* by Robert Bly

Do not laugh at my tower.   Warm Invitation, A.   Yüan Chiu-ts'ai.   WoPoe, *tr.* by Henry Hart

Do not let any woman read this verse!   Deirdre.   James Stephens.   AWP; OBMV; PoRA

Do Not Let Skeezix Go in There: Winslow's Villanelle.   Ron Hansen.   Unle

Do not look at me.   *Unknown.*   ArkPo, *tr.* by Edwin A. Cranston

Do not look for him.   Elegy.   Leonard Cohen.   HeIP-4

Do not lose sight.   You Who Occupy Our Land.   Maria Manuela Margarido.   HAWP; WPOW, *tr.* by Allan Francovich

Do not love me, cousin.   Flavien Ranaivo.   *See* Do not love me, my friend

Do not love me, my friend.   Love Song.   Flavien Ranaivo.   PBA

Do Not Make Things Too Easy.   Martha Baird.   LW

Do Not Ponder Too Much.   Stefan George.   WoPoe, *tr.* by Stanley Burnshaw

Do not press my hands.   Intimate.   Gabriela Mistral.   SpanPo, *tr.* by Kate Flores

Do Not Put Dead Monkeys in the Freezer.   Martín Espada.   TouFir

Do not ridicule the small.   On a Small Bath.   *Unknown.*   GrAn, *tr.* by Robin Skelton

Do not say "Godspeed" to me, wicked heart.   Callimachus.   HePo   *Fr.* Epigrams.

Do not seek too much fame.   Old Song.   *Unknown.*   RaBo

Do Not Show Your Love.   Sa'id 'Aql.   MAP, *tr.* by Naomi Shihab Nye and Matthew Sorenson

Do not smile to yourself.   Lady Otomo no Sakanoé.   OHPJ

Do not speak to us of dreams, speak to us of autumn in.   Gardens of Ravished Psyche, The.   George Barker.   OBGa

Do Not Stop Me!   Angela Miri.   NAfrP

Do not suddenly break the branch, or.   T. S. Eliot.   FaBoCh; NOCV; PeECV   *Fr.* Landscapes.

Do not take a bath in Jordan.   Scotch Rhapsody.   Dame Edith Sitwell.   TwCP

Do not tell me, my brother, to reach.   Keorapetse Kgositsile.   PBMAP   *Fr.* Present Is a Dangerous Place to Live, The.

Do not think anything alien to mankind which may befall one.   Certaine verses written by the said ladie Jane with a pinne.   Lady Jane Grey Dudley.   EMWP

Do not think I am not grateful for your small.   Gratitude.   Louise Glück.   FaBoWP; TRP

Do not torment me, lady.   *Unknown.*   NOIV

Do not try so hard.   Lesson.   Barbara Winder.   MiVo

Do Not Turn Away.   Kumeroa Ngoingoi Pewhairangi.   PeNZ, *tr.* by Sam Karetu

Do not weep maiden, for war is kind.   Stephen Crane.   APN-2; FaBoWar; NAAL-2v2; NOBA; OBWP; RaBo; TCAPo   *Fr.* War Is Kind.

Do parks get lonely.   Snowy Benches.   Aileen Fisher.   KaS

Do People moulder equally.   Emily Dickinson.   ChIV-2

Do sit down, Metro. Get up and set.   Friends in Private.   Herodas.   HePo, *tr.* by Barbara Hughes Fowler

Do Skyscrapers ever grow tired.   Skyscrapers.   Rachel Lyman Field.   ChAP; NOxBChV; SSCS

Do Something, Brother.   M. Gopalakrishna Adiga.   OMIP, *tr.* by A. K. Ramanujan

Do'st thou thinke we shall know one an other.   John Webster.   OxBEV   *Fr.* Duchess of Malfi, The.

Do Stella love. Fools, who doth it deny? (LL)   Sir Philip Sidney.   PoE; Son   *Fr.* Astrophil and Stella.

Do tell me, Hermes, what was it like when the soul.   Lucianus [*or* Lucian].   GrAn

Do the Baby Cake-Walk.   Clyde Watson.   NTCP

Do the Dead Know What Time It Is?   Kenneth Patchen.   MoAmPo

Do the Others Speak of Me Mockingly, Maliciously?   Delmore Schwartz.   APT-2; ChIV-1

Do the people.   Poem for Teacup Mantlepiece Poets Palpitating Poot Booty Plagiarists Imprisoned in Ivy League White Supremacist Mental Biological Warfare Labs.   Tony Medina.   InTrad

Do the wife and baby travelling to see.   Sick Nought, The.   Randall Jarrell.   OxBA

Do they call Virtue [*or* Vertue] there ungratefulness[e]? (LL)   Sir Philip Sidney.   AEP; AWP; BoLoP; CABP; EnLoPo; GSo; HAP; HeIP-4; NAEL-5v1; NAEL-6v1; NAEL-7v1; NPeEn; NoSic; OxAEP-1; OxBSo; PoE; PoRA; SCGP; Son; TFi; TRP   *Fr.* Astrophil and Stella.

Do they think of me now.   Making the Children Behave.   William Daniel Ehrhart.   CDa

Do they whisper behind my back? Do they speak.   Do the Others Speak of Me Mockingly, Maliciously?   Delmore Schwartz.   APT-2; ChIV-1

Do things then happen.   Melting Milk.   Bill Berkson.   PmAP

Do This Favour for Me.   Luis de Camões [*or* Camões].   BoLoP; WoPoe, *tr.* by Roy Campbell

Do this: so worship shall be thine and love. (LL)   Dante Alighieri.   AWP; EaItPo, *tr.* by Dante Gabriel Rossetti   *Fr.* La Vita Nuova.

Do We Not Hear Thy Footfall?   Amy Carmichael.   SacPr

Do we reach the sea with clocks.   Deaf and Blind, The.   Paul Éluard.   WoPoe, *tr.* by Paul Auster

Do we see in what we see.   In the Stealth of Stillness.   Thurayya Al-Urayyid.   PoArWo, *tr.* by Farouk Mustafa

Do what you are going to do, and I will tell about it. (LL)   I Go Back to May 1937.   Sharon Olds.   BLT; EmeKit; NIL-7

Do What You Can.   Lawrence Joseph.   PBCAP

Do what you come for, captain, with your news.   To Captain Hungry.   Ben Jonson.   FaBoWar

Do with me, God! as Thou didst deal with John.   To God.   Robert Herrick.   ChIV-2

Do, writing books, she also said that he smiles a lot and kinda got good teeth. (LL)   Poet: What Ever Happened to Luther?   Haki R. Madhubuti.   SpirFl; UnSA

Do ye hear the children weeping, O my brothers.   Elizabeth Barrett Browning.   EBVV; OxAEP-2; VWP; ViWPN

Do ye ken hoo to fush for the salmon?   Master and Man.   Sir Henry John Newbolt.   OxBTC

Do ye, o congregation.   Psalm 58.   *Unknown.*   NoP-4

Do you ask what the birds say?   Answer to a Child's Question.   Samuel Taylor Coleridge.   ITBLP; NOxBChV

Do you been or did you never? Ha!   Red-Headed Intern, Taking Notes.   Ramon Guthrie.   APT-2

Do you believe in a God.   Ordinary God.   Donald Davie.   InvLi

Do you believe in charms and spells.   It Could Happen to You.   Jimmy Van Heusen.   ReLy

Do you believe in evolution, oh, thing of easy answers?   Darwin Descending.   Russell Edson.   LCAP-2

Do you believe that I am like the autumn wind.   Alfred de Musset.   WoPoe, *tr.* by Claire Nicholas White   *Fr.* Night in May, A.

Do you blame me that I loved him?   Double Standard, A.   Frances Ellen Watkins Harper.   BlSi; NAAAL; PWR

Do you carrot all for me?   *Unknown.*   ChAP

Do you come to me to bend me to your will.   Woman to Her Lover, A.   Christina Walsh.   BrRo

Do you dare? (LL)   Love Poem: "In your quest or request God is remote."   Huda Na'mani.   BBASP; MAP, *tr.* by Samuel Hazo and Lena Jayyusi

Do you envy, my comrades-in-arms.   Viktor Aleksandrovich Sosnora.   TCRP; TCRusP, *tr.* by Daniel Weissbort

Do You Fear the Wind?   Hamlin Garland.   ITBLP

Do you give yourself to me utterly.   Sleep.   Kenneth Slessor.   BMAP

Do you have a sweet thought, Cerinthus.   Sulpicia.   BoWoP, *tr.* by Aliki Barnstone and Willis Barnstone

Do you have any scissors I could borrow? No, I'm sorry I don't. What about. No Sorry.   Catherine Bowman.   BAP-97

Do you have the Poems of Han-shan in your house?   Tahoe Nocturne.   Sherod Santos.   GeoHom

Do you have the poems of Han-shan in your house?   *Unknown.*   CoBCP

Do you know a dark man?   My Exorcist Mother.   Patricia Adelman.   Prnts

Do you know, Daphne, of this old romance.   To J—Y Colonna.   Gérard de Nerval.   WoPoe, *tr.* by Richard Sieburth

Do you know that once.   Overnight Guest.   Ramona Wilson.   VoR

Do you know that your soul is of my soul such part.   To My Son.   Margaret Johnston Grafflin.   PoToHe

Do you know the neighbor who lives in your block.   Your Neighbor.   H. Howard Biggar.   PoToHe

Do you know the old man who.   Wild Flower Man, The.   Lu Yu.   OHPC, *tr.* by Kenneth Rexroth

Do you know the story of Hamelin Town?   Rat Trap.   Mick Gowar.   NOxBChV

Do you know what.   Fancy.   Robert Creeley.   NOBA

Do you know what happened in August here?   Anna Deavere Smith.   OxWW   *Fr.* Fires in the Mirror.

Do you know what is bad?   Bad and Good.   Alexander Resnikoff.   NTCP

Do you know what was waiting beyond those steps of the harp calling you from another time, other days?   Sonata.   Alvaro Mutis.   TCLAP, *tr.* by Sophie Cabot Black and Maria Negroni

Do You Know What You're Saying.   Debby Barben.   IBA

Do you know why the old woman sings?   Why the Old Woman Limps.   Lupenga Mphande.   HBAPE

Do you know you have asked for the costliest thing. Woman's Question, A. Lena Lathrop. ITBLP; PoToHe

Do you lazily nurse your knee and muse? What Are You Doing? Edmund Vance Cooke. PWR

Do you look for a rainbow, Love, in this wet weather. Wet Weather. Patricia Low. VGW

Do you love her? Inquisition. Gloria Wade-Gayles. ISC

Do you make me notice you! (LL) Reminder, The. Thomas Hardy. ChAP; OBCP

Do you more than we? (LL) "Is It Nothing to You?" May Probyn. OBEV; SacPr

Do you need an explanation. Russian God, The. Prince P. A. Vyazemsky. WoPoe, *tr. by* Alan Meyers

"Do you not find something very strange about him?" Assassination, The. Robert Silliman Hillyer. MoAmPo

Do you not hear the Aziola cry? Aziola, The. Shelley. EBEV

Do You Not Know that I Need to Touch You. Frances Horovitz. LW

Do you not love me, do you not pity me. Do You Not Love Me. Sergey [*or* Sergei] Aleksandrovich Yesenin [*or* Essenin]. RusPo, *tr. by* Robert Arthur Douglas Ford

Do you not see that we pitched our tent on the banks of night. Female. Muhammad Al-Ghuzzi. MAP; NAfrP, *tr. by* John Heath-Stubbs and May Jayyusi

Do you not see the riverside grass. Pao Chao. ChinPo, *tr. by* Yip Wai-lim *Fr.* Weary Road, The.

Do you not see the Running Horse River flowing along the Sea of Snow. Song of the Running Horse River: Presented on Seeing General Feng Off on a Campaign to the West, A. Ts'en Shen. SuSp, *tr. by* Daniel Bryant

Do you not see the young men off to war. Pao Chao. ChinPo, *tr. by* Yip Wai-lim *Fr.* Weary Road, The.

Do you not wish to renounce the Devil? Epigram. Armand Lanusse. TTY, *tr. by* Langston Hughes

Do you remember. Friend. Hone Tuwhare. PeNZ, *tr. by* Kumeroa Ngoingoi Pewhairangi

Do you remember an Inn. Tarantella. Joseph Hilaire Pierre Belloc. FaBoCh; MoBrPo; OBMV; RB; UV

Do you remember an Inn. New Tarantella. Paul Griffin. UV

Do you remember an inn, Miranda? It lost its licence of course. Footnote to Belloc's "Tarantella." John Heath-Stubbs. OBCoV

Do you remember Don Quixote. Imagination. Johnny Burke. ReLy

Do you remember how I beat on the door. Door, A. W. S. Merwin. LCAP-2

Do you remember how we went. To Another Housewife. Judith Wright. NALW

Do you remember / How you won. Frank Horne. BPo *Fr.* Letters [*or* Notes] Found near a Suicide.

Do you remember Mr. Goodbeare, the carpenter. Elegy for Mr. Goodbeare. Sir Osbert Sitwell. MoBrPo

Do You Remember 1926? Idris Davies. AngWePo; OBWVE

Do you remember, O Delphic Apollo. Edgar Lee Masters. APT-1 *Fr.* Spoon River Anthology.

Do You Remember That Night. *Unknown.* WoPoe, *tr. by* George Petrie

Do You Remember That Night? *Unknown.* BIrV, *tr. by* Eugene O'Curry

Do you remember that you wanted to be a Marguerite. Marguerite. "Rubén Dario." SpanPo, *tr. by* Anita Volland

Do you remember the lizard? Lizard, The. Rona Murray. NOBC

Do you remember the ritual of candle-wax. Sliding. Sam Adams. AngWePo

Do you remember, when you were first a child. Message from Home. Kathleen Jessie Raine. WPE

Do you remember? We were in a room. Raiment We Put On, The. Kelly Cherry. FFC

Do you see me! One with this world. *Unknown.* FaBoA, *tr. by* A. L. Kroeber

Do you see that hummingbird. Grain of Sand. Fanny Carrión de Fierro. TANSG, *tr. by* Sally Cheney Bell

Do you see the town, how it rests over there. Do You See the Town? Hugo von Hofmannsthal. AmFaPo, *tr. by* Anne Adams

Do you see this grain of sand. Grain of Sand, A. Frances Ellen Watkins Harper. PWR

Do you see this square old yellow Book, I toss. Robert Browning. FaBoVe *Fr.* Ring and the Book, The.

Do you see? Evening falls. Seventh Eclogue. Miklós Radnóti. PFTM-1

Do you think I know what I'm doing? Jelaluddin [*or* Jalal al-Din] Rumi. LoL

Do you think of me as I think of you. L. E. L.'s Last Question. Elizabeth Barrett Browning. VWP

Do you think that odes and sermons. Edgar Lee Masters. GeoHom *Fr.* Spoon River Anthology.

Do you think we'll ever get to see Earth, sir? Sheenagh Pugh. TCAWP

Do you think we might go to hell too? Igor Vladimirovich Chinnov. TCRusP, *tr. by* John Glad

Do you think you will hug the shore, Captain, to-day? Hugging the Shore. Mary E. Tucker. CBWP-1

Do You Think? Josephine D. Henderson Heard. CBWP-4

Do you understand the concept? The marvel? Tender at the neck. Constant Bride, The. Mary Jo Bang. NAPBL

Do you want to know his name? Porch, The. Ronald Stuart Thomas. NOCV

Do you want to return. River Silence, The. Leonid Nikolaevich Martynov. TCRP, *tr. by* J. R. Rowland

Do You Wonder Why I Am Sleepy. James Purdy. CAGL

Do Your Best. Mrs. Henry Linden. CBWP-4

Do yuh hear that whistle down the line? On the Atchison, Topeka and the Santa Fe. Johnny Mercer. ReLy

Doan raise no kite is good friday. Mama Dot Warns against an Easter Rising. Frederick D'Aguiar. Oth

Dobbin. George Bowering. NOBC

Dobbs Ferry in autumn. I with my pen. With Walter and Amati. Gabriel Preil. FIT, *tr. by* Robert Friend

Dobbs Ferry possesses a rat which slips out of his lair at night and. Don Marquis. TCAPo

Dockens afore his Peers. Charles Murray. NePenScot

Docker. Seamus Heaney. HeIP-4; NOIV

Dockery and Son. Philip Larkin. PoetW

Dockery was junior to you. Dockery and Son. Philip Larkin. PoetW

Doctor, The. Dannie Abse. BloBone

Doctor, The. Roger Woddis. UV

Doctor asked him if he dreamed at night, The. Patient, The. Nicholas Moore. SPE

Doctor Faustus. Christopher Marlowe. NAEL-5v1; NAEL-7v1
  End of Doctor Faustus, The. FaBoVe; HeIP-4; PeECV
  "Had I as many souls as there be stars." SacPr
  Was This the Face. EBEV

Doctor Faustus was a good man. Mother Goose. LB

Doctor Fell. Thomas [*or* "Tom"] Brown. FaBoEE; NBLV; OBCoV; OBVE; OxBEV; OxNR
  (Non Amo Te.) AWP
  (On the Occasion of One Dr. Fell's Challenge to Translate an Epigram of Martial's.) WoPoe

Doctor Foster is a good man. Dr. Foster. *Unknown.* OxNR

Doctor Foster went to Gloucester. *Unknown.* OxBEV

Doctor Foster went to Gloucester [*or* Glo'ster]. Mother Goose. LB; OxBoLi; OxNR; ReMoGo

Doctor Frolic. Robert Pinsky. NoAM

Doctor gave them what they thought was enough, The. Between Worlds. Jacqueline Berger. AmPoNex

Doctor in a clean, starched band, The. Reasons That Induced Dr. Swift to Write a Poem Called "The Lady's Dressing-Room," The. Lady Mary Wortley Montagu. NAEL-7v1

Doctor Johnson. Soame Jenyns. FaBoEE; OBSV

Dr. King's photograph. Report from the Skull's Diorama. Yusef Komunyakaa. LTA

Doctor, Lawyer, Indian Chief. Paul Francis Webster. ReLy

Doctor loves the patient, The. Bed, The. Alec Derwent Hope. NoAM; OxBC; OxBSP

Doctor Meyers. Edgar Lee Masters. APT-1; IllVoic *Fr.* Spoon River Anthology.

Dr. Newman with the crooked pince-nez. Robert Graves. PeLV *Fr.* Grotesques.

Doctor, of great skill and fame, A. Fair and Softly Goes Far or, The Wary Physician. Laetitia Pilkington. PEW

Doctor put her on a soft diet, then, The. Death of Gladys Presley, The. Fleda Brown Jackson. AllShUp

Doctor's face on a December day, The. On Dutch's Death. Robert Coles. BloBone

Doctor's fortunate indeed, A. Physicians' Fortune, The. Friedrich von Logau. GePo, *tr. by* George C. Schoolfield

Doctor's Journal Entry for August 6, 1945, A. Vikram Seth. OMIP

Doctor to his retinue of interns and residents. Scene: A Bedside in the Witches' Kitchen. Ramon Guthrie. APT-2

Doctor Who Sits at the Bedside of a Rat, The. Josephine Miles. VGW

Doctor, you say there are no haloes. Monet Refuses the Operation. Lisel Mueller. IllVoic

Doctors' Row. Conrad Potter Aiken. HAP

Doctors tender of their fame, The. Jonathan Swift. NOBL *Fr.* Verses on the Death of Dr. Swift, D.S.P.D.

Doctors that learned be. John Skelton. OBSV *Fr.* Colin Clout.

Documentary. Claribel Alegría. LoL; VCWP

Documentary Film. "Ern Malley." BMAP

Dodder twines around the *huang-po* tree, The. Woman Née Wu, The. Wu Chia-chi. CoBLCP, *tr. by* Jonathan Chaves

Dodder vine trails with the long wind, The. Old *Chüeh-chü*. *Unknown*. CoBCP, *tr.* by Burton Watson

Doddledy, doodledy, doodledy, dan. *Unknown*. OxNR

Do[e] but consider this small dust. Hour-Glass [*or* Houre-Glasse], The. Ben Jonson. BeJo; EnLoPo; NIP-4

Do[e] not their profane orgies hear[e]. William Habington. BeJo *Fr.* Castara.

Doe of the mountains east. Mother / Deer / Lady. Harold Littlebird. VoR

Doe's leap, A. Peggy Lyles. HA

Doeg, though without knowing how or why. Dryden. FHYEP *Fr.* Absalom and Achitophel, Part 2.

Does a man ever give up hope, I wonder. Truth at Last. Edward Rowland Sill. APN-2

Does a word as a widow in the brain. Elegy for Sir Ifor Williams. Anthony Conran. AngWePo

Does anyone know this feeling: it's not the blues. Does Anyone Know This Feeling. J. Adwaita Dèr Mouw. TuT, *tr.* by Peter Van de Kamp

Does Charidas lie beneath you? If you mean. Callimachus. GrAn

Does he cock his weather-ear, enquiringly. David Jones. TCAWP *Fr.* Sleeping Lord, The.

Does he think of me in the merry throng. Question, The. Josephine D. Henderson Heard. CBWP-4

Does It Go Like this? Maura Dooley. NeBl

Does It Matter? Siegfried Sassoon. MoBrPo; PAI; PeFWW; PoWW

Does it really matter, really, if it's true or not. Singing to Tony Bennett's Cock. Victoria Redel. KGB

Does it wear a yarmulka. What Is a Jewish Poem? Myra Sklarew. CRP

Does man love Art? Man visits Art, but squirms. Gwendolyn Brooks. BPo *Fr.* Two Dedications.

Does mother get praised as often as she should. Woman Back in the Kitchen, The. Nicholas Lloyd Ingraham. PWR

Does my voice reach you? You are. Light Years and the Love Lost in the Oleanders. Alane Rollings. WeW-3

Does my voice sound strange? I am sitting. Talking to You Afterwards. Peter Porter. BMAP

Does not mean silence. To Play Pianissimo. Lola Haskins. MiVo

Does now like one of them appear. (LL) Andrew Marvell. BASC; GeHe; NAEL-7v1

Does That Answer Your Question, Mr Shakespeare? Stanley J. Sharpless. PeLV

Does the day break. Dawn. Nirmalprabha Bardoloi. OMIP, *tr.* by D. N. Bezbarua

Does the mouth refuse? Russians Breathing. Philip Hammial. NOBAu

Does the policeman sleep with his boots on. Song. Gerda Mayer. PeLV

Does the road wind up-hill all the way? Uphill. Christina Georgina Rossetti. CABP; EBVV; HAP; InPK-6; NAEL-5v2; NALW; NOBE; OBEV; PoE; PoRA; SacPr; TFi; TrCP; WPE; WeW-3

Does the sound or the silence make. Would You Think? John Wheelwright. APT-2

Does the Spearmint Lose Its Flavor on the Bedpost Overnight? Billy Rose. OBAL

Does the trick worth forty wenches. (LL) Song: "Love a woman? You're [*or* Y'are] an ass." John Wilmot, 2d Earl of Rochester. NBLV; NOBL; NOSC; PeLV; WoPoe

Does this water. At the Well. Leonard Nathan. PBCAP

Does thy life destroy. (LL) William Blake. AWP; BoLoP; ClHu; EnLoPo; FHYEP; HAP; InPK-4; NAEL-5v2; NAEL-6v2; NAWM-7v2; NIP-4; NOBE; NOBRP; NOEC; NPeEn; OPOU; OxAEP-2; OxBEV; OxBSP; PoE; RB; SCGP; SoSe-8; TFi; TRP; WeW-3 *Fr.* Songs of Experience.

Does your mother realize. You Must Have Been a Beautiful Baby. Johnny Mercer. ReLy

Doesn't he realize / that I am not / like the swaying kelp. Ono no Komachi. BoWoP; WPOW; WoPoe, *tr.* by Ikuko Atsumi and Kenneth Rexroth

Doesn't make any sense. (LL) Jelaluddin [*or* Jalal al-Din] Rumi. BLT; EnlH

Dog. Ingrid Jonker. HAWP, *tr.* by Jack Cope and William Plomer

Dog. Harold Monro. MoBrPo

Dog. John Crowe Ransom. OBAL

Dog, A. Gertrude Stein. TTTS *Fr.* Tender Buttons.

Dog, The. William Henry Davies. MoBrPo

Dog, The. Valentin Iremonger. BIrV

Dog, The. Stanley Moss. BodElec

Dog, The. Ogden Nash. Spl

Dog, The. Susan Fromberg Schaeffer. PoCoUp

Dog, The. Gerald Stern. Unle

Dog, The. Gerald Stern. WeW-3

Dog, The. C. K. Williams. BodElec

Dog Bark, The. Mary Jo Bang. NAPBL

Dog barked itself, The. Dog Which Barked Itself Out, The. Tymoteusz Karpowicz. PoSu, *tr.* by Rzej Busza and Bogdan Czaykowski

Dog barking, A. Buson. EH, *tr.* by Robert Hass

Dog barks amid the sound of water, A. Calling on a Taoist Priest in Tai-t'ien Mountain but Failing to See Him. Li Po. SuSp, *tr.* by Joseph J. Lee

Dog beneath the Skin, The. W. H. Auden. OxBTC "We are girls of different ages." UV

Dog Body and Cat Mind. Jenny Joseph. BrRo

Dog Creek Mainline. Charles Wright. LCAP-2

Dog Day Lesson. John Hughes. PNI

Dog Day Vespers. Charles Wright. LCAP-2

Dog Days. Derek Mahon. OPOU

Dog Days. Katherine Soniat. PoCoUp

Dog Days and Delta Nights. Franz Douskey. PasH

Dog Fight. Eric Rolls. NOBAu

Dog Fox Field. Les A. Murray. BMAP

Dog from Malta, The. Tymnes. *See* Epigrams

Dog-God. Robin Becker. ExTi

Dog in the River, The. Phaedrus. AWP, *tr.* by Christopher Smart

Dog it was that died, The. (LL) Oliver Goldsmith. FaBoCh; NBLV; NOEC; NOIV; OBNV; OxAEP-1; TFi *Fr.* Vicar of Wakefield, The.

Dog Kibble: A Villanelle. Charles Baxter. Unle

Dog must see your corpse, The. The last thing that you feel. Dog Prospectus. Peter Redgrove. OxBC

Dog of Art, The. Denise Levertov. NoAM

Dog Parted from Her Master. Hsüeh T'ao. WoPoe, *tr.* by Jeanne Larsen

Dog Prospectus. Peter Redgrove. OxBC

Dog's, A / body zipped. At the Crossroads. Thomas Kinsella. NoAM

Dog's Song. Robert Wallace. TLR

Dog's Vigil, A. Margaret E. Bruner. PoToHe

Dog scatters her body in sleep, The. Biography. Michael Ondaatje. NoAM

Dog searches until he finds me, The. Jane Kenyon. LoL *Fr.* Having It Out with Melancholy.

Dog Show. Laurie Anderson. OxWW

Dog Sleeping on My Feet, A. James Dickey. NAAL-2v2

Dog Sonnet. Sidney Wade. Unle

Dog Star. Gerry Gomez Pearlberg. WiU

Dog Suicide. Wanda Coleman. GeoHom

Dog-tired, suisired, will now my body down. Poet's Final Instructions, The. John Berryman. Son; VGW

Dog was in a hurry, The. It smelled the trees. Large raindrops were already falling. (LL) End of Dodona II, The. Yannis Ritsos. VCWP; WoPoe, *tr.* by Edmund Keeley

Dog was there, outside her door, The. Dog, The. William Henry Davies. MoBrPo

Dog Which Barked Itself Out, The. Tymoteusz Karpowicz. PoSu, *tr.* by Rzej Busza and Bogdan Czaykowski

Dog with daisies for eyes, The. Dog of Art, The. Denise Levertov. NoAM

Dogalypse. Andrey [*or* Andrei] Andreievich Voznesensky [*or* Voznesenskii]. CLPP

Dogen. Robert Bringhurst. "Under the sunrise the mountains." PoCoUp

Doggerel. Abigail Thomas. Unle

Doggerel by a Senior Citizen. W. H. Auden. NBLV; NOBL

Doggies went to the mill, The. *Unknown*. OxNR

Doggin the Rockman. Paul Beatty. InTrad

Dogknotting in Quezaltenango. Vincent O'Sullivan. PeNZ

Dogman, The. John Rybicki. Unle

Dogs. Laurie Duggan. South Coast Haiku. BMAP

Dogs, The. Michael S. Weaver. PBCAP

Dogs Are Shakespearean, Children Are Strangers. Delmore Schwartz. NoAM

Dogs bark ably, The: in Accra. Many Worlds Are Walked Once. Kojo Laing. HBAPE

Dogs bark in the midst of gurgling water. On Visiting Taoist Recluse of Tai-Tien-Shan and Not Finding Him. Li Po. ChinPo, *tr.* by Yip Wai-lim

Dogs bark where the river sings. Going to Visit a Taoist Recluse on Heaven's Mountain Only to find Him Gone. Li Po. CrYelRi, *tr.* by Sam Hamill

Dogs Gambol. Novica Tadic. VCWP, *tr.* by Charles Simic

Dogs, hogs, leaks in the bogs—we never went back. (LL) Itinerary. Edwin Morgan. HarvBoo; OBCoV

Dogs in the Morning Light. Bruce Dawe. NoAM

Dogs of New York, The. Lee Meitzen Grue. UrbNat

Dogs of war are loose and the rugged Russian bear, The. G. W. Hunt. FaBoWar *Fr.* McDermott's War Song.

Dogs on a leash. David Kherdian. UrbNat *Fr.* Taking the Soundings on Third Avenue.

Dogs on the Cliffs, The. Michael Burkard. BodElec

Dogs yap, sirens wail through the city. Lacrimae Rerum. Patricia Goedicke. ExTi

Dogtown. James Harms. GeoHom

Dogwood flakes / what is green. Variations Done for Gerald Van De Wiele. Charles Olson. APT-2; NOBA; NeAP; NoAM

Doing. Giancarlo Majorino. ItPo, *tr.* by Gayle Ridinger

Doing, a filthy pleasure is, and short. Fragment of Petronius Arbiter, A. Petronius Arbiter. ErotSp; OxBEV; WoPoe, *tr.* by Ben Jonson

Doing all she had to do, the sea going wild. (LL) Beehive Cell. Richard Murphy. CIP-2; OxBSo

Doing the Reactionary. Harold Rome. ReLy

Dol and Roger. Laetitia Pilkington. PEW

Dolce. Kennette Wilkes. PasH

Dolce Far Niente. Fidelito Cortes. ReBoTo

Dole of the King's Daughter, The. *Unknown.* AWP, *tr.* by Oscar Wilde

Doll. Myra Cohn Livingston. TLR

Doll. Josephine Miles. NALW

Doll. John Wieners. FTOS

Doll in the doll-maker's house, A. Dolls, The. W. B. Yeats. NoAM; PoE

Doll Museum, The. Carlyle Reedy. Oth

Doll Not Included. David Trinidad. WiU

Doll's hair concealing, A. Partial Resemblance. Denise Levertov. CoAP

Doll's House, A. Kit Wright. EmeKit

Dolls. David St. John. LCAP-2

Dolls, The. W. B. Yeats. NoAM; PoE

Dolls Museum in Dublin, The. Eavan Boland. NoP-4

Dolor. Josephine Miles. FaBoWP

Dolor. Theodore Roethke. HCAP; HeIP-4; NoAM; OPOU; OxBSP; TRP

Dolores. Algernon Charles Swinburne.
  "O lips full of lust and of laughter." UV

Dolorous, here he made his stand. He Who Loved Beauty. Alec Brock Stevenson. FuPo

Dolphin. Robert Lowell. NOBA; NoAM; VCAP

Dolphin, The. Maurya Simon. GeoHom

Dolphins. Bryn Griffiths. TCAWP

Dolphins play, The. Thom Gunn. NOxBChV *Fr.* Three for Children.

Domaine Public. Geoffrey Hill. OxBC *Fr.* Four Poems Regarding the Endurance of Poets.

Dome of Sunday, The [*or* A]. Karl Shapiro. CoAP; MoAmPo; NoAM; OxBA

Domestic Asides; or, Truth in Parentheses. Thomas Hood. PeLV

Domestic Blues. Teresa Calderón. TANSG, *tr.* by Celeste Kostopulos-Cooperman

Domestic carnage now filled the whole year. William Wordsworth. NAEL-6v2 *Fr.* Prelude; Growth of a Poet's Mind, The [1850 vers.].

Domestic Economy. Anna Wickham. ItWoWo

Domestic love! not in proud palace halls. Domestic Love. George Croly. TreFP

Domestic Mysticism. Lucie Brock-Broido. PoPoPo

Domestic Philosopher, The. *Unknown.* ECWP

Domestic Poems. Thomas Hood.
  Serenade, A. NBLV

Domestic Scene. Michael Hartnett. BIrV
  (Bread.) ModIr

Domestic Stones (fragment), The. Hans [*or* Jean] Arp. SPE, *tr.* by David Gascoyne

Domestic Storm, A. Priscilla Jane Thompson. CBWP-2

Domestic Tranquility. Gerald William Barrax. GT

Domestic Work, 1937. Natasha Trethewey. SpirFl

Domesticity of Giraffes, The. Judith Beveridge. BMAP

Domestics. Kattie M. Cumbo. BISi

Domi Solus. Danny Anderson. Unle

Domicilium. Thomas Hardy. OBGa

Domination of Black. Wallace Stevens. APT-1; MoAmPo; OWoS; OxBA; TCAPo

Domineering Eagle and the Inventive Bratling, The. Guy Wetmore Carryl. OBAL

Domingo Limón. Alberto A. Ríos. NAAL-5

Dominic Francis Xavier Brotherton-Chancery. Pastoral. Gavin Ewart. OxBC

Domino Theory (or Snoop Dogg Rules the World), The. Kenneth Carroll. SpirFl

Dominus Illuminatio Mea. Richard Doddridge Blackmore. OBEV; SacPr

Don and Dave and Di. Ballad of Don and Dave and Di, The. John Heath-Stubbs. EBNV

Don Baty, the Draft Resister. Muriel Rukeyser. NNaP

Don Giovanni. Lorenzo Da Ponte.
  Giovinette, Che Fate All'Amore. TrJP, *tr.* by Natalie MacFarren

Don José Gorostiza Encounters el Cordobés. Jay Wright. ESEAA

Don Juan. Byron.
  Canto the First. CABP; NAEL-5v2; NAEL-6v2; PoE; SCV
    "But now at thirty years my hair is grey." NOBE; SCV
    Growing Old. NOBE; SCV
    "If ever I should condescend to prose." OxBoLi; PeLV
    Juan's Puberty. NPeEn
    Poetical Commandments. OxBoLi; PeLV
    "Poor Julia's heart was in an awkward state." NOBRP
    "Sagest of women, even of widows, she." NOBL; PeLV
    "They tell me 'tis decided; you depart." NOBRP
    "What is the end of fame? 'Tis but to fill." OBCoV
    "Young Juan wandered by the glassy brooks." OBCoV
  Canto the Second.
    "Alas for Juan and Haidee! They were." NePenScot
    "Alas, they were so young, so beautiful." EroLit; OxBEV
    "At half-past eight o'clock, booms, hencoops, spars." NPeEn
    "But to our tale: the Donna Inez sent." NAEL-6v2
    "His eyes he opened, shut, again unclosed." EBNV
    "How long in his damp trance young Juan lay." NAEL-6v2
    Juan and Haïdée. EBNV
    "Nine souls more went in her: the long-boat still." OxBEV
    Shipwreck, The. NPeEn
    "Shore looked wild, without a trace of man, The." HAP
    "There, breathless, with his digging nails he clung." OxAEP-2
  Canto the Third.
    Evening. AWP
    "Haidée and Juan carpeted their feet." NOBRP
    "I know that what our neighbours call *longueurs*." OBSV
    "Isles of Greece, the isles of Greece!, The." AWP; NOBE; OBEV; OxAEP-2
    "Milton's the prince of poets—so we say." NOBL
    "O Hesperus! thou bringest all good things." AWP
  Canto the Fourth.
    "As boy, I thought myself a clever fellow." NAEL-6v2
    "I leave Don Juan for the present, safe." NOBRP
    "They were alone once more; for them to be." EBEV
  Canto the Seventh.
    "'Let there be light!' said God, and there was light!" OBWP
    "Oh, thou eternal Homer! I have now." FaBoWar
  Canto the Ninth.
    On Wellington. FaBoWar; OBSV; OxAEP-2; OxBoLi
    "To be or not to be! That is the question." OBCoV
  Canto the Tenth.
    "Lawyer and the critic but behold, The." NePenScot
  Canto the Eleventh. NOBRP
    "Don Juan had got out on Shooter's Hill." FaBoVe
    "In the great world—which, being interpreted." OxBoLi; PeLV
    Juan in England. FaBoVe
    "Over the stones still rattling, up Pall Mall." NOBL
    "To our theme. The man who has stood on the Acropolis." OBSV
    "When Bishop Berkeley said 'there was no matter'" NOBRP
  Canto the Twelfth.
    "Why call the miser miserable? as." UnPo
    "Young unmarried man, with a good name, A." NOBL
  Canto the Fourteenth.
    "You know, or you don't know, that great Bacon saith." NOBL
  Dedication: "Bob Southey! You're a poet—poet-laureate." CTC; OBSV
  Fragment: "I would to heaven that I were so much clay." CTC; NAEL-5v2; NAEL-6v2; NOBL; OxBEV; OxBSP

Don Juan had got out on Shooter's Hill. Byron. FaBoVe *Fr.* Don Juan.

Don Juan in Hell. Charles Baudelaire. AWP, *tr.* by James Elroy Flecker

Don Juan's Address to the Sunset. Robert Malise Bowyer Nichols. OBMV

Don Leon. *Unknown.*
  "Among the yeomen's sons on my estate." CAGL
  "Chance led me once, when idling through the street." CAGL
  "Sometimes I sauntered from my lone abode." CAGL
  "Statesmen, in your exalted station know." CAGL
  "Thou ermined judge, pull off that sable cap!" CAGL
  "Thus feverish fancies floated in my brain." CAGL
  "Tree we plant will, when its boughs are grown, The." CAGL
  "Women as women, me had never charmed." CAGL

Don Pullen at the Zanzibar Blue Jazz Cafe, 1994. Major L. Jackson. SpirFl

Don Quixote in England. Henry Fielding.
  Hunting Song. OxBoLi; PeLV

Don's Holiday. George Rostrevor Hamilton. OBCoV

Don Surly, to aspire the glorious name. On Don Surly. Ben Jonson. FaBoEE; NAEL-5v1; NAEL-6v1; NAEL-7v1

Don't anther. (LL) Panther, The. Ogden Nash. OBAL; OBCA; OxIBACP

Don't ape what must be born in one.   Donkey and the Lapdog, The.   Jean de La Fontaine.   OBVE, *tr. by* Marianne Moore

Don't ask about the Six Dynasties of the Sui Palace.   Wang T'ing-hsiang.   CoBLCP   *Fr.* Song of Wu-ch'eng.

Don't ask any questions!   Drunk among the Flowers.   Mao Wen-hsi.   ColAnChi, *tr. by* Lois Fusek

Don't ask me for a date.   Rendezvous in the Cave.   Ahmad 'Abd al-Mu'ti Hijazi.   MAP, *tr. by* Sargon Boulus and Peter Porter

Don't Ask Me for That Love Again.   Faiz Ahmad Faiz.   PoetW; VCWP, *tr. by* Agha Shahid Ali

Don't ask me just how it happened.   I Got Lost in His Arms.   Irving Berlin.   ReLy

Don't ask me, my love, for that love again. (LL)   Don't Ask Me for That Love Again.   Faiz Ahmad Faiz.   PoetW; VCWP, *tr. by* Agha Shahid Ali

Don't Ask Me Who I Am.   James A. Randall, Jr.   BPo

Don't ask suspiciously.   Muso Soseki.   EaWin, *tr. by* W. S. Merwin

Don't ask us for the word to frame.   Eugenio Montale.   PoetW, *tr. by* Jonathan Galassi

Don't assume each threat is uttered.   *Unknown*.   PriapPo, *tr. by* Richard W. Hooper   *Fr.* Priapus Poems, The.

Don't be afraid.   Matter of Control, A.   Diana García.   TouFir

Don't be afraid of the future.   Life Is a Song, Let's Sing It Together.   Fred E. Ahlert.   ReLy

Don't be dismayed, woman, by my fierce form.   Annunciation.   Primo Levi.   AF; GI

Don't be polite.   How to Eat a Poem.   Eve Merriam.   ChAP

Don't be too eager to ask.   Horace.   WoPoe, *tr. by* David Ferry   *Fr.* Odes.

Don't believe Nicole.   Zebra, The.   Marie Laurencin.   CuPo

Don't Believe the Hype.   Public Enemy.   NAAAL

Don't bite your nails, Amanda!   Amanda!   Robin Klein.   OTCP

Don't Blame Me.   Dorothy Fields.   ReLy

Don't blame me, ladies, if I've loved. No sneers.   Sonnet 24.   Louise Labé.   BoWoP

Don't block my way, friend.   Mirabai [*or* Mira Bai].   ErotSp, *tr. by* Andrew Schelling

Don't bother about the news!   Aleksandr Semionovich Kushner.   TCRusP, *tr. by* Daniel Weissbort

Don't bother telling me about the programs.   TV.   John Forbes.   CBAP

Don't Bring Lulu.   Ray Henderson.   ReLy

Don't Bring Out the Straw Mat.   Han Kwak.   WoPoe, *tr. by* Virginia Olsen Baron and Chung Seuk Park

Don't care didn't care.   *Unknown*.   OTCP

Don't. Crow and butcher bird. Sick Woman.   John Kinsella.   BMAP

Don't cry / over the happy dead.   *Unknown*.   GrAn

Don't Cry, Scream.   Haki R. Madhubuti.   SeSe

Don't cut it to make a flute.   Bamboo by Li Ch'e Yun's Window, The.   Po Chü-i.   OHMPC, *tr. by* Kenneth Rexroth

Don't die, Dad.   Last Hellos, The.   Les A. Murray.   HarvBoo

Don't dress it for it.   Chiyojo [*or* Chiyo *or* Chiyo-Ni *or* Kaga no Chiyo *or* Fukuda Chiyo-Ni].   BoWoP

Don't drive me out of my mind.   Second Honeymoon.   *Unknown*.   BIrV, *tr. by* Augustus Young

Don't even go to a movie show.   Keepin' Out of Mischief Now.   Andy Razaf.   ReLy

Don't Ever Leave Me.   Jerome Kern.   ReLy

Don't fash yourself, man! Don't complain.   Palladas [*or* Pallades].   GrAn

Don't fear me! There's the grey beginning. Zooks! (LL)   Robert Browning.   CTC; EBVV; FHYEP; NAEL-6v2; OxAEP-2

Don't Feel No Way.   Kevin Powell.   InTrad

Don't fly off, nightingale.   Issa.   ZenPo, *tr. by* Takashi Ikemoto and Lucien Stryk

Don't Forget.   Alice Sadongei.   HATNAP

Don't forget henna for the palms of your hands. (LL)   Mwana Kupona Msham.   HAWP; WPOW   *Fr.* Poem to Her Daughter.

Don't forget the crablike / hands.   Hands, The.   Denise Levertov.   NeAP; PoM

Don't forget to ask him to send me all of his. . . / I should have given.   Bernard Heidsieck.   PFTM-2, *tr. by* Nicholas Zürbrugg   *Fr.* Canal Street.

Don't forget to say no, baby, while I'm with your Uncle Sam.   Don't Forget to Say No, Baby.   Hoagy Carmichael.   ReLy

Don't forget when the sticks are ready for picking.   Don't Forget.   Alice Sadongei.   HATNAP

Don't founder, my ship, tomorrow's hero guides you.   On New Waters.   Endre Ady.   IQMS, *tr. by* Anton N. Nyerges

Don't frighten me with a terrible fate.   Don't Frighten Me.   Anna Andreyevna Akhmatova.   RusPo, *tr. by* Robert Arthur Douglas Ford

Don't Get Around Much Anymore.   Duke Ellington.   ReLy

Don't give everything.   David Foster.   NOBAu   *Fr.* Fleeing Atalanta, The.

Don't Give Up.   C. C. Cameron.   PoToHe   *Fr.* Success.

Don't go.   Larry Eigner.   PoM

Don't go back, Ma, don't go back, Mother.   Najrul Islām.   SinGod, *tr. by* Rachel Fell McDermott

Don't go hide in the deep mountains.   Po Chü-i.   CoBCP, *tr. by* Burton Watson   *Fr.* Better Come Drink Wine with Me.

Don't go 'round mopin', hopin'   (Up on Top of a Rainbow) Sweepin' the Clouds Away.   Sam Coslow.   ReLy

Don't halt your voyage, sailor, nor drop sail.   Johannes Barbucollas.   GrAn

Don't help-on the big chariot.   Big Chariot, The.   *Unknown*.   ChiP, *tr. by* Arthur Waley

Don't hitch your dear little cunt against that wall.   Strato [*or* Straton].   EroLit, *tr. by* Kenneth McLeish

Don't Hope to Gain by What Has Preceded.   Joanne Kyger.   PoM

Don't hunt too anxiously a wilful hound.   Advice to a Man Who Lost a Dog.   Howard Baker.   APT-2

Don't imitate me.   Basho.   EH, *tr. by* Robert Hass

Don't judge men by their gravestones.   Antipater of Thessalonica.   GrAn

Don't kill that fly!   Issa.   EH, *tr. by* Robert Hass

Don't kill that fly!   Avedik Issahakian.   ChAP

Don't kill that poor fly!   Issa.   SoOfWa, *tr. by* Sam Hamill

Don't Kill Yourself.   Carlos Drummond de Andrade.   TCLAP, *tr. by* Elizabeth Bishop

Don't Kill Yourself.   Carlos Drummond de Andrade.   WoPoe, *tr. by* Mark Strand

Don't Knock the Rawleigh's Man.   Vincent O'Sullivan.   PeNZ

Don't know a man or woman can do it, tell the truth about love.   She Attempts to Tell the Truth about True Romance.   Kathy Fagan.   ExTi

Don't know about the people.   Issa.   EH, *tr. by* Robert Hass

Don't know / Nice, though. (LL)   Ode on a Grecian Urn Summarized.   Desmond Skirrow.   NIL-7; NIP-4; NOBL

Don't Know No English.   Nicolás Guillén.   PFTM-1

Don't know why I.   Angola Question Mark.   Langston Hughes.   BPo; TTY

Don't know why / There's no sun up in the sky.   Stormy Weather (Keeps Rainin' All the Time).   Ted Koehler.   ReLy

Don't laugh because it's muddy—year-end wine brewed in country homes.   Trip to Mountain West Village, A.   Lu Yu.   CoBCP, *tr. by* Burton Watson

Don't let freezing hands play with these pearls.   Meng Chiao.   SuSp   *Fr.* Apricots Die Young.

Don't let it matter much, Philaenis.   Tymnes.   GrAn

Don't let me fall.   Prayers: I.   Kadya Molodovsky [*or* Molodowsky].   WPoS, *tr. by* Kathryn Hellerstein

Don't Let's Be Beastly to the Germans.   Noël Coward.   ReLy

Don't Let That Horse.   Lawrence Ferlinghetti.   RB

Don't let your dog curb you!   Warning: Augmented.   Langston Hughes.   APT-2

Don't lie down again.   Lying Down.   *Unknown*.   STP, *tr. by* Franz Boas

Don't lock me in wedlock, I want.   About Marriage.   Denise Levertov.   NALW

Don't love me, my dear.   Flavien Ranaivo.   *See* Don't love me, my sweet

Don't love me, my sweet.   Song of a Common Lover.   Flavien Ranaivo.   TTY, *tr. by* Alan Ryder

Don't lower your eyes.   Lady Freedom among Us.   Rita Dove.   LoL

Don't make me go out eat goose.   Ebenezer Californicus.   August Kleinzahler.   PmAP

Don't mind if you die. It's just your body's shape.   On Death.   Sándor Weöres.   IQMS, *tr. by* Alan Dixon

Don't mistake what you have for what you are. (LL)   Wang An-shih.   SuSp; WoPoe, *tr. by* Jan W. Walls   *Fr.* In the Style of Han Shan and Shih Te.

Don't obey me!—the Master ordered the perplexed Golem.   Ana Maria Shúa.   MirDau, *tr. by* Rhonda Buchanan   *Fr.* Golem and Rabbi.

Don't pay any attention.   Martial.   PGA

Don't pile cruel cares upon those griefs.   Stesichoros.   SaLy, *tr. by* Diane Rayor

Don't prepare for tomorrow, enter the narrow lane.   Yehuda Amichai [*or* Amikhai].   FIT, *tr. by* Robert Friend

Don't pretend I didn't warn you.   *Unknown*.   PriapPo, *tr. by* Richard W. Hooper   *Fr.* Priapus Poems, The.

Don't put your daughter on the stage. (LL)   Noël Coward.   ReLy; UV   *Fr.* Mrs Worthington.

Don't Rain on My Parade.   Jule Styne.   ReLy

Don't Read Books!   Yang Wan-li.   ColAnChi, *tr. by* Jonathan Chaves

Don't read odes, boy, timetables.   For a Senior College Textbook.   Hans Magnus Enzensberger.   PoSu

Don't remove the glasses and plates.   Instructions for a Waitress.   Yehuda Amichai [*or* Amikhai].   PoSu, *tr. by* Harold Schimmel

Don't Say Goodbye to the Pork-Pie Hat.   Larry Neal.   GT; ISC; SeSe
   (Again, this time from the chorus.) (LL)   ISC; SeSe

Don't Say Goodnight to Etheridge Knight.   Tony Medina.   InTrad

Don't say: How can Phoenix Hill.   Kuan Yün-shih.   SuSp, *tr. by* Richard John

Lynn *Fr.* Medley of Southern and Northern Tunes—Scenic Tour of West Lake.

Don't say the daily struggle will get you down. It's All Yours. Dorothy Fields. ReLy

Don't say there are only hills and slopes at West Lake. Abandoning the Plans of Visiting West Lake. Hsü Wei. SuSp, *tr. by* Irving Y. Lo

Don't say this to an old idol that's lost its nose. Paavo Haavikko. WoPoe, *tr. by* Anselm Hollo *Fr.* Fifteen Epigrams in Praise of the Tyrant.

Don't say to me. On Wishes. Mahmoud Darwish. VCWP, *tr. by* Denys Johnson-Davies

Don't seek me where the myrtles bloom! My Camping Ground. Morris Jacob Rosenfeld. TrJP, *tr. by* Aaron Kramer

DON'T set sail! Love-Poem. Fêng Mêng-lung. ChiP, *tr. by* Arthur Waley

Don't shoo the morning flies away. Han Yü. SuSp

Don't sing: a song. Drops of Gall. Gabriela Mistral. BoWoP, *tr. by* David Garrison

Don't sing "The Song of Everlasting Sorrow." Ma-wei. Yüan Mei. CoBLCP, *tr. by* Jonathan Chaves

Don't Sleep. Ingrid Jonker. WPOW, *tr. by* Elizabeth Jones

Don't sleep! for your paddle fell into the water and your spear. Song of Parents Who Want to Wake Up Their Son. *Unknown.* TTTS

Don't sleep, look! Don't Sleep. Ingrid Jonker. WPOW, *tr. by* Elizabeth Jones

Don't smile. So you won't become a Buddha. Paavo Haavikko. WoPoe, *tr. by* Anselm Hollo *Fr.* Fifteen Epigrams in Praise of the Tyrant.

Don't steal. Thou'lt never thus compete. Ambrose Bierce. NBLV

Don't stereotype an image of what you want me to be. Right to Be. Eva Johnson. IBA

Don't stop after beating the swords. Appendix to the Vision of Peace, An. Yehuda Amichai [*or* Amikhai]. PoSu, *tr. by* Glenda Abramson and Tudor Parfitt

Don't suppose that the weightless phantom. Titans, The. Betti Alver. BoWoP, *tr. by* Willis Barnstone and Felix Oinas

Don't sweep away this green after the rain. Moss below the Stairs. Kao Ch'i. CoBLCP, *tr. by* Jonathan Chaves

Don't talk to me about trees having branches and roots. On Trees. Alan Dugan. NoAM

Don't talk to me of love. I've had an earful. In Paris with You. James Fenton. NoP-4

Don't tell me. For Thieves Only. Lois Red Elk. ReEnLa

Don't tell me not to fly. Don't Rain on My Parade. Jule Styne. ReLy

Don't tell me what he did in some other country. Wife to a Friend, A. Kshetrayya. WoPoe, *tr. by* V. Narayana Rao, A. K. Ramanujan and David Shulman

Don't the moon look lonesome shining through the trees? Sent for You Yesterday. Jimmy Rushing. NAAAL

Don't thee think, Zurrr, I be zo amazin' Limerick. Elizabeth H. Lister. PeLi

Don't they really have. What She Said. Mamalatan. WoPoe, *tr. by* A. K. Ramanujan

Don't think, I said, that because I deny. Monodrama. Bill Knott. BodElec

Don't think it will fall to your lot. Limerick. Leslie Johnson. PeLi

Don't think / that I don't know. Sous-Entendu. Anne Stevenson. LW; OxBSP

Don't throw your arms around me in that way. Footnote to John II: 4. Ronald Allison Kells Mason. PeNZ

Don't Touch. Boris Leonidovich Pasternak. TCRusP, *tr. by* Bogdan Boychuk and Mark Rudman

Don't touch me. Hermaphrodite's Song, The. Lorna Mitchell. BrRo

Don't touch my corpse. Standing Coffin. Tamura Ryuichi. AF, *tr. by* Christopher Drake

"Don't touch!" my host cried. Tan Taigi. SoOfWa, *tr. by* Sam Hamill

Don't touch that. And stop your whining too. What I Heard at the Discount Department Store. David Budbill. RaBo; TRP

Don't touch that fruit, Eve. *Paradise Lost* as a Haiku. Stanley J. Sharpless. OBCoV

"Don't touch. Wet paint." the sign said. Don't Touch. Boris Leonidovich Pasternak. TCRusP, *tr. by* Bogdan Boychuk and Mark Rudman

Don't trace out your profile. Antonio Machado Ruiz. RaBo *Fr.* Moral Proverbs and Folk Songs.

Don't travel beyond. Immigrant. Arthur Nortje. PeSAV

Don't try and make that home made brew. Distress upon the Farm. Laury Wells. IBA

Don't turn around, don't look back. Olga Fiodorovna Berggolts [*or* Bergholts]. TCRusP, *tr. by* Daniel Weissbort

Don't Walk beside the Big Carriage. *Unknown.* CoBCP, *tr. by* Burton Watson

Don't Wanna Write about the South. Harold Rome. ReLy

Don't want any millions. I'm Sitting on Top of the World. Ray Henderson. ReLy

Don't waste yourself, dragging out the life of a vagrant. Leonidas of Tarentum. GrAn

Don't we talk of then are unsealed they efflorescing. Giant Philosophical Otters. Jackson Mac Low. FTOS

Don't weep for me—I'll live on. Incantation. Bella [*or* Izabella] Akhatovna Akhmadulina. TCRP, *tr. by* Albert C. Todd

Don't weep, insects / Lovers, stars, themselves. Issa. ZenPo, *tr. by* Takashi Ikemoto and Lucien Stryk

Don't worry. Philippe Jaccottet. MFP, *tr. by* Martin Sorrell

Don't worry about growing old. Prayerwheel: 2. David Meltzer. NeAP

Don't Worry 'bout Me. Ted Koehler. ReLy

Don't worry, nobody has the. Secret, The. Charles Bukowski. RaBo

Don't worry / One night we'll find that deserted kinema. If Life's a Lousy Picture, Why Not Leave before the End. Roger McGough. OxBTC

Don't worry please please how many times do I have to say it. Ikkyu Sojun. WoPoe, *tr. by* Stephen Berg *Fr.* Four Poems.

Don't worry, spiders. Issa. ChAP; EH, *tr. by* Robert Hass

Don't worry, you'll get there! You're close. Don't worry. Philippe Jaccottet. MFP, *tr. by* Martin Sorrell

Don't worry. You're in darkness. Instructions to a Seed. David Curzon. GI

Don't write poems about what's happening. Looking for Poetry. Carlos Drummond de Andrade. ChAP, *tr. by* Mark Strand

Don't You Be like the Foolish Virgin. *Unknown.* AH

Don't you believe it's enough that I'm stuck in this spot. *Unknown.* PriapPo, *tr. by* Richard W. Hooper *Fr.* Priapus Poems, The.

Don't you care for my love? she said bitterly. Intimates. D. H. Lawrence. BoLoP; NBLV; OxBSP; RaBo

Don't you cut the brush. Lady Otomo no Sakanoé. ArkPo, *tr. by* Edwin A. Cranston

Don't you feel it's like being in the midst of a long novel? On Being in the Midwest. Diana Chang. FSt

Don't you hear it? (LL) Desnos Reading the Palms of Men on Their Way to the Gas Chambers. Stephen Berg. GotH; TaR

Don't You Hear that Whistle Blowin' Denise Levertov. GM

Don't you know. Ox-Soldier, The. Oumar Ba. PBMAP

Don't you love my baby, mam. Infant Song. Charles Causley. NOxBChV; OxBC

Don't you remember sweet Alice, Ben Bolt. Ben Bolt. Thomas Dunn English. APN-1

Don't you see how the Running Horse River flows along the edge of the Sea of Snow. Song of the Running Horse River: Presented on Saying Farewell to the Army Going on Campaign to the West, A. Ts'en Shen. ColAnChi, *tr. by* Daniel Bryant

Don't you see, north of Ch'ang-an, by the bridge over Wei River. Weary Road, The. Lu Chao-lin. SuSp, *tr. by* Robin D. S. Yates

Don'ts. D. H. Lawrence. OxBoLi; PeLV

Doña Josefina Counsels Doña Concepción before Entering Sears. Maurice Kilwein Guevara. AmPoNex

Donagh MacDonagh. James Liddy. BiHa

Donahue's Sister. Thom Gunn. NoAM

Donal Og. *Unknown.* RB, *tr. by* Lady Augusta Gregory

Donald Evans. Witter Bynner. APT-1

Donald, he's come to this town. Dugall Quin. *Unknown.* ESPB

Donald of the Isles. *Unknown.* *See* Lizie Lindsay

Donal[l] Oge [*or* Og]: Grief of a Girl's Heart. *Unknown.* RB, *tr. by* Lady Augusta Gregory

Donatello's Saint George. Louise Imogen Guiney. *Fr.* Knight Errant, The.

Donatilia's Unrequited Love Remedy. Virgil Suárez. AmPoNex

Done is a battell on the dragon blak. On the Resurrection of Christ. William Dunbar. NPeEn; NePenScot; OxBEV

Done is a battle on the dragon black. William Dunbar. SacPr

Done to death by slanderous tongues. William Shakespeare. CTC *Fr.* Much Ado about Nothing.

Done with a long day's begging. Ryokan. WoPoe, *tr. by* Burton Watson

Dong, Sounds the Brass in the East. Henry David Thoreau. APN-1

Dong with a Luminous Nose, The. Edward Lear. EBNV; EBVV; NOBVV; NOxBChV; OxAEP-2; OxBEV

Donkey, The. Gilbert Keith Chesterton. ChIV-2; GI; InPK-6; MoBrPo; OBEV; RB

Donkey, The. Theodore Roethke. OBCA

Donkey, The. Stevie Smith. HarvBoo

Donkey and the Lapdog, The. Jean de La Fontaine. OBVE, *tr. by* Marianne Moore

Donkey, donkey, do not bray. *Unknown.* OxNR

Donkey, donkey, old and gray. *Unknown.* ReMoGo

Donkey's tail is very nice, A. Monotony Song, The. Theodore Roethke. ChAP

Donna Mi Priegha. Ezra Pound. *See* Cantos

Donne, the delight of Phoebus, and each Muse. To John Donne. Ben Jonson. BeJo; NAEL-5v1; NAEL-6v1; NAEL-7v1

Donought would have everything. Song. Ebenezer Elliott. NOBVV

Dont' tell me I'm getting gray. Paulus [or Paulos] Silentiarius. PGA

Dont Worry Yr Hair. Bill Bissett. NOBC

Doodle doodle doo, / The Princess lost her shoe. Lost Shoe, The. *Unknown.* ReMoGo

Dooley Is a Traitor. James Michie. OxBTC

Doom. "Rubén Dario." SpanPo, *tr. by* Kate Flores

Doom Ferry. Sir Arthur Thomas Quiller-Couch. EBVV

Doom is dark and deeper than any sea-dingle. Wanderer, The. W. H. Auden. HarvBoo; NoAM; RB; WeW-3; WoPoe

Doom of a City, The. James Thomson.
  "Thy Church has long been becoming the Fossil of a Faith." SacPr

Doom of Beauty, The. Michelangelo Buonarroti. AWP, *tr. by* John Addington Symonds

Doom of Devorgoil, The. Sir Walter Scott.
  Bonny [or Bonnie] Dundee. FaBoCh; OxBS; OxBoLi; UV

Doomed in the depths to dwell. Thanksgiving. David Abenatar Melo. TrJP, *tr. by* Henry Hart Milman

Doomsday. George Herbert. GeHe

Doomsday. Maurya Simon. ExTi

Doomsday. Elinor Wylie. NoP-4; SacPr

Doomsday Morning. Genevieve Taggard. MoAmPo

Doomsday of wind. Door of Roses. Munia Samara. PoArWo, *tr. by* Amal Amireh

Doomsday, the Mysteries. *Unknown.*
  Harrowing, The. WoPoe, *tr. by* Tony Harrison

Doon Deeside cam Inverey. Baron of Braikley, The. *Unknown.* OxBB

Door. Valerie Worth. CA

Door, A. U. A. Fanthorpe. NewEx

Door, A. W. S. Merwin. LCAP-2; SPE

Door, The. W. H. Auden. Son *Fr.* Quest, The.

Door, The. Robert Creeley. NAAL-5; NeAP; NoAM; PoM; VGW

Door, The. Mark Strand. NoAM

Door, The. Leonard Alfred George Strong. MoBrPo

Door, The. Charles Tomlinson. OxBEV

Door and the Window, The. Henry Reed. HarvBoo

Door and Window Bolted Fast. Mani Leib [or Leyb]. TrJP, *tr. by* Joseph Leftwich

Door behind me was you, The. Tom Clark. PmAP; SPE *Fr.* You.

Door-Bell, The. Charlotte Becker. PoToHe

Door by door. Jerusalem, Timeless. Luisa Futuransky. MirDau, *tr. by* Celeste Kostopulos-Cooperman

Door does not turn; in my window, no face, The. Purity. Avigdor Hame'iri. MHP, *tr. by* Ruth Finer Mintz

Door, friends, will not, The. Love Song of Audrey. Jim Shepard. Unle

Door is before you again and the shrieking, The. Door, The. Mark Strand. NoAM

Door is open, The. I shall not be intruding. Old Pump-house, Llanwrtyd Wells. Ruth Bidgood. TCAWP

Door isn't locked, The. You walk. In the Gloaming. Jennifer Maiden. BMAP

Door jambs still frames, The. Grandmother's Farm. Mark Todd. GeoH

Door of Hope, The. Lizelia Augusta Jenkins Moorer. CBWP-3

Door of Roses. Munia Samara. PoArWo, *tr. by* Amal Amireh

Door of the Cities. Munia Samara. PoArWo, *tr. by* Amal Amireh

Door slam, The. After the First Frost. Lew Blockcolski. VoR

Door still swinging to, and girls revive, The. Dream of Fair Women, A. Kingsley Amis. NoAM

Door sunk in a hillside, with a bolt, A. Icehouse in Summer, The. Howard Nemerov. NoAM

Door swung open, The. Kenneth Mackenzie. BMAP

Door that someone opened wide, The. Message, The. Jacques Prévert. WeW-3, *tr. by* John Frederick Nims

Door Thrown Open to Daisies. Rick Agran. AmPoNex

Door was shut, The. I looked between. Shut Out. Christina Georgina Rossetti. NALW

Doorbell buzzed, The. It was past three o'clock. Australian Dream, The. David Campbell. CBAP

Doorkeeper has feet seven fathoms long, The. Sappho. SaLy, *tr. by* Diane Rayor

Doors. Tom Clark. CoAmPo

Doors. Rosalie Moore. YaYoPo

Doors. Thérèse Plantier. BoWoP, *tr. by* Willis Barnstone and Elene Kolb

Doors are open, The. We must pass through. Preface to I Am Rain. Hilary Booth. SurWo

Doors of dead roses close stargazing lilies a garden we grew. As I Leave You. Chrystos. ReEnLa

Doors of Sleep, The. Marion Angus. NePenScot

Doors open by themselves, The. Chicken, The. Vladimir Holan. PoSu, *tr. by* Ian Milner and Jarmila Milner

Doors open on the sands, doors open on exile. "St.-John Perse." AF *Fr.* Exile.

Doors swing out, and spill you down the stair. After Carnival. Peter Rafferty. NLP

Doors, the little doors, swing wide, The. (LL) Jim Desterland. Hyam Plutzik. RB; VGW

Doors, where my heart was used to beat. Tennyson. FHYEP; NAEL-6v2; SCV *Fr.* In Memoriam A. H. H.

Dope. Imamu Amiri Baraka. APSN

Doper's Dream. Don Receveur. CDa

Dora Markus. Eugenio Montale. PoetW, *tr. by* William Arrowsmith

Dora Markus and Her Actors. Gregorio Scalise. ItPo, *tr. by* Gayle Ridinger

Dora versus Rose. Austin Dobson. NOBL

Dora Williams. Edgar Lee Masters. HAP *Fr.* Spoon River Anthology.

Dorcas. George Macdonald. SacPr

Dorcas, be off! & tell her this. Meleager. GrAn

Doreen had a round face. Doreen. Janice Mirikitani. UnSA

Doretha wore the short blue lace last night. Reception, The. June Jordan. FaBoWP

Doria. Ezra Pound. MoAmPo

Doricha. Poseidippus. AWP; FaBoEE; OBVE, *tr. by* E. A. Robinson

Doricha. *Var. authors.* AWP; FaBoEE; OBVE; WoPoe, *tr. by* Edwin Arlington Robinson *Fr.* Variations of Greek Themes.

Doricha, your soft bones are. Poseidippus. FaBoEE

Dorinda's sparkling wit, and eyes. On the Countess of Dorchester. Charles Sackville, 6th Earl of Dorset. OBEV

Doris. William Congreve. NOEC

Doris, I that could repell. Snow-Ball, The. Thomas Stanley. NPeEn

Dorkion, sweet little tomboy. Asclepiades. EroLit, *tr. by* Kenneth McLeish

Dornier, The. Gladys Mary Coles. TCAWP

Dorothy Q. Oliver Wendell Holmes. NOBA

Dorothy Wordsworth, dying, did not want to read. My Sisters, O My Sisters. May Sarton. NALW

Dos Geshray (The Scream). Jerome Rothenberg. FTOS; PFTM-2 *Fr.* Khurbn.

Dos Oysleydikn (The Emptying). Jerome Rothenberg. PFTM-2 *Fr.* Khurbn.

Dose of a mere, The. Discovery of LSD a True Story, The. Anselm Hollo. PoM

Dosn't thou 'ear my 'erse's legs, as they canters awaäy? Northern Farmer: New Style. Tennyson. NAEL-5v2; NAEL-6v2; OBCoV; OxAEP-2; PeVV

Dossers at the Imperial War Museum. Joyce Herbert. TCAWP

Dost see how unregarded me now. Sonnet. Sir John Suckling. BASC; BeJo; CaPo; CavPo; NOSC

Dost tha hear my horse's feet, as he canters away? Lord Tennyson and Lord Melchett. D. H. Lawrence. FaBoEE

Dost therefore swell and pout with pride. Tyrant in Sleep, Naught Differeth from a Common Man, A. Timothy Kendall. NoSic

Dost thou forget. William Shakespeare. OxAEP-1 *Fr.* Tempest, The.

Dost thou look back on what hath been. Tennyson. NAEL-6v2 *Fr.* In Memoriam A. H. H.

Dot a dot dot dot a dot dot. Weather. Eve Merriam. TLR

Dotage. George Herbert. SacPr

Dotes less on Nature, then on Art. (LL) Art above Nature, to Julia. Robert Herrick. BeJo; NOSC

Doth die unknown, dazed with dreadful face. (LL) Stand Whoso List. Sir Thomas Wyatt. NAEL-7v1; NoP-4

Doth dye unknow[e]n, dazed with dreadful[l] face. (LL) Seneca. NPeEn; NoSic; OBVE; OxBEV, *tr. by* Sir Thomas Wyatt *Fr.* Thyestes.

Doth Fortune play the huswife with me now? William Shakespeare. FaBoWar *Fr.* King Henry V.

Doth make my heart give to my tongue the lie! (LL) Sir Philip Sidney. NAEL-5v1; NAEL-6v1; NAEL-7v1; NoP-4 *Fr.* Astrophil and Stella.

Doth not thou, Castara, read. William Habington. BeJo *Fr.* Castara.

Doth then the world go thus, doth all thus move? William Drummond, of Hawthornden. GTBS-P

Doth time [or tyme] outlive. (LL) Bible, *O.T.* ChIV-1; OxBEV, *tr. by* Mary Sidney Herbert, Countess of Pembroke *Fr.* Psalms.

Doth warm our hands, and make them write of love. (LL) Love (1). George Herbert. GeHe; Son

Dotito Is Our Brother. Charles Mungoshi. PeSAV

Double, The. Joan Aleshire. OPRER

Double Acrostich on Mrs Svsanna Blvnt, A. Thomas Jordan. NPeEn

Double Autumn, The. James Reeves. OxBSP

Double Ballad of Good Counsel, A. François Villon. AWP, *tr. by* Algernon Charles Swinburne

Double Bed. Carol Rumens. LW

Double boiler fixed on fiery wheels, A. Alec Derwent Hope. OxBC *Fr.* Dunciad Minor.

Double Crossing. Eva Salzman. MFPA

Double Dactyl. Chris Wallace-Crabbe. OBCoV

Double Dactyls. Eric Salzman. OBCoV

Double Dactyls. E. William Seaman. OBCoV; WeW-3

Double Date. Lincoln Kirstein. PeLV

Double Elegy. Michael S. Harper. ESEAA; NoAM

Double Feature. Robert Earl Hayden. NoAM

Double Features. Ed Rossman. HHAm

Double flesh / Double way. Freud: Dying London, He Recalls the Smoke of His Cigar Beginning to Sing. James Schevill. TAP

Double Fortress, The. Alfred Noyes. SacPr

Double-Goer, The. Daryl Hine. MoCV

Double-headed Snake, The. John Newlove. MoCV

Double Helix. Sean Thomas Dougherty. AmPoNex

Double-horned, nocturnal Moon. Philodemus. GrAn

Double-lived in regions new! (LL) Ode: "Bards of passion and of mirth." John Keats. FHYEP; OBEV; OxAEP-2

Double Looking Glass, The. Alec Derwent Hope. CBAP

Double love torments me; I strain because of two boys, A. Angelo [*or* Andrea] Poliziano. CAGL, *tr. by* James J. Wilhelm *Fr.* Greek Epigrams.

Double Rock, The. Henry King, Bishop of Chichester. NOSC

Double Song. Frank Mkalawile Chipasula. NAfrP

Double Sonnet. Anthony Hecht. Son

Double sorwe of Troilus to tellen, The. Geoffrey Chaucer. MakPoe *Fr.* Troilus and Criseyde [*or* Criseide].

Double Standard, A. Frances Ellen Watkins Harper. BlSi; NAAAL; PWR

Double Standard, The. Franklin Pierce Adams. OBAL

Double Take at Relais de L'Espadon. Thadious M. Davis. BlSi

Double Transformation, The. Oliver Goldsmith. OBCoV; OBNV

Double Trouble. David Trinidad. PmAP

Double Vision of Manannan, The. *Unknown.* BIrV, *tr. by* John Montague

Double Writing. Stephen Knight. NeBl

Doubled at their feet. (LL) King Harald's Trance. George Meredith. EBNV; PeVV

Doubly unfortunate are those who dwell in Hell. Lucilius. GrAn

Doubt. Mary Elizabeth Coleridge. NALW; ViWPN

Doubt. Fanny Howe. BAP-01

Doubt. Clara Ann Thompson. CBWP-2

Doubt, A. Sarah Morgan Bryan Piatt. NCAP

Doubt crept into a heart one day, A. Doubt. Clara Ann Thompson. CBWP-2

Doubt, cypress crowned, upon a ruined arch. Elizabeth Oakes-Smith. TCAPo *Fr.* Atheism.

Doubt no longer miracles. Miracles. Arna Bontemps. NAAAL

Doubt of Future Foes. Elizabeth I, Queen of England. CTC; NAEL-5v1; NAEL-6v1; NAEL-7v1; NALW; NoSic; WPE

(Doubt of future foes exiles my present joy, The.) NoP-4

Doubt of Martyrdom, A. Sir John Suckling. *See* Sonnet: "O[h]! for some honest lover's ghost."

Doubt which ye misdeeme, fayre love, is vaine, The. Edmund Spenser. NAEL-5v1; NAEL-6v1; NAEL-7v1 *Fr.* Amoretti.

Doubt you to whom my Muse these notes intendeth [*or* entendeth]. Sir Philip Sidney. OxAEP-1 *Fr.* Astrophil and Stella.

Doubter's Prayer, The. Anne Brontë. SacPr

Doubtful divines, lawyers that wrangle most. Robert Hayman. NOSC *Fr.* Owen's Epigrams.

Doubtful, I chose a bronze chrysanthemum. Leavetaking. Veronica Rospigliosi. Prnts

Doubting. Louis Simpson. NNaP

Doubtless. Maggie O'Sullivan. NNaP

"Dancer, The." PFTM-2

Doubtless there are other roads. (LL) Stephen Crane. APN-2; MoAmPo *Fr.* War Is Kind.

Douglas and the Bruce's Heart. Sir Richard Holland. OxBS *Fr.* Buke of the Howlat, The.

Douglas, Douglas, Tender and True. Dinah Maria Mulock Craik. TreFP

(Could you come back to me, Douglas, Douglas.) LW

Douglas Tragedy, The. *Unknown.* OxBS

Douglass. Paul Laurence Dunbar. CBCWP; GSo; NAAAL; Son

Douglass was someone who. Frederick Douglass: 1817–1895. Langston Hughes. BPo; CBCWP; HHAm

Doun throu the sea. Cokkils. Sydney Goodsir Smith. OxBS

Dour thing in olive trees, The. Olive Trees. Bernard Spencer. NoAM

Dousing clean a thousand old cares. Night with a Friend, A. Li Po. CoBCP, *tr. by* Burton Watson

Dove, A. Ted Hughes. OxBC

Dove, The. Victor James Daley. NOBAu

Dove, The. Walter De la Mare. OWoS

Dove, The. Judah Halevi. TrJP, *tr. by* Amy Levy

Dove and the Wren, The. Mother Goose. OxNR; ReMoGo

Dove at Sundown. Catherine Bowman. MoASP

Dove-Breeder, The. Ted Hughes. PAI

Dove burned in its whiteness, The. Island in the Light. Sara de Ibáñez. TCLAP, *tr. by* Inés Probert

Dove-cries on the tower stones, The. Song of the Dove, The. Alexander Robertson. APT-1

Dove descending breaks the air, The. T. S. Eliot. SacPr *Fr.* Four Quartets.

Dove has brought an olive branch to eat, The. (LL) Where the Rainbow Ends. Robert Lowell. HCAP; MoAmPo; PoetW

Dove-Love. Judith Wright. NIL-7; NIP-4; NoAM

Dove of New Snow, The. Nicholas Vachel Lindsay. MoAmPo

Dove of rarest worth, A. Dove, The. Judah Halevi. TrJP, *tr. by* Amy Levy

Dove peered in the, The. Hymn to St. Maximinus, A. Hildegard von Bingen. NAWM-7v1, *tr. by* Peter Dronke

Dove purrs—over and over the dove, The. Dove-Love. Judith Wright. NIL-7; NIP-4; NoAM

Dove says, Coo, coo, The. Dove and the Wren, The. Mother Goose. OxNR; ReMoGo

Dove that ventured outside, flying far from the dovecote. Rainer Maria Rilke. EnlH

Dove walks with sticky feet, The. Pastoral. Kenneth Patchen. CLPP

Dover Beach. Matthew Arnold. AWP; AmFaPo; BRP; CABP; ClHu; EBVV; GTBS-P; HAP; HelP-4; ITBLP; InPK-6; MakPoe; NAEL-5v2; NAEL-6v2; NIL-7; NIP-4; NOBE; NOBVV; NPeEn; NoP-4; OxBEV; PAI; PeVV; PoE; PoPoPo; PoRA; SCGP; SCV; TFi; TOF; WoPoe

Dover Bitch, The. Anthony Hecht. NBLV; NIL-7; NIP-4; NOBA; NOBL; OBAL; PeLV; UnPo; VGW

(Dover Bitch: A Criticism of Life, The.) TRP

Dover Cliffs. William Lisle Bowles. OxAEP-2

(On Dover Cliffs. July 20, 1787.) CenSon

Dover to Munich. Charles Stuart Calverley. NOBL

Doves, The. Katharine Tynan. AWP

Doves in the rain. Sisters. Haunani-Kay Trask. ReEnLa

Doves love a dying palm. They nestle in the loud fronds. They hum. Los Angeles, the Angels. James Harms. NeAmPo; PuP-23

Dowager. John Montague. ModIr

Dowager Duchess of Spout, The. Limerick. Edward Gorey. PeLV; PeLi

Dowie Dens of Yarrow, The. *Unknown.* IBB

Dowie Houms o' Yarrow, The. *Unknown.* OBEV; OxBS

(Braes o' Yarrow, The.) ESPB

Down. George Minot. Unle

Down a broad river of the western wilds. Indian Woman's Death-Song, The. Felicia Dorothea Hemans. PEW

Down all the lanterned Bagdad of our youth. On Reading the Life of Haroun Er Reshid. Madison Cawein. APN-2

Down along the Iran River. Iranian Song. Velemir [*or* Viktor Vladimirovich] Khlebnikov. TCRusP, *tr. by* Kathy Lewis and Bob Perelman

Down among the roots like a half-. Nuchal, a Fragment. Thomas Kinsella. PBCIP

Down and Out. Langston Hughes. PoE

Down at the bottom. Madrigal. Giovanni Raboni. ItPo, *tr. by* Gayle Ridinger

Down at the Docks. Kenneth Koch. VGW

Down below, everywhere, all. Central Standard Time. Kevin Young. AmPoNex

Down by the brook which glides through yonder vale. Robin; a Pastoral Elegy. John Dobson. NOEC

Down by the Erie Canal. George M. Cohan. ReLy

Down by the gate of the orchard. Spring Whistles. Lucy Larcom. OBCA

Down by the river. *Unknown.* OxNR

Down by the Salley Gardens. W. B. Yeats. CTC; EBVV; EnLoPo; NAEL-5v2; NAEL-6v2; NPeEn; NoAM; OBEV; PoPoPo; SoSe-8

(Old Song Resung, An.) MoBrPo

Down by the sea lived a lonesome oyster. Tale of the Oyster, The. Cole Porter. ReLy

Down by the Station, Early in the Morning. John Ashbery. HCAP

Down by yon garden green. Laird of Wariston, The. *Unknown.* ESPB

Down! Down! Eleanor Farjeon. NTCP

Down, down, in millions, blending. Snow-Flakes, The. Priscilla Jane Thompson. CBWP-2

Down, down into the great world's flowering. (LL) Gardener to His God, The. Mona Van Duyn. RACG; TrCP; UnPo; WPE

Down drop of the blackbird, The. Three Spring Notations on Bipeds. Carl Sandburg. AWP

Down flew the shaft of the god. Love Affair, A. Arnold Bennett. OxBTC

Down from the bridge rail. Clement Hoyt. HA

Down from the Country. John Blight. BMAP; CBAP

Down from the north on the north wind flying. And Stands There Sighing. Elizabeth Jane Coatsworth. KaS

Down from the rain-soaked law. Barry MacSweeney. Oth *Fr.* Pearl.

Down from the window take the withered holly. Twelfth Night. Phyllis McGinley. APT-2

Down-Hearted Blues. Albert Hunter. NAAAL

Down here now / summer's burnt skeins. In Blanco County. Russell T. Fowler. NOBC

Down hills floating by heart on the bulldozed land. (LL) For Robert Frost. Galway Kinnell. NOBA; VGW

Down home / he sets on a stoop. Neighbor. Langston Hughes. APSN; PFTM-1

Down—I got it all. Almost. W. D. Snodgrass. BodElec *Fr.* Führer Bunker, The.

Down in a green and shady bed. Violet, The. Jane Taylor. WoRP

Down in a valley, by a forest's side. William Browne (1591–1643). OxBSo *Fr.* Visions.

Down in all the plain, in the tinder-dry cities. Children of the Atomic Age. Dominador I. Ilio. ReBoTo

Down in Atlanta. Slim in Atlanta. Sterling Allen Brown. APT-2; NoP-4

Down in Dumbarton there wonnd a rich merchant. Bonnie Annie. *Unknown.* ESPB

Down in front of Casey's old brown wooden stoop. Sidewalks of New York, The. James W. Blake. TCAPo

Down in Georgia there are peaches. Everything Is Peaches Down in Georgia. Grant Clarke. ReLy

Down in history we find it and in grandest works of art. Negro Heroines. Lizelia Augusta Jenkins Moorer. CBWP-3

Down in Kentucky. Blue Grass. Arthur Schwartz. ReLy

Down in the bass / That steady beat. Easy Boogie. Langston Hughes. APSN

Down in the bottom built for comfort. (LL) Impressions / of Chicago; For Howlin' Wolf. Quincy Troupe. NAAAL; NBV

Down in the cabin all things were gay. Thwarted. Priscilla Jane Thompson. CBWP-2

Down in the deep, dumb worlds are waiting, silent. Letter to My Wife. Miklós Radnóti. AF

Down in the dell. Henrietta Cordelia Ray. BlSi *Fr.* Idyl.

Down in the depth of mine iniquity. Fanny [*or* Frances] Macartney Greville. CABP *Fr.* Caelica.

Down in the depth of mine iniquity. Fulke Greville, 1st Baron Brooke. CABP; NOSC; NoSic *Fr.* Caelica.

Down in the Depths. Cole Porter. ReLy

Down in the depths of this fair church. Church Echoes. May Kendall. ViWPN

Down in the flood of remembrance, I weep like a child for the past. (LL) Piano. D. H. Lawrence. CABP; GTBS-P; HAP; HarvBoo; HeIP-4; InPK-6; MoBrPo; NAEL-5v2; NAEL-6v2; NIL-7; NOBE; NoAM; NoP-4; OPOU; OxBSP; PAI; PoE; RB; SCGP; TFi; TRP; UnPo; WeW-3

Down in the Frantic Mountains. Survey, A. William Stafford. RB

Down in the Lonesome Garden. *Unknown.* BPo

Down in the orchard. Félix Lope de Vega Carpio. HAP; WoPoe, *tr. by* Geoffrey Hill *Fr.* Pentecost Castle, The.

Down in the pool room. True Blue Lou. Sam Coslow. ReLy

Down in the south, by the waste without sail on it. Beyond Kerguelen. Henry Clarence Kendall. NOBAu

Down in Washington, D.C. Money Song, The. Harold Rome. ReLy

Down in yon garden sweet and gay. Willy Drowned in Yarrow. *Unknown.* GTBS-P

Down into the earth's womb. "Novalis." WoPoe, *tr. by* Dick Higgins *Fr.* Hymns to the Night.

Down mountain roads like scars across a fist. At Tripolis. Constance Carrier. WPE

Down near the river. Spring of Work Storm. Joseph Ceravolo. FTOS

Down 99, south from Portland, then. South. M. L. Williams. GeoHom

Down now into the dark earth's womb. Yearning for Death. "Novalis." NAWM-7v2, *tr. by* Charles E. Passage

Down on my knees again, on the linoleum outside room six. Outside Room Six. Lynn Emanuel. ReTh

Down on My Luck. Arthur Rex Dugard Fairburn. PeNZ

Down one of Baghdad's lanes I went. Both Strangers. Jamil Sidqi Al-Zahawi. MAP, *tr. by* Issa Boullata and Christopher Middleton

Down [*or* Downe] lay the shepherd swain. Hye Nonny Nonny Noe. *Unknown.* NOBL; PeLV

Down poured the rain; the closed window streamed. Storm, The. Margaret Stanley-Wrench. LW

Down rippling, The. Frank K. Robinson. HA

Down she comes from her vermilion tower, her face freshly adorned. Song of

Spring Replying to a Poem by Po Chü-yi, A. Liu Yu Hsi. SuSp, *tr. by* Daniel Bryant and Ronald C. Miao

Down Stream. Louise Imogen Guiney. SWaP

Down streams of centuries grown old. Women of My Land. Frankie Armstrong. BrRo

Down stucco sidestreets. Dublinesque. Philip Larkin. NoAM; OxBC

Down sunk the sun, nor shed one golden ray. Holbain. Anne Batten Cristall. RWP

Down the assembly line they roll and pass. Brides, The. Alec Derwent Hope. HAP; PAI

Down the billboard girl's bare belly. Leroy Gorman. HA

Down the blue night the unending columns press. Clouds. Rupert Brooke. OBEV; OBMV; OxBTC

Down the close, darkening lanes they sang their way. Send-Off, The. Wilfred Owen. HarvBoo; MoBrPo; NPeEn; OBWP; OBWVE; OxBEV; OxBTC; PeFWW; PoWW; RB; TCAWP

Down the cloud ladder, but the problem has not been solved. (LL) Our Youth. John Ashbery. CoAmPo; VGW

Down the coast south of here. Earth. Jim Tollerud. VoR

Down the dead streets of sun-stoned Frederiksted. Virgins, The. Derek Walcott. OxBC; SoSe-8

Down the dim aisle of standing pullman coaches. Departure. Mildred Weston. FFC

Down the green hill-side fro' the castle window. Lady Jane. Sir Arthur Thomas Quiller-Couch. PeLV

Down the imperturbable street. (LL) Aspect of Love, Alive in the Ice and Fire, An. Gwendolyn Brooks. BPo; PAI; TAP

Down the irrationally humped. Origins. Vincent Buckley. BMAP

Down the long hall she glistens like a star. Venus of the Louvre. Emma Lazarus. APN-2; GS

Down the M4. Dannie Abse. OxBC

Down the narrow Calle where the moonlight cannot enter. Venetian Nocturne. Agnes Mary Frances Robinson. VWP

Down the Nile. Robert Lowell. HCAP

Down the old high roads of inexhaustible light. (LL) Coal Fire in Winter, A. Thomas McGrath. ErotSp; GifTon; RaBo

Down the red stock route. Song for the Cattle. David Campbell. NOBAu

Down the road someone is practising scales. Sunday Morning. Louis MacNeice. FaBoMo; MoBrPo; NAEL-5v2; NAEL-6v2; NIP-4; OxAEP-2; Son

Down the rock chute into the tombs of the kings they grope these battling sandalled. This Is the Life. Louis MacNeice. NoAM

Down the slimy rope into the impossible! Poem Films Itself, The. J. S. Harry. BMAP

Down the street the ground is feeling so. Directions, The. Christopher Gilbert. GT

Down the street their script on every window! Drinking with the Nazis. Joseph Glazer. GotH

DOWN the valley gan he track. Palmer, The. Robert Greene. NoSic

Down the waves of the Yang-tse-Kiang. Ballade of the Chinese Lover. Stuart Merrill. APN-2

Down the white steps, into the night, she came. Victory. Lionel Pigot Johnson. NOBVV

Down the winding lanes of Moscow, down its hopeless. Elegies on the Cardinal Points. Yelena [*or* Elena] Shwarts [*or* Shvarts]. VCWP, *tr. by* Michael Molnar

Down the Wolf river. Feasts of Death, Feasts of Love. Stuart Z. Perkoff. NeAP

Down their carved [*or* chiselled] names the rain-drop ploughs. (LL) During Wind and Rain. Thomas Hardy. GTBS-P; HAP; HarvBoo; NAEL-5v2; NAEL-6v2; NIL-7; NPeEn; NoP-4; OxBEV; OxBTC; PeVV; PoE; TFi; TOF; TRP

Down there a poor woman. Potter, The. *Unknown.* TTY, *tr. by* Halim El-Dabh

Down there where I was. Story of My Life, The. Carroll Arnett. VoR

Down through the earth as a last gift. Meleager. PGA

Down through the tomb's inward arch. Ikon: The Harrowing of Hell. Denise Levertov. BodElec

Down to dark leaf-mold. O. Mabson Southard. HA

Down to me quickly, down! I am such dust. Mummy Invokes His Soul, The. "Michael Field." NPeEn; OxBSo; VWP

Down to the Dregs. César Vallejo. TCLAP, *tr. by* James Wright

Down to the Mire. *Unknown.* WPoS

Down to the Puritan marrow of my bones. Elinor Wylie. BoWoP; MoAmPo *Fr.* Wild Peaches.

Down to the river! into the street! (LL) Allen Ginsberg. CLPP; NeAP; TAP *Fr.* Howl.

Down to the Sacred Wave. Samuel Francis Smith. AH

Down to the vale this water steers; how merrily it goes! Old Man by the Brook, The. William Wordsworth. TreFP

Down under the bridge you.   Shakti.   Rae Desmond Jones.   BMAP

Down, up—a single dot of red.   Yang Chi.   CoBLCP, tr. by Jonathan Chaves   Fr. Ten Poems on the Tuan-yang Festival.

Down valley a smoke haze.   Mid-August at Sourdough Mountain Lookout.   Gary Snyder.   ColAP; HAP; InPK-6; LoL; NoP-4; TAP; VCAP

Down, Wanton, Down!   Robert Graves.   BoLoP; FaBoTw; HarvBoo; HeIP-4;   InPK-6; NAEL-5v2; NAEL-6v2; NoAM; PoE

Down with Love.   Harold Arlen.   ReLy

Down with the lambs.   Unknown.   OxNR

Down with the Money-Exchange.   Carlos German Belli.   TCLAP, tr. by   Maureen Ahern and David Tipton

Down with the Rosemary and Bay[e]s.   Ceremonies for Candlemas[se] Eve.   Robert Herrick.   BeJo; CaPo

Down with the rosemary, and so.   Ceremony upon Candlemas Eve.   Robert   Herrick.   OBCP

Down you go alone, so late, into the surge-black fissure. (LL)   You Will Know   When You Get There.   Allen Curnow.   EmeKit; NoP-4; PeNZ

Down, you mongrel, Death!   Poet and His Book, The.   Edna St. Vincent   Millay.   MoAmPo

Downe in the depth of mine iniquity.   Fulke Greville, 1st Baron Brooke.   SacPr   Fr. Caelica. See also Down in the depth of mine iniquity

Downe to the king's most bright-kept baths they went.   Homer.   CTC, tr. by   George Chapman   Fr. Odyssey.

Downed Black Pilot Learns How to Fly, A.   Horace Coleman.   CDa

Downfall.   Georg Trakl.   AF, tr. by Daniel Simko

Downfall of the Gael, The.   Fearflatha O'Gnive [or O'Gnimh].   AWP, tr. by Sir   Samuel Ferguson

Downhill [or Down hill] I came, hungry, and yet not starved.   Owl, The.   Edward Thomas.   AF; ChAP; EBEV; FaBoTw; GTBS-P; NAEL-5v2;   NAEL-6v2; NIP-4; NOBE; NoAM; NoP-4; OBWVE; OWoS; OxAEP-2;   PeFWW; PoE; RB; SCGP; TCAWP; TFi; TRP; UnPo

Downland Crisis, A.   Dominic Bevan Wyndham Lewis.   "Ale they drink in Giggleswick, The."   UV

Downpour.   Daisy Zamora.   CLPP, tr. by Barbara Paschke

Downriver, someone plays.   River Flute.   Po Chü-i.   CrYelRi, tr. by Sam   Hamill

Downstairs I laugh, I sport and jest with all.   L. E. L.   Christina Georgina   Rossetti.   VWP

Downstairs neighbors quicken.   Jesus Never Sleeps.   David Graham.   SwNoth

Downstream.   Thomas Kinsella.   HarvBoo   "Again in the mirrored dusk the paddles sank."   PBCIP

Downstream the raft plunged.   In the Torrent.   Johannes Bobrowski.   WoPoe,   tr. by Mark Rudman

Downtime.   Lisa Buscani.   AmPoNex

Downtown anywhere and between the roil.   Homo Will Not Inherit.   Mark   Doty.   HarvBoo; OPRER; WiU

Downtown Los Angeles / In the huge baroque lobby.   Bagpipes at the   Biltmore.   Robert Conquest.   OBCoV

Downtown, on the precinct wall.   Field Trip.   Carol Muske.   GeoHom

Downtown Seattle in the Fog.   Tina Koyama.   FSt

Downtown Sunday.   Robert Crawford.   OPRER

Downward Mobility.   Lewis Warsh.   BAP-97

Downward to darkness, on extended wings. (LL)   Sunday Morning.   Wallace   Stevens.   APT-1; BBASP; ColAP; HAP; HCAP; HarvBoo; HeIP-4;   MoAmPo; NAAL-2v2; NAAL-5; NAWM-7v2; NIL-7; NIP-4; NOBA;   NoAM; NoP-4; OxBA; PoE; PoPoPo; SAmP; SoSe-8; TAP; TCAPo; TFi;   TRP

Downy Hair.   Shinkichi Takahashi.   ZenPo, tr. by Takashi Ikemoto and Lucien   Stryk

Dowsed coals fume and hiss after your meal, The.   Book of Yolek, The.   Anthony Hecht.   HP; MakPoe; NoP-4; TaR; WeW-3

Dowser, The.   Edwin Morgan.   NPeEn; NoP-4

Doxology.   Josephine D. Henderson Heard.   CBWP-4

Doxology.   Bert Leston Taylor.   OBAL

Doxy, oh! thy glaziers shine.   Maunder's Praise of His Strowling Mort, The.   Unknown.   OxBoLi; PeLV

Doyen of walls.   Apologia (Nkomati).   Wole Soyinka.   HBAPE

Dozen Cocktails—Please, A.   Else Von Freytag-Loringhoven.   APT-1

Dozen dozen in her place, A. (LL)   Sir John Suckling.   BASC; BeJo; CavPo;   NAEL-6v1; NAEL-7v1; NBLV; NOSC; NPeEn; NoP-4; OxAEP-1; OxBEV;   PBRV; PeLV; PoE   Fr. Poem with the Answer, A.

Dozens of girls would storm up.   Embraceable You.   George Gershwin.   ReLy

Dozens of wrangling sparrows have built their.   Ian Wedde.   PeNZ   Fr.   Earthly: Sonnets for Carlos.

Dozing on horseback / smoke from tea-fires.   Basho.   ZenPo, tr. by Takashi   Ikemoto and Lucien Stryk

Dr. Bronowski stands in the marshes.   Visit, Auschwitz, 1971, The.   Lisa Ress.   GotH

Dr. Halley never eat any thing.   Edmond Halley.   Roy Fuller.   OxBC

Dr. Johnson's Ghost.   Elizabeth Moody.   ECWP

Dr. Johnson, when sober or pissed.   Limerick.   A. Cinna.   PeLi

Dr Szasz, professor, sir.   Footnote Extended, A.   Dannie Abse.   HP

Dr. Wasserman.   Brenda Coultas.   HeMarv

Dracula.   Salwa Al-Neimi.   PoArWo, tr. by Subhi Hadidi

Draft Board at Shih-hao, The.   Tu Fu.   CrYelRi, tr. by Sam Hamill

Draft Horse, The.   Robert Frost.   APT-1; EmeKit; HeIP-4; PAI; PoE; SAmP;   TRP; WoPoe

Draft of a Modern Love Poem.   Tadeusz Rózewicz.   PoSu; VCWP   (And yet white.)   VCWP   (And yet whiteness.)   BLT, tr. by Czeslaw Milosz   (In a modern love poem.) (LL)   BLT, tr. by Czeslaw Milosz

Draft of a Reparations Agreement.   Dan Pagis.   HP; PoSu; WoPoe, tr. by   Stephen Mitchell

Drafted.   Su Wu.   OHMPC, tr. by Kenneth Rexroth

Drafts for a Quatrain.   Edmund Wilson.   OBAL

Dragged, drenched, from sleep, by horror.   Mimesis.   Elizabeth Garrett.   MFPA

Dragging him up the stairs to one who lies dead. (LL)   Conversation of Prayer,   The.   Dylan Thomas.   EBEV; GTBS-P; OxAEP-2

Dragging his heart from one ruined soul to another. (LL)   Romania, Romania.   Gerald Stern.   LCAP-2; MiVo

Dragging his prize to land. (LL)   Discovery of America, The.   James Logie   Robertson.   NOBVV; NePenScot

Dragon.   Ruth Bidgood.   AngWePo

Dragon.   Olive Dove.   OTCP

Dragon-Fly, The.   Walter Savage Landor.   OBEV

Dragon Gate cuts a wide gorge.   Dragon Gate Gorge.   Tu Fu.   CrYelRi, tr. by   Sam Hamill

Dragon Gate Gorge.   Tu Fu.   CrYelRi, tr. by Sam Hamill

Dragon-Gate House.   Muso Soseki.   EaWin, tr. by W. S. Merwin

Dragon has come, A.   Dragon.   Olive Dove.   OTCP

Dragon never rears its head before sending down torrential rain.   Filled with   Emotions on the Moon-ferrying Bridge at Arashiyama.   Liu Ya-tzu.   SuSp, tr. by Wu-Chi Liu

Dragon Night.   Jane Yolen.   OTCP

Dragon of our dreams roared in the hills, The.   Y Ddraig Goch.   Henry Treece.   TCAWP

Dragon's Breath.   Hervey Allen.   YaYoPo

Dragon Skate.   Gladys Cardiff.   CDW

Dragon Slaying.   Zoltán Jékely.   IQMS, tr. by George Szirtes

Dragon sleeps three winter months, A.   Tu Fu.   CrYelRi, tr. by Sam Hamill   Fr. Random Pleasures.

Dragon Speaks, The.   Unknown.   NPeEn

Dragon-Steed, The.   Sándor Weöres.   IQMS, tr. by Adam Makkai and Donald   E. Morse

Dragon that our seas did raise his crest, The.   Of the Great and Famous. . .Sir   Francis Drake, and of My Little-Little Selfe.   Robert Hayman.   FaBoCh

Dragon-Tiger Terrace.   Yang Shih-ch'i.   CoBLCP, tr. by Jonathan Chaves

Dragon-Watching in St. Louis.   Carter Revard.   UrbNat

Dragonfish, The.   John Balaban.   CDa

Dragonfly.   Gary Snyder.   BLT

Dragonfly, The.   Basho.   EH, tr. by Robert Hass

Dragonfly, The.   Louise Bogan.   APT-2; HeIP-4

Dragonfly, The.   Issa.   EH, tr. by Robert Hass

Dragonfly, The.   Stanley Kunitz.   APT-2

Dragons and snakes tangle in my dream; they can hardly recoil.   Dragons and   Snakes.   Liu Ya-tzu.   SuSp, tr. by Wu-Chi Liu

Drags the loose knee, and intermitting step. (LL)   Sonnet: Ingratitude.   Anna   Seward.   CenSon; ECWP; NOEC

Drained Cup, The.   D. H. Lawrence.   FaBoVe

Drainlayer.   Duncan Bush.   AngWePo

Drake he's in his hammock an' a thousand mile away.   Drake's Drum.   Sir   Henry John Newbolt.   FaBoCh; FaBoWar; OBMV; PoRA; UV

Drake pays court to the duck, The.   Mikhail Yeryomin.   ItGoST, tr. by J. Kates

Drake's Drum.   Sir Henry John Newbolt.   FaBoCh; FaBoWar; OBMV; PoRA;   UV

Drake, who the world hast conquered like a scroll.   To the Noble Sir Francis   Drake.   Thomas Beedome.   OxBSP

Drama, The.   Suliaman El-Hadi.   SpirFl

Drama of our time is the coming of all men into one fate, The.   Robert Duncan.   PFTM-1   Fr. Rites of Participation.

Drama's Vitallest Expression Is the Common Day.   Emily Dickinson.   NOBA

Dramatic Fragments.   Trumbull Stickney.   ("I hear a river thro' the valley wander.")   NoP-4   "I heard a river thro' the valley wander."   APN-2   "Sir, say no more."   APN-2; InPK-6; OxBA; OxBSP

Dramatic Symphony, The.   Andrey [or Andrei] Bely [or Belyi].

"By-street was bathed in sun, The." PFTM-1

Drank lonesome water. Lonesome Water. Roy Helton. APT-1; MoAmPo

Dransfield, who wrote. Eight xx. Laurie Duggan. BMAP

Drapery Factory, Gulfport, Mississippi, 1956. Natasha Trethewey. SpirFl

Draw a bucket of water. *Unknown.* FaBoVe

Draw a little closer, comrades! Fisherman's Story, The. Henrietta Cordelia Ray. CBWP-3

Draw a pail of water. *Unknown.* FaBoVe; LB; OxNR

Draw closer to me, God, than were I one. Prayer of an Unbeliever. Lizette Woodworth Reese. SacPr

Draw in your head and sleep the long way home. (LL) Hart Crane. ColAP; NAAL-2v2; NAAL-5; PoE *Fr.* Voyages.

Draw me nere [*or* near], draw me nere [*or* near]. Jolly Jugger, The. *Unknown.* EBEV; NPeEn

"Draw me," the cypress said. Childhood Painting Lesson. Henry Rago. WHSW

Draw near, / And list what with our council we have done. William Shakespeare. OxAEP-1 *Fr.* King Richard II.

Draw near [*or* neer], / You lovers that complain. Exequies, The. Thomas Stanley. BeJo; MeLP

Draw up his venetians and welcome the moon. (LL) Moonlight and Gas. Constance Naden. VWP; ViWPN

Drawer. Zbigniew Herbert. VCWP, *tr.* by Czeslaw Miosz and Peter Dale Scott

Drawer of My Writing Desk, The. Boris Petrovich Kornilov. TCRP, *tr.* by Bernard Meares

Drawerful of obscure tools, A. Casino. Richard Tipping. BMAP

Drawing a bow you must draw a strong one. Tu Fu. WoPoe, *tr.* by David Lattimore *Fr.* Crossing the Border, First Series.

Drawing Hands. Greg Williamson. AmPoNex

Drawings of the Song Animals. Duane Niatum. HATNAP

Drawn by old Homer's hand, the rose. Evan Lloyd. AngWePo; OBWVE *Fr.* Powers of the Pen, The.

Drawn by Stones, by Earth, by Things That Have Been in the Fire. Marvin Bell. VCAP

Drawn on the blackboard. School and Nature. Jean Follain. BLT, *tr.* by W. S. Merwin

Drawn on the burden of light. Bleat. Barbara Guest. FTOS

Draws back his blade. (LL) Buson. WoPoe; ZenPo, *tr.* by Takashi Ikemoto and Lucien Stryk

Draws every wish to me. (LL) Song: "Through springtime walks, with flowers perfumed." Anne Batten Cristall. ECWP; RWP

Draws tears, or blood [*or* bloud], not want a[n] handkerchief. (LL) Dawning, The. George Herbert. ESCV; NOSC

Dread. Frederick D'Aguiar. WaCA

Dread. John Millington Synge. BoLoP; MoBrPo; OxBSP

Dread are the death-pale Kings. Still-Heart. Frank Pearce Sturm. OBMV

Dread of future foes exyle my present Joy, The. Elizabeth I, Queen of England. EMWP

Dread song. "Not one of my seed" the words said. So Jah Sey. Kendel Hippolyte. WaCA

Dread Soveraign Charles! O King of Most Renown! Exultationis Carmen To the Kings Most Excellent Majesty upon His Most Desired Return. Rachel Jevon. EMWP

Dreaded Road. 'Abd al-Razzaq 'Abd al-Wahid. MAP, *tr.* by Diana Der Hovanessian and Lena Jayyusi

Dreaded Task, The. Margaret E. Bruner. PoToHe

Dreadful and the desperate hate I bear, The. Cecco Angiolieri, da Siena. EaItPo, *tr.* by Dante Gabriel Rossetti

Dreadful are the happenings of our evil ages. András Szkhárosi Horvát. IQMS, *tr.* by Adam Makkai *Fr.* Curse, The.

Dreadful case of murder, A. Execution of Alice Holt. *Unknown.* OxBoLi

Dreadful Dinotherium he, The. Joseph Hilaire Pierre Belloc. NOBL *Fr.* Moral Alphabet, A.

Dreadful Fate of Naughty Nate, The. John Kendrick Bangs. OBCA

Dreadful Has Already Happened, The. Mark Strand. HCAP; NoAM; VCAP

Dreadlocks gone. For Bob Marley. John Agard. WaCA

Dreadtalk. Frederick D'Aguiar. WaCA

Dreadwalk. Dennis Scott. WaCA

Dream. Maria Arrillaga. TANSG

Dream. Richard Watson Dixon. EBEV; NOBVV; OxBEV; PeVV; SCGP

Dream. Nana Issaia. BoWoP, *tr.* by Helle Tzaopoulou Barnstone

Dream. Mikhail Yuryevich Lermontov. WoPoe, *tr.* by W. K. Matthews

Dream. Novella Nikolaevna Matveyeva [*or* Matveieva]. TCRP, *tr.* by Deming Brown

Dream. Vahan Tekeyan. AF, *tr.* by Diana Der Hovanessian and Marzbed Margossian

Dream. *Unknown.* STP, *tr.* by Armand Schwerner

Dream, A. Bella [*or* Izabella] Akhatovna Akhmadulina. BoWoP, *tr.* by Olga Carlisle and Jean Valentine

Dream, A. Anna Andreyevna Akhmatova. TCRusP, *tr.* by Daniel Weissbort

Dream, A. Muhammad Al-Ghuzzi. MAP, *tr.* by John Heath-Stubbs and May Jayyusi

Dream, A [*or* The]. William Allingham. BIrV; NOBVV

Dream, A. Matthew Arnold. GTBS-P *Fr.* Switzerland.

Dream, A. William Blake. FHYEP; NOBRP *Fr.* Songs of Innocence.

Dream, A. Maggie Pogue Johnson. CBWP-4

Dream, A. Evan Jones. NOBAu

Dream, A. Sir John Suckling. ChIV-2

Dream, A. Charles Tomlinson. OxBC

Dream, A. Charles Tennyson Turner. OxBSo

Dream, A. Charles Williams. OBEV

Dream, The. Aphra Behn. RACG *Fr.* Voyage to the Isle of Love, A.

Dream, The. "Brian Bendo." NOEC

Dream, The. Louise Bogan. InPK-6; MoAmPo; NALW; NoAM

Dream, The. Irving Feldman. TaR; VCAP

Dream, The. Robert Earl Hayden. ESEAA; NBV

Dream, The. David Ignatow. CoAP; NNaP; PAI

Dream, The. Paul Petrie. TAP

Dream, The. Felix Pollak. RaBo

Dream, The. Theodore Roethke. NIL-7; UnPo

Dream, The. Sir Edward Sherburne. OxBSP

Dream, The ("I dreamed that, buried in my fellow clay.") *Unknown.* NOEC

Dream, The ("Last night I supped on lobster; it nearly drove me mad.") *Unknown.* OxBoLi

Dream 2: Brian the Still-Hunter. Margaret Atwood. BoWoP

Dream, A / we dreamed. Perpetuum Mobile: The City. William Carlos Williams. APT-1

Dream about a Piano, A. Yury [*or* Iurii] Davydovich Levitansky [*or* Levitanskii]. TCRP, *tr.* by Sophie Lund

Dream about Our Master, William Shakespeare, The. Hyam Plutzik. RB

Dream after dream I see the wrecks that lie. Posted. John Masefield. Son

Dream, after Reading Dante's Episode of Paolo and Francesca, A. John Keats. NOBRP

Dream; An Epistle to Mr. Dryden, The. Elizabeth Thomas. EMWP

Dream and Poetry. Hu Shih. WoPoe, *tr.* by Kai-yu Hsu

Dream at Night, A. Mei Yao Ch'en. BLT; OHPC, *tr.* by Kenneth Rexroth

Dream Barker. Jean Valentine. VGW

Dream behind the. Here. Bob Orr. PeNZ

Dream Boogie. Langston Hughes. APSN; HCAP; NAAAL; PFTM-1; SSLK

Dream Boogie: Variation. Langston Hughes. APSN
  (Tinkling treble.) SSLK

Dream Broke, A. William Cartwright. NOSC

Dream Called Life, The. Pedro Calderón de la Barca. AWP, *tr.* by Edward Fitzgerald

Dream Cloud. Lindiwe Mabuza. HAWP

Dream Come True. Molly Peacock. RA

Dream Data. Robert Duncan. NeAP

Dream Deferred. Langston Hughes. *See* Lenox Avenue Mural

Dream Dream, The. Michael Davidson. FTOS

Dream/eaters on the edge. Dream/Eaters. Shirley Bradley LeFlore. SpirFl

Dream Fears. Bessie Rayner Parkes. PoBW

Dream Feast (Three Poems), The. Anita Endrezze. VoR

Dream: Flight of a Dragonfly. Gennady Aygi. ItGoST, *tr.* by Peter France

Dream fluently, still brothers, who when young. To the Etruscan Poets. Richard Wilbur. OxBC

Dream, half-illumined, half-obscure, A. (LL) Bits of Reminiscence. "Shu Ting." CarOv; VCWP, *tr.* by Carolyn Kizer and Y. H. Zhao

Dream House. Catherine Parmenter Newell. PoToHe

Dream in a dream the heavy soul somewhere. Canto Amor. John Berryman. CoAP; MoAmPo; VGW

Dream is living still. Old Ottakring. Josef Weinheber. AuPH, *tr.* by Lowell A. Bangerter

Dream it was in which I found myself, A. Dream Called Life, The. Pedro Calderón de la Barca. AWP, *tr.* by Edward Fitzgerald

Dream Land. Christina Georgina Rossetti. BrRo

Dream-Land [*or* Dreamland]. Edgar Allan Poe. APN-1; NAAL-2v1; NAAL-3; NCAP; NOBA; OxBA; TAP

Dream-Language of Fergus, The. Medbh McGuckian. CIP-2

Dream-Love. Christina Georgina Rossetti. HAP

Dream Lover. Mark DeFoe. SwNoth

Dream Maiden, A. Harriet Hamilton King. VWP

Dream May 18, 1958. Peter Orlovsky. BB

Dream not, O Soul, that easy is the task. Help. John Greenleaf Whittier. Son

Dream of a Baseball Star. Gregory Corso. BB; PmAP; VGW

Dream of a Black Fox. Brendan Kennelly. PBCIP

Dream of a Slave. Gavin Ewart. EmeKit

Dream of a summer day: a hearse. Summer Day, A. Robert Greacen. PNI

Dream of Birth, The. Judith Ortiz Cofer. PueRic

Dream of Blue Eyes, A. Frederick William Faber. CenSon

Dream of Christopher Columbus, The. Juan Felipe Herrera. TouFir

Dream of Comparison, A. Stevie Smith. BWW

Dream of Completion, The. Shirley Kaufman. LCAP-2

Dream of Dying, A. Leslie Monsour. FFC

Dream of Elfland, A. Henrietta Cordelia Ray. CBWP-3

Dream of Fair Women, A. Kingsley Amis. NoAM

Dream of Gerontius, The. John Henry, Cardinal Newman.
    Chorus of Angels. NOCV
    (Fifth Choir of Angelicals.) NOBVV

Dream of Glass Bangles, A. Agha Shahid Ali. OpBo

Dream of Hanging, A. Patricia Beer. EmeKit

Dream of Husbands, A. Alberto A. Ríos. NoAM

Dream of Instant Total Representation, The. Anselm Hollo. PmAP

Dream of Jealousy, A. Seamus Heaney. NoP-4

Dream of Judgement, A. Douglas Dunn. OxBC

Dream of Mimesis, A. Katherine Lederer. BodElec

Dream of Mountaineering, A. Po Chü-i. BLT; ChiP, tr. by Arthur Waley

Dream of Pairing. Ntozake Shange. GT

Dream of Rebirth. Roberta Hill Whiteman. CDW

Dream of Retarded Children, A. Robert Bly. LoL

Dream of Sappho, A. Ella Higginson. SWaP

Dream of the Artfairy. Carl Morse. GLP

Dream of the Caiman, The. José Santos Chocano. TCLAP, tr. by Andrew
    Rosing

Dream of the Condor, The. José Santos Chocano. TCLAP, tr. by Andrew
    Rosing

Dream of the Cross, The. *Unknown.* EBEV, tr. by Sally Purcell

Dream of the Evil Servant. Reetika Vazirani. NAPBL

Dream of the Forgotten Lover. Lucia Fox. BoWoP, tr. by R. Maghan

Dream of the Quartz Pebble, The. Vasco [or Vasko] Popa. PoSu   *Fr.* Quartz
    Pebble, The.

Dream of the Ring: The Great Jack Johnson, A. George Barlow. ESEAA;
    MoASP

Dream of the Rood, A. Cynewulf. AnOE, tr. by Charles W. Kennedy

Dream of the Rood, The. *Unknown.* NePenScot, tr. by Robert Crawford

Dream of the Rood, The. *Unknown.* NOCV, tr. by Michael Alexander

Dream of the Rood, The. *Unknown.* ASW, tr. by Kevin Crossley-Holland

Dream of the Unknown, The. Shelley. *See* Question, The

Dream of Trains, A. Mark Van Doren. GM

Dream of Tsuang Tsi, The. Lőrinc Szabó. IQMS, tr. by Adam Makkai

Dream of Venus, A. Bion. AWP, tr. by Leigh Hunt

Dream of Wearing Shorts Forever, The. Les A. Murray. EmeKit

Dream of William Carlos Williams, A. Robert Bly. BodElec

Dream of Winter. George Mackay Brown. FaBoTw

Dream On. James Tate. BodElec

Dream on the Same Mattress. Sharif Elmusa. GraLe

Dream, or the Type of the Rising Sun, A. Jean Adams. ECWP; NOEC

Dream-Pedlary. Thomas Lovell Beddoes. HAP; NOBE; OBEV; OxAEP-2

Dream, ploughman, of what agriculture brings. Elegy for the Lost Parish.
    Douglas Dunn. DiPo

Dream Poem. Mary Jo Bona. UnSA

Dream Question, A. Thomas Hardy. ChIV-1

Dream: Queue for Paraffin. Gennady Aygi. ItGoST, tr. by Peter France

Dream Recalling a Temptation, A. Maysoun Saqr Al-Qasimi. PoArWo, tr. by
    Subhi Hadidi and Nathalie Handal

Dream Record: June 8 1955. Allen Ginsberg. CoAmPo; NOBA

Dream Sequence, Part 9. Naomi Long Madgett. BPo

Dream Song. Lewis Alexander. WHSW

Dream Song. *Unknown.* OBVE, tr. by Francis Densmore

Dream Songs. John Berryman.
    April Fool's Day, or St. Mary Egypt. ChIV-2
    "At Henry's bier let some thing fall out well." NoP-4
    "Bats have no bankers and they do not drink." EmeKit
    "Chilled in this Irish pub I wish my loves." FaBoMo; LCAP-2
    "Deprived of his enemy, shrugged to a standstill." LCAP-2
    (Dream Song 4.) HarvBoo; PoPoPo

Dream Song 8. HarvBoo

Dream Song 14. ColAP; HAP; HCAP; HarvBoo; HeIP-4; NAAL-2v2;
    NOBA; NoAM; NoP-4; PoetW; TAP; TRP; TwCP; VCAP

Dream Song 26. HCAP; HarvBoo

Dream Song 29. HAP; HCAP; HarvBoo; NAAL-5; NoP-4; PoE; VCAP

Dream Song 45. HCAP; PoPoPo

Dream Song 55. ChIV-2

Dream Song 61. CoAP; HarvBoo

Dream Song 255. HarvBoo

Dream Song 384. HCAP; PoPoPo; VCAP

Elegy for W. C. W., the Lovely Man, An. MakPoe

4th Song. BoLoP; ColAP; EmeKit; HAP; HCAP; NoP-4; OBAL; VCAP

"He lay in the middle of the world, and twitcht." HCAP; PoE

(He stared at ruin.) NAAL-5

Henry's Confession. LCAP-2; NAAL-2v2; NoAM; PoE; TwCP; VCAP

"Henry's mind grew blacker the more he thought." FaBoMo; NOBA

"Henry's pelt was put on sundry walls." NoAM; TRP

Henry sats in de bar and was odd. HCAP; PoPoPo; VCAP

"How this woman came by the courage, how she got." TAP

"Huffy Henry hid the day." ColAP; HCAP; NAAL-2v2; NoP-4; PoE; VCAP

"I am, outside. Incredible panic rules." VCAP

"I can't get him out of my mind, out of my mind." NoP-4

"I have moved to Dublin to have it out with you." NoAM; TRP

"I'm cross with god who has wrecked this generation." FaBoMo

"I'm scared a lonely. Never see my son." NoP-4

"Ill lay he long, upon this last return." TAP

"Irish have the thickest ankles in the world, The." TAP

Lay of Ike, The. LCAP-2

"Love her he doesn't but the thought he puts." FaBoMo

Sabbath. LCAP-2

"Seedy Henry rose up shy in de world." HCAP; VCAP

So Long? Stevens. HAP; HCAP; NOBA

"Some good people, daring and subtle voices." HCAP

"Supreme my holdings, greater yet my need." CRP

"That dark brown rabbit, lightness in his ears." TwCP

"That's enough of that, Mr Bones. *Some* lady you make." NAAL-2v2;
    VCAP

This world is gradually becoming a place. NOBA; NoAM

"Three 'coons come at his garbage. He be cross." LCAP-2

(324. An Elegy for W.C.W., The Lovely Man.) NoP-4

"Three limbs, three seasons smashed; well, one to go." HCAP

"Thunder & the flaw of their great quarrel, The." VCAP

"Turning it over, considering, like a madman." NoAM

"Welcome, grinned Henry, welcome fifty-one!" TAP

"You couldn't bear to grow old, but we grow old." TAP

"Your face broods from my table, Suicide." TAP

Dream that stole o'er us in the time. Charlotte Brontë. PEW   *Fr.*
    Retrospection.

Dream Thief. Nathaniel Mackey. GT

Dream Time. Anthony Thwaite. DiPo

Dream tree, Polly's tree, A. Polly's Tree. Sylvia Plath. AmFaPo

Dream Variation[s]. Langston Hughes. APT-2; HAP; ISC; ITBLP; NAAAL;
    NAAL-2v2; NOBA; NoP-4; SAmP; SSLK

Dream within a Dream, A. Edgar Allan Poe. NCAP; NOBA; OxBA; TAP;
    TCAPo

Dream within a Song, A. Henrietta Cordelia Ray. CBWP-3

Dream you remember yet. (LL) Ave atque Vale. Rosamund Marriott Watson.
    NOBE; OBEV

Dreamcat. Fonk. What? Scurr. Ah. Nietzsche Possessed. Brooks Haxton.
    Unle

Dream[e], The. John Donne. ESCV; MeLP; OBEV; TOF

Dream[e], The. Ben Jonson. BeJo; NOBE; NOSC

Dreame, Ane. Alexander Montgomerie. NePenScot

Dream[e], The [or A]. Rachel Speght. BASC; WPE
    Disswasion hearing her assigne my helpe." PBRV
    "My grief, quoth I, is called Ignorance." NAEL-7v1
    "When splendent Sol, which riseth in the East." EMWP

Dreamed Realization, A. Gregory Corso. NeAP; PoM; VGW

Dreamer Meets Conscience and Reason. William Langland. NAEL-6v1;
    NAEL-7v1   *Fr.* Vision of Piers Plowman, The.

Dreamer's Holiday, A. Mabel Wayne. ReLy

Dreamer, visionary, green-eyed sluggard! Mikhail Valentinovich Kulchitsky [or
    Kulchitskii]. TCRP

Dreamers. Siegfried Sassoon. MoBrPo; NoAM; Son
    (Soldiers are citizens of death's gray land.) GSo

Dreamers? Louisa Sarah Bevington. VWP

Dream[e]s. Robert Herrick. BeJo; CaPo; HAP; KaS; NAEL-5v1; NAEL-6v1;
    NAEL-7v1; OPOU; OxBSP; Spl
    (Here we are all, by day; by night we are hurled.) KaS

Dreaming. Fleur Adcock. OxBSo

Dreaming. Larry Wiggin. HA

Dreaming at the Rexall Drug. Robin Becker. ReTh

Dreaming Child, The. Felicia Dorothea Hemans. NOBRP

Dreaming, dreaming the night, the street, the stairway. Nocturne of the Statue. Xavier Villaurrutia. TCLAP, *tr. by* Dana Stangel

Dreaming Horse. Silvia Curbelo. TouFir

Dreaming I sat by the fire last night. Saturday Tub, The. Mary Gilmore. NOBAu

Dreaming I see you infinitely superposed upon yourself. Dreaming I See You. André Breton. SurPaPo, *tr. by* Jean-Pierre Cauvin and Mary Ann Caws

Dreaming in the Shanghai Restaurant. Dennis Joseph Enright. EmeKit

Dreaming of a Dead Lady. Shên Yo. ChiP, *tr. by* Arthur Waley

Dreaming of French Fries behind the Projects in Far Rockaway. Dennis Bernstein. SpudSo

Dreaming of Hair. Li-Young Lee. BodElec

Dreaming of Li Po. Tu Fu. ChinPo, *tr. by* Yip Wai-lim

Dreaming of Li Po. Tu Fu. WoPoe, *tr. by* David Hinton

Dreaming of Li Po. Tu Fu. CoBCP, *tr. by* Burton Watson

Dreaming of Li Po. Tu Fu. CrYelRi, *tr. by* Sam Hamill

Dreaming of Li Po. Tu Fu.
"Drifting clouds pass by all day long." SuSp
"Parted by death, we swallow remorse." SuSp

Dreaming of Master Chung-lu. K'ang Hai. CoBLCP, *tr. by* Jonathan Chaves

Dreaming of My Wife. Yuan Chen. CrYelRi, *tr. by* Sam Hamill

Dreaming of Yüan Chên. Po Chü-i. ChiP, *tr. by* Arthur Waley

Dreaming that I went with Li and Yü to Visit Yüan Chên. Po Chü-i. ChiP, *tr. by* Arthur Waley

Dreaming the flower I have never seen. (LL) Moly. Thom Gunn. CABP; HAP; NPeEn; NoAM

Dreaming Up Mother. Robert Adamson. BMAP

Dreaming, waking, the beggar maid. Beggar Maid, The. Sydney E. Jerrold. SacPr

Dreamland. Edgar Allan Poe. *See* Dream-Land [*or* Dreamland]

Dreamlike leap, A. For the Record. Roy Blount, Jr. OBAL

Dreams. Cecil Frances Alexander. NOxBChV

Dreams. Robert Herrick. *See* Dream[e]s

Dreams. Helen Hunt Jackson. APN-2

Dreams. Myŏng'ok. WoPoe, *tr. by* Okhee Yoo and Michael Stephens

Dreams. Edgar Allan Poe. NCAP
"Oh! that my young life were a lasting dream!" OxBA; TAP

Dreams. Henry Timrod. APN-2

Dreams. *Unknown.* ReMoGo

Dreams. Israel Zangwill. TrJP

Dreams Ahead, The. Edwin Carlile Litsey. PoToHe

Dreams Are Also Wounds. Breyten Breytenbach. VCWP, *tr. by* André Brink

Dreams by No One's Daughter. Leslie Ullman. PBCAP

Dreams fled away, this country bedroom, came. Another September. Thomas Kinsella. BIrV; CABP; CIP-2; HarvBoo; NoP-4

Dreams in German. "David Martin." NOBAu

Dreams in Harrison Railroad Park. Nellie Wong. OpBo

Dreams in War Time. Amy Lowell.
"I dug a grave under an oak-tree." BoWoP

Dreams of a Rival. Mary Robinson. CenSon; RWP

Dreams of Beauty. Adah Isaacs Menken. CBWP-1

Dreams of the One, The. Lőrinc Szabó. IQMS, *tr. by* Edwin Morgan

Dreams of Water. Donald Justice. LCAP-2

Dreams that delude with flying shade men's minds. We Are Such Stuff as Dreams. Petronius Arbiter. AWP, *tr. by* Howard Mumford Jones

Dreams, whimseys [*or* whimsies], and no more. (LL) Seneca. EBEV; OBVE, *tr. by* John Wilmot, 2d Earl of Rochester *Fr.* Troades.

Dreamt I today [*or* to-day] the dream of yesternight. George Santayana. APN-2 *Fr.* Sonnets.

Dreamt I was a poet. La Bodega Sold Dreams. Miguel Piñero. PueRic

Dreamt Up. Dennis Cooper. WiU

Dreamtime, / The first ones lived, those of long ago. Lalai (Dreamtime). Sam Woolagoodjah. NOBAu

Dreamy and docile you sit. Grooming. Katie Donovan. NeBl

Dreamy Cars Graze on the Dewy Boulevard. James Tate. LCAP-2

Drear cell, along whose lonely bounds. Bastille, a Vision, The. Helen Maria Williams. RWP

Drearie trumpet blew a dreadfull blast, The. Torquato Tasso. PBRV, *tr. by* Edward Fairfax *Fr.* Godfrey of Bulloigne; or, The Recoverie of Jerusalem [Gerusalemme Liberata].

Dreary Change, The. Sir Walter Scott. NAEL-5v2; NAEL-6v2

Dreary days are over. Long Ago (And Far Away). George Gershwin. ReLy

Dredge of that gravity, being without experience, The. (LL) In the Yukon. Ralph Gustafson. MoCV; NoP-4

Dregs. Ernest Christopher Dowson. OBMV

Dreme, The. Sir David Lindsay [*or* Lyndsay].
("And thus as we wer talking to and fro.") PBRV

(Complaynt of the Comoun weill of Scotland, The.) PBRV

(Compleynt of the Comoun Weill of Scotland, The.) OxBS

Deuisioun of the Eirth, The. NePenScot

Of the Realme of Scotland. OxBS

Drenched with the silver salvage of the mornfrost. (LL) History. Robert Lowell. ColAP; HCAP; PoetW; TAP; VCAP

Drenching, The. Samuel Hazo. GraLe

Drenching night drags on: no sleep or snore, The. Egan [*or* Aodhagán] O'Rahilly [*or* O'Reilly *or* Ó Rathaille]. NOIV

Drenching rain hisses down, cooling the evening. Su Tung-p'o (Su Shih). CoBCP, *tr. by* Burton Watson *Fr.* Days of Rain; the Rivers Have Overflowed: Two Poems.

Dresden. Ciaran Carson. CIP-2; ModIr; NPeEn; PBCIP; PNI

Dresdener. Remembering Dresden. Van K. Brock. HP

Dress me in green. *Unknown.* BoWoP

Dress of Fire, A. Dahlia Ravikovitch [*or* Ravikovich]. VCWP

Dress that my brother has put on is thin, The. *Var. authors.* AWP *Fr.* Manyo Shu, Part 1 of 4.

Dress to know her socks off, spent all day looking for just the right. I Bought a New Red. Chrystos. WiU

Dressed as a drag queen. Tiger Lady. Yusef Komunyakaa. CDa

Dressed in his clumsy, stiff, aquatic clothes. Diver, The. Edward Leslie Mayo. CoAP

Dressed in the colours of a country day. From the Painting "Back from Market" by Chardin. Eavan Boland. PBCIP

Dressed mainly in black and with hair. Hopkins Enters the Roman Catholic Church. David Scott. NLP

Dressed man and a naked man, A. George Orwell. EBEV

Dressing. Henry Vaughan. ESCV

Drew trips over his shadow by the pool. Gwyneth Lewis. NeBl

Dried leaves as I bow and pass smiling. (LL) Young Housewife, The. William Carlos Williams. APT-1; ColAP; HeIP-4; NAAL-2v2; NAAL-5; TAP

Dried up old cactus. June. Elaine Feinstein. BrRo

Dried vines, an old tree, evening crows. Tune: "Sky-Pure Sand." Ma Chih-yüan. ChinPo, *tr. by* Yip Wai-lim

Drier than the sun-dried raisins. *Unknown.* PriapPo, *tr. by* Richard W. Hooper *Fr.* Priapus Poems, The.

Drift. Alberta Turner. LCAP-2

Drift-Wood. Clara Ann Thompson. CBWP-2

Drifter off Tarentum, A. Rudyard Kipling. FaBoEE; PeFWW; PoWW; WoPoe *Fr.* Epitaphs of the War [1914–1918].

Drifters. Bruce Dawe. BMAP; CBAP; NoAM

Drifting and innocent and like snow. Christmas Letter Home. George Sutherland Fraser. OxBTC

Drifting clouds disgorge a bright moon, The. Song of "Night After Night," A. Ou-yang Hsiu. SuSp, *tr. by* Irving Y. Lo

Drifting clouds, distant and vast, The. Hsü Kan. SuSp *Fr.* Boudoir Thoughts.

Drifting clouds pass by all day long. Tu Fu. SuSp *Fr.* Dreaming of Li Po.

Drifting from above, the palms seem to sink. Last Night in Havana. Richard Blanco. NAPBL

Drifting in casually, one by one. (LL) Icarus. Valentin Iremonger. BIrV; CIP-2; ModIr

Drifting night in the Georgia pines. O Daedalus, Fly Away Home. Robert Earl Hayden. HAP; NAAAL

Drifting off the wheel of a past. First Spring. Duane Niatum. HATNAP

Drifting officials alone. Harmonizing a Spring Poem by Premier Lu of Chin-Ling. Tu Shen-yen. ChinPo, *tr. by* Yip Wai-lim

Drifting to meet us on the darkening stage. Thomas Kinsella. HarvBoo

Drifts That Bar My Door. Adah Isaacs Menken. CBWP-1

Driftwood. Witter Bynner. APT-1

Driftwood and Seacoal. Andrew Crozier. Oth

Drill's the Thing. *Unknown.* FaBoWar

Drill sergeants break up the only road we've got, The. Good Science. Ken Edwards. Oth

Drilling in Russell Square. Edward Richard Burton Shanks. OBMV

Drimeh Kundan. *Unknown.*
"Queen wept but thought: It is not appropriate to show such grief, The." WoPoe, *tr. by* Armand Schwerner

Drink. William Carlos Williams. OxBA

Drink and Agriculture. Dave Etter. IllVoic

Drink and be merry, merry, merry boys. Song, The. Thomas Morton. NAAL-3

Drink and be whole again beyond confusion. (LL) Directive. Robert Frost. APT-1; ColAP; HAP; MakPoe; MoAmPo; NAAL-2v2; NOBA; NoAM; NoP-4; PoE; SAmP; TFi

Drink and dance and laugh and lie. Flaw in Paganism, The. Dorothy Parker. NBLV

Drink, Asklepiades. Asclepiades. GrAn

Drink deep, my heart, of brightest noon. Afternoon Light. Jacob [or Jakov] Fichman. MHP, tr. by Ruth Finer Mintz

Drink of Milk, A. John Montague. ModIr; PNI

Drink of Spring, A. John Ennis. CIP-2; PBCIP

Drink of Water, A. Seamus Heaney. OxBC; TRP

Drink On. Mary E. Tucker. CBWP-1

Drink to drown my sorrows and restart, A. Palladas [or Pallades]. GrAn

Drink to me only with thine eyes. Song: To Celia. Ben Jonson. AWP; AmFaPo; BeJo; ClHu; NAEL-5v1; NAEL-6v1; NAEL-7v1; NOSC; OxAEP-1; OxBEV; PoE; SoSe-8; UV

Drink was the end of you, Anacreon. Julianus of Egypt. GrAn

Drink. . .with me, Melanippos. Why (think that). Alcaeus [or Alkaios]. SaLy, tr. by Diane Rayor

Drink wonder, my heart, drink in the wonder. Drink Wonder. Shin Shalom. MHP, tr. by Ruth Finer Mintz

Drinke and be merry, merry, merry boyes. Song. Thomas Morton. SCAP

Drinke to me onley with thine eyes. Ben Jonson. See Drink to me only with thine eyes

Drinker, glutton supreme. Simonides. GrAn

Drinking. Anacreon. BeJo; NOBE; NPeEn; OBEV; OBVE; OxAEP-1; OxBEV; PAI, tr. by Abraham Cowley

Drinking. Chu Yün-ming. CoBLCP, tr. by Jonathan Chaves

Drinking against men, Kalliston. Dedication to Aphrodite, A. Hedylos. GrAn, tr. by William Moebius

Drinking All Night, Sleeping All Day. Li Ho. CrYelRi, tr. by Sam Hamill

Drinking Alone. Wang Fan-chih. CrYelRi, tr. by Sam Hamill

Drinking Alone beneath the Moon. Li Po.
"If Heaven weren't fond of wine." SuSp
"Pot of wine among the flowers, A." SuSp

Drinking Alone in Moonlight. Li Po. TAL

Drinking Alone in the Moonlight. Li Po. ColAnChi; WoPoe, tr. by Elling O. Eide

Drinking Alone in the Moonlight. Li Po. AWP

Drinking Alone in the Rainy Season. T'ao Ch'ien [or T'ao Yuan-ming]. CrYelRi, tr. by Sam Hamill

Drinking Alone under Moonlight. Li Po. TAL

Drinking Alone with the Moon. Witter Bynner. APT-1

Drinking Alone with the Moon. Li Po. CrYelRi, tr. by Sam Hamill

Drinking alone without knowing the coming of dusk. To Amuse Myself. Li Po. SuSp, tr. by Joseph J. Lee

Drinking Art, The. Robert Minhinnick. AngWePo; TCAWP

Drinking at Crooked River. Tu Fu. CrYelRi, tr. by Sam Hamill

Drinking at Night in the Western Pavilion of the Fa-hua Temple. Liu Tsung-yüan. SuSp, tr. by Jan W. Walls

Drinking at Night with Yen Kung-mou. Shen Chou. CoBLCP, tr. by Jonathan Chaves

Drinking at the Cave Mouth. Tsung Ch'en. CoBLCP, tr. by Jonathan Chaves

Drinking at the Lake, First It's Sunny, Then It Rains. Su Tung-p'o (Su Shih). SuSp, tr. by Irving Y. Lo

Drinking Back. Franz Wright. LCAP-2

Drinking Cold Water. Peter Everwine. NNaP

Drinking Fountain, The. Robert Duncan. CLPP

Drinking, I sing of peace and of equality. Drinking Song. Ts'ao Ts'ao. CrYelRi, tr. by Sam Hamill

Drinking into deep night at East Slope, sober then drunk. Tune: "Immortal by the River." Su Tung-p'o (Su Shih). ChnPo, tr. by Yip Wai-lim

Drinking is done, the lamps extinguished, The. New Year's Eve. Wen Cheng-ming. CoBLCP, tr. by Jonathan Chaves

Drinking on East Slope at night. Listening to the River. Su Tung-p'o (Su Shih). TAL

Drinking Sappho Brand Ouzo. Martin Johnston. BMAP Fr. In Transit: A Sonnet Square.

Drinking Song. Robert Burns. NPeEn; NePenScot; PoE Fr. Jolly Beggars, The.

Drinking Song. Silvia Curbelo. TouFir

Drinking Song. Robert Fergusson. OxAEP-1

Drinking Song. Richard Brinsley Sheridan. NOIV; NPeEn; OxBEV Fr. School for Scandal, The.

Drinking Song. James Kenneth Stephen. NOBL; PeLV

Drinking Song. Ts'ao Ts'ao. CrYelRi, tr. by Sam Hamill

Drinking Song ("She tells me with claret she cannot agree.") Unknown. NOBL

Drinking Song ("Tappster, fille another ale.") Unknown. MiEL

Drinking-Song, A. Henry Carey. OBEV

Drinking Song, A. "The Peniarth Poet."
"Loke that none of you departe." AngWePo

Drinking Song, A. William Shakespeare. NoSic Fr. Antony and Cleopatra.

Drinking Song, A. W. B. Yeats. BoLoP

Drinking Spree beneath the Open Sky. Slavko Mihalic. PoSu, tr. by Peter Kastmiler

Drinking the Wind. "Tan Ying." WPOW

Drinking There Alone. Tu Fu. CarOv, tr. by Carolyn Kizer Fr. Meandering River Poems, The.

Drinking together in the evening we are human. Antimedon [or Antomedon]. GrAn

Drinking until drunk, the day is nearly gone. Sobering Up. Yüan Chên. SuSp, tr. by Dell R. Hales

Drinking Wine. Ch'ien Ch'ien-i [or Ch'ien Ch'ien-yi]. SuSp, tr. by Irving Y. Lo

Drinking Wine. Lin Hung. SuSp, tr. by Irving Y. Lo

Drinking Wine. Mo Shih-lung. CoBLCP, tr. by Jonathan Chaves

Drinking Wine. T'ao Ch'ien [or T'ao Yuan-ming]. CoBCP, tr. by Burton Watson
"Autumn chrysanthemums have beautiful color." SuSp
"Green pine grows in eastern garden, A." SuSp
"I built my hut in a place where people live." CoBCP
"Old friends know what I like." SuSp
"Prosperity and decline have no fixed dwelling." CoBCP
"Unsettled, a bird lost from the flock." SuSp
"Way's been lost for a thousand years, The." CoBCP

Drinking Wine. Unknown. ChinPo, tr. by Yip Wai-lim

Drinking Wine with a Mountain Hermit. Li Po. CrYelRi, tr. by Sam Hamill

Drinking with Elder Cheng the Eighth at Crooked River. Tu Fu. CrYelRi, tr. by Sam Hamill

Drinking with Friends. Tu Fu. CarOv, tr. by Carolyn Kizer Fr. Meandering River Poems, The.

Drinking with Friends amongst the Blooming Peonies. Liu Yu Hsi. OHMPC, tr. by Kenneth Rexroth

Drinking with the Nazis. Joseph Glazer. GotH

Drinks are okay. Friendliest Thing (Two People Can Do), The. Ervin Drake. ReLy

Drinks in the Town Square. Rachel Wetzsteon. AmPoNex; NeAmPo

Drip Drip or Not Bloody Likely. Gerda Mayer. PeLV

Drip drip, the rain on paulownia leaves. Pouring Out My Feelings after Parting from Yüan Chen. Po Chü-i. CoBCP, tr. by Burton Watson

Drip in darkness like a leaking pipe in the cellar. (LL) Evening Hawk. Robert Penn Warren. APT-2; ColAP; NAAL-2v2; NoP-4; OWoS; VCAP

Dripping with sweat he bends down. One-Armed Man in the Undergrowth, The. Bertolt Brecht. PoSu, tr. by Derek Bowman

Dripping / words / off. (Ryokan's scroll). Louis Zukofsky. APT-2

Drips surprise, The. They talk too. Fag-End. Philip O'Connor. SPE

Drive. Maggie Hannan. NeBl

Drive a Tractor. Unknown. NBLV

Drive-In, The. R. S. Gwynn. RA

Drive-ins are out, to start with. Movie-Going. John Hollander. CoAP

Drive off that golden oriole. Spring Sorrow. Chin Ch'ang-hsü. OHMPC, tr. by Kenneth Rexroth

Drive on, sharp wings, and cry above. Redshanks, The. Julian Bell. OBMV

Drive to Lone Ranger, A. Ray A. Young Bear. AF

Driven by hunger I leave my home. Begging for Food. T'ao Ch'ien [or T'ao Yuan-ming]. SuSp, tr. by Wu-Chi Liu

Driver, The. James Dickey. VGW

Dríver, drive fáster and máke a good rún. Calypso. W. H. Auden. PeLV

Driver rubbed at his nettly chin, The. To the Four Courts, Please. James Stephens. BIrV; MoBrPo; UnPo

"Driver, what stream is it?" I asked, well knowing. Lordly Hudson, The. Paul Goodman. APT-2; CoAP; VGW

Drivers dread suicides. Rhythm. Yevgeny [or Evgenii] Mikhailovich Vinokurov. TCRP, tr. by Daniel Weissbort

Drivers, therefore, didn't do, The. (LL) Limerick: "Man hired by John Smith and Co., A." "Mark Twain." InPK-6; PeLi

Driving. Alan Pizzarelli. HA

Driving across the Bay Bridge at 50 m.p.h. Picnic on the Bay Bridge. Morton Marcus. GeoHom

Driving an orange bug, passes. At the Stop Light, the Braided Blond Man. Anthony R. Vigil. AmPoNex

Driving and Drinking. David Lee.
"This all happened before." GifTon

Driving around, I will waste more time. (LL) Driving to Town Late to Mail a Letter. Robert Bly. HeIP-4; InPK-6; VGW

Driving Cross-Country. X. J. Kennedy. TwCP

Driving down the concrete artery. White Man Pressed the Locks, The. James C. Kilgore. InPK-6

Driving Home the Cows. Kate Putnam Osgood. CBCWP

Driving, I come for a while. Late at Night. William Stafford. NNaP

Driving in a Snowstorm, King Salmon to Naknek. Richard Dauenhauer. GifTon

Driving in Oklahoma. Carter Revard. HATNAP; VoR

Driving in the Park. *Unknown.* OxBoLi; PeLV

Driving keel, cut from the forest—look—travels the current, The. Boat Song, A. Saint Columba. NOIV

Driving late at night I pass. Sleep. Dana Naone. CDW

Driving Montana. Richard Hugo. AmFaPo

Driving north out of town today. Wanting You. Terra Hunter. PasH

Driving on the road to Stinson Beach. Promising Author. Carolyn Kizer. GeoHom

Driving south and travelling. Maintrunk Country Roadsong. Sam Hunt. PeNZ

Driving the perfect fuel, its thermonuclear wings. Hummingbirds. Ruth Stone. ExTi

Driving the perfect length of Ireland. To a Cuckoo at Coolanlough. Medbh McGuckian. PBCIP

Driving through new england. Lucille Clifton. ESEAA

Driving to Katoomba. Merlinda Bobis. ReBoTo

Driving to the Winnebago pow-wow, across Iowa in the August evening. Indian Car. Catron Grieves. ReTh

Driving to Town Late to Mail a Letter. Robert Bly. HeIP-4; InPK-6; VGW

Driving to work. Fringe-Area Reception. Halvard Johnson. MiVo

Driving to work, planned day ahead. You Got You Got to Be Told. Elizabeth Brown. IBA

Driving toward the Lac Qui Parle River. Robert Bly. CoAmPo; LCAP-2

Driving up highway 99. Children in the Arbor. Glover Davis. GeoHom

Driving west in the afternoon. Sphinx. Van K. Brock. SwNoth

Driving Wheel. Shirley Anne Williams. BlSi

Drizzle. Shinkichi Takahashi. ZenPo, *tr. by* Takashi Ikemoto and Lucien Stryk

Drizzle, The. China Observed through Greek Rain in Turkish Coffee. Henrik Nordbrandt. VCWP, *tr. by* Henrik Norbrandt and Alexander Taylor

Drizzle, drizzle, drop, drop, the rain at Winding Pond. Tune: "Deva-like Barbarian." *Unknown.* SuSp, *tr. by* Hellmut Wilhelm

Drizzling rain, A. Michael McClintock. HA

Drizzling rain set in, A. (LL) Rosy Bosom'd Hours, The. Coventry Patmore. EnLoPo; NOBVV

Dromedary has one hump, The. How to Tell a Camel. J. Patrick Lewis. TLR

Drone of the mosquitoes. Motojo. JDP, *tr. by* Yoel Hoffmann

Drone v. Worker. Ebenezer Elliott. OBSV

Droning a drowsy syncopated tune. Weary Blues, The. Langston Hughes. ColAP; FaBoA; HarvBoo; ISC; NAAAL; NOBA; NoAM; NoP-4; PoPoPo; SAmP

Drooling Madness at St. Liz. Charles Bukowski. BodElec

Drop a Pebble in the Water. James William Foley. PoToHe

Drop a Stone. *Unknown.* PWR

Drop by bright red drop. (LL) Child Burial. Paula Meehan. EmeKit; MakPoe; ModIr

Drop dies in the river, The. Ghazal 5. Mirza Asadullah Khan Ghalib. EaWin, *tr. by* Aijaz Ahmad and W. S. Merwin

Drop, drop, slow tears, and bathe those beauteous feet. Hymn. Phineas Fletcher. OxBSP; SacPr

Drop from above. (LL) Grace. George Herbert. ChIV-1; GeHe

Drop of Dew, A. Shmuel Halkin. TrJP, *tr. by* Jacob Sonntag

Drop of dew on an autumn lotus leaf, A. On Dewdrop. Wei Ying-wu. SuSp, *tr. by* Irving Y. Lo

Drop of ocean. Alan Pizzarelli. HA

Drop of sepia in the fragrant vase, The. Dusk. Abraham Z. Lopez-Penha. TrJP, *tr. by* Thomas Walsh

Drop of water freezes instantly, A. Kaso Sodon. JDP, *tr. by* Yoel Hoffmann

Dropped by memory. (LL) Emily Dickinson. APN-2; AWP; OxBA

Dropped into the Ether Acre. Emily Dickinson. NCAP

Dropped off the tip of the tongue. Dialogue of Thunder. Christine Hume. AmPoNex

Dropped petals of a broken lotus-moon. No Less than Prisoners. Frederick Thomas Bennett Macartney. CBAP

Dropping the reins, we dismount from the ornate carriage. Hand in Hand; a Song. Shen Yüeh. SuSp, *tr. by* Richard B. Mather

Drops of blood drip on the earth. Where Are the Men Chased Away by that Mad Wind? Alda do Espirito Santo. HAWP, *tr. by* Jacques-Noël Gouat

Drops of Gall. Gabriela Mistral. BoWoP, *tr. by* David Garrison

Drops of Water. Ella Wheeler Wilcox.
  "And he held me fast, and he said, At last." VerBaPo

Drops on four feet. Yet he has bleeding paws. (LL) Allegory of the Wolf Boy, The. Thom Gunn. HarvBoo; OxBC

Drought. David Holbrook. OxBTC

Drought. J. G. Mocoancoeng. WoPoe, *tr. by* Philip Bryant and Mongane Wally Serote

Drought. Joan I. Siegel. PoCoUp

Drought. Sitanshu Yashashchandra. OMIP, *tr. by* Saleem Peeradina

Drought, The. Gary Soto. NoAM

Drought, malevolent stepmother. Natalya [*or* Natal'ia] Gorbanevskaya [*or* Gorbanyevskaya *or* Gorbanevskaia]. TCRusP, *tr. by* Daniel Weissbort

Drought seems to go on forever, The. Subterranean. Michael Hannon. GeoHom

Drought Year. Judith Wright. NoAM

Drouth, The. Jon Dressel. AngWePo

Drove all day from San Diego. August Fires. Glover Davis. GeoHom

Drove-Road, The. Wilfrid Wilson Gibson. OxBTC

Drover, A. Padraic Colum. AWP; MoBrPo; OBMV; RB

Drover's Boy, The. Ted Egan. NOBAu

Drowned, The. Norman MacCaig. OxBC

Drowned Children, The. Louise Glück. HCAP; VCAP

Drowned Sailor, The. Judith Ortiz Cofer. PueRic

Drowned Spaniel, The. Charles Tennyson Turner. PeVV

Drowned truck-driver was propped on the slab, A. Little Aster. Gottfried Benn. PFTM-1

Drowning. Epitaphs. Charles Reznikoff. APT-2

Drowning Horses. Joy Harjo. NAAL-5 *Fr.* She Had Some Horses.

Drowning in the Last Days of Luxury. Edwin Torres. HeMarv

Drowning is not so pitiful. Emily Dickinson. NCAP; OxBSP

Drowning of the Facts of a Life, The. Michael S. Harper. ESEAA

Drowsy sun went slowly to his rest, The. Evening. James Stephens. MoBrPo

Drug of the incomprehensible. Bad Habit, The. Charles Henri Ford. SPE

Drug Store. Karl Shapiro. OxBA; TwCP

Drugs. Dennis Cooper. PmAP

Drugs. Jacquie Jones. ISC

Drugs are a tuition. Going to School in France or America. Tom Clark. CoAmPo

Drugs Made Pauline Vague. Stevie Smith. FaBoWP

Drugs of War, The. Les A. Murray. BMAP

Druk. / Druker. / Druksome. Drukascripts. Vladimir Druk. TCRP, *tr. by* John High and Katya Olmsted

Drukascripts. Vladimir Druk. TCRP, *tr. by* John High and Katya Olmsted

Drum. Langston Hughes. APT-2; MoAmPo

Drum, The. John Scott of Amwell. *See* Ode: "I hate that drum's discordant sound."

Drum heartbeat is present / An external behavior. Unconsciously. Ken Edwards. Oth

Drum on your drums, batter on your banjos. Jazz Fantasia. Carl Sandburg. AiP; MoAmPo

Drum sounds from the high city wall as the lampwick burns out, The. Tune: "Song of Picking Mulberry." Wang Kuo-wei. SuSp, *tr. by* Ching-i Tu

Drum; the Narrative of the Demon of Tedworth, The. Dame Edith Sitwell. FaBoTw

Drumbeat is constant as surf, The. At Bon Odori. James Masao Mitsui. OpBo

Drumbeats. Yi Inbok. WoPoe, *tr. by* Kevin O'Rourke

Drumlin Prayer. Tom MacIntyre. CIP-2

Drumlin Woodchuck, A. Robert Frost. APT-1; NOBA; NoAM

Drummer, The. Bruce Beaver. BMAP

Drummer, The. Philip Dacey. MiVo

Drummer Hodge. Thomas Hardy. AWP; EBEV; FaBoWar; GTBS-P; HAP; HarvBoo; NAEL-5v2; NAEL-6v2; NOBVV; NoAM; NoP-4; OBWP; OxAEP-2; PAI; PeFWW; WeW-3

Drummond's Lover Sings the Blues. Norman Weinstein. WaCA

Drums mutter for war, and soon we must begin, The. Advice for a Journey. Sidney Keyes. PoWW

Drunk. Carroll Arnett. VoR

Drunk among the Flowers. Mao Wen-hsi. ColAnChi, *tr. by* Lois Fusek

Drunk as drunk on turpentine. Drunk As Drunk. Pablo Neruda. BoLoP; PasH; WoPoe, *tr. by* Christopher Logue

Drunk came in out of the cold, A. What Did They Have in Mind? Nikolai Ivanovich Glazkov. TCRP, *tr. by* Daniel Weissbort

Drunk, Climbing to the Peak of Iron Tomb on Wei Mountain. Li K'ai-hsien. CoBLCP, *tr. by* Jonathan Chaves

Drunk Dog. Erin McGraw. Unle

Drunk, Facing Crimson Leaves. Po Chü-i. CoBCP, *tr. by* Burton Watson

Drunk, I left the western pavilion. Tune: "Butterflies Lingering over Flowers." Yen Chi-tao. SuSp, *tr. by* An-yan Tang

Drunk, I let my skiff. Tune: "Rouged Lips." Ch'in Kuan. ColAnChi, *tr. by* Jiaosheng Wang

Drunk I observe the golden dance of stars. Argentarius. GrAn

Drunk, I scurry up a hillside. Climbing Yun-lung Mountain. Su Tung-p'o (Su Shih). CrYelRi, *tr. by* Sam Hamill

Drunk in the Furnace, The. W. S. Merwin. NAAL-2v2; NoAM; NoP-4; PoE; TwCP

Drunk in the kitchen, I ring God. Telephoning God. Gary Soto. PBCAP

Drunk Last Night with Friends, I Go to Work Anyway. Philip Dow. InPK-6

Drunk Man, The. *Unknown.* NOBAu

Drunk Man Looks at the Thistle, A. Hugh MacDiarmid.
"Dae what ye wull ye canna parry." EBEV; OxAEP-2
Farewell to Dostoevski. NAEL-5v2; NAEL-6v2
"Language that but sparely floo'ers, The." NePenScot
"O wha' the bride that cairries the bunch." NPeEn
"Yet ha'e I Silence left, the croon o' a'" NAEL-5v2; NAEL-6v2

Drunk on Dragon Hill tonight. On Dragon Hill. Li Po. CrYelRi, *tr. by* Sam Hamill

Drunk on the blossoming plum. To an Ancient Tune. Chu Tun-ju. CrYelRi, *tr. by* Sam Hamill

Drunk Too Soon. Yüan Chên. SuSp, *tr. by* Dell R. Hales

Drunk water cold and clear from an inexhaustible hidden fountain. (LL) Wilderness, The. Kathleen Jessie Raine. BoWoP; WPE

Drunk who lives across the street from us, The. Neighbor. Richard Hugo. GifTon

Drunk with wine, I slap my spring robe. Yen Chi-tao. SuSp

Drunkard, The. Bible, *O.T.* TrJP *Fr.* Proverbs.

Drunkard and the Pig, The. *Unknown.* OBAL

Drunkard's Nocturnes, A. "Sasha Chorny" [*or* Chiornyi]. TCRP, *tr. by* Bernard Meares

Drunkard's Wife, The. Mary E. Tucker. CBWP-1

Drunkards are rolling in slowly, The. Drunkards, The. Jelaluddin [*or* Jalal al-Din] Rumi. EnlH, *tr. by* Robert Bly

Drunken Americans. John Ashbery. HCAP

Drunken Boat. Arthur Rimbaud. SxFrPo, *tr. by* Martin Sorrell

Drunken Boat, The. Arthur Rimbaud. NAWM-7v2, *tr. by* Stephen Stepanchev
"Hearing the thunder of the intransitive weirs." WoPoe, *tr. by* Derek Mahon

Drunken Fisherman, The. Robert Lowell. ChIV-2; NOBA; OxBA; VGW

Drunken Memories of Anne Sexton. Alan Dugan. BodElec

Drunken Merchant, The. Milán Füst. IQMS, *tr. by* Jess Perlman

Drunken night in my house with a, A. Dream Record: June 8 1955. Allen Ginsberg. CoAmPo; NOBA

Drunken Poem. David Helwig. NOBC

Drunken Rose, The. Amarou. AWP, *tr. by* E. Powys Mathers

Drunken sun / totters among the clouds, The. Orgy (That Is, Vegetable Market, at Sarno). Gina Labriola. WPOW, *tr. by* Edgar Pauk

Drunkenness. "Anvari." WoPoe, *tr. by* Geoffrey Squires

Drunkenness. Friedrich von Logau. GePo, *tr. by* George C. Schoolfield

Dry as the first of August. Partitions. Franco Buffoni. ItPo, *tr. by* Gayle Ridinger

Dry birch tree stood, The. Maya Borisova. TCRusP, *tr. by* Daniel Weissbort

Dry brown coughing beneath their feet, The. Gwendolyn Brooks. ESEAA; VGW *Fr.* Womanhood, The.

Dry creekbeds littered with buckeyes, fallen. Like Memory, Caverns. Elizabeth Dodd. AmPoNex

Dry Eleven Months. John Berryman. BodElec

Dry heat of the Tassajara canyon. Letter to Jeanne (at Tassajara). Diane Di Prima. BB

Dry in the sun by corner of K'i. Bamboos Grow Well under Good Rule, The. *Unknown.* WoPoe, *tr. by* Ezra Pound

Dry Leaves, Dry Leaves. *Unknown.* CoBCP, *tr. by* Burton Watson

Dry Loaf. Wallace Stevens. NOBA; OxBA; PoRA; RaBo

Dry River. *Unknown.* FaBoVe

Dry River Bed. Andrew Salkey. WoPoe

Dry riverbed, A. Issa. EH, *tr. by* Robert Hass

Dry Root in a Wash. Simon J. Ortiz. HATNAP

Dry-rot at ease till the Judgment-day! (LL) Robert Browning. CTC; EBVV *Fr.* Garden Fancies.

Dry Salvages, The. T. S. Eliot. AiP; NoP-4; OxBA *Fr.* Four Quartets.

Dry Spell of Faith, A. Timothy Geiger. AmPoNex

Dry, summer day. Robert Spiess. HA

Dry Tree. Muso Soseki. EaWin, *tr. by* W. S. Merwin

Dry tree with an empty honeycomb, A. James McAuley. BMAP *Fr.* Hero and the Hydra, The.

Dry World. Dieter Weslowski. InvLad

Dry Your Tears, Africa! Bernard Dadié. TTY, *tr. by* Donatus Ibe Nwoga

Drying Clothes. Yang Wan-li. SuSp, *tr. by* Jonathan Chaves

Du Bartas: His Divine Weeks and Works. Joshua Sylvester.
Acrostichelliostichon. OxBSo
"If patience true could termine passions warr." OxBSo

"Rare type of gentrie, and true Vertues Starr." OxBSo

Du bist wie eine Blume. Heinrich Heine. AWP *Fr.* Homeward Bound.

Dual, The. Richard Lovelace. CaPo

Dual Site, The. Michael Hamburger. TwCP

Dualism. Ishmael Reed. ESEAA; NAAAL

Duan First. Robert Burns. *Fr.* Vision, The.

Dubbed Out. Jean Binta Breeze. WaCA

Dubious "Old Kriss, A." James Whitcomb Riley.
"Us-folks is purty pore—but Ma." VerBaPo

Dublin. Louis MacNeice. CIP-2; OxBTC *Fr.* Closing Album, The.

Dublin Girl, Mountjoy, 1984. Dermot Bolger. BiHa

Dublin Made Me. Donagh MacDonagh. OxBTC

Dublinesque. Philip Larkin. NoAM; OxBC

Duchess of Malfi, The. John Webster. NAEL-5v1; NAEL-7v1
"Do'st thou thinke we shall know one an other." OxBEV
Hark, Now Everything Is Still. HAP; SCGP
("Hearke, now every thing is still.") NPeEn; OxBEV
(Shrouding of the Duchess of Malfi, The.) NOBE; OBEV
"Thou wretched thing of blood." OxBEV
"What death?" OxBEV

Duchess's Lullaby, The. Lewis Carroll. FaBoCh; NBLV; UV *Fr.* Alice's Adventures in Wonderland.

Duchesses. David Campbell. NOBAu

Duck. John Lyle Donaghy. BIrV

Duck. Valerie Worth. NTCP

Duck, The. Ogden Nash. RB

Duck and a drake, A. Ducks and Drakes. Mother Goose. OxNR; ReMoGo

Duck-chasing. Galway Kinnell. TwCP; VGW

Duck fats rot in the roasting pan, The. Gwendolyn Brooks. ColAP *Fr.* Notes from the Childhood and the Girlhood.

Duck feathers. David Lloyd. HA

Duck lives forever. Braggart Duck. Shinkichi Takahashi. ZenPo, *tr. by* Takashi Ikemoto and Lucien Stryk

Duck patrol is waddling down the odd-number side of Raglan, The. Army. Ciaran Carson. BiHa; PBCIP

Duck's Ditty. Kenneth Grahame. NOxBChV; NTCP; OTCP; WHSW *Fr.* Wind in the Willows, The.

Duckling, Swan. Jim Elledge. SwNoth

Ducks and Drakes. Mother Goose. OxNR; ReMoGo

Ducks bobbing on the water. Issa. EH, *tr. by* Robert Hass

Ducks flew up from the Morton Pond, The. John Masefield. EBNV *Fr.* Reynard the Fox.

Ducks in pairs drowse on the warm sand. (LL) South Wind. Tu Fu. BLT; OHPC, *tr. by* Kenneth Rexroth

Ducks land, The. William J. Higginson. HA

Duckweed. Leopold Staff. PoSu, *tr. by* Adam Czerniawski

Duckweed Pond. Wang Wei. CoBCP, *tr. by* Burton Watson

Due of the Dead, The. William Makepeace Thackeray. FaBoWar; OBWP

Due the hilot, faithful to my father. From the Raw. Alejandrino Hufana. ReBoTo

Due to the tragic lowness of my brow. Red, Hot and Blue. Cole Porter. ReLy

Duel. H. C. ten Berge. TuT *Fr.* Lusitanian Variant, The.

Duel, The. Eugene Field. APN-2; ITBLP; NOxBChV; OBAL; OBCA; PoRA; TFi

Duel with Verses over a Great Man. *Unknown.* TrJP

Duellist, The. Charles Churchill.
"First (entitled to the place), The." OBSV

Duenna, The. Richard Brinsley Sheridan.
Air: "I ne'er could any lustre see." NOEC
"Oh, the days when I was young." OxAEP-1
Song: "Give Isaac the nymph who no beauty can boast.". NOIV

Duet. Lady Caroline Lamb. RWP

Duet. Theodore Roethke. OBCoV

Duet, A. Thomas Sturge Moore. OBEV

Duet for a Chair and a Table. Jack Spicer. APSN

Dufferin, Simcoe, Grey (4). Margaret Atwood. PoetW *Fr.* Four Small Elegies.

Dug-Out, The. Siegfried Sassoon. MoBrPo

Dugall Quin. *Unknown.* ESPB

Duh, duh, duh, Dum! (LL) Double Dactyls. E. William Seaman. OBCoV; WeW-3

Duino Elegies. Rainer Maria Rilke.
("Emptiness first / felt the vibration that now charms us and comforts and helps?") (LL) PFTM-1
"Not wooing, no longer shall wooing, voice that has outgrown it." EnlH
("Who, if I cried, would hear me among the angelic orders?") PFTM-1

"Why, if this interval of being can be spent serenely."   EnlH

Duke and I 2, The.   Charles Ducal.   TuT, *tr.* by Desmond Egan

Duke Ellington Dream, The.   Paul Zimmer.   PBCAP

Duke Is the Lad [to Frighten a Lass], The.   Thomas Moore.   OBCoV

Duke of Athole's Nurse, The.   *Unknown.*   ESPB; OxBB

Duke Of Buccleuch, The.   J. A. Phelp.   NOBAu

Duke of Buckingham, The.   Pope.   NOBE   *Fr.* Epistle III, to Allen Lord Bathurst.

Duke of Gordon's Daughter, The.   *Unknown.*   ESPB

Duke of York's Statue, The.   Walter Savage Landor.   FaBoEE

Duke: royall letcher; goe, gray hayrde adultery.   Cyril Tourneur.   OxBEV   *Fr.* Revenger's Tragedy, The.

Duke's Song, The.   Mary Sidney Wroth, Countess of Montgomery.   RACG; WPE   *Fr.* Urania.

Duke's World.   Imamu Amiri Baraka.   SpirFl

Duke was in his hammock and a thousand miles away, The.   Great Poll-Tax Victory of '88, The.   Noel Petty.   UV

Dulce et Decorum Est.   Wilfred Owen.   AmFaPo; CABP; FaBoTw; FaBoWar; HarvBoo; HeIP-4; InPK-6; MoBrPo; NAEL-5v2; NAEL-6v2; NIL-7; NIP-4; NoAM; NoP-4; OBWP; OxBEV; PeFWW; PoE; PoPoPo; PoWW; RaBo; TCAWP; TFi; TRP; UnPo

Dulce it is, and *decorum,* no doubt, for the country to fall, to.   Arthur Hugh Clough.   EBVV; FaBoWar; OxAEP-2   *Fr.* Amours de Voyage.

Dull and unthinking! had'st thou none but me.   Upon a Bookseller.   John Oldham.   BASC

Dull as a bat, said my mother.   Cousin Sidney.   Dannie Abse.   AngWePo

Dull as I was, to think that a Court Fly.   Black Patch on Lucasta's Face, A.   Richard Lovelace.   BeJo; CaPo

Dull. Dull indeed! What shall it e'er be thus?   Edward Taylor.   ChIV-1   *Fr.* Preparatory Meditations before My Approach to the Lord's Supper.

Dull evening in a run-down village, A.   Earth Poem.   Mahmoud Darwish.   AF, *tr.* by Abdullah Al-Udhari

Dull people, A.   From Colony to Nation.   Irving Layton.   NIL-7; NOBC

Dull rattle of shutters being lowered, The.   Anatoly Steiger.   TCRusP, *tr.* by Paul Schmidt

Dull sleep instructs, nor sport vain dreams in vain. (LL)   Edward Young.   NOEC; OxAEP-1   *Fr.* Night Thoughts.

Dull Sonnet.   Henry Reed.   OxBEV

Dull to myself [or my self] and almost dead to these.   Bad Season Makes the Poet Sad, The.   Robert Herrick.   BASC; BeJo; CaPo; CavPo; NAEL-5v1; NAEL-6v1; NAEL-7v1; SCGP

Dull unwashed windows of eyes.   Poem Some People Will Have to Understand, A.   Imamu Amiri Baraka.   BPo; GT; NOBA; RaBo

Dull water spirit—and Protean god.   Fog.   Henry David Thoreau.   APN-1

Dulled by the slow glare of the yellow bulb.   Wartime Dawn, A.   David Gascoyne.   NPeEn

Dulness[e].   George Herbert.   ESCV

Dulngulg Song Cycle, The.   *Unknown.*
   "Day breaks—the first rays of the rising Sun, stretching her arms, The."   NOBAu, *tr.* by Ronald M. Berndt
   Sunrise Sequence.   NOBAu, *tr.* by Ronald M. Berndt

Duluth, Minnesota.   Connie Wanek.   UrbNat

Dum Diana Vitrea.   *Unknown.*   WoPoe, *tr.* by Richmond Lattimore   *Fr.* Carmina Burana.

Dumas.   Jabari Asim.   InTrad

Dumb.   Hildegarde Flanner.   APT-2

Dumb are the trumpets, cymbals.   Solomon.   Heinrich Heine.   TrJP, *tr.* by Emma Lazarus

Dumb, / Bloodied, the severed.   Grafted Tongue, A.   John Montague.   BIrV; CIP-2; PBCIP

Dumb: for they flamed, and it was me they burned. (LL)   Some Eyes Condemn.   Edward Thomas.   NoAM; OxBSo

Dumb genius blows.   From Another Room.   Gregory Corso.   NeAP

Dumb herd scowled, The.   Cashier, The.   Andrey [or Andrei] Andreievich Voznesensky [or Voznesenskii].   TCRP, *tr.* by W. H. Auden

Dumb Insolence.   Adrian Mitchell.   NOxBChV

Dumb Oxen.   Sister Mary Madeleva.   CRP   *Fr.* Of Mary.

Dumb thing near a drunken man, A. (LL)   Dumb World, The.   William Henry Davies.   OBWVE; OxBTC

Dumb World, The.   William Henry Davies.   OBWVE; OxBTC

Dumbfounding, The.   Margaret Avison.   NOBC

Dummer the Shepherd Sacrific'd.   Cotton Mather.   SacPr; SCAP   *Fr.* Epitaph.

Dump, The.   Yelena [or Elena] Shwarts [or Shvarts].   ItGoST, *tr.* by Catriona Kelly and Michael Molnar

Dumping (left over from the autumn).   Enemy Encounter.   Padraic Fiacc.   PNI

Dumpy Ducky.   Lucy Larcom.   OBCA

Dun-Colour [or Dun-Color].   Ruth Pitter.   PoRA

Dun shades quiver down the lone long fallow.   Poem for Max Nordau, A.   Edwin Arlington Robinson.   APN-2

Dunbar.   Anne Spencer.   NAAAL

Dunbar Attacks His Rival.   William Dunbar.   NePenScot   *Fr.* Flyting of Dunbar and Kennedy, The.

Dunbar, 1650.   Sidney Keyes.   FaBoWar

Duncan Gray.   Robert Burns.   GTBS-P

Dunce, The.   Jacques Prévert.   MFP, *tr.* by Martin Sorrell

Dunce, The.   *Unknown.*   OxNR

Dunciad, The.   Pope.
   Book the Fourth.
      "O Muse! relate (for you can tell alone)."   OxBEV
   High on a gorgeous seat, that far out-shone.
      "This labour passed, by Bridewell all descend."   FHYEP
      "Three college sophs, and three pert templars came."   FHYEP
   To Dr. Jonathan Swift.   OxAEP-1
      "Here she beholds the chaos dark and deep."   FHYEP
   Yet, yet a moment, one dim ray of light.   NAEL-5v1; NAEL-6v1; NAEL-7v1
   Certain Type of Scientist Speaks, A.   ECEV
   Idle Pursuits.   ECEV; OBSV
   "In flowed [or flow'd] at once a gay embroidered [or embroider'd] race."   NOEC
   "In vain, in vain—the all-composing Hour."   EBEV; NoP-4; SCV
   "Let others creep by timid steps, and slow."   ECEV
   "More had she spoke, but yawn'd—All nature nods."   FHYEP
   "Next, bidding all draw near on bended knees."   ECEV; OBSV
   "Now crowds on crowds around the goddess press."   NAEL-6v1; NAEL-7v1
   Reign of Chaos, The.   EBEV; NoP-4; SCV
   "She comes! she comes! the sable throne behold."   ECEV
   "Then[,] blessing all, Go, children of my care!"   NAEL-6v1; NAEL-7v1; NOEC; NPeEn
   "Then thick as locusts black'ning the ground."   NOEC; NPeEn
   ("Then thick as locusts blackening the ground.")   NAEL-6v1; NAEL-7v1
   Triumph of Dullness, The.   NAEL-6v1; NAEL-7v1; NOBE; NOEC; NPeEn
   Young Traveller Is Presented to the Goddess Dulness, A.   NOEC
   "Yet, yet a moment, one dim ray of light."   NAEL-5v1; NAEL-6v1; NAEL-7v1

Dunciad Minor.   Alec Derwent Hope.
   On Shakespeare Critics.   OxBC

Dundee.   John Burnside.   NePenScot

Dunes stir sleepily, The.   Cities.   Grigory [or Grigorii] Mikhailovich Pozhenyan [or Pozhenian].   TCRP, *tr.* by Lubov Yakovleva

Dung-beetle.   Breyten Breytenbach.   PoetW, *tr.* by André Brink

Dunna thee tell me it's his'n, mother.   Whether or Not.   D. H. Lawrence.   MoBrPo

Duns Scotus's Oxford.   Gerard Manley Hopkins.   CABP; EBEV; GTBS-P; NAEL-5v2; NAEL-6v2; NoAM; OBMV; OxAEP-2; PeECV

Duns Scotus, say, with Scotus Eriugena. (LL)   Sushi.   Paul Muldoon.   CABP; CIP-2

Dunt Dunt Dunt Pittie Pattie.   *Unknown.*   FaBoVe

Duo-Tang.   Kenward Elmslie.   FTOS

Duomo, The.   Maria Luisa Spaziani.   NeIt, *tr.* by Beverly Allen

Durand of Blonden.   Ludwig Uhland.   AWP, *tr.* by James Clarence Mangan

Duration of Water.   Mei-Mei Berssenbrugge.   FSt

Durban, Birmingham.   Question and Answer.   Langston Hughes.   BPo

Dürer: Innsbruck, 1495.   "Ern Malley."   BMAP; CBAP

Dürer's 'Young Hare.'   Norah Hill.   Prnts

Dürer would have seen a reason for living.   Marianne Craig Moore.   APT-1; BoWoP; ColAP; FaBoMo; FaBoWP; HAP; HarvBoo; NOBA; NoAM; NoP-4; OxBA; PoPoPo; WPE   *Fr.* Part of a Novel, Part of a Poem, Part of a Play.

Duressor.   Larissa Szporluk.   AmPoNex

Durham.   Tony Harrison.   NoAM

Durham.   *Unknown.*   ASW, *tr.* by Kevin Crossley-Holland

"Durham," "Devonia," "Allendale,"—their houses, those.   Summer Cloud, A.   Waldo Williams.   OBWVE, *tr.* by Joseph P. Clancy

Durham Field.   *Unknown.*   ESPB

Duriesdyke.   Algernon Charles Swinburne.   OxBB

During a Bombardment by V-Weapons.   Roy Fuller.   OxBSP

During a cozy hour of rain, I wondered.   St. Bartholomew's Night.   Bella [or Izabella] Akhatovna Akhmadulina.   TCRP, *tr.* by Albert C. Todd

During a war the poets turn to war.   Ordonnance.   Thomas McGrath.   GifTon

During an Illness.   Vladimir Holan.   WoPoe, *tr.* by Ian Milner and Jarmila Milner

During His Courtship.   Charles Wesley.   NOCV

During his great speech the prosecutor. Trial, The. Zbigniew Herbert. PoetW, *tr.* by John Carpenter and Bogdana Carpenter

During his great speech the prosecutor. Trial, The. Zbigniew Herbert. AF, *tr.* by John Carpenter

During March while hoeing long rows. Hoeing. Gary Soto. PBCAP

During Music. Arthur Symons. NOBVV

During my sister's birth. Coming Down from Derry Hill. Maggie Hannan. NLP

During one period I remember. Eveningsong 2. Ramona Wilson. VoR

During our argument. Alexis Rotella. HA

During Recess. Giovanna Pollarolo. TANSG, *tr.* by Marjorie Agosin

During Saturn's reign I believe that Chastity still. Juvenal. RomPo, *tr.* by Peter Green *Fr.* Satires.

During the Depression my grandmother. One Foot in the Door. Anne Elder. CBAP

During the early winter. Poem for Shane on Her Brother's Birthday. Donald T. Sanders. TTTS

During the ebb I wrote words in the sand. Fame. Kahlil Gibran. MAP, *tr.* by Michael Beard and Adnan Haydar

During the Eichmann Trial. Denise Levertov.
   Crystal Night. TaR
   Peachtree, The. TaR
   When We Look Up. TaR

During the First International Elvis Conference in Oxford. Elvis Reads the Wild Swans at Coole. Fleda Brown Jackson. AllShUp

During the holidays. Holidays. Eva Mylonas. BoWoP, *tr.* by Kimon Friar

During the last nights of my father's life. My Father's Clothes. Pascale Petit. Prnts

During the Pageant at Medicine Lodge. Charles G. Ballard. VoR

During the plague I came into my own. Tarantula or the Dance of Death. Anthony Hecht. CoAP

During the winter of course. Elephant in Winter, The. Michael Van Walleghen. UrbNat

During War, the Timeless Air. John Seed. Oth

During Wind and Rain. Thomas Hardy. GTBS-P; HAP; HarvBoo; NAEL-5v2; NAEL-6v2; NIL-7; NPeEn; NoP-4; OxBEV; OxBTC; PeVV; PoE; TFi; TOF; TRP

During your absence, when I swept the floor. Roy Fuller. OxBSo *Fr.* Cancer Hospital, The.

Durst ye not stoop to play the fools for him? (LL) On Those That Deserve It. Francis Quarles. NOCV; NOSC

Dusk. Basho. EH, *tr.* by Robert Hass

Dusk. Frank Mkalawile Chipasula. HBAPE *Fr.* Nightsong.

Dusk. Angelina Weld Grimké. APT-1

Dusk. John Hollander. *See* Dusk. / Above the / water hang the

Dusk. Abraham Z. Lopez-Penha. TrJP, *tr.* by Thomas Walsh

Dusk. Gabriela Mistral. BoWoP, *tr.* by David Garrison

Dusk. Gabriela Mistral. TANSG, *tr.* by Maria Jacketti

Dusk. Summer Recital. Cynthia S. Pederson. MiVo

Dusk. Shuntaro Tanikawa. PoetW, *tr.* by Harold Wright

Dusk. *Unknown, fr. Terezin Concentration Camp.* INSAB

Dusk. Helen Welshimer. PoToHe

Dusk, The. Robert Gray. BMAP

Dusk. / Above the / water hang the. Swan and Shadow. John Hollander. InPK-6; VCAP

Dusk dark / On Railroad Avenue. Railroad Avenue. Langston Hughes. APT-2

Dusk flew in on the wings of evening, The. Dusk. *Unknown, fr. Terezin Concentration Camp.* INSAB

Dusk from rock to rock a waterthrush. John Wills. HA

Dusk-haired and gold-robed o'er the golden wine. For "The Wine of Circe" by Edward Burne-Jones. Dante Gabriel Rossetti. UV

Dusk in Creason's Park comes on slow. Late Afternoon, Late in the Twentieth Century. Jeffrey Skinner. PBCAP

Dusk in My Backyard. Keith Wilson. BLT

Dusk in the Country. Harry Edmund Martinson. RB, *tr.* by Robert Bly

Dusk in Winter. W. S. Merwin. BLT

Dusk, iridescent gasoline floats on the. Going Back to the River. Marilyn Hacker. WiU

Dusk: July. Marilyn Hacker. FFC

Dusk must become your light. Sitting with Lester Young. Paul Zimmer. SeSe

Dusk of Horses, The. James Dickey. ColAP

Dusk over the lake. Virgil Hutton. InPK-6

Dusk sifted into my breathless room, The. Deep Song. Antonio Machado Ruiz. SpanPo, *tr.* by John Crow

Dusk, the ivy thick with sparrows. Temple near Quang Tri, Not on the Map. Bruce Weigl. CDa

Dusking year, in cosmic measure, ushers in shorter days. Night up in the Tower. Tu Fu. ChinPo, *tr.* by Yip Wai-lim

Dusky night rides down the sky, The. Henry Fielding. OxBoLi; PeLV *Fr.* Don Quixote in England.

Dusky sky fades into blue, The. Paean to the Dawn, A. Bayard Taylor. CAGL

Dust. Rupert Brooke. MoBrPo; OxBTC

Dust. André Spire. TrJP, *tr.* by Jethro Bithell

Dust. Kathleen Spivack. BoWoP

Dust. Randolph Stow. CBAP

Dust. Judith Wright. HarvBoo *Fr.* Shadow of Fire: Ghazals, The.

Dust and clay. Ascension Hymn. Henry Vaughan. ESCV; GeHe; NOSC; TrCP

Dust and old plaster on our heads descend. In the Church of Marosszentimre. Zoltán Jékely. IQMS, *tr.* by John Gordon Nichols

Dust as we are, the immortal spirit grows. William Wordsworth. SCV *Fr.* Prelude; Growth of a Poet's Mind [1850 vers.], The.

Dust Bowl. P. Inman.
   "Field dodd." FTOS

Dust cools easily. South Texas Summer Rain. Rebecca Gonzales. AiP

Dust had covered us both, and the dust was white, The. (LL) George Robinson: Blues. Muriel Rukeyser. NNaP; RACG

Dust is the only Secret. Emily Dickinson. TCAPo

Dust may never settle, The. (LL) When I Think about America Sometimes (I Think of Ralph Kramden). Dorothy Barresi. ExTi; ReTh

Dust of all the saints of the ages, The. Cymru. David Gwenallt Jones. OBWVE, *tr.* by Gwyn Jones

Dust of Snow. Robert Frost. APT-1; ChAP; OxBA; OxBSP; PAI; SAmP; SoSe-8; TAP; UnPo; WeW-3

Dust of Timas, The. Sappho. AWP, *tr.* by E. A. Robinson

Dust of Timas, The. *Var. authors.* AWP *Fr.* Variations of Greek Themes.

Dust Storm. Gray Jacobik. BAP-97

Dust Storm. Beryl Philp-Carmichael (Yungha-Dhu). IBA

Dust Storm Disaster. Woody Guthrie. APT-2

Dust storms whipped. Putting an End to the War Stories. Larry Moffi. CDa

Dust takes you from the stranger's company. Gaius Valerius Flaccus. RomPo, *tr.* by Kenneth McLeish and Frederic Raphael *Fr.* Argonautica, The.

Dust to Dust. Thomas Hood. NBLV

Dust World. Adrian C. Louis. UnSA

Duster, dust away, my friend. Dust. André Spire. TrJP, *tr.* by Jethro Bithell

Dusting. Rita Dove. ESEAA; HCAP; HeIP-4; LCAP-2; NAAL-5 *Fr.* Thomas and Beulah.

Dusting. Daniel Hall. YaYoPo

Dusting off the board, I sit down happily to play. Wei-ch'i Chess. Li K'ai-hsien. CoBLCP, *tr.* by Jonathan Chaves

Dusty Miller, The. *Unknown.* ReMoGo

Dusty pickup, The. Richard Crist. HA

Dusty, with some skeleton of. Yahrtzeit Light, The. Lyn Lifshin. UnSA

Dutch, The. George Canning. PeLV
   (Epigram.) OxBoLi

Dutch Interiors. Jane Kenyon. ExTi

Dutch Lover, The. Aphra Behn.
   ("Ah who can guess the rest?") (LL) LW; PEW
   Song: "Ah false Amyntas, can that hour." WPE
   (Song: The Willing Mistriss.) PEW
   (Willing Mistress, The.) NALW
   (Willing Mistriss, The.) LW

Dutch Lullaby, A. Eugene Field. *See* Wynken, Blynken, and Nod

Dutch Proverb, A. Matthew Prior. FaBoEE; NOEC; OBCoV

Duty. Arthur Hugh Clough. EBVV

Duty, or Truth at Work. Lizelia Augusta Jenkins Moorer. CBWP-3

Duty Surviving Self-Love. Samuel Taylor Coleridge. NPeEn

Duty—that's to say, complying. Duty. Arthur Hugh Clough. EBVV

Duty to Tyrants. Robert Herrick. BASC

Duw gwyddiad mai da y gweddai. Dafydd [*or* David] ap Gwilym. CABP *Fr.* Mis Mai.

Dux Bellorum. Max Winter. NeAmPo

Dvonya. Louis Simpson. NNaP; NOBA

Dvora. Denyse Kirsch. GotH

Dwarf barefooted, chanting, The. Peasants, The. Alun Lewis. OxBEV; PoWW; TCAWP

Dwarf Birches. Yevgeny Aleksandrovich Yevtushenko [*or* Evtushenko]. TCRusP, *tr.* by Peter Levi and Robin Milner-Gulland

Dwell, awful Silence, on the shady hills. Pan Piping. Plato. FaBoEE, *tr.* by Thomas Stanley

Dwell in this stone who once was tenant of flesh. Design for a Tomb. John Ormond. TCAWP

Dwell of a sound for a while, The. Textures. William Stafford. BodElec

Dweller in hollow places, hills and rocks. Echo. Madison Cawein. APN-2

Dwelling. Emily Warn. GifTon

Dwelling-Place, The. Henry Vaughan. GeHe; MeLP; NOSC; PeECV

Dwells within the soul of every Artist. Unexpressed. Adelaide Anne Procter. SacPr

Dwelt with the joyful beauty that is fled. (LL) Dante Alighieri. AWP; EaItPo, tr. by Dante Gabriel Rossetti Fr. La Vita Nuova.

Dwindled and harsh, dead-white and cloudy-clear. (LL) Elinor Wylie. FaBoWP; NAAL-2v2; NALW; OxBA; WPE

Dyeing. Mabel Tobrise. NAfrP

Dyer, The. Unknown. OxNR

Dying. Adah Isaacs Menken. CBWP-1

Dying. Robert Pinsky. HCAP; VCAP

Dying. Tōge Sankichi. PFTM-2, tr. by Richard H. Minear Fr. Poems of the Atomic Bomb.

Dying. John Stigall. CRP

Dying Airman, The. Unknown. OxBoLi; PeLV; RB

Dying: An Introduction. Louis Edward Sissman.
 "Bruisingly cradled in a Harvard chair." NoP-4

Dying Art, A. Derek Mahon. ModIr

Dying at the Edge of Death. Hameed Sa'id. MAP, tr. by Diana Der Hovanessian and Lena Jayyusi

Dying Away. William Meredith. NoAM

Dying Child, The. Mary Howitt. VWP

Dying Child, The. Letitia [or Laetitia] Elizabeth Landon. VWP

Dying Child's Request, The. Hannah Flagg Gould. OBCA

Dying Christian to His Soul, The. Pope. See Ode: The Dying Christian to His Soul

Dying day pinches the tot. Daily News. Tom Clark. SPE

Dying firelight slides along the quirt, A. End of the Weekend, The. Anthony Hecht. CoAmPo; FaBoMo; HAP; WeW-3

Dying Gaul, The. Desmond O'Grady. BIrV; PBCIP
 "Day concludes burning, The." CIP-2

Dying Girl, The. Mary Weston Fordham. CBWP-2

Dying Gladiator, The. Byron. NOBE Fr. Childe Harold's Pilgrimage.

Dying Husband's Farewell, The. Phineas Fletcher. SacPr

Dying in Paris. Heinrich Heine.
 Death and Morphine. WoPoe, tr. by Robert Lowell
 "Every idle desire has died in my breast." WoPoe, tr. by Robert Lowell
 "My zenith was luckily happier than my night." WoPoe, tr. by Robert Lowell

Dying Indian, The. Joseph Warton. NOEC; OxAEP-1

Dying Man in His Garden, The. George Sewell. GTBS-P
 (Soliloquy.) OBGa

Dying Prostitute; an Elegy, The. Thomas Holcroft. NOEC

Dying Raven, The. Richard Henry Dana. APN-1

Dying Soldier, The. Karl Kraus. AuPH, tr. by Lowell A. Bangerter

Dying Song. Anton Ulrich. GePo, tr. by George C. Schoolfield

Dying Speech of an Old Philosopher. Walter Savage Landor. FaBoEE; GTBS-P; NOBVV; NoP-4 Fr. Last Fruit off an Old Tree, The.

Dying sun, shine warm a little longer! Lament for Pasiphaë. Robert Graves. FaBoTw

Dying Swan, The. Thomas Sturge Moore. OBMV

Dying Swan, The. Tennyson. OWoS

Dying Synagogue at South Terrace, The. Thomas McCarthy. BiHa

Dying Tiger—moaned for Drink, A. Emily Dickinson. InPK-6

Dying Viper, A. "Michael Field." CABP

Dying Wife to Her Husband, A. Moses Ibn Ezra. TrJP

Dying with Amish Uncles. Julia Kasdorf. PBCAP

Dying with the Wrong Name. Sam Hamod. GraLe; UnSA

Dying Words of Stonewall Jackson, The. Sidney Lanier. APN-2; CBCWP

Dying Year, The. Clara Ann Thompson. CBWP-2

Dyirringan is lost to the tribes of the Yuin. Lament for a Dialect. Mary Duroux. IBA

Dykes, The. Rudyard Kipling. HarvBoo; OBWP

Dylan is about the Individual against the whole of creation. Is About. Allen Ginsberg. BAP-97

Dylan Thomas at Tenby. Raymond Garlick. TCAWP

Dylan, Two Days. Patricia Smith. GT

Dynamic marking cuts through the fill-up. Allen Fisher. Oth Fr. Stepping Out.

Dynamizer and the Oscilloclast, The. Jack Coulehan. BloBone

Dynamo Stadium, 1980. Aleksandr Petrovich Tkachenko. ItGoST, tr. by Maia Tekses

Dynastic Hymn. Unknown. ChiP, tr. by Arthur Waley

Dynasts, The. Thomas Hardy.
 Albuera. FaBoWar

"Certain sort of bravery, A." FaBoWar
 Eve of Waterloo, The. FaBoWar; OBWP
 Night of Trafalgar, The. FaBoCh; MoBrPo; OBMV
 "What are you thinking, that you speak no word?" FaBoWar

Dynasts, Part 2, The. Thomas Hardy.
 "Something stands here to peril our advance." FaBoWar

Dyonea, nycht hyrd, and wach of day. Gawin [or Gavin] Douglas. NePenScot Fr. Eneados.

Dysraphism. Charles Bernstein. FTOS

Dzhansukh, the shepherd, met a devil. Devil and the Shepherd, The. Fazil Abdulovich Iskander. TCRP, tr. by Daniel Weissbort

Dzogbese Lisa has treated me thus. Songs of Sorrow. Kofi Awoonor. HBAPE; PBMAP

E

E. D. in Commendation of the Author and His Choise. "E. D." EMWP

E. D. in Prayse of Mr. W. Fouler Her Friend. "E. D." EMWP

E'en as a lovely flower. Heinrich Heine. AWP Fr. Homeward Bound.

E'en as the sculptor chisels patiently. Tireless Sculptor, The. Henrietta Cordelia Ray. CBWP-3; SWaP

E'en from my heart the strings do break. (LL) When to Her Lute Corinna [or Corrina] Sings. Thomas Campion. NAEL-5v1; NAEL-7v1; NoSic; PoE

E get one dream. I Wan Bi President. Ezenwa-Ohaeto. NAfrP

E- / gypt. Journeys, The. Edward Kamau Brathwaite. HarvBoo

E hó hì ura bhì. Waulking Song: Two. Minnie Bruce Pratt. GLP

E Is in Heaven. Dixie Salazar. GeoHom

E. Jarvis-Thribb (17) and Keith's Mum. On the Tercentenary of Milton's Death. Gavin Ewart. OxBC

E-Mail. Reetika Vazirani. NAPBL

E. P. Ode pour l'Election de Son Sepulchre. Ezra Pound. See Hugh Selwyn Mauberley (Life and Contacts)

E Pur Si Muove. George Bradley. YaYoPo

E Questa Vita Un Lampo. Peter Riley. Oth

E Questo il Nido in Che la Mia Fenice? Alec Derwent Hope. OxBC

E're I forget the zenith of your love. To My Cosen Mrs. Ellinor Evins. George Alsop. SCAP

E're since hath in her Sun-shine liv'd. (LL) Lucasta's World. Richard Lovelace. BeJo; CaPo

E-ri-e, The. Unknown. TCAPo

E. S. L. Charles Martin. RA

E stands for egg. Joseph Hilaire Pierre Belloc. NoAM Fr. Moral Alphabet, A.

E Tenebris. Oscar Wilde. ChIV-2; MoBrPo; NAEL-5v2; NAEL-6v2; OxAEP-2; Son

(E Tenebris².) GSo

È, the Feasting Florentines. Daniel Gerard Hoffman. VGW

E Uni Que A The Hi A Tho, Father. Roberta Hill Whiteman. VoR

'E was warned agin 'er. Sergeant's Weddin', The. Rudyard Kipling. OBCoV; OxBTC

Each afternoon draws to a close. Each Afternoon. Idea Vilariño. TANSG, tr. by Louise B. Popkin

Each and All. Ralph Waldo Emerson. APN-1; AWP; ColAP; NAAL-2v1; NAAL-3; NAAL-5; NCAP; NOBA; OxBA; TAP; TCAPo; TreFP

Each Bird Walking. Tess Gallagher. FaBoWP

Each blessed lady that in virtue spends. To All Virtuous Ladies in General. Aemilia Bassano Lanyer. BASC

Each blest drop, or each blest limb [or limme]. On the Water of Our Lord's Baptism[e]. Richard Crashaw. GeHe

Each body has its art, its precious prescribed. Gwendolyn Brooks. IllVoic Fr. Gay Chaps at the Bar.

Each burning deed and thought! (LL) Village Blacksmith, The. Henry Wadsworth Longfellow. APN-1; AiP; BRP; OBAL; OBCA; OxIBACP; PWR; UV

Each care decays, and yet my sorrow springs. (LL) Soote Season, The. Henry Howard, Earl of Surrey. NAEL-5v1; NAEL-6v1; NAEL-7v1; NoP-4; NoSic; Son

Each care-worn face is but a book. Strangers, The. Jones Very. APN-1; OxBA

Each certain kind of weather or of light. Black Cockatoos. Judith Wright. OWoS

Each Day. David Ignatow. BodElec; NNaP

Each Day. Sister Maura. CRP

Each day I grow poorer by the day. Written at Random. Lu Yu. SuSp, tr. by Irving Y. Lo

Each day I live, each day the sea of light. Poem against the Rich. Robert Bly. NOBA

Each day I long so much to see. One Who Is at Home, The. Franciso Albanez. RaBo, tr. by Robert Bly

Each day I see them carefully grow old and feed. Sunny Prestatyn. John Davies. TCAWP

Each day I sink in sleep, as into death. Of the Resurrection of the Body. Marbod of Rennes. MLL, tr. by Helen Waddell

Each day into the upper air. Election Reflection. M. Keel Jones. NBLV

Each day the absent grow. Ranseki. JDP, tr. by Yoel Hoffmann

Each day when Court is over, I skip to the pawnshop. Tu Fu. CarOv, tr. by Carolyn Kizer Fr. Meandering River Poems, The.

Each drifiting snowflake. Snow Valley. Muso Soseki. EaWin, tr. by W. S. Merwin

Each droplet contains a message. It Is Raining Today. Sandra Maria Esteves. PueRic

Each evening, ducks paddle, egrets fly. Venturing Out. Vietnamese Oral Tradition. CaDao, tr. by John Balaban

Each evening, I watch the clouds flying. Evening. Vietnamese Oral Tradition. CaDao, tr. by John Balaban

Each evening Master Lu sets his fish traps. Mandarin Who Couldn't Do Anything, The. Vietnamese Oral Tradition. CaDao, tr. by John Balaban

Each face in the street is a slice of bread. Bread. W. S. Merwin. SPE; VCAP

Each face its own phantom. Cartagena de Indias. Earle Birney. MoCV

Each fall this town empties, leaving me. Emptying Town. Nick Flynn. AmPoNex; NAPBL

Each falling petal diminishes spring. Crooked River Meditation. Tu Fu. CrYelRi, tr. by Sam Hamill

Each find in each a just, unshaken friend. (LL) Elegy on a Maiden Name, An. Jane Cave. CABP; ECWP

Each form of beauty's but the new disguise. Unimaginative, The. Madison Cawein. APN-2

Each Found Himself at the End Of. Ebbe Borregaard. NeAP

Each friend turned out to be an enemy. Hafiz [or Hafez]. WoPoe, tr. by Dick Davis Fr. Three Poems on Friendship.

Each grain of sand has an architecture, but. Proposition II. Keith Waldrop. InPK-6

Each Happiness Ringed by Lions. Jane Hirshfield. ExTi

Each hour has some glory all its own. Hour's Glory, The. Henrietta Cordelia Ray. CBWP-3

Each in a Place Apart. James McMichael.
  "My parents had teased that if I ever caught a fish I'd take it to bed." GeoHom

Each in her well-lighted picture window, reading a book or magazine. Karl Shapiro. BodElec Fr. Bourgeois Poet, The.

Each in His Own. "Angelus Silesius." GePo, tr. by George C. Schoolfield Fr. Cherubical Wanderer, The.

Each in his Proper gloom. My Own Fate. Lionel Pigot Johnson. SacPr

Each inmost peece in me is thine. Bible, O.T. NPeEn, tr. by Mary Sidney Herbert, Countess of Pembroke Fr. Psalms.

Each Life Converges to some Centre. Emily Dickinson. TCAPo

Each Lon was a notable man. Limerick. L. G. Udall. PeLi

Each lover's longing leads him naturally. To Dante Alighieri: He Interprets Dante's Dream. Cino da Pistoia. AWP; EaItPo, tr. by Dante Gabriel Rossetti

Each man is limited by inborn traits. Love Is Kind. Benjamin Keech. PoToHe

Each man on this slow train. Farewell to You. Elizabeth Alexander. GT

Each minute the last minute. (LL) Living. Denise Levertov. BLT; OPOU; VGW; WPE

Each Moment Is Surrounded. Ray DiPalma. PmAP

Each More Melodious Note I Hear. Henry David Thoreau. OxBSP

Each morn / From the straw raincoat. Ransetsu. ZenPo, tr. by Takashi Ikemoto and Lucien Stryk

Each Morning. Imamu Amiri Baraka. ESEAA Fr. Hymn for Lanie Poo.

Each morning a missionary advertise with neon sign. Civilization (Bongo, Bongo, Bongo). Bob Hilliard. ReLy

Each morning I finish my coffee. Lullaby. Jon Mukand. BloBone

Each morning she is wheeled into the picture. Living in the La Brea Tar Pits. Nancy Vieira Couto. PBCAP

Each morning the birds awake me. Morning Vigil. Phillip [or "Phil"] William George. VoR

Each morning they bring me the condemned man's brekker. Analogy. Brian Higgins. FaBoTw

Each morning they pass over. Starling Migration, The. Jeffrey Skinner. PBCAP

Each naked branch, the yellow leaf or brown. Robe, The. Jones Very. NCAP

Each new daybreak we are born again. Palladas [or Pallades]. GrAn

Each night a dark river flows over the edge. Currents. Tina Koyama. FSt

Each night father fills me with dread. Limerick. Edward Gorey. PeLi

Each night, I braid my daughter's hair. They Were Alone in the Winter. Luci Tapahonso. ItWoWo

Each night / the dead man. Twilight of Vanity. Vyacheslav Kupriyanov [or Kuprianov]. TCRP, tr. by Albert C. Todd

Each night with moist leaves. Bamboo Elegy: Two. Edmond Yi-teh Chang. OpBo

Each object by a few short years how changed! Richard Polwhele. NOEC Fr. Influence of Local Attachment, The.

Each of them must have terrified. In Memory of the Utah Stars. William Matthews. MoASP

Each of these microscopic points and lines is in itself a complete world. Universe of the Rose. Chimako Tada. VCWP, tr. by Kirsten Vidaeus

Each of us has some bodily trait that's well known. Unknown. PriapPo, tr. by Richard W. Hooper Fr. Priapus Poems, The.

Each of us holds a locked razor. (LL) Waking in the Blue. Robert Lowell. AmFaPo; CoAP; HCAP; MoAmPo; UnPo

Each of us like you. Adonis. "H. D." AWP

Each of us pursues his trade. Scholar and the Cat, The. Unknown. WoPoe, tr. by Frank O'Connor

Each one making possible the next. (LL) From a Survivor. Adrienne Rich. LoL; NALW; PAI

Each one showed me his gold medal. Viet Kong. William Trowbridge. ReTh

Each perfect rose that unfolded yesterday. Ecstasy. Amado Nervo. TCLAP, tr. by Sue Standing

Each photographed face. Valerio Magrelli. NeIt

Each picture was a painted memory. Hour in a Studio, An. Richard Watson Gilder. APN-2

Each Saturday, our father downtown to work. Arrowhead Christian Center and No-Smoking Luncheonette. Janet Sylvester. ReTh

Each Sentence Is into the Fast. Joe Wenderoth. BodElec

Each small gleam was a voice. Stephen Crane. APN-2 Fr. War Is Kind.

Each sockeye of adulterous claim. Little Hans. Steve McCaffery. FTOS

Each star a rung. Prison Evening, A. Faiz Ahmad Faiz. VCWP, tr. by Agha Shahid Ali

Each storm-soaked flower has a beautiful eye. Rain. Nicholas Vachel Lindsay. RaBo

Each subtlety hard for the pedant to solve. Coming Across. Mehri. WPOW, tr. by Deirdre Lashgari

Each Sunday I climb the mountain to picnic. Picnic. Nellie Wong. OpBo

Each Time. Edgar Anawrok. GifTon

Each time breath draws through me. This Body. Michael Cuddihy. GifTon

Each time I come over a rise. Sierra Noon. C. G. Hanzlicek. GeoHom

Each Tuesday above a roadway. Daniil Kharms. TCRP

Each volcano lifts its profile. Volcanoes, The. José Santos Chocano. TCLAP, tr. by Andrew Rosing

Each way the turn. Turn, The. Robert Creeley. FTOS; LCAP-2

Each week, our great Aunt Doris came to teach me piano. Largo. Deryn Rees-Jones. TCAWP

Each wishing for the sword that severs all. (LL) George Meredith. CABP; EnLoPo; GSo; NAEL-5v2; NAEL-6v2; NOBVV; NPeEn; NoP-4; PoE; Son Fr. Modern Love.

Each with each has borne in patience. To Edom. Heinrich Heine. TrJP

Each year for a short season. Folk Wisdom. Thomas Kinsella. TwCP

Each year it is but a peck of rice. Mukai Kyorai. WoPoe, tr. by Earl Miner Fr. Linked-Verse Sequence throughout the Town, The.

Each year, the court expands. Old Pro's Lament, The. Paul Petrie. TAP

Each year the monuments grew larger. Monuments, The. John Ash. EmeKit

Eadwacer. Unknown. WPE
  (Wulf and Eadwacer.) BoWoP; CIP-2, tr. by Willis Barnstone and Elene Kolb

Eager baby voice outside my door, The. (LL) Augusta Davies Webster. VWP; ViWPN Fr. Mother and Daughter.

Eager breath, An. First Portrait of My Son. Alaide Foppa. TANSG, tr. by Celeste Kostupulos-Cooperman

Eager note on my door said "Call me," The. Poem. Frank O'Hara. NOBA; NoAM; PmAP; SPE

Eager Spring. Gordon Bottomley. MoBrPo

Eager Street. Kendra Kopelke. AiP

Eagerness of objects to, The. Interior (With Jane). Frank O'Hara. LCAP-2

Eagle. Robin Skelton. NOBC

Eagle, An. 'Umar Abu Risha. MAP, tr. by Issa Boullata and Thomas G. Ezzy

Eagle, The. Tennyson. ChAP; ClHu; FHYEP; FaBoCh; GTBS-P; HeIP-4; ITBLP; InPK-6; NAEL-5v2; NAEL-6v2; NOBVV; NTCP; NoP-4; OWoS; OxBSP; PAI; SCGP; TFi; TRP; UnPo

Eagle, The. "Aleksandr Iakovlevich Yashin" [or "Iashin"]. TCRP, tr. by Daniel Weissbort

Eagle above Us, The. Santiago Altamirano. STP

Eagle above Us, The. *Unknown*. WoPoe, *tr. by* Willard Trask

Eagle and Me, The. Harold Arlen. ReLy

Eagle and the Beetle, The. Jean de La Fontaine. OBVE, *tr. by* Elizur Wright

Eagle and the Mole, The. Elinor Wylie. AWP; BoWoP; MoAmPo; NALW; UnPo

Eagle-Feather Fan, The. N. Scott Momaday. CDW; NoP-4

Eagle for an Emperor. Falconry. Anne Wilkinson. MoCV

Eagle has moved down to the foot of the mountain, The. Eagle, An. 'Umar Abu Risha. MAP, *tr. by* Issa Boullata and Thomas G. Ezzy

Eagle in the Land of Oz. Don Receveur. CDa

Eagle is my power, The. Eagle-Feather Fan, The. N. Scott Momaday. CDW; NoP-4

Eagle looked at this changing world, The. Mount Eagle. John Montague. BiHa

Eagle of Pengwern. *Unknown*. WoPoe, *tr. by* Gwyn Williams

Eagle of the tomb, whose tomb is this? Why. *Unknown*. GrAn

Eagle Poem. Joy Harjo. HATNAP; WeW-3

Eagle's nest on the head of an old redwood on one of the, An. Beaks of Eagles, The. Robinson Jeffers. NOBA

Eagle shall die, the. Dumas. Jabari Asim. InTrad

Eagle soars in the summit of heaven, The. T. S. Eliot. OBMV *Fr.* Choruses from "The Rock."

Eagle Song. Gordon Bottomley. MoBrPo *Fr.* Suilven and the Eagle.

Eagle That Is Forgotten, The. Nicholas Vachel Lindsay. APT-1; AWP; MoAmPo; NOBA; OxBA

Eagle Valor, Chicken Mind. Robinson Jeffers. OxBA; OxBSP

Eagle! why soarest thou above that tomb? Spirit of Plato. *Unknown*. AWP; OBVE

Eagles. James Dickey. BodElec

Eagles, The. Jones Very. TAP; TCAPo

Eagles and butterflies (and some other things). Nina Nikolaevna Berberova. TCRP

Eagles gather on the place of death, The. Eagles, The. Jones Very. TAP; TCAPo

Eagles, that wheel above our crests. Cedars of Lebanon, The. Alphonse Marie Louis de Lamartine. AWP, *tr. by* Toru Dutt

Eaper Weaper, chimney sweeper. *Unknown*. OxBoLi

Ear, The. Louis MacNeice. OxBSP

Ear Ear. Concrete Cat. Dorthi Charles. InPK-6

EAr eAr stripestripestripestripe. Dorthi Charles. *See* Ear Ear

Ear's Delight, The. George Chapman. NoSic *Fr.* Ovid's Banquet of Sense.

Ear-string, An. William Strode. NOSC

Ear struck from within, roaring. (LL) Paterson: The Falls. William Carlos Williams. APT-1; ColAP

Ear Training. Sekou Sundiata. SpirFl

Eardrums of the deaf are already broken; they like it loud, The. They. Deaf Dancing to Rock, The. Lisel Mueller. SwNoth

Earl Bothwell. *Unknown*. ESPB

Earl Brand ("Did ye ever hear o guid Earl o Bran.") *Unknown*. ESPB

Earl Brand ("O Did you ever hear of the brave Earl Brand.") *Unknown*. OxBB

Earl Crawford. *Unknown*. ESPB

Earl March look'd on his dying child. Maid of Neidpath, The. Thomas Campbell. GTBS-P

Earl Mertoun's Song. Robert Browning. OBEV *Fr.* Blot in the 'Scutcheon, A.

Earl of Aboyne, The. *Unknown*. ESPB

Earl of Errol, The. *Unknown*. ESPB

Earl of Mar's Daughter, The. *Unknown*. ESPB

Earl of Westmoreland, The. *Unknown*. ESPB

Earl of Wigton had three daughters, The. Richie Story. *Unknown*. ESPB

Earl Rothes. *Unknown*. ESPB

Earle of Somerset. Sir Henry Wotton. *See* Upon the Sudden Restraint of the Earl[e] of Somerset, Then Falling from Favor [*or* Favour]

Earlier in the evening the moon. Moon, The. Robert Creeley. VGW

Earlier, to be ready, I hoovered the carpet. On Reading Rumi. Mimi Khalvati. MFPA

Earliest Known Representation of a Storm in Western Art, The. Lavinia Greenlaw. MFPA

Earliest Spring. William Dean Howells. OBEV

(In Earliest Spring.) APN-2

Earliest Spring. Denise Levertov. LCAP-2

Earlobe. Leonid Andreievich Zavalnyuk [*or* Zaval'niuk]. TCRP, *tr. by* Albert C. Todd

Early. Jean-Baptiste Tati-Loutard. WoPoe, *tr. by* Eric Sellin

Early Affection. George Moses Horton. TCAPo

Early Afterlife, An. Linda Pastan. ExTi

Early April on Broadway, south of Union Square. Seeing Off a Friend. Stephen Dobyns. EmeKit

Early Arrival: Sydney. Vivian Smith. NOBAu

Early Aspirations. William Bell Scott. CenSon

Early Autumn. Ralph Burns. ReLy

Early autumn enters my rickety house. Thoughts in Early Autumn: Thirty Rhymes Sent to Lu-wang. P'i Jih-hsiu. SuSp, *tr. by* Irving Y. Lo

Early Autumn in the Mountains. Wen T'ing-yün. SuSp, *tr. by* William R. Schultz

Early autumn, white rabbits. Wang Chien. SuSp *Fr.* Palace Poems.

Early bird got up and whet his beak, The. Birthday Ode to Mr. Alfred Austin, A. Sir Owen Seaman. NOBL

Early bird may catch the worm, The. Samuel Hoffenstein. NBLV *Fr.* As the Crow Flies, Let Him Fly.

Early blossoms—could a single. Permanence in Change. Goethe. STV, *tr. by* John Frederick Nims

Early Copper. Carl Sandburg. HeIP-4

Early dawn shows the maroon and tan shell. Bedside. Clive Matson. PasH

Early Days. John Stuart Williams. TCAWP

Early Death. Hartley Coleridge. OBEV

Early dew woos the half-opened flowers, An. *Unknown*. AWP *Fr.* Thousand and One Nights, The.

Early Discoveries. David Malouf. CBAP

Early, each morning, Martha Blake. Martha Blake at Fifty-one. Austin Clarke. CIP-2; ModIr; NOIV; NPeEn

Early electric people had domesticated the wild ass, The. Electric Orchard, The. Paul Muldoon. HarvBoo

Early Electric! With what radiant hope. Metropolitan Railway, The. Sir John Betjeman. EBEV; OxAEP-2; OxBTC

Early evening hill is a lantern's lamp, The. Loop-the-Loop in Prospect Park (1905). Gerry Gomez Pearlberg. WiU

Early Evening Quarrel. Langston Hughes. SAmP; UnPo

Early fall. Basho. EH, *tr. by* Robert Hass

Early Frost. Leslie Norris. AngWePo

Early Geese. Tu Mu. SuSp

Early germ. Plague Victims Catapulted over Walls into Besieged City. Thomas Lux. KGB

Early Graves, The. Friedrich Gottlieb Klopstock. GePo, *tr. by* J. W. Thomas

Early History of a Writer. Charles Reznikoff.
"I had been bothered by a secret weariness." APT-2

Early I rose. Love Song: "Early I rose." *Unknown*. AWP, *tr. by* Mary Austin

Early in the morning. Lungi Crossing. Iyamide Hazeley. NAfrP

Early in the Morning. Li-Young Lee. LoL

Early in the Morning. Louis Simpson. CoAmPo; TRP

Early in the morning. Jules Supervielle. MFP, *tr. by* Martin Sorrell

Early in the morning I hear monkeys call from the mouth of the gorge. West Cliff. Chu Yi-tsun. SuSp, *tr. by* Chang Yin-nan

Early in the spring-time a huntsman full of sorrow. Miklós Zrínyi. IQMS, *tr. by* René Bonnerjea *Fr.* Idyll.

Early January. W. S. Merwin. VGW

Early Levée, An. Po Chü-i. ChiP, *tr. by* Arthur Waley

Early light of the rising sun shines on the beams of my house, The. Getting Up Early on a Spring Morning. Po Chü-i. ChiP, *tr. by* Arthur Waley

Early light on the meadow. Prey. Ken Gerner. GifTon

Early Losses: a Requiem. Alice Walker. BlSi

Early Lynching. Carl Sandburg. ChIV-2; MoAmPo

Early may fly the Babylonian wo[e]. (LL) On the Late Massacre [*or* Massacher] in Piedmont [*or* Piemont]. John Milton. AWP; CABP; GSo; GTBS-P; HAP; HeIP-4; NAEL-5v1; NAEL-6v1; NIL-7; NOBE; NOCV; NPeEn; NoP-4; OBWP; OxBEV; OxBSo; PoPoPo; SCGP; Son; TFi; TRP; UnPo; WeW-3

Early Morning, The. Joseph Hilaire Pierre Belloc. OxBSP; Spl; TLR

Early morning glows. *Unknown*. ErotSp, *tr. by* Sam Hamill

Early morning over Rouen, hopeful. Rouen. May Wedderburn Cannan. NAEL-5v2; NAEL-6v2; OBWP; OxBTC

Early Morning Test Light over Nevada, 1955. Robert Vasquez. GeoHom

Early morning, the day before yesterday. Green Snake. B. R. Lakshman Rao. OMIP, *tr. by* A. K. Ramanujan

Early mornings the baby nudges. Shotgun. Patti See. MPUn

Early Noon. Ingeborg Bachmann. AF, *tr. by* Mark Anderson

Early on a pleasant day. Mocking-Bird, The. Joseph Rodman Drake. APN-1

Early on I wished to seek out famous mountains. Returning to My Garden Home: In Respectful Response to the Master of Hua-yang. Shen Yüeh. ColAnChi, *tr. by* Richard Mather

Early on Lammas Morning. Nighean Dhonnchadh (The Daughter of Duncan Campbell of Glenlyon). EMWP

Early on the morning of Monday. Omens. *Unknown*. RB; WoPoe, *tr. by* Alexander Carmichael

Early on you introduced me to young women in bars.   To World War Two.   Kenneth Koch.   BAP-01

Early Pregnancy.   Penelope Shuttle.   BrRo

Early Rising.   Tu Fu.   CrYelRi, *tr.* by Sam Hamill

Early, sober, and alone. (LL)   Epitaph on a Party Girl.   Richard Usborne.   FaBoEE; OBCoV

Early Spring.   Eloise Bibb.   CBWP-4

Early Spring.   Hugo von Hofmannsthal.   AuPH, *tr.* by Lowell A. Bangerter

Early Spring.   Sidney Keyes.   MoBrPo

Early Spring.   Richard von Schaukal.   AuPH, *tr.* by Lowell A. Bangerter

Early spring's sweet blush, The.   Early Spring.   Eloise Bibb.   CBWP-4

Early Summer: At the Riverside, Seeing Off Li Chiu-ho as He Returns to Yeh with the Books I Lent Him.   Li K'ai-hsien.
   "Not a day goes by without someone borrowing books from me."   CoBLCP

Early Summer in the Year Jen-tzu (1672)—Playfully Painted in the Manner of Ts'ao Yün-hsi.   Yün Shou-p'ing.   CoBLCP, *tr.* by Jonathan Chaves

Early summer rain.   Buson.   EH, *tr.* by Robert Hass

Early Summer Sea-Tryst.   Frederick Thomas Bennett Macartney.   CBAP

Early Summer Waking from a Nap.   Yang Wan-li.   SuSp, *tr.* by Sherwin S. S. Fu

Early sun grazes.   Whale in the Web, The.   Bill O'Daly.   GifTon

Early sun on Beaulieu water.   Youth and Age on Beaulieu River, Hants.   Sir John Betjeman.   FaBoTw; TwCP

Early sun on fields.   Fast Car On Nebraska I-80: Visting Teacher.   Hilda Raz.   ExTi

Early Sunday Morning.   John A. Stone.   PoSol

Early this morning.   Rose Furuya Hawkins.   FSt   *Fr.* Proud upon an Alien Shore.

Early this morning when you knocked upon my door.   Me and the Devil Blues.   Robert Johnson.   APT-2

Early Thoughts of Winter.   Maxine W. Kumin.   ExTi

Early to bed and early to rise.   Early to Bed.   Mary Mapes Dodge.   SWaP

Early Triangles.   Ron Padgett.   FTOS

Early Unfinished Sketch.   Austin Clarke.   ModIr

Early Walk on Shang Mountain, An.   Wen T'ing-yün.   SuSp, *tr.* by William R. Schultz

Early we set out from Ch'en-hsi ferry.   Ch'en-hsi County.   Ho Ching-ming.   CoBLCP, *tr.* by Jonathan Chaves

Early worshipper at Nature's shrine, An.   Charlotte Smith.   MakPoe   *Fr.* Beachy Head.

Earnest, earthless, equal, attuneable, vaulty, voluminous, stupendous.   Spelt from Sibyl's Leaves.   Gerard Manley Hopkins.   FaBoMo; NOBVV; NPeEn; OxBEV; OxBSo; TOF

Earnest elements of nature. (LL)   Boats in a Fog.   Robinson Jeffers.   NAAL-2v2; NoP-4; OxBA

Earnest Liberal's Lament, The.   Ernest Hemingway.   OBAL; OBSV

Earnest to explore within and all around.   Dante Alighieri.   OBVE   *Fr.* Divina Commedia.

Earnest young leftie named Tariq.   Limerick.   Bernard Levin.   PeLi

Earning a Dinner.   Matthew Prior.   NBLV

Earning high wages? Yus.   Munition Wages.   Madeline Ida Bedford.   FaBoWar

Earrings.   Annette Bialik Harchik.   GotH

Earrings Dangling and Miles of Desert.   Gary Snyder.   APSN   *Fr.* Mountains and Rivers without End: The Market.

Ears.   Sonja Åkesson.   WPOW, *tr.* by Joanna Bankier

Ears in the Turrets Hear.   Dylan Thomas.   FaBoTw

Ears like a walnut's broken shell.   Babysitter's Devotion, The.   Kevin Prufer.   AmPoNex

Ears on the floor were pressed to the ground. (LL)   Colonel, The.   Carolyn Forché.   MakPoe; OBWP; SoSe-8

Earth.   Margaret Atwood.   PoE

Earth.   Kahlil Gibran.   MAP, *tr.* by Michael Beard and Adnan Haydar

Earth.   Yaroslav [*or* Iaroslav] Vasilevich Smelyakov [*or* Smeliakov].   TCRP, *tr.* by Albert C. Todd

Earth.   Jules Supervielle.   MFP, *tr.* by Martin Sorrell

Earth.   Ann Taylor.   NOxBChV

Earth.   Jim Tollerud.   VoR

Earth.   John Hall Wheelock.   MoAmPo; SoSe-8

Earth, The.   David Gwenallt Jones.   OBWVE, *tr.* by Dyfnallt Morgan

Earth, The.   Christopher Pilling.   NLP

Earth, The.   Jones Very.   APN-1; OxBA

Earth a flower.   For Nothing.   Gary Snyder.   NNaP

Earth and Goddess of Birth.   Macedonius.   GrAn

Earth and heaven endure forever.   Substance, Shadow, and Spirit.   T'ao Ch'ien [*or* T'ao Yuan-ming].   ColAnChi, *tr.* by J. R. Hightower

Earth and I Gave You Turquoise.   N. Scott Momaday.   CDW; HATNAP; UnPo

Earth and metal.   Atsujin.   JDP, *tr.* by Yoel Hoffmann

Earth and Rain, the Plants & Sun.   Simon J. Ortiz.   NAAL-5

Earth and Sky.   Joseph Miezan Bognini.   PBMAP

Earth and sky black.   Denis Glover.   PeNZ   *Fr.* Arawata Bill.

Earth and water, air and stars.   Immortality.   "Nicolai Maksimovich Minsky."   TrJP, *tr.* by Babette Deutsch

Earth Angel.   Jeffrey Skinner.   PBCAP

Earth between two lights.   Twilight under Pine Ridge.   Robert Mezey.   GeoHom

Earth bleeds / as a breast bleeds, The.   Kassak.   Birago Diop.   NegPo, *tr.* by Ellen Conroy Kennedy

Earth Breaks Up.   Robert Browning.   TrCP   *Fr.* Christmas-Eve.

Earth Buried.   Kenneth Mackenzie.   CBAP

Earth did tremble; and heaven's closed eye, The.   Francis Quarles.   PeECV   *Fr.* Divine Fancies.

Earth does not understand her child.   Return, The.   Edna St. Vincent Millay.   MoAmPo; NoAM; OxBA

Earth, Ephemera.   That Which Is Fugitive, That Which Is Medicinally Sweet or Alterable to Gold, That Which Is Substantiated by Unscientific Means.   Valerie Wohlfeld.   YaYoPo

Earth exhales, The. (LL)   Slough.   Sir John Betjeman.   HarvBoo; MoBrPo; NoAM; OxAEP-2

Earth expanding right hand and left hand, The.   Walt Whitman.   AmFaPo   *Fr.* Song of the Open Road.

Earth Felicities, Heavens Allowances.   Richard Steere.   SCAP

Earth for the sun her lover.   Spring Song.   John Milton.   MLL, *tr.* by Helen Waddell

Earth goes on the earth glittering in gold, The.   Inscribed in Melrose Abbey.   *Unknown.*   FaBoEE

Earth grown old, yet still so green.   Advent.   Christina Georgina Rossetti.   ChrPo; TrCP

Earth has many keys, The.   Emily Dickinson.   APN-2

Earth has not anything to show [*or* shew] more fair.   Composed upon Westminster Bridge, September 3, 1802.   William Wordsworth.   AWP; CABP; CenSon; ClHu; FaBoCh; GTBS-P; HAP; HeIP-4; ITBLP; InPK-6; MakPoe; NAEL-5v2; NAEL-6v2; NAWM-7v2; NOBRP; NPeEn; NoP-4; OPOU; OxBEV; OxBSo; PoE; SCGP; Son; TFi; UnPo

Earth holds the sunlit.   For Spring.   Douglas G. Jones.   NOBC

Earth in beauty dressed.   Her Anxiety.   W. B. Yeats.   OPOU

Earth in her mercy permits us to repeat.   Wedding Song.   Patricia Storace.   FFC

Earth in Spring, The.   Judah Halevi.   TrJP, *tr.* by Edward G. King

Earth is a beautiful place, The.   Third Sermon on the Warpland, The.   Gwendolyn Brooks.   BPo; SeSe

Earth is a living thing, The.   Lucille Clifton.   HW

Earth is a place on which England is found, The.   Gilbert Keith Chesterton.   OBSV   *Fr.* Songs of Education.

Earth is a prison to man all his life, The.   Prison, The.   Samuel Ha-Nagid.   WoPoe, *tr.* by T. Carmi

Earth is at the same time mother, The.   Hildegard von Bingen.   HW

Earth is fragrant, The.   Fuwa.   JDP, *tr.* by Yoel Hoffmann

Earth is full of anger, The.   Hymn before Action.   Rudyard Kipling.   FaBoWar

Earth is hard enough, The.   Moon's Cadaver, The.   Clara Silva.   TANSG, *tr.* by Celeste Kostopulos-Cooperman

Earth is raw with this one note.   Crows.   Lizette Woodworth Reese.   APT-1; TCAPo

Earth is sweet with roses, The.   Easter Eve.   Prudentius.   MLL, *tr.* by Helen Waddell

Earth is taken: this is not your home, The. (LL)   Travelogue for Exiles.   Karl Shapiro.   MoAmPo; TrJP

Earth is the Lord's and the fulness thereof, The.   Bible, *O.T.*   AWP; TrJP, *tr.* by Christopher Smart   *Fr.* Psalms.

Earth is weary of our foolish wars, The.   Let Us Have Peace.   Nancy Byrd Turner.   PoToHe

Earth issues forth from Earth forcibly.   Earth.   Kahlil Gibran.   MAP, *tr.* by Michael Beard and Adnan Haydar

Earth keeps some vibration going, The.   Edgar Lee Masters.   IllVoic; NoAM; OxBA; TAP   *Fr.* Spoon River Anthology.

Earth, like a girl, sipped the rains, The.   Summer.   Judah Halevi.   NAWM-7v1, *tr.* by William M. Davis

Earth Magician shapes this world.   Creation of the Earth, The.   *Navajo Oral Tradition.*   TCAPo

Earth Man.   Lynne Wycherley.   Prnts

Earth may change from summer green to winter white, The.   Nothing Ever Changes My Love for You.   Marvin Fisher.   ReLy

Earth Mother.   Sonia Sanchez.   ItWoWo

Earth, mountains, rivers—hidden in this nothingness.   On Joshu's Nothingness.   Saisho.   ZenPo, *tr.* by Takashi Ikemoto and Lucien Stryk

Earth Movers, The.   Christopher Cokinos.   UrbNat

Earth moves, The.   Good Nights.   Saundra Sharp.   SpirFl

Earth must burn, ere we for Christ can look, The. (LL) Fulke Greville, 1st Baron Brooke. NOCV; SacPr *Fr.* Caelica.

Earth, My Likeness. Walt Whitman. APN-1; OxBA

Earth, ocean, air, belovèd brotherhood! Shelley. NAEL-6v2

Earth offers its greeting, with a paternal kiss. Return, The. Julio Herrera y Reissig. TCLAP, *tr. by* Andrew Rosing

Earth Outside, The. Muzahim al-Ugaili. ArPe, *tr. by* Omar S. Pound

Earth owls in ancient burrows clumpt. Sentinels, The. Robert Duncan. HarvBoo

Earth Poem. Mahmoud Darwish. AF, *tr. by* Abdullah Al-Udhari

Earth Quake. Ruth Stone. ExTi

Earth quivers wherever I go, The. Thou Gaia Art I. Heide Göttner-Abendroth. HW

Earth rais'd up her head. William Blake. ChIV-1; FHYEP; NAEL-5v2; NAEL-6v2; NOBRP; NOEC; PoE *Fr.* Songs of Experience.

Earth rebelled, The. / The good and patient earth. And the Earth Rebelled. Yuri Suhl. TrJP, *tr. by* Max Rosenfeld

Earth, receive an honoured guest. W. H. Auden. FaBoTw *Fr.* In Memory of W. B. Yeats.

Earth revives, The. Earthquake. Kuo Mo-jo. WoPoe, *tr. by* Harold Acton and Ch'en Shih-hsiang

Earth, river, mountain. Dangai. ZenPo, *tr. by* Takashi Ikemoto and Lucien Stryk

Earth's Answer. William Blake. ChIV-1; FHYEP; NAEL-5v2; NAEL-6v2; NOBRP; NOEC; PoE *Fr.* Songs of Experience.

Earth's first Adam, he lay in the grass. Adam and Eve. Itsik [*or* Itzik *or* Itzig] Manger. TrJP, *tr. by* Jacob Sonntag

Earth's Immortalities. Robert Browning.
  Love. EnLoPo

Earth's Lyric. Bliss Carman. APN-2

Earth Said to Death. Helen Waddell. MLL

Earth Screaming. Esther Iverem. GT

Earth sees in thee. To Sultan Murad II. James Clarence Mangan. NOIV

Earth shows her face to the moon, The. Eclipse II. Linda Hogan. HATNAP

Earth smells dank, the weeds grow rank, The. Witch's Last Ride, The. Emily Jane Pfeiffer. ViWPN

Earth Song. Thomas Love Peacock. VoR

Earth spins to my finger-tips and, The. Globe in North Carolina, The. Derek Mahon. BiHa; PBCIP

Earth Spirit, The. William Ellery Channing.
  "Then spoke the Spirit of the Earth." TCAPo

Earth stopped. The Holy City hit a mountin. Joshua. X. J. Kennedy. ChIV-1

Earth, Take Me Back. John Hall Wheelock. APT-1

Earth that creates all that lives, The. Eternity. Sándor Weöres. IQMS, *tr. by* Adam Makkai and Donald E. Morse

Earth, that drinks rain, refreshes the trees. In Defence of Drunkards. Jan Kochanowski. WoPoe, *tr. by* Jerzy Peterkiewicz and Burns Singer

Earth that lightly covers her, The. (LL) Upon a Child That Died [*or* Dyed]. Robert Herrick. BeJo; CaPo; InPK-6; PAI

Earth turns / like a rainbow, The. When You Read This Poem. Pinkie Gordon Lane. BlSi

Earth was my home, but even there I was a stranger. Flight of Apollo, The. Stanley Kunitz. OPRER; TaR

Earth was young, the world was fair, The. Saxon Legend of Language, The. Mary Weston Fordham. CBWP-2

Earth which I breathe in the heavy night. Mole, The. Christine D'Haen. TuT, *tr. by* Dennis O'Driscoll

Earth will be going on a long time, The. Lute Music. Kenneth Rexroth. TAP

Earth with thunder torn[e], with fire blasted, The. Fulke Greville, 1st Baron Brooke. NoSic *Fr.* Caelica.

Earth Worm, The. Denise Levertov. NOBA

Earth wraps your body, Kallisto, in its lap. Epitaph from Piraeus. *Unknown.* GrAn, *tr. by* Peter Jay

Eartha my mother's name, now earth. Crinagoras. GrAn

Earthen Jugs. Gabriela Mistral. SpanPo, *tr. by* Kate Flores

Earthen Lot, The. Tony Harrison. NPeEn

Earthly Joy. Sydney E. Jerrold. SacPr

Earthly Light. Marcia Southwick. PuP-23

Earthly Paradise, The. William Morris. NoP-4
  Apology, An. AWP; EBVV; NAEL-5v2; NAEL-6v2
  Outlanders, The. EBVV
  Prologue: The Wanderers. EBVV

Earthly roses at God's call have made, The. On the Death of a Pious Lady. Olof Wexionius. AWP, *tr. by* Sir Edmund William Gosse

Earthly: Sonnets for Carlos. Ian Wedde.
  "By day and also by night and you are." PeNZ
  "Diesel trucks past the Scrovegni chapel." PeNZ

"If thy wife is small bend down to her and." PeNZ
  Power Transformer. PeNZ

Earthquake. Robert Arthur Douglas Ford. NOBC

Earthquake. Kuo Mo-jo. WoPoe, *tr. by* Harold Acton and Ch'en Shih-hsiang

Earthquake. Li K'ai-hsien.
  "Earthquake covered Shansi and Shensi, The." CoBLCP; ColAnChi, *tr. by* Jonathan Chaves

Earthquake of 1886, The. Josephine D. Henderson Heard. CBWP-4

Earthquake Weather. Janice Gould. GeoHom

Earthquaked, my house collapsed. Antiphilus [*or* Antiphilos]. GrAn

Earthquakes could be caused. Tabloid News. Blythe Nobleman. ReTh

Earthworker's God Is Healed, The. Bernadette Mayer. FTOS

Earthworm. Robert Francis. APT-2

Earthworm, The. Harry Edmund Martinson. RB; RaBo, *tr. by* Robert Bly

Earthworms. Parody. Martha Paley Francescato. BoWoP, *tr. by* Willis Barnstone

Earthy Anecdote. Wallace Stevens. RB; SAmP

Eartly [*or* Earthly] nourris [*or* nouris *or* nourrice] sits and sings, An. Great Silkie of Sule Skerry, The. *Unknown.* ESPB; FaBoCh

Earwigs. Edward Newman. VerBaPo

Ease. Po Chü-i. Spl, *tr. by* Arthur Waley

Ease is the pray'r of him who, in a whaleboat. Sapphics: At the Mohawk-Castle, Canada. Thomas Morris. NOEC

Ease your weary limbs, stranger, under this elm. Anyte [*or* Anytes]. GrAn

Easing a savior's birth. (LL) Cecil Day Lewis. MoBrPo; OBMV *Fr.* Magnetic Mountain, The.

East. Thomas Merton. *Fr.* Geography of Lograire, The.

East and West. Ernest Francisco Fenollosa.
  Separated East, The. APN-2
  Separated West, The.
    "Soul of my inner face, face of my race." APN-2
    "West provokes the East, The. The iron arm." APN-2

East Anglian Bathe. Sir John Betjeman. NoP-4

East Bronx. David Ignatow. CoAmPo

East Coast Journey. James Keir Baxter. NoP-4; PeNZ

East Coker. T. S. Eliot. HAP; VGW *Fr.* Four Quartets.

East Gate, The. *Unknown.* ChinPo, *tr. by* Yip Wai-lim

East is a clear violet mass, The. Street Scene, A. Lizette Woodworth Reese. OBCA

East London. Matthew Arnold. SCGP

East of the eastern ocean. Song of a Dream Journey over the Vast Sea. Yang Wei-chen. CoBLCP, *tr. by* Jonathan Chaves

East of the Palace Gates: Working Late. Tu Fu. CarOv, *tr. by* Carolyn Kizer *Fr.* Adviser to the Court.

East of the river there's a foul bird. Parable, A. Ch'en Tzu-lung. SuSp, *tr. by* Irving Y. Lo

East of the salt village, low and narrow. Wu Chia-chi. CoBLCP

East of the strait. Muso Soseki. EaWin, *tr. by* W. S. Merwin

East of the sun's slant, in the vineyard that never failed. Harvest. Gary Soto. PBCAP

East or West? Charles Tennyson Turner. OxBSo

East Peak. Muso Soseki. EaWin, *tr. by* W. S. Merwin

East Seventh Street. Mark Wunderlich. WiU

East Song. Alvaro Mutis. TCLAP, *tr. by* Sophie Cabot Black and Maria Negroni

East the ocean, west the Himalaya. Eulogy of the Sagely Virtue of His Imperial Majesty Emperor Shih-tsu, A. Chao Meng-fu. CoBLCP, *tr. by* Jonathan Chaves

East Utica. Eugene Paul Nasser.
  "Lebanon, land of our birth and hopefully of our dying." GraLe

East Wind. Ou-yang Hsiu. OHPC, *tr. by* Kenneth Rexroth

East Wind asperges Boston with Lynn's sulphurous brine, An. Father. John Wheelwright. UnPo

East wind blows gently, The. Begonias. Su Tung-p'o (Su Shih). OHPC, *tr. by* Kenneth Rexroth

East wind blows in the street to-day, The. March Day in London, A. Amy Levy. VWP

East wind finds the gap bringing rain, The. Return: An Elegy, The. Robert Penn Warren. APT-2

East wind, knowing I plan to walk through the hills, The. On the Road to Hsin-ch'eng. Su Tung-p'o (Su Shih). CoBCP, *tr. by* Burton Watson

East wind's whistlin' could an' shrill, The. Schule Laddie's Lament on the Lateness o' the Season, A. James Logie Robertson. NOBVV

East wind stirs fine dust on the roads. Rhyming with Tzu-yu's "Treading the Green." Su Tung-p'o (Su Shih). CoBCP, *tr. by* Burton Watson

East wind whirling, light clouds in strands, The. Tune: "Beautiful Lady Yü, The"—Spring Sorrow. Ch'en Liang. SuSp, *tr. by* Hellmut Wilhelm

East winds have blown the grass green in Ying-chou. Poem Composed at the Command of the Emperor. Li Po. ChinPo, *tr. by* Yip Wai-lim

Easter. George Herbert. ESCV; FHYEP; FaBoCh; GeHe; NAEL-5v1; NAEL-6v1; NOBE; NOSC; OBEV; OxBEV; PeECV; TrCP

  (Song, The.) NAEL-7v1

Easter. Herman Melville. APN-2 *Fr.* Clarel: A Poem and Pilgrimage in the Holy Land.

Easter. Howard Nemerov. NoP-4

Easter. Frank O'Hara. SPE

Easter. Adelia Prado. TANSG, *tr. by* Ellen Watson

Easter. Charles Hubert Sisson. OxBSP

Easter. Edmund Spenser. *See* Amoretti

Easter Afternoon. Rachel Hadas. UrbNat

Easter again, and a small rain falls. Other Side of the River, The. Charles Wright. VCAP

Easter at Christmas. Alun Lewis. PoWW

Easter Bonnet, The. Clara Ann Thompson. CBWP-2

Easter Carol. Henrietta Cordelia Ray. CBWP-3

Easter Dawn. Kofi Awoonor. PBMAP

Easter-Day. Henry Vaughan. ESCV; PeECV

Easter Day. Oscar Wilde. OxAEP-2

Easter Eve. Prudentius. MLL, *tr. by* Helen Waddell

Easter Eve. Muriel Rukeyser. VGW

Easter Garland, An. Carol Rumens. FaBoWP

Easter has come around. W. D. Snodgrass. VCAP *Fr.* Heart's Needle.

Easter Hymn. Alec Derwent Hope. ChIV-2; GI

Easter Hymn. A. E. Housman. EBEV; GI

Easter Hymn. Henry Vaughan. ChIV-2; ESCV; SacPr

Easter Light, The. Clara Ann Thompson. CBWP-2

Easter light in the convent garden. Latin Lesson, The. Eavan Boland. ModIr

Easter Monday. Christina Georgina Rossetti. NOCV

Easter Morn. Giles Fletcher, the Younger. NOCV *Fr.* Christ's Victory and Triumph.

Easter Morn. Josephine D. Henderson Heard. CBWP-4

Easter Morning. A. R. Ammons. HCAP; NAAL-2v2; NAAL-5; NoAM; PoetW

Easter Morning. Amy Clampitt. ChIV-2

Easter Night. Alice Thompson Meynell. BrRo; ChIV-2; SacPr

Easter 1984. Les A. Murray. ChIV-2

Easter 1916. W. B. Yeats. FaBoMo; HAP; HarvBoo; HeIP-4; NAEL-5v2; NAEL-6v2; NAWM-7v2; NIL-7; NIP-4; NOBE; NOIV; NPeEn; NoAM; NoP-4; OBWP; OxAEP-2; OxBTC; PoE; PoPoPo; TFi

Easter; or, Spring-Time. Lizelia Augusta Jenkins Moorer. CBWP-3

Easter Outing. Sally Carr. Prnts

Easter Parade. Irving Berlin. ReLy

Easter Revolt Painted on a Tablespoon, The. Maurice Kilwein Guevara. TouFir

Easter Roses. Robert Grenier. FTOS *Fr.* Phantom Anthems.

Easter '68. Basil T. Paquet. CDa

Easter Song, An. *Unknown.* MiEL

Easter stars are shining, The. Flight to the City. William Carlos Williams. APT-1

Easter Sunday. Allen Ginsberg. FTOS

Easter Sunday. Janice Gould. GeoHom

Easter Sunday and my father plans a visit to one of the old missions along the Camino Real. Easter Sunday. Janice Gould. GeoHom

Easter Sunday, 1985. Charles Martin. RA

Easter: Wahiawa, 1959. Cathy Song. OpBo

Easter Wings. George Herbert. AngWePo; BASC; CABP; ChIV-1; ESCV; FHYEP; FSCP; GeHe; HAP; HeIP-4; InPK-6; MakPoe; MeLP; NAEL-5v1; NAEL-6v1; NAEL-7v1; NIL-7; NIP-4; NOSC; NoP-4; PAI; PBRV; PoE; PoPoPo; SacPr; TFi; TOF; TRP; TrCP; WeW-3; WoPoe

Eastern Gate, The. *Unknown.* ChiP, *tr. by* Arthur Waley

Eastern guard tower. Haiku. Etheridge Knight. BPo; ESEAA; NIL-7; TAP

Eastern mountains / and western mountains. Yüan Hung-tao. CoBLCP *Fr.* Passing by the Hot Springs at Hua-ch'ing Palace.

Eastern neighbor, western neighbor. Yang Chi. CoBLCP *Fr.* Scenes.

Eastern Sea, 100 fathoms. Lobster, The. Lorine Niedecker. APT-2

Eastern Slope. Su Tung-p'o (Su Shih).

  "Abandoned earthworks nobody tends." CoBCP

  "I planted rice before Spring Festival." CoBCP; ColAnChi, *tr. by* Burton Watson

  "Little stream used to cross my land, A." CoBCP; ColAnChi, *tr. by* Burton Watson

Eastern spices I bring with me. Venio ex Oriente. Nuala Ni Dhomhnaill. BiHa

Eastern Tempest. Edmund Charles Blunden. MoBrPo

Eastern Wall stands high and long, The. *Unknown.* ChiP *Fr.* Seventeen Old Poems.

Eastern War Time. Adrienne Rich.

  "Memory lifts her smoky mirror: 1943." NoP-4

  "Memory says: Want to do right? Don't count on me." TaR

Eastmuir king, and Wastmuir king. Fause Foodrage. *Unknown.* ESPB

Eastward, etched in purple by a sun. Appalachian Convalescence. Robert Conquest. OxBC

Eastward goes the Yangtze! Tune: "Charming Nien-Nu." Su Tung-p'o (Su Shih). ChinPo, *tr. by* Yip Wai-lim

Eastward Ho! A Succession. David Bromige. FTOS

Eastward, overlooking the Monolith. View of the Blue Sea. Ts'ao Ts'ao. ChinPo, *tr. by* Yip Wai-lim

Eastward spurs tip backward from the sun, The. Nigger's Leap, New England. Judith Wright. NOBAu

Eastward, the faint glimmer of the early dawn. Starting Early from Yü-p'u Deep. Meng Hao Jan. SuSp, *tr. by* Daniel Bryant

Eastward the sea and sky, and a lengthening evening. Evening View at River Pavilion, Inviting Guest. Po Chü-i. SuSp, *tr. by* Irving Y. Lo

Easy as an eyelid, godless, and I write. (LL) Alone. Anna Andreyevna Akhmatova. BoWoP; GifTon, *tr. by* Stephen Berg

Easy Boogie. Langston Hughes. APSN

Easy Come, Easy Go. Edward Heyman. ReLy

Easy Exercises in the Use of Difficult Words. Edmund Wilson.

  Lakeside. OBCoV

  Nursery Vignette. OBCoV

  Scène de Boudoir. OBCoV

Easy in the presence of her lover. (LL) Laboratory Poem. James Merrill. InPK-6; TwCP

Easy live and quiet die. (LL) Sir Walter Scott. NAEL-6v2; NOBE; NPeEn; OBEV; OxAEP-2; OxBEV; OxBS; WoPoe *Fr.* Bride of Lammermoor, The.

Easy Living. Ralph Rainger. ReLy

Easy Living. Michael S. Weaver. SpirFl

Easy Morning's Ride, An. (LL) Hummingbird, A. Emily Dickinson. APN-2; HeIP-4; NAAL-2v1; NAAL-3; NoP-4; SoSe-8; TCAPo

Easy on your drums. Dark Girl. Arna Bontemps. APT-2

Easy Rider Blues. Blind Lemon Jefferson. GM

Easy task it is to tread, An. Path of Independence, The. *Unknown.* TreFP

Easy way out. Nayo-Barbara Watkins. NBV

Eat and drink, O you rich. Eat and Drink! Ilya Abu Madi. GraLe, *tr. by* George Dimitri Selim

Eat, Eat me, Soul, and thou shalt never die. (LL) Meditation Eight. Edward Taylor. ChIV-2; ColAP; NAAL-2v1; NAAL-3; NOBA; OxBA; SCAP; TAP *Fr.* Preparatory Meditations before My Approach to the Lord's Supper.

Eat me to the root. Vine *v.* Goat. Euenus. GrAn, *tr. by* Alistair Elliot

Eat the fire of the Lord. Pentecost. Gerrit Achterberg. TuT, *tr. by* Dennis O'Driscoll

Eat thou and drink; tomorrow thou shalt die. Choice, The. Dante Gabriel Rossetti. ChIV-2

Eat / 300 feet. Anthropophagites See a Sign on NC Highway 177 That Looks like Heaven, The. Jonathan Williams. OBAL

Eat what you wish; I'll teach ye all to die. George Chapman. NOSC *Fr.* Eugenia.

Eat ye this bread, eat ye this bread. Song of the Eucharist, A. James Ryman. SacPr

Eat your banana, Annie dear. Sales Talk for Annie. Morris Gilbert Bishop. NBLV

Eat Your Heart Out, Edward Lear! Roger Woddis. UV

Eaten away by light. (LL) Daguerreotype Taken in Old Age. Margaret Atwood. BoWoP; NoAM

Eater of Wives, The. Linda France. MFPA

Eaters saddened every heart in Tenejapa, The. Story of the Eaters, A. Santiago Mendes Zapata. STP

'Eathen, The. Rudyard Kipling. OxBTC

Eating Alone. Li-Young Lee. NAAL-5; TRP; WeW-3

Eating an apple, I think of Emerson. Windfall. William Heyen. PoCoUp

Eating Bamboo-Shoots. Po Chü-i. OBVE, *tr. by* Arthur Waley

Eating cherries off a plate. (LL) Mother Goose. LB; OxNR

Eating Clay. Minnie Bruce Pratt. ExTi

Eating in Hall. Alexander Barclay. NoSic *Fr.* Eclogues.

Eating meat, growing old in the capital! (LL) Following the Rhymes of Shao-pao Huang's Poem on Being Moved while Visiting the Farmers. Yang Shih-ch'i. CoBLCP; WoPoe, *tr. by* Jonathan Chaves

Eating Poetry. Mark Strand. NoAM; TAP

Eating Roasted *Matsutake* Mushrooms. Ishikawa Jōzan. WoPoe, *tr. by* Jonathan Chaves

Eating Shepherd's-purse. Mei Yao Ch'en. SuSp, *tr. by* Jonathan Chaves

Eating the Forest. D. F. Brown. CDa

Eating the living germs of grasses. Song of the Taste. Gary Snyder. LCAP-2

Eating the Pig. Donald Hall. BodElec

Eating Together. Li-Young Lee. IllVoic; InvLad; NAAL-5

Eating Wild Mushrooms. Gary Young. GeoHom

Eats the whole land at home. (LL) Sea Eats the Land at Home, The. Kofi Awoonor. EmeKit; PBMAP

Eau-Forte. Francis Stewart [or "Frank"] Flint. OxBTC

Eaves. Ellis Jones. OBWVE, tr. by Anthony Conran

Eavesdropper. Breyten Breytenbach. PeSAV; PoetW, tr. by Ernst Van Heerden

Eavesdropper, The. Jane O. Wayne. InvLad

Ebb. Sorley MacLean (Somhairle MacGill-Eain). NePenScot

Ebb and Flow, The. Edward Taylor. InvLi; SCAP

Ebb on, tide, moving swiftly outwards! Invalid's Song. Harata Tangikuku. PeNZ, tr. by Margaret Orbell

Ebb slips from the rock, the sunken, The. Night. Robinson Jeffers. AWP; ColAP; MoAmPo; NOBA; OxBA

Ebb tide has come for me. Unknown. BIrV, tr. by John Montague

Ebb-tide to me as to the sea; old age brings me reproach. Hag of Beare, The. Unknown. OBVE, tr. by Augusta, Lady Gregory

Ebb / with the flow. Daufuskie. Mari E. Evans. BISi

Ebbing of Kraft, The. Iain Sinclair.
  Serious of Photographs, A. Oth
  Snow Lip. Oth
  World's Oldest Comedian Is Dead. Oth

Ebbtide at Sundown. "Michael Field." OxBSo; VWP

Ebenezer Californicus. August Kleinzahler. PmAP

Ebony Wood. Jacques Roumain.
  "Negro peddler of revolt." NegPo

Ecce Homo. David Gascoyne. ChIV-2; NoP-4; OBWP; PeECV Fr. Miserere.

Ecce Homunculus. Ronald Allison Kells Mason. PeNZ

Ecce Puer. James Joyce. AmFaPo; BIrV; ChIV-2; EBEV; NoAM; TrCP

Eccentric propositions of its fate, The. (LL) Men Made out of Words. Wallace Stevens. APT-1; NOBA; OxBSP; TAP; VGW

Eccho, tell me: on what's religion grounded? . . .Roundhead. Eccho, An. Unknown. AngWePo

Eccho, what shall I do to my Nymphe, when I goe to behold her? Barnabe Barnes. MakPoe Fr. Parthenophil and Parthenophe.

Eccles Street, Bloomsday, 1982. Harry Clifton. PBCIP

Ecclesiastes. Bible, O.T.
  "Cast thy bread upon the waters." AWP; OBVE
  (Creator is to be remembrd in due time, The.) NPeEn
  It Is Better. TrJP
  Remember Now Thy Creator. AWP; OBVE
  ("To all things there is an appointed time, and a time to everie purpose under the heaven.") NPeEn
  To Everything There Is a Season. NAWM-5v1; OBVE
  "Vanity of vanities, saith the Preacher, vanity of vanities; all is vanity." NAWM-5v1; TrJP
  (Remember Then Thy Creator.) TrJP

Ecclesiastes. Gilbert Keith Chesterton. ChIV-1; MoBrPo; OxBSP

Ecclesiastes. Derek Mahon. BIrV; CIP-2; ChIV-1; ModIr; PNI

Ecclesiastical Chronicle, An. John Heath-Stubbs.
  "Year of Our Lord two thousand one hundred and seven, The." NOBL

Ecclesiastical Sonnets. William Wordsworth.
  ("From the Baptismal hour, thro' weal and woe.") SacPr
  Mutability. CenSon; EBEV; HeIP-4; InPK-6; NAEL-6v2; NOBE; NoP-4; OBEV
  Obligations of Civil to Religious Liberty. SacPr
  Persuasion. OWoS
  (Pilgrim Fathers, The.) AiP
  Point at Issue, The. SacPr
  Trepidation of the Druids. Son
  (Within King's College Chapel, Cambridge.) GTBS-P

Ecclesiasticus. Bible, Apocrypha.
  "All flesh waxeth old as a garment." OBVE
  "By his commandment hee maketh the snow to fall apace." OBVE
  Music. TrJP
  O Death. TrJP
  Our Fathers. OBVE; TrJP
  Test of Men, The. TrJP

Echo. Ausonius. NPeEn, tr. by George Sandys

Echo. Madison Cawein. APN-2

Echo. Robert Creeley. BodElec

Echo. Walter De la Mare. OBMV

Echo. Henriqueta Lisboa. TCLAP, tr. by Hélcio Veiga Costa

Echo. John Milton. OBEV Fr. Comus; a Masque Presented at Ludlow Castle.

Echo. Thomas Moore. GTBS-P; NOBE; NOBRP; OBEV
  (Echoes.) GTBS-P; OxAEP-2

Echo. Vasco [or Vasko] Popa. PoSu Fr. Besieged Serenity.

Echo. Christina Georgina Rossetti. BoLoP; EBVV; LW; NOBE; NoP-4; PEW; PoBW; PoE; VWP

Echo. George Santayana. APN-2

Echo. John Banister Tabb. APN-2

Echo, An. Sir William Alexander, Earl of Stirling. NOSC

Echo, The. William Barnes. SCGP

Echo and Narcissus. Gerda Mayer. PeLV

Echo and the Ferry. Jean Ingelow. EBVV

Echo Club, The. Bayard Taylor.
  Night the Second: All or Nothing. APN-2
  Night the Sixth: Hadramaut. APN-2
  Night the Eighth: Camerados. APN-2

Echo. Ever. (LL) Heaven. George Herbert. ESCV; GeHe; TTTS; TrCP; WoPoe

Echo from Willow-Wood, An. Christina Georgina Rossetti. CABP

Echo, I ween, will in the wood reply. Gentle Echo on Woman, A. Jonathan Swift. NBLV

Echo:/ mimic, / last sip. Euodos. GrAn

Echo of childhood stalks before me, An. J. P. Clark Bekedermo. PBMAP Fr. Reed in the Tide, A.

Echo of fireplace on the dividing wall, An. Echo of fireplace, An. Louise Herlin. MFP, tr. by Martin Sorrell

Echo of insects where the lamplight thins. At Ch'ang-ku, Reading: To Show to My Man Pa. Li Ho. CoBCP; ColAnChi, tr. by Burton Watson

Echo of the clocktower, footstep. Prayer. Dana Gioia. NoP-4

Echo Reverie. Henrietta Cordelia Ray. CBWP-3

Echo's Bones. Samuel Beckett. NoAM

Echo's Complaint. Henrietta Cordelia Ray. CBWP-3

Echo's Lament for Narcissus. Ben Jonson. See Cynthia's Revels.

Echo's [or Eccho's] Song. Ben Jonson. NOSC Fr. Cynthia's Revels.

Echo, tongueless, sings her sweet. Satyrus. GrAn

Echo your thought in ours? 'Destroy! Destroy!' (LL) Brother Fire. Louis MacNeice. AF; NOBE; NoAM

Echoes. William Ernest Henley.
  Blackbird, The. MoBrPo
  (I. M. Margaritae Sorori.) CABP
  Invictus. AmFaPo; BRP; CABP; MoBrPo; NAEL-6v2; NOBE; OBEV; OBMV
  (Late Lark, A.) PoRA
  Margaritæ Sorori [I. M.]. MoBrPo; NOBE; OBEV
  On the Way to Kew. MoBrPo
  We'll Go No More a-Roving. MoBrPo

Echoes. Emma Lazarus. APN-2; GSo

Echoes. Timothy Liu. ReTh

Echoes. Audre Lorde. NoP-4

Echoes. Naomi Long Madgett. SeSe

Echoes. Thomas Moore. See Echo

Echoes. John Banister Tabb. APN-2

Echoes. Ronald Stuart Thomas. OxAEP-2

Echoes, The. Raymond Mazisi Kunene. PBMAP

Echoes are soundless. Transformations. Orkhan Muyassar. MAP, tr. by Samuel Hazo and Lena Jayyusi

Echoes from Theocritus. Edward Cracroft Lefroy.
  Cleonicos. AWP
  Epitaph of Eusthenes, The. AWP
  Flute of Daphnis, The. AWP
  Grave of Hipponax, The. AWP
  Monument of Cleita, The. AWP
  Sacred Grove, A. AWP
  Sylvan Revel, A. AWP
  Thyrsis. AWP

Echoes of the Murder of Emmett Till. Ira B. Jones. InTrad

Echoes of wheels and singing lashes. Echoes of Wheels. "Furnley Maurice." NOBAu

Echoing Old Man Mu's Poem, "Inscribed on Shen Lang-ch'ien's Little Landscape, Autumn Willows at Stone Cliff." Wang Shih-chieng. CoBLCP, tr. by Jonathan Chaves

Echoing [or Ecchoing] Green, The. William Blake. AmFaPo; FHYEP; NAEL-5v2; NAEL-6v2; OxAEP-2; PoE; UnPo Fr. Songs of Innocence.

Eclipse. Anita Endrezze. CDW

Eclipse. John Haines. PoCoUp

Eclipse. Jonathan Johnson. AmPoNex

Eclipse. Ed Roberson. GT

Eclipse, The. Henry Vaughan. OxBSP

Eclipse II. Linda Hogan. HATNAP

Eclipse and glory of her kind?, The. (LL) On His Mistress [*or* Mistris], the Queen of Bohemia. Sir Henry Wotton. BASC; EnLoPo; HAP; MeLP; NOSC; NPeEn; OxBEV; SCGP; TFi

Eclipse, Kenwick, 1974. Tracy Ryan. NeBl

Eclipses. Nancy Sullivan. TAP

Eclogue 1. Baldomero Garcilaso de la Vega.
    "O waters running pure and crystal clear." SpanPo, *tr. by* Edwin Morgan

Eclogue 4: "Shell-bursting births, comas, and the mute." Andrea Zanzotto. ItPo, *tr. by* Gayle Ridinger

Eclogue IV: The Poet. Charles Jenner. AWP
    Soliloquy in the Suburbs, A. NOEC

Eclogue IV: Winter. Joseph Brodsky. TCRP, *tr. by* Joseph Brodsky

Eclogue 8. Francis Quarles. BASC

Eclogue: Clerk of the Weather. William Scammell. NLP

Eclogue for Christmas, An. Louis MacNeice. FaBoMo; NoAM; OBMV

Eclogue: "Industry undressing in front of Agriculture." Michael Hofmann. HarvBoo

Eclogue: "Men talking, The." George Oppen. APT-2; FTOS

Eclogues. Alexander Barclay.
    "Miseries of Courtiers" by Æneas Sylvius Ricolomini, The.
        Eating in Hall. NoSic
    Winter. PBRV

Eclogues. Titus Calpurnius Siculus. RomPo, *tr. by* Guy Lee
    Eclogue 1. RomPo, *tr. by* Guy Lee
    Eclogue 2. RomPo, *tr. by* Guy Lee
    Eclogue 3. RomPo, *tr. by* Guy Lee
    Eclogue 4. RomPo, *tr. by* Guy Lee
    Eclogue 5. RomPo, *tr. by* Guy Lee
    Eclogue 6. RomPo, *tr. by* Guy Lee
    Eclogue 7. RomPo, *tr. by* Guy Lee

Eclogues. Virgil [*or* Vergil].
    Corydon and Thyrsis. AWP, *tr. by* John Dryden
    Eclogue 2: The Lament of Corydon for His Faithless Alexis. CAGL, *tr. by* Byrne Fone
    Lycidas and Moeris. AWP, *tr. by* John Dryden
    Messiah, The. AWP
    Shepherd's Gratitude, The. AWP, *tr. by* Charles Stuart Calverley
    ("Sicilian Muses, sing we greater things.") OBVE, *tr. by* Sir John Beaumont

Ecologue. Eugenio Montale. WoPoe, *tr. by* William Arrowsmith

Ecology. Lionel Fogarty. IBA

Economy of Vegetation, The. Erasmus Darwin. *Fr.* Botanic Garden, The.

Ecstacy, An. Richard Crashaw. *See* Song: "Lord, when the sense of Thy sweet grace."

Ecstacy. Amado Nervo. TCLAP, *tr. by* Sue Standing

Ecstasy. Sharon Olds. EmeKit

Ecstasy. Hélène Swarth. WPOW, *tr. by* Jonathan Crewe

Ecstasy. *Unknown.* AH

Ecstasy, The. John Donne. BASC; BoLoP; CABP; FHYEP; FSCP; HAP; NAEL-5v1; NAEL-6v1; NAEL-7v1; NOBE; NoP-4; OBEV; OxBEV; PoE; TFi; TOF
    (Extasie, The.) NPeEn
    (Extasie, The.) ESCV; EnLoPo; MeLP

Ecstasy of St Saviour's Avenue, The. Neil Rollinson. EmeKit

Ecstasy of the moon. (LL) Mandoline. Paul Verlaine. AWP; OBMV, *tr. by* Arthur Symons

Ecstatic bird songs pound. Dawn. William Carlos Williams. APT-1; MoAmPo

Ecstatic Longing. Goethe. STV, *tr. by* John Frederick Nims

Ecstatic thought's the thing. Poetry. Mary Elizabeth Fullerton. GI; NOBAu

Ed ascoltando al leggier mormorio. Ezra Pound. *See* Zeus lies in Ceres' bosom

Eddi, priest of St. Wilfrid. Eddi's Service. Rudyard Kipling. OBCP

Eddi's Service. Rudyard Kipling. OBCP

Eddie and the Birthday. Michael Rosen. NOxBChV

Eddie Priest's Barbershop and Notary. Kevin Young. AmPoNex; ISC; SpirFl

Eddie was a cute boy. Realist of 1939–40, A. Wilma Elizabeth McDaniel. GeoHom

Eden. Emily Grosholz. FFC; RA

Eden. John Milton. PeECV *Fr.* Paradise Lost.

Eden. Claudia Rankine. GT

Eden. James Simmons. PNI

Eden. Thomas Traherne. ChIV-1; ESCV; GeHe

Eden. David Woo. OpBo

Eden after Dark. Richard Shelton. CDa

Eden Is a Zoo. Margaret Atwood. WPE

Eden is that Old-Fashioned House. Emily Dickinson. ChIV-1; NALW

Eden Rock. Charles Causley. NPeEn; NoP-4

Eden Says No. Robert Johnstone. PNI

"Eden," the First Part of the First Day of the Second Week. Guillaume de Salluste Du Bartas. *Fr.* Divine Weeks and Works, The.

Edenhall. "Susan Coolidge." OBCA

Edenic glory sequestered just outside. Brooklyn Botanic Garden, The. Timothy Liu. UrbNat

Edgar A. Guest Considers "The Old Woman Who Lived in a Shoe" and the Good Old Verities at the Same Time. Louis Untermeyer. OBAL *Fr.* Mother Goose Up-to-Date.

Edgar A. Guest Syndicates the Old Woman Who Lived in a Shoe. Louis Untermeyer. MoAmPo *Fr.* Mother Goose Up-to-Date.

Edge. Robert David Fitzgerald. CBAP

Edge. Sylvia Plath. FaBoWP; HCAP; NAAL-2v2; NALW; NPeEn; PoE; PoPoPo; TAP; VCAP

Edge, The. Robert Creeley. FTOS

Edge, The. Rosemary Dobson. NOBAu

Edge, The. Louise Glück. HarvBoo

Edge, The. Andrey [*or* Andrei] Andreievich Voznesensky [*or* Voznesenskii]. RusPo, *tr. by* Robert Arthur Douglas Ford

Edge-Hill; or, The Rural Prospect Delineated and Moralised. Richard Jago.
    Instructions on landscaping. OBGa
    Iron Industry in Birmingham, The. NOEC
    Sage Philosophy. ECEV

Edge of Autumn, The. Michael Anania. NoAM

Edge of Something, The. Linda Gregg. BodElec

Edge of the cancer, The. Front Lines. Gary Snyder. PoE

Edge of the light. (LL) How Poetry Comes to Me. Gary Snyder. LoL; PoPoPo

Edge of the sky, The. Songs and Chants. *Unknown.* APN-2, *tr. by* John Wesley Powell

Edge the word. Crow trembles in the knot. (LL) Narrative Charm for Ibbotroyd. Maggie O'Sullivan. Oth; PFTM-2

Edges of the gorges hack up sun and moon, The. Meng Chiao. SuSp *Fr.* Laments of the Gorges.

Edgewater Park. Ruth L. Schwartz. WiU

Edging each other towards consummation. In the Borghese Gardens. Charles Tomlinson. OBGa

Edible World, The. David Bromige. FTOS

Edinburgh after Flodden. William Edmonstoune [*or* Edmondstoune] Aytoun.
    "Then the Provost he uprose." OBWP

Edith, a Tale of the Woods. Felicia Dorothea Hemans. RWP

Edith B——and her mother on a Sunday afternoon. Liz Rosenberg. UnSA *Fr.* Prose Poems.

'Edith is fair,' the painter said. Two Artists, The. Constance Naden. VWP; ViWPN

Editing *Poetry*. Karl Shapiro. IllVoic

Editor's Wooing, The. "Orpheus C. Kerr." OBAL

Editor Whedon. Edgar Lee Masters. APT-1; FaBoEE; NOBA; OBSV; OxBA; PoE *Fr.* Spoon River Anthology.

Edlesborough. Anne Ridler. SacPr

Edmond Halley. Roy Fuller. OxBC

Edmonton, thy cemetery. Stevie Smith. OxBTC

Edmund Burke. Oliver Goldsmith. FaBoEE; NOEC; NPeEn; OxBEV *Fr.* Retaliation.

Edmund Davie 1682; Annagram. Benjamin Tompson. SCAP

Edna's Alphabet. Barry Humphries. OBCoV

Edna's Hymn. Barry Humphries. NOBAu

Edna St. Vincent Millay Exhorts Little Boy Blue. Louis Untermeyer. MoAmPo *Fr.* Mother Goose Up-to-Date.

Edom o' Gordon. *Unknown.* NePenScot; OxBB
    (Captain Car.) ESPB

Education by Stone. João Cabral de Melo Neto. TCLAP, *tr. by* James Wright
    (Education by stone: through lessons, An.) VCWP, *tr. by* James Wright

Education in Wales. Goronva Camlan. AngWePo

Education's Martyr. May Kendall. VWP

Edvard Munch. Charles Wright. HCAP

Edward. Honor Moore. WiU

Edward. *Unknown.* *See* Edward [*or* Edward, Edward]

Edward back from the Indian Sea. Neglectful Edward. Robert Graves. MoBrPo

Edward Hopper. Anthony Rudolf. PoSol

Edward Hopper and the House by the Railroad. Edward Hirsch. PoSol

Edward Hopper, "Hotel Room," 1931. Larry Levis. PoSol

Edward Hopper Retrospective, The. Tony Quagliano. PoSol

Edward Hopper's "Lighthouse at Two Lights." Tony Quagliano. PoSol

Edward Hopper's Nighthawks, 1942. Joyce Carol Oates. PoSol

Edward Hopper's Seven A.M. John Hollander. PoSol

Edward Lear. W. H. Auden. OxAEP-2; OxBSo

Edward Lear in February. Christopher Middleton. TwCP

Edward MacDermott. Mail King. Paul B. Janeczko. HHAm

Edward [or Edward, Edward]. *Unknown.* ClHu; EBEV; ESPB; HAP; InPK-6; NAEL-5v1; NOBE; NoP-4; OBEV; OxBB; OxBEV; OxBS; PAI; PoRA; SCGP; SoSe-8; TFi; TRP

(Why does your brand sae drap wi' bluid.) NoP-4

Edward / Paterson has grown older. William Carlos Williams. NoAM *Fr.* Paterson.

Edward the Dyke and Other Poems. Judy Grahn.

"In the place where." NALW

Edward the Second. Christopher Marlowe.

"Ah, wicked King! Accursed Gaveston!" CAGL

"He's gone, and for his absence thus I mourn." CAGL

"Here is the form of Gaveston's exile." CAGL

"My father is deceas'd. Come, Gaveston." CAGL

"Nephew, I must to Scotland. Thou stay'st here." CAGL

Edwin, the Minstrel. James Beattie. OxAEP-1

Edwin, your father has never ceased to be. Veterans of the Wars. Edgar Lee Masters. CBCWP

Ee calazi. Hammer-Song. *Unknown.* FaBoVe

E[e]astrich, thou feather[e]d fool[e] and easy [or easie] prey. Lucasta's Fan[ne], with a Looking-Glass[e] in It. Richard Lovelace. CaPo

Eeeveryyee time. Trips. Nikki Giovanni. CA

Eek! / Her legs are caught in something. Orlando Commercial, The. George MacBeth [or Macbeth]. NOBL; PeLV

Eel, The. Eugenio Montale. PoetW, *tr.* by William Arrowsmith; STV; WeW-3; WoPoe, *tr.* by Jonathan Galassi

(Eel, the siren, The.) PFTM-1

Eel, The. Ogden Nash. NTCP

Eel, coldwater, The. Eel, The. Eugenio Montale. PoetW, *tr.* by William Arrowsmith

Eel-Grass. Edna St. Vincent Millay. APT-1

Eels and Tortoises. William Diaper. *See* Halieutica

Eemis-Stane, The. Hugh MacDiarmid. NAEL-5v2; NAEL-6v2; NPeEn; NePenScot

Eena Mi Corner. Jean Binta Breeze. WaCA

Eenie, meenie, mackeracka. *Unknown.* OxNR

Eenie, meenie, minie, mo / Catch a thief by the toe. *Unknown.* OxNR *Fr.* Counting-out Rhymes.

Eenity, feenity, fickety, feg. *Unknown.* OxNR

Eeny meeny figgety fig. Tig. *Unknown.* FaBoVe

Eeny, weeny, winey, wo. *Unknown.* OxNR

Ef ah could, ah sholy would. Railroad Section Leader's Song. *Unknown.* GM

Ef I had wings like Noah's dove. Dink's Song. *Unknown.* OxBoLi

Ef you / Don't / Watch / Out! (LL) Little Orphant Annie. James Whitcomb Riley. APN-2; BRP; ChAP; ITBLP; NBLV; OBAL; OBCA; OxIBACP; TCAPo

Effects of Abstract Art, The. Gary Soto. GeoHom

Effeminate Englishmen. William Cowper. ECEV *Fr.* Task, The.

Effervescence and Evanescence. Keith Preston. OBAL

Effet de Neige. John Hollander. GS

Efficient Wife's Complaint, The. Confucius. CTC, *tr.* by Ezra Pound *Fr.* Airs of Pei.

Effigies, The. Felicia Dorothea Hemans. NOBRP

Efflux of the soul is happiness, here is happiness, The. Walt Whitman. AmFaPo *Fr.* Song of the Open Road.

Effort at Speech between Two People. Muriel Rukeyser. MoAmPo; NAAL-5; PAI; TrJP; TwCP

Effortlessly, / Love flows from God into man. Mechthild von Magdeburg. EnlH

Effulgent Autumn. Georg Trakl. AuPH, *tr.* by Lowell A. Bangerter

Effusions. Samuel Taylor Coleridge.

(Aeolian Harp, The.) NoP-4

("As erst that other fiend beneath great Michael's sword.") (LL) CenSon Burke. CenSon

("E'en so thou, Siddons! meltest my sad heart!") (LL) CenSon

Eolian Harp, The. FHYEP; NAEL-5v2; NAEL-6v2; NOBRP; NPeEn Koskiusko. OxBSo

La Fayette. CenSon

("My heart has thanked thee, Bowles! for those soft strains.") CenSon

On a Discovery Made Too Late. CenSon; GSo; Son

Pitt. CenSon

("Still glows wide Heaven with his distended blaze!") (LL) CenSon

("Though king-bred rage, with lawless uproar rude.") CenSon

To a Young Ass. OxAEP-2

To the Autumnal Moon. CenSon

To the Rev. [or Reverend] W. L. Bowles. Son

("Was it some Spirit, Sheridan! that breathed.") CenSon

EFT. Roberta Swann. PoCoUp

Eftsoones they heard a most melodious sound. Edmund Spenser. NOBE; OxBEV; PBRV; SCV *Fr.* Faerie Queene, The.

Egan O Rahilly. *Unknown.* EBEV; OBMV, *tr.* by James Stephens

Egeria! sweet creation of some heart. Byron. NOBRP *Fr.* Childe Harold's Pilgrimage.

Egg. Linda Pastan. InvLad

Egg, The. Clarence Day. NBLV

Egg and the Machine, The. Robert Frost. MoAmPo

Egg Hatches Out a Flame, An. Drahomira Vandas. SurWo, *tr.* by Guy Ducornet

Egg I have chosen is sandy brown, The. Boiling an Egg. Stanley Cook. OTCP

Egg is a grand thing for a journey, An. How the Hen Sold Her Eggs to the Stingy Priest. Nancy Willard. LCAP-2

Egg is always being made, The. Grand Grand Mother Is Returning. Judy Grahn. HW

Egg of fire, The. the egg of water. the egg of wind in the silk bag. the egg of air. Man, The. The Woman. Hans [or Jean] Arp. PFTM-1

Egg so round on the outside, An. To Beat or Not to Beat. Nina Iskrenko. TCRP, *tr.* by John High and Katya Olmsted

Egg Thoughts. Russell Hoban. NTCP; OTCP

Eggleston was a taxi-driver. Cynical Portraits. Louis Paul. NBLV

Eggomania. Felicia Lamport. NBLV

Eggplant. Ibn Sara. WoPoe, *tr.* by Leticia Garza-Falcón and Christopher Middleton

Eggplants Have Pins and Needles, The. Novella Nikolaevna Matveyeva [or Matveieva]. TCRusP; WPOW, *tr.* by Daniel Weissbort

Eggs. Susan Wood. SoSe-8

Egil's Saga. *Unknown.*

"I crossed the deep sea." WoPoe, *tr.* by John Lucas

Egles byrde hath spred his wings, The. John Heywood. PBRV *Fr.* Ballad on the Marriage of Philip and Mary, A.

Eglwys Newydd. John Tripp. AngWePo

Ego. Philip Booth. TwCP

Ego. Denise Duhamel. NeAmPo

Ego. Norman MacCaig. GTBS-P

Ego Flos. Guido Gezelle. TuT, *tr.* by Peter Van de Kamp

Ego Sum Vitis. William Alabaster. OxBEV *Fr.* Divine Meditations.

Ego Tripping [(There May Be a Reason Why)]. Nikki Giovanni. GT; ISC; RaBo

Egoisme à Deux. Louisa Sarah Bevington. VWP

Egoisme à Deux. Louisa S. Guggenberger. NOBVV

Egoist is not / good for himself. (LL) Immoral Proposition, The. Robert Creeley. NeAP; PoM

Egotist. Ambrose Bierce. APN-2; OBAL *Fr.* Devil's Dictionary, The.

Egret died the other night. Egret's Death and Funeral Preparations. *Vietnamese Oral Tradition.* CaDao, *tr.* by John Balaban

Egret's Death and Funeral Preparations. *Vietnamese Oral Tradition.* CaDao, *tr.* by John Balaban

Egrets. Tu Mu. WoPoe, *tr.* by A. C. Graham

Egrets. Tu Mu. SuSp

Egrets bear egret sons. Mother Egret. *Vietnamese Oral Tradition.* CaDao, *tr.* by John Balaban

Egypt. "H. D." APT-1

Egypt. Keith Douglas. HarvBoo

Egypt's Favorite. Sir Francis Hubert.

Joseph in Carcere. ChIV-1

Egyptian Dancer at Shubra. Bernard Spencer. NoAM

Egyptian Kites. Rex Warner. OWoS

Egyptian Passage, An. Theodore Weiss. TAP

Egyptian Pulled Glass Bottle in the Shape of a Fish, An. Marianne Craig Moore. APT-1; NALW

Egyptian Register. "Ern Malley." BMAP

Egyptian Serenade. 'Ali Mahmud Taha. MAP, *tr.* by Issa Boullata and Thomas G. Ezzy

Egyptian woman. Christian Epigram. *Unknown.* WoPoe, *tr.* by John Peck

Eh! Oranges, sweet little oranges / my lady! Marketwoman of Luanda. Maria Eugénia Lima. HAWP, *tr.* by Julia Kirst

Eh-Ros-ka, the Warrior's Dance. *Unknown.* APN-2 *Fr.* War Dance.

Eheu! "Rubén Dario." SpanPo, *tr.* by Anita Volland

Eheu Fugaces. "Thomas Ingoldsby." FaBoEE; OxBoLi

Eia, Domine Deus. (LL) A, a, a, Domine Deus. David Jones. FaBoTw; HarvBoo; NOCV

Eia, with handbells, jews' harps, risible. Geoffrey Hill. DiPo *Fr.* Hymns to Our Lady of Chartres.

Eidolons. Walt Whitman. APN-1

Eiffel Tower. Vincente Huidobro. CuPo

Eiffel tower, The. "Adonis" [*or* "Adunis"]. PFTM-2, *tr. by* Allen Hibbard and Osama Isber *Fr.* Desire Moving through the Maps of the Material.

Eiffel Tower, on the topmost platform, The. Going Down, Please. László Mécs. IQMS, *tr. by* Watson Kirkconnell

Eiga Monogatari, The. *Unknown.*
   "Which is worse." WoPoe, *tr. by* Helen Craig McCullough and William H. McCullough

8. Catullus. NAWM-7v1, *tr. by* Charles Martin

Eight Aspects of Melissa. Lawrence Durrell.
   Visitations. MoBrPo

Eight Ball. Richard Jackson. SwNoth

8-Ball at the Twilite. David Baker. ReTh

Eight Beds, Eight Lockers. Debby Barben. IBA

Eight Days in April. Marilyn Hacker. FFC

8:50 AM Ft. Lyons VAH. Simon J. Ortiz. NAAL-5 *Fr.* Poems from the Veterans Hospital.

Eight o'Clock. A. E. Housman. InPK-6; MoBrPo; NoAM; OxBSP; PAI; PoE; SoSe-8

Eight Pearle: Science, The. Lady Diana Primrose. EMWP *Fr.* Chain of Pearl, A.

Eight Phases of Contemplation. Giusi Busceti. ItPo, *tr. by* Gayle Ridinger

Eight Sandbars on the Takano River. Gary Snyder. NOBA; VGW

Eight Six Foxtrot—Eight Six Foxtrot. Gliding Baskets. Frank A. Cross, Jr. CDa

8-track clicked through tunes as we two, The. Playland. Richard Foerster. SwNoth

Eight Ways of Looking at Pussy. Letta Neely. WiU

Eight xx. Laurie Duggan. BMAP

Eight years ago this May. Gary Snyder. VGW *Fr.* Four Poems for Robin.

Eight years difference in age seems now, The. Terminal. Thom Gunn. CAGL; OxBEV

Eighteen. Maria Banus. BoWoP

Eighteen Dead, The. Jan Campert. TuT, *tr. by* Mary E. O'Donnell

1887. A. E. Housman. NIP-4; NOBVV; SCGP; UnPo

1815. Jeffrey Wainwright. NPeEn

1845. Jackson Mac Low. APSN *Fr.* Presidents of the United States of America, The.

1841 (I). Jackson Mac Low. APSN *Fr.* Presidents of the United States of America, The.

1841 (II). Jackson Mac Low. APSN *Fr.* Presidents of the United States of America, The.

Eighteen Hundred and Eleven[, A Poem]. Anna Laetitia Barbauld. NOBRP; RWP

1808 Wordsworth dies from fall while hiking in Scotland. Other Lives of the Romantics. Jane Flanders. PBCAP

1805. Robert Graves. FaBoCh; FaBoWar; OBCoV; OBSV; PeLV

1809. Jackson Mac Low. APSN *Fr.* Presidents of the United States of America, The.

1801. Jackson Mac Low. APSN *Fr.* Presidents of the United States of America, The.

1801. William Wordsworth. CenSon; Son

1802. Mary Tighe. CenSon

1817. Jackson Mac Low. APSN *Fr.* Presidents of the United States of America, The.

Eighteen-Seventy. Arthur Rimbaud.
   Evil. OBWP
   Napoleon after Sedan. OBWP, *tr. by* Robert Lowell
   Poster of Our Dazzling Victory at Saarbrucken, A. OBWP, *tr. by* Robert Lowell
   Sleeper in the Valley, The. OBWP
   ("There's a green hollow where a river sings.") AWP, *tr. by* Ludwig Lewisohn
   To the French of the Second Empire. OBWP, *tr. by* Robert Lowell

1871. J. D. McClatchy. WiU *Fr.* First Steps.

1837. Jackson Mac Low. APSN *Fr.* Presidents of the United States of America, The.

Eighteen to Twenty-One. David Trinidad.
   "As one young guy screwed another young guy." WiU
   "He said his name was Nick; later I learned." WiU
   "More than anything, I wanted Charlie." WiU
   "Tom used spit for lubricant and fucked me." WiU

1825. Jackson Mac Low. APSN *Fr.* Presidents of the United States of America, The.

1829. Jackson Mac Low. APSN *Fr.* Presidents of the United States of America, The.

Eighteen Verses Sung to a Tatar Reed Whistle. Ts'ai Yen.
   "I have no desire to live, but I am afraid of death." WPOW
   "I never believed that in my broken life." BoWoP; WPOW
   "I was born in a time of peace." BoWoP; WPOW
   "Seventeenth stanza, The. My heart aches, my tears fall." WPOW
   "Sun sets, The. The wind moans." BoWoP; WPOW
   "Tatar chief forced me to become his wife, A." WPOW

Eighteenth century, The. As I Sat in the Armchair of the Tsar. Bulat Shalvovich Okudzhava. TCRP, *tr. by* Deming Brown

Eighteenth-Century Medical Illustration: The Infant in its Little Room. Ann Townsend. AmPoNex

Eighteenth of October, The. Fire of Frendraught, The. *Unknown.* ESPB; OxBB

Eighth Air Force. Randall Jarrell. NOBA; NoAM; NoP-4; OBWP; PoWW; TRP; VCAP

Eighth and the Thirteenth, The. Alicia Ostriker. TaR

Eighth Eclogue. Miklós Radnóti. IQMS, *tr. by* Peter Zollman

Eighth Elegy. Children's Elegy. Muriel Rukeyser.
   "That is what they say, who were broken off from love." LCAP-2

Eighth Inning, The. Donald Hall. MoASP

Eighth of Shostakovich, The. Eighth and the Thirteenth, The. Alicia Ostriker. TaR

Eighth Sky. Michael Palmer. FTOS

Eighties Meditation. Kay Murphy. SwNoth

85. Catullus. NAWM-7v1, *tr. by* Charles Martin

84 01. Michael Haslam. Oth *Fr.* Continual Song.

'Eighty-nine was bad. Graves at Elkhorn. Richard Hugo. UnPo; VCAP

80 papers / was all there was. Delivering the Times, 1952–1944. David Huddle. PBCAP

87. Catullus. NAWM-7v1, *tr. by* Charles Martin

87. Fanny [*or* Frances] Macartney Greville. CABP *Fr.* Caelica.

86. Catullus. NAWM-7v1, *tr. by* Charles Martin

86 Pasteur Corner. Manuela Fingueret. MirDau, *tr. by* Celeste Kostopulos-Cooperman

83. Catullus. NAWM-7v1, *tr. by* Charles Martin

Eighty-three years—at last. Kyurin-Eki. ZenPo, *tr. by* Takashi Ikemoto and Lucien Stryk

Eild. Robert Tannahill. NePenScot

Eileen Aroon. Gerald Griffin.
   "When like the rising day." OBEV

Eileen's Vision. Eileen Myles. BodElec

Eileithyia, brought safe. Leonidas. PGA

Eileithyia, once more. Callimachus. GrAn

Ein Complaint. Virginia Graham. OBCoV

Ein feste Burg ist unser Gott. Martin Luther. CTC, *tr. by* M. Woolsey Stryker

Ein Fichtenbaum steht einsam. Heinrich Heine. AWP, *tr. by* James Thomson

Ein Leben. Dan Pagis. FIT, *tr. by* Robert Friend

Eine Kleine Snailmusik. May Sarton. NBLV

Einstein's Bathrobe. Howard Moss. VCAP

Eire. David [*or* Daibhi][*or* Daithi] O'Bruadair [*or* Ó Bruadair]. BIrV, *tr. by* Austin Clarke

Eireann. Osbert Lancaster. NOBL; PeLV *Fr.* Afternoons with Baedeker.

Eisenhower Years, The. Paul Zimmer. PBCAP

Either cockleshells from the Erythraian reef as gifts. Hedyla. SaLy, *tr. by* Diane Rayor

Either get out of the house or conform to my tastes, woman. Martial. FaBoEE, *tr. by* James Michie

Either heard or taught. Song for a Thin Sister. Audre Lorde. OxWW

Either I'm swimming toward a floating discotheque its dancers. Treason's Choice. Philip Hammial. BMAP

Either incognito and desperate. Lonely Tower, The. Tom Paulin. ModIr

Either my sight is getting worse. Recognition. Kate Clanchy. MFPA

Either now or tomorrow or the day after that. (LL) Girl in a Nightgown. Wallace Stevens. AmFaPo; OxBA

Either she was foul, or her attire was bad. Ovid. OBVE, *tr. by* Christopher Marlowe *Fr.* Elegies.

Either the lunches or the dead soldiers. (LL) Dead Soldiers. James Fenton. AF; FaBoWar; NoAM; NoP-4; OBWP

Either thou'dst die, or thou must run away. (LL) Sonnet: Of an Ill-Favored Lady. Guido Cavalcanti. AWP; EaltPo, *tr. by* Dante Gabriel Rossetti

Either Way. Tricia Corob. Prnts

Either you will / go through this door. Prospective Immigrants Please Note. Adrienne Rich. AiP; AmFaPo; VGW

Ejaculating into their vaginas—young girls of the western tribes. *Unknown.* NOBAu *Fr.* Goulburn Island Song Cycle.

Ejaculation. Elinor Wylie. APT-1

Ejected Wife, The. Yüan-ti. OBVE; OxBEV, *tr. by* Arthur Waley

El Aghir. Norman Cameron. *See* Green, Green Is El Aghir

El Alamein. Steve Crow. HATNAP

El Alamein. John Jarmain. FaBoWar

El Camino Verde. Paul Blackburn. PmAP

El Curandero. Rafael Campo. BloBone

El Desdichado. Gérard de Nerval. WoPoe, *tr. by* Robert Duncan

El Día de los Muertos. Rafael Campo. RA

El Dorado. Richard Ryan. BIrV

El Elvis. Wasabi Kanastoga. ReTh

El Greco: Espolio. Earle Birney. MoCV

El-Hajj Malik El-Shabazz. Robert Earl Hayden. ESEAA
    (El-Hajj Malik El-Shabazz (Malcolm X).) NAAAL

El Hombre. William Carlos Williams. SAmP

El; in the top of his head: to tell / him. (LL) Plato Told Him. E. E.
    Cummings. CTC; NOBA; NoAM; OxBA; PoE

El Jibarito Moderno. Miguel Algarin. PueRic

El Paso Monologue. Ishmael Reed. SpirFl

El Paso Times "World of Women," The. Catherine Bowman.
    "Bride wore a gown, The." ExTi

El periférico, or Sleep. Joshua Clover. NeAmPo

El Ropero. Antonio Di Montorio. TrJP

El Serape's floorshow finished at one. The lights. Elephant Hunt in
    Guadalajara. Jack Gilbert. BodElec

El Sueño de la Razón. Jane Cooper. FaBoWP *Fr.* March.

Elaine, pretending it was salt. E. Aitken. UV

Elaine sleeps most of the day. She's the prettiest invalid I've ever seen. True
    Bride, The. Amy Gerstler. PmAP

Elba. Gerrit Kouwenaar. PFTM-2, *tr. by* Peter Nijmeijer

Elbow in Dumberland, An. Edwin Torres. HeMarv

Elbows. Minnie Bruce Pratt. WiU

Elbows cut wind. Near the front. Dip in ground. Ballad of the Blue Envelope,
    The. Nikolai Semionovich Tikhonov. TCRP, *tr. by* Michael Frayn

Elder Brother, The. John Fletcher.
    "Beauty clear and fair." NOSC; OBEV

Elder Dubb. Edwin Torres. HeMarv

Elder Edda, The. *Unknown.*
    Counsels of Sigrdrifa. AWP
    First Lay of Gudrun, The. AWP, *tr. by* Eirikr Magnusson and William Morris
    Gudrun Laments over Sigurd. OBVE
    Lay [*or* Short Lay] of Sigurd, The. AWP, *tr. by* Eirikr Magnusson and
    William Morris
    "And now one prayer." OBVE
    (Part of the Lay of Sigrdrifa.) OBVE
    Voluspo. AWP, *tr. by* Henry Adams Bellows
    Words of the All-Wise, The. WoPoe, *tr. by* Wystan Hugh Auden and Paul B.
    Taylor
    "Say, Dwarf, for it seems to me." OBVE, *tr. by* Wystan Hugh Auden and
    Paul B. Taylor

Elder Father, though thine eyes. Holy of Holies, The. Gilbert Keith
    Chesterton. SacPr

Elder lives by the side of the river, An. Juan Chi. ColAnChi *Fr.* Songs of
    My Soul.

Elder's Reproof to his Wife, An. 'Abdillaahi Muuse. TTY, *tr. by* B. W.
    Andrejewski and I. M. Lewis

Elder Sister, The. Sharon Olds. NIL-7; NIP-4

Elder Stonegate treats the body like a dream. Written in Jest on Elder
    Stonegate's Eastern Balcony. Liu Tsung-yüan. SuSp, *tr. by* Jan W. Walls

Elderblossom. Johannes Bobrowski. AF

Elderly bride of Port Jervis, An. Limerick. Ogden Nash. PeLi

Elderly Lady Crossing on Green. Wyatt Prunty. RA

Elders and officers line the returning road. Good-bye to the People of
    Hangchow. Po Chü-i. ChiP, *tr. by* Arthur Waley

Elders Are Gods, The. Tijan M. Sallah. NAfrP

Eldorado. Edgar Allan Poe. APN-1; AWP; ColAP; FaBoCh; NOBA; OxBA;
    PAI; TAP; TCAPo
    (Gaily bedight.) ChAP; NCAP; NOxBChV; NoP-4

Eleanor (she spoiled in a British climate). Ezra Pound. NOBA; NoAM *Fr.*
    Cantos.

Eleanora Duse. Amy Lowell.
    Seeing You Stand Once More before My Eyes. Son

Eleazar Wheelock. Richard Hovey. OBAL

Elect. Mary Ursula Bethell. PeNZ

Elected Knight, The. *Unknown.* AWP, *tr. by* Henry Wadsworth Longfellow

Elected Silence. Siegfried Sassoon. MoBrPo

Elected Silence, sing to me. Habit of Perfection, The. Gerard Manley
Hopkins. ChIV-2; MoBrPo; NoAM; OBEV; OBMV; OxAEP-2; PoRA;
    RB; SacPr; TFi

Elected virgins, The. Wedding in Hanover. Lorna Goodison. GT

Election. Oswald de Andrade. TCLAP, *tr. by* Flavia Vidal

Election, The. Sitakant Mahapatra. OMIP, *tr. by* Sitakant Mahapatra

Election, The. Leonard Nathan. PBCAP

Election Day. R. Zamora-Linmark. ReBoTo

Election Day, 1984. Carolyn Kizer. ExTi; GifTon

Election Eve, with Cat. Alex Skovron. BMAP

Election Reflection. M. Keel Jones. NBLV

Election Time. Lamont B. Steptoe. UnSA

Election Time. *Unknown.* UV

Electra. György Petri. VCWP, *tr. by* George Gömöri and Clive Wilmer

Electric Elegy. Adam Zagajewski. VCWP, *tr. by* Renata Gorcyznski

Electric Orchard, The. Paul Muldoon. HarvBoo

Electrical Hierarchy, The. Konrad Bayer. PFTM-2, *tr. by* Walter Billeter *Fr.*
    Philosopher's Stone, The.

Electrical, naked in the hot marble that filters from skin to clothes. Beautiful
    Ones, The. Gonzalo Rojas. BLPSL, *tr. by* Rene de Costa, Rigas
    Kappatos and Eleni Paidoussi

Electricity Breadthwise. Marcel Duchamp. PFTM-1

Electricity of Blossoms. Lorenzo Thomas. FTOS

Electroconvulsive Therapy. Elspeth Cameron Ritchie. BloBone

Electrocution. Lola Ridge. WPE

Electronic Sound. May Swenson. APT-2

Elegance. Christopher Smart. NOCV *Fr.* Hymns for the Amusement of
    Children.

Elegance in the Extreme. Ntozake Shange. SeSe

Elegant use of foliage and grace, An. Gertrude Stein. TCAPo *Fr.* Tender
    Buttons.

Elegant Women, The. Tu Fu. SuSp, *tr. by* Mark Perlberg

Elegiac Ballad, An. Hannah Cowley. ECWP

Elegiac Sonnet to a Mopstick. William Beckford. CenSon

Elegiac Stanzas Suggested by a Picture of Peele Castle, in a Storm, Painted by
    Sir George Beaumont. William Wordsworth. GTBS-P; NAEL-5v2;
    NAEL-6v2; NOBRP; NoP-4; NPeEn; PoE
    (I was thy neighbor once, thou rugged Pile!) GS; NoP-4
    (Suggested by a Picture of Peele Castle, in a Storm, Painted by Sir George
    Beaumont.) GS

Elegiac Verse. Henry Wadsworth Longfellow.
    "Peradventure of old, some bard in Ionian Islands." APN-1

Elegiac Verse 12. Henry Wadsworth Longfellow. TCAPo

Elegiack Verse on Mr. Elijah Corlet, An. Nehemiah Walter. SCAP

Élegie. Pernette De [*or* Du] Guillet.
    "But if he came straight for me." EroLit, *tr. by* T. Anthony Perry

Elegie on the Deplorable Departure of the Honered and Truely Religious
    Chieftain John Hull, An. John Saffin. SCAP

Elegie upon the Death of the Deane of Pauls, Dr. John Donne, An. Thomas
    Carew. *See* Elegy upon the Death of the Dean of [St.] Paul's, Dr. John
    Donne, An

Elegie upon the Death of the Reverend. . .Mr. Thomas Shepard, An. Urian
    Oakes. SCAP
    "Away loose-reined careers of poetry!" NOCV

Elegie Written by the Lady A. S. to the Countesse of London Derrye
    Supposyenge Hir to be Dead by Hir Long Silence, An. Lady Anne Harris
    Southwell. EMWP

Elegies. André Marie de Chénier. AWP, *tr. by* Arthur Symons
    "Happy is he given to sage disciplines." WoPoe, *tr. by* David Curzon and
    Jeffrey Fiskin

Elegies. John Donne.
    ("As thou by comming neere, keep'st them from me.") (LL) RACG
    Autumnal[l], The. BASC; FSCP; NOSC
    Change. EBEV
    Comparison, The. BASC; PeLV
    His Parting from Her. EBEV
    His Picture. FSCP; MeLP; OxAEP-1; PBRV
    (Jealosie.) ESCV
    Love's Progress. BASC
    "Nature's lay idiot [*or* ideot], I taught thee to love." BASC; NoP-4; OxAEP-
    1; PeLV
    "Oh, let me not serve so, as those men serve." BASC
    On His Mistress [*or* Mistris]. BoLoP; CABP; EBEV; ESCV; FSCP; MeLP;
    NAEL-5v1; NAEL-6v1; NAEL-7v1; NPeEn; NoSic; OxAEP-1; SCGP
    Perfume, The. ESCV; FSCP; NoSic
    (Sapho To Philaenis.) RACG
    (To His Mistress Desiring to Travel with Him as His Page.) NOBE
    To His Mistress Going to Bed. BASC; BoLoP; FSCP; NAEL-6v1; NAEL-
    7v1; NoP-4; NoSic; PBRV; PoE
    (To His Mistris Going to Bed.) EroLit; OxAEP-1; OxBEV; WoPoe

Elegies. Douglas Dunn.
   "She sat up on her pillows, receiving guests." NoP-4
Elegies. Hugh Maxton. PBCIP
Elegies. Ovid.
   1.2.
   "What makes my bed seem hard seeing it is soft?" AWP, *tr. by* Christopher Marlowe
   1.3.
   "I ask but right: let her that caught me late." EBEV, *tr. by* Christopher Marlowe
   1.4.
   "Thy husband to a banquet goes with me." CABP; NoSic, *tr. by* Christopher Marlowe
   ("Your husband will be with us at the treat.") BoLoP, *tr. by* John Dryden
   1.5.
   (Elegy to His Mistress.) ErotSp
   "In summer's heat[e] and mid-time of the day." BoLoP; CABP; EBEV; NPeEn; NoSic; OBVE; OxAEP-1; OxBEV, *tr. by* Christopher Marlowe
   1.14.
   "Old man's fair-haired consort, whole dewy axle-tree, The." AWP, *tr. by* Kirby Flower Smith
   1.15.
   "Envy, why carp'st thou my time is spent so ill." CABP; NoSic, *tr. by* Christopher Marlowe
   2.1.
   "I, Ovid, poet of my wantonness." OBVE, *tr. by* Christopher Marlowe
   2.8.
   "Cypassis, that a thousand ways trim'st hair." EBEV, *tr. by* Christopher Marlowe
   2.10.
   "Graecinus (well I wot) thou told'st me once." EBEV, *tr. by* Christopher Marlowe
   3.1.
   "Old wood stands uncut, of long year's space, An." CABP, *tr. by* Christopher Marlowe
   3.6.
   "Either she was foul, or her attire was bad." CABP; OBVE, *tr. by* Christopher Marlowe
   3.13.
   "Seeing thou art fair, I bar not thy false playing." OBVE, *tr. by* Christopher Marlowe
   ("Seeing thou art faire, I barre not thy false playing.") NPeEn
Elegies. Propertius. AWP
   Ah Woe Is Me. AWP, *tr. by* F. A. Wright
   Hylas. AWP, *tr. by* F. A. Wright
   "Night's best of all. Night brings delight." EroLit, *tr. by* Kenneth McLeish
   Revenge to Come. AWP, *tr. by* Kirby Flower Smith
Elegies on the Cardinal Points. Yelena [*or* Elena] Shwarts [*or* Shvarts]. VCWP, *tr. by* Michael Molnar
Elegies, or the Stations of the Other Time. Ahmad 'Abd al-Mu'ti Hijazi. MAP, *tr. by* May Jayyusi and Naomi Shihab Nye
Elegist, The. Geoff Page. BMAP
Elegy. Yehuda Amichai [*or* Amikhai]. PFTM-2, *tr. by* Stephen Mitchell
Elegy. Frank Bidart. HCAP
Elegy. Joseph Brodsky. AF, *tr. by* Joseph Brodsky
Elegy. Constance Carrier. APT-2
Elegy. Arthur L. Clements. UnSA
Elegy. Black Autumn. Aida Cartagena de Portalatin. TANSG, *tr. by* Daisy Cocco De Filippis
Elegy. Carolyn Forché. ExTi; LoL
Elegy. Raymond Mazisi Kunene. PBMAP
Elegy: "My Prime of Youth Is but a Frost of Cares." Chidiock Tichborne [*or* Tichbourne]. *See* Tichborne's Elegy
Elegy. Tomas Tranströmer. WoPoe, *tr. by* Robert Bly
Elegy. *Unknown. See* Lament: "Cheek by cheek on our pillow[s]"
Elegy 2. Anacreon. CAGL, *tr. by* Peter Bing and Rip Cohen
Elegy V: [Separation of Man from God]. George Barker. FaBoTw
Elegy VII. Ezra Pound. VGW *Fr.* Homage to Sextus Propertius.
Elegy 11: "Ah me, my friend! it will not, will not last!" William Shenstone. NOEC
Elegy 11: Ford. Eric Mottram. Oth
Elegy 23: "How does it help me if, with flawless art." Louise Labé. WPOW, *tr. by* Raymond Oliver
Elegy: "Alone, with harsh marine aloneness." José Gorostiza. TCLAP, *tr. by* Rachel Benson
Elegy, An: "Love, give me leave to serve thee, and be wise." Thomas Randolph. BeJo; NOSC
Elegy, An: "She fell away in her first ages spring." Edmund Spenser. OBEV *Fr.* Daphnaïda.

Elegy, An: "Though beauty be the mark of praise." Ben Jonson. BeJo; NoP-4; OBEV
Elegy: "April again, and it is a year again." Sidney Keyes. NoP-4
Elegy as Evening, as Exodus. James Harms. GeoHom
Elegy: "At first the dead." Henriqueta Lisboa. TCLAP, *tr. by* Hélcio Veiga Costa
Elegy: "Cross between a bakehouse and a bell tower, A." Oleg Grigorevich Chukhonstev. TCRP, *tr. by* Simon Franklin
Elegy: "Cur foretells the knell of parting day, The." Ambrose Bierce. APN-2; OBAL *Fr.* Devil's Dictionary, The.
Elegy: "Death be not proud, thy hand gave not this blow." Lucy Harington, Countess of Bedford. EMWP; PeECV; WPE
Elegy: "Do not look for him." Leonard Cohen. HeIP-4
Elegy does not raise its wistful tone in downpour of southern shine, An. To Tarshish. Shimon Halkin. MHP, *tr. by* Ruth Finer Mintz
Elegy: "Fled is the swiftness of all the white-footed ones." Joseph Auslander. TrJP
Elegy: "Floods of tears well from my deepest heart, The." Immanuel di Roma. TrJP, *tr. by* J. Chotzner
Elegy for a Child. Gregory Orr. BodElec
Elegy for a Dead Soldier. Karl Shapiro. HAP; OBWP; OxBA
Elegy for a Forest Clear-Cut by the Weyerhaeuser Company. David Wagoner. NoAM
Elegy for a Man Who Died and Died. Mamdouh 'Udwan. MAP, *tr. by* May Jayyusi and Naomi Shihab Nye
Elegy for a Professor. Nicholas Samaras. TWW
Elegy for a School-Friend. Augustus Young. BIrV
Elegy for a Schoolmate. Vincent O'Sullivan. PeNZ
Elegy for a White Cock. Mei Yao Ch'en. SuSp, *tr. by* Jonathan Chaves
Elegy for a Woman of No Importance. Nazik Al-Mala'ika. ItWoWo, *tr. by* Chris Knipp, Mohammed Sadiq and Mohammad Sadiq
Elegy for Aisha. Abdul Wahab [*or* 'Abd al-Wahhab] Al-Bayati [*or* Al-Bayyati]. MAP, *tr. by* Sargon Boulus and Christopher Middleton
Elegy for Alto. Christopher Okigbo. HBAPE; VCWP
Elegy for Bob Marley, An. William Matthews. SwNoth
Elegy for Chief Sealth. Duane Niatum. CDW
Elegy for Chloe Nguyen. Marilyn Chin. UnSA
Elegy for David Beynon. Leslie Norris. AngWePo; TCAWP
Elegy for Drowned Children. Bruce Dawe. BMAP; NOBAu
Elegy for Elvis. Richard Blessing. AllShUp; SwNoth
Elegy for Faustina. Fergus Allen. ModIr
Elegy for Hassan Nasir. Faiz Ahmad Faiz. CarOv, *tr. by* Carolyn Kizer
Elegy for Her Brother Sakhr. Al-Khansa. BoWoP, *tr. by* Willis Barnstone
Elegy for Her Brother Sakhr. Al-Khansa. WPOW
Elegy for Himself. Chidiock Tichborne [*or* Tichbourne]. *See* Tichborne's Elegy
Elegy (for Himself). Moses Rimos of Majorca. TrJP, *tr. by* Israel Abrahams
Elegy for His Daughter Ellen. Goronwy Owen. OBWVE, *tr. by* George Borrow
Elegy for Jack Bowman. Joseph Bruchac. CDW
Elegy for Jane. Theodore Roethke. APT-2; CoAP; ColAP; HAP; HCAP; InPK-6; MoAmPo; NoP-4; PAI; PoE; PoPoPo; TAP; TFi; TRP; TwCP; WeW-3
Elegy for Jim Larkin. Patrick Kavanagh. ModIr
Elegy for Joan the Mad One. Federico García Lorca. BLPSL, *tr. by* Rene de Costa, Rigas Kappatos and Eleni Paidoussi
Elegy for Llywelyn Humphries. Meic Stephens. TCAWP
Elegy for Lyn James. Leslie Norris. OBWVE; TCAWP
Elegy for Mangochi Fishermen, An. Jack A. Mapanje. PBMAP
Elegy for Mélusine from the Intensive Care Ward. Ramon Guthrie. APT-2
Elegy for Minor Poets. Louis MacNeice. CABP; PNI
Elegy (for MOVE and Philadelphia). Sonia Sanchez. ESEAA
Elegy for Mr. Goodbeare. Sir Osbert Sitwell. MoBrPo
Elegy for My Father. Howard Moss. CoAP
Elegy for My Father. Mark Strand. HCAP; LCAP-2
   Empty Body, The. UnPo
   New Year, The. UnPo
Elegy for My Father, Who Is Not Dead. Andrew Hudgins. RA
Elegy for My Friend E. Galo. Raymond Mazisi Kunene. PoetW
Elegy for My Mother. Andrey [*or* Andrei] Andreievich Voznesensky [*or* Voznesenskii]. TCRP, *tr. by* F. D. Reeve and William Jay Smith
Elegy for My Sister. Howard Moss. VCAP
Elegy for Myself. Ki Joon. GifTon, *tr. by* Sung-Il Lee
Elegy for N. N. Czeslaw Milosz. BodElec, *tr. by* Larence Davis
Elegy for New York, The. Douglas Crase. MakPoe
Elegy for Sir Ifor Williams. Anthony Conran. AngWePo
Elegy for 6 So Far. Gig Ryan. BMAP
Elegy for Slit-Drum. Christopher Okigbo. HBAPE

Elegy for the Dead of Soweto. Thembinkosi Ndlovu. PeSAV, *tr. by* Chris Mann

Elegy for the Duke. Robert Dana. SeSe

Elegy for the Duke of Marmalade. Luis Palés Matos. TCLAP, *tr. by* Ellen G. Matilla and Diego de la Texera

Elegy for the Giant Tortoises. Margaret Atwood. BoWoP

Elegy for the Great Inca Atawallpa, The. *Unknown*.
"You all by yourself fulfilled." WoPoe, *tr. by* W. S. Merwin

Elegy for the Lost Parish. Douglas Dunn. DiPo

Elegy for the Monastery Barn. Thomas Merton. VGW

Elegy for the Nightbound. Anthony Cronin. PBCIP

Elegy for the Revolution. Kofi Anyidoho. NAfrP

Elegy for the Time at Hand. "Adonis" [*or* "Adunis"]. AF, *tr. by* Samuel Hazo

Elegy for the Unknown Soldier. Michael O'Loughlin. PBCIP

Elegy for the Welsh Dead, in the Falkland Islands, 1982. Anthony Conran. TCAWP

Elegy for the Wife of a Friend. Yü Hsüan-chi. BoWoP, *tr. by* Geoffrey Waters

Elegy for Thelonious. Yusef Komunyakaa. ESEAA

Elegy for Two Banjos. Karl Shapiro. TrJP

Elegy for W. C. W., the Lovely Man, An. John Berryman. MakPoe *Fr. Dream Songs.*

Elegy for William Soutar. William Montgomerie. OxBS

Elegy for Wright & Hugo. Norman Dubie. NoAM

Elegy for Your Absence. Eugenio Florit. TCLAP, *tr. by* Hoffman Reynolds Hays

Elegy: "Friend, whose unnatural early death." David Gascoyne. FaBoTw; TwCP

Elegy: "From the old settlements only the writings." Slavko Mihalic. PoSu, *tr. by* Charles Simic

Elegy: "I die for Your holy word without regret." Antonio Enriquez Gomez. TrJP

Elegy: "I expected him to look dead in the casket." Richard Hugo. GM

Elegy: "I know but will not tell." Alan Dugan. NIL-7; NIP-4

Elegy: "I must wait for a stranger to knock on my door." David Ignatow. NNaP

Elegy: "I've won (lost) my day." Carlos Drummond de Andrade. TCLAP, *tr. by* Virginia de Araújo

Elegy in a Country Churchyard. Gilbert Keith Chesterton. FaBoWar; MoBrPo; OBWP; OxBSP

Elegy in a Presbyterian Burying-Ground. Robert Noble Denison Wilson. BIrV

Elegy in a Spider's Web. Laura Riding Jackson. PFTM-1

Elegy in an Abandoned Boatyard. Dave Jeddie Smith. VCAP

Elegy in Memory of the Worshipful Major Thomas Leonard Esq, An. Samuel, Jr. Danforth. SCAP

Elegy in Newgate. William Cobbett. UV

Elegy: "In pain she bore the son who her embrace." Moses Ibn Ezra. TrJP, *tr. by* Solomon Solis-Cohen

Elegy in the Manner of a Requiem in Memory of D. H. Lawrence. Walter Lowenfels.
Among the Luminals. APT-2

Elegy: "In the May breeze." M. Safdar Mir. CarOv, *tr. by* Carolyn Kizer

Elegy Is Preparing Itself, An. Donald Justice. CRP

Elegy: Ise Lamenting the Death of Empress Onshi. Lady Ise. BoWoP, *tr. by* Etsuko Terasaki

Elegy Just in Case. John Ciardi. TwCP

Elegy: "Leaves have a sense of, The." Lewis Warsh. BodElec

Elegy: "Let them bury your big eyes." Edna St. Vincent Millay. APT-1; MoAmPo; OxBA; PoRA *Fr. Memorial to D. C.*

Elegy: "My thoughts impelled me to the resting-place." Moses Ibn Ezra. TrJP, *tr. by* Emma Lazarus

Elegy: "Newspaper appears in the morning, The." Khalifa Al-Wugayyan. MAP, *tr. by* John Heath-Stubbs and Lena Jayyusi

Elegy: "No more, no more Jewish townships in Poland." Antoni Slonimski. HP, *tr. by* Isaac Komen

Elegy: "Noon is beautiful: the perfect wheel, The." Yvor Winters. VGW

Elegy: "Nor Hammond's love nor Shenstone's was sincere." John Maclaurin, Lord Dreghorn. NOEC

Elegy: "O loveliest daughter of Hsieh." Yuan Chen. CrYelRi; ErotSp, *tr. by* Sam Hamill

Elegy: "O [*or* Oh] snatch'd away in beauty's bloom!" Byron. GTBS-P

Elegy of a Knight. Fadwa Tuqan [*or* Tuquan]. PoArWo, *tr. by* Samira Kawar

Elegy of Fortinbras. Zbigniew Herbert. PoSu; VCWP; WoPoe, *tr. by* Czeslaw Milosz

Elegy of Our Times. Eugenio Montale. ItPo, *tr. by* Gayle Ridinger

Elegy of the Wind. Christopher Okigbo. VCWP

Elegy on a Broom Bush. Árpád Tóth. IQMS, *tr. by* Neville Masterman

Elegy on a Favorite Cat, An. Anne Francis.

"When cats like him submit to fate." ECWP

Elegy on a Lady, Whom Grief for the Death of Her Betrothed Killed. Robert Bridges. OBEV

Elegy on a Maiden Name, An. Jane Cave. CABP; ECWP

Elegy on a Young Airedale Bitch Lost Two Years Since in the Salt-Marsh. Yvor Winters. APT-2

Elegy on a Young Lady. Anne Batten Cristall. RWP

Elegy on a Young Thrush Which Escaped from the Writer's Hand. Helen Maria Williams. ECWP

Elegy on a Young Warrior. Ponmutiyar. WoPoe

Elegy on an X-ray Photo of My Skull. Yelena [*or* Elena] Shwarts [*or* Shvarts]. ItGoST; VCWP, *tr. by* Catriona Kelly and Michael Molnar

Elegy on Any Lady by George Moore. Max Beerbohm. FaBoEE

Elegy on Ben Jonson, An. John Cleveland. MeLP

Elegy on Cynddylan, The. *Unknown*.
"Stand out, maids, and look on the land of Cynddylan." OBWVE

Elegy on D. D. Sidney Godolphin. BeJo

Elegy on Mael Mhedha, His Wife. Muireadhach Albanach Ó Dálaigh. NePenScot, *tr. by* Thomas Owen Clancy

Elegy on Reichenau. Walafrid Strabo. NAWM-7v1, *tr. by* Peter Godman

Elegy on the Death of a Mad Dog, An. Oliver Goldsmith. FaBoCh; NBLV; NOEC; NOIV; OBNV; OxAEP-1; TFi *Fr. Vicar of Wakefield, The.*

Elegy on the Death of Dobbin, the Butterwoman's Horse, An. Francis Fawkes. NOEC

Elegy on the Death of Her Husband. Anne Howard, Duchess of Arundel. *See* Good Shepherd's Sorrow for the Death of His Beloved Son, The

Elegy on the Death of Mr Sterne. Miles Peter Andrews. NOBRP

Elegy on the Dust. Thom Gunn. NoAM *Fr. Misanthropos.*

Elegy on the Earl of Rochester. Anne Wharton. NOSC

Elegy on the Pilot. Reuel Denney.
"Death in an ancient country was a simple passport." YaYoPo

Elegy on Thomas Hood. Martin Fagg. NOBL; UV

Elegy on Thyrza. Byron. GTBS-P

Elegy: "Outworn year has altered his apparel, The." Miklós Zrínyi. IQMS, *tr. by* Watson Kirkconnell

Elegy over a Tomb. Edward Herbert, 1st Baron Herbert of Cherbury. MeLP; NOBE; OBEV; OBWVE

Elegy Residence on Earth. Robert Hass. BodElec

Elegy: "There is a question." Max Winter. NeAmPo

Elegy: "They are lang deid, folk that I used to ken." Robert Garioch. NPeEn; NePenScot; OxBS

Elegy: "Those reckless hosts rush to the wells." Baruch of Worms. TrJP

Elegy to a Dissected Puppy, An. Georgia Bailey Parrington.
"Sweet Dog! now cold and stiff in death." VerBaPo

Elegy, to an Old Beauty, An. Thomas Parnell. ECEV; NOEC

Elegy to His Mistress. Ovid. *See* Elegies

Elegy: To Spring. Michael Bruce.
"Farewell, ye blooming fields! ye cheerful plains!" NOEC

Elegy to the Memory of an Unfortunate Lady. Pope. ECEV; NOBE; NOEC; OBEV; SCGP

Elegy: "Tonight the moon is high, to summon all." William Bell. FaBoTw

Elegy upon His Tomb in Herndon-Hill Church, Erected by His Wife, Who Speaks, An. James Howell. OBWVE

Elegy upon Old Freeman, An. Matthew Stevenson.
"Here in this homely cabinet." NOSC

Elegy upon S[ir] W[alter] R[aleigh], An. Henry King, Bishop of Chichester. NOSC

Elegy upon the Death of Doctor [*or* Dr.] Donne, Dean of Paul's, An. Thomas Carew. *See* Elegy upon the Death of the Dean of [St.] Paul's, Dr. John Donne, An

Elegy upon the Death of His Own Father, An. Richard Corbet [*or* Corbett]. BeJo; NOSC

Elegy upon the Death of Mrs. A. Behn, the Incomparable Astrea, An. *Unknown*. EMWP

Elegy upon the Death of the Dean of [St.] Paul's, Dr. John Donne, An. Thomas Carew. BASC; CABP; CaPo; CavPo; NAEL-6v1; NAEL-7v1; NoP-4
On the Death of Donne. NOBE

Elegy upon the Lady Venetia Digby, An. Thomas Randolph. BASC

Elegy: "Wander, my troubled soul, sigh mid the night thy pain." Anne Batten Cristall. RWP

Elegy: "We carved our names." Chang Chi. CrYelRi, *tr. by* Sam Hamill

Elegy: "We first lay down among flowers." Ikkyu Sojun. ErotSp, *tr. by* Sam Hamill

Elegy: "What remains of the suicide's voice is the last conversation." Edgar Silex. NAPBL

Elegy: "Who would I show it to." W. S. Merwin. HCAP

Elegy: "Wood is bare: a river-mist is steeping, The." Robert Bridges. EBVV

Elegy Written in a Country Churchyard. Thomas Gray. AWP; BRP; CABP;

ClHu; EBEV; FHYEP; GTBS-P; HAP; HeIP-4; InPK-6; MakPoe; NAEL-6v1; NAEL-7v1; NIL-7; NOBE; NOEC; NPeEn; NoP-4; OBEV; OxAEP-1; OxBEV; PoPoPo; SCGP; SCV; TFi; TreFP; UV; UnPo; WeW-3

"Curfew tolls the knell of parting day, The."   UV

Epitaph: "Here rests his head upon the lap of earth."   FHYEP; SCGP

Elegy Written in a Country Coal-Bin.   Christopher Darlington Morley.   OBAL

Elegy, Written with His Own Hand in the Tower before His Execution. Chidiock Tichborne [or Tichbourne].   See Tichborne's Elegy

Elegy Wrote in a Country Church Yard, An.   Thomas Gray.   See Elegy Written in a Country Churchyard

Element.   Patricia K. Page.   MoCV

Element Mother, The.   Lorine Niedecker.   FTOS

Element that utters doves, angels and cleft flames.   Air.   Kathleen Jessie Raine. MoBrPo

Elemental.   Marjorie M. Evasco.   ReBoTo

Elemental.   D. H. Lawrence.   NoP-4

Elementary.   Jim Tollerud.   VoR

Elementary Cosmogony.   Charles Simic.   NNaP

Elementary Scene, The.   Randall Jarrell.   PoE

Elementary School Classroom in a Slum, An.   Stephen Spender.   FaBoMo; MoBrPo; TwCP; UnPo

Elements, The.   William Henry Davies.   MoBrPo

Elements, The.   Tom Lehrer.   UV

Elements, The.   John Henry, Cardinal Newman.   SacPr

Elements have merged into solicitude, The.   Racer's Widow, The.   Louise Glück.   MoASP

Elements of Composition.   A. K. Ramanujan.   VCWP

Elements of San Joaquin, The.   Gary Soto.   GeoHom; PBCAP

Rain.   NoAM

Wind.   NoAM

Elena.   Pat Mora.   NIL-7; UnSA

Elena's Song.   Sir Henry Taylor.   OBEV; RACG   Fr. Philip van Artevelde.

Elene.   Cynewulf.   AnOE, tr. by Charles W. Kennedy

Elephant.   Pablo Neruda.

"Gross innocent."   TTTS

Elephant [I], The.   Unknown.   TTTS; TTY, tr. by Ulli Beier and Bakare Gbadamosi

Elephant [II], The.   Unknown.   TTY, tr. by C. M. Bowra

Elephant beaten with candy and little pops and chews.   Gertrude Stein.   TTTS Fr. Tender Buttons.

Elephant Hunt in Guadalajara.   Jack Gilbert.   BodElec

Elephant in his tub, An.   Twilight.   Philippe Soupault.   SurPaPo, tr. by Mary Ann Caws and Patricia Terry

Elephant in Winter, The.   Michael Van Walleghen.   UrbNat

Elephant of Moissel, hear my pious prayer.   Léopold Sédar Senghor.   NegPo Fr. Return of the Prodigal Son.

Elephant on a ball presents a Shakespearean spectacle, An.   Modern circus, The.   Pierre McOrlan.   MFP, tr. by Martin Sorrell

Elephant, or the Force of Habit, The.   A. E. Housman.   NOBL

Elephant Rocks.   Kay Ryan.   ExTi

Elephant who brings death.   Elephant [I], The.   Unknown.   TTTS; TTY, tr. by Ulli Beier and Bakare Gbadamosi

Elephants Are Different to Different People.   Carl Sandburg.   MoAmPo

Elephants Are in the Yard, The.   Indran Amirthanayagam.   OpBo

Elephants Dying, The.   Michael C. Blumenthal.   NoAM

"Elephants in bed," my daughter says.   Vision.   Louis Johnson.   PeNZ

Elephants of Thailand perform their bows extremely well, The.   Elephants of Thailand.   So Chong-Ju.   WoPoe, tr. by David R. McCann

Elephants walking.   Holding Hands.   Lenore M. Link.   NTCP

Eletelephony.   Laura Elizabeth Richards.   NBLV; NOxBChV; NTCP; OBCA; OxIBACP

Élévation.   Charles Baudelaire.   AWP, tr. by Arthur Symons

Elevator operator.   Mr. 'Gator.   N. M. Bodecker.   NTCP

11.   Catullus.   NAWM-7v1, tr. by Charles Martin

Eleven.   Archibald MacLeish.   HAP; WeW-3

Eleven A.M. on My Day Off, My Sister Phones Desperate for a Babysitter. Sharon Hashimoto.   FSt; OpBo

Eleven Addresses to the Lord.   John Berryman.   OxBC

"Master of beauty, craftsman of the snowflake."   InvLi; PAI; UnPo

"Sole watchman of the flying stars, guard me."   UnPo

Eleven he courts, twelve he marries. (LL)   Unknown.   LB; OxNR

Eleven o'clock and the bar is empty.   Hat Factory, The.   Paul Durcan.   BiHa; ModIr

Eleven Rock Poems.   Gustaf Sobin.   PmAP

11 rue Daguerre.   John Montague.   ModIr; NPeEn

Eleven Stars over Andalusia.   Mahmoud Darwish.

"On our last evening on this land we chop our days."   PoetW, tr. by Agha Shahid Ali, Mona Anis, Ahmad Dallal and Nigel Ryan

Eleven struck. Check the little clock.   Mighty Ocean, The.   Ilya [or Karl] L'vovich Selvinsky [or Sel'vinskii].   TCRP, tr. by Daniel Weissbort

11/10 Again.   Lucille Clifton.   GT

Eleven-thirty and hot.   Cyclist, The.   Marge Piercy.   NoAM

Eleventh Vertical Poetry.   Roberto Juarroz.

"Every word is a doubt."   VCWP

Elf Shots.   Peter Riley.   Oth

Elfer Hill.   Unknown.   AWP, tr. by Robert Jamieson

Elfin Knight, The.   Unknown.   ESPB

Elfrida.   László Arany.   IQMS, tr. by Watson Kirkconnell

Eli, Eli.   Judith Wright.   BMAP; CBAP; GI

Eliahu.   Tamara Kamenszain.   MirDau, tr. by Roberta Gordenstein

Elijah's Wagon knew no thill.   Emily Dickinson.   ChIV-1

Elijah Speaking.   Doug Fetherling.   NOBC

Elinda's [or Ellinda's] Glove.   Richard Lovelace.   CaPo; NOSC

(Thou snowy farm with thy five tenements!)   CavPo

Elinor Glyn.   Unknown.   OBCoV

Elinour Rumming.   John Skelton.

"Instead of coin and money."   NoSic

Elis.   Georg Trakl.   WoPoe, tr. by Robert Firmage

Elis, when the blackbird calls in the black forest.   To the Child Elis.   Georg Trakl.   WoPoe, tr. by Robert Firmage

Elise.   Alan Wearne.   BMAP   Fr. Nightmarkets, The.

Elite Syncopations.   Richard Garcia.   TouFir

Elitere Lyric Poetry.   Theresa Hak Kyung Cha.   PFTM-2   Fr. Dictée.

Elites, levels, proletariat.   Satis Passio.   Les A. Murray.   HarvBoo

Elixir.   Richard Murphy.   BiHa

Elixir [or Elixer], The.   George Herbert.   BASC; ESCV; EnlH; FaBoCh; GeHe; NOSC; NoP-4; SacPr

Eliza Harris.   Frances Ellen Watkins Harper.   NAAAL

Eliza in Uncle Tom's Cabin.   Eloise Bibb.   CBWP-4

Elizabeth.   Michael Ondaatje.   NoAM

Elizabeth.   Sylvia Townsend Warner.   MoBrPo

Elizabeth, Elspeth, Betsy, and Bess.   Mother Goose.   OxNR; ReMoGo

Elizabeth, frigidly stretched.   This Houre Her Vigill.   Valentin Iremonger.   CIP-2; ModIr; NOIV; OxBTC

Elizabeth Hoby, Wife, to Thomas Hoby, Knight, Her Husband.   Elizabeth Cooke Hoby.   EMWP

Elizabeth in Italy.   Richard Weber.   BoLoP

Elizabeth lies here (alas for my heart), thus fated.   Epicedium by Elizabeth Hoby, Their Mother, on the Death of Her Two Daughters Elizabeth and Anne, An.   Elizabeth Cooke Hoby.   EMWP

Elizabeth of Bohemia.   Sir Henry Wotton.   See On His Mistress [or Mistris], the Queen of Bohemia

Elizabeth's War with the Christmas Bear.   Norman Dubie.   LCAP-2; NoAM

Elizabeth / Szilágyi.   Mother of King Matthias, The.   János Arany.   IQMS, tr. by Neville Masterman

"Elizabeth the Beloved."   Elizabeth.   Sylvia Townsend Warner.   MoBrPo

Elizabeth Walters is my name.   Elizabeth Walters.   FaBoVe

Elizabethan & Nova Scotian Music.   Charles North.   PmAP

Elizabethans Called It Dying, The.   James Schuyler.   NeAP; PoM

Elk, The Whelk, The.   Robert Williams Wood.   NBLV

Elkhorn Slough.   Abigail Albrecht.   GeoHom

Ella, fell a / Maple tree.   Picnic.   Hugh Lofting.   OTCP

Ella, in a Square Apron, Along Highway 80.   Judy Grahn.   NALW   Fr. Common Woman, The.

Ella Mi Fu Rapita!   Gavin Ewart.   NoAM

Ellen Learning to Walk.   Frances Sargent Osgood.   ColAP

Ellen West.   Frank Bidart.   NAAL-2v2; RACG

Ellenore.   William Taylor.   NOBRP

Ellin Thorne Songe.   Ellin Thorne.   EMWP

Ellington is dead. Elegy for the Duke.   Robert Dana.   SeSe

Elliott Hawkins.   Edgar Lee Masters.   OxBA   Fr. Spoon River Anthology.

Ellis Britton was standing outside the churchhouse.   Benediction.   David Lee. GifTon

Ellis Island, September 1907.   Andrea Hollander Budy.   OPRER

Elm.   Robert Hass.   BodElec

Elm.   Sylvia Plath.   NOBA; NoAM; NoP-4

Elm, laburnum, hawthorn, oak.   Trees.   Fleur Adcock.   OBGa

Elm Tree in Paddington, An.   Robert Adamson.   BMAP

Elm Tree on Lafayette Street, The.   Rod Kessler.   OPRER

Elms.   Louise Glück.   NoAM

Elms have to fight, The.   Home Movies.   Carter Revard.   VoR

Elms here are easy to talk about, The.   Park Elms.   Charles Ghigna.   UrbNat

Eloi, Eloi, Lama Sabachthani?   D. H. Lawrence.   GI

Eloisa to Abelard.   Pope.   NAEL-5v1; NAEL-6v1; NAEL-7v1; RACG

(Life of a Nun.)   ECEV

Elopement and civil wedding . . . the sham squire. Distaff Side, The. Harry Clifton. PBCIP

Eloquent between the formal hedges. Affair of Honour. George Whalley. MoCV

Elphin knight sits on yon hill, The. Elfin Knight, The. *Unknown.* ESPB

Elsa Wertman. Edgar Lee Masters. NoAM; OxBA; PAI *Fr.* Spoon River Anthology.

Else a great Prince in prison lies. Denise Levertov. VGW

Else tears heap all within one clay-cold hill. (LL) To Emily Dickinson. Hart Crane. ColAP; NIL-7; NIP-4; NOBA; NoAM; NoP-4; Son; TAP

Elsewhere. Lynn Emanuel. BodElec

Elsewhere. "Michael Field." VWP

Elsewhere, Things Tend. Claudia Rankine. AmPoNex

Elsie Marley is grown so fine. *Unknown.* OxNR

Elude me still, keep ever just before. Mystery. Lizette Woodworth Reese. SWaP

Elusive Maid, The. Abraham Ibn-Chasdai. TrJP, *tr. by* J. Chotzner

Elusive Shadow of My Substance, Stay. Sister Juana Inés de la Cruz. SpanPo, *tr. by* Kate Flores

Elustrious Dame whose vertues rare doe shine. Acrostick on Mrs. Elizabeth Hull, An. John Saffin. SCAP

Elves and Fairies. John Gilbert Cooper. ECEV *Fr.* Call of Aristippus, The.

Elvin Jones Gretsch Freak. David Henderson. SeSe

Elvin's Blues. Michael S. Harper. BPo; LoL

Elvis. Sam Cornish. AllShUp

Elvis. Brian G. Gilmore. AllShUp

Elvis Acts as His Own Pallbearer. Fleda Brown Jackson. AllShUp

Elvis at the End of History. Fleda Brown Jackson. AllShUp

Elvis couldn't twitch a hip. All Shook Up. Don Bogen. AllShUp

Elvis Elevator, The. Terry Stokes. AllShUp

Elvis for the Ages, An. Lynne McMahon. AllShUp

Elvis from the Waist Up. Alice Fulton. AllShUp *Fr.* Wonder Stings Me More than the Bee.

Elvis Goes to the Army. Fleda Brown Jackson. AllShUp

Elvis, King of PTL TV. I Wannabe Your Queen. Susan Swartwout. SwNoth

Elvis lay cool in his thick shadow. Elegy for Elvis. Richard Blessing. AllShUp; SwNoth

Elvis Lives. Charles Bukowski. AllShUp

Elvis Moving a Small Cloud: The Desert Near Las Vegas, 1976. David Wojahn. AllShUp

Elvis P. and Emma B. Elizabeth Ash Vélez. AllShUp

Elvis Presley. Thom Gunn. AllShUp

Elvis Presley. Rochelle Nameroff. SwNoth

Elvis Presley is alive and well. Elvis. Brian G. Gilmore. AllShUp

Elvis Reads The Wild Swans at Coole. Fleda Brown Jackson. AllShUp

Elvis Sings Gospel. Fleda Brown Jackson. AllShUp

Elwha River, The. Gary Snyder. NoAM

Elwood Collins: Summer of 1932. Dave Etter. IllVoic

Flysee. Larry Eigner. VGW

Elysian Fields. Marilyn Hacker. RA

Elysium is as far as to. Suspense. Emily Dickinson. AWP; MoAmPo; OxBA; TCAPo; WPE

Em pom pee para me. Clapping Chant, A. *Unknown.* FaBoVe

Emaciated Teeth. Fatma Kandil. PoArWo, *tr. by* Khaled Mattawa

Emanations. Hameed Sa'id. MAP, *tr. by* Lena Jayyusi and Naomi Shihab Nye

Emancipation. Priscilla Jane Thompson. CBWP-2

Emancipation Day. Lizelia Augusta Jenkins Moorer. CBWP-3

Emancipation Proclamation. William Heyen. PoCoUp

Emaricdulfe. "E. C." Son

Embalmer. Rossana Ombres. Nelt, *tr. by* Ruth Feldman

Embalmment. "Michael Field." VWP

Embankment, The (The fantasia of a fallen gentleman on a cold, bitter night). Thomas Ernest Hulme. EBEV; FaBoMo; GTBS-P; OPOU; OxBSP; OxBTC

Embarcation. Thomas Hardy. OBWP

Embarkation for Cythera, The. David Ferry. GS

Embarkation, 1942. John Jarmain. PoWW

Embarrassed cold. Half-Season. Simone Yoyotte. SurWo, *tr. by* Myrna Bell Rochester

Embarrassed presently. Solitary. Samar Sen. WoPoe, *tr. by* Pritish Nandy

Embarrassed the moon with his curses & songs. (LL) Because of My Father's Job. James Masao Mitsui. NIL-7; OpBo; UnSA

Embarrassed, you reach God's door. Ceremony. Al-Munsif Al-Wahaybi. MAP, *tr. by* Salma Khadra Jayyusi and Naomi Shihab Nye

Embarrassing Episode of Little Miss Muffet, The. Guy Wetmore Carryl. OBCA

Embassy to Achilles, The. Homer. NAWM-7v1, *tr. by* Robert Fagles *Fr.* Iliad, The.

Embers of night flare up afresh. Twin Flames. James Broughton. PasH

Embers of the day are red, The. Evensong. Robert Louis Stevenson. ITBLP

Embers of wood in fire I'd be. Four Elements, The. Sándor Weöres. IQMS, *tr. by* Adam Makkai and Donald E. Morse

Emblazoned bleak in austral skies. Herman Melville. TCAPo *Fr.* Clarel: A Poem and Pilgrimage in the Holy Land.

Emblem 51. Zbigniew Morsztyn. WoPoe, *tr. by* Jerzy Peterkiewicz and Burns Singer

Emblems. Douglas Dunn. FaBoMo

Emblems. Francis Quarles.
  "At length, by flight, I over-went the Pack." ESCV
  "Before a Pack of deep-mouth'd Lusts I flee." ESCV
  "Behold thy darling, which thy lustfull care." ESCV
  "Come then, my soule, approach this royall Burse." ESCV
  (Divine Rapture, A.) OBEV
  "Ev'n [*or* E'en *or* Even] like two little bank-dividing brooks [*or* brookes]." MeLP; NOBE
  "How shall my tongue expresse that hallow'd fire." ESCV
  (I Am My Beloved's, and His Desire Is towards Me.) NPeEn; OxAEP-1; SacPr
  "If lust should chase my soule, made swift by fright." ESCV
  "Let Grace conduct thee to the paths of peace." ESCV
  Like to the Arctic Needle. EBEV; NOCV
  ("Like to the Artick needle, that doth guide.") SacPr
  My Beloved Is Mine, and I Am His; He Feedeth among the Lillies. MeLP; NOBE
  "My Soule is like a Bird; my Flesh, the Cage." ESCV
  "Not as the thirsty soyle desires soft showres." ESCV
  "This furnisht Ark presents the greedy view." ESCV
  "Whene'er the old exchange of profit rings." BASC; NOSC
  "Why dost thou shade thy lovely face? O[h] why." BASC; MeLP; NOSC; OxAEP-1; SacPr
  "World's a Floore, whose swelling heapes retaine, The." ESCV
  "Worldly wisdome of the foolish man, The." ESCV

Emblems. Allen Tate. AWP; VGW

Emblems of Love. Lascelles Abercrombie.
  Epilogue: "What shall we do for Love these days?" MoBrPo
  Hymn to Love. OBEV
  "We are thine, O Love, being in thee and made of thee." OBEV
  "What thing shall be held up to woman's beauty?" MoBrPo
  Woman's Beauty. MoBrPo

Embodied close, the lab'ring Grecian train. Homer. OBVE *Fr.* Iliad, The.

Embodiment of what, The. Lyric: "Embodiment of what, The." Arthur Gregor. TAP

Embrace. Dulce Maria Loynaz. TANSG, *tr. by* Alan West

Embrace, The. Mark Doty. AmFaPo

Embrace of the Electric Eel. Pascale Petit. Prnts

Embrace the Blade. Joyce Mansour. HAWP, *tr. by* Carol Cosman

Embraceable You. George Gershwin. ReLy

Embracing in the road. Hawk's Shadow. Louise Glück. HarvBoo

Embracing low-falutin. Countryman's Return, The. Dylan Thomas. OxBTC

Embro to the Ploy. Robert Garioch. OxBS

Embroidered Memory. Lorene Zarou-Zouzounis. PoArWo

Embroidery. Catherine Nomura Crystal. AiP

Emerald in big clusters. High the Mount of Wu. Li Ho. ChinPo, *tr. by* Yip Wai-lim

Emerald is as green as grass, An. Flint. Christina Georgina Rossetti. SacPr

Emeralds are singing on the grasses, The. How Many Heavens. Dame Edith Sitwell. TrCP

Emeralds big as half the county. (LL) Ireland Never Was Contented. Walter Savage Landor. FaBoEE; OxBSP; OxBoLi; PeLV

Emerge, and shine upon the Aral Sea. (LL) Matthew Arnold. EBNV; OBNV

Emergency. Julio Marzán. PueRic

Emergency Haying. Hayden Carruth. NNaP

Emergency Kit. Tanure Ojaide. EmeKit

Emergent Manner. Allen Fisher.
  "Correlation which unites the human condition." Oth
  Diary Theme, The. Oth
  Ditchley Portrait, The. Oth
  Machynlleth. Oth
  Murder One. Oth
  "Processes activities break drop and disappear, The." Oth
  "That that mind perceives how to fly alone." Oth
  "Virtually whole they perceive it and name it Anagallis tenella." Oth

Emerging hot and rosy. Anita Virgil. HA

Emerging through the automatic doors. Library, The. Timothy Steele. RA

Emerson. James Russell Lowell. APN-1; NOBA; OxBA; TAP; TCAPo *Fr.* Fable for Critics, A.

Emerson. Henrietta Cordelia Ray. CBWP-3

Emigrant, The. Alexander McLachlan.
  Arrival, The. NOBC
  Song: "Old England is eaten by Knaves." NOBC
  "Soon we entered in the woods." NOBC

Emigrant, The. Standish O'Grady.
  "Thou barren waste; unprofitable strand." NOBC
  Winter in Lower Canada. NOBC

Emigrant Irish, The. Eavan Boland. AmFaPo; EmeKit

Emigrant's Cabin, The. Thomas Pringle. PeSAV

Emigrant's Son, The. Luis Andrade Silva. NAfrP, *tr.* by Don Burness

Emigrant Song. "S. Ansky." TrJP, *tr.* by Joseph Leftwich

Emigrants. Jane Griffiths. NeBl

Emigrants. Berthold Viertel. AuPH, *tr.* by Lowell A. Bangerter

Emigrants, The. Charlotte Smith. RWP
  Long wintry months are past; the Moon that now.
    Disillusion with the French Revolution. ECWP
  "So many years have passed." ECWP

Emigration Trains, The. Thomas McCarthy. PBCIP

Emigravit. Helen Hunt Jackson. SWaP

Emily Brontë. Cecil Day Lewis. GTBS-P

Emily Carr. Wilfred Watson. MoCV; NOBC

Emily Dickinson. Wendy Cope. NIL-7

Emily Dickinson. Yury [*or* Iurii] Ivask. TCRusP, *tr.* by William Tjalsma

Emily Dickinson. Michael Longley. CIP-2

Emily Dickinson, Bismarck and the Roadrunner's Inquiry. Ray A. Young Bear. HATNAP

Emily Dickinson in Southern California. X. J. Kennedy. NBLV; OBCoV

Emily Dickinson's Defunct. Marilyn Nelson Waniek. ESEAA

Emily Hardcastle, Spinster. John Crowe Ransom. OxBSP

Emily's Words. Leslie Monsour. FFC

Emily Sparks. Edgar Lee Masters. APT-1 *Fr.* Spoon River Anthology.

Emily Writes Such a Good Letter. Stevie Smith. OBCoV

Eminent Public Figure. Dezső Kosztolányi. IQMS, *tr.* by Peter Zollman

Emmeline Grangerford's "Ode to Stephen Dowling Bots, Dec'd." "Mark Twain." NBLV; OBAL *Fr.* Adventures of Huckleberry Finn, The.

Emmet, The. Ogden Nash. OBCoV

Emmet is an ant (archaic), The. Emmet, The. Ogden Nash. OBCoV

Emmett Till. Wanda Coleman. NAAAL

Emmett Till. James A. Emanuel. NIL-7; NIP-4

Emotional the / fox at an am. Brill. Clark Coolidge. PmAP

Empedocles came coughing through the smoke. To the Thoughtful Reader. William Meredith. NoAM

Empedocles on Etna. Matthew Arnold.
  "Far far from here." GTBS-P
  Hymn of Empedocles. OBEV
  "It is so small a thing." OBEV
  Song of Callicles, The. GTBS-P; NOBE; OBEV
  "Through the black, rushing smoke-bursts." NOBE; OBEV

Empedocles' Sandal. Habib Tengour.
  "Traces/Renown/Shades/Urns/Life(s)/Epoch/Zenith." PFTM-2, *tr.* by Pierre Joris

Emperor, The. Jonathan Griffin. Oth

Emperor, The. Tu Fu. AWP, *tr.* by E. Powys Mathers

Emperor and his might—what are they to us!, The. (LL) Ground-Thumping Song. *Unknown.* CoBCP; ColAnChi, *tr.* by Burton Watson

Emperor Hadrian on his Soul. Emperor Hadrian. WoPoe, *tr.* by Frederick Morgan

Emperor Hadrian to his Soul, The. Emperor Hadrian. RomPo

Emperor Marcus Aurelius, The. Limerick: "Yorick." PeLi

Emperor of China, The. Shirley Kaufman. BAP-01

Emperor of Ice-Cream, The. Wallace Stevens. APT-1; FaBoMo; HAP; HCAP; HeIP-4; InPK-6; NAAL-2v2; NAAL-5; NAWM-7v2; NIL-7; NIP-4; NOBA; NoAM; NoP-4; OxBA; PoE; PoPoPo; TAP; TCAPo; TFi; TRP; WeW-3

Emperor of the Moon. Aphra Behn.
  Song: "All joy to mortals, joy and mirth." WPE
  Song: "Curse upon that faithless maid, A." WPE

Emperor prized beauty, and longed for a woman to topple a kingdom, The. Song of Everlasting Sorrow. Po Chü-i. WoPoe, *tr.* by Dore J. Levy

Emperor's city, a place of fame and profit, The. Quiet House in Ch'ang-lo Ward, A. Po Chü-i. CoBCP, *tr.* by Burton Watson

Emphasis Falls on Reality, An. Barbara Guest. FTOS; PmAP

Emphasis on the dull and the glossy, The. Portrait. Mary Leader. NAPBL

Emphasize the "h," you ignorant ass. On Being Told I Don't Speak Like a Black Person. Allison Joseph. OPRER

Empire Builders. Archibald MacLeish. OxBA
  (Museum Attendant, The.) GM

Empire of Dreams. Charles Simic. BLT; LCAP-2; VCAP

Empire Smoke, Forgeries, Salient and The Ritz. Ray DiPalma. FTOS

Employment (1). George Herbert. GeHe

Employment: "He that is weary, let him sit." George Herbert. FaBoVe
  (Employment (2).) GeHe

Employments of Life, The. John Gay. PeLV *Fr.* Begger's Opera.

Emplumada. Lorna Dee Cervantes. NoAM; PBCAP

Empowered image Baudrillard. Robert Sheppard. Oth *Fr.* Empty Diaries/Twentieth Century Blues 24.

Empress Brand Trim: Ruby Reminisces, The. Sherley Anne Williams. BlSi

Empress Herself Served Tea to Su Tung-Po, The. Lew Welch. BB

Empress Messalina, The. Juvenal. BASC, *tr.* by John Dryden *Fr.* Satires.

Empress of Imagined Fertility, The. Leah Aini. DTA, *tr.* by Miriyam Glazer

Empress of Sighs. Beth Lisick. AmPoNex; BAP-97

Empress Receives the Head of a Taiping Rebel, The. Sarah Gorham. FFC

Empress Shōtoku Invents Printing in 1770. Teresa D. Cader. ExTi

Empryce of prys, imperatrice. William Dunbar. EBEV *Fr.* Ballad of Our Lady.

Emptied with weeping. At the Badr Trench. Safiya bint Musafir. WPOW, *tr.* by Bridget Connelly and Deirdre Lashgari

Emptiness of being a man is not like, The. Emptiness of Being a Man, The. Joao Cabral de Melo Neto. PoetW, *tr.* by Galway Kinnell

Emptiness of Man, The. João Cabral de Melo Neto. TCLAP, *tr.* by Galway Kinnell
  (Emptiness of man is not like, The.) VCWP, *tr.* by Galway Kinnell

Emptiness of the day, The. Roberto Juarroz. VCWP *Fr.* Fifth Vertical Poetry.

Empty are. Sohoku. JDP, *tr.* by Yoel Hoffmann

Empty bag of skin filling with desire. Taoist Song: "Empty bag of skin filling with desire." Teng Yu-pin. CrYelRi, *tr.* by Sam Hamill

Empty Bed Blues. Bessie Smith. APT-2; OBAL; UnPo

Empty bed, hard to keep alone, An. (LL) *Unknown.* SuSp; WoPoe, *tr.* by Dell R. Hales

Empty bell, The. Secret. Pierre Reverdy. PFTM-1

Empty black haunted house. Empty Black Haunted House. Joyce Mansour. NAWM-7v2, *tr.* by Serge Gavronsky

Empty boat, floating, adrift, An. (LL) Written on the Wall at Chang's Hermitage. Tu Fu. EnlH; OHPC, *tr.* by Kenneth Rexroth

Empty Body, The. Mark Strand. UnPo *Fr.* Elegy for My Father.

Empty Cage, The. Lise Deharme. SurWo, *tr.* by Franklin Rosemont

Empty Church, The. Ronald Stuart Thomas. AngWePo; EmeKit

Empty cicada shell. Fukaku. JDP, *tr.* by Yoel Hoffmann

Empty Diaries/Twentieth Century Blues 24. Robert Sheppard.
  "Bees at my hive anticipate her hands." Oth
  "Empowered image Baudrillard." Oth
  Empty Diary 1905. Oth
  Empty Diary 1936. Oth
  Empty Diary 1944. Oth
  Empty Diary 1954. Oth
  Empty Diary 1968. Oth
  Empty Diary 1987. Oth
  Empty Diary 1990. Oth
  "For the man who." Oth
  "Past empty rooms full of men, the." Oth
  "She falls for him, conventional longing well." Oth
  "Vauxhall was grey she needed blocks of." Oth
  "We are statues of ourselves, stiffened eulogies." Oth

Empty elevator, An. Jack Cain. HA

Empty Glen, The. R. Crombie Saunders. OxBS

Empty-handed I entered the world. Kozan Ichikyo. JDP, *tr.* by Yoel Hoffmann

Empty-handed, I return home. After Delivering Your Lunch. Lynne Yamaguchi Fletcher. FSt

Empty highway, The. Nicholas Virgilio. HA

Empty holes in the fish-dying-becoming directions. Armand Schwerner. PFTM-2 *Fr.* Tablets, The.

Empty House. Yuan Chen. CrYelRi; ErotSp, *tr.* by Sam Hamill

Empty House, The. Aida Gelbtrunk. MirDau, *tr.* by Roberta Gordenstein

Empty House, The. William Dean Howells. APN-2

Empty House, The. Max Williams. CBAP

Empty, I echo to the least footfall. Barren Woman. Sylvia Plath. OxBSP

Empty, illusory life. Enchanted Region; or, Mistaken Pleasures, The. Walter Harte. EBEV

Empty Kettle. Louis Oliver. HATNAP

Empty mailbox.　Marlene Mountain.　HA

Empty mountain after fresh rains.　Autumn Dusk at a Mountain Lodge.　Wang Wei.　ChinPo, *tr. by* Yip Wai-lim

Empty mountain: no man.　Four Examples from the Poems of River Wang Deer Enclosure.　Wang Wei.　ChinPo, *tr. by* Yip Wai-lim

Empty of dreams. (LL)　Halsted Street Car.　Carl Sandburg.　IllVoic; NAAL-2v2

Empty out your pockets nighttime, Daddy.　Who I Think You Are.　Elizabeth Alexander.　FFC; RA

Empty Page, The.　Sara de Ibáñez.　TCLAP, *tr. by* Andrew Rosing

Empty Pain-Killer Bottles, The.　Tom Raworth.　SPE

Empty perfection, as I take you in.　James Merrill.　NoAM　*Fr.* Coda: The Higher Keys.

Empty Purse.　Tu Fu.　CrYelRi, *tr. by* Sam Hamill

Empty Purse, The.　George Meredith.
　"He cancelled the ravaging Plague."　VerBaPo

Empty Purse, The.　Tu Fu.　TAL

Empty room.　Jack Cain.　HA

Empty room begins to growl, The.　Vasco [or Vasko] Popa.　PoSu　*Fr.* Besieged Serenity.

Empty room is still the empty room, The.　Empty Room, The.　Hans Andreus.　TuT, *tr. by* Desmond Egan

Empty room is still the empty room, The.　Empty Room, The.　Hans Andreus.　TuT, *tr. by* Joan McBreen

Empty sky, a world of heather, An.　Divided.　Jean Ingelow.　VWP

Empty Tomb, The.　Clara Ann Thompson.　CBWP-2

Empty Vessel.　Hugh MacDiarmid.　FaBoTw; NPeEn; NePenScot; OxBEV; OxBS

Empty Walnut, The.　Gabriela Mistral.　TANSG, *tr. by* Maria Jacketti

Empty Warriors.　Haki R. Madhubuti.　RaBo

Empty your mind of all thoughts.　Lao Tzu.　EnlH　*Fr.* Tao Te Ching.

Emptying Town.　Nick Flynn.　AmPoNex; NAPBL

Emu Shot.　Tjinapirrgarri.　NOBAu, *tr. by* George von Brandenstein

Emulation, The.　Sarah Fyge Egerton.　CABP; ECWP; NOEC; PEW

Emulation, The: A Pindarick Ode.　*Unknown.*　EMWP

En Bateau.　Paul Verlaine.　AWP, *tr. by* Arthur Symons

En Cest Sonet Coind' a Leri.　Arnaut Daniel.　WoPoe
　(En Cest Sonet Coind' a Leri.)　WoPoe

En el Sol de Mi Barrio.　Sandra M. Castillo.　TouFir

En Famille.　Robert Creeley.　BAP-1

En Famille.　Dame Edith Sitwell.　NALW

En las Internas Entrañas.　Saint Theresa [or Teresa] of Avila.　WPOW, *tr. by* Father Benedict Zimmerman

En Monocle.　Donald Evans.　APT-1

En Route.　Alan Ross.　FaBoWar

En Route.　Duncan Campbell Scott.　NOBC

En un Vergier Soiz Folha D'Albespi.　*Unknown.*　WoPoe, *tr. by* Stanley Burnshaw

En-vi-RON-ment.　Lee Bennett Hopkins.　HHAm

Enacting someone's notion of themselves.　Aunt Jemima of the Ocean Waves.　Robert Earl Hayden.　LCAP-2

Enamel Girl, The.　Genevieve Taggard.　MoAmPo

Enamoured of the Miniscule.　Michael Hartnett.　BIrV

Encampment at Morning, An.　W. S. Merwin.　GifTon

Encased by winter.　Hou.　JDP, *tr. by* Yoel Hoffmann

Enchanted frame assures the image of a loved one, An.　Veil.　Marjorie Welish.　PmAP

Enchanted is what they were.　Animals Are Entering Our Lives.　Lisel Mueller.　ExTi

Enchanted Island, The.　Letitia [or Laetitia] Elizabeth Landon.　CABP; NOBRP

Enchanted Princess, An.　Rosamund Marriott Watson.　ViWPN

Enchanted Region; or, Mistaken Pleasures, The.　Walter Harte.　EBEV

Enchanted Shell, The.　Henrietta Cordelia Ray.　CBWP-3

Enchantment, The.　Thomas Otway.　OBEV

Enchantment, The.　Theocritus.　CTC; OBVE　*Fr.* Idylls.

Enchantress' Song, The.　Giles Fletcher, the Younger.　*See* Christ's Victory and Triumph

Enclosed, self-possessed one spreads his wings across the lake, The.　Flamingo, The.　Saleem Barakat.　MAP, *tr. by* Lena Jayyusi and Naomi Shihab Nye

Enclosed with a Letter to My Family—For Shu.　Yang Shih-ch'i.　CoBLCP, *tr. by* Jonathan Chaves

Enclosure.　Christopher Gilbert.　SwNoth

Encompass me, my lover.　Constant North, The.　J. F. Hendry.　OxBS

Encounter.　Denis Devlin.　BIrV

Encounter.　Rick Fournier.　PasH

Encounter.　Mary Low.　SurWo

Encounter.　Czeslaw Milosz.　BodElec; ChAP; PoetW; WoPoe, *tr. by* Lillian Vallee

Encounter.　Alfonsina Storni.　TANSG, *tr. by* Mark McCaffrey

Encounter.　August Stramm.　PFTM-1

Encounter.　Marion Strobel.　LW

Encounter, An.　Guido Cavalcanti.　NAWM-7v1, *tr. by* James J. Wilhelm

Encounter, The.　Paul Blackburn.　NeAP

Encounter, The.　Ezra Pound.　PAI

Encounter, The.　Edgell Rickword.　OxBTC

Encounter at St. Martin's.　Ken Smith.　OPOU

Encounter at the Post Office Counter.　Christopher Pilling.　NLP

Encountering a Snowstorm, I Stay with the Recluse of Mount Hibiscus.　Liu Ch'ang-ch'ing.　SuSp, *tr. by* Dell R. Hales

Encountering Sorrow.　*Unknown.*　CoBCP, *tr. by* Burton Watson

Encouragement.　János Batsányi.　IQMS, *tr. by* Matthew Mead

Encouragement.　Mrs. Henry Linden.　CBWP-4

Encouragement to Exile.　Petronius Arbiter.　AWP, *tr. by* Howard Mumford Jones

Encouraging.　Attila József.　WoPoe, *tr. by* John Batki

End.　Hugh Seidman.　BodElec

End, The.　Allen Ginsberg.　CoAmPo

End, The.　Wilfred Owen.　ChIV-1

End, The.　Mark Strand.　TRP

End and the Beginning, The.　Wislawa Szymborska.　VCWP, *tr. by* Stanislaw Baranczak

End came as I drove it down the road, The.　Last of the Poet's Car.　Tony Connor.　OxBTC

End came easy for most of us, The.　Man from Washington, The.　James Welch.　CDW; HATNAP; NoAM; PoPoPo; RaBo

End / conscience.　Stéphane Mallarmé.　PFTM-1　*Fr.* Le Livre.

End Is Near the Beginning, The.　David Gascoyne.　SPE

End, Middle, Beginning.　Anne Sexton.　PoE

End of a Campaign.　Hamish Henderson.　PoWW

End of a Course.　Ivor Armstrong Richards.　CRP

End of a line, The.　Wishon Line, The.　Sherley Anne Williams.　GeoHom

End of a long stillness.　Dawn in January.　Lance Henson.　CDW

End of a Love Affair, The.　Edward C. Redding.　ReLy

End of a Season.　Thomas McGrath.　BodElec

End of a thing, The.　December.　Lucille Clifton.　NOxBChV

End of a War, The.　Sir Herbert Read.　OBMV; PeFWW

End of a Year.　Robert Lowell.　HCAP

End of All History, The.　Ken Smith.　SpudSo

End of an Audience.　Tu Fu.　CarOv, *tr. by* Carolyn Kizer　*Fr.* Adviser to the Court.

End of an Ethnic Dream, The.　Jay Wright.　SeSe

End of Another Home Holiday.　D. H. Lawrence.　EBEV; FaBoMo; OxAEP-2

End of Art, The.　Reiner Kunze.　PoSu, *tr. by* Michael Hamburger

End of Civilization as We Know It, The.　Colleen J. McElroy.　UrbNat

End of Clonmacnois, The.　*Unknown.*　CIP-2; WoPoe, *tr. by* Frank O'Connor

End of Communism, The.　Rodney Jones.　IllVoic

End of Doctor Faustus, The.　Christopher Marlowe.　FaBoVe; HeIP-4; PeECV　*Fr.* Doctor Faustus.

End of Dodona II, The.　Yannis Ritsos.　VCWP; WoPoe, *tr. by* Edmund Keeley

End of Ends. . . in god's Beginnning's lost, The. (LL)　Sidney Lanier.　APN-2; ColAP

End of everything approaches, The.　Doomsday.　Elinor Wylie.　NoP-4; SacPr

End of His Work, The.　Robert Herrick.　CaPo

End of Human Reign on Bashan Hill, The.　Bernadette Mayer.　FTOS

End of It, The.　Francis Thompson.　NOBVV; OxBSP

End of July.　John Peck.　HarvBoo

End of love should be a big event, The.　End of Love, The.　Sophie Hannah.　MFPA

End of Man Is Death, The.　Moses Ibn Ezra.　TrJP, *tr. by* Solomon Solis-Cohen

End of May, The.　William Morris.　NOBVV

End of "Pain," The.　Amanda Ros.　VerBaPo

End of Play.　Robert Graves.　EBEV

End of spring, The.　Buson.　EH, *tr. by* Robert Hass

End of Summer.　Stanley Kunitz.　LoL; MoAmPo; VGW

(End) of Summer (1966).　Bill Knott.　*See* Two Vietnam Poems: (1966)

End of summer suggested the way, The.　Autumn Leaves.　James Cushing.　SeSe

End of the Affair, The.　E. San Juan, Jr.　ReBoTo

End of the Affair, The.　James Simmons.　PBCIP

End of the cold spell.　Marlene Mountain.　HA

End of the factory-window song. (LL)　Factory Windows Are Always Broken.　Nicholas Vachel Lindsay.　APT-1; OBCA; OxBSP

End of the Flower World (A.D. 2300).　Stanley Burnshaw.　APT-2; TrJP

End of the Game. Artur Miedzyrzecki. PoSu, *tr.* by John Batki and Artur Miedzyrzecki

End of the Journey, The. May Probyn. VWP

End of the Line, The. Thomas McGrath. GM

End of the Picnic. Francis Webb. BMAP; NOBAu

End of the Questionnaire. Dan Pagis. PoSu, *tr.* by Robert Friend

End of the Reagan Era, The. Peter Balakian. ReTh

End of the Row. Anne Born. Prnts

End of the Suitors, The. Homer. OBVE, *tr.* by George Chapman *Fr.* Odyssey.

End of the War, The. Ioan Alexandru. FaBoWar, *tr.* by Brenda Walker

End of the Weekend, The. Anthony Hecht. CoAmPo; FaBoMo; HAP; WeW-3

End of the World. Else Lasker-Schüler. BoWoP, *tr.* by Willis Barnstone and Michael Gillespie

End of the World, The. Gordon Bottomley. MoBrPo

End of the World, The. Archibald MacLeish. GSo; InPK-6; MoAmPo; NOBA; NoAM; OBAL; OxBA; OxBSo; PAI; Son; TAP; TFi; VGW

End of the World, The. Thomas McGrath. AF

End of the World, The. João Cabral de Melo Neto. VCWP

End of the Year. Paula Ludwig. AuPH, *tr.* by Lowell A. Bangerter

End of the Year, The. Su Tung-p'o (Su Shih). OHPC, *tr.* by Kenneth Rexroth

End of their journey, I descended too, The. (LL) Traveller, The. John Berryman. GM; VGW

End or a Beginning, An. Bei Dao. AF, *tr.* by Bonnie S. McDougall

End to Myth, An. Charles Buckmaster. BMAP

End to Spring, An. Li Ch'ing-chao. CrYelRi, *tr.* by Sam Hamill

End to Spring, An. Tzu Yeh. CrYelRi, *tr.* by Sam Hamill

End was more of a melting, The. Death of Will, The. Charles Tomlinson. OxBC

End was quick and bitter, The. Quick And Bitter. Yehuda Amichai [*or* Amikhai]. BoLoP; VCWP

End your groan, and come away. (LL) John Webster. HAP; SCGP *Fr.* Duchess of Malfi, The.

Endangered Nouns. David Antin. PFTM-2

Endangered Roots of a Person. Wendy Rose. ReEnLa

Endangered Species. Ai. ESEAA

Ended, ere it begun. Emily Dickinson. APN-2

Endimion. John Lyly.
   "Pinch him, pinch him black and blue." NoSic
   "Stand! Who goes there?" NoSic; OBCoV

Endimion Porter and Olivia. Sir William Davenant [*or* D'Avenant]. NOBE
   (Song: Endimion Porter and Olivia.) MeLP; NOSC; NPeEn

Ending. Gavin Ewart. NBLV; OxBSP; SoSe-8

Ending. Eugene McCarthy. HHAm *Fr.* Page of Short Poems, A.

Ending Poem. Aurora Levins Morales. PueRic

Ending up tending shop up in Fiesole. (LL) Tourists. Howard Moss. NoP-4; OBCoV; PeLV

Endless and indestructible. (LL) Descent, The. William Carlos Williams. APT-1; HAP; SAmP; WeW-3

Endless blue mountains disperse, The. On the Tower of Gathering Remoteness. Su Tung-p'o (Su Shih). TAL

Endless downpour; misty wood. Ivan Alekseievich Bunin. TCRP

Endless fields sit under snowy blankets, The. Farewell to Várad. Janus Pannonius. IQMS, *tr.* by Adam Makkai

Endless horizons of wheat and corn. End of the Reagan Era, The. Peter Balakian. ReTh

Endless infusions, silver strainers. Sean Dunne. ModIr *Fr.* Sydney Place.

Endless Journeys. Pierre Reverdy. WoPoe, *tr.* by John Ashbery

Endless lanes sunken in the clay. Trenches, The. Frederic Manning. NOBAu; PoWW

Endless sameness. Paul Verlaine. SxFrPo, *tr.* by Martin Sorrell

Endless Song, The. Ruth McEnery Stuart. OBAL

Endless, waterway toward the southwest. To Hsuan-Ch'eng, Past Hsin-Lin-P'u, Toward Pan-Ch'iao. Hsieh T'iao. ChinPo, *tr.* by Yip Wai-lim

Endless worlds. The. One Hut. Muso Soseki. EaWin, *tr.* by W. S. Merwin

Endlessly, endlessly the blue waves break. Sea Spray. Marion Margaret Boyd. YaYoPo

Endlessly gaze at Mount Wu. Mount Wu Is High. Lu Chao-lin. SuSp, *tr.* by Robin D. S. Yates

Endow the fool with sun and moon. Fool and Wise. Coventry Patmore. SacPr

Endowed fiction of a mouse ear. Mac Wellman. HeMarv *Fr.* Rat Minaret: Miniaturist-Divan, The.

Endowed with Ch———l's strength and Low———r's face. (LL) Epistle from Mrs. Yonge to Her Husband. Lady Mary Wortley Montagu. NAEL-5v1; NAEL-6v1; NAEL-7v1; NALW; NPeEn; NoP-4

Ends. Robert Frost. TRP

Endsight. Michael Dransfield. BMAP

Endurance. Elizabeth Akers Allen. PoToHe

Endurance. Dennis Brutus. VCWP

Endure Hardness. Christina Georgina Rossetti. NOBVV

Endure the wintry and the darkened days. (LL) To Honora Sneyd. Anna Seward. CenSon; ECWP; PoBW

Endure what life God gives and ask no longer span. Sophocles. OBMV *Fr.* Oedipus at Colonus.

Enduring is the bust of bronze. Duke of York's Statue, The. Walter Savage Landor. FaBoEE

Enduring like a tree under the curious stars. (LL) Peasant, A. Ronald Stuart Thomas. AngWePo; OBWVE; OxBEV

Enduring Witness, the Mosques of Kattankudi. Peter Michelson. OPRER

Endymion. Thomas Kinsella. PBCIP

Endymion: A Poetic Romance. John Keats.
   "But there are." NPeEn
   "O Sorrow!" OBEV
   "Peona! ever have I long'd to slake." NAEL-5v2; NAEL-6v2
   Song of the Indian Maid. OBEV
      "Beneath my palm-trees, by the riverside." NOBE
   "Thing of beauty is a joy forever, A." CTC; FHYEP; ITBLP; NAEL-5v2; NAEL-6v2; NIP-4; NOBRP; OPOU; OxAEP-2; OxBEV

Eneados. Gawin [*or* Gavin] Douglas.
   "As brycht Phebus, shene souerane, hevynnis e." NePenScot
   "Dyonea, nycht hyrd, and wach of day." NePenScot
   Proloug of the Sevynt Buik, The. NePenScot
   Proloug of the Twelt Buik, The. NePenScot

Eneas wonderit the greitnes of Cartaige. Virgil [*or* Vergil]. OBVE, *tr.* by Gawin [*or* Gavin] Douglas *Fr.* Aeneid [*or* Eneados, *Aeneis*], The.

Enemies. Charlotte Zolotow. HHAm

Enemies of Promise. Edmund Wilson. OBCoV

Enemy. Beau Sia. HeMarv

Enemy, The. Randolph Stow. NOBAu

Enemy Dead, The. Bernard Gutteridge. FaBoWar; PoWW

Enemy Encounter. Padraic Fiacc. PNI

Enemy Had Burned His Cottage Home, The. Mikhail Vasilevich Isakovsky [*or* Isakovskii]. TCRP, *tr.* by Lubov Yakovleva

Enemy in the Fortress, The. Marbod of Rennes. MLL, *tr.* by Helen Waddell

Enemy or en'my] of life, decayer of all kind, The [*or* Th']. Sir Thomas Wyatt. OxBSP

Enemy roamed the desert and everyone itched, The. (LL) Day with the Foreign Legion, A. Reed Whittemore. CoAP; CoAmPo

Enemy's Eyes, The. Emma Lee Warrior. HATNAP

Energy. Víctor Hernández Cruz. PueRic

Energy in Sweden. Kenneth Koch. NoP-4

Enfant perdu. Heinrich Heine. AWP, *tr.* by Lord Houghton

Enfidaville. Keith Douglas. PoWW

Engine, The. Ella Wheeler Wilcox. APN-2

Engine stops, The. Dust in a weary threat. Hunger. Attila József. IQMS, *tr.* by Watson Kirkconnell

Engineers' Corner. Wendy Cope. OBCoV

Engines of Gloom and Affection. John Yau. PmAP

England. Marianne Craig Moore. MoAmPo

England. Mary Jo Salter. DiPo

England. *Unknown.* FaBoEE; OxBSP

England and America. James Kenneth Stephen.
   "Britannia rules the waves." NOBL
   On a Parisian Boulevard. NOBL
   On a Rhine Steamer. FaBoA; NOBL; NOBVV; OBCoV; PeLV
   "Republic of the West." FaBoA; NOBL; NOBVV; OBCoV; PeLV

England and America, 1863. Richard Monckton, 1st Baron Houghton Milnes. EBVV

England and Switzerland 1802. William Wordsworth. *See* Thought[s] of a Briton on the Subjugation of Switzerland

England! Awake! Awake! Awake! William Blake. *See* Jerusalem; The Emanation of the Giant Albion

England be your sepulchre. (LL) Song to the Men of England. Shelley. CABP; NAEL-6v2; PAI

England, 1802. William Wordsworth. NOBE; OBEV

England, 1802, I. William Wordsworth. *See* Written in London, September, 1802

England, 1802, II. William Wordsworth. *See* London 1802

England, 1802, III. William Wordsworth. OBEV; Son

England, 1802, V. William Wordsworth. GTBS-P; OBEV

England Expects. Ogden Nash. PeLV

England Expects? Sir Owen Seaman. NOBL

England in 1819. Shelley. CenSon; NAEL-5v2; NAEL-6v2; NAWM-7v2; NOBE; OxAEP-2; OxBEV; OxBSo; Son; TFi; UnPo

(Old, mad, blind, despised, and dying king, An.) NoP-4; PoPoPo

(Sonnet: England in 1819.) GSo

England, My England. William Ernest Henley. MoBrPo; OBEV

England, my England—you have been my tutrix. W. H. Auden. OBSV *Fr.* Letter to Lord Byron.

England Nil. Anne Rouse. MFPA; NeBl

England's Alfred Abroad. Sir Owen Seaman. UV

England's Dead. Felicia Dorothea Hemans. NAEL-6v2; NoP-4

England's Heroical Epistles. Michael Drayton.

"Judge not a Princess' worth impeached hereby." NoSic

Owen Tudor to Queen Katherine. NoSic

Queen Katherine to Owen Tudor. NoSic

"When first mine eyes beheld your princely name." NoSic

England's ingratitude still blots. What Jenner Said on Hearing in Elysium That Complaints Had Been Made of His Having a Statue [in Trafalgar Square]. Shirley Brooks. FaBoEE

England's sun was slowly setting o'er the hill-tops far away. Curfew Must Not Ring Tonight [or To-Night]. Rose Hartwick Thorpe. APN-2; BRP; SWaP

England that was the glory of the earth. On the Death of Henry the Lion. Hildebert. MLL, *tr.* by Helen Waddell

England! the time is come when thou shouldst wean. Sonnet: "England! the time is come when thou shouldst wean." William Wordsworth. Son

England, unlike junior nations. Remember Suez? Adrian Mitchell. OxBTC

England! with all thy faults I love thee still. Byron. UnPo *Fr.* Beppo; a Venetian Story.

England, with all thy faults, I love thee still. William Cowper. ECEV *Fr.* Task, The.

English. Osbert Lancaster. NOBL; PeLV *Fr.* Afternoons with Baedeker.

English, The. Sándor Sík. IQMS, *tr.* by James Turner

English Are So Nice!, The. D. H. Lawrence. NoP-4; PoPoPo; RaBo

English Bards and Scotch Reviewers. Byron.

"As Sisyphus against the infernal steep." OBSV

"Illustrious Holland! hard would be his lot." OBSV

"Time has been, when yet the muse was young, The." FHYEP

"Time was, ere yet in these degenerate days." FHYEP

"When Vice triumphant holds her sov'reign sway." FHYEP

English Cousin Comes to Scotland. Jackie Kay. NOxBChV

English Earthquake, The. Eva Salzman. MFPA

English, French, Italian. Chinoiserie. Kay Sage. SurWo

English Garden, The. William Mason.

Alcander's Flower Garden. OBGa

Some Early gardenists. OBGa

Thomas Gray's View of Nature. NOEC

English Girl. *Unknown.* OBMV, *tr.* by E. Powys Mathers

English Graves, The. Gilbert Keith Chesterton. FaBoWar

English has all the sexual options. Hebrew. Yona Volach. DTA, *tr.* by Miriyam Glazer

English hymn writer. Anne Steele. Jean Balderston. MPUn

English Liberal. Geoffrey Taylor. FaBoEE

English muskets went bim! bim!, The. George Washington Cable. APN-2

English Poetry. Lőrinc Szabó. IQMS, *tr.* by John Gordon Nichols *Fr.* Cricket Music.

English Poets. James McIntyre.

"We have scarcely time to tell thee." VerBaPo

English professor named Brooks, An. Limerick: "English professor named Brooks, An." D. H. Cudmore. PeLi

English Queen, The. Henry Lawson. NOBAu

English Sampler, An. Frederick D'Aguiar. Oth

English-Speaking Persons Will Find Translations. Michael S. Glaser. UnSA

English Teeth, English Teeth! Teeth. Spike Milligan. OPOU

English Thornton. Edgar Lee Masters. OxBA *Fr.* Spoon River Anthology.

English Was Only a Second Language. Walta Borawski. GLP

Englishman, The. Sir William Schwenck Gilbert. NOBL *Fr.* H. M. S. Pinafore.

Englishman at the Table, The. James Cawthorn. ECEV; NOEC *Fr.* Of Taste; an Essay.

Englishman's Home, The. Harry Graham. PeLV *Fr.* Some Ruthless Rhymes.

Engraved on the Collar of a Dog, Which I Gave to His Royal Highness. Pope. *See* Epigram Engraved on the Collar of a Dog Given [or Which I Gave] to His Royal Highness

Engraving, An. Aleksandr Petrovich Tkachenko. ItGoST, *tr.* by Maia Tekses

Engraving of Blake, An. Mary Kinzie. MakPoe

Engraving Twenty-Nine. Fadhila Chabbi. PoArWo, *tr.* by Yaseen Noorani

Enhances Nature now. (LL) Emily Dickinson. APN-2; NOBA; NoP-4; PoE

Enheduanna and Goethe. Amal Al-Juburi. PoArWo, *tr.* by Salih J. Altoma

Enigma. Catherine Maria Fanshawe. OBCoV

Enigma. Matthew Prior. PeLV

Enigma, An. Edgar Allan Poe. Son

Enigma No. 6. Augusta Davies Webster. VWP

Enigmatical, tremulous. Barrel-Organ, The. Arthur Symons. NOBVV

Enjoy'd the lady. (LL) Angel, The. William Blake. NAEL-5v2; PoE

Enjoy it a', ye've nae mair for't. (LL) Ode to Mr. F— [or Mr. Forbes]. Allan Ramsay. NOEC; OBVE

Enjoy [or Injoy] such liberty. (LL) To Althea, from Prison. Richard Lovelace. AWP; BASC; BeJo; CaPo; CavPo; GTBS-P; HAP; ITBLP; MeLP; NAEL-5v1; NAEL-6v1; NAEL-7v1; NIL-7; NOBE; NOSC; NPeEn; NoP-4; OBEV; OxBEV; PBRV; PoE; PoRA; SCGP; TFi

Enjoy your fortune as if you were about to die. Lucianus [or Lucian]. GrAn

Enjoy your time, my soul! another race. Enjoyment. Theognis. AWP, *tr.* by John Hookham Frere

Enjoying Coolness. Wang Wei. SuSp, *tr.* by Hugh M. Stimson

Enjoying [or Injoying] of myself I lie [or lye]. (LL) Love Made in the First Age[; To Chloris]. Richard Lovelace. BeJo; CaPo; NAEL-5v1; NAEL-6v1; NAEL-7v1

Enjoyment. Theognis. AWP, *tr.* by John Hookham Frere

Enjoyment of sex, although great, The. Limerick: "Enjoyment of sex, although great, The." *Unknown.* PeLi

Enkindled Spring, The. D. H. Lawrence. NoAM

Enlarge my Life with Multitude of Days. Samuel Johnson. OxBEV *Fr.* Vanity of Human Wishes, The; The Tenth Satire of Juvenal Imitated.

Enlarge your fortifications, Zeus. Philip of Macedon. Alcaeus [or Alkaios]. GrAn, *tr.* by Alistair Elliot

Enlightenment. Shih Shu. WoPoe, *tr.* by James H. Sanford

Enlightment. Ch'en Yü-yi. OHMPC, *tr.* by Kenneth Rexroth

Enlisted Today. *Unknown.* CBCWP

Enlli. Christine Evans. TCAWP

Enmeshed in steel stands a stone. Captive Stone, The. Jim Barnes. CDW

Enmeshment. Lewis Warsh. FTOS

Enmeshment is an enter. Closure. Douglas Messerli. FTOS

Enniskillen. David Morley. NLP

Ennui. Langston Hughes. OBAL; OBCA

Enobarbus, Antony. William Shakespeare. OxAEP-1 *Fr.* Antony and Cleopatra.

Enoch. Bible, Pseudepigrapha. TrJP

Seven Metal Mountains. TrJP

Enoch. Jones Very. ChIV-1; HAP; TCAPo

Enormous and solid. Grove, The. Octavio Paz. TCLAP, *tr.* by Elizabeth Bishop

Enormous Bliss of American death, The. Reading Frank O'Hara in a Mexican Rainstorm. Michael McClure. BB

Enormous cloud-mountains that form over Point Lobos and into the sunset. Clouds of Evening. Robinson Jeffers. MoAmPo

Enormous engineering problems, The. Popular Mechanics. Charles Simic. EmeKit

Enormous Hand, The. Jorge de Lima. PFTM-1

Enormous rope of silence, An. (LL) Distance. Peter Everwine. GeoHom; NNaP

Enormous tragedy of the dream in the peasant's bent / shoulders, The. Ezra Pound. AF *Fr.* Pisan Canto 124.

Enormous tree-trunk crawling on the waves. Dream of the Caiman, The. José Santos Chocano. TCLAP, *tr.* by Andrew Rosing

Enos Page the youngest brother. Julia A. Moore. VerBaPo *Fr.* Brave Page Boys, The.

Enosis. Christopher Pearse Cranch. TCAPo

(Gnosis.) APN-1; ColAP

Enough. Digby Mackworth Dolben. EBVV

Enough. Arthur Gregor. TAP

Enough. Thomas Kinsella. ModIr *Fr.* One Fond Embrace.

Enough. Tom Masson. OBAL

Enough. Marianne Craig Moore. NOBA

Enough. Tracy Ryan. NeBl

Enough. Sara Teasdale. APT-1

Enough cloth is plenty and more, more is almost enough for that. Gertrude Stein. TCAPo *Fr.* Tender Buttons.

Enough complaining. Arab Chieftain to His Young Wife, An. Abid ibn al-Abras. ArPe, *tr.* by Omar S. Pound

Enough for you. (LL) For Bud. Michael S. Harper. ESEAA; PoE

Enough kind Heaven! to purpose I have liv'd. To Mrs. W. on Her Excellent Verses. Aphra Behn. EMWP

Enough! Let this season end. Enough. Arthur Gregor. TAP

Enough, my Muse, of earthly things. Christ's Passion. Abraham Cowley. ChIV-2; SacPr

Enough of air. A desert subject now. John Armstrong. VerBaPo *Fr.* Art of Preserving Health, The.

Enough of Grongar and the shady dales. John Dyer. AngWePo

Enough of snivelling! Shove our papers in the desk. Osip Emilevich Mandelstam [or Mandelshtam]. TCRP

Enough of those who study the oblique. Good Resolution, A. Roy Campbell. OBSV

Enough of Thought, Philosopher. Emily Jane Brontë. BWW

Enough Rain for Agnes Walquist. Allen Grossman. BAP-01

Enough's enough: don't wait, don't hope. Despair. Andrey [or Andrei] Bely [or Belyi]. TCRP, tr. by Bernard Meares

Enough seen. The vision has been met in every air. Departure. Arthur Rimbaud. SxFrPo, tr. by Martin Sorrell

"Enough," she said. But the dust still rained around [or about] her. Dust. Randolph Stow. CBAP

Enough snow over last night's ice. Mercy. Bruce Weigl. CDa

Enough! we're tired, my heart and I. My Heart and I. Elizabeth Barrett Browning. VWP

Enough! Why should a man bemoan. Per Iter Tenebricosum. Oliver St. John Gogarty. OBMV

Enough women over thirty are at Redbones. Raising a Humid Flag. Thylias Moss. GT

Enquiry, The. Katherine Philips. OxBEV

Enquiry after Peace. A Fragment. Anne Finch, Countess of Winchilsea. ECWP; PoE

Enquiry Concerning the Bat, An. José Emilio Pacheco. TCLAP, tr. by Alastair Reid

Enrica, 1865. Christina Georgina Rossetti. NALW

Ensconced now in your heart, our mother. Nigeria of the Seventies. Molara Ogundipe-Leslie. HAWP

Enslaved. Claude McKay. BPo; NAAAL

Enslaved by passions, swelled with pride. Execration, The. Elizabeth Thomas. ECWP

Ensnaring Flower of Psalms. Rossana Ombres. NeIt, tr. by Ruth Feldman

Ensuing Copy the Late Printer Hath Been Pleased to Honour, by Mistaking It Among Those of the Most Ingenious and Too Early Lost Sir John Suckling, The. Sir John Suckling. See Song: "When, dearest, I but think on [or of] thee."

Entailed Farm, The. John Glassco. MoCV; NOBC

Entangled. Mathilde Blind. VWP

Entangled. Jules Supervielle. BBASP, tr. by James Kirkup

Entanglement. Francis Sparshott. MoCV

Entelechy on the Libidinal Fringe. E. San Juan, Jr. ReBoTo

Enter and learn the story of the rulers. Unknown. AWP Fr. Thousand and One Nights, The.

Enter and see this tomb, sirs, do not fear. Epitaph on Some Bottles of Sack and Claret Laid in Sand. Robert Wild. NOSC

Enter here and find your home. Eight Ways of Looking at Pussy. Letta Neely. WiU

Enter in the circle. Edouard J. Maunick. NegPo Fr. As Far as Yoruba Land.

Enter mine host. To Whom. Peter Klappert. YaYoPo

Enter the dream-house, brothers and sisters, leaving. Newsreel. Cecil Day Lewis. MoBrPo

Enter the forest. Double Song. Frank Mkalawile Chipasula. NAfrP

Enter the story here: their battle lost. Story, The. Kevin Hart. BMAP

Enter with him. Legend. W. H. Auden. CAGL

Entered in the Minutes. Louis MacNeice.
  "After the legshows and the brandies." OxBSP
  Night Club. OxBSP

Entered [or Enter'd or Entred] for both, far[re] above their desert! (LL) Obedience. George Herbert. ESCV; GeHe

Entered that brilliant intimate. Only Alice. Josephine Jacobsen. FFC

Entered to race, Barabbas was scratched. Passion of Jesus Considered as an Uphill Race, The. Alfred Jarry. PFTM-1

Entering Detroit. Víctor Hernández Cruz. PueRic

Entering—takes away, The. (LL) Emily Dickinson. MoAmPo; NALW; SAmP; TCAPo; WPoS

Entering the churchyard. Steeplejack. Katherine Pierpoint. MFPA

Entering the Gardens of Doom. Sayf Al-Rahabi. MAP, tr. by Samuel Hazo and Lena Jayyusi

Entering the hall, she meets the new wife. Ejected Wife, The. Yüan-ti. OBVE; OxBEV, tr. by Arthur Waley

Entering the Mare. Katie Donovan. NeBl

Entering the Mouth of P'eng-li Lake. Hsieh Ling-yün. SuSp, tr. by Francis Westbrook

Entering the publisher's warehouse, a foreign young lady. Anecdote from William IV Street. Dennis Joseph Enright. OxBC

Entering your silence, my Lord. Troubled Awakening. Magdalena Gomez. PueRic

Enters—and is lost in Balms. (LL) Emily Dickinson. FaBoVe; NALW; NCAP; TCAPo

Entertained by song and dance here in this wine pavilion. Pleasures of Shinbashi. Liu E. CoBLCP, tr. by Jonathan Chaves

Entertainer, The. Bruce Beaver. NOBAu

Entertainment Industry, The. William Langland. NOCV Fr. Vision of Piers Plowman, The.

Entertainment of War, The. Roy Fisher. FaBoMo

Entertainment, or Porch-Verse, at the Marriage of Mr. Henry Northleigh [or Hen. Northly] and the Most Witty Mrs. Lettice Yard, The. Robert Herrick. CaPo

Enthrone thy Rosy-selfe within mine Eyes. (LL) Edward Taylor. ChIV-1; OxBA; TCAPo Fr. Preparatory Meditations Before My Approach to the Lord's Supper.

Enthusiast, The. Herman Melville. ChIV-1; NAAL-2v1; NAAL-3

Enthusiast: or, The Lover of Nature, The. Joseph Warton. NOEC

Enthusiast, The. Arla. Anne Batten Cristall. RWP

Enthusiast, The; or, The Lover of Nature. Joseph Warton.
  "Ye green-robed Dryads, oft at dusky eve." ECEV; NOEC

Enthusiastically hurting a clouded yellow bud and. Gertrude Stein. TTTS Fr. Tender Buttons.

Entire country is overrun with private property, The. Gypsy. Josephine Miles. NoAM

Entire, more than entire have we been devastated! Tears of the Fatherland, Anno Domini 1636. Andreas Gryphius. GePo, tr. by George C. Schoolfield

Entity of Its Word, An. Sam Pereira. BodElec

Entrain airport: New York, Chicago, west. Valediction to My Contemporaries. Horace Gregory. MoAmPo

Entrance. Rainer Maria Rilke. AmFaPo, tr. by Edward Snow

Entrance and exit wounds are silvered clean. Recalling War. Robert Graves. AF; HarvBoo; NoAM; OBWP; PeFWW; PoWW

Entreaty. Robert Fitzgerald. OxBSP

Entrepreneur chicken shed his tail feathers, surplus, The. Josephine Miles. NoAM

Entresol. Jaime Sabines. TCLAP, tr. by Claudine-Marie D'Angelo

Entries on Light. Mimi Khalvati.
  "Knocking on the door." Prnts

Entropic Villanelle. Thomas M. [or "Tom"] Disch. RA

Entry into Jerusalem. Dmitry [or Dmitrii] Aleksandrovich Prigov. ItGoST, tr. by Robert Reid

Entwined on the bed in the dark. Two Shapes. Arthur Gregor. TAP

Enueg I. Samuel Beckett. CIP-2

Enueg II. Samuel Beckett. NoAM

Enumeration. Ilse Aichinger. AF, tr. by Allen H. Chappel

Envelope, The. Maxine W. Kumin. NALW

Envelope looks so peculiar, The. Aleksandr Semionovich Kushner. TCRP

Enveloping Echo, The. Ion Caraion. AF, tr. by Marguerite Dorian

Enviable Isles, The. Herman Melville. NCAP

Envies, The. George Bowering. NOBC

Envious and foul disease, could there not be. Epigram. To the Small-Pox, An. Ben Jonson. NOSC

Envious wits, what hath been mine offence. Sir Philip Sidney. PoE; Son Fr. Astrophil and Stella.

Environment. Lionel Kearns. NOBC

Environs. Larry Eigner. FTOS; NeAP

Environs of Vanholt I. Charles Spear. PeNZ

Envoi. James McAuley. BMAP

Envoi: "Go, dumb-born book." Ezra Pound. See Hugh Selwyn Mauberley (Life and Contacts)

Envoi: "God, thou great symmetry." Anna Wickham. MoBrPo

Envoi: "Hear me, whom I betrayed." James Vincent Cunningham. VGW

Envoi: "My country is not a country." Eli W. Mandel. NOBC

Envoi (1919). Ezra Pound. HAP; TCAPo; UnPo; VGW Fr. Hugh Selwyn Mauberley (Life and Contacts).

Envoi: "Sun in the mouth of the day." Robley, Jr. Wilson. InvLad; PBCAP

Envoi: "Take of me what is not my own." Kathleen Jessie Raine. NOBE

Envoi: "There's a whisper down the field where the year has shot her yield." Rudyard Kipling. OBEV

Envoi: Waking After Snow. David Baker. PasH

Envoi: Washington Square Park. Myra Cohn Livingston. SSCS

Envoi: "What have want to give." Kathleen Jessie Raine. WPE

Envoy. May Kendall. ViWPN

Envoy: "Go, songs, for ended is our brief, sweet play." Francis Thompson. MoBrPo

Envoy: "Good Night, at last." Robert Duncan. VGW Fr. Passages.

Envoy: "I left. I'd finished raising you. I walked." Walter Kirn. Unle

Envoy: "If homely virtues draw from me a tune." James Weldon Johnson. SacPr

Envoy of Mr. Cogito, The. Zbigniew Herbert. PoetW; WoPoe, *tr. by* Carpenter Bogdana, John Carpenter and Bogdana Carpenter

Envoy: "They are not long, the weeping and the laughter." Ernest Christopher Dowson. *See* Vitae Summa Brevis Spem Nos Vetat Incohare Longam

Envoy to Scogan. Geoffrey Chaucer. NPeEn

Envy. "Naum Korzhavin." TCRP, *tr. by* Vladimir Lunis and Albert C. Todd

Envy. Charles Lamb. WoRP

Envy. Adelaide Anne Procter. NOBVV; NPeEn; VWP

Envy of Poor Lovers, The. Austin Clarke. CIP-2

Envy the mad killer who lies in the ditch and grieves. Crime. Robert Penn Warren. FuPo

Envy, why carp'st thou my time is spent so ill. Ovid. CABP; NoSic, *tr. by* Christopher Marlowe *Fr.* Elegies.

Envy with heavy heart asked for shrift. William Langland. NAEL-5v1; NAEL-6v1; NAEL-7v1 *Fr.* Vision of Piers Plowman, The.

Envy withered the last stars. (LL) Birth of the Foal. Ferenc Juhász. RB; WoPoe, *tr. by* David Wevill

Envying the Pelican. Richard Weber. CIP-2

Enzensberger at "Exiles." John Tranter. BMAP

Eolian Harp, The. Samuel Taylor Coleridge. FHYEP; NAEL-5v2; NAEL-6v2; NOBRP; NPeEn *Fr.* Effusions.

Eous. Oliver Reynolds. TCAWP *Fr.* Tone Poem.

Ephemera Today on "All My Children." Connie Deanovich.
"Natalie gets discovered in her pit by an old, drunken transient." ReTh

Ephemeridae. Daniel Gerard Hoffman. YaYoPo

Ephemeron. Annie Fields. PoBW

Ephesos. Duris. GrAn, *tr. by* Peter Jay

Ephraim Repenting. William Cowper. ChIV-1 *Fr.* Olney Hymns.

Epi-strauss-ium. Arthur Hugh Clough. NAEL-5v2; NAEL-6v2

Epic: "I have lived in important places, times." Patrick Kavanagh. BIrV; CABP; CIP-2; HarvBoo; MakPoe; ModIr; NOIV; NPeEn; NoP-4; OxBSo

Epic of Gilgamesh, The. *Unknown.*
Coming of Enkidu, The. CAGL, *tr. by* N. K. Sandars
Death of Enkidu, The. CAGL, *tr. by* N. K. Sandars
"Gilgamesh went abroad in the world, but he met with none who could withstand his arms till he came to Uruk." CAGL, *tr. by* N. K. Sandars
"Hear me, great ones of Uruk." CAGL, *tr. by* N. K. Sandars
"In the early hours of the next morning dawning." WoPoe, *tr. by* David Ferry
Lament of Gilgamesh for Enkidu, The. CAGL, *tr. by* N. K. Sandars
"When the daylight came Enkidu got up and cried to Gilgamesh, "O my brother, such a dream I had last night." CAGL, *tr. by* N. K. Sandars
"With the first light of the early morning dawning." WoPoe, *tr. by* David Ferry

Epic, The [Morte d'Arthur]. Tennyson. NAEL-5v2; NAEL-6v2 *Fr.* Morte d'Arthur.

Epicedium by Elizabeth Hoby, Their Mother, on the Death of Her Two Daughters Elizabeth and Anne, An. Elizabeth Cooke Hoby. EMWP

Epicoene; or, The Silent Woman. Ben Jonson.
(Simplex Munditiis.) AWP; NOBE; OBEV
(Simplicity and Sweet Neglect.) OxAEP-1
(Clerimont's Song.) BASC; NOSC; PoE
(Song.) OxBSP
"Still to be neat, still to be dressed [*or* Drest]." BeJo; HAP; NAEL-5v1; NAEL-6v1; NAEL-7v1; NIL-7; NPeEn; NoP-4; PAI; PoPoPo; TFi; WeW-3

Epicure, Dining at Crewe, An. Limerick: "Epicure, Dining at Crewe, An." *Unknown.* NTCP; PeLi; PeLV

Epicure, The, Sung by One in the Habit of a Town Gallant. Thomas Jordan. *See* Careless Gallant, The

Epicure, The. Abraham Cowley. AWP; BeJo; OBEV; OxAEP-1
"Crown me with roses whilest I live." OBVE

Epicurean. William James Linton. EBVV

Epicurean Ode, An. John Hall. MeLP; NOSC; NPeEn

Epicurean Reminiscences of a Sentimentalist. Thomas Hood. PeLV

Epidemic. Charles Reznikoff. APT-2

Epidemic / of freedom, An. Vyacheslav Kupriyanov [*or* Kuprianov]. TCRP

Epiderm. Michael Dransfield. BMAP; CBAP

Epigram. Callimachus. WoPoe, *tr. by* Stanley Lombardo and Diane Rayor

Epigram. Samuel Johnson. *See* Turnip Vendor, The

Epigram IV.v: Of Treason. Sir John Harington [*or* Harrington]. *See* Of Treason

Epigram 29: "Gentlewoman of the dealing trade, A." Samuel Rowlands. NOSC

Epigram, A Supposed Construction. John Taylor. NOSC

Epigram: "After some years Bohemian came to this." James Vincent Cunningham. VGW

Epigram: "And now I, Meleager, am among them." Meleager. GrAn, *tr. by* Peter Whigham

Epigram: "And what is love? Misunderstanding, pain." James Vincent Cunningham. CRP; HAP

Epigram: "As honey in wine / wine, honey." Meleager. GrAn, *tr. by* Peter Whigham

Epigram: "At ten a clock, when I the fire rake." Francis Daniel Pastorius. SCAP

Epigram: "At 12 o'clock in the afternoon." Meleager. GrAn; WoPoe, *tr. by* Peter Whigham

Epigram: "Because I am idolatrous and have besought." Ernest Christopher Dowson. OxBSP

Epigram: "Boy's cocks, Diodore." Strato [*or* Straton]. GrAn, *tr. by* Thomas Meyer

Epigram: "Breath of my life, The—no less." Meleager. GrAn, *tr. by* Peter Whigham

Epigram: "Broad and ample he warms himself." *Unknown.* NOIV, *tr. by* Thomas Kinsella

Epigram: "Could Beatrice have written like Dante." Anna Andreyevna Akhmatova. TCRP, *tr. by* Max Hayward and Stanley Kunitz

Epigram: "Dark thoughts are my companions. I have wined." James Vincent Cunningham. VGW

Epigram: "Dear, if unsocial privacies obsess me." James Vincent Cunningham. VGW

Epigram: "'Do you not wish to renounce the Devil?'" Armand Lanusse. TTY, *tr. by* Langston Hughes

Epigram: Dutch, The. George Canning. OxBoLi; PeLV

Epigram Engraved on the Collar of a Dog Given [*or* Which I Gave] to His Royal Highness. Pope. FaBoEE; InPK-6; KaS; NOEC; NTCP; OxBEV; OxBSP; PAI
(Engraved on the Collar of a Dog, Which I Gave to His Royal Highness.) OxBoLi; SoSe-8; TTTS

Epigram: "Fair Beatrice tucks her coat up somewhat high." John Taylor. NOSC

Epigram for a Worm. Daria Menicanti. CItWP, *tr. by* Cinzia Sartini Blum and Lara Trubowitz

Epigram: "Friend [*or* friends] on this scaffold Thomas More lies dead." James Vincent Cunningham. *See* Friend, on This Scaffold Thomas More Lies Dead

Epigram from the French: "Sir, I admit your general [*or* gen'ral] Rule." Pope. FaBoEE
(Fool and the Poet, The.) NBLV

Epigram: "Gold priests, wooden chalices." *Unknown.* NOIV, *tr. by* Thomas Kinsella

Epigram: "Golden casket I designed, A." John Swanwick [*or* Swanick] Drennan. BIrV

Epigram: "Good Fortune, when I hailed her recently." James Vincent Cunningham. APT-2; VCAP

Epigram: "Great woe, fire & war come on me." Skythinos. GrAn, *tr. by* Thomas Meyer

Epigram: "Heat goes deep as cold." *Unknown.* NOIV, *tr. by* Thomas Kinsella

Epigram: "Here lies my wife. Eternal peace." James Vincent Cunningham. NIP-4; OBAL

Epigram: "Here lies New Critic who would fox us." James Vincent Cunningham. APT-2; MoAmPo; OBAL

Epigram: "Hetero-sex is best for the man of a serious turn of mind." Argentarius. GrAn, *tr. by* Fleur Adcock

Epigram: "Homer was poor. His scholars live at ease." James Vincent Cunningham. VGW; WoPoe

Epigram: "How we desire desire! Joy of surcease." James Vincent Cunningham. VGW

Epigram: "I am provoked." Strato [*or* Straton]. GrAn, *tr. by* W. G. Shepherd

Epigram: "I delight in the prime of a boy of twelve." Strato [*or* Straton]. GrAn, *tr. by* Thomas Meyer

Epigram: "I had gone broke, and got set to come back." James Vincent Cunningham. MoAmPo; OxBSP; VCAP

Epigram: "I loved thee beautiful and kind." Robert Nugent. NOEC

Epigram: "I was thirsty." Meleager. GrAn, *tr. by* Peter Whigham

Epigram: "I who by day am function of the light." James Vincent Cunningham. VGW
(Motto for a Sun Dial.) APT-2

Epigram: "If men be judged wise." Joseph Solomon Del Medigo. TrJP

Epigram in a Maid of Honour's Prayer-Book. Pope. FaBoEE

Epigram: "In whose will is our peace? Thou happiness." James Vincent Cunningham. VGW

Epigram: "It is true that I held Thero fair." Meleager. GrAn, *tr. by* Peter Whigham

Epigram: "King to Oxford sent a troop of horse, The." Sir William Browne (1692–1774). FaBoEE; OxBEV

Epigram: "Kissing Hippomenes, I crave." Paulus [*or* Paulos] Silentiarius. GrAn, *tr.* by Andrew Miller

Epigram: "Lasses, like nuts at bottom brown." Allan Ramsay. FaBoEE

Epigram: "Life flows to death as rivers to the sea." James Vincent Cunningham. APT-2; VGW

Epigram: Likeness, The. Martial. RomPo, *tr.* by Brian Hill

Epigram: "Long hair, endless curls trained by the devoted." Strato [*or* Straton]. GrAn, *tr.* by Teddy Hogge

Epigram: "Look how yon lecher's legs are worn away." John Taylor. NOSC

Epigram: "Loss of our learning brought darkness, weakness and woe." *Unknown.* NOIV, *tr.* by Thomas Kinsella

Epigram: "Love signed the contract blithe and leal." John Swanick [*or* Swanick] Drennan. BIrV

Epigram: "Lusty wench as nimble as an eel, A." John Taylor. NOSC

Epigram: "Member of the modern great, A." John Cunningham. FaBoEE

Epigram: "Midas, they say, possessed the art of old." "Peter Pindar." NIL-7; NIP-4

Epigram: "Milo's from home; and, Milo being gone." Martial. OBVE, *tr.* by Elijah Fenton

Epigram: "My heart still hovering round about you." Robert Nugent. NOEC

Epigram: "My soul, sit thou a patient looker-on." Francis Quarles. NOBE; PoToHe

(Epigram: Respice Finem.) OBEV

(My Soul, Sit Thou a Patient Looker-on.) NIP-4

Epigram: "Naked I came, naked I leave the scene." James Vincent Cunningham. *See* Five Epigrams

Epigram: "Need from excess—excess from folly growing." Samuel Bishop. NOEC

Epigram: "Nicander, ooh, your leg's got hairs!" Alcaeus [*or* Alkaios]. GrAn, *tr.* by Tony Harrison

Epigram on a Lawyer's Desiring One of the Tribe to Look with Respect to a Gibbet. Robert Fergusson. OxBS

Epigram on an Academic Visit to the Continent. Richard Porson. *See* Porson's Visit to the Continent

Epigram on Fasting. Jonathan Swift. OBVE

Epigram on Florio. John Winstanley. FaBoEE

Epigram: On Inclosures. *Unknown.* OxBoLi

(Epigram: On Inclosures.) OxBoLi

(On Enclosures.) FaBoEE

Epigram on Milton. Dryden. *See* Lines Printed under the Engraved Portrait of Milton [In Tonson's Folio of the "Paradise Lost"]

Epigram on One Who Made Long Epitaphs. Pope. FaBoEE

Epigram: "On parent knees, a naked new-born child." Sir William Jones. FaBoEE; OBEV

(Moral Tetrastich, A.) OxBSP

Epigram on Scolding, An. Jonathan Swift. FaBoEE; FaBoVe; NPeEn

Epigram: On Sir Roger Phillimore. *Unknown.* NBLV

Epigram on the Feuds between Handel and Bononcini. John Byrom. FaBoEE; NOBL; NOEC

Epigram on the First of April. John Winstanley. NOEC

Epigram on Woman, An. Philip Ayres. FaBoEE

Epigram: Political Reflexion. Howard Nemerov. NIP-4 *Fr.* Epigrams.

Epigram: "Poverty? wealth? seek neither." Kassia. WPOW, *tr.* by Patrick Diehl

Epigram: "'Prepare to meet the King of Terrors,' cried." Ebenezer Elliott. NOBVV

Epigram: Respice Finem. Francis Quarles. *See* Epigram: "My soul, sit thou a patient looker-on."

Epigram: "Says a Reverend Priest to a less Rev'rend friend." *Unknown.* NOBRP

Epigram VII: Winifred. Hugh Crompton. NOSC

Epigram: "Since first you knew my am'rous smart." Robert Nugent. NOEC

Epigram LXVII: Time, the Interpreter. Hugh Crompton. NOSC

Epigram: "There chanced to meet together in an inn." John Taylor. NOSC

Epigram: "There was this gym-teacher." Strato [*or* Straton]. GrAn, *tr.* by Teddy Hogge

Epigram: "This *Humanist* Whom No Beliefs Constrained." James Vincent Cunningham. *See* This *Humanist* Whom No Beliefs Constrained

Epigram: "This is my curse, Pompous, I pray." James Vincent Cunningham. HAP

Epigram: "Those snooty boys in all their purple drag!" Strato [*or* Straton]. GrAn, *tr.* by Tony Harrison

Epigram: "Thy nags (the leanest things alive)." Matthew Prior. FaBoEE

Epigram: "Time heals not: it extends a sorrow's scope." James Vincent Cunningham. VGW; WoPoe

Epigram: "Time was when once upon a time, such toys." Glaukos. GrAn, *tr.* by Peter Jay

Epigram: "To John I ow'd great obligation." Matthew Prior. FaBoEE; OBVE; OxBEV

(Quits.) AWP

Epigram. To the Household. 1630, An. Ben Jonson. BeJo; Son

Epigram. To the Small-Pox, An. Ben Jonson. NOSC

Epigram: "Tom's sickness did his morals mend." Matthew Prior. FaBoEE

Epigram: "' 'Twas not so in my time,' surly Grumio exclaims." Samuel Bishop. NOEC

Epigram: "Wealth covers sin—the poor." Kassia. WPOW, *tr.* by Patrick Diehl

Epigram: "Were I a king, I could command content." Edward de Vere, 17th Earl of Oxford. *See* Were I a king, I could command content

Epigram: "What is a communist? One who hath yearnings." Ebenezer Elliott. NOBVV

(On Communists.) NBLV; NOBL

Epigram: "When Bibo thought fit from the world to retreat." Matthew Prior. FaBoEE

Epigram: "When other Ladies to the Shades go down." Pope. *See* On Certain Ladies

Epigram: "While Adam slept, from him his Eve arose." *Unknown.* FaBoEE

Epigram: "Whilst maudlin Whigs deplore their Cato's fate." Nicholas Rowe. ECEV

Epigram: "Why all the racket, you chattering birds?" *Unknown.* GrAn, *tr.* by Thomas Meyer

Epigram: "Within this mindless vault." James Vincent Cunningham. RB; VGW; WoPoe

Epigram: "Woman working hard and wisely, A." Kassia. WPOW, *tr.* by Patrick Diehl

Epigram: "Women, as some men say, unconstant be." George Wither. NOSC

Epigram: "World laid low, and the wind blew like a dust, The." *Unknown.* FaBoWar; NOIV, *tr.* by Thomas Kinsella

Epigram: "Yes, every poet is a fool." Matthew Prior. FaBoEE

Epigram: "You ask me how Contempt who claims to sleep." James Vincent Cunningham. VCAP

Epigram: "You were a pretty boy once, Archestratus, and." Philip of Thessalonica. GrAn, *tr.* by Edith Morgan

Epigram: "You wonder why Drab sells her love for gold?" James Vincent Cunningham. APT-2

Epigrams. Antipater of Sidon.
  "Artemeias, surely when you from the nether world's bark." HePo
  "Here beside the threshing floor, O hardworking ant." HePo
  "I, who used to ward off the starlings and that snatcher." HePo
  "Let the four-clustered ivy flourish about you, Anacreon." HePo
  "Myriad times, Ptolemy, your father, myriad times." HePo
  "Tell me, woman, your parents, your name, your land. B. Calliteles." HePo
  "This is the barrow of grizzled Maronis, on which you see." HePo
  "To Pallas, three girls, all of an age, skilled as the spider." HePo
  "To Pan three brothers hung up these tools of the trade." HePo

Epigrams. Anyte [*or* Anytes].
  "Children, billy goat, have put crimson reins, The." HePo
  "For her locust, nightingale of the fields, and her cricket that slept." HePo
  "No longer, as before, will you wake at dawn and flap." HePo
  "No longer shall I exult in the floating seas and arch." HePo
  "Often on this her daughter's tomb did Cleina grieve." HePo
  "This tomb Damis built for his courageous horse." HePo

Epigrams. Asclepiades.
  "I am not yet twenty-two and I am tired of living." HePo
  "Lysidice dedicated to you, Cypris." HePo
  "This is the sweet work of Erinna, not much, of course." HePo

Epigrams. Bassus [*or* Bassos].
  "I'm not planning to turn into gold. Somebody else." HePo

Epigrams. Callimachus.
  "At dawn we buried Melanippus. At sunset." HePo
  "Do not say 'Godspeed' to me, wicked heart." HePo
  "'Goodbye, O sun,' said Cleombrotus of Ambracia." HePo
  "Here Philip the father buried." HePo
  "Hesiod's is the theme and his the style." HePo
  "I hate the cyclic poem, nor do I rejoice." HePo
  "On the mountain, Epicydes the hunter seeks." HePo
  "Someone told me, Heracleitus." HePo
  "These gifts to Aphrodite." HePo
  "Timon, for you exist no more." HePo
  "Whoever passes by my tomb, know." HePo
  "Would that there had never been swift ships!" HePo
  "You pass the tomb of Battus' son, well skilled." HePo

Epigrams. Crinagoras.
  "You toss now to the left; you toss now to the right." HePo

Epigrams. Sir John Davies.
  "Amongst the poets Dacus numbered is." NoSic
  "Cosmus hath more discoursing in his head." NoSic

"Fine youth Ciprius is more terse and neat, The." NoSic
(In Cosmum.) NPeEn
"Philo the gentleman, the fortune teller." NoSic
"Titus the brave and valorous gallant." NoSic
Epigrams. Dioscorides. (fl. 1st cent. B.C. or A.D. 1st cent.)
"Call me Polyxena, the wife of Archelaus." HePo
"Eros, that bane of men, molded soft as marrow." HePo
"Lamisca, who breathed her last in lamentable pangs of labor." HePo
"They drive me mad, those rosy lips, forever prattling." HePo
Epigrams. Diotimus.
"Polyaenus' daughter, Scyllis, came to the wide gates." HePo
"What use to suffer in labor, give birth to children, if she." HePo
Epigrams. Erinna.
"I am the grave of Baucis the bride. Passing by." HePo
"Stele and my Sirens and mournful pitcher that hold." HePo
Epigrams. Leonidas of Tarentum.
Fisherman, The. AWP, tr. by Andrew Lang
"Forever brigands and pirates, the Cretans are never just." HePo
"Get out of my hut, you stealthy vermin! Leonidas'" HePo
"Gloomy minister of Hades who sail this stream." HePo
"His ball, beautiful leaved, and his noisy boxwood rattle." HePo
"If the tombstone placed over me is small to see and close." HePo
"Morning and evening, sleep she drove away." AWP, tr. by Andrew Lang
"Old Platthis often thrust away her morning's sleep." HePo
Spinning Woman, The. AWP, tr. by Andrew Lang
"Theris the old, the waves that harvested." AWP, tr. by Andrew Lang
"Theris, thrice-old, who got his living from." HePo
"Thundering sea, why in savage storm did you plunge." HePo
"To Gluttony and Guzzling, that fastidious gourmet." HePo
"To Pallas, Theris, cunning of hand, dedicated." HePo
"Wallet, the hide of a goat, tough and untanned, a stick, A." HePo
"Whoever then are you? Whose wretched bones are these." HePo
Epigrams. Martial.
"Artemidorus sold his land to buy a boy." CAGL, tr. by Richard O'Connell
"Bearded Callistratus wedded rugged Afer." CAGL, tr. by Richard E. Prior
"Chrestus, your balls are depilated." CAGL, tr. by Joseph S. Salemi
"Here he is whom you read and clamor for." WoPoe, tr. by William Matthews
"If by chance, Flaccus, someone could offer me for the asking." CAGL, tr. by Richard E. Prior
"Nasica raped the doctor's pretty lad." CAGL, tr. by Brian Hill
"Surrounded by eunuchs and limp as a tissue." WoPoe, tr. by William Matthews
"Ted's studio burnt down, with all his poems." WoPoe, tr. by William Matthews
"You lie and I concur. You 'give'" WoPoe, tr. by William Matthews
"You often say my work is coarse. It's true." CAGL, tr. by J. A. Pott
"You sold a slave just yesterday." WoPoe, tr. by William Matthews
"Your slave boy's cock is aching, Naevolus." CAGL, tr. by Joseph S. Salemi
Epigrams. Meleager.
"Cup takes its sweet joy and tells how it touches, The." HePo
"Did I not tell you, my soul, 'By Cypris, you will be caught'" HePo
"Flower-feasting bee, why do you touch upon." HePo
"I foster a Love fond of playing ball. It throws." HePo
"I'll weave in the white violet. I'll weave in." HePo
"I'm down. Step on my neck, you savage god, with your heel." HePo
"I say that my sweetly prattling Heliodora will someday." HePo
"I was a quick-footed, long-eared hare, just snatched from my mother's." HePo
"If you burn my scorched soul too often, Love, she'll fly." HePo
"Love fed Heliodora's fingernail and made." HePo
"Love-prone Asclepias with eyes like a summer's day." HePo
"Mosquito, may you fly, a swift courier for me." HePo
"Mosquitoes, shameless and shrill of voice, sucking the blood." HePo
"Now the white violet blooms and narcissus that loves." HePo
"Pour and say again and again and yet again." HePo
"Pour for Heliodora Persuasion and pour for Cypris." HePo
"Sell it, though it sleeps still at its mother's breast!" HePo
"Shrilling cicada, drunk on drops of dew, you sing." HePo
"Still in his mother's lap the baby Love played." HePo
"Tears beneath the earth, Heliodora, I give." HePo
"Within my heart Love himself made Heliodora." HePo
"Yes, I'd rather hear Heliodora's voice." HePo
"You're sleeping, Zenophila, my tender bloom. I wish." HePo
Epigrams. Mnasalcas.
"Say, stranger, that this is the tomb of the mare Aethyia." HePo

Epigrams. Howard Nemerov. OBAL
(Epigram: Political Reflexion.) NIP-4
Epigrams. Philodemus.
"I fell in love with Demo of Paphos. No big surprise." HePo
"I've been in love. Who hasn't? I went out and got drunk." HePo
"In the middle of the night I slipped away from my husband." HePo
"O foot, O leg, O thighs for which I rightly died." HePo
"O two-horned moon, you love the parties that last all night." HePo
"Philaenion is small and swart, but her hair curls more." HePo
"Xanthippe's strumming, her chatter, her speaking eye, her song." HePo
Epigrams. Tymnes.
(Dog from Malta, The.) GrAn, tr. by Edmund Charles Blunden
"He came from Malta." FaBoCh; FaBoEE; Spl; WoPoe, tr. by Edmund Charles Blunden
Maltese Dog, A. FaBoCh; FaBoEE; Spl; WoPoe, tr. by Edmund Charles Blunden
"Stone says that it covers here the white dog, The." HePo
Epigrams and Epitaphs. Clive Staples Lewis.
"Save yourself. Run and leave me. I must go back." EBEV
Epigrams must be curt, nor seem. Walter Savage Landor. FaBoEE
Epigrams of Martial, The. Laurie Duggan.
One xxxvii. BMAP
"You drink from crystal." BMAP
Epigrams on Lord Galloway. Robert Burns.
"Bright ran thy line, O Galloway." OxBoLi
Lord Galloway. OxBoLi
"No Stewart art thou, Galloway." FaBoEE
On Lord Galloway. FaBoEE
Epigraph. William Blake. Spl Fr. Jerusalem; The Emanation of the Giant Albion.
Epigraph to "Drum-Taps." Walt Whitman. PAI
Epil y Filiast. Harri Webb. AngWePo; TCAWP
Epilog: "Like the ears of wheat in a wheat-field growing." Heinrich Heine. See North Sea, The
Epilogue. Anna Andreyevna Akhmatova. PFTM-2, tr. by Lenore Mayhew and William McNaughton Fr. Poem without a Hero.
Epilogue. William Shakespeare. RB; UV Fr. Tempest, The.
Epilogue. Wallace Stevens. See Notes toward a Supreme Fiction
Epilogue. Tennyson. Fr. In Memoriam A. H. H.
Epilogue. Miklós Zrínyi. IQMS, tr. by Michael Hatwell
Epilogue: "At the midnight in the silence of the sleep-time." Robert Browning. NAEL-5v2; NAEL-6v2; NOBE
Epilogue (At the Proper Distance). Mariella Bettarini. CItWP, tr. by Cinzia Sartini Blum and Lara Trubowitz
Epilogue: "Away, for we are ready to a man!" James Elroy Flecker. NOBE Fr. Golden Journey to Samarkand, The.
Epilogue: "Carol, every violet has." Alfred Noyes. MoBrPo Fr. Flower of Old Japan, The.
Epilogue: "Child! we must quit these visionary scenes." Hannah More. ECWP Fr. Search after Happiness, The.
Epilogue: "He is not dead nor liveth." Dorothy Wellesley, Duchess of Wellington. OBMV Fr. Deserted House.
Epilogue: "Heaven, which man's generations draws." Francis Thompson. MoBrPo Fr. Judgment in Heaven, A.
Epilogue: "I have seen flowers come in stony places." John Masefield. FaBoEE; OxBEV; OxBTC
Epilogue: "I, the genius Severyanin." "Igor Severyanin" [or Severianin]. TCRP, tr. by Bernard Meares
Epilogue: "If Luther's day expand to Darwin's year." Herman Melville. APN-2; NCAP; TCAPo Fr. Clarel: A Poem and Pilgrimage in the Holy Land.
Epilogue: "Like the stalks of wheat in the fields." Heinrich Heine. TrJP Fr. North Sea, The.
Epilogue: "Nothing now to mark the spot." Rachel Lyman Field. OBCA Fr. Circus Garland, A.
Epilogue: "Now my charms are all o'erthrown." William Shakespeare. CTC Fr. Tempest, The.
Epilogue: "O chansons foregoing." Ezra Pound. OxBA
Epilogue: "'O where are you going?' said reader to rider." W. H. Auden. FaBoCh; NOBE; NoAM; OxBEV; UV Fr. Five Songs.
Epilogue: "On the first of the Feast of Feasts." Robert Browning. ChIV-2
Epilogue: "Terence, this is stupid stuff." A. E. Housman. See Terence, This Is Stupid Stuff
Epilogue: "That death might not be casual." Burns Singer. FaBoTw
Epilogue: "Those blessed structures, plot and rhyme." Robert Lowell. HCAP; NAAL-2v2; NAAL-5; PoetW; VCAP
(Those blessèd structures, plot and rhyme.) HarvBoo; NoAM; NoP-4; PoPoPo

Epilogue: "Thus far, with rough and all-unable pen."   William Shakespeare.
    CTC   *Fr.* King Henry V.
Epilogue: "Time is a thing."   Stephen Spender.   MoBrPo
Epilogue to a Human Drama.   Stephen Spender.   AF
Epilogue to a Poetry Reading.   M. K. Joseph.   PeNZ
Epilogue to Alun Mabon.   John Ceiriog Hughes.   OBWVE, *tr.* by H. Idris Bell
Epilogue to Casualties.   John Pepper Clark Bekedermo.   HBAPE
Epilogue to "The Parson's Wedding."   Thomas Killigrew.   NOSC
Epilogue to the Satires, in Two Dialogues.   Pope.
    Art of Satire, The.   ECEV; OBSV
    "Ask you what provocation I have had?"   ECEV; OBSV
    (Defence of Satire.)   NOEC
    (Power of Ridicule, The.)   NOBE
    "Spare then the person, and expose the vice."   OBSV
    Triumph of Vice, The.   NOBE; NPeEn; OBSV
    "Virtue may choose the high or low degree."   NOBE; NPeEn; OBSV
Epilogue to "The Sister."   Oliver Goldsmith.
    "Lud! what a group the motley scene discloses!"   OBSV
Epilogue to *Tyrannic[k] Love.*   Dryden.   OBCoV   *Fr.* Tyrannic Love.
Epilogue: "Truly my Satan thou art but a dunce."   William Blake.   HAP;
    PeECV; PoE; WeW-3   *Fr.* Gates of Paradise, The.
Epilogue: "Well, when all is said and done."   "Æ"   MoBrPo
Epilogue: "What shall we do for Love these days?"   Lascelles Abercrombie.
    MoBrPo   *Fr.* Emblems of Love.
Epilogue: "With heart at rest I climbed the citadel's."   Charles Baudelaire.
    AWP, *tr.* by Arthur Symons
Epiphanies of Light! (LL)   Lemon Trees, The.   Eugenio Montale.   PoetW;
    WoPoe, *tr.* by William Arrowsmith
Epiphanies of the Voodoo Gods.   René Depestre.
    Attibon Legba.   NegPo, *tr.* by Ellen Conroy Kennedy
    "I am Attibon Legba."   NegPo, *tr.* by Ellen Conroy Kennedy
    "It was a summer evening in an Alabama city."   NegPo, *tr.* by Ellen Conroy
        Kennedy
    Prelude.   NegPo, *tr.* by Ellen Conroy Kennedy
Epiphany.   Christine D'Haen.   TuT, *tr.* by Dennis O'Driscoll
Epiphany.   Robert Fitzgerald.   ChrPo
Epiphany.   Pem Kremer.   HW
Epiphany.   Christopher Smart.   NOCV   *Fr.* Hymns and Spiritual Songs for the
    Fasts and Festivals of the Church of England.
Epiphany.   Andrea Zanzotto.   VCWP, *tr.* by Ruth Feldman
Epipsychidion.   Shelley.
    "True Love in this differs from gold and clay."   FHYEP
Episode 17.   William Carlos Williams.   APT-1; OxBA   *Fr.* Paterson.
Episode of a Night of May.   Arthur Symons.   PeVV   *Fr.* Scènes de la Vie de
    Bohème.
Episode of Hands.   Hart Crane.   CAGL; NIL-7
Epistemology.   Richard Wilbur.   CRP; NOBA; NoAM; OxBSP
Epistemology, and all the afternoon.   Days like Prose.   Alan Michael Parker.
    NeAmPo
Epistle, An.   Elizabeth Hands.   PoBW
Epistle [II,] to a Lady[: of the Characters of Women].   Pope.   NAEL-5v1;
    NAEL-6v1; NAEL-7v1; NOEC
    (To a Lady.)   OxBoLi
Epistle [II,] to a Lady[: Of the Characters of Women].   Pope.   NAEL-5v1;
    NOEC
    C[h]loe.   AWP; NOBE; OBSV
    "Men, some to bus'ness, some to pleasure take."   NPeEn; OBSV; OxBEV
    "Yet C[h]loe sure was form'd without a Spot"   AWP; NOBE; OBSV
Epistle III, to Allen Lord Bathurst.   Pope.
    "Behold what blessings Wealth to life can lend!"   OxBEV
    Duke of Buckingham, The.   NOBE
    "In the worst inn's worst room, with mat half-hung."   NOBE
    Sir Balaam.   NPeEn
    "Where London's column, pointing at the skies."   NPeEn
Epistle IV, to Richard Boyle, Earl of Burlington.   Pope.
    (At Timon's Villa.)   OBSV
    "At Timon's villa let us pass a day."   NOEC; NPeEn; OxBEV
    Timon's Villa.   NOEC; NPeEn; OxBEV
Epistle Answering to One that Asked to Be Sealed of the Tribe of Ben, An.
    Ben Jonson.   BASC; BeJo
Epistle Containing the Strange Medical Experience of Karshish, the Arab
    Physician, An.   Robert Browning.   ChIV-2; NAEL-5v2; NAEL-6v2
Epistle from a Half-Pay Officer in the Country to His Friend in London, An.
    Richardson Pack.   NOEC
Epistle from Alexander to Hephaestion in His Sickness, An.   Anne Finch,
    Countess of Winchilsea.   EMWP
Epistle from Fern Hill.   Mary Jones.   ECWP

Epistle from Mr Murray to Dr Polidori.   Byron.   OBCoV
    (Epistle from Mr Murray to Dr Polidori.)   OBCoV
Epistle from Mr. Pope to Dr. Arbuthnot, An.   Pope.   *See* Epistle to Dr.
    Arbuthnot
Epistle from Mrs. Yonge to Her Husband.   Lady Mary Wortley Montagu.
    NAEL-5v1; NAEL-6v1; NAEL-7v1; NALW; NPeEn; NoP-4
Epistle: "How happy you who varied joys pursue."   Lady Mary Wortley
    Montagu.   ECWP
Epistle in Form of a Ballad to His Friends.   François Villon.   AWP, *tr.* by
    Algernon Charles Swinburne
Epistle of Deborah Dough, The.   Mary Leapor.   ECWP
Epistle of Love and of Consolation unto Israel, An.   Dorothy White.   EMWP
Epistle to a Friend, to Persuade [*or* Perswade] Him to the Wars, [*or* Warres] An.
    Ben Jonson.   FaBoWar
    "Wake, friend, from forth thy lethargy; the drum."   FaBoWar
Epistle to a Lady, An.   Mary Leapor.   BWW; CABP; ECWP; NOEC
Epistle to a Lady: Of the Characters of Women.   Pope.   *See* Epistle [II,] to a
    Lady[: Of the Characters of Women]
Epistle to a Patron, An.   Frank Templeton Prince.   HarvBoo; OxBEV
Epistle to a Young Friend.   Robert Burns.   EBEV
Epistle to Artemisia.   Mary Leapor.
    "Once Delpho read—sage Delpho, learned and wise."   ECWP
    Patrons of My Early Song, The.   ECWP
Epistle to Augusta.   Byron.   FHYEP
Epistle to Baron Delvig.   Oleg Grigorevich Chukhonstev.   TCRP, *tr.* by Simon
    Franklin
Epistle to Be Left in the Earth.   Archibald MacLeish.   APT-1; MoAmPo;
    NOBA
Epistle to Clemena, Occasioned by an Argument She Had Maintained Against
    the Author.   Elizabeth Thomas.   ECWP
Epistle to Dr. Arbuthnot.   Pope.   FHYEP; NAEL-6v1; NAEL-7v1; OxAEP-1;
    PoE; TFi
    Apologia pro Vita Sua.   NOBE
    Atticus ("Peace to all such! but were there one whose fires").   AWP; InPK-6;
        NOBE; OxBEV; TRP
    "Bard whom pilf'red pastorals reknown, The."   OBSV
    Bufo.   OBSV
    "Lash like mine no honest man shall dread, A."   NPeEn
    "Let Sporus tremble—'What? That thing of silk'   AWP; NOBE; OBSV;
        OxBEV; SCV
    "Not Fortune's worshipper, nor Fashion's fool."   NOBE
    "Peace to all such! but were there one whose fires."   AWP; InPK-6; NOBE;
        OxBEV; TRP
    "Peace to all such! but were there one whose fires."   NPeEn
    "Proud as Apollo on his forked hill."   OBSV
    Sporus.   AWP; NOBE; OBSV; OxBEV; SCV
    "Why did [*or* do] I write? what sin to me unknown."   EBEV; TOF
    "Yet let me flap this bug with gilded wings."   ECEV
    "You think this cruel? take it for a rule."   NPeEn
Epistle. To Enrique Caracciolo Trejo.   Donald Davie.   HarvBoo
Epistle to George Keats.   John Keats.
    "Ah, my dear friend and brother."   FHYEP
Epistle to Her Friends at Gartmore.   Susanna Blamire.   ECWP
Epistle to John Guthrie.   Sydney Goodsir Smith.   OxBS
Epistle to John Walker, Esq., An.   "Eliza."   ECWP   *Fr.* Tour to the Glaciers of
    Savoy, A.
Epistle. To Katharine, Lady Aubigny.   Ben Jonson.   BeJo
Epistle to Lady Bowyer, An.   Mary Jones.   ECWP
    (How much of paper's spoiled! what floods of ink!)   PEW
Epistle to Lord Burlington.   Pope.
Epistle to Lord Burlington.   OBGa
    "Oft have you hinted to your brother peer."   OBGa
Epistle to Lord Burlington.   Pope.   OBGa   *Fr.* Epistle to Lord Burlington.
Epistle to Master John Selden, An.   Ben Jonson.   BASC; BeJo
Epistle to Miss [*or* Miss Teresa] Blount, on Her Leaving the Town after the
    Coronation.   Pope.   BoLoP; EBEV; FHYEP; NAEL-5v1; NAEL-6v1;
    NAEL-7v1; NOBE; NOEC
    (Epistle to Miss Blount.)   NoP-4
Epistle to Mr. Pope Occasioned by His Characters of Women, An.   Anne
    Ingram, Viscountess Irwin.   NAEL-7v1
    "Female mind like a rude fallow lies, A."   ECWP
Epistle to Mrs Anne Griffiths.   Jane Brereton.
    "But should some snarling critic chance to view."   ECWP
Epistle to My Friend J. B, An.   Robert Dodsley.   NOEC
Epistle to My Gardener.   Nicolas Boileau-Despéaux.
    Epistle to My Gardener.   OBGa, *tr.* by John Ozell
    "Thou as laborious, as thy master kind."   OBGa, *tr.* by John Ozell
Epistle. To Prince Henrie.   Samuel Daniel.

"Theare be great Prince, such as will tell you howe." PBRV

Epistle to Robert Nugent, Esq. with a Picture of Doctor Swift in Old Age, An. William Dunkin.

"Hibernia's Helicon is dry." NOEC

Epistle to Sir Richard Temple. Pope.

Wharton ("Wharton! the scorn and wonder of our days"). AWP

Epistle to the Gentiles. Alfred Hayes. TrJP

Epistle to the King of Sweden, An. Susanna Centlivre.

"To thee—rude warrior, who, we once admired." ECWP

Epistle to the President of the Scottish Society of Antiquaries: On Being Chosen a Correspondent Member. Alexander Geddes. OxBS

Epistle to the Right Hon. Charles James Fox, An. Thomas Maurice.

"How cursed that country, how severe its doom." NOEC

Epistle to the Right Honourable William Pulteney, Esq. John Gay.

French Fops. ECEV

"What peer of France would let him duchess rove." ECEV

Epistle Written in the Country to the Right Honourable the Lord Lovelace, An. Soame Jenyns.

"In days, my Lord, when mother Time." OBSV

"Nor can I for my soul delight." ECEV

Epistles. Horace.

"Health from the lover of the country, me." AWP, tr. by Abraham Cowley

1.1. AWP, tr. by Abraham Cowley

Epistles to Mr. Pope. Edward Young.

"These labouring wits, like paviours, mend our ways." OBSV

Epitafio. Ece Ayhan. WoPoe, tr. by Murat Nemet-Nejat

Epitaph. Marie-Claire Bancquart. MFP, tr. by Martin Sorrell

Epitaph. A. E. Housman. FaBoEE; HarvBoo; NOBVV; OxBEV; Spl

(Here Dead Lie We Because We Did Not Choose.) NoP-4

Epitaph. Katherine Philips. See Epitaph on her Son H. P. at St. Syth's Church

Epitaph. Sir Walter Ralegh. See Even Such Is Time

Epitaph. Charles Reznikoff. APT-2

Epitaph. U Tam'si Tchicaya. PBMAP Fr. L'Arc Musical (1970).

Epitaph. Unknown. WoPoe

Epitaph, An. Thomas Carew. OBEV

(Another [Epitaph on Lady Mary Villiers].) BeJo; CaPo

(Another.) CavPo

(Epitaph, An.) OBEV

Epitaph after Reading Ronsard's Lines from Rabelais. John Millington Synge. FaBoEE

Epitaph: "Again, traveller, you have come a long way led by that star." Thomas McGrath. RaBo

Epitaph, An: "Erected by her sorrowing brothers." Clive Staples Lewis. OBCoV

Epitaph, An: "He worshipped at the altar of Romance." Colin Ellis. OxBTC

Epitaph, An: "Here lie I, once a witty fair." Samuel Wesley. NOEC

Epitaph, An: "Here lies a most beautiful lady." Walter De la Mare. MoBrPo; OBEV; RB

Epitaph, An: "Here lies Nachshon, a man of great renown." Isaac Benjacob. TrJP, tr. by Joseph Chotzner

Epitaph, An: "Here lies Stephen Pwanya." Julius Chingono. PeSAV

Epitaph, An: "Here lieth under this marble ston." Unknown. MiEL

Epitaph, An: "His friends he loved. His direst earthly foes." Sir William Watson. NOBVV

Epitaph, An: "I was buried near this dyke [or Dike]." William Blake. FaBoEE; OBCoV

Epitaph, An: "I was, I am not; smiled, that since did weep." Thomas Heywood. OxBSP

Epitaph, An: "Interred [or Interr'd] beneath this marble stone." Matthew Prior. FaBoEE; NAEL-5v1; NAEL-6v1; NAEL-7v1; OBCoV; OBSV

Epitaph, An: "Like thee I once have stemm'd the sea of life." James Beattie. OBEV

Epitaph, An: "My name—my country—what are they to thee." Paulus [or Paulos] Silentiarius. See No Matter

Epitaph, An: On a Man for Doing Nothing. John Hoskyns [or Hoskins]. NOSC

Epitaph, An: "When I am gone." Josephine D. Henderson Heard. CBWP-4

Epitaph: André Breton. Philippe Soupault. SurPaPo, tr. by Mary Ann Caws and Patricia Terry

Epitaph: "Angler rose, he took his rod, The." Robert Louis Stevenson. OBCoV

Epitaph: "Athenagoras begot Eubulus" Chairemon. GrAn, tr. by Richard Evans

Epitaph: Atticus. Paulus [or Paulos] Silentiarius. GrAn, tr. by Andrew Miller

Epitaph: "Beauty itself lies here, in whom alone." Thomas Randolph. BASC

Epitaph: "Beneath this stone lies William Burke." R. P. Weston. OBCoV

Epitaph: "Body / of / Benjamin Franklin, The." Benjamin Franklin. TCAPo

Epitaph: Chryseomallus the Mime. Paulus [or Paulos] Silentiarius. GrAn, tr. by Andrew Miller

Epitaph: "Daniel and Abigail." Miguel de Barrios. TrJP

Epitaph: "Done to death by slanderous tongues." William Shakespeare. CTC Fr. Much Ado about Nothing.

Epitaph: "Dummer the shepherd sacrific'd." Cotton Mather. SacPr; SCAP

Epitaph Ending in And, The. William Stafford. LCAP-2

Epitaph: "Fate to beauty still must give." Claudian. AWP, tr. by Howard Mumford Jones

Epitaph for a Beatnik Poet. Guy Owen. CRP

Epitaph for a Concord Boy. Stanley Young. ChAP

Epitaph for a Godly Man's Tomb, An. Robert Wild. FaBoEE

Epitaph for a Good Mouser. Anne Stevenson. Spl

Epitaph for a Judge. Benedict Jeitteles. TrJP, tr. by Joseph Chotzner

Epitaph for a Meat-Packer. Guy Owen. CRP

Epitaph for a Poet. Homero [or Umberto] Aridjis. PoetW; STV; TCLAP, tr. by John Frederick Nims

Epitaph for a Postal Clerk. X. J. Kennedy. NIL-7; NIP-4

Epitaph for a Scientist. Lex Banning. NOBAu

Epitaph for Bruno of Angers. Marbod of Rennes. MLL, tr. by Helen Waddell

Epitaph for Cleonicus. Alexander of Pleuron. GrAn

Epitaph for Cu Chuimne. Unknown. NOIV; WoPoe, tr. by Thomas Kinsella

Epitaph for Erotion. Martial. FaBoEE, tr. by James Michie

Epitaph for G. B. Shaw. Max Beerbohm. FaBoEE

Epitaph for George Moore. Thomas Hardy. FaBoEE

Epitaph for His Niece, Sophia. Paul the Deacon. MLL, tr. by Helen Waddell

Epitaph for James Smith. Robert Burns. EBEV

(Epitaph for James Smith.) EBEV

Epitaph for Jonathan Robbins. Philip Freneau. TCAPo

Epitaph for Mael Mhuru. Unknown. NOIV

Epitaph for Maria Wentworth. Thomas Carew. See Maria Wentworth

Epitaph for Mariana Gryphius, His Brother Paul's Little Daughter. Andreas Gryphius. WoPoe, tr. by Christopher Benfey

Epitaph for Mr. Moses Levy. Unknown. TrJP

Epitaph for My Cat. Jean Garrigue. TAP

Epitaph for One Killed at Roncesvalles. Unknown. MLL, tr. by Helen Waddell

Epitaph for One Who Would Not Be Buried in Westminster Abbey. Pope. FaBoEE; NPeEn

Epitaph for [or on] Thomas Clere. Henry Howard, Earl of Surrey. NoSic; OxBSo

(Epitaph on Thomas Clere.) OBWP

(Norfolk sprang thee, Lambeth holds thee dead.) PBRV

(Norfolk sprung thee, Lambeth holds thee dead.) NoP-4

Epitaph for Paulinus of Aquileia and Arno of Salzburg. Alcuin. MLL, tr. by Helen Waddell

Epitaph for Peter Stuyvesant. Henricus Selyns. SCAP

Epitaph for Richard Cavendish, Engraved on his Monument in Hornsey Church. Margaret Russell Clifford, Countess of Cumberland. EMWP

Epitaph for Sir Henry Lee. Unknown. FaBoEE

Epitaph for Sir Lawrence Tanfield. Lady Elizabeth Tanfield. NOSC; TOF

(Tomb of Sir Lawrence Tanfield obiit 30 Ap. 1625 erected by Lady Tanfield 1628.) EMWP

Epitaph for Someone or Other. James Vincent Cunningham. APT-2; OBAL; TRP; WoPoe Fr. Five Epigrams.

Epitaph for St. Amand, Bishop of Utrecht. Alcuin. MLL, tr. by Helen Waddell

Epitaph for the Old Howard. Byron Vazakas. APT-2

Epitaph for the Poet. George Barker. OxBSP

Epitaph for the Race of Man. Edna St. Vincent Millay.

"Here lies, and none to mourn him but the sea." HeIP-4

"O Earth, unhappy planet born to die." HeIP-4

"See where Capella with her golden kids." MoAmPo

Epitaph for the Western Intelligentsia. Richard Allen. NOBAu

Epitaph: "For this she starred her eyes with salt." Elinor Wylie. MoAmPo

Epitaph for Thomas Johnson, Huntsman. Charlton, Sussex. Unknown. NPeEn

Epitaph for Vysotsky. Andrey [or Andrei] Andreievich Voznesensky [or Voznesenskii]. TCRP, tr. by William Jay Smith

Epitaph for William Nicol. Robert Burns. FaBoEE

Epitaph for William Pitt. Byron. FaBoEE

Epitaph for Willie or Little Black Poet with No Future. Sibby Anderson-Thompkins. InTrad

Epitaph: "Fortune's darling, king's content." Unknown. BASC

Epitaph from a Tomb in Asia Minor. Unknown. GrAn, tr. by Peter Whigham

Epitaph from Athens. Unknown. GrAn, tr. by Richmond Lattimore

Epitaph from Athens. Unknown. GrAn, tr. by Peter Jay

Epitaph: "From out the stormy sea unto the shore." Azariah di Rossi. TrJP, *tr. by* A. B. Rhine

Epitaph from Piraeus. *Unknown.* GrAn, *tr. by* Peter Jay

Epitaph: "Glassblower lies here at rest, A." John Bingham Morton. FaBoEE

Epitaph: "Her grieving parents cradled here." Sylvia Townsend Warner. MoBrPo

Epitaph: "Here I / What does." Paulus [*or* Paulos] Silentiarius. GrAn, *tr. by* Andrew Miller

Epitaph: "Here lie John Hughes and Sarah Drew." Lady Mary Wortley Montagu. ECWP

Epitaph: "Here lies a simple Jew." "Sholom Aleichem." TrJP, *tr. by* Joseph Leftwich

Epitaph: "Here lies John Hughes and Sarah Drew." Lady Mary Wortley Montagu. CABP; FaBoEE

Epitaph: "Here lies Sir Tact, a diplomatic fellow." Timothy Steele. InPK-6; NBLV

Epitaph: "Here lies the body of Richard Hind." Francis, Lord Jeffrey Jeffrey. FaBoEE; OxBoLi

Epitaph: "Here rests his head upon the lap of earth." Thomas Gray. FHYEP; SCGP *Fr.* Elegy Written in a Country Churchyard.

Epitaph: "I am old." Christopher Logue. OxBTC

Epitaph: "I, an unwedded wandering dame." Sylvia Townsend Warner. MoBrPo

Epitaph: "I lived in those times. For a thousand years." Robert Desnos. PFTM-1

Epitaph: "I never cared for Life: Life cared for me." Thomas Hardy. FaBoEE

Epitaph: "I, Richard Kent, beneath these stones." Sylvia Townsend Warner. MoBrPo

Epitaph: "Implacable angel / Has shot his dart, The." Leone da Modena. TrJP

Epitaph in Christ Church, Bristol, on Thomas Turner, Twice Master of the Company of Bakers. Francis, Lord Jeffrey Jeffrey. *See* In Christ Church, Bristol, on Thomas Turner, Twice Master of the Company of Bakers

Epitaph in Dialogue on the Sceptic Philosopher Pyrrho. Julianus of Egypt. GrAn, *tr. by* Lee T. Pearcy

Epitaph in Form of a Ballad, The. François Villon. CTC, *tr. by* Algernon Charles Swinburne

[Epitaph] In Obitum M.S., X° Maij [*or* Maii], 1614. William Browne (1591–1643). FaBoEE; NOBE; OBEV

Epitaph: "In shadows of this willow rests." Marie von Ebner-Eschenbach. AuPH, *tr. by* Lowell A. Bangerter

Epitaph in St. Olave's, Southwark, on Mr. Munday. *Unknown.* OxBoLi

Epitaph in the Borghese Gardens. *Unknown.* GrAn, *tr. by* Peter Whigham

Epitaph Intended for Sir Isaac Newton, in Westminster Abbey. Pope. *See* Intended for Sir Isaac Newton

Epitaph: Iohannis Sande. Thomas Bastard. FaBoEE

Epitaph: "It was for you that the mountains shook at Sinai." *Unknown.* TrJP

Epitaph: "John Bird, a laborer, lies here." Sylvia Townsend Warner. MoBrPo

Epitaph: Justice. Theocritus. WoPoe, *tr. by* Fred Chappell

Epitaph: "Like silver dew are the tears of love." Alfred Edgar Coppard. OBMV

Epitaph: "Lo worms enjoy the seat of bliss." Robert Burns. FaBoEE

Epitaph: "Malcolm Lowry." Malcolm Lowry. OBCoV

Epitaph: "Man who in his life trusts in this world, A." *Unknown.* TrJP

Epitaph: "Meek Francis lies here, friend, without stop or stay." Matthew Prior. FaBoEE

Epitaph: "Mr. Heath-Stubbs as you must understand." John Heath-Stubbs. OxBTC

Epitaph: "My brother is skull and skeleton now." William Montgomerie. OxBS

Epitaph: "My friend, judge not me." *Unknown.* NOSC

Epitaph: "Nor practising virtue nor committing crime." Geoffrey Taylor. FaBoEE

Epitaph: "O King, give Angilbert thy rest." Angilbert. MLL, *tr. by* Helen Waddell

Epitaph of a Dog. *Unknown.* GrAn, *tr. by* Dudley Fitts

Epitaph of a Girl. *Unknown.* GrAn, *tr. by* Dudley Fitts

Epitaph of a Nicene Actor. *Unknown.* GrAn, *tr. by* Dudley Fitts

Epitaph of a Sailor. Antiphilus [*or* Antiphilos]. GrAn, *tr. by* Dudley Fitts

Epitaph of a Sailor. Damagetus. GrAn, *tr. by* Dudley Fitts

Epitaph of Cleonicus. Theocritus. FaBoEE, *tr. by* Charles Stuart Calverley

Epitaph of Dionysia. *Unknown.* OBEV

Epitaph of Eusthenes, The. Edward Cracroft Lefroy. AWP *Fr.* Echoes from Theocritus.

Epitaph of Graunde [*or* La Graunde] Amoure, The. Stephen Hawes. EBEV; NoSic; OBEV *Fr.* Pastime of Pleasure, The.

Epitaph of Hipponax. Theocritus. FaBoEE, *tr. by* Charles Stuart Calverley

Epitaph of John Jack. Daniel Bliss. TCAPo

Epitaph of Maister Win Drowned in the Sea, An. George Turberville. FaBoEE

Epitaph: "Of many things adulterate." Tristan Corbière. AWP, *tr. by* Joseph T. Shipley

Epitaph of Nearchos. Ammianus. WeW-3, *tr. by* Dudley Fitts

Epitaph of Our Late Queen Mary, An. George Cavendish. NoSic

Epitaph of Pyramus and Thisbe. Abraham Cowley. FaBoEE
   (Epitaph: "Underneath this marble stone") EnLoPo

Epitaph of Sardanapalos, The. *Unknown.* PGA, *tr. by* Kenneth Rexroth

Epitaph of Sir Griffith ap Rhys, The. *Unknown.* AngWePo

Epitaph of the Death of Nicholas Grimald, An. Barnabe Googe. SCGP
   (Beholde this fle.) NPeEn
   (Epytaphe of the Death of Nicolas Grimoald, An.) NPeEn

Epitaph on a Betrothed Girl. Erinna. GrAn, *tr. by* Lenore Mayhew

Epitaph on a Child Killed by Procured Abortion. *Unknown.* NOEC

Epitaph (On a Commonplace Person who Died in Bed). Amy Levy. *See* Epitaph: "This is the end of him, here he lies."

Epitaph on a Dentist. *Unknown. See* Dentist, A

Epitaph on a Diamond Digger. Albert Brodrick. PeSAV

Epitaph on a Fir-Tree. Richard Murphy. FaBoTw

Epitaph on a Great Sleeper. Sir Aston Cokayne. FaBoEE

Epitaph on a Hare. William Cowper. HAP; NOEC; NoP-4; PoPoPo

Epitaph on a Jacobite. Thomas Babington Macaulay, 1st Baron Macaulay. *See* Jacobite's Epitaph, A

Epitaph on a Living Woman. Angelina Weld Grimké. APT-1

Epitaph on a Party Girl. Richard Usborne. FaBoEE; OBCoV

Epitaph on a Pessimist. Thomas Hardy. FaBoEE; TRP

Epitaph on a Pet Cat. Joachim Du Bellay. TriCat, *tr. by* Ralph Nixon Currey

Epitaph on a Robin Redbreast, An. Samuel Rogers. FaBoEE

Epitaph on a Schoolmaster. Robert Burns. FaBoEE

Epitaph on a Tomb near Rome. *Unknown.* GrAn, *tr. by* Frank Kuenstler

Epitaph on a Tyrant. W. H. Auden. AF; HeIP-4; NoAM; OxBEV; OxBSP; RB

Epitaph on a Waiter. David McCord. APT-2; NBLV; NIP-4; OBAL; OBCoV

Epitaph on a Willing Girl. Thomas Rowlandson. FaBoEE

Epitaph on a Young Child. Ivor Gurney. FaBoEE

Epitaph on a Young Poet Who Died before Having Achieved Success. Amy Lowell. OBAL

Epitaph on Achilles. *Unknown.* AWP, *tr. by* William M. Hardinge

Epitaph on an Army of Mercenaries. A. E. Housman. FaBoWar; NAEL-6v2; NPeEn; NoP-4; OxBEV; SCGP; SoSe-8

Epitaph on an Infant. Crinagoras. AWP, *tr. by* John William Burgon

Epitaph on an Irish Priest. *Unknown.* FaBoEE

Epitaph on an Unfortunate Artist. Robert Graves. FaBoEE; NOBL; OBCoV

Epitaph on Charles I. James Graham, Marquess of Montrose. *See* His Metrical Vow

Epitaph on Charles II. John Wilmot, 2d Earl of Rochester. SCGP; WoPoe

Epitaph on Claudy Phillips, a Musician, An. Samuel Johnson. *See* Epitaph upon the Celebrated Claudy Phillips, Musician, Who Died Very Poor, An

Epitaph on Colonel Francis Chartres. John Arbuthnot. FaBoEE
   (Colonel Chartres.) OBSV

Epitaph on Dr. Donne, Dean of Paul's, An. Richard Corbet [*or* Corbett]. BeJo

Epitaph on Dr. Keene. Thomas Gray. FaBoEE

Epitaph on Dr. Keene's Wife. Thomas Gray. FaBoEE

Epitaph on Dr Samuel Johnson. Soame Jenyns. ECEV

Epitaph on Elizabeth, L. H. Ben Jonson. BeJo; FaBoEE; HAP; NAEL-5v1; NAEL-6v1; NIL-7; NIP-4; NOSC; NoP-4; OBEV; PoE; SCGP

Epitaph on Erotion. Martial. RomPo, *tr. by* Leigh Hunt

Epitaph on her Son H. P. at St. Syth's Church. Katherine Philips. MakPoe
   (Epitaph.) NoP-4
   (Epitaph on Her Son Hector Philips.) CABP
   (EPITAPH. On her Son H. P. at St. Syth's Church where her body also lies Interred.) NOSC; PBRV; PEW

Epitaph on Herself, An. Mehetabel Wright. ECWP

Epitaph on Himself. Samuel Taylor Coleridge. FaBoEE

Epitaph on the Himself. Pope. FaBoEE

Epitaph on Himself. Matthew Prior. *See* On Himself

Epitaph on Hogarth. Samuel Johnson. *See* Epitaph on William Hogarth, An

Epitaph on James Moore Smythe. Pope. FaBoEE

Epitaph on John Knott. *Unknown.* FaBoEE

Epitaph on Laurence Sterne. David Garrick. FaBoEE

Epitaph on M. H., An. Charles Cotton. EBEV; FaBoEE; NPeEn

Epitaph on Master Philip Gray, An. Ben Jonson. FaBoEE

Epitaph on Master Vincent Corbet[t], An. Ben Jonson. BeJo

Epitaph on Mr. Burton. Robert Burns. FaBoEE

Epitaph on Mr W—. Felicia Dorothea Hemans. ViWPN

Epitaph on Peter Robinson. Francis, Lord Jeffrey Jeffrey. *See* On Peter Robinson

Epitaph on Prince Frederick. *Unknown. See* On Prince Frederick

Epitaph on Prince Henry. Hugh Holland. FaBoEE
(Lo, where he shineth yonder.) AngWePo
Epitaph on Robert Southey. Thomas Moore. FaBoEE
Epitaph on S. P. [Salomon *or* Salathiel Pavy], a Child of Q[ueen] El[izabeth's] Chapel. Ben Jonson. BeJo; NAEL-5v1; NAEL-6v1; NAEL-7v1; NOSC; OBEV; OxBEV; SCGP; UnPo
(Epitaph on S. P.) TFi
(On Solomon Pavy, a Child of Queen Elizabeth's Chapel.) NOBE
Epitaph on Sir Philip Sidney. Fulke Greville, 1st Baron Brooke. SCGP
Epitaph on Sir Philip Sidney, An. James I, King of England. Son
Epitaph on Sir Philip Sidney Lying in St Paul's without a Monument, to be Fastned upon the Church Door. Edward Herbert, 1st Baron Herbert of Cherbury. NPeEn
Epitaph on Sir Thomas Wyatt. Henry Howard, Earl of Surrey. NAEL-5v1; NAEL-6v1
(Earth his bones, the heavens possess his ghost, The.) (LL) NAEL-7v1; NoP-4
(Epitaph on Sir Thomas Wyatt.) NAEL-5v1; NAEL-6v1
(Excellent Epitaph of Sir Thomas Wyatt, An.) NoSic
(Tribute to Wyatt.) PeECV
(Wyatt resteth here, that quick could never rest.) NoP-4; PeECV
Epitaph on Sir Walter Pye. John Hoskyns [*or* Hoskins]. FaBoEE
Epitaph on Sir William Dyer. Lady Catherine [*or* Katherine] Dyer. *See* Sir William Dyer, Knight
Epitaph on Some Bottles of Sack and Claret Laid in Sand. Robert Wild. NOSC
Epitaph on the Admirable Dramatic Poet, W. Shakespeare, An. John Milton. *See* On Shakespear[e]
Epitaph on the Countess[e] Dowager of Pembroke. William Browne (1591–1643). *See* On the Countess Dowager of Pembroke
Epitaph on the Duke of Buckingham. James Shirley. *See* On the Duke of Buckingham
Epitaph on the Duke of Buckingham. *Unknown.* BASC; NPeEn; PBRV
Epitaph on the Duke of Grafton. Sir Fleetwood Shepherd. FaBoEE
Epitaph on the Earl of Leicester [*or* Leceister]. Sir Walter Ralegh. RB
Epitaph on the Earl of Strafford. John Cleveland. BASC; FaBoEE; NOBE; NOSC; NPeEn; OxBEV; PeECV
Epitaph on the Fart in the Parliament House. John Hoskyns [*or* Hoskins]. FaBoEE
Epitaph on the Favourite Dog of a Politician. Joseph Hilaire Pierre Belloc. OBSV
Epitaph on the Lady Mary Villiers. Thomas Carew. BeJo; CaPo; FaBoEE; NOBE; OBEV
(Epitaph on the Lady Mary Villers.) CavPo; OxBEV; PBRV
(Lady Mary Villers lies, The.) CavPo
(Lady *Mary Villers* lyes, The.) NPeEn; OxBEV; PBRV
Epitaph on the Monument of Sir William Dyer at Colmworth, 1641. Lady Catherine [*or* Katherine] Dyer. BoLoP; EnLoPo *Fr.* Sir William Dyer, Knight.
Epitaph on the Monument of Sir William Strode. William Strode. NOSC
Epitaph: On the Near-Death Experience. Ellis Owen. WoPoe, *tr. by* Anthony Conran
Epitaph on the Politician Himself. Joseph Hilaire Pierre Belloc. FaBoEE; MoBrPo; NBLV; OBSV
Epitaph on the Stanton-Harcourt Lovers. Pope. FaBoEE *Fr.* Three Epitaphs on John Hewet and Sarah Drew.
Epitaph on the Tombstone of a Child, the Last of Seven That Died Before. Aphra Behn. CABP; NOSC; OxBSo
Epitaph on Thomas Clere. Henry Howard, Earl of Surrey. *See* Epitaph for [*or* on] Thomas Clere
Epitaph on Tuft-Hunter. Thomas Moore. FaBoEE
Epitaph on William Hogarth, An. Samuel Johnson. EBEV
(Epitaph on Hogarth.) OxAEP-1
Epitaph on William Jones. *Unknown.* FaBoEE
Epitaph on William Whitehead. *Unknown.* FaBoEE
Epitaph: "One whom I knew, a student and a poet." Alex Comfort. MoBrPo
Epitaph: "Or many things adulterate." Tristan Corbière. AWP, *tr. by* Joseph T. Shipley
Epitaph: "Roots of mankind are tangled in my hair, The." Wendy Rose. CDW
Epitaph: Sappho. Pinytos. GrAn, *tr. by* Lee T. Pearcy
Epitaph: "See here, nice Death, to please his palate." Pope. FaBoEE
Epitaph: "Sir, you should notice me: I am the Man." Lascelles Abercrombie. MoBrPo
Epitaph: Snake River. Lance Henson. VoR
Epitaph: "So I may say." "H. D." APT-1
Epitaph: "Stone cries from the wall, The." *Unknown.* TrJP
Epitaph: "Stop, Christian passer-by!—Stop, child of God." Samuel Taylor Coleridge. NAEL-5v2; NAEL-6v2; NOCV; PeECV; SacPr

Epitaph: "This is the end of him, here he lies." Amy Levy. NOBVV; NPeEn; PEW; TrJP
(Epitaph (On a Commonplace Person who Died in Bed).) CABP; VWP
Epitaph: "This stone, with not unpardonable pride." John Sparrow. OBCoV
Epitaph: "Time that brings [*or* bringes] all things to light." Thomas Morton. NOSC; SCAP
Epitaph: "Tread softly; bid a solemn music sound." John Bingham Morton. FaBoEE
Epitaph: Tristran Tzara. Philippe Soupault. SurPaPo, *tr. by* Mary Ann Caws and Patricia Terry
Epitaph: "Underneath this marble stone." Abraham Cowley. *See* Epitaph of Pyramus and Thisbe
Epitaph upon a Child, An. Robert Herrick. FaBoEE
Epitaph Upon a Child that Died. Robert Herrick. *See* Upon a Child That Died [*or* Dyed]
Epitaph upon a Sober Matron, An. Robert Herrick. CaPo
Epitaph upon a Virgin, An. Robert Herrick. CaPo; FaBoEE; OxBoLi
Epitaph upon a Young Married Couple, An. Richard Crashaw. *See* Epitaph Upon Husband and Wife Who Died and Were Buried Together, An
Epitaph Upon Husband and Wife Who Died and Were Buried Together, An. Richard Crashaw. EBEV; NOBE; OBEV; OxAEP-1
(Epitaph upon a Young Married Couple, An.) FaBoEE; NIL-7
Epitaph upon That Profound and Learned Casuist, the Late Ordinary of Newgate, An. Thomas [*or* "Tom"] Brown. OBSV
Epitaph upon the Celebrated Claudy Phillips, Musician, Who Died Very Poor, An. Samuel Johnson. NOEC
(Epitaph on Claudy Phillips, a Musician, An.) NPeEn; OxAEP-1
Epitaph Upon the Lady Elizabeth, Second Daughter to his Late Majesty, An. Henry Vaughan. BeJo
Epitaph upon Thomas, Lord Fairfax, An. George, 2d Duke of Buckingham Villiers. NOSC
Epitaph, uppon Cassandra Mac Willms Wife to Sr Thomas Ridgway Earle of London Derry by ye Lady A. S., An. Lady Anne Harris Southwell. EMWP
Epitaph: "When I shall be without regret." James Vincent Cunningham. InPK-6
Epitaph: "When Oxford gave thee two degrees in art." Mrs. Boughton. EMWP
Epitaph: "Young then, / we were bored already." Eleanor Wilner. ChIV-1
Epitaphium Citharistriae. Victor Gustave Plarr. EnLoPo; NBLV
(Stand Not Uttering Sedately.) PoRA
Epitaphium Meum. William Bradford. SCAP
Epitaphs. Robert Francis.
"Everyman / Preacher or lecher, saint or sot." CRP
Epitaphs. Charles Reznikoff. APT-2
Epitaphs. Edmund Wilson. APT-2
Epitaphs of the War [1914–1918]. Rudyard Kipling. OBWP
"A. 'I was a Have.' B. 'I was a "Have-not."'" FaBoTw
Batteries Out of Ammunition. WoPoe
Beginner, The. FaBoTw
"Blown sand heaps on me, that none may learn, The." PeFWW
Bombed in London. WoPoe
Bridegroom, The. FaBoEE
"Call me not false, beloved." FaBoEE
Common Form. FaBoEE; FaBoTw; HarvBoo; NPeEn; PeFWW; WoPoe
Convoy Escort. WoPoe
Coward, The. FaBoEE; FaBoTw; HarvBoo; NPeEn; PeFWW; WoPoe
Dead Statesman, A. FaBoEE; FaBoWar; NBLV; OPOU; PoWW; WoPoe
Drifter off Tarentum, A. FaBoEE; PeFWW; PoWW; WoPoe
Equality of Sacrifice. FaBoTw
Ex-Clerk. HarvBoo
"He from the wind-bitten North with ship and companions descended." FaBoEE; PeFWW; PoWW; WoPoe
"Headless, lacking foot and hand." PoWW
"I could not dig: I dared not rob." FaBoEE; FaBoWar; NBLV; OPOU; PoWW; WoPoe
"I could not look on Death, which being known." FaBoEE; FaBoTw; HarvBoo; NPeEn; PeFWW; WoPoe
"I was a shepherd to fools." WoPoe
"I was of delicate mind. I stepped aside for my needs." FaBoEE; FaBoTw; NPeEn; PeFWW
"If any mourn us in the workshop, say." WoPoe
"If any question why we died." FaBoEE; FaBoTw; HarvBoo; NPeEn; PeFWW; WoPoe
Journalists. HarvBoo
"Laughing through clouds, his milk-teeth still unshed." PoWW
"My son was killed while laughing at some jest. I would I knew." FaBoEE; NPeEn; PeFWW

"On land and sea I strove with anxious care." WoPoe

"On the first hour of my first day." FaBoTw

Pelicans in the Wilderness (A Grave near Halfa). PeFWW

"Pity not! The Army gave." HarvBoo

R.A.F. (Aged Eighteen). PoWW

Refined Man, The. FaBoEE; FaBoTw; NPeEn; PeFWW

Servant, A. HarvBoo; NPeEn; PeFWW

Son, A. FaBoEE; NPeEn; PeFWW

Unknown Female Corpse. PoWW

"We have served our day." HarvBoo

"We were together since the War began." HarvBoo; NPeEn; PeFWW

Epitaphs [or Epitaph] on Two Piping-Bullfinches of Lady Ossory's, Buried under a Rose-Bush in Her Garden. Horace Walpole, 4th Earl of Orford. FaBoEE; NOEC

Epitaphy of la Graunde Amoure. Stephen Hawes. See Pastime of Pleasure, The

Epith. Carol Muske. MakPoe

Epithalamion. Nancy Schoenberger. SwNoth

Epithalamion. Terese Svoboda. ExTi

Epithalamion I–IV. James Liddy.
  "I know nothing but this scene." BiHa

Epithalamion: "Hark, hearer, hear what I do; lend a thought now, make believe." Gerard Manley Hopkins. CAGL

Epithalamion: or, a Song. Ben Jonson. BeJo

Epithalamion: "Singing, today I married my white girl." Dannie Abse. OBWVE

Epithalamion Teratos. Christopher Marlowe. NoSic Fr. Hero and Leander.

Epithalamion: "These are the small hours when." Michael Longley. CIP-2

Epithalamion: "Ye learned sisters which have oftentimes." Edmund Spenser. BoLoP; FHYEP; NAEL-6v1; NAEL-7v1; NOBE; NoSic; OBEV; OxAEP-1

Epithalamium, An. Joan Murray. YaYoPo

Epithalamium: "Can the lover share his soul." Walter James Turner. OBMV

Epithalamium: "Come, virgin tapers of pure wax." Richard Crashaw. NOCV

Epithalamium for a Niece. Norman Nicholson. NLP

Epithalamium: "Hymen, god of marriage bed." Joseph Rutter. NOSC

Epithalamium: "Hymen hath together tied." R. Hatton. NOSC

Epithalamium: "Let mother Earth." Sir Philip Sidney. OxAEP-1, tr. by Robert Hass Fr. Arcadia.

Epithalamium: "Lo! Hymen passes through th' admiring crowds." Unknown. ECWP

Epithalamium: "So you are married, girl. It makes me sad." Roy McFadden. PNI

Epithalamium: To Mistress M. A. Martin Lluellyn [or Lluelyn]. NOSC

Epithalamium: "Voice that breathed o'er Eden, The." John Keble. NOCV

Epithalamy. Alexander Brome. NOSC

Epithalamy to Sir Thomas Southwell and His Lady, An. Robert Herrick. CaPo

Epitomé (1962). U Tam'si Tchicaya.
  "I was naked for the first kiss of my mother." PBMAP

Epitomé (1962). U Tam'si Tchicaya.
  "What do I want with a thousand stars in broad daylight." PBMAP

Epitomé (1962). U Tam'si Tchicaya.
  "I drink to your glory my god." PBMAP

Scorner, The. PBMAP

Epoch. Vladimir Holan. PoSu, tr. by Ian Milner and Jarmila Milner

Epochs. Juan Gelman. TCLAP, tr. by Robert Marquez and Elinore Randall

Epode: "Not to know vice at all, and keep[e] true state." Ben Jonson. BeJo

Epodes. Horace.
  Counterblast against Garlic, A. NBLV, tr. by Roswell Martin Field

  Country Life. AWP, tr. by John Dryden

  ("Happie is he, that from all Businesse cleere.") BASC; OBVE, tr. by Ben Jonson

  "How happy in his low degree." AWP, tr. by John Dryden

  "May the man who has cruelly murdered his sire." NBLV, tr. by Roswell Martin Field

  (Praises of a Countrie Life, The.) OBVE, tr. by Ben Jonson

  Praises of a Country Life, The. BASC, tr. by Ben Jonson

  To a Randy Old Woman. EroLit, tr. by Unknown

  'Why so droopy?' did I hear you say?" EroLit, tr. by Unknown

Eppie Morrie. Unknown. ESPB; OxBB

Epygrams. John Heywood.
  "Wilt thou use turners craft still? ye by my trouth." PBRV

Epytaphe of the Death of Nicolas Grimoald, An. Barnabe Googe. See Epitaph of the Death of Nicholas Grimald, An

Equal, An. Unknown. ReMoGo

Equal by the wind. (LL) Vox Angelica. Timothy Liu. NeAmPo; WiU

Equal Temperament. Lin Max. MiVo

Equal to the Gods. Sappho. AmFaPo, tr. by Edward Sanders

Equality. Edwin Emanuel Bradford. VerBaPo Fr. Tree of Knowledge, The.

Equality. Hal Sirowitz. KGB

Equality, Father. Edith Bruck. AF, tr. by Ruth Feldman
  (Let us commit a mortal sin / worthy of death.) (LL) AF

Equality of Sacrifice. Rudyard Kipling. FaBoTw Fr. Epitaphs of the War [1914–1918].

Equally with the gods above. (LL) Henry Vaughan. BeJo; NAEL-5v1; NAEL-6v1

Equanimity. Les A. Murray. NOBAu

Equation. Nizar Qabbani. MAP, tr. by Diana Der Hovanessian and Lena Jayyusi

Equestrienne. Rachel Lyman Field. OBCA Fr. Circus Garland, A.

Equilibrists, The. John Crowe Ransom. APT-1; FuPo; HAP; NAAL-2v2; NOBA; NoAM; OxBA; TAP

Equinox. Elizabeth Alexander. ExTi

Equinox. Mateja Matevski.
  "This is an hour of calm, a quiet hour." CarOv, tr. by Carolyn Kizer

Equinox 1980. Peter Davison. NoP-4

Equipment. Edgar Albert Guest. PoToHe

Equipoise: becalmed / Trees, a dome of kindness. Evening in Connecticut. Louis MacNeice. HarvBoo

Er-Heb beyond the Hills of Ao-Safai. Sacrifice of Er-Heb, The. Rudyard Kipling. PeVV

Era's End. Mairtin O Direain. ModIr, tr. by Patrick Crotty

Era un aire suave: the calm and gentle air. Visit to the House of the Poet—Nicaragua, 1987—Homage to Rubén Darío on His Birthday, A. Thomas McGrath. BodElec

Erasers. Unknown. PoToHe

Erasers are the nicest things! Erasers. Unknown. PoToHe

Erat Quaedam Mulier. Lady Mary Cheke. EMWP

Erce, Erce, Erce, mother of earth. Charms for Unfruitful Land. Unknown. AnOE, tr. by Charles W. Kennedy

Erd sould trymbill, the firmament sould schaik, The. Quod Dunbar to Kennedy. William Dunbar. OxBoLi

Erdywurble. Carole Satyamurti. Prnts

Ere all the world had grown so drear. Philosophy. Amy Levy. ViWPN

Ere famous Winthrops bones are laid to rest. Chelmsfords Fate. Benjamin Tompson. SCAP

Ere God had built the mountains. William Cowper. ChIV-1 Fr. Olney Hymns.

Ere I freeze, to sing bravely. Poem of the Frost and Snow. Lewis Morris. OBWVE, tr. by Anthony Conran

Ere I had told / Ten birthdays when among the mountain-slopes. William Wordsworth. TOF Fr. Prelude, The; Growth of a Poet's Mind [1850 vers.].

Ere I know it—next moment I dance at the King's! (LL) Laboratory, The (Ancien Régime). Robert Browning. NAEL-5v2; NAEL-6v2; OBEV

Ere, in the northern gale. Autumn Woods. William Cullen Bryant. APN-1

Ere it passes, barefoot boy! (LL) John Greenleaf Whittier. APN-1; BRP; OBAL; OBCA

Ere long they come, where that same wicked wight. Edmund Spenser. NOBE Fr. Faerie Queene, The.

Ere my heart beats too coldly and faintly. Truants, The. Walter De la Mare. MoBrPo

Ere on my bed my limbs I lay. Pains of Sleep, The. Samuel Taylor Coleridge. AWTN; FHYEP; NAEL-5v2; NAEL-6v2

Ere [or Or] that I wist[!] / Farewell, unkissed[!]. (LL) Sir Thomas Wyatt. NoSic; SCGP

Ere Sleep Comes Down to Soothe the Weary Eyes. Paul Laurence Dunbar. APN-2; ColAP; NAAAL

Ere space exists, or earth, or sky. Lord Is King, The. Unknown. TrJP, tr. by Solomon Solis-Cohen

Ere the beard of thistle sails. Seasons, The. Thomas Holcroft. NOEC

Ere the cock has crowed. Forsaken Girl, The. Eduard Friedrich Mörike [or Möricke]. WoPoe, tr. by Randall Jarrell

Ere the Golden Bowl Is Broken. Anna Hempstead Branch. TCAPo

Ere their story die. (LL) In Time of "The Breaking of Nations." Thomas Hardy. BoLoP; ChIV-1; EBEV; HAP; HarvBoo; MoBrPo; NAEL-5v2; NAEL-6v2; NOBE; NoAM; NoP-4; OBEV; OBWP; OPOU; OxAEP-2; PoWW; RB; TFi; WeW-3

Ere we had reached the wished-for place, night fell. Composed after a Journey across the Hamilton Hills, Yorkshire. William Wordsworth. CenSon

Ere yet our course was graced with social trees. William Wordsworth. CenSon Fr. River Duddon [A Series of Sonnets], The.

Ere yet they win that verge and line. Herman Melville. APN-2 Fr. Clarel: A Poem and Pilgrimage in the Holy Land.

Ere yet your footsteps quit the place. Verses Addressed to a Friend, Just Leaving a Favourite Retirement. Samuel Henley. NOEC

Ere you were born was beauty's summer dead. (LL)   William Shakespeare.   GTBS-P; HeIP-4; NoSic; OBEV; OxAEP-1; SCGP   *Fr.* Sonnets.

Erected by her sorrowing brothers.   Epitaph, An: "Erected by her sorrowing brothers."   Clive Staples Lewis.   OBCoV

Erections.   Erin Belieu.   ExTi

Erica.   Mary Ursula Bethell.   PeNZ

Eride.   Trumbull Stickney.
   "Now in the palace gardens warm with age."   APN-2

Erie Canal, The.   William S. Allen.   HHAm
   (I've got an old mule and her name is Sal.)   APN-2
   (Low Bridge, Everybody Down.)   APN-2

Erik Satie, accused.   Olga Broumas.   WiU   *Fr.* Caritas.

Erin's Daughter.   Lydia Huntley Sigourney.   SWaP

Erinna.   Antipater of Sidon.   AWP, *tr.* by A. J. Butler

Erinna's *Distaff.*   Antipater of Sidon.   GrAn, *tr.* by Peter Jay

Erinna's Spinning.   Margaret Junkin Preston.   SWaP

Erl-King.   Goethe.   WoPoe, *tr.* by John Frederick Nims

Erl-King, The.   Goethe.   AWP; OBVE; STV
   (Who is it that rides through the forest so fast?)   NOBRP, *tr.* by Matthew Gregory Lewis

Erlinton.   *Unknown.*   ESPB

Erminia's steed this while his mistress bore.   Torquato Tasso.   NoSic   *Fr.* Godfrey of Bulloigne; or, The Recoverie of Jerusalem [Gerusalemme Liberata].

Ernest.   Malcolm Cowley.   APT-2

Ernie Morgan found him, a small.   Barn Owl.   Leslie Norris.   AngWePo

Erol Güney's Cat.   Orban Veli Kanik.   WoPoe, *tr.* by Talat Sait Halman

Erolog.   Michael Palmer.   FTOS

Eros.   Robert Bridges.   CABP; NOBE

Eros.   Ralph Waldo Emerson.   APN-1

Eros.   "Michael Field."   VWP

Eros.   Timothy Steele.   RA

Eros at Temple Stream.   Denise Levertov.   NALW

[Eros] came from heaven wearing a purple cloak.   Sappho.   SaLy, *tr.* by Diane Rayor

Eros came near in the horned shape of a shaggy Silenos.   Nonnus.   CAGL, *tr.* by W. H. D. Rouse   *Fr.* Dionysiaca.

Eros has changed his quiver.   Paulus [or Paulos] Silentiarius.   PGA

Eros: have you never perchance felt.   Public Prayer.   Delmira Agustini.   TANSG, *tr.* by Mark McCaffrey

Eros in His Striped Blue Shirt.   Reginald Shepherd.   WiU

Eros, let me lead you, blind father.   Another Race.   Delmira Agustini.   TCLAP, *tr.* by Karl Kirchwey

Eros Poesis.   Tatiana Shcherbina.   ItGoST, *tr.* by J. Kates

Eros seizes and shakes my very soul.   Sappho.   ErotSp, *tr.* by Sam Hamill

Eros taught Pratalidas his adolescent beauty.   Leonidas of Tarentum.   GrAn

Eros, that bane of men, molded soft as marrow.   Dioscorides.   (*fl.* 1st cent. B.C. *or* A.D. 1st cent.)   HePo   *Fr.* Epigrams.

Eros, thou yet behold'st me?   William Shakespeare.   EBEV; OxAEP-1   *Fr.* Antony and Cleopatra.

Eros Turannos.   Edwin Arlington Robinson.   APT-1; AmFaPo; HAP; HeIP-4; MoAmPo; NAAL-2v2; NOBA; NoAM; NoP-4; OxBA; PoE; PoPoPo; TAP; TCAPo; TFi; TRP; WoPoe

Eros, why should one or two small notes.   Goad, The.   "Michael Field."   VWP

Erosion.   Claribel Alegría.   TANSG, *tr.* by Darwin Flakoll

Erosion.   Christopher Merrill.   OPRER

Erosion.   Linda Pastan.   NIP-4

Erosion of Utopia or Rigor of Patience?   Biancamaria Frabotta.   CItWP, *tr.* by Cinzia Sartini Blum and Lara Trubowitz

Erotic Collectibles.   Wayne Koestenbaum.
   1980.   WiU
   1992.   WiU
   1977.   WiU
   "One man's dick had the quaint."   WiU
   "Sedans cruised past our bench."   WiU
   "This is how I learned."   WiU

Erotic Suite.   Olga Nolla.   TANSG, *tr.* by Paula Vega

Erotic tension is almost palpable, The.   Big No-No, The.   Chris Greenhalgh.   NeBl

Erotica 12.   Yannis Ritsos.   PFTM-2, *tr.* by Kimon Friar

Erotion.   Martial.   AWP, *tr.* by Kirby Flower Smith

Erotion rests here, in the.   Martial.   PGA

Errand.   David Morley.   NLP

Errata.   Jane Griffiths.   NeBl

Errata.   Charles Simic.   NNaP

Erratic, complicated shape, like a tool for some obsolete task, An.   Bone.   C. K. Williams.   UrbNat

Erratum.   E. J. Thribb.   PeLV

Errore.   Pier Giorgio Di Cicco.   NOBC

Erskineville. The sun came round a corner.   Pioneer Lane.   Michael Dransfield.   NOBAu

Erst when I wandered far from those I loved.   Charles Lloyd.   CenSon

Erthe tok of erthe erthe with woh.   *Unknown.*   HAP; MiEL

Erudite demon, a fiend in topology, An.   Möbius Strip-Tease.   Alec Derwent Hope.   OBCoV

Erudîte, solemn / The pious bird.   Rev Owl.   Abraham Moses Klein.   TrJP

Eruption: Pu'u Ō'ō.   Garrett Kaoru Hongo.   LoL

Es fällt ein Stern herunter.   Heinrich Heine.   AWP, *tr.* by Richard Garnett

Es Stehen Unbeweglich.   Heinrich Heine.   AWP; TrJP, *tr.* by James Thomson

Es war einmal. . . No, it's too heavy.   Märchenbilder.   John Ashbery.   LCAP-2; NOBA

Esanzo.   Antoine-Roger Bolamba.   NegPo, *tr.* by Ellen Conroy Kennedy

Escape.   Kenneth Fearing.   APT-2

Escape.   Robert Graves.   MoBrPo

Escape.   Elinor Wylie.   MoAmPo

Escape, The.   Ivor Gurney.   OxBSP

Escape, The.   William Stafford.   NNaP

Escape, The.   Mark Van Doren.   MoAmPo

Escape Artist, The.   Kevin Young.   AmPoNex; GT   *Fr.* Escape Artist, The.

Escape at Bedtime.   Robert Louis Stevenson.   OTCP

Escape from the weekday time. Which deadens and endures. (LL)   Sunday Morning.   Louis MacNeice.   FaBoMo; MoBrPo; NAEL-5v2; NAEL-6v2; NIP-4; OxAEP-2; Son

Escape me? / Never.   Life in a Love.   Robert Browning.   FHYEP

Escape to Love.   Patrick MacDonogh.
   "Alone and Godless, stopped by the sudden edge."   BIrV

Escaped from Germany.   History and Reality.   Stephen Spender.   HP

Escaped the nets.   Buson.   EH, *tr.* by Robert Hass

Escapes unhurt beneath so warm a veil. (LL)   William Cowper.   NAEL-6v1; NAEL-7v1   *Fr.* Task, The.

Escaping from Autopia.   Chryss Yost.   GeoHom

Escort fish, Pompilos, sending sailors a fair sailing.   Erinna.   SaLy, *tr.* by Diane Rayor

Escorting Candidates to the Examination Hall.   Po Chü-i.   ChiP, *tr.* by Arthur Waley

Esenin's Suicide Note.   Sergey [*or* Sergei] Aleksandrovich Yesenin [*or* Essenin].   CAGL, *tr.* by Simon Karlinsky

Eshu.   Adesanya Alakoye.   ISC

Eskimo Girl, The.   David Ray.   LTA

Eskimo Occasion.   Judith Rodriguez.   CBAP; FaBoWP; ItWoWo; NOBAu

Eskimo's Woman, The.   Anabel Torres.   TANSG, *tr.* by Celeste Kostopulos-Cooperman

Eskimos in Manitoba.   Recital.   John Updike.   OBAL

Esope, myne authour, makis mentioun.   Robert Henryson.   *See* Aesop, mine author, makis mention

ESP.   Carter Revard.   VoR

España, Aparta de me Este Caliz.   César Vallejo.
   Masses.   RB, *tr.* by Robert Bly
   "When the battle was over."   RB, *tr.* by Robert Bly

Especially he loves.   God Poem.   Stanley Moss.   VGW

Especially in weeping.   Valerio Magrelli.   NeIt

Especially When the October Wind.   Dylan Thomas.   AngWePo; MoBrPo; OBWVE; OxAEP-2; OxBTC

Esperance! The twinge of moonlight in outer space.   Blank Abandon of Beds, The.   Star Black.   KGB

Esposito, Fiorani, Fogagnolo.   To the Fifteen of Piazzale Loreto.   Salvatore Quasimodo.   AF, *tr.* by Jack Bevan

Espresso.   Carol Lee Saffoti.   UnSA

Esprit d'Escalier.   John Wheelwright.   APT-2

Essay on Concrete, An.   Douglas Messerli.   FTOS

Essay on Criticism, An.   Pope.   NAEL-5v1; NAEL-6v1; NAEL-7v1; OBCoV; TFi
   ("Are Nature still, but Nature methodized.") (LL)   HAP
   Art of Poetry, The.   ECEV
   "Avoid extremes; and shun the fault of such."   FHYEP
   Bookful Blockhead, The.   OBSV
   ("But are not critics to their judgment too?") (LL)   HAP
   "But most by numbers judge a poet's song."   ECEV; FHYEP; HAP; NIL-7; NIP-4
   "But true expression, like th' unchanging sun."   FHYEP
   "But where's the man who counsel can bestow."   OxAEP-1

Essay on Criticism.   OBCoV
   "In wit, as nature, what affects our hearts."   HAP
   (Little Learning, A.)   NOBE

"Little learning is a dangerous [or dang'rous] thing, A." HAP; OxBEV

"Of all the causes which conspire to blind." MakPoe; NoP-4; OxAEP-1

Plain Fools. OBSV

Servile Herd, The. OBSV

("Shows most true mettle when you check his course.") (LL) FHYEP

"Some are bewildered in the maze of Schools." OBSV

"Some beauties yet no precepts can declare." HAP

"Some ne'er advance a judgment of their own." OBSV

"Some to Conceit alone their taste confine." OxAEP-1

"Such shameless bards we have; and yet 'tis true." OBSV

"True ease in writing comes from Art, not Chance." HAP; InPK-6

"True wit is Nature to advantage dressed." HAP

"Where'er you find 'the cooling western breeze'" OBCoV

"Words are like leaves; and where they most abound." ECEV

Essay on Death. Hayden Carruth. BodElec

Essay on Friendship. Mary Leapor.

"To Artemisia.—'Tis to her we sing." PEW

Essay on Language. Wanda Coleman. PmAP

Essay on Man. *Unknown.* PoToHe

Essay on Man, An. Pope.

"All are but parts of one stupendous whole." FHYEP

"All Nature is but art, unknown to thee." ECEV

"Awake, my St. John! leave all meaner things." NAEL-5v1; NAEL-6v1; NAWM-7v2

"Behold the child, by Nature's kindly law." ECEV

"Bliss of man, The (could pride that blessing find)." NOEC

"Far as creation's ample range extends." ECEV

"For forms of government let fools contest." ECEV

"Know then thyself, presume not God to scan." ECEV; FHYEP; NAEL-5v1; NAEL-6v1; NAEL-7v1; NOEC; PAI; SacPr; TFi

(Know Thyself.) NOBE

"Look round our world; behold the chain of love." FHYEP

Paragon of Animals, The. ECEV; FHYEP; NAEL-5v1; NAEL-6v1; NAEL-7v1; NOEC; PAI; SacPr; TFi

"Placed on this isthmus of a middle state." WeW-3

(Scale of Being, The.) WoPoe

"See, through this air, this ocean, and this earth." InvLi

"What's fame? A fancied life in others' breath." FHYEP

"What would this Man? Now upward will he soar." HeIP-4

Essay on Marriage. Anne Finch (b. 1908).

"O, love, in your sweet name enough." FaBoTw

Essay on Memory. Robert David Fitzgerald.

"Rain in my ears: impatiently there raps." CBAP

Essay on Psychiatrists. Robert Pinsky.

"As a rule, the patients I know do not pace." NoAM

"As to my own concerns, it seems odd, given." NoAM

Dionysus as Psychiatrist. HCAP

'Greek Tragedy" of course is the sort of thing.' NoAM

"In a certain sense, they are not serious." NoAM

"In a more hostile view, the psychiatrists." HCAP

Invocation: "It's crazy to think one could describe them." NoAM

"It's crazy to think one could describe them." NoAM

(Lakeside Identification, A.) NoP-4

Mad, The. NoAM

"Other patients are ill otherwise, and do." NoAM

Peroration, Concerning Genius. NoAM

Proposition. HCAP; NoAM

'Shrink' is a misnomer. The religious." HCAP

Some Terms. HCAP

"Terms of all kinds mellow with time, growing." NoAM

Their Patients. NoAM

Their Philistinism Considered. NoAM

Their Seriousness, with Further Comparisons. NoAM

Their Speech, Compared with Wisdom and Poetry. NoAM

"These are the first citizens of contingency." HCAP; NoAM

("Yes, crazy to suppose one could describe them.") NoP-4

Essay on William Carlos Williams, An. Víctor Hernández Cruz. PmAP

Essay on Woman. John Wilkes.

"Awake my Fanny! leave all meaner things." EroLit

"He who the hoop's immensity can pierce." EroLit

"Pleased to the last, she likes the luscious food." EroLit

"Then, in the scale of Pricks, 'tis plain." EroLit

"Then, say not Man's imperfect, Heaven in fault." EroLit

Essay on Woman, An. Mary Leapor. BWW; ECWP; NAEL-7v1; NOEC

Essay upon Good-Friday, An. Anne King. EMWP

Esse. Czeslaw Milosz. TOF

Essence Is Not in the Living, The. Mairtin O Direain. BiHa, *tr. by* Tomás MacSiomóin and Douglas Sealy

Essence of Existence, The. Jack Kerouac. NeAP *Fr.* Mexico City Blues.

Essence of ink, The. Yün Shou-p'ing. CoBLCP *Fr.* In My Boat, Painting a Picture of Going Home by Boat.

Essence of orchids in her tumbled hair, a goddess of / spring spring. Song Of Chang Ching-Yüan Picking Lotus Flowers, A. Wen T'ing-yün. SuSp, *tr. by* William R. Schultz

Essences. Antonio Porta.

"Nearby creatures of the air." ItPo, *tr. by* Gayle Ridinger

"To become a tree." ItPo, *tr. by* Gayle Ridinger

"White bars from the window." ItPo, *tr. by* Gayle Ridinger

Essential oils—are wrung. Emily Dickinson. APN-2; SWaP; TCAPo

Essential poem at the centre [or center] of things, The. Primitive like an Orb, A. Wallace Stevens. NOBA

Essentially description, night. (1978, Remembering 1962). C. S. Giscombe. GT

Essie Parrish in New York. Elsie Parrish. STP, *tr. by* George Quasha

Está Muy Caliente. George Bowering. MoCV

Establish thy serenity o'er the fields. (LL) Henry David Thoreau. NCAP; TAP *Fr.* Week on the Concord and Merrimack Rivers, A.

"Established" is a good word, much used in garden books. Time. Mary Ursula Bethell. FaBoWP; OBGa

Establishment has taken to the hills. First Letter to an Irish Novelist. Roy McFadden. PNI

Estadio Chile. Víctor Jara. TCLAP, *tr. by* Joan Jara

Estate. Agi Mishol. DTA, *tr. by* Tsipi Keller

Estate, The. Charles Brasch.

"What have you seen on the summits, the peaks that plunge their." PeNZ

Estate and an earldom at seventy-four, An! Horace Walpole, 4th Earl of Orford. FaBoEE

Estate bird, The. Loon, The. Michael S. Harper. ESEAA

Estel. Julia Alvarez. ExTi

Estelí / this mountain town means something. Resurrection. Joy Harjo. HATNAP

Estes' Backyard, The. Pamela Stewart. UrbNat

Esther. Eve Merriam. TaR

Esther [a Young Man's Tragedy]. Wilfrid Scawen Blunt.

"He who has once been happy is for aye." OBEV; OBMV

I Will Not Tell the Secrets. Son

"When I hear laughter from a tavern door." OBMV

With Esther. OBEV; OBMV

Esther K. Comes to America: 1931. Jerome Rothenberg. NNaP

Esther's Tomcat. Ted Hughes. OxBC; OxBEV

Esthete in Harlem. Langston Hughes. BPo; ColAP

Esthétique du Mal. Wallace Stevens.

"How red the rose that is the soldier's wound." NOBA

Soldier's Wound, The. NOBA

"Sun, in clownish yellow, but not a clown, The." NOBA

Esthonian Bridal Song. Johann Gottfried von Herder. AWP

Estonia. A private dacha. Irina Znamenskaya [or Znamenskaia]. TCRP

Estranged in site. Parthenon, The. Herman Melville. NCAP

Estrangement. Jane Cooper. ExTi

Estray, The. Forceythe Willson. APN-2

Estrella's Prophecies #47. David Baratier. AmPoNex

Estrellitas. Carlos Cumpian. IllVoic

Estrich, thou feather'd fool and easy prey. Richard Lovelace. *See* E[e]astrich, thou feather[e]d fool[e] and easy [or easie] prey

Estuarial Republic, The. Douglas Dunn. FaBoMo

Esyllt. Glyn Jones. AngWePo; OBWVE

Et Cetera. Léon Damas. NegPo, *tr. by* Ellen Conroy Kennedy

Et cetera. (LL) Cheerful Girls at Smiller's Bar, 1971, The. Jack A. Mapanje. HBAPE; NAfrP; PBMAP; PeSAV

Et cætera, et cætera, et cætera. (LL) Austrian Army, An. Alaric Alexander Watts. NOBL; PeLV

Et in Leucadia Ego. Michael Davidson. PmAP

Et Incarnatus Est. William Langland. NOBE *Fr.* Vision of Piers Plowman, The.

Et Nox Facta Est. Victor Hugo. NAWM-7v2, *tr. by* Mary Ann Caws

Et Quidquid Aspiciebam Mors Erat. Robert Fitzgerald. APT-2

Etched Away From. Paul Celan. OBVE, *tr. by* Michael Hamburger

Etching. Samuel Greenberg. APT-1

Eternal Aphrodite, Zeus's daugther, throne. Prayer to Aphrodite. Sappho. WoPoe, *tr. by* Alfred Corn

Eternal autumn rain—evening sounds. To the Tune: The Wine Spring: "Eternal autumn rain—evening sounds." Li Hsun. CrYelRi; ErotSp, *tr. by* Sam Hamill

Eternal City, The. A. R. Ammons. HCAP

Eternal Controversy, The. Dean B. Lyman, Jr. YaYoPo

Eternal Dice, The. César Vallejo. PoetW, *tr. by* James Wright

Eternal Farewell. Ricardo Jaimes Freyre. TCLAP, *tr. by* Victor Tulli

Eternal Father, Strong to Save. William Whiting. NOCV

Eternal Female ground! [*or* groan'd!] it was heard all over the Earth, The.
William Blake. NAEL-6v2 *Fr.* Marriage of Heaven and Hell, The.

Eternal gates lift up their heads, The. Hymn: "Eternal gates lift up their heads,
The." Cecil Frances Alexander. SacPr

Eternal gates' terrific porter lifted the northern bar, The. William Blake.
OxBEV *Fr.* Book of Thel, The.

Eternal God, How They're Increased. Cotton Mather. AH

Eternal God! maker of all. Book, The. Henry Vaughan. AngWePo; BASC;
GeHe; InvLi; PBRV

Eternal God, our life is but. Prayer, A: "Eternal God, our life is but."
"Yehoash." TrJP, *tr. by* Isidore Goldstick

Eternal God, Whose Power Upholds. Henry Hallam Tweedy. AH

Eternal Goodness, The. John Greenleaf Whittier.
"I know not what the future hath." NOCV

Eternal Image, The. Ruth Pitter. MoBrPo; OxBTC

Eternal Jew, The. Jacob Cohen. TrJP, *tr. by* I. M. Lask

Eternal King, grant me true quietness. Angilbert's Prayer. Angilbert. MLL,
tr. by Helen Waddell

Eternal Landscape, The. Lenard D. Moore. GT

Eternal Light! Thomas Binney. NOCV

Eternal lightning of Lenin's bones, The. (LL) Skeleton of the Future, The.
Hugh MacDiarmid. MoBrPo; OBMV

Eternal Love, maintain thy life in me. (LL) Leave Me O Love. Sir Philip
Sidney. AEP; GSo; HeIP-4; NIP-4; NOBE; NPeEn; OxAEP-1; PoE;
SacPr; Son; TFi

Eternal Masculine. William Rose Benét. AWP; MoAmPo

Eternal Moment. Sándor Weöres. IQMS, *tr. by* Edwin Morgan

Eternal pain! (LL) Philomela. Matthew Arnold. FHYEP; OBEV; OWoS;
UnPo

Eternal Paraclete, to thee. (LL) Veni Creator Spiritus. Charlemagne. AWP;
SacPr, *tr. by* John Dryden

Eternal power from whose allseeing eye. Baptina Palavicino Cromwell.
EMWP

Eternal Power, of earth and air! Doubter's Prayer, The. Anne Brontë. SacPr

Eternal Present, The. Gabriel Preil. FIT, *tr. by* Robert Friend

Eternal reciprocity of tears, The. (LL) Insensibility. Wilfred Owen.
FaBoTw; FaBoWar; NoP-4; OBWP; OxAEP-2; OxBTC; PeFWW; PoWW

Eternal Return, The. Robert Silliman Hillyer. AiP

Eternal Road, The. Franz Werfel.
Ye Sorrowers. TrJP, *tr. by* Ludwig Lewisohn

Eternal Sabbath. Isaac Leibush [*or* Yitskhok Leybush] Peretz [*or* Perets].
TrJP, *tr. by* Joseph Leftwich

Eternal Spirit of the chainless Mind! Byron. CenSon; GSo *Fr.* Prisoner of
Chillon, The.

Eternal Spirit, Source of Light. Samuel Davies. AH

Eternal sprite, which art in heaven the love. To God the Holy Ghost. Henry
Constable. NoSic

Eternal, Thou. Saint Ambrose. MLL

Eternal Three, The. Tove Ditlevsen. WoPoe, *tr. by* Martin Allwood, Inga
Allwood and John Hollander

Eternal Values. Grace Noll Crowell. PoToHe

Eternal Years, The. Frederick William Faber. PWR

Eternall Truth, almighty, infinite. Fulke Greville, 1st Baron Brooke. NoSic;
SacPr *Fr.* Caelica.

Eternities before the first-born day. Mother Night. James Weldon Johnson.
Son

Eternity. William Blake. AWP; AmFaPo; EBEV; EnlH; FaBoEE; NOBE;
NoP-4; OxBSP; RB; SCGP; SoSe-8; Spl *Fr.* Several Questions Answered.

Eternity. Josephine D. Henderson Heard. CBWP-4

Eternity. Robert Herrick. CavPo
(Eternity.) CavPo
(O Years! and Age! Farewell.) CavPo

Eternity. Kabir. WoPoe, *tr. by* Arvind Krishna Mehrotra

Eternity. James Whitcomb Riley. GSo

Eternity. Shinkichi Takahashi. ZenPo, *tr. by* Takashi Ikemoto and Lucien
Stryk

Eternity. Sándor Weöres. IQMS, *tr. by* Adam Makkai and Donald E. Morse

Eternity Affirms the Hour. Robert Browning. SacPr

Eternity is passion, girl or boy. Whence Had They Come? W. B. Yeats.
BoLoP

Eternity of God, The. Frederick William Faber. SacPr

Eternity of Love Protested. Thomas Carew. BeJo; MeLP; NOSC

Eternity of Nature, The. John Clare. EBEV

Eternity's Woods. Paul Zweig. BodElec

Eternity shall tell. (LL) Speak Gently. G. W. Langford. PoToHe; UV

Eternity, Thou Thunderous Word. Johann Rist.
"Eternity, thou thunderous word." GePo

Ethel in her crimson row boat. Chateaux en Espagne. Henrietta Cordelia Ray.
CBWP-3

Ether broke into the house. Red Dye. Barbara Guest. BodElec

Ether Insatiable. May Kendall. CABP

Ethical schizophrenia you called it. Goin' to the Territory. Michael S. Harper.
NAAAL

Ethick. Robert Bridges. OxBTC *Fr.* Testament of Beauty, The.

Ethics. Linda Pastan. InPK-6

Ethics for Everyman. Roger Woddis. NOBL

Ethiopia. Kate Daniels. PBCAP

Ethiopia. Frances Ellen Watkins Harper. NAAAL

Ethiopia Unda a Jamaican Mango Tree. Opal Palmer Adisa. WaCA

Ethiopian Apocalypse of Don, The. Norman Weinstein. WaCA

Ethnogenesis. Henry Timrod. APN-2; NOBA; OxBA; TCAPo

Ethnologists up with the Sioux. Limerick. *Unknown.* PeLi

Etiquette. Sir William Schwenck Gilbert. FaBoCh

Etosion achthos aroures. Robert Bridges. OxBEV

Etrick Forest is a fair forest[e]. Outlaw Murray, The. *Unknown.* ESPB;
OxBB

Etruscan Notebook. Elena Clementelli.
"Bend of the gulf." CItWP, *tr. by* Cinzia Sartini Blum and Lara Trubowitz
"Subterranean geography." CItWP, *tr. by* Cinzia Sartini Blum and Lara
Trubowitz

Etruscan Tombs. Agnes Mary Frances Robinson. PeVV

Ettrick. Lady John Scott. LW; SoSe-8; WPE

Ettricke Foreste is a feir forestle. Sang of the Outlaw Murray, The. *Unknown.*
IBB

Étude Réaliste. Algernon Charles Swinburne.
"Baby's feet, like sea-shells pink, A." WeW-3

Etudes. Dennis Phillips.
"Because a thermal motif heard." FTOS
If It's Only Rhythm. FTOS

Etymolgy. Olga Broumas. WiU

Etymological Dirge. Heather McHugh. ExTi

Eucalyptus, his mouth. Into the Next One. Valerie Martínez. AmPoNex

"Euclid Alone Has Looked on Beauty Bare." Edna St. Vincent Millay. APT-
1; BRP; GSo; HeIP-4; MoAmPo; NAAL-2v2; NoP-4; Son; TAP

Euclid Avenue. Harry Clifton. PBCIP

Eudiades. John Addington Symonds.
"In years of old." CAGL

Eugene Onegin Stanza, The. Vladimir Vladimirovich Nabokov. *See* On
Translating "Eugene Onegin."

Eugenia. George Chapman.
Death Described by His True Effects. NOSC
"Eat what you wish; I'll teach ye all to die." NOSC

Eugenist, The. Robert Graves. FaBoEE

Eulogy, The. Carol Muske. PBCAP

Eulogy for Hasdai ibn Shaprut. *Unknown.* TrJP, *tr. by* Israel Abrahams

Eulogy of the Sagely Virtue of His Imperial Majesty Emperor Shih-tsu, A.
Chao Meng-fu. CoBLCP, *tr. by* Jonathan Chaves

Eulogy on My Own Portrait, A. Yang Shih-ch'i. CoBLCP, *tr. by* Jonathan
Chaves

Eulogy to W.H. Auden. Derek Walcott. ESEAA

Eumares. Asclepiades. AWP, *tr. by* Richard Garnett

Eumelos had a Maltese dog. Tymnes. PGA

Eumenides, The. Aeschylus. NAWM-5v1

Eunica scorned [*or* skornde] me, when her I would have sweetly kissed [*or* kist].
Theocritus. NoSic; OBVE, *tr. by* Unknown *Fr.* Idylls.

Eunuch Unique. Francis Picabia.
Eunuch Unique. PFTM-1
"Let's try the present hour." PFTM-1

Eupheme. Ben Jonson.
Picture of the Body, The. NOSC
"Sitting, and ready to be drawn." NOSC

Euphony. Yusef Komunyakaa. ESEAA

Eureka. Maureen Duffy. PoBW

Euripides. Thucydides. GrAn, *tr. by* Peter Jay

Euripides the Athenian. George Seferis. PoetW, *tr. by* Edmund Keeley and
Philip Sherrard

Europa. Rolfe Humphries. APT-2

Europa. Moschus. HePo, *tr. by* Barbara Hughes Fowler

Europa. Anatol Stern. PFTM-1

Europa and Jove. Ovid. NAWM-7v1, *tr. by* Allen Mandelbaum *Fr.*
Metamorphoses.

Europa (in Athens) does business / at truly reasonable rates. Antipater of Thessalonica. GrAn

Europa's kiss / even if. Rufinus. GrAn

Europe. Calvin Forbes. NBV

Europe and America. David Ignatow. NNaP; UnPo

Europe / Is endowed with the first move. Europe. Calvin Forbes. NBV

Europe, Late. Dan Pagis. HP, *tr.* by Stephen Mitchell

Europe's Prisoners. Sidney Keyes. PoWW

Europe, the 72d and 73d Year of These States. Walt Whitman. TCAPo (Leaves of Grass (1855).) APN-1

European Shoe, The. Michael Benedikt. TwCP

(European Shoe is constructed of grass and reed, bound, The.) CoAmPo

Eurotas said to the goddess of love. Leonidas of Tarentum. GrAn

Euryalus and Nisus Meet Their Deaths. Virgil [*or* Vergil]. NoSic, *tr.* by Thomas Phaer [*or* Phayer] *Fr.* Aeneid [*or* Eneados, *Aeneis*], The.

Eurydice. Rosita Copioli. CItWP, *tr.* by Cinzia Sartini Blum and Lara Trubowitz

Eurydice. "H. D."
"So you have swept me back." NALW; VGW

Eurydice. Luciana Frezza. CItWP, *tr.* by Cinzia Sartini Blum and Lara Trubowitz

Eurydice. Louise Glück. BodElec

Eurydice went back to hell. Eurydice. Louise Glück. BodElec

Eutawville Lynching, The. Lizelia Augusta Jenkins Moorer. CBWP-3

Euthymiae Raptus; or, The Teares of Peace. George Chapman.
Justice. NOSC
Learning ("So Learned Men in Controversies Spend"). NOSC
Peace Discovers the Poet. NOSC
Peace of Death, The. NOSC
"Peaceful and young, Herculean silence bore." NOSC
"Thou wretched man, whom I discover, born." NOSC
"Wretched estate of men by fortune blessed." NOSC

Eutopia. Francis Turner Palgrave. EBVV; OBGa

Eutychides. Edwin Arlington Robinson. OBAL

Eutychides. *Var. authors.* OBAL *Fr.* Variations of Greek Themes.

Eutychides the thief was in a rare. Lucilius. GrAn

Eutychus. Rosemary Dobson. ChIV-2

Eutychus the painter / Fathered twenty sons. Lucilius. GrAn

Ev'n for your sake. (LL) Address to the Deil. Robert Burns. NOEC; NePenScot; OxBS

Ev'n God himself, being pressed for my sake. (LL) Bunch of Grapes, The. George Herbert. ChIV-1; ESCV; GeHe; NAEL-5v1; NAEL-6v1; NAEL-7v1; NOSC; TOF

Ev'n [*or* E'en *or* Even] like two little bank-dividing brooks [*or* brookes]. Francis Quarles. MeLP; NOBE *Fr.* Emblems.

Ev'n sated with variety [*or* Varietie]. (LL) Scrutiny [*or* Scrutinie], The. Richard Lovelace. BeJo; BoLoP; CaPo; EnLoPo; MeLP

Ev'ry day is a brand new day. If There Is Someone Lovelier Than You. Howard Dietz. ReLy

Ev'ry day seems like a year. Sometimes I'm Happy. Irving Caesar. ReLy

Ev'ry rolling stone gets to feel alone. Sentimental Journey. Les Brown. ReLy

Ev'ry state has something. Rhode Island Is Famous for You. Howard Dietz. ReLy

Ev'ry Time. Ralph Blane. ReLy

Ev'ry Time We Say Good-bye. Cole Porter. ReLy

Ev'rybody's building the big ships and the boats. Quinn the Eskimo. "Bob Dylan." RaBo

Ev'ryone is on the make for something. Make with the Feet. Harold Adamson. ReLy

Ev'rything seems lovely. Because My Baby Don't Mean Maybe Now. Walter Donaldson. ReLy

Ev'rything that happens in life. That's Entertainment. Howard Dietz. ReLy

Ev'rything went wrong. Always. Irving Berlin. ReLy

Ev'rytime I hear that march from Lohengrin. Walter Donaldson. *See* Every time I hear that march from Lohengrin

"Eva!" again. (LL) Eve. Ralph Hodgson. ChIV-1; MoBrPo; TrCP; UnPo

Eva Braun. W. D. Snodgrass. BodElec *Fr.* Führer Bunker, The.

Eva, forma futuri. Andrea Zanzotto. ItPo, *tr.* by Gayle Ridinger *Fr.* Prophecies or Memories or Display-Board Newspapers.

Evacuation. Pol N Ndu. PBMAP

Evading believers, he hurries off down Pitt Street. (LL) Absolutely Ordinary Rainbow, An. Les A. Murray. CBAP; HarvBoo

Evadne. "H. D." BoWoP; LW

Evan just had the white birch lined up. Fear and Anger in the Mindless Universe. Hayden Carruth. NNaP

Evanescent hue whose pearly gleam, An. Ideal, An. Henrietta Cordelia Ray. CBWP-3

Evangelical vicar in want. Limerick. Ronald Arbuthnott Knox. PeLi

Evangeline, a Tale of Acadie. Henry Wadsworth Longfellow.
Tale of Acadie, A. APN-1; NoP-4; TCAPo; UV
"This is the forest primeval. The murmuring pines and the hemlocks." APN-1; NoP-4; TCAPo; UV

Evangeline made her. Straight Talk from Plain Women. Sherley Anne Williams. GT

Evangelist St John my patron was, The. William Wordsworth. HAP *Fr.* Prelude, The; Growth of a Poet's Mind [1850 vers.].

Evanishings. Mary E. Tucker. CBWP-1

Evans. Ronald Stuart Thomas. OxBEV

Evans Country, The. Kingsley Amis.
Aberdarcy: The Chaucer Road. NOBL
Aberdarcy: The Main Square. NOBL; NoAM; OxBTC
Aldport (Mystery Tour). NOBL
Brynbwrla. NOBL
"By the new Boot's, a tool-chest with flagpoles." NOBL; NoAM; OxBTC
Fforestfawr. NOBL
"5.40. The Bay View. After the office." NOBL
"Hearing how tourists, dazed with reverence." NOBL
Langwell. NOBL; OxBC
"Love is like butter, Evans mused, and stuck." NOBL
"Love's domain, supernal Zion." NOBL
"Now then, what are you up to, Dai?" NOBL; OxBC
Pendydd. NOBL
"When they saw off Dai Evan's da." NOBL

Evans? Yes, many a time. Evans. Ronald Stuart Thomas. OxBEV

Evarra and His Gods. Rudyard Kipling. MoBrPo

Evasive souls, of whom the wise lose track. Imaginative Life, The. Geoffrey Hill. NoAM

Eve. Arthur J. Bull. UnPo

Eve. Jacob [*or* Jakov] Fichman. FIT, *tr.* by Robert Friend

Eve. David Gascoyne. GTBS-P

Eve. Oliver Herford. OBAL

Eve. Ella Higginson. SWaP

Eve. Ralph Hodgson. ChIV-1; MoBrPo; TrCP; UnPo

Eve. Dorothy Livesay. ItWoWo; NALW

Eve. Julio Marzán. PueRic

Eve. Howard Nemerov. CRP

Eve. Christina Georgina Rossetti. ChIV-1; GTBS-P; NALW; NIL-7; NIP-4

Eve. *Unknown.* BIrV, *tr.* by Thomas Macdonagh

Eve am I, great Adam's wife. *Unknown.* NOIV

Eve & her envy roving slammed me down. Gislebertus' Eve. John Berryman. LCAP-2

Eve descends with radiant streaks, The. Song: "Eve descends with radiant streaks, The." Anne Batten Cristall. RWP

Eve Falling. Jane McVeigh. HW

Eve in Eden. Manuela Fingueret. MirDau, *tr.* by Roberta Gordenstein

Eve is madly in love with Hugh. Office Friendships. Gavin Ewart. PeLV

Eve Names the Animals. Susan Donnelly. NIL-7

Eve of Christmas had arrived, The. Christmas Ghost, A. Priscilla Jane Thompson. CBWP-2

Eve of St Agnes, The. John Keats. CABP; EBNV; FHYEP; HAP; NAEL-5v2; NAEL-6v2; NOBRP; NPeEn; NoP-4; OBNV; OxAEP-2; PoE; TFi; TRP

Eve of St. Agnes, The. John Keats.
"Her faltering hand upon the balustrade." OxBEV
"Sudden a thought came like a full-blown rose." EroLit

Eve of St Mark, The. Geoffrey Hill. NPeEn; OxBEV *Fr.* Apology for the Revival of Christian Architecture in England, An.

Eve of Waterloo, The. Byron. *See* Childe Harold's Pilgrimage

Eve of Waterloo, The. Thomas Hardy. FaBoWar; OBWP *Fr.* Dynasts, The.

Eve Oh Eve. Taslima Nasrin. VCWP

Eve (Rachel). Michael S. Harper. ESEAA

Eve's Apology in Defense of Women. Emilia [*or* Aemelia] Lanier [*or* Lanyer]. NAEL-7v1 *Fr.* Salve Deus Rex Judaeorum.

Eve's Monologue. Bella Abramovna Dizhur. ItGoST, *tr.* by Sarah Bliumis

Eve's Striptease. Julia Kasdorf. NeAmPo

Eve's tinted shadows slowly fill the fane. Sir Walter Scott at the Tomb of the Stuarts in St. Peter's. Richard Monckton, 1st Baron Houghton Milnes. EBVV

Eve-Song. Mary Gilmore. CBAP; LW

Eve to Adam. John Milton. UV; WoPoe *Fr.* Paradise Lost.

Eve to Her Daughters. Judith Wright. NALW; NoP-4

Eve, with her basket, was. Eve. Ralph Hodgson. ChIV-1; MoBrPo; TrCP; UnPo

Evelyn. Priscilla Jane Thompson. CBWP-2

Evelýn Hope.   Robert Browning.   TreFP

Even.   Anne Morrow Lindbergh.   AiP

Even a feather in flight can sketch.   Day and Night.   Eugenio Montale.   AF, *tr. by* William Arrowsmith

Even a fleabite.   Issa.   EH, *tr.* by Robert Hass

Even a Pyrrhonist.   Lot of Night Music, A.   Anthony Hecht.   OxBC

Even a rock.   How I Come to You.   Molly Peacock.   RA

Even after Confession.   On a Catholic Childhood.   Janet Campbell Hale.   VoR

Even after his death he did not return.   Dante.   Anna Andreyevna Akhmatova.   PoetW, *tr. by* Max Hayward and Stanley Kunitz

Even an old landscape has a moment of birth.   Moon.   Nathan [*or* Natan] Alterman.   FIT, *tr. by* Robert Friend

Even as a beast of Epicurus' sty. (LL)   To Dante Alighieri (He Commends the Work of Dante's Life).   Giovanni Quirino.   AWP; EaItPo, *tr. by* Dante Gabriel Rossetti

Even as a child I could.   Tea Mind.   Chase Twichell.   ExTi

Even as a holy martyr sheds her blood. (LL)   Stanzas on Mutability.   Hugo von Hofmannsthal.   AWP; TrJP, *tr. by* Jethro Bithell

Even as a river,—partly (it might seem).   William Wordsworth.   NAEL-6v2 *Fr.* Prelude, The; Growth of a Poet's Mind [1850 vers.].

Even as a young man.   Once More Fields and Gardens.   T'ao Ch'ien [*or* T'ao Yuan-ming].   AWP, *tr. by* Florence Ayscough and Amy Lowell

Even as children they were late sleepers.   Undead, The.   Richard Wilbur.   CoAP; CoAmPo; OxBC

Even as he was. (LL)   Jolly Jugger, The.   *Unknown.*   EBEV; NPeEn

Even as I Hold You.   Alice Walker.   WeW-3

Even as I stand or sit passing faster than you. (LL)   Walt Whitman.   HAP; NAWM-7v2; SAmP; WeW-3   *Fr.* Song of Myself.

Even as the cattle in the winter woods.   For France.   Claudian.   MLL, *tr. by* Helen Waddell

Even as the day into this room. (LL)   Room, The.   William Soutar.   EBEV; NePenScot

Even as the day when it is yet at dawning.   Canzone: Of His Love, with the Figure of a Sudden Storm.   Prinzivalle Doria.   AWP; EaItPo, *tr. by* Dante Gabriel Rossetti

Even as the moon amid the stars doth shed.   Tommaso Buzzuola.   EaItPo, *tr. by* Dante Gabriel Rossetti

Even as the others mock, thou mockest me.   Dante Alighieri.   AWP; EaItPo, *tr. by* Dante Gabriel Rossetti   *Fr.* La Vita Nuova.

Even as the praying statues of the sainted.   Psychologia Christiana.   Mihály Babits.   IQMS, *tr. by* Peter Zollman

Even as the Wandering Traveler.   John Hall.   ChIV-1

Even as the wandering traveler doth stray.   Even as the Wandering Traveler.   John Hall.   ChIV-1

Even as this Globe Shall Gleam and Disappear.   Katharine Lee Bates.   PoBW

Even ashes of lovers find no rest. (LL)   Hour-Glass [*or* Houre-Glasse], The.   Ben Jonson.   BeJo; EnLoPo; NIP-4

Even at prayer, our eyes look inward.   Mirza Asadullah Khan Ghalib.   EnIH

Even at this late date, sometimes I have to look up.   Fuel.   Naomi Shihab Nye.   ExTi

Even at 26, the hush when.   Paul Laurence Dunbar in The Tenderloin.   Ishmael Reed.   ESEAA

Even barely enough light to find a mouth.   Grammar of Light, The.   Carol Ann Duffy.   HarvBoo

Even before I speak, she serves. (LL)   Nani.   Alberto A. Ríos.   MakPoe; SoSe-8; UnSA

Even before the flat yellow sail of the sun.   Shades.   Minnie Bruce Pratt.   ExTi

Even before the Renaissance they realized that there was a simplicity in keeping.   I'm Sending You Saint Francis Preaching to the Birds.   Karen Kipp.   BodElec

Even before we begin, the sound of wind.   Dancing a Spell.   Marjorie M. Evasco.   ReBoTo

Even birds help.   Little Invitation in a Hushed Voice.   Tess Gallagher.   PasH

Even Buddha is lost in this land.   Tassajara, 1969.   Diane Di Prima.   BB

Even clothed in wrinkles, dear Philinna.   Paulus [*or* Paulos] Silentiarius.   ErotSp, *tr. by* Sam Hamill

Even considered.   Issa.   EH, *tr. by* Robert Hass

Even dead the old man grows.   Hipponax.   Alcaeus [*or* Alkaios].   GrAn, *tr. by* Alistair Elliot

Even dew distilled.   Tojun.   JDP, *tr. by* Yoel Hoffmann

Even during war, moments of delicate peace.   Muriel Rukeyser.   TrJP   *Fr.* Letter to the Front.

Even flow of neuronal pattern was visible, The.   Neuroanatomy Summer.   Marc J. Straus.   BloBone

Even for the wind there was no room.   Way the Bird Sat, The.   Ray A. Young Bear.   CDW; VoR

Even Forsaken They'd Flower.   Raúl Zurita.   TCLAP, *tr. by* Jack Schmitt

Even from a distance, this picture is known.   Nossis.   SaLy, *tr. by* Diane Rayor

Even from earthly love thy face avert not.   Nuru'ddin Abdu 'R-Rahman Jami.   TOF

Even gods resent my paradise.   Hors de Combat.   "Anvari."   ArPe, *tr. by* Omar S. Pound

Even He Was Abashed.   *Unknown.*   WoPoe, *tr. by* Martha Ann Selby   *Fr.* Gathasaptasati, The.

Even here I taste, having eaten it / all these years. (LL)   Red Dust.   Philip Levine.   NNaP; NoAM

Even here in Cincinnati.   Elvis Elevator, The.   Terry Stokes.   AllShUp

Even here, thousands of miles.   Snowy Owl.   Matthew J. Spireng.   PoCoUp

Even if God did not exist, religion would still be holy and divine.   Fuses I and II.   Charles Baudelaire.   PFTM-1

Even if I am only more dust.   Pompeius.   GrAn

Even if I am too late. (LL)   I Did Not Manage To Save.   Jerzy Ficowski.   HP; PoSu, *tr. by* Keith Bosley and Krystyna Wandycz Bosley

Even if the geraniums are artificial.   Geraniums, The.   Genevieve Taggard.   VGW

Even if you are killed, you die.   Bus-Stop on the Somme, The.   David Rowbotham.   NOBAu

Even if you can't shape your life the way you want.   As Much As You Can.   Constantine P. Cavafy.   RB

Even in bed I pose: desire may grow.   Carnal Knowledge.   Thom Gunn.   BoLoP

Even in bronze curtains, I pierce the white ceiling.   Stone Will Talk, The.   Houda Al-Na'mani.   PoArWo

Even in Kyoto.   Basho.   SoOfWa, *tr. by* Sam Hamill

Even in Kyoto.   Basho.   EH, *tr. by* Robert Hass

Even in my dreams / I must no longer meet you.   Lady Ise.   BoWoP

Even in my town / Now, I sleep.   Mukai Kyorai.   ZenPo, *tr. by* Takashi Ikemoto and Lucien Stryk

Even in repentance there is pleasure.   Elizaveta Kuzmina-Karavayeva.   TCRP

Even in the age.   Narihira (Ariwara no Narihira).   OHPJ

Even in the bluest noonday of July.   To Mrs. Will H. Low.   Robert Louis Stevenson.   NOBVV; NPeEn

Even in the moment of our earliest kiss.   Edna St. Vincent Millay.   HeIP-4; VGW

Even is come; and from the dark Park, hark.   Nocturnal Sketch, A.   Thomas Hood.   PeLV

Even my loves are measured by wars.   Yehuda Amichai [*or* Amikhai].   PoSu   *Fr.* Patriotic Songs.

Even naturalists are uninterested in pigeons.   Pigeons.   Baron Wormser.   UrbNat

Even now.   Bilhana.   EroLit, *tr. by* Barbara Stoler Miller *Fr.* Fantasies of a Love-Thief.

Even now, after twice her lifetime of grief.   Anne Frank Huis.   Andrew Motion.   HarvBoo

Even now, angle-poised over a desk.   Exact Fares.   David Morley.   NLP

Even now, at the end of the century.   Edgewater Park.   Ruth L. Schwartz.   WiU

Even now I cannot help thinking of them.   George Szirtes.   NewEx

Even now I wish that you had been there.   Swans Mating.   Michael Longley.   PNI

Even now my breast bone's aching.   Part of a Bird.   Nina Cassian.   PoSu, *tr. by* Andrea Deletant and Brenda Walker

Even now / My thought is all of this gold-tinted king's daughter.   Black Marigolds.   Bilhana.   AWP, *tr. by* E. Powys Mathers

Even now that care which on thy crown[e] attends.   To the Thrice-Sacred Queen Elizabeth.   Mary Sidney Herbert, Countess of Pembroke.   NALW; NoP-4

Even now the devastation is begun.   Oliver Goldsmith.   EBEV   *Fr.* Deserted Village, The.

Even now the fragrant darkness of her hair.   Terre Promise.   Ernest Christopher Dowson.   NOBVV

Even now there are places where a thought might grow.   Disused Shed in Co. Wexford, A.   Derek Mahon.   BiHa; CABP; CIP-2; EmeKit; ModIr; NOIV; NPeEn; NoP-4; OxBC; PBCIP; PNI

Even now this landscape is assembling.   All Hallows.   Louise Glück.   HCAP; PoPoPo

Even on clear nights, lead the most supple children.   Great Bear, The.   John Hollander.   ColAP; NoAM; TwCP

Even on Sunday.   Robin Blaser.   FTOS

Even on the quietest days the distant.   Ford Manor.   Derek Mahon.   PBCIP

Even on the smallest islands.   Issa.   EH, *tr. by* Robert Hass

Even or odd, of all days in the year.   William Shakespeare.   SCV   *Fr.* Romeo and Juliet.

Even ordinarily, parting is difficult.   Yang Shih-ch'i.   CoBLCP   *Fr.* Inscribed on a Painting of Bamboo Presented to Lecturer Ch'en Upon His Departure to Resume His Duties at Nanking.

Even so. (LL)   Dirge in Woods.   George Meredith.   NAEL-5v2; NAEL-6v2; OBEV

Even So. Dante Gabriel Rossetti. NOBE; NOBVV

Even so deep in the jungle they were not safe. Garden of Ships, The. Douglas Stewart. CBAP

Even so distant, I can taste the grief. Deceptions. Philip Larkin. GTBS-P; HarvBoo; OxAEP-2

'Even so!' said the Queen. (LL) Jealousy. Mary Elizabeth Coleridge. EnLoPo; LW; WPE

Even Such Is Time. Sir Walter Ralegh. HAP; OxBSP; PoRA; RB; TFi
  (Author's Epitaph, Made By Himself, The.) NAEL-5v1; NAEL-6v1; NAEL-7v1; NIL-7
  (Conclusion, The.) OBEV
  (Epitaph.) FaBoEE; NOBE; PeECV; SCGP
  (Even such is Time, which takes in trust.) NAEL-6v1; NIL-7; PeECV
  (Even suche is tyme that takes in trust.) NPeEn
  (Verses Made the Night before He Died [or Dyed].) NoSic
  (Verses Written the Night before His Execution.) TRP

Even such is Time, which takes in trust. Authours Epitaph, Made by Himself, The. Sir Walter Ralegh. NIL-7

Even the abandoned husk of a person can sometimes. Figure in the Carpet, The. James Tate. BodElec

Even the air could kill us. (LL) Angels in Winter. Nancy Willard. ColAP; LCAP-2

Even the bad news came slowly and was afraid. Washington Heights, 1959. Michael C. Blumenthal. HCAP

Even the barnacle has certain rights. This Octopus Exploits Women. James Fenton. NoAM

Even the Beating Heart Is Already Indicated. Ernst Waldinger. AuPH, tr. by Lowell A. Bangerter

Even the dark end of Belmont Avenue. Walking by the Cliffside Dyeworks. Robert Carnevale. UnSA

Even the dirt kept breathing a small breath. (LL) Root Cellar. Theodore Roethke. ColAP; HarvBoo; HeIP-4; InPK-6; NoP-4; PAI; VCAP

Even the dissident ones speak. America. John Newlove. NOBC

Even the dumplings / Are smaller. Morikawa Kyoroku. ZenPo, tr. by Takashi Ikemoto and Lucien Stryk

Even the Eagles Must Gather. Alma Villanueva. FFC

Even the fat slug. Everything in the Garden is Lovely. Alasdair Aston. OBGa

Even the graves are not tended in Russia. Georgy [or Georgii] Vladimirovich Ivanov. TCRP

Even the last few, weeks off yet, misshapen as toes. (LL) Broad Bean Sermon, The. Les A. Murray. BMAP; EmeKit; HarvBoo; MakPoe

Even the liveliest of us had. Another and Another and. Theodore Weiss. DiPo

Even the long-dead are willing to move. Gentle Communion. Pat Mora. NIL-7; NIP-4

Even the man who is happy. Kalidasa. EaWin, tr. by J. Moussaieff Masson and W. S. Merwin

Even the most die-hard liberals. Lonely Affair, A. Reuben Jackson. GT

Even the night will blossom as the rose. (LL) On Growing Old. John Masefield. MoBrPo; PoRA

Even the sun-clouds this morning cannot manage such skirts. Poppies in October. Sylvia Plath. FaBoWP; HCAP; LCAP-2; NoAM

Even the tallest didn't remember. Gentleness of the Very Tall, The. Linda France. MFPA

Even the Trees. Jackie Kay. MFPA

Even the trees outside feel it, their fine branches. Even the Trees. Jackie Kay. MFPA

Even the walls are flowing, even the ceiling. Variation on Heraclitus. Louis MacNeice. NoAM

Even the Whales. Tom Matthews. PNI

Even the wind that should listen hums something lovely. Letter. Margit Szécsi. IQMS, tr. by Kenneth McRobbie

Even the worst intelligence must needs ride. Sir Gelli to R.S. Roland Mathias. AngWePo

Even the wrist's fast jack. Bone Die, The. Maggie Hannan. NLP

Even then I said. Antiphilus [or Antiphilos]. GrAn

Even these long days. Basho. SoOfWa, tr. by Sam Hamill

Even this far from that burning place. History. Alpay Ulku. AmPoNex

Even this far, with two paper cups and miles of taut string, I could describe a ghost of myself. From San Diego. Chryss Yost. GeoHom

Even this late it happens. Coming of Light, The. Mark Strand. HCAP

Even this love's heat must be its curb and rein. (LL) Cantica: Our Lord Christ: Of Order. Saint Francis of Assisi. AWP; EaItPo; OBVE, tr. by Dante Gabriel Rossetti

Even this suburb has overcome Death. Easter. Howard Nemerov. NoP-4

Even though he lies underground. Erucius [or Erycius] of Cyzicus. GrAn

Even though I'm angry. Tenderness. Belinda Zubicueta Carmona. TANSG, tr. by Celeste Kostopulos-Cooperman

Even though it's dark. Race. Orkhan Muyassar. MAP, tr. by Samuel Hazo and Lena Jayyusi

Even though my hands / are rough from much rice-pounding. *Unknown.* BoWoP

Even though she don't have a job, Mami still words. Unemployed Mami. Willie Perdomo. InTrad

Even thus, and never cease to moan Ay me? (LL) Canzone: His Lament for Selvaggia. Cino da Pistoia. AWP; EaItPo, tr. by Dante Gabriel Rossetti

Even to each other. Merely to be mere, ly to be. (LL) Song Form. Imamu Amiri Baraka. ChAP; TTTS

Even to the children / on the disenchanted shore. Leah Goldberg. TrJP, tr. by Robert Friend Fr. Songs of the Stream.

Even to the icy winter, and the siege. (LL) Leningrad Cemetery, Winter of 1941. Sharon Olds. NIL-7; NIP-4

Even to thy pure and most most loving breast. (LL) William Shakespeare. EBEV; NAEL-6v1; NAEL-7v1; NoSic; OxAEP-1 Fr. Sonnets.

Even tonight and I need to take a walk and clear. Poem About My Rights. June Jordan. GLP; ISC; NAAAL; NoAM

Even two weeks after her fall. Death in Mexico. Denise Levertov. NAAL-5

Even what the hungry Wolf in Field would do. Mary Mollineux. EMWP, tr. by Henry Mollineux

Even when cross planks are nailed down. Leaving the Village. *Vietnamese Oral Tradition.* CaDao, tr. by John Balaban

Even when first her face. Someone Talking to Himself. Richard Wilbur. HarvBoo

Even when I fall asleep early. Insomnia. Lu Yu. OHMPC, tr. by Kenneth Rexroth

Even when they destroy you it will still be beautiful. Odysseus Elytis. GifTon, tr. by Olga Broumas Fr. With Light and With Death.

Even when you see through the lies, the lies they. Once a Shoot of Heaven. Beckian Fritz Goldberg. PuP-23

Even whilst I watch him I am remembering. To T.A.R.H. Stephen Spender. CAGL

Even with insects. Issa. EH, tr. by Robert Hass

Even with insects. Avedik Issahakian. ChAP

Even with the good knight Charlemain. (LL) Ballad of the Lords of Old Time. François Villon. AWP; PeVV, tr. by Algernon Charles Swinburne

Even yet, perhaps, a trifle piqued—who knows? (LL) Troll's Nosegay, The. Robert Graves. OxBSo; Son

Even Your Escape Is a Bit Special. Anna Cascella. CItWP, tr. by Cinzia Sartini Blum and Lara Trubowitz

Evenen in the Village. William Barnes. EBVV

Evenfall, so slow on hills, hath shot, The. Lights of London, The. Louise Imogen Guiney. APN-2

Evening. Richard Aldington. MoBrPo

Evening. Joanna Baillie. ECWP Fr. Summer Day, A.

Evening. Byron. AWP Fr. Don Juan.

Evening. John Clare. NOBVV

Evening. "H. D." APT-1; FaBoMo; HarvBoo; VGW; WPE

Evening. Andreas Gryphius. GePo, tr. by George C. Schoolfield

Evening. Kiyu. JDP, tr. by Yoel Hoffmann

Evening. Willem Kloos. TuT, tr. by Desmond Egan

Evening. King D. Kuka. VoR

Evening. Emma Lazarus. APN-2 Fr. Phantasies.

Evening. Mark McMorris. AmPoNex

Evening. W. S. Merwin. NAAL-2v2

Evening. Thomas Miller. NOxBChV

Evening. John Milton. See Paradise Lost

Evening. Khalil Mutran. MAP, tr. by Issa Boullata and Thomas G. Ezzy

Evening. James Stephens. MoBrPo

Evening. Ronald Stuart Thomas. HarvBoo

Evening. Victor Van Vriesland. TrJP, tr. by Adriaan J. Barnouw

Evening. *Vietnamese Oral Tradition.* CaDao, tr. by John Balaban

Evening. Mihály Csokonai Vitéz. IQMS, tr. by Madeline Mason

Evening. Karen Volkman. NIL-7

Evening. James Wright (1927–80). NOBA

Evening, An. William Allingham. EnLoPo; NOBVV

Evening, An. Robert Mezey. GeoHom

Evening, The. Georg Trakl. PFTM-1

Evening! A flight of pigeons in clear sky! Flute; a Pastoral, The. José-Maria de Heredia. AWP, tr. by H. J. C. Grierson

Evening after Rain. Tu Fu. CrYelRi, tr. by Sam Hamill

Evening, and Maidens. William Barnes. OBEV

Evening and morning old Platthis kept. Leonidas. PGA

Evening and Night. James Thomson. NAEL-6v1; NAEL-7v1 Fr. Seasons, The.

Evening—another evening—and the lights flare. Thomas McGrath. NNaP Fr. Letter to an Imaginary Friend.

Evening, as slow thy placid shades descend. Sonnet 5. William Lisle Bowles. NOBRP; NOEC

Evening before, The. (LL) Michael Wigglesworth. ColAP; TCAPo Fr. Day of Doom, The.

Evening before Rain. Leonard Alfred George Strong. OxBTC

Evening, before the King's pavilion. At the Exiled King's River Pavilion. U'ng Bình. CaDao, tr. by John Balaban

Evening Bell from a Misty Temple. Wen Cheng-ming. CoBLCP, tr. by Jonathan Chaves

Evening bell / Persimmons pelt. Masaoka Shiki. ZenPo, tr. by Takashi Ikemoto and Lucien Stryk

Evening Bells near a Temple. Ma Chih-yüan. CrYelRi, tr. by Sam Hamill

Evening breeze, The. Tenderly. Walter Gross. ReLy

Evening bridge / A thousand hands. Kikaku. ZenPo, tr. by Takashi Ikemoto and Lucien Stryk

Evening brings all home. For that we wait, The. Horatius Bonar. SacPr Fr. My Old Letters.

Evening calm envelops the cold city. Listening to the Washblock in the Moonlight. Liu Ch'ang-ch'ing. SuSp, tr. by Dell R. Hales

Evening came, a child was missing. Little Bell. Mary E. Tucker. CBWP-1

Evening Change. John Haines. GifTon

Evening cherry-blossoms. Kaisho. JDP, tr. by Yoel Hoffmann

Evening clears, The. Issa. EH, tr. by Robert Hass

Evening cloudburst, An. Buson. SoOfWa, tr. by Sam Hamill

Evening clouds dispersed. Tune: "Joy All Under Heaven"—Sunset on the Western Hill. Hsü Tsai-ssu. SuSp, tr. by Sherwin S. S. Fu

Evening Comes. Li Shang-yin. OHMPC, tr. by Kenneth Rexroth

Evening comes and everything is hushed, The. Family Circle. János Arany. IQMS, tr. by Neville Masterman

Evening comes. My mind is troubled. Evening Comes. Li Shang-yin. OHMPC, tr. by Kenneth Rexroth

Evening comes with an onslaught of wind and rain. Tune: Song of Picking Mulberry. Li Ch'ing-chao. CoBCP, tr. by Burton Watson

Evening Contemplation. George Washington Doane. AH

Evening Dance of the Grey Flies. Patricia K. Page. NOBC

Evening Darkens Over, The. Robert Bridges. HAP; NOBVV; SCGP

Evening darkens until. Unknown. OHMPJ

Evening Ebb. Robinson Jeffers. NoAM
  (Ocean has not been so quiet for a long while; five night- / herons, The.) BLT

Evening falls on the smoky walls. Ballad of the Londoner. James Elroy Flecker. EnLoPo

Evening, Gertrude. Anne Batten Cristall. ECWP; RWP

Evening Halo of Light, An. Árpád Tóth. IQMS, tr. by Thomas Kabdebo

Evening has brought its. Witnesses. W. S. Merwin. LCAP-2

Evening has passed and the moon will soon vanish, The. Visitor Who Never Came, The. Nazik Al-Mala'ika. MAP, tr. by Christopher Middleton and Matthew Sorenson

Evening Hawk. Robert Penn Warren. APT-2; ColAP; NAAL-2v2; NoP-4; OWoS; VCAP

Evening Hymn in the Hovels. Francis Lauderdale Adams. OxBS

Evening in Connecticut. Louis MacNeice. HarvBoo

Evening in Paradise. John Milton. NOBE Fr. Paradise Lost.

Evening in Terezin, An. Eva Schulzová. INSAB

Evening in the Garden Clear after Rain. Ch'u Ch'uang I. OHMPC

Evening in the Sanitarium. Louise Bogan. FaBoWP; NALW; NIL-7; TwCP

Evening in the Village. Lu Yu. OHPC, tr. by Kenneth Rexroth

Evening is clogged with gnats as the light fails. Alceste in the Wilderness. Anthony Hecht. CoAmPo

Evening is coming, the day wears on. Unknown. WoPoe, tr. by Charles Hubert Sisson Fr. Song of Roland, The.

Evening is part of the jig-saw truth of her. Ode in Honour. Francis Scarfe. SPE

Evening Land, The. D. H. Lawrence. FaBoA

Evening lecture. Scott Montgomery. HA

Evening Lights on the River. Chiang Shih-ch'üan. OHMPC, tr. by Kenneth Rexroth

Evening Lull, An. Walt Whitman. NAAL-2v1; NAAL-3

Evening Meal in the Twentieth Century. John Holmes (1904–62). AiP

Evening moon. Issa. EH, tr. by Robert Hass

Evening Musicale. Phyllis McGinley. OBAL; OBCoV; Son

Evening near Serpent River. Tu Fu. CrYelRi, tr. by Sam Hamill

Evening Nixon called his last troops off, The. April 30, 1975. John Balaban. CDa

Evening oer the meadow seems to stoop, The. Mist in the Meadows. John Clare. NPeEn

Evening of My Birthday, The. Yang Shih-ch'i. CoBLCP, tr. by Jonathan Chaves

Evening of the Mind, The. Donald Justice. VCAP

Evening of the Sixth Day, The. Rose Drachler. APT-2

Evening of the Whirlwind. Amir Gilbo'a. MHP, tr. by Ruth Finer Mintz

Evening on Calais Beach. William Wordsworth. See It is a beauteous evening

Evening on Lesbos. Edna St. Vincent Millay. PoBW

Evening on the Mountain: Song to the Moon in the Well. Yi Kyubo. WoPoe, tr. by Kevin O'Rourke

Evening on the Potomac. Richard Hovey. APN-2

Evening Out, The. Ogden Nash. MoAmPo

Evening outdoors is only a larger lobby. One-Night Expensive Hotel. Ronald G. Everson. NOBC

Evening Prayer. Arthur Fitger. AWP, tr. by Jethro Bithell

Evening Prayer. Thomas Merton. ChIV-1

Evening Prayer. Henrietta Cordelia Ray. CBWP-3

Evening Prayer. Unknown. TrJP, tr. by Solomon Solis-Cohen

Evening Prayer, at a Girls' School. Felicia Dorothea Hemans. VWP

Evening primrose. Buson. EH, tr. by Robert Hass

Evening Primrose, The. Christopher Pearse Cranch. APN-1

Evening primrose dressed. Pollen. Wyn Cooper. UrbNat

Evening Quatrains. Charles Cotton. NOSC; NPeEn; OxBEV; SCGP

Evening rain drips on the steps. Tune: "Joy of Returning to the Fields." Huang T'ing-chien. ColAnChi, tr. by J. R. Hightower

Evening red and morning gray. Unknown. FaBoVe; OxNR

Evening rises toward the mountain trails. Night in a Room by the River. Tu Fu. AWTN; CrYelRi, tr. by Sam Hamill

Evening river is level and motionless, The. Flowers and Moonlight on the Spring River. Yang-Ti, Emperor of Sui Dynasty. ChiP, tr. by Arthur Waley

Evening's End. Leon Stokesbury. BAP-97

Evening's getting cold and old, The. Valse Triste. Sándor Weöres. IQMS, tr. by W. Arthur Boggs

Evening's late November, clouds hump and streak, The. Wild Night at Treweithan. Gwyn Williams. AngWePo; TCAWP

Evening's Love, An. Dryden.
  After the Pangs of a Desperate Lover. PeLV

Evening—Sail. Ian Hamilton Finlay. NePenScot

Evening Sail, The. George Crabbe. TreFP Fr. Borough, The.

Evening Scene, An. Zhao Zhenkai. VCWP, tr. by Chen Maiping and Bonnie S. McDougall

Evening Scene at Twin Forests. Chin Nung. CoBLCP, tr. by Jonathan Chaves

Evening shadows steal. Roka. JDP, tr. by Yoel Hoffmann

Evening Song. Sherwood Anderson. GM

Evening Song. Kenneth Fearing. SPE
  (Go to sleep McKade.) APT-2

Evening Song. Sidney Lanier. UnPo

Evening Song. Ralph J. Mills, Jr. IllVoic

Evening Song. Elizabeth Madox Roberts. APT-1

Evening Song. Jean Toomer. APT-2; BPo; GT

Evening Song. Philipp von Zesen. GePo, tr. by George C. Schoolfield

Evening-Star. Louise Bogan. APT-2

Evening star. William J. Higginson. HA

Evening star. Hal Roth. HA

Evening star, The. Nick Avis. HA

Evening Star, The. Pablo Antonio Cuadra. TCLAP, tr. by Ann McCarthy de Zavala and Grace Schulman

Evening Star, The. Henry Wadsworth Longfellow. APN-1

Evening star that in the vaulted skies, The. Verse Written in the Album of Mademoiselle. Pierre Dalcour. TTY, tr. by Langston Hughes

Evening Star who gathers everything. Sappho. SaLy; WPoS, tr. by Diane Rayor

Evening Stroll. Ema Saiko. WoPoe, tr. by Conrad Totman

Evening sun, The. John Wills. HA

Evening sun sets beyond the western ranges, The. Spending the Night at the Hillside Lodge of Master Yeh and Waiting for My Friend Ting. Meng Hao Jan. SuSp, tr. by Daniel Bryant

Evening swallows keep twittering by my curtain. Late Spring. Yüan Chên. SuSp, tr. by Dell R. Hales

Evening, the heather, The. Invasion Summer. Laurie Lee. OxBSP

Evening Twilight. Heinrich Heine. AWP, tr. by John Todhunter Fr. North Sea, The.

Evening View as the Snow Clears. Chia Tao. SuSp, tr. by Stephen Owen

Evening View at River Pavilion, Inviting Guest. Po Chü-i. SuSp, tr. by Irving Y. Lo

Evening View from Grass Hill. Gensei. WoPoe, tr. by Burton Watson

Evening View from the Bell Tower at P'ing-ch'ang. T'ang Hsien-tsu. CoBLCP, tr. by Jonathan Chaves

Evening Walk. Sonja Åkesson. WPOW, tr. by Joanna Bankier

Evening Walk, An. J. H. Prynne. PFTM-2

Evening Walk, The. Nazim Hikmet. AF

Evening-Watch, The. Henry Vaughan. ESCV

Evening will come. Evening—Sail. Ian Hamilton Finlay. NePenScot

Evening wind. Buson. EH, tr. by Robert Hass

Evening Wind. William Carpenter. PoSol

Evening Wind. Robert Mezey. PoSol

Evening without Angels. Wallace Stevens. VGW

Evenings ever more willing lapse into my world's evening. Denis Devlin. ModIr; NOIV Fr. Memoirs of a Turcoman Diplomat.

Evenings I hear. Plague of Starlings, A. Robert Earl Hayden. ESEAA; NoAM

Evenings, listening hard. Backgrounds. Moniza Alvi. NeBl

Evenings we went out alone to that long field. Digging Potatoes, 1950. Stanley Plumly. SpudSo

Eveningsong. Ramona Wilson. VoR

Eveningsong 2. Ramona Wilson. VoR

Evenlode, The. Joseph Hilaire Pierre Belloc. OxAEP-2

Evensong. Marc Cohen. KGB

Evensong. Paul Gerhardt. GePo, tr. by Ingrid Waløe-Engel

Evensong. Robert Herrick. BASC

Evensong. Clive Staples Lewis. TrCP

Evensong. Robert Louis Stevenson. ITBLP

Evensong [or Even-Song]. George Herbert. ESCV

Event. Kim Addonizio. MoASP

Event. Sylvia Plath. NOBA

Event, An. Edward Field. CoAP

Event, The. Rita Dove. ESEAA; NAAL-5; NoAM Fr. Thomas and Beulah.

Event, The. Thomas Sturge Moore. OBMV

Event on the Street, An. Daniil Kharms. AF

Events Like Palaces. Paz Molina. TANSG, tr. by Steven F. White

Eventual Proteus. Margaret Atwood. MoCV

Ever a toiling *child* doth make us sad. Caroline Elizabeth Norton. VWP Fr. Voice from the Factories, A.

Ever at night have I looked up for thee. Planet Jupiter, The. Epes Sargent. APN-1

Ever been kidnapped. Kidnap Poem. Nikki Giovanni. BPo; TAP

Ever-blissful Kali. Kamalākānta Bhattācārya. SinGod, tr. by Rachel Fell McDermott

Ever-Fixed Mark, An. Kingsley Amis. NoAM

Ever gratefully, Your little friend. (LL) Matinees. James Merrill. HCAP; NOBA

Ever let the Fancy roam. Fancy. John Keats. OBEV

Ever mine [or myn] hap[pe] is slack and slo[w] in coming [or commyng]. Petrarch. OBVE

Ever moulded by the lips of man. (LL) To Virgil [or Vergil]. Tennyson. AWP; GTBS-P; NAEL-6v2

Ever perfect, ever in them- / selves eternal [or eternall]. (LL) Thomas Campion. EnLoPo; InPK-6; NAEL-5v1; NAEL-6v1; NAEL-7v1; NOSC; NoP-4; PoE; TFi; TRP Fr. Observations in the Art of English Poesie.

Ever Present. Philip Ayres. OxBSP

Ever seem them close. (LL) Gary Snyder. HAP; VGW; WeW-3 Fr. Four Poems for Robin.

Ever since I left home. Unknown. ColAnChi, tr. by Red Pine

Ever since I realized there was someone callt. Ntozake Shange. BlSi Fr. For Colored Girls Who Have Considered Suicide When the Rainbow Is Enuf.

Ever since i was knee high to a grasshopper they said i had cute cheeks. Marble surfaces. Joanne Burns. BMAP

Ever since Miss Susan Johnson lost her jockey, Lee. Yellow Dog Blues. William Christopher Handy. NAAAL

Ever since my heart took such a tumble. Will You Still Be Mine? Matt Dennis. ReLy

Ever since school. My Last Name. Nicolás Guillén. TCLAP, tr. by Robert Marquez and David Arthur McMurray

Ever since T'ien-pao, this silence and desolation. Man with No Family to Take Leave of, The. Tu Fu. CoBCP, tr. by Burton Watson

Ever since the lucky night I found you. Don't Blame Me. Dorothy Fields. ReLy

Ever since the time when I was a lusty boy. Realizing the Futility of Life. Po Chü-i. ChiP, tr. by Arthur Waley

Ever since they'd left the Tennessee ridge. Event, The. Rita Dove. ESEAA; NAAL-5, NoAM Fr. Thomas and Beulah.

Ever singing "Die, oh die" (LL) Phantom-Wooer, The. Thomas Lovell Beddoes. NAEL-5v2; NAEL-6v2

Ever So, Between. Valerie Martínez. NAPBL

Ever the poet *from* the land. Ralph Waldo Emerson. TCAPo Fr. Quatrains.

Ever upward like a kite. If We Try. George Sands Johnson. PWR

Ever Watchful. Ta' Abbata Sharra. AWP, tr. by W. G. Palgrave

Evergreen, The. John Frederick Nims. APT-2

Evergreen Cemetery. Alfred Wellington Purdy. MoCV

Evergreen shadow and the pale magnolia, The. Souls Lake. Robert Fitzgerald. APT-2; TwCP

Everlasting Forests, The. Dahlia Ravikovitch [or Ravikovich]. BoWoP, tr. by Chana Bloch

Everlasting Gospel, The. William Blake.
  "Vision of Christ that thou dost see, The." ChIV-2
  "Was Jesus Chaste? or did he." ChIV-2
  "Was Jesus Humble? or did he." ChIV-2

Everlasting Mercy, The. John Masefield.
  "From '41 to '51." SacPr

Everlasting night, An. (LL) John Donne. BASC; EBEV; ESCV; MeLP; NAEL-5v1; NAEL-6v1; NAEL-7v1; NOSC; NPeEn; OxAEP-1; PeECV; SacPr

Everlasting omen of what is. (LL) Often I Am Permitted to Return to a Meadow. Robert Duncan. ColAP; HarvBoo; NOBA; PFTM-2; PmAP

Everlasting Quail. Sam Witt. NeAmPo

Everlasting universe of things, The. Mont Blanc. Shelley. NAEL-5v2; NAEL-6v2; NIP-4; NOBRP; NoP-4

Everlasting Voices, The. W. B. Yeats. AWP

Everly Brothers, The. Floyd Skloot. SwNoth

Evermore, wher-so-evere I be. Unknown. OHMEL

Everness. Jorge Luis Borges. TCLAP, tr. by Richard Wilbur

Every being in the universe. Lao Tzu. EnlH Fr. Tao Te Ching.

Every being is immortal, says the first Goddess. Goddesses, The. Janine Canan. HW

Every boy knows what it's like. What Every Boy Knows. "Antler." GLP

Every branch big with it. Snow in the Suburbs. Thomas Hardy. MoBrPo; OBMV; OxBTC

Every Bullet Has Its Billet. Unknown. FaBoWar

Every Cache. Robert Johnstone.
  "He's a high clear forehead." PNI
  "Various instants I'm not with you." PNI

Every child may joy to hear. (LL) William Blake. ClHu; FaBoCh; HeIP-4; NAEL-5v2; NOBE; NOEC; NOxBChV; PoE; SoSe-8; TFi Fr. Songs of Innocence.

Every Christian Born of God. Unknown. AH

Every city in America is approached. Kissing Stieglitz Goodbye. Gerald Stern. LCAP-2

Every Day. Ingeborg Bachmann. BoWoP, tr. by Christopher Middleton

Every Day. Ingeborg Bachmann. PoSu, tr. by Daniel Huws

Every day. Sun-Dial, The. Adelaide Crapsey. APT-1

Every day. Outside the Furnace. Aziz Qaisi. OMIP, tr. by Baidar Bakht

Every day. Heart and Soul. Assotto Saint. CAGL

Every day a wilderness—no. Dusting. Rita Dove. ESEAA; HCAP; HeIP-4; LCAP-2; NAAL-5 Fr. Thomas and Beulah.

Every day another broken heart. Fat Chance. Beth Gylys. AmPoNex

Every day brings a ship. Letters. Ralph Waldo Emerson. OxBSP

Every-Day Characters. Winthrop Mackworth Praed.
  Belle of the Ball-Room, The. NOBRP
  Portrait of a Lady in the Exhibition of the Royal Academy. NOBL; PeLV
  "Some years ago, ere time and taste." OBEV; OxAEP-2
  Vicar, The. OBEV; OxAEP-2
  "What are you, Lady?—naught is here." NOBL; PeLV
  "Years, years ago,— ere yet my dreams." NOBRP

Every day I burn a stick of incense. Joanne Kyger. BB

Every day I meet the horses. Horses at Valley Store. Leslie Marmon Silko. VoR

Every day I peruse the box scores for hours. Baseball and Classicism. Tom Clark. PmAP

Every day I receive the Imperial favor. Enclosed with a Letter to My Family—For Shu. Yang Shih-ch'i. CoBLCP, tr. by Jonathan Chaves

Every day I see from my window. Wild Oats. Norman MacCaig. NPeEn; NePenScot; OxBTC

Every day is a long pause without seams. Silence, The. Vern Rutsala. CDa

Every Day, Matilde. Pablo Neruda. GifTon, tr. by William O'Daly

Every day on the way home from. By the Winding River I. Tu Fu. OHPC, tr. by Kenneth Rexroth

Every day our bodies separate. Villanelle. Marilyn Hacker. MakPoe

Every evening before the sea departs from Beirut. Sea Desires. Laila Al-Saih. MAP, tr. by Patricia Alanah Byrne and Salma Khadra Jayyusi

Every evening, bent over the bright. Valerio Magrelli. NeIt

Every evening, down into the hardweed. Hardweed Path Going. A. R. Ammons. HCAP; UnPo; VGW

Every evening now throughout the summer. (LL) Cold Spring, A. Elizabeth Bishop. ColAP; TwCP

Every family has a genius. Invaders from Mars. Robert Glück. WiU

Every few months / I dream of Nazis. Every Few Months. Alina Tugend. GotH

Every few weeks or so, I make. Queen of Swords, The. Joanne Limburg. NeBl

Every few years, down at the Florida Keys. Death of the Pilot Whales, The. Peter Meinke. PBCAP

Every foolish drunken poet. Female Genitals, The. Gwerfyl Mechain. EroLit, *tr.* by Dafydd Johnston

Every game that Harvey plays. Harvey Always Wins. Jack Prelutsky. NTCP

Every girl, without delay, listen intently. Debate between Jane Vaughan of Caergai and Cadwaladr the Poet. Jane Vaughan. EMWP

Every hour and every minute. Vow for New Year's, A. Mary Carolyn Davies. PoToHe

Every hour, every moment. "H. D." NALW; NoAM *Fr.* Tribute to the Angels.

Every idle desire has died in my breast. Heinrich Heine. WoPoe, *tr.* by Robert Lowell *Fr.* Dying in Paris.

Every inch of you, a terrible vision, not bear, but virgin! (LL) Elizabeth's War with the Christmas Bear. Norman Dubie. LCAP-2; NoAM

Every lady in this land. Mother Goose. OxNR; ReMoGo

Every last morsel of it, is bought with such toil? (LL) Pitying the Farmer. Li Shen. CoBCP; ColAnChi, *tr.* by Burton Watson

Every letter you've read in this whole book was written. Ovid. RomPo, *tr.* by Peter Green *Fr.* Tristia.

Every Life. Brenda Hillman. BodElec

Every long and wide expanse of sea. Every Wide and Long Expanse of Sea. Maurice Scève. WoPoe, *tr.* by Richard Sieburth

Every man can be like that. Old Man Is Like Moses, The. Vicente Aleixandre. GifTon, *tr.* by Lewis Hyde

Every man wants to be a stud. Cocks and Mares. Ruth Stone. RaBo

Every Metaphor. Milo De Angelis. ItPo, *tr.* by Gayle Ridinger

Every moment we were together. First Meetings. Arseny [*or* Arsenii] Aleksandrovich Tarkovsky [*or* Tarkovskii]. TCRP, *tr.* by Albert C. Todd

Every Month. Teresa Porzecanski. MirDau, *tr.* by Roberta Gordenstein

Every morn I lift my head. Ralph Waldo Emerson. APN-1 *Fr.* Monadnoc.

Every morning. Work We Hate and Dreams We Love. Jimmy Santiago Baca. LoL

Every morning. Claire Malroux. VCWP, *tr.* by Marilyn Hacker

Every morning. Marichiko. OHMPJ

Every morning. Daily Habits. Heberto Padilla. VCWP

Every Morning After Killing Thousands of Angels. Tamura Ryuichi. VCWP, *tr.* by Christopher Drake

Every morning after sleep. Beautiful World, The. Albert Verwey. TuT, *tr.* by Tony Curtis

Every morning, emerald trees. Tune: "Sheep on the Mountain Slope." Liu Chih. ChinPo, *tr.* by Yip Wai-lim

Every morning he is astounded again. Terminally Ill. Anna Swirszczynska. PoSu

Every morning, I. Kenneth Rexroth. APSN; APT-2 *Fr.* Love Poems of Marichiko, The.

Every morning I break trail. Changeling VIII. Kristjana Gunnars. NOBC

Every morning I do this. I stop work, and through. Ghosts. William Carpenter. ReTh

Every morning I forget how it is. Poem. Charles Simic. NNaP

Every morning I get up. To the Tune "A Floating Cloud Crosses Enchanted Mountain." Huang O [*or* Huang Ho]. BoWoP; WoPoe, *tr.* by Chung Ling and Kenneth Rexroth

Every morning I went to her charity and learned. To a Red-headed Do-good Waitress. Alan Dugan. Son

Every morning, in the dust. Sparrow in the Dust, A. Ruth Domino. BoWoP, *tr.* by Daniel Hoffman and Jerre Mangione

Every morning the curtain rises. Every morning. Claire Malroux. VCWP, *tr.* by Marilyn Hacker

Every morning the sun comes, the sun. (LL) Arc Inside and Out, The. A. R. Ammons. NoAM; NoP-4

Every morning there is war again. Clearing Station. Wilhelm Klemm. PeFWW

Every morning they hold hands. Suburban Lovers. Bruce Dawe. NOBAu

Every morning you return from a long. Morning Roar of the City, The. Slavko Mihalic. PoSu, *tr.* by Charles Simic

Every need analyzed, each personal problem weighed, carefully, and solved according to the circumstance of. Bryce & Tomlins. Kenneth Fearing. APT-2

Every night. Gary Hotham. HA

Every night, as my grandfather sat. Guild, The. Sharon Olds. RaBo

Every night at this place. Ted's Bar and Grill. Jim Daniels. ReTh

Every night death counts on her fingers. Nocturnal. Romelia Alarcón de Folgar. TANSG, *tr.* by Alison Ridley

Every night I dream we're fighting, armies raised. Jill Breckenridge. CBCWP *Fr.* Civil Blood.

Every night my prayers I say. System. Robert Louis Stevenson. PWR

Every night when I went to bed. Brian [*or* Bryan] Merriman [*or* Merryman]. OBVE, *tr.* by Frank O'Connor *Fr.* Midnight Court, The.

Every nymph may read thee here. (LL) Sigh, A. Anne Finch, Countess of Winchilsea. ECWP; OxBEV

Every October it becomes important, no, *necessary*. Leaves. Lloyd Schwartz. UrbNat

Every October millions of little fish come along the shore. Birds and Fishes. Robinson Jeffers. NAAL-2v2; NAAL-5; NoP-4

Every old man I see. Memory of My Father. Patrick Kavanagh. RB

Every one loved King Matthias, when his charger he rode. King Matthias in Gömör. János Garay. IQMS, *tr.* by James Turner

Every one of these bodies, those in drag, those. Cotillion. Carl Phillips. WiU

Every one of these, stood, separate, upright, above ground. David Jones. PeECV *Fr.* In Parenthesis.

Every [*or* Ev'ry] Time I Feel the [*or* de] Spirit. Unknown. APN-2

Every path a green lady. Four Songs from the Book of Samuel. Eli W. Mandel. MoCV

Every peak is a crater. This is the law of volcanoes. Adrienne Rich. NAAL-2v2; NALW; NoAM *Fr.* Twenty-one Love Poems.

Every plant is burnt yellow. War Lament. Unknown. CrYelRi, *tr.* by Sam Hamill

Every poem. Regeneration. Leo Vroman. TuT, *tr.* by James Liddy

Every poem is a hesitation of history. Tenth.9. Roberto Juarroz. PoetW, *tr.* by Mary Crow

Every poem is made of air. Noise. Ferreira Gullar. TCLAP, *tr.* by Renato Rezende

Every season has its dead. Maurizio Cucchi. ItPo, *tr.* by Gayle Ridinger

Every Second Thought. Theodore Weiss.
  "Grey and dankish thing, A." DiPo

Every silver. 9.1.59: VI. Pablo Picasso. CLPP, *tr.* by Paul Blackburn

Every single instant begins another new year. At the New Year. John Hollander. TaR

Every stance seemed crooked. He had. Saint Ras. Anthony McNeill. WaCA

Every store keeps a book for complaints. Yevgeny [*or* Evgenii] Mikhailovich Vinokurov. TCRP

Every summer. Lemonade Stand. Myra Cohn Livingston. TLR

Every summer. Braly Street. Gary Soto. GeoHom; UnSA

Every Sunday she prepared the brown oak table. Poet of the Mountains, The. Thomas McCarthy. CIP-2

Every Thing. Harold Monro. MoBrPo

Every thing that gains a shape. Plasnewydd Square. Christopher Meredith. TCAWP

Every thread of summer is at last unwoven. Puella Parvula. Wallace Stevens. HCAP; LCAP-2

Every time I am bound towards you. Choking. Saniyya Salih. PoArWo, *tr.* by Kamal Boullata

Every time I climb a tree. Five Chants. David McCord. NOxBChV; NTCP

Every time I hear that march from Lohengrin. Makin' Whoopee. Walter Donaldson. OBCoV

Every time I think about us women. Sacred Trees. Jayne Cortez. SurWo

Every time I tried to put the eight ball. Eight Ball. Richard Jackson. SwNoth

Every time Lady Lowbodice swoons. Lady Lowbodice. Unknown. PeLV; PeLi

Every time the bucks went clattering. Earthy Anecdote. Wallace Stevens. RB; SAmP

Every Time We Say Goodbye. James Cushing. SeSe

Every time you hear me sing this song. Railroad Blues, The. Unknown. GM

Every time you weep, I feel the surface of a river. Letters from Home. Elmaz Abinader. PoArWo

Every town with black Catholics has a St. Peter Claver's. St. Peter Claver. Toi Derricotte. LTA; PBCAP

Every village has its village idiot. It Took a Village. Stephanie Brown. AmPoNex

Every weekday morning heading east. Silver-Paced. Bruce Berger. UrbNat

Every Where and Every When. Arthur Sze. OpBo

Every Wide and Long Expanse of Sea. Maurice Scève. WoPoe, *tr.* by Richard Sieburth

Every wild she-bird has nest and mate in the warm April weather. Virgin Martyr, The. Ada Cambridge. NOBAu

Every word is a doubt. Roberto Juarroz. VCWP *Fr.* Eleventh Vertical Poetry.

Every year in June—up here, that's the month for lilacs. What the Light Was Like. Amy Clampitt. FaBoWP

Every year men harvest grapes, not seeing. Macedonius. GrAn

Every year the harvest of its flowers will be reaped by others. (LL) Fêng

Mêng-lung. ColAnChi; WoPoe, *tr. by* Richard W. Bodman *Fr.* Mountain Songs.

Every year they try to rob us. Berlin Metro. Desmond O'Grady. BiHa

Every year without knowing it I have passed the day. For the Anniversary of My Death. W. S. Merwin. CoAP; ColAP; HCAP; InPK-6; NAAL-2v2; NOBA; PAI; PoPoPo; VCAP

Every young woman in the world. Young Woman's Complaint about Her Sweetheart, A. Elen Gwdman. EMWP

Everybody. Mark Levine. AmPoNex

Everybody but Me. Margaret Goss Burroughs. BlSi

Everybody dug a hole and lived in it. Theory. David Huddle. CDa

Everybody else, then, going. Exeunt Omnes. Thomas Hardy. FaBoVe; UV

Everybody knows her, for they see her every day. Pay Your Debts. Mrs. Henry Linden. CBWP-4

Everybody loved Chick Lorimer in our town. Gone. Carl Sandburg. NOBA

Everybody loved Yona. Real Love Isn't What It Seems. Dahlia Ravikovitch [*or* Ravikovich]. DTA, *tr. by* Chana Bloch

Everybody's singing, they call it that. Singing. Geoff Hattersley. NeBl

Everybody said it was useless. All of Them. Qasim Haddad. MAP, *tr. by* Charles Doria and Sharif Elmusa

Everybody says don't. Everybody Says Don't. Stephen Sondheim. ReLy

Everybody wants an intelligent son. At the Washing of My Son. Su Tung-p'o (Su Shih). OHPC, *tr. by* Kenneth Rexroth

Everybody who's anybody longs to be a tree. Horse and Tree. Rita Dove. TRP

Everyday. Indian Girl. Lenard D. Moore. GT

Everyday Alchemy. Genevieve Taggard. APT-2

Everyday / I think about dying. Survivor. Roger McGough. OBCoV

Everyday is a reenactment of the creation story. Postcolonial Tale, A. Joy Harjo. BodElec

Everydays homecoming at sidewalk university / harlem campus. Independent Study. Paul Beatty. AmPoNex

Everymaid. John Oxenham. TrCP

Everyman. Siegfried Sassoon. MoBrPo

Everyman. *Unknown.* NAEL-5v1; NAWM-5v1

Everyman/ Preacher or lecher, saint or sot. Robert Francis. CRP *Fr.* Epitaphs.

Everyone at Lake Kearney had a nickname. Sway. Louis Simpson. NoAM

Everyone cheered her on. Grandmother, Dead at 99 Years and 10 Months. William Matthews. PuP-23

Everyone complains about the nose. Nose, The. Ruth Stone. InvLad

Everyone else may leave you, I will never leave you, fugitive. (LL) Under Voice, The. Jean Valentine. BodElec; ExTi

Everyone has only one leg. Great Infirmities. Charles Simic. ChAP

Everyone hates the gaudy slave trader, with good reason. Gaudy Slave Trader. Wayne Koestenbaum. KGB

Everyone here wears a full head of dark hair. Mornings. Midlife. Robin Becker. BodElec

Everyone in Genthe's famous photographs of the San Francisco earthquake and fire is well dressed. Images of the San Francisco Disaster. Larry Kramer. GeoHom

Everyone in here hates. That is why this place is called a clinic. Cure, The. Eugene Wildman. OPRER

Everyone in me is a bird. In Celebration of My Uterus. Anne Sexton. NALW

Everyone in this room. Conference, A. Renée Weiss. BodElec

Everyone is young, young, young. David Davidovich Burlyuk [*or* Burliuk]. TCRP

Everyone's born with an empty body. Drinking Alone. Wang Fan-chih. CrYelRi, *tr. by* Sam Hamill

Everyone's dancing where I live. Zali Gurevitch. FIT, *tr. by* Robert Friend

Everyone's flocking to Gajan. Mahendranāth Bhattācārya. SinGod, *tr. by* Rachel Fell McDermott

Everyone's here, and because I love old things, I've rented a grand. Old House Blues. William Kulik. BodElec

Everyone's on about Walter's willy. Underneath the Archers *or* What's All This about Walter's Willy? Kit Wright. OBCoV

Everyone Sang. Siegfried Sassoon. GTBS-P; MoBrPo; NAEL-5v2; NAEL-6v2; NOBE; NPeEn; NoAM; NoP-4; OBEV; OBWP; OPOU; OxBSP; OxBTC; TrJP

Everyone says / what they do. Life Is a Killer. John Giorno. PmAP

Everyone seems to be waiting for it. It. Roger Mitchell. PoCoUp

Everyone sees. Mugoku Osho's Snow Poem. Muso Soseki. EaWin, *tr. by* W. S. Merwin

Everyone silent, moving . . . .Take my hand. Speak to me. (LL) Effort at Speech between Two People. Muriel Rukeyser. MoAmPo; NAAL-5; PAI; TrJP; TwCP

Everyone speaks of the sad autumn with a heavy heart. Sounds of Autumn. Lu Yu. SuSp, *tr. by* Irving Y. Lo

Everyone stands alone at the heart of this earth. And Suddenly It Is Evening. Salvatore Quasimodo. WoPoe, *tr. by* J. Ruth Gendler

Everyone suddenly burst out singing. Everyone Sang. Siegfried Sassoon. GTBS-P; MoBrPo; NAEL-5v2; NAEL-6v2; NOBE; NPeEn; NoAM; NoP-4; OBEV; OBWP; OPOU; OxBSP; OxBTC; TrJP

Everyone talking at once. Alexis Rotella. HA

Everyone thinks I am poisonous. I am not. Tarantula, The. Reed Whittemore. CoAP

Everyone thinks me a cannibal. When Negro Teeth Speak. Ouologuem Yambo. PBMAP

Everyone wants to meet *him*. (LL) T. S. Eliot. NBLV; OBAL; PeLV *Fr.* Five-Finger Exercises.

Everyone Who Wants to Work Can. Brooke Wiese. OPRER

Everything and Nothing. Jorge Luis Borges. PoetW, *tr. by* Anthony Kerrigan

Everything as in a good old-fashioned novel. Vladimir Nikolaevich Sokolov. TCRP

Everything but everything. Snapshot. Lajos Kassák. IQMS, *tr. by* Edwin Morgan

Everything but mere being just like this. (LL) Two Parents, The. Hugh MacDiarmid. FaBoTw; OxBTC

Everything can be grown from seed—only stipulation. Summer Seeming. John Riley. Oth

Everything / can be retouched. Need for Censorship, The. Reiner Kunze. PoSu, *tr. by* Michael Hamburger

Everything Changes. Cicely Herbert. OPOU

Everything! Counter and scales. Business Reverses. Edgar Lee Masters. ChIV-2

Everything: Eloy, Arizona, 1956. Ai. BodElec

Everything else remained the same. This is why, you said, there was no fiction. (LL) Rosmarie Waldrop. FTOS; PFTM-2 *Fr.* Reproduction of Profiles, The.

Everything ended with the Honeymoon. Loyal Housewife. Daisy Zamora. LoL, *tr. by* Margaret Randall

Everything fades away beyond oneself. Looking in a Mirror the Day before the Advent of Autumn. Li Yi. SuSp, *tr. by* William H. Nienhauser

Everything fades, turning into grey. What Will Come of This? Jenő Dsida. IQMS, *tr. by* Adam Makkai

Everything falls asleep with sleep. Passenger Opposite, The. Elma Mitchell. NePenScot

Everything flows. Denise Levertov. NAAL-2v2 *Fr.* Olga Poems.

Everything gets forgotten. Vyacheslav Kupriyanov [*or* Kuprianov]. TCRusP, *tr. by* Pamela Davidson

Everything Happens to Me. Matt Dennis. ReLy

Everything Happens to (Monk and) Me. Brenda Marie Osbey. BodElec

Everything has a place. Landscape. Johanna Kruit. TuT, *tr. by* Micheal O'Siadhail

Everything has been checked. My inventory is ready. Elizaveta Kuzmina-Karavayeva. TCRP

Everything has come true. The punishment fits the crime. Svetlana Kekova. ItGoST, *tr. by* Judith Hemschemeyer

Everything has its limit, including sorrow. To Urania. Joseph Brodsky. AF, *tr. by* Joseph Brodsky

Everything has lasted till today. Unknown Soldier, The. Alun Lewis. MoBrPo

Everything has ripened. Listening to Dvorak's Serenade in E. Colette Inez. MiVo

Everything here is curtained in darkness. Bulat Shalvovich Okudzhava. TCRP

Everything I do is against meaning. Against Meaning. Andrei Codrescu. PmAP

Everything I do is stitched with its color. (LL) Separation. W. S. Merwin. HAP; NoP-4

Everything I Have Is Yours. Burton Lane. ReLy

Everything I Need to Know I Learned in Kindergarten. Martin Jude Farawell. OPRER

Everything I say / is a garment. (LL) Sous-Entendu. Anne Stevenson. LW; OxBSP

Everything I steal, I give away. Gift of Tongues, The. Sam Hamill. GifTon

Everything I want to say. Stinking Rose, The. Sujata Bhatt. HarvBoo

Everything in Its Place. Arthur Guiterman. NBLV; OBAL; OBCoV

Everything in motion! Wind of Our Going: Adagio Ma Non Troppo. Patricia Goedicke. MiVo

Everything in the Garden is Lovely. Alasdair Aston. OBGa

Everything Is Going to Be All Right. Derek Mahon. PBCIP

Everything Is Peaches Down in Georgia. Grant Clarke. ReLy

Everything Is Plundered. Anna Andreyevna Akhmatova. WPOW
  (Everything is plundered, betrayed, sold.) WPoS, *tr. by* Max Hayward and Stanley Jasspon Kunitz

Everything is swept away by the brief year. Everything Is Swept Away by the Brief Year. Francisco de Quevedo y Villegas. SpanPo, *tr. by* Kate Flores

Everything is Your wish, Tara. Naracandra Rāy. SinGod, *tr. by* Rachel Fell McDermott

Everything leans, like tottering, hunched old women. Closed Town, The. *Unknown, fr. Terezin Concentration Camp.* INSAB

Everything lives and nothing is dead. Fugs, The. Edward Sanders. PoM

Everything opauqe about us, perhaps. Anthony Wilson. NewEx

Everything passes and vanishes. William Allingham. NOBVV; NPeEn; OxBEV

Everything rubs me the wrong way. I can't stand dancing any more. Ghost Street. Milán Füst. IQMS, *tr. by* Jess Perlman

Everything's a metaphor, some wise. History. Rita Dove. ExTi; FFC; NAAAL *Fr.* Mother Love.

Everything's Coming Up Roses. Stephen Sondheim. ReLy

Everything's equal now. Blue leash blue bike. School of Fish. Eileen Myles. WiU

Everything's just as it was: fine hard snow. Guest, The. Anna Andreyevna Akhmatova. RaBo; WoPoe, *tr. by* Vera Dunham and Jane Kenyon

Everything's laughter / everything dust. Glycon. GrAn

Everything's / so far away. Sadness of Leaving, The. Eileen Myles. PmAP

"Everything's the same old way," she said tenderly. Same Old Way, The. "Igor Severyanin [*or.*" Severianin]. TCRP, *tr. by* Bernard Meares

Everything she wants she sees. Traveler. Valerie Martínez. TouFir

Everything sounds funny in a funny magazine. Paper on Humor. Andrei Codrescu. PmAP

Everything That Acts Is Actual. Denise Levertov. NoAM

Everything that happens to me these days. Julia Alvarez. FFC *Fr.* ("33").

Everything that lives has its own proper pride. Proper Pride. D. H. Lawrence. FaBoEE

Everything the power of the world does. Everything the Power of the World Does is Done in a Circle. Black Elk. AmFaPo

Everything this generation has told me. (LL) Isaiah by Kerosene Lantern Light. Robert Harris. ChIV-1; NOBAu

Everything to Declare. Frank Mkalawile Chipasula. NAfrP

Everything was happening for the first time. As we travelled through. There. Philip Mead. BMAP

Everything was put to use. Seven Words, The. Jerzy Ficowski. PoSu, *tr. by* Keith Bosley and Krystyna Wandycz

Everything was simple, yet triumphant. For the Unveiling of a Memorial. Daniil Leonidovich Andreyev [*or* Andreiev]. TCRP, *tr. by* Bradley Jordan

Everything we know about death. Altruism. Dionisio D. Martinez. TouFir

Everything we look upon is blest. (LL) Dialogue of Self and Soul, A. W. B. Yeats. FaBoMo; MoBrPo; NAEL-5v2; NAEL-6v2; NoAM; PoE

Everything we say. (LL) Antipater of Thessalonica. GrAn; PGA

Everything we stand up in. Spectrum. Aidan Carl Mathews. PBCIP

Everything white, the lake's cheek, turns. Trompe L'Oeil in Winter. Mary Ann Samyn. AmPoNex

Everything will be forsaken then. Apocrypha. János Pilinszky. PoSu, *tr. by* Ted Hughes

Everything You Own. Gerald Costanzo. GifTon

Everything you see, Reader, in the little book before you. To the Reader. Elizabeth Jane Leon. EMWP

Everytime a thunderstorm comes. My Mother is a God Fearing Woman. Cornelius Eady. ISC

Everytime you weep, I feel the surface. Letters from Home. Elmaz Abinader. GraLe

Everywhere, a reason for caution. Wedding Gifts. Adrienne Su. NAPBL

Everywhere about is landscape as far as foot can feel. Homage to Paul Delvaux. Ramon Guthrie. PoE

Everywhere / At once. (LL) As for Poets. Gary Snyder. BB; PmAP

Everywhere, everywhere, Christmas tonight! Christmas Everywhere. Phillips Brooks. PWR

Everywhere, everywhere, following me. Camerados. Bayard Taylor. UnPo

Everywhere, everywhere, following me. Bayard Taylor. APN-2 *Fr.* Echo Club, The.

Everywhere, *everywhere,* snow sifting down. Manna. Joseph Stroud. GeoHom

Everywhere I look in the garden. Déjeuner Sur l'Herbe. Bruce Beaver. BMAP

Everywhere of Silver, An. Emily Dickinson. TCAPo

Everywhere petals are flying. By the Winding River II. Tu Fu. OHPC, *tr. by* Kenneth Rexroth

Everywhere / soft breeze warm sunshine. Spring Cliff. Muso Soseki. EaWin, *tr. by* W. S. Merwin

Everywhere the material world is speaking to me. One Explanation of Beauty. Mark Wunderlich. AmPoNex

Everywhere we are either moving away from. For the Woman with the Radio. Malena Mörling. AmPoNex

Everywhere You Eat. Kalamu ya Salaam. SpirFl *Fr.* New Orleans Haiku.

Eves Apologie. Emilia [*or* Aemelia] Lanier [*or* Lanyer]. BoWoP *Fr.* Salve Deus Rex Judaeorum.

Eves of autumn. Brambleberry, The. Sándor Weöres. IQMS, *tr. by* Adam Makkai and Valerie Becker Makkai

Eviction. Lucille Clifton. NTCP

Eviction. Michelle T. Clinton. ISC

Eviction, The. William Allingham. BIrV; NOIV *Fr.* Laurence Bloomfield in Ireland.

Evidence. Joanna Fuhrman. AmPoNex

Evidence. Dan Pagis. FIT, *tr. by* Robert Friend

Evidence, The. Tom Leonard. Oth

Evidence at the Witch Trials. James Keir Baxter. OxBC

Evidence everywhere: accumulation. On That Mountain. Rachel Hadas. ExTi

Evidence of *a woman's hard life.* Old Women. Judith Ortiz Cofer. PueRic

Evidence on Film, The. Ron Charach. BloBone

Evidence Read at the Trial of the Knave of Hearts. Lewis Carroll. GTBS-P; NOBVV; NPeEn; OxBoLi; PeLV *Fr.* Alice's Adventures in Wonderland.

Evil. Langston Hughes. APT-2

Evil. Arthur Rimbaud. FaBoWar, *tr. by* Norman Cameron

Evil. Arthur Rimbaud. OBWP *Fr.* Eighteen-Seventy.

Evil Days, The. Dennis Joseph Enright. OBCoV

Evil Days, The. Boris Leonidovich Pasternak. GI, *tr. by* Nina Kossman

Evil, if rightly understood. On the Origin of Evil. John Byrom. NOEC; NPeEn

Evil Man, An! Richard Beer-Hofmann. TrJP *Fr.* Graf von Charolais, Der.

Evil Nigger Waits for Lightnin' Imamu Amiri Baraka. NOBA

Evil [*or* Evill] spirit, your beauty, haunts me still, An. Michael Drayton. NOBE; NoSic *Fr.* Idea.

Evil Raven, have paper pity upon those. Mac Wellman. HeMarv *Fr.* Rat Minaret: Miniaturist-Divan, The.

Evil That Men Do, The. Queen Latifah. NAAAL

Evil was active in the land. "H. D." HarvBoo; NAAL-5 *Fr.* Walls Do Not Fall, The.

Evil word it is, / This Love, An. (LL) In Memory of Radio. Imamu Amiri Baraka. BB; NAAAL; NAAL-2v2; NeAP; PoM

Evoba. Steve McCaffery.
"Can there be a collision between picture and application?" FTOS

Evocation of Recife. Manuel Bandeira. TCLAP, *tr. by* Candace Slater

Evohé. Cristina Peri Rossi.
"Tired of women." TANSG, *tr. by* Diana P. Decker

Evolution. Sherman Alexie. NeAmPo; PoPoPo

Evolution. John Blight. CBAP

Evolution. Langdon Smith. BRP

Evolution. John Banister Tabb. APN-2

Evolution. Israel Zangwill. TrJP

Evolution from the Fish. Robert Bly. NOBA; NoAM

Evolution of Appetite. Kelleen Zubick. OPRER

Evolution of Lather, The. Michael Portnoy. HeMarv

Evolution on 38th Street. Jack Brannon. UrbNat

Evolutionary Erotics. Constance Naden. ViWPN
"I had found out a gift for my fair." VWP
"I was a youth of studious mind." VWP
Natural Selection. VWP
Scientific Wooing. VWP
Solomon Redivivus, 1886. VWP
"What am I? Ah, you know it." VWP

Evolutionary Hymn. Clive Staples Lewis. NOBL

Evolving Similarities. Ralph Angel. BodElec

Evyn as mery as I make myght. *Unknown.* EMWP

Ewes and lambs, loving the far hillplaces, The. Ad Limina. Joseph Campbell. BIrV

Ewigkeit. Jorge Luis Borges. WoPoe, *tr. by* Richard Wilbur

Ex-Basketball Player. John Updike. InPK-6; TRP

Ex-Boyfriends Named Michael. Justin Chin. WiU

Ex-Clerk. Rudyard Kipling. HarvBoo *Fr.* Epitaphs of the War [1914–1918].

Ex-Deputy Sheriff Remembers the Eastern Oklahoma Murderers, An. Jim Barnes.
Summerfield. HATNAP
"They took a tire tool to his head." HATNAP

Ex-Judge at the Bar, An. Melvin B. Tolson. NAAAL

Ex Nihilo. David Gascoyne. GTBS-P *Fr.* Miserere.

Ex-Queen Among the Astronomers, The. Fleur Adcock. FaBoWP; NAEL-6v2; NALW; NoP-4

Ex Vermibus. Hugh MacDiarmid. CABP

Ex-Voto for a Shipwreck. Aimé Césaire. PFTM-1

Exact Fares. David Morley. NLP

Exactly like the upper life sleep has. As Endymion. Odysseus Elytis. GifTon, *tr. by* Olga Broumas

Exaggeration of Despair, The. Sherman Alexie. BAP-97; NeAmPo

Exaltatio Humanae Naturae. William Alabaster. NoSic

Exaltation. Franz Werfel. TrJP, *tr. by* Edith Abercrombie Snow

Examination, The. Priscilla Jane Thompson. CBWP-2

Examination at the Womb-Door. Ted Hughes. NAEL-5v2; NAEL-6v2; NoP-4; OxBC

Examination Question. *Unknown.* OBCoV

Examining the I. Jean V. Gier. ReBoTo

Example, An. M. Wyrebek. AmPoNex

Example, The. William Henry Davies. MoBrPo

Example, The. Paul Zimmer. OPRER

Example of Kant's sterling wit, An. Limerick: "Example of Kant's sterling wit, An." Victor Gray. PeLi

Excavation, The. Carl Hancock Rux. HeMarv

Exceeding brightness of this early sun, The. Sun This March, The. Wallace Stevens. APT-1; HarvBoo

Exceeding sorrow / Consumeth my sad heart! O Mors! Quam Amara Est Memoria Tua Homini Pacem Habenti In Substantiis Suis. Ernest Christopher Dowson. OBMV

Excelente Balade of Charitie, An. Thomas Chatterton. EBEV; NOEC; OxAEP-1

Excellent Brutus, of all human race. Brutus. Abraham Cowley. BASC

Excellent Epitaffe of Syr Thomas Wyat, An. Henry Howard, Earl of Surrey. NoSic; NPeEn

  (Earth his bones, the heavens possess his ghost, The.) (LL) NAEL-7v1; NoP-4

  (Epitaph on Sir Thomas Wyatt.) NAEL-5v1; NAEL-6v1

  (Excellent Epitaph of Sir Thomas Wyatt, An.) NoSic

  (Tribute to Wyatt.) PeECV

  (Wyatt resteth here, that quick could never rest.) NoP-4; PeECV

Excellent Wigglesworth, Remembered by some Good Tokens, The. Cotton Mather. SacPr

Excelsior. Henry Wadsworth Longfellow. BRP; NAAL-2v1; NAAL-3; OBCA; OBSP; TCAPo; UV

Except a certain awful look / of terrible depression. (LL) Lawrence Ferlinghetti. PmAP; RB

Except for shoes. Impediment. Stephen Dunn. PoSol

Except for the dog, that she wouldn't have him put away, wouldn't let him die, I'd have liked her. Dog, The. C. K. Williams. BodElec

Except home. (LL) William Carlos Williams. APT-1; PoRA *Fr.* Folded Skyscraper, A.

Except my h[e]art which you bestowed [*or* beestow'd] be[e]fore. (LL) Mary Sidney Wroth, Countess of Montgomery. BASC; EMWP *Fr.* Pamphilia to Amphilanthus.

Except seeing the world's self submerged. (LL) He Is Out of Heart with His Time. Guerzo di Montecanti. AWP; EaItPo, *tr. by* Dante Gabriel Rossetti

Except ourselves, we have no other prayer. Without Ceremony. Vassar Miller. MoAmPo

Except the Heaven had come so near. Emily Dickinson. SAmP

Except the Lord, That He for Us Had Been. Henry Ainsworth. AH

Except to prove the sweetness of a shower. (LL) Tall Nettles. Edward Thomas. FaBoTw; FaBoVe; MoBrPo; NPeEn; OxBEV; OxBSP

Excerpt from a Report to the Galactic Council. Robert Conquest. OxBC

Excerpts from the Sabbath Dream Book. Esther Ettinger. DTA, *tr. by* Mariana Barr

Excess of lemon, whether on the phone. Lair, The. Rachel Hadas. FFC

Exchange. George Rostrevor Hamilton. FaBoEE

Exchange in greed the ungraceful signs. Thrust. Violent Space, The. Etheridge Knight. BPo

Exchange of Feelings. Paul Verlaine. SxFrPo, *tr. by* Martin Sorrell

Exchange of Hats, An. Stanley Moss. BodElec

Exchange of Letters. Wendy Cope. OBCoV

Exchange of Poems by Tung-yang Stream, An. Hsieh Ling-yün. CoBCP, *tr. by* Burton Watson

  "How fetching! Somebody's wife." CoBCP, *tr. by* Burton Watson

Exchanges. Ernest Christopher Dowson. OBMV

Exchanging Hats. Elizabeth Bishop. NIL-7

Excitation. Lorenzo Thomas. FTOS

Excite my breasts. Feathers. Jayne Cortez. SurWo

Excited as a sophisticated boy at his first. Matins and Lauds. Marie Ponsot. CLPP

Excited woodwinds, staccato strings in noisy clamor. Kuan Yün-shih. SuSp, *tr. by* Richard John Lynn *Fr.* Medley of Southern and Northern Tunes— Scenic Tour of West Lake.

Excitement. Polly Clark. NeBl

Exciting at first. Basho. EH, *tr. by* Robert Hass

Exclamation. Octavio Paz. ChAP, *tr. by* Eliot Weinberger

Exclusive Blue. Robert Francis. CRP

Excrement Poem, The. Maxine W. Kumin. FaBoWP

Excursion. Niyi Osundare. HBAPE

Excursion, The. Tu Fu. AWP, *tr. by* Florence Ayscough and Amy Lowell

Excursion, The. William Wordsworth.

  Despondency Corrected.

    "I have seen / A curious child, who dwelt upon a tract." ITBLP

  "On Man, on Nature, and on Human Life." FHYEP; PoE

  Prospectus. FHYEP; PoE

  Wanderer, The.

    "Supine the Wanderer lay." NOBRP

Excursion, The. William Wordsworth.

  "Her cottage, then a cheerful object, wore." OBGa

Excursion of the Speech and Hearing Class, The. David Wagoner. VCAP

Excursion to Ravenna of A Young Girl with Her Parents. Rossana Ombres.

  Afternoon Hours. PeFWW

    "Among the drinking doves, Galla Placidia." PeFWW

  Morning Hours. NeIt

    "One needs sand from the sea, we have known." NeIt

Excursion to the Suburbs, An. Tsung Ch'en.

  "Side by side, we ride out of the city." CoBLCP

Excuse, The. Carl H. Greene. NBV

Excuse, The. Morgan Llwyd. AngWePo *Fr.* 1648.

Excuse for Not Returning the Visit of a Friend, An. Mei Yao Ch'en. OHPC, *tr. by* Kenneth Rexroth

Excuse me. Half-caste. John Agard. Oth

Excuse me. I thought for a moment you were someone I know. I Thought It Was Harry. William Bronk. APSN

Excuse me, isn't that you I see concealed underneath there. Thoughts. Michael Benedikt. CoAmPo

Excuse me, pilgrim. Art of Getting Lost, The. Art Goodtimes. GeoH

Excuse of Absence, An. Thomas Carew. CaPo

Exeat. Stevie Smith. NAEL-5v2; NAEL-6v2; NoAM

Execration, The. Elizabeth Thomas. ECWP

Execration upon Vulcan, An. Ben Jonson. BeJo

Execution. James A., Jr. Randall. BPo

Execution, The. Vladimir Vladimirovich Nabokov. TCRP, *tr. by* Vladimir Nabokov

Execution of Alice Holt. *Unknown.* OxBoLi

Execution of King Charles, The. Andrew Marvell. PoRA

Execution of Madame du Barry, The. J. J. Bray. NOBAu

Execution of Memory, The. Jerzy Ficowski. HP, *tr. by* Keith Bosley

Execution of Montrose, The. William Edmonstoune [*or* Edmondstoune] Aytoun.

  "Morning dawned full darkly, The." NePenScot

Execution of the faithless maids. Homer. OBVE, *tr. by* Alexander Pope *Fr.* Odyssey.

Executioner of Flowers. Muhammad Al-Maghut. PFTM-2, *tr. by* May Jayyusi and Naomi Shihab Nye

Executioner yawned. From his axe the blood was still dripping, The. Imagerie d'Epinal. Aleksander Wat. AF

Executive. Sir John Betjeman. NOBL

Executive Geochrone. Daniel Anderson. AmPoNex

Executive's Death, The. Robert Bly. CoAP

Exempla. James Fenton.

  "For the context of the basidiocarp Singer states." PeLV

  "Is shut / 22 hours a day and all day Sunday." FaBoMo

  ("Of globose, vesiculate, hyaline conidia.") (LL) PeLV

  Pitt-Rivers Museum, Oxford, The. FaBoMo

Exeo in a spasm. Enueg I. Samuel Beckett. CIP-2

Exequies, The. Thomas Stanley. BeJo; MeLP

Exequy, An. Peter Porter. NoAM; NoP-4; OxBC

Exequy, The. Henry King, Bishop of Chichester. HAP; MeLP; NAEL-6v1; SCGP

Exequy on [*or* upon] His Wife. Henry King, Bishop of Chichester. *See* Exequy, The

Exequy to His Matchless[e] Never to be Forgotten Friend [*or* Freind], An. Henry King, Bishop of Chichester. *See* Exequy, The

Exercise. W. S. Merwin. NOBA

Exercise No. 2. William Carlos Williams. SAmP

Exercises in Scriptural Writing. Carl Rakosi.

  Sandalwood Comes to My Mind. ChIV-1

Exert thy voice, sweet harbinger of Spring! To the Nightingale. Anne Finch, Countess of Winchilsea. ECWP; NALW; WPE

Exerted by this grey and shuttered town. (LL) Osbert Lancaster. NOBL; PeLV *Fr.* Afternoons with Baedeker.

Exeter Riddle, An. Gavin Ewart. OxBC

Exeunt. Richard Wilbur. HeIP-4

Exeunt Omnes. Thomas Hardy. FaBoVe; UV

Exhausted Bug, The. Robert Bly. BodElec

Exhausted from depression. Ilya Krichevsky [*or* Krichevskii]. TCRP

Exhausted, I sought. Basho. SoOfWa, *tr.* by Sam Hamill

Exhausted Inconsistency Floats Here, An. Giusi Busceti. ItPo, *tr.* by Gayle Ridinger

Exhausted now her sighs, and dry her tears. Walter Savage Landor. FaBoEE

Exhibits, The. Tracey Herd. MFPA

Exhilerating, something I can't explain. Anthuriums, Pahoa. Joan Swift. PoCoUp

Exhortation to Learn of Others' Trouble. Henry Howard, Earl of Surrey. FaBoEE

Exhortation to Prayer. William Cowper. NOCV   *Fr.* Olney Hymns.

Exhorting Myself. Ssu-k'ung Shu. SuSp, *tr.* by Hellmut Wilhelm

Exile. Ingeborg Bachmann. PoSu, *tr.* by Daniel Huws

Exile. Teresa Calderón. TANSG, *tr.* by Celeste Kostopulos-Cooperman

Exile. Hart Crane. *See* Carrier Letter

Exile. Mbella Sonne Dipoko. PBMAP

Exile. Stephen Dobyns. OPRER

Exile. Ernest Christopher Dowson. BoLoP

Exile. Erich Fried. AF, *tr.* by Georg Rapp

Exile. Donald Hall. NoP-4

Exile. George Rostrevor Hamilton. FaBoEE

Exile. Anthony Hecht. TaR

Exile. John Milton. NOSC   *Fr.* Paradise Lost.

Exile. Amjad Nasir. MAP, *tr.* by Charles Doria and May Jayyusi

Exile. "St.-John Perse."

    "Doors open on the sands, doors open on exile." AF

Exile. Dennis Phillips.

    "But perfectly random and coastal." FTOS

    From Arena. FTOS

Exile. Alejandra Pizarnik. TCLAP, *tr.* by Frank Graziano and María Rosa Fort

Exile. Danton R. Remoto. ReBoTo

Exile. Saniyya Salih. PoArWo, *tr.* by Kamal Boullata

Exile. Karl Shapiro. CRP   *Fr.* Adam and Eve.

Exile. Ellen Bryant Voigt. AWTN

Exile, The. Pablo Medina. OPRER

Exile in Japan. Su Man-shu. BLT, *tr.* by Kenneth Rexroth

Exile in Nigeria. Ezekiel Mphahlele. PBA

Exile lingering here, An. (LL) Infelix. Adah Isaacs Menken. CBWP-1; TCAPo

Exile of Erin, The. *Unknown.* NOBAu

Exile of Rákóczi, The. *Unknown.* IQMS, *tr.* by Watson Kirkconnell

Exile of the Sons of Uisliu. *Unknown.* NOIV, *tr.* by Thomas Kinsella

Exile, Representative. Breyten Breytenbach. AF, *tr.* by Denis Hirson

Exile's Letter. Li Po. CTC; FaBoMo; OxBA, *tr.* by Ezra Pound

Exile's Letter. Rihaku. APT-1, *tr.* by Ezra Pound

Exile's Letter (Or: An Essay on Assimilation). Marilyn Chin. OpBo

Exile's Return, The. Robert Lowell. OxBA

Exile's Return, The. Slavko Mihalic. PoSu, *tr.* by Peter Kastmiler and Charles Simic

Exile's Reverie, The. Mary Weston Fordham. CBWP-2

Exile's Reveries, The. James Kennedy.

    "Chased from my calling to this hackneyed trade." NOEC

Exile's Song, The. Robert Gilfillan. TreFP

Exile: Welsh Service from Daventry. Llewelyn Wyn Griffith. AngWePo

Exiled. Edna St. Vincent Millay. PoRA

Exiled Heart, The. Maurice Lindsay. OxBS

Exiles. "Æ" BIrV; MoBrPo

Exiles. Abena Busia. NAfrP

Exiles. Diana Der Hovanessian. OPRER

Exiles, The. W. H. Auden. OxBTC

Exiles, The. Iain Crichton Smith. HarvBoo; NePenScot

Exist, without a man cook. (LL) Coming Woman, The. Mary Weston Fordham. CBWP-2; SWaP

Existing. Alejandra Piznarnick. MirDau, *tr.* by Roberta Gordenstein

Existing Psychically. Andrea Zanzotto. ItPo, *tr.* by Gayle Ridinger

Exists, like blinder or mistake. Doors. Rosalie Moore. YaYoPo

Exists there one, who carelessly can view. Second Evening. Mary F. Johnson. CenSon

Exit. Rita Dove. ExTi

Exit. Edwin Arlington Robinson. MoAmPo; OxBSP

Exit Amor. Virginia Hamilton Adair. APT-2

Exits. Jean Earle. TCAWP

Exits. Patricia Pogson. NLP

Exits and Entrances. Naomi Long Madgett. BlSi

Exodus. Bible, *O.T.*

    "Let us synge unto the Lorde, for he is become glorious." OBVE

    Then Sang Moses. OBWP

    "Then sang Moses and the children of Israel this song." OBWP

Exodus. Horst Bienek. AF

Exodus. Anita Endrezze. CDW

Exodus. George Oppen. ChIV-1

Exodus. Charles Reznikoff. ChIV-1

Exodus. Robyn Selman. WiU

Exodus. Jaime Torres Bodet. TCLAP, *tr.* by Sonja Karsen

Exodus. *Unknown.*

    "Band of the bold were gathered together, The." AnOE, *tr.* by Charles W. Kennedy

    Parting of the Red Sea, The. AnOE, *tr.* by Charles W. Kennedy

Exodus from Egypt, The. Ezechiel of Alexandria. TrJP, *tr.* by E. H. Gifford

Exorcism. Dorothy Nimmo. Prnts

Exorcism of the Straight/Man/Demon. Aaron Shurin. GLP

Expanding in the chill. Cold-Weather Love. Ronald G. Everson. MoCV

Expansive puppets percolate self-unction. Canadian Authors Meet, The. Francis Reginald Scott. NOBC

Expatriates. Sharif Elmusa. GraLe

Expatriates. Ronald Stuart Thomas. AngWePo

Expatriates. David Woo. OpBo

Expect Nothing Else from Me. Rita Joe. ReEnLa

Expectans Expectavi. Charles Hamilton Sorley. FaBoCh

Expectant Mother. Penelope Shuttle. BrRo

Expectation. Ida G. M. Gerhardt. TuT, *tr.* by Peter Van de Kamp

Expectation. Thomas Stanley. BeJo

Expectation: Night and Day. Christian Dotremont and Pierre Joris. MAP, *tr.* by Diana Der Hovanessian and Lena Jayyusi

Expected Guest, The. Sidney Keyes. PoWW

Expected, the handsome, the one who needs us, The. (LL) Beauty and the Beast. Rita Dove. ESEAA; NoAM

Expecting no miracle, we found none. Return to DeKalb. Lucien Stryk. IllVoic

Expecting to see him anytime. Between Days. Yusef Komunyakaa. ESEAA

Expence of Spirit in a waste of shame, Th' William Shakespeare. *See* Expense of spirit in a waste of shame, The [*or* Th']

Expense of spirit in a waste of shame, The [*or* Th']. William Shakespeare. AWP; EBEV; ErotSp; HAP; HeIP-4; NAEL-5v1; NAEL-6v1; NAEL-7v1; NIL-7; NIP-4; NOBE; NoSic; OBEV; OxAEP-1; OxBEV; PAI; PoE; SCGP; SCV; Son; TFi; UnPo; WoPoe   *Fr.* Sonnets.

Expensive Wife, The. Judah ibn Sabbatai. TrJP   *Fr.* Gift of Judah the Woman-Hater, The.

Experience. Ralph Waldo Emerson. APN-1; TAP; TCAPo

Experience. Lesbia Harford. CBAP

Experience. Dorothy Parker. NAAL-2v2

Experience. James Simmons. BIrV

Experience. Edith Wharton. APN-2

Experience, The. Bruce Bennett. PeECV

Experience, though all authority. Geoffrey Chaucer. NAWM-7v1, *tr.* by Theodore Morrison   *Fr.* Canterbury Tales, The.

Experience, though noon auctoritee. Geoffrey Chaucer. FHYEP; NAEL-5v1; NAEL-6v1; NAEL-7v1   *Fr.* Canterbury Tales, The.

Experience, though noon auctoritee. Geoffrey Chaucer. OxBEV; OxBoLi; PeLV   *Fr.* Canterbury Tales, The.

Experience Too Late. Letitia [*or* Laetitia] Elizabeth Landon. RWP

Experienced wife, An. Midwife's Story; Two, A. Anne Szumigalski. NOBC

Experiences as a taxi-driver in Venezuela. *Unknown.*

    "When I start my fast driving." EroLit

Experiment. Wislawa Szymborska. PoSu, *tr.* by Magnus F. Krynski

Experiment Degustatory. Ogden Nash. ChAP

Experiment escorts us last. Emily Dickinson. APN-2

Experiments in the Impersonal. Steve Wilson. AmPoNex

Experiments with God. Karen Gershon. HP

Experts, The. Jack Myers. BodElec

Experts say for me to do it well. Running. Brendan Galvin. MoASP

Expiation. Victor Hugo.

    "It was snowing. For the first time, conquered." WoPoe, *tr.* by Louis Simpson

    "Waterloo! Waterloo! Waterloo! dismal plain!" WoPoe, *tr.* by Phillip Holland

Expiration, The. John Donne. MeLP; OxBSP

Explain given to. Underneath (3). Jorie Graham. BodElec

Explaining everything. (LL) Last Gods. Galway Kinnell. PasH; RaBo

Explaining the Origin of My Name. Fatima Lim-Wilson. AmPoNex

Explanation. William Barber. CAGL

Explanation. Explanation / tangent things. Larry Eigner. PFTM-2

Explanation of a Sign. Pyotr Vegin. TCRusP, *tr.* by Daniel Weissbort

Explanation of America, An. Robert Pinsky.
"In something you have written in school, you say." ColAP
"Mile more down the flat fast road, the homestead, A." NAAL-2v2
Serpent Knowledge. ColAP
Serpent Knowledge. NAAL-2v2

Explanation / tangent things. Larry Eigner. PFTM-2

Explanatory Note. Yevgeny [*or* Evgenii] Bunimovich. TCRP, *tr.* by Albert C. Todd

Exploded. To the ground. On his back. Arms apart. He. Eyes. Yevgeny [*or* Evgenii] Mikhailovich Vinokurov. TCRusP, *tr.* by Anthony Rudolf

Exploding before my very eyes. Peyote Vision. Lew Blockcolski. VoR

Exploiter of the shadows. Fox. Clifford Dyment. OxBSP

Exploration. Daniel Gerard Hoffman. CoAP

Explore the beauty of our land. Odyssey, The. Sipho Sepamla. AF

Explorers as Seen by the Natives. Doug Fetherling. NOBC

Explorers will come, The. Explorers, The. Margaret Atwood. MoCV

Explosion. Shinkichi Takahashi. ZenPo, *tr.* by Takashi Ikemoto and Lucien Stryk

Explosion, The. Philip Larkin. EBEV; EmeKit; FaBoMo; HAP; MakPoe; NAEL-5v2; NAEL-6v2; NPeEn; NoAM; NoP-4; OxAEP-2; OxBC; PeECV; RB; SCV; WeW-3

Explosion names, An. 86 Pasteur Corner. Manuela Fingueret. MirDau, *tr.* by Celeste Kostopulos-Cooperman

Explosion your death, An. Silence. Claribel Alegría. TANSG, *tr.* by Darwin Flakoll

Explosive posters lit at night. Break of Dawn, The. Thomas Sayers Ellis. InTrad

Exposing his plate to the air. Limerick: "Exposing his plate to the air." Joyce Johnson. PeLi

Expostulation, An. Isaac Bickerstaffe. OBCoV

Expostulation, The. Elizabeth Singer Rowe. PEW

Expostulation and Reply. William Wordsworth. FHYEP; NAEL-5v2; NAEL-6v2; NOBRP

Exposure. Seamus Heaney. NPeEn; PBCIP; PNI

Exposure. Wilfred Owen. FaBoMo; NoAM; OBWP; PeFWW; PoWW; RB; TCAWP

Express. William Allingham. NOBVV

Express. Vincente Huidobro. PFTM-1

Express, The. Stephen Spender. HeIP-4; MoBrPo; NIL-7; NoAM; TwCP

Express Train. Rolf Jacobsen. BLT, *tr.* by Roger Greenwald

Express Train. Karl Kraus. TrJP, *tr.* by Albert Bloch

Express train 1256 races alongside hidden, remote villages. House. Express Train. Rolf Jacobsen. BLT, *tr.* by Roger Greenwald

Expressing My Feelings. Meng Chiao. SuSp, *tr.* by Stephen Owen

Expression. Thom Gunn. OxBC

Expression. Isaac Rosenberg. MoBrPo

Expression is the need of my soul. Don Marquis. APT-1 *Fr.* Coming of Archy, The.

Expulsion. Lisa Sewell. AmPoNex

Expulsion, The. Gerald Stern. LCAP-2

Expulsion from Eden, The. John Milton. OPOU *Fr.* Paradise Lost.

Expulsion of Hagar, The. Eloise Bibb. CBWP-4

Exquisite Alchemy. Debra Taub. SurWo

Exquisite bartender at Sweeney's, The. Limerick. *Unknown.* PeLi

Exquisite stillness! What serenities. Don Juan's Address to the Sunset. Robert Malise Bowyer Nichols. OBMV

Exquisite torment, dainty Mrs. Hargreaves. Sapphics. Dominic Bevan Wyndham Lewis. NOBL; PeLV

Exquisite world, powerful, joyous, splendid. To the Natural World: at 37. Genevieve Taggard. APT-2

Exstasie, The. John Donne. *See* Ecstasy, The

Extasie, The. John Donne. *See* Ecstasy, The

Extempore Effusion upon the Death of James Hogg. William Wordsworth. EBEV; NAEL-6v2; NOBE; SCV

Extempore—On Being Shown a Beautiful Country Seat Belonging to Maxwell of Cardoness. Robert Burns. OBGa

Extempore [Verses] Intended to Allay the Violence of Party-Spirit. John Byrom. *See* Jacobite Toast

Extend, there where you venture and come back. Walk on the Moon. N. Scott Momaday. CRP

Extending from her left ear down her jaw. S. W. Rafael Campo. BloBone

Extensive the lands flanking that southern mountain. *Unknown.* ColAnChi, *tr.* by Jeffrey Riegel *Fr.* Classic of Odes.

Exterior formed in measure to match his mind, An. (LL) Marbod of Rennes. CAGL; EroLit, *tr.* by John Boswell *Fr.* Unyielding Youth, The.

Exterior—to Time. (LL) Emily Dickinson. APN-2; NAAL-2v1; NAAL-3; NAAL-5; NCAP; NOBA; TCAPo

Extermination of the Jews, The. Marvin Bell. GotH; TaR

External rituals mean nothing. Kamalākānta Bhattācārya. SinGod, *tr.* by Rachel Fell McDermott

Extinguish, One by One. Vicki Raymond. NOBAu

Extinguish that delight. (LL) Last Confession, A. W. B. Yeats. BoLoP; HAP; NIP-4

Extra Joyful Chorus for Those Who Have Read This Far, An. Robert Bly. SPE

Extract from a Diary. János Pilinszky. PoSu, *tr.* by Peter Jay

Extract from Memoirs. Howard Nemerov. OxBC

Extract the quint-essence. Francis Daniel Pastorius. SCAP

Extraordinary patience of things!, The. Carmel Point. Robinson Jeffers. APT-1; BLT; NAAL-2v2; NAAL-5; NoAM; NoP-4

Extravagance of Zoos, The. Craig Arnold. AmPoNex

Extravagant Drunkard's Wish, The. Edward Ward. NOEC

Extreme Unction. Ernest Christopher Dowson. MoBrPo; OBMV; PeECV; PeVV

Exuberant, restless. West Lake. Kenneth O. Hanson. CoAP

Exult each patriot heart!—this night is shewn. Royall Tyler. NAAL-3 *Fr.* Contrast, The.

Exultant and wise. The born child cries. (LL) Multipara: Gravida 5. Marie Ponsot. CLPP; VGW

Exultation. Hywel ab Owain Gwynedd. OBWVE, *tr.* by Gwyn Williams

Exultation is the going. Emily Dickinson. APN-2; TCAPo

Exultationis Carmen To the Kings Most Excellent Majesty upon His Most Desired Return. Rachel Jevon. EMWP

Exulting in his Strength, he seems to dare. Virgil [*or* Vergil]. OBVE, *tr.* by John Dryden *Fr.* Aeneid [*or* Eneados, *Aeneis*], The.

Eyam. Anna Seward. ECWP; RWP
"In scenes paternal, not beheld through years." NOEC

Eye, The. Michael Benedikt. CoAmPo

Eye, The. Robert Herrick. CaPo

Eye, The. Robinson Jeffers. NOBA; NoAM; OxBA

Eye after countless eye of the bomb. Vision of Hiroshima. Oscar Hahn. TCLAP, *tr.* by Sandy McKinney

Eye and Ear, The. Jones Very. APN-1

Eye and Tooth. Robert Lowell. NAAL-2v2

Eye Blade. George Evans. AF

Eye can hardly pick them out, The. At Grass. Philip Larkin. HAP; HarvBoo; NPeEn; OxBEV; OxBTC; RB; WeW-3

Eye-flattering fortune, look thou never so fair. Fortune. Sir Thomas More. SacPr

Eye for an Eye, An. Christine M. Donald. GLP

Eye is meant to see things, An. Someone Digging in the Ground. Jelaluddin [*or* Jalal al-Din] Rumi. RaBo, *tr.* by Coleman Barks

Eye Mask. Denise Levertov. BLT

Eye, murdered, is not yet dead, The. Blindman's Cries, The. Tristan Corbière. WoPoe, *tr.* by Martin James

Eye of Creation, The. Angelina Muñiz Huberman. MirDau, *tr.* by Aurora Camacho

Eye of God. Jim Tollerud. VoR

Eye of the earth; and what it watches is not our wars. (LL) Eye, The. Robinson Jeffers. NOBA; NoAM; OxBA

Eye of the future, gazing back, The. (LL) Answer. Bei Dao. PoetW; VCWP, *tr.* by Donald Finkel

Eye of this storm is not quiet, The. To a Gone Era. Irma McClaurin. BlSi

Eye-Opener. Malcolm Lowry. NoP-4

Eye opening is a mouth seeing, The. Eyesight II. Robert Duncan. SPE

Eye's roundness between the bars. Language Mesh. Paul Celan. VCWP, *tr.* by Michael Hamburger

Eye sees, but not itself, The. 4th Witness—The Petty Thieves. Ifi Amadiume. NAfrP

Eye sit here, now, inside my fast thickening breath. Reflections on Growing Older. Quincy Troupe. GT

Eye standing up eye lying down eye sitting. Making Feet and Hands. Benjamin Péret. SPE, *tr.* by David Gascoyne

Eye that sees, The. Another Poetics. Octavio Armand. TCLAP, *tr.* by Carol Maier

Eye, the cauldron of morning. (LL) Ariel. Sylvia Plath. HCAP; HeIP-4; LCAP-2; NAAL-2v2; NALW; NOBA; NoAM; NoP-4; PoE; VCAP

Eye unacquitted by whatever it holds in allegiance, The. Didactic Piece. Louise Bogan. NoAM

Eye use to write poems about burning. Boomerang: A Blatantly Political Poem. Quincy Troupe. AF

Eye winker. *Unknown.* OxNR

Eye You See Isn't, The. Antonio Machado Ruiz. SpanPo, *tr.* by William M. Davis

Eye you see isn't, The.　Eye You See Isn't, The.　Antonio Machado Ruiz.　SpanPo, *tr.* by William M. Davis

Eyeball Works, The.　Stephen Knight.　NeBl

Eyebrow mounds dark, facing the spluttering lamp.　Mating.　Yang Wei-chen.　ColAnChi, *tr.* by John Timothy Wixted

Eyeful Glances.　Niyi Osundare.　HBAPE

Eyeglasses.　Tom Clark.　CoAmPo

Eyeing the Eyes of One's Mistress.　Ebenezer Jones.　NOBVV

Eyeless labourer in the night, The.　Woman to Man.　Judith Wright.　BMAP; CBAP; NoP-4; WPE

Eyelid is twitching. From the open mouth, An.　Sextet.　Joseph Brodsky.　TCRP, *tr.* by Joseph Brodsky

Eyelids glowing, some chill morning, The.　Monet: "Les Nymphéas."　W. D. Snodgrass.　CoAP; CoAmPo

Eyelids meet. He'll catch a little nap, The.　In the Smoking-Car.　Richard Wilbur.　CoAmPo; GM; MoAmPo

Eyelids of eve fall together at last, The.　Thomas Hardy.　FaBoWar; OBWP　*Fr.* Dynasts, The.

Eyes.　Juan Gelman.　TCLAP, *tr.* by Robert Marquez and Elinore Randall

Eyes.　Vladimir Dmitrievich Tsybin.　TCRP, *tr.* by Lubov Yakovleva

Eyes.　Yevgeny [*or* Evgenii] Mikhailovich Vinokurov.　TCRusP, *tr.* by Anthony Rudolf

EYES always open eyes.　Eyewash.　Niall Montgomery.　SPE

Eyes and Tears.　Andrew Marvell.　FSCP; GeHe

Eyes, Calm beside Thee (Lady, Could'st Thou Know!).　Robert Browning.　Son

Eyes caught by beauty, fancy by eyes caught.　Husband of To-Day, The.　Edith Nesbit.　VWP

Eyes Fastened with Pins.　Charles Simic.　VCAP

Eyes filled with speaking fire.　Irenaeus Referendarius.　GrAn

Eyes / flatterers of Soul.　Meleager.　GrAn

Eyes in this place droop, The.　Pastime Café.　W. M. Ransom.　GifTon

Eyes knees and of your Etcetera. (LL)　E. E. Cummings.　HeIP-4; OBAL; OBWP; OxBA; PAI; PeFWW

Eyes look front in humans, The.　Teleology.　May Swenson.　VCAP

Eyes: . . . . . .Medium.　All There Is to Know about Adolph Eichmann.　Leonard Cohen.　InPK-6

Eyes of clear serenity.　Madrigal: Eyes of Clear Serenity.　Gutierre de Cetina.　SpanPo, *tr.* by Kate Flores

Eyes of heavenly essence, O breasts of the purity of breasts.　Poem for a Lost Lover.　Syl Cheney-Coker.　PBMAP

Eyes of men running, falling, screaming.　*Unknown.*　OBWP

Eyes of mother-of-pearl, smell of quince.　To Die.　Sándor Weöres.　IQMS, *tr.* by Edwin Morgan

Eyes of Night-Time.　Muriel Rukeyser.　BoWoP

Eyes of [*or* the] body, being blindfold by night, The.　Valentine Ackland.　PoBW

Eyes of slain stag.　In Some Seer's Cloud Car.　Christopher Middleton.　TwCP

Eyes of twenty centuries, The.　Judas Iscariot.　Stephen Spender.　MoBrPo; NIP-4

Eyes open on the beach.　Christopher Okigbo.　PBMAP　*Fr.* Heavensgate (1961).

Eyes open to a cry of pulleys, The.　Love Calls Us to the Things of This World.　Richard Wilbur.　AmFaPo; HAP; HeIP-4; MoAmPo; NAAL-5; NIL-7; NIP-4; NoAM; PoE; PoRA; TAP; TFi; UnPo; VCAP; VGW

Eyes red, the lips blue, The.　Three Seamstresses, The.　Isaac Leibush [*or* Yitskhok Leybush] Peretz [*or* Perets].　TrJP, *tr.* by Joseph Leftwich

Eyes shining without mystery.　Pantoum.　John Ashbery.　CoAmPo

Eyes shut tight.　Madness.　Sachiko Yoshihara.　BoWoP, *tr.* by James Kirkup and Shozo Tokunaga

Eyes So Tristful.　Diego de Saldaña.　AWP, *tr.* by Henry Wadsworth Longfellow

Eyes that drew from me such fervent praise, The.　Petrarch.　NAWM-5v1　*Fr.* Sonnets to Laura.

Eyes that glass fear, though fear on furtive foot.　Hare, A.　Walter De la Mare.　EBEV

Eyes That Last I Saw in Tears.　T. S. Eliot.　NOBE

Eyes that mock me sign the way, The.　Bahnhofstrasse.　James Joyce.　NPeEn

Eyes that weep for pity of the heart, The.　Dante Alighieri.　AWP　*Fr.* La Vita Nuova.

Eyes, the Blood, The.　David Meltzer.　PoM

Eyes turn topaz, The. (LL)　Ezra Pound.　APT-1; NOBA; NoAM; TAP

Eyes Watch the Stars.　Christopher Okigbo.　PBMAP　*Fr.* Heavensgate (1961).

Eyesight II.　Robert Duncan.　SPE

Eyewash.　Niall Montgomery.　SPE

Ez Malindy sings. (LL)　When Malindy Sings.　Paul Laurence Dunbar.　APN-2; ISC; NAAAL

Ezekiel.　Bible, *O.T.*
　"Hand of the Lord held me transported, The."　WoPoe, *tr.* by David Curzon
　"How was thy mother a lioness."　TrJP
　Lamentation.　TrJP
　Thy Mother Was like a Vine.　TrJP
　Valley of Dry Bones, The.　WoPoe, *tr.* by David Curzon

Ezekiel.　John Greenleaf Whittier.　ChIV-1

Ezekiel Saw de [*or* the] Wheel.　*Unknown.*　APN-2
　(Ezek'el saw the wheel.)　NoP-4
　(Ezekiel Saw the Wheel.)　NoP-4

Ezra Pound.　Robert Lowell.　NAAL-2v2; NOBA; NoAM

F

F.B.I. swooped in early, The.　Lawson Fusao Inada.　GeoHom　*Fr.* Legends from Camp.

F.D.R. Jones.　Harold Rome.　ReLy

F. de Samara to A. G. A.　Emily Jane Brontë.　NALW

Fa la la! (LL)　Sing We and Chant It.　Thomas Morley.　EBEV; NoSic

Fa la la! (LL)　Now Is the Month of Maying.　*Unknown.*　EBEV; NoSic

Fa, Mi, Fa, Re, La, Mi.　*Unknown.*　InPK-6

Fa'se Footrage.　*Unknown.*　*See* Fause Foodrage

Fab Four Tour Deutschland: Hamburg, 1961.　David Wojahn.　PBCAP　*Fr.* Mystery Train: A Sequence.

Fable.　Eugenio de Andrade.　VCWP, *tr.* by Alexis Levitin

Fable.　James Facos.　NBLV

Fable, A.　John Hookham Frere.　UV

Fable, The.　Yvor Winters.　APT-2

Fable XXI: The Rat-catcher and Cats.　John Gay.　OxAEP-1

Fable, A: "In Æsop's tales an honest wretch we find."　Matthew Prior.　NoP-4

Fable: "Animal understands itself, The."　Luiza Neto Jorge.　SurWo, *tr.* by Jean R. Longland

Fable at the beginning of the monsoon, The.　Monsoon Day Fable, A.　Jayanta Mahapatra.　VCWP

Fable for Critics, A.　James Russell Lowell.　NAAL-2v1; NAAL-3
　Alcott.　TCAPo
　Bryant.　NOBA; TAP
　Channing and Thoreau.　TCAPo
　Cooper.　NOBA; OxBA; TAP; TCAPo
　Emerson.　APN-1; NOBA; OxBA; TAP; TCAPo
　(Fable for Critics, A.)　NCAP
　Hawthorne.　NOBA; TAP; TCAPo
　"Here's Cooper, who's written six volumes to show."　NOBA; OxBA; TAP; TCAPo
　Holmes.　NOBA; TCAPo
　Irving.　TAP
　Lowell.　NOBA; OxBA; TAP; TCAPo
　Philothea (Lydia Child).　TCAPo
　Phoebus.　TCAPo
　"Phoebus, sitting one day in a laurel tree's shade."　TCAPo
　(Poe.)　TAP
　Poe and Longfellow.　APN-1; OxBA; TCAPo
　"There are truths you Americans need to be told."　OBSV
　"There comes Emerson first, whose rich words, every one."　APN-1; NOBA; OxBA; TAP; TCAPo
　"There comes ———, for instance; to see him's rare sport."　TCAPo
　"There comes Philothea, her face all aglow."　TCAPo
　"There comes Poe, with his raven, like fudge."　APN-1; OxBA; TCAPo
　"There is Bryant, as quiet, as cool, and as dignified."　NOBA; TAP
　"There is Hawthorne, with genius so shrinking and rare."　NOBA; TAP; TCAPo
　"There is Lowell, who's striving Parnassus to climb."　NOBA; OxBA; TAP; TCAPo
　"There is Whittier, whose swelling and vehement heart."　NOBA; OxBA
　"There's Holmes, who is matchless among you for wit."　NOBA; TCAPo
　"What! Irving? thrice welcome, warm heart, and fine brain."　TAP
　Whittier.　NOBA; OxBA
　"Yonder, calm as a cloud, Alcott stalks in a dream."　TCAPo

Fable for Critics, A.　James Russell Lowell.　*See* Fable for Critics, A

Fable: "Mountain and the squirrel, The."　Ralph Waldo Emerson.　APN-1; NBLV; OBAL; OBCA; OxIBACP; TFi

Fable of Polyphemus and Galatea.　Luis de Góngora y Argote.
　Dedication: to the Count of Niebla.　SpanPo, *tr.* by Frances Fletcher
　"Now that your nebula, O noble Count, sheds."　SpanPo, *tr.* by Frances Fletcher
　"O lovely Galatea, sweeter than."　SpanPo, *tr.* by Frances Fletcher

Polyphemus' Love Song. SpanPo, *tr.* by Frances Fletcher

Fable of the War, A. Howard Nemerov. OBWP

Fable of the Young Man and His Cat, The. Christopher Pitt. ECEV

Fable: "Once upon a time / there was a lonely wolf." János Pilinszky. OBVE; PoSu; RB

Fable: "Under a dung-cake." D. J. Opperman. PeSAV, *tr.* by Jack Cope

Fabled queen of love, The. (LL) Sonnet: "When Phoebe formed a wanton smile." William Collins. EnLoPo; OxBSP

Fables. John Gay.
  "Against an elm a sheep was tied [*or* ty'd]." NOEC; NPeEn
  "Give me a son. The blessing sent." PeLV
  "I hate the man who builds his name." PeLV
  Mother, the Nurse, and the Fairy, The. PeLV
  Poet and the Rose, The. PeLV
  Wild Boar and the Ram, The. NOEC; NPeEn

Fabrication of Ancestors. Alan Dugan. CBCWP; NoAM

Fabulary Satire IV. Daryl Hine. NOBC

Fabulists, The. Rudyard Kipling. OxBEV

Fabulous Wizard of Oz, The. Limerick: "Fabulous Wizard of Oz, The." *Unknown.* PeLi

Façade. Dame Edith Sitwell.
  Hornpipe. FaBoMo; GTBS-P
  "Long steel grass." NAEL-5v2; NAEL-6v2
  "Sailors come / To the drum." FaBoMo; GTBS-P
  Sir Beelzebub. BoWoP; FaBoMo; FaBoWP; MoBrPo; NALW; OBCoV; OxBTC
  Trio for Two Cats and a Trombone. NAEL-5v2; NAEL-6v2
  "When / Sir / Beelzebub called for his syllabub in the hotel in Hell." BoWoP; FaBoMo; FaBoWP; MoBrPo; NALW; OBCoV; OxBTC

Façade. Dame Edith Sitwell.
  "I Do Like To Be Beside the Seaside" PFTM-1
  "When." PFTM-1

Face. Sounds. Wassily Kandinsky [*or* Kandinskii]. PFTM-1

Face, A. Robert Browning. CTC

Face, A. Marianne Craig Moore. OxBSP

Face, The. Anthony Euwer. OBAL; PeLi

Face, The. Edwin Muir. GTBS-P

Face, A? There. Between Us. James Merrill. PoE

Face damp on a lover's thigh and scratchy. Eating Clay. Minnie Bruce Pratt. ExTi

Face-down; odor. Terror. Denise Levertov. PoE

Face from the Past, A. Menella Bute Smedley. VWP

Face, huge face on the screen. Scene-Script. Giancarlo Majorino. ItPo, *tr.* by Gayle Ridinger

Face in the Mirror, The. Robert Graves. CABP

Face in the mirror, / my tiny nightmare. (LL) Landcrab I. Margaret Atwood. LCAP-2; NIP-4

Face is turned to Mecca, The. Prayer. Rudaki. WoPoe, *tr.* by Geoffrey Squires

Face like a chocolate bar. 125th Street. Langston Hughes. APT-2

Face Lost in the Wilderness. Fadwa Tuqan [*or* Tuquan]. MAP, *tr.* by Patricia Alanah Byrne, Salma Khadra Jayyusi and Naomi Shihab Nye

Face Lost in the Wilderness. Fadwa Tuqan [*or* Tuquan]. AF, *tr.* by Naomi Shihab Nye

Face Mask. Patricia Pogson. NLP

Face of a Horse, The. Nikolai Alekseievich Zabolotsky [*or* Zabolotskii]. TCRusP, *tr.* by Kathy Lewis and Bob Perelman

Face of all the world is changed, I think, The. Elizabeth Barrett Browning. CTC; CenSon *Fr.* Sonnets from the Portuguese.

Face of azure beams on the face, The. As With Them. Boris Leonidovich Pasternak. TCRusP, *tr.* by Bogdan Boychuk and Mark Rudman

Face of Love, The. Ingrid Jonker. HAWP, *tr.* by Jack Cope

Face of the Horse, The. Nikolai Alekseievich Zabolotsky [*or* Zabolotskii]. RB; TCRP, *tr.* by Daniel Weissbort

Face of the landscape is a mask, The. Mask. Stephen Spender. MoBrPo

Face of the precipice is black with lovers, The. Salvador Dali. David Gascoyne. OxBTC; SPE

Face of the spring moon. Issa. EH, *tr.* by Robert Hass

Face of the Waters, The. Robert David Fitzgerald. CBAP

Face reigned on the water, A. Two Hands on the Water. Zuhur Dixon. MAP, *tr.* by Patricia Alanah Byrne and Salma Khadra Jayyusi

Face shines, anchored in fog, A. Things of the Blind. Paz Molina. TANSG, *tr.* by Steven F. White

Face sings, alone, The. Poem for Willie Best, A. Imamu Amiri Baraka. NAAL-5

Face sweaty and hot with chagrin. (LL) Dappled Horse, The. Mei Yao Ch'en. CoBCP; ColAnChi, *tr.* by Burton Watson

Face that should content me wonders [*or* wondrous] well, A. Sir Thomas Wyatt. CTC; EnLoPo

Face the Animal. Jean Follain. BLT, *tr.* by Heather McHugh

Face to Face. Adrienne Rich. NAAL-2v2; NoAM

Face to Face. K. V. Tirumalesh. OMIP, *tr.* by A. K. Ramanujan

Face to Face with My Lover on Daito's Anniversary. Ikkyu Sojun. ErotSp, *tr.* by Sam Hamill

Face wrapping a champagne glass. Bob Boldman. HA

Face yellowed, The. Betrayal, The. "Nirala." OMIP, *tr.* by Arvind Krishna Mehrotra

Faces. John Ciardi. WeW-3

Faces, The. Robert Creeley. NoAM

Faces greying faster than loam-crumbs on a harrow. Judge Not. Theodore Roethke. ChIV-2; GI

Faces I Love, The. Gerald Stern. LoL

Faces in the Street. Henry Lawson. CBAP

Faces may alter, names can't change. Nathaniel Lee to Sir Roger L'Estrange. Nathaniel Lee. FaBoEE

Faces of dolls, The. Seifū. NIL-7, *tr.* by Daniel C. Buchanan

Faces of the counted years. Naked Face, The. Andrée Chedid. HAWP, *tr.* by Mirène Ghossein and Samuel Hazo

Faces surround me that have no smell or color no time. Chain. Audre Lorde. BlSi

Faceted grains of wisdom. Mikhail Yeryomin. TCRusP, *tr.* by John Glad

Facing Bonnard. Aleksander Wat. BLT

Facing His Own Death. Narihira (Ariwara no Narihira). WoPoe, *tr.* by F. Vos *Fr.* Ise Monogatari, The.

Facing It. Yusef Komunyakaa. AmFaPo; ESEAA; NAAAL; PoPoPo; TRP

Facing me, the blustering evening rain besprinkles the sky over the river. Tune: "Eight Beats of a Kan-chou Song." Liu Yung. ColAnChi; SuSp, *tr.* by James J. Y. Liu

Facing the Chair. Hugh MacDiarmid. FaBoMo

Facing the palm of fire. Meditation for this Day. Antonio Machado Ruiz. CLPP, *tr.* by Kenneth Rexroth

Facing the Snow. Tu Fu. CrYelRi, *tr.* by Sam Hamill

Facing the sun, untalkative, out of reach. (LL) Here. Philip Larkin. NPeEn; PoE

Facing West from California's Shores. Walt Whitman. MoAmPo; NAAL-2v1; NAAL-3; NAAL-5; NIL-7; TAP

Facing Wine with Memories of Lord Ho. CoBCP Li Po.
  "Wild man of Ssu-ming Mountain." CoBCP

Facing Wine with Memories of Lord Ho. Li Po. CoBCP *Fr.* Facing Wine with Memories of Lord Ho.

Facing you, on the wall, across from your bed. Yün Shou-p'ing. CoBLCP *Fr.* Mourning for Lü Hui-chiu.

Fact. Langston Hughes. APSN; PFTM-1

Fact. Kenneth Rexroth. OBAL

Fact of life is it's no life-or-death matter, The. There Is No Real Peace in the World. Douglas Crase. BodElec

Fact of the matter is, Jack, The. Limerick: "Fact of the matter is, Jack, The." John Stanley. PeLi

Fact that we survive it compels us, The. Beyond Fear. Odia Ofeimun. HBAPE

Factory. "Antler."
  "Machines waited for me, The." CLPP
  "Ungag our souls!! Unstrangle our souls!! Unsmother our souls!!" CLPP

"Factory." André Breton. PFTM-1 *Fr.* Magnetic Fields, The.

Factory, The. Aleksandr Aleksandrovich Blok. TCRP, *tr.* by Yakov Hornstein

Factory, The. Lajos Kassák. IQMS, *tr.* by Michael Kitka

Factory Girl's Come-All-Ye, The. *Unknown.* OBAL

Factory Windows Are Always Broken. Nicholas Vachel Lindsay. APT-1; OBCA; OxBSP

Factory Workers' Song. *Unknown.* FaBoVe

Facts of Life, The. Ronald Wallace. PBCAP

Facts of Life, Ballymoney. Eamon Grennan. PBCIP

Fade the kingfisher blue, trim the red, blend the colors. Yüan Hao-wen. SuSp *Fr.* On Poetry.

Faded. Augusta Davies Webster. VWP

Faded, and the hill slept. (LL) He Fell among Thieves. Sir Henry John Newbolt. EBVV; OBEV; OBWP; OxBTC

Faded back last night. Talking. Robert Creeley. FTOS

Faded flowers of the bed sheets autumn night. Marlene Mountain. HA

Faded hibiscus and its leaves. Tune: "Sand of Silk-Washing Brook." Wang Kuo-wei. ColAnChi, *tr.* by Jiaosheng Wang

Faded Pictures. William Vaughn Moody. TCAPo

Faded the last red blossoms. Tune: "Butterflies Lingering over Flowers." Su Tung-p'o (Su Shih). ColAnChi, *tr.* by Jiaosheng Wang

Fading Beauty. Giambattista [*or* Giovanni Battista] Marino. AWP, *tr. by* Samuel Daniel

Fading Beauty. *Unknown.* FaBoEE

Fading dream lingers by the hills on the screen. Tune: "Song of Divination." Chu Yi-tsun. SuSp, *tr. by* Irving Y. Lo

Fading-Leaf and Fallen-Leaf. Richard Garnett. EBVV

Fading Skiff, The. Henrietta Cordelia Ray. CBWP-3

Fado Singer. Wole Soyinka. HBAPE

Faerie Queene, The. Edmund Spenser.

Address to Venus. AWP

("And death instead of life have sucked from our Nurse.") (LL) AEP

"And is there care in heauen [*or* heaven]? and is there loue [*or* love]." NOCV; NoSic

("And Nature's self did vanish, whither no man wist.") (LL) AEP

Arthur's Fight with Orgoglio and Duessa. EBNV

"As when a ship, that flyes faire under saile." FHYEP

"Ay me, how many perils doe unfold [*or* enfold]." FHYEP

"Behold I see the haven nigh at hand." FHYEP

Book 1. NAEL-6v1; NAEL-7v1

"By vew of her he ginneth to revive." CAGL

"That darkesome cave they enter, where they find." OxBEV

Bower of Bliss, The.

Bower of Bliss, The. NAEL-6v1; NAEL-7v1; OBGa

(Bower of Blisse Destroyed, The.) NPeEn

"Eftsoones they heard a most melodious sound." NOBE; OxBEV; PBRV; SCV

"Thence passing forth, they shortly do arrive." NAEL-6v1; NAEL-7v1; OBGa

Britomart at Isis' Church. PoE

"By her the heaven is in his course contained." PoE

"By this the Northerne wagoner had set." FHYEP; NoSic

Cave of Despair, The. OBNV

"Ere long they come, where that same wicked wight." NOBE

Faerie Queene Book 2, The.

"And in the midst of all, a fountaine stood." EroLit

Faerie Queene Book 3, The.

Belphoebe and Timias. NAEL-6v1; NAEL-7v1

Britomart chaseth Ollyphant. NAEL-6v1; NAEL-7v1

"First was Fancy, like a lovely boy, The." CAGL

"Great enimy to it, and to all the rest." OxBEV

Maske of Cupid, The. NAEL-6v1; NAEL-7v1

"Most sacred fire, that burnest mightily." NAEL-6v1; NAEL-7v1

"O hatefull hellish snake, what furie furst." NAEL-6v1; NAEL-7v1

"Providence heavenly passeth living thought." NAEL-6v1; NAEL-7v1

"There now he lives in everlasting joy." CAGL

"Tho when as chearelesse night ycovered had." NAEL-6v1; NAEL-7v1

Visit to Merlin, The. NAEL-6v1; NAEL-7v1

Faerie Queene Book 4, The.

"But farre away from these, another sort." CAGL

"Hard is the doubt, and difficult to deeme." CAGL

Fight of the Red Cross Knight and the Heathen Sansjoy, The. FHYEP; NoSic

"For other beds the priests there used none." PoE

Garden of Adonis, The. NOBE

Gardin of Adonis, The. NOBE; NPeEn

"In that same gardin all the goodly flowres." NOBE; NPeEn

"Gentle knight was pricking on the plaine, A." EBEV; FHYEP; NAEL-5v1

Guardian Angels. NOCV; NoSic

Guyon's Voyage to the Bower of Bliss. NoSic

"He making speedy way through spersed ayre." NoSic

"He was to weet a man of full ripe years." UV

"High time now gan it wex for Una faire." FHYEP

Hill of the Graces, The. NOBE

House of Busyrane, The. NoSic

In the Bower of Bliss. EBEV

"It falles me here to write of Chastity." NAEL-5v1; NAEL-6v1; NAEL-7v1

("It was a chosen plot of fertile land.") AEP

Legend of Britomartis, or of Chastitie, The. NAEL-5v1; NAEL-6v1; NAEL-7v1

"And at the upper end of that faire rowme." NPeEn

Britomart in the House of the Enchanter Busyrane. NPeEn

Legend of the Knight of the Red Crosse, or of Holinesse, The. FHYEP; NAEL-5v1; NAEL-7v1

"Lo I the man, whose muse whilome did maske." NAEL-6v1; NAEL-7v1

"Lo I the man, whose Muse whilome [*or* whylome] did maske." FHYEP; NAEL-5v1; NAEL-7v1

Mutability Claims to Rule the World. NoSic

(Nature.) AEP

Nature's Reply to Mutability. MakPoe; NOBE

"Then since within this wide great Universe." NPeEn

"Noble hart, that harbours vertuous [*or* virtuous] thought, The." FHYEP; NoSic

"Nought is there under heav'ns wide hollownesse." FHYEP

"Nought vnder heauen so strongly doth allure." NoSic

"O goodly golden chaine, wherewith yfere." FHYEP

"One day as he did raunge the fields abroad." NoSic

(Pageant of the Seasons and the Months, The.) OxAEP-1

(Phaedria's Island: The Faerie Queene II.vi. 12–17.) AEP

"Right well I w[r]ote most mighty Soueraine [*or* soveraine]." NoSic

Scudamor in the Temple of Venus. PoE

("She brought her to her ioyous Paradize.") OBGa

"Shee brought her to her joyous paradise." NOBE

"So forth she comes, and to her coche does clyme." NAEL-5v1

"So having ended, silence long ensewed." MakPoe; NOBE

Song of Bliss. OBVE

("Then forth issued (great goddess) great Dame Nature.") AEP

"There the most daintie Paradise on ground." EBEV

"They sadly travelled thus, until they went." EBNV

"This great Grandmother of all creatures bred." NoSic

"Thus been they parted, Arthur on his way." OBNV

"Two dayes now in that sea he sayled has." NoSic

"Unto this place when as the Elfin Knight." NOBE

Vision of the Graces, The. NoSic

"What man is he, that boasts of fleshly might." FHYEP

"What man so wise, what earthly wit so ware." FHYEP

("What man that sees the ever-whirling wheel.") AEP

("When I bethink me on that speech whilere.") SacPr

"When I bethinke me on that speech whyleare." NPeEn; NoSic

"Whiles someone did chant this lovely lay, The." OBVE

"Who travels [*or* trauels] by the wearie wandring way." OxAEP-1

"With huge impatience, he inly swelt." NoSic

"Young knight, what ever that dost armes professe." FHYEP

Faerie Queene Book 2, The. Edmund Spenser. *Fr.* Faerie Queene, The.

Faerie Queene Book 3, The. Edmund Spenser.

"For round about, the wals yclothed were." PBRV

Faerie Queene Book 3, The. Edmund Spenser. *Fr.* Faerie Queene, The.

Faerie Queene Book 4, The. Edmund Spenser. *Fr.* Faerie Queene, The.

Faerie Queene Book 5, The. Edmund Spenser.

"Tho when they came to the sea coast, they found." PBRV

Faery Beam upon You, The. Ben Jonson. BeJo; EBEV *Fr.* Gypsies Metamorphosed, The.

Faery Chasm, The. William Wordsworth. CenSon; OxBSo *Fr.* River Duddon [A Series of Sonnets], The.

Fafnir. Alec Derwent Hope. BMAP

Fag art sucks. Fag Art. John Iozia. CAGL

Fag-End. Philip O'Connor. SPE

(Drips surprise. They talk too, The.) SPE

Faggots and their friends now live in Ramrod, The. Larry Mitchell. GLP

Faggots created a rite of cleansing, The. The faggots sit in a circle. Sons and Fathers. Larry Mitchell. GLP

Fail to meet by a moment, and a word. (LL) World and I, The. Laura Riding Jackson. APT-2; ColAP; HarvBoo

Failing the Examination. Meng Chiao. SuSp, *tr. by* Stephen Owen

Failure. Dana Gioia. KGB

Failure. Kate Tucker Goode. PWR

Failure. Henrietta Cordelia Ray. CBWP-3

Failure. Lina Tibi. PoArWo, *tr. by* Subhi Hadidi and Nathalie Handal

Failure. Natan Zach. FIT, *tr. by* Robert Friend

Failure, A. Cecil Day Lewis. NOBE

Failure and Success. Richard Watson Gilder. PWR

Failure of an Invention. Safiya Henderson-Holmes. UnSA

Failure, the longed-for valley, takes him in. (LL) In the Smoking-Car. Richard Wilbur. CoAmPo; GM; MoAmPo

Failures. May Kendall. VWP; ViWPN

Fain would I be sleeping, dreaming. Plaint of the Wife, The. *Unknown.* AWP, *tr. by* W. R. S. Ralston

Fain would I have a pretty thing. Proper Song, Entitled: Fain Would I Have a Pretty Thing to Give unto My Lady, A. *Unknown.* NoSic

Fain would I kiss my Julia's dainty leg. Her Legs. Robert Herrick. NOSC

Fain would I rival thee. To the Eagle. Mary Weston Fordham. CBWP-2

Fain Would I Wed. Thomas Campion. NAEL-5v1; NAEL-6v1; NAEL-7v1

Fain would my Muse the flow'ry Treasures sing. Garden, The. Pope. OBGa

Faint, and final. (LL) Butcher's Wife, The. Louise Erdrich. HATNAP; NoP-
4

Faint clouds caress the mountains. Farewell Song. Ch'in Kuan. CrYelRi, *tr. by* Sam Hamill

Faint Falls the Gentle Voice. Henry Timrod. AH

Faint flush spread all over her cheeks, still sleepy-eyed, A. Tune: "Sand of Silk-washing Stream." Wu Wei-yeh. SuSp, *tr. by* Irving Y. Lo

Faint-flushed buds awake within the cup, The. Awakening. Henrietta Cordelia Ray. CBWP-3

Faint Honey. James Purdy. CAGL

Faint Love. Arthur Symons. CABP

Faint Music. Walter De la Mare. FaBoCh

Faint not—fight on! To-morrow comes the song. (LL) Be Strong. Maltbie Davenport Babcock. AH; ITBLP; PWR; SoSe-8

Faint now in the evening pallor. Silver Jubilee. Llewelyn Wyn Griffith. OBWVE

Faint shines the far moon. Road, The. Nikolay Platonovich Ogarev. AWP, *tr. by* P. E. Matheson

Faint Thunder Drifts beneath the Willow. Ou-yang Hsiu. ErotSp, *tr. by* Jerome P. Seaton

Faint thunder drifts . . . / beneath the willow. Faint Thunder Drifts beneath the Willow. Ou-yang Hsiu. ErotSp, *tr. by* Jerome P. Seaton

Faint yellow rose, A. Issa. SoOfWa, *tr. by* Sam Hamill

Faint yet pursuing, faint yet still pursuing / Ever. (LL) Life's Parallels, A. Christina Georgina Rossetti. NAEL-5v2; NAEL-6v2

Faintheart in a Railway Train. Thomas Hardy. CTC; EnLoPo

Faintly answering still the notes that once were so dear. (LL) Echo. Thomas Moore. GTBS-P; NOBE; OBEV

Faintly as tolls the evening chime. Canadian Boat Song, A. Thomas Moore. TreFP

Fair am I, mortals, as a stone-carved dream. Beauté, La. Charles Baudelaire. AWP, *tr. by* Lord Alfred Bruce Douglas

Fair Amazon of Heaven who tookst in hand. To Saint Margaret. Henry Constable. NoSic

Fair Amoret is gone astray. Hue and Cry after Fair Amoret, A. William Congreve. NOEC; NPeEn; OBEV; OxBEV

Fair and bright assembly, A: never strode. Thomas Lovell Beddoes. CTC *Fr.* Death's Jest Book.

Fair and Fair. George Peele. OBEV *Fr.* Arraignment of Paris, The.

Fair and Scornful. *Unknown.* OBCoV

Fair and Softly goes fair or, The Wary Physician. Laetitia Pilkington. PEW

Fair and Unfair. Robert Francis. VGW

Fair Annie. *Unknown.* ESPB; OxBB

Fair Annie an Sweet Willie. Lord Thomas and Fair Annet. *Unknown.* ESPB

Fair Annie had a costly bower. Holy Nunnery, The. *Unknown.* ESPB

Fair are the bells of this bright-flowering weed. Poet and Botanist. Constance Naden. VWP; ViWPN

Fair at Windgap, The. Austin Clarke. OxBTC

Fair Beatrice tucks her coat up somewhat high. Epigram. John Taylor. NOSC

Fair Beggar, The. Richard Lovelace. BeJo

Fair bosom! fraught with virtue's richest treasure. Edmund Spenser. NIP-4 *Fr.* Amoretti.

Fair boy, alas, why fliest thou me. Black Maid to the Fair Boy, The. Henry Reynolds. NOSC

Fair Cassidy. *Unknown.* BIrV, *tr. by* Donagh MacDonagh

Fair cheek under a merry blue eye, two brows, A. Beloved, The. David Roberts. OBWVE, *tr. by* H. Idris Bell

Fair Chunda smiles amid the burning waste. Erasmus Darwin. NOBRP *Fr.* Botanic Garden, The.

Fair Cop, A. Robert Garioch. OBCoV

Fair copy of my Celia's face. To T. H., a Lady Resembling My Mistress. Thomas Carew. CaPo

Fair Cynthia, all the Homage that I may. Thoughts on the Sight of the Moon. Sarah Kemble Knight. SCAP

Fair Cynthia mounted on her sprightly pad. Cynthia on Horseback. Philip Ayres. EnLoPo; OxBSo

Fair Danubie is praised for being wide. Rivers. Thomas Storer. FaBoCh

Fair daughter of that fleeting race. Nymph of the Fountain to Charlotte, The. Anne Grant. PoBW

Fair eastern star, that art ordained to run. Of the Epiphany. John Beaumont. SacPr

Fair Exchange. Aileen Fisher. NOxBChV

Fair fa' your honest, sonsie face. To a Haggis. Robert Burns. FaBoVe; NePenScot

Fair famous flood, which sometimes did divide. Sonnet: On the River Tweed. Sir Robert Aytoun [*or* Ayton]. NOSC

Fair Flower! Tune: "Partridge Sky." Li Ch'ing-chao. ColAnChi, *tr. by* Jiaosheng Wang

Fair flower of fifteen springs, that still. To His Young Mistress. Pierre de Ronsard. AWP, *tr. by* Andrew Lang

Fair Flower of Northumberland, The. *Unknown.* ESPB; OxBB

Fair flower, that dost so comely grow. Wild Honey Suckle, The. Philip Freneau. ColAP; ITBLP; NAAL-2v1; NAAL-3; NOBA; OxBA; TAP; TCAPo

Fair, fragile Una, golden-haired. Enchanted Shell, The. Henrietta Cordelia Ray. CBWP-3

Fair friend, 'tis true, your beauties move. Ben Jonson. NOSC

Fair girl tripping out to meet her love, A. Power of Interval, The. John Byrne Leicester Warren, 3d Baron De Tabley. NOBVV; OxBSP

Fair Golden Age! When milk was th' on[e]ly food. Sir Richard Fanshawe. NOSC; OBVE *Fr.* Il Pastor Fido.

Fair, great, and good, since seeing you, we see. To the Countess of Salisbury. John Donne. PeECV

Fair gull on the water's bank. Seagull, The. Siôn Phylip. OBWVE, *tr. by* Joseph P. Clancy

Fair Helen. *Unknown. See* Helen of Kirconnell

Fair Hills of Ireland, The. *Unknown.* OBEV, *tr. by* Sir Samuel Ferguson

Fair Hope with lucent light in her glad eyes. Quest of the Ideal, The. Henrietta Cordelia Ray. CBWP-3; SWaP

Fair Ilonka. Mihály Vörösmarty. IQMS, *tr. by* Watson Kirkconnell

Fair Ines. Thomas Hood. OBEV

Fair Iris I love, and hourly I die. Dryden. AWP *Fr.* Amphitryon.

"Fair is Alexis," I no sooner said. On Alexis. Plato. AWP, *tr. by* Thomas Stanley

Fair is my dove, my loved one. Marriage Song. Judah Halevi. TrJP, *tr. by* Alice Lucas

"Fair is my Love and cruel as she's fair." Samuel Daniel. *See* To Delia

"Fair is my love, when her fair golden hairs." Edmund Spenser. *See* Amoretti

Fair Is Too Foul an Epithet. Christopher Marlowe. EBEV *Fr.* Tamburlaine the Great.

Fair Isabel sat in her bower door. Hind Etin. *Unknown.* OxBB

Fair Isabell of Rochroyall. *Unknown.* OxBB

Fair Isle at Sea—thy lovely name. Robert Louis Stevenson. NOBVV

Fair Janet. *Unknown.* ESPB; OxBB

Fair lady Isabel sits in her bower sewing. Lady Isabel and the Elf-Knight. *Unknown.* ESPB

Fair lady, on that snowy neck and half-clad bosom. More Care for the Neck Than for the Intellect. J. Gordon Coogler. VerBaPo

Fair lady, what's your face to me? Love for Enjoying. James Shirley. BeJo

Fair lady, will you travel. Wooing of Etain, The. *Unknown.* BIrV, *tr. by* John Montague

Fair lake, thy lovely and thy haunted shore. Castle of Chillon, The. Letitia [*or* Laetitia] Elizabeth Landon. CenSon

Fair Lass of Islington, The. *Unknown.* OxBB

Fair lovely maid, or if that title be. To the Fair Clarinda [*or* Clorinda], Who Made Love to Me, Imagined [*or* Imagin'd] More Than Woman. Aphra Behn. BASC; CABP; EMWP; NALW; NIL-7; NoP-4; PEW; PoBW

Fair maid, had I not heard thy baby cries. To a Lofty Beauty, from Her Poor Kinsman. Hartley Coleridge. OxAEP-2

Fair Maid of Amsterdam, The. *Unknown.* OxBoLi; PeLV; RB

Fair maid sat in her bower-door, A. False Lover Won Back, The. *Unknown.* ESPB

Fair maid who, the first of May. First of May, The. *Unknown.* ReMoGo

Fair maiden, fair maiden. Invocation to the Muse. Richard Hughes. MoBrPo

Fair maiden, white and red. George Peele. FaBoCh; NOBE; OxBoLi *Fr.* Old Wives' [*or* Wife's] Tale, The.

Fair Margaret and Sweet William. *Unknown.* ESPB; OxBB

Fair Margret was a young ladye. Proud Margret. *Unknown.* OxBB

Fair Marjorie sat i her bower-door. Young Benjie. *Unknown.* ESPB

Fair Mary of Wallington. *Unknown.* ESPB
  (Bonny Earl of Livingston, The.) OxBB

Fair Mary of Wallington. *Unknown.* ESPB
  (Bonny Earl of Livingston, The.) OxBB

Fair Melody: To Be Sung by Good Christians, A. Hans Sachs. GePo, *tr. by* Catherine Winkworth

Fair Mildred wide her lattice threw. Mildred's Doves. Henrietta Cordelia Ray. CBWP-3

Fair Moon! You shining lady of the sombre night. To The Moon. Dávid Baróti Szabó. IQMS, *tr. by* Adam Makkai

Fair morn unbars her gates of gold. Dawn's Carol. Henrietta Cordelia Ray. CBWP-3

Fair Morning, The. Jones Very. GSo; NOBA

Fair mouth's broken tooth, A. (LL) August 1914. Isaac Rosenberg. EBEV; HarvBoo; NOBE; NPeEn; OBWP; OxBEV; OxBTC; PeFWW

Fair Musidora starry-eyed. Musidora's Vision. Henrietta Cordelia Ray. CBWP-3

Fair nights beneath the mellow moon. Maid of Ehrenthal, The. Henrietta Cordelia Ray. CBWP-3

Fair of face, full of pride. Lyke-Wake Song, A. Algernon Charles Swinburne. PAI

Fair one, to you this monitor I send. Mira to Octavia. Mary Leapor. ECWP

Fair [or Faire] stood the wind for France. Battle of Agincourt, The. Michael Drayton. EBNV

Fair [or Fayre] is my love, when her fair [or fayre] golden heares. Edmund Spenser. Son Fr. Amoretti.

Fair[e] pledges of a fruitful tree. To Blossoms. Robert Herrick. BeJo; CaPo; GTBS-P; NAEL-5v1; NAEL-6v1; NOSC; OBEV; SCGP; TreFP

Fair princess[e] of the spacious air. Falcon, The. Richard Lovelace. CaPo

Fair Protarchus doesn't want to. Alcaeus [or Alkaios]. GrAn

Fair proud, now tell me, why should fair be proud. Edmund Spenser. Son Fr. Amoretti.

Fair Raiment. John Oxenham. SacPr

Fair rebel to thyself and time. Revenge, The. Pierre de Ronsard. AWP, tr. by Thomas Stanley

Fair, Rich, and Young. Sir John Harington [or Harrington]. NIP-4 (Of a Fair Shrew.) FaBoEE

Fair rosa. Unknown. FaBoVe

Fair Rosa was a lovely child. Fair rosa. Unknown. FaBoVe

Fair Salamis, the billow's roar. Sophocles. AWP, tr. by Winthrop Mackworth Praed Fr. Ajax.

Fair seagull on the water's edge, bright-feathered breast, rich your state. Siôn Phylip. See Fair gull on the water's bank

Fair seed-time had my soul, and I grew up. William Wordsworth. OxAEP-2 Fr. Prelude, The; Growth of a Poet's Mind [1805 vers.].

Fair shadow, faithless as my sun! Dream, The. Sir Edward Sherburne. OxBSP

Fair ship, that from the Italian shore. Tennyson. CAGL; EBVV; NAEL-6v2 Fr. In Memoriam A. H. H.

Fair Singer, The. Andrew Marvell. EnLoPo; FSCP; MeLP; NOBE; NoP-4; SCGP

Fair sinks the summer evening now. Emily Jane Brontë. BWW

Fair sir, this love of ours. Saladino da Pavia. EaItPo, tr. by Dante Gabriel Rossetti

Fair slim boy not made for this world's pain, A. Wasted Days. Oscar Wilde. CAGL

Fair Star of evening, Splendo[u]r of the west. Composed by the Sea-Side, near Calais, August, 1802. William Wordsworth. CenSon; Son

Fair summer droops, droop men and beasts therefore. Thomas Nashe [or Nash]. NoSic Fr. Summer's Last Will and Testament.

Fair, the young acacia, thick with leaves. Young Acacia, The. Hayyim Nahman [or Khayim Nakhman or Chaim Nachman] Bialik. TrJP, tr. by Helena Frank

Fair these broad meads—these hoary woods are grand. Canadian Boat Song. John Galt. FaBoCh; OBEV; OxBS

Fair Thou Art. Mordecai ben Isaac. TrJP, tr. by Herbert Loewe

Fair Ursly, in a merry mood. Annibal Cruceius. FaBoEE

Fair Virtue, the Mistress of Philarete. George Wither.
   (Author's Resolution, The.) AWP; OBEV
   (Lover's Resolution, A.) BoLoP; NOBE
   Shall I, Wasting in Despair. OxAEP-1; SCGP
   ("Shall I wasting in Dispaire.") OxBEV
   (Manly Heart, The.) GTBS-P
   Sonnet: "I wandered out a while agone." NOSC

Fair was this yonge wyf, and therwithal. Geoffrey Chaucer. EBEV Fr. Canterbury Tales, The.

Fair witch crept to a young man's side, A. Witch-Bride, The. William Allingham. NOBVV

Fair ye be sure, but cruel and unkind. Edmund Spenser. Son Fr. Amoretti.

Fair young face o'er which is only cast, A. Princess Victoria, The. Letitia [or Laetitia] Elizabeth Landon. RWP

Fair young fine-browed lass, A. When Her Father a Widower Asked What She Would Say to His Intention of Marrying a Young Girl. Alis Ferch Gruffyd ab Ieuan ap Lleywelyn Fychan. EMWP

Fair young wanton lady, A. (LL) Gypsy Laddie, The. Unknown. ESPB; HAP

Fair[e] as unshaded light; or as the day. To the Queen[e], Entertain[e]d at Night by the Countess[e] of Anglesey. Sir William Davenant [or D'Avenant]. MeLP; NOSC

Fair[e] daffodils [or daffadills], we weep to see. To Daffodils [or Daffadills]. Robert Herrick. AWP; BASC; BeJo; CaPo; FaBoCh; GTBS-P; NOBE; NOSC; NoP-4; OBEV; OxAEP-1; PoRA; SCGP; TFi; TTTS; TreFP; UnPo

Fair[e] Days; or, Dawn[e]s Deceitful[l]. Robert Herrick. CaPo

Faire famous flood, which sometyme did devyde. Sir Robert Aytoun [or Ayton]. See Fair famous flood, which sometimes did divide

Faire, fresshest erthly creature. Unknown. OHMEL

Faire Friend, 'tis true, your beauties move. Sidney Godolphin. NPeEn

Faire [or fayre] soule, how long shall veyles thy graces shroud? At Home in Heaven. Robert Southwell. ESCV

Fair[e] was the dawn[e], and but e'ne now the skies. Fair[e] Days; or, Dawn[e]s Deceitful[l]. Robert Herrick. CaPo

Fairer and fairer apple of beauty. Between Gaeta and Capua. Franz Grillparzer. AuPH, tr. by Lowell A. Bangerter

Fairest day that ever yet has shone, The. Lost, The. Jones Very. APN-1; NOBA; NoP-4

Fairest flower, all flowers excelling. To a Child [of] Five Years Old. Nathaniel Cotton. ECEV

Fairest isle, all isles excelling. Dryden. OxBoLi Fr. King Arthur.

Fairest of trees under heaven and on earth. Hymn to the Orange. Unknown. SuSp, tr. by Wu-Chi Liu

Fairest summer hath its sudden showers, The. Shadows. John Clare. CenSon

Fairest thing I leave behind is sunlight, The. Praxilla. SaLy, tr. by Diane Rayor

Fairest things are those which live, The. Song. Mary Russell Mitford. NOBRP

Fairfax, whose name in arm[e]s through Europe rings. On the Lord Gen[eral] Fairfax at the Siege of Colchester. John Milton. NOSC

Fairies, The. William Allingham. FaBoCh; NOBE; NOBVV; NOxBChV; OBEV; OTCP; TFi

Fairies Are Dancing All Over the World, The. Michael Rumaker. CAGL; GLP

Fairies are taken into the world, The. Scenes of Childhood. Carl Morse. GLP

Fairies break their dances, The. Fairies Break Their Dances, The. A. E. Housman. OxBSP; PeVV

Fairies' Farewell, The. Richard Corbet [or Corbett]. See Proper New Ballad Entitled [or Intituled] The Fairies' [or Faeryes] Farewell, or God-a-Mercy Will, A

Fairies' Lullaby, The. William Shakespeare. NOBE; NoSic; PoRA; SCGP Fr. Midsummer Night's Dream, A.

Fairies' Song, The. Jane Taylor. NOBRP

Fairweill. Unknown. OxBS

Fairy Blessing, The. William Shakespeare. See Midsummer Night's Dream, A

Fairy Land, 1. William Shakespeare. OBEV Fr. Midsummer Night's Dream, A.

Fairy Land, 2. William Shakespeare. See Midsummer Night's Dream, A

Fairy Maimounè, The. John Moultrie. NOBRP

Fairy [or Faery or Faiery] beam[e] upon you, The. Ben Jonson. BeJo; EBEV Fr. Gypsies Metamorphosed, The.

Fairy Ring, The. Andrew Young. Spl

Fairy Scene. Jean Cocteau. CuPo

Fairy Song. W. B. Yeats. See Land of Heart's Desire, The

Fairy Song ("Over hill, over dale"). William Shakespeare. NOBE Fr. Midsummer Night's Dream, A.

Fairy Story. Stevie Smith. NOxBChV; OBSP

Fairy Straighttalk. Carl Morse. GLP

Fairy Tale. Miroslav Holub. RB, tr. by George Theiner

Fairy Tale, A. Bogdan Boychuk. WoPoe, tr. by David Ignatow

Fairy Tale about Rain, A. Bella [or Izabella] Akhatovna Akhmadulina. TCRP, tr. by Albert C. Todd

Fairy Tales. "Shu Ting." VCWP

Fairy tales can come true. Young at Heart. Carolyn Leigh. ReLy

Fairy Temple; or, Oberon's Chapel, The. Robert Herrick. CaPo

Fairyland [or Fairy-Land]. Edgar Allan Poe. APN-1; NAAL-2v1; NAAL-3

Fait Accompli. Anne Waldman. BodElec

Faith. Frances Anne [or "Fanny"] Kemble. SWaP

Faith. Friedrich von Logau. GePo, tr. by George C. Schoolfield

Faith. Czeslaw Milosz. RaBo, tr. by Renata Gorcynski, Robert Hass and Robert Pinsky

Faith. Christopher Smart. ChIV-1 Fr. Hymns for the Amusement of Children.

Faith. Unknown. PoToHe

Faith. Jones Very. SacPr

Faith. Ella Wheeler Wilcox. PoToHe

Faith Above Reason. William Drummond, of Hawthornden. SacPr

Faith and Works. Muriel Spark. OxBSP

"Faith" bleats—to understand! (LL) Emily Dickinson. APN-2; NOCV; SacPr

Faith for Tomorrow. Thomas Curtis Clark. PoToHe

Faith hasn't got no eyes, but she long-legged. Zora Neale Hurston. NAAAL

Faith Healing. Philip Larkin. ChIV-2; GI; NoAM; OxBEV

Faith, Hope, and Charity Are the Prospects of Manhood. Leigh Hunt. ChIV-2

"Faith" is a fine invention. Emily Dickinson. APN-2; NAAL-2v1; NAAL-3; NAAL-5; NCAP; NOBA; NoP-4; OxBA; TAP; TCAPo

Faith—is the Pierless Bridge. Emily Dickinson. NCAP

"Faith, master, whither you will." Captain Car; or, Edom o Gordon. *Unknown.* ESPB

Faith #1. Esther Iverem. InTrad

Faith Upon the Waters. Laura Riding Jackson. APT-2

Faith (wench) I cannot court thy sprightly eyes. Sir John Davies. PBRV

Faithful as enemy, or friend. (LL) Roosters. Elizabeth Bishop. APT-2; ChIV-2; NALW

Faithful Daughter Dreams of Spring Break While Installing a Bird Feeder for Her Mother by a Window in the Courtyard of Safe Harbour, The. Vivian Shipley. ExTi

Faithful friend from flattering foe. (LL) *Var. authors.* NOBE; OBEV *Fr.* Passionate Pilgrim, The.

Faithful Mirror. Gyula Illyés. IQMS, *tr. by* Adam Makkai and Donald E. Morse

Faithful mother tongue. My Faithful Mother Tongue. Czeslaw Milosz. VCWP

Faithful Shepherdess, The. John Fletcher.
    "All ye woods, and trees, and bowers." FaBoCh
    "Do not fear to put thy feet." NOSC
    God of Sheep, The. FaBoCh
    Hymn to Pan. NOBE; OBEV
    River[-]God's Song, The. NOSC
    Satyr's Song, The ("Softly Gliding as I Go"). NOSC
    (See, the Day Begins to Break.) SCGP
    "Sing his praises that doth keep." NOBE; OBEV
    "Softly gliding I go." NOSC
    (Song: "Do not fear to put thy feet") SCGP

Faithful watcher sits alone, A. Watcher, The. Clara Ann Thompson. CBWP-2

Faithful Wife, A. Chang Chi. OHMPC, *tr. by* Kenneth Rexroth

Faithful Wife, The. Patricia Beer. LW

Faithless Nelly Gray. Thomas Hood. NOBL; NOBRP; UV

Faithless, perverse, and blind. Unbelief. Phoebe Cary. SacPr

Faithless Sally Brown. Thomas Hood. NOBL; OBNV

Faithless Shepherdess, The. *Unknown. See* Unfaithful Shepherdess, The

Faithless Wife, The. Federico García Lorca. BoLoP, *tr. by* A. L. Lloyd

Faithless Wife, The. Federico García Lorca. SpanPo, *tr. by* Robert O'Brien and Robert O'Brien

Faking Boy, The. *Unknown.* RB

Fakir, The. Richard Owen Cambridge. ECEV

Fakir (a religious well known in the East), A. Fakir, The. Richard Owen Cambridge. ECEV

Falcon. Rachel Hadas. ExTi

Falcon, The. Richard Lovelace. CaPo

Falcon and the Dove, The. Sir Herbert Read. FaBoMo

Falcon Drinking. Dimitris Tsaloumas. BMAP

Falcon gone to the gloom. Long Wind, the Dawn Wind. Ezra Pound. APT-1

Falcon hovers at the edge of the sky, A. I Stand Alone. Tu Fu. CrYelRi, *tr. by* Sam Hamill

Falcon soars, The. Angelica the Doorkeeper. *Unknown.* RB, *tr. by* Anne Pennington

Falconry. Anne Wilkinson. MoCV

Falero, lero, loo. (LL) I Loved a Lass. George Wither. NOBE; OBEV; VerBaPo

Falkland at Newbury, 1643. Hugh Conway. EBVV

Fall. Robert Francis. VGW

Fall. George Cabot Lodge. APN-2

Fall. Ferdinand von Saar. AuPH, *tr. by* Lowell A. Bangerter

Fall. Michael Smith. CIP-2

Fall, The. Malak' Abd Al-Aziz. HAWP, *tr. by* Pamela Vittorio

Fall, The. Fergus Allen. ModIr

Fall, The. Michael Anania. IllVoic

Fall, The. Russell Edson. LCAP-2

Fall, The. Sir Richard Fanshawe. NOSC, *tr. by* Sir Richard Fanshawe *Fr.* Il Pastor Fido.

Fall, The. John Kinsella. NeBl

Fall, The. Sarah Maguire. LW

Fall, The. John Wilmot, 2d Earl of Rochester. ChIV-1; EnLoPo

Fall, The. Edmund Waller. NOSC

Fall Again, The. Howard Nemerov. CoAmPo

Fall asleepe, or hearing dye. (LL) John Fletcher. FaBoCh; NOSC *Fr.* King Henry VIII.

Fall Comes in Back-Country Vermont. Robert Penn Warren. VGW

Fall days are not entirely free of heat. Sitting at Night on the Moonlit Terrace. Yang Wan-li. CoBCP, *tr. by* Burton Watson

Fall from these beclouded skies. (LL) One Foot in Eden. Edwin Muir. GTBS-P; NOBE; NoAM

Fall, gáll themsélves, and gásh góld-vermílion. (LL) Windhover, The. Gerard

Manley Hopkins. AmFaPo; CABP; ClHu; EBVV; GTBS-P; HAP; InPK-6; MoBrPo; NAEL-5v2; NAEL-6v2; NIL-7; NOBE; NOBVV; NPeEn; NoAM; NoP-4; OWoS; OxAEP-2; OxBEV; OxBSo; PeECV; PoE; PoPoPo; PoRA; RB; SCGP; SCV; SacPr; TFi; TOF; TRP; UnPo

Fall going. Basho. EH, *tr. by* Robert Hass

Fall golden on the patience of the dead. (LL) Many Are Called. Edwin Arlington Robinson. GI; OxBA

Fall in Long Island. Lake Success. Robert Conquest. OxBC

Fall Is Here, The. Mrs. Henry Linden. CBWP-4

Fall, leaves, fall; die, flowers, away. Song. Emily Jane Brontë. FaBoCh; NPeEn; OxBSP

Fall 1961. Robert Lowell. OBWP; VGW

Fall of Because, The. David Baratier. AmPoNex

Fall of Da Nang, The. Gerald McCarthy. CDa

Fall of Hyperion; A Dream, The. John Keats. NAEL-6v2
    "Then the tall shade, in drooping linens veiled." OxBEV
    "Towards the altar sober-paced I went." TOF

Fall of J. W. Beane, The. Oliver Herford. OBAL

Fall of leaves, The. Shozan. JDP, *tr. by* Yoel Hoffmann

Fall of Leaves, The. Yvor Winters. APT-2

Fall of night. Basho. TAL

Fall of Rock, A. William Plomer. PeSAV

Fall of Rome, The. W. H. Auden. NPeEn; OxBEV; OxBTC; UnPo

Fall of / velvet plum points and umber aureolae, The. Mastectomy. Wanda Coleman. NAAAL

Fall of Zolnok, The. Sebestyén Tinódi. IQMS, *tr. by* George Borrow

Fall, plum petals. Minteisengan. JDP, *tr. by* Yoel Hoffmann

Fall River. David Rivard. PBCAP

Fall River Song. Li Po. CrYelRi, *tr. by* Sam Hamill

Fall silent! Cease to sing your tale. On Mankind. Mihály Vörösmarty. IQMS, *tr. by* Valerie Becker Makkai and Neville Masterman

Fall wind blows through yellow leas, The. Autumn Evening. Adalbert Stifter. AuPH, *tr. by* Lowell A. Bangerter

Fall wind in pinyons. Foster Jewell. HA

Fall winds wail in mulberry branches. Castleside Song. Wang Ch'ang-ling. CoBCP, *tr. by* Burton Watson

Fallen / angels. Homework Assignment on the Subject of Angels. Tadeusz Rózewicz. VCWP

Fallen birch leaf. Virginia Brady Young. HA

Fallen Blossoms. Yang Wan-li. SuSp, *tr. by* Sherwin S. S. Fu

Fallen cold and dead. (LL) Walt Whitman. APN-1; BRP; CBCWP; ChAP; FaBoCh; HHAm; InPK-6; MakPoe; MoAmPo; OBCA; SAmP; TAP; TCAPo; TFi *Fr.* Memories of President Lincoln.

Fallen Elm, The. John Clare. FHYEP

Fallen Flowers. Li Shang-yin. SuSp, *tr. by* James J. Y. Liu

Fallen flowers rise. Haiku: "Fallen flowers rise." Arakida Moritaké. SoSe-8, *tr. by* Harold G. Henderson

Fallen flowers should still be mourned. In Heaven. Ssu-k'ung Shu. SuSp, *tr. by* Irving Y. Lo

Fallen from heaven, lies across. River. Ted Hughes. NAEL-5v2; NAEL-6v2; NoP-4

Fallen horse. Geraldine Clinton Little. HA

Fallen leaves are scattered by evening rain. Regretful Thoughts. Yü Hsüan-chi. BoWoP, *tr. by* Geoffrey Waters

Fallen leaves / Raking. Tan Taigi. ZenPo, *tr. by* Takashi Ikemoto and Lucien Stryk

Fallen on a turf grown green. (LL) Somewhere Or Other. Christina Georgina Rossetti. FaBoVe; NOBE; NOBVV; OxBEV

Fallen petals carpet the garden walk. Tune: "Spring in the Painted Hall." Ch'in Kuan. ColAnChi, *tr. by* Jiaosheng Wang

Fallen petals of red plum. Buson. EH, *tr. by* Robert Hass

Fallen pile! I ask not what has been thy fate. Netley Abbey. William Lisle Bowles. Son

Fallen red blossoms. Buson. SoOfWa, *tr. by* Sam Hamill

Fallen, so freshly fallen. Dragonfly, The. Stanley Kunitz. APT-2

Fallen Star, The. George Darley. OBEV

Fallen Tower of Siloam, The. Robert Graves. ChIV-2

Fallen Yew, A. Francis Thompson. MoBrPo

Fallin' Bobbi Sykes. IBA

Falling. Lesley Dauer. AmPoNex; NAPBL

Falling. James Dickey. LCAP-2; NoAM

Falling. Joy Katz. NeAmPo

Falling Asleep. Siegfried Sassoon. MoBrPo; OxBTC

Falling Asleep over the Aeneid. Robert Lowell. MoAmPo; OxBA

Falling flower, The. Arakida Moritaké. NIL-7, *tr. by* Babette Deutsch

Falling flower, The. Haiku: "Falling flower, The." Arakida Moritaké. SoSe-8, *tr. by* Babette Deutsch

Falling for Jesus. Enid Shomer. OPRER

Falling forever. Oche Iron. Peter Blue Cloud. HATNAP
Falling from a sleeve. Wild Sleeve. Marjorie Welish. FTOS
Falling from the ridge. Yozei Emperor. OHPJ
Falling, I caught the curtain. On the Other Side. Czeslaw Milosz. PoSu, *tr.* by Jan Darowski
Falling in Love after Forty. Ruth L. Schwartz. NeAmPo
Falling in Love at Sixty-Five. Mona Van Duyn. NoP-4
Falling in Love with Love. Richard Rodgers. ReLy
Falling in the wind. Ippu. JDP, *tr.* by Yoel Hoffmann
Falling leaves leave the trees. Poem on Falling Leaves. Liu E. CoBLCP, *tr.* by Jonathan Chaves
Falling Moon. Roberta Hill Whiteman. CDW
Falling separate into the dark. Late at Night. William Stafford. NNaP
Falling Snow. Amy Lowell. ColAP
Falling Star, The. Sara Teasdale. ChAP; OBCA
Falling tears in my heart. Paul Verlaine. SxFrPo, *tr.* by Martin Sorrell
Fallow Deer at the Lonely House, The. Thomas Hardy. AWP; OxBSP; RB; TTTS
Fallow fields, dark pewter sky. Winter Drive. James McAuley. BMAP
Falls from mine eyes, which she dissolves in showers. (LL) Henry Constable. NIL-7; NIP-4; OBGa *Fr.* Diana.
Falls Funeral. John Montague. CIP-2
Falls of Glomach, The. Andrew Young. OxBS
Falmouth. William Ernest Henley. MoBrPo
  (Falmouth.) MoBrPo
Fals fox came unto our croft, The. *Unknown.* MiEL
False Arrest. Cornelius Eady. LTA
False Bay. Frank Templeton Prince. HarvBoo
False beauty who, although in semblance fair. Ballade to His Mistress. François Villon. WeW-3, *tr.* by Norman Cameron
False dreams, all false. Iliad. Humbert Wolfe. MoBrPo
False Enchantment. Jean Starr Untermeyer. MoAmPo
False, ere I come, to two or three. (LL) Song: "Go and catch a falling star." John Donne. AWP; ClHu; EBEV; FHYEP; FSCP; HAP; HeIP-4; InPK-6; NAEL-5v1; NAEL-6v1; NAEL-7v1; NAWM-5v1; NIL-7; NIP-4; NOBE; NOSC; NoP-4; NoSic; OBEV; OxAEP-1; PoE; SoSe-8; TFi; WoPoe
False . . . False. Thurayya Malhas. PoArWo, *tr.* by Nasser Farghaly
False Friends-like. William Barnes. NOBVV; NPeEn; OxBSo
False glozing pleasures, casks of happiness. Dotage. George Herbert. SacPr
False Heart, The. Joseph Hilaire Pierre Belloc. FaBoCh; FaBoEE; OxBSP
  (For False Heart.) MoBrPo
False Knight upon [*or* on] the Road, The. *Unknown.* ESPB
  (False Knight and the Wee Boy, The.) FaBoCh; OxBS; OxBoLi
False life! a foil and no more. Quickness. Thomas Stanley. GeHe; MeLP; NOBE; NOCV; NOSC
False life! a foil and no more, when. Quickness. Henry Vaughan. BBASP
False Love. John Lilliat. EBEV
False Lover Won Back, The. *Unknown.* ESPB; OxBB
False Move. Grace Schulman. ExTi
False [*or* Faulce] hope which feeds but[t] to destroy, and spill. Mary Sidney Wroth, Countess of Montgomery. BASC; NAEL-5v1; NAEL-6v1; NAEL-7v1; PEW *Fr.* Pamphilia to Amphilanthus.
False or true? Ev'ry Time. Ralph Blane. ReLy
False Poets and True. Thomas Hood. CenSon
False Prophet, The. Ernst Waldinger. AuPH, *tr.* by Lowell A. Bangerter
False Report, A. Robert Graves. OxBEV
False Security. Sir John Betjeman. NoAM; NoP-4
False Sir John a wooing came. May Colven [*or* May Colvin]. *Unknown.* OxBB
False Though She Be. William Congreve. BoLoP; NOBE; OBEV; OxBSP
  (Song.) EnLoPo; OxBEV
False world, good night: since thou hast brought. To the World [A Farewell for a Gentlewoman, Virtuous and Noble]. Ben Jonson. BeJo
Falsehood. William Cartwright. OBEV
Falso Brilhante. Nathaniel Mackey. NAAAL
Fam'ly cares call next upon the wife, The. Joanna Baillie. NePenScot *Fr.* Winter Day, A.
Fame. Kahlil Gibran. MAP, *tr.* by Michael Beard and Adnan Haydar
Fame. Josephine D. Henderson Heard. CBWP-4
Fame. Robert Herrick. FaBoEE
Fame. Charlotte Mew. BrRo; HarvBoo; InPK-6; NPeEn; VWP
Fame. Vladimir Vladimirovich Nabokov. TCRP, *tr.* by Vladimir Nabokov
Fame. Virgil [*or* Vergil]. NPeEn; OBVE, *tr.* by John Dryden *Fr.* Aeneid [*or* Eneados, *Aeneis*], The.
Fame and Friendship. Austin Dobson. OBEV
Fame is a bee. Emily Dickinson. NoP-4
Fame is a fickle food. Emily Dickinson. SAmP; TAP

Fame is a food that dead men eat. Fame and Friendship. Austin Dobson. OBEV
Fame, like a wayward girl, will still be coy. John Keats. CenSon *Fr.* Two Sonnets on Fame.
Fame Makes Us Forward. Robert Herrick. CaPo
Fame's pillar here at last we set. Pillar of Fame, The. Robert Herrick. BeJo; CaPo; NIP-4
Fame, wisdom, love, and power were mine. "All Is Vanity, Saith the Preacher." Byron. ChIV-1; TrCP
Famed big-hitter in cricket, A. Limerick: "Famed big-hitter in cricket, A." Douglas Catley. PoCo
Famed Telethusa, of the downtown mob. *Unknown.* PriapPo, *tr.* by Richard W. Hooper *Fr.* Priapus Poems, The.
Familial. Jacques Prévert. CLPP; FaBoWar, *tr.* by Lawrence Ferlinghetti
Familiar. Maria Luisa B. Aguilar-Cariño. ReBoTo
Familiar Epistle, A. Ann Murry. WPE
Familiar Epistle to J. B. Esq, A. Robert Lloyd.
  "Mark yon round parson, fat and sleek." ECEV; OBSV
  Public Schools. NOEC
Familiar Oxen. Oumar Ba. PBMAP
Familiar Poem from Nisa to Fulvia of the Vale. Ann Yearsley. ECWP
Familiar Story. Alan Shapiro. DiPo; NIP-4
Familiar with, the tune. Something I'm Not. Liz Lochhead. NePenScot
Families. Thomas Blackburn. OxBSP
Families, when a child is born. On the Birth of His Son. Su Tung-p'o (Su Shih). AWP; OBVE; WoPoe, *tr.* by Arthur Waley
Family. Nissim Ezekiel. OBCoV *Fr.* Songs for Nandu Bhende.
Family. Josephine Miles. FaBoWP
Family, The. Donna R. Lydston. PoToHe
Family Album. Amos Neufeld. GotH
Family Album, A. Alter Brody. TaR
Family Album, The. Lisa Ress. GotH
Family Cat, The. Roy Fuller. OxBC
Family Circle. János Arany. IQMS, *tr.* by Neville Masterman
Family Conference. John Montague. ModIr
Family Court. Ogden Nash. PeLV
Family Fool, The. Sir William Schwenck Gilbert. NBLV *Fr.* Yeoman of the Guard.
Family Fortunes. Charles Hubert Sisson. OxBC
Family Goldschmitt, The. Henri Coulette. CoAP
Family Grove. Albert Goldbarth. HCAP
Family History. Irving Feldman. VCAP
Family History, The. Nicole Cooley. AmPoNex
Family Is All There Is, The. Pattiann Rogers. NIP-4
Family Jewels. Essex Hemphill. GLP; GT
Family Man, A. Maxine W. Kumin. TAP
Family Man, The. Bruce Dawe. BMAP
Family Name, The. Charles Lamb. CenSon; Son
Family of Love, The. James Philip McAuley.
  Song of Shem. ChIV-1
  "When our beasts low in their stalls." ChIV-1
Family [*or* Familie], The. George Herbert. ESCV
Family Outing—a Celebration. Nicki Jackowska. BrRo
Family Photograph. Gerald Vizenor. VoR
Family Photograph, The. Vona Groarke. MFPA
Family Photograph 1939, A. James Keir Baxter. OxBC
Family Photos: Black and White: 1960. Virginia Cerenio. FSt
Family Portrait. Shuntaro Tanikawa. VCWP, *tr.* by Harold Wright
Family Portraits. Mary E. Tucker. CBWP-1
Family Pride. T. S. Venugopalan. OMIP, *tr.* by Rajagopal Parthasarathy
Family Prime. Mark Van Doren. VGW
Family Procession, A. John Pepper Clark Bekedermo. HBAPE
Family Reunion. Louise Erdrich. HATNAP; NoAM
Family reunion—. Haiku. Lenard D. Moore. SpirFl
Family Reunion—Aunt Vern's Two Cents. Beth Gylys. AmPoNex
Family Romance. Joshua Clover. AmPoNex
Family Romance. Paul Hoover. IllVoic
Family Romance. Larry Levis. BodElec
Family Secrets. Toi Derricotte. SpirFl
Family Secrets. Sharon Kessler. GotH
Family Stories. Dacia Maraini. CItWP, *tr.* by Cinzia Sartini Blum and Lara Trubowitz
Family story tells, and it was told true, The. Funnel. Anne Sexton. MoAmPo
Family tombs, The. Inscribed on Sun An-chih's "Painting of Pines and Catalpas." Chao Meng-fu. CoBLCP, *tr.* by Jonathan Chaves
Family Tree, The. Catalina Cariaga. ReBoTo

Family were gathered, The.   Kisimiso.   Musaemura Bonus Zimunya.
  HBAPE; NAfrP

Family whispers.   Jikko.   JDP, *tr.* by Yoel Hoffmann

Famine.   David Citino.   SpudSo

Famine, The.   Henry Wadsworth Longfellow.   TreFP   *Fr.* Song of Hiawatha,
  The.

Famine Road, The.   Eavan Boland.   FaBoWP

Famine's End.   Judy Longley.   SpudSo

Famished end to my tale this night, A.   Maghnas O Domhnaill.   NOIV

Famished plain, The.   Come Back, Alexander.   Sati Kumar.   OMIP, *tr.* by
  Manohar Bandopadhyay

Famous.   Naomi Shihab Nye.   LoL

Famous Flower of Serving-Men; or, The Lady Turn'd Serving-Man, The.
  Unknown.   ESPB; OxBB

Famous might have been this scholar.   Scholar's Cat, The.   János Arany.
  IQMS, *tr.* by Neville Masterman

Famous monk dropped to this knees before a giant image and cried, A.   Robert
  Glück.   WiU   *Fr.* Visit, The.

Famous philosopher, Kant, The.   Limerick.   C. S. Cook.   PeLi

Famous Tay Whale, The.   William McGonagall.   PeVV
  "And my opinion is that God sent the whale in time of need."   VerBaPo

Famous theatrical actress, A.   Limerick.   *Unknown.*   PeLi

Famous Women—Claudette Colbert.   Kathleen de Azevedo.   ReTh

Famous Writers School Opens Its Arms in the Next Best Thing to Welcome,
  The.   Rosellen Brown.   WWork

Famously she descended, her red hair.   Recollection, A.   John Peale Bishop.
  Son

Fan, The.   Eugenio Montale.   AF, *tr.* by William Arrowsmith

Fan from Korea, A.   Chu Yün-ming.   CoBLCP; ColAnChi, *tr.* by Jonathan
  Chaves

Fan Letter, A.   Amy Gerstler.   BAP-97; BodElec

Fan of smoke in the long, green-white revery of the sky, A.   Death.   Maxwell
  Bodenheim.   APT-1

Fan-Piece, for Her Imperial Lord.   Ezra Pound.   APT-1

Fanaticism? No. Writing is exciting.   Baseball and Writing.   Marianne Craig
  Moore.   BoWoP; FaBoA; MoASP

Fanatics have their dreams, wherewith they weave.   John Keats.   NAEL-6v2

Fancies at Navesink.   Walt Whitman.
  By That Long Scan of Waves.   NAAL-2v1; NAAL-3
  Had I the Choice.   SoSe-8

Fancy.   Robert Creeley.   NOBA

Fancy.   John Keats.   OBEV
  (Realm of Fancy, The.)   GTBS-P

Fancy.   Thomas Moore.   CenSon

Fancy.   Jonathan Smedley.   OxBSP

Fancy, A.   Thomas Carew.   BeJo; NOSC
  (Marke how this polisht Easterne sheet.)   PBRV

Fancy, and I, last Evening walkt.   To Amoret Gone from Him.   Henry
  Vaughan.   BeJo; EnLoPo; MeLP

Fancy and Imagination.   Henrietta Cordelia Ray.   CBWP-3

Fancy Another Day Gone.   Lorine Niedecker.   FTOS   *Fr.* This Condensery:
  The Complete Writing of Lorine Niedecker, 1985.

Fancy Dress.   Dorothea MacKellar.   NOBAu

Fancy in Nubibus.   Samuel Taylor Coleridge.   CenSon

Fancy (quoth he) farewell, whose badge I long did bear.   Green Knight's
  Farewell to Fancy, The.   George Gascoigne.   NoSic

Fancy's Knell.   A. E. Housman.   FaBoCh; PoRA

Fancy, that Sleeping makes us reenjoy.   On my Visitt to WS Which I Dreamt of
  That Night.   Lucy Hutchinson.   EMWP

Fancy the Copt.   Coptic Socks.   Roy Fuller.   OBCoV

Fancy the Sunrise—left the door ajar! (LL)   Emily Dickinson.   APN-2;
  MoAmPo; OxBA; PoRA

Fancy! to thee, I pour a votive strain.   To Fancy.   Martha Hanson.   CenSon

Fane Wald I Luve.   Sir John, of Penicuik Clerk.   OxBS

Fanfare.   U. A. Fanthorpe.   Prnts

Fanfare for the Makers, A.   Louis MacNeice.   NOBE   *Fr.* Autumn Sequel.

FANFARE of drums, wooden bells: iron chapter.   Thunder Can Break.
  Christopher Okigbo.   HBAPE

Fanfare of glory. . . And which of us dares to deny him?, A. (LL)   Tetélestai.
  Conrad Potter Aiken.   APT-1; MoAmPo

Fannie.   Thomas Bailey Aldrich.   OBAL

Fanning away the heat.   Friend Comes to Visit on a Summer Night, A.   Mo
  Shih-lung.   CoBLCP, *tr.* by Jonathan Chaves

Fanny.   Fitz-Greene Halleck.
  "Fanny was younger once than she is now."   CTC
  "We owe the ancients something. You have read."   OBAL

Fanny was younger once than she is now.   Fitz-Greene Halleck.   CTC   *Fr.*
  Fanny.

Fanny's Removal in 1714.   John Winstanley.   NOEC

Fans.   Baron Wormser.   SwNoth

Fans of the oldest living tree.   Wave.   Gregory Orfalea.   GraLe

Fantasia.   Gilbert Keith Chesterton.   SacPr

Fantasia.   Dorothy Livesay.   MoCV

Fantasie Metropolitan.   Janet Holmes.   ExTi

Fantasies of a Love-Thief.   Bilhana.   EroLit, *tr.* by Barbara Stoler Miller
  "Even now."   EroLit, *tr.* by Barbara Stoler Miller

Fantasies of old age.   Merced.   Adrienne Rich.   NOBA

Fantastic!   "Eduard Veniaminovich Limonov."   TCRusP, *tr.* by William
  Tjalsma   *Fr.* Secret Notebook.

Fantastic Rock, The.   Wu Chen.   CoBLCP, *tr.* by Jonathan Chaves

Fantastic Simile, A.   Thomas Lovell Beddoes.   Son

Fantasy.   Gwendolyn B. Bennett.   BlSi

Fantasy.   Gérard de Nerval.   WoPoe, *tr.* by Geoffrey Wagner

Fantasy, A.   Mathilde Blind.   PoBW; VWP; ViWPN

Fantasy of an African Boy.   James Berry.
  "Such a peculiar lot."   EmeKit

Fantasy spaceman, The.   Star Trek III.   Richard Harteis.   GLP

Fantasy under the Moon.   Emmanuel Boundzekei-Dongala.   TTY, *tr.* by Ulli
  Beier and Gerald Moore

Fantasy under the Moon.   Emmanuel Dongala.   PBMAP

Fantoches.   Paul Verlaine.   AWP; OBMV, *tr.* by Arthur Symons

Far across the waves, the wing of a gull.   Voices, The.   Jean-Baptiste Tati-
  Loutard.   PBMAP

Far and near, and now, from never.   Beauty.   Isaac Rosenberg.   TrJP

Far as creation's ample range extends.   Pope.   ECEV   *Fr.* Essay on Man, An.

Far as man can see.   Song of the Rain Chant.   *Unknown.*   AWP, *tr.* by Natalie
  Curtis Burlin

Far Away.   *Unknown.*   FaBoWar

Far Away and Long Ago.   "Rubén Dario."   PFTM-1; SpanPo, *tr.* by Denise
  Levertov

Far away from my heart. (LL)   Nobody Riding the Roads Today.   June Jordan.
  BPo; NoAM

Far away from those.   Only the Sun.   István Sinka.   IQMS, *tr.* by William
  Price Turner

Far away on a state farm called Victory.   Griboyedov's Waltz.   Aleksandr
  Bashlachov [*or* Bashlachev].   TCRP, *tr.* by Sarah W. Bliumis

Far away, still I was with you.   Eugenio Montale.   WoPoe, *tr.* by Dana Gioia
  Fr. Motets, The.

Far away the spring comes down among clustered peaks.   Cold Spring.   Kao
  Ch'i.   SuSp, *tr.* by Irving Y. Lo

Far away, we saw three chimneys in the trees.   Chimneys.   Ruth Bidgood.
  AngWePo

Far back under a ledge.   Elizabeth Searle Lamb.   HA

Far back when I went zig-zagging.   Orion.   Adrienne Rich.   NAAL-2v2; NIP-
  4; NoAM; NoP-4; WPE

Far be remov'd each painted scene!   Invocation. To Horror.   Hannah Cowley.
  NOBRP

Far beyond all the girls of Pirelli.   Limerick.   I. D. M. Morley.   PeLi

Far beyond the chalky pain.   Cyclones.   Anna Hajnal.   IQMS, *tr.* by Laurence
  James

Far brighter than this gaudy melon-flower! (LL)   Home-Thoughts, From
  Abroad.   Robert Browning.   AWP; CABP; ClHu; EBVV; FHYEP; HeIP-
  4; NAEL-5v2; NAEL-6v2; NOBE; NOBVV; NoP-4; OBEV; PoRA; TFi;
  UV

Far but near.   End.   Hugh Seidman.   BodElec

Far cliff Babylon, your natty dread future is a dole card.   Far Cliff Babylon.
  Barry MacSweeney.   Oth

Far Cry after a Close Call, A.   Richard Howard.   UnPo

Far Cry from Africa, A.   Derek Walcott.   AmFaPo; ESEAA; HeIP-4; NAEL-
  5v2; NAEL-6v2; NIL-7; NoAM; NoP-4; TTY; UnPo

Far down, down through the city's great gaunt gut.   Subway Wind.   Claude
  McKay.   APT-1

Far down, in the pool below me.   Seal Cave.   Brenda Chamberlain.   TCAWP

"Far enough down is China," somebody said.   Digging for China.   Richard
  Wilbur.   TwCP

Far, far.   Abba Kovner.   HP, *tr.* by Shirley Kaufman   *Fr.* "My Little Sister."

Far, Far a City Lies.   Abba Kovner.   HP, *tr.* by Shirley Kaufman   *Fr.* 'My
  Little Sister."

Far far away, the Herdboy Star.   *Unknown.*   CoBCP

Far, far, far are my silver waters drawn.   Song of the Oktahutchee.   Alexander
  L. Posey.   APN-2

Far far from gusty waves these children's faces.   Elementary School Classroom
  in a Slum, An.   Stephen Spender.   FaBoMo; MoBrPo; TwCP; UnPo

Far far from here.   Matthew Arnold.   GTBS-P   *Fr.* Empedocles on Etna.

Far, far from home they rode on their excursions.   Two Englishmen.   Douglas
  Stewart.   CBAP

Far, far out lie the white sails all at rest. Ocean Musing, An. Henrietta Cordelia Ray. CBWP-3; SWaP

Far, far sea (its waters blue and cool), The. Robinson Crusoe. Soubhagya Kumar Mishra. OMIP, tr. by Jayanta Mahapatra

Far far the least of all, in want. Prisoners, The. Stephen Spender. FaBoMo; MoBrPo

Far, faraway, steep mountain paths. Shih Te. SuSp

Far Field, The. Theodore Roethke. NAAL-2v2; NoAM

Far Field, The. Theodore Roethke. ColAP; NAAL-2v2; NoAM   Fr. North American Sequence.

Far footfalls died away till none were left. (LL) Ball's Bluff. Herman Melville. CBCWP; FaBoWar; OBWP

Far from a cultural centre he was used. W. H. Auden. NoAM   Fr. Sonnets from China.

Far from Africa: Four Poems. Margaret Danner. BPo
    Garnishing the Aviary. BPo
    "Our moulting days are in the twilight stage." BPo

Far from Home. Nicholas Christopher. NoP-4

Far from Italy, far from my native Tarentum. Leonidas of Tarentum. GrAn

Far from kingdoms. Patrizia Cavalli. NeIt; VCWP, tr. by Judith Baumel

Far from Love the Heavenly Father. Emily Dickinson. APN-2

Far from me and like the stars, the sea, and all the props of poetic legend. If You Knew. Robert Desnos. SurPaPo, tr. by Mary Ann Caws

Far from Our Friends. Jeremy Belknap. AH

Far from our garden at the edge of a gulf. Gulf, The. Denise Levertov. NNaP

Far from the Beach. Alda do Espírito Santo. HAWP, tr. by Jacques-Noël Gouat

Far from the deep roar of the Aegean main. Farewell. Plato. AWP, tr. by Charles Whibley

Far from the happy homeland I adore. (LL) On a Shipmate, Pero Moniz, Dying at Sea. Luis de Camões [or Camões]. OxBEV; PeSAV; WoPoe, tr. by Roy Campbell

Far from the Kingdoms. Patrizia Cavalli. CItWP, tr. by Cinzia Sartini Blum and Lara Trubowitz

Far from the parlour have your kitchen placed. William King. ECEV   Fr. Art of Cookery, The.

Far from the Rappahannock, the silent. Into the Dusk-Charged Air. John Ashbery. APSN

Far from the thronged luxurious town. On Honour. Bernard Mandeville. NOEC

Far from the Vistula, along the northern plain. Auschwitz. Salvatore Quasimodo. AF, tr. by Jack Bevan

Far from the vulgar haunts of men. On the Same. Roy Campbell. OBCoV; OxBTC

Far from the world, O Lord, I flee. William Cowper. SacPr   Fr. Olney Hymns.

Far from this atmosphere that music sounds. Music. Henry David Thoreau. APN-1

Far from thy dearest self, the scope. To His Mistress in Absence. Torquato Tasso. AWP, tr. by Thomas Stanley

Far greater numbers have been lost by hopes. Samuel Butler (1612–80). FaBoEE

Far have I clamored in my mind. Charity and Humility. Henry More. SacPr

Far In. Rachel Loden. PaSH

Far in a western brookland. A. E. Housman. AWP; NPeEn

Far in the east, far below. House Song to the East. Unknown. TTTS

Far in the Heavens my God retires. Incomprehensible, The. Isaac Watts. SacPr

Far in the land of sunny South. Southern Scene, A. Priscilla Jane Thompson. CBWP-2

Far in the past, dimly it comes back to me. White Night. Boris Leonidovich Pasternak. RusPo, tr. by Robert Arthur Douglas Ford

Far in the purple valleys of illusion. Purple Valleys, The. Madison Cawein. APN-2

Far inland from the sea the onion fields. Onion Fields. Robert Francis. APT-2

Far inland / go my sad thoughts. Unknown. BoWoP

Far moon maketh lovers wise, The. Moonlight. Walter De la Mare. EnLoPo

Far o'er the waves my lofty bark shall glide. Describes her Bark. Mary Robinson. CenSon; RWP

Far off a lonely hound. Hounds, The. John Freeman. OBMV; OxBSP

Far-off a young State rises, full of might. Farther. John James Piatt. APN-2

Far off, above the plain the summer dries. Second Air Force. Randall Jarrell. NAAL-2v2; NAAL-5

Far off and deep in woodlands ways. In the Forest of Vaal. János Vajda. IQMS, tr. by Watson Kirkconnell

Far-off / at the core of space. Swan. D. H. Lawrence. PoE

Far off brough, A. Unknown. FaBoVe

Far off I see the River at Meng Ford. Song of the Breaking of the Willow. Unknown. CoBCP; ColAnChi, tr. by Burton Watson

Far-off, most secret, and inviolate Rose. Secret Rose, The. W. B. Yeats. NAEL-5v2; NAEL-6v2

Far-off mountains hide you from me, The. Absent Lover. Unknown. PBA, tr. by A. C. Jordan

Far-Off Rose, A. Josephine Preston Peabody. TCAPo

Far off the sea is grey and still as the sky. Week-End by the Sea. Edgar Lee Masters. MoAmPo

Far, oh, far is the Mango island. Constant Cannibal Maiden, The. Wallace Irwin. OBAL

Far out of sight forever stands the sea. Slow Pacific Swell, The. Yvor Winters. APT-2; ColAP; HarvBoo; NOBA

Far reach. Lorine Niedecker. APT-2

Far Rockaway. Delmore Schwartz. APT-2

Far shore, The. Elizabeth Searle Lamb. HA

Far Side of Introspection, The. Alfred M. [or "Al"] Lee. CoAP

Far Sweeter than Honey. Abraham Ibn Ezra. TrJP, tr. by Israel Abrahams

Far up the dim twilight fluttered. Unknown God, The. "Æ" MoBrPo

Far Up the River. Tu Fu. OHPC, tr. by Kenneth Rexroth

Far up the River—hark! 'tis the loud shock. Flight of Wild Ducks, A. Charles Harpur. NOBAu

Far Within Us. Vasco [or Vasko] Popa.
    "Look that is that uninvited." PoSu
    "Streets of your glances, The." PoSu
    "These are your lips." PoSu

Fara Diddle Dyno. Thomas Weelkes. FaBoCh; OBCoV
    (Madrigal.) OxBoLi; PeLV

Farasa. Nicholas Samaras. TWW

Faraway Landscape. Richard Michelson. GotH

Faraway Places. Walter McDonald. CDa

Farce was ended, The. Get Out of Town. Cole Porter. ReLy

Fare, The. Molly Peacock. ExTi

Fare Thee Well. Byron. NOBRP

Fare Well. Walter De la Mare. GTBS-P; NOBE; NoP-4; OBEV; OxBEV

Fareweel to a' our Scotish fame. Such a Parcel of Rogues in a Nation. Robert Burns. NePenScot; OxBS

Farewel, dear daughter Sara; now Thou'rt gone. In Saram. John Cotton. SCAP

Farewell, this world! I take my leve for evere,—. Unknown. See Farewell, this world! I take my leve for ever

Farewel to the World, A. Michael Wigglesworth. SacPr

Farewel to Worldly Joyes, A. Anne Killigrew. See Farewell to Worldly Joys, A

Farewel ye guilded follies, pleasing troubles. Unknown. MeLP

Farewele Advent; Cristemas [or Christemas] is cum [or come]. Farewell Advent. James Ryman. MiEL

Farewell. Banzan. JDP, tr. by Yoel Hoffmann

Farewell. Robert Fitzgerald. APT-2

Farewell. Enrique Lihn. BLPSL, tr. by Rene de Costa, Rigas Kappatos and Eleni Paidoussi

Farewell. Adriaan Morriën. TuT, tr. by Peter Van de Kamp

Farewell. Ferdinand Raimund. AuPH, tr. by Lowell A. Bangerter

Farewell. Arthur Rimbaud. SxFrPo, tr. by Martin Sorrell

Farewell, A. George Gascoigne. EBEV; HAP; NOBE; SCGP   Fr. Adventures of Master F. I, The.

Farewell, A. Coventry Patmore. BoLoP; EnLoPo; GTBS-P; NOBE; OBEV   Fr. Unknown Eros, The.

Farewell, A. Sir Philip Sidney. NOBE

Farewell! Farewell, The. Letitia [or Laetitia] Elizabeth Landon. VWP

Farewell, A: "Farewell thou little Nook of mountain-ground." William Wordsworth. OBGa

Farewell, A: "My fairest child, I have no song to give you." Charles Kingsley. EBVV

Farewell, A [or The]. Robert Burns. OBEV

Farewell, A: "Venus, take my votive glass." Matthew Prior. See Lady Who Offers Her Looking-Glass to Venus, The

Farewell, A: "What is there left to be said?" Arthur Rex Dugard Fairburn. PeNZ

Farewell, The. Rosario Castellanos. TANSG, tr. by Magda Bogin

Farewell, The. Letitia [or Laetitia] Elizabeth Landon. RWP; WWP

Farewell, The: "Gone, gone,—sold and gone." John Greenleaf Whittier. AWP; NCAP

Farewell, adieu, that courtly life. John Pickering [or Pikerying]. NoSic   Fr. Horestes.

Farewell Advent. James Ryman. MiEL

Farewell and adieu to you noble hearties. Tom Deadlight. Herman Melville. APN-2; NCAP

Farewell and adieu to you, Spanish ladies.   Spanish Ladies.   *Unknown.*
FaBoCh

Farewell!—and never think of me.   Song.   Letitia [*or* Laetitia] Elizabeth
Landon.   VWP

Farewell—and though there be.   Hakusai.   JDP, *tr. by* Yoel Hoffmann

Farewell at the Moment of Parting.   Agostinho Neto.   PBMAP

Farewell awhile, beautiful Italy!   Farewell to Italy.   Frances Anne [*or* "Fanny"]
Kemble.   VWP

Farewell, Captain. In bygone days.   Vladimir L'vovich Korvin-Piotrovsky.
TCRP

Farewell dear babe, my heart's too much content.   In Memory of My Dear
Grandchild Elizabeth Bradstreet Who Deceased August, 1665, Being a Year
and Half Old.   Anne Bradstreet.   BASC; ColAP; NAAL-2v1; NAAL-3;
NAAL-5; NOCV; SCAP; WPE

Farewell, dear love! Since thou wilt needs be gone.   *Unknown.*   NoSic

Farewell, dear scenes, for ever closed to me.   Lines Written upon a Window-
Shutter at Weston.   William Cowper.   NOEC

Farewell, false Friend!—our scenes of kindness close!   Sonnet 019.   Anna
Seward.   CenSon

Farewell, False Love.   Sir Walter Ralegh.   *See* Farewell to False Love, A

Farewell, false love, the oracle of lies.   Farewell to False Love, A.   Sir Walter
Ralegh.   BoLoP; NAEL-5v1; NoSic

Farewell, "Far from the deep roar of the Aegean main."   Plato.   AWP, *tr. by*
Charles Whibley

Farewell, farewell! Before our prow.   Dover to Munich.   Charles Stuart
Calverley.   NOBL

Farewell: "Farewell to the bushy clump close to the river."   John Clare.   NoP-4

Farewell, farewell, Your Royal Highness. (LL)   Luncheon, A.   Max Beerbohm.
NOBL; OBSV; OxBTC; PeLV

Farewell for ever to last night.   Niall Mor MacMuireadach.   NePenScot, *tr. by*
Derick Thomson

Farewell, for Two Years, to England, A. A Poem.   Helen Maria Williams.
RWP

Farewell Frost; or, Welcome the Spring.   Robert Herrick.   CaPo

Farewell! gay Summer! now the changing wind.   On the Approach of Autumn.
Amelia Alderson Opie.   CenSon

Farewell, German radio with your green eye.   Electric Elegy.   Adam
Zagajewski.   VCWP, *tr. by* Renata Gorcyznski

Farewell has long been said; I have forgone thee.   After a Parting.   Alice
Thompson Meynell.   NOBVV

Farewell! I goe to sleep; but when.   Evening-Watch, The.   Henry Vaughan.
ESCV

Farewell, I say, farewell to the incomplete.   Leonid Lavrov.   TCRP   *Fr.* Notes
on the Impossible.

Farewell in a Dream.   Stephen Spender.   MoBrPo

Farewell, incomparable element.   Hymn to Earth.   Elinor Wylie.   MoAmPo

Farewell: "Leave me, my love, it's time to part."   Ibrahim Naji.   MAP, *tr. by*
Issa Boullata and John Heath-Stubbs

Farewell: "Linden blossomed, the nightingale sang, The."   Heinrich Heine.
AWP, *tr. by* John Todhunter

Farewell, love, and all thy law[e]s forever [*or* for ever].   Sonnet: "Farewell,
Love."   Sir Thomas Wyatt.   GSo; NAEL-5v1; NAEL-6v1; NAEL-7v1;
NoSic; OxBSo; SCGP

Farewell my Betty, and farewell my Annie.   Song, A: "Farewell my Betty, and
farewell my Annie."   Christian Carstairs.   ECWP

Farewell: "My boat goes west, yours east."   Ch'ao Li-houa [*or* Chao Li-hua].
BoWoP

Farewell my dearer half, joy of my heart.   First Farewell to J.G G.   "Ephelia."
NOSC

Farewell, my lute!—and would that I.   Letitia [*or* Laetitia] Elizabeth Landon.
RWP; VWP   *Fr.* Improvisatrice, The.

Farewell, my younger brother!   *Unknown.*   APN-2, *tr. by* Washington
Matthews   *Fr.* Mountain Chant, The.

Farewell, my Youth! for now we needs must part.   Ave atque Vale.   Rosamund
Marriott Watson.   NOBE; OBEV

Farewell now, poesy's secret cell, thy ordered grace.   Farewell to Hendre
Fechan.   William Phylip.   OBWVE, *tr. by* H. Idris Bell

Farewell, O Prince, farewell, O sorely tried!   Theodor Herzl.   Israel Zangwill.
TrJP

Farewell of an Old Man.   Tu Fu.   SuSp, *tr. by* Michael E. Workman

Farewell of the Attendant Spirit.   John Milton.   OBEV; OxAEP-1   *Fr.* Comus;
a Masque Presented at Ludlow Castle.

Farewell, old friend, we part at last.   My Old Straw Hat.   Eliza Cook.   BrRo

Farewell once more,—and yet again farewell!   George Henry Boker.   APN-2
Fr. Sonnets: A Sequence on Profane Love.

Farewell Once More to My Friend Yen at Feng Chi Station.   Tu Fu.   OHPC, *tr.*
by Kenneth Rexroth

Farewell Poem.   *Unknown.*   CrYelRi, *tr. by* Sam Hamill

Farewell poor Turkeys I must say. (LL)   Melancholy Lay, A.   Marjory
Fleming.   FaBoCh; NBLV

Farewell, Rewards and Fairies.   Richard Corbet [*or* Corbett].   *See* Proper New
Ballad Entitled [*or* Intituled] The Fairies' [*or* Faeryes] Farewell, or God-a-
Mercy Will, A

Farewell, rewards and fairies [*or* faeries].   Richard Corbet [*or* Corbett].
BASC; BeJo; NOSC; OxBEV; PBRV; PeLV

Farewell Rhyme.   Tu Fu.   CrYelRi, *tr. by* Sam Hamill

"Farewell, Romance!" the Cave-men said.   King, The.   Rudyard Kipling.
CABP

Farewell: "Shores of my native land."   Isaac Toussaint L'Ouverture.   TTY, *tr.*
by Edna Worthley Underwood

Farewell, sire.   Konishi Raizan.   JDP, *tr. by* Yoel Hoffmann

Farewell: "Smell of death was in the air, The."   John Press.   PoRA

Farewell Song.   Ch'in Kuan.   CrYelRi, *tr. by* Sam Hamill

Farewell Song.   Nikolai Mikhailovich Rubtsov.   TCRP, *tr. by* Bradley Jordan
and Katya Zubritskaya

Farewell, sweet boy; complain not of my truth.   Fulke Greville, 1st Baron
Brooke.   Son   *Fr.* Caelica.

Farewell (sweet Cooke-ham [*or* Cookham]) where I first obtained [*or* obtain'd].
Aemilia Bassano Lanyer.   BASC; CABP; NAEL-6v1; NAEL-7v1; NoP-4;
PBRV

Farewell, that was my lef so dere.   *Unknown.*   EMWP

Farewell, the bell upon a ram's neck hung.   Corydon's Farewell, on Sailing in
the Late Expedition Fleet.   *Unknown.*   NOEC

Farewell, then. It is finished. I forego.   Wilfrid Scawen Blunt.   OxBSo

Farewell, this world! I take my leve for ever.   *Unknown.*   MiEL; NPeEn

Farewell! Thou art too dear[e] for my possessing.   William Shakespeare.
CAGL; EBEV; GTBS-P; NAEL-5v1; NAEL-6v1; NOBE; NoSic; OBEV;
OxAEP-1; Son; TFi   *Fr.* Sonnets.

Farewell, thou child of my right hand and joy.   On My First Son[ne].   Ben
Jonson.   AWP; AmFaPo; BASC; BeJo; CABP; ClHu; EBEV; FaBoEE;
HAP; InPK-6; MakPoe; NAEL-5v1; NAEL-6v1; NAEL-7v1; NIL-7; NIP-4;
NOSC; NPeEn; NoP-4; OxBEV; OxBSP; PBRV; PoE; PoPoPo; RB; RaBo;
SCGP; TFi; TRP; WeW-3; WoPoe

Farewell thou little Nook of mountain-ground.   Farewell, A: "Farewell thou
little Nook of mountain-ground."   William Wordsworth.   OBGa

Farewell, thou Thing, time-past so knowne, so dear.   His Farewell [*or* Fare-
well] to Sack.   Robert Herrick.   BeJo; CaPo; NAEL-5v1; NAEL-6v1;
NAEL-7v1

Farewell to a Friend.   Hsüeh T'ao.   SuSp, *tr. by* Eric Johnson

Farewell to a Southern Melody, A.   Huang O [*or* Huang Ho].   BoWoP;
WoPoe, *tr. by* Chung Ling and Kenneth Rexroth

Farewell to Allen University.   Josephine D. Henderson Heard.   CBWP-4

Farewell to America. To Mrs. S. W, A.   Phillis Wheatley.   NoP-4

Farewell to an idea . . . A cabin stands.   Wallace Stevens.   HCAP; PoE   *Fr.*
Auroras of Autumn, The.

Farewell to an idea . . . The mother's face.   Wallace Stevens.   HCAP; PoE   *Fr.*
Auroras of Autumn, The.

Farewell to Anactoria.   Sappho.   AWP, *tr. by* Allen Tate

Farewell to Arms, A.   Aleksandr Petrovich Mezhirov.   TCRP, *tr. by* Deming
Browm

Farewell to Arms, A.   George Peele.   *See* Polyhymnia

Farewell to Autumn.   Oleg Grigorevich Chukhonstev.   TCRP, *tr. by* Simon
Franklin

Farewell to barn and stack and tree.   A. E. Housman.   HarvBoo; MoBrPo;
UnPo

Farewell to Bath.   Lady Mary Wortley Montagu.   WPE

Farewell to "Blessed be."   Shigan.   JDP, *tr. by* Yoel Hoffmann

Farewell to Cupid.   Fulke Greville, 1st Baron Brooke.   Son   *Fr.* Caelica.

Farewell to Dostoevski.   Hugh MacDiarmid.   NAEL-5v2; NAEL-6v2   *Fr.*
Drunk Man Looks at the Thistle, A.

Farewell to English, A.   Michael Hartnett.
"Chef Yeats, that master of the use of herbs."   NOIV
"Gaelic is the conscience of our leaders."   CIP-2
"Half afraid to break a promise."   NOIV
"Her eyes were coins of porter and her West."   ModIr

Farewell to False Love, A.   Sir Walter Ralegh.   BoLoP; NAEL-5v1; NoSic
(Farewell, False Love.)   NAEL-6v1; NAEL-7v1

Farewell to Fan Yun at An Ch'eng.   Shen Yüeh.   OHMPC, *tr. by* Kenneth
Rexroth

Farewell to Florida.   Wallace Stevens.   NoAM

Farewell to Folly.   Robert Greene.
Maesia's Song.   CTC; UnPo
"Sweet are the thoughts that savo[u]r of content."   CTC; UnPo

Farewell to France.   Sarah Hamilton.   CenSon

Farewell to Hendre Fechan.   William Phylip.   OBWVE, *tr. by* H. Idris Bell

Farewell to Hiruharama.   Haere Ra.   James Keir Baxter.   PeNZ

Farewell to Ireland.   Saint Columcille [*or* Columba].   AWP, *tr. by* Douglas
Hyde

Farewell to Italy.   Frances Anne [*or* "Fanny"] Kemble.   VWP

Farewell to Juliet. Wilfrid Scawen Blunt. *Fr.* Love Sonnets of Proteus, The.

Farewell to Juliet ("I see you, Juliet, still, with your straw hat"). Wilfrid Scawen Blunt. BoLoP; EnLoPo; OxBTC *Fr.* Love Sonnets of Proteus, The.

Farewell to Kingsbridge. *Unknown.* ECEV

Farewell to Kurdistan. Rosemary Tonks. OxBTC

Farewell to London in the Year 1715, A. Pope. OBCoV

Farewell to Love. John Donne. BASC

Farewell to Love. Michael Drayton. MakPoe; NOSC *Fr.* Idea.

Farewell to Love. Sir John Suckling. CaPo

(Well-shadow'd landskip, fare ye well.) CavPo

Farewell to Maria. Tadeusz Borowski. HP, *tr. by* Tadeuszt Pióro

Farewell to My Mother. "Placido". TTY, *tr. by* James Weldon Johnson

Farewell to My Scooter. Mbuyiseni Oswald Mtshali. PeSAV

Farewell to New Zealand. Wynford Vaughan-Thomas. NOBL

Farewell to one now silenced quite. Parted. Alice Thompson Meynell. PeVV

Farewell to Russia. Lev Mak. TCRusP, *tr. by* Daniel Weissbort

Farewell to Shen Yueh. Fan Yun. OHMPC, *tr. by* Kenneth Rexroth

Farewell to the bushy clump close to the river. Farewell. John Clare. NoP-4

Farewell to the Court. George Peele. *See* Polyhymnia

Farewell to the Court. Sir Walter Ralegh. NoSic

(Like Truthless Dreams.) Son

Farewell to the Highlands. Robert Burns. *See* My Heart's in the Highlands

Farewell to the Highlands, farewell to the North. Robert Burns. *See* My heart's in the Highlands, my heart is not here

Farewell to the Muse, A. Maria Jane Jewsbury. VWP

Farewell to the world, and to the night farewell. Chikamatsu Monzaemon. WoPoe, *tr. by* Donald Keene *Fr.* Love Suicides at Sonezaki, The.

Farewell to Tobacco, A. Charles Lamb. OxBoLi

Farewell to Van Gogh. Charles Tomlinson. GTBS-P; NoP-4; PoE

Farewell to Várad. Janus Pannonius. IQMS, *tr. by* Adam Makkai

Farewell to Worldly Joys, A. Anne Killigrew. BASC; CABP

(Farewel to unsubstantial joyes.) BoWoP

(Farewell to Worldly Joyes, A.) BoWoP

Farewell to Yin Shu. Li Po. CrYelRi, *tr. by* Sam Hamill

Farewell to You. Elizabeth Alexander. GT

Farewell, too little and too lately known. To the Memory of Mr Oldham. Dryden. AWP; BASC; EBEV; HAP; InPK-6; NAEL-6v1; NAEL-7v1; NIL-7; NIP-4; NOBE; NOSC; NPeEn; NoP-4; OxAEP-1; OxBEV; PAI; PoE; PoPoPo; SCGP; TFi; TRP

Farewell, twin sons of Neokles. On Epicurus and Themistokles. Menander. GrAn, *tr. by* Alan Marshfield

Farewell, ungrateful traitor! Dryden. *See* Farewell ungrateful[l] traitor [*or* traytor], / Farewell my perjured swain

Farewell ungrateful[l] traitor [*or* traytor], / Farewell my perjured swain. Dryden. BoLoP; EnLoPo; HAP; NOBE *Fr.* Spanish Friar [*or* Fryar], The.

Farewell, Unkind! Farewell! to me, no more a father! *Unknown.* EnLoPo

Farewell: "What should I say." Sir Thomas Wyatt. NOBE

(Revocation, A.) OBEV

(What Should I Say.) NoP-4

Farewell, ye blooming fields! ye cheerful plains! Michael Bruce. NOEC *Fr.* Elegy: To Spring.

Farewell, ye coral caves, ye pearly sands. Suspects his Constancy. Mary Robinson. CenSon; RWP

Farewell, ye towering cedars, in whose shade. Determines to Follow Phaon. Mary Robinson. CenSon; RWP

Farewell you everlasting hills! I'm cast. Mans Fall, and Recovery. Henry Vaughan. ESCV

Farewell: "You sang round-dance songs." Liz Sohappy Bahe. CDW

Farewells from Paradise. Elizabeth Barrett Browning. OBEV

Farm, A. A cannon on a hill. Cannon Hill. Sandra Hochman. YaYoPo

Farm and black wood-stack stand, The. Tristitia Ante. Maurice Gilliams. TuT, *tr. by* Sean Dunne

Farm Boy after Summer. Robert Francis. APT-2

Farm boys wild to couple. Sheep Child, The. James Dickey. EmeKit; HCAP; NOBA; NoAM; TAP; VCAP

Farm by the Lake, The. Chu Hsi. OHPC, *tr. by* Kenneth Rexroth

Farm Families. Lu Yu. CoBCP, *tr. by* Burton Watson

"Snug—the robe sewn from coarse cotton." CoBCP

Farm families have few leisure months. Watching the Wheat-Reapers. Po Chü-i. SuSp, *tr. by* Irving Lo

Farm Implements and Rutabagas in a Landscape. John Ashbery. CoAP; HarvBoo; PmAP

Farm never seemed the same after gramps died, The. Memories. Charles Bernstein. BodElec

Farm on the Great Plains, The. William Stafford. HAP; VGW

Farm Picture, A. Walt Whitman. BLT; TRP

Farm Routine. Ch'u Kuang-hsi. SuSp, *tr. by* Joseph J. Lee

Farm Wife. Ellen Bryant Voigt. WWork

Farm within farm, and in the centre, me. (LL) Summer Farm. Norman MacCaig. NPeEn; NePenScot; OxBTC

Farmer. Prince Redcloud. HHAm

Farmer, The. Mary Elizabeth Fullerton. CBAP

Farmer, The. Kees Ouwens. TuT, *tr. by* Peter Van de Kamp

Farmer, The. Fredegond Maitland Shove. SacPr

Farmer, The. Ellen Bryant Voigt. WeW-3

Farmer and the Farmer's Wife, The. Paul Gerhardt Hiebert. NBLV

Farmer and the Raven, The. *Unknown. See* Mischievous Raven, The

Farmer drives by, A. Arizona Zipper. HA

Farmer Goes Beserk. Anne Elder. CBAP

Farmer has got a receipt, but the yamen still presses for tax payment. Fan Ch'eng-ta. SuSp, *tr. by* Wu-Chi Liu *Fr.* Four Songs in Imitation of Wang Chien.

Farmer John. John Townsend Trowbridge. PWR

Farmer Kalligenes sowed his wheat. Astrologer, The. Agathias. GrAn, *tr. by* Guy Davenport

Farmer Nguyen. William Daniel Ehrhart. CDa

Farmer of Tilsbury Vale, The. William Wordsworth. EBEV

Farmer / Pointing the way. Issa. ZenPo, *tr. by* Takashi Ikemoto and Lucien Stryk

Farmer puts his field under the plow, The. Sándor Petőfi. IQMS, *tr. by* Peter Zollman *Fr.* Clouds, The.

Farmer Remembers the Somme, The. Vance Palmer. NOBAu

Farmer's Bride, The. Charlotte Mew. BWW; BoLoP; EBNV; FaBoWP; MoBrPo; NALW; OxBTC; WPE

Farmer's clothes are soaked through and never dried, The. Ise Tayu. WPOW

Farmer's Curst Wife, The. *Unknown.* ESPB

Farmer's goose, who in the stubble, The. Progress of Poetry, The. Jonathan Swift. NOIV

Farmer's Pride, The. *Unknown.* WoPoe, *tr. by* Nguyen Ngoc Bich

Farmer's roadside, The. Basho. SoOfWa, *tr. by* Sam Hamill

Farmer's son is good and mad, The. Recitative. Ronald McCuaig. NOBAu

Farmer's Son Writes from the City, A. Herbert Strutz. AuPH, *tr. by* Lowell A. Bangerter

Farmer's Song at Can Tho. Herbert Krohn. CDa

Farmer's Thoughts, A. Ch'u Kuang-hsi. CoBCP, *tr. by* Burton Watson

Farmer's wife looked out of the dairy, The. Rival, The. Sylvia Townsend Warner. MoBrPo

Farmer say to de weevil, De. Ballet [*or* Ballit] of de Boll Weevil, De. *Unknown.* NOBA

Farmer Seth Atwood was past eighty when. Well, The. Howard Phillips Lovecraft. APT-1

Farmer sleeps under a printed stone, The. Apple-Tree Man, The. Charles Causley. OBSP

Farmer went trotting on [*or* upon] his grey mare. Mischievous Raven, The. *Unknown.* OxNR

Farmer, what's the point complaining. *Unknown.* PriapPo, *tr. by* Richard W. Hooper *Fr.* Priapus Poems, The.

Farmer, worn from, The. Farmer. Prince Redcloud. HHAm

Farmers. Liu Tsung-yüan.

"Beyond the bamboo fence, cooking fire and smoke." SuSp

"By an ancient road, abundant thistle plants." SuSp

Farmers. Thomas Lux. LCAP-2

Farmers. Kathleen Peirce. PBCAP

Farmers are practical people, all right. Music for the Cows. Jim Johnson. MiVo

Farmers on the Gorge lead a hard life. Consoling the Yü Farmers. Fan Ch'eng-ta. SuSp, *tr. by* Wu-Chi Liu

Farmhand lay all hidden, A. Steinmar. GePo

Farmhouse lingers, though averse to square, The. Brook in the City, A. Robert Frost. OxBA

Farming Family Invites the Guest to Stay Overnight, A. Fan Ch'eng-ta. SuSp, *tr. by* Wu-Chi Liu *Fr.* Four Songs in Imitation of Wang Chien.

Farms at Wei River, The. Wang Wei. SuSp, *tr. by* Paul W. Kroll

Farragut, Farragut. William Tuckey Meredith. CBCWP

Farrar! to thee these early lays I owe. Studley Park. John Langhorne. OBGa

Farrell O'Reilly. Oliver St. John Gogarty. OxBTC

Farther. John James Piatt. APN-2

Farther and farther. Lenard D. Moore. HA

Farther east it wouldn't be on the map. Midwest Town. Ruth Delong Peterson. CA

Farther he went the farther home grew, The. For the Grave of Daniel Boone. William Stafford. PAI

Farther than I have been. Kathleen Jessie Raine. OxBS *Fr.* Beinn Naomh.

Farthest from any war, unique in time. Hollywood. Karl Shapiro. OxBA

Farthest Thunder that I heard, The. Emily Dickinson. NAAL-2v1; NAAL-3

Farthing, A. *Unknown.* OxNR

Fascicle 34 Poem 9. Emily Dickinson. PFTM-1
(My Life had stood—a.) PFTM-1

Fascinating Rhythm. George Gershwin. ReLy

Fascinating the way our dreams. In the Chariot Drawn by Dragons. Michael Van Walleghen. IllVoic

Fascination of What's Difficult, The. W. B. Yeats. BIrV; NAEL-5v2; NAEL-6v2; OxAEP-2

Fascist, erect and irate, A. Limerick. Thomas Thorneley. PeLi

Fashion. Ada Cambridge. NOBAu

Fashionable blood. Drip Drip or Not Bloody Likely. Gerda Mayer. PeLV

Fashionable women in luxurious homes. Anti-Suffragists, The. Charlotte Perkins Stetson Gilman. SWaP

Fashioned After the Manner of Master Geoffrey Chaucer in His Assembly of Fowls. Thomas Warton, the Elder. ChIV-1

Fast-Anchor'd Eternal O Love! Walt Whitman. APN-1

Fast asleep on the wooden bench. Warru. Jack Davis. BMAP

Fast Ball. Jonathan Williams. NeAP

Fast Break. Edward Hirsch. DiPo; MoASP; VCAP

Fast breaks. Lay ups. With Mercury's. Slam, Dunk, and Hook. Yusef Komunyakaa. ISC; MoASP

Fast Car On Nebraska I-80: Visting Teacher. Hilda Raz. ExTi

Fast falls the snow, O lady mine. To F. C. Mortimer Collins. NOBVV

Fast Gas. Dorianne Laux. GeoHom

Fast rode the knight. Stephen Crane. NAAL-2v2 *Fr.* War Is Kind.

Fasten the chamber! Bluebeard's Closet. Rose Terry Cooke. APN-2; TCAPo

Faster, Earth, Faster. Juan Ramón Jiménez. SpanPo, *tr. by* Eloise Roach

Faster, earth, faster. Faster, Earth, Faster. Juan Ramón Jiménez. SpanPo, *tr. by* Eloise Roach

Faster I find to the war[re] they arme them. (LL) Bible, *O.T.* BASC; OxBEV, *tr. by* Mary Sidney Herbert, Countess of Pembroke *Fr.* Psalms.

Faster than fairies, faster than witches. From a Railway Carriage. Robert Louis Stevenson. NePenScot

Fastidiously, with gloved and careful fingers. Lady Selecting Her Christmas Cards. Phyllis McGinley. ChrPo

Fat black bucks in a wine-barrel room. Congo, The. Nicholas Vachel Lindsay. APT-1; MoAmPo; NOBA; OxBA; PoRA; TAP

Fat Budgie, The. John Lennon. NBLV

Fat cat came into my drawing room, A. Face to Face. K. V. Tirumalesh. OMIP, *tr. by* A. K. Ramanujan

Fat Chance. Beth Gylys. AmPoNex

Fat friar stroking golf balls, The. Walking along the Hudson. Donald Petersen. CoAP

Fat in America. Heid E. Erdrich. AmPoNex

Fat-kneed god! Feeder of mangy leopards! You Also, Gaius Valerius Catullus. Archibald MacLeish. noAM; TAP

Fat lady, The. Alan Pizzarelli. HA

Fat men go about the streets, The. Ballade of the Poetic Life. Sir John Collings Squire. OBMV

Fat priest, The. Issa. EH, *tr. by* Robert Hass

Fat-tailed Dwarf Lemur, in bed, A. Limerick: "Fat-tailed Dwarf Lemur, in bed, A." Gerry Hamill. PeLi

Fat White Woman Speaks, The. Gilbert Keith Chesterton. OBCoV; UV

Fata Morgana in Flanders. Willem M. Roggeman. TuT, *tr. by* Gabriel Rosenstock

Fatal Birth, The. Ebenezer Elliott. OxBSo

Fatal Dream; or, The Unhappy Favourite, The. Emanuel Collins. NOEC

Fatal Interview. Edna St. Vincent Millay.
Love Is Not All. Son

Fatal Love. Matthew Prior. NBLV

Fatal sisters—death and cards and women, The. Dark Fates, The. Dezső Kosztolányi. IQMS, *tr. by* Lydia Pasternak-Slater

Fatal Volume, The. Marina Ivanovna Tsvetayeva [*or* Tsvetaeva]. GI, *tr. by* Nina Kossman

Fatales Poetae. Henry Parrot. FaBoEE

Fatality. "Rubén Dario." TCLAP, *tr. by* Lysander Kemp

Fatality. D. H. Lawrence. PeECV

Fate. Ralph Waldo Emerson. APN-1; NoP-4 *Fr.* Quatrains.

Fate. Susan Marr Spalding. PoToHe

Fate. Carolyn Wells. SWaP

Fate and the Younger Generation. D. H. Lawrence. OxBoLi

Fate brought three men to birth. Petronius Arbiter. MLL *Fr.* Satyricon.

Fate didn't hustle Gessius to his death. Palladas [*or* Pallades]. GrAn

Fate, give me space to breathe, let me do. Sándor Petőfi. IQMS, *tr. by* Edwin Morgan

Fate in Incognito. Michael Benedikt. OBAL

Fate is a cruel. Fate Is a Cruel and Proficient Potter. Vidya. WoPoe, *tr. by* Andrew Schelling

Fate of Vultures, The. Tanure Ojaide. NAfrP

Fate's sister, fortune, favours those. Christopher Logue. FaBoWar *Fr.* War Music.

Fate / Sent her to me. She's a Latin from Manhattan. Harry Warren. ReLy

Fate to beauty still must give. Epitaph: "Fate to beauty still must give." Claudian. AWP, *tr. by* Howard Mumford Jones

Fateful slumber floats and flows, The. For the Briar Rose. William Morris. NOBVV

Fates of Men (Exeter Book). *Unknown.* AnOE, *tr. by* Charles W. Kennedy

Fates of the Apostles. Cynewulf.
"Now I pray the man who may love this lay." AnOE

Father. Paul Carroll. NeAP

Father. Ralph Dickey. ESEAA

Father. Myra Cohn Livingston. NTCP

Father. Anne Sexton. NAAL-5 *Fr.* Death of the Fathers, The.

Father. John Tripp. TCAWP

Father. John Wheelwright. UnPo

Father. Paul Zweig. BodElec

Father, The. John Donne. NOCV *Fr.* Litany, A.

Father, The. Donald Finkel. PAI

Father, The. Joshua Sylvester. InvLi; SacPr

Father, and bard revered! to whom I owe. Dedicatory Sonnet to S. T. Coleridge. Hartley Coleridge. CenSon; Son

Father and Child. Gwen Harwood. CBAP; WPE

Father and Daughter. Sonia Sanchez. FFC; GT

Father and Daughter. Cathy Song. OpBo

Father and Farther. Sherman Alexie. AmPoNex

Father and I drove to the sand-quarry across the ruined marshlands. Sand-Quarry with Moving Figures. Muriel Rukeyser. NoP-4

Father and I went down to camp. Yankee Doodle. *Unknown.* TCAPo

Father and I went to camp. Royall Tyler. NAAL-3 *Fr.* Contrast, The.

Father and Son. Robert Greacen. PNI

Father and Son. Frederick Robert Higgins. BIrV; OBMV

Father and Son. Stanley Kunitz. AF; TaR; TwCP, *tr. by* Jack Bevan

Father calls me William, sister calls me Will. Jest 'fore Christmas. Eugene Field. ChrPo

Father dead and mother dead. Female Principle, The. Alec Derwent Hope. OxBC

Father dead, loved one dead. Motionless Faces. Carlos Drummond de Andrade. PFTM-1

Father, dear father, come home with me now! Come Home, Father[!]. Henry Clay Work. APN-2

Father, father, where are you going? William Blake. FHYEP *Fr.* Songs of Innocence.

Father from Asia. Shirley Lim. UnSA

Father, grant me yourself from Elysian springs. Publius Papinius Statius. RomPo, *tr. by* W. G. Shepherd *Fr.* Sylvae.

Father grew up here. Red Hills of Home. Chenjerai Hove. HBAPE; NAfrP

Father has a bus'ness. Second Hand Rose. Grant Clarke. ReLy

Father, have pity on me. *Unknown.* NAAL-5 *Fr.* Ghost-Dance Songs.

Father, he cried, after the critics' chewing. Howard Nemerov. GI *Fr.* Gnomes.

Father, Hear the Prayer We Offer. Love Maria Willis. AH

Father heard his children scream. Harry Graham. PeLV *Fr.* Some Ruthless Rhymes.

Father, hello and goodbye. (LL) Elegy: "I know but will not tell." Alan Dugan. NIL-7; NIP-4

Father! I bless thy name that I do live. In Him We Live [& Move & Have Our Being]. Jones Very. APN-1; OxBA

Father, I have launched my bark. Pilgrim, The. Emma Catherine Embury. OBCA

Father, I know that all my life. My Times Are in Thy Hand. Anna L. Waring. PWR; SacPr

Father! I Own Thy Voice. Samuel Wolcott. AH

Father! I wait thy word—the sun doth stand. Son, The. Jones Very. NCAP

Father in heaven, after each lost day. Petrarch. NAWM-5v1; NAWM-7v1, *tr. by* Bernard Bergonzi *Fr.* Sonnets to Laura.

Father in the Railway Buffet. U. A. Fanthorpe. FaBoWP

Father, in Thy Mysterious Presence Kneeling. Samuel Johnson. AH

Father, it was an honor to be there, in the dugout. Poem for My Father; for Quincy Trouppe, Sr. Quincy Troupe. MoASP

Father John's bread was made of rye. Rye Bread. William Stanley Braithwaite. GT

Father Lullabies the Unborn. Sharif Elmusa. GraLe

Father Malloy. Edgar Lee Masters. OxBA *Fr.* Spoon River Anthology.

Father Mat. Patrick Kavanagh. CIP-2; ModIr; PoE

Father, Mother. Father, Mother. Carlos German Belli. TCLAP, *tr. by* Maureen Ahern and David Tipton

Father, Mother, and me. Rudyard Kipling. NoAM *Fr.* Debits and Credits.

Father, 1952. Christopher Buckley. GeoHom

Father! no amaranths e'er shall wreathe my brow. Sara Coleridge. VWP

Father of all! in every [*or* ev'ry] age. Universal Prayer [Deo Opt. Max.], The. Pope. InvLi

Father of Famine. Richard Ryan. PBCIP

Father of heaven, and him, by whom. John Donne. NOCV *Fr.* Litany, A.

Father of Light! great God of Heaven! Prayer of Nature, The. Byron. TreFP

Father of lights! what sunny [*or* sunnie] seed. Cock-crowing. Henry Vaughan. BASC; ESCV; GeHe; NAEL-7v1; NPeEn; PBRV

Father of love! Evening Prayer. Henrietta Cordelia Ray. CBWP-3

Father of My Country, The. Diane Wakoski. NoAM; TAP

Father of My Father. Lawson Fusao Inada. UnSA

Father of Rivers! standing by thy side. Richard Henry Wilde. APN-1 *Fr.* Hesperia.

Father of the Faithful said, The. Christopher Smart. ChIV-1 *Fr.* Hymns for the Amusement of Children.

Father of the Man. David Graham. SwNoth

Father of the Stethoscope, The. Back-Up Singer, The. Dorothy Barresi. SwNoth

Father of Women, A [Ad Sororem E. B.]. Alice Thompson Meynell. BrRo; NALW; VWP; WPE

Father, on the first day on the Hunting Moon. First Day of the Hunting Moon, The. Patricia Low. VGW

Father or Son. James Schuyler. FTOS

Father Poem. Joel Oppenheimer. PoM

Father Riley's Horse. Andrew Barton Paterson. NOBAu

Father's Belt. Shalin Hai-Jew. FSt

Father's Day. Gloria Vando. TouFir

Father's Death, A. John Hewitt. PNI

Father's gone a-flailing. *Unknown.* OxNR

Father's Hymn for the Mother to Sing. George Macdonald. SacPr

Father's Love, The. Mary E. Tucker. CBWP-1

Father's sickle is hanging. *Unknown.* WoPoe, *tr. by* Siv Cedering Fox *Fr.* Two Swedish Riddles.

Father's Testament, A. Judah ibn Tibbon. TrJP, *tr. by* Israel Abrahams

Father's Things. R. V. Bailey. Prnts

Father sat by the chimney-post, A. Good and Better. *Unknown.* TreFP

Father says so—E'yayo!, The. *Unknown.* NAAL-5 *Fr.* Ghost-Dance Songs.

Father says so, the father says so, The. (LL) *Unknown.* NAAL-5; TCAPo *Fr.* Ghost-Dance Songs.

Father-Sequence. Luigi Fontanella. NeIt, *tr. by* Michael Palma

Father Short came down the lane. *Unknown.* OxNR

Father Son and Holy Ghost. Audre Lorde. ESEAA; NAAAL; NoAM

Father studied theology through the mail. Book Full of Pictures, A. Charles Simic. NoP-4

Father, this year's jinx rides us apart. All My Pretty Ones. Anne Sexton. NAAL-2v2; NoAM

Father! Thy wonders do not singly stand. Spirit Land, The. Jones Very. HAP

Father! Thy wonders do not singly stand. God Not Afar Off. Jones Very. InvLi

Father was a serf, seldom came home at night. Self-Portrait. So Chong-Ju. WoPoe, *tr. by* Peter H. Lee

Father was to her, and to me. Fever. Judith Ortiz Cofer. PueRic

Father, when I am in my grave, kind Father. Christina. Dora Greenwell. VWP

Father, who designs his babe a priest, The. William Cowper. OBSV *Fr.* Tirocinium; or, A Review of Schools.

Father, Who Mak'st Thy Suff'ring Sons. Arthur Cleveland Coxe. AH

Father, whom I murdered every night but one. Elegy for My Father. Howard Moss. CoAP

Father! whose hard and cruel law. Death of Grant, The. Ambrose Bierce. CBCWP

Father will descend, The. *Unknown.* APN-2, *tr. by* James Mooney *Fr.* Ghost-Dance Songs.

Father William. Lewis Carroll. ChAP; NOBL; NOBVV; NPeEn; OBCoV; OxBEV; PoRA; TFi; UnPo *Fr.* Alice's Adventures in Wonderland.

Father, you must have been. Offering. Thomas McGrath. RaBo

Father, you turn your hands toward me. Father from Asia. Shirley Lim. UnSA

Father, your hallowed ghost. Stopping at the Mayflower. Joseph Awad. GraLe

Fatherhood. Joan Waddleton. Prnts

Fatherland in the Heights. Gyula Illyés. IQMS, *tr. by* Vernon Watkins

Fatherland Song. Bjørnstjerne Bjørnson. AWP, *tr. by* William Ellery Leonard

Fatherless boy, thirteen, walks and weeps, The. Ballad of the Fatherless Boy. Wang Chiu-ssu. CoBLCP, *tr. by* Jonathan Chaves

Fathers. Robert Creeley. FTOS

Fathers, The. Edwin Muir. OxBS

Fathers and Sons. Tom Leonard. CABP; NePenScot

Fathers: naked, you stand for their big faces. This Is a Poem for the Dead. Michael Ryan. YaYoPo

Fatigue. Joseph Hilaire Pierre Belloc. NBLV; NOBL; OxBTC; UV

Fatima. Laura Kasischke. AmPoNex

Fatima. Tennyson. UnPo

Fatness. Alan Ansen. CoAP

Fatted on herbs, swollen on crabapples. Porcupine, The. Galway Kinnell. NAAL-5; NOBA

Faucet she is dripping, The. Mañana (Is Soon Enough for Me). Peggy Lee. ReLy

Fault, The. Carol Muske. GeoHom

Fault of the Age, The. Ella Wheeler Wilcox. PWR

Faun, The. Ezra Pound. FaBoCh; FaBoTw

Faun Sees Snow for the First Time, The. Richard Aldington. MoBrPo

Fause Foodrage. *Unknown.* ESPB
   (Fa'se Footrage.) OxBB

Faust. John Ashbery. TwCP

Faust. Goethe.
   "All that is past of us." WoPoe, *tr. by* Louis MacNeice
   "Castles with lofty." AWP, *tr. by* Bayard Taylor
   Christ Is Arisen. TrCP, *tr. by* Bayard Taylor
   Mystical Chorus. WoPoe, *tr. by* Louis MacNeice
   Prologue in Heaven.
      Chorus of the Archangels, The. AWP; OBVE
   Soldier's Song. AWP, *tr. by* Bayard Taylor

Faust's Servant. Roy Fuller. OxBTC

Faustina hath a spot upon her face. De Naevo in Facie Faustinae. Thomas Bastard. FaBoEE

Faustina, if that was your name, you are dead. Elegy for Faustina. Fergus Allen. ModIr

Faustina, or Rock Roses. Elizabeth Bishop. FaBoMo

Faustus. Alec Derwent Hope. NOBAu

Faustus Triumphant. Thom Gunn. FaBoMo

Fauviste. Donald Revell. BodElec

Favn in the Afternoon, A. Stéphane Mallarmé. SxFrPo, *tr. by* E. H. Blackmore and A. M. Blackmore

Favola di Orfeo. Angelo [*or* Andrea] Poliziano.
   "What song will ever be so sorrowful." CAGL, *tr. by* Elizabeth Basset Welles

Favored by Heaven are those, ordained to taste. Sonnet Introductory. Mary Robinson. CenSon; RWP

Favorite Flower, The. Celia Laighton Thaxter. AiP

Favorite Grandson Braid. Phillip [*or* "Phil"] William George. VoR

Favorite Little Shrine, A. Enrique Lihn. VCWP

Favorite Slave's Story, The. Priscilla Jane Thompson. CBWP-2; RACG

Favour. Robert David Fitzgerald. CBAP

Favourite Swain, The. Elizabeth Hands. WoRP

Favourite Village, The. James Hurdis.
   "Forth goes the weeding dame; her daily task." ECEV
   Peasants at Work. ECEV

Fawn frolics, A. Chiyojo [*or* Chiyo *or* Chiyo-Ni *or* Kaga no Chiyo *or* Fukuda Chiyo-Ni]. JDP, *tr. by* Yoel Hoffmann

Fawn in the Snow, The. William Rose Benét. MoAmPo

Fawn's Foster-Mother. Robinson Jeffers. NOBA; NoAM

Fawnia. Robert Greene. OBEV

Fayre is my love, when her fayre golden heares. Edmund Spenser. *See* Fair [*or* Fayre] is my love, when her fair [*or* fayre] golden heares

Fayre Summer droops, droope men and beasts therefore. Thomas Nashe [*or* Nash]. *See* Fair summer droops, droop men and beasts therefore

Fazal / all eyes on the clock. Fazal. Chiqui Vicioso. TANSG, *tr. by* Emma Jane Robinett

FB Eye Blues, The. Richard Wright. APT-2

Fear. Marjorie Agosin. ExTi

Fear. Devdas Chhotray. OMIP, *tr. by* Jayanta Mahapatra

Fear. Anna Hajnal. BoWoP, *tr. by* Daniel Hoffman

Fear. George Oppen. BodElec

Fear. Thomas Love Peacock. VoR

Fear. Eva Picková. INSAB; ItWoWo

Fear. Charles Simic. HCAP; WeW-3

Fear, A. Francis Ledwidge. NOIV

Fear, The. Lascelles Abercrombie. OBMV

Fear 2. Marjorie Agosin. ExTi

Fear and Anger in the Mindless Universe. Hayden Carruth. NNaP

Fear and dreams. Rest Is Grace, The. János Pilinszky. IQMS, *tr. by* Adam Makkai

Fear and the Monkey. William S. Burroughs. PFTM-2

Fear, as I see the spring go. Kuan Han-ch'ing. SuSp *Fr.* Tune: "Green Jade Flute."

Fear death?—to feel the fog in my throat. Prospice. Robert Browning. FHYEP; ITBLP; NAEL-5v2; NAEL-6v2; PoRA; TrCP

Fear (Extracts). Yevgeny Aleksandrovich Yevtushenko [*or* Evtushenko]. RusPo, *tr. by* Robert Arthur Douglas Ford

Fear God—obey his just decrees. Christopher Smart. ChIV-1 *Fr.* Hymns for the Amusement of Children.

Fear it has faded and the night. Schoolgirls Hastening. John Shaw Neilson. NOBAu

Fear, jealousy and murder are the same. Gamecock. James Dickey. UnPo

Fear me, virgin whosoever. Herman Melville. *See* Behind the house the upland falls

Fear / nested. Fear. Marjorie Agosin. ExTi

Fear no longer for the lone grey birds. End of the Flower World (A.D. 2300). Stanley Burnshaw. APT-2; TrJP

Fear No More the Heat o' the Sun. William Shakespeare. *See* Cymbeline

Fear not, dear love, that I'll reveal. Secrecy [*or* Secresie] Protested. Thomas Carew. CaPo

Fear Not: For They That Be With Us. Jones Very. ChIV-1

Fear Not, Poor Weary One. Thomas Cogswell Upham. AH

Fear not, shepherds, for I bring. Angel's Song. Charles Causley. OBCP

Fear of Death. John Ashbery. FaBoMo; TAP

Fear of death disturbs me constantly, The. Prayer. Gabrielle de Coignard. WPOW, *tr. by* Raymond Oliver

Fear of loneliness, the wish, The. Price, The. Anne Stevenson. DiPo

Fear of Madness, The. Lucretia Davidson. TCAPo

Fear of poetry is the, The. Reading Time : 1 Minute 26 Seconds. Muriel Rukeyser. NIL-7

Fear of Shoplifting. Maureen Seaton. FFC

Fear of Subways. Maureen Seaton. FFC

Fear of the Earth. Alex Comfort. MoBrPo

Fear of the Future. Gillian Ferguson. NeBl

Fear of the Lord, The. Bible, *O.T.* TrJP *Fr.* Proverbs.

Fear Test: Integrity of Heroes. James Simmons. CIP-2

Fear the one who has sharp weapons. Song of the Lioness for Her Cub. *Unknown.* BoWoP

Fear turns objects over in the darkness. Anna Andreyevna Akhmatova. ARWW, *tr. by* Catriona Kelly

Fear ws no longer that continuous presence that took pleasure in appropriating our surroundngs. Fear 2. Marjorie Agosin. ExTi

Feare no more the heat o'th'Sun. William Shakespeare. *See* Fear no more the heat o' the Sun

Feare not, litle flocke, for it is your fathers good pleasure to give you the kingdome. Bible, *N.T.* OBVE *Fr.* St. Luke.

Fearful night sinks, The. Hymn to the Sun. *Unknown.* TTTS

Fearful of beauty, I always went. Enamel Girl, The. Genevieve Taggard. MoAmPo

Fearful the chamber's quiet; the veiled windows. Development of Idiotcy, A. Ebenezer Jones. PeVV

Fearful Women. Carolyn Kizer. ExTi

Fearless One. Genrik Veniaminovich Sapgir. TCRP, *tr. by* Albert C. Todd

Fears and sorrows of this day, The. (LL) Lucasia, Rosania and Orinda Parting at a Fountain, July 1663. Katherine Philips. EMWP; PEW

Fears and Tears. *Unknown.* ReMoGo

Fears any one his bride lest she a virgin be not. Reasons for and against Marrying Widows. Henricus Selyns. SCAP

Fears in Solitude. Samuel Taylor Coleridge. FHYEP; OBWP
"Thankless too for peace." FaBoWar

Fears of the Eighth Grade. Toi Derricotte. GT

Feast, The. Robert Duncan. APSN *Fr.* Passages.

Feast and noon grew high, and Sacrifice, The. John Milton. EBEV *Fr.* Samson Agonistes.

Feast Day. W. S. Merwin. BodElec

Feast o' Saint [*or* St.] Stephen, The. Ruth Sawyer. OBCP

Feast of Blood, The. Joseph Fawcett. NOEC *Fr.* Art of War, The.

Feast of San Silvestro, The. V. Penelope Pelizzon. AmPoNex

Feast of St. Tortoise, The. Nancy Willard. LCAP-2

Feast of Stephen, The. Anthony Hecht. HAP; NoAM; VCAP

Feast of Stephen, The. Kevin Nichols. OBCP

Feast of the dead. Shinga. JDP, *tr. by* Yoel Hoffmann

Feast of the Monkeys, The. John Philip Sousa. OBAL

Feast of the Ram's Horn. Harvey Shapiro. VGW

Feast's begun / And the wine is done, The. Water Song. Solomon ibn Gabirol. TrJP, *tr. by* Israel Abrahams

Feastful sight, A. Rain at Noon-time. Molara Ogundipe-Leslie. HAWP

Feasting with Etang a Hundred Times Around. Al Robles. ReBoTo

Feasts, The. Boris Leonidovich Pasternak. TCRP, *tr. by* Yakov Hornstein

Feasts of Death, Feasts of Love. Stuart Z. Perkoff. NeAP

Feat of Gardening, The. John Gardner.
Feat of Gardening, The. OBGa
"How so well a gardener be." OBGa

Feat of Gardening, The. John Gardner. OBGa *Fr.* Feat of Gardening, The.

Feather, The. Lilian Bowes-Lyon. LW

Feather, The. Vernon Watkins. FaBoTw

"Feathered fowl's in your orchard, father, A." Brown Robin. *Unknown.* ESPB

Feathered songster chaunticleer, The. Bristowe Tragedie: or, The Dethe of Syr Charles Bawdin. Thomas Chatterton. OxBB

Feathered Dances. Kenward Elmslie. PmAP

Feathered discs of asters trace, The. Maritime Pastoral. Ted Benttinen. PoCoUp

Feathered Robe, The. Gary Snyder. BodElec

Feathers. Jayne Cortez. SurWo

Feathers blacken against the sun. Manifest Destiny. Anita Endrezze. CDW

Feathers fan the spade. Nearness. David Lindley. NLP

Feathers in a fan, The. Man. Humbert Wolfe. MoBrPo

Feathers of the willow, The. Song. Richard Watson Dixon. FaBoCh; GTBS-P; NOBE

Feathers or Lead? James Richard Broughton. NeAP

Feathers up fast, and steeples; then in clods. Fountain, The. Donald Davie. GTBS-P; NoP-4; OxBTC

Feathery forests are blown back, frost rends, The. Winter. John Lyle Donaghy. BIrV

Feats of Arms, and famed heroick Host, The. Luis de Camões [*or* Camões]. FaBoWar, *tr. by* Richard Burton *Fr.* Lusiads, The.

February. John Clare. NOBE *Fr.* Shepherd's [*or* Shepheards] Calendar, The.

February. John Heath-Stubbs. OBCP

February. Lisa Lewis. BodElec

February. W. S. Merwin. NNaP

February. Henrietta Cordelia Ray. CBWP-3

February. Folgore da San Geminiano [*or* Gimignano]. EaItPo, *tr. by* Dante Gabriel Rossetti *Fr.* Sonnets of the Months.

February. James Schuyler. NeAP

February. Berthold Viertel. AuPH, *tr. by* Lowell A. Bangerter

February 8, 1980: And No One Has Warned Me. Stanislaw Baranczak. AF, *tr. by* Magnus J. Krynski

February 11, 1977. Frederick Morgan. DiPo

February Afternoon. Edward Thomas. NoAM; PeFWW; PoWW

February Days. May Sarton. APT-2

February Evening in Boston, 1971. Denise Levertov. TaR

February Evening in New York. Denise Levertov. NoAM

February, from a nook in the wall. Seasons. Giampiero Neri. ItPo, *tr. by* Gayle Ridinger

February. Get your ink and weep. Boris Leonidovich Pasternak. TCRP

February Ground. Edward Dahlberg. APT-2

February Ice Years. Melinda Goodman. WiU

February in Sydney. Yusef Komunyakaa. ESEAA; NAAAL

February is the love and wrath of weather. Blizzard. Bella [*or* Izabella] Akhatovna Akhmadulina. TCRP, *tr. by* Albert C. Todd

February Morning. King D. Kuka. VoR

February Park. Gerald Vizenor. VoR

February: Pemaquid Point. Ira Sadoff. PoSol

February's Forgotten Mitts. Raymond Knister. NOBC

February 17th. Ted Hughes. NPeEn

February Sun. Paul Rodenko. TuT, *tr. by* Mary E. O'Donnell

February; the Boy Breughel. Norman Dubie. LCAP-2

February: Thinking of Flowers. Jane Kenyon. LoL

February Twilight. Sara Teasdale. OBCA

Feckless Dinner-Party, The. Walter De la Mare. FaBoTw

Fed back to the dot. Loopy Dupes. Andrew Crozier. Oth

Fedele and Fortunio. Anthony Munday.
I Serve a Mistress. HAP; SCGP

Federation. W. T. Goodge. NOBAu

Fee, fi, fo, fum. *Unknown.* OxNR

Feeble Little Voice: All It Takes Is Barely Opening the Shutter, A. Amelia Roselli. CItWP, *tr. by* Cinzia Sartini Blum and Lara Trubowitz

Feed, silly sheep, although your keeper pineth. William Smith. Son *Fr.* Chloris [*or* the Complaint of the Passionate Despised Shepheard].

Feed still thy self, thou fondling, with belief. *Unknown.* NoSic

Feed the Mexican Back into Her. Cherríe Moraga. GLP

Feed them with red flamboyán. Take the Hearts of Children. Sandra Maria Esteves. PueRic

Feed Thou my feeble shoots. (LL) Long Barren. Christina Georgina Rossetti. TrCP; ViWPN

Feeder is red with sugared water, The. Chuparosa. Juan Delgado. AmPoNex

Feeding, The. Lou Lipsitz. CDa

Feeding, The. Joel Oppenheimer. NeAP

Feeding a Child. Nuala Ni Dhomhnaill. CIP-2, *tr. by* Michael Hartnett

Feeding Ducks. Norman MacCaig. HarvBoo; OxBS

Feeding Frenzies. C. G. Hanzlicek. GeoHom

Feeding Ground. Thomas McCarthy. CIP-2

Feeding the Bat. Hilary Llewellyn-Williams. TCAWP

Feeding the Dog. Russell Edson. RaBo

Feeding the Dove. Velemir [*or* Viktor Vladimirovich] Khlebnikov. TCRP, *tr. by* Gary Kern

Feeding the Sun. Bill Knott. PBCAP

Feel and hear. Billie Holiday. Sterling Plumpp. IllVoic

Feel for your bad fall how could I fail. Sympathy, A Welcome, A. John Berryman. NoP-4

Feel Free. Natasha Tarpley. ISC

Feel my eye breaking. (LL) Window, The. Robert Creeley. FTOS; NOBA; NoAM; PmAP; TAP; VGW

Feel of Hands, The. Thom Gunn. OxBEV

Feel the sharpness. Meeting, The. Ramona Wilson. VoR

Feel their age, and sigh for liberation. (LL) Seed-Picture, The. Medbh McGuckian. Modlr; PNI

Feel, you said. How does this feel? On the Line. Ruth Padel. MFPA

Feelin' fine, feelin' great. Haven't Got a Worry. Ray Evans. ReLy

Feeling. Bolivia: Another End of Ace. Tom Raworth. PFTM-2

Feeling, The. William Bronk. VGW

Feeling and Form. Marilyn Hacker. NoAM

Feeling constricted by the dusty city. In the Second Month of Summer, Taking My Family to the Villages East of the City. Li K'ai-hsien. CoBLCP, *tr. by* Jonathan Chaves

Feeling down. No One to Guide Us. Charmaine Papertalk-Green. IBA

Feeling Fucked/Up Up. Etheridge Knight. GT; NNaP; PBCAP; RaBo

Feeling Her End Would Come with Summer's End. Rosalía de Castro. SpanPo, *tr. by* Kate Flores

Feeling it with me. Walking on Water. James Dickey. ChIV-2

Feeling its way to air. (LL) South Country. Kenneth Slessor. BMAP; CBAP

Feeling Jon is far more anxious for her, A. Group. John Berryman. BodElec

Feeling my face has the terrible shine of fish. Element. Patricia K. Page. MoCV

Feeling Old Age. Liu Tsung-yüan. SuSp, *tr. by* Jan W. Walls

Feeling Sorry for Myself. Lu Yu. CoBCP, *tr. by* Burton Watson

Feeling that it is vaguely undignified. Science and Human Behavior. John Hollander. YaYoPo

Feeling the Itch. Fêng Mêng-lung. ColAnChi; WoPoe, *tr. by* Richard W. Bodman *Fr.* Mountain Songs.

Feeling the urge my mother. Birth. Edith Bruck. BoWoP, *tr. by* Ruth Feldman

Feeling Type and His Friends, The. Michael Davidson. FTOS

Feelings Come As I Pass through Wu-chiang. Wu Wei-yeh. CoBLCP, *tr. by* Jonathan Chaves

Feelings go up into the air, The. Some Feelings. Michael Benedikt. CoAmPo

Feelings I don't have I don't have, The. To Women, as Far as I'm Concerned. D. H. Lawrence. NPeEn; OxBSP; RaBo

Feelings of a Republican on the Fall of Bonaparte. Shelley. CenSon; Son

Feelings Wakened by a Mirror. Po Chü-i. CoBCP, *tr. by* Burton Watson

Feels the dampness of the garden like a caress. (LL) Poem: "We think to create festivals." Antonio Machado Ruiz. AWP; WoPoe, *tr. by* John Dos Passos

Feet and butthole. I love. Rosie. Andrew Hudgins. Unle

Feet covered with mud, the smell of meat on their breath. Making Fun of the Well at the Inn below the Mountain. Chu Yün-ming. CoBLCP, *tr. by* Jonathan Chaves

Feet incorrigible / ragging the world. (LL) E. E. Cummings. NBLV; OxBA

Feet O' Jesus. Langston Hughes. ISC

Feet of morning the feet of noon and the feet of evening, The. Domestic Stones (fragment), The. Hans [*or* Jean] Arp. SPE, *tr. by* David Gascoyne

Feet of Spring Are on the Stair, The. Rosalía de Castro. NAWM-7v2, *tr. by* S. Griswold Morley

Feet of spring are on the stair, the. Feet of Spring Are on the Stair, The. Rosalía de Castro. NAWM-7v2, *tr. by* S. Griswold Morley

Feet pulled in, sparrow dead. Sparrow in Withered Field. Shinkichi Takahashi. ZenPo, *tr. by* Takashi Ikemoto and Lucien Stryk

Felicitous Life, A. Czeslaw Milosz. PoSu

Felicitous phenomenon! (LL) O to be a Dragon. Marianne Craig Moore. APT-1; CTC; ChIV-1; NAAL-5; NALW

Felicity. Isaac Watts. SacPr

Felicity the healer isn't young. Doctor Frolic. Robert Pinsky. NoAM

Feliks Skrzynecki. Peter Skrzynecki. CBAP

Felines. Daria Menicanti. CItWP, *tr. by* Cinzia Sartini Blum and Lara Trubowitz

Felipa, La Filosofa de Rincon que Nació a los 98 Años. Jose Angel Figueroa. PueRic

Felix Holt, the Radical. "George Eliot."
  "Why, there are maidens of heroic touch." LW
  "This man's metallic; at a sudden blow." LW

Felix Randal. Gerard Manley Hopkins. EBEV; EBVV; FaBoMo; FaBoVe; GTBS-P; HAP; MoBrPo; NAEL-5v2; NAEL-6v2; NOBE; NoAM; NoP-4; OBEV; OxAEP-2; OxBSo; PeECV; PoE; PoRA; SCGP; Son; TFi; WeW-3; WoPoe
  (Felix Randal the farrier, O is he dead then?) PoPoPo
  (Felix Randal the farrier, O he is dead then? my duty all ended.) CABP

Felix White Sr.'s Introduction to Wakjankaga. *Winnebago Oral Tradition.* NAAL-5

Felixstowe, or, The Last of Her Order. Sir John Betjeman. OxBTC

Fell fast I loitered still. (LL) Apple Gathering, An. Christina Georgina Rossetti. NAEL-5v2; NAEL-6v2

Fell the edge of the knife. Shoriken. Charles Brasch. PeNZ

Fell through the parlor floor today. (LL) Termite, The. Ogden Nash. KaS; OBCA

Felled Plane Tree, The. Anna Hajnal. BoWoP, *tr. by* William Jay Smith

Felling a tree. Basho. EH, *tr. by* Robert Hass

Felling a Tree. Ivor Gurney. FaBoVe

Fellow countrymen. He Was a Man of Jokes outside Office. Oswald Basize Dube. PeSAV

Fellow from far Erewhon, A. Limerick: "Fellow from far Erewhon, A." W. F. N. Watson. PeLi

Fellow has a screw loose, The. Conversation with a New York Poet. Lev Vladimir Loseff [*or* Losev]. TCRusP, *tr. by* Henry Pickford

Fellow Mortal, A. John Masefield. OxAEP-2

Fellow-trees, bell so frail and brown. Forest Divers. Frank O'Hara. BodElec

Fellow who fucked but as few can, A. Limerick. *Unknown.* PeLi

Fellow who sits in the air-conditioned office, The. At the Back of Progress. . . . Taslima Nasrin. VCWP

Fellow, you have no flair for art, I fear. Sitting Bard, The. Sir Owen Seaman. NOBL

Fellows, if you're on. Nagasaki. Harry Warren. ReLy

Fellowship. "Michael Field." VWP

Felo de Se. Thomas Blackburn. OxBTC

Felo de Se. Richard Hughes. OBMV

Felo de Se. Amy Levy. VWP

Felt for thee as a lover or a child! (LL) England, 1802, V. William Wordsworth. GTBS-P; OBEV

Feltons Epitaph. *Unknown.* NPeEn; PBRV

Felucca and Pinnace. Waterfront Girls, The. Rufinus. GrAn, *tr. by* Alan Marshfield

Female. Muhammad Al-Ghuzzi. MAP; NAfrP, *tr. by* John Heath-Stubbs and May Jayyusi

Female Advocate Or, An Answer to a Late Satyr*, The. Sarah Fyge Egerton.
  "Blasphemous wretch! How canst thou think or say." PEW

Female and the Silence of a Man, The. June Jordan. NAAAL

Female Dancer. James Camp. Son

Female Figure. Olga Sedakova. ItGoST, *tr. by* Catriona Kelly

Female Genitals, The. Gwerfyl Mechain. EroLit, *tr. by* Dafydd Johnston

Female giants, fauna of women. Women of Rubens, The. Wislawa Szymborska. WPOW, *tr. by* Celina Wieniewska

Female God, The. Isaac Rosenberg. FaBoTw

Female is fertile, and discipline, The. Praise for Sick Women. Gary Snyder. NeAP

Female mind like a rude fallow lies, A. Anne Ingram, Viscountess Irwin. ECWP *Fr.* Epistle to Mr. Pope Occasioned by His Characters of Women, An.

Female of the Species. Maureen Watson. IBA

Female Philosopher, The. Charlotte Dacre. NOBRP; RWP

Female Principle, The. Alec Derwent Hope. OxBC

Female's Lamentations, The; or, The Village in Mourning. Hannah Wallis. ECWP

Female Scriptural Characters. Rebekah Gumpert Hyneman.
  "Midnight in the Assyrian camp! No sound." SWaP
  No. 5, Judith. SWaP

Female Socket. Nicole Espagnol. SurWo, *tr. by* Myrna Bell Rochester

Female spider / swept her legends into her palms. Roots of Blue Bells. Nia Francisco. HATNAP

Female Transport, The. *Unknown.* NOBAu

Female Wits, The: A Song by a Lady of Quality. *Unknown.* NOSC

Femina. Daphne Marlatt. NOBC

Femina Contra Mundum. Gilbert Keith Chesterton. OxAEP-2

Feminine Intuition. Stephanie Brown. AmPoNex; BAP-97

Feminine mouth in Utopia, The. Limerick. W. F. N. Watson. PeLi

Femininity. Jay Livingston. ReLy

Feminism, baby, feminism. Male Rage Poem. Pier Giorgio Di Cicco. NOBC

Feminist Poem Number One. Elizabeth Alexander. NAPBL

Femme et Chatte. Paul Verlaine. AWP; OBVE

Femmemasochism. Alicia Galaz Vivar. TANSG, *tr. by* Dave Oliphant

Fence beyond fence from breakfast. Names of the Humble, The. Les A. Murray. CBAP

Fence can be seen from afar, The. Edmond Jabès. PFTM-2, *tr. by* Rosmarie Waldrop *Fr.* Book of Questions, The.

Fence Wire. James Dickey. VGW

Fencing. Anthony Lawrence. NOBAu

Fencing instructor named Fisk, A. Limerick. *Unknown.* PeLi

Fencing School. John Streeter Manifold. CBAP

Fennel. David Lindley. NLP

Feral Pioneers, The. Ishmael Reed. UnPo

Ferdia of the hosts. *Unknown.* WoPoe, *tr. by* Thomas Kinsella *Fr.* Táin, The.

Ferdinand De Soto lies. Distant Runners, The. Mark Van Doren. MoAmPo

Ferdinando and Elvira; or, The Gentle Pieman. Sir William Schwenck Gilbert. OBCoV

Fergus attempts to make off with the Sheild of Dunottar. William Malveisin. NePenScot, *tr. by* Mick Imlah *Fr.* Fergus of Galloway: Knight of King Arthur.

Fergus of Galloway: Knight of King Arthur. William Malveisin.
  Fergus attempts to make off with the Sheild of Dunottar. NePenScot, *tr. by* Mick Imlah
  "When Fergus drew his favourite blade." NePenScot, *tr. by* Mick Imlah

Ferishtah's Fancies. Robert Browning.
  When I Vexed You. OxBSP

Fern Hill. Dylan Thomas. AmFaPo; AngWePo; CABP; ChAP; ClHu; GTBS-P; HAP; HarvBoo; HeIP-4; InPK-6; MoBrPo; NAEL-5v2; NAEL-6v2; NIL-7; NIP-4; NOBE; NoAM; NoP-4; OBWVE; OxBTC; PAI; PoE; PoPoPo; PoRA; SoSe-8; TCAWP; TFi; TRP; TwCP

Fern Song. Hildegarde Flanner. APT-2

Fernando. Marci Ridlon. NTCP

Ferniehirst Castle. Richard Hugo. NoAM

Ferns and the Night. John Ash. HarvBoo

Ferns in a hollow of absence. Ferns in a Hollow of Absence. Alice Rahon. SurWo, *tr. by* Myrna Bell Rochester

Ferris Wheel, The. Wyatt Prunty. RA

Ferry. Louis Zukofsky. APT-2 *Fr.* 29 Poems.

Ferry departs, The. Buson. SoOfWa, *tr. by* Sam Hamill

Ferry drags, The. For the Lover. María Luisa B. Aguilar-Cariño. ReBoTo

Ferry Me Across. B. P. Nichol. FTOS

Ferry Me across the Water. Christina Georgina Rossetti. TLR *Fr.* Sing-Song.

Ferry of Lead, The. Iwan [*or* Yvan] Goll. WoPoe, *tr. by* Galway Kinnell

Ferry wades across the kyle, The. I drive. Return to Scalpay. Norman MacCaig. NePenScot

Ferryman's Song at Binh Minh. Herbert Krohn. CDa

Fertile and rank and rich the coastal rains. Advent. William Everson. NeAP; TrCP

Fertile Muck, The. Irving Layton. NOBC; NoAM

Fervent lover and the sage austere, The. Cats. Charles Baudelaire. TriCat, *tr. by* Dugald Sutherland MacColl

Fervid breath of our flushed Southern May, The. Evening on the Potomac. Richard Hovey. APN-2

Festal Song. *Unknown.* CrYelRi, *tr. by* Sam Hamill

Feste Burg Ist Unser Gott, Ein. Frederic Henry Hedge. *See* Mighty Fortress Is Our God, A

Feste's Song. William Shakespeare. *See* Twelfth Night

Festival of massacre: how make it vivid?, The. Bangla Desh: 1. Faiz Ahmad Faiz. CarOv, *tr. by* Carolyn Kizer

Festival of Souls. Sofu. JDP, *tr. by* Yoel Hoffmann

Festive draperies override the claims of. Naming Day, A. Odia Ofeimun. HBAPE; PBMAP

Festus Conrad. Melvin B. Tolson. GT

Fetch me a red flower from that meadow. Speech Warts. Myra Sklarew. CRP

Fetch? Balls and sticks engage my attention. Beau: Golden Retrievals. Mark Doty. Unle

Fetching Cows. Norman MacCaig. NoP-4; OxBC

Fete. Guillaume Apollinaire. CuPo

Fete, A. Larry Eigner. NeAP

Fete on the Lake. Molly Bendall. NAPBL

Feud, The. Sydney Lea. RA

Feuerzauber. Louis Untermeyer. TrJP

Feuilles d'Automne. Victor Hugo.
  "Have you sometimes, calm, silent let your tread aspirant rise." AWP, *tr. by* Francis Thompson
  Heard on the Mountain. AWP, *tr. by* Francis Thompson
  "I love the evenings, passionless and fair, I love the evens." AWP, *tr. by* Francis Thompson
  Sunset, A. AWP, *tr. by* Francis Thompson

Fever. Bella [*or* Izabela] Akhatovna Akhmadulina. TCRP, *tr. by* Elaine Feinstein

Fever. Judith Ortiz Cofer. PueRic

Fever. Sean O Riordain. ModIr, *tr. by* Patrick Crotty

Fever, The. Rosemary Dobson. FaBoWP

Fever and ague. (LL) Canzonetta: A Bitter Song to His Lady. Pier Moronelli da Fiorenza. AWP; EaItPo; OBVE, *tr. by* Dante Gabriel Rossetti

Fever 103°. Sylvia Plath. FaBoWP; NOBA; NoAM; VCAP; VGW

Fever Tune. Karel Van de Woestijne. TuT, *tr. by* Tony Curtis

Feverish Propositions. Rosmarie Waldrop. FTOS; PFTM-2 *Fr.* Reproduction of Profiles, The.

Feverish psyche gropes for an, A. Elegy for the Revolution. Kofi Anyidoho. NAfrP

Feverish room and that white bed, The. White Heliotrope. Arthur Symons. BoLoP; EBEV; NPeEn; PeVV

Fevers and plagues, and all their noxious stores. (LL) Philip Freneau. NAAL-2v1; NAAL-3 *Fr.* House of Night, The.

Few are the moonlit nights that I've cared for. Last Stop. George Seferis. AF

Few Autobiographical Facts, A. Anna Barkova. ARWW, *tr. by* Catriona Kelly

Few beds are stonier than one shared by a sleeper. Bed Time. Peter Davison. UnPo

Few dark notes from a jade flute, A. Listening to a Flute on a Spring Night in Lo-yang. Li Po. CrYelRi, *tr. by* Sam Hamill

Few Days in the South in February, a. Eleanor Ross Taylor. CBCWP

Few days to turn the pages, A. Dirt to Dirt. Hugh Seidman. BodElec

Few ever came to help you speak or sell. Peter Dale. NOCV *Fr.* Fragments, The.

Few Facts about Me, A. Charles North. PmAP

Few flakes appear, A. Chuck Brickley. HA

Few hairs, made fewer by the comb. Master Liu Painted a Portrait of Me in My Old Age and Asked Me to Write a Poem About the Picture. Yang Wan-li. SuSp, *tr. by* Jonathan Chaves

Few Happy Matches. Isaac Watts. NOEC

Few Helpful Hints, A. Peter Sirr. ModIr

Few hours ago a woman went on a walk, A. Legend of Hell, The. C. D. Wright. LCAP-2

Few Lines to Fill up a Vacant Page, A. John Danforth. SCAP

Few men in any age have second sight. To a Reviewer Who Admired My Book. John Ciardi. OBAL

Few miles from here, they've unearthed, A. Brandy Station, Virginia. David Moolten. BloBone

Few minutes ago, I stepped onto the deck, A. Cobweb, The. Raymond Carver. BLT

Few months obliterate, A. (LL) Basil Bunting. HarvBoo; NPeEn; NoAM; NoP-4; PoE *Fr.* Briggflatts [An Autobiography].

Few of the Bird-Family, a. James Whitcomb Riley. NOxBChV

Few people are talking low in a boat, A. (LL) Driving toward the Lac Qui Parle River. Robert Bly. CoAmPo; LCAP-2

Few people could hope to compare. Limerick. J. Endersby. PeLi

Few Picnics in Illinois, a. Maura Stanton. IllVoic

Few puffs of white cloud, A. Suzan Oshos's Visit to My West Mountain Hut. Muso Soseki. EaWin, *tr. by* W. S. Merwin

Few, save the poor, feel for the poor. Poor, The. Letitia [*or* Laetitia] Elizabeth Landon. VWP

Few strokes of ink and there it is, A. Reading the Japanese Poet Issa: (1762–1826). Czeslaw Milosz. WoPoe, *tr. by* Robert K. Haas

Few Things, A. Gerhard Rühm. PFTM-2, *tr. by* Rosmarie Waldrop

Few Things Can More Inflame. Cecil Day Lewis. OBMV

Few things for themselves, A. O Florida, Venereal Soil. Wallace Stevens. TCAPo

Few things to desire can so prod us. Limerick. W. F. N. Watson. PeLi

Few thought he was even a starter. Clement Attlee. OBCoV

Few times only, then away, A. Night Song for a Woman. Alfred Wellington Purdy. NOBC

Few words are best; I wish you well. To Mr. C., St. James's Place, London, October 22nd. Pope. OxBSP

Few year back and they told me Black, A. Poem about Intelligence for My Brothers and Sisters, A. June Jordan. PAI

Ffarwell sweet infant; blissfull babe adieu. Greifes Farwell, to an Inherritor of Joy. Ann Williams. EMWP

Fforestfawr. Kingsley Amis. NOBL *Fr.* Evans Country, The.

F[f]rom depth of[f] sin[n] and from a deep [*or* diepe] despair [*or* dispaire]. Bible, *O.T. See* Out of the deep [*or* depths] have I called [*or* cried unto] thee, O Lord

Fiascherino. Charles Tomlinson. NoAM

Fib Detected, A. Catullus. AWP, *tr. by* John Hookham Frere *Fr.* Carmina.

Fickle Fortune. Ferenc Faludi. IQMS, *tr. by* Watson Kirkconnell and John Gordon Nichols

Fickle winter shower. Shinseki. JDP, *tr. by* Yoel Hoffmann

Fiction: A Message. Gavin Ewart. OxBC

Fiction and the Reading Public. Philip Larkin. NOBL; OBSV

Fiction-Makers, The. Anne Stevenson. DiPo

Fiction: The House Party. Gavin Ewart. PeLV

Fictions. William Kulik. BodElec

Fiddle, we know, is diddle: and diddle, we take it, is dee. (LL) Algernon Charles Swinburne. CABP; PeVV *Fr.* Heptalogia, The.

Fiddleheads. Maureen Seaton. BAP-97

Fiddler and his wife, The. *Unknown.* OxNR

Fiddler Jones. Edgar Lee Masters. IllVoic; NoAM; OxBA; TAP *Fr.* Spoon River Anthology.

Fiddler of Dooney, The. W. B. Yeats. EBVV; FaBoCh; NBLV; OxAEP-2

Fiddler settles in, The. Lament for the O'Neills. John Montague. CIP-2

Fidel in Ohio. Martín Espada. TouFir

Fidele. William Collins. *See* Fidele, A

Fidele, A. William Collins. NOEC

  (Dirge in "Cymbeline") NOBE; SCGP

  (Fidele.) OBEV

  (Song from Shakespeare's Cymbeline, A.) CABP

Fidele's Dirge. William Shakespeare. *See* Cymbeline

Fidelity Rewarded. Dora Greenwell. VWP

Fidessa, More Chaste than Kind[e]. Bartholomew Griffin.
  Care-Charmer Sleep. NoSic; SCGP
  "Care-charmer sleepe, sweet ease in restles miserie." NoSic; SCGP

Fie fie fie fie fie! (LL) Madrigal: "Ay me, alas, heigh ho, heigh ho!" Thomas Weelkes. FaBoCh; NPeEn; OxBoLi

Fie on all courtesy, and unruly winds. Coxcomb, The. Joseph Hall. OxAEP-1

Fie on Eastern Luxury. Horace. InPK-6, *tr. by* Hartley Coleridge *Fr.* Odes.

Fie on Love. James Shirley. OxBSP

Fie [*or* Fy] tedious Hope, why do[e] you still rebel[l]? Mary Sidney Wroth, Countess of Montgomery. NOSC *Fr.* Pamphilia to Amphilanthus.

Fie [*or* Fye], foolish Earth, think[e] you the heaven wants glory. Fulke Greville, 1st Baron Brooke. Son *Fr.* Caelica.

Fie, school of Patience, fie; your lesson is. Sir Philip Sidney. NAEL-5v1; NAEL-6v1; NAEL-7v1 *Fr.* Astrophil and Stella.

Fie upon hearts that burn with mutual fire[!]. Against Fruition. Sir John Suckling. BeJo; CaPo

Field. Annie Foster. NLP

Field. Dana Levin. AmPoNex

Field, A. *Unknown.* GrAn, *tr. by* Peter Jay

Field, The. Mary Barnard. APT-2

Field, The. Christopher Pilling. NLP

Field, The. Jean Valentine. LCAP-2

Field and Forest. Randall Jarrell. LCAP-2; VGW

Field daisies, with lichens—each a mint coin. Stanza Written in Jest. Yang Wan-li. SuSp, *tr. by* Sherwin S. S. Fu

Field Day. William Robert Rodgers. BIrV; PNI

Field dodd. P. Inman. FTOS *Fr.* Dust Bowl.

Field Full of Folk, The. William Langland. PoE *Fr.* Vision of Piers Plowman, The.

Field-Glasses. Andrew Young. GTBS-P; RB

Field his arms, The. (LL) Christopher Marlowe. NOBE; OBEV *Fr.* Hero and Leander.

Field Hospital, The. Paul Muldoon. CIP-2; PNI

Field is large, the barn at hand, The. Morgan Llwyd. AngWePo *Fr.* 1648.

Field Manoeuvres. Richard Aldington. PeFWW

Field mouse follows its own shadow, The. Snowfall; a Poem about Spring. James Wright (1927–80). NoAM

Field of bright mustard. Buson. EH, *tr. by* Robert Hass

Field of bright mustard. Buson. EH, *tr. by* Yoel Hoffmann

Field of cotton, A. Basho. EH, *tr. by* Robert Hass

Field of Folk, The. William Langland. *See* Vision of Piers Plowman, The

Field of Glory, The. Edwin Arlington Robinson. MoAmPo

Field of golden wheat there grows, A. Harvest Song. Richard Dehmel. AWP, *tr. by* Ludwig Lewisohn

Field of Light, A. Theodore Roethke. TwCP

Field of mustard, A. Buson. EH, *tr. by* Yoel Hoffmann

Field of oilseed rape, The. Field. Annie Foster. NLP

Field of the Cloth of Gold, The. Patrick Joseph Hartigan. NOBAu

Field Path. John Clare. OxBSP

Field Poem. Gary Soto. PBCAP

Field Trip. Carol Muske. GeoHom

Field Trip. Kevin Young. GT

Field Upon Field Upon Field. Sergey [*or* Sergei] Aleksandrovich Yesenin [*or* Essenin]. TCRusP, *tr. by* Nigel Stott

Fields, The. W. S. Merwin. HCAP

Fields and mountains. Naito Joso. OHMPJ

Fields and mountains turn. Ransetsu. OHMPJ

Fields are chill, The; the sparse rain has stopped. Clearing at Dawn. Li Po. AWP, *tr. by* Arthur Waley

Fields belong to woman, The. In her body, woman carries. Fields Belong to Woman, The. Betty De Shong Meador. HW

Fields dying off. Gokei. JDP, *tr. by* Yoel Hoffmann

Fields flame with it, endless, blue, The. Indigo. Chitra Divakaruni. OpBo

Fields from Islington to Marybone, The. William Blake. OBNV *Fr.* Jerusalem; The Emanation of the Giant Albion.

Fields of Learning. Josephine Miles. NoAM

Fields of Sorrow, The. Ausonius. WoPoe, *tr. by* Helen Waddell

Fields, Teruko-san, are threshed, The. A good. Hibakusha's Letter (1955), The. David Mura. OpBo

Fields were bleached white, The. Patrick Kavanagh. NPeEn *Fr.* Great Hunger, The.

Fields Where We Slept. Muriel Rukeyser. NNaP

Fierce Dream, The. Jeffrey Wainwright. DiPo

Fierce musical cries of a couple of sparrowhawks hunting on the headland, The. Birds. Robinson Jeffers. APT-1; VGW

Fierce passions discompose the mind. William Cowper. ChIV-2 *Fr.* Olney Hymns.

Fierce they drove on, impatient to destroy. Homer. OBVE *Fr.* Iliad, The.

Fierce was the wild billow, Dark was the night. Anatolius. SacPr, *tr. by* John Mason Neale

Fierce west wind. Tune: "Remembering the Lady of Ch'in"—Loushan Pass. Mao Tse-tung [*or* Mao Zedong]. SuSp, *tr. by* Eugene Eoyang

Fierce wind urges me to change into my quilted cotton gown. Strolling in the Countryside. Chao Yi. SuSp, *tr. by* Chang Yin-nan

Fierce wrath of Solomon. Burning of the Temple, The. Isaac Rosenberg. FaBoMo; PeFWW; TrJP

Fiercely the battle raged and, sad to tell. Ambrose Bierce. APN-2; OBAL *Fr.* Devil's Dictionary, The.

Fiery ball takes on oxygen, burning off, The. Reconciled Flame. Alessandro Ceni. ItPo, *tr. by* Gayle Ridinger

Fiery Darts of Satan stob my heart, The. Edward Taylor. TCAPo *Fr.* Preparatory Meditations Before My Approach to the Lord's Supper.

Fiery palm tree in front of me, The. Today's Meditation. Antonio Machado. AF, *tr. by* Robert Bly

Fiery unicorn snapped, The. Daichu. ZenPo, *tr. by* Takashi Ikemoto and Lucien Stryk

Fiery wheel without beginning. Sunflower. Tuvia Rivner. MHP, *tr. by* Ruth Finer Mintz

Fiery young fellow called Bryant, A. Barney Blackley. PeLi

Fife Tune. John Streeter Manifold. CBAP; FaBoWar; NBLV; NOBAu

Fifteen. Jan Freeman. OxWW *Fr.* Autumn Sequence.

Fifteen. Patricia Pogson. NLP

15. Sir Philip Sidney. *See* Astrophil and Stella

Fifteen beds. Fifteen chairs with names. Pain Strikes Sparks on Me, the Pain of Terezin. *Unknown, fr. Terezin Concentration Camp.* INSAB

Fifteen Days of Judgment, The. Sebastian Evans. NOBVV

Fifteen dogs prowled. Mum. Kevin Gilbert. IBA

Fifteen Epigrams in Praise of the Tyrant. Paavo Haavikko.
  "Before you ask for justice. Make sure." WoPoe, *tr. by* Anselm Hollo
  "Don't say this to an old idol that's lost its nose." WoPoe, *tr. by* Anselm Hollo
  "Don't smile. So you won't become a Buddha." WoPoe, *tr. by* Anselm Hollo
  "Hades is an even worse place." WoPoe, *tr. by* Anselm Hollo
  "How decisively." WoPoe, *tr. by* Anselm Hollo
  "I always bow down deep before a small tree and a great tyrant." WoPoe, *tr. by* Anselm Hollo
  "It has been proposed that the stars should be removed from sight." WoPoe, *tr. by* Anselm Hollo
  "Look, life has been constructed this way to make sure." WoPoe, *tr. by* Anselm Hollo

"Plant trees. Exactly against this tree." WoPoe, *tr. by* Anselm Hollo

"Precisely the way you divide your small change between two." WoPoe, *tr. by* Anselm Hollo

"Take heart, Ovid. No sentence." WoPoe, *tr. by* Anselm Hollo

"Twice, three times." WoPoe, *tr. by* Anselm Hollo

"Tyrant inspires small poems, The." WoPoe, *tr. by* Anselm Hollo

"When the tyrant is young. Everyone waits." WoPoe, *tr. by* Anselm Hollo

"When you go to the tyrant. Keep your head on a platter." WoPoe, *tr. by* Anselm Hollo

Fifteen foresters in the Braid alow. Johnie Cock. *Unknown.* ESPB

Fifteen men on the Dead Man's Chest. Robert Louis Stevenson. NOBVV; NPeEn *Fr.* Treasure Island.

Fifteen Million Plastic Bags. Adrian Mitchell. EmeKit; OBSV; OxBTC

Fifteen minutes or thereabouts. Thomas Kinsella. ModIr *Fr.* Anniversaries.

Fifteen to Eighteen. Marilyn Hacker. GLP

Fifteen years ago the edict came: peace with the invader. Border Mountain Moon. Lu Yu. CoBCP, *tr. by* Burton Watson

Fifteen years old and naked, quivering. Tower. David Biespiel. NAPBL

15th Kühl-Psalm, The. Quirinus Kuhlmann. GePo, *tr. by* George C. Schoolfield

Fifteenth of May. Cherry blossom. The swifts. Swifts. Ted Hughes. OWoS

Fifteenth passes with drums and in armour, The. Centuries. Ronald Stuart Thomas. CABP

Fifteenth Volume, The. Po Chü-i. ChiP, *tr. by* Arthur Waley

Fifth Amendment, The. Susan Hahn. ExTi

Fifth Book. Elizabeth Barrett Browning. PEW

Fifth Book: On Limitation. Nanni Cagnone. ItPo, *tr. by* Gayle Ridinger *Fr.* Vaticinio.

Fifth Choir of Angelicals. John Henry, Cardinal Newman. *See* Dream of Gerontius, The

Fifth day of the fifth month. Hsü Wei. CoBLCP *Fr.* Lotus.

Fifth-Floor Window, The. Lola Ridge. APT-1; WPE

Fifth Grade Autobiography. Rita Dove. ISC; NIL-7; NIP-4

Fifth Inning, The. Donald Hall. MoASP

Fifth month, golden plums are ripe. Evening in the Garden Clear after Rain. Ch'u Ch'uang I. OHMPC

Fifth Movement: Autobiography. Louis Zukofsky. PFTM-1; TaR *Fr.* Poem Beginning "The."

Fifth Ode of Horace, The. Horace. EBEV; EnLoPo, *tr. by* Milton *Fr.* Odes.

Fifth Ode of Horace. Lib. I, The. Horace. NPeEn; OxBEV; PBRV, *tr. by* John Milton *Fr.* Odes.

Fifth Philosopher's Song. Aldous Leonard Huxley. OBCoV

Fifth Prose. Michael Palmer. NoP-4; PmAP

Fifth Stanzas. De Arte Poetica. Olga Sedakova. ARWW; ItGoST, *tr. by* Catriona Kelly

Fifth Vertical Poetry. Roberto Juarroz.
"Emptiness of the day, The." VCWP

Fifth Villancico, in Alternating Voices, Written for the Feast of the Nativity in Puebla, 1689, The. Sister Juana Inés de la Cruz.
"Because my Lord was born to suffer." WPoS; WoPoe, *tr. by* Alan S. Trueblood

Fifties Rock Party, 1985. Judith Berke. SwNoth

Fifty. Kenneth Rexroth. TAP

Fifty American cheerleaders booking uphill on Rue LePic. Bloodletting. Anselm Berrigan. HeMarv

Fifty cents apiece. Good Hot Dogs. Sandra Cisneros. NOxBChV; OxIBACP

58. Catullus. NAWM-7v1, *tr. by* Charles Martin

Fifty Faggots. Edward Thomas. MoBrPo; PeFWW; PoWW

50–50. Langston Hughes. NOBA; NoAM; PoE

Fifty-Fifty. Al Young. SpirFl

Fifty foot trombone blows, A. Whale Breathing: Bartlett Cove, Alaska. Bill Holm. MiVo

54. Sir Philip Sidney. *See* Astrophil and Stella

54. Edmund Spenser. *See* Amoretti

Fifty Gunner, The. Frank A. Cross. CDa

59 / And the / Cancer creeped. Don't Say Goodnight to Etheridge Knight. Tony Medina. InTrad

59th Light Poem: for La Monte Young and Marian Zazeela—6 November 1982. Jackson Mac Low. PmAP

51. Catullus. NAWM-7v1, *tr. by* Charles Martin

Fifty Quatrains. "Michael Field." VWP

56 Westervelt. Maggie Nelson. AmPoNex

Fifty thousand people uprooted by mfecane. Mantatee Horde, The. Mtutuzeli Matshoba. PeSAV

Fifty-three years / This clumsy ox has managed. Sekishitsu-Soei. ZenPo, *tr. by* Takashi Ikemoto and Lucien Stryk

Fifty times the rose has flower'd and faded. On the Jubilee of Queen Victoria. Tennyson. UnPo

52. Gavin Selerie. Oth *Fr.* Roxy.

Fifty years have passed. Problem of Anxiety, The. John Ashbery. BAP-97

50 Years in the Career of an Aspiring Thug. Suzanne Wise. AmPoNex

Fig Curtain of Atherton, The. Michael Spence. PoCoUp

Fig for the Lower House, A. Patrick Carey [*or* Cary]. NOSC

Fig for Thee, Oh! Death, A. Edward Taylor. NAAL-2v1; NAAL-3

Fig-tree, a falling woolshed, a filled-in well, A. Mullabinda. David Rowbotham. CBAP

Fig-trees, weird fig-trees. Bare Fig-trees. D. H. Lawrence. FaBoVe

Figgie Hobbin. Charles Causley. NOxBChV

Fight at Rorke's Drift, The. Emily Jane Pfeiffer. ViWPN

Fight of the Red Cross Knight and the Heathen Sansjoy, The. Edmund Spenser. FHYEP; NoSic *Fr.* Faerie Queene, The.

Fight of the Year, The. Roger McGough. OBCP

Fight on brave soldiers for the cause. Saints' Encouragement, The. Alexander Brome. BASC

Fight thou with shafts of silver, and o'[e]rcome. Money Gets the Mastery [*or* Masterie]. Robert Herrick. CaPo

Fight was at its hottest, The. Rev. Andrew Brown, over the Hill to Rest. Josephine D. Henderson Heard. CBWP-4

Fight was over, and the battle won, The. Allegory, An. Barcroft Henry Boake. CBAP

Fight with a Water-Spirit. Norman Cameron. OxBSo

Fight With An Angel. Tadeusz Rózewicz. PoSu, *tr. by* Victor Contoski

Fight your little fight, my boy. Don'ts. D. H. Lawrence. OxBoLi; PeLV

Fighters come, The. Libyan/Egyptian Acrobats/Israeli Air Circus. Sam Hamod. GraLe

Fighting Fire. Hamlin Garland. APN-2

Fighting on the South Frontier. Li Po. TAL

Fighting South of the Castle. *Unknown.* AWP, *tr. by* Arthur Waley

Fighting, south of the ramparts. *Unknown.* ChinPo, *tr. by* Yip Wai-lim

Fighting South of the Ramparts. *Unknown.* ChiP, *tr. by* Arthur Waley

Fighting South of the Wall. Li Po. WoPoe, *tr. by* Elling O. Eide

Fights, The. Milton Acorn. MoCV; NOBC

Fights After School. Norman J. Loftis. SpirFl

Fights God for cursed Amalek? That hand. Meditatio Septima. Francis Quarles. ChIV-1

Figlio Maggiore. Robert Fitzgerald. NoP-4

Figs. D. H. Lawrence. EroLit

FigTree. Stephanie Strickland. ExTi

Figure, A/ perhaps John the Evangelist. Vision at Knock. Gerry Murphy. BiHa

Figure in the Carpet, The. James Tate. BodElec

Figure is not anatomical, The. Limerick. Thomas Thorneley. PeLi

Figure it out for yourself, my lad. Equipment. Edgar Albert Guest. PoToHe

Figure Motioned with Its Mangled Hand Toward the Wall Behind It, The. Kenneth Patchen. APT-2

Figure of Eight. Louis MacNeice. OxBSP

Figure stood a crucifix against the door, The. Message from a Cross. Max Harris. NOBAu

Figure who stands on the beach, A. Vincent O'Sullivan. PeNZ *Fr.* Brother Jonathan, Brother Kafka.

Figured Wheel, The. Robert Pinsky. NoAM

Figurehead, The. Léonie Adams. APT-2; WPE

Figurehead, The. Maria Luisa Spaziani. NeIt, *tr. by* Beverly Allen

Figures, The. Robert Creeley. UnPo

Figures in a Ruined Ballroom. George Hitchcock. VGW

Figures in an Ancient Ink. Carl Rakosi. APT-2

Figures in the fields against the sky! Poem. Antonio Machado Ruiz. AWP; WoPoe, *tr. by* John Dos Passos

Figures of light and dark, these two are walking. Effet de Neige. John Hollander. GS

Filaments of light. In the New Sun. Philip Levine. NNaP

File-Hewer's Lamentation, The. Joseph Mather. NOEC

File into yellow candle light, fair choristers of King's. Sunday Morning, King's Cambridge. Sir John Betjeman. PeECV

Filene's department store. Ladders. Elizabeth Alexander. FFC

Filipino Boogie. Jessica Tarahata Hagedorn. UnSA

Fill and Illumined. Joseph Ceravolo. ChIV-1

Fill High the Bowl. John Keble. NOCV

Fill the bowl with rosie [*or* rosy] wine. Epicure, The. Abraham Cowley. BeJo

Fill thou my life, O Lord my God. Horatius Bonar. SacPr

Fill up my glass again! The anodyne. Tibullus. WoPoe, *tr. by* Rachel Hadas *Fr.* Adde Merum Vinoque.

Filled out gourd rots, the, The. Motion's Holdings. A. R. Ammons. NoAM

Filled with Emotions on the Moon-ferrying Bridge at Arashiyama. Liu Ya-tzu. SuSp, *tr. by* Wu-Chi Liu

Filled with His goodness, lost in His love. (LL)   Blessed Assurance.   Fanny Crosby.   AH; SWaP

Filled with myself, walled up in my skin.   José Gorostiza.   TCLAP, *tr.* by Rachel Benson   *Fr.* Death Without End.

Filled with old lovers, in the clutch of the chair.   Girlfriends, The.   Elizabeth Woody.   ReEnLa

Filled with the final weariness.   Boris Abramovich Slutsky [*or* Slutskii].   TCRP

Filled with water.   Family Portrait.   Shuntaro Tanikawa.   VCWP, *tr.* by Harold Wright

Filling an Order.   John Townsend Trowbridge.   OBAL

Filling her compact and delicious body.   John Berryman.   BoLoP; ColAP; EmeKit; HAP; HCAP; NoP-4; OBAL; VCAP   *Fr.* Dream Songs.

Filling Station.   Elizabeth Bishop.   FaBoMo; HAP; HCAP; InPK-6; NoP-4; PoetW; VCAP; WeW-3

Filling the Gap.   Lawson Fusao Inada.   OpBo

Filling the hollow of my throat. (LL)   To My Father.   Tony Curtis.   AngWePo; TCAWP

Filling the mind.   Clouds, The.   William Carlos Williams.   VGW

Filthy young fellow called Lawrence, A.   Limerick.   Bill Greenwell.   PeLi

Fin, A.   Bob Boldman.   HA

Fin de Siècle.   Joe Bolton.   AmPoNex

Fin-de-Siècle Cat.   Oscar Wilde.   TriCat   *Fr.* Sphinx, The.

Fin-de-Siècle Identikit.   Pierre Joris.   PFTM-2

Final.   Pablo Neruda.   WoPoe, *tr.* by Ben Belitt

Final adventure of Skinny Marcus—.   Lucilius.   GrAn

Final Count.   Bobbi Sykes.   IBA

Final Curtain.   Roger Woddis.   UV

Final Inch, The.   Emily Dickinson.   APN-2; NCAP; PoE

Final Knowledge.   Anton Wildgans.   AuPH, *tr.* by Lowell A. Bangerter

Final Manuscript.   Giannina Braschi.   TANSG, *tr.* by Alan West

Final Moments, The.   Edwin John Pratt.   NOBC   *Fr.* Titanic, The.

Final Painting, The.   Lee Harwood.   SPE

Final Prayer.   Enheduanna.   BoWoP, *tr.* by Aliki Barnstone and Willis Barnstone

Final reductions.   M. R. Peacocke.   NLP

Final shadow that will close my eyes, The.   Love Constant Beyond Death.   Francisco de Quevedo y Villegas.   AmFaPo, *tr.* by Willis Barnstone

Final Signs, The.   Lenze L. Bouwers.   TuT, *tr.* by Pat Boran

Final signs are weariness and might, The.   Final Signs, The.   Lenze L. Bouwers.   TuT, *tr.* by Pat Boran

Final Soliloquy of the Interior Paramour.   Wallace Stevens.   APT-1; BBASP; ColAP; HAP; HCAP; HarvBoo; LCAP-2

Final Solution: Jobs, Leaving.   Simon J. Ortiz.   PFTM-2

Final Sonnet.   Miguel Hernández.   BLPSL, *tr.* by Rene de Costa, Rigas Kappatos and Eleni Paidoussi

Final Sonnet, A.   Ted Berrigan.   FTOS; PFTM-2; PmAP   *Fr.* Sonnets, The.

Final Tree.   Gabriela Mistral.   TCLAP, *tr.* by Doris Dana

Final Vigil.   Georg Heym.   WoPoe, *tr.* by Peter Viereck

Finale.   Sue Lenier.   LW

Finale.   Judith Wright.   EmeKit

Finally.   Meret Oppenheim.   SurPaPo, *tr.* by Catherine Schelbert

Finally found a fellow.   Murder, He Says.   Frank Loesser.   ReLy

Finally, from your house there is no view.   Water Island.   Howard Moss.   CoAP; NoP-4

Finally, one arrives at the place.   Golgotha.   Andrew Lansdown.   ChIV-2

Finally out of reach.   Tessho.   ZenPo, *tr.* by Takashi Ikemoto and Lucien Stryk

Finally retired pensionless.   Big Momma.   Haki R. Madhubuti.   AmFaPo; BPo

Finally stays no more away.   Consolation Aria.   Johann Christian Günther.   GePo, *tr.* by George C. Schoolfield

Finally / The butcher dog snaps at the golden ring. The.   Finally.   Meret Oppenheim.   SurPaPo, *tr.* by Catherine Schelbert

Finally / the only one I want.   Privacy.   Olga Broumas.   PasH

Finally the Rain.   Carrington McDuffie.   PoCoUp

Finally there are enough people to hug!   At Mother Teresa's.   Naomi Shihab Nye.   OPRER

Finally, to forgo love is to kiss a leaf.   Rescue the Dead.   David Ignatow.   VGW; WoPoe

Finally to make his mind up to go home. (LL)   Prodigal, The.   Elizabeth Bishop.   APT-2; ChIV-2; CoAP; LCAP-2; TwCP

Find.   Josephine Miles.   WPE

Find easy voice to utter each aright. (LL)   Once Alien Here.   John Hewitt.   CABP; CIP-2; PNI

Find Heaven and thee. (LL)   Silence and Stealth of Day[e]s!   Henry Vaughan.   ESCV; NAEL-5v1; NAEL-6v1; NAEL-7v1; NPeEn

Find me, and turn thy back on heaven. (LL)   Brahma.   Ralph Waldo Emerson.

APN-1; AWP; ColAP; HAP; NOBA; NoP-4; OBEV; OxBA; PAI; PoE; PoRA; TAP; TCAPo; TFi; UV; UnPo

Find me in the grass.   Spirit of the Place, The.   Tony Curtis.   AngWePo

Find out cursed policies of man. (LL)   Heart Is Deep, The.   Roger Wolcott.   ChIV-1; SCAP

"Find rest in Him!"   One knows the parsons' tags.   Charlotte Mew.   ChIV-2   *Fr.* Madeleine in Church.

Find the fair Pierides! (LL)   Garden Song, A.   Austin Dobson.   OBEV; OBGa

Find their sole voice [*or* speech] in that victorious brow. (LL)   Shakespeare.   Matthew Arnold.   FHYEP; HeIP-4; OBEV; OxAEP-2; OxBSo; SCGP; Son

Find thy body by the wall! (LL)   Last Word, The.   Matthew Arnold.   NOBE; SCGP

Find Uncle Fred's photograph.   Well You Needn't.   Dave Etter.   SeSe

Finder, The.   Robin Blaser.   FTOS

Finder of a Horseshoe, The.   Osip Emilevich Mandelstam [*or* Mandelshtam].   TCRP, *tr.* by Bernard Meares

Finding.   Celia Barry.   Prnts

Finding a Horseshoe.   Osip Emilevich Mandelstam [*or* Mandelshtam].   RusPo, *tr.* by Robert Arthur Douglas Ford

Finding a Long Gray Hair.   Jane Kenyon.   LoL

Finding a Teacher.   W. S. Merwin.   NNaP

Finding all of the stops. (LL)   San Sepolcro.   Jorie Graham.   HCAP; VCAP

Finding God's taboos totalitarian.   Limerick.   Basil Ransome-Davies.   PeLi

Finding gold *A* left.   Exchange.   George Rostrevor Hamilton.   FaBoEE

Finding His Fist.   Patricia Smith.   SpirFl

Finding is the first Act.   Emily Dickinson.   NOBA; TCAPo

Finding Serenity.   Yüan Mei.   CoBLCP, *tr.* by Jonathan Chaves

Finding the stars over and over again.   County.   Katayoon Zandvakili.   AmPoNex

Finding the Way Back.   Gerald McCarthy.   CDa

Finding Them Lost.   Howard Moss.   CoAP

Finding this cavern.   Foster Jewell.   HA

Finding What's Lost.   Dorianne Laux.   GeoHom

Finds a tree of unrecorded species.   Literary Excellence.   Robert Harris.   BMAP

Finds ways enough to ease thine heaviness. (LL)   Of Money.   Barnabe Googe.   NBLV; NoSic; SoSe-8

Fine and Dandy.   Paul James.   ReLy

Fine and Mellow.   Billie Holiday.   NAAAL

Fine as wine! / Life is fine! (LL)   Life Is Fine.   Langston Hughes.   NBLV; SAmP

Fine breeze blows through the temple halls, A.   Wen Cheng-ming.   CoBLCP   *Fr.* Chung-i Temple, The.

Fine day! A good sign, A.   April in Town.   Yury [*or* Iurii] Ryashentsev [*or* Riashentsev].   TCRP, *tr.* by Daniel Weissbort

Fine delight that fathers thought; the strong, The.   To R. B.   Gerard Manley Hopkins.   GTBS-P; OxAEP-2

Fine evening may I have.   Courtship.   Rita Dove.   LCAP-2

Fine feelings under blockade! Cargoes just in from Kamschatka!   Winter Coming On.   Martin Bell.   FaBoMo; OBVE; OxBTC

Fine! Fine!   Isaac Rosenberg.   PeFWW   *Fr.* Moses.

Fine fish to net.   Ezra Pound.   OBVE

Fine game is grab-bag, a fine game to see, A!   Grab-Bag.   Helen Hunt Jackson.   OBCA

Fine knacks for ladies, cheap, choice, brave and new!   Fine Knacks for Ladies.   *Unknown.*   EBEV; HAP; NoP-4; NoSic

Fine knacks for ladies, cheape choise brave and new.   John Dowland.   NPeEn; PBRV

Fine Madam Would-Be, wherefore° should you fear.   To Fine Lady Would-Be.   Ben Jonson.   FaBoEE; NOSC; NoP-4; OxBSP

Fine Old English Gentleman; New Version, The.   Charles Dickens.   NOBVV; OBSV

Fine rain, gentle thunder.   Tune: "Full River Red"—A Four-season Song on the Hardships and Joys of Farming Life.   Cheng Hsieh.   SuSp, *tr.* by Irving Y. Lo

Fine Romance, A.   Dorothy Fields.   OBCoV; ReLy

Fine suicide fled victoriously, The.   Stéphane Mallarmé.   SxFrPo, *tr.* by E. H. Blackmore and A. M. Blackmore

Fine view, but I'm still getting thinner.Tune.   Huang T'ing-chien.   SuSp, *tr.* by James J. Y. Liu

Fine youth Ciprius is more terse and neat, The.   Sir John Davies.   NoSic   *Fr.* Epigrams.

Fineness of midnight.   Midnight.   Gabriela Mistral.   BoWoP, *tr.* by David Garrison

Finger lifted to the eye, A.   Music of the Spheres.   Anthony Barnett.   Oth

Finger-nails.   Paolo Buzzi.   PFTM-1

Finger of death touched me, The.   He Is Gone.   Anna Swirszczynska.   PoSu

Fingers lie in the lap, The.   Year's End.   Ellen Bryant Voigt.   NoAM

Fingers over the hedge, you move around. Near Speech, The. Mark McMorris. AmPoNex

Fingers probe. Fingers probe. Claire Malroux. VCWP, *tr.* by Marilyn Hacker

Fings Ain't Wot They Used t'Be. Lionel Bart. ReLy

Finis. Walter Savage Landor. OBEV *Fr.* Last Fruit Off an Old Tree, The.

FINIS. (LL) Michael Wigglesworth. NAAL-2v1; SCAP

Finished. Kate Llewellyn. NOBAu

Finished Gentleman, A. Geoffrey Dutton. NOBAu

Finished the stranger, with whom, late. César Vallejo. WoPoe, *tr.* by Rebecca Seiferle

Finite Intuition. Milo De Angelis. NeIt, *tr.* by Lawrence Venuti

Finite—to fail, but infinite to Venture. Emily Dickinson. TCAPo

Finn's Wishes. Desmond O'Grady. CIP-2, *tr.* by the author

Finnegan's Wake. Unknown. NBLV

Finnegans Wake. James Joyce.
  Ballad of Persse O'Reilly, The. PeLV
  "Have you heard of one Humpty Dumpty." PeLV
  "He larved ond he larved on he merd such a nauses." BIrV
  "Hear, O hear, Iseult la belle! Tristan, sad hero, hear! The Lambeg drum." PFTM-2
  Ondt and the Gracehoper, The. BIrV

Finnesburh Fragment, The. Unknown. ASW; OBWP, *tr.* by Kevin Crossley-Holland

Fir. T.E. Jay. GifTon

Fire. Amiya Chakravarty. OMIP, *tr.* by Sujit Mukherjee

Fire. Fazil Hüsnü Daglarca. CRP

Fire. Langston Hughes. NOBA

Fire. Mark O'Connor. NOBAu

Fire. Luis J. Rodriguez. UnSA

Fire. Ann Taylor. NOxBChV

Fire. Unknown. WoPoe, *tr.* by Keith Bosley *Fr.* Kalevala, The.

Fire. Dorothy Wellesley, Duchess of Wellington. OBMV

Fire, The. Robert Creeley. NOBA

Fire, The. Robert Duncan. APSN; VGW *Fr.* Passages.

Fire, The. Sir Walter Scott. OBCP

Fire! Willy Bal. WoPoe, *tr.* by Yann Lovelock

Fire alight / in the other window as it. Open Air Where. Larry Eigner. PmAP

Fire and Brimstone; or, The Destruction of Sodom. George Lestey.
  "Behold, how Sodom swaggers in its Pride." CAGL

Fire and Embers. Leonor Scliar-Cabral. MirDau, *tr.* by Regina Igel

Fire and Ice. Robert Frost. APT-1; BRP; ColAP; FaBoEE; HeIP-4; InPK-6; MoAmPo; NAAL-2v2; NAAL-5; NOBA; NoAM; OxBA; PAI; RaBo; SoSe-8; TAP; TFi

Fire and Rope, Bullet and Axe. Nikolai Semionovich Tikhonov. TCRusP, *tr.* by John Glad

Fire and sword with ease subdues. (LL) Beauty. Thomas Stanley. AWP; OBVE

Fire at Alexandria, The. Theodore Weiss. NoAM; SAmP; TAP

Fire Barns. Jordan Davis. HeMarv

Fire-blade split the known roof and the white ceiling, The. Vision of St. Michael and St. John, The. Jeremy Ingalls. YaYoPo

Fire-Bringer, The. William Vaughn Moody.
  I Stood within the Heart of God. AH

Fire burns bright on my hearth to-night, The. Fire Guest, The. George Alfred Townsend. PWR

Fire Burns Low, The. John Leax. TrCP

Fire-charms of summer's flaming legion, The. Hungarian Summer [1918]. Gyula Juhász. IQMS, *tr.* by Adam Makkai

Fire darkens, the wood turns black, The. Song for the Sun That Disappeared behind the Rainclouds. *Hottentot Oral Tradition.* TTTS; TTY, *tr.* by Ulli Beier

Fire darkens, the wood turns black, The. Song for the Sun That Disappeared behind the Rainclouds. Unknown. ChAP

Fire-Dragon and the Treasure, The. Unknown. AnOE, *tr.* by Charles W. Kennedy *Fr.* Beowulf.

Fire falls, the night, The. Summer Is a Poem by Ovid. Douglas G. Jones. NIP-4

Fire, Famine, and Slaughter. Samuel Taylor Coleridge. FaBoWar

Fire, fire, fire, fire! Thomas Campion. WoPoe

Fire! Fire! said [*or* says] the town crier. Unknown. OxNR

Fire-fly, fire-fly! bright little thing. Chant to the Fire-fly. William Ellery Channing. TCAPo

Fire-fly, fire-fly, light me to bed. Chant to the Fire-Fly. Unknown. APN-2; OxIBACP, *tr.* by Henry Rowe Schoolcraft

Fire Guest, The. George Alfred Townsend. PWR

Fire high up in air, The. Bird's Song, A. Dame Edith Sitwell. NALW

Fire in Early Morning. Christiane Jacox Kyle. YaYoPo

Fire in leaf and grass, The. Living. Denise Levertov. BLT; OPOU; VGW; WPE

Fire in My Meditation Burned. Henry Ainsworth. AH; ChIV-1

Fire in the Heavens. Christopher John Brennan. CBAP; NOBAu *Fr.* Quest of Silence, The.

Fire in the heavens, and fire along the hills. Christopher John Brennan. CBAP; NOBAu *Fr.* Quest of Silence, The.

Fire in the Hole. Gary Snyder. NAAL-2v2

Fire in the olive groves throughout the night. Vineta. Charles Spear. PeNZ

Fire in the Stone, The. Tuvia Rivner. MHP, *tr.* by Ruth Finer Mintz

Fire in the window! flashes in the pane! Fire in the window. Mary Mapes Dodge. SWaP

Fire is burning clear and blithely, The. Darkened Mind, The. James Russell Lowell. NCAP

Fire Is Laid, The. *Hungarian Oral Tradition.* IQMS, *tr.* by Dermot Spence

Fire is out, and spent the warmth thereof, The. Dregs. Ernest Christopher Dowson. OBMV

Fire is out, the house dark, The. (LL) Nurse's Lament, The. Mary Elizabeth Coleridge. NOBVV; OxBSP

Fire is passing up through the soles of my feet!, A. (LL) Evolution from the Fish. Robert Bly. NOBA; NoAM

Fire Island. May Swenson. TAP

Fire Keeper. Bahiyyih Maroon. SpirFl

Fire more priceless than diamonds rare. Father's Love, The. Mary E. Tucker. CBWP-1

Fire of Drift-Wood, The. Henry Wadsworth Longfellow. APN-1; ITBLP; MakPoe; NAAL-2v1; NAAL-3; NCAP; NOBA; OxBA; TAP

Fire of Frendraught, The. Unknown. ESPB; OxBB

Fire of Meditation burns, The. Præfatory Poem to the Little Book, Entituled, Christianus per Ignem, A. Nicholas Noyes. SCAP

Fire of our victims, The. Knell, The. Muhammad Al-Faituri [*or* Al-Fituri *or* Al-Fayturi]. TTY, *tr.* by Samir M. Zoghby

Fire: On earth there's a warrior of curious origin. Cynewulf. ASW *Fr.* Riddles (Exeter Book).

Fire on the Hills. Robinson Jeffers. RaBo

Fire Poem, The. Theodore Enslin. CRP

Fire rides calmly in the air. At War. Charles Madge. FaBoMo

Fire's army overruns Topanga's hills. Arson. Charles Harper Webb. GeoHom

Fire's here, that won't be forgotten. Log. David Bromige. FTOS

Fire Sermon, The. T. S. Eliot. HarvBoo *Fr.* Waste Land, The.

Fire Seven Times Tried This, The. William Shakespeare. CTC *Fr.* Merchant of Venice, The.

Fire Side, The; a Pastoral Soliloquy. Isaac Hawkins Browne. NOEC *Fr.* Foundling Hospital for Wit, The.

Fire, Sixth Month, 408. T'ao Ch'ien [*or* T'ao Yuan-ming]. CrYelRi, *tr.* by Sam Hamill

Fire Station's Delight, The. Susan Hampton. NOBAu

Fire Support Burk. Steve Denning. CDa

Fire, the lamp, and I, were alone together, The. Mary Elizabeth Coleridge. VWP; ViWPN

Fire: The People. Alfred Corn. NAAL-2v2; VCAP *Fr.* Call in the Midst of the Crowd, A.

Fire the river that is to say, the. Brush-Fire. U Tam'si Tchicaya. NegPo, *tr.* by Sangodare Akanji

Fire, the rope, the bullet, and the ax, The. Nikolai Semionovich Tikhonov. TCRP

Fire threatens, The. Hyena Addressing Her Young Ones, The. Unknown. PeSAV, *tr.* by W. H. I. Bleek

Fire-Truck, A. Richard Wilbur. AiP

Fire Us with Ice, Burn Us with Snow. Mary Monk. LW

Fire was furry as a bear, The. Dark Song. Dame Edith Sitwell. FaBoTw

Fire, water, woman, are man's ruin! Dutch Proverb, A. Matthew Prior. FaBoEE; NOEC; OBCoV

Fire will not ask me to make its bed, The. Asseverations. Arthur Nortje. HBAPE

Fire, with well-dried logs supplied, The. Fire, The. Sir Walter Scott. OBCP

Fire within fire, desire in deity. (LL) Dante Gabriel Rossetti. NOBVV; Son *Fr.* House of Life, The.

Firebell for Peace. Joyce Lee. NOBAu

Fireblade / Flame scimitar's cutting edge. Suncoming. Oliver La Grone. NBV

Firebombing, The. James Dickey. OBWP

Firebowl. Sydney Clouts. PeSAV

Firebrand. Harry Crosby. SPE
  (What is your feeling about the revolutionary spirit of your age.) SPE

Firecrackers thundering day and night, and lightning silences. Any Two Wheels. Jane Miller. BodElec

Fired Pot, The. Anna Wickham. FaBoTw; FaBoWP; LW; NPeEn; OxBTC

Fired up over the chess, cards, poems. Having Led a Charmed Life, He Had to be Hanged Twice. Mac Wellman. FTOS

Fired with the music, Aikin, of thy lays. On Anna Laetitia Aikin. Mary Scott. RWP

Firefighters of Chernobyl, The. Xochiquetzal. Pauline Stainer. NeBl

Fireflies. Paul Fleischman. NOxBChV

Fireflies. José Gorostiza. TCLAP, *tr. by* Rachel Benson

Fireflies / Entering my house. Issa. ZenPo, *tr. by* Takashi Ikemoto and Lucien Stryk

Fireflies float noiseless. Canicula. Mary Kinzie. FFC

Fireflies floated up from the grass, The. On a Summer Night. Elmaz Abinader. GraLe

Fireflies in the Garden. Robert Frost. OxBSP; SAmP

Firefly. Elizabeth Madox Roberts. NTCP

Firefly. Tu Fu. CrYelRi, *tr. by* Sam Hamill

Firefly, airplane, satellite, star—. Back Yard, July Night. William Cole. KaS

Firefly light. Summer. Ramona Wilson. VoR

Firelight. Edwin Arlington Robinson. NoAM

Firelight. John Greenleaf Whittier. OBCP *Fr.* Snow-Bound [*or* Snow-Bound; a Winter Idyl].

Firemen, The. James Keir Baxter. NOxBChV

Firemen, firemen! Help! X. J. Kennedy. CA

Fireplace, The. Michael S. Harper. GT

Fires. József Kiss. IQMS, *tr. by* Peter Zollman

Fires / Burn in my heart. Kenneth Rexroth. APSN *Fr.* Love Poems of Marichiko, The.

Fires in Illinois. John James Piatt. APN-2

Fires in the Mirror. Anna Deavere Smith.
  "Do you know what happened in August here?" OxWW
  Roslyn Malamud the Coup. OxWW

Fires run through my body—the pain of loving you. *Kwakiutl Oral Tradition.* ErotSp, *tr. by* Sam Hamill

Firestone. David Rivard. PBCAP

Firewing. Breyten Breytenbach. VCWP, *tr. by* Ernst Van Heerden

Firewood, iron-ware, and cheap tin trays. (LL) Cargoes. John Masefield. BRP; CABP; InPK-6; MoBrPo; NOBE; OBEV; OBMV; PAI; PoRA; TFi

Fireworks. Valerie Worth. NTCP

Fireworks explode like thunderclaps all over Chungking. On Hearing the News of the Japanese Surrender. Liu Ya-tzu. SuSp, *tr. by* Wu-Chi Liu

Fireworks in steel. Fete. Guillaume Apollinaire. CuPo

Fireworks on the Grass. Archilochus. WoPoe, *tr. by* Guy Davenport

Firing back at my heavy heart. Aleksandr Rudolfovich Gangnus. TCRP

Firm as young bones, fine as blown spume, still. Paradigm. Babette Deutsch. TrJP

Firm Belief. *Unknown.* PoToHe

Firm desire which enters, The. Arnaut Daniel. EroLit, *tr. by* Anthony Bonner

Firm of Happiness, Limited, The. Norman Cameron. FaBoTw

Firmament breaks up. In black eclipse, The. Word for the Hour, A. John Greenleaf Whittier. NCAP

Firmness. Anthony Hecht. OBAL

Firs / born Xmas day. Christopher Reid. FaBoVe *Fr.* Memres of Alfred Stoker.

First. Douglas Florian. NOxBChV

First. Sharon Olds. ExTi

First. Mother's Song to a Baby. *Unknown.* OxIBACP

First, The. Grace Cavalieri. UnSA

First / A far thud. Fireworks. Valerie Worth. NTCP

First a monkey, then a man. Dawn of the Space Age. John Ciardi. OBAL

First a razor then a fact. (LL) Fifth Prose. Michael Palmer. NoP-4; PmAP

First a sea: soft sands, muds, and marls. What Happened Here Before. Gary Snyder. APSN; NNaP; PoM

First Adventurer for her fame I stand, The. Delariviere Manley. EMWP *Fr.* Lost Lover, The.

First agency we went to, The. Waiting Lists, The. Jackie Kay. NeBl

First Aid at 4 A.M. Christopher Bursk. InPK-6

First Americans, The. (LL) When Something Happens. James A., Jr. Randall. BPo; SSLK

First and last time I met, The. Drunken Memories of Anne Sexton. Alan Dugan. BodElec

First Anniversary of the Government under His Highness the Lord Protector, 1655, The. Andrew Marvell. BASC

First Anniversary of the Government under O.C., The. Andrew Marvell.
  "Is this, saith one, the Nation that we read." PBRV

First Anniversary [*or* Anniversarie], The. John Donne. *Fr.* Anatomy [*or* Anatomie] of the World, An[: The First Anniversary].

First, are you our sort of a person? Applicant, The. Sylvia Plath. EmeKit; NAAL-2v2; NOBA; PoPoPo; TwCP

First, at a window of the vacant house. Windows, The. Chris Wallace-Crabbe. BMAP

First Atlantic Telegraph, The. Jones Very. NCAP

First Attempt in Rhyme, A. Thomas Hood. OBCoV

First Autumn Night. Katie Donovan. BiHa

First Beating. Lorna Dee Cervantes. TouFir

First Birthday, The. Hartley Coleridge. CenSon

First blossom was the best blossom, The. Apple Blossom. Louis MacNeice. PeECV; RB

First blow caught me sideways, my jaw, The. Beating, The. Ann Stanford. SoSe-8; WPE

First Book, The. Rita Dove. LoL

First Book: Young Aurora's Fostermother. Elizabeth Barrett Browning. NALW *Fr.* Aurora Leigh.

First-born, The. Jack Davis. BMAP; IBA

First born of Chaos, who so fair didst come. Hymn: To Light. Abraham Cowley. MeLP; OxAEP-1

First bout of Shanghai flu, sweat the bed without you. So Get Over It, Honey. Belle Waring. ExTi

First box held tiny yellow apples, The. Boat Down the River of Yellow Silt, A. Kimiko Hahn. ExTi

First came the legions, then the colonists. Colony, The. John Hewitt. ModIr

First came the primrose. Sydney Thompson Dobell. OBEV *Fr.* Balder.

First Canzone. Nikolai Stepanovich Gumilyov [*or* Gumiliov *or* Gumilev]. TCRusP, *tr. by* Mary Jane White

First Canzone of the Convito, The. Dante Alighieri. OBVE, *tr. by* Percy Bysshe Shelley

First Carolina Said-Song. A. R. Ammons. OBAL

First cat that was ever killed by Care, The. (LL) New England. Edwin Arlington Robinson. HeIP-4; MoAmPo; NAAL-2v2; NOBA; OxBA; PoPoPo; TAP

First chairs, east, west: meadowlarks. Morning Chamber Orchestra Near Piney Crick, Wyoming, 7 A.M., The. William Borden. MiVo

First Chance Twice. Fanny Howe. FTOS

First chap to fuck little Sophie, The. Limerick. Victor Gray. PeLi

First cherry blossoms. Sanpu. SoOfWa, *tr. by* Sam Hamill

First cicada / Life is. Issa. ZenPo, *tr. by* Takashi Ikemoto and Lucien Stryk

First Circle, The. Kofi Awoonor. HBAPE; PBMAP; VCWP

First Circle, The. S. K. Kelen. BMAP

First Claims Poem. Víctor Hernández Cruz. NBV

First clan of autumn, thistleball on a stem. Thistledown. James Merrill. UnPo

First clear afternoon of Spring bursts, The. Games with My Daughter. Tony Curtis. TCAWP

First cold rain. Basho. TTTS

First colour? Just like a captive, The. Three-Coloured Banner. János Pilinszky. PoSu, *tr. by* Peter Jay

First come I. My name is Jowett. *Var. authors.* FaBoEE; NOBL; PeLV *Fr.* Balliol Rhymes.

First comes the logic of substitution. Secret Life of Gilbert Bond, The. Joan Retallack. FTOS

First Communiqué from One Returning from the Zanj Revolt. Abd al-Aziz Al-Maqalih. MAP, *tr. by* John Heath-Stubbs and Lena Jayyusi

First Confession. X. J. Kennedy. CoAmPo

First Corinthians at the Crossroads. Bruce Dawe. NoAM

First country to die was normal in the evening, The. Last War, The. Kingsley Amis. OBSV; OxBC

First cries were, The. Mother Poem. Joel Oppenheimer. PoM

First crops. Chiri (d. 1716). JDP, *tr. by* Yoel Hoffmann

First Cycle of Love Poems. George Barker.
  My Joy, My Jockey, My Gabriel. MoBrPo

1st Dance—Making Things New—6 February 1964. Jackson Mac Low. FTOS; PFTM-2; PmAP *Fr.* Pronouns, The—A Collection of 40 Dances—For the Dancers.

First dawn comes, The. *Unknown.* OHMPJ

First day he had gone, The. Space in the Air, A. Jon Silkin. TrJP

First day he was travelling in Asia, The. Shape-Changer, The. Chris Wallace-Crabbe. NOBAu

First day I shot dope, The. Summer Words of [*or* for] a Sistuh [*or* Sister] Addict. Sonia Sanchez. BPo; BlSi; UnPo

First day of Christmas, The. Twelve Days of Christmas, The. *Unknown.* OxBoLi; OxNR

First day of false spring, I hit the street, The. Green Market, New York. Julia Kasdorf. NeAmPo

First day of kindergarten I slice my four-years' thumb. Susans. Susan Clements. UnSA

First day of spring. Basho. EH, *tr. by* Robert Hass

First Day of Spring, The. Pien Kung. CoBLCP, *tr. by* Jonathan Chaves

First Day of Spring, The. Pedro Juan Pietri. PueRic

First Day of the Hunting Moon, The. Patricia Low. VGW

First day of the week he spoke to them, The. Eutychus. Rosemary Dobson. ChIV-2

First day of this month I saw. Snowdrops. George MacBeth [*or* Macbeth]. OBCP

First Day's Night had come, The. Emily Dickinson. NCAP; OxBA; PoE; TRP; WPOW

First day she passed up and down through the Heavens, The. Petrarch. OBMV *Fr.* Sonnets to Laura.

First day the Germans came into the city, The. Charles Reznikoff. APSN

First day the radiator, The. Heat in October. Kyoko Mori. FSt

First-Day Thoughts. John Greenleaf Whittier. APN-1; TrCP

First day we stood in gradations of high and low, The. Concert Choir. Beth McGrath. MiVo

First day when water, The. Winter Mirror. Judith Mok. TuT, *tr. by* Michael O'Loughlin

First daylight on the bittersweet-hung. Meridian. Amy Clampitt. NIL-7

First Daylight Song. *Unknown.* APN-2, *tr. by* Washington Matthews *Fr.* Mountain Chant, The.

First Days, The. James Wright (1927–80). *See* Mantova

First Days of Spring. Ryokan. EnlH; WoPoe, *tr. by* Stephen Mitchell

First days of spring—the sky. First Days of Spring. Ryokan. EnlH; WoPoe, *tr. by* Stephen Mitchell

First Death. Ann Townsend. NeAmPo

First Death in Nova Scotia. Elizabeth Bishop. CoAP; FaBoWP; HarvBoo; LCAP-2; NOBA

First, delicate apple-greens, The. Easter Outing. Sally Carr. Prnts

First did I fear, when first my love began. Giles Fletcher, the Elder. Son *Fr.* Licia.

First Dimension of Skunk, The. Ray A. Young Bear. HATNAP

First Dream. Sister Juana Inés de la Cruz.
 "But Venus first." BoWoP

First Drift. Ron Padgett. FTOS

First Early Mornings Together. Robert Pinsky. ColAP

First Eclogue. Baldomero Garcilaso de la Vega.
 "Oh, to my sobs, Galatea, you are harder than a stone." BLPSL, *tr. by* Rene de Costa, Rigas Kappatos and Eleni Paidoussi

First Elegy for the Dead in Cyrenaica. Hamish Henderson. OxBS

First English Wildcat, The. Colin Simms. Oth

First enters wearing the neon armour, The. Ten Types of Hospital Visitor. Charles Causley. OxBC

First (entitled to the place), The. Charles Churchill. OBSV *Fr.* Duellist, The.

First Epistle of the First Book of Horace Imitated, The. Pope.
 Profiteers. ECEV; OBSV
 "Well, if a King's a lion, at the least." ECEV; OBSV

First Epistle of the Second Book of Horace Imitated, The. Pope.
 "Of little use the man you may suppose." EBEV

First, / erase your name. Who Remains Standing? Andrée Chedid. HAWP; WoPoe, *tr. by* Mirène Ghossein and Samuel Haze

First Extra, The. Amy Levy. ViWPN

First Farewell to J.G G. "Ephelia." NOSC

First, feel, then feel, then. Young Soul. Imamu Amiri Baraka. BPo

First Fig. Edna St. Vincent Millay. APT-1; AiP; BRP; ChAP; FaBoWP; NALW; NIL-7; NoAM; NoP-4; TAP

First Fight. Then Fiddle. Gwendolyn Brooks. InPK-6; NIL-7; NIP-4 *Fr.* Womanhood, The.

First firefly / Why turn away. Issa. ZenPo, *tr. by* Takashi Ikemoto and Lucien Stryk

First, for effusions due unto the dead. Upon His Sister-in-Law, Mistress Elizabeth Herrick. Robert Herrick. CaPo

First, for kindness, we must assume the dark. Love Among Lepers. Richard Ronan. BodElec

First forget what time it is. Exercise. W. S. Merwin. NOBA

First form your artful looks with studious care. Charlotte Lennox. ECWP; LW *Fr.* Art of Coquetry, The.

First fruits from her fruitful bed, The. Dioscorides. GrAn

First full moon of overgrown buffalo. America's Wounded Knee. Phillip [*or* "Phil"] William George. VoR

First Grade. Phillip [*or* "Phil"] William George. VoR

First Grey Hair, The. Mary E. Tucker. CBWP-1

First having read the book of myths. Diving into the Wreck. Adrienne Rich. ColAP; EmeKit; HCAP; HarvBoo; HeIP-4; InPK-6; MakPoe; NAAL-2v2; NAAL-5; NALW; NIL-7; NIP-4; NOBA; NoAM; NoP-4; OxWW; PoPoPo

First hazelnut trundles down from above, The. Squirrel, The. Saleem Barakat. MAP, *tr. by* Lena Jayyusi and Naomi Shihab Nye

First hear, then repeat what I say: it's rhymed. Mene Tekel. Frigyes Karinthy. IQMS, *tr. by* Aaron Kramer

First horn lifts its arm over the dew-lit grass, The. House Slave, The. Rita Dove. NoAM

First horse I ever saw, The. Horse. Michael Waters. UrbNat

First hot night, The. Anita Virgil. HA

First Hour. Sarah Josepha Buell Hale. *Fr.* Three Hours; or, The Vigil of Love.

First I am one. Mystery, The. Jeni Couzyn. HAWP

First I looked on, after a long time far from home, The. American Change. Allen Ginsberg. HCAP

First I lowered my head. Woman's Song, about Men, A. *Unknown.* STP, *tr. by* Armand Schwerner and Paul-Emile Victor

First I saw the white bear, then I saw the black. At the Zoo. William Makepeace Thackeray. NTCP

First I was born and it was tough on Mom. Story Often Told in Bars, A: The *Reader's Digest* Version. William Matthews. ReTh

First I went down to the street. Ballad of Going Down to the Store, A. Miron Bialoszewski. BLT, *tr. by* Czeslaw Milosz

First I would have a face exactly fair. How to Choose a Mistress. Edmond Prestwich. NOSC

First, I would have her be beautiful. Selecting a Reader. Ted Kooser. PBCAP

First Ice, The. Andrey [*or* Andrei] Andreievich Voznesensky [*or* Voznesenskii]. RusPo, *tr. by* Robert Arthur Douglas Ford

First idea was not our own, The. Adam. Wallace Stevens. NOBA *Fr.* Notes toward a Supreme Fiction.

First Impression. Joe Wenderoth. NAPBL

First Impressions. Alfred Grant Walton. PoToHe

First in a carriage. *Unknown.* OxNR

First in his pride the orient sun's display. Joseph Hilaire Pierre Belloc. FaBoEE

First in the North. The black sea-tangle beaches. Mythical Journey, The. Edwin Muir. NoAM; OxBS

First indication was this repeated tic, The, the latch jigging and clicking. Asylum. Ciaran Carson. PNI

First inroads were made in our 19-aughts. Contemporary Culture and the Letter "K." Alfred Corn. NoP-4

First Invasion of Ireland, The. *Unknown.* BIrV, *tr. by* John Montague

First is a park, The. Four-Light Window, A. Ágnes Nemes Nagy. VCWP, *tr. by* Hugh Maxton

First Kingdom, The. Seamus Heaney. PoetW *Fr.* Sweeney Redivivus.

First know, my friend, I do not mean. Matthew Green. ECEV; NOEC *Fr.* Spleen, The.

First lady of the throne room, The. Restoration of Enheduanna to Her Former Station, The. Enheduanna. BoWoP

First Lawcase, The. *Unknown.* BIrV, *tr. by* John Montague

First Lay of Gudrun, The. *Unknown.* AWP, *tr. by* Eirikr Magnusson and William Morris *Fr.* Elder Edda, The.

First Lesson. Philip Booth. TwCP

First lesson is electricity, The. Art of Kissing, The. Mary Ann Samyn. AmPoNex

First let me show you with the pointer. Map. Martin Sorescu. VCWP, *tr. by* Michael Longley and Russell-Gebbett

First, let me view what noxious nonsense reigns. Richard Savage. OBSV *Fr.* Authors of the Town, The.

First let there be a tree, roots taking ground. Design for a Quilt. John Ormond. AngWePo; TCAWP

First Letter From Tamara A. Reiner Kunze. PoSu, *tr. by* Ewald Osers

First Letter to an Irish Novelist. Roy McFadden. PNI

First Light. Thomas Kinsella. BIrV; PoE

First Light. Lisa Suhair Majaj. PoArWo

First light of morning, it gives you no warning. Those Which Were Pomp and Delight. Pedro Calderón de la Barca. WoPoe, *tr. by* Katherine Washburn

First light shook with ax blows to the frozen pond. Winter. Judy Jordan. AmPoNex

First Limick. Ogden Nash. PeLi

First Lord's Song, The. Sir William Schwenck Gilbert. PeLV *Fr.* H. M. S. Pinafore.

First Love. Thomas Campion. OxBoLi

First Love. John Clare. BoLoP; EnLoPo; HAP; NOBVV; NoP-4; PoPoPo

First Love. Mary Dorcey. BrRo

First Love. Elizabeth Jennings. LW

First Love. Edwin Rolfe. APT-2

First Love. Vidyapati. ErotSp, *tr. by* Sam Hamill

First Maccabees. Bible, Apocrypha.
 "And his son Judas, who was called Maccabeus." TrJP
 "And there was great mourning in Israel in every place." TrJP
 Dirge: "Her house is become like a man dishonored." TrJP
 Great Mourning. TrJP
 Judas Maccabeus. TrJP

First, make a letter like a monument. Book of Kells, The. Padraic Colum. BlrV

First man—you are his child, he is your child, The. Song of the Flood. *Unknown.* TTTS

First Mango. Vince Gotera. ReBoTo

First March. Ivor Gurney. OxBEV

First Meditation. Theodore Roethke. LCAP-2; NOBA *Fr.* Meditations of an Old Woman.

First Meetings. Arseny [*or* Arsenii] Aleksandrovich Tarkovsky [*or* Tarkovskii]. TCRP, *tr. by* Albert C. Todd

First melt, The. Michael McClintock. HA

First Men on Mercury, The. Edwin Morgan. NePenScot; PeLV

First Merseburg Spell. *Unknown.* GePo, *tr. by* Carroll Hightower

First month, early auspicious, Dinghai day, The. Yun'er's Bell. Yun'er. WoPoe, *tr. by* Constance A. Cook

First month of his absence, The. Song (On Seeing Dead Bodies Floating Off the Cape). Alun Lewis. NAEL-5v2; NAEL-6v2; OBWP

First month of winter: cold air comes. *Unknown.* CoBCP

First month of winter the blood of ours sons, The. Lament for Ch'en T'ao. Tu Fu. CrYelRi, *tr. by* Sam Hamill

First Morning. George Keithley. PoCoUp

First morning after anyone's death, is it important, The. Thomas Hardy. Norman Dubie. LCAP-2

First morning of Three Mile Island: those first disquieting, uncertain, mystifying hours, The. Tar. C. K. Williams. VCAP

First Movement. Padraic Fiacc. PNI

First-name-only business beggars history, The. Larkin. Gibbons Ruark. DiPo

First Night. Julia H. Ackerman. PasH

First Night, A. Peter Kane Dufault. DiPo; NoP-4

First night, the first night, The. Carol for the Last Christmas Eve. Norman Nicholson. NOxBChV; OBCP

First night you were gone. Place, Places. Melvin Dixon. ISC

1st. No other God exists than Mighty Me. Ten New Commandments. Robert Greacen. PeLV

First nobody liked us; they said we smelled. American Dream: First Report. Joseph Papaleo. UnSA

First Nowell, The. *Unknown.* ChrPo

First Nowell the angel did say, The. First Nowell, The. *Unknown.* ChrPo

First of all do you remember the way a bear goes through. Destruction. Joanne Kyger. BLT

First of all, I could never get a straight answer. I'd ask, what day is it. Why He Had to Go. Justin Chin. AmPoNex

First of all it has to be anecdotal; ideas don't exist. Canadian Prairie's View of Literature, The. David Donnell. NOBC

"First of all, it's all true." Creation. Simon J. Ortiz. CDW; ColAP; HATNAP

First of all, it's being nine years old and. What It's Like to Be a Black Girl (For Those of You Who Aren't). Patricia Smith. UnSA

First of all my dreams was of, The. E. E. Cummings. VGW

First of all people was Adam, The. Moira Blyth. PeLi

First of Autumn, The. Meng Hao Jan. SuSp, *tr. by* Paul W. Kroll

First of December, The. Publius Papinius Statius. RomPo, *tr. by* W. G. Shepherd *Fr.* Sylvae.

First of May, The. *Unknown.* ReMoGo

First of summer, lovely sight. *Unknown.* NOIV

First of that train which cursed the wave. To the First Slave Ship. Lydia Huntley Sigourney. ColAP

First of the gods I honor in my prayer is Mother Earth. Eumenides, The. Aeschylus. NAWM-5v1

First of the undecoded messages read: Popeye sits in thunder, The. Farm Implements and Rutabagas in a Landscape. John Ashbery. CoAP; HarvBoo; PmAP

First of walkers come the Earwigs. Earwigs. Edward Newman. VerBaPo

First on Offense. David Lehman. PmAP

First on TV, A. David Ignatow. RaBo

First pains came slow, The. First Death. Ann Townsend. NeAmPo

First pale shoots, The. On a Picture of Your House. Douglas G. Jones. NOBC

First Party at Ken Kesey's with Hell's Angels. Allen Ginsberg. PmAP; TRP (Cool black night thru redwoods.) CoAmPo

First Payment. Jon Mukand. BloBone

First Performance of the Rock 'n Roll Band *Puce Exit*. Kevin Stein. SwNoth

First Person—1981. D. F. Brown. CDa

First person to set foot on land was Noah's daughter, The. Ballad of Noah's Daughter. Rossana Ombres. Nelt, *tr. by* Ruth Feldman

First Philosopher's Song. Aldous Leonard Huxley. AWP

First, Plaintiff contracted with Defendant. Anonymous Wedding Photo. Jennifer O'Grady. AmPoNex

First Poem, The. Paavo Haavikko. PFTM-2, *tr. by* Anselm Hollo *Fr.* Winter Palace, The.

First Poem, The. Mark Van Doren. APT-2

1st Poem for Cuba. Sandra Maria Esteves. PueRic

First Portrait of My Son. Alaide Foppa. TANSG, *tr. by* Celeste Kostopulos-Cooperman

First Praise. William Carlos Williams. VGW

First Prayer for the Hottentotsgod. Breyten Breytenbach. AF, *tr. by* Denis Hirson

First Prelude. Francis J. Smith. CRP

First Problem. Aimé Césaire. NegPo, *tr. by* Ellen Conroy Kennedy

First Psalm (Posthumous). Bertolt Brecht. PFTM-1

First Quilt. Ann Townsend. AmPoNex

First Radio. Michael McFee. SwNoth

First Reader Santee Training School, 1873, The. Diane Glancy. LTA

First real grip I ever got on things, The. Wheels within Wheels. Seamus Heaney. ModIr

First rehearse the easy things. How to Disappear. Amanda Dalton. NeBl

First Resurrection. Géza Páskándi. IQMS, *tr. by* Neville Masterman

First resurrection, move forward. First Resurrection. Géza Páskándi. IQMS, *tr. by* Neville Masterman

First retainer / he gave to her, The. Marriage, A. Robert Creeley. NeAP; RaBo

First Robin. Jane Yolen. NOxBChV

First Rock and Roll Song of 1970, The. Pedro Juan Pietri. ReTh

First Rondeau: After a French Poet of the Fourteenth Century. Johann Nikolaus Götz. GePo, *tr. by* George C. Schoolfield

First Rule. Maurice Kenny. HATNAP

First rule is to pacify the wives, The. Gwyneth Lewis. MFPA *Fr.* Welsh Espionage.

First Samuel. Bible, *O.T.*
  "And Hannah prayed, and said." BoWoP
  Hannah's Song of Thanksgiving. AWP
  Hannah's Thanksgiving. BoWoP
  "My heart doth in the Lord rejoice [*or* rejoiceth in the Lord], that living Lord of might." AWP
  (Song of Hannah, The.) TrCP

First Satire of the Second Book of Horace [Imitated], The. Pope. "With all a woman's virtues but the pox." OBSV

First Second, The. Ian Duhig. NeBl

First see those ample melons—brindled o'er. Basket of Summer Fruit, A. Charles Harpur. NOBAu

First sentence: Her cheap perfume. Seduced by Analogy. Bob Perelman. FTOS

First Sex. Richard Tayson. WiU

First Shaman Song. Gary Snyder. NOBA; PFTM-2 *Fr.* Myths and Texts.

First she heard a sound. Sound, The. Robert Kelly. PoM

First shot out of that sling, The. After Goliath. Kingsley Amis. NOBL; OxBTC

First Sight. Philip Larkin. NTCP

First Sight of Her and After. Thomas Hardy. FaBoVe

First sign of fall: yellow chalk. School of Denial. Mary Ruefle. ExTi

First silver work of kindness, The. First Station, The. Jean Valentine. ExTi

First Six Verses of the Ninetieth Psalm, The. Robert Burns. ChIV-1

First Smile. Nathan [*or* Natan] Alterman. FIT, *tr. by* Robert Friend

First Snow. Joseph Awad. GraLe

First snow. Basho. EH; NIL-7, *tr. by* Robert Hass

First snow, The. Tanko (d. 1735). JDP, *tr. by* Yoel Hoffmann

First snow comes in on lorries from the north. Weather Report. Charles Tomlinson. HarvBoo

First Snow-fall, The. James Russell Lowell. ITBLP

First snow / Head clear. Etsujin. ZenPo, *tr. by* Takashi Ikemoto and Lucien Stryk

First Snow in Alsace. Richard Wilbur. NoP-4; OBWP

First snow, unrolling scrim, my dogs running. Aubade: Opal and Silver. Mark Doty. HarvBoo

First snow was sleet, The. It swished heavily. Sleet. Norman MacCaig. OBCP

First snow wet against the windshield. In the Third Month. David Ray. RaBo

First Snowfall, The. James Russell Lowell. TAP

First Snowfall [*or* Snow-Fall], The. James Russell Lowell. AmFaPo; TAP

First Snowflake. N. M. Bodecker. TLR

First Solitude, The. Luis de Góngora y Argote. OBVE, *tr. by* Edward Meryon Wilson

First Song. T. Carmi. MHP, *tr. by* Ruth Finer Mintz *Fr.* René's Songs.

First Song. Galway Kinnell. NoP-4; TwCP

First Song of Moses, The. George Wither. ChIV-1

First Song of the Exploding Stick. *Unknown.* APN-2, *tr. by* Washington Matthews *Fr.* Mountain Chant, The.

First Song of the Thunder. *Unknown.* APN-2; TCAPo, *tr. by* Washington Matthews *Fr.* Mountain Chant, The.

First sorrow of autumn, The. Seven Sorrows, The. Ted Hughes. NAEL-5v2; NAEL-6v2

First Spring. Duane Niatum. HATNAP

First Spring Day, The. Christina Georgina Rossetti. FaBoVe

First Spring in California, 1936. Wilma Elizabeth McDaniel. GeoHom

First Station, The. Jean Valentine. ExTi

First Steps. J. D. McClatchy. WiU

  "Chasing on the margins of pond-waters, the sun." WiU

  1871. WiU

  "How to put this exactly? I mean without." WiU

  1946, 1957. WiU

  1971. WiU

  "Spirit sets about its task, but slowly, The." WiU

  "What do *you* think?" The question my head." WiU

First Steps Up Parnassus. Michael Drayton. NOBE

  (And so my deare friend, for this time adue.) (LL) PBRV

  (First Steps Up Parnassus.) NOBE

  (My dearely loved friend how oft have we.) PBRV

  (To my most dearely-loved friend Henery Reynolds Esquire, of Poets and Poesie.) PBRV

First Stone of the New Castle, The. *Unknown.* PeSAV, *tr. by* H. C. V. Leibbrandt

First strawberry, The. Original Strawberry. Nancy Willard. LCAP-2

First Sunday I missed Mass on purpose, The. Day Zimmer Lost Religion, The. Paul Zimmer. InPK-6; PBCAP

First surprise: I like it, The. Getting Older. Elaine Feinstein. HarvBoo

First / tale of Gotham City, the Beggar, The. Beggar at the Gate, The. Ian Wedde. PeNZ

First Thanksgiving. Myra Cohn Livingston. HHAm

First Thanksgiving, The. Jack Prelutsky. NTCP

First Thanksgiving of All. Nancy Byrd Turner. ChAP

First the chemistry that made their atoms wobble. Sadness of Couples, The. Barbara Ras. NAPBL

First the goat. Making of the Drum, The. Edward Kamau Brathwaite. EmeKit

First the melody, clean and hard. How High the Moon. Lance Jeffers. SeSe

First the outer gate. Truth Hall. Muso Soseki. EaWin, *tr. by* W. S. Merwin

First the pleasures fire the heart. From Belfast to Suffolk. William Peskett. PNI

First the snare crack. Some Tentative Definitions 1. Kwame Dawes. WaCA

First, the two men stand pondering. Verona. James Wright (1927–80). NNaP

First there came the general's wife. Army Dance, The. *Unknown.* FaBoWar

First there was putting hot-water bottles to it. Inevitable. Sir John Betjeman. MoBrPo

First there was the island. Sea and Other Stories, The. Jennifer Rankin. NOBAu

First, there was the waking. Migration. Jane Griffiths. NeBl

First there were two of us, then there were three of us. Storm, The. Walter De la Mare. NOxBChV

First they came for the Jews. First They Came for the Jews. Pastor Niemoller. HP

First They Slaughtered the Angels. Lenore Kandel. BB

First they taught us earth. The Napoleonic death. Ballad of the Bayonet, A. Ernest Bryll. FaBoWar, *tr. by* Czeslaw Milosz

First Thing. Kit Robinson. FTOS

First Thing, The. Mohja Kahf. PoArWo

First thing I saw in the morning, The. Mantova. James Wright (1927–80). NNaP

First Things. Lucienne Desnoues. WPOW, *tr. by* Miller Williams

First things first. First. Douglas Florian. NOxBChV

First think, my soul, if I have foes. George Wither. SacPr *Fr.* Prisoner's Lay, A.

First, this one: "Peetah, Peetah, Peetah!" Kong Breaks a Leg at the William Morris Agency. William Trowbridge. ReTh

First time, The. Bare Floors. Melanie Hope. WiU

First Time, The. Karl Shapiro. APT-2; VGW

First time he kissed me, he but only kissed. Elizabeth Barrett Browning. CTC; CenSon; ITBLP; LW *Fr.* Sonnets from the Portuguese.

First time I flew over Florida I was amazed, The. Distinct Call of the Alligator, The. Betsy Sholl. PBCAP

First time I got high I stood in a circle, The. Blunts. Major L. Jackson. SpirFl

First time I heard, The. Big Words, The. Brendan Kennelly. EmeKit

First time I held a gun, The. Gun, The. Jacqueline Berger. AmPoNex

First time I lied to my baby, I told him that it was his face on the baby food jar, The. How Lies Grow. Maxine Chernoff. IllVoic; PmAP

First time I saw her between her embroidered curtains, The. Tune: "Joy in Spring's Coming"—Seven Songs. *Unknown.* SuSp, *tr. by* Wayne Schlepp

First time I saw hundreds of fiddlehead ferns boiling. Fiddleheads. Maureen Seaton. BAP-97

First time I saw you, The. *Unknown.* OHMPJ

First time I see, The. Carmelita. D. A. Feinfeld. BloBone

First time I walked, The. Oranges. Gary Soto. NoAM; WeW-3

First time I was sweet sixteen. Nayo-Barbara Watkins. NBV

First Time In. Ivor Gurney. FaBoVe

First Time: 1950. Honor Moore. FFC; GLP

First time out. Lives. Derek Mahon. EmeKit; ModIr; PBCIP

First time that the sun rose on thine oath, The. Elizabeth Barrett Browning. CenSon; NAEL-5v2; NAEL-6v2; WPE *Fr.* Sonnets from the Portuguese.

First to come, The. Song of the Crows. *Chippewa Oral Tradition.* NAAL-5

First to feast is love, The. On the scraps of love the fever feasts. Margherita Guidacci. CItWP, *tr. by* Cinzia Sartini Blum and Lara Trubowitz *Fr.* Meditations and Maxims.

First Tooth, The. Charles Lamb. WoRP

First touch of hand in hand—Did one but know! (LL) Christina Georgina Rossetti. BoLoP; LW; OxBSo; Son *Fr.* Monna Innominata.

First Trimester, The. Campbell McGrath. NeAmPo; UrbNat

First Turn to Me. Bernadette Mayer. PmAP

First TV in a Mennonite Family. Julia Kasdorf. AmPoNex

First unexpected pain is beautiful, The. Ivano Fermini. ItPo, *tr. by* Gayle Ridinger

1st Untitled Poem. Pedro Juan Pietri. PueRic

First View of the Islands, A. Jean V. Gier. ReBoTo

First Villancico, Written for the Nativity of Our Lord, Puebla, 1689, The. Sister Juana Inés de la Cruz.

  "Since Love is shivering." WPoS

First Walk on the Moon. May Swenson. RACG

First war resembles. First War. Samuel Ha-Nagid. WoPoe, *tr. by* Peter Cole

First Warning Sign: Epiphany. Edoardo Cacciatore. ItPo, *tr. by* Gayle Ridinger *Fr.* Full Powers: Five Warning Signs.

First was Fancy, like a lovely boy, The. Edmund Spenser. CAGL *Fr.* Faerie Queene, The.

First we locked our fingers, wove them. My Blood Brother. Frank Mkalawile Chipasula. HBAPE

First week the soil was clean, The. Digging for Indians. Gary Gildner. PBCAP

First when Maggie [*or* Maggy] was my care. Whistle o'er the Lave o't. Robert Burns. OxBS

First William the Norman. *Unknown.* OxNR

First Winter: Joy. Peggy Shumaker. PBCAP

First winter rain. Basho. EH, *tr. by* Robert Hass

First World War Poets. Edward Bond. FaBoWar

First Year, The. Edith Jay Scovell.

  Days Drawing In. FaBoWP

  "Days fail: night broods over afternoon, The." FaBoWP

First you bite your fingernails. And then you comb your hair again. And then you wait. And wait. American Rhapsody. Kenneth Fearing. APT-2; MoAmPo

First you must blow a bottle round your sleep. Directions for Dreamfishing. Martin Johnston. CBAP

First you must have. Instructions for Building Straw Huts. Yusef Komunyakaa. GT

First, you think they are dead. Lobsters in the Window. W. D. Snodgrass. TAP; TRP

First, you took the parakeet out of its cage. Harm. Vickie Karp. KGB

Firstborn. Louise Glück. HarvBoo

Firstborn Land, The. Ingeborg Bachmann. BoWoP, *tr. by* Daniel Huws

First—Chill—then Stupor—then the letting go. (LL) Emily Dickinson. APN-2; BoWoP; HAP; HeIP-4; MoAmPo; NAAL-2v1; NAAL-3; NAAL-5; NALW; NAWM-7v2; NIL-7; NIP-4; NOBA; NoAM; NoP-4; OxWW; PAI; PoE; PoPoPo; SAmP; TAP; TCAPo; TFi; TRP; UnPo

Firste stok, fader of gentilesse, The. Gentilesse. Geoffrey Chaucer. AWP; MiEL; NAEL-5v1

Fisbo. Robert Malise Bowyer Nichols.

  "Talking of Ezra Pound and long-dead pantos." OBSV

Fish. Moniza Alvi. NeBl

Fish. Bhanuji Rao. OMIP, *tr. by* Jayanta Mahapatra

Fish. Mariana Romo-Carmona. WiU

Fish. Joe Rosenblatt. NOBC

Fish. W. W. Eustace Ross. MoCV

Fish. Shinkichi Takahashi. ZenPo, *tr.* by Takashi Ikemoto and Lucien Stryk

Fish, The. Elizabeth Bishop. APT-2; ChAP; FaBoWP; HAP; HarvBoo; HeIP-4; InPK-6; MoASP; MoAmPo; NAAL-2v2; NALW; NOBA; NoAM; NoP-4; PAI; PoE; PoPoPo; PoetW; RB; TFi; TRP

Fish, The. Marianne Craig Moore. APT-1; ColAP; FaBoWP; MoAmPo; NAAL-2v2; NoAM; NoP-4; OxBA

Fish 2. Fidelito Cortes. ReBoTo

Fish and Chips on the Merry-Go-Round. K. O. Arvidson. PeNZ

Fish Answers, A. Leigh Hunt. NBLV; NPeEn; SCGP   *Fr.* Fish, the Man, and the Spirit, The.

Fish at Mass, The. *Unknown.* BIrV, *tr.* by J. F. Webb

Fish bones walked the waves off Hatteras. Cottonmouth Country. Louise Glück. CoAP

Fish cannot drown in water, A. Mechthild von Magdeburg. EnIH; WPoS

Fish Cove. Blaise Cendrars. BLT, *tr.* by Monique Chefdor

Fish Crier. Carl Sandburg. OxBA

Fish dripping, A. Fish. W. W. Eustace Ross. MoCV

Fish (fly-replete, in depth of June). Heaven. Rupert Brooke. EBEV; MoBrPo; NOBE; NPeEn; OxBEV; PoRA

Fish Food. John Wheelwright. APT-2

Fish / fowl. Lorine Niedecker. *See* And the place was water

Fish-Hawk, The. John Hall Wheelock. APT-1

Fish in a Painting. Ho Ching-ming. CoBLCP, *tr.* by Jonathan Chaves

Fish in River: "My house is not quiet, I am not loud." Cynewulf. AnOE, *tr.* by Charles W. Kennedy   *Fr.* Riddles (Exeter Book).

Fish in the Net. János Pilinszky. IQMS, *tr.* by Adam Makkai

Fish in the Stone, The. Rita Dove. EmeKit; HCAP

Fish in the unruffled lakes. W. H. Auden. BoLoP; MoBrPo   *Fr.* Twelve Songs.

Fish man chats with the passers by, The. Fish Peddler. Mei Yao Ch'en. OHPC, *tr.* by Kenneth Rexroth

Fish Peddler. Mei Yao Ch'en. OHPC, *tr.* by Kenneth Rexroth

Fish Peddler and Cobbler. Kenneth Rexroth. NNaP

Fish Replies, A. Leigh Hunt. *See* Fish, the Man, and the Spirit, The

Fish's Nightsong. Christian Morgenstern. WeW-3

Fish shop. Basho. WoPoe; ZenPo, *tr.* by Takashi Ikemoto and Lucien Stryk

Fish Shop Windows. Geoffrey Dutton. NOBAu

Fish Tea Rice. Linda Gregg. ExTi

Fish, the Man, and the Spirit, The. Leigh Hunt. HAP; NOBL; OBEV; OxBSo

  "Amazing monster! that, for aught I know." NBLV; NPeEn; SCGP

  Fish Answers, A. NBLV; NPeEn; SCGP

  (Fish Replies, A.) PeLV

  "Man's life is warm, glad, sad, 'twixt loves and graves." NPeEn

  To a Fish. NBLV; NPeEn; PeLV; SCGP

  "You strange, astonished-looking, angle-faced." NBLV; NPeEn; PeLV; SCGP

Fish took a notion, A. Tip-Toe Tail. Dixie Willson. NTCP

Fish wade / through blade jade, The. Fish, The. Marianne Craig Moore. FaBoWP; MoAmPo; NoAM; OxBA

Fish weeps in the, The. Fish Weeps, The. *Unknown.* OHMPC, *tr.* by Kenneth Rexroth

Fisher, The. Roderic Quinn. CBAP

Fisher Street. Thylias Moss. GT

Fisheris are gon to the sea, The. For Cadging Fish. Isabel Gowdie. EMWP

Fisherman. Ou-yang Hsiu. BLT; OHPC, *tr.* by Kenneth Rexroth

Fisherman. Ts'en Shen. SuSp, *tr.* by C. H. Wang

Fisherman, The. Goethe. STV, *tr.* by John Frederick Nims

Fisherman, The. Leonidas of Tarentum. AWP, *tr.* by Andrew Lang   *Fr.* Epigrams.

Fisherman, The. Jay Macpherson. NOBC

Fisherman, The. Janice Mirikitani. OpBo

Fisherman, The. Yunna Petrovna [*or* Iunna Pinkhusovna] Moritz [*or* Morits]. TCRusP, *tr.* by Daniel Weissbort

Fisherman, The. Su Tung-p'o (Su Shih).

  "Fisherman drinks, The." SuSp

  "Fisherman, laughing, The." SuSp

  "Fisherman's drunk, The." SuSp

  "Fisherman wakes, The." SuSp

Fisherman, The. W. B. Yeats. HAP; NoAM

Fisherman drinks, The. Su Tung-p'o (Su Shih). SuSp   *Fr.* Fisherman, The.

Fisherman, Hey! *Hungarian Oral Tradition.* IQMS, *tr.* by Dermot Spence

Fisherman in wellingtons, A. Gaelic Stories. Iain Crichton Smith. NePenScot

Fisherman, laughing, The. Su Tung-p'o (Su Shih). SuSp   *Fr.* Fisherman, The.

Fisherman on a Southern Stream. Lu Kuei Meng. SuSp, *tr.* by Robin D. S. Yates

Fisherman's drunk, The. Su Tung-p'o (Su Shih). SuSp   *Fr.* Fisherman, The.

"Fisherman's Honor," The. Li Ch'ing-chao. WPoS, *tr.* by Jane Hirshfield (Written to the Tune "The Fisherman's Honor") WoPoe

Fisherman's hut, by the mouth of the river. Coming at Night to a Fisherman's Hut. Chang Chi. BLT

Fisherman's Lyric. Chao Meng-fu. CoBLCP, *tr.* by Jonathan Chaves

Fisherman's Rhyme. *Unknown.* FaBoVe

Fisherman's Song, The. Thomas D'Urfey [*or* Durfey]. NOSC

Fisherman's Songs. Chang Chih-ho.

  "Before dusk on the lake, the moon just full." SuSp

  "Near the rim of Hsi-sai Mountain, white egrets fly." SuSp

  "Oh, about the joy of owning a crab hut at Sung-chiang!" SuSp

Fisherman's Story, The. Henrietta Cordelia Ray. CBWP-3

Fisherman's Wife, The. Jody Gladding. YaYoPo

Fisherman's Wife, The. Amy Lowell. BoWoP

Fisherman wakes, The. Su Tung-p'o (Su Shih). SuSp   *Fr.* Fisherman, The.

Fishermen. Song. Primus St. John. GT

Fishermen, The. Theocritus. AWP; OBVE, *tr.* by Charles Stuart Calverley   *Fr.* Idylls.

Fishermen among the fireweed, The. By Rail through the Earthly Paradise, Perhaps Bedfordshire. Denise Levertov. NNaP

Fishermen at Ballyshannon. Limbo. Seamus Heaney. CIP-2; NoAM; OxBC

Fishermen, Drowned beyond the West Coast. Vivian Smith. CBAP

Fishermen from Ma Yuan. "Lucebert." TuT, *tr.* by Peter Van de Kamp

Fishermen, hey! Fishermen, hey! Fisherman, Hey! *Hungarian Oral Tradition.* IQMS, *tr.* by Dermot Spence

Fishermen's fires glitter and fade. Staying Overnight on the Banks of Embroidered River. Li K'ai-hsien. CoBLCP, *tr.* by Jonathan Chaves

Fishermen's Song. *Unknown.* PeNZ, *tr.* by Margaret Orbell

Fishermen will relate that in the South. Lord of the Isle, The. Stefan George. AWP, *tr.* by Ludwig Lewisohn

Fishes are born in water. Man Is Born in Tao. Chuang Tzu. BLT, *tr.* by Thomas Merton

Fishes swim in water clear. *Unknown.* OxNR

Fishing. Paula McLain. AmPoNex

Fishing. Dorothy Wellesley, Duchess of Wellington. OBMV

Fishing Among the Learned. Nikky Finney. SpirFl

Fishing at dawn, trap them east of town. Fishing Trapping Song, A. Wen T'ing-yün. SuSp, *tr.* by William R. Schultz

Fishing boat driving water. After Source of the Peach Blossom Stream. Wang Wei. ChinPo, *tr.* by Yip Wai-lim

Fishing Boats in Martigues. Roy Campbell. FaBoEE; OxBSP

Fishing cove and long lines of fishermen's huts, A. Ch'ien Ch'ien-i [*or* Ch'ien Ch'ien-yi]. SuSp   *Fr.* Poems Written in Prison.

Fishing in the Keep of Silence. Linda Gregg. BodElec

Fishing in the Wei River. Po Chü-i. ChiP, *tr.* by Arthur Waley

Fishing in Winter. Ralph Burns. MoASP

Fishing Lass of Hakin, The. Lewis Morris. AngWePo

Fishing on a wide river from a boat. Supreme Death. Douglas Dunn. FaBoMo

Fishing Rod, The. Shen Yüeh. SuSp, *tr.* by Richard B. Mather

Fishing-Tackle, The. Bertolt Brecht. PoSu, *tr.* by Lee Baxendall

Fishing the Dream. Mike Delp. MoASP

Fishing the White Water. Audre Lorde. GT

Fishing Trapping Song, A. Wen T'ing-yün. SuSp, *tr.* by William R. Schultz

Fishing with Elvis. Dabney Stuart. AllShUp

Fishmarket closed, the fishes gone into flesh, The. Galway Kinnell. CoAmPo   *Fr.* Avenue Bearing the Initial of Christ into the New World, The.

Fishmonger. Marsden Hartley. APT-1

Fishnet. Robert Lowell. HCAP; PoetW; VCAP

Fishy smell, A. Basho. EH, *tr.* by Robert Hass

Fist, The. Derek Walcott. ESEAA

Fist meets the face as the stone meets water, The. Battery. Robin Morgan. GifTon

Fist of red fire, a flower, A. First Love. Elizabeth Jennings. LW

Fistful of News, A. Antoine-Roger Bolamba. PBMAP

Fists. Peter Finch. TCAWP

Fists in their pockets, daggers in their eyes. (LL) Drinks in the Town Square. Rachel Wetzsteon. AmPoNex; NeAmPo

Fit As a Fiddle. Arthur Freed. ReLy

Fit of Rhyme [*or* Rime] against Rhyme [*or* Rime], A. Ben Jonson. BeJo

  (Fit of Rhyme Against Rhyme, A.) NoP-4

  (Fit of Rime against Rime, A.) PBRV

  (Rhyme, the rack of finest wits.) NoP-4

  (Rime, the rack of finest wits.) PBRV

Fit only for barbarians. (LL) Translation. Roy Fuller. NOBE; OxBTC

Fit place to observe the transit of Venus, A. Tahiti. Louis Johnson. PeNZ

Fit the Second: The Bellman's Speech. Lewis Carroll. OBCoV *Fr.* Hunting of the Snark, The.

Fit the Sixth: The Barrister's Dream. Lewis Carroll. EBNV *Fr.* Hunting of the Snark, The.

Fitness expert. Big gym-man. Strato [*or* Straton]. EroLit, *tr. by* Kenneth McLeish

Fitting. Pauline Prior-Pitt. Prnts

Fitting, The. Edna St. Vincent Millay. NALW

Fitz-Eustace's Song. Sir Walter Scott. GTBS-P *Fr.* Marmion.

Fitzroy. Andrew Taylor. BMAP

5. Catullus. NAWM-7v1; WoPoe, *tr. by* Charles Martin

Five. Dennis Phillips. FTOS *Fr.* Twenty Questions.

Five a.m., and I've been. Dawn. Lucien Stryk. InvLad

Five Arabic Verses in Praise of Wine. *Unknown.* TrJP, *tr. by* Hartwig Hirschfeld

Five barrels of flour seventy sticks. Making Old Bones. Alberta Turner. LCAP-2

Five bells. Five bells coldly ringing out. / Five bells. (LL) Five Bells. Kenneth Slessor. CBAP; NOBAu; PoRA

Five best doctors anywhere, The. Five Best Doctors, The. O. S. Hoffman. PoToHe

Five bolts of hanging silk. Returning from the Seventy-Two Mountains. Hsü Wei. CoBLCP, *tr. by* Jonathan Chaves

Five buds were on the parent tree. Family Portraits. Mary E. Tucker. CBWP-1

Five Chants. David McCord. NOxBChV

Five-Color. Yang Chi. CoBLCP; WoPoe, *tr. by* Jonathan Chaves

Five daughters, in the slant light on the porch. Daughters, 1900. Marilyn Nelson Waniek. FFC

Five Dawn Skies in November. David Wagoner. VCAP

Five-Day Rain, The. Denise Levertov. NeAP

Five Domestic Interiors. Vernon Scannell. OxBC

5.8.1942 / In Memory of Janusz Korczak*. Jerzy Ficowski. HP, *tr. by* Keith Bosley

Five Epigrams. James Vincent Cunningham.
And Now You're Ready Who While She Was Here. GrAn; OBVE, *tr. by* James Vincent Cunningham
"Bride loved old words, and found her pleasure marred." OBAL
(Epigram: "Naked I came, naked I leave the scene") VGW
Epitaph for Someone or Other. APT-2; OBAL; TRP; WoPoe
Lip. OBAL
"Lip was a man who used his head." OBAL
"Naked I came, naked I leave the scene." APT-2; OBAL; TRP; WoPoe
(Too Late.) WoPoe

515 Madison Avenue. Rhapsody. Frank O'Hara. NoAM

Five-Finger Exercises. T. S. Eliot.
"How delightful to meet Mr. Hodgson!" NBLV; OBAL; PeLV
"How unpleasant to meet Mr. Eliot!" NBLV; OBAL; OBCoV; PeLV; UV
Lines for Cuscuscaraway and Mirza Murad Ali Beg. NBLV; OBAL; OBCoV; PeLV; UV
Lines to Ralph Hodgson Esqre. NBLV; OBAL; PeLV

Five Flower World Variations. *Unknown.* STP, *tr. by* Jerome Rothenberg

Five Foot Two, Eyes of Blue (Has Anybody Seen My girl?). Joe Young. ReLy

Five for the Grace of Man. Winfield Townley Scott. VGW

5.40. The Bay View. After the office. Kingsley Amis. NOBL *Fr.* Evans Country, The.

Five geese deploy mysteriously. Bas-Relief. Carl Sandburg. ColAP

Five Ghost Songs. *Ambo Oral Tradition.* TTTS

Five gleaming crows. In Air. Peter Clarke. PBA

Five Groups of Verse. Charles Reznikoff.
After I Had Worked All Day. VGW

Five hours, (and who can do it less in?). Lady's Dressing Room, The. Jonathan Swift. NAEL-7v1

Five Hundred Points of Good Husbandry. Thomas Tusser.
Advice of Housewives. NoSic
December's Husbandry. NoSic
"Make company break." NoSic
"When frost will not suffer to dike and to hedge." NoSic

Five Hymns to Pain. Nazik Al-Malaika. PoArWo, *tr. by* Husain Haddawy

Five inches from. Desire. Paul Hoover. PmAP

Five Men. Zbigniew Herbert. PoSu, *tr. by* Czeslaw Milosz and Peter Dale Scott

Five men pull straws. Fragging. Yusef Komunyakaa. ESEAA

Five miles beneath the fuselage I see. First View of the Islands, A. Jean V. Gier. ReBoTo

Five-Minute Orlando Macbeth, The. George MacBeth [*or* Macbeth]. NOBL; PeLV

Five Minutes. Norman Nicholson. NLP

Five minutes, five minutes more, please! Bedtime. Eleanor Farjeon. OTCP

"5 Minutes, Mr. Salaam." Kalamu ya Salaam. SpirFl

Five minutes with his paintings and I remember. Fauviste. Donald Revell. BodElec

Five months after your death, I come like the others. Elegy for a Forest Clear-Cut by the Weyerhaeuser Company. David Wagoner. NoAM

Five months have passed. Hair. Yusuf Al-Sa'igh. MAP, *tr. by* Diana Der Hovanessian and Salma Khadra Jayyusi

Five Nights of Bleeding. Linton Kwesi Johnson. WaCA

Five Nocturnes. Robert Frost.
Were I in Trouble. OxBSP
"Where I could think of no thoroughfare." OxBSP

Five Nocturnes, after Derek Jarman. Ken Edwards.
"About this time streetlamps flicker up like." Oth
"Art of definition—is this, An." Oth
"De—um majorettes." Oth
"Night falls on single vision zombies everywhere." Oth
"This juxtaposition of events without." Oth

Five Notebooks for Exit Art. Cecilia Vicuña. PFTM-2

Five-0. Ras Baraka. InTrad

Five O'Clock Opera. Lavinia Greenlaw. MFPA

Five Old Favorites. James Merrill.
Midnight Snack, The. OxBSo
"When I was little and he was riled." OxBSo

Five. One. Laurie Duggan. BMAP *Fr.* Ash Range, The.

Five oxen, grazing in a flowery mead. On a Seal. Plato. AWP; FaBoEE, *tr. by* Thomas Stanley

5 Poems. Robert Gray. CBAP

Five Poems about Poetry. George Oppen.
From Virgil. NNaP
Gesture, The. NNaP
"I, says the buzzard." NNaP
"Question is: how does one hold an apple, The." NNaP

Five Poems on Returning to Hangchou. Yüan Mei. CoBLCP, *tr. by* Jonathan Chaves

Five rice dumplings. Ransetsu. ZenPo, *tr. by* Takashi Ikemoto and Lucien Stryk

Five rivers, like the fingers of a hand. Ebenezer Elliott. NOBRP *Fr.* Village Patriarch, The.

Five seasons without traveling to a festival, without walking. Homage to Lester Flatt. David Bottoms. SwNoth

Five Sestinas. James Keir Baxter.
Dark Welcome, The. PeNZ
"In the rains of winter the pa children." PeNZ

Five Smooth Stones. Deborah Digges. ExTi

Five soldiers fixed by Mathew Brady's eye. Looking into History. Richard Wilbur. VCAP; VGW

Five Songs. W. H. Auden.
Epilogue: "'O where are you going?' said reader to rider." FaBoCh; NOBE; NoAM; OxBEV; UV
Love Song: "For what as easy." PeLV
"That night when joy began." OxBTC; PAI; SoSe-8
(Three Companions, The.) WoPoe

Five Songs. W. H. Auden.
Song: "Deftly, admiral, cast your fly." GTBS-P
"Starling and a willow-wren, A." FaBoMo

Five Sorrowful Mysteries, The. Francis Jammes. GI, *tr. by* Jeffrey Fiskin

Five-string, The. Po Chü-i. ChiP, *tr. by* Arthur Waley

Five Students, The. Thomas Hardy. GTBS-P

Five summer days, five summer nights. Blue-Fly, The. Robert Graves. NAEL-5v2; NAEL-6v2; NoAM

Five Things Sought For—In the Manner of Han Wo. Hsü Pen. CoBLCP, *tr. by* Jonathan Chaves

Five Things White. Edward May. FaBoEE

5:30 A.M. Adrienne Rich. NOBA

Five-thirty light fell onto the dining room table, The. Leaving Home. Sarah Rosenblatt. AmPoNex

5:32, The. Phyllis McGinley. APT-2; WPE *Fr.* I Know a Village.

529 1983. Gerda Mayer. Spl

Five Unmistakable Marks, The. David Jones. *Fr.* In Parenthesis.

Five Urban Love Songs. Kate Light.
"If safety can be had from hollow men." AmPoNex
Safe-T-Man. AmPoNex

Five Weeks. Lee Ranaldo. HeMarv

Five Were Foolish. Arthur J. Hodge. AH

Five Wishes. Anne Porter. KGB

Five Words for Joe Dunn on His 22nd Birthday.   Jack Spicer.   PoM

Five years ago we knew such ecstasies.   Interim.   Frank Ormsby.   CIP-2

Five summers have passed [or past]; five summers, with the length.   William Wordsworth.   AmFaPo; CABP; FHYEP; HeIP-4; NAEL-6v2; NAWM-7v2; NIL-7; NPeEn; NoP-4; OxAEP-2; OxBEV; PoPoPo; SCGP; TFi

Five years since you died and I am.   Letter to a Dead Father.   Richard Shelton.   PBCAP

Five yen each / A cup of tea.   Issa.   ZenPo, tr. by Takashi Ikemoto and Lucien Stryk

Fix.   Michael Dransfield.   NOBAu

Fix bayonets, and die, as English soldiers do.   Isandula.   Hume Nisbet.   FaBoWar

Fixed Ideas.   Kenneth Slessor.   BMAP

Fixed in the fireplace.   Fireplace, The.   Michael S. Harper.   GT

Fixer of Midnight.   Reuel Denney.   OBAL

Fixin' to Die.   Bukka White.   APT-2

Flaccus gave me, the silver lamp.   Statilius Flaccus.   GrAn

Flag, The.   Pablo Neruda.   PoetW, tr. by Nathaniel Tarn

Flag-covered coffin.   Nicholas Virgilio.   HA

Flag Goes By, The.   Henry Holcomb Bennett.   PWR

Flag of Chile, The.   Teresa de Jesús.   AF, tr. by Maria Proser

Flagpole Sitter, The.   Donald Finkel.   CoAP

Flags of all sorts.   Things We Dreamt We Died For.   Marvin Bell.   CoAP

Flags of war like storm-birds fly, The.   Battle Autumn of 1862, The.   John Greenleaf Whittier.   CBCWP

Flags Vex a Dying Face.   Emily Dickinson.   MoAmPo

Flailed from the heart of water in a bow.   Ballade for the Duke of Orléans.   Richard Wilbur.   WoPoe

Flailing like a foal giraffe to keep his balance.   Sailing.   Richard Kenney.   YaYoPo

Flake diamond of / the sea.   Larry Eigner.   PoM

Flakes not of fabric but of words of fabric of words—scraps—remnants.   Bernard Heidsieck.   PFTM-2, tr. by Nicholas Zürbrugg   Fr. Canal Street.

Flakes pour to the black dead.   In the Camp There Was One Alive.   Randall Jarrell.   HP

Flame burns in the morning, A.   Le Chariot.   John Wieners.   VGW

Flame-flower, day-torch, Mauna Loa.   Lines to a Nasturtium.   Anne Spencer.   APT-1

Flame Ode.   Barry MacSweeney.   Oth

Flame out, you glorious skies.   Dead Heroes, The.   Isaac Rosenberg.   MoBrPo

Flame's speech is confused, The. The muttering of the water is hollow.   A. Velichansky.   TCRusP, tr. by Daniel Weissbort

Flamenco Guitar.   Ruth L. Schwartz.   WiU

Flames.   Tōge Sankichi.   FaBoWar, tr. by Richard H. Minear

Flames and Dangling Wire.   Robert Gray.   BMAP; NOBAu

Flames are shooting.   Song of the Fire-Charm.   Unknown.   STP, tr. by Frances Densmore and Jerome Rothenberg

Flames from sun.   Magnificent Tomorrows.   Haki R. Madhubuti.   SpirFl

Flames?, The. (LL)   Another Night in the Ruins.   Galway Kinnell.   CoAP; InvLad

Flaming Heart, The.   Richard Crashaw.   NAEL-5v1; NAEL-6v1; NAEL-7v1
   "Live in these conquering leaves; live all the same."   OxAEP-1
   "O Heart! the equal poise of love's both parts."   GeHe
   "O sweet incendiary! shew here thy art."   NPeEn
   "O thou undaunted daughter of desires!"   HAP; NOBE; OBEV; WoPoe
   Upon the Book and Picture of the Seraphical Saint Teresa.   HAP; NOBE; OBEV; WoPoe

Flaming Terrapin, The.   Roy Campbell.
   "Maternal Earth stirs redly from beneath."   MoBrPo

Flaming with anger and despair, Perseus is hunting Medusa.   Apotheosis of Medusa.   Pat Parnell.   HW

Flamingo, The.   Saleem Barakat.   MAP, tr. by Lena Jayyusi and Naomi Shihab Nye

Flamingo delouses its belly with the easy speed.   Seriema Song.   Albert Goldbarth.   UrbNat

Flamingos, The.   Rainer Maria Rilke.   OWoS, tr. by Stephen Mitchell

Flammonde.   Edwin Arlington Robinson.   NoAM

Flaneur, The.   Oliver Wendell Holmes.   APN-1

Flanking Sheep in Mosedale.   David Scott.   NLP

Flannan Isle.   Wilfrid Wilson Gibson.   PoRA

Flannery O'Connor.   Dorothy Walters.   PoRA

Flap, flap, the captive bird in the cage.   Scholar in the Narrow Street, The.   Tso Ssu.   AWP; ChiP, tr. by Arthur Waley

Flap, flap, the sounds of autumn.   Spending the Night in an Inn at Swatow and Writing about My Feelings, Sent to Liang Shih-wu.   Huang Tsun-hsien.   SuSp, tr. by An-yan Tang

Flap, flap, you curtain in front of our bed!   Curtain of the Wedding Bed, The.   Liu Hsün's Wife.   ChiP, tr. by Arthur Waley

Flap we our lips, praise Big Man.   Cywydd o Fawl.   Harri Webb.   AngWePo; TCAWP

Flap your wings on my bare trees.   Little Tales.   Zakiyya Malallah.   PoArWo, tr. by Wen Chin Ouyang

Flapping of ducks' wings, The.   Autumn.   Andrey [or Andrei] Andreievich Voznesensky [or Voznesenskii].   TCRP

Flash.   Lee Bennett Hopkins.   SSCS

Flash, A.   May Muzaffar.   PoArWo, tr. by Tahia Abdel Nasser

Flash Cards.   Rita Dove.   ESEAA; LoL; PoPoPo

Flash Colonial Barman, The.   William W. Coxon.   NOBAu

Flash Crimson.   Carl Sandburg.   MoAmPo

Flash lights from the wild gardens. (LL)   Wild Gardens Overlooked by Night Lights.   Barbara Guest.   FTOS; PmAP

Flash me.   Lee Ranaldo.   HeMarv

Flash of lightning does not satisfy thirst, A.   Modern Love Songs.   Unknown.   TTY, tr. by B. W. Andrzejewski and I. M. Lewis

Flash, sort belts, dresses, shirts, baby clothes. (LL)   First Time: 1950.   Honor Moore.   FFC; GLP

Flashed [or flasht] out between the middle and extre[a]me. (LL)   Definition of Beauty, The.   Robert Herrick.   BeJo; CaPo

Flashing and glimmering at the edge of the horizon. (LL)   East Coast Journey.   James Keir Baxter.   NoP-4; PeNZ

Flashing light, this ancient mirror.   Song of the Ch'in-Dynasty Mirror—Written for Yüan Sung-li.   Wang Shih-chieng.   CoBLCP, tr. by Jonathan Chaves

Flashing their angry tears, here in Live Oak. (LL)   Walking Down the Road.   Adrienne Rich.   NIL-7; NIP-4

Flashing wild horses of Europe.   Ten to One to No.   Joyce Mansour.   SurWo, tr. by Mary Beach

Flask of Brandy, A.   Padraic Fallon.   ModIr

Flat.   St. Louis.   Amy Lowell.   NAAL-5

Flat end of sorrow here, The.   First Circle, The.   Kofi Awoonor.   HBAPE; PBMAP; VCWP

Flat Mountain.   Muso Soseki.   EaWin, tr. by W. S. Merwin

Flat on the bank I parted.   Trout, The.   John Montague.   ModIr; NoP-4; PBCIP; PNI; PoE

Flattened your words against your speaking mouth. (LL)   Hearing Your Words, and Not a Word Among Them.   Edna St. Vincent Millay.   ColAP; NoAM; VGW

Flaubert in Egypt.   Robert Penn Warren.   NoAM

Flaubert wanted to write a novel.   Style.   Howard Nemerov.   NoAM

Flautist boasts but God's enraged—, The.   Elegy on an X-ray Photo of My Skull.   Yelena [or Elena] Shwarts [or Shvarts].   ItGoST; VCWP, tr. by Catriona Kelly and Michael Molnar

Flavia's a name a deal too free.   Unknown.   FaBoEE

Flavor of vanilla drifts, A.   Dark Romance.   Lucha Corpi.   WPOW, tr. by Catherine Rodriguez-Nieto

Flaw, A.   "Michael Field."   VWP; ViWPN

Flaw, The.   Robert Lowell.   HarvBoo

Flaw in Paganism, The.   Dorothy Parker.   NBLV

"Flawless" is the word, no doubt, for this third of May.   Hourglass.   Josephine Jacobsen.   NoP-4

Flax.   Ivan Alekseievich Bunin.   AWP, tr. by Babette Deutsch and Avrahm Yarmolinsky

Flaxen-headed cow-boy, as simple as may be, A.   Air.   John O'Keefe [or O'Keeffe].   NOEC

Flaxman.   Margaret Fuller.   APN-1

Flay the square with crowds.   Girl with the Bad Rep, The.   Kay Murphy.   SwNoth

Flea.   Raymond Roseliep.   HA

Flea, The.   John Donne.   AmFaPo; BASC; BoLoP; EBEV; ESCV; FSCP; InPK-6; NAEL-5v1; NAEL-6v1; NAEL-7v1; NBLV; NIL-7; NIP-4; NoP-4; NoSic; OxAEP-1; PAI; PoE; SCV; TFi

Flea flew by a bee, A. The bee.   Mary Ann Hoberman.   OBSP   Fr. Bugs.

Flea's Hymn.   Oodgeroo of the tribe Noonuccal (Kath Walker).   Unle

Fleadh Cheoil.   Pearse Hutchinson.   PBCIP

Fleance.   Michael Longley.   CIP-2; PNI

Fleas in my hut.   Issa.   EH, tr. by Robert Hass

Fleas, lice.   Basho.   EH, tr. by Robert Hass

Fleas, stink, pigs, mold.   Rondeau.   Eustache Deschamps.   WoPoe, tr. by David Curzon and Jeffrey Fiskin

Fleche.   Larry Eigner.   VGW

Flecknoe, an English Priest at Rome.   Andrew Marvell.   BASC

Fled are the frosts, and now the fields appear[e].   Farewell Frost; or, Welcome the Spring.   Robert Herrick.   CaPo

Fled are those times, when, in harmonious strains.   George Crabbe.   FHYEP   Fr. Village, The.

Fled gasping from the House. (LL)   Emily Dickinson.   NOBA; OxBA; PoRA; SAmP

Fled is that music—Do I wake or sleep? (LL)   John Keats.   AWP; AmFaPo;

BRP; CABP; ClHu; EBEV; GTBS-P; HAP; HeIP-4; NAEL-5v2; NAEL-6v2; NAWM-7v2; NIL-7; NOBE; NOBRP; NPeeEn; NoP-4; OBEV; OWoS; OxBEV; PoE; PoPoPo; PoRA; RB; SCGP; SoSe-8; TFi; TOF; UnPo

Fled is the swiftness of all the white-footed ones. Elegy: "Fled is the swiftness of all the white-footed ones." Joseph Auslander. TrJP

Fledgling. Anthony Conran. AngWePo

Fle[e] alway[i]s from[e] the snare [or snair]. (LL) Rondel of Luve [or Love], A. Alexander Scott. BoLoP; OBEV; OxBEV; OxBS

Flee every friendship and live: a greater truth. Seneca. RomPo, tr. by Anthony James Boyle

Flee—into yourself, into the Churches, to the lavatories, to the Egypts, to Haiti. Beatnik's Monologue, The. Andrey [or Andrei] Andreievich Voznesensky [or Voznesenskii]. TCRusP, tr. by Daniel Weissbort

Flee, lovers, from Love, flee from his fire. Michelangelo Buonarroti. CAGL, tr. by James M. Saslow

Flee, stately Juno, Samos fro. Ludovic Lloyd. AngWePo Fr. Sidanen.

Flee trouble, as you desire: it will catch you and hold you in bondage. Soul of a Man, The. Ferenc Kazinczy. IQMS, tr. by Adam Makkai

Fleece, The. John Dyer.
  Happy Workhouse and the Good Effects of Industry, The. NOEC
  "In cold stiff soils the bleaters oft complain." ECEV
  "O when, through ev'ry province, shall be raised." NOEC
  Treating Sheep Ailments. ECEV
  (Urban Progress.) ECEV

Fleeing across the roofs. (LL) Roofwalker, The. Adrienne Rich. CoAP; NAAL-2v2

Fleeing Atalanta, The. David Foster.
  "Alchemists say the Stone turns lead to gold." NOBAu
  "Don't give everything." NOBAu
  "Seeking heat men become cold, and look for meaning." NOBAu

Fleeing from my fellow-countrymen. 1940. Bertolt Brecht. HP, tr. by John Willet

Fleeing from threatened flood, they sailed. First Invasion of Ireland, The. Unknown. BIrV, tr. by John Montague

Fleeing sandpipers, The. J. W. Hackett. HA

Fleering snow, The. Winter (January / February 1978). Larry Eigner. PFTM-2

Flees the outhouse and a baby inherits the pain. (LL) Southern Birth. Kevin Powell. AmPoNex; InTrad

Fleet Astronomer can bore, The. Vanity [or Vanitie] (1). George Herbert. BASC; FSCP; GeHe; NOSC; NoP-4

Fleet ships encountering on the high seas. Good Ships. John Crowe Ransom. OxBSo; WeW-3

Fleeting birds may soon in ocean swim, The. To Miss Laetitia Van Lewen. Constantia Grierson. ECWP; WPE

Fleeting glory or decay—are wind and lightning. Monk of Auspicious Fortune Monastery Asking Me to Name a Pavilion, A. Su Tung-p'o (Su Shih). SuSp, tr. by Chiang Yee

Fleeting Return. Juan Ramón Jiménez. BLPSL, tr. by Rene de Costa, Rigas Kappatos and Eleni Paidoussi

Fleetly hath passed the year; the seasons came. New Year, The. Nathaniel Parker Willis. TreFP

Fleggit Bride, The. Hugh MacDiarmid. OxBS

Fleming Helphenstine. Edwin Arlington Robinson. OxBSo

Flemington Racecourse. Kevin Hart. NOBAu

Flemish Beauty. Talvikki Ansel. AmPoNex

Flesh, and cars, tar, dug holes beneath stone. Contract. (For The Destruction and Rebuilding of Paterson), A. Imamu Amiri Baraka. FTOS

Flesh and the Spirit, The. Anne Bradstreet. BASC; ChIV-2; NAAL-2v1; NAAL-3; NOBA; OxBA; OxWW; SCAP; TAP

Flesh chase night, weather booming and dark. Major Bowes' Diary. Imamu Amiri Baraka. NAAL-2v2

Flesh, considered as cognitive region, as opposed to undifferentiated. Rosmarie Waldrop. PFTM-2 Fr. Key into the Language of America, A.

Flesh-Fly and the Bee, The. Coventry Patmore. FaBoEE

Flesh is sad, alas, The! and all the books are read. Sea-Wind. Stéphane Mallarmé. AWP, tr. by Arthur Symons

Flesh is sad, alas, The! And I have read. Sea Breeze. Stéphane Mallarmé. WoPoe, tr. by Louis Simpson

Flesh is sad—and I've read every book, The. Sea Breeze. Stéphane Mallarmé. SxFrPo, tr. by E. H. Blackmore and A. M. Blackmore

Flesh of dark, The. Caliban. Edward Kamau Brathwaite. HarvBoo

Flesh to feed hell's worm upon. (LL) After Death. Algernon Charles Swinburne. NOBVV; PeVV

Flesh will heal and pain will fade. Claire Richcreek Thomas. PoToHe

Fleshes his dirty hunka tin I am right. Burroughs. Robert Glück. WiU

Fleshing his dream of the beautiful, needful thing. (LL) Frederick Douglass. Robert Earl Hayden. CBCWP; ESEAA; HCAP; ISC; NAAAL; NIL-7; NIP-4; PoPoPo; Son; TTY; VCAP

Flexible. William Kulik. BodElec

Flexion of God. Anne Carson. BodElec Fr. Truth About God, The.

Flicker, The. Lew Blockcolski. VoR

Flicker flies by. Bend in the River. Simon J. Ortiz. HATNAP; PoPoPo

Flickering curtain, scintillations, junebugs. Wavering. Denise Levertov. PmAP

Flickering shades, / Stick figures, lithe game. Hunt by Night, The. Derek Mahon. HarvBoo

Flies. Jack Kerouac. CLPP

Flies a finch o'er the path. Early Spring. Richard von Schaukal. AuPH, tr. by Lowell A. Bangerter

Flies and butterflies, children, bees. At a Grave. Martinus Nijhoff. TuT, tr. by Desmond Egan

Flies, flies are on the plane tree, on the streets. (LL) As a Plane Tree by the Water. Robert Lowell. CoAP; MoAMPo; NOBA; OxBA

Flies in the temple, The. Issa. EH, tr. by Robert Hass

Flies screaming like a jay. (LL) Deaf-Mute in the Pear Tree. Patricia K. Page. NoAM; NoP-4; PoE

Flies swarming / What do they want of. Issa. ZenPo, tr. by Takashi Ikemoto and Lucien Stryk

Flight. Charles Stuart Calverley. OBCoV

Flight. Jorge Guillén. BLT, tr. by Reginald Gibbons

Flight, The. John Haines. SPE

Flight, The. Theodore Roethke. RB Fr. Lost Son, The.

Flight, The. Sara Teasdale. LW

Flight from Bootle, The. Sir John Betjeman. PeLV

Flight from Manhattan, The. Les A. Murray. BMAP Fr. Sydney Highrise Variations, The.

Flight from the Marriage Bed. Lisa M. Carbone. PasH

Flight in the Desert, The. William Everson. ChIV-2; VGW

Flight into Egypt, The. W. H. Auden. Fr. For the Time Being; a Christmas Oratorio.

Flight is past: and man forgot, The. (LL) Sic Vita. Henry King, Bishop of Chichester. BASC; NOBE; NOSC; OxBSP; PAI; SCGP

Flight of Apollo, The. Stanley Kunitz. OPRER; TaR

Flight of Love, The. Shelley. See Lines: "When the lamp is shattered [or shatter'd]"

Flight of migrating birds froze in full sky, The. It Was a Season Tattooed on the Forehead of the Earth. Venus Khoury-Gata. PoArWo, tr. by Lucy McNair

Flight of the Duchess, The. Robert Browning.
  "And were I not, as a man may say, cautious." OBCoV

Flight of the Earls, The, 1607. Fearghal Og MacWard.
  "All Ireland's now one vessel's company." BIrV

Flight of the Itzás. Chilam Balam. WoPoe, tr. by Christopher Sawyer-Lauçanno

Flight of the Roller Coaster. Raymond Souster. NOBC

Flight of the Sparrow. Shinkichi Takahashi. ZenPo, tr. by Takashi Ikemoto and Lucien Stryk

Flight of the Spirit. Felicia Dorothea Hemans. Son

Flight of the White South Africans, The. Christopher Hope. PeSAV

Flight of Wild Ducks, A. Charles Harpur. NOBAu

Flight of Zalán, The. Mihály Vörösmarty. IQMS, tr. by Watson Kirkconnell

Flight out of Time. Hugo Ball.
  "I have invented a new species of poetry, 'verse without words' or sound." PFTM-1

Flight out of Time. Hugo Ball. PFTM-1 Fr. Flight out of Time.

Flight to Italy. Cecil Day Lewis.
  "Winged bull trundles to the wired perimeter, The." OxBTC

Flight to the City. William Carlos Williams. APT-1

Flights. Roger McDonald. CBAP

Flights of strings above the orange trees! (LL) Childhood in Jacksonville, Florida. Jane Cooper. ExTi; TAP

Flighty young lady from Loddon, A. Limerick. Ida Thurtle. PeLi

Fling Out the Banner! George Washington Doane. AH

Fling this useless book away. Written in a Lady's Prayer Book. John Wilmot, 2d Earl of Rochester. BoLoP

Flinging the frisbee. Alan Pizzarelli. HA

Flint. Christina Georgina Rossetti. SacPr

Flint Hills, The. Lew Blockcolski. VoR

Flip, clack! The windscreen wipers clear. Seven Rainy Months. William Plomer. OxBTC

Flip, Flop. Denise Riley. Oth Fr. Seven Strangely Exciting Lies.

Flip-top with brain. Bird. Frieda Hughes. NeBl

Flippancies. Richard Wilbur.
  "If fictive music fails your lyre, confess." NBLV
  Star System, The. NBLV
  What's Good for the Soul is Good for Sales. NBLV

"While you're a white-hot youth, emit the rays." NBLV

Flipping eck, cor blimey, strewth. Taking the Plunge. John Mole. NOxBChV

Flirt, The. William Henry Davies. EnLoPo

Flirtation. Li Ch'ing-chao. *See* To the Tune "I Paint My Lips Red."

Flitting, The. John Clare. OxAEP-2

Flitting, The. Medbh McGuckian. PBCIP; PNI

Float over us, Florence, your banners. History as Decoration. Rosanna Warren. DiPo

Floating. Kenneth Rexroth. BodElec

Floating along the tops of the Sangre de Christos. Give. Mark Irwin. PoCoUp

Floating clouds and worldly affairs. Wen Cheng-ming. CoBLCP *Fr.* Improvised on Horseback to Say Good-bye to Those Who Are Seeing Me Off.

Floating clouds, before my eyes. Inscribed on a Painting of Sailboats on the River—Seeing Off Yen-chi on His Journey to Ch'ang-an. Yün Shou-p'ing. CoBLCP, *tr. by* Jonathan Chaves

Floating Epitaphs, Their Possible Explanations in Poro Point. Alejandrino Hufana. ReBoTo

Floating, floating on misty waves. Fisherman's Lyric. Chao Meng-fu. CoBLCP, *tr. by* Jonathan Chaves

Floating, floating, the river waters. Wang Chiu-ssu. WoPoe, *tr. by* Jonathan Chaves *Fr.* After Reading the Poems of Master Han Shan.

Floating, floating weightless. Swimming Pool. Myra Cohn Livingston. NOxBChV

Floating, floating, your boat sets sail. Song of the Merchant's Wife. Yang Wei-chen. CoBLCP, *tr. by* Jonathan Chaves

Floating in the sac. Learning to Smile. Art Goodtimes. GeoH

Floating Island at Hawkshead. Dorothy Wordsworth. NPeEn; PEW

Floating on the River Han. Wang Wei. ChinPo, *tr. by* Yip Wai-lim

Floating perfectly through the net. (LL) Fast Break. Edward Hirsch. DiPo; MoASP; VCAP

Floating Petals. Jan Barry. CDa

Floating Poem, Unnumbered, The. Adrienne Rich. EroLit; NALW; NoAM *Fr.* Twenty-one Love Poems.

Floating scent encircles the curved shore. Lotuses on the Crooked Pond. Lu Chao-lin. SuSp, *tr. by* Paul W. Kroll

Floating that cypress boat. Cypress Boat. *Unknown.* WoPoe, *tr. by* Constance A. Cook

Floating threads of spider webs hang. Wen Cheng-ming. CoBLCP *Fr.* Chung-i Temple, The.

Flock. Lance Henson. VoR

Flock of bright red lanterns / Has settle, A. (LL) About an Excavation. Charles Reznikoff. NTCP; VGW

Flock of crows high from the Northland flies, A. Autumn. Detlev, Freiherr von Liliencron. AWP, *tr. by* Ludwig Lewisohn

Flock of sheep that leisurely pass by, A. To Sleep. William Wordsworth. GTBS-P

Flock of winds came winging [*or* flying] from the North, A. Roaring Frost, The. Alice Thompson Meynell. EBVV; WPE

Flocks of birds fly high and vanish. Sitting Alone in Ching-t'ing Mountain. Li Po. SuSp, *tr. by* Irving Y. Lo

Flocks of chicken clucking from every corner. Tu Fu. SuSp *Fr.* Ch'iang Village.

Flocks of Doves. Carlos Pellicer. TCLAP, *tr. by* Alexandra Migoya

Flocks of doves, The. Flocks of Doves. Carlos Pellicer. TCLAP, *tr. by* Alexandra Migoya

Flocks of the wandering waves I hold, The. Alfred Austin. VerBaPo *Fr.* Wind Speaks, The.

Flocks were bleating; the roads, The. Sorrowful Shadow, The. Julio Herrera y Reissig. TCLAP, *tr. by* Andrew Rosing

Flodden Field. *Unknown.* ESPB

Flood. Ch'ien T'ao. ChiP, *tr. by* Arthur Waley

Flood. James Joyce. MoBrPo

Flood, The. Patricia Beer. HarvBoo

Flood, The. John Clare. RB

Flood, The. John Milton. NOSC *Fr.* Paradise Lost.

Flood at the International Writer's Workshop. Bogomil Gjuzel. CarOv, *tr. by* Carolyn Kizer

Flood of Is in Brittany, The. Augusta Davies Webster. ViWPN

Flood-Tide below me! I see you face to face! Walt Whitman. APN-1; ColAP; FaBoA; NAAL-2v1; NAAL-3; NAAL-5; NCAP; NOBA; NoAM; NoP-4; TAP

Flood-tide below me! I see you face to face! Walt Whitman. WoPoe *Fr.* Crossing Brooklyn Ferry.

Flood Water. *Unknown.* NOBAu, *tr. by* Mungayana Nundhirribala

Flood Year. Judith Wright. NoAM

Flooded Mind. Norman MacCaig. OxBC

Flooded Valley, The. Roland Mathias. AngWePo

Flooding with a brilliant mist. To the Moon. Goethe. STV, *tr. by* John Frederick Nims

Floods all the soul with its melodious seas. (LL) Milton. Henry Wadsworth Longfellow. AWP; GSo; TAP

Floods, by nature enemies to land, The. Ovid. OBVE *Fr.* Metamorphoses.

Floods of men. All the Spirit Powers Went to Their Dancing Place. Gary Snyder. UnPo

Floods of tears well from my deepest heart, The. Elegy. Immanuel di Roma. TrJP, *tr. by* J. Chotzner

Floods Swell around Me, Angry, Appalling. Zachary Eddy. AH

Flooer o the Gean. George Campbell Hay. OxBS

Floor, The. Yolanda Palis. ReBoTo

Floor and the Ceiling, The. William Jay Smith. OBCA; OxIBACP

Floor Is Dirty, The. Edward Field. NeAP
  (Dirty Floor, The.) CoAP

Floor / of the temple, The. Trance. "H. D." APT-1

Floor Plans. Maxine Scates. PBCAP

Floor Scrapers. Daniel Tobin. NAPBL

Floor tilts, The. I'm trying to go tell Him. Drunk Dog. Erin McGraw. Unle

Floorboards creak, The. New Apartment. Linda Hogan. HATNAP; UnSA

Flopped on the fan. Issa. EH, *tr. by* Robert Hass

Flora's Plea to Mary. Juan Delgado. TouFir

Floral Apron, The. Marilyn Chin. LoL

Florence Vane. Philip Pendleton Cooke. APN-1

Florida. Dannie Abse. OxBC

Florida. Elizabeth Bishop. TwCP

Florida. Campbell McGrath. NAPBL

Florida. Carl Rakosi. TAP

Florida Anasazi, The. Campbell McGrath. NAPBL

Florida Beach, The. Constance Fenimore Woolson. APN-2

Florida Road Workers. Langston Hughes. MoAmPo

Florin for the willing guard, A. Rosy Bosom'd Hours, The. Coventry Patmore. EnLoPo; NOBVV

Florio: A Tale, and The Bas-bleu; or, Conversation. Hannah More. RWP

Florio, one ev'ning, brisk, and gay. Epigram on Florio. John Winstanley. FaBoEE

Florist's Vade-Mecum, The. Samuel Gilbert.
  "Were I employ'd a garden to contrive." OBGa

Florist was told, cyclamèn or azalea, The. Lines to Accompany Flowers for Eve. Carolyn Kizer. BoWoP

Florus, canst thou define that innate spark. To Mr. ———, an Unlettered Poet, on Genius Unimproved. Ann Yearsley. NOEC

Flos Lunae. Ernest Christopher Dowson. OBMV; PeVV

Flossie Cabanis. Edgar Lee Masters. APT-1 *Fr.* Spoon River Anthology.

Flounder. Natasha Trethewey. TWW

Flounders in mud. O Jesus, make it stop! (LL) Attack. Siegfried Sassoon. MoBrPo; NOBE; OxBTC

Flour is exhaustion. Kitchen. Laura Jensen. LCAP-2

Flour of England, fruit of Spain. Plum Pudding, A. Mother Goose. OxNR; ReMoGo

Flourish of silver, A. Deer Park. John Montague. PBCIP

Flourish of sunlight in the room where, A. Claud Cockburn. Thomas McCarthy. PBCIP

Flow Chart. John Ashbery.
  "Still in the published city but not yet." PmAP
  "Suddenly they all stopped talking about it. Yet I." PFTM-2

Flow, flow—he's often near water. Inscribed on a Painting of Bamboo. Wu Chen. CoBLCP, *tr. by* Jonathan Chaves

Flow, flow the waves hated. Illusions. Ralph Waldo Emerson. APN-1

Flow Gently, Sweet Afton. Robert Burns. AWP
  (Afton Water.) NAEL-5v2; NAEL-6v2

Flow swiftly into thee, and in thee ever end. (LL) Upon Nothing. John Wilmot, 2d Earl of Rochester. NOSC; OBSV; OxAEP-1; OxBEV

Flower, A. Po Chü-i. TAL

Flower, The. Robert Creeley. PAI; PmAP

Flower, The. George Herbert. AWP; AngWePo; BASC; ESCV; FSCP; GeHe; NAEL-5v1; NAEL-6v1; NAEL-7v1; NOBE; NOCV; NPeEn; NoP-4; OBGa; OxBEV; PBRV

Flower and the Leaf, The. The Lady of the Arbour.
  "And at the last I cast my mine eye aside." WPE
  "Wherefore I marvel greatly of myself." OBGa

Flower, and yet not a flower, A. Tune: "Flower unlike Flower." Po Chü-i. SuSp, *tr. by* Eugene Eoyang

Flower bursts from stone. Stone Wall. Shinkichi Takahashi. ZenPo, *tr. by* Takashi Ikemoto and Lucien Stryk

Flower child. Statue, The. Luz Maria Umpierre. PueRic

Flower Ensnarer of Psalms. Rossana Ombres. BoWoP, *tr. by* I. L. Salomon

Flower-feasting bee, why do you touch upon. Meleager. HePo *Fr.* Epigrams.

Flower-fed buffaloes of the spring, The. Flower-fed Buffaloes, The. Nicholas Vachel Lindsay. GM; MoAmPo; NOBA; OBCA; PoE; RB; TRP; VGW

(Flower-fed buffalos of the spring, The.) CA

Flower Given to My Daughter, A. James Joyce. OBMV; RB; RaBo

Flower Herding on Mount Monadnock. Galway Kinnell. HeIP-4; LCAP-2; NOBA; NoAM

(Flower-herding Pictures on Mount Monadnock.) CoAmPo

Flower in the Crannied Wall. Tennyson. BBASP; BRP; ITBLP; InPK-6; NAEL-5v2; NAEL-6v2; TFi

Flower Is Looking, A. Harold Monro. MoBrPo *Fr.* Strange Meetings.

Flower is not visible, The. Sang Yi. PFTM-1 *Fr.* Critical Condition.

Flower is withered on the stem, The. Nurse's Lament, The. Mary Elizabeth Coleridge. NOBVV; OxBSP

Flower Market, The. Po Chü-i. ChiP, *tr. by* Arthur Waley

Flower Master, The. Medbh McGuckian. ModIr; PNI

Flower / my heart, The. Poem to Be Recited Every 8 Years While Eating Unleavened Tamales. *Unknown.* STP, *tr. by* Anselm Hollo

Flower No More Than Itself, A. Linda Gregg. BBASP

Flower of Air, The. Gabriela Mistral. TCLAP, *tr. by* Doris Dana

Flower of drowsiness. Menace of the Flower, The. Alfonso Reyes. TCLAP, *tr. by* Samuel Beckett

Flower of Flame, The. Robert Malise Bowyer Nichols. "Before I woke I knew her gone." OBMV

Flower of Mullein, A. Lizette Woodworth Reese. MoAmPo

Flower of Old Japan, The. Alfred Noyes. Epilogue: "Carol, every violet has." MoBrPo

FLOWER of roses, angels' joy. Hymn to the Virgin. *Unknown.* NoSic

Flower of the flock. On Sweet Killen Hill. Tom MacIntyre. CIP-2

Flower of the pear-tree gathers and turns to fruit, The. At the End of Spring. Po Chü-i. ChiP, *tr. by* Arthur Waley

Flower of the race, The. Gentlemen. Geoffrey Taylor. FaBoEE

Flower of the vine! Stornelli and Strambotti. Agnes Mary Frances Robinson. VWP

Flower of This Purple Dye. William Shakespeare. CTC *Fr.* Midsummer Night's Dream, A.

Flower of Virtue is the heart's content, The. Sonnet: Of Virtue. Folgore da San Geminiano [*or* Gimignano]. AWP; EaItPo, *tr. by* Dante Gabriel Rossetti

Flower of waves, A. Lady Ise. BoWoP; WoPoe, *tr. by* Irma Brandeis and Etsuko Terasaki

Flower-Patterned Snake. So Chong-Ju. VCWP, *tr. by* David R. McCann

Flower Piece. Gerhard Rühm. PFTM-2, *tr. by* Rosmarie Waldrop

Flower Poem. Alec Derwent Hope. BMAP

Flower Pot, The. David Shimoni. MHP, *tr. by* Ruth Finer Mintz

Flower-Rain Terrace, The. Tao-chi. CoBLCP, *tr. by* Jonathan Chaves

Flower's fragrance is a woman's virtue, A. Orchid House, The. Medbh McGuckian. CABP

Flower's Name, The. Robert Browning. CTC *Fr.* Garden Fancies.

Flower-sellers, Budapest. Kathleen Jamie. NePenScot

Flower Shadows. Mo Shih-lung. CoBLCP, *tr. by* Jonathan Chaves

Flower that smiles today, The. Mutability. Shelley. NAEL-5v2; NAEL-6v2; NoP-4

Flower-tinted cheek, the flowery close, A. Hafiz [*or* Hafez]. TAL *Fr.* Odes.

Flower was offered [*or* offerd] to me, A. William Blake. BoLoP; FHYEP; NAEL-5v2; NAEL-6v2; NOBRP *Fr.* Songs of Experience.

Flowering Absence, A. John Montague. BiHa; CIP-2; PBCIP

Flowering Bars, The. Charles Donnelly. CIP-2

Flowering Cherry, The. Janet Frame. PeNZ

Flowering of the Rod, The. "H. D."
"Blue-geese, white-geese, you may say." APT-1; NOBA
"I go where I love and where I am loved." APT-1; HarvBoo
"In resurrection, there is confusion." APT-1
"It is no madness to say." FaBoMo
"O the beautiful garment." HarvBoo
"Satisfied, unsatisfied." APT-1
"So I would rather drown, remembering." APT-1
"Yet resurrection is a sense of direction." APT-1

Flowering plum, A. Issa. SoOfWa, *tr. by* Sam Hamill

Flowering Quince. Winfield Townley Scott. APT-2

Flowering Tree, The. Wang T'ing-hsiang. CoBLCP, *tr. by* Jonathan Chaves

Flowering War, The. *Unknown.* STP, *tr. by* Jerome Rothenberg

Flowerpot. (LL) Poem: "As the cat." William Carlos Williams. ChAP; HarvBoo; KaS; NoP-4; PAI; PoPoPo; SoSe-8; TTTS

Flowers. Margaret Atwood. NoP-4

Flowers. Roo Borson. NOBC

Flowers. Wendy Cope. NoP-4

Flowers. Dennis Joseph Enright. OBGa

Flowers. Julie Fay. NAPBL

Flowers. Leo Vroman. TuT, *tr. by* James Liddy

Flowers. William Wordsworth. CenSon *Fr.* River Duddon [A Series of Sonnets], The.

Flowers along the palace, The. Waiting for Audience on a Spring Night. Tu Fu. OHPC, *tr. by* Kenneth Rexroth

Flowers and Men. D. H. Lawrence. FaBoEE

Flowers and Moonlight on the Spring River. Yang-Ti, Emperor of Sui Dynasty. ChiP, *tr. by* Arthur Waley

Flowers, and tall-stalked grasses, and a bee. Ivan Alekseievich Bunin. GI; WoPoe, *tr. by* David Curzon and Vladislav L. Gucrassev

Flowers and Trees. Sir Walter Scott. OxAEP-2 *Fr.* Lady of the Lake, The.

Flowers—at ease and tall. The king is dead. (LL) No Swan So Fine. Marianne Craig Moore. NALW; OxBA; UnPo

Flowers beside the palace fade. Passing the Night. Tu Fu. CrYelRi, *tr. by* Sam Hamill

Flowers bloom. Gazing at Spring. Hsüeh T'ao. WoPoe, *tr. by* Jeanne Larsen

Flowers bloom a score of days. Tairyu. JDP, *tr. by* Yoel Hoffmann

Flowers bloom, flowers fall. To Send Away Melancholy. Huang Tsun-hsien. SuSp, *tr. by* An-yan Tang

Flowers bloomed yesterday. Shoshun. JDP, *tr. by* Yoel Hoffmann

Flowers by the Sea. William Carlos Williams. APT-1; MoAmPo; NoAM; RB; TAP

Flowers did not seem to unfurl from slow bulbs, The. Easter Garland, An. Carol Rumens. FaBoWP

Flowers for Luis Bunuel. Stuart Z. Perkoff. NeAP

Flowers from growing, your flowers. (LL) For James Dean. Frank O'Hara. NNaP; NeAP

Flowers hast thou in thyself, and foliage. Sonnet: To His Lady Joan, of Florence. Guido Cavalcanti. AWP; EaItPo, *tr. by* Dante Gabriel Rossetti

Flowers have fenced-in. Clearing, The. Peter Everwine. NNaP

Flowers have lost their withered red, The. Spring Scene. Su Tung-p'o (Su Shih). TAL

Flowers I called Christ's when I was four, The. (LL) Supernatural Love. Gjertrud Schnackenberg. DiPo; MakPoe; NoAM; NoP-4; VCAP

Flowers in bud on the trees, The. On the Death of a New Born Child. Mei Yao Ch'en. OHPC; WoPoe, *tr. by* Kenneth Rexroth

Flowers in legions bloomed around in forest, scrub, and marsh. Tasmanian Scenes. Louisa Meredith. NOBAu

Flowers in the Valley. *Unknown.* OxBoLi

Flowers in the Ward. John Shaw Neilson. CBAP

Flowers leaves stems / lips hands eyes. Still Life. "Shahryar." OMIP, *tr. by* Gopi Chand Narang

Flowers left thick at nightfall in the wood, The. In Memoriam (Easter, 1915). Edward Thomas. GTBS-P; NOBE; OBWP; OBWVE; OxBTC; PeFWW; Spl

Flowers lurk in the dusk by the palace walls. Spring Vigil in the Imperial Chancellery. Tu Fu. ChinPo, *tr. by* Yip Wai-lim

Flowers. Masquerading as words. Confrontation with a Bouquet. Maggie Bevan. Prnts

Flowers need irrigation, The. Busy. Yüan Mei. CoBLCP, *tr. by* Jonathan Chaves

Flowers need the sunshine. You're Gonna Lose Your Gal. Joe Young. ReLy

Flowers nodding gaily, scent in air. Duet, A. Thomas Sturge Moore. OBEV

Flowers of autumn still bloom in the garden, The. At the End of September. Sándor Petőfi. IQMS, *tr. by* Adam Makkai and Valerie Becker Makkai

Flowers of fire. (LL) To the tune "Soaring Clouds." Huang O [*or* Huang Ho]. BoWoP; EroLit; WPOW

Flowers of ice. Snow. Muso Soseki. EaWin, *tr. by* W. S. Merwin

Flowers of Love and Persuasion. (LL) Asclepiades. GrAn; PGA

Flowers of Mildew. Tudor Arghezi. WoPoe, *tr. by* Michael Impey and Brian Swann

Flowers of Politics, I, The. Michael McClure. NeAP

Flowers of Politics, II, The. Michael McClure. NeAP

Flowers of Red and Blue. Nezahualcoyotl. WoPoe, *tr. by* Stephen Berg

Flowers of red and blue. Flowers of Red and Blue. Nezahualcoyotl. WoPoe, *tr. by* Stephen Berg

Flowers of the Field. John Keble. SacPr

Flowers of the Forest, The. Alison Rutherford Cockburn. ECWP

Flowers of the Forest, The. Jane [*or* Jean] Elliot. ECWP; FaBoCh; NePenScot; OxBEV; OxBS; SCGP; WPE

(I've heard the lilting at our yowe-milking.) NoP-4

(Lament for Flodden, The.) GTBS-P; OBEV

Flowers of the Forest are a' wede away, The. (LL) Flowers of the Forest, The. Jane [*or* Jean] Elliot. ECWP; FaBoCh; NePenScot; OxBEV; OxBS; SCGP; WPE

Flowers of the grass. Asei. JDP, *tr. by* Yoel Hoffmann

Flowers of the willow, light, fluffy by the second moon. Willow Catkins. Hsüeh T'ao. SuSp, *tr. by* Eric W. Johnson

Flowers offered to the Buddha. Buson. EH, *tr. by* Robert Hass

Flowers on one tree have opened, The. Plum Window. Muso Soseki. EaWin, *tr. by* W. S. Merwin

Flowers say goodbye to me, The. Sergey [*or* Sergei] Aleksandrovich Yesenin [*or* Essenin]. TCRP

Flowers shall hang upon the palls. Death. John Clare. GTBS-P

Flowers that in thy garden rise, The. Song. Sir Henry John Newbolt. FaBoTw

Flowers through the window. Nantucket. William Carlos Williams. HAP; HarvBoo; OxBA; TAP; TRP; WeW-3

Flowers upon the rosemary spray, The. Rosemary Spray, The. Luis de Góngora y Argote. AWP, *tr. by* E. Churton

Flowers whirl away, The. Kintsune. OHPJ

Flowers will do us no good on our tombstones. *Unknown.* PGA

Flowers with six petals. Snow Garden. Muso Soseki. EaWin, *tr. by* W. S. Merwin

Flowing winds brush Meandering Islet. Orchid Pavilion. Sun Ch'o. ChinPo, *tr. by* Yip Wai-lim

Flowrets—wreaths—thy banks along. To a Gentleman, Who Desired Proper Materials for a Monody. *Unknown.* NOEC

Fluency. Adelia Prado. TCLAP, *tr. by* Marcia Kirinus

Flukum couldn't stand the strain. Flukum. Etheridge Knight. ESEAA; NNaP *Fr.* Two Poems for Black Relocation Centers.

Flung outward and up—disappearing suddenly! (LL) Spring Strains. William Carlos Williams. APT-1; TCAPo

Flunked out and laid-off. Eisenhower Years, The. Paul Zimmer. PBCAP

Flunkeyed and trumpeting Sea[!], The. (LL) Said King Pompey. Dame Edith Sitwell. BWW; UV

Flush / a Play. Leslie Scalapino. PmAP

Flush of fever in spring. The heart's. Rose Quartz. Leslie Ullman. ExTi

Flush or Faunus. Elizabeth Barrett Browning. VWP

Flushed by the spirit of the genial year. James Thomson. OxAEP-1 *Fr.* Seasons, The.

Flushed, from my restless pillow I arose. Song of Arla, Written During Her Enthusiasm, A. Anne Batten Cristall. RWP

Flute, The. Sophia De Mello Breyner. VCWP, *tr. by* Ruth Fainlight

Flute, The. Oktay Rifat. WoPoe, *tr. by* Talat Sait Halman

Flute; a Pastoral, The. José-Maria de Heredia. AWP, *tr. by* H. J. C. Grierson

Flute and Wind in the Hermit's Cell. Khalil Hawi. MAP, *tr. by* Sharif Elmusa and Diana Der Hovanessian

Flute-music. Rabindranath Tagore. OMIP, *tr. by* William Radice

Flute Notes from a Reedy Pond. Sylvia Plath. FaBoMo

Flute of Daphnis, The. Edward Cracroft Lefroy. AWP *Fr.* Echoes from Theocritus.

Fluteplayers from Finmarken. Carl Rakosi. FTOS

Flutes, and the harp on the plain. Home on the Range, February 1962. Edward Dorn. CoAmPo

Flutes echo from the far shore. At Lake Yi. Wang Wei. CrYelRi, *tr. by* Sam Hamill

Flutter flutter on clothes and cap, jujube flowers fall. Tune: Sand of Silk-washing Stream. Su Tung-p'o (Su Shih). CoBCP, *tr. by* Burton Watson

Flux. Richard Eberhart. VGW

Flux dehydrates my flesh, The. Common. 1668. Dom Moraes. EmeKit

Fly. W. S. Merwin. ChAP; NNaP; OWoS

Fly. Larry Wiggin. HA

Fly, The. Philip Ayres. OBVE

Fly, The. William Blake. *See* Songs of Experience

Fly, The. Walter De la Mare. OTCP

Fly, The. Miroslav Holub. NPeEn; PoSu; PoetW; RB, *tr. by* Ian Milner and George Theiner

(She sat on the willow bark.) VCWP, *tr. by* Stuart Friebert

Fly, The. William Oldys. *See* On a Fly Drinking out of [*or* from] His Cup

Fly, The. Karl Shapiro. NoAM; SoSe-8

Fly about a Glass[e] of Burnt Claret, A. Richard Lovelace. CaPo

Fly Away, Fly Away. Christina Georgina Rossetti. Spl

Fly by night / black galaxy / friendly galaxy. Lee Morgan. David Henderson. SeSe

Fly Caught in a Cobweb, A. Richard Lovelace. BeJo; CaPo

Fly, dare take / The rice grain. Ransetsu. ZenPo, *tr. by* Takashi Ikemoto and Lucien Stryk

Fly down, Death: call me. Madboy's Song. Muriel Rukeyser. MoAmPo; TrJP

Fly envious Time, till thou run out thy race. On Time. John Milton. OBEV; SCGP; SacPr

Fly, fly, my friends. Sir Philip Sidney. NAEL-7v1; NoSic *Fr.* Astrophil and Stella.

Fly from the soil whose desolating creed. To Persecuted Foreigners. Penina Moise. SWaP

Fly hence, shadows, that do keep. John Ford. OBEV *Fr.* Lover's Melancholy, The.

Fly is giving another sermon, The. Benediction. Stuart Dybek. UrbNat

Fly Me to the Moon (In Other Words). Bart Howard. ReLy

Fly or beetle on their track, The. Shepherd Boy, The. John Clare. NOBVV

Fly [*or* Flie] hand in hand to heav'n! (LL) Sunday. George Herbert. GeHe; PeECV; TrCP

Fly That Flew into My Mistress'[s] Eye, A. Thomas Carew. CaPo

Fly to the desert, fly with me. Thomas Moore. BIrV *Fr.* Lalla Rookh.

Flyer's Fall. Wallace Stevens. SAmP

Flying. Michael Dransfield. BMAP

Flying arrow hardly was aware, The. Deceiver Time. Luis de Góngora y Argote. SpanPo, *tr. by* James Edward Tobin

Flying at Night. Ted Kooser. InPK-6; PBCAP

Flying Bells. Yüan Mei. CoBLCP, *tr. by* Jonathan Chaves

Flying catkins, flying floss, where have they gone? Tune: "Immortal at the River"—Winter Willow. Na-lan Hsing-te. SuSp, *tr. by* Irving Y. Lo

Flying Crooked. Robert Graves. FaBoMo; OxBSP; PeLV; RB; TwCP

Flying Deeper into the Century. Pier Giorgio Di Cicco. NOBC

Flying Down to Rio. Vincent Youmans. ReLy

Flying Dutchman, The. Ian D. Colvin. PeSAV

Flying Fish, The. John Gray. NOBVV

Flying Fowl, and Creeping Things, Praise Ye the Lord. Isaac Watts. ChIV-1

Flying Fox. Thomas William Shapcott. CBAP

Flying from the dry pall of the city. Gray Woods Exploding, The. Earle Birney. NoAM

Flying full tilt already. (LL) Running. Richard Wilbur. CoAP; MoASP

Flying Home from Utah. May Swenson. WPE

Flying Horse was in jail. Urban Experience: Part Two, The. Lew Blockcolski. VoR

Flying Inn, The. Gilbert Keith Chesterton.

"Old Noah he had an ostrich farm and fowls on the largest scale." ChIV-1; MoBrPo

Wine and Water. ChIV-1; MoBrPo

Flying Kangaroos. Coral Hull. PoCoUp

Flying light, flying light. Flying Light. Li Ho. WoPoe, *tr. by* Arthur Sze

Flying-man, Flying-man. Flying-Man. Mother Goose. HHAm

Flying Noises. Thomas Lux. LCAP-2

Flying out from. Issa. EnlH

Flying Petals. Hsiao Kang. OHMPC, *tr. by* Kenneth Rexroth

Flying Scrolls. Ralph Hodgson. FaBoTw

Flying skeleton. Pãhkahkos. Louise Bernice Halfe. ReEnLa

Flying south, south, into the deepest south, there was the feeling of. South. Aurora Levins Morales. PueRic

Flying squirrel, A. Buson. SoOfWa, *tr. by* Sam Hamill

Flying squirrel, A. Buson. EH, *tr. by* Robert Hass

Flying up a valley in the Alps where the rock. Lufthansa. John Tranter. BMAP; NOBAu

Flying word from here and there, A. Master, The. Edwin Arlington Robinson. CBCWP; MoAmPo

Flyover Elegies. Gwyneth Lewis. MFPA

Flypaper. Theodore Weiss. BodElec

Flyting o' Life and Daith, The. Hamish Henderson. OxBS

Flyting of Dunbar and Kennedy, The. William Dunbar.

Dunbar Attacks his Rival. NePenScot

"Iersche brybour baird, vyle beggar with thy brattis." NePenScot

Fo' yeah or mo' on this roof I'se layed. Aeschylus. CTC, *tr. by* Dallam Simpson *Fr.* Agamemnon.

Fo'c'sle had gone under the creep, The. Edwin John Pratt. NOBC *Fr.* Titanic, The.

Foal. Vernon Watkins. AngWePo; OxBTC

Foal, The. William Renton. NOBVV

Foam. Roland Jones. WoPoe, *tr. by* Anthony Conran

Foam fluttered on the sea like birds' wings. Hills of Salt. Dahlia Ravikovitch [*or* Ravikovich]. WPOW, *tr. by* Chana Bloch

Foam on the last water, The. Mitoku. JDP, *tr. by* Yoel Hoffmann

Foaming white wave washes over a grave, A. Exultation. Hywel ab Owain Gwynedd. OBWVE, *tr. by* Gwyn Williams

Focus. Adrienne Rich. FaBoWP

Foetus kicks. Janice Bostok. HA

Fog. Michelle Boisseau. ExTi

Fog. Amy Clampitt. MakPoe

Fog. Louise Imogen Guiney. APN-2

Fog. Gary Hotham. HA

Fog. Lizette Woodworth Reese. APT-1

Fog. György Sárközi. IQMS, *tr. by* Roy Fuller

Fog. Carl Sandburg. APT-1; BRP; ChAP; HeIP-4; ITBLP; InPK-6; MoAmPo; NAAL-2v2; NAAL-5; OBCA; OxIBACP; PAI; Spl; TAP; TCAPo; TFi; TTTS

Fog. Henry David Thoreau. APN-1

Fog and thaw make the garden smell like Christmas. It's February But. Janet Fisher. MFPA

Fog at Liang-hsiang. Yüan Mei. CoBLCP, *tr. by* Jonathan Chaves

Fog: big doped cats lazily. Fog. György Sárközi. IQMS, *tr. by* Roy Fuller

Fog comes, The. Fog. Carl Sandburg. APT-1; BRP; ChAP; HeIP-4; ITBLP; InPK-6; MoAmPo; NAAL-2v2; NAAL-5; OBCA; OxIBACP; PAI; Spl; TAP; TCAPo; TFi; TTTS

Fog descends over the tidal surge and the shallow lagoons. Gary Young. GeoHom *Fr.* If He Had.

Fog hanged over the park, the night cold, and, clean. And, Hinges. Ted Greenwald. FTOS

Fog has settled, The. Claire Pratt. HA

Fog. He can see only this deep still fog. Winslow Homer. Winfield Townley Scott. APT-2

Fog Land. Ingeborg Bachmann. WoPoe, *tr. by* Michael Hamburger

Fog lifting above the fields. Mussel Rock/Lowtide—Santa Cruz, California 1959. Jeff Tagami. OpBo

Fog obscures the deserted mountain. Man in Hangchou Spread Word that I Had Died. Chen-chü Heard of This and Was Upset, So I Have Written This To Send Him, A. Ni Tsan. CoBLCP, *tr. by* Jonathan Chaves

Fog of night envelops the flowering trees, The. T'ang Yin. CoBLCP *Fr.* Spring—River—Flower—Moon—Night.

Fog over the base: the beams ranging. Front, A. Randall Jarrell. NoP-4; OBWP; OxBC; PoWW; VGW

Fog smog fog smog. Windshield Wiper. Eve Merriam. KaS

Fog-Talk. Philip Booth. BodElec

Fog. The road I usually wander down. Georgy [*or* Georgii] Vladimirovich Ivanov. TCRP

Fog veils the river and the mountains. Taking the Ferry at Ta-kao at Dawn. Yang Wei-chen. SuSp, *tr. by* Jonathan Chaves

Fog-wreaths of doubt in blinding eddies drifted. One Reality, The. Frances Ridley Havergal. SacPr

Foggy Day (in London Town), A. George Gershwin. ReLy

Foggy, Foggy Dew, The. *Unknown.* OxBoLi; PeLV

Foggy moon, bird-calls in the flowers at dawn. Twenty-first Day of the Seventh Month. Henry Vaughan. CoBLCP, *tr. by* Jonathan Chaves

Foghorns. Gillian Clarke. TCAWP

Fol de riddle, lol de riddle, hi ding do. (LL) Mother Goose. LB; OxNR; ReMoGo

Fold away all your bright-tinted dresses. Hospital Duties. *Unknown.* CBCWP

Fold home, fast fold thy child. (LL) Blessed Virgin Compared to the Air We Breathe, The. Gerard Manley Hopkins. NOBVV; PeVV

Fold it up carefully, lay it aside. Jacket of Gray, The. Caroline Augusta Ball. CBCWP

Folded close under deepening snow. (LL) First Snowfall [*or* Snow-Fall], The. James Russell Lowell. AmFaPo; TAP

Folded hands and darkened eyes. Stone, The. Walter De la Mare. WeW-3

Folded Skyscraper, A. William Carlos Williams.

    Hemmed-in Males. APT-1; PoRA

    "Saloon is gone up the creek, The." APT-1; PoRA

Folders, papers, proofs, maps. Artists' Letters. Thomas Kinsella. BiHa

Folding clothes / I think of folding you. Sorting Laundry. Elisavietta Ritchie. SoSe-8

Folding the paper money, tearing the bills. (LL) Struggle, The. Toi Derricotte. LTA; PBCAP

Folding the Sheets. Rosemary Dobson. ItWoWo; NOBAu *Fr.* Daily Living.

Foley Artist, The. Nick Drake. NeBl

Foliage of Vision. James Merrill. VGW

Folk Museum, The. Medbh McGuckian. CIP-2

Folk Song: "O I'm off to Hullaboola where the climate's never cooler." Bruce Beaver. OBCoV

Folk-Songs. Chan Fang-sheng. ChiP, *tr. by* Arthur Waley

Folk Tune. Esther Raab. FIT, *tr. by* Robert Friend and Shimon Sandbank

Folk Who Live in Backward Town, The. Mary Ann Hoberman. OBCA; OxIBACP

Folk Wisdom. Thomas Kinsella. TwCP

Folks ain't got no right to censuah othah [*or* uthah] folks about dey habits. Accountability. Paul Laurence Dunbar. APN-2

Folks and Me. Lucile Crites. PWR

Folks are blessed who make the best of ev'ry day. Give Me the Simple Life. Harry Ruby. ReLy

Folks downstairs brought him home, The. Dylan, Two Days. Patricia Smith. GT

Folks, I'm telling you. Advice. Langston Hughes. NBLV; SAmP

Folks in Georgia's 'bout to go insane. Ballin' the Jack. Christopher Smith. ReLy

Folks need a lot of loving in the morning. Need of Loving. Strickland W. Gillilan. PoToHe

Folks Who Live on the Hill, The. Jerome Kern. ReLy

Folks, you've heard of scandalous vamps. Louisville Lou (The Vampin' Lady). Milton Ager. ReLy

Follies of Adam, The. Theodore Roethke. ChIV-1

Follow a shadow [*or* shadow], it still flies you. Song. That Women Are But Men's Shadows. Ben Jonson. BeJo; OxBSP

Follow back from the gull's bright arc and the osprey's plunge. Water Ouzel. William H. Matchett. CoAP

Follow, follow[e] / Though with mischiefe. Thomas Campion. EnLoPo *Fr.* Observations in the Art of English Poesie.

Follow Me. Nada El-Hage. PoArWo, *tr. by* Nathalie El-Hani

Follow my Bangalorey Man. *Unknown.* OxNR

Follow the clews. Song for Annie. Harry Gilonis. Oth

Follow the yellow brick road. We're Off to See the Wizard (The Wonderful Wizard of Oz). Harold Arlen. ReLy

Follow Thy Fair Sun[ne] [Unhappy Shadow]. Thomas Campion. EnLoPo; NOBE; NOSC; NoSic; SCGP; UnPo

(Devotion.) OBEV

(Follow Thy Fair Sun.) NoP-4

(Followe thy faire sunne unhappy shaddowe.) NPeEn; OxBEV

Follow your nose. Segue O Teu Destino. Fernando Pessoa. WoPoe, *tr. by* David Wright

Followed mountains over a thousand miles. Night: Setting out from Shih-Kuan Pavilion. Hsieh Ling-yün. ChinPo, *tr. by* Yip Wai-lim

Follower. Seamus Heaney. CABP; PNI

Following a Man. John Ash. HarvBoo

Following forbidden streets. Wraith-Friend, The. George Barker. OBMV

Following Her to Sleep. Jeffrey McDaniel. NeAmPo

Following His Rhymes and Answering the Poems of My Friend Next Door on Recent Events. Tai Piao-yüan.

    "South of the house, north of the house." CoBLCP

Following the Army on Campaign. Wang Ch'ang-ling.

    "At Jade Gate Pass mountain ridges several thousand-fold." SuSp

    "In the citadel of Jade Gate Pass, elm leaves early scatter yellow." SuSp

    "P'i-p'a begins the dance, midst changing new sounds, The." SuSp

Following the Rhymes of Chiang Hui-shu. Su Tung-p'o (Su Shih). CoBCP, *tr. by* Burton Watson

Following the Rhymes of Autumn Night Song by Meng Tzu-chou, Signatory Official of the Board of Rites. Yü Chi. CoBLCP, *tr. by* Jonathan Chaves

Following the Rhymes of Bamboo Branch Songs in Response to Yüan Po-chang. Yü Chi. CoBLCP, *tr. by* Jonathan Chaves

Following the Rhymes of Chang Hsün, in My Study in Late Spring. Huang T'ing-chien. SuSp, *tr. by* Michael E. Workman

Following the Rhymes of Chiang Hui-shu. Su Tung-p'o (Su Shih). CoBCP, *tr. by* Burton Watson

(Following the Rhumes of Chiang Hui-shu.) CoBCP

(Following the Rhymes of Chiang Hui-shu.) CoBCP, *tr. by* Burton Watson

Following the Rhymes of Fellow Graduate P'ei Chung-mou. Huang T'ing-chien. SuSp, *tr. by* Michael E. Workman

Following the Rhymes of Kao Chi-ti's Poem: "We Had Planned to Travel to Cloud Cliff But Couldn't Because of Rain." Hsü Pen. CoBLCP, *tr. by* Jonathan Chaves

Following the Rhymes of Magistrate Liu's Poems on Entertaining Two Assistant Premiers at Pine-Snow Temple. Hsü Chung-hsing.

    "Trees are ancient, thick with patterns of moss, The." CoBLCP

Following the Rhymes of Shao-pao Huang's Poem on Being Moved while Visiting the Farmers. Yang Shih-ch'i. CoBLCP; WoPoe, *tr. by* Jonathan Chaves

Following the Rhymes of the Six Poems "Thinking of the Past at Ku-Su and Ch'ien-t'ang." Ni Tsan. CoBLCP, *tr. by* Jonathan Chaves

Following the Rhymes of Wang An-shih's Poem "Inscribed on the Wall of the Temple of Western Great Unity." Huang T'ing-chien. SuSp, *tr. by* Michael E. Workman

Following the Rhymes of Yang T'ing-ho's Poem, "On the Road Back, Accompanying the Imperial Retinue on a Visit to the Tombs of Former Emperors." Li Tung-yang. CoBLCP, *tr. by* Jonathan Chaves

Following the Rhymes of Yü-chai's Poems on Autumn. Ni Tsan.

    "You ask when I will go back home." CoBLCP

Following the roads. Ono no Komachi. OHMPJ

Following their road of exit, they stooped over and came out. *Zuni Oral Tradition.* APN-2 *Fr.* History Myth of the Coming of the A′ shiwi as Narrated by ʼKiäklo.

Follows the naked work, profoundly moved by it. (LL) Story of a Hotel Room. Rosemary Tonks. LW; OxBTC

Folly—. What is the Word. Samuel Beckett. OxBEV

Folly and error, stinginess and sin. To the Reader. Charles Baudelaire. SxFrPo, *tr. by* James McGowan

Folly of Being Comforted, The. W. B. Yeats. HeIP-4; NAEL-5v2; NAEL-6v2

Folly's Song. Thomas Dekker. NOSC

Fond greeting, hillock there, A. Laoiseach Mac an Bhaird. NOIV

Fond man *Musophilus*, that thus dost spend. Samuel Daniel. NoSic; PBRV *Fr.* Musophilus; or, Defence of All Learning.

Fond Memory. Eavan Boland. ModIr

Fond nymphs, from us true pleasure learn. In Derision of a Country Life. Edward Ravenscroft. NOSC

Fond Painter, why woulds't thou my picture draw? Echo. Ausonius. NPeEn, *tr. by* George Sandys

Fond words have oft been spoken to thee, sleep! To Sleep. William Wordsworth. Son

Fondle me. Marrow of My Bone. Mari E. Evans. BPo

Fondling and snuggling. Love Song: "Fondling and snuggling." Kuan Yün-shih. CrYelRi, *tr. by* Sam Hamill

Food and Drink. Louis Untermeyer. MoAmPo

Food-Factory Kitchen. Vladimir Salimon. TCRP, *tr. by* Vera Dunham

Food for Fire, Food for Thought. Robert Duncan. NeAP

Food for Thought. Val Ferdinand. NBV

Food is steaming. Toho. JDP, *tr. by* Yoel Hoffmann

Food of Birds, The. Brewster Ghiselin. APT-2

Food of Love. Carolyn Kizer. RaBo

Food of the North. D. H. Lawrence. FaBoEE

Food Packages: 1947. Adrienne Rich. TaR

Fool, The. Kenneth Mackenzie. BMAP

Fool, a fool! I met a fool i' the forest, A. William Shakespeare. OBCoV *Fr.* As You Like It.

Fool and the Poet, The. Pope. *See* Epigram from the French: "Sir, I admit your general [*or* gen'ral] Rule."

Fool and Wise. Coventry Patmore. SacPr

Fool hath said in his heart, The, There is no God. Bible, *O.T.* TrJP *Fr.* Psalms.

Fool much bit by fleas put out the light, A. Richard Lovelace. FaBoEE

Fool's Prayer, The. Edward Rowland Sill. APN-2; ITBLP

Fool's Preferment, A. Thomas D'Urfey [*or* Durfey]. I'll Sail upon the Dog-Star. FaBoCh; OxBoLi

Fool's Song. Thomas Holcroft. NOEC

Fool, said my Muse to me, look in thy heart and write. (LL) Sir Philip Sidney. AWP; CABP; EBEV; HAP; NAEL-5v1; NAEL-6v1; NAEL-7v1; NPeEn; NoP-4; NoSic; OxAEP-1; OxBSo; PoE; SCGP; Son; TFi *Fr.* Astrophil and Stella.

Fool, take up thy shaft again. Song. Thomas Stanley. EnLoPo

Fool there was and he made his prayer, A. Vampire, The. Rudyard Kipling. NOBVV; OxBEV

Fool, to put up four crosses at your door. Jonathan Swift. FaBoEE

Foolin' Myself. Jack Lawrence. ReLy

Fooling God. Louise Erdrich. ReEnLa

Fooling Mom. Fêng Mêng-lung. ColAnChi, *tr. by* Richard W. Bodman *Fr.* Mountain Songs.

Foolish Child. *Unknown.* PBA, *tr. by* J. B. Danquah

Foolish eyes, thy streams give over. Song. Martha Sansom. ECWP

Foolish gods are doing poppers while they sing along, The. Gods at Three A.M., The. Reginald Shepherd. NeAmPo; WiU

Foolish man rides here, A. In the Heart of the Desert. Al-Tirimmah. ArPe, *tr. by* Omar S. Pound

Foolish men who accuse. She Proves the Inconsistency of the Desires and Criticism of Men Who Accuse Women of What They Themselves Cause. Sister Juana Inés de la Cruz. BoWoP, *tr. by* Aliki and Willis Barnstone

Foolish prater, what dost thou. Swallow, The. Abraham Cowley. EBEV; OBEV; OxAEP-1

Foolish rhythm turns in my idle head, A. Tune, A. Arthur Symons. BoLoP

Foolish Thing. Michael Burkard. BodElec

Foolish useless man who had done nothing, A. Brummell at Calais. John Glassco. MoCV

Foolishness. Nizar Qabbani. MAP, *tr. by* Diana Der Hovanessian and Lena Jayyusi

Fools and Wise Men. Friedrich von Logau. GePo, *tr. by* George C. Schoolfield

Fools Fall in Love. Irving Berlin. ReLy

Fools have power over wise men: each transactions, each affair. Fools and Wise Men. Friedrich von Logau. GePo, *tr. by* George C. Schoolfield

Fools! Sit down and wait for them to crumble! (LL) On the Fly-Leaf of Pound's Cantos. Basil Bunting. FaBoTw; HarvBoo; NoAM; OxBTC

Foot, and gazing into the future. (LL) Why Brownlee Left. Paul Muldoon. DiPo; EmeKit; NPeEn; NoP-4; OxBSo; PBCIP

Foot of the tower. An angle where the darkness, The. Thomas Kinsella. PBCIP *Fr.* Nightwalker.

Foot Race Song. *Unknown.* OBVE, *tr. by* Frank Russell

Foot Soldiers. John Banister Tabb. OBAL

Foot-Washing, The. A. R. Ammons. ChIV-2

Foot-Washing, The. George Ella Lyon. OxWW

Football. Louis Jenkins. MoASP; RaBo

Football. "Nikolai Karpovich Otrada." TCRP, *tr. by* Daniel Weissbort

Football, The. Arizona Zipper. HA

Football thuds upon the green field, The. Footballers. Zoltán Jékely. IQMS, *tr. by* John Gordon Nichols

Footballers. Zoltán Jékely. IQMS, *tr. by* John Gordon Nichols

Footbinding. Patricia Beer. NoP-4

Footnote at "Figure of Speech." Tina Darragh. FTOS

Footnote Extended, A. Dannie Abse. HP

Footnote on Monasticism, A: Dingle Peninsula. John Montague. BBASP

Footnote to Belloc's "Tarantella." John Heath-Stubbs. OBCoV

Footnote to Enright's "Apocalypse." Martin Bell. FaBoMo

Footnote to John II: 4. Ronald Allison Kells Mason. PeNZ

Footnote to Tennyson. Gerald Bullett. UV

Footnote to the Amnesty Report on Torture. Margaret Atwood. NoAM

Footnote to the Lord's Prayer. Kay Smith. "Heaven which art in Heaven Our Father in Heaven." TrCP

Footnotes. Arkadii Dragomoschenko. ItGoST, *tr. by* Elena Balashova and Lyn Hejinian

Footnotes to "The Autobiography of Bertrand Russell." Mona Van Duyn. "This seems, in a world where love must take its chances." HAP

Footpath. Stella Ngatho. WPOW

Footpath would have been enough, A. Entailed Farm, The. John Glassco. MoCV; NOBC

Footprint on the Air, A. Naomi Lewis. NOxBChV

Footprints. Dan Pagis. VCWP, *tr. by* Stephen Mitchell

Footprints on the Glacier. W. S. Merwin. NoAM

Footprints tread. Distance. Luciana Notari. CItWP, *tr. by* Cinzia Sartini Blum and Lara Trubowitz

Footsole to scalp alive facing the window's black mirror. Late Ghazal. Adrienne Rich. HarvBoo

Footsteps of an Owl and His Lament, The. Viktor Aleksandrovich Sosnora. TCRusP, *tr. by* Kathy Lewis

For a Birthday. Sophie Jewett. PoBW

For a Black Child. David Diop. NegPo, *tr. by* Ellen Conroy Kennedy

For a Black Poet. Gerald William Barrax. NBV

For a Child Expected. Anne Ridler. SacPr

For a Coming Extinction. W. S. Merwin. GifTon; HCAP; NNaP; PoE; VCAP (Gray whale.) PoPoPo

For a creed that will not let you dance? (LL) Magalu. Helene Johnson. APT-2; BISi

For a Daughter Gone Away. Brendan Galvin. GM

For a dawn moon, hard to hold its light. Failing the Examination. Meng Chiao. SuSp, *tr. by* Stephen Owen

For a day and a night. Rock, The. Elizabeth Spires. ExTi

For a Dead Lady. Edwin Arlington Robinson. APT-1; HeIP-4; MoAmPo; NOBA; NoAM; OxBA; PoRA; TCAPo; TFi

For a dream's sake. (LL) Mirage. Christina Georgina Rossetti. BoLoP; PoRA

For a face, and dark lines for arms. (LL) Sonnet: "Now I see them sitting me before a mirror." Michael Palmer. HarvBoo; MakPoe

For a Far-out Friend. Gary Snyder. BB; NeAP; PoM

For a Father. Anthony Cronin. FaBoTw

For a few thousand battered books. (LL) Ezra Pound. HarvBoo; MoAmPo; NOBE; NPeEn; OxBA; PoE; TRP; UnPo *Fr.* Hugh Selwyn Mauberley (Life and Contacts).

For a Fountain. "Barry Cornwall." OBEV

For a Friend in Travail. Adrienne Rich. NAAL-5

For a good decade. Drunk in the Furnace, The. W. S. Merwin. NAAL-2v2; NoAM; NoP-4; PoE; TwCP

For a hundred days grenades have been piercing. Lieutenant, The. Konstantin Mikhailovich Simonov. TCRP, *tr. by* Lubov Yakovleva

For a hundred miles the west wind carries the fragrance of millet. Yün Shou-p'ing. CoBLCP *Fr.* On the Painting "Joys of Village Life."

For a kid that's black? (LL) Merry-Go-Round. Langston Hughes. AmFaPo; PAI; SAmP

For a Lady I Know. Countee Cullen. APT-2; HeIP-4; InPK-6; NIL-7; NIP-4; OBAL; SSLK; TAP; TRP *Fr.* Four Epitaphs.

For a Lady's Summons of Non-Entry. William Drummond, of Hawthornden. NOSC

For a Lamb. Richard Eberhart. ColAP; OxBSP; RB; SoSe-8

For a long day and a night we read the names.   Reading the Names of the Vietnam War Dead.   Thomas McGrath.   CDa

For a long time.   For Tetsu the New Head Priest of Erin-ji.   Muso Soseki.   EaWin, *tr.* by W. S. Merwin

For a long time he tried to survive.   Vyacheslav Kupriyanov [*or* Kuprianov].   TCRusP, *tr.* by Pamela Davidson

For a long time I haven't seen such a young face.   Faina Grimberg.   TCRP

For a long time, not a year, not two.   Valentin Petrovich Katayev [*or* Kataev].   TCRP

For a long time we've been apart.   While It Was Raining.   Wen Cheng-ming.   CoBLCP, *tr.* by Jonathan Chaves

For a long time we've called ourselves grown-ups.   Prospectors' Little Waltz, The.   Aleksandr Arkadevich Galich.   TCRP, *tr.* by Gene Sosin

For a long while I have lived with the hope.   Wish, A.   Olga Fiodorovna Berggolts [*or* Bergholts].   TCRusP, *tr.* by Daniel Weissbort

For a maid again I'll never be. (LL)   Waly, Waly [Love Be Bonny].   *Unknown*.   EnLoPo; HAP; NOSC; OBEV; OxBS; TFi

For a man that's dedicated.   Vote for Lunn.   *Unknown*.   FaBoVe

For a Masseuse and Prostitute.   Kenneth Rexroth.   NNaP

For a minute, daughter, for an afternoon.   Prevention of Stacy Miller, The.   Peter Miller.   MoCV

For a moment all that it touches back to wonder. (LL)   Beautiful Changes, The.   Richard Wilbur.   CoAP; HCAP; NAAL-5; NIL-7; PoE

For a moment I saw a surging river.   Impermanence.   Lal Ded [*or* Lalla].   BoWoP

For a moment pause.   Mound, The.   Thomas Hardy.   OxBTC

For a moment, the idiot inside me who shouts death constantly blacks out.   Talking About Things.   Michael Ryan.   YaYoPo

For a moment there.   Rando.   JDP, *tr.* by Yoel Hoffmann

For a moment there is no periphery.   Camera Obscura.   Valerie Martínez.   NAPBL

For a Monk Going West.   Muso Soseki.   EaWin, *tr.* by W. S. Merwin

For a Mouthy Woman.   Countee Cullen.   ChIV-1; OBAL

For a Neighbor Girl.   Yü Hsüan-chi.   BoWoP, *tr.* by Geoffrey Waters

For a New Home.   Rosa Zagnoni Marinoni.   PoToHe

For a night—any night—that bends.   Poem of the Dawn and the Night.   Rodolfo Di Biasio.   NeIt, *tr.* by Stephen Sartarelli

For a particular size of stone about the size of your fist.   There Are Words.   Gael Turnbull.   Oth

For a Pastoral Family.   Judith Wright.

    I to my Brothers.   BMAP

For a Picture Where a Queen Laments over the Tomb of a Slain Knight.   Thomas Carew.   CaPo

For a Poet.   Countee Cullen.   TTY

For a Poet.   George Wither.   ChIV-2

For a Portrait of Annette Vallon.   Andrey [*or* Andrei] Andreievich Voznesensky [*or* Voznesenskii].   RusPo, *tr.* by Robert Arthur Douglas Ford

For a Quick Exit.   Norma Farber.   KaS

For a ráinbow fóoting it nor hé for his bónes rísen. (LL)   Caged Skylark, The.   Gerard Manley Hopkins.   MoBrPo; OBMV; OWoS; SoSe-8; Son

For a saving grace, we didn't see our dead.   War in the Air, The.   Howard Nemerov.   ColAP; DiPo; VCAP

For a Senior College Textbook.   Hans Magnus Enzensberger.   PoSu

For a single beautiful word. (LL)   Parsley.   Rita Dove.   ESEAA; HCAP; LoL; NAAAL; NAAL-5; NIL-7; NoAM; NoP-4; PoPoPo; VCAP

For a Six Year Old.   Ben Scammell.   NLP

For a solemn opening.   We Survived Them.   Anna Swirszczynska.   AF, *tr.* by Czeslaw Milosz

For a Stone Girl at Sanchi.   Gary Snyder.   BB

For a Swarm of Bees.   *Unknown*.   ASW, *tr.* by Kevin Crossley-Holland

For A' That and A' That.   Shirley Brooks.   NOBL; UV

For A' That and A' That ["Is there, for honest poverty"].   Robert Burns.   NAEL-5v2; NAEL-6v2; OxAEP-2; TFi; TreFP; UV

    (Is There for Honest Poverty.)   BRP; NePenScot; OxBEV

    (Man's a Man for A' That, A.)   CABP; NOEC

    (Song: For A' That and A' That.)   CABP; NOEC

For a' the gowd in Christentie. (LL)   Kinmont Willie.   *Unknown*.   ESPB; IBB; OxBB

For a thing done, repentance is no good.   Sonnet: He Is Past All Help.   Cecco Angiolieri, da Siena.   AWP; EaItPo, *tr.* by Dante Gabriel Rossetti

For a thousand years, you, African, suffered like a beast.   Dawn in the Heart of Africa.   Patrice Emery Lumumba.   PBA; TTY

For a trophy on this pine tree. (LL)   Leonidas.   GrAn; PGA

For A Venetian Pastoral By Giorgone (In the Louvre).   Dante Gabriel Rossetti.   GS

    (Water, for anguish of the solstice,—yea.)   CenSon

For a Violin, Somewhat Nervously.   Vladimir Vladimirovich Mayakovsky [*or* Maiakovskii].   TCRP, *tr.* by Bernard Meares

For a Virgin Lady.   Countee Cullen.   MoAmPo

For a War Memorial.   Gilbert Keith Chesterton.   PoWW

For a Wedding.   Kate Clanchy.   MFPA

For a while a year is a long time.   Wholes.   Larry Eigner.   PmAP

For a while there we had 25-inch Chinese peasant families.   Not-so-good Earth, The.   Bruce Dawe.   CBAP

For a whole week.   Roma Higgins.   Dave Etter.   IllVoic

For a Wife in Jizzen.   Douglas Young.   OxBS

For a Wine Festival.   Vernon Watkins.   OxBTC

For a Winnebago Brave.   Joseph Bruchac.   CDW

For a Woman's Rights.   Joette Harland-Watts.   InTrad

For a year he'd collect.   Milkman and His Son, The.   Thomas Lux.   LCAP-2

For a Young Artist.   Robert Earl Hayden.   NoAM

For aa da scraimin stars at hing.   Gallow Hill.   William J. Tait.   OxBS

For Adelaide.   Bessie Rayner Parkes.   VWP

For Adolf Eichmann.   Primo Levi.   AF, *tr.* by Ruth Feldman

For age is opportunity no less.   Henry Wadsworth Longfellow.   PoToHe   *Fr.* Morituri Salutamus.

For ages and ages.   When Your Lover Has Gone.   E. A. Swan.   ReLy

For ages and ages, they couldn't have seemed less simpatico.   Nature of Things, The.   Kathleen Ossip.   BAP-01

For Albert, the Terrible.   Carlota Caulfield.   TANSG, *tr.* by Chris Allen

For All Blasphemers.   Stephen Vincent Benét.   OxBA

For All Mary Magdalenes.   Desanka Maksimovic.   WPOW, *tr.* by Vasa D. Mihailovich

For All My Brothers and Sisters.   Dick Lourie.   CDa

For all of us destiny is undivided.   Nikolai Stefanovich.   TCRP

For all one flag, one flag for all. (LL)   Atlanta Exposition Ode.   Mary Weston Fordham.   CBWP-2; SWaP

For all that [*or* this] lady's hire. (LL)   Dapple-gray.   Mother Goose.   LB; OxNR; ReMoGo

For all the saints who from their labors rest.   Funeral Hymn.   William Walsham Howe.   SacPr

For all the scenes that Day's bright eye pervades! (LL)   Night.   Ann Radcliffe.   NOBRP; WPE

For all the vision that took fire this night.   Burning Bush.   Martin Feinstein.   TrJP

For all these years, my certain Zen.   Ryushu Shutaku.   ZenPo, *tr.* by Takashi Ikemoto and Lucien Stryk

For all this wast[e] of wealth, and loss of blood. (LL)   On the Detraction Which Followed upon My Writing Certain Treatises.   John Milton.   NoP-4; Son

For all those beaten, for the broken heads.   Litany for Dictatorships.   Stephen Vincent Benét.   OxBA

For all true poetry is cruel.   Constipation.   Breyten Breytenbach.   PoetW, *tr.* by A. J. Coetzee

For All Unwed Mothers.   Robert Fleming.   ISC

For All We Know.   Sam M. Lewis.   ReLy

For all we know / We may never meet again.   For All We Know.   Sam M. Lewis.   ReLy

For all your days prepare.   Preparedness.   Edwin Markham.   MoAmPo

For Alva Benson, and for Those Who Have Learned to Speak.   Joy Harjo.   HATNAP; UnSA

For America is a lady rocking on a porch in an unpainted house on an.   Sixth Psalm.   Anne Sexton.   LCAP-2

For among My People are found wicked men.   Bible, *O.T.*   TrJP   *Fr.* Jeremiah.

For an Album.   Adrienne Rich.   VCAP

For "An Allegorical Dance of Women" by Andrea Mantegna.   Dante Gabriel Rossetti.   CenSon

For An Amorous Lady.   Theodore Roethke.   NBLV

For an Approving God. (LL)   Emily Dickinson.   NAAL-2v1; NAAL-3; NAAL-5; SAmP; SoSe-8; TCAPo

For an Asian Woman Who Says My Poetry Gives Her a Stomachache.   Nellie Wong.   FSt

For an Emigrant.   Randall Jarrell.   OxBA

For an Epitaph at Fiesole.   Walter Savage Landor.   FaBoEE

For an Ex-Far East Prisoner of War.   Charles Causley.   OxBC

For an officer / in the old Capital, fox fur.   Ezra Pound.   OBVE

For and Against the Environment.   D. M. Black.   EmeKit

For Andy Goodman—Michael Schwerner—and James Chaney.   Margaret Abigail Walker.   BPo

For Angus MacLeod.   Iain Crichton Smith.   OxBS

For Ann Scott-Moncrieff.   Edwin Muir.   GTBS-P

For Anne Gregory.   W. B. Yeats.   NAEL-5v2; NAEL-6v2; OxAEP-2

For Annie.   Edgar Allan Poe.   APN-1; ColAP; NOBA; OBEV; OxBA; TCAPo

For anyone who is tired and still has to walk. (LL)   Kinaxixi.   Agostinho Neto.   PoetW; WoPoe, *tr.* by W. S. Merwin

For Ares, gold-exchanger for the dead.   Aeschylus.   FaBoWar, *tr.* by Robert Browning   *Fr.* Agamemnon.

For Art Blakey and the Jazz Messengers. Keorapetse Kgositsile. SeSe

For Artaud. Michael McClure. NeAP

For as the harmony which sense admires. Fulke Greville, 1st Baron Brooke. NOSC *Fr.* Treatise of Monarchy, A.

For as the Soul's essential powers are three. Three Kinds of Life Answerable to the Three Powers of the Soul. John Davies. SacPr

For at midnight brake forth a Light. Michael Wigglesworth. TCAPo *Fr.* Day of Doom, The.

For at the window of my house. Bible, *O.T.* TrJP *Fr.* Proverbs.

For aught that a lie saith, fear. (LL) Lake of Gaube, The. Algernon Charles Swinburne. CABP; NAEL-5v2; NAEL-6v2

For August, be your dwelling thirty towers. Folgore da San Geminiano [*or* Gimignano]. CTC; EaItPo, *tr. by* Dante Gabriel Rossetti *Fr.* Sonnets of the Months.

For auld lang syne. (LL) Auld Lang Syne. Robert Burns. AWP; NAEL-5v2; NAEL-6v2; NOBE; NOSC; NePenScot; OBEV; OxAEP-2; OxBEV; OxBS; SCGP

For auld Robin Gray he is kind unto me. (LL) Auld Robin Gray. Lady Anne Lindsay. ECWP; GTBS-P; NOEC; OBEV; OxBEV; PeSAV; WPE

For Aunt Cathy. Kevin Powell. InTrad

For authorities whose hopes. Paper Nautilus, The. Marianne Craig Moore. FaBoWP; HarvBoo; MakPoe; NAAL-5; NALW; VGW

For awhile I too was haunted by. Amnesiac. Mark Osaki. CDa

For aye unsought-for slept among his ashes cold. (LL) Eve of St Agnes, The. John Keats. CABP; EBNV; FHYEP; HAP; NAEL-5v2; NAEL-6v2; NOBRP; NPeEn; NoP-4; OBNV; OxAEP-2; PoE; TFi; TRP

For Babies Unborn. Tracy Clarke. InTrad

For Baby. *Unknown.* ReMoGo

For bards, like these, who neither sing nor say. Charles Churchill. NOEC *Fr.* Prophecy of Famine, The.

For Beauty. Susan Hahn. ExTi

For being unfaithful though ever true. Christopher Cook. NewEx

For Beirut I write. Beirut. Claire Gebeyli. PoArWo, *tr. by* Mona Takyeddine Amyuni

For best of bone and blood. (LL) Fowls [*or* Foweles *or* Fowles] in the Frith. *Unknown.* FaBoVe; HAP; MiEL; NAEL-5v1; OxBSP

For best work. Lorine Niedecker. VGW

For better waters now the little bark. Dante Alighieri. NAWM-5v1 *Fr.* Divina Commedia.

For Black Poets Who Think of Suicide. Etheridge Knight. HeIP-4; InPK-6; LTA; NAAAL

For Black Women Who Are Afraid. Toi Derricotte. ExTi

For Bob Marley. John Agard. WaCA

For Both of You, the Divorce Being Final. John Hollander. YaYoPo

For brave comportment, wit without offence. To His Honoured and Most Ingenious Friend Mr. Charles Cotton. Robert Herrick. CaPo; NOSC

For breakfast—war and coffee. Pilots. Battle News. Samuel Hazo. CDa

For, Brother, What Are We? Thomas Clayton Wolfe. RaBo

For Bud. Michael S. Harper. ESEAA; PoE

For by tomorrow [*or* to morrow], I may think[e] so too. (LL) Woman's Constancy. John Donne. ESCV; NBLV; NOSC

For C. Philip Whalen. NeAP; VGW

For C., Who Died of Childbirth at the Age of One Year and Eleven Months. Giovanni Raboni. ItPo, *tr. by* Gayle Ridinger

For Cadging Fish. Isabel Gowdie. EMWP

For Carlos Charles Bucillio. Alice Sadongei. HATNAP

For centuries sadhus live and die. Circumambulating Arunachala. Gary Snyder. BB

For certain he hath seen all perfectness. Dante Alighieri. AWP; EaItPo, *tr. by* Dante Gabriel Rossetti *Fr.* La Vita Nuova.

For certain, I did not live thus in this world. "Naum Korzhavin." TCRP

For change of solitude. (LL) Happiness Makes Up in Height for What It Lacks in Length. Robert Frost. MoAmPo; SoSe-8

For Christmas Day. Joseph Hall. SacPr

For Christopher Isherwood and Chester Kallman. W. H. Auden. SacPr

For City Spring. Stephen Vincent Benét. NBLV

For Colored Girls Who Have Considered Suicide When the Rainbow Is Enuf. Ntozake Shange.

  "At 4:30 AM/ she rose." BoWoP

  Dark Phrases. BlSi

  No More Love Poems #1. BlSi

For comfort on bad nights. Barton in the Beans. Joanne Limburg. NeBl

For Consciousness. Mervyn Morris. WaCA

For Contemporary Artist Pien Wei-Ch'I. Cheng Hsieh. SuSp

For conversation when we meet again. (LL) I, Being Born A Woman. Edna St. Vincent Millay. APT-1; BoLoP; HarvBoo; LW; NALW; NIL-7; NIP-4; NoP-4

For Cool Papa Bell. Tom Dent. ISC

For cover—the tall forest. Landscape Painted on a Fan—Echoing a Poem by Wen Cheng-ming, A. Chu Yün-ming. CoBLCP, *tr. by* Jonathan Chaves

For Craig Who Leapt Off a Cliff in to Hummingbird Light. Diane Wakoski. PmAP

For Crethis' store of tales and pleasant chat. Crethis. Callimachus. AWP, *tr. by* Richard Garnett

For dame and doodle-doo. (LL) Mother Goose. LB; OxNR; ReMoGo

For Daniel Beels, Third Generation Bricklayer. John Rybicki. AmPoNex

For, Dante, I'm the goad and you're the bull. (LL) Sonnet: To Dante Alighieri (He Writes to Dante, Then in Exile at Verona, Defying Him as No Better Than Himself). Cecco Angiolieri, da Siena. AWP; EaItPo, *tr. by* Dante Gabriel Rossetti

For Danton. Charles Tomlinson. HarvBoo

For dateless consummation dateless days. To My Lady. E. S. Miller. Son

For Daughters of Magdalen. Countee Cullen. ChIV-2

For dawn, wind. Crow Jane. Imamu Amiri Baraka. PoM

For days after the wedding. Balloon Heart. Beth Gylys. AmPoNex

For days he has dumped a trail of tuna blood. Great White Shark, The. Arthur Sze. GifTon

For days now, / It's been a real binge. Tune: "Distant Red Window." Chou Pang-yen. SuSp, *tr. by* Irving Y. Lo

For days you find it one long zero hour. Marking Time. Peter Steele. NOBAu

For de Lawd. Lucille Clifton. TAP; TwCP

For Dear Life. Alane Rollings. OPRER

For Death, he taketh all away, but them he cannot take. (LL) Heraclitus. William Johnson Cory. AWP; EBVV; FaBoEE; InPK-6; NOBE; OBEV; OxAEP-2; OxBSP; PoRA; SCGP; UV

For Death thou art a Mower too. (LL) Damon the Mower. Andrew Marvell. BASC; ESCV; GeHe; NAEL-5v1; NAEL-6v1; NAEL-7v1; NOSC

For deep deer-copse beneath Mount Han. Ezra Pound. OBVE

For Deliverance from a Fever. Anne Bradstreet. NAAL-2v1; NAAL-3; NALW

For Demeter winnowing, for the Hours who haunt the furrows. Diodorus Zonas. GrAn

For Don Drummond. Lorna Goodison. WaCA

For Douglas whom the cloud and eddy rejected. Funeral Oration, A. Drummond Allison. PoWW

For Dr. and Mrs. Dresser. Margaret Avison. MoCV

For Drum Hadley. Harold Littlebird. VoR

For duke ellington. Reuben Jackson. ESEAA

For dwelling in milk. (LL) Jack Kerouac. NeAP; PmAP *Fr.* Mexico City Blues.

For each breath of the south-wind makes a new bamboo! (LL) Eating Bamboo-Shoots. Po Chü-i. ChiP; OBVE, *tr. by* Arthur Waley

For each ecstatic instant. Emily Dickinson. NAAL-2v1; NAAL-3

For each morning a tune. Interior Music, The. Patricia Goedicke. MiVo

For Easter Island or Another Island. William Dickey. YaYoPo

For Edward Hicks. David Helwig. NOBC

For Edward Hopper, from the Floor. Lucia Maria Perillo. ExTi

For eight and fifty years. Tanko (d. 1884). JDP, *tr. by* Yoel Hoffmann

For Elaine de Kooning. Hilda Morley. PmAP

For Eleanor and Bill Monahan. William Carlos Williams. CRP; VGW

For Eli Jacobson. Kenneth Rexroth. RaBo

For Emily (Dickinson). Maureen Owen. PmAP; ReTh

For Emma. Luigi Fontanella. NeIt, *tr. by* Michael Palma

For Esther. Stanley Plumly. GM; LCAP-2

For Etheridge Knight. Jackie Warren-Moore. SpirFl

For ev'ry man there's a woman. For Every Man There's a Woman. Leo Robin. ReLy

For ever cursed be this detested day. Pope. EroLit *Fr.* Rape of the Lock, The.

For ever, Fortune, wilt thou prove. To Fortune. James Thomson. GTBS-P

For ever shall I be called virgin. Epitaph of a Girl. *Unknown.* GrAn, *tr. by* Dudley Fitts

For every bird there is this last migration. Death of the Bird, The. Alec Derwent Hope. BMAP

For every chekeh of the guitar. Some Tentative Definitions 11. Kwame Dawes. WaCA

For every evil under the sun. Mother Goose. LB; OxNR; ReMoGo

For Every Heart. Olga Broumas. ErotSp

For Every Man There's a Woman. Leo Robin. ReLy

For every parcel I stoop down to seize. Armful, The. Robert Frost. OxBSP

For every year, he grew a new tooth. Man Who Became Old, The. Alberto A. Ríos. NoAM

For every year of life we light. Birthday Poem, A. James Simmons. OxBSP; PNI

For everyone. Swimmer's Moment, The. Margaret Avison. NOBC

For example, taking the cement onto palettes, for the hoist.   Bill Griffiths.   Oth *Fr.* Building: The New London Hospital.

For Exmoor.   Jean Ingelow.   OBEV

For eyes he waves greentipped.   Slug in Woods.   Earle Birney.   NOBC; NoP-4

For F. M. Who Did Not Get Killed Yesterday on 57th Street.   Malena Mörling.   AmPoNex

For False Heart.   Joseph Hilaire Pierre Belloc.   *See* False Heart, The

For Fawzi in Jerusalem.   Samuel Hazo.   GraLe

For fear of finding something worse. (LL)   Jim Who Ran Away from His Nurse, and Was Eaten by a Lion.   Joseph Hilaire Pierre Belloc.   EBNV; NOxBChV; OBSP; OxAEP-2

For fear that she wyle your fancy frae me. (LL)   Whistle, and I'll Come to You, My Lad.   Robert Burns.   OxAEP-2; OxBoLi

For fear they burn a hole through two-foot steel. (LL)   Spoils.   Robert Graves.   HAP; Son; WeW-3

For fellowship—at night. (LL)   Emily Dickinson.   MoAmPo; SWaP

FOR few nights' solace in delicious bed.   To St Mary Magdalen.   Henry Constable.   ChIV-2; NoSic

For Fidel Castro.   Sandra Maria Esteves.   PueRic

For 5p at a village fête I bought.   On First Looking into Chapman's Hesiod.   Peter Porter.   NOBAu

For forms of government let fools contest.   Pope.   ECEV   *Fr.* Essay on Man, An.

For forty million years a warm, warm rain.   Formation of Soils, The.   Brenda Hillman.   BAP-01

For forty years I shunned the lust.   For a Virgin Lady.   Countee Cullen.   MoAmPo

For France.   Claudian.   MLL, *tr.* by Helen Waddell

For Freckle-Faced Gerald.   Etheridge Knight.   BPo; ESEAA

For Friendship.   Robert Creeley.   VCAP

For Fugitives.   Frank Templeton Prince.   HarvBoo

For gay bard, barren summer.   Lament for Lleucu Llwyd.   Llywelyn Goch ap Meurig Hen.   OBWVE, *tr.* by Joseph P. Clancy

For Gen the New Head Priest of Erin-ji.   Muso Soseki.   EaWin, *tr.* by W. S. Merwin

For George Santayana.   Robert Lowell.   NAAL-2v2; VGW

For Gil and Other Incurables.   Renée Weiss.   BodElec

For giving me my madness back, or nearly. (LL)   Come Dance with Kitty Stobling.   Patrick Kavanagh.   HarvBoo; NPeEn; NoAM

For Glaukos, for the Nereids.   Lucianus [*or* Lucian].   PGA

For God, our God is a gallant foe.   Ballad for Gloom.   Ezra Pound.   MoAmPo

For God's sake be careful or someone will hear you! (LL)   Sacred and Profane Love, or, There's Nothing New under the Moon Either.   Peter De Vries.   NBLV; OBCoV

For God's sake mark that fly.   Nulla Fides.   Patrick Carey [*or* Cary].   SCGP

For God's sake [*or* Godsake] hold your tongue, and let me love.   Canonization, The.   John Donne.   BASC; CABP; ESCV; EnLoPo; FHYEP; FSCP; FaBoVe; HAP; NAEL-5v1; NAEL-6v1; NAEL-7v1; NAWM-5v1; NIL-7; NIP-4; NOBE; NOSC; NPeEn; NoP-4; PBRV; PoE; PoPoPo; SCGP; SoSe-8; TFi; TRP; UnPo; WoPoe

For God's sake, reader! take them not for mine! (LL)   Byron.   NAEL-5v2; NAEL-6v2; PoE   *Fr.* Don Juan.

For going up or coming down.   For a Quick Exit.   Norma Farber.   KaS

For good is the life ending faithfully. (LL)   Long love that in my thought doth harbo[u]r, The.   Sir Thomas Wyatt.   GSo; NAEL-5v1; NAEL-6v1; NAEL-7v1

For Granny (from Hospital).   J. P. Clark Bekederemo.   PBMAP   *Fr.* Reed in the Tide, A.

For grief.   Exile.   Saniyya Salih.   PoArWo, *tr.* by Kamal Boullata

For grief I am about to sing.   Emperor Frederick II.   EaItPo, *tr.* by Dante Gabriel Rossetti

For Grizzel McNaught (1709–1792).   Anne Finch (b. 1908).   FFC

For Guests after Their Visit.   Liu Ya-tzu.   SuSp, *tr.* by Wu-Chi Liu

For Guillaume Apollinaire.   William Meredith.   CoAP

For guilty men an axe is what I am.   Julianus Sees a Magistrate's Axe.   Julianus of Egypt.   GrAn, *tr.* by Lee T. Pearcy

For H. W. Fuller.   Carolyn M. Rodgers.   BPo

For half a century.   Roller Coaster.   Nicanor Parra.   TCLAP, *tr.* by Miller Williams

For Harper, Killed in Action.   Walter McDonald.   CDa

For harvest once again. (LL)   Scarecrow, The.   Walter De la Mare.   MoBrPo; OxBTC

For Hazel Hall, American Poet.   Countee Cullen.   APT-2

For H.D.   Diane Di Prima.   PmAP

For he was a shrub among the poplars.   Christopher Okigbo.   PBMAP   *Fr.* Limits (1962).

For he was drowned, and I've the ague. (LL)   Written After Swimming from Sestos to Abydos.   Byron.   NAEL-5v2; NAEL-6v2; NBLV; NoP-4

For he was wounder amiabill.   Sir David Lindsay [*or* Lyndsay].   OxBS   *Fr.* Historie of Squyer William Meldrum, The.

For Heather, Entering Kindergarten.   Roberta Hill Whiteman.   HATNAP; NoAM

For Heaven and the future's sakes. (LL)   Two Tramps in Mud Time.   Robert Frost.   APT-1; MoAmPo; NAAL-2v2; NoAM; SAmP

For Hekabé and the women of Ilion.   Dion.   Plato.   GrAn, *tr.* by Peter Jay

For her gait, if she be walking.   Song.   William Browne (1591–1643).   OBEV

For her locust, nightingale of the fields, and her cricket that slept.   Anyte [*or* Anytes].   HePo   *Fr.* Epigrams.

For her sake that died for me. (LL)   Helen of Kirconnell.   *Unknown.*   AWP; OBEV; OxBEV; SCGP

For Hermann Heyen.   William Heyen.   GotH

For Hettie.   Imamu Amiri Baraka.   GT; NOBA; NeAP

For Hidden Mist Pavilion.   Yü Hsüan-chi.   BoWoP, *tr.* by Geoffrey Waters

For him also I powrit out mony teiris.   Mary Stuart, Queen of Scots.   NePenScot, *tr.* by *Unknown*   *Fr.* Sonnets to Bothwell.

For him, it seems, everything was molten. Court-ladies flow in gentle streams.   Laughing Hyena, after [*or* by] Hokusai, The.   Dennis Joseph Enright.   TwCP

For him the Shannon opens.   Swimmer, The.   Brendan Kennelly.   PBCIP

For his Campbell's Soup screen-prints, society's.   Limerick.   Bill Greenwell.   PeLi

For His Friends.   Alcuin.   MLL, *tr.* by Helen Waddell

For his mind, I do[e] not care.   Ben Jonson.   NAEL-6v1; NAEL-7v1   *Fr.* Celebration of Charis in Ten Lyric[k] Pieces [*or* Peeces], A.

For His Own Epitaph.   Matthew Prior.   *See* For My Own Monument

For his own soul, to wear for evermore. (LL)   What the Sonnet Is.   Eugene Lee-Hamilton.   GSo; Son

For his religion it was fit.   Samuel Butler (1612–80).   OBCoV; OBSV; OxBEV   *Fr.* Hudibras.

For His Ring and Watch on the Night Stand.   Gladys Cardiff.   HATNAP

For His Wife, on Her Birthday.   Charles Wesley.   NOCV

For Hokey and Henrietta.   Norman Nicholson.   NoP-4

For hours I sat on our driveway beneath the dogwood tree.   St. Francis Speaks to Me at a Young Age.   Vic Coccimiglio.   InvLad

For hours my wife says "Goodbye."   Limerick.   Frank Gelett Burgess.   PeLi

For how long known this boundless wash of light.   Summer Beach.   Frances Darwin Cornford.   BrRo

For human nature Hope remains alone.   Hope.   Theognis.   AWP, *tr.* by John Hookham Frere

For I am rightful fellow of their band.   Mentors.   Gwendolyn Brooks.   ESEAA

For I can snore like a bullhorn.   After Making Love We Hear Footsteps.   Galway Kinnell.   ColAP; NAAL-5; NIL-7; NIP-4; NoAM; NoP-4; PasH; RaBo; VCAP

For I Have Done a Good and Kindly Deed.   Franz Werfel.   TrJP, *tr.* by Edith Abercrombie Snow

For I have read.   Of Earthly Love.   Susanna Valentine Mitchell.   LW

For I have seen the false mermaid. (LL)   Clerk Colvill.   *Unknown.*   ESPB; OxBB

For I Have Taught the Japanese.   Lucia Maria Perillo.   ExTi

For I inhabit a wood.   Marban, a Hermit Speaks.   *Unknown.*   BIrV; CIP-2, *tr.* by Michael Hartnett

For I lull nobody, and you will never understand me. (LL)   To a Certain Civilian.   Walt Whitman.   CBCWP; FaBoWar

For I'm going to do nothing for ever and ever. (LL)   *Unknown.*   FaBoEE; OBCoV

For I'm wearied with hunting and fain would lie down. (LL)   Lord Randal[l].   *Unknown.*   AWP; EBEV; EBNV; ESPB; HAP; HeIP-4; OxBB; OxBEV; OxBS; PAI; SCGP; TFi; TRP; WeW-3

For I'me a parting now from you. (LL)   To My Husband.   "Eliza."   EMWP; LW; PBRV

For I prophesy that they will understand the blessing and virtue of the rain.   Christopher Smart.   ECEV   *Fr.* Jubilate Agno.

For I prophesy that we shall have our horns again.   Christopher Smart.   ChIV-1   *Fr.* Jubilate Agno.

For I rejoice in my cat Matty.   Jubilate Matteo.   Gavin Ewart.   UV

For I shall love the very scorne which for my sake you do put on. (LL)   Song: "Or love me less, or love me more."   Sidney Godolphin.   BeJo; NOSC

For I will consider my Cat Jeoffry.   Christopher Smart.   CABP; CTC; FaBoCh; HAP; HeIP-4; NAEL-5v1; NAEL-6v1; NAEL-7v1; NOEC; NPeEn; NoP-4; OBWVE; OxAEP-1; PAI; PoE; PoPoPo; RB; SCV; TRP; TTTS; TriCat; WeW-3   *Fr.* Jubilate Agno.

For I will dare none. Good lord, walk dead still. (LL)   On Something, that Walk[e]s Somewhere.   Ben Jonson.   BASC; BeJo; NAEL-5v1; NAEL-6v1; NAEL-7v1; OxBSP; PAI; PoE; SCGP

For if it prosper, none dare call it Treason. (LL)   Of Treason.   Sir John Harington [*or* Harrington].   FaBoEE; InPK-6; NPeEn; NoSic; OBCoV; OxBEV; OxBoLi; SoSe-8

For if you knew our hardships you'd never poach again. (LL) Van Dieman's Land. *Unknown.* NOBAu; PeVV

"For if your boone be askeable." Thomas Cromwell. *Unknown.* ESPB

For Imelda. James Simmons. PNI

For in much wisdom is much grief: and he that increaseth knowledge increaseth sorrow. (LL) Bible, *O.T.* NAWM-5v1; TrJP *Fr.* Ecclesiastes.

For Innocents' Day. Luke Wadding [*or* Waddinge]. NOIV

For instance, the child skipping. No Boundaries. Liz Rosenberg. InvLad

For it's up with the bonnets of Bonny Dundee. (LL) Sir Walter Scott. FaBoCh; OxBS; OxBoLi; UV *Fr.* Doom of Devorgoil, The.

For it seems to us worthy of record. (LL) Les Millwin. Ezra Pound. APT-1; OBCoV

For J. W. Rafael Campo. RA

For James Dean. Frank O'Hara. NNaP; NeAP

For Jan as the End Draws Near. Carolyn Kizer. GeoHom

For Jan, in Bar Maria. Carolyn Kizer. VGW

For Jan, with Love. David Lee. GifTon

For Jane Myers. Louise Glück. FaBoWP

For January I give you vests of skin. Folgore da San Geminiano [*or* Gimignano]. EaItPo, *tr. by* Dante Gabriel Rossetti *Fr.* Sonnets of the Months.

For Jean Vincent d'Abbadie, Baron St.-Castin. Alden Nowlan. NOBC

For Joe Brainard. David Trinidad. WiU

For John Berryman. Robert Lowell. NOBA

For John Chappell. Gary Snyder. NNaP

For John Clare. John Ashbery. HarvBoo

For John Donne: Master Metaphysical. Alexander Trocchi. EroLit

For Johnny. John Pudney. OBWP

For Jose Mercado Vasquez and Frances Roman Vasquez. Robert Vasquez. GeoHom

For joy. (LL) Upon a Spider Catching a Fly. Edward Taylor. NOBA; NoP-4; OxBA; OxBEV; PeECV; SCAP; TAP; TCAPo

For Jude's Lebanon. Joseph Awad. GraLe

For July, in Siena, by the willow-tree. Folgore da San Geminiano [*or* Gimignano]. EaItPo, *tr. by* Dante Gabriel Rossetti *Fr.* Sonnets of the Months.

For just a brief while every day. Rendezvous. Mary Scott Fitzgerald. PoToHe

For Just Men Light Is Sown. Michael Wigglesworth. AH

For Kai Snyder. Philip Whalen. PoM

For Karen. Elizabeth Robinson. AmPoNex

For Kelly, Missing in Action. Walter McDonald. CDa

For Kinna 2. Christine Ama Ata Aidoo. HAWP

For knighthood is not in the feats of war. Stephen Hawes. OBEV *Fr.* Pastime of Pleasure, The.

For Ko Who Has Come Back from China. Muso Soseki. EaWin, *tr. by* W. S. Merwin

For Ku Yen-hsien, A Poem for Him to Give to His Wife. Lu Yün. CoBCP, *tr. by* Burton Watson

For Kuo Hsiang. Yü Hsüan-chi. BoWoP, *tr. by* Geoffrey Waters

For lack of knowledge do my people die! My People Are Destroyed for Lack of Knowledge. Jones Very. ChIV-1

For Langston Hughes. Etheridge Knight. NBV

For Larry Levis in Memory. Luis Omar Salinas. GeoHom

For Laura. Mihály Vörösmarty. IQMS, *tr. by* Adam Makkai

For Li Po. Tu Fu. SuSp, *tr. by* Eugene Eoyang

For Life I Had Never Cared Greatly. Thomas Hardy. NoAM

For listening and instructional purposes. Drive to Lone Ranger, A. Ray A. Young Bear. AF

For Lo! My Jonah How He Slumped. John Wilson. AH

For lo! the board with cups and spoons is crown'd. Pope. UV *Fr.* Rape of the Lock, The; an Heroi-Comical Poem.

For Lolita Lebron. Sandra Maria Esteves. PueRic

For long and in loneliness. (LL) Stephen Crane. APN-2; TCAPo *Fr.* War Is Kind.

For long between the trenches a dead man lay in view. Brothers. Heinrich Lersch. FaBoWar, *tr. by* Christopher Middleton

For, Lord, the Crowded Cities Be. Rainer Maria Rilke. AWP; TrJP, *tr. by* Ludwig Lewisohn

For Lorine Niedecker in Heaven. Ralph J. Mills, Jr. IllVoic

For Lost and Found Brothers. Naomi Shihab Nye. GraLe

For lost honour among thieves. (LL) Thieves, The. Robert Graves. BoLoP; GTBS-P

For lost parents / their own age. (LL) Lost Parents. Lawrence Ferlinghetti. PoM; ReTh

For Lotus Flower. Li Shang-yin. SuSp, *tr. by* Eugene Eoyang

For Louis Armstrong, A Ju-Ju. Sarah Webster Fabio. SeSe

For Love. Robert Creeley. CoAmPo; NOBA; PmAP; VCAP

For love he offered me his perfect world. Gift to a Jade. Anna Wickham. OxBSP

For love—I would. Warning, The. Robert Creeley. NeAP; TAP; VGW

For love no time has she, or inclination. Soame Jenyns. OBSV *Fr.* Modern Fine Lady, The.

For love of mayde and moder thyn benigne. Amen. (LL) Geoffrey Chaucer. NOCV; SacPr *Fr.* Troilus and Criseyde [*or* Criseide].

For Love's sake, kiss[e] me once again[e]. Ben Jonson. NAEL-6v1; NAEL-7v1 *Fr.* Celebration of Charis in Ten Lyric[k] Pieces [*or* Peeces], A.

For Love's Sake Only. Elizabeth Barrett Browning. *See* Sonnets from the Portuguese

For love there is no other drug, Nicias. Theocritus. *See* And so an easier life our Cyclops drew

For M.S. Singing *Fruhlingsglaube* in 1945. Frances Darwin Cornford. BrRo

For Malcolm X. Margaret Abigail Walker. BPo; NAAAL; Son

For Malcolm's eyes, when they broke. Poem for Black Hearts, A. Imamu Amiri Baraka. NAAAL; PoM

For Malcolm's eyes, when they broke. Poem for Black Hearts, A. LeRoi Jones. SSLK

For man is between the pinchers while his soul is shaping and purifying. Christopher Smart. ChIV-1 *Fr.* Jubilate Agno.

For man to tell how human life began. John Milton. ChIV-1 *Fr.* Paradise Lost.

For Man will hearken to his glozing lies. John Milton. InvLi *Fr.* Paradise Lost.

For many distant travelers. Acoma. William Oandasan. HATNAP

For many, many days together. Riding Together. William Morris. NOBE

For many thousand ages. Es Stehen Unbeweglich. Heinrich Heine. AWP; TrJP, *tr. by* James Thomson

For many unsuccessful years. Advice to a Lover. Thomas Yalden. ECEV

For many years. For a Monk Going West. Muso Soseki. EaWin, *tr. by* W. S. Merwin

For many years. (LL) Kisimiso. Musaemura Bonus Zimunya. HBAPE; NAfrP

For many years I did not make migration. Tougaloo Blues. Kelly Norman Ellis. SpirFl

For Mao Tse-tung; a Meditation on Flies and Kings. Irving Layton. NOBC

For maple and for pine. Maple and the Pine, The. Robert Garioch. NPeEn

For Martin Luther King. Charles Fort. LTA

For Maulana Karenga & Pharoah Sanders. Imamu Amiri Baraka. APSN

For me a perfectly ordinary. Routine Day Sonnet. A. K. Ramanujan. EmeKit

For me a tragedy's most important act is the sixth. Theater Impressions. Wislawa Szymborska. VCWP

For Me and My Gal. Edgar Leslie. ReLy

For me, for me, two horses wait. Wizard's Funeral, The. Richard Watson Dixon. NOBVV; PeVV

For me neither honey nor bee. Sappho. SaLy, *tr. by* Diane Rayor

For me the Muse a simple band design'd. To Mr. Hayley, on Receiving Some Elegant Lines from Him. Charlotte Smith. RWP

For me, the naked and the nude. Naked and the Nude, The. Robert Graves. SoSe-8

For me to lose you and for you to lose me, we both lose. Ernesto Cardenal. BLPSL, *tr. by* Rene de Costa, Rigas Kappatos and Eleni Paidoussi

For Medgar Evers. David Ignatow. LTA

For men and women soon the day draws near. Abu Sa'id Abul Khayr. WoPoe, *tr. by* Dick Davis *Fr.* Four Poems on Death.

For Meng Hao-Jan. Li Po. WoPoe, *tr. by* Greg Whincup

For mercy, courage, kindness, mirth. Song, A. Laurence Binyon. MoBrPo

For Midas, the Man from Akragas First in the Flute Match. Pindar. WoPoe, *tr. by* Thomas Meyer *Fr.* Pythian Odes.

For Miriam. Marjorie Oludhe Macgoye. HAWP; WPOW

For Miss Tin in Hue. John Balaban. CDa

For Monk. Michael McClure. SeSe

For months / my books were stacked. February Park. Gerald Vizenor. VoR

For more than five thousand years. At the Jewish New Year. Adrienne Rich. TaR

For more than sixty years he has been blind. War Blinded. Douglas Dunn. DiPo; NePenScot; OBWP

For more than thirty years we hadn't met. Reunion. Carolyn Kizer. ExTi

For mortal love, that might not die of it. (LL) "Oh, sleep forever in the Latmian cave." Edna St. Vincent Millay. GSo; MoAmPo; NALW; NoAM

For mortals, mortal things. And all things leave us. Lucianus [*or* Lucian]. GrAn

For "Mr. Dudley," a Black Spy. James A. Emanuel. BPo; NBV

For Mrs. Cam, Whose Name Means "Printed Silk." John Balaban. CDa

For Musia's Grandchildren. Irving Layton. NOBC

For My Ancestors. Rolfe Humphries. PoRA

For my beautiful, dutiful Lily Adair. (LL)   Lily Adair.   Thomas Holley Chivers.   APN-1; OBAL

For my bed. (LL)   Calling the Doctor (1000 A.D.).   Nizami Arudi.   ArPe; WoPoe, *tr. by* Omar Pound and Omar S. Pound

For My Birthday.   Attila József.   IQMS, *tr. by* Istvan Fekete

For My Birthday.   Attila József.   IQMS, *tr. by* Anton N. Nyerges

For My Birthday.   Attila József.   IQMS, *tr. by* Earl M. Herrick

For My Birthday.   Attila József.   IQMS, *tr. by* Adam Makkai

For My Brother Hagok.   Ho Nansorhon.   WoPoe, *tr. by* Kichung Kim

For My Contemporaries.   James Vincent Cunningham.   APT-2; CoAP; VCAP

For My Daughter.   Weldon Kees.   CoAP; OxBSo

For My Daughter.   John Logan.   CRP

For My Father.   Duriel Harris.   SpirFl

For My Father.   Paul Potts.   FaBoTw

For My Father.   Philip Schultz.   TaR

For My Father's Grave.   Yvor Winters.   IllVoic

For my first poem there are specific images.   Mr. Nabokov's Memory.   Thomas McCarthy.   ModIr

For My Grandmother.   Countee Cullen.   APT-2; MoAmPo; SSLK; VGW   *Fr.* Four Epitaphs.

For My Grandmother, Bridget Halpin.   Michael Hartnett.   BIrV; ModIr; PBCIP

For My Great-Grandfather: A Message Long Overdue.   Maxine W. Kumin.   UnSA

For My Lover, Returning to His Wife.   Anne Sexton.   HCAP; UnPo; WPE

For My Mother.   Doris Brett.   NOBAu

For My Mother.   David Diop.   NegPo, *tr. by* Ellen Conroy Kennedy

For My Mother.   Louise Glück.   UnPo

For My Mother.   June Jordan.   BoWoP

For My Mother.   Iain Crichton Smith.   OxBS

For My Mother: Ellen Bryant Voigt.   NIP-4

For My Mother: Genevieve Jules Creeley.   Robert Creeley.   PoM; TRP

For My Own Monument.   Matthew Prior.   OBEV

(For His Own Epitaph.)   FaBoEE

For my part, I'le not meddle with the cause.   Homer.   CTC   *Fr.* Odyssey.

For my part, I never care.   Lips Tongueless[e].   Robert Herrick.   CaPo

For My People.   Wendy Rose.   CDW

For my poor passage to the stall of Night? (LL)   On an Anniversary.   John Millington Synge.   FaBoEE; NOIV; OBMV

For my sister's sake.   *Var. authors.*   AWP   *Fr.* Manyo Shu, Part 1 of 4.

For My Sister Shura.   Sergey [*or* Sergei] Aleksandrovich Yesenin [*or* Essenin].   TCRusP, *tr. by* Nigel Stott

For My Son.   Muriel Rukeyser.   TaR

For My Son Noah, Ten Years Old.   Robert Bly.   LoL; RaBo

For my sorrowful life. (LL)   Thanking Doctor Jen.   Li K'ai-hsien.   CoBLCP; ColAnChi, *tr. by* Jonathan Chaves

For my torturer, Lieutenant D.   Leila Djabali.   HAWP; WPOW, *tr. by* Anita Barrows

For Myo's Departure for Anzen-ji.   Muso Soseki.   EaWin, *tr. by* W. S. Merwin

For Myo's Departure for Shofuku-ji.   Muso Soseki.   EaWin, *tr. by* W. S. Merwin

For Napoleon. (LL)   Napoleon.   Miroslav Holub.   ChAP; PoSu, *tr. by* Kaca Plakova

For nations vague as weed.   Nothing to Be Said.   Philip Larkin.   OxBTC

For nearly a month.   Drought.   Sitanshu Yashashchandra.   OMIP, *tr. by* Saleem Peeradina

For nearly a week that open-aired autumn.   Ground Elder.   Leonard Clark.   OBGa

For never a begger need now despair, And every rogue has a chance. (LL)   Speculators, The.   William Makepeace Thackeray.   OBCoV; OBSV

For New Year, Postumus, ten years ago.   Roman Thank-You Letter, A.   Martial.   OBCP, *tr. by* James Michie

For nine months I had borne him in my womb.   Labour.   Kristina Rungano.   HAWP

For No Clear Reason.   Robert Creeley.   VGW

For No Good Reason.   Peter Redgrove.   PoE

For no love borne by me.   *Unknown.*   EaItPo, *tr. by* Dante Gabriel Rossetti

For no reason.   Short Circuit.   Daniel Hall.   OWoS

For no reason that I can tell. (LL)   Little Elegy.   Denis Devlin.   ModIr; NOIV

For noble minds, the worst of miseries.   Poverty.   Theognis.   AWP, *tr. by* John Hookham Frere

For none can call again the passed time. (LL)   Edmund Spenser.   AWP; HAP; OBEV; PoE; Son   *Fr.* Amoretti.

For None see God and live. (LL)   Emily Dickinson.   APN-2; NCAP

For Norman Nicholson.   David Scott.   NLP

For not honoring my parents.   Isan.   JDP, *tr. by* Yoel Hoffmann

For Nothing.   Gary Snyder.   NNaP

For nothing now can ever come to any good. (LL)   W. H. Auden.   CAGL; MoBrPo; OPOU; RB   *Fr.* Twelve Songs.

For now, and since first break of dawne the Fiend.   John Milton.   NPeEn   *Fr.* Paradise Lost.

For oak and elm have pleasant leaves.   Oscar Wilde.   MakPoe; NoAM   *Fr.* Ballad of Reading Gaol, The.

For once.   Portrait of Jonah with woman.   Marie-Claire Bancquart.   MFP, *tr. by* Martin Sorrell

For once, I hardly noticed what I ate.   Runaways CaféII.   Marilyn Hacker.   NoAM

For once it doesn't matter that you've gone.   Troubadour.   Peter Sirr.   BiHa

For Once, Then, Something.   Robert Frost.   APT-1; NOBA; NoAM

For one brief day, did Queenie stay.   Queenie.   Mary Weston Fordham.   CBWP-2

For One Lately Bereft.   Margaret E. Bruner.   PoToHe

For one long term, or e'er her trial came.   Inscription.   George Canning.   FaBoEE

For One Moment.   David Ignatow.   NNaP

For One Must Want / To Shut the Other's Gaze.   Jorie Graham.   BodElec

For one short week I leave, with anxious heart.   Eyam.   Anna Seward.   ECWP; RWP

For One Who Died Young.   Hoffman Reynolds Hays.   SPE

For One Who Gayly Sowed His Oats.   Countee Cullen.   APT-2

For One Who Is Serene.   Margaret E. Bruner.   PoToHe

For one who says he feels.   Petra von Morstein.   BoWoP

For other beds the priests there used none.   Edmund Spenser.   PoE   *Fr.* Faerie Queene, The.

For other fruits my father was indifferent.   My Father and the Fig Tree.   Naomi Shihab Nye.   GraLe

For our Dragon hath vanquish'd [*or* vanquished] the St. *George*. (LL)   Mock Song, A.   Richard Lovelace.   BeJo; CaPo

For "Our Lady of the Rocks."   Dante Gabriel Rossetti.   EBEV

(For Our Lady of the Rocks By Leonardo da Vinci.)   GS

For our own lady's dying, brother dear. (LL)   Sonnet: On the 9th of June 1290.   Dante Alighieri.   AWP; EaItPo, *tr. by* Dante Gabriel Rossetti

For over a week now, again and again.   Mother.   Attila József.   IQMS, *tr. by* Vernon Watkins

For over sixty years.   Kokei Sochin.   JDP, *tr. by* Yoel Hoffmann

For P—Celtic: found text from Machen.   Bill Griffiths.   Oth

For Paddy Mac.   Padraic Fallon.   CIP-2

For Paul.   Eve Triem.   APT-2

For Paul Celan and Primo Levi.   Harvey Shapiro.   TaR

For Paul Laurence Dunbar.   Countee Cullen.   SSLK   *Fr.* Four Epitaphs.

For Paula Cooper.   Jackie Warren-Moore.   SpirFl

For Period exhaled. (LL)   Emily Dickinson.   APN-2; NOCV

For physic and farces his equal there scarce is.   On Sir John Hill, M. D., Playwright.   David Garrick.   FaBoEE; NBLV

For plucking out the feathers of rigid archangels.   Final Sonnet.   Miguel Hernández.   BLPSL, *tr. by* Rene de Costa, Rigas Kappatos and Eleni Paidoussi

For poor Cock Robin. (LL)   Who Killed Cock Robin.   Mother Goose.   OxNR; ReMoGo; UV

For P[ope] has wrote upon their tomb. (LL)   Epitaph: "Here lies John Hughes and Sarah Drew."   Lady Mary Wortley Montagu.   CABP; FaBoEE

For prodigal read generous.   E. E. Cummings.   FaBoEE

For purposes of illusion.   Theorem.   Walter Conrad Arensberg.   APT-1

For Raftery.   Alan Alexander.   NOBAu

For rage and dignity no words compare.   Classical Quatrain, A.   Paul Goodman.   VGW

For rank, descent and title famed.   Martial.   RomPo, *tr. by* J. P. Sullivan

For reading I can recommend.   Domaine Public.   Geoffrey Hill.   OxBC

For reasons any.   Irapuato.   Earle Birney.   NIL-7

For repose I have sighed and have struggled; have sigh'd and have struggled in vain.   Felo de Se.   Amy Levy.   VWP

For Rhoda.   Delmore Schwartz.   MoAmPo; OxBA   *Fr.* Repetitive Heart, The.

For rice-planting women.   Konishi Raizan.   SoOfWa, *tr. by* Sam Hamill

For Richer, For Poorer.   Emily Hickey.   PoBW

For rigorous teachers seized my youth.   Matthew Arnold.   FHYEP   *Fr.* Stanzas from the Grande Chartreuse.

For Robert Desnos.   Tristan Tzara.   AF

For Robert Frost.   Galway Kinnell.   NOBA; VGW

For round about, the wals yclothed were.   Edmund Spenser.   PBRV   *Fr.* Faerie Queene Book 3, The.

For Sale.   Robert Lowell.   CoAmPo

For Sale or Rent.   *Unknown.*   PoToHe

For sale what the Jews have not sold, what neither nobility nor.   Sales.   Arthur Rimbaud.   SxFrPo, *tr. by* Martin Sorrell

For Santacruze the glad fleet takes her way.   Andrew Marvell.   FaBoWar   *Fr.* Victory Obtained by Blake over the Spaniards, in the Bay of Santa Cruz in the Island of Teneriffe, 1657.

For Sappho/After Sappho. Carolyn Kizer. GifTon
For Saturday. Christopher Smart. NOEC *Fr.* Hymns for the Amusement of Children.
For Saundra. Nikki Giovanni. BPo; NAAAL; TTY
For, see! where Winter comes, himself, confest. James Thomson. NePenScot *Fr.* Seasons, The.
For seeing / brightness within, A. New Light, A. William Hawkins. MoCV
For sentimental reasons. Last Apple, The. Carol Coiffait. Prnts
For Services Rendered. F. G. Butterfield. FaBoWar
For seven long years I had declared my passion. Cywdd to Morvydd, The. Dafydd [*or* David] ap Gwilym. NOEC
For seven years at school I named. Song of the Dead Soldier, The. Christopher Logue. FaBoWar
For seven years now Uludağ and I have been staring each other in the eye. About Mount Uludağ. Nazim Hikmet. WoPoe, *tr. by* Randy Blasing and Mutlu Konuk
For seventy-two years / I've kept the ox well under. Bokuo. ZenPo, *tr. by* Takashi Ikemoto and Lucien Stryk
For Several Days I Have Not Visited the Garden Pavilion—A Poem Sent to My Pet Crane. Wang Chiu-ssu. CoBLCP, *tr. by* Jonathan Chaves
For several miles I have heard the chill waters. Passing by a Mountain Village: Evening. Chia Tao. SuSp, *tr. by* Stephen Owen
For several months. P.C. Plod versus the Dale St. Dog Strangler. Roger McGough. OBSP
For several weeks I have been reading. Expression. Thom Gunn. OxBC
For Several Years I Have Wanted To Grow a Garden, But Have Never Finished One. This Year It Is Already Halfway Through Summer, and This Has Made Me Despondent. Chu Yün-ming. CoBLCP, *tr. by* Jonathan Chaves
For shame, thou everlasting wooer. Antiplatonic[k], The. John Cleveland. NOSC
For she came of the better kin. (LL) Little Musgrave and Lady Barnard. *Unknown.* ESPB; OxBB
For Sheridan. Robert Lowell. HCAP; PoetW
For Sho the New Head Priest of Erin-ji. Muso Soseki. EaWin, *tr. by* W. S. Merwin
For Sidney Bechet. Philip Larkin. NoP-4
For Signs. Thom Gunn. PoE
For Simon Rodia: The sudden appearance, at once, of. Time Traveler's Potlatch. Philip Lamantia. CLPP
For Singing In Good Mood. Lebert Bethune. GT
For Sister Sue Ellen and Her Special Messenger. Toi Derricotte. ExTi
For Sistuhs Wearin' Straight Hair. Carolyn M. Rodgers. NAAAL
For six hundred years I have travelled. Clever Daughter, The. Susan Wicks. MFPA
For six months now I've washed her clothes. Service Wash. Deryn Rees-Jones. MFPA
For six years sitting alone. Buddha's Satori. Muso Soseki. EaWin, *tr. by* W. S. Merwin
For Sleep. Larry Eigner. FTOS
For Soldiers. Humphrey [*or* Humfrey] Gifford. FaBoWar; NoSic
For Some Future Day. Hans Andreus. TuT, *tr. by* Peter Van de Kamp
For some semitropical reason. Tarantulas on the Lifebuoy. Thomas Lux. LCAP-2
For some the shuttle leaping in the sun. Rosa Luxembourg. Eileen Duggan. PeNZ
For some twisted reason I. Juniper. Abbie Huston Evans. APT-1
For some we loved, the loveliest and the best. Omar Khayyám. TRP, *tr. by* Edward Fitzgerald *Fr.* Rubáiyát of Omar Khayyám [of Naishápúr], The.
For some years he still would harden as he. Fall, The. Sarah Maguire. LW
For Song. Gerald Stern. BBASP
For South Bronx. Sandra Maria Esteves. PueRic
For spoiling her nice new clothes. (LL) Mother Goose. LB; OxNR; ReMoGo
For sport my *Julia* threw a Lace. Silken Snake, The. Robert Herrick. OxBSP; PBRV
For Spring. Douglas G. Jones. NOBC
For Spring By Sandro Botticelli. Dante Gabriel Rossetti. GS
For Starters. Victoria McCabe. CRP
For Steph. Wendy Rose. CDW
For Stuart Porter, Who Asked for a Poem That Would Not Depress Him Further. Jeffrey Skinner. PBCAP
For sunlight on the garden. (LL) Sunlight on the Garden, The. Louis MacNeice. EBEV; GTBS-P; HAP; HarvBoo; NAEL-5v2; NAEL-6v2; NOBE; NOIV; NPeEn; NoP-4; OxAEP-2; OxBTC; PNI; TRP; TwCP; WoPoe
For sure, *circa Regna tonat.* (LL) *V. Innocentia Veritas Viat Fides Circumdederunt me inimici mei.* Sir Thomas Wyatt. NAEL-7v1; NoSic
For surfeits sooner kill than fasts. (LL) Against Absence. Sir John Suckling. CaPo; CavPo
For Survival. Andrée Chedid. HAWP, *tr. by* Marie Ponsot

For sweet things dying. (LL) Dirge, A: "Why were you born when the snow was falling?" Christina Georgina Rossetti. EBVV; NOBVV; OxBEV; SCGP
For T.S.E. Only. Hyam Plutzik. APT-2; TaR
For Taihei Osho. Muso Soseki. EaWin, *tr. by* W. S. Merwin
For Talking. Denise Nico Leto. UnSA
For ten miles the mountains rise. Farm by the Lake, The. Chu Hsi. OHPC, *tr. by* Kenneth Rexroth
For ten miles, till day at last breaks. (LL) Starting Early from the Ch'u-ch'êng Inn. Po Chü-i. ChiP; OBVE, *tr. by* Arthur Waley
For ten years I never left my books. After Passing the Examination. Po Chü-i. ChiP, *tr. by* Arthur Waley
For Tetsu the New Head Priest of Erin-ji. Muso Soseki. EaWin, *tr. by* W. S. Merwin
For that goatfucker, goatfooted. Leonidas. GrAn; PGA
For That He Looked Not upon Her. George Gascoigne. NoP-4 ("You must not wonder, though you think it strange") GSo
For that I never knew you, I only learned to dread you. St. Roach. Muriel Rukeyser. GLP
For that is his knock at the door! (LL) Love Versus Learning. Constance Naden. VWP; ViWPN
For that noble princess pressed him so hard. *Unknown.* EroLit *Fr.* Sir Gawain and the Green Knight.
For that rare, random descent. (LL) Black Rook in Rainy Weather. Sylvia Plath. NAAL-2v2; NIL-7; NoP-4
For that reason / I am a true Russian! (LL) Babii Yar. Yevgeny Aleksandrovich Yevtushenko [*or* Evtushenko]. HP; VCWP, *tr. by* George Reavey
For that's the best cure for a little pussy cat. (LL) *Unknown.* FaBoCh; OxNR
For that the sonnet no doubt was my own true. Late Sonnet. Hayden Carruth. Son
For that they housed Him from the cold! (LL) Christmas Folk-Song, A. Lizette Woodworth Reese. OBCA; TrCP
For the Anniversary Day of One's Conversion. Charles Wesley. SacPr
For the Anniversary of My Death. W. S. Merwin. CoAP; ColAP; HCAP; InPK-6; NAAL-2v2; NOBA; PAI; PoPoPo; VCAP
For the Athenian Dead at Plataia. Simonides. GrAn, *tr. by* Peter Jay
For the Baptiste. William Drummond, of Hawthornden. NPeEn; OxBEV; PBRV
For the Barn at Bread Loaf. William Stafford. BodElec
For the Barren Woman. Desanka Maksimovic. GI, *tr. by* Ivo Soljan
For the beauty of the earth. F. S. Pierpoint. SacPr
For the bees keep buzzing around the meat. City's Coat of Arms, The. László Nagy. IQMS, *tr. by* Adam Makkai
For the black plunge-line nightdress. (LL) Skunk, The. Seamus Heaney. NAEL-5v2; NAEL-6v2; NoP-4; OxBC; PoE
For the blue flash and the moments. Ezra Pound. APT-1 *Fr.* Cantos.
For the Bones of Josef Mengele, Disinterred June 1985. Robert Bringhurst. NIP-4
For the Book of Love. Jules Laforgue. AWP, *tr. by* Jethro Bithell
For the Briar Rose. William Morris. NOBVV
For the Brothers Who Aint Here. Ras Baraka. InTrad
For the bumps bangs and scratches of. Auto Mobile. A. R. Ammons. OBAL
For the Candle Light. Angelina Weld Grimké. BlSi; NAAAL
For the Cenotaph of a Lost Soldier. Theon. GrAn, *tr. by* Dudley Fitts
For the child of her love is no longer a slave. (LL) She's Free! Frances Ellen Watkins Harper. BlSi; Son
For the Children. Thomas Love Peacock. VoR
For the Children. Gary Snyder. PAI
For the Children or the Grown-ups? *Unknown.* OBCP
For the clouds above the garden in Papenburg. Homesick. Helmut Heissenbüttel. CLPP, *tr. by* Jerome Rothenberg
For the Color of My Mother. Cherríe Moraga. UnSA
For the Common Market. Michael Burn. OBCoV
For the Company Underground. Francis MacNamara. NOBAu
For the context of the basidiocarp Singer states. James Fenton. PeLV *Fr.* Exempla.
For the country will bring us no peace. (LL) Raleigh Was Right. William Carlos Williams. NIL-7; NIP-4; NoAM; RB; WoPoe
For the Courtesan Ch'ing Lin. Wu Tsao. BoWoP; WPOW; WoPoe, *tr. by* Chung Ling and Kenneth Rexroth
For the cracked dish. Still Life with Endings. Ray Gonzalez. TouFir
For the cricket (nightingale of the field) and oak. Anyte [*or* Anytes]. SaLy, *tr. by* Diane Rayor
For the cry from the well of "mama!" Irina Ratushinskaya [*or* Ratushinskaia]. ItGoST, *tr. by* David McDuff
For the D. Anthony McNeill. WaCA
For the Dancer of the King of Wu. Li Po. TAL
For the Dead. Kevin Prufer. AmPoNex

For the Dead. Adrienne Rich. NAAL-2v2

For the Dead Lecturer. Diane Di Prima. BB

For the Death of a Monk. Muso Soseki. EaWin, tr. by W. S. Merwin

For the Death of Vince Lombardi. James Dickey. MoASP

For the dim regions whence my fathers came. Outcast. Claude McKay. APT-1

For the doubling of flowers is the improvement of the gard'ner's talent. Christopher Smart. ChIV-2; NOEC; NPeEn Fr. Jubilate Agno.

For the Drunk. Carole Oles. OPRER

For the end of the story sucks. Not air. Ground Beneath Us, The. Patricia Goedicke. ExTi

For the Examination at Ho-nan-fu: Songs of the Twelve Months. Li Ho. "Stars rest cold by shoals of cloud." CoBCP

For the expectant is the glory. Zealots of Yearning. David Rokeah [or Rokeakh]. MHP, tr. by Ruth Finer Mintz

For the eyes of the children. Sorrow Song. Lucille Clifton. BodElec

For the fairest maid in Hampton. Changeling, The. John Greenleaf Whittier. MakPoe

For the Fallen. Laurence Binyon. NOBE; NPeEn; OBEV; OBWP; OxBTC "They went with songs to the battle, they were young." FaBoWar

For the Family of Cuchonnacht O Dalaigh. David [or Daibhi][or Daithi] O'Bruadair [or Ó Bruadair]. NOIV, tr. by Thomas Kinsella

For the Far-Out Experimental Writer. Víctor Hernández Cruz. PueRic

For the Father of Sandro Gulotta. Janet Lewis. APT-2

For the Field. Robyn Selman. TaR

For the First Manned Moon Orbit. James Dickey. "So long." AiP

For the first time, I listen to a lost. Then. Roddy Lumsden. NeBl

For the first time in what must be. Evening's End. Leon Stokesbury. BAP-97

For the first time, now for the first time seen. (LL) Green. D. H. Lawrence. HarvBoo; MoBrPo

For the first time, on the road north of Tampico. Making a Fist. Naomi Shihab Nye. GraLe

For the first time since anyone remembers. Rhapsody on Main Street. Patrick Williams. PNI

For the first time the only. Rescue. James Tate. YaYoPo

For the first twenty years [or yeares], since yesterday. Computation, The. John Donne. NoSic; OxBSP; SoSe-8

For the floating world? (LL) Akazome Emon. BoWoP; WPOW

For the Fly-Leaf of a School-Book. Norman Cameron. OxBS

For the forced-fire / of roses. (LL) Porcupine, The. Galway Kinnell. NAAL-5; NOBA

For the fount of life undying. Paradise. Peter Damian. MLL, tr. by Helen Waddell

For the Fourth of July. Eliza Lee Cabot Follen. SWaP

For the Girls 'cause They Know. Harold Littlebird. VoR

For the God of Peyote. Unknown. STP, tr. by Jerome Rothenberg

For the Good of the Pythian Order. Mrs. Henry Linden. CBWP-4

For the Grave of a Peace-Loving Man. Hans Magnus Enzensberger. VCWP, tr. by Hans Magnus Enzensberger and Michael Hamburger

For the Grave of Daniel Boone. William Stafford. PAI

For the great-eyed sunflower you gave us. Song of the Tower of Skulls. Vasco [or Vasko] Popa. WoPoe, tr. by Anne Pennington

For the great flint to come singing into his heart. (LL) Bushed. Earle Birney. MoCV; NOBC; NoAM; NoP-4

For the green turtle with her pulsing burden. Lament. Gillian Clarke. HarvBoo; TCAWP

For the Holy Family by Michelangelo. Dante Gabriel Rossetti. SacPr

For the huge. Whirl Wind Must, The. George Oppen. BodElec

For the Intellectuals. Jeremy Ingalls. YaYoPo

For the Kindling of the Light on Easter Eve. Prudentius. MLL, tr. by Helen Waddell

For the Lady Olivia Porter; a Present upon a New Year's Day. Sir William Davenant [or D'Avenant]. MeLP; NOSC

For the Last Summer. Robert Wrigley. SwNoth

For the last time Beowulf uttered his boast. Unknown. AnOE, tr. by Charles W. Kennedy Fr. Beowulf.

For the last time I wash the shirt. I Wash the Shirt. Anna Swirszczynska. BLT

For the Last Time on My Native Estate. Ilya Iankelevich Gabai. TCRP, tr. by Albert C. Todd

For the life. My Least Skirtable Deficiency. HeidiLynn Nilsson. NeAmPo

For the Lord of Caves. Allama Prabhu. PFTM-1

For the Lordes parte is his folke. Bible, O.T. OBVE Fr. Deuteronomy.

For the Lost Generation. Galway Kinnell. PAI

For the love of Mike! Café du Dôme. Else Von Freytag-Loringhoven. APT-1; SurPaPo

For the Lover. Maria Luisa B. Aguilar-Cariño. ReBoTo

For the Magdalene. William Drummond, of Hawthornden. ChIV-2

For the man was she made by the Eden tree. Ballade of Lovers. May Probyn. VWP

For the man who. Robert Sheppard. Oth Fr. Empty Diaries/Twentieth Century Blues 24.

For the Market. Jane Mayhall. TAP

For the Marriage of Faustus and Helen. Hart Crane. APT-2; NOBA; NoAM ("Brazen hypnotics glitter here.") SeSe "Capped arbiter of beauty in this street." FaBoMo

For the mighty wind arises, roaring seaward, and I go. (LL) Tennyson. EBEV; NAEL-5v2; NAEL-6v2

For the Missing in Action. John Balaban. AF

For the Moment. Belkis Cuza Malé. TANSG, tr. by Pamela Carmell

For the Moment. Pierre Reverdy. TTTS, tr. by Ron Padgett

For the moment, we've run out of starry nights. For the Moment. Belkis Cuza Malé. TANSG, tr. by Pamela Carmell

For the Monk San-tsang on His Return to the Western Regions. Li Tung. CoBCP, tr. by Burton Watson

For the Nativity. John Heath-Stubbs. ChrPo

For the New Union Dead in Alabama. Edward Dorn. PoM

For the New York City Poet Who Informed Me that Few People Live This Way. Jeff Gundy. IllVoic

For the next legation I bite. Melanin. J. H. Prynne. PFTM-2

For the nightemare. Unknown. MiEL

For the Nightly Ascent of the Hunter Orion over a Forest Clearing. James Dickey. TwCP

For the one. 'No' Madonnas, The. Gwyneth Lewis. TCAWP

For the One Who Would Take Man's Life in His Hands. Delmore Schwartz. MoAmPo; VGW

For the Opening of the William Dinsmore Briggs Room. Yvor Winters. CRP

For the Palace that lies desolate. We Sit Solitary. Unknown. TrJP

For the poet's biography. Poet's Biography. Belkis Cuza Malé. TANSG, tr. by Pamela Carmell

For the Poet Who Said Poets Are Struck by Lightning Only Two or Three Times. Peter Klappert. NBLV

For the Poets. Jayne Cortez. PmAP

For the Poorman's nosegay is an introduction to a Prince. (LL) Christopher Smart. ChIV-2; NOEC; NPeEn Fr. Jubilate Agno.

For the raindrop, joy is in entering the river. Mirza Asadullah Khan Ghalib. EnlH

For the Reader (Blank Book). Laura Mullen. ExTi

For the Record. Roy Blount, Jr. OBAL

For the Record. George Jonas. MoCV

For the Record. Audre Lorde. ESEAA

For the Record. Roy McFadden. PNI

For the Record. Adrienne Rich. NIL-7; NIP-4; VCAP

For the resounding wave of milennia to come. Osip Emilevich Mandelstam [or Mandelshtam]. TCRP

For the sake of a night. Stewardess of the Empress Kōka. OHPJ

For the self you did not value? (LL) To a Comrade in Arms. Alun Lewis. FaBoTw; MoBrPo

For the seven lakes, and by no man these verses. Canto 49. Ezra Pound. PFTM-1

For the seven lakes, and by no man these verses. Ezra Pound. APT-1 Fr. Cantos.

For the Sin. Unknown. TrJP

For the Sisters of the Hôtel Dieu. Abraham Moses Klein. NoP-4

For the site of the Kingdom of Heaven. (LL) Emily Dickinson. ChIV-2; NALW; NCAP

For the Sleepwalkers. Edward Hirsch. IllVoic

For the smell. Leroy Gorman. HA

For the sound we revere. For Art Blakey and the Jazz Messengers. Keorapetse Kgositsile. SeSe

For the Spartan Dead at Plataia. Simonides. GrAn, tr. by Peter Jay

For the Spartan Dead at Thermopylai (480 B.C.). Simonides. See On the Spartan Dead at Thermopylae

For the spiritual musick is as follows. Christopher Smart. NOEC Fr. Jubilate Agno.

For the Stepford Girl Groups. Gwynne Garfinkle. MiVo

For the Student Strikers. Richard Wilbur. OxBC

For the Sun Declined. Yitzhak Lamdan. "Where am I, O awesome friend?" TrJP

"For the tenth time, dull Daphnis," said Chloe. Limerick. Unknown. PeLi

For the Theft of Cattle. Unknown. ASW, tr. by Kevin Crossley-Holland

For the Thing we call Moon contains. Chords Passages 14. Robert Duncan. FTOS

For the three dead children. (LL) Lament for Tadhg Cronin's Children.

Aodhagán O Rathaille.   ModIr; PBCIP; RB; WoPoe, *tr. by* Michael Hartnett

For the Time Being; a Christmas Oratorio.   W. H. Auden.
  Flight into Egypt, The.
    After Christmas.   ChrPo; MoBrPo; OBCP
    "Well, so that is that. Now we must dismantle the tree."   ChrPo; MoBrPo; OBCP

For the Tree to Sing . . . .   Vladimir Alekseievich Soloukhin.   TCRusP, *tr. by* Daniel Weissbort

For the Twentieth Century.   Frank Bidart.   KGB

For the unbidden swish of morning curtains.   Thankyou Note.   Dannie Abse.   TCAWP

For the Union Dead.   Robert Lowell.   CBCWP; CoAP; ColAP; HAP; HCAP; HarvBoo; HeIP-4; LCAP-2; NAAL-2v2; NAAL-5; NOBA; NoAM; NoP-4; OBWP; PoE; PoetW; SCV; TFi; TRP; TwCP; UnPo; VCAP; WeW-3

For the Unveiling of a Memorial.   Daniil Leonidovich Andreyev [*or* Andreiev].   TCRP, *tr. by* Bradley Jordan

For the voyage of oblivion awaits you. (LL)   Ship of Death, The.   D. H. Lawrence.   FaBoTw; GTBS-P; MoBrPo; NAEL-5v2; NAEL-6v2; NoAM; NoP-4; OxAEP-2; OxBEV

For the Wandering Jews.   Philip Schultz.   TaR

For the White Lady Holding Me.   Crystal Williams.   AmPoNex

For the white-limbed heroes of Hellas ride by upon their horses.   Ford Madox Ford.   FaBoWar   *Fr.* Antwerp.

For "The Wine of Circe" by Edward Burne-Jones.   Dante Gabriel Rossetti.   UV

For the woman / African in ancestry.   Freedom Song for the Black Woman, A.   Carole C. Gregory Clemmons.   BlSi

For the Woman Who Dressed Up to Listen to Gigli on the Radio.   Jane Duran.   MFPA

For the Woman with the Radio.   Malena Mörling.   AmPoNex

For the Word Is Flesh.   Stanley Kunitz.   VGW

For the word of God is a sword on my side—no matter what other weapon a stick or a straw.   Christopher Smart.   BBASP   *Fr.* Jubilate Agno.

For the word which burns like Joan at the stake.   Humble Litany.   Aida Cartagena de Portalatin.   TANSG, *tr. by* Emma Jane Robinett

For thee and for myself no quiet find. (LL)   William Shakespeare.   AWTN; CAGL; HeIP-4; NoSic; SCGP   *Fr.* Sonnets.

For thee to wear, but this of thine own Blood. (LL)   Upon the Body of Our Blessed Lord, Naked and Bloody.   Richard Crashaw.   NOSC; PAI

For thee was a house built.   Henry Wadsworth Longfellow.   TCAPo   *Fr.* From the Anglo-Saxon.

For them to move. I want to see them again. (LL)   Joy Addict, The.   James Harms.   NAPBL; NeAmPo

For there is an African virtue of the tree.   Edouard J. Maunick.   NegPo   *Fr.* As Far as Yoruba Land.

For there is no God found stronger than death; and death is a sleep. (LL)   Hymn to Proserpine.   Algernon Charles Swinburne.   EBVV; NAEL-5v2; NAEL-6v2

For these dead Birds sigh a prayer. (LL)   Phoenix and the Turtle, The.   William Shakespeare.   NOBE; NoSic; OBEV; OxAEP-1; OxBEV; PeECV; SCGP

For these I feel,—and feel that they are Love. (LL)   Describes the Characteristics of Love.   Mary Robinson.   CenSon; RWP

For they appeal from tyranny to God. (LL)   Byron.   CenSon; GSo   *Fr.* Prisoner of Chillon, The.

For they know when their Shepherd is nigh. (LL)   William Blake.   ChAP; FHYEP   *Fr.* Songs of Innocence.

For They Shall See God.   Luci Shaw.   TrCP

For Thieves Only.   Lois Red Elk.   ReEnLa

For thine is the kingdom.   Lord's Prayer.   D. H. Lawrence.   PeECV

For thine own Duplicity. (LL)   Emily Dickinson.   APN-2; InvLi

For things we never mention.   Broken Men, The.   Rudyard Kipling.   HarvBoo

For thinking that thou art not ill. (LL)   England.   *Unknown.*   FaBoEE; OxBSP

For thirteen days / she had threatened / and forced me dark.   Friendly Town #3.   Safiya Henderson-Holmes.   UnSA

For thirty-five years, Father, you were a numb-fish.   Embrace of the Electric Eel.   Pascale Petit.   Prnts

For this agility chance found.   Ezra Pound.   TCAPo   *Fr.* Hugh Selwyn Mauberley (Life and Contacts).

For this and for all enclosures like it the archetype.   Cave of Making, The.   W. H. Auden.   FaBoVe; OxAEP-2

For this, as well, I love black cypress; and I love.   Cypress.   Aleksandr Semionovich Kushner.   ItGoST, *tr. by* Paul Graves and Carol Ueland

For this hell.   Garden.   Marina Ivanovna Tsvetaeva [*or* Tsvetaeva].   RusPo, *tr. by* Robert Arthur Douglas Ford

For this I will be thine, my love! for this I will be thine! (LL)   Chamois Hunter's Love, The.   Felicia Dorothea Hemans.   RWP; VWP

For this is Christ. (LL)   On the Swag.   Ronald Allison Kells Mason.   PeNZ; SacPr

For this is not the road against which stand enemy lines.   Piyyut for Rosh Hashana.   Haim [*or* Chaim *or* Khayim] Guri [*or* Gouri].   MHP, *tr. by* Ruth Finer Mintz

For this is the day of joy.   Gaudeamus Igitur: A Valediction.   John A. Stone.   BloBone

For this particular silence. (LL)   Memory of Elena, The.   Carolyn Forché.   LoL; NoAM

For this poor wreath, give Thee a crown of praise. (LL)   Wreath, A.   George Herbert.   GeHe; NOSC; NPeEn; OxBSP

For this present, hard.   Ralph Waldo Emerson.   NOBA

"For this same night att [Bucklesfeildberry]"   Little Musgrave and Lady Barnard.   *Unknown.*   ESPB

For this she starred her eyes with salt.   Epitaph.   Elinor Wylie.   MoAmPo

For this the ancient stars were hurled.   Evolution.   Israel Zangwill.   TrJP

For this the monk is to blame. (LL)   Weak Monk, The.   Stevie Smith.   BoWoP; FaBoTw

For this your mother sweated in the cold.   To Jesus on His Birthday.   Edna St. Vincent Millay.   ChIV-2; HeIP-4; TrCP

For Thomas Moore.   James Simmons.   BiHa; PBCIP

For Those Dead, Our Dead.   Ernesto Cardenal.   PoetW, *tr. by* Jonathan Cohen

For Those my unbaptized Rhymes [*or* Rhimes].   His Prayer for Absolution.   Robert Herrick.   BeJo; SacPr

For those of us who live at the shoreline.   Litany for Survival, A.   Audre Lorde.   NAAAL

For those parallel destinies.   Alice Rahon.   SurWo, *tr. by* Nancy Deffebach and Vanina Deler

For those that never know the light.   Children of the Night, The.   Edwin Arlington Robinson.   APN-2; OxBA

For those vicissitudes by which men die. (LL)   La Gioconda; Leonardo Da Vinci, The Louvre.   "Michael Field."   CABP; PeVV; ViWPN

For Those Who Always Fear the Worst.   *Unknown.*   NBLV

For Those Who Fail.   Joaquin Miller.   PoToHe

For those who place their blooms on new-made graves.   Time's Hand Is Kind.   Margaret E. Bruner.   PoToHe

For those who worship Thee there is no death.   Trees of Life, The.   Jones Very.   NOBA

For Those Whom the Gods Love Less.   Denise Levertov.   BodElec

For thou art not beloved. (LL)   Revenge.   Letitia [*or* Laetitia] Elizabeth Landon.   NOBRP; NPeEn

For thou didst die for me, O Son of God!   Henry Hart Milman.   SacPr   *Fr.* Martyr of Antioch, The.

For though my rhyme be ragged.   John Skelton.   OBCoV   *Fr.* Colin Clout.

For Though the Eaves [*or* Caves] Were Rabbeted [*or* Rabbited].   Henry David Thoreau.   OxBSP

  (For Though the Eaves were Rabbeted.)   NCAP

For though ye be true of your tongue and honestly earn.   William Langland.   NOCV   *Fr.* Vision of Piers Plowman, The.

For thoughts that curve like winging birds.   I Yield Thee Praise.   Philip Jerome Cleveland.   SacPr

For three hours I have been doing accounts.   To Know Me?   Jolanda Insana.   CItWP, *tr. by* Cinzia Sartini Blum and Lara Trubowitz

For three years, diabolus in the scale.   Ezra Pound.   TCAPo   *Fr.* Hugh Selwyn Mauberley (Life and Contacts).

For three years I sadly listened.   Wen Cheng-ming.   CoBLCP   *Fr.* Improvised on Horseback to Say Good-bye to Those Who Are Seeing Me Off.

For three years, out of key with his time.   Ezra Pound.   APT-1; NOBA; NoAM; TAP

For Thurman Thomas.   Reuben Jackson.   ISC

For Thursday be the tournament prepar'd.   Folgore da San Geminiano [*or* Gimignano].   EaItPo, *tr. by* Dante Gabriel Rossetti

For thus I leave the world, the flesh, and devil. (LL)   John Donne.   BASC; EBEV; FaBoVe; MeLP; PAI; Son   *Fr.* Holy Sonnets.

For Thus saith The Lord to the men of Judah and Jerusalem.   Bible, *O.T.*   OBVE   *Fr.* Jeremiah.

For thy names sake, be my refuge.   Voyce of Anne Askewe out of the 54. Psalme of David, Called, Deus in Nomine Tuo, The.   Anne Askew.   EMWP

For thy rich blood, which is my Drink-Indeed. (LL)   Edward Taylor.   OxBA; SacPr   *Fr.* Preparatory Meditations Before My Approach to the Lord's Supper.

For Thy Sake Let the World Call Me Fool.   *Unknown.*   SacPr

For thy soul's health to shed his dearest blood. (LL)   Emilia [*or* Aemelia] Lanier [*or* Lanyer].   EMWP; NAEL-6v1; NALW; NOSC   *Fr.* Salve Deus Rex Judaeorum.

For to a torche or to a taper the Trinite is likened.   William Langland.   SacPr   *Fr.* Vision of Piers Plowman, The.

For to Admire.   Rudyard Kipling.   MoBrPo

For to please ourselves, truly, is more than we can. (LL)   On an Unsociable Family.   Elizabeth Hands.   ECWP; NPeEn; WoRP

For to sit upon a serpent's knee' (LL)   Dives and Lazarus.   *Unknown.*   ESPB; OxBB

For today we have naming of parts. (LL)   Henry Reed.   AmFaPo; FaBoWar; MoBrPo; NAEL-6v2; NOBE; NoP-4; OxBEV; OxBTC; PAI; PoPoPo; PoRA; RaBo; SoSe-8; TFi; UV; UnPo   *Fr.* Lessons of the War.

For Tom.   Richard Caddel.   Oth

For Tom Numkena, Hopi/Spokane.   Harold Littlebird.   VoR

For Tony, Embarking in Spring.   Haniel Long.   APT-1

For Travelers Going Sidereal.Limerick.   Robert Frost.   OBAL

For treuthe [*or* trewthe] telleth that love [*or* loue] is triacle to abate sinne [*or* of hevene].   William Langland.   OBEV   *Fr.* Vision of Piers Plowman, The.

For true report rung in his royall eares.   Thomas Deloney.   FaBoWar   *Fr.* Destruction of Jerusalem, The.

For truth, and like the Preacher found it not. (LL)   Sonnet: Lift Not the Painted Veil: "Lift not the painted veil which those who live."   Shelley.   CenSon; FHYEP; GSo; NOBRP; Son

For twelve days.   German Army, Russia, 1943, The.   Ai.   MakPoe

For twenty years and more surviving after.   Widows.   Edgar Lee Masters.   MoAmPo

For Two Children.   David Malouf.   BMAP

For two days I have not said a word.   Seamstress, The.   Zinaida Nikolayevna [*or* Nikolaevna] Gippius.   ARWW, *tr.* by Catriona Kelly

For two days I've been crying.   Novel, The.   Richard Jones.   GifTon

For two months the dust of the capital.   On First Returning from Taking the Examinations: Feelings at Cloud-Stop Pavilion.   Wen Cheng-ming.   CoBLCP, *tr.* by Jonathan Chaves

For two nights.   Fire Support Burk.   Steve Denning.   CDa

For Two Voices.   Luis Cernuda.   CAGL, *tr.* by Rick Lipinski

For two years I looked forward.   Breakfast.   Thom Gunn.   OxBC

For Una.   Robinson Jeffers.   APT-1

For Uncle Jim's deep-fried, all-fat, real gone / whale steaks. (LL)   Naughty Boy.   Robert Creeley.   HeIP-4; NOBA; NoAM

For *Under the Volcano.*   Malcolm Lowry.   NOBC

For us, five writers, it's partly.   Women Watching Basketball.   Marisa De Los Santos.   NAPBL

For us, his creatures and his foes, hath died. (LL)   John Donne.   BASC; NOCV; PoE; TrCP   *Fr.* Holy Sonnets.

For us like any other fugitive.   Another Time.   W. H. Auden.   OxBA

For Us No Night Can Be Happier.   Nikolaus [*or* Nicolaus] Ludwig, Graf von Zinzendorf.   AH

For us repeopled were the solitary shore. (LL)   Byron.   NAEL-5v2; NAEL-6v2   *Fr.* Childe Harold's Pilgrimage.

For vacant hours of man's destructive leisure.   To a Gentleman Who Invited Me to Go A-Fishing.   Elizabeth Moody.   ECWP

For vanished Hellas and Hebraic pain. (LL)   Venus of the Louvre.   Emma Lazarus.   APN-2; GS

For vein honour or for the worldes good.   John Gower.   SacPr   *Fr.* Address to the King, An.

For vengeance, and the ashes of language. (LL)   Lament: "For the green turtle with her pulsing burden."   Gillian Clarke.   HarvBoo; TCAWP

For Venus' ceston every line you make. (LL)   Sonnet to the Noble Lady, the Lady Mary Wroth, A.   Ben Jonson.   BeJo; NAEL-7v1; NoP-4

For vulgar praise, doth it too dearly [*or* dearely] buy. (LL)   To My Book.   Ben Jonson.   BeJo; FaBoVe; NAEL-5v1; NAEL-6v1; NAEL-7v1

For Walter Lowenfels.   Wendy Rose.   CDW

For Walter Washington.   Tom Dent.   NBV

For Want.   Talvikki Ansel.   NeAmPo

For want of a flashlight.   For Want.   Talvikki Ansel.   NeAmPo

For want of a nail.   Mother Goose.   OxNR; ReMoGo

For wars his life and half a world away.   Lullaby, A.   Randall Jarrell.   HCAP; OxBC

For water-ices, cheap but good.   Grace for Ice-Cream, A.   Allan M. Laing.   OBCoV

For W.C.W.   Robert Creeley.   FTOS; LCAP-2

For We Are Thy People.   *Unknown.*   TrJP

For we know that in Heaven above at this moment *he's* saving *God.* (LL)   Addition to Kipling's "The Dead King (Edward VII), 1910"   Max Beerbohm.   FaBoEE; OBCoV

For weariness of life, not love of thee. (LL)   To Heaven.   Ben Jonson.   BASC; BeJo; ChIV-2; HAP; InvLi; NAEL-5v1; NAEL-6v1; NAEL-7v1; NOCV; NOSC; NPeEn; SCGP; SacPr; TRP; UnPo

For weeks and weeks the autumn world stood still.   How One Winter Came in the Lake Region.   Wilfred Campbell.   NOBC

For weeks before it comes I feel excited, yet when it.   Afterthought.   Elizabeth Jennings.   NOxBChV; OBCP

For weeks now.   Haciendo Apenas la Recolección.   Tino Villanueva.   UnSA

For wele or wo I wyl not flee.   *Unknown.*   OHMEL

For wha ere had a lealer luve.   Brown Adam.   *Unknown.*   ESPB

For what are husbands for, but to praise their wives? (LL)   Divorce Referendum, Ireland, 1986, The.   Paul Durcan.   BiHa; PBCIP

For what as easy.   W. H. Auden.   PeLV   *Fr.* Five Songs.

For what contend the wise?—for nothing less.   William Wordsworth.   SacPr   *Fr.* Ecclesiastical Sonnets.

For what emperor.   Bowl.   Wallace Stevens.   PAI

For What For Whom Unwanted.   Brian Coffey.
   "And where no snow had."   ModIr
   "Consider his song."   ModIr

For what the world admires I'll wish no more.   Resolve, The.   Mary Lee, Lady Chudleigh.   ECWP; WPE

For what to-morrow shall disclose.   Quid Sit Futurum Cras Fuge Quaerere.   Matthew Prior.   FaBoEE

For what we owe to other days.   Exit.   Edwin Arlington Robinson.   MoAmPo; OxBSP

For what we still had to lose. (LL)   Take Good Care of Yourself.   Mark Wunderlich.   NeAmPo; ReTh; WiU

For whatever animals dwell on earth.   For Whatever Animals Dwell On Earth.   Petrarch.   AWTN, *tr.* by Robert M. Durling

For whatever did it—the cider.   Cure at Porlock, A.   Amy Clampitt.   NoAM

For when they meet, the tensile air.   Paradigm, The.   Allen Tate.   NOBA

For which all long has never yet been built. (LL)   Peace in the Welsh Hills.   Vernon Watkins.   GTBS-P; OxBTC

For Whigs admit no force but argument. (LL)   Epigram: "King to Oxford sent a troop of horse, The."   Sir William Browne (1692–1774).   FaBoEE; OxBEV

For whisper and orchestra.   "Eduard Veniaminovich Limonov."   TCRusP, *tr.* by William Tjalsma   *Fr.* Secret Notebook.

For Whitsuntide.   Hildebert.   MLL, *tr.* by Helen Waddell

For Who?   Mary Weston Fordham.   CBWP-2

For whom no envy can make dim the truth. (LL)   Giovanni Boccaccio.   AWP; EaItPo, *tr.* by Dante Gabriel Rossetti   *Fr.* Sonnets.

For whom now will you comb your hair in lover's fashion?   Paulus [*or* Paulos] Silentiarius.   GrAn

For Whom the Bells Toll and Toll and Toll.   John Nelson.   GeoH

For whom the possessed sea littered, on both shores.   Requiem for the Plantagenet Kings.   Geoffrey Hill.   CABP; NAEL-5v2; NAEL-6v2; NoAM

For whom there is no ornament. (LL)   Nativity Poem.   Louise Glück.   GI; HarvBoo

For whore and rogue; and dog and bitch. (LL)   Epigram on Scolding, An.   Jonathan Swift.   FaBoEE; FaBoVe; NPeEn

For why? The gains doth seldom quit the change.   George Gascoigne.   Son   *Fr.* Gascoigne's Memories.

For Widower—wanted, house-keeper.   Limerick.   *Unknown.*   PeLi

For Willyce.   Patricia Parker.   PoBW

For Wine Drinkers.   Bálint Balassi.   IQMS, *tr.* by René Bonnerjea

For with his nail[e]s he'll dig them up again [*or* agen]. (LL)   John Webster.   EBEV; FaBoCh; HAP; NOSC; NPeEn; OxAEP-1; OxBEV; PoRA; RB; SCGP; TFi   *Fr.* White Devil, The.

For women grieve to think they must be old. (LL)   Samuel Daniel.   NOBE; NoSic; OBEV   *Fr.* To Delia.

For Women shall you Taylors have.   Isabella Whitney.   BWW   *Fr.* Manner of Her Will and What She Left to London and to All Those in It, at Her Departing, The.

For words want art and art wants words to praise her.   George Chapman.   OxBSo   *Fr.* Coronet for His Mistress Philosophy, A.

For X.   Louis MacNeice.   BoLoP; EnLoPo   *Fr.* Trilogy for X.

For years after we left Puerto Rico for the last time, I would wake.   Immigrants.   Aurora Levins Morales.   PueRic

For years he had heard his father talk about work, about carbon.   Black Light.   Peter Markus.   AmPoNex

For years he's gone over her parting words.   No, Go On.   Maura Dooley.   LW

For years I dug in the earth.   Muso Soseki.   EaWin, *tr.* by W. S. Merwin

For years I fantasized pain.   Beauty and the Beast.   Olga Broumas.   YaYoPo

For years I had not seen such a town.   Reunion.   Judith Herzberg.   BoWoP, *tr.* by Shirley Kaufman

For years I thought I knew, at the bottom of the dream.   Meeting, The.   Louise Bogan.   NoAM

For years I've heard.   Poem.   Robin Blaser.   NeAP

For years I've suffered from extreme poverty.   Writing Poetry in the Back Garden.   Chao Yi.   SuSp, *tr.* by Chang Yin-nan

For years I wanted to trade.   Falling for Jesus.   Enid Shomer.   OPRER

For years I was doomed to worship a contemptible woman.   Viper, The.   Nicanor Parra.   TCLAP, *tr.* by W. S. Merwin

For years my heart asked me for Jamshid's cup.   Ghazal 24: For Years My Heart Asked Me for Jamshid's Cup.   Hafiz [*or* Hafez].   WoPoe, *tr.* by Elizabeth Gray

For years now I have heard the cracking of.   Studying Physics with My Daughter.   Jeanne Murray Walker.   WeW-3

For years, so long, I had imagined. West Pitch at the Falls. Marsden Hartley. APT-1

For years the dead. Change, The. Denise Levertov. BAP-97

For years the drops of belladonna in our eyes. Possible Man, The. A. V. Christie. NAPBL

For years we endured his insolence. Mask-Maker. Michael Jackson. PeNZ

For You. Carl Sandburg. MoAmPo

For You. James Harvey Spencer. PWR

For you. (LL) Vladimir Uflyand [or Ufliand]. TCRP; TCRusP, tr. by Daniel Weissbort

For you, be there. (LL) My Spirit Will Not Haunt the Mound. Thomas Hardy. FaBoVe; MoBrPo

For you beautiful ones my mind. Sappho. SaLy, tr. by Diane Rayor

For you fleas too. Avedik Issahakian. ChAP

For you, for you I am trilling these songs. (LL) For You O Democracy. Walt Whitman. APN-1; CAGL; UV

For you, I cry this paper down into words on Black feminism. For a Woman's Rights. Joette Harland-Watts. InTrad

For you I have emptied the meaning. Louis Zukofsky. NoAM

For you I have slept. Michael Ondaatje. NoP-4 Fr. Rock Bottom.

For you / I will be a ghetto jew. Genius, The. Leonard Cohen. MoCV

For You, Mamá. Cherríe Moraga. GLP

For You, My Son. Horace Gregory. MoAmPo

For You O Democracy. Walt Whitman. APN-1; CAGL; UV

For you, O gulls. Richard Wright. APT-2

For you too, my fleas. Issa. SoOfWa, tr. by Sam Hamill

For you who loved me too. For Fugitives. Frank Templeton Prince. HarvBoo

For your fleas too. Issa. EH, tr. by Robert Hass

For your offence. (LL) Thomas Lodge. NOBE; NoSic; OBEV Fr. Rosalynde; or Euphues' Golden Legacy.

For Zion's Sake. Bible, O.T. TrJP Fr. Isaiah.

Forbear bold Youth. Answer to Another Persuading a Lady to Marriage, An. Katherine Philips. HAP; WeW-3

Forbear this liquid fire, fly. Fly about a Glass[e] of Burnt Claret, A. Richard Lovelace. CaPo

Forbear, thou great good husband, little ant. Ant, The. Richard Lovelace. BASC; CaPo

Forbearance. Samuel Taylor Coleridge. ChIV-2

Forbearance. Ralph Waldo Emerson. TAP

Forbecause a prisoner lies. Ja Nul Homs Pris Ne Ira a Raison. Richard I, Coeur de Lion. WoPoe, tr. by Frank Templeton Prince

Forbid! Marcelijus Martinaitis. TWW, tr. by Laima Sruoginis

Forbid / Kukutis to drive. Forbid! Marcelijus Martinaitis. TWW, tr. by Laima Sruoginis

Forbidden gate, palace trees, a moon's flitting trace. Presented to a Lady within the Palace. Chang Yü. SuSP, tr. by Ronald C. Miao

Forbidden Love. Elizabeth Daryush. PoBW

Forc'd from home, and all its pleasures. Negro's Complaint, The. William Cowper. CABP

Force. Unknown. OBCoV

Force. Unknown. OBCoV Fr. Advertising Rhymes.

Force. Derek Walcott. OxBC

Force-feeding swans—let me tell. Farmers. Thomas Lux. LCAP-2

Force of Gravity, The. Luiza Neto Jorge. SurWo, tr. by Jean R. Longland

Force of Love, The. Samuel Jones. NOEC; NPeEn

Force that through the green fuse drives the flower, The. Dylan Thomas. CABP; EBEV; FaBoMo; HarvBoo; MoBrPo; NAEL-5v2; NAEL-6v2; NOBE; NPeEn; NoAM; NoP-4; OBWVE; OxAEP-2; OxBEV; OxBTC; PoE; RB; SCV; TFi; UnPo

Forced by soft violence of prayer. Matthew Green. ECEV Fr. Spleen, The.

Forced Feelings. Wang Chiu-ssu.
   "You think I am happy." CoBLCP

Forced March. Miklós Radnóti. AF

Forced March. Miklós Radnóti. IQMS, tr. by Peter Zollman

Forced Music, A. Robert Graves. MoBrPo

Forced Recruit, The. Elizabeth Barrett Browning. FaBoWar

Ford Castle: The Borders. Geoffrey Holloway. NLP

Ford Madox Ford. Robert Lowell. OxBC; TwCP

Ford Manor. Derek Mahon. PBCIP

Ford o' Kabul River. Rudyard Kipling. FaBoTw; PeVV

Ford of Ch'u, knot for three Hsiang waters. Floating on the River Han. Wang Wei. ChinPo, tr. by Yip Wai-lim

Fording the River. Seamus Deane. PBCIP; PNI

'Fore I'll return again. (LL) Son David. Unknown. OxBB; OxBS

Foreboding. John Haines. CoAmPo

Forecast. Josephine Miles. NoAM

Forefathers. Edmund Charles Blunden. NOBE; NoP-4; OBEV; OBMV; OxBTC

Forehead, Eyes, Cheeks, Nose, Mouth, and Chin. Mother Goose. FaBoVe; LB; OxNR; ReMoGo

Forehead without scalp, dry shell without yolk of eye. Crinagoras. GrAn

Foreign. Kate Clanchy. MFPA

Foreign. Carol Ann Duffy. HarvBoo

Foreign Aid. Lionel Kearns. NOBC

Foreign Gate, The. Sidney Keyes.
   "Moon is a poor woman, The." NoP-4; OBWP

Foreign Land. Greta Knutson. SurWo, tr. by Penelope Rosemont

Foreign room, slab faces, dusty panes, A. Rebel General, The. Chris Wallace-Crabbe. CBAP

Foreign Ruler, A. Walter Savage Landor. OBSV; OxBEV

Foreign thing desertless in origin, A. (LL) Apologia pro Vita Sua. A. R. Ammons. HCAP; NOBA

Foreign Ways. Diana Chang. UnSA

Foreign Woman. Rosario Castellanos. WPOW, tr. by J. M. Cohen

Foreigner, A. Witter Bynner. APT-1

Foreigner Who Died in Juchitán, The. Pancho Na'car. WoPoe, tr. by Brian Swann

Foreigners, The. John Tutchin. BASC

Foreigners at the Fair. Fred Emerson Brooks. OBAL

Foreman drives by the fields counting his pickers, A. Campesinos. Juan Delgado. GeoHom

Foremost of false philosophies. Sea, False Philosophy. Laura Riding Jackson. APT-2

Forenoon. Summer Insects Described. James Thomson. NPeEn Fr. Seasons, The.

Forensic Jocularities. Sir George Rose. OxBoLi

Forensic Medicine. Gieve Patel. OMIP

Foreplay. Natasha Josefowitz. PasH

Forerunners. Ralph Waldo Emerson. APN-1; OBEV; OxBA

Forerunners, The. George Herbert. AngWePo; ESCV; GeHe; NAEL-5v1; NAEL-6v1; NAEL-7v1; NoP-4; TOF

Foreseen for so many years: these evils, this monstrous violence. May-June, 1940. Robinson Jeffers. MoAmPo

Foresees her Death. Mary Robinson. CenSon; RWP

Foresight. Lincoln Kirstein. OBWP; PoWW

Forest. Priscilla Borthwick. Prnts

Forest. Jean Garrigue. NOBA

Forest, The. Miroslav Holub. PoSu, tr. by George Theiner

Forest Birds (A Woman Speaks). Chu Yün-ming. CoBLCP, tr. by Jonathan Chaves

Forest Divers. Frank O'Hara. BodElec

Forest drips and glows with green, The. Rainforest. Judith Wright. OPOU

Forest Fire. Vadim Sergeievich Shefner. TCRP, tr. by Daniel Weissbort

Forest Hymn. William Cullen Bryant. TreFP Fr. Forest Hymn, A.

Forest Hymn, A. William Cullen Bryant. APN-1; TAP
   Forest Hymn. TreFP

Forest in winter, The! From edge to edge. Konstantin Iakovlevich Vanshenkin. TCRusP, tr. by Daniel Weissbort

Forest is crowded and a wounded, The. Chicago Blues. Rohan B. Preston. AmPoNex

Forest Lake. Edith Södergran. WPoS, tr. by Stina Katchadourian

Forest Leaves in Autumn. John Keble. November. OBEV

Forest Murmurs. Eduard Friedrich Mörike [or Möricke]. WoPoe, tr. by Randall Jarrell

Forest of the Dead, The. James Griffyth Fairfax. PoWW

Forest of yellow bamboo trees, The. Forest of Yellow Bamboo Trees, The. B. S. Mardhekar. OMIP, tr. by Vinay Dharwadker

Forest Road, The. Charlotte Mew. VWP

Forest road, The. Forest Road, The. Charlotte Mew. VWP

Forest stands, The. John Wills. HA

Forest Trees of the Sea. Unknown. WoPoe, tr. by Alfons L. Korn and Mary Kawena Pukui

Forest was fair and wide, The. Thomas of Erceldoune. OxBS Fr. Sir Tristrem.

Forests and Caverns. Eleanor Percy Lee. SWaP

Forests are branches of a tree lying down. Flying Home from Utah. May Swenson. WPE

Forests break off. Mountains stretch on still. River Song, The. Wang Yung. ChinPo, tr. by Yip Wai-lim

Forests grow pink and lacy in the dawn, The. Russian Woman. "Igor Severyanin" [or "Severianin"]. TCRP, tr. by Bernard Meares

Forests of Lithuania, The. Donald Davie.
   "But this, so feminine?" OxBTC

Forests were on fire, The. Two Drops. Zbigniew Herbert. RB, *tr. by* Czeslaw Milosz

Foresworn now the love-vows! Meleager. GrAn

Foretold Futures. Giovanna Pollarolo. TANSG, *tr. by* Marjorie Agosin

"Forever." Charles Stuart Calverley. NOBL; NOBVV

Forever Ambrosia. Christopher Darlington Morley. OBAL

Forever Arima. Cheryl Boyce Taylor. WiU

Forever brigands and pirates, the Cretans are never just. Leonidas of Tarentum. HePo *Fr.* Epigrams.

Forever Dead. Sappho. AWP, *tr. by* William Ellery Leonard

Forever intervene! (LL) Emily Dickinson. APN-2; NOBA; TAP

Forever / it dwells in the windows and doors. Time for Dejection. Hamda Khamees. PoArWo, *tr. by* Joseph T. Zeidan

Forever, life-long. (LL) To O.E.A E. A. Claude McKay. BPo; GT

Forever Martial. *Unknown.* WoPoe, *tr. by* John S. Major

Forever over now, forever, forever gone. Cameo, The. Edna St. Vincent Millay. MoAmPo; UnPo; WPE

Forever Parted: Graveyard. Gu Cheng. VCWP, *tr. by* Jerome P. Seaton

Forever the Snake. Jennifer Rankin. BMAP

Forever; 'tis a single word! "Forever." Charles Stuart Calverley. NOBL; NOBVV

Forevermore. Jones Very. NCAP

Foreword to New Numbers. Christopher Logue. OxBTC

Forfeit their Paradise by their pride. (LL) Flower, The. George Herbert. AWP; AngWePo; BASC; ESCV; FSCP; GeHe; NAEL-5v1; NAEL-6v1; NAEL-7v1; NOBE; NOCV; NPeEn; NoP-4; OBGa; OxBEV; PBRV

Forfeiture, The. Henry King, Bishop of Chichester. NOSC

Forge, The. Seamus Heaney. NAEL-5v2; NAEL-6v2; NoP-4; OxAEP-2

Forge me a tool, my Seamus. His Request. Owen Roe O'Sullivan. BIrV, *tr. by* Joan Keefe

Forge the contrary of this world. Movement. Andrée Chedid. HAWP, *tr. by* Mirène Ghossein and Samuel Hazo

Forget each kindness that you do. Memory System, A. *Unknown.* PWR

Forget him and forget her. (LL) To the Tune of The Coventry Carol. Stevie Smith. FaBoTw; WoPoe

Forget maps at 10F each. Those before. Strangers: An Essay. Jim Elledge. SwNoth

Forget Me Not. Austin Clarke. CIP-2

Forget-Me-Not, The. Mary Russell Mitford. CenSon

Forget-Me-Nots. Yevgeny [*or* Evgenii] Mikhailovich Vinokurov. TCRP, *tr. by* Daniel Weissbort

Forget me then; but ne'er believe that thou canst be forgot! (LL) Forget Thee? John Moultrie. ITBLP; PoToHe

Forget not this. (LL) Steadfastness. Sir Thomas Wyatt. FaBoVe; HAP; NAEL-5v1; NOBE; NoSic; OBEV; SCGP

Forget Not Yet. Sir Thomas Wyatt. *See* Steadfastness

Forget not yet the tried intent. Steadfastness. Sir Thomas Wyatt. FaBoVe; HAP; NAEL-5v1; NOBE; NoSic; OBEV; SCGP

Forget our pride, our faces, our common love. (LL) Do the Others Speak of Me Mockingly, Maliciously? Delmore Schwartz. APT-2; ChIV-1

Forget six counties overhung with smoke. William Morris. EBVV *Fr.* Earthly Paradise, The.

Forget the past and live the present hour. Now. Sarah Knowles Bolton. PWR

"Forget thee?" If to dream by night and muse on thee by day. Forget Thee? John Moultrie. ITBLP; PoToHe

Forget thine anguish. Meditations. Solomon ibn Gabirol. TrJP, *tr. by* Emma Lazarus

Forget to mail my letter to my friend Death. Overdue Balance Sheet. Thérèse Plantier. BoWoP, *tr. by* Maxine W. Kumin and Judith Kumin

Forget What Did. Philip Larkin. NoAM

Forget your life. Say *God is Great.* Get up. Say Yes Quickly. Jelaluddin [*or* Jalal al-Din] Rumi. EnlH; RaBo

Forgetfulness. Hart Crane. HarvBoo; NIL-7

Forgetfulness! Josephine D. Henderson Heard. CBWP-4

Forgetfulness Is Not. Anna Cascella. CItWP, *tr. by* Cinzia Sartini Blum and Lara Trubowitz

Forgetting. Air. Pierre Reverdy. CuPo

Forgetting. Vahan Tekeyan. AF, *tr. by* Diana Der Hovanessian and Marzbed Margossian

Forgetting God. Sir Thomas Seymour. NoSic

FORGETTING God. Forgetting God. Sir Thomas Seymour. NoSic

Forgetting, Love. Nathalie Handal. PoArWo

Forgetting the Sixties. Mark DeFoe. SwNoth

Forgetting. Yes, I will forget it all. Forgetting. Vahan Tekeyan. AF, *tr. by* Diana Der Hovanessian and Marzbed Margossian

Forgive a hick unable to compete. *Unknown.* PriapPo, *tr. by* Richard W. Hooper *Fr.* Priapus Poems, The.

Forgive and Live. Yusef Komunyakaa. BodElec

Forgive, But Do Not Forget. Ernst Waldinger. AuPH, *tr. by* Lowell A. Bangerter

Forgive Me. Shakti Chattopadhyay. OMIP, *tr. by* Prithvindra Chakravarty

Forgive Me! Andrey [*or* Andrei] Andreievich Voznesensky [*or* Voznesenskii]. RusPo, *tr. by* Robert Arthur Douglas Ford

Forgive me if I speak possessively of him. To a New Daughter-in-Law. *Unknown.* PoToHe

Forgive me, if I wound your ear. In a Letter to A.R.C. on Her Wishing to Be Called Anna. Matilda Barbara Betham-Edwards. ECWP; PoBW; WoRP

Forgive me if my eyes see. Pablo Neruda. GifTon, *tr. by* William O'Daly

Forgive me, my God, and overlook my sins. His Illness. Solomon ibn Gabirol. TOF, *tr. by* David Goldstein

Forgive Me, Sire. Norman Cameron. FaBoEE; GTBS-P; OxBEV; OxBS; OxBSP

Forgive me that I pitch your praise too low. Apology for Understatement. John Wain. OxBTC

Forgive me, you whom they cast in a name. Prayer. Avraham Shlonsky. MHP

Forgive, O Lord, my little jokes on Thee. Robert Frost. SAmP

Forgive the hours spent listening to radios. Looking at a Dead Wren in My Hand. Robert Bly. NNaP

Forgive these nigguhs that know not what they do. (LL) Riot. Gwendolyn Brooks. BPo; NAAAL; NALW; NBV; SSLK; TAP

Forgive your son! (LL) Ecce Puer. James Joyce. AmFaPo; BIrV; ChIV-2; EBEV; NoAM; TrCP

Forgiven. Margaret Elizabeth Munson Sangster. PoToHe

Forgiveness. John Greenleaf Whittier. GSo; TrCP

Forgiveness Dream. Jean Valentine. LCAP-2

Forgiving. Tennyson. SacPr

Forgo the charming Muses! No, in spite. Elizabeth Singer Rowe. PEW *Fr.* To one that persuades me to leave the Muses.

Forgotten. *Unknown, fr. Terezin Concentration Camp.* INSAB

Forgotten Girlhood. Laura Riding Jackson. RB

Forgotten Song. John Ashbery. HarvBoo

Forgotten? / What it was about? / What the matter was? ((((((Hollanditis)))))). Simon Vinkenoog. CLPP, *tr. by* Charles McGeehan

Fork. Charles Simic. ChAP; ColAP; HCAP; LCAP-2; PoPoPo; TRP; WeW-3

Fork of the Road, The. William Renton. NOBVV

Forlorn. William Dean Howells. APN-2

Forlorn and glum the couples go. Houses, The. Eden Phillpotts. OxBTC

Forlorn and lonely, my time will never come. Parting from Wang Wei. Meng Hao Jan. SuSp, *tr. by* Daniel Bryant

Forlorn Saphira, with reclining head. Thomas Gilbert. NOEC *Fr.* View of the Town, A. In an Epistle to a Friend.

Form, as any taper, fine, A. Modern Female Fashions. Mary Robinson. NOBRP

Form in Void. Ikkyu Sojun. ZenPo, *tr. by* Takashi Ikemoto and Lucien Stryk

Form is the woods: the beast. Poem. James [*or* Jim] Harrison. VGW

Form of Chiasmus; The Chiasmus of Forms, The. Michael Davidson. PmAP

Form of Epitaph, A. Laurence Whistler. GTBS-P

Form of Passion, A. David McFadden. NOBC

Form of Women, A. Robert Creeley. ErotSp

Form of youth without blemish, is not such the form divine?, The. Song of My Soul. Ralph Chubb. CAGL

Formal as a minuet or sonnet. Mystery Story. Howard Nemerov. NBLV

Formal exercise for withered fingers, A. Old Fisherman with Guitar. George Mackay Brown. OxBC

Formal Poem, A. Amal Moussa. PoArWo, *tr. by* Khaled Mattawa

Formalized / by middle age. Song of Bullets, The. Jessica Hagedon. FSt

Formation of Soils, The. Brenda Hillman. BAP-01

Formed long ago, yet made today. Mother Goose. OxNR

Former Barn Lot. Mark Van Doren. MoAmPo

Former Beauties. Thomas Hardy. NoAM; OBMV *Fr.* At Casterbridge Fair.

Former girlfriend praises my new place, A. Tourists, Potatoes, and Genocide. Rush Rankin. SpudSo

Former Love, a Lover of Form, A. Carol Muske. BodElec

Formerly a Slave. Herman Melville. APN-2; TAP

Formerly he had been a well-loved god. Naked among the Trees. Norman Cameron. OxBEV

Formerly I thought of you twice. Four Notions of Love and Marriage. N. Scott Momaday. HATNAP

Forming Child Poems. Simon J. Ortiz. CDW

Forms, flames, and the flakes of flames. (LL) Nomad Exquisite. Wallace Stevens. APT-1; ColAP

Forms of Love, The. George Oppen. NNaP

Forms of the Earth at Abiquiu. N. Scott Momaday. CDW

Formulaires. Mohammed Dib.

"Language sovereign secret incompatible submerged in the universal wound." PFTM-2, *tr. by* Carol Lettieri and Paul Vangelisti

Fornication is a filthy business. Petronius Arbiter. PGA

Fornicator. A New Song, The. Robert Burns. NPeEn

Forsaken. Zalman Schneour. TrJP, *tr. by* Joseph Leftwich

Forsaken, The. Duncan Campbell Scott. NOBC

Forsaken, The. Agnes Strickland. CenSon

Forsaken Bride, The. *Unknown. See* Waly, Waly [Love Be Bonny]

Forsaken Garden, A. Algernon Charles Swinburne. EBEV; GTBS-P; NOBE; NOBVV; NPeEn; NoP-4; OBGa; OxAEP-2; SCGP

Forsaken Girl, The. Eduard Friedrich Mörike [*or* Möricke]. WoPoe, *tr. by* Randall Jarrell

Forsaken Merman, The. Matthew Arnold. EBEV; FHYEP; FaBoCh; NAEL-5v2; NAEL-6v2; OBNV; OBSP

Forsaken of all comforts but these two. Upone Tabacco. Sir Robert Aytoun [*or* Ayton]. OxBS

Forsaken they would not see the prairies but only a cry. Even Forsaken They'd Flower. Raúl Zurita. TCLAP, *tr. by* Jack Schmitt

Forsaken Wife, The. Elizabeth Thomas. ECWP; LW

Forsaken Wife, The. Ts'ao Chih. CoBCP, *tr. by* Burton Watson

Forsaken woods, trees with sharp storms opressed. Robert Sidney. NoSic

"Forsaking all"—You mean. Word, The. Margaret Avison. MoCV

Forsee or more control than robin or wren. (LL) Fifty Faggots. Edward Thomas. MoBrPo; PeFWW; PoWW

Forster says in Aspects of the Novel. In the Grove. Rachel Hadas. KGB

Forsythia. Mary Ellen Solt. BoWoP

Fort by the oak trees there, The. Fort of Rathangan, The. Berchan. FaBoCh, *tr. by* Kuno Meyer

Fort of Ard Ruide, The. *Unknown.* NOIV

Fort of Rathangan, The. Berchan. FaBoCh, *tr. by* Kuno Meyer

Fort of Rathangan, The. *Unknown.* WoPoe, *tr. by* Kuno Meyer

Fort or Castle of Hope, The. Margaret Lucas Cavendish, Duchess of Newcastle.
"Some with sharp swords, to tell O most accursed!" PEW

Fort over against the oak-wood, The. Fort of Rathangan, The. *Unknown.* WoPoe, *tr. by* Kuno Meyer

Forth Feasting. William Drummond, of Hawthornden.
"What blust'ring noise now interrupts my sleep." NOSC

Forth from its scabbard, pure and bright. Sword of Robert Lee, The. Abram Joseph Ryan. CBCWP

Forth from my literal door I'm greeted. Report to the Stockholders. Reg Saner. PoCoUp

Forth from the east, up the ascent of Heaven. Matthew Arnold. PeVV *Fr.* Balder Dead.

Forth goes the weeding dame; her daily task. James Hurdis. ECEV *Fr.* Favourite Village, The.

Forth into the warm darkness faring wide. Wings in the Dark. John Gray. NOBVV

Forth, to the alien gravity. Launch, The. Alice Thompson Meynell. PeVV; WPE

Forth went the candid man. Stephen Crane. MoAmPo *Fr.* War Is Kind.

Forthwith the sounds and seas, each creek and bay. John Milton. ChIV-1 *Fr.* Paradise Lost.

Forties, The. "David Samuilovich Samoylov" [*or* "Samoilov"]. TCRP, *tr. by* Lubov Yakovleva

Forties Flick. John Ashbery. FTOS; NoAM

Fortification of New Ross, The. *Unknown.*
"I have a whim to speak in verse." NOIV

Fortitude. Christopher Smart. ChIV-2 *Fr.* Hymns for the Amusement of Children.

Fortnight before Christmas Gypsies were everywhere, A. Gypsy, The. Edward Thomas. NoAM; NoP-4

Fortress of stone, as unmoved as the arm and the beast of our builder! Vajdahunyad. Ferenc Kazinczy. IQMS, *tr. by* Watson Kirkconnell

Fortunate, / Being articulate. Nocturne of the Self-evident Presence. Thomas MacGreevy [*or* McGreevy]. BIrV; CIP-2

Fortunate Traveller, The. Derek Walcott. NoAM

Fortunately the skins. Judy Grahn. PasH

Fortune. Mary Ursula Bethell. PoBW

Fortune. Charles Madge. FaBoMo

Fortune. Sir Thomas More. SacPr

Fortune. *Unknown.* HeIP-2
(Lady Fortune is bothe frend and fo, The.) OHMEL

Fortune always boosts the dumb. Weighing-In, The. Ibn al-Rumi. ArPe, *tr. by* Omar S. Pound

Fortune and Virtue. Thomas Dekker. NoSic *Fr.* Old Fortunatus.

Fortune-Bringing Misfortune. Catharina Regina von Greiffenberg. AuPH, *tr. by* Lowell A. Bangerter and George C. Schoolfield

Fortune Cookie Blues. Amy Uyematsu. LTA

Fortune did not mean to give you promotion. On a Worthless Politician. *Unknown.* GrAn, *tr. by* Peter Jay

Fortune doth frown. Sir Thomas Wyatt. NoSic

Fortune favours the Brave, old Proverbs say. Mr Cromek to Mr Stothard. William Blake. FaBoEE

Fortune has brought me down--her wonted way. Hittan of Tayyi. AWP *Fr.* Hamasah.

Fortune Hath Taken Away. Sir Walter Ralegh. NoSic
(Fortune hath taken thee away, my love.) NoP-4

Fortune hath taken the away my love. Sir Walter Ralegh.
"Thus now I leave my love in fortunes {handes / bandes}." PBRV

Fortune is Bardolph's foe, and frowns on him. William Shakespeare. FaBoWar *Fr.* King Henry V.

Fortune, Nature, Love. Sir Philip Sidney. PoE *Fr.* Arcadia.

Fortune, Nature, Love, long have contended about me. Sir Philip Sidney. PoE *Fr.* Arcadia.

Fortune's darling, king's content. Epitaph. *Unknown.* BASC

Fortune's Legacy. *Unknown.* NOSC

Fortune's Treachery. Judah Halevi. TrJP, *tr. by* Solomon Solis-Cohen

Fortune smiles, cry holy day! [*or* holiday]. Thomas Dekker. NoSic *Fr.* Old Fortunatus.

Fortune Teller, The. Fu'ad [*or* Fuad] Rifqa [*or* Rifka]. BBASP; MAP, *tr. by* Sargon Boulus and Samuel Hazo

Fortune-tellers say I won't last long. Antipater of Thessalonica. PGA

Fortunes in knee breeches. H. C. ten Berge. TuT *Fr.* Lusitanian Variant, The.

Fortunes locked in the Hua-kai stars, why seek anything. Self-mockery. "Lu Hsün." SuSp, *tr. by* William R. Schultz

Fortunes of Men, The. *Unknown.* ASW, *tr. by* Kevin Crossley-Holland

Fortunes of War. Kit Wright. PeLV

Fortunes of War, I Tell You Plain, The. *Unknown.* InPK-6

Forty Augusts—aye, and several more—ago. Voice of Things, The. Thomas Hardy. HarvBoo

Forty Days. John Wheelwright.
Second Ascension of Christ, The. NOCV

40 Days and 40 Nights. Henri Cole. PoPoPo

48 Words for a Woman's Dance Song. Jerome Rothenberg. PoM

Forty-five Minutes from Broadway. George M. Cohan. ReLy

Forty-five Years Since the Fall of the Ch'ing Dynasty. Philip Whalen. *See* 10:X:57, 45 Years Since the Fall of the Ch'ing Dynasty

Forty Fungi. Harry Gilonis.
"Hunting with." Oth
Orange Birch Bolete (Leccinum versipelle). Oth

Forty *li* through Chü-yang Pass. Yang Shih-ch'i. CoBLCP *Fr.* Ten Miscellaneous Poems Written as a Member of the Imperial Retinue on an Inspection Tour of the Frontier—We Reached Hsüan-fu and Then Returned.

40. Love. Roger McGough. OBCoV

'49 dawn set me high on a roaring yellow tractor, The. In Kansas. Carter Revard. HATNAP

49 Stomp, The. Lew Blockcolski. VoR

Forty-nine years / —What a din! Uncho. ZenPo, *tr. by* Takashi Ikemoto and Lucien Stryk

Forty-one Seconds on a Sunday in June, in Salt Lake City, Utah. Quincy Troupe. MoASP

Forty-second Street. Harry Warren. ReLy

47. Gavin Selerie. Oth *Fr.* Roxy.

46. Samuel Daniel. *See* To Delia

Forty—that's not so old! Written for the Pavilion of the Drunken Old Man at Ch'u-chou. Ou-yang Hsiu. CoBCP, *tr. by* Burton Watson

Forty Three Years After Hitler My Parents Visit Eugene. Joan Dobbie. GotH

Forty-two years ago (to me if to no one else. Star-Gazer. Louis MacNeice. ModIr; NAEL-5v2; NAEL-6v2; NoP-4

Forty years / How sharp. Kaya Shirao. ZenPo, *tr. by* Takashi Ikemoto and Lucien Stryk

Forward! Announce the dust cloud's coming. Second Coming, The. Mohammad Bennis. MAP, *tr. by* Charles Doria and Sharif Elmusa

Forward exults on the run, The. Soccer. Nikolai Alekseievich Zabolotsky [*or* Zabolotskii]. TCRP, *tr. by* Daniel Weissbort

Forward or Back. Aaron Shurin. FTOS

Forward, sons of the tribe! Tambourine song for Soldiers Going into Battle. Hind bint Utba. WPOW, *tr. by* Bridget Connelly and Deirdre Lashgari

Forward violet thus did I chide, The. William Shakespeare. OxAEP-1 *Fr.* Sonnets.

Forward Youth that would appear, The. Andrew Marvell. BASC; CABP; EBEV; ESCV; FSCP; GTBS-P; GeHe; HAP; NAEL-6v1; NAEL-7v1; NOBE; NOSC; NPeEn; NoP-4; OBEV; OBWP; OxAEP-1; OxBEV; PBRV; PoPoPo; SCGP; TFi

Fossil. E. D. Blodgett. NOBC

Fossil, A. May Kendall. VWP

Fossil, The. Boynton, Jr. Merrill. CRP

Fossil, 1975. Janet Lewis. CRP

Fossil Raindrops, The. Harriet Prescott Spofford. OBCA

Foul canker of fair virtuous action. John Marston. NoSic *Fr.* Scourge of Villainy [*or* Villanie], The.

Foul fa' the breast first treason bred in. Hobie [*or* Hobbie] Noble. *Unknown.* ESPB; IBB; OxBB

Foul Line—1987. Colleen J. McElroy. LTA

Foul parent of fair child, swoll'n Breadtax! thou. Fatal Birth, The. Ebenezer Elliott. OxBSo

Foul Shots: A Clinic. William Matthews. MoASP

Foul sod covers a bad one here. Crinagoras. GrAn

Found. Goethe. STV, *tr. by* John Frederick Nims

Found a family, build a state. Fragments of a Lost Gnostic Poem of the Twelfth [*or* 12th] Century. Herman Melville. APN-2; NOBA; NoP-4; OxBSP; PoPoPo; TCAPo

Found a hole with a light in it, and saying. Little Random Creatures, The. *Unknown.* STP, *tr. by* Armand Schwerner

Found dead a rat—no case could sure be harder. *Unknown.* FaBoEE

Found he had worsted God! (LL) Emily Dickinson. ChIV-1; NoP-4

Found him, and set to barking. (LL) Bicycle Racers, The. Ann Townsend. AmPoNex; NeAmPo

Found him with crabs upon his face. (LL) Newcomer's Wife, The. Thomas Hardy. BoLoP; OxBTC

Found—my little angel. Sandro Penna. CAGL, *tr. by* John McRae

Found—Who Lost? Mary E. Tucker. CBWP-1

Foundation. Henry Van Dyke. SacPr

Foundation Stone. Alejandra Piznarnick. TANSG, *tr. by* Susan Bassnett

Foundations. Leopold Staff. BLT, *tr. by* Czeslaw Milosz

Foundations. Leopold Staff. PoSu, *tr. by* Adam Czerniawski

Foundations, The. Jennifer Maiden. BMAP

Foundations of Being, The. Patrizia Vicinelli.
Crossing the River. ItPo, *tr. by* Gayle Ridinger

Founder thou; these are thy race!, The. (LL) Experience. Ralph Waldo Emerson. APN-1; TAP; TCAPo

Foundered Star. Jane Miller. ExTi

Founding of New Hampshire, The. Carl Rakosi. FTOS

Founding of Yuba City, The. Chitra Divakaruni. GeoHom

Foundling Hospital for Wit, The. Isaac Hawkins Browne.
Fire Side, The; a Pastoral Soliloquy. NOEC

Foundlings in the Yukon. A. K. Ramanujan. PoetW

Fount, The. "Rubén Dario." SpanPo, *tr. by* William M. Davis

Fount there is, doth overfling, A. At the Fountain. Marcabrun. AWP, *tr. by* Harriet Waters Preston

Fountain. Elizabeth Jennings. WPE

Fountain. Elizabeth Robinson. AmPoNex

Fountain, The. William Cullen Bryant. APN-1

Fountain, The. William Cowper. *See* Olney Hymns

Fountain, The. Donald Davie. GTBS-P; NoP-4; OxBTC

Fountain, The. Don Allen Johnson. AWP, *tr. by* Dulcie L. Smith

Fountain, The. James Russell Lowell. OBCA; TreFP

Fountain, The. William Wordsworth. GTBS-P; OxAEP-2

Fountain, a Bottle, a Donkey's Ears and Some Books, A. Robert Frost. VGW

Fountain, a house of stone, A. Fountain, a House of Stone, A. Heberto Padilla. VCWP

Fountain at the Tomb, The. Nicias. AWP, *tr. by* Charles Merivale

Fountain, coolest fountain. Ballad of the Cool Fountain. *Unknown.* BoWoP, *tr. by* Edwin Honig

Fountain from Wilderness Stone, A. Bible, *O.T.* CRP *Fr.* Psalms.

Fountain-head that is so bright to see, The. Guido Cavalcanti. EaItPo, *tr. by* Dante Gabriel Rossetti

Fountain in the plaza cascaded dirty water, The. San Jacinto Plaza. Ray Gonzalez. UrbNat

Fountain of Cyanë, The. Donald Davie. HarvBoo

Fountain of light, Light, Source of light. Prayer at Night. Alcuin. MLL, *tr. by* Helen Waddell

Fountain of living light. Hymn to Su'rya, A. Sir William Jones. NOBRP

Fountain of tears, river of grief. Christine de Pisan. WPOW

Fountain plays, The. Memorial Fountain, The. Roy Fisher. NPeEn

Fountain, that springest on this grassy slope. Fountain, The. William Cullen Bryant. APN-1

Fountain to which we, The. Bath. John Godfrey. FTOS

Fountains. Sacheverell Sitwell. MoBrPo

Fountains. Sir Osbert Sitwell. MoBrPo

Fountains are dry and the roses over, The. Manor Garden, The. Sylvia Plath. FaBoWP; HarvBoo; LCAP-2

Fountains in the Sea. Martin Sorescu. VCWP, *tr. by* Seamus Heaney and Joana Russell-Gebbett

Fountains mingle with the river, The. Love's Philosophy. Shelley. BoLoP; FHYEP; GTBS-P; OxAEP-2; PoToHe; SCGP

Fountains of the boiling stars, the flowers on the foreland, the ever-returning roses of dawn, The. (LL) Apology for Bad Dreams. Robinson Jeffers. APT-1; MoAmPo; NOBA; OxBA

Fountains that frisk and sprinkle. Ballade Made in the Hot Weather. William Ernest Henley. MoBrPo

IV. Allen Ginsberg. BB *Fr.* Kaddish.

Four III. E. E. Cummings. FaBoMo; TTTS

Four a.m. in summertime. Lovely Morning Thought. Arthur Rimbaud. SxFrPo, *tr. by* Martin Sorrell

Four adobe walls. Bougainvillaeas. Stanzas for an Imaginary Garden. Octavio Paz. OBGa

Four Ages of Man, The. Anne Bradstreet.
Old Age. TCAPo

Four Ages of Man, The. W. B. Yeats. PAI; TrCP

4 A.M. Kenneth Fearing. APT-2

Four a.m. At the reactor an alarm begins. Glow-boys. John Tranter. BMAP

4 a.m. freight comes pounding and shaking through the fall night, The. Don't You Hear that Whistle Blowin' Denise Levertov. GM

Four and a Half. John Holmes (1904–62). APT-2

4½ Months: Halfway Song. George Barlow. ISC

Four and twenty bonny boys. Sir Hugh; or, The Jew's Daughter. *Unknown.* ESPB

Four-and-twenty Highland men. Eppie Morrie. *Unknown.* ESPB; OxBB

Four-and-twenty ladies fair. Bonny Baby Livingston. *Unknown.* ESPB

Four and twenty noblemen they rode thro Banchory fair. Glenlogie; or, Jean o Bethelnie. *Unknown.* ESPB

Four and twenty nobles sits in the king's ha. Glenlogie; or, Jean o Bethelnie. *Unknown.* ESPB

Four and twenty tailors / went to kill a snail. Snail, The. Mother Goose. LB; OxNR; ReMoGo

Four be the things I am wiser to know. Inventory. Dorothy Parker. NBLV

Four Best Things, The. Robert Herrick. *See* Four[e] Things Make Us Happy Here

Four Bird Songs. Simon J. Ortiz. HATNAP

Four Black Bogmen, The. Elder Olson. APT-2

Four blue stones in this thrush's nest. Nest, The. Andrew Young. Spl

Four boards of the coffin lid, The. After Death. Algernon Charles Swinburne. NOBVV; PeVV

Four centuries of sleep they say. African Sleeping Sickness. Wanda Coleman. PmAP

Four days to go until the twelfth, and the bonfire is fourteen feet high. Thoughts in a Black Taxi. Sinéad Morrissey. MFPA

Four days with you, my father three months dead. Stream, The. Mona Van Duyn. VCAP

Four dazzling points of phosphor gleamed. (LL) Femme et Chatte. Paul Verlaine. AWP; OBVE

Four Dead Sons. James Wright (1927–80). BodElec

Four decades, I've aroused the southeast with flute and sword. To a Friend, Using the Same Rhymes of a Peom He Sent Me. Liu Ya-tzu. SuSp, *tr. by* Wu-Chi Liu

Four Deer. Eamon Grennan. ModIr

Four deer lift up their lovely heads to me. Four Deer. Eamon Grennan. ModIr

Four Divine Animals. Shinkichi Takahashi. ZenPo, *tr. by* Takashi Ikemoto and Lucien Stryk

Four Ducks on a Pond. William Allingham. NOBVV; NOIV; OxAEP-2

Four Elements, The. Sándor Weöres. IQMS, *tr. by* Adam Makkai and Donald E. Morse

Four Epigrams on the Naturalization Bill. John Byrom. NOBL

Four Epitaphs. Countee Cullen.
For a Lady I Know. APT-2; HeIP-4; InPK-6; NIL-7; NIP-4; OBAL; SSLK; TAP; TRP

For My Grandmother. APT-2; MoAmPo; SSLK; VGW

For Paul Laurence Dunbar. SSLK

(Lady I Know, A.) MoAmPo

Four Examples from the Poems of River Wang Deer Enclosure. Wang Wei. ChinPo, *tr. by* Yip Wai-lim

Four feet up, under the bruise-blue. Small Woman on Swallow Street. W. S. Merwin. CoAmPo; CoAP

Four fingers o' his right han' (LL) Brown Adam. *Unknown.* ESPB; OxBB

Four foot box, a foot for every year, A. (LL) Mid-Term Break. Seamus Heaney. AmFaPo; NIL-7; PoPoPo

Four for Sir John Davies. Theodore Roethke. APT-2; MoAmPo; NOBA; NoAM

Four Glosses. *Unknown.* NOIV

"Bird is calling from the willow, A." NOIV

"How lovely it is today!" NOIV, *tr. by* Thomas Kinsella

"Little bird, The." NOIV, *tr. by* Thomas Kinsella

"Wall of woodland overlooks me, A." NOIV, *tr. by* Thomas Kinsella

Four Good Things. James McMichael.

"Cat came, A." GeoHom

Four Heads & How to Do Them. John Forbes. CBAP

(Classical Head, The.) BMAP

Four Horses, The. James Reeves. TLR

4 hours into the climb. Climbing Sears Tower. Dennis Schmitz. IllVoic

400-Meter Freestyle. Maxine W. Kumin. MoASP

Four hundred years ago. Good Luck. Oswald de Andrade. TCLAP, *tr. by* Flavia Vidal

Four in the Morning. Wislawa Szymborska. BLT

Four-Leaf Clover. Ella Higginson. SWaP

Four-Light Window, A. Ágnes Nemes Nagy. VCWP, *tr. by* Hugh Maxton

Four Lines of a Black Love Letter Between Teachers. Ed Roberson. NBV

Four little children. Lost Angel, The. Philip Levine. NOBA

Four little words I send, indeed, mark them well. To your own son. One For a Keepsake Album. Ferenc Kölcsey. IQMS, *tr. by* Adam Makkai

Four May Poems. *Unknown. See* Lusty May

Four May Poems. *Unknown.* OxBS

(Quhen Flora Had O'erfret the Firth.) OBEV

Four May Poems, II. *Unknown.* OxBS

Four May Poems: "Be glaid, al ye that luvaris bene." *Unknown.* OxBS

Four Minute History of Getting It Together in Order to Be Fabulous, Briefly, A. Anselm Berrigan. HeMarv

Four Mountain Wolves. Leslie Marmon Silko. VoR

Four Nights' Drunk, The. *Unknown.* OBAL

(Four Nights' Drunk, The.) OBAL

Four Notions of Love and Marriage. N. Scott Momaday. HATNAP

Four o'clock. Letters from Chankiri Prison. Nazim Hikmet. PFTM-1

Four of July. Robert Newton Peck. CA

Four on a Sidewalk. *Unknown.* CA

IV, 1. To Venus. Horace. OBVE *Fr.* Odes.

4 or 5 Tadpoles. Kusano Shimpei. PFTM-1

4 Part Geometry Lesson, A. Robin Blaser. NeAP

Four Paths. Nikolai Ivanovich Glazkov. TCRP, *tr. by* Daniel Weissbort

Four pelicans went over the house. Pelicans. Robinson Jeffers. MoAmPo

Four Poems. Ikkyu Sojun.

"Don't worry please please how many times do I have to say it." WoPoe, *tr. by* Stephen Berg

"Nobody told the flowers to come up nobody." WoPoe, *tr. by* Stephen Berg

"Oh green green willow wonderfully red flower." WoPoe, *tr. by* Stephen Berg

"Ten years of whorehouse joy I'm alone now in the mountains." WoPoe, *tr. by* Stephen Berg

Four Poems. Velemir [*or* Viktor Vladimirovich] Khlebnikov. PFTM-1

Four Poems for Robin. Gary Snyder. NNaP; NOBA; NoAM

Autumn Morning in Shokoku-ji, An. HAP; VGW; WeW-3

(Four Poems for Robin.) BB

("Karma demands.") (LL) BB

Spring Night in Shokoku-ji, A. VGW

Four Poems for Robin. Gary Snyder. BB *Fr.* Four Poems for Robin.

Four Poems for *The St. Louis Sporting News.* Jack Spicer. PoM

Four Poems from the Sequence "Singing of the Moon." Yang Shen. CoBLCP, *tr. by* Jonathan Chaves

Four Poems on Death. Abu Sa'id Abul Khayr.

"For men and women soon the day draws near." WoPoe, *tr. by* Dick Davis

"His absence is the knife that cuts your throat?" WoPoe, *tr. by* Dick Davis

"I'm going to tell You something that is true." WoPoe, *tr. by* Dick Davis

"If I've been dead for twenty years or so." WoPoe, *tr. by* Dick Davis

Four Poems On the Ch'ung-wu Festival. Chang Yü. CoBLCP, *tr. by* Jonathan Chaves

Four Poems Regarding the Endurance of Poets. Geoffrey Hill.

Domaine Public. OxBC

Four Poems to the Tune "Ch'ing-chiang yin." Ma Chih-yüan. CoBLCP, *tr. by* Jonathan Chaves

Four Preludes on Playthings of the Wind. Carl Sandburg. MoAmPo; NOBA

Four Quartets. T. S. Eliot.

Burnt Norton. APT-1; HarvBoo; MoAmPo; NAAL-2v2; NAAL-5; PoE

Dry Salvages, The. AiP; NoP-4; OxBA

"Where is there an end of it, the soundless wailing." AmFaPo

East Coker. HAP; VGW

Little Gidding. CABP; FaBoMo; FaBoTw; GTBS-P; NAEL-5v2; NAEL-6v2; NAWM-7v2; NOBA; NOBE; NoAM; OxAEP-2; OxBTC; PeECV; TAP; TFi

"Ash on an old man's sleeve." FaBoTw; NPeEn; OxBEV

"Dove descending breaks the air, The." SacPr

Four Quartz Crystal Clocks. Marianne Craig Moore. TwCP

Four Quatrains. Jelaluddin [*or* Jalal al-Din] Rumi.

"In the shambles of love, they kill only the best," RaBo

"Tonight with wine being poured." RaBo

"Two strong impulses: One." RaBo

"Where is a foot worthy to walk a garden," RaBo

Four Recollections. Shen Yüeh. SuSp, *tr. by* Richard B. Mather

Four Resurrections in the Valley of the Ghosts. Yehuda Amichai [*or* Amikhai]. VCWP, *tr. by* Benjamin Harshav

Four Roads, The. Alice Greene. PeSAV

Four roads lead out of the town. Four Roads, The. Alice Greene. PeSAV

Four Saints in Three Acts. Gertrude Stein.

"Pigeons on the grass alas." OWoS; TAP

Four-score and seven, so the papers say. Old Boatman of Death's River, The. R. Williams Parry. OBWVE, *tr. by* Joseph P. Clancy

Four Screen Shots. John Cayley. PFTM-2 *Fr.* Reveal Code: Indra's Net 8.

Four seasons fill the measure of the year. Human Seasons, The. John Keats. GTBS-P

Four Seasons in the Mountains, The. Chang Yü. CoBLCP, *tr. by* Jonathan Chaves

Four Seasons of the Year, The. Anne Bradstreet. SCAP

4.7. Horace. NAEL-5v1; NAEL-6v1; NAEL-7v1, *tr. by* Samuel Johnson *Fr.* Odes.

4.7. Horace. WoPoe, *tr. by* Michael O'Brien *Fr.* Odes.

Four Sheets to the Wind and a One-Way Ticket to France. Conrad Kent Rivers. BPo

Four Small Elegies. Margaret Atwood. PoetW

Beauharnois (1). PoetW

Beauharnois (3). PoetW

Beauharnois, Glengarry (2). PoetW

Dufferin, Simcoe, Grey (4). PoetW

Four Songs from the Book of Samuel. Eli W. Mandel. MoCV

Four Songs in Imitation of Wang Chien. Fan Ch'eng-ta.

"Autumn wheat turns green and lush as spring wheat yellows." SuSp, *tr. by* Wu-Chi Liu

"Farmer has got a receipt, but the yamen still presses for tax payment." SuSp, *tr. by* Wu-Chi Liu

Farming Family Invites the Guest to Stay Overnight, A. SuSp, *tr. by* Wu-Chi Liu

"Pig's leg fills the plate, wine overflowing the cups, A." SuSp, *tr. by* Wu-Chi Liu

Pressing for Tax Payment. SuSp, *tr. by* Wu-Chi Liu

Reeling Silk. SuSp, *tr. by* Wu-Chi Liu

Rejoicing the Spirits. SuSp, *tr. by* Wu-Chi Liu

"Traveler, don't ridicule this farming house as too small." SuSp, *tr. by* Wu-Chi Liu

Four Sonnets About Food. Adrienne Su. NAPBL

4 squirrels / are as busy as monks. Maine Vastly Covered with Much Snow. John Tagliabue. InPK-6

Four Stanzas Written in Anxiety. George Jonas. MoCV

Four stiff-standers. *Unknown.* LB; OxNR

Four talked about the pine tree. One defined it by genus, species, and. Conversation. Dan Pagis. VCWP, *tr. by* Stephen Mitchell

Four Tao philosophers as cedar waxwings. Waxwings. Robert Francis. APT-2; BLT; LCAP-2; RaBo

4. The Satisfaction. Lu Chi. WoPoe, *tr. by* Sam Hamill *Fr.* Art of Writing, The.

Four Things. Henry Van Dyke. PoToHe

Four things are white, the fifth exceeds the rest. Five Things White. Edward May. FaBoEE

Four Things Choctaw. Jim Barnes. HATNAP

4.13: Revenge ("Audivere, Lyce"). Horace. AWP, *tr. by* Louis Untermeyer *Fr.* Odes.

(4) THOUGHT AND SPEECH CANNOT KEEP UP WITH THE EMO-. Declaration of the Word as Such. Aleksei Eliseievich Kruchyonykh [*or* Kruchionykh *or* Kruchenykh]. PFTM-1

Four times during the night your eyes like white butterflies. Four times during the night. Jeannette Miller. TANSG, *tr. by* Paula Vega

Four times the pitch is outside the strike zone. Aesthetics of the Bases Loaded Walk. Joe Wenderoth. AmPoNex

Four Trees—upon a solitary Acre. Emily Dickinson. APN-2

Four *Tz'u* from Tun-huang. *Unknown.* CoBCP, *tr. by* Burton Watson

"He was a traveler west of the river,/ only he knew how lonely he was." ColAnChi, *tr. by* Burton Watson

"He was a traveler west of the river,/ then he took sick, lay an inch away from death." ColAnChi, *tr. by* Elling O. Eide

"He was a traveler west of the river,/ with wealth and eminence rare in this world." ColAnChi, *tr. by* Burton Watson

"I can't stand the wily magpie and all his extravagant stories!" CoBCP; ColAnChi, *tr. by* Burton Watson

Tune: Eternal Longing. ColAnChi, *tr. by* Burton Watson

Tune: Eternal Longing. ColAnChi, *tr. by* Elling O. Eide

Tune: Eternal Longing. ColAnChi, *tr. by* Burton Watson

Tune: Magpie on the Branch. CoBCP; ColAnChi, *tr. by* Burton Watson

4 Variations On. Gerrit Kouwenaar. PFTM-2, *tr. by* Peter Nijmeijer

4-Way Stop. Myra Cohn Livingston. KaS

Four Ways of Dying. Steve Chimombo. HBAPE; NAfrP

Four wet winters and now the dry. Runoff. William Everson. NoAM

Four white heifers with sprawling hooves. Orotava Road, The. Basil Bunting. NoAM

Four white walls. Four White Walls. Debby Barben. IBA

Four Winds. Hal Porter. NOBAu

Four Winds, The. Henry Wadsworth Longfellow. *Fr.* Song of Hiawatha, The.

Four winds and seven seas have called me friend. From Life to Love. Countee Cullen. ChIV-1

Four winds contend on the sea's face. Vision of Beasts, A. John Heath-Stubbs. ChIV-1

Four Winds dry their wooden shoes, The. (LL) Fishing Boats in Martigues. Roy Campbell. FaBoEE; OxBSP

Four-Word Lines. May Swenson. GLP; WPE

Four words have the coins of Van-Lich. Coins of Van-Lich. *Vietnamese Oral Tradition.* CaDao, *tr. by* John Balaban

Four years. Immortality. Samuel Marshak. RusPo, *tr. by* Robert Arthur Douglas Ford

Four years ago I met your death here. Letter from Chicago. May Sarton. NALW

Four years ago I started reading Proust. Bookmark, A. Thomas M. [*or* "Tom"] Disch. RA

Four years!—and didst thou stay above. Geist's Grave. Matthew Arnold. NOBVV

Four[e] Things Make Us Happy Here. Robert Herrick. CaPo; Spl (Four Best Things, The.) Spl

Fourfold Exercise for the Believer in His Lodging on Earth, A. Ralph Erskine. SacPr

Fourier what have they done with your keyboard. André Breton. PFTM-2, *tr. by* Kenneth White *Fr.* Ode to Charles Fourier.

Fourscore and seven years ago. Gettysburg Address, The. Abraham Lincoln. HHAm

Fourteen, a sonneteer thy praises sings. Sonnet upon Sonnets, A. Robert Burns. GSo; Son

Fourteen and still a boy. Hundred Worries, A. Tu Fu. CrYelRi, *tr. by* Sam Hamill

Fourteen good measur'd verses make a sonnet. (LL) Sonnet upon Sonnets, A. Robert Burns. GSo; Son

Fourteen Men. Mary Gilmore. CBAP

1492. Emma Lazarus. APN-2; SWaP; WPE

14 Reasons Why I Mention Mario Lanza to the Man I Love Every Chance I Get Tonight. Jim Elledge. IllVoic

Fourteen small broidered berries on the hem. What the Sonnet Is. Eugene Lee-Hamilton. GSo; Son

14 Songs and 1 Riddle. Robert Filliou. "Homage in dance, An." PFTM-2

(1422 amsterdam avenue). Old Buildings, The. Pedro Juan Pietri. UnSA

Fourteen-year-old boy is out rambling alone, A. Backside to the Wind. Paul Durcan. PBCIP

14-Year-Old Convalescent Cat in the Winter, A. Gavin Ewart. OPOU; OxBSP

Fourteen years after you snuck. En el Sol de Mi Barrio. Sandra M. Castillo. TouFir

Fourteen years old, learning the alphabet. Reading Lesson, The. Richard Murphy. PBCIP

Fourteenth Ode. Sekeena Shaben. PoArWo

14th Street Was Gutted in 1968. Cheryl Clarke. UnSA

Fourth and fifth months are when the tea is best in mountain groves, The. On Hearing that Holders of the *Chin-shih* Degree Are Dealing in Tea. Mei Yao Ch'en. SuSp, *tr. by* Jonathan Chaves

4th Base. Gary Gildner. MoASP

Fourth Book, Concerning the Nature of Love, The. Lucretius. *Fr.* De Rerum Natura (On the Nature of Things).

Fourth Book of Sibylline Oracles, The. "The Jewish Sibyl." There Is a City. TrJP, *tr. by* Bohn

Fourth day, The. Aki-No-Bo. JDP, *tr. by* Yoel Hoffmann

Fourth Day of the First Week, The. Guillaume de Salluste Du Bartas. *Fr.* Divine Weeks and Works, The.

Fourth Eclogue, The. Miklós Radnóti. IQMS, *tr. by* John Wain

Fourth Ecologue: Pollio, The. Virgil [*or* Vergil]. WoPoe, *tr. by* David R. Slavitt

Fourth Floor, Dawn, Up All Night Writing Letters. Allen Ginsberg. HarvBoo; InvLad

Fourth Month, The. *Unknown.* SuSp, *tr. by* C. H. Wang

Fourth month: summer already, The. Fourth Month, The. *Unknown.* SuSp, *tr. by* C. H. Wang

Fourth Pearl, The: Temperance. Lady Diana Primrose. WPE *Fr.* Chain of Pearl, A.

Fourth Poem of a Canto of Accusation. Costa Andrade. PBMAP (There are on the earth 50,000 dead whom no one mourned.) PBMAP

Fourth Rome, The. Nikolai Alekseievich Klyuyev [*or* Kliuev *or* Klyuev]. CAGL, *tr. by* Simon Karlinsky

4th Song. John Berryman. BoLoP; ColAP; EmeKit; HAP; HCAP; NoP-4; OBAL; VCAP *Fr.* Dream Songs.

Fourth Song, The. Francis Beaumont. NOSC *Fr.* Masque of the Inner Temple and Gray's Inne, The.

Fourth Song the Night Nurse Sang. Robert Duncan. VGW

Fourth watch, the moon sinks, paper window calm. Inscribed on a Painting of Bamboo. T'ang Yin. CoBLCP, *tr. by* Jonathan Chaves

4th Weekend. John Berryman. BodElec

Fourth Wish. Alberta Turner. LCAP-2

4th Witness—The Petty Thieves. Ifi Amadiume. NAfrP

Fowls [*or* Foweles *or* Fowles] in the Frith. *Unknown.* FaBoVe; HAP; MiEL; NAEL-5v1; OxBSP

Fowre Hymnes. Edmund Spenser. Hymne of Heavenly Beautie, An. PeECV "Rapt with the rage of mine own ravisht thought." PeECV

Fowre muckle angels wi their trumpets, stalkin. Judgment Day. Robert Garioch. OBVE

Fox. David Campbell. CBAP

Fox. Clifford Dyment. OxBSP

Fox. Kenneth Rexroth. NNaP *Fr.* Bestiary, A.

Fox, The. Dafydd [*or* David] ap Gwilym. NAWM-7v1, *tr. by* Richard Morgan Loomis

Fox, The. Kahlil Gibran. GraLe

Fox, The. Philip Levine. SoSe-8

Fox, The. Mary Oliver. PoCoUp

Fox, The. R. Williams Parry. OBWVE, *tr. by* Gwyn Williams

Fox, The. *Unknown.* OxNR (Fox set out in hungry plight, The.) ChAP (Visit from Mr. Fox, A.) ChAP

Fox and crow, their dirty business finished, The. Fabulary Satire IV. Daryl Hine. NOBC

Fox and the Ape Go to Court, The. Edmund Spenser. NoSic *Fr.* Mother Hubbard's Tale.

Fox and the Crow, The. Jean de La Fontaine. OBVE, *tr. by* Marianne Moore

Fox and the Goose, The. *Unknown.* MiEL

Fox at your neck and snakeskin on your feet, A. Leaving Something Behind. David Wagoner. CoAP

Fox Came into my Garden, A. Charles Causley. OTCP

Fox chewed his thoughtful paw, gnawed, The. Different Voice, The. Frieda Hughes. NeBl

Fox Dancing. Suzanne Knowles. RB

Fox don't make a fauz pas! A. John Fuller. PeLV *Fr.* Fox-Trot.

Fox Glove Song. Christina Beer. PeNZ

Fox is after dinner, too, The. (LL) Sycophantic Fox and the Gullible Raven, The. Guy Wetmore Carryl. NBLV; OBCA

Fox is very clever, The. Kenneth Rexroth. NNaP *Fr.* Bestiary, A.

Fox jumped up one winter's night, A. Fox, The. *Unknown.* OxNR

Fox knew well, that before they tore him, The. John Masefield. OBNV *Fr.* Reynard the Fox.

Fox knows many. Strategy. Archilochus. WoPoe, *tr. by* Guy Davenport

Fox knows many things, The. Archilochus. SaLy, *tr. by* Diane Rayor

Fox looked at his shadow at sunrise and said, I will have, A. Fox, The. Kahlil Gibran. GraLe

Fox may steal your hens, sir, A. John Gay. NOEC *Fr.* Begger's Opera.

Fox's Counsel, The. Huw Llwyd. OBWVE, *tr. by* Joseph P. Clancy

Fox set out in hungry plight, The. *Unknown.* *See* Fox jumped up one winter's night, A

Fox-Trot. John Fuller. Can-Can. PeLV Polka. PeLV

Fox Who Watched for the Midnight Sun, The. Norman Dubie. LCAP-2

Fox woman / dances, string of blue beads. Second Skins—a Peyote Song. Joseph Bruchac. CDW

Fox you didn't know you had, The. Scotch. Ruth Padel. MFPA

Foxes. Frieda Hughes. NeBl

Foxes, The. Janet Frame. WPE

Foxes move in pairs. *Unknown.* ColAnChi, *tr.* by Jeffrey Riegel *Fr.* Classic of Odes.

Foxes there in the dark. (LL) Vidya. EaWin; WPOW, *tr.* by J. Moussaieff Masson and W. S. Merwin

Foxfire. Dominique Parker. SpirFl

Fra Bank to Bank, Fra Wood to Wood I Rin. Mark Alexander Boyd. OxBEV; Son; WoPoe

  (Cupid and Venus.) InPK-6

  (Sonet.) NPeEn; PBRV

  (Sonet: "Fra bank [*or* banc] to bank [*or* banc], fra wood [*or* wod] to wood [*or* wod] I rin") EBEV; OBEV

  (Venus and Cupid.) HAP; NePenScot

Fra Lippo Lippi. Robert Browning. CTC; EBVV; FHYEP; NAEL-6v2; OxAEP-2

Fractal Audition. Pimone Triplett. NAPBL

Fradel Schtok. Irena Klepfisz. TaR

Frae great Apollo, poet say. Poet's Wish; an Ode, The. Allan Ramsay. OBVE

Frae nirly, nippin', Eas'lan' breeze. Ille Terrarum. Robert Louis Stevenson. OxBS

Fragging. Yusef Komunyakaa. ESEAA

Fragile. U Tam'si Tchicaya.

  "I am no longer master of my tears." NegPo

Fragile as a spider's web. Love. May Sarton. PoBW

Fragment. Alessandro Ceni. ItPo, *tr.* by Gayle Ridinger

Fragment. Adelaide Crapsey. APT-1

Fragment. Ray DiPalma. FTOS

Fragment, A. Anne Brontë. VWP

Fragment, A. Christopher Smart. *Fr.* Jubilate Agno.

Fragment, A. William Wordsworth. NOBRP

  (Fragment, A.) NOBRP

Fragment 1. Bill Griffiths. Oth *Fr.* Building: The New London Hospital.

Fragment 4. Bill Griffiths. Oth *Fr.* Building: The New London Hospital.

Fragment 9. Bill Griffiths. Oth *Fr.* Building: The New London Hospital.

Fragment 10. The Boudoir. Sydney Owenson, Lady Morgan. RWP *Fr.* Lay of an Irish Harp, or Metrical Fragments, The.

Fragment 11. Bill Griffiths. Oth *Fr.* Building: The New London Hospital.

Fragment 12. Bill Griffiths. Oth *Fr.* Building: The New London Hospital.

Fragment 13. Bill Griffiths. Oth *Fr.* Building: The New London Hospital.

Fragment 17. Anacreon. CAGL, *tr.* by Eugene O'Connor

Fragment 18. Bill Griffiths. Oth *Fr.* Building: The New London Hospital.

Fragment 19. L'Amant Mutin. Sydney Owenson, Lady Morgan. RWP *Fr.* Lay of an Irish Harp, or Metrical Fragments, The.

Fragment 35. The Irish Jig. Sydney Owenson, Lady Morgan. RWP *Fr.* Lay of an Irish Harp, or Metrical Fragments, The.

Fragment 36 [*or* Thirty-Six]: "I know not what to do." "H. D." NALW; OxBA; PoBW; VGW

Fragment 58: Night and Sleep. Alcman. WoPoe, *tr.* by Rosanna Warren

Fragment 113: "Not honey, / not the plunder of the bee." "H. D." APT-1; NAAL-2v2

Fragment 360. Anacreon. CAGL, *tr.* by Alfred Corn

Fragment 652. Euripides. CAGL, *tr.* by John Addington Symonds

Fragment, A: "I saw the Sibly at Cumæ." Dante Gabriel Rossetti. PeVV

Fragment, A: "I walked [*or* walk'd] along a stream for pureness rare." Gervase Markham. CTC

Fragment, A: "In Cloe's chamber, she and I." John Bancks. NOEC

Fragment, A: "Our fancies are but joys all unexprest." Henrietta Cordelia Ray. CBWP-3

Fragment, A: The Blind Man. Anne Batten Cristall. *See* Blind Man, The

Fragment, A: "Thou strainest through the mountain fern." Robert Louis Stevenson. NOBVV

Fragment: "As for him who." William Carlos Williams. Spl

Fragment: August 4, 1856. Henry Wadsworth Longfellow. TCAPo

Fragment B. Christopher Smart. *Fr.* Jubilate Agno.

Fragment C. Christopher Smart. *Fr.* Jubilate Agno.

Fragment: "Cold chain of life presseth heavily on me tonight, The." Adah Isaacs Menken. CBWP-1

Fragment: December 18, 1847. Henry Wadsworth Longfellow. APN-1; TCAPo

Fragment Descriptive of the Miseries of War. Charlotte Smith. ECWP

Fragment for the Dark. Elizabeth Jennings. FaBoWP

Fragment for the Mother. Mariella Bettarini. CItWP, *tr.* by Cinzia Sartini Blum and Lara Trubowitz

Fragment (Found Inside My Mother). Nick Flynn. AmPoNex

Fragment from "The Maladjusted: A Tragedy." Morris Gilbert Bishop. NBLV

Fragment: "I cannot find my way to Nazareth." Yvor Winters. OBSV

Fragment: "I lived on this earth in an age." Miklós Radnóti. IQMS, *tr.* by George Gömöri and Clive Wilmer

Fragment: "I would to heaven that I were so much clay." Byron. CTC; NAEL-5v2; NAEL-6v2; NOBL; OxBEV; OxBSP *Fr.* Don Juan.

Fragment: "Language has not the power to speak what love indites." John Clare. FaBoEE; OxBSP

Fragment: "Mountain summits sleep, glens, cliffs, and caves, The." Alcman. AWP

Fragment of a Greek Tragedy. A. E. Housman. NOBL; PeLV; WoPoe

Fragment of a Poem on Hunting, A. Thomas Tickell.

  "Such be the dog, I charge, thou mean'st to train." ECEV

Fragment of a rainbow bright, A. Rainbow, The. John Keble. TreFP

Fragment of a Song on the Beautiful Wife of Dr. John Overall. *Unknown.* BoLoP

Fragment of a Sonnet. Pierre de Ronsard. AWP; OBVE, *tr.* by Keats

Fragment of an English Opera. A. E. Housman. OBCoV

Fragment of an Ode to Maia Written on May Day, 1818. John Keats. OBEV

Fragment of Death. François Villon. *See* Fragment on Death, A

Fragment of Petronius, A. Petronius Arbiter. BoLoP; OBVE; OxBSP

  (Fragment of Petronius Arbiter, A.) NPeEn, *tr.* by Ben Jonson

Fragment on Death, A. François Villon. CTC; PeVV, *tr.* by Algernon Charles Swinburne

  (Fragment of Death.) AWP

Fragment 3. Sydney Owenson, Lady Morgan. PoBW

Fragment: "Wake the serpent not—lest he." Shelley. SCGP

Fragment: Where Is Tangwen Now? Glyn Jones. TCAWP

Fragmentary Stars. Léonie Adams. APT-2

Fragmented Address to the FBI. Diane Di Prima. BB

Fragments. Gottfried Benn. AF, *tr.* by Vernon Watkins

Fragments. Gerard Manley Hopkins.

  How Looks the Night? OxBSP

Fragments. Letitia [*or* Laetitia] Elizabeth Landon.

  Secrets. VWP

Fragments, The. Peter Dale.

  "Few ever came to help you speak or sell." NOCV

Fragments join in me with their own music, The. (LL) Poem as Mask, The. Muriel Rukeyser. APT-2; NAAL-5; NALW

Fragments: "Locke sank into a swoon." W. B. Yeats. NoAM

Fragments 1920–1921. Nikolai Stepanovich Gumilyov [*or* Gumiliov *or* Gumilev]. TCRusP, *tr.* by Mary Jane White

Fragments of a Lost Gnostic Poem of the Twelfth [*or* 12th] Century. Herman Melville. APN-2; NOBA; NoP-4; OxBSP; PoPoPo; TCAPo

Fragments of Ancient Poetry, Collected in the Highlands of Scotland. James Macpherson.

  "I sit by the mossy fountain; on the top of the hill of winds." NOEC; NePenScot

Fragments of the Night, The. José Lezama Lima. TCLAP, *tr.* by Willis Barnstone

Fragments, / Refuse of the soul. Fragments. Gottfried Benn. AF, *tr.* by Vernon Watkins

Fragments to Overcome Silence. Alejandra Piznarnick. TANSG, *tr.* by Susan Bassnett

Fragrance. Kay Sage. SurWo

Fragrance comes from the scent I wear, The. *Unknown.* CoBCP *Fr.* Tzu Yeh Songs.

Fragrance is due to perfumes. *Unknown.* ChinPo, *tr.* by Yip Wai-lim

Fragrance of Life, Odor of Death. Denise Levertov. AF

Fragrance of men. (LL) Kirkyard. George Mackay Brown. NPeEn; NePenScot

Fragrance of red lotuses has faded, The. Plum Blossoms. Li Ch'ing-chao. ErotSp, *tr.* by Sam Hamill

Fragrance of the large old farmhouse cool and sour, The. Grandparents' House. Arthur Zanker. AuPH, *tr.* by Lowell A. Bangerter

Fragrance of the red lotus fades, The. Poem to the Tune of "Yi chian mei." Li Ch'ing-chao. WPOW, *tr.* by Marsha Wagner

Fragrance of the Udumbara, The. Muso Soseki. EaWin, *tr.* by W. S. Merwin

Fragrance would call me out of the house, A. Catching Webs. Judith Beveridge. NOBAP

Fragrances that like a wind disturb. Islands Where I Was Born, The. Gloria Rawlinson. PeNZ

Fragrant firewood grows in the rain. Country Road, A. Li Ho. CrYelRi, *tr.* by Sam Hamill

Fragrant grass in front of the courtyard. Spoken to Pines and Bamboos. Wei Chuang. SuSp, *tr.* by Robin D. S. Yates

Fragrant Hands. Faiz Ahmad Faiz. VCWP, *tr.* by Agha Shahid Ali

Fragrant mignonettes place on the table, The. All Souls' Day. Herman von Gilm zu Rosenegg. AuPH, *tr.* by Lowell A. Bangerter

Fragrant prayer upon the air, A. Poem to Be Said on Hearing the Birds Sing, A. Biddy Crummy. AWP, *tr.* by Douglas Hyde

Fragrant Thy Memories. "Judah." TrJP, *tr. by* Herbert Loewe

Fragrant Tree, The. Shen Yüeh. SuSp, *tr. by* Richard B. Mather

Fragrant with powder, moist with perspiration. Creamy Breasts. Chao Luan-luan. EroLit, *tr. by* Chung Ling and Kenneth Rexroth

Frail and tenuous mist lingers on baffled and intricate branches, A. Leaves. Frederic Manning. NOBAu

Frail as the leaves that quiver on the sprays. Homer. OBVE *Fr.* Iliad, The.

Frail branches of the arbor, The. When the Moon is in the River of Heaven. Ou-yang Hsiu. OHPC, *tr. by* Kenneth Rexroth

Frail duration of a flower, The. (LL) Wild Honey Suckle, The. Philip Freneau. ColAP; ITBLP; NAAL-2v1; NAAL-3; NOBA; OxBA; TAP; TCAPo

Frail, frail, lone-growing bamboo. *Unknown.* CoBCP; ColAnChi, *tr. by* Burton Watson

Frail multitude, whose giddy law is list. Crucify Him! Giles Fletcher, the Elder. SacPr

Frail sound of a tunic trailing, A. Poem. Antonio Machado Ruiz. AWP; WoPoe, *tr. by* John Dos Passos

Frail the white rose and frail are. Flower Given to My Daughter, A. James Joyce. OBMV; RB; RaBo

Frail[e] as our flesh, crumble to dust. (LL) Maria Wentworth. Thomas Carew. CaPo; MeLP; NPeEn; PeECV

Frailty. George Herbert. NOCV

Frailty and Hurtfulness of Beauty, The. Henry Howard, Earl of Surrey. EnLoPo

Frailty, Thy Name is Woman. William Shakespeare. OxAEP-1; SCV *Fr.* Hamlet.

Frame for the Angels, A. Paul Smyth.
"Spring that I was six I found in the woods, The." CRP

Frame of the world is suddenly rotated, The. Pin's Fee, or Painting with Star, A. David Shapiro. BodElec

Frame within frame, the evolving conversation. Dancers Exercising. Amy Clampitt. NoAM

Framed in her phoenix fire-screen, Edna Ward. Cottage Street, 1953. Richard Wilbur. BodElec; FaBoMo; HCAP; PoPoPo

Framer of the earth and sky. Hymn. Saint Ambrose. TrCP

Framing. Michael Davidson. FTOS

Fran. Christopher Pilling. NLP

France aids them now, a desperate game I play. Philip Freneau. TCAPo *Fr.* George the Third's Soliloquy.

France (Concluded). William Wordsworth. *Fr.* Prelude, The; Growth of a Poet's Mind [1850 vers.].

France's I am; my lookout's glum. Quatrain. François Villon. WoPoe, *tr. by* Richard Wilbur

France underfoot like a worn-out carpet spread. Night at Dunkirk. Louis Aragon. FaBoWar, *tr. by* Malcolm Cowley and Rolfe Humphries

Francie-the-Possessed. Oswald Durand. NegPo, *tr. by* Ellen Conroy Kennedy

Francine's Room. Louise Erdrich. NoAM

Francis Ford Coppola and Anthropologist Interpreter Teaching Gartewienna Tribesmen to Sing "Light My Fire," Philippine Jungle, 1978. David Wojahn. ReTh

Francisco Velarde was here. Lolo Panchito was here. (LL) Madarika. Vince Gotera. OpBo; ReBoTo

François Villon. Bulat Shalvovich Okudzhava. TCRusP, *tr. by* Denis Johnson, Aleksandar Petrov and Shirley Rihner

François Villon. Bulat Shalvovich Okudzhava. TCRP, *tr. by* Deming Brown

Francus. Sir John Davies. *See* In Francum

Frandus fell in the Po and, struggling, cried to Olympus. About the Shipwrecked Frandus. Janus Pannonius. IQMS, *tr. by* Iain MacLeod

Frank Albert and Viola Benzena Owens. Ntozake Shange. BISi

Frank Baker's my name, and a bachelor I am. *Unknown. See* My name is Frank Taylor, a bachelor I am

Frank Costello eating spaghetti in a cell at San Quentin. Mafioso. Sandra M. Gilbert. UnSA

Frank O'Hara Five, Geoffrey Chaucer Nil. Geoff Hattersley. NeBl

Frank Plume, a spark about the town. Inquisitive Bridegroom, The. William Somerville [*or* Somerville]. ECEV

Frank, will[']t live handsomely? Trust not too far. Advice to My Best Brother, Colonel Francis Lovelace. Richard Lovelace. BeJo

Frankenstein. Connie Deanovich. ReTh

Frankfurt. János Pilinszky. PoSu
(Frankfurt 1945.) AF

Frankie and Albert. *Unknown.* APN-2

Frankie and Johnny [*or* Johnnie *or* Albert]. *Unknown.* EBNV; FaBoA; NAAAL; NIP-4; NOBA; OxBoLi; RB; TCAPo; UnPo

Frankie was a good waoman. Frankie and Albert. *Unknown.* APN-2

Franklin Hyde. Joseph Hilaire Pierre Belloc. NBLV

Franklin's Prologue, The. Geoffrey Chaucer. NAEL-5v1; NAEL-6v1 *Fr.* Canterbury Tales, The.

Franklin's Tale, The. Geoffrey Chaucer. NAEL-5v1; NAEL-6v1 *Fr.* Canterbury Tales, The.

Franklin sailed a key-hung kite. Fable. James Facos. NBLV

Franks come down the hill with a random course, The. *Unknown.* FaBoWar, *tr. by* John Hookham Frere *Fr.* Poem of the Cid, The.

Frantic as a prentice poet. Niyi Osundare. HBAPE *Fr.* Moonsongs.

Frantic elk climb from the valleys to escape the flies, The. On the Elk, Unwitnessed. Alan Dugan. YaYoPo

Frater Ave Atque Vale. Tennyson. EBVV; GTBS-P; HAP; NAEL-5v2; NAEL-6v2; NoP-4; OxBSP

Fraternitas. Confucius. CTC; OBVE *Fr.* Deer Sing.

Frau Bauman, Frau Schmidt, and Frau Schwartze. Theodore Roethke. APT-2; CoAP; NAAL-2v2; NOBA; NoAM; TAP

Fraudulent perhaps in that they gave. Swans. Lawrence Durrell. MoBrPo

Fray of Suport, The. *Unknown.* IBB

Freak. Chandrashekhar Patil. OMIP, *tr. by* A. K. Ramanujan

Freaks at Spurgin Road Field, The. Richard Hugo. LCAP-2; NoAM; SoSe-8

Freckled and frivolous cake there was, A. Frivolous Cake, The. Mervyn Laurence Peake. PeLV

Freckles numberless as stars on my forehead. My Portrait. Moyshe-Leyb [*or* Moishe-Leib *or* Leyb] Halpern. TrJP, *tr. by* Joseph Leftwich

Fred. Ian Duhig. NeBl

Fred Pickering never asked why. Playground, The. Gregory Harrison. NOxBChV

"Fred, where is north?" West-Running Brook. Robert Frost. APT-1; MoAmPo; NOBA; NoP-4

Freddie Hubbard's music / is an hour late. Left Bank Jazz Society, The. Michael S. Weaver. UnSA

Freddy. Stevie Smith. LW

Fredensborg. Friedrich Gottlieb Klopstock. GePo, *tr. by* George C. Schoolfield

Frederick Douglass. Paul Laurence Dunbar. CBCWP

Frederick Douglass. Robert Earl Hayden. CBCWP; ESEAA; HCAP; ISC; NAAAL; NIL-7; NIP-4; PoPoPo; Son; TTY; VCAP

Frederick Douglass: 1817–1895. Langston Hughes. BPo; CBCWP; HHAm

Fredericksburg. Thomas Bailey Aldrich. TCAPo

Frederiksted, Dusk. Derek Walcott. NoAM

Fredman's Epistlar, 1790. Carl Michael Bellman.
Fredman's Epistle No. 23. WoPoe, *tr. by* Rika Lesser

Free Abandonment Blues, The. Jean Valentine. BodElec

Free at last [*or* las'], free at last [*or* las']. I Thank God I'm Free at Las' *Unknown.* BPo; TAP

Free bird leaps / on the back of the wind, A. Caged Bird. Maya Angelou. WeW-3

Free-booter, The. George Darley. OxBSo

Free-coursing wind from the sky. Wind, The. Dafydd [*or* David] ap Gwilym. WoPoe, *tr. by* Daniel Huws

Free evening fades, outside the windows fastened with decorative iron grilles, The. Evening in the Sanitarium. Louise Bogan. FaBoWP; NALW; NIL-7; TwCP

Free Fantasia on Japanese Themes. Amy Lowell. MoAmPo

Free Fantasia: Tiger Flowers. Robert Earl Hayden. ESEAA

Free Fire Zone. Igor Bobrowsky. CDa

Free from all fogs but[t] shining fair[e], and clear [*or* cleere]. Mary Sidney Wroth, Countess of Montgomery. BASC; EMWP *Fr.* Pamphilia to Amphilanthus.

Free Grace. Charles Wesley. NOCV; SacPr

Free hands. Hands. Bernard Dadié. NegPo, *tr. by* Ellen Conroy Kennedy

Free Harbor. Su'ad al-Mubarak Al-Sabah. MAP, *tr. by* John Heath-Stubbs and May Jayyusi

Free I have my own self-reliance. I Drift in the Wind. Ingrid Jonker. HAWP; WPOW, *tr. by* Jack Cope

Free Old Man. Muso Soseki. EaWin, *tr. by* W. S. Merwin

Free One, A. W. H. Auden. *See* Watch Any Day

Free Parliament Litany, A. *Unknown.* OxBoLi

Free Puerto Rico. Puerta Rica. Víctor Hernández Cruz. LoL

Free Radicals. James Sherry. FTOS

Free Thought. Algernon Charles Swinburne. NPeEn

Free Thoughts on Several Eminent Composers. Charles Lamb. OxBoLi; PeLV

Free Throw. Mark Kraushaar. MoASP

Free Union. André Breton. NAWM-7v2, *tr. by* Mary Ann Caws

Free Union. André Breton. PFTM-1; TTTS
(Freedom of Love.) SPE, *tr. by* Edouard Roditi
(My wife with the hair of a wood fire.) SPE, *tr. by* Edouard Roditi

Free Verse. Charles Reznikoff. APT-2

Free will-star is a hendiadys for dream. To the Readers. Maria Luisa Spaziani. CItWP, *tr. by* Cinzia Sartini Blum and Lara Trubowitz

Free woman, A. At last free! The mother of Sumangala. BoWoP

Freeborn Pindaric never does refuse. Samuel Wesley. NOBL; VerBaPo *Fr.* Pindaricque on the Grunting of a Hog, A.

Freediving thirty to forty feet, only a few seconds to spare. Lobsters in the Brain Coral. Laurence Lieberman. IllVoic

Freedom. Ambrose Bierce. APN-2 *Fr.* Devil's Dictionary, The.

Freedom. Wimal Dissanayake. ChAP

Freedom. Ralph Waldo Emerson. APN-1

Freedom. Abraham Ibn Ezra. TrJP, *tr. by* Solomon Solis-Cohen

Freedom. Friedrich von Logau. GePo, *tr. by* George C. Schoolfield

Freedom. "Jan Struther." LW

Freedom. Anthony Thwaite. OxBSo

Freedom a Come Oh! *Unknown.* FaBoVe

Freedom; a Poem, Written in Time of Recess from the Rapacious Claws of Bailiffs. Andrew Brice.

   Poet's Terror at the Bailiffs of Exeter, The. NOEC

Freedom and Love. Thomas Campbell. GTBS-P

Freedom, as every schoolboy knows. Ambrose Bierce. APN-2 *Fr.* Devil's Dictionary, The.

Freedom at last. Cincinnati. Mitsuye Yamada. UnSA

Freedom at McNealy's. Priscilla Jane Thompson. CBWP-2; SWaP

Freedom Fighter. Antigone Kefala. BMAP; ItWoWo

Freedom Hair. Raymond Washington. NBV

Freedom in Peril. "Sagittarius." UV

Freedom in the Air. *Unknown.* NAAAL

Freedom is a dream. Dark Testament. Pauli Murray. BlSi

Freedom is more than a word, more than the base coinage. *Nabara,* The. Cecil Day Lewis. EBNV; OBNV

Freedom, New Hampshire. Galway Kinnell. LCAP-2

Freedom of Love. André Breton. *See* Free Union

Freedom of the Moon, The. Robert Frost. APT-1

Freedom of the wholly mad, The. Phenomenology of Anger, The. Adrienne Rich. PFTM-2; PoE

Freedom [*or* Fredome]. John Barbour. FaBoCh; NePenScot; OBEV; OxBS; TreFP *Fr.* Bruce, The.

Freedom Song, A. Marjorie Oludhe Macgoye. HAWP; ItWoWo; WoPoe

Freedom Song for the Black Woman, A. Carole C. Gregory Clemmons. BlSi

Freedom to worship God. (LL) Landing of the Pilgrim Fathers [in New England], The. Felicia Dorothea Hemans. BRP; HHAm; ITBLP; NAEL-6v2; NoP-4; WPE

Freehold. John Hewitt.

   Lonely Heart, The.

     "Once in a seaside town with time to kill." ModIr

Freely Espousing. James Schuyler. FTOS; NeAP; NoP-4

Freely in Hidden Fire. Mirza Asadullah Khan Ghalib. WoPoe, *tr. by* Frances W. Pritchett

Freely the dead bracken breaks to your stride. Argenteuil County. Peter Dale Scott. MoCV

Freeman Field. Marilyn Nelson Waniek. ESEAA

Freeman, I treat tonight, and treat your friends. Invitation, The. Leonard Welsted. NOEC

Freestyle, on the First of Tishri. Enid Shomer. TaR

Freeway 280. Lorna Dee Cervantes. NoAM; WeW-3

Freeze-up annexes the sea even, The. Freeze-Up. Michael Longley. CABP

Freezing Night. T'ao Hung Ching. OHMPC, *tr. by* Kenneth Rexroth

Freight. John Frederick Nims. GM

Freight Cars. Stephen Dobyns. GM

Freight Train, Freight Train. Alvin Greenberg. GM

Freight trains are pulling in. Freight Trains. Attila József. AF, *tr. by* John Batki

Freighter, gay with rust, The. Jews at Haifa. Randall Jarrell. MoAmPo

Freind! for your epitaphs I'm griev'd. Epigram on One Who Made Long Epitaphs. Pope. FaBoEE

Frelimo Oya. Let It Be. Musaemura Bonus Zimunya. NAfrP

French. Osbert Lancaster. NOBL; PeLV *Fr.* Afternoons with Baedeker.

French are a race among races, The. Limerick. *Unknown.* PeLi

French are glad to die for love, The. Diamonds Are a Girl's Best Friend. Leo Robin. ReLy

French Dress. Friedrich von Logau. GePo, *tr. by* George C. Schoolfield

French, 1870–1871, The. *Unknown.* FaBoEE

French Fops. John Gay. ECEV *Fr.* Epistle to the Right Honourable William Pulteney, Esq.

French Garden. Léopold Sédar Senghor. NegPo, *tr. by* Ellen Conroy Kennedy

French Generals, The. Robert Bly. BAP-01

French Historie, The. Anne Dowriche.

   "So him at first *De Nance* commanded was to kill;" PBRV

French Lisette: A Ballad of Maida Vale. William Plomer. OBCoV

French Noel. William Morris. ChrPo

French poodle espied in the hall, A. Limerick. *Unknown.* PeLi

French Prisoner, The. János Pilinszky. IQMS, *tr. by* Peter Zollman

French Prisoner, The. János Pilinszky. PoSu, *tr. by* Janos Csokits

French Quarter Intimacies. Kalamu ya Salaam. SpirFl *Fr.* New Orleans Haiku.

French ships run in the new canal, The. Difficulties at Love. *Vietnamese Oral Tradition.* CaDao, *tr. by* John Balaban

Frenchie. Stephen Dobyns. BodElec

Frenzy. George Crabbe. NOBE *Fr.* Sir Eustace Grey.

Frenzy softens the air. Radiant Silhouette IV. John Yau. OpBo

Frenzy, Sweet Little Child, You Sleep. Marcelle Ferry. SurWo, *tr. by* Myrna Bell Rochester

Frequent oil your safety-clutch. (LL) Ambrose Bierce. APN-2; OBAL *Fr.* Devil's Dictionary, The.

Frequently the moonlight's flame. Moon, The. Abraham A Santa Clara. AuPH, *tr. by* George C. Schoolfield

Fresco. Martin Sorescu. VCWP, *tr. by* D. J Enright and Joana Russell-Gebbett

Fresco Come to Life. Boris Leonidovich Pasternak. AF

Fresco: Departure for an Imperialist War. Thomas McGrath. AF

Fresco-Sonnets to Christian Sethe. Heinrich Heine. AWP, *tr. by* John Todhunter

Fresh Air. Kenneth Koch. NNaP; NeAP"

   "Supposing that one walks out into the air." OBCoV

Fresh and fair the morn awaketh. Morn. Josephine D. Henderson Heard. CBWP-4

Fresh breezes waft across march orchid fragrance as. Kuan Yün-shih. SuSp, *tr. by* Richard John Lynn *Fr.* Medley of Southern and Northern Tunes—Scenic Tour of West Lake.

Fresh, changeful, constant, upward, like thee! (LL) Fountain, The. James Russell Lowell. OBCA; TreFP

Fresh Cheese and Cream. Robert Herrick. BASC

Fresh content of fresh enamouring, A. Ser Pace. EaItPo, *tr. by* Dante Gabriel Rossetti

Fresh fields and woods! the Earth's fair face. Retirement. Henry Vaughan. ChIV-1

Fresh Flowers. Wang An-shih. CoBCP, *tr. by* Burton Watson

Fresh from the dewy hill, the merry year. Song. William Blake. PeECV

Fresh From the Void. Masaoka Shiki. OHMPJ, *tr. by* Kenneth Rexroth

Fresh in their new wraps, earth and heaven. On New Year's Day. Nantembo. ZenPo, *tr. by* Takashi Ikemoto and Lucien Stryk

Fresh Mussels. Charles McDonald. NLP

Fresh night, The. (LL) God is Good. It Is a Beautiful Night. Wallace Stevens. APT-1; SAmP

Fresh Paint. Boris Leonidovich Pasternak. TrJP, *tr. by* Babette Deutsch

Fresh peaks of salt and pepper hair. Vallejo. Maggie Nelson. HeMarv

Fresh savannas of the Sangamon, The. Painted Cup, The. William Cullen Bryant. APN-1

Fresh Spring the herald of love's mighty king. Edmund Spenser. AWP; HAP; OBEV; PoE; Son *Fr.* Amoretti.

Fresh Stain. Tess Gallagher. ExTi

Fresh strewings [*or* strowings] allow. Peter-penny, The. Robert Herrick. CaPo

Fresh were the breathings of the nightborn gale. Charles Newton. NOEC *Fr.* Stanzas.

Fresh wind strains. Azov's shallow sea. Watermelon. "Eduard Georgievich Bagritzky [*or* Bagritsky]." TCRP, *tr. by* Vera Dunham

Fresher and fresher comes the air. The blue. John Neal. APN-1 *Fr.* Battle of Niagara, The.

Freshly fallen snow. Nick Avis. HA

Freshly lit cigarette in his mouth. Improvisation for Piano. Michael S. Weaver. UnSA

Fresno Truth, The. Lawson Fusao Inada. GeoHom

Fressh lusty beautee joyned wyth gentilesse. *Unknown.* OHMEL

Freud: Dying London, He Recalls the Smoke of His Cigar Beginning to Sing. James Schevill. TAP

Freud's Butcher. Charles Bernstein. BodElec

Friar had said his paternosters duly, The. Necrological. John Crowe Ransom. FuPo

Friar in the Well, The. *Unknown.* ESPB

Friar Lubin. Clément Marot. AWP, *tr. by* Henry Wadsworth Longfellow

Friar of Orders Gray, The. *Unknown.* NOEC

Friar's Prologue, The. Geoffrey Chaucer. PoE *Fr.* Canterbury Tales, The.

Friar's Tale, The. Geoffrey Chaucer. PoE *Fr.* Canterbury Tales, The.

Friday before Labor Day, The. In the Way Back. Debra Kang Dean. UnSA

Friday Evening. Sean Lucy. CIP-2

Friday Night at the End of a Millennium, A. Clare Pollard.

   "I enjoy dancing." NeBl

"On the first of January."   NeBl

Friday night's dream, on Saturday told.   Dreams.   *Unknown.*   ReMoGo

Friday the Thirteenth.   Allen Ginsberg.   NNaP

Friday. Wet Dusk.   Christopher Logue.   OxBTC

Fridge clicks, hums; light flows across, The.   Joseph.   Timothy Steele.   RA

Friend.   Hone Tuwhare.   PeNZ, *tr. by* Kumeroa Ngoingoi Pewhairangi

Friend, A.   Santob [*or* Shem-Tob] De Carrion.   TrJP   *Fr.* Proverbios Morales.

Friend, A.   Paul Klee.   PFTM-1

Friend, A.   Sir Thomas N. Talfourd.   PoToHe

Friend, A.   *Unknown.*   PoToHe

Friend, The.   Marge Piercy.   NALW

Friend, a poet, wrote me near the end, A.   Drouth, The.   Jon Dressel.   AngWePo

Friend after friend departs.   On the Loss of Friends.   James Montgomery.   SacPr

Friend, Ah You Have Changed!   Frank Mkalawile Chipasula.   HBAPE

Friend calls, says, A.   Suzy Wong's Been Dead a Long Time.   Kitty Tsui.   ReTh

Friend Cato.   Anna Wickham.   MoBrPo

Friend Col and I, both full of whim.   David Garrick.   FaBoEE

Friend Comes to Visit on a Summer Night, A.   Mo Shih-lung.   CoBLCP, *tr. by* Jonathan Chaves

Friend, coming in a friendly wise.   If Any Be Pleased to Walk into My Poor Garden.   Francis Daniel Pastorius.   SCAP

Friend dies one night, A.   Drugs.   Dennis Cooper.   PmAP

Friend, do you remember the time we went.   Breaking of the Glass, The.   'Abdallah Al-Tayyib.   MAP, *tr. by* Salma Khadra Jayyusi and Christopher Middleton

Friend, don't be angry.   Mirabai [*or* Mira Bai].   BoWoP

Friend, henceforth to be reckoned the foremost among my comrades.   Ovid.   RomPo, *tr. by* Peter Green   *Fr.* Tristia.

Friend, hope for the Guest while you are alive.   To Be a Slave of Intensity.   Kabir.   RaBo, *tr. by* Robert Bly

Friend, how can I meet my lord?   Mirabai [*or* Mira Bai].   BoWoP

Friend I can trust is the one who will let me have my death, The.   Ghazal.   Adrienne Rich.   WoPoe

Friend, I'm reading your old poems on the north terrace.   Antonio Cisneros.   TCLAP, *tr. by* Maureen Ahern and David Tipton   *Fr.* Loneliness.

Friend in a tipi in the, A.   Two Fawns That Didn't See the Light This Spring.   Gary Snyder.   HCAP

Friend in my mountain-side demesne.   To A Gardener.   Robert Louis Stevenson.   OBGa

Friend is sometimes desert, A.   Eugenio de Andrade.   VCWP   *Fr.* White on White.

Friend, now for ever gone.   To One Who Died in a Garret in Cardiff.   Huw Menai.   AngWePo

Friend of Humanity and the Knife Grinder, The.   George Canning.   OBCoV; UV

    (Sapphics.)   NOBRP; NOEC; NPeEn

Friend of mine, A. See, I hold her face in trembling, passionate hands. (LL)   Small Female Skull.   Carol Ann Duffy.   EmeKit; HarvBoo

Friend of my father came to stay, A.   Stranger to a Small Child.   Ben Scammell.   NLP

Friend of Ronsard, Nashe and Beaumont.   On a Birthday.   John Millington Synge.   OBMV

Friend of that poor queen, The. (LL)   Deirdre.   James Stephens.   AWP; OBMV; PoRA

Friend of the arts and artists, scholar, generous patron.   Ovid.   WoPoe, *tr. by* David R. Slavitt   *Fr.* Tristia.

Friend of the Family, A.   Louis Simpson.   NNaP

Friend of the wise! and teacher of the good!   To William Wordsworth.   Samuel Taylor Coleridge.   FHYEP; NAEL-5v2; NAEL-6v2

Friend of the wretched! wherefore should the eye.   Ode to Death.   Charlotte Smith.   NoP-4

Friend, on This Scaffold Thomas More Lies Dead.   James Vincent Cunningham.   InPK-6

    (Epigram: "Friend [*or* friends] on this scaffold Thomas More lies dead.")   CRP

Friend, Ortho of Syracuse gives thee this charge.   Ortho's Epitaph.   Theocritus.   FaBoEE, *tr. by* Charles Stuart Calverley

Friend! / Poor, foolish blossom!   Beauty.   Peter Hille.   AWP, *tr. by* Jethro Bithell

Friend remarks to the Prophet, "Why is it," A.   Jelaluddin [*or* Jalal al-Din] Rumi.   LoL

Friend sparrow, do not eat, I pray.   Basho.   AWP

Friend—the face I wallow toward.   What I Like.   Alice Fulton.   WeW-3

Friend, the Old Man that was last year.   Than, Mau.   John Balaban.   CDa

Friend, there be they on whom mishap.   Contentment.   Charles Stuart Calverley.   NOBVV

Friend thinks he knows best, A.   Late Victorian Girl, The.   Bill Manhire.   PeNZ

Friend told me, A.   Alone.   Michael S. Harper.   ISC

Friend, well I know thou knowest well to bear.   Guido Orlandi.   EaItPo, *tr. by* Dante Gabriel Rossetti

Friend Who Just Stands By, The.   Bertye Young Williams.   PoToHe

Friend, whose unnatural early death.   Elegy.   David Gascoyne.   FaBoTw; TwCP

Friend, with regard to this same hare.   To the Rev. Mr. Powell.   Christopher Smart.   OBWVE

Friend, you seem thoughtful. I not wonder much.   Sea Dialogue, A.   Oliver Wendell Holmes.   OBAL

Friendless and faint, with martyred steps and slow.   Calvary.   Edwin Arlington Robinson.   GI; MoAmPo; Son

Friendliest Thing (Two People Can Do), The.   Ervin Drake.   ReLy

Friendly Cinnamon Bun, The.   Russell Hoban.   OTCP

Friendly cow all red and white, The.   Cow, The.   Robert Louis Stevenson.   NTCP; PWR; TLR; WHSW

Friendly Game of Football, A.   Edward Dyson.   CBAP

Friendly Town #1.   Safiya Henderson-Holmes.   UnSA

Friendly Town #3.   Safiya Henderson-Holmes.   UnSA

Friends.   John Ashbery.   LCAP-2

Friends.   Thomas Curtis Clark.   PoToHe

Friends.   Helen Hunt Jackson.   PoBW

Friends.   May Muzaffar.   PoArWo, *tr. by* Tahia Abdel Nasser

Friends.   Mikhail Arkadyevich [*or* Arkad'evich] Svetlov.   TCRP, *tr. by* Daniel Weissbort

Friends.   W. B. Yeats.   NoAM

Friends, The.   Bertolt Brecht.   PoSu, *tr. by* Michael Hamburger

Friends are unhappy; their long night.   Winter Work.   Peter Fallon.   CIP-2; PBCIP

Friends Beyond.   Thomas Hardy.   EBVV; FaBoVe; GTBS-P; NOBVV; OBEV

Friends Departed.   Henry Vaughan.   *See* They Are All Gone into the World of Light!

Friends fail and Love grow cold. (LL)   Song Set by John Farmer.   *Unknown.*   CTC; NoSic

Friends in Private.   Herodas.   HePo, *tr. by* Barbara Hughes Fowler

Friends, last night I carefully watched my love.   Caring for My Lover.   Jelaluddin [*or* Jalal al-Din] Rumi.   WoPoe, *tr. by* Willis Barnstone

Friends my own age all have kids they can't wait.   Without.   Bruce Berger.   OPRER

Friends of faces unknown and a land.   Only a Curl.   Elizabeth Barrett Browning.   TreFP

Friends / our dear sister.   Goodbye Party for Miss Pushpa T. S.   Nissim Ezekiel.   OBCoV

Friends repeat: "All means are good."   Olga Fiodorovna Berggolts [*or* Bergholts].   TCRP

Friends, Romans, countrymen, lend me your ears.   William Shakespeare.   MakPoe; OxAEP-1; OxBEV   *Fr.* Julius Caesar.

Friends, there has to be a limit.   *Unknown.*   PriapPo, *tr. by* Richard W. Hooper   *Fr.* Priapus Poems, The.

Friends, when my latest bed of rest is made.   Thomas Doubleday.   CenSon

Friends who come to see you, The.   Sleep.   James Schuyler.   GLP

Friends whose names smell powdery.   Healthy Remedies.   Georges Henein.   SurPaPo, *tr. by* Mary Ann Caws

Friends—With a Difference.   Mary Elizabeth Coleridge.   VWP

Friends, / you are lucky you can talk.   Vidya.   BoWoP

Friendship.   Hartley Coleridge.   *See* To a Friend

Friendship.   Florence Converse.   PoBW

Friendship.   Dinah Maria Mulock Craik.   ITBLP; PoToHe

Friendship.   Ralph Waldo Emerson.   CAGL

Friendship.   Margaretta Faugeres.   PoBW

Friendship.   Katherine Mansfield.   PoBW

Friendship.   Cole Porter.   ReLy

Friendship.   Sadi [*or* Saadi *or* Sa'di].   AWP, *tr. by* L. Cranmer-Byng   *Fr.* Gulistan, The.

Friendship.   Shel [*or* Shelley] Silverstein.   NTCP

Friendship.   Anatoly Steiger.   TCRusP, *tr. by* Paul Schmidt

Friendship.   *Unknown.*   PoToHe

Friendship.   Ella Wheeler Wilcox.   PoToHe

Friendship.   Mary Julia Young.   CenSon

Friendship, The.   Toi Derricotte.   PBCAP

Friendship After Love.   Ella Wheeler Wilcox.   APN-2; LW

Friendship, as some sage poet sings.   On the Aphorism "L'Amitié est l'Amour sans Ailes."   Charlotte Smith.   CABP; PEW

Friendship Between Ephelia and Ardelia.   Anne Finch, Countess of Winchilsea.   BWW; ECWP; NALW; NoP-4; PoBW

Friendship for a Woman of Grace.   J. Greshoff.   TuT, *tr. by* Dennis O'Driscoll

Friendship! I hate thy name—my rankled heart. Friendship. Margaretta Faugeres. PoBW

Friendship in Emblem[e], or the Seal[e], to my dearest Lucasia. Katherine Philips. CABP; EMWP; PBRV

Friendship in Perfection. Andrew Michael Ramsay. NOEC

Friendship needs no studied phrases. Friendship. *Unknown.* PoToHe

Friendship's folly, to utter. Miscarriage. Joseph P. Clancy. AngWePo

Friendship's Mystery[s], to my dearest Lucasia. Katherine Philips. BASC; NAEL-7v1; PBRV; PEW

Frigate Jones, the Pussyfooter. Kenneth Burke. OBAL

Frightened / by the sound of my own voice. Lawrence Ferlinghetti. TAP

Frightened Flier Goes North, The. Judith Kazantzis. BrRo

Frightened Man, The. Louise Bogan. FaBoWP

Frightful Release, A. Gertrude Stein. TCAPo *Fr.* Tender Buttons.

Frigidity the hesitant. Cold, The. Yvor Winters. APT-2

Fringe-Area Reception. Halvard Johnson. MiVo

Fringed Gentians. Abbie Huston Evans. APT-1

Frisbees. Giulia Niccolai.
"Careful that these *Frisbees.*" ItPo, *tr. by* Gayle Ridinger

Frisbees '88. Giulia Niccolai.
"What's that? the boy asks his mother, pointing to the flag." ItPo, *tr. by* Gayle Ridinger

Frisbees on Light. Giulia Niccolai. CItWP, *tr. by* Cinzia Sartini Blum and Lara Trubowitz

Frisco-City. Blaise Cendrars. BLT, *tr. by* Monique Chefdor

Frisky Lamb, A. Christina Georgina Rossetti. WHSW

Frithiof's Saga. Esaias Tegnér. AWP, *tr. by* Henry Wadsworth Longfellow

Fritz. Gerald Stern. MiVo

Frivolous Cake, The. Mervyn Laurence Peake. PeLV

Fro Niz - nil - imbo. (LL) Metamorphosis. Wallace Stevens. InPK-6; VGW

Frog. Issa. WoPoe, *tr. by* Conrad Totman

Frog. Marlene Mountain. HA

Frog, A. Friedrich von Logau. GePo, *tr. by* George C. Schoolfield

Frog, The. Joseph Hilaire Pierre Belloc. ChAP; NOxBChV; NTCP

Frog, The. Francis Ponge. BLT, *tr. by* Beth Archer

Frog, The. *Unknown.* NBLV; NOxBChV; NTCP; RB

Frog and I. Lucien Stryk. IllVoic *Fr.* Issa: A Suite of Haiku.

Frog Autumn. Sylvia Plath. OxBSP

Frog He Would a-Wooing Go, A. Mother Goose. OxNR

Frog in the Swimming Pool, The. Debora Greger. NoP-4

Frog Prince, The. Stevie Smith. HAP

Frog's Fate, A. Christina Georgina Rossetti. NOBVV

Frog Song. Hildegarde Flanner. APT-2

Frogologist, The. Brian Patten. OTCP

Frogs. Buddhadeva Bose. OMIP, *tr. by* Buddhadeva Bose

Frogs and snakes and a dead cat or two. Our Spring Needs Shoveling. Haniel Long. APT-1

Frogs time out of mind, The. Aesop's Fable of the Frogs. Jean de La Fontaine. OBVE, *tr. by* John Hookham Frere

Frolic. "Æ" MoBrPo

Frolic architecture of the snow, The. (LL) Snow-Storm [*or* Snowstorm], The. Ralph Waldo Emerson. APN-1; ITBLP; NAAL-2v1; NAAL-3; NCAP; NOBA; NoP-4; OxBA; PoE; PoPoPo; TAP; TCAPo; TFi; TreFP; UnPo

Frolic[k], A. Robert Herrick. FaBoEE

From 115. Ezra Pound. APSN; FaBoMo *Fr.* Cantos.

From a battle lost come riders three. Three, The. Nikolaus Lenau. AuPH, *tr. by* Winthrop H. Root

From a Boat at Coniston. Norman Nicholson. NLP

From a branch / The bird called. Bird, The. Max Michelson. TrJP

From a Childhood. Rainer Maria Rilke. TrJP
(Darkening was like riches in the room, The.) TTTS, *tr. by* M. D. Herter Norton
(Darkness in the room was like enormous riches, The.) RaBo, *tr. by* Robert Bly

From a Conversation During Divorce. Carol Rumens. EmeKit

From a Correct Address in a Suburb of a Major City. Helen Sorrells. PAI; WPE

From a crumpled wartime diary. Aleksandr Trifonovich Tvardovsky [*or* Tvardovskii]. TCRP

From a determinable horizon. Axiom. Walter Conrad Arensberg. APT-1

From a distance—twilight's distance, which is measureless. Night Fishing. Caroline Price. Prnts

From a donkey, excuse me, one lesson is given. Fanny Howe. FTOS

From a Dream. Ch'in Kuan. CrYelRi, *tr. by* Sam Hamill

From a friend's friend I taste friendship. Dirge. Stevie Smith. HarvBoo; NPeEn

From A Funeral Song, Upon the Decease of Annes His Mother. Nicholas

Grimald. NoP-4 *Fr.* Funeral Song, Upon the Decease of Annes His Mother, A.

From a German War Primer. Bertolt Brecht. AF

From a hummock in the Malookas. Hummock in the Malookas, A. Matthew Rohrer. AmPoNex

From a junto that labour for absolute power. Libera nos, Domine—Deliver Us, O Lord. Philip Freneau. OxBEV

From a Late Diary. Gabriel Preil. FIT, *tr. by* Robert Friend

From a Lavatory Wall. *Unknown.* FaBoEE

From a Letter: About Snow. Toi Derricotte. SpirFl

From a letter thrown on the table a line comes. Lines of the Hand, The. Julio Cortázar. TCLAP, *tr. by* Paul Blackburn and Pal Blackburn

From a libation cup. Shang Cup. Louis Zukofsky. APT-2

From a little basket on the kitchen shelf I was about to. Concerning a Girl. Shuntaro Tanikawa. VCWP, *tr. by* Harold Wright

From a little town quickly passed over. (LL) Twirling. Jane Flanders. ItWoWo; PBCAP

From a London Bookshop. *Unknown.* NBLV

From a lonesome old house, near Holbeach Wash-way. From the Country, to Mr. Rowe in Town. Susanna Centlivre. ECWP

From a long way off I can see the cross. Blueprints. Madeline DeFrees. ExTi

From a Museum Man's Album. John Hewitt. OxBTC

From a new peony. Sonnet for Minimalists. Mona Van Duyn. FFC; WeW-3

From a passing train at twilight. Renewal Notice. Bruce Dawe. BMAP

From a Photograph. George Oppen. FTOS

From a place I came. Kathleen Jessie Raine. OxBTC *Fr.* Two Invocations of Death.

From a pot of wine among the flowers. Drinking Alone with the Moon. Witter Bynner. APT-1

From a precipitous cliff, a withered pine hangs upside down. Tune: "Intoxication in the East Wind" Autumn Scenery. Lu Chih. SuSp, *tr. by* Sherwin S. S. Fu

From a Railway Carriage. Robert Louis Stevenson. NePenScot

From a red tile roof. Richard Wright. APT-2

From a Republican Grave: Daniel Henry Deniehy, 1828–1865. Philip Mead. NOBAu

From a Revolutionary to J. L. Borges. Roque Dalton. TCLAP, *tr. by* Julie Schumacher

From a rived tree, that stands beside the grave. Sonnet. Anna Seward. ECWP

From a ruler that's a curse. Litany. Charles Cotton. OBSV

From a Sick Poetesse to Mrs St George on Her Feeding the Swans. *Poets of the Tixall Circle.* EMWP

From a Spanish Cloister. Gilbert Keith Chesterton. UV

From a Survivor. Adrienne Rich. LoL; NALW; PAI

From a Talk. Yevgeny Aleksandrovich Yevtushenko [*or* Evtushenko]. CLPP, *tr. by* Anselm Hollo

From a thousand Chinese dinners, one cookie. Robert Mezey. RaBo *Fr.* Thousand Chinese Dinners, A.

From a thousand hills, bird flights have vanished. River Snow. Liu Tsung-yüan. CoBCP, *tr. by* Burton Watson

From a thread in space, endless and unbroken. Without unravelling. Jacques Dupin. VCWP *Fr.* Songs of Rescue.

From a Train Window. Edna St. Vincent Millay. GM

From a Vacant House. Mark Wunderlich. NeAmPo

From a Very Little Sphinx. Edna St. Vincent Millay. NOxBChV; OBAL

From a well you mount up, dear child. Your head a pyre. Whisper in the Dark. Sándor Weöres. IQMS, *tr. by* Edwin Morgan

From a Window in Princes Street. William Ernest Henley. EBVV

From a woman, the gods turned me into stone. Niobe. *Unknown.* GrAn, *tr. by* Peter Jay

From a Woman to a Greedy Lover. Norman Cameron. FaBoEE *Fr.* Three Love Poems.

From a world more full of weeping than he can understand. (LL) Stolen Child, The. W. B. Yeats. NAEL-5v2; NAEL-6v2; NoP-4

From a Young Woman to an Old Officer Who Courted Her. Elizabeth Frances Amherst. ECWP

From Abertillery and Aberdare. Angry Summer, The. Idris Davies. AngWePo

From above it's a dickie or a verdant tie skewed sideways, banana or schlong. Florida Anasazi, The. Campbell McGrath. NAPBL

From across the stream, on the side of the opposite hill. Not Seeing Is Believing. Paul Petrie. TAP

From afar I beheld him. What Am I Chasing! Hala Mohammad. PoArWo, *tr. by* Cornelia Al-Khaled

From Age to Age They Gather. Frederick Lucian Hosmer. AH

From all my lame defeats and oh! much more. Apologist's Evening Prayer, The. Clive Staples Lewis. SacPr; TrCP

From All Peoples. Nathan [or Natan] Alterman.
"When our children cried in the shadow of the gallows." TrJP

From All Sides Laughter Shall Strike Them. Amir Gilbo'a. MHP, tr. by Ruth Finer Mintz

From all the circle of the hills. (LL) Tennyson. EBVV; FHYEP; GTBS-P; OBGa; PeECV; SCV Fr. In Memoriam A. H. H.

From all the rooms, my father suddenly. Death of My Father, The. Yehuda Amichai [or Amikhai]. FIT, tr. by Robert Friend

From all these trees. Basho. EH; SoOfWa, tr. by Sam Hamill

From Altitude, the Diamonds. Richard Hugo. MoASP

From America. James M. Whitfield. APN-2; BPo

From America comes the little huming-bird. Vermont Apollinaire. William Corbett. PmAP

From among ten thousand trees autumn wind rises. Sent in Lieu of a Letter to Shih-wu, Lan-ku, and Other Friends. Huang Tsun-hsien. SuSp, tr. by An-yan Tang

From among the miserable soldiers. (LL) George Oppen. APSN; NNaP Fr. Some San Francisco Poems.

From an Afternoon Caller. Sister Mary Madeleva. CRP

From an airtight office window. Downpour. Daisy Zamora. CLPP, tr. by Barbara Paschke

From an Album. Genrik Veniaminovich Sapgir. ItGoST, tr. by J. Kates

From an Apocryphal Gospel. Jorge Luis Borges. GI, tr. by Norman Thomas Di Giovanni Fr. Apocryphal Gospel, An.

From an ass to an analyst and back. Joyce Mansour. MFP, tr. by Martin Sorrell

From an Asylum; Kathy Chattle to Her Mother, Ruth Arbeiter. Anne Stevenson. BrRo

From an Old House in America. Adrienne Rich. NNaP; TRP

From an old house shaded with macrocarpas. James Keir Baxter. PeNZ Fr. Pig Island Letters.

From an overspilling jar. (LL) Mechthild von Magdeburg. EnlH; WPoS

From anger into the pit of sleep. Wife to Husband. Fleur Adcock. PeNZ

From Another Room. Gregory Corso. NeAP

From Arena. Dennis Phillips. FTOS Fr. Exile.

From Ariadne's Crown. Shooting Star, A. Edith Matilda Thomas. ChAP

From Asia, the stony Rife. Roadside Weeds. John Haines. PoCoUp

From Battle Clamour. Samuele Romanelli. TrJP, tr. by Nina Davis Salaman

From Beachy Head. Charlotte Smith. NOBRP; NoP-4 Fr. Beachy Head.

From before the beginning of the universe. (LL) Say Yes Quickly. Jelaluddin [or Jalal al-Din] Rumi. EnlH; RaBo

From behind a crag, as though round a corner. Eagle, The. "Aleksandr Iakovlevich Yashin [or Iashin]." TCRP, tr. by Daniel Weissbort

From behind he looks like a man. China. Dorianne Laux. LW

From behind me. Cor Van den Heuvel. HA

From behind the Bars. Fadwa Tuqan [or Tuquan].
From the Diary of———. WPOW, tr. by Hatem Hossaini

From Belfast to Suffolk. William Peskett. PNI

From below, the waist-thick pine. Yggdrasill. Paul Muldoon. PBCIP

From Belsen a crate of gold teeth. Riddle. William Heyen. HP; SoSe-8

From Beowulf. Unknown.
"How that glory remains in remembrance." NoP-4

From between my own teeth I come out smoking. Hungry Man's Wheel, The. César Vallejo. PFTM-1

From bill to breast a snake. Swan. Edward Lowbury. GTBS-P

From Bindle's opera house in the village. Edgar Lee Masters. APT-1 Fr. Spoon River Anthology.

From black branches. (LL) Love Song: "Sweep the house clean." William Carlos Williams. MoAmPo; SAmP

From blacked-out streets. Denise Levertov. TaR Fr. During the Eichmann Trial.

From Blenheim's clocktower a cheerful bell bangs out. Distilled Water. M. K. Joseph. PeNZ

From Blossoms. Li-Young Lee. TRP

From blossoms. Ode to the Lemon. Pablo Neruda. PoetW, tr. by Margaret Sayers Peden

From blossoms comes. From Blossoms. Li-Young Lee. TRP

From blue Loch Carron rise white and sheer. Among the Hebrides. Emily Jane Pfeiffer. ViWPN

From blue sky birds come. Like the White. Qasim Haddad. MAP, tr. by Charles Doria and Sharif Elmusa

From blue sky to green forest, bathing. Susannah Bathing. Ödön Palasovszky. IQMS, tr. by Kenneth McRobbie

From Bowling Green. Al Young. ESEAA

From breakfast on through all the day. Land of Nod, The. Robert Louis Stevenson. PWR

From breezeway or through front porch screen. Sheets, The. Timothy Steele. DiPo

From Brooklyn, over the Brooklyn Bridge, on this fine morning. Invitation to Miss Marianne Moore. Elizabeth Bishop. NALW

From Bulgaria thick, wild cannon pounding rolls. Picture Postcards. Miklós Radnóti. AF

From burweed / Such a butterfly. Issa. ZenPo, tr. by Takashi Ikemoto and Lucien Stryk

From buttered gold to. Kalamu ya Salaam. SpirFl Fr. New Orleans Haiku.

From Caelica. Fulke Greville, 1st Baron Brooke. NoP-4 Fr. Caelica.

From Calpe's rock, with loss of leg. Soldier That Has Seen Service, The. Unknown. NOEC

From Canaan Joseph shall return, whose face. Hafiz [or Hafez]. TAL Fr. Odes.

From cavities of bones. From the Cavities of Bones. Patricia Parker. BlSi

From Chekiang I Went to Hsin-an and Climbed Even-with-the-Clouds Mountain. On the Way Back There Were Many Beautiful Sights at the Inns Where I Stayed and Yet I Could Not Write One Word of Poetry. When I Got Back to the Main Road I Wrote These Four L. Hsü Wei. CoBLCP, tr. by Jonathan Chaves

From child to youth; from youth to arduous man. Heart of the Night, The. Richard Doddridge Blackmore. SacPr

From childhood's hour I have not been. "Alone." Edgar Allan Poe. APN-1; NAAL-2v1; NAAL-3

From Chin-Chu Creek, Past the Ridge, Along the Stream. Hsieh Ling-yün. ChinPo, tr. by Yip Wai-lim

From Clee to heaven the beacon burns. 1887. A. E. Housman. NIP-4; NOBVV; SCGP; UnPo

From Colony to Nation. Irving Layton. NIL-7; NOBC

From Countless Hearts. Gail Brook Burket. AH

From Creature to Ghost. Pauline Hanson. TAP

From darkness / I go onto the road / of darkness. Lady Izumi. BoWoP

From darkness where no stars shine. Observed Observer, The. Alan Gould. BMAP

From dawn to dark, and back from dark to dawn. Hedylos. GrAn

From death to life thou mightst him yet recover. (LL) Michael Drayton. AEP; AWP; BASC; BoLoP; ClHu; EnLoPo; GSo; HAP; HeIP-4; NAEL-5v1; NAEL-6v1; NAEL-7v1; NOBE; OPOU; OxBSo; SCGP; SoSe-8; Son; TFi Fr. Idea.

From deep below a world of eerie silence. Letter to My Spouse. Miklós Radnóti. IQMS, tr. by Peter Zollman

From deep in my heart. Issho. JDP, tr. by Yoel Hoffmann

From deep sleep. Nightmare. James A. Emanuel. BPo

From deepest need cry out, oh hungered heart! From Deepest Need. Quirinus Kuhlmann. GePo, tr. by George C. Schoolfield

From depth of dole, wherein my soul doth dwell. George Gascoigne. ChIV-1; SacPr Fr. De Profundis.

From depth of grief. Bible, O.T. EMWP Fr. Psalms.

From depth of sinn and from a diepe despaire. Bible, O.T. OxBEV, tr. by Sir Thomas Wyatt Fr. Psalms.

From Depths of Woe I Cry to You. Martin Luther. GePo, tr. by F. Samuel Janow

From Disaster. George Oppen. APT-2

From distant grove I hear the occasional knell of a monastery bell. Inscribed on the Painting of "Garden for Retirement:" Pavilion of Sincerity, on Rocky Mountain. Chu Yi-tsun. SuSp, tr. by Chang Yin-nan

From drear decays of age, outlive the old! (LL) December Morning. Anna Seward. CenSon; ECWP

From Drogheda all along the coast, the Irish sea. Back to Dublin. Robert Arthur Douglas Ford. MoCV

From dusk to dawn I sit under the canopy of a pine. In the Country. Ssu-k'ung Shu. SuSp, tr. by Hellmut Wilhelm

From early dusk the day was inscrutable. Bread. Mahmoud Darwish. MAP, tr. by Lena Jayyusi and Christopher Middleton

From Eastertide to Eastertide. Ballad of a Nun, A. John Davidson. MoBrPo; UV

'From Escomb, County Durham:' July 1990. John Seed. Oth

From every direction. Basho. SoOfWa, tr. by Sam Hamill

From every limb the leaves are cast. De Ramis Cadunt Folia (Love in Winter). Unknown. WoPoe, tr. by Phillip Holland

From every place you cast your wandering eyes. Anne Ingram, Viscountess Irwin. OBGa Fr. Castle Howard, the Seat of the Rt. Hon. Charles, Earl of Carlisle.

From every swimming hole, from every pool, Ophelia. (LL) Broken Doll, The. Nuala Ni Dhomhnaill. BiHa; ModIr, tr. by John Montague

From everything a little remained. Residue. Carlos Drummond de Andrade. PoetW; VCWP, tr. by Mark Strand

From Exile. Dafydd [or David] Benfras. OBWVE, tr. by Anthony Conran

From Exile to Exile. 'Abd-Allah Al-Baraduni. MAP, tr. by Sharif Elmusa and Diana Der Hovanessian

From fair Jamaica's fertile plains. Lines. "Ada" (Sarah Louisa Forten). BlSi

From fairest creatures we desire increase. William Shakespeare. CTC; HeIP-4; NAEL-6v1; NAEL-7v1 *Fr.* Sonnets.

From Fanon. Sandra Maria Esteves. PueRic

From far away, a mile or so. Bayonet Training. Vernon Scannell. FaBoWar

From Far, from Eve and Morning. A. E. Housman. HAP; MoBrPo; NoP-4

From far off I have brought medicines, she watches me because I am her son. Saitō Mokichi. WoPoe, *tr. by* Hiroaki Sato and Burton Watson *Fr.* Mother Dies.

From far she's come, and very old. Age in Youth. Trumbull Stickney. ColAP

From far the music rings, we'll listen, hear. Mozart. Eugenie Fink. AuPH, *tr. by* Lowell A. Bangerter

From Father to Son. Emyr Humphreys. AngWePo; OBWVE; TCAWP

From fealty to light. (LL) Enthusiast, The. Herman Melville. ChIV-1; NAAL-2v1; NAAL-3

From Feathers to Iron. Cecil Day Lewis.
     Now She Is like the White Tree-Rose. FaBoTw; MoBrPo

From first light we fear falling. Hotel Fire: New Orleans. Paul Ruffin. InPK-6

From flesh into phantom. Christopher Okigbo. PBMAP *Fr.* Distances (1964).

From Florrie Abraham Witness, December 1972. Jack A. Mapanje. HBAPE

From [fly] those Windings and that Shade! (LL) Anne Finch, Countess of Winchilsea. ECWP; NOSC *Fr.* Petition for an Absolute Retreat, The.

From '41 to '51. John Masefield. SacPr *Fr.* Everlasting Mercy, The.

From frozen climes, and endless tracks [*or* tracts] of snow. Winter-Piece, A. Ambrose Philips. NOEC; NPeEn

From furthest Spirit—God. (LL) Emily Dickinson. APN-2; NoP-4

From Generation to Generation. Sir Henry John Newbolt. FaBoTw

From ghoulies and ghosties. Things That Go Bump in the Night. *Unknown.* NTCP

From Gloucester Out. Edward Dorn. NOBA; PmAP; PoM

From God's side even of such a simple thing? (LL) To a Daisy. Alice Thompson Meynell. MoBrPo; SacPr; Son; VWP

From green and blue things and arguments that cannot be proven. (LL) Canal Bank Walk. Patrick Kavanagh. CIP-2; FaBoTw; MoBrPo; NoAM; NoP-4

From Green Mountain. William Reed Huntington. APN-2

From green to grey. Alexis Rotella. HA

From Greenland's Icy Mountains. Reginald Heber. SacPr

From heav'n, from heavenly [*or* heav'nly] harmony. Dryden. AWP; BASC; FHYEP; FaBoTw; GTBS-P; HAP; NAEL-6v1; NAEL-7v1; NOSC; OBEV; OxAEP-1; SCGP; TFi; TreFP; WoPoe

From Harvest to January. Charles Tennyson Turner. NOBVV

From haunt of man, from day's obtrusive glare. To the Bat. Ann Radcliffe. CenSon

From having done nothing up to now. Reality. Léon Damas. NegPo, *tr. by* Ellen Conroy Kennedy

From heaped-up mound of earth and from the heart. Poem of Jacobus Sadoletus on the Statue of Laocoon, The. Jacopo Sadoleto. GS, *tr. by* H. S. Wilkinson

From Hear to Air. Douglas Messerli. FTOS

From Heart to Heart. William Channing Gannett. AH

From Heaven Above to Earth I Come. Martin Luther. GePo

From Heaven's Gate to Hampstead Heath. Ballad of Hampstead Heath, The. James Elroy Flecker. MoBrPo

From her autumn-lotus mouth. Kamalākānta Bhaṭṭācārya. SinGod, *tr. by* Rachel Fell McDermott

From her bed's high and odoriferous roome. Homer. CTC *Fr.* Odyssey.

From her neon window. Alexis Rotella. HA

From her room in Fu-chou tonight. Moonlight Night. Tu Fu. CoBCP, *tr. by* Burton Watson

From here an empty echo penetrates to Hades. Erinna. SaLy, *tr. by* Diane Rayor

From here do I send. Medicine Songs. *Unknown.* APN-2, *tr. by* Francis La Flesche

From here it is necessary to ship all bodies east. Thomas McGrath. GifTon *Fr.* Letter to an Imaginary Friend.

From here, the quay, one looks above to mark. Harbour Bridge, The. Thomas Hardy. NoAM

From here through tunnelled gloom the track. Railway Junction, The. Walter De la Mare. OxBTC

From here to the frontiers of this world. Panther, The. *Unknown.* ASW, *tr. by* Kevin Crossley-Holland

From here to there / To Washington Square. *Unknown.* OxNR

From his brimstone bed at break of day. Devil's Thoughts, The. Samuel Taylor Coleridge. OBSV; OxBoLi; PeLV

From his brimstone bed at the break of day. Devil, The. Robert Southey. NOxBChV

From his circuits round the district. Lady Macbeth. Nikolai Nikolaevich Ushakov. TCRP, *tr. by* Daniel Weissbort

From his garden bed our Lord. Harvesting of the Roses, The. Menahem ben Jacob. TrJP

From his heavenly Father, our Fortress and Strength. (LL) Wanderer, The. *Unknown.* AnOE; NAWM-5v1, *tr. by* Charles William Kennedy and Charles W. Kennedy

From his library in Surrey. Nothing Sacred. Roger Woddis. NOBL

From his own solitude to the world unheeding. Llewelyn Wyn Griffith. OBWVE *Fr.* Barren Tree, The.

From his shoulder Hiawatha. Hiawatha's Photographing. Lewis Carroll. NOBL; PeLV

From his wanderings far to eastward. Henry Wadsworth Longfellow. NCAP *Fr.* Song of Hiawatha, The.

From holy flower to holy flower. Study of a Spider, The. John Byrne Leicester Warren, 3d Baron De Tabley. NOBVV

From Homegrown: An Asian-American Anthology of Writers. Colleen J. McElroy. LTA

From honey-dew of milking. Feeding a Child. Nuala Ni Dhomhnaill. CIP-2, *tr. by* Michael Hartnett

From inside the bird a dream hums itself out and turns. These Horses Came. Ray A. Young Bear. CDW

From inside the room. Climbing Down the Snowy Mountain. Muso Soseki. EaWin, *tr. by* W. S. Merwin

From its unknown source, a resurrection, a new spirit? (LL) Agony . . . A Resurrection, An. Assumpta Acam-Oturu. HAWP; NAfrP

From it[t] self[e] never turning [*or* turnynge]. (LL) As You Came from the Holy Land [of Walsingham]. *Unknown, sometimes at. to* Sir Walter Ralegh. EnLoPo; HAP; NPeEn; NoSic; OBEV; OxAEP-2; OxBEV; PBRV; RB; TFi

From just on puberty, I lived in funeral. Burning Want. Les A. Murray. HarvBoo

From knight, robber, and ghost-stories. (LL) United States, The. Goethe. AiP; FaBoA, *tr. by* Robert Bly

From lake-caves the tortoise-heads protrude. Fantastic Rock, The. Wu Chen. CoBLCP, *tr. by* Jonathan Chaves

From lake Tung-t'ing we travel west. On the Way to Pa-ling. Yüan Mei. CoBLCP; ColAnChi, *tr. by* Jonathan Chaves

From left to right, she leads the eye. Myth on Mediterranean Beach: Aphrodite as Logos. Robert Penn Warren. HAP

From Life to Love. Countee Cullen. ChIV-1

From Lines of Swinburne. Charles Bernstein. FTOS

From lips notched in the pinebranch bled. His Long Home. Rosanna Warren. ExTi

From Los Angeles Looking South. Eloise Klein Healy. WiU

From loud sound and still chance. Baroque Comment. Louise Bogan. APT-2

From low to high doth dissolution climb. William Wordsworth. CenSon; EBEV; HeIP-4; InPK-6; NAEL-6v2; NOBE; NoP-4; OBEV *Fr.* Ecclesiastical Sonnets.

From many a lip came sounds of praise. Letitia [*or* Laetitia] Elizabeth Landon. RWP *Fr.* Improvisatrice, The.

From marrying in haste, and repenting at leisure. New Litany, Occasioned by an Invitation to a Wedding, A. Elizabeth Thomas. ECWP

From masons laying up brick. Mason's Trick. James Hayford. InPK-6

From me far off, with others all too near. (LL) William Shakespeare. AWTN; CAGL *Fr.* Sonnets.

From me, who whilom sung the town. Ballad to Mrs. Catherine Fleming in London from Malshanger Farm in Hampshire, A. Anne Finch, Countess of Winchilsea. ECWP

From mental mists to purge a nation's eyes. George Canning. NOEC *Fr.* New Morality.

From Miss Biddy Fudge to Miss Dorothy———. Thomas Moore. PeLV *Fr.* Fudge Family in Paris, The.

From moccasins to shoes. First Grade. Phillip [*or* "Phil"] William George. VoR

From Mohawk's mouth, far westing with the sun. Joel Barlow. APN-1 *Fr.* Columbiad, The.

From Molepolole and Morogoro. Reflexions on the Seizure of the Suez, and on a Proposal to Line the Banks of That Canal with Billboard Advertisements. Howard Nemerov. NBLV

From Momentary Work, A Wrench. Jean Day. FTOS

From moonwater, from mirror mist, a slender porcelain. Gift Hour. Maria Banus. BoWoP

From morn to [*or* till] midnight, all day through. Expectans Expectavi. Charles Hamilton Sorley. FaBoCh

From morning on Rain wouldn't leave my side. Fairy Tale about Rain, A. Bella [*or* Izabella] Akhatovna Akhmadulina. TCRP, *tr. by* Albert C. Todd

From morning slumber a stir a shift a spinning motion of tossing. Maya Bejerano. DTA, *tr. by* Tsipi Keller *Fr.* Hymns of Job.

From Mustapha. Fulke Greville, 1st Baron Brooke. *See* Mustapha

From My Diary. Yaroslav [*or* Iaroslav] Vasilevich Smelyakov [*or*Smeliakov]. TCRP, *tr.* by Simon Franklin

From My Diary, 3. Vera Bulich. ARWW, *tr.* by Catriona Kelly

From My Diary, July 1914. Wilfred Owen. FaBoMo; MoBrPo

From my disease's danger, and from thee. (LL) To Doctor Empiric[k]. Ben Jonson. FaBoEE; WoPoe

From my face. And will obtain a blush. (LL) But first one must free oneself. Patrizia Cavalli. NeIt; VCWP, *tr.* by Patrizia Cavalli and Robert McCraken

From my father and mother I inherited land enough. Han-shan. ChiP

From my father my strong heart. Gifts. Ronald Stuart Thomas. NPeEn

From my favorite place in the Chung-nan Mountains. Oxhead Temple. Ssu-k'ung Shu. ColAnChi; SuSp, *tr.* by Hellmut Wilhelm

From my feet. (LL) Charles Olson. APT-2; NAAL-5; NOBA; NeAP; PmAP; PoE; PoM; VGW *Fr.* Maximus Poems, The.

From My High Love. Kenneth Patchen. MoAmPo

From my high window I can watch. Winter in Minneapolis. Richard Ryan. PBCIP

From My Hut in Miura. Muso Soseki. EaWin, *tr.* by W. S. Merwin

From My Lai the Thunder Went West. Richard Ryan. CIP-2

From my lyre within the sky. (LL) Israfel. Edgar Allan Poe. APN-1; AWP; NAAL-2v1; NAAL-3; NOBA; OxBA; PoE; TAP; TCAPo

From My Mother's Home. Leah Goldberg. FIT, *tr.* by Robert Friend

From my mother, the antique mirror. Heritage. Linda Hogan. UnSA

From my mother's sleep I fell into the State. Death of the Ball Turret Gunner, The. Randall Jarrell. ClHu; ColAP; HAP; HarvBoo; HeIP-4; InPK-6; LCAP-2; MoAmPo; NAAL-2v2; NAAL-5; NIL-7; NIP-4; NOBA; NoAM; NoP-4; OBWP; OxBA; PAI; PoE; PoPoPo; PoWW; RB; SoSe-8; TAP; TFi; UnPo; VCAP; VGW

From my neighbor's ashcan. Richard Wilbur. *See* Axe angles / from my neighbor's ashcan, An

From My Parisian Diary. Mbella Sonne Dipoko. PBMAP

From my window I can see the moonlight stroking the smooth surface of the river. Dissonance. Amy Lowell. APT-1

From my years young in dayes of youth. Epitaphium Meum. William Bradford. SCAP

From my youth up I never liked the city. I Return to the Place I Was Born. T'ao Ch'ien [*or* T'ao Yuan-ming]. OHMPC, *tr.* by Kenneth Rexroth

From narrow provinces. Moose, The. Elizabeth Bishop. DiPo; FaBoWP; NAAL-2v2; NAAL-5; NALW

From near the sea, like Whitman my great predecessor, I call. Ode: Salute to the French Negro Poets. Frank O'Hara. GLP; NNaP; NeAP; PFTM-2; PoM

From noise of scare-fires rest ye free. Bellman, The. Robert Herrick. CaPo

From non-being into being: the cloud peaks gather. Sent to a Ch'an Master. Han Wo. SuSp, *tr.* by Irving Y. Lo

From now on. Kamalākānta Bhattācārya. SinGod, *tr.* by Rachel Fell McDermott

From Now On. James Harms. AmPoNex

From now on. Issa. EH, *tr.* by Robert Hass

From now on let birds tell you of our life. Letter of the 26th June. Philippe Jaccottet. MFP, *tr.* by Martin Sorrell

From Now Until Chile. Emma Sepúlveda-Pulvirenti. TANSG, *tr.* by Shaun Griffin

From Number Nine, Penwiper Mews. Edward Gorey. OBCoV; PeLi

From Oberon, in fairy land. Robin Goodfellow. *Unknown*. FaBoCh

From Olney Hymns. William Cowper. *See* Olney Hymns

From one basin. Issa. JDP, *tr.* by Yoel Hoffmann

From one darkness. Lady Izumi. WoPoe, *tr.* by Steven D. Carter

From one of the white throats which it hid among? (LL) Vision by Sweetwater. John Crowe Ransom. FaBoMo; HarvBoo; NOBA; OxBA; RB

From one shaft at Cleator Moor. Cleator Moor. Norman Nicholson. FaBoTw

From one that's base but merely has succeeded. (LL) W. H. Auden. OxBSP; PeLV *Fr.* Shorts [1939–1947].

From one unus'd in pomp of words to raise. To My Venerable Friend, the President of the Royal Academy. Washington Allston. APN-1

From One Who Stays. Amy Lowell. BoWoP

From Orford Ness to Shingle Street. Dawn on the East Coast. Alun Lewis. OBWP

From out a book into my lap. Withered Rose, A. "Yehoash." TrJP, *tr.* by Isidore Goldstick

From out his secret altar touched [*or* toucht] with hallowed [*or* hallow'd] fire. (LL) John Milton. FaBoCh; SacPr *Fr.* On the Morning of Christ's Nativity.

From out of the waters it came with a moan. Beast in Man, The. George Clutesi. HATNAP

From out the crowd of vanity and noise. New Cantata, A. Clara Reeve. ECWP

From out the font of being, undefiled. Mathilde Blind. ViWPN *Fr.* Ascent of Man, The.

From out the heart of Summer's joy. (LL) Pomona. William Morris. NOBVV; NPeEn; OxBEV; WoPoe

From out the stormy sea unto the shore. Epitaph. Azariah di Rossi. TrJP, *tr.* by A. B. Rhine

From Pa-Ling, the sight of Ch'ang-an. Ascend the Three Mountains Toward the Evening: Looking Back at the Capital. Hsieh T'iao. ChinPo, *tr.* by Yip Wai-lim

From Pent-up Aching Rivers. Walt Whitman. APN-1; BoLoP; EroLit; NAAL-2v1; NAAL-3; NOBA *Fr.* Song of Myself.

From Persian looms the silk *he* wove. To Mr. Blanchard, the Celebrated Aeronaut in America. Philip Freneau. APN-1

From plains that reel to southward, dim. Heat. Archibald Lampman. NOBC

From plane of light to plane, wings dipping through. Evening Hawk. Robert Penn Warren. APT-2; ColAP; NAAL-2v2; NoP-4; OWoS; VCAP

From Plane to Plane. Robert Frost. MoAmPo

From Poetical Sketches. William Blake. *See* To the Muses

From point A a wind is blowing to point B. After the Broken Arm. Ron Padgett. CoAmPo; SPE

From prehistoric distance, beyond clocks. Street Fight. Harold Monro. FaBoTw

From Prison. Todros ben Judah Abulafia. TOF, *tr.* by David Goldstein

From Psyche. Mary Tighe. NoP-4 *Fr.* Psyche.

From purple rhetoric of evening skies. (LL) Cecil Day Lewis. FaBoTw; MoBrPo *Fr.* Magnetic Mountain, The.

From red to green all the yellow dies away. Windows. Guillaume Apollinaire. CuPo

From relief to relief, the white lines, the white paper. Amelia Rosselli. ItPo, *tr.* by Gayle Ridinger

From Rich Uneasy America to My Friend Christopher Logue. Adrian Mitchell. SeSe

From rivers, and from the earth itself. James Purdy. CAGL

From Rooftops, Kenji Takezo Throws Himself. Rick Noguchi. NeAmPo

From Room to Room. Jane Kenyon. LoL

From Rosary. Barbara Tran. PuP-23

From rude darkness the heroes rose. Passing Chao-ling Again. Tu Fu. CoBCP, *tr.* by Burton Watson

From San Diego. Chryss Yost. GeoHom

From Sand Creek. Simon J. Ortiz.
"At the Salvation Army." NAAL-5

From Sand River to Ts'ai Rock. Yang Chi.
"After my illness, so hard to be a traveler." CoBLCP

From Sappho to myself, consider the fate of women. Carolyn Kizer. VCAP *Fr.* Pro Femina.

From say, the sea, a purity of space. (LL) Metonymy as an Approach to a Real World. William Bronk. APSN; VGW

From sea to shining sea! (LL) America the Beautiful. Katharine Lee Bates. APN-2; FaBoA; HHAm; TAP

From Sex, This Sea. Douglas G. Jones. NOBC

From shores of Senegal, from Lake Omandaba. O My Swallows! Ernst Toller. TrJP, *tr.* by Ashley Dukes

From side to side the sufferer tossed. Message, The. Mathilde Blind. ViWPN

From six o'clock I traversed to and fro. Verses to Miss———. J. Wilde. NOEC

From 66 to 70 A.D. Rome and Palestine tore. Wars of Imperialism. John Foulcher. NOBAu

From slavery then your rising realms to save. Joel Barlow. TCAPo *Fr.* Columbiad, The.

From snow that melted only yesterday. (LL) Spring Pools. Robert Frost. APT-1; ColAP; HarvBoo; NoAM; OxBA

From *So* Mountain. *Vietnamese Oral Tradition.* CaDao, *tr.* by John Balaban

From some unsought somewhere. Pain, The. John Graham-Pole. BloBone

From some void. Saturday Morning, A. Manuel A. Viray. ReBoTo

From somewhere over the houses, through the silence. Lovers. Witter Bynner. APT-1

From "Songs of a Wanderer." Aleksander Wat. BLT

From Sorrow Sorrow Yet Is Born. Tennyson. OxBSP

From Soul to Soul. Árpád Tóth. IQMS, *tr.* by Watson Kirkconnell

From *Spoke / Aug 19.* Hannah Weiner. FTOS

From squandering, the day at length grew weary. Autumn Fullness. Ernst Goll. AuPH, *tr.* by Lowell A. Bangerter

From stainless steel basins of water. Operation, The. W. D. Snodgrass. InPK-6; TAP

From Stanzas in Meditation. Gertrude Stein. NoP-4 *Fr.* Stanzas in Meditation.

From Stirling Castle we had seen. Yarrow Unvisited [1803]. William Wordsworth. GTBS-P; PoRA

From Stone to Steel. Edwin John Pratt. NoP-4

From sultry Mobile's gulf-indented shore. Joel Barlow. APN-1 *Fr.* Columbiad, The.

From Sunset to Star Rise. Christina Georgina Rossetti. VWP

From Superstition. Boris Leonidovich Pasternak. TCRP, *tr. by* Yakov Hornstein

From Susquehanna's farthest springs. Indian Student; or, Force of Nature, The. Philip Freneau. OxBA

From sweet weeping to a painful smile. Michelangelo Buonarroti. CAGL, *tr. by* James M. Saslow

From tape 2 "Kitch's Last Meal." Interior Scroll. Carolee Schneemann. PFTM-2

From 10. (LL) All Shook Up. Dan Sicoli. AllShUp; SwNoth

From that blest bed the hero came. Andrew Marvell. OBGa *Fr.* Upon Appleton House [To My Lord Fairfax].

From that dire era, bane to Sarum's pride. On Bishop Burnet's Being Set on Fire in His Closet. Thomas Parnell. ECEV

From that far land to him? (LL) Indian Names. Lydia Huntley Sigourney. APN-1; ColAP; SWaP

From that first flash when awful Love took flame. Sonnet 4. Louise Labé. BoWoP, *tr. by* Willis Barnstone

From that high apple-tree, my love. Apple Tree, The. James Keir Baxter. OxBC

From that last acre on oblivion's heap. Louis Untermeyer. MoAmPo *Fr.* Mother Goose Up-to-Date.

From that prominent bar in Secaucus, N.J. (LL) In a Prominent Bar in Secaucus [One Day]. X. J. Kennedy. AiP; CoAmPo; NBLV; NIL-7; NIP-4; OBAL; TRP

From that they found most lovely, most abhorred. Beginning. Alden Nowlan. NOBC

From that woman. Issa. SoOfWa, *tr. by* Sam Hamill

From the Admonitions of St. Theresa of Avila. István Vas. IQMS, *tr. by* George Szirtes

From the Anglo-Saxon. Henry Wadsworth Longfellow. Grave, The. TCAPo

From the Antique. Christina Georgina Rossetti. EnLoPo; OxBEV; PEW

From the Arabic: An Imitation. Shelley. OBEV

From the archaic ships the green and red. Mathilde in Normandy. Adrienne Rich. YaYoPo

From the ash-colored steel of images. Spring and the Ashura. Miyazawa Kenji. PFTM-1

From the back it looks like a porch. For Esther. Stanley Plumly. GM; LCAP-2

From the barbed body, wires. Yearbook. Milo De Angelis. NeIt, *tr. by* Lawrence Venuti

From the bathing machine came a din. Limerick. Edward Gorey. OBAL; OBCoV; PeLi

From the beginning. Fujiwara no Teika. OHMPJ

From the beginning. East Peak. Muso Soseki. EaWin, *tr. by* W. S. Merwin

From the beginning of time: just this! just this! (LL) First Days of Spring. Ryokan. EnlH; WoPoe, *tr. by* Stephen Mitchell

From the beginning, / We have been with you. Ancient Ones, The. Patricia Reis. HW

From the besieged hills. Vasco [*or* Vasko] Popa. PoSu, *tr. by* Anne Pennington *Fr.* St Sava's Spring.

From the black beach and broad expanse of sea. Thomas Parnell. ChIV-1 *Fr.* Hezekiah.

From the black forests inside my mother long ago. (LL) Of Poor B.B. Bertolt Brecht. RB; WoPoe, *tr. by* Michael Hamburger

From the black trunk I shake out. Yuba City School. Chitra Divakaruni. GeoHom; LTA; OpBo

From "The Blue Notebook" No. 12. Daniil Kharms. TCRP, *tr. by* Bradley Jordan

From the Boat. Patricia Goedicke. ExTi

From the bottomless waterhole. Archie Weller. IBA

From the bough. Issa. BLT; ZenPo, *tr. by* Takashi Ikemoto and Lucien Stryk

From the boy's identification. Myself, Rousseau, a Few Others. William Meredith. YaYoPo

From the breath of these marble fish. From Their Eyes Adorned With Vitreous Sands. Coral Bracho. TANSG, *tr. by* Celeste Kostopulos-Cooperman

From the Bridge. Claribel Alegría. AF

From the bright realms, and happy fields above. To Cleone. Elizabeth Singer Rowe. PoBW

From the bright stars, or from the viewless air. To a Departed Spirit. Felicia Dorothea Hemans. RWP

From the bus I see graffiti. Kevin of the N.E. Crew. Elizabeth Alexander. FFC

From the Canton of Expectation. Seamus Heaney. CIP-2; ModIr

From the Cavities of Bones. Patricia Parker. BlSi

From the ceiling near the roof. Engraving of Blake, An. Mary Kinzie. MakPoe

From the Childhood of Jesus. Robert Pinsky. EmeKit; HarvBoo

From the Chinese. Michael Smith. CIP-2; PBCIP

From the cliff-top it appeared a place of defeat. Cave, The. Arthur Rex Dugard Fairburn. PeNZ

From the cold hands of guards. Letters Come to Prison. Shahid. GLP

From the colour the nature. Ezra Pound. APSN; APT-1; VGW *Fr.* Cantos.

From the conception the increase. Cosmogony. *Unknown.* WoPoe, *tr. by* Richard Taylor

From the cool electric gaze of a Hollywood enigma. California. Paul Hoover. BAP-97

From the Country, to Mr. Rowe in Town. Susanna Centlivre. ECWP

From The Cradle to the Graave, or, through working and sweating, suffering and hardship, even through prayyer into damnation. Adolf Wolfli. "And now: And now: here begins Our Voyage, hunters and naturalists of indefatigable enthusiasm." PFTM-1

From the crypt of the church of St. Giles. Limerick. *Unknown.* PeLi

From the dark mood's control. Recovery, The. Edmund Charles Blunden. MoBrPo

From the Dark Tower. Countee Cullen. APT-2; BPo; ColAP; MakPoe; NAAL-2v2; Son

(We shall not always plant what others reap.) NAAAL

From the dark woods that breathe of fallen showers. Zebras, The. Roy Campbell. MoBrPo; OxBSo

From the day of my coming hither. Tsugen Jakurei. JDP, *tr. by* Yoel Hoffmann

From the day you retired to this home of three paths. Retreat of Liu Kuo-pao, The. Chang Yü. CoBLCP, *tr. by* Jonathan Chaves

From the deep shadow of the still fir-groves. Chamouni at Sunrise. Frederike Brün. SacPr, *tr. by* Timothy Dwight

From the depth of the dreamy decline of the dawn through a notable nimbus of nebulous moonshine. Algernon Charles Swinburne. PeVV *Fr.* Heptalogia, The.

From the desert I come to thee. Bedouin Song. Bayard Taylor. APN-2; TCAPo

From the Diary of————. Fadwa Tuqan [*or* Tuquan]. WPOW, *tr. by* Hatem Hossaini *Fr.* From behind the Bars.

From the Domain of Arnheim. Edwin Morgan. EmeKit

From the dress-box's plashing tis. Catch, The. Richard Wilbur. DiPo; WeW-3

From the dry, rattle-like dahlias. Forgive Me! Andrey [*or* Andrei] Andreievich Voznesensky [*or* Voznesenskii]. RusPo, *tr. by* Robert Arthur Douglas Ford

From the dull confines of the drooping West. His Return to London. Robert Herrick. BASC; BeJo; CaPo; NAEL-5v1; NAEL-6v1; NAEL-7v1

From the dust of my bosom! (LL) Edgar Lee Masters. CBCWP; HAP; MoAmPo; NOBA; NoAM; OxBA; PAI; TFi *Fr.* Spoon River Anthology.

From the earliest poets, the fashion stands. Satire 5. Persius. RomPo, *tr. by* Richard Emil Braun

From the elephant paddock one day. Limerick. Frank Richards. PeLi

From the end of the nose. Issa. EH, *tr. by* Robert Hass

From the explosion to the iron split. Pablo Neruda. GifTon, *tr. by* James Nolan

From the eyes endlessly falls. Diamond of Character, The. Kabita Sinha. OMIP, *tr. by* Swapna Mitra

From the fair head, for ever, and for ever! (LL) Pope. EBNV; OBSV; OxBoLi *Fr.* Rape of the Lock, The; an Heroi-Comical Poem.

From the false brand of incapacity. (LL) To Almystrea, on Her Divine Works. Elizabeth Thomas. ECWP; EMWP

From the Field. Lenard D. Moore. GT

From the field's plane tree. Diodorus Zonas. GrAn

From the fires of Estrées. (LL) Fly, The. Miroslav Holub. NPeEn; PoSu; PoetW; RB, *tr. by* Ian Milner and George Theiner

From the first cave, the first farm, the first sage. Violence. Robert Lowell. NoAM

From the first it had been like a. Bronzeville Mother Loiters in Mississippi, A. Meanwhile, a Mississippi Mother Burns Bacon. Gwendolyn Brooks. ESEAA; IllVoic

From the first shock of leaves their alliance. Park Poem. Paul Blackburn. PmAP

From the first thou wert; in the end thou art. (LL) Algernon Charles Swinburne. NAEL-5v2; NAEL-6v2 *Fr.* Triumph of Time, The.

From the Flats. Sidney Lanier. APN-2; NOBA; NoP-4; OxBA

From the flower vendor I bought. Tune: "Magnolia Flowers." Jiaosheng Wang. ColAnChi

From the forests and highlands. Hymn of Pan. Shelley. FaBoCh; OBEV

From the frantic weather into his creaking tomb. His Necessary Darkness. Nancy Sullivan. TAP

From the French. Charles North. FTOS

From the Frontier of Writing. Seamus Heaney. CABP; ModIr; PoPoPo; PoetW

From the Garden. Anne Sexton. LW

From the Garden of the Women Once Fallen. Lorna Goodison. VCWP

From the geyser ventilators. Business Girls. Sir John Betjeman. UV

From the grasp of Pharaoh. Kahlil Gibran. GraLe, *tr. by* Suheil B. Bushrui *Fr.* Khalil the Heretic.

From the Great Buddha's. Issa. SoOfWa, *tr. by* Sam Hamill

From the great trees the locusts cry. In August. Hamlin Garland. APN-2

From the Greek. Ptolemy. GrAn, *tr. by* Robert Bridges

From the Greek Anthology. Crinagoras. PGA, *tr. by* Kenneth Rexroth

From the Green Book of Yfan. Rolfe Humphries. APT-2

From the grey fires of South-east Asia. (LL) Newscast, The. Ian Hamilton. FaBoWar; NPeEn

From the Grove Press. Anthony Hecht. OBAL; OBCoV

From the hag[g] and hungry [*or* hungrie] goblin. Tom o' Bedlam's Song. *Unknown.* BASC; EBEV; FaBoCh; NPeEn; NoP-4; OxBoLi; PoRA; TFi

From the half / of the sky. Approach of the Storm, The. *Chippewa Oral Tradition.* NAAL-5; OBVE; TTTS, *tr. by* Frances Densmore

From the Hazel Bough. Earle Birney. HeIP-4; NIP-4

From the Healing Dark. Alma Villanueva. HW

From the heart of a flower. Leave It to Me Blues. Joel Oppenheimer. VGW

From the heart of the earth. Wind of Liberty. Amélia Veiga. HAWP, *tr. by* Julia Kirst

From the hector of France to the cully of Britain. (LL) Satire on Charles II, A. John Wilmot, 2d Earl of Rochester. NOSC; PeLV

From the heel / Of a half loaf. Austerities. Charles Simic. EmeKit

From the Heights. Li Shang-yin. CrYelRi, *tr. by* Sam Hamill

From the high Alpine pass. Petronius Arbiter. MLL *Fr.* Satyricon.

From the high line spun over us, we hang on to. Confluences at San Francisco. Elton Glaser. PBCAP

From the high terrace porch I watch the dawn. On a View of Pasadena from the Hills. Yvor Winters. HarvBoo

From the Highest Camp. Thom Gunn. Son; TwCP

From the House of Yemanjá. Audre Lorde. NALW; NoAM; NoP-4

From The Hymn to Inanna. Enheduanna. WPoS

From the icy niche where men placed you. Death Sonnet I. Gabriela Mistral. BoWoP, *tr. by* David Garrisonf

Bro Duncanson. C. S. Giscombe. GT

From the Indians who welcomed the pilgrims. Winter in America. Gil Scott-Heron. ISC

From the Irish. Ian Duhig. NeBl

From the Irish. James Simmons. ModIr; PBCIP; PNI

From the Island of Manhattan to the Coast of Gold. Of Thee I Sing. George Gershwin. ReLy

From the Island to Europe. Island and Europe, The. Luis Andrade Silva. NAfrP, *tr. by* Don Burness

From the jagged edges of purple clouds to the west. Tu Fu. SuSp *Fr.* Ch'iang Village.

From the Joke Shop. Roy Fuller. OxBC

From the land of refuge. Week-Seek. Jim Tollerud. VoR

From the local office, orders flying thicker than comb's teeth. Confiscating Salt. Wang An-shih. CoBCP; ColAnChi, *tr. by* Burton Watson

From the loutishness of learning. (LL) Gnome. Samuel Beckett. BIrV; OxBSP

From the Meadow. Peter Everwine. GeoHom

From the meadows of bliss even the angel goes. Fredensborg. Friedrich Gottlieb Klopstock. GePo, *tr. by* George C. Schoolfield

From the mind. Chiyojo [*or* Chiyo *or* Chiyo-Ni *or* Kaga no Chiyo *or* Fukuda Chiyo-Ni]. WPoS

From the Moment I Picked Up Your Book. Ann Sansom. MFPA

From the Monkey House and Other Cages: Monkey II. Irena Klepfisz. GLP

From the Most Distant Time. Emperor Wu of Han [*or* Wu Ti *or* Ou-ty *or* Liu Ch'e *or* Liu Ch'u]. OHMPC, *tr. by* Kenneth Rexroth

From the mountain's end, sight of coming smoke. Wu Yun. ChinPo, *tr. by* Yip Wai-lim

From the mountains we come. Warrior Nation Trilogy. Lance Henson. VoR

From the Nativity. Adoration of the Kings, The. William Carlos Williams. ChrPo

From the North Saskatchewan. Eli W. Mandel. NOBC

From the Novissimi. Giulia Niccolai. PFTM-2, *tr. by* Paul Vangelisti

From the Nursery. Jane Kenyon. LoL *Fr.* Having It Out With Melancholy.

From the old settlements only the writings. Elegy. Slavko Mihalic. PoSu, *tr. by* Charles Simic

From the old slave shack I chose my lady. Trellie. Lance Jeffers. NBV

From the ominous petulance of the sea. (LL) Severn Bore. Catherine Fisher. AngWePo; TCAWP

From the other world. (LL) Milkweed. James Wright (1927–80). ColAP; LCAP-2; NOBA; RaBo

From the Outland. Peter Davison. UrbNat

From the Outside. Mafika Pascal Gwala. NAfrP

From the Painting "Back from Market" by Chardin. Eavan Boland. PBCIP

From the pier, at dusk, the dim. Buried Graves, The. Brad Leithauser. NoP-4

From the piling's kelp I drew. After You Left. Heather McHugh. BodElec

From the pole of the flower vendor. Tune: "Magnolia Blossoms, Abbreviated." Li Ch'ing-chao. SuSp, *tr. by* Eugene Eoyang

From the Porch. John Koethe. MakPoe

From the porch; from the hayrick where her prickled. Mood Indigo. William Matthews. WeW-3

From the Prison House. Adrienne Rich. NNap

From the private ease of Mother's womb. Thom Gunn. AmFaPo; RB *Fr.* Three Songs.

From the Provençal of William of Poitiers. William of Aquitaine. MLL, *tr. by* Helen Waddell

From the Provinces. Ben Scammell. NLP

From the Rain Forest. Desiré Flynn. BrRo

From the ravine pours silent angry darkness. Fadwa Tuqan [*or* Tuquan]. WPOW, *tr. by* Hatem Hossaini *Fr.* From behind the Bars.

From the Raw. Alejandrino Hufana. ReBoTo

From the Republic of Conscience. Seamus Heaney. BodElec

From the river bank she saw the fields. Heifer, The. Andrew Crozier. Oth

From the riverbank / She hails a boat. Tune: "River Messages." Wen T'ing-yün. SuSp, *tr. by* William R. Schultz

From the rocky-bound Atlantic to the south Pacific shore. Wabash Cannonball, The. Delmore Brothers. GM

From the ruins of that place. (LL) Voice and Address. Michael Palmer. FTOS; PmAP

From the scaffold. Last Platform, The. Yury [*or* Iurii] Timofeievich Galanskov. TCRusP, *tr. by* Olive Dehn

From the Seashore. Anna Petrovna Bunina. NAWM-7v2, *tr. by* Pamela Perkins

From the seven small windows of my room. For the Field. Robyn Selman. TaR

From the shiny iron stove. Easy Living. Michael S. Weaver. SpirFl

From the slopes of the mountain. Clear Bright. Li Ch'ing-chao. BoWoP, *tr. by* Kenneth Rexroth

From the small life that loves with tooth and nail. Coventry Patmore. FaBoEE

From the sombre clouds fell slow. Snow Song. Henrietta Cordelia Ray. CBWP-3

From the soul of a man who was homeless. Peace at the Goal. Ella Wheeler Wilcox. PWR

From the south they came, Birds of War. From the South: 2. *Unknown.* TCAPo, *tr. by* William Ellery Channing

From the south they come. From the South. *Unknown.* TCAPo, *tr. by* William Ellery Channing

From the south they come. War Songs. *Unknown.* APN-2, *tr. by* Henry Rowe Schoolcraft

From the sphere of our sorrow? (LL) To————: "One word is too often profaned." Shelley. BoLoP; GTBS-P; NOBE; OBEV; OxAEP-2; TFi

From the Spotted Night. Ray A. Young Bear. HATNAP
(In the blizzard / while chopping wood.) AF

From the spreading sepsis that was once my balls. (LL) Basket Case. Basil T. Paquet. CDa; FaBoWar

From the start, each living thing's. Sergey [*or* Sergei] Aleksandrovich Yesenin [*or* Essenin]. TCRP

From the stately violence of the State. Broken Mirror, The. Bob Perelman. FTOS

From the Suburbs. Louise Glück. FaBoWP; NALW *Fr.* Dedication to Hunger.

From the sun. (LL) Easter Morning. A. R. Ammons. HCAP; NAAL-2v2; NAAL-5; NoAM; PoetW

From the Sun Itself. Roberta Hill Whiteman. HATNAP

From the sustaining air. Larry Eigner. PoM

From the tall pavilion the guests have all departed. Fallen Flowers. Li Shang-yin. SuSp, *tr. by* James J. Y. Liu

From the tawny light. Everything That Acts Is Actual. Denise Levertov. NoAM

From the Telephone. Florence Ripley Mastin. LW

From the temple, deep in its tender bamboos. On Parting with the Buddhist Pilgrim Ling-Ch'ê. Liu Ch'ang-ch'ing. WoPoe, *tr. by* Witter Bynner

From the Theater of Wine. Cyrus Cassells. GifTon

From the thin slats of the Venetian blinds. Underwood. Howard Moss. TwCP

From the Threshold to the Sky. Muhammad Al-Maghut. MAP, *tr. by* John Heath-Stubbs and May Jayyusi

From the Tibetan. John Hewitt. PNI

From the time of the womb. Dīnrām. SinGod, *tr. by* Rachel Fell McDermott

From the time you came into my house. Sad Remembrance. Mei Yao Ch'en. CoBCP; ColAnChi, *tr. by* Burton Watson

From the top here. X L E B. Jack Hirschman. CLPP

From the top of Dragon Gate. Inscribed on My Ink Landscape Painting. Tao-chi. CoBLCP, *tr. by* Jonathan Chaves

From the top of this bank I am able. Daybreak. Christiania Whitehead. NeBl

From "The Torah of the Void." Rabbi Nahman [*or* Nachman] of Bratzlav. BLT, *tr. by* Zalman Schachter

From the tragic-est novels at Mudie's. Dora versus Rose. Austin Dobson. NOBL

From the train window at daybreak. At Daybreak. Adam Zagajewski. VCWP, *tr. by* Renata Gorczynski

From the Travels of Gulliver. Suniti Namjoshi. GLP

From the trucks we see. Graves Registration. Basil T. Paquet. CDa

From the union of power and money. Mad Farmer, Flying the Flag of Rough Branch, Secedes from the Union, The. Wendell Berry. PoCoUp

From the uttermost part of the earth. Bible, *O.T.* TrJP *Fr.* Isaiah.

From the very first coming down. Letter, The. W. H. Auden. FaBoTw; NoAM

From the Viking Museum. John Peck. HarvBoo

From the Wailing Wall. Enid Shomer. TaR

From the War. Aleksandr Petrovich Mezhirov. TCRP, *tr. by* Deming Brown

From the Wave. Thom Gunn. NAEL-5v2; NAEL-6v2; NoP-4

From the west. African Thunderstorm, An. James David Rubadiri. PBMAP

From the west comes Harold, with a bitter smile. Harold. David Ignatow. LTA

From the west to the fabulous east. Limerick. *Unknown.* PeLi

From the White Day to Take Me. Francisco de Quevedo y Villegas. SpanPo, *tr. by* Kate Flores

From the wilderness remote he breaks. Red-Man, The. Frank Prewett. HATNAP

From the Willow Branches. Salvatore Quasimodo. WoPoe, *tr. by* Michael Egan

From the window. Alexis Rotella. HA

From the window. Dog Days. Katherine Soniat. PoCoUp

From the Window of a Plane. Andrey [*or* Andrei] Andreievich Voznesensky [*or* Voznesenskii]. TCRusP, *tr. by* Daniel Weissbort

From the window of a train. Night Coach. Phillis Levin. RA

From the window of my grandfather's. Late Gothic. Phyllis Gotlieb. NOBC

From the Window of the Beverly Wilshire Hotel. Michael McClure. SPE

From the windows of a standing train. Standing Trains, The. Thomas McCarthy. ModIr

From the winter wind. Michael Rosen. Spl

From the woods at night. Richard Wright. APT-2

From the world submerged beneath the ground, in a maze. Man of the Stone City. Mahmoud Al-Buraikan. MAP, *tr. by* Lena Jayyusi and Naomi Shihab Nye

From Thee to Thee. Solomon ibn Gabirol. TrJP, *tr. by* Israel Abrahams

From Their Eyes Adorned With Vitreous Sands. Coral Bracho. TANSG, *tr. by* Celeste Kostopulos-Cooperman

From their journeys our dreams return. Pavel Grigoryevich Antokolsky. TCRP

From thence took first their Rise, thither at last must Flow. (LL) Hymn: To Light. Abraham Cowley. MeLP; OxAEP-1

From these bare trees. Chinese Winter. Frederick Robert Higgins. BIrV

From these high walls I look at the town below. After Collecting the Autumn Taxes. Po Chü-i. BLT; ChiP, *tr. by* Arthur Waley

From thine eyrie, the crag. Fred Emerson Brooks. VerBaPo *Fr.* Old Eagle.

From this contriving flesh-land. Existing Psychically. Andrea Zanzotto. ItPo, *tr. by* Gayle Ridinger

From this deep chasm, where quivering sunbeams play. William Wordsworth. CenSon *Fr.* River Duddon [A Series of Sonnets], The.

From this depth—I came only to draw water. Song of the Brightness of Water. Karol Wojtyla. CRP

From this high quarried ledge I see. Mountain over Aberdare, The. Alun Lewis. AngWePo; TCAWP

From this I will not swerve nor fall nor falter. Ready for Flight. Eavan Boland. OxBSo

From this lone village rises dimly a wisp of smoke. Chanting These Verses on My Way to Yodoe. Su Man-shu. SuSp, *tr. by* Wu-Chi Liu

From This Moment On. Cole Porter. ReLy

From this swaying city. Birthday Poem from Venice. Patricia Beer. OxBC

From this this father's quality. (LL) Cradle Song: "Come, little babe." Nicholas Breton. NOBE; OBEV

From this tree-finned hill. Hill Fort, Caerleon. Sam Adams. AngWePo

From this ultimate dim Thule. (LL) Dream-Land [*or* Dreamland]. Edgar Allan Poe. APN-1; NAAL-2v1; NAAL-3; NOBA; OxBA; TAP

From this, unto the last of daies. (LL) Easter Hymn. Henry Vaughan. ChIV-2; ESCV; SacPr

From those theaters, Claudia, from those feasts. Ernesto Cardenal. BLPSL, *tr. by* Rene de Costa, Rigas Kappatos and Eleni Paidoussi

From three dark places Christ came forth this day. Upon Christ's Nativity or Christmas. Rowland Watkyns. OBWVE

From three sources, / vital sources flowing in dull shades of red. Oleg Khlebnikov. TCRP *Fr.* Miracle Workers.

From thy patient, who while here. Accompanying a Gift. Lizelia Augusta Jenkins Moorer. CBWP-3

From time to time our love is like a sail. Wedding. Alice Oswald. MFPA

From today thou shalt have a (certain) time of dying. Horse Cursed by the Sun, The. *Unknown.* PeSAV, *tr. by* W. H. I. Bleek

From Tomorrow On. *Unknown.* TrJP, *tr. by* Joseph Leftwich

From tomorrow's mist-fall till Time be sped! (LL) Thomas Hardy. FaBoWar; OBWP *Fr.* Dynasts, The.

From Transylvanian peaks to far Tibet. Song about Kőrösi Csoma. Gyula Juhász. IQMS, *tr. by* Watson Kirkconnell

From Travancore to Tripoli. Ballad of the Oedipus Complex. Lawrence Durrell. OBCoV

From Trollope's Journal. Elizabeth Bishop. CBCWP

From two voices I learned some words. Out. Anderson Ferrell. Unle

From under the ground. Digging Out the Buddha Relic. Muso Soseki. EaWin, *tr. by* W. S. Merwin

From under the house. Richard Wright. APT-2

From up here in the crow's nest. Jesus Dies. Anne Sexton. PFTM-2; RACG

From up here, the insomniac. Distance. Mary Jo Salter. ExTi

From us, like appendicitis. Poem. Andrey [*or* Andrei] Andreievich Voznesensky [*or* Voznesenskii]. RusPo, *tr. by* Robert Arthur Douglas Ford

From V. C. (a Gentleman of Verona). Gavin Ewart. OxBC

From Venice Was That Afternoon. Jean Garrigue. NOBA

From Virgil. George Oppen. NNaP *Fr.* Five Poems about Poetry.

From Water-Tower Hill to the brick prison. Point Shirley. Sylvia Plath. NIL-7; NIP-4

From what I've been hearing. Letter. Keith Gilyard. SpirFl

From what proud star I know not, but I found. Giant Puffball, The. Edmund Charles Blunden. FaBoTw

From Whence Doth This Union Arise? Thomas Baldwin. AH

From whence no paths return. Other World, The. Dmitry [*or* Dmitrii] Vasil'evich Bobyshev. ItGoST, *tr. by* Michael Van Walleghen

From where dark clouds of curling smoke arise. Susanna Blamire. ECWP; NOEC *Fr.* Stoklewath; or, The Cumbrian Village.

From where, from whom? Why ask, in torment. Gift, The. John Ormond. TCAWP

From where I am. Drinking Back. Franz Wright. LCAP-2

From where I live, from windows on four sides. Juniper. Robert Francis. VGW

From Where I Stand. Elena Georgiou. WiU

From where I stand now. 12 October. Myra Cohn Livingston. NTCP

From where I stand, Professor Pagels. Proton Decay. Robert Pack. ColAP

From where I stand the sheep stand still. Sheep. Robert Francis. LCAP-2

From where you have come. Ana Istarú. TANSG, *tr. by* Shaun Griffin and Emma Sepúlveda-Pulvirenti

From white silk a whiff of wind and frost. Hawk in a Painting, A. Tu Fu. WoPoe, *tr. by* David Lattimore

From Whitehall Stairs, whence oft with distant view. Whitehall Stairs. Aaron Hill. NOEC

From Whitsuntide to Whitsuntide. Ballad of a Bun, A. Sir Owen Seaman. UV

From whom, in happier hours, we wept to part. (LL) To the River Itchin, near Winton. William Lisle Bowles. CenSon; NAAL-6v2; OxBSo

From Wibbleton to Wobbleton is fifteen miles. *Unknown.* OxNR

From Winchester, twenty miles away! (LL) Sheridan's Ride. Thomas Buchanan Read. APN-2; CBCWP

From winter, plague, and pestilence, good Lord, deliver us! (LL) Thomas Nashe [*or* Nash]. NoSic; SCGP *Fr.* Summer's Last Will and Testament.

From witty men and mad. Poet, The. Thomas Randolph. OxBSP

From wonder to wonder. Jolanda Insana. CItWP, *tr. by* Cinzia Sartini Blum and Lara Trubowitz *Fr.* Scream of Abû Nuwàs, The.

From Wynyard's Gap the livelong day. Trampwoman's Tragedy, A. Thomas Hardy. NAEL-5v2; NAEL-6v2; OBNV

From Year to Year the Contest Grew. James M. Whitfield. CBCWP *Fr.* Poem Written for the Celebration of the Fourth Anniversary of President Lincoln's Emancipation Proclamation, A.

From yon fair hill, whose woody crest. Verses Written in the Spring. Anne Batten Cristall. RWP

From Yoshino / Mountain the autumn. Fujiwara no Masatsune. OHPJ

From you have I been absent in the spring. William Shakespeare. AWP; EBEV; NAEL-5v1; NAEL-6v1; NAEL-7v1; NOBE; NoSic; OBEV; OxAEP-1 *Fr.* Sonnets.

From you I want more than I've ever asked. Adrienne Rich. AmFaPo; LoL *Fr.* Not Somewhere Else, But Here.

From you I would love a child who could be a sword. Genesis. Alda Merini. CItWP, *tr. by* Cinzia Sartini Blum and Lara Trubowitz

From you, Ianthe, little troubles pass. Walter Savage Landor. NOBE *Fr.* Ianthe.

From you, Rose, I do not like. Rondeau for You. Mário de Andrade. TTY, *tr. by* John Nist

"From Your Depths and Kneeling." Teresa Calderón. TANSG, *tr. by* Celeste Kostopulos-Cooperman

From your eyes I thought. Silences; a Dream of Governments. Jean Valentine. LCAP-2

From your mouth, from the well of your eyes I drink, from your belly, at your flanks. On Contact Opens Its Indigo Pit. Coral Bracho. PFTM-2, *tr. by* Forrest Gander

From Zeus let us begin, him we mortals never. Aratus. HePo, *tr. by* Barbara Hughes Fowler *Fr.* Phaenomena.

From its dancers circulates among the other / dancers. Dance, The. Robert Duncan. NeAP

Front, A. Randall Jarrell. NoP-4; OBWP; OxBC; PoWW; VGW

Front Lines. Gary Snyder. PoE

Front wheel's off the mountainside, The. Either Way. Tricia Corob. Prnts

Front Window, The. Rae Desmond Jones. BMAP

Frontera / Border. Francisco Alarcon. GeoHom

Frontier. Oswald de Andrade. TCLAP, *tr. by* Flavia Vidal

Frontier, The. John Hewitt. BIrV

Frontier of Rage, The. Askia M. Toure. ISC

Frontier Songs. Lu Lun.
"Moon blackens, geese fly high." SuSp
"Select fine arrows and call for falcons." SuSp
"Woods darken, grasses startled by wind." SuSp

Frontier Songs, First Series. Tu Fu.
"If you draw a bow, draw the strongest." SuSp
"Sad, sad they leave their old village." SuSp
"Sharpen the sword in the Sobbing Waters." SuSp

Frontispiece. May Swenson. CoAP; WPE

Fronto, Father, Flaccilla, Mother, extend. Martial. RomPo, *tr. by* Peter Whigham

Frost. Stella Benson. OxBTC

Frost, a star edges with its fire. (LL) Sea Violet. "H. D." APT-1; NoP-4

Frost and snow, frost and snow. Ariel. David Campbell. CBAP

Frost at Midnight. Samuel Taylor Coleridge. CABP; EBEV; FHYEP; HAP; NAEL-5v2; NAEL-6v2; NOBE; NPeEn; NoP-4; PoE; TFi; TOF
"Frost performs its secret ministry, The." OPOU

Frost at Midnight. Mary Jo Salter. RA

Frost bit deep, The. When heavy guns were dragged. Winter, Before the War. Waclaw Potocki. WoPoe, *tr. by* Jerzy Peterkiewicz and Burns Singer

Frost covers the reeds of the marsh. Kenneth Rexroth. APSN *Fr.* Love Poems of Marichiko, The.

Frost falls only to melt in the valley. Living in Exile at Ch'ien-nan. Huang T'ing-chien. SuSp, *tr. by* Michael E. Workman

Frost has sealed. Tree in December. Melville Cane. MoAmPo

Frost in the Corn, The. Robert McAlmon. AiP

Frost is All Over, The. Pearse Hutchinson. PBCIP

Frost lies white, The. Yakamochi (Otomo no Yakamochi). OHPJ

Frost of separation / Father, child. Ome Shushiki. ZenPo, *tr. by* Takashi Ikemoto and Lucien Stryk

Frost on a summer day. Shutei. JDP, *tr. by* Yoel Hoffmann

Frost on grass. Zaishiki. JDP, *tr. by* Yoel Hoffmann

Frost on the windowpanes; the sick. Eugenio Montale. WoPoe, *tr. by* Dana Gioia *Fr.* Motets, The.

Frost performs its secret ministry, The. Samuel Taylor Coleridge. CABP; EBEV; FHYEP; HAP; NAEL-5v2; NAEL-6v2; NOBE; NPeEn; NoP-4; OPOU; PoE; TFi; TOF *Fr.* Frost at Midnight.

Frost-sad, clouds of white hair. Miscellaneous Poems Written While in Jail. Ch'ien Ch'ien-i [*or* Ch'ien Ch'ien-yi]. CoBLCP, *tr. by* Jonathan Chaves

Frost shall freeze; fire melt wood. Maxims (Exeter Book). *Unknown.* AnOE

Frost, 1654, The: To Mr. W.L. Thomas Shipman.
"Streams are fettered, and with us as rare, The." NOSC

Frost To-night. Edith Matilda Thomas. TCAPo

Frosts are Coming. László Nagy. IQMS, *tr. by* Alan Dixon

Frosty Christmas Eve, A. Noel; Christmas Eve, 1913. Robert Bridges. ChrPo; NOCV; OBCP; SacPr

Frosty Morning, A. William Cowper. NOEC *Fr.* Task, The.

Frosty Night, A. Robert Graves. MoBrPo; OxBTC

Frottage. Dean Young. BAP-97

Froude informs the Scottish youth. Hymn on Froude and Kingsley, A. William Stubbs. FaBoEE

Frowardness of the Elect in the Work of Conversion, The. Edward Taylor. SCAP *Fr.* God's Determinations [touching his Elect].

Frozen breaths, The. George Swede. HA

Frozen clouds in the dark gloomy air. Tune: "Midnight Music." Liu Yung. SuSp, *tr. by* James J. Y. Liu

Frozen Field, The. Sheenagh Pugh. TCAWP

Frozen Greenhouse, The. Thomas Hardy. OBGa

Frozen Hands. Joseph Bruchac. CDW

Frozen in the ice. Masaoka Shiki. OHMPJ

Frozen Logger, The. *Unknown.* OBAL

Frozen lost dead with hunger. August Bank Holiday. Jacques Prévert. MFP, *tr. by* Martin Sorrell

Frozen Rain. Michael Longley. PBCIP

Frozen river is drifted deep with snow, The. In the Evening I Walk by the River. Ou-yang Hsiu. OHPC, *tr. by* Kenneth Rexroth

Frozen Stiff. Sean O Riordain. ModIr, *tr. by* Patrick Crotty

Frozen Tarn. Catherine Fisher. TCAWP

Frozen Witness, The. Nick Piombino. FTOS

Frozen Zone; or, Julia Disdainful, The. Robert Herrick. CaPo (Julia Disdainful: or, The Frozen Zone.) CavPo

Fructus. Genevieve Taggard. APT-2

Fruit. Kenward Elmslie. FTOS

Fruit. Philippe Jaccottet. MFP, *tr. by* Martin Sorrell

Fruit and Flower Painter. Herman Melville. NCAP

Fruit-Gift, The. John Greenleaf Whittier. TCAPo

Fruit is ruined, but the bread is baked, The. Oven. Laura Kasischke. NAPBL

Fruit of Knowledge, The. Robert Johnstone. PNI

Fruit of Sin, or a Lamentation for England, The. Julea Palmer. EMWP

Fruit on the trees is aging fast, The. Words to a Song. Ágnes Nemes Nagy. BoWoP, *tr. by* Bruce Berlind

Fruit Plummets from the Plum Tree. *Unknown.* WoPoe, *tr. by* Tony Barnstone and Chou Ping

Fruit-vender church. Sunday. Jorge Carrera Andrade. TCLAP, *tr. by* Muna Lee

Fruit white and lustrous as a pearl. Lychee, The. Wang I. FaBoCh, *tr. by* Arthur Waley

Fruited Month, The. Zalman Schneour. MHP, *tr. by* Ruth Finer Mintz

Fruitful earth drinks up the rain. All Things Drink. Thomas Stanley. AWP

Fruits of War, The. George Gascoigne.
"Conference among ourselves we called, A." OBWP
"I set aside to tell the restless toil." FaBoWar
"Soldiers, behold, and captains, mark it well." FaBoWar

Fruits you give me are more savory than others, The. Marguerite Burnat-Provins. BoWoP

Frustrated. May Probyn. VWP

Frutta di Mare. Geoffrey Scott. OBMV

Fry says a word. Brown Rosellen. FFC

Fryar was walking in Exeter-Street, A. Crafty Miss of London; or, The Fryar Well Fitted, The. *Unknown.* OxBB

Fúar liom an adhaighsi dh'Aodh. Winter Campaign, A. Eochaidh Ó Heóghusa. CABP

Fuck European girls. Things to Do in Holland. Beau Sia. HeMarv

Fuck I want to be bound by devotion! Tortured. African Sunday. Maureen Owen. PmAP

(Fuck Ode). Michael McClure. BB *Fr.* Dark Brown.

Fucking. Frederick Seidel. BodElec

Fucking, I feel at one with the world. Christian Karlson Stead. PeNZ *Fr.* Clodian Songbook.

Fudge Family in Paris, The. Thomas Moore.
"After dreaming some hours of the land of Cockaigne." BIrV
"At length, my Lord, I have the bliss." OBSV
From Miss Biddy Fudge to Miss Dorothy———— PeLV Letter 1. NOBRP
"Oh Dick! You may talk of your writing and reading." OBCoV

Fuel. Naomi Shihab Nye. ExTi

Fugitive, The. Amin Al-Rihani.
"I ran and still I run away from Thee." GraLe

Fugitive, The. Alice Thompson Meynell. NOCV

Fugitive, The. Priscilla Jane Thompson. CBWP-2

Fugitive Pieces and Reminiscences of Lord Byron with Some Original Poetry, Letters and Recollections of Lady Caroline Lamb, ed. I. Nathan. Lady Caroline Lamb.
"Let the harp be mute for ever." RWP

William Lamb's Return from Paris, Asking Me My Wish. RWP

"You ask my wish—the boon I crave." RWP

Fugitive returned on New Year's Eve, The. Festus Conrad. Melvin B. Tolson. GT

Fugitive Slave's Apostrophe to the North Star, The. John Pierpont. APN-1

Fugitive Slaves. Gale Jackson. SpirFl

Fugitive Slaves, The. Jones Very. TAP

Fugs, The. Edward Sanders. PoM

Fugue. Shauqi Abi Shaqra. MAP, tr. by Sargon Boulus and Peter Porter

Fugue. Shara McCallum. NAPBL

Fugue. Howard Nemerov. TAP

Fugue. Stephen Perry. MiVo

Fugue for Tinhorns. Frank Loesser. ReLy

Fugue of Death. Paul Celan. OBVE; PoetW, tr. by Christopher Middleton

Fugue of Death. Paul Celan. See Death Fugue, A

Führer Bunker, The. W. D. Snodgrass.

Adolf Hitler ———1 April, 1945. BodElec

Adolf Hitler ———20 April, 1934; 1900 hours. BodElec

Eva Braun. BodElec

Hermann Fegelein. BodElec

Fuimus Fumus. Joshua Sylvester. FaBoEE

Full and True Account of a Dreaded Fire, that Lately Broke out in the Pope's Breeches, A. Unknown. EroLit

Full and True Account of a Horrid and Barbarous Robbery, A. John Byrom.

"Dear Martin Folkes, dear scholar, brother, friend." NOBL

Full autumn moon. Sodo. JDP, tr. by Yoel Hoffmann

Full autumn moon, A. Jim Handlin. HA

Full autumn moon / On the straw mat. Kikaku. ZenPo, tr. by Takashi Ikemoto and Lucien Stryk

Full be the year, abundant be the grain. Ezra Pound. OBVE

Full clear and bright the Christmas night range. Christmas Rede. Jane Barlow. SacPr

Full day. Today Tutu Is Beating the Same Burru As Me. Lebert Bethune. GT

Full days come striding with measured, The. Concerning the Awakening of My Soul. Henriëtte Roland-Holst. WPOW, tr. by Jonathan Crewe

Full deck gusts outside the playground, The. Mutability Checkers. Randolph Healy. Oth

Full doelful Tales have oft been told. Samuel Wesley. VerBaPo Fr. On Two Souldiers Killing One Another for a Groat.

Full eighteen years in sorrow I did lye. Revelation 8, March 31. Anne Wentworth. EMWP

Full face. Andrée Chedid. PoArWo, tr. by Lucy McNair

Full Fathom Five. Arthur Rex Dugard Fairburn. PeNZ

Full Fathom Five. William Shakespeare. AWP; ClHu; EBEV; FaBoCh; HAP; InPK-6; NAEL-5v1; NAEL-6v1; NoP-4; NoSic; OBEV; OxBEV; OxBSP; PoE; PoPoPo; PoRA; TFi Fr. Tempest, The.

Full fathom five thy father lies. June Mercer Langfield. SCGP

Full in her glory, she as Tirzah fair. Prophet Jeremiah and the Personification of Israel, The. Eleazar ben Kalir. TrJP, tr. by Nina Davis Salaman

Full in the hand, heavy. September Afternoon at Four O'Clock. Marge Piercy. NIP-4

Full little he thinks who has life's joy. Seafarer, The. Unknown. SacPr, tr. by Margaret Williams

Full Many a Glorious Morning. William Shakespeare. See Sonnets

Full many a glorious morning have I seen[e]. William Shakespeare. AWP; EBEV; HAP; NAEL-7v1; NIP-4; NoP-4; NoSic; OxAEP-1; PoRA; SCGP; Son; TFi; WeW-3 Fr. Sonnets.

Full Moon. Robert Graves. NOBE

Full Moon. Robert Earl Hayden. BPo; GT

Full moon. Issa. EH, tr. by Robert Hass

Full Moon. Sappho. AWP, tr. by William Ellery Leonard

Full Moon. Tu Fu. OHPC

Full Moon. Elinor Wylie. NALW; NoP-4

Full Moon and Little Frieda. Ted Hughes. HarvBoo; NPeEn; OPOU; OxBC; OxBSP

Full Moon at Tierz; before the Storming of Huesca. John Cornford. OBWP

Full moon creates a crystalpath, The. Landscape. Paul Van Ostaijen. TuT, tr. by Tony Curtis

Full moon dominates the dark, The. (LL) Full Moon. Robert Earl Hayden. BPo; GT

Full moon easterly rising, furious, The. Love Story, A. Robert Graves. FaBoTw; NAEL-5v2; NAEL-6v2

Full moon illuminated large initial for letter M. Appalachian Book of the Dead III, The. Charles Wright. AWTN

Full Moon in Malta. "Asphodel." BrRo

Full Moon in Salzburg. Lilly Sauter. AuPH, tr. by Lowell A. Bangerter

Full moon is partly hidden by cloud, The. Fable of the War, A. Howard Nemerov. OBWP

Full Moon: New Guinea. Karl Shapiro. APT-2

Full moon on the Colosseum, The. Colosseum. Harold Norse. TrJP

Full moon on the night of the seventeenth, A. Night of the Seventeenth, The. Li K'ai-hsien. CoBLCP, tr. by Jonathan Chaves

Full moon. Our Narragansett gales subside. John Berryman. CoAP; HarvBoo Fr. Dream Songs.

Full moon ringed, The. Prince Shiki. SoOfWa, tr. by Sam Hamill

Full moon rising on the waters of my heart. Evening Song. Jean Toomer. APT-2; BPo; GT

Full Moon; Santa Barbara. Sara Teasdale. OBCA

Full moon slip swim. Moon and Farmstead. Sándor Weöres. IQMS, tr. by Edwin Morgan

Full moon was rising, The. Sappho. SaLy, tr. by Diane Rayor

Full moonlit night people. Net of Moon, The. Unknown. STP, tr. by Jerome Rothenberg

Full-nelsoned in earth's arms the Crusher sleeps. Last Lines on a Wrestler. X. J. Kennedy. CRP

Full Neurological Work-up. Padgett Powell. Unle

Full of beauty, full of tension, to effort a stranger, a stripling. On the Statue of a Player at Svaika. Alexander Sergeyevich Pushkin. CAGL, tr. by Michael Green

Full of courage and promise like the geese gone away. Prince Enters the Forest, The. Henri Cole. DiPo

Full of fear in my doubt, never at rest my pain. One for Balassi. Ferenc Kölcsey. IQMS, tr. by George Sutherland Fraser

Full of great changes. Tetsugen Doko. JDP, tr. by Yoel Hoffmann

Full of her long white arms and milky skin. Equilibrists, The. John Crowe Ransom. APT-1; FuPo; HAP; NAAL-2v2; NOBA; NoAM; OxBA; TAP

Full of Life Now. Walt Whitman. APN-1

Full of mercy, full of love. Prayer for Charity, A. Jeremy Taylor. SacPr

Full of old stories that still go walking in my sleep. (LL) South of My Days. Judith Wright. FaBoWP; WPE

Full of sentiment, clever at mechanics, and we love our luxuries. (LL) Ave Caesar. Robinson Jeffers. NOBA; NoAM; OxBA; OxBSP

Full of simple sweetness and repetition. (LL) Supremes, The. Mark Jarman. GeoHom; SwNoth

Full of years and seasoned like a salt timber. Islandman. Brenda Chamberlain. AngWePo; OBWVE

Full oft doth Mat. with Topaz dine. Earning a Dinner. Matthew Prior. NBLV

Full oft of old the islands changed their name. Epitaph on an Infant. Crinagoras. AWP, tr. by John William Burgon

Full often as I rove by path or stile. Wind on the Corn. Charles Tennyson Turner. EBVV

Full Orchestra. Kenneth Slessor. OxBSo

Full Powers: Five Warning Signs. Edoardo Cacciatore.

"Blast of anniversary excitement, true." ItPo, tr. by Gayle Ridinger

First Warning Sign: Epiphany.

"Here—they've all started moving at once." ItPo, tr. by Gayle Ridinger

"Let's try another hand, let's redo the count." ItPo, tr. by Gayle Ridinger

Second Warning Sign: the Game Heats Up.

"There's nothing truer than fake fruit, let's say." ItPo, tr. by Gayle Ridinger

Third Warning Sign: An Endless Surprise.

"Where do I stand and where do you? Seems like." ItPo, tr. by Gayle Ridinger

Full September moon sheds floods of light, The. September Night, A. George Marion McClellan. TCAPo

Full stop. Let's not. Far In. Rachel Loden. PasH

Full summer and at noon; from a waste bed. Noon. "Michael Field." NOBVV

Full Tide. Paraire Henare Tomoana. PeNZ, tr. by Margaret Orbell

Full Vision. Henrietta Cordelia Ray. CBWP-3

Full Well I Know. Hartley Coleridge. Son

Full well, my gentle sir, I know. Lorenzo Da Ponte. TrJP, tr. by John Mazzinghi Fr. Il Capriccio Dramatico.

Full well, Tibaldi, did thy kindred mind. On Seeing the Picture of Æolus by Pelegrino Tibalbi, in the Institute at Bologna. Washington Allston. APN-1

Full white the Bourbon lily blows. Thistle's Grown aboon the Rose, The. Allan Cunningham. NePenScot

Full year since, I took this eager city, A. Irishman in Coventry, An. John Hewitt. BIrV; CIP-2; ModIr; PNI

Fullfillment. Eunice Tietjens. PoToHe

Fulling Cloth for Clothes. Hsieh Hui-lien. CoBCP, tr. by Burton Watson

Fulvia, our Consul bids me thank thee: why. Familiar Poem from Nisa to Fulvia of the Vale. Ann Yearsley. ECWP

Fum and Hum, the Two Birds of Royalty. Thomas Moore. OBSV

Fumbling for the live nerve. Winter. Rae Armantrout. FTOS

Fumes from all kinds, The. Coming Down Cleveland Avenue. James Tate. YaYoPo

Fun to be Fooled. Harold Arlen. ReLy

Fundamentals. Ian Duhig. NeBl

Funeral. Clarence Major. BodElec

Funeral, The. John Donne. *See* Funeral[l], The

Funeral, The. Norman Dubie. InPK-6; NoAM

Funeral, The. Donald Hall. Son

Funeral, The. "M. J." TrJP, *tr. by* A. Glanz-Leyeles

Funeral, The. Stephen Spender. MoBrPo; NoAM

Funeral, The. Sir Richard Steele.
Trim's Song: The Fair Kitchen-Maid. OxBSP

Funeral Elegy Upon that Pattern and Patron of Virtue, A. John Norton. SCAP

Funeral Eva. Koroneu. RaBo

Funeral gent led us, The. Choosing Coffins. Raymond Souster. MoCV

Funeral Hymn. William Walsham Howe. SacPr

Funeral in Soweto. Wole Soyinka.
"We wish only to bury our dead. Shorn." PoetW

Funeral in the East. Pablo Neruda. TRP, *tr. by* Robert Bly

Funeral Lament (Kommos) from Epiros. *Unknown.* BoWoP, *tr. by* Elene Margot Kolb

Funeral March in B Flat. Female Socket. Nicole Espagnol. SurWo, *tr. by* Myrna Bell Rochester

Funeral Music. Geoffrey Hill.
"My little son, when you could command marvels." NoAM
"Not as we are but as we must appear." NoAM

Funeral of Martin Luther King, Jr, The. Nikki Giovanni. BPo

Funeral of Poetry, The. Karl Shapiro. APT-2

Funeral of the German Emperor, The. William McGonagall.
"As the procession passes the palace the blinds are drawn." VerBaPo

Funeral Oration. Dezső Kosztolányi. IQMS, *tr. by* George Gömöri and Clive Wilmer

Funeral Oration. *Unknown.* IQMS, *tr. by* Alan Jenkins

Funeral Oration, A. Drummond Allison. PoWW

Funeral Oration, A. David Wright. PeSAV

Funeral Oration for a Mouse. Alan Dugan. HAP

Funeral Plainsong from a Younger Woman to an Older Woman, A. Judy Grahn. GLP

Funeral Pyre, The. *Unknown.* AnOE, *tr. by* Charles W. Kennedy *Fr.* Beowulf.

Funeral Rites. Seamus Heaney. BiHa; ModIr; PBCIP; PoetW

Funeral Sermon, Soweto. Wole Soyinka. VCWP

Funeral Song. Hayiaku. STP, *tr. by* James Koller

Funeral Song, Upon the Decease of Annes His Mother, A. Nicholas Grimald.
"Yea, and a good cause why thus should I plain." NoP-4

Funeraled Fare Well. Kalamu ya Salaam. SpirFl *Fr.* New Orleans Haiku.

Funeral[l], The. John Donne. AWP; BoLoP; EBEV; ESCV; EnLoPo; FSCP; HeIP-4; MeLP; NAEL-5v1; NAEL-6v1; NAEL-7v1; NAWM-5v1; NoP-4; OBEV; PoRA; SCGP; TFi
(Whoever comes to shroud me, do not harm.) FSCP; NoP-4

Funeral[l] Rites of the Rose, The. Robert Herrick. CaPo; NOSC; OBEV

Funerall song, upon the deceas of Annes his moother, A. Nicholas Grimald.
"I, in your frutefull woomb conceyved, born was." PBRV

Funeral[l] stone, A. To Laurels. Robert Herrick. CaPo

Funerals are important. Exiles. Abena Busia. NAfrP

Funerary Portraits. Rosanna Warren. NoAM

Funereal, phosphorescent light. (LL) Insects. Isidor Schneider. APT-2; TrJP

Funfair, henhouse of pleasure. Peoples House. Nikolai Alekseievich Zabolotsky [*or* Zabolotskii]. TCRP, *tr. by* Daniel Weissbort

Funicello at 50. Klipschutz. ReTh

Funk. Mary Weems. SpirFl

Funk Lore. Imamu Amiri Baraka. UnSA

Funky Football. Ruby C. Saunders. BlSi

Funnel. Anne Sexton. MoAmPo

Funnel-web spider, snake and octopus. Pelicans. Judith Wright. BMAP; OWoS

Funny how the kid you always punched. Dogtown. James Harms. GeoHom

Funny Poem. Bill Knott. PBCAP

Funny thing is that he's reading a paper, The. Sandwich Man, The. Ron Padgett. CoAmPo

Fur in see bi west Spayngne. Land of Cokaygne, The. *Unknown.* NOIV

Fürchte dich nicht, ich bin bei dir. (LL) Exequy, An. Peter Porter. NoAM; NoP-4; OxBC

Furies, The. Anne Sexton. BodElec
Fury of Abandonment, The. BodElec
Fury of Beautiful Bones, The. BodElec
Fury of Cocks, The. BodElec
Fury of Earth, The. BodElec
Fury of Flowers and Worms, The. BoWoP; BodElec
Fury of God's Good-bye, The. BodElec
Fury of Guitars and Sopranos, The. BodElec
Fury of Hating Eyes, The. BodElec
Fury of Jewels and Coal, The. BodElec
Fury of Overshoes, The. NIL-7
Fury of Sundays, The. BodElec
Fury of Sunrises, The. BodElec
Fury of Sunsets, The. BodElec

Furious Clarity, A. Gabriel Zaid. TCLAP, *tr. by* George McWhirter

Furious Gun, The. Sir Thomas Wyatt. PoE

Furious words and minerals which destroy, The. (LL) Two Armies. Stephen Spender. OBWP; OxBTC

Furiously a crane. Shock. C. K. Williams. UrbNat

Furiously along the banks stormed Hannibal. Catius As Conius Silius Italicus. RomPo, *tr. by* Marcus Wilson *Fr.* Punica, The.

Furius and Aurelius, aides to Catullus. Farewell. Robert Fitzgerald. APT-2

Furius and Aurelius, loyal friends. Carmen: 11. Catullus. WoPoe, *tr. by* Frederick Morgan

Furl sails into fishermen's cove. Tune: "Full Court of Fragrance." Yao Sui. ChinPo, *tr. by* Yip Wai-lim

Furnace, The. Thomas Kinsella. BiHa

Furnace Blast, The. John Greenleaf Whittier. CBCWP

Furnace fire lights up earth and sky, The. Li Po. SuSp *Fr.* Songs of Ch'iu-p'u.

Furnace tolls the knell of falling steam, The. Elegy Written in a Country Coal-Bin. Christopher Darlington Morley. OBAL

Furnished Room, The. James Merrill. NOBA

Further, advancing further. (LL) Louis MacNeice. BoLoP; EnLoPo *Fr.* Trilogy for X.

Further Advantages of Learning. Kenneth Rexroth. TAP

Further adventure of Skinny Marcus. Lucilius. GrAn

Further Adventures with You. C. D. Wright. LCAP-2

Further in Summer than the Birds. Emily Dickinson. APN-2; NOBA; NoP-4; PoE

Further Instructions. Ezra Pound. TwCP *Fr.* Lustra.

Further Language from Truthful James. Bret Harte. NOBL

Further Notice. Philip Whalen. PoM; VGW

Further off is the measured force the word of the sea. Edouard J. Maunick. PBMAP *Fr.* Les Manèges de la Mer (1964).

Further Proposal, A. Allen Ginsberg. NIL-7

Furtherness. Mary Ruefle. BAP-01

Furtive blow, more like, A. There was I. Leda's Version. James [*or* Jim] Harrison. NIP-4

Fury. Lucille Clifton. LoL

Fury against the Moslems at Uhud. Hind bint Utba. WPOW, *tr. by* Bridget Connelly and Deirdre Lashgari

Fury of Abandonment, The. Anne Sexton. BodElec *Fr.* Furies, The.

Fury of Aerial Bombardment, The. Richard Eberhart. APT-2; FaBoMo; HeIP-4; InPK-6; NIL-7; NIP-4; NoAM; NoP-4; OBWP; PAI; PoWW; RB; TAP; TwCP; UnPo; VGW

Fury of Beautiful Bones, The. Anne Sexton. BodElec *Fr.* Furies, The.

Fury of Cocks, The. Anne Sexton. BodElec *Fr.* Furies, The.

Fury of Earth, The. Anne Sexton. BodElec *Fr.* Furies, The.

Fury of Flowers and Worms, The. Anne Sexton. BoWoP; BodElec *Fr.* Furies, The.

Fury of God's Good-bye, The. Anne Sexton. BodElec *Fr.* Furies, The.

Fury of Guitars and Sopranos, The. Anne Sexton. BodElec *Fr.* Furies, The.

Fury of Hating Eyes, The. Anne Sexton. BodElec *Fr.* Furies, The.

Fury of Jewels and Coal, The. Anne Sexton. BodElec *Fr.* Furies, The.

Fury of Overshoes. Anne Sexton. LCAP-2; NIP-4

Fury of Overshoes, The. Anne Sexton. NIL-7 *Fr.* Furies, The.

Fury of Sundays, The. Anne Sexton. BodElec *Fr.* Furies, The.

Fury of Sunrises, The. Anne Sexton. BodElec *Fr.* Furies, The.

Fury of Sunsets, The. Anne Sexton. BodElec *Fr.* Furies, The.

Fury said to a mouse. Lewis Carroll. *See* Alice's Adventures in Wonderland

Fury said to a mouse, That. Long Tale, A. Lewis Carroll. OBCoV

Fury this Friday broke through my wall, The. In Memory of a Friend. George Barker. OxBTC

Fus time dem kar me go a Bellevue was fi di dactar an de lanlord operate, De. Riddym Ravings (The Mad Woman's Poem). Jean Binta Breeze. WaCA

Fuscus is free, and hath the world at will. In Fuscum. Sir John Davies. FaBoEE

Fuselage Installation. Juan Felipe Herrera. BodElec

Fuses I and II. Charles Baudelaire. PFTM-1

Fusty Christopher. (LL) To Christopher North. Tennyson. FaBoEE; PeLV

Futile Flight, Futile Fugue. Dulce Maria Loynaz. TANSG, *tr.* by Alan West

Futile Poem, A. Remco Campert. TuT, *tr.* by Theo Dorgan

Futility. Wilfred Owen. FaBoMo; GTBS-P; HarvBoo; MoBrPo; NAEL-5v2; NAEL-6v2; NPeEn; NoAM; NoP-4; OBWP; PAI; PeFWW; RB; TCAWP

Future. Vicki Viidikas. BMAP

Future, The. Angel González. VCWP, *tr.* by Steven Ford Brown

Future, The. James Oppenheim. TrJP

Future ain't what it used to be, The. Pharaoh. Jane Kenyon. LoL

Future and the Ancestor, The. Andrée Chedid. HAWP; WPOW, *tr.* by Mirène Ghossein and Samuel Hazo

Future Debris. Heid E. Erdrich. AmPoNex

Future is for Tomorrow, The. Anna Gréki. HAWP; WPOW, *tr.* by Mildred P. Mortimer

Future Martyr of Supersonic Waves. Juan Felipe Herrera. TouFir

Future Models May Have Infra-Red Sensors. Tom Raworth. Oth

Future of which we dream, The. S.L.A.M. Giovanna Pollarolo. TANSG, *tr.* by Marjorie Agosin

Future, past, the sea. Sea of Oblivion. Shinkichi Takahashi. ZenPo, *tr.* by Takashi Ikemoto and Lucien Stryk

Future Peace and Glory of the Church, The. William Cowper. InvLi *Fr.* Olney Hymns.

Future Verdict, The. Ada Cambridge. NOBAu

Future Work. Fleur Adcock. DiPo

Future—turned his back, and walked away, The. (LL) Great Artist Reconsiders the Homeric Simile, The. John Tranter. BMAP; NOBAu; NoAM

Futurism Wants to Transform the Variety Theater into a Theater of Amazement, Record-setting, and Body-madness. Filippo Tommaso Marinetti. PFTM-1 *Fr.* Variety Theater Manifesto, The.

Fuzzy fellow, without feet, A. Caterpillar. Emily Dickinson. TAP

Fuzzy-Wuzzy. Rudyard Kipling. MoBrPo

Fuzzy Wuzzy was a bear. *Unknown.* NTCP

Fwap! Alan Pizzarelli. HA

G

G. B. Shaw wrote to Yeats: "P'raps it's mad of me." Limerick. W. A. Rathkey. PeLi

G. K. Chesterton. Humbert Wolfe. TrJP

G. K. Chesterton on His Birth. A. E. Housman. NBLV

G. M. B. Donald Davie. OxBC

G'uggery G'uggery Nunc. Limerick. Sir John Betjeman. PeLi

Ga-wash-truht in Mesita, in early fall. Hunter's Dance in Early Fall. Debra Haaland Toya. ReEnLa

Gaa-a-Muna, a Mountain Flower. Harold Littlebird. VoR

Gaberlunzie Man, The. *Unknown.* OxBB; OxBS

Gabey's comin' Lonely Town. Betty Comden. ReLy

Gabi. Maria Luisa B. Aguilar-Cariño. ReBoTo

"Gables are not burning, The." Finnesburh Fragment, The. *Unknown.* ASW; OBWP, *tr.* by Kevin Crossley-Holland

Gabriel. Adrienne Rich. VGW

Gabriel's Appearance. Abraham Cowley. NOSC *Fr.* Davideis.

Gabriel the rain-lover. Rain Poem. Gabriel Preil. FIT, *tr.* by Robert Friend

Gabriel turned at last into old Mr Preil. From a Late Diary. Gabriel Preil. FIT, *tr.* by Robert Friend

Gabrielle, the terrapin, whose tiny eyes. Terrapin, The. Elizabeth Smither. PeNZ

Gaelic is alive. Aonghas Macneacail. NePenScot

Gaelic is the conscience of our leaders. Michael Hartnett. CIP-2 *Fr.* Farewell to English, A.

Gaelic Stories. Iain Crichton Smith. NePenScot

Gaeltacht. Pearse Hutchinson. BIrV; ModIr; PBCIP

Gaeta from wool and weaving first began. In Gaetam. Thomas Bastard. FaBoEE

Gaffer Gray. Thomas Holcroft. NOEC; OxAEP-1

Gaffer Speaks. Ghulam-Reza Ruhani. WoPoe, *tr.* by Omar Pound

Gaia. Gary Snyder. GifTon

Gaia, first-born daughter of Chaos. Czeslaw Milosz. BodElec *Fr.* Lithuania, After Fifty-Two Years.

Gaiety of Form, The. Robert Bly. BodElec

Gail. Hugh Seidman. KGB

Gaily bedight / A gallant knight. Eldorado. Edgar Allan Poe. APN-1; AWP; ColAP; FaBoCh; NOBA; OxBA; PAI; TAP; TCAPo

Gaily into Ruislip Gardens. Middlesex. Sir John Betjeman. OxBTC

Gaily they grow, the quiet throng. Heather Flowers. Eliseus Williams. OBWVE, *tr.* by Kenneth Hurlstone Jackson

Gain without gladness. Liadain. *Unknown.* WPOW, *tr.* by Frank O'Connor

Gal's Cry for a Dying Lover. Langston Hughes. NAAAL

Galapagos. Neil Curry. NLP

Galataea. Callimachus.

"Or rather the sacred fish with the golden faces." HePo

Galatea and Pygmalion. Robert Graves. PAI

Galatians 6.14. Francis Quarles. ChIV-2

Galaxies. Alan Gould. NOBAu

Galaxy, The. Henry Wadsworth Longfellow. OxBSo

Gale at Dawn. William Everson. APT-2

Gale in April. Robinson Jeffers. MoAmPo

Gale: tiles, roofs whirling. Beach. Shinkichi Takahashi. ZenPo, *tr.* by Takashi Ikemoto and Lucien Stryk

Gales. Anne Stevenson. Spl

Galilee Shore. Allen Ginsberg. ChIV-2

(With the blue-dark dome old-starred at night, green boat-lights purring over.) FTOS

Galileo. János Székely. IQMS, *tr.* by George Gömöri and Adam Makkai

Gallant Château. Wallace Stevens. MoAmPo

Gallant foeman in the fight, A. Robert E. Lee. Julia Ward Howe. CBCWP

Gallant laird of Lamington, The. Katharine Jaffray. *Unknown.* ESPB

Gallantry. Keith Douglas. NAEL-5v2; NAEL-6v2; NoAM; OBWP

Gallants attend, and hear a friend. Battle of the Kegs, The. Francis Hopkinson. OBAL

(Galleons in sea-pomp) sails. Armada of Thirty Whales, An. Daniel Gerard Hoffman. YaYoPo

Gallery. Albert Goldbarth. TaR

Gallery, The. Andrew Marvell. BASC; ESCV; MeLP; NoP-4; PBRV; PoE

Gallery, The. Tomas Tranströmer. PFTM-2, *tr.* by Robin Fulton

Gallery of My Heart. King D. Kuka. VoR

Gallery Shepherds. Patricia Beer. OxBC

Galley, The. Petrarch. HAP; OBVE; OxBEV; SCGP; Son; WeW-3, *tr.* by Sir Thomas Wyatt *Fr.* Sonnets to Laura.

Galley Oars. Ali ibn Hariq. WoPoe, *tr.* by Christopher Middleton

Galley of Count Arnaldos, The. Henry Wadsworth Longfellow. OBEV

Galley-Slave, The. Rudyard Kipling. PeVV

Galliass, The. Walter De la Mare. FaBoTw

Gallio's Song. Rudyard Kipling. ChIV-2

Gallon of gin and a flitch of pork, A. Obsequy for Dylan Thomas. James Keir Baxter. PeLV

Gallop a dreary dun. (LL) Master and Man. Mother Goose. OxNR; ReMoGo

Galloping around, north and south. T'ang Yin. CoBLCP *Fr.* Miscellaneous Feelings.

Galloping Cat, The. Stevie Smith. BrRo

Galloping collection of boards, The. Somewhere. Robert Creeley. NoAM

Gallow Hill. William J. Tait. OxBS

Gallows, The. Edward Thomas. MoBrPo; NoAM; PAI; SCGP; UnPo

Gallows in my garden, people say, The. Ballade of Suicide, A. Gilbert Keith Chesterton. NBLV; OBCoV

Gallowstree drops, The. Jesus Unborn. Anne Sexton. PFTM-2

Galoots, you hairy, hankering. Galoots. Carl Sandburg. APT-1

Galoshes. Rhoda Warner Bacmeister. NTCP

Galway is a blackguard place. Clonakilty. *Unknown.* FaBoEE

Galway Races. *Unknown.* OxBoLi

Galya, Mother, and My Daughter Anna. Yevgeny [*or* Evgenii] Borisovich Rein. TCRP, *tr.* by Bernard Meares

Gambier. Joe Osterhaus. AmPoNex; NAPBL

Gambit. Tony Curtis. AngWePo

Gamble. Linda Hogan. HATNAP

Gambling. Vince Gotera. OpBo

Gambling. Royall Tyler. TAP

Game, The. Edvard Kocbek. PoSu, *tr.* by Michael Scammell and Veno Taufer

Game after Supper. Margaret Atwood. FaBoWP; LCAP-2

Game at Salzburg, A. Randall Jarrell. NoAM

Game of Chess, A. T. S. Eliot. HarvBoo; SCV *Fr.* Waste Land, The.

Game of Chess, A. Gwen Harwood. MakPoe

Game of Consequences, A. Paul Dehn. NOBL

Game of "just supposing," The. Make Believe. Jerome Kern. ReLy

Game Trail, The. Mark Todd. GeoH

Gamebagkeeper dealt detachable breath. TM. Ulli Freer. Oth

Gameboy. Regie Cabico. WiU

Gamecock. James Dickey. UnPo

Gamekeeper of Lady Chatterley, The. Limerick. Gerry Hamill. PeLi

Gamelia. Susan M. Whitmore. AmPoNex

Games. Sandra McPherson. LCAP-2

Games. Vasco [*or* Vasko] Popa. RB, *tr.* by Anne Pennington

He. PoSu, *tr.* by Anne Pennington

Nail, The. PoSu

Seed, The. PoSu

Games at the Hour of the Desert. Manuela Fingueret. MirDau, *tr. by* Roberta Gordenstein

Games were over now. The gathered armies scattered, The. Homer. NAWM-7v1, *tr. by* Robert Fagles *Fr.* Iliad, The.

Games with My Daughter. Tony Curtis. TCAWP

Gammer Gurton's Needle. William Stevenson.

  Back and Side Go Bare, Go Bare. HeIP-4; NAEL-5v1; NAEL-6v1, *tr. by* John Still

  Jolly Good Ale and Old. OBEV

  (Song of Ale, A.) SCGP

Gang Girls. Gwendolyn Brooks. IllVoic *Fr.* Blackstone Rangers, The.

Gang of labourers on the piled wet timber, A. Morning Work. D. H. Lawrence. MoBrPo

Gang wanted to give Oedipus Rex a going away present, The. Oedipus. Josephine Miles. SoSe-8; WPE

Gang was there when midnight came, The. Joseph Moncure March. APT-2 *Fr.* Wild Party, The.

Ganges, The. Norman Dubie. LCAP-2

Gangrel Rymour and the Pairdon of Sanct Anne, The. Sydney Goodsir Smith. "But ae braithless note." OBVE

Gangrene. Philip Levine. VGW

Gap, The. Annie Foster. NLP

Gape, gape, gorlin' Ex Vermibus. Hugh MacDiarmid. CABP

Garage in Co. Cork, A. Derek Mahon. DiPo; PBCIP

Garage Sale. Brian Henry. AmPoNex

Garage Sale as a Spiritual Exercise, The. Thomas M. [*or* "Tom"] Disch. GI

Garbage. A. R. Ammons.

  "Garbage has to be the poem of our time because." NAAL-5

Garbage is bagged, deposited in the dump, and several, The. Little Cape Cod Landscape. Charles North. FTOS

Garbage went over the fantail, boiling into blue. Memories of Mess Duty and the War. Christopher Howell. CDa

García Lorca. Louis Dudek. MoCV; NOBC

García Lorca Murdered in Granada. John Streeter Manifold. CBAP

García Lorca tasted. Drinking Fountain, The. Robert Duncan. CLPP

Garden. Michael Bullock. OBGa

Garden. "H. D." APT-1; NoAM

Garden. Marina Ivanovna Tsvetayeva [*or* Tsvetaeva]. RusPo, *tr. by* Robert Arthur Douglas Ford

Garden. John Greenleaf Whittier. OBGa

Garden, A. Andrew Marvell. OBEV *Fr.* Upon Appleton House [To My Lord Fairfax].

Garden, The. Rae Armantrout. FTOS

Garden, The. Franta Bass. INSAB

Garden, The. Joseph Beaumont. NOSC

  (Garden's quit with me: as yesterday, The.) OBGa

Garden, The. Abraham Cowley.

  ("Happy art thou, whom God does bless.") OBGa

Garden, The. William Cowper. *Fr.* Task, The.

Garden, The. "H. D." NoAM

  Heat. HeIP-4; InPK-6; MoAmPo; OxBA; TAP; TCAPo; TRP; UnPo

Garden, The. Louise Glück. HCAP; NAAL-2v2; NoP-4; VCAP

Garden, The. Andrew Marvell. AWP; BASC; ClHu; ESCV; FSCP; GeHe; HAP; MakPoe; MeLP; NAEL-5v1; NAEL-6v1; NAEL-7v1; NIL-7; NIP-4; NOBE; NOSC; NPeEn; OBGa; OxBEV; PBRV; PoE; PoPoPo; PoRA; SCGP; TFi; TOF; TRP

  (Thoughts in a Garden.) GTBS-P; OBEV

Garden, The. Bernadette Mayer. FTOS

Garden, The. Harriet Monroe. IllVoic

Garden, The. Pope. OBGa

Garden, The. Ezra Pound. APT-1; AWP; HeIP-4; MoAmPo; NIL-7; NIP-4; OxBSP; TwCP

Garden, The. Victoria Mary Sackville-West. OBGa

Garden, The. James Shirley. BeJo; NOSC

Garden, The. Mark Strand. ColAP; NoAM

Garden, The. Joshua Sylvester. OBGa

Garden, The. Jones Very. APN-1; OxBA; TAP

Garden, The. Oscar Wilde. PoRA *Fr.* Impressions.

Garden Abstract. Hart Crane. OBGa

Garden at the General's Residence, The. Muso Soseki. EaWin, *tr. by* W. S. Merwin

Garden-boy is leading the cranes home, The. (LL) Cranes, The. Po Chü-i. ChiP; OBVE; OWoS, *tr. by* Arthur Waley

Garden butterfly. Issa. EH, *tr. by* Robert Hass

Garden By The Sea, A. William Morris. NOBE *Fr.* Life and Death of Jason, The.

Garden Calendar. N. M. Bodecker. TLR

Garden called Gethsemane, The. Gethsemane. Rudyard Kipling. FaBoTw; NPeEn; PeFWW

Garden Chidings. Louise Imogen Guiney. SWaP

Garden did not bloom, The. Gethsemane A. D. Dolores Kendrick. FFC

Garden Fancies. Robert Browning.

  Flower's Name, The. CTC

  (Garden Fancies.) OBGa

  Sibrandus Schafnaburgensis. CTC; EBVV; OBGa

Garden flew round with the angel, The. Pleasures of Merely Circulating, The. Wallace Stevens. OBAL

Garden God, The. Richard Eberhart. OBGa

Garden Hose, The. Beatrice Janosco. NTCP

Garden in September, The. Robert Bridges. OBGa

Garden in the middle of a hundred acres is half-covered with moss, The. Tune: "Sand of Silk-washing Stream." Wang An-shih. SuSp, *tr. by* James J. Y. Liu

Garden inclosed is my sister, my spouse; a spring shut up, a fountain / sealed, A. Bible, *O.T.* OBGa *Fr.* Song of Solomon, The.

Garden is a loathsome thing, God wot, A. My Garden. P. R. Hines. UV

Garden is a lovesome thing, God wot!, A. My Garden. Thomas Edward Brown. InPK-6; OBEV; OBGa; UV

Garden is a *lovesome* thing? What rot!, A. My Garden. J. A. Lindon. InPK-6

Garden Living. Wu Wei-yeh. CoBLCP, *tr. by* Jonathan Chaves

Garden Note I, Los Altos. Janet Lewis. APT-2

Garden Note II, March. Janet Lewis. APT-2

Garden. Nothing catches fire, The. (LL) Public Garden, The. Robert Lowell. OBGa; PoRA; TAP

Garden of Adonis, The. Edmund Spenser. NOBE *Fr.* Faerie Queene, The.

Garden of Appleton House, The ("When in the east the morning ray"). Andrew Marvell. NOBE *Fr.* Upon Appleton House [To My Lord Fairfax].

Garden of Eden, The. Ágnes Nemes Nagy. IQMS, *tr. by* Hugh Maxton

Garden of Eden (described in the Bible), The. Fall, The. Fergus Allen. ModIr

Garden of Friendship, The. Frances Sargent Osgood. PoBW

Garden of Gethsemane, The. Boris Leonidovich Pasternak. GI, *tr. by* Nina Kossman

Garden of Love, The. William Blake. AWP; EnLoPo; FHYEP; HAP; NAEL-5v2; NAEL-6v2; NPeEn; NoP-4; OBGa; OxAEP-2; OxBEV; PoE; PoPoPo; RB; SCGP; TFi; TOF; TRP *Fr.* Songs of Experience.

Garden of Proserpine, The. Algernon Charles Swinburne. AWP; CABP; HAP; NAEL-5v2; NAEL-6v2; NOBE; NOBVV; NoP-4; OxBEV; PeVV; PoE; PoRA; SCV; TFi

Garden of Shanah. Sara Riwka Erlich. MirDau, *tr. by* Auristela Xavier

Garden of Ships, The. Douglas Stewart. CBAP

Garden of Shushan! Before the Feast of Shushan. Anne Spencer. BlSi; NAAAL

Garden of Song, The. Moses Ibn Ezra. TOF, *tr. by* David Goldstein

Garden of the Muses: Iopas' Song, The. John Skelton. NPeEn *Fr.* Garland [*or* Garlande *or* Garlands] of Laurel[l], The.

Garden of Theophrastus, The. Peter Huchel. AF, *tr. by* Daniel Simko

Garden Party. Sir Herbert Read. OBGa

Garden Party, The. Donald Davie. OxBEV

Garden Poem. Ian Hamilton Finlay. OBGa

Garden's quit with me, The. As yesterday. Garden, The. Joseph Beaumont. NOSC

Garden Seat, The. Thomas Hardy. HAP; RB

Garden Shukkei-en, The. Carolyn Forché. ExTi

Garden Song, A. Austin Dobson. OBEV; OBGa

Garden Song, A. George R. Sims. NOBVV; OBCoV; OBGa

Garden, The ("How vainly men themselves amaze"). Andrew Marvell. AWP; HAP; MeLP; NIP-4; NOBE; PoRA

Garden we walked in, The. Green Grass and Yellow Balloons. Etheridge Knight. GT

Garden where he broods is like a riddle, The. Wartburg, 1521–22, The. Timothy Steele. RA

Garden, Wilderness. Michael Hamburger. OBGa

Garden Window, The. Aaron Hill. OBGa

Garden Year, The. Sara Coleridge. ChAP; OTCP

Gardener. Ralph Waldo Emerson. OxBA *Fr.* Quatrains.

Gardener. Robert Graves. OBGa

Gardener. Dom Moraes. OBGa

Gardener. A. H. Snow. OBGa

Gardener, The. Sidney Keyes. MoBrPo

Gardener, The. Craig Raine. UV

Gardener, The. Robert Louis Stevenson. OBGa

Gardener, The. Rabindranath Tagore. OBMV

Gardener, The. *Unknown.* ESPB

Gardener, The. Rowland Watkyns. NOSC

Gardener came running, The. Incident in a Rose Garden. Donald Justice. CRP

Gardener does not love to talk, The. Gardener, The. Robert Louis Stevenson. OBGa

Gardener Janus Catches a Naiad. Dame Edith Sitwell. MoBrPo; OBGa

Gardener's Daughter, The. Tennyson.
"Lightly he laughed, as one that read my thought." OBGa

Gardener's rule applies to youth and age, The. Adage. Henry James Byron. NBLV

Gardener stands in his bower-door, The. Gardener, The. *Unknown.* ESPB

Gardener to His God, The. Mona Van Duyn. RACG; TrCP; UnPo; WPE

Gardener wi' His Paidle; or, The Gardener's March, The. Robert Burns. OBGa

Gardeners. Douglas Dunn. OBGa

Gardeners, The. Christopher Reid. DiPo

Gardening Chrysanthemums, I Think of [T'ao] Yüan-Ming. Ishikawa Jōzan. WoPoe, *tr. by* Jonathan Chaves

Gardening in the Tropics, you never know. Brief Lives. Olive Senior. EmeKit

Gardens. Neil Curry. OBGa

Gardens, The. Abbé Jacques de Lille.
"Velvet ground we now with pleasure tread, The." OBGa

Gardens for the Fire and the Rain. Muhammad Al-As'ad. MAP, *tr. by* Charles Doria and Lena Jayyusi

Gardens, gardens, and we are gardeners. Gardeners. Douglas Dunn. OBGa

Gardens No Emblems. Donald Davie. OBGa

Gardens of Alcinous, The. Homer. OBGa; OBVE, *tr. by* Alexander Pope *Fr.* Odyssey.

Gardens of Alcinous, The. Homer. OBVE, *tr. by* George Chapman *Fr.* Odyssey.

Gardens of Ravished Psyche, The. George Barker. OBGa

Gardens of the Villa D'Este, The. Anthony Hecht. ColAP; OBGa

Gardens of Zuñi, The. W. S. Merwin. GifTon

Gardens We Have Left. David Mura. OpBo

Gardin of Adonis, The. Edmund Spenser. NOBE; NPeEn *Fr.* Faerie Queene, The.

Gardner of the World, he goes, The. (LL) Summer Sun. Robert Louis Stevenson. MoBrPo; PWR

Gare du Midi. W. H. Auden. OxBSP

Garfish. John Blight. BMAP

Gargoyle. Carl Sandburg. NOBA; NoAM

Gargoyle. Robert B. Shaw. CRP

Garland, The. Vladimir Nikolaevich Sokolov. TCRP, *tr. by* Albert C. Todd

Garland and the Girdle, The. Michelangelo Buonarroti. AWP, *tr. by* John Addington Symonds

Garland briefer than a girl's, The. (LL) To an Athlete Dying Young. A. E. Housman. ChAP; HAP; HeIP-4; InPK-6; MoBrPo; NAEL-5v2; NAEL-6v2; NIP-4; NoAM; NoP-4; PoE; PoRA; SCGP; SoSe-8; TFi; TRP; UnPo; WeW-3

Garland for a Propagandist. Ted Pauker. NOBL

Garland for Advancing Years, A. William Bell Scott. GSo

Garland for Heliodora, A. Meleager. AWP, *tr. by* "Christopher North."

Garland of Precepts, A. Phyllis McGinley. NBLV

Garland of roses, whether you come. Martial. FaBoEE

Garland [or Garlande or Garlands] of Laurel[l], The. John Skelton.
Garden of the Muses: Iopas' Song, The. NPeEn
(Mistress Margaret Hussey.) FaBoCh
(To Mastres Margery Wentworthe.) OxBEV
To Mistress Margery Wentworth. EBEV; EnLoPo; NOBE; OBEV
To Mistress [or Maystres] Isabell Pennell. NOBE; NPeEn; NoSic; OBEV; OxBoLi; SCGP; TTTS
To Mistress [or Maystres] Margaret Hussey. EBEV; EnLoPo; NAEL-5v1; NAEL-6v1; NBLV; NOBE; NoP-4; NoSic; OBEV; OxBEV; PeLV; PoE; PoRA; SCGP; SCV; TFi
Lullay, Lullay, Like a Child. NAEL-6v1; NAEL-7v1; NoSic; SCGP

Garlands fade that Spring so lately wove, The. Sonnet Written at the Close of Spring [or Elegiac Sonnet]. Charlotte Smith. CenSon; ECWP; RWP

Garlands of fatted words are strung through the city. Silence. Miroslav Holub. PoSu, *tr. by* Ian Milner and Jarmila Milner

Garments of God, The. Jessica Agnes Powers. InvLi

Garments worn in flying dreams, The. Windy City. Stuart Dybek. IllVoic

Garnishing the Aviary. Margaret Danner. BPo *Fr.* Far from Africa: Four Poems.

Garrisons pent up in a little fort. Sonnet of Brotherhood. Ronald Allison Kells Mason. PeNZ

Garrulous to the very last. (LL) After the Supper and Talk. Walt Whitman. MoAmPo; NAAL-2v1; NAAL-3

Garvey's Head as Value. Norman Weinstein. WaCA

Gas. Gerry Gordon. MiVo

Gas. Sidney Wade. PoSol

Gas and Hot Air. Morris Gilbert Bishop. OBAL

Gas Drill. Tom Rawling. FaBoWar

Gas fire, The. Persian, The. Stevie Smith. FaBoWP

Gas is good, The. Petit Guignol. Philip Hammial. BMAP

Gas-lamps abandoned by the night burn on. Baudelaire in Brussels. Anthony Cronin. BIrV

Gas Station, The. C. K. Williams. VCAP

Gas Station Attendant. Brian G. Gilmore. SpirFl

Gas was on in the Institute, The. Shropshire Lad, A. Sir John Betjeman. HarvBoo

Gasa, the aggressive one. Praises of Field-marshal J. C. Smuts, The. Nongejeni Zuma. PeSAV, *tr. by* Harry C. Lugg

Gasbags. *Unknown.* NOBL

Gasco. Günter Grass. CLPP, *tr. by* Jerome Rothenberg

Gascoigne's Good-Morrow. George Gascoigne. NOCV; NoSic

Gascoigne's Lullaby [or Lullabie]. George Gascoigne. *See* Lullaby [or Lullabie] of a Lover, The

Gascoigne's Memories. George Gascoigne.
"All were to[o] little for the merchant's [or merchauntes] hand[e]." Son
"And every year a world my will did deem." Son
"Before mine eye to feed my greedy will." Son
"For why? The gains doth seldom quit the change." Son
"In haste poste haste, when first my wandering [or wandring] mind[e]." NoSic; Son
No Hast But Good. NoSic; Son
"No haste but good, where wisdome makes the waye." Son
"To prink me up and make me higher placed." Son

Gascoigne's [or Gascoygnes] Good-Night. George Gascoigne. NOCV; NoSic

Gascoigne's Woodmanship. George Gascoigne. NoSic
(Gascoignes wodmanship.) PBRV
(My worthy Lord, I pray you wonder not.) CABP; PBRV
(Woodmanship.) NAEL-7v1

Gascoignes wodmanship. George Gascoigne. *See* Gascoigne's Woodmanship

Gasholders, russet among fields. Milldams, marpools that lay unstirring. Eel-swarms. Coagulations of frogs; once, with branches and half-bricks, he battered a ditchful; then sidled away from the stillness and silence. Geoffrey Hill. HAP; NPeEn; NoAM; NoP-4 *Fr.* Mercian Hymns.

Gaslight. Rolf Jacobsen. WoPoe, *tr. by* Roger Greenwald

Gasp sounded, The. Poem, A. Mongane Wally Serote. PeSAV

Gassing the woodchucks didn't turn out right. Woodchucks. Maxine W. Kumin. NIL-7; NIP-4

Gate closed, The. Key to Dreams. Georg Nikolic. IllVoic

Gate Lodge. Richard Murphy. PBCIP

Gate of Universal Light, The. Muso Soseki. EaWin, *tr. by* W. S. Merwin

Gate, red lights revolving in the leaves. (LL) First Party at Ken Kesey's with Hell's Angels. Allen Ginsberg. PmAP; TRP

Gate's Open, The. John Blight. CBAP

Gate was open; the fence under the aspens, fallen, The. Mountain Corral. Helen Sorrells. WPE

Gatehouse Salutation, The. Eleanor Touchet Davies. EMWP

Gateposts. Medbh McGuckian. BiHa; MakPoe; ModIr; PBCIP

Gates, The. Muriel Rukeyser. BodElec

Gates clanged and they walked you into jail, The. Conscientious Objector, The. Karl Shapiro. OxBA

Gates fly open with a pretty sound, The. Under the Hill. Daryl Hine. MakPoe; MoCV

Gates of Paradise, The. William Blake.
Epilogue: "Truly my Satan thou art but a dunce." HAP; PeECV; PoE; WeW-3
(To the Accuser Who Is the God of This World.) FHYEP; NPeEn; OxBEV; OxBSP; SCGP

Gates of the town are closed. The princes, The. Prayer to the Gods of the Night. *Unknown.* WoPoe, *tr. by* David Ferry

Gateway, The. Alec Derwent Hope. BoLoP

Gateway buried deep in flowers. Tune: "Sand of Silk-Washing Brook" A Reminiscence. Wu Wen-ying. ColAnChi, *tr. by* Jiaosheng Wang

Gathasaptasati, The. *Unknown.*
Even He Was Abashed. WoPoe, *tr. by* Martha Ann Selby
Lone Buck. WoPoe, *tr. by* Andrew Schelling
Newly Wed Girl, The. WoPoe, *tr. by* David Ray
These Women Plunder My Husband. WoPoe, *tr. by* David Ray
Those Women. WoPoe, *tr. by* Martha Ann Selby
You Love Her. WoPoe, *tr. by* David Ray

Gather a body to me. Charles Olson. BodElec *Fr.* Maximus Poems, The.

Gather for festival. "H. D." MoAmPo *Fr.* Songs from Cyprus.

Gather noble death. Cumae. Merrill Moore. FuPo

Gather or take fierce degree. Short Poem for Armistice Day, A. Sir Herbert Read. PeFWW

Gather 'round me. Accentuate the Positive. Johnny Mercer. ReLy

Gather round while I sing you of Wernher von Braun. Wernher von Braun. Tom Lehrer. OBCoV

Gather the sacred dust. Lines. Abram Joseph Ryan. APN-2

Gather while you may. Rose. Kathleen Jessie Raine. WPE

Gather ye bank-notes while ye may. Election Time. Unknown. UV

Gather, ye brave sons of Ukadi Awaka! Moon Song. Chuba Nweke. PBA

Gather ye rose-buds while ye may. To the Virgins, to Make Much of Time. Robert Herrick. AWP; BASC; BeJo; BoLoP; CaPo; CavPo; ClHu; EnLoPo; HAP; HeIP-4; ITBLP; InPK-6; NAEL-5v1; NAEL-6v1; NAEL-7v1; NBLV; NIL-7; NIP-4; NOBE; NOSC; NPeEn; NoP-4; OBEV; OxAEP-1; OxBEV; PAI; PoE; PoPoPo; SCGP; SCV; SoSe-8; TFi; UV

Gather ye rosebuds while ye may. On Lady A———. Nicolas Bentley. OBCoV

Gathered at the nation's sickbed. Conga. Allen Fisher. PFTM-2

Gathered in inter-admiration. When the Five Prominent Poets. Josephine Jacobsen. TAP

Gathering. Basho. EH, tr. by Robert Hass

Gathering, The. Edwin John Pratt. MoCV Fr. Towards the Last Spike.

Gathering at the River. Anne Caston. NAPBL

Gathering in the Days. Gareth Owen. NOxBChV

Gathering Leaves. Robert Frost. RB; VGW

Gathering Lotus. Chu Ch'ing-yü. SuSp, tr. by Irving Y. Lo

Gathering Lotus with Singing Girls. Mo Shih-lung. CoBLCP, tr. by Jonathan Chaves

Gathering lotuses by Yeh River. Li Po. CrYelRi; ErotSp, tr. by Sam Hamill Fr. Women of Yueh.

Gathering Mushrooms. Paul Muldoon. BiHa; CIP-2; HarvBoo; ModIr; NoP-4; PBCIP; PNI

Gathering Place, The. Alan Alexander. NOBAu

Gathering Song of Donald the Black. Sir Walter Scott. See Pibroch of Donuil Dhu

Gaudeamus Igitur: A Valediction. John A. Stone. BloBone

Gaudy boat with wine on board: West Lake is at its best, A. Tune: "Gathering Mulberry Leaves." Ou-yang Hsiu. ColAnChi, tr. by J. R. Hightower

Gaudy Gossip, The. Juvenal. BASC, tr. by John Dryden Fr. Satires.

Gaudy gossip, when she's set agog, The. Juvenal. BASC, tr. by John Dryden Fr. Satires.

Gaudy Slave Trader. Wayne Koestenbaum. KGB

Gauge. Langston Hughes. APSN

Gauguin. Derek Walcott. NoAM Fr. Midsummer.

Gauguin's White Horse. Vicki Hearne. GS

Gauley Bridge. Muriel Rukeyser. NNaP

Gauley Bridge is a good town for Negroes, they let us stand. George Robinson: Blues. Muriel Rukeyser. NNaP; RACG

Gauls Sacrifice, The. Charles Montague Doughty. FaBoTw Fr. Dawn in Britain, The.

Gaunt brown walls, The. William Ernest Henley. NPeEn Fr. In Hospital.

Gaunt thing, The. Babylon Revisited. Imamu Amiri Baraka. BPo; NoAM

Gaurus, you have a fault for which. Martial. RomPo, tr. by Dorothea Wender

Gave me things I. Swallow the Lake. Clarence Major. ESEAA; FTOS; GT; NAAAL; PmAP

Gave proof through the night. Poem to My Sister, Ethel Ennis, Who Sang "The Star-spangled Banner" at the Second Inauguration of Richard Milhous Nixon. June Jordan. TAP

Gave to the dim harmonics voice and tongue? (LL) Harmonics. William Vaughn Moody. APN-2; AmFaPo

Gawain and the Lady of the Castle. Unknown. EBEV Fr. Sir Gawain and the Green Knight.

Gawain Journeys North. Unknown. NPeEn Fr. Sir Gawain and the Green Knight.

Gay, The. "Æ" OBMV

Gay and audacious crime glints in his eyes. In the Vices. Donald Evans. APT-1

Gay blade on the gentle hedgerow. Daffodil. Waldo Williams. OBWVE, tr. by Gwyn Jones

Gay Chaps at the Bar. Gwendolyn Brooks.
    My Dreams, My Works, Must Wait Till After Hell. IllVoic
    Still Do I Keep My Look, My Identity. IllVoic
    "We knew how to order. Just the dash." IllVoic

Gay Full Story. Bernadette Mayer. PmAP

Gay Goshawk [or Goss-Hawk], The. Anna Gordon Brown. ESPB; OxBB; WPE

Gay little Girl-of-the-Diving-Tank. At the Carnival. Anne Spencer. APT-1; BlSi

Gay Love and the Movies. Ralph Pomeroy. CAGL

Gay Old Hag, The. Unknown. BIrV

Gay Poet, The. William Barber. CAGL

Gay Psalm from Fort Valley, A. Louie Crew. GLP

Gay soccer spectator from Wix, A. Limerick. Cyril Mountjoy. PeLi

Gay Summer's Bliss, Good-bye. Dietmar, von Aist [or Eist]. GePo, tr. by J. W. Thomas

Gaylen got them to sit. Meeting Gaylen's 5th Grade Class. Miguel Algarin. PueRic

Gaza, creeps. Moment of Mourning, A. Donia El-Amal Ismail. PoArWo

Gaza, Undated. Rachel Tzvia Back. DTA

Gaze is no longer leveled, The. Cassiopeia at Noon. Michelle Boisseau. ExTi

Gaze North-east. Unknown. BIrV, tr. by John Montague

Gaze not upon my outside, friend. Apple Dumplings. Mary E. Tucker. CBWP-1

Gaze penetrates through the glass. Reflection on El Train Glass. Luis J. Rodriguez. IllVoic

Gazelle, The. Samuel Ha-Nagid. WoPoe, tr. by Peter Cole

Gazelle, The. Yasin Taha Hafiz. MAP, tr. by Sharif Elmusa and Christopher Middleton

Gazelle Calf, The. D. H. Lawrence. OxBTC; RB

Gazelle-girl / gazelle. King Solomon Vistas. Ian Wedde. PeNZ

Gazelles, The. Thomas Sturge Moore. OBMV

Gazing at Ch'ang-po Mountain. Li K'ai-hsien. CoBLCP, tr. by Jonathan Chaves

Gazing at Spring. Hsüeh T'ao. WoPoe, tr. by Jeanne Larsen

Gazing thro' her chamber window. Reflection. Christina Georgina Rossetti. VWP

Gazing upon him now, severe and dead. Edna St. Vincent Millay. APT-1 Fr. Sonnets from an Ungrafted Tree.

Gazing west—the isles of paradise. Waiting for the Ferry at Inchŏn. Liu E. CoBLCP, tr. by Jonathan Chaves

GDR. Frederick D'Aguiar.
    Now the Two Are One. WaCA

Gebir. Walter Savage Landor.
    "Now to Aurora, borne by dappled steeds." NOBRP
    "Sleepless, with pleasure and expiring fears." NOBRP

Gee, but it's hard to love someone, when that someone don't love you. Down-Hearted Blues. Albert Hunter. NAAAL

Gee, but it's tough to be broke, kid. I Can't Give You Anything but Love. Dorothy Fields. APT-2; ReLy

Gee! It's great, after bein' our late. Walkin' My Baby Back Home. Fred E. Ahlert. ReLy

Gee, Officer Krupke. Stephen Sondheim. OBAL; ReLy

Gee, that poor shine! (LL) Bottled [New York]. Helene Johnson. APT-2; BlSi

Gee up, Neddy, to the fair. Unknown. OxNR

Geese, The. Jorie Graham. HCAP

Geese Blood. Barbara Guest. FTOS

Geese flew by as you entered me, The. Aubade. Kate C. Richardson. PasH

Geese, fresh greens / Wait for you. Issa. ZenPo, tr. by Takashi Ikemoto and Lucien Stryk

Geese Gone Beyond. Gary Snyder. NoAM

Geese have gone, The. Cor Van den Heuvel. HA

Gegard. Fazil Abdulovich Iskander. ItGoST, tr. by Avril Pyman

Geist's Grave. Matthew Arnold. NOBVV

Gem Creek. Muso Soseki. EaWin, tr. by W. S. Merwin

Gem Forest. Muso Soseki. EaWin, tr. by W. S. Merwin

Gem Mountain. Muso Soseki. EaWin, tr. by W. S. Merwin

Gem of all isthmuses and isles that lie. Catullus. See Apple of islands, Sirmio, & bright peninsulas, set

Gem of the crimson-colour'd Even. To the Evening Star. Thomas Campbell. GTBS-P

Gems and jewels let them heap. In a Garret. Herman Melville. OBAL

Genaro was standing. Appointment, The. Louis Simpson. BodElec

Genau'r Glyn, Tywyn, each day from these to Rhys's halls. Ode to Rhys ap Maredudd of Tywyn. Dafydd [or David] Nanmor. OBWVE, tr. by H. Idris Bell

Gene sat on a rock, dangling our map. Route of the Táin, The. Thomas Kinsella. PBCIP

Genealogical Reflection. Ogden Nash. OBAL

Genealogy of Crosses, The. Andrey [or Andrei] Andreievich Voznesensky [or Voznesenskij]. PFTM-2, tr. by Richard McKane

Genealogy of Women, The. Semonides.
    "God in His Wisdom from the start." WoPoe, tr. by Peter Whigham

Geneology. Bob Kaufman. NBV

General, The. Siegfried Sassoon. FaBoWar; NAEL-5v2; NAEL-6v2; NPeEn; NoAM; NoP-4; OBWP; OxBEV; OxBSP; OxBTC; OxBoLi; PoE

General B. F. Butler. Ambrose Bierce. CBCWP

General becomes a sword, The. Having Died. Kim Kwangsŏp. WoPoe, tr. by David R. McCann

General Communion, A. Alice Thompson Meynell. NOCV; WPE

General conquers Russia, The. Honest with Oneself. "Don Aminado." TCRP, tr. by Albert C. Todd

General Description of Men and Things in Cape Town, A. Frederic Brooks. PeSAV

General Eclipse, The. John Cleveland. BASC

General Elliott, The. Robert Graves. PeLV

General Grant—the Hero of the War. George Moses Horton. CBCWP

General inspecting the trenches, The. Sir Alan Patrick Herbert. PoWW

General John Cabell Breckinridge. Jill Breckinridge. CBCWP Fr. Civil Blood.

General names, no other. Nanni Cagnone. ItPo, tr. by Gayle Ridinger

General once lived named de Gaulle, A. Limerick. Paul Bristow. PeLi

General Prologue. Geoffrey Chaucer. NAWM-5v1; NAWM-7v1, tr. by Theodore Morrison Fr. Canterbury Tales, The.

General Prologue, The. Geoffrey Chaucer. FHYEP; NAEL-6v1; NAEL-7v1; NAWM-5v1; PoE Fr. Canterbury Tales, The.

General Review of the Sex Situation. Dorothy Parker. NAAL-2v2

General Robert Smalls. Josephine D. Henderson Heard. CBWP-4

General's Plaque, The. Ho Xuan Hong. FaBoWar, tr. by Graeme Wilson

General Secretary's feet whispered over the red carpet, The. Anteroom: Geneva. Denis Devlin. CIP-2

General Store. Rachel Lyman Field. ChAP

General Strike. Nancy Joyce Peters. SurWo

General, there's a battle / between your orders and my songs. Song of the Juggler. Heberto Padilla. AF, tr. by Alastair Reid

General will be shot in the face, The. Respect for Law and Order, A. John Hughes. PNI

General William Booth Enters into Heaven. Nicholas Vachel Lindsay. APT-1; ChIV-2; ColAP; MoAmPo; NOBA; OxBA; PoE; TAP; TCAPo

General wonder in our land. Unknown. NOIV

Generalities. Robert Conquest. OxBC

Generals Ride in Cars. Unknown. FaBoWar

Generation. Rae Armantrout. FTOS

Generation. Audre Lorde. NBV

Generation, A. Gu Cheng. PFTM-2, VCWP, tr. by Sam Hamill

Generation Gap, The. Ruby C. Saunders. BlSi

Generation of the Seeds, or the Origin of Corn, The. Unknown.
  "Lo! ye children of men and the Mother." APN-2

Generations. Joseph Awad. GraLe

Generations. Rachel [or Rokhl] Korn. CarOv, tr. by Carolyn Kizer

Generations 1. Sam Cornish. GT

Generations 2. Sam Cornish. GT

Generations of the virgin are tattooed on her unblemished belly, The. Poem of any Virgin. Jorge de Lima. PFTM-1

Generations unfold from our faces. Bones and Drums. Ron Welburn. SeSe

Generic Elbows. Bernadette Mayer. FTOS

Genes confessing. (LL) Weakness, The. Toi Derricotte. GT; LTA

Genesis. Buland Al-Haidari [or Al-Haydari]. MAP, tr. by Patricia Alanah Byrne and Salma Khadra Jayyusi

Genesis. Bible, O.T.
  "And God saw that the wickedness of man was great." NAWM-5v1
  "And the Lord God planted a garden eastward in Eden." OBGa
  "And Joseph was brought down to Egypt." NAWM-5v1
  "And Noah was six hundred years old when the flood of waters." NAWM-5v1
  "And the whole earth was of one language, and of one speech." NAWM-5v1
  "In the beginning God created the heaven and the earth." NAWM-5v1
  "Joseph, being seventeen years old, was feeding the flock with his brethren." NAWM-5v1
  "See, the smelle of my sone is as the smell of a feld." OBVEr

Genesis. OBGa

Genesis. Caedmon.
  Noah's Flood. AnOE, tr. by C. W. Kennedy
  Temptation and Fall of Man, The. AnOE, tr. by C. W. Kennedy

Genesis. Brian Higgins. FaBoTw

Genesis. Geoffrey Hill. ChIV-1; HAP; HarvBoo; OxBC; PeECV; TOF

Genesis. Alda Merini. CItWP, tr. by Cinzia Sartini Blum and Lara Trubowitz

Genesis. K. Satchidanandan. OMIP, tr. by K. Satchidanandan

Genesis. Delmore Schwartz.
  "And then one day Hershey played by the door." TrJP
  You Are a Jew! TrJP

Genesis. Ali Smith. PoBW

Genesis. Jules Alan Wein. TrJP

Genesis 2. Etheridge Knight. BodElec

Genesis XXIV. Arthur Hugh Clough. ChIV-1

Genesis (Chapter 7, Verse 5). Manuela Fingueret. MirDau, tr. by Roberta Gordenstein

Genesis of Butterflies, The. Victor Hugo. AWP, tr. by Andrew Lang

Geneva was the wild one. Ballad of Aunt Geneva, The. Marilyn Nelson Waniek. FFC; GT; RA

Génèvres Hérissez, et Vous, Houx Espineux. Pierre de Ronsard. WoPoe, tr. by Donald Davie

Genial poets, pink-faced. Goodbye to Tolerance. Denise Levertov. NoAM

Genie in the Jar, The. Nikki Giovanni. SeSe

Genie's Prayer Under the Kitchen Sink. Rita Dove. RACG

Genie serves a continental breakfast, angel brings the desired, A. Zealous. Joshua Clover. PuP-23

Genius. R. J. P. Hewison. PeLi

Genius. Philip Levine. NoAM

Genius. Adah Isaacs Menken. CBWP-1; ViWPN

Genius. Margit Szécsi. IQMS, tr. by Agnes Arany-Makkai

Genius, The. Leonard Cohen. MoCV

Genius Child. Langston Hughes. PoPoPo

Genius Child. Kevin Powell. AmPoNex

Genius is power. Genius. Adah Isaacs Menken. CBWP-1; ViWPN

Genius Loci. Margaret Louisa Woods. OBEV

Genius of Fog at Ecola Creek Mouth. Sandra McPherson. ExTi

Genius, or Muse, whate'er thou art! whose thrill. Robert Merry. NOBRP Fr. Laurel of Liberty. A Poem, The.

Genius, technique—you'd swear the pair unsuited. Nature and Art. Goethe. STV, tr. by John Frederick Nims

Genius, that power which dazzles mortal eyes. Success. C. C. Cameron. PoToHe

Genius was 81, The. Cutting Prow, The. Edward Sanders. PmAP

Genoa. Dino Campana. PFTM-1

Gent, Nugget, Swank, and Dude. Thirteen. Ronald Wallace. PBCAP

Genteel in personage, / Conduct and equipage. Maid's Husband, The. Henry Carey. ECEV

Gentian weaves her fringes, The. Emily Dickinson. PoRA

Gentilesse. Geoffrey Chaucer. AWP; MiEL; NAEL-5v1
  (Firste fader and findere of gentilesse, The.) NAEL-6v1

Gentle Anarchist, The. Brunton Stephens. NOBAu

Gentle and smiling as before. Wheel, The. Robert Earl Hayden. BPo

Gentle Annie, willow wind, the West, A. Four Winds. Hal Porter. NOBAu

Gentle as a maiden's dream. Snow Storm, The. Mary Weston Fordham. CBWP-2

Gentle at last, and as clean as ever. Grandfather in the Old Men's Home. W.S. Merwin. CoAmPo

Gentle breeze has died down, The. To the Tune "Spring at Wu Ling." Li Ch'ing-chao. OHMPC, tr. by Kenneth Rexroth

Gentle breeze, morning dew. I Wake Up Alone. Li Shang-yin. OHMPC, tr. by Kenneth Rexroth

Gentle breeze rustles through reeds and rushes, A. In a Boat, Getting Up at Night. Su Tung-p'o (Su Shih). SuSp, tr. by Irving Y. Lo

Gentle Breeze with a Whispered Cry, The. Gustavo Adolfo Bécquer. SpanPo, tr. by Alice Jane McVan

Gentle Check, The. Joseph Beaumont. NOSC

Gentle, cheerful ticking of a clock, The. Quiet Days. Mildred T. Mey. PoToHe

Gentle Christ? (LL) Marban, a Hermit Speaks. Unknown. BIrV; CIP-2, tr. by Michael Hartnett

Gentle Communion. Pat Mora. NIL-7; NIP-4

Gentle East wind is blowing, A. On the Siu Cheng Road. Su Tung-p'o (Su Shih). OHPC, tr. by Kenneth Rexroth

Gentle Echo on Woman, A. Jonathan Swift. NBLV

Gentle footsteps on the sand. Crows, The. Maria Valli. CBAP

Gentle ghost. Marina Ivanovna Tsvetayeva [or Tsvetaeva]. TCRusP, tr. by Bob Perelman, Aleksandar Petrov and Shirley Rihner Fr. Poems to Blok.

Gentle hands that never weary. Lines to Mother. Rose M. Stein. PWR

Gentle Heart Two: A. Judith Johnson Sherwin. BoWoP

Gentle knight was pricking on the plaine, A. Edmund Spenser. EBEV; FHYEP; NAEL-5v1 Fr. Faerie Queene, The.

Gentle Locke sits down to write his famous treatise. At Work. Artur Miedzyrzecki. PoSu, tr. by John Batki and Artur Miedzyrzecki

Gentle lords and ladies gay. (LL) Hunting Song. Sir Walter Scott. GTBS-P; SCGP

Gentle of hand, the Dean of St. Patrick's guided. Sermon on Swift, A. Austin Clarke. BIrV

Gentle Owen was a man well set, The. Owen Tudor. Hugh Holland. AngWePo

Gentle River, Gentle River. Unknown. AWP, tr. by Thomas Percy

Gentle Shepherd, The. Allan Ramsay.
(Peggy.) OBEV
(Sang.) OxBEV
Wawking of the Fauld, The. OxBS; SCGP

Gentle slopes are green to remind you, The. David Jones. NAEL-5v2; NAEL-6v2 *Fr.* In Parenthesis.

Gentle squire would gladly entertain, A. Joseph Hall. NoSic *Fr.* Virgidemiarum.

Gentle thought there is will often start, A. Dante Alighieri. AWP; EaItPo, *tr. by* Dante Gabriel Rossetti *Fr.* La Vita Nuova.

Gentle Wind, A. Fu Hsüan. AWP, *tr. by* Arthur Waley
(GENTLE wind fans the calm night, A.) ChiP, *tr. by* Arthur Waley

Gentle Word, A. *Unknown.* PoToHe

Gentleman, The. Menahem ben Judah Lonzano. TrJP, *tr. by* A. B. Rhine

Gentleman and the Lady, The. Vivian Lamarque. CItWP, *tr. by* Cinzia Sartini Blum and Lara Trubowitz

Gentleman cam oure the sea, A. Cruel Brother, The. *Unknown.* ESPB

Gentleman in Front, The. Vivian Lamarque. CItWP, *tr. by* Cinzia Sartini Blum and Lara Trubowitz

Gentleman in hunting rode astray, A. Beggar Woman, The. William King. ECEV; NOEC

Gentleman in the Heart, The. Vivian Lamarque. CItWP, *tr. by* Cinzia Sartini Blum and Lara Trubowitz

Gentleman Is a Dope, The. Richard Rodgers. ReLy

Gentleman makes his way among clouds and moons, The. Brief Note from Jerusalem, A. Gabriel Preil. FIT, *tr. by* Robert Friend

Gentleman, most wretched in his lot, A. Reformation. Anne Finch, Countess of Winchilsea. ECWP

Gentleman's Study, in Answer to The Lady's Dressing-Room, The. "Miss W——." ECWP

Gentlemen. Geoffrey Taylor. FaBoEE

Gentlemen, as we take our seats. Rehearsal, The. Horace Gregory. VGW

Gentlemen, for this day's work our chance has not been ill. *Unknown.* FaBoWar, *tr. by* John Hookham Frere *Fr.* Poem of the Cid, The.

"Gentlemen, look on this wonder." Adhesive Autopsy of Walt Whitman, The. Jonathan Williams. PoM

Gentlemen-Rankers. Rudyard Kipling. FaBoWar; NOBVV

Gentlemen, / the situation is tragic. State of the Union. Aimé Césaire. NegPo, *tr. by* Denis Kelly

Gentlemen who have got to be classics and are now old, The. Letter to the Academy. Langston Hughes. AF

Gentleness of the slant October light, The. Where It Ends. William Bronk. APSN

Gentleness of the Very Tall, The. Linda France. MFPA

Gentlest air, thou breath of lovers. Sigh, A. Anne Finch, Countess of Winchilsea. ECWP; OxBEV

Gentlest fair, mourn, mourn no moe. (LL) John Fletcher. OBEV; OxAEP-1 *Fr.* Queen of Corinth, The.

Gentlest of women, put your weapons by. Lay Your Arms Aside. Pierce Ferriter. BIrV, *tr. by* Eiléan Ní Chuilleanáin

Gentlewoman of the dealing trade, A. Epigram 29. Samuel Rowlands. NOSC

Gentlewoman yt Married a Yonge Gent Who After Forsooke Whereuppon She Tooke Hir Needle in Which She Was Excelent and Worked upon Hir Sampler Thus, A. *Unknown.* EMWP

Gentlewomans Answer to One, that Sayd He Should Dye, if Shee Refuse His Desires, A. *Unknown.* EMWP

Gently about this tomb wind gently O Ivy. At the Tomb of Sophokles. Simmias [*or* Simias] of Rhodes. GrAn, *tr. by* Dudley Fitts

Gently, gently prithee, time. *Unknown.* NOSC

Gently I stir a white feather fan. In the Mountains on a Summer Day. Li Po. AWP, *tr. by* Arthur Waley

Gently I took that which ungently came. Forbearance. Samuel Taylor Coleridge. ChIV-2

Gently I wave the visible world away. Absinthe-Drinker, The. Arthur Symons. FaBoTw; NOBVV

Gently, so as not to rouse / His skinny girl. Lucilius. GrAn

Gently stroke a wound. Joyce Mansour. MFP, *tr. by* Martin Sorrell

Gently to hear, kindly to judge, our play. (LL) William Shakespeare. OxAEP-1; SCV *Fr.* King Henry V.

Gentry, The. Elmaz Abinader. GraLe

Genuine Jewish Flesh. Richard Michelson. GotH

Genuine Poem, Found on a Blackboard in a Bowling Alley in Story City, Iowa. Ted Kooser. KaS

Genuine, you are interested in poetry. (LL) Poetry: "I, too, dislike it: there are things that are important beyond all this fiddle." Marianne Craig Moore. APT-1; AmFaPo; BoWoP; ColAP; FaBoWP; HAP; HeIP-4; MoAmPo; NAAL-2v2; NAAL-5; NALW; NIP-4; NOBA; NoAM; NoP-4; OxBA; PAI; PoE; PoPoPo; TAP; TCAPo; TFi; UnPo

Genus Infoelix Vitae. Queen of England Elizabeth I. EMWP

Geode, the troll's melon. James Merrill. HCAP *Fr.* In Nine Sleep Valley.

Geographers, The. Karl Shapiro. OxBA

Geographical History, The. Giulia Niccolai. CItWP, *tr. by* Cinzia Sartini Blum and Lara Trubowitz

Geography. Gilbert Keith Chesterton. OBSV *Fr.* Songs of Education.

Geography. Michael Dransfield.
"In the forest, in unexplored." CBAP
"Sky ceases. There is only." CBAP

Geography. Kenneth Koch. NoAM

Geography. Brenda Marie Osbey. BodElec

Geography: a Song. Howard Moss. OBCoV

Geography I am learning, The. Geography. Brenda Marie Osbey. BodElec

Geography Lesson. Carol Rumens. FaBoWP

Geography of dream is complex, The. Difference Between Night and Day, The. Bin Ramke. YaYoPo

Geography of Lograire, The. Thomas Merton.
East.
Place Names. ChIV-1

Geological Hymn. Joseph Ceravolo. PmAP

Geology, A. Brenda Hillman. GeoHom

Geometric, deformed, unnatural. (LL) Venus Hottentot, The. Elizabeth Alexander. ESEAA; InTrad

Geometrical Place. Günter Eich. AF, *tr. by* David Young

Geometry. Rita Dove. HCAP; HeIP-4

Geometry Class. Mark Bibbins. AmPoNex; WiU

Geometry of the Soul. Fawziyya Abu Khalid. PoArWo, *tr. by* Farouk Mustafa

Geordie [An Old Ballad]. *Unknown.* ESPB; OxBB

Georg Heym—The Almost Metaphysical Adventure. Zbigniew Herbert. PoetW, *tr. by* John Carpenter and Bogdana Carpenter

Georg Trakl. Else Lasker-Schüler. PFTM-1

George. Dudley Randall. BPo; CoAmPo; NoAM

George III. Edmund Clerihew Bentley. NOBL; NPeEn; OxBoLi; PeLV *Fr.* Clerihews.

George III and the Sailor. "Peter Pindar." NOEC *Fr.* Royal Tour, and Weymouth Amusements, The.

George III Visits Whitbread's Brewery. "Peter Pindar." NOEC *Fr.* Instructions to a Celebrated Laureat.

George Aloe and the *Sweepstake*, The. *Unknown.* ESPB

George and Genevieve. George Hugnet. Gertrude Stein. NoAM

George and me. Letter to a Boy at School. Anna Wickham. NOxBChV

George Burns likes to insist that he always. Of Time and the Line. Charles Bernstein. NIL-7; PFTM-2; PmAP; ReTh

George Copway's Dream Song. *Unknown.* APN-2, *tr. by* George Copway

George Crabbe. Edwin Arlington Robinson. APN-2; MoAmPo; NAAL-2v2; NOBA; NoP-4; OxBA; TAP

George Gissing. Dorothy Parker. APT-1 *Fr.* Pig's-Eye View of Literature, A.

George Grosz. Else Lasker-Schüler. PFTM-1

George Hugnet. Gertrude Stein. NoAM

George! I dunno how you do it George. Toronto Board of Trade Goes Abroad. Earle Birney. PeLV

George Moses Horton, Myself. George Moses Horton. NAAAL

George Robinson: Blues. Muriel Rukeyser. NNaP; RACG

George Sand. Dorothy Parker. APT-1; NALW *Fr.* Pig's-Eye View of Literature, A.

George Stephenson said: "These repairs." Limerick. Frank Richards. PeLi

George the First was always reckoned. Georges, The. Walter Savage Landor. FaBoEE; NIP-4; OBCoV; OBSV

George the Third. Edmund Clerihew Bentley. NOBL; NPeEn; OxBoLi; PeLV *Fr.* Clerihews.

George the Third's Soliloquy. Philip Freneau. NOBA
"France aids them now, a desperate game I play." TCAPo

George Washington and the Loss of His Teeth. Diane Wakoski. PFTM-2

George Washington never owned a camel. Jackson Mac Low. APSN *Fr.* Presidents of the United States of America, The.

George Washington said to his dad. Limerick. Frank Richards. PeLi

George Washington, your name is on my lips. Patriotic Poem. Diane Wakoski. VGW

Georges, The. Walter Savage Landor. FaBoEE; NIP-4; OBCoV; OBSV

Georges, The. William Makepeace Thackeray. FaBoEE

Georgia. Philippe Soupault. SurPaPo, *tr. by* Mary Ann Caws and Patricia Terry

Georgia Dusk. Jean Toomer. APT-2; BPo; NAAL-2v2; NAAL-5; NoAM; NoP-4

Georgia on My Mind. Hoagy Carmichael. ReLy

Georgiad, The. Roy Campbell.
"Hail, mediocrity, beneath whose spell." MoBrPo
"Next him Jack Squire through his own tear-drops sploshes." OxBTC

Georgian Spring.   Roy Campbell.   OBSV

Georgics.   Virgil [*or* Vergil].

  Georgics 1.

    "Therefore Philippi saw once more the Roman battalions."   APT-2, *tr. by* Richmond Lattimore

    "Who dares deny the burning truth of the sun?"   WoPoe, *tr. by* David R. Slavitt

    "What makes a plenteous harvest."   AWP

Georgics of Heisod, The.   Hesiod.

  Winter.   NOSC, *tr. by* George Chapman

Georgie Porgie, pudding and pie.   Mother Goose.   LB; OxNR; ReMoGo

Georgina Trevellyn to Luisa: "Dearest Louisa, Enquire if you please about Mr. Claude."   Arthur Hugh Clough.   FaBoVe   *Fr.* Amours de Voyage.

"Gerald's here!" my mother called.   Voice in the Garden, A.   Selima Hill.   FaBoWP

Gerald the Bitter, with your polished smile.   Widow's Curse, The.   *Unknown.*   NOIV, *tr. by* Thomas Kinsella

Geranium.   Edward Dorn.   PmAP

Geranium, The.   Theodore Roethke.   CoAP; EmeKit; UnPo; WeW-3

Geranium, The.   Richard Brinsley Sheridan.   BoLoP

Geranium and the Child.   Ece Ayhan.   PFTM-2, *tr. by* Murat Nemet-Nejat

Geranium, houseleek, laid in oblong beds.   Poem.   John Gray.   NOBVV

Geranium needs, The.   Holm Oak, The.   Mariella Bettarini.   CItWP, *tr. by* Cinzia Sartini Blum and Lara Trubowitz

Geraniums, The.   Genevieve Taggard.   VGW

Gerarde.   Eloise Bibb.   CBWP-4

Gereint ab Erbin.   *Unknown.*   OBWVE, *tr. by* Joseph P. Clancy

Gereint Son of Erbin.   *Unknown.*   WoPoe, *tr. by* Gwyn Williams   *Fr.* Black Book of Carmarthen, The.

Geriatric.   Ronald Stuart Thomas.   TCAWP

Geriatric, wizened, ancient man.   Trickster 1 (for Winston Rodney).   Kwame Dawes.   WaCA

Germ, The.   Ogden Nash.   APT-2; RB

Germ of new life, whose powers expanding slow.   To a Little Invisible Being Who Is Expected Soon to Become Visible.   Anna Laetitia Barbauld.   ECWP; NAEL-6v2; WoRP

German Army, Russia, 1943, The.   Ai.   MakPoe

German Frontier at Basel: 1942 and 1992, The.   Hilda Schiff.   HP

German Language, The.   Friedrich von Logau.   GePo, *tr. by* George C. Schoolfield

German Language, The.   Berthold Viertel.   AuPH, *tr. by* Lowell A. Bangerter

German Prisoners.   Joseph Lee.   FaBoWar

German Requiem, A.   James Fenton.   HarvBoo; NAEL-5v2; NAEL-6v2; NPeEn; NoAM

"His wife nods, and a secret smile."   HP

Germans in Greek, The.   Porson on German Scholarship.   Richard Porson.   FaBoEE

Germans stood together under guard, The.   1945.   Ed Leeflang.   TuT, *tr. by* Peter Van de Kamp

Germany, 1981.   Phyllis Kahaney.   GotH

Germany of three confessions now shall keep a single one.   One Faith and No Faith.   Friedrich von Logau.   GePo, *tr. by* George C. Schoolfield

Germinal.   "Æ"   BIrV; MoBrPo; OBEV; OBMV

Gerontion.   T. S. Eliot.   APT-1; ColAP; EBEV; GTBS-P; HAP; NAAL-2v2; NAAL-5; NOBA; NPeEn; NoAM; OxAEP-2; OxBA; PAI; TAP; TCAPo; TFi

Gertrude and Gulielma, sister-twins.   Frederick Goddard Tuckerman.   HAP   *Fr.* Sonnets.

Gertrude, or Fidelity Till Death.   Felicia Dorothea Hemans.   RWP

Gertrude Stein.   Mina Loy.   APT-1

Gertrude Stein at Snails Bay.   Peter Porter.   OxBC

Gest of Robyn Hode.   *Unknown.*   ESPB; OxBB

  "Lythe and listin, gentilmen."   NAEL-6v1

  "They toke togyder theyr counsell."   PeECV

Gestalt Me Out!   Bruce Andrews.   FTOS

Gesture.   Donald Finkel.   InPK-6

Gesture, The.   George Oppen.   NNaP   *Fr.* Five Poems about Poetry.

Gesture and Flight.   Ann Lauterbach.   BodElec

Gesture by a Lady with an Assumed Name, A.   James Wright (1927–80).   CoAmPo

Gesture of an Ionic column returning your face.   Noli Me Tangere.   Jan Polkowski.   AF, *tr. by* Michael March

Gesture the gesture the gesture the gesture, The.   Michael McClure.   NeAP; PmAP   *Fr.* Hymn to St. Geryon.

Gestures from My Window.   Yolanda Bedregal.   TANSG, *tr. by* Carolyne Wright

Get a load.   Lorine Niedecker.   APT-2

Get-Away.   Robert Malise Bowyer Nichols.

"Beginning when I was six I became my father's accomplice."   CLPP

"Get away from Eros!"   Archias.   GrAn

Get away, they're all gone.   Chops Are Flyin.   Stanley Crouch.   GT

Get Drunk.   Ho Ch'i-fang.   WoPoe, *tr. by* Kai-yu Hsu

Get drunk, my boy, don't weep, you're.   Asclepiades.   PGA

Get drunk / Walk on water.   Things to Do in the Bible.   Elaine Equi.   IllVoic

Get free, and so thou shalt even all admire. (LL)   Preparative, The.   Thomas Traherne.   BASC; ESCV; GeHe

Get him up and be gone as one shaped awry; he disturbs the order here. (LL)   Thomas Hardy.   ChIV-1; NoAM; OxBTC   *Fr.* In Tenebris.

Get it, / she said, so it's unknown which parent.   John Cage.   APSN   *Fr.* Diary: How to Improve the World (You Will Only Make Matters Worse).

Get on top.   On Top of It All.   Keith Gilyard.   SpirFl

Get out of me a little.   Death Is Your Salvation.   Nidaa Khoury.   DTA, *tr. by* Shirley Kaufman and Roger Tavor

Get out of my hut, you stealthy vermin! Leonidas'   Leonidas of Tarentum.   HePo   *Fr.* Epigrams.

Get Out of Town.   Cole Porter.   ReLy

Get put gat eisnin monocotyledon.   Like Pornography.   Rob MacKenzie.   Oth

Get ready. (LL)   La Migra.   Pat Mora.   NIL-7; UnSA

Get ready your money and come to me.   *Unknown.*   OxNR

Get the Gasworks.   David Ignatow.   InPK-6

Get thee a ship well-rigged and tight.   In Praise of Fidelia.   Mildmay Fane, 2d Earl of Westmorland.   BeJo; NOSC; OxBSP

Get thee behind me. Even as heavy-curled,   "Retro Me, Sathana."   Dante Gabriel Rossetti.   ChIV-2

Get this.   Descriptive Poetry.   Friedrich Hölderlin.   WoPoe, *tr. by* Vyt Bakaitis

Get this straight, Joe, and don't get me wrong.   How Do I Feel?   Kenneth Fearing.   APT-2

Get up!   Joseph Skipsey.   InPK-6; NOBVV; NPeEn

Get Up and Bar the Door.   *Unknown.*   ESPB; HeIP-4; NePenScot; NoP-4; OxBS

Get Up, Get Up.   *Unknown.*   NTCP

Get up, get up for shame! the blooming morn[e].   Corinna's Going a-Maying.   Robert Herrick.   AEP; BASC; BeJo; CABP; CaPo; HAP; NAEL-5v1; NAEL-6v1; NAEL-7v1; NIP-4; NOBE; NOSC; NoP-4; OBEV; OxBEV; PBRV; PoE; PoPoPo; SCGP; TFi

Get up, get up, Mountain: no more sleep for you!   Āśutos Bhattācārya.   SinGod, *tr. by* Rachel Fell McDermott

Get up, get up, you lazy-head.   Get Up, Get Up.   *Unknown.*   NTCP

"Get up! Marlene?" I smell the April rain.   Mark Stern Wakes Up.   Frederick Feirstein.   RA

Get up, Mountain, get up!   *Unknown.*   SinGod, *tr. by* Rachel Fell McDermott

"Get up!" the caller calls, "Get up!"   Get Up!   Joseph Skipsey.   InPK-6; NOBVV; NPeEn

Get up, you old dog.   To the Man Inside.   Carl Rakosi.   BodElec

Get ye hence, rebellious spirits.   Incantation.   Zinaida Nikolayevna [*or* Nikolaevna] Gippius.   ARWW, *tr. by* Catriona Kelly

Get ye up from the wrath of God's terrible day!   Cities of the Plain, The.   John Greenleaf Whittier.   ChIV-1; NCAP

Get your flag out of my face, it tickles!   Last Will and Testament.   Hans Magnus Enzensberger.   PoSu

(Get Your Kicks On) Route 66!   Bobby Troup.   ReLy

Get your purse, have you got your keys? (LL)   Secondhand Coat.   Ruth Stone.   NALW; NIL-7; NIP-4

Gethsemane.   Rudyard Kipling.   FaBoTw; NPeEn; PeFWW

  (Garden called Gethsemane / In Picardy it was, The.)   GI

Gethsemane A. D.   Dolores Kendrick.   FFC

Gethsemani, KY.   Ernesto Cardenal.

  Like Empty Beer Cans.   TCLAP, *tr. by* Thomas Merton

Gettin' Straight.   Mcavoy Layne.   CDa

Getting Across.   Carter Revard.   VoR

Getting Away: Verses and Choruses for Various Voices.   Wendell Berry.   PoCoUp

Getting Berries.   *Unknown.*   STP, *tr. by* Franz Boas

Getting Dirty.   Dorthi Charles.   TLR

Getting Down to Get Over.   June Jordan.   TAP

Getting Even.   Mark Fleckenstein.   MiVo

Getting Firewood.   *Unknown.*   STP, *tr. by* Franz Boas

Getting in the Wood.   Gary Snyder.   NoAM

Getting Inside the Miracle.   Luci Shaw.   TrCP

Getting It Wrong, Again.   Steve Griffiths.   AngWePo

Getting Lost in Nazi Germany.   Marvin Bell.   GotH; TaR

Getting old, I retire to this little mountain district.   Late in the Year K'uei-yu (1333), Staying at the Temple of the Upper Regions.   Yü Chi.   CoBLCP, *tr. by* Jonathan Chaves

Getting Older.   Elaine Feinstein.   HarvBoo

Getting on Horseback.   Yü Chi.   CoBLCP, *tr. by* Jonathan Chaves

Getting Out. Cleopatra Mathis. SoSe-8

Getting Out Alive. Rosario Morales. PueRic

Getting out of bed one day, you broke. Elegy for My Sister. Howard Moss. VCAP

Getting Ready. Jack Gilbert. BodElec

Getting the Mail. Galway Kinnell. UnPo

Getting the Message. Maxine W. Kumin. TaR

Getting the News. Helen Chasin. YaYoPo

Getting There. Sylvia Plath. GM

Getting through with the world. Approach to a City. William Carlos Williams. PoRA

Getting to Know Her. Jacqueline Berger. AmPoNex

Getting to Rome. *Unknown.* NOIV

Getting to Sleep in New Jersey. John A. Stone. BloBone

Getting Up Early on a Spring Morning. Po Chü-i. ChiP, *tr. by* Arthur Waley

Getting Up in Winter. Emperor Ch'ien-wen of Liang. BLT, *tr. by* Kenneth Rexroth

Getting Warm. Rae Armantrout. FTOS

Getting Your Rocks Off. Melvin Dixon. CAGL

Gettysburg. Edgar Lee Masters. CBCWP

Gettysburg Address, The. Abraham Lincoln. HHAm

Gettysburg, July 1, 1863. Jane Kenyon. CBCWP

Gettysburg Ode. Bayard Taylor. CBCWP

Geyser, The. Ágnes Nemes Nagy. PoSu, *tr. by* Bruce Berlind

Ghaflah—the sin of forgetfulness. Dima Hilal. PoArWo

Ghaists; a Kirk-yard Eclogue, The. Robert Fergusson. OxBS

Ghastly ordeal it was, A. In. No Title. David Schubert. APT-2

Ghazal. Mirza Asadullah Khan Ghalib. WoPoe, *tr. by* Frances W. Pritchett

Ghazal. Adrienne Rich. WoPoe

Ghazal 5. Mirza Asadullah Khan Ghalib. EaWin, *tr. by* Aijaz Ahmad and W. S. Merwin

Ghazal 12. Mirza Asadullah Khan Ghalib. EaWin, *tr. by* Aijaz Ahmad and W. S. Merwin

Ghazal 15. Mirza Asadullah Khan Ghalib. EaWin, *tr. by* Aijaz Ahmad and W. S. Merwin

Ghazal 21. Mirza Asadullah Khan Ghalib. EaWin, *tr. by* Aijaz Ahmad and W. S. Merwin

Ghazal 24: For Years My Heart Asked Me for Jamshid's Cup. Hafiz [*or* Hafez]. WoPoe, *tr. by* Elizabeth Gray

Ghazal 25. Mirza Asadullah Khan Ghalib. EaWin, *tr. by* Aijaz Ahmad and W. S. Merwin .

Ghazal 34. Mirza Asadullah Khan Ghalib. EaWin, *tr. by* Aijaz Ahmad and W. S. Merwin

Ghazal: Comet. Jacqueline Osherow. ExTi

Ghazal: Half-Way Through the Night. Hafiz [*or* Hafez]. WoPoe, *tr. by* Geoffrey Squires

Ghazal of the Better-Unbegun. Heather McHugh. ExTi

Ghazal on signs of Love and Occupation. Philip Salom. BMAP

Ghede Poem. Nathaniel Mackey. PmAP

Ghetto. Michael Longley. EmeKit; NoP-4; PNI

Ghetto. Guy Tirolien. NegPo, *tr. by* Ellen Conroy Kennedy

Ghetto, The. Lola Ridge.
   "Cool inaccessible air." APT-1
   "In this dingy café" APT-1

Ghetto Twilight. Alter Brody. TaR

Ghona Widow's Lullaby, The. Thomas Pringle. PeSAV

Ghost. Nina Cassian. PoSu, *tr. by* Christopher Hewitt

Ghost, The. Charles Churchill.
   "Pomposo (insolent and loud)." OBSV

Ghost, The. Walter De la Mare. EnLoPo; MoBrPo; NOBE; OxBTC

Ghost, The. Ágnes Nemes Nagy. PoSu, *tr. by* Bruce Berlind

Ghost, The. Fitz-James O'Brien. FaBoVe; NOEC

Ghost, The. Propertius. WoPoe, *tr. by* Robert Lowell

Ghost, The. Iain Crichton Smith. NOxBChV

Ghost & Shaman. *Unknown.* STP, *tr. by* Franz Boas

Ghost appears in the dark of winter, The. Ghost of Soul-making, The. Michael S. Harper. NAAAL

Ghost at Anlaby, The. Randolph Stow. NOBAu

Ghost-Dance Songs. *Unknown.*
   "I'yehe! my children." STP
   Songs of the Arapaho. APN-2, *tr. by* James Mooney
     "Father, have pity on me." NAAL-5
     "*He!* When I met him approaching." NAAL-5
   Songs of the Kiowa. APN-2, *tr. by* James Mooney
   Songs of the Paiute. APN-2
   Songs of the Sioux. APN-2
     "Father says so—E'yayo!, The." NAAL-5

     "Give me my knife." NAAL-5
     "Whole world is coming, The." NAAL-5; TCAPo
     "We shall live again." STP

Ghost in the Martini, The. Anthony Hecht. DiPo; NoP-4; OxBC

Ghost is someone: death has left a hole, A. Ghost, The. Propertius. WoPoe, *tr. by* Robert Lowell

Ghost of a Ghost, The. Brad Leithauser. RA

Ghost of a mouldy larder is one thing, A: whiskery bread. Corposant. Peter Redgrove. OxBTC

Ghost of Abel, The. William Blake. ChIV-1

Ghost of another comes to visit and we hold, The. Dance, The. Mark Strand. LCAP-2

Ghost of Edward. Joanna Baillie. ECWP *Fr.* Night Scenes of Other Times.

Ghost of Fadon, The. Joanna Baillie. NOBRP

Ghost of Ninon would be sorry now, The. Veteran Sirens. Edwin Arlington Robinson. NOBA

Ghost of our blood, I worship You. Adoramus Te, Christe. David [*or* Daibhi][*or* Daithi] O'Bruadair [*or* Ó Bruadair]. NOIV, *tr. by* Thomas Kinsella

Ghost of Santo Domingo, The. Suzanne Gardinier. NeAmPo

Ghost of Soul-making, The. Michael S. Harper. NAAAL

Ghost rose when the waves rose, A. Faith Upon the Waters. Laura Riding Jackson. APT-2

Ghost's Song, The. *Unknown. See* Cauld Lad of Hilton, The *or* The Wandering Spectre

Ghost Shirt, The. Lucia Maria Perillo. BAP-01

Ghost Song. Jack Spicer. APSN

Ghost Story. Dylan Thomas. OBCP

Ghost Street. Milán Füst. IQMS, *tr. by* Jess Perlman

Ghost Tantras. Michael McClure.
   "Pleasure fears me, foot rose, foot breath." BB
   "Silence the eyes! Becalm the senses!" PFTM-2
   "Trees are elephants' heads, the." PFTM-2

Ghost that loved a lady fair, A. Phantom-Wooer, The. Thomas Lovell Beddoes. NAEL-5v2; NAEL-6v2

Ghost Town. Michael Longley. ModIr

Ghost-Who-Walks, The. Colleen J. McElroy. GT

Ghost with PCP eyes, A. On Display. Thomas Sayers Ellis. InTrad

Ghostly Gladness. Richard Rolle of Hampole. HAP

Ghostly Tree. Léonie Adams. APT-2; MoAmPo

Ghosts. Robert Bridges. OxBEV

Ghosts. William Carpenter. ReTh

Ghosts, The. Thomas Love Peacock. OBCoV

Ghosts, The. Edith Jay Scovell. HarvBoo

Ghosts II. Lauris Edmond. PeNZ

Ghosts are attacking me, crowding up from. Poet Haunted, The. Wendy Rose. ReEnLa

Ghosts not having. Underneath (2). Jorie Graham. BodElec

Ghosts of hedgers and ditchers. Ash Keys. Michael Longley. PBCIP

Ghosts of the Buffaloes, The. Nicholas Vachel Lindsay. MoAmPo

Ghosts, Places, Stories, Questions. Vincent Buckley. NOBAu

Ghoul, The. Jack Prelutsky. OBCA

Ghoul Care. Ralph Hodgson. MoBrPo

Ghurba. Rawia Morra.
   "Powerless." PoArWo, *tr. by* Magdi Abdelhadi

Gi'e me a lass with a lump of land. Lass with a Lump of Land. Allan Ramsay. NOEC; OxBEV

Gia. Tracey Herd. MFPA

Gia's Song. Nora Naranjo-Morse. ReEnLa

Giant Decorative Dahlias. Molly Holden. OxBTC

Giant Killer. George Garrett. CRP

Giant Otters. Jackson Mac Low. FTOS

Giant Philosophical Otters. Jackson Mac Low. FTOS

Giant-Power from earth's remotest caves, The. Erasmus Darwin. NOEC *Fr.* Botanic Garden, The.

Giant Puffball, The. Edmund Charles Blunden. FaBoTw

Giant Red Woman. Clarence Major. GT

Giant Rocket. Wes Magee. NOxBChV

Giant sparkler, / Lights of the river. Louis Zukofsky. VGW *Fr.* A.

Giant swan descends: the winter weather, A. In Winter. Anastasius Grün. AuPH, *tr. by* Lowell A. Bangerter

Giant Thunder. James Reeves. OTCP
   (Giant Thunder, striding home.) NOxBChV

Giant Yellow. Maggie O'Sullivan. Oth

Giantess, The. Charles Baudelaire. OBVE, *tr. by* Roy Campbell

Giantesses, female fauna. Women of Rubens, The. Wislawa Szymborska. PoSu; VCWP

Giants. Jane Miller. ExTi

Giaour, The. Byron. NOBRP

Gibraltar. Wilfrid Scawen Blunt. OBEV

Gibran. Amin Al-Rihani.
 "On the Mediterranean coast, between the estuary and Jubail." GraLe, *tr. by* Sharif Elmusa

"Gie corn to my horse, mither." Mother's Malison; or, Clyde's Water, The. *Unknown.* ESPB

Gie her a *Haggis*! (LL) To a Haggis. Robert Burns. FaBoVe; NePenScot

Gif ye kip the schule. I Winna Let On. James King Annand. NOxBChV

Gife Langour. Henry Stuart [*or* Stewart], Lord Darnley. OxBS

Gift. Rabindranath Tagore. AmFaPo, *tr. by* William Radice

Gift, A. *Unknown.* GrAn, *tr. by* Guy Davenport

Gift, The. Margaret E. Bruner. PoToHe

Gift, The. Robert Creeley. NOBA

Gift, The. Ann Darr. PAI

Gift, The. Greg Delanty. BiHa

Gift, The. Louise Glück. FaBoWP; TaR

Gift, The. Li-Young Lee. BodElec; LoL; OpBo; RaBo; UnSA

Gift, The. N. Scott Momaday. NoP-4

Gift, The. Amado Nervo. TCLAP, *tr. by* Sue Standing

Gift, The. John Ormond. TCAWP

Gift, The. Edgar Silex. NAPBL

Gift, The. Sara Teasdale. LW

Gift, The. William Carlos Williams. ChIV-2
 (As the wise men of old brought gifts / guided by a star.) GI

Gift for the Queen. *Unknown.* OxNR

Gift for you should not be vulgar, A. Inscribed on a Painting of Windy Bamboo, to Be Presented to Tzu-kan. Hsü Wei. SuSp, *tr. by* Chiang Yee

Gift from Him who lifts our ev'ry care, A. (LL) Self-Mastery. Henrietta Cordelia Ray. CBWP-3; SWaP

Gift from Kenya. May Miller. BlSi

Gift Horse. Yusef Komunyakaa. GT

Gift Hour. Maria Banus. BoWoP

Gift of Children, The. Tiruvalluvar. WoPoe, *tr. by* Emmons E. White *Fr.* Kural, The.

Gift of God, The. Edwin Arlington Robinson. MoAmPo; OxBA

Gift of Great Value, A. Robert Creeley. LCAP-2

Gift of Judah the Woman-Hater, The. Judah ibn Sabbatai.
 Expensive Wife, The. TrJP
 "Up! Up! the time for sleep is past!" TrJP

Gift of Speech, The. Sadi [*or* Saadi *or* Sa'di]. AWP, *tr. by* L. Cranmer-Byng *Fr.* Gulistan, The.

Gift of the Poem. Stéphane Mallarmé. AWTN, *tr. by* Kate Flores

Gift of Tongues, The. Peter Davison. YaYoPo *Fr.* Breaking of the Day, The.

Gift of Tongues, The. Sam Hamill. GifTon

Gift Outright, The. Robert Frost. AiP; ColAP; FaBoA; HHAm; HarvBoo; MoAmPo; NAAL-2v2; NAAL-5; NOBA; NoAM; NoP-4; OxBA; PoPoPo; TFi; TRP

Gift to a Jade. Anna Wickham. OxBSP

Gift to Be Simple, The. Howard Moss. TwCP

Gift You Must Lose, A. Gregory Orfalea. GraLe

Gifted with vision the snowman would see. Frank Fell. NewEx

Gifts. Mary Elizabeth Coleridge. VWP

Gifts. Juliana Horatia Ewing. LW

Gifts. Emma Lazarus. TrJP

Gifts. Lenard D. Moore. SpirFl

Gifts. "Shu Ting." VCWP

Gifts. Ronald Stuart Thomas. NPeEn

Gifts. James Thomson. OBEV *Fr.* Sunday up the River.

Gifts. Thelma Tyfield. PoBW

Gifts, The. John Heath-Stubbs. OxBC

Gifts her kinship and our loves reveal, The. (LL) Chicago. Bret Harte. APN-2; AiP

Gifts Misused. Letitia [*or* Laetitia] Elizabeth Landon. VWP

Gifts of God, The. George Herbert. See Pulley, The

Gifts to a Lady. Antiphilus [*or* Antiphilos]. GrAn

Gigabyte Me—How Much RAM in Your Summer of Love? Edwin Torres. HeMarv

Gil Brenton. *Unknown.* ESPB; OxBB

Gil Morrice. *Unknown.* OxBB

Gilbertian Cats. Sir William Schwenck Gilbert. TriCat

Gilbertus Glanvil, whose heart was a hard as an anvil. *Unknown.* FaBoEE

Giles Collin he said to his mother one day. Lady Alice. *Unknown.* ESPB

Giles Collins he said to his old mother. Lady Alice. *Unknown.* ESPB

Giles Johnson, Ph.D. Frank Marshall Davis. BPo

Gilgamesh went abroad in the world, but he met with none who could withstand his arms till he came to Uruk. *Unknown.* CAGL, *tr. by* N. K. Sandars *Fr.* Epic of Gilgamesh, The.

Gill Morice stood in stable-door. Childe Maurice. *Unknown.* ESPB

Gillespie. Sir Henry John Newbolt. PeVV

Gilligan's Island. Tim Dlugos. ReTh

Gilly Silly Jarter. *Unknown.* OxNR

Gimme a Little Kiss (Will Ya, Huh?). Jack Smith. ReLy

Gimme $25.00. Request. Langston Hughes. APT-2

Gin a body meet a body. Comin' thro' the Rye. Robert Burns. UV

Gin a body meet a body. Rigid Body Sings. James Clerk Maxwell. UV

Gin I were on my milkwhite steed. Bents and Broom, The. *Unknown.* OxBB

Gin she this sight did see! (LL) Rose the Red and White Lil[l]y. *Unknown.* ESPB; OxBB

Gin-Shop, The; A Peep into Prison. Hannah More.
 "Come, neighbour, take a walk with me." ECWP

Gin the Goodwife Stint. Basil Bunting. CTC

Gin-weary, temple on the pane. Up in the Air. Greg Williamson. AmPoNex

Ginevra. Samuel Rogers. OxAEP-2

Ginger Bread Mama. Doughtry Long. BPo

Ginger-flowers. Kenneth Mackenzie. BMAP

Ginger-Haired Girl, The. Novella Nikolaevna Matveyeva [*or* Matveieva]. TCRusP, *tr. by* Daniel Weissbort

Gingerbread man gave a gingery shout, The. Gingerbread Man, The. Rowena Bastin Bennett. ChAP

Gingerly walked the hare. Two Laments. *Unknown.* ChiP, *tr. by* Arthur Waley

Gingham dog and the calico cat, The. Duel, The. Eugene Field. APN-2; ITBLP; NOxBChV; OBAL; OBCA; PoRA; TFi

Gingilee. Moyshe-Leyb [*or* Moishe-Leib *or* Leyb] Halpern. TrJP, *tr. by* Joseph Leftwich
 (Oh, Gingilee, my aching heart.) TrJP, *tr. by* Joseph Leftwich
 (To himself "Good morning" said.) (LL) TrJP, *tr. by* Joseph Leftwich

Ginkgoes in Fall. Howard Nemerov. HCAP

Ginny at a table of young men belly dancing. Soup Kitchen. Betsy Sholl. PBCAP

Giorno dei Morti. D. H. Lawrence. NOBE

Giotto. Rafael Alberti. WoPoe, *tr. by* Carolyn Tipton

Giovanni Azania. Don Mattera. PeSAV

Giovanni da Fiesole on the Sublime. Richard Howard. GS

"Giovinette, Che Fate All'Amore." Lorenzo Da Ponte. TrJP, *tr. by* Natalie MacFarren *Fr.* Don Giovanni.

Gipsies: "Gipsies seek wide sheltering woods again, The." John Clare. FHYEP

Gipsies tell me my life-line's a short one, The. Antipater of Thessalonica. GrAn

Gipsy Girl, The. Ralph Hodgson. MoBrPo

Gipsy Laddie, The. *Unknown.* FaBoCh; OxBoLi

Gipsy-Night. Richard Hughes. OBWVE

Gipsy of the sea. Stormpetrel. Richard Murphy. ModIr

Gipsy Queen. John Alexander Chapman. OBEV

Gipsy's Malison, The. Charles Lamb. OxBSo

Gipsy Song. Ben Jonson.See Gypsies Metamorphosed, The

Gipsy Trail, The. Rudyard Kipling. PoRA

Giraffe. Stanley Plumly. ChAP

Giraffe, The. Nikolai Stepanovich Gumilyov [*or* Gumiliov *or* Gumilev]. TCRP, *tr. by* Yakov Hornstein

Giraffes, yes, even the strongest. Limerick. Frank Davies. PeLi

Girandole. Gustaf Sobin. APSN

Gird up thy loins now like a man. Bible, *O.T.* AWP *Fr.* Job.

Girdle, A. William Strode. NOSC

Girdle round the Earth, A. Anthony Thwaite. PeLV

Girdle the world with peace. (LL) Songs for the People. Frances Ellen Watkins Harper. NAAAL; PWR

Girl. Kelly Norman Ellis. SpirFl

Girl. Octavio Paz. STV, *tr. by* John Frederick Nims

Girl. *Unknown.* RB, *tr. by* Anne Pennington

Girl, A. "Michael Field." VWP; ViWPN

Girl, A. Ezra Pound. MoAmPo; NOxBChV

Girl and Baby Florist Sidewalk Pram Nineteen Seventy Something. Kenneth Koch. NoP-4

Girl at Her Devotions, A. Letitia [*or* Laetitia] Elizabeth Landon. VWP

Girl at the Chu Lai Laundry. Bruce Weigl. CDa

Girl at the Seaside. Richard Murphy. BIrV

Girl at the Window. Pinkie Gordon Lane. GT

Girl attacked me once with a number 2 Eagle pencil, A. Blasphemy, A. Rodney Jones. IllVoic; WeW-3

Girl, Boy, Flower, Bicycle. M. K. Joseph. PeNZ

Girl by Green River, The. *Unknown.* OHMPC, *tr.* by Kenneth Rexroth

Girl by the River, The. Alton Delmore. APT-2

Girl (captured; later, freed), The. For Miss Tin in Hue. John Balaban. CDa

Girl cat / So thin. Basho. ZenPo, *tr.* by Takashi Ikemoto and Lucien Stryk

Girl comes out of a doorway in the morning, A. Arthur Rex Dugard Fairburn. PeNZ *Fr.* Album Leaves.

Girl dreams of her lover at night, The. Konstantin Iakovlevich Vanshenkin. TCRusP, *tr.* by Daniel Weissbort

Girl fishes up the sea, The. Greek Girl at Riis Beach, A. Frank O'Hara. BodElec

Girl fits her body, The. Night Vision. Lucille Clifton. BodElec; GifTon; UnSA

Girl from Ch'ang-kan, The. Cheng Hsieh. CoBLCP, *tr.* by Jonathan Chaves

Girl from Flower Mountain, The. Han Yü. SuSp, *tr.* by Charles Hartman

Girl from Rafah. Samih Al-Qasim. MAP, *tr.* by Charles Doria and Sharif Elmusa

Girl from the realm of birds florid and fleet. Something Like a Sonnet for Phillis Miracle Wheatley. June Jordan. NIL-7

Girl gathering lotus upon a brook, A. Upon a Brook. Ku K'uang. SuSp, *tr.* by Irving Y. Lo

Girl grew up to become a woman, The. Twenty Years. Đỗ Tấn Xuân. WoPoe, *tr.* by Nguyen Ngoc Bich

Girl grows up hidden in far-off rooms, A. In a Boat on a Summer Evening. Lu Yu. CoBCP, *tr.* by Burton Watson

Girl grows up hidden in innermost rooms, A. In a Boat on a Summer Evening, I Heard the Cry of a Water Bird. Lu Yu. SuSp, *tr.* by Burton Watson

Girl Held without Bail. Margaret Abigail Walker. BPo; WWork

Girl Help. Janet Lewis. APT-2; HeIP-4; InPK-6

Girl, / Her soul a deep-wave pearl, A. Girl, A. "Michael Field." VWP; ViWPN

Girl in a Fur-Trimmed Dress. Honor Moore. WiU

Girl in a Library, A. Randall Jarrell. NAAL-2v2; NOBA; NoAM

Girl in a Nightgown. Wallace Stevens. AmFaPo; OxBA

Girl in poor clothes, her skin lustrous as jade, A. Teahouse at Hoshioka, A. Liu E. CoBLCP, *tr.* by Jonathan Chaves

Girl in the Kitchen. "Vaidehi." OMIP, *tr.* by A. K. Ramanujan

Girl in the lane, The. Mother Goose. OxNR; ReMoGo

Girl in the tea shop, The. Tea Shop, The. Ezra Pound. HeIP-4

Girl in trousers wheeling a red baby, The. Metamorphoses. Roy Fuller. OxBTC

Girl is freezing in the telephone, A. First Ice, The. Andrey [or Andrei] Andreievich Voznesensky [or Voznesenskii]. RusPo, *tr.* by Robert Arthur Douglas Ford

Girl / loosens her bra, The. Alan Pizzarelli. HA

Girl Named Spring, A. Betsy Sholl. PBCAP

Girl no whiter than the Moors are. *Unknown.* PriapPo, *tr.* by Richard W. Hooper *Fr.* Priapus Poems, The.

Girl of Fifteen. James Weldon Johnson. GT

Girl of Mount Hua, The. Han Yü. CoBCP; ColAnChi, *tr.* by Burton Watson

Girl of Six from the Ghetto Begging in Smolna Street in 1942, A. Jerzy Ficowski. HP, *tr.* by Keith Bosley

Girl of Yueh, The. Li Po. TAL

Girl on the Land, The. Alice Thompson Meynell. VWP

Girl plays the piano, The. Capriccios. Jaime Sabines. TCLAP, *tr.* by Claudine-Marie D'Angelo

Girl Powdering Her Neck. Cathy Song. NoP-4

Girl Refugee, The. Matilde Salganicoff. MirDau, *tr.* by Celeste Kostopulos-Cooperman

Girl's Desire Moves Among Her Bangles, The. Gagan Gill. OMIP, *tr.* by Mrinal Pande

Girl's far treble, muted to the heat, The. Milkmaid. Laurie Lee. BoLoP; FaBoTw

Girl's Hair, A. Dafydd [or David] ab Edmwnd. OBWVE, *tr.* by Gwyn Williams

Girl's Head, A. Katherine Gallagher. NOBAu

Girl's Song. *Unknown.* WoPoe, *tr.* by Edwin Gladding Burrows

Girl's Song, A. *Unknown.* APN-2, *tr.* by Franz Boas *Fr.* Songs of the Kwakiutl Indians.

Girl Sings to the Stream, The. Leah Goldberg. MHP, *tr.* by Ruth Finer Mintz *Fr.* Songs of the Stream.

Girl/Spit. Lisa Coffman. AmPoNex

Girl, stop pretending tragedy. Wicked Women. *Vietnamese Oral Tradition.* CaDao, *tr.* by John Balaban

Girl them a shock out, The. Some Tentative Definitions 4. Kwame Dawes. WaCA

Girl thinks if I can only manage, The. Marie Luise Kaschnitz. ItWoWo, *tr.* by Beatrice Cameron *Fr.* Return to Frankfurt.

Girl threw an apple to a cloud, A. *Unknown.* WoPoe, *tr.* by Charles Simic

Girl to Soldier on Leave. Isaac Rosenberg. PeFWW

Girl today, dreaming, A. Auf dem Wasser zu Singen. Stephen Spender. EnLoPo

Girl was singing in the choir with fervor, A. Aleksandr Aleksandrovich Blok. TCRP

Girl, watch your cunt; boy, keep your ass from grief. *Unknown.* PriapPo, *tr.* by Richard W. Hooper *Fr.* Priapus Poems, The.

Girl, when rejecting me you never guessed. To a Jilt. Martin Donisthorpe Armstrong. FaBoEE

Girl who is bespectacled, A. Lines Written to Console Those Ladies Distressed by the Lines "Men Never Make Passes, etc." Ogden Nash. PeLV

Girl Who Loved the Sky, The. Anita Endrezze. HATNAP

Girl who sells melons beside the stream, The. Melon Girl. Mei Yao Ch'en. OHPC, *tr.* by Kenneth Rexroth

Girl who was touring Zambesi, A. Limerick. *Unknown.* PeLi

Girl with all that raising, A. Ballad of the Girl Whose Name Is Mud. Langston Hughes. SAmP

Girl with Mind Wandering. Paul Valéry. STV, *tr.* by John Frederick Nims

Girl with Pitcher. Ruth Dallas. PeNZ

Girl with the Bad Rep, The. Kay Murphy. SwNoth

Girl with the beautiful legs, The. Tides, The. Paul Blackburn. PoM

Girl with the Binh Tien Hairdo, The. *Vietnamese Oral Tradition.* CaDao, *tr.* by John Balaban

Girl with the Dark Hair. *Unknown.* WoPoe, *tr.* by W. S. Merwin

Girl with the Green Skirt. Dana Naone. CDW

Girl working the xerox in the stationery store, The. For Emily (Dickinson). Maureen Owen. PmAP; ReTh

Girl would be a fool to run away, A. (LL) Giovanni Boccaccio. AWP; EaItPo, *tr.* by Dante Gabriel Rossetti *Fr.* Sonnets.

Girl, you cut me up inside. To a Beauty, White, Pure, and Constant. Abu Bakr ibn Abd al-Malik Ibn Quzman. WoPoe, *tr.* by Leticia Garza-Falcón and Christopher Middleton

Girlfriends. Carol Ann Duffy. HarvBoo

Girlfriends, The. Elizabeth Woody. ReEnLa

Girls, The. Nights in Nha Trang. Jan Barry. CDa

Girls and Boys Come out to Play. *Unknown.* LB; ReMoGo

Girls are drifting in their ponytails, The. He or She That's Got the Limb, That Holds Me Out on It. Susan Wheeler. ExTi

Girls are simply the prettiest things. My Cat and I. Roger McGough. OxBTC

Girls / Brides / Tortoise. Erinna. SaLy, *tr.* by Diane Rayor

Girls, brighter than wine, are clothed and naked, The. Night Club. Francis Reginald Scott. NOBC

Girls Can We Educate We Dads? James Berry. NOxBChV

Girls, don't ever marry students! Good Scholars Make Bad Husbands. *Unknown.* WoPoe, *tr.* by Nguyen Ngoc Bich

Girls go by in their sailor suits, The. Sailor. Gerry Gomez Pearlberg. WiU

Girls in Their Seasons. Derek Mahon. BoLoP

Girls of Llanbadarn, The. Dafydd [or David] ap Gwilym. OBWVE, *tr.* by Rolfe Humphries

Girls of Llanbadarn, The. Dafydd [or David] ap Gwilym. DiPo, *tr.* by Leslie Norris

Girls of the Light, The. José María Eguren. TCLAP, *tr.* by Iver Lofving

Girls of the riverside, Nereids, did you see. Pan Asks about Daphnis. Diodorus Zonas. GrAn, *tr.* by Alistair Elliot

Girls of Yueh, The. Li Po. TAL

Girls on mopeds rode to Fécamp parties. Musical Orchard, The. Douglas Dunn. FaBoMo

Girls planting paddy. Konishi Raizan. OxBEV, *tr.* by Anthony Thwaite

Girls' School. Alan Moore. BiHa

Girls scream. School's Out. William Henry Davies. OBMV

Girls Sitting Together Like Dolls. Christiania Whitehead. NeBl

Girls today in society, The. Brush Up Your Shakespeare. Cole Porter. OBAL; OBCoV; ReLy

Girls Working in Banks. Karl Shapiro. WeW-3

Girly, womanly, female, feminine dame!, A. (LL) There Is Nothin' like a Dame. Oscar Hammerstein, II. OBAL; ReLy

Gisela, I went to the wall. Being Modern in Jerusalem. Evelyn Posamentier. GotH

Gislebertus' Eve. John Berryman. LCAP-2

Gist of the Story, The. Salah Abd al-Sabur. MAP, *tr.* by John Heath-Stubbs and Lena Jayyusi

Git out o' bed, you rascals. Call Boy. Sterling Allen Brown. GM

Gita Govinda, The. Jayadeva.

   Hymn to Vishnu. AWP, *tr.* by Sir Edwin Arnold

   "Sandal and garment of yellow and lotus garlands upon his body of blue." TAL

   Song of Krishna: The Fourth Song, Sung with Raga "Ramakari" WoPoe, *tr.* by Barbara Stoler Miller

Gita says three *gunas*, The.   To Phil Dow, in Oregon.   Robert Hass.   BodElec

Gitanjali.   Rabindranath Tagore.

Day after Day.   OBMV

I Have Got My Leave.   OBMV

If It Is Not My Portion.   OBMV

On the Slope of the Desolate River.   OBMV

Thou Art the Sky.   OBMV

Giuseppe, da barber, ees greata for "mash."   Mia Carlotta.   Thomas Augustin Daly.   NBLV

Give.   Mark Irwin.   PoCoUp

Give a man a horse he can ride.   James Thomson.   OBEV   *Fr.* Sunday up the River.

Give a man his.   Wait for Me.   Robert Creeley.   NOBA

Give: A Sequence Reimagining Daphne & Apollo.   Alice Fulton.   "What they had in common went beyond the I'm cool-are-you."   AllShUp

Give All to Love.   Ralph Waldo Emerson.   APN-1; AWP; ColAP; NOBA; OBEV; OxBA; TAP; TCAPo

Give all you have been, or could be. (LL)   Barter.   Sara Teasdale.   ITBLP; SoSe-8

Give, and take the cash.   Strato [*or* Straton].   GrAn

Give back my dead!   Cry of South Africa, The.   Olive Schreiner.   PeSAV

Give changing moods to even halcyon days. (LL)   Ocean Musing, An.   Henrietta Cordelia Ray.   CBWP-3; SWaP

Give ear my children to my words.   *Unknown.*   OBCA   *Fr.* New England Primer, The.

Give Ear, O God, to My Loud Cry.   Thomas Prince.   AH

Give Ear, O Heavens, to That Which I Declare.   Henry Ainsworth.   AH; ChIV-1

Give ear to my prayer, O God.   Bible, *O.T.*   AWP   *Fr.* Psalms.

Give ear to my words, O Lord.   Psalm 5.   Ernesto Cardenal.   TCLAP, *tr. by* Robert Marquez

Give Ear, Ye Heavens.   Bible, *O.T.*   TrJP   *Fr.* Deuteronomy.

Give, give me back that Trifle you despise.   Request of Alexis, The.   Sarah Dixon.   LW

Give God thy heart.   Motto for a Sundial.   *Unknown.*   FaBoEE

Give him coffee, said the general.   Ainadamar.   Nigel Jenkins.   TCAWP

Give him the darkest inch your shelf allows.   George Crabbe.   Edwin Arlington Robinson.   APN-2; MoAmPo; NAAL-2v2; NOBA; NoP-4; OxBA; TAP

Give Honour unto Luke Evangelist.   Saint Luke the Painter.   Dante Gabriel Rossetti.   SacPr

Give Isaac the nymph who no beauty can boast.   Richard Brinsley Sheridan.   NOIV   *Fr.* Duenna, The.

Give it all back, even what you were just handed.   Lover Man.   James Cushing.   SeSe

Give it up! / Give it up!   There Must Be Somethin' Better Than Love.   Dorothy Fields.   ReLy

Give Lucinda pearl nor stone.   To the New Year [For the Countess of Carlisle].   Thomas Carew.   CaPo

Give me a chair.   Song of the Poor Man.   *Unknown.*   TTY, *tr. by* Anselm Hollo

Give me a color.   America.   Wendy Rose.   CDW

Give me a cottage on some Cambrian wild.   Henry Kirke White.   CenSon

Give me a doctor, partridge-plump.   W. H. Auden.   OBCoV   *Fr.* Shorts [1948–1957].

Give me a girl[e] (if one I needs must meet).   Women.   William Cartwright.   BeJo

Give me a golden pen, and let me lean.   On Leaving Some Friends at an Early Hour.   John Keats.   CenSon

Give me a happy heart and suasive tongue.   Happy Heart, A.   Josephine D. Henderson Heard.   CBWP-4

Give me a harsh land to wring music from.   This Land.   Ian Mudie.   NOBAu

Give Me a Heart to Sing To.   Victor Young.   ReLy

Give me a heart where no impure.   William Habington.   BeJo   *Fr.* Castara.

Give me a homeland.   Issa.   SoOfWa, *tr. by* Sam Hamill

Give me a man that is not dull.   His Desire.   Robert Herrick.   OxBSP

Give me a mattress on the ship's poop some day.   Antiphilus [*or* Antiphilos].   GrAn

Give me a mind to suit my slavish state. (LL)   Humble Wish, The.   B–ll M–rt– n.   ECWP; LW

Give me a pen.   Testament of a Rebel.   Breyten Breytenbach.   PeSAV, *tr. by* André Brink

Give me a son. The blessing sent.   John Gay.   PeLV   *Fr.* Fables.

Give me a thrill, says the reader.   Fiction and the Reading Public.   Philip Larkin.   NOBL; OBSV

Give me all the kisses of your mouth.   Bible, *O.T.*   ErotSp, *tr. by* Sam Hamill   *Fr.* Song of Solomon, The [*or* The Song of Songs].

Give me back my stones! (LL)   Testing-Tree, The.   Stanley Kunitz.   APT-2; UnPo

Give me, fair sweet, the map, well-colourèd.   John Davies of Hereford.   OxBSo   *Fr.* Wit's Pilgrimage.

Give me food.   Mahārāja Rāmkrsna Rāy.   SinGod, *tr. by* Rachel Fell McDermott

Give me, give me Buriano.   Francesco Redi.   AWP; OBVE   *Fr.* Bacchus in Tuscany.

Give me, great God! said I, a little farm.   Verses Written in the Chiosk [of the British Palace], at Pera, Overlooking [the City of] Constantinople.   Lady Mary Wortley Montagu.   ECEV; ECWP

Give me hunger / O you gods that sit and give.   At a Window.   Carl Sandburg.   PoToHe

Give Me Jesus.   *Unknown.*   BPo; SacPr

Give me leave to rail at you.   Song.   John Wilmot, 2d Earl of Rochester.   NOSC

Give me Maeonian Homer's resonant tongue.   Catius As Conius Silius Italicus.   RomPo, *tr. by* Marcus Wilson   *Fr.* Punica, The.

Give me more love or more disdain.   Mediocrity in Love Rejected.   Thomas Carew.   BeJo; NoP-4

Give me my captive soul, or take.   Church Lock-and-Key.   George Herbert.   GeHe

Give me my knife.   *Unknown.*   NAAL-5   *Fr.* Ghost-Dance Songs.

Give me, my love, that billing kiss.   Kiss, The.   Thomas Moore.   EnLoPo

Give me my robe, put on my crown; I have.   William Shakespeare.   OxAEP-1   *Fr.* Antony and Cleopatra.

Give me my Scallop[-]shell of quiet.   Passionate Man['s] Pilgrimage, The.   Sir Walter Ralegh.   ChIV-2; NOBE; NPeEn; NoSic; OxBEV; PeECV; PoE; PoRA; RB; SCGP; TFi

Give me new Phœnix wings to fly at my desire. (LL)   On Sitting Down to Read "King Lear" Once Again.   John Keats.   CABP; EBEV; GSo; NAEL-5v2; NAEL-6v2; NoP-4; PoPoPo

Give me no gift! Less than thyself were nought.   Broken Friendship.   Mary Elizabeth Coleridge.   VWP

Give me, O friend, the secret of thy heart.   Rosa Rosarum.   Agnes Mary Frances Robinson.   PoBW

Give me, O indulgent fate!   Anne Finch, Countess of Winchilsea.   ECWP; NOSC   *Fr.* Petition for an Absolute Retreat, The.

Give me on earth, Lord, only as much room.   To the Dear Lord.   Christine Busta.   AuPH, *tr. by* Lowell A. Bangerter

Give me one kiss.   To Dianeme.   Robert Herrick.   CaPo

Give me one small smothering of earth.   Leonidas of Tarentum.   GrAn

Give Me Peace.   Andrey [*or* Andrei] Andreievich Voznesensky [*or* Voznesenskii].   TCRP

Give me something to eat.   Poor Crow!   Mary Mapes Dodge.   OBCA; SWaP

Give me sweet nectar in a kiss.   *Unknown.*   FaBoEE

Give me that man that dares bestride.   His Cavalier.   Robert Herrick.   CaPo

Give me that old-time religion.   Old-Time Religion.   *Unknown.*   APN-2

Give me the Daulian bird and Locrian Arsinoë.   From V. C. (a Gentleman of Verona).   Gavin Ewart.   OxBC

Give me the lowest place: not that I dare.   Lowest Place, The.   Christina Georgina Rossetti.   NOBVV

Give me the priest these graces shall possess.   Priest of Christ, The.   Thomas Ken.   SacPr

Give me the Red on the Black of the Bullet (for Claude Reece Jr.).   Jayne Cortez.   LTA

Give me the right of way.   Irish.   Paul Celan.   OBVE, *tr. by* Michael Hamburger

Give me the sea-breath from your mouths to breathe a while! (LL)   Morning Call.   Richard Murphy.   BiHa; ModIr

Give Me the Simple Life.   Harry Ruby.   ReLy

Give Me the Splendid Silent Sun.   Walt Whitman.   CBCWP; HAP; MoAmPo; NOBA

Give me the woman here. (LL)   Sonnet: "O[h]! for some honest lover's ghost."   Sir John Suckling.   BASC; BeJo; CavPo; MeLP; OxBEV

Give me those flowers there, Dorcas. Reverend sirs.   William Shakespeare.   OxAEP-1   *Fr.* Winter's Tale, The.

Give Me Thy Heart.   Adelaide Anne Procter.   SacPr

Give me truths / For I am weary of the surfaces.   Blight.   Ralph Waldo Emerson.   APN-1; NCAP; NOBA; TCAPo

Give me wide walls to build my house of Life.   Wide Walls.   *Unknown.*   PoToHe

Give me your hand old Revolutionary.   Centenarian's Story, The.   Walt Whitman.   CTC

Give me your hand. Place it on my bare breast.   She Teaches Him to Reach Out.   Martha Elizabeth.   PasH

Give mee my Escallope shell of Quiett.   Sir Walter Ralegh.   *See* Give me my Scallop[-]shell of quiet

Give *Mee* the *Free* and *Noble Stile.*   Claspe, The.   Margaret Lucas Cavendish, Duchess of Newcastle.   BWW; PBRV

Give money me, take friendship whoso list.   Of Money.   Barnabe Googe.   NBLV; NoSic; SoSe-8

Give my dream back. Onitsura. JDP, *tr. by* Yoel Hoffmann

Give my heart. (LL) Christina Georgina Rossetti. NOBVV; OxBEV; SacPr; VWP

Give My Regards to Broadway. George M. Cohan. ReLy; TCAPo

Give Not Our Blankets, Tax-Fed Squire. Ebenezer Elliott. Son *Fr.* Year of Seeds, The.

Give oftener what is heard of than received. (LL) For the Lady Olivia Porter; a Present upon a New Year's Day. Sir William Davenant [*or* D'Avenant]. MeLP; NOSC

Give over, now, red roses. Warning of Winter. Mary Ursula Bethell. FaBoWP; PeNZ

Give pardon, blessèd soul, to my bold cries. On the Death of Sir Philip Sidney. Henry Constable. OBEV

Give patient eare to something I man saye. Admonition to Montgomerie. James I, King of England. GTBS-P; OxBS

Give Peace in These Our Days, O Lord. Edmund Grindal. AH

Give Peace, O God, the Nations Cry. John W. Norris. AH

Give place, you ladies, and be gone! Praise of His Lady, A. John Heywood. OBEV

Give store of days, good Jove, give length of years. Juvenal. OBSV *Fr.* Satires.

Give thanks for this turn for the better. Change in Style, A. Eochadh [*or* Eochy] O'Hussey [*or* O'Heughusa]. NOIV

Give the barber a pinch of snuff. (LL) Mother Goose. LB; OxNR; ReMoGo

Give the mourning doves any sun. Ruined Motel, The. Reginald Gibbons. BodElec

Give the sounds of the curved mated phonographs. Three Found Poems. George Hitchcock. OBAL

Give them back / to me. Blues. Léon Damas. NegPo, *tr. by* Ellen Conroy Kennedy

Give them my regards when you go to the school reunion. More of a Corpse Than a Woman. Muriel Rukeyser. NALW

Give them thy fingers, me thy lips to kiss. (LL) William Shakespeare. NAEL-5v1; NAEL-6v1; NAEL-7v1; OxAEP-1; PoE *Fr.* Sonnets.

Give this to my mother. For Babies Unborn. Tracy Clarke. InTrad

Give thou my sacred relics burial [*or* Reliques Buriall]. (LL) His Return to London. Robert Herrick. BASC; BeJo; CaPo; NAEL-5v1; NAEL-6v1; NAEL-7v1

Give to barrows, trays, and pans. Art. Ralph Waldo Emerson. APN-1

Give to me the life I love. Vagabond, The. Robert Louis Stevenson. OxAEP-2

Give unto the Lord, O ye mighty. Bible, *O.T.* AWP *Fr.* Psalms.

Give up erotic games, Kabir. Kabir. ErotSp, *tr. by* Sam Hamill

Give up on friends. No Pardon. Friedrich Hölderlin. WoPoe, *tr. by* Vyt Bakaitis

Give us that grand word woman once again. Woman. Ella Wheeler Wilcox. SWaP

"Give us your very best table," I swaggered, taking the head waiter aside and. Jet Set Melodrama. Michael Brownstein. FTOS

Give way, and be ye ravished by the sun. To Marygolds. Robert Herrick. NAEL-5v1

Give way, give way ye Gates, and win. Wassaile, The. Robert Herrick. PBRV

Giveaway, The. Phyllis McGinley. PoRA

Given all my worries over each day's trivia. Joachim Du Bellay. WoPoe, *tr. by* David Curzon *Fr.* Regrets.

Given away in poems, only their solitude kept. (LL) Correspondence School Instructor Says Goodbye to His Poetry Students, The. Galway Kinnell. NOBA; NoAM; NoP-4; TAP

"Given faith," sighed the vicar of Deneham. Limerick. *Unknown.* PeLi

Given Flesh Returns Nothing but Bread, The. Aileen Kelly. ChIV-2

Given in Person Only. Mark Wunderlich. WiU

Given, not lent. Unto Us a Son Is Given. Alice Thompson Meynell. SacPr

Given to a Lady Who Asked Me to Write a Poem. Janet Little. ECWP

Given to love. (LL) Agony, An. As Now. Imamu Amiri Baraka. BPo; NAAL-2v2; PoE

Given What Manages. Cleopatra Mathis. ExTi *Fr.* Lessons.

Giving. Nora B. Cunningham. LW

Giving. *Unknown.* PoToHe

Giving and Forgiving. Thomas Grant Springer. PoToHe

Giving Back the Flower. Sarah Morgan Bryan Piatt. APN-2

Giving brilliant gourd-shell rattles / to everyone who comes. (LL) Grandfather at the Indian Health Clinic. Elizabeth Cook-Lynn. HATNAP; UnSA

Giving her mother's / zealous eye. Paulus [*or* Paulos] Silentiarius. GrAn

Giving in Marriage. Jean Ingelow. TreFP *Fr.* Songs of Seven.

Giving oneself to the dentist or doctor who is a good one. Kind of Act Of, The. Robert Creeley. NeAP

Giving Potatoes. Adrian Mitchell. NBLV; RB

Giving Rabbit to My Cat Bonnie. Anne Stevenson. FaBoWP

Giving Thanks. Anne K. Smith. PasH

Giving up women is worse than animal laxatives. John Tranter. NoAM *Fr.* Crying in Early Infancy.

Giving Way. Johanna Kruit. TuT, *tr. by* Medbh McGuckian

Giving, while the rain lasts, soft noises. Eaves. Ellis Jones. OBWVE, *tr. by* Anthony Conran

Gizzard and some ruby inner parts, A. Lament. Margaret Avison. HAP

Glad. W. H. Auden. CAGL *Fr.* Three Posthumous Poems.

Glad at the Cold (1955). Alan Dugan. NoAM

Glad, but not flush'd with gladness. Algernon Charles Swinburne. OBEV *Fr.* Before the Mirror.

Glad Christmas comes, and every hearth. John Clare. ChrPo; OBCP *Fr.* December.

Glad Day. Louis Untermeyer. TrJP

Glad Eye, The. Paul Muldoon. NoAM

Glad Rag Doll. Dan Dougherty. ReLy

Glad that I live am I. Little Song of Life, A. Lizette Woodworth Reese. OBCA

Glad to Be Unhappy. Lorenz Hart. ReLy

Gladioli by the Sea. Oscar Hahn. TCLAP, *tr. by* Isabel Bize

Gladstone was still respected. Ezra Pound. MoAmPo *Fr.* Hugh Selwyn Mauberley (Life and Contacts).

Glamis thou art, andd Cawdor; and shalt be. William Shakespeare. OxAEP-1 *Fr.* Macbeth.

Glance. Dhabya Khamees. PoArWo, *tr. by* Clarissa C. Burt

Glance. Belkis Cuza Malé. TANSG, *tr. by* Pamela Carmell

Glance, A. *Unknown.* NOIV, *tr. by* Thomas Kinsella

Glance, The. George Herbert. ESCV

Glance in White Space. Clark Coolidge. FTOS

Glanced down at Shannon from the sky-way. Irish-American Dignitary. Austin Clarke. BIrV

Glances changed their source. Alice Rahon. SurWo, *tr. by* Nancy Deffebach and Vanina Deler

Glancing at the train from hills touched with autumn. Anguish. Andrey [*or* Andrei] Andreievich Voznesensky [*or* Voznesenskii]. RusPo, *tr. by* Robert Arthur Douglas Ford

Glancing at the wicker. Elite Syncopations. Richard Garcia. TouFir

Glanmore Revisited. Seamus Heaney.
    Skylight, The. OxBSo

Glans, high point of the soul. Balanide 2. Paul Verlaine. CAGL, *tr. by* Alan Stone

Glare from the brass horn makes sun-brown satin fit smoothly the girl by the, The. Lorine Niedecker. FTOS *Fr.* This Condensery: The Complete Writing of Lorine Niedecker, 1985.

Glaring headlights. (LL) Nicholas Virgilio. HA; InPK-6

Glasgerion. *Unknown.* ESPB

Glasgow. Alexander Smith.
    "Sing, Poet, 'tis a merry world." NePenScot

Glasgow Peggie. *Unknown.* ESPB

Glasgow Schoolboys, Running Backwards. Douglas Dunn. OxBC

Glasgow Street. William Montgomerie. OxBS

Glasnevin Cemetery. Michael O'Loughlin. PBCIP

Glass. Gillian Clarke.
    Migraine. Prnts

Glass. W. S. Merwin. SPE

Glass. Anne Rouse. NeBl

Glass. Takako Uchino Lento. BoWoP, *tr. by* the author

Glass. Anne Finch, Countess of Winchilsea. OxBEV

Glass, The. Esther Ettinger. DTA, *tr. by* Mariana Barr

Glass, The. Carolyn Kizer. ErotSp

Glass, The. Edwin Morgan. HarvBoo

Glass, The. Sharon Olds. NIL-7; NIP-4

Glass Blower, The. James Scully. TwCP

Glass Bubbles, The. Samuel Greenberg. APT-1

Glass Canyons. David Romtvedt. UrbNat

Glass Enclosure, The. Michael Brownstein. FTOS

Glass falls lower, The. Sad Green. Sylvia Townsend Warner. MoBrPo

Glass has been falling all the afternoon, The. Storm Warnings. Adrienne Rich. AiP; NAAL-2v2; NAAL-5; NIL-7; NIP-4; YaYoPo

Glass House. Diane Ward. PmAP

Glass I've wanted to live. Through You. Edwin Honig. TAP

Glass in her hand is the only thing moving, The. Photograph of a Bawd Drinking Raleigh Rye. Natasha Trethewey. NeAmPo

Glass King, The. Eavan Boland. CIP-2

Glass man, without external reference, The. (LL) Asides on the Oboe. Wallace Stevens. FaBoMo; MoAmPo

Glass of Beer, A. James Stephens. InPK-6; NBLV; OBCoV; OBMV; OxBEV; OxBS; OxBTC; RB

(Righteous Anger.) MoBrPo

Glass of Pure Water, The. Hugh MacDiarmid. PFTM-2

Glass of Water, The. Wallace Stevens. MoAmPo; OxBA; TAP

Glass on the picture from the Bible, The. Darkening Hotel Room. Alfred Corn. VCAP

Glass was the Street—in tinsel Peril. Emily Dickinson. OxBA

Glassblower lies here at rest, A. Epitaph. John Bingham Morton. FaBoEE

Glassed with cold sleep and dazzled by the moon. Train Journey. Judith Wright. NoP-4

Glassily strand the sea. (LL) Undead, The. Richard Wilbur. CoAP; CoAmPo; OxBC

Glassine envelopes trampoline the pigmeat into a final awakening. Glass Enclosure, The. Michael Brownstein. FTOS

Glassworks. Margit Mikes. IQMS, *tr.* by Suzanne K. Walther

Glassy Sea. W. S. Merwin. BodElec

Glaucopis. Richard Hughes. OBMV

Glaucus, pilot of the Nessus strait, born. On the Death of the Ferryman, Glaucus. Antiphilus [*or* Antiphilos]. GrAn; WoPoe, *tr.* by W. S. Merwin

Glaukon and Korydon, mountain herdsmen. Erucius [*or* Erycius] of Cyzicus. GrAn

Glaukos, look: already the deep sea is troubled. Archilochus. SaLy, *tr.* by Diane Rayor

Glazier, The. Stéphane Mallarmé. OBVE, *tr.* by Keith Bosley

Glazing the pale hair, the duplicate gray [*or* grey] standard faces. (LL) Dolor. Theodore Roethke. HCAP; HeIP-4; NoAM; OPOU; OxBSP; TRP

Glazunoviana. John Ashbery. LCAP-2; VCAP

Gleam of irrecoverable gold, The. (LL) Sunken Gold. Eugene Lee-Hamilton. GSo; NOBVV

Gleamed a resplendent star. At Christmas-Tide. Henrietta Cordelia Ray. CBWP-3

Gleaming—sunken stones. O. Mabson Southard. HA

Gleams a green lamp. Louis Zukofsky. APT-2 *Fr.* 29 Poems.

Gleaners of grain they did not sow. Rooks: December. Huw Menai. AngWePo

Gleaning. David Shimoni. MHP, *tr.* by Ruth Finer Mintz

Gleaning the rice field. Buson. EH, *tr.* by Robert Hass

Glee-fulfiller, fruit-producer, cook who glad the year can feed. Concerning the Fruit-bringing Autumn Season. Catharina Regina von Greiffenberg. GePo, *tr.* by George C. Schoolfield

Glee—The great storm is over. Emily Dickinson. APN-2

Glenaradale. Walter Chalmers Smith. OBEV; PeVV

Glenaveril. "Owen Meredith."
   Tears. EBVV

Glencoe. Douglas Stewart.
   "Sigh, wind in the pine." CBAP

Glengormley. Derek Mahon. CIP-2

Glenkindie was ance a harper gude. Glasgerion. *Unknown.* ESPB

Glenlogie; or, Jean o Bethelnie. *Unknown.* ESPB

Glenn Miller and I were heroes. Jack Kerouac. NeAP *Fr.* Mexico City Blues.

Glib little beer-buff from Troon, A. Limerick. Bill Greenwell. PeLi

Glides white through the phosphorus sea. (LL) Commemorative of a Naval Victory. Herman Melville. HAP; UnPo

Gliding Baskets. Frank A. Cross, Jr. CDa

Gliding through the still air, he made no sound;. Return of Persephone, The. Alec Derwent Hope. BMAP

Gliding toward the Lamps. Matthew Rohrer. NeAmPo

Glimmer farther away than the head, The. Adieu. Pierre Reverdy. CuPo

Glimmering morning. Michael McClintock. HA

Glimpse, A. Frances Darwin Cornford. OBMV

Glimpse, A. Robert Duncan. FTOS

Glimpse, A. Walt Whitman. APN-1; OxBA; RaBo

Glimpse, A. John Wieners. FTOS

Glimpse from the Past. Ilse Aichinger. AF, *tr.* by Allen H. Chappel

Glimpse of a once-loved face, The. What Do They Say. Gary Snyder. NNaP

Glimpse of Terrain. Thomas Bolt. YaYoPo

Glimpse of your body, A. Mirabai [*or* Mira Bai]. ErotSp, *tr.* by Andrew Schelling

Glimpse through an interstice caught, A. Glimpse, A. Walt Whitman. APN-1; OxBA; RaBo

Glimpsed. Vladimir Holan. PoSu, *tr.* by Ian Milner and Jarmila Milner

Glimpsed from the train, which takes shadow for truth. Glimpsed. Vladimir Holan. PoSu, *tr.* by Ian Milner and Jarmila Milner

Glimpsed through a Lens. Yevgeny [*or* Evgenii] Borisovich Rein. TCRP, *tr.* by Bernard Meares

Glimpsed world, halfway through the film, A. Malice of Innocence, The. Denise Levertov. BodElec; NNaP

Glimpses. Christopher Gilbert. GT

Glimpses. Philippe Jaccottet. VCWP, *tr.* by Derek Mahon

Glimpses. William Stafford. BodElec

Glimpses of Infancy. Priscilla Jane Thompson. CBWP-2

Glinting like water. Mary Kinzie. FFC

Glistening, The. Deema K. Shehabi. PoArWo

Glistening at my core. (LL) Four-Word Lines. May Swenson. GLP; WPE

Glistening like drops of copper in our path. (LL) Chrysalides. Thomas Kinsella. BIrV; ModIr

Glitt'ring colors of the day are fled, The. Helen Maria Williams. *See* Glittering colors of the day are fled, The

Glitter of a northern kingdom. Mao Tse-tung [*or* Mao Zedong]. WoPoe, *tr.* by David Lattimore

Glittering and still shall come the awful night. (LL) Winter Evening. Archibald Lampman. NIL-7; NOBC

Glittering bridge. Bridge, The. Charlotte Zolotow. CA

Glittering colors of the day are fled, The. To the Moon. Helen Maria Williams. NoP-4

Glittering leaves of the rhododendrons, The. Green Symphony. John Gould Fletcher. MoAmPo

Glittering of air, it glitters. Mystery. Octavio Paz. TCLAP, *tr.* by Muriel Rukeyser

Glittering rises in flocks, The. Approaches, The. W. S. Merwin. NOBA

Glittering topaz in your glass, The. At a Danse Macabre. Charles Spear. PeNZ

Gloat, glittering talmudist. Talmudist. Stanley Burnshaw. DiPo

Globe, a paper of the Tories, The. Suggestion Made by the Posters of the *Globe*, A. J. E. Thorold Rogers. FaBoEE

Globe in North Carolina, The. Derek Mahon. BiHa; PBCIP

Globe of th'earth on which we dwell, The. On the Tack. Thomas Hearne. ECEV

Gloire de Dijon. D. H. Lawrence. EnLoPo; NoAM; PAI

Glom: Labrador, 110 pounds. Karen Shepard. Unle

Gloom of death is on the raven's wing, The. Raven, The. Edwin Arlington Robinson. AWP; FaBoEE; OBAL

Gloom of death is on the raven's wing, The. *Var. authors.* AWP; FaBoEE; OBAL *Fr.* Variations of Greek Themes.

Gloom of night had overspread the land, The. Nativity, The. Mary Weston Fordham. CBWP-2

Glooms of the live-oaks, beautiful-braided and woven. Marshes of Glynn, The. Sidney Lanier. NOBA; OxBA; TCAPo

Glooms of the live-oaks, beautiful-braided and woven. Sidney Lanier. NOBA; OxBA *Fr.* Hymns of the Marshes.

Gloomy am I, oppressed and sad. Poet's Arbour in the Birchwood, The. Edward Williams. OBWVE, *tr.* by Kenneth Hurlstone Jackson

Gloomy cripple with his empty eyes, The. Cripple, The. Khalil Khouri. MAP, *tr.* by Sharif Elmusa and Christopher Middleton

Gloomy hulls, in armour [*or* armor] grim, The. *Temeraire*, The. Herman Melville. APN-2; FaBoWar

Gloomy lowering of the sky, The. Written on a Gloomy Day, in Sickness. Susanna Blamire. ECWP

Gloomy minister of Hades who sail this stream. Leonidas of Tarentum. HePo *Fr.* Epigrams.

Gloomy night embraced the place. Richard Crashaw. NOBE *Fr.* In the Holy Nativity of Our Lord God.

Gloomy Night of Sadness, The. *Unknown.* AH

Gloomy thought, Ben Bulben, A. Deserted Mountain, The. *Unknown.* BIrV, *tr.* by John Montague

Gloria. Lincoln Kirstein. APT-2

Gloria mundi est. *Unknown.* NPeEn

Gloriana Dying. Sylvia Townsend Warner. FaBoWP

Glories of the world struck me, made me aria, once, The. John Berryman. HCAP; HarvBoo *Fr.* Dream Songs.

Glorified in full release upward—/ songs cease. (LL) Dawn. William Carlos Williams. APT-1; MoAmPo

Glorious days he had, and a chivalrous spirit. Old White Russian, An. Ch'en Meng-chia. WoPoe, *tr.* by Harold Acton and Ch'en Shih-hsiang

Glorious greks dois prayse their Homers quill, The. E. D. in Prayse of Mr. W. Fouler Her Friend. "E. D." EMWP

Glorious image of the Maker's beauty, The. Edmund Spenser. SacPr; Son *Fr.* Amoretti.

Glorious Judge will priviledge, The. Michael Wigglesworth. TCAPo *Fr.* Day of Doom, The.

Glorious night! / The giant moon, the tiny evening star. Sándor Petőfi. IQMS, *tr.* by Peter Zollman *Fr.* Clouds, The.

Glorious Strike of the Builders, The. *Unknown.* FaBoVe

Glorious the sun in mid career. Christopher Smart. FaBoCh *Fr.* Song to David, A.

Glorious Things of Thee Are Spoken. John Newton. NOCV
(Zion, or the City of God.) NOEC

Glorious Vision you adore, The. (LL)   Love's Mirror.   Constance Naden.   VWP; ViWPN

Glorious Wonders of the DEITY, The. (LL)   Eden.   Thomas Traherne.   ChIV-1; ESCV; GeHe

Glory.   D. H. Lawrence.   OxBSP

Glory.   Joseph Wise.   AH

Glory, A.   Hymn to the Sun.   Akhenaton [or Akhnaton].   WoPoe, tr. by John Perlman

Glory, The.   Edward Thomas.   HarvBoo; OxBTC; TOF

Glory and Enduring Fame.   William Gilmore Simms   Son

Glory and loveliness have passed away.   To Leigh Hunt, Esq.   John Keats.   Son

Glory Be to Chingwe's Hole.   Jack A. Mapanje.   HBAPE

Glory be to God for dappled things.   Pied Beauty.   Gerard Manley Hopkins.   AWP; AmFaPo; CABP; ChAP; ClHu; EBVV; EnlH; FaBoMo; GTBS-P; HAP; HeIP-4; ITBLP; InPK-6; InvLi; MoBrPo; NAEL-5v2; NAEL-6v2; NIL-7; NOBE; NOBVV; NPeEn; NoAM; NoP-4; OBEV; OBMV; OxAEP-2; OxBEV; OxBSP; PoE; PoPoPo; PoRA; RB; RaBo; SCGP; SCV; SacPr; SoSe-8; TFi; TTTS; UV; WeW-3

Glory be to God for Hopkins' verse.   Pied Beauty.   Stanley J. Sharpless.   UV

Glory be to God on high.   Incarnation, The.   Charles Wesley.   NOCV

Glory, Glory, Glory to the heroes!!!   On Trash.   Vladimir Vladimirovich Mayakovsky [or Maiakovskii].   TCRP, tr. by Daniel Weissbort

Glory here Diggers all. (LL)   Digger's Song, The.   Gerrard Winstanley.   BASC; NOSC

Glory of God, The.   Bible, O.T.   See Psalms

Glory of Him who moves all things rays forth, The.   Dante Alighieri.   NAWM-5v1   Fr. Divina Commedia.

Glory of Love, The.   Billy Hill.   ReLy

Glory of my Work, and Me, The. (LL)   His Prayer for Absolution.   Robert Herrick.   BeJo; SacPr

Glory of the beauty of the morning, The.   Glory, The.   Edward Thomas.   HarvBoo; OxBTC; TOF

Glory of the Garden, The.   Rudyard Kipling.   OBGa

Glory of Women.   Siegfried Sassoon.   FaBoWar; NAEL-5v2; NAEL-6v2; NoP-4; OBWP; OxAEP-2; OxBSo; PeFWW

Glory to caesar! and glory to God in the highest!   Viktor Krivulin.   ItGoST, tr. by Michael Molnar

Glory to God, and praise, and love Be ever, ever given.   For the Anniversary Day of One's Conversion.   Charles Wesley.   SacPr

Glory to God and to God's Mother chaste.   To Dante Alighieri (He Commends the Work of Dante's Life).   Giovanni Quirino.   AWP; EaItPo, tr. by Dante Gabriel Rossetti

Glory to Osiris, the Prince of Everlastingness.   Unknown.   AWP   Fr. Book of the Dead.

Glory to Thee, My God, This Night.   Thomas Ken.   NOCV

Glory to you, red star hero.   Last Page of the Civil War.   Vladimir Vladimirovich Mayakovsky [or Maiakovskii].   RusPo, tr. by Robert Arthur Douglas Ford

Glory Trumpeter, The.   Derek Walcott.   GT; NAEL-5v2; NAEL-6v2; NoP-4; SeSe

Gloss.   Padraic Fiacc.   CIP-2; PNI

Gloss.   David McCord.   OBAL

Gloss to Matthew V 27–28.   Alec Derwent Hope.   GI

Gloucester Moors.   William Vaughn Moody.   APN-2; NOBA; OxBA; TCAPo

Glow and beauty of the stars, The.   Sappho.   BoWoP

Glow-boys.   John Tranter.   BMAP

Glow, little glow-worm, fly of fire.   Glow-Worm, The.   Johnny Mercer.   OBAL; ReLy

Glow of my campfire is dark red and flameless, The.   Spring, Coast Range.   Kenneth Rexroth.   APT-2

Glow-Worm, The.   Johnny Mercer.   OBAL; ReLy

Glow-Worm, The.   Charlotte Smith.   BWW

Glowworm.   David McCord.   NTCP

Glowworm, The.   Thomas Stanley.   BeJo; NOSC

Glowworm scatters flashes through the moss, A.   Glowworm Scatters Flashes, A.   Rosalía de Castro.   NAWM-7v2, tr. by S. Griswold Morley

Gloze Upon This Text, Dominus iis opus habet, A.   George Gascoigne.   ChIV-2

Glue and a small amount of alum.   Pictures of the Floating World.   Miyazawa Kenji.   PFTM-1

Glutton [or Glutton in the Tavern], The.   William Langland.   PoE   Fr. Vision of Piers Plowman, The.

Gluttony in the Ale-house.   William Langland.   See Vision of Piers Plowman, The

Glycine's Song.   Samuel Taylor Coleridge.   OBEV   Fr. Zapolya.

Glykon, glory of Asia / born in Pergamum.   Antipater of Thessalonica.   GrAn

Glyn Cynon Wood.   Unknown.   OBWVE, tr. by Gwyn Williams

Glyndwr, see thy comet flaming.   Glyndwr's War Song.   John Jones.   AngWePo

Gnarly and bent and deaf's a pos'   Zeke.   Leonard Alfred George Strong.   MoBrPo

Gnat, The.   Joseph Beaumont.   NOSC

Gnat on My Paper.   Richard Eberhart.   APT-2

Gnawed at by lichens.   Meditation Rock, The.   Mo Shih-lung.   CoBLCP, tr. by Jonathan Chaves

Gnawed by a beetle. (LL)   What She Said.   Kaccipettu Nannakaiyar.   BoWoP; WPOW, tr. by A. K. Ramanujan

Gnawing the Breast.   Sandra McPherson.   LCAP-2

Gnawing the guts of men. (LL)   End of Clonmacnois, The.   Unknown.   CIP-2; WoPoe, tr. by Frank O'Connor

Gnome.   Samuel Beckett.   BIrV; OxBSP

Gnomes.   Howard Nemerov.

  Sacrificed Author, A.   GI

Gnomic Verses.   William Blake.

  Abstinence Sows Sand All Over.   EBEV; FaBoEE; OxBEV

  "Angel that presided o'er my birth, The."   InPK-6; OxBSP; RB

  Great Things [Are Done].   OxBSP

  Sword and the Sickle, The.   FaBoEE

Gnosis.   Christopher Pearse Cranch.   APN-1; ColAP

  (Enosis.)   TCAPo

Gnostic Prelude.   James McAuley.   BMAP

Go ahead. Call me Zacko, Hound Thing, Gray Beard.   Pet Names.   Bernard Cooper.   Unle

Go and ask Robin to bring the girls over.   Vision by Sweetwater.   John Crowe Ransom.   FaBoMo; HarvBoo; NOBA; OxBA; RB

Go and catch a falling star.   Song.   John Donne.   AWP; ClHu; EBEV; FHYEP; FSCP; HAP; HeIP-4; InPK-6; NAEL-5v1; NAEL-6v1; NAEL-7v1; NAWM-5v1; NIL-7; NIP-4; NOBE; NOSC; NoP-4; NoSic; OBEV; OxAEP-1; PoE; SoSe-8; TFi; WoPoe

Go and find work. (LL)   What the Chairman Told Tom.   Basil Bunting.   EmeKit; NoP-4; OxBTC

Go Ask the Dead.   Thomas McGrath.   AF

Go away a bit my sadness.   Time to Shine.   Hamda Khamees.   PoArWo, tr. by Joseph T. Zeidan

Go Away, Death!   Alfred Austin.   VerBaPo

Go bet, penny, go bet, go!   Unknown.   MiEL

Go bind thou up young dangling apricots.   William Shakespeare.   OBGa   Fr. King Richard II.

Go bow thy head in gentle spite.   To a Lily.   James Matthew Legaré.   APN-2

"Go Bring Me," Said the Dying Fair.   William Hunter.   AH

Go By.   Tennyson.   PeVV

Go by! linked fin by fin! most odiously. (LL)   Leigh Hunt.   NBLV; NPeEn; SCGP   Fr. Fish, the Man, and the Spirit, The.

Go call a careful painter, let him show.   Of the French Kings Nativity.   Benjamin Harris.   SCAP

Go, cruel tyrant of the human breast!   Supposed to Be Written by Werter.   Charlotte Smith.   CenSon; RWP

Go, daughters of Zion.   Death of Tammuz, The.   Saul [or Shaul] Tchernichowsky [or Tchernichovsky].   TrJP, tr. by L. V. Snowman

Go Down Death.   James Weldon Johnson.   ISC; SacPr

Go Down, Moses.   Unknown.   BPo; NAAAL; NoP-4

  (When Israel was in Egypt land.)   PeECV

  (When Israel Was in Egypt's Land.)   AH; NOBA

Go Down, O Sun, Out from the Motu River.   Te Aomuhurangi te Maaka.   PeNZ, tr. by the author

Go down obscurely.   Be of Good Cheer.   Robert Creeley.   BodElec

Go Down, Old Hannah.   Unknown.   NAAAL

Go down to Kew in lilac-time, in lilac-time, in lilac-time.   Barrel-Organ, The.   Alfred Noyes.   MoBrPo; PoRA

Go, draw aside the curtain, and discover.   William Shakespeare.   OxAEP-1   Fr. Merchant of Venice, The.

Go, dumb-born book.   Ezra Pound.   HAP; TCAPo; UnPo; VGW   Fr. Hugh Selwyn Mauberley (Life and Contacts).

Go farther! let it serve to trample on. (LL)   Elizabeth Barrett Browning.   BWW; CenSon; OxAEP-2   Fr. Sonnets from the Portuguese.

Go fetch to me a pint o' [or of] wine.   Silver Tassie, The.   Robert Burns.   NOBE; OBEV; WoPoe

Go find Avicenna.   Calling the Doctor (1000 A.D.).   Nizami Arudi.   ArPe; WoPoe, tr. by Omar Pound and Omar S. Pound

"Go, Flee?"—A man like me does not flee!   Prophet, Go, Flee!   Hayyim Nahman [or Khayim Nakhman or Chaim Nachman] Bialik.   MHP, tr. by Ruth Finer Mintz

Go fly a kite he writes.   Ted Berrigan.   BodElec

Go For Broke.   André Breton.   PFTM-1

Go, for they call you, Shepherd, from the hill.   Matthew Arnold.   EBEV;

EBVV; FHYEP; HAP; NAEL-5v2; NAEL-6v2; NOBE; NOBVV; NoP-4; OBEV; OxAEP-1; PoE; SCGP; TFi

Go;—for 'tis Memorial morning. Memorial Day. Clara Ann Thompson. CBWP-2

Go forth from life in guise of mendicants. (LL) For, Lord, the Crowded Cities Be. Rainer Maria Rilke. AWP; TrJP, *tr. by* Ludwig Lewisohn

Go forth myn hert wyth my lady. Charles, Duc d' Orléans. NPeEn

Go from me: I am one of those who fall. Mystic and Cavalier. Lionel Pigot Johnson. MoBrPo

Go from me, summer friends, and tarry not. From Sunset to Star Rise. Christina Georgina Rossetti. VWP

Go from me. Yet I feel that I shall stand. Elizabeth Barrett Browning. BWW; CenSon; LW; OBEV; OxAEP-2 *Fr.* Sonnets from the Portuguese.

Go from the must-laden room. Advance of the Grizzly, The. Barbara Guest. BodElec

Go, go, queint folies, sugred sin. Idle Verse. Henry Vaughan. MiEL

Go, grieving rimes of mine, to that hard stone. Petrarch. NAWM-5v1; NAWM-7v1, *tr. by* Morris Gilbert Bishop *Fr.* Sonnets to Laura.

Go, Hart. *Unknown.* OxBS

(Go, heart, unto thy Saviour.) (LL) SacPr

Go her way, her quiet, quiet way. Relinquishment. Elsa Gidlow. PoBW

Go hert, hurt with adversité. *Unknown.* MiEL

Go herte, hurt wyth adversitee. *Unknown. See* Go hert, hurt with adversité

Go home, stupid. Ultimatum: Kid to Kid. Langston Hughes. NOxBChV

Go! hunt the whiter ermine, and present. For the Lady Olivia Porter; a Present upon a New Year's Day. Sir William Davenant [*or* D'Avenant]. MeLP; NOSC

Go, idle Boy! I quit thy pow'r. Adieu and Recall to Love, The. Robert Merry. NOBRP

Go Idle Lines. Thomas Watson. Son *Fr.* Tears of Fancy, The.

Go, ill-sped book, and whisper to her or. John Berryman. BoLoP

Go inside a stone. Stone. Charles Simic. ChAP

Go into the Highways and Hedges, And Compel Them to Come In. Aleister Crowley. CAGL

Go, keep holiday far away. Publius Papinius Statius. RomPo, *tr. by* W. G. Shepherd *Fr.* Sylvae.

Go, let the fatted calf be killed. Abraham Cowley. BoLoP *Fr.* Mistress, The.

Go, litel bille, and do me recomaunde. *Unknown.* OHMEL

Go, litel ryng, to that ilke swete. *Unknown.* OHMEL

Go Little Book. Robert Louis Stevenson. *See* Wishes

Go, little book, my little tragedy. Geoffrey Chaucer. WoPoe, *tr. by* Burton Raffel and Selden Rodman *Fr.* Troilus and Criseyde [*or* Criseide].

Go love without the help of any thing [*or* King] on Earth. (LL) William Blake. InPK-6; OxBSP; RB *Fr.* Gnomic Verses.

Go[e], lovely rose. Song. Edmund Waller. AWP; BASC; BeJo; BoLoP; CABP; CTC; ClHu; EnLoPo; GTBS-P; HAP; HeIP-4; InPK-6; NAEL-5v1; NAEL-6v1; NAEL-7v1; NIL-7; NOBE; NOSC; NPeEn; NoP-4; OBEV; OxAEP-1; OxBEV; PBRV; PoE; PoPoPo; PoRA; SoSe-8; TFi; UnPo; WeW-3; WoPoe

Go measure the distance from Cape Town to Pretoria. Measure for Measure. Sipho Sepamla. AF; PeSAV

Go, my flock, go get you hence. Sir Philip Sidney. NoSic *Fr.* Astrophil and Stella.

Go, my Lord of the Mountains. Kamalākānta Bhattācārya. SinGod, *tr. by* Rachel Fell McDermott

Go, my songs, seek your praise from the young and from the intolerant. Ité. Ezra Pound. HAP; MoAmPo

Go, my songs, to the lonely and the unsatisfied. Commission. Ezra Pound. BoLoP; TwCP

Go, my thought, as long as a word clear enough for flight. Go, My Thought. Ingeborg Bachmann. PoSu, *tr. by* Mark Anderson

Go north up the T'ai-heng Mountains. Bitter Cold: A Song. Ts'ao Ts'ao. ChinPo, *tr. by* Yip Wai-lim

Go not, happy day. Tennyson. EBVV *Fr.* Maud [A Monodrama].

Go not to the hills of Erinn. Wind on the Hills, The. Dora Sigerson Shorter. NOBVV

Go not too frequently thy friends to see. Advice to Bores. Abraham Ibn-Chasdai. TrJP, *tr. by* J. Chotzner

Go not too near a House of Rose. Emily Dickinson. MoAmPo; NIL-7; NIP-4

Go on! Go on! Sermon at Clevedon, A. Thomas Edward Brown. NOBVV

Go on, high ship, since now, upon the shore. Farewell to Florida. Wallace Stevens. NoAM

Go on; I'll follow thee. (LL) William Shakespeare. EBEV; OxAEP-1 *Fr.* Hamlet.

Go on, / Muses, / and sing the Moon with her big wings. *Unknown.* HW, *tr. by* Charles Boer *Fr.* Homeric Hymns.

Go on, tell me the season is over. Alan Wearne. BMAP

Go on the Scout they say. Thorow. Susan Howe. APSN

Go out and camp somewhere. You're lying down. Mapooram. *Aborigine Oral Tradition.* NOBAu, *tr. by* Fred Biggs

Go out in the midday sun. (LL) Mad Dogs and Englishmen. Noël Coward. NBLV; NOBL; PeLV; ReLy

Go out in this dear summertide. Paul Gerhardt. GePo, *tr. by* George C. Schoolfield

Go peni go. (LL) Penny. *Unknown.* FaBoVe; MiEL

Go, perjured youth, and court what nymph you please. To Philaster. Sarah Fyge Egerton. ECWP

Go pretty [*or* prettie] child and bear[e] this flower. To His Saviour, a Child; a Present, by a Child. Robert Herrick. BeJo; ChIV-2; PeECV; TrCP

Go Right along the Seashore. *Unknown.* PeNZ

Go, rose, my Chloe's bosom grace. Love's Emblem. John Clare. NIL-7; NIP-4

Go, rural Naiad! wind thy stream along. To the Naiad of the Arun. Charlotte Smith. CenSon; RWP

Go sad or sweet or riotous with beer. Old Women, The. George Mackay Brown. NoP-4; OxBS

Go, said old Lyce, senseless lover, go. Lyce. William Walsh. BoLoP

Go, silly worm, drudge, trudge, and travell. Omnia Somnia. Joshua Sylvester. FaBoEE

Go sit yo ass down. We Are the Young Magicians. Ruth Forman. AmPoNex

Go slow, my soul, to feed thyself. Emily Dickinson. APN-2

Go slowly, go slowly, oh moon, upon your way. We are sowing by your light. They That Sow at Night. Shin Shalom. MHP, *tr. by* Ruth Finer Mintz

Go, smiling souls, your new-built cages break. Richard Crashaw.*See* Go[e], smiling soul[e]s, your new-built cages break[e]

Go softly past the graveyard where. Leonidas of Tarentum. GrAn

Go, solitary wood, and henceforth be. On the Death of a Nightingale. Thomas Randolph. BASC; BeJo

Go, songs, for ended is our brief, sweet play. Envoy. Francis Thompson. MoBrPo

Go, Soul [*or* Goe soule], the body's [*or* bodies] guest. Lie, The. Sir Walter Ralegh. CTC; EBEV; HAP; NAEL-5v1; NAEL-6v1; NAEL-7v1; NOBE; NPeEn; NoSic; OxBEV; RB; SCGP; SCV; TFi

Go soule, go sweetest soule for ever blest. Ludovico Ariosto. OBVE *Fr.* Orlando Furioso.

Go t' School. Day at School, A. Andrea M. Wren. InTrad

Go Take the World. Jay Macpherson. MoCV

Go talk with those who are rumored to be unlike you. For the Student Strikers. Richard Wilbur. OxBC

Go tell at Sparta, traveler passing by. On the Spartan Dead at Thermopylae. Simonides. WeW-3, *tr. by* Peter Jay

Go tell the king—the carven hall is felled. *Unknown.* GrAn

Go tell the king: the daedal. Last Utterance of the Delphic Oracle, The. *Unknown.* OBVE, *tr. by* Kenneth Rexroth

Go tell the Spartans, thou that passest by. Thermopylae. Simonides. AWP; OBEV; OBWP; WoPoe, *tr. by* William Lisle Bowles

Go, the rich *Chariot* instantly prepare;. Muse, The. Abraham Cowley. CABP; PBRV

Go, then, and join the murmuring city's throng! To a Friend. William Lisle Bowles. Son

Go then, my dove, but now no longer mine. Cotton Mather. AiP; SCAP

Go thou forth, my book, though late. To His Book. Robert Herrick. CaPo

Go thou gentle whispering wind. Prayer to the Wind, A. Thomas Carew. BeJo; CavPo

Go, thou that vainly dost mine eyes invite. Sonnet. Henry King, Bishop of Chichester. OxBSP

Go through the pockets of the enemy wounded. Love Letters of the Dead. Douglas Street. FaBoWar

Go to Ahmedabad. Sujata Bhatt. FSt

Go to bed first. Go to Bed. *Unknown.* OxNR

Go to bed late. *Unknown.* OxNR

Go to bed, Tom. *Unknown.* OxNR

Go to sleep McKade. Kenneth Fearing. *See* Sleep, McKade

Go to sleep, my baby goblin. Mother Goblin's Lullaby. Jack Prelutsky. NOxBChV

Go to sleep—though of course you will not. Goodnight, A. William Carlos Williams. MoAmPo

Go to sleepy, little baby. (LL) All the Pretty Little Horses. *Unknown.* OxBoLi; TTTS

"Go to the Ant." Stanley J. Sharpless. NOBL

Go to the Ant [Thou Sluggard]. Bible, *O.T.* TrJP *Fr.* Proverbs.

Go to the ant, you sluggard. Proverbs 6:6. David Curzon. ChIV-1

Go to the moon / white folks going to the moon / going to. Moon Bound. Raymond Washington. NBV

Go to the patch some afternoon. How to Make Rhubarb Wine. Ted Kooser. PBCAP

Go to the sea. How to Get a Baby. Judith Ortiz Cofer. NIL-7; PueRic

Go to the western gate, Luke Havergal. Luke Havergal. Edwin Arlington Robinson. APN-2; AWP; MoAmPo; NAAL-2v2; NAAL-5; NOBA; NoAM; TCAPo; TFi; UnPo

Go under. Swimming Lesson. Wyatt Townley. SpudSo

Go underneath the ancient rooms. Search, The. Inge Hoogerhuis. HW

Go, Valentine. Robert Southey. Son

Go wailing verse, the infants of my love. Samuel Daniel. NoP-4

Go walk the streets of Baroda. Go to Ahmedabad. Sujata Bhatt. FSt

Go, wash thyself in Jordan—go, wash thee and be clean! Naaman's Song. Rudyard Kipling. ChIV-1

Go 'way from dat window, "My Honey, My Love." Song to the Runaway Slave. Unknown. BPo

Go when the friendly moon permits the tides. Advice to a Clam-Digger. Wilbert Snow. APT-1

Go where my mind will. Tune: "Four Pieces of Jade"—Idle Leisure. Kuan Han-ch'ing. SuSp, tr. by Jerome Seaton

Go where the waters fall. John Keble. SacPr Fr. Waterfall, The.

Go where those others went to the dark boundary. Envoy of Mr. Cogito, The. Zbigniew Herbert. PoetW; WoPoe, tr. by Carpenter Bogdana, John Carpenter and Bogdana Carpenter

Go where we will, at ev'ry time and place. Charles Churchill. ECEV Fr. Times, The.

Go with a perm or a duck tail. How to Dress Like a Femmy Dyke. Jane Barnes. GLP

Go Work in My Vineyard. Frances Ellen Watkins Harper. PWR

Goad, The. "Michael Field." VWP

Goanna chases grasshopper. Goanna. Unknown. NOBAu, tr. by Mungayana Nundhirribala

Goat, The. Umberto Saba. WoPoe, tr. by Stephen Sartarelli

Goat and a sheep, with a fat pig, are, A. Pig, Goat, Sheep. Jean de La Fontaine. WoPoe, tr. by Bruce Boone and Robert Glück

Goat-foot choros the. Japanese Presentation I and II. Joan Retallack. FTOS

Goat-foot Pan has quit his flocks. Meleager. GrAn

Goat God, The. Cesare Pavese. WoPoe, tr. by William Arrowsmith

Goat Paths, The. James Stephens. AWP; SCGP; UnPo

Goat that used to bleat in our yard, The. San Juan. Myrna Peña Reyes. FSt

Goat was nibbling on a vine, A. Vine and the Goat, The. Aesop. AWP, tr. by William Ellery Leonard

Goats on the roof. John Wills. HA

Gobble the news with seven grains. Landing on the Moon. Odia Ofeimun. EmeKit

Goblet, The. Bayard Taylor. TreFP

Goblet of wine, A. Tune: "Sand of Silk-Washing Brook." Yen Shu. ColAnChi, tr. by Jiaosheng Wang

Goblin, The. Rose Fyleman. NTCP

Goblin, The. Jack Prelutsky. TLR

Goblin lives in our house, in our house, in our house, A. Goblin, The. Rose Fyleman. NTCP

Goblin Market. Christina Georgina Rossetti. EBEV; NAEL-5v2; NAEL-6v2; NALW; NOBVV; NOxBChV; OBNV; OxAEP-2; OxBEV; VWP; ViWPN

"Good folk," said Lizzie. FaBoVe

"Laughed every goblin." BrRo

God. Bella [or Izabella] Akhatovna Akhmadulina. RusPo, tr. by Robert Arthur Douglas Ford

God. Samuel Greenberg. APT-1

God. Isaac Rosenberg. OxBEV

God. Boris Abramovich Slutsky [or Slutskii]. TCRusP, tr. by Daniel Weissbort

God. Boris Abramovich Slutsky [or Slutskii]. TCRP, tr. by J. R. Rowland

God. Unknown. See I Vision God

God, A. Ted Hughes. GI

God (3). Marina Ivanovna Tsvetaeva [or Tsvetaeva]. WPoS, tr. by Paul Graves

God a great railway to heaven has planned. Beulah Railway, The. Unknown. GM

God, A Poem. James Fenton. DiPo; NoAM; NoP-4; OBCoV

God aloft in majesty. God Supreme. Abraham Ibn Ezra. TOF, tr. by David Goldstein

God alone is God! Mohammed rassoul Allah!. Desert. Birago Diop. NegPo, tr. by Ellen Conroy Kennedy

God alone suffices. (LL) Poem: "Nothing move thee." Saint Theresa [or Teresa] of Avila. CRP; WoPoe, tr. by Yvor Winters

God and Man Set as One. Unknown. SacPr

God and Saint [or Sanct] Peter was gangand be the way. How the First Hielandman of God Was Made. Unknown. OBSV

God and the devil in these letters. Postman's Bell Is Answered Everywhere, The. Horace Gregory. MoAmPo

God and the devil still are wrangling. For a Mouthy Woman. Countee Cullen. ChIV-1; OBAL

God and the Holy Stones. Annie Foster. NLP

God and Yet a Man, A? Unknown. HAP; MiEL

God banish from your house. Benediction. Stanley Kunitz. VGW

God be here, God be there. Unknown. OxNR

God be in my head. Knight's Prayer, The. Unknown. InvLi

(God be praised!) the Georges ended. (LL) Georges, The. Walter Savage Landor. FaBoEE; NIP-4; OBCoV; OBSV

God Be with You. Unknown. PoToHe

God Be with You till We Meet Again. Jeremiah Eames Rankin. AH

God being with thee when we know it not. (LL) It is a beauteous evening. William Wordsworth. AWP; BRP; CenSon; FHYEP; GSo; GTBS-P; HeIP-4; NAEL-5v2; NAEL-6v2; NIP-4; NOBRP; NoP-4; OxAEP-2; PAI; SCGP; Son; TFi

God Bless America. John Fuller. OBSV; PeLV

God Bless Our Father-Land. Oliver Wendell Holmes. TreFP

God bless our good and gracious King. Impromptu on Charles II. John Wilmot, 2d Earl of Rochester. BASC; FaBoEE; NBLV; NOBL; OBSV; OxAEP-1; PeLV

God bless our meat. Unknown. OxNR

God Bless Our Native Land. Frances Ellen Watkins Harper. PWR

God Bless the Child. Arthur, Jr. Herzog. ReLy

God bless the king, God bless our faith's defender. John Byrom. See God bless the King!—I mean the Faith's Defender

God bless the King!—I mean the Faith's Defender. Jacobite Toast. John Byrom. FaBoEE

God bless the little feet that never go astray. My Darlings' Shoes. Unknown. TreFP

God bless this house from thatch to floor. Unknown. OxNR

God Bless You. Unknown. PoToHe

God bless you! (LL) Unknown. NTCP; OxNR; ReMoGo

God-born before the Sons of God, she hurled. Music. Madison Cawein. APN-2

God braced me with His firm hand. Tool of Fate, The. "Yehoash." TrJP, tr. by Isidore Goldstick

God breathed. Creation. Robin Gurr. NOBAu

God broke into my house last night. Scapegoat. William Robert Rodgers. CIP-2

God broke upon this upturned field; trees. Body of a Rook. David Wevill. MoCV

God brought perfect man to fruition. Limerick. Douglas Catley. PeLi

God, but I do. Paganly. Trinidad Tarrosa Subido. InvLi

God by his Wisdome, and all seeing Pow'r. Alice Sutcliffe. EMWP Fr. Meditations of Man's Mortalitie; or, A Way to True Blessedness.

God caught his eye. (LL) Epitaph on a Waiter. David McCord. APT-2; NBLV; NIP-4; OBAL; OBCoV

God, consider the soul's need. Death Song for Owain ab Urien. Taliesin. OBWVE, tr. by Anthony Conran

God Correctly Understood. J. Gordon Coogler. VerBaPo

God Coup, The. Anne Carson. BodElec Fr. Truth About God, The.

God created his image. Fill and Illumined. Joseph Ceravolo. ChIV-1

God decided he was tired. Budgie Finds His Voice. Wendy Cope. UV

God did forbid the Israelites, to bring. Ass[e], The. Robert Herrick. ChIV-1

God does for virtue goal and urge and crown afford. "Angelus Silesius." GePo, tr. by George C. Schoolfield Fr. Cherubical Wanderer, The.

God doth dwell in men, from th' blessed seats, A. In Consort to Wednesday, Jan. 1st. 1701. Richard Henchman. SCAP

God doubtless makes her, and doth make her good. Sir John Davies. SacPr Fr. Nosce Teipsum.

God, ever gracious God! Here I myself debase. Night Thoughts Concerning a Dream. Daniel Casper von Lohenstein. GePo, tr. by George C. Schoolfield

God Everywhere. Abraham Ibn Ezra. TrJP, tr. by D. E. de L

God exists. Instead. Fatima. Laura Kasischke. AmPoNex

God exists, though he doesn't exist. Phallus. Kazuko Shiraishi. BoWoP, tr. by Ikuko Atsumi

God Fit, The. Anne Carson. BodElec Fr. Truth About God, The.

God, for a man that solicits insurance! (LL) Bohemia. Dorothy Parker. APT-1; NBLV

God, / for Mercy's sake. From "The Torah of the Void." Rabbi Nahman [or Nachman] of Bratzlav. BLT, tr. by Zalman Schachter

God Forgotten. Nick Flynn. AmPoNex

God-Forgotten. Thomas Hardy. InvLi

God from His Throne with Piercing Eye. Joseph Steward. AH

God Gave Us Trees to Cut Down. W. Les Russell. IBA

God, give me back the simple faith that I so long have clung to. Prayer for Faith, A. Margaret Elizabeth Sangster. PoToHe

God give me strength to lead a double life. Prayer. Hugo Williams. EmeKit; NPeEn

God give me strength to lead a double life. (LL) Prayer. Hugo Williams. EmeKit; NPeEn

God give the yellow man. God Give to Men. Arna Bontemps. BPo; ColAP

God give us men! A time like this demands. Wanted. Josiah Gilbert Holland. SacPr

God gives them sleep on ground, on straw. Roger Williams. SCAP

God gives us joy that we may give. Giving. *Unknown.* PoToHe

God! / glad I'm black. Blue Black. Bloke Modisane. PBA

God grant thee thine own wish, and grant thee mine. John Donne. OBVE

God ha' mercy on such as we, / Baa! Yah! Bah! (LL) Gentlemen-Rankers. Rudyard Kipling. FaBoWar; NOBVV

God had no name. Anne Carson. BodElec *Fr.* Truth About God, The.

God had released her. (LL) Widow, The. Robert Southey. NOBRP; NOEC; UV

God has a Right Hand, but is quite bereft. Right Hand, The. Robert Herrick. CavPo

God has foure keyes, which He reserves alone. Gods Keyes. Robert Herrick. SacPr

God has, of old, been speaking to you through his Seers. To the Hungarian People. János Edrosi Sylvester. IQMS, *tr. by* Adam Makkai

God hath the whole world perfect made, and free. Pleasd with thy Place. Epictetus. NPeEn, *tr. by* George Chapman

God hath yeuen, of myghtis most. Seven Gifts of the Holy Ghost, The. John Audelay [*or* Awdelay]. SacPr

God help me, liberal mothers. Russ Joy Little League. Douglas Carlson. MoASP

God help thee, Traveler, on thy journey far. Winter Traveler, The. Henry Kirke White. CenSon

God help who follows his father's craft! Passing of the Poets, The. Fearflatha O'Gnive [*or* O'Gnimh]. NOIV

God help who looks upon Enniskillen. Visit to Enniskillen, A. Tadhg Dall O'Huiginn. NOIV

God help you on that fatal day. (LL) Be Frugal. Richard Church. OxBSP; OxBTC

God Himself, in all His righteous wrath. Our Father. Barbara Goldberg. GotH

God, how I envy you these great oak roots. Jew Walks in Westminster Abbey, A. Aubrey Hodes. TrJP

God! How I Long for You. Kenneth Mackenzie. CBAP

God how is it that we surrender. Nizar Qabbani. MAP

God, how my mouth swam. Sparrow Hills. Robley, Jr. Wilson. PBCAP

God! how they plague his life, the three damned sisters. Little Brother, The. James Reeves. OxBTC

God Hunger. Michael Ryan. BodElec

God, I know nothing, my sense is all nonsense. Grace, A. Donald Hall. LoL

God I love my master. I love my master I love my master. Lynda Barry. Unle

God I love thee in Thy robe of roses. Zebaoth. Else Lasker-Schüler. TrJP, *tr. by* Jethro Bithell

God, I need a job because I need money. Prayer. Alan Dugan. NoAM

God if he exists. Man Root, The. Kazuko Shiraishi. PFTM-2, *tr. by* Ikuko Atsumi and Kenneth Rexroth

God if he isn't is. Phallic Root. Kazuko Shiraishi. WPOW

GOD-IN-HIMSELF / I feel the evil of absence in my eternal heart. Preface or The Drama of Absence in an Eternal Heart. Roger Gilbert-Lecomte. PFTM-1

God in His Wisdom from the start. Semonides. WoPoe, *tr. by* Peter Whigham *Fr.* Genealogy of Women, The.

God in Wrath, A. Stephen Crane. OxBSP; TAP *Fr.* Black Riders [and Other Lines], The.

God Is. Roland Mathias. CRP

God is a distant—stately Lover. Emily Dickinson. APN-2; NCAP

God is a grand heart cut. Anne Carson. BodElec *Fr.* Truth About God, The.

God is a pure no-thing. "Angelus Silesius." EnlH

God is a zealous pruner. Pruner, The. John Oxenham. SacPr

God is above the sphere of our esteem. What God Is. Robert Herrick. BeJo; NOSC

God Is Dead—Nietzche. Elizabeth Bartlett. Prnts

God is Good. It Is a Beautiful Night. Wallace Stevens. APT-1; SAmP

God is indeed a jealous God. Emily Dickinson. NOBA

God is love. Then by inversion. History of Ideas. James Vincent Cunningham. NIP-4; VCAP

God is my staff, my path, my goal, my game, my fire. "Angelus Silesius." GePo, *tr. by* George C. Schoolfield *Fr.* Cherubical Wanderer, The.

God is near, and, The / difficult to grasp. Patmos. Friedrich Hölderlin. OBVE; WoPoe, *tr. by* David Gascoyne

God is no botcher, but when God wrought you two. On Botching. John Heywood. FaBoEE

God is not dumb, that he should speak no more. James Russell Lowell. ChIV-1 *Fr.* Bibliolaters.

God is not on[e]ly merciful, to call. Calling, and Correcting. Robert Herrick. BeJo

God Is Nothing Physical. "Angelus Silesius." GePo, *tr. by* George C. Schoolfield *Fr.* Cherubical Wanderer, The.

God is older than the sun and moon. Maximus. D. H. Lawrence. BLT; TOF

God is our refuge and strength, a very present help in trouble. Bible, *O.T.* AWP *Fr.* Psalms.

God is our strength and our refuge: therefore will we not tremble. Hexameters[; Paraphrase of Psalm XLVI]. Samuel Taylor Coleridge. ChIV-1

God is praise and glory. *Unknown.* AWP *Fr.* Thousand and One Nights, The.

God is still glorified. Building in Stone. Sylvia Townsend Warner. MoBrPo

God is the great urge that has not yet found a body. Body of God, The. D. H. Lawrence. ChIV-2

God is the Most High. Muhammedan Call to Prayer. Bilal. TTY, *tr. by* Raoul Abdul

God Is to Me What I Desire. "Angelus Silesius." GePo, *tr. by* George C. Schoolfield *Fr.* Cherubical Wanderer, The.

God, keep me still unsatisfied. (LL) Prayer: "God, though [*or* although] this life is but a wraith." Louis Untermeyer. MoAmPo; TrJP

God knows, teaching the Renaissance I could use it. Why I Don't Speak Italian. Arthur L. Clements. UnSA

God knows / We have our troubles, too. High to Low. Langston Hughes. APT-2; HCAP; PoPoPo

God knows what beat him down into that deadland. At the Entrance. Douglas Stewart. CBAP

God knows what happened to the candlestick. Candlestick, The. Jaroslav Seifert. AF, *tr. by* Ewald Osers

God lay dead in Heaven. Stephen Crane. APN-2 *Fr.* Black Riders [and Other Lines], The.

God leaned out of himself one day. Whole New Scene, A. John Fuller. NOxBChV

God, let me be a giver, and not one. Let Me Be a Giver. Mary Carolyn Davies. PoToHe

God let me find the lonely ones. Prayer for a Day's Walk. Grace Noll Crowell. PoToHe

God let never soe old a man. Old Robin of Portingale. *Unknown.* ESPB

God like a kiss, God like a welcoming. Mark Jarman. InvLi *Fr.* Unholy Sonnets.

God Looks on Nature With a Glorious Eye. John Clare. BBASP

God love you. Poem for the Old Man, A. John Wieners. NeAP

God love you now, if no one else will ever. Ode for the American Dead in Korea. Thomas McGrath. VGW

God loves us all, I'm pleased to say. God's Love. Vikram Seth. TRP

God Lyaeus, Ever Young. John Fletcher. OBEV *Fr.* Tragedy of Valentinian, The.

God made the bees. Mother Goose. Spl

God made the sex-shop keeper. Fiona Pitt-Kethley. UV

God made the sugar cane grow where it's hot. Bundaberg Rum. W. N. Scott. NOBAu

God made the wicked grocer. Song against Grocers, The. Gilbert Keith Chesterton. OBCoV

God makes a path, provides a guide. Roger Williams. SacPr

God makes all things for good; 'tis man. Man Leavens the Batch. Mildmay Fane, 2d Earl of Westmorland. BeJo

God makes sech nights all white an' still. James Russell Lowell. NOBA; OBAL *Fr.* Biglow Papers, The.

God mercifully forgets us for a few hours. God Forgotten. Nick Flynn. AmPoNex

God moves in a mysterious way. William Cowper. CABP; EBEV; ECEV; FHYEP; FaBoCh; NOBE; NOCV; NOEC; NPeEn; OxBEV; PWR; SCGP; SacPr; TFi; TOF *Fr.* Olney Hymns.

God must have a big eye to see everything. Jack Spicer. NeAP; PmAP *Fr.* Imaginary Elegies.

God my father spoke in the calm of evening. Peter Davison. YaYoPo *Fr.* Breaking of the Day, The.

God Not Afar Off. Jones Very. InvLi

God, O God, whom I have begged. Poem in Praise of Colum Cille, A. Dallán Forgaill. NOIV

God of Abraham, of Isaac, and of Jacob. *Unknown.* TrJP, *tr. by* Olga Marx

God of Abraham praise, The. Thomas Olivers. SacPr

God of Bethel Heard Her Cries, The. Richard Allen. AH

God of day rolls his car up the slopes, The. Guido's Aurora. Henry David Thoreau. APN-1

God of his goodnes, praysed that he be. *Unknown.* NOIV *Fr.* Praise of Waterford, The.

God of Love, The. George MacBeth [*or* Macbeth]. EmeKit

God of Mercy. Kadya Molodovsky [or Molodowsky]. WPOW, tr. by Irving Howe

God of Might, God of Right. Unknown. TrJP

God of mine, I am weeping for the life that I live. Eternal Dice, The. César Vallejo. PoetW, tr. by James Wright

God of My Life! Benjamin Colman. AH

God of Nature in the field of Grace, The. (LL) Abraham Cowley. MeLP; NOSC Fr. Mistress, The.

God of Our Fathers. Melanchton Woolsey Stryker. AH

God of Our Fathers, Bless This Our Land. John Henry, Jr. Hopkins. AH

God of our fathers, known of old. Recessional. Rudyard Kipling. AWP; BRP; CABP; InvLi; MoBrPo; NAEL-6v2; NOBE; NOBVV; NPeEn; NoAM; NoP-4; OBEV; OxAEP-2; OxBEV; PWR; SCGP; TFi; UV; UnPo

God of Our Fathers, Whose Almighty Hand. Daniel C. Roberts. AH

God of Peace, in Peace Preserve Us. Ernst W. Olson. AH

God of Pepper, The. Alan Michael Parker. NeAmPo

God of Sheep, The. John Fletcher. FaBoCh Fr. Faithful Shepherdess, The.

God of Smoke listens idly in the heat, The. Backyard. John Tranter. BMAP

God of song and laughter long ago, The. But. Vladimir Holan. PoSu, tr. by Ian Milner and Jarmila Milner

God of the Flies. John Rimington. FaBoWar

God of the Nations. Walter Russell Bowie. AH

God of the Nations, Near and Far. John Haynes Holmes. AH

God of the Prophets! Bless the Prophets' Sons. Denis Wortman. AH

God of the Strong, God of the Weak. Richard Watson Gilder. AH

God of the World. Israel Najara. TrJP, tr. by Israel Abrahams

God of the World, Thy Glories Shine. Sewall Sylvester Cutting. AH

God of Visions. Emily Jane Brontë. BrRo

(O! thy bright eyes must answer now.) PEW; VWP

God of War, The. Bertolt Brecht. AF, tr. by Michael Hamburger

God of your fathers, known of old. Post-Recessional. Gilbert Keith Chesterton. UV

God Once Commanded Us, A. Leah Goldberg. FIT, tr. by Robert Friend

God only, who made us rich, can make us poor. (LL) Elizabeth Barrett Browning. CenSon; NOBVV; OxBEV Fr. Sonnets from the Portuguese.

God ordered motion, but ordained no rest. (LL) Man. Henry Vaughan. ESCV; GeHe; MeLP; NOBE; NOCV; OBEV; SCGP

God our fathers formerly knew. Headlined in Heaven. Paul Grano. NOBAu

God our Refuge. Richard Chenevix Trench. SacPr

God, pity broken little families. Prayer for Broken Little Families, A. Violet Alleyn Storey. PoToHe

God pity me whom (god distinctly has). E. E. Cummings. SeSe

God pity the wretched prisoners. In Prison. Michael Smith. PWR

God Poem. Stanley Moss. VGW

God prosper long our Gracious King. Ode for the New Year, An. John Gay. OxBoLi

God rest that Jewy woman. Song for the Clatter-Bones. Frederick Robert Higgins. ChIV-1; OBMV

God rest the soul of Ireland. After the Flight of the Earls. Fearflatha O'Gnive [or O'Gnimh]. NOIV

God rest ye merry, gentlemen. Unknown. SacPr

God Rest You Merry. Dinah Maria Mulock Craik. UV

God rest you merry gentlemen. Christmas Carol, A. Gilbert Keith Chesterton. UV

God rot the guts and the guts' indulgences. Palladas [or Pallades]. GrAn

God's a-Gonna Trouble the Water. Unknown. NAAAL

God's Absence. Mechthild von Magdeburg. WPoS, tr. by Oliver Davies

God's all-unfathomed plan is quite fulfilled. (LL) Tireless Sculptor, The. Henrietta Cordelia Ray. CBWP-3; SWaP

God's armies of Heaven, with pinions extended. Pro Patria. Adah Isaacs Menken. CBWP-1

God's Blessing. Len Roberts. BodElec

God's blessing on poor ship-folk! Peace and prayer. Wanderers, The. Robert Williams Buchanan. OxBSo

God's blessings all are uniform. They Are the Same. Priscilla Jane Thompson. CBWP-2

God's Body. Sara Klugman. HW

God's boundless mercy is, to sinful man. God's Mercy. Robert Herrick. BeJo

God's child in Christ adopted—Christ my all. My Baptismal Birthday [or Birth-Day]. Samuel Taylor Coleridge. ChIV-2; NOCV

God's City. Francis Turner Palgrave. SacPr

God's Controversy with New-England. Michael Wigglesworth. SCAP

God's Determinations [touching his Elect]. Edward Taylor.

Christ's Reply. NAAL-2v1; NAAL-3

Frowardness of the Elect in the Work of Conversion, The. SCAP

(In Heaven Soaring Up.) AH

Joy of Church Fellowship Rightly Attended, The. NAAL-2v1; NAAL-3; OxBA; SCAP

Preface, The: "Infinity, when all things it beheld.". HAP; NAAL-2v1; NAAL-3; NOBA; NOSC; OxBA; OxBEV; SCAP; TCAPo

Soul's Groan to Christ for Succo[u]r, The. NAAL-2v1; NAAL-3

God's Electric Power. Mrs. Henry Linden. CBWP-4

God's evident, and may be said to be. Gods Presence. Robert Herrick. SacPr

God's favour like the sun, whose beams appear. Francis Quarles. PeECV Fr. Divine Fancies.

God's Gifts. Albrecht von Johannsdorf. GePo, tr. by F. C. Nicholson

God's grace has surely been overabundant. To My Friends. Yuly [or Iulii] Markovich Daniel. TCRP, tr. by Arthur Boyars and David Burg

God's Grandeur. Gerard Manley Hopkins. AWP; AmFaPo; BBASP; CABP; ChAP; ClHu; EBVV; EnlH; GSo; HAP; ITBLP; InPK-6; MoBrPo; NAEL-5v2; NAEL-6v2; NIL-7; NIP-4; NOBE; NOBVV; NoAM; NoP-4; OxBEV; OxBSo; PeVV; PoE; PoPoPo; RaBo; SCGP; SacPr; SoSe-8; Son; TFi; TrCP; UnPo; WeW-3

God's Handiwork. Anne Carson. BodElec Fr. Truth About God, The.

God's Harp. Gustav Falke. AWP, tr. by Ludwig Lewisohn

God's head for a paperweight, A. Desk, The. Cid Corman. VGW

God's Love. Vikram Seth. TRP

God's Measurements. Laurence Lieberman. IllVoic

God's Mercy. Robert Herrick. BeJo

God's Mercy. William Langland. NOCV Fr. Vision of Piers Plowman, The.

God's Name. Anne Carson. BodElec Fr. Truth About God, The.

God's old angels made us peaceful. My New Angels. Sinéad Morrissey. MFPA

God's other eye is good and gold. So bright. Jack Spicer. NeAP; PmAP Fr. Imaginary Elegies.

God's philosophical and so can wait. Palladas [or Pallades]. GrAn

God's plan made a hopeful beginning. Limerick. Unknown. PeLi

God's querulous calling. (LL) Theology. Ted Hughes. FaBoMo; NAEL-5v2; NAEL-6v2; NoAM; NoP-4; PAI

God's Residence. Emily Dickinson. SAmP; WPoS

God's shadow. (LL) Ahmad al-Mushari Al-'Udwani. BBASP; MAP, tr. by Charles Doria and Hilary Kilpatrick Fr. Signs.

God's touch will keep its one chord quivering. (LL) L'Envoi. Edwin Arlington Robinson. ITBLP; TrCP

God's twins (the testaments) speak loud. Morgan Llwyd. AngWePo Fr. 1648.

God's Two Dwellings. Thomas Washbourne. SacPr

God's undivided, One in Persons Three. To God. Robert Herrick. SacPr

God's unfinished work. (LL) Campesino's Lament, The. Judith Ortiz Cofer. PueRic; TouFir

God's Virtue. Barnabe Barnes. NOCV Fr. Divine Century of Spiritual Sonnets, A.

God's Ways Are Strange. Margaret E. Bruner. PoToHe

God's Ways, Not Our Ways. Henrietta Cordelia Ray. CBWP-3

God's Will for You and Me. Unknown. SoSe-8

God's Work. Anne Carson. BodElec Fr. Truth About God, The.

God's World. Edna St. Vincent Millay. APT-1; ITBLP; MoAmPo; TrCP

GOD said, Let Newton be! and All was Light. (LL) Intended for Sir Isaac Newton. Pope. ECEV; FaBoEE; InPK-6; WeW-3

God said, "Let there be light, and there was light." Mysteries of Life. Mary E. Tucker. CBWP-1

God said to Abraham. Aida Gelbtrunk. MirDau, tr. by Roberta Gordenstein

God Save Great Thomas Paine. Joseph Mather. NOEC

God save the King, that King that sav'd the land. Benjamin Harris. SCAP

God Save the Plough. Lydia Huntley Sigourney. OBAL

God save this troop! That's all I have to tell. (LL) Geoffrey Chaucer. NAWM-5v1; NAWM-7v1, tr. by Theodore Morrison Fr. Canterbury Tales, The.

God Scatters Beauty. Walter Savage Landor. InvLi

("God scatters beauty as he scatters flowers") FaBoEE

God send euerie Preist ane wyfe. Unknown. NePenScot Fr. Gude and Godlie Ballatis, The.

God send her well to speede! (LL) Boy and the Mantle, The. Unknown. ESPB; OxBB

God send the Devil is a gentleman. Knight Fallen on Evil Days, The. Elinor Wylie. MoAmPo

God send the land deliverance. Unknown. See Liddesdale Crosiers hae ridden a race, The.

God sende hem so[o]ne [a] verray pestilence[!]. (LL) Geoffrey Chaucer. FHYEP; NAEL-5v1; NAEL-6v1; NAEL-7v1 Fr. Canterbury Tales, The.

God sends his tasks. Visitation, The. Brigit Pegeen Kelly. YaYoPo

God sent us here to make mistakes. Mistakes. Ella Wheeler Wilcox. PoToHe

God Set Us Here. Nicasius de Sillè. AH

God Shed His Grace. Philip Stephens. AmPoNex

God sits on a chair of darkness in my soul. Garments of God, The. Jessica Agnes Powers. InvLi

God sits on the firmament arch. Creation of Light, The. Sister Maura. CRP

God Sour the Milk of the Knacking Wench. Alden Nowlan. MoCV

God Speaks to the Soul. Mechthild von Magdeburg. WPoS, *tr. by* Oliver Davies

God spoke once in the dark. Precision, The. Yvor Winters. SPE

God stopped and the car. Not Singing. Kate Daniels. PBCAP

God strengthen me to bear myself. Who Shall Deliver Me? Christina Georgina Rossetti. SacPr; TOF

God strikes His Church, But 'tis to this intent. Persecutions Purifie. Robert Herrick. SacPr

God Supreme. Abraham Ibn Ezra. TOF, *tr. by* David Goldstein

God Supreme! To Thee We Pray. Penina Moise. AH

God tempteth no one (as S. Aug'stine saith). Temptation. Robert Herrick. SacPr

God, that all this mightes may. *Unknown.* MiEL

God That Doest Wondrously. Moses Ibn Ezra. TrJP, *tr. by* Solomon Solis-Cohen

God, that mad'st her well regard her. Dieu Qu'il la Fait. Charles, Duc d' Orléans. AWP, *tr. by* Ezra Pound

God the Artist. Angela Morgan. PoToHe

God the Eater. Stevie Smith. BWW

God the mother. Spell for Birth. Jeni Couzyn. HAWP

God, the Port of Peace. John Walton. SacPr

God, the rabbis tell us, never assigns. Getting the Message. Maxine W. Kumin. TaR

God— / they fear you, they hold you so. Testimony. Carolyn M. Rodgers. BPo

God, thou great symmetry. Envoi. Anna Wickham. MoBrPo

God, though [*or* although] this life is but a wraith. Prayer. Louis Untermeyer. MoAmPo; TrJP

God thought of you, and so I am here. (LL) George Macdonald. ITBLP; WHSW *Fr.* At the Back of the North Wind.

God through the wrong end of a telescope. (LL) Of John Davidson. Hugh MacDiarmid. HarvBoo; NePenScot; OxBEV

God to Thee We Humbly Bow. George Henry Boker. AH

God tole Hezykiah. Little Black Train Is a-Comin' *Unknown.* GM

God tried to teach Crow how to talk. Crow's First Lesson. Ted Hughes. NoAM

God, we don't like to complain. Caliban in the Coal Mines. Louis Untermeyer. MoAmPo; TrJP

God when He's angry here with any one. Gods Anger without Affection. Robert Herrick. InvLi

God, when you thought of a pine tree. God the Artist. Angela Morgan. PoToHe

God who also watched over me / was my old granny's friend. (LL) To the Anxious Mother. Valente Goenha Malangatana. PBA; PBMAP, *tr. by* Dorothy Guedes and Philippa Rumsey

God who created me. Prayers. Henry Charles Beeching. OBEV; SacPr

God who mounts the winged winds, The. Homer. OBVE *Fr.* Odyssey.

God, Whom Shall I Compare to Thee? Judah Halevi. TrJP, *tr. by* Alice Lucas

God, whose love and joy. "Angelus Silesius." EnlH

God will cheat no one, not even the world of its triumph. (LL) W. H. Auden. ChrPo; MoBrPo; OBCP *Fr.* For the Time Being; a Christmas Oratorio.

God will have all or none; serve Him, or fall. Neutrality Loathsome. Robert Herrick. ChIV-1

God wills us free; man wills us slaves. Epitaph of John Jack. Daniel Bliss. TCAPo

God / you aint. I Wonta Thank Ya. Tejumola Ologboni. NBV

God, you could grow to love it, God-fearing, God. Ecclesiastes. Derek Mahon. BIrV; CIP-2; ChIV-1; ModIr; PNI

Goddam Street, The. Robert Coles. BloBone

Goddès mother be. (LL) I Sing of a Maiden. *Unknown.* ChIV-2; EBEV; FaBoCh; InPK-6; MiEL; NAEL-5v1; NOBE; NOCV; PoE; SCGP; SCV; TFi; TOF

Goddess. Judith Johnson Sherwin. BoWoP

Goddess, A. Czeslaw Milosz. BodElec *Fr.* Lithuania, After Fifty-Two Years.

Goddess, The. Denise Levertov. NALW; NOBA; NeAP; PoM

Goddess, The. M. R. Peacocke. NLP

Goddess adored! who gained my early love. Housewife's Prayer on the Morning Preceding a Fete, The. Elizabeth Moody. ECWP

Goddess capricious is Fame, A. Limerick. Langford Reed. PeLi

Goddess Chiao, The. *Unknown.* CoBCP, *tr. by* Burton Watson

Goddess Corn Finds Her Dress in Disarray, The. Terese Svoboda. ExTi

Goddess Fortune be praised (on her toothed wheel), The. Unpredicted, The. John Heath-Stubbs. BoLoP; OxBC

Goddess intervenes between Achilles and Agamemnon, The. Homer. OBVE, *tr. by* John Dryden *Fr.* Iliad, The.

Goddess Laksmi, The. Cosmology. *Unknown.* WoPoe, *tr. by* J. Moussaieff Masson and W. S. Merwin

Goddess of chain link fences. City Goddess. Leah Korican. HW

Goddess of poetry. To the Moon. Yvor Winters. APT-2

Goddesse bade the nymphs remove, The. *Unknown.* OBVE *Fr.* Vigil of Venus, The.

Goddesses, The. Janine Canan. HW

Godfrey of Bulloigne; or, The Recoverie of Jerusalem [Gerusalemme Liberata]. Torquato Tasso.
  "All wilie sleights, that subtile women know." OxBEV, *tr. by* Edward Fairfax
  "Drearie trumpet blew a dreadfull blast, The." PBRV, *tr. by* Edward Fairfax
  "Erminia's steed this while his mistress bore." NoSic
  "Joyous birds, hid under greenewood shade, The." OBVE
  "Palace great is builded rich and round." NoSic
  "Sweet Armida tooke this charge on hand, The." OBVE

Godhorse. Kojo Laing. HBAPE

Godlie Instruction for Old and Young, Ane. *Unknown.* EMWP

Godlike. Anselm Hollo. PmAP

Godlings are born racily. Nativities. U. A. Fanthorpe. NoP-4

Godly Dream, A. Elizabeth Melville, Lady Culross. WPE

Godmother. Dorothy Parker. PoRA

Gododdin, The. Aneirin.
  "Lord of Gododdin will be praised in song, A." NePenScot, *tr. by* Joseph P. Clancy
  "Men went to Catraeth, keen their war-band." OBWVE
  "Men went to Gododdin, laughter-loving." OBWP
  "To Cattraeth's vale in glitt'ring row." OBVE
  "When a crowd of cares." NePenScot, *tr. by* Joseph P. Clancy
  "Youth." WoPoe, *tr. by* Desmond O'Grady

Gods. Shinkichi Takahashi. ZenPo, *tr. by* Takashi Ikemoto and Lucien Stryk

Gods, The. Dennis Lee. NOBC

Gods, The. Les A. Murray. WoPoe

Gods Anger without Affection. Robert Herrick. InvLi

Gods are dead: no longer do we bring, The. Santa Decca. Oscar Wilde. OxBSo

Gods are everywhere. Gods. Shinkichi Takahashi. ZenPo, *tr. by* Takashi Ikemoto and Lucien Stryk

Gods are happy, The. Matthew Arnold. OBEV *Fr.* Strayed Reveller, The.

Gods Are Here, The. Jean Toomer. APT-2

Gods arrive, The. (LL) Give All to Love. Ralph Waldo Emerson. APN-1; AWP; ColAP; NOBA; OBEV; OxBA; TAP; TCAPo

Gods Ash Their Cigarettes, The. S. K. Kelen. BMAP

Gods at Three A.M., The. Reginald Shepherd. NeAmPo; WiU

Gods boundles bownties gods promise ever abyding. Bible, *O.T.* PBRV, *tr. by* Mary Sidney Herbert, Countess of Pembroke *Fr.* Psalms.

Gods, by right of Nature, must possess, The. Lucretius. NPeEn, *tr. by* John Wilmot, 2d Earl of Rochester *Fr.* De Rerum Natura (On the Nature of Things).

Gods chase / Round vase. Ode on a Grecian Urn Summarized. Desmond Skirrow. NIL-7; NIP-4; NOBL

Gods have heard me, Lyce, The. Horace. AWP, *tr. by* Louis Untermeyer *Fr.* Odes.

Gods have taken alien shapes upon them, The. Exiles. "Æ" BIrV; MoBrPo

Gods *Houses,* almost like *Troyes Ilion.* John Taylor. PBRV *Fr.* Here followeth the unfashionable fashion, or the too too homely Worshipping of God.

Gods it is I ask to release me from this watch, The. Agamemnon. Aeschylus. NAWM-5v1

Gods Keyes. Robert Herrick. SacPr

Gods of old are silent on their shore, The. Aristomenes. Byron. NPeEn

Gods of the Copybook Headings, The. Rudyard Kipling. NoAM; OBSV; OxBTC

Gods of the storm and the giants of the earth, The. Ascent of Vasco da Gama, The. Fernando Pessoa. PeSAV, *tr. by* F.E.G. Quintanilha

Gods Presence. Robert Herrick. SacPr

Gods Providence. Robert Herrick. SacPr

Gods their god-like fun. (LL) Letter to My Sister. Anne Spencer. BlSi; NAAAL; TCAPo

Gods themselves with us do dwell, The. (LL) Mower Against Gardens, The. Andrew Marvell. BASC; CABP; EBEV; ESCV; NAEL-5v1; NAEL-6v1; NAEL-7v1; NIL-7; NOSC; NPeEn; NoP-4; OBGa; OxAEP-1; PBRV; PoE

Gods who rule the ghosts; all silent shades. Virgil [*or* Vergil]. NAWM-5v1; NAWM-7v1, *tr. by* Robert Fitzgerald *Fr.* Aeneid [*or* Eneados, *Aeneis*], The.

Gods! with what pride I see the titled slave. Charles Churchill. OBSV *Fr.* Author, The.

Gods Wrote, The. Keorapetse Kgositsile. GT

Godspeed. John Greenleaf Whittier. GSo; Son

Goe and catche a falling starre. John Donne. *See* Go and catch a falling star

Go[e] forth, and be a knight. (LL) Ben Jonson. EBEV; OxBEV *Fr.* Alchemist, The.

Goe hurtles soules, whom mischiefe hath opprest. Seneca. NPeEn, *tr. by* Jasper Heywood *Fr.* Hercules Furens.

Goe little book, and once a week shake hands. Ad Librum. Samuel, Jr. Danforth. SCAP

Goe little booke: thy selfe present. Edmund Spenser. NAEL-6v1; NAEL-7v1 *Fr.* Shepheardes [*or* Shepeards *or* Shepherd's] Calender, The.

Go[e], perjured [*or* perjur'd] man, and if thou e'er [*or* ere] return. Curse. A Song, The. Robert Herrick. CaPo

Go[e], smiling soul[e]s, your new-built cages break[e]. To the Infant Martyrs. Richard Crashaw. ChIV-2; GeHe; NAEL-5v1; NAEL-6v1; NAEL-7v1; OxBSP; PAI

Goe soule the bodies guest. Sir Walter Ralegh. *See* Go, Soul [*or* Goe soule], the body's [*or* bodies] guest

Goe turne away those Cruell Eyes. Song. Barbara Syms. EMWP

Goes all right. Korean Figures. *Unknown.* EaWin, *tr. by* W. S. Merwin

Goes all the way down. (LL) Lament: "Someone is dead." Anne Sexton. CoAmPo; WPE

Goes flaring down to Baggot Street. (LL) Baggot Street Deserta. Thomas Kinsella. CIP-2; NoAM

Goes on, and the moon in the breast of man is cold. (LL) Moon and the Night and the Men, The. John Berryman. CoAP; VCAP; VGW

Goes out. Issa. EH, *tr. by* Robert Hass

Goes straight up to heaven and nothing more is heard of it. (LL) Her Husband. Ted Hughes. HarvBoo; OxBC

Goes through the mud. *Unknown.* OxNR

Goes way back to the days / my father a young man. Cousin Mary. Wanda Coleman. GT

Goethe and Brentano. Andrew Taylor. BMAP *Fr.* Travelling to Gleis-Binario.

Goethe in Weimar sleeps, and Greece. Matthew Arnold. CABP; NAEL-5v2; NAEL-6v2

Goethe's Blues. Denise Levertov. FaBoWP

Goff; an Heroi-comical Poem, The. Thomas Mathison. Victory on the Last Green. NOEC

Gogol (his namesake). Personal Histories, The. Michael Burkard. BodElec

Goin' Back T'morrer. Hamlin Garland. OBAL

Goin' to Chicago Blues. *Unknown.* NAAAL

Goin' to the Territory. Michael S. Harper. NAAAL

Goin' up State Street, comin' down Main. Take a Whiff on Me. *Unknown.* NOBA

Going. Bruce Dawe. BMAP

Going. Peter Everwine. NNaP

Going. Philip Larkin. WoPoe

Going, The. Thomas Hardy. EBEV; HarvBoo; NOBE; OxAEP-2; PAI; SCGP; UnPo

Going Alone to Spend a Night at the Hsien-Yu Temple. Po Chü-i. ChiP, *tr. by* Arthur Waley

Going and Coming of Sequins. Joyce Mansour. PFTM-2, *tr. by* Molly Bendall

Going and Staying. Thomas Hardy. NoAM

Going Back Again. "Owen Meredith." VerBaPo

Going Back Patiently. Frank Mkalawile Chipasula. HBAPE

Going Back to the River. Marilyn Hacker. WiU

Going Baroque. Jean V. Gier. ReBoTo

Going Blind. Rainer Maria Rilke. BLT, *tr. by* Walter Arndt

Going Down Hill on a Bicycle. Henry Charles Beeching. NOxBChV; OBEV

Going Down, Please. László Mécs. IQMS, *tr. by* Watson Kirkconnell

Going-elsewhere of ripples incessantly shaping, The. (LL) Swimming Chenango Lake. Charles Tomlinson. FaBoMo; NoAM

Going for Peaches, Fredericksburg, Texas. Naomi Shihab Nye. GraLe

Going Forth. Andrée Chedid. PoArWo, *tr. by* Lucy McNair

Going from us at last. Escape, The. Mark Van Doren. MoAmPo

Going, Going. Philip Larkin. NoAM; OxAEP-2

Going Home. Catherine Obianuju Acholonu. HAWP

Going home. Buson. EH, *tr. by* Robert Hass

Going Home. Wing Tek Lum. UnSA

Going Home. Derek Mahon. HarvBoo

Going Home. Patricia Pogson. NLP

Going Home Madly. Brooke Wiese. UrbNat

Going Home to Mayo, Winter, 1949. Paul Durcan. CIP-2; PBCIP

Going In to Dinner. Edward Richard Burton Shanks. OBMV; OxBTC

Going north meant Opal Fruits and Aztec bars. Legacy. Siobhan Campbell. MFPA

Going on always on and on. *Unknown.* SuSp; WoPoe, *tr. by* Charles O. Hartman

Going on boats but. Leslie Scalapino. PmAP *Fr.* Crowd and Not Evening Or Light.

Going Out and Coming In. Mary [*or* Mollie] Evelyn Moore Davis. SWaP

Going Out for Cigarettes. Billy Collins. OPRER

Going out that evening with the garbage. Death in Larkspur Canyon, A. Richard Garcia. UrbNat

Going Out Through the North Gate of Chi. Pao Chao. ColAnChi; SuSp, *tr. by* Daniel Bryant

Going out to fame and triumph. Going Out and Coming In. Mary [*or* Mollie] Evelyn Moore Davis. SWaP

Going Out to the Country on a Boat Trip, Sheltering from Rain Beneath a Tree. Kao Ch'i. CoBLCP, *tr. by* Jonathan Chaves

Going Rate, The. Michael Lassell. GLP *Fr.* Times Square Poems.

Going the Rounds; a Sort of Love Poem. Anthony Hecht. BoLoP

Going to Chicago, sorry that I can't take you. Goin' to Chicago Blues. *Unknown.* NAAAL

Going to Church. Coventry Patmore. PeVV *Fr.* Angel in the House, The.

Going to Europe. Michael Lassell. WiU

Going to his room one night. Householder Departs from the City, The. Nathan [*or* Natan] Alterman. FIT, *tr. by* Robert Friend

Going to Mass after Fifteen Years. Maxine Scates. PBCAP

Going to Mass Last Sunday. Donagh MacDonagh. BIrV

Going to Remake This World. James Welch. CDW

Going to School. Karl Shapiro. TrJP

Going to School in France or America. Tom Clark. CoAmPo

Going to Sea. Douglas Messerli. FTOS

Going to sleep, I cross my hands on my chest. Death. Bill Knott. PBCAP; SPE

Going to Sleep in Childhood. Gennady Aygi. ItGoST, *tr. by* Peter France

Going to Tend Our Family Graves. Issa. WoPoe, *tr. by* Harold Stewart

Going to the Ministry with Chao Tzu-ch'i. Yü Chi. CoBLCP, *tr. by* Jonathan Chaves

Going to the Mountains with a Little Dancing Girl, Aged Fifteen. Po Chü-i. ChiP, *tr. by* Arthur Waley

Going to the Palace with a Friend at Dawn. Tu Fu. CrYelRi, *tr. by* Sam Hamill

Going to Visit a Taoist Recluse on Heaven's Mountain Only to Find Him Gone. Li Po. CrYelRi, *tr. by* Sam Hamill

Going up for the assault that morning. Walt. Ted Hughes. NoP-4

Going up for the jump shot. I Try to Turn in My Jock. David Hilton. MoASP

Going up the river, or down, their tuneless look. Barges on the Hudson. Babette Deutsch. WPE

Going up through the hill called the vineyard. Vineyard, The. W. S. Merwin. NNaP

Going Uptown to Visit Miriam. Víctor Hernández Cruz. PueRic (On the train.) LoL

Golagros and Gawane. *Unknown.* "Thai passit in thare pilgramage." OxBS

Gold and al this worldës wyn. *Unknown. See* Gold and all this werdis [werldes] win

Gold and all this werdis [werldes] win. I Would Be Clad in Christ's Skin. *Unknown.* MiEL

Gold and whores a thousand years announced that. Kingdom, The. Barry Silesky. IllVoic

Gold armchair is witness to his calm, The. Boy's Afraid of the Live Tiger, The. Cesare Greppi. ItPo, *tr. by* Gayle Ridinger

Gold-armoured ghost from the Roman road, The. Youth with Red-gold Hair, The. Dame Edith Sitwell. FaBoTw

Gold Coast Customs. Dame Edith Sitwell. "One fantee wave." OBMV

Gold-colored [*or* coloured] skin of my Lebanese friends, The. Trip to Four or Five Towns, A. John Logan. CoAP; NNaP

Gold cut the knot of otherwise. Paulus [*or* Paulos] Silentiarius. GrAn

Gold Digger's Song (We're in the Money), The. Harry Warren. ReLy

Gold Glade. Robert Penn Warren. CRP; TRP

Gold I've none, for use or show. Lyric[k] for Legacies. Robert Herrick. BeJo

Gold in *Jesus and the Stone* fell, The. Diptych: Jesus and the Stone. Charles Baxter. BBASP

Gold Is the Son of Zeus: Neither Moth nor Worm May Gnaw It. "Michael Field." OBMV

Gold Leaves. Gilbert Keith Chesterton. OxBTC

Gold on Oak Leaves Said Young. George Oppen. BodElec; FTOS

Gold or iv'ry's not intended. Horace. OBVE, *tr. by* Christopher Smart *Fr.* Odes.

Gold priests, wooden chalices. Epigram. *Unknown.* NOIV, *tr. by* Thomas Kinsella

Gold said her golden. Gold on Oak Leaves. George Oppen. FTOS

Gold, / Silver. *Unknown.* OxNR

Gold survives the fire that's hot enough. Tony Harrison. EmeKit; HarvBoo *Fr.* School of Eloquence, The.

Gold tane from the kings harbengers. Robin Hood and Queen Katherine. *Unknown.* ESPB

Gold tape gently billowing with her breathing. Mars and Venus. Rachel Hadas. GS

Gold that was my hair has turned, The. Marina Ivanovna Tsvetayeva [*or* Tsvetaeva]. WPoS

Gold Tooth Blues. Tennessee Williams. OBAL

Gold triangle is my enemy, The. Resurrection of the Flesh, The. Juan Felipe Herrera. TouFir

Gold will not buy this voyage. Looking for a Country under Its Original Name. Colleen J. McElroy. BlSi

Goldbrown upon the sated flood. Flood. James Joyce. MoBrPo

Golden Age, The. William Browne (1591–1643). NOSC *Fr.* Britannia's Pastorals.

Golden Age, The. Sir Richard Fanshawe. NOSC; OBVE *Fr.* Il Pastor Fido.

Golden Age, The. Artur Miedzyrzecki. PoSu, *tr. by* Stanislaw Baranczak

Golden Age, The. Ovid. NAEL-5v1; NAEL-6v1; NAEL-7v1, *tr. by* Arthur Golding *Fr.* Metamorphoses.

Golden Age, The. Torquato Tasso. AWP; OBVE, *tr. by* Leigh Hunt *Fr.* Aminta.

Golden Age: Flower-weaving, The. William Browne (1591–1643). NPeEn *Fr.* Britannia's Pastorals.

Golden Age, The. A Paraphrase on a Translation out of French. Torquato Tasso. BASC, *tr. by* Aphra Behn *Fr.* Aminta.

Golden apples of the sun, The. (LL) Song Of Wandering Aengus, The. W. B. Yeats. ChAP; FaBoCh; MoBrPo; OTCP; PoRA; RaBo; TFi; TTTS

Golden Bells. Po Chü-i. BLT; ChiP, *tr. by* Arthur Waley

Golden Birch Grove's, The. Sergey [*or* Sergei] Aleksandrovich Yesenin [*or* Essenin]. TCRusP, *tr. by* Nigel Stott

Golden Bough. Elinor Wylie. MoAmPo

Golden Bough: The Feather Palm. Susan Mitchell. ExTi

Golden bridle of Bellerephon [*or* Bellerophon], The. Lady Diana Primrose. WPE *Fr.* Chain of Pearl, A.

Golden Calf. Norman MacCaig. ChIV-1; OxBS

Golden casket I designed, A. Epigram. John Swanwick [*or* Swanick] Drennan. BIrV

Golden chrysanthemums just in bloom. Tune: "On the Trail of Sweet Incense." Li Ch'ing-chao. ColAnChi, *tr. by* Jiaosheng Wang

Golden cloud slept for her pleasure, A. Mountain, The. Mikhail Yuryevich Lermontov. AWP, *tr. by* Max Eastman

Golden cradle under you, and you young, A. He Meditates on the Life of a Rich Man. Douglas Hyde. OBMV, *tr. by* Augusta, Lady Gregory and Lady Gregory

Golden dawn and trembling dusk find our brig lying off the coast opposite that villa and its outbuildings. Promontory. Arthur Rimbaud. SxFrPo, *tr. by* Martin Sorrell

Golden eagle swooped out of the sky, The. Salmon Drowns Eagle. Malcolm Lowry. MoCV

Golden Gate, The. Vikram Seth.
　"How ugly babies are! How heedless." OBCoV
　Week ago, when I had finished, A.

Golden girl / in a golden gown. College Formal: Renaissance Casino. Langston Hughes. APT-2

Golden God, the Self, the immortal Swan, The. *Unknown.* EnlH, *tr. by* Stephen Mitchell *Fr.* Upanishads, the.

Golden Grove, The. Sergey [*or* Sergei] Aleksandrovich Yesenin [*or* Essenin]. RusPo, *tr. by* Robert Arthur Douglas Ford and R.A.D. Ford

Golden Grove, Carmarthen. Rowland Watkyns. AngWePo

Golden grove was whispered its last, The. Rowan Tree Fire, The. Sergey [*or* Sergei] Aleksandrovich Yesenin [*or* Essenin]. TCRP, *tr. by* Geoffrey Thurley

Golden hair that Gulla wears, The. Bought Locks. Martial. AWP, *tr. by* Sir John Harington \VP/[*or* Harrington]

Golden hinges of the year have turned, The. Parting. Frances Anne [*or* "Fanny"] Kemble. PoBW

Golden Island, The; or, the Darian Song. *Unknown.* EMWP

Golden Journey to Samarkand, The. James Elroy Flecker.
　"And how beguile you? Death has no repose." OxBTC
　Epilogue: "Away, for we are ready to a man!" NOBE
　Prologue: "We Who with Songs Beguile Your Pilgrimage" OBMV; OxBTC; UV

Golden Jubilee of Wilberforce. Mrs. Henry Linden. CBWP-4

Golden light has presently, The. Evening Song. Philipp von Zesen. GePo, *tr. by* George C. Schoolfield

Golden Mean, The. Henry Howard, Earl of Surrey. OBVE

Golden Mile-Stone, The. Henry Wadsworth Longfellow. NCAP

Golden mists o'er Cloudland wreathing. Fancy and Imagination. Henrietta Cordelia Ray. CBWP-3

Golden [*or* Goldyn] Targe, The. William Dunbar. OxBS

Golden Palace, The. *Unknown.* ChiP, *tr. by* Arthur Waley

Golden Pheasant. Mating Pair. Golden Pheasant. William Hart-Smith. NOBAu

Golden prince of pictorial war, A. (LL) Uccello. Gregory Corso. NeAP; PoM

Golden Road to Barcelona: 1992, The. Martin Fagg. UV

Golden Sayings. Gérard de Nerval. WoPoe, *tr. by* Richard Sieburth

Golden Shower, The. Roy Campbell.
　"Here, where relumed by changing seasons, burn." OxBTC

Golden Slumbers. Thomas Dekker. NoSic; OxAEP-1; OxBEV *Fr.* Pleasant Comedy of Patient Grissell [*or* Grissel *or* Grissill], The.

Golden spider of the sky, The. Solar Myth. Genevieve Taggard. MoAmPo

Golden State. Frank Bidart. NoAM

Golden sun that brings the day, The. In Praise of the Sun. "A. W." CTC

Golden sun upon his fiery wheels, The. Michael Drayton. NoSic *Fr.* Idea's Mirrour.

Golden Vanity, The. *Unknown.* FaBoCh
　(Sweet Trinity), The.) ESPB

Golden Violet, The. Letitia [*or* Laetitia] Elizabeth Landon.
　Song: "My heart is like the failing hearth." NOBRP
　Song: "Where, O! where's the chain to fling." NOBRP

Golden with fruit of a man's body. (LL) In a Country Church. Ronald Stuart Thomas. FaBoMo; HarvBoo; TOF

Golden, within this golden hive. Danaë. Barbara Howes. WPE

Goldenrod. Mary Oliver. NIL-7

Goldenrod [*or* Golden-rod] is yellow, The. September [Days Are Here]. Helen Hunt Jackson. APN-2

Goldfinger. Anthony Newley. ReLy

Goldfish. Barrie Wade. OTCP

Goldfish in the Charles River. Lewis Hyde. UrbNat

Goldfish in the Garden Pond. Valerie Worth. NOxBChV

Goldfish on the Writing Desk. Max Brod. TrJP, *tr. by* Babette Deutsch and Avrahm Yarmolinsky

Goldfish Wife, The. Sandra Hochman. UnPo

Goldie Sapiens. P. J. Kavanagh. OBCoV

Goldminers' Waltz, The. Aleksandr Arkadevich Galich. TCRusP, *tr. by* Gerry Smith

Golem, The. Jorge Luis Borges. PoetW, *tr. by* John Hollander

Golem and Rabbi. Ana Maria Shúa.
　"Don't obey me!—the Master ordered the perplexed Golem." MirDau, *tr. by* Rhonda Buchanan
　Golem and Rabbi 3. MirDau, *tr. by* Rhonda Buchanan
　Golem and Rabbi 4. MirDau, *tr. by* Rhonda Buchanan
　Golem and Rabbi 5. MirDau, *tr. by* Rhonda Buchanan

Golf Links, The. Sarah Norcliffe Cleghorn. InPK-6; PAI
　(Golf links lie so near The mill, The.) APT-1; KaS; NIP-4
　(Quatrain.) NIP-4

Golgotha. Andrew Lansdown. ChIV-2

Goliardic Song. Anthony Hecht. OBCoV

Goliath and David. Robert Graves. FaBoWar

Goliath and David. Louis Untermeyer. TrJP

Goliath Poem. Terrance Hayes. AmPoNex

Goliath was known for ferocity. Limerick. Frank Richards. PeLi

Goliathus goliathus, the one banana. Zoo, The. Gilbert Sorrentino. NeAP

Goll Mac Morna Parts from His Wife. *Unknown.* NOIV, *tr. by* Thomas Kinsella

Gollihar / Burned the winter grass from his fields. Rahab. Diane Glancy. CRP

Golly, How Truth Will Out. Ogden Nash. MoAmPo

Gombeen, The. Joseph Campbell. BIrV

Gondibert. Sir William Davenant [*or* D'Avenant].
　City Morning, The. NOSC
　Praise and Prayer. OBEV; PBRV

Gondibert Book 2. Sir William Davenant [*or* D'Avenant].
　"There, when they thought they saw in well sought Books." PBRV

Gondoliers, The. Sir William Schwenck Gilbert.
　There Lived a King. OBCoV

Gone. Mary Elizabeth Coleridge. OBEV; PoBW; VWP

Gone. Carl Sandburg. NOBA

Gone. Mary E. Tucker. CBWP-1

Gone, A. Larry Eigner. NeAP

Gone are my blues. Gold Digger's Song (We're in the Money), The. Harry Warren. ReLy

Gone are my people, but I exist yet. Dead Are My People. Kahlil Gibran. GraLe, tr. by Anthony Rizcallah Ferris

Gone are the coloured princes, gone echo, gone laughter. Ruin, The. Richard Hughes. OBMV

Gone Are the Days. Norman MacCaig. CABP; OxBC

Gone are the drab monosyllabic days. Tilth. Robert Graves. FaBoEE; OBSV

Gone are the games we played all night. Mahsati. WPOW

Gone are those three, those sisters rare. Three Sisters, The. Arthur Davison Ficke. TCAPo

Gone as his mouth's last sighs. (LL) Burning of the Temple, The. Isaac Rosenberg. FaBoMo; PeFWW; TrJP

Gone Before. Christina Georgina Rossetti. PoBW

Gone from this bruk-spirit, kiss-me-arse place. (LL) Nigger Sweat. Edward Baugh. EmeKit; WaCA

Gone, Gone Again. Edward Thomas. OxAEP-2; PeFWW; PoWW (Blenheim Oranges.) NPeEn

Gone Gone / Another weaver of black dreams has gone. For Langston Hughes. Etheridge Knight. NBV

Gone, gone,—sold and gone. Farewell, The. John Greenleaf Whittier. AWP; NCAP

Gone, I say and walk from church. Truth the Dead Know, The. Anne Sexton. ColAP; LCAP-2; MoAmPo; NoAM; NoP-4; TAP; VCAP

Gone is *Elizabeth*. Short and Sweet Sonnet Made by One of the Maids of Honour, upon the Death of Queen Elizabeth, Which She Sewed upon a Sampler, in Red Silke, A. *Unknown*. EMWP

Gone is the city, gone the day. Right Kind of People, The. Edwin Markham. PoToHe

Gone is the romance that was so divine. What'll I Do? Irving Berlin. ReLy

Gone Is the Sleepgiver. Penelope Shuttle. BrRo

Gone is the sound of my favorite misfortune, which even yesterday. Bakhyt Kenjeev. ItGoST, tr. by Nina Kossman

Gone Ladies. François Villon. WoPoe, tr. by Christopher Logue

Gone now the baby's nurse. Home After Three Months Away. Robert Lowell. HCAP; PoetW

Gone she is a long, long way. Upon a Maid. Robert Herrick. CaPo

Gone the three ancient ladies. Frau Bauman, Frau Schmidt, and Frau Schwartze. Theodore Roethke. APT-2; CoAP; NAAL-2v2; NOBA; NoAM; TAP

Gone to seed, ailanthus, the poverty. Ornithology. Lynda Hull. SeSe

Gone up in flames. Hokushi. JDP, tr. by Yoel Hoffmann

Gone were but the Winter. Christina Georgina Rossetti. GTBS-P; PoE; WPE Fr. Spring Fancies.

Gone, with all her sparkling beauty. Gone. Mary E. Tucker. CBWP-1

Gone with the Wind. Herb Magidson. ReLy

"Goneys an' gullies an' all o' the birds o' the sea." Sea Change. John Masefield. FaBoTw; OBMV; RB

Gong, A. Odia Ofeimun. PBMAP

Gongula. (LL) Papyrus. Ezra Pound. APT-1; PFTM-1

Gongyla. Sappho. SaLy, tr. by Diane Rayor

Gonna be so slammin. This Poem. Ruth Forman. SpirFl

Gonsalves. Ron Welburn. SeSe

Gonzales will always be. Poem for Gonzales, California, The. Morton Marcus. GeoHom

Gooboora, Gooboora, the Water of Fear. Gooboora, the Silent Pool. Oodgeroo of the tribe Noonuccal (Kath Walker). IBA

Good Advice. Mother Goose. OxNR; ReMoGo

Good advice speaks from unlikely places, so you follow it. Radio Nebraska. Erin Belieu. NAPBL

Good afternoon, General Ball. Collect Call. Mcavoy Layne. CDa

Good aged Bale, that with thy hoary hairs. To Doctor Bale. Barnabe Googe. NoSic

Good and bad and right and wrong. Good and Bad. James Stephens. MoBrPo

Good and bad are in my heart. Twins, The. James Stephens. RaBo

Good and Bad Children. Robert Louis Stevenson. ChAP; EBVV; FaBoCh; OBCoV

Good and Bad Luck. John Milton Hay. *See* Good Luck and Bad

Good and Better. *Unknown*. TreFP

Good and Clever. Elizabeth Wordsworth. OxBTC

Good, and great God, can I not think[e] of thee. To Heaven. Ben Jonson. BASC; BeJo; ChIV-2; HAP; InvLi; NAEL-5v1; NAEL-6v1; NAEL-7v1; NOCV; NOSC; NPeEn; SCGP; SacPr; TRP; UnPo

Good and great God! How should [or sho'd] I fear[e]. No Coming to God without Christ. Robert Herrick. OxBSP; SacPr

Good Appetite. Mark Van Doren. OxBSP; Spl

Good Attitude to Horses, A. Vladimir Vladimirovich Mayakovsky [or Maiakovskii]. TCRusP, tr. by P. Lemke

Good bailiff of my farm, that snug domain. Horace. OBVE

Good, better, best. Comparatives. *Unknown*. OxNR

Good board, and absolute isolation from hellish life. (LL) What Mr. Cogito Thinks About Hell. Zbigniew Herbert. VCWP; WoPoe, tr. by John Carpenter and Bogdana Carpenter

Good Boy, A. Robert Louis Stevenson. PWR

Good-By. Grace Denio Litchfield. PoToHe

Good-by can be a happy word. Good-By. Margaret E. Bruner. PoToHe

Good-by er Howdy-do. James Whitcomb Riley. CTC

Good-by, my son, good-by. Wayward Son, The. Mrs. Henry Linden. CBWP-4

Good-by now to the streets and the clash of wheels and locking hubs. Teamster's Farewell, A. Carl Sandburg. IllVoic

Good-by, sweetheart, our days of bliss. Parting Lovers, The. Mrs. Henry Linden. CBWP-4

Good-by, the tears are in my eyes. Rondel. François Villon. AWP, tr. by Andrew Lang

Good-bye. Ralph Waldo Emerson. PWR; PoToHe; TAP

Good-Bye. Joan Larkin. WiU

Good-bye—and hail! my Fancy. (LL) Good-Bye, My Fancy! Walt Whitman. NAAL-2v1; SAmP; TAP

Good-Bye, My Fancy! Walt Whitman. NAAL-2v1; NAAL-3; SAmP; TAP; TCAPo

Good-bye / No use leading with our chins. I Wish You Love (Que Reste-t-il de Nos Amours?). Charles Trenet. ReLy, tr. by Albert A. Beach

Good-bye, proud world! I'm going home. Good-bye. Ralph Waldo Emerson. PWR; PoToHe; TAP

"Good-bye," said the river, "I'm going downstream." Howard Nemerov. WeW-3

Good-Bye to the Mezzogiorno. W. H. Auden. OxBTC

Good-bye to the People of Hangchow. Po Chü-i. ChiP, tr. by Arthur Waley

Good-bye to Winter, I'll see you next year. Ho Hum. Edward Heyman. ReLy

Good-Bye, Valentine. Leslie Anne McIlroy. AmPoNex

Good Captain, Maker of the light. For the Kindling of the Light on Easter Eve. Prudentius. MLL, tr. by Helen Waddell

Good Catholic girl, she didn't mind the cleaning. Snow White and the Seven Deadly Sins. R. S. Gwynn. SoSe-8

Good Christian men, rejoice. *Unknown*. SacPr, tr. by John Mason Neale

Good christian Reader judge me not. God's Controversy with New-England. Michael Wigglesworth. SCAP

Good Company. William Matthews. BodElec

Good Counsail. Geoffrey Chaucer. TreFP

   (And Trouthe shal delivere, it is no drede.) (LL) NoP-4; SacPr

   (And Truthe shall deliver, it is no dread.) (LL) MiEL; SCGP

   (Flee fro the prees and dwelle with soothfastnesse.) NAEL-6v1; NAEL-7v1; NoP-4; SacPr

   (Truth.) AWP; NAEL-5v1; NoP-4

Good Counsel. *Unknown*. OBWVE, tr. by Glyn Jones

Good Counsel. *Unknown*. NOIV, tr. by James Clarence Mangan

Good Counsel to a Young Maid. Thomas Carew. CavPo

   (Song)

Good creatures, do you love your lives. I Counsel You Beware. A. E. Housman. PeVV

Good Creed, A. *Unknown*. *See* Little Word, The

Good "D." James McKean. MoASP

Good dame looked from her cottage, The. Leak in the Dike, The. Phoebe Cary. ITBLP

Good Day's Work, A. Naomi Replansky. WWork

Good day's work, two contracts made, A. Between a Contractor and His Wife. *Unknown*. NOEC

Good Devil, The. Kurt Brown. OPRER

Good Dream, The. Denise Levertov. NNaP

Good evening, daddy! Boogie: 1 A.M. Langston Hughes. APSN; APT-2

Good faith, Mr. Parson, excuse me from that! (LL) On Marriage. Thomas Flatman. NOBL; PeLV

Good Filya. Nikolai Mikhailovich Rubtsov. TCRP, tr. by Lubov Yakovleva

Good folk, go gain. God's Gifts. Albrecht von Johannsdorf. GePo, tr. by F. C. Nicholson

Good folk [or folke], for gold or hire [or hyre]. Crier, The. Michael Drayton. NOSC

"Good folk," said Lizzie. Christina Georgina Rossetti. FaBoVe Fr. Goblin Market.

Good for good is only fair. Good Counsel. *Unknown*. OBWVE, tr. by Glyn Jones

Good for Nothin' Joe. Ted Koehler. ReLy

Good for the wind, good for the night, good for the cold. Waltz of the Twenty-

Year-Olds, The. Louis Aragon. FaBoWar, _tr._ by Malcolm Cowley and Rolfe Humphries

Good Fortune, when I hailed her recently. Epigram. James Vincent Cunningham. APT-2; VCAP

Good Frend. "H. D."

"Time has an end, they say." NOBA; VGW

Good Friday. Rofel G. Brion. ReBoTo

Good Friday. João da Cruz e Sousa. TCLAP, _tr._ by Flavia Vidal

Good Friday. George Herbert. GeHe

Good Friday. Kathleen Jessie Raine. BBASP

Good Friday. Christina Georgina Rossetti. ChIV-2

Good Friday and the Present Crucifixion. Vincent Buckley. CBAP

Good Friday: For Lack of an Orchestra. Jack Spicer. APSN

Good Friday: Rex Tragicus, or, Christ Going to His Cross[e]. Robert Herrick. NOSC

Good Friday [or Goodfriday], 1613. Riding Westward. John Donne. BASC; BBASP; ChIV-2; ESCV; FSCP; MeLP; NAEL-5v1; NAEL-6v1; NAEL-7v1; NOCV; NOSC; NoP-4; PBRV; PeECV; PoE; SacPr; TFi

Good Friday. Somewhere a death. Good Friday and the Present Crucifixion. Vincent Buckley. CBAP

Good Friday was the day. Martyr, The. Herman Melville. CBCWP; ColAP; NCAP; TAP; TCAPo

Good Gad! who's this? What's this, my son? Democratic Barber; or, Country Gentleman's Surprise, The. John Parrish. NOEC

Good Girl. Molly Peacock. FFC

Good glory, give a look at Sporting Beasley. Sporting Beasley. Sterling Allen Brown. APT-2; NAAAL

Good god, make me for thi love and thi desyre. Make Me Loathe Earthly Likings. _Unknown._ SacPr

Good God, What a Night That Was. Petronius Arbiter. BoLoP; PGA; PasH, _tr._ by Kenneth Rexroth

Good gray [or grey] guardians of art, The. Museum Piece. Richard Wilbur. FaBoMo; InPK-6; NIL-7; NIP-4; TAP; TRP

Good Grease. Mary Tallmountain. UnSA

Good Great Man, The. Samuel Taylor Coleridge. PWR

Good grey guardians of art, The. Richard Wilbur. _See_ Good gray [or grey] guardians of art, The

Good heaven, I thank thee since it was designed. On Myself. Anne Finch, Countess of Winchilsea. OxBSP

Good Heaven! this mystery of life explain. Ad Coelum. William Pattison. OxBSP

Good Hot Dogs. Sandra Cisneros. NOxBChV; OxIBACP

Good house. Basho. EH, _tr._ by Robert Hass

Good house, and ground whereon, A. Salt Garden, The. Howard Nemerov. OBGa

Good hunting, rabbit-catcher and bird-catcher. Leonidas of Tarentum. GrAn

Good in Everything. William Shakespeare. PoToHe _Fr._ As You Like It.

Good in graves as heavenly seed are sown, The. Sir William Davenant [or D'Avenant]. MeLP

Good is an orchard, the saint saith. Of an Orchard. Katharine Tynan. SacPr

Good is the wine that is in love with us. Sixth Sense, The. Nikolai Stepanovich Gumilyov [or Gumiliov or Gumilev]. TCRP, _tr._ by Yakov Hornstein

Good King Matthias, whom we mourn. On The Death of King Matthias. _Unknown._ IQMS, _tr._ by Joseph Leftwich

Good King Wenceslas. _Unknown._ ChrPo; SacPr, _tr._ by John Mason Neale

Good King Wenceslas went out. Children's Rhymes and Parodies. _Unknown._ NOBAu

Good Kosciusko, thy great name alone. To Kosciusko. John Keats. CenSon

Good-looking, I'll never stoop for you. Mahsati. WPOW

Good Lord. Good Lord in That Heaven. _Unknown._ WPoS

Good Lord, behold this dreadful[l] enemy. Edward Taylor. NAAL-2v1; NAAL-3 _Fr._ God's Determinations [touching his Elect].

Good Lord in That Heaven. _Unknown._ WPoS

Good Lord Nelson had a swollen gland, The. Ballad of the Good Lord Nelson, A. Lawrence Durrell. PeLV

"Good lord of the land, will you stay thane." Lord Maxwell's Last Goodnight. _Unknown._ ESPB; OxBB

Good Lord Saved Her, The. Anna Swirszczynska. PoSu

Good Loser, The. Sophie Hannah. HarvBoo

Good Luck. Oswald de Andrade. TCLAP, _tr._ by Flavia Vidal

Good Luck and Bad. John Milton Hay. FaBoEE; NBLV; OBAL

Good Luck Gold. Janet S. Wong. NOxBChV; OxIBACP

Good madam, when ladies are willing. To a Lady Making Love. Lady Mary Wortley Montagu. LW

Good Man in Hell, The. Edwin Muir. MoBrPo

Good man ther[e] was of religioun [or religion], A. Geoffrey Chaucer. NOCV _Fr._ Canterbury Tales, The.

Good manners may in Seven Words be found. Of Courtesy. Arthur Guiterman. Spl

Good Marriage, A. Giovanna Pollarolo. TANSG, _tr._ by Marjorie Agosin

Good mechanics are all of one mind. Limerick. Douglas Catley. PeLi

Good medicin for sor eyen. _Unknown._ MiEL

Good Medicine. _Unknown._ PWR

Good Men. Roberta Spear. GeoHom

Good men and women gone too soon to bed. (LL) Dear Uncle Stranger. Conrad Potter Aiken. ColAP; NOBA; NoAM

Good Mistress Dishclout, what's the matter? Written by Desire of a Lady, on an Angry, Petulant Kitchen-Maid. Jane Cave. ECWP

Good Moolly Cow, The. Eliza Lee Cabot Follen. OBCA

Good mornin', blues. Good Morning, Blues. Jimmy Rushing. NAAAL

Good Morning. Arthur Freed. ReLy

Good Morning. Langston Hughes. APSN; APT-2 _Fr._ Lenox Avenue Mural.

Good Morning. Carl Rakosi. FTOS

Good morning, Algernon: Good morning, Percy. On Mundane Acquaintances. Joseph Hilaire Pierre Belloc. FaBoEE; OBCoV; OxBTC

Good morning, and How do you do? Ninety-Nine. Elizabeth Godley. NOxBChV

Good morning, Blues. Jimmy Rushing. NAAAL

Good morning daddy! Dream Boogie. Langston Hughes. APSN; HCAP; NAAAL; PFTM-1; SSLK

Good morning, daddy! / Ain't you heard? (LL) Langston Hughes. APT-2; HCAP _Fr._ Lenox Avenue Mural.

Good morning, Father Francis. _Unknown._ OxNR

Good morning, fox of the cave. Fox's Counsel, The. Huw Llwyd. OBWVE, _tr._ by Joseph P. Clancy

Good-morning; good-morning! the General said. General, The. Siegfried Sassoon. FaBoWar; NAEL-5v2; NAEL-6v2; NPeEn; NoAM; NoP-4; OBWP; OxBEV; OxBSP; OxBTC; OxBoLi; PoE

Good morning, Life—and all. Greeting, A. William Henry Davies. MoBrPo

Good Morning—Midnight. Emily Dickinson. NALW

Good morning, Mistress and Master. _Unknown._ OxNR

Good morning, Mrs Roebeck. Christ have mercy! (LL) On Mundane Acquaintances. Joseph Hilaire Pierre Belloc. FaBoEE; OBCoV; OxBTC

Good morning Pearl, good morning John. Barry MacSweeney. Oth _Fr._ Pearl.

Good morning, sad priestess. Letters to Lebanon. Ben Bennani. GraLe

Good morning to the day; and, next, my gold. Ben Jonson. OxBEV _Fr._ Volpone.

Good morning to You, Almighty God. Kaddish. Levi-Yitzhok [or Levi-Isaac] of Berditchev. TrJP, _tr._ by Joseph Leftwich

Good Morrow. Thomas Heywood. GTBS-P _Fr._ Rape of Lucrece, The.

Good-Morrow, The. John Donne. AWP; BASC; BoLoP; CABP; ClHu; EBEV; ESCV; EnLoPo; FHYEP; FSCP; FaBoVe; MeLP; NAEL-5v1; NAEL-6v1; NAEL-7v1; NAWM-5v1; NIL-7; NOSC; NoP-4; OxAEP-1; OxBEV; PoE; PoRA; SCV; SoSe-8; TFi

Good morrow bids the cock, th' owl bids good night. Of a Husbandman. Joshua Sylvester. NOSC

Good morrow to the day so fair. Mad Maid's Song, The. Robert Herrick. AWP; CaPo; EnLoPo; OBEV; RACG

Good morrow to thy sable beak. Blackcock, The [or The Black Cock]. Joanna Baillie. WoRP

Good morrow to you, Valentine. _Unknown._ OxNR

Good Mr. Peeps or Peps or Pips. Gospel of Mr. Pepys, The. Christopher Darlington Morley. NBLV

Good name is better than precious oil, A. Bible, _O.T._ TrJP _Fr._ Ecclesiastes.

Good-nature is thy sterling name. Christopher Smart. NOCV _Fr._ Hymns for the Amusement of Children.

Good News from New England. Edward Johnson. SCAP

Good news from the windy city: Thomas Edison's. Muddy Waters and the Chicago Blues. Cornelius Eady. ESEAA

Good news, good news. (LL) Letter Written on a Ferry While Crossing Long Island Sound. Anne Sexton. CoAP; NAAL-2v2; TwCP

Good news. It seems he loved them after all. Song about Major Eatherly, A. John Wain. OxBTC

Good Night. Eleanor Farjeon. NOxBChV; OTCP

Good Night. Thomas Hood. OTCP; Spl

Good-night. James Shirley. BeJo

(Goodnight.) NOSC

Good Night. William Carlos Williams. SAmP

Good Night! Gilbert Sorrentino. FTOS

Good Night, at last. Robert Duncan. VGW _Fr._ Passages.

Good night, big world. Back to the Ghetto. Jacob Glatstein [or Glatsteyn]. TrJP, _tr._ by Joseph Leftwich

Good-night; ensured release. Parta Quies. A. E. Housman. NOBE

Good night for the fireplace to be, A. Heat in the Room, The. Weldon Kees. SPE

Good night, God bless you. *Unknown.* OxNR

Good Night! Good Night! John Holmes (1904–62). PoToHe

Good night, ladies, good night, sweet ladies, good night, good night. (LL) T. S. Eliot. HarvBoo; SCV *Fr.* Waste Land, The.

Good night Marcus put out the light. To Marcus Aurelius. Zbigniew Herbert. VCWP, *tr. by* Czeslaw Miosz and Peter Dale Scott

Good night, my two little cloud ladies. For the Girls 'cause They Know. Harold Littlebird. VoR

Good-Night, or Blessing, The. Robert Herrick. CaPo

Good night, sweet repose. *Unknown.* OxNR

Good Night, Sweetheart. Jimmy Campbell. ReLy

Good night to the Year Academic. Grouchy Good Night to the Academic Year, A. Ted Pauker. NOBL; PeLV

Good Night, Willie Lee, I'll See You in the Morning. Alice Walker. WeW-3 (Looking down into my father's.) ISC; NAAAL

Good Nights. Saundra Sharp. SpirFl

Good of the Chaplain to enter Lone Bay. Herman Melville. APN-2; HAP; NAAL-2v1; NCAP; NOBA; OxBoLi; WoPoe *Fr.* Billy Budd, Foretopman.

Good Old Days, The. Stephen Clayton. IBA

Good Old Days, The. Barbara Fried. NBLV

Good old, honest Deacon Brown. Deacon Brown's Conclusion. George Sands Johnson. PWR

Good old Mother Fairie. To Mother Fairie. Alice Cary. OBCA

Good Omen. Lewis Warsh. BodElec

Good Parson, The. Geoffrey Chaucer. NOCV *Fr.* Canterbury Tales, The.

Good people all, of every sort. Oliver Goldsmith. FaBoCh; NBLV; NOEC; NOIV; OBNV; OxAEP-1; TFi *Fr.* Vicar of Wakefield, The.

Good people draw near as you pass along. Alphabetical Song on the Corn Law Bill. *Unknown.* OxBoLi

Good people, give attention, a story you shall hear. Lord Delamere. *Unknown.* ESPB

Good people give attention, and listen for a while. Queen's Dream, The. *Unknown.* PeVV

Good people I pray. Orange, The. Matthew Prior. PeLV

Good people, what, will you of all be bereft. Ballad on the Taxes, A. Edward Ward. OxBoLi

Good Play, A. Robert Louis Stevenson. OTCP; PWR

Good prince, what? The dog that keeps, A. Of a Good Prince and an Evil. Timothy Kendall. NoSic

Good prince? (Guardian of Flocks.) His bark. Good Princes and Bad. Sir Thomas More. WoPoe, *tr. by* Katherine Washburn

Good Princes must be pray'd for: for the bad. Duty to Tyrants. Robert Herrick. BASC

Good rain knows its season, A. Spring Rain. Tu Fu. OHMPC, *tr. by* Kenneth Rexroth

Good rain knows its season, A. Spring Night, A—Rejoicing in Rain. Tu Fu. SuSp, *tr. by* William H. Nienhauser

Good reader! if you e'er have seen. Nonsense. Thomas Moore. FaBoEE

Good repute is water carried in a sieve. Lalleswari. WPOW

Good Resolution, A. Roy Campbell. OBSV

Good Samaritan et Al, The. Stephen Mitchell. GI

Good Scholars Make Bad Husbands. *Unknown.* WoPoe, *tr. by* Nguyen Ngoc Bich

Good Science. Ken Edwards. Oth

Good Sense. César Vallejo. PoetW, *tr. by* Clayton Eshleman

Good Shepherd, The. Richard Baxter. SacPr

Good Shepherd: Atlanta, 1981, The. Ai. RACG

Good Shepherd, have You skipped away, to leave. At the Ascension. Luís De León. SpanPo, *tr. by* James Edward Tobin

Good Shepherd's Sorrow for the Death of His Beloved Son, The. Anne, Duchess of Arundel Howard. NOSC
(Elegy on the Death of Her Husband.) WPE

Good Ships. John Crowe Ransom. OxBSo; WeW-3

Good show, A. Atomic Bride. Thomas Sayers Ellis. BAP-97; NeAmPo

Good snowman. Winter's End. Dan Pagis. FIT, *tr. by* Robert Friend

Good speech is rarer than jade. It is rarer. Song of Ptahhotep, The. Robert Bringhurst. GifTon

Good Taste. Christopher Logue. OBSP

Good Teachers, The. Carol Ann Duffy. ItWoWo

Good Thing, A. Ray Mathew. CBAP

Good Thing Is, We Know, The. Antonio Machado Ruiz. SpanPo, *tr. by* William M. Davis

Good things go by so softly, The. Back to It. Larry Eigner. FTOS

Good things, that come of course, far less[e] do[e] please. Casualties. Robert Herrick. BASC

Good thoughts are the threads. Good Thoughts. Katherine Maurine Haaff. PoToHe

Good Tidings of Great Joy to All People. James Montgomery. *See* Nativity

Good Time Charlie. Jimmy Van Heusen. ReLy

Good time of the year, The. Bernard [*or* Bernart] de Ventadour [*or* Ventadorn]. STV

Good time will never come back again, The. Parting from Su Wu. Li Ling. ChiP, *tr. by* Arthur Waley

Good Times. Lucille Clifton. BPo; HHAm; PAI; SoSe-8; TAP; TRP; TwCP

Good times and bum times. I'm Still Here. Stephen Sondheim. ReLy

Good times were drunk times, The. Mardi Gras Premortem. Ann Townsend. NeAmPo

Good traveler has no fixed plans, A. Lao Tzu. EnlH *Fr.* Tao Te Ching.

Good Vibrations Sound Studio. Miguel Algarin. PueRic *Fr.* Angelitos Negros: A Salsa Ballet.

Good Water. Patty Seyburn. AmPoNex

Good Will to Men—Christmas Greetings in Six Languages. Dorothy Brown Thompson. OBCP

Good Wish. *Unknown.* FaBoCh

Good wood. Food for Fire, Food for Thought. Robert Duncan. NeAP

Good Works. William Langland. NOCV *Fr.* Vision of Piers Plowman, The.

Good World. Velemir [*or* Viktor Vladimirovich] Khlebnikov.
"And so the castles of world trade." TCRP

Good world, A. Issa. EH; ZenPo, *tr. by* Takashi Ikemoto and Lucien Stryk

Good writing, the book tells you. Famous Writers School Opens Its Arms in the Next Best Thing to Welcome, The. Rosellen Brown. WWork

Good Wyf [*or* Wif] was ther of bisyde [*or* biside] Bathe, A. Geoffrey Chaucer. EBEV *Fr.* Canterbury Tales, The.

Good, your worship, cast your eyes. Maunding Soldier; or, The Fruits of Warre Is Beggery, The. Martin Parker. FaBoWar

Goodby Betty,don't remember me. E. E. Cummings. PoE

Goodby, you long black sonofabitch, he says. Elvis Goes to the Army. Fleda Brown Jackson. AllShUp

Goodbye. Bella [*or* Izabella] Akhatovna Akhmadulina. BoWoP, *tr. by* Barbara Einzig

Goodbye. (LL) Phone Call to Rutherford. Paul Blackburn. PFTM-2; PoM

Goodbye. Bill Knott. SPE

Goodbye. Alun Lewis. AngWePo; BoLoP; NAEL-5v2; NAEL-6v2; NoP-4; OBWP; OxBTC; PoWW; TCAWP

Goodbye. Adrian Mitchell. OPOU

Goodbye. (LL) To a Daughter Leaving Home. Linda Pastan. ItWoWo; NIL-7; NIP-4

Goodbye, bright creature. In the Cloud of Unknowing. Carol Rumens. DiPo

Goodbye David Tamunoemi West. Margaret Danner. BPo

Goodbye, Goldeneye. May Swenson. NoP-4

Goodbye: I bite the word back. Paulus [*or* Paulos] Silentiarius. GrAn

Goodbye. I willgo. Buson. SoOfWa, *tr. by* Sam Hamill

"Goodbye" is not quite true; we'll meet tonight. Letter to My Mother. Suzanne Gardinier. NeAmPo

Goodbye, lady in Bangor, who sent me. Correspondence School Instructor Says Goodbye to His Poetry Students, The. Galway Kinnell. NOBA; NoAM; NoP-4; TAP

Goodbye, my friend, goodbye. Esenin's Suicide Note. Sergey [*or* Sergei] Aleksandrovich Yesenin [*or* Essenin]. CAGL, *tr. by* Simon Karlinsky

Goodbye, my friend, goodbye. Sergey [*or* Sergei] Aleksandrovich Yesenin [*or* Essenin]. TCRP

Goodbye Nkrumah. Diane Di Prima. PoM

"Goodbye, O sun," said Cleombrotus of Ambracia. Callimachus. HePo *Fr.* Epigrams.

Goodbye Party for Miss Pushpa T. S. Nissim Ezekiel. OBCoV

Goodbye, Sally. James Simmons. BIrV

"Goodbye Sun!" said the Ambracian. Callimachus. GrAn

Goodbye to Brigid / An Agnus Dei. Padraic Fiacc. CIP-2

Goodbye to London. Louis MacNeice. PeECV

Goodbye to Tolerance. Denise Levertov. NoAM

Goodbye, Winter, / The days are getting longer. Prognosis. Louis MacNeice. NOBE

Goodbye, Zenobia. Saniyya Salih. MAP, *tr. by* Patricia Alanah Byrne, Charles Doria and Salma Khadra Jayyusi

Goodhousekeeping #17. Safiya Henderson-Holmes. ISC

Goodnight. John Ciardi. OBAL

Goodnight. James Shirley. *See* Good-night

Goodnight. Stevie Smith. FaBoWP

Goodnight, A. William Carlos Williams. MoAmPo

Goodnight, Achilles. Enrique Lihn. VCWP, *tr. by* Alastair Reid

Goodnight, Mary. (LL) Tullynoe: Tête-à-Tête in the Parish Priest's Parlour. Paul Durcan. ModIr; NPeEn; OBCoV

Goodnight to the Season! Winthrop Mackworth Praed. NOBE; NOBL; NPeEn; OBCoV; OxBEV; OxBoLi; PeLV

Goodtime Jesus. James Tate. LCAP-2

Goodyere, I am [*or* I'm] glad and grateful to report. To Sir Henry Goodyere. Ben Jonson. NOSC

Gooing babies, helpless pygmies. J. W. Scholl. VerBaPo *Fr.* Light-Bearer of Liberty, The.

Goops they lick their fingers, The. Table Manners. Frank Gelett Burgess. OBCA

Goose. Richard Emil Braun. NoAM

Goose and the Gander, The. *Unknown.* RB

Goose Fish, The. Howard Nemerov. HeIP-4; NIL-7; NIP-4; NoAM; NoP-4; PoE

Goose-Girl, The. Edith Nesbit. VWP

Gooseberry Fool. Amy Clampitt. NoAM

Gooseflesh. Janet Fisher. MFPA

Goosey, goosey, gander, where [*or* whither] shall I wander? shall I wander? Mother Goose. LB; OxNR; ReMoGo

Goosey, goosey gander, / Who stands yonder? Betsy Baker. *Unknown.* OxNR

Goran's Whispers. Nathalie Handal. PoArWo

Gorcheanu: Three Laments, The. Aneirin. WoPoe, *tr.* by Desmond O'Grady

Goree. Harriet Jacobs. SpirFl

Goree. Niyi Osundare. HBAPE

Gorée ten miles offshore beckons. Gorée. Everett Hoagland. GT

Gorey at the Biennale. Martin Johnston. BMAP

Gorg, a Detective Story. B. P. Nichol. NOBC

Gorgeous, and on fire. I have my kingdom. (LL) Homo Will Not Inherit. Mark Doty. HarvBoo; OPRER; WiU

Gorgeous blossoms of that magic tree, The. To a Persian Boy in the Bazaar at Smyrna. Bayard Taylor. CAGL

Gorgeous grew the common walls about me. Impromptu. Mary Elizabeth Coleridge. VWP

Gorges of Wu are hoary and dim in the season of mist and rain, The. Liu Yu Hsi. SuSp *Fr.* Bamboo Branch Song.

Gorgo, a Cretan bitch, on a deer's track. Antipater of Thessalonica. GrAn

Gorgo and Praxinoa. Theocritus. HePo, *tr.* by Barbara Hughes Fowler *Fr.* Idylls.

Gorgon. Ambrose Bierce. APN-2 *Fr.* Devil's Dictionary, The.

Gorilla Gorilla. Bruce Dawe. NoAM

Gorilla lay on his back, The. Au Jardin des Plantes. John Wain. OxBTC

Goring and the Death, The. Federico García Lorca. WoPoe, *tr.* by Alan S. Trueblood *Fr.* Lament for Ignacio Sanchez Mejias.

Gorse Fires. Michael Longley. NoP-4

Gorselight, yellow, the slopes. Matière de Bretagne. Paul Celan. WoPoe, *tr.* by Margaret Guillemin and Katherine Washburn

Gorselight, yellow, the slopes. Matière de Bretagne. Paul Celan. VCWP, *tr.* by Michael Hamburger

Gosling following its neck to the bug. Marlene Mountain. HA

Gospel of Labor, The. Henry Van Dyke. SacPr

Gospel of Mr. Pepys, The. Christopher Darlington Morley. NBLV

Gospel train is moving, The. Gospel Train, The. *Unknown.* GM

Gossip. Mrs. Henry Linden. CBWP-4

Gossip. Angela Sorby. AmPoNex

Gossip grows like weeds. Kakinomoto no Hitomaro. OHPJ, *tr.* by Kenneth Rexroth

Got a Home in That Rock. *Unknown.* APN-2

Got a little rhythm, a rhythm, a rhythm. Fascinating Rhythm. George Gershwin. ReLy

Got No Shame. Selwyn Hughes. IBA

Got up. Passage, The. Rita Dove. ESEAA

Got up and dressed up. Jack Kerouac. NeAP; PmAP *Fr.* Mexico City Blues.

Got up, went to school. Diary. Mary Wilson. Spl

Gotham. Charles Churchill. NOEC

Gothic columns of petrified motion. M. G. Mainwaring. TOF

Gothic flowers bedded themselves. Book of Sharp Silhouettes, The. Molly Bendall. NAPBL

Gothic Landscape. Irving Layton. TrJP

Gothic looks solemn, The. On Oxford. John Keats. SCGP

Götterdämmerung. Rita Dove. ExTi

Goulburn Island Song Cycle. *Unknown.*

    "Bird saw the young Burara girls, twisting their strings, making string figures, The." NOBAu

    "Ejaculating into their vaginas—young girls of the western tribes." NOBAu

    "They saw the young girls twisting their strings, Goulburn Island." NOBAu

    "They seize the young girls of the western tribes, with their swaying." NOBAu

Gourd Dancer, The. N. Scott Momaday. CDW

Gourd has still lost its bitter leaves, The. *Unknown.* AWP, *tr.* by Helen Waddell *Fr.* Shi King.

Gourmand, The. Harry Graham. UV

Gourmet challenged me to eat, A. Experiment Degustatory. Ogden Nash. ChAP

Gourmet's Love-Song, The. P. G. Wodehouse. NOBL

Gout. Lewis Warsh. FTOS

Gout and Wings. Charles Tennyson Turner. NOBVV

Gouzeaucourt: The Deceitful Calm. Edmund Charles Blunden. PeFWW

Govern a life. (LL) Words. Sylvia Plath. CoAmPo; HCAP; NAAL-2v2; NALW; PoE; VCAP

Governante, The. Dame Edith Sitwell. BWW *Fr.* Sleeping Beauty, The.

Governess, The. Evelyn Wexler. GotH

Government asks me to "check one," The. Check One. Regie Cabico. ReBoTo; WiU

Government building, not my own home, A. Written when Governor of Soochow. Po Chü-i. ChiP, *tr.* by Arthur Waley

Government-bull yoked to a government-cart, A! Chancellor's Gravel-Drive, The. Po Chü-i. WoPoe, *tr.* by Arthur Waley

Government wine of Peking is sweeter than honey, The. Hsieh Chin. CoBLCP *Fr.* Things Experienced upon Withdrawal from Court.

Governor loves to go mapping—round and round, The. Sydney Cove, 1788. Peter Porter. NoAM

Governor your husband lived so long, The. John Berryman. NOBA *Fr.* Homage to Mistress Bradstreet.

Gowan glitters on the sward, The. Trysting Bush, The. Joanna Baillie. WPE

Goyng towards Spayne. Barnabe Googe. PBRV

    (Farewell thou fertyll soyle.) PBRV

Gr-r-r—there go, my heart's abhorrence! Soliloquy of the Spanish Cloister. Robert Browning. FHYEP; FaBoVe; InPK-6; NAEL-5v2; NAEL-6v2; NIL-7; NIP-4; NOBL; NOBVV; NoP-4; OxBEV; PAI; PeVV; TOF; UV

Grab-Bag. Helen Hunt Jackson. OBCA

Grab each other. (LL) Love Poem. Linda Pastan. NIL-7; NIP-4

Grab the beast by the horns. Stuart Henson. NewEx

Grab whatever cash he has. Madam to a Young Courtesan, The. Sarangapani. WoPoe, *tr.* by V. Narayana Rao, A. K. Ramanujan and David Shulman

Grace. Ralph Waldo Emerson. APN-1; InvLi; NCAP

Grace. George Herbert. ChIV-1; GeHe

Grace. Laura Kasischke. NAPBL

Grace. Adelia Prado. TCLAP, *tr.* by Marcia Kirinus

Grace, A. Donald Hall. LoL

Grace Abounding. A. R. Ammons. HCAP

Grace after Dinner. Robert Burns. FaBoEE *Fr.* Graces—the Globe Tavern.

Grace after Meals. *Unknown.* TrJP, *tr.* by Alice Lucas

Grace at Kirkudbright. Robert Burns. OxBEV; OxBSP

Grace before Meat. Robert David Fitzgerald. NOBAu

Grace by his priest; *The feast is ended.* (LL) Oberon's Feast. Robert Herrick. BeJo; CaPo; NOSC

Grace for a Child. Robert Herrick. AWP; NAEL-5v1; NAEL-6v1; PoE; TFi

    (Another Grace for a Child.) BeJo; NAEL-7v1; NOSC; SCGP

    (Child's Grace, A.) FaBoCh; OBEV; OxAEP-1

Grace for Ice-Cream, A. Allan M. Laing. OBCoV

Grace, Majesty, and the calm bliss of life. Two Worlds. Richard Watson Gilder. GS

Grace-Note, The. Denise Levertov. CoAmPo

Grace of Animals, The. Richard Harteis. GLP

Grace of God and the Meth-Drinker, The. Sydney Goodsir Smith. NePenScot

Grace of old Greece the divine and the greatness of Rome the majestic. Our Tongue. Ferenc Kazinczy. IQMS, *tr.* by Watson Kirkconnell

Grace of the Homeland. Herbert Strutz. AuPH, *tr.* by Lowell A. Bangerter

Grace of the Way. Francis Thompson.

    "Now of that vision I, bereaven." MoBrPo

Grace of Tullies eloquence doth excell, The. Tony Harrison. NoP-4 *Fr.* School of Eloquence, The.

Grace, thou source of each perfection. Christopher Smart. NOCV *Fr.* Hymns and Spiritual Songs for the Fasts and Festivals of the Church of England.

Grace to be born and live as variously as possible. Ted Berrigan. FTOS; PFTM-2 *Fr.* Sonnets, The.

Grace to Be Said at the Supermarket. Howard Nemerov. SoSe-8

Graceful error may correct the cave, A. (LL) Mind. Richard Wilbur. HCAP; OxBSP; SoSe-8; VCAP

Graceful handsome youth, A. *Unknown.* ColAnChi, *tr.* by Red Pine

Graces—at the Globe Tavern. Robert Burns.

    After Dinner.

    Grace after Dinner. FaBoEE

Graces da[u]nced and Apollo played, The. (LL) Gratiana Dancing [*or* Dauncing] and [*or*&] Singing. Richard Lovelace. BeJo; CaPo; MeLP; OBEV

Graces, if the beautiful Dionysios. *Unknown.* GrAn

Gracey Nugent. Turlough Carolan [*or* O'Carolan]. OxBEV, *tr.* by Austin Clarke

Graciela. Gary Soto. NoAM

Graciela wouldn't fuck me. De Ambiente. Tatiana De la Tierra. GLP

Gracing the tide-warmth, this seagull. Seagull, The. Dafydd [*or* David] ap Gwilym. OBWVE; TCAWP, *tr.* by Glyn Jones

Gracious Lady / Simple as when I asked your aid before. Prayer to the Virgin of Chartres. Henry Adams. APT-1

Gracious Saviour let me make. Thou Lovest Me. Josephine D. Henderson Heard. CBWP-4

Gracious Saviour, We Adore Thee. Sewall Sylvester Cutting. AH

Gracius and gay. *Unknown.* MiEL

Grackle, The. Ogden Nash. NBLV

Gradation. Charles Bernstein. FTOS

Gradual self-effacement of the dead, The. (LL) Song (On Seeing Dead Bodies Floating Off the Cape). Alun Lewis. NAEL-5v2; NAEL-6v2; OBWP

Gradually. Elvira Levy. MirDau, *tr.* by Roberta Gordenstein

Graecinus (well I wot) thou told'st me once. Ovid. EBEV, *tr.* by Christopher Marlowe *Fr.* Elegies.

Graf von Charolais, Der. Richard Beer-Hofmann. "Evil Man, An!" TrJP

Graffiti. Julian Croft. NOBAu

Graffiti. Alice Archer Sewall James. NBLV

Graffiti. Jane Yolen. SSCS

Grafted Bud, The. Mary Weston Fordham. CBWP-2

Grafted Tongue, A. John Montague. BIrV; CIP-2; PBCIP

Grail, The. Sidney Keyes. FaBoTw

Grain-Barge Wife, The. Wu Chia-chi. CoBLCP; ColAnChi, *tr.* by Jonathan Chaves

Grain of Sand. Fanny Carrión de Fierro. TANSG, *tr.* by Sally Cheney Bell

Grain of Sand, A. Frances Ellen Watkins Harper. PWR

Grain of sand, the beginning of the desert, The. Grain of Sand, The. Maria Luisa Spaziani. NeIt, *tr.* by Beverly Allen

Grainfield. Ibn 'Iyad. WoPoe, *tr.* by Cola Franzen

Grains of snow ride down here as bits. Letter from a Black Soldier. Bill Anderson. VGW

Gramercy, Death, as you've my love to win. Sonnet: He Argues His Case with Death. Cecco Angiolieri, da Siena. AWP; EaItPo, *tr.* by Dante Gabriel Rossetti

Grammar, A. Andrei Codrescu. SPE

Grammar commences with a 5-line curse. Palladas [*or* Pallades]. OBVE, *tr.* by Tony Harrison

Grammar of Light, The. Carol Ann Duffy. HarvBoo

Grammarian's daughter, The. Palladas [*or* Pallades]. GrAn

Grammarian's Funeral, A. Robert Browning. NAEL-5v2; NAEL-6v2; NOBVV; PeECV

Grammer's Shoes. William Barnes. EBVV

Granada (1000 A.D.). Abu Ishaq al-Ilbin. ArPe, *tr.* by Omar S. Pound

Grand Abacus. John Ashbery. SPE

Grand ancient, Gothic, mark this ample dome. Lake, The; Or, Modern Improvement in Landscape. Anna Seward. OBGa

Grand Army Plaza. June Jordan. ISC

Grand attempt some Amazonian dames, An. On a Fortification at Boston Begun by Women. Benjamin Tompson. NOSC; SCAP

Grand Canyon, The. Jean Garrigue. APT-2

Grand Canyon, The. James Merrill. TAP

Grand Central Hotel, The. Roy McFadden. PNI

Grand Central Station, 20 December 1987. Bruce Bawer. RA

Grand conglomerate hills of Araby, The. Bayard Taylor. APN-2 *Fr.* Echo Club, The.

Grand-Dad, they say you're old and frail. Child to His Sick Grandfather, A. Joanna Baillie. CABP; ECWP; NOEC; RACG; WoRP

Grand Entry, The. Gary Snyder. NoAM

Grand Finale. Irving Layton. NOBC

Grand Grand Mother is returning. Judy Grahn. HW

Grand Houses at Lo-yang, The. Po Chü-i. ChiP, *tr.* by Arthur Waley

Grand Rapids. Julia A. Moore. OBAL

Grand Rapids Cricket Club, The. Julia A. Moore. "When Mr. Dennis does well play." VerBaPo

Grand rough old Martin Luther. Twins, The. Robert Browning. FaBoVe

Grand Testament. François Villon. "I love and serve my lady with a will." EroLit, *tr.* by Peter Dale

Granddaddy longlegs did twilight, The. Ohio Valley Swains. James Wright (1927–80). NNaP

Granddaughter was a guerilla, The. Dream. Maria Arrillaga. TANSG

Granddaughters' bright smiles, chili dogs, and lemonade in the shade start. Baseball. Christopher Stanard. SpirFl

Grandest ship-of-war which e'er to sea was known, The. She Is the Greatest Wealth. Georg Rudolph Weckherlin. GePo, *tr.* by George C. Schoolfield

Grandest writer of late ages, The. Distribution of Honours for Literature. Walter Savage Landor. FaBoEE

Grandeur of Ghosts. Siegfried Sassoon. MoBrPo; OBMV

Grandeurs of his Babylonian heart, The. (LL) Francis Thompson. MoBrPo; OBMV; Son *Fr.* Heart, The.

Grandfa' Grig / Had a pig. *Unknown.* OxNR

Grandfather. George Bowering. NOBC

Grandfather. Michael S. Harper. ESEAA; LCAP-2; NAAAL; TAP; VCAP

Grandfather. Lance Henson. CDW; HATNAP, *tr.* by Lance Henson

Grandfather. Derek Mahon. OxBC; OxBSo

Grandfather. Joseph Stroud. GeoHom

Grandfather and Grandmother in Love. David Mura. TRP

Grandfather at the Indian Health Clinic. Elizabeth Cook-Lynn. HATNAP; UnSA

Grandfather: Frailty Is Not the Story. Diana Helen Melhem. GraLe

Grandfather Grandfather. Marlon D. Satchell. InTrad

Grandfather-in-law. David Mura. LoL

Grandfather in the Garden. Robert Minhinnick. OBGa

Grandfather in the Old Men's Home. W.S. Merwin. CoAmPo

Grandfather puts down his tea-glass. Night in Odessa, A. Louis Simpson. NNaP

Grandfather's Cap, My. David St. John. MoASP

Grandfather's Clock. Henry Clay Work. ITBLP

Grandfather's Mint. Edward Cortez Garrett. ReBoTo

Grandfather's Rockery. David Woo. OpBo

Grandfather, sleepless in a room upstairs. John Berryman. VGW *Fr.* Black Book, The.

Grandfather Was Queer, Too. Bob Kaufman. NAAAL

Grandfather, we come to you now. Yahrzeit. Susan Fromberg Schaeffer. TaR

Grandma and I used to go. Double Features. Ed Rossman. HHAm

Grandma, come back, I forgot. Morning Baking, The. Carolyn Forché. LoL

Grandma Fire. Charles G. Ballard. VoR

Grandma in the Shower. Dale M. Kushner. UnSA

Grandma Jenny never learned. Observance. Barbara Unger. TWW

Grandma lit the stove. History. Gary Soto. PBCAP

Grandma Mariana, washerwoman. Grandma Mariana. Alda do Espirito Santo. HAWP, *tr.* by Julia Kirst

Grandma's Bureau. Robert Morgan. WeW-3

Grandma's Lost Balance. Sydney Dayre. OBCA

Grandma's Man. James Welch. NoAM

Grandma sleeps with / my sick. Medicine. Alice Walker. PAI

Grandma Talk. Sonya Brooks. InTrad

Grandmither, Think Not I Forget. Willa Sibert Cather. AmFaPo; WPE

Grandmother. Grace Cavalieri. UnSA

Grandmother. Regina DeCormier-Shekerjian. TWW

Grandmother. Siv Cedering Fox. PBCAP

Grandmother. Eva Salzman. MFPA

Grandmother. Fily-Dabo Sissoko. NegPo, *tr.* by Ellen Conroy Kennedy

Grandmother, The. Claribel Alegría. TANSG, *tr.* by Darwin Flakoll

Grandmother, The. Victor Hugo. TreFP

Grandmother, a Caribbean Indian, Described by My Father. Yvonne Sapia. NIL-7; UnSA

Grandmother Came Down to Visit Us, The. Joseph Bruchac. CDW

Grandmother: Crossing Jordan. Melvin Dixon. ESEAA

Grandmother, Dead at 99 Years and 10 Months. William Matthews. PuP-23

Grandmother, I dreamed of you again. Visit, The. Phillip [*or* "Phil"] William George. VoR

Grandmother Jackson. David Jackson. OBCP

Grandmother of Russian Poetry: A Self-Portrait, The. Vera Merkureva. ARWW, *tr.* by Catriona Kelly

Grandmother Remembers, A. Janet Lewis. IllVoic

Grandmother's Farm. Mark Todd. GeoH

Grandmother's love. Love Necessitates. Eugene B. Redmond. ISC

Grandmother's mother: her age, I guess. Dorothy Q. Oliver Wendell Holmes. NOBA

Grandmother Sleeps. Liz Sohappy Bahe. CDW

Grandmother, the same hot night you died. May Levine. Susan Fromberg Schaeffer. TaR

Grandmother Watching at Her Window. W. S. Merwin. VGW

Grandmothers. Adrienne Rich. HCAP; NAAL-2v2; NoAM

Grandmothers, The. Mary Oliver. WPE

Grandmothers in Green and Orange. Frank R. Maloney. GifTon

Grandmothers Land. William Oandasan. HATNAP

Grandmother's mirror. Penny Harter. HA

Grandmothers sing their song. Grandmothers' Song. Nellie Wong. FFC; MakPoe

Grandmothers who wring the necks. Classic Ballroom Dances. Charles Simic. LCAP-2; WeW-3

Grandpa, I saw you die in the Indian hospital at Pawnee. Hartico. Anna Walters. VoR

Grandpa Is Ashamed. Ogden Nash. OBCoV

Grandpapa. Harry Graham. OBCoV

Grandparents. Robert Lowell. ColAP

Grandparents' House. Arthur Zanker. AuPH, tr. by Lowell A. Bangerter

Grandpa's .45. W. M. Ransom. CDW

Grandson Is a Hoticeberg, A. Margaret Danner. BlSi

Grandson of György Dózsa, The. Endre Ady. IQMS, tr. by Sir Maurice Bowra

Grange, The. Stevie Smith. OBCoV

Grania's Song to Diarmuid. Unknown. WoPoe, tr. by Frank O'Connor

Granite and Cypress. Robinson Jeffers. APT-1

Granite and Grass. Donald Hall. DiPo

Grannie's Birthday. Eliza Ogilvy. VWP

Granny Crack. James Reaney. NOBC

Granny's here. Her mother's voice was bright. Big Girls. Tracey Herd. MFPA

Granny's House. Phoebe Cary. APN-2

Grant, I thee pray, such heat into mine heart. Prayer, A. Sir Thomas More. InvLi

Grant me a single summer, you lords of all. To the Fates. Friedrich Hölderlin. NAWM-7v2, tr. by Christopher Middleton

Grant me, indulgent Heaven, a rural seat. Choice, The. Nahum Tate. OxBSP

Grant me the great and solemn breath withdrawn. Invocation and Prelude. Stefan George. AWP, tr. by Ludwig Lewisohn

Grant that no Hobgoblins fright me.Prayer John Day. Spl

Grant us, O God! great Ruler of the Skies! Translation of "Pax Bello Potior." Unknown. NOBRP, tr. by Unknown

Granted, we die for good. Table Talk. Wallace Stevens. NoP-4

Grape-gathering. Avraham Shlonsky. TrJP, tr. by I. M. Lask

Grapes. Unknown. AWP, tr. by Alma Strettell

Grapes Making. Léonie Adams. APT-2; UnPo

Graphemics. Jack Spicer. VGW

"Walden Pond / All those noxious gases rising from it." VGW

Grappa in September. Cesare Pavese. RaBo, tr. by William Arrowsmith

Grashopper, The. Abraham Cowley. See Grasshopper, The

Grasmere—a Fragment. Dorothy Wordsworth. See Peaceful Our Valley, Fair and Green

Grasping my flying cane, several feet of wood. Drunk, Climbing to the Peak of Iron Tomb on Wei Mountain. Li K'ai-hsien. CoBLCP, tr. by Jonathan Chaves

Grasping with opposite hand the side of his pram. Outside the Supermarket. Roy Fuller. OxBC

Grass. Byok Namkung. WoPoe, tr. by Kevin O'Rourke

Grass. Carl Sandburg. AWP; ColAP; FaBoWar; MoAmPo; NAAL-2v2; NOBA; NoAM; OBWP; OxBA; PeFWW; TCAPo; TFi

Grass, The. George Bowering. MoCV

Grass and the Sin, The. Larissa Szporluk. AmPoNex

Grass below—above the vaulted sky, The. (LL) I Am. John Clare. BBASP; CABP; EBEV; EBVV; FHYEP; GTBS-P; HAP; NAEL-5v2; NAEL-6v2; NOBE; NOBVV; NoP-4; NPeEn; OxBEV; PeECV; PoPoPo; TFi; TOF; TRP; WoPoe

Grass bends: blades crack from a wind, The. Camping Out on Rainy Mountain. Jim Barnes. CDW

Grass caught in willow tells the flood's height that has subsided. Basil Bunting. FaBoMo Fr. Briggflatts [An Autobiography].

Grass Crust, The. Christiania Whitehead. NeBl

Grass cut trees need pruning. Maya to Herself and Then to Her Gardener. Reetika Vazirani. NAPBL

Grass cuts our feet as we wend our way, The. Young Prince and the Young Princess, The. John Ashbery. CoAmPo

Grass Fingers. Angelina Weld Grimké. APT-1

Grass-green and aspen-green. Variables of Green. Robert Graves. FaBoEE

Grass grew in vain, The. Bride, The. Vladislav Felitsianovich Khodasevich. TCRusP, tr. by Daniel Weissbort

Grass grows wild by Red Bird Bridge. Blacktail Row. Liu Yu Hsi. CrYelRi, tr. by Sam Hamill

Grass has not yellowed on the paths by the river, The. In Imitation of Ancient-style Poetry. Pao Chao. SuSp, tr. by Daniel Bryant

Grass hovel filled with wind and dust. Wang Fan-chih. SuSp

Grass is half-covered with snow, The. Snowfall in the Afternoon. Robert Bly. NOBA; SPE

Grass is very green, my friend, The. Unison, A. William Carlos Williams. NOBA

Grass manoeuvres under passing swans. Picnic. Kenward Elmslie. FTOS

Grass on Ancient Plain, a Song of Farewell. Po Chü-i. SuSp, tr. by Irving Y. Lo

Grass on the Mountain, The. Unknown. APT-1; AWP, tr. by Mary Austin

Grass Path Lasts. Anita Virgil. KaS

Grass people bow, The. To Turn Back. John Haines. CoAmPo; TRP

Grass purpled by fallen Judas flowers. In the Spring Garden. Geoffrey Grigson. OBGa

Grass resurrects to mask, to strangle. Distant Fury of Battle, The. Geoffrey Hill. FaBoWar; NoP-4

Grass shakes. / Smoke streaks, no, The. Growing Dark. James Schuyler. GLP

Grass singed and low. Chickory. Zerubavel Gal'ed. TrJP

Grass, summer grass. Grass. Byok Namkung. WoPoe, tr. by Kevin O'Rourke

Grass Widows. Robert B. Shaw. CRP

Grasse-Hopper, The. Richard Lovelace. See Grasshopper, The

Grasse: The Olive Trees. Richard Wilbur. NAAL-2v2; NOBA; NoAM

Grassehopper, The. Thomas Stanley. See Grasshopper, The

Grasses and trees. Joy Mountain. Muso Soseki. EaWin, tr. by W. S. Merwin

Grasses enclose the old palaces as waning sunlight shifts. Chin-ling Post Station. Wen T'ien-hsiang. ColAnChi, tr. by Michael A. Fuller

Grasshopper, A. Tropicalia. Margaret Haley. YaYoPo

Grasshopper, A. Michael McClintock. HA

Grasshopper, A. Richard Wilbur. HAP

Grasshopper, The. Abraham Cowley. AWP; BASC; BeJo; NOSC; NPeEn; OBVE; OxAEP-1

Grasshopper, The. Richard Lovelace. BASC; BeJo; CaPo; CavPo; EBEV; NAEL-5v1; NAEL-6v1; NAEL-7v1; NOBE; NOSC; NoP-4; OBEV; SCGP; TFi

(Grasse-Hopper, The.) MeLP; NPeEn; PBRV

(To the Grasshopper.) OxAEP-1

Grasshopper, The. Thomas Stanley. NOSC; OBVE

(Grassehopper, The.) NPeEn

Grasshopper and the Bird, The. James Reeves. OTCP

Grasshopper and the Cricket, The. Leigh Hunt. See To the Grasshopper and the Cricket

Grasshopper and the Cricket, The. Olga Sedakova. ItGoST, tr. by Catriona Kelly

Grasshopper and the Glowworm, The. William Wilkie. True Knowledge. ECEV

Grasshopper Is a Burden. D. H. Lawrence. FaBoVe

Grasshopper's among some grassy hills, The. (LL) On the Grasshopper and [the] Cricket. John Keats. CenSon; FHYEP; NIL-7; NIP-4; OxAEP-2; Son; TTTS

Grasshopper said, The. Grasshopper and the Bird, The. James Reeves. OTCP

Grasshopper thrice-happy! who. Grasshopper, The. Thomas Stanley. NOSC; OBVE

Grasshopper Wings. Unknown. CoBCP, tr. by Burton Watson

Grasshopper, your fairy [or tiny] song. Earth. John Hall Wheelock. MoAmPo

Grasshoppers. John Clare. TTTS

Grasshoppers. Roland Mathias. TCAWP

Grasshoppers / Chirping in the sleeves. Kawai Chigetsu-Ni. WPOW

Grasshoppers click and whirr. Carnal Knowledge 2. Gwen Harwood. HarvBoo

Grasshoppers on the Bell. László Nagy. IQMS, tr. by Júlia Kada and Kenneth McRobbie

Gratiana Dancing [or Dauncing] and [or&] Singing. Richard Lovelace. BeJo; CaPo; CavPo; MeLP; OBEV; PBRV

Gratitude. Ilya Abu Madi.

"What is poetry?" GraLe, tr. by George Dimitri Selim

Gratitude. William Cornish. See Pleasure It Is

Gratitude. Louise Glück. FaBoWP; TRP

Gratitude. György Petri. VCWP, tr. by George Gömöri and Clive Wilmer

Gratitude. Christopher Smart. NOEC Fr. Hymns for the Amusement of Children.

Gratitude for gifts. Issa. SoOfWa, tr. by Sam Hamill

Gratitude to Life. Eugenie Fink. AuPH, tr. by Lowell A. Bangerter

Gratitude to Mother Earth, sailing through night and day. Prayer for the Great Family. Gary Snyder. HAP; WeW-3

Gratitude to the Unknown Instructors. W. B. Yeats. EnlH

Gratulatory to Mr. Ben Johnson for His Adopting of Him to Be His Son, A. Thomas Randolph. BeJo; NPeEn

Grauballe Man, The. Seamus Heaney. OxBEV; PoetW

Grave, A. Herman von Gilm zu Rosenegg. AuPH, tr. by Lowell A. Bangerter

Grave, A.   Marianne Craig Moore.   APT-1; FaBoWP; HAP; HeIP-4; NAAL-2v2; NOBA; NoAM; NoP-4; PoE; TAP; TFi; TRP; UnPo; WPE; WeW-3

Grave, The.   Robert Blair.
All Impelled Onward Alike.   OxAEP-1
"But see! the well-plumed hearse comes nodding on."   ECEV
Grave-yard on a Stormy Night, The.   OxAEP-1
"Oft in the lone church-yard at night I've seen."   OxAEP-1
Peace the End of the Good Man.
"Sickly taper / By glimmering through thy low-browed misty vaults, The."   ECEV
("Whilst some affect the sun, and some the shade.")   NOEC

Grave, The.   Henry Wadsworth Longfellow.   TCAPo   *Fr.* From the Anglo-Saxon.

Grave, The.   *Unknown.*   MiEL
(Whan the turf is thy tour.)   OHMEL

Grave and the Rose, The.   Victor Hugo.   AWP, *tr. by* Andrew Lang

Grave Bird, that sheltered in thy lonely bower.   To the Owl.   Thomas Russell.   CenSon

Grave but ends the struggle!—Follows then, The.   Triumph, The.   William Gilmore Simms.   Son

Grave charge in Mayfair bathroom case.   Headline History.   William Plomer.   OBCoV

Grave Doubts.   Patricia Beer.   NoP-4

Grave for New York, A.   "Adonis" [*or* "Adunis"].   MAP, *tr. by* Alan Brownjohn and Lena Jayyusi

Grave has the bones and dumb name of Sappho, The.   Epitaph: Sappho.   Pinytos.   GrAn, *tr. by* Lee T. Pearcy

Grave in Hollywood Cemetery, Richmond, A.   Margaret Junkin Preston.   CBCWP

Grave in Ukraine, A.   Saul [*or* Shaul] Tchernichowsky [*or* Tchernichovsky].   TrJP, *tr. by* Robert Mezey, L. V. Snowman and Shula Starkman

Grave no conquest gets, Death hath no sting, The. (LL)   Elegy: "Death be not proud, thy hand gave not this blow."   Lucy, Countess of Bedford   Harington.   EMWP; PeECV; WPE

Grave number twenty-four.   Udude.   Pol N Ndu.   PBMAP

Grave of a Poetess, The.   Felicia Dorothea Hemans.   RWP; VWP

Grave of Hipponax, The.   Edward Cracroft Lefroy.   AWP   *Fr.* Echoes from Theocritus.

Grave of Little Su, The.   Li Ho.   WoPoe, *tr. by* A. C. Graham

Grave of Love, The.   Thomas Love Peacock.   OxAEP-2; OxBSP

Grave, on which to rest from singing? . . . choose, A. (LL)   Elizabeth Barrett Browning.   BrRo; CenSon   *Fr.* Sonnets from the Portuguese.

Grave said to the Rose, The.   Grave and the Rose, The.   Victor Hugo.   AWP, *tr. by* Andrew Lang

Grave wise man that had a great rich lady, A.   Of an Heroical Answer of a Great Roman Lady to Her Husband.   Sir John Harington [*or* Harrington].   BoLoP

Grave-Yard, The.   Jones Very.   NOBA

Grave-yard on a Stormy Night, The.   Robert Blair.   OxAEP-1   *Fr.* Grave, The.

Gravedigger, The.   Kahlil Gibran.   GraLe, *tr. by* Andrew Ghareeb

Gravel rattles against the fenders of the van.   Once on a Night in the Delta: A Report From Hell.   Etheridge Knight.   BodElec

Gravelly Run.   A. R. Ammons.   CoAP; NAAL-2v2; NoAM; VCAP

Gravely. (LL)   Have You Anything to Say in Your Defense?   César Vallejo.   PoetW; RaBo, *tr. by* James Wright

Graves.   Orkhan Muyassar.   MAP, *tr. by* Samuel Hazo and Lena Jayyusi

Graves, The.   Lorine Niedecker.   APT-2

Graves at Elkhorn.   Richard Hugo.   UnPo; VCAP

Graves by the Sea, The.   Paul Valéry.   WoPoe, *tr. by* John Finlay

Graves grow deeper, The.   Dead, The.   Mark Strand.   HeIP-4

Graves of a Household, The.   Felicia Dorothea Hemans.   NOBRP; RWP; TreFP; WPE

Graves Registration.   Basil T. Paquet.   CDa

Graves the rain makes wet and sleek, The.   *Unknown.*   OBWVE   *Fr.* Stanzas of the Graves, The.

Graves! Where in dust are laid our dearest hopes!   Vigilantius, or a Servant of the Lord Found Ready.   Cotton Mather.   SCAP

Gravestone, The.   'Abd al-Karim Kassid.   MAP, *tr. by* Lena Jayyusi and Anthony Thwaite

Gravestone at Corinth, A.   *Unknown.*   GrAn, *tr. by* Peter Jay

Gravestone, August 8, 1968, A.   Paul Goodman.   BodElec

Gravestone upon the Floor in the Cloisters of Worcester Cathedral, A.   William Wordsworth.   SacPr

Graveyard, A.   Gensho.   JDP, *tr. by* Yoel Hoffmann

Graveyard, The.   Hayyim Nahman [*or* Khayim Nakhman *or* Chaim Nachman] Bialik.   TrJP, *tr. by* Bertha Beinkinstadt

Graveyard at Bald Eagle Ridge.   John Balaban.   CDa

Graveyard by the Sea, The.   Paul Valéry.   STV, *tr. by* John Frederick Nims

Graveyard crows.   Tune: "Unbroken."   Chang K'o-chiu.   ChinPo, *tr. by* Yip Wai-lim

Gravity and Grace.   Claudia Keelan.   BodElec

Gravity, Death.   Agi Mishol.   DTA, *tr. by* Tsipi Keller

Gravity is one of the oldest tricks in the book.   Defying Gravity.   Roger McGough.   EmeKit

Gravy Train, The.   R. R. Davidson.   NOBAu

Gray bark of the street. (LL)   Street, The.   Robert Pinsky.   NAAL-5; NoP-4

Gray-blue shadows lift.   Starlight Scope Myopia.   Yusef Komunyakaa.   MakPoe

Gray brick, ash, hand-bent railings, steps so big.   Cumberland Station.   Dave Jeddie Smith.   HCAP

Gray despair.   Old Mare, The.   Elizabeth Jane Coatsworth.   MoAmPo

Gray Folk, The.   Edith Nesbit.   NOBVV; PEW

Gray Glove.   Roo Borson.   NOBC

Gray gray of frosty grasses, insects chirp-chirping.   Village Night.   Po Chü-i.   CoBCP, *tr. by* Burton Watson

Gray hairs being plucked.   Basho.   SoOfWa, *tr. by* Sam Hamill

Gray hairs, unwelcome monitors, begin.   Dial, The.   Thomas Cole.   APN-1

Gray Heron, The.   Galway Kinnell.   OWoS

Gray heron flies past, A.   Splitting Wood Near Morris, Oklahoma on Robbie and Lesa McMurtry's Farm.   Lance Henson.   HATNAP

Gray Hills Taught Me Patience, The.   Allen Eastman Cross.   AH

Gray maidservant lets me in, A.   Matinees.   James Merrill.   HCAP; NOBA

Gray mist wolf.   Four Mountain Wolves.   Leslie Marmon Silko.   VoR

Gray Morning.   Aleksandr Aleksandrovich Blok.   TCRP, *tr. by* Geoffrey Thurley

Gray Nights.   Ernest Christopher Dowson.   Son

Gray of the sea, and the gray of the sky, The.   Her Thought and His.   Paul Laurence Dunbar.   NAAAL

Gray on gray post, this silent little bird.   Spotted Flycatcher, The.   Walter De la Mare.   OxBSP

Gray [*or* Grey] Goose and Gander.   *Unknown.*   OxBoLi; OxNR

Gray Poem.   Peter Everwine.   GeoHom

Gray rainwater lay on the grass in the late afternoon.   Wednesday.   Marvin Bell.   VCAP

Gray She-Wolf, The.   *Unknown.*   WoPoe, *tr. by* W. S. Merwin

Gray skies are gonna clear up.   Put on a Happy Face.   Lee Adams.   ReLy

Gray sky, mist, the trees black and wet.   November Woods.   S. J. Marks.   BodElec

Gray smoke rose from the morning ground.   Actual Vision of Morning's Extrusion.   Alan Dugan.   YaYoPo

Gray Squirrel, The.   Humbert Wolfe.   MoBrPo

Gray steel, cloud-shadow-stained.   Watch the Lights Fade.   Robinson Jeffers.   NOBA

Gray Stones and Gray Pigeons.   Wallace Stevens.   SAmP

Gray suit.   Wrong Color.   Christopher Stanard.   SpirFl

Gray Thrums.   Clara Doty Bates.   OBCA

Gray tide flows and flounders in the rocks, The.   At Sainte-Marguerite.   Trumbull Stickney.   APN-2; OxBA; TCAPo

Gray Waves.   Leopoldo Lugones.   TCLAP, *tr. by* Julie Schumacher

Gray whale / Now that we are sending you to the end.   For a Coming Extinction.   W. S. Merwin.   GifTon; HCAP; NNaP; PoE; VCAP

Gray Woods Exploding, The.   Earle Birney.   NoAM

Graze on, my sheep; and let your souls defy.   Eclogue 8.   Francis Quarles.   BASC

Grazing.   Chiyojo [*or* Chiyo *or* Chiyo-Ni *or* Kaga no Chiyo *or* Fukuda Chiyo-Ni].   WPoS

Grazing.   Ira Sadoff.   BodElec

Grazing Locomotives.   Archibald MacLeish.   GM

Great.   Great frog race.   Ian Hamilton Finlay.   KaS

Great A, little a.   Pancake Day.   Mother Goose.   LB; OxNR; ReMoGo

Great A was alarmed at B's bad behavior.   Alphabet.   *Unknown.*   OxNR

Great Adventure, The.   *Unknown.*   *See* Love Will Find Out the Way

Great Alexander sailing was from his true course turned.   Speaking Tree, The.   Muriel Rukeyser.   VGW

Great all-seeing burning eye of day, The.   Libra, September.   John Taylor.   NOSC

Great and bounteous Benefactor.   Christopher Smart.   ChIV-2   *Fr.* Hymns and Spiritual Songs for the Fasts and Festivals of the Church of England.

Great and glorious thing it is, A.   Arithmetic on the Frontier.   Rudyard Kipling.   OBWP

Great and Strong.   Miroslav Holub.   RB, *tr. by* George Theiner

Great Arbiter of Fate, The.   Ch'u Yüan.   SuSp, *tr. by* Wu-Chi Liu

Great are the fallen of Thermopylae.   Greek Dead at Thermopylae, The.   Simonides.   FaBoWar, *tr. by* T. F. Higham

Great are the Hittites.   Concerning My Neighbors, the Hittites.   Charles Simic.   VCAP

Great Artist Reconsiders the Homeric Simile, The. John Tranter. BMAP; NOBAu; NoAM

Great-Aunt Rebecca. Elizabeth Brewster. NOBC

Great-aunts have a corner, and wrinkled skin, The. Language of Great-Aunts, The. Alberto A. Ríos. UnSA

Great Bassist, The. Lawson Fusao Inada. OpBo

Great Bear, The. John Hollander. ColAP; NoAM; TwCP

Great Bear, come down, shaggy night. Invocation of the Great Bear. Ingeborg Bachmann. VCWP, *tr. by* Mark Anderson

Great Bear Lake Meditations, The. J. Michael Yates.
  "I persist in a little fabric between me and the world." NOBC

Great Big Bunch of You, A. Harry Warren. ReLy

Great big houses with great big rooms. Little Things in Life, The. Irving Berlin. ReLy

Great Bird, The. Li Po. CrYelRi, *tr. by* Sam Hamill

Great blue ceremony of the air, The. Mary and the Bramble. Lascelles Abercrombie. OBMV

Great Blue Heron, The. Carolyn Kizer. CoAP; InvLad; WPE

Great blue mountain! Ghost. Mount Kearsarge. Donald Hall. LoL

Great Breath, The. "Æ" MoBrPo; OBEV; OBMV

Great Britain Through the Ice: Or, Premature Patriotism. Charles Tennyson Turner. OxBSo; Son

Great buck-wagon, our 'desert ship,' The. Song of the Wagon-whip, A. Samuel Cron Cronwright. PeSAV

Great captain if you will! great Duke! great Slave! Wellington. Charles Harpur. NOBAu

Great city fell asleep, The. What Her Friend Said. Kollan Alici. WoPoe, *tr. by* A. K. Ramanujan

Great city has a hundred million rooms so any combination, The. Day at a Time. Michael Dransfield. BMAP

Great cup tumbled, ringing like a bell, The. Grail, The. Sidney Keyes. FaBoTw

Great dark work, The. Toward a Poetics. Onwuchekwa Jemie. PBMAP

Great Day. Vincent Youmans. ReLy

Great Day, The. W. B. Yeats. BIrV; OxBSP

Great death has made all his for evermore. (LL) Sonnet: "When you see millions of the mouthless dead." Charles Hamilton Sorley. FaBoWar; NPeEn; OBWP; OxBSo; PeFWW; PoWW

Great desert, let your sweetness wake. (LL) Dowser, The. Edwin Morgan. NPeEn; NoP-4

Great Digest, The. Confucius.
  "In letters of gold on T'ang's bathtub." PFTM-1

Great Digest of Confucius, The. Ezra Pound. GifTon

Great Doubters of History, The. Stephen Dobyns.
  "Woman who kicked out the back window, The." BodElec

Great enimy to it, and to all the rest. Edmund Spenser. OxBEV *Fr.* Faerie Queene, The.

Great-enough both accepts and subdues; the great frame takes all creatures. Phenomena. Robinson Jeffers. NOBA; OxBA

Great Expectations. Charles Dickens.
  Joe Gargery's Epitaph on His Father. FaBoVe

Great fame can be obtained. Autumn Thoughts. Lu Yu. OHPC, *tr. by* Kenneth Rexroth

Great Farter, The. Nakasuk. STP, *tr. by* Jerome Rothenberg

"Great father Alighier, if from the skies." To Dante. Vittorio Alfieri. AWP

Great Father Eating His Children, The. Hesiod. RaBo, *tr. by* Richmond Lattimore *Fr.* Theogony.

Great Favorit Beheaded, A. Sir Richard Fanshawe. *See* Il Pastor Fido

Great Fetishes, The. Blaise Cendrars. PFTM-1

Great Figure, The. William Carlos Williams. AiP; HeIP-4; InPK-6; NoAM; SAmP; TTTS

Great fish's eyes never shut, The. Rosario Castellanos. BoWoP

Great folks are of a finer mould. Epigram on Scolding, An. Jonathan Swift. FaBoEE; FaBoVe; NPeEn

Great Foreign Writer Visits Age-Old Temple, Greeted by Venerable Abbess, 1955. Anthony Thwaite. OBCoV

Great Fortune is an hungry thing. Aeschylus. AWP, *tr. by* Gilbert Murray *Fr.* Agamemnon.

Great Fountains, The. Anne Hébert. BoWoP, *tr. by* Willis Barnstone

Great freight of the summer now is loaded, The. Great Freight, The. Ingeborg Bachmann. AuPH, *tr. by* Lowell A. Bangerter

Great frog race. Ian Hamilton Finlay. KaS

Great Giver has ended His disposing, The. Day of Atonement. Charles Reznikoff. ChIV-1

Great God accept our gratitude. Doxology. Josephine D. Henderson Heard. CBWP-4

Great God, How Frail a Thing Is Man. Mather Byles. AH

Great God, how short's mans time; each minute speaks. Meditations for July 19, 1666. Philip Pain. SCAP

Great God, I Ask Thee for No Meaner Pelf. Henry David Thoreau. NOBA

Great God, our King! (LL) America. Samuel Francis Smith. AiP; TCAPo

Great God, Preserver of All Things. Francis Daniel Pastorius. AH

Great God, the Followers of Thy Son. Henry, Jr. Ware. AH

Great God, Thy Works. Mather Byles. AH

Great, good and just, could I but rate. His Metrical Vow. James Graham, Marquess of Montrose. OxBS

Great Grandame Wales, from whom those ancestors. John Davies of Hereford. AngWePo *Fr.* Cambria.

Great-Grandfather. Freda Downie. FaBoWP

Great-grandfather at Waterloo. Limerick. Frank Richards. PeLi

Great-Grandfathers, blessed by great-grandmothers. Geneology. Bob Kaufman. NBV

Great-great-grandmother. Guy Butler. PeSAV

Great Helmsman, The. David Woo. OpBo

Great Horse Fair, The. Desmond O'Grady. PBCIP

Great horse running in the fields. Horse. Gloria Anzaldúa. UnSA

Great horses of Yilderin, The. Horses of Yilderin, The. Kenneth Patchen. APT-2

Great humility fills me. Thank You, My Fate. Anna Swirszczynska. BLT

Great Hunger, The. Patrick Kavanagh.
  "Cards are shuffled and the deck, The." NPeEn
  "Clay is the word and clay is the flesh." ModIr; NPeEn; NoAM; NoP-4; OxBTC
  "Fields were bleached white, The." NPeEn
  "He gave himself another year." BIrV
  "Maguire is not afraid of death, the Church will light him a candle." CIP-2
  "Poor Paddy Maguire, a fourteen-hour day." ModIr; NPeEn
  "We may come out into the October reality, Imagination." ModIr

Great Hymn. Ntsikana Gaba. PeSAV, *tr. by* John Knox Bokwe

Great Hymn. Ntsikana Gaba. PeSAV, *tr. by* Thomas Pringle

Great Industrial Centre, A. Edith Nesbit. VWP

Great Infirmities. Charles Simic. ChAP

Great is a drink of snow. Asclepiades. GrAn

Great is my envy of you, earth, in your greed. Petrarch. NAWM-5v1 *Fr.* Sonnets to Laura.

Great is the folly of a feeble brain. Joseph Hall. EBEV *Fr.* Virgidemiarum.

Great is the sun, and wide [*or* wise] he goes. Summer Sun. Robert Louis Stevenson. MoBrPo; PWR

Great Is Thy Faithfulness. Thomas O. Chisholm. SacPr

Great is thy worke in Wildernesse, Oh man. Mr. Eliot Pastor of the Church of Christ at Roxbury. Edward Johnson. SCAP

Great It May Be. Ceraman Kottampalattut. WoPoe, *tr. by* George L. III Hart

Great Jehova's working word effecting wondrously, The. Edward Johnson. SCAP

Great joy be to the sailor if he chart. Heureux Qui, Comme Ulysse, A Fait un Beau Voyage. Joachim Du Bellay. WoPoe, *tr. by* Anthony Hecht

Great King. Tuini Ngawai. PeNZ, *tr. by* Margaret Orbell

Great labor was always to efface oneself, The. Lives of Alchemists, The. Charles Simic. KGB

Great Lament of my Obscurity Three, The. Tristan Tzara. PFTM-1

Great land and a wide land was the east land, A. *Unknown.* OBVE; TCAPo *Fr.* Walam Olum; or, Red Score [of the Lenâpé], The [*or* The Wallam Olum; The Red Score or Painted History of the Lenni Lenape].

Great learned lady, whom I long have known. To the Lady Arabella. Emilia [*or* Aemelia] Lanier [*or* Lanyer]. NOSC

Great learning (adult study, grinding corn in the head's mortar to fit), The. Great Digest of Confucius, The. Ezra Pound. GifTon

Great legend of the railways and reservoirs, the weariness of carriage, The. André Breton. PFTM-1 *Fr.* Magnetic Fields, The.

Great light of compassion, The. Gate of Universal Light, The. Muso Soseki. EaWin, *tr. by* W. S. Merwin

Great light was born in Athens when, A. Simonides. PGA

Gret Lord of All, Whose Work of Love. Jacob Duché. AH

Great lords, wise men ne'er sit and wail their loss. William Shakespeare. FaBoWar *Fr.* King Henry VI, Pt. III.

Great love may seem like none at all. Sent in Parting. Tu Mu. CoBCP, *tr. by* Burton Watson

Great Lover, The. Rupert Brooke. MoBrPo; PoRA

Great machete blow of red pleasure right in the face there was blood, The. Miraculous Weapons, The. Aimé Césaire. PFTM-1

Great man once said to me, A. White Paper. V. Narayana Rao. OMIP, *tr. by* V. Narayana Rao

Great master! Boyish, sympathetic man! To John Keats. Amy Lowell. Son

Great Masturbator, The. Salvador Dali. PFTM-1

Great men have been among us; hands that penned. England, 1802, III. William Wordsworth. OBEV; Son

Great men want the four seas. I've only. Untitled. T'ao Ch'ien [*or* T'ao Yuan-ming]. WoPoe, *tr. by* David Hinton

Great Monarch, whose feared hands the thunder fling. Paraphrase Upon Part of the CXXXIX Psalm, A. Thomas Stanley. ChIV-1

Great Moth, The. Robert Gittings. OxBTC

Great Mourning. Bible, Apocrypha. TrJP *Fr.* First Maccabees.

Great Mutando, The. Deryn Rees-Jones. TCAWP

Great Nature clothes the soul, which is but thin. Soul's Garment, The. Margaret Lucas Cavendish, Duchess of Newcastle. WPE

Great Nature she doth clothe the soul within. Soul and Body. Margaret Lucas Cavendish, Duchess of Newcastle. OxBSP

Great New York bridges reflect its faces, The. New York Face, A. Edwin Denby. APT-2

Great Northern. Dave Etter. GM

Great odes have had no revival, The. Ancient Airs. Li Po. SuSp, *tr. by* Joseph J. Lee

Great or small, you furnish your parts toward the soul. (LL) Walt Whitman. APN-1; ColAP; FaBoA; NAAL-2v1; NAAL-3; NAAL-5; NCAP; NOBA; NoAM; NoP-4; TAP

Great Overdog, The. Canis Major. Robert Frost. KaS; MoAmPo

Great Pacific railway, The. Railroad Cars Are Coming, The. *Unknown.* HHAm

Great Painter! to thy soul aglow with thought. Raphael. Henrietta Cordelia Ray. CBWP-3

Great Palaces of Versailles, The. Rita Dove. ESEAA; NoAM

Great Pan is not dead. Different History, A. Sujata Bhatt. HarvBoo

Great Panjandrum [Himself], The. Samuel Foote. FaBoCh

Great philosopher did choke, A. Samuel Butler (1612–80). FaBoEE

Great Physician, The. Sadi [*or* Saadi *or* Sa'di]. AWP, *tr. by* Sir Edward Arnold *Fr.* Gulistan, The.

Great pleasure of laziness . . . as it slides. Hibernation. Maurizio Cucchi. ItPo, *tr. by* Gayle Ridinger

Great poets are not in the language but in business, The. Poetry Paper. Andrei Codrescu. SPE

Great Poll-Tax Victory of '88, The. Noel Petty. UV

Great Prayer. Alfonso Cortes. TCLAP, *tr. by* Thomas Merton

Great princes have great playthings. Some have played. William Cowper. FaBoWar *Fr.* Task, The.

Great pulsation passed. Glass lay around me, The. Rejoice in the Abyss. Stephen Spender. AF

Great recluse lives in market and court, The. Half-recluse, The. Po Chü-i. ChiP, *tr. by* Arthur Waley

Great River wraps an arm, The. On the River. Yü Hsüan-chi. SuSp, *tr. by* Jan W. Walls

Great Sadness, The. Federico García Lorca. PFTM-1

Great Santa Barbara Oil Disaster OR, The. Conyus. NBV

Great sea, The. Shaman Song. Uvavnuk. WoPoe, *tr. by* Jane Hirshfield

Great sea has set me in motion, The. Uvavnuk. EnlH

Great Silkie of Sule Skerry, The. *Unknown.* ESPB; FaBoCh

  (Grey Selchie of Sule Skerry, The.) OxBB

  (I am a man, upo da land.) NePenScot

Great Sir, having just had the good luck to catch. Copy of an Intercepted Despatch from His Excellency Don Strepitoso Diabolo. Thomas Moore. OBSV

Great sleeves of air, The. Between. Ágnes Nemes Nagy. VCWP, *tr. by* Hugh Maxton

Great Society, The. Robert Bly. NoAM; PAI

Great soul, thou sittest with me in my room. To the Spirit of Keats. James Russell Lowell. Son

Great South Land, The. Rex Ingamells.

  "Cook admired the native courage, made." NOBAu

  "They made impudent inspection of our coast." CBAP

Great Spaces. Howard Moss. TwCP

Great Spirit. *Unknown.* FHYEP *Fr.* U.N. Environmental Sabbath Program.

Great Spirit's lodge—you have heard of it. I will enter it, The. Meda Songs. *Unknown.* APN-2, *tr. by* Henry Rowe Schoolcraft

Great Spirit, whose dry lands thirst, help us to find. *Unknown.* FHYEP *Fr.* U.N. Environmental Sabbath Program.

Great Spirits Now on Earth. John Keats. CenSon; Son

Great stone hearth has gone, The. Fire. Dorothy Wellesley, Duchess of Wellington. OBMV

Great Streets of silence led away. Emily Dickinson. APN-2; NOCV

Great success need not be proud. Tseng Jui. SuSp *Fr.* Tune: "Sheep on Mountain Slope"—Lamenting the Times.

Great Summons, The. Ch'u Yüan. AWP, *tr. by* Arthur Waley

Great Summons, The. *Unknown.* ChiP, *tr. by* Arthur Waley

Great tempest on the Plain of Ler, A. *Unknown.* NOIV

Great, the charming Strephon is no more, The. (LL) On the Death of the Late Earl of Rochester. Aphra Behn. BASC; EMWP; NoP-4

Great thing is a refuge for itself, A. Fifth Stanzas. De Arte Poetica. Olga Sedakova. ARWW; ItGoST, *tr. by* Catriona Kelly

Great Things. Thomas Hardy. NOBE

Great things are done when Men and Mountains meet. William Blake. OxBSP *Fr.* Gnomic Verses.

Great thrushes have not appeared this year, The. Unremarkable Year, The. Roy Fuller. OxBC

Great tiger, The. Folk Tune. Esther Raab. FIT, *tr. by* Robert Friend and Shimon Sandbank

Great Time, A. William Henry Davies. MoBrPo

Great Tom. Richard Corbet [*or* Corbett]. OxBoLi

Great trouble and vexation. Necessitie and Benefit of Affliction, The. Anne Lok [*or* Locke]. EMWP

Great Unaffected Vampires and the Moon. Stevie Smith. NoAM

Great Uncle Joe. Apology. Duane Niatum. HATNAP

Great Unrestrained Sadist, The. Hans [*or* Jean] Arp. PFTM-1

Great Venus, Queene [*or* Queen] of Beautie [*or* Beauty] and of grace. Lucretius. AWP *Fr.* De Rerum Natura (On the Nature of Things).

Great Wager, The. Geoffrey Anketell Studdert-Kennedy. TrCP

Great Wall, The. Chu Ch'ing-yü. SuSp, *tr. by* Irving Y. Lo

Great wall of china, The. Yellow River, The. Nabaneeta Dev Sen. OMIP, *tr. by* Nabaneeta Dev Sen

Great War, The. Vernon Scannell. OBWP

Great War Dance, The. *Unknown.* WoPoe, *tr. by* Constance A. Cook

Great Waves Breaking with a Roar. Gustavo Adolfo Bécquer. SpanPo, *tr. by* John Haines

Great Way has no gate, The. Wu-Men. EnlH

Great Way isn't difficult, The. Mind of Absolute Trust, The. Seng-ts'an. EnlH, *tr. by* Stephen Mitchell

Great Way—simple as it is, The. Speaking My Mind. Chung-ch'ang T'ung. CoBCP, *tr. by* Burton Watson

Great Wheel, The. Hugh MacDiarmid. OxBS

Great white lilies in the grass, The. Pallor. Agnes Mary Frances Robinson. NOBVV; VWP

Great White Shark, The. Arthur Sze. GifTon

Great whorl-centered sun, The. Helianthus. Constance Carrier. APT-2

Great wind arises—billowing clouds fly, A. Song of the Great Wind. Liu Pang. ColAnChi, *tr. by* Victor H. Mair

Great wind kill my little shell with sound, The. (LL) Trumbull Stickney. OxBA; Son *Fr.* Sonnets from Greece.

Great wind rises, A. Song of the Great Wind. Liu Pang. SuSp, *tr. by* Ronald C. Miao

Great woe, fire & war come on me. Epigram. Skythinos. GrAn, *tr. by* Thomas Meyer

Great Women Composers, The. Gavin Ewart. OBCoV

Great you call Demosthenes. Self-Portrait. Moses Mendelssohn. TrJP

Great Zeus was reared in Krete and no one. Moiro. SaLy, *tr. by* Diane Rayor

Greater cats with golden eyes, The. Greater Cats, The. Victoria Mary Sackville-West. OBMV; OTCP; Spl

Greater cities are, The. Poem. Víctor Hernández Cruz. PueRic

Greater Courage. Natan Zach. PoSu, *tr. by* Peter Everwine and Shulamit Yasny-Starkman

Greater Friendship Baptist Church, The. Carole C. Gregory Clemmons. BlSi

Greater Gift, The. Margaret E. Bruner. PoToHe

Greater Love. Wilfred Owen. EnLoPo; FaBoMo; GTBS-P; MoBrPo; NoAM; TFi

Greater than the Spring. (LL) Two Springs. Li Ch'ing-chao. BoWoP; OHPC, *tr. by* Kenneth Rexroth

Greater was our gain, our losse the more, The. (LL) Anne Bradstreet. OxBEV; TCAPo *Fr.* In Honour of that High and Mighty Princess Queen Elizabeth of Happy Memory.

Greatest bliss, The. Kiss, The. Charlotte Dacre. CABP; NOBRP

Greatest delight, I sense, The. Betrayal. Adam Zagajewski. VCWP, *tr. by* Renata Gorczynski

Greatest in many things, in some the least. On a Distinguished Politician. J. E. Thorold Rogers. FaBoEE

Greatest living poet, The. Traffic Misdirector. Pedro Juan Pietri. PueRic

Greatest Love, The. Anna Swirszczynska. PoSu

Greatest of all forms of wealth. Tiruvalluvar. WoPoe, *tr. by* Emmons E. White *Fr.* Kural, The.

Greatest saints and sinners have been made, The. Samuel Butler (1612–80). FaBoEE

Greatest self-made man in the world today, The. Our Noble Booker T. Washington. Mrs. Henry Linden. CBWP-4

Greatly shining / The autumn moon floats in the thin sky. Wind and Silver. Amy Lowell. BoWoP; HeIP-4; KaS; MoAmPo; PAI; Spl; TCAPo

Greatness in Little. Richard Leigh. NOSC

Grecian Kindness. John Wilmot, 2d Earl of Rochester. OxBSP

Grecian soldiers, tired with ten years' war. Christopher Marlowe. FaBoWar *Fr.* Dido, Queen of Carthage.

Greece. Gunnar Ekelof. BLT

Greed. Giuseppe Gioacchino Belli. WoPoe, *tr. by* Anthony Burgess

Greed. *Unknown.* OxNR

Greed and Aggression. Sharon Olds. RaBo

Greedy Man, The. *Unknown.* ReMoGo

Greedy the people, The. E. E. Cummings. SoSe-8

Greedy Tom. *Unknown.* OxNR

Greedyguts. Kit Wright. OTCP

Greek Architecture. Herman Melville. NoP-4

Greek Dead at Thermopylae, The. Simonides. FaBoWar, *tr. by* T. F. Higham

Greek Epigram. Ezra Pound. MoAmPo

Greek Epigrams. Angelo [*or* Andrea] Poliziano.
    Love Song for Chrysokomos (Goldenlocks). CAGL, *tr. by* James J. Wilhelm
    On the Love of Two Boys. CAGL, *tr. by* James J. Wilhelm
    To Giovan Battista Buoninsegni. CAGL, *tr. by* James J. Wilhelm

Greek Girl at Riis Beach, A. Frank O'Hara. BodElec

Greek History. Olga Nolla. TANSG, *tr. by* Paula Vega

Greek Metamorphosis. Belkis Cuza Malé. TANSG, *tr. by* Pamela Carmell

Greek Room, The. James W. Thompson. BPo

"Greek Tragedy" of course is the sort of thing. Robert Pinsky. NoAM *Fr.* Essay on Psychiatrists.

Greeks Like Clouds, The. Homer. OBVE, *tr. by* George Chapman *Fr.* Iliad, The.

Green. D. H. Lawrence. HarvBoo; MoBrPo

Green. Paul Verlaine. SxFrPo, *tr. by* Martin Sorrell

Green. Paul Verlaine. WoPoe, *tr. by* Yvor Winters

Green Afternoon, The. Henry Rago. VGW

Green and blue the reedy shallows. At Yuen Yang Lake. Wu Wei-yeh. OHMPC, *tr. by* Kenneth Rexroth

Green and Red, Verde y Rojo. Martín Espada. PueRic

Green and silent spot amid the hills. Samuel Taylor Coleridge. FHYEP; OBWP

Green arbor that I once knew, A. Green Arbor, A. Linda Beatrice Brown. GT

Green arch of the bridge says sleep, The. Sleep. Jane Holland. NeBl

Green arsenic smeared on an egg-white cloth. L'Art, 1910. Ezra Pound. HeIP-4; OxBA; TCAPo

Green as an afterthought. (LL) Weathering Out. Rita Dove. ESEAA; LCAP-2; NoAM

Green as that summer fly. Silk Robe. Jeffrey Skinner. PBCAP

Green Automobile, The. Allen Ginsberg. BB

Green Banana Leaves. Yün Shou-p'ing. CoBLCP, *tr. by* Jonathan Chaves

Green be the turf above thee. On the Death of Joseph Rodman Drake. Fitz-Greene Halleck. APN-1

Green Beret. Ho Thien. FaBoWar, *tr. by Unknown*

Green beyond green, the grass along the river. *Unknown.* ChinPo, *tr. by* Yip Wai-lim

Green-blue ground, The. On Gay Wallpaper. William Carlos Williams. APT-1; MoAmPo; TAP

Green, blue, yellow, and red. One, The. Patrick Kavanagh. MoBrPo

Green-bodied, with small eyes of crimson fire. Moon-talk. Edgell Rickword. OxBSo

Green Boots n Lil Honeys. Ruth Forman. SpirFl

Green bubbles—new brewed wine. Question Addressed to Liu Shih-chiu, A. Po Chü-i. CoBLCP, *tr. by* Burton Watson

Green Buddhas / On the fruit stand. Watermelons. Charles Simic. OBAL; VCAP

Green bushes are bursting with giant flowers. Asphyxiated Man, The. Victor Serge. AF, *tr. by* James Brook

Green Candles. Humbert Wolfe. MoBrPo

Green catalpa tree has turned, The. April Inventory. W. D. Snodgrass. CoAP; ColAP; HAP; NoAM; NoP-4; PAI; TAP; TRP; TwCP; VCAP

Green cheese, yellow laces. *Unknown.* OxNR

Green Chile. Jimmy Santiago Baca. NIL-7

Green cockleburs, The. Haiku. Richard Wright. KaS

Green Corn Season. Diana García. TouFir

Green-darkened lake, surrounded closely, steeply. Old Aussee. Martha Hoffmann. AuPH, *tr. by* Lowell A. Bangerter

Green elm with the one great bough of gold, The. October. Edward Thomas. CABP; HarvBoo; NoAM

Green embellishment of human life. Hope. Sister Juana Inés de la Cruz. SpanPo, *tr. by* Kate Flores

Green Enravishment of Human Life. Sister Juana Inés de la Cruz. WPOW

Green Eye of the Yellow God, The. J. Milton Hayes. EBNV

Green-eyed and could not give them to her children. About this Woman. Judith Rodriguez. BMAP

Green-eyed Care. Old Cat Care. Richard Hughes. OBMV

Green Eyed Monsters of the Valley Dusk, The. Sherley Anne Williams. GeoHom

Green Family, The. Colleen Thibaudeau. NOBC

Green fields are like constructions of the mind which have / suddenly, The. At Parting. Duo Duo (Li Shizheng). AF, *tr. by* Gregory Lee

Green figures move forward and the objects grow larger, The. North. Tony Towle. PmAP

Green fingers, green hand, by now green man. Garden, Wilderness. Michael Hamburger. OBGa

Green first thing each day sees waves. Green Sees Things in Waves. August Kleinzahler. EmeKit

Green Frog at Roadstead, Wisconsin. James Schevill. TAP

Green garden of growing weeds, A. Playing with Fire. James Simmons. CIP-2

Green gossip of the maidenhair, The. Bruce Beaver. BMAP *Fr.* Odes and Days.

Green gourd, A. Somaru. JDP, *tr. by* Yoel Hoffmann

Green grape, and you refused me. Brief Autumnal. *Unknown.* GrAn; PAI; WeW-3, *tr. by* Dudley Fitts

Green Grass. *Unknown.* FaBoVe; OxBoLi; OxNR

Green Grass and Yellow Balloons. Etheridge Knight. GT

Green grass tendrils like silk. Wandering Gentleman, The. *Unknown.* SuSp, *tr. by* Ronald C. Miao

Green Gravel. *Unknown.* FaBoVe

Green, green. ChiP *Fr.* Seventeen Old Poems.

Green, green, green / Herbs splash. Konishi Raizan. ZenPo, *tr. by* Takashi Ikemoto and Lucien Stryk

Green, green Is El Aghir. Norman Cameron. NPeEn; NePenScot; OBWP; OxBTC

(El Aghir.) FaBoTw

Green green, river bank grasses. *Unknown.* CoBCP

Green, green riverside grass. *Unknown.* ColAnChi, *tr. by* Anne Birrell *Fr.* Nineteen Old Poems, The.

Green green the cypress on the ridge. *Unknown.* CoBCP

Green, green willows hang, The. Farewell Poem. *Unknown.* CrYelRi, *tr. by* Sam Hamill

Green Grow the Rashes [A Fragment]. Robert Burns. AWP; CTC; NAEL-5v2; NAEL-6v2; NoP-4; OxAEP-2; PeLV; SCGP
    Song

Green Grow the Rushes O. *Unknown.* OxBoLi

Green Hair. Elinor Wylie. APT-1

Green Hammock, White Magnolia Tree. Ruth Gilbert. PeNZ

Green has suddenly, The. Fall of Leaves, The. Yvor Winters. APT-2

Green hell of the jungle. Green Hell, Green Death. Jan Barry. CDa

Green hills on both banks—mounds of rice kernels. Inscribed on a Painting. Cheng Hsieh. SuSp, *tr. by* Irving Y. Lo

Green hills sloping from the nothern wall. Seeing a Friend Off. Li Po. CoBCP, *tr. by* Burton Watson

Green, how I love you, green. Sleepwalking Ballad, The. Federico García Lorca. WoPoe, *tr. by* Michael Hartnett

Green I love you green. Sleepwalkers' Ballad. Federico García Lorca. WeW-3, *tr. by* John Frederick Nims

Green. I want you green. Somnambulist Ballad. Federico García Lorca. SpanPo, *tr. by* Robert O'Brien

Green Ice. Vivienne Finch. BrRo

Green is the color of everything. One West Coast. Al Young. GeoHom

Green is the grass on riverbanks. *Unknown.* SuSp; WoPoe, *tr. by* Dell R. Hales

Green is the night, green kindled and apparelled. Candle a Saint, The. Wallace Stevens. PoRA

Green is the plane-tree in the square. London Plane-Tree, A. Amy Levy. PEW; ViWPN

Green is the valley, and fair the slopes around it. Ruined Altar, A. Rosamund Marriott Watson. ViWPN

Green it's your green I love. Sleepwalkers' Ballad. Federico García Lorca. STV, *tr. by* John Frederick Nims

Green Jade Plum Trees in Spring. Ou-yang Hsiu. OHPC, *tr. by* Kenneth Rexroth

Green Knight's Farewell to Fancy, The. George Gascoigne. NoSic

Green lamp flares on the table, The. This Life. Rita Dove. GT

Green lawn / a picket fence. Alice Walker. BlSi

Green leaf that will outlast the winter. Louis Zukofsky. VGW

Green leaves. Buson. EH, *tr. by* Robert Hass

Green level of lily leaves, A. To Paint a Water Lily. Ted Hughes. CABP

Green Light. Kenneth Fearing. PoE; VGW

Green Linnet, The. William Wordsworth. GTBS-P

Green little vaulter in the sunny grass. To the Grasshopper and the Cricket. Leigh Hunt. CenSon; GSo; OxBSo; Son

Green lotus on waves of transparent blue, A. Lotus Lover, The. Tzu Yeh. CrYelRi, *tr. by* Sam Hamill

Green Market, New York. Julia Kasdorf. NeAmPo

Green Martyrs. Richard Murphy. NOIV *Fr.* Battle of Aughrim, The.

Green Mistletoe! / Oh, I remember now. Winter. Walter De la Mare. OBMV

Green mothering of moss knits shadow and light, The. Rain Forest. Dave Jeddie Smith. HCAP

Green mountain lies beyond the north wall of the city, The. Saying Farewell to a Friend. Li Po. TAL

Green mountains. Muso Soseki. EaWin, *tr. by* W. S. Merwin

Green mountains lie across the north wall. Taking Leave of a Friend. Li Po. ChinPo, *tr. by* Yip Wai-lim

Green mountains on three sides, a bamboo fence all around. Sitting on a Rock by Mountain Stream. Ch'en Yü-yi. SuSp, *tr. by* Irving Y. Lo

Green mountains rise to the north. Taking Leave of a Friend. Li Po. CrYelRi, *tr. by* Sam Hamill

Green Nostalgia. Thế Lữ WoPoe, *tr. by* Nguyen Ngoc Bich

Green nut tree, The. Fruited Month, The. Zalman Schneour. MHP, *tr. by* Ruth Finer Mintz

Green of the distant meadows, lightly. Tadeusz Borowski. HP

Green parrot. Echo. Henriqueta Lisboa. TCLAP, *tr. by* Hélcio Veiga Costa

Green pine grows in eastern garden, A. T'ao Ch'ien [*or* T'ao Yuan-ming]. SuSp *Fr.* Drinking Wine.

Green Place, A. Honor Moore. FFC

Green plum. Buson. EH, *tr. by* Robert Hass

Green Plumes of Royal Palms. LeRoy V. Brant. AH

Green Rain. Dorothy Livesay. NALW; NIP-4; NOBC; NoP-4

Green Red Brown and White. May Swenson. VGW

Green Refrain, The. Avraham Huss. MHP, *tr. by* Ruth Finer Mintz

Green Revolutions. Barbara Guest. FaBoWP

Green River. William Cullen Bryant. APN-1; NOBA; OxBA; TCAPo "When breezes are soft and skies are fair." ITBLP

Green River, The. Lord Alfred Bruce Douglas. OBEV

Green road lies this way, The. El Camino Verde. Paul Blackburn. PmAP

Green Roads, The. Edward Thomas. NoAM

Green robe, green robe, lined with yellow. Ezra Pound. APSN

Green rushes with red shoots. Plucking The Rushes. *Unknown.* BoLoP; ChiP; OBVE, *tr. by* Arthur Waley

Green rustlings, more-than-regal charities. Royal Palm. Hart Crane. MoAmPo; NoAM

Green scapulars to wear over your shroud. (LL) Strand at Lough Beg, The. Seamus Heaney. CIP-2; NPeEn; NoAM; OBWP

Green sea clothes on. Hints. Giancarlo Majorino. ItPo, *tr. by* Gayle Ridinger

Green Sees Things in Waves. August Kleinzahler. EmeKit

Green-shadowed people sit, or walk in rings. Spring. Philip Larkin. MoBrPo

Green shingles of rest homes unfold revealing, The. United States Prepare for the Permanent Revolution, The. George Hitchcock. SPE

Green shutters, shut your shutters! Windyridge. Sir John Betjeman. OxBTC *Fr.* Beside the Seaside.

Green Side, The. Jennifer Maiden. BMAP

Green Sleeves [and Tartan Ties]. Robert Burns. FaBoVe

Green Snake. B. R. Lakshman Rao. OMIP, *tr. by* A. K. Ramanujan

Green Snake, when I hung you round my neck. To the Snake. Denise Levertov. NAAL-5; PAI

Green soaks into the dark trees. Twilight in West Virginia: Six O'Clock Mine Report. Irene McKinney. PBCAP

Green Song. Dame Edith Sitwell. BWW

Green Spring receiveth. Great Summons, The. Ch'u Yüan. AWP, *tr. by* Arthur Waley

Green Spring receiveth. Great Summons, The. *Unknown.* ChiP, *tr. by* Arthur Waley

Green Symphony. John Gould Fletcher. MoAmPo

Green-tinged pink tones fade. Brussels: Simple Frescos 1. Paul Verlaine. SxFrPo, *tr. by* Martin Sorrell

Green trees form shade, the path is covered with moss. Recording My Happiness upon Returning Home. Wen Cheng-ming. CoBLCP, *tr. by* Jonathan Chaves

Green Trees that in the Forest grew. (LL) Dialogue between the Soul and [the] Body, A. Andrew Marvell. BASC; ESCV; FSCP; GeHe; HAP; MeLP; NAEL-5v1; NAEL-6v1; NAEL-7v1; NoP-4; OxAEP-1; OxBEV; SoSe-8; TFi

Green upon green, grass along the river. Water the Horses at a Breach in the Great Wall. *Unknown.* ChinPo, *tr. by* Yip Wai-lim

Green Valley, The. Sylvia Townsend Warner. MoBrPo

Green Willow, The. *Unknown.* SCGP

Green willows and fragrant grass by the posthouse road. Tune: "Spring in the Jade House." Yen Shu. ColAnChi, *tr. by* J. R. Hightower

Green willows, fragrant grass, the many-stationed road. Tune: "Spring in Jade Pavilion." Yen Shu. SuSp, *tr. by* An-yan Tang

Green woodpecker flying up and down, The. Green Woodpecker's Nest, The. John Clare. FaBoVe

Green yellow dog up. I have not. I am. green red cat down. I is not. I is. Scraptures: 7th Sequence. B. P. Nichol. FTOS

Greene's Farewell to Folly. Robert Greene. Song: "Sweet are the thoughts that savour of content." PoToHe

Greene's Mourning Garment. Robert Greene. Shepherd's Wife's Song, The. HAP; NoSic; RACG

Greene's Vision. Robert Greene. Description of Sir Geoffrey Chaucer, The. CTC; NoSic; SCGP (Sir Geoffrey Chaucer.) FaBoCh

Greenest jade for a clothes-pounding stone. Ch'ing-yang Ford. *Unknown.* CoBCP, *tr. by* Burton Watson

Greengrocer, The. Michael Longley. BiHa; ModIr *Fr.* Wreaths.

Greenhalgh's Pub. Julian Croft. NOBAu

Greenhouse Vanity, The. Les A. Murray. FaBoVe

Greens. David Ray. VGW

Greensleeves. *Unknown.* TTTS (New Courtly Sonnet of the Lady Greensleeves, A.) FaBoCh

Greenwich Observatory. Sidney Keyes. MoBrPo

Greenwood's. Michael Sharkey. NOBAu

Greeting. Henrietta Cordelia Ray. CBWP-3

Greeting, A. William Henry Davies. MoBrPo

Greeting Shekinah. Lynn Gottlieb. HW

Greeting to Queen Elizabeth, the Rare White Heron of Single Flight, A. Wiremu Kingi Kerekere. PeNZ, *tr. by* Wiremu Kingi Kerekere

Greeting to thee, O most trusty friend!, A. To My Own Face. Caroline Lindsay. VWP

Greeting you on the street that day. Zhoukoudian Bride's Harvest. Carolyn Lau. FSt

Greetings, Blaise Cendrars. Sonia Delaunay. CuPo

Greetings from the Chateau. James Schuyler. FTOS

Greetings, great evangelist! Lines on the Return to Britain of Billy Graham. E. J. Thribb. PeLV

Greetings ladies, kith and kin. Judah Halevi. WoPoe, *tr. by* Gabriel Levin *Fr.* On the Sea.

Greetings, 260 thousand ccm. Murder Machine 43. Kurt Schwitters. PFTM-1

Greetings! you seven students of Professor Aristides. *Unknown.* GrAn

Gregory Griggs, Gregory Griggs. *Unknown.* OxNR

Gregory's House. David Huddle. PBCAP

Greifes Farwell, to an Inherritor of Joy. Ann Williams. EMWP

Grenada. Mikhail Arkadyevich [*or*Arkad'evich] Svetlov. TCRP, *tr. by* Daniel Weissbort

Grenade. Francis Scarfe. FaBoWar

Grenadier. A. E. Housman. OBMV; OBWP

Grenadier, The. *Unknown.* OxNR

Grenadiers, The. Heinrich Heine. FaBoWar, *tr. by* Unknown

Grenoble Café. Jean Garrigue. APT-2

Greta's Song. Matthew Graham. Unle

Gretel in Darkness. Louise Glück. NoAM; NoP-4

Gretsch love / gretsch hate. Elvin Jones Gretsch Freak. David Henderson. SeSe

Grew wilder. (LL) Bag of Mice. Nick Flynn. AmPoNex; NAPBL

Grey afternoon clouds, The. Sea-Sickness. Heinrich Heine. WoPoe, *tr. by* Vernon Watkins

Grey already the hair at my temples. Strato [*or* Straton]. GrAn

Grey and dankish thing, A. Theodore Weiss. DiPo *Fr.* Every Second Thought.

Grey and Green. Arthur Symons. NOBVV; PeVV *Fr.* At Dieppe.

Grey beards wag, the bald heads nod, The. Miniature. Eden Phillpotts. OxBSP

Grey brick upon brick. Louis MacNeice. CIP-2; OxBTC *Fr.* Closing Album, The.

Grey Cock, or, Saw You My Father?, The. *Unknown.* ESPB

Grey courtyards where the imprisoned. Via Margutta. Maria Luisa Spaziani. NeIt, *tr. by* Beverly Allen

Grey Dawn. Julio Herrera y Reissig. TCLAP, *tr. by* Andrew Rosing

Grey Eye Weeping, A. Egan [*or* Aodhagán] O'Rahilly [*or* O'Reilly *or* Ó Rathaille]. OBMV, *tr. by* Frank O'Connor

Grey flies, fragile, slender-winged and slender-legged. Evening Dance of the Grey Flies. Patricia K. Page. NOBC

Grey gaunt days dividing us in twain, The. Minute before Meeting, The. Thomas Hardy. OxBSo

Grey goose and gander. *Unknown.* LB

Grey-green stretch of sandy grass, The. Arthur Symons. NOBVV; PeVV *Fr.* At Dieppe.

Grey Hair, The. Judah Halevi. TrJP, *tr. by* J. Chotzner

Grey haunted eyes, absent-mindedly glaring. Face in the Mirror, The. Robert Graves. CABP

Grey hills of that country fall away, The. Cadaver Politic. Tom Paulin. PNI

Grey horse, Death, in profile bears the young Titus, The. Polish Rider, The. Derek Walcott. WoPoe

Grey. Intangible drops. Sea. Marie-Claire Bancquart. MFP, *tr. by* Martin Sorrell

Grey is her sleep to-night. (LL) Highland Woman, A. Sorley MacLean (Somhairle MacGill-Eain). HarvBoo; NePenScot

Grey Monk, The. William Blake. PeECV

Grey monkeys gibber, ignorant and wise. Alun Lewis. FaBoWar *Fr.* Jungle, The.

Grey mountains, sea and sky. Even the misty. Sea Anemones, The. Gwen Harwood. BMAP

Grey [*or* Gray] sea and the long black land, The. Meeting At Night. Robert Browning. AWP; BRP; BoLoP; FHYEP; FaBoVe; HeIP-4; ITBLP; NAEL-5v2; NAEL-6v2; NOBE; NOBVV; OBEV; OPOU; OxBEV; OxBSP; PAI; PeVV; PoRA; SCGP; SCV; SoSe-8; TFi; UnPo

Grey over Riddrie the clouds piled up. King Billy. Edwin Morgan. NePenScot; NoP-4

Grey psychopath in her season, The. Cat. Joe Rosenblatt. NOBC

Grey sea and the long black land, The. Robert Browning. *See* Grey [*or* Gray] sea and the long black land, The

Grey sea turns in its sleep, The. Aberdeen. Robin Robertson. NePenScot

Grey Selchie of Sule Skerry, The. *Unknown. See* Great Silkie of Sule Skerry, The

Grey Selchie of Sule Skerry, The. *Unknown.* OxBB

Grey sky, grey city-smoke. 9th July, 1932. Mary Ursula Bethell. PeNZ

Grey the sky, and growing dimmer. Twilight. Louisa Sarah Bevington. PEW

Grey the sky, and growing dimmer. Twilight. Louisa S. Guggenberger. NOBVV

Grey Time moves silently, and creeping on. *Unknown.* GrAn

Grey, to the low grass cropping. Wole Soyinka. PBMAP *Fr.* Idanre and Other Poems (1967).

Grey trees, grey skies, and not a star. Dawn. Angelina Weld Grimké. APT-1

Grey Wagtail on the Tyne. Colin Simms. Oth

Grey water tanks in grey mist. Bayonne Turnpike to Tuscarora. Allen Ginsberg. NNaP

Grey Wolf, The. Arthur Symons. FaBoTw

Grey Woman. Gladys Cardiff. CDW; GifTon

Greyer than the tide below, the tower. Homage to Jack Yeats. Thomas MacGreevy [*or* McGreevy]. OBMV

Greyhound, The. Saleem Barakat. MAP, *tr. by* Lena Jayyusi and Naomi Shihab Nye

Greyhound should be headed like a snake, A. Properties of a Good Greyhound, The. Dame Juliana Berners. RB; WoPoe, *tr. by* Seamus Heaney

Griboyedov's Waltz. Aleksandr Bashlachov [*or* Bashlachev]. TCRP, *tr. by* Sarah W. Bliumis

Grid Erectile. Christopher Dewdney. FTOS

Grief. Robin Becker. TaR

Grief. Elizabeth Barrett Browning. HeIP-4; InPK-6; NALW; NOBVV; NPeEn; OBEV; VWP; WPE

Grief. Catullus. RaBo, *tr. by* Jacob Rabinowitz *Fr.* Carmina.

Grief. Ruth L. Schwartz. AmPoNex

Grief. Siamanto. AF, *tr. by* Peter Balakian

Grief. *Unknown.* OBWVE, *tr. by* Aneirin Talfan Davies

Grief: I've grieved as a solitary phoenix grieves. Kuan Han-ch'ing. SuSp *Fr.* Tune: "Intoxication in the East Wind."

Grief is not apparel. Homicide. Essex Hemphill. GT

Grief isn't empty it's black and material I've seen it. 1—Towards a Definition. Alice Notley. ExTi

Grief / o grief. Alarum. Urszula Koziol. WPOW, *tr. by* Czeslaw Milosz

Grief of Love, The. *Unknown.* AWP, *tr. by* Wilfrid Scawen Blunt

Grief of the coyote seems to make, The. Arizona Midnight. Robert Penn Warren. AmFaPo

Grief's prodigals, where are you? Unthrifts, where? Upon Mr. Hopton's Death. Henry Halswell. NOSC

Grief that troubled your life, The. (LL) Elegy: "O loveliest daughter of Hsieh." Yuan Chen. CrYelRi; ErotSp, *tr. by* Sam Hamill

Griefe was common, common were the Cryes, The. Miserable Estate of the World Before the Incarnation of God. William Drummond, of Hawthornden. SacPr

Griefs of a little boy are forever, The. Four and a Half. John Holmes (1904–62). APT-2

Griesly Wife, The. John Streeter Manifold. MoBrPo

Grieve, ladies, so may God keep you. Lament for the Death of Guillén Peraza. *Unknown.* WoPoe, *tr. by* W. S. Merwin

Grieve not, dear love, although we often part. Grieve Not, Dear Love. John Digby. NOSC; OxBSP

Grieve not, my wife—grieve not for me. Joshua McCarter Simpson. TCAPo *Fr.* Away to Canada.

Grieve Not the Holy Spirit, etc. George Herbert. ESCV

Grieved, I idle and doze. Tu Fu. CrYelRi, *tr. by* Sam Hamill *Fr.* Random Pleasures.

Grieved lands of Africa, The. Grieved Lands, The. Agostinho Neto. PBMAP; PoetW, *tr. by* Michael Wolfers

Grieving the sapless limbs, the shorn and shaken. (LL) Dead Boy. John Crowe Ransom. FaBoMo; FuPo; HarvBoo; NoAM; NoP-4; OxBA; PoE; TwCP

Grievous folly shames my sixtieth year, A. Hafiz [*or* Hafez]. AWP *Fr.* Odes.

"Grill me some bones," said the Cobbler. At the Keyhole. Walter De la Mare. MoBrPo

Grim bulwarked hatred between heart and heart! (LL) 1492. Emma Lazarus. APN-2; SWaP; WPE

Grim Cotton Mather. Cotton Mather. Stephen Vincent Benét. APT-2

Grim monarch! see, deprived of vital breath. To a Lady on the Death of Her Husband. Phillis Wheatley. TAP

Grim Sisters, The. Liz Lochhead. CABP

Grim Skeleton come back and put me out of Action. Grim Skeleton. Allen Ginsberg. BodElec

Grimalkin. Thomas Lynch. EmeKit

Grimes Golden Greening Yellow Transparent. Counting-out Rhyme. Eve Merriam. KaS

Grin, A. Ted Hughes. EmeKit

Grinder's art has been known so long, The. Glimpsed through a Lens. Yevgeny [*or* Evgenii] Borisovich Rein. TCRP, *tr. by* Bernard Meares

Grinder, who serenely grindest. Lines on Hearing the Organ. Charles Stuart Calverley. NOBL

Grinding Vibrato. Jayne Cortez. BlSi

Grinding yoke from Israel's neck he tore, The. Eulogy for Hasdai ibn Shaprut. *Unknown.* TrJP, *tr. by* Israel Abrahams

Griots Who Know Brer Fox, The. Colleen J. McElroy. NAAAL

Gripe. Lincoln Kirstein. PoWW

Gripped on the shoulder of the man in front. (LL) War Blinded. Douglas Dunn. DiPo; NePenScot; OBWP

Gription. Paul Beatty. InTrad

Griselda's dead, and so's her patience. Geoffrey Chaucer. PoRA *Fr.* Canterbury Tales, The.

Griselda stands at the window. Griselda. Evangeline Paterson. Prnts

Grit. Geoff Page. NOBAu

Grizzel Grimme. *Unknown.* FaBoEE

Grizzly Bear is huge and wild, The. Infant Innocence. A. E. Housman. FaBoCh; NOBL; OxBoLi; PeLV; Spl

Gro-ink. Kopita, kopita, ko-pi-ta. . .*konk.* Nub. Chris Wallace-Crabbe. BMAP

Grocer's Dream, The. Giovanna Pollarolo. TANSG, *tr. by* Marjorie Agosin

Grodek. Georg Trakl. PeFWW
   (In the evening the autumn woods ring.) AF, *tr. by* Daniel S. Simko

Groin, come of age, his [']state sold out of hand. On Groin. Ben Jonson. NOSC

Groins, for his fleshly burglary of late. Upon Groins: Epigram. Robert Herrick. CaPo

Grongar Hill. John Dyer. CABP; NOEC; NoP-4; OxAEP-1
   "Now, I gain the Mountain's Brow." NPeEn

Groom of the Chamber's Religion in King Henry the Eighth's Time, A. John Harington. NoSic

Groom retails the favours of his lord, The. (LL) Samuel Johnson. NOEC; NPeEn; OBSV; OxAEP-1 *Fr.* London: A Poem in Imitation of the Third Satire of Juvenal.

Groome of the Chambers religion in King Henry the eights time, A. Sir John Harington [*or* Harrington]. PBRV

Grooming. Katie Donovan. NeBl

Groove in black plastic got deeper, The. Rock 'n Roll. Peter Balakian. SwNoth

Groping along the tunnel, step by step. Rear-Guard, The. Siegfried Sassoon. MoBrPo; NAEL-5v2; NAEL-6v2; NoAM; OBWP; PoWW

Groping back to bed after a piss. Sad Steps. Philip Larkin. NAEL-6v2; NoAM; NoP-4

"Gross, Coarse, Hideous" (Police Description of My Pictures). D. H. Lawrence. FaBoEE

Gross innocent. Pablo Neruda. TTTS *Fr.* Elephant.

Grossdaadi's Funeral. Julia Kasdorf. NeAmPo

Grotesque. Amy Lowell. BoWoP

Grotesque. Frederic Manning. PeFWW

Grotesque. William Carlos Williams. TCAPo

Grotesque and queerly huddled. Troop ship, The. Isaac Rosenberg. OxBEV; PoWW

Grotesques. Robert Graves. OBCoV

  "Dr. Newman with the crooked pince-nez." PeLV

  "Sir John addressed the Snake-god in his temple." PeLV

Grouchy Good Night to the Academic Year, A. Ted Pauker. NOBL; PeLV

Ground beneath my feet is cracked, The. Day Twenty-three. Victor Coleman. NOBC

Ground Beneath Us, The. Patricia Goedicke. ExTi

Ground drops back, The. Aeroplane. Pudjipangu. NOBAu, tr. by George von Brandenstein

Ground Elder. Leonard Clark. OBGa

Ground Glass. Irina Odoyevtseva [or Odoevtseva]. TCRP, tr. by Bradley Jordan

Ground / itself would / hint, The. Kiche Manitou. Nathaniel Mackey. FTOS

Ground lapis for the sky, and scrolls of gold. Illumination. Anthony Hecht. ChrPo

Ground-Squirrel Song. Navajo Oral Tradition. TTTS

Ground Swell. Mark Jarman. GeoHom; MoASP

Ground-Thumping Song. Unknown. CoBCP; ColAnChi, tr. by Burton Watson

Ground was frozen so hard, The. Dying with Amish Uncles. Julia Kasdorf. PBCAP

Groundhog, The. Richard Eberhart. APT-2; FaBoMo; MoAmPo; NoAM; PAI; RaBo; TAP; TFi; TRP; UnPo

Groundhog is, at best, a simple soul, The. Groundhog, The. Luci Shaw. TrCP

Groundhog on the mountain did not run, The. Incommunicado. Sylvia Plath. BodElec

Group. John Berryman. BodElec

Group of Musings, A. Henrietta Cordelia Ray. CBWP-3

Group of Officials, A. Yang Shih-ch'i.

  "Beyond the temple, a hidden cliff." CoBLCP

Group of professional, A. Physics of Ochun, The. Víctor Hernández Cruz. PueRic

Group of them, A. Basho. EH, tr. by Robert Hass

Group Photo from Pretoria Local on the Occasion of a Fourth Anniversary (Never Taken). Jeremy Cronin. PeSAV

  (Uprooted tree leaves / behind it a hole in the ground, An.) AF

Group Shot. Basil T. Paquet. CDa

Group Therapy. Carolyn M. Rodgers. ISC

Groups of God, The. Rainmakers, The. Robert Kelly. PmAP

Grove, The. Octavio Paz. TCLAP, tr. by Elizabeth Bishop

Grove at Nemi, The. Susan Mitchell. ExTi

Grove beyond the Barley, The. Alden Nowlan. MoCV

Grove of small trees, branches thick with berries, A. Charles Reznikoff. APT-2

Groves of Blarney, The. Richard Alfred Millikin. OBGa; OxBoLi

Groves were God's first temples. Ere man learned, The. William Cullen Bryant. APN-1; TAP; TreFP Fr. Forest Hymn, A.

Grow. Joseph Ceravolo. BodElec

Grow not too high, grow not too far from home. Edna St. Vincent Millay. OxBSo

Grow old along with me! Robert Browning. ITBLP; NAEL-5v2; NAEL-6v2; PoToHe Fr. Rabbi Ben Ezra.

Grow to my lip, thou sacred kiss. Kiss, The. Thomas Moore. NOBRP

Growing, The. Mongane Wally Serote. PBMAP

Growing Dark. James Schuyler. GLP

Growing Days, The. Rick Alley. AmPoNex

Growing, he saw his friends increase. Tony White. Richard Murphy. BiHa

Growing in Grace. Jack R. Clemo. NOCV

Growing into my name. Harriet Jacobs. SpirFl

Growing Old. Matthew Arnold. FHYEP; NAEL-5v2; NAEL-6v2; NOBVV; NPeEn

Growing Old. Byron. NOBE; SCV Fr. Don Juan.

Growing Old (1). Yüan Mei. WoPoe, tr. by Arthur Waley

Growing Old (2). Yüan Mei. WoPoe, tr. by Arthur Waley

Growing older, I grow into the Tao. Hermitage at Chung-nan Mountain. Wang Wei. CrYelRi, tr. by Sam Hamill

Growing tired of her hysterical gestures. On the Glittering Beaches. Tracey Herd. MFPA

Growing Up Haunted. Marge Piercy. TaR

Growing Up in a Jewish Neighborhood. Richard Chess. TaR

Growing Up Italian. Maria Gillan. UnSA

Growltiger's Last Stand. T. S. Eliot. FaBoCh; OBCA

Grown and Flown. Christina Georgina Rossetti. NOBVV

Grown old are these strong elements of tragedy. One Hundred Lines for the Coast. Kojo Laing. HBAPE

Grown old in Love from Seven till Seven times Seven. William Blake. FaBoEE

Grown still loud voices of the day. Lullaby. Ferdinand von Saar. AuPH, tr. by Lowell A. Bangerter

Grown-up. Edna St. Vincent Millay. NoAM; PAI

Grown-ups. Geoffrey Holloway. OTCP

Grown-ups say things like. Chivvy. Michael Rosen. OTCP

Grown violent, do's either die, or tire. (LL) Love Me Little, Love Me Long. Robert Herrick. CaPo; SCGP

Grows deathless by the sacrifice [or sacrifise]. (LL) Friendship's Mystery[s], to my dearest Lucasia. Katherine Philips. BASC; NAEL-7v1; PBRV; PEW

Grows fainter and fades away. (LL) Kenneth Rexroth. APSN; APT-2 Fr. Love Poems of Marichiko, The.

Growth. Shuntaro Tanikawa. PoetW, tr. by Harold Wright

Growth of Love, The. Robert Bridges.

  "Man that sees by chance his picture made, A." NoAM

  "My lady pleases me and I please her." Son

  "O weary pilgrims, chanting of your woe." MoBrPo

  "They that in play can do the thing they would." NoAM

  "Whole world now is but the minister, The." Son

Grr—what's that? A dog? A poet? From a Spanish Cloister. Gilbert Keith Chesterton. UV

Grudge, The. Dimitris Tsaloumas. BMAP

Grudges mend and wear and turn in winter. Household. Laura Jensen. LCAP-2

Gruel heaped / In a perfect bowl. Naito Joso. ZenPo, tr. by Takashi Ikemoto and Lucien Stryk

Gruesome ghoul, the grisly ghoul, The. Ghoul, The. Jack Prelutsky. OBCA

Grumble Family, The. Unknown. PWR

Grunion. Wendy Rose. CDW

Grunts, and drains it clean. (LL) Drink of Milk, A. John Montague. ModIr; PNI

Gruoch. Marion Lomax. NeBl

Gruyere—is being cleared of its forest—the mountains. End to Myth, An. Charles Buckmaster. BMAP

Gryll Grange. Thomas Love Peacock.

  Love and Age. NOBVV; OBEV

Gryll / Had his fill. Gryll's State. Roy Blount, Jr. OBAL

Gryll's State. Roy Blount, Jr. OBAL

Guadalupe, W.I. Nicolás Guillén. TTY, tr. by Anselm Hollo

Guaranteed the canopy of the firmament above us. (LL) Picnic, an Homage to Civil Rights, The. Michael S. Weaver. LTA; PoPoPo

Guard. Viktor Krivulin. TCRusP, tr. by Daniel Weissbort

Guard, The. Lyn Hejinian.

  "Can one take captives by writing." FTOS

Guard at the Binh Thuy Bridge, The. John Balaban. AF; CDa

Guard-Duty. August Stramm. PeFWW, tr. by Patrick Bridgwater

Guard me, Oh God, from hating man my brother. Guard Me, Oh God. Shin Shalom. MHP, tr. by Ruth Finer Mintz

Guard me, oh God, from the cold winds that blow. Woman's Prayer, A. Yehuda Karni. MHP, tr. by Ruth Finer Mintz

Guard picks dead leaves from plants, The. In an Urban School. Toi Derricotte. PBCAP

Guarded Wound, The. Adelaide Crapsey. APT-1; WPE

Guardian Angel. Rolf Jacobsen. RaBo, tr. by Robert Bly

Guardian-Angel, The. Robert Browning. PeECV

Guardian Angel, The. Stephen Dunn. OPRER

Guardian Angel of Not Feeling, The. Jorie Graham. ExTi

Guardian Angels. Edmund Spenser. NOCV; NoSic Fr. Faerie Queene, The.

Guardian Life. Michael Klein. WiU

Guardian of heavenly gates, self-portrait, neon retort. New York Airport at Night. Andrey [or Andrei] Andreievich Voznesensky [or Voznesenskii]. TCRP, tr. by William Jay Smith

Guardian of the gate. Kanemasa. OHPJ

Guardians, The. Geoffrey Hill. NoP-4

Gubbinal. Wallace Stevens. NAAL-2v2

Gud Ber. Unknown. FaBoVe

Gude and Godlie Ballatis, The. Unknown.

  "God send euerie Preist ane wyfe." NePenScot

  Till Christ ("Till Christ, quhome I am haldin for to lufe"). OxBS

  "With huntis vp, with huntis vp." NePenScot

Gude guide me, are ye hame again, and hae ye got nae wark? Last Sark, The. Ellen Johnston. NePenScot

Gude Lord Graeme is to Carlisle gane. Bewick and the Graeme, The. Unknown. OxBB

Gude Lord Scroop[e]'s to the huntin[g] gane. Hughie [the] Gra[e]me. *Unknown.* ESPB; IBB

Gude Wallace. *Unknown.* ESPB

Gudewife sits i' the chimney-neuk, The. Ballad of the Were-Wolf, A. Rosamund Marriott Watson. VWP; ViWPN

Gudrun Laments over Sigurd. *Unknown.* OBVE *Fr.* Elder Edda, The.

Gudrun of old days. *Unknown.* AWP, *tr. by* Eirikr Magnusson and William Morris *Fr.* Elder Edda, The.

Guélowâr! / We have listened to you, we have heard you. Camp 1940. Léopold Sédar Senghor. PoetW, *tr. by* Melvin Dixon

Guerilla Fighter. Jofre Rocha. NAfrP, *tr. by* Don Burness

Guerillas. Seamus Deane. BiHa

Guerrilla-Cong, The. Michael S. Harper. NBV

Guerrilla War. William Daniel Ehrhart. CDa

Guess I'll Hang My Tears Out to Dry. Jule Styne. ReLy

Guess well, and that is well. Our age can find. Tennyson. OxBSo

Guess! / Where do you think I'm goin' when the winds start blowin' strong? Way Down Yonder in New Orleans. Henry Creamer. ReLy

Guess Who. Fred Chappell. NBLV

'Guess who I saw last night?' was all she said. Your Street Again. Sophie Hannah. MFPA

Guess Who I Saw Today. Murray Grand. ReLy

Guess who is this creature. Song to the Wind, A. Taliesin. FaBoCh, *tr. by* A. P. Graves

Guess Who's in Town? (Nobody but That Gal of Mine). J. C. Johnson. ReLy

Guest. Dennis Joseph Enright. OxBC

Guest, A. Tu Fu. ChinPo, *tr. by* Yip Wai-lim

Guest, The. Anna Andreyevna Akhmatova. ErotSp, *tr. by* Max Hayward and Stanley Kunitz

Guest, The. Anna Andreyevna Akhmatova. RaBo; WoPoe, *tr. by* Vera Dunham and Jane Kenyon

Guest, The. Sheenagh Pugh. TCAWP

Guest, The. *Unknown.* FaBoCh; PoRA; SacPr; TrCP

  (Preparations.) NOBE; OBEV

  (Yet if his Majestie our Sovaraigne lord.) PBRV

  (Yet If His Majesty, Our Sovereign Lord.) NoP-4

Guest Arrives, A. Tu Fu. ColAnChi, *tr. by* Victor H. Mair

Guest Arrives, A. Tu Fu. CoBCP, *tr. by* Burton Watson

Guest Ellen at the Supper for Street People, The. David Ferry. NIP-4

Guest gone / I stroke the brazier. Shozan. ZenPo, *tr. by* Takashi Ikemoto and Lucien Stryk

Guest is inside you, and also inside me, The. Guest Is Inside, The. Kabir. RaBo, *tr. by* Robert Bly

Guests in their summer colors have fled, The. Last Picnic, The. Stanley Kunitz. AF

Guests moved restless, The. Party, The. Antigone Kefala. BMAP

Guests on the sea: Our visit is short. Guests on the Sea. Mahmoud Darwish. VCWP, *tr. by* Lena Jayyusi

Guide and Guard. Herman Melville. NCAP

Guide, and support, and cheer me to the end! (LL) William Wordsworth. FHYEP; PoE *Fr.* Excursion, The.

Guide from St. Stephen the Sabaite, The. John Mason Neale. SacPr

Guide Me, O Thou Great Jehovah. William Williams. OBWVE

  Christian Pilgrim's Hymn. SacPr

  "Guide me, O thou great Redeemer." SacPr

Guide me on my way. Princess Shokushi. ArkPo, *tr. by* Robert H. Brower and Earl Miner

Guide to Holland, A. Peter Sirr. PBCIP

Guide to the Other Gallery. Dana Gioia. RA

Guide to the Perplexed. David Malouf. NOBAu

Guide to the Symphony. Weldon Kees. VGW

Guide to the Underworld. Gunnar Ekelof.

  "Alone in the quiet night." WoPoe, *tr. by* Rika Lesser

Guide to Urban Birds, A. David B. Axelrod. UrbNat

Guide us to Thy perfect light. (LL) We Three Kings of Orient Are. John Henry, Jr. Hopkins. AH; ChrPo

Guided Missiles Experimental Range. Robert Conquest. OxBC

Guiding hand raised, A. When Asked to Lie Down on the Altar. Eleanor Wilner. TaR

Guido, an image of my lady dwells. Guido Cavalcanti. EaItPo, *tr. by* Dante Gabriel Rossetti

Guido, I wish that Lapo, thou, and I. Dante Alighieri. EaItPo, *tr. by* Dante Gabriel Rossetti

Guido, I wish that you and Lapo and I. Love and Poetry. Dante Alighieri. NAWM-7v1, *tr. by* James J. Wilhelm

Guido, I wish that you and Lapo and I. Sonnet. Dante Alighieri. RB; TTTS, *tr. by* Kenneth Koch

Guido, I would that Lapo, thou, and I. Sonnet: To Guido Cavalcanti. Dante Alighieri. AWP

Guido's Aurora. Henry David Thoreau. APN-1

Guido, that Gianni who, a day agone. Gianni Alfani. EaItPo, *tr. by* Dante Gabriel Rossetti

Guidon flags flutter gaily [or gayly] in the wind, The. (LL) Cavalry Crossing a Ford. Walt Whitman. AiP; CBCWP; HeIP-4; InPK-6; NAAL-2v1; NAAL-3; NAAL-5; NoAM; OxBA; PAI; SAmP; TAP; TCAPo; TFi; TRP; UnPo

Guiffre's Nightmusic. Thomas McGrath. SeSe

Guild, The. Sharon Olds. RaBo

Guile and softness of the Saxon race, The. On the Welch. *Unknown.* AngWePo

Guillotine is the masterpiece of the plastic arts, The. Head, The. Blaise Cendrars. CuPo

Guillotine's / Sharp blade, The? "V. Ropshin." TCRP

Guilt, Desire and Love. James Baldwin. CAGL; GLP

Guilty. Harry Akst. ReLy

Guilty, he does not always like his patients. Doctor, The. Dannie Abse. BloBone

Guilty, my Lord, what can I more declare? Edward Taylor. ChIV-1; TCAPo *Fr.* Preparatory Meditations Before My Approach to the Lord's Supper.

Guinea. Jacques Roumain. NegPo; TTY, *tr. by* Langston Hughes

Guitar. Federico García Lorca. InPK-6, *tr. by* Keith Waldrop

Guitar. David St. John. InvLad

Guitar, The. Federico García Lorca. SpanPo, *tr. by* Rachel Benson and Robert O'Brien

Guitar / makes dreams cry, The. Six Strings, The. Federico García Lorca. RB, *tr. by* Donald Hall

Guitarist Tunes Up, The. Frances Darwin Cornford. SoSe-8

Gularwundul's Wish. Kevin Gilbert. IBA

Gulf. Dhabya Khamees. PoArWo, *tr. by* Clarissa C. Burt

Gulf. Marion Lomax. NeBl

Gulf, The. Denise Levertov. NNaP

Gulf, The. Derek Walcott. NoP-4; PoPoPo; PoetW

Gulf Coast Blues. Clarence Williams. NAAAL

Gulistan, The. Sadi [*or* Saadi *or* Sa'di].

  Alas! AWP, *tr. by* L. Cranmer-Byng

  Courage. AWP, *tr. by* Sir Edwin Arnold

  Dancer, The. AWP, *tr. by* Sir Edward Arnold

  Friendship. AWP, *tr. by* L. Cranmer-Byng

  Gift of Speech, The. AWP, *tr. by* L. Cranmer-Byng

  Great Physician, The. AWP, *tr. by* Sir Edward Arnold

  He Hath No Parallel. AWP, *tr. by* L. Cranmer-Byng

  Help. AWP, *tr. by* Sir Edwin Arnold

  Love's Last Resource. AWP, *tr. by* L. Cranmer-Byng

  Mesnevi. AWP, *tr. by* L. Cranmer-Byng

  On the Deception of Appearances. AWP, *tr. by* L. Cranmer-Byng

  Sooth-Sayer, The. AWP, *tr. by* Sir Edwin Arnold

  Take the Crust. AWP, *tr. by* L. Cranmer-Byng

  Wealth. AWP, *tr. by* Sir Edwin Arnold

Gull flies low across the darkening bay, A. Nocturne. James McAuley. BMAP

Gull's Flight, The. Nigel Roberts. NOBAu

Gull Goes Up, A. Léonie Adams. OWoS

Gull inch-perfect over water, The. Louise Herlin. MFP, *tr. by* Martin Sorrell

Gull inch-perfect over water, the busy crane, The. Gull inch-perfect over water, The. Louise Herlin. MFP, *tr. by* Martin Sorrell

Gull Lake set in the rolling prairie. At Gull Lake; August, 1810. Duncan Campbell Scott. NOBC

Gull on a post form. Gull on a Post. Jeremy Hooker. AngWePo

Gull rides on the ripples of a dream, A. Walk in Late Summer, A. Theodore Roethke. APT-2

Gull shanty red rot. Vase of the Universe, The. Edwin Torres. HeMarv

Gull shrieks guided us, The. Seagulls. Judith Herzberg. TuT, *tr. by* Greg Delanty

Gull, up close, A. Seagulls. John Updike. OWoS

Gulling[e] Sonnets, The. Sir John Davies. Son

  "As when the bright[e] Crulean firmament." NoSic

  "My case is this." NoSic

  "Sacred muse that first[e] made love divine [*or* devine], The." NoSic; OxBSo; PBRV

  "What eagle can beho[u]ld her sunbright[e] eye." NoSic

Gulliver. Sylvia Plath. NOBA

Gulliver Plays Cards. Nikolai Semionovich Tikhonov. TCRP, *tr. by* Michael Frayn

Gulls. Jorie Graham. BAP-01

Gulls. William Carlos Williams. OxBA

Haidée and Juan carpeted their feet. Byron. NOBRP *Fr.* Don Juan.

Haif hairt in hairt ye hairt of hairtis haill. *Unknown.* EMWP

Haiku. Lenard D. Moore. SpirFl

Haiku. Sonia Sanchez. ISC

Haiku Ambulance. Richard Brautigan. InPK-6

Haiku: "August heat." Gerald Vizenor. VoR

Haiku: "Bitter morning, A." J. W. Hackett. HA

Haiku: "Coming from the woods." Richard Wright. KaS

Haiku: "Eastern guard tower." Etheridge Knight. BPo; ESEAA; TAP

Haiku: "Fallen flowers rise." Arakida Moritaké. SoSe-8, *tr. by* Harold G. Henderson

Haiku: "Falling flower, The." Arakida Moritaké. SoSe-8, *tr. by* Babette Deutsch

Haiku: "Green cockleburs, The." Richard Wright. KaS

Haiku: "Just enough of rain." Richard Wright. APT-2

Haiku: "Lightning flashes, The!" Basho. SoSe-8, *tr. by* Earl Miner

Haiku: "Lightning gleam, A." Basho. SoSe-8, *tr. by* Harold G. Henderson

Haiku #3. Kim C. Lee. InTrad

Haiku: "Was it yesterday." Sonia Sanchez. FFC

Haiku: "Your voice unwrapping." Sonia Sanchez. FFC

Hail, aged God who lookest on thy Father. *Unknown.* AWP *Fr.* Book of the Dead.

Hail and beware the dead who will talk life until you are blue. Newly Discovered "Homeric" Hymn, A. Charles Olson. NeAP; NoAM; PoM

Hail beauteous Chiswick! hail, sequestered seat! Thomas Maurice. OBGa *Fr.* Richmond Hill.

Hail, beauteous stranger of the grove [*or* wood]! To the Cuckoo. Michael Bruce. OBEV

Hail, Blushing Goddess, Beauteous Spring! Esther Vanhomrigh. LW

Hail, curious wights! to whom so fair. To the Virtuosos. William Shenstone. ECEV

Hail! Dawn is shining glory doing. Kilaben Bay Song. *Unknown.* NOBAu, *tr. by* Perce Haslam

Hail, Derwent's beauteous pride! Ode to Borrowdale in Cumberland. Amelia Alderson Opie. RWP

Hail, Devon! In thy bosom let me rest. Written in Devonshire, Near the Dart. Anne Batten Cristall. RWP

Hail, Dionysos. Dudley Randall. BPo

Hail, ever-pleasing Solitude! Hymn on Solitude. James Thomson. NOEC

Hail, fair youth, who seeks no bribe. To an English Boy. Hilary. CAGL, *tr. by* John Boswell

Hail Flag of the Union! Hail Flag of the free! Stars and Stripes. Mary Weston Fordham. CBWP-2

Hail, forest nymphs, daughters of the river. Moiro. GrAn

Hail, gentle spirits, who with magic wing. To Dreams. Mary Julia Young. CenSon

Hail! gentle youth, and do not deem me rude. Lines: To a Young Gentleman of Surpassing Beauty. Ellen Johnston. VWP

Hail, glorious day; mayst thou be writ in gold. Simon Ford. NOSC *Fr.* London's Resurrection.

HAIL graceful morning of eternal day. To the Blessed Virgin. William Alabaster. NoSic

Hail, happy bride, for thou art truly blest! On the Death of Mrs. Bowes. Lady Mary Wortley Montagu. BoWoP; LW

Hail, happy day, when smiling like the morn. To the Right Honourable William, Earl of Dartmouth, His Majesty's Principal Secretary of State for North America. Phillis Wheatley. NAAAL; NAAL-5; NALW

Hail, happy lot of the laborious man. Poverty, in Imitation of Milton. Samuel Jones. NOEC

Hail, happy saint, on thine immortal throne. On the Death of the Rev. Mr. George Whitefield, 1770. Phillis Wheatley. NAAL-2v1; NAAL-3; NAAL-5; SacPr

Hail, happy virgin! of celestial race. To Almystrea, on her Divine Works. Elizabeth Thomas. ECWP; EMWP

Hail, Holy Land. Thomas Tillam. *See* Upon the First Sight of New England, June 29, 1638

Hail, holy Lead!—of human feuds the great. Ambrose Bierce. APN-2; OBAL *Fr.* Devil's Dictionary, The.

Hail holy Light, ofspring [*or* offspring] of Heav'n [*or* Heaven] first-born. John Milton. NAEL-5v1; NAEL-6v1; OxBEV; PeECV; SCV; TOF *Fr.* Paradise Lost.

Hail Ihesu, my creator, of the sorrowing, medicine! Cantus Amoris 2. Richard Rolle of Hampole. SacPr

Hail Matrimony, made of Love! William Blake. OxBEV *Fr.* Island in the Moon, An.

Hail, May Day, dedicated to holy delights, to joy as full as unadulterated. May Morning. George Buchanan. PBRV

Hail, mediocrity, beneath whose spell. Roy Campbell. MoBrPo *Fr.* Georgiad, The.

Hail, meek-eyed maiden, clad in sober grey. Ode to Evening. Joseph Warton. OxAEP-1

Hail Mother full of grace power is with thee. Jennifer Berezan. HW

Hail, Oh Hail to the King. Beatrice Quickenden. AH

Hail, old patrician trees, so great and good! Abraham Cowley. BASC

Hail Our Incarnate God! William Duke. AH

Hail! Oure patron and lady of erthe. Salve Regina. *Unknown.* MiEL

Hail peaceful Shade, whose sacred verdant side. Alicia D'Anvers. NOSC *Fr.* Academia; or The Humours of the University of Oxford.

Hail, Priapus, primal father. Corpus Inscriptionum Latinarum 14.3565. *Unknown.* PriapPo, *tr. by* Richard W. Hooper

Hail, Queen of Heaven. *Unknown.* OxBSP

Hail! Richmond, hail! thy matchless beauties. *Unknown.* OBGa *Fr.* Richmond Gardens: A Poem.

Hail, Roma, daughter of Ares. Melinno. SaLy, *tr. by* Diane Rayor

Hail, sacred shades! cool, leafy house! Upon the Priory Grove, His Usual Retirement. Henry Vaughan. BeJo

Hail, Sana'i, the Moon of the Soul. Amin Al-Rihani. GraLe *Fr.* Chant of Mystics, A.

Hail, Silimela! Pleiades, The. S. E. K. Mqhayi. PeSAV, *tr. by* Jeff Opland

Hail, sister springs! Weeper, The. Richard Crashaw. FSCP

Hail South Australia! blessed clime. Hail South Australia! *Unknown.* NOBAu

Hail! the Glorious Golden City. Felix Adler. AH

Hail then ye daring few! who proudly soar. Henry James Pye. NOEC *Fr.* Aerophorion.

Hail, thou Great God in thy Boat. *Unknown.* AWP *Fr.* Book of the Dead.

Hail, Thou my Native Soil. William Browne (1591–1643). OxAEP-1 *Fr.* Britannia's Pastorals.

Hail, thou once despised Jesus. *Unknown.* SacPr

Hail, thou sole Empress of the Land of wit. Pindarick to Mrs. Behn on her Poem on the Coronation, A. *Unknown.* EMWP

Hail, thou who shinest from the moon. *Unknown.* AWP *Fr.* Book of the Dead.

Hail to *Clarinda*, dear Euterpe Hail. To Mrs S. F. on Her Poems. Mary Pix. EMWP

Hail to the black! (LL) Song of the Smoke, The. William Edward Burghardt DuBois. ISC; SSLK; UnPo

Hail to the Brightness of Zion's Glad Morning. Thomas Hastings. AH

Hail to the coming time! (LL) Fine Old English Gentleman; New Version, The. Charles Dickens. NOBVV; OBSV

Hail to the fields—with Dwellings sprinkled o'er. William Wordsworth. CenSon *Fr.* River Duddon [A Series of Sonnets], The.

Hail to the hero! Ernest Crosby. FaBoWar *Fr.* War and Hell.

Hail to the Joyous Day. Royall Tyler. AH

Hail to the Queen. *Unknown.* AH

Hail to the Sabbath Day. Stephen Greenleaf Bulfinch. AH

Hail to the sage divine of Milan's plains! On Hearing That Torture Was Suppressed throughout the Austrian Dominions. John Codrington Bampfylde. Son

Hail to Thee, Blithe Owl. Ring Lardner. OBAL

Hail to thee, blithe Spirit! To a Skylark. Shelley. BRP; FHYEP; GTBS-P; HAP; NAEL-5v2; NAEL-6v2; NOBRP; NoP-4; OBEV; OWoS; OxAEP-2; SCGP; TFi

Hail to thee, merciful King, Saint Ladislas! Lay of King Saint Ladislas, The. *Unknown.* IQMS, *tr. by* Anthony Edkins

Hail to thy pencil! Well its glowing art. To Mr. Opie, On His Having Painted for Me the Picture of Mrs Twiss. Amelia Alderson Opie. RWP

Hail to thy puggy nose, my Darling. Natal Address to My Child, March 19th 1844, A. Eliza Ogilvy. VWP

Hail, Tranquil Hour of Closing Day. Leonard Bacon. AH

Hail, universal mother! lightly rest. Ovid. NOBRP, *tr. by* John Herman Merivale *Fr.* Metamorphoses.

Hail Wedded Love! Jay Macpherson. MoCV

Hail, ye indomitable heroes, hail! Crimean Heroes, The. Walter Savage Landor. FaBoWar

Haile from the dead, or from eternity. Lines on a Purple Cap Received as a Present from My Brother. George Alsop. SCAP

Haile gracefull morning of eternall Daye. William Alabaster. ESCV *Fr.* Divine Meditations.

Hail[e] great Redeemer, man, and God, all hail[e]. Hymn[e] to Our Saviour on the Cross[e], A. George Chapman. PeECV

Hail[e], sister springs! Saint Mary Magdalene or The Weeper. Richard Crashaw. BASC; ChIV-2; GeHe; MeLP

Haill clanjamfrie!, The. (LL) Bonnie Broukit Bairn, The. Hugh MacDiarmid. FaBoCh; FaBoVe; HAP; HarvBoo; NePenScot

Hailstone, The. Peter Didsbury. NPeEn

Hailstones. Basho. EH, *tr. by* Robert Hass

Hailstones falling like sharp blue sky chips. Crazy Horse Monument. Peter Blue Cloud. HATNAP; UnSA

Hailstorm in May. Gerard Manley Hopkins. Spl

Hain't no use to weep, hain't no use to moan. Down in the Lonesome Garden. *Unknown*. BPo

Hair. Yusuf Al-Sa'igh. MAP, *tr. by* Diana Der Hovanessian and Salma Khadra Jayyusi

Hair. Rémy de Gourmont. AWP, *tr. by* Jethro Bithell

Hair. Nina Iskrenko. ItGoST, *tr. by* Patrick Henry, John High and Katya Olmsted

Hair. Breda Sullivan. Prnts

Hair and bacon grease, pearl button. Genie's Prayer Under the Kitchen Sink. Rita Dove. RACG

Hair beneath, The. Stand farther [*or* further] off then! Go. (LL) Elizabeth Barrett Browning. CenSon; LW; NALW; PEW; VWP *Fr.* Sonnets from the Portuguese.

Hair-bowed Rose, deep in lush grass of the river. Profile of Rose. Glyn Jones. OBWVE

Hair—braided chestnut. Portrait in Georgia. Jean Toomer. APT-2; NoP-4

Hair fanning out, he'll float upside down. Necromancy: The Last Days of Brian Jones, 1968. David Wojahn. SwNoth

Hair half gone grey, half blinded. Grandmother of Russian Poetry: A Self-Portrait, The. Vera Merkureva. ARWW, *tr. by* Catriona Kelly

Hair, in my comb's teeth. Clement Hoyt. HA

Hair is heaven's water flowing eerily over us. Hair Poem. Bill Knott. SPE

Hair oil, boiled sweets, chalk dust, squid's ink. Caliban's Books. Michael Donaghy. EmeKit

Hair on our shoulders dangles and shines, The. (LL) Natives, The. David Mura. CDa; WeW-3

Hair on your body, The. David Hart. NewEx

Hair ornament of the sun, The. Takajo Mitsuhashi. BoWoP

Hair Poem. Bill Knott. SPE

Hair that I gloss down. Just Like the Legend. Léon Damas. PFTM-1

Hair the color of. Powwow. Carroll Arnett. LTA

Hair Tonic. Gisèle Prassinos. PFTM-1

Hair-Tonic Bottle, The. Ben King. OBAL

Hair unbound, in this. Akiko Yosano. OHMPJ

Hair which boldly speaks in Bernice's despite, A. Description of Perfect Beauty. Christian Hofmann von Hofmannswaldau. GePo, *tr. by* George C. Schoolfield

Hairband, homespun, opera-hat, afghan. Motley. Peter Davison. NBLV

Hairbrush, The. Sandra Hochman. YaYoPo

Haircut. Karl Shapiro. TwCP

Hairdo and ornaments all the latest fashion. Beginning of Spring—A Stroll with My Wife. Hsü Chün-ch'ien. CoBCP, *tr. by* Burton Watson

Hairdresser's, The. Pierre McOrlan. MFP, *tr. by* Martin Sorrell

Hairdressing. Patricia Pogson. NLP

Hairline Fracture, A. Amy Clampitt. NoAM

Hairs less in sight, or any hairs but these! (LL) Pope. EBNV; OxAEP-1 *Fr.* Rape of the Lock, The; an Heroi-Comical Poem.

Hairs rush out of his nose and ears. Old Man. Geoffrey Holloway. NLP

Hairy Toe, The. *Unknown*. OBSP

Haiseau has yet another thing. Ring That Controlled Erections, The. *Unknown*. NAWM-7v1, *tr. by* Ned Dubin

Haiti. Chiqui Vicioso. TANSG, *tr. by* Daisy Cocco De Filippis

Hajj Abbass Habhab: my grandfather. After the Funeral of Assam Hamady. Sam Hamod. GraLe

Haka: Hinemotu. Te Aomuhurangi te Maaka. PeNZ

Haka: The Blossoming. Pita Sharples. PeNZ, *tr. by* Pita Sharples

Haka: The Feathered Albatross. Muru Walters. PeNZ, *tr. by the author*

Hakeldama. Zbigniew Herbert. GI, *tr. by* John Carpenter

Hako, The. *Unknown*.

Mother Corn Assumes Leadership.

"Mother with the life-giving power now comes." APN-2

Song of the Promise of the Buffalo. APN-2, *tr. by* Alice C. Fletcher

Song to the Trees and Streams. APN-2, *tr. by* Alice C. Fletcher

Halcion. R. T. Smith. AWTN

Halcyon. "H. D."

"I'm not here." MoAmPo

Halcyon Days. Jim Barnes. CDW; VCAP

Halcyon Days. Walt Whitman. OxBA

Half. Julia Park Rodrigues. TWW

Half a bar, half a bar. Village Choir, The. *Unknown*. UV

Half a basin. Two Prison Poems. Ho Chi Minh. PoetW, *tr. by* Burton Raffel

Half a Double Sonnet. Mary Jo Salter. MakPoe

Half a league, half a league. Tennyson. BRP; CABP; ChAP; FHYEP; FaBoWar; NAEL-5v2; NAEL-6v2; NOBVV; NoP-4; OBWP; OxAEP-2; OxBEV; PeVV; TFi; UV

Half a lifetime now, I've played my art on the stage. Tune: "Slow Chant." Ma Chih-yüan. SuSp, *tr. by* Sherwin S. S. Fu

Half afraid to break a promise. Michael Hartnett. NOIV *Fr.* Farewell to English, A.

Half an hour after our heads were cut off. (LL) She and I. Norman Cameron. OxBSP; RB

Half an hour north of Grand Central. In Cheever Country. Dana Gioia. GM

Half-and-half affair, I grew from the union, A. Peter Davison. YaYoPo *Fr.* Breaking of the Day, The.

Half-and-Half Song, The. Li Mi-an. ColAnChi, *tr. by* Lin Yutang

Half asleep. Fishing the Dream. Mike Delp. MoASP

Half Asleep. Gareth Owen. OTCP

Half asleep on the cold grass. For a Stone Girl at Sanchi. Gary Snyder. BB

Half-Ballad of Waterval. Rudyard Kipling. FaBoWar; PeSAV

Half-blind, hands shaking. Blues for Aunt Ruth. Norita Dittberner-Jax. MiVo

Half-blown Rose, The. Samuel Daniel. NoSic; SCGP *Fr.* To Delia.

Half-Breed. Cherríe Moraga. UnSA

Half-bridge over nothingness. Northhanger Ridge. Charles Wright. HCAP

Half-caste. John Agard. Oth

Half-Caste Girl. Judith Wright. NALW

Half Choakt ith' Dust of our lewd Town. Alicia D'Anvers. EMWP *Fr.* Oxford-Act, The.

Half close your eyelids, loosen your hair. He Thinks of Those Who Have Spoken Evil of His Beloved. W. B. Yeats. NoAM

Half cracked open, my hands are stained with it. (LL) West Willow. Reginald Shepherd. AmPoNex; IllVoic

"Half-cracked" to Higginson, living. I Am in Danger—Sir. Adrienne Rich. HCAP; HarvBoo; NAAL-5; NALW; NOBA

Half-dead comatose, The. They Do Not Go Gentle. Basil T. Paquet. CDa

Half heedlessly ironical. (LL) At the Cavour. Arthur Symons. NOBVV; NPeEn; OxBSP

Half-hidden in a graveyard. Stranger, The. Walter De la Mare. OxBTC

Half-high, or tapering off at Summer's end. (LL) Frederick Goddard Tuckerman. APN-2; NoP-4; Son *Fr.* Sonnets.

Half in a dream. Kenneth Rexroth. APSN; APT-2 *Fr.* Love Poems of Marichiko, The.

Half in the Family, Half Out. Po Chü-i. CoBCP, *tr. by* Burton Watson

Half into the mountains—a mountain monastery. Climbing to a Mountain Monastery. Tu Hsün-ho. SuSp, *tr. by* Edward H. Schafer

Half Measures. Thomas McGrath. BodElec

Half-Measures. Yevgeny Aleksandrovich Yevtushenko [*or* Evtushenko]. TCRP, *tr. by* Albert C. Todd

Half-moon hangs on sparse *wu-t'ung* tree. Tune: "Song of Divination." Su Tung-p'o (Su Shih). SuSp, *tr. by* Eugene Eoyang

Half my friends are dead. Sea Canes. Derek Walcott. HeIP-4

Half-numb, guzzling bourbon and Coke from coffee mugs. Body and Soul. B. H. Fairchild. MoASP

Half of America doubtless has the whole. Line Drive Caught by the Grace of God. Linda Gregerson. ExTi; MoASP

Half of his / body hung in. Spirits. Víctor Hernández Cruz. PueRic

Half of Life. Friedrich Hölderlin. OBVE

Half of Life, The. Friedrich Hölderlin. NAWM-7v2, *tr. by* Christopher Middleton

Half of my life is gone, and I have let. Mezzo Cammin. Henry Wadsworth Longfellow. APN-1; NAAL-2v1; NAAL-3; NCAP; PoE; TAP; TCAPo

Half of our borders, rivers and mountains were gone. In the Home of the Scholar Wu Su-chiang. Wu Tsao. BoWoP; WPOW

Half of the minnows. J. W. Hackett. HA

Half of the people in the world. Yehuda Amichai [*or* Amikhai]. FIT, *tr. by* Robert Friend

Half-past eight Don Pullen just arrived. Don Pullen at the Zanzibar Blue Jazz Cafe, 1994. Major L. Jackson. SpirFl

Half Past Four, October. Anna Hajnal. BoWoP, *tr. by* Daniel Hoffman

Half past nine—high time for supper. In Praise of Cocoa, Cupid's Nightcap. Stanley J. Sharpless. NBLV; PeLV

Half-past three in the morning! Louise on the Door-Step. Charles MacKay. EBVV

Half-recluse, The. Po Chü-i. ChiP, *tr. by* Arthur Waley

Half remembering, yet not remembering, just waked up from a dream. Song on Being Too Lazy to Get Up. Shao Yung. CoBCP, *tr. by* Burton Watson

Half-Season. Simone Yoyotte. SurWo, *tr. by* Myrna Bell Rochester

Half Sigh. *Unknown*. PBA, *tr. by* Miriam Koshl

Half-sleeping, / my body pulls toward yours. Jane Hirshfield. PasH

Half spirit, the older. Jest, The. Austin Clarke. BIrV

Half squatter, half tenant (no rent). Manuelzinho. Elizabeth Bishop. FaBoWP

Half the spring has gone by since our parting. Tune: "Pure Serene Music." Li Yü. SuSp, *tr. by* Daniel Bryant

Half the time they munched the grass, and all the time they lay. Cows. James Reeves. NOxBChV; NTCP

Half-way across the racing river. Midstream. Dennis Joseph Enright. OxBC

Half-way down you lose the sense of falling. Peacetime. Peter McDonald. ModIr

Half-way, for one commandment broken. A. E. Housman. OxBSP

Half-Way Pause, A. Dante Gabriel Rossetti. NOBVV; OxBEV

Half-way through the night. Ghazal. Hafiz [or Hafez]. WoPoe, tr. by Geoffrey Squires

Halflife. Friedrich Hölderlin. WoPoe, tr. by Vyt Bakaitis

Halftime. Adam Lefevre. MoASP

Halfway Street, Sidcup. Fleur Adcock. Spl

Halfway through an afternoon. Hot Comb. Natasha Trethewey. SpirFl

Halfway Through the Book I'm Writing. Lynn Emanuel. ExTi

Halibut Cove Harvest. Kenneth Leslie. NOBC

Halieutica. Oppian, tr. by William Diaper.

  "Lamprey, glowing with uncommon fires, The." ECEV; OBVE

  Sex-life of Fish, The. ECEV; OBVE

  (Eels and Tortoises.) NOEC

  (Loves of the Fishes, The.) NPeEn

  Loves of the Tortoise, The. NPeEn

  "When they in throngs a safe retirement seek." OBVE

Hall by the water where flowers grow dense, A. Occasional Poem, An. Ssu-k'ung Shu. SuSp, tr. by Irving Y. Lo

Hall of Ifor Hael, The. Evan Evans. OBWVE, tr. by Gwyn Williams

Hall of the Guardian God. Muso Soseki. EaWin, tr. by W. S. Merwin

Hallaig. Sorley MacLean (Somhairle MacGill-Eain). HarvBoo; NPeEn; NePenScot; WoPoe

Hallelujah! Vincent Youmans. ReLy

Hallelujah, Bum Again. Unknown. GM

Hallelujah! Praise the Lord. Edwin Francis Hatfield. AH

Hallelujah Terrible. Matthew Lippman. BAP-97

"Hallelujah!" was the only observation. Hallelujah! A. E. Housman. PeLV

Halley's Comet. Norman Nicholson. NoP-4

Halley's Comet crossed the jungle sky. Talvikki Ansel. YaYoPo Fr. In Fragments, In Streams.

Hallo My Fancy. William Cleland. OxBoLi

Hallow days o Yule are come, The. Wife of Usher's Well, The. Unknown. ESPB

Hallow-Fair. Robert Fergusson. OxBS

Hallow the threshold, crown the posts anew! On the Queen's Return from the Low Countries. William Cartwright. OBEV

Hallowe'en. Lizelia Augusta Jenkins Moorer. CBWP-3

Hallowe'en mask, A. Clement Hoyt. HA

Hallowed be the Sabbaoth. Epitaph in St. Olave's, Southwark, on Mr. Munday. Unknown. OxBoLi

Hallowed be Thy name—Halleluiah! Human Cry, The. Tennyson. InvLi

Halloween. Robert Burns. NOBRP; TreFP

Hallowing of Hell, The. Robin Morgan.

  "And blessed be the women who get you through." GLP

Hallucinogenic Bullfighter. Juan Felipe Herrera. BodElec

Halsted Street Car. Carl Sandburg. IllVoic; NAAL-2v2

Halt! Shoulder arms! Recover! As you were! Sonnet to Britain. William Edmonstoune [or Edmondstoune] Aytoun. OxBSo

Halted against the shade of a last hill. Spring Offensive. Wilfred Owen. GTBS-P; PeFWW

Haltersick's Song. John Pickering [or Pikerying]. NoSic Fr. Horestes.

Hamasah. Hittan of Tayyi.

  His Children. AWP

Hamatreya. Ralph Waldo Emerson. APN-1; NAAL-3; NCAP; TCAPo

Hambone and the Heart, The. Dame Edith Sitwell. OBMV

Hamburg: the clock hands move upon their star. Galaxies. Alan Gould. NOBAu

Hamburger. August Kleinzahler. PmAP

Hamburger Hill. Michael McClintock. HA Fr. Vietnam.

Hame came our goodman. Our Goodman. Unknown. ESPB

Hame, Hame, Hame. Allan Cunningham. OBEV

Hameed. Salah Niyazi [or Niazi]. MAP, tr. by Charles Doria and Lena Jayyusi

Hamelin Town's in Brunswick. Robert Browning. EBNV; FaBoCh; NOxBChV; OBNV; OBSP; PeLV

Hamilton Greene. Edgar Lee Masters. NoAM; OxBA; PAI Fr. Spoon River Anthology.

Hamlen Brook. Richard Wilbur. HarvBoo; VCAP; WeW-3

Hamlet. Ciaran Carson. FaBoVe; ModIr; PNI

Hamlet. Boris Leonidovich Pasternak. GI; WoPoe, tr. by Nina Kossman

Hamlet. Boris Leonidovich Pasternak. TCRP

(Buzz subsides. I have come on stage, The.) AF

Hamlet. William Shakespeare. NAWM-5v1

  "Angels and ministers of grace defend us!" EBEV; OxAEP-1

  "Ay, so, God be wi' ye! Now I am alone." OxAEP-1

  Frailty, Thy Name is Woman. OxAEP-1; SCV

  "It faded on the crowing of the cock." PeECV; TOF

  "Look here, upon this picture, and on this." OxAEP-1

  "Mote it is to trouble the mind's eye, A." OxAEP-1

  "My lord, as I was sewing in my closet." OxAEP-1

  "O! my offense is rank, it smells to heaven." OxAEP-1

  Ophelia's Death. OxAEP-1; RB

  Ophelia's Song. EBEV; EnLoPo; NoSic; PoRA; SCGP

  Ophelia's Songs, 2 ("And will he not come again"). NoSic

  Song: "Tomorrow is Saint Valentine's Day." EnLoPo; NoSic; NTCP

  "To be, or not to be, that is the question." OxAEP-1; OxBEV; TreFP; UV

  "What ceremony else?" EBEV

  "Why, let the strucken deer go weep." NoSic

Hamlet. Stanley J. Sharpless. NBLV; PeLi

Hamlet. Yevgeny [or Evgenii] Mikhailovich Vinokurov. TCRP, tr. by Daniel Weissbort

Hamlet's Lost Monologue. László Kálnoky. IQMS, tr. by Kenneth McRobbie and Zita McRobbie

Hammer, hammer. Hammer and Anvil. John Oxenham. SacPr

Hammer-Song. Unknown. FaBoVe

Hammer struck my nail, instead of nail, The. Almanac. May Swenson. APT-2

Hammers, The. Ralph Hodgson. MoBrPo; NOBE; OxBTC

Hammers pound there above. Along Galeana Street. Octavio Paz. VCWP, tr. by Elizabeth Bishop

Hammock. Blaise Cendrars. CuPo

Hammock was a blue cocoon, The. Dream of Dying, A. Leslie Monsour. FFC

Hamnavoe Market. George Mackay Brown. EmeKit; NePenScot

Hampstead Highgate Finchley Hendon Muswell hill: rage loud. William Blake. NOBRP Fr. Jerusalem; The Emanation of the Giant Albion.

Hampton Court. Antonio Cisneros. TCLAP, tr. by William Rowe Fr. Loneliness.

Hampton Court. Pope. EBNV; OBSV; OxBoLi Fr. Rape of the Lock, The; an Heroi-Comical Poem.

Hamra Night. Sa'di Yusuf. FaBoWar, tr. by Abdullah Al-Udhari

Han court honors clever eunuchs, The. Inscription on a Tree atop mount Sacrifice (Ssu Shan) and Sent to Censor Ch'iao. Ch'en Tzu-ang. SuSp, tr. by Geoffrey R. Waters

Han-shan. Unknown. CoBCP, tr. by Burton Watson

Hand. Robert E. Penn. WiU

Hand. Edouard Roditi. SPE

Hand. Shinkichi Takahashi. ZenPo, tr. by Takashi Ikemoto and Lucien Stryk

Hand, The. Brian Fawcett. NOBC

Hand, The. Frank Lima. BodElec

Hand, The. Howard Moss. TAP

Hand, The. Ronald Stuart Thomas. NOCV; OxBC

Hand a shade of moonlight on the pillow, The. Non Ti Fidar. Louis Zukofsky. VGW

Hand and Foot, The [or Hand and the Foot, The]. Jones Very. APN-1; OxBA; SacPr; TAP

Hand appeared out of the earth, A. Vasco [or Vasko] Popa. PoSu Fr. Quartz Pebble, The.

Hand burns resinous in the evening sky, The. Egyptian Register. "Ern Malley." BMAP

Hand by Hand We Shall Us Take. Unknown. OHMEL; SacPr

Hand-clapping Rhyme. Unknown. NTCP

Hand for Some Others, A. Geoffrey Holloway. NLP

Hand Further, The. Clark Coolidge. PmAP

Hand has her hair, A. Libido. Larissa Szporluk. AmPoNex

Hand in Hand; a Song. Shen Yüeh. SuSp, tr. by Richard B. Mather

Hand in the breast pocket, The. (LL) Marriage. Marianne Craig Moore. APT-1; ColAP; NALW; NOBA

Hand is all heart, The. It hops around like a toad to prove its. Hand, The. Frank Lima. BodElec

Hand Me Down Blues. Calvin Forbes. GT

Hand Mirror. Daisy Zamora. LoL, tr. by Barbara Paschke

Hand-Mirror, A. Walt Whitman. NAAL-2v1; NAAL-3; OxBA; PoPoPo

Hand moves, and the fire's whirling takes different shapes, A. Singing Image of Fire. Kukai. EnlH, tr. by Stephen Mitchell

Hand of Art here torpid lies, The. Epitaph on William Hogarth, An. Samuel Johnson. EBEV

Hand of Snapshots, A. Louis MacNeice.

  Once-in-Passing, The. ModIr

Hand of Solo, A. Thomas Kinsella. CIP-2; NOIV

Hand of the Lord held me transported, The. Bible, *O.T.* WoPoe, *tr. by* David Curzon   *Fr.* Ezekiel.

Hand of the wind's own lover, The. Caroline von Günderode. Alejandra Pizarnik. SurWo, *tr. by* Natalie Kenvin

Hand on the Prophet, God. Birth (al-Maulid). Muhammad al-Mahdi Al-Majdhoub. MAP, *tr. by* Charles Doria and Salma Khadra Jayyusi

Hand over hungry hand. (LL) Climbing. Lucille Clifton. GT; LoL

Hand reaches for the cocktail, it's in darkness, The. Glass House. Diane Ward. PmAP

Hand reaches up, A. Ruth Latta. HA

Hand-Rolled Cigarettes. Yevgeny Aleksandrovich Yevtushenko [*or* Evtushenko]. VCWP

Hand's / writing the, A. Out of the Identical. Gustaf Sobin. PmAP

Hand-Shadows. Jarold Ramsey. NIP-4

Hand swinging the loops of paint—splashes—drips. Ode to Jackson Pollock. Michael McClure. PmAP

Hand tells the bowstring, The. Japanese Archery. Aleksander Wat. TOF, *tr. by* Richard Lourie

Hand that made us is Divine, The. (LL) Ode: "Spacious firmament on high, The." Joseph Addison. ChIV-1; ECEV; NOCV; NOEC; NPeEn; OxBEV; TOF

Hand That Rocks the Cradle Is the Hand That Rules the World, The. William Ross Wallace. ITBLP

Hand That Signed the Paper, The. Dylan Thomas. FaBoWar; MoBrPo; NOBE; NoAM; NoP-4; OBWP; RB; TCAWP

Hand-tinted, creamy olive skin. Taking It Back. Dixie Salazar. UnSA

Hand trembling towards hand; the amazing lights. Sonnet Reversed. Rupert Brooke. NOBL; OxBSo; PeLV

Hand triumphant to disaster. (LL) Parable of the Blind, The. William Carlos Williams. LCAP-2; SAmP

Hand triumphant to disaster. (LL) William Carlos Williams. LCAP-2; SAmP *Fr.* Pictures from Brueghel.

Handbag. Ruth Fainlight. OPOU

Handball Players at Brighton Beach, The. Irving Feldman. TaR

Handbell Choir, The. Jane Flanders. PBCAP

Handbook of Sex of the Plain Girl, The. Marian Yee. FSt

Handful of Dust, A. James Oppenheim. TrJP

Handful of red sand, from the hot clime, A. Sand of the Desert in an Hour-Glass. Henry Wadsworth Longfellow. NCAP

Handful of thatch, A. Old Hut. Muso Soseki. EaWin, *tr. by* W. S. Merwin

Handfuls of Wind. Laila Halaby. PoArWo

Handfuls of Wind. Yekhi'el [*or* Yehiel] Mar. MHP, *tr. by* Ruth Finer Mintz

Handicraft—After Marina Tsvetaeva. Duo Duo (Li Shizheng). PoetW, *tr. by* Michelle Yeh

Handing me the bread / dipped in the dish. Judas' Reproach. Nina Kossman. GI

Handing out anti-war leaflets at United Aircraft. Home Front. Bill Tremblay. CDa

Handle for the Flutist, A. Odia Ofeimun. HBAPE

Handless Clock. Raymond Radiguet. CuPo

Handling Sin. Robert Mannyng [*or* Manning]. Dancers of Colbek, The. PoE

Handloom, The. Judith Rodriguez. FaBoWP

Handmaid of Religion, The. Edgell Rickword. OBSV

Handnotes. Lyn Moir. Prnts

Hands. Bernard Dadié. NegPo, *tr. by* Ellen Conroy Kennedy

Hands. Donald Finkel. CoAP

Hands. Rin Ishigaki. WoPoe, *tr. by* Naoshi Koriyama and Edward Lueders

Hands. Edvard Kocbek. PoSu, *tr. by* Michael Scammell and Veno Taufer

Hands. Victor Serge. AF, *tr. by* James Brook

Hands, The. Tony Harrison. FaBoTw

Hands, The. Denise Levertov. NeAP; PoM

Hands explore tentatively, The. Feel of Hands, The. Thom Gunn. OxBEV

Hands full of sun are in spring's longing for you. Hands Full of Sun. David Rokeah [*or* Rokeakh]. MHP, *tr. by* Ruth Finer Mintz

Hands gripped hard on the desert, The. (LL) At the Bomb Testing Site. William Stafford. CoAP; NIL-7; NIP-4; NoAM; OBWP; RB

Hands have no tears to flow. (LL) Hand That Signed the Paper, The. Dylan Thomas. FaBoWar; MoBrPo; NOBE; NoAM; NoP-4; OBWP; RB; TCAWP

Hands in the Motion of Prayer. Sojourner Kincaid Rolle. GeoHom

Hands in the Wind. Ted Kooser. UrbNat

Hands make love to thigh, breast, clavicle. Euphony. Yusef Komunyakaa. ESEAA

Hands must touch and handle many things, The. New Man, The. Jones Very. APN-1; NOBA; TCAPo

Hands of God, The. D. H. Lawrence. ChIV-2; InvLi

Hands of Mary Joe, The. Mary Tallmountain. LoL

Hands of the Old Métis, The. Maurice Kilwein Guevara. NAPBL

Hands that eased my mother's labor drew, The. Rhyme for the Child as a Wet Dog. Judith Johnson Sherwin. TAP

Hands were yours, the arms were yours, The. Mark Strand. UnPo   *Fr.* Elegy for My Father.

HANDSAWWWWWWWWWWWWWWWWWW. Richard Lebovitz. KaS

Handsome friend, charming and kind. Beatrice [*or* Beatritz *or* Beatriz], Countess de Die [*or* Dia]. WPOW

Handsome Heart, The. Gerard Manley Hopkins. FaBoVe

Handsome horses O shiver and admire. Anaktoria. Sappho. WoPoe, *tr. by* Guy Davenport

Handsome Is as Handsome Does. James Wright (1927–80). BodElec

Handsome man is good to look at, A. Sappho. SaLy, *tr. by* Diane Rayor

Handsome young airman lay dying, A. Dying Airman, The. *Unknown.* OxBoLi; PeLV; RB

Handsome young monk in a wood, A. Limerick. *Unknown.* PeLi

Handsome youth with a golden whip, A. Tune: "Mountain Hawthorns." Yen Chi-tao. SuSp, *tr. by* James J. Y. Liu

Handy dandy. *Unknown.* OxNR

Handy Mole who plied no shovel, A. Christina Georgina Rossetti. VWP

Hang and swinging hang and swinging. Eugen Gomringer. PFTM-2, *tr. by* Jerome Rothenberg

Hang at my hand as I write now. Verses for a First Birthday. George Barker. MoBrPo

HANG him, base gull; I'll stab him, by the Lord. Boreas. Samuel Rowlands. NoSic

Hang it all, Robert Browning. Ezra Pound. APT-1; HAP; MoAmPo; NOBA; NoAM; OxBA   *Fr.* Cantos.

Hang my hearts, like a string of onions. (LL) Viktor Aleksandrovich Sosnora. TCRP; TCRusP, *tr. by* Daniel Weissbort

Hang new heavens with new birds, all be renewed. (LL) Shiva. Robinson Jeffers. NOBA; NoAM; Son

Hang Out the Flag. James Sterling Tippett. CA

Hang sorrow, cast away care. Song. *Unknown.* NOSC

Hang that day with black, that night, sinister, moonless. Hegesippus. GrAn

Hang up Hooks, and shears [*or* Sheers] to scare. Another Charme for Stables. Robert Herrick. BeJo

Hang Up the Baby's Stocking! *Unknown.* OBCP

Hang up those dull, and envious fools. Another. In Defense of Their Inconstancy [*or* Inconstancie]. A Song. Ben Jonson. BeJo

Hanging Fire. Audre Lorde. NIL-7; NIP-4; NoAM; NoP-4; PoPoPo; TRP

Hanging from the beam. Portent, The. Herman Melville. APN-2; CBCWP; ColAP; InPK-6; NAAL-2v1; NAAL-3; NCAP; NOBA; NoP-4; OBWP; OxBA; PoE; TAP; TCAPo

Hanging from the branches of a green / willow tree. Lady Ise. BoWoP

Hanging luggage disturbs shadows in the water. Ascend Lu-Shan. Pao Chao. ChinPo, *tr. by* Yip Wai-lim

Hanging Man, The. Sylvia Plath. HCAP; VCAP

Hanging on the wall, an iron face watches me. Mask, The. Irma McClaurin. BlSi

Hanging on the walls. Gallery of My Heart. King D. Kuka. VoR

Hanging out of the train, I. Autumn in Sigulda. Andrey [*or* Andrei] Andreievich Voznesensky [*or* Voznesenskii]. TCRP, *tr. by* W. H. Auden

Hanging / out under the bridge. Getting Across. Carter Revard. VoR

Hanging raindrops, The. Jakuren. OHPJ

Hanging, Zomba Central Prison, A. Frank Mkalawile Chipasula. PeSAV

Hangman. Gunnar Ekelof. PFTM-1

Hangman. Philip Stephens. AmPoNex

Hangman's Love Song, The. Stanley Moss. VGW

Hangman's Room, The. János Pilinszky. PoSu, *tr. by* Peter Jay

Hangman / what will you do with my arms? Hangman. Gunnar Ekelof. PFTM-1

Hangover. Jeffery Conway. WiU

Hangover Mass. X. J. Kennedy. DiPo

Hangs and cannot wake itself. (LL) Laser. A. R. Ammons. NAAL-2v2; NOBA; NoAM

Hangs on and howls, biting at air. (LL) Vacuum, The. Howard Nemerov. NIL-7; NIP-4; RB

Hangs. / whipped / blood. Biography. Imamu Amiri Baraka. TAP

Hank Mobley's. Cornelius Eady. SeSe

Hannah Bantry. *Unknown.* OxNR

Hannah's Song of Thanksgiving. Bible, *O.T.* AWP   *Fr.* First Samuel.

Hannah's Thanksgiving. Bible, *O.T.* BoWoP   *Fr.* First Samuel.

Hannibal ("Produce the urn that Hannibal contains"). Juvenal. OBVE, *tr. by* William Gifford   *Fr.* Satires.

Hannibal ("Put Hannibal i' th' scale"). Juvenal. OBVE, *tr. by* Henry Vaughan *Fr.* Satires.

Hannibal ("Throw Hannibal on the scales, how many pounds"). Juvenal. OBVE, *tr.* by Robert Lowell *Fr.* Satires.

Hannoi Hanna. Yusef Komunyakaa. SwNoth

Hans Breitmann as a Politician. Charles Godfrey Leland. "There's a liddle fact of hishdory vitch few hafe oondershtand." APN-2

Hans Breitmann gife a barty. Hans Breitmann's Party [*or* Barty]. Charles Godfrey Leland. NOBL; OBAL; OBCoV

Hans Carvel, Impotent and Old. Hans Carvel. Matthew Prior. PeLV

Hansel and Gretel. Barbara Noel-Scott. Prnts

Hansel, Gretel and Ruby Redlips. Anita Endrezze. HATNAP

Hap. Thomas Hardy. AWP; CABP; EBVV; GSo; MoBrPo; NAEL-5v2; NAEL-6v2; NoAM; NoP-4; OxBSo; Son

Hapless youth, whom fates averse had drove, A. Fable of the Young Man and His Cat, The. Christopher Pitt. ECEV

Happen you come on your own. Seven Sides and Seven Syllables. Edouard J. Maunick. CarOV; NegPo; VCWP, *tr.* by Carolyn Kizer

Happening, The. Eight Phases of Contemplation. Giusi Busceti. ItPo, *tr.* by Gayle Ridinger

Happening at Sordid Creek. Peter Porter. NoAM

Happening to pass a Roman Catholic church. Moment of Eschatological Doubt, A. Stanley J. Sharpless. PeLV

Happenings / (the telephone). (LL) Discrete Series. George Oppen. APT-2; PFTM-1

Happie is he, that from all Businesse cleere. Horace. *See* Happy is he, that from all business clear

Happie newyear god grant may ever stande. Sisters Newyearsgift from Elizabeth to Mary a Happie Mother of Good Children, The. Elizabeth Cromwell. EMWP

Happiest Day, the Happiest Hour, The. Edgar Allan Poe. OxBA

Happiness. Louise Glück. HarvBoo

Happiness. John Keble. TreFP

Happiness. Priscilla Leonard. PoToHe

Happiness. Alan Alexander Milne. AmFaPo; NOxBChV

Happiness. Robert Pollok. TreFP

Happiness. Carl Sandburg. IllVoic; OxBA

Happiness. Mihály Csokonai Vitéz. IQMS, *tr.* by Paul Tabori

Happiness amidst Troubles. Immanuel di Roma. TrJP, *tr.* by J. Chotzner

Happiness comes with success. I've Got a Pocketful of Dreams. Johnny Burke. ReLy

Happiness doesn't have any songs. Pain. Edith Södergran. WPOW, *tr.* by Samuel Charters

Happiness Is Just a Thing Called Joe. Harold Arlen. ReLy

Happiness is like a crystal. Happiness. Priscilla Leonard. PoToHe

Happiness Is the Art of Being Broken. Bruce Dawe. NoAM

Happiness is when. Tachibana Akemi. WoPoe, *tr.* by Burton Watson *Fr.* Thirty Tanka.

Happiness Makes Up in Height for What It Lacks in Length. Robert Frost. MoAmPo; SoSe-8

Happy about Being Old. Yüan Mei. CoBLCP, *tr.* by Jonathan Chaves

Happy and Contented in Your Hut. Francisco de Quevedo y Villegas. SpanPo, *tr.* by William M. Davis

Happy and mournful were the memories. Present, The. Maria Luisa Spaziani. CItWP, *tr.* by Cinzia Sartini Blum and Lara Trubowitz

Happy and Unhappy Families 1. Lisel Mueller. ExTi

Happy and Unhappy Families 2. Lisel Mueller. ExTi

Happy Arabia. Tom Matthews. PNI

Happy are men who yet before they are killed. Insensibility. Wilfred Owen. FaBoTw; FaBoWar; NoP-4; OBWP; OxAEP-2; OxBTC; PeFWW; PoWW

Happy are they and charmed in life. Memorial on the Slain at Chickamauga. Herman Melville. CBCWP

Happy are those of simple ways who still bless the light. Song Yet Song. Amir Gilbo'a. MHP, *tr.* by Ruth Finer Mintz

Happy are you, whom Quantock overlooks. William Diaper. NOEC; OBSV *Fr.* Brent; a Poem to Thomas Palmer Esq.

Happy As the Day Is Long. Ted Koehler. ReLy

Happy band on the hill slope, A. Battle of Waun Gaseg, The. Llywelyn ab y Moel. OBWVE, *tr.* by H. Idris Bell

Happy be they which will believe, and never seek the rest. (LL) Sir Philip Sidney. NoP-4; PoE *Fr.* Arcadia.

Happy Birthday. Frank Bidart. HCAP; VCAP

Happy bridegroom, the marriage that you prayed for. Sappho. SaLy, *tr.* by Diane Rayor

Happy choristers of air. Pastoral[l] Hymn[e], A. John Hall. MeLP

"Happy Christmas to all, and to all a good night!" (LL) Visit from St Nicholas, A. Clement Clarke Moore. APN-1; AiP; BRP; ChAP; ChrPo; NTCP; OBAL; OBCA; OBCP; OxIBACP; TCAPo; TFi

Happy Day Will Soon Appear, The. *Unknown.* AH

Happy Days Are Here Again. Jack Yellen. ReLy

Happy Ending. Fleur Adcock. LW

Happy Farmer, The. Edward Williams. "I live on my farm in a beautiful vale." AngWePo

Happy genius of my household?, The. (LL) Danse Russe. William Carlos Williams. AmFaPo; NoP-4

Happy have no notion how time passes, The. Brontë Sisters, The. Anna Semionovna Prismanova. ARWW, *tr.* by Catriona Kelly

Happy he who has found wisdom. Bible, *O.T.* HW *Fr.* Proverbs.

Happy he whose eyes have view'd. Boethius. OBVE *Fr.* Consolation of Philosophy, The ("De Consolacione Philosophie").

Happy Heart, A. Josephine D. Henderson Heard. CBWP-4

Happy Heart, The. Thomas Dekker. GTBS-P; HAP; NoSic; RB; SCGP; UnPo *Fr.* Pleasant Comedy of Patient Grissell [*or* Grissel *or* Grissill], The.

Happy Hour. Walid Bitar. KGB

Happy Hours that Hurry Away. Gutierre de Cetina. SpanPo, *tr.* by Kate Flores

Happy hunters are coming back, The. Lion Lion. Tom Raworth. PFTM-2

Happy insect, what can be. Grasshopper, The. Abraham Cowley. AWP; BASC; BeJo; NOSC; OBVE; OxAEP-1

Happy Insensibility. John Keats. GTBS-P (Stanzas.) OBEV

Happy Is England! I Could Be Content. John Keats. CenSon; OxAEP-2

Happy is he given to sage disciplines. André Marie de Chénier. WoPoe, *tr.* by David Curzon and Jeffrey Fiskin *Fr.* Elegies.

Happy is he, that from all business clear. Horace. BASC, *tr.* by Ben Jonson *Fr.* Epodes.

Happy is the day which saw me when I was joined to my boyfriend. Pacifico Massimi. CAGL, *tr.* by James J. Wilhelm *Fr.* Hecateleguim.

Happy Is the Man. Bible, *O.T.* TrJP *Fr.* Proverbs.

Happy Is the Man. Bible, *O.T.* *See* Psalms

Happy is the man whom Thou hast set apart. Psalm. "Yehoash." TrJP, *tr.* by Isidore Goldstick

Happy Life, A. Martial. OBVE, *tr.* by Sir Richard Fanshawe

Happy Life, A. Mildmay Fane, 2d Earl of Westmorland. BeJo (Happy Life (Martial X. xlvii), A.) NOSC

Happy Life, The. Martial. NOBE; NoSic; OBVE, *tr.* by Henry Howard, Earl of Surrey (Martial, the things that do attain.) NAEL-7v1 (Means to Attain the Happy Life, The.) FaBoEE; OBEV (My Friend, the Things That Do Attain.) NAEL-5v1; NAEL-6v1

Happy Life, The. William Thompson. ECEV

Happy Life of a Country Parson, The. Pope. UV

Happy Little Cripple, The. James Whitcomb Riley. "I'm thist a little crippled boy, an' never goin' to grow." VerBaPo

Happy lover who has come, A. Tennyson. NAEL-6v2 *Fr.* In Memoriam A. H. H.

Happy Man, A. Carphyllides. AWP, *tr.* by E. A. Robinson

Happy Man, A. *Var. authors.* AWP *Fr.* Variations of Greek Themes.

Happy me! o happy sheepe! Bible, *O.T.* *See* Lord is my shepherd; I shall not want, The

Happy men that lose their heads, The. Fantasia. Gilbert Keith Chesterton. SacPr

Happy moments tell me, pray. Birth of Time, The. Josephine D. Henderson Heard. CBWP-4

Happy New Year. Miguel Algarin. PueRic

Happy New Year, A. W. H. Auden. OBSV

Happy New Year, Anyway. Joanna Cole. NTCP

Happy one, who is almost / an idiot, The. Happy One, The. Paul Klee. PFTM-1

Happy Pair, A. Priscilla Jane Thompson. CBWP-2

Happy Pair, The. Sir Charles Sedley. Marriage and Money. OBSV

Happy people die whole, they are all dissolved in a moment, they have had what they wanted. Post Mortem. Robinson Jeffers. MoAmPo

Happy Returns! the children say. Grannie's Birthday. Eliza Ogilvy. VWP

Happy's the man whose pleasant labours with the lark. Ploughman, in Imitation of Milton, The. Samuel Jones. NOEC

Happy, Saviour, Would I Be. Edwin H. Nevin. AH

Happy shall he be, that taketh and dasheth thy little ones against the stone. (LL) Bible, *O.T.* AWP; NAWM-5v1; TrJP *Fr.* Psalms.

Happy, so she lived. (LL) Air: "The Love of a Woman." Robert Creeley. VCAP; VGW

Happy Swain, The. Ambrose Philips. EnLoPo

Happy talk / Keep talkin' happy talk. Happy Talk. Richard Rodgers. ReLy

Happy that first white age! when wee. Boethius. NOSC; OBVE; PAI, *tr.* by Henry Vaughan *Fr.* Consolation of Philosophy, The ("De Consolacione Philosophie").

Happy the hare at morning, for she cannot read. Cultural Presupposition, The. W. H. Auden. PAI

Happy the man which, far from city care. Second Epode of Horace Translated, The. Thomas Randolph. BASC

Happy the man, who free as air. Widower, The. Royall Tyler. OBAL

Happy the Man, who his whole time doth bound. Old Man of Verona, The. Claudian. AWP; OBVE, *tr. by* Abraham Cowley

Happy the man who, safe on shore. Hurricane, The. Philip Freneau. TAP; TCAPo

Happy the man, who, void of cares and strife. John Phillips. NOEC *Fr.* Splendid Shilling, The.

Happy the man whose wish and care. Ode on Solitude. Pope. AWP; FHYEP; HeIP-4; NAEL-5v1; NAEL-6v1; NIL-7; NOSC; PAI; PoRA; SacPr; SCGP

Happy the one who sighs for you by your side. Imitating an Ode by Sapho. Gertrudis Gomez de Avellaneda. BLPSL, *tr. by* Rene de Costa, Rigas Kappatos and Eleni Paidoussi

Happy the tree, that scarcely feels. Doom. "Rubén Dario." SpanPo, *tr. by* Kate Flores

Happy the wild birds that can soar. Unfair to Men. *Unknown.* OBWVE, *tr. by* Gwyn Jones

Happy those early days [*or* dayes]! when I. Retreat[e], The. Henry Vaughan. AWP; BASC; CABP; ClHu; ESCV; FSCP; GTBS-P; GeHe; HAP; InPK-6; MeLP; NAEL-5v1; NAEL-6v1; NAEL-7v1; NIP-4; NOBE; NOCV; NOSC; NPeEn; NoP-4; OBEV; OBWVE; OxBEV; PBRV; PeECV; PoE; PoRA; SCGP; TFi; TOF

Happy Thought. Robert Louis Stevenson. BRP; PWR; Spl

Happy Time, The. John Kander. ReLy

Happy to have these fish! Catch, The. Raymond Carver. MoASP

Happy, too happy was the world. Boethius. MLL *Fr.* Consolation of Philosophy, The ("De Consolacione Philosophie").

Happy Too Much. Boethius. CTC, *tr. by* Queen of England Elizabeth I *Fr.* Consolation of Philosophy, The ("De Consolacione Philosophie").

Happy traveler / Mosquito wick. Buson. ZenPo, *tr. by* Takashi Ikemoto and Lucien Stryk

Happy Warrior, The. Sir Herbert Read. FaBoWar; PeFWW

Happy were he could finish forth his fare. Happy Were He. Robert Devereux, 2d Earl of Essex. NoSic; OxBSP

Happy who like Ulysses, or that lord. Heureux Qui, comme Ulysse, A Fait un Beau Voyage. Joachim Du Bellay. AWP, *tr. by* Gilbert Keith Chesterton

Happy who near you sigh, for you alone. Verses Made by Sappho, Done from the Greek by Boyleau, and from the French by a Lady of Quality. Sappho. EMWP

Happy Workhouse and the Good Effects of Industry, The. John Dyer. NOEC *Fr.* Fleece, The.

"Happy ye leaves! whenas those lily hands." Edmund Spenser. *See* Amoretti

Happyer those times were, when the Flaxen clew. William Browne (1591–1643). PBRV *Fr.* Brittania's Pastorals Book 2.

Hara came and made off with my Gauri. Kamalākānta Bhattācārya. SinGod, *tr. by* Rachel Fell McDermott

Harangue on the Death of Hayyim Nahman Bialik. César Tiempo. TrJP, *tr. by* Donald Devenish Walsh

Harbach 1944. János Pilinszky. AF; HP; PoSu; WoPoe, *tr. by* Janos Csokits and Ted Hughes

Harbingers are come. See, see their mark, The. Forerunners, The. George Herbert. AngWePo; ESCV; GeHe; NAEL-5v1; NAEL-6v1; NAEL-7v1; NoP-4; TOF

Harbor, The. William Ellery Channing. APN-1

Harbor, The. Carl Sandburg. APT-1; ColAP; TAP

Harbor Dawn, The. Hart Crane. MoAmPo; NOBA; NoAM; OxBA *Fr.* Bridge, The.

Harbored inside a much-thumbed Joy of Cooking. Potatoes Coriander. Elise Paschen. SpudSo

Harbour Bridge, The. Thomas Hardy. NoAM

Harbour of Fowey, The. Sir Arthur Thomas Quiller-Couch. OBCoV

Harbour roars out, The. Creide's Lament for Cael. *Unknown.* NOIV

Hard Against the Soul. Dionne Brand.
"Then it is this simple. I felt the unordinary romance of." PoBW

Hard and Easy. Ferenc Kazinczy. IQMS, *tr. by* Watson Kirkconnell

Hard as hurdle arms, with a broth of goldish flue. Harry Ploughman. Gerard Manley Hopkins. EroLit; FaBoMo

Hard as mine with another man? (LL) Attempt at Jealousy, An. Marina Ivanovna Tsvetayeva [*or* Tsvetaeva]. OxBEV; TCRP; WoPoe, *tr. by* Elaine Feinstein

Hard, but you can polish it. Donald Justice. CRP *Fr.* Things.

Hard by the lilied Nile I saw. Thomas Lovell Beddoes. NOBVV; NPeEn; OxBEV; RB *Fr.* Last Man, The.

Hard by the tall elms and a wooded hill. Old Rustic Mill, The. George Sands Johnson. PWR

Hard calloused dreams. Wild Glee from Elsewhere. Joyce Mansour. SurWo

Hard captains of industry, The. Still Century. Tom Paulin. BiHa

Hard cold fire of the northerner, The. Belfast. Louis MacNeice. PeECV

Hard core nights are so. Kalamu ya Salaam. SpirFl *Fr.* New Orleans Haiku.

Hard Country. Philip Booth. CoAP

Hard Daddy. Langston Hughes. NAAAL

Hard Drive. Paul Muldoon. KGB

Hard energy, like the stars. (LL) My Sad Captains. Thom Gunn. FaBoMo; NAEL-5v2; NAEL-6v2; NPeEn; NoAM; NoP-4; PoPoPo

Hard frosts march together. Frosts are Coming. László Nagy. IQMS, *tr. by* Alan Dixon

Hard heart of a child, The. (LL) Beauty. Elinor Wylie. APT-1; NAAL-2v2; OxBA

Hard Heart of Mine. Henry Alline. AH

Hard-Hearted Hannah (The Vamp of Savannah). Milton Ager. ReLy

Hard hook-finger clutching down to the bottom. Creature Has a Purpose, The. Thomas Lux. BodElec

Hard is it for a man to please all men. Siciliano Inghilfredi. EaItPo, *tr. by* Dante Gabriel Rossetti

Hard is my fate, thus to want bread. Between an Unemployed Artist and His Wife. *Unknown.* NOEC

Hard is the doubt, and difficult to deeme. Edmund Spenser. CAGL *Fr.* Faerie Queene, The.

Hard is the stone, but harder still. Image-Maker, The. Oliver St. John Gogarty. OBEV; OBMV; PoRA

Hard it is, very hard. Dorothy Leigh Sayers. TrCP *Fr.* Devil to Pay, The.

Hard Journey, A. Yes. Hayden Carruth. VGW

Hard life of the young, The. (LL) Album. Josephine Miles. APT-2; ColAP; FaBoWP

Hard Listener, The. William Carlos Williams. OxBSP

Hard Put. Catie Rosemurgy. AmPoNex

Hard Road Blues. *Unknown.* FaBoVe

Hard Rock / was / known not to take no shit. Hard Rock Returns to Prison from the Hospital for the Criminal Insane. Etheridge Knight. CoAmPo; ESEAA; NAAAL; NIL-7; NIP-4; NNaP; PBCAP; TAP; TRP; UnPo

Hard sand breaks, The. Hermes of the Ways. "H. D.". WPE

Hard shape to describe—not circular, not square, A. Playful Poem on a Chicken Egg, A. Hsieh Chin. CoBLCP, *tr. by* Jonathan Chaves

Hard Structure of the World, The. Richard Eberhart. NoAM

Hard Times. John Ashbery. NoAM

Hard times, bad year, and a family dispossessed. On a Moonlit Night, Sent to My Brothers and Sisters. Po Chü-i. SuSp, *tr. by* Irving Lo

Hard to Bear. Tudor Jenks. OBCA

Hard to image. Anacapa. Abigail Albrecht. GeoHom

Hard to Place. Elaine Randell. Oth

Hard to pronounce and play, the OBOE. Oboe. Laurence McKinney. NBLV

Hard to say why some of us have come this far. Tourist, The. Jane Schapiro. GotH

Hard water and square wheels. Written While Riding the Long Island Rail Road. May Swenson. GM

Hard? You don't know what hard is, boy. Childhood of the Ancients. Andrew Hudgins. InvLad

Hardened in a leaf? (LL) Sea Rose. "H. D.". APT-1; FaBoMo; HeIP-4; NIL-7; NoAM; NoP-4; OxWW; TRP

Hardening of the World, and the First Settlement of Men, The. *Unknown.* "That the earth be made safer for men, and more stable." APN-2

Hardening through the mind and night of the first freeze. (LL) Hardweed Path Going. A. R. Ammons. HCAP; UnPo; VGW

Harder time is coming, A. Respite, The. Ingeborg Bachmann. WPOW, *tr. by* Michael Hamburger

Hardest knife ill used doth lose his edge, The. (LL) William Shakespeare. HeIP-4; SCGP *Fr.* Sonnets.

Hardly a day goes by I don't think of him. Damien. George Young. BloBone

Hardly a ghost left to talk with. The slavs moved on. River Now, The. Richard Hugo. VCAP

Hardly a Man Is Now Alive. Ring Lardner. OBAL

Hardly a shot from the gate we stormed. Sir Alfred Comyn Lyall. PeVV *Fr.* Studies at Delhi, 1876.

Hardly can disagree. (LL) You Would Have Understood Me. Paul Verlaine. BoLoP; MoBrPo; NOBVV, *tr. by* Ernest Dowson

Hardly spring, with ice. Chiyojo [*or* Chiyo *or* Chiyo-Ni *or* Kaga no Chiyo *or* Fukuda Chiyo-Ni]. BoWoP

Hardly visible they rock, on a sigh of light. Evening. Willem Kloos. TuT, *tr. by* Desmond Egan

Hardness Scale, The. Joyce Peseroff. TRP

Hardon ("Get One Today"). Ian Wedde. PeNZ

Hardship of Accounting, The. Robert Frost. FaBoCh; OBAL *Fr.* Ten Mills.

Hardships of tomorrow are put off, The. Procession, The. Sarah Rosenblatt. AmPoNex

Hardware formed relationship from just creating. Worker Who, the Human Who, the Abo Who, The. Lionel Fogarty. IBA

Hardweed Path Going. A. R. Ammons. HCAP; UnPo; VGW

Hardwood sheathing, A. Great Fetishes, The. Blaise Cendrars. PFTM-1

Hardy Perennial. Richard Eberhart. AiP

Hardy's "Shelley's Skylark." Daniel Hall. YaYoPo

Hare, A. Walter De la Mare. EBEV

Hare, The. Gillian Clarke. TCAWP

Hare-hunting. William Somervile [or Somerville]. NOEC   *Fr.* Chase, The.

Hare we had run over, The. Interruption to a Journey. Norman MacCaig. RB

Harebell and Pansy. Laurence Binyon. CABP

Hares, The. Susan Miles. LW

Hares at Play. John Clare. RB; WoPoe

Hares on the Mountain. *Unknown.* PeLV

Hares on their forms at dusk were not so still. "Robin Hyde." PeNZ   *Fr.* Houses, The.

Hari helps his people. Mirabai [or Mira Bai]. BoWoP

Hari, look at me a while. Mirabai [or Mira Bai]. BoWoP

Hark! Sacrifice, A. Robert Davenport. NOSC

Hark! ah, the nightingale. Philomela. Matthew Arnold. FHYEP; OBEV; OWoS; UnPo

Hark, All Ye Lovely Saints. *Unknown.* NPeEn

Hark, and Hear My Trumpet Sounding. *Unknown.* AH

Hark! for the beetle winds his horn. Fairies' Song, The. Jane Taylor. NOBRP

Hark! from yon covert, where those tow'ring oaks. William Somervile [or Somerville]. NOEC   *Fr.* Chase, The.

Hark! hark! that pig—that pig! the hideous note. Ode to a Pig While His Nose Was Being Bored. Robert Southey. NOBL

Hark, hark, the bark as Fido springs. Dawn Chorus. Mary Holtby. UV

"Hark, Hark, the Dogs Do Bark." Mother Goose. OxNR; ReMoGo

Hark, hark! the lark at heaven's gate sings. William Shakespeare. AWP; FaBoCh; ITBLP; NIL-7; NIP-4; NoSic; TFi; UV   *Fr.* Cymbeline.

Hark! Hark! with Harps of Gold. Edwin Hubbell Chapin. AH

Hark!—heard ye the signals of triumph afar? Caffer Commando, The. Thomas Pringle. PeSAV

Hark, hearer, hear what I do; lend a thought now, make believe. Epithalamion. Gerard Manley Hopkins. CAGL

Hark, how all the welkin rings! Glory to the King of Kings. Charles Wesley. SacPr

Hark how the Mower Damon sung. Damon the Mower. Andrew Marvell. BASC; ESCV; GeHe; NAEL-5v1; NAEL-6v1; NAEL-7v1

Hark, I hear the bells of Westgate. Westgate-on-Sea. Sir John Betjeman. OxBoLi

Hark! My Beloved! Bible, *O.T.* TrJP, *tr. by* Willis Barnstone   *Fr.* Song of Solomon, The [or The Song of Songs].

Hark, my Flora! Love doth call us. Song of Dalliance, A. William Cartwright. NOSC

Hark, my soul! it is the Lord. William Cowper. ChIV-2   *Fr.* Olney Hymns.

Hark, Now Everything Is Still. John Webster. HAP; SCGP   *Fr.* Duchess of Malfi, The.

Hark, now the drums beat up again. Over the Hills and Far Away. *Unknown.* FaBoWar

Hark! one saith: "Proclaim!" Bible, *O.T.* TrJP   *Fr.* Isaiah.

Hark, plaintful ghosts! Infernal furies, hark. Sir Philip Sidney.   *Fr.* Arcadia.

Hark, reader! wilt be learn'd i' th' wars? To My Truly Valiant, Learned Friend, Who in His Book Resolved the Art Gladiatory into the Mathematics. Richard Lovelace. CaPo

Hark! that's the nightingale. Pain or Joy. Christina Georgina Rossetti. OWoS

Hark! the flow of the four rivers. Farewells from Paradise. Elizabeth Barrett Browning. OBEV

Hark, the glad sound! the Saviour comes. Philip Doddridge. SacPr

Hark! the herald angels sing, Glory to the newborn King. Charles Wesley. SacPr

Hark! the herald angels sing / timidly. Dean Inge. Humbert Wolfe. FaBoEE

Hark! the Mavis. Robert Burns. OBEV

Hark the sound of holy voices, chanting at the crystal sea. All Saints' Day, Nov. 1. Christopher Wordsworth. SacPr

Hark! the wood doves' moan. Lai. May Probyn. VWP

Hark! 'Tis the Saviour of Mankind. John Murray. AH

Hark to the blackbird's pleasing note. Bullfinch in Town, The. Henrietta, Lady Luxborough Knight. ECWP

Hark, to the snow-fiend's voice afar. Snow-Fiend, The. Anne Batten Cristall. RWP

Hark to the whimper of the sea-gull. Sea-Gull, The. Ogden Nash. OWoS

Hark what a sound, and too divine for hearing. Hymn. Frederic William Henry Myers. OBEV

Hark[e]! now I hear[e] them—ding-dong, bell. (LL) William Shakespeare. AWP; ClHu; EBEV; FaBoCh; HAP; InPK-6; NAEL-5v1; NAEL-6v1; NoP-4; NoSic; OBEV; OxBEV; OxBSP; PoE; PoPoPo; PoRA; TFi   *Fr.* Tempest, The.

Harlackenden, among these men of note Christ hath thee seated. Among These Troopes of Christs Souldiers, Came. . . Mr. Roger Harlackenden. Edward Johnson. SCAP

Harlech Castle. John Corben. Spl

Harlem. Jean Brierre. TTY, *tr. by* John F. Matheus

Harlem. Langston Hughes. APSN; APT-2; AiP; GLP; GT; HCAP; HeIP-4; NAAAL; NoP-4; RaBo; SAmP; SSLK   *Fr.* Lenox Avenue Mural.

Harlem (A Dream Deferred). Langston Hughes. *See* Lenox Avenue Mural

Harlem Dancer, The. Claude McKay. APT-1; BPo; ISC; NAAL-5; NIL-7; NIP-4; NoAM; Son; TAP; TCAPo

Harlem dud. For "Mr. Dudley," a Black Spy. James A. Emanuel. BPo; NBV

Harlem Freeze Frame. Lebert Bethune. GT

Harlem Gallery. Melvin B. Tolson.

  Alpha. APT-2

  Birth of John Henry, The. BPo; NAAAL; TTY

  Mu. APT-2; PFTM-1

Harlem Gallery, an Afric pepper bird, The. Melvin B. Tolson. APT-2   *Fr.* Harlem Gallery.

Harlem Gallery: From the Inside. Larry Neal. BPo; NBV

Harlem Haiku: A Scrapbook. Jabari Asim. InTrad

Harlem is vicious / modernism. BangClash. Return of the Native. Imamu Amiri Baraka. APSN; BPo

Harlem, Montana. James Welch. CDW; HATNAP

  (Harlem, Montana: Just Off the Reservation.) PoPoPo

Harlem: Neo-Image. Kevin Powell. AmPoNex

Harlem Shadows. Claude McKay. APT-1; ColAP; NAAAL; NAAL-5; TCAPo

Harlem Sweeties. Langston Hughes. NoP-4; TTY

Harlot's Catch. Robert Malise Bowyer Nichols. FaBoTw

Harlot's House, The. Oscar Wilde. EBVV; MoBrPo; NAEL-5v2; NAEL-6v2; NoAM

Harm. Vickie Karp. KGB

Harmonics. William Vaughn Moody. APN-2; AmFaPo

Harmonie du Soir. Charles Baudelaire. AWP, *tr. by* Lord Alfred Bruce Douglas

Harmonies. Thomas Kinsella. ModIr   *Fr.* Out of Ireland.

Harmonious powers with Nature work. Floating Island at Hawkshead. Dorothy Wordsworth. NPeEn; PEW

Harmonizing a Spring Poem by Premier Lu of Chin-Ling. Tu Shen-yen. ChinPo, *tr. by* Yip Wai-lim

Harmonizing with a Poem by Left Assistant Yu Kao-chih Requesting Sick Leave. Shen Yüeh. ColAnChi, *tr. by* Richard Mather

Harmony. Thomas Grant Springer. PoToHe

Harmony. *Unknown.* GrAn, *tr. by* William J. Philbin

Harmony. Andrea M. Wren. InTrad

Harmony in the Kingdom. *Vietnamese Oral Tradition.* CaDao, *tr. by* John Balaban

Harmony of Evening, The. Charles Baudelaire. SxFrPo, *tr. by* James McGowan

Harold. David Ignatow. LTA

Harold and Imogene. Paul Violi. ReTh

Harold's Bowl and Food. Denis Johnson. Unle

Harold's Walk. Geoffrey Lehmann. EmeKit

Harold Wilson's Selected Poems. Mary Wilson.

  "I went out of the conf'rence to get a pint of beer." UV

Haroun Al-Rachid for Heart's-Life. *Unknown.* AWP   *Fr.* Thousand and One Nights, The.

Haroun's Favorite Song. *Unknown.* AWP   *Fr.* Thousand and One Nights, The.

Harp, The. Ralph Waldo Emerson. APN-1

Harp, The. Ralph Knevet. ChIV-2

Harp, The. Po Chü-i. TAL

Harp/Desire. Katherine Soniat. MiVo

Harp music blows off the stand, The. Music in the Meadow. Alice Wirth Gray. MiVo

Harp of David, The. Jacob Cohen. TrJP, *tr. by* Sholom J. Kahn

Harp of David, The. "Yehoash." TrJP, *tr. by* Alter Brody

Harp of the North, Farewell! Sir Walter Scott. OxAEP-2   *Fr.* Lady of the Lake, The.

Harp of the North! that mouldering long hast hung. Sir Walter Scott. NePenScot   *Fr.* Lady of the Lake, The.

Harp Song. Lu Yu. CoBCP, *tr. by* Burton Watson

Harp Song of the Dane Women. Rudyard Kipling. HAP; HarvBoo; PoRA; RACG   *Fr.* Puck of Pook's Hill.

Harp That Once through Tara's Halls, The. Thomas Moore. CABP; NAEL-5v2; NAEL-6v2

Harp the Monarch Minstrel Swept, The. Byron. ChIV-1

Harpe's Head. John Knoepfle. IllVoic

Harper's Song for Inherkhawy, The. *Unknown.* WoPoe, *tr. by* John L. Foster

Harpers Ferry. Adrienne Rich. BodElec

Harpies, The. Virgil [*or* Vergil]. OWoS, *tr. by* John Dryden *Fr.* Aeneid (Dryden translation).

Harpist believes there is music, The. Concert, The. Lisel Mueller. MiVo

Harpkin gaed up t'the hill. Harpkin. *Unknown.* FaBoVe

Harried / earth is swept, The. Wind Increases, The. William Carlos Williams. NAAL-2v2

Harriet. Robert Lowell. NoP-4

Harriet Beecher Stowe. Paul Laurence Dunbar. BPo; PoPoPo

Harriet Beecher Stowe. Dorothy Parker. APT-1; NALW *Fr.* Pig's-Eye View of Literature, A.

Harriet there was always somebody calling us crazy. Harriet. Audre Lorde. BlSi; NAAL-5

Harriet Tubman. *Unknown.* HHAm

Harriet Tubman aka Moses. Samuel Allen. ISC

Harrison Street Court. Carl Sandburg. APT-1

Harrowing. Douglas Messerli. FTOS

Harrowing, The. *Unknown.* WoPoe, *tr. by* Tony Harrison *Fr.* Doomsday, the Mysteries.

Harry Fat and Uncle Sam. James Keir Baxter. PeLV

Harry Parry. *Unknown.* OxNR

Harry Ploughman. Gerard Manley Hopkins. EroLit; FaBoMo

Harry Pollit Was a Bolshie. *Unknown.* OBCoV

Harry's Bar Ballad. Giulia Niccolai. CItWP, *tr. by* Cinzia Sartini Blum and Lara Trubowitz

Harry Vaughan. John L. Thomas.
   "His father did intend that Harry should." AngWePo

Harry, whose tuneful[l] and well-measured [*or* well-measur'd] song. To Mr. H. Lawes On His Airs. John Milton. AWP

Harry Williams. Edgar Lee Masters. APT-1 *Fr.* Spoon River Anthology.

Harsh Climate. Charles Simic. LCAP-2

Harsh cry the crows. Solitary, The. Friedrich Wilhelm Nietzsche. AWP, *tr. by* Ludwig Lewisohn

Harsh Metropolitan Season. Luciana Notari. CItWP, *tr. by* Cinzia Sartini Blum and Lara Trubowitz

Harsh russet of dried blood, The. (LL) Buried at Springs. James Schuyler. CoAP; PoM

Harsh with salt of the sea. (LL) Drover, A. Padraic Colum. AWP; MoBrPo; OBMV; RB

Hart Crane. Paul Engle. YaYoPo

Hart he loves the high wood, The. Mother Goose. FaBoCh; OxNR; ReMoGo

Hart Loves the High Wood, The. *Unknown.* RB

Hartico. Anna Walters. VoR

Hartnett, the poet, might as well be dead. Michael Hartnett. BiHa *Fr.* Purge, The.

Hartwell Gardens. A. of Aylesbury Merrick. OBGa

Harum Scarum. Roger McGough. OTCP

Harvard, Cambridge, Mass. Harvard. Julian Symons. PeLV

Harvest. Blaise Cendrars. BLT, *tr. by* Monique Chefdor

Harvest. Gary Soto. PBCAP

Harvest, The. Shafiq Al-Kamali. MAP, *tr. by* Sargon Boulus

Harvest, The. Morgan Llwyd. AngWePo *Fr.* 1648.

Harvest, The. Jones Very. SacPr

Harvest Bow, The. Seamus Heaney. BiHa; HarvBoo; ModIr; NoAM; PBCIP; PNI

Harvest Dawn Is Near, The. George Burgess. AH

Harvest Gathering. Phoebe Cary. SWaP

Harvest Home. Henry Alford. SacPr

Harvest-Home. Theocritus. AWP *Fr.* Idylls.

Harvest Moon. Jan Barry. CDa

Harvest moon. Basho. EH, *tr. by* Robert Hass

Harvest moon. Buson. EH, *tr. by* Robert Hass

Harvest Moon, The. Henry Wadsworth Longfellow. APN-1

Harvest-mouse with caution walks, The. Rustler. William Stroud. Spl

Harvest of Hate. Wole Soyinka. AF

Harvest of War. Catherine Obianuju Acholonu. HAWP; NAfrP

Harvest ripe, the farmers rejoice, The. Hastily Composed on the Mo-ling Road. Wang An-shih. SuSp, *tr. by* Jan W. Walls

Harvest Sacrifice. Su Tung-p'o (Su Shih). OHPC, *tr. by* Kenneth Rexroth

Harvest shall flourish in wintry weather, The. Merlins Prophecy. William Blake. WoPoe

Harvest shall stop? The. (LL) Gathering Leaves. Robert Frost. RB; VGW

Harvest Song. Richard Dehmel. AWP, *tr. by* Ludwig Lewisohn

Harvest Song. Ludwig Heinrich Christoph Hölty. AWP, *tr. by* Charles T. Brooks

Harvest Song. Jean Toomer. NoP-4

Harvest Song. *Unknown.* OxNR

Harvesters, The. Mary Gilmore. NOBAu

Harvesting of the Roses, The. Menahem ben Jacob. TrJP

Harvesting Wheat for the Public Share. Li Chü. BoWoP

Harvey Always Wins. Jack Prelutsky. NTCP

Harvey, the happy above happiest men. To the Right Worshipfull, My Singular Good Friend, Master Gabriel Harvey, Doctor of the Lawes. Edmund Spenser. NoSic

Harvey, the happy above happiest men. Edmund Spenser. NoSic *Fr.* Commendatory Sonnets.

Has a gold tooth, sits long hours. Black Bourgeoisie. Imamu Amiri Baraka. BPo; ESEAA

Has a packet of chocolate and a souvenir of Tripoli. (LL) Cairo Jag. Keith Douglas. HarvBoo; PoWW

Has any one supposed it lucky to be born? Walt Whitman. NAWM-7v2 *Fr.* Song of Myself.

Has Anyone Seen the Boy? Jelaluddin [*or* Jalal al-Din] Rumi. RaBo; WoPoe, *tr. by* Coleman Barks and John Moyne

Has been hauled away. (LL) As the Dead Prey upon Us. Charles Olson. APT-2; NeAP

Has done the lover mortal hurt. (LL) Vergissmeinicht. Keith Douglas. FaBoMo; FaBoWar; GTBS-P; HarvBoo; NAEL-5v2; NAEL-6v2; NPeEn; NoAM; NoP-4; OBWP; OxBEV; OxBTC; PoWW; RB; SoSe-8; WoPoe

Has Faded in Part but Magnificent Also Late for RC / Mirrors. Robert Grenier. PmAP

Has fixed my mother and father in a garden. Photograph, The. Myra Schneider. Prnts

Has he tempered the viol's wood. Ezra Pound. *See* Zeus lies in Ceres' bosom

Has it ever happened. Interlaced Lines for the Same Moment. Ghada El-Shafa'i. PoArWo, *tr. by* Atef Abu-Seif and Nathalie Handal

Has it really been thirty years? To Abbot Min the Compassionate. Tu Fu. CrYelRi, *tr. by* Sam Hamill

Has left a note saying GONE AWAY. (LL) Ending. Gavin Ewart. NBLV; OxBSP; SoSe-8

Has my life been a failure? I wonder. "Ivan Venediktovich Elagin." TCRP

Has no feeling but because he has so much. (LL) Student, The. Marianne Craig Moore. NAAL-2v2; TwCP

Has not altered. Spenser's Ireland. Marianne Craig Moore. FaBoWP; NOBA; NoAM; OxBA; TAP

Has not his flying-crooked gift. (LL) Flying Crooked. Robert Graves. FaBoMo; OxBSP; PeLV; RB; TwCP

Has not the night been as a drunken rose. Drunken Rose, The. Amarou. AWP, *tr. by* E. Powys Mathers

Has only just / begun. (LL) Charles Olson. APSN; ColAP *Fr.* Maximus Poems, The.

Has painted his hands blue. Logical Positivist, The. David Bromige. FTOS

Has Sabine winter brought you to your fireside. Satire 6. Persius. RomPo, *tr. by* Richard Emil Braun

Has set me softly down beside you. The poem is you. (LL) Paradoxes and Oxymorons. John Ashbery. FTOS; HeIP-4; NoAM; PmAP; PoPoPo

Has the age of psychology really passed? Whatever Became Of: Freud? Edward Field. BodElec

Has the time come to draw up the accounts? Yevgeny [*or* Evgenii] Mikhailovich Vinokurov. TCRusP, *tr. by* Daniel Weissbort

Hasbrouck and the Rose. Howard Phelps Putnam. APT-2; OxBA

Haschish, The. John Greenleaf Whittier. APN-1; NCAP; OBAL

Haskell. Witter Bynner. NoP-4

Hassan. James Elroy Flecker.
   Hassan's Serenade. OBEV
   War Song of the Saracens. MoBrPo

Hast Never Come to Thee an Hour. Walt Whitman. SAmP

Hast power to say the Time in terms of tone. (LL) Sidney Lanier. APN-2; NCAP *Fr.* Street Cries.

Hast then sweet Love our wished flight. (LL) Come Away, Come, Sweet Love. John Dowland. NAEL-5v1; NoSic

Hast thou a charm to stay the morning-star. Hymn before Sunrise, in the Vale of Chamouni. Samuel Taylor Coleridge. SacPr

Hast thou a cunning instrument of play. Preparation. Thomas Edward Brown. OBEV

Hast thou come with the heart of thy childhood back? Return, The. Felicia Dorothea Hemans. RWP

Hast Thou Heard It, O My Brother. Theodore Chickering Williams. AH

Hast thou named all the birds without a gun? Forbearance. Ralph Waldo Emerson. TAP

Hast thou no Arm for Me? (LL) Emily Dickinson. APN-2; NCAP; TCAPo

Hast thou no mercy, wind, that thou should'st tear from me.   Mother's Lament, The.   Mary E. Tucker.   CBWP-1

Hast Thou seen her, great Jew.   Highland Woman, A.   Sorley MacLean (Somhairle MacGill-Eain).   HarvBoo; NePenScot

Hast thou seen reversed the prophet's miracle.   Frederick Goddard Tuckerman.   NOBA   Fr. Sonnets.

"Hast thou seen that lordly castle."   Castle by the Sea, The.   Ludwig Uhland.   AWP, tr. by Henry Wadsworth Longfellow

Hast thou seen the down i' th' air.   Song to a Lute, A.   Sir John Suckling.   BeJo; CaPo

Hast thou, spirit.   William Shakespeare.   OxAEP-1   Fr. Tempest, The.

Hasta luego and over you go and it's not.   Border, The.   Martha Collins.   ExTi

Haste, hoist the sails! Fair blows the wind.   Negro Boy's Tale, The.   Amelia Alderson Opie.   RWP

Haste Not! Rest Not!   Goethe.   TreFP, tr. by Unknown

Haste to the mighty ocean.   August.   Henrietta Cordelia Ray.   CBWP-3

Hasten hither, little book.   Company in Loneliness.   Unknown.   NOIV

Hasten on your childhood to the hour when white.   Poem.   Pablo Picasso.   SPE, tr. by David Gascoyne

Hasten toward immense and earthly joy, the eyelids blinking as they.   Waking.   Tristan Tzara.   AF

Hastening on, the wanderer strode.   Wanderer, The.   "Yehoash."   TrJP, tr. by Isidore Goldstick

Hastily Composed on the Mo-ling Road.   Wang An-shih.   SuSp, tr. by Jan W. Walls

Hasty Pudding, The.   Joel Barlow.   NAAL-3; NOBA; OBAL; OxBA; TAP; TCAPo

Hat.   Tomasz Jastrun.   AF, tr. by Daniel Bourne

Hat Factory, The.   Paul Durcan.   BiHa; ModIr

Hat Given to the Poet by Li Chien, The.   Po Chü-i.   ChiP, tr. by Arthur Waley

Hat Lady, The.   Linda Pastan.   SoSe-8

Hat pulled low at work.   One of the Years.   William Stafford.   KaS

Hatchet was buried, the table made ready, The.   Two Kinds of Welsh Bards.   Endre Ady.   IQMS, tr. by Neville Masterman

Hate.   James Stephens.   MoBrPo

Hate and the Love of the World, The.   Max Ehrmann.   PoToHe

Hate, be a faithful prop, and find.   Hate!   Pavel Grigoryevich Antokolsky.   TrJP, tr. by Babette Deutsch

Hate Hitler? No, I spared him hardly a thought.   IFF.   Howard Nemerov.   BodElec

Hate is only one of many responses.   Poem.   Frank O'Hara.   NeAP

Hate me or love, I care not, as I pass.   Unicorn, The.   Ruth Pitter.   MoBrPo

Hate-Song, A.   Shelley.   EnLoPo

Hate the Idle Pleasures.   William Shakespeare.   PoE   Fr. King Richard III.

Hated by the Muses!   B kw rm.   Euenus.   GrAn, tr. by Alistair Elliot

Hated Rats, The.   Nguyen Binh Khiem.   WoPoe, tr. by Nguyen Ngoc Bich

Hateful Old Age.   Unknown.
   "Before my back was bent I was eloquent."   OBWVE

Hater he came and sat by a ditch, A.   Hate-Song, A.   Shelley.   EnLoPo

Hath any loved you well, down there.   Marie de France.   AWP; EnLoPo; WPOW   Fr. Chartivel.

Hath cared to look upon thy face. (LL)   Eros.   Robert Bridges.   CABP; NOBE

Hath God, who freely gave you his own Son.   To the Rev'd Mr. Jno. Sparhawk on the Birth of his Son.   Samuel Sewall.   SCAP

Hath melted like snow in the glance of the Lord! (LL)   Destruction of Sennacherib, The.   Byron.   BRP; CABP; ChAP; ChIV-1; FHYEP; FaBoCh; FaBoWar; HAP; HeIP-4; NoP-4; OBWP; OxAEP-2; PAI; RB; SCGP; TFi; TrCP; WeW-3; WoPoe

Hath no misfortune, but that Rich she is. (LL)   Sir Philip Sidney.   NAEL-5v1; NAEL-6v1; NAEL-7v1; Son   Fr. Astrophil and Stella.

Hath not the morning dawned with added light?   Ethnogenesis.   Henry Timrod.   APN-2; NOBA; OxBA; TCAPo

Hath oftener left me mourning. (LL)   Simon Lee [the Old Huntsman].   William Wordsworth.   GTBS-P; NAEL-5v2; NAEL-6v2

Hath onely Anger an Omnipotence.   Upon the Asse That Bore Our Saviour.   Richard Crashaw.   ChIV-2; GeHe

Hath the Rain a Father?   Jones Very.   ChIV-1

Hath this world aught so fair as Stella is? (LL)   Sir Philip Sidney.   NAEL-5v1; NAEL-7v1; NoSic; PoE   Fr. Astrophil and Stella.

Hatikvah—a Song of Hope.   Naphtali Herz Imber.   TrJP, tr. by Henry Snowman

Hating Jews.   Tom Wayman.   LTA

Hating the air! (LL)   Poets Hitchhiking on the Highway.   Gregory Corso.   BB; NeAP; PoM

Hatred.   Gwendolyn B. Bennett.   BlSi; RaBo

Hatred and vengeance, my eternal portion.   Lines Written During a Period of Insanity.   William Cowper.   EBEV; HAP; NOEC; NPeEn; NoP-4

Hatred I reserve for thee, The.   Invective Against Denise, a Witch.   Pierre de Ronsard.   WoPoe, tr. by Anthony Hecht

Hatred's swift repulsions play. (LL)   Visit, The.   Ralph Waldo Emerson.   APN-1; NOBA

Hatred Surely Does Not Kiss.   Kaspar Stieler.   GePo, tr. by George C. Schoolfield

Hats.   Jean Pedrick.   WWork

Hats off! / Along the street there comes.   Flag Goes By, The.   Henry Holcomb Bennett.   PWR

Hatteras Calling.   Conrad Potter Aiken.   ColAP; NOBA; TAP

Hatters, The.   Nan McDonald.   NOBAu

Hattie House.   Julia A. Moore.
   "She had blue eyes and light flaxen hair."   VerBaPo

Hattie Went to Market.   Leslie Simon.   FFC

Haud ictus sapio. (LL)   Gascoigne's Good-Morrow.   George Gascoigne.   NOCV; NoSic

Haud ictus sapio. (LL)   Gascoigne's [or Gascoygnes] Good-Night.   George Gascoigne.   NOCV; NoSic

Haul the mainsail down. I have reached the harbour.   My Portion.   Dániel Berzsenyi.   IQMS, tr. by Peter Zollman

Haul up the flag, you mourners.   Elegy for Two Banjos.   Karl Shapiro.   TrJP

Haul Your Paper Boats.   Eugenio Montale.   WoPoe, tr. by William Arrowsmith

Hauled hay bales all afternoon.   Appaloosa Hail Storm.   Gerald Hausman.   GifTon

Haulier's Wife Meets Jesus on the Road Near Moone, The.   Paul Durcan.   ModIr

Hauling Over Wolf Creek Pass in Winter.   Walter McDonald.   CDa

Haunch under the whip of douches in the slime.   Spermal Chimney.   Francis Picabia.   PFTM-1

Haunted.   Edith Nesbit.   VWP

Haunted, The.   Brad Leithauser.   RA

Haunted Beach, The.   Mary Robinson.   ECWP; RWP

Haunted by poems beginning with I.   Prologue.   Audre Lorde.   ESEAA

Haunted Country.   Robinson Jeffers.   APT-1; OxBA

Haunted Heart.   Arthur Schwartz.   ReLy

Haunted House, The.   Thomas Hood.   EBEV

Haunted Houses.   Henry Wadsworth Longfellow.   PWR; TCAPo

Haunted Oak, The.   Paul Laurence Dunbar.   ColAP; NAAAL; UnPo

Haunted Palace, The.   Edgar Allan Poe.   APN-1; NAAL-3; NOBA; OxBA; TAP; TCAPo; TFi

Haunted Streets.   Mathilde Blind.   ViWPN

Haunter, The.   Thomas Hardy.   NOBE

Haunting the page of my passport.   Paris Is Not the Same.   James Strachey.   ReLy

Haunting the Western Moor. (LL)   Trampwoman's Tragedy, A.   Thomas Hardy.   NAEL-5v2; NAEL-6v2; OBNV

Haunting velvet blanket, A.   Velvet Blanket.   Marlon D. Satchell.   InTrad

Haunts me night and day. (LL)   Look, The.   Sara Teasdale.   APT-1; LW

Haunts of the Mirage.   Bruce Berger.   GeoH

Havana Harbor.   Nancy Morejón.   TANSG, tr. by Joy Renjilian-Burgy

Have a being less durable even than he. (LL)   Poplar Field, The.   William Cowper.   FHYEP; HAP; NOBE; NOEC; OxBEV

Have actually pardoned me. (LL)   Amnesty.   "Ivan Venediktovich Elagin."   TCRP; TCRusP, tr. by Bertram D. Wolfe

Have all built their nests in my beard! (LL)   There Was an Old Man With a Beard.   Edward Lear.   NOBL; NOxBChV; NPeEn; OPOU; PeLV; PeLi; TLR

Have ascended to the Sixth Heaven of Desire? (LL)   On the Day of Washing the Buddha in the Year Ting-wei (1607), I Dreamed That My Late Son Shih-ch'ü Was Holding a Book, and Appeared to Be Quite Happy. He Said That He Had Earned His Chin-shih Degree in the Underworld.   T'ang Hsien-tsu.   CoBLCP; ColAnChi, tr. by Jonathan Chaves

Have certain periods set, and hidden fates. (LL)   Sonnet: "Dost see how unregarded now."   Sir John Suckling.   BASC; BeJo; CaPo; CavPo; NOSC

Have crawled too far! (LL)   Emily Dickinson.   APN-2; NCAP

Have died, the Present teaches, but in vain! (LL)   Robert Gould Shaw.   Paul Laurence Dunbar.   CBCWP; PoPoPo; Son

Have ending. (LL)   White Island.   Robert Herrick.   BeJo; NOSC; TOF

Have eyes to wonder, but lack tongues to praise. (LL)   William Shakespeare.   AWP; CTC; EnLoPo; FaBoCh; NAEL-5v1; NAEL-6v1; NAEL-7v1; NOBE; NoSic; OBEV; OxAEP-1; PoRA; SCGP; Son; WoPoe   Fr. Sonnets.

Have Feet, Will Dance.   Dorothy Fields.   ReLy

Have gathered them and will do never again. (LL)   In Memoriam (Easter, 1915).   Edward Thomas.   GTBS-P; NOBE; OBWP; OBWVE; OxBTC; PeFWW; Spl

Have good day, now, Mergerete.   Unknown.   MiEL

Have, have ye no regard, all ye.   His Saviour['s] Words, Going to the Cross[e].   Robert Herrick.   ChIV-2; NOCV; SacPr

Have heard a kitten in the wilderness. (LL) Chaplinesque. Hart Crane. APT-2; HeIP-4; NAAL-2v2; NAAL-5; NOBA; NoAM; OxBA; VGW

Have heard her massive sandal set on stone. (LL) "Euclid Alone Has Looked on Beauty Bare." Edna St. Vincent Millay. APT-1; BRP; GSo; HeIP-4; MoAmPo; NAAL-2v2; NoP-4; Son; TAP

Have I a body or have I none? *Unknown.* CoBCP

Have I a wife? Bedam I have! Brewer's Man, The. Leonard Alfred George Strong. OBCoV; PeLV

Have I caught my heav'nly jewel. Sir Philip Sidney. NoSic *Fr.* Astrophil and Stella.

Have I got a hut! Kukutis Describes His Hut. Marcelijus Martinaitis. TWW, *tr. by* Laima Sruoginis.

Have I let my love. Kasa no Iratsume. ArkPo, *tr. by* Edwin A. Cranston

Have I no weapon-word for thee—some message brief and fierce? To the Pending Year. Walt Whitman. OxBSP

Have I not blessed [*or* blest] thee? Then go forth; nor fear. To His Book[e]. Robert Herrick. BASC; CaPo

Have I not seen the hills of Candahar. Albery Allson Whitman. APN-2 *Fr.* Twasinta's Seminoles; Or Rape of Florida.

Have I renounc't my faith, or basely sold. Upon an Unhandsome Gentlewoman, Who Made Love unto Him. Richard Corbet [*or* Corbett]. BASC

Have I spent all my life turning. Simon and the Tarantula. James Wright (1927–80). NNaP

Have I the power to bid the frost not melt. To Barba. Edward May. FaBoEE

Have I told you the name of a lady? Have You Seen the Lady? John Philip Sousa. OBAL

Have mynde how I mankynde have take. James Ryman. OHMEL

Have neither part nor lot in me. (LL) Magdalen. Amy Levy. VWP; ViWPN

Have no use for any sweets of any kind. Honeysuckle Rose. Andy Razaf. ReLy

Have oon god in worship. *Unknown.* OHMEL

Have peace, O restless, sorrow-laden heart! Solemn Vow, A. Mikhail Naimy. GraLe

Have pity, God, on one you cast down here. Wilderness. Ilyas Farhat. MAP, *tr. by* John Heath-Stubbs and Salma Khadra Jayyusi

Have pity on our brother. Have Pity. Claribel Alegría. TANSG, *tr. by* Darwin Flakoll

Have pity, pity, friends, have pity on me. Epistle in Form of a Ballad to His Friends. François Villon. AWP, *tr. by* Algernon Charles Swinburne

Have power to cure all sadness—but despair. (LL) To Spring. Charlotte Smith. BWW; RWP; WPE

Have saved them from the gas. (LL) "It Out-Herods Herod. Pray You, Avoid It." Anthony Hecht. AF; CoAP; NIP-4; NOBA; NoAM; OxBC

Have Some Madeira, M'dear? Michael Flanders. OBCoV

Have the gods then loved me here on earth? Retreat. Árpád Tóth. IQMS, *tr. by* Watson Kirkconnell

Have the poets left a place. Black Night, The. Antar [*or* Antara]. WoPoe, *tr. by* Desmond O'Grady

Have the poets left a single spot for a patch to be sewn? Var. authors. TTY *Fr.* Mu'allaqat, The.

Have thine own way, Lord! Have thine own way! Adelaide A. Pollard. SacPr

Have this wish I wish tonight. (LL) Wishing Poem. *Unknown.* NTCP; OxNR

Have to leave the city. Intermission from Monday. Pedro Juan Pietri. PueRic

Have to work after all. (LL) Necessity. Langston Hughes. APSN; NOBA; RaBo

Have ye beheld (with much delight). Upon the Nipples of Julia's Breast. Robert Herrick. CaPo; ErotSp; NAEL-5v1; NAEL-6v1; NAEL-7v1; NOSC; PeLV

Have ye e'er heard of gallant like young Lochinvar? (LL) Sir Walter Scott. EBNV; NAEL-6v2; NOBE; NePenScot; OxAEP-2; OxBS; PoRA; TFi *Fr.* Marmion.

Have ye seen the morning sky. Happy Swain, The. Ambrose Philips. EnLoPo

Have you a gold cup. Question, The. Robert Duncan. NeAP

Have you any idea. the Mother of Michitsuna. OHPJ

Have You Anything to Say in Your Defense? César Vallejo. PoetW; RaBo, *tr. by* James Wright

Have You Been at Carrick? *Unknown.* BIrV, *tr. by* Edward Walsh

Have you been in our wild west country? then. West Country, The. Alice Cary. APN-2; SWaP

Have you dug the spill. Harlem Sweeties. Langston Hughes. NoP-4; TTY

Have you ever awakened to find that you're glad to be awake? You're in Love. Bobby Troup. ReLy

Have you ever been ordered to strip. Solitary Confinement. Robert Walker. IBA; NOBAu

Have You Ever Faked an Orgasm? Molly Peacock. RA

Have you ever heard of lynching in the great United States? Lynching. Lizelia Augusta Jenkins Moorer. CBWP-3

Have you ever heard of the Sugar-Plum Tree? Sugar-Plum Tree, The. Eugene Field. ITBLP; NBLV; OTCP

Have you ever heard that a tailor was ill? Tailor, The. Joseph Leftwich. TrJP

Have you ever noticed how her toes tickle. Her Eyes a Thousand Times Over. Chani DiPrima. HW

Have you ever seen. Gut Catcher. Stan Platke. FaBoWar

Have you ever seen the dawn of love? Lady's in Love with You, The. Burton Lane. ReLy

Have you ever smelled summer? That Was Summer. Marci Ridlon. NTCP

Have you ever watched your old mother. Mother. Vladimir Holan. PoSu, *tr. by* Ian Milner and Jarmila Milner

Have you forgotten what we were like then. Animals. Frank O'Hara. HarvBoo

Have you forgotten yet? Aftermath. Siegfried Sassoon. MoBrPo; PoWW; TrJP

Have you had a kindness shown? Pass It On. Henry Burton. PWR

Have you heard how the Taipan. Taipan. Kevin Gilbert. IBA

Have you heard Howard's tape? War Stories. Perry Oldham. CDa

Have you heard, my dear Anne, how my spirits are sunk? Lines by a Lady on the Loss of Her Trunk. Richard Brinsley Sheridan. OBCoV

Have you heard, my friend, the slander that the Negro has to face? Immortality. Lizelia Augusta Jenkins Moorer. CBWP-3

Have you heard of a collier of honest renown. Patient Joe; or, The Newcastle Collier. Hannah More. ECWP; WoRP

Have You Heard of Artemisia? Heather McPherson. PeNZ

Have you heard of one Humpty Dumpty. James Joyce. PeLV *Fr.* Finnegans Wake.

Have you heard of the dreadful fate. Ashtabula Disaster, The. Julia A. Moore. OBAL; VerBaPo

Have you heard of the wonderful one-hoss shay. Oliver Wendell Holmes. APN-1; BRP; ITBLP; NAAL-3; NOBA; OBAL; OBCA; OxBA; PoRA; TAP; TCAPo; TFi *Fr.* Autocrat of the Breakfast Table, The.

Have you heard the latest miser story. Nicarchus of Alexandria. GrAn

Have you heard the story that gossips tell. John Burns of Gettysburg. Bret Harte. CBCWP

Have you heard? The troubles. Sulpicia. BoWoP

Have you his lovely image still in mind. Stefan George. EroLit, *tr. by* Ernst Morwitz and Carol North Valhope

Have you listened for the things I have left out? Unsaid. A. R. Ammons. NOBA

Have you lived long, sir, in these parts? Interview, An. K. W. Grandsen. OxBTC

Have you made your life worth? (LL) After Experience Taught Me. W. D. Snodgrass. CoAP; OBWP

Have You Met Miss Jones? Richard Rodgers. ReLy

Have you never seen. Bring the Wine! Li Po. CoBCP, *tr. by* Burton Watson

Have you no thought O dreamer that it may be all maya, illusion? (LL) Are You the New Person Drawn toward Me? Walt Whitman. APN-1; OxBSP

Have you not heard the gossip and the rumour going around. Raphael de Leon. EroLit

Have you not in a chimney seen. Description of Maidenhead, A. John Wilmot, 2d Earl of Rochester. NOBL

Have you not noted, in some family. Dante Gabriel Rossetti. Son *Fr.* House of Life, The.

Have you not seen the grasses on the riverbank? Pao Chao. SuSp *Fr.* Weary Road, The.

Have you not seen (you must remember). Henry Luttrell. NOBRP *Fr.* Letter to Julia, in Rhyme.

Have you noticed. Angels. Anne Szumigalski. NOBC

Have you read in the Talmud of old. Sandalphon. Henry Wadsworth Longfellow. TCAPo

Have you really come home? (LL) Father of My Country, The. Diane Wakoski. NoAM; TAP

Have you seen. Seashore, The. Leonid Nikolaevich Martynov. TCRP, *tr. by* J. R. Rowland

Have you seen a little dog anywhere about? My Dog. Emily Lewis. OTCP

Have you seen an apple orchard in the spring? Apple Orchard in the Spring, An. William Martin. PWR

Have you seen but a bright lily grow. Ben Jonson. FaBoCh *Fr.* Devil Is an Ass, The.

Have you seen how a word is born and dies? Edmond Jabès. PFTM-2, *tr. by* Rosmarie Waldrop *Fr.* Book of Questions, The.

Have you seen my cousin? William Shakespeare. OxAEP-1 *Fr.* Troilus and Cressida.

Have you seen that Vigilante Man? Vigilante Man. Woody Guthrie. APT-2

Have You Seen the Lady? John Philip Sousa. OBAL

Have you seen the listening snake? Vines, The. John Gray. NOBVV

Have you seen the well-to-do. Puttin' on the Ritz (Original Version). Irving Berlin. ReLy

Have you seen the well-to-do. Puttin' on the Ritz (Revised Version). Irving Berlin. ReLy

Have you sometimes, calm, silent let your tread aspirant rise. Victor Hugo. AWP, tr. by Francis Thompson Fr. Feuilles d'Automne.

Have you starved? Are We the Same. Charmaine Papertalk-Green. IBA

Have you time for a story. Charity Overcoming Envy. Marianne Craig Moore. GS

Have Yourself a Merry Little Christmas. Ralph Blane. ReLy

Haven of Rest. Mihály Tompa. IQMS, tr. by Doreen Bell

Haven't Got a Worry. Ray Evans. ReLy

Haven't I told you enough? (LL) When I Was Growing Up. Nellie Wong. OxWW; UnSA

Haven't seen my friend Li Po for some time. No Word. Tu Fu. SuSp, tr. by Eugene Eoyang

Haven't you already filled. On Poetry. Franco Buffoni. ItPo, tr. by Gayle Ridinger

Having a Coke with You. Frank O'Hara. GLP; VCAP

Having a crush was how I existed. Suburban Childhood, A. Liz Rosenberg. PBCAP

Having a fine new suit. Apologue. Tony Connor. BoLoP

Having allowed my willow to dry out. Halcion. R. T. Smith. AWTN

Having attained success in business. Robert Whitmore. Frank Marshall Davis. BPo

Having been tenant long to a rich Lord. Redemption. George Herbert. BASC; CABP; ESCV; FSCP; GSo; GeHe; HAP; InPK-6; MeLP; NAEL-5v1; NAEL-6v1; NAEL-7v1; NOBE; NOCV; NOSC; NPeEn; NoP-4; OxBEV; OxBSo; PBRV; PeECV; PoE; PoPoPo; SCGP; SCV; SoSe-8; TFi; TrCP; WeW-3

Having built my city and named my god. Lenaia. Susan M. Whitmore. AmPoNex

Having Climbed to the Topmost Peak of the Incense-Burner Mountain. Po Chü-i. ChiP, tr. by Arthur Waley

Having come to this place. This Place in the Ways. Muriel Rukeyser. AiP

Having commanded Adam to bestow. Naming the Animals. Anthony Hecht. ChIV-1

Having Completed My Fortieth Year. John Tranter. BMAP

Having crossed the threshold. Threshold, The. Fu'ad [or Fuad] Rifqa [or Rifka]. MAP, tr. by Sargon Boulus and Samuel Hazo

Having Died. Kim Kwangsŏp. WoPoe, tr. by David R. McCann

Having dined yesterday on a goat's foot. Automedon. GrAn

Having done most shameful, unjust things. Alcaeus [or Alkaios]. SaLy, tr. by Diane Rayor

Having done things, a thing, along that line myself. (LL) Scholars at the Orchid Pavilion. John Berryman. HarvBoo; PoE

Having endured them all. (LL) To an Artist, to Take Heart. Louise Bogan. PAI; TRP

Having enjoyed his shower, the cake of soap. On His Birthday. Greg Williamson. NAPBL

Having fallen not knowing. Conscript Goes, The. William Sydney Graham. FaBoWar

Having given up hope for a high-wire act. Learning to Swim at Forty-Five. Colleen J. McElroy. GT

Having gone out through the west city wall in the chilly dawn. Arriving after Rain at the Temple of Heavenly Peace. Wang Shih-cheng. SuSp, tr. by Richard John Lynn

Having gone upstairs. Mirror, A. Jean Follain. BLT

Having heard that an official was coming to investigate the disaster. Ballad on the Investigation of a Disaster. Yao Chen. ColAnChi, tr. by Victor H. Mair

Having heard the instruction. One Modern Poet. Carl Sandburg. OBAL

Having hooded my face with hair. Sibyl's Song, The. Michele Roberts. BrRo

Having interred [or interr'd] her infant-birth. Ode, upon a Question Moved, Whether Love Should Continue Forever?, An. Edward Herbert, 1st Baron Herbert of Cherbury. BASC; MeLP; NOBE; OxAEP-1; OxBEV

Having invented a new Holocaust. U. S. 1946 King's X. Robert Frost. NIP-4

Having It Out With Melancholy. Jane Kenyon. ExTi

  From the Nursery. LoL

  In and Out. LoL

  Often. LoL

  Once There Was Light. LoL

  Pardon. LoL

  Suggestion from a Friend. LoL

Having Led a Charmed Life, He Had to be Hanged Twice. Mac Wellman. FTOS

Having left behind its cutting. Unknown. RomPo, tr. by Eugene O'Connor Fr. Priapeic Corpus, The.

Having left hard [or solid] ground behind. Insular Celts, The. Ciaran Carson. BIrV; CIP-2

Having left the great mean city, I make. Goodbye to London. Louis MacNeice. PeECV

Having lost my leather purse. My Son. Ruth Stone. WPE

Having Lost My Sons, I Confront the Wreckage of the Moon: Christmas, 1960. James Wright. CoAP; HCAP; NAAL-2v2

Having myself been scared silly when I was young. Thief, The. Alden Nowlan. RaBo

Having never been. On Trying to Imagine the Kiwi Pregnant. Clarence Major. GT

Having no force to fly. (LL) Ezra Pound. APSN; APT-1; OBVE

Having planted a banana tree. Basho. EH, tr. by Robert Hass

Having power is nothing to be concerned about. Wang Fan-chih. SuSp

Having Prayed for, and Made Much Mention of the Merchants, She Sings the Following Hymn to Them. Anna Trapnell. EMWP

Having put yourself on the way. Spirits, Dancing. Arthur Gregor. VGW

Having read up on the subject. Jane Holland. NeBl

Having reddened the plum blossoms. Buson. EH, tr. by Robert Hass

Having rid Hamelin town of its vermin. Limerick. Ted Thompson. PeLi

Having sat all morning at the bay window. Late Mr Charles Lynch Digresses, The. Paul Durcan. ModIr

Having seen thy salvation. (LL) Song for Simeon, A. T. S. Eliot. ChIV-2; NOCV

Having slept, the cat gets up. Issa. EH, tr. by Robert Hass

Having Slept with a Man. Palladas [or Pallades]. WoPoe, tr. by Peter Jay

Having so rich a treasury, so fine a hoard. Daisy, The. Marya Alexandrovna Zaturenska. MoAmPo

Having spelt it out in blood. National Bird. N. Pichamurti. OMIP, tr. by Rajagopal Parthasarathy

Having split up the chaparral. Wide Land, The. A. R. Ammons. TwCP

Having submitted your petition for dismissal. Svetlana Kekova. ItGoST, tr. by Judith Hemschemeyer

Having the Wrong Name for Mr. Wright. Helen Barolini. UnSA

Having this day my horse, my hand, my lance. Sir Philip Sidney. HAP; NAEL-5v1; NAEL-6v1; NAEL-7v1; PoE; Son Fr. Astrophil and Stella.

Having to Part From His Mistress at Dawn. Bálint Balassi. IQMS, tr. by Yakov Hornstein

Having traveled ten li from the high city walls. Traveling at Break of Day. Huang Ching-jen. SuSp, tr. by Chang Yin-nan

Having tried to use the. It Is Deep. Carolyn M. Rodgers. NAAAL; SSLK

Having used every subterfuge. Renewal, A. James Merrill. OxBSP; VCAP

Having wet me with love. Mirabai [or Mira Bai]. ErotSp, tr. by Andrew Schelling

Having written every kind of poem. Tired Hunter, The. Gabriel Preil. FIT, tr. by Robert Friend

Having written several poems which I will not publish. Baedeker for Metaphysicians. Brian Higgins. FaBoTw

Haw Lantern, The. Seamus Heaney. HarvBoo; MakPoe; NoAM; PNI

Hawaii Dantesca. Charles Wright. HCAP; LCAP-2

Hawk. Mary Oliver. NAAL-5; OWoS

Hawk, The. George Mackay Brown. NoP-4; RB

Hawk and Snake. Leslie Marmon Silko. VoR

Hawk Chant of the Saginaws. Unknown. APN-2, tr. by Henry Rowe Schoolcraft

Hawk hovers in air, A. Loneliness. Tu Fu. OHPC, tr. by Kenneth Rexroth

Hawk in a Painting, A. Tu Fu. WoPoe, tr. by David Lattimore

Hawk Is a Woman. Hildegarde Flanner. WPE

Hawk Nailed to a Barn Door. Peter Blue Cloud. VoR

Hawk Roosting. Ted Hughes. GTBS-P; HAP; HeIP-4; OWoS; OxBEV; OxBTC; TwCP; UnPo

Hawk's Cry in Autumn, The. Joseph Brodsky. TCRP, tr. by Joseph Brodsky and Alan Myers

Hawk's Shadow. Louise Glück. HarvBoo

Hawk turns into the sun. Net of Place, The. Paul Blackburn. PFTM-2; PmAP

Hawking for the Partridge. Thomas Ravenscroft. OxBoLi

Hawks turn their heads nimbly round, The. Hawk Chant of the Saginaws. Unknown. APN-2, tr. by Henry Rowe Schoolcraft

Hawktree. Dave Jeddie Smith. HCAP

Hawthorn, The. Unknown. MiEL

Hawthorn at Digiff. Ruth Bidgood. TCAWP

Hawthorn Hedge, The. Judith Wright. WPE

Hawthorn morning moving, The. Renewal by Her Element. Denis Devlin. CIP-2; ModIr

Hawthorne. James Russell Lowell. NOBA; TAP; TCAPo Fr. Fable for Critics, A.

Hawthorne berries, The. David Kherdian. UrbNat Fr. Taking the Soundings on Third Avenue.

Hawthorne Garland, A.   Richard Harter Fogle.   OBAL

Hay.   Maxine W. Kumin.   BodElec

Hay, ay, hay, ay.   *Unknown*.   MiEL

Hay Fever.   Alec Derwent Hope.   NoAM

Hay for the Horses.   Gary Snyder.   BB; CoAmPo; LoL; TRP

Hay has long been built into the stack, The.   From Harvest to January.   Charles Tennyson Turner.   NOBVV

Hay Hotel, The.   Oliver St. John Gogarty.   BIrV

Hay is for horses.   *Unknown*.   OxNR

Hay making.   Joanna Baillie.   OxAEP-2

Hay-Making.   Gillian Clarke.   AngWePo

Hay scented, The. The cinnamon, the horsetail.   Understory.   Pamela Alexander.   ExTi

Hay-Time; or, The Constant Lovers. A Pastoral.   Josiah Relph.   NOEC

Hay wagon passed through the town at night, The.   Hay Wagon.   Lőrinc Szabó.   IQMS, *tr. by* Godfrey Turton

Haydon! forgive me that I cannot speak.   To B. R. Haydon, with a Sonnet Written on Seeing the Elgin Marbles.   John Keats.   CenSon

Hayle holy-land wherein our holy lord.   Uppon the First Sight of New England, June 29, 1638.   Thomas Tillam.   SCAP

Haylle, Comly and Clene.   *Unknown*.   OBEV; OxBoLi   *Fr.* Second Shepherd's Play, The.

Haymakers.   Deborah Randall.   NeBl

Haymaking.   Edward Thomas.   MoBrPo

Haymaking.   William Carlos Williams.   NoAM   *Fr.* Pictures from Brueghel.

Haystack in the Floods, The.   William Morris.   CABP; EBEV; EBNV; EBVV; HAP; NAEL-5v2; NAEL-6v2; NoP-4; OBNV; OxAEP-2; PeVV; PoRA

Hazard's friend Elliot is homosexual.   Wholesome.   William Meredith.   TAP

Hazardous Waste.   James Sherry.   FTOS

Hazards of Imagery, The.   Paul Violi.   KGB

Haze.   Carl Sandburg.   TCAPo

Haze, char, and the weather of All Souls'   In the Elegy Season.   Richard Wilbur.   InPK-6

Haze of gold, the Occident lights up, A.   Baruch Spinoza.   Jorge Luis Borges.   WoPoe, *tr. by* Willis Barnstone

Hazed with harvest dust and heat.   For the Missing in Action.   John Balaban.   AF

Hazel.   Oliver Reynolds.   FaBoWar

Hazel Goodwin Morrissey Brown.   Sinéad Morrissey.   MFPA

Hazel Stick for Catherine Ann, A.   Seamus Heaney.   NoAM

Hazel Tells LaVerne.   Katharyn Howd Machan.   ReTh

Hazy mountain temple hides away behind the setting sun, A.   Tune: "Sand of Silk-Washing Brook."   Wang Kuo-wei.   ColAnChi, *tr. by* Jiaosheng Wang

He.   Lawrence Ferlinghetti.   NeAP; PoM

He.   Stanley Kunitz.   NoP-4; VGW

He.   Vasco [*or* Vasko] Popa.   PoSu, *tr. by* Anne Pennington   *Fr.* Games.

He.   *Unknown*.   WoPoe, *tr. by* Paul Blackburn   *Fr.* Poem of the Cid, The.

He accepts the circle, speech and so.   Anne-Marie Albiach.   BoWoP

He adored the desk, its brown-oak inlaid with ebony, assorted prize pens, the seals of gold and base metal into which he had sunk his name.   Geoffrey Hill.   HAP; NoAM; NoP-4   *Fr.* Mercian Hymns.

He: Age Doesn't Matter When You're Both in Love.   Julia Alvarez.   Son   *Fr.* 33.

He ahold of my hand has completely satisfied me. (LL)   Of the Terrible Doubt of Appearances.   Walt Whitman.   APN-1; CAGL

He aims. At her. Then drops his aim. Idly. (LL)   Guard at the Binh Thuy Bridge, The.   John Balaban.   AF; CDa

He all that time among the sewers of Troy.   Troy.   Edwin Muir.   HarvBoo

He also told them a parable.   William Carlos Williams.   GI   *Fr.* St. Matthew; He also told them a parable.

He always blinked too much.   Remembering Dennis's Eyes.   Geoff Hattersley.   NeBl

He ambles along like a walking pin cushion.   Hedgehog.   Chu Chen Po.   OHMPC, *tr. by* Kenneth Rexroth

He and his, unwashed all winter.   Native, The.   W. S. Merwin.   PoRA

He and I.   End of a Course.   Ivor Armstrong Richards.   CRP

He and I.   Dante Gabriel Rossetti.   OxBSo

He applies for a job.   Variations on a Poem by Reznikoff.   Louis Simpson.   BodElec

He approaches her, trailing his whole fortune.   Peacock Display.   David Wagoner.   OWoS

He Approacheth the Hall of Judgment.   *Unknown*.   AWP   *Fr.* Book of the Dead.

He arises. Oriane / the lurcher wants.   Red Brick and Brown Stone.   James Schuyler.   BodElec

He arrived, towing a crowd, and slept.   David Constantine.   HarvBoo

He ascended from a lonely crag in winter.   On the Death of Karl Barth.   Jack R. Clemo.   NOCV

He ask'd, and hoped, through Christ. Do thou the same! (LL)   Epitaph: "Stop, Christian passer-by!—Stop, child of God."   Samuel Taylor Coleridge.   NAEL-5v2; NAEL-6v2; NOCV; SacPr

He asked for bread, and he received a stone. (LL)   On the Setting Up of Mr. Butler's Monument in Westminster Abbey.   Samuel Wesley.   NBLV; NOEC; OxBSP

He Asked Them What Did They Know & They Told Him.   *Unknown*.   STP, *tr. by* Richard Johnny John and Jerome Rothenberg

He Asketh Absolution of God.   *Unknown*.   AWP   *Fr.* Book of the Dead.

He ate and drank the precious Words.   Emily Dickinson.   APN-2

He attempted *texas red light*.   Random (Re-arrangeable) Study for *Views*.   Tony Towle.   PmAP

He avoids the momentous rhythm.   Last Man, The.   Thom Gunn.   OxAEP-2   *Fr.* Misanthropos.

He awoke this morning from a strange dream.   Chief Leschi of the Nisqually.   Duane Niatum.   CDW

He bade me "Be Happy," he whisper'd "Forget me."   He Bade Me Be Happy.   Frances Sargent Osgood.   TCAPo

He bare him [*or* hym] up, he bare him [*or* hym] down.   *Unknown*.   HAP; OxBEV

He bathes his soul in women's wrath.   Irish Patriarch, The.   Ruth Pitter.   NALW

He beat me with the hem of a kimono.   Club, The.   Mitsuye Yamada.   FSt

He best can paint 'em, who shall feel 'em most. (LL)   Pope.   NAEL-5v1; NAEL-6v1; NAEL-7v1; RACG

He Biddeth Osiris to Arise from the Dead.   *Unknown*.   AWP   *Fr.* Book of the Dead.

He blinks upon the hearth-rug.   On a Cat Aging.   Sir Alexander Gray.   TriCat

He bought me the fur thing five Winters ago.   Take Back Your Mink.   Frank Loesser.   ReLy

He bows because he is nobody.   Tennessee Waltz, The.   James Haug.   OPRER

He breathed deeply.   Circle.   'Enayat Jaber.   PoArWo, *tr. by* Wen Chin Ouyang

He breathed in air, he breathed out light.   Goodbye.   Adrian Mitchell.   OPOU

He broods of pleasant days gone by.   Sorcerer, The.   Laury Wells.   IBA

He brought a light so she could see.   Strains of Sight.   Robert Duncan.   PoE

He brought our saviour to the western side.   John Milton.   NOSC   *Fr.* Paradise Regained [*or* Regain'd].

He brushed against me, Father. Very gently. (LL)   Cuba.   Paul Muldoon.   CIP-2; ModIr; PNI

He built a house, time laid it in the dust.   His Monument.   Sarah Knowles Bolton.   PWR

He built himself a house.   Fairy Tale.   Miroslav Holub.   RB, *tr. by* George Theiner

He burnt up his desire. (LL)   Adonis.   *Unknown*.   NPeEn; NoSic, *tr. by* Theocritus

He buys me a glass.   Gameboy.   Regie Cabico.   WiU

He called a conquered land his own.   Wolfe Tone.   Austin Clarke.   CIP-2

He calleth to me out of Seir, Watchman, what of the night?   Bible, *O.T.*   AWP   *Fr.* Isaiah.

He calls it their stage which echoes our first misrecognition of unity.   Instances.   Swan, The.   Mei-Mei Berssenbrugge.   OpBo

He calls you in his wedding coat.   Wedding Coat, The.   Harriet Rose.   BrRo

He came after the reading, when all.   Belonging.   Leslie Norris.   TCAWP

He came and took me by the hand.   Mystery, The.   Ralph Hodgson.   InvLi; MoBrPo

He came apart in the open.   Martin's Blues.   Michael S. Harper.   HCAP; NAAL-5

He came back.   Dry River Bed.   Andrew Salkey.   WoPoe

He came back and shot. He shot him. When he came.   Incident.   Imamu Amiri Baraka.   AF; NoAM

He came from hills to comfortable plains.   Mountaineer, The.   Robert Nathan.   TrJP

He came from Malta.   Tymnes.   FaBoCh; FaBoEE; Spl; WoPoe, *tr. by* Edmund Charles Blunden   *Fr.* Epigrams.

He came in she said he had come in.   Adelaide's Dream.   Christopher Middleton.   PeLV

He came lilting down the brae with a blackthorn stick the thick of a shotgun.   Bagpipe Music.   Ciaran Carson.   ModIr

He came of a sharecrop farm family.   Corporal Kevin Spina, U. S. M. C.   Bryan Alec Floyd.   CDa

He came over to London and straight away strode.   Dinky Di.   *Unknown*.   NOBAu

He came to deliver the secret of the sun.   U Tam'si Tchicaya.   *See* He had just surrendered the secret of the sun

He came to my desk with a quivering lip.   New Leaf, A [*or* The].   Helen Field Fischer.   PoToHe

He came to the depot a figure of shame.   Conchie, The.   R. F. Palmer.   FaBoWar

He came to the desert of London town. William Blake. James Thomson. CABP

He Came to Visit Me. Martin Seymour-Smith. FaBoTw

He Came Unto His Own, and His Own Received Him Not. Mary Elizabeth Coleridge. ViWPN

He can build, and once more fire. (LL) John Fletcher. NOBE; OBEV *Fr.* Tragedy of Valentinian, The.

He can only drink tea now, screwed and filed. Pink Slip at Tool & Dye. Dave Jeddie Smith. NoAM

He can snuggle back in the telephone pole. (LL) Woodpecker, The. Elizabeth Madox Roberts. OBCA; TLR

He cancelled the ravaging Plague. George Meredith. VerBaPo *Fr.* Empty Purse, The.

He cannot imagine a doorknob. Feeling Type and His Friends, The. Michael Davidson. FTOS

He cannot make, if that's a thing He can. (LL) Sonnet: Of the Making of Master Messerin. Rustico Di Filippo. AWP; EaItPo, *tr. by* Dante Gabriel Rossetti

He captured many thousand guns. Napoleon. William Makepeace Thackeray. FaBoWar

He carried the spit to the nearest urn. Citizen's Way, The. Vladimir Burich. TCRP, *tr. by* Albert C. Todd

He cast his net at morn where fishers toiled. Failure. Kate Tucker Goode. PWR

He catch'd at love, and fill'd his arm with bayes. (LL) Story of Phoebus and Daphne Applied, [etc.], The. Edmund Waller. NAEL-5v1; NOSC

He catches salamanders two centimeters long. Sarah Kirsch. PFTM-2, *tr. by* Wayne Kvam *Fr.* Kite-Flying.

He changes into a bird, and that's. Gout. Lewis Warsh. FTOS

He circles slowly and the walls of the room. Baba Mostafa. Mimi Khalvati. Prnts

He clasps the crag with crookèd hands. Eagle, The. Tennyson. ChAP; ClHu; FHYEP; FaBoCh; GTBS-P; HeIP-4; ITBLP; InPK-6; NAEL-5v2; NAEL-6v2; NOBVV; NTCP; NoP-4; OWoS; OxBSP; PAI; SCGP; TFi; TRP; UnPo

He clicks off the reading lamp, and it is almost morning. Night Person, The. Richard Frost. AWTN

He climbed and, under the gray leaves. Olive Garden, The. Rainer Maria Rilke. GI

He climbed, devoured. In her mouth. Cat in the Dovecote. Avner Trainin. MHP, *tr. by* Ruth Finer Mintz

He climbs the stair. Waterchew! Gregory Corso. VGW

He closed the deal on the night. A real. Nocturnes. Dionisio D. Martinez. TouFir

He closes his eyes. Wink. Roger Gilbert-Lecomte. PFTM-1

He Comes Among. George Barker. OBMV

He comes from the mountains, he stands in the grove! Antichrist, The. Stefan George. WoPoe, *tr. by* Peter Viereck

He comes from the north. Three for Bear. Aimé Césaire. PFTM-1

He Comes Not To-night. Josephine D. Henderson Heard. CBWP-4

He comes running. Poem about a Wolf Maybe Two Wolves, A. *Unknown.* STP, *tr. by* Richard Johnny John and Jerome Rothenberg

He comes to brood and sit. (LL) Peace. Gerard Manley Hopkins. GTBS-P; OxBSP; TrCP

He comes to near that comes to be denied. (LL) Lady's Resolve, The. Lady Mary Wortley Montagu. BoWoP; OxBSP

He comes unknown and heard and stands there. Man into a Churchyard. Bernard Gutteridge. SPE

He comes with autumn, when the leaves flake. Shoni Onions. Sheenagh Pugh. AngWePo

He Cometh Forth into the Day. *Unknown.* AWP *Fr.* Book of the Dead.

He cometh, O bliss! He Cometh. Judah Halevi. TrJP, *tr. by* Emma Lazarus

He Commandeth a Fair Wind. *Unknown.* AWP *Fr.* Book of the Dead.

He Considers the Birds of the Air. Karl Kirchwey. GI

He could barely tell one from the other. (LL) Milkweed and Monarch. Paul Muldoon. NoP-4; PoetW

He could have come to tell us. Never Give a Bum an Even Break. James Welch. NoAM

He could help us out. Tennis in the City. Frank Higgins. MoASP

He could not imagine himself a hero at all. Country or Western Music. Gerald Early. BodElec

He could see the little lake. Lake, The. James Stephens. MoBrPo

He could sing sweetly on a string. Orpheus. Elizabeth Madox Roberts. MoAmPo

He couldn't remember what propelled him. Man on a Fire Escape. Edward Hirsch. UrbNat

He courts her up there on the roof. Muse Is Always the Other Woman, The. Constance Urdang. PBCAP

He cracked them in half. Cracking Walnuts. Maria Jastrzebska. Prnts

He crawls to the edge of the foaming creek. Meeting the Mountains. Gary Snyder. NoAM; TAP

He crouches, and buries his face on his knees, / And hides in the dark of his hair. Last of His Tribe, The. Henry Clarence Kendall. CBAP

He cut a sappy sucker from the muckle rodden-tree. Whistle, The. Charles Murray. OxBS

He dances on a toe. L'indifférent. "Michael Field." ViWPN

He debated whether. Arthur Ridgewood, M.D. Frank Marshall Davis. BPo

He Defendeth His Heart against the Destroyer. *Unknown.* AWP *Fr.* Book of the Dead.

He delights to play. Musical Saw. David Kresh. MiVo

He did his duty both by peers and peasants. King George V. Charles W. Hayward. NOBAu

He did not come / A gnostic. Incarnation Poem. John Leax. TrCP

He did not come of a long line of stone-cutters. Man Who Went Absent from the Native Literature, The. Anthony Cronin. CIP-2

He did not lie to us, that spirit, mournfully severe. Progeny of Cain, The. Nikolai Stepanovich Gumilyov [*or* Gumiliov *or* Gumilev]. TCRP, *tr. by* Simon Franklin

He did not think me strange or older, Nor I, him. (LL) All Souls' Night. Frances Darwin Cornford. EnLoPo; OxBSP; OxBTC

He did not wear his scarlet coat. Oscar Wilde. CABP; EBNV; MoBrPo; NOBE; NOBVV; NPeEn; NoAM; OBMV; OBNV; OxAEP-2; OxBEV; TFi; UV *Fr.* Ballad of Reading Gaol, The.

He did not wear his swallow tail. Gourmand, The. Harry Graham. UV

He didn't, no he didn't think continually. Hand for Some Others, A. Geoffrey Holloway. NLP

He didn't say. Malcolm Spoke / Who Listened? Haki R. Madhubuti. ESEAA; NAAAL

He died, in our land where he came to stay. Foreigner Who Died in Juchitán, The. Pancho Na'car. WoPoe, *tr. by* Brian Swann

He died privately. Ram. Gillian Clarke. AngWePo

He dies vicariously on "Carol Burnett." Assassination of Robert Goulet as Performed by Elvis Presley: Memphis, 1968, The. David Wojahn. AllShUp; IllVoic

He "Digesteth Harde Yron." Marianne Craig Moore. APT-1; NoAM; OWoS

He dines alone surrounded by reflections. Witch Doctor. Robert Earl Hayden. NoAM; PAI

He disagrees with Simone de Beauvoir. His Plans for Old Age. William Meredith. TAP

He disappeared in the dead of winter. W. H. Auden. AmFaPo; HAP; HeIP-4; MakPoe; MoBrPo; NAEL-6v2; NIL-7; NOBE; NPeEn; NoAM; NoP-4; OxAEP-2; OxBTC; PAI; TFi; TRP; UnPo; WeW-3

He discovered the age of the sun and he knows. To a Mathematician. Jan Kochanowski. WoPoe, *tr. by* Jerzy Peterkiewicz and Burns Singer

He discovers himself on an old airfield. Old Pilot, The. Donald Hall. LCAP-2

He does not sit with silent men. Oscar Wilde. NPeEn; OxBEV *Fr.* Ballad of Reading Gaol, The.

He does not think that I haunt here nightly. Haunter, The. Thomas Hardy. NOBE

He doesn't act as though he cares. As Long As He Needs Me. Lionel Bart. ReLy

He doesn't know the world at all. Birdsong. *Unknown, fr. Terezin Concentration Camp.* INSAB

He doesn't like it, of course. His Body. Sandra McPherson. LoL

He doesn't mind breathing dust. Mowing. Stuart Dybek. UrbNat

He Doeth All Things Well. Anne Brontë. SacPr

He Done His Level Best. "Mark Twain." AiP

He doth not crave less time, but more. (LL) Time. George Herbert. NAEL-5v1; NAEL-6v1; NAEL-7v1

He doth sit by us and moan. (LL) William Blake. AWP; FHYEP; InvLi; OxAEP-2 *Fr.* Songs of Innocence.

He draws a man. Picture of a Man. Calvin Forbes. ISC

He draws memory out of me with hands of fire. Penelope Shuttle. LW *Fr.* Passion.

He dreamed of / an open window. Dream, The. Felix Pollak. RaBo

He dreams of saxophones and hounds. Lugs Benedict on the Coast, 1934. Tom Rea. GifTon

He drew a circle that shut me out. Outwitted. Edwin Markham. MoAmPo; PoToHe

He drew hundreds of women. Beauty and Sadness. Cathy Song. NoAM

He drifts into a room of strangers. Leaving the Country. Wyn Cooper. OPRER

He drifts on blue water. Blue Water. Li Po. CrYelRi; ErotSp, *tr. by* Sam Hamill

He drinks because she scolds, he thinks. Which the Chicken, Which the Egg? Ogden Nash. APT-2

He drowsed and was aware of silence heaped. Death-Bed, The. Siegfried Sassoon. AF; PeFWW

He dwelt among "apartments let." Jacob. Phoebe Cary. APN-2; OBAL

He dwelt there all that day, and at dawn on the morrow. *Unknown.* FaBoWar *Fr.* Sir Gawain and the Green Knight.

He dyes / his white hair black. Compromise, The. Ibn al-Rumi. ArPe, *tr. by* Omar S. Pound

He eats of the fruits of the great Speckle. Ted Berrigan. FTOS *Fr.* Sonnets, The.

He eats rain. Fir. T.E. Jay. GifTon

He Embarketh in the Boat of Ra. *Unknown.* AWP *Fr.* Book of the Dead.

He ended, and they both descend the hill. John Milton. NAWM-5v1; NAWM-7v1 *Fr.* Paradise Lost.

He ended; and thus *Adam* last reply'd. John Milton. HeIP-4 *Fr.* Paradise Lost.

He ended, nor the Argicide refus'd. Homer. OBVE *Fr.* Odyssey.

He enjoyed making masks. Mask. Sapardi Djoko Damono. WoPoe, *tr. by* John H. McGlynn

He Entereth the House of the Goddess Hathor. *Unknown.* AWP *Fr.* Book of the Dead.

He escape the lynch days. He survives. Wole Soyinka. HBAPE

He Establisheth His Triumph. *Unknown.* AWP *Fr.* Book of the Dead.

He fails who climbs to power and place. Failure and Success. Richard Watson Gilder. PWR

He feared money so much he was known. Usual Immigrant Uncle Poem, The. Askold Melnyczuk. OPRER

He fed them generously who were his flocks. W. D. Snodgrass. Son

He feels small as he awakens. Awakening, The. Robert Creeley. NeAP

He Fell among Thieves. Sir Henry John Newbolt. EBVV; OBEV; OBWP; OxBTC

He fell for a beautiful. Vasco [*or Vasko*] Popa. PoSu, *tr. by* Anne Pennington *Fr.* Quartz Pebble, The.

He fell in love with the butcher's daughter. Street. Eiléan Ní Chuilleanáin. EmeKit

He fell in victory's fierce pursuit. General Elliott, The. Robert Graves. PeLV

He fell off a barn on his head. Captains Courageous. Frank O'Hara. FTOS

He felt at first. Roman Study. Louise Glück. BodElec

He felt the wild beast in him betweenwhiles. George Meredith. NOBVV *Fr.* Modern Love.

He finds it in the yard. Bird. Kim Addonizio. UrbNat

He finds the God there far unlike his books. (LL) Fulke Greville, 1st Baron Brooke. HAP; NAEL-5v1; NAEL-6v1; NAEL-7v1; NOBE; OxBEV *Fr.* Mustapha.

He first deceased [*or* deceas'd]; she for a little tried [*or* tri'd]. Upon the Death of Sir Albert Morton's Wife. Sir Henry Wotton. BASC; BoLoP; EnLoPo; FaBoEE; NPeEn; OBEV; OxBEV; PBRV; WeW-3

He flies not—but he coolly walks away. (LL) On the Aphorism "L'Amitié est l'Amour sans Ailes." Charlotte Smith. CABP; PEW

He flies so easy, when he sings. (LL) Driving in Oklahoma. Carter Revard. HATNAP; VoR

He floated upwards, and regain'd the steep. (LL) White Horse of Westbury, The. Charles Tennyson Turner. EBEV; PeVV

He followed his own mind. *Unknown.* STP

He followed their lilting stanzas. Local Poet, A. John Hewitt. ModIr; PNI

He forced his way into it, a near shave. Life, A. Janet Fisher. MFPA

He found a formula for drawing comic rabbits. Epitaph on an Unfortunate Artist. Robert Graves. FaBoEE; NOBL; OBCoV

He found her by the ocean's moaning verge. George Meredith. NAEL-6v2; NoP-4 *Fr.* Modern Love.

He frightens all the witches and the dragons in their lair. Black Cock, The. Ishmael Reed. ISC

He from the wind-bitten North with ship and companions descended. Rudyard Kipling. FaBoEE; PeFWW; PoWW; WoPoe *Fr.* Epitaphs of the War [1914–1918].

He fumbles at your Spirit. Emily Dickinson. APN-2; LW; NAAL-2v1; NAAL-3; NCAP; NOCV; TCAPo; TRP

He gathered for His own delight. Ere the Golden Bowl Is Broken. Anna Hempstead Branch. TCAPo

He gave himself another year. Patrick Kavanagh. BIrV *Fr.* Great Hunger, The.

He gave his strength and his loveliness for his country. On a Soldier Killed in the Great War. R. Williams Parry. OBWVE, *tr. by* H. Idris Bell

He gave joy to men & more joy. Krantor. Theaitetus. GrAn, *tr. by* Dennis Schmitz

He gave silver shoes to the rabbit. Blake Leads a Walk on the Milky Way. Nancy Willard. OBCA

He gave the solid rail a hateful kick. Egg and the Machine, The. Robert Frost. MoAmPo

He gave us all a good-bye cheerily. Messmates. Sir Henry John Newbolt. EBVV; PeVV

He gave us eyes to see them, and lips that we might tell, How great is God

Almighty, Who has made all things well. (LL) All Things Bright and Beautiful. Cecil Frances Alexander. SacPr; UV

He gazed and gazed and gazed and gazed. Rhyme for a Child Viewing a Naked Venus in a Painting [of "The Judgement of Paris"]. Robert Browning. NPeEn; OBCoV

He gazed on the face of the high-born maid. George R. Sims. VerBaPo *Fr.* Beauty and the Beast.

He gives her all the configurations. Configurations. Grace Nichols. LW

He gives me a handshake. Big Chill Variations. Reuben Jackson. UnSA

He giveth his beloved-sleep. (LL) Sleep, The. Elizabeth Barrett Browning. ChIV-1; OxAEP-2

He glanced at me one day—but then his mean. Sadi [*or Saadi or* Sa'di]. WoPoe, *tr. by* Dick Davis

He gloried in the feats. My Father's Heroes. Allison Joseph. SeSe

He gossips like my grandmother, this man. Cleaving, The. Li-Young Lee. OpBo

He gossips like my grandmother, this man. Li-Young Lee. OpBo; IllVoic *Fr.* Cleaving, The.

He got hauled in. Autobiography of John Doe, The. Jon Lavieri. OPRER

He grew old between the fires of Troy. Euripides the Athenian. George Seferis. PoetW, *tr. by* Edmund Keeley and Philip Sherrard

He had a name. Generations 1. Sam Cornish. GT

He Had a Quality of Growth. Muriel Rukeyser. NNaP

He had a tall cedar he wanted to cut for posts. Old Man Climbs a Tree, The. Wendell Berry. PoCoUp

He had always supposed he would die first. Soon. James Harms. NeAmPo

He had been falling in the abyss some four thousand years. Et Nox Facta Est. Victor Hugo. NAWM-7v2, *tr. by* Mary Ann Caws

He had been there all his life, at the Corner. Old Co'es. Jim Everett. IBA

He had contempt that was divine. Mess Boy, The. Sydney Wilmer. CAGL

He had determined to dance the presence of the dance. He had been in fact determined. Presence of the Dance / The Resolution of the Music, The. Robert Duncan. FTOS

He had driven half the night. Hay for the Horses. Gary Snyder. BB; CoAmPo; LoL; TRP

He had entered her heart. Gentleman in the Heart, The. Vivian Lamarque. ClItWP, *tr. by* Cinzia Sartini Blum and Lara Trubowitz

He had got, finally. Poem for Speculative Hipsters, A. Imamu Amiri Baraka. NOBA; NoAM

He had his Thirty-nine Articles. Fossil, A. May Kendall. VWP

He had just surrendered the secret of the sun. Mat to Weave, A. U Tam'si Tchicaya. NegPo, *tr. by* Ellen Conroy Kennedy

He had need of a way. Being Somebody. Edwin Honig. TAP

He "Had Not Where to Lay His Head." Frances Ellen Watkins Harper. PWR

He had passed it. Disconcerting Object. J. Bernlef. TuT, *tr. by* Peter Van de Kamp

He had the nerve to say *Let's be grown-up about this.* New York Spring. Linda France. MFPA

He had to be four times cuckold. (LL) Temperaments, The. Ezra Pound. BoLoP; NOBA; NoAM; OBCoV; PAI

He had to die they say. Heaven's Ring. Vasco [*or Vasko*] Popa. VCWP, *tr. by* Charles Simic

He halted in the wind, and—what was that. Boundless Moment, A. Robert Frost. NAAL-2v2

He hands / down the gift. Gift, The. Robert Creeley. NOBA

He hands them back when he sees they are done. (LL) Toaster, The. William Jay Smith. NOxBChV; OTCP

He has a rather plain wife. My Neighbor. Roque Dalton. AF, *tr. by* Richard Schaaf

He has a ticking in his soul, and prays. Peter Klappert. YaYoPo *Fr.* Pieces of the One and a Half Legged Man.

He has an eye for cities. Among his rows. Lewis Mumford. George Buchanan. PNI

He has become as / talkative as Bottom a weaver and says for. Louis Zukofsky. APSN *Fr.* A.

He has been awake. My Father, Counting Sheep. Kate Foley. Prnts

He has built himself a cottage in the wood. Cottage in the Wood, A. Russell Edson. LCAP-2

He has chopped wood (very badly too) and carried logs for one. Caliban's Journal. Suniti Namjoshi. RACG

He has finished a day's work. Pornographer, The. Robert Hass. YaYoPo

He has gone. Last Journey. Enrique Gonzáles Martínez. TCLAP, *tr. by* Samuel Beckett

He has gone into the forest. Journey to the Interior. William Jay Smith. DiPo

He has hanged himself—the Sun. November. Frederick William Harvey. OxBTC

He has lain here for a terrible, motionless. David Wojahn. PBCAP; SwNoth *Fr.* Mystery Train: A Sequence.

He has married again. His wife. Pot Burial. Tom Paulin. ModIr

He has not woo'd, but he has lost his heart. Country Dance, A. Charles Tennyson Turner. NOBVV; OxBEV

He has taken flight through the tropic day and the night. Perchance to Dream. Mary Low. SurWo

He has taught the Universe to realize itself. Alcoholic in the 3rd Week of the 3rd Treatment, The. John Berryman. BodElec

He has the lower part. Man with a Hole in His Face, The. Jack Coulehan. BloBone

He has three singles on the charts and in. David Wojahn. PBCAP *Fr.* Mystery Train: A Sequence.

He has two antennae. Gnat on My Paper. Richard Eberhart. APT-2

He has woven rose-vines. C33. Hart Crane. CAGL

He hasn't gone to work. Poem Circling Hamtramck, Michigan, All Night in Search of You, The. Philip Levine. NNaP

He hath abolished the old drouth. Gerard Manley Hopkins. SacPr

He Hath Need of Rest. Josephine D. Henderson Heard. CBWP-4

He Hath No Parallel. Sadi [*or* Saadi *or* Sa'di]. AWP, *tr. by* L. Cranmer-Byng *Fr.* Gulistan, The.

He hath no place to rest his head. Judaeus Errans. Louis Golding. TrJP

He hears it not now, but used to notice such things? (LL) Afterwards. Thomas Hardy. EBEV; GTBS-P; HarvBoo; MoBrPo; NOBE; NoP-4; OxAEP-2; OxBEV; PoPoPo; TFi; TOF; WoPoe

He Hears the Cry of the Sedge. W. B. Yeats. OxBTC; RB

He hears with gladdened heart the thunder. Robert Louis Stevenson. ITBLP

He Held Radical Light. A. R. Ammons. PoE; VCAP

He Hides within the Lily. William Channing Gannett. AH

He hie fie finger / speak in simple sound. Man, The. Robert Creeley. OBAL

He hoes the grain under a midday sun. Pitying the Farmer. Li Shen. CoBCP; ColAnChi, *tr. by* Burton Watson

He Hola. Keri Hulme. PeNZ

He Holdeth Fast to the Memory of His Identity. *Unknown.* AWP *Fr.* Book of the Dead.

He holds a volume open in his hands. Boy with Book of Knowledge. Howard Nemerov. NoP-4

He hunched a broomstick. Canary Man and You, The. Rick Alley. AmPoNex

He in Christ's doctrine deals by way of trade. Portrait of a Bishop. Evan Lloyd. AngWePo

He: In the long river, the fish swim off without a trace. Replies. *Vietnamese Oral Tradition.* CaDao, *tr. by* John Balaban

He Intercedes with Charlemagne for His Brother in Exile. Paul the Deacon. MLL, *tr. by* Helen Waddell

He invented a rainbow but lightning struck it. Bushed. Earle Birney. MoCV; NOBC; NoAM; NoP-4

He is a parricide to his mother's name. In Praise of Women in General. Thomas Randolph. NOSC

He is a tower unleaning. But how will he not break. Vaunting Oak. John Crowe Ransom. OxBA; VGW

He is a very inoffensive man. Sonnet 43. Eleanor Brown. MFPA

He is a young knight from the south of Han-tan. Youth of Han-tan, The; a Song. Kao Shih. SuSp, *tr. by* Joseph J. Lee

He is almost a god, a man beside you. Sappho. ErotSp, *tr. by* Sam Hamill

He is always right. Interrogator, The. Elizabeth Jennings. WPE

He is an Englishman! Sir William Schwenck Gilbert. NOBL *Fr.* H. M. S. Pinafore.

He is an utter failure as a devil. Devil, A. Zbigniew Herbert. RB, *tr. by* Czeslaw Milosz

He is blood, himself. Water of the Flowery Mill (II), The. Jerome Rothenberg. FTOS

He is breathing his last, my rebellion is dying. Surrender. "Rachel" [*or* "Rahel"]. FIT, *tr. by* Robert Friend

He is coming, Adzed-Head. *Unknown.* NOIV

He is coming, my long-desired lord. *Var. authors.* AWP, *tr. by* Lafcadio Hearn *Fr.* Manyo Shu, Part 3 of 4.

He is dead, the beautiful youth. Killed at the Ford. Henry Wadsworth Longfellow. CBCWP

He Is Declared True of Word. *Unknown.* AWP *Fr.* Book of the Dead.

He Is Far. *Unknown.* MiEL

He is firm and strong. Oriki Erinle. *Unknown.* PBA; TTY, *tr. by* Ulli Beier

He is going to stop thinking. Dandelion. Juan Delgado. AmPoNex

He is gone. Tune: "Dreaming of Southland" Thinking of Someone. Liu Shih. ColAnChi, *tr. by* Kang-i Sun Chang

He Is Gone. Anna Swirszczynska. PoSu

He is having his hair cut. Towels are tucked. Alex at the Barber's. John Fuller. PeLV

He is, in truth, lacking in civility. Mary Stuart, Queen of Scots. EMWP

He is knit with his doom. (LL) Germinal. "Æ" BIrV; MoBrPo; OBEV; OBMV

He is knit with his doom. (LL) Exiles. "Æ" BIrV; MoBrPo

He is learning at a rate of knots. For a Six Year Old. Ben Scammell. NLP

He Is Lightning. Jordan Davis. HeMarv

He is like a god. Catullus. ErotSp, *tr. by* Sam Hamill

He Is like the Lotus. *Unknown.* AWP, *tr. by* Ulli Beier *Fr.* Book of the Dead.

He Is like the Serpent Saka. *Unknown.* AWP *Fr.* Book of the Dead.

He is lonely then within the pale of the palace. Commentary. Hyam Plutzik. TaR

He is lost to the small farms, lane by lane. (LL) Day in August, A. Frank Ormsby. PBCIP; PNI

He Is My Countryman. Antoni Slonimski. TrJP, *tr. by* Frances Notley

He is my love / my sweet nutgrove. *Unknown.* BIrV

He is my shadow. Veronique Tadjo. NAfrP, *tr. by* Faustine Boateng Gyima

He is no friend who in thine hour of pride. Sadi [*or* Saadi *or* Sa'di]. AWP, *tr. by* L. Cranmer-Byng *Fr.* Gulistan, The.

He is not a brother to me. Brother, The. Semion Yakovlevich Nadson. TrJP, *tr. by* H. Badanes

He is not dead. (LL) Frederick Douglass: 1817–1895. Langston Hughes. BPo; CBCWP; HHAm

He is not dead nor liveth. Dorothy Wellesley, Duchess of Wellington. OBMV *Fr.* Deserted House.

He is not de[a]d that sometime [*or* somtyme] hath a fall. Sir Thomas Wyatt. OBVE

He is not here, the old sun. No Possum, No Sop, No Taters. Wallace Stevens. HCAP; OxBA; TAP; VGW

He is not quite dead. Armand Schwerner. PFTM-2; WoPoe *Fr.* Tablets, The.

He is not the man who goes over the wall. Man on the Edge. Heberto Padilla. VCWP

He is older than the naval side of British history. Chief Petty Officer. Charles Causley. OxBTC

He is one of the prophets come back. He. Lawrence Ferlinghetti. NeAP; PoM

He Is Out of Heart with His Time. Guerzo di Montecanti. AWP; EaItPo, *tr. by* Dante Gabriel Rossetti

He is quick, thinking in clear images. In Broken Images. Robert Graves. HarvBoo; NoP-4; TRP

He is repulsed [*or* repuls'd] indeed—but you are [*or* you're *or* you'r] undone. (LL) To the Noblest and Best of Ladies, the Countess of Denbigh. Richard Crashaw. GeHe; MeLP; NAEL-6v1; NAEL-7v1

He is risen now that was so long asleep. War. Georg Heym. PeFWW, *tr. by* Patrick Bridgwater

He is rust / in moonlight. Coyote Fragments. Lance Henson. HATNAP

He is Shaka the unshakable. *Unknown.* PBA; TTY, *tr. by* A. C. Jordan

He is sherrier. Thinnest Shadow, The. John Ashbery. TTTS

He is stark mad, who ever says. Broken Heart, The. John Donne. EBEV; FSCP

He is sun-bright myth and Cosmic Light. O Lord of Light! A Mystic Sage Returns to Realms of Eternity! Askia Muhammad Touré. SeSe; SpirFl

He, is the Great God, Who is in heaven. Great Hymm. Ntsikana Gaba. PeSAV, *tr. by* John Knox Bokwe

He is the King amang us three! (LL) Willie Brew'd [*or* Brewed] a Peck o' Maut. Robert Burns. AWP; OxBS

He is the love-wolf. *Unknown, fr. Egyptian hieroglyphics.* ErotSp, *tr. by* Barbara Hughes Fowler

He is the oldest grandfather. Memory Sire, The. Barney Bush. HATNAP

He is the one who waves. (LL) Salt Water Story. Richard Hugo. NAAL-2v2; NoAM

He is the source of hot forests. Cusp of Desire, The. Maysoun Saqr Al-Qasimi. PoArWo, *tr. by* Subhi Hadidi and Nathalie Handal

He is very busy with his looking. Young Heroes. Gwendolyn Brooks. BPo; NAAAL

He is very old. At his sunken brow. Derzhavin. Georgy [*or* Georgii] Arkadevich Shengeli. TCRP, *tr. by* Daniel Weissbort

He is your friend. (LL) Turtle, The. William Carlos Williams. EmeKit; RaBo; SAmP

He jests at scars [that never felt a wound]. William Shakespeare. PAI *Fr.* Romeo and Juliet.

He journeys over the dark land. Vasco [*or* Vasko] Popa. PoSu; WoPoe, *tr. by* Anne Pennington *Fr.* St Sava's Spring.

He jumped me while I was asleep. Assailant. John Raven. BPo

He jumps from behind, flying like a shard. Sarah Gorham. FFC *Fr.* Notes From a Chinese Love Manual.

He kicked the world, and lunging long ago. Horse, The. James Wright (1927–80). YaYoPo

"He killed his parents." Majeski Plays the Saxophone. Martín Espada. SeSe

He Kindleth a Fire. *Unknown.* AWP *Fr.* Book of the Dead.

He kneels on the rumpled bed. Gail Morse. PasH

He knelt, the Savior knelt and prayed. Agony in the Garden, The. Felicia Dorothea Hemans. TrCP

He knew how death hunts / at distance. Epitaph: Atticus. Paulus [*or* Paulos] Silentiarius. GrAn, *tr.* by Andrew Miller

He knew it was waiting for him somewhere. My Father's Death. Constance Urdang. PBCAP

He Knew Joy on Earth. Unsi Al-Haj [*or* Hajj]. MAP, *tr.* by Sargon Boulus and Alistair Elliot

He knew what I wanted. O Dirty Bird Yr Gizzard's Too Big & Full of Sand. James Koller. PoM

He Knoweth the Souls of the East. *Unknown.* AWP *Fr.* Book of the Dead.

He Knoweth the Souls of the West. *Unknown.* AWP *Fr.* Book of the Dead.

He knows the depths of smokestacks. Survivor. Florence Weinberger. GotH

He larved ond he larved on he merd such a nauses. James Joyce. BIrV *Fr.* Finnegans Wake.

He lay, and those who watched him were amazed. Sprig of Lime, The. Robert Malise Bowyer Nichols. GTBS-P

He lay in the middle of the world, and twitcht. John Berryman. HCAP; PoE *Fr.* Dream Songs.

He lay like someone fallen from a high. Request, The. Sharon Olds. BodElec

He lay on the bed, thinking. Man on the Bed, The. Debora Greger. PoSol

He lay on the couch night after night. Saturn. Sharon Olds. RaBo

He lay on the floor covered in shit. 999 Call. Elizabeth Bartlett. FaBoWP

He lay with quiet heart in the stern asleep. Prayer at Night. Alcuin. MLL, *tr.* by Helen Waddell

He Leadeth Me. Joseph Henry Gilmore. AH; SacPr

He leans on the gate going staying. Marlene Mountain. HA

He left behind coins, for his lodging, and traces of red mud. (LL) Geoffrey Hill. NoAM; NoP-4 *Fr.* Mercian Hymns.

He left his application forms. Non-Emigrant, The. Lotte Kramer. Prnts

He left his pants upon a chair. Theodore Roethke. OBCoV *Fr.* Three Epigrams.

He left not faction, but of that was left. (LL) Dryden. NOBE; OBSV *Fr.* Absalom and Achitophel.

He left the Court in mere despair. (LL) Jonathan Swift. NOBE; NOEC; OxBoLi; PeLV *Fr.* Verses on the Death of Dr. Swift, D.S.P.D.

He lies / Beside me. On Death and Love. Janet Campbell Hale. VoR

He lies groaning on his bed. Radio Gibberish. Genrikh Sabgir. TCRusP, *tr.* by Daniel Weissbort

He lies on the sofa, listening to the baroness. Last Solo: Charlie Parker, Hotel Stanhope, March 12, 1955. David Jauss. MiVo

He lifted the wicker lid. Man Who Invented Pain, The. Craig Raine. EmeKit

He lifted up, among the actuaries. John Berryman. HAP; HCAP; NOBA *Fr.* Dream Songs.

He lifts his small hands. Mantis. Ruth Miller. PeSAV

He Liked the Dead. Malcolm Lowry. OxBTC

He likes to do the kind of thing that shows. Beauty and the Prince Formerly Known as Beast. Eleanor Brown. NeBl

He listened at the porch that day. Year's Spinning, A. Elizabeth Barrett Browning. NAEL-5v2; NAEL-6v2

He Lived a Life. H. N. Fifer.
    "What was his creed?" PoToHe

He Lived amidst th' Untrodden Ways. Hartley Coleridge. UV (Wordsworth Unvisited.) NOBL; PeLV

He lived—childhood summers. Lorine Niedecker. APT-2

He lived in a small farm-house. Refusal to Mourn, A. Derek Mahon. ModIr; PNI

He lived in a tin hut with a hard dirt floor. Black Rat, The. Iris Clayton. IBA

He lived so little: only forty years. "Nikolai Nikolaevich Morshen." TCRP

He lives—he then unties the string. (LL) Warning to Children. Robert Graves. FaBoCh; NOxBChV; NPeEn; NoP-4; OxBEV

He lives in the sky. Eagle above Us, The. Santiago Altamirano. STP

He Lives Long Who Lives Well. Thomas Randolph. TreFP

He lives, who last night flopped from a log. Burning. Galway Kinnell. CoAP

He liveth long who liveth well. Length of Days. Horatius Bonar. PWR

He'll grow into his sleep so sound again. (LL) Ten Days Leave. W. D. Snodgrass. MoAmPo; UnPo

He'll never rise again but he is ready. Ash Plant, The. Seamus Heaney. BiHa

He'll shoot baith my young son and me. (LL) Great Silkie of Sule Skerry, The. *Unknown.* ESPB; FaBoCh

He loathed the fraud, yet would not bed alone. (LL) Ulysses. Robert Graves. FaBoTw; NoAM

He lolls in the supermarket. Portrait of a House Detective. Hans Magnus Enzensberger. HP; PoSu, *tr.* by Michael Hamburger

He longs / He strokes with words the place of longing. I Remember Having Loved. Hasan 'Abdallah. MAP, *tr.* by Lena Jayyusi and Christopher Middleton

He looked about six or seven, only much too thin. Forgiveness Dream. Jean Valentine. LCAP-2

He looked for her and found her. He Knew Joy on Earth. Unsi Al-Haj [*or* Hajj]. MAP, *tr.* by Sargon Boulus and Alistair Elliot

He looks back at me. Guerrilla-Cong, The. Michael S. Harper. NBV

He looks back over the last metaphor. Great Artist Reconsiders the Homeric Simile, The. John Tranter. BMAP; NOBAu; NoAM

He looks into a glass. Lord, What is Man? Carl Rakosi. FTOS

He looks like a fat little old man. Dead Seal. Alfred Wellington Purdy. MoCV

He loved her so he wrote. Body Language. Sylvia Kantaris. LW

He loved his cabin: there. Salt Water Story. Richard Hugo. NAAL-2v2; NoAM

He loved peculiar plants and rare. Education's Martyr. May Kendall. VWP

He loved statues with broken noses. Ancient Signs. Edward Hirsch. TaR

He loved the brook's soft sound. Peasant Poet, The. John Clare. FHYEP

He Loved Three Things. Anna Andreyevna Akhmatova. BoWoP
    (He loved three things.) RaBo, *tr.* by Jerome Bullitt

He loved three things in life. He Loved Three Things. Anna Andreyevna Akhmatova. BoWoP

He loved to pull out his clasp-knife. Gardener. A. H. Snow. OBGa

He Loves. David Schirmer. GePo, *tr.* by George C. Schoolfield

He loves, but hates equally. (LL) Self-Portrait. Robert Creeley. NoAM; PmAP

He Loves in Vain. Christian Hofmann von Hofmannswaldau. GePo, *tr.* by George C. Schoolfield

He loves me. *Unknown.* OxNR

He made her do the same scene. Marilyn Climbs Out of the Pool. Tracey Herd. NeBl

He made peace with eternity. Second-Class Citizen. Slavko Mihalic. PoSu, *tr.* by Charles Simic

He made the whole Fleet love him, damn his eyes! (LL) 1805. Robert Graves. FaBoCh; FaBoWar; OBCoV; OBSV; PeLV

He Makes a House Call. John A. Stone. BloBone

He makes himself comfortable. Jackson Mac Low. FTOS; PFTM-2; PmAP *Fr.* Pronouns, The—A Collection of 40 Dances—For the Dancers.

He Maketh Himself One with Osiris. *Unknown.* AWP *Fr.* Book of the Dead.

He Maketh Himself One with the God Ra. *Unknown.* AWP, *tr.* by Robert Hillyer *Fr.* Book of the Dead.

He Maketh Himself One with the Only God, Whose Limbs Are the Many Gods. *Unknown.* AWP *Fr.* Book of the Dead.

He making speedy way through spersed ayre. Edmund Spenser. NoSic *Fr.* Faerie Queene, The.

Hé mandu / It was me. Ay, Bashful Thou! Mor Nighean Uisdein. EMWP

He marries the lilac from the Taurus Mountains. Mixed Marriage. Diana Der Hovanessian. NeBl

He may go. (LL) Exeat. Stevie Smith. NAEL-5v2; NAEL-6v2; NoAM

He Measured Out His Spirit Tower. *Unknown.* SuSp, *tr.* by Heng Kuan

He Meditates on the Life of a Rich Man. Douglas Hyde. OBMV, *tr.* by Augusta, Lady Gregory and Lady Gregory

He meets, by heavenly chance express. Coventry Patmore. OxAEP-2 *Fr.* Angel in the House, The.

He met a lady. From the Hazel Bough. Earle Birney. HeIP-4

He might be tethered. Self-Examination. Elaine Terranova. GifTon

He might be weak enough to suffer woe. (LL) John Donne. BASC; Son; TOF *Fr.* Holy Sonnets.

He might happen to take thee for one, my dear. (LL) Young May Moon, The. Thomas Moore. OBEV; PeLV

He mounts his favorite steed of war. Mandan Chief, The. Fanny Crosby. SWaP

He moves his hips. One Night With a Stranger at 30. Lisa Glatt. AmPoNex

He must attend two dozen funerals. Eminent Public Figure. Dezső Kosztolányi. IQMS, *tr.* by Peter Zollman

He must be 30 or 31. Father, 1952. Christopher Buckley. GeoHom

He Na Tye Woman. Paula Gunn Allen. HW

He Never Did That to Me. Noël Coward. NBLV

He Never Expected Much. Thomas Hardy. NAEL-5v2; NAEL-6v2; NoAM; OxBTC; SCV

He never felt twice the same about the flecked river. This Solitude of Cataracts. Wallace Stevens. LCAP-2

He Never Said a Mumblin' Word. *Unknown.* APN-2

He never smiled, his friends said. Scott Joplin. Bill Holm. MiVo

He never spoke a word to me. Simon the Cyrenian Speaks. Countee Cullen. BPo; ChIV-2; HAP; MoAmPo; TTY; TrCP

He nice frum far, but far frum nice. Vicious Circle. Marsha Prescod. LW

He, of his gentleness. In the Wilderness. Robert Graves. MoBrPo; PeECV

He often came and stood outside my door. Lonely Dog, The. Margaret E. Bruner. PoToHe

He often would ask us. Choirmaster's Burial, The. Thomas Hardy. PeECV

He only happy is, and wise. How to Ride Out a Storm. Mildmay Fane, 2d Earl of Westmorland. NOSC

He only wanted me for happiness. Wiederkehr. Rita Dove. BodElec

He only wanted to sleep, that wakeful. Anti-dithyrambics. John Peck. HarvBoo

He opened the car door. There was a low rumble. Meeting, The. Nicki Jackowska. BrRo

He opens his eyes with a cry of delight. Child's Christmas Day, A. Unknown. OBCP

He Opens Wide a Third Eye. Bei Dao. PFTM-2, tr. by Chen Maiping and Bonnie S. McDougall

He opens wide a third eye. He Opens Wide a Third Eye. Bei Dao. PFTM-2, tr. by Chen Maiping and Bonnie S. McDougall

He or She That's Got the Limb, That Holds Me Out on It. Susan Wheeler. ExTi

He [or When he] killed the noble Mudjokivis. George A. Strong. OBCoV; PeLV; UV Fr. Song of Milkanwatha, The.

He Overcometh the Serpent of Evil in the Name of Ra. Unknown. AWP Fr. Book of the Dead.

He Paid Me Seven. Unknown. BPo

He painted the mountain over and over again. Dearest Reader. Michael Palmer. FTOS

He paints words with the past. Roy Fisher. Oth Fr. Cut Pages, The.

He pales at pleasure. Prometheus. Robert Horan. YaYoPo

He paused on the sill of a door ajar. Newcomer's Wife, The. Thomas Hardy. BoLoP; OxBTC

He pays the whole, and yet I am not free. (LL) William Shakespeare. HeIP-4; OxAEP-1 Fr. Sonnets.

He Perceives His Rashness in Love, but Has No Choice. Guido Guinicelli. AWP; EaItPo, tr. by Dante Gabriel Rossetti

He pitied her, and wept in vanishing. (LL) To Dante Alighieri: He Interprets Dante's Dream. Cino da Pistoia. AWP; EaItPo, tr. by Dante Gabriel Rossetti

He placed all rest, and had no resting place. Mary Sidney Herbert, Countess of Pembroke. SacPr Fr. Our Saviour's Passion.

He planked down sixpence and he took his drink. Henry Turnbull. Wilfrid Wilson Gibson. FaBoTw

He plays. Advice. Lee Cataldi. BMAP

He Pleads for Forgiveness Before His Intended Marriage. Bálint Balassi. IQMS, tr. by Joseph Leftwich

He plodded away through drifts of ice. Susan Howe. FTOS

He Points Out the Brevity of Life, Unthinking and Suffering, Surprised by Death. Francisco de Quevedo y Villegas. WoPoe, tr. by Willis Barnstone

He Praises the Trees. Unknown. BIrV, tr. by Robin Skelton

He prayed for patience; Care and Sorrow came. His Answer. Clara Ann Thompson. BlSi; CBWP-2

He Prayeth for Ink and Palette That He May Write. Unknown. AWP Fr. Book of the Dead.

He preached upon "Breadth" till it argued him narrow. Emily Dickinson. NAWM-7v2; NOCV; SacPr

He preaches to the crowd that power is lent. Dryden. NOBE Fr. Medal [or Medall], The.

He preferred his glass eye to be of itself. Millefiori. Lavinia Greenlaw. MFPA

He protested all his life long. Edgar Lee Masters. APT-1; IllVoic Fr. Spoon River Anthology.

He pushes behind the words. Waiting. Robert Creeley. VGW

He Put the Belt Around My Life. Emily Dickinson. TRP

He puts four dimes into the slot. Vending Machine. Hans Magnus Enzensberger. PoSu

He Puts Me to Rest. David Ignatow. VGW

He Raise a Poor Lazarus. Unknown. AH

He ran a good shop, and he died. Michael Longley. BiHa; ModIr Fr. Wreaths.

He ran the course and as he ran he grew. Innocence. Thom Gunn. HP

He rang me up. Dream of Hanging, A. Patricia Beer. EmeKit

He raped. In the Tradition of Bobbitt. Saundra Sharp. SpirFl

He reaches Weymouththreads the Esplanade. Royal Tour, The. "Peter Pindar." OxBoLi; PeLV

He Remembers Forgotten Beauty. W. B. Yeats. CTC

He removes his glove. Raymond Roseliep. HA

He Resigns. John Berryman. HarvBoo; OxBSP; WeW-3

He rested through the winter, watched the rain. Death of a Gardener. Phoebe Hesketh. OBGa

He retains a slight "Martian" accent, from the years of single phrases. It Allows a Portrait in Line Scan at Fifteen. Les A. Murray. HarvBoo

He returned to grass two feet tall. Exile, The. Pablo Medina. OPRER

He rides at their head. College Colonel, The. Herman Melville. CBCWP; FaBoWar; NCAP; OBWP

He roars in the swamp. Alligator, The. Beatrice Witte Ravenel. WPE

He rode a white horse. Colonel. Kate Llewellyn. NOBAu

He rode into town upon a wild-eyed mountain horse. Yellowjacket. Peter Blue Cloud. HATNAP

He rose again behind the stone. (LL) Easter Night. Alice Thompson Meynell. BrRo; ChIV-2; SacPr

He rose at dawn, and fired with hope. Sailor Boy, The. Tennyson. SCGP

He rose the morrow morn. (LL) Samuel Taylor Coleridge. CABP; EBEV; EBNV; FHYEP; FaBoCh; HAP; HeIP-4; NAEL-6v2; NOBE; NoP-4; OBEV; OBNV; OxAEP-2; OxBEV; PeECV; PoE; PoPoPo; SCGP; TFi; TOF

He rose up on his dying bed. Hope. Langston Hughes. APSN; OBAL; PFTM-1

He runs before the wise men: He. He. Stanley Kunitz. NoP-4; VGW

He runs free in the furrow, flutters his wings in the air. I Love, Love. Gabriela Mistral. BLPSL, tr. by Rene de Costa, Rigas Kappatos and Eleni Paidoussi

He's a Cousin of Mine. Cecil Mack. ReLy

He's a dragon, see. Strato [or Straton]. GrAn

He's a fool, and don't I know it. Lorenz Hart. See After one whole quart of brandy

He's a high clear forehead. Robert Johnstone. PNI Fr. Every Cache.

He's about 300 pounds and knows martial arts, boxing and wrestling. I'm Dealing with My Pain. Denise Duhamel. NeAmPo

He's an awkward bedfellow and I love to keep. Paul Verlaine. EroLit, tr. by Alistair Elliot

He's an old grey horse, with his head bowed sadly. Old Whim Horse, The. Edward Dyson. CBAP

He's at the window now. V's Farmhouse. Lisa Fishman. AmPoNex

He's carrying on with a distracting song. Redwing Sonnets. Julia Alvarez. BodElec

He's dead / the dog won't have to. Death. William Carlos Williams. NAAL-2v2; OxBA; VGW

He's diving off the front of the stage! Performance Poem. Bob Holman. KGB

He's down again, aswim in a dream. Liam. Mary Jo Salter. ExTi

He's driving a truck, and we know. Young Elvis. Cornelius Eady. AllShUp

He's filled himself with himself. Vasco [or Vasko] Popa. PoSu, tr. by Anne Pennington Fr. Quartz Pebble, The.

He's going around with your letter. Ghazal 34. Mirza Asadullah Khan Ghalib. EaWin, tr. by Aijaz Ahmad and W. S. Merwin

He's gone, and all our plans. To His Love. Ivor Gurney. MakPoe; NAEL-5v2; NPeEn; OBWP; PeFWW; PoWW

He's gone, and for his absence thus I mourn. Christopher Marlowe. CAGL Fr. Edward the Second.

He's gone to bed at last, that flaring, glaring. My Stearine Candles. James Henry. NOBVV

He's got a radio on his shoulder. Street Music. Greg Pape. PBCAP

He's had. Hypochondriac. Geoffrey Holloway. NLP

He's had enough of the circle. Vasco [or Vasko] Popa. PoSu, tr. by Anne Pennington Fr. Quartz Pebble, The.

He's Jus' de Same Today. Unknown. InvLi

He's knelt to fish her face up from the sidewalk. Rebirth of Venus, The. Mary Jo Salter. FFC

He's lost him completely. And he now tries to find. In Despair. Constantine P. Cavafy. CAGL, tr. by Edmund Keeley and Philip Sherrard

He's lost / in the wilderness of his future, or his past. (LL) Armenian Language Is the Home of the Armenian, The. Moushegh Ishkhan. BLT; WoPoe, tr. by Diana Der Hovanessian

He's lying in poor water, a yard or so depth of poor safety. October Salmon, An. Ted Hughes. EmeKit

He's mad, who lying half dead gets up to march again. Forced March. Miklós Radnóti. IQMS, tr. by Peter Zollman

He's metamorphosed [or metamorphos'd] me into an ass! (LL) Metamorphosis, The. Sir John Suckling. CaPo; FaBoEE

He's now the ruler of the country which once exiled him. Exile's Return, The. Slavko Mihalic. PoSu, tr. by Peter Kastmiler and Charles Simic

He's obsessed with clocks, she with politics. Small Lochs. Norman MacCaig. NePenScot

He's on the porch. Buson. EH, tr. by Robert Hass

He's only a talented man! (LL) Talented Man, The. Winthrop Mackworth Praed. CABP; NOBL; PeLV

He's only rich that cannot tell his store. (LL) Against Fruition. Sir John Suckling. BeJo; CaPo; CavPo; NOSC

He's part of all, yet all's transcended. Chikusen. ZenPo, tr. by Takashi Ikemoto and Lucien Stryk

He's played hookey to see the flick again.   David Wojahn.   PBCAP   *Fr.* Mystery Train: A Sequence.

He's polite looking over the polaroids.   Warhol at Wetlands.   John Kinsella.   NeBl

He's still among us.   Elegy for a Man Who Died and Died.   Mamdouh 'Udwan.   MAP, *tr. by* May Jayyusi and Naomi Shihab Nye

He's still young—; thirty, but looks younger.   Self-Portrait.   Frank Bidart.   HCAP

He's sunk forever. There's no doubt.   Dictator, The.   Lajos Kassák.   IQMS, *tr. by* Paul Tabori

He's the man who climbs his barn.   Man in the Moon.   Linda Hogan.   HATNAP

He's walked each path beneath the pines.   Little Landscape by Yen Wen-kuei, A.   Yü Chi.   CoBLCP, *tr. by* Jonathan Chaves

He Said.   Jean Valentine.   TAP

He said: "Darling, I pay through the nose." (LL)   Limerick: "There was a young man of Montrose."   Arnold Bennett.   OxBoLi; PeLi

He said he would be back and we'd drink wine together.   Waiting for Icarus.   Muriel Rukeyser.   LCAP-2; NNaP

He said his name was Nick; later I learned.   David Trinidad.   WiU   *Fr.* Eighteen to Twenty-One.

He said I should try something harder.   Mask of Anger, A.   Lyn Hejinian.   FTOS

He Said: "If in His Image I Was Made."   Trumbull Stickney.   APN-2; TCAPo

He said in his mother's house, growing up.   Wallpaper.   Julia Alvarez.   BodElec

He said it doesn't look good.   What the Doctor Said.   Raymond Carver.   EmeKit

He said it two days ago.   Emmett Williams.   PFTM-2   *Fr.* Red Chair (for three voices), The.

He said / "Let's stay here."   Party Piece.   Brian Patten.   BoLoP

He said to them, Look at this: You see.   Tall Wind, The.   K. O. Arvidson.   PeNZ

He sang / How the swan blanched forever.   Owl's Song.   Ted Hughes.   PAI

He sang of life, serenely sweet.   Poet, The.   Paul Laurence Dunbar.   BPo; NAAAL; TCAPo

He sat; and in the assembly next upstood.   John Milton.   FaBoWar   *Fr.* Paradise Lost.

He sat by the boot shop window.   Playing for England.   David Scott.   NLP

He sat in a wheeled chair, waiting for dark.   Disabled.   Wilfred Owen.   FaBoWar; NAEL-5v2; NAEL-6v2; NIL-7; NoAM; OBWVE; OxBTC; PeFWW; PoPoPo; SCGP

He sat in his cell staring.   Baboon, The.   Rhydwen Williams.   OBWVE, *tr. by* R. Gerallt Jones

He sat up slowly, and around his left side.   Lazarus.   Ágnes Nemes Nagy.   PoSu, *tr. by* Frederic Will

He sate like winter o'er the wasted year.   Thomas Tod Stoddart.   NOBRP   *Fr.* Death-Wake, The; or, Lunacy.

He saw her from the bottom of the stairs.   Robert Frost.   APT-1; ColAP; NAAL-2v2; SoSe-8; TAP; TRP

He saw the skull within the looping.   Epitaph for a Scientist.   Lex Banning.   NOBAu

He saw the sun, the Light-giver, step down behind the oak.   Ballad of the Homing Man, The.   Ernest Rhys.   AngWePo

He saw thee Lord of all his creatures stand. (LL)   Created, The.   Jones Very.   APN-1; InvLi; NOCV

He says again, "Good fences make good neighbors." (LL)   Mending Wall.   Robert Frost.   APT-1; BRP; ChAP; ClHu; HAP; HarvBoo; HeIP-4; ITBLP; MoAmPo; NAAL-2v2; NAAL-5; NOBA; NoAM; NoP-4; OxBA; PAI; PoE; PoPoPo; SAmP; SCV; SoSe-8; TAP; TCAPo; TFi; VGW; WeW-3

He says he doesn't feel like working today.   My Erotic Double.   John Ashbery.   LCAP-2; PoE; VCAP

He says, *My reign is in peace*, so slays.   Foreign Ruler, A.   Walter Savage Landor.   OBSV; OxBEV

He says that home is here.   At the Olive Grove of the Resistance.   Robert Hedin.   GifTon

He says the waves in the ship's wake.   Leaving Forever.   Denise Levertov.   InPK-6

He says / When they made this place.   Outside the Hospital.   Joe Wenderoth.   BodElec

He says you're a blackberry, dropped into his mouth.   Willing.   Paula McLain.   AmPoNex

He scanned me closely, Rufus, just as.   Martial.   RomPo, *tr. by* Peter Whigham

He scattered tarantulas over the roads.   Devil in Texas, The.   *Unknown.*   NBLV; RB

He scorned his land, his tongue denied.   Dic Siôn Dafydd.   Thomas Jacob Thomas.   OBWVE, *tr. by* H. Idris Bell

He seemed to know the harbour.   Shark, The.   Edwin John Pratt.   NOBC

He seems to be a god, that man.   Arbor, The.   Sappho.   WoPoe, *tr. by* Guy Davenport

He Seems to Me Almost a God.   Catullus.   WoPoe, *tr. by* Robert Mezey

He sees the gentle stir of birth.   Matthew Arnold.   NPeEn   *Fr.* Resignation.

He Sees through Stone.   Etheridge Knight.   CoAmPo; GT; NNaP; PBCAP

He seized me by the waist and kissed my throat.   Charleston in the Eighteen-Sixties.   Adrienne Rich.   CoAP; NAAL-2v2

He served his God so faithfully and well.   On a Puritan.   Joseph Hilaire Pierre Belloc.   FaBoEE

He served his master well from youth to age.   Old Stephen.   Charles Tennyson Turner.   EBVV

He set her on her steede, and forward forth did beare. (LL)   Edmund Spenser.   FHYEP; NoSic   *Fr.* Faerie Queene, The.

He set out and kept hunting.   Hunter, The.   Frank O'Hara.   NNaP

He shakes the dust from off his feet.   Battle of Murfreesboro.   Allen Tate.   FaBoA

He shall feed his flock like a shepherd: he shall gather the lambs with his arm and carry them in his bosom, and shall gently lead those that are young. (LL)   Bible, *O.T.*   OBVE; TrJP   *Fr.* Isaiah.

He shall not hear the bittern cry.   Lament for Thomas MacDonagh.   Francis Ledwidge.   BIrV

He shifted his trumpet, and only took snuff. (LL)   Oliver Goldsmith.   FaBoEE; NOEC; NOIV; OBCoV; OxBEV; OxBoLi   *Fr.* Retaliation.

He shifts on the bed carefully, so as.   Man on the Hotel Room Bed, The.   Galway Kinnell.   VCAP

He Shook off the Beast.   Charles Wesley.   ChIV-2

He should, he could, he would, he did the best. (LL)   Look[e] Home.   Robert Southwell.   ESCV; NOCV; NoSic

He should not have sent his son.   Meditations of Mr. Cogito on Redemption.   Zbigniew Herbert.   GI, *tr. by* John Carpenter

He showed me hights I never saw.   Emily Dickinson.   PoE

He shows me tonight.   Nobody.   Novica Tadic.   VCWP, *tr. by* Charles Simic

He shuddered briefly and stared down the long valley.   Return of Robinson Jeffers, The.   Robert Hass.   GeoHom

He shudders. . . feeling on the shaven spot.   Electrocution.   Lola Ridge.   WPE

He shuffled my file.   Lilith and the Doctor.   Kathleen Norris.   HW

He Singeth a Hymn to Osiris, the Lord of Eternity.   *Unknown.*   AWP   *Fr.* Book of the Dead.

He Singeth in the Underworld.   *Unknown.*   AWP   *Fr.* Book of the Dead.

He sipped at a weak hock and seltzer.   Arrest of Oscar Wilde at the Cadogan Hotel, The.   Sir John Betjeman.   EBEV; MoBrPo; NPeEn; NoAM; NoP-4; OxBTC

He sits at the bar in the Alhambra.   Simple.   Naomi Long Madgett.   GT

He sits in front of the bright, blazing grate.   Old Freedman, The.   Priscilla Jane Thompson.   CBWP-2

He sits in the corner.   Corner.   Amal Dunqul.   MAP, *tr. by* Sharif Elmusa and Thomas G. Ezzy

He sits on a bench.   Taxidermist at the Zoo, The.   Ruth Anderson Barnett.   UrbNat

He slammed the door shut. From under trees.   Outside in the Open.   Adriann Roland Holst.   TuT, *tr. by* Desmond Egan

He sleeps in the room next to mine, a wall between us.   Solitude Exercises.   Iman Mersal.   PoArWo, *tr. by* Khaled Mattawa

He sleeps on the top of a mast.   Unbeliever, The.   Elizabeth Bishop.   NAAL-2v2; NAAL-5; NoAM

He slept in my bed.   Drugs.   Jacquie Jones.   ISC

He slept like a rock or a man that's dead. (LL)   Weary Blues, The.   Langston Hughes.   ColAP; FaBoA; HarvBoo; ISC; NAAAL; NOBA; NoAM; NoP-4; PoPoPo; SAmP

He slew the noble Mudjekeewis.   What Hiawatha Probably Did.   *Unknown.*   NBLV

He slid out of the skin, leaving it.   Summer.   Diane Wakoski.   VGW

He smashed all the glass in the room (Bill:50) $50). (LL)   Malcolm Lowry.   FaBoTw; NoP-4; OxBTC   *Fr.* Cantinas, The.

He smelled bad and was red-eyed with the miseries.   Portrait from the Infantry.   Alan Dugan.   AF

He smiles from his statue.   Sri Nityananda Mandir (The Temple of Nityananda).   Elsa Cross.   TANSG, *tr. by* Patricia Dubrava

He smorit thame with smuke. (LL)   Dance of the Sevin Deidly Synnis, The.   William Dunbar.   MiEL; NePenScot; OxBS; PoE

He snuggles his fingers.   After Winter.   Sterling Allen Brown.   GT

He sought the mountain and the loneliest height,   Jesus Praying.   Hartley Coleridge.   ChIV-2

He spake no dream, for as his words had end.   John Milton.   NOSC   *Fr.* Paradise Regained [*or* Regain'd].

He speaks of voyages.   Tour Guide: La Maison des Esclaves.   Melvin Dixon.   ESEAA

He spins about (laughing) then shows.   Silvana Colonna.   ItPo, *tr. by* Gayle Ridinger

He spoke. And drank rapidly a glass of water. (LL)   E. E. Cummings.   FaBoA; InPK-6; NAAL-2v2; NAAL-5; NBLV; NoP-4; OBWP; OxBA; PAI; PoWW; RaBo; TAP; TFi; VGW

He spoke; and silent tow'rd the northern sky. Joel Barlow. APN-1 *Fr.* Columbiad, The.

He spoke, and what he spoke was soon obeyed. London Subverted by the Furies. Abraham Cowley. NOSC

He spoke of undying love. Talker, The. Benjamin Appel. TrJP

He spoke while sitting on what seemed to be. Memory 2. George Seferis. PoetW, *tr.* by Edmund Keeley and Philip Sherrard

He stalks in his vivid stripes. Tiger in the Zoo, A. Leslie Norris. OTCP

He stalls above me like an elephant. (LL) To Speak of Woe That Is in Marriage. Robert Lowell. NAAL-2v2; NoAM

He stands against what looks like the other side. David Ferry. FaBoA

He stands before a red-hot furnace. Worker, The. Nikolai Stepanovich Gumilyov [*or* Gumiliov *or* Gumilev]. TCRP, *tr.* by Simon Franklin

He stands beside his ancient, lovely mistress. Old Fisherman, The. Emily Grosholz. RA

He stands, cold in the morning wind. Roll-Call in the Concentration Camp. Dan Pagis. FIT; PoSu, *tr.* by Robert Friend

He stands on the bridge. Survivor. Barry Sternlieb. GotH

He stands, stamps a little in his boots. Roll Call, The. Dan Pagis. HP, *tr.* by Stephen Mitchell

He stands / Up and all. He Is Lightning. Jordan Davis. HeMarv

He stands with his forefeet on the drum. Two Performing Elephants. D. H. Lawrence. RB

He stared at ruin. Ruin stared straight back. John Berryman. HCAP; PoPoPo *Fr.* Dream Songs.

He started coming on to me. Unfaithful Wife, The. Nuala Ni Dhomhnaill. ModIr, *tr.* by Paul Muldoon

He starts a landslide shooting a. Rabbit Shoeshine. S. K. Kelen. BMAP

He stepped ino the night aware. Tired Man, The. Suliaman El-Hadi. SpirFl

He stepped on a land mine. Private Ian Godwin, U. S. M. C. Bryan Alec Floyd. CDa

He steps down from the dark train, blinking; stares. Ten Days Leave. W. D. Snodgrass. MoAmPo; UnPo

He steps out from the others. Passion of Ravensbrück. János Pilinszky. AF; GI; HP; IQMS; PoSu, *tr.* by Ted Hughes

He still believes by middle-age. Traveler, The. Duane Niatum. HATNAP

He still may leave thy garland green. (LL) Love and Friendship. Emily Jane Brontë. EBVV; InPK-6; LW; PoBW

He still wore the OD tee shirt. When Chicken Man Came Home to Roost. Frank A. Cross. CDa

He stood, a worn-out City clerk. Peace. Charles Stuart Calverley. EBVV

He stood alone within the spacious square. James Thomson. NOBVV *Fr.* City of Dreadful Night, The.

He stood among a crowd at Drumahair [*or* Dromahair]. Man Who Dreamed of Faeryland, The. W. B. Yeats. NAEL-5v2; NAEL-6v2; NoAM

He stood, and heard the steeple. Eight O'Clock. A. E. Housman. InPK-6; MoBrPo; NoAM; OxBSP; PAI; PoE; SoSe-8

He stood before my heart's closed door. Refiner's Gold, The. Frances Ellen Watkins Harper. PWR

He stood by the piano for an hour, every Wednesday. Mr Teller the Piano Teacher. Jane Duran. MFPA

He stood in his shoes / And he wondered. (LL) John Keats. FHYEP; FaBoCh; OBCoV *Fr.* Song about Myself, A.

He stood in the sulphur baths, his calves. First. Sharon Olds. ExTi

He stood, the last—the last of all. William Bingham Tappan. VerBaPo *Fr.* Last Drunkard, The.

He stood wrapped in air. Annunciation. Anna Kamienska. GI, *tr.* by David Curzon and Grażyna Drabik

He stopped on the irreproachable sidewalk. Elysee. Larry Eigner. VGW

He straight perceav'd himselfe to be my Lover. (LL) Richard Barnfield [*or* Barnefield]. CAGL; PBRV *Fr.* Cynthia, with Certain[e] Sonnets.

He strides across the grassy corn. Scarecrow, The. Andrew Young. FaBoTw

He sucks with greed the treacherous attraction. Death of a Fly. Goethe. STV, *tr.* by John Frederick Nims

He swayed in sunlight, in mild dreams. He tested the little pears. He smeared catmint on his palm for his cat Smut to lick. He wept, attempting to master *ancilla* and *servus*. (LL) Geoffrey Hill. HAP; NoAM; NoP-4 *Fr.* Mercian Hymns.

He switched on the electric light and laughed. Intimate Supper. Peter Redgrove. FaBoMo; OxBC

He takes Earl Grey tea. Taking Tea with My Father and Mother. Pam Zinnemann-Hope. Prnts

He takes the long review of things. To a Certain Most Certainly Certain Critic. David McCord. OBAL

He talked of Delhi brothels half the night. Long Tom. Wilfrid Wilson Gibson. OxBTC

He tells me in Bangkok he's robbed. Baby Villon. Philip Levine. CoAP

He tempted me to. Akiko Yosano. OHMPJ

He thanked me for my kindness, disagreed. William Wetmore Story. APN-1 *Fr.* Contemporary Criticism, A.

He Thanks His Woodpile. Lew Welch. BB

He that but once too nearly hears. Coventry Patmore. NPeEn *Fr.* Victories of Love, The.

He that can trace a ship making her way. Heart Is Deep, The. Roger Wolcott. ChIV-1; SCAP

He that dwelleth in the secret place of the most High. Bible, *O.T.* AWP *Fr.* Psalms.

He that for fear his Master did deny. To St. Peter and St. Paul. Henry Constable. NoSic; Son

He that had come that morning. Ballad of John Cable and Three Gentlemen. W. S. Merwin. CoAP; MakPoe; NOBA; YaYoPo

He that has grown to wisdom hurries not. Sonnet: Of Moderation and Tolerance. Guido Guinicelli. AWP; EaltPo, *tr.* by Dante Gabriel Rossetti

He That Hath No Mistress. *Unknown.* OxBSP

He that hath set his headlong heart. Boethius. MLL *Fr.* Consolation of Philosophy, The ("De Consolacione Philosophie").

He that holds fast the golden mean. Horace. PoToHe, *tr.* by William Cowper *Fr.* Odes.

He that in youthe no vertu will yowes. *Unknown.* MiEL

He that is by Mooni now. Mooni. Henry Clarence Kendall. OBEV

He that is down, needs fear no fall. John Bunyan. EBEV; NOBE; OBEV; SacPr *Fr.* Pilgrim's Progress, The.

He that is weary, let him sit. Employment. George Herbert. FaBoVe

He that lies at the stock. Rock, Ball, Fiddle. *Unknown.* OxBoLi; OxNR

He that loves a rosy cheek. Thomas Carew. BASC; BeJo; CavPo; GTBS-P *Fr.* Disdain Returned.

He That Loves a Rosy Cheek. Heinrich von Rugge. AWP, *tr.* by Jethro Bithell

He That None Can Capture. May Swenson. LW

He that of such a height hath built his mind. To the Lady Margaret, Countess [*or* Countesse] of Cumberland. Samuel Daniel. NOSC

He that owns wealth, in mountain, wold, or waste. Sadi [*or* Saadi *or* Sa'di]. AWP, *tr.* by Sir Edwin Arnold *Fr.* Gulistan, The.

He that saw hell in his melancholy dream. John Cleveland. NOSC *Fr.* Rebel Scot, The.

He that spendes muche and getes nothing. *Unknown.* MiEL

He that to God's law doth cling. Freedom. Abraham Ibn Ezra. TrJP, *tr.* by Solomon Solis-Cohen

He that to number all the stars would seek. Guillaume de Salluste Du Bartas. NOSC, *tr.* by Joshua Sylvester *Fr.* Divine Weeks and Works, The.

He that will not love must be. Not To Love. Robert Herrick. CaPo

He that would thrive must rise at five. *Unknown.* OxNR

He that would write an epitaph for thee. Epitaph on Dr. Donne, Dean of Paul's, An. Richard Corbet [*or* Corbett]. BeJo

He the Beloved. Qorratu'l-Ayn. "Cupbearer, O victorious Falcon, come!" WPOW

He Thinks of Those Who Have Spoken Evil of His Beloved. W. B. Yeats. NoAM

He thinks when we die we'll go to China. Heaven. Cathy Song. NAAL-5; NIL-7; NoAM

He thought he kept the universe alone. Most of It, The. Robert Frost. APT-1; BLT; HAP; NAAL-2v2; NoP-4; TOF; TRP; WeW-3

He thought he saw an elephant [*or* a banker's clerk *or* a buffalo]. Lewis Carroll. WoPoe *Fr.* Sylvie and Bruno.

He thought I thought he thought I slept. (LL) Coventry Patmore. BoLoP; EnLoPo; NOBVV *Fr.* Angel in the House, The.

He thought it humanity's lot for ever to be persuading a huge rock up a mountainside. David Bromige. FTOS *Fr.* Tight Corners.

He thought to quell the stubborn hearts of oak. Buonaparte. Tennyson. Son

He threw his cigarette in silence, then he said. L.R.D.G. J. G. Meddemmen. FaBoWar

He threw them out and slammed the gate shut. Eden. James Simmons. PNI

He thrust his joy against the weight of the sea. Surfer, The. Judith Wright. WPE

He tips his boy baby's hand in an icy. Three Sonnets for Iva. Marilyn Hacker. GLP

He tiptoes into the room almost as if he were an intruder. Annunciation, The. Stephen Mitchell. GI

He Told His Life Story to Mrs. Courtly. Stevie Smith. NBLV (Autumn.) FaBoWP; LW

He told me he had spent. Shortening the Road. Michael Davitt. PBCIP, *tr.* by Philip Casey

He told the crowd "The devils." John Logan. CRP *Fr.* Short Life of the Hermit, A.

He too has an eternal part to play. Historical Judas, The. Howard Nemerov. NoP-4

He too must with me wash his body, though. Anniversary of Death, An. John Wieners. PoM

He too will soon go away. "Rachel" [*or* "Rahel"]. FIT, *tr.* by Robert Friend

He took / flight. Exile. Erich Fried. AF, *tr.* by Georg Rapp

He Took Her. Tom Masson. OBAL

He took her through a fire hydrant. Sex—A Five-Minute Briefing. Nina Iskrenko. ItGoST, *tr.* by Patrick Henry, John High and Katya Olmsted

He took her with a sigh. (LL) Love's Secret. William Blake. EnLoPo; ITBLP; NOBE; NPeEn; OxBEV; SCGP

He took one step. Blood Heifer. Dahlia Ravikovitch [*or* Ravikovich]. DTA, *tr.* by Chana Bloch and Ariel Bloch

He touched me, so I live to know. Emily Dickinson. NCAP

He tramped in the fading light. Monk, The. Thomas Kinsella. BBASP

He travels after a winter sun. Tilly. James Joyce. RB

He tried to / climb a / ladder of light. Written for Love of an Ascension—Coltrane. Carolyn M. Rodgers. SeSe

He Tries out the Concords Gently. "Eduard Georgievich Bagritzky" [*or* "Bagritsky"]. TrJP, *tr.* by C. M. Bowra

He trudges the street of Blantyre. Tramp. Frank Mkalawile Chipasula. HBAPE; PeSAV

He turned and waved. Harold's Walk. Geoffrey Lehmann. EmeKit

He turned his field into a meeting-place. W. H. Auden. SCV *Fr.* Sonnets from China.

He turned up in benighted villages. Prince Foma. Pavel Nikolaevich Vasilyev [*or* Vasil'ev]. TCRP, *tr.* by David Macduff

He turns his back to dress; i've lost him. Memoirs of a Velvet Urinal. Michael Dransfield. BMAP

He Understands the Great Cruelty of Death. Petrarch. BIrV; OBMV; OxBEV; WoPoe, *tr.* by John Millington Synge and J. M. Synge *Fr.* Sonnets to Laura.

He unto whom thou art so partial. Post-Obits and the Poets. Martial. AWP; FaBoEE; OBVE; RomPo, *tr.* by George Gordon Noel Byron, 6th Baron

He wades in neoprene boots the tank's. Wild Salmon: Stillaguamish Tribal Hatchery. Joan Swift. PoCoUp

He waits at dusk, bamboo walking stick in hand. Visiting the Mountain Hermitage of a Monk at Gan-hua Monastery. Wang Wei. CrYelRi, *tr.* by Sam Hamill

He wakes; speak to him. William Shakespeare. SCV *Fr.* King Lear.

He walked out and left me flat. T'Ain't No Use. Burton Lane. ReLy

He Walketh by Day. *Unknown.* AWP *Fr.* Book of the Dead.

He walks among us. He's a gentle soul. Revolutionary, The. Dezső Kosztolányi. IQMS, *tr.* by Peter Zollman

He walks around here. Berlioz in the Madhouse. Halvard Johnson. MiVo

He waltzes into the lane. Makin' Jump Shots. Michael S. Harper. ISC; MoASP; PoE

He wanted to rise up to the moment. Poet Lied, The. Odia Ofeimun. HBAPE

He wants to be. Self-Portrait. Robert Creeley. NoAM; PmAP

He wants to go. Growing up in a Jewish Neighborhood. Richard Chess. TaR

He wants to wonder not look so. Jerome in His Study. Clark Coolidge. FTOS

He warranted no better, I don't know. (LL) Mr Bleaney. Philip Larkin. NPeEn; OxBC; OxBEV; PoE; PoPoPo; TRP; UV

He was a big man, says the size of his shoes. Abandoned Farmhouse. Ted Kooser. WeW-3

He was a blessing one never prays for—. Obituary. Steve Chimombo. HBAPE

He was a boy when first we met. Love Returned. Bayard Taylor. CAGL

He was a famous trumpet man from out Chicago way. Boogie Woogie Bugle Boy. Hughie Prince. ReLy

He was a farmer, he didn't think much of towns. Stephen Vincent Benét. AiP *Fr.* John Brown's Body.

He was a gentleman sitting in front of a lady seated in. Gentleman in Front, The. Vivian Lamarque. CItWP, *tr.* by Cinzia Sartini Blum and Lara Trubowitz

He was a good boy. Uncle's First Rabbit. Lorna Dee Cervantes. NoAM

He was a huge. Time Heals All Wounds—But One. Vernon Rowe. BloBone

He was a large-eyed, Hunnish youth. Poet of the Hortobágy, The. Endre Ady. IQMS, *tr.* by Anton N. Nyerges

He Was a Man of Jokes Outside Office. Oswald Basize Dube. PeSAV

He was a mighty hunter in his youth. White Cat of Trenarren, The. Alfred Leslie Rowse. OxBTC

He was a rat, and she was a rat. What Became of Them? *Unknown.* OBCA

He was a reprobate I grant. Deceased, The. Keith Douglas. FaBoTw

He was a selfish shellfish. Idyll. Stoddard King. NBLV

He was a soldier in the army. Casualty. Langston Hughes. APT-2

He was a soldier or a Shaker. At least he was doing *something*. Chapter 2, Book 35. John Ashbery. BodElec

He was a South-of-Watford man. Looking North. Pamela Gillilan. Prnts

He was a traveler west of the river/ only he knew how lonely he was. *Unknown.* ColAnChi, *tr.* by Burton Watson *Fr.* Four *Tz'u* from Tun-huang.

He was a traveler west of the river/ then he took sick, lay an inch away from death. *Unknown.* ColAnChi, *tr.* by Elling O. Eide *Fr.* Four *Tz'u* from Tun-huang.

He was a traveler west of the river/ with wealth and eminence rare in this world. *Unknown.* ColAnChi, *tr.* by Burton Watson *Fr.* Four *Tz'u* from Tun-huang.

He Was Acquainted with Grief. Jones Very. SacPr

He was alive with death. Sergeant Brandon Just, U. S. M. C. Bryan Alec Floyd. CDa

He was always the same. Portrait. Leopold Staff. PoSu, *tr.* by Adam Czerniawski

He was an Indiana corporal. At Chancellorsville. Andrew Hudgins. CBCWP

He was an upright man, a too-tight man. Woman Who Mistook her Father for an Irishman, The. Nicki Jackowska. Prnts

He was arrested and detained. Soft Targets. Essex Hemphill. GT

He was back. Said nothing. Homecoming. Wislawa Szymborska. PoSu, *tr.* by Adam Czerniawski

He was bad at torture. Flubbed his first flaying. Good Devil, The. Kurt Brown. OPRER

He was born in Alabama. Gwendolyn Brooks. ESEAA; NOBA; NoAM *Fr.* Street in Bronzeville, A.

He was born with the fingerpads of the blind. Prodigy, The. Lola Haskins. MiVo

He was but dust: How could he stand before him? Giles Fletcher, the Younger. SacPr *Fr.* Christ's Victory and Triumph.

He was captured in the Valley of Women. Man in the Valley of Women, A. Chris Greenhalgh. NeBl

He was caught in the whirlpool of dismay. Whirlpool, The. *Unknown.* PoToHe

He was digging; his fingers. Of Mohenjo Daro at Oxford. Keki N. Daruwalla. OMIP

He was dreaming of the factories across the water's fog. What Cannot Be Kept. Reginald Shepherd. GT

He was dying on the cross. On the Cross. Anna Kamienska. GI, *tr.* by David Curzon and Grażyna Drabik

He was first seen in a Louisiana bayou. Grandfather Was Queer, Too. Bob Kaufman. NAAAL

He was found by the Bureau of Statistics to be. Unknown Citizen, The. W. H. Auden. HeIP-4; InPK-6; NBLV; NIP-4; NOBL; OBSV; PAI; PoRA; SoSe-8; TRP; UnPo

He was heroic, fugitive, in love with the machinery. Marco Polo. Marvin Bell. BodElec

He was holding clean globes in his hands. (LL) Medgar Evers. Gwendolyn Brooks. ESEAA; NoP-4

He was in logic[k] a great critic. Samuel Butler. MeLP; PeLV *Fr.* Hudibras.

He was just back. Vietnam. Clarence Major. HHAm

He was lodging above in Coom. 'Mergency Man, The. John Millington Synge. NPeEn

He was lost!—not a shade of doubt of that. Little Lost Pup. Arthur Guiterman. ITBLP

He Was Lucky. Anna Swirszczynska. HP; PoSu

He was my servant—and the better man. (LL) Rudyard Kipling. HarvBoo; NPeEn; PeFWW *Fr.* Epitaphs of the War [1914–1918].

He was no longer my father. Mirror, The. Michael Davitt. BiHa; CIP-2; PBCIP, *tr.* by Paul Muldoon

He was not a wise man. My Father. Manuela Fingueret. MirDau, *tr.* by Roberta Gordenstein

He was not bad, as emperors go, not really—. Apology for Domitian. Robert Penn Warren. NOBA; PAI

He was once a tiny, helpless thing. Aaron Nicholas, Almost Ten. Janet Campbell Hale. VoR

He was out of work that year. Days of 1908. Constantine P. Cavafy. PFTM-1

He was preparing an Ulster fry for breakfast. Michael Longley. BiHa; ModIr *Fr.* Wreaths.

He was quite a guy how he laughed like oh what's the name of the guy. Famous Women—Claudette Colbert. Kathleen de Azevedo. ReTh

He was reading late, at Richard's, down in Maine. Henry's Understanding. John Berryman. NOBA; NoAM; WoPoe

He was short and sturdy, one of dim Picton's Silurians. In Memory of Idris Davies. John Tripp. AngWePo

He was sixty [years old]. . . Still teaching. Lessons in Parsing. Rashid Husain [*or* Hussein]. MAP

He was still Uncle. Empress Brand Trim: Ruby Reminisces, The. Sherley Anne Williams. BlSi

He was straight and strong, and his eyes were blue. Lynmouth Widow, A. Amelia Josephine Burr. LW

He was strange weather, this luther. he read books, mainly poetry and sometimes. Poet: What Ever Happened to Luther? Haki R. Madhubuti. SpirFl; UnSA

He was strolling with another woman. Ballad. Gabriela Mistral. BLPSL, *tr. by* Rene de Costa, Rigas Kappatos and Eleni Paidoussi

He was such a curious lover of shells. Full Fathom Five. Arthur Rex Dugard Fairburn. PeNZ

He was the best postilion. Postilion Has Been Struck by Lightning, The. Patricia Beer. OxBC

He was the doctor up to Combe. Coroner's Jury. Leonard Alfred George Strong. OxBTC

He was the first always: Fortune. Envy. Adelaide Anne Procter. NOBVV; NPeEn; VWP

He was the first to see the snow. (LL) First Snow in Alsace. Richard Wilbur. NoP-4; OBWP

He was the last. Truly the last. Butterfly, The. Pavel Friedmann. HP, *tr. by* Dennis Silk

He was the terror of the district. Urchin, The. Konstantin Iakovlevich Vanshenkin. TCRP, *tr. by* Daniel Weissbort

He was the Word that Spake it. *Unknown.* OxBEV

He was the youngest son of a strange brood. Otto. Theodore Roethke. HarvBoo

He was there / Old Man Coyote. Medicine-Tail. STP

He was to weet a man of full ripe years. Edmund Spenser. UV *Fr.* Faerie Queene, The.

He Was Too Good to Me. Richard Rodgers. ReLy

He was twelve years old. Green Beret. Ho Thien. FaBoWar, *tr. by Unknown*

He was walking a frozen road. Music of Spheres. Jean Follain. BLT

He was walking from Bethany to Jerusalem. Miracle, The. Boris Leonidovich Pasternak. GI, *tr. by* Nina Kossman

He watch her like a coonhound watch a tree. Balance. Marilyn Nelson Waniek. FFC; RA

He watched them as they walked towards the tree. Dorothy Auchterlonie. NOBAu

He wears Clarks Movers, his new shoes. News of the Changes. Bryan Aspden. AngWePo

He Wears Old Socks. Florence Weinberger. GotH

He went by with another. Ballad. Gabriela Mistral. SpanPo, *tr. by* Muriel Kittel

He went down to the woodshed. No One Heard Him Call. Dorothy Aldis. TLR

He went home when the new replacements arrived. Lance Corporal Purdue Grace, U. S. M. C. Bryan Alec Floyd. CDa

He went in with his fur coat flung open. Subject for a Story. Nikolai Ivanovich Glazkov. TCRP, *tr. by* Daniel Weissbort

He went into a grey day. For One Who Died Young. Hoffman Reynolds Hays. SPE

He went into his harvest barn. Farmer, The. Mary Elizabeth Fullerton. CBAP

He went there. Poem of the Conscripted Warrior. "Rui Nogar." TTY, *tr. by* Dorothy Guedes and Philippa Rumsey

He went to fix the awning. Fixer of Midnight. Reuel Denney. OBAL

He went to the wood and caught it. Riddle. *Unknown.* OxNR

He! When I met him approaching. *Unknown.* NAAL-5 *Fr.* Ghost-Dance Songs.

He whittled scallops for a hardy thatch. Thatcher, The. Brendan Kennelly. CIP-2

He who appointed weight to the wind. Semyon [*or* Semion] Izrailevich Lipkin. TCRP

He who at first a womans mind. Inconstancy. James Harrington. PBRV

He who began from brick and rime. In Obitum Ben. Jons. Mildmay Fane, 2d Earl of Westmorland. OxBSP

He who believes that absence. Sonnet 41. Francisco de Medrano. BLPSL, *tr. by* Rene de Costa, Rigas Kappatos and Eleni Paidoussi

He who binds to himself a joy. William Blake. AWP; AmFaPo; EBEV; EnlH; FaBoEE; NOBE; NoP-4; OxBSP; RB; SCGP; SoSe-8; Spl *Fr.* Several Questions Answered.

He-who-came-forth was. Son, The. Denise Levertov. NALW

He who comes knows only his coming. Sengai Gibon. JDP, *tr. by* Yoel Hoffmann

He who could win the girl I love. Girl's Hair, A. Dafydd [*or* David] ab Edmwnd. OBWVE, *tr. by* Gwyn Williams

He who discovered. My Father Recounts a Story from His Youth. Kevin Prufer. AmPoNex

He who doesn't dance still dances. Aleksandr Semionovich Kushner. TCRP

He who first stretched his nerves of subtile wire. Science and Poetry. James Russell Lowell. NCAP

He who gave weight to the wind. Yury [*or* Iurii] Mikhailovich Kublanovsky [*or* Kublanovskii]. TCRP

He who has a yod in his name. Bella and the Golem. Rossana Ombres. CItWP, *tr. by* Cinzia Sartini Blum and Lara Trubowitz

He who has compared himself to the eye of a horse. Boris Pasternak. Anna Andreyevna Akhmatova. TCRP, *tr. by* Max Hayward and Stanley Kunitz

He Who Has Lost All. David Diop. TTY, *tr. by* Anne Atik

He who has lost soul's liberty. Soul's Liberty. Anna Wickham. MoBrPo; OxBSP

He who has made his reckoning with life. Boethius. MLL *Fr.* Consolation of Philosophy, The ("De Consolacione Philosophie".)

He who has no hands. Ralph Waldo Emerson. OxBA *Fr.* Quatrains.

He who has once been happy is for aye. Wilfrid Scawen Blunt. OBEV; OBMV *Fr.* Esther [a Young Man's Tragedy].

He who has seen my Mother. Najrul Islām. SinGod, *tr. by* Rachel Fell McDermott

He who has toiled and bought for himself books. Proverbs. Samuel Ha-Nagid. TrJP, *tr. by* Israel Abrahams

He who holds that nothingness. Inscription over His Door. Gido. ZenPo, *tr. by* Takashi Ikemoto and Lucien Stryk

He, who in his youth. William Wordsworth. TOF *Fr.* Prelude, The; Growth of a Poet's Mind [1850 vers.].

He who knows how to shave the razor, will know how to erase the. Henri Michaux. PFTM-1 *Fr.* Slices of Knowledge.

He who knows not the Oba. Praise Song for the Oba of Benin. *Unknown.* WoPoe, *tr. by* John Bradbury

He Who Loved Beauty. Alec Brock Stevenson. FuPo

He who made a feast of dew, drink from a rock. Inscription in Monastic Refectory. Alcuin. MLL, *tr. by* Helen Waddell

He, who navigated with success. Death of a Young Son by Drowning. Margaret Atwood. BoWoP; NIL-7; NOBC

He who plucked land. J. P. Clark Bekedermo. PBMAP *Fr.* Reed in the Tide, A.

He who saved Ankoma Oh nature. Prelude to Akwasidae. *Unknown.* TTY, *tr. by* Halim El-Dabh

He who shot my maternal grandfather, Aaron. In Memory of Aaron, Murdered Grandfather. Seymour Mayne. GotH

He who shuts off the rain. July. Margit Szécsi. IQMS, *tr. by* Agnes Arany-Makkai

He who sits from day to day. On a Similar Occasion for the Year 1790. William Cowper. NOCV

He Who splashed a thousand worlds with color. Quatrain. Ayn Al-Qozat Hamadani. BBASP, *tr. by* Nasrollah Pourjavady and Peter Lamborn Wilson

He who stole my virginity / is the same man. Silabhattarika. WPOW

He who the hoop's immensity can pierce. John Wilkes. EroLit *Fr.* Essay on Woman.

He who thinks perchance to drown. Drunkenness. Friedrich von Logau. GePo, *tr. by* George C. Schoolfield

He Who Weeps Goes Not Alone. Rosalía de Castro. SpanPo, *tr. by* Kate Flores

He who would acclaim Cleanness in becoming style. *Unknown.* NOCV *Fr.* Cleanness.

He who writ [*or* wrote] this, not without pains and thought. Dryden. PeLV *Fr.* Secret Love; or, The Maiden Queen.

He Whose Hand and Eye Are Gentle. *Unknown.* OBWVE, *tr. by* Kenneth Hurlstone Jackson

He whose not too honest fingers. *Unknown.* PriapPo, *tr. by* Richard W. Hooper *Fr.* Priapus Poems, The.

He will be an uncle / if we are lucky. (LL) Game after Supper. Margaret Atwood. FaBoWP; LCAP-2

He will go over and tell the king. Over the Wall: Berlin, May 1975. Charles Hubert Sisson. OxBC

He will have turned. Old Story. Lance Henson. VoR

He will insist on. Bath, The. Joel Oppenheimer. NeAP

He will sit at the bare table, reading a dictionary. Time of Waiting. Geoffrey Dutton. CBAP

He will walk in as you're sitting down to a meal. (LL) Book of Yolek, The. Anthony Hecht. HP; MakPoe; NoP-4; TaR; WeW-3

He Wishes for the Cloths of Heaven. W. B. Yeats. ChAP; MoBrPo; NoAM; OBEV

He wishes he could hug them like big friends from home. (LL) Stalin Epigram, The. Osip Emilevich Mandelstam [*or* Mandelshtam]. AF; WoPoe, *tr. by* Clarence Brown and W. S. Merwin

He with body waged a fight. Four Ages of Man, The. W. B. Yeats. PAI; TrCP

He with the beating wings. Dead Language. Johannes Bobrowski. WoPoe, *tr. by* Matthew Mead and Ruth Mead

He with whom I ran hand in hand. Woman Meets an Old Lover, A. Denise Levertov. BLT

He woke, and wondered more: For there she lay. (LL) Dante Gabriel Rossetti. EBVV; NAEL-5v2; NAEL-6v2; NOBVV *Fr.* House of Life, The.

He woke from slumber rubbing his eyes. Memories of the Village School. Al-Tijani Yusuf Bashir. MAP, *tr. by* Issa Boullata and John Heath-Stubbs

He works / stone to.   Rock Painting.   Carroll Arnett.   VoR

He worshipped at the altar of Romance.   Epitaph, An.   Colin Ellis.   OxBTC

He would come back and sing. (LL)   Last Word of a Bluebird, The.   Robert Frost.   NOxBChV; OxIBACP

He would declare and could himself believe.   Never Again Would Birds' Song Be The Same.   Robert Frost.   APT-1; HAP; InPK-6; NIP-4; NoAM; NoP-4; OWoS; SoSe-8; Son; VGW

He would drink by himself.   Casualty.   Seamus Heaney.   ModIr; NAEL-5v2; NAEL-6v2; PBCIP; PoE

He would get the gold.   Stroke.   Hugh Seidman.   BodElec

He would Have His Lady Sing.   Digby Mackworth Dolben.   EBEV

He would like not to kill. He would like.   Robber Bridegroom, The.   Margaret Atwood.   LCAP-2

He would not lie uncovered.   Burial of the Dog.   Susan Musgrave.   NoAM

He would not stay for me; and who can wonder?   A. E. Housman.   CAGL

He writes down something that he crosses out. (LL)   Boy, The.   Marilyn Hacker.   ExTi; WiU

He Wrote the History Book.   Marianne Craig Moore.   APT-1

He wrote *The I and the It*.   On the Death of a German Philosopher.   Stevie Smith.   OBCoV

He yawned and watched the lilac horns of his island.   Derek Walcott.   NoP-4   *Fr.* Omeros.

Head, A.   James Schuyler.   PoM

Head, The.   Blaise Cendrars.   CuPo

Head, The.   Padraic Fallon.   CIP-2

Head-Ache, The; An Ode to Health.   Jane Cave.
   "Ah! why from me art thou for ever flown."   ECWP

Head bumper.   *Unknown.*   OxNR

Head in a cloud Moses stands.   Moses.   Sydney Tremayne.   OxBS

Head Is a Paltry Matter, The.   Pier Giorgio Di Cicco.   NOBC

Head of a White Woman Winking.   James Tate.   BodElec

Head of Hair.   Charles Baudelaire.   SxFrPo, *tr.* by James McGowan

Head of Medusa.   Marya Alexandrovna Zaturenska.   MoAmPo

Head of Medusa on a Rotella of Michelangelo da Caravaggio, in the Gallery of the Grand Duke of Tuscany, The.   Marino Giambattista.   GS, *tr.* by *Unknown*

Head or Tail—which does he lack?, A.   Hippo, The.   Theodore Roethke.   VGW

Head over Heels in Love.   Mack Gordon.   ReLy

Head pillowed on arm.   Buson.   SoOfWa, *tr.* by Sam Hamill

Head pressed against the shoulder, thirty times, The.   Tape Mark.   Nanni Balestrini.   PFTM-2, *tr.* by Lawrence R. Smith

Head pure, sinless quite of brain or soul, A.   Robert Burns.   FaBoEE   *Fr.* Versicles on Sign-Posts.

Head That Once Was Crowned with Thorns, The.   Thomas Kelly.   SacPr

Head thrusts in as for the view, A.   All Revelation.   Robert Frost.   APT-1

Head to limp head, the sunk-eyed wounded scanned.   Smile, Smile, Smile.   Wilfred Owen.   PeFWW

Headache, The.   Mary Leapor.   ECWP; PEW

Heading East or West, down the.   Farewell to Shen Yueh.   Fan Yun.   OHMPC, *tr.* by Kenneth Rexroth

Heading for the Heights.   Merryn Williams.   Prnts

Heading Out West.   John Balaban.   OPRER

Heading over to Bulaan Alaaga's.   Cutting Back the Ifugao Past.   Al Robles.   ReBoTo

Heading South.   Tu Fu.   CrYelRi, *tr.* by Sam Hamill

Headlands.   Jack Hirschman.   CLPP

Headless, lacking foot and hand.   Rudyard Kipling.   PoWW   *Fr.* Epitaphs of the War [1914–1918].

Headless limbless / it appears.   Vasco [*or* Vasko] Popa.   PoSu, *tr.* by Anne Pennington   *Fr.* Quartz Pebble, The.

Headless torsos, faceless lovers, friends of mine. (LL)   Onion, Memory, The.   Craig Raine.   NAEL-5v2; NAEL-6v2; NoAM; NoP-4

Headline History.   William Plomer.   OBCoV

Headline to Summarize a Passion.   U Tam'si Tchicaya.   NegPo, *tr.* by Ellen Conroy Kennedy

Headlined in Heaven.   Paul Grano.   NOBAu

Headmaster.   John Tripp.   AngWePo

Headmaster addresses the Assembly, The.   Private School for Girls, May 14, 1948, New York City, A.   Florence W. Freed.   GotH

Headrock.   Brian Coffey.   CIP-2

Heads, impenetrable / And the slow bulk, The.   Oxen: Ploughing at Fiesole.   Charles Tomlinson.   OxBTC

Heads of strong old age are beautiful, The.   Promise of Peace.   Robinson Jeffers.   MoAmPo

Heads or Tails?   Kit Wright.   OTCP

Headstrong young lady of Ealing, A.   Limerick.   Edward Gorey.   PeLi

Headwaters.   N. Scott Momaday.   NoP-4

Heal Me, My God.   Judah Halevi.   TOF, *tr.* by David Goldstein

Healer of broken bones. (LL)   Elegy for Her Brother Sakhr.   Al-Khansa.   BoWoP; WPOW

Healing.   D. H. Lawrence.   RaBo

Healing.   Alicia Ostriker.   ExTi   *Fr.* Mastectomy Poems, The.

Healing.   Abraham Reisen.   TrJP, *tr.* by Joseph Leftwich

Healing Animal.   Joy Harjo.   SeSe

Healing Logic, A.   M. Wyrebek.   AmPoNex

Healing Notebooks, The.   Kenny Fries.
   "I bed next to you, I feel your heartbeat."   AmPoNex
   "Who knows the precise moment when the stream."   AmPoNex

Healing of the Leper, The.   Vernon Watkins.   FaBoTw

Healing Songs.   Tohono O'odham (Owl Woman) (Juana Manwell).   SWaP, *tr.* by Frances Densmore

Healing the Mare.   Linda McCarriston.   LoL

Health, A.   Edward Coote [*or* Coate] Pinkney.   APN-1

Health from the lover of the country, me.   Horace.   AWP, *tr.* by Abraham Cowley   *Fr.* Epistles.

Health in his rags, Content upon his face.   On Seeing a Bird-Catcher.   Eliza Cook.   VWP

Health is the first good lent to men.   Four[e] Things Make Us Happy Here.   Robert Herrick.   CaPo; Spl

Health to great Gloucester—from a man unknown.   Dedication.   Charles Churchill.   OBSV

Health to my fair Odelia! Some that know.   To Odelia.   James Shirley.   BeJo

Healthy Remedies.   Georges Henein.   SurPaPo, *tr.* by Mary Ann Caws

Healthy Spot, A.   W. H. Auden.   AiP

Heap cassia, sandal-buds and stripes.   Robert Browning.   OBEV   *Fr.* Paracelsus.

Heap earth upon it. (LL)   Requiescat.   Oscar Wilde.   EBVV; MoBrPo; PeVV

Heap on more grass was his request.   Joseph Gwyer.   VerBaPo   *Fr.* On the Funeral of Dr. Livingston.

"Heap on more wood!—the wind is chill."   Sir Walter Scott.   ChrPo; OBCP   *Fr.* Marmion.

Hear all, the new moon new in all / the ancient sky. (LL)   Charles Olson.   NAAL-5; PoM   *Fr.* Maximus Poems, The.

Hear and make example too. (LL)   Ben Jonson.   NAEL-6v1; NAEL-7v1   *Fr.* Celebration of Charis in Ten Lyric[k] Pieces [*or* Peeces], A.

Hear father yet thou Long-Armed Lord! these latest words I say.   *Unknown.*   TAL   *Fr.* Bhagavad-Gita, The.

Hear hear hear hear.   Ronald Johnson.   APSN   *Fr.* Ark.

Hear! hear! hear! / Listen! the word.   Mocking-Bird, The.   Richard Hovey.   APN-2

Hear, Hear, O Ye Nations.   Frederick Lucian Hosmer.   AH

Hear Icenian, Catieuchlanian, hear Coritanian, Trinobant!   Tennyson.   FaBoWar   *Fr.* Boädicea.

Hear in the sea, Thetis, Memnon's alive.   Asclepiodotus.   GrAn

Hear it! Eventless inmesh. A stick collapses.   Truth Put It.   Marianne Vitale.   HeMarv

Hear, Jehovah / May the eternal serpent's curse be on him!   Byron.   NOBRP   *Fr.* Cain: A Mystery.

Hear me, great ones of Uruk.   *Unknown.*   CAGL, *tr.* by N. K. Sandars   *Fr.* Epic of Gilgamesh, The.

Hear me / helper of mankind.   *Unknown.*   RaBo, *tr.* by Charles Boer   *Fr.* Homeric Hymns.

Hear me, my God, and hear me soon.   Petition, The.   Thomas Beedome.   NOSC

Hear me [*or* Heare mee], O God!   Hymn[e] to God the Father, A.   Ben Jonson.   BeJo; InvLi; NOSC; OxAEP-1; SacPr; TrCP

Hear me propitious, and defend my lays. (LL)   To Mæcenas.   Phillis Wheatley.   NAAAL; NAAL-5

Hear me, whom I betrayed.   Envoi.   James Vincent Cunningham.   VGW

Hear me, ye smokeless skies and grass-green earth.   Charles Mair.   NOBC   *Fr.* Last Bison, The.

Hear my voice, birds of war!   Ojibwa War Songs.   *Unknown.*   AWP, *tr.* by H. H. Schoolcraft

Hear my voice where you are.   Come Back to Me.   Burton Lane.   ReLy

Hear now a curious dream I dreamed last night.   My Dream.   Christina Georgina Rossetti.   BrRo; VWP; ViWPN

Hear now a sound of floods.   Song for Ilva Mackay and Mongane.   Keorapetse Kgositsile.   PBMAP

Hear, O hear, Iseult la belle! Tristan, sad hero, hear! The Lambeg drum.   James Joyce.   PFTM-2   *Fr.* Finnegans Wake.

Hear, O Israel.   Shema Yisrael.   *Unknown.*   TrJP

Hear, O Israel! and plead my cause against the ungodly nation.   Adah Isaacs Menken.   CBWP-1

Hear, O Israel, Jehovah, the Lord our God is one.   Israel.   Israel Zangwill.   TrJP

Hear, O Israel, the commandments of life. Bible, Apocrypha. TrJP *Fr.* Baruch.

Hear, O Israel / Will you never tire of repeating in your prayers. Hear, O Israel! André Spire. TrJP, *tr. by* Stanley Burnshaw

Hear, O my people, and I will speak. Bible, *O.T.* InvLi, *tr. by* New Revised Standard Version *Fr.* Psalms.

Hear, sweet spirit, hear the spell. Samuel Taylor Coleridge. PeECV *Fr.* Remorse.

Hear that echo, children. Swan Sequence, The. *Unknown.* WoPoe, *tr. by* Denis Goacher

Hear that tree-lizard singin' out. Jarrangulli. Roland Robinson. NOxBChV

Hear the Bird of Day. David Campbell. NOBAu

Hear the dreary, dreary rain. Voices of the Rain. Henrietta Cordelia Ray. CBWP-3

Hear the music, the thunder of the wings. Love the wild swan. (LL) Love the Wild Swan. Robinson Jeffers. APT-1; MoAmPo; NoAM; Son

Hear the sledges with the bells. Bells, The. Edgar Allan Poe. APN-1; BRP; ChAP; ITBLP; OBAL; OBCA; TAP; TCAPo; TFi; TreFP

Hear the Voice. William Blake. *See* Songs of Experience

Hear the Word of the Lord. Bible, *O.T.* TrJP *Fr.* Isaiah.

Hear the word that Jesus spake. Lost Word of Jesus, A. Henry Van Dyke. TrCP

Hear them, hear them—all. Cage of Voices, The. Horace Gregory. APT-2

Hear them whisper. (LL) Jack Spicer. NeAP; PmAP *Fr.* Imaginary Elegies.

Hear this, and tremble, all. Upon My Lord Chief Justice's Election of My Lady Anne Wentworth [*or* A.W.] for His Mistress. Thomas Carew. CaPo

Hear! this is what I. For John Donne: Master Metaphysical. Alexander Trocchi. EroLit

Hear what God the Lord hath spoken. William Cowper. InvLi *Fr.* Olney Hymns.

Hear, ye children, the instruction of a father. Bible, *O.T.* TrJP *Fr.* Proverbs.

Hear, Ye Ladies [That Despise]. John Fletcher. NOBE; OBEV *Fr.* Tragedy of Valentinian, The.

Heard by a Girl. Louise Bogan. APT-2

Heard de owl a hootin'. Gal's Cry for a Dying Lover. Langston Hughes. NAAAL

Heard him gladly. Waldere 1. *Unknown.* AnOE, *tr. by* Charles W. Kennedy

Heard in a Violent Ward. Theodore Roethke. HCAP

Heard in the Cougate. Robert Garioch. OxBTC

Heard, not seen. Basho. SoOfWa, *tr. by* Sam Hamill

Heard on a Boat. T'an Yüan-ch'un. SuSp, *tr. by* Irving Y. Lo

Heard on the Mountain. Victor Hugo. AWP, *tr. by* Francis Thompson *Fr.* Feuilles d'Automne.

Heard the pulse of you when all was still ringing little bells last night under my ear. (LL) I Heard You Solemn-Sweet Pipes of the Organ. Walt Whitman. APN-1; OxBA; SAmP

Heard ye eer of the silly blind harper. Lochmaben Harper, The. *Unknown.* ESPB; OxBB

Hear[e] ye Virgins, and I'll [*or* Ile] teach. To Virgins. Robert Herrick. CaPo

Hearing. Michael McClintock. HA

Hearing. W. S. Merwin. NoAM

Hearing a Flute at Broken Bridge. Yün Shou-p'ing. CoBLCP, *tr. by* Jonathan Chaves

Hearing a Flute on the River Chi. Wen Cheng-ming. CoBLCP, *tr. by* Jonathan Chaves

Hearing a Song from My Boat. Chang Yü. CoBLCP, *tr. by* Jonathan Chaves

Hearing a Startled Bird during Stayover at Chin-Ch'ang Pavilion. Li Shang-yin. ChinPo, *tr. by* Yip Wai-lim

Hearing a thud, as though a ball had struck. False Move. Grace Schulman. ExTi

Hearing how tourists, dazed with reverence. Kingsley Amis. NOBL *Fr.* Evans Country, The.

Hearing I ask from the holy races. *Unknown.* AWP, *tr. by* Henry Adams Bellows *Fr.* Elder Edda, The.

Hearing Impairment. Les A. Murray. OBCoV

Hearing Loom and Shuttle. Yü Chi. CoBLCP, *tr. by* Jonathan Chaves

Hearing Loss. Christian Wiman. AmPoNex

Hearing loss? Yes, loss is what we hear. Hearing Impairment. Les A. Murray. OBCoV

Hearing of harvests rotting in the valleys. Paysage Moralisé. W. H. Auden. HarvBoo; MoBrPo; UnPo

Hearing of Imperial Forces Retaking Ho-Nan and Ho-Pei. Tu Fu. ChinPo, *tr. by* Yip Wai-lim

Hearing of past actions. John Cage. APSN *Fr.* Diary: How to Improve the World (You Will Only Make Matters Worse).

Hearing of Reagan's Trip to Bitburg. Lyn Lifshin. GotH

Hearing one saga, we enact the next. Remembering the 'Thirties. Donald Davie. HarvBoo; NoP-4; OxBTC

Hearing Russian Spoken. Donald Davie. GTBS-P

Hearing Steps. Charles Simic. HCAP

Hearing That His Friend Was Coming Back from the War. Wang Chien. ChiP, *tr. by* Arthur Waley

Hearing the Early Oriole. Po Chü-i. ChiP, *tr. by* Arthur Waley

Hearing the Flute in the City of Loyang in a Spring Night. Li Po. ChinPo, *tr. by* Yip Wai-lim

Hearing the judges' well-considered sentence. After the Trial. Weldon Kees. MakPoe

Hearing the organ stray. Service. Peter Scupham. HarvBoo

Hearing the rain at last, I stepped out and saw the dark day. Finally the Rain. Carrington McDuffie. PoCoUp

Hearing the stones cry out under the horizons. (LL) Wind. Ted Hughes. HarvBoo; NAEL-5v2; NAEL-6v2; NoP-4

Hearing the thunder of the intransitive weirs. Arthur Rimbaud. WoPoe, *tr. by* Derek Mahon *Fr.* Drunken Boat, The.

Hearing, this June day, the thin thunder. Home Thoughts from Abroad. William Robert Rodgers. OBCoV

Hearing Your Words, and Not a Word among Them. Edna St. Vincent Millay. ColAP; NoAM; VGW

H[e]ark! O h[e]ark, you guilty trees. Orpheus to Woods. Richard Lovelace. CaPo

Hearken all ye, 'tis the feast o' Saint Stephen. Feast o' Saint [*or* St.] Stephen, The. Ruth Sawyer. OBCP

Hearken, Lady Betty, hearken. Christopher Anstey. NOEC *Fr.* New Bath Guide, The.

Hearken, thou craggy ocean pyramid! To Ailsa Rock. John Keats. CenSon

Hearken to me, gentlemen. King Estmere. *Unknown.* ESPB; OBNV; OxBB

Hears not my Phillis how the birds. Song. Sir Charles Sedley. EnLoPo

Hears't thou, my soul, what serious things. Dies Irae. Thomas of Celano. AWP, *tr. by* Richard Crashaw

Hears thy voice right, now he is gone. (LL) Matthew Arnold. CABP; NAEL-5v2; NAEL-6v2

Hearse Song, The. *Unknown.* OxBoLi; RB

Hearse was the oven of the crematory, The. Funeral, The. "M. J." TrJP, *tr. by* A. Glanz-Leyeles

Heart. Guillaume Apollinaire. TTTS, *tr. by* Roger Shattuck *Fr.* Heart, Crown, and Mirror.

Heart. Catherine Bowman. ExTi

Heart. Maura Dooley. NeBl

Heart. Jerry Ross. ReLy *Fr.* Damn Yankees.

Heart. Dieter Weslowski. InvLad

Heart, The. Stephen Crane. APN-2; MoAmPo; NoP-4; TCAPo *Fr.* Black Riders [and Other Lines], The.

Heart, The. Michael Drayton. NOSC

Heart, The. Jakov [*or* Jacob] Steinberg. TrJP, *tr. by* Harry H. Fein

Heart, The. Francis Thompson.
  All's Vast. MoBrPo; OBMV; Son
  (Correlated Greatness.) GTBS-P
  "Heart you hold too small and local thing, The." OBMV

Heart-affluence in discursive talk. Tennyson. NAEL-6v2 *Fr.* In Memoriam A. H. H.

Heart and flesh. (LL) Same Gesture, The. John Montague. BIrV; Modlr; PNI

Heart and Mind. Dame Edith Sitwell. LW; OxBTC; TwCP

Heart and Soul. Assotto Saint. CAGL

Heart and the Severed Head, The. Rosita Copioli. CItWP, *tr. by* Lara Trubowitz

Heart asks Pleasure—first, The. Emily Dickinson. APN-2; MoAmPo; NAAL-2v1; NAAL-3; NOBA; NoP-4; OxBA; PoPoPo; TCAPo; WPE

Heart be content, though she be gone. Ostella forth of Town: To My Heart. John Tatham. NOSC

Heart beating, beating inside what I say en inglés. (LL) Bilingual Sestina. Julia Alvarez. ExTi; FFC

Heart burns—but has to keep out of face how heart burns, The. (LL) Strange Hells. Ivor Gurney. FaBoWar; OxBTC; PeFWW

Heart cold in the breast with terror, grieving. Lament for Llywelyn ap Gruffudd. Gruffudd ab yr Ynad Coch. OBWVE, *tr. by* Joseph P. Clancy

Heart, Crown, and Mirror. Guillaume Apollinaire.
  Heart. TTTS, *tr. by* Roger Shattuck

Heart dies of this sweetness, The. (LL) Brigit Pegeen Kelly. ExTi; IllVoic *Fr.* Southern Review, The.

Heart Escaping. László Kálnoky. IQMS, *tr. by* Kenneth McRobbie and Zita McRobbie

Heart free, hand free. Sic Vita. William Stanley Braithwaite. NAAAL

Heart has need of some deceit, The. Only the Polished Skeleton. Countee Cullen. VGW

Heart-Hungry. Josephine D. Henderson Heard. CBWP-4

Heart Is Deep, The. Roger Wolcott. ChIV-1; SCAP

Heart is sensual, though five eyes break, The. (LL)   When All My Five and Country Senses See.   Dylan Thomas.   MoBrPo; NoAM; Son

Heart made full of thought, A.   Maghnas O Domhnaill.   NOIV

Heart, my heart churning with fathomless cares.   Archilochus.   SaLy, *tr. by* Diane Rayor

Heart, My Lovely Hobo.   Sandra Cisneros.   IllVoic

Heart of a Woman, The.   Georgia Douglas Johnson.   BlSi

Heart of Autumn.   Robert Penn Warren.   APT-2; ColAP; FuPo

Heart of autumn!   Chipmunk, The.   Herman Melville.   NCAP

Heart of Herakles, The.   Kenneth Rexroth.   BLT   *Fr.* Lights in the Sky are Stars, The.

Heart of Midlothian, The.   Sir Walter Scott.
  (Madge Wildfire's Death Song.)   HAP
  (Madge Wildfire's Song.)   NOBE
  (Madge Wildfire Sings.)   NPeEn
  (Pride of Youth, The.)   GTBS-P
  Proud Maisie.   CABP; FaBoCh; NAEL-5v2; NAEL-6v2; NOBRP; NePenScot; OBEV; OxBEV; OxBS; RACG; SCGP; TFi; UnPo

Heart of O'Leary, S.J., The.   Limerick.   David Phillips.   PeLi

Heart of Oak.   David Garrick.   FaBoWar; NOEC; OxBoLi

Heart of Rice Straw, A.   Nellie Wong.
  "Ma, my heart must be made of rice straw."   UnSA

Heart of standing is we cannot fly, The. (LL)   Aubade: "Hours before dawn we were woken by the quake."   William Empson.   FaBoMo; FaBoTw; OxAEP-2; OxBEV; OxBTC

Heart of the heartless world.   Huesca.   John Cornford.   BoLoP

Heart of the Matter.   Susan Prospere.   AmPoNex

Heart of the Night, The.   Richard Doddridge Blackmore.   SacPr

Heart of the Quartz Pebble, The.   Vasco [*or* Vasko] Popa.   PoSu, *tr. by* Anne Pennington   *Fr.* Quartz Pebble, The.

Heart of the World, The.   Rabbi Nahman [*or* Nachman] of Bratzlav.   TrJP, *tr. by* Joseph Leftwich

Heart of Time.   Fanny Carrión de Fierro.   TANSG, *tr. by* Sally Cheney Bell

Heart on the Hill, The.   Petrarch.   AWP   *Fr.* Sonnets to Laura.

Heart's Abysses, The.   Walter Savage Landor.   FaBoEE; OBSV

Heart's Anchor, The.   William Winter.   PoToHe

Heart's Desire.   Adelia Prado.   TANSG, *tr. by* Ellen Watson

Heart's Ease.   Paul Hoover.   PmAP

Heart's Ease.   Mary E. Tucker.   CBWP-1

Heart's Fine Gold, The.   W. O. Bourne.   TreFP

Heart's Haven.   Dante Gabriel Rossetti.   Son   *Fr.* House of Life, The.

Heart's Music.   Thomas Campion.   OBEV

Heart's Needle.   W. D. Snodgrass.
  Child of My Winter Born.   MoAmPo
  "Easter has come around."   VCAP
  "I thumped on you the best I could."   NoAM
  "Late April and you are three; today."   VCAP

Heart stood at the helm that night, The.   Departure.   Gerrit Achterberg.   TuT, *tr. by* Peter Van de Kamp

Heart, The / a canned tulip.   Surplus.   Rebecca Reynolds.   AmPoNex

Heart! We [*or* Heart, we] will forget him!   Emily Dickinson.   SAmP

Heart whose love is innocent, A. (LL)   She Walks In Beauty.   Byron.   AWP; AmFaPo; BRP; BoLoP; CABP; FHYEP; GTBS-P; HeIP-4; ITBLP; NAEL-5v2; NAEL-6v2; NOBE; NOBRP; NePenScot; NoP-4; OBEV; OxAEP-2; OxBEV; PoE; PoPoPo; SCGP; TFi

Heart with Little or No Bedrock for Anchor, A.   Vivian Shipley.   ExTi

Heart Wounds.   Claire Richcreek Thomas.   PoToHe

Heart, you bully, you punk, I'm wrecked, I'm shocked.   One is One.   Marie Ponsot.   ExTi

Heart you hold too small and local thing, The.   Francis Thompson.   OBMV   *Fr.* Heart, The.

Heartbeats.   Melvin Dixon.   ESEAA

Heartbreak Camp.   Roy Campbell.   OxBTC

Heartbreak Hotel Piano-Bar.   Richard Speakes.   SwNoth

Heartease 3.   Lorna Goodison.   WaCA

Hearted Americans are.   Kind-, The.   James Laughlin.   CDa

Hearth and Home.   Stoddard King.   OBAL

Hearth Song.   John Montague.   PNI

Hearthstone.   Harold Monro.   OBMV

Heartland.   Jim Barnes.   HATNAP

Heartland.   Trent Busch.   BAP-01

Heartland.   Linda Hogan.   UrbNat

Heartless Art, The.   Tony Harrison.   NoP-4

Hearts, The.   Robert Pinsky.   VCAP

Hearts-Ease.   Walter Savage Landor.   OxBEV

Hearts, like doors, will ope with ease.   *Unknown.*   OxNR

Hearts (1983).   Laurie Duggan.   BMAP   *Fr.* Three Found Poems.

Hearts that are great beat never loud.   Thought, A.   Abram Joseph Ryan.   PWR

Hearts thus intermixed speak, The.   Friendship in Emblem[e], or the Seal[e], to my dearest Lucasia.   Katherine Philips.   CABP; EMWP; PBRV

Heartsong.   Jeni Couzyn.   HAWP

Heartsong.   Khaled Mattawa.   BAP-97; NAPBL; NeAmPo

Heartstopping.   Nicole Espagnol.   SurWo, *tr. by* Myrna Bell Rochester

Heat.   Maura Dooley.   NeBl

Heat.   "H. D."   HeIP-4; InPK-6; MoAmPo; OxBA; TAP; TCAPo; TRP; UnPo   *Fr.* Garden, The.

Heat.   Denis Johnson.   MakPoe; SwNoth

Heat.   Archibald Lampman.   NOBC

Heat.   Kenneth Mackenzie.   BMAP; CBAP

Heat before the storm.   Nicholas Virgilio.   HA

Heat goes deep as cold.   Epigram.   *Unknown.*   NOIV, *tr. by* Thomas Kinsella

Heat-heavy creatures.   Mary Kinzie.   FFC

Heat in October.   Kyoko Mori.   FSt

Heat in the Room, The.   Weldon Kees.   SPE

Heat-lightning streak.   Basho.   InPK-6

Heat of Midnight Tears, The.   Mirabai [*or* Mira Bai].   WPoS, *tr. by* Robert Bly

Heat of the oven, The.   Breaded Meat, Breaded Hands.   Michael S. Harper.   ISC

Heat's on the hooker, The.   Translations from the English.   George Starbuck.   VGW

Heat Sours, The.   David Biespiel.   AmPoNex

Heat that feb ice. Spell melt.   La Tormenta.   Geraldine Monk.   Oth

Heat wave, A / Blew right into town last week.   Heat Wave.   Irving Berlin.   ReLy

Heat waves shimmering.   Basho.   EH, *tr. by* Robert Hass

Heath grass / Sandals.   Masaoka Shiki.   ZenPo, *tr. by* Takashi Ikemoto and Lucien Stryk

Heathen Are Come into Thine Inheritance, The.   Bible, *O.T.*   TrJP   *Fr.* Psalms.

Heathen Pass-ee, The.   Arthur Clement Hilton.   NOBL; UV

Heather Flowers.   Eliseus Williams.   OBWVE, *tr. by* Kenneth Hurlstone Jackson

Heather on the Hill, The.   Frederick Loewe.   ReLy

Heav'n it self would stoop to her. (LL)   John Milton.   OBEV; OxAEP-1   *Fr.* Comus; a Masque Presented at Ludlow Castle.

Heaven.   Chairil Anwar.   PoetW, *tr. by* Burton Raffel

Heaven.   Rupert Brooke.   EBEV; MoBrPo; NOBE; NPeEn; OxBEV; PoRA

Heaven.   George Herbert.   ESCV; GeHe; TTTS; TrCP; WoPoe

Heaven.   Langston Hughes.   *See* Heaven, Heaven, Heaven Is the Place

Heaven.   Philip Levine.   LCAP-2

Heaven.   Cathy Song.   NAAL-5; NIL-7; NoAM

Heaven.   Gary Soto.   SwNoth

Heaven.   Isaac Watts.   TOF
  (Prospect of Heaven Makes Death Easy, A.)   NOCV; NoP-4; PeECV

Heaven and earth a rotating ball.   Tune: "Wild Geese Have Come down; Song of Victory"—Idle Leisure.   Teng Yu-pin.   SuSp, *tr. by* Hellmut Wilhelm

Heaven and Earth exist for ever;.   Substance, Shadow, and Spirit.   Ch'ien T'ao.   ChiP, *tr. by* Arthur Waley

Heaven and earth to peace beguiles. (LL)   William Blake.   FHYEP; OBCP   *Fr.* Songs of Innocence.

Heaven and Hell.   Nalungiaq.   STP, *tr. by* Edward Field

Heaven and Hell.   Willie Nelson.   InPK-6

Heaven and Hell.   Francis Thompson.   OxBSP; SacPr

Heaven and hell are men's unhappy inventions.   Taoist Song.   Teng Yu-pin.   CrYelRi, *tr. by* Sam Hamill

Heaven conserve thy course in quietness.   Ezra Pound.   APSN

Heaven expands, autumn arcs high, the night still long.   Following the Rhymes of Autumn Night Song by Meng Tzu-chou, Signatory Official of the Board of Rites.   Yü Chi.   CoBLCP, *tr. by* Jonathan Chaves

Heaven had not won, nor earth so timely lost. (LL)   Epitaph for [*or* on] Thomas Clere.   Henry Howard, Earl of Surrey.   NoSic; OxBSo

Heaven-Haven.   Gerard Manley Hopkins.   HeIP-4; MoBrPo; NOBE; NOCV; NoAM; OBEV; OxAEP-2; OxBSP; PAI; PeECV; RB; SoSe-8; TFi; TOF

Heaven, Heaven, Heaven Is the Place.   Langston Hughes.   AH
  (Heaven.)   NOBA

Heaven / I'm in heaven.   Cheek to Cheek.   Irving Berlin.   ReLy

Heaven in the South, earth Northward.   Kuan Han-ch'ing.   SuSp   *Fr.* Tune: "Intoxication in the East Wind."

Heaven Is Here.   John G. Adams.   AH

Heaven is Hers! / Earth is Hers!   Inanna's Chant.   Janine Canan.   HW

Heaven Is Just Another Country.   Jaime Jacinto.   ReBoTo

"Heaven"—is what I cannot reach!   Emily Dickinson.   NOCV; PoBW

Heaven of Animals, The.   James Dickey.   CoAP; ColAP; EmeKit; HeIP-4; NAAL-2v2; NOBA; NoAM; PoE; TAP; TRP; VCAP; WoPoe

Heaven opened wide / Her ever during gates, harmonious sound. John Milton. ChIV-1; TreFP *Fr.* Paradise Lost.

Heaven Peak. Muso Soseki. EaWin, *tr.* by W. S. Merwin

Heaven Questions, The. Ch'u Yüan. "In the beginning of old." WoPoe, *tr.* by Stephen Field

Heaven's mercy shines, wonders and glorys meet. Mercies of the Year, The. John Danforth. SCAP

Heaven's mills are grinding slowly, but they grind exceeding small. Divine Revenge. Friedrich von Logau. GePo, *tr.* by George C. Schoolfield

Heaven's Ring. Vasco [*or* Vasko] Popa. VCWP, *tr.* by Charles Simic

Heaven shall forgive you Bridge at dawn. Ballade D'une Grande Dame. Gilbert Keith Chesterton. OxBoLi

Heaven, the earth, and all the liquid main [*or* mayne], The. Virgil [*or* Vergil]. OBVE *Fr.* Aeneid [*or* Eneados, *Aeneis*], The.

Heaven took my wife. Now it. Sorrow. Mei Yao Ch'en. OHPC; WoPoe, *tr.* by Kenneth Rexroth

Heaven, unmoved, weeps on forever. Sunday Piece. Jules Laforgue. WoPoe, *tr.* by William Jay Smith

Heaven vows to keep him. (LL) Epitaph on S. P. [Salomon *or* Salathiel Pavy], a Child of Q[ueen] El[izabeth's] Chapel. Ben Jonson. BeJo; NAEL-5v1; NAEL-6v1; NAEL-7v1; NOSC; OBEV; OxBEV; SCGP; UnPo

Heaven / was only half as far that night. 21. Lawrence Ferlinghetti. CLPP

Heaven which art in Heaven Our Father in Heaven. Kay Smith. TrCP *Fr.* Footnote to the Lord's Prayer.

Heaven, which man's generations draws. Francis Thompson. MoBrPo *Fr.* Judgment in Heaven, A.

Heaven Will Protect the Working-Girl. Edgar Smith. ReLy

Heavenly Aeroplane, The. *Unknown.* NOCV

Heavenly City, The. Stevie Smith. FaBoTw

Heavenly Eloquence. Samuel Daniel. *See* Musophilus; or, Defence of All Learning

"Heavenly Father"—take to thee. Emily Dickinson. APN-2; InvLi

Heavenly Foreigner, The. Denis Devlin. "Spires, firm on their monster feet rose light and thin, The." CIP-2

Heavenly Jerusalem, Jerusalem of the Earth. Leah Goldberg. FIT, *tr.* by Robert Friend

Heavenly labials in a world of gutturals. / It will undo him. (LL) Plot against the Giant, The. Wallace Stevens. OxBA; SAmP

Heavenly Questions. Ch'u Yüan. ColAnChi, *tr.* by Victor H. Mair

Heavenly Rhetoric, The. William Shakespeare. Son *Fr.* Love's Labour's Lost.

Heavenly River is muddy year-round. Heavenly River. Tu Fu. CrYelRi, *tr.* by Sam Hamill

Heavens! all China's on the ground, in pieces! Broken Vase, The. Victor Hugo. SxFrPo, *tr.* by E. H. Blackmore and A. M. Blackmore

Heavens allowed me, The. At Whole-World-In-View-Hut. Muso Soseki. EaWin, *tr.* by W. S. Merwin

Heavens bright lamp, shine forth some of thy light. George Alsop. SCAP

Heavens Cherubim High Horsed or The Meeting of the Two Sevens (May 1977). Velma Pollard. WaCA

Heavens declare the glory of God, The. Bible, *O.T.* AWP; NAWM-5v1 *Fr.* Psalms.

Heavens Do Declare, The. *Unknown.* AH

Heavens doe declare/ The majesty of God, The. Bible, *O.T.* SCAP *Fr.* Bay Psalm Book, The.

Heavens glorious Eie, which all the world surveyes. Another on the Sun Shine. Lucy Hutchinson. EMWP

Heavens, ocean, and all earth, rejoice! Sedulius Scottus. NOIV *Fr.* Defeat of the Norsemen, The.

Heavens sense our burden, The. Storm, The. Jirka Polak. INSAB

Heavensgate (1961). Christopher Okigbo.
Bridge. PBMAP
Eyes Watch the Stars. PBMAP
Lustra. PBMAP
Overture. PBMAP
Passion Flower. PBMAP

Heaviest wheel rolls across our foreheads, The. Terezin. Mif. INSAB

Heavily Flapping Are the Bustards' Plumes. *Unknown.* SuSp, *tr.* by C. H. Wang

Heaviness May Endure for a Night, But Joy Cometh in the Morning. Christina Georgina Rossetti. SacPr

Heaving roses of the hedge are stirred, The. Winter Will Follow. Richard Watson Dixon. GTBS-P

Heavnly Frame sets forth the Fame, The. Bible, *O.T. See* Heavens declare the glory of God, The

Heavy and dull, the motionless clouds. Motionless Clouds. T'ao Ch'ien [*or* T'ao Yuan-ming]. CoBCP, *tr.* by Burton Watson

Heavy Bear Who Goes with Me, The. Delmore Schwartz. APT-2; ColAP; NOBA; NoAM; TAP; TrJP; TwCP; UnPo *Fr.* Repetitive Heart, The.

Heavy blue veins streaked across my mother's legs, some of them bunched up into dark lumps at her ankles. Heavy Blue Veins. Luis J. Rodriguez. UnSA

Heavy bodies lunge, the broken language, The. Old Men Playing Basketball. B. H. Fairchild. MoASP

Heavy cart rumbles by, A. Buson. EH, *tr.* by Robert Hass

Heavy curtains in the waiting rooms. Waiting-rooms. David Vogel. FIT, *tr.* by Robert Friend

Heavy dew. Thick mist. Dense grass. Passing a Ruined Palace. Wen T'ing-yün. OHMPC, *tr.* by Kenneth Rexroth

Heavy glacier and the terrifying Alps, The. Long Lines. Paul Goodman. VGW

Heavy gray and white clouds surrounding the dark green mountaintops, The. Chinese Landscape above Caracas. John Yau. BodElec

Heavy Headed Dance, The. Jayne Cortez. BAP-97

Heavy heart, Beloved, have I borne, A. Elizabeth Barrett Browning. CenSon *Fr.* Sonnets from the Portuguese.

Heavy-hearted. Judah Al-Harizi. TrJP

Heavy, heavy, heavy, hand and heart. Tenebrae. Denise Levertov. NoP-4

Heavy hippity hoppity hipster. Arts Are Black, The. Charlie R. Braxton. InTrad

Heavy-Laden Is My Soul. Kahlil Gibran. GraLe

Heavy mahogany door with its wrought-iron screen, The. Devonshire Street W.1. Sir John Betjeman. NPeEn

Heavy mirror carried. Miracle Glass Co. Charles Simic. MakPoe

Heavy mist, A. A muffled sea. Atheling Grange; or, The Apotheosis of Lotte Nussbaum. William Plomer. OBNV

Heavy-Petting Zoo, The. Clare Pollard. NeBl

Heavy rain crumbles a wall of my house, A. Night Rain: A Wall Collapses—Sent To My Neighbors. Yang Shih-ch'i. CoBLCP; ColAnChi, *tr.* by Jonathan Chaves

Heavy reggae beat thumps. Reggae Prophecy. Marion Bethel. WaCA

Heavy shower bends her to the earth, The. Little Birch Tree, The. Stepan Petrovich Shchipachov [*or* Shchipachiov]. TCRP, *tr.* by Daniel Weissbort

Heavy smells of Spring, The. Jack. Louis Golding. TrJP

Heavy sounds are over-sweet, The. City-Storm. Harold Monro. MoBrPo

Heavy, to hurt those sacred seeds of thee. (LL) To His Dying Brother, Master William Herrick. Robert Herrick. CaPo; CavPo; NOSC

Heavy umbrellas / aren't worth their weight, The. Crocus Night. James Schuyler. PoM

Heavy Violets. Barbara Guest. FTOS

Heavy Water Blues. Bob Kaufman. NBV
(Radio is teaching my goldfish Jujuitsu, The.) CLPP

Heavy with leaves the garden bushes again. Clear View in Summer. Valentin Iremonger. ModIr

Heavy with the heat and silence. Henry Wadsworth Longfellow. APN-1 *Fr.* Song of Hiawatha, The.

Heavyweight champ of Seattle, The. *Unknown.* OBAL

Heavyweight champion of the world Mike Tyson. Today's News. Elizabeth Alexander. ISC; InTrad

Hebe and Ganymede. *Unknown.* CAGL, *tr.* by John Boswell

Hebrew. Yona Volach. DTA, *tr.* by Miriyam Glazer

Hebrew, Greek or Latin, I have not. To Cotton Mather, from a Quaker. Thomas Maule. TCAPo

Hebrew Melodies. Heinrich Heine.
By the Waters of Babylon. TrJP, *tr.* by Charles Godfrey Leland

Hebrew of Your Poets, Zion, The. Charles Reznikoff. APT-2; ChIV-1; VGW

Hebrews. James Oppenheim. TrJP

Hebrides, The. Michael Longley. PBCIP

Hecale. Callimachus.
"As long as it was still noon and the earth." HePo
"South wind does not shed so great a cast, The." HePo
"They fell asleep but not for long, for soon." HePo

Hecateleguim. Pacifico Massimi.
Book 1.
Advice to Paulinus. CAGL, *tr.* by James J. Wilhelm
Book 2.
Love Song for Marcus, A. CAGL, *tr.* by James J. Wilhelm
Book 5.
On Happiness. CAGL, *tr.* by James J. Wilhelm

Hecatodistichon. Jane Seymour.
"This sacred urn holds the ashes of the Queen of Navarre." EMWP

Hector. Valentin Iremonger. CIP-2

Hector Arms. Homer. NOSC, *tr.* by George Chapman *Fr.* Iliad, The.

Hector Flees before Achilles. Homer. OBVE, *tr.* by Alexander Pope *Fr.* Iliad, The.

Hector Protector was dressed all in green. Mother Goose. OxNR; ReMoGo

Hector Returns to Troy. Homer. NAWM-7v1, *tr.* by Robert Fagles *Fr.* Iliad, The.

Hector's Child and the Plume. Homer. OBVE, *tr.* by George Chapman *Fr.* Iliad, The.

Hector's Defiance. Homer. NOSC, *tr.* by George Chapman *Fr.* Iliad, The.

Hector, the captain bronzed, from simple fight. Geoffrey Scott. OBMV *Fr.* Skaian Gate, The.

Hecuba's Testament. Rosario Castellanos. STV, *tr.* by John Frederick Nims

Hedda Gabler is lighting the lamps in a fury. Act One. Chana Bloch. ExTi

Hedge, A. Pine Shade. Muso Soseki. EaWin, *tr.* by W. S. Merwin

Hedge, The. Gwyneth Lewis. MFPA

Hedge before me, one behind, A. *Unknown.* BIrV

Hedge breaks out in bud, The. Elaine Randell. Oth *Fr.* Snoad Hill Poems, The.

Hedge Life. James Dickey. LCAP-2

Hedge Schoolmaster, A. Padraic Fallon. CIP-2

Hedgehog. Chu Chen Po. OHMPC, *tr.* by Kenneth Rexroth

Hedgehog. Paul Muldoon. BIrV; NoAM; PBCIP

Hedges are dazed as cock-crow, heaps of leaves, The. Departure in Middle Age. Roland Mathias. CRP; OBWVE

Hedges Freaked With Snow. Robert Graves. OxBTC *Fr.* Three Songs for the Lute.

Heed us when we turn our eyes to heaven. Song to Heaven. Uri Zvi Greenberg. FIT, *tr.* by Robert Friend

Heedless and wilful, took their knights to bed. (LL) Edna St. Vincent Millay. HeIP-4; NALW; NIL-7

Heedless of where the next bright bolt may fall. (LL) White Goddess, The. Robert Graves. HarvBoo; MoBrPo; NAEL-5v2; NAEL-6v2; NoP-4

Heemi. Hone Tuwhare. PeNZ

Heenie Majeski, Johnny Gee. Van Lingle Mungo. Dave Frishberg. ReLy

Heere uninterr'd suspendes though not to save. Feltons Epitaph. *Unknown.* NPeEn; PBRV

Heere we doe not lynger; thee vowd sollemnitye finnisht. Virgil [*or* Vergil]. NoSic, *tr.* by Richard Stanyhurst *Fr.* Aeneid [*or* Eneados, *Aeneis*], The.

Heidi men call me when their homes I visit. Song of the Seeress. *Unknown.* NAWM-5v1

Heifer, The. Andrew Crozier. Oth

Heifer Clambers Up, A. Gary Snyder. NOBA

Heigh ho! my heart is low. *Unknown.* OxNR

Heigh ho, my heart! would God that she were mine! (LL) Thomas Lodge. GTBS-P; OBEV *Fr.* Rosalynde; or Euphues' Golden Legacy.

Heigh-ho on a Winter Afternoon. Donald Davie. OxBTC

Heigh-ho / Summer comes along. Summer Is a-Comin' In. Vernon Duke. ReLy

Heigh ho thats life andc. (LL) Babbitt and the Bromide, The. George Gershwin. OBCoV; ReLy

Heigh in the hevynnis figure circulere. James I, King of Scotland. NePenScot *Fr.* Kingis Quair, The.

Heigho, dot and go one. (LL) Lover's Arithmetic, The. *Unknown.* OxBoLi; PeLV

Height. Rosalie Moore. APT-2

Height, Breadth, Depth. Kalamu ya Salaam. SpirFl *Fr.* New Orleans Haiku.

Height of the Ridiculous, The. Oliver Wendell Holmes. OBAL; OBCA

Height of the Season, The. Maxine W. Kumin. FFC

Height of trees. Geese Blood. Barbara Guest. FTOS

Heights of Macchu Picchu, The. Pablo Neruda.
  "Come up with me, American love." PFTM-2, *tr.* by Nathaniel Tarn
  "Rise up, brother, be born with me." TCLAP, *tr.* by David Young
  "Stone upon stone, and man, where was he?" TCLAP, *tr.* by John Felstiner
  "Stone within stone, and man, where was he?" VCWP
  "Then up the ladder of the earth I climbed." TCLAP, *tr.* by Nathaniel Tarn

Heimkehr, Die. Heinrich Heine. AWP, *tr.* by Ezra Pound

Heine's mother was a monster. Century Piece for Poor Heine, A. John Logan. NNaP

Heinrich Heine. Ludwig Lewisohn. TrJP

Heir, The. Joseph Georg Oberkofler. AuPH, *tr.* by Lowell A. Bangerter

Heir of Linne, The. *Unknown.* ESPB

Heiress, The. Raymond Garlick. TCAWP

Heiress, The. Carolina Oliphant, Baroness Nairne. NePenScot

Heirloom. Leonard Cohen. NOBC

Heirloom. Abraham Moses Klein. NIL-7; NOBC; TrJP

Heirloom. Kathleen Jessie Raine. NALW

Heirlooms. Geoffrey Philp. WaCA

Heirs of Stalin, The. Yevgeny Aleksandrovich Yevtushenko [*or* Evtushenko]. TCRP, *tr.* by George Reavey
  (Mute was the marble. / Mutely glimmered the glass.) VCWP, *tr.* by George Reavey

Heirs to these marshy lowlands. Cors-y-Gwaed: Fenland of Blood. A. G. Prys-Jones. AngWePo

Hektor of Troy. Archias of Macedon. GrAn, *tr.* by Dudley Fitts

Hélas! Oscar Wilde. CAGL; MoBrPo; NAEL-5v2; NAEL-6v2; Son (Hélas[1].) GSo

Helbatrawss, The. Kingsley Amis. NOBL

Held Back, Like a Bow Drawn Tight. Walter Höllerer. CLPP, *tr.* by Jerome Rothenberg

Held between wars / my lifetime. Käthe Kollwitz. Muriel Rukeyser. NALW

Held it. Martin Shea. HA

Held them captive. (LL) Lake Baskunchak. Andrey Alekseievich Amalrik. TCRP; TCRusP, *tr.* by John Glad

Heledd and Inge, when the torches are red. In Berlin, August 1945: Lehrte Bahnhof. Alun Llywelyn-Williams. OBWVE, *tr.* by Joseph P. Clancy

Helen. "H. D." APT-1; BoWoP; ColAP; FaBoWP; MoAmPo; NAAL-2v2; NAAL-5; NALW; NIL-7; NOBA; NoAM; NoP-4; PAI; TAP

Helen. James [*or* Jim] Harrison. NBLV

Helen. Mary Lamb. NOBRP

Helen. Peter Meinke. PBCAP

Helen. Paul Valéry. OBVE, *tr.* by Robert Lowell

Helen. Paul Valéry. WoPoe, *tr.* by Richard Wilbur

Helen and the Elders. Homer. NPeEn, *tr.* by George Chapman *Fr.* Iliad, The.

Helen Grown Old. Janet Lewis. APT-2

Helen in Egypt. "H. D."
  "Alas, my brothers." NOBA
  "Another shout from the wharves." NOBA
  "This is the spread of wings." WoPoe

Helen like the Rose. Evan Lloyd. AngWePo; OBWVE *Fr.* Powers of the Pen, The.

Helen of Kirconnell. *Unknown.* AWP; OBEV; OxBEV; SCGP
  (Fair Helen.) GTBS-P

Helen Paints a Room (1984). John A. Scott. BMAP

Helen's Burning. Laura Riding Jackson. ColAP

Helen's Lamentation. Homer. OBVE, *tr.* by William Congreve *Fr.* Iliad, The.

Helen suddenly saw a divine omen. Stesichoros. SaLy, *tr.* by Diane Rayor

Helen, the Sad Queen. Paul Valéry. AWP, *tr.* by Joseph T. Shipley

Helen, thy beauty is to me. To Helen. Edgar Allan Poe. APN-1; AWP; BRP; BoLoP; ClHu; ColAP; HAP; HeIP-4; NAAL-2v1; NAAL-3; NAAL-5; NIP-4; NOBA; NOBE; NoP-4; OBEV; OxBA; PoE; PoPoPo; PoRA; TAP; TCAPo; TFi; WeW-3

Helen Todd: My Birthname. Sandra McPherson. LCAP-2; LoL

Helianthus. Constance Carrier. APT-2

Helicopter cameras, The. Looters, The. Robert Minhinnick. TCAWP

Helicopter of the hill. Lark. Tom Earley. AngWePo

Helicopter Wrecked on a Hill. Christine Hume. BAP-97

Heliodora's Brows. Meleager. GrAn, *tr.* by Peter Whigham

Heliogabalus. John Hollander. NBLV; OBAL

Helioptér of a skyscraper hotel. Mikhail Yeryomin. ItGoST, *tr.* by J. Kates

Heliotrope sprouts from your shoes, brother. Blue Suede Shoes. Ai. ReTh

Hell. Andreas Gryphius. WoPoe, *tr.* by Michael Hamburger

Hell. Robert Herrick. SacPr

Hell. Edith Södergran. PFTM-1

Hell. Mátyás Nyéki Vörös.
  "Of what avail are palaces in hell." IQMS, *tr.* by Watson Kirkconnell

Hell and Heaven. *Unknown.* OxBoLi
  (I Been Rebuked and I Been Scorned.) NAAAL

Hell blot black for alway the thought "Peace"! (LL) Sestina: Altaforte. Ezra Pound. APT-1; ColAP; FaBoTw; MakPoe; MoAmPo; NOBA; TCAPo

Hell Gate. A. E. Housman. NoAM; SCGP; UnPo

Hell is a city much like London. Shelley. OBSV *Fr.* Peter Bell the Third.

Hell is a red barn on a hill. Curse, The. Robert Francis. APT-2

Hell is no other, but a soundlesse pit. Hell. Robert Herrick. SacPr

"Hell" said the Devil, as it might have been. Reborn. Kingsley Amis. OxBC

Hell to Pay. Susanne Doyle. FFC

Hell, Well, Heaven. Mongane Wally Serote. PBMAP

Hell where youth and laughter go. (LL) Suicide in [the] Trenches. Siegfried Sassoon. FaBoWar; PoWW

Hellas. Desmond O'Grady.
  "Here, because of the shock, the sudden." PBCIP

Hellas. Shelley.
  (Chorus.) EBEV; HAP; NOBE; OxBEV
  (Chorus from "Hellas") AWP
  (Chorus: "Worlds on worlds are rolling ever") NAEL-5v2
  (Hellas.) OBEV
  World's Great Age, The. HeIP-4; NAEL-5v2; NoP-4; PoE
  Worlds on Worlds. HeIP-4; NAEL-6v2

Hellas. Shelley. *See* Hellas

Hellenistic Period, The. Hedylos. GrAn, *tr.* by Adrian Wright

Hellhound on My Trail. Robert Johnson. APT-2; NAAAL; PFTM-2

Hello. Gregory Corso. PoM

Hello, daffodil, saffron-yellow exclamation. Yellow Gramophone. Sheila Cussons. PeSAV, *tr.* by the author

Hello, Dolly! Jerry Herman. ReLy

"Hello, hello, hello, sir." Jump-Rope Rhyme. *Unknown.* NTCP

Hello. Hello. What's your name? Philodemus. PGA

Hello sir i'm glad you're here we. Kentucky. M. Loncar. NAPBL

Hello There. Philodemus. GrAn, *tr.* by William Moebius

Hello up There. Marge Piercy. NBLV

Hello, Young Lovers. Richard Rodgers. ReLy

Helmet and rifle, pack and overcoat. Battle, The. Louis Simpson. OBWP; PoWW

Helmet now an hive for bees becomes, The. Vote, The. Ralph Knevet. FaBoWar; NOSC

Helmets; a Fragment, The. Thomas Penrose. NOEC

Helmett now an hive for Bees becomes, The. Ralph Knevet. *See* Helmet now an hive for bees becomes, The

Helmsman, The. "H. D." OxBA

Heloise. Biancamaria Frabotta.
  "Here dwells the whole and scattered." CItWP, *tr.* by Cinzia Sartini Blum and Lara Trubowitz

Help. Sadi [*or* Saadi *or* Sa'di]. AWP, *tr.* by Sir Edwin Arnold *Fr.* Gulistan, The.

Help. John Greenleaf Whittier. Son

Help! X. J. Kennedy. CA

Help, a love, a you, a wife. (LL) Love Song: I and Thou. Alan Dugan. AmFaPo; InPK-6; NoAM

Help, help all tongues to celebrate this wonder. Ben Jonson. NOSC *Fr.* Masque of Queens, The.

Help! How Minne has deserted me. Friedrich von Hausen. GePo

Help, Lord, because the Godly Man. Francis Rous. AH

Help me down Cemetery Road. (LL) Toads Revisited. Philip Larkin. NOBL; OxAEP-2

Help Me Today. Elsie Robinson. PoToHe

Help Thy Servant. Andrew Broaddus. AH

Help us, oh God, we're rich. (LL) Harlem, Montana. James Welch. CDW; HATNAP

Helpe, crosse, fairest of timbres three. *Unknown.* MiEL

Help[e] me! help[e] me! now I call. To His Mistress[es]. Robert Herrick. CaPo; ErotSp

Helping Hand, A. Miroslav Holub. PoSu, *tr.* by George Theiner

Helpless like this. Edward Kamau Brathwaite. NoP-4 *Fr.* Arrivants: A New World Trilogy, The.

Helpless on the meathook. Choice, Inanna and the Galla. Pem Kremer. HW

Hemlock at Sunset, A. Alec Brock Stevenson. FuPo

Hemlock in the Furrows. Adah Isaacs Menken. CBWP-1

Hemlock shakes in the rafter, the oak in the driving keel, The. (LL) Misgivings. Herman Melville. APN-2; NAAL-2v1; NAAL-3; NCAP; NOBA; OxBA; TCAPo

Hemlocks in Autumn. Edward Weismiller. YaYoPo

Hemlocks slumped, The. Bonus. A. R. Ammons. HCAP

Hemmed-in Males. William Carlos Williams. APT-1; PoRA *Fr.* Folded Skyscraper, A.

Hemp / A stick. Gauge. Langston Hughes. APSN

Hems gathered up, sash not yet tied. *Unknown.* CoBCP *Fr.* Tzu Yeh Songs.

Hen. Zbigniew Herbert. VCWP, *tr.* by Czeslaw Milosz and Peter Dale Scott

Hen, The. Christian Morgenstern. RB, *tr.* by Lore Segal and W. D. Snodgrass

Hen Flower, The. Galway Kinnell. NNaP

Hen is the best example of what living constantly with humans, The. Hen. Zbigniew Herbert. VCWP, *tr.* by Czeslaw Milosz and Peter Dale Scott

Hen It Is a Noble Beast, The. William McGonagall. NBLV

Hen, one who could have brought more geese, a female, a wild one, dead, A. Wings of a Wild Goose, The. Chrystos. GLP

Hen remarked to the mooley cow, The. Art. *Unknown.* NBLV

Hen's Nest. John Clare. Son

Hen under Bay-Tree. Ruth Pitter. OxBTC

Hen Woman. Thomas Kinsella. CIP-2; ModIr; NPeEn; PBCIP

Hence, all you vain delights. John Fletcher. GTBS-P; OBEV *Fr.* Nice Valor, The.

Hence Cupid! with your cheating toys. Against Love. Katherine Philips. BoWoP; WPE

Hence, heart, with her that must depart. Alexander Scott. NePenScot; OBEV

Hence, hence, all you vain delights. Melancholy. Thomas Middleton. NOSC

Hence loathèd Melancholy. John Milton. AWP; BASC; FHYEP; GTBS-P; HAP; NAEL-6v1; NAEL-7v1; NOSC; NoP-4; OBEV; PBRV; PoPoPo; TFi

Hence, stupid Peace! thy pride and song. Age of War, The. *Unknown.* NOBRP

Hence thro' the windings of the mazy wood. Gilbert West. OBGa *Fr.* Stowe, the Gardens of the Rt. Hon. Richard Lord Viscount Cobham.

Hence to deep Acheron they take their way. Virgil [*or* Vergil]. NPeEn, *tr.* by John Dryden *Fr.* Aeneid [*or* Eneados, *Aeneis*], The.

Hence vain deluding joy[e]s. John Milton. AWP; BASC; FHYEP; GTBS-P; HAP; NAEL-6v1; NAEL-7v1; NOSC; NoP-4; OBEV; TFi

Hence, vain intruder, haste away. To My Rival. Thomas Carew. OxBSo

Hence with your jeerings, petulant and low. Charles Tennyson Turner. CenSon

Hence ye profane: mell not with holy things. Satire VIII. Joseph Hall. ChIV-2

Henceforth, from the Mind. Louise Bogan. WPE

Henchman, The. John Greenleaf Whittier. OBEV

Hendecasyllabics. Tennyson. EBEV; NOBL; PeLV

Henley's a special regatta. Limerick. Jim Anthony. PeLi

Henpecked Husband, A. *Unknown.* PeLV

Henri Toussaints. Cheryl Savageau. TWW

Henry V at the Siege of Harfleur. William Shakespeare. OxAEP-1 *Fr.* King Henry V.

Henry Adams / Was mortally afraid of Madams. W. H. Auden. OBAL *Fr.* Academic Graffiti.

Henry and King Pedro, clasping. Death of Don Pedro, The. *Unknown.* AWP, *tr.* by John Gibson Lockhart

Henry and Mary. Robert Graves. NOxBChV

Henry by Night. John Berryman. EmeKit

Henry C. Calhoun. Edgar Lee Masters. *Fr.* Spoon River Anthology.

Henry got me with child. Edgar Lee Masters. APT-1; NoAM *Fr.* Spoon River Anthology.

Henry I to the Sea. Eugene Lee-Hamilton. PeVV

Henry in Ireland to Bill underground. John Berryman. MakPoe *Fr.* Dream Songs.

Henry King, Who Chewed Bits of String, and Was Early Cut Off in Dreadful Agonies. Joseph Hilaire Pierre Belloc. NBLV; OBCoV; OxAEP-2; PeLV

Henry Martyn. *Unknown.* ESPB

Henry Morgan's March on Panama. A. G. Prys-Jones. AngWePo

Henry nodded, un-. (LL) John Berryman. HCAP; PoPoPo *Fr.* Dream Songs.

Henry Porter wore good clothes for his journey. Passage. Elizabeth Alexander. ISC

Henry's Confession. John Berryman. LCAP-2; NAAL-2v2; NoAM; PoE; TwCP; VCAP *Fr.* Dream Songs.

Henry's Fate. John Berryman. ColAP

Henry's mind grew blacker the more he thought. John Berryman. FaBoMo; NOBA *Fr.* Dream Songs.

Henry's nocturnal habits were the terror of his women. Henry by Night. John Berryman. EmeKit

Henry's pelt was put on sundry walls. John Berryman. NoAM; TRP *Fr.* Dream Songs.

Henry's Understanding. John Berryman. NOBA; NoAM; WoPoe

Henry sats in de bar and was odd. John Berryman. HCAP; PoPoPo; VCAP *Fr.* Dream Songs.

HENRY THE GRANDFATHER. Hannah Weiner. FTOS *Fr.* Little Books / Indians.

Henry Turnbull. Wilfrid Wilson Gibson. FaBoTw

Henry was a young king. Henry and Mary. Robert Graves. NOxBChV

Henry went over the edge of the bridge first; he always did. Death of John Berryman, The. William Dickey. BAP-97

Hens, The. Elizabeth Madox Roberts. OBCA

Heptalogia, The. Algernon Charles Swinburne.
  Higher Pantheism in a Nutshell, The. CABP; PeVV
  Nephelidia. PeVV
  Sonnet for a Picture. OxBSo; UV

Heptonstall. Ted Hughes. OxAEP-2

Her Accident. Thomas Hood. EBVV *Fr.* Miss Kilmansegg and Her Precious Leg.

Her Address to the Moon. Mary Robinson. CenSon; RWP

Hēr Æeolstān cyning, eorla drihten. *Unknown.* CABP *Fr.* Battle of Brunanburh.

Her alien eyes. (LL) Cradle-Song at Twilight. Alice Thompson Meynell. NOBVV; NPeEn; VWP

Her angel looked upon God's face. Eternal Image, The. Ruth Pitter. MoBrPo; OxBTC

Her Answer. John Bennett. ITBLP

Her Anxiety. W. B. Yeats. OPOU

Her arms are gravelled at the undertow. Airport. Martin Johnston. CBAP

Her arms around me—child—. From a Photograph. George Oppen. FTOS

Her arms have the beauty. What He Said. Orerulavanar. WoPoe, *tr.* by A. K. Ramanujan

Her auld father to see. (LL) Brown Robin. *Unknown.* ESPB; OxBB

Her back in a line straight. Foul Line—1987. Colleen J. McElroy. LTA

Her Back to Me. Ed Stever. PasH

Her bare feet tell the neurasthenic: fake moustaches on that ostrich. Metal Coughdrops. Tristan Tzara. PFTM-1

Her beautiful hair for Yom Kippur festively tied. Torah Braids. Tamara Kamenszain. MirDau, *tr. by* Roberta Gordenstein

Her beauty conquers all. (LL) Love's Emblem. John Clare. NIL-7; NIP-4

Her beauty is hidden by a cloudy screen. Her Beauty Is Hidden. Li Shang-yin. OHMPC, *tr. by* Kenneth Rexroth

Her beauty, passive in despair. Philanthropist and the Jelly-fish, The. May Kendall. VWP; ViWPN

Her beauty, which we talk of. Helen's Burning. Laura Riding Jackson. ColAP

Her Bed. Robert Herrick. PBRV

Her black negligee. Hal Roth. HA

Her blacks crackle and drag. (LL) Edge. Sylvia Plath. FaBoWP; HCAP; NAAL-2v2; NALW; NPeEn; PoE; PoPoPo; TAP; VCAP

Her blows did make you blue. (LL) How Violets Came Blue. Robert Herrick. BeJo; CaPo; TTTS

Her Body. Daniel Halpern. BAP-97

Her body is not so white as. Queen-Anne's-Lace. William Carlos Williams. APT-1; MoAmPo; NAAL-2v2; NOBA; NoAM; TAP

Her Body Is Private. Eleanor Wilner. ExTi

Her boredom took her away. So simple. Ella Mi Fu Rapita! Gavin Ewart. NoAM

Her bracelets tinkle. *Unknown.* OHMPJ

Her breast is fit for pearls. Emily Dickinson. HeIP-4; PoBW

Her breasts are still filling with milk. (LL) On the Death of a New Born Child. Mei Yao Ch'en. OHPC; WoPoe, *tr. by* Kenneth Rexroth

Her breasts lift with her arms. Rod Willmot. HA

Her breath, I feel it still upon my face. On Transitoriness. Hugo von Hofmannsthal. AuPH, *tr. by* Lowell A. Bangerter

Her burning eyes on her forgetful hands. (LL) Power of Interval, The. John Byrne Leicester Warren, 3d Baron De Tabley. NOBVV; OxBSP

Her chair drawn to the door. Laundress, The. Thomas Kinsella. HarvBoo

Her charming steel-horse could not miss. J. Gordon Coogler. VerBaPo *Fr.* Lover's Return on a Bicycle, The.

Her chaunging lookes no colour longe can holde. Seneca. OBVE, *tr. by* John Studley *Fr.* Medea.

Her cheek is flush'd with fever red. Dying Child, The. Letitia [*or* Laetitia] Elizabeth Landon. VWP

Her cheeks are hot, her cheeks are white. Bianca. Arthur Symons. PeVV

Her cheeks were white, her eyes were wild. Sea, The. William Henry Davies. FaBoTw

Her Christening. Thomas Hood. NOBVV *Fr.* Miss Kilmansegg and Her Precious Leg.

Her Confirmed Despair. Mary Robinson. CenSon; RWP

Her cottage, then a cheerful object, wore. William Wordsworth. OBGa *Fr.* Excursion, The.

Her Dancing Days. Anna Adams. BrRo

Her day out from the workhouse-ward, she stands. Ice, The. Wilfrid Wilson Gibson. OxBTC

Her Death. Thomas Hood. NOBVV *Fr.* Miss Kilmansegg and Her Precious Leg.

Her Descending Down. Margaret Lucas Cavendish, Duchess of Newcastle. BASC; NOSC

Her Dilemma. Thomas Hardy. NOBVV

Her door opened on the white water. Little Lady of Ch'ing-ch'i, The. *Unknown.* ChiP, *tr. by* Arthur Waley

Her dress is soft green and deep scarlet. Oriole. Yuan Chen. CrYelRi, *tr. by* Sam Hamill

Her drooping flowers dabble upon. Betty by the Sea. Ronald McCuaig. NOBAu

Her Education. Thomas Hood. EBVV *Fr.* Miss Kilmansegg and Her Precious Leg.

Her Elegy. *Unknown.* BoWoP; STP

Her even lines her steady temper show. On a Lady's Writing. Anna Laetitia Barbauld. PEW

Her exquisite yellow youth. . . . (LL) Jessie Mitchell's Mother. Gwendolyn Brooks. BoWoP; ColAP; NALW

Her eyebrows are arched willows. To the Tune: Southern Song. Wen T'ing-yün. CrYelRi, *tr. by* Sam Hamill

Her Eyes. Helen Hunt Jackson. PoBW; TCAPo

Her Eyes. Daniel Casper von Lohenstein. GePo, *tr. by* George C. Schoolfield

Her Eyes. John Crowe Ransom. OBAL

Her Eyes a Thousand Times Over. Chani DiPrima. HW

Her eyes are bright as sparkling stars. Mine. Mary E. Tucker. CBWP-1

Her eyes are fixed; they seek the skies. Murillo's Magdalen. William Ellery Channing. APN-1

Her eyes are gold. Rufinus. GrAn

Her eyes are velvet, soft and fine. My Poker Girl. Tom Masson. OBAL

Her eyes flood lickes his feets faire staine. Bible, *N.T.* NOSC; SacPr, *tr. by* Richard Crashaw *Fr.* St. Luke.

Her eyes still closed. Hal Roth. HA

Her eyes the glow-worm[e] lend thee. Night-Piece, to Julia, The. Robert Herrick. BeJo; CaPo; NAEL-5v1; NAEL-6v1; NAEL-7v1; NOSC; OBEV; PoE; PoRA; SCGP; TFi

Her eyes were coins of porter and her West. Michael Hartnett. ModIr *Fr.* Farewell to English, A.

Her eyes were gentle; her voice was for soft singing. Old Woman Remembers, An. Sterling Allen Brown. ISC

Her face has made my life most proud and glad. Of His Lady's Face. Jacopo da Lentino. EaItPo, *tr. by* Dante Gabriel Rossetti

Her Face, Her Tongue, Her Wit. Sir Arthur Gorges. WoPoe

Her face / Is a spotless moon. Rāmprasād Sen. SinGod, *tr. by* Rachel Fell McDermott

Her face thins almost. Each Day. Sister Maura. CRP

Her face was in a bed of raint. Emily Dickinson. PoBW

Her face was like sad things: was like the lights. Stranger, A. Lionel Pigot Johnson. NOBVV

Her Faith. Joseph Hilaire Pierre Belloc. SacPr

Her faltering hand upon the balustrade. John Keats. OxBEV *Fr.* Eve of St. Agnes, The.

Her father blended truth and myth. Singing down the Breadfruit. Pauline Stewart. NOxBChV

Her father is sick. He dozes most afternoons. Anastasia McLaughlin. Tom Paulin. PBCIP

Her father lessons me I at times am hard. Augusta Davies Webster. ViWPN *Fr.* Mother and Daughter.

Her father lov'd me; oft invited me. William Shakespeare. EBEV; FaBoWar; OxAEP-1; SCV *Fr.* Othello.

Her father's brother rapes her! Fountain of Cyanë, The. Donald Davie. HarvBoo

Her filthie parbreake all the place defiled has. (LL) Edmund Spenser. EBEV; FHYEP; NAEL-5v1 *Fr.* Faerie Queene, The.

Her Final Show. Rafael Campo. BloBone

Her fingers bore the winecup in. Two of Them, The. Hugo von Hofmannsthal. STV, *tr. by* John Frederick Nims

Her First Week. Sharon Olds. ExTi

Her flowers were exclusive blue. Exclusive Blue. Robert Francis. CRP

Her foot sparkled like silver. Rufinus. ErotSp, *tr. by* Sam Hamill

Her for a mistress would I fain enjoy. How to Choose a Mistress. *Unknown.* NOSC

Her future, all in her, presented an avenue of gloom, as if to say Go on, do what you. Seeking Out His face in a Cup. Fanny Howe. FTOS

Her Garden. Meena Alexander. OMIP

Her Garden. Freda Downie. FaBoWP

Her Garden. Donald Hall. BAP-01

Her Gift. Annie Hindle. PoBW

Her going through changes. Seth Bingham. William W. Cook. SpirFl

Her goodness leaves scores on the skin. Marian Hymn. Christiania Whitehead. NeBl

Her grieving parents cradled here. Epitaph. Sylvia Townsend Warner. MoBrPo

Her Habit. Lucie Brock-Broido. ExTi

Her Hair. Charles Baudelaire. NAWM-7v2, *tr. by* Doreen Bell

Her hair is long, very, very long. Country, A. Fawziyya Abu Khalid. PoArWo, *tr. by* Farouk Mustafa

Her hand a goblet bore for him. Two, The. Hugo von Hofmannsthal. AWP, *tr. by* Ludwig Lewisohn

Her hand in my hand. Suddenly. Yusuf Al-Sa'igh. MAP, *tr. by* Diana Der Hovanessian and Salma Khadra Jayyusi

Her hand on the doorknob. Rod Willmot. HA

Her hands feed striped cloth into the machine. First Quilt. Ann Townsend. AmPoNex

Her hands lift and tend King Salmon. Hands of Mary Joe, The. Mary Tallmountain. LoL

Her hands were clasped, her dark eyes raised. Gertrude, or Fidelity Till Death. Felicia Dorothea Hemans. RWP

Her health is good. She owns to forty-one. Phyllis McGinley. WPE *Fr.* I Know a Village.

Her Heart Is a Rose Petal and Her Skin Is Granite. Lorene Zarou-Zouzounis. PoArWo

Her heart it brak in twa O. (LL) Willie and Lady Margerie [*or* Maisry]. *Unknown.* ESPB; OxBB

Her heart so stricken, Helen. Alcaeus [*or* Alkaios]. WoPoe, *tr. by* Sam Hamill

Her heart that loved me once is rottenness. Two Thoughts of Death. Christina Georgina Rossetti. ViWPN

Her / him. (LL) Landscape with Next of Kin. Olga Broumas. BoWoP; WiU

Her house is become like a man dishonored. Bible, Apocrypha. TrJP *Fr.* First Maccabees.

Her house loomed at the end of a Berkshire lane. Not at Home. Robert Graves. CABP

Her Husband. Ted Hughes. HarvBoo; OxBC

Her Husband Asks Her to Buy a Bolt of Silk. Ch'en Tao. OHMPC, *tr. by* Kenneth Rexroth

Her husband was *hors de combat.* Limerick. C. Vita-Finzi. PeLi

Her I was and her I drank. Gud Ber. *Unknown.* FaBoVe

Her imaginary playmate was a grown-up. Cinderella. Randall Jarrell. LCAP-2; NAAL-2v2; VCAP

Her iron beats. Domestic Scene. Michael Hartnett. BIrV

Her job was to sort through the eyes. Perla at the Mexican Border Assembly Line of Dolls. Rigoberto González. AmPoNex

Her Kind. Anne Sexton. CoAP; HCAP; HeIP-4; NALW; PoPoPo; TAP; TwCP; VCAP; WPOW

Her knees and [*or* &] elbows are only glued together. (LL) Marriage. William Blake. OxBoLi; PeLV

Her Last Appeal to Phaon. Mary Robinson. CenSon; RWP

Her last breath, disappointed. (LL) Martha Blake at Fifty-one. Austin Clarke. CIP-2; ModIr; NOIV; NPeEn

Her—"last Poems." Emily Dickinson. NALW

Her last words wandered across the ceiling. Death in the Evening. Miroslav Holub. PoSu, *tr. by* George Theiner

Her leggings could burn. Of Three Friendly Warnings This Is the Third. *Unknown.* STP, *tr. by* Richard Johnny John and Jerome Rothenberg

Her Legs. Robert Herrick. NOSC
   (I fain would kiss my Julia's dainty leg.) CavPo

Her legs were retrieved from a fen. (LL) Limerick: "Incautious young woman named Venn, An." Edward Gorey. PeLV; PeLi

Her Life Runs Like a Red Silk Flag. Bruce Weigl. AF

Her limp lover Maud couldn't pardon. Limerick. Kit Wright. PeLi

Her Lips Are Copper Wire. Jean Toomer. APT-2; GT; NoAM

Her lips disclosed to view. Solyman Brown. VerBaPo *Fr.* Dentologia; a Poem on the Diseases of the Teeth and Their Proper Remedies.

Her List. Sharon Olds. BodElec

Her little boy weeping sought. (LL) William Blake. FHYEP; NoP-4 *Fr.* Songs of Innocence.

Her long paper legs. Leroy Gorman. HA

Her long with ardent look his Eye pursu'd. John Milton. UnPo *Fr.* Paradise Lost.

Her Longing. Theodore Roethke. NAAL-2v2

Her look doth promise and her life assure. George Chapman. OxBSo *Fr.* Coronet for His Mistress Philosophy, A.

Her Losses make our Gains ashamed. Emily Dickinson. NALW

Her "love" for whose dear love I rise and fall. (LL) William Shakespeare. EBEV; HeIP-4; NoSic; OxAEP-1; PoE *Fr.* Sonnets.

Her love in all her honor. (LL) Louis Zukofsky. APSN; APT-2; ColAP; VGW *Fr.* A.

Her magnificent eyes alone. Gustave Thibon, How Simone Weil Appeared to Me 2. Stephanie Strickland. ExTi

Her Majestie resembled to the crowned piller. Ye must read upward. George Puttenham. PBRV

Her Man Described by Her Own[e] Dictamen. Ben Jonson. NAEL-6v1; NAEL-7v1 *Fr.* Celebration of Charis in Ten Lyric[k] Pieces [*or* Peeces], A.

Her mascara makes butterfly patterns on my pillowcase. Lizzie. Cheryl Burke. WiU

Her mate devoured. Kikaku. SoOfWa, *tr. by* Sam Hamill

Her, Me, and Yochanan. Chava Pinchas-Cohen. DTA, *tr. by* Miriyam Glazer

Her melodious tongue lights up. Once Again, Anne Frank. Elina Wechsler. MirDau, *tr. by* Darrell Lockhart

Her memory fragmented like a necklace. Broken Necklace. Jill Bamber. Prnts

Her men's boots wore out. Portrait. Yaroslav [*or* Iaroslav] Vasilevich Smelyakov [*or* Smeliakov]. TCRP, *tr. by* Simon Franklin

Her Merriment. William Henry Davies. EnLoPo

Her mind, adorned with virtues manifold. (LL) Edmund Spenser. HeIP-4; NIP-4; Son *Fr.* Amoretti.

Her morning adornment finished now. Tune: "Casket of Pearls, A." Li Yü. SuSp, *tr. by* Daniel Bryant

Her mother died when she was young. Kemp Owyne. Alice Cary. ESPB

Her mouth: The tiger, the leap, the toll. Woman 12, A. Hugo Claus. TuT, *tr. by* Peter Van de Kamp

Her Muffe. Richard Lovelace. PBRV

Her name is at my tongue whene'er I speak. Ever Present. Philip Ayres. OxBSP

Her Name Is Helen. Beth Brant. GLP

Her name is in the books I've bought at Oxfam. Fran. Christopher Pilling. NLP

Her Name like the Hours. Gloria Evans Davies. OBWVE

Her name tells of how. Quiet Until the Thaw. Jacob Nibenegenesabe. AmFaPo, *tr. by* Howard Norman

Her nerves awry, importunate. For a Violin, Somewhat Nervously. Vladimir Vladimirovich Mayakovsky [*or* Maiakovskii]. TCRP, *tr. by* Bernard Meares

Her own clasped hands. (LL) Preface to a Twenty Volume Suicide Note. Imamu Amiri Baraka. AmFaPo; BB; ESEAA; NAAAL; PoM; TTY

Her own self-will made void her own self's will. (LL) End of It, The. Francis Thompson. NOBVV; OxBSP

Her pale head heavy as metal. (LL) Snowdrop. Ted Hughes. FaBoMo; HarvBoo

Her Passing. William Drummond, of Hawthornden. OBEV

Her Passion Increases. Mary Robinson. CenSon; RWP

Her perfect naked breast. Argentarius. ErotSp, *tr. by* Sam Hamill

Her planted eye today controls. Ralph Waldo Emerson. NoP-4 *Fr.* Quatrains.

Her poets die for the mountains. After Asia. Michael Stephens. CDa

Her Precious Leg. Thomas Hood. NOBVV *Fr.* Miss Kilmansegg and Her Precious Leg.

Her pretty feet. Upon Her Feet. Robert Herrick. BeJo; CaPo; OxBSP; PoE

Her purple shoes know the way, and the metal band on her ankle knows it. Sacrifice, The. Gertrud Kolmar. AF, *tr. by* David Kipp

Her Reflections on the Leucadian Rock before She Perishes. Mary Robinson. CenSon; RWP

Her refusal to accept a room of solitude. Pieces. Duane Niatum. HATNAP

Her remembered frailty had strengthened his. Private First Class Brooks Morgenstein, U. S. M. C. Bryan Alec Floyd. CDa

Her Reply. Sir Walter Ralegh. *See* Nymph's [*or* Nimphs] Reply to the Shepherd [*or* Sheepheard], The.

Her Resurrection has again with Thee. (LL) Upon M. Ben Jo[h]nson: Epigram. Robert Herrick. BeJo; CaPo

Her Reticence. Theodore Roethke. RACG

Her Retirement. Anne Rouse. NeBl

Her ringlets glistened like the gold of morn. Picture, A. Henrietta Cordelia Ray. CBWP-3

Her Rival for Aziza. *Unknown.* AWP *Fr.* Thousand and One Nights, The.

Her Rose Tattoo. Gerry LaFemina. AmPoNex

Her row veering off. Issa. EH, *tr. by* Robert Hass

Her saffron gown. *Unknown.* GrAn

Her scarf *à la* Bardot. Twice Shy. Seamus Heaney. TwCP

Her sense of humor has no gold stop. Telephonist. Janet Frame. WPE

Her Seventeenth Winter. John Leax. CRP

Her shadow races with slanting moonbeams. Written for My Neighbor. Shen Yüeh. CoBCP, *tr. by* Burton Watson

Her shadow races with slanting moonbeams. Written for My Neighbor. Wang Seng-ta. CoBCP, *tr. by* Burton Watson

Her shoes could burn. Of Three Friendly Warnings This Is the Second. *Unknown.* STP, *tr. by* Richard Johnny John and Jerome Rothenberg

Her sight is short, she comes quite near. Jenny Wren. William Henry Davies. MoBrPo

Her silence at dinner. Scott Montgomery. HA

Her silken gown rustles. Wang Chien. SuSp *Fr.* Palace Poems.

Her sins to her Saviour! (LL) Bridge of Sighs, The. Thomas Hood. BRP; EBEV; GTBS-P; OBEV; OxAEP-2; TreFP

Her Sister. "Moira O'Neill." OxBTC

Her sleeping head with its great gelid mass. Perseus. Robert Earl Hayden. NoAM

Her small feet walk a mossy path. Year's End. Chang K'o-chiu. CrYelRi, *tr. by* Sam Hamill

Her smock in the entrails of the ministrants. . . . (LL) Christopher Okigbo. PBMAP; TTY *Fr.* Distances.

Her Son. Ebba M. Leaf. PWR

Her songs died on the air. (LL) Song: "She sat and sang alway." Christina Georgina Rossetti. NAEL-5v2; NAEL-6v2

Her soul is a select district. Paysage Choisi. Francis Sparshott. MoCV

Her spirit stands unhoused before my door. (LL) Grey Woman. Gladys Cardiff. CDW; GifTon

Her Story. Leah Korican. HW

Her street is dark. The tall housetops now shade. Her Street Is Dark. Antonio Machado Ruiz. SpanPo, *tr. by* John Crow

Her Strong Enchantments Failing. A. E. Housman. FaBoTw; NOBE; NOBVV; OxBEV; PeVV; WoPoe

Her / strong / white / legs. Romp. Dave Etter. WeW-3

Her sweet converts to gall. (LL) Judah in Exile Wanders. George Sandys. AH; ChIV-1

Her Sweet turn to leave the Homestead. Emily Dickinson. SWaP

Her sweet Weight on my Heart at Night. Emily Dickinson. TCAPo

Her terrace was the sand. Infanta Marina. Wallace Stevens. APT-1

Her thin puny little body. Clinic Day. Jo Barnes. BrRo

Her Thought and His. Paul Laurence Dunbar. NAAAL

Her Time. Theodore Roethke. NAAL-2v2

Her toes, bite her arch, trail my tongue along the inside of her leg and. I Suck. Chrystos. WiU

Her towel up, turban-style, about her hair. (LL) Aubade, An: "As she is showering, I wake to see." Timothy Steele. PasH; RA

Her Triumph. Ben Jonson. BASC; CTC; EBEV; NAEL-6v1; NAEL-7v1; NOSC; NPeEn; NoP-4 *Fr.* Celebration of Charis in Ten Lyric[k] Pieces [*or* Peeces], A.

Her udder shrivels and the milk goes dry. (LL) Cow in Apple Time, The. Robert Frost. MoAmPo; OxBSP

Her Voice. Barney Bush. HATNAP

Her Voice Could Not Be Softer. Austin Clarke. NOIV

Her voice forever match to dry wood. Dirge in Jazz Time. Vassar Miller. FFC

Her voice is like some angel picking at the door. Alan Brunton. PeNZ

Her voice roosts in my memory. Route. Philippe Soupault. PFTM-1

Her white arms became my entire horizon. Rooster and the Pearl, The. Max Jacob. CuPo

Her whole life is an Epigram smack smooth & neatly pend. Character, A. William Blake. FaBoEE; InPK-6

Her window ringed by moonlight. To a Young Widow. Po Chü-i. CrYelRi, *tr.* by Sam Hamill

Her wings inferring. Mail from Right Here, The. Brendan Galvin. PoCoUp

Her Word of Reproach. Sarah Morgan Bryan Piatt. NCAP

Her work was to count linings—. Charles Reznikoff. APT-2

Her wounds came from the same source as her power. (LL) Power. Adrienne Rich. ColAP; NALW; TAP

Her young employers, having got in late. Summer Morning, A. Richard Wilbur. FaBoMo; NBLV

Hera, Hung from the Sky. Carolyn Kizer. WPE

Heraclitus. William Johnson Cory. AWP; EBVV; FaBoEE; InPK-6; NOBE; OBEV; OxAEP-2; OxBSP; PoRA; SCGP; UV

Herakles. Parrhasios. GrAn, *tr.* by Peter Jay

Herakles' rebuttal was too much. Philodemus. PGA

Herald came, The. Sappho. SaLy, *tr.* by Diane Rayor

Heraldic Decoration. Julio Herrera y Reissig. TCLAP, *tr.* by Andrew Rosing

Heraldic Decoration. Julio Herrera y Reissig. BLPSL, *tr.* by Rene de Costa, Rigas Kappatos and Eleni Paidoussi

Heralds of Christ. Laura S. Copenhaver. AH

Herb-Garden, The. Charles Hubert Sisson. HarvBoo

Herba Santa. Herman Melville. NCAP

Herbe Féconde (1973). Joseph Miezan Bognini.
 "We are men of the new world a tree prompts us to harmony." PBMAP
 "Suddenly an old man on the threshold of the age." PBMAP

Herbert's a hard and horrid man. One for the Anthologies. Gavin Ewart. OBCoV

Herbert Street Revisited. John Montague. CIP-2; ModIr; PBCIP; PNI

Herbertson telephoned. For the Record. Roy McFadden. PNI

Herbie. David Alpaugh. OPRER

Hercules Furens. Seneca.
 Chorus. NPeEn, *tr.* by Jasper Heywood
 "Let oken club now strike, and poast of might." OBVE

Hercules Oetaeus. Seneca.
 "Let other mount aloft, let other sore." OBVE

Herd, The. Peter Fallon. PBCIP

Herd-Boy, The. Lu Yu. ChiP, *tr.* by Arthur Waley

Herdboy returns, none too early, The. Yang Shih-ch'i. CoBLCP *Fr.* Painting of Water Buffaloes, A.

Herder who hailed from Terre Haute, A. Limerick. *Unknown.* PeLi

Herding cows by his side. (LL) Mirabai [*or* Mira Bai]. WPoS; WoPoe, *tr.* by Jane Hirshfield

Herdmen, The. William Byrd. *See* Quiet Life, The

Herdsman's Song. *Unknown.* ChiP, *tr.* by Arthur Waley

Herdsmen, The. Theocritus. AWP, *tr.* by Charles Stuart Calverley *Fr.* Idylls.

Herdsmen crush under their feet. Sappho. SaLy, *tr.* by Diane Rayor

Here. Robert Creeley. NOBA

Here. Sandra Maria Esteves. PueRic

Here. Issa. EH, *tr.* by Robert Hass

Here. Lawrence Joseph. UrbNat

Here. Jane Kenyon. LoL

Here. Philip Larkin. NPeEn; PoE

Here. Glenna Luschei. GeoHom

Here. Bob Orr. PeNZ

Here. Grace Paley. BAP-01

Here. Octavio Paz. STV, *tr.* by Nims, John Fredrick

Here. Octavio Paz. TCLAP, *tr.* by Charles Tomlinson

Here. Ronald Stuart Thomas. GTBS-P; NPeEn; RB

Here a false face won't help you. (LL) Kenneth Rexroth. KaS; NNaP *Fr.* Bestiary, A.

Here a little child I stand. Grace for a Child. Robert Herrick. AWP; NAEL-5v1; NAEL-6v1; PoE; TFi

Here a mile down at Betharram. At Betharram. Robert Hedin. GifTon

Here a pretty Baby lies. Upon a child. Robert Herrick. OBEV

Here, a sheer hulk, lies poor Tom Bowling. Poor Tom. Charles Dibdin. NOEC; OxBoLi

Here a solemn[e] fast keep[e]. Epitaph upon a Virgin, An. Robert Herrick. CaPo; FaBoEE; OxBoLi

Here, above / cracks in the buildings are filled with battered moonlight. Man-Moth, The. Elizabeth Bishop. APT-2; MoAmPo; NALW; NOBA; NoAM

Here all alone in silence might I mourne. Mary Sidney Wroth, Countess of Montgomery. NAEL-7v1 *Fr.* Urania.

(Here Am I) Broken Hearted. Lew Brown. ReLy

Here am I, little [J]jumping Joan. Little Jumping Joan. Mother Goose. NTCP; ReMoGo

Here am I now cast down. David Gascoyne. GTBS-P *Fr.* Miserere.

Here am I yet, another twelvemonth spent. Arthur Hugh Clough. CenSon *Fr.* Blank Misgivings of a Creature Moving about in Worlds Not Realized.

Here, Amanda, gently bending. Garden Window, The. Aaron Hill. OBGa

Here among long-discarded cassocks. Diary of a Church Mouse. Sir John Betjeman. OxBTC

Here among them the americans this baffling. [American Journal]. Robert Earl Hayden. ESEAA; ISC

Here and hereafter, touch a Paradise. (LL) To Ned. Herman Melville. APN-2; NAAL-2v1; NAAL-3; NOBA; TCAPo

Here and in hell. (LL) Nameless One, The. James Clarence Mangan. BIrV; NOIV; OBEV

Here and now I have to dilute myself into many things. Vincente Huidobro. TCLAP, *tr.* by Stephen Fredman *Fr.* Altazor.

Here and now is clear so we. 20-200 on 737. Heather McHugh. NIP-4

Here and There. Ann Lauterbach. BodElec; PmAP

Here and there. Elephant Rocks. Kay Ryan. ExTi

Here and there little breezes stir the rushes. Woodcutter on His Way Home, A. *Unknown.* EaWin, *tr.* by W. S. Merwin and Nguyen Ngoc Bich

Here are / blue teapot. Components. Roger McDonald. CBAP

Here are cakes for thy body. *Unknown.* AWP, *tr.* by Robert Silliman Hillyer *Fr.* Book of the Dead.

Here are consoling pieties. Elegy for a Child. Gregory Orr. BodElec

Here are fine gifts, children. Sappho. BoWoP

Here are grapes ready to turn to wine. Crinagoras. GrAn

Here are my lady's knives and forks. *Unknown.* LB

Here are no signs of festival. African Christmas. John Press. OBCP

Here are only cliffs and crags. Outpost Soldier, The. *Vietnamese Oral Tradition.* CaDao, *tr.* by John Balaban

Here are sweet peas, on tiptoe for a flight. John Keats. FHYEP *Fr.* I Stood Tip-Toe upon a Little Hill.

Here are the brains here the hearts. One o'Clock. Philippe Soupault. AF, *tr.* by Eden Paul

Here are the homeless black men begging small coins. Man Named Troy, A. Reginald Shepherd. IllVoic

Here are the lady's knives and forks. *Unknown.* OxNR

Here are the Schubert *Lieder.* Now begin. For M.S. Singing *Fruhlingsglaube* in 1945. Frances Darwin Cornford. BrRo

Here are those who are challenged by. Jewish Singles Event, The. Stewart Florsheim. GotH; UnSA

Here are two half-grown black cats perched on a / lump. Walking beside the Kamogawa, Remembering Nansen and Fudo and Gary's Poem. Philip Whalen. BB

Here are two pictures from my father's head. Wounds. Michael Longley. ModIr; NPeEn; PBCIP; PNI

Here are weeds about his mouth. Wide Empty Landscape with a Death in the Foreground. N. Scott Momaday. CDW

"Here are your magic glasses. Ballad of the Magic Glasses. Maura Stanton. FFC

Here, as in a painting, yellow noon burns [*or* noon burns yellow]. Natalya [*or* Natal'ia] Gorbanevskaya [*or* Gorbanyevskaya *or* Gorbanevskaia]. BoWoP

Here, as one breathes, one writes. In the Mountains. Andrey [*or* Andrei] Andreievich Voznesensky [*or* Voznesenskii]. RusPo, *tr.* by Robert Arthur Douglas Ford

Here at the center of the turning year. New Year. Stephen Spender. AWP

Here at the seashore they use the clouds over and over. Rhode Island. William Meredith. NoP-4

Here at the Vespasian-Carlton, it's just one. Boom! Howard Nemerov. NBLV; NIL-7; NIP-4

Here at the wayside station, as many a morning. Wayside Station, The. Edwin Muir. FaBoTw

Here be dragons, and bitter. Bitter Wood. Martin Carter. WoPoe

Here, because of the shock, the sudden. Desmond O'Grady. PBCIP *Fr.* Hellas.

[Here before the sunrise blue and in this solitude]. Janine Pommy-Vega. CLPP

Here begin dreams of flight, the wallpaper. Fog. Michelle Boisseau. ExTi

Here, beside the Latin sea. Eheu! "Rubén Dario." SpanPo, *tr.* by Anita Volland

Here beside the threshing floor, O hardworking ant. Antipater of Sidon. HePo *Fr.* Epigrams.

Here birds fly south. At the Lighthouse. "Nikolai Nikolaevich Morshen." TCRusP, *tr.* by John Glad

Here blooms the legend fed by [*or* with] Time and Chance. Rouen, Place de la Pucelle. Maria White Lowell. APN-2

Here bounds the gaudy, gilded chair. Birth-Day, The. Mary Robinson. ECWP; WoRP

Here by a snowbound river. To Robert Nichols. Robert Graves. PeFWW

Here by the ample river's argent sweep. Two Backgrounds. Edith Wharton. APN-2

Here by the grey north sea. Northern Vigil, A. Bliss Carman. OBEV

Here, by the seashore, there lies / Archilochus. Gaetulicus. GrAn

Here, by this brook, we parted; I to the East. Tennyson. OxAEP-2

Here by this crumbling wall. Butterfly Garden, The. Alfred Noyes. OBGa

Here, Caelia [*or* Celia], for thy sake I part. To the Mutable Fair. Edmund Waller. BeJo

Here, calling to mind what then I saw. William Wordsworth. NAEL-6v2 *Fr.* Prelude, The; Growth of a Poet's Mind [1850 vers.].

Here, Charmian, take my bracelets. Cleopatra. William Wetmore Story. APN-1

Here circling trees, which form a shade. Joseph Giles. OBGa *Fr.* Leasowes: Or, A Poetical Description of the Late Mr. Shenstone's Rural Retirement, The.

Here Cleita sleeps. You ask her life and race? Edward Cracroft Lefroy. AWP *Fr.* Echoes from Theocritus.

Here come I to my own again. Rudyard Kipling. NoAM *Fr.* Kim.

Here come my night thoughts. Something, The. Charles Simic. BAP-97

Here come real stars to fill the upper skies. Fireflies in the Garden. Robert Frost. OxBSP; SAmP

Here come the capybaras on their bikes. James Fenton. PeLV *Fr.* Wild Life Studies.

Here Come the Dreamers. Hugh Martin. ReLy

Here come the line-gang pioneering by. Line-Gang, The. Robert Frost. OxBSP

Here comes a cropper. That's what I said. (LL) American Lights, Seen from off Abroad. John Berryman. LCAP-2; OBAL; OBCoV

Here Comes a Lusty Wooer. *Unknown.* OxNR

Here comes a new storm, roiling and black. Kerosene. Chase Twichell. ExTi

Here comes / Babel, Isaak. Elderblossom. Johannes Bobrowski. AF

Here comes my husband from his whist. (LL) Dîs Aliter Visum; or, Le Byron de Nos Jours. Robert Browning. NAEL-5v2; NAEL-6v2

Here comes my lady with her little baby. *Unknown.* OxNR

Here comes one more looking pale. Man from the Death Institute. Novica Tadic. VCWP, *tr.* by Charles Simic

Here comes one who in silence. When Love's Perished. Dambudzo Marechera. NAfrP

Here comes someone soft as goose down. *Unknown.* PriapPo, *tr.* by Richard W. Hooper *Fr.* Priapus Poems, The.

Here comes the question. Prerogative of Lieder, The. Ray DiPalma. FTOS

Here comes the shadow not looking where it is going. Sire. W. S. Merwin. CoAP; VGW

—Here comes the smoking Bouillabaisse! (LL) William Makepeace Thackeray. OBEV; OxAEP-2

Here continueth to rot. Epitaph on Colonel Francis Chartres. John Arbuthnot. FaBoEE

Here costive many minutes did I strain. Privy-Love for My Landlady. George Farewell. NOEC; OBCoV

Here cursing swearing Burton lies. Epitaph on Mr. Burton. Robert Burns. FaBoEE

Here Dead Lie We Because We Did Not Choose. A. E. Housman. *See* Epitaph

Here, decayed, an old. Harlech Castle. John Corben. Spl

Here Delia's buried at fourscore. Hildebrand Jacob. FaBoEE

Here did his fathers live and pass. Ploughman: In Welsh Uplands, The. A. G. Prys-Jones. AngWePo

Here died St. Amand, shepherd of his sheep. Epitaph for St. Amand, Bishop of Utrecht. Alcuin. MLL, *tr.* by Helen Waddell

Here dock and tare. In the Grave No Flower. Edna St. Vincent Millay. NAAL-2v2; NAAL-5

Here doth Dionysia lie. Epitaph of Dionysia. *Unknown.* OBEV

Here down my wearied [*or* wearyed] limbs I'll [*or* Ile] lay. On Himself[e]. Robert Herrick. BASC

Here droops the muse! while from her glowing mind. [Sonnet] Conclusive. Mary Robinson. CenSon; RWP

Here dwells the whole and scattered. Biancamaria Frabotta. CItWP, *tr.* by Cinzia Sartini Blum and Lara Trubowitz *Fr.* Heloise.

Here, dying for the world, the world's life hung. On the Cross. Alcuin. MLL, *tr.* by Helen Waddell

Here earth and sky are reduced to an ultimate simplicity. Nullarbor. William Hart-Smith. BMAP

Here ended Hall, and our last light, that long. Tennyson. NAEL-5v2 *Fr.* Morte d'Arthur.

Here envying and lies. On Leaving Prison. Luís De León. SpanPo, *tr.* by Brenda M. Sackett

Here erect I guard the land / and Phrikon's crops and hut. Priapus the Scarecrow. Antistius Vetus. GrAn, *tr.* by Alistair Elliot

Here, ever since you went abroad. What News. Walter Savage Landor. BoLoP

Here, everything gets eaten: drippings, marinade. Olesya [*or* Olesia] Nikolayeva [*or* Nikolaeva]. ItGoST, *tr.* by Paul Graves and Carol Ueland

Here, few signs distinguish dawns from nights. Prisoner's Dream, The. Eugenio Montale. PoetW, *tr.* by Jonathan Galassi

Here, five feet deep, lies on his back. On the Astrologer and Almanac Maker, John Partridge. Jonathan Swift. FaBoEE

Here followeth the unfashionable fashion, or the too too homely Worshipping of God. John Taylor.
"Gods *Houses,* almost like *Troyes Ilion.*" PBRV

Here Follows Some Verses upon the Burning of Our House [July 10th, 1666. Copied Out of a Loose Paper]. Anne Bradstreet. AiP; BASC; BoWoP; ColAP; EMWP; MakPoe; NAAL-2v1; NAAL-3; NAAL-5; NALW; NOBA; NOSC; NoP-4; OxBA; PEW; SCAP; SacPr; TAP; TCAPo; WPE

Here for a few short years. To a Young Winter. Yvor Winters. APT-2

Here for a little we pause. Benicasim. Sylvia Townsend Warner. OBWP

Here. Forget. Poem. Charles Bernstein. FTOS

Here from his prominent but thankfully. Old Bachelor Brother. Brad Leithauser. NoP-4; RA

Here, from laborious art, proud towns, ye rose! On Catania and Syracuse Swallowed up by an Earthquake, from the Italian of Filicaja. Anna Seward. Son

Here from the castle's terraced site. Scene on the Northern Shore of Sicily. Ann Radcliffe. RWP

Here from the start, from our first of days, look. Tally Stick, The. Jarold Ramsey. NIL-7; NIP-4

Here Goes My Lord. *Unknown.* ReMoGo

Here have I seen the king, when great affairs. Sir John Denham. PoE *Fr.* Cooper's Hill.

Here he is whom you read and clamor for. Martial. WoPoe, *tr.* by William Matthews *Fr.* Epigrams.

Here he's at it, spading toward a. Ditchdigger, The. Igor Moiseievich Irtenev. TCRP, *tr.* by John High

Here, here are our enjoyments done. Lucasia, Rosania and Orinda Parting at a Fountain, July 1663. Katherine Philips. EMWP; PEW

Here, here I live with what my board. His Content in the Country. Robert Herrick. CaPo; CavPo

Here, here, oh here Eurydice [*or* Euridice]. Orpheus to Beasts. Richard Lovelace. CaPo

Here Hermes, says Jove who with nectar was mellow. Jupiter and Mercury. David Garrick. ECEV

Here hills and vales, the woodland and the plain. Pope. ECEV *Fr.* Windsor-Forest [*or* Windsor Forest].

Here, Home. John Powell Ward. TCAWP

Here I am. Ode on Arrival. Carl Rakosi. BodElec

Here I Am. Abraham Sutskever [*or* Sutzkever]. TrJP, *tr.* by Joseph Leftwich

Here I am again with my sickle, spade, hoe. Weeding. Michael Hamburger. OBGa

Here I am, an industry without chimneys. Perfection of Dentistry, The. Marvin Bell. CoAP

Here I am, an old man in a dry month. Gerontion. T. S. Eliot. APT-1; ColAP; EBEV; GTBS-P; HAP; NAAL-2v2; NAAL-5; NOBA; NPeEn; NoAM; OxAEP-2; OxBA; PAI; TAP; TCAPo; TFi

Here I am and forth I must. Prayer for the Journey. *Unknown.* SacPr

Here I am, awakened by accident. Brother Body. Peter Cooley. OPRER

Here I am, full-grown, flourishing. Here I Am. Abraham Sutskever [*or* Sutzkever]. TrJP

Here I am in Europe. Promenade, The. U Tam'si Tchicaya. NegPo, *tr. by* Ellen Conroy Kennedy

Here I am in the garden laughing. Here. Grace Paley. BAP-01

Here I am launching my Second Book of Epigrams—. Lucilius. GrAn

Here I am once more before the sea. Here I am Once More. Rachida Madani. HAWP; NAfrP, *tr. by* Eric Sellin

Here I am, sprouted to my full height. Here I Am. Abraham Sutskever [*or* Sutzkever]. TrJP, *tr. by* Joseph Leftwich

Here I am / The same old fervent plea. You May Not Love Me. Jimmy Van Heusen. ReLy

Here I am with my rabbits. *Unknown.* OxNR

Here I am writing my first villanelle. Saturday at the Border. Hayden Carruth. MakPoe

Here I ame and fourthe I mouste. *Unknown.* MiEL

Here I find refuge, though the woman. In the Bookstore. Allison Joseph. IllVoic

Here I go again. Starting from San Francisco. Lawrence Ferlinghetti. GM

Here I have enough to eat. Thanks for Daisen Osho's Visit. Muso Soseki. EaWin, *tr. by* W. S. Merwin

Here I lie at the chancel door. On Elizabeth Ireland. *Unknown.* FaBoEE

Here I lie for the last time. Epitaph on an Irish Priest. *Unknown.* FaBoEE

Here i lie in chinatown. My Ship Does Not Need a Helmsman. Alan Chong Lau. OBWVE

Here I ligg, Sydney Slugabed Godless Smith. Sydney Goodsir Smith. OxBS *Fr.* Under the Eildon Tree.

Here I'm perched on a sheer cliff. Ode. Attila József. IQMS, *tr. by* Suzanne K. Walther

Here I myself [*or* my selfe] might likewise die. Poetry Perpetuates the Poet. Robert Herrick. BeJo; FaBoEE

Here I read Biggles; in this chair, *Ulysses*. Latitudes of Home, The. Alistair Elliot. OxBSo

Here, I said, Here. These parts. (LL) In my country. Jackie Kay. MFPA; NeBl

Here, I Say. Joanna Fuhrman. AmPoNex

Here I say again: the heart of the city has not yet died. Love, Attributed City. Nancy Morejón. TCLAP, *tr. by* Kathleen Weaver

Here I sing / of the Hesperides. Hesperides, The. Burleigh Mutén. HW

Here I sing / of the Muses. Queen Medusa. Burleigh Mutén. HW

Here I sing / of Urania. Urania. Burleigh Mutén. HW

Here / I sing th green branch. At Pakiri Beach. David Mitchell. PeNZ

Here I sit. Bad Morning. Langston Hughes. OBAL

Here I sit on a rock. Campfire. Anna Lindtová. INSAB

Here I slept with my face turned. Prospect Beach. Lou Lipsitz. VGW

Here I stand / Replacing another, who has been murdered. End or a Beginning, An. Bei Dao. AF, *tr. by* Bonnie S. McDougall

Here I stand with life ahead of me. Today Is the First Day of the Rest of My Life. David Shire. ReLy

Here I was and here I drank. *Unknown.* MiEL

Here I / What does. Epitaph. Paulus [*or* Paulos] Silentiarius. GrAn, *tr. by* Andrew Miller

Here, if the road shall bring thee back. Boethius. MLL, *tr. by* Helen Waddell *Fr.* Consolation of Philosophy, The ("De Consolacione Philosophie").

Here in a distant place I hold my tongue. Egan O Rahilly. *Unknown.* EBEV; OBMV, *tr. by* James Stephens

Here in caterpillar country. Hornworm: Summer Reverie. Stanley Kunitz. BodElec

Here in foreign land this rose. To Her Far Away. Nikolaus Lenau. AuPH, *tr. by* Alexander Gode

Here in his lamp-lit parable, he'll scan. Garden, The. Victoria Mary Sackville-West. OBGa

Here, in huge cauldrons, the rough mass they stow. Richard Jago. NOEC *Fr.* Edge-Hill; or, The Rural Prospect Delineated and Moralised.

Here, in July, in Jana's weedy garden. In Jana's Garden. Joyce Carol Oates. SpudSo

Here in Kansas is a school. Haskell. Witter Bynner. NoP-4

Here in Katmandu. Donald Justice. CoAmPo; CoAP; HeIP-40

Here, in late spring, the summer is on us already. Hot Afternoons Have Been in West 15th Street. Paul Blackburn. VGW

Here in my curving hands I cup. This Quiet Dust. John Hall Wheelock. MoAmPo

Here in my garden. *Unknown.* ArkPo, *tr. by* Edwin A. Cranston

Here in my head, the home that is left for you. Burning the Letters. Randall Jarrell. MoAmPo

Here in my heart I am Helen. Song of One of the Girls. Dorothy Parker. NALW

Here in our moment of darkness. We'll Be Together Again. Frankie Laine. ReLy

Here in Shinano. Issa. SoOfWa, *tr. by* Sam Hamill

Here in the country's heart. Country Faith, The. Norman Gale. OBEV

Here in the dark, O heart. Second Best. Rupert Brooke. MoBrPo

Here, in the darkness, where this plaster saint. Madeleine in Church. Charlotte Mew. VWP

Here in the dry consump. Extravagance of Zoos, The. Craig Arnold. AmPoNex

Here, in the ear of the earth. Our Skin Is Paper. Hilary Booth. SurWo

Here in the electric dusk your naked lover. Heat. Denis Johnson. MakPoe; SwNoth

Here in the good old U.S.A. In the Good Old U.S.A. José Angel Sr. Villalongo. UnSA

Here in the green scooped valley I walk to and fro. Green Valley, The. Sylvia Townsend Warner. MoBrPo

Here, in the half-dark of the sauna. Bodies, The. Elizabeth Spires. NIL-7

Here in the half-darkness of a basement. Chinese Laundry. Yury [*or* Iurii] Kazarnovsky [*or* Kazarnovskii]. TCRP, *tr. by* Bradley Jordan

Here, in the hollow caverns of the rocks. Wily Fox, The. Edward Davies. OBWVE, *tr. by* Joseph P. Clancy

Here, in the lather of sebum, of the decomposed, the misconstrued, the. Evolution of Lather, The. Michael Portnoy. HeMarv

Here in the middle of London. South African Exhibition, 1907. Kingsley Fairbridge. PeSAV

Here, in the most Unchristian basement. Men's Room in the College Chapel, The. W. D. Snodgrass. MoAmPo

Here in the mountain village. Evening in the Village. Lu Yu. OHPC, *tr. by* Kenneth Rexroth

Here in the new white neighborhood. Beloved Spic. Martín Espada. OPRER

Here in the North I chase an old despair. Trumbull Stickney. APN-2

Here in the quiet of my room. Prayer of an Unemployed Man. W. C. Ackerly. PoToHe

Here in the room of my life. Room of My Life, The. Anne Sexton. VCAP

Here in the self is all that men can know. John Masefield. AWP *Fr.* Lollingdon Downs.

Here in the shadow of death it is hard. Dokyo Etan. JDP, *tr. by* Yoel Hoffmann

Here in the slack of night. Camphor Laurel. Judith Wright. BMAP

Here, in the terraced. Aquarium du Trocadéro. Duncan Bush. AngWePo; TCAWP

Here in the uplands. Scotland. Sir Alexander Gray. OxBS

Here, in the withered arbor, like the arrested wind. Statue and Birds. Louise Bogan. MoAmPo

Here in these fretted caverns whence the sea. Sir Lewis Morris. AngWePo *Fr.* Lydstep Caverns.

Here in this bleak city of Rochester. Sestina d'Inverno. Anthony Hecht. NoAM

Here in this carload. Written in Pencil in the Sealed Railway-Car. Dan Pagis. AF, *tr. by* Stephen Mitchell

Here in this great house in the barrack square. Hambone and the Heart, The. Dame Edith Sitwell. OBMV

Here in this homely cabinet. Matthew Stevenson. NOSC *Fr.* Elegy upon Old Freeman, An.

Here in this house, among photographs. From Room to Room. Jane Kenyon. LoL

Here in this leafy place. Before Sedan. Austin Dobson. PeVV

Here in this rough trench lies. Poseidippus. GrAn

Here in this sequestered close. Garden Song, A. Austin Dobson. OBEV; OBGa

Here in this transport. Scrawled in Pencil in a Sealed Car. Dan Pagis. PoSu, *tr. by* Robert Friend

Here in this world / I won't live. Lady Izumi. BoWoP

Here in West Philadelphia. Black Man's Sonata, A. Michael S. Weaver. UnSA

Here is. Jean-Joseph Rabéarivelo [*or* Rebéarivelo]. NegPo

Here is a coast; here is a harbor. Arrival at Santos. Elizabeth Bishop. FaBoWP; OxBC

Here is a cup left empty in their. Broken Home. William Stafford. NNaP

Here is a ditch of hopelessly dead water. Dead Water. Wen Yi-tuo or Wen I-to. PFTM-1; WoPoe, *tr. by* Arthur Sze

Here is a fable men tell. Archilochus. SaLy, *tr. by* Diane Rayor

Here is a family so little famous. Photograph in a Stockholm Newspaper for March 13, 1910. Don Coles. NOBC

Here is a green Jew. Soap. Gerald Stern. TaR

Here is a heart-shaped leaf. Maple Leaf. "Shu Ting." VCWP

Here is a map of our country. Adrienne Rich. NAAL-5 *Fr.* Atlas of the Difficult World, An.

Here is a Mudwall tent, whose Matters are. Edward Taylor. TCAPo *Fr.* Preparatory Meditations before My Approach to the Lord's Supper.

Here is a painting on wood. Hazards of Imagery, The. Paul Violi. KGB

Here is a rarity. Know Thyself. Kenneth Burke. OBAL

Here is a room to come to. Portinaio. Julie Agoos. YaYoPo

Here Is a Song. John Peck. AH

Here is a story. Tess's Torch Song (I Had a Man). Ted Koehler. ReLy

Here is a symbol in which. Rock and Hawk. Robinson Jeffers. APT-1; ColAP; NOBA; NoAM; OxBA

Here is a tiny, hard-shelled thing. He is the length of a child's tooth. Exhausted Bug, The. Robert Bly. BodElec

Here is an island. Here is a house on stilts. Bella Abramovna Dizhur. ItGoST, tr. by Sarah Bliumis

Here is another bone to pick with you. Lucille Clifton. BodElec

Here is another poem in a picture. Daryl Hine. GS; NoAM

Here is Joe Blow the poet. On Being Asked for a Peace Poem. Howard Nemerov. OxBC

Here is Klito's little shack. Kenneth Rexroth. GrAn; NNaP; PGA

Here is much burning anger, mighty hate. Here Is Much Burning Anger. Shimon Halkin. MHP, tr. by Ruth Finer Mintz

Here is my gift, not roses on your grave. In Memory of M. B. Anna Andreyevna Akhmatova. PoetW, tr. by Max Hayward and Stanley Kunitz

Here is my horse Abstraction. Winged Horse, The. Louise Glück. BodElec

Here is my soul, with its strange. Way It Must Be, The. Enrique Molina. TCLAP, tr. by Naomi Lindstrom

Here is my uncle, a rice ball in his mouth. Nisei Picnic: From an Album, A. David Mura. LoL

Here is no peace, although the air has fainted. Innocent Landscape. Elinor Wylie. OxBA

Here is Peter. Here is Jane. They like fun. Reading Scheme. Wendy Cope. MakPoe

Here is poor Villon's final word. Ballade to End With, A. François Villon. WoPoe, tr. by Richard Wilbur

Here is the ancient floor. Self-Unseeing, The. Thomas Hardy. EBEV; HAP; MoBrPo; NOBE; NOBVV; OxAEP-2; OxBEV; RB; WeW-3

Here is the black sheep, master. Black Sheep, The. Gojko Djogo. AF, tr. by Michael March

Here is the church, and here is the steeple. Unknown. OxNR

Here is the crossroads where the slain. Dead Man's Corner. Robert Silliman Hillyer. APT-2

Here is the form of Gaveston's exile. Christopher Marlowe. CAGL Fr. Edward the Second.

Here is the haven: Pain touched with soft magic. Hospital. Wilfred John Funk. PoToHe

Here is the house, in readiness for you. To the New Owner. Lucile Hargrove Reynolds. PoToHe

Here is the lantern and the key. Demeter's Blessing. Burleigh Mutén. HW

Here is the long-bided hour: the labor of years is accomplished. Work. Alexander Sergeyevich Pushkin. AWP, tr. by Babette Deutsch and Avrahm Yarmolinsky

Here is the machine, the dynamizer. Dynamizer and the Oscilloclast, The. Jack Coulehan. BloBone

Here is the mother all boobed and bodicey. Victorian Family Photograph. Kit Wright. OBCoV

Here is the News. Michael Rosen. OBSP

Here is the phial; here I turn the key. Minor Poet, A. Amy Levy. VWP

Here is the place, my lord; good my lord, enter. William Shakespeare. OxAEP-1 Fr. King Lear.

Here is the place; right over the hill. Telling the Bees. John Greenleaf Whittier. APN-1; AWP; ColAP; NOBA; NoP-4; TAP; TCAPo

Here is the proposition that heals. Snail River. James Bertolino. PoCoUp

Here is the queen. Adrian Brooks. CAGL

Here is the scene: She follows him. Hameed Sa'id. MAP, tr. by Diana Der Hovanessian and Lena Jayyusi

Here is the Scripture, for your mind. Vanitatum Vanitas. Ferenc Kölcsey. IQMS, tr. by Watson Kirkconnell

Here is the shadow of its joy. (LL) Monet's "Waterlilies." Robert Earl Hayden. AmFaPo; GT

Here is the shadow of truth, for only the shadow is true. Way to Love God, A. Robert Penn Warren. NAAL-2v2

Here is the sign: It trembles. Eugenio Montale. WoPoe, tr. by Dana Gioia Fr. Motets, The.

Here is the soundless cypress on the lawn. Nightingale near the House, The. Harold Monro. MoBrPo

Here is the stream again under the rainbow. U Tam'si Tchicaya. PBA Fr. Debout.

Here is the tale of Carrousel. Ballad of a Barber, The. Aubrey Beardsley. NOBVV; PAI

Here is the yoke, with arrow and share near by. Laborer, The. José-Maria de Heredia. AWP, tr. by Wilfrid Thorley

Here it comes again, imagination of myself. International Date Line, Monday/ Monday 27:XI:67. Philip Whalen. BB

Here it comes again: Vision bevel-edged. Gillian Clarke. Prnts Fr. Glass.

Here it is ever Sunday. Festively. Prater's Tree-Lined Boulevard. Friedrich Torberg. AuPH, tr. by Lowell A. Bangerter

Here it is, near the house. Right in the Trail. Gary Snyder. PmAP

Here it is night: I stay at the Summit Temple. Summit Temple, The. Li Po. TAL

Here it is spring again. Late Singer, The. William Carlos Williams. SAmP

Here it's a fortnight to Carnival. Divorce Referendum, The. Sarah Maguire. MFPA

Here it's rose-time again, chick-peas in season. Philodemus. GrAn

Here Johnson lies; what human can deny. Epitaph for Thomas Johnson, Huntsman. Charlton, Sussex. Unknown. NPeEn

Here Klito spent eighty years. (LL) Kenneth Rexroth. GrAn; NNaP; PGA

Here lapped in hallowed slumber Saon lies. Saon of Acanthus. Callimachus. AWP, tr. by John Addington Symonds

Here lay a fair fat land. Culbin Sands. Andrew Young. GTBS-P; OxBS; OxBTC

Here lay dark Pittsburgh, from whose site there broke. James Kirke Paulding. APN-1 Fr. Backwoodsman, The.

Here let me rest me feet! Reverie of a Mum. Nancy Keesing. CBAP; NOBAu

Here let me sit, in this empty, cool, terraced hall. Ernest Francisco Fenollosa. APN-2 Fr. Ode on Reincarnation.

Here let my Lord hang up his conquering lance. Giles Fletcher, the Younger. ChIV-2; NOSC; SacPr Fr. Christ's Victory and Triumph.

Here let's jump rope together here. Picnic to the Earth. Shuntaro Tanikawa. PoetW, tr. by Harold Wright

Here let the Muse perform the painter's art. Unknown. ECWP Fr. Clio's Picture.

Here let us pause:—The opening prospect view. John Pierpont. APN-1 Fr. Airs of Palestine.

Here let us rest, while with meridian blaze. Written at the Eagle's Nest, Killarney. July 26, 1800. Mary Tighe. CenSon; OxBSo

Here lie a grasshopper and a / Cicada. Argentarius. GrAn

Here lie Ciardi's pearly bones. Elegy Just in Case. John Ciardi. TwCP

Here lie I, Martin Elginbrodde. At Aberdeen. George Macdonald. FaBoEE

Here lie I, once a witty fair. Epitaph, An. Samuel Wesley. NOEC

Here lie I, Timon. William Shakespeare. AWP Fr. Timon of Athens.

Here lie John Hughes and Sarah Drew. Epitaph. Lady Mary Wortley Montagu. ECWP

Here lie my old bones: My vexation now ends. Messenger Mounsey. FaBoEE

Here lie the banes o' Tammy Messer. Tammy Messer. Unknown. FaBoEE

Here lie two poor lovers, who had the mishap. Pope. FaBoEE Fr. Three Epitaphs on John Hewet and Sarah Drew.

Here lie Willie Michie's [or M—hie's] banes. Epitaph on a Schoolmaster. Robert Burns. FaBoEE

Here lies a bard, Hipponax--honored name! Edward Cracroft Lefroy. AWP Fr. Echoes from Theocritus.

Here lies a bard, let epitaphs be true. My Epitaph. H. J. Daniel. FaBoEE

Here lies a Bond under this tomb. On Bond the Usurer. Unknown. NOSC

Here lies a clerk who half his life had spent. Volunteer, The. Herbert Asquith. OBWP; OxBTC

Here lies a digger, all his chips departed. Epitaph on a Diamond Digger. Albert Brodrick. PeSAV

Here lies a Doctor of Divinity. On a Doctor of Divinity. Richard Porson. FaBoEE

Here lies a dog: May every dog that dies. Epitaph on the Favourite Dog of a Politician. Joseph Hilaire Pierre Belloc. OBSV

Here lies a great sleeper, as everybody knows. Epitaph on a Great Sleeper. Sir Aston Cokayne. FaBoEE

Here Lies a Lady. John Crowe Ransom. APT-1; AWP; HAP; MoAmPo; NAAL-2v2; NoAM; PoRA; RB; TAP; VGW Fr. Sixteen Poems in Eight Pairings.

Here lies a man. And here, a girl. They live. Memorial. Robert Pinsky. HCAP

Here lies a man who was killed by lightning. At Great Torrington, Devon. Unknown. FaBoEE

Here lies a most beautiful lady. Epitaph, An. Walter De la Mare. MoBrPo; OBEV; RB

Here lies a peer. Epitaph on the Duke of Grafton. Sir Fleetwood Shepherd. FaBoEE

Here lies a piece of Christ; a star in dust. Epitaph for a Godly Man's Tomb, An. Robert Wild. FaBoEE

Here lies a poet—where's the great surprise! "Z. Z." FaBoEE

Here lies a poor woman who always was tired. Unknown. FaBoEE; OBCoV

Here Lies a Prisoner. Charlotte Mew. MoBrPo

Here lies a shoe-maker whose knife and hammer. At His Father's Grave. John Ormond. FaBoTw; OBWVE

Here lies a simple Jew. Epitaph. "Sholom Aleichem." TrJP, tr. by Joseph Leftwich

Here lies a true maid, deformed and old. My Own Epitaph. Mary Chandler. ECWP

Here lies Anacreon. Simonides. PGA

Here lies, and none to mourn him but the sea. Edna St. Vincent Millay. HeIP-4 *Fr.* Epitaph for the Race of Man.

Here Lies Archeanassa. Asclepiades. WoPoe, *tr.* by Frederick Morgan

Here lies Arkheanassa of Kolophon. Arkheanassa. Asclepiades. GrAn, *tr.* by Peter Jay

Here lies Bogus, beatnik bard. Epitaph for a Beatnik Poet. Guy Owen. CRP

Here lies Cock Robbin dead and cold. Death and Burial of Cock Robbin, The. *Unknown.* OWoS

Here lies David Garrick, describe me who can. Oliver Goldsmith. NOEC; NPeEn; OxBEV *Fr.* Retaliation.

Here lies Dr. Keene, the good Bishop of Chester. Epitaph on Dr. Keene. Thomas Gray. FaBoEE

Here lies Fred. On Prince Frederick. *Unknown.* FaBoEE; NOBL

Here lies free from blood and slaughter. In Memory of Captain Underwood Who Was Drowned. *Unknown.* FaBoEE

Here lies Hilaire Belloc, who. Hilaire Belloc. Humbert Wolfe. FaBoEE

Here lies I, no wonder I'm dead. *Unknown.* FaBoEE

Here lies in death, who living always lied. On Ryneveld, an Unpopular Dutch Judge. *Unknown.* FaBoEE

Here lies intombed / Beneath these bricks. Epitaph on a Willing Girl. Thomas Rowlandson. FaBoEE

Here lies John Bun. John Bun. *Unknown.* NBLV

Here lies John Hughes and Sarah Drew. Epitaph. Lady Mary Wortley Montagu. CABP; FaBoEE

Here lies John Knott. Epitaph on John Knott. *Unknown.* FaBoEE

Here lies John Trot, the Friend of all mankind. Another [Epitaph]. William Blake. FaBoEE

Here lies Jonson [*or* lyes Johnson] with the rest. Upon Ben Jo[h]nson. Robert Herrick. BeJo; CaPo; FaBoEE

Here lies Judge A——, he's done with legal tort. Epitaph for a Judge. Benedict Jeitteles. TrJP, *tr.* by Joseph Chotzner

Here lies Landor. Walter Savage Landor.

Here lies Lord Coningsby—be civil. Lord Coningsby's Epitaph. Pope. FaBoEE

Here lies magnanimous Humility. Upon the Tomb of the Most Reverend Mr. John Cotton. Benjamin Woodbridge. SCAP

Here lies Miss Havisham. Miss Havisham. Olga Orozco. TCLAP, *tr.* by Stephen Tapscott

Here lies Mistress Keene the Bishop of Chester. Epitaph on Dr. Keene's Wife. Thomas Gray. FaBoEE

Here lies Mr. Chesterton. G. K. Chesterton. Humbert Wolfe. TrJP

Here lies my dear wife, a sad slattern and a shrew. *Unknown.* FaBoEE

Here lies my poor wife, much lamented. *Unknown.* FaBoEE

Here lies my poor wife, without bed or blanket. *Unknown.* FaBoEE

Here lies my wife. Susannah Prout. Walter De la Mare. FaBoEE

Here lies my wife. Eternal peace. Epigram. James Vincent Cunningham. NIP-4; OBAL

Here lies Nachshon, a man of great renown. Epitaph, An. Isaac Benjacob. TrJP, *tr.* by Joseph Chotzner

Here lies New Critic who would fox us. Epigram. James Vincent Cunningham. APT-2; MoAmPo; OBAL

Here lies Nolly Goldsmith, for shortness call'd Noll. On Oliver Goldsmith. David Garrick. FaBoEE; OxBEV

Here lies old Forty-five Per Cent. Old Forty-five Per Cent. *Unknown.* FaBoEE

Here lies old *Hobson*, Death hath broke his girt. On the University Carrier Who Sick'n'd [*or* Sickened] in the Time of His Vacancy [, Being Forbid to go to London, by Reason of the Plague]. John Milton. EBEV; FaBoCh; FaBoEE; NOSC; OxAEP-1

Here lies one sweet of heart. For My Father's Grave. Yvor Winters. IllVoic

Here lies our good Edmund, whose genius was such. Oliver Goldsmith. FaBoEE; NOEC; NPeEn; OxBEV *Fr.* Retaliation.

Here lies our Sovereign Lord the King. Epitaph on Charles II. John Wilmot, 2d Earl of Rochester. SCGP; WoPoe

Here lies Piron—a man of no position. Alexis Piron. FaBoEE

Here lies poor Johnson. Reader! have a care. Doctor Johnson. Soame Jenyns. FaBoEE; OBSV

Here lies resting, out of breath. Little Elegy. X. J. Kennedy. CoAP; CoAmPo

Here lies Sam Johnson:—Reader, have a care. Epitaph on Dr Samuel Johnson. Soame Jenyns. ECEV

Here lies Sir John Plumpudding of the Grange. *Unknown.* FaBoEE

Here lies Sir Tact, a diplomatic fellow. Epitaph. Timothy Steele. InPK-6; NBLV

Here lies Stephen Pwanya. Epitaph, An. Julius Chingono. PeSAV

Here lies that poet, buried in the night. On a Poet. Henry Parrot. FaBoEE

Here lies the author of the "Apparition." Author's Epitaph, Written by Himself, An. Abel Evans. FaBoEE

Here lies the best and worst of fate. On the Duke of Buckingham. James Shirley. FaBoEE

Here lies the body of Daniel Saul. *Unknown.* FaBoEE

Here lies the body of Edith Bone. On Myself. Edith Bone. FaBoEE

Here lies the body of Richard Hind. Epitaph. Francis, Lord Jeffrey Jeffrey. FaBoEE; OxBoLi

Here lies the body of Sir John Guise. *Unknown.* FaBoEE

Here lies the body of W. W. On William Wilson, Tailor. *Unknown.* FaBoEE

Here lies the body of William Jones. Epitaph on William Jones. *Unknown.* FaBoEE

Here lies the clerk who half his life had spent. Herbert Asquith. *See* Here lies a clerk who half his life had spent

Here lies the corpse of Doctor Chard. *Unknown.* FaBoEE

Here lies the corpse of William Prynne. On William Prynne. Samuel Butler. FaBoEE

Here lies the fairest flower, that stood. David's Epitaph on Jonathan. Francis Quarles. ChIV-1

Here lies the good old knight Sir Harry. Epitaph for Sir Henry Lee. *Unknown.* FaBoEE

Here lies the great. False marble, where? *Unknown.* FaBoEE

Here lies, the Lord have mercy upon her. Upon One of the Maids of Honour to Queen Elizabeth. John Hoskyns [*or* Hoskins]. FaBoEE

Here lies the man that madly slain. John Hoskyns [*or* Hoskins]. FaBoEE

Here lies the man was born and cried. Epitaph, An: On a Man for Doing Nothing. John Hoskyns [*or* Hoskins]. NOSC

Here lies the man who in life. On a Contentious Companion. John Hoskyns [*or* Hoskins]. FaBoEE

Here lies the man who stripp'd Sin bare. Ebenezer Elliott. FaBoEE

Here lies the noble flesh of Spartacus the knave. Daniel Casper von Lohenstein. GePo *Fr.* Arminius.

Here lies [*or* lyes] the noble warrior [*or* Warryor] that never blunted sword. Epitaph on the Earl of Leicester [*or* Leceister]. Sir Walter Ralegh. RB

Here lies the preacher, judge, and poet, Peter. On Peter Robinson. Francis, Lord Jeffrey Jeffrey. FaBoEE; NBLV

Here lies the pride of Queens, pattern of Kings. Anne Bradstreet. TCAPo *Fr.* In Honour of that High and Mighty Princess Queen Elizabeth of Happy Memory.

Here lies the Reverend Jonathan Doe. On the Reverend Jonathan Doe. *Unknown.* FaBoEE

Here lies Thomas Logge—a Rascally Dogge. Thomas Logge. Walter De la Mare. FaBoEE

Here lies to each her parent's ruth. On My First Daughter. Ben Jonson. BASC; BeJo; EBEV; FaBoEE; NAEL-5v1; NAEL-6v1; NAEL-7v1; NOBE; NOSC; NoP-4; PoE

Here lies what had not birth, nor shape, nor frame. Epitaph on James Moore Smythe. Pope. FaBoEE

Here lies, whom hound did ne'er pursue. Epitaph on a Hare. William Cowper. HAP; NOEC; NoP-4; PoPoPo

Here lies Wise and Valiant Dust. Epitaph on the Earl of Strafford. John Cleveland. BASC; FaBoEE; NOBE; NOSC; NPeEn; OxBEV; PeECV

Here lies with Death auld Grizzel Grimme. Grizzel Grimme. *Unknown.* FaBoEE

Here lies, within his tomb, so calm. On the Clerk of a Country Parish. William Shenstone. FaBoEE

Here lies wrapped up in forty thousand towels. On Queen Caroline's Deathbed. Pope. NPeEn

Here lies wrapped up tight in sod. Epitaph for a Postal Clerk. X. J. Kennedy. NIL-7; NIP-4

Here lieth John Cruker, a maker of bellows. Bellows Maker of Oxford, The. John Hoskyns [*or* Hoskins]. FaBoEE

Here lieth the worthy warrior / Who never bloodied sword. On the Earl of Leicester. *Unknown.* FaBoEE

Here lieth Thom Nick's body. Upon a Fool. John Hoskyns [*or* Hoskins]. FaBoEE

Here lieth under this marble ston. Epitaph, An. *Unknown.* MiEL

Here, Lord, Retired, I Bow in Prayer. Matthew Bolles. AH

Here luxury's the common lot. The light. Grasse: The Olive Trees. Richard Wilbur. NAAL-2v2; NOBA; NoAM

Here lyes a Boy the finest Child from me. On My Boy Henry. Elizabeth, Lady Brackley Egerton. EMWP

Here lyeth he, who was born and cried. On One That Lived Ingloriously. John Hoskyns [*or* Hoskins]. FaBoEE

Here Lysis set an empty tomb. Phanias. GrAn

Here make an end of singing? (LL) If All the World Were Paper. *Unknown.* NOSC; NTCP; OBCoV; OxNR; TTTS

Here may Paulinus rest, for ever rest. Epitaph for Paulinus of Aquileia and Arno of Salzburg. Alcuin. MLL, *tr.* by Helen Waddell

Here must we pause; this only let me add.   William Wordsworth.   NAEL-6v2   *Fr.* Prelude, The; Growth of a Poet's Mind [1850 vers.].

Here my garden is growing, the flowers of Eros I tend here.   Goethe.   EroLit, *tr. by* David Luke   *Fr.* Roman Elegies, The.

Here my meat is, clean and dressed.   Epitaph for a Meat-Packer.   Guy Owen.   CRP

Here, next the mountain, the cold comes early.   Early Autumn in the Mountains.   Wen T'ing-yün.   SuSp, *tr. by* William R. Schultz

Here no bugles sound reveille. (LL)   Sir Walter Scott.   AWP; NOBE; PoRA   *Fr.* Lady of the Lake, The.

Here none think of wealth or fame.   Daigu.   ZenPo, *tr. by* Takashi Ikemoto and Lucien Stryk

Here not the flags, the rhythmic.   Neutrality.   Sidney Keyes.   MoBrPo

Here, O my Lord, I see Thee face to face.   Horatius Bonar.   SacPr   *Fr.* This Do in Remembrance of Me.

Here often, when a child, I lay reclined.   Lines.   Tennyson.   PAI

Here on Earth.   "Rachel" [*or* "Rahel"].   MHP, *tr. by* Ruth Finer Mintz

Here on Mondays, after the.   Anglo-Saxon Comedy.   Peter Rose.   BMAP

Here on the earth—not in high clouds.   Here on Earth.   "Rachel" [*or* "Rahel"].   MHP, *tr. by* Ruth Finer Mintz

Here, on the forest's edge, I have pitched camp.   In Camp.   Jibanananda Das.   OMIP, *tr. by* Clinton B. Seely

Here on the west edge, the town turned its back on the west.   City Limits.   Ted Kooser.   GM

Here on this patio, lonely as a mushroom, which way should I look.   Antonio Cisneros.   TCLAP, *tr. by* William Rowe   *Fr.* Loneliness.

Here on this stretcher now he coldly lies.   Mort, Le.   Howard Buck.   YaYoPo

Here once did sound sweet words, a-spoke.   Vield Path, The.   William Barnes.   NOBVV

Here once flint walls.   Edward Thomas.   OxBEV

Here once the evenings sobbed.   Pear-Tree, The.   Iwan [*or* Yvan] Goll.   TrJP, *tr. by* Babette Deutsch and Avrahm Yarmolinsky

Here [*or* How] richly, with ridiculous display.   Epitaph on the Politician Himself.   Joseph Hilaire Pierre Belloc.   FaBoEE; MoBrPo; NBLV; OBSV

Here Philip the father buried.   Callimachus.   HePo   *Fr.* Epigrams.

Here, Queen of the Mountains.   Kamalākānta Bhaṭṭācārya.   SinGod, *tr. by* Rachel Fell McDermott

Here, reader, turn your weeping eyes.   Orator's Epitaph, The.   Henry Peter Brougham, 1st Baron Brougham and Vaux.   NBLV

Here rests his head upon the lap of earth.   Thomas Gray.   FHYEP; SCGP   *Fr.* Elegy Written in a Country Churchyard.

Here rests poor Stella's restless part.   Stella's Epitaph.   Mary Jones.   ECWP

Here Reynolds is laid, and to tell you my mind.   Oliver Goldsmith.   FaBoEE; NOEC; OBCoV; OxBEV   *Fr.* Retaliation.

Here Rhodoklea / is a garland.   Rufinus.   GrAn

Here's a ball for baby.   *Unknown.*   LB

Here's a body—there's a bed!   Good Night.   Thomas Hood.   OTCP; Spl

Here's a fine bag of meat.   Bags of Meat.   Thomas Hardy.   RB

Here's a girl from a dangerous town.   Belfast Tune.   Joseph Brodsky.   VCWP

Here's a good piece of cheese (I perhaps might have kept it).   Cheese for the Archdeacon, A.   Thomas Hughes.   AngWePo

Here's a good rule of thumb.   Reflection on Ingenuity.   Ogden Nash.   RB

Here's a guy.   Michael McClintock.   HA

Here's a hotel where even the stairs.   Hot Springs.   Earle Birney.   OxBC

Here's a jolly couple! Oh the jolly jolly cuple!   *Unknown.*   NOSC

Here's a large one for the lady.   Broom Squire's Song, The.   *Unknown.*   OxNR

Here's a little mouse) and.   Four III.   E. E. Cummings.   FaBoMo; TTTS

Here's a live one.   Evidence on Film, The.   Ron Charach.   BloBone

Here's a picture of me.   Photographs.   Alec Wilder.   ReLy

Here's a poor widow from Babylon.   *Unknown.*   OxNR

Here's a song.   Season Song.   *Unknown.*   RB; WoPoe, *tr. by* Flann O'Brien and Flann O'Brien

Here's a song of praise for all those people.   Those Who Make Paths.   Catherine Fisher.   TCAWP

Here's a song that I've created.   Remember Me?   Harry Warren.   ReLy

Here's an example from / A Butterfly.   Example, The.   William Henry Davies.   MoBrPo

Here's an old lady, almost ninety-one.   Two Old Ladies.   Siegfried Sassoon.   OxBTC

Here's another Spaniard! Welcome!   Antonio Machado Ruiz.   STV

Here's another window.   Marina Ivanovna Tsvetayeva [*or* Tsvetaeva].   AWTN, *tr. by* Elaine Feinstein   *Fr.* Insomnia.

Here's Cooper, who's written six volumes to show.   James Russell Lowell.   NOBA; OxBA; TAP; TCAPo   *Fr.* Fable for Critics, A.

Here's Dog Diogenes, you ferryman.   *Unknown.*   GrAn

Here's fine rosemary, sage, and thyme.   Cries of London, The.   *Unknown.*   OPOU

Here's Finiky Hawkes.   *Unknown.*   OxNR

Here's how it was: I caught you by the throat.   To Eros.   Alfonsina Storni.   TANSG, *tr. by* Mark McCaffrey

Here's Looking at You Francis Bacon.   Joan Retallack.   FTOS

Here's my dream of a final exam.   Two Apes of Brueghel, The.   Wisława Szymborska.   WoPoe, *tr. by* Sharon Olds

Here's my mom and dad leaving.   Roc, The.   Mohja Kahf.   PoArWo

Here's no more news, than virtue, I may as well.   To Sir Henry Wotton.   John Donne.   OxAEP-1

Here's one in whom Nature feared—faint at such vying.   Cardinal Bembo's Epitaph on Raphael.   Thomas Hardy.   FaBoEE

Here's proof—as if one needed any.   Dedicatory Epistle, with a Book of 1949.   Roy Fuller.   PeLV

Here's Sulky Sue.   Sulky Sue.   Mother Goose.   OxNR; ReMoGo

Here's That Rainy Day.   Johnny Burke.   ReLy

Here's the garden she walked across.   Robert Browning.   CTC   *Fr.* Garden Fancies.

Here's the little dressmaker.   Epith.   Carol Muske.   MakPoe

Here's the long trough, covered by a screen.   China Camp, California.   Kim Addonizio.   GeoHom

Here's to Life.   Violeta Parra.   TCLAP, *tr. by* Joan Baez and James Upton

Here's to Lysidice: Pour in ten ladles, boy.   Argentarius.   GrAn

Here's to my best romance.   Hooray for Love.   Leo Robin.   ReLy

Here's to the building trade.   To the Building Trade.   Matthew Sweeney.   ModIr

Here's to the ladies who lunch.   Ladies Who Lunch, The.   Stephen Sondheim.   ReLy

Here's to the maiden [*or* maid] of Bashful fifteen.   Richard Brinsley Sheridan.   NOIV; NPeEn; OxBEV   *Fr.* School for Scandal, The.

Here's to thee, MY HERO, MY SODGER LADDIE. (LL)   Robert Burns.   NBLV; OxBoLi   *Fr.* Jolly Beggars, The.

Here's to thee, old apple tree.   *Unknown.*   OxNR

Here's to women for they bear such / lovely kiddies! (LL)   Uncle Henry.   W. H. Auden.   NOBL; PeLV

Here's two or three jolly boys.   *Unknown.*   OxNR

Here's what I see.   Dogs Gambol.   Novica Tadic.   VCWP, *tr. by* Charles Simic

Here's where I wanted to put the streetcars.   Old Postcards.   Günter Eich.   AF, *tr. by* Stuart Friebert

Here's witts extraction morall and divine.   One Presenting a Rare Book to Madame Hull.   John Saffin.   SCAP

"Here," said the Cloud-gatherer Zeus, "that is a journey you may well postpone.   Homer.   EroLit, *tr. by* Emile Victor Rieu   *Fr.* Iliad, The.

Here Saon of Akanthos, Dikon's son.   Callimachus.   GrAn

Here shadow[e] lie.   Epitaph for Sir Lawrence Tanfield.   Lady Elizabeth Tanfield.   NOSC; TOF

Here she beholds the chaos dark and deep.   Pope.   FHYEP   *Fr.* Dunciad, The.

Here she lies, a pretty bud.   Upon a Child That Died [*or* Dyed].   Robert Herrick.   BeJo; CaPo; InPK-6; PAI

Here she lies [*or* lyes] (in Bed of Spice).   Upon a Maid[e].   Robert Herrick.   CaPo; FaBoCh; FaBoEE; OxBoLi

Here, she said, is your deepest well in Madras.   Deepest Well in Madras, The.   N.V.M. Gonzalez.   ReBoTo

Here, she said, put this on your head.   Flounder.   Natasha Trethewey.   TWW

Here She Stands.   Jean-Joseph Rabéarivelo [*or* Rebéarivelo].   PBA, *tr. by* Miriam Koshl

Here She Was Wont to Go.   Ben Jonson.   BeJo; OxBSP   *Fr.* Sad Shepherd, The.

Here shift the scene, to represent.   Jonathan Swift.   OxBEV   *Fr.* Verses on the Death of Dr. Swift, D.S.P.D.

Here should my wonder dwell, and here my praise.   Sir John Denham.   NAEL-5v1; NAEL-6v1; NOSC; NPeEn   *Fr.* Cooper's Hill.

Here silken twines, there locks you see.   Ear-string, An.   William Strode.   NOSC

Here sits the Lord Mayor.   Forehead, Eyes, Cheeks, Nose, Mouth, and Chin.   Mother Goose.   FaBoVe; LB; OxNR; ReMoGo

Here, six years old, by Destiny's crime.   Epitaph for Erotion.   Martial.   FaBoEE, *tr. by* James Michie

Here sleeps at length poor Col, and without screaming.   Epitaph on Himself.   Samuel Taylor Coleridge.   FaBoEE

Here sleeps the Queen, this is the royall bed.   Anne Bradstreet.   OxBEV; TCAPo   *Fr.* In Honour of that High and Mighty Princess Queen Elizabeth of Happy Memory.

Here stand I, for whores as great.   *Unknown.*   FaBoEE

Here stands death, a bluish decoction in a cup with no saucer.   Death.   Rainer Maria Rilke.   PFTM-1

Here, still sequestered, Penmon's sacred dome.   Richard Llwyd.   AngWePo   *Fr.* Beaumaris Bay.

Here stood a lofty church—there is a steeple.   Pleasant Delusion of a Sumpteous Citty.   Sarah Kemble Knight.   SCAP

Here stood Hypocrisy, in sober brown. Timothy Dwight. NOCV *Fr.* Triumph of Infidelity, The.

Here, take again thy sackcloth! and thank heaven. Henry Vaughan. AngWePo; BASC *Fr.* Upon a Cloak [*or* Cloke] Lent Him by Mr. J. Ridsley.

Here / Take it home and give it to your wife. Wooden Handle, The. Gojko Djogo. AF, *tr.* by Michael March

Here take my Picture, though I bid farewell. John Donne. FSCP; MeLP; OxAEP-1; PBRV *Fr.* Elegies.

Here take no care, take here no care, my Muse. Discontent, The. Anne Killigrew. BASC

Here, take this gift. To a Certain Cantatrice. Walt Whitman. AmFaPo

Here the boat set me down, and I wait. Queen of the River. Elizabeth Nannestad. PeNZ

Here, the bones of the Geblites. Israel Revisited. Luisa Futuransky. MirDau, *tr.* by Celeste Kostopulos-Cooperman

Here the crow starves, here the patient stag. T. S. Eliot. NAEL-5v2; NAEL-6v2 *Fr.* Landscapes.

Here the delicate dance of silence. Woodtown Manor. John Montague. PBCIP

Here the eye is inevitably cast. Sakhara. Robert Arthur Douglas Ford. NOBC

Here the foot prints stop;. After Twenty Years. Fadwa Tuqan [or Tuquan]. AF, *tr.* by Unknown

Here the Frailest Leaves of Me. Walt Whitman. APN-1; CAGL; NAAL-2v1; NAAL-3; NAAL-5

Here the green vein of life. Places. Luciana Frezza. CItWP, *tr.* by Cinzia Sartini Blum and Lara Trubowitz

Here the hangman stops his cart. Carpenter's Son, The. A. E. Housman. ChIV-2; MoBrPo; OxAEP-2; UV

Here the hills are earth's bones. Asian Desert. Dorothy Wellesley, Duchess of Wellington. OBMV

Here the horse-mushrooms make a fairy ring. Fairy Ring, The. Andrew Young. Spl

Here the human past is dim and feeble and alien to us. Haunted Country. Robinson Jeffers. APT-1; OxBA

Here the image of a child on a hill. Michael Palmer. APSN *Fr.* Baudelaire Series.

Here the jack-hammer jabs into the ocean. Colloquy in Black Rock. Robert Lowell. MoAmPo; NAAL-2v2

Here the moutain joins the sea. Brief Ectasy. Luciana Notari. CItWP, *tr.* by Cinzia Sartini Blum and Lara Trubowitz

Here the part played by color is the inconsistency. Risk of Abstraction, The. Adriano Spatola. PFTM-2, *tr.* by Paul Vangelisti

Here the picture is less gloomy. All That Glitters. Maureen Owen. PmAP

Here, the ribs end, they—divide, into. Recumbent. Carl Phillips. NAPBL

Here the round begins again. Traveller, A. J. R. Rowland. CBAP

Here the savoury roast and pungent sauce. Latrine in a Suburb of Smyrna, A. Agathias. GrAn, *tr.* by Guy Davenport

Here the white-rayed anemone is born. In a Spring Grove. William Allingham. OxBSo

Here then is the life-giving activity given to every man: the sexual / act, vivificator. Stefan Brecht. CLPP *Fr.* Sex.

Here they all come to die. Country of a Thousand Years of Peace, The. James Merrill. NoP-4

Here they are. The soft eyes open. Heaven of Animals, The. James Dickey. CoAP; ColAP; EmeKit; HeIP-4; NAAL-2v2; NOBA; NoAM; PoE; TAP; TRP; VCAP; WoPoe

Here they caper all over the scarred bronze. Grasshoppers on the Bell. László Nagy. IQMS, *tr.* by Júlia Kada and Kenneth McRobbie

Here they come past High Street station, everyone I've ever known. Big Parade, The. Stephen Knight. NeBl; TCAWP

Here they lie mottled to the ground unseen. Partridges. John Masefield. OxBTC

Here they stand, rotund, and undiluted by grief. Ever So, Between. Valerie Martínez. NAPBL

Here they stood, whom the Kecoughtan first believed. Elegy in an Abandoned Boatyard. Dave Jeddie Smith. VCAP

Here—they've all started moving at once. Edoardo Cacciatore. ItPo, *tr.* by Gayle Ridinger *Fr.* Full Powers: Five Warning Signs.

Here they went with smock and crook. Forefathers. Edmund Charles Blunden. NOBE; NoP-4; OBEV; OBMV; OxBTC

Here those of us who really understand. Osbert Lancaster. NOBL; PeLV *Fr.* Afternoons with Baedeker.

Here to the leisured side of life. Lamplighter, The. "Seumas O'Sullivan." BIrV

Here Today. Andrew Elliott. PNI

Here Together Met. Louis Johnson. PeNZ

Here too are dreaming landscapes. In the Miscroscope. Miroslav Holub. PoSu; WoPoe, *tr.* by Ian Milner and Jarmila Milner

Here too, 'tis sung, of old Diana stray'd. Pope. OxAEP-1 *Fr.* Windsor-Forest [*or* Windsor Forest].

Here under leafy bowers. Under Leafy Bowers. Judah Al-Harizi. TrJP

Here, under Pear-trees. David Campbell. BMAP

Here under the radiant rays of the sun. Facing the Chair. Hugh MacDiarmid. FaBoMo

Here Usually Comes the Bride. Ogden Nash. NIL-7

Here war is harmless like a monument. W. H. Auden. OBWP *Fr.* Sonnets from China.

Here war is simple like a monument. W. H. Auden. *See* Here war is harmless like a monument

Here was raised. Plain of Adoration, The. *Unknown.* BIrV, *tr.* by John Montague

Here was the sound of water falling only. Owl, The. Robert Penn Warren. MoAmPo

Here, watching T.V. Hunting the Dugong. Gladys Cardiff. HATNAP

Here we are all, by day; by night we are [*or* w'are] hurled. Dream[e]s. Robert Herrick. BeJo; CaPo; HAP; NAEL-5v1; NAEL-6v1; NAEL-7v1; OPOU; OxBSP; Spl

Here we are, picking the first fern-shoots. Song of the Bowmen of Shu. Ezra Pound. FaBoWar; OBVE

Here we are, see? At the Well. Paul Blackburn. APSN; PFTM-2

Here we are together. Good Morning. Arthur Freed. ReLy

Here we bring new water. New Year Carol, A. *Unknown.* OxBoLi

Here we broached the Christmas barrel. House of Hospitalities, The. Thomas Hardy. RB

Here We Come A-wassailing. *Unknown.* ChrPo

Here we come gathering nuts an' [*or* in] May. Nuts an' May. *Unknown.* LB

Here we come looby loo. Lubin. *Unknown.* FaBoVe

Here we enact the opening of the world. Australian Garden, An. Peter Porter. OBGa

Here we go round ring by ring. *Unknown.* OxNR

Here we go round the mulberry bush, The. Mulberry Bush, The. *Unknown.* LB

Here We have No Firm Dwelling-Place. Eugène Marais. PeSAV, *tr.* by Hugh Finn

Here we have the sea of children; here. Geography Lesson. Carol Rumens. FaBoWP

Here we have thirst. Egyptian Pulled Glass Bottle in the Shape of a Fish, An. Marianne Craig Moore. APT-1; NALW

Here We Loved. Yehuda Amichai [*or* Amikhai]. "My father was four years at their war." MHP

Here we must rest; and where else should we rest? Sepulchrum Domus Mea Est. William Austin. NOSC

Here we part. Farewell Once More to My Friend Yen at Feng Chi Station. Tu Fu. OHPC, *tr.* by Kenneth Rexroth

Here we raise the dead. Kalamu ya Salaam. SpirFl *Fr.* New Orleans Haiku.

Here we're set upon the green grass. Green Grass. *Unknown.* FaBoVe

Here We Stand before the Temporal World. Joan Murray. YaYoPo

Here we stand on the brink of tomorrow. Year after Year. Bart Howard. ReLy

Here We Will Stay. Tawfiq Zayyad. MAP, *tr.* by Charles Doria and Sharif Elmusa

Here Where Coltrane Is. Michael S. Harper. ESEAA; NAAL

Here, where fecundity of Babel frames. Babylon and Sion (Goa and Lisbon). Luis de Camões [*or* Camões]. AWP, *tr.* by Richard Garnett

Here where our Lord once laid his head. Upon the Holy Sepulchre. Richard Crashaw. FaBoEE

Here, where relumed by changing seasons, burn. Roy Campbell. OxBTC *Fr.* Golden Shower, The.

Here, where summer slips. Red and the Green, The. Anne Wilkinson. MoCV

Here, where the baby paddles in the gutter. Lean Street. George Sutherland Fraser. OxBS

Here, where the creek culls sand and silt. Sandbar at Moore's Creek. Judy Jordan. AmPoNex

Here, where the Danube pour its tawny waters. Hungary. Dániel Berzsenyi. IQMS, *tr.* by Watson Kirkconnell

Here where the elm trees were. Elegy. Constance Carrier. APT-2

Here where the end of bone is no end of song. Poet's Corner, The. Laura Riding Jackson. FuPo

Here, where the noises of the busy town. In the Jewish Synagogue at Newport. Emma Lazarus. TaR

Here Where the Path. Gabriella Leto. CItWP, *tr.* by Cinzia Sartini Blum and Lara Trubowitz

Here, where the red man swept the leaves away. Frederick Goddard Tuckerman. NOBA; TAP *Fr.* Sonnets.

Here, where the taut wave hangs. Life's Circumnavigators. William Robert Rodgers. GTBS-P

Here where the wind is always north-north-east. New England. Edwin Arlington Robinson. HeIP-4; MoAmPo; NAAL-2v2; NOBA; OxBA; PoPoPo; TAP

Here, where the world is quiet. Algernon Charles Swinburne. AWP; CABP; HAP; NAEL-5v2; NAEL-6v2; NOBE; NOBVV; NoP-4; OxBEV; PeVV; PoE; PoRA; SCV; TFi

Here, where Vespasian's legions struck the sands. Embarcation. Thomas Hardy. OBWP

Here with a Loaf of Bread beneath the Bough. Omar Khayyám. UV, *tr. by* Edward Fitzgerald *Fr.* Rubáiyát of Omar Khayyám [of Naishápúr], The.

Here / With my beer / I sit. Beer. George Arnold. OBAL

Here with roses in bloom, with woodbine twining the laurel. Anacreon's Grave. Goethe. STV, *tr. by* John Frederick Nims

Here with the desert so austere that only. Burial Flags. Ralph Nixon Currey. PoWW

Here X. lies dead, but God's forgiving. J. E. Thorold Rogers. FaBoEE

Here you are beside me again. Shadow. Guillaume Apollinaire. PeFWW, *tr. by* Christopher Middleton

Here you are, grand old sensualist! Rubens. Harriet Monroe. IllVoic

Here you can find joy in cloudy weather or bright, day or night. Kuan Yün-shih. SuSp, *tr. by* Richard John Lynn *Fr.* Medley of Southern and Northern Tunes—Scenic Tour of West Lake.

Here you could pass your holidays. Kyoto Garden, A. Dennis Joseph Enright. OBGa

Here you have fruits and flowers and boughs with leaves. Green. Paul Verlaine. WoPoe, *tr. by* Yvor Winters

Here! You sons of the men. Edgar Lee Masters. OxBA *Fr.* Spoon River Anthology.

Here you've got time to think. In Line at the Supermarket. Greg Pape. PBCAP

Hereafter, The. Andrew Hudgins. RA

Hereafter, shall smell of the lamp, not thee. (LL) His Farewell [*or* Fare-well] to Sack. Robert Herrick. BeJo; CaPo; NAEL-5v1; NAEL-6v1; NAEL-7v1

Heredity. Arthur Guiterman. OBAL; PeLi

Heredity. Thomas Hardy. CTC; EBEV; HarvBoo; RB

Heredity. Tony Harrison. HarvBoo; NAEL-6v2 *Fr.* School of Eloquence, The.

Heredom. Kenneth Irby. FTOS

Hereto I come to view a voiceless ghost. After a Journey. Thomas Hardy. EBEV; EnLoPo; GTBS-P; HarvBoo; NPeEn; OxAEP-2; OxBEV; OxBTC; PoE

Herezsometobaccozhere. We Got Everything We Needed Here and Aint It Something. *Unknown.* STP, *tr. by* Richard Johnny John and Jerome Rothenberg

Heriger and the False Prophet. *Unknown.* WoPoe, *tr. by* Fred Chappell *Fr.* Cambridge Songs.

Heriger the bishop of Mainz once encountered. *Unknown.* WoPoe, *tr. by* Fred Chappell *Fr.* Cambridge Songs.

Heriot's Ford. Rudyard Kipling. PoRA *Fr.* Light That Failed, The.

Heritage. Gwendolyn B. Bennett. BlSi; ColAP; NAAAL

Heritage. Countee Cullen. APT-2; BPo; ColAP; HeIP-4; MoAmPo; NAAAL; NAAL-2v2; NAAL-5; NoAM; NoP-4; PoPoPo; SSLK; TTY

Heritage. Mary Gilmore. CBAP

Heritage. Haim Gouri. HP

Heritage. Linda Hogan. UnSA

Heritage. Dorothea MacKellar. NOBAu

Heritage. Augustus Young. CIP-2

Herkeneth, lordinges, grete and smale. *Unknown.* MiEL

Herman Altman. Edgar Lee Masters. OxBA *Fr.* Spoon River Anthology.

Herman Melville. Conrad Potter Aiken. NoAM; TAP

Herman Melville. W. H. Auden. OxBA

Hermann Fegelein. W. D. Snodgrass. BodElec *Fr.* Führer Bunker, The.

Hermann, the Channel was blue-green. For Hermann Heyen. William Heyen. GotH

Hermaphrodite's Song, The. Lorna Mitchell. BrRo

Hermaphroditus, a delight, a. Ovid, Meet a Metamorphodite. Jonathan Williams. PoM

Hermes. André Marie de Chénier.

"When the Euxine goddess with astonished eyes." WoPoe, *tr. by* Paul Schmidt

Hermes came to me in a dream. I said. Sappho. BoWoP, *tr. by* Willis Barnstone

Hermes, god / of crossed sticks. Prayer to Hermes. Robert Creeley. PoM

Hermes, lord of the dead, look down and guard the fathers' power. Libation Bearers, The. Aeschylus. NAWM-5v1

Hermes of the Ways. "H. D." WPE

Hermes Trismegistus. "H. D." NALW *Fr.* Tribute to the Angels.

Hermetic Bird. Philip Lamantia. VGW

Hermetic Definition. "H. D."

Red Rose and a Beggar. PFTM-2

Hermit, The. Eloise Bibb. CBWP-4

Hermit, The. William Henry Davies. MoBrPo

Hermit and Politician. Po Chü-i. ChiP, *tr. by* Arthur Waley

Hermit and the Soul, The. Henrietta Cordelia Ray. CBWP-3

Hermit Cackleberry Brown, on Human Vanity, The. Jonathan Williams. OBAL; PoM

Hermit Feng's Residence on the Lake. Hsü Pen. CoBLCP, *tr. by* Jonathan Chaves

Hermit Has a Visitor, The. Maxine W. Kumin. BoWoP

Hermit Hoar. Samuel Johnson. NBLV

(Idyll.) NOBL; PeLV

Hermit in his cave beside the sea, The. Hermit and the Soul, The. Henrietta Cordelia Ray. CBWP-3

Hermit Li's Herb Garden Retreat at T'ung-ch'uan. Hsü Pen. CoBLCP, *tr. by* Jonathan Chaves

Hermit Marbán, The. *Unknown.* NOIV

Hermit's chapel, the pilgrim's prayer, The. (LL) T. S. Eliot. FaBoCh; NOCV; PeECV *Fr.* Landscapes.

Hermit's Song, A. *Unknown.* BIrV, *tr. by* James Simmons

Hermit with Landscape. Daniel Hall. YaYoPo

Hermitage. Donald Davidson.

Descending Chestnut Ridge. FuPo

Hermitage at Chung-nan Mountain. Wang Wei. CrYelRi, *tr. by* Sam Hamill

Hermogenes is rather short. Lucilius. GrAn

Hernando De Soto. Rosemary Benét. NBLV

Hernando's Hideaway. Jerry Ross. ReLy

Hero. Yevgeny [*or* Evgenii] Aronovich Dolmatovsky [*or* Dolmatovskii]. TCRP, *tr. by* Daniel Weissbort

Hero, The. Marianne Craig Moore. NOBA; OxBA *Fr.* Part of a Novel, Part of a Poem, Part of a Play.

Hero, The. Pablo Neruda. GifTon, *tr. by* William O'Daly

Hero, The. Siegfried Sassoon. OBWP

Hero and Leander. John Donne. NoSic; SoSe-8

Hero and Leander. Christopher Marlowe. NAEL-6v1; NAEL-7v1

"Amorous Leander, beautiful and young." CAGL

Amorous Neptune. NOBE

"And as her silver body downeward went." OxBEV

Bridal Song: "O come, soft rest of cares, come Night." NOBE; OBEV

"By this Leander being near the land." EBEV; NPeEn

Epithalamion Teratos. NoSic

"His bodie was as straight as Circes wand." NPeEn; OxBEV

Leander's Return. EBNV

Love at First Sight. NOBE

"Men of wealthy Sestos, every year, The." AEP

"New light gives new directions, Fortunes new." NoSic; PBRV

"Now from Leander's place she rose, and found." EBEV

"O Hero, Hero!" thus he cried full oft. EroLit

"O none but gods have power their love to hide." OxAEP-1

"On Hellespont, guilty of true love's blood." NoSic; PoE

"So on she goes, and in her idle flight." PoE

Hero and the Hydra, The. James McAuley.

Tomb of Heracles, The. BMAP

Hero and Thief. Kofi Anyidoho. PBMAP

Hero first thought it, The. Truth. "Æ" MoBrPo

Hero in the Land of Dough, A. Robert Clairmont. KaS

Hero is a good lad, The. He causes no anxiety. On the Tomb of the Unknown Soldier. László Mécs. IQMS, *tr. by* Watson Kirkconnell

Hero/Lil. David Meltzer.

Third Shell, The. PFTM-2

Hero of the Mirages, The. László Arany.

"Albion, teach me (and not with loud, unsubtle)." IQMS, *tr. by* John Gordon Nichols

Hero's Portion. John Montague. NOIV

Herod's Palace. Gwyneth Lewis. HarvBoo

Herod the King came sounding through. In Galilee. Jessie Mackay. SacPr

Herodes, thou wikked foe, wharof is thy dredinge? William Herebert. MiEL

Herodotus, while gossiping. Behind the Headlines. Raymond Garlick. TCAWP

Heroes. Robert Creeley. NOBA; NoP-4

Heroes. Sorley MacLean (Somhairle MacGill-Eain). FaBoTC; FaBoWar

Heroes. Kathleen Jessie Raine. FaBoWar

Heroes. Walt Whitman. SAmP *Fr.* Song of Myself.

Heroes, The. Louis Simpson. OBWP

Heroes, and Kings! your distance keep. Epitaph for One Who Would Not Be Buried in Westminster Abbey. Pope. FaBoEE; NPeEn

Héroes del Cinco de Mayo. Zaragoza Clubs.

"My heart tells me." SWaP, *tr.* by Luis A. Torres

Heroes paused upon the plain, The. Byrnies, The. Thom Gunn. NoAM; OxBTC

Heroes screamed from my fingertips. Bard. Gavin Bantock. FaBoTw

Heroic Epistle to Sir William Chambers, An. William Mason.

"There was a time, in Esher's peaceful grove." OBGa

Heroic Simile. Robert Hass. VCAP

Heroides. Ovid.

"To Paris that was once her owne though now it be not so." OBVE

Heroides: Dedicated to the Muses. Ekaterina Urusova.

"O Muses! I beseech you, fire my heart with song." ARWW, *tr.* by Catriona Kelly

Heroin. Jim Carroll. OBCoV

Heroin. Bob Hicok. AmPoNex; BAP-97

Heroine. Paul Groves. AngWePo

Heron. James King Annand. NOxBChV

Heron, The. Theodore Roethke. APT-2; OWoS

Heron, The. Vernon Watkins. AngWePo; GTBS-P; TCAWP; TwCP; UnPo

Heron in the Alyn. Gladys Mary Coles. TCAWP

Heron moonlight feathers the full air, The. Height. Rosalie Moore. APT-2

Heron stalks, The. Sunset at Twin Lake. Anita Endrezze. HATNAP

Heron-Woman. Marjorie M. Evasco. ReBoTo

Herons. Robin Blaser. NeAP

Herostratos and Herostratos. Sergey Stratanovsky. ItGoST, *tr.* by J. Kates

Herr Bruckner often wandered into church. Lives of the Great Composers. Dana Gioia. RA

Herr Direktor, ich sent Sei ein cable. Ein Complaint. Virginia Graham. OBCoV

Herrick, thou art too coarse to love. (LL) Vision, The. Robert Herrick. CaPo; CavPo; SCGP

Herring Girls, The. Iain Crichton Smith. NePenScot

Herring Girls, The. Derick Thomson. NePenScot

Herring loves the merry moonlight, The. Sir Walter Scott. FaBoCh *Fr.* Antiquary, The.

Herring Weir, The. Sir Charles G. D. Roberts. NOBC *Fr.* Songs of the Common Day.

Hers was the vacant seat by the door. Illness. David Scott. NLP

Hersilia. William Johnson Cory. NOBVV

Hervenis, harping on the hackneyed text. Sunday: A Fragment Transcribed from a Ms. in Chatterton's Handwriting. Thomas Chatterton. ECEV

He's / most definitely / (my father died meanwhile) / against parting. (LL) Against Parting. Natan Zach. HP; PoSu

Hesiod's is the theme and his the style. Callimachus. HePo *Fr.* Epigrams.

Hesiod's style and themes: the poet from Soloi. Callimachus. GrAn

Hesitate to Call. Louise Glück. LW

Hesitating Veteran, The. Ambrose Bierce. CBCWP

Hesitation. "Lu Hsün." SuSp; WoPoe, *tr.* by William R. Schultz

Hesperia. Richard Henry Wilde.

"Across the Prairie's silent waste I stray." APN-1

"Beyond Vermont's green hills, against the skies." APN-1

"Change blots out change,—their very memory dies." APN-1

"Father of Rivers! standing by thy side." APN-1

"If the romantic land whose soil I tread." APN-1

"Mount Auburn! loveliest city of the dead." APN-1

"Saint Augustine, thy praise was sung by one." APN-1

"Where dost thou lie, great Nimrod of the West!" APN-1

Hesperides, The. Burleigh Mutén. HW

Hesperos, you bring home all the bright dawn disperses. Sappho. BoWoP

Hesperus. John Clare. EBVV; GTBS-P; NOBVV

Hesperus. Star of Evening. Sappho. WoPoe, *tr.* by Paul Roche

Hesperus! the day is gone. Hesperus. John Clare. EBVV; GTBS-P; NOBVV

Hessian in his last letter home, The. Christmas. Steve Hassett. CDa

Hester. Charles Lamb. GTBS-P; OBEV

Hestia / you who have received the highest honor. *Unknown.* HW, *tr.* by Charles Boer *Fr.* Homeric Hymns.

Hetero-sex is best for the man of a serious turn of mind. Epigram. Argentarius. GrAn, *tr.* by Fleur Adcock

Heterosexual Poem. Strato [*or* Straton]. GrAn, *tr.* by Teddy Hogge

Heterosexuals can get AIDS too. Alarming New Development, An. Ron Schreiber. GLP

"Heu Quam Praecipih Mersa Profundo." Boethius. MLL, *tr.* by Helen Waddell *Fr.* Consolation of Philosophy, The ("De Consolacione Philosophie").

Heu Quam Precipiti. Boethius. OBMV, *tr.* by John Walton *Fr.* Consolation of Philosophy, The ("De Consolacione Philosophie").

Heureux Qui, Comme Ulysse, a Fait un Beau Voyage. Joachim Du Bellay. WoPoe, *tr.* by Anthony Hecht

Heureux Qui, comme Ulysse, A Fait un Beau Voyage. Joachim Du Bellay. AWP, *tr.* by Gilbert Keith Chesterton

Heven, it es a riche ture. *Unknown.* MiEL

Hewn out of faith and composite politics. Towards Springtime. Ágnes Nemes Nagy. IQMS, *tr.* by Ila Egon

Hexameters[; Paraphrase of Psalm XLVI]. Samuel Taylor Coleridge. ChIV-1

Hey, Boys! Up Go We! *Unknown.* NOBAu

Hey Cool Papa. For Cool Papa Bell. Tom Dent. ISC

Hey diddle diddle. *Unknown.* LB; OxBEV; OxNR

Hey diddle dinkety, poppety, pet. Merchants of London, The. Mother Goose. OxNR; ReMoGo

Hey diddle dout / My candle's out. *Unknown.* OxNR

Hey ding a ding. *Unknown.* OxNR

Hey, dorolot, dorolot! *Unknown.* OxNR

Hey, ey, hey, ey / Make we myrie as we may. *Unknown.* OHMEL

Hey, feller, with a million smackers. Are You Havin' Any Fun? Sammy Fain. ReLy

Hey, Hara, Ganges-Holder. Kamalākānta Bhattācārya. SinGod, *tr.* by Rachel Fell McDermott

Hey, hey, hey, hey! *Unknown.* MiEL

Hey! Ho! Hurrah! Kamatari. OHMPJ

Hey-How for Hallowe'en. Witches, The. *Unknown.* FaBoCh

Hey, it's not wine I drink. Rāmprasād Sen. SinGod, *tr.* by Rachel Fell McDermott

Hey, Johnnie Cope, are ye wauking yet. Johnnie Cope. Adam Skirving. NePenScot; OxBS

Hey let's fight that shaman, let's fight that ghost first & then that shaman. Ghost & Shaman. *Unknown.* STP, *tr.* by Franz Boas

Hey! listen to my story 'bout. Daddy. Bobby Troup. ReLy

Hey, Look Me Over. Cy Coleman. ReLy

Hey Mama, what's revolution? Bedtime Story. Nayo-Barbara Watkins. NBV

Hey, Mountain King, Gauri is sulking. Kamalākānta Bhattācārya. SinGod, *tr.* by Rachel Fell McDermott

Hey, my kitten, my kitten. My Kitten. Mother Goose. OxNR; ReMoGo

Hey Nellie / how long you been here? did you. Smokey's Getting Old. Jessica Tarahata Hagedorn. OpBo

Hey Nonny No! *Unknown.* EBEV; OBEV

(Round, A.) FaBoCh

Hey noyney! I will love our Sir John and I love eny. *Unknown.* MiEL

Hey! [*or* Hay!] now [*or* nou] the day dawis [*or* daunss]. Night Is Near [*or* Neir] Gone, The. Alexander Montgomerie. OBEV; OxBS

Hey [*or* Sing hey], diddle, diddle, / The cat and the fiddle. Mother Goose. OxBoLi; OxNR; ReMoGo

Hey Robin. Joseph Skipsey. EBVV

Hey Shabaka. Gwendolyn Brooks. ESEAA *Fr.* Winnie.

Hey, sparrow! Issa. EH, *tr.* by Robert Hass

Hey There. Jerry Ross. ReLy

Hey There, Peacock. *Hungarian Oral Tradition.* IQMS, *tr.* by Dermot Spence

Hey there poleece. Poem to a Nigger Cop. Bobb Hamilton. TTY

Hey there, taxi, do your stuff. My Cutey's Due at Two-to-Two Today. Leo Robin. ReLy

Hey there / You with the stars in your eyes. Hey There. Jerry Ross. ReLy

Hey, this little kid gets roller skates. 74th Street. Myra Cohn Livingston. SSCS

Hey! Who is She, dark as clouds. Rāmprasād Sen. SinGod, *tr.* by Rachel Fell McDermott

Hey, Willie. What are you, man? Boricua? Moreno? Que? Nigger-Reecan Blues. Willie Perdomo. InTrad

Hey, woman in the white, transparent dress. Camelia. Igor Moiseievich Irtenev. TCRP, *tr.* by Bradley Jordan

Hey . . . y! Uh . . . hm!, covered with sweat. Velemir [*or* Viktor Vladimirovich] Khlebnikov. TCRusP, *tr.* by Kathy Lewis and Bob Perelman

Hey yo I'm a savage in fake braids who races. I Bring You Greetings: How. Chrystos. WiU

Hey, you sharp little con men! Stop Fooling. Velemir [*or* Viktor Vladimirovich] Khlebnikov. TCRP, *tr.* by Gary Kern

Hey, you, *you slant-eyed, luscious brown-skinned / broad,.* Words and Thoughts. John Clark Pratt. CDa

Heye Louerd, thou here my bone. *Unknown.* MiEL

Heyl, Levedy, see-sterre bright. William Herebert. MiEL

Hezekiah. Thomas Parnell.

"From the black beach and broad expanse of sea." ChIV-1

Hezekiah's Display. John Keble. ChIV-1

Hi. William Kulik. BodElec

Hi! Walter De la Mare. NOxBChV

Hi! handsome hunting man. Hi! Walter De la Mare. NOxBChV

Hi Kali, come on in. Oh Kali. Janine Canan. HW

Hi! shoo aller birds. Bird Starver's Cry. *Unknown.* FaBoVe

Hi there. My name is George. Notes on the Peanut. June Jordan. NoAM

Hialmar Speaks to the Raven. Charles Marie René Leconte de Lisle. AWP, *tr. by* James Elroy Flecker

Hiatus. Margaret Avison. HAP

Hiawatha's Departure. Henry Wadsworth Longfellow. *Fr.* Song of Hiawatha, The.

Hiawatha's Fasting. Henry Wadsworth Longfellow. *Fr.* Song of Hiawatha, The.

Hiawatha's Photographing. Lewis Carroll. NOBL; PeLV

Hiawatha's Wooing. Henry Wadsworth Longfellow. EBNV *Fr.* Song of Hiawatha, The.

Hiawatha: The White Man's Foot. Henry Wadsworth Longfellow. NCAP *Fr.* Song of Hiawatha, The.

Hibakusha's Letter (1955), The. David Mura. OpBo

Hibernation. Maurizio Cucchi. ItPo, *tr. by* Gayle Ridinger

Hibernia. Stuart Howard-Jones. NOBL

Hibernia's Helicon is dry. William Dunkin. NOEC *Fr.* Epistle to Robert Nugent, Esq. with a Picture of Doctor Swift in Old Age, An.

Hibiscus. Su Tung-p'o (Su Shih). SuSp, *tr. by* Irving Y. Lo *Fr.* On Chao Ch'ang's Flower Paintings in Wang Po-yang's Collection.

Hibiscus Flowers. Li Shang-yin. SuSp, *tr. by* Eugene Eoyang

Hibiscus grows lushly on the grave mounds, The. Juan Chi. ColAnChi *Fr.* Songs of My Soul.

Hibiscus is flaming and frillier. Limerick. Ruth Silcock. PeLi

Hic, Hoc, the Carrion Crow. *Unknown.* OxBoLi

Hic Jacet. Rosamund Marriott Watson. ViWPN

Hic jacet Tom Shorthose. *Unknown.* FaBoEE

Hic Vir, Hic Est. Charles Stuart Calverley. OxBoLi; PeLV

Hiccups. Léon Damas. NegPo; PFTM-1, *tr. by* Ellen Conroy Kennedy

Hick-a-more, Hack-a-more. Sunshine. Mother Goose. OxNR; ReMoGo

Hickamore hackamore. Riddle. *Unknown.* FaBoVe

Hickery, dickery, 6 and 7. Counting-out Rhyme, A. *Unknown.* ReMoGo

Hickety pickety i sillickety [*or* i-silicity]. *Unknown.* OxNR

Hickety, pickety, my black hen. Black Hen, The. Mother Goose. LB; OxNR; ReMoGo

Hickie, The. Liz Lochhead. LW

Hickory, dickory, dock. Mother Goose. LB; OxNR; ReMoGo

Hid by the august foliage and fruit of the grape vine. To a Chameleon. Marianne Craig Moore. APT-1

"Hid! Hid!" the fish-hawk saith. Ezra Pound. APSN

Hid in a close and lowly nook. City Garden, A. William Stanley Braithwaite. GT

Hidden. Ron Silliman.
"Lucky my ears 'pop' at the hilltop." FTOS

Hidden among the roots. Otsuin. JDP, *tr. by* Yoel Hoffmann

Hidden behind a rustic gate. To My Cousin, Ching-yuan, Twelfth Month, 403. T'ao Ch'ien [*or* T'ao Yuan-ming]. CrYelRi, *tr. by* Sam Hamill

Hidden by a minstrel-smile. (LL) Heritage. Gwendolyn B. Bennett. BlSi; ColAP; NAAAL

Hidden dragons entice with their mysterious forms. Climbing the Tower by the Pond. Hsieh Ling-yün. SuSp, *tr. by* Francis Westbrook

Hidden Essence. Henrietta Cordelia Ray. CBWP-3

Hidden Flame. Dryden. *See* Secret Love; or, The Maiden Queen

Hidden immortal. Near a Waterfall at Ryumon. Lady Ise. BoWoP, *tr. by* Etsuko Terasaki

Hidden in a mother-of-pearl drawer. Legend. Anne Ethuin. SurWo, *tr. by* Guy Ducornet

Hidden in hidden rooms. Hide and Seek. Mudrooroo Narogin. BMAP

Hidden in my trousers, winter lice have all been wiped out. Recuperating in Chang Villa. Huang Tsun-hsien. SuSp, *tr. by* Irving Y. Lo

Hidden in the clouds. Oyake. ArkPo, *tr. by* Edwin A. Cranston

Hidden-in-winter. *Unknown.* ArkPo, *tr. by* Edwin A. Cranston

Hidden in wonder and snow, or sudden with summer. Laurentian Shield. Francis Reginald Scott. NOBC

Hidden language, not that of hands or eyes, a language beyond gesture. Desert, The. Edmond Jabès. AF, *tr. by* Rosmarie Waldrop

Hidden lovers' woes. His Own True Wife. Wolfram von Eschenbach. AWP, *tr. by* Jethro Bithell

Hidden Meaning. Susan Musgrave. NIL-7

Hidden Name. Victor Segalen. BBASP, *tr. by* Nathaniel Tarn

Hidden, oh hidden. Song for the Rainy Season. Elizabeth Bishop. APT-2

Hidden People and the Star People, The. *Unknown.* STP, *tr. by* Barbara Tedlock *Fr.* Ceremony of Sending.

Hidden Pleasure. Fanny Carrión de Fierro. TANSG, *tr. by* Sally Cheney Bell

Hide, Absalom, thy gilte tresses clear. Geoffrey Chaucer. WoPoe, *tr. by* Burton Raffel and Selden Rodman *Fr.* Legend of Good Women, The.

Hide and Seek. Robert Graves. KaS; NTCP

Hide and Seek. Mudrooroo Narogin. BMAP

Hide and Seek. Vernon Scannell. NOxBChV

Hide not thy talent in the earth. One Talent, The. William Cutler. PWR

Hide of My Mother, The. Edward Dorn. NeAP

Hide of the black cow is stretched, The. Jean-Joseph Rabéarivelo [*or* Rebéarivelo]. PBMAP *Fr.* Traduits de la Nuit.

Hide [*or* Hyd], Absalon, thy gilte tresses clere. Geoffrey Chaucer. AWP; EBEV; HAP; NOBE; OBEV; SCGP *Fr.* Legend of Good Women, The.

Hide this one night thy crescent, kindly Moon. To the Moon. Pierre de Ronsard. AWP, *tr. by* Andrew Lang

Hide your daughters, lock your doors! (LL) We Are Americans Now, We Live in the Tundra. Marilyn Chin. FSt; NIL-7; OPRER; UnSA

Hideho Heights. Melvin B. Tolson. APT-2; PFTM-1 *Fr.* Harlem Gallery.

Hideous hue which William is, The. Purple William or The Liar's Doom. A. E. Housman. NOxBChV

Hideous laughter, The. Because the Wind Remembers. Frank Mkalawile Chipasula. HBAPE

Hidesong. Aig Higo. PBMAP; TTY

Hiding. Dorothy Aldis. ChAP

Hiding in the. Vidya. EaWin; WPOW, *tr. by* J. Moussaieff Masson and W. S. Merwin

Hiding in the church of an abandoned stone. Confession to J. Edgar Hoover. James Wright (1927–80). CoAmPo

Hiding Place. Richard Armour. NIL-7; NIP-4

Hiding under the hill. Garden, The. Harriet Monroe. IllVoic

Hie Away, Hie Away. Sir Walter Scott. OxAEP-2 *Fr.* Waverley.

Hie, hie, says Anthony. Mother Goose. OxNR

Hie prudence, and wirking mervelous, the. Preiching of the Swallow, The. Robert Henryson. OxBS

Hie to the market, Jenny come trot. *Unknown.* OxNR

Hie upon Hielands [*or* High up on highland *or* High upon Highlands]. Bonnie [*or* Bonny] George [*or* James] Campbell. *Unknown.* OxBB; OxBoLi; SCGP

Hiems. William Shakespeare. *See* Love's Labour's Lost

Hiero's former Nurse. (*fl.* 1st cent. B.C. *or* A.D. 1st cent.) Dioscorides. GrAn

Hierofant. Oswald de Andrade. TCLAP, *tr. by* Flavia Vidal

Hieronymus Bosch. Pavel Grigoryevich Antokolsky. TCRP, *tr. by* Bernard Meares

Hierusalem, my happy [*or* happie] home. Hierusalem. *Unknown.* NOBE; PeECV; SCGP; SacPr; TOF

(New Jerusalem, The.) OBEV

Higashiyama Crematorium, November 6, 1983. Lynne Yamaguchi Fletcher. FSt

Higgledy-piggledy. Emily Dickinson. Wendy Cope. NIL-7

Higgledy-piggledy / Andrea Doria. Last Words. John Hollander. OBAL

Higgledy-piggledy / Anna Karenina. Russian Soul II, The. John Hollander. NBLV

Higgledy-piggledy / Archangel Raphael. Paradise Lost, Book V: An Epitome. Anthony Hecht. NBLV

Higgledy-piggledy, / Benjamin Harrison. Historical Reflections. John Hollander. OBAL; OBCoV

Higgledy-piggledy / Franklin D. Roosevelt. Danish Wit. John Hollander. NBLV

Higgledy, piggledy / Gloria Vanderbilt. Poor Kid. William Cole. OBAL

Higgledy-piggledy / Heliogabalus. Heliogabalus. John Hollander. NBLV; OBAL

Higgledy-Piggledy here we lie. Charade. *Unknown.* OxNR

Higgledy-piggledy / John Simon Guggenheim. No Foundation. John Hollander. OBAL; OBCoV

Higgledy-piggledy / Josephine Bonaparte. Appearance and Reality. John Hollander. OBAL

Higgledy-piggledy / Ludwig van Beethoven. Double Dactyls. E. William Seaman. OBCoV; WeW-3

Higgledy-piggledy / Mme. de Maintenon. Firmness. Anthony Hecht. OBAL

Higgledy, piggledy, my black hen. Hickety, pickety, my black hen. Mother Goose. OxNR

Higgledy-piggledy / President Jefferson. Twilight's Last Gleaming. Arthur W. Monks. NIP-4

Higgledy-piggledy / Ralph Waldo Emerson. From the Grove Press. Anthony Hecht. OBAL; OBCoV

Higgledy-piggledy / Thomas Stearns Eliot. Vice. Anthony Hecht. OBAL

Higgledy-Piggledy / Thomas Stearns Eliot. Double Dactyl. Chris Wallace-Crabbe. OBCoV

Higglety, Pigglety, Pop! Samuel Griswold Goodrich. NOxBChV; OxNR

High above the lake a bomber flies. This Summer's Sky. Bertolt Brecht. PoSu, *tr. by* Michael Hamburger

High above you some fool. In the Aviary. Gerald Costanzo. UrbNat

High Adventure. A. W. Spalding. ITBLP

High and solemn mountains guard Rioupéroux. Rioupéroux. James Elroy Flecker. OBEV

High as a star, yet lowly as a flower. Beauty. Madison Cawein. APN-2

High as the sky it flies. Riddle. *Unknown.* FaBoVe

High at the window in her cage. Caged Bird, A. Sarah Orne Jewett. APN-2; ColAP

High autumn days. Sad Birds, The. Harry Mathews. PmAP

High bare field, brown from the plough, and borne, A. Potato Harvest, The. Sir Charles G. D. Roberts. NIL-7; NOBC

High-born Helen, round your dwelling. Helen. Mary Lamb. NOBRP

High Bridge above the Tagus River at Toledo, The. William Carlos Williams. CTC

High-Class Bananas, The. Gary Gildner. PBCAP

High Cliffs lashed by icy polar winds. Aleutian Islands. Blaise Cendrars. BLT, *tr. by* Monique Chefdor

High-coiffed the muse in green brocade. Remark. Charles Spear. PeNZ

High Country. Tim Thorne. BMAP

High Diddle Diddle. Mother Goose. OxBoLi; OxNR; NPeEn; ReMoGo

High diddle doubt, my candle's out. My Little Maid. *Unknown.* ReMoGo

High dome, The. Seamen's Mission. Gerald Dawe. PNI

High Embrace, The. William Everson. GeoHom

High Flight. John Gillespie, Jr. Magee. ITBLP; PoWW

High Germany. Edward Richard Burton Shanks. OBMV

High hard one—up, the. Chin Music. Alan Soldofsky. MoASP

High-hearted Surrey! I do love your ways. Salutation, A. Louise Imogen Guiney. APN-2

High heels fought a battle with long skirts. Without Guile. Paul Verlaine. SxFrPo, *tr. by* Martin Sorrell

High-heels were struggling with a full-length dress. Young Fools, The. Paul Verlaine. WoPoe, *tr. by* Louis Simpson

High Hills, The. Ivor Gurney. NPeEn

High, hollowed in green. Quest, The. Denise Levertov. LW

High Holy Days. Jane Shore. NoP-4

High in the air exposed the slave is hung. Robert Southey. CenSon

High in the darkening heavens. Harriet Tubman aka Moses. Samuel Allen. ISC

High in the esteem of He. Hind and Her Mother. "Al-Akhtal al-Saghir." MAP, *tr. by* Issa Boullata and Thomas G. Ezzy

High in the mountain mist, a world apart. English, The. Sándor Sík. IQMS, *tr. by* James Turner

High in the mountains. Magic City Monastery. Wang Yang-ming. CrYelRi, *tr. by* Sam Hamill

High in the woodland, on the mountain-side. Ant-Heap, The. Arthur Christopher Benson. EBVV

High in their other heaven, pardon love. (LL) To a Nun. John Ormond. EBEV; FaBoTw; NoP-4

High is the dark clouds. Caught in the Swamp. Joseph Ceravolo. BodElec

High Island. Richard Murphy. CIP-2; NOIV

High King of Glory permit her to get the mange, The. (LL) Glass of Beer, A. James Stephens. InPK-6; NBLV; OBCoV; OBMV; OxBEV; OxBS; OxBTC; RB

High King, wilt hear me plead? He Intercedes with Charlemagne for His Brother in Exile. Paul the Deacon. MLL, *tr. by* Helen Waddell

High-loping Cowboy, The. Curley W. Fletcher. AiP

High Midnight was garlanding her head, The. Moonlight. Jacques Tahureau. AWP, *tr. by* Andrew Lang

High Modes: Vision as Ritual: Confirmation. Michael S. Harper. NBV

High mountain, A. Poem on Dry Mountain (A Zen Garden). Muso Soseki. EaWin, *tr. by* W. S. Merwin

High mountains, a million feet, skyward. Sailing Back to the Capital. Chan Fang-sheng. ChinPo, *tr. by* Yip Wai-lim

High Noon at Los Alamos. Eleanor Wilner. NoP-4

High noon in Daghestan; a lonely valley. Dream. Mikhail Yuryevich Lermontov. WoPoe, *tr. by* W. K. Matthews

High o'er his moldering castle walls. Voice from the Invisible World, A. Goethe. AWP, *tr. by* James Clarence Mangan

High o'er the Hills. William Walker. AH

High on a gorgeous seat, that far out-shone. Pope. *Fr.* Dunciad, The.

High on a rock, coeval with the skies. Temple of Chastity, The. Mary Robinson. CenSon; RWP

High on a Throne of Royal State, which far. John Milton. FHYEP; NAEL-5v1; NAEL-6v1; NIL-7; NIP-4; OxAEP-1 *Fr.* Paradise Lost.

High on his figured couch beyond the waves. Theseus and Ariadne. Robert Graves. HAP

High on his stockroom ladder like a dunce. Playboy. Richard Wilbur. NOBA; NoAM

High on the Mount of Rama a yaksha dwelt, who for. Kalidasa. WoPoe, *tr. by* Franklin Edgerton and Eleanor Edgerton *Fr.* Cloud Messenger, The.

High on the mountain of sunrise where standeth the Temple of Sebek. *Unknown.* AWP *Fr.* Book of the Dead.

High on tree-tips, the hibiscus. Hsin-I Village. Wang Wei. ChinPo, *tr. by* Yip Wai-lim

High overhead. Thomas Edward Brown. NOBVV

High pink wall; plaster in map shapes peeling, A. Blue Arm. Bernard Spencer. NoAM

High poets are gone, The. For the Family of Cuchonnacht O Dalaigh. David [*or* Daibhi][*or* Daithi] O'Bruadair [*or* Ó Bruadair]. NOIV, *tr. by* Thomas Kinsella

High Priest, The. *Unknown.* TrJP, *tr. by* Arthur Davis

High Priests of telescopes and cyclotrons, The. Ode to Terminus. W. H. Auden. HAP

High propositions of barrenness. Creation. Eunice Odio. TCLAP, *tr. by* Martha Collins

High Renaissance. George Starbuck. NBLV; OBAL

High Resolve. *Unknown.* PoToHe

High Seas on the Caspian. Boris Petrovich Kornilov. TCRP, *tr. by* Bernard Meares

High sheriff tol' de deputy, "Go out an' bring me Laz'us." Poor Lazarus. *Unknown.* NAAAL

High Skip, The. *Unknown.* LB

High Speed. Debra Gregerman. AmPoNex

High-speed metal snake switches its tail, A. Chief of the West, Darkling, The. David Knight. MoCV

High-spirited friend / I send not balms, nor corsives to your wound. Ode, An. Ben Jonson. BeJo

High stretched upon the swinging yard. Disguises. Thomas Edward Brown. SacPr

High Summer. Ebenezer Jones. NOBVV

High Summer on the Mountains. Idris Davies. OxBTC

High summer's sheen upon all things. Web, The. Theodore Weiss. CoAP

High Talk. W. B. Yeats. FaBoVe; RaBo

High tensile wire, when strained. Fencing. Anthony Lawrence. NOBAu

High the Mount of Wu. Li Ho. ChinPo, *tr. by* Yip Wai-lim

High the vanes of Shrewsbury gleam. Welsh Marches, The. A. E. Housman. FaBoTw; SCGP

High tide. William J. Higginson. HA

High Tide. Jean Starr Untermeyer. MoAmPo

High Tide at Gettysburg, The. Will Henry Thompson. CBCWP

High Tide on the Coast of Lincolnshire, 1571, The. Jean Ingelow. EBVV; OxAEP-2

High time now gan it wex for Una faire. Edmund Spenser. FHYEP *Fr.* Faerie Queene, The.

High to Low. Langston Hughes. APT-2; HCAP; PoPoPo

High-Toned Old Christian Woman, A. Wallace Stevens. NAAL-2v2; NAAL-5; NOBA; NoAM; TAP

High Treason. José Emilio Pacheco. TCLAP, *tr. by* Alastair Reid

High up among the mountains, through a lovely grove of cedars. Bears. Arthur Guiterman. PoRA

High up here I live. My Room. Marceline Desbordes-Valmore. WoPoe, *tr. by* Edmund Charles Blunden

High up on a snowy peak. Ivan Alekseievich Bunin. TCRP

High up there she saw what. Stuff. Linda Gregg. ExTi

High Water Everywhere. Charlie Patton. APT-1

High Way to the Spital House, The. Robert Copland. "To write of Sol in his exaltation." NoSic

High wind, cold moon. Shokaku. ZenPo, *tr. by* Takashi Ikemoto and Lucien Stryk

High wind . . . They turn their backs to it, and push. Glasgow Schoolboys, Running Backwards. Douglas Dunn. OxBC

High Windows. Philip Larkin. FaBoMo; HarvBoo; NAEL-5v2; NAEL-6v2; NoAM; PoPoPo; PoetW

High Wood. Philip Johnstone. FaBoWar

High / yellow / black / girl. To Anita. Sonia Sanchez. ISC

High-yellow of my heart, with breasts like tangerines. Peasant Declares His Love, The. Emile Roumer. NegPo; TTY, *tr. by* John Peale Bishop

Higher Argument. John Milton. NOSC *Fr.* Paradise Lost.

Higher Pantheism, The. Tennyson. CABP; InvLi

Higher Pantheism in a Nutshell, The. Algernon Charles Swinburne. CABP; PeVV *Fr.* Heptalogia, The.

Higher than a house / Higher than a tree. Mother Goose. OxNR; ReMoGo

Highest Bidder, The. Witter Bynner. TCAPo

Highest Divinity. *Unknown.* TrJP, *tr. by* Israel Zangwill

Highest of Immortals bright. *Unknown.* AWP *Fr.* Vedic Hymns.

Highest Sickness, The. Boris Leonidovich Pasternak. TCRP

Highest things are easiest to be shown, The. Demonstration, The. Thomas Traherne. BASC

Highland Glen near Loch Ericht, A.   Arthur Hugh Clough.   FaBoVe   *Fr.* Bothie of Tober-na-Vuolich, The [A Long-Vacation Pastoral].

Highland Harry Back Again.   Robert Burns.   EBEV

Highland Mary.   Robert Burns.   AWP; GTBS-P; OBEV

Highland Mary.   Mary Weston Fordham.   CBWP-2

Highland, 1955.   Kevin Fitzpatrick.   MiVo

Highland Poor, The.   Anne Grant.   RWP   *Fr.* Highlanders, The.

Highland Woman, A.   Sorley MacLean (Somhairle MacGill-Eain).   HarvBoo; NePenScot

Highlanders, The.   Anne Grant.
Part 2.
Highland Poor, The.   RWP

Highlandmen hae a' come down, The.   Lady of Arngosk, The.   *Unknown.* ESPB

Highly bored damsel called Brown, A.   Limerick.   *Unknown.*   PeLi

Highmindedness, a jealousy for good.   Addressed to Haydon.   John Keats. CenSon

Highty, tighty, paradighty, clothed [all] in green.   Riddle.   *Unknown.*   OxNR

Highway, The.   Sir Philip Sidney.   *See* Astrophil and Stella

Highway I was walking on, The.   Charles Reznikoff.   FTOS   *Fr.* By the Well of Living and Seeing.

Highway is full of big cars, The.   Come, and Be My Baby.   Maya Angelou. OPOU

Highway is narrow, the curves dangerous, The.   Passing Piedras Blancas. Abigail Albrecht.   GeoHom

Highway Poems.   Lisel Mueller.   IllVoic

Highway, since you my chief Parnassus be.   Sir Philip Sidney.   SCGP   *Fr.* Astrophil and Stella.

Highway 6.   Timothy Liu.   AmPoNex

Highwayman, The.   Alfred Noyes.   BRP; ChAP; EBNV; ITBLP; NOxBChV; OBNV; OBSP

Highwayman, The.   *Unknown.*   ECEV

Hike on the Downs, A.   Sir John Betjeman.   OBCoV

Hiking.   Joseph Bruchac.   CDW

Hiking a levee through the salt marsh.   Wings and Seeds.   Sandra McPherson. LoL

Hilaire Belloc.   Humbert Wolfe.   FaBoEE

Hilbert's Program.   Milo De Angelis.   NeIt, *tr. by* Lawrence Venuti

Hildegund eagerly urged him.   Waldere 1.   *Unknown.*   ASW, *tr. by* Kevin Crossley-Holland

Hill, A.   Anthony Hecht.   CoAP; NIL-7; NoP-4; VCAP

Hill, The.   Rupert Brooke.   MoBrPo; OxBSo; OxBTC; Son

Hill, The.   Robert Creeley.   CRP; RaBo; TRP
(It is sometime since I have been.)   CoAmPo

Hill, The.   Edgar Lee Masters.   ColAP; IllVoic; NOBA; NoAM; OxBA; TAP *Fr.* Spoon River Anthology.

Hill beside the wood had dressed in green, The.   After the Battle.   Anton Malczewski.   WoPoe, *tr. by* Jerzy Peterkiewicz and Burns Singer

Hill-billy, hill-billy come to buy.   Confucius.   CTC; OBVE, *tr. by* Ezra Pound *Fr.* Wei Wind.

Hill Farmer Speaks, The.   Ronald Stuart Thomas.   GTBS-P; OBWVE

Hill Field, The.   Donald Davie.   NPeEn

Hill Figures.   Maggie O'Sullivan.   Oth

Hill Fort, Caerleon.   Sam Adams.   AngWePo

Hill full, a hole full, A.   Mist, The.   *Unknown.*   ReMoGo

Hill of the Graces, The.   Edmund Spenser.   NOBE   *Fr.* Faerie Queene, The.

Hill of Truth, The.   John Donne.   OBSV   *Fr.* Satires.

Hill-Shade, The.   William Barnes.   OxBEV

Hill-Side Park, The.   William Henry Davies.   OBGa

Hill Songs of Saint Orm, The.   B. P. Nichol.   PFTM-2   *Fr.* Martyrology 7, The.

Hill Wife, The.   Robert Frost.   HAP; NoP-4; RACG
House Fear.   VGW
Impulse, The.   RaBo; TCAPo
Loneliness.   VGW
Oft-Repeated Dream, The.   TCAPo

Hillcrest.   Edwin Arlington Robinson.   APT-1; OxBA

Hills, The.   Frances Darwin Cornford.   MoBrPo

Hills, The.   D. H. Lawrence.   ChIV-1

Hills, The.   John Wills.   HA

Hills afloat across the water are.   Lamentation on Ninety-Mile Beach.   Barry Mitcalfe.   PeNZ

Hills all glowed with a festive light, The.   Illuminated City, The.   Felicia Dorothea Hemans.   RWP

Hills and leafless forests slowly yield, The.   In November.   Archibald Lampman.   NIL-7

Hills and rivers of the lowland country, The.   Protest in the Sixth Year of Ch'ien Fu, A.   Ts'ao Sung.   ChiP, *tr. by* Arthur Waley

Hills are white, but not with snow, The.   Orchard at Avignon, An.   Agnes Mary Frances Robinson.   NOBVV

Hills are white with snow, The.   Lament.   Cho Wen-chun.   CrYelRi, *tr. by* Sam Hamill

Hills fled from our sight; but left his golden load. (LL)   To Autumn.   William Blake.   NAEL-5v2; NAEL-6v2

Hills hunch their backs, The.   Fistful of News, A.   Antoine-Roger Bolamba. PBMAP

Hills in emerald robes of richest dye, The.   Among the Berkshire Hills. Henrietta Cordelia Ray.   CBWP-3

Hills like burnt pages, The.   Or anything resembling it.   Michael Palmer. BodElec

Hills moved. I watched their shadows.   Beetle on the Shasta Daylight.   Shirley Kaufman.   WPE

Hills of God, Break Forth in Singing.   John Wright Buckham.   AH

Hills of Salt.   Dahlia Ravikovitch [*or* Ravikovich].   WPOW, *tr. by* Chana Bloch

Hills picking up the / moonlight like.   Nina Cassian.   BoWoP

Hills sink to plains, and man returns to dust.   Philip Freneau.   TCAPo   *Fr.* House of Night, The.

Hills slide eastward into the desert, The.   Mount of Olives, The.   Shirley Kaufman.   DTA

Hills step off into whiteness, The.   Sheep in Fog.   Sylvia Plath.   FaBoWP; HCAP; LCAP-2; NPeEn

Hills stirring under their woven, The.   Goethe's Blues.   Denise Levertov. FaBoWP

Hills, the bridge, the country, the squeaking wheelbarrow, The.   Bobbin Stops, The.   István Sinka.   IQMS, *tr. by* Adam Makkai

Hills turn hugely in their sleep, The.   Robert Silliman Hillyer.   MoAmPo   *Fr.* Prothalamion.

Hills were lush, The.   Monterey.   David Schubert.   APT-2

Hillside Thaw, A.   Robert Frost.   AmFaPo

Hilly Pavlovsk still I can see before me.   Pavlovsk.   Anna Andreyevna Akhmatova.   RusPo, *tr. by* Robert Arthur Douglas Ford

Hilo: First Night Back.   Garrett Kaoru Hongo.   LoL

Him, His Place.   Liam Rector.   BodElec

Him I'm thinking of.   *Unknown.*   ChinPo, *tr. by* Yip Wai-lim

Him, on the Bicycle.   Bruce Weigl.   CDa

Him strong Genius urged to roam.   Ralph Waldo Emerson.   TCAPo   *Fr.* Life.

Him that I love I wish to be.   Even.   Anne Morrow Lindbergh.   AiP

Him the way we leave a porchlight on.   She Wants.   David Baratier. AmPoNex

Himalayan Balsam.   Anne Stevenson.   FaBoWP; OxAEP-2

Himself.   Edwin John Ellis.
"At Golgotha I stood alone."   OBMV

Himself.   Peter Fallon.   PBCIP

Himself it was who wrote.   Ralph Waldo Emerson.   APN-1

Hind and Her Mother.   "Al-Akhtal al-Saghir."   MAP, *tr. by* Issa Boullata and Thomas G. Ezzy

Hind and the Panther, The.   Dryden.
Churches of Rome and of England, The.   UV
(Confessio Fidei.)   NOBE
"Portly prince, and goodly to the sight, A."   OBSV
Presbyterians, The.   NOSC

Hind Etin.   *Unknown.*   ESPB; OxBB

Hind Horn.   *Unknown.*   ESPB

Hindoo: He Doesn't Hurt a Fly or a Spider Either, The.   A. K. Ramanujan. OxBC

Hindu to His Body, A.   A. K. Ramanujan.   PoetW

Hinge of the year, The.   Nicholas Virgilio.   HA

Hinglish.   Gerald Stern.   BodElec

Hinny / by / stallion, An.   Louis Zukofsky.   APSN   *Fr.* A.

Hint for the Incomplete Angler.   Kendrick Smithyman.   PeNZ

Hint from Voiture.   William Shenstone.   EnLoPo

Hinted Wish, A.   Martial.   AWP, *tr. by* Francis Lewis

Hinterland.   Margaret Stanley-Wrench.   OBGa

Hints.   Giancarlo Majorino.   ItPo, *tr. by* Gayle Ridinger

Hints at Distance.   Michael Portnoy.   HeMarv

Hinx! minx! / The old witch winks!   *Unknown.*   OxNR

Hip Hop Bop.   Jabari Asim.   InTrad

Hippo, The.   Theodore Roethke.   VGW

Hippodramania; or, Whiffs from the Pipe.   Adam Lindsay Gordon.
"Rest, and be thankful! On the verge."   CBAP

Hippolytus.   Euripides.
"No more, O my spirit."   AWP
O for the Wings of a Dove.   AWP, *tr. by* Gilbert Murray

Hippolytus Temporizes.   "H. D."   APT-1; HarvBoo; RACG

Hipponax.   Alcaeus [*or* Alkaios].   GrAn, *tr. by* Alistair Elliot

Hippopotamus. Joanna Cole. NTCP

Hippopotamus, The. Joseph Hilaire Pierre Belloc. InPK-6

Hippopotamus, The. T. S. Eliot. AWP; NAEL-5v2; NAEL-6v2; OBMV; PAI; SacPr; TCAPo; VGW

Hippopotamus is strong, The. Habits of the Hippopotamus. Arthur Guiterman. OBCA; OxIBACP

Hiraeth. *Unknown.* OBWVE, *tr.* by Aneirin Talfan Davies

Hiraeth in N.W.3. Wynford Vaughan-Thomas. NOBL

Hiram Helsel. Julia A. Moore. VerBaPo

"Hiram, I think the sump is backing up." Mending Sump. Kenneth Koch. InPK-6; NeAP; NoAM

Hiram Powers'"Greek Slave." Elizabeth Barrett Browning. GS; NALW; ViWPN

Hired Hand. David Lee. GifTon

Hired Man's Way, The. John Kendrick Bangs. OBCA

Hireling's wages to the priest are paid, A. Poet vs. Parson. Ebenezer Elliott. Son

Hirmophrodite in sense in Art a monster. Railing Rimes Returned upon the Author by Mistress Mary Wrothe. Mary Sidney Wroth, Countess of Montgomery. EMWP

Hiroshima. "Agyeya." OMIP; WoPoe, *tr.* by Agyeya and Leonard Nathan

Hirsute hell chimney-spouts, black thunderthroes. To My First White Hairs. Wole Soyinka. OPOU

His absence is the knife that cuts your throat? Abu Sa'id Abul Khayr. WoPoe, *tr.* by Dick Davis *Fr.* Four Poems on Death.

His acre. His arbour. Alan Halsey. Oth *Fr.* Robin Hood Book, A.

His Age, Dedicated to His Peculiar Friend, Master John Wickes, under the Name of Posthumus. Robert Herrick. CaPo

His all the mercy and the power. (LL) Herman Melville. APN-2; ChIV-1 *Fr.* Moby Dick.

His anchor, seaweed-probing, boat-securing. Philip of Thessalonica. GrAn

His Answer. Clara Ann Thompson. BlSi; CBWP-2

His Anthem, to Christ on the Cross. Robert Herrick. CavPo

His arm grew heavy on me as he slept, the oaks' California Poem. Chryss Yost. GeoHom

His art is eccentricity, his aim. Pitcher, The. Robert Francis. MoASP; OxBSP; RaBo; WeW-3

His artificial feet calumped in holy rhythm. Deacon Morgan. Naomi Long Madgett. BlSi

His attractive face a bit pale. In the Street. Constantine P. Cavafy. CAGL, *tr.* by Edmund Keeley and Philip Sherrard

His baby cry. Birth of Shaka, The. Mbuyiseni Oswald Mtshali. PBMAP

His back and clavicles are draped. Antonio Banderas in His Underwear. Regie Cabico. WiU

His ball, beautiful leaved, and his noisy boxwood rattle. Leonidas of Tarentum. HePo *Fr.* Epigrams.

His balls: It sure was pleasant to spend a day in the country. (LL) Farm Implements and Rutabagas in a Landscape. John Ashbery. CoAP; HarvBoo; PmAP

His Banquets Cure Most Ills. Al-Lajjam al-Harrani. ArPe, *tr.* by Omar S. Pound

His bare feet warmed by the thick black dust. Shelly Beach. Christopher Koch. NOBAu

His bed is like his death. Genesis. Buland Al-Haidari [or Al-Haydari]. MAP, *tr.* by Patricia Alanah Byrne and Salma Khadra Jayyusi

His being gone is a gift to my people. Wulf and Eadwacer. *Unknown.* BoWoP, *tr.* by Willis Barnstone and Elene Kolb

His Being Was in Her Alone. Sir Philip Sidney. PAI

His best / were the two. My Father's Fights. Stuart Dybek. PBCAP

His bicycle stood at the window-sill. Seamus Heaney. EmeKit; NOIV *Fr.* Singing School.

His blood is on us. In Memory of Izziddin al-Qalaq. Ahmad Dahbur. MAP, *tr.* by Charles Doria and Lena Jayyusi

His blood's sweet current much more loud to be. (LL) Church-Lock and Key. George Herbert. ESCV; GeHe; OxBSP

His blood will not be traced while I live. (LL) Hallaig. Sorley MacLean (Somhairle MacGill-Eain). HarvBoo; NPeEn; NePenScot; WoPoe

His bodie was as straight as Circes wand. Christopher Marlowe. NPeEn; OxBEV *Fr.* Hero and Leander.

His Body. Sandra McPherson. LoL

His body: A perfect shock absorber. (LL) Passage. Billy Marshall-Stoneking. BMAP; NOBAu

His body doubled. On the Swag. Ronald Allison Kells Mason. PeNZ; SacPr

His Body Books. Robert Southey. *See* Scholar, The

His bride to the fair island. (LL) Enchanted Island, The. Letitia [or Laetitia] Elizabeth Landon. CABP; NOBRP

His cauldrons seethe. This Man. G. S. Shivarudrappa. OMIP, *tr.* by A. K. Ramanujan

His Cavalier. Robert Herrick. CaPo

His changing eyes. (LL) Cat and the Moon, The. W. B. Yeats. FaBoCh; HarvBoo; TTTS; WHSW

His Children. Hittan of Tayyi. AWP *Fr.* Hamasah.

His children tuckered out, tucked in (three girls). Frost at Midnight. Mary Jo Salter. RA

His clumsy body is a golden fruit. Deaf-Mute in the Pear Tree. Patricia K. Page. NoAM; NoP-4; PoE

His collar is frayed, and his trousers unpressed. Shabby Old Dad. Anne Campbell. PoToHe

His compassionate face, slightly wan. On the Street. Constantine P. Cavafy. BoLoP, *tr.* by Rae Dalven

His Confession. *Unknown.* NAWM-7v1, *tr.* by Helen Waddell

His conscience may remain unriven. (LL) To His Importunate Mistress. Peter De Vries. NBLV; NIL-7; NIP-4

His Content in the Country. Robert Herrick. CaPo; CavPo

His corpse below. (LL) Spirit of Plato. *Unknown.* AWP; OBVE

His corpse owre a' the city lies. Dead Liebknecht, The. Hugh MacDiarmid. OBVE

His corpse was returned. Captain James Leson, U. S. M. C. Bryan Alec Floyd. CDa

His Costume. Sharon Olds. BAP-01

His Creed. Robert Herrick. BeJo

His cycle kerbed, the peeler found. Roy McFadden. PNI *Fr.* Memories of Chinatown.

His daughter Charlotte said to Mr. Brontë. Sampler from Haworth. Frances Minturn Howard. WPE

His Dawn Vision. Seamus Heaney. PoetW

His day was not really complete until. Letters from Baron Von Hügel to a Niece. David Scott. NLP

His Defence against the Idle Critic. Michael Drayton. NOSC

His Desire. Robert Herrick. OxBSP

His dinner on the stove, Grandpa smirked at our jar. Leftover Blessings. Julia Kasdorf. PBCAP

His Discourse with Cupid. Ben Jonson. NAEL-6v1 *Fr.* Celebration of Charis in Ten Lyric[k] Pieces [or Peeces], A.

His eight children and their mother. Death of the Shoemaker, The. Ahmad Dahbur. MAP, *tr.* by Charles Doria and Lena Jayyusi

His endless look. (LL) This Lunar Beauty. W. H. Auden. MoBrPo; NPeEn; OBMV; OxBTC; RB

His establishing most broad and pervasive! (LL) Journey North. Tu Fu. ColAnChi; SuSp, *tr.* by Hugh M. Stimson

His Excuse for Loving. Ben Jonson. NAEL-6v1; NAEL-7v1; NOSC *Fr.* Celebration of Charis in Ten Lyric[k] Pieces [or Peeces], A.

His Eye Is on the Sparrow. C. D. Martin. TCAPo

His eyes are green and his nose is brown. King of the Hobbledygoblins, The. Laura Elizabeth Richards. OBCA

His eyes are mournful, but the long lined palm. Creatures in the Zoo. Babette Deutsch. APT-2

His eyes are quickened so with grief. Lost Love. Robert Graves. AWP; FaBoCh; MoBrPo

His eyes burned shrewdly as emerging stars. (LL) Star Watcher, The. Peter Davison. TwCP; YaYoPo

His eyes he opened, shut, again unclosed. Byron. EBNV *Fr.* Don Juan.

His eyes were so distant. Georg Trakl. Else Lasker-Schüler. PFTM-1

His face is streaked with prepared tears. Clown, The. Janet Frame. PeNZ

His face is trodden deeper in the mud. (LL) Glory of Women. Siegfried Sassoon. FaBoWar; NAEL-5v2; NAEL-6v2; NoP-4; OBWP; OxAEP-2; OxBSo; PeFWW

His face severe in clouds above the waters of childhood. Remembering My Father. Zbigniew Herbert. VCWP, *tr.* by John Carpenter

His fame stole his real name. 'Abd-Allah Al-Baraduni. MAP *Fr.* Rose from al-Mutanabbi's Blood, A.

His family roots are in the mountains. Prosperous Villager, The. Li K'ai-hsien. CoBLCP, *tr.* by Jonathan Chaves

His farces are physic; his physic a farce is. (LL) On Sir John Hill, M. D., Playwright. David Garrick. FaBoEE; NBLV

His Farewell [or Fare-well] to Sack. Robert Herrick. BeJo; CaPo; CavPo; NAEL-5v1; NAEL-6v1; NAEL-7v1

His father and grandfather before him were coachmen. Birth of a Coachman. Paul Durcan. PBCIP

His father did intend that Harry should. John L. Thomas. AngWePo *Fr.* Harry Vaughan.

His father gave him a box of truisms. Truisms, The. Louis MacNeice. NOBE; OBSV; PNI

His Father's Hands. Thomas Kinsella. PoE

His father's steel, piercing the wholesome fruit. King Honour's Eldest Son. Elinor Wylie. SacPr

His Father, Singing. Leslie Norris. TCAWP

His Favourite Seat. Deborah Randall. NeBl

His Feet are shod with Gauze. Emily Dickinson. SAmP

His fingers are caterpillars balanced. Blue Movies. Maurya Simon. GifTon

His fingers leaned. Sun House. Haki R. Madhubuti. ESEAA

His Fingers Seem to Sing. Sam Cornish. GT

His fingers wake, and flutter; up the bed. Conscious. Wilfred Owen. PoWW

His first bullet is a present, a mark of intelligence that will. Knee, The. Ciaran Carson. PNI

His fists beating time. Then the hands giving way. (LL) "It's Only Rock and Roll but I Like It": The Fall of Saigon, 1975. David Wojahn. IllVoic; ReTh

His flames ar[e] joy[e]s, his bands true lovers' might. (LL) Mary Sidney Wroth, Countess of Montgomery. BASC; EMWP Fr. Pamphilia to Amphilanthus.

His flames ar[e] joy[e]s, his bands true lovers' might. Mary Sidney Wroth, Countess of Montgomery. BASC Fr. Pamphilia to Amphilanthus.

His footsteps in the room. Alexis Rotella. HA

His Friend's Last Battle. Theodore Nicholl. AngWePo

His friend the watchman was still awake. Leave-Taking, A. Arno Holz. AWP, tr. by Jethro Bithell

His friends he loved. His direst earthly foes. Epitaph, An. Sir William Watson. NOBVV

His glory and his monuments are gone. (LL) Meru. W. B. Yeats. GSo; NoAM; OxBSo; PoPoPo

His Golden Lock[e]s [Time Hath to Silver Turned]. George Peele. NIP-4; NPeEn; NoP-4; OxBEV; SCGP; TFi Fr. Polyhymnia.

His Grace! impossible! what dead! Satirical Elegy on the Death of a Late Famous General, A. Jonathan Swift. NBLV; NPeEn; OBSV; PoE

His Grange, or Private Wealth. Robert Herrick. BASC; BeJo; CaPo; CavPo

HIS GRATEFUL OPPONENTS SET UP THIS STATUE OF APIS THE BOXER. Lucilius. GrAn, tr. by Peter Porter

His green eyes on the homestead of another man. Snake, The. Andrew Suknaski. NOBC

His green garden's twytined digging fork. To Priapos. Unknown. GrAn, tr. by Guy Davenport

His hand came out of the east. Homer. OBVE, tr. by Christopher Logue Fr. Iliad, The.

His Hand Shall Cover Us. Isaac ben Samuel of Dampière. TrJP, tr. by Nina Davis Salaman

His hat is rammed on. Near the School for Handicapped Children. Thomas William Shapcott. CBAP

His head appeared in the hand. Orpheus. John Kinsella. BMAP

His head like a fist rooted in his abdomen. Agents, The. Robert Conquest. SPE

His head split in four parts. Promenade. David Ignatow. TrJP

His headstone said. Funeral of Martin Luther King, Jr, The. Nikki Giovanni. BPo

His heart, to me, was a place of palaces and pinnacles and shining towers. I Have Been through the Gates. Charlotte Mew. MoBrPo

His heart to the darkness and into the sadness of joy. (LL) First Song. Galway Kinnell. NoP-4; TwCP

His heart unbiassed, and his mind his own. (LL) Richard Savage. NOEC; OBSV Fr. Bastard, The.

His heart was in his garden; but his brain. Frederick Goddard Tuckerman. APN-2; NoP-4; TCAPo Fr. Sonnets.

His holy / slowly. Darwin. Lorine Niedecker. APSN; APT-2

His Hope or Sheet-Anchor. Robert Herrick. CaPo

His howls flow patient and slow. Deserted Angel, The. Anna Hajnal. IQMS, tr. by Jeannette Nichols

His Illness. Solomon ibn Gabirol. TOF, tr. by David Goldstein

His kingdom is forever. (LL) Mighty Fortress Is Our God, A. Frederic Henry Hedge. AWP; GePo; PWR; SacPr

His Lady's Cruelty. Sir Philip Sidney. See Astrophil and Stella

His Lady's Death. Pierre de Ronsard. AWP, tr. by Andrew Lang

His Lady's Tomb. Pierre de Ronsard. AWP, tr. by Andrew Lang

His lamp, his bow, and quiver laid aside. Cupid Turned Plowman. Moschus. AWP, tr. by Matthew Prior

His Lamp Near Daybreak. Yannis Ritsos. AWTN, tr. by Martin McKinsey

His last breath was drawn. (LL) Siberia. James Clarence Mangan. BIrV; NOBVV; NOIV; NPeEn

His last days linger in that low attic. Old Jockey, The. Frederick Robert Higgins. OBMV; OxBTC

His last glimpse of the former wife. After Eden. James Simmons. PNI

His last white eärms, an' they stood still. (LL) Turnstile, The. William Barnes. NOBVV; NPeEn; OxBEV

His Late Wife's Wedding-Ring. George Crabbe. See Marriage Ring, The

His laugh. Spell of Blazing Trees, The. Sa'adyya Muffareh. PoArWo, tr. by Mona Fayad

His left hand, in heat of noonday. Ann Griffiths. WPoS

His Legs Strong and Lithe. Itaikkunrurkilar. WoPoe, tr. by George L. III Hart

His Letanie, to the Holy Spirit. Robert Herrick. See His Litany to the Holy Spirit

His life is in the body of the living. Soul and Body of John Brown, The. Muriel Rukeyser. CBCWP; MoAmPo

His lips move ceaselessly. Humped Ox, The. Flavien Ranaivo. NegPo, tr. by Ellen Conroy Kennedy

His Litany to the Holy Spirit. Robert Herrick. BASC; BeJo; NOSC; PeECV
(His Letanie, to the Holy Spirit.) SacPr
(Litany to the Holy Spirit.) OBEV

His little fleet floated in a trio. Columbus. J. Slauerhoff. TuT, tr. by Desmond Egan

His living name. (LL) Epilogue: "Those blessed structures, plot and rhyme." Robert Lowell. HCAP; NAAL-2v2; NAAL-5; PoetW; VCAP

His Long Home. Rosanna Warren. ExTi

His look will flow like oil over us. (LL) Ank'hor Vat. Denis Devlin. BIrV; CIP-2; ModIr; NOIV

His Mansion in the Pool. Emily Dickinson. OBAL

His merry Companions returned in a Throng. (LL) Butterfly's Ball [and the Grasshopper's Feast], The. William Roscoe. NOBRP; OxBEV

His Metrical Prayer. James Graham, Marquess of Montrose. See On Himself, upon Hearing What Was His Sentence

His Metrical Vow. James Graham, Marquess of Montrose. OxBS
(Epitaph on Charles I.) NOBE

His mind is as high as a mountain. Unknown. ColAnChi, tr. by Red Pine

His mind moves upon silence. (LL) Long-Legged Fly. W. B. Yeats. FaBoMo; FaBoTw; NAEL-5v2; NAEL-6v2; NOBE; NPeEn; NoAM; NoP-4; PAI; PoE

His Monument. Sarah Knowles Bolton. PWR

His morning posture is sketched naked. Painting the Nude. Eric Dyer. BloBone

His Mother. Haim [or Chaim or Khayim] Guri [or Gouri]. MHP, tr. by Ruth Finer Mintz

His mother, a petrol pump attendant, was said by those who knew her. Hard to Place. Elaine Randell. Oth

His Mother Drinks. Edwin Emanuel Bradford. VerBaPo

His Mother's Service to Our Lady. François Villon. AWP; CTC, tr. by Dante Gabriel Rossetti

His mother weaves silk for a living. Morsel. Ali Sardar Jafri. OMIP, tr. by Kathleen Grant Jaeger

His mother wept so bitterly. Mother of Judas, The. Yevgeny [or Evgenii] Mikhailovich Vinokurov. GI, tr. by Anthony Rudolf

His mouth was like the heart of a pomegranate, and the shadows. Mary Magdalen. Kahlil Gibran. GraLe

His moving likeness on the page. (LL) Lens. Anne Wilkinson. MoCV; NOBC

His naked skin clothed in the torrid mist. Serf, The. Roy Campbell. GTBS-P; MoBrPo; OBMV

His name is Jason, he's. Michael Lassell. GLP Fr. Times Square Poems.

His name is Mister Snow. Mister Snow. Richard Rodgers. ReLy

His name was Chance, Jack Chance, he said. Ballad of a Strange Thing. Howard Phelps Putnam. OxBA

His name was Yuba! When Yuba Plays the Rumba on the Tuba. Herman Hupfeld. ReLy

His Necessary Darkness. Nancy Sullivan. TAP

His new-fangled rifle, his green new steel helmet. (LL) March 1, The. Robert Lowell. PoPoPo; PoetW

His night job is insomnia. Dissecting Uncle Sorrow. Rick Alley. AmPoNex

His nights in the aunts' house, their talk and tea. Provincial Adolescence, A. Michael Foley. PNI

His nose is short and scrubby. My Dog. Marchette Chute. WHSW

His Offering, with the Rest, at the Sepulcher. Robert Herrick. ChIV-2

His old age fell on years of abundant harvest. Felicitous Life, A. Czeslaw Milosz. PoSu

His only beauty to be / all moose. (LL) Poetry, a Natural Thing. Robert Duncan. NOBA; NoAM; PmAP; TRP

His original way. Free Old Man. Muso Soseki. EaWin, tr. by W. S. Merwin

His overalls hung on the hook by his hat, and I noticed. Treasures. Claire Richcreek Thomas. PoToHe

His Own Epitaph. Robert Herrick. CaPo

His Own Epitaph, When He Was Sick. John Hoskyns [or Hoskins]. FaBoEE

His Own True Wife. Wolfram von Eschenbach. AWP, tr. by Jethro Bithell

His pads furring the scarp's rime. Snow-Leopard, The. Randall Jarrell. TwCP

His pains so racked my heart. Sympathy. Viola Meynell. LW

His paper propped against the electric toaster. Daniel at Breakfast. Phyllis McGinley. OBSV

His Parting from Her. John Donne. EBEV Fr. Elegies.

His Pen did once meat from the eater fetch. Excellent Wigglesworth, Remembered by some Good Tokens, The. Cotton Mather. SacPr

His pendulous stomach hangs a-shaking. (LL) Wagner. Rupert Brooke. FaBoTw; NOBL; PeLV

His penis erect with / Fantasy. (LL) Along History. Muriel Rukeyser. NALW; NNaP

His penis rises before him, a compulsion. He would take hormones if. Barbie's Molester. Denise Duhamel. ReTh

His photograph, yellowed by the years. Big John. Norman J. Loftis. SpirFl

His Picture. John Donne. FSCP; MeLP; OxAEP-1; PBRV *Fr.* Elegies.

His piercing pince-nez. Some dim frieze. Ted Berrigan. FTOS *Fr.* Sonnets, The.

His Pilgrimage. Sir Walter Ralegh. *See* Passionate Man[']s Pilgrimage, The

His place, as he sat and as he thought, was not. Quiet Normal Life, A. Wallace Stevens. NAAL-2v2; NAAL-5; NoAM

His place is before, not in, the National Gallery. London Pavement Artist. James Schevill. TAP

His Plans for Old Age. William Meredith. TAP

His plumage is dun. Jailbird. Vernon Scannell. OxBC

His poems, yellow, torn and fading. Langston Hughes. Lew Blockcolski. VoR

His Poetry His Pillar. Robert Herrick. BeJo; CaPo; NOSC

His poor mother gives Mikythos' Leonidas. PGA

His Praises. Swidi-Nonkamfela Mhlongo. PeSAV, *tr. by* Elizabeth Gunner

His praises hymned in Masses by throaty Russian priests. Paul the First. Pavel Grigoryevich Antokolsky. TCRP, *tr. by* Bernard Meares

His Prayer for Absolution. Robert Herrick. BeJo; SacPr
(For those my unbaptized rhymes.) CavPo

His Prayer to Ben Jonson. Robert Herrick. BASC; BeJo; CaPo; NAEL-5v1; NAEL-6v1; NAEL-7v1; NOSC; NoP-4; OxBSP; OxBoLi; PeLV

His Promise. Aaron Shurin. FTOS

His Request. Owen Roe O'Sullivan. BIrV, *tr. by* Joan Keefe

His Request to Julia. Robert Herrick. BeJo; CaPo; CavPo; NOSC

His rest, and on his lips their honey made. (LL) Love Sleeping. Plato. AWP; FaBoEE, *tr. by* Thomas Stanley

His Return to London. Robert Herrick. BASC; BeJo; CaPo; NAEL-5v1; NAEL-6v1; NAEL-7v1

His Reward. Sir Thomas Wyatt. InPK-6; NoSic

His role is to invert the fairy tale. Psychiatrist. Peter De Vries. OBAL

His Rule of Behaviour: If You Are Civil, I Am Sober. James Carkesse. NOSC

His Saviour[']s Words, Going to the Cross[e]. Robert Herrick. ChIV-2; NOCV; SacPr

His shadow monstrous on the palace wall. Oedipus. Thomas Blackburn. FaBoTw

His Shield. Marianne Craig Moore. NALW

His shoulder did I hold. Any Saint. Francis Thompson. MoBrPo

His simple is. Drive. Maggie Hannan. NeBl

His sins were scarlet, but his books were read. (LL) On His Books. Joseph Hilaire Pierre Belloc. FaBoEE; MoBrPo; NBLV; OxBoLi; WeW-3

His sister named [*or* called] Lucy O'Finner. Limerick. Lewis Carroll. PeLi

His skin like cream is free of wrinkles. Rosa Filí. Maria Arrillaga. TANSG

His snores / protect the sleeping hut. Wife of the Husband. Micere Githae Mugo. HAWP

His snout intimate with worms and leaves. (LL) Geoffrey Hill. FaBoMo; HAP; NoAM *Fr.* Mercian Hymns.

His solid flesh had never been away. Alienation. Howard Phillips Lovecraft. APT-1

His Son. Callimachus. AWP, *tr. by* G. B. Grundy

His Son's / A Jew. *Unknown.* OBCoV

His soul is gone aloft. (LL) Poor Tom. Charles Dibdin. NOEC; OxBoLi

His soul is with the saints, I trust. (LL) Knight's Tomb, The. Samuel Taylor Coleridge. FaBoCh; NPeEn; RB

His soul stretched tight across the skies. T. S. Eliot. TCAPo *Fr.* Preludes (I–IV).

His sovereignty is o'er my gathered throng. His Sovereignty. Kalonymos ben Moses of Lucca. TrJP, *tr. by* Nina Davis Salaman

His speculation be regretted. I Want a Tenant; a Satire. John O'Keefe [*or* O'Keeffe]. NOEC

His spirit fled into the gloom below. (LL) Virgil [*or* Vergil]. NAWM-5v1; NAWM-7v1, *tr. by* Robert Fitzgerald *Fr.* Aeneid [*or* Eneados, Aeneis], The.

His Spirit in smoke ascended to high heaven. Lynching, The. Claude McKay. APT-1; ColAP; GT; NAAL-5

His stars eternally. (LL) Drummer Hodge. Thomas Hardy. AWP; EBEV; FaBoWar; GTBS-P; HAP; HarvBoo; NAEL-5v2; NAEL-6v2; NOBVV; NoAM; NoP-4; OBWP; OxAEP-2; PAI; PeFWW; WeW-3

His startled life with lead, and all went out. (LL) Working Party, A. Siegfried Sassoon. AF; PeFWW

His stature was not very tall. Robert Greene. CTC; NoSic; SCGP *Fr.* Greene's Vision.

HIS:STORY. Lee Ranaldo. HeMarv

His sullen kinsmen, by the winter sea. Santa Claus. Dom Moraes. NoAM

His sun's arms and grappling. Isaac: a Poise. Peter Cole. ChIV-1

His sun went down in the morning. Our Ernest. "Elmo." PWR

His Tears to Thamesis [*or* Thamasis]. Robert Herrick. NOSC

His theme / over and over. Williams: An Essay. Denise Levertov. PmAP

His thing is singing. Elvis. Sam Cornish. AllShUp

His Throne Is with the Outcast. James Russell Lowell. TrCP

His tongue out with its fork. (LL) Eve. Christina Georgina Rossetti. ChIV-1; GTBS-P; NALW; NIL-7; NIP-4

His trousers are wind. Song to a Lover. *Unknown.* BoWoP, *tr. by* Willis Barnstone

His trowel catches the light and becomes precious. (LL) On Roofs of Terry Street. Douglas Dunn. NPeEn; OxBTC

His twelve-year-old / son. Callimachus. GrAn

His Uncle came on Franklin Hyde. Franklin Hyde. Joseph Hilaire Pierre Belloc. NBLV

His vast frame splayed on an uneasy chair. Confrontation with an Artist. Elisabeth Eybers. PeSAV

His vision, from the constantly passing bars. Panther, The. Rainer Maria Rilke. NAWM-7v2, *tr. by* Stephen Mitchell

His Visitor. Thomas Hardy. HarvBoo

His waiting becomes a time to hear thoughts, the sound. Picture of a Japanese Farmer, Woodland, California, May 20, 1942. James Masao Mitsui. OpBo

His was a chamber in the topmost tower. Charles Tennyson Turner. CenSon

His was the first corpse I had ever seen. My Wicked Uncle. Derek Mahon. OxBC

His Waves. Rick Noguchi. AmPoNex

His way home to the mark. (LL) Boston Hymn. Ralph Waldo Emerson. CBCWP; InvLi; TCAPo

His whiskers didn't come, his mustache is gone. Mustacheless Bard, A. J. Gordon Coogler. OBAL

His Wife. Shirley Kaufman. LCAP-2

His Wife. "Rachel" [*or* "Rahel"]. WPOW, *tr. by* Sholom J. Kahn

His wife and he enter. Labour and Delivery. Ron Charach. BloBone

His wife looked it up in her dream book / and played it. (LL) Hope. Langston Hughes. APSN; OBAL; PFTM-1

His wife nods, and a secret smile. James Fenton. HP *Fr.* German Requiem, A.

His wife then composed a poem with the names of medicines its theme and. Poem of Medicine Puns. *Unknown.* ColAnChi; WoPoe, *tr. by* Victor H. Mair

His wild heart beats with painful sobs. Happy Warrior, The. Sir Herbert Read. FaBoWar; PeFWW

His Winding-Sheet. Robert Herrick. BASC; CaPo; OBEV

His window frames our pictured, distanced city. Very Rich Hours, The. Nick Drake. NeBl

His words were magic and his heart was true. Uncle Ananias. Edwin Arlington Robinson. MoAmPo; NIP-4

His works are the apocalypse of verse. (LL) On the Death of Mr. Pope. *Unknown.* NOEC; NPeEn

Hiss, hiss—the north wind blows. Commiserating with the Poor. Li K'ai-hsien. CoBLCP, *tr. by* Jonathan Chaves

Hissed offstage / mocked by the batteries. Ode on the Revolution. Vladimir Vladimirovich Mayakovsky [*or* Maiakovskii]. TCRP, *tr. by* Daniel Weissbort

Hist   whist / little ghostthings. E. E. Cummings. NOxBChV

Histoire. Harry Mathews. NIP-4; PmAP

Historic, side-long, implicating eyes. La Gioconda; Leonardo Da Vinci, The Louvre. "Michael Field." CABP; PeVV; ViWPN

Historical Judas, The. Howard Nemerov. NoP-4

Historical Reflections. John Hollander. OBAL; OBCoV

Historically these people have been noted for a strange dish called. Okeydokey Tribe, The. Chrystos. WiU

Historie of Squyer William Meldrum, The. Sir David Lindsay [*or* Lyndsay]. Squire Meldrum at Carrickfergus. OxBS

Histories of Bodies. Mariko Nagai. PuP-23

Historiography. Lorenzo Thomas. SeSe

History. Kelly Cherry. FFC

History. Gilbert Keith Chesterton. OBSV *Fr.* Songs of Education.

History. Carl Dennis. BAP-97

History. Maura Dooley. NeBl

History. Rita Dove. ExTi; FFC

History. Rita Dove. NAAAL *Fr.* Mother Love.

History. Ralph Waldo Emerson. APN-1

History. Robert Fitzgerald. APT-2

History. Juan Gelman. TCLAP, *tr. by* Robert Marquez

History. Jorie Graham. HarvBoo

History. Arthur Gregor. TAP

History. D. H. Lawrence. RaBo

History. James Liddy. CIP-2 *Fr.* Love Songs of Corca Bascinn.

History. Robert Lowell. ColAP; HCAP; PoetW; TAP; VCAP

History. Heberto Padilla. AF, *tr.* by Alastair Reid

History. Adrienne Rich. NIL-7 *Fr.* Inscriptions.

History. Gary Soto. PBCAP

History. Alpay Ulku. AmPoNex

History. Yevgeny [*or* Evgenii] Mikhailovich Vinokurov. Objects. TCRusP, *tr.* by Daniel Weissbort

History among the Rocks. Robert Penn Warren. CBCWP; MoAmPo *Fr.* Kentucky Mountain Farm.

History and Reality. Stephen Spender. HP

History as Decoration. Rosanna Warren. DiPo

History as Trash. Michelle T. Clinton. SpirFl

History during Nocturnal Snowfall. Robert Penn Warren. DiPo

History Goes to Work. Elizabeth Garrett. MFPA; NeBl

History has to live with what was here. History. Robert Lowell. ColAP; HCAP; PoetW; TAP; VCAP

History hibernates here. Maridunum. Douglas Phillips. AngWePo

History Lesson, A. Miroslav Holub. PoSu; RB, *tr.* by George Theiner

History Lessons. Seamus Deane. BiHa; PBCIP; PNI

History Myth of the Coming of the A' shiwi as Narrated by 'Kiäklo. *Zuni Oral Tradition.*
  "Following their road of exit, they stooped over and came out." APN-2

History of a Literary Movement. Howard Nemerov. PoE

History of Civilization, A. Albert Goldbarth. HCAP

History of Costume, A. Michelle Cliff. OxWW

History of Dub Poetry, The. "Mbala". WaCA

History of Education. David McCord. APT-2; OBAL

History of Ideas. James Vincent Cunningham. NIP-4; VCAP

History of Lesbianism, A. Judy Grahn. GLP

History of Love, A. William Carlos Williams. VGW

History of My Face. Khaled Mattawa. AmPoNex

History of My Father's House, The. Vona Groarke. MFPA

History of Sexual Preference, A. Robin Becker. BodElec; ExTi

History of the Caesars, A. Isidor Schneider. APT-2

History of the Flood, The. John Heath-Stubbs. NOxBChV; OxBTC

History of the Invisible. Rodger Kamenetz. TaR

History of the Lyre, A. Letitia [*or* Laetitia] Elizabeth Landon. VWP

History of Truth, The. W. H. Auden. FaBoMo

History of World Languages. Dennis Joseph Enright. OxBC

History repeats a work of. One Man's Potato Chip. Dina von Zweck. SpudSo

History, the angel, was stirred. Northern Ireland: Two Comments. Seamus Deane. CIP-2

History theirs whose language is the sun. (LL) Elementary School Classroom in a Slum, An. Stephen Spender. FaBoMo; MoBrPo; TwCP; UnPo

Hit and hit and hit and hit and fallen. Like Her Body The World. Martha Collins. ExTi

Hit me! Jab me! Third Degree. Langston Hughes. BPo

Hit Men, The. Philippa Lawrence. Prnts

Hit wes upon a Scere-thorsday that vre louerd aros. Judas. *Unknown.* ESPB

Hitch Haiku. Gary Snyder. LCAP-2
  "After weeks of watching the roof leak." InPK-6; KaS

Hitchcock would have loved 136. Woman Hanging from Lightpole, Illinois Route 136. Lucia Cordell Getsi. IllVoic

Hitcher. Simon Armitage. EmeKit

Hitchhikers, The. Diane Wakoski. NoAM

Hither, Ardelia, I your steps pursue. Some Reflections. Anne Finch, Countess of Winchilsea. ChIV-1

Hither, O captives, hither let you come. Boethius. MLL *Fr.* Consolation of Philosophy, The ("De Consolacione Philosophie").

Hither the heroes and the nymphs resort. Pope. ECEV *Fr.* Rape of the Lock, The; an Heroi-Comical Poem.

Hither thou com'st: the busy [*or* busie] wind all night. Bird, The. Henry Vaughan. ESCV; GeHe; OBEV; PoE

Hither We Come, Our Dearest Lord. Enoch W. Freeman. AH

Hither, where tangled thickets of the acacia. Babiaantje, The. Frank Templeton Prince. MoBrPo

Hitler Speaks. Helen Waddell. MLL

Hits and Runs. Carl Sandburg. MoASP

Hitting Golfballs off the Bluff. Jeffrey Harrison. MoASP

Hitting the nail at last. (LL) Structural Study of Myth, The. Jerome Rothenberg. FTOS; PoM

Hittites, The. Roy Fuller. OxBSP

Hitty Pitty within the wall. *Unknown.* OxNR

HMS *Glory.* Charles Causley. FaBoWar

Ho, all you cats in all the street. Cat's Meat. Harold Monro. OBMV

Ho! Brother. Archie Weller. IBA

Ho! brother [*or* broder] Teague, dost hear de decree. Lilli Burlero [A New Song]. Thomas Wharton, 1st Marquess of Wharton. BASC; NOIV; OxBoLi

Ho! Cupid calls, come Lovers, come. Cupid's Call. James Shirley. BeJo; NOSC

Ho, everyone that thirsteth. A. E. Housman. ChIV-1

Ho, for the Pirate Don Durk of Dowdee! Pirate Don Durk of Dowdee, The. Mildred Plew Meigs. ChAP

Ho, Giant! This is I! Bean-Stalk, The. Edna St. Vincent Millay. NOxBChV

Ho Ho Ho Caribou. Joseph Ceravolo. PmAP

Ho Hum. Edward Heyman. ReLy

Ho, Moeris! Whether on thy way so fast? Virgil [*or* Vergil]. AWP, *tr.* by John Dryden *Fr.* Eclogues.

Ho! Persephone brings flowers, to them. Old Men, The. Irving Feldman. TwCP

'Ho!' said the child, 'how fine the horses go." Mother, The. Dora Sigerson Shorter. VWP

Ho, why dost thou shiver and shake. Gaffer Gray. Thomas Holcroft. NOEC; OxAEP-1

Hoar-Frost. Amy Lowell. ColAP

Hoar frost has congealed. Along the Grand Canal. Ch'in Kuan. BLT, *tr.* by Kenneth Rexroth

Hoar with salt-sleet and chalkings of the birds. (LL) Frederick Goddard Tuckerman. APN-2; NOBA *Fr.* Sonnets.

Hoardings screened the landscape from his sight. Copy-writer's Dream, The. Bruce Dawe. BMAP

Hoarfrost and Fog. Barton Sutter. UrbNat

Hoarse is the husky tickling's muffled chant. Pendulum, The. Árpád Tóth. IQMS, *tr.* by Watson Kirkconnell

Hoarse with fulfillment, I never made promises. (LL) Noah's Raven. W. S. Merwin. ChIV-1; HCAP

Hoatchunk' Narwoanar, or Winnebago War Song. *Unknown.* APN-2, *tr.* by Caleb Atwater

Hob Gobbling's Song. James Russell Lowell. OBCA

Hob, shoe, hob; hob, shoe, hob. *Unknown.* OxNR

Hob upon a Holiday. *Unknown.* NOEC

Hobart Town, Van Diemen's Land (11th June, 1837). Hal Porter. NOBAu

Hobbes clearly proves that every creature. Jonathan Swift. HAP; SCV *Fr.* On Poetry: A Rhapsody.

Hobbinol. William Somervile [*or* Somerville].
  On the Village Green. ECEV

Hobie [*or* Hobbie] Noble. *Unknown.* ESPB; IBB; OxBB

Hobson has supt, and's newly gon to bed. (LL) On the University Carrier Who Sick'n'd [*or* Sickened] in the Time of His Vacancy [Being Forbid to go to London, by Reason of the Plague]. John Milton. EBEV; FaBoCh; FaBoEE; NOSC; OxAEP-1

Hoccleve Remembers His Madness. Thomas Hoccleve [*or* Occleve]. NPeEn *Fr.* Complaint, The.

Hock-Cart, or Harvest Home, The. Robert Herrick. BASC; BeJo; CaPo; EBEV; NAEL-5v1; NAEL-6v1; NAEL-7v1; NOSC; OxAEP-1

Hoddley, poddley, puddle and fogs. *Unknown.* OxNR

Hoddy doddy. *Unknown.* OxNR

Hoeing. Gary Soto. PBCAP

Hog Butcher for the World. Chicago. Carl Sandburg. APT-1; AiP; AmFaPo; BRP; ColAP; IllVoic; MoAmPo; NAAL-2v2; NOBA; NoAM; OxBA; TAP; TFi; TRP; UnPo; VGW

Hog, the Sheep and Goat, Carrying to a Fair, The. Anne Finch, Countess of Winchilsea. ECWP

Hogarcito de La Madrugada, El. Anthony R. Vigil. AmPoNex

Hogging it down like a pig I call the feeding of corpses. (LL) Mystic. D. H. Lawrence. BLT; PAI

Hogwash. Robert Francis. LCAP-2; NIL-7; NIP-4; TRP

Hogyn cam to bowers dore. Hogyn. *Unknown.* MiEL

Hohenlinden. Thomas Campbell. CABP; FaBoCh; GTBS-P; NOBE; NOBRP; OBWP; TFi

Hoireann o. Blue Song. Mary Macleod (Màiri Nighean Alasdair Ruaidh). NePenScot, *tr.* by Robert Crawford

Hoise up the sail, cried they who understand. Sea-Voyage from Tenby to Bristol, A. Katherine Philips. WPE

Hoist your burdens, get on down the road. (LL) Gravelly Run. A. R. Ammons. CoAP; NAAL-2v2; NoAM; VCAP

Hoisting the tuba, like a golden. Strolling Musicians. Nikolai Alekseievich Zabolotsky [*or* Zabolotskii]. TCRP, *tr.* by Daniel Weissbort

Hokey, pokey, whisky, thum. *Unknown.* OxNR

Holbain. Anne Batten Cristall. RWP

Hold a glass of pure water to the eye of the sun!   Glass of Pure Water, The.   Hugh MacDiarmid.   PFTM-2

Hold a hand held out without a protective glove.   Your Figure or the War against Fat.   Joyce Mansour.   SurPaPo, *tr.* by Mary Ann Caws

Hold, are you mad? you damned [*or* damn'd] confounded dog.   Dryden.   OBCoV   *Fr.* Tyrannic Love.

Hold back completely.   Archilochus.   SaLy, *tr.* by Diane Rayor

Hold back the hand that works the mill.   Water-mill, A.   Antipater of Thessalonica.   GrAn, *tr.* by Alistair Elliot

Hold fast—hold fast your dreams! (LL)   Hold Fast Your Dreams.   Louise Driscoll.   ChAP; ITBLP

Hold Fast Your Dreams.   Louise Driscoll.   ChAP; ITBLP

Hold hard, Ned! Lift me down once more, and lay me in the shade.   Sick Stockrider, The.   Adam Lindsay Gordon.   CBAP

Hold high the woof, dear friends, that we may see.   On a Piece of Tapestry.   George Santayana.   APN-2

Hold, hold it tight.   Song for a Girl on Her First Menstruation.   *Unknown.*   BoWoP, *tr.* by Joe Prentuo

Hold, hold your hand, hold; mercy, mercy, spare.   Sonnet on Sir William Alexander's Harsh Verses after the English Fashion, A.   James I, King of England.   Son

Hold it up sternly—see this it sends back, (who is it? is it you?).   Hand-Mirror, A.   Walt Whitman.   NAAL-2v1; NAAL-3; OxBA; PoPoPo

Hold me / let me lay my head.   Place Setting.   Johari M. Rashad.   PasH

Hold me here / till only, these are my.   White Fish in Reeds.   Joseph Ceravolo.   BodElec

Hold my Rooster.   *Unknown.*   FaBoVe

(Precious Things.)   TTY

Hold not your lips so close; dispense.   Kiss 1656, The. To Mrs. C.   Thomas Shipman.   NOSC

Hold of the land. (LL)   Battle of Brunanburh.   *Unknown.*   FaBoWar; OBVE; OBWP; PeVV, *tr.* by Alfred Tennyson, 1st Baron Tennyson

Hold on!   Shayo.   JDP, *tr.* by Yoel Hoffmann

Hold on or let go. (LL)   Variations on the Word *Love*.   Margaret Atwood.   LW; NoAM

Hold out a handful of snow.   Natalya [*or* Natal'ia] Gorbanevskaya [*or* Gorbanyevskaya *or* Gorbanevskaia].   TCRusP, *tr.* by Daniel Weissbort

"Hold the horse's head" the farmer said.   Horse's Head, The.   Brendan Kennelly.   CIP-2

Hold the pen close to your ear.   Thin Prison, The.   Leslie Norris.   OTCP

Hold them now, Earth, now hand of man cannot.   *Unknown.*   NAEL-5v1   *Fr.* Beowulf.

Hold thy tonge stille. (LL)   Tell Me, Wight in the Broom.   *Unknown.*   MiEL; NAEL-5v1; NAEL-6v1

Hold up the right corner of the sea.   When He Believed Himself to Be a Young Girl Lifting the Skin of the Water.   Juan Felipe Herrera.   TouFir

Hold up the universe, good girl. Hold up.   Good Girl.   Molly Peacock.   FFC

Hold up your head.   *Unknown.*   OxNR

Hold your hand in your ear.   Polar.   Jacqueline Senard.   SurWo, *tr.* by Myrna Bell Rochester

"Hold your hand, Lord Judge," she says.   Maid Freed from the Gallows, The.   *Unknown.*   ESPB

Hold your mad hands! for ever on your plain.   Robert Southey.   CenSon

Holding a jug of wine among the flowers.   Drinking Alone under Moonlight.   Li Po.   TAL

Holding a keepsake of the wind in its hand.   On the Sand Dune.   Kawamura Yoichi.   GifTon, *tr.* by Naoshi Koriyama and Edward Lueders

Holding Hands.   Lenore M. Link.   NTCP

Holding her picture in his hands, he whispered:.   Eurydice.   Rosita Copioli.   CItWP, *tr.* by Cinzia Sartini Blum and Lara Trubowitz

Holding his gaze.   Alexis Rotella.   HA

Holding My Beads.   Grace Nichols.   ItWoWo

Holding the feathered dancing string.   Koel (Rainbird) and Effigy.   *Unknown.*   NOBAu, *tr.* by Mungayana Nundhirribala

Holding the Sky.   William Stafford.   GM

Holding the water.   William J. Higginson.   HA

Holding us all at once, I watch.   Spin.   Tracy Ryan.   NeBl

Holding you.   Anita Virgil.   HA

Holds steady in my right hand.   My Pen.   Tom Pickard.   Oth

Hole.   Leonard Nathan.   PBCAP

Hole in the Floor, A.   Richard Wilbur.   NOBA

Hole, Where Once in Passion We Swam.   Dave Jeddie Smith.   NoAM

Holes Commence Falling.   David Huddle.   PBCAP

Holes in the wall, The.   Issa.   EH, *tr.* by Robert Hass

Holes you made, The.   Coal Miners, The.   James Ballowe.   IllVoic

Holiday, The.   Hans Magnus Enzensberger.   VCWP, *tr.* by Hans Magnus Enzensberger and Michael Hamburger

Holiday, The.   Stevie Smith.   BWW

Holiday at Hampton Court.   John Davidson.   EBVV

Holiday Gown.   John Cunningham.   ECEV

Holiday in Reality.   Wallace Stevens.   OxBA

Holiday Present.   Ilya Abu Madi.   GraLe, *tr.* by George Dimitri Selim

Holidays.   Eva Mylonas.   BoWoP, *tr.* by Kimon Friar

Holiest of all holidays are those, The.   Henry Wadsworth Longfellow.   PoToHe

Holiness[e] on the head.   Aaron.   George Herbert.   BASC; ChIV-1; FSCP; GeHe; MeLP; NOSC; PeECV; SacPr

Holla, Approach.   William Shakespeare.   NPeEn   *Fr.* Love's Labour's Lost.

Holland.   Hendrik Marsman.   TuT, *tr.* by Michael Longley

Holland Brick, A.   Wallace Bruce.   VerBaPo

Holland, that scarce deserves the name of land.   Andrew Marvell.   BASC; NOBL; PeLV

((((((Hollanditis)))))).   Simon Vinkenoog.   CLPP, *tr.* by Charles McGeehan

Hollis laughed.   Johnna at the Windmill.   Diane Glancy.   CRP

Hollo! keep it up, boys—and push around the glass.   Drinking Song.   Robert Fergusson.   OxAEP-1

Hollow Echo.   Fazil Hüsnü Daglarca.   CRP

Hollow eyes of shock remain, The.   Two Years Later.   John Wieners.   PmAP; PoM; RaBo

Hollow Men, The.   T. S. Eliot.   APT-1; MoAmPo; NAAL-2v2; NAAL-5; OBMV

Hollow Thesaurus, The.   Roger McDonald.   BMAP; CBAP

Hollow Tree, A.   Robert Bly.   NNaP

Hollow winds of night no more, The.   Poem on the Bill Lately Passed for Regulating the Slave-Trade, A.   Helen Maria Williams.   RWP

Hollow Wood, The.   Edward Thomas.   OWoS

Hollowness.   Mac Wellman.

"Two hollow eyes follow a cat's crie."   FTOS

Holly and Ivy.   *Unknown.*   MiEL; NPeEn

Holly and the Ivy, The.   *Unknown.*   ChRPo; PeECV

Holly gone I discover.   Holly Gone.   Gloria Evans Davies.   AngWePo

Hollyhocks, The.   Basho.   EH, *tr.* by Robert Hass

Hollywood.   Karl Shapiro.   OxBA

Hollywood Finch, The.   A. V. Christie.   NAPBL

Holm Oak, The.   Mariella Bettarini.   CItWP, *tr.* by Cinzia Sartini Blum and Lara Trubowitz

Holmes.   James Russell Lowell.   NOBA; TCAPo   *Fr.* Fable for Critics, A.

Holocaust.   Charles Reznikoff.

"When the Second World War began."   HP

Holocaust.   Myra Sklarew.   CRP

Holocaust 1944.   Anne Ranasinghe.   GotH

(I do not know.)   HP

Holstenwall.   Sidney Keyes.   FaBoTw

Holver and Hivy made a gret party.   Holly and Ivy.   *Unknown.*   MiEL

Holy and hokey, Hallowe'en.   Trick or Treat.   John Frederick Nims.   IllVoic

Holy angels, in envy I cast no sigh.   Gaspara Stampa.   BoWoP, *tr.* by J. Vitiello

Holy Baptism (1).   George Herbert.   GeHe

Holy Baptism (2).   George Herbert.   ChIV-2

Holy Book like the Eighth Sphere, does shine, The.   Reason.   Abraham Cowley.   SacPr

Holy boy, The.   Children of Love.   Harold Monro.   MoBrPo

H[oly] Communion, The.   George Herbert.   ChIV-1; ESCV

Holy Communion, The.   Henry Vaughan.   ESCV

Holy Cross.   Venantius Fortunatus.   MiEL

Holy earth is overspread with leaves, The.   On Visiting Sokei, Where the Sixth Patriarch Lived.   Tesshu.   ZenPo, *tr.* by Takashi Ikemoto and Lucien Stryk

Holy Fair, The.   Robert Burns.   OBSV

Holy Family.   Muriel Rukeyser.   ChIV-2; MoAmPo

Holy Father, Great Creator.   Alexander V. Griswold.   AH

Holy Field, The.   Henry Hart Milman.   SacPr

Holy Ghost.   Larissa Szporluk.   NeAmPo

Holy Ghost, The.   John Donne.   NOCV   *Fr.* Litany, A.

Holy Ghost first knocks, so high extold, shews the end come, The.   Gatehouse Salutation, The.   Eleanor Touchet Davies.   EMWP

Holy God, We Praise Thy Name.   Clarence A. Walworth.   AH

Holy Goddess Tellus / Mother of Living Nature.   Holy Goddess Tellus.   *Unknown.*   HW

Holy Grail, The.   Jack Spicer.

Book of Gawain, The.   PoM

Holy Grail, The.   Tennyson.   *Fr.* Idylls of the King.

Holy Hill, A.   "Æ"   AWP

Holy, Holy, Holy.   Reginald Heber.   SacPr

"Holy, holy, holy!" the choir chants sweet and low.   Opening Service, An.   Clara Ann Thompson.   CBWP-2

Holy Innocents, The.   Robert Lowell.   CoAmPo; MoAmPo; OBCP; OxBC

Holy is the moon and our own Selene.   *Unknown.*   GrAn

Holy Light.   John Milton.   *See* Paradise Lost

Holy Longing, The. Goethe. RaBo; WoPoe, tr. by Robert Bly

Holy man, ungird your gabardeen. Rest. Roots. Seymour Mayne. NOBC

Holy moder, that bere Crist. William Herebert. MiEL

Holy Moses! Have a look! On Visiting Westminster Abbey. Amanda Ros. VerBaPo

Holy Night. Lucille Clifton. NALW

Holy Nunnery, The. *Unknown.* ESPB

Holy of Holies, The. Gilbert Keith Chesterton. SacPr

Holy Office, The. James Joyce. FaBoTw; NoAM; OxBTC

Holy Ones, the Young Ones, The. Chayyim Zeldis. TrJP

Holy Order. Gemino H. Abad. ReBoTo

Holy Priestess of Heaven, The. *Unknown.* HW, tr. by Samuel Noah Kramer and Diane Wolkstein

Holy Rood, The. John Davies of Hereford.
   "Although we do not all the good we love." Son

Holy Rose, The. Vyacheslav Ivanovich Ivanov. AWP, tr. by Babette Deutsch and Avrahm Yarmolinsky

Holy Russia. Maksimilian Aleksandrovich Voloshin. TCRusP, tr. by Bob Perelman

Holy Russia. Maksimilian Aleksandrovich Voloshin. TCRP, tr. by Bernard Meares

Holy Satyr. "H. D.". MoAmPo

Holy Scripture, Writ Divine. From a London Bookshop. *Unknown.* NBLV

Holy Sepulchre, The. Rowland Watkyns. BASC

Holy Shechina, / are You that gentle female Voice. Poem for the Shechina. Cassia Berman. HW

Holy Skirts. Else Von Freytag-Loringhoven. PFTM-1

Holy Solitude, in the skies above you. Solitude. Dániel Berzsenyi. IQMS, tr. by Watson Kirkconnell

Holy Sonnets. John Donne. ESCV
  Divine Meditations.
    "At the round earth's imagined corners, blow." BASC; ChIV-2; ClHu; EBEV; FHYEP; HAP; HeIP-4; MakPoe; MeLP; NAEL-5v1; NAEL-6v1; NAEL-7v1; NAWM-5v1; NOBE; NOSC; OxAEP-1; OxBEV; OxBSo; PAI; PeECV; PoE; SCGP; Son; TFi; TOF; WoPoe
    ("At the round earths imagin'd corners, blow.") NPeEn; SacPr
    "Batter my heart, three-personed [or three person'd] God; for you." BASC; CABP; ClHu; EBEV; FHYEP; FSCP; GSo; HAP; HeIP-4; InPK-6; InvLi; MeLP; NAEL-5v1; NAEL-6v1; NAEL-7v1; NIL-7; NIP-4; NOBE; NOSC; NPeEn; NoP-4; OxAEP-1; OxBSo; PAI; PBRV; PeECV; PoE; PoPoPo; SacPr; SoSe-8; Son; TFi; TOF; TrCP
    "Death be not proud, though some have called thee." BASC; FHYEP; HAP; HeIP-4; ITBLP; InPK-6; MeLP; NAEL-5v1; NAEL-6v1; NAEL-7v1; NAWM-5v1; NIL-7; NIP-4; NOBE; NOSC; NPeEn; OPOU; OxAEP-1; OxBEV; OxBSo; PAI; PoE; PoRA; SCGP; SCV; SacPr; SoSe-8; TRP; TrCP; WeW-3
    "I am a little world made cunningly." BASC; ChIV-1; NAEL-5v1; NAEL-6v1; NAEL-7v1; NIP-4; NoP-4; OxBSo; PoE; Son
    "If poisonous [or poysonous] mineral[l]s, and if that tree." BASC; EBEV; FaBoVe; NAEL-5v1; NAEL-6v1; NAEL-7v1; NoP-4; OxAEP-1; SCGP; Son; UnPo
    "O might those sigh[e]s and tear[e]s return[e] again[e]." SacPr
    "Oh my black[e] soul[e]! now thou art summoned." EBEV; OxAEP-1; Son; TOF
    "Oh, to vex me, contraries [or contraryes] meet in one." BASC; ChIV-2; NAEL-7v1; NOSC; Son
    "Show me dear[e] Christ, thy spouse, so bright and clear[e]." BASC; FSCP; MeLP; NAEL-5v1; NAEL-6v1; NAEL-7v1; NOSC; OxBSo; PeECV; PoE; Son
    "Since she whom[e] I loved [or lov'd or lovd] hath paid [or payd] her last debt." BASC; FSCP; NAEL-5v1; NAEL-6v1; NAEL-7v1; NOSC; PBRV; Son
    "Spit in my face ye [or you] Jew[e]s, and pierce my side." BASC; Son; TOF
    "This is my play's [or playes] last scene, here heavens appoint." BASC; EBEV; FaBoVe; MeLP; PAI; Son
    "Thou hast made me, and shall thy work[e] decay?" EBEV; GSo; InvLi; MeLP; NAEL-5v1; NAEL-6v1; NAEL-7v1; NOBE; NOCV; NOSC; NoP-4; OxAEP-1; SCGP; Son
    "What if this present were the world's last night?" BASC; EBEV; HeIP-4; MeLP; NAEL-5v1; NAEL-6v1; NAEL-7v1; NOCV; NOSC; OxAEP-1; PeECV; PoE; Son
    "Why are we[e] by all creatures waited on?" BASC; NOCV; PoE; TrCP
    "Wilt thou love God, as he doe? [or thee!] then digest." TrCP
  La Corona. ChIV-2; ESCV; Son
    Annunciation. TrCP
    Crown, The. ChIV-2
    ("Moyst with one drop of thy blood, my dry soule.") ESCV
    Nativity [or Nativitie]. ChrPo

Holy Spirit, Faithful Guide. Marcus Morris Wells. AH

Holy Spirit / giving life to all life. Hildegard von Bingen. EnlH

Holy Spirit, Lord of light. Hymn to the Holy Spirit. Stephen Langton. TrCP

Holy Spirit, Truth Divine. Samuel Longfellow. AH

Holy Thursday [1]. William Blake. FHYEP; NAEL-5v2; NAEL-6v2; NAWM-7v2; NOBE; NOBRP; NOEC; NPeEn; NoP-4; PeECV; PoE; SCV; TFi; TrCP *Fr.* Songs of Innocence.

Holy Thursday [2]. William Blake. FHYEP; NAEL-5v2; NAEL-6v2; NOBRP; NOEC; NoP-4 *Fr.* Songs of Experience.

Holy Thursday (Experience). William Blake. *See* Songs of Experience

Holy Thursday (Innocence). William Blake. *See* Songs of Innocence

Holy Tide, The. Frederick Tennyson. OBEV; SacPr

Holy Was Demeter Walking th' Corn Furrow. Edward Sanders. PoM

Holy Water. Hayan Charara. AmPoNex

Holy Water come and bring. Spell, The. Robert Herrick. CaPo

Holy Well. Padraic Fallon. BBASP

Holy Well, The. *Unknown.* FaBoCh; NOCV

Holy Willie's Prayer. Robert Burns. EBEV; NAEL-6v2; NOBRP; NOEC; OBCoV; OBSV; OxBS; PoE; TFi
  (O Thou, wha in the heavens dost dwell.) NePenScot; NoP-4; OxBoLi

Holy Wroughte of sterres bright. William Herebert. MiEL

Holyhead. September 25, 1727. Jonathan Swift. BIrV; NOIV

Holywell. John Jones.
  "Now slowly winding from the mountain's head." AngWePo

Homage. Gustave Kahn. TrJP, tr. by Jethro Bithell

Homage and Lament for Ezra Pound in Captivity. Robert Duncan. NOBA

Homage in dance, An. Robert Filliou. PFTM-2 *Fr.* 14 Songs and 1 Riddle.

Homage: Light from the Hall. David Wojahn. PBCAP *Fr.* Mystery Train: A Sequence.

Homage: Summer/Winter, Shay Creek. Joseph Stroud. GeoHom

Homage to a Bellhop. Yusef Komunyakaa. BodElec

Homage to a Government. Philip Larkin. EBEV; NoAM; OxBEV

Homage to Chagall. Duane Niatum. CDW

Homage to Claudius Ptolemy. Brotherhood. Octavio Paz. LoL, tr. by Eliot Weinberger

Homage to Diana. Sir Walter Ralegh. NPeEn; NoSic

Homage to Elvis, Homage to the Fathers. Bruce Weigl. ReTh

Homage to Faiz Ahmed Faiz. Agha Shahid Ali. OpBo

Homage to Ferd. Holthausen. Gwen Harwood. NOBAu

Homage to Hieronymus Bosch. Thomas MacGreevy [or McGreevy]. BIrV; ModIr; SPE

Homage to Issac Newton. János Pilinszky. IQMS, tr. by Peter Jay

Homage to Jack Yeats. Thomas MacGreevy [or McGreevy]. OBMV

Homage to John Millington Synge. Mairtin O Direain. NOIV, tr. by Thomas Kinsella

Homage to Lester Flatt. David Bottoms. SwNoth

Homage to Literature. Muriel Rukeyser. SeSe

Homage to Mallarmé. Daniel Mark Epstein.
  Barrel Organ, The. DiPo

Homage to Marcel Proust. Thomas MacGreevy [or McGreevy]. CIP-2

Homage to Mistress Bradstreet. John Berryman.
  "Governor your husband lived so long, The." NOBA
  "I trundle the bodies, on the iron bars." NOBA
  "O all your ages at the mercy of my loves." NOBA
  "Winters close, Springs open, no child stirs, The." NAAL-2v2; NAAL-5; NoP-4t
  "When by me in the dusk my child sits down." ColAP

Homage to My Hips. Lucille Clifton. NAAAL

Homage to Paul Cézanne. Charles Wright. VCAP
  "Dead are a cadmium blue, The." HCAP

Homage to Paul Delvaux. Ramon Guthrie. PoE

Homage to René Magritte. George Melly. SPE

Homage to Robert Johnson. David St. John. SwNoth

Homage to Sextus Propertius. Ezra Pound.
  Elegy VII. VGW
  "Now if ever it is time to cleanse Helicon." VGW
  "Shades of Callimachus, Coan ghosts of Philetas." APT-1; HAP; NOBA; OBVE; OxBA; WoPoe
  "When, when, and whenever death closes our eyelids." APT-1; NPeEn; OBMV
  "Who, who will be the next man to entrust his girl to a friend?" FaBoMo

Homage to Sharon Stone. Lynn Emanuel. BodElec

Homage to Tara Our Mother. *Unknown.* HW

Homage to the British Museum. William Empson. FaBoMo; MoBrPo; NPeEn; OxBEV; PoE

Homage to the Brown Bomber. Michael S. Harper. MoASP

Homage to the Canal People. Andrew Sant. NOBAu

Homage to the Empress of the Blues. Robert Earl Hayden. APT-2; ESEAA; HCAP; LCAP-2; NAAAL; NAAL-5

Homage to the New World. Michael S. Harper. ESEAA; LCAP-2

Homage to the Painter General Ts'ao. Tu Fu. CrYelRi, *tr. by* Sam Hamill

Homage to the Philosopher. Babette Deutsch. TrJP

Homage to thee, O Ra, at thy tremendous rising! *Unknown.* AWP *Fr.* Book of the Dead.

Home. Franta Bass. INSAB

Home. Anne Brontë. VWP

Home. Henry Cuyler Bunner.
   "As sea-foam blown of the winds, as blossom of brine that is drifted." OBAL

   "Home, Sweet Home," with Variations ("As sea-foam blown of the winds, as blossom of brine that is drifted"). OBAL

   "Home, Sweet Home," with Variations ("Brown o' San Juan"). OBAL

   "Home, Sweet Home," with Variations ("Mid pleasures and palaces though we may roam"). OBAL

Home. Matilda Caroline Edwards. PWR

Home. Calvin Forbes. GT

Home. Edgar Albert Guest. BRP; ITBLP; OBAL; PWR

Home. June Brown Harris. PoToHe

Home. Nellie Womack Hines. PoToHe

Home. Robinson Jeffers. BodElec

Home. Pauline Kaldas. PoArWo

Home. Vincent O'Sullivan. PeNZ

Home. Frank Ormsby. ModIr; PBCIP; PNI

Home. *Unknown.* OHMPC, *tr. by* Kenneth Rexroth

Home. Ivan Zhdanov. TCRP, *tr. by* John High

Home, A. "Susan Coolidge." SWaP

Home address: galaxy and star number. End of the Questionnaire. Dan Pagis. PoSu, *tr. by* Robert Friend

Home after Three Months Away. Robert Lowell. HCAP; PoetW

Home again, home again, joggety jog [*or* jiggety-jog]. (LL) *Unknown.* LB; OxNR; ReMoGo

Home again in dreams, I'm walking that foothill road. Sycamore Canyon Nocturne. Christopher Buckley. GeoHom

Home and Mother. Hettye Rayburn Ramsey. PWR

Home! at the word, what blissful visions rise. Home, Sweet Home, with Variations. Henry Cuyler Bunner. OBAL

Home Burial. Robert Frost. APT-1; ColAP; NAAL-2v2; SoSe-8; TAP; TRP

Home-coming. Léonie Adams. MoAmPo

Home-Coming. Albert Ehrenstein. TrJP, *tr. by* Babette Deutsch and Avrahm Yarmolinsky

Home Coming. Lenrie Peters. HBAPE
   (Homecoming.) PBMAP

Home early. Gary Hotham. HA

Home for receiving those from whom God has withdrawn. On the Bell Frieze of a Roman Church. René Char. WoPoe, *tr. by* Mark Rudman

Home for Thanksgiving. W. S. Merwin. NoAM

Home for Winter. Marcia Falk. TaR

Home from Guatemala, back at the Waldorf. Arrival at the Waldorf. Wallace Stevens. HCAP

Home from his journey Farmer John. Farmer John. John Townsend Trowbridge. PWR

Home Front. Bill Tremblay. CDa

Home furthest off grows dearer from the way. Soldier, The. John Clare. FaBoWar

Home Greeting, A. Priscilla Jane Thompson. CBWP-2

Home Ground. Charles Brasch. PeNZ

Home, home from the horizon far and clear. At Night. Alice Thompson Meynell. OxAEP-2

Home in Three Days. Don't Wash. Linda Smukler. WiU

Home is more than just four walls. Hearth and Home. Stoddard King. OBAL

Home is mysterious: a place to die, a place to breed. Destinations. Josephine Jacobsen. WPE

Home Is So Sad. Philip Larkin. InPK-6; OxBSP; PoetW

Home Is Where There Is One to Love Us. Charles Swain. PoToHe

Home late. Michael Dudley. HA

Home Leave. Barbara Howes. TwCP

Home Movies. Carter Revard. VoR

Home News. Ahmed Tidjani-Cissé. NAfrP; PBMAP

Home no more home to me, whither must I wander? Robert Louis Stevenson. AmFaPo

Home of Aphrodite, The. Euripides. AWP, *tr. by* Gilbert Murray *Fr.* Bacchae.

Home of the Percys' high-born race. Alnwick Castle. Fitz-Greene Halleck. APN-1

Home on Palm. Selwyn Hughes. IBA

Home on the Range, A. *Unknown.* APN-2
   (O give me a home where the buffalo roam.) TCAPo

Home on the Range, February 1962. Edward Dorn. CoAmPo

Home's not merely four square walls. Home Is Where There Is One to Love Us. Charles Swain. PoToHe

Home's the place we head for in our sleep. Indian Boarding School: The Runaways. Louise Erdrich. HATNAP; NoAM; UnSA

Home-Sickness. Justinus Kerner. AWP, *tr. by* James Clarence Mangan

Home-Sickness. Hedwig Lachmann. TrJP, *tr. by* Jethro Bithell

Home, Sweet Home! John Howard Payne. APN-1; BRP; TCAPo *Fr.* Clari, the Maid of Milan.

Home, Sweet Home, with Variations. Henry Cuyler Bunner. OBAL

Home, Sweet Home, with Variations, III. Henry Cuyler Bunner. OBAL

"Home, Sweet Home," with Variations ("As sea-foam blown of the winds, as blossom of brine that is drifted"). Henry Cuyler Bunner. OBAL *Fr.* Home.

"Home, Sweet Home," with Variations ("Brown o' San Juan"). Henry Cuyler Bunner. OBAL *Fr.* Home.

"Home, Sweet Home," with Variations ("Mid pleasures and palaces though we may roam"). Henry Cuyler Bunner. OBAL *Fr.* Home.

Home the dark prisoner in his shroud of coats. (LL) Blood Donor. Robert Morgan. AngWePo; TCAWP

Home, The Spare Room, The. Robert Adamson. BMAP

Home they brought her warrior dead. Tennyson. OxAEP-2 *Fr.* Princess, The.

H[ome], thou return'st from Thames, whose naiads long. William Collins. NOEC; OxAEP-1

Home Thoughts. Denis Glover. PeNZ

Home-Thoughts, from Abroad. Robert Browning. AWP; CABP; ClHu; EBVV; FHYEP; HeIP-4; NAEL-5v2; NAEL-6v2; NOBE; NOBVV; NoP-4; OBEV; PoRA; TFi; UV

Home Thoughts from Abroad. William Robert Rodgers. OBCoV

Home-Thoughts, from the Sea. Robert Browning. NAEL-5v2; NAEL-6v2; SCGP

Home to Farm. *Unknown.* ChinPo, *tr. by* Yip Wai-lim

Home to me is laughter. Home. June Brown Harris. PoToHe

Home, too, was out there. Lawson Fusao Inada. GeoHom *Fr.* Legends from Camp.

Home Truths from Abroad. *Unknown.* UV

Home when he came, he seemed not to be there. Christopher Marlowe. EBNV *Fr.* Hero and Leander.

Homecoming. Bruce Dawe. BMAP; CBAP; EmeKit

Homecoming. Ho Ch'e Ch'ang. OHMPC, *tr. by* Kenneth Rexroth

Homecoming. Langston Hughes. SAmP; TRP

Homecoming. Dorianne Laux. ExTi

Homecoming. Joao Pedro. NAfrP, *tr. by* Don Burness

Homecoming. Lenrie Peters. *See* Home Coming

Homecoming. Linda Reuther.
   "And the Great Mother said." HW

Homecoming. Edith Södergran. WPoS

Homecoming. Karl Shapiro. APT-2

Homecoming. Wislawa Szymborska. PoSu, *tr. by* Adam Czerniawski

Homecoming. Peter Viereck. CoAP

Homecoming—Late at Night. Tu Fu. OHPC, *tr. by* Kenneth Rexroth

Homecoming of Love Amongst Illustrious Ruins. Rafael Alberti. CLPP, *tr. by* Kenneth Rexroth

Homecoming Singer, The. Jay Wright. VCAP

Homecomings. Pablo Neruda. GifTon, *tr. by* William O'Daly

Homeland. Max Mell. AuPH, *tr. by* Lowell A. Bangerter

Homeland beckons you, The. Homeland. Max Mell. AuPH, *tr. by* Lowell A. Bangerter

Homeland! O beloved village. My Country. Elolongue Epanya Yondo. NegPo, *tr. by* Ellen Conroy Kennedy

Homeless. Beatrix Gates. WiU *Fr.* Triptych.

Homeless. Michael Hannon. GeoHom

Homeless. Adelaide Anne Procter. VWP

Homeless Compleynt. Allen Ginsberg. BodElec

Homeless on Cold Food Festival Day. Moon on the Cold Flood Festival. Tu Fu. CrYelRi, *tr. by* Sam Hamill

Homeless people. En-vi-RON-ment. Lee Bennett Hopkins. HHAm

Homeless / The Living Bread. Despised and Rejected. Katharine Lee Bates. TrCP

Homely Meats. John Davies of Hereford. *See* Scourge of Folly, The

Homemade Smiles. Jose Angel Figueroa. PueRic

Homenajes de Gratitud. Zaragoza Clubs.
   "When the French, to their shame." SWaP, *tr. by* Luis A. Torres

Homeostasis finally. System oscillation over. All parameters at rest.   Middle Manager in Paradise, The.   Michael Foley.   PNI

Homeowners unite.   Firebombing, The.   James Dickey.   OBWP

Homeplace, The.   Lenard D. Moore.   GT

Homer.   Albert Ehrenstein.   TrJP, *tr. by* Babette Deutsch and Avrahm Yarmolinsky

Homer and the Brazen Head of Rumour.   George Chapman.   NOSC

Homer's Gift of Fame.   Homer.   NOSC, *tr. by* George Chapman   *Fr.* Iliad, The.

Homer's Iliad, To the Reader.   George Chapman.

    "And, for our tongue, that still is so empayr'd."   PBRV

Homer said everything beautifully, but to call.   Antipater of Thessalonica.   GrAn

Homer Travestie.   Thomas Bridges.

    "Squabbling gods the fight forsake, The."   FaBoWar

Homer was poor. His scholars live at ease.   Epigram.   James Vincent Cunningham.   VGW; WoPoe

Homer where born where buried of whom the son.   Brian Coffey.   BiHa; ModIr   *Fr.* Death of Hektor, The.

Homeric Hexameter, The.   Samuel Taylor Coleridge.   OxAEP-2

Homeric Hymn to Ares, The.   *Unknown.*   *Fr.* Homeric Hymns.

Homeric Hymn to Hermes.   *Unknown.*   *Fr.* Homeric Hymns.

Homeric Hymns.   *Unknown.*

    Homeric Hymn to Ares, The.

        "Hear me, / helper of mankind."   RaBo, *tr. by* Charles Boer

    Homeric Hymn to Hermes.

        Stealing of Apollo's Cattle, The.   WoPoe, *tr. by* Padraic Fallon

    Hymn to Aphrodite.   HW, *tr. by* Patricia Monaghan

    Hymn to Athena.   AWP, *tr. by* Percy Bysshe Shelley

    Hymn to Castor and Pollux.   AWP, *tr. by* Percy Bysshe Shelley

    Hymn to Earth the Mother of All.   AWP, *tr. by* Percy Bysshe Shelley

    Hymn to Hestia, The.

        "Hestia, / you who have received the highest honor."   HW, *tr. by* Charles Boer

    Hymn to Mercury.

        "Seized with a sudden fancy for fresh meat."   OBVE, *tr. by* Percy Bysshe Shelley

    Hymn to Selene.   AWP, *tr. by* Percy Bysshe Shelley

    Hymn to the Earth, The.   HW, *tr. by* Charles Boer

    Hymn to the Moon, The.

        "Go on, / Muses, / and sing the Moon with her big wings."   HW, *tr. by* Charles Boer

    "I sing of Aphrodite, the lover's goddess."   HW, *tr. by* Patricia Monaghan

Homes.   Charlotte Perkins Stetson Gilman.   SWaP

Homes for All.   Phoebe Cary.   SWaP

Homes of England, The.   Felicia Dorothea Hemans.   NOBRP; PEW; RWP; UV; ViWPN; WPE

Homesick.   Helmut Heissenbüttel.   CLPP, *tr. by* Jerome Rothenberg

Homesick.   *Unknown, fr. Terezín Concentration Camp.*   INSAB

Homesick Blues.   Langston Hughes.   GM; MoAmPo; NAAAL

Homesick Bride, The.   *Vietnamese Oral Tradition.*   CaDao, *tr. by* John Balaban

Homesickness.   Marina Ivanovna Tsvetayeva [*or* Tsvetaeva].   TCRP, *tr. by* Elaine Feinstein

Homestead.   Tu Fu.   CrYelRi, *tr. by* Sam Hamill

Homesteading.   Eva Salzman.   MFPA

Hometown.   Salih Michael Fisher.   CAGL

Hometown Piece for Messrs. Alston and Reese.   Marianne Craig Moore.   OBAL

"Hometown"; well, most admit an affection for a city.   Return to Cardiff.   Dannie Abse.   AngWePo; TCAWP

Homeward at evening through the drifted snow.   Cold Pastoral.   Diotimus.   GrAn, *tr. by* Dudley Fitts

Homeward Bound.   Heinrich Heine.

    And When I Lamented.   TrJP, *tr. by* Emma Lazarus

    Dearest Friend, Thou Art in Love.   TrJP, *tr. by* Emma Lazarus

    Du bist wie eine Blume.   AWP

    I, a Most Wretched Atlas.   TrJP, *tr. by* Emma Lazarus

    Mortal, Sneer Not at the Devil.   TrJP, *tr. by* Emma Lazarus

    Thou Hast Diamonds.   TrJP, *tr. by* Emma Lazarus

    ("Thou Seemest Like a flower.")   TrJP, *tr. by* Emma Lazarus

Homeward Bound.   Ezekiel Mphahlele.   AF

Homeward-Bound Passenger Ship, The.   Edward Edwin Foot.

    "Captain scans the ruffled zone, The."   VerBaPo

Homeward Journey, The.   Leonard [*or* Lazarus] Aaronson.   TrJP

Homewards.   Tomas Tranströmer.   WoPoe, *tr. by* Robin Fulton

Homework.   Allen Ginsberg.   NoAM

Homework.   Mona Van Duyn.   FFC; VCAP

Homework Assignment on the Subject of Angels.   Tadeusz Rózewicz.   VCWP

Homework! Oh, Homework!   Jack Prelutsky.   ChAP

Homines qouque si taceant, vocem invenient libri.   Steve McCaffery.   FTOS   *Fr.* Panopticon.

Homing at dusk—the snow falls on them—cattle.   Diotimus.   GrAn

Homo called sapiens. (LL)   Apostrophe to Man.   Edna St. Vincent Millay.   NAAL-5; NALW

Homo Erectus, Cerne Abbas.   Mercer Simpson.   TCAWP

Homo Sapiens.   John Wilmot, 2d Earl of Rochester.   *See* Satire [*or* Satyre *or* Satyr] against [Reason and] Mankind, A

Homo Suburbiensis.   Bruce Dawe.   BMAP

Homo Will Not Inherit.   Mark Doty.   HarvBoo; OPRER; WiU

Homocide.   Essex Hemphill.   GT

Homosexuality.   Frank O'Hara.   CAGL; LCAP-2; PFTM-2; TAP

Homunculus et la Belle Étoile.   Wallace Stevens.   MoAmPo

Honest Abe Lincoln.   Max Shulman.   OBAL

Honest man was Deacon Ray, An.   Honest Deacon, The.   Isaac Hinton Brown.   PWR

Honest matrons, pray retire.   *Unknown.*   PriapPo, *tr. by* Richard W. Hooper   *Fr.* Priapus Poems, The.

Honest ox, rejoiced, into the shade. (LL)   My Ox Duke.   John Dyer.   NOEC; NPeEn

Honest with Oneself.   "Don Aminado."   TCRP, *tr. by* Albert C. Todd

Honestly I'd as soon be dead!   Sappho.   STV

Honestly I wish I were dead!   Sappho.   BoWoP

Honesty.   Sir Thomas Wyatt.   NoSic; OxBSP

Honesty-Stones.   J. S. Harry.   NOBAu

Honey.   Sterling Allen Brown.   *See* Honey / When de man

Honey.   Robert Morgan.   BLT

Honey in the Honeycomb.   Vernon Duke.   ReLy

Honey Lamb, The.   Jonathan Williams.   PoM

Honey-Mead: "I am valued by men, fetched from afar."   Cynewulf.   AnOE, *tr. by* Charles W. Kennedy   *Fr.* Riddles (Exeter Book).

Honey Moon.   Kathleen Leland Baker.   NBLV

Honey of peace in old poems, The. (LL)   To the Stone-Cutters.   Robinson Jeffers.   ColAP; MoAmPo; NAAL-2v2; NAAL-5; NOBA; OxBA; PAI; PoRA

Honey people murder mercy U.S.A.   In Memoriam: Martin Luther King, Jr.   June Jordan.   NAAAL

Honey, pepper, leaf-green limes.   Jamaica Market.   Agnes Maxwell-Hall.   TTY; WHSW

Honey, Take a Whiff on Me.   *Unknown.*   OxBoLi

Honey / When de man.   Sister Lou.   Sterling Allen Brown.   APT-2

Honeycomb, The.   Pauline Stainer.   NeBl

Honeyed by time.   Wooden Chamber, The.   Anne Hébert.   WPOW, *tr. by* Birgit Swenson

Honeymoon.   Alice R. Friman.   MPUn

Honeymoon, The.   James Simmons.   PNI

Honeymoon is Over, The.   Judith Viorst.   LW

Honeymoon Postcard.   Paul Durcan.   OBCoV

Honeymooning couples blithely hanging out.   ITMA.   Roddy Lumsden.   NeBl

Honeystain / the rhetoricians of blackness.   Anti-Semanticist, The.   Everett Hoagland.   BPo; NBV

Honeysuckle.   J. C. Bloem.   TuT, *tr. by* Desmond Egan

Honeysuckle (Chevrefoil).   Marie de France.   BoWoP, *tr. by* Patricia Terry

Honeysuckle Rose.   Andy Razaf.   ReLy

"Honeysuckle Was the Saddest Odor of All, I Think."   Thadious M. Davis.   BlSi

Honeysuckles tap soil.   Nocturne: My Sister Life.   Erin Belieu.   NeAmPo

Hong Kong Blues.   Hoagy Carmichael.   ReLy

Hongo Store 29 Miles Volcano Hilo, Hawaii, The.   Garrett Kaoru Hongo.   PoPoPo

Honky-Tonk Blues.   Walter McDonald.   SwNoth

Honnd by honnd we schulle ous take.   Hand by Hand We Shall Us Take.   *Unknown.*   SacPr

Honor a going thing, goldfinch, corporation, tree.   Mechanism.   A. R. Ammons.   HAP

Honor be to Mudjekeewis!   Henry Wadsworth Longfellow.   UV   *Fr.* Song of Hiawatha, The.

Honor (1969).   Allston James.   CDa

"Honor," said the man.   Definitions.   Joseph Joel Keith.   PoToHe

Honora, should that cruel time arrive.   To Honora Sneyd.   Anna Seward.   CenSon; ECWP; PoBW

Honorable woodland snake.   Poem about Rain.   Nikolai Alekseievich Zabolotsky [*or* Zabolotskii].   TCRusP, *tr. by* Daniel Weissbort

Honored Counselor, Ornament of Heaven, Joy of An! Lady of the Morning, The.   *Unknown.*   HW, *tr. by* Samuel Noah Kramer and Diane Wolkstein

Honour.   Abraham Cowley.   BoLoP

Honour Dishonoured. Wilfrid Scawen Blunt. OBMV

Honour is flashed off exploit, so we say. In Honour of St. Alphonsus Rodriguez. Gerard Manley Hopkins. EBEV; OxAEP-2

Honour past all bens. Duncan Ban MacIntyre. NePenScot, *tr. by* Iain Crichton Smith *Fr.* Last Farewell to the Hills.

Honour plays a bubble's part. John Gay. PeLV *Fr.* Polly; an Opera.

Honour, that Guardian Angel, can alone. Martha Sansom. LW *Fr.* Clio.

Honour with Age. Walter Kennedy. OxBS

Honourable Entertainment Given to the Queen's Majesty in Progress at Elvetham, 1591, The. *Var. authors.*

    Phillida and Coridon. NoSic; OBEV; TTTS

    (Ploughman's Song, The.) NOBE

Honourable Winifred Wemyss, The. Limerick. *Unknown.* PeLi

Honoured I lived e'erwhile with honoured men. Honour Dishonoured. Wilfrid Scawen Blunt. OBMV

Honours that the people give always, The. Thespians at Thermopylae, The. Norman Cameron. GTBS-P

Honure, joy, helthe, and plesaunce. Charles, Duc d' Orléans. MiEL

Hoochie Coochie. Muddy Waters. NAAAL

Hooded Legion, The. Gerald McCarthy. CDa

Hoofbeats pounded. Good Attitude to Horses, A. Vladimir Vladimirovich Mayakovsky [*or* Maiakovskii]. TCRusP, *tr. by* P. Lemke

Hoofer, The. A. K. Redwing. VoR

Hook. Floyd Skloot. MoASP

Hook, The. Duncan Bush. TCAWP

Hook-nosed, longsighted he was, like me. Baltic Summer. Yunna Petrovna [*or* Iunna Pinkhusovna] Moritz [*or* Morits]. TCRP, *tr. by* Bernard Meares

Hook shot kisses the rim and, A. Fast Break. Edward Hirsch. DiPo; MoASP; VCAP

Hooly and Fairly. Joanna Baillie. RACG; WoRP

Hoopla. Star Black. KGB

Hoopoe Bird, The. Saleem Barakat. MAP, *tr. by* Lena Jayyusi and Naomi Shihab Nye

Hooray for Hollywood. Johnny Mercer. ReLy

Hooray for Love. Leo Robin. ReLy

Hoot. Marlene Mountain. HA

Hooters. Meic Stephens. AngWePo; TCAWP

Hoover, in grim silence, sat, The. Limerick. David Woodsford. PeLi

Hooves drummed / Seeming to say. On Being Kind to Horses. Vladimir Vladimirovich Mayakovsky [*or* Maiakovskii]. TCRP, *tr. by* Bernard Meares

Hop hop, thump thump. Stevie Smith. WPE *Fr.* Dedicated Dancing Bull and the Water Maid, The.

Hop-poles stand in cones, The. Midnight Skaters, The. Edmund Charles Blunden. FaBoTw; GTBS-P; MoBrPo; NOBE; NPeEn; PeFWW; WoPoe

Hop, Skip, and Jump. Gary Snyder. LCAP-2

Hope. Emily Jane Brontë. NoP-4

Hope. Opus 2. Witter Bynner. APT-1, *tr. by* Emanuel Morgan

Hope. Josephine D. Henderson Heard. CBWP-4

Hope. George Herbert. ChIV-2; NPeEn; OxBEV; WeW-3

Hope. Langston Hughes. APSN; OBAL; OBCA; OxIBACP; PFTM-1; TRP

Hope. Dolores de Iruretagoyena de Humphrey. ReBoTo

Hope. Randall Jarrell. MoAmPo

Hope. Sydney E. Jerrold. SacPr

Hope. Sister Juana Inés de la Cruz. SpanPo, *tr. by* Kate Flores

Hope. Christopher Smart. ChIV-1 *Fr.* Hymns for the Amusement of Children.

Hope. Theognis. AWP, *tr. by* John Hookham Frere

Hope. Clara Ann Thompson. CBWP-2

Hope. Mary E. Tucker. CBWP-1

Hope. *Unknown.* CIP-2, *tr. by* Frank O'Connor

Hope and Despair. Lascelles Abercrombie. OBMV

Hope and Faith. Isaac Leibush [*or* Yitskhok Leybush] Peretz [*or* Perets]. TrJP, *tr. by* Henry Goodman

Hope appears. Where Hope Lives. Carol Bell. GeoH

Hope Deferred. Clara Ann Thompson. CBWP-2

Hope for a Miracle. György Sárközi. IQMS, *tr. by* Roy Fuller

Hope! Fortune! Je m'en fous! Palladas [*or* Pallades]. GrAn

Hope I dreamed of was a dream, The. Mirage. Christina Georgina Rossetti. BoLoP; PoRA

Hope I handed Alfred, The. Azalea Poem, The. Jack Coulehan. BloBone

Hope is agony. Mikhail Naimy. GraLe, *tr. by* Sharif Elmusa and Gregory Orfalea *Fr.* Cord of Hope, The.

"Hope" is the thing with feathers. Emily Dickinson. APN-2; AmFaPo; ChAP; MoAmPo; NOBA; NoP-4; OxBA; SAmP; TAP; TCAPo

Hope is what skims time always from our lives. Julius Polyaenus. GrAn

Hope like a wisp of straw shines in the stable. Paul Verlaine. SxFrPo, *tr. by* Martin Sorrell

Hope, like the hyaena [*or* hyena], coming to be old. Henry Constable. EnLoPo; SCGP; Son *Fr.* Diana.

Hope! Not distant is the Springtime. Hope and Faith. Isaac Leibush [*or* Yitskhok Leybush] Peretz [*or* Perets]. TrJP, *tr. by* Henry Goodman

Hope, of all ills that men endure. In Praise of Hope. Abraham Cowley. OxAEP-1

Hope of burning off at least the top layer of the time's uncleanness, from the acid-bottles. (LL) Prescription of Painful Ends. Robinson Jeffers. APT-1; MoAmPo; OxBA

Hope's Okay. A. R. Ammons. HCAP

Hope Thou in God. Josephine D. Henderson Heard. CBWP-4

Hope thou in God: For I shall yet praise him, who is the health of my countenance, and my God. (LL) Bible, *O.T.* AWP; TrJP *Fr.* Psalms.

Hope! Thou vain, delusive maiden. Josephine D. Henderson Heard. CBWP-4

Hope was but a timid friend. Hope. Emily Jane Brontë. NoP-4

Hope, whose weak[e] being ruined [*or* ruin'd] is. Abraham Cowley. MeLP; NOSC *Fr.* Mistress, The.

Hope ye, my verses, that posterity. Joachim Du Bellay. PoE *Fr.* Ruins of Rome.

Hopeful old fellow called Rousseau, A. Limerick. John Fay. PeLi

Hopeful Spiritual Athlete, The. Kabir. RaBo, *tr. by* Robert Bly

Hopeless Desire Soon Withers and Dies. "A. W." NoSic

Hopelessly handcuffed to a mysterious butterfly. Lost Mohican Visits Hell's Kitchen, A. A. K. Redwing. VoR

Hopelessness. Li Ch'ing-chao. BLT, *tr. by* Kenneth Rexroth

Hopi Prophet Chooses a Pop. Heid E. Erdrich. AmPoNex

Hoping all the time. *Var. authors.* AWP *Fr.* Kokin Shu.

Hoping it might be so. (LL) Oxen, The. Thomas Hardy. CABP; ChAP; ChrPo; EBEV; HAP; HarvBoo; InPK-6; MoBrPo; NOBE; NoAM; OBCP; OxAEP-2; OxBTC; PeECV; RB; SoSe-8; TFi; TOF; TRP; WeW-3

Hoping publicly to humiliate her husband. Of Love, Death and the Sea-Squirt. Chris Greenhalgh. NeBl

Hopkins Enters the Roman Catholic Church. David Scott. NLP

Hopkins wrote, punning bird and verb. All quail to the wallowing. Lynne McMahon. ExTi

Hopper: In the Cafe. W.R. Elton. PoSol

Hopper never painted this, but here. American Solitude. Grace Schulman. PoSol

Hopper o'ditches, A. Riddle. *Unknown.* FaBoVe

Hopper painted this one empty of people. Cobb's Barns. Anne Babson Carter. PoSol

Hopper's "Nighthawks" (1942). Ira Sadoff. PoSol

Hopper's Women. Sue Standing. PoSol

Hopping frog, hop here and be seen. Christina Georgina Rossetti. VWP

Hopping Toad Blues. Raymond R. Patterson. SeSe

Hoppity. Alan Alexander Milne. NTCP

Hoppy. Reginald Gibbons. DiPo

Hops. Boris Leonidovich Pasternak. BoLoP; TTTS

Hops are a menace on the moon, a nuisance crop. Moon-Hops. Ted Hughes. CABP

Horace. Dániel Berzsenyi. IQMS, *tr. by* Peter Zollman

Horace composed an ode about a certain boy. Marbod of Rennes. CAGL; EroLit, *tr. by* John Boswell *Fr.* Unyielding Youth, The.

Horae. Robert Fitzgerald. APT-2

Horae Canonicae. W. H. Auden.

    Lauds. BBASP; TrCP

    Prime. PoE

    Terce. GI; PoE

    Vespers. FaBoMo

Horae Canonicae. Donald Davie. CRP

Horatian Epode to the Duchess of Malfi. Allen Tate. FaBoMo

Horat. Ode 29. Book 3. Horace. NPeEn *Fr.* Odes.

Horatian Ode upon Cromwell's Return from Ireland, An. Andrew Marvell. BASC; CABP; EBEV; ESCV; FSCP; GTBS-P; GeHe; HAP; NAEL-6v1; NAEL-7v1; NOBE; NOSC; NPeEn; NoP-4; OBEV; OBWP; OxAEP-1; OxBEV; PBRV; PoPoPo; SCGP; TFi

Horatius [*or* Horatius at the Bridge]. Thomas Babington Macaulay, 1st Baron Macaulay. CABP; EBNV; FaBoCh; FaBoWar; OBNV; OBWP; OxAEP-2 *Fr.* Lays of Ancient Rome.

Horeb's mountain top of old. Mountain Tops. Lizelia Augusta Jenkins Moorer. CBWP-3

Horestes. John Pickering [*or* Pikerying].

    Haltersick's Song. NoSic

    Song Sung by Egistus and Clytemnestra. NoSic

    Vice's Song, The. NoSic

Horizon. David Emrys James. WoPoe, *tr. by* Anthony Conran

Horizon, The. Kevin Hart. NOBAu

Horizon Blues. David Henderson. GT

Horizon line. Poem. Raymond Radiguet. CuPo

Horizon of Expectations, A. Only Indirectly. Giulia Niccolai. CItWP, *tr. by* Cinzia Sartini Blum and Lara Trubowitz

Horizon of islands shifting. Outer Banks, The. Muriel Rukeyser. APT-2

Horizon slopes away, The. Departure. Pierre Reverdy. CuPo

Horizons release skies. Rules and Ranges for Ian Tyson. Roy Fisher. Oth

Horizontal in a deckchair on the bleak ward [*or* Horizontal on a deckchair in the Ward]. Ezra Pound. Robert Lowell. NAAL-2v2; NOBA; NoAM

Horn, The. Léonie Adams. MoAmPo

(While coming to the feast I found.) APT-2

Horn, The. James Reeves. OTCP

Horn for weapon, and wool for shield. Zodiac Song, The. John Ruskin. NOBVV

Horn hung on an oak, A. Bit of Brass, A. Padraic Fallon. ModIr; NPeEn

Horn: I'm loved by my lord, and his shoulder. Cynewulf. ASW *Fr.* Riddles (Exeter Book).

Horn of doom is blaring, The! Sergey [*or* Sergei] Aleksandrovich Yesenin [*or* Essenin]. CAGL, *tr. by* Simon Karlinsky

Horn of Roland, The. Marina Ivanovna Tsvetayeva [*or* Tsvetaeva]. TCRusP, *tr. by* William Tjalsma

Horn: "Time was when I was weapon and warrior." Cynewulf. AnOE, *tr. by* Charles W. Kennedy *Fr.* Riddles (Exeter Book).

Horned Snake, The. Louis Oliver. HATNAP

Hornets collect on the side of the sun. Beetle Light. Madeline DeFrees. GifTon

Hornets occasionally build their nests near roads. Homer. OBVE, *tr. by* Christopher Logue *Fr.* Iliad, The.

Hornless hart carries off the harem, The. Royal Stag, The. Hugh MacDiarmid. FaBoMo

Hornlike at the top. (LL) Young Sycamore. William Carlos Williams. APT-1; TAP

Hornpipe. Dame Edith Sitwell. FaBoMo; GTBS-P *Fr.* Façade.

Horns [*or* Hornes] to bulls wise Nature lends. Beauty. Thomas Stanley. AWP; OBVE

Horns protruded from the. Rising, The. Jayne Cortez. NBV

Hornworm: Autumn Lamentation. Stanley Kunitz. AmFaPo; BodElec

Hornworm: Summer Reverie. Stanley Kunitz. BodElec

Horny-Goloch, The. *Unknown.* FaBoCh

Horny or Harm seems an ordinary home. Various Readings of an Illegible Postcard. Christine Hume. AmPoNex

Horoscope. Colleen J. McElroy. GT

Horowitz debuted a Schumann piece. What I Heard on the Radio Today. Marc J. Straus. BloBone

Horrible Decree, The. Charles Wesley.

"Sinners, abhor the Fiend." NOCV

Horrible Today, The. Max Jacob. AF, *tr. by* Ron Padgett

Horror. Peter Baum. AWP, *tr. by* Jethro Bithell

Horror. Gyula Illyés. IQMS, *tr. by* Anthony Edkins

Horror. Henry Treece. SPE

Horror Comic. Robert Conquest. OxBTC

Hors de Combat. "Anvari." ArPe, *tr. by* Omar S. Pound

Horse. Gloria Anzaldúa. UnSA

Horse. Louise Glück. NALW

Horse. Kenneth Rexroth. NNaP *Fr.* Bestiary, A.

Horse. Chase Twichell. ExTi

Horse. Michael Waters. UrbNat

Horse, The. Marie Laurencin. CuPo

Horse, The. Philip Levine. CoAP; VCAP

Horse, The. Valerie Patterson Napanangka. IBA

Horse, The. James Wright (1927–80). YaYoPo

Horse and a flea and three blind mice, A. Whoops! *Unknown.* NTCP

Horse and His Rider, The. Joanna Baillie. ECWP; NOEC

Horse and Tree. Rita Dove. TRP

Horse Boyle was called Horse Boyle because of his brother Mule. Dresden. Ciaran Carson. CIP-2; ModIr; NPeEn; PBCIP; PNI

Horse butcher, The. Pierre McOrlan. MFP, *tr. by* Martin Sorrell

Horse Calligram. Guillaume Apollinaire. PFTM-1

Horse can't pull while kicking, A. Horse Sense. *Unknown.* PWR

Horse Chestnut Tree, The. Richard Eberhart. MoAmPo

Horse Cursed by the Sun, The. *Unknown.* PeSAV, *tr. by* W. H. I. Bleek

Horse he sits on its saddless, The. Young Horseman. Lajos Kassák. IQMS, *tr. by* Edwin Morgan

Horse is running, A. Horse, The. Valerie Patterson Napanangka. IBA

Horse is white, The. Or it. Saving the Appearances. Charles Tomlinson. OxBEV

Horse meadow quarters roots as large, The. Genius of Fog at Ecola Creek Mouth. Sandra McPherson. ExTi

Horse on a Fence. George Evans. PmAP

Horse's Head, The. Brendan Kennelly. CIP-2

Horse's mind, The. Unity. Fazil Hüsnü Daglarca. RaBo, *tr. by* Tâlat S. Halman

Horse Sense. *Unknown.* PWR

Horse Show, The. William Carlos Williams. NOBA; TAP; VGW

Horse that carried Miss Kilmansegg, The. Thomas Hood. EBVV *Fr.* Miss Kilmansegg and Her Precious Leg.

Horse Thief, The. William Rose Benét. MoAmPo

Horse-Watering Hole, The. Yang Wei-chen. CoBLCP, *tr. by* Jonathan Chaves

Horse with a chestnut mane reflected in the green waves of the spring river. Tune: "Echoing Heaven's Everlastingness." Wang Kuo-wei. SuSp, *tr. by* Ching-i Tu

Horse with birds on its mane, doubt on its tail, The. Godhorse. Kojo Laing. HBAPE

Horseback. Carolyn Kizer. MoASP

Horseback on Sunday morning. Wild Geese, The. Wendell Berry. TRP

Horseman at the Roadside, The. Yang Wei-chen. CoBLCP, *tr. by* Jonathan Chaves

Horseman on the Skyline, The. Henry Lawson. CBAP

Horseman, pass by! (LL) W. B. Yeats. HAP; NAEL-5v2; NAEL-6v2; NoAM; NoP-4; OxBTC

Horses. Witter Bynner. APT-1

Horses. Edwin Muir. FaBoCh

Horses. Gwyn Thomas. OBWVE, *tr. by* Joseph P. Clancy

Horses. Dorothy Wellesley, Duchess of Wellington. OBMV; OxBTC

Horses, The. Ted Hughes. NoAM

Horses, The. Edwin Muir. CABP; EmeKit; HAP; HeIP-4; MoBrPo; NOBE; NPeEn; NePenScot; NoAM; OxBTC; PoE; RB; TRP; WeW-3

Horses at a Breach in the Great Wall. Ch'en Lin. ChinPo, *tr. by* Yip Wai-lim

Horses at Valley Store. Leslie Marmon Silko. VoR

Horses Chawin' Hay. Hamlin Garland. OBAL

Horses go down at dawn, The. Horses in the Lake. Pablo Antonio Cuadra. TCLAP, *tr. by* Ann McCarthy de Zavala and Grace Schulman

Horses in Flowers. Sappho. OBVE; WoPoe, *tr. by* Guy Davenport

Horses in Snow. Roberta Hill Whiteman. NoAM

Horses in the Lake. Pablo Antonio Cuadra. TCLAP, *tr. by* Ann McCarthy de Zavala and Grace Schulman

Horses in the Ocean. Boris Abramovich Slutsky [*or* Slutskii]. TCRusP, *tr. by* Daniel Weissbort

Horses in the Sea. Boris Abramovich Slutsky [*or* Slutskii]. TCRP, *tr. by* J. R. Rowland

Horses know how to swim. Horses in the Ocean. Boris Abramovich Slutsky [*or* Slutskii]. TCRusP, *tr. by* Daniel Weissbort

Horses of the sea, The. Christina Georgina Rossetti. NTCP *Fr.* Sing-Song.

Horses of Yilderin, The. Kenneth Patchen. APT-2

Horses on the Camargue. Roy Campbell. GTBS-P

Horses out of their brains bored all, The. Flying Noises. Thomas Lux. LCAP-2

Horses which Titan when discharged for the night, The. Catius As Conius Silius Italicus. RomPo, *tr. by* Marcus Wilson *Fr.* Punica, The.

Horsewoman of charm at Uttoxeter, A. Limerick. R. D. Condon. PeLi

Hos Ego Versiculos. Francis Quarles. NOSC *Fr.* Argalus and Parthenia.

Hosanna. Thomas Traherne. ChIV-2

Hosanna to Christ. Isaac Watts. NOCV

Hosannah! *Christus natus est.* (LL) Christus Natus Est. Countee Cullen. ChIV-2; ChrPo

Hosannah the home run! (LL) Dream of a Baseball Star. Gregory Corso. BB; PmAP

Hospital. Wilfred John Funk. PoToHe

Hospital. Charles North. FTOS

Hospital. Karl Shapiro. VGW

Hospital. Boris Abramovich Slutsky [*or* Slutskii]. TCRP, *tr. by* J. R. Rowland

Hospital, The. Patrick Kavanagh. BIrV; CABP; CIP-2; EmeKit; ModIr; NPeEn

Hospital, The. Sofiya [*or* Sofiia] Iul'evna Preygel [*or* Preigel']. TCRP, *tr. by* Bradley Jordan

Hospital, The. Boris Abramovich Slutsky [*or* Slutskii]. TCRusP, *tr. by* Daniel Weissbort

Hospital / All in white. My Friends. Mikhail Kuz'mich Lukonin. TCRP, *tr. by* Albert C. Todd

Hospital Barge at Cérisy. Wilfred Owen. HarvBoo; RB; TCAWP

Hospital Duties. *Unknown.* CBCWP

Hospital Evening. Gwen Harwood. EmeKit; FaBoWP

Hospital for Defectives. Thomas Blackburn. GTBS-P; OxBTC

Hospital for sick and needy Jews, A. New Jewish Hospital at Hamburg, The. Heinrich Heine. TrJP, *tr. by* Charles Godfrey Leland

Hospital Gypsy Song. Aleksandr Arkadevich Galich. TCRusP, *tr. by* Gerry Smith

Hospital Interiors. Giovanni Raboni. ItPo, tr. by Gayle Ridinger

Hospital Night. Francis Webb. BMAP

Hospital Poem. Sonia Sanchez. BPo

Hospital—Retrospections, The. Kenneth Mackenzie. CBAP (New Arrival.) BMAP

Hospital Soliloquy, A. Rose Terry Cooke. SWaP

Hospital State, The. Betsy Sholl. PBCAP

Hospital Window, The. James Dickey. HCAP; NoAM; VCAP

Host is riding from Knocknarea, The. Hosting of the Sidhe, The. W. B. Yeats. NoAM

Host of peaks rear up into the color of cold, A. Spending the Night at a Mountain Temple. Chia Tao. SuSp, tr. by Stephen Owen

Host set forth, and pour'd his steel waves far out of the fleet, The. Homer. FaBoWar, tr. by George Chapman Fr. Iliad, The.

Hostage to the phalli. Queynt. Anne Rouse. NeBl

Hostages, The. Muriel Rukeyser. AF

Hostel, The. Herman Melville. APN-2 Fr. Clarel: A Poem and Pilgrimage in the Holy Land.

Hostess' Daughter, The. Ludwig Uhland. AWP, tr. by Margarete Münsterberg

Hostess of the Ferry Inn, The. Gwerfyl Mechain. OBWVE, tr. by H. Idris Bell

Hosting of the Sidhe, The. W. B. Yeats. NoAM

Hot afternoon. Anita Virgil. HA

Hot Afternoons Have Been in West 15th Street. Paul Blackburn. VGW

Hot air balloon convention floats, The. Looking Up. Sujata Bhatt. EmeKit

Hot and Cold. Silvio Giussani. ItPo, tr. by Gayle Ridinger

Hot Anger stirs the soup; Grief moves the dust. Sisters, The. Melissa Cannon. FFC

Hot Boiled Beans. Unknown. ReMoGo

Hot Cake. Shu Hsi. ChiP, tr. by Arthur Waley

Hot Codlins. Unknown. ReMoGo

Hot Comb. Natasha Trethewey. SpirFl

Hot cross buns! Hot-cross buns! / One a penny, two a penny. Mother Goose. OxNR; ReMoGo

Hot Day at the Races. Tom Raworth. SPE

Hot day. Dying of thirst. Slake myself. Meleager. EroLit, tr. by Kenneth McLeish

Hot Day in Sydney, A. Unknown. NOBAu

Hot Dog Poem, The. Jane Barnes. GLP

Hot Evening, A. Sa'di Yusuf. MAP, tr. by Lena Jayyusi and Naomi Shihab Nye

Hot Flame of My Grief, The. Moses Ibn Ezra. TrJP, tr. by Solomon Solis-Cohen

Hot, humid, the smell of sewage. Greenhalgh's Pub. Julian Croft. NOBAu

Hot ice shoots (it seems) through. Epiphany. Christine D'Haen. TuT, tr. by Dennis O'Driscoll

Hot in June a narrow winged. Nameless One, A. Margaret Avison. HeIP-4; NOBC

Hot midsummer night on Water Street, A. Hot Night on Water Street. Louis Simpson. TwCP

Hot night. Cor Van den Heuvel. HA

Hot night makes us keep our bedroom windows open, The. To Speak of Woe That Is in Marriage. Robert Lowell. NAAL-2v2; NoAM

Hot night of the ramparts. Embrace the Blade. Joyce Mansour. HAWP, tr. by Carol Cosman

Hot Night on Water Street. Louis Simpson. TwCP

Hot Noon in Malabar. Kamala Das. OMIP

Hot Pease Man, The. Mother Goose. OxNR; ReMoGo

Hot Springs. Earle Birney. OxBC

Hot. Steaming hot. Sex and the Single Spud. Ann Slegman. SpudSo

Hot stink of skunk. Camino Real. Adrienne Rich. BodElec

Hot summer wind, A. Lorraine Ellis Harr. HA

Hot sun[ne], cool[e] fire, temper[e]d with sweet air[e]. George Peele. ChIV-1; NOBE; NPeEn; NoSic; OxBEV; OxBSP; OxBoLi; RB Fr. David and [Fair] Bethsabe.

Hot thumb, The. Just after Michael's Death, the Game of Pool. Richard Tipping. BMAP

Hotel and again! My friend Paul is a prisoner of the Germans My, The. In Search of the Traitor. Max Jacob. AF, tr. by Michael Brownstein

Hotel Ameridemocratogrando. Black Man, 13th Floor. James A. Emanuel. NBV

Hotel de Dream. Jane Cooper. ExTi

Hotel de L'Etoile. Matthew Rohrer. AmPoNex

Hotel Fire: New Orleans. Paul Ruffin. InPK-6

Hôtel Fraternité. Hans Magnus Enzensberger. CLPP, tr. by Jerome Rothenberg

Hotel Fresno. Dixie Salazar. GeoHom

Hotel Lautréamont. John Ashbery. FTOS; HarvBoo

Hotel Marine. David Campbell. BMAP

Hotel Normandie Pool, The. Derek Walcott. VCWP

Hotel Paradiso e Commerciale. John Malcolm Brinnin. TwCP

Hôtel Transylvanie. Frank O'Hara. NeAP; PoM

Hotpink crimplene petunias. Matching Flowers. Kate Foley. Prnts

Hots, The. Michael Sharkey. NOBAu

Hottentot Venus. Stephen Gray. PeSAV

Houdini. Moniza Alvi. EmeKit; MFPA

Houdini. Eli W. Mandel. NIP-4; NOBC

Hound, The. Robert Francis. SoSe-8

Hound, The. Kaye Starbird. KaS

Hound / Could never be called refined, The. Angry Poet, The. Frank O'Connor. CIP-2

Hound of Heaven, The. Francis Thompson. CABP; ChIV-2; InvLi; MoBrPo; NAEL-5v2; NAEL-6v2; OBMV; SacPr; TFi

"I fled Him, down the nights and down the days." EroLit; ITBLP

Hounds, The. John Freeman. OBMV; OxBSP

Hounds are breathing at my trail, The. John Fuller. PeLV Fr. Fox-Trot.

Hounds are either the work of wind, The. Dennis Phillips. FTOS Fr. Means.

Hounds of the Soul, The. Louis Ginsberg. TrJP

Hour, The. Juana de Ibarbourou. TCLAP, tr. by Sophie Cabot Black

Hour after Hour, Day after Day. Rosalía de Castro. SpanPo, tr. by Muriel Kittel

Hour at last come round, The. Dying Gaul, The. Desmond O'Grady. BIrV; PBCIP

Hour farther witch art in Heaven. Hour farther. Robert Desnos. MFP, tr. by Martin Sorrell

Hour from night to day, The. Four in the Morning. Wislawa Szymborska. BLT

"Hour gets later, the times get worse, The." Preliminary Poem. John Heath-Stubbs. OxBC

Hour-Glass, The. Robert Herrick. BeJo; CaPo

Hour Glass, The. Edward Quillinan. NOBRP

Hour-Glass [or Houre-Glasse], The. Ben Jonson. BeJo; EnLoPo; NIP-4

Hour has struck, though I heard not the bell!, The. (LL) George Meredith. NAEL-6v2; Son Fr. Modern Love.

Hour in a Studio, An. Richard Watson Gilder. APN-2

Hour is dark. The river comes to its end, The. Mary Ursula Bethell. PeNZ Fr. By the River Ashley.

Hour is held deep, in the underneath of time, An. Naming Souls. Uri Zvi Greenberg. PeFWW, tr. by Jon Silkin and Exra Spicehandler

"Hour is late, The," the shepherds said. Shepherd Left Behind, The. Mildred Plew Meigs. TrCP

Hour is tired as if it were time for bed, The. Uri Zvi Greenberg. FIT, tr. by Robert Friend

Hour of Death, The. Felicia Dorothea Hemans. NOBRP

Hour of Magic, The. William Henry Davies. MoBrPo

Hour of Sleep, The. Robert Ellis. OBWVE, tr. by H. Idris Bell

Hour of the Angel, The. Rudyard Kipling. OxBSo Fr. Land and Sea Tales.

Hour of the Siesta, The. Judith Ortiz Cofer. PueRic

Hour's Glory, The. Henrietta Cordelia Ray. CBWP-3

Hour ten he rose, ten-sworded, every finger. Timoshenko. Sidney Keyes. OBWP

Hour, the spot, are here at last, The. At Harper's Ferry Just before the Attack. Edward W. Williams. CBCWP

Hour was: A child's legs, The. Jerusalem and the Hour. Rashid Husain [or Hussein]. MAP, tr. by Lena Jayyusi and Peter Porter

Hour when the moon mists over. Dawn. Philippe Jaccottet. VCWP

Hour with Thee, An. Sir Walter Scott. BoLoP

Hourglass. Josephine Jacobsen. NoP-4

Hourglass, The. Joseph Beaumont. NOSC

Hourglass Lying Down. Alice Rahon. SurWo, tr. by Nancy Deffebach and Vanina Deler

Hours, The. John Peale Bishop. OxBA

Hours, The. Christopher Pearse Cranch. PWR

Hours, The. David Diop. NegPo, tr. by Ellen Conroy Kennedy

Hours, The. Paul Ramsey. CRP

Hours ago he woke up the sky. Bird on a Jaunt. T. Harri Jones. TCAWP

Hours are viewless angels, The. Hours, The. Christopher Pearse Cranch. PWR

Hours before dawn we were woken by the quake. Aubade. William Empson. FaBoMo; FaBoTw; OxAEP-2; OxBEV; OxBTC

Hours glide, the. Midnight. Vicente Huidobro. CuPo

Hours Musicians Keep, The. Aleda Shirley. SwNoth

Hours of rest are over, The. To-Day. Lessie M. Drown. PWR

Hours of Sleep. Unknown. NBLV

Hours of the Day, The. George Dillon. IllVoic

Hours of the Day, The. Richard Kenney.

In Retrospect.   Son

Hours of the Passion, The.   *Unknown.*   MiEL

Hours pass / slowly as a snail.   Clockface.   Judith Thurman.   Spl

Hours rise up putting off stars and it is, The.   Impression.   E. E. Cummings.   MoAmPo; OxBA

Hours that kept looking at us, The.   Handless Clock.   Raymond Radiguet.   CuPo

Hous-keeping's dead, *Saturio:* wot'st thou where?   Joseph Hall.   PBRV   *Fr.* Virgidemiarum Book 5.

House.   Robert Browning.   NAEL-5v2; NAEL-6v2

House.   Murray Edmond.   PeNZ

House.   Robert Hass.   LoL

House.   Laura Mullen.   ExTi

House, A.   Yuly [*or* Iulii] Markovich Daniel.   TCRP, *tr. by* Arthur Boyars and David Burg

House, The.   George Bowering.   NOBC

House, The.   Robert Creeley.   FTOS

House, The.   Robert Minhinnick.   AngWePo

House, The.   Gabriela Mistral.   BBASP; TCLAP, *tr. by* Doris Dana

House, The.   William Carlos Williams.   VGW

House across the Way, The.   Ralph Hodgson.   FaBoTw

House and Land.   Allen Curnow.   PeNZ

House and the Road, The.   Josephine Preston Peabody.   ITBLP

House Beautiful, The.   Robert Louis Stevenson.   NOBE

House beside the Sea, The.   Rachel Hadas.   FFC

House Blessing.   *Zuni Oral Tradition.*   NAWM-7v2, *tr. by* Ruth L. Bunzel   *Fr.* Shalako.

House (Blown Apart).   David Shapiro.   BodElec

House built within men's reach, A.   Drinking Wine.   *Unknown.*   ChinPo, *tr. by* Yip Wai-lim

House by the Sea.   Johanna Kruit.   TuT, *tr. by* Micheal O'Siadhail

House by the Sea, The.   Elizabeth Stoddard.   SWaP

House by the Side of the Road, The.   Sam Walter Foss.   BRP; ITBLP

House Call to a Man with Parkinson's Disease, A.   Michael O'Reilly.   BloBone

House can be haunted by those who were never there, A.   Selva Oscura.   Louis MacNeice.   HarvBoo

House Cap.   Bernadette Mayer.   FTOS

House cat has never seen the sea, The.   Woman asleep.   Marie-Claire Bancquart.   MFP, *tr. by* Martin Sorrell

House catch on fire and ain't no water 'round.   Southern Blues.   *Unknown.*   APT-1

House Divided, A.   Michael Ondaatje.   MoCV

House Fear.   Robert Frost.   VGW   *Fr.* Hill Wife, The.

House fell head-first, quietly crushing all but a child, The.   Bianor.   GrAn

House full, a hole full, A.   *Unknown.*   OxNR

House full, [a] yard full, [A].   Riddle.   *Unknown.*   LB; NTCP

House gives way to dimmer shades of dim, The.   Domi Solus.   Danny Anderson.   Unle

House Guest.   Elizabeth Bishop.   TAP

House had gone to bring again, The.   Need of Being Versed in Country Things, The.   Robert Frost.   APT-1; NOBA; NoAM; OxBA; SAmP; TCAPo; TRP; UnPo

House in Broad Street, red brick, with nine rooms, The.   Things, The.   Conrad Potter Aiken.   HAP; WeW-3

House in Byzantium, A.   Agathias.   GrAn, *tr. by* Fleur Adcock

House in Krasnogruda.   Czeslaw Milosz.   BodElec

House in St. Petersburg.   Stanley Burnshaw.   WoPoe

House in Taos, A.   Langston Hughes.   APT-2

House in the Green Well, The.   John Hall Wheelock.   MoAmPo

House in the long ago, The.   House by the Sea.   Johanna Kruit.   TuT, *tr. by* Micheal O'Siadhail

House in the Wood, The.   Randall Jarrell.   LCAP-2

House Is an Enigma.   Laura Jensen.   LCAP-2

House is cold. It's raining, The.   Joseph Come Back as the Dusk.   Franz Wright.   LCAP-2

House is crammed: Tier beyond tier they grin, The.   Blighters.   Siegfried Sassoon.   FaBoTw; NoAM; OxBEV; OxBSP; PoWW

House is filled. The last heartthrob, The.   Near the Ocean.   Robert Lowell.   NOBA

House is haunted; when the little feet, The.   Haunted.   Edith Nesbit.   VWP

House Is Old, The.   Ron Schreiber.   GLP

House is so quiet now, The.   Vacuum, The.   Howard Nemerov.   NIL-7; NIP-4; RB

House Martins: This wind wafts little creatures.   Cynewulf.   ASW   *Fr.* Riddles (Exeter Book).

House-Mates.   Leon Gellert.   CBAP; NOBAu

House my earthly parent left, The.   Cottage, The.   Jones Very.   APN-1; OxBA

House Next Door, The.   Douglas Dunn.   OxBC

House next door has yellow windows, The.   Factory, The.   Aleksandr Aleksandrovich Blok.   TCRP, *tr. by* Yakov Hornstein

House of Alvargonzález, The.   Antonio Machado Ruiz.   SpanPo, *tr. by* Denise Levertov

House of Breath.   Ken Gerner.   GifTon

House of Broughton Street, The.   Mary Ann Larkin.   AiP

House of Busyrane, The.   Edmund Spenser.   NoSic   *Fr.* Faerie Queene, The.

House of Christmas, The.   Gilbert Keith Chesterton.   ChrPo; MoBrPo; SacPr

House of Desire, The.   Sherley Anne Williams.   BlSi

House of Falling Leaves, The.   William Stanley Braithwaite.   NAAAL

House of five fires, you never raised me.   In the Longhouse, Oneida Museum.   Roberta Hill Whiteman.   NoAM

House of God, The.   Alec Derwent Hope.   OxBC

House of God, The.   Bishop Richard Mant.   SacPr

House of God is due to be converted, The.   Development.   Dennis Joseph Enright.   OxBSP

House of Hospitalities, The.   Thomas Hardy.   RB

House of Life, The.   Dante Gabriel Rossetti.

("And the last bird fly into the last light.") (LL)   NoP-4

Barren Spring.   EBVV; NoP-4

Birth-Bond, The.   Son

Body's Beauty.   Son

Bridal Birth.   Son

Choice, The.   GTBS-P; OBEV

Heart's Haven.   Son

Inclusiveness.   NAEL-5v2; NAEL-6v2

Kiss, The.   NOBVV; Son

Life-in-Love.   HAP

Lost Days.   SacPr

Lost on Both Sides.   NoP-4

Lovesight.   EBVV; GTBS-P; NAEL-5v2; NAEL-6v2

Nuptial Sleep.   EBVV; NAEL-5v2; NAEL-6v2; NOBVV

One Hope, The.   GSo; NAEL-5v2; NAEL-6v2

Sea-Limits, The.   NAEL-5v2; NAEL-6v2

Severed Selves.   BoLoP

(Sibylla Palmifera.)   OxAEP-2

Silent Noon.   GSo; HAP; NAEL-5v2; NAEL-6v2; NoP-4

Sonnet, A [*or* "A Sonnet is a moment's monument"].   GSo; NIL-7; Son

(Sonnet, The.)   NAEL-5v2; NAEL-6v2

Soul's Beauty.   OBEV

Superscription, A.   EBVV; GSo; GTBS-P; NAEL-5v2; NAEL-6v2; NoP-4

Willowwood ("And now love sang: but his was such a song").   NAEL-5v2; NAEL-6v2; OxBSo

Willowwood ("I sat with Love upon a woodside well").   CABP; NAEL-5v2; NAEL-6v2; OxBSo

Willowwood ("O ye, all ye that walk in Willowwood").   NAEL-5v2; NAEL-6v2; OxBSo

Willowwood ("So sang he: and as meeting rose and rose").   NAEL-5v2; NAEL-6v2; OxBSo

Without Her.   Son

Woodspurge, The.   CABP; EBEV; GTBS-P; HAP; HelP-4; NAEL-6v2; NOBE; NPeEn; NoP-4; OBEV; OxBEV; SCGP; TFi; UnPo

House of Madam Juju, The.   Mieko Kanai.   BoWoP, *tr. by* Christopher Drake

House of Mercy, A.   Stevie Smith.   FaBoWP; HarvBoo

House of Night, The.   Philip Freneau.

"And by that light around the dome appear'd."   NAAL-3; TCAPo

"And from the woods the late resounding note."   TCAPo

"And from within the howls of Death I heard."   TCAPo

"And here and there with laurel shrubs between."   NAAL-3

"At distance far approaching to the tomb."   NAAL-2v1; NAAL-3; TCAPo

"At last, by chance and guardian fancy led."   NAAL-2v1; NAAL-3; TCAPo

"Before the hearse Death's chaplain seem'd to go."   TCAPo

"But now this man of hell toward me turned."   NAAL-2v1; NAAL-3

"By some sad means, when reason holds no sway."   TCAPo

"Dark was the sky, and not one friendly star."   TCAPo

"Dim burnt the lamp, and now the phantom Death."   TCAPo

"Hills sink to plains, and man returns to dust."   TCAPo

"Meantime from an adjoining chamber came."   NAAL-3

"Much spoke he of the myrtle and the yew."   NAAL-2v1; NAAL-3

"No pleasant fruit or blossom gaily smiled."   NAAL-3

"Nor look'd I back, till to a far off wood."   TCAPo

"O'er a dark field I held my dubious way."   TCAPo

"Pathetic were their words, and well they aimed."   TCAPo

"Peace to this awful dome!—when straight I heard."   NAAL-3

"Poppy there, companion to repose, The."   NAAL-3

"Primrose there, the violet darkly blue, The."   NAAL-3

"Rude, from the wide extended Chesapeke." TCAPo

"Sad was his countenance, if we can call." NAAL-2v1; NAAL-3

"Then up three winding stairs my feet were brought." NAAL-2v1; NAAL-3

"There cedars dark, the osier, and the pine." NAAL-3

"Too nearly join'd to sickness, toils, and pains." TCAPo

"Towering Alps, the haughty Appenine, The." TCAPo

"Trembling, across the plain my course I held." TCAPo

"Trembling I write my dream, and recollect." NAAL-2v1; NAAL-3; TCAPo

"Up rushed a band, with compasses and scales." NAAL-2v1; NAAL-3

Vision of the Night, The. NAAL-2v1; NAAL-3

"What is this Death, ye deep read sophists, say?" TCAPo

"When Nature bids thee from the world retire." TCAPo

House of Prayer, The. William Cowper. ChIV-2 *Fr.* Olney Hymns.

House of Pride, The. William James Dawson. PoToHe

House of Red Leaves, The. Liu E. CoBLCP, *tr. by* Jonathan Chaves

House of Rest. Sir John Betjeman. OxAEP-2

House of Rest, The. Julia Ward Howe. SWaP

House of Spring. Muso Soseki. EaWin, *tr. by* W. S. Merwin

House of the Mouse, The. Lucy Sprague Mitchell. NTCP

House on a Cliff. Louis MacNeice. HarvBoo; ModIr; NOIV; NPeEn

House on Bentalou Street, The. Beginnings. Michael S. Weaver. PBCAP

House on Buder Street, The. Gary Gildner. TAP

House on fire, A! We stumbled over the snow. Houses Burning; Quebec. Patrick Anderson. NOBC

House on Moscow Street, The. Marilyn Nelson Waniek. UnSA

House on the Hill, The. Edwin Arlington Robinson. APN-2; MakPoe; MoAmPo; NAAL-2v2; NCAP

House over the garden is a bouquet of evening windows, The. Mikhail Yeryomin. ItGoST, *tr. by* J. Kates

House Plants. David McFadden. NOBC

House ringed round with trees and in the trees, A. Asylum. John Freeman. OBMV

House Slave, The. Rita Dove. NoAM

House-snake dwells here still, The. Closed World, The. Denise Levertov. NoP-4

House Song to the East. *Unknown.* TTTS

House Sparrows. Anthony Hecht. OWoS

House Style, The. Elizabeth Macklin. KGB

House That Fear Built: Warsaw, 1943, The. Jane Flanders. PBCAP

House That Jack Built, The. Mother Goose. LB; OxBEV; OxBoLi; OxNR; ReMoGo

House That Jack Built, The. *Unknown.* NBLV; OxBoLi

House That Was, The. Laurence Binyon. MoBrPo

House-Top, The. Herman Melville. APN-2; CBCWP; NAAL-2v1; NAAL-3; NCAP; NOBA; TCAPo

House, village, city, land, and empire harvest hurt. Women's Rule. Friedrich von Logau. GePo, *tr. by* George C. Schoolfield

House was empty and, The. Music in an Empty House. Hugh Sykes Davies. SPE

House Was Quiet and the World Was Calm, The. Wallace Stevens. AiP; HAP; NoP-4; SAmP; VGW

House was shaken by a rising wind, The. Brainstorm. Howard Nemerov. HAP; TRP

House was still—the room was still, The. Charlotte Brontë. NOBVV

House where I was born, The. Doves, The. Katharine Tynan. AWP

House, with blind unhappy face, The. Gray Folk, The. Edith Nesbit. NOBVV; PEW

House with Nobody in It, The. Joyce Kilmer. ChAP

House-wreckers have left the door and a staircase, The. House-wreckers, The. Charles Reznikoff. APT-2; KaS

Housebound. Amy Gerstler. ExTi

Household. Laura Jensen. LCAP-2

Household Cavalry, Llanstephan. Sally Roberts Jones. TCAWP

Household Fires. Indira Sant. OMIP, *tr. by* Vinay Dharwadker

Household Gods. Jim Elledge. SwNoth

Household of Eight. Abraham Reisen. WoPoe, *tr. by* Nathan Halper

Household of Ruth, The. Mrs. Henry Linden. CBWP-4

Household Rules. Farewell Avenue, Chicago, 1946. Lisa Ress. GotH

Household words, no more depart. (LL) Seaweed. Henry Wadsworth Longfellow. APN-1; ColAP; OxBA; TAP

Householder Departs from the City, The. Nathan [*or* Natan] Alterman. FIT, *tr. by* Robert Friend

Housekeeping. Lucie Brock-Broido. ExTi

Houseplant. Felicity Napier. BrRo

Houses. Agha Shahid Ali. NIP-4

Houses. Aileen Fisher. NTCP

Houses, The. "Robin Hyde."

"Adolicus; that's a creeper rug, its small." PeNZ

"Hares on their forms at dusk were not so still." PeNZ

"None of it true; for Christ's sake, spill the ink." PeNZ

Houses, The. Eden Phillpotts. OxBTC

Houses, The. October. Yvor Winters. APT-2

Houses, an embassy, the hospital. Days of 1964. James Merrill. CoAP; HCAP; NAAL-2v2; PoE; VCAP

Houses and rooms are full of perfumes. Walt Whitman. CAGL; UnPo *Fr.* Song of Myself.

Houses and the haystacks are on fire, The. Razglednica (2). Miklós Radnóti. IQMS, *tr. by* Peter Zollman

Houses are faces. Houses. Aileen Fisher. NTCP

Houses are haunted, The. Disillusionment of Ten O'Clock. Wallace Stevens. APT-1; NAAL-2v2; NoAM; OxBA; PAI; RB; SAmP; SoSe-8; TCAPo; TRP; TTTS

Houses Burning; Quebec. Patrick Anderson. NOBC

Houses, churches, mixed together. Description of London, A. John Bancks. NOEC; OBCoV

Houses die, and will not die, The. Heartland. Jim Barnes. HATNAP

Houses in country and city. Requiem. Wang Fan-chih. CrYelRi, *tr. by* Sam Hamill

Houses like Angels. Jorge Luis Borges. TCLAP, *tr. by* Robert Fitzgerald

Houses of Corr an Chait are cold, The. Seamas Dall Mac Cuarta. NOIV

Houses of Emily Dickinson, The. Larry Rubin. NIP-4

Housewife. Josephine Miles. APT-2

Housewife. Anne Sexton. NALW

Housewife's Prayer on the Morning Preceding a Fete, The. Elizabeth Moody. ECWP

Housewifery. Edward Taylor. *See* Huswifery

Housework. Amanda Berenguer. WPOW, *tr. by* Priscilla Joslin

Housework. Joan Larkin. WiU

Housing Poem, The. Dian Million. ReEnLa

Hovering clouds scatter over the islet. Arriving at North Pond by Stupid Brook on a Morning Walk after the Rain. Liu Tsung-yüan. SuSp, *tr. by* Jan W. Walls

How. Joanne Burns. BMAP

How a Girl Got Her Chinese Name. Nellie Wong. WPOW

How a Girl Was Too Reckless of Grammar [by Far]. Guy Wetmore Carryl. OBAL

How-a! How-a! / O-ta-pa! / I am proud of being at home! *Unknown.* APN-2 *Fr.* War Dance.

How about that! (LL) To Satch. Samuel Allen. ISC; MoASP; PAI; TTY

How about the Mount of Mounts? Looking at Mount T'ai-Shan. Tu Fu. ChinPo, *tr. by* Yip Wai-lim

How about You. Ralph Freed. ReLy

How absence becomes presence. Presence, The. Elder Olson. IllVoic

How admirable! Basho. EH, *tr. by* Robert Hass

How am I hitched. Suffering. Albert Ehrenstein. TrJP, *tr. by* Babette Deutsch

How an Old Man Can Regain His Youth through Sexual Potency. Ibn Kamal. EroLit, *tr. by* Jo Lakeland

How Annandale Went Out. Edwin Arlington Robinson. APT-1; GSo; MoAmPo; NOBA; NoAM; SoSe-8

How Apollo's laurel sapling shakes. Callimachus. HePo, *tr. by* Barbara Hughes Fowler *Fr.* Hymns.

How are the mighty fallen, and the weapons of war perished! (LL) Bible, *O.T.* NPeEn; OBVE; OBWP; TrJP *Fr.* Second Samuel.

How Are Things in Glocca Morra? Burton Lane. ReLy

How Are You, Dear World, This Morning? Horace Logo Traubel. TrJP

How are you faring, Uma. Rām Basu. SinGod, *tr. by* Rachel Fell McDermott

How are you so smooth-faced. Girl. *Unknown.* RB, *tr. by* Anne Pennington

How at my sheet goes the same crooked worm. (LL) Dylan Thomas. CABP; EBEV; FaBoMo; HarvBoo; MoBrPo; NAEL-5v2; NAEL-6v2; NOBE; NPeEn; NoAM; NoP-4; OBWVE; OxAEP-2; OxBEV; OxBTC; PoE; RB; SCV; TFi; UnPo

How Awful. Idea Vilariño. TANSG, *tr. by* Louise B. Popkin

How awful, how sublime this view. Written on the Sea-Shore. Felicia Dorothea Hemans. RWP

How awkward it looks. Buson. EH, *tr. by* Robert Hass

"How bare! How all the lion-desert lies." Macrinus against Trees. "Michael Field." WPE

How Beastly the Bourgeois Is. D. H. Lawrence. NAEL-5v2; NAEL-6v2; OBSV; PAI

How beauteous is the bond. Peau de Chagrin of State Street, The. Oliver Wendell Holmes. TCAPo

How beautiful and calm how crimson pale. Spirit Craft, The. Charles G. Ballard. VoR

How beautiful are both these nothings. (LL) Shane O'Neill's Cairn. Robinson Jeffers. NOBA; NoAM

How beautiful are thy feet with shoes. Bible, *O.T.* EroLit, *tr. by* King James Version *Fr.* Song of Solomon, The [*or* The Song of Songs].

How beautiful, how beautiful you streamed upon my sight. Corinne's Last Love-Song. Lady Jane Francesca Wilde. VWP

How beautiful is the rain! Rain in Summer. Henry Wadsworth Longfellow. TreFP

How beautiful the river is in spring. Sunset. Tu Fu. CrYelRi, *tr. by* Sam Hamill

How Beautiful upon the Mountains. Bible, *O.T.* TrJP *Fr.* Isaiah.

How beautiful you are, my love. Canticle for Abba Jacob, A. Marilyn Nelson Waniek. FFC

How beautifully they remembered beauty. (LL) Silver Sands, The. Richard Blanco. AmPoNex; NAPBL

How bitter for these border men! Call to Arms. Tso Yen-nien. CoBCP, *tr. by* Burton Watson

How bittersweet it is on winter nights. Cracked Bell, The. Charles Baudelaire. SxFrPo, *tr. by* James McGowan

How black it is, how fast it is, below? (LL) Neurasthenia. Agnes Mary Frances Robinson. NOBVV; NPeEn

How blessed [*or* blest] was the created state. Fall, The. John Wilmot, 2d Earl of Rochester. ChIV-1; EnLoPo

How blest are lovers in disguise! Song, A. George Farquhar. NOSC

How blest art thou, canst love the country [*or* countrey], Wroth. To Sir Robert Wroth. Ben Jonson. BeJo

How blest be[e] they then, who his favo[u]rs prove. Mary Sidney Wroth, Countess of Montgomery. BASC *Fr.* Pamphilia to Amphilanthus.

How blest is he, who for his country dies. To the Earl of Oxford, Late Lord Treasurer. Jonathan Swift. FaBoWar; OBVE

How blest the land that counts among. Statesmen, The. Ambrose Bierce. APN-2

How blest would be Ïerne's isle. Written in Ireland. Mary Alcock. ECWP; NOEC

How blind men are! We surely cannot know. Understanding. H. W. Bliss. PoToHe

How brave is the hunter who nobly will dare. Manly Sports. Marion Bernstein. NePenScot

How brave the peasant who lives beside the lake. Hsü Chung-hsing. CoBLCP *Fr.* Song of Catching Tigers.

"How brent is your brow, my Lady Elspat!" Lady Elspat. *Unknown.* ESPB

How bright this weird autumnal eve. Fires in Illinois. John James Piatt. APN-2

How brightly glistening in the sun. Home. Anne Brontë. VWP

How brittle are the Piers. Emily Dickinson. NCAP; SacPr

How busie are the sonnes of men? Roger Williams. SCAP

How busied's man. My CLose-Committee. Mildmay Fane, 2d Earl of Westmorland. BeJo

How, butler, how! bevis a tout! *Unknown.* MiEL

How Callum Innes Paints. Peter Finch. Oth

How Came What Came Alas. HeidiLynn Nilsson. NeAmPo

How can a girl with such a big belly be so desirable? Mrs. Loewinsohn etc. Ron Loewinsohn. NeAP

How can I be bitter? Second-Hand Elegy, A. Michael Anania. CDa

How can I call out! How can I shout? At Night. Bella [*or* Izabella] Akhatovna Akhmadulina. BoWoP, *tr. by* Daniel Halpern and Albert Todd

How can I climb the Mount of Purgatory? Cato. Charles Hubert Sisson. NOCV

How can I describe anything when all these interruptions keep *arriving* and then. Hannah Weiner. PmAP *Fr.* Clairvoyant Journal.

How can I give thee up, my child, my dearest, earliest born. Wail of the Divorced. Mary E. Tucker. CBWP-1

How can I hope a wise heart to attain. Dietmar, von Aist [*or* Eist]. GePo

How can I make myself stony like you? (LL) Stone on the Hilltop, The. Lu Yu. CoBCP; ColAnChi, *tr. by* Burton Watson

How can I regret my life. Signal, The. David Ignatow. NNaP

How Can I See You, Love. David Vogel. HP, *tr. by* A. C. Jacobs

How Can I Sing. Odia Ofeimun. HBAPE

How can I sleep, when in the window glow. Full Moon in Salzburg. Lilly Sauter. AuPH, *tr. by* Lowell A. Bangerter

How can I speak your spirit. Earth Man. Lynne Wycherley. Prnts

How can I tell you of the terrible cries. Wars, The. Howard Moss. VCAP

How can I tell you what is in my heart. How Deep Is the Ocean? (How High Is the Sky?). Irving Berlin. ReLy

How can I thank you B, for your ear, your mind, your affection? Inn at Kirchstetten, The. James Laughlin. PmAP

How can I, that girl standing there. Politics. W. B. Yeats. AmFaPo; HeIP-4; OxBTC; PoE; SCV

How can I then return in happy plight. William Shakespeare. AWTN *Fr.* Sonnets.

How can I turn from Africa and live? (LL) Far Cry from Africa, A. Derek Walcott. AmFaPo; ESEAA; HeIP-4; NAEL-5v2; NAEL-6v2; NIL-7; NoAM; NoP-4; TTY; UnPo

How can I turn this wheel that turns my life. Wheel, The. Edwin Muir. NoAM

How can I, who cannot control. Blind Steersmen. Francis Ernest Kobina Parkes. PBA

How can I write about you. My True Love Hath My Heart. Naomi Mitchison. LW

How can one make an absence flower. Flowering Absence, A. John Montague. BiHa; CIP-2; PBCIP

How can she live till in her blood He live! (LL) Ribh Considers Christian Love Insufficient. W. B. Yeats. BBASP; RaBo

How can that black woman be so beautiful? Kamalākānta Bhattācārya. SinGod, *tr. by* Rachel Fell McDermott

How can the tide of the river be compared to your love? Po Chü-i. SuSp *Fr.* Tune: "Ripples Sifting Sand."

How can there be heroic feelings, as in bygone days? Lamenting Yang Ch'uan. "Lu Hsün." SuSp, *tr. by* William R. Schultz

How can they stand it, going out in the world with only $10 and a hydrogen bomb? (LL) Yiddishe Kopf. Allen Ginsberg. BodElec; TaR

How can they write or paint. Observations in a Cornish Teashop. Kenneth Rexroth. OBAL

How can we know the dancer from the dance? (LL) Among School Children. W. B. Yeats. CABP; GTBS-P; HAP; HarvBoo; MoBrPo; NAEL-5v2; NAEL-6v2; NAWM-7v2; NIL-7; NIP-4; NOBE; NPeEn; NoAM; NoP-4; OxBEV; OxBTC; PoE; PoPoPo; SCGP; TFi; TRP

How can we live without the unknown in front of us? Argument. René Char. AF

How / Can you. On South Africa. Kim C. Lee. InTrad

How can you be quite so uncouth? After sharing. Ode to the Diencephalon. W. H. Auden. OxAEP-2

How can you forget me? Low to High. Langston Hughes. APT-2

How can you live, how exist. Likeness, The. Arthur Gregor. VGW

How can you look at the Neva. Anna Andreyevna Akhmatova. BoWoP

How! Canst thou see the basket wherein lay. Moses in Infancy. Jones Very. ChIV-1

How certain the mule's step in the abyss. Rhapsody for the Mule. José Lezama Lima. TCLAP, *tr. by* Dudley Fitts, José Rodríguez Feo and Donald D. Walsh

How changed is here each spot man makes or fills! Matthew Arnold. FHYEP; NAEL-5v2; NAEL-6v2; NOBE; OBEV

How cold are thy baths, Apollo! Jugurtha. Henry Wadsworth Longfellow. TCAPo

How come a thickish tree. View, A. James Schuyler. BodElec

How come alle ye that ben i-broght. *Unknown.* OHMEL

How come, Henry dear. Mamma Goes Where Papa Goes. Jack Yellen. ReLy

How come / I wanna know. To the Latin Lover I Left at the Candy Store. Magdalena Gomez. PueRic

How come nobody is being bombed today? All Quiet. David Ignatow. CoAmPo

How come the inlaid lute has fifty strings? Inlaid Lute, The. Li Shang-yin. ChinPo, *tr. by* Yip Wai-lim

How Come the Truck-Loads? Judith Rodriguez. FaBoWP

How comely glisten the rounded cheeks. Fatness. Alan Ansen. CoAP

How comes it, Flora, that, whenever we. Queen of Hearts, The. Christina Georgina Rossetti. NPeEn; PeVV

How comest thou, O flower so fair. Snowdrop, The. Mary Weston Fordham. CBWP-2

How comforting. Day They Cleaned Up the Border El Salvador, February, 1981, The. Wendy Rose. HATNAP

How compare either of this grim twain? Thomas Hardy and A. E. Housman. Max Beerbohm. NBLV

How cool / forehead touched. Sono-Jo, Lady. ZenPo, *tr. by* Takashi Ikemoto and Lucien Stryk

How cool it feels. Basho. TTTS

How could I ever be untrue? (LL) *Unknown.* CoBCP; ColAnChi, *tr. by* Burton Watson

How could I have known. Rufinus. ErotSp, *tr. by* Sam Hamill

How could I seek the empty world again? (LL) Remembrance. Emily Jane Brontë. BoLoP; BoWoP; CABP; EBEV; EnLoPo; HAP; MakPoe; NAEL-5v2; NAEL-6v2; NOBE; NOBVV; NPeEn; NoP-4; OxAEP-2; OxBEV; PEW; PoE; PoPoPo; TFi; VWP; WPE; WeW-3

How could I wake from childhood. To Be. Marvin Bell. BodElec

How could she not take pride in him. On the Marriage at Cana. Rainer Maria Rilke. GI

How could you have forgotten her. Kamalākānta Bhattācārya. SinGod, *tr. by* Rachel Fell McDermott

How crowded and bustling it is over there. Kuan Yün-shih. SuSp, *tr. by*

Richard John Lynn *Fr.* Medley of Southern and Northern Tunes—Scenic Tour of West Lake.

How Cruel Is the Story of Eve. Stevie Smith. NALW

How cursed that country, how severe its doom. Thomas Maurice. NOEC *Fr.* Epistle to the Right Hon. Charles James Fox, An.

"How'd I solve de Negro Problum?" Uncle Rube on the Race Problem. Clara Ann Thompson. CBWP-2

How dare I in thy courts appear. Hymn. Phoebe Cary. SacPr

How dare we now be anything but numb? (LL) Rejoinder to a Critic. Donald Davie. CABP; NoP-4

How dare you! To the Police Officer Who Refused to Sit in the Same Room as My Son because He's a "Gang Banger." Luis J. Rodriguez. IllVoic

How dare you say that still you love? Unfaithful Lover, The. Charlotte Dacre. RWP

How dark the veins of your temples. Final Vigil. Georg Heym. WoPoe, *tr.* by Peter Viereck

How daur ye ca' me "Howlet-face." Keekin' Glass, The. Robert Burns. FaBoEE

How dear to my heart are the grand politicians. Old Hokum Buncombe, The. Robert E. Sherwood. NBLV

How dear to my heart is the old village drugstore. Hair-Tonic Bottle, The. Ben King. OBAL

How dear to this heart are the scenes of my childhood. Old Oaken Bucket, The. Samuel Woodworth. BRP; TCAPo

How Death Came. *Unknown.* TTY, *tr.* by W. H. I. Bleek

How decisively. Paavo Haavikko. WoPoe, *tr.* by Anselm Hollo *Fr.* Fifteen Epigrams in Praise of the Tyrant.

How Deep Is the Ocean? (How High Is the Sky?). Irving Berlin. ReLy

How deep the woods are. (LL) Jacklight. Louise Erdrich. HATNAP; NIL-7; WeW-3

How deep yon azure dyes the sky! Thomas Parnell. OxAEP-1 *Fr.* Night Piece on Death.

How delectable are the attributes of Virginity! Meditation, Followed by Excellent Advice. Eratosthenes. GrAn, *tr.* by Dudley Fitts

How delicious is the winning. Freedom and Love. Thomas Campbell. GTBS-P

How delicious to walk into the stillness. To Go Through Life Is to Walk Across a Field. S. J. Marks. BodElec

How delightful, at sunset, to loosen the boat! Excursion, The. Tu Fu. AWP, *tr.* by Florence Ayscough and Amy Lowell

How delightful to meet Mr. Hodgson! T. S. Eliot. NBLV; OBAL; PeLV *Fr.* Five-Finger Exercises.

How did a great Red-tailed Hawk. Dead by the Side of the Road, The. Gary Snyder. HAP

How did decay work its way into the theater of water. Synchronized Swimming. Angela Sorby. AmPoNex

How did the grapes come to know. Pablo Neruda. GifTon, *tr.* by William O'Daly *Fr.* Book of Questions, The.

How did the party go in Portman Square? Juliet. Joseph Hilaire Pierre Belloc. BoLoP; EnLoPo

How did the stones vote. Election, The. Leonard Nathan. PBCAP

How Did They Kill My Grandmother? Boris Abramovich Slutsky [*or* Slutskii]. FaBoWar, *tr.* by Elaine Feinstein

How did they kill my grandmother? How They Killed My Grandmother. Boris Abramovich Slutsky [*or* Slutskii]. HP, *tr.* by Daniel Weissbort

How did they understand Livy my grandfather my great grandfather. Transformations of Livy. Zbigniew Herbert. PoetW, *tr.* by John Carpenter and Bogdana Carpenter

How Did You Die? Edmund Vance Cooke. PWR

How died my master, Strato? William Shakespeare. OxAEP-1 *Fr.* Julius Caesar.

How Different! Ebenezer Elliott. EBEV

How difficult for me is Hebrew. Charles Reznikoff. APT-2

How difficult to live without you! "Naum Korzhavin." TCRP

How disgusting. Idea Vilariño. TANSG, *tr.* by Louise B. Popkin

How dishonest the sun. Seeing through the Sun. Linda Hogan. HATNAP

How do I enter the silence of stones. Mona Sa'udi. WPOW

How Do I Feel? Kenneth Fearing. APT-2

How do I hate you? Let me count the ways. Sonnet. Stanley J. Sharpless. UV

How do I know the sound. Crows. Mariana Romo-Carmona. WiU

How do I know why you ask me, "How *are* you?" Cross Questions. John Wheelwright. APT-2

How do I love thee? Beyond Compare. David Ross. ReLy

How do I pity that proud wealthy clown. My Estate. John Norris. NOSC

How do I spin my time away. On the Spirit Adulterated by the Flesh. Thomas Warton, the Elder. ChIV-1

How do I thank thee, death, and bless thy power. On the Lady Arabella. Richard Corbet [*or* Corbett]. NOSC

How do people feel. Stolen Away. Joseph Ceravolo. FTOS

How do they do it, the ones who make love. Sex without Love. Sharon Olds. HeIP-4; NIL-7; NIP-4; TRP

How do we break the habit of big words. Anatoly Steiger. TCRusP, *tr.* by Paul Schmidt

How do we know, by the bank-high river. Rudyard Kipling. OxBTC *Fr.* Land and Sea Tales.

How do you account for things: Take night. Above the Fray Is Only Thin Air. A. R. Ammons. BodElec

How do you cut an ax-handle? *Unknown.* ColAnChi, *tr.* by Jeffrey Riegel *Fr.* Classic of Odes.

How do you know that the pilgrim track. Year's Awakening, The. Thomas Hardy. OxBTC

How do you like to go up in a swing. Swing, The. Robert Louis Stevenson. ChAP; NOxBChV; NTCP; TLR

How do you like what you have. Gertrude Stein. AiP *Fr.* Portraits and Repetition.

How do you make a black man red. Plan of the Klan. Michelle T. Clinton. InTrad

How do you make bread talk, this old treasure all wrapped. Bread Is Born. Anne Hébert. BoWoP, *tr.* by Maxine W. Kumin

How do you move? Conversation with Isadora Duncan. Molly Bendall. AmPoNex

How do you recognize death? Minor Elegy. Henriqueta Lisboa. BoWoP, *tr.* by Willis Barnstone and Nelson Cerqueira

How Do You Shape an Axe Handle? Gary Snyder. NoAM

How do you spell change brother like frayed slogan underwear. New York City 1970. Audre Lorde. NBV

How Do Your Eggs Want You (?) Pedro Juan Pietri. PueRic

How does a person get to be a capable liar? Golly, How Truth Will Out. Ogden Nash. MoAmPo

How does it feel to be. Nude Woman Spotted in Cappuccino Cup as Advertising Dollar co-opts another life. Bahiyyih Maroon. SpirFl

How does it happen, tell me. Edgar Lee Masters. FaBoEE; OBSV *Fr.* Spoon River Anthology.

How does it help me if, with flawless art. Elegy 23. Louise Labé. WPOW, *tr.* by Raymond Oliver

How does one get outside. Dear Miss. Herman Gladwin. PeNZ

How does one stand. American Sublime, The. Wallace Stevens. FaBoA

How does the water / Come down at Lodore? Robert Southey. NOxBChV *Fr.* Cataract of Lodore, The.

How does thy mercies stil renew. Dec. 5th 1644 Upon Robin Austins Recovery of the Smal Pox and General Popams Son John Diing of Them. Katherine Austen. EMWP

How doth the city sit solitary that was full of people. Bible, *O.T.* WoPoe, *tr.* by Susan Stewart *Fr.* Lamentations.

How doth the city sit solitary, that was full of people! Bible, *O.T.* AWP *Fr.* Lamentations.

How Doth the Little Busy Bee. Isaac Watts. ChAP
  (Against Idleness and Mischief.) OxAEP-1; OxBEV; UV

How drunk I got tonight. Drinking Spree beneath the Open Sky. Slavko Mihalic. PoSu, *tr.* by Peter Kastmiler

How dully in the evening. Calendar of the Air. Yevgeny [*or* Evgenii] Borisovich Rein. TCRP, *tr.* by Lubov Yakovleva

How easily happiness begins by. Onions. William Matthews. EmeKit

How easily the ripe grain. Widow, The. W. S. Merwin. UnPo; VGW

How Elizabeth Foole and Her Husband Parted by Means of Her Sister in Law. Elizabeth With. EMWP

How empty seems the town now you are gone! From One Who Stays. Amy Lowell. BoWoP

How entrancing are the 124 ways. Larousse Gastronomique. Anne Stevenson. PeLV

How everything gets tamed. Mountain, Fire, Thornbush. Harvey Shapiro. VGW

How Everything Happens. May Swenson. APT-2; HAP

How fair a flower is sown. Coventry Patmore. FaBoEE

How fair is youth that flies so fast! Then be happy, ye who may. Lorenzo de' Medici. CTC, *tr.* by Richard Aldington *Fr.* Carnival Songs.

How Far. Gertrud Fussenegger. AuPH, *tr.* by Lowell A. Bangerter

How far are they deceived, that hope in vain. In the Person of a Lady, to Bajazet, Her Unconstant Gallant. "Ephelia." PEW

How far from enough. *Unknown.* ArkPo, *tr.* by Helen Craig McCullough

How far is it to you by foot? How Far? Vassar Miller. FFC

How far is it? Getting There. Sylvia Plath. GM

How far is St. Helena from a little child at play? St. Helena Lullaby, A. Rudyard Kipling. EBEV; FaBoCh; FaBoWar; OBMV

How far, ye Nymphs and Dryads! must we stray. On the Rapid Extension of the Suburbs. John Thelwall. CenSon

How Far? Vassar Miller. FFC

"How fared you when you mortal were?" After. Ralph Hodgson. MoBrPo

How Fast. Martha Rhodes. NAPBL

How fast thou fliest, O Time, on loves swift wings. Mary Sidney Wroth, Countess of Montgomery. NOSC *Fr.* Pamphilia to Amphilanthus.

How fetching! Somebody's wife. Hsieh Ling-yün. CoBCP, *tr. by* Burton Watson *Fr.* Exchange of Poems by Tung-yang Stream, An.

How fickle's health! when sickness thus. Upon a Friend's Pet Cat, Being Sick. John Winstanley. TriCat

How fierce in its loyalties the beat of the heart. Coronary Thrombosis. William Price Turner. OxBS

How fierce was I, when I did see. Upon Julia['s] Washing Herself in the River. Robert Herrick. CaPo

How fine a light on. May Song. Goethe. STV, *tr. by* John Frederick Nims

How Firm a Foundation. "K." SacPr

How first we met do you still remember? Brussels and Oxford. William Hurrell Mallock. EBVV

How foolish men on expeditions go! On Riding to See Dean Swift in the Mist of the Morning. Pope. FaBoEE

How forlorn and lost. Heart of the Matter. Susan Prospere. MakPoe

How found you him? William Shakespeare. OxAEP-1 *Fr.* Cymbeline.

How frail / Above the bulk. Niagara. Adelaide Crapsey. APT-1; PAI

How frail is human life! How fleet our breath. On the Death of an Infant of Five Days Old. Elizabeth Boyd. ECWP

How fresh, O[h] Lord, how sweet and clean. Flower, The. George Herbert. AWP; AngWePo; BASC; ESCV; FSCP; GeHe; NAEL-5v1; NAEL-6v1; NAEL-7v1; NOBE; NOCV; NPeEn; NoP-4; OBGa; OxBEV; PBRV

How fresh the air, the birds how busy now! Birds' Nest. John Clare. OWoS

How funny you are today New York. Steps. Frank O'Hara. CoAmPo; PmAP

How funny your name would be. Myrtle. John Ashbery. NAAL-5

How gaily is at first begun. Life's Progress. Anne Finch, Countess of Winchilsea. ECWP

How Garnett Mims and the Enchanters Came into Your Life. Bruce Smith. SwNoth

How gladly would I lay my aching head. Jane Alice Sargant. CenSon

How Glorious Are the Morning Stars. Benjamin Keach. AH

How Glorious Is Thy Name. Bible, *O.T.* See Psalms

How God Answers the Soul. Mechthild von Magdeburg. WPoS, *tr. by* Oliver Davies

How God Comes to the Soul. Mechthild von Magdeburg. WPoS, *tr. by* Oliver Davies

How God speeds the tax-bribed plough. Drone v. Worker. Ebenezer Elliott. OBSV

How Goes the Night? *Unknown.* AWP, *tr. by* Helen Waddell *Fr.* Shi King.

How good it would be if our surroundings always. Dinner at Le Caprice. Rachel Wetzsteon. RA

How good of Mrs. Metz! The blur. Snapshots. John Updike. NoP-4

How goodly are the tentes of Jacob and thine habitacions Israel. Bible, *O.T.* OBVE, *tr. by* William Tyndale *Fr.* Numbers.

How Goodly Is Thy House. Henry S. Jacobs. AH

How goofy and horrible is life. Just. Frottage. Dean Young. BAP-97

How grace this hallowed day? Christmas. Henry Timrod. APN-2

How green / Flowering slopes. Naito Joso. ZenPo, *tr. by* Takashi Ikemoto and Lucien Stryk

How happy a thing were a wedding. On Marriage. Thomas Flatman. NOBL; PeLV

How happy for us, that it is not at home! (LL) Place of the Damned [*or* Damn'd], The. Jonathan Swift. ChIV-2; FaBoEE; OBSV

How happy I can be with my love away! Absence, The. Sylvia Townsend Warner. MoBrPo

How happy in his low degree. Horace. AWP, *tr. by* John Dryden *Fr.* Epodes.

How happy is he born and taught. Character of a Happy Life, The. Sir Henry Wotton. BASC; GTBS-P; NOBE; NOSC; OBEV; OxBEV; SacPr

How happy is the little Stone. Emily Dickinson. APN-2; RB

How happy the animals seem just now. October, Yellowstone Park. Maxine W. Kumin. ExTi

How happy uncle us'd to be. Uncle an' Aunt. William Barnes. NOBVV

How happy you who varied joys pursue. Epistle. Lady Mary Wortley Montagu. ECWP

How hard a fate enthrals the wretched maid. Virgil [*or* Vergil]. ECWP *Fr.* Aeneid [*or* Eneados, *Aeneis*], The.

How hard it is! To the Memory of G. N. Obolduyev. Yelena [*or* Elena] Blaginina. TCRP, *tr. by* Vera Dunham

How hard it is to take September. Absolute September. Mary Jo Salter. ExTi

How hard it is, we say. Clothes Maketh the Man. Theodore Weiss. NoAM

How hard to control the route. Orientation from Afar. Silvana Colonna. ItPo, *tr. by* Gayle Ridinger

How have I served you? I have let you waste. John Hewitt. PNI *Fr.* Sonnets for Roberta (1954).

How he found his life long ago. How Just One Poor Man Lives. Alonzo Gonzales Mó. STP, *tr. by* Allan F. Burns

How He Saw Her. Ben Jonson. NAEL-6v1; NAEL-7v1 *Fr.* Celebration of Charis in Ten Lyric[k] Pieces [*or* Peeces], A.

How He Should Like to Be Kissed. Paul Fleming. GePo, *tr. by* Harold B. Segel

How heal the phantom body of its phantom ill. Tesshu. ZenPo, *tr. by* Takashi Ikemoto and Lucien Stryk

How heavy do I journey on the way. William Shakespeare. OxAEP-1 *Fr.* Sonnets.

How Her Teeth Were Pulled. *Unknown.* STP, *tr. by* Jarold Ramsey

How, hey! It is none les. Henpecked Husband, A. *Unknown.* MiEL; PeLV

How High the Moon. Nancy Hamilton. ReLy

How High the Moon. Lance Jeffers. SeSe

How his body stood against a thicket rich in hardwood gentry: Ponderous and gloomy. D. A. Powell. NAPBL

How his own members bloat and shrink again. (LL) Ogres and Pygmies. Robert Graves. FaBoMo; NoAM

"How, how," he said. "Friend Chang," I said. Chinese Nightingale, The. Nicholas Vachel Lindsay. MoAmPo

How I Became a Dog. Vladimir Vladimirovich Mayakovsky [*or* Maiakovskii]. TCRP, *tr. by* Bernard Meares

How I Brought the Good News from Aix to Ghent (or Vice Versa). R. J. Yeatman. UV

How I Came to Have a Man's Name. Emma Lee Warrior. HATNAP

(Before a January dawn, under a moondog sky.) ReEnLa

How I Changed My Name, Felice. Felix Stefanile. UnSA

How I Come to You. Molly Peacock. RA

How I cut the fresh branches of succulent rhyme. Poet Grows Old, The. Oliver Wendell Holmes. TCAPo

How I Discovered Poetry. Marilyn Nelson. ExTi

How I do[e] love thee, Beaumont, and thy Muse. To Francis Beaumont. Ben Jonson. BeJo

How I forsook Elias and Pisa after, and betook. Sir Richard Fanshawe. AWP *Fr.* Il Pastor Fido.

How I Got That Name. Marilyn Chin. GeoHom; LoL

How I Got the Word. Marvin Bell. BodElec

How I Had to Act. Molly Peacock. FFC

How I hate myself, this body which is me. Eloi, Eloi, Lama Sabachthani? D. H. Lawrence. GI

How I Learned English. Gregory Djanikian. UnSA

How I Learned to Sweep. Julia Alvarez. FFC; RA

How I love this girl who until. It Is Sticky in the Subway. David Schubert. APT-2

How I regret being late to see the flowers blossom. Sighing over Flowers. Tu Mu. SuSp, *tr. by* Eddie Tsang

How I Sailed on the Lake till I Came to the Eastern Stream. Lu Yu. ChiP, *tr. by* Arthur Waley

How I See It. Kit Wright. OTCP

How I See Things. Yusef Komunyakaa. ESEAA

How I succeed, you kindly ask. Mary Barber. ECWP *Fr.* To a Lady, Who Commanded Me to Send Her an Account in Verse.

How I wish I had known / beforehand of this journey. *Unknown.* BoWoP

How I wish the Argo had never reached the land. Euripides. NAWM-5v1

How I would have the poem rest. Mahogany Ship, The. Judith Rodriguez. BMAP

How I Wrote It. David Dooley. TRP

How ill doth he deserve a lover's name. Eternity of Love Protested. Thomas Carew. BeJo; MeLP

How in the sad depths of old centuries. Song about Benedek Virág. Dezső Kosztolányi. IQMS, *tr. by* Watson Kirkconnell

How Infinite Are Thy Ways. William Force Stead. OBMV *Fr.* Uriel.

How innocent their lives look. Photos of a Salt Mine. Patricia K. Page. NIP-4; NOBC; NoAM

How intelligent he looks! Changing Diapers. Gary Snyder. RaBo

How intimate was the earth in days gone by. Earth, The. David Gwenallt Jones. OBWVE, *tr. by* Dyfnallt Morgan

How Is He Coming Then. Lucille Clifton. NALW

How is it. Wall, The. Witter Bynner. APT-1

How is it all gonna turn out. "Haida Charlie." STP

How is it I can eat bread here and cut meat. Evening Meal in the Twentieth Century. John Holmes. AiP

How is it I was not raised. In the Dark Backward. Gloria Vando. TouFir

How is it proved? Great Wager, The. Geoffrey Anketell Studdert-Kennedy. TrCP

How is it, Salma, that when you are near me. Salma. Ilyas Farhat. MAP, *tr. by* John Heath-Stubbs and Salma Khadra Jayyusi

How is it that. Kuan Yün-shih. SuSp, *tr. by* Richard John Lynn *Fr.* Medley of Southern and Northern Tunes—Scenic Tour of West Lake.

How is it that Fortune now always ignores me? Las, Où Est Maintenant Ce Mespris de Fortune. Joachim Du Bellay. WoPoe, *tr. by* Fred Beake

How is it that I am so careless here. Meditation 62. Philip Pain. NOBA

How is it the stomach knows first. David Hall. CDa

How is it with another woman? Attempt at Jealousy, An. Marina Ivanovna Tsvetayeva [*or* Tsvetaeva]. WPOW, *tr. by* Robert Perelman and Aleksandar Petrov

How is man parcell'd out? how ev'ry hour. Tempest, The. Henry Vaughan. ESCV

How Is the Night? *Unknown.* CoBCP, *tr. by* Burton Watson

How is your life with the other one. Attempt at Jealousy, An. Marina Ivanovna Tsvetayeva [*or* Tsvetaeva]. OxBEV; TCRP; WoPoe, *tr. by* Elaine Feinstein

How It Comes. Dorothy Barresi. SwNoth

How It Comes About. Larry Eigner. PmAP

How it feels to be touching. We Become New. Marge Piercy. TAP

How it goes. Severance. Kit Robinson. FTOS

How It Is. Maxine W. Kumin. NALW; NoAM

How It Strikes a Contemporary. Robert Browning. CTC; GTBS-P; NPeEn

How It Will Always Seem. David Rivard. PBCAP

How joyous his neigh! Song of the Horse. *Unknown.* AWP, *tr. by* Natalie Curtis Burlin

How Just One Poor Man Lives. Alonzo Gonzales Mó. STP, *tr. by* Allan F. Burns

How keen the nights / were. Fluteplayers from Finmarken. Carl Rakosi. FTOS

How lacking in permanence the minds of the sentient. Hakuin. ZenPo, *tr. by* Takashi Ikemoto and Lucien Stryk

How large unto the tiny fly. Fly, The. Walter De la Mare. OTCP

How larger is remembrance than desire! Ebbtide at Sundown. "Michael Field." OxBSo; VWP

How Late Desire Looks. Katrina Roberts. NAPBL

How leisurely the cherry. Kin'u. JDP, *tr. by* Yoel Hoffmann

How Lies Grow. Maxine Chernoff. IllVoic; PmAP

How life and death in Thee. To Our Blessed Lord upon the Choice of His Sepulchre. Richard Crashaw. GeHe; NOSC

How like a bolt of white silk is this water. Li Po. SuSp *Fr.* Songs of Ch'iu-p'u.

How like a fire doth love increase in me[e]. Mary Sidney Wroth, Countess of Montgomery. NOSC *Fr.* Pamphilia to Amphilanthus.

How like a man, is Man, who rises late. Eye-Opener. Malcolm Lowry. NoP-4

How like a rich and gorgeous picture hung. November Landscape, A. Sarah Helen Whitman. ColAP

How like a winter hath my absence been[e]. William Shakespeare. AWP; EnLoPo; GTBS-P; HeIP-4; NAEL-5v1; NAEL-6v1; NAEL-7v1; NOBE; NoSic; OBEV; OxAEP-1; PoRA; SCGP; Son; TFi *Fr.* Sonnets.

How like an angel came I down! Wonder. Thomas Traherne. BASC; ESCV; GeHe; HAP; NAEL-5v1; NAEL-6v1; NAEL-7v1; NPeEn; NoP-4; OxBEV; PoE; TOF

How like her! But 'tis she herself. In the Mile End Road. Amy Levy. PEW; RACG; ViWPN

How like the leper, with his own sad cry. Buoy-Bell, The. Charles Tennyson Turner. GSo; PeVV; Son

How Lillies Came White. Robert Herrick. BeJo; CaPo

How Lisa Loved the King. "George Eliot."
 "She watched all day that she might see him pass." LW

How little does history manage to tell? Lessons in History. Robert Penn Warren. BodElec

How little of God's grace caresses you, Massadah. Yitzhak Lamdan. MHP *Fr.* In the Khamsin.

How little of the world had been left dry! (LL) "Michael Field." VWP; ViWPN

How Little We Know. Johnny Mercer. ReLy

How Little We Know (How Little It Matters). Carolyn Leigh. ReLy

How Long. Andrea Zanzotto. VCWP, *tr. by* Ruth Feldman

How long ago Hector took off his plume. Parting in Wartime. Frances Darwin Cornford. FaBoWP; NIP-4

How long ago she planted the hawthorn hedge. Hawthorn Hedge, The. Judith Wright. WPE

How long ago we dreamed. Carol of the Three Kings. W. S. Merwin. ChrPo

How long, and yet how long. How Long? Emma Lazarus. SWaP

How long before light welds us together? Gift You Must Lose, A. Gregory Orfalea. GraLe

How long between the grain and the wind. How Long. Andrea Zanzotto. VCWP, *tr. by* Ruth Feldman

How Long Blues. Leroy Carr. NAAAL

How long can one man live. Mourning for Yin Yao. Wang Wei. CrYelRi, *tr. by* Sam Hamill

How long, despondent birds, with silent throats. Bird, to Its Young, The. Mihály Tompa. IQMS, *tr. by* Watson Kirkconnell

How Long Does the Curator Dance For? Edwin Torres. HeMarv

How long for the small yellow flowers. Time. Robert Creeley. BodElec

How long, great God, a wretched captive here. Expostulation, The. Elizabeth Singer Rowe. PEW

How Long Has This Been Going On? George Gershwin. ReLy

How Long Has Trane Been Gone. Joe Corrie. NAAAL

How Long Has Trane Been Gone. Jayne Cortez. ISC

How Long Have We Forgotten How to Listen! Nelly Sachs. WPoS, *tr. by* Matthew Mead and Ruth Mead

How long, how long, has that evenin' train gone? How Long Blues. Leroy Carr. NAAAL

How long, how long must I regret? Lost Tribe, The. Ruth Pitter. WPOW

How Long I Sailed. Hartley Coleridge. Son

How long in his damp trance young Juan lay. Byron. NAEL-6v2 *Fr.* Don Juan.

How long in these empty thermals near the cold. Crinagoras. GrAn

How Long, Jehovah? Henry Ainsworth. AH

How long, long ago. Kenneth Rexroth. APSN *Fr.* Love Poems of Marichiko, The.

How long must we two hide the burning gaze. United. Paulus [*or* Paulos] Silentiarius. AWP, *tr. by* W. H. D. Rouse

How long, O lion, hast thou fleshless lain? Lion's Skeleton, The. Charles Tennyson Turner. NOBVV

"How long shall fortune faile me now." Earl of Westmoreland, The. *Unknown.* ESPB

How long she waited for her executioner! Head of Medusa. Marya Alexandrovna Zaturenska. MoAmPo

How Long the Lord. Attila József. IQMS, *tr. by* Anton N. Nyerges

How long the tree's been barren. Hoge. ZenPo, *tr. by* Takashi Ikemoto and Lucien Stryk

How long will it last? Lady Horikawa. WPOW

How long will your eyes be with you? Oh, do you know? How Long? Felix Braun. AuPH, *tr. by* Lowell A. Bangerter

How Long? Felix Braun. AuPH, *tr. by* Lowell A. Bangerter

How Long? Emma Lazarus. SWaP

How looks the night? There does not miss a star. Gerard Manley Hopkins. OxBSP *Fr.* Fragments.

How lovely are the tombs of the dead nymphs. Panope. Dame Edith Sitwell. MoBrPo

How lovely are thy tabernacles. Bible, *O.T.* TrJP *Fr.* Psalms.

How lovely is thy dwelling. Bible, *O.T.* CABP, *tr. by* Mary Sidney Herbert, Countess of Pembroke *Fr.* Psalms.

How lovely it is today! *Unknown.* NOIV, *tr. by* Thomas Kinsella *Fr.* Four Glosses.

How lovely the Imperial Mound, but when can I visit it? On the Road to Western Hill. Ch'ien Ch'ien-i [*or* Ch'ien Ch'ien-yi]. SuSp, *tr. by* Irving Y. Lo

How lovely the Russian lady. Its Pliancy. Hans Lodeizen. TuT, *tr. by* Eamon Grennan

How lumpy and warlike you all looked. Land Army Photographs. Tony Curtis. TCAWP

How many a day in various hues arrayed. To My Eldest Brother, With the British Army in Portugal. Felicia Dorothea Hemans. RWP

How many a throb of the young poet-heart. Early Aspirations. William Bell Scott. CenSon

How many apples grow on the tree? George Barker. NOxBChV

'How Many Bards Gild the Lapses of Time'! John Keats. CenSon; OxAEP-2

How many blessed groups this hour are bending. Sabbath Sonnet. Felicia Dorothea Hemans. Son

How many children must have come to pass. Walter Parmer. Greg Williamson. RA

How many constants should there be? Native. Rae Armantrout. PFTM-2

How many dawns, chill from his rippling rest. Hart Crane. AiP; AmFaPo; APT-2; ChIV-1; CIHu; ColAP; FaBoA; HarvBoo; MakPoe; MoAmPo; NAAL-2v2; NAAL-5; NOBA; NoP-4; OxBA; PoE; PoPoPo; TFi; TRP *Fr.* Bridge, The.

How many days has my baby to play? Mother Goose. OxNR; ReMoGo

How many doors will this man open. Death. Roy Fuller. NoAM

How many drops has the ocean sea? Sándor Petőfi. IQMS, *tr. by* Peter Zollman *Fr.* Clouds, The.

How many empty hotel rooms. Sea Sprite, Hermosa Beach, The. Maurya Simon. GeoHom

How many evenings in the arbor by the river. Tune: "As in a Dream; a Song." Li Ch'ing-chao. BoWP; SuSp, *tr. by* Eugene Eoyang

How many faults you might accuse me of. Sonnet. Elinor Wylie. NAAL-2v2

How many fields which like a sponge.   Amelia Rosselli.   ItPo, *tr.* by Gayle Ridinger

"How many fires."   George Reavey.   SPE

How Many Heavens.   Dame Edith Sitwell.   TrCP

How many lives ago.   Kenneth Rexroth.   APSN; APT-2   *Fr.* Love Poems of Marichiko, The.

How many loves had I.   Doll.   John Wieners.   FTOS

How many men are killed by power, by power.   Juvenal.   OBVE, *tr.* by Robert Lowell   *Fr.* Satires.

How many miles to Babylon?   Mother Goose.   LB; OxBSP; OxNR

(How many miles to Barley-Bridge?)   OxBoLi

(To Babylon.)   ReMoGo

How many notes written. . . .   Suicide Note.   Janice Mirikitani.   OxWW

How many of you are there?   Map.   Raymond Radiguet.   CuPo

How many pallid Christs, with painted blood.   All Around Us.   Constance Urdang.   PBCAP

How Many Paltry, Foolish, Painted Things.   Michael Drayton.   EnLoPo; HAP; HeIP-4; NAEL-5v1; NAEL-7v1; NIP-4; NOSC; SCGP   *Fr.* Idea.

How many pounds does the baby weigh.   Weighing the Baby.   Ethel Lynn Beers.   PoToHe

How many prompters! what a chorus! (LL)   Plays.   Walter Savage Landor.   NBLV; OxBSP; OxBoLi; PeLV

How many scenes, O sun.   Ode to the Sun.   Eloise Bibb.   CBWP-4

How many shoelaces will they make of that! (LL)   Mad Yak, The.   Gregory Corso.   BB; PFTM-2; PmAP

How many thousand of my poorest subjects.   William Shakespeare.   AWTN   *Fr.* King Henry IV, Pt. II.

How many times, Death.   O All down within the Pretty Meadow.   Kenneth Patchen.   HAP; WeW-3

How many times do I love thee, dear?   Thomas Lovell Beddoes.   NAEL-6v2   *Fr.* Torrismond.

How many times God will remember.   Silence, The.   Robert Mezey.   TaR

How many times has the moon shone full?   Tune: "Water Mode Song."   Su Tung-p'o (Su Shih).   ColAnChi, *tr.* by J. R. Hightower

How many times have I traveled.   Commuter.   Lisel Mueller.   GM

How many times Nights silent Queene her Face.   Sonnet.   William Drummond, of Hawthornden.   NPeEn

How many times these low feet staggered.   Emily Dickinson.   HAP; NAAL-2v1; NAAL-3; TCAPo; WeW-3

How many voices can I plum in this poem?   Serpentine Voices.   Diana García.   TouFir

How many were going to St. Ives? (LL)   Mother Goose.   LB; NTCP; OxNR; ReMoGo

How many will her coldness kill! (LL)   William Congreve.   NOEC; OxBSP

How many wise men and heroes.   To the Tune "The River Is Red."   Ch'iu Chin.   AiP; BoWoP; ItWoWo, *tr.* by Chung Ling and Kenneth Rexroth

How many years can a man possess?   Weeping for Ying Yao.   Wang Wei.   WoPoe, *tr.* by Willis Barnstone, Tony Barnstone and Xu Haixin

How many years, decades, since I'd even thought of Gary.   Basement, The.   Alan Shapiro.   TaR

How many years since 1619 have I been singing Spirituals?   Since 1619.   Margaret Abigail Walker.   NoP-4

How Marigolds Came Yellow.   Robert Herrick.   TTTS

How massively, with what a fine stiff rise.   Erucius [*or* Erycius] of Cyzicus.   GrAn

How may one be spared the sorrow and regret of human life?   Tune: "Song of Tzu-yeh."   Li Yü.   SuSp, *tr.* by Daniel Bryant

How memory cuts away the years.   Autumn.   Jean Starr Untermeyer.   MoAmPo

How Metaphor Can Save Your Life.   Myra Sklarew.   CRP

How *much.*   Issa.   EH, *tr.* by Robert Hass

How much are they deceived who vainly strive.   Love and Jealousy.   William Walsh.   BoLoP

How much better it seems now.   Next Poem, The.   Dana Gioia.   DiPo; NoP-4

How much death works.   Eyes Fastened with Pins.   Charles Simic.   VCAP

How Much Earth.   Philip Levine.   NNaP

How much I should like to begin.   At the Edge.   Denise Levertov.   NAAL-2v2

How Much Is Not True.   Kabir.   RaBo

How Much Is This Poem Going to Cost Me?   Denise Duhamel.   NeAmPo

How Much Longer Will I Be Able to Inhabit the Divine Sepulcher.   John Ashbery.   FTOS; HarvBoo; NeAP; PoM

How Much Longer?   Robert Mezey.   OBWP

How much more / Of wind and rain?   Tune: "Groping for Fish."   Hsin Ch'i-chi.   SuSp, *tr.* by Irving Y. Lo

How much mystery this atom bears in the universe.   Tormented Mystic.   Al-Tijani Yusuf Bashir.   MAP, *tr.* by Patricia Alanah Byrne and Matthew Sorenson

How much of paper's soiled! what floods of ink!   Epistle to Lady Bowyer, An.   Mary Jones.   ECWP

How much, Preventing God! how much I owe.   Grace.   Ralph Waldo Emerson.   APN-1; InvLi; NCAP

How much regret in my dream last night?   Tune: "Butterflies Lingering over Flowers."   Wang Kuo-wei.   SuSp, *tr.* by Ching-i Tu

"How much," sighed the gentle Narcissus.   Limerick.   Stephen Sylvester.   PeLi

How much the heart may bear and yet not break!   Endurance.   Elizabeth Akers Allen.   PoToHe

How much there was of everything: kettledrums and horns and bells!   Nikolai Ivanovich Tryapkin [*or* Triapkin].   TCRP

How much wood would a woodchuck chuck?   *Unknown.*   TLR

How much work.   Hating Jews.   Tom Wayman.   LTA

How near me came the hand of Death.   Widow's Hymn, A.   George Wither.   OBEV

How Near Vietnam Came to Us.   Paul Zarzyski.   SwNoth

How neatly this world divides.   Near Sheridan.   Robin Becker.   PoCoUp

How nice! How convenient!   Marvelous Land of Indefinitions, The.   Lorenzo Thomas.   PmAP

How nice to know Mr MacBeth.   With a Presentation Copy of Verses.   Martin Bell.   PeLV

How noteless Men, and Pleiads, stand.   Emily Dickinson.   PoE

How now! is he dead?   William Shakespeare.   OxAEP-1   *Fr.* Antony and Cleopatra.

How odd / Of God.   Chosen People, The.   W. N. Ewer.   OBCoV

How oft alas my brother have I warned thee to beware.   Lines Written for a Friend on the Death of His Brother, Caused by a Railway Train Running over Him Whilst He Was in a State of Inebriation.   James Henry Powell.   VerBaPo

How oft, ere morning lit the eastern steep.   Richard Hall.   AngWePo   *Fr.* Venni-Vach Revisited.

How Oft Has the Banshee Cried.   Thomas Moore.   AWP

How oft I've watch'd thee from the garden croft.   Orion.   Charles Tennyson Turner.   GSo

How oft in schoolboy-days, from the school's sway.   Frederick Goddard Tuckerman.   APN-2; NoP-4; Son   *Fr.* Sonnets.

How oft the distant mountains capped with snow.   They Killed Our Longing for Our Homeland.   Ernst Waldinger.   AuPH, *tr.* by Lowell A. Bangerter

How oft 'tis said, "this is a songless Land."   Songless Land, The.   Francis Carey Slater.   PeSAV

How oft we see the female sex.   School for Satire, The.   Lady Sophia Burrell.   ECWP

How oft, when thou, my music, music play'st.   William Shakespeare.   NAEL-5v1; NAEL-6v1; NAEL-7v1; OxAEP-1; PoE   *Fr.* Sonnets.

How often and often I wish.   Limerick.   Frances Darwin Cornford.   PeLi

How often does a man need to see a woman?   Word Made Flesh, The.   Walter James Turner.   OBMV

How often, for some trivial wrong.   Retaliation.   Margaret E. Bruner.   PoToHe

How often have I carried our family word.   Quoof.   Paul Muldoon.   FaBoVe; NPeEn; PBCIP; PNI

How often have I started out.   Inspiration.   Robert W. Service.   WeW-3

How often have my tears.   In Allusion to the French Song.   Richard Lovelace.   CaPo

How often have we known a dog to be.   Beyond the Grave.   Margaret E. Bruner.   PoToHe

How often my grandparents allude to death, now.   Behind the Veil.   Andrew Lansdown.   NOBAu

How often should we think of this, that we.   Meditations for August 1, 1666.   Philip Pain.   SCAP

How often, these hours, have I heard the monotonous crool of a dove.   Dove, The.   Walter De la Mare.   OWoS

How often we forget all time, when lone.   Stanzas.   Edgar Allan Poe.   APN-1

How often we neglect a friend.   Atonement.   Margaret E. Bruner.   PoToHe

How often, when life's summer day.   Walter Savage Landor.   FaBoEE

How Old Are You?   H. S. Fritsch.   PoToHe

How Old Is Pilar?   Manuel González Prada.   SpanPo, *tr.* by William M. Davis

How Old Is the Old Mole?   Marie-Dominique Massoni.   SurWo, *tr.* by Myrna Bell Rochester

How old may Phillis [*or* Phyllis] be, you ask.   Phillis's Age.   Matthew Prior.   EnLoPo

How old was Mary out of whom you cast.   Charlotte Mew.   MoBrPo   *Fr.* Madeleine in Church.

How, on a summer night.   Music like Water, The.   Jane Hirshfield.   PasH

How on Solemn Fields of Space.   Elizabeth Daryush.   NOCV

How One Winter Came in the Lake Region.   Wilfred Campbell.   NOBC

How painful, dear, how strange it is.   Ballad about a Smoke-Filled Railway Carriage.   Aleksandr Kochetkov.   TCRP, *tr.* by Lubov Yakovleva

How pitiful is her sleep. In Memory of Kathleen. Kenneth Patchen. MoAmPo

How pleasant are the green. Lying in Bed on a Summer Morning. Carl Rakosi. APT-2

How Pleasant It Is to Have Money. Arthur Hugh Clough. GTBS-P; NOBE; NOBVV; OBCoV; OBSV; OxBoLi *Fr.* Dipsychus [and the Spirit].

How Pleasant to Know Mr. Lear. Edward Lear. EBEV; HAP; NAEL-6v2; NOBE; NOBL; NOBVV; NoP-4; OxAEP-2; OxBEV; PAI; PoPoPo; UV

(By Way of Preface.) GTBS-P; NBLV; PeLV

(Self-Portrait of the Laureate of Nonsense.) FaBoCh

How Poetry Comes to Me. Gary Snyder. LoL; PoPoPo

How pointless this straining. Patrizia Cavalli. ItPo, *tr.* by Gayle Ridinger

How poor was Jacob's motion, and how strange. On Jacob's Purchase. Francis Quarles. ChIV-1

How possibly could I. Cameo in Sudden Light. Lorenzo Thomas. FTOS

How probable to the eye, this collation. Lakes, The. David Wright. NLP

How prone we are to sin, how sweet were made. And Forgive Us Our Trespasses. Aphra Behn. EBEV

How proudly Man usurps the power to reign. Martha Hanson. CenSon

How pure at heart and sound in head. Tennyson. NAEL-6v2 *Fr.* In Memoriam A. H. H.

"How Quick You Are!" *Unknown.* CoBCP, *tr.* by Burton Watson

How quickly we age. Not so the heavens. Tune: "Song of Picking Mulberry" Double-Ninth Festival. Mao Tse-tung [or Mao Zedong]. SuSp, *tr.* by Eugene Eoyang

How quiet and how still to-day old Bethel's corners 'round. Day after Conference, The. Josephine D. Henderson Heard. CBWP-4

How quiet is the morning in the hills! Morning in the Hills. Bliss Carman. NOBC

How red the rose that is the soldier's wound. Wallace Stevens. NOBA *Fr.* Esthétique du Mal.

How reluctantly. Basho. SoOfWa, *tr.* by Sam Hamill

How rich and pleasing thou, my Julia, art. To Julia. Robert Herrick. CaPo

How rich, O Lord! how fresh thy visits are! Unprofitablenes. Henry Vaughan. ESCV; GeHe; NAEL-7v1; NOSC

How Roses Came Red. Robert Herrick. BeJo; CaPo; NAEL-7v1; SoSe-8

How rough a sea. Basho. TAL

How sacred and how innocent. Country Life, A. Katherine Philips. BASC

How sad. Sakyoku. JDP, *tr.* by Yoel Hoffmann

How sad: Cherry blossoms. Kari. JDP, *tr.* by Yoel Hoffmann

How sad it is to be framed in woman's form! Woman. Fu Hsüan. ChiP, *tr.* by Arthur Waley

How sad it must be. Poem for My Father, A. Sonia Sanchez. BPo

How say that by law we may torture and chase. She's Free! Frances Ellen Watkins Harper. BlSi; Son

How seldom, friend, a good, great man inherits. Good Great Man, The. Samuel Taylor Coleridge. PWR

"How shall I a habit break?" Builder's Lesson, A. John Boyle O'Reilly. PWR; PoToHe

How shall I array my love? Question, The. Frederick Goddard Tuckerman. APN-2; ColAP

How shall I be a poet? Poeta Fit, Non Nascitur. Lewis Carroll. OBSV

How shall I begin my song. Songs for the Four Parts of the Night. Tohono O'odham (Owl Woman) (Juana Manwell). WPoS, *tr.* by Frances Densmore

How shall I behold the face. John Milton. TOF *Fr.* Paradise Lost.

How shall I forsake wisdom? In Praise of Wisdom. Solomon ibn Gabirol. TrJP, *tr.* by Solomon Solis-Cohen

How shall I guard my soul so that it be. Song of Love, The. Rainer Maria Rilke. AWP, *tr.* by Ludwig Lewisohn

How shall I hold my spirit, that it not. Love Song. Marilyn Nelson. ExTi

How shall I paint thee?—Be this naked stone. William Wordsworth. CenSon *Fr.* River Duddon [A Series of Sonnets], The.

How shall I tell the torments of that hour. Francis Hawling. NOEC *Fr.* Signal; or, A Satire against Modesty, The.

How shall I tell you. Nikolai Nikolaievich Aseyev [or Aseiev]. TCRP

How shall my tongue express that hallow'd fire. Francis Quarles. ESCV *Fr.* Emblems.

How shall the river learn. Max Schmitt in a Single Scull. Richmond Lattimore. AiP

How shall the wine be drunk, or the woman known? Voice from under the Table, A. Richard Wilbur. HAP; NOBA

How shall we adorn. Angle of Geese. N. Scott Momaday. CDW; HATNAP

How shall we bring our dying heart up. Leah Goldberg. MHP *Fr.* On Blossoming.

How Shall We Mourn You Who Are Killed and Wasted. Charles Reznikoff. APT-2

How shall we please this age? If in a song. To Nysus. Sir Charles Sedley. FaBoEE; OBSV

How shall we praise the magnificence of the dead. Tetélestai. Conrad Potter Aiken. APT-1; MoAmPo

How Shall We Rise to Greet the Dawn? Sir Osbert Sitwell. "Continually they cackle thus." PoWW

How shall we speak of Canada. W. L. M. K. Francis Reginald Scott. NOBC

How shall your name go down in history. To Youth. Josephine D. Henderson Heard. CBWP-4

How shalt thou bear the Cross that now. Eternal Years, The. Frederick William Faber. PWR

How she got yr number baby, i'm sorry. (LL) Ntozake Shange. NAAAL; WPOW

How she let her long hair down over her shoulders, making a love. O Best of All Nights, Return and Return Again. James Laughlin. GifTon

How She Resolved to Act. Merrill Moore. MoAmPo

How she sat there. Rosa. Rita Dove. ExTi

How should I direct my steps to her now? Woman, A. Sa'di Yusuf. MAP, *tr.* by Lena Jayyusi and Naomi Shihab Nye

How should I, even if I could. To Catulinus That He Cannot Write Him an Epithalamium because of the Enemy Hosts. Apollinaris Sidonius. MLL, *tr.* by Helen Waddell

How should I not be glad to contemplate. Everything Is Going to Be All Right. Derek Mahon. PBCIP

How should I praise thee, Lord! how should my r[h]ymes. Temper (1), The. George Herbert. ESCV; GeHe; NOCV

How Should I Say This? Robert Dow. BAP-97

How should I your true love know. Old Song Ended, An. Dante Gabriel Rossetti. BoLoP; EBVV

How should I your true love know. William Shakespeare. EBEV; EnLoPo; NoSic; PoRA; SCGP *Fr.* Hamlet.

How shril are silent tears? when sin got head. Admission. Henry Vaughan. ESCV

How sick I get. Father. Paul Carroll. NeAP

How silent is the world. In the Night. Robert Ivanovich Rozhdestvensky [or Rozhdestvenskii]. RusPo, *tr.* by Robert Arthur Douglas Ford

How silently the years have sped away. To My Dead Brother. Clara Ann Thompson. CBWP-2

How silly that soldier is pointing his gun at the wood. Russians. Keith Douglas. OxBTC

How silly were those sages heretofore. Samuel Butler. NOBL *Fr.* Satire upon the Licentious Age of Charles II.

How Sleep the Brave. William Collins. CABP; NOBE; OBEV; OxAEP-1; TFi

(Ode.) SCGP

(Ode Written in MDCCXLVI.) GTBS-P

(Ode Written in the Beginning of the Year 1746.) AWP; HAP; NAEL-5v1; NAEL-6v1; NAEL-7v1; NOEC; NPeEn; NoP-4; OxBEV; OxBSP; PoE

How slow they are awakening, these trees. Plain Fare. Daryl Hine. CoAP

How slowly glide the hours by, the minutes hours seem. Drunkard's Wife, The. Mary E. Tucker. CBWP-1

How slowly learns the child at school. Citizenship; Form 8889512, Sub-Section Q. Gilbert Keith Chesterton. OxBoLi

How small, of all that human hearts endure. Lines Contributed to Goldsmith's "The Traveller." Samuel Johnson. NPeEn

How smooth that lake expands its ample breast! Stanzas. Ann Radcliffe. WPE

How so well a gardener be. John Gardner. OBGa *Fr.* Feat of Gardening, The.

How Socratic is Somerset Maugham! Limerick. R. B. S. Instone. PeLi

How soft a Caterpillar steps—. Caterpillar. Emily Dickinson. SAmP

How soft the pause! the notes melodious cease. Written at Killarney. July 29, 1800. Mary Tighe. CenSon

How Some of It Happened. Marie Howe. ExTi

How soon doth man decay! Mortification. George Herbert. ESCV; FSCP; GeHe; NOSC

How soon hath Time the subtle [or suttle] thief [or theef] of youth. Sonnet 7. John Milton. HeIP-4; NAEL-5v1; NAEL-6v1; NOSC; NoP-4; PAI; PoE; SCGP; Son

How soon shall I be stretched at yours! (LL) La Belle Juive. Henry Timrod. APN-2; TCAPo

How speak of the not-I without screaming? (LL) Man Walks by with a Loaf of Bread on His Shoulder, A. César Vallejo. PoetW; TCLAP, *tr.* by Clayton Eshleman

How splendid in the morning glows. James Elroy Flecker. OBEV *Fr.* Hassan.

How Spring Comes. Alice Notley. PmAP

How Stars Start. Al Young. ESEAA

How startling to find the portraits of the gods. Roy Fuller. Son *Fr.* Mythological Sonnets.

How still. Sea Calm. Langston Hughes. APT-2

How still he stands as mists begin to move.   Guard at the Binh Thuy Bridge, The.   John Balaban.   AF; CDa

How still, how happy! These [or Those] are words.   Emily Jane Brontë.   BWW; NOBVV; SCGP

How still the Riddle lies! (LL)   Emily Dickinson.   NCAP; OxBA

How strange a thing was friendship, long ago.   Friendship.   Florence Converse.   PoBW

How Strange Are Dreams.   J. Gordon Coogler.

How strange are dreams! I dreamed the other night.   J. Gordon Coogler.   VerBaPo   Fr. How Strange Are Dreams.

How strange at night [or it is] to wake.   Night and Sleep.   Coventry Patmore.   EBVV

How strange is Love; I am not one.   Gourmet's Love-Song, The.   P. G. Wodehouse.   NOBL

How strange is this herald who arrives.   Tapestry of the Heart, The.   Jolanda Insana.   CItWP, tr. by Cinzia Sartini Blum and Lara Trubowitz

How strange it seems! These Hebrews in their graves.   Jewish Cemetery at Newport, The.   Henry Wadsworth Longfellow.   APN-1; ChIV-1; ColAP; FaBoA; HAP; HeIP-4; NAAL-5; NCAP; NOBA; NoP-4; OxBA; PoPoPo; TAP; TCAPo

How strange the pride of many Irishmen!   New Style, The.   David [or Daibhi][or Daithi] O'Bruadair [or Ó Bruadair].   BIrV, tr. by John Montague

How strange to be gone in a minute? A man.   Ted Berrigan.   FTOS; PFTM-2; PmAP   Fr. Sonnets, The.

How strangely beats my troubled heart.   Nostalgia.   Lajos Áprily.   IQMS, tr. by Watson Kirkconnell

How strangely blind is prejudice, the Negro's greatest foe!   Prejudice.   Lizelia Augusta Jenkins Moorer.   CBWP-3

How strong does my passion flow.   On Her Loving Two Equally.   Aphra Behn.   NALW; NIL-7; NIP-4

How struts my love my cavalier.   Cock-a-Hoop.   Isabella Gardner.   WPE

How sublime.   Kozan.   JDP, tr. by Yoel Hoffmann

How subtle-secret is your smile! Did you love none then? Nay, I know.   Oscar Wilde.   MoBrPo   Fr. Sphinx, The.

How sweet and awful is the place.   Isaac Watts.   SacPr

How sweet and innocent are country sports.   James Thomson.   UV   Fr. Of a Country Life.

How sweet and lovely dost thou make the shame.   William Shakespeare.   HeIP-4; SCGP   Fr. Sonnets.

How Sweet I Roamed [or Roam'd] from Field to Field.   William Blake.   EnLoPo; NAEL-5v2; NOEC; TFi
   (Prince of Love, The.)   NOBE
   (Song.)   NAEL-6v2; NoP-4

How sweet is harmless solitude!   Solitude.   Mary Mollineux.   NOSC

'How sweet is mortal Sovranty!'— think some.   Omar Khayyám.   UV, tr. by Edward Fitzgerald   Fr. Rubáiyát of Omar Khayyám [of Naishápúr], The.

How Sweet Is the Language of Love.   Oliver Holden.   AH

How sweet is the Shepherd's sweet lot!   William Blake.   ChAP; FHYEP   Fr. Songs of Innocence.

How sweet it is, when mother Fancy rocks.   William Wordsworth.   CenSon

How sweet the answer Echo makes.   Echo.   Thomas Moore.   NOBRP

How sweet the chime of the Sabbath bells!   Creeds of the Bells.   George W. Bungay.   PWR

How sweet the moonlight sleeps upon this bank!   William Shakespeare.   OxAEP-1; TreFP   Fr. Merchant of Venice, The.

How sweet the name of Jesus sounds.   John Newton.   ECEV; NOEC; SacPr

How Sweet Thy Precious Gift of Rest.   Menahem ben Makhir of Ratisbon.   TrJP, tr. by Herbert Loewe

How sweet to weight the line with all these vowels!   Gaiety of Form, The.   Robert Bly.   BodElec

How sweetly did the moments glide.   Cottager's Complaint, on the Intended Bill for Enclosing Sutton-Coldfield, The.   John Freeth.   NOEC

How sweetly now like a boy I dawdle by ditches.   Widespread Implications.   A. R. Ammons.   BodElec

How swiftly it dries.   Burial Songs.   Unknown.   ChiP, tr. by Arthur Waley

How swiftly time doth passe away.   To Her Husband, on New Year's Day 1651.   Gertrude Aston Thimelby.   EMWP

How terrible it is to trust no one.   Unknown.   TCRP

How terrifying at night is the convex face of the black.   First Psalm (Posthumous).   Bertolt Brecht.   PFTM-1

How that girl can move.   Dog Star.   Gerry Gomez Pearlberg.   WiU

How that glory remains in remembrance.   Unknown.   NoP-4   Fr. FROM Beowulf.

How that great work of Love enhances Nature's. (LL)   Elizabeth Barrett Browning.   BWW; CTC; CenSon; OxAEP-2   Fr. Sonnets from the Portuguese.

How the Abbey of Saint Werewulf Juxta Slingsby Came by Brother Fabian's Manuscript.   Sebastian Evans.   PeVV

How the Bulls Were Begotten.   Unknown.

Two Bulls, The.   NOIV, tr. by Thomas Kinsella

How the Camel Got His Hump.   Rudyard Kipling.   Fr. Just-So Stories.

How the days went.   Now That I Am Forever with Child.   Audre Lorde.   NAAAL; NALW

How the Death of a City Is Never More than the Sum of the Deaths of Those Who Inhabit Its Spaces.   Victor Coleman.   NOBC

How the Doughty Duke of Albany like a Coward Knight Ran Away Shamefully.   John Skelton.
   "O ye wretched Scots."   OBSV

How the Elderly Drive.   Erin Belieu.   AmPoNex

How the elements solidify!   Event.   Sylvia Plath.   NOBA

How the First Hielandman of God Was Made.   Unknown.   OBSV
   (How the first Helandman of god was maid of Ane hors turd in argylle as is said.)   NePenScot

How the Heart Aches.   N.V.M. Gonzalez.   ReBoTo

How the Hen Sold Her Eggs to the Stingy Priest.   Nancy Willard.   LCAP-2

How the Last Act Begins.   Chana Bloch.   ExTi

How the Lover Perisheth in His Delight, As the Fly in the Fire.   Petrarch.   SCGP, tr. by Sir Thomas Wyatt   Fr. Sonnets to Laura.

How the majestic stellar lights of Heav'n.   Compensation.   Henrietta Cordelia Ray.   CBWP-3

How the melody of a single ice cream truck.   Desire.   Kathy Fagan.   GeoHom

How the moon triumphs through the endless nights!   James Thomson.   NePenScot   Fr. City of Dreadful Night, The.

How the New Teacher Got Her Nickname.   Brian Patten.   NOxBChV

How the old Mountains drip with Sunset.   Emily Dickinson.   RB

How the rain-day froze.   Child Christ at the Top of the Stairs.   James Ragan.   TWW

How the Rainbow Works.   Al Young.   ESEAA

How the red road stretched before us, mile on mile.   Independence.   Nancy Cato.   WPE

How the river cools your blood is something you can't.   Autobiography, Chapter XVII: Floating the Big Piney.   Jim Barnes.   HATNAP

How the Soul Speaks to God.   Mechthild von Magdeburg.   WPoS, tr. by Oliver Davies

How the splendour of these veils and of this dress.   Phaedra.   Osip Emilevich Mandelstam [or Mandelshtam].   OBVE, tr. by James Greene

How the tenor warbles in April!   Madrigal.   Mary Leader.   NAPBL

How the Tortoise Knew It Was Her Time.   Joan I. Siegel.   PoCoUp

How the Wild South East Was Lost.   Kit Wright.   OBCoV

How the wind howls this morn.   End of May, The.   William Morris.   NOBVV

How the Women Will Stop War.   Aristophanes.   FaBoWar   Fr. Lysistrata.

How the world changes! How I myself change!   Metamorphoses.   Nikolai Alekseievich Zabolotsky [or Zabolotskii].   TCRusP, tr. by John Glad

How the young attempt / and are broken.   Generation.   Audre Lorde.   NBV

How the young flutist smiles.   Bulat Shalvovich Okudzhava.   ItGoST, tr. by Ronnie Apter and Mark Herman

How these pieces of paper: Lined unlined small large crinkled smooth.   How.   Joanne Burns.   BMAP

How They Brought the Good News from Ghent to Aix.   Robert Browning.   EBNV; FHYEP; NAEL-5v2; NAEL-6v2; OBSP; PeVV; UV

How they came into the world.   History of Lesbianism, A.   Judy Grahn.   GLP

How They Killed My Grandmother.   Boris Abramovich Slutsky [or Slutskii].   HP, tr. by Daniel Weissbort

How They Made the Golem.   John Robert Colombo.   MoCV

How They Took the City.   Virgil [or Vergil].   NAWM-5v1; NAWM-7v1, tr. by Robert Fitzgerald   Fr. Aeneid [or Eneados, Aeneis], The.

How thin and sharp is the moon tonight!   Winter Moon.   Langston Hughes.   KaS; SAmP

How Things Bear Their Telling.   Ann Lauterbach.   ExTi

How Things Work.   Gary Soto.   NoAM

How this woman came by the courage, how she got.   John Berryman.   TAP   Fr. Dream Songs.

How thought you that this thing could captivate?   Tennyson.   OxBSo

How time reverses.   For My Contemporaries.   James Vincent Cunningham.   APT-2; CoAP; VCAP

How to Approach Your Lover's Wife.   Amy Bottke.   OPRER

How to Be Old.   May Swenson.   UnPo

How to behold what cannot be held?   Giovanni da Fiesole on the Sublime.   Richard Howard.   GS

How to Change a Flat.   Leslie Anne McIlroy.   AmPoNex

How to Choose a Mistress.   Edmond Prestwich.   NOSC

How to Choose a Mistress.   Unknown.   NOSC

How to deal with these hours.   Midnight Saving Time.   Adrien Stoutenburg.   AWTN

How to Disappear.   Amanda Dalton.   NeBl

How to Do It.   Martial.   WoPoe, tr. by Fred Chappell

How to Dress Like a Femmy Dyke.   Jane Barnes.   GLP

How to Dress like a Scary Dyke. Jane Barnes. GLP

How to Drink the Sun. Vladimir Alekseievich Soloukhin. TCRusP, *tr. by* Daniel Weissbort

How to Eat a Poem. Eve Merriam. ChAP

How to Find Love in an Instant. Michael Lassell. GLP *Fr.* Times Square Poems.

How to Forget. Rebecca Foresman. PoToHe

How to Get a Baby. Judith Ortiz Cofer. NIL-7; PueRic

How to Get Grizzly Spirit. *Unknown.* STP, *tr. by* James Koller

How to Get on in Society. Sir John Betjeman. NOBL; OBSV; OxBTC; UV

How to isolate the fragments of the night. Fragments of the Night, The. José Lezama Lima. TCLAP, *tr. by* Willis Barnstone

How to keep—is there ány any, is there none such, nowhere known. Leaden Echo and the Golden Echo, The. Gerard Manley Hopkins. GTBS-P; MoBrPo; NOBVV; OBMV

How to Kill. Keith Douglas. FaBoMo; HarvBoo; NOBE; NPeEn; PoWW; RB

How To leave you. (LL) Les Luths. Frank O'Hara. NOBA; NoAM

How To Like It. Stephen Dobyns. Unle

How to live as a single natural being. Plan for a Curriculum of the Soul, A. Charles Olson. PFTM-2

How to Live in the Elegy. Tracy Philpot. AmPoNex

How To Live through This Night (A Dream). Nina Iskrenko. ItGoST, *tr. by* Patrick Henry, John High and Katya Olmsted

How to live? How be simple and literal? How? Vladimir Holan. PoSu, *tr. by* Ian Milner and Jarmila Milner

How To Make Good Baked Salmon from the River. Nora Dauenhauer. ReEnLa

How to Make Rhubarb Wine. Ted Kooser. PBCAP

How to make this impure. Empty Page, The. Sara de Ibáñez. TCLAP, *tr. by* Andrew Rosing

How to Meditate. Jack Kerouac. BB; PoM

(—lights out—/ fall, hands a-clasped, into instantaneous.) CLPP

How to Obtain Her. *Unknown.* NoSic

How to Paint a Perfect Christmas. Miroslav Holub. OBCP, *tr. by* Ian Milner and George Theiner

How to Play Night Baseball. Jonathan Holden. MoASP

How to put it . . . without offence. Thomas Kinsella. BiHa *Fr.* Technical Supplement, A.

How to put this exactly? I mean without. J. D. McClatchy. WiU *Fr.* First Steps.

How to Reach the Sun. . . on a Piece of Paper. Wes Magee. NOxBChV

How to Read Me. Walter Savage Landor. NOBVV

How To Ride Out a Storm. Mildmay Fane, 2d Earl of Westmorland. NOSC

How to say hate was in rancorous bloom. Upon Finding a Black Woman's Door Sprayed with Swastikas, I Tell Her This Story of Hands. Kevin Stein. SwNoth

How to say the distance, not the difference. Black English. Richard Katrovas. LTA

How to serve you, and you trust me. (LL) To Lucasta, from Prison. Richard Lovelace. BASC; BeJo; CaPo; CavPo

How to shrug off. Idea Vilariño. TANSG, *tr. by* Louise B. Popkin

How to Start a War. Phyllis McGinley. OBSV

How to Tell a Camel. J. Patrick Lewis. TLR

How To Tell the Wild Animals. Carolyn Wells. NBLV

How to the invisible. Elementary Cosmogony. Charles Simic. NNaP

How to Treat Elves. Morris Gilbert Bishop. OBAL; OBCA

How to Watch Your Brother Die. Michael Lassell. CAGL; GLP; WiU

How to Write Anglo-Welsh Poetry. John Davies. AngWePo; TCAWP

How tranquil is man's life. Life Withdrawn, The. Luís De León. SpanPo, *tr. by* Edwin Morgan

How true it is when I am sad. Work. J. W. Thompson. PoToHe

How ugly babies are! How heedless. Vikram Seth. OBCoV *Fr.* Golden Gate, The.

How unpleasant to meet Mr. Eliot! T. S. Eliot. NBLV; OBAL; OBCoV; PeLV; UV *Fr.* Five-Finger Exercises.

How unpurposed, how inconsequential. Gouzeaucourt: The Deceitful Calm. Edmund Charles Blunden. PeFWW

How vainly men themselves amaze. Garden, The. Andrew Marvell. AWP; BASC; ClHu; ESCV; FSCP; GeHe; HAP; MakPoe; MeLP; NAEL-5v1; NAEL-6v1; NAEL-7v1; NIL-7; NIP-4; NOBE; NOSC; NPeEn; OBGa; OxBEV; PBRV; PoE; PoPoPo; PoRA; SCGP; TFi; TOF; TRP

How varied the family Sen! Limerick. Roy Fuller. PeLi

How vast a world is figured by a word! Word: Man, A. Washington Allston. APN-1

How vast, how dread, o'erwhelming is the thought. On a Falling Group in the Last Judgement of Michael Angelo, in the Cappella Sistina. Washington Allston. APN-1

How vast karma. Seigen-yuiin. ZenPo *tr. by* Takashi Ikemoto and Lucien Stryk

How vastly we improve our style! (LL) Word of Encouragement, A. J. R. Pope. NBLV; NOBL

How very noble! Basho. SoOfWa, *tr. by* Sam Hamill

How vigilant was Spenser. Edmund Clerihew Bentley. OBCoV *Fr.* Clerihews.

How Violets Came Blue. Robert Herrick. BeJo; CaPo; TTTS

How warm this woodland wild Recess! Recollections of Love. Samuel Taylor Coleridge. NAEL-5v2; NAEL-6v2

How was I born? Where from? Why did I come. *Unknown.* GrAn

How was it? / Sweet. (LL) Rudaki. BoLoP; OBVE; OxBEV; WoPoe, *tr. by* Basil Bunting

How was she, my God, how was she? Fleeting Return. Juan Ramón Jiménez. BLPSL, *tr. by* Rene de Costa, Rigas Kappatos and Eleni Paidoussi

How was thy mother a lioness. Bible, *O.T.* TrJP *Fr.* Ezekiel.

How We Beat the Favourite. Adam Lindsay Gordon. CBAP; PeVV

How We Carry Ourselves. Jimmy Santiago Baca. AF

How We Danced. Anne Sexton. NAAL-5 *Fr.* Death of the Fathers, The.

How we desire desire! Joy of surcease. Epigram. James Vincent Cunningham. VGW

How We Drove the Trotter. W. T. Goodge. NOBAu

How we envy their not caring. Card-Players, The. David Ray. VGW

How we go on. (LL) Axe Handles. Gary Snyder. ColAP; LoL; NoAM; PmAP; PoPoPo; VCAP

How We Heard the Name. Alan Dugan. CoAP; NoAM; YaYoPo

How We See. Edward Bond. HP

How weak his will to resist has become. Gravity, Death. Agi Mishol. DTA, *tr. by* Tsipi Keller

How welcome it is, how sweet that the old stories do not always. Rhiannon. Christine Furnival. TCAWP

How well (dear Brother) art thou called Stone? To My Reverend Dear Brother, M. Samuel Stone. John Cotton. SCAP

How well do I recall that walk in state. Frederick Goddard Tuckerman. APN-2 *Fr.* Sonnets.

How well he knows he must lift out. Sea Inside the Sea. Tess Gallagher. PasH

How well her name an *Army* doth present. Anagram. George Herbert. ChIV-2; GeHe

How well I know that fountain's rushing flow. St John of the Cross: Song of the Soul That Is Glad to Know God by Faith. Roy Campbell. PeECV

How well I know what I mean to do. By the Fire-Side. Robert Browning. EBVV

How well the brittle boat doth personate. On the Same [Death of My Dear Brother, Mr. H.S., Drowned]: The Boat. William Hammond. NOSC

How when one entered a cottage. Answer, The. John Montague. CIP-2

How wild the sea is. Basho. SoOfWa

How will he hear the bell at school. Mutterings over the Crib of a Deaf Child. James Wright (1927–80). LCAP-2

How will I hide? (LL) Question. May Swenson. APT-2; VGW

How will I think of you. December 21st. Jean Valentine. LCAP-2

How will it be, the day death comes? Day Death Comes, The. Faiz Ahmad Faiz. PoetW, *tr. by* Naomi Lazard

How will it be with me in time of love? (LL) After Communion. Christina Georgina Rossetti. SacPr; WPoS

How will it go, crumbling earthquake, towering inferno, juggernaut, volcano, smashup. New Reality Is Better Than a New Movie, A! Imamu Amiri Baraka. NoAM

How will our unborn children scoff at us. Future Verdict, The. Ada Cambridge. NOBAu

How will the earth die? . . . will she freeze? will she burn? Sándor Petőfi. IQMS, *tr. by* Peter Zollman *Fr.* Clouds, The.

How Will You Call Me, Brother. Mari E. Evans. BlSi

How will you cross the autumn mountain alone? Princess Oku. BoWoP

How will you fill your goblet? How? Abraham Sutskever [or Sutzkever]. HP

How will you manage. *Var. authors.* AWP *Fr.* Manyo Shu, Part 2 of 4.

How will You rescue me, Tara? Kamalākānta Bhattācārya. SinGod, *tr. by* Rachel Fell McDermott

How will you your Christmas keep? Keeping Christmas. Eleanor Farjeon. OBCP

How wisely Nature did decree. Eyes and Tears. Andrew Marvell. FSCP; GeHe

How Woeful It Is For Me. Péter Bornemisza. IQMS, *tr. by* Paul Tabori

How wonderful! Look what. Rāmprasād Sen. SinGod, *tr. by* Rachel Fell McDermott

How wonderful, Tomasito! Celebration. Thomas McGrath. GifTon

How would it all end? Both Earth and Heaven. Huda Na'mani. MAP, *tr. by* John Heath-Stubbs and Lena Jayyusi

How would you. To the Far Corners of Fractured Worlds. Susan Griffin. GifTon

How would you have us, as we are? To America. James Weldon Johnson. APT-1

How wretched is a woman's fate. Woman's Hard Fate. *Unknown*. ECWP

How 'Ya Gonna Keep 'Em Down on the Farm? (After They've Seen Paree). Sam M. Lewis. ReLy

How yet resolves the Governor of the town? William Shakespeare. FaBoWar *Fr.* King Henry V.

How you became a poet's a mystery! Tony Harrison. HarvBoo; NAEL-6v2 *Fr.* School of Eloquence, The.

How You Get Born. Erica Jong. UnPo

How you go along all day. Strange. Kirby Doyle. NeAP

How, you said, you used to sleep—the way. At the Egyptian Exhibit. Daniel Tobin. NAPBL

How Zenists carry on. Gekko-Sojo. ZenPo, *tr. by* Takashi Ikemoto and Lucien Stryk

How? Vladimir Holan. PoSu, *tr. by* Ian Milner and Jarmila Milner

How? Abraham Sutskever [*or* Sutzkever]. HP

How? 'Providence', and yet a Scottish crew? John Cleveland. BASC; NOSC *Fr.* Rebel Scot, The.

However. Jane Mead. NAPBL

However difficult the cliff. On Climbing the Mountain Where Buddha Trained. Mokusen. ZenPo, *tr. by* Takashi Ikemoto and Lucien Stryk

However, Eumolpus, our champion in time of trouble and the author of the present harmony. Petronius Arbiter. EroLit, *tr. by* J. P. Sullivan *Fr.* Satyricon.

However heaped the fire. Fire Is Laid, The. *Hungarian Oral Tradition.* IQMS, *tr. by* Dermot Spence

However, imperceptibly you'll grow up. Shows. Yevgeny [*or* Evgenii] Mikhailovich Vinokurov. TCRP, *tr. by* Daniel Weissbort

However sure a fate may seem to be. Sayings in Verse. Arthur Schnitzler. AuPH, *tr. by* Lowell A. Bangerter

However the battle is ended. Inspiration, An. Ella Wheeler Wilcox. ITBLP

However the image enters. Afterimages. Audre Lorde. LTA; VCAP

However we wrangled with Britain awhile. Literary Importation. Philip Freneau. TAP

However you look at it. Secular, The. Chris Wallace-Crabbe. NOBAu

Howie gave sentence of slaughter. Desertion of the Women and Seals, The. George Mackay Brown. OxBC

Howl. Allen Ginsberg. HarvBoo; LCAP-2; NAAL-5; PoM

"I saw the best minds of my generation destroyed by madness." NoAM; NoP-4; PmAP; VCAP

"What sphinx of cement and aluminum bashed open their skulls." CLPP; NeAP; TAP

Howl. Beau Sia. HeMarv

Howl, Howl. Christopher Reid. OBCoV

Howl, howl, howl! O! you are men of stones. William Shakespeare. OxAEP-1 *Fr.* King Lear.

Howling Babe, The. (LL) La Préface. Charles Olson. APT-2; PFTM-2; PoM

Howling of Wolves, The. Ted Hughes. OxBTC

Howling storm is brewing, A. Storm, The. Heinrich Heine. AWP, *tr. by* Louis Untermeyer

Howres for the Hours of Matines, The. Richard Crashaw. PeECV

Hrothgar answered helm of the Shield-Danes. *Unknown.* WoPoe, *tr. by* Frederick Rebsamen *Fr.* Beowulf.

Hsi-li Echoed My Poems, and I Respond to Him, Using the Same Rhymes— Also Sent to Tsung-lien. Yang Shih-ch'i.

"Not sobered up from my muddy Kao-yang drunk." CoBLCP

Hsi Shih received the favor of Wu. Following the Rhymes of the Six Poems "Thinking of the Past at Ku-Su and Ch'ien-t'ang." Ni Tsan. CoBLCP, *tr. by* Jonathan Chaves

Hsin-I Village. Wang Wei. ChinPo, *tr. by* Yip Wai-lim

Hsiu-chou. T'ang Hsien-tsu. CoBLCP, *tr. by* Jonathan Chaves

Hsün-yang on the Yangtze, seeing off a guest at night. Song of the Lute. Po Chü-i. CoBCP, *tr. by* Burton Watson

Hub of the Universe, The. Walt Whitman. EnlH *Fr.* Song of Myself.

Hubert's Museum. Louis Simpson. OxBC

Hubris. Mary Karr. NIL-7

Huc omnes pariter. Boethius. OBMV, *tr. by* John Walton *Fr.* Consolation of Philosophy, The ("De Consolacione Philosophie").

Huck Finn at Ninety, Dying in a Chicago Boarding House Room. James Schevill. TAP

Huckster at Noontime. James Ragan. TWW

Hucksters haggle in the mart, The. For a War Memorial. Gilbert Keith Chesterton. PoWW

Hudibras. Samuel Butler (1612–80).

Argument, The. BASC; EBEV; NAEL-5v1; NAEL-6v1; NAEL-7v1

Arms and the Man. NOSC

"For his religion it was fit." OBCoV; OBSV; OxBEV

(Hudibras, the Presbyterian Knight.) OxBoLi

"In mathematic[k]s he was greater." NOBL

Independent Squire. NOBE

Metaphysical Sectarian, The. MeLP; PeLV

"Question then, to state it first, The." NOBL

"Quoth he, My faith as adamantine." OBSV

"Quoth he, to bid me not to love." NOBL

Sidrophel, the Rosicrucian Conjurer. OxBoLi

"Sir Hudibras his passing worth." BASC; EBEV; NAEL-5v1; NAEL-6v1; NAEL-7v1

"Some were for setting up a king." EBEV

"There is a tall long-sided dame." OBSV

"This place (quoth she) they say's enchanted." NOBL

"What makes a knave a child of God." NOBL; OBSV

"When civil fury [*or* dudgeon] first grew high." BASC; CABP; EBEV; NAEL-5v1; NAEL-6v1; NAEL-7v1

Hudibras and Milton Reconciled. William Somervile [*or* Somerville]. NOEC

Hudibras, the Presbyterian Knight. Samuel Butler (1612–80). *See* Hudibras

Hudney, Sutej IX, X, XI, 7, 9, 25, 58, 60, 61, 64. Index. Paul Violi. PmAP

Hudson is angry, white-capped, splashing, The. Three Poems. Michael Lassell. WiU

Hudson tells us of them. Hudson's Geese. Leslie Norris. TCAWP

Hue and Cry after Fair Amoret, A. William Congreve. NOEC; NPeEn; OBEV; OxBEV

Hue is as rich, The. Ki no Tsurayuki. WoPoe, *tr. by* Helen Craig McCullough

Huelsenbeck / janko, chant / tzara. L'amiral cherche une maison à louer. Richard Huelsenbeck. PFTM-1

Huesca. John Cornford. BoLoP
    (To Margot Heinemann.) OBWP; OxBTC

Huey. Etheridge Knight. NNaP

Huffing puffing upstairs downstairs telephone. Not Dead Yet. Allen Ginsberg. BodElec

Huffy Henry hid the day. John Berryman. ColAP; HCAP; NAAL-2v2; NoP-4; PoE; VCAP *Fr.* Dream Songs.

Hug, The. Thom Gunn. HarvBoo; NPeEn

Hug o' War. Shel [*or* Shelley] Silverstein. NTCP

Huge Car with the Sad Voice, The. Kojo Laing. HBAPE

Huge dog, Broderick, and, The. Messengers, The. Robert Creeley. NAAL-5

Huge doll of my body, The. My Life. Mark Strand. NoAM

Huge elm, with rifted trunk all notched and scarred. Shepherd's Tree, The. John Clare. CenSon

HUGE FIGURES FUCKING THE HUGE FIGURES / FUCKING, THE. Michael McClure. BB *Fr.* Dark Brown.

Huge fish, bold and noble, A. Fish in a Painting. Ho Ching-ming. CoBLCP, *tr. by* Jonathan Chaves

Huge frog and I, A. Issa. EH, *tr. by* Robert Hass

Huge frogs and curses. Gu Cheng. PFTM-2, *tr. by* Eva Hung *Fr.* Bulin File, The.

Huge glaring maps the walls surround. Domestic Philosopher, The. *Unknown.* ECWP

Huge-headed oak. He Praises the Trees. *Unknown.* BIrV, *tr. by* Robin Skelton

Huge shards of glass and ice slash through the North Sea. North Sea. Duo Duo (Li Shizheng). PFTM-2, *tr. by* Tony Barnstone and Newton Liu

Huge shoe mounts up from the horizon, A. Wounded Breakfast, The. Russell Edson. LCAP-2

Huge summer afternoon with no sign of rain, A. Basketball. Louis Jenkins. MoASP

Huge upon the hazy plain. Grazing Locomotives. Archibald MacLeish. GM

Huge, viewless, ocean into which we cast. To Silence. Thomas Lovell Beddoes. Son

Huge with Time, a wombfruit lanced. Wole Soyinka. HBAPE

Huge wound in my head began to heal, The. Wound, The. Thom Gunn. NPeEn

Hugerl, for a decade now. W. H. Auden. CAGL *Fr.* Three Posthumous Poems.

Hugging the Shore. Mary E. Tucker. CBWP-1

Hugh of Lincoln. *Unknown. See* Sir Hugh; or, The Jew's Daughter

Hugh Selwyn Mauberley (Life and Contacts). Ezra Pound. APT-1; NOBA; NoAM; OxBA; TAP; UnPo

"Age demanded an image, The." HAP; HarvBoo; MoAmPo; NPeEn; VGW

"Beneath the sagging roof." MoAmPo

Brennbaum. MoAmPo

(E. P. Ode Pour l'Election de Son Sepulchre.) HAP; MoAmPo; NAAL-2v2; NoAM; TCAPo; VGW

(Envoi: "Go, dumb-born book") MoAmPo; OxBA

Envoi (1919). HAP; TCAPo; UnPo; VGW

Hugh Selwyn Mauberley. OxBA; UnPo

Mauberly (1920).

Age Demanded, The. TCAPo

"For this agility chance found." TCAPo

"For three years, diabolus in the scale." TCAPo

"Luini in porcelain!" TCAPo

"Scattered Moluccas." TCAPo

Mr. Nixon. MoAmPo

(Pour l'Election de Son Sepulchre, I-V.) FaBoMo

Siena Mi Fe'; Disfecemi Maremma. MoAmPo

"Tea-rose tea-gown, etc., The." ColAP; HarvBoo; MoAmPo; NOBE

"There died a myriad." HarvBoo; MoAmPo; NOBE; NPeEn; PoE; TRP

"These fought in any case." HarvBoo; HeIP-4; MoAmPo; NOBE; NPeEn; OBWP; PoE; PoWW; TRP; VGW

Yeux Glauques. MoAmPo

Hugh Spencer's Feats in France. *Unknown.* ESPB

Hughie at the Inn. Elinor Wylie. WPE

Hughie Graham. Robert Burns. OxBB

Hughie Grame. *Unknown.* ESPB; IBB

Hugs! Hugs! Damn these hugs! Hugs. Pearson Marx. Unle

Huguenot, A. Mary Elizabeth Coleridge. SacPr

Huguenot Graveyard at the Heart of the City, The. Eavan Boland. HarvBoo

Huh!—*For All?*. (LL) Children's Rhymes. Langston Hughes. BPo; NOxBChV

Huh-huh huh-huh huh-huh huh-huh. Complacencies of the Fenced Yard. William Tester. Unle

Huh uh! Chillun, let us pray! (LL) Ante-Bellum Sermon, An. Paul Laurence Dunbar. APN-2; BPo; NAAAL

Hui-chu Temple, Mount K'un. Wang An-shih. CrYelRi, *tr. by* Sam Hamill

Hui-neng's Pond. Muso Soseki. EaWin, *tr. by* W. S. Merwin

Hula Skirt, 1959, The. Kimiko Hahn. UnSA

"Hullo!" Sam Walter Foss. VerBaPo

Hullo hullo one more night stop guessing it's me the cave man there are cicadas which. Automatic Crystal, The. Aimé Césaire. SurPaPo, *tr. by* Clayton Eshleman and Annette Smith

Hullo, Inside. Max Fatchen. NOxBChV

Hulls jut out of sand, sink, emerge as if from black holes. Heart with Little or No Bedrock for Anchor, A. Vivian Shipley. ExTi

Hully Gully. Rita Dove. SwNoth

Human Abstract, The. William Blake. FHYEP; NAEL-5v2; NAEL-6v2; NOBRP; NOEC; OxAEP-2; PoE *Fr.* Songs of Experience.

Human Affection. Stevie Smith. NALW

Human and Divine. Phoebe Cary. SacPr

Human Animal, The. Jane Mayhall. TAP

Human body is a little universe, The. Enlightenment. Shih Shu. WoPoe, *tr. by* James H. Sanford

Human Clay, The. Ilya Abu Madi. MAP, *tr. by* Issa Boullata and Naomi Shihab Nye

Human contours are so easily lost, The. Human Form Divine, The. Kathleen Jessie Raine. WPE

Human Cry, The. Tennyson. InvLi

Human cunt, like the eye, dilates, The. Tryst. Olga Broumas. WiU

Human Debasement; a Fragment. Edward Rushton. NOEC

Human eye, a sphere of waters and tissue, absorbs an energy that, The. Ronald Johnson. APSN *Fr.* Ark.

Human Form Divine, The. Kathleen Jessie Raine. WPE

Human Geography. Gloria Fuertes. BoWoP, *tr. by* Willis Barnstone

Human Greatness. Edwin Barclay. PBA

Human Heart, The. Frank Carleton Nelson. PoToHe

Human Heart its hungry Gorge, The. (LL) William Blake. ChIV-1; NAEL-5v2; NAEL-6v2; NoP-4; RB *Fr.* Songs of Experience.

Human House. Tamura Ryuichi. VCWP, *tr. by* Christopher Drake

Human Life. Matthew Prior. FaBoEE; OBCoV; OxBEV

Human life does not reach a hundred. Roaming Immortal. Ts'ao Chih. SuSp, *tr. by* Ronald C. Miao

Human Mind, The. Ai Shih-te. TrJP, *tr. by* William C. White

Human Misery. Andreas Gryphius. GePo, *tr. by* George C. Schoolfield

Human Museum, The. Brenda Coultas. HeMarv

Human race is going to the cemetery, The. Etel Adnan. WPOW *Fr.* Beirut-Hell Express, The.

Human race would die out all, The. Bondage. Gyula Illyés. IQMS, *tr. by* Doreen Bell

Human reason is beautiful and invincible. Incantation. Czeslaw Milosz. VCWP

Human Seasons, The. John Keats. GTBS-P

Human shape is a ghost, The. Jelaluddin [*or* Jalal al-Din] Rumi. LoL

Human sigh commuted to life imprisonment, The. Sonnet against Nuclear Weapons. Jane Miller. ExTi

Human Soul. René Maran. TTY, *tr. by* Mercer Cook

Human spirits saw I on a day, The. Questioning Spirit, The. Arthur Hugh Clough. SacPr

Human strength. Simonides. SaLy, *tr. by* Diane Rayor

Human torch / races through Prague, A. Ballad of Jan Palach, Student and Heretic. Ondra Lysohorsky. AF, *tr. by* Ewald Osers

Human Touch, The. Spencer Michael Free. PoToHe

Human Tragedy, The. Alfred Austin.

"And do they wear that lubricating lie." VerBaPo

"But the fleet hours pass pitilessly fleeter." VerBaPo

Human Universe, The. Valerie Martínez. TouFir

Humanities Lecture. William Stafford. NNaP; NoAM

HUMANITY, the field of miseries. Exaltatio Humanae Naturae. William Alabaster. NoSic

Humankind has not declined! Sándor Petőfi. IQMS, *tr. by* Peter Zollman *Fr.* Clouds, The.

Humankind, that my broken mother, fooled. On Mankind. Attila József. IQMS, *tr. by* Adam Makkai

Humans. Attila József. IQMS, *tr. by* Vernon Watkins

Humble-Bee, The. Ralph Waldo Emerson. APN-1; NCAP; NOBA; OxBA

Humble Beginnings. Thomas Lovell Beddoes. NOBVV

Humble Heart, A. Alfred Norris. PWR

Humble life of dull and easy work, The. Paul Verlaine. SxFrPo, *tr. by* Martin Sorrell

Humble Litany. Aida Cartagena de Portalatin. TANSG, *tr. by* Emma Jane Robinett

Humble Petition of the British Jacobins to their Brethren of France, The. *Unknown.* NOBRP

Humble springs of stately Plimouth Beach, The. Upon the Springs Issuing out from the Foot of Plimouth Beach. Samuel Sewall. SCAP

Humble Wish, The. B–ll M–rt–n. ECWP; LW

Humble Wish; off Porto-Sancto, March 29, 1779, An. Edward Thompson. I've served my country nine and twenty years. NOEC

Humbly, He Speaks to His Tools. Venus Khoury-Gata. PoArWo, *tr. by* Lucy McNair

Humiliated again. Rod Willmot. HA

Humiliating the Laser-Beam. Ödön Palasovszky. IQMS, *tr. by* Kenneth McRobbie

Humiliation. Kaifi A'Zmi. OMIP, *tr. by* Mumtaz Jahan

Humility. George Herbert. NOSC

Humility. Marie Luise Kaschnitz. WPOW, *tr. by* Michael Hamburger

Humility is the eye of the needle. Yelena [*or* Elena] Rubisova. TCRP

Humm Tee Dim Tay. Humpty Dumpty. Michael Rosen. NOxBChV

Humming bee purrs softly o'er his flower, The. Cricket, The. Frederick Goddard Tuckerman. APN-2; NCAP; NOBA; TCAPo

Humming-Bird. D. H. Lawrence. NoAM; OWoS; OxBEV; RB

Humming-Bird, The. Mary E. Tucker. CBWP-1

Humming wll put you to sleep, The. Your Death and Mine. János Pilinszky. IQMS, *tr. by* Adam Makkai

Hummingbird. X. J. Kennedy. NOxBChV

Hummingbird. Harold Littlebird. VoR

Hummingbird, A. Emily Dickinson. APN-2; HeIP-4; NAAL-2v1; NAAL-3; NoP-4; SoSe-8; TCAPo

Hummingbird Light. Diane Wakoski. PmAP

Hummingbird Pauses at the Trumpet Vine. Mary Oliver. NAAL-5

Hummingbirds. Norman Dubie. BodElec; LCAP-2

Hummingbirds. Ruth Stone. ExTi

Hummock in the Malookas, A. Matthew Rohrer. AmPoNex

Humorous Lovers, The. William Cavendish, Duke of Newcastle. Song: "We'll, placed in Love's triumphant chariot high.". OxBSP

Humorous Verse. Abu Dulama. TTY, *tr. by* Raoul Abdul

Humours. John Marston. NoSic *Fr.* Satires.

Humours of the King's Bench Prison, a Ballad, The. Leonard Howard. NOEC

Hump, The. Rudyard Kipling. NOxBChV *Fr.* Just-So Stories.

Hump-Backed Flute Player, The. Gary Snyder. APSN; PFTM-2 *Fr.* Mountains and Rivers without End: The Market.

Humped Ox, The. Flavien Ranaivo. NegPo, *tr. by* Ellen Conroy Kennedy

Humphy-backit heron, A. Heron. James King Annand. NOxBChV

Humpty Dumpty. Michael Rosen. NOxBChV

Humpty Dumpty's Poetic Recitation. Lewis Carroll. EBEV; NOBVV; NPeEn *Fr.* Through the Looking-Glass.

Humpty Dumpty sat on a wall. Mother Goose. LB; OxBEV; OxBoLi; OxNR; ReMoGo

Hunchback Girl: She Thinks of Heaven. Gwendolyn Brooks. ChAP *Fr.* Street in Bronzeville, A.

Hunchback in the Park, The. Dylan Thomas. AngWePo; EBEV; FaBoTw; MoBrPo; NAEL-5v2; NAEL-6v2; NoAM; NoP-4; OxBEV; TCAWP; TwCP

Hunchback of Dugbe, The. Wole Soyinka. VCWP

Hunchback on the corner, with gum and shoelaces, The. Pursuit. Robert Penn Warren. FuPo; HAP; MoAmPo; TwCP

Hunchèd camels of the night, The. Arab Love-Song, An. Francis Thompson. AWP; MoBrPo

Hunched, hump-backed, gigantic. Blues. Edward Kamau Brathwaite. GT

Hunched I make my way, uncertainly. On the Back of a Photograph. János Pilinszky. PoSu, tr. by Peter Jay

Hunched in a corner seat, I'd watch him pass. Notes from Underground: W. H. Auden on the Lexington Avenue IRT. Grace Schulman. ExTi

Hunched like poker players at my kitchen table. Corpses, The. Lynn Emanuel. ExTi

Hunder pipers canna blaw, A. Calvinist Sang. Alexander Scott. OxBS

Hundred buffalo, A. Bone Yard. Jim Barnes. CDW

Hundred-gated City! thou. George Darley. NOBE Fr. Nepenthe.

Hundred-gated Thebes. George Darley. NOBE Fr. Nepenthe.

Hundred Headless Woman, The. Max Ernst.

Hundred houses were in ruins, A. Never Again. Jaroslav Seifert. AF, tr. by Ewald Osers

Hundred hundred kisses, A. "Johannes Secundus." EroLit, tr. by Wayland Young Fr. Basia.

Hundred mares, all white! their manes, A. Frédéric Mistral. AWP, tr. by George Meredith Fr. Mirèio.

Hundred men shouting at once, helping to rattle the oars, A. Blue Rapids. Lu Yu. CoBCP; ColAnChi; SuSp, tr. by Burton Watson

Hundred miles from the capital city of hope, A. Yevgeny Aleksandrovich Yevtushenko [or Evtushenko]. TCRusP, tr. by Peter Levi and Robin Milner-Gulland

Hundred rivers day and night flow on, The. Beginning of Autumn: A Poem to Send to Tzu-yu. Su Tung-p'o (Su Shih). CoBCP, tr. by Burton Watson

Hundred ruddy peach-moons ring the grass, A. Under the September Peach. Robert Wallace. Son

Hundred spirits whisper "Peace", A. (LL) Tennyson. EBVV; NAEL-6v2 Fr. In Memoriam A. H. H.

Hundred-sunned Phenix. George Darley. OWoS Fr. Nepenthe.

Hundred thousand li of journey, how many dangers?, A. For the Monk San-tsang on His Return to the Western Regions. Li Tung. CoBCP, tr. by Burton Watson

Hundred Thousand Million Mites, A. Charles Hamilton Sorley. PoWW

Hundred Ways of Playing Solitaire, A. Belle Randall.
Mabel Woo. CRP

Hundred Worries, A. Tu Fu. CrYelRi, tr. by Sam Hamill

Hundred years, and half have passed already, A. Sent to the Magistrate of P'eng-chou. Tu Fu. CrYelRi, tr. by Sam Hamill

Hundred years are but a butterflys dream, A. Tune: "Sailing at Night"—A Song Sequence. Ma Chih-yüan. SuSp, tr. by Sherwin S. S. Fu

Hundred years from now, dear heart, A. In a Rose Garden. John Bennett. ITBLP

Hundred Years from Today, A. Victor Young. ReLy

Hundred years the Ark in the building was, A. Michael Drayton. ChIV-1 Fr. Noah's Flood.

Hundreds of birds are singing in the square. Marché aux Oiseaux. Richard Wilbur. OWoS

Hundreds of houses, thousands of houses—like a great chess-board. Climbing the Terrace of Kuan-yin and Looking at the City of Ch'ang-an. Po Chü-i. ChiP, tr. by Arthur Waley

Hundreds of open flowers. House of Spring. Muso Soseki. EaWin, tr. by W. S. Merwin

Hung be the heavens with black, yield day to night. William Shakespeare. OxAEP-1 Fr. King Henry VI, Pt. I.

Hung between thief and thief. Impropriea. Francis Sparshott. MoCV

Hung clouded in the dragon-guarded shrine. (LL) Christopher Pearse Cranch. APN-1; GM Fr. Seven Wonders of the World.

Hung outside the door to dry. (LL) Caravan. Michael Longley. CIP-2; ModIr; PNI

Hung there in the thermal. Vultures. Margaret Atwood. LCAP-2; OWoS

Hungarian Medical Student, The: 1928. Evelyn Posamentier. GotH

Hungarian Summer [1918]. Gyula Juhász. IQMS, tr. by Adam Makkai

Hungarian Winter. Gyula Juhász. IQMS, tr. by Jess Perlman

Hungarian Writer, The. János Batsányi. IQMS, tr. by Adam Makkai

Hungary. Dániel Berzsenyi. IQMS, tr. by Watson Kirkconnell

Hungary. Sándor Petőfi. IQMS, tr. by Peter Zollman

Hunger. Laurence Binyon. OxBTC

Hunger. Attila József. IQMS, tr. by Watson Kirkconnell

Hunger. Mikhail Naimy. GraLe

Hunger. Arthur Rimbaud. AWP, tr. by Louise Varese

Hunger. Jerome Rothenberg. APSN

Hunger. Samik. STP, tr. by Edward Field

Hunger. Charles Simic. NNaP

Hunger. Gaspara Stampa. WPOW, tr. by Brenda Webster

Hunger. Unknown. PBA; TTY, tr. by Ulli Beier

Hunger and Imagination. Teresa Whitman. MiVo

Hunger Camp at Jaso. Wislawa Szymborska. See Starvation Camp near Jaslo

Hunger makes a person climb up to the ceiling. Hunger. Unknown. PBA; TTY, tr. by Ulli Beier

Hunger of the Lemur, The. Matthew Rohrer. NeAmPo

Hunger of the Suffering Man, The. Syl Cheney-Coker. PBMAP

Hungering Hearts. Unknown. PoToHe

Hungering on the gray plain of its birth. Lion Named Passion, A. John Hollander. NoAM

Hungrier than I / thot. (LL) Dualism. Ishmael Reed. ESEAA; NAAAL

Hungry, and plucking / the fruit. (LL) O Taste and See. Denise Levertov. ChIV-1; TAP

Hungry and thirsty for holiness. Vasco [or Vasko] Popa. PoSu, tr. by Anne Pennington Fr. St Sava's Spring.

Hungry Black Child, The. Adam David Miller. NBV

Hungry bower of drolleries—. Gavin Selerie. Oth Fr. Roxy.

Hungry crows sit and guard. Song of the Maidens. Yüan Hao-wen. SuSp, tr. by Stephen West

Hungry Grass, The. Donagh MacDonagh. BIrV

Hungry Man's Wheel, The. César Vallejo. PFTM-1

Hungry Master and Hungry Cat. Shamaqmaq, Abu. TriCat

Hungry winter, this winter. To Hell with It. Frank O'Hara. NeAP

Hungry / without money—. Michael McClintock. HA

Hunner funnels bleezin', reekin', A. Oor Location. Janet Hamilton. NePenScot

Hunnish horse / Hunnish horse. Tune: "Song of Flirtatious Laughter." Wei Ying-wu. SuSp, tr. by Hellmut Wilhelm

Hunt by Night, The. Derek Mahon. HarvBoo

Hunt ceases, The. St. Eustace. Derek Mahon. BiHa

Hunt-Cup, The. Daniel Tobin. NAPBL

Hunt in the Black Forest, A. Randall Jarrell. CoAP; LCAP-2

Hunt not, fish not, shoot not. Bishop Blomfield's First Charge to His Clergy. Sydney Goodsir Smith. FaBoEE

Hunt the Thimble. Dannie Abse. TCAWP

Hunt was up, the hunt was up, The. Capture of Edwin Alonzo Boyd, The. Peter Miller. MoCV

Hunter, The. Frank O'Hara. NNaP

Hunter, The. Raymond Souster. NOBC

Hunter friend of mine. Daydream of Ants, The. Tanure Ojaide. NAfrP

Hunter Poems of the Yoruba. Unknown. RB, tr. by Ulli Beier

Hunter's Dance in Early Fall. Debra Haaland Toya. ReEnLa

Hunter's Song. Unknown. APN-2, tr. by Albert S. Gatschet

Hunter's Song at Nightfall, The. Goethe. STV, tr. by John Frederick Nims

Hunter to the husbandman, The. Valentine, A. Robert Graves. FuPo

Hunter Trials. Sir John Betjeman. OBCoV

Hunters, The. Ruth Temple Lindsay. SacPr

Hunters are back / from beating the winter's face, The. Woman Thing, The. Audre Lorde. BlSi

Hunters in the Snow, The. William Carlos Williams. LCAP-2 Fr. Pictures from Brueghel.

Hunters of the Deer, The. Dale Zieroth. NOBC

Hunters went out with guns. Good Grease. Mary Tallmountain. UnSA

Hunting. William Daniel Ehrhart. CDa

Hunting. Tymoteusz Karpowicz. PoSu, tr. by Jan Darowski

Hunting. Gary Snyder. Fr. Myths and Texts.

Hunting. "Yehoash." TrJP, tr. by Isidore Goldstick

Hunting a Hare. Andrey [or Andrei] Andreievich Voznesensky [or Voznesenskii]. TCRP, tr. by W. H. Auden

Hunting Accident. Alicia Muñoz. Unle

Hunting and Fishing. Pope. ECEV; FHYEP Fr. Windsor-Forest [or Windsor Forest].

Hunting Civil War Relics at Nimblewill Creek. James Dickey. CoAmPo

Hunting horn upon the plain, A. Mystery of the Three Horns, The. Jules Laforgue. WoPoe, tr. by William Jay Smith

Hunting in Twilight. David Scott Ward. AmPoNex

Hunting of a Stag, The. Margaret Lucas Cavendish, Duchess of Newcastle. EMWP

Hunting of the Gods, The. Unknown. OxBoLi

Hunting of the Hare, The. Margaret Lucas Cavendish, Duchess of Newcastle. BASC; BWW; FaBoVe; NAEL-7v1; NOSC

Hunting of the Snark, The. Lewis Carroll. OBNV

Baker's Tale, The. EBEV; NAEL-5v2; NAEL-6v2; OxAEP-2

Fit the Second: The Bellman's Speech. OBCoV

Fit the Sixth: The Barrister's Dream. EBNV

Vanishing, The. OxAEP-2

Hunting Pheasants in a Cornfield. Robert Bly. CoAmPo; TRP

Hunting Rabbits. Peter Skrzynecki. BMAP

Hunting season / Once every year, the Deer catch human beings. They. Long Hair. Gary Snyder. NOBA

Hunting Song. Henry Fielding. OxBoLi; PeLV *Fr.* Don Quixote in England.

Hunting Song. Sir Walter Scott. GTBS-P; SCGP

Hunting-Song. *Unknown.* AWP; PAI, *tr. by* Natalie Curtis

Hunting Song. *Unknown.* STP, *tr. by* Jerome Rothenberg

Hunting Song. Paul Whitehead. OxBoLi *Fr.* Apollo and Daphne.

Hunting the Dugong. Gladys Cardiff. HATNAP

Hunting the Wren. *Unknown.* FaBoVe

Hunting with. Harry Gilonis. Oth *Fr.* Forty Fungi.

Huntington sleeps in a house six feet long. Southern Pacific. Carl Sandburg. GM

Hunts—through clear glass windows. Indoor Cat, The. Paul Petrie. PoCoUp

Huntsman, The. Helen Adam. APT-2

Huntsman, The. Edward Lowbury. OBSP

Huntsman waits with watchful eye, The. Fair Ilonka. Mihály Vörösmarty. IQMS, *tr. by* Watson Kirkconnell

Hurley High. Paul Zarzyski. SwNoth

Hurly, hurly, roon the table. *Unknown.* FaBoCh *Fr.* Two Graces.

Hurlygush. Maurice Lindsay. OxBS

Huron, The. Ruth Herschberger. WPE

Huron Carol, The. Jesse Edgar Middleton. OBCP

Hurrah for revolution and more cannon-shot! Great Day, The. W. B. Yeats. BIrV; OxBSP

Hurra[h] for the pumpkin pie! (LL) Thanksgiving Day. Lydia Maria Child. NTCP; WHSW

Hurrah for Thunder. Christopher Okigbo. HBAPE

Hurrahing in Harvest. Gerard Manley Hopkins. MoBrPo; NAEL-5v2; NAEL-6v2; OxBSo; PeECV; PoE; SacPr; TOF

Hurray, hurray, the jade's away. Witch o' Fife, The. James Hogg. NePenScot

Hurricane. John Balaban. UrbNat

Hurricane, The. Hart Crane. MoAmPo; OxBA; TrCP

Hurricane, The. Philip Freneau. TAP; TCAPo

Hurrier, The. Harold Monro. MoBrPo

Hurry, Hurry, Mary Dear! N. M. Bodecker. TLR

Hurry me Nymphs! O, hurry me. George Darley. NPeEn *Fr.* Nepenthe.

Hurry of the Spirits, in a Fever and Nervous Disorders, The. Isaac Watts. NOEC

Hurry on, My Weary Soul. *Unknown.* AH

Hurry, take pleasure in the oblique caress of rain while the sun shines. Natalya [*or* Natal'ia] Gorbanevskaya [*or* Gorbanyevskaya *or* Gorbanevskaia]. TCRusP, *tr. by* Daniel Weissbort

Hurry up, Christendom, think about salvation. András Szkhárosi Horvát. IQMS, *tr. by* Adam Makkai *Fr.* About Two Kinds of Faith: That of Christ and That of the Pope's Ragged Patchwork.

Hurrying to catch my Comet. Naturally the Foundation Will Bear Your Expenses. Philip Larkin. PeLV

Hurt. Marcie Hans. CA

Hurt Hawks. Robinson Jeffers. APT-1; ChAP; ColAP; HarvBoo; MoAmPo; NAAL-2v2; NOBA; NoAM; NoP-4; OWoS; OxBA; RB; TAP; TFi; TRP; UnPo

Hurt No Living Thing. Christina Georgina Rossetti. OTCP *Fr.* Sing-Song.

"Hurt not the trees" (LL) Trees Are Down, The. Charlotte Mew. BrRo; ChIV-2; MoBrPo; OxAEP-2; TrCP; VWP; WPE; WPOW

Hurt of Love, The. George Macdonald. TrCP

Hurt people crawl as if they. These Days. William Stafford. NNaP

Hurtled under the lover-sundering river. Traveling Boy. William Meredith. YaYoPo

Hurtling between hedges now, I see. Limerick Train, The. Brendan Kennelly. PBCIP

Hurtling past us in an old Volvo are women who speak with forked. Women who Speak with Steak Knives. Susan Hampton. BMAP

Husband. Popati Hiranandani. OMIP, *tr. by* Popati Hiranandani

Husband and Heathen. Sam Walter Foss. OBAL

Husband and Wife. Arthur Guiterman. PoToHe

Husband and Wife. Edward Hirsch. IllVoic

Husband and Wife. *Vietnamese Oral Tradition.* CaDao, *tr. by* John Balaban

Husband and wife! No converse now ye hold. Husband's and Wife's Grave, The. Richard Henry Dana. APN-1

Husband and wife we loved each other then. Old Man's Song, about His Wife, The. *Unknown.* STP, *tr. by* Armand Schwerner

Husband, if you will be my dear. Wife to Husband. John Harington. NoSic

Husband of to-Day, The. Edith Nesbit. VWP

Husband or a lover has run this one out, A. People at the Pay Telephone, The. Victoria McCabe. OPRER

Husband, put down Spinoza, Pericles. Put off Constricting Day. Mary Stanley. PeNZ

Husband's and Wife's Grave, The. Richard Henry Dana. APN-1

Husband's Lament, The. Brian [*or* Bryan] Merriman [*or* Merryman]. OBVE, *tr. by* Frank O'Connor *Fr.* Midnight Court, The.

Husband's Message, The. *Unknown.* AnOE, *tr. by* Charles W. Kennedy (Now that we are on our own I can explain this secret stave.) ASW

Husband's Return, The. Priscilla Jane Thompson. CBWP-2

Husband to Wife. John Harington. NoSic

Husband, today could you and I behold. Wife Speaks, The. Elizabeth Stoddard. SWaP

Husband who lived in Tiberias, A. Limerick. *Unknown.* PeLi

Husbandman, The. George Wither. NOSC *Fr.* Collection of Emblemes, Ancient and Moderne, A.

Husbands and Wives. Miriam Hershenson. NTCP

Hush. Mary Elizabeth Coleridge. PoBW

Hush. David St. John. LCAP-2

Hush-a-ba birdie [*or* burdie], croon, croon. *Unknown.* OxNR

Hush-a-baa, baby / Dinna mak' a din. *Unknown.* OxNR

Hush-a-Bye. *Unknown.* ReMoGo

Hush-a-bye a baa lamb. *Unknown.* OxNR

Hush-a-bye, baby, on the tree-top. Mother Goose. OxBEV; OxNR; ReMoGo

Hush-a-bye, baby / The beggar shan't have 'ee. *Unknown.* OxNR

Hush-a-bye, baby, they're gone to milk. *Unknown.* OxNR

Hush, baby, my dolly, I pray you don't cry. Baby Dolly. *Unknown.* ReMoGo

Hush'd Be the Camps to-Day. Walt Whitman. SAmP *Fr.* Memories of President Lincoln.

Hush Honey. Ruby C. Saunders. BlSi

Hush, Hush. Mani Leib [*or* Leyb]. TrJP, *tr. by* Joseph Leftwich

Hush, Hush. John Bingham Morton. UV *Fr.* When We Were Very Silly.

Hush, hush, do not speak. Hush, Hush. Mani Leib [*or* Leyb]. TrJP, *tr. by* Joseph Leftwich

Hush, hush / Nobody cares! John Bingham Morton. UV *Fr.* When We Were Very Silly.

Hush! Hush! Whisper who dares! Alan Alexander Milne. UV *Fr.* Vespers.

Hush! hush! wild heart. (LL) Beauty Rohtraut. Eduard Friedrich Mörike [*or* Möricke]. AWP; OBVE, *tr. by* George Meredith

Hush is over all the teeming lists, A. Frederick Douglass. Paul Laurence Dunbar. CBCWP

Hush, little baby, don't say a word. *Unknown.* OxNR; TLR

Hush little Lily. Chillen Get Shoes. Sterling Allen Brown. APT-2; NoP-4

Hush, lullay. Lullaby. Léonie Adams. MoAmPo

Hush, my baby, do not cry. *Unknown.* OxNR

Hush! my dear, lie still and slumber. Cradle Hymn, A. Isaac Watts. OBEV; SCGP

Hush now. You cannot describe it. Hunt the Thimble. Dannie Abse. TCAWP

Hush of / the river, The. Canoer, The. Diane Wakoski. HeIP-4

Hush, Suzanne! Mouse in the Wainscot, The. Ian Serraillier. OTCP

Hush thee, my babby. *Unknown.* OxNR

Hush Thee, Princeling. Anna Elizabeth Bennett. AH

Hush! 'tis a holy hour—the quiet room. Evening Prayer, at a Girls' School. Felicia Dorothea Hemans. VWP

Hush! 'tis the gap between two lightnings. Room. Non Pax—Expectatio. Francis Thompson. OxBSo

Hush ye, hush ye! honey, darlin'. Lullaby. Clara Ann Thompson. CBWP-2

Hush Yo Mouf. Thomas Sayers Ellis. InTrad

Hush! Yo' mouth. Hush Honey. Ruby C. Saunders. BlSi

Hushaby / Don't you cry. All the Pretty Little Horses. *Unknown.* OxBoLi; TTTS

Hushed, the lake-shore's pines. O. Mabson Southard. HA

Hushed was the courtyard of the temple. Cicada, The. Ou-yang Hsiu. ChiP, *tr. by* Arthur Waley

Hushie ba, burdie beeton. *Unknown.* OxNR

Huswifery. Edward Taylor. ColAP; ITBLP; InVLi; NAAL-2v1; NAAL-3; NAAL-5; NIP-4; NOBA; NOBE; OxBA; SCAP; SacPr; TAP; TCAPo; TFi (Housewifery.) NoP-4

Huszt. Ferenc Kölcsey. IQMS, *tr. by* Watson Kirkconnell

Hut in Harmony. Muso Soseki. EaWin, *tr. by* W. S. Merwin

Hut in the bush of bark or rusty tin, The. Hatters, The. Nan McDonald. NOBAu

Huts that stand like plaited baskets. Village and Factory. Alexander Ilyich Bezymensky [*or* Bezymenskii]. TrJP, *tr. by* Babette Deutsch

Huts were of mud and hay, The. In the Refugee Camp. Sharif Elmusa. GraLe

Huxley Hall. Sir John Betjeman. CABP; OBSV

Huy Nguyen: Brothers, Drowning Cries. David Mura. CDa

Huzza! Hodgson, we are going. Lines to Mr Hodgson. Byron. OBCoV

Hwaet! / A dream came to me. Dream of the Rood, The. *Unknown*. NOCV, *tr. by* Michael Alexander

Hwæt, wē gār-dena in gēardagum. *Unknown*. CABP *Fr.* Beowulf (c. 8th century).

Hyacinth. Louise Glück. NoAM

Hyacinth I wished me in her hand, A. (LL) Madrigal: "Like the Idalian Queen[e]." William Drummond, of Hawthornden. NOSC; SCGP

Hyænas [*or* Hyenas], The. Rudyard Kipling. NAEL-5v2; NAEL-6v2; OBSV

Hyaku-Nin-Isshu. *Var. authors*. AWP, *tr. by* Curtis Hidden Page

Hyder Iddle. *Unknown*. OxNR

Hydrocarbons of flesh and stone. (LL) Lyell's Hypothesis Again. Kenneth Rexroth. APSN; APT-2

Hydrologist tells me, The. You Live on a Drifting Road. Robert Ivanovich Rozhdestvensky [*or* Rozhdestvenskii]. TCRP, *tr. by* J. R. Rowland

Hydromaniac. Rosemary Tonks. EmeKit

Hye Nonny Nonny Noe. *Unknown*. NOBL; PeLV

Hyena. *Unknown*. TTY, *tr. by* George Economou

Hyena, The. Cees Buddingh' TuT, *tr. by* John Hughes

Hyena Addressing Her Young Ones, The. *Unknown*. PeSAV, *tr. by* W. H. I. Bleek

Hygiene. Reginald Shepherd. ReTh

Hyla Brook. Robert Frost. APT-1; TCAPo

Hylas. Propertius. AWP, *tr. by* F. A. Wright *Fr.* Elegies.

Hylas. Bayard Taylor. CAGL
    "Storm-wearied Argo slept upon the water." CAGL

Hylas. Bayard Taylor. CAGL *Fr.* Hylas.

Hylas. Theocritus. HePo, *tr. by* Barbara Hughes Fowler *Fr.* Idylls.

Hymen. "H. D.".
    "Never more will the wind." CTC

Hymen, god of marriage bed. Epithalamium. Joseph Rutter. NOSC

Hymen hath together tied. Epithalamium. R. Hatton. NOSC

Hymen's Triumph. Samuel Daniel.
    Love Is a Sickness. NOBE; OBEV

Hymeneal Song on the Nuptials of the Lady Anne Wentworth and the Lord Lovelace, An. Thomas Carew. CaPo

Hymn. Joseph Addison. OxAEP-1

Hymn. Saint Francis Xavier. ChIV-2

Hymn. Jack Kerouac. CLPP

Hymn. Christopher Smart. *See* Hymns and Spiritual Songs for the Fasts and Festivals of the Church of England

Crucifixion to the World by the Cross of Christ. Isaac Watts. *See* Hymn: "When I survey the wondrous cross."

Hymn. John Wesley. *See* Hymn: "Thou hidden love of God, whose height."

Hymn. John Greenleaf Whittier. NOxBChV
    (Thy perfected praise!) (LL) NOxBChV

Hymn, A. Phineas Fletcher. *See* Hymn: "Drop, drop, slow tears, and bathe those beauteous feet."

Hymn, The. Denise Levertov. BodElec

Hymn 10. William Cowper. *See* Olney Hymns

Hymn, A: "Lead gently, Lord, and slow." Paul Laurence Dunbar. SacPr

Hymn, a snare, and an exceeding sun. (LL) Boy Breaking Glass. Gwendolyn Brooks. AiP; ESEAA; NAAL-2v2; NoAM; NoP-4

Hymn among the Ruins. Octavio Paz. PFTM-1; TCLAP, *tr. by* William Carlos Williams

Hymn, An: "Wake, O my soul; awake, and raise." Phineas Fletcher. NOSC

Hymn: "And many voices marshalled in one hymn." Thomas Lovell Beddoes. NOBVV

Hymn before Action. Rudyard Kipling. FaBoWar

Hymn before Sunrise, in the Vale of Chamouni. Samuel Taylor Coleridge. SacPr

Hymn: "Blest are the moments, doubly blest." William Wordsworth. SacPr

Hymn: "Christians, awake, salute the happy morn." John Byrom. ECEV; NOCV; SacPr

Hymn: "Drop, drop, slow tears, and bathe those beauteous feet." Phineas Fletcher. OxBSP; PeECV; SacPr

Hymn: "Eternal gates lift up their heads, The." Cecil Frances Alexander. SacPr

Hymn for Advent. Jeremy Taylor. SacPr

Hymn for All Seasons. László Nagy. IQMS, *tr. by* Adam Makkai

Hymn for Atonement Day. Judah Halevi. TrJP, *tr. by* Solomon Solis-Cohen

Hymn for Christmas Day, A. John Byrom. ECEV; NOCV

Hymn for Easter Morn. John Mason Neale. TrCP

Hymn for Lanie Poo. Imamu Amiri Baraka. BB
    Each Morning. ESEAA

Hymn for Morning. Prudentius. MLL, *tr. by* Helen Waddell

Hymn for Seedtime and a Safe Harvest (Arval Hymn). *Unknown*. WoPoe, *tr. by* Janet Lembke

Hymn for St. John's Eve. *Unknown*. AWP, *tr. by* John Dryden

Hymn for the Boatmen, as They Approach the Rapids under the Castle of Heidelberg. William Wordsworth. SacPr *Fr.* Memorials of a Tour of the Continent; 1820.

Hymn for the Close of the Week. Peter Abelard. TrCP

Hymn for the Eve of the New Year. Abraham Gerondi. TrJP, *tr. by* Solomon Solis-Cohen

Hymn: "Framer of the earth and sky." Saint Ambrose. TrCP

Hymn: "Hark what a sound, and too divine for hearing." Frederic William Henry Myers. SacPr

Hymn: "How dare I in thy courts appear." Phoebe Cary. SacPr

Hymn: "Hymn of glory let us sing, A." The Venerable Bede. SacPr, *tr. by* Elizabeth Rundle Charles and Elizabeth Charles

Hymn: "I know if I find you I will have to leave the earth." A. R. Ammons. CoAmPo

Hymn: "If in my womb and mind You placed." Alda Merini. CItWP, *tr. by* Cinzia Sartini Blum and Lara Trubowitz

Hymn in Adoration of the Blessed Sacrament. Richard Crashaw. MeLP

Hymn in Columbus Circle. Stephen Vincent Benét. OBAL

Hymn in Praise of Neptune, A. Thomas Campion. NOBE; OBEV

Hymn: "In vain the dusky night retires." Elizabeth Singer Rowe. ECWP

Hymn: "Inspirer and hearer of prayer." Augustus Montague Toplady. SacPr

Hymn: "Jesus these eyes have never seen." Ray Palmer. SacPr

Hymn: "Jesus, where'er thy people meet." William Cowper. SacPr *Fr.* Olney Hymns.

Hymn: "Lord, when the wise men came from far[r]." Sidney Godolphin. BeJo; HAP; MeLP; NOCV; NPeEn; OxBEV; PBRV; PeECV; SacPr
    (Maditation on the Nativity.) NOSC
    (Wise Men and Shepherds.) NOBE

Hymn: "Lord, within thy fold I be." Priscilla Jane Thompson. CBWP-2

Hymn: "Now the day is over." Sabine Baring-Gould. SacPr; WHSW

Hymn: "Now the shadows flee and vanish." William Williams. AngWePo

Hymn: "Now we should praise Heaven-kingdom's guard." Caedmon. PAI, *tr. by* D. K. Fry

Hymn: "O God of Hosts, thine Ear incline." *Unknown*. NOBRP

Hymn: "O Love of God, how strong and true." Horatius Bonar. SacPr

Hymn of Empedocles. Matthew Arnold. OBEV *Fr.* Empedocles on Etna.

Hymn of glory let us sing, A. Hymn. The Venerable Bede. SacPr, *tr. by* Elizabeth Rundle Charles and Elizabeth Charles

Hymn of Heavenly Love, An. Edmund Spenser. SacPr

Hymn of Love, The. György Sárközi. IQMS, *tr. by* Adam Makkai

Hymn of Pan. Shelley. FaBoCh; OBEV

Hymn of the Earth. William Ellery Channing. APN-1

Hymn of the Fairest Fair, The. William Drummond, of Hawthornden.
    "In those vast fields of light, ethereal plains." NOSC

Hymn of the Magdalen. Marbod of Rennes. MLL, *tr. by* Helen Waddell

Hymn of the Patriotic War Veterans. Benjamin Péret. AF, *tr. by* Keith Hollaman

Hymn of Unity. *Unknown*. TrJP, *tr. by* H. M. Adler

Hymn of Weeping. Amittai ben Shefatiah. TrJP, *tr. by* Nina Davis Salaman

Hymn on Froude and Kingsley, A. William Stubbs. FaBoEE

Hymn on Solitude. James Thomson. NOEC

Hymn on the Morning of Christ's Nativity. John Milton. NOBE; OBEV *Fr.* On the Morning of Christ's Nativity.

Hymn on the Seasons, A. James Thomson. CABP *Fr.* Seasons, The.

Hymn[:] Sung at the Completion of the Concord Monument, April 19, 1836. Ralph Waldo Emerson. *See* Concord Hymn

Hymn, The: "To the Almighty on his radiant throne." Anne Finch, Countess of Winchilsea. ChIV-1 *Fr.* Pindaric Poem, A.

Hymn: "Thou hidden love of God, whose height." John Wesley. ECEV; NOEC

Hymn to a Woman under Interrogation. Reiner Kunze. PoSu, *tr. by* Ewald Osers

Hymn to Adversity. Thomas Gray. GTBS-P

Hymn to Aphrodite. *Unknown*. HW, *tr. by* Patricia Monaghan *Fr.* Homeric Hymns.

Hymn to Apollo. Callimachus. HePo, *tr. by* Barbara Hughes Fowler *Fr.* Hymns.

Hymn to Artemis. Callimachus. HePo, *tr. by* Barbara Hughes Fowler *Fr.* Hymns.

Hymn to Athena. *Unknown*. AWP, *tr. by* Percy Bysshe Shelley *Fr.* Homeric Hymns.

Hymn to Castor and Pollux. *Unknown*. AWP, *tr. by* Percy Bysshe Shelley *Fr.* Homeric Hymns.

Hymn to Comus. Ben Jonson. NOSC; SCGP *Fr.* Pleasure Reconciled to Virtue.

Hymn to Contentment, A. Thomas Parnell. NOEC

Hymn to Cynthia. Ben Jonson. NOSC; PoE; SCGP *Fr.* Cynthia's Revels.

Hymn to Demeter. Callimachus. HePo, *tr. by* Barbara Hughes Fowler *Fr.* Hymns.

Hymn to Diana. Catullus. AWP, *tr. by* Richard Claverhouse Jebb *Fr.* Carmina.

Hymn to Diana. Ben Jonson. AWP; GTBS-P; HAP; NOBE; OBEV; PoRA; TFi *Fr.* Cynthia's Revels.

Hymn to Earth. Elinor Wylie. MoAmPo

Hymn to Earth the Mother of All. *Unknown.* AWP, *tr. by* Percy Bysshe Shelley *Fr.* Homeric Hymns.

Hymn to Eros. Denise Levertov. LW

Hymn to God the Father, A. Ben Jonson. *See* Hymn[e] to God the Father, A

Hymn to Her Unknown. Walter James Turner. OBMV

Hymn to Hestia, The. *Unknown. Fr.* Homeric Hymns.

Hymn to Him, A. Frederick Loewe. ReLy

Hymn to Holy Women, A. Notker Balbulus. NAWM-7v1, *tr. by* Peter Dronke

Hymn to Indra, A. Sir William Jones. NOBRP

Hymn to Intellectual Beauty. Shelley. FHYEP; HAP; HeIP-4; NAEL-5v2; NAEL-6v2; NOBRP; NoP-4; PoE; TOF

Hymn to Ishtar. Ashur-Nasir-Pal, King of Assyria. HW

Hymn: To Light. Abraham Cowley. MeLP; OxAEP-1

Hymn to Love. Lascelles Abercrombie. OBEV *Fr.* Emblems of Love.

Hymn to Mercury. *Unknown. Fr.* Homeric Hymns.

Hymn to Moloch. Ralph Hodgson. OxBTC

Hymn to My God in a Night of My Late Sickness[e], A. Sir Henry Wotton. MeLP; NOSC; SacPr

Hymn to Na'ra'yena, A. Sir William Jones. NOBRP

Hymn to Night. Melville Cane. MoAmPo

Hymn to Night. *Unknown.* WoPoe, *tr. by* Peter Dent and Edwin Gerow *Fr.* Vedic Hymns.

Hymn to Night, A. Max Michelson. TrJP

Hymn to Nut. *Unknown.* HW

Hymn to Pan. John Fletcher. NOBE; OBEV *Fr.* Faithful Shepherdess, The.

Hymn to Priapus. D. H. Lawrence. OBMV; PoE; SCGP

Hymn to Proserpine. Algernon Charles Swinburne. EBVV; NAEL-5v2; NAEL-6v2

Hymn to Saint Geryon. Michael McClure. PmAP

Hymn to Science. Mark Akenside. ECEV

Hymn to Selene. *Unknown.* AWP, *tr. by* Percy Bysshe Shelley *Fr.* Homeric Hymns.

Hymn to St. Geryon. Michael McClure.
"Gesture the gesture the gesture the gesture, The." NeAP

Hymn to St. Maximinus, A. Hildegard von Bingen. NAWM-7v1, *tr. by* Peter Dronke

Hymn to Su'rya, A. Sir William Jones. NOBRP

Hymn to the Creator. John Clare. NOBVV

Hymn to the Earth, The. *Unknown.* HW, *tr. by* Charles Boer *Fr.* Homeric Hymns.

Hymn to the Evening, An. Phillis Wheatley. WPE

Hymn to the Fairest Fair, A. William Drummond, of Hawthornden.
"O king, whose greatness none can comprehend." SacPr

Hymn to the Fallen. *Unknown.* ChiP; FaBoWar; OBWP, *tr. by* Arthur Waley

Hymn to the Graces, A. Robert Herrick. NOSC

Hymn to the Guilotine. "Peter Pindar." NOBRP

Hymn to the Holy Spirit. Stephen Langton. TrCP

Hymn to the Moon. Lady Mary Wortley Montagu. ECWP

Hymn to the Moon, The. *Unknown. Fr.* Homeric Hymns.

Hymn to the Morning, An. Phillis Wheatley. TAP

Hymn to the Name and Hono[u]r of the Admirable Saint[e] Teresa, A. Richard Crashaw. BASC; FSCP; NOBE; NoP-4; OBEV
"Love, thou art absolute sole lord." EBEV; ESCV; GeHe; HAP; MeLP; NOSC; OxBEV
"Thou art love's victim; and must die." EroLit

Hymn to the Night. Henry Wadsworth Longfellow. APN-1; NOBA; OxBA; PWR; TAP; TCAPo

Hymn to the North Star. William Cullen Bryant. NCAP

Hymn to the Orange. *Unknown.* SuSp, *tr. by* Wu-Chi Liu

Hymn to the Pepper. Novella Nikolaevna Matveyeva [*or* Matveieva]. TCRP, *tr. by* Deming Brown

Hymn to the Sacred Mushroom. Bob Cobbing. Oth

Hymn to the Saints, and to Marquis Hamilton[, An]. John Donne. NOSC

Hymn to the Spirit of Nature. Shelley. *See* Prometheus Unbound [A Lyrical Drama in Four Acts]

Hymn to the Sun. Akhenaton [*or* Akhnaton]. WoPoe, *tr. by* John Perlman

Hymn to the Sun. Charles Montague Doughty. FaBoTw *Fr.* Dawn in Britain, The.

Hymn to the Sun. Michael Roberts. FaBoCh; OxBTC

Hymn to the Sun. *Unknown.* TTTS

Hymn to the Sun, The. Akhenaton [*or* Akhnaton]. TTY, *tr. by* J. E. Manchip White

Hymn to the Supreme Being. Christopher Smart. ChIV-1
"But, O immortals! What had I to plead." NOEC

Hymn to the Thousand Islands. Henrietta Cordelia Ray. CBWP-3

Hymn to the Virgin. *Unknown.* NoSic

Hymn to the Virgin, The. Ieuan ap Hywel Swrdwal.
("O michti ladi, owr leding/tw haf.") AngWePo
("To the queen of might.") (LL) AngWePo

Hymn to the Winds. Joachim Du Bellay. AWP, *tr. by* Andrew Lang

Hymn to Venus, The. *Unknown, formerly at. to* Homer.
"Among the springs which flow from Ida's head." OBVE
"But when the golden-thron'd Aurora made." OBVE

Hymn to Vishnu. Jayadeva. AWP, *tr. by* Sir Edwin Arnold *Fr.* Gita Govinda, The.

Hymn to Yellow. Genevieve Taggard. APT-2

Hymn upon St. Bartholomew's Day, An. Thomas Traherne. SacPr

Hymn: "What conscience dictates to be done." Pope. SacPr

Hymn: "What is the world, and what is life." William Williams. AngWePo

Hymn: "When I survey the wondrous cross." Isaac Watts. OxAEP-1; SacPr
(Crucifixion to the World by the Cross of Christ.) ECEV; NOCV; NOEC; NPeEn; OxBEV; PeECV

Hymn: "When our heads are bowed with woe." Henry Hart Milman. SacPr

Hymn: "When storms arise." Paul Laurence Dunbar. SacPr

Hymn: "When winds are raging." Harriet Beecher Stowe. AH; PoToHe

Hymn Written at the Holy Sepulchre in Jerusalem. George Sandys. SacPr

Hymn Written in Windsor Forest, A. Pope. *See* Lines Written in Windsor Forest

Hymn: "Ye golden lamps of heaven, farewell." Philip Doddridge. ECEV; SacPr

Hymne for the Epiphanie, Sung as by the three Kings, A. Richard Crashaw. ESCV
(Bright BABE! Whose awfull beautyes make.) FSCP
(In the Gloriovs Epiphanie of Ovr Lord God, A Hymn. Svng as by the Three Kings.) FSCP

Hymn[e] of Heavenly Beauty [*or* Beautie], An. Edmund Spenser. PeECV, *Fr.* Fowre Hymnes.
"Cease then my tongue, and lend unto my mind." InvLi

Hymne of the Daie of Judgment, The. Lady Elizabeth Tyrwhit. EMWP

Hymn[e] of the Nativity, An. Richard Crashaw. *See* In the Holy Nativity of Our Lord God

Hymne of the State of all Adams Posteritie, An. Lady Elizabeth Tyrwhit. EMWP

Hymn[e] on the Nativity [*or* Nativitie] of My Saviour, A. Ben Jonson. BeJo; ChIV-2; SacPr; TrCP

Hymn[e] the Nativity [Sung as by the Shepheards]. Richard Crashaw. *See* In the Holy Nativity of Our Lord God

Hymn[e] to Christ, at the Author's Last Going Into Germany, A. John Donne. BASC; EBEV; ESCV; MeLP; NAEL-5v1; NAEL-6v1; NAEL-7v1; NOSC; NPeEn; OxAEP-1; PeECV; SacPr

Hymn[e] to God My God, in My Sickness[e], A. John Donne. BASC; EBEV; ESCV; HeIP-4; MeLP; NAEL-5v1; NAEL-6v1; NAEL-7v1; NOSC; NoP-4; OxAEP-1; PBRV; PoE; SoSe-8; TFi; TOF

Hymn[e] to God the Father, A. John Donne. AWP; BASC; EBEV; FSCP; HAP; InPK-4; MeLP; NAEL-5v1; NAEL-6v1; NAEL-7v1; NOBE; NOSC; NPeEn; OxBEV; PeECV; PoRA; SCGP; SCV; SacPr; SoSe-8; TFi; TOF

Hymn[e] to God the Father, A. Ben Jonson. BeJo; InvLi; NoP-4; NOSC; OxAEP-1; SacPr; TrCP
(Hear me, O God!) NoP-4

Hymne to Love, An. Robert Herrick. NOSC

Hymn[e] to Our Saviour on the Cross[e], A. George Chapman. PeECV

Hymns. Callimachus.
Hymn to Apollo. HePo, *tr. by* Barbara Hughes Fowler
Hymn to Artemis. HePo, *tr. by* Barbara Hughes Fowler
Hymn to Demeter. HePo, *tr. by* Barbara Hughes Fowler
On the Bath of Pallas. HePo, *tr. by* Barbara Hughes Fowler

Hymns and Fragments. Friedrich Hölderlin.
"But speech." WoPoe, *tr. by* Richard Sieburth

Hymns and Spiritual Songs for the Fasts and Festivals of the Church of England. Christopher Smart.
Ascension of Our Lord Jesus Christ, The. NOCV
Crucifixion of Our Blessed Lord. ChIV-2
Epiphany. NOCV
(Hymn.) NOEC
Nativity of Our Lord and Saviour Jesus Christ, The. ChrPo; NOCV; NPeEn; OxBEV; SacPr
Christmas Day. OBCP

(Nativity of Our Lord, The.)   EBEV; HAP; NOBE; SCGP

Nativity of St. John the Baptist, The.   ChIV-2

New Year.   ChrPo

St. Philip and St. James.   NOCV; NOEC

St. Thomas.   ChIV-2

Hymns for the Amusement of Children.   Christopher Smart.

Beauty.   SacPr

Conclusion of the Matter, The.   ChIV-1

Elegance.   NOCV

Faith.   ChIV-1

For Saturday.   NOEC

Fortitude.   ChIV-2

Gratitude.   NOEC

Hope.   ChIV-1

(Hymns for Saturday.)   NOxBChV

(Lark's Nest, A.)   FaBoCh

Long-Suffering of God.   NOCV

Loveliness.   NOCV

Moderation.   NOCV

Mutual Subjection.   NOCV

Pray Remember the Poor.   NOEC

Taste.   ChIV-1; NOCV

Hymns in Darkness.   Nissim Ezekiel.

"I met a man once."   WoPoe

"There's only this."   OMIP

Hymns of Job.   Maya Bejerano.

"From morning slumber a stir a shift a spinning motion of tossing."   DTA, tr. by Tsipi Keller

"In a slick, black bodysuit Job stood before me."   DTA, tr. by Tsipi Keller

"Interlude."   DTA, tr. by Tsipi Keller

"It has all begun with still waters."   DTA, tr. by Tsipi Keller

"Job: I was cast onto a new life cycle."   DTA, tr. by Tsipi Keller

"Noon. 12:45 already."   DTA, tr. by Tsipi Keller

"Oh spare me, spare me."   DTA, tr. by Tsipi Keller

"Suddenly I was stabbed from behind."   DTA, tr. by Tsipi Keller

Hymns of the Marshes.   Sidney Lanier.   APN-2

Marsh Song—At Sunset.   NOBA; TCAPo

Marshes of Glynn, The.   NOBA; OxBA

Sunrise.

"In my sleep I was fain of their fellowship, fain."   TCAPo

Hymns to Our Lady of Chartres.   Geoffrey Hill.

"Eia, with handbells, jews' harps, risible."   DiPo

Hymns to the Night.   "Novalis."

Longing for Death.   WoPoe, tr. by Dick Higgins

Hymnus Ad Patrem Sinensis.   Philip Whalen.   BB

Hypatia.   Elizabeth Tollet.

"What cruel laws depress the female kind."   ECWP; NOEC

Hyped up on caffeine and Thorazine.   Something to Say.   Betsy Sholl.   ExTi

Hyperbola, The.   Footnote at "Figure of Speech."   Tina Darragh.   FTOS

Hyperbole! Can't you arise.   Prose for Des Esseintes.   Donald Davie.   OBVE

Hyperboreans, The.   Pindar.   WoPoe, tr. by Padraic Fallon   Fr. Pythian Odes.

Hyperion.   Friedrich Hölderlin.

Schicksalslied.   WoPoe, tr. by M. L. Rosenthal

"You wander above in brightness."   WoPoe, tr. by M. L. Rosenthal

Hyperion.   John Keats.

Saturn.   FHYEP; NOBRP; OxAEP-2; OxBEV

"So ended Saturn; and the God of the Sea."   FHYEP

"Thus in alternate uproar and sad peace."   FHYEP

Hyperion.   Leslie Norris.   TCAWP

Hyperion's Bones.   Tracey Herd.   NeBl

Hyperion's Song of Fate.   Friedrich Hölderlin.   NAWM-7v2, tr. by Christopher Middleton

Hypochondriac.   Geoffrey Holloway.   NLP

Hypochondriasis.   Ambrose Bierce.   APN-2   Fr. Devil's Dictionary, The.

Hypocrisy will serve as well.   Samuel Butler (1612–80).   FaBoEE

Hypocrite Women.   Denise Levertov.   NALW; PoM

Hypocrites shed tears.   On Watching Politicians Perform at Martin Luther King's Funeral.   Etheridge Knight.   NNaP

Hypothesis.   Ted Olson.   YaYoPo

Hysteria.   Chu Shu-chen.   OHPC, tr. by Kenneth Rexroth

Hysteria.   T. S. Eliot.   OxBEV

Hywel and Blodwen.   Idris Davies.   AngWePo

I

I.   Jan Arends.   TuT, tr. by Peter Van de Kamp

"I."   Louis Golding.   TrJP

I.   Gabriella Sica.   CItWP, tr. by Cinzia Sartini Blum and Lara Trubowitz

I, a boat with a bony keel.   Dentist's Window, A.   James Keir Baxter.   OxBC

I, a Most Wretched Atlas.   Heinrich Heine.   TrJP, tr. by Emma Lazarus   Fr. Homeward Bound.

I, a princess, king-descended, decked with jewels, gilded, drest.   Royal Princess, A.   Christina Georgina Rossetti.   BrRo

I, a ship, built on the profits / from my master's amorous trade.   Philip of Thessalonica.   GrAn

I, a traveler, came from south of the river.   Traveler's Moon, A.   Po Chü-i.   SuSp, tr. by Chiang Yee

I, a wanderer north of Tu-ling.   Parting from the Courtier Sung.   Yin Shih.   CoBCP, tr. by Burton Watson

I abdicate my daily self that bled.   Vita Nuova.   Stanley Kunitz.   VGW

I abhor the slimy [or slimie] kiss [or kisse].   Kisses Loathesome.   Robert Herrick.   CaPo; OxBSP

I abide and abide and better abide.   Sir Thomas Wyatt.   BoLoP; EnLoPo

I abide in a goodly museum.   Ballad of the Ichthyosaurus.   May Kendall.   ViWPN

I accompanied you as far as the village of granaries.   Nocturne.   Léopold Sédar Senghor.   WoPoe, tr. by Melvin Dixon

I admire the quixotic display of your paramountcy.   On His Royal Blindness Paramount Chief Kwangala.   Jack A. Mapanje.   AF

I admire your felicitous phrasing.   Limerick.   A. M. Sayers.   PeLi

I admit I have always wanted.   10th Untitled Poem.   Pedro Juan Pietri.   PueRic

I advance for as long as forever is. (LL)   Twenty-four Years.   Dylan Thomas.   OxBEV; OxBSP

I advise rest; the farmhouse.   To a Print of Queen Victoria.   James Keir Baxter.   OxBC

I ain't going to hurry up for the white man no more.   I Ain't Going to Hurry No More.   Jesse F. García.   UnSA

I ain't got long to stay here. (LL)   Steal Away to Jesus.   Unknown.   BPo; NAAAL; NoP-4

I Ain't Got Nothin' but the Blues.   Duke Ellington.   ReLy

I ain't quite so sure. (LL)   For Hettie.   Imamu Amiri Baraka.   GT; NOBA; NeAP

I ain't superstitious.   Superstitions.   Maggie Pogue Johnson.   CBWP-4

I aint jokin people, I aint playin around.   Concentration Camp Blues.   Henry Dumas.   SeSe

I almost ruined the stew and where.   Pigs for Circe in May, The.   Joanne Kyger.   PoM

I, Alphonso, live and learn.   Alphonso of Castile.   Ralph Waldo Emerson.   NOBA

I already knew the secrets of light.   Someone Is Probably Dead.   Marvin Bell.   BodElec

I always bow down deep before a small tree and a great tyrant.   Paavo Haavikko.   WoPoe, tr. by Anselm Hollo   Fr. Fifteen Epigrams in Praise of the Tyrant.

I always choose the plainest food.   Matthew Green.   VerBaPo   Fr. Spleen, The.

I always felt like a bird blown through the world.   Stripping and Putting On.   May Swenson.   WeW-3

I always had such a good time, good time girl. Each and.   Little Red Riding Hood.   Ania Walwicz.   BMAP

I always knew / you were singing!   Throat Song: The Whirling Earth.   Wendy Rose.   HATNAP

I always lay before my rushing heart.   And Look for God.   Else Lasker-Schüler.   BBASP, tr. by Robert P. Newton

I always like summer.   Knoxville, Tennessee.   Nikki Giovanni.   BPo; BlSi; OxIBACP

I always loved this solitary hill.   Infinito, L'   Giacomo Leopardi.   AWP

I always remember West Lake.   Tune: "Song of the Wine Spring."   P'an Lang.   SuSp, tr. by James J. Y. Liu

I always remember your beautiful flowers.   Pad, Pad.   Stevie Smith.   NPeEn; OxBEV

I always saw, I always said.   Red Dress, The.   Dorothy Parker.   APT-1

I always say I won't go back to the mountains.   Sourdough Mountain Lookout.   Philip Whalen.   BB; NeAP; PoM

I always see, I don't know why.   Knowledgeable Child, The.   Leonard Alfred George Strong.   OBMV

I always talk of living in the mountains.   For Several Years I Have Wanted To Grow a Garden, But Have Never Finished One. This Year It Is Already Halfway through Summer, and This Has Made Me Despondent.   Chu Yün-ming.   CoBLCP, tr. by Jonathan Chaves

I always try to dislike my poets.   It's Hard to Dislike Ewart.   Gavin Ewart.
OBCoV

I always was afraid of Somes's Pond.   Atavism.   Elinor Wylie.   NALW

I Am.   John Clare.   BBASP; EBEV; EBVV; FHYEP; GTBS-P; HAP; NAEL-
5v2; NAEL-6v2; NOBE; NOBVV; OxBEV; PeECV; TFi; TOF; TRP
(Written in Northampton County Asylum.)   OBEV; OxAEP-2

I Am.   John Clare.   CABP; NPeEn; NoP-4; PoPoPo; WoPoe

I am. (LL)   Both Your Mothers.   Jerzy Ficowski.   HP; PoSu, tr. by Keith
Bosley

I am.   Yevgeny Aleksandrovich Yevtushenko [or Evtushenko].   HP

I am a babe of royalty.   Royal Education.   Winthrop Mackworth Praed.
OBSV

I am a bairn.   De.   Robert Alan Jamieson.   FaBoVe

I am a Bard of no regard.   Robert Burns.   PoE   Fr. Jolly Beggars, The.

I Am a Black Woman.   Mari E. Evans.   PAI

I am a blue fox on a gray farm.   Monologue of a Blue Fox.   Yevgeny
Aleksandrovich Yevtushenko [or Evtushenko].   TCRP, tr. by Albert C.
Todd and John Updike

I am a bold Coachman, and drive a good hack.   Hackney Coachman, The; Or,
The Way to Get a Good Fare.   Hannah More.   WoRP

I Am a Book I neither Wrote nor Read.   Delmore Schwartz.   TAP

I am a book with a cover of blue.   Solo with Chorus.   Rose Fyleman.
NOxBChV

I am a broken-hearted milkman, in grief I'm arrayed.   Polly Perkins.
Unknown.   OBCoV; OxBoLi; PeLV

I am a bunch of red roses.   Love Song.   Unknown.   BoWoP, tr. by Reza
Baraheni and Zahra-Soltan Shokoohtaezeh

I am a Camera.   Bob Kaufman.   PFTM-2

I Am a Cameraman.   Douglas Dunn.   EmeKit

I am a child.   Survivals.   Ruth Behar.   MirDau

I am a child of the Dreamtime People.   Spiritual Song of the Aborigine.
Hyllus Maris.   IBA

I am a child of the valley.   Delta.   Margaret Abigail Walker.   YaYoPo

I am a city child—and folks agree.   I Am a City Child.   Anton Wildgans.
AuPH, tr. by Lowell A. Bangerter

I Am a Cowboy in the Boat of Ra.   Ishmael Reed.   ESEAA; NAAAL; NIL-7;
NIP-4

I Am a Creature.   Giuseppe Ungaretti.   PeFWW, tr. by David McDuff

I am a daughter of that land.   Letitia [or Laetitia] Elizabeth Landon.   RWP
Fr. Improvisatrice, The.

I am a dispossessed Ontario wood.   Silverthorn Bush.   Robert Finch.   NOBC

I am a false philosopher of this.   Radiating Naïveté.   Lucie Brock-Broido.
OPRER

I am a feather on the bright sky.   Delight Song of Tsoai-Talee, The.   N. Scott
Momaday.   CDW; InPK-6

I Am A Finn.   James Tate.

"I am standing in the post office, about."   EmeKit

"I failed my exam, which is difficult."   EmeKit

I am a flower.   Ego Flos.   Guido Gezelle.   TuT, tr. by Peter Van de Kamp

I am a frill necked lizard.   Ecology.   Lionel Fogarty.   IBA

I am a frog.   Frog Prince, The.   Stevie Smith.   HAP

I am a gentle Anarchist.   Gentle Anarchist, The.   Brunton Stephens.   NOBAu

I am a gentleman in a dustcoat trying.   Piazza Piece.   John Crowe Ransom.
APT-1; BoLoP; ColAP; FuPo; HarvBoo; HeIP-4; MoAmPo; NAAL-2v2;
NOBA; NoAM; NoP-4; OxBA; PAI; Son; TAP; TFi

I am a glider on time's thermals.   John Hawkhead.   NewEx

I am a God in the depths of my thought.   Sonnet.   Willem Kloos.   TuT, tr. by
Tony Curtis

"I am a gold lock."   Lock and Key.   Unknown.   ReMoGo

I am a great inventor, did you but know it.   Ernest Crosby.   FaBoWar   Fr. War
and Hell.

I Am a Hunchback.   Robert Louis Stevenson.   OxBSP

I am a Jew.   Franta Bass.   INSAB

I am a Jew among sunflowers, a Jew.   Insomnia Litany.   Joan Logghe.
OPRER

I am a Jew and will be a Jew forever.   I am a Jew.   Franta Bass.   INSAB

I am a jolly soldier.   Bunker's Hill, or the Soldier's Lamentation.   John Freeth.
NOEC

I am a jovial miner.   Miner's Ballad, The.   Lewis Morris.   AngWePo

I am a kindred spirit to death.   Kinsman of Death, The.   Endre Ady.   IQMS,
tr. by Peter Zollman

I am a king's daughter, you a king's wife.   Letter to Her Mother, A.   Eristi-
Aya.   BoWoP, tr. by Willis Barnstone

I am a lady young in beauty waiting. (LL)   Piazza Piece.   John Crowe
Ransom.   APT-1; BoLoP; ColAP; FuPo; HarvBoo; HeIP-4; MoAmPo;
NAAL-2v2; NOBA; NoAM; NoP-4; OxBA; PAI; Son; TAP; TFi

I am a lamp, a lamp that is out.   She Warns Him.   Frances Darwin Cornford.
EnLoPo

I am a lioness.   'Aisha bint Ahmad al-Qurtubiyya.   WPOW

I am a little girl with my pants pulled down around my ankles.   Pants.   Lisa
Vice.   GLP

I am a little orphan girl.   Orphan Girl, An.   Mrs. Henry Linden.   CBWP-4

I am a little world made cunningly.   John Donne.   BASC; ChIV-1; NAEL-5v1;
NAEL-6v1; NAEL-7v1; NIP-4; NoP-4; OxBSo; PoE; Son   Fr. Holy
Sonnets.

I am a lone, unfathered chick.   Orphan Born.   Robert Jones Burdette.   OBAL

I am a lonely being, scarred by swords.   Riddles.   Unknown.   NoP-4

I am a mad mother.   Projected Scenario of a Performance to Be Given before
the UN.   Lawson Fusao Inada.   FaBoA

I am a man defeated in his loins.   Beggar to Burgher.   Arthur Rex Dugard
Fairburn.   PeNZ

I am a man now.   Here.   Ronald Stuart Thomas.   GTBS-P; NPeEn; RB

I am a man of war and might.   Soldier, A.   Sir John Suckling.   PoE

I am a man, upo da land.   Unknown.   See Eartly [or Earthly] nourris [or nouris
or nourrice] sits and sings, An

I am a miner. The light burns blue.   Nick and the Candlestick.   Sylvia Plath.
CoAP; LCAP-2; NALW

I am a Mo Village Girl.   Ke-Mo Village Girl.   Vietnamese Oral Tradition.
CaDao, tr. by John Balaban

I Am a Most Fleshly Man.   Robert Duncan.   CAGL

I Am a Negro.   Muhammad Al-Faituri [or Al-Fituri or Al-Fayturi].   TTY, tr. by
Halim El-Dabh

I Am a Parcel of Vain Strivings Tied.   Henry David Thoreau.   APN-1; ColAP;
TAP; TCAPo

(Sic Vita.)   NCAP; OxBA

I am a Peeping Tom Girl, and from my seat on the downtown bus.   Peeping
Tom Tom Girl.   Marisela Norte.   GeoHom

I am a plane-tree. I was sound and strong when the blasts.   Philip of
Thessalonica.   GrAn

I am a poet.   Uncertainty of the Poet, The.   Wendy Cope.   OPOU

I am a poet, a unanimous.   Italy.   Giuseppe Ungaretti.   PeFWW, tr. by David
McDuff

I am a poet—so why should I care.   Ars Poetica.   Attila József.   IQMS, tr. by
Michael Beevor

I am a poor pilgrim of sorrow.   City Called Heaven.   Unknown.   NAAAL

I am a poor wayfaring stranger.   Poor Wayfaring Stranger.   Unknown.   SacPr

I am a pretty wench.   Unknown.   OxNR

I AM a prisoner in the hands of the enemy.   Other Side of the Valley, The.
Unknown.   ChiP, tr. by Arthur Waley

I am a purse.   Yevgeny Aleksandrovich Yevtushenko [or Evtushenko].   TCRP

I am a reaper whose muscles set at sundown. All my oats are cradled.   Harvest
Song.   Jean Toomer.   NoP-4

I am a sea-shell flung.   Frutta di Mare.   Geoffrey Scott.   OBMV

I am a servant of the War Lord.   Archilochus.   SaLy, tr. by Diane Rayor

I am a service.   Family Romance.   Joshua Clover.   AmPoNex

I am a skinny girl.   Skinny Girl, The.   Anne Hébert.   BoWoP, tr. by Willis
Barnstone

I am a sleeping body.   Jay Macpherson.   NOBC   Fr. Ark, The.

I am a solitary man, not a democracy.   Yehuda Amichai [or Amikhai].   PoSu
Fr. Travels of a Latter-Day Benjamin of Tudela.

I Am a Son of the German Language.   Ernst Waldinger.   AuPH, tr. by Lowell
A. Bangerter

I am a soul in the world: In.   Invention of Comics, The.   Imamu Amiri Baraka.
CRP; GT; NAAAL

I am a spring.   Well, The.   Thomas Edward Brown.   NOBVV

I am a stag: Of seven tines.   Alphabet Calendar of Amergin, The.   Unknown.
BIrV, tr. by Robert Graves

I am a sundial, and I make a botch.   On a Sundial.   Joseph Hilaire Pierre
Belloc.   FaBoEE

I am a sundial. Ordinary words.   Joseph Hilaire Pierre Belloc.   FaBoEE

I am a sundial, turned the wrong way round.   Joseph Hilaire Pierre Belloc.
FaBoEE

I am a tethered fuck-angel.   Of My Nipple Ring Halos.   Edwin Torres.
HeMarv

I am a thief.   Listen.   Jessica Tarahata Hagedorn.   WPOW

I am a tree on the margin.   Union.   Annie Foster.   NLP

I am a very old pussy.   Old Cat's Confessions, An.   Christopher Pearse
Cranch.   APN-1; OBCA

I Am a Victim of Telephone.   Allen Ginsberg.   NBLV

I am a wandering child.   Women at the Crossroad / (May Elegba Forever Guard
the Right Doors).   Opal Palmer Adisa.   GT

I am a white girl gone brown to the blood color of my mother.   For the Color of
My Mother.   Cherríe Moraga.   UnSA

I am a widow, robed in black, alone.   Christine de Pisan.   BoWoP

I am a winged creature, flightless.   Su Jarwood.   NewEx

I Am a Woman.   Akhtar Amiri.

"My home is the mountain."   WPOW

I am a woman and my poems. Practice of Magical Evocation, The. Diane Di Prima. PmAP; PoM

I am a word hunter. Collective Search. Patrick Sylvain. InTrad

I am a young executive. No cuffs than mine are cleaner. Executive. Sir John Betjeman. NOBL

I am a young girl, gay. *Unknown.* BoWoP

I am a young jolly brisk sailor. Tarpauling Jacket. *Unknown.* OxBoLi; PeVV

I am absent but deep in this absence. Poetry Is a Heavenly Crime. Vincente Huidobro. TCLAP, *tr. by* W. S. Merwin

I am Accused of Tending to the Past. Lucille Clifton. ISC

I am afar, but near thee is my heart. Carnino Ghiberti. EaItPo, *tr. by* Dante Gabriel Rossetti

I am afraid. Wedding Day. Seamus Heaney. OxAEP-2

I am afraid I may be Ilia. Fear. Anna Hajnal. BoWoP, *tr. by* Daniel Hoffman

I Am Afraid of Fire. Anna Swirszczynska. AF, *tr. by* Czeslaw Milosz

I am afraid of losing the marvel of your eyes of a statue, and the accent the solitary rose of your breath lays on my cheek at night. Federico García Lorca. CAGL, *tr. by* David William Foster *Fr.* Sonetos del Amor Oscuro [Sonnets of Dark Love].

I am afraid of the unknown. You Called to Me, Prison Windows. Danièle Amrane. HAWP, *tr. by* Eric Sellin

I am afraid to. Nizar Qabbani. MAP

I am afraid to lose the marvel. Sonnet of Sweet Complaint. Federico García Lorca. BLPSL, *tr. by* Rene de Costa, Rigas Kappatos and Eleni Paidoussi

I am afraid to own a Body. Emily Dickinson. NCAP

I am afraid to think about my death. No Coward's Song. James Elroy Flecker. OxBSP

I Am Africa. Kimberly Ann Collins. InTrad

I am Alice of Daphne, and my heart clogs for John Pounden. Alice of Daphne, 1799. John Ennis. PBCIP

I am alive—I guess. Emily Dickinson. NOBA

I am all bent to glean the golden ore. To His Lady Selvaggia Vergiolesi; Likening His Love to a Search for Gold. Cino da Pistoia. AWP; EaItPo, *tr. by* Dante Gabriel Rossetti

I am all things. Some Magic. James Koller. PoM

I Am Almost Asleep. Eldon Grier. MoCV

I Am Alone. Léopold Sédar Senghor. PoetW; VCWP, *tr. by* Melvin Dixon

I am alone in the garden, separated. Perfect Heart, The. Shara McCallum. AmPoNex

I am alone in the plains. I Am Alone. Léopold Sédar Senghor. PoetW; VCWP, *tr. by* Melvin Dixon

I am already a singing flower. Singing Flower, The. "Shu Ting." CarOv, *tr. by* Carolyn Kizer and Y. H. Zhao

I am already quite scarce. For years [*or* now]. Last Ones, The. Dan Pagis. PoSu

I am always aware of my mother. Mother. Kiyoko Nagase. BoWoP

I am always behind. Jo Shapcott. NewEx

I am always sorry for the big ape falling. Goliath Poem. Terrance Hayes. AmPoNex

I am an ancient reluctant conscript. Old Timers. Carl Sandburg. NoAM

I am an apple, tossed. Sokrates to Xanthippé. Plato. GrAn, *tr. by* Peter Jay

I am an April Woman. April Woman. Salma Khadra Jayyusi. MAP, *tr. by* Charles Doria and the author

I Am an Atheist Who Says His Prayers. Karl Shapiro. APT-2

I am an end and a beginning. Monument, The. Vladislav Felitsianovich Khodasevich. TCRP, *tr. by* Michael Frayn

I am an entry in all kinds of books. Dezső Kosztolányi. IQMS, *tr. by* Leslie A. Kery *Fr.* Laments of a Sad Man.

I am an ephemeral and none too discontented citizen of a metropolis thought to be modern. City. Arthur Rimbaud. SxFrPo, *tr. by* Martin Sorrell

I am an honest man. Sonnet. Octavio Armand. TCLAP, *tr. by* Jason Shinder

I am an honest man. José Martí. TCLAP, *tr. by* Elinore Randall *Fr.* Simple Verses.

I am an orphan. Orphan, An. Thurayya Malhas. PoArWo, *tr. by* Nasser Farghaly

"I am an owl of orders gray." Song of the Owl, The. Richard Kendall Munkittrick. OBCA

I Am Ardent, I Am Brunette. Gustavo Adolfo Bécquer. SpanPo, *tr. by* Kate Flores

"I am as brown as brown can be." Brown Girl, The. *Unknown.* ESPB

I Am As God And God As I. "Angelus Silesius." GePo, *tr. by* George C. Schoolfield *Fr.* Cherubical Wanderer, The.

I Am as Happy as a Queen on Her Throne. Mrs. Henry Linden. CBWP-4

I am as I am and so will I be. Sir Thomas Wyatt. NoSic

I am as large as God, and God as small as I. "Angelus Silesius." GePo, *tr. by* George C. Schoolfield *Fr.* Cherubical Wanderer, The.

I am as light as any roe. *Unknown.* MiEL

I am as virtuous as a rabbinical student. Spiritual Morning. Robin Becker. TaR

I am ashamed before the earth. Therefore I Must Tell the Truth. Torlino. STP, *tr. by* Washington Matthews

I am asking about the way ahead. Lenrie Peters. HBAPE

I am asking for understanding / for the women who have not given. For the Barren Woman. Desanka Maksimovic. GI, *tr. by* Ivo Soljan

I Am Asking You to Come Back Home. Jo Carson. RaBo

I am astounded at their mouthful names. Building Nicole's Mama. Patricia Smith. SpirFl

I am at a retreat house, Still Point, not too far from Yaddo. From a Letter: About Snow. Toi Derricotte. SpirFl

I am at Deep Well where the spirit-trees. Roland Robinson. CBAP; NOBAu *Fr.* Deep Well.

I am at last that thing, a stranger in my own life. Diary. Gerald Stern. OPRER

I am Athenian, that was my city. Erucius [*or* Erycius] of Cyzicus. GrAn

I am Attibon Legba. René Depestre. NegPo, *tr. by* Ellen Conroy Kennedy *Fr.* Epiphanies of the Voodoo Gods.

I am away from home. Faithful Wife, The. Patricia Beer. LW

I am back from up the country—very sorry that I went. Up the Country. Henry Lawson. CBAP

I am bathing. All my greyness. El Curandero. Rafael Campo. BloBone

I am Baukis the bride's. Epitaph on a Betrothed Girl. Erinna. GrAn, *tr. by* Lenore Mayhew

I am become a shell of delicate alleys. Airliner. Francis Webb. CBAP; NOBAu

I Am Becoming My Mother. Lorna Goodison. OPOU

(Yellow/brown woman.) GT

I am being carried on great winds across the sky. (LL) Sometimes I Go about Pitying Myself. *Unknown.* RaBo; WoPoe, *tr. by* Robert Bly and Frances Densmore

I am being followed by a table. Intermission from Thursday. Pedro Juan Pietri. PueRic

I Am Beset with a Dream of Fair Woman. Maureen Duffy. LW

I am big, I am gigantic, look at me way up here. Sally. Cynthia Heimel. Unle

I am black and I have seen black hands, millions and millions of them. I Have Seen Black Hands. Richard Wright. APT-2

I am black-browed. Pauline Stainer. NewEx

I am bleeding. Song of the Woman with Her Parts Coming Out, The. Susan Griffin. GLP

I am Bog-Face. (LL) Bog-Face. Stevie Smith. NPeEn; RB

I Am Bound, I Am Bound. Henry David Thoreau. TCAPo

I am Brahman. But we're stuck for a maid. I am Brahman. J. Adwaita Dèr Mouw. TuT, *tr. by* Peter Van de Kamp

I am Branson; Nature's laws. *Var. authors.* FaBoEE *Fr.* Balliol Rhymes.

I am bright with the wonder of you. Brightness. Denis Glover. PeNZ

I am built of my thoughts. Resistance. Susan Dambroff. GotH

I am busy doing drawings. David's Rumor. Liam Rector. OPRER

"I am but clay," the sinner plead. Distinction. Paul Laurence Dunbar. SacPr

I am, by fate, slave to your will. To My More Than Meritorious Wife. John Wilmot, 2d Earl of Rochester. OxBSP

I am Cap'tain Zombi. René Depestre. PFTM-2, *tr. by* Joan Dayan *Fr.* Rainbow for the Christian West, A.

I am chained. Lotte Kramer. NewEx

I am Chango hurler of thunder. René Depestre. PFTM-2, *tr. by* Joan Dayan *Fr.* Rainbow for the Christian West, A.

I am Charlotte. I don't say hello. Charlotte, Her Book. Elizabeth Bartlett. FaBoWP

I Am Cherry Alive. Delmore Schwartz. NOxBChV; TTTS

I am Chiang Liang. Old Leaves from the Chinese Earth. Sadanand Rege. OMIP; WoPoe, *tr. by* Dilip Chitre

I am Child of sand and sun. Child of the Sun. Lillian M. Fisher. HHAm

I am child to no one, mother to a few. Self-Portrait. Linda Pastan. ExTi

I am climbing. *Unknown.* STP

I am cold and alone. Boy Fishing, The. Edith Jay Scovell. FaBoWP

I am come into my garden, my sister, my spouse. Bible, *O.T.* EroLit; OBVE; TOF, *tr. by* King James Version *Fr.* Song of Solomon, The [*or* The Song of Songs].

I Am Consecrated to the Coming One. Wafaa' Lamrani. PoArWo, *tr. by* Richard McKane and Tahia Abdel Nasser

I am constantly wounded. *Unknown.* PGA; WoPoe, *tr. by* Kenneth Rexroth *Fr.* Carmina Burana.

I am content. Fossil, The. Boynton, Jr. Merrill. CRP

I am content, I do not care. Careless Content. John Byrom. NOEC; OBCoV

I am content to live the patient day. Tuckanuck, I. George Cabot Lodge. APN-2

I am convinced that finally. Apple, The. Vladimir Alekseievich Soloukhin. TCRusP, *tr. by* Daniel Weissbort

I am cuddle-shaped and freckled. James Berry. NewEx

I am curiously stirred. Courtship, The. Ann Beresford. LW

I am dancing and. Heavy Headed Dance, The. Jayne Cortez. BAP-97

I am dangerous. Scissor-Man. George MacBeth [*or* Macbeth]. FaBoMo

I am dark, daughters of Jerusalem. Bible, *O.T.* WPoS *Fr.* Song of Solomon, The.

I am dead. Larva, The. Tadeusz Rózewicz. PoSu, *tr. by* Magnus F. Krynski

I Am Dead But I Know the Dead Are Not Like This. Charles Bukowski. PmAP

I am dead, to be sure. Small Fig Tree, A. Donald Hall. ChIV-2; GI

I Am Deaf. Osip Emilevich Mandelstam [*or* Mandelshtam]. TCRusP, *tr. by* John Glad

I am deeply convinced that objects. Yevgeny [*or* Evgenii] Mikhailovich Vinokurov. TCRusP, *tr. by* Daniel Weissbort *Fr.* History.

I Am Disquieted When I See Many Hills. Hyam Plutzik. VGW

I am dreaming. Let Me Call You Sweetheart. Beth Slater Whitson. TCAPo

I am Drink, carved by a skilled hand. On a Ring. Asclepiades. GrAn, *tr. by* Alan Marshfield

I am driving; it is dusk; Minnesota. Driving toward the Lac Qui Parle River. Robert Bly. CoAmPo; LCAP-2

I am driving to you and I will drive all the way to New York. Home in Three Days. Don't Wash. Linda Smukler. WiU

I am driving west in the afternoon. Sphinx. Van K. Brock. AllShUp

I am dying now because I do not die. James Keir Baxter. HarvBoo *Fr.* Jerusalem Sonnets.

I am dying somehow strangely . . . Life is not killing me. Ineffable, The. Delmira Agustini. TANSG, *tr. by* Mark McCaffrey

I am dying strangely . . . it is not life. Ineffable, The. Delmira Agustini. TCLAP, *tr. by* Karl Kirchwey

I am dying under this heat. Almost a God. Emanuel Carnevali. APT-2

I am ebbing—but not like the sea. Hag of Béara, The. *Unknown.* NOIV, *tr. by* Thomas Kinsella

I am egg-shell fragile and grapefruit sour. Breakfast Poem. Clare Pollard. NeBl

I am enamored, and yet not so much. Sonnet: He Will Not Be Too Deeply in Love. Cecco Angiolieri, da Siena. AWP; EaItPo, *tr. by* Dante Gabriel Rossetti

I am Eve, great Adam's wife. Eve. *Unknown.* BIrV, *tr. by* Thomas Macdonagh

I am exceedingly green: Chillgreen. Twelve Faces of the Emerald. Dan Pagis. WoPoe, *tr. by* Stephen Mitchell

I am far from sentimental or romantic. Very Soft Shoes. Mary Rodgers. ReLy

I Am Fashion's Toy. Mary E. Tucker. CBWP-1

I am fated to perform a heroic deed. "Aleksandr Iakovlevich Yashin" [*or* "Iashin"]. TCRP

I am featly-tripping Lee. *Var. authors.* FaBoEE *Fr.* Balliol Rhymes.

I am fevered with the sunset. Sea Gypsy, The. Richard Hovey. BRP; TCAPo

I am filled with love like a melon. Morning Love Song. Marge Piercy. PasH

I am filthy. Lice gnaw me. Swine, when they look at me, vomit. The scabs. Comte de Lautréamont. PFTM-1 *Fr.* Maldoror.

I am fire and water, honestly combined, on free terms. (LL) Vierge Moderne. Edith Södergran. ItWoWo; PFTM-1, *tr. by* Stina Katchadourian

I am first mouth, then hand. Edwyna Prior. NewEx

I am fixed in waiting. Sagimusume: The White Heron Maiden. Jonny Kyoko Sullivan. WPOW

I am forbidden to look back. Remembering Love. Aleksandr Semionovich Kushner. TCRP, *tr. by* Paul Graves and Carol Uel

I am four monkeys. Tree, The. Alfred Kreymborg. APT-1

I am four years older than you but scarcely an unwobbling. James [*or* Jim] Harrison. BodElec *Fr.* Letters to Yesenin.

I am fourteen. Hanging Fire. Audre Lorde. NIL-7; NIP-4; NoAM; NoP-4; PoPoPo; TRP

I am from everywhere. Edouard J. Maunick. NegPo *Fr.* As Far as Yoruba Land.

I am from Warsaw. Oratorio for a Concentration Camp. János Pilinszky. IQMS, *tr. by* Adam Makkai

I am full of grief, and the tear runs from my eye. Five Arabic Verses in Praise of Wine. *Unknown.* TrJP, *tr. by* Hartwig Hirschfeld

I am fully qualified to work as a doorkeeper, and for this reason. Rabi'a al-Adawiyya. WPoS

I am furious with myself. Elsa Tió. BoWoP

I am giving a lecture on poetry. In English in a Poem. Lynn Emanuel. ExTi

I am glad daylong for the gift of song. Rhapsody. William Stanley Braithwaite. TCAPo

I am glad that I am not one of those. Side 32. Víctor Hernández Cruz. PueRic

I am going to be your host tonight. My Name Is Dimitri. John Ashbery. BodElec

I am going to keep things like this. (LL) Hawk Roosting. Ted Hughes. GTBS-P; HAP; HeIP-4; OWoS; OxBEV; OxBTC; TwCP; UnPo

I am going to rise. Vive Noir! Mari E. Evans. NBV

I Am Going to Sleep (Suicide Poem). Alfonsina Storni. BoWoP, *tr. by* Aliki Barnstone and Willis Barnstone

I Am Going to Speak of Hope. César Vallejo. PoetW, *tr. by* Clayton Eshleman

I Am Going to Talk about Hope. César Vallejo. TCLAP, *tr. by* Robert Bly

I Am Goya. Andrey [*or* Andrei] Andreievich Voznesensky [*or* Voznesenskii]. OBWP; TCRP; VCWP

I am green and replete like a song that has blown through the grass. Song of the Strange Woman. Leah Goldberg. FIT, *tr. by* Robert Friend

I am growing calmer. Rimma Fiodorovna Kazakova. TCRP

I Am Growing Old. George Sands Johnson. PWR

I am growing on a woman's corpse. Origin. Rosario Castellanos. TANSG, *tr. by* Magda Bogin

I am Hajar the immigrant. First Thing, The. Mohja Kahf. PoArWo

I am half, my children half again. Half. Julia Park Rodrigues. TWW

I am happy. Utitia'q's Song. *Inuit Oral Tradition.* AWTN, *tr. by* Franz Boas and Brian Swann

I am happy in my love. Girl's Song. *Unknown.* WoPoe, *tr. by* Edwin Gladding Burrows

I am happy to live correctly and simply. Marina Ivanovna Tsvetayeva [*or* Tsvetaeva]. BBASP, *tr. by* Mary Jane White

I am harum. Harum Scarum. Roger McGough. OTCP

I Am He That Aches with Love. Walt Whitman. ErotSp

I am he who aches with amorous love. Pact, A. Robert Hass. BodElec

I am her thin owen child, I wil don as thu wilt. (LL) Christ's Prayer in Gethsemane. *Unknown.* MiEL; SacPr

I am here, and shells are quaking over the cracked city. To a War Correspondent. Star Black. KGB

I am here, and there is nothing to say. Lecture on Nothing. John Cage. FTOS; PFTM-2

I am here / and will follow. (LL) For My Mother: Genevieve Jules Creeley. Robert Creeley. PoM; TRP

I am here, I have traversed the Tomb. *Unknown.* AWP *Fr.* Book of the Dead.

I am Hermes. I stand in the crossroads by a windy. Anyte [*or* Anytes]. BoWoP

I am his Highness' dog at Kew. Epigram Engraved on the Collar of a Dog Given [*or* Which I Gave] to His Royal Highness. Pope. FaBoEE; InPK-6; KaS; NOEC; NTCP; OxBEV; OxBSP; PAI

I am holding this turquoise. Serenity in Stones, The. Simon J. Ortiz. CDW; ColAP

I am homesick now for middle age, as then. Listening to Collared Doves. Edith Jay Scovell. HarvBoo

I am / I am from and of The Mother. Creed for Free Women, A. Elsa Gidlow. HW

I am I, but also the other. *Unknown.* WoPoe, *tr. by* Patrick Olivelle *Fr.* Upanishads, The.

I am I, old Father Fisheye that begat the ocean, the worm. End, The. Allen Ginsberg. CoAmPo

I am immortal in Cheyenne! Norman Rosten. YaYoPo

I am in a daydream of my uncle. Thirteen Years. Erin Mouré. NIL-7

I am in a desert. Bushed. Barry McKinnon. NOBC

I Am in a Novel. D. H. Lawrence. OBCoV

I am in Danger—Sir. Adrienne Rich. HCAP; HarvBoo; NAAL-5; NALW; NOBA

I am in great misery tonight. Suibne Geilt. NOIV

I am in love, meantime, you think; no doubt you would think so. Arthur Hugh Clough. FaBoVe; NPeEn *Fr.* Amours de Voyage.

I am in love with the laughing sickness. Zizi's Lament. Gregory Corso. BB; NeAP; VGW

I am in love, you say; I do not think so exactly. (LL) Arthur Hugh Clough. FaBoVe; NPeEn *Fr.* Amours de Voyage.

I am in my Eskimo-hunting-song mood. Eskimo Occasion. Judith Rodriguez. CBAP; FaBoWP; ItWoWo; NOBAu

I am in my room observing my record player covered with dust. Analysis. Syl Cheney-Coker. NAfrP

I am in pain. Yury [*or* Iurii] Timofeievich Galanskov. TCRusP, *tr. by* Olive Dehn

I am in the book. Dream Dream, The. Michael Davidson. FTOS

I am in the castle, my younger brother is beyond. Other Side of the Valley, The. *Unknown.* CoBCP, *tr. by* Burton Watson

I am in the most exquisite distress. Laura H. Kennedy. PasH

I am in the rain, with black writing. Womb. Sonia Sekula. SurWo

I am in the tub with my body. To My Body. Nancy Sullivan. TAP

I am inside someone. Agony, An. As Now. Imamu Amiri Baraka. BPo; NAAL-2v2; PoE

I am invited to enter these gardens. Welshman at St. James' Park, A. Ronald Stuart Thomas. AngWePo

I Am Ireland. Padraic Pearse. OBMV, tr. by Augusta, Lady Gregory and Lady Gregory

I am irradiated by the room through which a tram runs. X-Rays. I. K. Bonset. TuT, tr. by Desmond Egan

I am jealous! I am jealous! which I ne'er have been before. Lines / Suggested by the Song of a Nightingale. Eliza Cook. VWP

I am Jesu that cum to fight. Undo Your Heart. Unknown. MiEL

I am John Reed. John Reed's Monologue. Yevgeny Aleksandrovich Yevtushenko [or Evtushenko]. RusPo, tr. by Robert Arthur Douglas Ford

I am Judas. W. B. Yeats. GI Fr. "Calvary."

I am just going outside and may be some time. Antarctica. Derek Mahon. NPeEn; PBCIP

I am king. Vincente Huidobro. TCLAP, tr. by Stephen Fredman Fr. Altazor.

I am knotted in pain. Obeah Mama Dot. Frederick D'Aguiar. Oth

I am leading a quiet life. Autobiography. Sonja Åkesson. BoWoP, tr. by Ingrid Claréus

I am like a flag unfurled in space. Presaging. Rainer Maria Rilke. AWP; TrJP, tr. by Jessie Lemont

I Am like a Rose. D. H. Lawrence. OxBSP

I am like a sliced-up worm. Chaadayev on Basmannaya. Oleg Grigorevich Chukhonstev. TCRP, tr. by Simon Franklin

I am like a train. City of Yes and the City of No, The. Yevgeny Aleksandrovich Yevtushenko [or Evtushenko]. TCRP, tr. by Geoffrey Dutton, Igor Mezhakoff-Koriakin and Tina Tupkina-Glaessner

I am Lilith, grandmother of Mary Magdalene. Liturgy for Lilith. Cosi Fabian. HW

I am listening for your footsteps death. Body Inside the Soul, The. Bell Hooks. ISC

I am listening to Istanbul with my eyes closed. I Am Listening to Istanbul. Orban Veli Kanik. WoPoe, tr. by Murat Nemet-Nejat

I am living more alone now than I did. Last Chapter, The. Walter De la Mare. MoBrPo

I am locked in a little cedar box. Satan Says. Sharon Olds. PBCAP

I am lonely. Poem for Some Black Women. Carolyn M. Rodgers. BlSi

I am / look / ing at. You Too? Me Too—Why Not? Soda Pop. Robert Hollander. NIL-7; NIP-4

I am looking for the photo that would make all the difference in my life. Lost and Found. Maxine Chernoff. PmAP

I am looking for the women of my house. Lineage. Daisy Zamora. LoL, tr. by Margaret Randall

"I am Lot's pillar, caught in turning." Columns and Caryatids. Carolyn Kizer. WPE

I am love. (LL) On Being Head of the English Department. Pinkie Gordon Lane. BlSi; GT

I am made all things to all men. At His Execution. Rudyard Kipling. ChIV-2

I am making / a wind come here. Unknown. STP

I am Marilyn Mei Ling Chin. How I Got That Name. Marilyn Chin. GeoHom; LoL

"I am master of the chivalric idiom" Spenser said. Master. Brendan Kennelly. BiHa

I am Mawu of the Waters. Mawu of the Waters. Abena Busia. HAWP; NAfrP

I am mighty melancholy. Vandunk's Four Humours, in Quality and Quantity. Richard Brathwaite [or Brathwait]. NOSC

I am Minerva, the village poetess. Edgar Lee Masters. APT-1; IllVoic Fr. Spoon River Anthology.

I am Miss Stein. Gertrude Stein at Snails Bay. Peter Porter. OxBC

I am monarch of all I survey. Verses Supposed to Be Written by Alexander Selkirk during His Solitary Abode on the Island of Juan Fernandez. William Cowper. NOEC

I am monarch of troubles a host. Verses. Maria Jane Jewsbury. VWP

I am Moses awaiting. Video Victim. Luis H. Francia. ReBoTo

I am most honoured. Great Foreign Writer Visits Age-Old Temple, Greeted by Venerable Abbess, 1955. Anthony Thwaite. OBCoV

I am moved often, and easily. Few Facts about Me, A. Charles North. PmAP

I Am My Beloved's. Bible, O.T. BoWoP; TrJP, tr. by Willis Barnstone Fr. Song of Solomon, The [or The Song of Songs].

I Am My Beloved's, and His Desire Is towards Me. Francis Quarles. See Emblems

I am my lover's and he desires me. Bible, O.T. BoWoP; TrJP, tr. by Willis Barnstone Fr. Song of Solomon, The [or The Song of Songs].

I am my own. As I Am My Father's. Rose Drachler. TaR

I am myself at last; now I achieve. I Am like a Rose. D. H. Lawrence. OxBSP

I Am New York City. Jayne Cortez. BoWoP

I am 1939 and cold air. Katyn Forest. Steven Sherrill. BAP-97

I am no brazen face to hale the Lord. Rabbi Yom-Tob of Mayence Petitions His God. Abraham Moses Klein. TrJP

I am no disciple of Audubon. Survivors. Sterling Plumpp. UrbNat

I am no heir, no proud ancestor. I Want to Be Loved. Endre Ady. IQMS, tr. by Peter Zollman

I am no longer master of my tears. U Tam'si Tchicaya. NegPo Fr. Fragile.

I am no longer sure of anything. To the Ocean. S. J. Marks. BodElec

I am no shepherd of a child's surmises. Montana Pastoral. James Vincent Cunningham. APT-2; MoAmPo; VGW

I am no woman. I am a neuter. Vierge Moderne. Edith Södergran. ItWoWo; PFTM-1, tr. by Stina Katchadourian

I am nobody. Richard Wright. APT-2

I Am Not a Conspiracy Everything Is Not Paranoid The Drug Enforcement Administration Is Not Everywhere. Susan Musgrave. NIL-7; NoAM

I am not a flower of song. Ghazal 12. Mirza Asadullah Khan Ghalib. EaWin, tr. by Aijaz Ahmad and W. S. Merwin

I am not a handsome man. Eclipse. Ed Roberson. GT

I am not a mechanism, an assembly of various sections. Healing. D. H. Lawrence. RaBo

I am not a metaphor or symbol. Distant Drum, The. Calvin C. Hernton. GT; TTY

I am not a painter, I am a poet. Why I Am Not a Painter. Frank O'Hara. CoAmPo; HCAP; NOBA; NeAP; NoAM; NoP-4; PoE; PoM; PoPoPo; VCAP

I am not a person. Waka. Lindley Williams Hubbell. APT-2

I am not a poet. Explanatory Note. Yevgeny [or Evgenii] Bunimovich. TCRP, tr. by Albert C. Todd

I am not a sparrow or a rat. On the Thirteenth Day of the Eleventh Month I Went to the Granary for the First Time since My Illness. Mei Yao Ch'en. SuSp, tr. by Jonathan Chaves

I am not afraid of loving, I am afraid of forgetting I loved. Forgetting, Love. Nathalie Handal. PoArWo

I am not any of the faces. Failure of an Invention. Safiya Henderson-Holmes. UnSA

I am not blind. For Steph. Wendy Rose. CDW

I am not certain I love him. Bluebeard. Mark Bibbins. WiU

I am not eagle ey'd to face the Sun. To the Reader. Rowland Watkyns. BASC

I am not even my own ghost. (LL) Luis de Góngora y Argote. SpanPo; WoPoe, tr. by Roy Campbell Fr. Spectre of the Rose, The.

I am not gay by your definition. Explanation. William Barber. CAGL

I am not going to invite you. Blond. Joseph De Roche. HeIP-4

I am not going to turn into gold. Bassus [or Bassos]. PGA

I am not here now. 7th Untitled Poem. Pedro Juan Pietri. PueRic

I Am Not I. Juan Ramón Jiménez. RaBo, tr. by Robert Bly

I am not I; pity the tale of me. (LL) Sir Philip Sidney. NAEL-5v1; NAEL-6v1; NAEL-7v1; NoSic; PoE Fr. Astrophil and Stella.

I Am Not Just a Body for You. Shakuntala Hawoldar. HAWP

I am not Mahomet. Edmund Clerihew Bentley. NOBL Fr. Clerihews.

I am not moved (O Thou my God!) to love Thee. To Christ Crucified. Miguel de Guevara. SpanPo, tr. by Ian Fletcher

I am not my body. Madame X. Margherita Guidacci. CItWP, tr. by Cinzia Sartini Blum and Lara Trubowitz

I am not myself, I am my sisters. Monologue of the Magdalene. John Peck. HarvBoo

I am not one of those who believe that a city must not rise to catastrophe one more back. Virgin Forest, The. Aimé Césaire. SurPaPo, tr. by Clayton Eshleman and Annette Smith

I am not one of those who left the land. Anna Andreyevna Akhmatova. TCRP

I am not one who much or oft delight. Personal Talk. William Wordsworth. NOBE

I am not resigned to the shutting away of loving hearts in the hard ground. Dirge Without Music. Edna St. Vincent Millay. AmFaPo

I am not shaving, I'm writing about it. Shaving. Richard Blanco. AmPoNex; NAPBL

I am not striving with the tree that will not bend for me. Ebb. Sorley MacLean (Somhairle MacGill-Eain). NePenScot

I am not such a clever one. I'm Old-Fashioned. Johnny Mercer. ReLy

I am not sure I would always fight for my life. What Would You Fight For? D. H. Lawrence. OxBSP

I am not sure if I knew the truth. Youth. "Laurence Hope." WeW-3

I am not the first one infatuated with the glorious maiden. Phoenix, The. Ilya Abu Madi. MAP, tr. by Issa Boullata and Naomi Shihab Nye

I am not the walrus. Ishmael Reed. SpirFl

I am not the wind, nor the sail. Song of Pursuit. Gabriel Zaid. TCLAP, tr. by Mónica Hernández-Cancio

I am not to be trifled with. Hoatchunk' Narwoanar, or Winnebago War Song. *Unknown*. APN-2, tr. by Caleb Atwater

I am not treacherous, callous, jealous, superstitious. Face, A. Marianne Craig Moore. OxBSP

I am not what my lips explain. Utterance. Donald Davidson. FuPo

I am not wiser for my age. Ralph Waldo Emerson. TCAPo *Fr.* Quatrains.

I am not worthy. Kyohaku. JDP, tr. by Yoel Hoffmann

I am not yet born; O hear me. Prayer before Birth. Louis MacNeice. FaBoVe; GTBS-P; HarvBoo; PNI; TwCP

I am not yet twenty-two and I am tired of living. Asclepiades. HePo *Fr.* Epigrams.

I am not you. Africa's Plea. Roland Tombekai Dempster. TTY

I am not your God. African Easter. Abioseh Nicol. PBA

I am not your lover and you will never know me. Minutiae 3. P. F. Widdows. FaBoWar

"I Am Not Yours." Sara Teasdale. VGW

I am now so weary with waiting. Gaspara Stampa. WPOW

I am now utterly translated into Macedonian, after two days and nights, non-stop in Skopje. Translation. Carolyn Kizer. CarOv

I am now very high upon the tree of the seasons. Jean-Baptiste Tati-Loutard. PBMAP *Fr.* Poèmes de la Mer (1968).

I am obnoxious to each carping tongue. Anne Bradstreet. WoPoe *Fr.* Prologue, The.

I am of little worth and poor, apart. Song of Loneliness. Judah Halevi. TrJP, tr. by Nina Davis Salaman

I am of old and young, of the foolish as much as the wise. Walt Whitman. NAWM-7v2 *Fr.* Song of Myself.

I am of one that hath the wings of Love. (LL) Sonnet: A Trance of Love. Cino da Pistoia. AWP; EaItPo, tr. by Dante Gabriel Rossetti

I Am of the Earth. Anna Walters. VoR

I Am of the Tribe of Yehuda. Rosita Kalina. MirDau, tr. by Maria Xirinachs

I am of this world. *Var. authors*. BoWoP *Fr.* Manyo Shu, Part 2 of 4.

I am Ojistoh, I am she, the wife. Ojistoh. Emily Pauline Johnson. NOBC

I am old. Epitaph. Christopher Logue. OxBTC

I am old, sick and lonely. Verses. Su Tung-p'o (Su Shih). TAL

I am olde whan age doth apele. *Unknown*. MiEL

I am on my way running. Song for a Young Girl's Puberty Ceremony. *Unknown*. ChAP; ItWoWo, tr. by Frances Densmore

I am one of passion's asses. Girls of Llanbadarn, The. Dafydd [*or* David] ap Gwilym. OBWVE, tr. by Rolfe Humphries

I am one of those troubled hearts. Human Soul. René Maran. TTY, tr. by Mercer Cook

I am one of you, though you do not. Buying Fish. Susan Wicks. MFPA

I am, outside. Incredible panic rules. John Berryman. VCAP *Fr.* Dream Songs.

I am outside of. Dualism. Ishmael Reed. ESEAA; NAAAL

I am peasant. Transfiguration. Jack Hirschman. CLPP

I am picking wild grapes last year. Winemaker's Beat-étude, The. Alfred Wellington Purdy. MoCV

I am pleased with a frame of four lights. My Greenhouse. Edwin Morgan. OBGa

I am plural. My intents are manifold. Nondescript, The. Peter Scupham. HarvBoo

I am poor and old and blind. Belisarius. Henry Wadsworth Longfellow. APN-1

I am poor brother Lippo, by your leave! Robert Browning. CTC; EBVV; FHYEP; NAEL-6v2; OxAEP-2

I am poor once more! (LL) I Never Lost as Much. Emily Dickinson. HeIP-4; MoAmPo; NAAL-2v1; NAAL-3; NCAP; NOBA; NoAM; NoP-4; TAP; TCAPo

I am powerless against the world. (LL) Night in a Room by the River. Tu Fu. AWTN; CrYelRi, tr. by Sam Hamill

I am Priapus. I was put here according to custom. Lucianus [*or* Lucian]. GrAn

I am provoked. Epigram. Strato [*or* Straton]. GrAn, tr. by W. G. Shepherd

I am quiet, like this, stubbornly quiet. Attitude. Magda Portal. TANSG, tr. by Shaun Griffin and Emma Sepúlveda-Pulvirenti

I am quite mad and you are wholly sane. Mad Woman. Su'ad al-Mubarak Al-Sabah. MAP; PoArWo, tr. by John Heath-Stubbs and May Jayyusi

I Am Raftery. Derek Mahon. OxBC

I am Raftery [*or* Raferty]. Anthony [*or* Antoine] Raftery [*or* Raifteiri]. AWP; WoPoe, tr. by Douglas Hyde

I am Raifteiri, the poet, full of courage and love. Anthony [*or* Antoine] Raftery [*or* Raifteiri]. NOIV

I am rather tall and stately. *Var. authors*. FaBoEE; NOBL *Fr.* Balliol Rhymes.

I am reading a diary at night. Discovering Lasseter. Conal Fitzpatrick. NOBAu

I am reminded of the vestment. I'm Not Here / Never Was. Constanta Buzea. BoWoP, tr. by Stavros Deligiorgis

I am resolved, this charming day. John Dyer. ECEV *Fr.* Country Walk, The.

I am restored in beauty. (LL) Shootingway Ceremony Prayer. *Unknown*. WPoS; WoPoe, tr. by Gladys A. Reichard

I am riding on a limited express, one of the crack trains of the nation. Limited. Carl Sandburg. HAP; MoAmPo; OxBA

I Am Root. Claribel Alegría. PoetW; VCWP, tr. by Carolyn Forché

I am Rose like anything. (LL) I Am Rose. Gertrude Stein. OBCA; TrJP (I am Rose my eyes are blue.) APT-1; KaS

I Am Sad. Le Ngoc Hiep. WoPoe, tr. by John Balaban and T. L. Nguyen

I am sad this morning. Kenneth Rexroth. APSN *Fr.* Love Poems of Marichiko, The.

I am saying goodbye to the trees. Going Home. Derek Mahon. HarvBoo

I am scorned by patterns which hold. Moon at Three A.M. Lance Henson. CDW

I am sending you this letter. Line from St. David's, A. Ronald Stuart Thomas. AngWePo

I am set off. Luxembourg Garden. Michael S. Weaver. GT

I am shaking life a leaf in the orchard. Orchard in the Spring. Jane Rohrer. BodElec

I am silver and exact. I have no preconceptions. Mirror. Sylvia Plath. FaBoWP; HAP; NIL-7; NIP-4; PAI

I am simple like the light. Transmutation. Julia de Burgos. TANSG, tr. by Heather Rosario Sievert

I Am Singing Now. Luci Tapahonso. UnSA

I Am Singing the Cold Rain. Lance Henson. HATNAP; STP

I am singing to the heavens above. Incantations of Modoc Conjurers. *Unknown*. APN-2, tr. by Albert S. Gatschet

I am single and I am just. Photo Genic. Olga Broumas. ExTi

I am sitting across the table. Sunday at the State Hospital. David Ignatow. RaBo

I am sitting again on the steps of the burned out barrack. On the Far Edge of Kilmer. Gerald Stern. LoL

I am sitting alone among the silence of the animals. Sleep of Beasts, The. Peter Cooley. UrbNat

I am sitting here. Poor Girl's Meditation, The. *Unknown*. BIrV; OBMV, tr. by Padraic Colum

I am sitting in a cell with a view of evil parallels. Jail Poems. Bob Kaufman. NAAAL

I am sitting in a strange room listening. Baby-Sitting. Gillian Clarke. FaBoWP; TCAWP

I am sitting in Mike's Place trying to figure out. One Thousand Fearful Words for Fidel Castro. Lawrence Ferlinghetti. VGW

I am sitting sad and lonely. Lines to Florence. Mary Weston Fordham. CBWP-2

I am sitting thirty feet above the water. For Song. Gerald Stern. BBASP

I am sixteen you are my first love. Gail. Hugh Seidman. KGB

I am sleepless in the glow and shadow of the lamplight. Visiting Tsan, Abbot of Ta-Yun. Tu Fu. OHPC, tr. by Kenneth Rexroth

I am sleepy, and the oozy weeds about me twist. (LL) Herman Melville. APN-2; HAP; NAAL-2v1; NCAP; NOBA; OxBoLi; WoPoe *Fr.* Billy Budd, Foretopman.

I am slowly dying, water evaporating. George Bowering. NOBC *Fr.* Summer Solstice.

I am so fair that wheresoe'er I wend. Beauty Accurst. Richard Le Gallienne. RACG

I Am So in Love I Grow a New Hymen. Sandra Cisneros. IllVoic

I am so out of love through poverty. Sonnet: Of Why He Would Be a Scullion. Cecco Angiolieri, da Siena. AWP; EaItPo, tr. by Dante Gabriel Rossetti

I am so passing rich in poverty. Sonnet: He Jests Concerning His Poverty. Bartolomeo di Sant' Angelo. AWP; EaItPo, tr. by Dante Gabriel Rossetti

I am sorry, my little cat, I am sorry—. War Cat. Dorothy Leigh Sayers. TriCat

I am sorry to speak of death again. Poetics against the Angel of Death. Phyllis Webb. MoCV; NOBC

I am sorry you are. Roots. Charlotte Watson Sherman. ISC

I am space. On reading the new physics—Creation and Cosmology. Cosi Fabian. HW

I am speaking of that hollow-eyed race. They Never Grew Old. Judith Ortiz Cofer. PueRic

I am standing above you and tide. Christopher Okigbo. PBMAP *Fr.* Heavensgate (1961).

I am standing for peace and non-violence. Patriot, The. Nissim Ezekiel. EmeKit; FaBoVe

I am standing in the post office, about. James Tate. EmeKit *Fr.* I Am A Finn.

I am standing tensely at the desk. Current "Now, Voyager" Fantasy. Remy Holzer. OPRER

I am staring out the window. African Sculpture. Christopher Gilbert. ESEAA

I Am Still a Finn. James Tate. EmeKit *Fr.* I Am A Finn.

I am still bitter about the last place we stayed. Codicil. Ruth Stone. BoWoP

I am still on fire. Distance. Eugene B. Redmond. SeSe

I Am Still Rich. Thomas Curtis Clark. PoToHe

I am storing at heart a bundle of grass. Nightmare 3. Abdul Maqsoud Abdul Karim. NAfrP, *tr. by* Clarissa C. Burt

I am strange here and often I am still trying. Evening. W. S. Merwin. NAAL-2v2

I am Suibne the wanderer. Suibne Geilt. NOIV

I am surprised to see. Letter Written on a Ferry While Crossing Long Island Sound. Anne Sexton. CoAP; NAAL-2v2; TwCP

I Am Taliesin. I Sing Perfect Metre. *Unknown.* OBWVE, *tr. by* Ifor Williams

I am Te-ngau-reka-a-tu. Taiaha Haka Poem. Apirana Taylor. PeNZ

I am telling you a number of half-conditioned ideas. Sunday Evening. Barbara Guest. NeAP

I am tempted by rumors, by history. Coming off a Depression, She Prepares for Venice. A. V. Christie. NAPBL

I am tempted to think of you. Poem of Villeneuve St Georges, A. Mbella Sonne Dipoko. PBMAP

I am that Dido which thou here do'st see. Ausonius. NoSic; OBVE

I am that man with helmet made of thorn. For an Ex-Far East Prisoner of War. Charles Causley. OxBC

I am that Savior that vouchsafed to die. On the Inscription over the Head of Christ on the Cross. Henry Colman. ChIV-2

I am that serpent-haunted cave. Pythoness, The. Kathleen Jessie Raine. MoBrPo

I am that woman whose works are good. Sovereign Queen. Padeshah Khatun. WPOW, *tr. by* Deirdre Lashgari

I am the acorn. Journey. Judith Nicholls. OBSP

I am the American heartbreak. American Heartbreak. Langston Hughes. APT-2; BPo

I am the ancient Apple-Queen. Pomona. William Morris. NOBVV; NPeEn; OxBEV; WoPoe

I Am the Autumn. Itsik [*or* Itzik *or* Itzig] Manger. TrJP, *tr. by* Joseph Leftwich

I am the Babe of Joseph Stalin's Daughter. Rochelle Owens. PFTM-2

I am the bird that flutters against your window in the. Guardian Angel. Rolf Jacobsen. RaBo, *tr. by* Robert Bly

I Am the Blood. Isaac Rosenberg. MoBrPo

I am the blossom pressed in a book. Briefly It Enters, and Briefly Speaks. Jane Kenyon. HW

I am the blue! I come from the lower world. Helen. Paul Valéry. OBVE, *tr. by* Robert Lowell

I am the boy with his hands raised over his head. House That Fear Built: Warsaw, 1943, The. Jane Flanders. PBCAP

I am the broken reed in this deathly organ. How We Carry Ourselves. Jimmy Santiago Baca. AF

I am the captain of my soul. (LL) William Ernest Henley. AmFaPo; BRP; CABP; MoBrPo; NAEL-6v2; NOBE; OBEV; OBMV *Fr.* Echoes.

I am the captain of my soul. Probably. Keith Preston. NBLV

I Am the Cat. Leila Usher. ITBLP

I am the cat of cats. I am. Cat of Cats, The. William Brighty Rands. NOxBChV

I am the chaunt-rann of a Singer. Poet, The. Padraic Fiacc. CIP-2

I am the dark one,—the widower,—the unconsoled. El Desdichado. Gérard de Nerval. WoPoe, *tr. by* Robert Duncan

I am the Dean of Christ Church, Sir. *Var. authors.* FaBoEE; NOBL *Fr.* Balliol Rhymes.

I am the desert. Carthage. Najaat Al-Udwany. PoArWo, *tr. by* Moulouk Berry and Ali Farghaly

I am the difficult silk that slides from your grasp. Elizabeth Garrett. NewEx

I Am the Door [*or* Doore]. Richard Crashaw. GeHe; NAEL-5v1; NAEL-6v1; NAEL-7v1

I am the family face. Heredity. Thomas Hardy. CTC; EBEV; HarvBoo; RB

I am the farmer, stripped of love. Hill Farmer Speaks, The. Ronald Stuart Thomas. GTBS-P; OBWVE

I am the feast-maker. William Ernest Henley. FaBoWar *Fr.* Song of the Sword.

I am the first. Paul Celan. VCWP, *tr. by* Michael Hamburger

I am the first and I am the last. Bible, *O.T.* InvLi, *tr. by* New Revised Standard Version *Fr.* Isaiah.

I am the first to drink of the blue that still looks for its eye. I am the first. Paul Celan. VCWP, *tr. by* Michael Hamburger

I am the flute of Daphnis. On this wall. Edward Cracroft Lefroy. AWP *Fr.* Echoes from Theocritus.

I Am the Freshly Dead Husband. Kojo Laing. HBAPE; NAfrP

I am the fruit of Adams hands, through sin lockt in satans bands. Hymne of the State of all Adams Posteritie, An. Lady Elizabeth Tyrwhit. EMWP

I am the ghost of Shadwell Stair. Shadwell Stair. Wilfred Owen. FaBoTw

I am the grandson of György Dózsa. Grandson of György Dózsa, The. Endre Ady. IQMS, *tr. by* Sir Maurice Bowra

I am the grass. / Let me work. (LL) Grass. Carl Sandburg. AWP; ColAP; FaBoWar; MoAmPo; NAAL-2v2; NOBA; NoAM; OBWP; OxBA; PeFWW; TCAPo; TFi

I am the grave of Baucis the bride. Passing by. Erinna. HePo *Fr.* Epigrams.

I am the great Baron-Samedi. René Depestre. PFTM-2, *tr. by* Joan Dayan *Fr.* Rainbow for the Christian West, A.

I am the Great Bassist. Great Bassist, The. Lawson Fusao Inada. OpBo

I Am the Great Sun. Charles Causley. OxBSo; PeECV; TOF

I am the great sun, but you do not see me. Charles Causley. OxBSo; PeECV; TOF

I am the hazel-nut. An anaemic worm. I Am the Hazel-Nut. Karel Van de Woestijne. TuT, *tr. by* Michael Longley

I am the keeper of the earth and air. Keeper. Esther Iverem. GT

I am the least. Mite, The. Boynton, Jr. Merrill. CRP

I am the living body of the Great Spirit above. Chants to the Deity. *Unknown.* APN-2, *tr. by* Henry Rowe Schoolcraft

I am the Living Quetzalcoatl. Living Quetzalcoatl, The. D. H. Lawrence. OWoS

I Am the Lord. Alexander Mack. AH, *tr. by* Sheema Z. Buehne

I am the Lord of Light, the self-begotten Youth. *Unknown.* AWP, *tr. by* Robert Hillyer *Fr.* Book of the Dead.

I am the magical mouse. Magical Mouse, The. Kenneth Patchen. KaS

I am the maiden in bronze set over the tomb of Midas. Cleoboulos. GrAn

I am the man that hath seen affliction. Bible, *O.T.* TrJP *Fr.* Lamentations.

I am the man who looked for peace and found. War Poet. Sidney Keyes. FaBoWar; NoP-4; PoWW

I am the month when roses. June. Mary Weston Fordham. CBWP-2

I am the mother of sorrows. Paradox, The. Paul Laurence Dunbar. TCAPo

I Am the Mountainy Singer. Joseph Campbell. MoBrPo

I am the mover of other eyes. Dirge for the Living. Rosalie Moore. YaYoPo

I am the Muse who sung alway. Solution. Ralph Waldo Emerson. OBAL

I am the night watchman of rue de Flandre. Night Watchman of Pont-au-Change, The. Robert Desnos. AF, *tr. by* Carolyn Forché

I am the October lady. Horoscope. Colleen J. McElroy. GT

I Am the One. Thomas Hardy. OxBTC

I am the one in your dreams. Dark Lord of Savaiki, The. Alistair Campbell. PeNZ

I am the one who gnawed the blanket through. Message from Outside. Gary Snyder. BodElec

I am the one who looks the other way. Bystander, The. Rosemary Dobson. CBAP

I am the one who talks with the mountains. Dear Webster. Connie Fife. ReEnLa

I am the one whose praise. Hildegard von Bingen. HW, *tr. by* Gabriele Uhlein

I am the one whose thought. Death. William Bell Scott. NOBVV

I am the only being whose doom. Emily Jane Brontë. NALW

I am the only hero of my verses. Lyric Poet's Epilogue, The. Mihály Babits. IQMS, *tr. by* Peter Zollman

I am the only one, the only one left. *Unknown.* APN-2, *tr. by* Stephen Powers *Fr.* Sacred Songs of the Konkau.

I am the people—the mob—the crowd—the mass. I Am the People, the Mob. Carl Sandburg. IllVoic; OxBA; TAP

I Am the Poet. Walt Whitman. BLT

I Am the Poet Davies, William. William Henry Davies. OxBSP

I am the poet of reality. I Am the Poet. Walt Whitman. BLT

I am the poet of the Body and I am the poet of the Soul. Walt Whitman. CAGL; ColAP; NAWM-7v2; WeW-3 *Fr.* Song of Myself.

I am the poet of the spare room. Home, the Spare Room, The. Robert Adamson. BMAP

I am the Prince in the Field. *Unknown.* AWP *Fr.* Book of the Dead.

I am the pure lotus. *Unknown.* AWP, *tr. by* Ulli Beier *Fr.* Book of the Dead.

I am the pure red witch. Moi-Même. Carmen Bruna. SurWo, *tr. by* Natalie Kenvin

I am the pure, the true of word, triumphant. *Unknown.* AWP *Fr.* Book of the Dead.

I am the pure traveler. *Unknown.* AWP *Fr.* Book of the Dead.

I am the reasonable one. I am the one you can say your spite to, the. I Am the Reasonable One. Rosario Morales. PueRic

I am the Red Cloud. *Unknown.* APN-2, *tr. by* Stephen Powers *Fr.* Sacred Songs of the Konkau.

I am the rose of Sharon, and the lily of the valleys. Bible, *O.T.* BoLoP; OBVE *Fr.* Song of Solomon, The [*or* The Song of Songs].

I am the self-appointed guardian of English literature. Souvenir de Monsieur Poop. Stevie Smith. NALW

I am the serpent, fat with years. *Unknown.* AWP *Fr.* Book of the Dead.

I am the seventh son of the son. Malcolm X—an Autobiography. Larry Neal. BPo

I am the sister of him. Little. Dorothy Aldis. NTCP; WHSW

I am the Smoke King. Song of the Smoke, The. William Edward Burghardt DuBois. ISC; SSLK; UnPO

I am the snake-woman kneeling at Knossos. Power of the Soul. Sheilah Glover. HW

I am the sole homosexual. Power of One. Walta Borawski. CAGL

I Am the Son of King Gog of Magog. Gyula Reviczky. IQMS, *tr. by* Adam Makkai

I am the song that sings the bird. I am the Song. Charles Causley. NOxBChV

I am the stage, impassive, mute and cold. Nature. Alfred de Vigny. AWP, *tr. by* Margaret Jourdain

I am the still rain falling. Moods. Sara Teasdale. APT-1

I am the stone that kills me. (LL) Stone. Edward Kamau Brathwaite. PFTM-2; WaCA

I am the stone the Persians put to bear. Statue of Nemesis at Rhamnus, The. Parmenion of Macedon. GrAn, *tr. by* Alistair Elliot

I am the swift scribble. Patricia Hawkhead. NewEx

I am the teacher of athletes. Walt Whitman. CAGL; ColAP *Fr.* Song of Myself.

I am the thought on the bath in the room without mirrors. Blue Wind, The. Nadja. SurWo, *tr. by* Richard Howard

I am the thunder of my tribe. *Unknown.* APN-2, *tr. by* Franz Boas *Fr.* Songs of the Kwakiutl Indians.

I am the tomb of a shipwrecked man. Sail on. Theodoridas. GrAn

I am the tomb of Crethon; here you read. Tomb of Crethon, The. Leonidas of Tarentum. AWP, *tr. by* John Hermann Merivale

I am the tomb of Tellen, I contain. Leonidas of Tarentum. GrAn

I Am the Tropical Night's High Noon. Maria Martins. SurWo, *tr. by* Rachel Blackwell

I am the true vine, and my Father is the husbandman. Bible, *N.T.* OBVE *Fr.* St. John.

I am the trumpet blown by time [*or* Time]. Trumpet, The. Ilya Grigoryevich Ehrenburg [*or* Erenburg]. TCRP; TrJP, *tr. by* Yakov Hornstein

I am the Turquoise Woman's son. War God's Horse Song, The. *Unknown.* RB; TTTS, *tr. by* Louis Watchman

I am the used-arrow collector. Actor Speaks, An. Ben Scammell. NLP

I Am the Very Model [*or* Pattern] of a Modern Major-General. Sir William Schwenck Gilbert. NOBL *Fr.* Pirates of Penzance, The.

I am the very pattern of a modern major-giral. Sir William Schwenck Gilbert. UV *Fr.* Pirates of Penzance, The.

I am the voice of music and the ended dance. (LL) Judith Wright. BMAP; CBAP *Fr.* Blind Man, The.

"I Am the Way." Alice Thompson Meynell. NOBVV; OBMV; OxBSP

I am the wealthy one. Demeter's Song. Starhawk. HW

I am the wee falorie man. Wee Falorie Man, The. *Unknown.* FaBoVe

I am the whistling of night. Second Portrait. Manuela Fingueret. MirDau, *tr. by* Roberta Gordenstein

I am the woman always too young to be. I've Been around: It Gets Me Nowhere. Marie Ponsot. ExTi

I am the woman, and about to enter. (LL) Alicia Ostriker. PBCAP; TaR

I am the woman of the great expanse of the water. María Sabina. PFTM-1 *Fr.* Midnight Velada, The.

I am the woman of the principal fountain. Shaman. María Sabina. WPOW, *tr. by* Henry Munn

I am Thine, O Lord, I have heard Thy voice. I Am Thine, O Lord. Fanny Crosby. SWaP

I am thinking of tents and tentage, tents through the ages. Thinking of Tents. Reed Whittemore. TAP

I am thinking of that boy who bragged about the day he threw. Boy at the Paterson Falls. Toi Derricotte. PBCAP

I am thirty-two and wise. For My Birthday. Attila József. IQMS, *tr. by* Anton N. Nyerges

I Am thy Charge, thy Care! "Michael Field." PoBW

I am thy fugitive, thy votary. To the Lord Love. "Michael Field." OBMV

I am Thy grass, O Lord! Trust. Lizette Woodworth Reese. SWaP

I am thy other self, what thou wilt be. Thy Better Self. Jones Very. TCAPo

I am tired of civilization. (LL) Tired. Fenton Johnson. APT-1; NAAAL; PAI; TCAPo; TTY

"I am tired of this barn!" said the colt. Barn, The. Elizabeth Jane Coatsworth. OBCP

I am tired of work; I am tired of building up somebody else's civilization. Tired. Fenton Johnson. APT-1; NAAAL; PAI; TCAPo; TTY

I am to follow her. There is much grace. George Meredith. NAEL-5v2; NAEL-6v2; NOBVV *Fr.* Modern Love.

I am to see to it that I do not lose you. (LL) To a Stranger. Walt Whitman. APN-1; NOBA; SAmP

I am told. Ingredients of Glass. Margaret Speak. Prnts

I am told that the best people have begun saying. War Has Been Given a Bad Name. Bertolt Brecht. HP; PoSu

I Am Too Near. Wisława Szymborska. BoWoP, *tr. by* Czeslaw Milosz

I am too near, too clear a thing for you. Flower of Mullein, A. Lizette Woodworth Reese. MoAmPo

I am too old to burn ships, even if I am a pirate don't mind me. Old Pirate in These Waters, An. Ali Püsküllüoğlu. WoPoe, *tr. by* Murat Nemet-Nejat

I am too young to grow a beard. Street Song. Thom Gunn. HeIP-4; OxBC

I am troubled, I'm dissatisfied, I'm Irish. (LL) Spenser's Ireland. Marianne Craig Moore. FaBoWP; NOBA; NoAM; OxBA; TAP

I am true in the land of ancient sounds. Susan Taylor. NewEx

I am trusting Thee, Lord Jesus. Trusting Jesus. Frances Ridley Havergal. SacPr

I am trying to decide to go swimming. Wind Is Blowing West, The. Joseph Ceravolo. TTTS

I am trying to drain my mind. Prelude to Nothing. Sonia Sanchez. GT

I am trying to imagine. Re-forming the Crystal. Adrienne Rich. TAP

I am trying / to learn to walk again. Walk. Frank Horne. BPo

I am trying to pry open your casket. Dear Reader. James Tate. SPE

I am twelve years old, my hair in braids. Music Mother. Naomi Feigelson Chase. MiVo

I am 25 years old. My Poem. Nikki Giovanni. BPo; NBV

I am twenty-four. Survivor, The. Tadeusz Rózewicz. HP; PoSu, *tr. by* Adam Czerniawski

I am twenty-two years old. Chirst. Portrait. Miklós Radnóti. IQMS, *tr. by* Thomas Land

I Am Two. Dacia Maraini. CItWP, *tr. by* Cinzia Sartini Blum and Lara Trubowitz

I am two fools, I know. Triple Fool, The. John Donne. FSCP; NOSC; SoSe-8

I am two parts / a person. Here. Sandra Maria Esteves. PueRic

I am unable to recapture the allbody poured. Jolanda Insana. CItWP, *tr. by* Cinzia Sartini Blum and Lara Trubowitz *Fr.* Parabola of the Heart, The.

"I am unable," yonder beggar cries. Lame Beggar, A. John Donne. NoSic; PeLV

I am unhappy / I do not care what happens. Motoyoshi Prince. OHPJ

I am unhappy that I am not God. He Puts Me to Rest. David Ignatow. VGW

I am unity on high. Leah Goldberg. MHP, *tr. by* Ruth Finer Mintz *Fr.* Songs of the Stream.

I am unjust, but I can strive for justice. Why I Voted the Socialist Ticket. Nicholas Vachel Lindsay. MoAmPo

I am useless. New Heavens for Old. Amy Lowell. APT-1

I am valued by men, fetched from afar. Cynewulf. AnOE, *tr. by* Charles W. Kennedy *Fr.* Riddles (Exeter Book).

I am virtually gone. Blue Diamond. Claudia Keelan. BodElec

I am waetch. Archie Weller. IBA

I am waiting. (LL) Yet Still. Rashidah Ismaili. HAWP; ItWoWo

I am waiting for my case to come up. Lawrence Ferlinghetti. AiP; PmAP *Fr.* Oral Messages.

I am waiting for news, let it come. Snow Poem. Rodolfo Di Biasio. NeIt, *tr. by* Stephen Sartarelli

I Am Walking. Frances Densmore. APT-1 *Fr.* Chippewa Music.

I am walking a trail. Intimidations of an Autobiography. James Tate. NoAM

I am walking and I. Ray A. Young Bear. STP

I am walking backwards into the future like a Greek. River and Fountain. Michael Longley. ModIr

I am walking rapidly through striations of light and dark thrown under an arcade. I Dream I'm the Death of Orpheus. Adrienne Rich. NALW

I am wandering. Margaret Haskell Indian School. Carolyn Marie Dunn. ReEnLa

I am warm. Promise, The. Jewel C. Latimore. BlSi

I am watching them churn the last milk. Mad Yak, The. Gregory Corso. BB; PFTM-2; PmAP

I am wearing absent-minded red. Spots of Blood. Phyllis Webb. NOBC

I am Weary, Mother. Mary E. Tucker. CBWP-1

I am weary of lying within the chase. Ballade de Marguerite. *Unknown.* AWP, *tr. by* Oscar Wilde

I am weary of salmon dawns. Opus 131. Arthur Davison Ficke. APT-1, *tr. by* Anne Knish

I Am Weary of Straying. Sarah E. York. AH

I am weary of the working. To Solitude. Alice Cary. APN-2

I am weaving a song of waters. Song. Gwendolyn B. Bennett. BlSi

I am whale-in. Bill Griffiths. Oth *Fr.* Building: The New London Hospital.

I am what I am. Ending Poem. Aurora Levins Morales. PueRic

I Am White, Darling. Semyon [or Semion] Isaakovich Kirsanov. RusPo, tr. by Robert Arthur Douglas Ford

I am who the trail took. Exploration. Daniel Gerard Hoffman. CoAP

I am wild for love and suffer a hunger for hearts. Wild for Love. Delmira Agustini. TANSG, tr. by Mark McCaffrey

I am William Bronk, have been raised to believe. Plainest Narrative, The. William Bronk. APSN

I am with thee, and Most take all. (LL) Quidditie [or Quiddity], The. George Herbert. GeHe; NOSC

I Am with Those. Ingrid Jonker. BoWoP; HAWP, tr. by Jack Cope and William Plomer

I Am With You. Lajos Kassák. IQMS, tr. by Edwin Morgan

I am wondering what became of all those tall abstractions. Death of Allegory, The. Billy Collins. WeW-3

I am worn out with dreams. Men Improve with the Years. W. B. Yeats. OxAEP-2

I am yesterday, to-day and to-morrow. Unknown. AWP Fr. Book of the Dead.

I am: Yet what I am none cares or knows. I Am. John Clare. BBASP; CABP; EBEV; EBVV; FHYEP; GTBS-P; HAP; NAEL-5v2; NAEL-6v2; NOBE; NPeEn; NoP-4; PoPoPo; WoPoe; OxBEV; PeECV; TFi; TOF; TRP

I am you are he she it is. Monkey. Bruce Weigl. CDa

I am your mother, your mother's mother. Jelaluddin [or Jalal al-Din] Rumi. OBVE

I am your servant and your thrall. (LL) John Fletcher. NOSC; OBEV Fr. Elder Brother, The.

I am your son, white man! Mulatto. Langston Hughes. NAAL-2v2; NAAL-5

I Am Your Wife. Unknown. PoToHe

I am your wisdom. (LL) Kenneth Rexroth. APSN; APT-2 Fr. Love Poems of Marichiko, The.

I am yours, you are mine. Frau Ava. BoWoP

I ame not she by proweff of syt. Unknown. EMWP

I, an unwedded wandering dame. Epitaph. Sylvia Townsend Warner. MoBrPo

I and I. Khalil-ur-Rahman Azmi. OMIP, tr. by C. M. Naim

I and myself swore enmity. Alack. Interior. Sir John Collings Squire. OxBSP

I and Pangur Ban, my cat. Pangur Ban. Unknown. TriCat, tr. by Robin Ernest William Flower

I and Pangur Bán, my cat. Pangur Bán. Unknown. FaBoCh; RB

I and the other intruders. Of Objects Considered as Fortresses in a Baleful Place. Hyam Plutzik. VGW

I and the shore are lovers. Song of the Wave. Kahlil Gibran. GraLe, tr. by H. M. Nahmad

I and You. Nikolai Stepanovich Gumilyov [or Gumiliov or Gumilev]. TCRP, tr. by Yakov Hornstein

I apologize to coincidence for calling it necessity. Under a Certain Little Star. Wislawa Szymborska. PoetW; VCWP, tr. by Magnus J. Krynski and Robert A. Maguire

I appear like a bird from nowhere. Below Hekla. Selima Hill. FaBoWP

I Applied for the Board. Jimmy Santiago Baca. LoL

I approach gianthood warily. Up. Nigel Wells. AngWePo

I approached Moses and said to him. Moses. Amir Gilbo'a. MHP, tr. by Ruth Finer Mintz

I argue / that where the body is concerned. Saddle and Cell. The Three Marias. BoWoP, tr. by Helen R. Lane

I arise and unbuild it again. (LL) Cloud, The. Shelley. CABP; FHYEP; NAEL-5v2; NAEL-6v2; NoP-4; PWR

I arise from dreams of thee. Indian Serenade, The. Shelley. AWP; OBEV; RaBo; TTTS; TreFP

I arose early and stepped outside. February Morning. King D. Kuka. VoR

I arose swiftly that night, for I heard a knock at my door. Future, The. James Oppenheim. TrJP

I Arrived in that Town, Everyone Greeted Me and I Recognized No One. When I Was Going to Read My Verses, the Devil, Hidden behind a Tree, Called Out to Me Sarcastically and Filled My Hands with Newspaper Clippings. J. V. Foix. PFTM-1

I as in love with the word "aloha." Poem for George Helm: Aloha Week 1980. Eric Chock. OpBo

I ask a man in the smoker where he is going and he answers: /"Omaha Omaha." (LL) Limited. Carl Sandburg. HAP; MoAmPo; OxBA

I ask all blessings. Unknown. EnlH

I ask but right: Let her that caught me late. Ovid. EBEV, tr. by Christopher Marlowe Fr. Elegies.

I Ask My Mother to Sing. Li-Young Lee. IllVoic; InvLad; LoL; OpBo; UnSA

I Ask My Teachers. Sister Mary Madeleva. CRP Fr. Concerning Death.

I ask no kind return of love. Fanny [or Frances] Macartney Greville. OBEV Fr. Prayer for Indifference, A.

I ask not out of sorrow, but in wonder. (LL) Encounter. Czeslaw Milosz. BodElec; ChAP; PoetW; WoPoe, tr. by Lillian Vallee

I ask not wit, nor beauty do I crave. Humble Wish, The. B–ll M–rt–n. ECWP; LW

I ask not wit, nor beauty do I crave. Wish, by a Young Lady, The. Laetitia Pilkington. PEW

I ask the clerk to show me children's books. I say. Bookstore. Toi Derricotte. ExTi

I ask the mountain, but it does not say. (LL) Miscellaneous Feelings in the Sui Garden. Yüan Mei. CoBLCP; ColAnChi, tr. by Jonathan Chaves

I ask thee whence those ashes were. Question, A. Unknown. NOSC

I ask thy aid, O potent rum! Resentments Composed because of the Clamor of Town Topers Outside My Apartment. Sarah Kemble Knight. AiP; SCAP

I ask, who will buy a poem? Who Will Buy a Poem? Mahon O'Heffernan. NOIV

I ask you. Pindar. WoPoe, tr. by Thomas Meyer Fr. Pythian Odes.

I ask you: Has the Singer sung. Non Omnis Moriar. Allen Tate. FuPo

I ask you, Is our soul still open? All Soul's Day. Maurya Simon. ExTi

I ask you to witness, Priapus. Unknown. RomPo, tr. by Eugene O'Connor Fr. Priapean Corpus, The.

I askéd a thief to steal me a peach. Angel, The. William Blake. NAEL-5v2; PoE See Angel, The

I asked an aged man, a man of cares. What Is Time? James Marsden. PWR

I asked if I got sick and died, would you. Question, A. John Millington Synge. MoBrPo; NOIV; OBMV; OxBTC; PAI

I asked if I should pray. Mohini Chatterjee. W. B. Yeats. NoAM

I asked my dead to tea. Tea Party, The. Jean Earle. TCAWP

I asked my love: "Why do you make yourself so beautiful?" I Asked My Love. Abu Sa'id. EroLit

I asked my mother for fifty cents. Unknown. OxBoLi

I asked no other thing. Emily Dickinson. APN-2; NOBA; OxBA

I asked [or ask't] thee oft what poets thou hast read. Upon the Same. Robert Herrick. CaPo

I asked [or askd] my Dear Friend, Orator Prigg. Orator Prigg. William Blake. OBSV

I asked professors who teach the meaning of life to tell me what is happiness. Happiness. Carl Sandburg. IllVoic; OxBA

I asked the grave-digger, "Do you have." Ahmad al-Mushari Al-'Udwani. MAP Fr. Personal Reflections.

I asked the heaven of stars. Night Song at Amalfi. Sara Teasdale. APT-1; MakPoe; MoAmPo

I asked the Lord: "Sire, is this true." Dream Question, A. Thomas Hardy. ChIV-1

I asked the maid in dulcet tone. Scones. Unknown. OBCoV

I associate hours and days. Monotomy. Gabriella Sica. CItWP, tr. by Cinzia Sartini Blum and Lara Trubowitz

I assume that we are talking about saving a few young men from suicide and a few others from becoming cops or firemen. Rhetoric. Francis Ponge. WoPoe, tr. by Serge Gavronsky

I at my window sit, and see. Autumn. Unknown. NOEC

I / at one time. Self-Hatred of Don L. Lee, The. Haki R. Madhubuti. BPo; ESEAA

I ate and drank with you, fellow men. Yevgeny [or Evgenii] Mikhailovich Vinokurov. TCRP

I ate pancakes one night in a Pancake House. Player Piano, The. Randall Jarrell. NAAL-2v2

I attach no importance to life. Spectral Attitudes, The. André Breton. SPE, tr. by David Gascoyne

I attended the burial of all my rosy feelings. Transaction. A. R. Ammons. HCAP

I awoke happy, the house. Revelation, The. William Carlos Williams. SAmP

I awoke in profuse sweat, arms aching. Hag-Ridden. Robert Graves. BIrV

I awoke in the midsummer not-to-call night, in the white and the walk of the morning. Moonrise. Gerard Manley Hopkins. MoBrPo; NOBVV; RB

I bade make ready for our guests to-night. (LL) Augusta Davies Webster. PeVV; VWP Fr. Circe.

I bargained with life for a penny. My Wage. Jessie Belle Rittenhouse. PoToHe

I bathe in orchid water. Unknown. CoBCP, tr. by Burton Watson Fr. Nine Songs, The.

I bear a little more than I can bear. (LL) Elinor Wylie. NAAL-2v2; OxBA; Son Fr. One Person.

I bear the sucker-torch to the western tree-ridge. Songs of Spirits. Unknown. APN-2, tr. by Jeremiah Curtin

I beat like a deaf man on the door of the dead. Son of the Bone Speaks, The. Roger Gilbert-Lecomte. PFTM-1

I become them, sometimes. Pure fight. Pure fantasy. Lean. (LL)   Turncoat, The. Imamu Amiri Baraka. NeAP; PoE

I bed next to you, I feel your heartbeat.   Kenny Fries. AmPoNex   *Fr.* Healing Notebooks, The.

I been 'buked an' I been scorned.   Hell and Heaven.   *Unknown.* OxBoLi   *See* Hell and Heaven

I been ridin' fer cattle the most of my life.   High-loping Cowboy, The.   Curley W. Fletcher. AiP

I been scarred and battered.   Langston Hughes.   *See* I've been scarred and battered

I been t'inkin"bout de preachah; whut he said de othah night.   Philosophy. Paul Laurence Dunbar. BPo; NAAAL

I Been Working on the Railroad.   *Unknown.* TCAPo

I beg death's pardon now. And mourn the dead. (LL)   Pardon, The.   Richard Wilbur. NIL-7; NOBA; NoAM; PAI

I beg God's grace, guardian of the parish.   In Praise of Tenby.   *Unknown.* OBWVE, *tr. by* Joseph P. Clancy

I beg of you, Chung Tzu.   Chung Tzu.   *Unknown.* WoPoe, *tr. by* Arthur Waley

I beg you, beg you, mother.   *Unknown.* WoPoe, *tr. by* Konstantinos Lardas   *Fr.* Mourning Songs of Greece.

I began in Ohio.   Stages on a Journey Westward.   James Wright (1927–80). LCAP-2

I began losing the battles.   Domestic Blues.   Teresa Calderón. TANSG, *tr. by* Celeste Kostopulos-Cooperman

I begin each day.   Kikaku.   SoOfWa, *tr. by* Sam Hamill

I begin through the grass once again to·be bound to the Lord.   Reconciliation. "Æ"   OBMV; TrCP

I begin with the hills.   This House.   Ray A. Young Bear. CDW

I beheld her and was conquered at the start.   I Guess I'll Have to Change My Plan.   Howard Dietz. ReLy

I beheld her, on a day.   Ben Jonson. NAEL-6v1; NAEL-7v1   *Fr.* Celebration of Charis in Ten Lyric[k] Pieces [*or* Peeces], A.

I behold her there.   Together Again.   Victor Vroomkoning. TuT, *tr. by* Anne Kennedy

I, Being Born A Woman.   Edna St. Vincent Millay. APT-1; BoLoP; HarvBoo; LW; NALW; NIL-7; NIP-4; NoP-4

I Believe.   Saul [*or* Shaul] Tchernichowsky [*or* Tchernichovsky].   TrJP, *tr. by* Reginald V. Feldman

I Believe.   *Unknown.* HP

I believe a leaf of grass is no less than the journey-work of the stars.   Walt Whitman. SAmP   *Fr.* Song of Myself.

I believe in magic. I believe in the rights.   Credo.   Maxine W. Kumin. ExTi

I believe in the chance behind which God smiles.   My Dear Little Fellow. László Mécs. IQMS, *tr. by* Watson Kirkconnell

I believe in the heretical teachings of a degenerate age, the witchcraft of the Christian God.   Secret Song of the Heretics.   Kitahara Hakushū. WoPoe, *tr. by* Donald Keene

I believe in the increasing of life: Whatever.   Escape, The.   Ivor Gurney. OxBSP

I believe in the sun.   I Believe.   *Unknown.* HP

I believe in this stalled magnificence.   Snowbound City, The.   John Haines. SPE

I Believe in You.   Frank Loesser. ReLy

I believe in you my soul.   Walt Whitman. CAGL   *Fr.* Song of Myself.

I believe it was a calm evening.   Widower.   Julia Copus. NeBl

I believe the Blacks are bad.   Sun, The.   Benjamin Zephaniah. Oth

I believe the dose will do. (LL)   Receipt to Cure [*or* for] the Vapours, A.   Lady Mary Wortley Montagu. ECWP; NOEC; NPeEn; OxBEV; PEW

I believe there is no one alive who weeps for my sorrow.   Heinrich von Morungen. GePo

I belt out "I feel pretty, oh, so pretty" in the best Ethel Merman I can muster. (LL)   Man I Love and I Shop at Jewel, The.   Jim Elledge. IllVoic; ReTh

I bend over an old hollow cottonwood stump.   Hollow Tree, A.   Robert Bly. NNaP

I bend over the woman.   Country Midwife: A Day, The.   Ai. GT

I Bended unto Me.   Thomas Edward Brown. NOBVV; NTCP

I bequeath my notes to my successors and heirs.   Hieronymus Bosch.   Pavel Grigoryevich Antokolsky. TCRP, *tr. by* Bernard Meares

I, Bertolt Brecht, came out of the black forests.   Of Poor B.B.   Bertolt Brecht. RB; WoPoe, *tr. by* Michael Hamburger

I beseech God's favour, faultless your gift.   Petition for Reconciliation. Cynddelw Brydydd Mawr. OBWVE, *tr. by* Joseph P. Clancy

I bespeak words.   Introduction: "I bespeak words."   Clere Parsons. FaBoTw

"I bet I can hold my breath."   One-Upmanship.   Miriam Chaikin. NTCP

I bet you don't wear shoulder pads in bed.   Wagers.   Marilyn Hacker. RA

I bind unto myself to-day.   St Patrick's Breastplate.   Saint Patrick. FaBoCh; SacPr, *tr. by* Frances Alexander

I blame even clear-voiced.   Korinna [*or* Corinna].   SaLy, *tr. by* Diane Rayor

I blame old women for buying paper roses.   Look, No Hands.   Pearse Hutchinson. PBCIP

"I bleed by the black stream."   Haemorrhage.   Padraic Fiacc. CIP-2

I Bless the Daily Labor.   Marina Ivanovna Tsvetayeva [*or* Tsvetaeva].   WPoS

I bless the daily labor of my hands.   Marina Ivanovna Tsvetayeva [*or* Tsvetaeva).   WPoS

I bless the everyday labor.   Marina Ivanovna Tsvetayeva [*or* Tsvetaeva]. BBASP, *tr. by* Mary Jane White

I Bless Thee, Lord, for Sorrows Sent.   Samuel Johnson. AH

I bless[e] thee, Lord, because I GROW.   Paradise.   George Herbert. AngWePo; BASC; GeHe; NOSC

I blink and half my life is over.   Pete Winslow. CLPP

I block out the midday brightness with a screen depicting dark woods. Impromptu on a Hangover.   P'i Jih-hsiu. CoBCP; ColAnChi, *tr. by* Burton Watson

I blow tobacco smoke.   Mushroom.   Shinkichi Takahashi. ZenPo, *tr. by* Takashi Ikemoto and Lucien Stryk

I borrow moonlight.   Saikaku.   JDP, *tr. by* Yoel Hoffmann

I bought a dollar and a half's worth of small red potatoes.   Simple Truth, The. Philip Levine. NoP-4

I bought a great big hat.   Would You Believe It?   Bart Howard. ReLy

I Bought a New Red.   Chrystos. WiU

I bought a red-brick villa.   Song for Straphangers.   George Buchanan. PNI

I bought a spray of blossoms from a vendor.   To the Tune: Magnolia Blossoms. Li Ch'ing-chao. CrYelRi, *tr. by* Sam Hamill

I bowed my head, and heard the sea far off / Washing its hands. (LL)   At the Slackening of the Tide.   James Wright (1927–80). UnPo; VGW

I break off a branch, and prod my lazy donkey.   Trip to a Mountain Village, A. Li K'ai-hsien. CoBLCP, *tr. by* Jonathan Chaves

I BREAK up cypress and make a book-box.   On a Box Containing his Own Works.   Po Chü-i. ChiP, *tr. by* Arthur Waley

I breathe, sweet Gib [*or* Ghib], the temperate air of Wrest.   To my Friend G.N. from Wrest.   Thomas Carew. BeJo; CaPo

I breathe the air of another country.   Australia.   Gary Catalano. NOBAu

I breathed my fill—and then breathed out.   Tatiana Bek.   ItGoST, *tr. by* Richard McKane

I breathed upon the aluminum microphone-stand a body's length away.   Thus Crosslegged on Round Pillow Sat in Space.   Allen Ginsberg. NNaP

I bring back the petticoat and the bottle of scent. (LL)   Lent.   William Robert Rodgers. ModIr; PNI

I bring fresh showers for the thirsting flowers.   Cloud, The.   Shelley. CABP; FHYEP; NAEL-5v2; NAEL-6v2; NoP-4; PWR

I bring myself back from the streets that open like long.   Home for Thanksgiving.   W. S. Merwin. NoAM

I bring ye love. Quest. What will love do?   Upon Love, by Way of Question and Answer.   Robert Herrick. CaPo

I bring you a bit of seaweed which was tangled with the sea.   Obsession. Robert Desnos. SurPaPo, *tr. by* Mary Ann Caws

I bring you a goat.   Hroswitha von Gandersheim (or, Hroswitha).   WPOW   *Fr.* Paphnutius.

I bring you along with me.   Theatre, The.   Remco Campert. TuT, *tr. by* Desmond Egan

I bring you as offering. (LL)   Orchard.   "H. D." APT-1; MoAmPo; OxBA

I Bring You Greetings: How.   Chrystos. WiU

I bring you news.   *Unknown.* NOIV

I bring you the offspring of an Idumæan night!   Gift of the Poem.   Stéphane Mallarmé. AWTN, *tr. by* Kate Flores

I bring you words freshly.   Word Gifts for an Australian Critic.   Merlinda Bobis. ReBoTo

I brocht my love a cherry.   Auld Sang.   William Soutar. OxBS

I broke a glass, got bloodstains on the sheet.   Eight Days in April.   Marilyn Hacker. FFC

I broke bread.   Under the Williamsburg Bridge.   Galway Kinnell. UrbNat

I Brood about Some Concepts, for Example.   Alicia Ostriker. PBCAP

I brood on the uselessness of letters. (LL)   Snow Storm.   Tu Fu. BLT; OHPC, *tr. by* Kenneth Rexroth

I Brotachos of Gortyn lie here. This.   Simonides. GrAn

I brought a little wolf cub home.   Wolf Cub.   Sergey [*or* Sergei] Sergeievich Narovchatov. TCRP, *tr. by* Lubov Yakovleva

I brought my children to the mound.   Anniversaries of War.   Yehuda Amichai [*or* Amikhai]. VCWP, *tr. by* Benjamin Harshav

I brought my life this far.   Anniversary.   Odysseus Elytis. AF

I brought my love.   Beloved.   Iyamide Hazeley. NAfrP

I brush the spider webs from the dismantled sky.   Housewife.   Amanda Berenguer. WPOW, *tr. by* Priscilla Joslin

I build the perfect silence with my hands.   Wavelength.   Jane Holland. NeBl

I built her a tower when I was young.   For Una.   Robinson Jeffers. APT-1

I built my house near where others dwell.   Written While Drunk.   Ch'ien T'ao. WoPoe, *tr. by* William Acker and Cyril Birch

I built my house upon the solid rock.   Here We have No Firm Dwelling-Place. Eugène Marais.   PeSAV, *tr. by* Hugh Finn

I Built My Hut.   José Juan Tablada.   AWP, *tr. by* Arthur Waley   *Fr.* Two Drinking Songs.

I built my hut beside a traveled road.   Poems after Drinking Wine.   Ch'ien T'ao.   ColAnChi, *tr. by* J. R. Hightower

I built my hut in a place where people live.   T'ao Ch'ien [*or* T'ao Yuan-ming].   CoBCP   *Fr.* Drinking Wine.

I BUILT my hut in a zone of human habitation.   Ch'ien T'ao.   ChiP

I built my hut near where people live.   José Juan Tablada.   AWP, *tr. by* Arthur Waley   *Fr.* Two Drinking Songs.

I built my soul a lordly pleasurehouse.   Tennyson.   NOBRP

I built on the sand.   Foundations.   Leopold Staff.   BLT, *tr. by* Czeslaw Milosz

I burned my life, that I might find.   Alchemist, The.   Louise Bogan.   APT-2; AWP; MoAmPo

I burst out laughing. (LL)   Lesson, The.   Charles Simic.   AF; HCAP

I buy the dark with my last fifteen cents.   Depression Days.   Pat Mora.   UnSA

I buzz through two security doors.   Visiting Father.   Juan Delgado.   TouFir

I, Caesar, when I learned of the fame.   Limerick.   *Unknown.*   PeLi

I Cain't Say No.   Richard Rodgers.   ReLy

I call that parent rash and wild.   Velvet Hand, The.   Phyllis McGinley.   OBCoV

I call you with honest words.   Bláthmac Mac Con Brettan.   NOIV   *Fr.* Poem to Mary, A.

I called at your.   From an Afternoon Caller.   Sister Mary Madeleva.   CRP

I called him to come in.   Evening.   James Wright (1927–80).   NOBA

I called one day—on Eden's strand.   Emily Dickinson in Southern California.   X. J. Kennedy.   NBLV; OBCoV

I called out of mine affliction.   Bible, *O.T.*   TrJP   *Fr.* Jonah.

I called the white donkey who hurt my left shoulder.   Calling the White Donkey.   Ray Gonzalez.   TouFir

I called today, Peter, and you were away.   Thermal Stair, The.   William Sydney Graham.   FaBoMo; HarvBoo

I called you because I could not stand alone.   Burden.   Peter Kane Dufault.   NoP-4

I came.   Riddles.   Ilya Abu Madi.   GraLe, *tr. by* Andrew Ghareeb

I Came a-Riding.   Reinmar von Zweter.   AWP, *tr. by* Jethro Bithell

I came a thousand miles to share your dream.   To Yuan Chen.   Po Chü-i.   CrYelRi, *tr. by* Sam Hamill

I came across a little demon.   Little Demon, The.   Zinaida Nikolayevna [*or* Nikolaevna] Gippius.   TCRP, *tr. by* Lubov Yakovleva

I came, alas! to conquer—not to die! (LL)   Philip Freneau.   NAAL-2v1; NAAL-3   *Fr.* House of Night, The.

I came as a question.   Harvest, The.   Shafiq Al-Kamali.   MAP, *tr. by* Sargon Boulus

I came at night to the dark house.   Survivors, The.   Tracey Herd.   NeBl

I came back from home yesterday, spent.   Consolation.   Tanure Ojaide.   EmeKit

I came, doctor, because my head hurts.   Poems from the Erotic Left.   Ana María Rodas.   TANSG, *tr. by* Zoë Anglesey

I came east to pay a son's respects.   Yen-chou City Wall Tower.   Tu Fu.   CrYelRi, *tr. by* Sam Hamill

I came first through the warm grass.   Bee's Last Journey to the Rose, The.   Brian Patten.   OTCP

I came from somewhere.   Poem of the Future Citizen.   José Craveirinha.   TTY, *tr. by* Dorothy Guedes and Philippa Rumsey

I came from the banks of the Ganges.   On the Tisza.   Endre Ady.   IQMS, *tr. by* Anton N. Nyerges

I Came from under the Earth.   *Unknown.*   WoPoe, *tr. by* Jean Guiart

I came / heavy with child in the fierce sun.   Waiheke 1972—Rocky Bay.   Christina Beer.   PeNZ

I came here as a wanderer.   Listening to a Flute in Yellow Crane Pavilion.   Li Po.   CrYelRi, *tr. by* Sam Hamill

I came here. I don't know you here.   Clark Coolidge.   PmAP   *Fr.* At Egypt.

I came home and found a lion in my living room.   Lion for Real, The.   Allen Ginsberg.   EmeKit; GLP; HCAP; RB

I came home from Vietnam.   Anna Grasa.   Bruce Weigl.   CDa

I came in the blinding sweep.   Frank Horne.   BPo   *Fr.* Letters [*or* Notes] Found near a Suicide.

I came in tonight and my building sighed.   Sleepless.   Eileen Myles.   WiU

I came into the City and none knew me.   Upper Chamber, An.   Frances Bannerman.   OBEV

I came into the pasture-ground.   Settlement.   Ingeborg Bachmann.   PoSu, *tr. by* Daniel Huws

I came into the world after Buddha.   Ungo Kiyo.   JDP, *tr. by* Yoel Hoffmann

I came late to the dharma.   Meal for the Monks, A.   Wang Wei.   CrYelRi, *tr. by* Sam Hamill

I came once to sit on Cold Mountain.   *Unknown.*   CoBCP

I came out a winner.   O Realm Bejewelled.   Forugh Farrokhzad.   WPOW, *tr. by* Amin Banani and Jascha Kessler

I came then to the city of my brethren.   Shore of Life, The.   Robert Fitzgerald.   VGW

I came to a field.   Pastoral.   Charles Simic.   NNaP

I came to a place where buildings were going up.   Errand.   David Morley.   NLP

I Came to a Valley in the Wilderness.   Baldomero Garcilaso de la Vega.   SpanPo, *tr. by* Edwin Morgan

I came to love, I came into my own. (LL)   Dream, The.   Theodore Roethke.   NIL-7; UnPo

I came to the east. I Come from a South.   Ruy Duarte de Carvalho.   PBMAP

I came to the end at an inappropriate midnight.   Post Operative.   Thomas William Shapcott.   BMAP

I came to the lake and six cranes were there.   Six Cranes at Dusk.   Henri Faust.   YaYoPo

I came to this world.   Rāmprasād Sen.   SinGod, *tr. by* Rachel Fell McDermott

I came to visit my friend.   Birds of Detroit.   Greg Pape.   PBCAP

I came to you with a greeting.   Morning Song.   Afanasi Afanasievich Fet [*or* Foeth].   AWP, *tr. by* Max Eastman

I came too late to the hills: They were swept bare.   Wilderness, The.   Kathleen Jessie Raine.   BoWoP; WPE

I came, yes, dear, dear.   Kore in Hades.   Kathleen Jessie Raine.   NALW

I came, you know, but your gate was locked.   Old Friend.   Dimitris Tsaloumas.   BMAP

I can afford to discriminate.   Discriminator, The.   Vernon Scannell.   OxBC

I can almost see.   On the Rouge.   Raymond Souster.   NOBC

I can barely imagine my mother.   Roses, The.   Jennifer Snyder.   BodElec

I can be.   Anything.   Brenda Brooks.   PoBW

I can be no more than four or five.   Auschwitz.   János Pilinszky.   IQMS, *tr. by* Peter Jay

I can break your heart. (LL)   Kid, The.   Ai.   GT; NoAM

I can close my eyes one heartbeat.   My Father's Country.   Joyce Lee.   NOBAu

I Can Cook, Too.   Betty Comden.   ReLy

I Can Dream, Can't I?   Irving Kahal.   ReLy

I can feel the loneliness.   Muneyuki.   OHPJ

I can feel the tug.   Punishment.   Seamus Heaney.   EmeKit; NAEL-5v2; NAEL-6v2; NoAM; NoP-4; OxAEP-2; PBCIP; PoPoPo

I Can Fly.   Felice Holman.   NTCP

I can give myself to her.   Akiko Yosano.   WPOW

I can hear it hum in silence.   Red Clock.   A., Jr. Poulin.   OPRER

I can hear the evening bell.   Returning by Night to Lu-Men.   Meng Hao Jan.   OHMPC, *tr. by* Kenneth Rexroth

I can hear the voice of Boris Vian, which is something because of course I never.   Paris Visitation.   Michael Brownstein.   FTOS

I can hear voices. Through my eyelids, light.   Open Windows.   Victor Hugo.   SxFrPo, *tr. by* E. H. Blackmore and A. M. Blackmore

I can imagine, in some otherworld.   Humming-Bird.   D. H. Lawrence.   NoAM; OWoS; OxBEV; RB

I can imagine someone who found.   California Hills in August.   Dana Gioia.   DiPo; InPK-6

I can lift gravity's stern glower.   Libby Houston.   NewEx

I can love both fair[e] and brown[e].   John Donne.   BASC; BoLoP; ESCV; NAEL-5v1; NAEL-6v1; NAEL-7v1; NAWM-5v1; NOSC; SoSe-8

I can make out the rigging of a schooner.   North Haven.   Elizabeth Bishop.   HCAP; PAI

I can manage so few of you.   Persons Unknown.   Aidan Carl Mathews.   BiHa

I can meet you.   Reservation Love Song.   Sherman Alexie.   PoPoPo

I Can Neither Hold You Nor Let You Go.   Sister Juana Inés de la Cruz.   SpanPo, *tr. by* Kate Flores

"I" Can Never Be a Great Man, An.   Stephen Spender.   OBMV

I can no longer ask how it feels.   Making of a Servant, The.   J. J. R. Jolobe.   PeSAV

I Can No Longer Care for the Dying.   Brenda J. Moossy.   PoArWo

I can no longer hold, my body grows.   Lover that Durst Not Speak to His M[istress], A.   James Shirley.   NOSC

I Can No Longer Untangle My Hair.   *Unknown.*   OHMPC, *tr. by* Kenneth Rexroth

I can not invent it,   "H. D."   NALW   *Fr.* Tribute to the Angels.

I can only say I have waited for you.   Time of Waiting in Amsterdam.   Ingrid Jonker.   BoWoP, *tr. by* Jack Cope and William Plomer

I can only think of him as.   As My Cat Eats the Head of a Field Mouse He Has Caught.   M. Loncar.   NAPBL

I can [*or* kan] nam[o]ore; my tale is at an ende. (LL)   Geoffrey Chaucer.   NAEL-5v1; NAEL-6v1   *Fr.* Canterbury Tales, The.

I can remember. I can remember.   Boy Actor, The.   Noël Coward.   OxBTC

I can remember looking up at him.   King Billy on the Walls.   Sheenagh Pugh.   AngWePo

I can remember wind-swept streets of cities.   Memory.   Margaret Walker Alexander.   GT

I can rest me where I am. (LL)   Ben Jonson.   NAEL-6v1; NAEL-7v1   *Fr.* Celebration of Charis in Ten Lyric[k] Pieces [*or* Peeces], A.

I can see buckra a come.   Italist Chant.   Rohan B. Preston.   WaCA

I can see he's not one of us. (LL)   Nazis.   Ira Sadoff.   LTA; OPRER

I can see how Abraham answered.   After Years of Feasting and No Sacrifice.   Linda Zisquit.   DTA

I can see the stones.   Masaoka Shiki.   OHMPJ

I can see the traces of old work.   House (Blown Apart).   David Shapiro.   BodElec

I can see your house, babe.   Curious.   Langston Hughes.   APT-2

I can sing a true song about myself.   *Unknown.*   ASW   *Fr.* Seafarer, The.

I can sing of myself a true song.   *Unknown.*   PoRA   *Fr.* Seafarer, The.

I can still hear Simone's voice in the deserted.   Gustave Thibon, How Simone Weil Appeared to Me 5.   Stephanie Strickland.   ExTi

I can still recall their laughter.   Spring's Last Drop, The.   Catherine Obianuju Acholonu.   HAWP; NAfrP

I can still remember my great aunt's old house and that pair of etchings.   Karl Marx Died 1883 Aged 65.   Antonio Cisneros.   TCLAP, *tr. by* Maureen Ahern and David Tipton

I can support it no longer.   Flower Herding on Mount Monadnock.   Galway Kinnell.   HeIP-4; LCAP-2; NOBA; NoAM

I can't answer because they are still there. (LL)   Louis MacNeice.   NOBL; NPeEn   *Fr.* Autumn Journal.

I can't appease Ashimbabbar, the moon god An.   Crimes of Lugalanne.   Enheduanna.   BoWoP

I can't bear a journey to the village.   Listless.   Tu Fu.   CrYelRi, *tr. by* Sam Hamill

I can't bear to watch your hips.   Argentarius.   ErotSp, *tr. by* Sam Hamill

I Can't Become a Buddhist.   Adrienne Su.   NAPBL

I Can't Believe That You're in Love with Me.   Clarence Gaskill.   ReLy

I can't believe you've come back.   Rise.   Brenda Shaughnessy.   AmPoNex

I can't break with the Dark One.   Mirabai [*or* Mira Bai].   BoWoP

I can't, Celinda, say I love.   To Celinda.   Elizabeth Singer Rowe.   BASC; PEW

I can't concentrate on poetry.   Kevin and Nicole.   Amanda Nazario.   HeMarv

I Can't Even Remember the Name.   Robert Penn Warren.   CRP   *Fr.* Ballad: Between the Boxcars.

I can't even see my hands in front of my face.   Diver for the NYPD Talks to His Girlfriend, A.   Richard Garcia.   TouFir; UrbNat

I can't feel the sunshine.   Lesbia Harford.   PoBW

I can't figure it out.   Stalker.   Jeanne Schinto.   Unle

I can't forget / How she stood at the top of that long marble stair.   Piazza di Spagna, Early Morning.   Richard Wilbur.   OxBSP; VGW

I can't get him out of my mind, out of my mind.   John Berryman.   NoP-4   *Fr.* Dream Songs.

I Can't Get Started.   Ai.   GT

I can't get started with you. (LL)   I Can't Get Started.   Vernon Duke.   APT-2; ReLy

I Can't Give You Anything but Love.   Dorothy Fields.   APT-2; ReLy

I Can't Have a Martini, Dear, but You Take One, or, Are You Going to Sit There Guzzling All Night?   Ogden Nash.   PoRA

I can't hear myself think in America no more!   Spearo's Blues (or: Ode to a Grecian Yearn).   Eugene B. Redmond.   NBV

I Can't Help You.   Ryszard Krynicki.   BLT, *tr. by* Stanisław Barańczak

I can't hold it, keep it.   Lake.   Ronald Albert Simpson.   CBAP

I can't just sit here.   Today Is Not the Day.   Audre Lorde.   AfrBLW

I can't keep my hands from stones.   Archeology.   Lorna Dee Cervantes.   TouFir

I can't keep my verbs straight. That's part of.   Part of What I Mean.   Frank Gaspar.   UrbNat

I can't live in this world.   Further Notice.   Philip Whalen.   PoM; VGW

I can't look at all at these lush fields of Hoho.   Walking the Plateau.   Lupenga Mphande.   NAfrP

I can't really remember now. The soundless foamed.   Thinking.   Jorie Graham.   BAP-97; ExTi

I can't remember.   Biology Teacher.   Zbigniew Herbert.   PoSu, *tr. by* John Carpenter

I can't remember—.   Origin.   "Eduard Georgievich Bagritzky [*or.*" Bagritsky].   TCRP, *tr. by* Vera Dunham

I can't remember how it happened.   Father and Son.   Robert Greacen.   PNI

I can't remember much forgetfulness. (LL)   Forgetfulness.   Hart Crane.   HarvBoo; NIL-7

I can't remember really envying them.   Fatherhood.   Joan Waddleton.   Prnts

I can't remember the name of the gaunt monk.   Deep Shit.   Daniel Tobin.   NAPBL

I can't remember why I stepped outside.   Pepper.   Joe Osterhaus.   NAPBL

I can't ridge it back again from char.   Death of the Kapowsin Tavern.   Richard Hugo.   NAAL-2v2

I can't say much about Richie Savalo.   Motorcycle Ward.   David Moolten.   BloBone

I can't say our garden is a delight.   Louisiana.   Steve Crow.   HATNAP

I can't say words like *kiss, cuss, miss,* or *bless.*   *Unknown.*   PriapPo, *tr. by* Richard W. Hooper   *Fr.* Priapus Poems, The.

I can't show my face.   It's the Talk of the Town.   A. J. Neiburg.   ReLy

I can't sleep Georgia.   Georgia.   Philippe Soupault.   SurPaPo, *tr. by* Mary Ann Caws and Patricia Terry

I can't sleep; no light burns.   Lines Written at Night During Insomnia.   Alexander Sergeyevich Pushkin.   AWTN, *tr. by* D. M. Thomas

I can't solve this.   How Callum Innes Paints.   Peter Finch.   Oth

I can't stand it, said the old man.   In the End.   Peter Everwine.   NNaP

I can't stand the wily magpie and all his extravagant stories!   *Unknown.*   CoBCP; ColAnChi, *tr. by* Burton Watson   *Fr.* Four *Tz'u* from Tun-huang.

I can't stand Willy wet-leg.   Willy Wet-Leg.   D. H. Lawrence.   RB

I can't stop eating sweets!   Candy Man, The.   Leslie Bricusse.   ReLy

I can't stuff myself anymore! (arguments in the form of noble people.   Not-France.   Carla Harryman.   PFTM-2

I can't talk to you now.   Failure.   Lina Tibi.   PoArWo, *tr. by* Subhi Hadidi and Nathalie Handal

I can tell by the way the trees beat, after.   Man Watching, The.   Rainer Maria Rilke.   RaBo, *tr. by* Robert Bly

I can tell you about this because I have held in my hand.   Drawn by Stones, by Earth, by Things That Have Been in the Fire.   Marvin Bell.   VCAP

I can think of William of Orange.   Centaurs, The.   Paul Muldoon.   BiHa

I can understand the haggard eyes.   Ted Hughes.   NoAM   *Fr.* Stations.

I can use it.   Song of the Crab Medicine-Bag.   *Unknown.*   STP, *tr. by* Jerome Rothenberg

I can usually feel at home in rooms.   Aleksandr Petrovich Mezhirov.   TCRP

I Can Wade Grief.   Emily Dickinson.   APN-2; ColAP; HeIP-4; NOBA

I can write the saddest verses tonight.   Poem 20.   Pablo Neruda.   BLPSL, *tr. by* Rene de Costa, Rigas Kappatos and Eleni Paidoussi

I canceled your funeral, Mother.   Elegy for My Mother.   Andrey [*or* Andrei] Andreievich Voznesensky [*or* Voznesenskii].   TCRP, *tr. by* F. D. Reeve and William Jay Smith

I canna tell what has come ower me.   Ich Weiss Nicht Was Soll es Bedeuten.   Heinrich Heine.   AWP, *tr. by* Alexander Macmillan

I Cannot.   Sara de Ibáñez.   TCLAP, *tr. by* Andrew Rosing

I cannot be ashamed.   Emily Dickinson.   TCAPo

I cannot be positive which. (LL)   Yak, The.   Joseph Hilaire Pierre Belloc.   MoBrPo; NBLV; NOBL; NoAM

I cannot be shaken into explanations for my life.   Pit, The.   David Ignatow.   BodElec

I cannot be sure what.   Testament.   Roland Mathias.   AngWePo

I cannot bear to put away.   Bamboo Mat.   Yuan Chen.   CrYelRi; ErotSp, *tr. by* Sam Hamill

I cannot blind myself.   How Can I Sing.   Odia Ofeimun.   HBAPE

I cannot bring a world quite round.   Wallace Stevens.   RaBo   *Fr.* Man with the Blue Guitar, The.

I cannot but ask, in the park and the streets.   Arthur Hugh Clough.   OBCoV   *Fr.* Spectator ab Extra.

I cannot change as others do.   Constancy.   John Wilmot, 2d Earl of Rochester.   OBEV

I Cannot Choose but Think upon the Time.   "George Eliot."   Son   *Fr.* Brother and Sister.

I cannot close my doors.   I Cannot.   Sara de Ibáñez.   TCLAP, *tr. by* Andrew Rosing

I cannot dance, O Lord.   Mechthild von Magdeburg.   WPoS

I cannot dance upon my Toes.   Emily Dickinson.   APN-2; NCAP; TCAPo

I cannot disclaim that string-thin, five-year-old boy.   Naval Base (Part III), The.   Jeremy Cronin.   AF

I cannot eat such little meat.   William Stevenson.   OBEV   *Fr.* Gammer Gurton's Needle.

I cannot find my way.   Credo.   Edwin Arlington Robinson.   ITBLP; MoAmPo; NAAL-2v2; OxBA; TAP; TrCP

I cannot find my way to Nazareth.   Fragment.   Yvor Winters.   OBSV

I cannot find such great delight.   Scorpions, The.   Alfonso X.   NAWM-7v1, *tr. by* Peter Dronke

I cannot forget.   Marichiko.   OHMPJ

I cannot forget.   Kenneth Rexroth.   APSN; APT-2   *Fr.* Love Poems of Marichiko, The.

I cannot forget my jo.   Poor French Sailor's Scottish Sweetheart, A.   William Johnson Cory.   EBVV

I Cannot Forget with What Fervid Devotion.   William Cullen Bryant.   APN-1

I cannot give the reasons.   Mervyn Laurence Peake.   NOxBChV

I cannot give you the Metropolitan Tower. Parting Gift. Elinor Wylie. APT-1; OxBA

I cannot go back now. Considering Poverty and Homelessness. Robert Sund. GifTon

"I cannot go to school today." Sick. Shel [or Shelley] Silverstein. ChAP

I cannot go to the bazaar. Prokosch in Tehran, 1978. Dominador I. Ilio. ReBoTo

I cannot go to you. Unknown. OHMPJ

I Cannot Grow. W. H. Auden. RB

I Cannot Lie Here Anymore. Nuala Ni Dhomhnaill. BiHa, tr. by Michael Hartnett

I cannot like you. Amaryllis Belladonna. Patricia Pogson. NLP

I cannot live with You. Emily Dickinson. APN-2; MoAmPo; NAAL-2v1; NAAL-3; NAAL-5; NOBA; OxBA; TCAPo; TRP

I cannot live without thee! (LL) To His Coy Love, A Canzonet. Michael Drayton. NOSC; PBRV

I cannot move. Malcolm. Welton Smith. BPo

I cannot ope mine eyes. Mattens. George Herbert. ESCV

I cannot praise the Doctor's eyes. On Hearing a Lady Praise a Certain Rev. Doctor's Eyes. George Outram. EBVV

I cannot praise Thee. By his instrument. Shall the Dead Praise Thee? George Macdonald. TrCP

I cannot reach it; and my striving eye. Childhood. Henry Vaughan. NOSC

I cannot say. Lady Izumi. WPoS

I Cannot Say the Name of the City. Slavko Mihalic. PoSu, tr. by Peter Kastmiler

I cannot see him plain, that far-off sire. Immigrant, The. Donald Davidson. FuPo

I cannot see the features right. Tennyson. NAEL-6v2 Fr. In Memoriam A. H. H.

I cannot see the short, white curls. Dumb World, The. William Henry Davies. OBWVE; OxBTC

I cannot send you back my hart. Answeare to my Lady Alice Edgertons Songe, Of I prethy send mee back my Hart, An. Lady Jane Cavendish. EMWP

I cannot sleep or take the air. Snowy Day, A. Unknown. OBWVE, tr. by H. Idris Bell

I cannot sleep. The long, long. Night Thoughts. Lu Yu. OHPC; WoPoe, tr. by Kenneth Rexroth

I cannot spare water or wine. Mithridates. Ralph Waldo Emerson. APN-1; NCAP

I cannot speak with my voice but with my voices. Foundation Stone. Alejandra Piznarnick. TANSG, tr. by Susan Bassnett

I cannot stand the man who wears. Ringless. Diane Wakoski. NALW

I cannot stay / And if I could it would be senseless. Tune: "Paying Homage at the Golden Gate." Sun Kuang-hsien. SuSp, tr. by Hellmut Wilhelm

I cannot stop thinking of Srirangam. Speaking of Places. Rajagopal Parthasarathy. OMIP

I cannot stop thinking of that old hat. My Grandfather's Hat. Judith Ortiz Cofer. TouFir

I cannot tell! (LL) On the Departure Platform. Thomas Hardy. NOBE; OxBTC

I cannot tell for I do not know. (LL) Two Pigeons. Unknown. OxNR; ReMoGo

I cannot tell the sorrows that I feel. He Was Acquainted with Grief. Jones Very. SacPr

I cannot tell who loves the skeleton. La Bella Bona-Roba. Richard Lovelace. BeJo; CaPo; EBEV; NOSC; OxBEV

I cannot tell you how it was. May. Christina Georgina Rossetti. NOBVV; NPeEn; OxBEV

I cannot think the thing farewell. (LL) Tennyson. HAP; NAEL-6v2; NOBE Fr. In Memoriam A. H. H.

I cannot view the bloom upon the rose. Blind. Norman V. Pearce. PoToHe

I care not a curse though from birth he inherit. Worker, The. Gerald Massey. EBVV

I care not for my Lady's soul. Lust of the Eyes, The. Elizabeth Siddal. VWP

I Care Not for These Ladies. Thomas Campion. HAP; NAEL-5v1; NAEL-7v1; NoP-4; NoSic; PoE; SCGP

I care nothing for battle odes. Anna Andreyevna Akhmatova. TCRP

I caressed your face with my fingers. Faithful Mirror. Gyula Illyés. IQMS, tr. by Adam Makkai and Donald E. Morse

I carouse all night. Song. Cho-yong. WoPoe, tr. by Okhee Yoo and Michael Stephens

I carried my wife inside me. Carrying My Wife. Moniza Alvi. NeBl

I Carried Statues. Ágnes Nemes Nagy. BoWoP; PoSu

I carried you to an island. Sea-bundle. Jennifer Rankin. BMAP

I carry a dead relationship around everywhere with me. This Dead Relationship. Katherine Pierpoint. EmeKit

I carry in the vases the yearning. Yearning of Karakashian, The. Chava Pinchas-Cohen. DTA, tr. by Miriyam Glazer

I carry me on my fingertips. Love Me. Amal Moussa. PoArWo, tr. by Khaled Mattawa

I carry the ground-hog along by the tail. Hunter, The. Raymond Souster. NOBC

I carry your heart with me (i carry it in). E. E. Cummings. TAP

I cartwheel like a knife. These Last Days. Katie Donovan. NeBl

I carve my defiant, raging pulse. Judas and Jesus. Endre Ady. IQMS, tr. by Peter Zollman

I carved your name on my watchband. Letters from a Man in Solitary. Nazim Hikmet. AF

I cast from me the medications. Loneliness. Franz Werfel. TrJP, tr. by Edith Abercrombie Snow

I cast the brush aside. Koha. JDP, tr. by Yoel Hoffmann

I catch. John Wills. HA

I catch myself trying. Untitled Blues; after a Photograph by Yevgeni Yevtushenko. Yusef Komunyakaa. ESEAA; GT; UnSA

I catch sight of the promised land. (LL) Ars Poetica. Claribel Alegría. LoL; TANSG, tr. by Darwin Flakoll

I caught a fella last night in the South Pacific. Radio. Harriet Monroe. APT-1

I Caught a Glimpse. Philip Levine. GeoHom

I caught a little ladybird. Christina Georgina Rossetti. FaBoVe; NPeEn

I caught a tremendous fish. Fish, The. Elizabeth Bishop. APT-2; ChAP; FaBoWP; HAP; HarvBoo; HeIP-4; InPK-6; MoASP; MoAmPo; NAAL-2v2; NAAL-5; NALW; NOBA; NoAM; NoP-4; PAI; PoE; PoPoPo; PoetW; RB; TFi; TRP

I caught this morning morning's mínion, king-. Windhover, The. Gerard Manley Hopkins. AmFaPo; CABP; ClHu; EBVV; GTBS-P; HAP; InPK-6; MoBrPo; NAEL-5v2; NAEL-6v2; NIL-7; NOBE; NOBVV; NPeEn; NoAM; NoP-4; OWoS; OxAEP-2; OxBEV; OxBSo; PeECV; PoE; PoPoPo; PoRA; RB; SCGP; SCV; SacPr; TFi; TOF; TRP; UnPo

I caught you, sir, having a look at her. Once in Love with Amy. Frank Loesser. ReLy

I cease not from desire till my desire. Hafiz [or Hafez]. AWP; TAL Fr. Odes.

I celebrate myself, and sing myself. Walt Whitman. ColAP; FaBoVe; MoAmPo; NAAL-3; NAAL-5; NAWM-7v2; NCAP; NIL-7; NoAM; NOBA; OxBA; PoE; PoPoPo; RaBo; SAmP; TCAPo Fr. Song of Myself.

I celebrate racquetball and sing racquetball. Song of Racquetball. David Allan Evans. MoASP

I celebrate Rhegion, Italy's tip. Tomb of Ibykos, The. Unknown. GrAn, tr. by Peter Jay

I certainly have lost something. Kenneth Koch. NoAM Fr. Days and Nights.

I chanced upon a new book yesterday. To Edward FitzGerald. Robert Browning. NAEL-5v2; NAEL-6v2; OxBSP

I, Chang P'ing-tzu, had traversed the Nine Wilds and seen their wonders. Bones of Chuang Tzu, The. Chang Heng. AWP, tr. by Arthur Waley

I change, and so do women too. Written on a Looking-Glass. Unknown. FaBoEE

I changed a grown man's clothes on a stripped ward. In a Building Named for a Governor. Christopher L. Dornin. CRP

I Chant of the Miracle Stag (Christian Version). Hungarian Oral Tradition. IQMS, tr. by Adam Makkai

I Chant of the "Miracle Stag" (Shamanistic Version). Hungarian Oral Tradition. IQMS, tr. by Adam Makkai

I charge you, O daughters of Jerusalem, if ye find my beloved, that ye tell him, that I am sick of love. (LL) Bible, O.T. OBVE; TOF Fr. Song of Solomon, The [or The Song of Songs].

I charge you, O winds of the West, O. Mathilde Blind. TrJP Fr. Love in Exile.

I charm thy life. Robert Southey. NOBRP Fr. Curse of Kehama, The.

I Cherish That Love. Kabir. WoPoe, tr. by Pritish Nandy

I chew a bitter cud, lying. Green Nostalgia. Thê Lũ' WoPoe, tr. by Nguyen Ngoc Bich

I Ching. Diane Di Prima. SeSe

I Ching, The. Unknown.
Marrying Maiden, The. PFTM-1

I choose a place that is unfrequented by men. (LL) Madly Singing in the Mountains. Po Chü-i. BLT; ChiP; WoPoe, tr. by Arthur Waley

I choose at random, knowing less and less. Old Atheist Pauses by the Sea, An. Thomas Kinsella. PAI

I choose back lanes for the pace they will impose. Sunday Morning. Robert Minhinnick. TCAWP

I choose to come every noon. Sauna 2. Karina Africa-Bolasco. ReBoTo

I chopped down the house that you had been saving to live in next summer. Variations on a Theme by William Carlos Williams. Kenneth Koch. NBLV; NIL-7; NIP-4; NoAM; PmAP; PoM

I chose the bed down-stairs by the sea-window for a good death-bed. Bed by the Window, The. Robinson Jeffers. APT-1

I chose the blonde from the chemist's, thirty-six.   Happening at Sordid Creek.   Peter Porter.   NoAM

I chose this. To be this.   Meteor.   Larissa Szporluk.   BAP-01

I chuck my Bible in the parlour fire.   Song.   Peter Redgrove.   EmeKit

I chuck their chins.   Anne Born.   NewEx

I clasp in the hot pit and bed.   Memorial Couplets for the Dying Ego.   George Barker.   EBEV

I clasp them, is because they die. (LL)   Mimnermus in Church.   William Johnson Cory.   NOBE; OBEV

I classed, appraising once.   Loved Once.   Elizabeth Barrett Browning.   ViWPN

I cleansed the mirror.   Renseki.   JDP, tr. by Yoel Hoffmann

I cleared mother's apartment of her urine-soaked rags today, while she wept.   When the Gods Put on Meter.   Cal Bedient.   BAP-01

I clearly hear the crowing of a rooster.   I Don't Know That Man.   Jan Polkowski.   AF, tr. by Michael March

I climb high to look out upon the world.   Ancient Airs.   Li Po.   CrYelRi, tr. by Sam Hamill

I Climb That Barren Ridge.   Unknown.   CoBCP, tr. by Burton Watson

I climb the black rock mountain.   Where Mountain Lion Lay [or Laid] down with Deer.   Leslie Marmon Silko.   TRP; VoR; WPOW

I climb the cold mountain by.   View from the Cliffs.   Tu Mu.   OHMPC, tr. by Kenneth Rexroth

I climb the hill: From end to end.   Tennyson.   EBVV; FHYEP   Fr. In Memoriam A. H. H.

I climb the road to Cold Mountain.   Unknown.   CoBCP

I CLIMB to the ridge of the Pei-mang Hills.   Ruins of Lo-yang, The.   Ts'ao Chih.   ChiP, tr. by Arthur Waley

I climbed a hill as light fell short.   Song of Honor [or Honour], The.   Ralph Hodgson.   MoBrPo

I climbed Lotus Mountain in the west.   Old Style Poem.   Li Po.   CrYelRi, tr. by Sam Hamill

I climbed the hillside to the lady's house.   Visiting Father and Friends.   Allen Ginsberg.   TaR

I climbed through woods in the hour-before-dawn dark.   Horses, The.   Ted Hughes.   NoAM

I climbed towards you on a ray of moonlight.   Fantasy under the Moon.   Emmanuel Boundzekei-Dongala.   PBMAP; TTY, tr. by Ulli Beier and Gerald Moore

I cling to the funk.   Funk.   Mary Weems.   SpirFl

I cling to this crippled tree.   Rivers, The.   Giuseppe Ungaretti.   PFTM-1

I close my door and trace the transformations of nature.   Ch'en Tzu-ang.   ColAnChi, tr. by Victor H. Mair   Fr. Poems of Reflection on the Vicissitudes of Life.

I close my eyes; waves blow against the pillow.   Moored for the Night at the Lan-chi Riverside Courier Station.   Yang Wan-li.   GifTon, tr. by Paul Hansen

I close the book on Crime and Punishment.   Crime and Punishment.   Paul Lake.   RA

I closed my book to listen.   Church Bells.   Clara Ann Thompson.   CBWP-2

I closed my eyes as I sat in the jet.   Day Flight.   Jack Davis.   CBAP

I Closed My Eyes to-Day and Saw.   William Force Stead.   OBMV

I collected the ears in my apron.   Ruth.   Elizaveta Kuzmina-Karavayeva.   ARWW, tr. by Catriona Kelly

I collide with sun and foam, a fierce.   L'Agulhas, A Walk.   Wilma Stockenström.   PeSAV, tr. by Rosa Keet

I come across from Mellstock while the moon wastes weaker.   His Visitor.   Thomas Hardy.   HarvBoo

I come among the peoples like a shadow.   Hunger.   Laurence Binyon.   OxBTC

I come back to the cottage in.   Only Years.   Kenneth Rexroth.   TAP

I come back to the geography of it.   Charles Olson.   NOBA; PoE   Fr. Maximus Poems, The.

I come from a family of businessmen, teachers, priests.   Origins.   Leonard Nolens.   TuT, tr. by Michael O'Loughlin

I Come from a South.   Ruy Duarte de Carvalho.   PBMAP

I come from Alabama wid [or with] my Banjo on my knee.   Oh! Susanna.   Stephen Collins Foster.   OBAL; TCAPo

I come from far away. I have forgotten my country.   Foreign Woman.   Rosario Castellanos.   WPOW, tr. by J. M. Cohen

I come from haunts of coot and hern.   Tennyson.   FHYEP   Fr. Brook; An Idyl, The.

I come from nothing.   Song of Derivations, A.   Alice Thompson Meynell.   CABP

I come from Salem County.   Cowboy Song.   Charles Causley.   PoRA

I come from the city of Boston.   Boston.   John Collins Bossidy.   FaBoEE; NBLV; OBAL; OBCoV; OxBoLi; PeLV

I come from Tu Ling, an unimportant man.   Testament.   Tu Fu.   CarOv, tr. by Carolyn Kizer

I come home at the end of four years of research.   Rice.   Chemmanam Chacko.   OMIP, tr. by K. Ayyappa Paniker

I come home from you through the early light of spring.   Adrienne Rich.   BoWoP   Fr. Twenty-one Love Poems.

I come home in the evening.   Nissim Ezekiel.   OBCoV   Fr. Songs for Nandu Bhende.

I come, I come–ye have called me long.   Voice of Spring, The.   Felicia Dorothea Hemans.   RWP

I come of a mighty race.   Hebrews.   James Oppenheim.   TrJP

I come off a little bit ventilated.   Wings.   John Godfrey.   PmAP

I come quietly.   Tree Stillness.   Karen L. Mitchell.   GT

I come the rushing wind that shook the place.   Promise, The.   Jones Very.   NCAP

I come to, knocking on the door of the cellar.   Moonshine Sonata.   John Tranter.   KGB

I come to read them poems.   In White America.   Lucille Clifton.   LTA

I Come to Supplicate.   Simeon ben, of Mainz Isaac ben Abun.   TrJP, tr. by Nina Davis Salaman

I come to tell you that my son is dead.   Prince, The.   Edgar Bowers.   CoAmPo

I come to the simplest things.   Retired Pilot to Himself, The.   Walter McDonald.   CDa

I come / to the White Painted Woman.   Puberty Rite Dance Song (Traditional).   Unknown.   BoWoP, tr. by Willis Barnstone

I come to thee by daytime constantly.   Guido Cavalcanti.   EaItPo, tr. by Dante Gabriel Rossetti

I come to thee, O God long since forgot.   Before the Statue of Apollo.   Saul [or Shaul] Tchernichowsky [or Tchernichovsky].   TrJP, tr. by L. V. Snowman

I come to you.   Prayer of a Woman in Charge of Berry Picking in Knights Inlet.   Unknown.   WPoS

I come to you with the vertigoes of the source.   Yvonne Caroutch.   BoWoP

I come upon it suddenly, alone.   Country Pathway, A.   James Whitcomb Riley.   CA

I compare the awesome flight of Nungesser to the limitless work of Picasso.   Painting.   André Salmon.   CuPo

I Concentrate on You.   Cole Porter.   ReLy

I confess.   Banners of the Heart.   Fawziyya Al-Sindi.   PoArWo, tr. by Joseph T. Zeidan

I confess, my friend, I am puzzled. (LL)   Meditatio.   Ezra Pound.   FaBoCh; OBAL

I conjour hem in the name of the Fader, and Sone.   Unknown.   MiEL

I Conquer the World with Words.   Nizar Qabbani.   MAP, tr. by Diana Der Hovanessian and Lena Jayyusi

I, Conscience, know this Mother-Wit me it taught.   William Langland.   NOCV   Fr. Vision of Piers Plowman, The.

I consecrate to thee. (LL)   Rose Aylmer.   Walter Savage Landor.   AWP; BoLoP; EnLoPo; HAP; NAEL-5v2; NAEL-6v2; NOBE; NOBRP; OBEV; OxAEP-2; SCGP; TFi; UnPo; WeW-3

I consider I really am through.   Limerick.   Elizabeth H. Lister.   PeLi

I consider myself a poet but im not reading poetry as you see.   Private Occasion in a Public Place, A.   David Antin.   PmAP

I consoled myself for not being able to describe.   No Consolation.   Norman MacCaig.   HarvBoo

I constantly aspire.   Mokudo.   JDP, tr. by Yoel Hoffmann

I consumed nights inside books.   Readings.   Armanda Guiducci.   CItWP, tr. by Cinzia Sartini Blum and Lara Trubowitz

I converse with my uncle.   Middle Age.   Luis Omar Salinas.   GeoHom

I could be a heart patient in my forties, waiting out winter.   Bad Karma.   Mary Crockett Hill.   AmPoNex

I could be in Paris or Vienna.   "Naum Korzhavin."   TCRP

I could become a great grinning host.   Poem.   Jack Kerouac.   CLPP

I could bring You Jewels—had I a mind to.   Emily Dickinson.   TAP

I could divide a leaf.   Propositions.   Phyllis Webb.   MoCV

I could do nothing: Nothing. Do you.   Child Taken from the Mother, The.   Minnie Bruce Pratt.   GLP

I could do wid one o' dem boogie tonight.   Antonette's Boogie.   Kendel Hippolyte.   WaCA

I could draw its map by heart.   Amor Loci.   W. H. Auden.   NOCV

I could eat you. (LL)   "Dove-Love."   Judith Wright.   NIL-7; NIP-4; NoAM

I could go seeking some secret part of nature, the bulbous tumor.   Abomination.   Mary Crockett Hill.   AmPoNex

I COULD have a job, but am too lazy to choose it;.   Lazy Man's Song.   Po Chü-i.   ChiP; OBVE, tr. by Arthur Waley

I could have been Lord Dacre or a balalaika-maker.   Peter Norman.   UV

I Could Have Danced All Night.   Frederick Loewe.   ReLy

I could have loved the winter.   Snow.   Innokenty Fiodorovich Annensky.   TCRP, tr. by Daniel Weissbort and Lubov Yakovleva

I could have painted pictures like that youth's. Pictor Ignotus. Robert Browning. CTC

I could have said obscurely: Cast about. *Unknown*. PriapPo, *tr. by* Richard W. Hooper *Fr.* Priapus Poems, The.

I could hear the music as I waited to be born. Aragon Ballroom, The. John Dickson. IllVoic

I could just as easily be nine years old. Night Beach. Vic Coccimiglio. InvLad

I could kill you right now. Lobo. Charles Lillard. NOBC

I could lie down in all that blue. Dreaming Horse. Silvia Curbelo. TouFir

I could love thee till I die. Platonic Lady, The. John Wilmot, 2d Earl of Rochester. NOSC

I could no deeper love. (LL) Song: "Love still has something of the sea." Sir Charles Sedley. NOBE; OxAEP-1; OxBEV

I could not dig: I dared not rob. Rudyard Kipling. FaBoEE; FaBoWar; NBLV; OPOU; PoWW; WoPoe *Fr.* Epitaphs of the War [1914–1918].

I could not hope / to touch the sky. Sappho. BoWoP

I could not look on Death, which being known. Rudyard Kipling. FaBoEE; FaBoTw; HarvBoo; NPeEn; PeFWW; WoPoe *Fr.* Epitaphs of the War [1914–1918].

I could not name a single blessing. Neither Shadow of Turning. Jack R. Clemo. NOCV

I could not see to see. (LL) Emily Dickinson. APN-2; BoWoP; ClHu; ColAP; HAP; HeIP-4; InPK-6; MoAmPo; NAAL-2v1; NAAL-3; NAAL-5; NALW; NAWM-7v2; NOBA; NoAM; NoP-4; OxBA; PAI; PoE; PoPoPo; PoRA; SAmP; SCV; SoSe-8; TAP; TCAPo; TFi; TOF; TRP; WeW-3

I could not swallow the lake. (LL) Swallow the Lake. Clarence Major. ESEAA; FTOS; GT; NAAAL; PmAP

I could resign that eye of blue. To Cloe. Martial. AWP; NBLV, *tr. by* Thomas Moore

I could say it's the happiest period of my life. Ongoing Story, The. John Ashbery. HCAP

I could see, far above my head, a black speck. Victor Hugo. SxFrPo, *tr. by* E. H. Blackmore and A. M. Blackmore

I could simply die, Priapus. *Unknown*. PriapPo, *tr. by* Richard W. Hooper *Fr.* Priapus Poems, The.

I could take the Harlem night. Juke Box Love Song. Langston Hughes. NAAAL; SAmP; TTTS

I could wish to be dead! Tragic Mary Queen of Scots, II, The. "Michael Field." OBMV

I couldn't do it again. Garden, The. Louise Glück. NoP-4

I couldn't have liked it more. (LL) I've Been to a Marvelous Party. Noël Coward. NBLV; ReLy

I couldn't stand sitting around reading. Can't Stand It. Vladimir Vladimirovich Mayakovsky [*or* Maiakovskii]. TCRP, *tr. by* Bernard Meares

I couldn't touch a stop and turn a screw. Thirty Bob a Week. John Davidson. CABP; EBEV; EBVV; FaBoTw; NOBE; NOBVV; NPeEn; NePenScot; OxBEV; OxBS; OxBTC

I Counsel You Beware. A. E. Housman. PeVV

I Count the Days Until I See You, Dear. Lesbia Harford. PoBW

I count your quick life by the minute, day, and year. Xenia: Stranger/Guest. David Gewanter. NAPBL

I Cover the Waterfront. Edward Heyman. ReLy

I crave an ampler, worthier sphere. Anno 1829. Heinrich Heine. AWP; OBVE, *tr. by* Charles Stuart Calverley

I craved for flash of eye and sword. Dreams. Israel Zangwill. TrJP

I crawl up the couch leg feeling. Whose Scene? Ruth Stone. BoWoP

I crawled in. Sorry. Julie Watson Nungarrayi. IBA

I crawled out of the wreckage whistling. Witness. Rachel Wetzsteon. AmPoNex

I cremated Sam McGee! (LL) Cremation of Sam McGee, The. Robert W. Service. BRP; NOBC; OBCoV; OBNV; TCAPo

I Cried for You. Abe Lyman. ReLy

I cried on my mother's breast, cried sore. Lament. Cathal Ó Searcaigh. ModIr, *tr. by* Seamus Heaney

I cried to dream again. (LL) William Shakespeare. OxAEP-1; RB *Fr.* Tempest, The.

I cried unto God with my voice, even unto God with my voice. Bible, *O.T.* AWP *Fr.* Psalms.

I crisscrossed with Monk. Jazz Fan Looks Back. Jayne Cortez. ESEAA

I cross a stream, cross another stream. Seeking out Hermit Hu. Kao Ch'i. CoBLCP, *tr. by* Jonathan Chaves

I cross the river to pluck hibiscus. *Unknown*. SuSp

I crossed. Thomas Bolt. YaYoPo *Fr.* Way Out of the Wood, The.

I crossed from last. Bunzan. JDP, *tr. by* Yoel Hoffmann

I crossed the deep sea. *Unknown*. WoPoe, *tr. by* John Lucas *Fr.* Egil's Saga.

I crouch over my radio. Speech. Henry Taylor. NBLV

I crowd all earth into a traveller's eye. Shillong. Bernard Gutteridge. PoWW

I cry. Woman's Mourning Song, The. Bell Hooks. ISC

I cry: / but you want comforting. Quatrain. Jelaluddin [*or* Jalal al-Din] Rumi. ArPe, *tr. by* Omar S. Pound

I cry I cry. No Categories! Stevie Smith. NoP-4

I cry to you beyond upon this bitter air. (LL) Immortal Autumn. Archibald MacLeish. MoAmPo; NAAL-2v2

I Cry Your Mercy, Pity, Love—Ay, Love! John Keats. CenSon (To Fanny.) BoLoP; EBEV; Son

I cup my ears. Senchojo. JDP, *tr. by* Yoel Hoffmann

I cupboard these pickled peaches in Time's despite. (LL) Homework. Mona Van Duyn. FFC; VCAP

I Curse in the Highest Sky. Violeta Parra. TANSG, *tr. by* Shaun Griffin and Emma Sepúlveda-Pulvirenti

I curse my bearing, childhood, youth. John Millington Synge. FaBoEE

I curse the optimistic views of Haig. Scribbled at a Cabinet Meeting. Sir Edward Carlson. FaBoVe

I cut the deck. Valentine for Ben Franklin Who Drives a Truck in California, A. Diane Wakoski. NoAM

I'd a dream to-night. Mater Dolorosa. William Barnes. NOBE; OBEV

I'd almost know, the nights I snuck in late. Fifteen to Eighteen. Marilyn Hacker. GLP

I'd already lost my hair. Now my sun. Corn, The. Daniel David Moses. HATNAP

I'd be better off bride to the River Lord! (LL) Lament of the Farm Wife of Wu. Su Tung-p'o (Su Shih). CoBCP; ColAnChi, *tr. by* Burton Watson

I'd been browsing the poetry section at Cody's. Berkeley, Late Spring. Forrest Hamer. GeoHom

I'd been on duty from two till four. Stand-to: Good Friday Morning. Siegfried Sassoon. FaBoTw

I'd been tired, under. Hitcher. Simon Armitage. EmeKit

I'd Buy You, Wisdom. Jan Kochanowski. WoPoe, *tr. by* Stanislaw Barańczak and Seamus Heaney *Fr.* Laments, The.

I'd buy you, Wisdom, with all of the world's gold. Jan Kochanowski. WoPoe, *tr. by* Stanislaw Barańczak and Seamus Heaney *Fr.* Laments, The.

I'd change his course forever. (LL) Danger, Men in Trees. Doris Safie. GraLe; PoArWo

I'd decided I initiate most. Sonnet 37. Phyllis Koestenbaum. FFC

I'd draw all this into a fine element,—a color. Rug, The. Michael McClure. NeAP

I'd gie them a' to King Charlie.' (LL) Bonnie House o' Airlie, The. *Unknown*. ESPB; OBEV; OxBB; OxBS

I'd Give a Dollar for a Dime. Eubie Blake. ReLy

I'd give everything I own for that gazelle. Gazelle, The. Samuel Ha-Nagid. WoPoe, *tr. by* Peter Cole

I'd give it five stars. Revelation: The Movie. Elton Glaser. PBCAP

I'd have to ask the grass to let me sleep. (LL) To Dorothy. Marvin Bell. InvLad; VCAP

I'd have to piss through my eyes to cry for you. I Just Missed the Bus and I'll Be Late for Work. Ariel Dorfman. AF

I'd heard so much good. Desert Reservation. Barry Lopez. GifTon

I'd like to be a tree. My father clinked. Tree. Andrew Hudgins. InvLad

I'd like to be with you. Longing. Lilly Sauter. AuPH, *tr. by* Lowell A. Bangerter

I'd like to get away, Junior. There's a Small Hotel. Richard Rodgers. ReLy

I'd like to go away alone. I'd Like to Go Alone. Alena Synková. INSAB

I'd like to go home. Summer Nostalgia. Virginia E. Escandor. ReBoTo

I'd like to have a wild bird. Five Wishes. Anne Porter. KGB

I'd like to have a word. Book of Lies, The. James Tate. YaYoPo

I'd like to know everything. Jazz. Angela Ball. BAP-01

I'd like to live with you. Marina Ivanovna Tsvetayeva [*or* Tsvetaeva]. BoWoP

I'd like to paint monkey-eaters. Monkey-eaters. Takahashi Mutsuo. PFTM-2, *tr. by* Hiroaki Sato

I'd like to / Pull. Intelligent Sheepman and the New Cars, The. William Carlos Williams. OBAL

I'd like to taste my life again in little. Return to Paris. Jules Supervielle. MFP, *tr. by* Martin Sorrell

I'd like to write one poem but darkness is down. In the Red Book. Kelvin Corcoran. Oth

I'd Love to Be a Fairy's Child. Robert Graves. ChAP

I'd love to make them linger on, those nymphs. Faun in the Afternoon, A. Stéphane Mallarmé. SxFrPo, *tr. by* E. H. Blackmore and A. M. Blackmore

I'd make a bed for you. Labasheedy (The Silken Bed). Nuala Ni Dhomhnaill. CABP; CIP-2, *tr. by the* author

I'd rather be the ship that sails. Ship That Sails, The. *Unknown*. PoToHe

I'd rather have fingers than toes. On Digital Extremities. Frank Gelett Burgess. PeLi

I'd rather my fist be made of steel. Last Word, The. Imamu Amiri Baraka. UnSA

I'd rather see than be one! (LL)   Purple Cow, The.   Frank Gelett Burgess. BRP; NBLV; NTCP; OBAL; OBCA; OBCoV; OxIBACP; TCAPo; TFi; TLR

I'd run about / on the desert.   Her Elegy.   *Unknown.*   BoWoP; STP

I'd say goodbye to the business of living. (LL)   Good God, What a Night That Was.   Petronius Arbiter.   BoLoP; PGA; PasH, *tr. by* Kenneth Rexroth

I'd say he'd had too much.   Runaway Cow, A.   Cathal Ó Searcaigh.   ModIr, *tr. by* Patrick Crotty

I'd sell my soul for that fawn.   Samuel Ha-Nagid.   ErotSp, *tr. by* Harris Lenowitz and Jerome Rothenberg

I'd shoot the man who pulled up slowly in his hot car this morning.   If I Had a Gun.   Gig Ryan.   BMAP

I'd smoke in the freezer.   Shoplifters.   Maura Stanton.   ReTh

I'd still have been their song. (LL)   Ahmad al-Mushari Al-'Udwani.   BBASP; MAP, *tr. by* Charles Doria and Hilary Kilpatrick   *Fr.* Signs.

I'd thwack you well to cure your pride, my Woman of Three Cows! (LL)   Woman of Three Cows, The.   *Unknown.*   NOIV; OBCoV, *tr. by* James Clarence Mangan

I'd toddle safely home and die—in bed. (LL)   Base Details.   Siegfried Sassoon.   FaBoWar; MoBrPo; NPeEn; OxBEV; OxBSP; PeFWW

I'd 20/20 the dogs.   Happy Hour.   Walid Bitar.   KGB

I'd wake up starved on the day of the match.   Reflections on Hillsborough in Memoriam.   T. H. Naisby.   NOBAu

I'd wed you without herds, without money, or rich array.   Cashel of Munster.   William English.   BIrV; OBEV, *tr. by* Sir Samuel Ferguson

I damn such fools!—Go, go you're bit. (LL)   Day of Judgement, The.   Jonathan Swift.   BIrV; ChIV-1; NOBE; NOEC; NPeEn; OBSV; OxBEV; SCGP

I dance on all the mountains.   Gary Snyder.   GeoHom; NOBA   *Fr.* Myths and Texts.

I danced on "Shop Around."   Boppin' is Safer than Grindin'   Thulani Davis.   GT

I Danced to the Rumble of the Drum.   Elevena Burbank.   AiP

I dare not ask a kiss[e].   To Electra.   Robert Herrick.   CaPo; OBEV

I dare not tell it in words, not even in these songs. (LL)   Earth, My Likeness.   Walt Whitman.   APN-1; OxBA

I dashed around on a Dragon-Steed.   Dragon-Steed, The.   Sándor Weöres.   IQMS, *tr. by* Adam Makkai and Donald E. Morse

I daydream, melancholy at the windowsill.   Remembering.   Yuan Chen.   CrYelRi; ErotSp, *tr. by* Sam Hamill

I ddin't know what estrangement.   In Emily's Manner.   Armanda Guiducci.   CItWP, *tr. by* Cinzia Sartini Blum and Lara Trubowitz

I declare myself.   Nu-plastik Fanfare Red.   Judith Rodriguez.   BMAP

I dedicate this poem.   Daughters.   "Astra."   BrRo

I defended Genet on the subject of terror in London.   Edoardo Sanguineti.   ItPo, *tr. by* Gayle Ridinger   *Fr.* Reisebilder.

I defy you Wallace Stevens.   I Defy You.   Shirley Lim.   UnSA

I delight in the prime of a boy of twelve.   Epigram.   Strato [*or* Straton].   GrAn, *tr. by* Thomas Meyer

I demand a thatched house.   Poet's Request, The.   *Unknown.*   BIrV, *tr. by* John Montague

I demand that the human race.   Poem.   Jack Kerouac.   CLPP

I depend on the stars.   For Sleep.   Larry Eigner.   FTOS

I derive endless satisfaction from thinking, saying, and singing the follow.   Of of Titmouse.   Michael Portnoy.   HeMarv

I descend on my love.   How God Comes to the Soul.   Mechthild von Magdeburg.   WPoS, *tr. by* Oliver Davies

I desire that my body be.   When I Am Dead.   George MacBeth [*or* Macbeth].   OxBTC

I Despair Because I Don't Have Words.   Patrizia Valduga.   CItWP, *tr. by* Cinzia Sartini Blum and Lara Trubowitz

I despise my friends more than you.   To an Enemy.   Maxwell Bodenheim.   TrJP

I despise neo-epic verse sagas.   Callimachus.   GrAn

I detest innocent women.   Thoughts on Innocence.   Olga Nolla.   TANSG, *tr. by* Paula Vega

I did but look and love awhile.   Enchantment, The.   Thomas Otway.   OBEV

I did but prompt the age to quit their [*or* thir] clogs.   On the Detraction Which Followed upon My Writing Certain Treatises.   John Milton.   NoP-4; Son

I did expect a ring. (LL)   Hope.   George Herbert.   ChIV-2; NPeEn; OxBEV; WeW-3

I did my best; / farewell. (LL)   Sparrow, The.   William Carlos Williams.   LCAP-2; VGW

I did not cry, my good mother, the song in my hand burst in tears.   Silent Words, The.   Haim [*or* Chaim *or* Khayim] Guri [*or* Gouri].   MHP, *tr. by* Ruth Finer Mintz

I did not fall from the sky.   Women of Dan Dance with Swords in Their Hands to Mark the Time When They Were Warriors, The.   Audre Lorde.   NAAL-2v2; NALW; NoAM

I did not know death was so strange. (LL)   Child Dying, The.   Edwin Muir.   FaBoTw; GTBS-P; PoWW; RB; WoPoe

I did not know where you kept your heart.   "Case of Assault", A.   Lydia Stephanou.   BoWoP, *tr. by* Kimon Friar

I did not live until this time.   To My Excellent Lucasia, On Our Friendship.   Katherine Philips.   BASC; LW; MeLP; NALW; NOSC; NPeEn; NoP-4; OxBEV; PBRV; PEW; PoBW; WPE; WPOW

I did not love him for myself alone.   Trinity.   "Michael Field."   VWP

I did not love you anymore, yet I never stopped.   Sadistic Love.   Julio Herrera y Reissig.   BLPSL, *tr. by* Rene de Costa, Rigas Kappatos and Eleni Paidoussi

I Did Not Manage To Save.   Jerzy Ficowski.   HP; PoSu, *tr. by* Keith Bosley and Krystyna Wandycz Bosley

I Did Not Notice.   Franz Wright.   LCAP-2

I did not see Lannes at Ratisbon.   Heroes.   Sorley MacLean (Somhairle MacGill-Eain).   FaBoTC; FaBoWar

I did not stand at the altar, I stood.   Wedding Vow, The.   Sharon Olds.   MPUn

I did not take the road to the capital.   Tune: "Partridge Sky"—Written at the Po-shan Monastery.   Hsin Ch'i-chi.   SuSp, *tr. by* Irving Y. Lo

I did not think that I should find them there.   Clerks, The.   Edwin Arlington Robinson.   APN-2; MoAmPo; NAAL-2v2

I did not touch your night, or your air, or dawn.   Pablo Neruda.   TCLAP, *tr. by* Stephen Tapscott

I did not want to be old Mr. Uncle Dog; the Poet at 9.   Robert Sward.   CoAP; VGW

I didn't come out my mummy's tummy.   What Jenny Knows.   Jackie Kay.   NOxBChV

I didn't expect you today.   Letter.   Iosif Pavlovich Utkin.   TCRP, *tr. by* Lubov Yakovleva

I didn't get much sleep last night.   Underwear.   Lawrence Ferlinghetti.   EmeKit; OBAL

I didn't have anything to think about. (LL)   Kenneth Rexroth.   APSN; APT-2   *Fr.* Love Poems of Marichiko, The.

I didn't have this face then.   Portrait.   Cecília Meireles.   TCLAP, *tr. by* Luiz Fernández García

I didn't just read the Bible, I lived it.   Charisma.   Ai.   ExTi

I Didn't Know About You.   Duke Ellington.   ReLy

I didn't know him.   Suicide on Pentwyn Bridge.   Gillian Clarke.   AngWePo

I didn't know my own face.   On a Portrait of the Poet.   Po Chü-i.   CrYelRi, *tr. by* Sam Hamill

I Didn't Know What Time It Was.   Richard Rodgers.   ReLy

I didn't know where the temple was.   Visiting the Temple of Accumulated Fragrance.   Wang Wei.   CoBCP, *tr. by* Burton Watson

I didn't know whether from Phoenician sands.   Glass, The.   Esther Ettinger.   DTA, *tr. by* Mariana Barr

I didn't let the blue ship run aground a wreck.   Noah.   Margit Szécsi.   IQMS, *tr. by* Agnes Arany-Makkai

I didn't make you know how glad I was.   Servant to Servants, A.   Robert Frost.   NAAL-2v2

I didn't think about the house much.   Honeysuckle.   J. C. Bloem.   TuT, *tr. by* Desmond Egan

I didn't want a monument.   Invasion of Grenada, The.   William Daniel Ehrhart.   CDa

I didn't want this, not.   Marina Ivanovna Tsvetayeva [*or* Tsvetaeva].   OBVE   *Fr.* Poem of the End.

I didnt thing I'd.   I Was Surprised to Find Myself Out Here & Acting like a Crow.   *Unknown.*   STP, *tr. by* Johnny John and Jerome Rothenberg

I die.   Koson.   JDP, *tr. by* Yoel Hoffmann

I die, and yet not dies in me.   Dhu 'l-Nún.   TOF

I Die because I Do Not Die.   Saint Theresa [*or* Teresa] of Avila.   TOF, *tr. by* E. Allison Peers

I die for Your holy word without regret.   Elegy.   Antonio Enriquez Gomez.   TrJP

I die I die the Mother said.   Grey Monk, The.   William Blake.   PeECV

I Die of Thirst While at the Fountain Side.   François Villon.   WoPoe, *tr. by* David Curzon and Jeffrey Fiskin

I died as mineral and became a plant.   Jelaluddin [*or* Jalal al-Din] Rumi.   TOF

I died for Beauty—but was scarce.   Emily Dickinson.   APN-2; AWP; BoWoP; MakPoe; MoAmPo; NAAL-2v2; NAAL-3; NAAL-5; NAWM-7v2; NOBA; PAI; SAmP

I died with the first blow and was buried.   Autobiography.   Dan Pagis.   PoSu, *tr. by* Stephen Mitchell

I died with the first blow and was buried.   Autobiography.   Dan Pagis.   FIT, *tr. by* Robert Friend

I dig my teeth into the crust of this land.   Leave in Mid-Winter.   John Short.   FaBoWar

I dine at Blenheim twice a week. (LL)   *Var. authors.*   FaBoEE; NOBL; OBCoV; PeLV   *Fr.* Balliol Rhymes.

I disapprove even of eloquent / Myrtis.   Korinna [*or* Corinna].   WPOW

I discovered the evidence.   Crazy Horse Speaks.   Sherman Alexie.   UnSA

I discovered the sweet lovely lady.   Albrecht von Johannsdorf.   GePo

I Discuss the Past and Not the Present. What Men of Today Are Worth Discussing? May the Men of the Past Not Blame Me for My Discussion of Them.   Chin Nung.

"Who bought a mountain and became a hermit there?"   CoBLCP

I DISMOUNT from my horse at the Hsi-lin Temple.   Visiting the Hsi-lin Temple.   Po Chü-i.   ChiP, *tr.* by Arthur Waley

I do believe. (LL)   Mother Goose.   FaBoVe; OxNR

I do believe that die I must.   His Creed.   Robert Herrick.   BeJo

I do but ask that you be always fair.   Edna St. Vincent Millay.   Son

I do confess thou'rt smooth and fair.   To His Forsaken Mistress.   Sir Robert Aytoun [*or* Ayton].   OBEV

I do direct the night.   Portrait of Myself with Arshile Gorky and Gertrude Stein.   Jerome Rothenberg.   FTOS

I do errands early.   Siesta.   Leslie Anne McIlroy.   AmPoNex

I do in thee delight. (LL)   Edward Taylor.   NAAL-2v1; NAAL-3   *Fr.* God's Determinations [touching his Elect].

"I Do Like To Be Beside the Seaside."   Dame Edith Sitwell.   PFTM-1   *Fr.* Façade.

I Do Love My Charlie So.   Zelda Sayre Fitzgerald.   AiP

I do my best to smile at spring, small flowers.   White Days.   Reginald Shepherd.   GT

I Do Not.   Michael Palmer.   BodElec

I do not ask—for you are fair.   Ovid.   AWP, *tr.* by F. A. Wright   *Fr.* Amores.

I Do Not Believe That David Killed Goliath.   Charles Reznikoff.   ChIV-1

I do not call it his sign.   Mahadevi.   WPoS; WoPoe, *tr.* by Jane Hirshfield

I do not care if.   *Unknown.*   OHMPJ

I do not care; some day I *shall* not think; I shall not *be*! (LL)   Quiet House, The.   Charlotte Mew.   BrRo; EBEV; HarvBoo; NALW; NPeEn

I do not catch these subtle shades of feeling.   Wife of All Ages, The.   Edith Nesbit.   VWP

I do not complain of suffering for Love.   Knowing Love in Herself.   Hadewijch.   WPoS, *tr.* by Oliver Davies

I do not count the hours I spend.   Waldeinsamkeit.   Ralph Waldo Emerson.   APN-1; NOBA

I do not do nature.   Manifesto.   Peter E. Murphy.   UrbNat

I do not, do not think I can. (LL)   Infant Song.   Charles Causley.   NOxBChV; OxBC

I do not doubt you would have liked.   Mother's Day.   Daisy Zamora.   LoL, *tr.* by Margaret Randall

I do not dream of Sussex downs.   Home Thoughts.   Denis Glover.   PeNZ

I do not enjoy.   Rufinus.   GrAn

I do not feel the peace of the saints.   Bird in the Hand, A.   Vassar Miller.   CRP

I do not feel this suffering as Cesar Vallejo. I am not.   I Am Going to Talk About Hope.   César Vallejo.   TCLAP, *tr.* by Robert Bly

I do not have a body.   Bill Herbert.   NewEx

I do not hold a mirage in my hand—.   What's Not in the Heart.   Abba Kovner.   AF, *tr.* by Shirley Kaufman

I do not know English.   I Do Not.   Michael Palmer.   BodElec

I do not know if, climbing some steep hill.   Opportunity.   Helen Hunt Jackson.   SWaP

I do not know if the color of the day.   Poem of Attrition, A.   Etheridge Knight.   GT

I do not know / In what strange far off earth.   Holocaust 1944.   Anne Ranasinghe.   GotH

I do not know it for sure, but I suppose.   I Do Not Know It for Sure.   Jaime Sabines.   TCLAP, *tr.* by Isabel Bize

I do not know more than the Sea tells me.   Achilles' Song.   Robert Duncan.   FTOS

I do not know much about gods; but I think that the river.   T. S. Eliot.   AiP; NoP-4; OxBA   *Fr.* Four Quartets.

I do not know the power of my hand.   When I Know the Power of my Black Hand.   Lance Jeffers.   ISC; NBV

I do not know what has destroyed you.   Destruction.   Shakuntala Hawoldar.   HAWP

I do not know what promise it makes to him. (LL)   Birth of Love.   Robert Penn Warren.   APT-2; UnPo; VCAP

I do not know where I have been.   Hell, Well, Heaven.   Mongane Wally Serote.   PBMAP

I do not know which god sent me.   Kofi Awoonor.   PBMAP; VCWP   *Fr.* Night of My Blood (1971).

I do not know your name, I have never seen.   Lyrical Letter to the Other Woman.   Alfonsina Storni.   TCLAP, *tr.* by Dana Stangel

I do not like my state of mind.   Symptom Recital.   Dorothy Parker.   APT-1

I do not like the circus.   Yevgeny [*or* Evgenii] Mikhailovich Vinokurov.   TCRusP, *tr.* by Anthony Rudolf

I do not like the empty vocabulary.   In the Dunes.   Aleksandr Aleksandrovich Blok.   TCRP, *tr.* by Geoffrey Thurley

I do not like the way you slide.   Egg Thoughts.   Russell Hoban.   NTCP; OTCP

I do not live in the depthless cool.   Turning of the Year, The.   Delaina Thomas.   OpBo

I do not love my country. Its abstract splendour.   High Treason.   José Emilio Pacheco.   TCLAP, *tr.* by Alastair Reid

I do not love [*or* like] thee, Doctor Fell.   Doctor Fell.   Thomas [*or* "Tom"] Brown.   FaBoEE; NBLV; OBCoV; OBVE; OxBEV; OxNR

I do not love thee, Dr. Fell.   Truth at Last, The.   Fred Chappell.   WoPoe

I do not love thee!—no! I do not love thee!   I Do Not Love Thee.   Caroline Elizabeth Norton.   OBEV

I do not love to wed.   Poet Loves a Mistress, but Not to Marry, The.   Robert Herrick.   CaPo

I do not mean the symbol.   Woman Who Could Not Live With Her Faulty Heart, The.   Margaret Atwood.   LCAP-2

I do not need thy food, but thou dost mine.   My Meat and Drink.   Jones Very.   InvLi

I do not regret, complain, or weep.   Sergey [*or* Sergei] Aleksandrovich Yesenin [*or* Essenin].   TCRP

I do not suffer this pain as Vallejo.   I Am Going to Speak of Hope.   César Vallejo.   PoetW, *tr.* by Clayton Eshleman

I do not thank Thee, Lord.   Thanks Be to God.   Janie Alford.   PoToHe

I do not think Grandmother or Grandfather.   Favorite Grandson Braid.   Phillip [*or* "Phil"] William George.   VoR

I do not think of you lying in the wet clay.   In Memory of My Mother.   Patrick Kavanagh.   BIrV; CIP-2; NoAM; RaBo

I do not think the ending can be right.   But That Is Another Story.   Donald Justice.   CoAP; NoP-4

I do not think you will.   Challenge to the Reader, A.   Tad Richards.   SwNoth

I do not understand.   In the Synagogue.   Cynthia Ozick.   TaR

I do not understand the world, father.   On the Subject of Poetry.   W. S. Merwin.   PAI

I do not visit his grave. He is not there.   Peachstone.   Dannie Abse.   AngWePo; OxBC; WeW-3

I do not want only.   Poem.   Colleen Thibaudeau.   NOBC

I Do Not Want the Ceiling of the Sistine Chapel.   Felicity Napier.   Prnts

I do not want to be reflective any more.   Wolves.   Louis MacNeice.   NoAM; OxBTC

I do not want to pour out my heart any more.   Marcus Aurelius.   Charles Hubert Sisson.   OxBC

I do not waste what is wild.   Empty Kettle.   Louis Oliver.   HATNAP

I do not wear white as a general rule.   Trousseau.   Vona Groarke.   MFPA

I do not weep over this hooted blood.   Refusal to Inter.   Mohammed Khaïr-Eddine.   PFTM-2, *tr.* by Pierre Joris

I do not wish that anyone were here.   Postcard from a Travel Snob.   Sophie Hannah.   MFPA

I do not wish you joy without a sorrow.   Birthday Wish, A.   Dorothy Nell McDonald.   PoToHe

I do not witness myself.   Fifth Amendment, The.   Susan Hahn.   ExTi

I do remember some things.   Manna.   James Tate.   GM

I do seem to zee Grammer as she did use.   Grammer's Shoes.   William Barnes.   EBVV

I do something consciously.   Jackson Mac Low.   PmAP   *Fr.* Pronouns, The—A Collection of 40 Dances—For the Dancers.

I do tricks in order to know.   With My Crowbar Key.   William Stafford.   CoAmPo

I do want to be a famous poet.   Fourth Rome, The.   Nikolai Alekseievich Klyuyev [*or* Kliuev *or* Klyuev].   CAGL, *tr.* by Simon Karlinsky

I don't ask to be forgiven.   How Stars Start.   Al Young.   ESEAA

I don't believe in anything.   California Dreaming.   Rochelle Nameroff.   SwNoth

I don't believe in becoming a Buddha.   Drinking Wine.   Mo Shih-lung.   CoBLCP, *tr.* by Jonathan Chaves

I don't believe in God and fate.   Bulat Shalvovich Okudzhava.   TCRP

I Don't Believe in Human-tales.   Brian Patten.   OTCP

I don't believe the sleepers in this house.   Cabin in the Clearing, A.   Robert Frost.   APT-1

I don't believe there's such a thing.   I Don't Believe in Human-tales.   Brian Patten.   OTCP

I don't blow the trumpet or step up to the speaker's platform.   Revolution.   Enrique Lihn.   TCLAP, *tr.* by Jonathan Cohen

I don't care.   *Unknown.*   OHMPJ

I don't care if there's powder on my nose.   It Never Entered My Mind.   Richard Rodgers.   ReLy

I don't care if you're married, I'll still get you.   *Unknown.*   STP   *Fr.* Kiowa "49" Songs.

I don't care what the weatherman says.   Jeepers Creepers.   Johnny Mercer.   ReLy

I don't care who.   I Gotta Right to Sing the Blues.   Ted Koehler.   ReLy

I don't complain that time passes too soon. Tune: "Green Jade Cup." Kung Tzu-chen. SuSp, *tr. by* An-yan Tang

I don't dare start thinking in the morning. Blues at Dawn. Langston Hughes. SAmP

I don't enclose the universe in my grasp. Vladimir Shchirovsky [*or* Shchirovskii*]*. TCRP

I don't even know. Saigyo. WoPoe, *tr. by* Steven D. Carter

I don't expect to touch heaven. Sappho. SaLy, *tr. by* Diane Rayor

I don't feel like reading another book. Yang Wan-li. ColAnChi; SuSp, *tr. by* Jonathan Chaves   *Fr.* Songs of Depression.

I don't for example consider that poets are. Iain Sinclair. Oth   *Fr.* Ebbing of Kraft, The.

I don't give a damn if some Thracian ape strut. Archilochus. GrAn; WoPoe, *tr. by* Stuart Silverman

I don't give a duck. (LL) Poem in Time of Winter. Ray Mathew. NOBAu; OBCoV

I don't go out. Reply to Reizan Osho. Muso Soseki. EaWin, *tr. by* W. S. Merwin

I don't have any medals. I feel their lack. James [*or* Jim] Harrison. BodElec   *Fr.* Letters to Yesenin.

I don't have any place to come up through. Shaman Song. Luswat. STP, *tr. by* James Koller

I don't have any seed to cast about the world. Patrizia Cavalli. ItPo, *tr. by* Gayle Ridinger

I Don't Have the Energy. Artie Gold. NOBC

I don't imagine I'll manage to express Sunyata. I Fail as a Dharma Teacher. Diane Di Prima. BB

I don't kiss the guy who guzzles wine beside the brimming bowl and talks battles and tearful war. Elegy 2. Anacreon. CAGL, *tr. by* Peter Bing and Rip Cohen

I don't know. Basho. EH, *tr. by* Robert Hass

I Don't Know. Daria Menicanti. CItWP, *tr. by* Cinzia Sartini Blum and Lara Trubowitz

I don't know. After Seeing Paintings in a Small Book by T. C. Cannon (1946–1978). Alice Sadongei. HATNAP

I don't know about you, / but I'm sick of good poems. A. R. Ammons. HCAP   *Fr.* Sphere.

I don't know any greatest treat. Parterre, The. E. Harriet Palmer. NOBL; PeLV

I don't know anymore the night terrible anonymity of death. Sun the First. Odysseus Elytis. GifTon, *tr. by* Olga Broumas

I don't know anything about God but what the human record tells. Even on Sunday. Robin Blaser. FTOS

I don't know as I get what D. H. Lawrence is driving at. Poem. Frank O'Hara. LCAP-2

I Don't Know Enough About You. Peggy Lee. ReLy

I Don't Know Exactly. Eva Svankmajerová. SurWo, *tr. by* Katerina Pinosová

I don't know exactly how it started. You're Getting to Be a Habit with Me. Harry Warren. ReLy

I don't know how he came. Osawatomie. Carl Sandburg. OxBA

I don't know how I lost my amulets. Nujoum Al-Ghanim. PoArWo, *tr. by* Clarissa C. Burt   *Fr.* Trespasses.

I don't know how it was. Mystery. "Yehoash." TrJP, *tr. by* Marie Syrkin

I don't know. I wonder how long this life of mine. I Don't Know. Daria Menicanti. CItWP, *tr. by* Cinzia Sartini Blum and Lara Trubowitz

I don't know if the old people will return one day. Legacies. Heberto Padilla. TCLAP, *tr. by* Andrew Hurley and Alastair Reid

I don't know now if it was kindness—we do. Fresh Stain. Tess Gallagher. ExTi

I don't know politics but I know the names. Introduction. Kamala Das. NALW; WPOW

I don't know somehow it seems sufficient. Gravelly Run. A. R. Ammons. CoAP; NAAL-2v2; NoAM; VCAP

I Don't Know That Man. Jan Polkowski. AF, *tr. by* Michael March

I don't know the wisdom others seem to need. Konstantin Dmitrievich Balmont. TCRP

I don't know what day it is. Ship Without a Sail, A. Richard Rodgers. ReLy

I don't know what I should do—I'm of two minds. Sappho. SaLy, *tr. by* Diane Rayor

I don't know what it was you gave my husband to eat. Horse butcher, The. Pierre McOrlan. MFP, *tr. by* Martin Sorrell

I don't know what the final buzzer means. Triple Overtime. Lucinda Roy. GT

I don't know what to say to you, neighbor. Winter. Marie Ponsot. ExTi

I don't know where the owls go when they leave this place. Gary Young. GeoHom   *Fr.* Days.

I don't know where you come from. Letter to a Roving Poet. Amadou Lamine Sall. NAfrP

I don't know who I am or was I know only my chaos. Eyes. Juan Gelman. TCLAP, *tr. by* Robert Marquez and Elinore Randall

I don't know who it is. Lovely Étan, The.   *Unknown.* NOIV

I don't know who that man is. Pilate's Wife. Nina Kossman. GI

I Don't Know Why (I Just Do). Fred E. Ahlert. ReLy

I don't know why I'm so crazy. Why? Myra Cohn Livingston. CA

I don't know why you tell me I'm drunk. Toxaoci. STP

I don't know your stories. This one here. Feud, The. Sydney Lea. RA

I don't like a tall general, swaggering. Archilochus. SaLy, *tr. by* Diane Rayor

I don't like my teeth. I feel they are too small. They give the wrong impression. First Impression. Joe Wenderoth. NAPBL

I don't like this, being carried sideways. Sleeping Compartment. Norman MacCaig. EmeKit

I don't like weddings. Wedding in the Courthouse, The. Kathleen Norris. MPUn

I don't love flowers / I love women. Lilac by the Museum on St. Wenceslas Square, The. Vitĕzslav Nezval. AF, *tr. by* Ewald Osers

I don't love you. Imamu Amiri Baraka. NAAAL

I don't mind eels. Eel, The. Ogden Nash. NTCP

I don't need to know any more about death. White Crane. Dean Young. IllVoic

I don't need your photograph. Very Thought of You, The. Ray Noble. ReLy

I don't / pity this man, I love him. Vanzetti. Charles Buckmaster. CBAP

I don't plow my southern acre. Thinking of the Way Home, a Song. Lo Yin. SuSp, *tr. by* Geoffrey R. Waters

I don't recall his name. Contra, The. Sandra M. Castillo. TouFir

I don't remember being very, very good or horrid. But I do. "C" ing in Colors: Red. Safiya Henderson-Holmes. SpirFl

I Don't Remember Christmas. Richard Maltby, Jr. ReLy

I don't remember him. Yevgeny [*or* Evgenii] Mikhailovich Vinokurov. TCRusP, *tr. by* Daniel Weissbort

I don't remember seeing it at night. It would look like. Remembering the Pacific. Diane Wakoski. GeoHom

I don't remember train whistles. Narrative of the Life and Times of John Coltrane: Played by Himself, A. Michael S. Harper. SeSe

I don't remember where he was taking us. Chase, The. Richard Tayson. AmPoNex

I don't seek salvation in poetry. Khikhimora. Nikolai Ivanovich Glazkov. TCRP, *tr. by* Daniel Weissbort

I don't sell for nothing less. (LL) Lady in the Pink Mustang, The. Louise Erdrich. HATNAP; OPRER; ReTh

I don't / share my recipes with them. Only the Hand That Stirs Knows What's in the Pot. Luz Maria Umpierre. PueRic

I don't sleep. All night. Mirabai [*or* Mira Bai]. BoWoP

I don't think that I believe in "gay life." Sonnet No. 22. Mark Ameen. GLP

I don't travel much in these parts. Passing Ch'ien-hsi as Military Adviser in the Third Month of the Year Yi-ssu. T'ao Ch'ien [*or* T'ao Yuan-ming]. SuSp, *tr. by* Eugene Eoyang

I don't understand how Janis Joplin did it, how she made her voice. Penalty for Bigamy Is Two Wives, The. William Matthews. SwNoth

I don't understand it myself. Too Lazy to Write Poetry. Chu Yün-ming. CoBLCP, *tr. by* Jonathan Chaves

I don't understand the conflict of the winds. Alcaeus [*or* Alkaios]. SaLy, *tr. by* Diane Rayor

I Don't Want Any More Visitors. Ingrid Jonker. HAWP, *tr. by* Ingrid Jonker

I don't want to be a nun.   *Unknown.* BoWoP

I Don't Want to be a Soldier.   *Unknown.* PoWW   *Fr.* Soldiers' Songs of the First World War.

I don't want to hear you beg. Isn't It Funny? Essex Hemphill. GLP

I don't want to return a sad spirit. Luis Cernuda. CAGL, *tr. by* Rick Lipinski

I don't want to see you. Erosion. Claribel Alegría. TANSG, *tr. by* Darwin Flakoll

I Don't Want to Walk Without You. Jule Styne. ReLy

I don't want trouble, but the rutabagas. Potato. Michelle Boisseau. SpudSo

I don't wish you were. Never Land. Yusef Komunyakaa. ReTh

I don't wonder where you are anymore. Vespers. Louise Glück. HarvBoo

I don't write haiku. I'm no good at silence. Phantom Haiku/Silent Film. Jacqueline Osherow. ExTi

I done been 'roun' to evvy spot. Belle Layotte. George Washington Cable. APN-2

I Done Got So Thirsty That My Mouth Waters at the Thought of Rain. Patricia Jones. BlSi

I done try go to church, I done go for court. One Wife for One Man. Frank Aig-Imoukhuede. PBA

I doubt if you knew. Rescue, The. John Logan. CoAP

I doubt not God is good, well-meaning, kind. Yet Do I Marvel. Countee Cullen. APT-2; AmFaPo; BPo; InvLi; NAAAL; NAAL-2v2; NAAL-5; NIL-7; NoAM; SSLK; Son; TAP; TTY

I drag a boat over the ocean. Lal Ded [*or* Lalla]. BoWoP; WPoS

I drag my heavy heart. From the Heights. Li Shang-yin. CrYelRi, *tr. by* Sam Hamill

I drag my shirt across the floor. Eager Street. Kendra Kopelke. AiP

I drank at night on East Slope, sobered up, got drunk again. Tune: "Immortal by the River." Su Tung-p'o (Su Shih). ColAnChi, *tr.* by J. R. Hightower

I drank cool water from the fountain. Raisin, The. Donald Hall. TAP

I drank firmly. His Father's Hands. Thomas Kinsella. PoE

I draw aside flowery bedside curtains. To the Tune: Sands of the Washing Stream. Li Ch'ing-chao. CrYelRi, *tr.* by Sam Hamill

I draw hats on rabbits, sew women back. Prestidigitator 2, The. Al Young. NBV

I draw my sight in when I sleep. Evening Song. Elizabeth Madox Roberts. APT-1

I draw the willow. Masumi Kato. JDP, *tr.* by Yoel Hoffmann

I dreaded that first Robin, so. Emily Dickinson. APN-2; HAP; MoAmPo; NAAL-2v1; NAAL-3; NAAL-5

I Dream. Valentine Penrose. SurWo, *tr.* by Roy Edwards

I Dream Awake. José Martí. TCLAP, *tr.* by Elinore Randall

I dream'd a morning dream—a torrent brought. Dream, A. Charles Tennyson Turner. OxBSo

I dream'd I lost a pearl, and so it prov'd. On the Death of My Dear Friend and Play-Fellow Mrs. E. D. Having Dream'd the Night Before I Heard Thereof that I Had Lost a Pearl. Jane Barker. EMWP; PoBW

I Dream'd in a Dream. Walt Whitman. APN-1

I dream'd that I walk'd in Italy. Going Back Again. "Owen Meredith." VerBaPo

I Dream I'm the Death of Orpheus. Adrienne Rich. NALW

I dream in the intimate semi-darkness of an afternoon. Visit. Léopold Sédar Senghor. PBMAP

I dream my love goes riding out. Song for a Dancer. Kenneth Rexroth. TAP

I dream no ill of death. (LL) Confession of Faith. Elinor Wylie. APT-1; MoAmPo

I dream of. Memory of a Dream From the Year 1963. Tadeusz Rózewicz. PoSu

I dream of a headless man. Richard Murphy. NOIV *Fr.* Battle of Aughrim, The.

I dream of a red-rose tree. Women and Roses. Robert Browning. NAEL-5v2; NAEL-6v2

I dream of coupling. Dream of Pairing. Ntozake Shange. GT

I dream of Jeanie with the light brown hair. Jeanie with the Light Brown Hair. Stephen Collins Foster. APN-2

I dream of journeys repeatedly. Far Field, The. Theodore Roethke. ColAP; NAAL-2v2; NoAM *Fr.* North American Sequence.

I Dream of St. Francis. Peter Orlovsky. BB

I dream of Serenity. I'm a Dreamer. Kattie M. Cumbo. BISi

I dream of you to wake: would that I might. Christina Georgina Rossetti. OxBSo *Fr.* Monna Innominata.

I dream with open eyes. I Dream Awake. José Martí. TCLAP, *tr.* by Elinore Randall

I dream. Youth is beyond the rain she arrives. I Dream. Valentine Penrose. SurWo, *tr.* by Roy Edwards

I dreamed a dream, and in my dream, I heard. Snapping of the Bow, The. James David Corrothers. NAAAL

I dreamed a dream: I dreamt that I espied. Arthur Hugh Clough. NOBVV

I dreamed a dreary dream this night. Braes of Yarrow, The. *Unknown.* ESPB; OxBB

I dreamed a man unknown to me in a city no. 30th Year Dream. Gregory Corso. BodElec

I dreamed all my dreams. If I Had You. Ted Shapiro. ReLy

I dreamed, and saw a modern Hell, more dread. Pessimist's Vision, The. Constance Naden. VWP; ViWPN

I dreamed I called you on the telephone. For the Dead. Adrienne Rich. NAAL-2v2

I dreamed I held / A sword against my flesh. Kasa no Iratsume. BoWoP; OHPJ; WPOW

I dreamed I lay in a little gray boat. Waking. Katharine Pyle. OBCA

I dreamed I met you beside the wall. Heraldic Decoration. Julio Herrera y Reissig. TCLAP, *tr.* by Andrew Rosing

I Dreamed I Moved among the Elysian Fields. Edna St. Vincent Millay. NoP-4

I dreamed I saw a little brook. Vision of Children, A. Thomas Ashe. EBVV

I dreamed I saw Joe Hill last night. Joe Hill. Alfred Hayes. UnPo

I dreamed I stood upon a little hill. Two Loves. Lord Alfred Bruce Douglas. CAGL

I dreamed I was a barber; and there went. Barber, The. John Gray. NOBVV

I dreamed I was a dog in a dog show. Dog Show. Laurie Anderson. OxWW

I dreamed it rose. Black Buoy. Robert H. Davis. HATNAP

I dreamed last night. Sit Down, You're Rockin' the Boat. Frank Loesser. ReLy

I dreamed last night I dreamed, and in that sleep. Le Rêve. Edgar Bowers. CoAmPo

I dreamed last night / that I was married. Journey Away, A. Carl Rakosi. PFTM-1

I dreamed of him last night, I saw his face. Dead Poet, The. Lord Alfred Bruce Douglas. GSo

I dreamed of Ted Williams. Dream of a Baseball Star. Gregory Corso. VGW

I dreamed of war-heroes, of wounded war-heroes. Heroes, The. Louis Simpson. OBWP

I dreamed [*or* dream'd] that, as I wandered [*or* wander'd] by the way. Question, The. Shelley. OBEV; OxBEV

I dreamed [*or* dream'd] this mortal part of mine. Vine, The. Robert Herrick. BeJo; CaPo; EroLit; NAEL-5v2; NAEL-6v1; NAEL-7v1

I dreamed [*or* dreamt] a dream the other night. Lowlands. *Unknown.* OxBoLi

I dreamed Ted Williams. Dream of a Baseball Star. Gregory Corso. BB; PmAP

I dreamed that, buried in my fellow clay. Dream, The. *Unknown.* NOEC

I Dreamed That in a City Dark as Paris. Louis Simpson. CoAP

I dreamed that someone's coming. Someone like No One Else. Forugh Farrokhzad. WPOW, *tr.* by Deirdre Lashgari

I dreamed that you were standing. Heraldic Decoration. Julio Herrera y Reissig. BLPSL, *tr.* by Rene de Costa, Rigas Kappatos and Eleni Paidoussi

I dreamed the heavy sky suddenly opened a gate. Dream. Vahan Tekeyan. AF, *tr.* by Diana Der Hovanessian and Marzbed Margossian

I dreamed the nymph that o'er my fancy reigns. Sir William Alexander, Earl of Stirling. NOSC *Fr.* Aurora.

I dreamed: the world had grown quiet and was awaiting the end. Dream. Novella Nikolaevna Matveyeva [*or* Matveieva]. TCRP, *tr.* by Deming Brown

I dreamed there was a bird. Bird, The. Susan M. Whitmore. AmPoNex

I dreamed there was an Emperor Antony. William Shakespeare. UnPo *Fr.* Antony and Cleopatra.

I dreamed there would be Spring no more. Tennyson. NOBE *Fr.* In Memoriam A. H. H.

I dreamed you were my child, and I had come. Dream, The. Paul Petrie. TAP

I dreamt a dream the other night. Lowlands. *Unknown.* OxBoLi

I dreamt a dream; till morning light. Arthur Hugh Clough. NAEL-5v2; NAEL-6v2 *Fr.* Dipsychus [and the Spirit].

I Dreamt a Dream—What can it mean? William Blake. FHYEP; RACG *Fr.* Songs of Experience.

I Dreamt a Pig. Dacia Maraini. CItWP, *tr.* by Cinzia Sartini Blum and Lara Trubowitz

I dreamt about you last night. Dream. *Unknown.* STP, *tr.* by Armand Schwerner

I dreamt ane dreame, o that my dreame wer trew! Dreame, Ane. Alexander Montgomerie. NePenScot

I dreamt her sensual proportions. Death of Venus, The. Robert Creeley. NOBA

I DREAMT I climbed to a high, high plain. Pitcher, The. Yüan Chên. AWP; ChiP, *tr.* by Arthur Waley

I dreamt I drank too much lemonade. Cruising. Gig Ryan. BMAP

I dreamt I held the laughter-loving girl. Macedonius. GrAn

I dreamt I saw great Venus by me stand. Dream of Venus, A. Bion. AWP, *tr.* by Leigh Hunt

I dreamt. I saw three ladies in a tree. Three Ladies, The. Robert Creeley. NeAP

I Dreamt I Was a Donkey Boy Again. Amin Al-Rihani. GraLe

I dreamt it all, from end to end, the carriageway. Dublin Girl, Mountjoy, 1984. Dermot Bolger. BiHa

I dreamt last night. For No Clear Reason. Robert Creeley. VGW

I dreamt last night. Fierce Dream, The. Jeffrey Wainwright. DiPo

I dreamt last night of you, John-John. John-John. Thomas Macdonagh. AWP

I dreamt (no "dream" awake—a dream indeed). In Sleep. Alice Thompson Meynell. BrRo

I dreamt of cooking roast pig. I Dreamt a Pig. Dacia Maraini. CItWP, *tr.* by Cinzia Sartini Blum and Lara Trubowitz

I dreamt of the old house. To My Sister. Olga Fiodorovna Berggolts [*or* Bergholts]. BoWoP; TCRusP, *tr.* by Daniel Weissbort

I Dreamt of Visiting Relatives. Amelia Rosselli. CItWP, *tr.* by Cinzia Sartini Blum and Lara Trubowitz

I dreamt one night—it was a horrid dream. Out of the Frying Pan into the Fire. James Henry. NOBVV

I dreamt that I was God Himself. Ezra Pound. FaBoEE

I dreamt you stood upon the trap of the world. On the Death of Ronald Ryan. Bruce Dawe. BMAP

I dreamt your suicide note. Bag of Mice. Nick Flynn. AmPoNex; NAPBL

I dremt that madness passes like a dream. (LL)   That Which We Call a Rose. Michael Dransfield. CBAP; NOBAu

I dressed my father in his little clothes.   Boat, The.   Robert Pack.   CoAP

I Drift in the Wind.   Ingrid Jonker.   HAWP; WPOW, *tr. by* Jack Cope

I drift off in a panel van waiting for Isolda.   Spread Rhythm.   C. D. Wright. LCAP-2

I drink but don't get drunk.   Drunkenness.   "Anvari."   WoPoe, *tr. by* Geoffrey Squires

I drink champagne early in the morning.   Cordon Negro.   Essex Hemphill. CAGL; GLP

I drink the bitterness of primroses and autumn skies.   Feasts, The.   Boris Leonidovich Pasternak.   TCRP, *tr. by* Yakov Hornstein

I drink to military asters, to all that I'm censured about.   Osip Emilevich Mandelstam [*or* Mandelshtam].   TCRP

I drink to the asters of war, to everything for which I stand accused.   I Drink to the Asters of War.   Osip Emilevich Mandelstam [*or* Mandelshtam]. TCRusP, *tr. by* John Glad

I drink to your glory my god.   U Tam'si Tchicaya.   PBMAP; TTY   *Fr.* Epitomé (1962).

I drink, wherever I go, to the charms.   Gracey Nugent.   Turlough Carolan [*or* O'Carolan].   OxBEV, *tr. by* Austin Clarke

I drink your love.   Luke Roma.   IBA

I drive fast, uphill.   Coming Over Coldwater.   Carol Muske.   GeoHom

I drive home with the books that I will read.   Edgar Bowers.   VCAP   *Fr.* Autumn Shade.

I drive my carriage from the Upper East Gate.   Unknown.   CoBCP

I drive round the dirty streets of Freetown.   Poet Among Those Who Are Also Poets.   Syl Cheney-Coker.   NAfrP

I drive Westward. Tumble and loco weed.   James Vincent Cunningham.   APT-2; NoAM

I drop the torch of rags in a bucket of water.   New Crops for a Free Man.   Ai. BodElec

I dropp'd here three weeks ago, yes—I know.   Mad Soldier, The.   Edward Wyndham Tennant.   FaBoWar

I dropped beside him. Taut as is the cord.   Razglednica (4).   Miklós Radnóti. IQMS, *tr. by* Iain MacLeod

I dropped my sail and dried my dropping seines.   Mass at Dawn.   Roy Campbell.   OxAEP-2

I drops in to see young Ben.   Chorus of a Song That Might Have Been Written by Albert Chevalier.   Max Beerbohm.   OBCoV; UV

I droun twa. (LL)   Tweed and Till.   Unknown.   FaBoCh; NPeEn; OxBSP

I drove three thousand miles to ask a question. No answer, naturally.   Karl Shapiro.   BodElec   *Fr.* Bourgeois Poet, The.

I drove to Little Hunger promontory.   Little Hunger.   Richard Murphy.   BIrV

I drove today along the foothills.   Los Angeles.   James Harms.   GeoHom

I du believe in Freedom's cause.   James Russell Lowell.   APN-1; NCAP   *Fr.* Biglow Papers, The.

I dug a grave under an oak-tree.   Amy Lowell.   BoWoP   *Fr.* Dreams in War Time.

I dug and dug amongst the snow.   Christina Georgina Rossetti.   FaBoEE

I dug, beneath the cypress shade.   Grave of Love, The.   Thomas Love Peacock.   OxAEP-2; OxBSP

I dug in with all the spirit of spring.   Knowing.   Mary Coghill.   BrRo

I dug you artless, I dug you out. Did you re-do? You dug me less, art.   Music for Homemade Instruments.   Harryette Mullen.   BAP-01

I dug your bull.   Saturday Night Decades.   Sterling Plumpp.   IllVoic

I dwell alone—I dwell alone, alone.   Autumn.   Christina Georgina Rossetti. BrRo; VWP

I dwell in Grace's court[e].   Robert Southwell.   ChIV-2; NoSic

I dwell in Possibility.   Emily Dickinson.   APN-2; EnlH; HeIP-4; NALW; NAWM-7v2; NCAP; NOBA; NoAM; OxBA; TCAPo

I dwell in seclusion and observe the creative process.   Ch'en Tzu-ang. ColAnChi, *tr. by* Victor H. Mair   *Fr.* Poems of Reflection on the Vicissitudes of Life.

I dwell in the forest nursing a long illness.   Ch'en Tzu-ang.   ColAnChi, *tr. by* Victor H. Mair   *Fr.* Poems of Reflection on the Vicissitudes of Life.

I dwell in this leaky Western castle.   Dowager.   John Montague.   ModIr

I dwell, who fain would be where she is gone. (LL)   Giovanni Boccaccio. AWP; EaltPo, *tr. by* Dante Gabriel Rossetti   *Fr.* Sonnets.

I Dye Alive.   Robert Southwell.   SacPr

I, E—S—J—, poet by vocation, now make my first will and.   Owl of Minerva Takes Flight in the Evening, The.   E. San Juan, Jr.   ReBoTo

I eat alone.   Michael McClintock.   HA

I Eat Kids Yum Yum!   Dennis Lee.   TLR

I eat my peas with honey.   Peas.   Unknown.   NTCP

I eat oatmeal for breakfast.   Oatmeal.   Galway Kinnell.   EmeKit

I eat with them at table.   From the Viking Museum.   John Peck.   HarvBoo

I edged back against the night.   High Tide.   Jean Starr Untermeyer.   MoAmPo

I embraced the summer dawn.   Arthur Rimbaud.   TTTS, *tr. by* Enid Rhodes Peschal   *Fr.* Illuminations.

I employ the blind mandolin player.   Music, A.   Wendell Berry.   VGW

I encountered the crowd returning from amusements.   Resolution of Dependence.   George Barker.   FaBoTw

I end in shadow.   Bob Boldman.   HA

I end the only lit and waitful thing in miles of / darkened houses. (LL)   Lew Welch.   NeAP; PoM   *Fr.* Taxi Suite.

I enjoy dancing.   Clare Pollard.   NeBl   *Fr.* Friday Night at the End of a Millennium, A.

I enter the lit house. (LL)   Parliament Hill Fields.   Sylvia Plath.   HCAP; NALW

I enter this moment in retrospect, already.   Narcissus Learning the Words to This Song.   Reginald Shepherd.   WiU

I entered into unknowning.   Stanzas Concerning an Ecstasy Experienced in High Contemplation.   Saint John of the Cross.   TOF, *tr. by* K. Kavanaugh and O. Rodrigues

I entered it before I understood it.   Spring at Nant Dywelan.   Bobi Jones. OBWVE, *tr. by* Joseph P. Clancy

I entered my parlor one bright summer morn.   Humming-Bird, The.   Mary E. Tucker.   CBWP-1

I entered the streetcar of poetry.   Streetcar Named Poetry, A.   Yevgeny Aleksandrovich Yevtushenko [*or* Evtushenko].   RusPo, *tr. by* Robert Arthur Douglas Ford

I Entered Where I Did Not Know.   Saint John of the Cross.   SpanPo, *tr. by* Willis Barnstone

I entered where I did not know.   I Entered Where I Did Not Know.   Saint John of the Cross.   SpanPo, *tr. by* Willis Barnstone

I entered with a torch before me.   Fleance.   Michael Longley.   CIP-2; PNI

I envied my wife her nightly visions.   Fish.   Moniza Alvi.   NeBl

I envy.   Issa.   EH, *tr. by* Robert Hass

I Envy Not Endymion.   Sir William Alexander, Earl of Stirling.   Son   *Fr.* Aurora.

I envy not in any moods.   Tennyson.   CABP; CAGL; FHYEP; NAEL-6v2; NAWM-7v2   *Fr.* In Memoriam A. H. H.

I envy not the dead that rest.   Mary Elizabeth Coleridge.   VWP

I Envy the Cracked, Black Basalt.   Katrina Porteous.   NeBl

I Epiktetos was born a slave, deformed.   On Epiktetos the Stoic.   Unknown. GrAn, *tr. by* Peter Jay

I escort.   Praises of the Bantu Kings (1–10).   Jerome Rothenberg.   FTOS

I even embrace the pain. (LL)   Remembering.   Yuan Chen.   CrYelRi; ErotSp, *tr. by* Sam Hamill

I even feel sure you will assist me again, Master of insight and beauty. (LL)   John Berryman.   InvLi; PAI; UnPo   *Fr.* Eleven Addresses to the Lord.

I, even I, am he who knoweth the roads.   De Aegypto.   Ezra Pound.   APT-1; VGW

I even I know the Eastern Gate of Heaven.   Unknown.   AWP   *Fr.* Book of the Dead.

I exchange eyes with the Mad Queen.   Harry Crosby.   APT-2; SPE   *Fr.* Vision.

I expand my heart so that.   Dawn.   Gabriela Mistral.   TANSG, *tr. by* Maria Jacketti

I expect every one.   Wonderful Guy, A.   Richard Rodgers.   ReLy

I expect to be praised.   Intermission from Wednesday.   Pedro Juan Pietri. PueRic

I Expect You Think This Huge Dark Coat.   Christine M. Donald.   GLP

I expected him to look dead in the casket.   Elegy.   Richard Hugo.   GM

I Expected My Skin and My Blood to Ripen.   Wendy Rose.   WPOW

I expected this face but did not predict it.   Elijah Speaking.   Doug Fetherling. NOBC

I Explain a Few Things.   Pablo Neruda.   PoetW, *tr. by* Nathaniel Tarn

I explain the silvered passing of a ship at night.   Stephen Crane.   APN-2; TCAPo   *Fr.* War Is Kind.

I explore you, my flesh, my gold, my body, that I spy on you, my raw naked paper.   Last Stroll, The: Homage to Pascoli.   Edoardo Sanguineti. PFTM-2, *tr. by* Richard Collins

I explored the grounds with monks this evening.   Visiting the Monastery at Lung-men.   Tu Fu.   CrYelRi, *tr. by* Sam Hamill

I face the yellow flowers.   Painting of Chrysanthemums in the Boneless Style of Hsü Ch'ung-ssu, A.   Yün Shou-p'ing.   CoBLCP, *tr. by* Jonathan Chaves

I Fail as a Dharma Teacher.   Diane Di Prima.   BB

I fail to cut your hands.   Matisse: Blue Nude, 1952.   Dionisio D. Martinez. TouFir

I fail to see the ancients before my time.   Song on Climbing the Gate Tower at Yu-chou, A.   Ch'en Tzu-ang.   SuSp, *tr. by* Wu-Chi Liu

I failed my exam, which is difficult.   James Tate.   EmeKit   *Fr.* I Am a Finn.

I fain would kiss my Julia's dainty leg.   Robert Herrick.   *See* Fain would kiss my Julia's dainty leg

I Fall in Love Too Easily.   Jule Styne.   ReLy

I, Fan-chih, wear my socks inside out.   Wang Fan-chih.   SuSp

I fasted for some forty days on bread and buttermilk. Pilgrim, The. W. B. Yeats. RB

I fasted three canonical hours. Brian [or Bryan] Merriman [or Merryman]. BIrV, tr. by Frank O'Connor Fr. Midnight Court, The.

"I favor your enterprise," the soup ladle says. You Know What I'm Saying? Irving Feldman. BAP-97

I fear at night he will not come again. (LL) Bartholomew Griffin. NoSic; SCGP Fr. Fidessa, More Chaste than Kind[e].

I fear, Mr. Lear, you're a clot. Limerick. Eric Swainson. PeLi

I fear that appearances are worshipped throughout France. Rat and the Elephant, The. Jean de La Fontaine. OBVE, tr. by Marianne Moore

I fear that I shall never make. Poet-Tree. Earle Birney. OxBC

I fear that you will never know or guess. (LL) Unknown. BoWoP; ChiP

I fear thee, ancient Mariner! Samuel Taylor Coleridge. NPeEn Fr. Rime of the Ancient Mariner, The.

I fear thy kisses, gentle maiden. To ———: "I fear thy kisses, gentle maiden." Shelley. GTBS-P

I fear to love thee, Sweet, because. To Olivia. Francis Thompson. MoBrPo

I feare, I shall begin to grow in love. Ben Jonson. OxBEV Fr. Volpone.

I fear[e] no Earthly Powers. On Himselfe. Robert Herrick. CaPo

I fear[e] no more. (LL) Hymn[e] to God the Father, A. John Donne. AWP; BASC; EBEV; FSCP; HAP; InPK-6; MeLP; NAEL-5v1; NAEL-6v1; NAEL-7v1; NOBE; NOSC; NPeEn; OxBEV; PeECV; PoRA; SCGP; SCV; SacPr; SoSe-8; TFi; TOF

I feared bacchantic rages in that house. Bronx Park. Richard Foerster. UrbNat

I feed a flame within, which so torments me. Dryden. AWP Fr. Secret Love; or, The Maiden Queen.

I feel a breath from other planets blowing. Rapture. Stefan George. AWP, tr. by Ludwig Lewisohn

I feel a little better today. Master Carpenter, The. G. Shankara Kurup. OMIP, tr. by K. M. George

I feel a sudden urge to sing. It's De-Lovely. Cole Porter. ReLy

I feel an apparition. Wallace Stevens. OBVE

I feel as if I ne'er could sing again! (LL) To Elizabeth Barrett Browning, in 1851. Dora Greenwell. PoBW; VWP

I feel groggy and weary and tragic. But Alive. Charles Strouse. ReLy

I feel I am; I only know I am. John Clare. FHYEP; NOBVV; OxBSo

I feel I am alone tonight. City a Wrecked Ship, The. Amal Dunqul. MAP; NAfrP, tr. by Sharif Elmusa and Thomas G. Ezzy

I feel I know what you have worked through, you. For John Berryman. Robert Lowell. NOBA

I feel / in her pockets; she wore nice cotton gloves. Secondhand Coat. Ruth Stone. NALW; NIL-7; NIP-4

I feel it when the game is done. Footnote to Tennyson. Gerald Bullett. UV

I feel like a mango. Mango, A. Joyce Mansour. SurWo, tr. by Mary Beach

I feel like a stranger. Return to the Homeland. Adelina da Silva. NAfrP, tr. by Don Burness

I feel like dancin', baby. Sunday by the Combination. Langston Hughes. APT-2

I feel like I've buried somebody inside of me. Death Asphodel. Jean Valentine. ExTi

I feel like the Emperor Nero. Crazy Rhythm. Irving Caesar. ReLy

I feel like your umbilical cord. Umbilical Cord. Ellyn Maybe. AmPoNex

I feel my heart melt. Dusk. Gabriela Mistral. TANSG, tr. by Maria Jacketti

I feel my heart melting. Dusk. Gabriela Mistral. BoWoP, tr. by David Garrison

I feel my limbs. Samih Al-Qasim. MAP Fr. After the Apocalypse.

I feel myself in need. George Moses Horton, Myself. George Moses Horton. NAAAL

I feel, O Laudanum, thy power divine. In Praise of Laudanum. William Harrison. NOEC

I feel pity for that girl Polya. To Kolya Otrada. Mikhail Kuz'mich Lukonin. TCRP, tr. by Albert C. Todd

I feel remorse for all that time has done. Love's Remorse. Edwin Muir. OxBTC

I feel ridiculous. Put Down. Léon Damas. TTY, tr. by Seth L. Wolitz

I feel ridiculous / in their shoes. Sell Out. Léon Damas. NegPo, tr. by Ellen Conroy Kennedy

I feel the cold this night for Aodh. Mag Uidhir's Winter Campaign. Eochadh [or Eochy] O'Hussey [or O'Heughusa]. NOIV

I feel the coming glory of the Light. (LL) Credo. Edwin Arlington Robinson. ITBLP; MoAmPo; NAAL-2v2; OxBA; TAP; TrCP

I feel the dead in the cold of violets. I Feel the Dead. Sophia De Mello Breyner. VCWP, tr. by Ruth Fainlight

I feel the flames of hottest summer day. (LL) Sir Philip Sidney. NAEL-5v1; NAEL-6v1; NAEL-7v1 Fr. Astrophil and Stella.

I feel the reasonableness of existence. Yevgeny [or Evgenii] Mikhailovich Vinokurov. TCRP

I feel the stubborn humming. Swift Floods. Kata Szidónia Petröczy [or Petröczi]. WPOW, tr. by Laura Schiff

I feel the texture of her complexion with both hand and heart. Errol West. IBA

I feel the truth; so let the world surmise. (LL) George Meredith. NAEL-5v2; NAEL-6v2; NoP-4; SCGP Fr. Modern Love.

I feel their absence and I burn. (LL) Warming Her Pearls. Carol Ann Duffy. MakPoe; NePenScot; NoP-4; PoBW

I feel unexpectedly. Fragrance. Kay Sage. SurWo

I feel warm. Jubilee. Sabah As-Sabah. InTrad

I feel within myself a life. Mother, The. Caroline Clive. VWP

I fell. Makeda (Queen of Sheba). WPoS

I fell asleep, and had a dream. Unromantic Awakening, An. Priscilla Jane Thompson. CBWP-2

I fell asleep in the daytime. Recording a Dream. Yang Shih-ch'i. CoBLCP, tr. by Jonathan Chaves

I fell beside him and his corpse turned over. Razglednica (4). Miklós Radnóti. IQMS, tr. by Zsuzsanna Ozsváth and Frederick Turner

I fell beside him. His body—which was taut. Razglednica (4). Miklós Radnóti. IQMS, tr. by George Gömöri and Clive Wilmer

I fell down. Three Ways to Screw Up on Your Way to the Doings Three Ways. Unknown. STP, tr. by Richard Johnny John and Jerome Rothenberg

I fell in love. I kissed her. Unknown. GrAn

I fell in love with Demo of Paphos. No big surprise. Philodemus. HePo Fr. Epigrams.

I fell in love with you, Atthis. Sappho. PGA

I fell next to him. His body rolled over. Postcard (Found on His body after He Was Killed by the Nazis). Miklós Radnóti. RaBo, tr. by Stephen Berg, S. J. Marks and Steven Polgar

I felt a Cleaving in my Mind. Emily Dickinson. APN-2

I Felt a Funeral in My Brain. Emily Dickinson. APN-2; BoWoP; HeIP-4; NAAL-2v1; NAAL-3; NALW; NOBA; NoP-4; OxBA; PoE; PoRA; RaBo; SCV; SoSe-8; TAP; TCAPo; TFi

I felt a spirit of love begin to stir. Dante Alighieri. AWP; EaItPo, tr. by Dante Gabriel Rossetti Fr. La Vita Nuova.

I felt no tremor and I caught no sounds. White Dust, The. Wilfrid Wilson Gibson. MoBrPo

I felt some folded paper in my pocket. Solo Palabras. Magdalena Gomez. PueRic

I felt such love for you. Poem for My Wet Nurse, A. Cheng Hsieh. CoBLCP, tr. by Jonathan Chaves

I felt the lurch and halt of her heart. Lightning. D. H. Lawrence. MoBrPo

I felt the season changing in the yard today. Man and the Tree, The. Philip Mead. NOBAu

I fight and fight. / I wake up. Grow. Joseph Ceravolo. BodElec

I figured / anything anybody. Mrs. Sadie Grindstaff, Weaver and Factotum. Jonathan Williams. OBAL

I fill'd [or filld] with woes the passing Wind. (LL) Crystal Cabinet, The. William Blake. FaBoCh; NPeEn; PAI

I fill this cup to one made up. Health, A. Edward Coote [or Coate] Pinkney. APN-1

I find her huddled on the bed. Rod Willmot. HA

I find him in the garden. Staked tomato-plants are what. Early Discoveries. David Malouf. CBAP

I find his feet. He is what is left of my life. (LL) "Dreadful Has Already Happened, The." Mark Strand. HCAP; NoAM; VCAP

I find my love fishing. Unknown. BoWoP

I find my vessel fast. (LL) My Bed Is a Boat. Robert Louis Stevenson. PWR; PeVV

I find no fault in this just man. (LL) Eighth Air Force. Randall Jarrell. NOBA; NoAM; NoP-4; OBWP; PoWW; TRP; VCAP

I find no peace and all my war[r] is done. Petrarch. OBVE; Son, tr. by Sir Thomas Wyatt Fr. Sonnets to Laura.

I Find You, Lord, All Things and In All. Rainer Maria Rilke. BBASP, tr. by Stephen Mitchell

I finde hou whilom ther was on. John Gower. NPeEn; OxBEV Fr. Confessio Amantis.

I finish chanting my new poems. Yang Wan-li. SuSp Fr. Songs of Depression.

I first learnt to swim at home in my father's study. Swim Right Up to Me. Katherine Pierpoint. MFPA

I first remember you in Paris, blaze. Memoir. Honor Moore. GLP

I first tasted under Apollo's lips. Evadne. "H. D." BoWoP; LW

I first would have him understand. On His Garden Book. Francis Daniel Pastorius. SCAP

I fish for minnows in the lake. Epigram. Su Tung-p'o (Su Shih). OHPC

I fish until the clouds turn blue. Shifting Colors. Robert Lowell. BodElec; HCAP

I-5 Incident. Juan Delgado. AmPoNex; GeoHom

I flash for megabucks. Diana Gittins. NewEx

I fled Him, down the nights and down the days. Hound of Heaven, The. Francis Thompson. CABP; ChIV-2; InvLi; MoBrPo; NAEL-5v2; NAEL-6v2; OBMV; SacPr; TFi

I fled Him, down the nights and down the days. Francis Thompson. EroLit; ITBLP *Fr.* Hound of Heaven, The.

I flee the city, temples, and each place. Sonnet 17. Louise Labé. BoWoP; WoPoe, *tr. by* Willis Barnstone

I flew into New York. Milk. Eileen Myles. KGB

I float / On the wind. Tamaki of a Hundred Lovers. Hirini Melbourne. PeNZ

I floated on a cloud one day. Cloud Fantasy. Henrietta Cordelia Ray. CBWP-3

I flourish between pleasure and pain. Michael Longley. NewEx

I fly the flag of the menstruating black dog. Dog, The. Stanley Moss. BodElec

I fly, to seek my lover, or my grave! (LL) Bids Farewell to Lesbos. Mary Robinson. CenSon; RWP

I folded myself and sent me to you. Long Distance. Laila Halaby. PoArWo

I follow her down the night, begging her not to depart. (LL) Aware. D. H. Lawrence. MoBrPo; NoAM

I follow her into the front room. Bill Griffiths. Oth *Fr.* Building: The New London Hospital.

I follow my mother in from the car. In Chapel. John Pook. AngWePo

I follow the army to campaign on distant roads. Joining the Army: A Song. Wang Ts'an. SuSp, *tr. by* Ronald C. Miao

I follow the moon into the mountains. In the Mountains. Wang An-shih. SuSp, *tr. by* Jan W. Walls

I follow the river, heron-seeking. Heron in the Alyn. Gladys Mary Coles. TCAWP

I Followed a Path. Patricia Parker. BlSi

I followed and breathed in silence. God. Samuel Greenberg. APT-1

I followed deadpan rivers down and down. Drunken Boat. Arthur Rimbaud. SxFrPo, *tr. by* Martin Sorrell

I followed her to the station, with her suitcase in my hand. Love in Vain. Robert Johnson. UnPo

I followed, o splendid season. Poem to Show the Trouble That Befell Him When He Was at Sea, A. Thomas Prys. OBWVE, *tr. by* Gwyn Williams

I followed the narrow cliffside trail half way up the mountain. Deer Lay Down Their Bones, The. Robinson Jeffers. APT-1; NoAM

I followed the winding path. Cutting, A. Ou-yang Hsiu. CrYelRi, *tr. by* Sam Hamill

I followed where they led. His Throne Is with the Outcast. James Russell Lowell. TrCP

I ford a river to play with autumn water. In Imitation of Ancient Songs. Li Po. SuSp, *tr. by* Joseph J. Lee

I Forgive You. Stevie Smith. BWW

I forgot for a moment France! I forgot England; I forgot my care. I Forgot for a Moment. Edna St. Vincent Millay. NAAL-5

I forgot I forgot the other heritage the other strain refrain. Other Heritage, The. Aurora Levins Morales. PueRic

I forgot to tell you about the red sheets my sister bought for us that were. Sign. Linda Smukler. WiU

I foster a Love fond of playing ball. It throws. Meleager. HePo *Fr.* Epigrams.

I fought on foot in every quarter. Semyon [*or* Semion] Petrovich Gudzenko. TCRP

I found a ball of grass among the hay. Mouse's Nest. John Clare. InPK-6; NAEL-5v2; NAEL-6v2; NPeEn; PAI; RB

I found a corpse, with golden hair. "Owen Meredith." VerBaPo *Fr.* Vampyre, The.

I found a dimpled spider, fat and white. Design. Robert Frost. APT-1; ColAP; HeIP-4; InPK-6; NAAL-2v2; NAAL-5; NIL-7; NOBA; NoAM; NoP-4; OxBSo; PAI; PoPoPo; RaBo; SAmP; SoSe-8; Son; TAP; TFi; TRP

I found a fox, caught by the leg. Fellow Mortal, A. John Masefield. OxAEP-2

I found a golden seashell on the beach. Seashell, The. "Rubén Dario." TCLAP, *tr. by* Lysander Kemp

I found a / hummingbird. Container, The. Cid Corman. VGW

I Found a Million Dollar Baby (In a Five and Ten Cent Store). Harry Warren. ReLy

I found a pigeon's skull on the machair. Perfect. Hugh MacDiarmid. NePenScot; NoP-4; OxBEV; RB; WoPoe

I found a torrent falling in a glen. Torrent, The. Edwin Arlington Robinson. APN-2

I found a / weed. Reflective. A. R. Ammons. HCAP; VCAP

I found again in the heart of a friend. (LL) Arrow and the Song, The. Henry Wadsworth Longfellow. BRP; ColAP; PWR; PoToHe; TCAPo; UV

I found her deep in the forest. Enchanted Princess, An. Rosamund Marriott Watson. ViWPN

I found her in the shade of spring. Rose Wreaths, The. Friedrich Gottlieb Klopstock. GePo, *tr. by* J. W. Thomas

I Found Her Out There. Thomas Hardy. NOBE; NoAM; OxAEP-2; PAI; PoE

I found him in the guard-room at the Base. Lamentations. Siegfried Sassoon. OBSV; OxAEP-2; PeFWW

I found his wool face, I went away. Reading Walt Whitman. Calvin Forbes. ESEAA; NBV

I found in Munster, unfettered of any. *Unknown.* BIrV *Fr.* Prince Alfrid's Itinerary.

I Found It. Fadwa Tuqan [*or* Tuquan]. BBASP; MAP, *tr. by* Patricia Alanah Byrne, Salma Khadra Jayyusi and Naomi Shihab Nye

I Found My Love by the Secret Canal. *Unknown.* WoPoe, *tr. by* John L. Foster

I found myself in this house. Siege. Sargon Boulus. MAP, *tr. by* Sargon Boulus and Alistair Elliot

I found one word. Thérèse 'Awwad. PoArWo, *tr. by* Kamal Boullata

I Found Orpheus Levitating. Nick Carbó. NAPBL; ReBoTo

I found that ivory image there. Crazy Jane Grown Old Looks at the Dancers. W. B. Yeats. EBEV

I found the colour of your. At Castor Bay. Sam Hunt. PeNZ

I found the land above the river, where. In Memory of H. F. Peter Klappert. YaYoPo

I found the letter in a book I bought at an outdoor theatre turned flea market every weekend. Letter, The. Morton Marcus. GeoHom

I found the packets of seed in a cobwebbed drawer. Lost Seed. Patrick Williams. PNI

I found the task that I had dreaded so. Dreaded Task, The. Margaret E. Bruner. PoToHe

I found the words to every thought. Emily Dickinson. APN-2

I found them between far hills, by a frozen lake. God of Love, The. George MacBeth [*or* Macbeth]. EmeKit

I found them here when I came. We Call Them Greasers. Gloria Anzaldúa. GLP

I found this jawbone at the sea's edge. Relic. Ted Hughes. NAEL-5v2; NAEL-6v2; NoP-4

I found this photograph. Returning to the Town Where We Used to Live. Susan Musgrave. NOBC

I found you in a newspaper. Idea of a Swimmer. Jean-Richard Bloch. TrJP, *tr. by* "S. P."

I found you on a rainy morning. Nansen. Gary Snyder. BB

I found your Horace with the writing in it. On First Looking into Loeb's Horace. Lawrence Durrell. FaBoMo

I frightened a little mouse under the [*or* her] chair. (LL) Mother Goose. LB; OxNR; ReMoGo

I, from my chamber window, mark. Autumn Thoughts. Mary E. Tucker. CBWP-1

I from my window looked at early dawning. Bereft. Josephine D. Henderson Heard. CBWP-4

I gaed to spend a week in Fife. Annuity, The. George Outram. PeVV

I gat your letter, winsome Willie. To William Simpson, Ochiltree. Robert Burns. OxBS

I gave chase. Evidence, The. Tom Leonard. Oth

I gave myself to Him—. Emily Dickinson. APN-2

I gave myself to Love Divine. Saint Theresa [*or* Teresa] of Avila. TOF

I gave the surge of myself to the dawn. Alejandra Piznarnick. TANSG, *tr. by* Susan Bassnett *Fr.* Tree of Diana.

I gave to Hope a watch of mine: but he. Hope. George Herbert. ChIV-2; NPeEn; OxBEV; WeW-3

I gave you wings. Black stone, blue heave shall take. Captive. Theognis. WoPoe, *tr. by* Richmond Lattimore

I Gaze across the Distant Hills. William Williams. OBWVE, *tr. by* H. Idris Bell

I gaze at you. Tattooed Man, The. Robert Earl Hayden. NoAM

I gaze far and long. Fujiwara no Teika. OHMPJ

I gaze over the landscape, clouded and dark. Shepherd's Wife's Farewell to the Old Pasture, The. István Sinka. IQMS, *tr. by* Gavin Ewart

I Gaze Upon My Country's Walls. Francisco de Quevedo y Villegas. SpanPo, *tr. by* Kate Flores

I gaze upon the beauty of the stars. Beauty of the Stars, The. Moses Ibn Ezra. TrJP, *tr. by* Solomon Solis-Cohen

I gaze upon the roast. Pot Roast. Mark Strand. AmFaPo

I gaze, where August's sunbeam falls. Newark Abbey. Thomas Love Peacock. NOBE

I gaze with grief upon our generation. Thought, A. Mikhail Yuryevich Lermontov. AWP, *tr. by* Max Eastman

I gazed through the darkness, one very dark night. Light in the Window, The. C. L. Erickson. PWR

I gazed upon thy face,—and beating life. Beauty. Jones Very. SacPr

I gently touched her hand: she gave. I Pressed Her Rebel Lips. *Unknown.* BoLoP

I genuinely wanted them to come. What Song the Syrens Sang. Eleanor Brown. MFPA

I Get a Kick Out of You. Cole Porter. APT-1

(My story is much too sad to be told.) ReLy

I Get Along Without You Very Well. Hoagy Carmichael. ReLy

I get as far as the park. Veteran. Walter McDonald. CDa

I get her up on the curb, two wheels off the street. Changing the Oil. Eloise Klein Healy. WiU

I get my degree. Lawd, Dese Colored Chillum. Ruby C. Saunders. BlSi; LTA

I get so drunk, I could be called the Earl of Dissipation! Chin Nung. CoBLCP Fr. Thirty Poems of Longing for People.

I get them in range and shoot. Photo Safari. Bruce Berger. PoCoUp

I Get Up at Dawn. Lu Yu. OHPC, tr. by Kenneth Rexroth

I get up. I am sick of / Rouging my cheeks. Morning. Chu Shu-chen. BoWoP, tr. by Kenneth Rexroth

I give my name back. Inseki. JDP, tr. by Yoel Hoffmann

I give my word on it. There is no way. Still and All. Burns Singer. HarvBoo; OxBS

I give thee all, I can no more. Sum, A. Lewis Carroll. Spl

I give thee back, when all the rest is spent. (LL) Michael Drayton. SCGP; Son Fr. Idea.

I give thee thanks, Adonai! Unknown. TrJP, tr. by E. Margaret Rowley Fr. Dead Sea Scrolls, The.

I give Thee thanks, my King. Mael Isu O Brolchain. NOIV

I give you a house of snow. Dove of New Snow, The. Nicholas Vachel Lindsay. MoAmPo

I Give You Back. Joy Harjo. HATNAP; LoL

I give you horses for your games in May. Folgore da San Geminiano [or Gimignano]. EaItPo, tr. by Dante Gabriel Rossetti Fr. Sonnets of the Months.

I give you meadow-lands in April, fair. Folgore da San Geminiano [or Gimignano]. EaItPo, tr. by Dante Gabriel Rossetti Fr. Sonnets of the Months.

I give you no greeting, Geoffrey. I Give You No Greeting. Marbod of Rennes. MLL, tr. by Helen Waddell

I give you now Professor Twist. Purist, The. Ogden Nash. KaS; MoAmPo; NBLV; OBCA

I Give You Thanks My God. Bernard Dadié. PoetW; TTY, tr. by Donatus Ibe Nwoga

I give you thanks my God for having created me black. (LL) I Give You Thanks My God. Bernard Dadié. PoetW; TTY, tr. by Donatus Ibe Nwoga

I give you the end of a golden string. William Blake. Spl Fr. Jerusalem; The Emanation of the Giant Albion.

I give you this Bible and more to take. Inscription on the Flyleaf of a Bible. Dannie Abse. TrJP

I glance down at my shoe and—there's the lace! To Be Said Over and Over Again. György Petri. VCWP, tr. by George Gömöri and Clive Wilmer

I go. Buson. ChAP; EH, tr. by Robert Hass

I go a road / among the upturned. In the Underworld. Muriel Rukeyser. APSN

I go along chanting the wayhouse poem. Inscribed on the Wall of Hsü Hsüan-Ping's Retreat. Li Po. WoPoe, tr. by Elling O. Eide

I go back. Tojaku. JDP, tr. by Yoel Hoffmann

I go back again. Hawk and Snake. Leslie Marmon Silko. VoR

I Go Back to May 1937. Sharon Olds. BLT; EmeKit; NIL-7

I go back ways to hurl rooftops. In My Mind. Norman MacCaig. OxBC

I Go before, my darling. Unknown. NoSic

I Go, but Where? Oh Gods! Patrizia Cavalli. CItWP, tr. by Cinzia Sartini Blum and Lara Trubowitz

I Go by Road. Catulle Mendès. AWP; TrJP, tr. by Alice Meynell

I go digging for clams once every two or three years. Clamming. Reed Whittemore. TAP

I go down step by step. Midnight Flowers. Eavan Boland. ModIr

I Go Dreaming Roads in My Youth. Luis Omar Salinas. AiP

I go for voting clean. (LL) Aunt Chloe's Politics. Frances Ellen Watkins Harper. NAAAL; NALW

I go. I go. I go. Ngungalari. Archie Weller. RACG

I go on dreaming. Antonio Machado Ruiz. BLPSL, tr. by Rene de Costa, Rigas Kappatos and Eleni Paidoussi

I go on in the dark, lit from within; does day exist? I Go on in the Dark, Lit from Within. Miguel Hernández. AF, tr. by Timothy Baland

I go out. Top of the World, The. Yves Bonnefoy. VCWP, tr. by John Naughton

I go out alone. Buson. SoOfWa, tr. by Sam Hamill

I go out of darkness / Onto a road of darkness. Lady Izumi. WPOW

I go out to find whatever comes. Slow. Marvin Bell. MoASP

I go separately. Santa Fe Trail. Barbara Guest. FTOS; NeAP; PoM

I go, the wind pushing me along. I Go, the Wind Pushing Me Along. Fanny Beznos. SurWo, tr. by Myrna Bell Rochester

I go through hollyhocks. Las Trampas U. S. A. Charles Tomlinson. TwCP

I go through the wood in silence. Kit Wright. NewEx

I go to concert, party, ball. My Rival. Rudyard Kipling. OxBTC

I go to say goodbye to the Cailleach. Wild Dog Rose, The. John Montague. BIrV; CIP-2; PBCIP; PoE

I go to school in the morning. Embroidery. Catherine Nomura Crystal. AiP

I go to sleep on one beach. Quiet Nights. Raymond Carver. EmeKit

I go to work. Workday. Linda Hogan. HATNAP

I Go Too. Tu Fu. CarOv, tr. by Carolyn Kizer Fr. Meandering River Poems, The.

I go where I love and where I am loved. "H. D." APT-1; HarvBoo Fr. Flowering of the Rod, The.

I go, with your good grace, lords and kinsmen. Hartmann von Aue. GePo

I got a gal at the head of the creek. Cripple Creek. Unknown. APN-2

I Got a Home in Dat Rock. Unknown. BPo

I got a one-eyed wife, a headless child. Guess Who. Fred Chappell. NBLV

I got an island in the Pacific. Occasional Man, An. Hugh Martin. ReLy

I got caught staring out the window when the bells were ringing. Once When I Was in the Eighth Grade. Maurice Kilwein Guevara. AmPoNex

I got fucked and it wasn't no thang. Black Rape. Michelle T. Clinton. InTrad

I got his name and phone. On Finding Out that the One You Slept with the Night Before Was Murdered the Next Day. Chuck Ortleb. GLP

I got home, very late, and parked the. Here, Home. John Powell Ward. TCAWP

I Got It Bad and That Ain't Good. Duke Ellington. ReLy

I Got Lost in His Arms. Irving Berlin. ReLy

I got me flowers to straw [or strew or strow] Thy [or the] way. Easter. George Herbert. FHYEP; FaBoCh; NAEL-5v1; NOBE; OBEV; OxBEV

I got myself a military man. My Man o' War. Spencer Williams. ReLy

I got one good look. Coon Song. A. R. Ammons. NOBA

I got out of bed. Otherwise. Jane Kenyon. AmFaPo; LoL

I Got Plenty o' Nuthin' George Gershwin. ReLy

I Got Rhythm. George Gershwin. ReLy

I got so I could take his name. Emily Dickinson. APN-2

I got some news from Kailasa! Īśvarcandra Gupta. SinGod, tr. by Rachel Fell McDermott

I got stones in my passway. Stones in my Passway. Robert Johnson. APT-2

I Got the Blues. Unknown. TTY

I got the horse right here. Fugue for Tinhorns. Frank Loesser. ReLy

I Got the Sun in the Morning. Irving Berlin. ReLy

I got to Kansas City on a Frid'y. Kansas City. Oscar Hammerstein, II. OBAL

I got to keep on dancing. Alvin Cash/Keep on Dancin' David Henderson. GT

I got up early and faced the east. Early. Jean-Baptiste Tati-Loutard. WoPoe, tr. by Eric Sellin

I got up early Sunday morning. Who and Each. Ron Padgett. PmAP

I got up. My legs too. Was I here? Yes. In the Library. Hamutal Bar Yosef. DTA, tr. by Shirley Kaufman

I gotta / buy me a new. Après le Bain. William Carlos Williams. OBAL

I Gotta Right to Sing the Blues. Ted Koehler. ReLy

I grant indeed that fields and flocks have charms. George Crabbe. NOBE Fr. Village, The.

I greatly need your friendship: leave it me. (LL) Am I to Lose You? Louisa Sarah Bevington. NOBVV; OxBSo

I greet my love with virtue and gladsome lay. Sabbath, My Love. Judah Halevi. TrJP, tr. by Solomon Solis-Cohen

I Greet You. J. Greshoff. TuT, tr. by Dennis O'Driscoll

I greet you, friend and neighbour. I Greet You. J. Greshoff. TuT, tr. by Dennis O'Driscoll

I greet you, son, with joy and winter rue. Muse in Late November. Jonathan Henderson Brooks. ChIV-1

I grew. Strong Bond, The. Juana de Ibarbourou. TCLAP, tr. by Sophie Cabot Black, Maria Negroni and Linda Scheer

I grew from the earth. Unknown. PGA

I Grew Up. Lenore Keeshig-Tobias. FFC

I grew up bent over. Prodigy. Charles Simic. VCAP

I GREW up near the town of Jung-yang. Stopping the Night at Jung-yang. Po Chü-i. ChiP, tr. by Arthur Waley

I grew up on the reserve. I Grew Up. Lenore Keeshig-Tobias. FFC

I grew up staring at the picture of him. Cousin. David Huddle. CDa

I grew up with the language of electrics. My Father Makes a Lightbox for Vivienne Westwood. Nicolette Golding. Prnts

I grieve and dare not show my discontent. On Monsieur's Departure. Queen of England Elizabeth I.   CABP; NAEL-5v1; NAEL-6v1; NAEL-7v1; NALW; WPE

I grieve for my second daughter.   Written on Seeing the Flowers, and Remembering My Daughter.   Kao Ch'i.   ColAnChi, *tr.* by F. W. Mote

I grieved for Buonaparté, with a vain.   1801.   William Wordsworth.   CenSon; Son

I grow old under an intensity.   Mirror.   James Merrill.   CoAP

I Guard Your Eyes.   Endre Ady.   IQMS, *tr.* by Adam Makkai

I guess an' fear! (LL)   To a Mouse; On Turning Her up in Her Nest, with the Plough, November, 1785.   Robert Burns.   BRP; CABP; FaBoVe; HAP; HeIP-4; NAEL-5v2; NAEL-6v2; NOEC; NPeEn; NePenScot; NoP-4; OxAEP-2; OxBEV; OxBS; PoE; SCGP; TFi; UV

I guess I'll be back late.   Human House.   Tamura Ryuichi.   VCWP, *tr.* by Christopher Drake

I Guess I'll Have to Change My Plan.   Howard Dietz.   ReLy

I guess I'm sick, because this is the third day.   Chills.   Bella [*or* Izabella] Akhatovna Akhmadulina.   ItGoST, *tr.* by F. D. Reeve

I guess it is ever green.   Evergreen Cemetery.   Alfred Wellington Purdy.   MoCV

I guess it was because it was the first time I had been anyplace.   Wo/man's Voice Must Be Heard, A.   Lorena M. Craighead.   InTrad

I guess there is a garden named.   Mirror Perilous, The.   Alan Dugan.   TwCP

I guess we haven't got a sense.   Two Sleepy People.   Hoagy Carmichael.   ReLy

I guess you love me now.   Songs of Divorce.   Jane Green.   WPOW, *tr.* by Frances Densmore

I guess you were the winter, a din that hid.   Fractal Audition.   Pimone Triplett.   NAPBL

I guide my boat to mooring by a misty islet.   Passing the Night on a River in Chien-te.   Meng Hao Jan.   SuSp, *tr.* by Paul W. Kroll

I gulp down seven drinks of water.   Hiccups.   Léon Damas.   NegPo; PFTM-1, *tr.* by Ellen Conroy Kennedy

I gurgled straight out of my.   In Gurgle Veritas.   Luis H. Francia.   ReBoTo

I had a bear that danced.   Song in Sligo.   Jean Garrigue.   APT-2

I Had a Black Man.   *Unknown.*   OxBoLi

I had a cat and the cat pleased me.   *Unknown.*   OxNR

I had a chair at every hearth.   Lamentation of the Old Pensioner, The.   W. B. Yeats.   HAP; InPK-6; NoAM; TRP; WeW-3

I had a conversation with a goat.   Goat, The.   Umberto Saba.   WoPoe, *tr.* by Stephen Sartarelli

I had a crisis at the supermarket, yesterday.   My Androgynous Years.   James Harms.   NeAmPo

I had a dog / Whose name was Buff.   *Unknown.*   OxNR

I had a Donkey, that was all right.   Donkey, The.   Theodore Roethke.   OBCA

I had a dream.   Nightmare Boogie.   Langston Hughes.   APSN; APT-2

I had a dream.   Death Survey.   Mongane Wally Serote.   PeSAV

I had a dream / A dream about you, Baby!   Everything's Coming Up Roses.   Stephen Sondheim.   ReLy

I had a dream: Columbia the Great.   Albery Allson Whitman.   APN-2   *Fr.* Idyll of the South, An.

I had a dream. I walked in a field of feather grass.   Aleksey [*or* Aleksei] Petrovich Tsvetkov.   TCRP

I had a dream in my mother's womb three days before I was born.   Reader of This Page.   Maurice Kilwein Guevara.   NAPBL

I had a dream one winter's night.   Dream, A.   Maggie Pogue Johnson.   CBWP-4

I had a dream: that I was cast in iron.   Monument, The.   Yaroslav [*or* Iaroslav] Vasilevich Smelyakov [*or* Smeliakov].   TCRP, *tr.* by Simon Franklin

I had a dream three walls stood up wherein a raven bird.   Anger's Freeing Power.   Stevie Smith.   OxBC

I had a dream, which was not all a dream.   Darkness.   Byron.   CABP; NAEL-5v2; NAEL-6v2; PoE; TreFP

I Had a Duck-billed Platypus.   Patrick Barrington.   OBCoV; PeLV

I Had a Future.   Patrick Kavanagh.   BIrV; NoAM

I had a good dream last night.   Rām Basu.   SinGod, *tr.* by Rachel Fell McDermott

I had a hippopotamus; I loved him as a friend.   I Had a Hippopotamus.   Patrick Barrington.   ITBLP

I had a house; I had a yard.   Fog.   Lizette Woodworth Reese.   APT-1

I had a little boy.   Blue Bell Boy.   *Unknown.*   ReMoGo

I had a little cow.   *Unknown.*   OxNR

I had a little dog and his name was Blue Bell.   *Unknown.*   OxNR

I had a little dog, and my dog was very small.   Child's Dream, A.   Frances Darwin Cornford.   NOxBChV

I had a little hen, the prettiest ever seen.   Clever Hen, The.   *Unknown.*   LB; ReMoGo

I had a little hobby-horse.   *Unknown.*   ReMoGo

I had a little hobby horse, it was well shod.   Mother Goose.   OxNR

I had a little horse, his name was Dappled Grey.   *Unknown.*   OxNR

I had a little husband.   *Unknown.*   OxNR; ReMoGo

I had a little moppet.   Little Moppet, The.   Mother Goose.   OxNR; ReMoGo

I had a little nag.   *Unknown.*   OxNR

I had a little nut-tree.   *Unknown.*   TTTS

I had a little nut-tree, / nothing would it bear.   Nut Tree, A.   Mother Goose.   OxBoLi; OxNR; TTTS

I had a little pony.   Dapple-gray.   Mother Goose.   LB; OxNR; ReMoGo

I had a most marvellous piece of luck. I died. (LL)   John Berryman.   HCAP; HarvBoo   *Fr.* Dream Songs.

I had a silver penny.   Nursery Rhyme of Innocence and Experience.   Charles Causley.   NOxBChV

I had a son and his name was John.   Rundown Church (Ballad of the First World War).   Federico García Lorca.   RaBo, *tr.* by Robert Bly

I had almost forgotten the singing in the streets.   Singing in the Streets.   Leonard Clark.   NOxBChV

I had almost lost.   Eugenio Montale.   WoPoe, *tr.* by Dana Gioia   *Fr.* Motets, The.

I had already looked at the coco-palms, the tamarinds.   Manuscript in a Bottle.   Pablo Antonio Cuadra.   BLPSL, *tr.* by Rene de Costa, Rigas Kappatos and Eleni Paidoussi

I had ambition, by which sin.   Ambition.   William Henry Davies.   MoBrPo

I had as lief be embraced by the porter at the hotel.   Two Figures in Dense Violet Night.   Wallace Stevens.   MoAmPo

I had become callous like most.   On the Death of Lisa Lyman.   Della Burt.   BlSi

I had been bothered by a secret weariness.   Charles Reznikoff.   APT-2   *Fr.* Early History of a Writer.

I had been hungry, all the Years.   Emily Dickinson.   MoAmPo; NALW; SAmP; TCAPo; WPoS

I had been sitting for days.   Long Distance.   Dana Naone.   CDW

I had been thinking of Gabriel.   "H. D."   NALW   *Fr.* Tribute to the Angels.

I had been trying to get through all day.   Diaries.   Ben Scammell.   NLP

I had been vexed, if vexed I had not been. (LL)   Sir Philip Sidney.   NAEL-5v1; NAEL-6v1; NAEL-7v1   *Fr.* Astrophil and Stella.

I had been watching them drift up and down.   North.   Roger Mitchell.   PoCoUp

I Had But Fifty Cents.   *Unknown.*   NBLV; WHSW

I had climbed the long slope of the spur from Capel Madog to Banc-y-Darren.   I Had Climbed the Long Slope.   John Barnie.   TCAWP

I had come from a dying man's room.   Line Drive.   Arthur Ginsberg.   BloBone

I had come to the edge of the water.   Seamus Heaney.   NPeEn; PBCIP   *Fr.* Station Island.

I had come to the house, in a cave of trees.   Medusa.   Louise Bogan.   APT-2; AWP; BoWoP; MoAmPo; NALW; NoAM; NoP-4; PAI; WPE

I had eight birds hatcht [*or* hatched] in one nest.   In Reference to Her Children, 23 June, 1659 [*or* 1659].   Anne Bradstreet.   BoWoP; NAAL-3; TAP

I had finally obtained my goal.   Recollections of the Cross.   Vladimir Nikolaevich Sokolov.   TCRP, *tr.* by Albert C. Todd

I had found out a gift for my fair.   Constance Naden.   VWP   *Fr.* Evolutional Erotics.

I had gone broke, and got set to come back.   Epigram.   James Vincent Cunningham.   MoAmPo; OxBSP; VCAP

I had heard / before, of an / American who would have preferred.   Mr. Brodsky.   Charles Tomlinson.   NoAM; OxBC

I had heard the bird's name, and searched with intent.   Oyster-Eaters, The.   John Blight.   NOBAu

I had just gone to bed.   Petronius Arbiter.   PGA

I had just turned the classic page.   To A. H.   James M. Whitfield.   APN-2

I had lots of fun today.   Through the Window.   Vladislav Felitsianovich Khodasevich.   TCRP, *tr.* by Yakov Hornstein

I had my good and my.   *Unknown.*   MiEL

I had never seen a cornfield in my life.   In the Elementary School Choir.   Gregory Djanikian.   OPRER; UnSA

I had no desire for life.   Writing My Feelings.   Yüan Mei.   CoBLCP, *tr.* by Jonathan Chaves

I had no gift for it.   Padraic Fallon.   ModIr   *Fr.* Three Houses.

I had no God but these.   Christ and the Pagan.   John Banister Tabb.   TrCP

I had no thought of violets of late.   Sonnet.   Alice Moore Dunbar-Nelson.   BlSi; Son

I had no time to Hate.   Emily Dickinson.   SWaP

I had no wish to be stone-hearted.   Perplexity.   Ibrahim Tuqan.   MAP, *tr.* by John Heath-Stubbs and Christopher Tingley

I had no witnesses.   Disappeared Woman V.   Marjorie Agosin.   TANSG, *tr.* by Cola Franzen

I had not an evil end in view.   True Dream, A.   Elizabeth Barrett Browning.   NALW

I had not fastened my sash over my gown.   Tzu Yeh.   EroLit; WPOW; WoPoe, *tr.* by Chung Ling and Kenneth Rexroth

I had not known of Hsiang-chi Monastery. Visiting Hsiang-Chi Monastery. Wang Wei. WoPoe, *tr. by* Eva Shan Chou

I had not minded—Walls. Emily Dickinson. AWP

I had not thought that it would be like this. (LL) Eden Rock. Charles Causley. NPeEn; NoP-4

I Had Occasion to Tell a Visitor about an Old Trip I Took. Lu Yu. CoBCP; WoPoe, *tr. by* Burton Watson

I had often, cowled in the slumberous heavy air. Dürer: Innsbruck, 1495. "Ern Malley." BMAP; CBAP

I had over-prepared the event. Villanelle: The Psychological Hour. Ezra Pound. CTC; NAAL-2v2

I had pelted the robot with all. Space Parable. Max Winter. NeAmPo

I had seen, as dawn was breaking. La Nuit Blanche. Rudyard Kipling. MoBrPo; UV

I had seen coconut trees and tamarinds. Manuscript in a Bottle. Pablo Antonio Cuadra. TCLAP, *tr. by* Ann McCarthy de Zavala and Grace Schulman

I had sex with a famous poet last night. Sex with a Famous Poet. Denise Duhamel. KGB; NeAmPo

I had some cards printed. Madam's Calling Cards. Langston Hughes. SAmP

I had the lab science, the ecology of texts. Other Syllabus, The. Chenjerai Hove. HBAPE

I had this dream. My Dream. Lew Blockcolski. VoR

I had three friends. Three Friends. *Unknown.* BoWoP; PBA, *tr. by* Ulli Beier

I had time to think about things. After I Was Dead. Laura Mullen. ExTi

I had to give a great speech to a filled hall, beginning. Impossible, The. Jane Miller. BodElec

I had to let my cutman go. (LL) Moorer Denies Holyfield in Twelve. Olena Kalytiak Davis. AmPoNex; MoASP

I had to write my. Spofford Hall. Alison Stone. SwNoth

I had two pigeons bright and gay. Two Pigeons. *Unknown.* OxNR; ReMoGo

I had two pillows and one was England. Laughing Moon, The. Moniza Alvi. MFPA

I had walked since dawn and lay down to rest on a bare hillside. Vulture. Robinson Jeffers. APT-1; NAAL-2v2; NOBA; NoAM

I had wanted a daughter. Mothers of Sons. Lesley Saunders. BrRo

I had wanted to go hunt. H. C. ten Berge. TuT   *Fr.* Lusitanian Variant, The.

I had written to Aunt Maud. Waste. Harry Graham. OBCoV; UV

I Hadn't Anyone Till You. Ray Noble. ReLy

I hadn't seen my first ocean yet. Still. Jack Marshall. GraLe

I hammer a nail. Bob Boldman. HA

I hang by my heels from the sky. Hera, Hung from the Sky. Carolyn Kizer. WPE

I hang from a thin green rope. Elizabeth Rapp. NewEx

I hang on to the hem of her dress like a child hanging. Two Little Girls. Fawziyya Abu Khalid. PoArWo, *tr. by* Farouk Mustafa

I happened once upon a time. James Hatley. *Unknown.* ESPB

I happened to come to the foot of a pine tree. In Reply to Questions. T'ai-shang. CoBCP, *tr. by* Burton Watson

I happy am if well with you. (LL) In Reference to Her Children, 23 June, 1659. Anne Bradstreet. BoWoP; NAAL-3; TAP

I hardly ever tire of love or rhyme. Variation on Belloc's "Fatigue." Wendy Cope. UV

I hardly saw His Face. John in Prison. Sydney E. Jerrold. SacPr

I hate an easy woman. Rufinus. GrAn

I hate and love. And if you should ask how I can do both. 85. Catullus. NAWM-7v1, *tr. by* Charles Martin

I hate and love. Ignorant fish, who even. Odi et Amo. Catullus. WoPoe, *tr. by* Frank Bidart

I hate and love. Why? You may ask but. Odi et Amo. Catullus. CTC, *tr. by* Ezra Pound

I hate and love, wouldst thou the reason know? De Amore Suo. Catullus. OBVE, *tr. by* Richard Lovelace

I hate Eros. He is loathsome and will not. Alcaeus [*or* Alkaios]. GrAn

I hate feeling. Taxing. Eileen Myles. BodElec

I hate it when grown-ups say. Frogologist, The. Brian Patten. OTCP

I hate my verses, every line, every word. Love the Wild Swan. Robinson Jeffers. APT-1; MoAmPo; NoAM; Son

I hate that drum's discordant sound. Ode. John Scott of Amwell. NIP-4; NOEC; OxAEP-1; PAI

I hate that particular dream. My Own Little Piece of Hollywood. James Harms. AmPoNex

I hate the cyclic poem, nor do I rejoice. Callimachus. HePo   *Fr.* Epigrams.

I Hate the Light. Osip Emilevich Mandelstam [*or* Mandelshtam]. TCRusP, *tr. by* John Glad

I hate the man who builds his name. John Gay. PeLV   *Fr.* Fables.

I hate the Spring in parti-coloured vest. Sonnet. Mary Locke. CenSon; ECWP

I hate the travel logs that tell you. Thoughts While Walking. Rachel Wetzsteon. ExTi

I hate these phrases: Of power absolute. Joshua Sylvester. FaBoEE

I hate this shadow of a ghost. Kenneth Rexroth. APT-2   *Fr.* Love Poems of Marichiko, The.

I hate to hear those crazy cocks crowing around a thatched inn. Rising Early in the Morning. Chao Yi. SuSp, *tr. by* Chang Yin-nan

I hate war. I'm worried, of course. Worried. Nguyen Binh Khiem. WoPoe, *tr. by* Nguyen Ngoc Bich

I hate wide mouth black girls. Illusion. Colleen J. McElroy. ISC

I hate your laces. Teasing Toads, The. Michael Rosen. OTCP

I hated thee, fallen tyrant! I did groan. Feelings of a Republican on the Fall of Bonaparte. Shelley. CenSon; Son

I hated you; I confess I hated you. I Do Not Want the Ceiling of the Sistine Chapel. Felicity Napier. Prnts

I Have. Jan Arends. TuT, *tr. by* Peter Van de Kamp

I have a beautiful child, her form. Sappho. SaLy, *tr. by* Diane Rayor

I have a bird in my head and a pig in my stomach. Alive for an Instant. Kenneth Koch. PmAP

I Have a Blue Piano. Else Lasker-Schüler. TrJP, *tr. by* Ralph Manheim

I have a bowl of paper whites. Window Ledge in the Atom Age. Elwyn Brooks White. NBLV; OBAL

I have a brain populated by women. Valerio Magrelli. ItPo, *tr. by* Gayle Ridinger

I have a couple acres of land. Wang Fan-chih. ColAnChi, *tr. by* Victor H. Mair

I have a daughter / mozambique. Bocas: A Daughter's Geography. Ntozake Shange. NAAAL

I have a delicious problem. Giant Red Woman. Clarence Major. GT

I have a feeling. Let's Fall in Love. Ted Koehler. ReLy

I have a feeling that beneath the little halo on your noble head. You Fascinate Me So. Cy Coleman. ReLy

I have a fifth of therapy. Interview with Doctor Drink. James Vincent Cunningham. OxBSP; VGW; WoPoe

I have a fish's tail, so I'm not qualified to love you. Siren. Amy Gerstler. ExTi

I have a friend. Black March. Stevie Smith. EmeKit

I have a friend who. Haiku #3. Kim C. Lee. InTrad

I have a friend who is red hot with pain. Anne Carson. BodElec   *Fr.* Truth About God, The.

I have a friend who still believes in heaven. Celestial Music. Louise Glück. BBASP

I have a garden and I have a well. I Have a Garden. Hayyim Nahman [*or* Khayim Nakhman *or* Chaim Nachman] Bialik. MHP, *tr. by* Ruth Finer Mintz

I have a garden of my own. Child's Song. Sir Thomas More. ChAP

I Have a Gentle Cock [*or* Gentil Cok]. *Unknown.* MiEL; NOBE; NoP-4; OPOU; PeLV

I have a great desire to move elsewhere. (LL) Work. Andrei Codrescu. PmAP; SPE

I have a grief. John Crowe Ransom. OxBA   *Fr.* Sixteen Poems in Eight Pairings.

I have a kindly neighbor, one who stands. Kindly Neighbor, The. Edgar Albert Guest. PoToHe

I have a life. I stand abandoned. Unmarked Stop in Front of Westmond General Store, Westmond, Idaho. Jonathan Johnson. AmPoNex

I have a life that did not become. Easter Morning. A. R. Ammons. HCAP; NAAL-2v2; NAAL-5; NoAM; PoetW

I have a little budgie. Fat Budgie, The. John Lennon. NBLV

I have a little pipe that I. Last Will and Testament. Géza Páskándi. IQMS, *tr. by* John Gordon Nichols

I have a little shadow that goes in and out with me. My Shadow. Robert Louis Stevenson. ChAP; ITBLP; OTCP; PWR; UV

I have a little shadow that goes out sometimes with me. My Shadow. W. Hodgson Burnett. UV

I have a little sister, they call her Peep-Peep. Mother Goose. OxNR

I have a little windmill on my head. Sliding Trombone. Georges Ribemont-Dessaignes. SPE, *tr. by* David Gascoyne

I have a lover. Tuesday Night Affair. Sandra Turner Bond. ISC

I have a mistress, for perfections rare. Devout Lover, A. Thomas Randolph. OBEV

I have a name of my own. Gruoch. Gruoch. Marion Lomax. NeBl

I have a neighbor. Brown Rosellen. FFC

I Have a New Garden. *Unknown.* MiEL; OBGa

I have a new home. A roaring Sparring Partner like a sunspot. Newark Public Library Reading Room, The. Sotère Torregian. NBV

I have a pretty little flow'r. Francis Daniel Pastorius. SCAP

I Have a Rendezvous with Death. Alan Seeger. APT-1; AiP; BRP; FaBoWar; TCAPo

(Rendezvous.) PeFWW

I have a seamstress, making a shirt for me. Seamstress, The. Harry Clifton. BiHa

I have a silence in the rain. Michael Burkard. BodElec

I have a sister, little sister, living in Chung-li. Tu Fu. CoBCP *Fr.* Seven Songs Written During the Ch'ien-yüan Era.

I have a smiling face, she said. Mask, The. Elizabeth Barrett Browning. VWP

I Have a Stage in My Head. Yona Volach. DTA, *tr. by* Miriyam Glazer

I have a suit, blessings upon it. Describing a Suit. Hafiz Ibrahim. MAP, *tr. by* Christopher Middleton and Christopher Tingley

I have a terrible fear of being an animal. César Vallejo. SPE, *tr. by* Robert Bly

I have a theory about motion. Jazz Dancer. Cornelius Eady. SeSe

I have a tree, a graft of love. Arbor Amoris. François Villon. AWP, *tr. by* Andrew Lang

I have a voice in my head that talks backwards. Lemn Sissay. NewEx

I have a whim to speak in verse. *Unknown.* NOIV *Fr.* Fortification of New Ross, The.

I have a word to say to you as men and as a man speaking to. David Jones. TCAWP *Fr.* Tribune's Visitation, The.

I have a young love. Sailor, The. Sylvia Townsend Warner. OBMV

I Have a Young Sister. *Unknown.* EBEV; FaBoVe; MiEL; NAEL-5v1; PeLV

I have all / my mother's habits. Mother's Habits. Nikki Giovanni. BlSi

I have allowed my family to scatter. Autumn. Boris Leonidovich Pasternak. TCRP, *tr. by* Henry Kamen

I have almost ev'rything. Something to Live For. Billy Strayhorn. ReLy

I have already come to the verge of. Unborn Child, An. Derek Mahon. CABP; PNI; WoPoe

I have already lost the style and maze of language. Sabah Al-Kharrat Zwein. PoArWo, *tr. by* Kaissar Afif *Fr.* Inclined House, The.

I have always been remarkably impressed. Dull Sonnet. Henry Reed. OxBEV

I have always been sorry. To the Tune "Glittering Sword Hilts." Liu Yu Hsi. OHMPC, *tr. by* Kenneth Rexroth

I have always known / That at last I would. Narihira (Ariwara no Narihira). OHPJ

I have always loved particulars: the angels. On Muranowska Street. Myra Sklarew. TaR

I have always loved the word *guitar*. Guitar. David St. John. InvLad

I have always regretted the shallowness of words. Looking at My Knife-hilt Ring, a Song. Liu Yu Hsi. SuSp, *tr. by* Daniel Bryant

I have an appointment with elsewhere. Wedding Day. Mark Levine. AmPoNex; BAP-01

I have an arrow that will find its mark. Ralph Waldo Emerson. TCAPo

I have an ear for music. Pretty Girl Is Like a Melody, A. Irving Berlin. ReLy

I have (and long shall have) a white great nimble cat. White Great Nimble Cat, A. Sir Philip Sidney. TriCat

I have armoured my feelings. Rufinus. GrAn

I have assumed a conscious sociability. Garden Party. Sir Herbert Read. OBGa

I have at times seen all the eastern sky. Dante Alighieri. NAWM-7v1, *tr. by* Allen Mandelbaum *Fr.* Divine Comedy, The (Mandelbaum Translation).

I have avoided your wide English eyes. Sweet William. "Ern Malley." BMAP

I have awakened at Missoula, Montana, utterly happy. (LL) In a Train. Robert Bly. InvLad; TTTS

I have baptized thee Withy, because of thy slender limbs. To ———? Richard Dehmel. AWP, *tr. by* Jethro Bithell

I have beaten him often, head and heel. Poète Manqué. Ernest Sandeen. CRP

I have beaten out my exile. (LL) Ezra Pound. MoAmPo; NOBA; NoAM; OxBA *Fr.* Lustra.

I have been a censor for fifteen months. Censorship. Arthur Waley. OxBTC

I Have Been a Foster. *Unknown.* EBEV; OxBSP

I have been a movie fan. He Never Did That to Me. Noël Coward. NBLV

I have been a privileged spectator at innumerable acts of vandalism. Drummer, The. Bruce Beaver. BMAP

I have been a rover. Breezin' Along with the Breeze. Haven Gillespie. ReLy

I have been all men known to history. Taliesin 1952. Ronald Stuart Thomas. HarvBoo

I have been all my lovers. Desire 1. Thulani Davis. ISC

I have been bitter with you, my brother. Colloquy with John Keats. "Ern Malley." BMAP

I have been brought into darkness. Bible, *O.T.* WoPoe, *tr. by* Susan Stewart *Fr.* Lamentations.

I have been cruel to a fat pigeon. Fly. W. S. Merwin. ChAP; NNaP; OWoS

I have been dying a long time. Earth, Take Me Back. John Hall Wheelock. APT-1

I have been encouraged to wait. Yet Still. Rashidah Ismaili. HAWP; ItWoWo

I have been faithful to thee, Cynara! in my fashion. (LL) Non Sum Qualis Eram Bonae sub Regno Cynarae. Ernest Christopher Dowson. AWP; BoLoP; CABP; ClHu; EBVV; EnLoPo; GTBS-P; HAP; HeIP-4; MoBrPo; NOBE; NoP-4; OBEV; OBMV; PeVV; PoRA; TFi; UnPo

I have been having an affair. Affair of the Heart. Peter Porter. BMAP

I have been her kind. (LL) Her Kind. Anne Sexton. CoAP; HCAP; HeIP-4; NALW; PoPoPo; TAP; TwCP; VCAP; WPOW

I have been here before. Sudden Light. Dante Gabriel Rossetti. BoLoP; CABP; CTC; NOBE; NOBVV; NPeEn; NoP-4; OxBEV

I have been here. Dispersed in meditation. Agnosco Veteris Vestigia Flammae. James Vincent Cunningham. VGW

I have been here for a half hour. Library, The. Aidan Carl Mathews. CIP-2

I HAVE been ill so long that I do not count the days. Being Visited by a Friend During Illness. Po Chü-i. ChiP, *tr. by* Arthur Waley

I have been in a marine aquarium and I have seen. Louis Dudek. MoCV *Fr.* Atlantis.

I have been in great distress. Lover's Prize, A. Beatrice [*or* Beatritz *or* Beatriz], Countess de Die [*or* Dia]. EroLit; NAWM-7v1, *tr. by* Peter Dronke

I have been in this bar. Man Who Married Magdalene, The. Anthony Hecht. ChIV-2; PeLV

I have been kissed before, she added, blushing slightly. Arthur Hugh Clough. FaBoVe *Fr.* Bothie of Tober-na-Vuolich, The [A Long-Vacation Pastoral].

I have been lazy. Thanks Sent to Taihei Osho. Muso Soseki. EaWin, *tr. by* W. S. Merwin

I have been looking these pages over, my dearest wife. Ovid. WoPoe, *tr. by* David R. Slavitt *Fr.* Tristia.

I have been noting events for forty years. Basil Bunting. NPeEn *Fr.* Chomei at Toyama.

I have been one acquainted with the night. Acquainted with the Night. Robert Frost. APT-1; AWTN; AmFaPo; GSo; HAP; HarvBoo; MoAmPo; NOBA; NoAM; NoP-4; PoE; SAmP; Son; TAP; TFi; TRP; TwCP; VGW; WeW-3

I have been profligate of happiness. To Olive. Lord Alfred Bruce Douglas. OBEV

I have been proud and said, "My Love, my own." (LL) Elizabeth Barrett Browning. CTC; CenSon; ITBLP; LW *Fr.* Sonnets from the Portuguese.

I have been so great a lover. Great Lover, The. Rupert Brooke. MoBrPo; PoRA

I have been studying how I may compare. William Shakespeare. OxAEP-1; WoPoe *Fr.* King Richard III.

I have been tempted to rush the job. Chairmaker, The. Siobhan Campbell. MFPA

I have been the woman on the subway. Release. Lisa Sewell. AmPoNex

I have been there again, and seen the backs. Again. Jon Stallworthy. OxBC

I have been thinking. Lilies. Mary Oliver. BBASP

I have been thinking of the difference between water. Kabir. EnlH

I Have Been Through the Gates. Charlotte Mew. MoBrPo

I have been to my God like the iris and the anemone. Saul [*or* Shaul] Tchernichowsky [*or* Tchernichovsky]. MHP *Fr.* To the Sun.

I have been to Paris since we parted. (LL) As Children Together. Carolyn Forché. NoAM; OxWW

I have been treading on leaves all day until I am autumn-tired. Leaf-Treader, A. Robert Frost. MoAmPo

I have been urged by earnest violins. Music. Wilfred Owen. CAGL

I have been waiting to speak to you. Eve (Rachel). Michael S. Harper. ESEAA

I have been walking above Cwmchwefri. Cwmchwefri. T. Harri Jones. AngWePo

I have been warned. It is more than thirty years since I wrote. But I Am Growing Old and Indolent. Robinson Jeffers. APT-1; ColAP; NOBA; TAP

I have been watching her for a long time. I have been watching. Public Place (After Olga Broumas), The. Achy Obejas. WiU

I have been watching slow things the long afternoon. Slow. Robert Francis. APT-2

I have been with you, and I have thought of you. Chinese Villanelle. John Yau. PmAP

I have been wondering. Letter, A. Anthony Hecht. OxBC

I have been young, and now am not too old. Report on Experience. Edmund Charles Blunden. FaBoTw; GTBS-P; NOBE; NPeEn; OBMV; OBWP; OxBEV; PeFWW

I have begged the angels. Good-Bye, Valentine. Leslie Anne McIlroy. AmPoNex

I have beginning and end. Monument, A. Vladislav Felitsianovich Khodasevich. TCRusP, *tr. by* John Glad

I have begun to die. Sentry, The. Alun Lewis. AngWePo; PoWW; TCAWP

I have borne the anguish of love, which ask me not to describe. Hafiz [or Hafez]. AWP *Fr.* Odes.

I Have Bowed before the Sun. Anna Walters. WPOW

I have braved, for want of wild beasts, steel cages. May 24, 1980. Joseph Brodsky. TCRP, *tr. by* Joseph Brodsky.

I have broken the sound barrier of morality. Gay Poet, The. William Barber. CAGL

I have brothers, younger brothers in a place far away. Tu Fu. CoBCP *Fr.* Seven Songs Written During the Ch'ien-yüan Era.

I HAVE brought my pillow and am lying at the northern. Folk-Songs. Chan Fang-sheng. ChiP, *tr. by* Arthur Waley

I have burned ten thousand volumes. On the Day of Washing the Buddha in the Year Ting-wei (1607), I Dreamed That My Late Son Shih-ch'ü Was Holding a Book, and Appeared To Be Quite Happy. T'ang Hsien-tsu. CoBLCP; ColAnChi, *tr. by* Jonathan Chaves

I have but four, the treasures of my soul. Slave Mother, The. Frances Ellen Watkins Harper. ColAP

I have but one chance left,—and that is going to Florence. Arthur Hugh Clough. FaBoVe *Fr.* Amours de Voyage.

I have carried it with me each day: that morning I took. Morning, A. Mark Strand. HCAP

I have carried my pillow to the windowsill. Summer near the River. Carolyn Kizer. CoAP; VGW

I have cast in here a soul. War Songs. *Unknown.* APN-2, *tr. by* Alfred Longley Riggs

I have changed my mind; or my mind is changed in me. Philoctetes. Henry Reed. HarvBoo

I have chosen to live near the rebuilt walls of my memory. Porte Dorée. Léopold Sédar Senghor. PoetW, *tr. by* Melvin Dixon

I have cleared this space of you, for you, for you. (LL) Sweet Reader, Flanneled and Tulled. Olena Kalytiak Davis. BAP-01; NAPBL

I have climbed all the way to the summit. Auditor Thinks about Female Nature, An. Jamie Grant. NOBAu

I have come down. Prologue. Odia Ofeimun. HBAPE; NAfrP

I have come far enough. Form of Women, A. Robert Creeley. ErotSp

I have come far to have found nothing. Cid Corman. VGW *Fr.* Three Tiny Songs.

I have come in my own time. California Light. Sherley Anne Williams. GeoHom

I have come out to smell the hyacinths which again in this. For and Against the Environment. D. M. Black. EmeKit

I have come to catch birds. Bird Catcher, The. *Unknown.* TTY, *tr. by* Ulli Beier

I have come to claim. I Have Come to Claim Marilyn Monroe's Body. Judy Grahn. ReTh

I have come to my end, but you. Wind, The. Boris Leonidovich Pasternak. RusPo, *tr. by* Robert Arthur Douglas Ford

I have come to the borders of sleep. Lights Out. Edward Thomas. HarvBoo; NOBE; OxAEP-2; PoWW; WoPoe

I have come to you tonite out of the depths. Reflections After the June 12th March for Disarmament. Sonia Sanchez. ESEAA

I have come upon the visage again. Wood Floor Dreams. Lance Henson. VoR

I have confidence, Peacock, and my eyes are soft. Lincoln Bedroom, The. Donald Berger. NAPBL

I have consider'd it; and find. Resolve, The. Henry Vaughan. ESCV

I have considered [*or* consider'd] it, and find[e]. Reprisal[l], The. George Herbert. ESCV; GeHe

I have constructed a labyrinth without a Minotaur. In My Labyrinth (The Minotaur's Game). Carlota Caulfield. TANSG, *tr. by* Chris Allen

I have courage and hardihood. Besieged. Zalman Schneour. TrJP, *tr. by* Joseph Leftwich

I have cultivated. Jewel Field. Muso Soseki. EaWin, *tr. by* W. S. Merwin

I Have Cut an Eagle. James Koller. PoM

I have cut the plaintain grove. Witch, The. Santal. RaBo

I have decided I'm divine. Ballade of the New God. Thomas M. [*or* "Tom"] Disch. RA

I have decided I will not be like John Hu anymore. Edge of Something, The. Linda Gregg. BodElec

I have desired to go. Heaven-Haven. Gerard Manley Hopkins. HeIP-4; MoBrPo; NOBE; NOCV; NoAM; OBEV; OxAEP-2; OxBSP; PAI; PeECV; RB; SoSe-8; TFi; TOF

I have discovered that I'm like Raquel. Like Raquel. Maria Arrillaga. TANSG

I have discovered that most of. January Morning. William Carlos Williams. APT-1

I have done all I could. Tree and the Lady, The. Thomas Hardy. MoBrPo

I have done it again. Lady Lazarus. Sylvia Plath. AmFaPo; ChIV-2; CoAmPo; FaBoWP; HCAP; HarvBoo; NAAL-2v2; NAAL-5; NALW; NIL-7; NIP-4; NOBA; NoAM; NoP-4; OxWW; PoPoPo; PoetW; TAP; TRP; VCAP; VGW

I Have Done My Reckoning. Attila József. IQMS, *tr. by* Michael Hatwell

I have done one braver thing. Undertaking, The. John Donne. NAEL-5v1; NAEL-7v1; NOBE

I have done the deed. Didst thou not hear a noise? William Shakespeare. EBEV; OxAEP-1 *Fr.* Macbeth.

I have done this with a loving heart for my father Amun. Queen Hatshepsut. HAWP *Fr.* Obelisk Inscriptions.

I have dreamt a dream of fulfillment, of freedom. Disciples Asleep at Gethsemane. Paul Kane. GI

I have dreamt it again: standing suddenly still. Wormwood. Thomas Kinsella. CIP-2; PBCIP

I have eaten. This Is Just to Say. William Carlos Williams. APT-1; ChAP; HarvBoo; HeIP-4; InPK-6; KaS; NAAL-2v2; NAAL-5; NIL-7; NIP-4; NOBA; NoAM; NoP-4; OPOU; PAI; PoPoPo; TAP; TRP

I have eaten the city. Manhattan. Hoffman Reynolds Hays. SPE

I have electricity in me. Intimate Mixture. Elena Georgiou. WiU

I have embraced the summer dawn. Dawn. Arthur Rimbaud. SxFrPo, *tr. by* Martin Sorrell

I have encountered a valley, in ragged bast matting. Elena Ignatova. ItGoST, *tr. by* Sibelan Forrester

I have entered into the Desert, the place of desolation. Charles Erskine Scott Wood. APT-1 *Fr.* Poet in the Desert, The.

I have examin'd and do find. To Mrs M. A. at Parting. Katherine Philips. NAEL-6v1; NAEL-7v1

I Have Exhausted the Delighted Range. Michael Hartnett. CIP-2; ModIr

I have faith in all those things that are not yet said. I Have Faith. Rainer Maria Rilke. BBASP, *tr. by* Robert Bly

I have fallen in love with American names. American Names. Stephen Vincent Benét. APT-2; FaBoA; OBAL; OxBA

I have fathered. Father Poem. Joel Oppenheimer. PoM

I have felt it as they've said. Larry Eigner. PoM

I have finally learned. Valerio Magrelli. NeIt

"I have finished another year," said God. New Year's Eve. Thomas Hardy. MoBrPo; NoAM

I have followed to this strand the scent of their blood. Pilgrimage to Loango Strand. Jean-Baptiste Tati-Loutard. PBMAP

I have followed you model. Ode to a Model. Vladimir Vladimirovich Nabokov. OBAL

I have forsworn[e] it whil[e] I live [*or* life]. Wake at the Well, The. *Unknown.* MiEL

I Have Fought the Good Fight. Jared Bell Waterbury. AH

I have found God. Discovery. Hilda Schiff. HP

I Have Found My Lover. Frances Densmore. APT-1 *Fr.* Chippewa Music.

I have found myself. DC Nocturne. Kenneth Carroll. AmPoNex

I have found out a gift for my Erin. Pastoral Ballad by John Bull, A. Thomas Moore. BIrV; OBSV

I have found such joy in simple things. I Have Found Such Joy. Grace Noll Crowell. PoToHe

I have freed myself at last. From the Bridge. Claribel Alegría. AF

I have from you this red. Valerio Magrelli. NeIt

I have given you my true love. I'm Through with Love. Gustave Kahn. ReLy

I have gone far from my beloved ones. Uri Zvi Greenberg. TrJP, *tr. by* Charles A. Cowen *Fr.* Jerusalem.

I have gone into my eyes. Depression. Sonia Sanchez. ESEAA

I Have Gone into My Prison Cell. Shakuntala Hawoldar. HAWP

I have gone out, a possessed witch. Her Kind. Anne Sexton. CoAP; HCAP; HeIP-4; NALW; PoPoPo; TAP; TwCP; VCAP; WPOW

I have gone through. Sharyu. JDP, *tr. by* Yoel Hoffmann

I have gone through life quietly. Earth. Yaroslav [*or* Iaroslav] Vasilevich Smelyakov [*or* Smeliakov]. TCRP, *tr. by* Albert C. Todd

I have got into the slow train. In the Stopping Train. Donald Davie. NPeEn

I Have Got My Leave. Rabindranath Tagore. OBMV *Fr.* Gitanjali.

I have great need that the Saint grant help. Cynewulf. AnOE *Fr.* Juliana.

I have grown past hate and bitterness. Nationality. Mary Gilmore. CBAP

I have had a companion on the road. Daio. EaWin, *tr. by* W. S. Merwin

I have had asthma for a. Visitors. Tu Fu. BLT; OHPC, *tr. by* Kenneth Rexroth

I have had my dream—like others. Thursday. William Carlos Williams. APT-1

I have had my ups and downs. Song of Mehitabel, The. Don Marquis. TriCat

I have had playmates, I have had companions. Old Familiar Faces, The. Charles Lamb. AWP; GTBS-P; NOBE; OBEV; OxAEP-2; RB

I have had to learn the simplest things. Charles Olson. APT-2; NAAL-5; NOBA; NeAP; PmAP; PoE; PoM; VGW *Fr.* Maximus Poems, The.

I have heard ingenuous Indians say. Roger Williams. SCAP

I have heard it said. To the Muse. Denise Levertov. APSN

"I have heard," said a maid from Montclair. Limerick. Morris Gilbert Bishop. PeLi

I have heard talk of bold Robin Hood. Robin Hood's Golden Prize. Unknown. ESPB

I have heard tell somewhere. Old Dog in the Ruins of the Graves at Arles, The. James Wright (1927–80). NNaP

I have heard that far from here. Unknown. ASW Fr. Phoenix, The.

I have heard that hysterical women say. Lapis Lazuli. W. B. Yeats. CABP; EnlH; FaBoMo; FaBoTw; HeIP-4; NAEL-5v2; NAEL-6v2; NAWM-7v2; NOBE; NoAM; NoP-4; TFi

I have heard the affairs in Ch'ang-an are like a game of chess. Tu Fu. SuSp Fr. Autumn Thoughts.

I have heard the pigeons of the Seven Woods. In the Seven Woods. W. B. Yeats. NoAM

I have heard the silvery note. Song. Sándor Kisfaludy. IQMS, tr. by Anthony Edkins

I Have Heard Them Knock. Michael Hartnett. NOIV

I have heard what the talkers were talking . . . . the talk of the beginning and the end. Walt Whitman. CAGL; ColAP Fr. Song of Myself.

I have hoped, I have planned, I have striven. Unsubdued. Samuel Ellsworth Kiser. PoToHe

I have hopped, when properly wound up. Tin Frog, The. Russell Hoban. Spl

I have horns, but am not beast. Gordon Wardman. NewEx

I have imagined all this. Sleeping, The. Lynn Emanuel. AiP

I have in my throat one word. One Word. Gabriela Mistral. TCLAP, tr. by Doris Dana

I have invented a new species of poetry, "verse without words" or sound-. Hugo Ball. PFTM-1 Fr. Flight out of Time.

I have invented new worlds. I have dreamed. Birth of the Sun, The. Pablo Antonio Cuadra. TCLAP, tr. by Thomas Merton

I have it in my heart to serve God so. Of His Lady in Heaven. Jacopo da Lentino. AWP; EaItPo, tr. by Dante Gabriel Rossetti

I have it, looking to my left, the cars of this. Not Much Singing. Charles Bukowski. BodElec

I have it now. Stone, The. Henry Vaughan. ChIV-1

I have it underfoot; I have found it. For a Swarm of Bees. Unknown. ASW, tr. by Kevin Crossley-Holland

I have just come down from my father. Hospital Window, The. James Dickey. HCAP; NoAM; VCAP

I have just flown 1100 miles from Australia. Christchurch, N. Z. Earle Birney. OxBC

I have just realized that the stakes are myself. Revolutionary Letter #1. Diane Di Prima. CLPP

I have just seen you go down the mountain. Departure. Wang Wei. TAL

I have killed a virgin by being born. Géza Páskándi. IQMS, tr. by Agnes Arany-Makkai Fr. Language Memory.

I have killed the moth flying around. Moth-Terror. Benjamin De Casseres. TrJP

I have kissed your son's feet. Flora's Plea to Mary. Juan Delgado. TouFir

I have known the inexorable sadness of pencils. Dolor. Theodore Roethke. HCAP; HeIP-4; NoAM; OPOU; OxBSP; TRP

I have known the silence of the stars and of the sea. Silence. Edgar Lee Masters. MoAmPo; PoToHe

I have known the strange nurses of Kindness. But I Do Not Need Kindness. Gregory Corso. NeAP

I have lain awake in the darkness many nights. Darkness, The. Charles E. Butler. YaYoPo

I have learn'd. William Shakespeare. OxAEP-1 Fr. King Henry IV, Pt. I.

I have learned. Rāmprasād Sen. SinGod, tr. by Rachel Fell McDermott

I have learned that love is not a picnic. Blue Again. Dorothy Fields. ReLy

I have learnt by heart the lesson of goodbyes. Tristia. Osip Emilevich Mandelstam [or Mandelshtam]. WoPoe, tr. by James Greene

I have learnt the Hebrew blessing before eating bread. Charles Reznikoff. APT-2

I have led her home, my love, my only friend. Tennyson. EBVV; NAEL-5v2; NAEL-6v2; NOBVV Fr. Maud [A Monodrama].

I have lighted the candles, Mary. Kenneth Patchen. TrCP

I have lived. Remembering the Past. Al Robles. ReBoTo

I Have Lived and I Have Loved. Unknown. TTTS

I have lived between my two hands. Hands. Edvard Kocbek. PoSu, tr. by Michael Scammell and Veno Taufer

I have lived in circles of solitude. Consultation. Jayne Cortez. SurWo

I have lived in important places, times. Epic. Patrick Kavanagh. BIrV; CABP; CIP-2; HarvBoo; MakPoe; ModIr; NOIV; NPeEn; NoP-4; OxBSo

I have lived long enough, having seen one thing, that love hath an end. Hymn to Proserpine. Algernon Charles Swinburne. EBVV; NAEL-5v2; NAEL-6v2

I have lived on the lip. Jelaluddin [or Jalal al-Din] Rumi. EnlH

I Have Lived This Way for Years and Do Not Wish to Change. Michael C. Blumenthal. HCAP

I have located it, my ghost town. Ghost Town. Michael Longley. ModIr

I Have Longed to Move Away. Dylan Thomas. OxBEV

I Have Longings for My Dead. Devorah Amir. DTA, tr. by Miriyam Glazer

I have looked at you as Christ, imagine, Veronica and they separated. To Forget the Image. Michel Deguy. PFTM-2, tr. by Clayton Eshleman

I Have Lost A Verse. Julia de Burgos. TANSG, tr. by Heather Rosario Sievert

I have lost all regret of evil with the years gone by. Three Stars. Robert Desnos. SurPaPo, tr. by Mary Ann Caws

I have lost, and lately, these. Upon the Loss[e] of His Mistresses. Robert Herrick. BASC; BeJo; CaPo; CavPo; NAEL-5v1; NAEL-6v1; NAEL-7v1; NOSC; PoE

I have lost my friend. The semi trucks out there. Stubble Burning, The. Sarah Ruden. AmPoNex

I have lost this wager. Time wins. Time Wins. Benoy Majumdar. OMIP, tr. by Jyotirmoy Dutta

I Have Loved Flowers. Robert Bridges. MoBrPo

I have loved the air outside Shop-Rite Liquor. Poetics. August Kleinzahler. PmAP

I have made a footprint, a sacred one. Planting Initiation Song. Unknown. WPoS; WoPoe, tr. by Francis La Flesche

I have made a footprint, I live in the light of day. (LL) Planting Initiation Song. Unknown. WPoS; WoPoe, tr. by Francis La Flesche

I have made a mistake, someone tells me. Beaten Track, The. Steve Benson. FTOS

I have made a sirventes against the city of Toulouse. Sirventes. Paul Blackburn. NeAP; PoM

I have made silken verses. Re-Conversion. Novella Nikolaevna Matveyeva [or Matveieva]. TCRusP, tr. by Nigel Stott

I have made tales in verse, but this man made. Waggon-Maker, The. John Masefield. EBEV

I have made you smile. (LL) On the Road to the Sea. Charlotte Mew. BrRo; FaBoWP; PoBW

I have marked, as on the heather now I strayed. As on the Heather. Reinmar von Hagenau. AWP, tr. by Jethro Bithell

I have (may I always keep!) blonde Minerva's protection: my vessel. Ovid. RomPo, tr. by Peter Green Fr. Tristia.

I have mentioned it by name. Edouard J. Maunick. NegPo Fr. As Far as Yoruba Land.

I have met them at close of day. Easter 1916. W. B. Yeats. FaBoMo; HAP; HarvBoo; HeIP-4; NAEL-5v2; NAEL-6v2; NAWM-7v2; NIL-7; NIP-4; NOBE; NOIV; NPeEn; NoAM; NoP-4; OBWP; OxAEP-2; OxBTC; PoE; PoPoPo; TFi

I have mislaid the torment and the fear. Success. William Empson. OxBTC

I have moved to Dublin to have it out with you. John Berryman. NoAM; TRP Fr. Dream Songs.

I have moved to this home of Immortals. Living in the Summer Mountains. Yü Hsüan-chi. WoPoe, tr. by Chung Ling and Kenneth Rexroth

I have my gri-gri. Portrait. Antoine-Roger Bolamba. PBMAP

I have my piety too, which could. Epitaph on Master Vincent Corbet[t], An. Ben Jonson. BeJo

I have neither Plummes nor Cherries. Nicholas Breton. NPeEn Fr. Solemne Long Enduring Passion, A.

I have never been at the top of wind-played Olympus. Uri Zvi Greenberg. FIT, tr. by Robert Friend

I have never been rich before. To My Friend. Anne Campbell. PoToHe

I have never seen him, this invisible member of the panel, this thirteenth juror. People vs. the People, The. Kenneth Fearing. MoAmPo

I have never seen the place where I was born. Birthplace. Tahereh Saffarzadeh. WPOW, tr. by Deirdre Lashgari

I have never soared, never soared. Bulat Shalvovich Okudzhava. TCRP

I have no Brother—they who meet me now. Thy Brother's Blood. Jones Very. APN-1; NOBA; TAP

I have no daughter. I desire none. (LL) For My Daughter. Weldon Kees. CoAP; OxBSo

I have no desire to live, but I am afraid of death. Ts'ai Yen. WPOW Fr. Eighteen Verses Sung to a Tatar Reed Whistle.

I have no dog, but it must be. My Dog. John Kendrick Bangs. ITBLP

I have no ears or eyes. Tugged Hand, The. William Henry Davies. TCAWP

I have no embroidered headband. Sappho. BoWoP

I have no God, I have no land. Songs of Innocence. Attila József. IQMS, tr. by Thomas Kabdebo and Anton N. Nyerges

I have no illusions. Visibility. Maura Stanton. BodElec

I have no Life but this. Emily Dickinson. FaBoVe

I have no memories or photograph of my father. O-Bon: Dance for the Dead. Garrett Kaoru Hongo. LoL

I have no mockings or arguments, I witness and wait. (LL) Walt Whitman. CAGL; ColAP; EnlH; NAWM-7v2; UnPo Fr. Song of Myself.

I have no name. William Blake. FHYEP; NAEL-5v2; OxAEP-2; OxBSP *Fr.* Songs of Innocence.

I have no name for the nameless thing. Nameless Thing. Robert Penn Warren. BodElec

I have no opinion. Opinion of Hagar, The. Alicia Ostriker. TaR

I have no other earthly friend! (LL) Affliction of Margaret— The. William Wordsworth. GTBS-P; RACG

I have no pain, dear mother, now. *Unknown.* OBCoV *Fr.* Soldiers' Songs of the First World War.

I have no seed to spread over the world. I Have No Seed to Scatter through the World. Patrizia Cavalli. NeIt, *tr.* by Robert McCracken

I have no shame, no regret. Cosmopolitan Poetry. János Arany. IQMS, *tr.* by Madeline Mason

I Have No Strength for Mine. Joanne Kyger. PoM

I have no substance and no form. Nigel Cameron. NewEx

I have no wit, no words, no tears. Better Resurrection, A. Christina Georgina Rossetti. NOBVV; VWP; ViWPN

I have not come within their frozen. Twilight in the Library. John Tripp. TCAWP

I have not experienced the true. Lighthouse. Novella Nikolaevna Matveyeva [*or* Matveieva]. TCRP, *tr.* by Deming Brown

I Have Not Lingered in European Monasteries. Leonard Cohen. NOBC

I have not ridden a horse much. Sharing, The. Bruce Weigl. CDa

I have not seen your writing. Letter, The. Patricia Beer. OxBC

I Have Not Signed a Treaty with the United States Government. Chrystos. UnSA

I have not slept for a week. Death of the Race Car Driver, The. Norman Dubie. MoASP

I have not stood at this grave nor have I. After a Time. Elizabeth Jennings. HarvBoo

I have not used my darkness well. Squall. Stanley Moss. CoAP

I have not woken from a dream nor arrived by express train. Prague in the Midday Sun. Vitězslav Nezval. AF, *tr.* by Ewald Osers

I have not yet grown weary. Gofu. JDP, *tr.* by Yoel Hoffmann

I have nothing new to ask of you. Another Year Come. W. S. Merwin. PAI

I have nothing to give you, but my anger. Love Poem for My Country, A. Frank Mkalawile Chipasula. HBAPE; NAfrP

I have nothing to say about the war. Yehuda Amichai [*or* Amikhai]. PoSu *Fr.* Patriotic Songs.

I have nothing to say to you, Billie Holiday. Billie in Silk. Angela Jackson. ReTh; SeSe

I have often imagined that glances. Valerio Magrelli. NeIt

I have paid my price to live with myself on the terms that I willed. (LL) Rudyard Kipling. FaBoEE; FaBoTw; NPeEn; PeFWW *Fr.* Epitaphs of the War [1914–1918].

I have perceiv'd that to be with those I like is enough. Walt Whitman. SAmP *Fr.* I Sing the Body Electric.

I have pietie thow suld fall sic mischance. (LL) Robert Henryson. EBEV; PoE *Fr.* Testament of Cresseid, The.

I have pined for the sight of the sea for years. Beautiful Sea, The. Mary E. Tucker. CBWP-1

I have planted a cedar in my garden. Cedar, The. Han G. Hoekstra. TuT, *tr.* by Peter Van de Kamp

I have played with her when a child. Tennyson. NAEL-6v2 *Fr.* Maud [A Monodrama].

I have *poetic* licence, i WriTe thE way i waNt. According to my Mood. Benjamin Zephaniah. NOxBChV

I have portrayed temptation as amusing. Good Loser, The. Sophie Hannah. HarvBoo

I have prayed for the end of his breath. Fay Zwicky. BMAP *Fr.* Three Songs of Love and Hate.

I have problems. Division of Labor. Feyyaz Kayacan. WoPoe, *tr.* by Feyyaz Fergar

I have put on a grotesque mask. Last Poem. Hugo Williams. NPeEn

I have put upon my wall. For the Intellectuals. Jeremy Ingalls. YaYoPo

I have raked [*or* accrued] up a golden and stinking blaze. (LL) Geoffrey Hill. EmeKit; PoE *Fr.* Mercian Hymns.

I have reached, alas, the long shadow. Sestina. Dante Alighieri. WoPoe, *tr.* by James Schuyler

I have read my name on a rock. In the Arab Maghreb. Badr Shakir Al-Sayyab. MAP, *tr.* by Lena Jayyusi and Christopher Middleton

I Have Recently Edited My Unworthy Poems in Four Chapters, Copied Them Out in My Own Hand, and Entrusted Them to My Daughter to Keep. Five Miscellaneous Poems. Chin Nung.
  "In the silences between peals of the bell." CoBLCP

I have risen from your body. Onion, The. John Thompson. NOBC

I have said / She 's adulteress; I have said with whom. William Shakespeare. OxAEP-1 *Fr.* Winter's Tale, The.

I have said that the soul is not more than the body. Walt Whitman. EnlH *Fr.* Song of Myself.

I have sailed the south rivers of China and prayed to the hillside Buddhas. In Search of Aunt Jemima. Crystal Williams. AmPoNex

I have seen a court, and a dozen courts. Christmas Revel, A. Dafydd [*or* David] Bach ap Madog Wladaidd. OBWVE

I have seen / A curious child, who dwelt upon a tract. William Wordsworth. ITBLP *Fr.* Excursion, The.

I have seen a lovely thing. Blight. Arna Bontemps. ColAP

I have seen a robin cock his head so. Botticelli's St. Sebastian. Brigit Pegeen Kelly. ExTi

I Have Seen Black Hands. Richard Wright. APT-2
  (I am black and I have seen black hands, millions and millions of / them.) AF

I have seen flowers come in stony places. Epilogue. John Masefield. FaBoEE; OxBEV; OxBTC

I have seen full many a sight. Dinah Kneading Dough. Paul Laurence Dunbar. NAAAL

I have seen her, wonderful! This Version of Love. Dorothy Hewett. BMAP; CBAP

I have seen lines on a paper. Borders. Michael S. Weaver. GT

I have seen men binding their brothers in chains, and crafty. Hate and the Love of the World, The. Max Ehrmann. PoToHe

I have seen, O desolate one, the voice has its tower. Bell Tower. Léonie Adams. MoAmPo

I have seen old ships sail like swans asleep. Old Ships, The. James Elroy Flecker. MoBoPo; OBMV; PoRA

I have seen rare sunshine held in the first birch leaves. Annunciation. Ken Etheridge. AngWePo

I have seen the black Vedas. One Book, The. Velemir [*or* Viktor Vladimirovich] Khlebnikov. TCRusP, *tr.* by Kathy Lewis and Bob Perelman

I have seen the paschal men today. Easter '68. Basil T. Paquet. CDa

I have seen the rain speak. New Dream, A (Wuski A-Baw-Tan). Jennifer Pierce Eyen. ReEnLa

I have seen the rosebud blow. On Viewing Her Sleeping Infant. Maria Frances Cecelia Cowper. ECWP

I have seen the soft light flicker. Message from Ohanapecosh Glacier. W. M. Ransom. CDW; GifTon

I have seen the sun break through. Bright Field, The. Ronald Stuart Thomas. AngWePo; TCAWP

I have seen the white horsemen riding to hell. Apocalypse and Resurrection. John Clifford Bayliss. SPE

I have seen them trying. I Have Seen Them. Norman Jordan. NBV

I have seen this picture before. Colleen J. McElroy. LTA

I have seen you, little mouse. Little Mouse, The. *Unknown.* ReMoGo

I have seen you, my erect morning, bare chested with tree-top tousled head. Morning in My City. Avraham Shlonsky. MHP, *tr.* by Ruth Finer Mintz

I have seen you suffer in the midst of winters. Harlem. Jean Brierre. TTY, *tr.* by John F. Matheus

I have seen your feet gilded by morning. Metamorphoses of M. John Peale Bishop. APT-1

I have shut my balcony door. Casida of Sobbing. Federico García Lorca. AF, *tr.* by Robert Bly

I have slept and I awaken . . . Or I haven't awakened. Dulce Maria Loynaz. TANSG, *tr.* by Alan West *Fr.* Last Days of Home.

I have slept by the cold window. Snow at Rohatsu Sesshin. Muso Soseki. EaWin, *tr.* by W. S. Merwin

I have snapped off my burning. Maui. Meg Campbell. PeNZ

I have so fiercely dreamed of you. Last Poem. Robert Desnos. AmFaPo, *tr.* by X. J. Kennedy

I have so little sorrow. Song. Patricia Jones. ISC

I Have So Often Dreamed of You. Robert Desnos. SurPaPo, *tr.* by Mary Ann Caws

I have so often dreamed of you that you have become unreal. I Have So Often Dreamed of You. Robert Desnos. SurPaPo, *tr.* by Mary Ann Caws

I Have Some Friends before Me Gone. *Unknown.* AH

I have sown beside all waters in my day. Black Man Talks of Reaping, A. Arna Bontemps. APT-2; BPo; ColAP; NAAAL; SSLK

I have spent my life. "Stephany." NBV

I have spread wet linen. Today. Ethel Romig Fuller. PoToHe

I have staked out my ground. My Ground. Marie Luise Kaschnitz. PFTM-2, *tr.* by Lisel Mueller

I have stood in forests, so old and vast. Forests and Caverns. Eleanor Percy Lee. SWaP

I have strolled the long groves of the Classics and Canons. Rhyme-Prose on the Idle Life. P'an Yüeh. CoBCP, *tr.* by Burton Watson

I have studied the tight curls. Movement Song. Audre Lorde. VCAP

I have supposed my past is a part of myself. Past, The. Ha Jin. NIL-7

I have swallowed a mighty gulp of poison. Night in Hell. Arthur Rimbaud. SxFrPo, *tr.* by Martin Sorrell

I have sworn ten thousand times. Kenneth Rexroth. NNaP; PGA

I have taken scales from off. Fishmonger. Marsden Hartley. APT-1

I have taken that vow. Red-haired Man's Wife, The. James Stephens. MoBrPo

I Have Taken the Suits and Shoes to Oxfam. Felicity Napier. Prnts

I have taken the woman of beauty. *Unknown.* AWP, *tr. by* Constance Lindsay Skinner *Fr.* Three Songs from the Haida.

I have the address exactly. I know her name. At the Exhibition of Parables. Donald Revell. BodElec

I have the blues. Left All Alone Again Blues. Anne Caldwell. ReLy

I have the itch on my nape. Pain. Lupenga Mphande. NAfrP

I have the net into which all fishes go. Net, The. Edith Södergran. WoPoe, *tr. by* David McDuff

I have the same. December 9th. Eileen Myles. PmAP

I have thee, thou hast me. *Unknown.* GePo, *tr. by* Alexander Gode

I have this deal of death about my hands. Blood. Ray Bremser. NeAP

I have this large tattoo on my chest. It is like a dream I have. Confessional Poem. Louis Jenkins. RaBo

I have this need to feel you. Love/a Many Splintered Thing. Kevin Powell. InTrad

I Have This Vision of Madness. Perry Brass. CAGL

I have thought of beaches, fields. Bundles. Carl Sandburg. MoAmPo

I have thought so much about the girl. Muliebrity. Sujata Bhatt. FSt; HarvBoo

I have thrown wide my window. Midnight. Michael Roberts. OBMV

I Have to Go Now. Maggie Estep. HeMarv

I have to live with myself, and so. Myself. *Unknown.* PWR

I have to say poetry and is that nothing and am I saying it. Opening the Cage. Edwin Morgan. NIL-7

I have to sing. Orpingalik's My Breath: Eskimo Song. Stephen Berg. GifTon

I have to thank God I'm a woman. Affinity, The. Anna Wickham. NALW

I have to write a page. Vladimir Leonovich. TCRP

I have told you. Tenth Symphony. John Ashbery. NOBA

I have tossed hours upon the tides of fever. Bout with Burning. Vassar Miller. MoAmPo

I Have Touched. Patti Tana. PasH

I have traveled, I have traveled. Consumptive, The. Priscilla Jane Thompson. CBWP-2

I have tried earnestly to express. Gertrude Stein. APT-1 *Fr.* Stanzas in Meditation.

I Have Tried Hard. Zindzi Mandela. HAWP; NAfrP

I have tried to shift the stars. Juniper Moon Pulls at My Bones, The. Earle Thompson. HATNAP

I have turned into a little shrine, a favorite. Favorite Little Shrine, A. Enrique Lihn. VCWP

I have turned to the landscape because men disappoint me. Ram's Horn, The. John Hewitt. BIrV; ModIr; PNI

I have twelve oxen that be faire and brown. *Unknown.* MiEL

I have two countries: Cuba and the night. Two Countries. José Martí. TCLAP, *tr. by* Elinore Randall

I have two sicknesses, Love. *Unknown.* PGA

I Have Two Sons and the One I Love Best Is Robert. Paula Tatarunis. BloBone

I have understood nothing. Edouard J. Maunick. NegPo *Fr.* As Far as Yoruba Land.

I have walked a great while over the snow. Witch, The. Mary Elizabeth Coleridge. BrRo; CABP; NALW; PoBW; VWP; ViWPN; WPE

I have walked here before. Stand Still. Jim Peterson. PoCoUp

I have walked the distance of the earth. Names and sorrows. D. Rubin Green. CAGL

I have walked through many lives. Layers, The. Stanley Kunitz. BodElec

I have wanted excellence in the knife-throw. Language of the Brag, The. Sharon Olds. MakPoe; PBCAP

I have wasted my life. (LL) Lying in a Hammock at William Duffy's Farm in Pine Island, Minnesota. James Wright (1927–80). CoAmPo; ColAP; HAP; HCAP; MakPoe; NOBA; TRP; VCAP

I have watched the summer day come up from the top of a pier of the Williamsburgh Bridge. John Reed. APT-1 *Fr.* America in 1918.

I have watched your fingers drum. Hand, The. Howard Moss. TAP

I have wished a bird would fly away. Minor Bird, A. Robert Frost. APT-1; OWoS; SAmP

I have with fishing-rod and line. Wounded Hawk, The. Herbert Edward Palmer. FaBoTw

I have wrapped my dreams in a silken cloth. For a Poet. Countee Cullen. TTY

I have written. Woman Who Wrote Too Much, The. Kay Ryan. ExTi

I have wrought these words together out of a wryed existence. Wife's Complaint, The. *Unknown.* BoLoP, *tr. by* Michael Alexander

I haven't a clue where I've been. Limerick. Sydney Bernard Smith. PeLi

I haven't learned to live abandonedly yet, Mother. Scenes for an Elegy. Michael Klein. WiU

I haven't the heart to poke poor Billy. (LL) Harry Graham. NBLV; NOxBChV; PeLV *Fr.* Some Ruthless Rhymes.

I haven't the heart to say. To an Unknown Poet. Carolyn Kizer. OPRER

I haveta turn my television down sometimes cuz. Ntozake Shange. UnSA *Fr.* Okra to Greens.

I, he says, am not a warrior. Novella Nikolaevna Matveyeva [*or* Matveieva]. TCRP

I hear a bird. How Are Things in Glocca Morra? Burton Lane. ReLy

I hear a river thro' the valley wander. Variations on a Fragment by Trumbull Stickney. John Hollander. NoP-4

I Hear a Step. Ted Greenwald. FTOS

I hear a sudden cry of pain! Snare, The. James Stephens. SCGP

I hear a whistling. Emmett Till. James A. Emanuel. NIL-7; NIP-4

I hear again the tread of war go thundering through the land. Albert Sidney Johnston. Kate Brownlee Sherwood. CBCWP

I hear America singing, the varied carols I hear. I Hear America Singing. Walt Whitman. AWP; AiP; HAP; HHAm; ITBLP; MoAmPo; NIL-7; SAmP; TFi; WeW-3

I hear and is my heart not badly shaken? (LL) Shancoduff. Patrick Kavanagh. BIrV; CIP-2; FaBoTw; HarvBoo; WoPoe

I hear eating. Night Fun. Judith Viorst. TLR

I hear footsteps over my head all night. Walker, The. Arturo Giovannitti. APT-1

I hear / he won't give horses for poems. Insult, An. *Unknown.* NOIV

I hear her sew. Leroy Gorman. HA

I hear her voice like. Her Voice. Barney Bush. HATNAP

I hear in my heart, I hear in its ominous pulses. Wild Ride, The. Louise Imogen Guiney. ColAP; RACG; TCAPo

I hear it in the deep heart's core. (LL) Lake-Isle of Innisfree, The. W. B. Yeats. CABP; ChAP; ClHu; HeIP-4; InPK-6; MoBrPo; NAEL-5v2; NAEL-6v2; NOBE; NoAM; NoP-4; OBEV; OxAEP-2; OxBTC; PAI; PoE; PoPoPo; PoRA; TFi; UV

I Hear It Was Charged against Me. Walt Whitman. APN-1; CAGL; MoAmPo

I hear leaves drinking rain. Rain, The. William Henry Davies. OxBTC

I hear many voices. To Adhiambo. Gabriel Okara. PBA

I Hear Music. Burton Lane. ReLy

I hear music when I look at you. Song Is You, The. Jerome Kern. ReLy

I hear [*or* heare] the whistling ploughman [*or* plough-man] all day long. On the Ploughman [*or* Plough-Man]. Francis Quarles. NOSC; SacPr

I hear people waiting for the riot to begin in their hearts. Ray Charles at Mississippi State. Tom Dent. NBV

I hear singing and there's no one there. You're Just in Love. Irving Berlin. ReLy

I hear something coming. Breathing. James Tate. LCAP-2

I hear tapping in your silence. Looking Deep. Magdalena Gomez. PueRic

I hear tell there's a stranger in the Jones household. F. D. R. Jones. Harold Rome. ReLy

I HEAR THAT THE AXE HAS FLOWERED. Paul Celan. PoSu

I hear that the peonies are magnificent. To Hsü Shih-t'ing. Hsü Wei. CoBLCP, *tr. by* Jonathan Chaves

I hear that you have burned ten thousand of your poems. Twenty-eight Characters Sent to Tung-ts'un on the Subject of the Poems He Burned. Cheng Hsieh. CoBLCP, *tr. by* Jonathan Chaves

I hear the apes howl sadly. Written for Old Friends in Yang-Jou City While Spending the Night on the Tung-Lu River. Meng Hao Jan. WoPoe, *tr. by* Greg Whincup

I hear the beat. Talking Drums, The. Kojo Gyinaye Kyei. PBA

I hear the halting footsteps of a lass. Harlem Shadows. Claude McKay. APT-1; ColAP; NAAAL; NAAL-5; TCAPo

I hear the man downstairs slapping the hell out of his stupid wife again. .38, The. Ted Joans. WeW-3

I hear the noise about thy keel. Tennyson. EBVV; NAEL-6v2; NAWM-7v2 *Fr.* In Memoriam A. H. H.

I hear the Shadowy Horses, their long manes a-shake. Michael Robartes Bids His Beloved Be at Peace. W. B. Yeats. NoAM

I hear the trumpets of flying angels. Trumpets, The. Jorge de Lima. TCLAP, *tr. by* Luiz Fernández García

I hear the voice. Israel. Carl Rakosi. ChIV-1

I hear the wood slats wince on the back porch. After the Wedding. David Biespiel. NAPBL

I hear they're hoping to run trips. 'Do you think we'll ever get to see Earth, sir?' Sheenagh Pugh. TCAWP

I hear voices. I hear them often. I've heard them. Be Quiet, Go Away. Wanda Coleman. NAAAL

I hear voices in the next room. In the Bluemist Motel. Greg Pape. ReTh

I hear you call. Call of the River Nun, The. Gabriel Okara. PBA

I hear you have gone to live among the village mounds.   Visiting the Hermit Cheng.   Po Chü-i.   TAL

I hear you, I will come. (LL)   Bredon Hill.   A. E. Housman.   EBVV; MoBrPo; NAEL-5v2; NAEL-6v2; OxAEP-2; SoSe-8; UV

I hear you Trane.   Afreeka Brass.   Mwatabu Okantah.   SeSe

I Hear You've Let Go.   Rosario Ferré.   BoWoP, tr. by Willis Barnstone

I hear you were.   How I See Things.   Yusef Komunyakaa.   ESEAA

I hear your familiar footsteps all about me.   Second Life of My Mother.   Jorge Carrera Andrade.   TCLAP, tr. by Muna Lee

I heard a bird at dawn.   Rivals, The.   James Stephens.   OBEV; OBMV

I Heard a Bird Sing.   Oliver Herford.   NTCP

I heard a brooklet gushing.   Wilhelm Müller.   AWP, tr. by Henry Wadsworth Longfellow   Fr. Beautiful Maid of the Mill, The.

I heard a cow low, a bonnie cow low.   Unknown.   FaBoCh   Fr. Queen of Elfan's [or Elfland's] Nourice [or Nourrice], The.

I heard a gentle maiden, in the spring.   Time, Hope, and Memory.   Thomas Hood.   TreFP

I heard a herald's note announce the coming of a king.   Rex Mundi.   David Gascoyne.   NoP-4

I Heard a Linnet Courting.   Robert Bridges.   OBMV
    (Linnet, The.)   OBEV

I heard a mouse.   Mouse, The.   Elizabeth Jane Coatsworth.   NOxBChV; OBCA

I Heard a Noise and Wishèd for a Sight.   Thomas Bateson.   EBEV; HAP

I heard a river thro' the valley wander.   Trumbull Stickney.   APN-2   Fr. Dramatic Fragments.

I heard a thousand blended notes.   Lines Written in Early Spring.   William Wordsworth.   FHYEP; NAEL-5v2; NAEL-6v2; NOBRP; PAI; SacPr

I heard a voice, within me, call.   Anna Andreyevna Akhmatova.   TCRP

I heard a winter tree in song.   Conceit.   Mervyn Laurence Peake.   Spl

I heard a woman's lips.   Harrison Street Court.   Carl Sandburg.   APT-1

I heard a woman's voice that wailed.   In Ruin Reconciled.   Aubrey Thomas De Vere.   BIrV

I heard a wood thrush in the dusk.   Wood Song.   Sara Teasdale.   APT-1

I heard an angel speak last night.   Curse for a Nation, A.   Elizabeth Barrett Browning.   NALW; ViWPN; WPE; WPOW

I heard an ignorant crow call, "Life is now."   Old Snapshot.   Ronald G. Everson.   MoCV

I heard an old farm-wife.   Son, The.   Frederic Ridgely Torrence.   TCAPo

I heard an owl at midday.   Como lo Siento.   Lorna Dee Cervantes.   NoAM

I heard Andrew Jackson say, as he closed his Virgil.   Andrew Jackson's Speech.   Robert Bly.   CoAmPo

I HEARD at nights your long sighs.   Dreaming of a Dead Lady.   Shên Yo.   ChiP, tr. by Arthur Waley

I heard Christ sing quhile roond him dar.   I Heard Christ Sing.   Hugh MacDiarmid.   ChIV-2

I heard from a decent man the other day.   On Hearing It Has Been Ordered in the Chapterhouse of Ireland That the Friars Make No More Songs or Verses.   Pádraigín Haicéad.   NOIV, tr. by Thomas Kinsella

I heard from Pablo Neruda.   Pablo Neruda.   Jose Angel Figueroa.   PueRic

I heard him in the autumn winds.   Life in Death.   Ellice Hopkins.   PeVV

I heard how, to the beat of some quick tune.   Sadi [or Saadi or Sa'di].   AWP, tr. by Sir Edward Arnold   Fr. Gulistan, The.

I Heard Immanuel Singing.   Nicholas Vachel Lindsay.   HAP

I heard in the night the pigeons.   No Child.   Padraic Colum.   OBMV

I heard last night a little child go singing.   Elizabeth Barrett Browning.   PEW; VWP   Fr. Casa Guidi Windows.

I heard last night a lovely lute.   Summer Eve's Vision, A.   Maria Jane Jewsbury.   VWP

I heard my love was going to Yang-chou.   Unknown.   BoWoP   Fr. Tzu Yeh Songs.

I heard my love was gone on garrison at Chin-wei Mountain.   Tune: "Immortal at the River."   Wang Kuo-wei.   SuSp, tr. by Ching-i Tu

I heard my meatless bones.   Night Fear.   Don Receveur.   CDa

I heard my mother say it once.   Lesson of the Teeth, The.   Judith Ortiz Cofer.   TouFir

I heard my name, the day rose and disappear over the beach.   City of Men.   Aaron Shurin.   FTOS

I heard my son burst out of his room.   Rightful One, The.   David Ignatow.   TaR

I heard new words prayed at cows.   Seamus Heaney.   ModIr   Fr. Sweeney Redivivus.

I heard of poor.   Poor.   Myra Cohn Livingston.   KaS

I heard on the meadow.   Heinrich von Morungen.   GePo

I heard one who said: "Verily."   Cassandra.   Edwin Arlington Robinson.   APT-1; NoAM; OxBA

I heard or seemed to hear the chiding Sea.   Sea-Shore.   Ralph Waldo Emerson.   APN-1; ColAP; OxBA

I heard that south of the capital city.   Southern Mountains.   Han Yü.   SuSp, tr. by Charles Hartman

I Heard the Byrd.   Oliver Lagrone.   SeSe

I heard the carping [or herde a carpyng] of a clerk.   Robyn and Gandeleyn.   Unknown.   ESPB; OxBB

I heard the dead men singing in the sun. (LL)   Supremacy.   Edwin Arlington Robinson.   APN-2; NoAM

I heard the dogs howl in the moonlight night.   Dream, A [or The].   William Allingham.   BIrV; NOBVV

I heard the dust falling between the walls. (LL)   Redeployment.   Howard Nemerov.   OBWP; PoWW; TrJP

I heard the Indian Agent say.   Old Man's Lazy, The.   Peter Blue Cloud.   HATNAP; LTA

I heard the old, old men say.   Old Men Admiring Themselves in the Water, The.   W. B. Yeats.   FaBoCh; KaS

I heard the Poor Old Woman say.   Lament for the Poets: 1916.   Francis Ledwidge.   AWP

I heard the pulse of the besieging sea.   To S. C.   Robert Louis Stevenson.   NePenScot; PeVV

I heard the trailing garments of the Night.   Hymn to the Night.   Henry Wadsworth Longfellow.   APN-1; NOBA; OxBA; PWR; TAP; TCAPo

I heard the weeping of the newly born in its mother's bosom.   Circle of Weeping, The.   Amir Gilbo'a.   MHP, tr. by Ruth Finer Mintz

I heard them say I'm ugly.   Ugly Child, The.   Elizabeth Jennings.   NOxBChV

I heard this morning.   Summer nineteen seventy.   Lindiwe Mabuza.   WPOW

I heard two workers say, "This chaos / Will soon be ended."   Idiom of the Hero.   Wallace Stevens.   OxBA

I heard you park by the road.   Hunting Accident.   Alicia Muñoz.   Unle

I Heard You Solemn-Sweet Pipes of the Organ.   Walt Whitman.   APN-1; OxBA; SAmP

I heard your heartbeat.   Heartsong.   Jeni Couzyn.   HAWP

I heave my morning like a sack.   Norbert Dentressangle Van, The.   Sophie Hannah.   HarvBoo

I heed the warning not to "sit beneath the eaves."   Passing Seven-League Rapids.   Meng Hao Jan.   ColAnChi, tr. by Daniel Bryant

I Held a Shelley Manuscript.   Gregory Corso.   BB; PmAP; VGW

I Held His Name.   Alberto A. Ríos.   NoAM

I held it truth, with him who sings.   Tennyson.   CAGL; EBVV; HeIP-4; NAEL-6v2; NAWM-7v2   Fr. In Memoriam A. H. H.

I held the briefcase at arm's length from me.   Briefcase, The.   Paul Muldoon.   CABP

I held the man for nothing in my arms. (LL)   Saint Judas.   James Wright (1927–80).   CoAmPo; GI; LCAP-2; NOBA; PAI

I Held the Vein, But Death.   Dennis Phillips.   FTOS

I held you / through all your shifts.   Eventual Proteus.   Margaret Atwood.   MoCV

I here, thou there, yet both but one. (LL)   Letter to Her Husband, Absent upon Public[k] Employment, A.   Anne Bradstreet.   HAP; HeIP-4; NAAL-2v1; NAAL-3; NAAL-5; NALW; SCAP

I hereby swear that to uphold your house.   Elinor Wylie.   NAAL-2v2; OxBA; Son   Fr. One Person.

I, Hermes, guard Cyllene's wooded slopes.   Nicias.   GrAn

I, Hermes, have been set up.   Anyte [or Anytes].   GrAn; OBVE; PGA; WoPoe, tr. by Kenneth Rexroth

I, Hermes, stand here by the windy tree-lined.   Anyte [or Anytes].   SaLy, tr. by Diane Rayor

I hid my love when young while [or till] I.   Secret Love.   John Clare.   FHYEP; PoE; SCGP

I hide behind simple things that you may find me.   Meaning of Simplicity, The.   Yannis Ritsos.   PFTM-2, tr. by Kimon Friar

I hoard a little spring of secret tears.   On Shooting a Swallow in Early Youth.   Charles Tennyson Turner.   NOBVV

I hoboed off to escape the dogman, slipping onto the grass.   Dogman, The.   John Rybicki.   Unle

I hoed and trenched and weeded.   A. E. Housman.   MoBrPo; UnPo; WeW-3

I hold a chipped bowl in my hands.   Game, The.   Edvard Kocbek.   PoSu, tr. by Michael Scammell and Veno Taufer

I Hold A Lust To See People.   Out of the Wailing.   Stephen Caldwell Wright.   ISC

I hold a newspaper, reading.   Fish.   Shinkichi Takahashi.   ZenPo, tr. by Takashi Ikemoto and Lucien Stryk

I hold him, verily, of mean emprise.   He Perceives His Rashness in Love, but Has No Choice.   Guido Guinicelli.   AWP; EaItPo, tr. by Dante Gabriel Rossetti

I hold it good—as who shall hold it bad?   Columbia's Agony.   "Orpheus C. Kerr."   OBAL

I hold it towards you. (LL)   This Living Hand, Now Warm and Capable.   John Keats.   AmFaPo; BoLoP; InPK-6; TRP

I hold it true that thoughts are things.   Secret Thoughts.   Ella Wheeler Wilcox.   PWR

I hold it true, whate're befall. Tennyson. UV *Fr.* In Memoriam A. H. H.

I hold my bet for the clouds. Fete on the Lake. Molly Bendall. NAPBL

I hold my breath and balance on a cliff. Prognosis. Debra Bruce. IllVoic

I hold my cut finger to the ice water. In Peru, the Quechuans Have a Thousand Words for Potato. Ray Gonzalez. SpudSo

I hold my honey and I store my bread. My Dreams, My Works Must Wait Till after Hell. Gwendolyn Brooks. IllVoic; NoP-4

I hold that Christian grace abounds. My Creed. Alice Cary. TreFP

I hold up my chin. Little Red Riding Hood and the Wolf. Gillie Bolton. Prnts

I hold your head tight. Marichiko. OHMPJ *tr. by* Kenneth Rexroth

I hold your head tight between. Kenneth Rexroth. APSN; APT-2 *Fr.* Love Poems of Marichiko, The.

I hold your love up as a lantern. The blackness of night. Clover Flower, The. 'Ali 'Abdallah Khalifa. MAP, *tr. by* Alistair Elliot and Lena Jayyusi

I Hope and Fear. Thomas Lodge. Son *Fr.* Phyllis.

I hope he doesn't see me walking past his bed. Letter. Alexander Bergman. TrJP

I hope I do not sound boasting. Rubai. Nazim Hikmet. WoPoe, *tr. by* Taner Baybars

I Hope, I Fear. Sir William Alexander, Earl of Stirling. Son *Fr.* Aurora.

I hope the old Romans. Ancient History. Arthur Guiterman. KaS; OBCA

I hope when I am dead that I shall lie. Oblivion. Jessie Redmond Fauset. NegPo

I hope you'll forgive the black paint. I Have Lived This Way for Years and Do Not Wish to Change. Michael C. Blumenthal. HCAP

I hope you'll make sense of the notes. (LL) Waste Land Limericks. Wendy Cope. FaBoWP; HarvBoo

I hoped that with the brave and strong. He Doeth All Things Well. Anne Brontë. SacPr

I HUG my pillow and do not speak a word. Poems in Depression, at Wei Village. Po Chü-i. ChiP, *tr. by* Arthur Waley

I hung his coat and trousers to roast before a fire. (LL) Mother Goose. OxNR; RB; ReMoGo

I hung my verses in the wind. Test, The. Ralph Waldo Emerson. OBAL

I hungered so for life! (LL) Edgar Lee Masters. APT-1; IllVoic *Fr.* Spoon River Anthology.

I hunt among stones. (LL) Kingfishers, The. Charles Olson. APSN; HarvBoo; NAAL-2v2; NOBA; NeaP; PoM; VCAP

"I, I, I." What a strange word he's saying! In Front of the Mirror. Vladislav Felitsianovich Khodasevich. TCRP, *tr. by* Michael Frayn

I, Icarus. Alden Nowlan. NOxBChV

I idly cut a parsley stalk.—On a Midsummer Eve. Thomas Hardy. FaBoVe

"I, if I perish, perish"—Esther spake. Christina Georgina Rossetti. OxBSo *Fr.* Monna Innominata.

I ignore their mouth smells voices touch. To the Readers Who Write to Me. Daria Menicanti. CItWP, *tr. by* Cinzia Sartini Blum and Lara Trubowitz

I imagine everything wrapped in a beatific mist. Georgy [*or* Georgii] Vladimirovich Ivanov. TCRP

I imagine her couplings and uncouplings. Foxfire. Dominique Parker. SpirFl

I imagine him still with heavy brow. Beethoven's Death Mask. Stephen Spender. OxBTC

I imagine it, a land. Sir Gelli Meurig. Ronald Stuart Thomas. AngWePo

I imagine that these thousand. Descent, The. James Tate. YaYoPo

I imagine the time of our meeting. Forms of the Earth at Abiquiu. N. Scott Momaday. CDW

I imagine this [*or* the] midnight moment's forest. Thought-Fox, The. Ted Hughes. FaBoMo; HeIP-4; MakPoe; NoP-4; NeAmP; NoAM; SCV

I imagine where God has never been. Peter Levi. TOF

I imagine you a virgin. Haiti. Chiqui Vicioso. TANSG, *tr. by* Daisy Cocco De Filippis

I implore Neptune to claim his child to-day! (LL) At the Carnival. Anne Spencer. APT-1; BlSi

I implore you, deer-shooter. Anacreon. SaLy, *tr. by* Diane Rayor

I impose on myself the costly punishment. Purple Spot, The. Ramón López Velarde. BLPSL, *tr. by* Rene de Costa, Rigas Kappatos and Eleni Paidoussi

I in a new understanding of my confusion. (LL) In Broken Images. Robert Graves. HarvBoo; NoP-4; TRP

I in My Bed of Thistles. Rosalía de Castro. SpanPo, *tr. by* Edwin Morgan

I, in My Intricate Image. Dylan Thomas. SPE

I, in your frutefull woomb conceyved, born was. Nicholas Grimald. PBRV *Fr.* Funerall song, upon the deceas of Annes his moother, A.

I inhabit a sacred wound. Lagoonal Calendar. Aimé Césaire. VCWP

I inhale my baby's. Inhaling His Hair. Gillian Ferguson. NeBl

I insert the blue and silver. Chembank Card. David S. Mills. InTrad

I intended an ode. Austin Dobson. OBEV *Fr.* Rose-Leaves.

I is the ghost of Stevey Fizzlegig. Ghost, The. Fitz-James O'Brien. FaBoVe; NOEC

I / is the total black. Coal. Audre Lorde. BlSi; ESEAA; NAAL-5; NALW; NBV; NoAM; VCAP

I itched inside and caught my lover's eye. Fêng Mêng-lung. ColAnChi; WoPoe, *tr. by* Richard W. Bodman *Fr.* Mountain Songs.

I jiggled it. This Tooth. Lee Bennett Hopkins. TLR

I Jocky Bell o'Braikenbrow lyes under this stane. On Jocky Bell. *Unknown.* FaBoEE

I John saw. I testify. "H. D." NALW *Fr.* Tribute to the Angels.

I journey / And the highway journeys too. Vasco [*or* Vasko] Popa. PoSu *Fr.* Besieged Serenity.

I journeyed to the suburbs, and there I was told. T. S. Eliot. UV *Fr.* Choruses from "The Rock."

I joy, dear[e] Mother, when I view. British Church, The. George Herbert. AngWePo; ESCV; PeECV

I joy not in no earthly bliss. Quiet Mind, The. *Unknown.* NoSic

I joy to see how in your drawen work. Edmund Spenser. NoP-4; PBRV; PoE *Fr.* Amoretti.

I just came back from a lovely trip. Santa Claus Is Comin' to Town. J. Fred Coots. ReLy

I just came by the prison-door. Christopher Smart. NOEC *Fr.* Hymns for the Amusement of Children.

I just can't seem to get that campus bloom. Lonely Coed, A. Billy Strayhorn. ReLy

I just didn't get it—. Ego. Denise Duhamel. NeAmPo

I just fell / Hook, line and sinker. What a Perfect Combination. Irving Caesar. ReLy

I Just Found Out About Love. Harold Adamson. ReLy

I just got an invitation through the mails. Top Hat, White Tie, and Tails. Irving Berlin. ReLy

I Just Heard John Buffington Died. Kalamu ya Salaam. SpirFl

I just knew it when we swept above the old roofs of Dijon. Elizabeth Barrett Browning. PeVV *Fr.* Aurora Leigh.

I Just Missed the Bus and I'll Be Late for Work. Ariel Dorfman. AF

I just said I didn't know. Parachutes, My Love, Could Carry Us Higher. Barbara Guest. NeAP

I just saw a maniac. Five Foot Two, Eyes of Blue (Has Anybody Seen My Girl?). Joe Young. ReLy

I just think it will happen, soon. (LL) Going, Going. Philip Larkin. NoAM; OxAEP-2

I keep a blue bottle. Melancholy inside Families. Pablo Neruda. RaBo

I keep a TV monitor on my chest. Shorts / Excerpts. Bill Knott. PBCAP

I keep dreaming I'm dead. Qaqatcguk. STP

I keep falling in love. Jack Kerouac. PmAP *Fr.* Mexico City Blues.

I keep feeling all space as my image. Poem. Sanders Russell. SPE

I Keep Forgetting. Lily Brett. HP

I Keep Going Back to Joe's. Jack Segal. ReLy

I keep him waiting, tuck in the curtains. Rita Dove. GT *Fr.* Suite for Augustus, A.

I keep meaning to tell you. Zohar. Tom Carey. KGB

I keep my parents in a garden. Eden Is a Zoo. Margaret Atwood. WPE

I keep running around. Song. *Unknown.* STP, *tr. by* Jerome Rothenberg

I keep saying. Salsabíl. Jamíl. ArPe, *tr. by* Omar S. Pound

I keep the custom of the Ferry. Hostess of the Ferry Inn, The. Gwerfyl Mechain. OBWVE, *tr. by* H. Idris Bell

I keep the rustic gate closed. Idleness. Lu Yu. OHPC, *tr. by* Kenneth Rexroth

I keep the taste of feasting. Epitaph of Sardanapalos, The. *Unknown.* PGA, *tr. by* Kenneth Rexroth

I Keep to Myself Such Measures. Robert Creeley. NoAM; PmAP

I kenning [*or* kening] through astronomy divine. Edward Taylor. ChIV-2; ColAP; NAAL-2v1; NAAL-3; NAAL-5; NOBA; NoP-4; OxBA; SCAP; TAP *Fr.* Preparatory Meditations Before My Approach to the Lord's Supper.

I kept it hidden, it was easy. Fragment (Found Inside My Mother). Nick Flynn. AmPoNex

I kept my answers small and kept them near. Answers. Elizabeth Jennings. OxBSP; OxBTC

I kept my hide intact. Good shields can be bought. (LL) Archilochus. GrAn; WoPoe, *tr. by* Stuart Silverman

I kept singing this, and I will call it out from the grave. Julianus of Egypt. GrAn

I kept the house on the corner of Linden and Pineapple Streets. Birdie McReynolds. Samuel Hoffenstein. NBLV

I kept the memory, like a miracle. Good Filya. Nikolai Mikhailovich Rubtsov. TCRP, *tr. by* Lubov Yakovleva

I killed a snake this morning in the grass. Snake, The. Vance Palmer. NOBAu

I killed them, but they would not die. Immortals, The. Isaac Rosenberg. FaBoTw; TrJP

I killed you Malcolm. Confession to Malcolm. Conyus. NBV

I kiss my Russian Revolution. "Eduard Veniaminovich Limonov." TCRusP, *tr. by* William Tjalsma *Fr.* Secret Notebook.

I kissed my father. (LL) Gift, The. Li-Young Lee. BodElec; LoL; OpBo; RaBo; UnSA

I Kissed Pa Twice after His Death. Mattie J. Peterson. VerBaPo

I kissed the cold earth that is heaven. Mea Shearim. Tamara Kamenszain. MirDau, *tr. by* Roberta Gordenstein

I kissed the warm live hand that held the thing. (LL) Maundy Thursday. Wilfred Owen. NPeEn; OxBSo

I kissed them in fancy as I came. Two Lips. Thomas Hardy. BoLoP

I kissed you, bride and lost, and went. Loser, The. Adrienne Rich. RACG

I kneel down to peer into a culvert. Kneeling Down to Look [*or* Peer] into a Culvert. Robert Bly. NoAM

I knew a cuckold once. I grieve for him. My Friend the Cuckold. Morris Gilbert Bishop. OBCoV

I knew a guerilla fighter. Guerilla Fighter. Jofre Rocha. NAfrP, *tr. by* Don Burness

I knew a man, a common farmer, the father of five sons. Walt Whitman. BLT *Fr.* I Sing the Body Electric.

I knew a man, he was my chum. Trench Poets. Edgell Rickword. FaBoWar

I knew a man who used to say. Statesman, The. Joseph Hilaire Pierre Belloc. NOBE

I knew a simple soldier boy. Suicide in [the] Trenches. Siegfried Sassoon. FaBoWar; PoWW

I Knew a Woman. Theodore Roethke. APT-2; BoLoP; HAP; HeIP-4; InPK-6; MoAmPo; NAAL-2v2; NAAL-5; NIL-7; NOBA; NoAM; PoE; RaBo; SoSe-8; TAP; TFi; TRP; TwCP; UnPo; VCAP

I knew, all the rest of my life. To Get Clear. J. P. Ward. AngWePo

I knew her self was not in that strange place. (LL) Harlem Dancer, The. Claude McKay. APT-1; BPo; ISC; NAAL-5; NIL-7; NIP-4; NoAM; Son; TAP; TCAPo

I knew him as a friend: married. She was older. Rowing in Familiar January. Milo De Angelis. NeIt, *tr. by* Lawrence Venuti

I knew how to make myself feel. Warmness. Anabel Torres. TANSG, *tr. by* Celeste Kostopulos-Cooperman

I knew Ibrahim. Deserted Well, The. Yusuf Al-Khal. MAP, *tr. by* Sargon Boulus and Naomi Shihab Nye

I knew it was love, and I felt it was glory. (LL) Stanzas Written on the Road between Florence and Pisa. Byron. NAEL-5v2; NAEL-6v2

I knew like a song your vows weren't strong. Mahsati. WPOW

I knew not grief. Lament of Mary, The. *Unknown.* IQMS, *tr. by* Michael Beevor

I knew not who had wrought with skill so fine. Before a Painting. James Weldon Johnson. GT

I knew that in winter it would snow. Plumbers. Susan Miles. NOxBChV

I knew the dick size of every boy in my class. Sixth Grade. Melanie Hope. WiU

I knew the length of an average penis. Size of It, The. Timothy Liu. WiU

I knew the time had come. Nevertheless (I'm in Love with You). Harry Ruby. ReLy

I knew too that through them I knew too that he was through, I knew. Valentine to Sherwood Anderson, A. Gertrude Stein. NoAM

I knew when I said. Nizar Qabbani. MAP

I knew you forever and you were always old. Some Foreign Letters. Anne Sexton. MoAmPo

I know. Male Grownups. Hoda Hussein. PoArWo, *tr. by* Cornelia Al-Khaled

I know. Wall, The. Ismail. OMIP, *tr. by* V. Narayana Rao

I know a bundle of humanity. Young and Healthy. Harry Warren. ReLy

I know a couple of newlyweds. Okay, Toots. Walter Donaldson. ReLy

I know a dark secluded place. Hernando's Hideaway. Jerry Ross. ReLy

I know a flower of beauty rare. Lay of the Captive Count, The. Goethe. AWP, *tr. by* James Clarence Mangan

I Know a Flower So Fair and Fine. Nicolai Frederik Severin Grundtvig. AH, *tr. by* Olav Lee

I know a forest and in that forest. Pool, The. Hayyim Nahman [*or* Khayim Nakhman *or* Chaim Nachman] Bialik. MHP, *tr. by* Ruth Finer Mintz

I know a funny little man. Mr Nobody. *Unknown.* ITBLP

I know a green grass path that leaves the field. Green River, The. Lord Alfred Bruce Douglas. OBEV

I know a Jew fish crier down on Maxwell Street. Fish Crier. Carl Sandburg. OxBA

I know a little bit about a lot of things. I Don't Know Enough About You. Peggy Lee. ReLy

I know a little cupboard. Cupboard, The. Walter De la Mare. NTCP

I know a little garden-close. William Morris. NOBE *Fr.* Life and Death of Jason, The.

I know a little language of my cat, tho Dante says. Robert Duncan. PoM *Fr.* Dante.

I know a little man both ept and ert. Gloss. David McCord. OBAL

I Know a Man. Robert Creeley. AmFaPo; NIP-4; NOBA; OxBSP; PoM; VCAP

(As I sd to my.) CoAmPo; NoP-4

I know a place where the sun is like gold. Four-Leaf Clover. Ella Higginson. SWaP

I know a pool where nightshade preens. Crazed. Walter De la Mare. OxBSP

I know a spot where Love delights to dream. Edward Cracroft Lefroy. AWP *Fr.* Echoes from Theocritus.

I Know a Strange, Gigantic Hymn. Gustavo Adolfo Bécquer. NAWM-7v2, *tr. by* Bruce Phenix

I Know a Village. Phyllis McGinley.

5:32, The. APT-2; WPE

Occupation: Housewife. WPE

I know all. He Asked Them What Did They Know & They Told Him. *Unknown.* STP, *tr. by* Richard Johnny John and Jerome Rothenberg

I know all about boys, I do. All about Boys and Girls. John Ciardi. NOxBChV

"I know all," you say; of incompleteness, you have enough. Palladas [*or* Pallades]. GrAn

I know an ice handler who wears a flannel shirt. Ice Handler. Carl Sandburg. OxBA

I know—and yet I cannot share, as once. August the First; Court Martial. The Mother Speaks. Marjorie Oludhe Macgoye. HBAPE

I know, as my life grows older. Whatever Is—Is Best. Ella Wheeler Wilcox. PWR

I know at least some of my upper teeth could have been saved. Romeo, Grown Old. James Wright (1927–80). BodElec

I know but will not tell. Elegy. Alan Dugan. NIL-7; NIP-4

I Know de Moonlight. *Unknown.* BPo

I know everyone. Jeep Driver, The. Martín Espada. PueRic

I Know Exactly the Sort of Woman I'd Like to Fall in Love With. Deryn Rees-Jones. MFPA

I know exactly what I want to say. For J. W. Rafael Campo. RA

I know exactly what I want to say. Two Hundred and Sixty-Five Words. Sophie Hannah. HarvBoo

I know, fair lady, how to love the lover well. Philodemus. GrAn

I know: from flesh. José Martí. TCLAP, *tr. by* Elinore Randall *Fr.* Simple Verses.

I Know Full Well the Water's Flowing Power. Saint John of the Cross. SpanPo, *tr. by* James Edward Tobin

I know her children. Goddam Street, The. Robert Coles. BloBone

I know her not! Her hand has been in mine. Lady in the White Dress, Whom I Helped into the Omnibus, The. Nathaniel Parker Willis. APN-1

I know him; / He'll give no horse for a poem. *Unknown.* BIrV

I know / how fascinated we are with clarity. Poem. Salah Fa'iq. MAP, *tr. by* Patricia Alanah Byrne and Salma Khadra Jayyusi

I know how people get treated when they die. Andeyek. STP

I know how worthless this poem will be. Shuntaro Tanikawa. PFTM-2, *tr. by* William I. Elliott and Kazuo Kawamura *Fr.* With Silence My Companion.

I know I am. Dinner Guest: Me. Langston Hughes. BPo; LTA; SSLK

I know I am but summer to your heart. Edna St. Vincent Millay. HeIP-4

I know I am poor. *Unknown.* PGA

I know I change / have changed. Daguerreotype Taken in Old Age. Margaret Atwood. BoWoP; NoAM

I know I dreamed again last night. At Dawn. Michael Patrick Hearn. CA

I know I have the best of time and space, and was never measured and will never be measured. Walt Whitman. ColAP; NAWM-7v2; NoAM *Fr.* Song of Myself.

I know, I know, Mother. Kamalākānta Bhattācārya. SinGod, *tr. by* Rachel Fell McDermott

I know I know short conviction. Silence Wager Stories. Susan Howe. BodElec; FTOS

I know, I know—though the evidence. Blow, West Wind. Robert Penn Warren. ColAP

I know I'm more alone than ever. Entering the Gardens of Doom. Sayf Al-Rahabi. MAP, *tr. by* Samuel Hazo and Lena Jayyusi

I Know I'm Not Sufficiently Obscure. Ray Durem. BPo

I know I shall never write poems. Drawer of My Writing Desk, The. Boris Petrovich Kornilov. TCRP, *tr. by* Bernard Meares

I know I should pity me. I Should Care. Sammy Cahn. ReLy

I know if I find you I will have to leave the earth. Hymn. A. R. Ammons. CoAmPo

I Know Inside. Yüan Mei. CoBLCP, *tr. by* Jonathan Chaves

I know it by thy song! (LL) To a Wandering Female Singer. Felicia Dorothea Hemans. VWP; ViWPN

I know it is my sin[ne] which locks thine ear[e]s. Church-Lock and Key. George Herbert. ESCV; GeHe; OxBSP

I know it now, once more 'tis spring. Lilacs. Karl Kraus. AuPH, *tr. by* Lowell A. Bangerter

I know / it's no easy joy. Wine. Nikolai Nikolaevich Ushakov. TCRP, *tr. by* Daniel Weissbort

I know just how you feel. Young Don't Want to Be Born. James Wright (1927–80). BodElec

I know monks masturbate at night. Earnest Liberal's Lament, The. Ernest Hemingway. OBAL; OBSV

I Know Moon-Rise [*or* Moonrise]. *Unknown*. APN-2; NAAAL; UnPo

I Know My Soul. Claude McKay. BPo

I know my soul hath power to know all things. Sir John Davies. OBEV *Fr.* Nosce Teipsum.

I know my upper arms will grow. Life I Led, The. Nikki Giovanni. GT

I know no couple better can agree! (LL) On Giles and Joan. Ben Jonson. NAEL-5v1; NAEL-6v1; NAEL-7v1; NOBL

I know no paint of poetry. On Fairford Windows. William Strode. NOSC

I know not, Dante, in what refuge dwells. Cino da Pistoia. EaItPo, *tr. by* Dante Gabriel Rossetti

I know not how, dear heart, I came to love you as I do. Nathaniel to Ruth. Emily Jane Pfeiffer. ViWPN

I know not how it falls on me. Emily Jane Brontë. NOBVV

I know not how it may be with others. Old Furniture. Thomas Hardy. OxBTC

I know not if it was a dream. I viewed. Passing Show, The. Ambrose Bierce. APN-2

I know not of what we ponder'd. Companions. Charles Stuart Calverley. NOBL

I know not that the men of old. Men of Old, The. Richard Monckton, 1st Baron Houghton Milnes. OBEV; TreFP

I know / Not these my hands. Amaze. Adelaide Crapsey. APT-1

I know not what awaits me. Last Hymn. Philip Paul Bliss. SacPr

I know not what I am, and what I know, I'm not. "Angelus Silesius." GePo, *tr. by* George C. Schoolfield *Fr.* Cherubical Wanderer, The.

I Know Not What I Seek Eternally. Rosalía de Castro. SpanPo, *tr. by* Muriel Kittel

I know not what spell is o'er me. Lorelei. Heinrich Heine. TrJP

I know not what the future hath. John Greenleaf Whittier. NOCV *Fr.* Eternal Goodness, The.

I know not what to do. Fragment 36. Hilda Doolittle. NALW; OxBA; PoBW; VGW

I know not when it was, I still confuse childhood and Eden. I Know Not When It Was. Léopold Sédar Senghor. NegPo, *tr. by* Ellen Conroy Kennedy

I know not when this tiresome man. Sundowner, The. John Shaw Neilson. CBAP

I Know Not Where the Road Will Lead. Evelyn Atwater Cummins. AH

I know not who thou art, oh lovely one! To the Lady in the Chemisette with Black Buttons. Nathaniel Parker Willis. OBAL

I know not why, but all this weary day. Henry Timrod. APN-2

I know not why my soul is rack'd [*or* racked]. Changed. Charles Stuart Calverley. NOBVV

I know nothing but this scene. James Liddy. BiHa *Fr.* Epithalamion I–IV.

I know now that once I longed to be white. When I Was Growing Up. Nellie Wong. OxWW; UnSA

I know of course. I, the Survivor. Bertolt Brecht. HP; PoSu

I know some lonely Houses off the Road. Emily Dickinson. APN-2; MoAmPo; OxBA; PoRA

I know something / But I can't express it. S'posin' Paul Denniker. ReLy

I Know Something Good about You. Louis C. Shimon. PoToHe

I know that a gangster will not murder me. "Ivan Venediktovich Elagin." TCRP

I know that any weed can tell. Song. Louis Ginsberg. TrJP

I know that He exists. Emily Dickinson. APN-2; NCAP

I know that he told that I snared his soul. Edgar Lee Masters. APT-1 *Fr.* Spoon River Anthology.

I know that his eyes look into mine. Assurance. Josephine D. Henderson Heard. CBWP-4

I know that I am. Jacky Sings His Songs. Mudrooroo Narogin. IBA

I Know That I Am a Great Sinner. Swami Purohit. OBMV

I Know That I Must Die Soon. Else Lasker-Schüler. TrJP, *tr. by* Ralph Manheim

I know that I shall meet my fate. Irish Airman Foresees His Death, An. W. B. Yeats. ChAP; FaBoCh; FaBoMo; FaBoWar; GTBS-P; HarvBoo; HeIP-4; MoBrPo; NOBE; NoAM; NoP-4; OBMV; OBWP; PoPoPo; PoWW; SCV; TFi; WeW-3

I know that mind. ESP. Carter Revard. VoR

I know that peace is soon coming, and love of common object. Geranium. Edward Dorn. PmAP

I know that the sun rising. Pindar's Revenge. Edward Sanders. PoM

I know that this my crying, like the crying. Night. Hayyim Nahman [*or* Khayim Nakhman *or* Chaim Nachman] Bialik. AWP, *tr. by* Maurice Samuel

I know that this was Life—the track. Tennyson. CAGL; NAEL-6v2 *Fr.* In Memoriam A. H. H.

I know that what our neighbours call *longueurs*. Byron. OBSV *Fr.* Don Juan.

I know / that when a grumbling old woman. Superstition. Minji Karibo. WPOW

I Know That You Know. Anne Caldwell. ReLy

I know the bottom, she says. I know it with my great tap root. Elm. Sylvia Plath. NOBA; NoAM; NoP-4

I know the colour rose, and it is lovely. Pathology of Colours. Dannie Abse. BloBone; NIP-4; NoAM; TCAWP

I know the force of words, I know their clarion call. Vladimir Vladimirovich Mayakovsky [*or* Maiakovskii]. TCRP

I know the incapacity of dream. Compassion's Bird. Jay Wright. ESEAA

I know the injured pride of sleep. Night and Morning. Austin Clarke. CIP-2

I know the limitations of my body. Realist, The. Carl H. Greene. NBV

I know the man who eavesdrops. Last Call. Silvia Curbelo. TouFir

I know—the Mongol yoke, the years of famine. Lev Vladimir Loseff [*or* Losev]. TCRusP, *tr. by* Henry Pickford

I know the [*or* a] thing that's most uncommon. On a Certain Lady at Court. Pope. NOBE; NOEC; OBEV; OxBSP

I know the reputation / of the idle ways. Lady Ki [*or* Kii]. WPOW

I know the reward of the secret tear as it humbly falls. Reward. Shimon Halkin. MHP, *tr. by* Ruth Finer Mintz

I know the rituals, the spells of grapes. Garrett Kaoru Hongo. GeoHom *Fr.* Cruising 99.

I know the spring that spurts and flows. Spring. Margherita Guidacci. CItWP, *tr. by* Cinzia Sartini Blum and Lara Trubowitz

I know the sun shines, and the lilacs are blowing. Enlisted Today. *Unknown*. CBCWP

I know the things I've lost are so many that I could not begin to count them. Possession of Yesterday. Jorge Luis Borges. WoPoe, *tr. by* Nicomedes Suarez Arauz

I know the truth—give up all other truths! Marina Ivanovna Tsvetayeva [*or* Tsvetaeva]. OPOU; WPoS, *tr. by* Elaine Feinstein

I know the way[e]s of learning; both the head. Pearl, The. Matth. 13:45. George Herbert. BASC; ChIV-2; EBEV; ESCV; FHYEP; FSCP; GeHe; HAP; NOCV; NOSC; OxBEV

I know thee. My name is Tom. Archaic Song of Dr. Tom the Shaman. *Unknown*. STP, *tr. by* Jerome Rothenberg

I know thee not, bright creature, ne'er shall know. Charles Johnston. CenSon

I know there are pigeons smaller than we are. Evolving Similarities. Ralph Angel. BodElec

I know there is a person. Poem to Be Read and Sung. César Vallejo. TCLAP, *tr. by* Clayton Eshleman

I know there is someone. Poem to Be Read and Sung. César Vallejo. SPE

I know these trees. Upper Marlboro. Kenneth Carroll. SpirFl

I know thou art a senseless thing. Old Crib, The. Mary E. Tucker. CBWP-1

I know 'tis vain ye mountains, and ye woods. Painter, A. Thomas Cole. APN-1

I know to whom I write. Here, I am sure. Ben Jonson. BASC; BeJo

I know two women / and the one. Wife, The. Robert Creeley. VGW

I know very well I could not. (LL) I Saw in Louisiana a Live-Oak Growing. Walt Whitman. APN-1; AWP; AiP; ColAP; InPK-6; NAAL-2v1; NAAL-3; NCAP; NIP-4; NOBA; NoAM; NoP-4; OxBA; PoPoPo; SAmP; TCAPo

I know what I am not. Governess, The. Evelyn Wexler. GotH

I know what I see. I Think That I Shall Never See. Jim Heynen. UrbNat

I know what it's like to be looked at. Kids on Television Imagine Me, The. Jordan Davis. HeMarv

I know what the caged bird feels, alas! Sympathy. Paul Laurence Dunbar. APN-2; GT; NAAAL; NIL-7; NoP-4; SSLK; TCAPo

I know where I'm going. Dog Sonnet. Sidney Wade. Unle

I know why the caged bird sings! (LL) Sympathy. Paul Laurence Dunbar. APN-2; GT; NAAAL; NIL-7; NoP-4; SSLK; TCAPo

I Know You Are, But What Am I? Paul Beatty. InTrad

I know you are reading this poem. Adrienne Rich. NAAL-5 *Fr.* Atlas of the Difficult World, An.

I know you are there. The sweat is, I am here. (LL) Certainty Before Lunch. John Berryman. LCAP-2; OxBC

I know you. I recognise the stumbling sway. From the Moment I Picked Up Your Book. Ann Sansom. MFPA

I know you little, I love you lots. My Love For You. *Unknown*. Spl

I know you: solitary griefs. Precept of Silence, The. Lionel Pigot Johnson. MoBrPo; SacPr

I know you think of me when you are lonely. Plea for My Heart's Sake. Naomi Long Madgett. SeSe

I know, you told me. Death and the Good Citizen. A. K. Ramanujan. PoetW

I know you wonder why I wear. Green Hair. Elinor Wylie. APT-1

I knowed a man, which he lived in Jones. Thar's More in the Man than Thar Is in the Land. Sidney Lanier. NOBA

I Korinna am here to sing the courage. Korinna [or Corinna]. BoWoP

I laboured these six years. Mazzeo di Ricco da Messina. EaItPo, tr. by Dante Gabriel Rossetti

I lack the braver mind. Confession of Faith. Elinor Wylie. APT-1; MoAmPo

I laid down my long net in the big tide. Net Breaker, The. Brewster Ghiselin. APT-2

I laid me down upon a bank. William Blake. EnLoPo

I laid my haffet on Elfer Hill. Elfer Hill. Unknown. AWP, tr. by Robert Jamieson

I Lais, once an arrow. Kenneth Rexroth. NNaP; PGA

I, Lais, who laughed disdainfully at Greece. Lais' Mirror. Unknown. GrAn, tr. by Peter Jay

I laks yo' kin' of lovin' Long Gone. Sterling Allen Brown. APT-2; BPo; NAAAL

I landed on Iona's holy isle. Iona. Frederick Tennyson. SacPr

I lang hae thought, my youthfu' friend. Epistle to a Young Friend. Robert Burns. EBEV

I language want, to dress[e] my fancies in. Imagination. Margaret Lucas Cavendish, Duchess of Newcastle. BASC; NOSC

I lately lost a preposition. Naughty Preposition, The. Morris Gilbert Bishop. NBLV; PeLV

I laugh at each dull bore, taste's parasite. Fresco-Sonnets to Christian Sethe. Heinrich Heine. AWP, tr. by John Todhunter

I laugh at my failing strength in old age. Shih Te. SuSp

I laughed at sweethearts I met at schools. My Heart Stood Still. Richard Rodgers. ReLy

I laughed at that boy. Stuck. Cheryl Clarke. WiU

I laved my hands. Lost for a Rose's Sake. Unknown. AWP, tr. by Andrew Lang

I lay at rest in the violet-fragrant. Persephone's Journey. Patricia Monaghan. HW

I lay at the edge of a well. Underground Stream, The. James Dickey. NOBA

I Lay Awake, Wandering in that Limbo. Gustavo Adolfo Bécquer. SpanPo, tr. by John Haines

I lay dear treasure for you. Pack, The. Frank Prewett. HATNAP

I lay down with my love and there was song. Armorial. Ralph Gustafson. MoCV

I lay face-downward on the grass. Barrier, The. Louis Lavater. NOBAu

I lay i' the bosom of the sun. Palabras Grandiosas. Bayard Taylor. OBAL

I lay in my coffin under the sod. Post Mortem. Arthur Joseph Munby. NOBVV

I lay in the Holy Cross. Reginald Pugh, The Man Who Came from the Army. Emma Lee Warrior. HATNAP

I lay my harp on the curved table. Harp, The. Po Chü-i. TAL

I lay on that rock where the storms have their dwelling. Rock of Cader Idris, The. Felicia Dorothea Hemans. RWP

I lay out the sheet. Dr. Wasserman. Brenda Coultas. HeMarv

I lay paralyzed. Suppression. Jayne Cortez. NBV

I lay waiting. Bog Queen. Seamus Heaney. NoAM; PAI; RACG

I lay with an acupuncture needle. Even the Eagles Must Gather. Alma Villanueva. FFC

I'le be at lest a Martyr in desire. (LL) In Emulation of Mr Cowleys Poem Call'd The Motto. Mary Astell. EMWP; NOSC

I lean against. Gazen. JDP, tr. by Yoel Hoffmann

I lean on a lighthouse rock. Girl at the Seaside. Richard Murphy. BIrV

I lean on my rustic gate. Twilight in the River Pavilion. Chiang Shih-ch'üan. OHMPC, tr. by Kenneth Rexroth

I lean on my staff, gaze at the sunlit snow. Evening View as the Snow Clears. Chia Tao. SuSp, tr. by Stephen Owen

I leaned out of window, I smelt the white clover. Jean Ingelow. TreFP Fr. Songs of Seven.

I leant [or leaned] upon a coppice gate. Darkling Thrush, The. Thomas Hardy. AmFaPo; CABP; ClHu; EBVV; HAP; HarvBoo; MoBrPo; NAEL-5v2; NAEL-6v2; NIL-7; NIP-4; NOBE; NOBVV; NPeEn; NoAM; NoP-4; OBEV; OWoS; OxBEV; PAI; PoE; PoPoPo; RB; SoSe-8; TFi; TOF; UnPo; WoPoe

I leap from depths. Ginka. JDP, tr. by Yoel Hoffmann

I Learn a Lesson About Our Society. Janice Gould. GeoHom

I learn by going where I have to go. (LL) Waking, The. Theodore Roethke. APT-2; AmFaPo; CRP; CoAP; HAP; HCAP; HeIP-4; ITBLP; InPK-6; MakPoe; MoAmPo; NAAL-2v2; NAAL-5; NIL-7; NIP-4; NOBA; NoAM; NoP-4; PoPoPo; RaBo; TAP; TFi; TwCP; VCAP; WeW-3; WoPoe

I learn to live by guile, to do without love. Book of Routh. Carolyn Beard Whitlow. FFC

I learned from my mother how to love. What I Learned from My Mother. Julia Kasdorf. AmPoNex; PBCAP

I learned it from my teacher way back in Sunday School. Reciprocity. Walter Kent. ReLy

I learned of your death over spiced tea. For Etheridge Knight. Jackie Warren-Moore. SpirFl

I learned the spoons from. Musician Talks About "Process," The. Rita Dove. ESEAA

I learned to be honest. Question of Climate, A. Audre Lorde. NoAM

I learned to name them—brown-nut-warm, wide. Afterwards: Caliban. Talvikki Ansel. AmPoNex

I learned to read in the dark. Song of the Third Generation. Julia Lisella. UnSA

I learned to shoot. Casting. Kevin Young. GT

I learned two things. Riding Lesson. Henry Taylor. NBLV

I learned yesterday. Antonin Artaud. PFTM-2, tr. by Clayton Eshleman and Norman Glass Fr. To Have Done with the Judgment of God.

I leave Don Juan for the present, safe. Byron. NOBRP Fr. Don Juan.

I leave him pleading. There's too much to do. (LL) Towards Curing AIDS. Rafael Campo. NeAmPo

I leave it for you to say why it is. Pietà. Allen Afterman. NOBAu

I leave my empty house at dawn. Empty House. Yuan Chen. CrYelRi; ErotSp, tr. by Sam Hamill

I leave the child to grow up by itself as a beggar from the killing. Fawaz Turki. GraLe Fr. Tel Zaatar Was the Hill of Thyme.

I leave the English Department for my second life. Her Rose Tattoo. Gerry LaFemina. AmPoNex

I leave thy praises unexpressed. Tennyson. NAEL-6v2 Fr. In Memoriam A. H. H.

I leave to the highborn. Reizan Osho Visits Me. Muso Soseki. EaWin, tr. by W. S. Merwin

I leave you in your garden. To Yvor Winters, 1955. Thom Gunn. GTBS-P

I Leave You These Imprints on the Earth. Alda Merini. CItWP, tr. by Cinzia Sartini Blum and Lara Trubowitz

I led my Silvia to a grove. Song. Aphra Behn. BASC

I left by the front door. Difference, The. Jackie Hardy. NeBl

I left Cornell / with half a wit; six mismated socks. Prayer. Daniel Berrigan. AF

I left home as a youth and am returning an old man. Written Impromptu upon Returning to My Hometown. Ho Ch'e Ch'ang. ColAnChi, tr. by Victor H. Mair

I left. I'd finished raising you. I walked. Envoy. Walter Kirn. Unle

I Left My Hat in Haiti. Burton Lane. ReLy

I left my hills. Lady Izumi. BoWoP

I left my home in a fair land. I Left My Home. Hungarian Oral Tradition. IQMS, tr. by Dermot Spence

I left my locked mouth. No-Word Hut. Muso Soseki. EaWin, tr. by W. S. Merwin

I Left My Low amd Humble Home. Nathaniel Hawthorne. APN-1

I left my prayers and the kneeling pilgrims. Fair Cassidy. Unknown. BIrV, tr. by Donagh MacDonagh

I left nothing behind me. Engraving Twenty-Nine. Fadhila Chabbi. PoArWo, tr. by Yaseen Noorani

I left the farm I loved. I went. Exile. George Rostrevor Hamilton. FaBoEE

I left thee when the midnight bell had tolled. Dream of Blue Eyes, A. Frederick William Faber. CenSon

I Left Those Walls. Nina Cassian. PoSu, tr. by Nina Cassian and Naomi Lazard

I left untilled by the force of gravity and passing especially quickly into. Transit. Prageeta Sharma. HeMarv

I lend a deck of cards to someone passing by. Headline to Summarize a Passion. U Tam'si Tchicaya. NegPo, tr. by Ellen Conroy Kennedy

I let her garden go. Her Garden. Donald Hall. BAP-01

I let the incense grow cold. Li Ch'ing-chao. BoWoP; OHMPC

I lie across the rafters of the loft. House, The. Robert Minhinnick. AngWePo

I lie and imagine a first light gleam in the bay. Achill. Derek Mahon. BiHa; PBCIP; PNI

I lie at ease where cassia blossoms fall. Birdsong Valley. Wang Wei. CrYelRi, tr. by Sam Hamill

I lie beneath my patchwork blanket at the southern window. Rising from Sleep. Wang Chiu-ssu. CoBLCP, tr. by Jonathan Chaves

I lie for a long time on my left side and my right side. Dead Color. Charles Wright. HCAP; LCAP-2

I lie in my crib midday this is. Baby's Pantoum. Anne Waldman. FFC

I lie in the palm of its hand. I wake in the quiet. Unknowing, The. Linda Gregg. ExTi

I lie in you, my space of love. Brevity of Embraces. Armanda Guiducci. CItWP, tr. by Cinzia Sartini Blum and Lara Trubowitz

I lie like a stone on the hill. In the Jerusalem Hills. Leah Goldberg. FIT, tr. by Robert Friend

I lie long abed. Yakamochi (Otomo no Yakamochi). OHPJ

I lie out flat on the river pavilion. River Pavilion. Tu Fu. CrYelRi, *tr. by* Sam Hamill

I lie quiet, musing, torn from dreams. Conversation with the Moon. Ludwig Goldscheider. AuPH, *tr. by* Lowell A. Bangerter

I lie slain. (LL) Félix Lope de Vega Carpio. HAP; WoPoe, *tr. by* Geoffrey Hill *Fr.* Pentecost Castle, The.

I lie under the crust of the night singing. Pregnant Woman. Ingrid Jonker. HAWP, *tr. by* Jack Cope and William Plomer

I lie under your hand—a cur. Dog. Ingrid Jonker. HAWP, *tr. by* Jack Cope and William Plomer

I Lift My Eyes Up to the Hills. Cotton Mather. AH

I lift my head and watch. Thoughts in Exile. Su Tung-p'o (Su Shih). OHPC, *tr. by* Kenneth Rexroth

I Lift My Heart to Thee. Thomas Sternhold. AH

I lift my heavy heart up solemnly. Elizabeth Barrett Browning. CenSon; LW; NALW; PEW; VWP *Fr.* Sonnets from the Portuguese.

I lift my lamp beside the golden door! (LL) New Colossus, The. Emma Lazarus. APN-2; AiP; AmFaPo; CA; FaBoA; GS; GSo; HHAm; NIL-7; NoP-4; SWaP; Son; TCAPo; WPE

I lift my songs. Battle Song. Macuilxochitl. WPOW, *tr. by* Catherine Rodriguez-Nieto

I lift the boy's body. Good Shepherd: Atlanta, 1981, The. Ai. RACG

I lift the Lord on high. Père Lalement. Marjorie Lowry Christie Pickthall. NOBC

I lift the toilet seat. Surprise. Richard Brautigan. KaS

I lift up mine eyes unto the hills. Hills, The. D. H. Lawrence. ChIV-1

I light my candles. Ritual. Rosita Kalina. MirDau, *tr. by* Roberta Gordenstein

I like a church; I like a cowl. Ralph Waldo Emerson. APN-1; AWP; NAAL-2v1; NAAL-3; NOBA; OxBA; TAP

I like a look of Agony. Emily Dickinson. APN-2; HeIP-4; NAAL-2v1; NAAL-3; NoP-4; OxBSP; PoE; PoPoPo; TAP; TCAPo

I like a pinto bean now and then. Brightness. Maggie Nelson. HeMarv

I like a woman built on ample lines. Nicarchus of Alexandria. GrAn

I like being in your apartment, and not disturbing anything. Staying at Ed's Place. May Swenson. VCAP

I like crack-seed. Sewing Woman. Alison Kim. FSt

I like it here. Under the Apple Tree. Diana Rivera. InvLad

I like it here just fine. Girl Held without Bail. Margaret Abigail Walker. BPo; WWork

I like it when my friend has lovers, their happy moans. For Every Heart. Olga Broumas. ErotSp

I like lazy weather. Lazy River. Hoagy Carmichael. ReLy

I like learning useless things. Learning. Michael Casey. YaYoPo

I like movies because. Why I Like Movies. Patricia Jones. BlSi

I like my body when it is with your. E. E. Cummings. BoLoP; PasH; Son; VGW

I like my body when you hover over me. Moonburn. Laura H. Kennedy. PasH

I like old houses, with steps that sag. Old Houses. Jennie Romano. PoToHe

I like people. Trombone Solo. Stoddard King. NBLV

I like poems that resemble a tram. Imitation of Boileau. Yelena [*or* Elena] Shwarts [*or* Shvarts]. TCRusP, *tr. by* Anna Barker and Daniel Weissbort

I like rust on a nail. And the Same Words. David Ignatow. NNaP

I like sitting alone when the moon is shining. Song of the pines. Po Chü-i. TAL

I like sleeping with somebody. *Unknown*. EaWin, *tr. by* J. Moussaieff Masson and W. S. Merwin

I like Sunday evenings after you're here. To H. John Wieners. FTOS

I like the articulate crack. Pool is a Godless Sport. James Haug. MoASP

I like the backs of houses. Fronts are smug. Hinterland. Margaret Stanley-Wrench. OBGa

I like the clattering of hoof on street. Metrics. Rhina P. Espaillat. FFC

I like the cold rooms of autumn, sitting. Morning Coffee. György Petri. VCWP, *tr. by* George Gömöri and Clive Wilmer

I like the cool and heft of it, dull metal on the palm. Smoking. Elton Glaser. BAP-97

I like the hunting of the hare. Old Squire, The. Wilfrid Scawen Blunt. OBEV; SCGP

I like the idea that nothing. For Jose Mercado Vasquez and Frances Roman Vasquez. Robert Vasquez. GeoHom

I Like the Likes of You. Vernon Duke. ReLy

I like the story of the circus waif. Road, The. Herbert Morris. DiPo

I like the way they look together. Photograph of My Parents. Silvia Curbelo. TouFir

I Like Them Fluffy. Sir Alan Patrick Herbert. NBLV

I like these foreign shores and I have never. "Ivan Venediktovich Elagin." TCRP

I like this secret walking. Charles Reznikoff. APT-2

I like to crawl around the house after my brother's wife. *Unknown*. STP

I like to find. Pleasures. Denise Levertov. NOBA; NeAP; NoAM; PoE

I like to get off with people. Conviction IV. Stevie Smith. LW

I like to hear of wealth and gold. Common Things. Paul Laurence Dunbar. GT

I like to look at you. You Touch Me. Andrena Zawinski. PasH

I like to play close by my father's den. Are You There? Strickland W. Gillilan. PoToHe

I Like to See It Lap the Miles. Emily Dickinson. GM

I like to think of a day for all those. Coming into Their Own. Sheenagh Pugh. AngWePo

I Like to Think of Harriet Tubman. Susan Griffin. NALW

I like to think that ours will be more than just another story. Wishful Thinking. Michael C. Blumenthal. HCAP

I like to walk / And hear the black crows talk. Crows. David McCord. MoAmPo

I like to walk down Fisher Street. Fisher Street. Thylias Moss. GT

I like to watch. Bath, The. Robin Becker. PBCAP

I like working near a door. I like to have my work-bench close by. Monologue. Hone Tuwhare. PeNZ

I like you when you are silent and you look as if you are absent. Poem 15. Pablo Neruda. BLPSL, *tr. by* Rene de Costa, Rigas Kappatos and Eleni Paidoussi

I like your muse because she's gay and witty. W. H. Auden. NOBL *Fr.* Letter to Lord Byron.

'I liked that,' said Offa, 'sing it again.' (LL) Geoffrey Hill. HAP; NPeEn; NoAM; WoPoe *Fr.* Mercian Hymns.

I likes a woman. Preference. Langston Hughes. APSN; HCAP; NOBA

I likes to take it real slow. (LL) Reactionary Poet, The. Ishmael Reed. ESEAA; GT

I limp along, looking for feathers. Stuffy Turkey. Dave Etter. SeSe

I 'listed at home for a lancer. Lancer. A. E. Housman. MoBrPo; OBWP

I listen for the sounds of cannon, cries. On Lookout Mountain. Robert Earl Hayden. PoE

I listen through underground walls like prisoners signaling. Gloria Gervitz. MirDau, *tr. by* Stephen Tapscott *Fr.* Yiskor.

I listened, heartwise, for the knock. (LL) Sweep Me through Your Many-Chambered Heart. Diane Ackerman. NIL-7; NIP-4

I listened, there was not a sound to hear. Full Moon; Santa Barbara. Sara Teasdale. OBCA

I listened to the Phantom by Ontario's shore. Walt Whitman. MoAmPo *Fr.* By Blue Ontario's Shore.

I listened to the voices that shattered. Enmeshment. Lewis Warsh. FTOS

I little thought (my Damon) once, that you. Irreconcilable, The. Damaris, Lady Masham. EMWP

I live a modest life. I don't suppose. Parrot, The. Oleg Grigorevich Chukhonstev. TCRP, *tr. by* Simon Franklin

I live alone where echoes roost. Charles Bennett. NewEx

I live amidst hills of desolate buildings. For South Bronx. Sandra Maria Esteves. PueRic

I live among the Pigmies and the Cranes. Pigmies and Cranes. Walter Savage Landor. NOBVV

I Live and Do Not Live in Myself. Saint John of the Cross. SpanPo, *tr. by* Stephen Stepanchev

I live at the head of the Long River. Tune: "The Diviner." Li Chih-yi. ColAnChi, *tr. by* Victor H. Mair

I live between heaven and earth. Lone Wild Goose, A. Lu Kuei Meng. SuSp, *tr. by* Robin D. S. Yates

I live between. I stalk space of these authors shunt. This Garden Being: The Hanging of Books. Clark Coolidge. FTOS

I live but in the present,—where art thou? Today. Jones Very. TAP

I live, but not in myself. Stanzas of the Soul that Suffers with Longing to See God. Saint John of the Cross. TOF, *tr. by* K. Kavanaugh and O. Rodrigues

I live for books. Light. Diane Wakoski. OPOU

I live, I die, I burn myself and drown. Sonnet 8. Louise Labé. BoWoP, *tr. by* Willis Barnstone

I live in a doorway. Sonrisas. Pat Mora. NIL-7; NIP-4

I live in a little country village. Han-shan. WoPoe, *tr. by* Robert Henricks

I live in a room named East. Suddenly. Robin Blaser. FTOS; PoM

I live in a town. Family Jewels. Essex Hemphill. GLP; GT

I live in an orchard. Confetti of bruised petals. Postcard from the Garden. Marge Piercy. NoAM

I Live in Music. Ntozake Shange. ISC

I live in sin, and dying to myself I live. Michelangelo Buonarroti. CAGL, *tr. by* James M. Saslow

I Live in the Mouth of History. Kalamu ya Salaam. SpirFl

I live in the town of Cahir. Haulier's Wife Meets Jesus on the Road Near Moone, The. Paul Durcan. ModIr

I live in this house, walls being plastered. Keep Me Still, for I Do Not Want to Dream. Larry Eigner. NeAP

I live invisible (in my whole sky). Too Bright a Day. Norman MacCaig. GTBS-P

I live my life day today as if. To My Bones. Zoltán Jékely. IQMS, tr. by George Szirtes

I live my life in growing orbits. Rainer Maria Rilke. RaBo

I live on my farm in a beautiful vale. Edward Williams. AngWePo Fr. Happy Farmer, The.

I live on the water. Winding Up. Derek Walcott. NoAM

I live on this depraved and lonely cliff. Vittoria da Colonna, Marchesa di Pescara. BoWoP

I live quietly and go nowhere. My Father's House. Calvin Forbes. ESEAA

I live where darkness / is not. Mukta Bai. BoWoP

I live / with a bullet in my heart. Margarita Iosifovna Aliger. ItWoWo; TCRP, tr. by Daniel Weissbort

I live with love encompassed round. Love's Mirror. Constance Naden. VWP; ViWPN

I live without inhabiting / Myself. Saint John of the Cross. OBVE Fr. Coplas about the Soul Which Suffers with Impatience to See God.

I live, yet no true life I know. I Die because I Do Not Die. Saint Theresa [or Teresa] of Avila. TOF, tr. by E. Allison Peers

I live; yet 'tis not I. He lives in me. Devotion. Paul Fleming. GePo, tr. by F. Warnke

I lived alone as happy as Larry. Brian [or Bryan] Merriman [or Merryman]. OBVE, tr. by Frank O'Connor Fr. Midnight Court, The.

I lived among great houses. Statesman's Holiday, The. W. B. Yeats. OxBTC

I lived for many years in the bush—far out—and I starved for lack of rain. Gravy Train, The. R. R. Davidson. NOBAu

I lived here nearly 5 years before I could. Chicago Poem. Lew Welch. NeAP; PoM

I lived here, too. On prison fare and water. On the Wall of My Age. Lajos Áprily. IQMS, tr. by Paul Tabori

I lived in a tree. The dream specified. Condo. Louise Glück. BodElec

I lived in the first century of world wars. Poem. Muriel Rukeyser. UnPo

I lived in those times. For a thousand years. Epitaph. Robert Desnos. PFTM-1

I lived inside a machine. On Being a Householder. Alan Dugan. NoAM

I lived obscurely and uncertainly. Ilya Grigoryevich Ehrenburg [or Erenburg]. TCRP

I lived on drugs and understood the pushers. Passing Through Experiences. Robert Adamson. BMAP

I lived on this earth in an age. Fragment. Miklós Radnóti. IQMS, tr. by George Gömöri and Clive Wilmer

I lived with Mr. Punch, they said my name was Judy. Variations. Randall Jarrell. VGW; WoPoe

I lived with my old man full nigh ten year. How Elizabeth Foole and Her Husband Parted by Means of Her Sister in Law. Elizabeth With. EMWP

I lived with Pride; the house was hung. House of Pride, The. William James Dawson. PoToHe

I lived with visions for my company. Elizabeth Barrett Browning. BWW; CenSon Fr. Sonnets from the Portuguese.

I'll act out a weird dream. Marie-Francoise Prager. BoWoP

I'll admit an occasional affair. I Hadn't Anyone Till You. Ray Noble. ReLy

I'll always dress in black and rave. Christine de Pisan. BoWoP

I'll always remember my town by the sea. (LL) Block City. Robert Louis Stevenson. AmFaPo; NTCP

I'll bark against the Dog-star. Loving Mad Tom. Unknown. NOSC

I'll be a tree, if you are its flower. Sándor Petőfi. IQMS, tr. by Egon F. Kunz

I'll be an otter, and I'll let you swim. River-Mates. Padraic Colum. AWP

I'll be around / No matter how. I'll Be Around. Alec Wilder. ReLy

I'll be finished, if I'll survive—. Boris Alekseievich Chichibabin. TCRP

I'll Be Seeing You. Sammy Fain. ReLy

I'll be the first. Dream of the Ring: The Great Jack Johnson, A. George Barlow. ESEAA; MoASP

I'll be the strongest amid you. Strongest, The. "Yehoash." TrJP, tr. by Marie Syrkin

I'll be the Vicar of Bray, Sir. (LL) Vicar of Bray, The. Unknown. NOBE; NOBL; OBSV; OxBEV; OxBoLi

I'll be tired of you. Then I'll Be Tired of You. Arthur Schwartz. ReLy

I'll be your Gigadibs,—despise. To Mr. Maunder Maunder, Professional Poet. Genevieve Taggard. APT-2

I'll bequeath no goods to you when I am dead. Testament. Tudor Arghezi. AF, tr. by Andrei Bantas

I'll bugger you and fuck you in the mouth. To Aurelius and Furius. Catullus. CAGL, tr. by Eugene O'Connor

I'll burn my books!—Ah, Mephistophilis! (LL) Christopher Marlowe. FaBoVe; HeIP-4; PeECV Fr. Doctor Faustus.

I'll buy you a tartan bonnet. Unknown. OxNR

I'll chase through the gypsy camp of dark streets. Osip Emilevich Mandelstam [or Mandelshtam]. TCRP

I'll check "other." (LL) Check One. Regie Cabico. ReBoTo; WiU

I'll cross the ridge. Saimaro. JDP, tr. by Yoel Hoffmann

I'll die for him tomorrow. (LL) Bonny Barbara Allan ("In Scarlet Town where I was born"). Unknown. AWP; BoLoP; ESPB; HeIP-4; InPK-6; NAEL-5v1; NAEL-6v1; NAEL-7v1; NePenScot; OxBB; PAI

I'll die in Paris on a rainy day. Black Stone on a White Stone. César Vallejo. WoPoe, tr. by Willis Barnstone

I'll die of mental anguish. Rāmprasād Sen. SinGod, tr. by Rachel Fell McDermott

I'll dig with it. (LL) Digging. Seamus Heaney. BIrV; CIP-2; NAEL-5v2; NAEL-6v2; NoP-4; SpudSo; TwCP

I'll do what the raids suggest. Boy, A. John Ashbery. NeAP

I'll dress you. Love Poem for Three for Kaye & Me. Gregory Corso. PmAP

I'll drown my book. (LL) William Shakespeare. AWP; EBEV; OxAEP-1; SCV Fr. Tempest, The.

I'll eat when I'm hungry, I'll drink when I'm dry. Rye Whisky. Unknown. OxBoLi

I'll faint no more beneath the burden. Submission. Clara Ann Thompson. CBWP-2

I'll find the stable and pull out the bolt. (LL) Fascination of What's Difficult, The. W. B. Yeats. BIrV; NAEL-5v2; NAEL-6v2; OxAEP-2

I'll follow and bring you back by force. I will!— (LL) Robert Frost. APT-1; ColAP; NAAL-2v2; SoSe-8; TAP; TRP

I'll Follow Thee. Clara Ann Thompson. CBWP-2

I'll frame, my Heliodora! a garland for thy hair. Garland for Heliodora, A. Meleager. AWP, tr. by "Christopher North."

I'll gather some by spells, and incantation. (LL) To ———: "Had I a man's fair form, then might my sighs." John Keats. CenSon; OxAEP-2

I'll Get By (As Long As I Have You). Fred E. Ahlert. ReLy

I'll get up soon, and leave my bed unmade. Widower in the Country, The. Les A. Murray. DiPo

I'll give a candle. Fair Exchange. Aileen Fisher. NOxBChV

I'll go among the dead to see my friend. Afternoon at the Beach, An. Edgar Bowers. VCAP

I'll go, said I, to the woods and hills. Apostate, The. Alfred Edgar Coppard. OBMV

I'll grant thee mine with all the powers I know. (LL) Female Philosopher, The. Charlotte Dacre. NOBRP; RWP

I'll greet the sun once more. Once More. Forugh Farrokhzad. BoWoP, tr. by Amin Banani and Jascha Kessler

I'll hold my candle high, and then. High Resolve. Unknown. PoToHe

I'll just stand here till you notice me, sir. Buddy. Andrew Hudgins. Unle

I'll keep your shirt white. Death Song. Unknown. BoWoP, tr. by Reza Baraheni and Zahra-Soltan Shokoohtaezeh

I'll Kill you if you Quote it! (LL) Cinq Ans Après. Frank Gelett Burgess. OBAL; OBCoV; TFi

I'll lay me doun an' dee. (LL) Siller Croun, The. Susanna Blamire. ECWP; LW

I'll lay this halfway me, which we the body name. Martin Opitz. GePo

I'll lay you five hundred pounds. Broomfield Hill, The. Unknown. ESPB; OxBB

I'll leave thy heart a-dying. (LL) Cheat of Cupid; or, The Ungentle Guest, The. Robert Herrick. AWP; OBVE

I'll live, and as he pulls me down mount higher. (LL) Ovid. CABP; NoSic, tr. by Christopher Marlowe Fr. Elegies.

(I'll Marry) the Very Next Man. Sheldon Harnick. ReLy

I'll meet thee, Pyramus, at Ninny's tomb. Ninny's Tomb. Patricia Beer. HarvBoo

I'll mock those thoughts of yours. Vladimir Vladimirovich Mayakovsky [or Maiakovskii]. TCRP, tr. by Bernard Meares Fr. Cloud in Trousers, The.

I'll never forget the boy who slept here last night. Memory, A. Yi Chŏngbo. WoPoe, tr. by Kevin O'Rourke

I'll Never Know No Sunday in This Weekday Room. Sabah As-Sabah. InTrad

I'll never know now! Well, goodbye. (LL) About the Teeth of Sharks. John Ciardi. OBCA; OxIBACP

I'll Never Love Thee More. James Graham, Marquess of Montrose. See My Dear and Only Love

"I'll never reach forty," my mother would say. She'd Say. Frank Davey. NOBC

I'll never see a tree at all. (LL) Song of the Open Road. Ogden Nash. APT-2; OBAL

I'll no be had for naething. Heiress, The. Carolina Oliphant, Baroness Nairne. NePenScot

I'll not be silent, though you put your finger. Francisco de Quevedo y Villegas. SpanPo, tr. by Denise Levertov Fr. Satiric and Censorious Epistle.

I'll not touch wood nor, fingers crossed. Favour. Robert David Fitzgerald. CBAP

I'll not weep that thou art going to leave me. Stanzas. Emily Jane Brontë. WPE

I'll only show your lines, and say, 'Tis this. (LL) Ode: Of Wit. Abraham Cowley. BeJo; MeLP; NAEL-5v1; NAEL-6v1; NAEL-7v1; NOSC

I'll only tell the story once. Bitter Mangoes, The. George Scurfield. FaBoWar

I'll [or Il'e] write no more of Love; but now repent. On Himselfe. Robert Herrick. CaPo

I'll [or Ile] come to thee in all those shapes. To Electra. Robert Herrick. CaPo

I'll [or Ile] write, because I'll [or Ile] give. To Critic[k]s. Robert Herrick. CaPo

I'll pass as a man today and take up public space with my urges in. Passing. Cheryl Clarke. WiU

I'll put a trinket on. (LL) Morns are meeker than they were, The. Emily Dickinson. ChAP; OBCA; SAmP

I'll Remember April. Don Raye. ReLy

I'll remember how in 6th-grade English class, always. Mrs. Frye and the Pencilsharpener. Bill Knott. BodElec

I'll rest me in this sheltered bower. Arbour, The. Anne Brontë. EBVV

I'll sacrifice in flames of love to Thee. (LL) Edward Taylor. NAAL-2v1; NAAL-3; NAAL-5 Fr. Preparatory Meditations Before My Approach to the Lord's Supper.

I'll Sail upon the Dog-Star. Thomas D'Urfey [or Durfey]. FaBoCh; OxBoLi Fr. Fool's Preferment, A.

I'll Say She Does. B. G. DeSylva. ReLy

I'll say. So no more now, from your loving husband, Wilfred. (LL) Jungle Husband, The. Stevie Smith. FaBoWP; HarvBoo; NBLV; NIL-7; NIP-4; RB

I'll See You Again. Noël Coward. ReLy

I'll See You Down the Lane. Alison Pryde. Prnts

I'll See You in My Dreams. Isham Jones. ReLy

I'll shoot a little bird for little brother. Unknown. STP

I'll sing of heroes, and of kings. Love. Abraham Cowley. AWP; BeJo; OBVE

I'll sing you a new ballad, and I'll warrant it first-rate. Fine Old English Gentleman; New Version, The. Charles Dickens. NOBVV; OBSV

I'll sing you a song. Bar on the Piccola Marina, A. Noël Coward. NBLV

I'll sing you a song / Nine verses long. Unknown. OxNR

I'll sing you a song / The days are long. Unknown. OxNR

I'll sink my roots far down. Returning Spring. Pauli Murray. GT

I'll stare at something less prepoceros. (LL) Rhinoceros, The. Ogden Nash. MoAmPo; OBAL

I'll still follow you, primordial. Tortoise and Badger. Cheryl Clarke. FFC

I'll still write on, and you shall rail. (LL) Headache, The. Mary Leapor. ECWP; PEW

I'll String Along with You. Harry Warren. ReLy

I'll Take Romance. Ben Oakland. ReLy

I'll teach my sons. My Sons. Ron Loewinsohn. NeAP

I'll tell as briefly as I can. Wild Dreams, The. Unknown. NAWM-7v1, tr. by Ned Dubin

I'll tell it You. (LL) Emily Dickinson. APN-2; NOCV

I'll tell my own daddy. Unknown. OxNR

I'll tell thee everything I can. Lewis Carroll. FaBoCh; NAEL-5v2; NAEL-6v2; NOBE; NOBL; NoAM; NoP-4; PeLV; TFi; UV Fr. Through the Looking-Glass.

I'll tell ye of ane great occasioun. Did Ye See Me? Robert Garioch. OBCoV

I'll tell you a story, a story anon. King John and the Bishop. Unknown. ESPB

I'll tell you a story / About Jack a Nory. Mother Goose. LB; OxNR; ReMoGo

I'll tell you a story / concerning John and Joan. Ballad. Peter Reading. PeLV

I'll tell you bluntly. Osip Emilevich Mandelstam [or Mandelshtam]. TCRP

I'll tell you how I speak a piece. Way To Do It, The. Mary Mapes Dodge. SWaP

I'll tell you how the Sun rose. Emily Dickinson. APN-2; ITBLP; TAP

I'll tell you how you were born, forbidden pleasures. I'll Tell You How You Were Born. Luis Cernuda. CAGL, tr. by Rick Lipinski

I'll tell you the story of Jimmy Jet. Jimmy Jet and His TV Set. Shel [or Shelley] Silverstein. OBCA; OBCoV

I'll tell you two fortunes, my fine little lad. Telling Fortunes. Alice Cary. SWaP

I'll test my power. Song of the Man Who Succeeded. Unknown. STP, tr. by Jerome Rothenberg

I'll think of the Leech-gatherer on the lonely moor. (LL) William Wordsworth. EBEV; FHYEP; HAP; NAEL-6v2; NOBE; NOBRP; NOCV; NoP-4; OxAEP-2; TFi

I'll think of thee, mine own, dear one. To a Loved One. Mary Weston Fordham. CBWP-2

I'll try counting raindrop stains on the oilcloth window. (LL) Yang Wan-li. ColAnChi; SuSp, tr. by Jonathan Chaves Fr. Songs of Depression.

I'll try / the whole / cause, / and / condemn / you / to / death.' (LL) Lewis Carroll. NoAM; OBCoV Fr. Alice's Adventures in Wonderland.

I'll try to hide my smile. (LL) Smile, A. Tzu Yeh. CrYelRi; ErotSp, tr. by Sam Hamill

I'll Twine White Violets. Meleager. See Epigrams

I'll wager, I'll wager, I'll wager with you. Broomfield Hill, The. Unknown. ESPB

I'll wagonloads of love and glory bring. (LL) Edward Taylor. NAAL-2v1; NAAL-3; NOBA; OxBA Fr. Preparatory Meditations Before My Approach to the Lord's Supper.

I'll wake you and shake you. To the Laggards. Joseph Bovshover. TrJP, tr. by Joseph Bovshover

I'll Walk Alone. Sammy Cahn. ReLy

I'll Wear Me a Cotton Dress. Unknown. BPo

I'll weave in the white violet. I'll weave in. Meleager. HePo Fr. Epigrams.

I'll worship You with tears, Ma. Ganapti Pāthak. SinGod, tr. by Rachel Fell McDermott

I'll write a book to prove I wrote these lines. (LL) Epigram: "Homer was poor. His scholars live at ease." James Vincent Cunningham. VGW; WoPoe

I'll write no more verses—plague take 'em! Those Flapjacks of Brown's. Bert Leston Taylor. OBAL

I loathe a boy who won't be hugged and kissed. Strato [or Straton]. CAGL, tr. by Daryl Hine

I loathe [or lothe] that I did love. Aged Lover Renounceth Love, The. Thomas Vaux, 2d Baron Vaux of Harrowden. NoSic; SCGP

I loathe the twin seas. Unknown. OHMPJ

I loathe you: keep your distance, you lowly crowd! Against Horace. Mihály Babits. IQMS, tr. by Adam Makkai and John Gordon Nichols

I loathed you, Spoon River. I tried to rise above you. Edgar Lee Masters. APT-1 Fr. Spoon River Anthology.

I loed you for yir kindness. Deean Tractorman, Clear, The. Edith Anne Robertson. OxBS

I long for him most. Ono no Komachi. ErotSp, tr. by Sam Hamill

I long for people. Chogo. JDP, tr. by Yoel Hoffmann

I long for the call to council. Alcaeus [or Alkaios]. WoPoe, tr. by Sam Hamill

I long to kisse the Image of my Death. (LL) Sleep, Silence' Child. William Drummond, of Hawthornden. NePenScot; Son

I long to talk[e] with some old lover's ghost. Love's Deity [or Deitie]. John Donne. AWP; ESCV; SoSe-8

I longed for your lips, dreamed of their roses. We Who Were Executed. Faiz Ahmad Faiz. PoetW, tr. by Agha Shahid Ali

I look. Catharina Regina von Greiffenberg. WPoS Fr. On the Sweet Comfort Brought by Grace.

I look after you as you go. Weingarten Travel Blessing, The. Unknown. GePo, tr. by Carroll Hightower

I look along the valley of my gun. Possibility That Has Been Overlooked Is the Future, The. Michael Hartnett. NOIV

I look at my face in the glass   and see / a halfborn woman. (LL) Upper Broadway. Adrienne Rich. HCAP; ItWoWo

I look at my mother's photograph on the wall. Depression. János Pilinszky. IQMS, tr. by Peter Jay

I look at my shadow over and over in the lake. Looking in the Lake. Po Chü-i. TAL

I look at the crisp golden-threaded hair. Canzone: His Portrait of His Lady, Angiola of Verona. Fazio degli Uberti. AWP; EaItPo, tr. by Dante Gabriel Rossetti

I look at the sky and stars scattered everywhere. Bare Rocks and Stars. Vietnamese Oral Tradition. CaDao, tr. by John Balaban

I look at the swaling sunset. In Trouble and Shame. D. H. Lawrence. OBMV

I / Look at you and suddenly. Old Devil Moon. Burton Lane. ReLy

I look at you from such deep graves. Aleksandr Yeryomenko [or Eremenko]. TCRP

I look at you so old and unaccomplished. I Look at You So Old. Armanda Guiducci. CItWP, tr. by Cinzia Sartini Blum and Lara Trubowitz

I look far off at T'ien-t'ai's summit. Unknown. CoBCP

I look for a way of writing. Valerio Magrelli. NeIt

I look, I look. Home. Franta Bass. INSAB

I look in that one kind of dwindled. And in this. Album—A Runthru. Clark Coolidge. FTOS

I Look into My Glass. Thomas Hardy. EBEV; FaBoTw; HAP; HarvBoo; NAEL-5v2; NAEL-6v2; NOBE; NOBVV; NoP-4; OxAEP-2; OxBSP; SCV; WeW-3

I look into the eyes of loved women. Savior. Ray Gonzalez. TouFir

I look into the lake (the lacquered water). From a Boat at Coniston. Norman Nicholson. NLP

I look now at the very moment. Tetto Giko. JDP, *tr. by* Yoel Hoffmann

I look now within myself. Poem for Mankind and Its Hope. Clementina Suárez. TANSG, *tr. by* Janet N. Gold

I look onto an alley here. Day for Anne Frank, A. C. K. Williams. GotH; TaR

I look out at the white sleet covering the still streets. Sleet Storm on the Merritt Parkway. Robert Bly. CoAmPo; NOBA

I look out the window: spring is coming. To Robert Lowell and Osip Mandelstam. Frederick Seidel. BodElec

I look over my own shoulder. Zen of Housework, The. Al Zolynas. BLT

I look up. William J. Higginson. HA

I LOOK up and see his curtains and bed. On the Death of his Father. Wei Wên-Ti. ChiP, *tr. by* Arthur Waley

I Look Up to the Sky. Samuel Ha-Nagid. TOF, *tr. by* David Goldstein

I look upon the world—and she resembles a garden. End of Man Is Death, The. Moses Ibn Ezra. TrJP, *tr. by* Solomon Solis-Cohen

I looked across the water. Loon upon the Lake, The. *Ojibwa Oral Tradition.* APN-2; OWoS, *tr. by* Charles Fenno Hoffman

I looked and I saw. Who But the Lord? Langston Hughes. BPo

I looked at my days and saw that. Purpose. Desmond O'Grady. PBCIP

I looked at my horoscope. It's a Good Day. Peggy Lee. ReLy

I looked at that face, dumbfounded. Esse. Czeslaw Milosz. TOF

I Looked for a Sounding-Board. Henriëtte Roland-Holst. WPOW, *tr. by* Jonathan Crewe

I looked for Beauty:—on a throne. Beauty and Her Visitors. Winthrop Mackworth Praed. NOBRP

I looked for that which is not, nor can be. Christina Georgina Rossetti. NOBE *Fr.* Three Stages.

I looked for you everywhere yet nowhere. Cloak of Dawn. Amadou Lamine Sall. NAfrP

I looked in my heart while the wild swans went over. Wild Swans. Edna St. Vincent Millay. HarvBoo; MoAmPo; OWoS; UnPo

I looked in the first glass. Three Mirrors, The. Edwin Muir. NoAM

I looked into my heart to write. Summer Song I. George Barker. HarvBoo

I looked like Abraham Lincoln. Edgar Lee Masters. OxBA *Fr.* Spoon River Anthology.

I looked on that prophetic land. Presences Perfected. Siegfried Sassoon. MoBrPo

I looked over Jordan and [*or* an'] what did I see. Swing Low, Sweet Chariot. *Unknown.* UnPo

I looked through the window and I saw a house. House, A. Yuly [*or* Iulii] Markovich Daniel. TCRP, *tr. by* Arthur Boyars and David Burg

I looked to find a man who walked with God. Enoch. Jones Very. ChIV-1; HAP; TCAPo

I looked to find Spring's early flowers. Lament of the Flowers, The. Jones Very. APN-1; ColAP; NOBA; OxBA

I Looked Up from My Writing. Thomas Hardy. NoAM

I lose myself within thy mind—from room. To Elizabeth Barrett Browning, in 1851. Dora Greenwell. PoBW; VWP

I lost my friend. Talin of the Pasta Factory. Rossana Ombres. CItWP, *tr. by* Cinzia Sartini Blum and Lara Trubowitz

I lost: my Joy turn'd to a Blaze. (LL) Apostacy, The. Thomas Traherne. OxBEV; SacPr

I lost my mare in Lincoln Lane. *Unknown.* OxNR

I lost the love, of heaven above. Vision, A. John Clare. EBVV; GTBS-P; NAEL-5v2; NAEL-6v2; NOBVV; OxBEV; PoE

I lounge on the jetty in the fragrance of catalpa. Quatrain. Tu Fu. SuSp, *tr. by* Jerome Seaton

I lov'd thee from the earliest dawn. Early Affection. George Moses Horton. TCAPo

I lovd thee living and lament thee dead. Mrs. Winchcombe. EMWP

I love a girl named Madelin' Paddlin' Madelin' Home. Harry Woods. ReLy

I love a still conservatory. Magic. Walter James Turner. OBGa

I love Adam. He is brave of heart. Eve. Jacob [*or* Jakov] Fichman. FIT, *tr. by* Robert Friend

I Love All Beauteous Things. Robert Bridges. EBEV; OxAEP-2; TrCP

I love all sights of earth and skies. Flaneur, The. Oliver Wendell Holmes. APN-1

I love America. Ham bones and shoes. In the New Country. Barbara Ras. OPRER

I love and fear him. Kasa no Iratsume. BoWoP; OHPJ; WoPoe, *tr. by* Kenneth Rexroth

I love, and he loves me again. Nymph's Passion, A. Ben Jonson. BeJo

I love, and must: So far[e]well liberty. (LL) Mary Sidney Wroth, Countess of Montgomery. BASC; CABP; NAEL-5v1; NAEL-6v1; NAEL-7v1; NOSC *Fr.* Pamphilia to Amphilanthus.

I love and serve my lady with a will. François Villon. EroLit, *tr. by* Peter Dale *Fr.* Grand Testament.

I love being a woman. Manifest, The. Olga Nolla. TANSG, *tr. by* Paula Vega

I Love Being Here with You. Bill Schluger. ReLy

I love breasts, hard. Breasts. Charles Simic. NNaP; RaBo

I Love But Thee. Heinrich Heine. AWP, *tr. by* Louis Untermeyer

I love desire, the state of want and thought. Why I Am Not a Buddhist. Molly Peacock. ExTi

I love hanging out laundry, bright linens. Past, The. Betsy Sholl. ExTi

I love her with the seasons, with the winds. Constancy. "Michael Field." VWP; ViWPN

I love him not; but shew no reason can. Antipathy. Rowland Watkyns. FaBoEE

I Love in White Ink. Siham Da'oud. PoArWo, *tr. by* Helen Knox and Smadar Lavie

I love it, I love it. Old Arm-Chair, The. Eliza Cook. BrRo; InPK-6; VWP

I love jukeboxes in dark, middle aged bars. Lucky 7. Katharine Harer. MiVo

I Love Little Pussy. Jane Taylor. OxNR

I love little pussy, her coat is so warm. *Unknown.* LB

I Love, Love. Gabriela Mistral. BLPSL, *tr. by* Rene de Costa, Rigas Kappatos and Eleni Paidoussi

I love / love's delicacy. Sappho. ErotSp, *tr. by* Sam Hamill

I love Master Meng. For Meng Hao-Jan. Li Po. WoPoe, *tr. by* Greg Whincup

I Love My Enemies. Leonid Andreievich Zavalniuk. GI, *tr. by* Magda Bogin

I love my friend's. My Friend's Dog. Meret Oppenheim. SurPaPo, *tr. by* Catherine Schelbert

I Love My Jean. Robert Burns. *See* Of A' the Airts [the Wind Can Blaw]

I Love My Jesus Quite Alone. Johannes Kelpius. AH, *tr. by* Christopher Witt

I love my little son, and yet when he was ill. Two Parents, The. Hugh MacDiarmid. FaBoTw; OxBTC

I Love My Love. Helen Adam. NeAP; WPOW

I love my master I love my master. Lynda Barry. Unle

I love my neighbour. Love Thy Neighbour. D. H. Lawrence. ChIV-2

I love my work and my children. God. Ovid in the Third Reich. Geoffrey Hill. CABP; FaBoMo; HP; HarvBoo; NPeEn; NoAM; OxBEV

I love not thy perfections. When I hear. Wilfrid Scawen Blunt. OBMV *Fr.* Love Sonnets of Proteus, The.

I love nothing better than my wife. (LL) Mother Goose. LB; OxNR

I love old mothers—mothers with white hair. Old Mothers. Charles Sarsfield Ross. PoToHe

I love or I don't—despair comes easily to me. She Loves Me, She Loves Me Not. Dmitry [*or* Dmitrii] Sergeievich Merezhkovsky [*or* Merezhkovskii]. TCRP, *tr. by* Albert C. Todd

I love roads. Roads. Edward Thomas. HarvBoo; PeFWW

I love Russia. Mikhail Valentinovich Kulchitsky [*or* Kulchitskii]. TCRP *Fr.* That's What It's Like.

I LOVE SEAHORSES, TEDDYBEARS, AFRICAN VIOLETS. Mad Sonnet: Grace. Michael McClure. BB

I love sixpence, jolly [*or* pretty] little sixpence. Mother Goose. LB; OxNR

I love sweets. Ellen West. Frank Bidart. NAAL-2v2; RACG

I love the bars and taverns. Bars. Nicolás Guillén. TCLAP, *tr. by* Eric Orozco

I love the bronze, the crystal and the porcelains. My Loves. Julián de Casal. BLPSL, *tr. by* Rene de Costa, Rigas Kappatos and Eleni Paidoussi

I love the cows best when they are a few feet away. Cow Worship. Gerald Stern. LoL

I love the days of long ago. My Africa. Michael Dei-Anang. PBA

I love the east, I love the west. I Love Being Here with You. Bill Schluger. ReLy

I love the evenings, passionless and fair, I love the evens. Victor Hugo. AWP, *tr. by* Francis Thompson *Fr.* Feuilles d'Automne.

I love the Fall, I love the endless tumbling. Eve Falling. Jane McVeigh. HW

I love the handful of the earth you are. Pablo Neruda. TCLAP, *tr. by* Stephen Tapscott

I love the hour before takeoff. Vacation. Rita Dove. SpirFl

I love the indolence of lying on the grass. Ballad of Indolence. Herman De Coninck. TuT, *tr. by* Eamon Grennan

I love the joyful time of Easter. In Praise of War. Bertrans [*or* Bertran *or* Bertrand] de Born. NAWM-7v1, *tr. by* Frederick Goldin

I love the lit corners of your kerosine smile. Senior Lady Sells Garden Eggs. Kojo Laing. HBAPE

I Love the Lord. *Unknown.* AH

I love the man whose lofty mind. Self-Reliance. James M. Whitfield. NAAAL

I love the master, Meng Hao-jan. To Meng Hao-jan. Li Po. ColAnChi, *tr. by* Stephen Owen

I Love the Night. Matilda Caroline Edwards. PWR

I love the old melodious lays. Proem. John Greenleaf Whittier. APN-1; OxBA; TAP

I love the quality of the. Essay on William Carlos Williams, An. Víctor Hernández Cruz. PmAP

I love the serenity of living in the woods. Wang Chiu-ssu. CoBLCP *Fr.* Living in the Woods.

I love the silent hour of night. Night. Anne Brontë. VWP

I love the small hours of the night. Pleasant Joys of Brotherhood, The. James Simmons. OBCoV; PBCIP

I love the sound of the horn in the deep, dim woodland. Sound of the Horn, The. Alfred de Vigny. AWP, *tr. by* Wilfred Thorley

I love the thought of his anger. Seamus Heaney. PoetW *Fr.* Sweeney Redivivus.

I love the word. Yes. Brendan Kennelly. CIP-2

I love Thee. (LL) Emily Dickinson. APN-2; LW

I Love Thee. Josephine D. Henderson Heard. CBWP-4

I love thee, Betty. *Unknown.* OxNR

I love thee for thy fickleness. *Unknown.* NOSC

I love thee, I love thee, and life will depart. Mother's Love, A. Ellen Johnston. VWP

I love thee, mournful, sober-suited Night! To Night. Charlotte Smith. NAEL-6v2

I love thee; never dream that I am dumb. Penetration. "Michael Field." VWP

I love them, I listen to them. Bells, The. Rosalía de Castro. SpanPo, *tr. by* Edwin Morgan

I love these gardens, all their show. Gardeners, The. Christopher Reid. DiPo

I love this body of mine that has lived a life. Celebration of the Body. Daisy Zamora. LoL, *tr. by* Dinah Livingston

I love this byre. Shadows are kindly here. Innkeeper's Wife, The. Clive Sansom. OBCP

I Love Thy Kingdom, Lord. Timothy Dwight. AH; TCAPo

I love to drive women's cars. Eclipse. Jonathan Johnson. AmPoNex

I love to encounter you in strange cities. Edouard J. Maunick. PBMAP *Fr.* Les Manèges de la Mer (1964).

I love to find a door. Like the spinal tap. Tap. Alice Jones. BloBone

I love to go out in late September. Blackberry Eating. Galway Kinnell. InPK-6; InvLad; NIL-7; NIP-4; SoSe-8

I love to hear the cock crow in. Cock-a-Doo. Stevie Smith. OWoS

I love to pass my fingers. J. P. Clark Bekedermo. PBMAP *Fr.* Reed in the Tide, A.

I love to ride the D train just to emerge from the tunnel. East Seventh Street. Mark Wunderlich. WiU

I love to rise ere gleams the tardy light. December Morning. Anna Seward. CenSon; ECWP

I love to rise in a summer morn. William Blake. FHYEP; FaBoCh; OxAEP-2 *Fr.* Songs of Experience.

I Love to See a Lady Nice and Natural at Any Price. Amanda Ros. VerBaPo

I love to see the starry flag. Our Flag. *Unknown.* CA

I love to see those loving and beloved. Lonely Love. Edmund Charles Blunden. OxBTC

I love to see, when leaves depart. Autumn. Roy Campbell. GTBS-P; MoBrPo; OBMV; OxBTC

I Love to Steal Awhile Away. Phoebe Hinsdale Brown. AH

I love to tell the story. Katherine Hankey.

"I love to tell the story." SacPr

I love to watch, while you are lazing. Snake that Dances, The. Charles Baudelaire. EroLit

I love uncertain gestures. Valerio Magrelli. NeIt

I love when you take over. Lumens. Olga Broumas. ExTi

I love wine but have no wine to drink. On Hearing That San-p'ing's Newly Brewed Chrysanthemum Wine Is Ready to Drink—Investigating with a Poem. Pien Kung. CoBLCP, *tr. by* Jonathan Chaves

I Love You. Ilyas Abu Shabaka. MAP, *tr. by* Michael Beard and Adnan Haydar

I love you. Equation. Nizar Qabbani. MAP, *tr. by* Diana Der Hovanessian and Lena Jayyusi

I love *you.* (LL) Dance of the Infidels. Al Young. ESEAA; NBV; SeSe

I love you better than I love my race. Charles Mair. NOBC *Fr.* Tecumseh.

I love you first because your face is fair. V-Letter. Karl Shapiro. IllVoic; NoAM; TrJP

I love you for your brownness. To a Dark Girl. Gwendolyn B. Bennett. BlSi; ColAP; NAAAL

I love you ginger bread mama. Ginger Bread Mama. Doughtry Long. BPo

I love you, great new Titan! Soldier: Twentieth Century. Isaac Rosenberg. PoWW

I love you he said but saying it took twenty years. Sources of the Delaware. Dean Young. BAP-01

I love you, I love you, is my song. Love Song. Pablo Neruda. ErotSp; GifTon, *tr. by* William O'Daly

I love you in the glow of cloudbanks faring. Grace of the Homeland. Herbert Strutz. AuPH, *tr. by* Lowell A. Bangerter

I love you in the newly born. Finger-nails. Paolo Buzzi. PFTM-1

I Love, You Love. "Rubén Darío." BLPSL, *tr. by* Rene de Costa, Rigas Kappatos and Eleni Paidoussi

I love you more than human heart can bear. I Love You. Ilyas Abu Shabaka. MAP, *tr. by* Michael Beard and Adnan Haydar

I love you, / Not only for what you are. Love. Roy Croft. ITBLP

I love you, rotten. Medlars and Sorb-Apples. D. H. Lawrence. FaBoVe; NPeEn; NoAM

I love you—Titan lover. Girl to Soldier on Leave. Isaac Rosenberg. PeFWW

I love you well, my steel-white dagger. Dagger. Mikhail Yuryevich Lermontov. AWP, *tr. by* Max Eastman

I love you, which is easy to see. You're Laughing at Me. Irving Berlin. ReLy

I Love You . . . Why Do You Hate Me? Rosalía de Castro. SpanPo, *tr. by* Edwin Morgan

I love you with my life. "Michael Field." VWP

"I love you," you said between two mouthfuls of pudding. Considered Reply to a Child, A. Jonathan Price. BoLoP

I love your eyebrows, said one. You Must Have Been a Sensational Baby. Harold Norse. GLP

I love your eyes. It's Got to Be Love. Richard Rodgers. ReLy

I love your plumpness. Sally Young. NewEx

I Loved a Lass. George Wither. NOBE; OBEV; VerBaPo (Love Sonnet, A.) NOSC

I loved booze. Clifton. Joan Larkin. GLP

I loved her softness, her warm human smell. Lion's Bride, The. Gwen Harwood. BoWoP

I loved him not; and yet, now he is gone. Walter Savage Landor. OBEV; TreFP *Fr.* Citation and Examination of William Shakespeare, The.

I loved Him not, yet I did not hate Him. I listened to Him not. Cobbler in Jerusalem, A. Kahlil Gibran. GraLe

I loved him three storms ere he loved me again. Love's Flight. Else Lasker-Schüler. TrJP, *tr. by* Jethro Bithell

I loved my friend. Poem. Langston Hughes. NTCP

I loved my lord, my black-haired lord, my young love. Magnet, The. Ruth Stone. MoAmPo

I loved my love from green of Spring. Grown and Flown. Christina Georgina Rossetti. NOBVV

I loved / secretly. *Unknown.* BoWoP *Fr.* Carmina Burana.

I loved the Supremes as much as baseball. Allegiance. Forrest Hamer. MoASP

I loved the way it felt once, practically invincible. Outside the Depot. Betsy Sholl. LTA

I loved thee beautiful and kind. Epigram. Robert Nugent. NOEC

I loved thee long and dearly. Florence Vane. Philip Pendleton Cooke. APN-1

I loved Theotormon. William Blake. CABP; NAEL-6v2

I loved—who hasn't? I worshipped—hasn't. I Loved—Who Hasn't? Philodemus. WoPoe, *tr. by* George Economou

I loved you. Disposition No. 1. Shafiq Al-Kamali. MAP, *tr. by* Sargon Boulus and Christopher Middleton

I Loved You. Alexander Sergeyevich Pushkin. AmFaPo, *tr. by* D. M. Thomas

I loved you; and perhaps I love you still. I Loved You. Alexander Sergeyevich Pushkin. AmFaPo, *tr. by* D. M. Thomas

I loved you Atthis once long ago. Sappho. SaLy, *tr. by* Diane Rayor

I LOVED you dearly, Stone Fish Lake. Stone Fish Lake. Yüan Chieh. ChiP, *tr. by* Arthur Waley

I loved you first: but afterwards your love. Christina Georgina Rossetti. OxBSo *Fr.* Monna Innominata.

I loved you first the time I saw you last. Letting Go. Daryl Hine. NoP-4

I lower sail at river mouth. At the Chiang-ning River Mouth. Wang An-shih. SuSp, *tr. by* Jan W. Walls

I lu-love you very well. Stuttering Lover, The. Fred Emerson Brooks. VerBaPo

I luikit up unto that Castell fair. Elizabeth Melville, Lady Culross. EMWP *Fr.* Ane Godly Dream.

I lurk on the floor of silence. Hunting. Tymoteusz Karpowicz. PoSu, *tr. by* Jan Darowski

I'm a bad, bad man. Bad Man. Langston Hughes. NAAAL

I'm a broken-hearted miner, who loves his cup to drain. Stringybark Cockatoo, The. *Unknown.* NOBAu

I'm a dead dog for real now. Buster's Visitation. Stephen Dunn. Unle

I'm a Dreamer. Kattie M. Cumbo. BlSi

I'm a fortunate tree. Once I stood drinking wind and bird-song, in the wood.

Julianus Sees the Chair of the Sophist Craterus.   Julianus of Egypt. GrAn, *tr.* by Lee T. Pearcy

I'm a Gigolo.   Cole Porter.   OBCoV; ReLy

I'm a glum one; it's explainable.   I Can't Get Started.   Vernon Duke.   APT-2; ReLy

I'm a lean dog, a keen dog, a wild dog and lone.   Lone Dog.   Irene McLeod. NOxBChV

I'm a little bit off.   Little Bit Off, A.   Richard Maltby, Jr.   ReLy

I'm a little butterfly.   *Unknown.*   OxNR

I'm a little gentleman.   One Little Boy.   *Unknown.*   NOxBChV

I'm a little husbandman.   Another Little Boy.   *Unknown.*   NOxBChV

I'm a mad immortal between heaven and earth.   To the Tune "Nan-hsiang-tzu." Shen Chou.   CoBLCP, *tr.* by Jonathan Chaves

I'm a man.   Transition #2.   Sabah As-Sabah.   InTrad

I'm a peevish old man with a penny-whistle.   Beggar's Serenade.   John Heath-Stubbs.   BoLoP

I'm a penny fallen from heaven's.   Motive.   Reginald Shepherd.   NeAmPo

I'm a quince, saved over from last year, still fresh.   Quince Preserved through the Winter, Given to a Lady, A.   Antiphilus [*or* Antiphilos].   GrAn *Fr.* Riddles (Exeter Book).

I'm a riddle in nine syllables.   Metaphors.   Sylvia Plath.   HeIP-4; InPK-6; SoSe-8

I'm a-Rollin'   *Unknown.*   NAAAL

I'm a strange composition as e'er was in nature.   Prize Riddle on Herself When 24, A.   Elizabeth Frances Amherst.   ECWP

I'm a strange creature, for I satisfy women.   Cynewulf.   ASW, *tr.* by Kevin Crossley-Holland   *Fr.* Riddles (Exeter Book).

I'm a Stranger Here Myself.   Ogden Nash.   ReLy

I'm a tough true-hearted sailor.   Every Bullet Has Its Billet.   *Unknown.* FaBoWar

I'm a very ordinary man.   I Want to Be Happy.   Irving Caesar.   ReLy

I'm a wanderer.   Basho.   SoOfWa, *tr.* by Sam Hamill

I'm a Worker.   Jayne Cortez.   NBV

I'm about to go shopping.   Song.   James Schuyler.   TTTS

(I'm Afraid) The Masquerade Is Over.   Herb Magidson.   ReLy

I'm afraid to close my eyes.   Menace of the Sick.   Breyten Breytenbach. PeSAV, *tr.* by Stephen Gray

I'm Ageing to Lay Down My Sword.   *Unknown.*   AH

I'm all afire and from bright blaze annealed.   Concerning Himself.   Paul Fleming.   GePo, *tr.* by George C. Schoolfield

I'm all alone. (LL)   Little Jumping Joan.   Mother Goose.   NTCP; ReMoGo

I'm all alone in this world, she said.   50–50.   Langston Hughes.   NOBA; NoAM; PoE

I'm Always Chasing Rainbows.   Joseph McCarthy.   ReLy

I'm always / most surprised.   Justice.   Petra von Morstein.   BoWoP, *tr.* by Rosmarie Waldrop

I'm an African, that's what he said. He was standing on the corner.   Another Impostor.   Bruce Jackson.   AmPoNex

I'm an Old Cowhand.   Johnny Mercer.   OBAL

I'm an unthinking dog.   Explosion.   Shinkichi Takahashi.   ZenPo, *tr.* by Takashi Ikemoto and Lucien Stryk

I'm ashamed of my thoughts.   *Unknown.*   NOIV

I'm at the bottom again. The baron's there.   Yury [*or* Iurii] Osipovich Dombrovsky [*or* Dombrovskii].   TCRP

I'm at the point of hurting myself and listening to myself.   Eunice Odio. TANSG, *tr.* by Arthur Natella   *Fr.* Creation.

I'm back after twenty years of baiting the trap of the past.   At the House of Ghosts.   Adrian C. Louis.   MoASP

I'm back in my town—excruciatingly familiar.   Leningrad.   Osip Emilevich Mandelstam [*or* Mandelshtam].   TCRusP, *tr.* by John Glad

I'm Beginning to See the Light.   Johnny Hodges.   ReLy

I'm beginning to talk to myself.   But My Blood.   Rose Romano.   UnSA

I'm Bert, p'rhaps you've heard of me, Bert, you've had word of me. Burlington Bertie from Bow.   William Hargreaves.   OBCoV

I'm big for ten years old.   Dumb Insolence.   Adrian Mitchell.   NOxBChV

I'm Black and Blue.   Heinrich Heine.   AWP, *tr.* by John Todhunter

I'm bored to extinction with Harrison.   Limericks and Puns.   *Unknown.*   PeLi

I'm bound to the hills. (LL)   Lonesome Water.   Roy Helton.   APT-1; MoAmPo

I'm building a nest in the garden.   Amanda Dalton.   NeBl   *Fr.* Room of Leaves.

I'm called by the name of a man.   *Unknown.*   OxNR

I'm careful of the words I say.   Be Careful.   *Unknown.*   NBLV

I'm caught, like any thrush the nets surprise.   Cecco Angiolieri, da Siena. EaItPo, *tr.* by Dante Gabriel Rossetti

I'm ceded—I've stopped being Theirs.   Emily Dickinson.   APN-2; NALW; SacPr; TRP; WPOW; WPoS

I'm cheerful, whatever happens.   Cloud.   Shinkichi Takahashi.   ZenPo, *tr.* by Takashi Ikemoto and Lucien Stryk

I'm cold. I'm destitute and absurd.   Konstantin Konstantinovich Kuzminsky [*or* Kuzminskii].   TCRP

I'm coming, coming out of space.   Three Octets.   Osip Emilevich Mandelstam [*or* Mandelshtam].   RusPo, *tr.* by Robert Arthur Douglas Ford

"I'm corrupt," he said to me in the French.   Corrupt Man in the French Pub, The.   Brian Higgins.   OxBTC

I'm Craving for That Kind of Love.   Eubie Blake.   ReLy

I'm cross with god who has wrecked this generation.   John Berryman. FaBoMo   *Fr.* Dream Songs.

I'm curled into a ball.   Poetry Reading.   Anna Swirszczynska.   BLT

I'm deaf? (LL)   Issa.   ChAP; EH, *tr.* by Robert Hass

I'm Dealing with My Pain.   Denise Duhamel.   NeAmPo

I'm delighted by the velocity of money as it whistles.   Velocity of Money. Allen Ginsberg.   NIL-7

I'm digging holes for three wilted saplings.   Noon.   Perry Oldham.   CDa

I'm discontented with homes that are rented.   Irving Caesar.   ReLy

I'm doing it again.   Reading, The.   Gabriel Gbadamosi.   HBAPE

I'm down. Step on my neck, you savage god, with your heel.   Meleager.   HePo *Fr.* Epigrams.

I'm dreaming geographically these days.   Rafael Campo.   WiU   *Fr.* Song for My Lover.

I'm dropping out. (LL)   Marks.   Linda Pastan.   NIL-7; NIP-4

I'm Explaining a Few Things.   Pablo Neruda.   TCLAP, *tr.* by Nathaniel Tarn

I'm Far From What I Call My Home.   John Campbell.   PeSAV

I'm feelin' mighty lonesome.   Black Coffee.   Paul Francis Webster.   ReLy

I'm flying to South Carolina.   Long Distance Moan.   Blind Lemon Jefferson. APT-2

I'm folding up my little dreams.   My Little Dreams.   Georgia Douglas Johnson.   BlSi; NAAAL

I'm Fond of Doctors.   Samuel Hoffenstein.   OBCoV

I'm 41st in line for Plisetskaya.   Chorus of Nymphs, A.   Andrey [*or* Andrei] Andreievich Voznesensky [*or* Voznesenskii].   VCWP, *tr.* by Vera Dunham

I'm forty-one. I was twenty-three then.   Vermont.   David Huddle.   CDa

I'm frightened at night.   At Night.   Elizabeth Jennings.   OTCP

I'm full of everything I do not want.   Sonnet: Of the 20th of June 1291. Cecco Angiolieri, da Siena.   AWP; EaItPo, *tr.* by Dante Gabriel Rossetti

I'm getting deep lines on my forehead.   Limerick.   Ron Rubin.   PeLi

I'm getting used to not understanding.   At the Protestant Museum.   Hugh Maxton.   CIP-2

I'm glad I'm not getting old like that.   Staying Young.   Bob Merrill.   ReLy

I'm Glad I'm Not Young Any More.   Frederick Loewe.   ReLy

"I'm glad pigs can't fly," said young Sellers.   Limerick.   Ron Rubin.   PeLi

I'm Glad There Is You (In This World of Ordinary People).   Paul Madeira. ReLy

I'm goin' to buy a paper doll that I can call my own.   Paper Doll.   Johnny S. Black.   ReLy

I'm goin' to whoop you, Sammy Taylor.   Domestic Storm, A.   Priscilla Jane Thompson.   CBWP-2

I'm going, all along. (LL)   Emily Dickinson.   HeIP-4; MoAmPo; PAI; TCAPo

I'm going out.   Issa.   EH, *tr.* by Robert Hass

I'm going out and get something.   Riot Act, April 29, 1992.   Ai.   ESEAA; NIL-7

I'm going out to clean the pasture spring.   Pasture, The.   Robert Frost.   APT-1; MoAmPo; NAAL-2v2; NAAL-5; NOBA; OxBA; PoE; SAmP; TLR; TRP; TTTS; WHSW

I'm going out to dine at Gray's.   Ballade of Hell and of Mrs. Roebeck.   Joseph Hilaire Pierre Belloc.   NPeEn

I'm going stark, staring mad because of the guns. (LL)   Repression of War Experience.   Siegfried Sassoon.   AF; NoAM; PeFWW; PoE

I'm going to be just like you, Ma.   Dance For Ma Rainey, A.   Al Young. NBV

I'm going to bring you something.   Conversations in Mayan.   Alonzo Gonzales Mó.   STP, *tr.* by Allan F. Burns

I'm going to die, he says.   Heaven Is Just Another Country.   Jaime Jacinto. ReBoTo

I'm going to England. And France.   Going to Europe.   Michael Lassell.   WiU

I'm going to move ahead.   Border.   Taslima Nasrin.   VCWP

I'm going to push it. (LL)   Precision German Craftsmanship.   Matthew Rohrer. NAPBL; NeAmPo

I'm going to put Johnny Dominguez right here.   Photograph: Migrant Worker, Parlier, California, 1967.   Larry Levis.   GeoHom

I'm going to roll over.   Issa.   EH, *tr.* by Robert Hass

I'm Going to Sleep.   Alfonsina Storni.   TCLAP, *tr.* by Andrew Rosing

I'm going to tell You something that is true.   Abu Sa'id Abul Khayr.   WoPoe, *tr.* by Dick Davis   *Fr.* Four Poems on Death.

I'm going to try and overcome my limitation.   Serious Concerns.   Wendy Cope.   OBCoV

I'm going under were the last words.   Teen Drowns in Rehabilitation Camp

Days Before 17th Birthday, Questions Persist. Gaylord Brewer. AmPoNex

I'm gong to murder you with love. Food of Love. Carolyn Kizer. RaBo

I'm gonna die & won't see you all any more. Tsakak. STP

I'm Gonna Go Fishin' Peggy Lee. ReLy

I'm Gonna Laugh You Right Out of My Life. Cy Coleman. ReLy

I'm gonna love you. Come Rain or Come Shine. Johnny Mercer. ReLy

I'm gonna marry my brother's wife. Unknown. STP

I'm Gonna Sit Right Down and Write Myself a Letter. Fred E. Ahlert. ReLy

I'm Gonna Slap Those Doctors. Jack Coulehan. BloBone

I'm gonna walk to the graveyard. Young Gal's Blues. Langston Hughes. NAAL-2v2

I'm grateful for the past. (LL) False Though She Be. William Congreve. BoLoP; NOBE; OBEV; OxBSP

I'm growing my beard from the turret room. Haymakers. Deborah Randall. NeBl

I'm happiest when most away. Emily Jane Brontë. NAEL-5v2; NAEL-6v2

I'm happy, Kerouac, your madman Allen's. Malest Cornifici Tuo Catullo. Allen Ginsberg. BB; NeAP

I'm happy through and through. Rifu. JDP, tr. by Yoel Hoffmann

"I'm having five minutes," he said. Five Minutes. Norman Nicholson. NLP

I'm heading off to Pasárgada. Off to Pasárgada. Manuel Bandeira. TCLAP, tr. by Candace Slater

I'm Here. Theodore Roethke. CoAP Fr. Meditations of an Old Woman.

I'm here, on the dark porch, restyled in my mother's chair. Sitting at Night on the Front Porch. Charles Wright. ColAP; GeoHom; LCAP-2

I'm hiding, I'm hiding. Hiding. Dorothy Aldis. ChAP

I'm hip / I'm no square. I'm Hip. Dave Frishberg. ReLy

I'm holding my cigarette out the car window. Smoking. Ronald Wallace. SwNoth

I'm Honest Abe. Honest Abe Lincoln. Max Shulman. OBAL

I'm in a car marked blueberry. Poetry Detective. Edwin Torres. HeMarv

I'm in a mirrorless room. Poem No. XV. Sang Yi. PFTM-1

I'm in love with a girl from Uttoxeter. Limerick. Gerard Benson. PeLi

I'm in love with a man. Party's Over, The. Jule Styne. ReLy

(I'm In Love With) The Honorable Mr. So and So. Sam Coslow. ReLy

I'm in the Mood for Love. Dorothy Fields. ReLy

I'm incorrect: the learned say. On Being Charged with Writing Incorrectly. "The Amorous Lady." ECWV

I'm introducing it as a hunchback. Yury [or Iurii] Arabov. TCRP

I'm Jewish because love my family Matzoh ball soup. Yiddishe Kopf. Allen Ginsberg. BodElec; TaR

I'm jilted, forsaken, outwitted. Jilted Nymph, The. Thomas Campbell. EnLoPo

I'm just a little "Jackie Horner." When I Take My Sugar to Tea. Pierre Norman. ReLy

I'm Just a Lucky So-and-So. Duke Ellington. ReLy

I'm just a poor wayfaring stranger. Unknown. See I am a poor wayfaring stranger

I'm just a woman. Am I Blue? Grant Clarke. ReLy

I'm just about as solitary. No Love, No Nothin' Harry Warren. ReLy

I'm just going to school. (LL) Soul Make a Path Through Shouting. Cyrus Cassells. GT; GifTon; OPRER; UnSA

I'm just Miss Blues'es child! (LL) Miss Blues'es Child. Langston Hughes. ChAP; SAmP; TTTS

I'm Just Wild About Harry. Noble Sissle. ReLy

I'm keeping to myself on my little porch. Soundtracks. Timothy Geiger. AmPoNex

I'm King of the cabbages green. Old King Cabbage. Richard Kendall Munkittrick. OBCA

I'm learning how to read the rocks. Indian Ruins Along Rio de Flag. Greg Pape. PBCAP

I'm leaving / Now you can make love. Issa. ZenPo, tr. by Takashi Ikemoto and Lucien Stryk

I'm like a skiff on the ocean tost. John Gay. EnLoPo

I'm like a vine supported on a stick. Leonidas of Tarentum. GrAn

I'm like all lovers, wanting love to be. Poem. Lesbia Harford. NOBAu

I'm Livin' in a Great Big Way. Dorothy Fields. ReLy

I'm living in a cave. Song. Unknown. STP, tr. by Jerome Rothenberg

I'm lookin' far in mind, b'lieve I'm fixin' to die, b'lieve I'm fixin' to die. Fixin' to Die. Bukka White. APT-2

I'm looking for a blue door. Sleep. Mary Crockett Hill. AmPoNex

I'm looking out of the window. Invention of a Garden, The. Jay Wright. GT

I'm / lost / among a / maze of cans. Supermarket. Felice Holman. OTCP

I'm made in sport by Nature, when. On an Indian Tomineois, the Least of Birds. Thomas Heyrick. NOSC

I'm makin' a road. Florida Road Workers. Langston Hughes. MoAmPo

I. M. Margaritae Sorori. William Ernest Henley. See Echoes

"I'm Mark's alone!" you swore. Given cause to doubt you. Contemplation. John Frederick Nims. InPK-6

I'm melted down into a black ooze. In a Remote Cloister Bordering the Empyrean. Joel Sloman. VGW

I'm middle-aged. Political Activist Living Alone. Pat Arrowsmith. BrRo

I'm Mighty Glad I'm Living and That's All. George M. Cohan. ReLy

I'm My Own Mother, Now. Stella P. Chipasula. HAWP

I'm naebody noo, though in days that are gane. I'm Naebody Noo. William Anderson. NePenScot

I'm naturally lazy, carefree. Fisherman on a Southern Stream. Lu Kuei Meng. SuSp, tr. by Robin D. S. Yates

I'm Neither the Loosening of Song nor the Close-Drawn Tent of Music. Mirza Asadullah Khan Ghalib. WoPoe, tr. by Adrienne Rich

I'm nervous and upset. Tonight at Eight. Sheldon Harnick. ReLy

I'm no artist but in bed. Artist, The. Han Yongwun. WoPoe, tr. by Bruce Taylor

I'm no fighting man, he says. Novella Nikolaevna Matveyeva [or Matveieva]. TCRusP, tr. by Daniel Weissbort

I'm no longer the bitter girl. Love Which Frees. Gloria Fuertes. WPOW, tr. by Philip Levine

I'm no matron, mother of warriors, Cornelia. Heart's Desire. Adelia Prado. TANSG, tr. by Ellen Watson

I'm no reformer; for I see more light. Optimism. Ella Wheeler Wilcox. PWR

I'm Nobody's Baby. Benny Davis. ReLy

I'm Nobody! Who are you? Emily Dickinson. APN-2; AmFaPo; BoWoP; ChAP; HeIP-4; NALW; NBLV; NOBA; OBCA; OBCoV; OTCP; OxBSP; OxIBACP; PoPoPo; SAmP; TAP; TCAPo; WPE

I'm not a child any more, Syama. Bhadreśvar Mandal. SinGod, tr. by Rachel Fell McDermott

I'm Not a Man. Harold Norse. CAGL; GLP

I'm not a man. I don't want to destroy you. (LL) I'm Not a Man. Harold Norse. CAGL; GLP

I'm not a poet / How well I know it. You're the Cream in My Coffee. Ray Henderson. ReLy

I'm not at all scared of the Pleiades setting. Antipater of Thessalonica. GrAn

I'm not at home if people call. (LL) Arrivals at a Watering-Place. Winthrop Mackworth Praed. NOBL; NOBRP; NPeEn; PeLV

I'm Not Complaining. Philip Schultz. SoSe-8

I'm not going to tell you everything. Closed Mill. Maggie Anderson. PBCAP

I'm not here. "H. D." MoAmPo Fr. Halcyon.

I'm Not Here / Never Was. Constanta Buzea. BoWoP, tr. by Stavros Deligiorgis

I'm not in court to be judged. Jenny Lewis. NewEx

I'm not interested in the poverty. I Go Dreaming Roads in My Youth. Luis Omar Salinas. AiP

I'm not looking at you, though it might seem that I am. Dreamt Up. Dennis Cooper. WiU

I'm not planning to turn into gold. Somebody else. Bassus [or Bassos]. HePo Fr. Epigrams.

I'm not sleeping now. Maysoun Saqr Al-Qasimi. PoArWo, tr. by Subhi Hadidi Fr. Morning of Every Sin, The.

I'm not so deep in it. Muso Soseki. EaWin, tr. by W. S. Merwin

I'm not sure at what point. Honor (1969). Allston James. CDa

I'm not sure it happened. Through the branches. Canto Eleven. Tomas Venclova. WoPoe, tr. by Vyt Bakaitis

I'm not sure of my age; descending pale. Fourteenth Ode. Sekeena Shaben. PoArWo

I'm not the branch, only the prebranchness. Ivan Zhdanov. TCRP

I'm not without you. Place of O, The. Ray A. Young Bear. VoR

I'm now a legend underneath this porch. Max Who Caught a Car. Ron Carlson. Unle

I'm now arriv'd the soul desired port. Edmund Davie 1682; Annagram. Benjamin Tompson. SCAP

I'm of no interest to myself. Dissolving Presence, A. Sándor Weöres. IQMS, tr. by Adam Makkai and Donald E. Morse

"I'm of no use," said a little brown seed. Little Brown Seed, The. Harriett Mulford Lothrop. PWR

I'm offering for sale today. Bargain Sale, A. Samuel Ellsworth Kiser. PoToHe

I'm old and you're going away. Sending Tzu-lung Off to a Post in Chi-chou. Lu Yu. CoBCP, tr. by Burton Watson

I'm Old-Fashioned. Johnny Mercer. ReLy

I'm Older than You, Please Listen. Arthur Rex Dugard Fairburn. PeNZ

I'm on a straight path with the sun gone down. Luigi Fontanella. NeIt

I'm on My Way to Canaan. Unknown. AH

I'm on the ledge. Paparazzi, The. Ai. ExTi

I'm on the way.   Prose of the Trans-Siberian and Little Jean of France.   Blaise Cendrars.   CuPo

I'm only a consumer, and it really doesn't matter.   Cheer for the Consumer.   Nixon Waterman.   OBAL

I'm only a poor little mouse, ma'am.   Mouse, The.   Laura Elizabeth Richards.   OBCA

I'm persistent as the pink locust.   Pink Locust, The.   William Carlos Williams.   SAmP

"I'm pregnant," I wrote to her in delight.   1973.   Marilyn Hacker.   GLP

I'm pretending not to see him so I can eat my lunch.   Poets on Poets.   Nin Andrews.   KGB

I'm quintessential female.   Doggerel.   Abigail Thomas.   Unle

I'm quite the opposite of my clever master.   Faust's Servant.   Roy Fuller.   OxBTC

I'm recallin' / Times when I was small, in.   Hallelujah!   Vincent Youmans.   ReLy

I'm red pepper in a shaker.   Sugar in the Cane.   Tennessee Williams.   OBAL

I'm round at Heliodorus' place—.   Lucilius.   GrAn

I'm Sad.   Forugh Farrokhzad.   BoWoP, tr. by Reza Baraheni

I'm scared a lonely. Never see my son.   John Berryman.   NoP-4   Fr. Dream Songs.

I'm Sending You Saint Francis Preaching to the Birds.   Karen Kipp.   BodElec

I'm sentimental, so I walk in the rain.   Why Try to Change Me Now?   Cy Coleman.   ReLy

I'm sewing on new buttons.   Invisible Mender, The.   Sarah Maguire.   MFPA

I'm sick. I hear the cranes.   1915.   Anna Andreyevna Akhmatova.   WoPoe, tr. by Stephen Berg

I'm sick of cautious lyricism.   Poetics.   Manuel Bandeira.   TCLAP, tr. by Candace Slater

I'm sick of celestial whodunits, wherein God.   Search, The.   Maurya Simon.   ExTi

I'm sick of love; O let me lie.   To Sycamores.   Robert Herrick.   CaPo

I'm sick of love songs.   Happy As the Day Is Long.   Ted Koehler.   ReLy

I'm sick of poems with Brueghel.   In the Middle of Reading One More Poem with Brueghel as a Metaphor.   Doris Safie.   GraLe

I'm sitting by the hearthstone now.   Twilight Musings.   Mary Weston Fordham.   CBWP-2

I'm sitting by the pool at the Mondrian.   Sunset Stripping: Visiting L.A.   Michael Lassell.   WiU

I'm sitting in the sunshine.   Postponed Nightmare.   Sandor Csoori.   VCWP, tr. by Len Roberts and László Vértes

I'm sitting on the stile, Mary.   Countess of Dufferin, The.   Helen Selina Blackwood, Countess of Dufferin.   OxAEP-2

I'm Sitting on Top of the World.   Ray Henderson.   ReLy

I'm skulking by the scandal and the handle on the door.   John Hegley.   NewEx

I'm Smith of Stoke, aged sixty-odd.   Epitaph on a Pessimist.   Thomas Hardy.   FaBoEE; TRP

I'm so blue I don't know what to do.   If I Could Be with You.   James P. Johnson.   ReLy

I'm so happy since the day.   My Baby Just Cares for Me.   Walter Donaldson.   ReLy

I'm so in love.   At Long Last Love.   Cole Porter.   ReLy

I'm so out of it I can't remember.   Apiary.   B. H. Boston.   GeoHom

I'm so sad to / Think that I have had to.   Till the Clouds Roll By.   P. G. Wodehouse.   ReLy

I'm so tired of this dull routine.   Let's Get Away from It All.   Matt Dennis.   ReLy

(I'm So) Weary of It All.   Noël Coward.   ReLy

I'm sorry but we can't go to the immersions tonight.   Ganges, The.   Norman Dubie.   LCAP-2

I'm sorry for the Dead—Today.   Emily Dickinson.   SAmP

I'm sorry I done it, Major.   Deserter, The.   Gilbert Frankau.   FaBoWar

I'm sorry I'm late.   Apology and Explanation.   John Sparrow.   OBCoV

I'm sorry it's slushy when it's going. (LL)   Winter Morning.   Ogden Nash.   OTCP; TLR

I'm sorry, officer. I didn't see the sign.   First Offense.   David Lehman.   PmAP

I'm sorry to say my dear wife is a dreamer.   Be Off!   Stevie Smith.   OxBC

I'm sound asleep, when a knock at the gate wakes me.   Recording My Happiness.   Wang Chiu-ssu.   CoBLCP, tr. by Jonathan Chaves

I'm speaking again.   Speaking.   Michael Ryan.   SoSe-8

I'm spending my nights in the doss house.   Soup Kitchen Song.   Unknown.   NOBAu

I'm Standing, Lord.   Stand Still, and See.   Betty Scott Stam.   SacPr

I'm stepping out, don't mess about.   Stepping Out.   Maureen Watson.   IBA

I'm Still Here.   Stephen Sondheim.   ReLy

I'm still struck (as when I saw my first Pasque-flower).   Black Train, The.   Thomas McGrath.   GM

I'm sure if I were a woman I should hate.   Sonnet: Equality of the Sexes.   Gavin Ewart.   Son

I'm sure we should all be as happy as kings. (LL)   Happy Thought.   Robert Louis Stevenson.   BRP; PWR; Spl

I'm swimming in vast stretches of dry ocean.   Ackermann Steppe, The.   Adam Mickiewicz.   WoPoe, tr. by Vyt Bakaitis

I'm taught P-l-o-u-g-h.   O-U-G-H.   Charles Battell Loomis.   NBLV

I'm thankful that the sun and moon.   Gasbags.   Unknown.   NOBL

I'm the bloke that's trained to sit behind the public stamp machines.   Song of the GPO, A.   Gerry Hamill.   NOBL

I'm the great Sir William Anson.   Var. authors.   FaBoEE   Fr. Balliol Rhymes.

I'm the individual.   Individual's Soliloquy, The.   Nicanor Parra.   PFTM-2, tr. by Lawrence Ferlinghetti and Allen Ginsberg

I'm the kid that's all the candy.   Yankee Doodle Boy, The.   George M. Cohan.   ReLy

I'm the Kilfenora teaboy.   Kilfenora Teaboy, The.   Paul Durcan.   PBCIP

I'm the king of the castle.   King of the Castle.   Unknown.   OxNR

"I'm the naked power-grab!" yodel the latecomers.   Confessional.   Tom Breidenbach.   KGB

I'm the snow on mountains.   Death Songs.   Unknown.   BoWoP, tr. by Reza Baraheni and Zahra-Soltan Shokoohtaezeh

I'm the tomb of Baukis, a bride; passing the deeply lamented.   Erinna.   SaLy, tr. by Diane Rayor

I'm the Way I Am.   Jacques Prévert.   STV, tr. by John Frederick Nims

I'm thinking about you. What else can I say?   Postcard.   Margaret Atwood.   NoAM

I'm thinking of your sex.   César Vallejo.   TCLAP, tr. by Sandy McKinney

I'm thist a little crippled boy, an' never goin' to grow.   James Whitcomb Riley.   VerBaPo   Fr. Happy Little Cripple, The.

I'm through with acid and with praise.   Recantation.   Minuchihri.   ArPe, tr. by Omar S. Pound

I'm Through with Love.   Gustave Kahn.   ReLy

I'm tired of Love: I'm still more tired of Rhyme.   Fatigue.   Joseph Hilaire Pierre Belloc.   NBLV; NOBL; OxBTC; UV

I'm tired of murdering children.   Two Vietnam Poems: (1966).   Bill Knott.   PBCAP; SPE

I'm tired of seeing sights south of the river.   Climbing a Solitary Islet in the River.   Hsieh Ling-yün.   SuSp, tr. by Francis Westbrook

I'm tired of symbols, of laws divine.   To My Generation.   Benyamin [or Benjamin] Galai.   TrJP, tr. by Jacob Sonntag

I'm tired of these grim wastes of snow and ice.   Imre Madách.   IQMS, tr. by Iain MacLeod   Fr. Tragedy of Man.

I'm tired of town and suburb life.   Tristan da Cunha.   Ian D. Colvin.   PeSAV

I'm troubled by one thought—to die.   Sándor Petőfi.   IQMS, tr. by Adam Makkai

I'm trying to pray; one of the voices of my mind says, "God, please help me do this."   Vessel, The.   C. K. Williams.   TaR

I'm ugly but I don't know why.   Sandra Tappenden.   NewEx

I'm unhappy / So unhappy.   One I Love (Belongs to Someone Else), The.   Walter Donaldson.   ReLy

I'm up against the wall.   Wall, The.   William Hawkins.   MoCV

"I'm very drowsy," said the Bear.   Hard to Bear.   Tudor Jenks.   OBCA

I'm waiting for sleep, but it won't come.   Svidrigailov's Last Night.   László Kálnoky.   IQMS, tr. by Kenneth McRobbie and Zita McRobbie

I'm walking out on Rome.   Antonio Porta.   CLPP

I'm watching and waiting.   Thanks a Lot, but No Thanks.   Adolph Green.   ReLy

I'm wearin' [or wearing] awa', John [or Jean].   Land o' the Leal, The.   Carolina Oliphant, Baroness Nairne.   GTBS-P; NOBRP; NPeEn; NePenScot; OBEV; OxBEV; OxBS

I'm weary o' the rose as o' my brain.   Great Wheel, The.   Hugh MacDiarmid.   OxBS

I'm weary of towns, it seems a'most a pity.   Tired of Towns.   Andrew Lang.   EBVV

I'm what is missing.   Valerio Magrelli.   ItPo, tr. by Gayle Ridinger

I'm wiser now. So what? It's like the rack.   Youth.   David J. Rothman.   GeoH

I'm wishing and fishing.   I'm Craving for That Kind of Love.   Eubie Blake.   ReLy

I'm working like a dog, testing my memory.   Expulsion, The.   Gerald Stern.   LCAP-2

I'm writing from the Botanic Garden at Tilden Park.   Tilden Park.   Alison Deming.   UrbNat

I'm writing just after an encounter.   Whatever You Say Say Nothing.   Seamus Heaney.   OBWP; OxBC

I'm writing this for love.   Lovepoem Writing Me.   Madeline J. Tiger.   MiVo

I Made a House of Houselessness.   Rose Cecil O'Neill.   LW

I Made a New Memory for You.   Maya Bejerano.   DTA, tr. by Miriyam Glazer

I made a posy for my love.   Posies.   Agnes Mary Frances Robinson.   VWP

I made a posy [or posie], while the day ran by.   Life.   George Herbert.   BASC; ESCV; FSCP; GeHe; MeLP; NOSC; NoP-4

I made another garden, yea. Song. Arthur William Edgar O'Shaughnessy. OBEV

I made car batteries new. Awakened in a Field. Juan Delgado. GeoHom

I made love with a man—hugely muscled, lean— the body. Trick, The. Mark Wunderlich. WiU

I made my song a coat. Coat, A. W. B. Yeats. NAEL-5v2; NAEL-6v2; NoAM; OxAEP-2; OxBSP

I made myself a path on the side of a hill. I Made Myself a Path. N.V.M. Gonzalez. ReBoTo

I made myself as a tree. March Hares. Andrew Young. SAmP

I made myself into armored concrete against the worms that graw us and suck us dry. Season of Anger. René Depestre. PFTM-2, tr. by Pierre Joris

I made no choice / I decided nothing. Margaret Atwood. NALW Fr. Circe / Mud Poems.

I made the motions of the sacred place. Edouard J. Maunick. NegPo Fr. As Far as Yoruba Land.

I made the Muses sick. Death of the Gods; an Ode Written in Imitation of Pindar, The. L. Ker. NOEC

I made the pilgrimage again. Derailment: A Delirium. Steve Chimombo. HBAPE

I made these mountains. Drainlayer. Duncan Bush. AngWePo

I, Maister Andro Kennedy. Testament of Mr. Andro Kennedy, The. William Dunbar. OxBS

I make a pact with you, Walt Whitman. Pact, A. Ezra Pound. APT-1; ColAP; NAAL-2v2; NAAL-5; NOBA; NoAM; OxBA; PAI; TAP

I make a simple assertion. Working with Tools. A. R. Ammons. TRP

I make all the poetic pauses. Dana Naone. CDW

I make free with old albums. At the Wailing Wall. Aidan Carl Mathews. BiHa; CIP-2

I make my shroud but no one knows. Song. Adelaide Crapsey. APT-1

I make no moan or outcry, just don't sleep. For Paul. Eve Triem. APT-2

I make this dirge for you Miss Mary Binning I miss you. Dirge. Unknown. BoWoP, tr. by Armand Schwerner

I make this song about me full sadly. Wife's Lament, The. Unknown. WPE, tr. by Ann Stanford

I make this song sadly about myself. Unknown. See I make this song about me full sadly

I make tiny, tiny huts. Miniaturist, The. Maurice Kilwein Guevara. AmPoNex; TouFir

I make up things to say. I've Told Ev'ry Little Star. Jerome Kern. ReLy

I marked where lovely Venus and her court. Venus's Looking-Glass. Christina Georgina Rossetti. NALW

I Married. Lorine Niedecker. APT-2

I married a man from County Roscommon. Overheard in County Sligo. Gillian Clarke. HarvBoo; TCAWP

I married a man of the Croydon class. Nervous Prostration. Anna Wickham. FaBoWP

I married a second time the other day. Second Marriage. Mei Yao Ch'en. SuSp, tr. by Jonathan Chaves

I married in my youth a wife. James Vincent Cunningham. MoAmPo

I marveled at the sight of you who without knowing. Whole two weeks after The Million Man March, A; and still, if you'd ask me, this is all I could say about it. Richard Rykard. SpirFl

I mastered pastoral theology, the Greek of the Apostles. Minister, The. Fenton Johnson. APT-1

I maun feed frae common trough ana' Vision of Myself, A. Hugh MacDiarmid. OxBEV

I, Maximus of Gloucester, to You ("By ear, she sd"). Charles Olson. NeAP Fr. Maximus Poems, The.

I, Maximus of Gloucester, to You ("Off-shore, by islands hidden in the blood"). Charles Olson. NOBA; NoAM; PmAP; PoM Fr. Maximus Poems, The.

I may be dead to-morrow, uncaressed. For the Book of Love. Jules Laforgue. AWP, tr. by Jethro Bithell

I may be following you! (LL) Award. Ray Durem. BPo; TTY

I may be smelly and I may be old. River God, The. Stevie Smith. BrRo; FaBoTw; FaBoWP

I may be too old to run a mile. It's Never Too Late to Fall in Love. Sandy Wilson. ReLy

I May Be Wrong (But I Think You're Wonderful). Henry Sullivan. ReLy

I may even be. Power and Light. James Dickey. NAAL-2v2

I May, I Might, I Must. Marianne Craig Moore. AmFaPo; ChAP; FaBoWP; OBAL; OxBSP

I may live on until. Fujiwara no Kiyosuke. OHPJ

I may not ope again. (LL) Get Up! Joseph Skipsey. InPK-6; NOBVV; NPeEn

I may picture her there. (LL) Thoughts of Phena. Thomas Hardy. EBVV; HarvBoo; NOBVV; NPeEn; NoP-4; OxBTC

I may wel sike for grevous is my peyne. Unknown. OHMEL

I mean that too, but yet a hidden strength. John Milton. NOSC Fr. Comus; a Masque Presented at Ludlow Castle.

I measure every Grief I meet. Emily Dickinson. MoAmPo

I measure time by how a body sways. (LL) I Knew A Woman. Theodore Roethke. APT-2; BoLoP; HAP; HeIP-4; InPK-6; MoAmPo; NAAL-2v2; NAAL-5; NIL-7; NOBA; NoAM; PoE; RaBo; SoSe-8; TAP; TFi; TRP; TwCP; UnPo; VCAP

I meditate upon a swallow's flight. Coole Park, 1929. W. B. Yeats. CABP; OBMV

I meet two soldiers sometimes here in Hell. That Exploit of Yours. Ford Madox Ford. PeFWW; PoWW

I meet you, but once. Shadow of Life, The. Vicki Davey. IBA

I meet you in an evil time. Eclogue for Christmas, An. Louis MacNeice. FaBoMo; NoAM; OBMV

I member we went to the hospital that day. Killing of the Birds, The. Shirley Williams. BoWoP

I mend the fyre and beikit me about. Robert Henryson. EBEV; PoE Fr. Testament of Cresseid, The.

I met a fair maiden so sweet and so fair. Girl by the River, The. Alton Delmore. APT-2

I met a girl from Derrygarve. New Song, A. Seamus Heaney. CABP; CIP-2; FaBoTw

I met a guy I used to know, who said. Ozymandias II. Howard Nemerov. Son

I met a King this afternoon! Emily Dickinson. ChAP

I met a lady / on a lazy street. From the Hazel Bough. Earle Birney. NIP-4

I met a little cottage-girl. Wordsworth on Lloyd George. Mary Visick. UV

I met a little cottage Girl. William Wordsworth. UV Fr. We Are Seven.

I met a little Elf-man, once. Little Elf, The. John Kendrick Bangs. NTCP; OBCA

I met a man in South Street, tall. Hart Crane. FaBoMo Fr. Bridge, The.

I met a man my age running a greenhouse. Scarlet Crown. Marc J. Straus. BloBone

I met a man once. Nissim Ezekiel. WoPoe Fr. Hymns in Darkness.

I met a man with a triple-chin. Man Who Sang the Sillies, The. John Ciardi. OBCA

I met a seer. Stephen Crane. MoAmPo Fr. Black Riders [and Other Lines], The.

I met a seer. Eidolons. Walt Whitman. APN-1

I met a tall broadchest. Murmuring. Kofi Anyidoho. NAfrP

I met a traveler [or traveller] from an antique land. Ozymandias. Shelley. AWP; BRP; CABP; CenSon; ChAP; ClHu; FaBoCh; GSo; GTBS-P; HAP; HeIP-4; InPK-6; MakPoe; NAAL-5v2; NAAL-6v2; NIL-7; NIP-4; NOBE; NPeEn; NoP-4; OPOU; OxBEV; OxBSo; PAI; PoE; PoPoPo; PoRA; RB; SCGP; SCV; SoSe-8; Son; TFi; UV

I met a traveller from an antique land. Ozymandias Revisited. Morris Gilbert Bishop. NBLV; UV

I met a woman, weeping by the sea. Cavour. Menella Bute Smedley. VWP

I met an elf-man in the woods. How to Treat Elves. Morris Gilbert Bishop. OBAL; OBCA

I met an honest man today. Alien. William Price Turner. OxBS

I met ayont the cairney. Empty Vessel. Hugh MacDiarmid. FaBoTw; NPeEn; NePenScot; OxBEV; OxBS

I Met by Chance. Heinrich Heine. AWP, tr. by John Todhunter

I met Death—he was a sportsman—on Cole's. Charles Olson. PoM Fr. Maximus Poems, The.

I met her as a blossom on a stem. Dream, The. Theodore Roethke. NIL-7; UnPo

I met her, not by chance. Flower of Air, The. Gabriela Mistral. TCLAP, tr. by Doris Dana

I met him at a party just a couple of years ago. Mad About the Boy. Noël Coward. ReLy

I met in a merchant's place. Charles Reznikoff. APT-2

I met in Mesilla. Edward Dorn. PFTM-2 Fr. Gunslinger.

I met Jack on a Friday night. Tip for Saturday, A. Francis Webb. BMAP

I met Musette / In the water-closet. Vague Lyric by G. M. Max Beerbohm. FaBoEE

I Met My Solitude. Naomi Replansky. BrRo

I met the Angel Sus on the Skin Bridge. Kenneth Irby. PFTM-2

I met the Bishop on the road. Crazy Jane Talks with the Bishop. W. B. Yeats. BoLoP; CABP; EBEV; InPK-6; NAEL-5v2; NAEL-6v2; NoAM; NoP-4; OxAEP-2; PAI; PoE; PoPoPo; TOF; TRP

I met the Love-Talker one eve in the glen. Love-Talker, The. "Ethna Carbery." WPE

I met the thieving miss magpie, number 123. I Met the Thieving Miss Magpie. Patrizia Vicinelli. ItPo, tr. by Gayle Ridinger

I met this lovely scene once before, on horseback. Gazing at Ch'ang-po Mountain. Li K'ai-hsien. CoBLCP, tr. by Jonathan Chaves

I met Tu Fu on a mountaintop. About Tu Fu. Li Po. CrYelRi, *tr.* by Sam Hamill

I met up with him on a corner on Florida Street. Encounter. Alfonsina Storni. TANSG, *tr.* by Mark McCaffrey

I met wizened wood-woman. Old Woman and the Sandwiches, The. Libby Houston. OBSP

I might as well be king of rainy lands. Spleen LXXVII. Charles Baudelaire. SxFrPo, *tr.* by James McGowan

I might have been born in Beirut. Curriculum Vitae. Lawrence Joseph. GraLe; PBCAP

I might have died when I was young. Song of the Old Man. Richard Jones. IllVoic

I might not have known his voice. Last Letter. Gerald William Barrax. ESEAA

I might, unhappy word, O me, I might. Sir Philip Sidney. NPeEn *Fr.* Astrophil and Stella.

I mind as 'ow the night afore that show. Chances, The. Wilfred Owen. OxBTC

I mind me of a morning while the mountains yet were grey. Mooimeisjes. Perceval Gibbon. PeSAV

I mind o' the Ponnage Pule. Ponnage Pool, The. Helen B. Cruickshank. NePenScot

I mind them or the show or resonance of them—I come and I depart. (LL) Walt Whitman. ColAP; SAmP *Fr.* Song of Myself.

I Minded God. Henry Ainsworth. AH

I mingle with the young and gay. I Smile, but Oh! My Heart Is Breaking. Mary E. Tucker. CBWP-1

I mingle with your bones. One Lost, The. Isaac Rosenberg. MoBrPo

I miss my grandmother. Dream Poem. Mary Jo Bona. UnSA

I miss our lizards. The one who watched us. Lizards in Sardinia. Eamon Grennan. BiHa

I miss you in the morning, dear. Miss You. *Unknown.* PoToHe

I missed. Empty Cage, The. Lise Deharme. SurWo, *tr.* by Franklin Rosemont

I missed him when the sun began to bend. Lost and Found. George Macdonald. SacPr

I Missed His Book, but I Read His Name. John Updike. OBAL

I missed / the last transport. Abandoned, The. Zbigniew Herbert. PoSu, *tr.* by Michael March

I mix my men and booze. Sally: Twelfth Street. Naomi Long Madgett. NBV

I mock thee not, though I by thee am mocked. To Flaxman. William Blake. FaBoEE; OxBoLi

I moot go walke the wode so wilde. Sir Thomas Wyatt. *See* I must go walk the woods so wild

I mope the new spring away in a white coat. Spring Rain. Li Shang-yin. ChinPo, *tr.* by Yip Wai-lim

I mourn for Antibia the virgin. Anyte [*or* Anytes]. GrAn

I mourn maiden Antibia: desiring her, many. Anyte [*or* Anytes]. SaLy, *tr.* by Diane Rayor

I mourn with thee, and yet rejoice. Penitent, The. Anne Brontë. SacPr

I mouth. Hickie, The. Liz Lochhead. LW

I Move the Meeting Be Adjourned. Nicanor Parra. TCLAP, *tr.* by Allen Ginsberg

I move to the window. Threading the Miles. Alfred Encarnacion. OpBo

I moved across the Dharma-nature. Getsudo. ZenPo, *tr.* by Takashi Ikemoto and Lucien Stryk

I moved into my house one day. Moving In. May Sarton. APT-2

I Muriel stood at the altar-table. Don Baty, the Draft Resister. Muriel Rukeyser. NNaP

I muse, alone, on Ararat. (LL) Lakeshore. Francis Reginald Scott. MoCV; NOBC

I must admit to this outright theft. Robo. Nick Carbó. NAPBL

I must be. (LL) All but Blind. Walter De la Mare. MoBrPo; WeW-3

I Must Be Able to Protect You. 'Marnia. LW

I must be careful about such things as these. Sonnet. Ed Roberson. GT

I must be dreaming through the days. Experience. Lesbia Harford. CBAP

I must be ill, of course. I've been shivering. Fever. Bella [*or* Izabella] Akhatovna Akhmadulina. TCRP, *tr.* by Elaine Feinstein

I must be mad, or very tired. Meeting-House Hill. Amy Lowell. APT-1; ColAP; MoAmPo; OxBA; PoRA; TCAPo

I must become a child again. (LL) Innocence. Thomas Traherne. BASC; CABP; ChIV-2; ESCV; MiEL; NOSC

I Must Become a Menace to My Enemies. June Jordan. NAAAL

I must become small and hide where he cannot reach. Fooling God. Louise Erdrich. ReEnLa

I must explain why it is that at night, in my own house. Still Life. Reed Whittemore. CoAP; CoAmPo

I must feel this soil again. Digging Soil. Peter Gruffydd. AngWePo

I must get those jeans taken up. (LL) My House. Robert Adamson. BMAP; CBAP

I must go back to winter. Two Decisions. Vernon Watkins. OxBTC

I must go down to the seas again, to the lonely sea and the sky. Sea Fever. John Masefield. BRP; CABP; ChAP; ITBLP; MoBrPo; OxAEP-2; OxBTC; UV

I must go down to the seas again, where the billows romp and reel. Sea-Chill. Arthur Guiterman. UV

I must go on, till in my tearful line. Cross, The. Jones Very. NCAP

I must go walk the woods so wild. Sir Thomas Wyatt. MiEL

I must have back this breath. Dealing Scraps. Ruth Garnett. ISC

I must have been dozing in the tub. Soap-Pig, The. Paul Muldoon. PBCIP

I must have passed the crest a while ago. Long Hill, The. Sara Teasdale. MoAmPo; TCAPo

I must hide him down in my deepest veins. Totem. Léopold Sédar Senghor. PoetW, *tr.* by Melvin Dixon

I must, I will have gin!—that skillet take. Strip Me Naked, or Royal Gin for Ever; a Picture. *Unknown.* NOEC

"I must leave here," said Lady De Vere. Limerick. *Unknown.* PeLi

I must leave you, but. Ariwara no Yukihira. OHPJ

I must lie down with them all soon and sleep. Thomas Kinsella. BIrV *Fr.* Nightwalker.

I must not dare to sleep. (LL) Coora Flower, The. Gwendolyn Brooks. IllVoic; NAAL-5; NIL-7; NoP-4

I must not grieve my love, whose eyes would read. Samuel Daniel. OBEV *Fr.* To Delia.

I must not think of thee; and, tired yet strong. Renouncement. Alice Thompson Meynell. BoLoP; GSo; LW; MoBrPo; NOBE; OBEV; OBMV; OxBSo; PEW; Son; VWP; WPE

I must / Not trust. Anacreontic. Robert Herrick. CaPo

I must possess you utterly. Possession. Richard Aldington. MoBrPo

I must read only children's books. Osip Emilievich Mandelstam [*or* Mandelshtam]. TCRP

I must remember. Spreading Wings on Wind. Simon J. Ortiz. HATNAP

I must see the lighthouse keeper. Pious One, The. Gabriela Mistral. BBASP, *tr.* by Doris Dana

I must stay here with my hurt. (LL) Here. Ronald Stuart Thomas. GTBS-P; NPeEn; RB

I must tell her, or die. (LL) Tennyson. NAEL-5v2; NAEL-6v2 *Fr.* Maud [A Monodrama].

I must tell you. Grass, The. George Bowering. MoCV

I must tell you. Young Sycamore. William Carlos Williams. APT-1; TAP

I must tell you, my dear. Love in Mayfair. May Probyn. VWP

I must wait for a stranger to knock on my door. Elegy. David Ignatow. NNaP

I mustn't ask about him. Tune: Drunk among the Flowers. Mao Wen-hsi. CoBCP, *tr.* by Burton Watson

I, my dear, was born to-day. On My Birthday, July 21. Matthew Prior. OBEV

I, my mother, my two brothers. Segregation #1. Carlos German Belli. TCLAP, *tr.* by Isabel Bize

I myself. (Invocation for Storing Corn). *Unknown.* WPoS, *tr.* by Francisco X. Alarcón

I myself am a complete orchestra / So long. (LL) Gilbert Keith Chesterton. NOBL; UV *Fr.* Variations on an Air Composed on Having to Appear in a Pageant as Old King Cole.

I myself and Pangur Bán. Pangur Bán. *Unknown.* NOIV

I myself have rolled the pearl screens up to their jade hooks. Tune: "Sand of Silk-washing Stream." Li Ching. SuSp, *tr.* by Daniel Bryant

I myself saw furious with blood. Aeneas at Washington. Allen Tate. APT-2; FuPo; NOBA; NoAM; OxBA

I nail Picasso's girl with a mirror. Notes from an Analyst's Couch. Anita Endrezze. CDW

I name you Evening, O ambiguous Evening, you fluttering leaf. Man and Beast. Léopold Sédar Senghor. PFTM-1

I named it sickle. But he. Hook, The. Duncan Bush. TCAWP

I ne'er could any lustre see. Richard Brinsley Sheridan. NOEC *Fr.* Duenna, The.

I ne'er was struck before that hour. First Love. John Clare. BoLoP; EnLoPo; HAP; NOBVV; NoP-4; PoPoPo

I ne have joy, plesauns, nor comfort. *Unknown.* MiEL

I need a ritual to perform, / clean and sane, for this perfect washday. Domestic Tranquility. Gerald William Barrax. GT

I need appreciation. Jim Carlson. IBA

I need but little! A crust of bread. Velemir [*or* Viktor Vladimirovich] Khlebnikov. TCRP

I need huge trees to grow within me. Secrecy of Mirrors, The. Al-Zahra Al-Mansouri. PoArWo, *tr.* by Nathalie Handal, Richard McKane and Tahia Abdel Nasser

I need kai kai ah. For the Poets. Jayne Cortez. PmAP

I need me a house like that.   Where the Heart Is.   Ntozake Shange.   GT

I Need Not Go.   Thomas Hardy.   NOBE; OBEV; OxBTC

I need not your needles.   *Unknown.*   OxNR

I need nothing but God's mercy.   Question.   Edith Södergran.   WPoS

I need only fall asleep / to return.   Ana Blandiana.   BoWoP, *tr. by* Stavros Deligiorgis

I need something easy.   Honey Moon.   Kathleen Leland Baker.   NBLV

I need to know their names.   Lost Women, The.   Lucille Clifton.   BodElec

I need to learn a language but not english.   Language.   Jennifer Maiden.   BMAP

I need to worship someone.   Bulat Shalvovich Okudzhava.   TCRP

I needed to point to the buildings, as if they all stood.   Thirty Years Rising.   Olena Kalytiak Davis.   AmPoNex

I never barked when out of season.   On a Dog of Lord Eglinton's.   Robert Burns.   OxBSP

I never believed in mirages.   Vladimir Semionovich Vysotsky [*or* Vysotskii].   TCRP

I never believed that in my broken life.   Ts'ai Yen.   BoWoP; WPOW   *Fr.* Eighteen Verses Sung to a Tatar Reed Whistle.

I never cared for Life: Life cared for me.   Epitaph.   Thomas Hardy.   FaBoEE

I never cared much for moonlit skies.   I'm Beginning to See the Light.   Johnny Hodges.   ReLy

I never could qualify as a saint.   Maybe I Should Change My Ways.   Duke Ellington.   ReLy

I never crossed your threshold with a grief.   Closed Door, The.   Theodosia Pickering Garrison.   PoToHe

I never did on cleft Parnassus dream.   Persius.   AWP, *tr. by* John Dryden   *Fr.* Satires.

I Never Do Anything Twice (Madam's Song).   Stephen Sondheim.   ReLy

I never drank of Aganippe well.   Sir Philip Sidney.   NAEL-5v1; NAEL-6v1; NAEL-7v1; NoSic; Son   *Fr.* Astrophil and Stella.

I never feel a thing is real.   It's Only a Paper Moon.   Harold Arlen.   ReLy

I Never Felt Better.   Hugh Martin.   ReLy

I never follow an inferior way.   (LL)   George Wither.   NOSC; SacPr   *Fr.* Collection of Emblemes, Ancient and Moderne, A.

I never gave a lock of hair away.   Elizabeth Barrett Browning.   CenSon; EBVV; HAP; OxBSo   *Fr.* Sonnets from the Portuguese.

I never hear it ring without.   Door-Bell, The.   Charlotte Becker.   PoToHe

I never hear the word "escape."   Emily Dickinson.   NCAP; NOBA; SAmP

I never knew. (LL)   Willy Lyons.   James Wright (1927–80).   HCAP; NNaP; PoE

I Never Knew a Night So Black.   John Kendrick Bangs.   PoToHe

I Never Knew I Was Jewish.   Irene Reti.   GotH

I never knew that by August.   Losing My Sight.   Lisel Mueller.   ExTi

I never knew the earth had so much gold.   Feuerzauber.   Louis Untermeyer.   TrJP

I never knew the worth of him / Until he died. (LL)   Old Story, An.   Edwin Arlington Robinson.   MoAmPo; OxBSP

I never knew you.   Pictures and Stories.   Amos Neufeld.   GotH

I never look upon the sea.   Aunt Zillah Speaks.   Herbert Edward Palmer.   FaBoTW

I Never Lost as Much.   Emily Dickinson.   HeIP-4; MoAmPo; NAAL-2v1; NAAL-3; NCAP; NOBA; NoAM; NoP-4; TAP; TCAPo

I never made friends faster.   Learning the War.   Wendy Wilder Larsen.   OPRER

I never painted myself yellow.   Children are Colorblind.   Genny Lim.   FSt

I never played for you. You'd have thrown.   For the Death of Vince Lombardi.   James Dickey.   MoASP

I Never rested on the Muses bed.   To William Drummond of Hawthornden.   Mary, of Morpeth Oxlie.   EMWP

I never said I loved you, John.   No, Thank You, John.   Christina Georgina Rossetti.   NAEL-5v2; NAEL-6v2

I Never Saw a Goddess Go.   Austin Hummell.   AmPoNex

I never saw a man in all my days—.   Rural Scenes.   John Clare.   CenSon

I never saw a Moor.   Emily Dickinson.   AmFaPo; HeIP-4; ITBLP; MoAmPo; SAmP; TAP; TFi; WPoS

I never saw a Purple Cow.   Purple Cow, The.   Frank Gelett Burgess.   BRP; NBLV; NTCP; OBAL; OBCA; OBCoV; OxIBACP; TCAPo; TFi; TLR

I never saw a wild thing.   Self-Pity.   D. H. Lawrence.   OxBTC; RB

I Never Saw Great Lakes.   Nancy Morejón.   TANSG, *tr. by* Joy Renjilian-Burgy

I never saw such a place as this.   Estes' Backyard, The.   Pamela Stewart.   UrbNat

I never saw that land before.   Edward Thomas.   HarvBoo

I Never Saw You.   Jyoti Lanjewar.   OMIP, *tr. by* Vinay Dharwadker

I never see you.   Buddha, The.   Daya Pawar.   OMIP, *tr. by* Eleanor Zelliot

I never set my two eyes on a head was so fine as your head.   Walther [*or* Walter] von der Vogelweide.   MoBrPo, *tr. by* J. M. Synge

I never shall forget thee—'tis a word.   To Mrs. Norton.   Frances Anne [*or* "Fanny"] Kemble.   VWP

I never soared, and never did I soar.   Bulat Shalvovich Okudzhava.   TCRusP, *tr. by* Denis Johnson, Aleksandar Petrov and Shirley Rihner

I never tasted the Pierian spring.   Priscilla Pointon.   ECWP   *Fr.* To the Critics.

I never thought for a moment.   Emily Dickinson, Bismarck and the Roadrunner's Inquiry.   Ray A. Young Bear.   HATNAP

I never thought frogs.   One Morning Beside a Pond.   Rofel G. Brion.   ReBoTo

I never thought that you could mourn.   Mistaken.   Mary Elizabeth Coleridge.   PoBW

I never tire in my search of solitude.   In Search of Solitude.   Chao Yi.   SuSp, *tr. by* Chang Yin-nan

I never told you.   What They Do to You in Distant Places.   Marvin Bell.   MoASP

I never touched thy royal hand, dead queen.   Lost Light, The.   Emily Jane Pfeiffer.   VWP

I never travel'd further north.   Let's Take a Walk Around the Block.   Harold Arlen.   ReLy

I never wanted the red of fire, the black at midnight.   Miracle.   Wen Yi-tuo [*or* Wen I-to].   PFTM-1

I never wanted to be a star.   On Earth.   Forugh Farrokhzad.   BoWoP, *tr. by* Girdhard Tikku

I never wholly feel that summer is high.   High Summer.   Ebenezer Jones.   NOBVV

I never writ, nor no man ever loved [*or* lov'd].   (LL)   William Shakespeare.   AEP; AWP; CABP; ClHu; EnLoPo; GSo; HAP; HeIP-4; NAEL-5v1; NAEL-6v1; NAEL-7v1; NIP-4; NOBE; NPeEn; NoSic; OBEV; OxAEP-1; OxBEV; OxBSo; PoE; PoPoPo; PoRA; SCGP; SCV; SoSe-8; Son; TFi; TRP; UnPo; WeW-3   *Fr.* Sonnets.

I no longer have to choose between.   Ismailia Eclipse.   Khaled Mattawa.   NAPBL

I no longer wonder.   After Reading *Poems to Einhir*.   Gwyn Williams.   TCAWP

I nod and nod to my own shadow and thrust.   Climbing Suilven.   Norman MacCaig.   HarvBoo

I not only was burned by love.   Put 'Em in a Box, Tie 'Em with a Ribbon (And Throw 'Em in the Deep Blue Sea).   Sammy Cahn.   ReLy

I not see you long time now, I not see you long time now.   Letter to My Mother, A.   Eva Johnson.   IBA

I, now at Carthage. He, shot dead at Rome.   *Vale* from Carthage.   Peter Viereck.   MoAmPo; WoPoe

I now had only to retrace.   Charlotte Brontë.   NOBVV

I now solicit not the Muses nine.   William Woty.   NOEC   *Fr.* Mock Invocation to Genius, A.

I now think[e], Love is rather deaf[e], than blind.   My Picture Left in Scotland.   Ben Jonson.   BeJo; NAEL-5v1; NAEL-6v1; NAEL-7v1; NPeEn

I now will throw myself down.   Dialogue, A.   David Ignatow.   NNaP

I observe: "Our sentimental friend the moon!"   Conversation Galante.   T. S. Eliot.   TCAPo

I offer my back to the silken net.   Allegory, An.   David Ignatow.   VGW

I offer these verses to you, Claudia, because you are their mistress.   Ernesto Cardenal.   BLPSL, *tr. by* Rene de Costa, Rigas Kappatos and Eleni Paidoussi

I offer you four things.   Roselle Angwin.   NewEx

I offer you the golden flagon.   Offering Wine.   Yü Wu-ling.   CoBCP, *tr. by* Burton Watson

I often go to Melano.   Geographical History, The.   Giulia Niccolai.   CItWP, *tr. by* Cinzia Sartini Blum and Lara Trubowitz

I Often Meet a Monster.   Max Fatchen.   OTCP

I often read the writings of the sages.   Words from the Goblet of Wisdom.   Yüan Mei.   CoBLCP, *tr. by* Jonathan Chaves

I often think of my old age.   Fragments 1920–1921.   Nikolai Stepanovich Gumilyov [*or* Gumiliov *or* Gumilev].   TCRusP, *tr. by* Mary Jane White

I often wonder as the fairy-story.   Lucky Marriage, The.   Thomas Blackburn.   GTBS-P

I often wonder how it is.   My Playmate.   Mary I. Osborn.   OTCP

I often wonder who will find.   Sándor Petőfi.   IQMS, *tr. by* Peter Zollman   *Fr.* Clouds, The.

I, Olga Orozco, tell everyone, from your heart, that I am dying.   Olga Orozco.   Olga Orozco.   TCLAP, *tr. by* Stephen Tapscott

I on my horse, and Love on me doth try.   Sir Philip Sidney.   NAEL-5v1; NAEL-6v1; NAEL-7v1; NoP-4; PoE   *Fr.* Astrophil and Stella.

I on the sunny side of Three Rivers.   For Ku Yen-hsien, A Poem for Him to Give to His Wife.   Lu Yün.   CoBCP, *tr. by* Burton Watson

I once broke evening bread with the brown-faced, white-smiled Prince of Siam.   Words of Oblivion and Peace.   Gabriel Preil.   FIT, *tr. by* Robert Friend

I once conjectur'd that those tygers hard.   Seaconk or Rehoboths Fate.   Benjamin Tompson.   SCAP

I Once Did a Bamboo Painting for Somebody—Now He Wants Me To Do

Another. I Have Written This To Answer Him. Hsü Wei. CoBLCP, tr. by Jonathan Chaves

I once drove to Atlantic City. Zoom (The Commodores). Thulani Davis. ISC

I once had. Wings, The. Delmira Agustini. TCLAP, tr. by Elizabeth Gordon

I once had a cat called Maria. Limerick. Paul Griffin. PeLi

I once had a gown, it was almost new. Alice Blue Gown. Harry Tierney. ReLy

I once had a lover. Bookishness. Sharif Elmusa. GraLe

I once heard the survivors. Don Marquis. NBLV Fr. Certain Maxims of Archy.

I once knew a spinster of Staines. Limerick. Plaiwon. PeLi

I once knew a woman named Benedicta, who infused everything. Which One Is Genuine? Charles Baudelaire. RaBo, tr. by Robert Bly

I once knowed an ole Sexion Boss but he done been laid low. Old Section Boss, The. Unknown. BPo

I once saw my grandma with her hair undone. Katherine's Hair. David Marlatt. AmPoNex

I once spent an evening in a village. Man Upright, The. Thomas Macdonagh. BIrV

I once took my girl to Southend. Limerick. Veronica Nicolson. PeLi

I Once Was a Maid. Robert Burns. NBLV; OxBoLi Fr. Jolly Beggars, The.

I once was a Pirate what sailed the 'igh seas. Cat Morgan Introduces Himself. T. S. Eliot. NOBL; PeLV

I once was happy, when while yet a child. Charlotte Smith. PEW; WPE Fr. Beachy Head.

I once wrote a letter as follows. Invoice, The. Robert Creeley. VGW

I Only Am Escaped Alone to Tell Thee. Howard Nemerov. CoAP; HeIP-4; NoAM

I Only Have Eyes for You. Harry Warren. ReLy

I only knew one poet in my life. How It Strikes a Contemporary. Robert Browning. CTC; GTBS-P; NPeEn

I Open the Cigarette. Alda Merini. CItWP, tr. by Cinzia Sartini Blum and Lara Trubowitz

I open the door. Exaggeration of Despair, The. Sherman Alexie. BAP-97; NeAmPo

I open the first door. Elegy. Tomas Tranströmer. WoPoe, tr. by Robert Bly

I open the top. Walking at Night. Brian Swann. PoCoUp

I open the wrong door. Kiss, The. Angela Ball. ExTi

I opened the door so my last look. One More Brevity. Robert Frost. APT-1

I Opened Your Head. Joyce Mansour. NAWM-7v2, tr. by Serge Gavronsky

I order the carriage to stop for a while. (LL) On the Road through Chang-te. Sun Yün-feng. BoWoP; WPOW

I ordered this, this clean wood box. Arrival of the Bee Box, The. Sylvia Plath. FaBoMo; FaBoWP; HCAP; NALW; NPeEn

I ought to be glad. Louis MacNeice. OBCoV Fr. Autumn Journal.

I ought to hurry up in order to save what can be saved. My Poetry. Lajos Kassák. IQMS, tr. by Adam Makkai

I overheard the other night / standing by the window. Imamu Amiri Baraka. BB Fr. Wise/Whys.

I, Ovid, poet of my wantonness. Ovid. OBVE, tr. by Christopher Marlowe Fr. Elegies.

I owe my living to the abattoir. My father, the manager, sat in the office. Abattoir, The. Ania Walwicz. BMAP

I owe nothing to winter. My Winter Past. Eldon Grier. NOBC

I owe you an apology. Question of Form and Content, A. Jon Stallworthy. OxBC

I owed my second birth. My Father's Workshop. Anna Swir. GifTon, tr. by Czeslaw Milosz and Leonard Nathan

I own a print of cows on a green hill. City Beneath the City, The. Eloise Klein Healy. GeoHom

I own nigger, I purchased it with the blood of my fathers. I stole it. In Exchange for Forty Acres. Bruce Jackson. AmPoNex

I own Pandora's box. For Albert, the Terrible. Carlota Caulfield. TANSG, tr. by Chris Allen

I pace the sounding sea-beach and behold. Milton. Henry Wadsworth Longfellow. AWP; GSo; TAP

I paced the length of it—one hundred and forty-three. On Seeing the Reformation Memorial in Geneva. Gyula Illyés. IQMS, tr. by John Wilkinson

I paid a spring-time visit to your country. Jean West. NewEx

I paid for the blooding of Hobson's hide. Account, An. Mick North. NLP

I Paint What I See. Elwyn Brooks White. NBLV

I painted my eyes with black antimony. Love Song. Unknown. BoWoP; WoPoe, tr. by Ulli Beier and H. Gaden

I painted rouge on my lips. Lover of Love. Hagiwara Sakutaro. PFTM-1

I painted the mailbox. That was fun. Painting the Gate. May Swenson. TLR; WeW-3

I park the car because I'm happy. Now. Christopher Gilbert. GT

I parted from my life last night. On the Death of His Wife. Muireadhach Albanach O'Dalaigh. BIrV; CIP-2, tr. by Frank O'Connor

I pass a / door. Daily Task. Belinda Zubicueta Carmona. TANSG, tr. by Celeste Kostopulos-Cooperman

I pass beneath. Yaitsu. JDP, tr. by Yoel Hoffmann

I pass the day tense, day-. Kenneth Rexroth. APSN Fr. Love Poems of Marichiko, The.

I Pass the Night at General Headquarters. Tu Fu. OHPC, tr. by Kenneth Rexroth

I pass the swamp borders. Raul Bopp. TCLAP, tr. by Renato Rezende Fr. Black Snake.

I pass two women in the hall. Pilgrimage. Yoshioka Minoru. PFTM-2, tr. by Eric Selland

I passed a tomb among green shades. Unknown. AWP Fr. Thousand and One Nights, The.

I passed along the water's edge below the humid trees. Indian upon God, The. W. B. Yeats. MoBrPo

I passed beside the reverend walls. Tennyson. EBVV; NAEL-6v2 Fr. In Memoriam A. H. H.

I passed by the beach. Akahito. OHPJ

I passed by the house of the young man who loves me. Love Song. Unknown. TTY, tr. by J. E. Manchip White

I passed Slimgullion, Morgan Mine. Philip Levine. GeoHom

I passed the window and saw their lovely flash of wings. Regret for the Mourning Doves Who Failed to Mate. Bruce Weigl. UrbNat

I passed thurgh a gardyn grene. Unknown. OHMEL

I patched my coat with sunlight. Coat, The. Dennis Lee. TLR

I peeled bits of straw and I got switches too. Song. John Clare. NAEL-5v2; NAEL-6v2

I peeped through the window. Unknown. OxNR

I peer adown a shining group. Tribute. Eloise Bibb. CBWP-4

I perch on the riverbank, forgetting to go back. Tu Fu. CarOv, tr. by Carolyn Kizer Fr. Meandering River Poems, The.

I persist in a little fabric between me and the world. J. Michael Yates. NOBC Fr. Great Bear Lake Meditations, The.

I pick a daimen icker from the thrave. Sir James Murray. Edwin Morgan. HarvBoo

I picked an azalea. Izumi Shikibu. OHMPJ

I picture your face. Luke Roma. IBA

I pitched my day's leazings in Crimmercrock Lane. Dark-Eyed Gentleman, The. Thomas Hardy. MoBrPo; NBLV; UnPo

I pitied him for his small strategy. (LL) Compassionate Fool, The. Norman Cameron. GTBS-P; OxBSP; OxBTC; RB

I pitied you. To ———. "Shu Ting." CarOv, tr. by Carolyn Kizer and Y. H. Zhao

I place my hope on the water. Language Issue, The. Nuala Ni Dhomhnaill. ModIr; NPeEn, tr. by Paul Muldoon

I place these numbed wrists to the pane. Nightmare Begins Responsibility. Michael S. Harper. ESEAA; GT; HCAP; LCAP-2; LoL; PoPoPo; TAP; VCAP

I placed a jar in Tennessee. Anecdote of the Jar. Wallace Stevens. ColAP; FaBoA; HCAP; HeIP-4; InPK-6; MoAmPo; NAAL-2v2; NAAL-5; NAWM-7v2; NIL-7; NOBA; NoAM; NoP-4; OxBA; OxBSP; PAI; PoPoPo; SAmP; TAP; TCAPo; TFi; UnPo

I placed my dream in a boat. Song. Cecília Meireles. WPOW, tr. by Eloah F. Giacomelli

I placed my hand cupped. Return of an Ikon. Dimitris Tsaloumas. BMAP

I planned to have a border of lavender. Paul Goodman. GLP; VGW

I plant beans at the foot of the southern hill. T'ao Ch'ien [or T'ao Yuan-ming]. SuSp Fr. On Returning to My Garden and Field.

I planted a hundred mulberry trees. Country House. Ch'u Ch'uang I. OHMPC, tr. by Kenneth Rexroth

I planted him in this country / like a flag. (LL) Death of a Young Son by Drowning. Margaret Atwood. BoWoP; NIL-7; NOBC

I planted rice before Spring Festival. Su Tung-p'o (Su Shih). CoBCP; ColAnChi, tr. by Burton Watson Fr. Eastern Slope.

I plaster myself with ashes. Gìríscandra Ghos. SinGod, tr. by Rachel Fell McDermott

I play a spade:—Such strange new faces. Arrivals at a Watering-Place. Winthrop Mackworth Praed. NOBL; NOBRP; NPeEn; PeLV

I play for Seasons; not Eternities! George Meredith. SCGP Fr. Modern Love.

I play marimba on your rib cage. Los Amantes. Richard Garcia. TouFir

I play pool. I aim toward the faces. Games. Sandra McPherson. LCAP-2

I play tennis with the shells. Poem. "Paul Dermée." CuPo

I play this sweet prelude. Ruggieri di Amici. EaItPo, tr. by Dante Gabriel Rossetti

I played piano while my daddy knelt. Southern Crescent Was on Time, The. Andrew Hudgins. GM

I played with you 'mid cowslips blowing.   Thomas Love Peacock.   NOBVV; OBEV   *Fr.* Gryll Grange.

I pledge allegiance to the Earth.   Pledge of Allegiance to the Family of Earth, A.   Mim Kelber.   HW

I pledge myself through thick and thin.   Tory Pledges.   Thomas Moore.   OBSV

I pluck the clustering flowers from the wall.   Tune: "Sprig of Flowers, A"—Not Bowing to Old Age.   Kuan Han-ch'ing.   SuSp, *tr. by* Jerome P. Seaton

I plucked my soul out of its secret place.   I Know My Soul.   Claude McKay.   BPo

I plucked pink blossoms from mine apple tree.   Apple Gathering, An.   Christina Georgina Rossetti.   NAEL-5v2; NAEL-6v2

I plunged my beak in the marbling cheek.   Eliza Cook.   VerBaPo   *Fr.* Carrion Crow, The.

I, / poet by trade.   Ars Poetica.   Claribel Alegría.   LoL; TANSG, *tr. by* Darwin Flakoll

I polish your skin. It is that of a woman.   Song in Praise of a Favourite Humming-Top, A.   Hone Tuwhare.   PeNZ

I Ponder on Life.   Max Ehrmann.   PoToHe

I ponder you in clamor and in silence.   Psalm.   Tudor Arghezi.   AF, *tr. by* Andrei Bantas

I pondered Buddha's teaching.   Zoso Royo.   JDP, *tr. by* Yoel Hoffmann

I pour out wine in a libation to the river god.   Meeting My Fellow Countryman, Yü Wu-chung.   Yang Chi.   CoBLCP, *tr. by* Jonathan Chaves

I practiced the piano all afternoon.   Involuntary Music.   D. Nurske.   MiVo

I praise a patron high-hearted in strife.   In Praise of Owain Gwynedd.   Cynddelw Brydydd Mawr.   OBWVE, *tr. by* Joseph P. Clancy

I praise a prince, lord of king's country.   Spoils of Annwn, The.   *Unknown.*   WoPoe, *tr. by* Anthony Conran

I praise God's mankind in an old woman.   Lines.   Wilfred Watson.   NOBC

I praise him not.   James Russell Lowell.   AiP   *Fr.* Ode Recited at the Harvard Commemoration (July 21, 1865).

I praise Saint Everyman, his house and home.   Here Together Met.   Louis Johnson.   PeNZ

I praise the country women.   Grit.   Geoff Page.   NOBAu

I praise the disk of the rising sun.   Vidya.   WPOW   *Fr.* Sun, The.

I praise the speech, but cannot now abide it.   Of the Wars in Ireland.   John Harington.   NoSic

I praise the tortilla in honor of El Panzón.   Praise the Tortilla, Praise the Menudo, Praise the Chorizo.   Ray Gonzales.   UnSA

I praise those ancient Chinamen.   Hymnus Ad Patrem Sinensis.   Philip Whalen.   BB

I praised the daisies on my lawn.   J is for Jealousy.   William Henry Davies.   TCAWP

I praised thee not while living; what to thee.   To Elizabeth Barrett Browning, in 1861.   Dora Greenwell.   PoBW; VWP

I pray and weep in my bed at night (craving sleep).   Praise Poem to Christ, A.   Catrin Ferch Gruffydd ab Ieuan ap Llywelyn Fychan.   EMWP

I pray that my will may be attuned to / Your will for & with me. (LL)   Alcoholic.   John Berryman.   BodElec; NOCV

I pray that the great world's flowering stay as it is.   Gardener to His God, The.   Mona Van Duyn.   RACG; TrCP; UnPo; WPE

I pray the Lord my soul to take.   Ogden Nash.   NBLV   *Fr.* One from One Leaves Two.

I pray thee by the soul of her that bore thee.   Iris, Her Book.   Oliver Wendell Holmes.   NCAP

I pray thee, Dante, shouldst thou meet with Love.   To Dante Alighieri: He Mistrusts the Love of Lapo Gianni.   Guido Cavalcanti.   AWP; EaItPo, *tr. by* Dante Gabriel Rossetti

I pray thee leave, love me no more.   To His Coy Love, A Canzonet.   Michael Drayton.   NOSC; PBRV

I pray thee Nymph Penaeis stay, I chase not as a fo.   Ovid.   OBVE, *tr. by* Arthur Golding   *Fr.* Metamorphoses.

I pray Thee O Lord.   Prayer, A: "I pray Thee O Lord."   Julian [*or* Juljan] Tuwim.   TrJP, *tr. by* Wanda Dynowska

I pray you all give [*or* gyve] your audience [*or* audyence].   *Unknown.*   NAEL-5v1; NAWM-5v1

I pray you, be mery and synge with me.   *Unknown.*   SacPr

I pray you, cum kiss me.   My Little Pretty Mopsy.   *Unknown.*   MiEL

I prayed for riches, and achieved success.   Answered Prayers.   Ella Wheeler Wilcox.   PWR

I prayed to the ghost of Carrie.   Ian Duhig.   NeBl

I prefer a young man for coition, and him only.   How an Old Man Can Regain His Youth Through Sexual Potency.   Ibn Kamal.   EroLit, *tr. by* Mary Jo Lakeland

I prefer red chile over my eggs.   Green Chile.   Jimmy Santiago Baca.   NIL-7

I prefer to come from silence to talk.   Valerio Magrelli.   ItPo, *tr. by* Gayle Ridinger

I Prefer Your Uneasiness Like a Dark Lantern.   Laurence Iché.   SurWo, *tr. by* Myrna Bell Rochester

I prepare for you the way I plan.   Simplest and the Hardest, The.   Margaret Lloyd.   OPRER

I Present Myself to the World.   Amina Said.   PoArWo, *tr. by* Lucy McNair

I press[e] not to the choir [*or* quire], nor dare I greet.   To My Worthy Friend Master George Sands [*or* Sandys], on His Translation of the Psalms.   Thomas Carew.   BeJo; CaPo; MeLP

I Pressed Her Rebel Lips.   *Unknown.*   BoLoP

I pretend to wait for you to enlarge the minutes.   Patrizia Cavalli.   NeIt

I prithee, daughter, do not make me mad.   William Shakespeare.   OxAEP-1   *Fr.* King Lear.

I prithee let my heart alone.   Song.   Thomas Stanley.   BeJo

I prithee spare me, gentle boy.   Song.   Sir John Suckling.   BeJo; CavPo

I promise you these days and an understanding.   Tourist Death.   Archibald MacLeish.   NAAL-2v2

I promised once if I got hold of.   Written in a Copy of Swift's Poems, for Wayne Burns.   James Wright (1927–80).   NOBA

I propose to you.   Statue, The.   Robert Creeley.   LCAP-2

I prove a theorem and the house expands.   Geometry.   Rita Dove.   HCAP; HeIP-4

I puff my breast out, my neck swells.   Cynewulf.   RB   *Fr.* Riddles (Exeter Book).

I pull opposites together.   Guida Swan.   NewEx

I pull the huge book down from the bookcase.   Automobiles of the Asylum.   Philip Hammial.   BMAP

I pulled a hummingbird out of the sky one day but let it go.   Wind.   Dionne Brand.   NOxBChV

I pulled on a suit of mail.   Precautions.   Martin Sorescu.   VCWP, *tr. by* Paul Muldoon and Joana Russell-Gebbett

I pulled the street up as you suggested.   Something for Easter.   Robert Creeley.   InvLad

I pump him full of lost watches. (LL)   Birthplace Revisited.   Gregory Corso.   NeAP; PoM; VGW

I purged my sins in a blaze of kisses.   Visit, The.   "Badawi al-Jabal."   MAP, *tr. by* John Heath-Stubbs and Matthew Sorenson

I pursue a form that does not fit my style.   I Pursue a Form.   "Rubén Dario."   SpanPo, *tr. by* Doreen Bell

I push out of Customs, stumble, almost fall, legs numb from.   Restroom.   Chitra Divakaruni.   UnSA

I put aside the swim team ribbons.   Belongings.   A. V. Christie.   AmPoNex

I put my cameleer off two thousand and one times.   Sand in Flames.   Nujoum Al-Ghanim.   PoArWo, *tr. by* Clarissa C. Burt

I put my cap in the cage.   Quartier Libre.   Jacques Prévert.   CLPP, *tr. by* Lawrence Ferlinghetti

I put my hat upon my head.   Ballad.   Samuel Johnson.   NOBL; OxAEP-1; UV

I put my hat upon my head.   Peter Veale.   NBLV

I put on a pair of overshoes.   Around My Room.   William Jay Smith.   TLR

I put on La Pathétique.   La Pathétique.   Lily Brett.   HP

I put on my new suit, the wind and fire.   My Burned Suit.   Ilyas Farhat.   MAP, *tr. by* John Heath-Stubbs and Salma Khadra Jayyusi

I put your leaves aside.   Weather-Cock Points South, The.   Amy Lowell.   APT-1; NALW; NoP-4

I quail, lean to beginnings, sheath-wet. (LL)   Cuttings.   Theodore Roethke.   APT-2; HCAP; LCAP-2; NAAL-2v2; NAAL-5; NOBA; NoAM; OBGa; TAP; TRP; UnPo; VCAP

I quake like Satan.   Herbert Lomas.   NewEx

I quarreled with kings till the Sabbath.   Song of the Sabbath.   Kadya Molodovsky [*or* Molodowsky].   WPOW, *tr. by* Jean Valentine

I quit med school when I found out the stiff they gave me.   Dangerous Life.   Lucia Maria Perillo.   IllVoic

I quitted and betook myself to France.   William Wordsworth.   OxAEP-2   *Fr.* Prelude, The; Growth of a Poet's Mind [1805 vers.].

I'r Hen Iaith a'i Chaneuon.   Ian Duhig.   ModIr

I rage, I melt, I burn.   John Gay.   NAEL-5v1; NAEL-6v1   *Fr.* Acis and Galatea.

I, Rainey Betha, 22.   Plaint.   Charles Henri Ford.   SPE

I raise my cup and invite.   Moon, Flowers, Man.   Su Tung-p'o (Su Shih).   OHPC, *tr. by* Kenneth Rexroth

I raise my hat.   John Mole.   OBCoV   *Fr.* Penny Toys.

I raise my winecup to the flowers.   To the Tune "Stopping My Horse to Listen."   Yang Shen.   CoBLCP, *tr. by* Jonathan Chaves

I raise the curtains and go out.   Alone.   Chu Shu-chen.   BoWoP; OHPC, *tr. by* Kenneth Rexroth

I raise the mirror of my life.   Taigen Sofu.   JDP, *tr. by* Yoel Hoffmann

I raised my glass, and—solid, pungent, like the soot-encrusted.   Calvin Klein's Obsession.   Ciaran Carson.   EmeKit

I raised myself a falcon trained him more than a year.   I Raised Myself a Falcon.   Lowell A. Bangerter.   AuPH, *tr. by* Lowell A. Bangerter

I ran.   Whipping, The.   Samuel F. Reynolds.   SpirFl

I ran across. New York Notebooks, The. Howard Moss. BodElec

I ran and still I run away from Thee. Amin Al-Rihani. GraLe *Fr.* Fugitive, The.

I ran into Tu Fu by a Rice Grain Mountain. To Send to Tu Fu as a Joke. Li Po. ColAnChi, *tr. by* Elling O. Eide

I ran out in the morning, when the air was clean and new. Autumn Morning at Cambridge. Frances Darwin Cornford. PoRA

I ran to the church. Journey Back to Christmas. Gwen Dunn. OBCP

I ran up and grabbed your arm, the way a man. At the Washing of My Son. David Ray. RaBo

I ran up six flights of stairs. Whole Mess. . . Almost, The. Gregory Corso. BB

I ran upon life unknowing, without or science or art. Tennyson. FaBoEE

I rang them up, while touring Timbuctoo. To Someone Who Insisted I Look up Someone. X. J. Kennedy. OBCoV

I reach from pain. Reuben, Reuben. Michael S. Harper. LoL; PoE

I reached heaven and it was syrupy. Transformation and Escape. Gregory Corso. PFTM-2

I reached that waterhole, its mud designed. Roland Robinson. CBAP *Fr.* Wanderer, The.

I reached the end, but you live on. Wind, The. Boris Leonidovich Pasternak. TCRP, *tr. by* Yakov Hornstein

I reached the middle of the mount. Dirge. Ralph Waldo Emerson. TCAPo

I read. Bob Boldman. HA

I read a boy's poem called. Every Morning After Killing Thousands of Angels. Tamura Ryuichi. VCWP, *tr. by* Christopher Drake

I read a novel by a friend of mine. I Am in a Novel. D. H. Lawrence. OBCoV

I read a sad poem / on the wall. Graffiti. Jane Yolen. SSCS

I read about the Blaskets and Dunquin. John Millington Synge. FaBoEE

I read for wolftooth and bearclaw. *Unknown*. WoPoe, *tr. by* Siv Cedering Fox *Fr.* Three Swedish Spells.

I read how Quixote in his random ride. Parable. Richard Wilbur. HarvBoo; OxBSP

I read in unforgettable books. Constant Memories. Patrick Sylvain. InTrad

I read last night of the Grand Review. Second Review of the Grand Army, A. Bret Harte. CBCWP

I read my face on smooth stones. Moraine Lake. Brian Henry. PoCoUp

I read of a Confessor, and a King. Upon the mournful death of our late Soveraign Lord Charles the first, King of England, etc. Rowland Watkyns. BASC

I read of a thousand killed. Thousand Killed, A. Bernard Spencer. FaBoWar; OBWP

I read once of a valley. After Babel. Peter Goldsworthy. NOBAu

I read or write, I teach or wonder what is truth. Apologia pro Vita Sua. Sedulius Scottus. BIrV, *tr. by* Helen Waddell

I read / Sand Creek massacre. Brief Wyoming Meditation. Diane Di Prima. BB

I Read That It Was All a Chain. Marianne Vitale. HeMarv

I read the marble-lettered name. Grave in Hollywood Cemetery, Richmond, A. Margaret Junkin Preston. CBCWP

I read the poems of the dead. Blood of Others, The. Gioconda Belli. TANSG, *tr. by* Steven F. White

I read you the soft verses of antiquity. 19 January 1944. Salvatore Quasimodo. AF, *tr. by* Jack Bevan

I realize the horse seen from an airplane looks like a violin. Art of a Cold Sun. G. E. Murray. IllVoic

I really can't stay! Baby, It's Cold Outside. Frank Loesser. ReLy

I really don't want to die now. Vladimir Shchirovsky [*or* Shchirovskii]. TCRP

I really hate to say it but I need a lady's room. (LL) Motorcyclists, The. James Tate. NoAM; ReTh

I really love you, / believe me. It is something I inherited. Attila József. AF, *tr. by* John Batki

I really take it very kind. Domestic Asides; or, Truth in Parentheses. Thomas Hood. PeLV

I really thought that drinking here would. Knocking Around. John Ashbery. NoAM

I reason, Earth is short. Emily Dickinson. APN-2; NCAP; TAP; TCAPo

I recall a drinking party on the bridge, the Meridian Bridge. Tune: "Immortal at the River"—Ascending a Little Tower at Night. Ch'en Yü-yi. SuSp, *tr. by* James J. Y. Liu

I recall everything, but more than all. Double Sonnet. Anthony Hecht. Son

I recall the times she came. Four Recollections. Shen Yüeh. SuSp, *tr. by* Richard B. Mather

I reckon—when I count at all. Emily Dickinson. APN-2; MoAmPo; NIL-7; NIP-4; NoP-4; TCAPo

I reclaim the moment, call the madness madness. Emanations. Hameed Sa'id. MAP, *tr. by* Lena Jayyusi and Naomi Shihab Nye

I recognize you. Spitting out four, five, six-syllable English words. I Recognize You. Rosario Morales. PueRic

I recognized him by his skips and hops. Pan and the Cherries. Paul Fort. AWP, *tr. by* Jethro Bithell

I recognized the voice. (LL) Old Leaves from the Chinese Earth. Sadanand Rege. OMIP; WoPoe, *tr. by* Dilip Chitre

I recollect a nurse call'd Ann. Terrible Infant, A. Frederick Locker-Lampson. OBCoV

I recommend herbs for you. Conversation in Front of a Helicopter. Rosario Murillo. CLPP, *tr. by* Alejandro Murguía

I recover now the time I drove. Art McCooey. Patrick Kavanagh. CIP-2

I reel off a little revolution. I Reel Off. "Lucebert." TuT, *tr. by* Mary E. O'Donnell

I refuse to turn into gold. Bassus [*or* Bassos]. GrAn

I refuted it all. Therapy. Giovanna. SurWo, *tr. by* Myrna Bell Rochester

I regret nothing, neither do I complain nor weep. I Regret Nothing. Sergey [*or* Sergei] Aleksandrovich Yesenin [*or* Essenin]. TCRusP, *tr. by* Nigel Stott

I regret the passing, the dying, of the vague dream. Return to Shaoshan. Mao Tse-tung [*or* Mao Zedong]. WoPoe, *tr. by* Willis Barnstone and Ko Ching-po

I regretted the arrival of my death. What Profit? Immanuel di Roma. TrJP, *tr. by* J. Chotzner

I rein in my horse. Fujiwara no Teika. OHMPJ

I release you, my beautiful and terrible. I Give You Back. Joy Harjo. HATNAP; LoL

I Remain. Nina Nikolaevna Berberova. TCRP, *tr. by* Albert C. Todd

I rememba. Rayboy Blk & Bluz. Shirley Bradley LeFlore. SpirFl

I remember. Birth. Gioconda Belli. TANSG, *tr. by* Steven F. White

I Remember. Eavan Boland. PBCIP

I Remember. Joe Brainard. CAGL

I Remember. Liu E. CoBLCP, *tr. by* Jonathan Chaves

I Remember. Anne Sexton. LW

I Remember. Stevie Smith. BoLoP; BoWoP; FaBoWP; InPK-6; NIL-7; OxBC

I remember a dead man. Forget-Me-Nots. Yevgeny [*or* Evgenii] Mikhailovich Vinokurov. TCRP, *tr. by* Daniel Weissbort

I remember a dim evening in Kishinyov [*or* Kishinev]. Woman from the Book of Genesis, A. "Dovid Knut." TCRP; TCRusP, *tr. by* John Glad

I remember a former day when I and a friend. Coming Again to Heng-yang, I Mourn for Liu Tsung-yüan. Liu Yu Hsi. SuSp, *tr. by* Daniel Bryant

I remember a grass hut. Fujiwara No Toshinari. OHMPJ

I remember a house where all were good. In the Valley of the Elwy. Gerard Manley Hopkins. NOBVV; NOCV; OxAEP-2; TOF

I remember a waterfall at the bottom of grottoes. Someone I knew, a. Trance Event. Robert Desnos. PFTM-1

I remember an ancient Chinese picture kept over there in Daitokuji. Ernest Francisco Fenollosa. APN-2 *Fr.* Ode on Reincarnation.

I remember at times. Scholar II. Seamus Deane. CIP-2; NOIV

I remember being ashamed of my father. Fathers and Sons. Tom Leonard. CABP; NePenScot

I remember being late. At the final minute. With My Mother, Missing the Train. Helena Nelson. Prnts

I remember coming up. Breath. Reginald Gibbons. BodElec

I remember dancing in July on the banks of the Hudson in the City. Journal of the Plague Years, A. Walter Holland. CAGL

I remember despotic times. Gaffer Speaks. Ghulam-Reza Ruhani. WoPoe, *tr. by* Omar Pound

I Remember Dexedrine. 1970. Pamela Brown. BMAP

I remember fleeing the rebels. P'eng-ya Road. Tu Fu. CrYelRi, *tr. by* Sam Hamill

I remember God as an eccentric millionaire. Quite Apart from the Holy Ghost. Adrian Mitchell. OBSV

I remember, gracious, graceful moon. To the Moon. Giacomo Leopardi. TTTS, *tr. by* Kenneth Koch

I Remember Haifa Being Lovely But. Lyn Lifshin. GotH; UnSA

I Remember Having Loved. Hasan 'Abdallah. MAP, *tr. by* Lena Jayyusi and Christopher Middleton

I remember him falling beside me. Litany, A. Gregory Orr. BodElec

I remember how, at that time, in this meadow. When We Were Children. Alexander the Wild. WoPoe, *tr. by* David Ferry

I remember how I came here. Winter Evening Poem. Laura Jensen. LCAP-2

I remember how in Spain. Musica. Philip Dacey. MiVo

I remember how, long ago, I found. Crystals like Blood. Hugh MacDiarmid. HAP; HarvBoo; RB

I Remember, I Remember. Thomas Hood. ITBLP; NOBE; OxAEP-2; OxBEV; TFi; TreFP (Past and Present.) GTBS-P

I Remember, I Remember. Philip Larkin. HarvBoo; NOBL

I Remember It Well. Frederick Loewe. ReLy

I remember / Joal! Joal. Léopold Sédar Senghor. NegPo, tr. by Ellen Conroy Kennedy

I remember kicking the bales down. Zoo. Polly Clark. NeBl

I remember little of myself. Patrizia Cavalli. ItPo, tr. by Gayle Ridinger

I remember long veils of green rain. Green Rain. Dorothy Livesay. NALW; NIP-4; NOBC; NoP-4

I remember lying awake. Endangered Roots of a Person. Wendy Rose. ReEnLa

I Remember Malcolm. Ras Baraka. InTrad

I remember my childhood bedroom. Little Poem. Max Jacob. CuPo

I remember / my first confession. Confession. Alice Lee. ReEnLa

I remember my mother's Aunt Rebecca. Great-Aunt Rebecca. Elizabeth Brewster. NOBC

I remember once, on a journey to the west. I Remember the River at Wu Sung. Mei Yao Ch'en. OHPC

I remember one death in my boyhood. Of John Davidson. Hugh MacDiarmid. HarvBoo; NePenScot; OxBEV

I remember other days. I Cried for You. Abe Lyman. ReLy

I remember rooms that have had their part. Rooms. Charlotte Mew. HarvBoo; PoBW

I Remember Sharpeville. Sipho Sepamla. AF

I remember / Sitting on his lap. Grandfather Grandfather. Marlon D. Satchell. InTrad

I remember sitting together in parks. Love's Advocate. Phoebe Hesketh. LW

I remember striding through the August twilight. Calling on Peadar O'Donnell at Dungloe. John Hewitt. CIP-2

I remember Sulayma when the passion. In Battle. Abu-l-Hasan Ibn Al-Qabturnuh. NAWM-7v1, tr. by Lysander Kemp

I remember sun. Penance. Sherman Alexie. MoASP

I remember that he wrote them backwards. My Grandfather's Poems. Edward Hirsch. TaR

I remember that once. Reply to Bukko Zenji's Poem at Seiken-ji. Muso Soseki. EaWin, tr. by W. S. Merwin

I remember that year, under the blossoms. Tune: Lotus-leaf Cup. Wei Chuang. CoBCP, tr. by Burton Watson

I remember that year, under the blossoms. Wen T'ing-yün. CoBCP

I remember the birth. Birth, 1975. Cheryl Van Dyke. GifTon

I remember the bliss. Do, Do, Do. George Gershwin. ReLy

I Remember the Blue River. Mei Yao Ch'en. OHPC, tr. by Kenneth Rexroth

I remember the Chillicothe ball players grappling the Rock. Hits and Runs. Carl Sandburg. MoASP

I remember the cities I have never seen. Tomorrow, Tomorrow. Derek Walcott. PoetW

I remember the day I arrived. Doubting. Louis Simpson. NNaP

I remember the day when we first met among the flowers. Offering Congratulations to the Enlightened Reign. Ou-yang Chiung. ColAnChi, tr. by Lois Fusek

I remember the dread with which I at a quarter past four. False Security. Sir John Betjeman. NoAM; NoP-4

I remember the evening. Swarming Bees, The. James Laughlin. VGW

I remember the forehead born. Uncle. Philip Levine. NNaP

I remember the fragrance of. Snaps of Immigration. Víctor Hernández Cruz. TouFir

I remember the log of Pi, the battle. Log of Pi, The. Marc J. Straus. BloBone

I remember the long corridors where the shadow was continuous. I remember the long corridors. Jeannette Miller. TANSG, tr. by Paula Vega

I remember the neckcurls, limp and damp as tendrils. Elegy for Jane. Theodore Roethke. APT-2; CoAP; ColAP; HAP; HCAP; InPK-6; MoAmPo; NoP-4; PAI; PoE; PoPoPo; TAP; TFi; TRP; TwCP; WeW-3

I remember the night. Aleksandr [or Viktor Fyodorovich] Vertinsky [or Vertinskii]. TCRusP, tr. by John Glad

I remember the old joke. Cliff, The. David Rowbotham. NOBAu

I remember the rain as the feathery fringe of her shawl. (LL) Green Rain. Dorothy Livesay. NALW; NIP-4; NOBC; NoP-4

I Remember the River at Wu Sung. Mei Yao Ch'en. OHPC

I remember the Roman Emperor, one of the cruellest of them. Exeat. Stevie Smith. NAEL-5v2; NAEL-6v2; NoAM

I remember the room in which he held. My Father with Cigarette Twelve Years Before the Nazis Could Break His Heart. Philip Levine. TaR

I remember the time. Little Girl's Dream World, A. Della Burt. BlSi

I remember the time I was called. Civilizing the Filipino. Nick Carbó. AmPoNex

I remember the way the big windows washed. I Remember. Eavan Boland. PBCIP

I remember, they sent. Corpse-bearing. Thomas Ashe. EBVV; NOBVV

I remember those years when we shared the joy of love. To the Tune "Heavenly Immortal." Yang Shen. CoBLCP, tr. by Jonathan Chaves

I remember today a Quebec roadside, the crucifix. Crucifix, The. Daniel Berrigan. CRP

I remember two dwarfs, back there in our country home. Nicaraguan Triptych. "Rubén Dario." TCLAP, tr. by Lysander Kemp

I remember watching Benjie. Potato Garden. Jeanette Redenius. SpudSo

I remember when he took me on a trip to this place. Chin Nung. CoBLCP
    Fr. On Twisting River Is the Old Home of My Father. Now That My Illness Has Eased Up, I Have Written These Six Poems About the Place.

I remember when I met Joe Brainard. For Joe Brainard. David Trinidad. WiU

I remember when I wrote The Circus. Circus, The. Kenneth Koch. PmAP

I remember when, in high school if you wore green and yellow on Thursday it meant that you were queer. I Remember. Joe Brainard. CAGL

I remember when the unicorns. Days of the Unicorns, The. Phyllis Webb. NOBC

I remember when we first fled the rebels. Song of P'eng-ya. Tu Fu. CoBCP, tr. by Burton Watson

I remember when we made our first promises of love. I Remember. Liu E. CoBLCP, tr. by Jonathan Chaves

I remember when you shared my insomnia. Broken Lampstand, The. Wu Wei-yeh. CoBLCP; ColAnChi, tr. by Jonathan Chaves

I Remember You. Johnny Mercer. ReLy

I remember you as you were that last autumn—. Poem. Pablo Neruda. CLPP, tr. by Kenneth Rexroth

I remember you in young peaches like jade. Elegy for the Wife of a Friend. Yü Hsüan-chi. BoWoP, tr. by Geoffrey Waters

I remember you were. Marisel. Juan Gonzalo Rose. BLPSL, tr. by Rene de Costa, Rigas Kappatos and Eleni Paidoussi

I remember your neck, its strength. Night. Mary Dorcey. PoBW

I remember your strut. Toward Guinea: For Larry Neal, 1937–1981. Houston A. Baker, Jr. ISC

I remembered Tung Tsao-chiu of Lo-yang. Remembering Our Excursion in the Past. Li Po. ChinPo, tr. by Yip Wai-lim

I remove my court gown and part from the Emperor's precincts. Wen Cheng-ming. CoBLCP Fr. Improvised on Horseback to Say Good-bye to Those Who Are Seeing Me Off.

I repeat. Vsevolod Nekrasov. ItGoST, tr. by Gerald Janecek

I repeat I'm ready, but ready for what? Eugenio Montale. ItPo, tr. by Gayle Ridinger

I resemble everyone. Self-Portrait. A. K. Ramanujan. NoP-4; PoetW

I reside at Table Mountain and my name is Truthful James. Society Upon the Stanislaus, The. Bret Harte. OBAL

I respect the dumb bastards. Billy's Famous Lounge. Joe Wenderoth. NAPBL

I return from my second T'ien-t'ai trip. On the Twenty-First Day of the Fifth Month, I Reached Home. Yüan Mei. CoBLCP, tr. by Jonathan Chaves

I Return to the Place I Was Born. T'ao Ch'ien [or T'ao Yuan-ming]. OHMPC, tr. by Kenneth Rexroth

I Return unto Zion. Bible, O.T. TrJP Fr. Zechariah.

I returned to my city, familiar as tears. Leningrad. Osip Emilevich Mandelstam [or Mandelshtam]. TCRP

I returned to the church. Of All There Is. C. Mikal Oness. GeoHom

I returned with a bottle of wine, with a deck of cards, with flowers. Return, The. Dalia Hertz. FIT, tr. by Robert Friend

I. RICE CHILD. Mama. Claire Kageyama. UnSA

I, Richard Kent, beneath these stones. Epitaph. Sylvia Townsend Warner. MoBrPo

I ride. May Swenson. APT-2; GM

I ride the heathen sea to my ache crouching in the heights; some of. Wail of Heights, The. Wafaa' Lamrani. PoArWo, tr. by Richard McKane and Tahia Abdel Nasser

I ride through a dark, dark land by night. Ichabod! The Glory Has Departed. Ludwig Uhland. AWP, tr. by James Clarence Mangan

I ride through Queens. Invitation to Madison County, An. Jay Wright. ESEAA

I rise about eight if the morning is warm. To Miss A[——]a M[——]a Tra[——]s; an Epistle from Scotland. Charlotte Brereton. ECWP

I rise at dawn, and stumble up steep, crumbling. At Summer's End. Charles Harper Webb. GeoHom

I rise at 2 a.m. these mornings, to. Feral Pioneers, The. Ishmael Reed. UnPo

I rise from the depths of my resemblance. I rise from the depths. Jean Daive. MFP, tr. by Martin Sorrell

I rise / I rise / I rise. (LL) Still I Rise. Maya Angelou. BlSi; NAAAL

I rise in the dawn, and I kneel and blow. Song of the Old Mother, The. W. B. Yeats. MoBrPo

I rise on Sugar-loaf Mountain. Molasses River. Richard Kendall Munkittrick. OBCA

I rise to gaze upon southern hills. Song of Wildfire, A. Wen T'ing-yün. SuSp, tr. by William R. Schultz

I rise with an effort and look out.   I Rise with an Effort.   Philippe Jaccottet. VCWP, *tr. by* Derek Mahon

I roamed the woods today and seemed to hear.   Fear, A.   Francis Ledwidge. NOIV

I rode my horse to the hostel gate.   Both Less and More.   Richard Watson Dixon.   SCGP

I rode one evening with Count Maddalo.   Shelley.   NPeEn   *Fr.* Julian and Maddalo; A Conversation.

I rode till I reached the House of Wealth.   Rest Only in the Grave.   James Clarence Mangan.   BIrV

I rode to Streatham Common on a tram.   Mind Reborn in Streatham Common, A.   Richard Percival Lister.   OBCoV

I Rode with Geronimo.   Conyus.   NBV

I Rode With My Darling.   Stevie Smith.   BrRo

I roll awake on the carpet over.   In Directions.   John Rybicki.   AmPoNex

I romp with joy in the bookish dark. (LL)   Eating Poetry.   Mark Strand. NoAM; TAP

I rose at the dead of night.   Chilly Night, A.   Christina Georgina Rossetti. VWP

I rose betimes to go I knew not where.   Poor Man's Province, The.   John Wright.   NOEC

I rose from daylong desk at last.   Vision.   James Devaney.   NOBAu

I rose from marsh mud.   Lorine Niedecker.   APT-2

I rose while yet the cattle, heat-opprest [*or* oppressed].   William Wordsworth. CenSon   *Fr.* River Duddon [A Series of Sonnets], The.

I rub my head and find a turtle shell.   Neo-Classical Urn, The.   Robert Lowell. NAAL-2v2

I run, I run, I am gathered to thy heart. (LL)   Renouncement.   Alice Thompson Meynell.   BoLoP; GSo; LW; MoBrPo; NOBE; OBEV; OBMV; OxBSo; PEW; Son; VWP; WPE

I rush to the office when I'm in the city.   Staying Overnight at T'ien-ning Ch'an Temple.   Chang Yü.   CoBLCP, *tr. by* Jonathan Chaves

I rush to your dwelling.   Pursuit.   Julian [*or* Juljan] Tuwim.   TrJP, *tr. by* Watson Kirkconnell

I said a while back.   Acknowledgement.   Keorapetse Kgositsile.   SeSe

I said, Ah! what shall I write?   A, a, a, Domine Deus.   David Jones. FaBoTw; HarvBoo; NOCV

I said, "Be mine."   Archilochus.   EroLit, *tr. by* Kenneth McLeish   *Fr.* Seduction, The.

I said bismillah in your name, Singer.   Standing Worship.   Dhabya Khamees. PoArWo, *tr. by* Clarissa C. Burt

I said fate plays a game without a score.   I Sit by the Window.   Joseph Brodsky.   VCWP, *tr. by* Howard Moss

I said, "I have shut my heart."   Over the Roofs.   Sara Teasdale.   ColAP

I said: I will go into the garden and consider roses.   Discipline.   Mary Ursula Bethell.   PoBW

I said I would always live for her.   Hartmann von Aue.   GePo

I said in my youth.   Primer, The.   Josephine Jacobsen.   NoP-4

I said: On all these, Death, with gentleness, come down. (LL)   Judge Not. Theodore Roethke.   ChIV-2; GI

I said petals from an appletree. (LL)   Portrait of a Lady.   William Carlos Williams.   HarvBoo; NAAL-2v2; NAAL-5; NOBA; NoAM; OxBA

I said, / take my belly.   Madonna of the Peaches.   Joan Logghe.   HW

I said—Then, dearest, since 'tis so.   Last Ride Together, The.   Robert Browning.   BoLoP; EroLit; FHYEP; ITBLP; NAEL-5v2; NAEL-6v2; OBEV; UnPo

I said to Heart, "How goes it?" Heart replied.   False Heart, The.   Joseph Hilaire Pierre Belloc.   FaBoCh; FaBoEE; OxBSP

I said to heaven that glowed above.   Hafiz [*or* Hafez].   AWP   *Fr.* Odes.

I said to her tears: "I am fallible and hungry."   Plea.   John Ciardi.   OxBSP

I said to him, you melt me.   Melt me.   Amanda Nazario.   HeMarv

I said to my baby.   Langston Hughes.   APSN; APT-2; SSLK   *Fr.* Lenox Avenue Mural.

I said to my companion, this is walking.   Victoria Market.   Francis Brabazon. NOBAu

I Said to My Heart.   Charles Mordaunt, Earl of Peterborough.   NOEC; OxBEV

I said to the stream, Be still, and it was still.   Miracles.   Julia Randall.   CRP

I sailed in my dreams to the Land of Night.   Fantasy.   Gwendolyn B. Bennett. BISi

I sall goe intill ane haire.   Shapeshifting.   Isabel Gowdie.   EMWP

I salute God, asylum's gift.   Poem on His Death-Bed.   Cynddelw Brydydd Mawr.   OBWVE, *tr. by* Joseph P. Clancy

I salute the most high lord.   Poet's Loves, The.   Hywel ab Owain Gwynedd. OBWVE, *tr. by* Gwyn Williams

I salute you.   Cedars.   Nadia Tuéni.   PoArWo

I salvaged one photograph form the general clear-out, plucked.   Hazel Goodwin Morrissey Brown.   Sinéad Morrissey.   MFPA

I sang as one.   Conflict, The.   Cecil Day Lewis.   MoBrPo; NoP-4

I sang in the sun.   Race Relations.   Carolyn Kizer.   CarOv; LTA

I sang the songs of red revenge.   Homer.   Albert Ehrenstein.   TrJP, *tr. by* Babette Deutsch and Avrahm Yarmolinsky

I sang the songs of red ripped-up vengeance.   Poet and War, The.   Albert Ehrenstein.   PeFWW, *tr. by* Christopher Middleton

I sat.   At the Door of Anticipation.   Hala Mohammad.   PoArWo, *tr. by* Cornelia Al-Khaled

I sat across, behind my desk.   Two Suffering Men.   Eugene Hirsch.   BloBone

I sat all morning in the college sick bay.   Mid-Term Break.   Seamus Heaney. AmFaPo; NIL-7; PoPoPo

I sat alone at my window.   Retrospect.   Josephine D. Henderson Heard. CBWP-4

I sat before my glass one day.   Other Side of a Mirror, The.   Mary Elizabeth Coleridge.   BoWoP; NALW; VWP; ViWPN

I sat behind the glowing grate, fresh heaped.   Meditation on Rhode Island Coal, A.   William Cullen Bryant.   TAP

I sat beside the glassy evening sea.   Departure, The.   William Vaughn Moody. APN-2

I sat between Grandmother.   Where I Sat.   Richard Michelson.   GotH

I sat by a stream in a.   Classic.   A. R. Ammons.   NOBA

I sat by the edge of the field.   Kim Roberts.   AmPoNex   *Fr.* Constellation Frigidaire, The.

I sat by the granite pillar, and sunlight fell.   Commemoration.   Sir Henry John Newbolt.   FaBoTw

I sat down in the colored section.   Segregated Railway Diner—1946.   Robert Winner.   LTA

I sat down on a rock.   Walther [*or* Walter] von der Vogelweide.   GePo

I sat down to remember.   Sediment of Lukewarm and Radiant Rain.   Coral Bracho.   TANSG, *tr. by* Celeste Kostopulos-Cooperman

I SAT drinking and did not notice the dusk.   Self-abandonment.   Li Po.   ChiP, *tr. by* Arthur Waley

I sat in the café and sipped at a Coke.   Greedyguts.   Kit Wright.   OTCP

I sat in the cold limbs of a tree.   Man in the Tree, The.   Mark Strand.   SPE

I sat in the door of our cottage.   Autumn Day, An.   Clara Ann Thompson. CBWP-2

I sat me down upon a green bank-side.   Bronx.   Joseph Rodman Drake. APN-1

I sat next to the Duchess at tea.   Limerick.   *Unknown.*   SoSe-8

I sat on cushioned otter-skin.   Madness of King Goll, The.   W. B. Yeats. NAEL-5v2; NAEL-6v2

I sat on my stool.   Father.   Ralph Dickey.   ESEAA

I sat on the couch. Sullen, young.   Cup of Coffee, The.   Carole Bernstein. AmPoNex

I sat on the Dogana's steps.   Ezra Pound.   TAP   *Fr.* Cantos.

I sat there on the quayside by the landing.   By the Danube.   Attila József. IQMS, *tr. by* Peter Zollman

I sat there singing her.   Songs.   Langston Hughes.   APT-2

I sat under my father's clothesline.   Con Los Pájaros.   Juan Delgado. AmPoNex

I sat up all night and watched you sleep. I did.   To Beth On Her Forty-Second Birthday.   Jane Chambers.   PoBW

I Sat Upon a Stone.   Walther [*or* Walter] von der Vogelweide.   AuPH, *tr. by* Lowell A. Bangerter

I sat with John Brown. That night moonlight framed.   Narrative.   Russell Atkins.   GT

I sat with Love upon a woodside well.   Dante Gabriel Rossetti.   CABP; NAEL-5v2; NAEL-6v2; OxBSo   *Fr.* House of Life, The.

I sat within a window, looking west.   East or West?   Charles Tennyson Turner. OxBSo

I save your grace inside.   Fire Keeper.   Bahiyyih Maroon.   SpirFl

I saved a life once.   Lipsticktion.   Edwin Torres.   HeMarv

I saved seventy dollars to buy Jan a present.   Jan's Birthday.   David Lee. GifTon

I savour on my own. (LL)   Pleasant Joys of Brotherhood, The.   James Simmons.   OBCoV; PBCIP

I saw a band of warriors coming on.   War Dance.   Miidhu.   NOBAu, *tr. by* George von Brandenstein

I saw a boy with eager eye.   Two Boys, The.   Mary Lamb.   WoRP

I Saw a Cave of Sable Depth Profound.   Thomas Cole.   APN-1

I saw a cottage in the sky.   Friends.   John Ashbery.   LCAP-2

I saw a famous man eating soup.   Soup.   Carl Sandburg.   HHAm; NOBA; NOBE; OBCA

I Saw a Fish-Pond All on Fire.   *Unknown.*   NOBL; OxBEV; OxNR

I saw a flat space.   Frozen Field, The.   Sheenagh Pugh.   TCAWP

I saw a fly [*or* Flie] within a Bead[e].   Amber Bead, The.   Robert Herrick. BeJo; CaPo

I saw a garden with a thousand rills.   Education in Wales.   Goronva Camlan. AngWePo

I saw a gardener with a watering can.   Progress of Poetry, The.   "Christopher Caudwell."   OxBTC

I saw a gold pillar from earth to heaven.   Message of King Sakis and the Legend of the Twelve Dreams He Had in One Night, The.   *Unknown.*   WoPoe, *tr. by* Charles Simic

I saw a great building with many storeys piled high.   Tony Charles.   NewEx

I saw a gull that slipped on the ice.   Town a Bird Sanctuary, The.   Jan Eijkelboom.   TuT, *tr. by* Peter Van de Kamp

I saw a hawk devour a screaming bird.   Hawk Is a Woman.   Hildegarde Flanner.   WPE

I saw a headless she-mule.   Good Friday: For Lack of an Orchestra.   Jack Spicer.   APSN

I Saw a Jolly Hunter.   Charles Causley.   EBNV; NOxBChV; OPOU

I saw a little girl.   Heart's Fine Gold, The.   W. O. Bourne.   TreFP

I saw a little tailor sitting stitch, stitch, stitching.   Tailor.   Eleanor Farjeon.   OTCP

I saw a maiden, fairest of the fair.   Charity.   Henrietta Cordelia Ray.   CBWP-3

I saw a man pursuing the horizon.   Stephen Crane.   APN-2; ChAP; MoAmPo; NOBA; NoP-4; TCAPo   *Fr.* Black Riders [and Other Lines], The.

I saw a mesa.   Leaving Port Authority for the St. Regis Rezz.   Wendy Rose.   HATNAP

I saw a mouth jeering.   Gargoyle.   Carl Sandburg.   NOBA; NoAM

I saw a pale tree, the leafless boughs—but two.   Ecstasy.   Hélène Swarth.   WPOW, *tr. by* Jonathan Crewe

I Saw a Peacock [with a Fiery Tail].   *Unknown.*   FaBoCh; OPOU; OTCP; OWoS; OxBSP; OxBoLi; OxNR; RB

(I saw a peacock with a flaming tail.)   AngWePo

I saw a people rise before the sun.   Yom Kippur.   Israel Zangwill.   TrJP

I saw a Phoenix in the Wood Alone.   Petrarch.   AWP, *tr. by* Edmund Spenser   *Fr.* Sonnets to Laura.

I saw a proud, mysterious cat.   Mysterious Cat, The.   Nicholas Vachel Lindsay.   OBCA

I saw a shadow on the ground.   Sky, The.   Elizabeth Madox Roberts.   MoAmPo

I saw a ship a-sailing.   Mother Goose.   LB; NTCP; OxNR; ReMoGo

I saw a Ship of martial build.   Berg, The.   Herman Melville.   ColAP; NCAP; NOBA; NoP-4; PoPoPo; TAP; TCAPo

I saw a sky of stars that rolled in grime.   Sidney Lanier.   APN-2; NCAP   *Fr.* Street Cries.

I saw / a specialist a cook.   To the Heart.   Tadeusz Rózewicz.   PoSu, *tr. by* Victor Contoski

I saw a stable low and very bare.   I Saw a Stable.   Mary Elizabeth Coleridge.   ChIV-2; OBCP; OxBSP; SacPr

I saw a star slide down the sky.   Falling Star, The.   Sara Teasdale.   ChAP; OBCA

I saw a staring virgin stand.   W. B. Yeats.   FaBoTw; HAP; NOBE; PoE   *Fr.* Resurrection, The.

I saw a strange creature.   Cynewulf.   ASW; WoPoe, *tr. by* Kevin Crossley-Holland   *Fr.* Riddles (Exeter Book).

I saw a trash-pit, filled and topped with earth.   Where Lie All the Slain.   Harry Morris.   CRP

I saw a tree.   Piece of Bone, The.   Katerina Pinosová.   SurWo

I saw a vision.   Gwyneth Lewis.   NeBl   *Fr.* Parables & Faxes.

I saw a vulture in the sky.   Life and Death.   Walter James Turner.   FaBoTw

I saw a woman sitting on a beast.   Sonnet 13.   Edmund Spenser.   ChIV-2

I saw a word in the air.   Cecilia Vicuña.   TANSG, *tr. by* Suzanne Jill Levine   *Fr.* Palabrarmás.

I saw a young deer standing.   Moment.   Hildegarde Flanner.   APT-2

I saw a young snake glide.   Snake.   Theodore Roethke.   NOBA

I saw about her spotless wrist.   Upon a Black Twist, Rounding the Arm of the Countess of Carlisle.   Robert Herrick.   CaPo

I saw among the clouds a monstrous trumpet.   Trumpet of Judgement, The.   Victor Hugo.   SxFrPo, *tr. by* E. H. Blackmore and A. M. Blackmore

I saw an eagle sweep to the sky.   Sun-Struck Eagle, The.   Eleanor Percy Lee.   SWaP

I saw an infant—health, and joy, and light.   Infant, The.   Agnes Strickland.   CenSon

I saw an ugly beast come from the sea.   Sonnet 12.   Edmund Spenser.   ChIV-2

I saw, and trembled for the day.   Warning, A.   Coventry Patmore.   EnLoPo

I saw another man die.   Wang Fan-chih.   SuSp

I Saw as a Child.   Zindzi Mandela.   NAfrP

I saw Aurora bouncing down the street.   Wish Fulfillment.   Maggie Nelson.   HeMarv

I saw before me a stormy condition.   I'm Livin' in a Great Big Way.   Dorothy Fields.   ReLy

I saw bleak Arrogance, with brows of brass.   Arrogance.   Walter De la Mare.   OxBSP

I saw Budapest burning.   Horror.   Gyula Illyés.   IQMS, *tr. by* Anthony Edkins

I saw children at Christmas in 1945.   Children at Christmas in 1945.   Vladimir Holan.   AF, *tr. by* C. G. Hanzlicek

I saw cold thunder in the grass.   Herons.   Robin Blaser.   NeAP

I saw dawn creep across the sky.   Summer Morning, A.   Rachel Lyman Field.   ChAP

I saw each soul as light, each single body.   Night of Souls.   Ann Stanford.   WPE

I saw Esau sawing wood.   *Unknown.*   Spl

I saw Eternity the other night.   Experience, The.   Bruce Bennett.   PeECV

I Saw Eternity the other night.   World, The (1).   Henry Vaughan.   AWP; ChIV-2; EBEV; ESCV; FSCP; HAP; NAEL-5v1; NAEL-6v1; NAEL-7v1; NOBE; NOCV; NOSC; NPeEn; OxAEP-1; OxBEV; PBRV; PeECV; SCGP; SacPr; TFi; TrCP

I saw fair[e] Chloris [*or* Cloris] walk alone.   On Chloris Walking in the Snow.   William Strode.   NPeEn

I saw God! Do you doubt it?   What Thomas an Buile Said in a Pub.   James Stephens.   MoBrPo; PoRA

I saw her amid the dunghill debris.   Tinker's Wife.   Patrick Kavanagh.   CIP-2; NoAM

I saw her first in Cabbage time.   I Saw Her in Cabbage Time.   Slocum Slugs.   VerBaPo

I saw her first in gleams.   Spirit's Odyssey, The.   M. Krishnamurti.   InPK-6

I saw her in a cluttered basement store.   Note, The.   Melvin B. Tolson.   GT

I Saw Her in Cabbage Time.   Slocum Slugs.   VerBaPo

I saw her in the fleeting wind.   To Echo.   Anna Maria Jones.   CenSon

I saw her near Anaheim by the fence.   Orphan, The.   Glover Davis.   GeoHom

I saw her once, one little while, and then no more.   And Then No More.   Friedrich Rückert.   BIrV, *tr. by* James Clarence Mangan

I saw him.   When I Passed in the Afternoon.   Laura Riesco.   TANSG, *tr. by* Shaun Griffin and Emma Sepúlveda-Pulvirenti

I saw him a squat man with red hair.   Off Brighton Pier.   Alan Ross.   OBWP

I saw him dead; I saw his Body fall.   Francis Quarles.   PBRV   *Fr.* Divine Fancies.

I saw him forging link by link his chain.   Slave, The.   Jones Very.   TAP

I saw him in the Airstrip Gardens.   Betjeman, 1984.   Charles Causley.   NOBL; OxBTC; PeLV; UV

I saw him in the Café Royal.   On Seeing an Old Poet in the Café Royal.   Sir John Betjeman.   OxBEV; UV

I saw him once before.   Last Leaf, The.   Oliver Wendell Holmes.   BRP; ITBLP; NAAL-2v1; NAAL-3; PWR; TCAPo

I saw him sitting in his door.   Philosopher, The.   Sara Teasdale.   PoToHe

I saw him to the last, the grey.   Painting of My Father.   Padraic Fallon.   NOIV

I saw him yesterday.   Quarrel, The.   Josephine D. Henderson Heard.   CBWP-4

I saw Hsiao-lien by the river.   Lute Player, The.   Li Ho.   CrYelRi, *tr. by* Sam Hamill

I saw in dream a dapper mannikin.   Im Traum sah ich ein Männchen klein und putzig.   Heinrich Heine.   AWP, *tr. by* Sir Theodore Martin

I Saw in Louisiana a Live-Oak Growing.   Walt Whitman.   APN-1; AWP; AiP; ColAP; InPK-6; NAAL-2v1; NAAL-3; NCAP; NIP-4; NOBA; NoAM; NoP-4; OxBA; PoPoPo; SAmP; TCAPo

I Saw It.   Ilya [*or* Karl] L'vovich Selvinsky [*or* Sel'vinskii].   TCRP, *tr. by* Daniel Weissbort

I Saw It!   Ilya [*or* Karl] L'vovich Selvinsky [*or* Sel'vinskii].   TCRusP, *tr. by* Denis Johnson

I saw it all, Polly, how when you had call'd for sop.   Poor Poll.   Robert Bridges.   EBEV; OxBTC; OxBoLi

I saw its periscope in the tide.   Mangrove.   John Blight.   NOBAu

I saw little tracks in the snow.   Invisible Tree.   Tamura Ryuichi.   WoPoe, *tr. by* Naoshi Koriyama and Edward Lueders

I saw magic on a green country road.   Michael Hartnett.   BIrV; PBCIP   *Fr.* Thirteen Sonnets.

I Saw My Darling.   Frederick Morgan.   UnPo

I Saw My Father Drowning.   David Vogel.   HP, *tr. by* A. C. Jacobs

I saw my grandad late last evening.   Gathering in the Days.   Gareth Owen.   NOxBChV

I Saw My Lady Weep.   *Unknown.*   EnLoPo; NoSic

(My Lady's Tears.)   EBEV; NOBE; OBEV

I saw my own children leaning.   To the Dregs.   Betsy Sholl.   ExTi

I saw my soul at rest upon a day.   Sestina.   Algernon Charles Swinburne.   MakPoe

I saw my toes the other day.   In Extremis.   John Updike.   OBCoV

I saw new Earth, new Heaven, said Saint John.   Sonnet 15.   Edmund Spenser.   ChIV-2

I saw new worlds beneath the water lie.   On Leaping over the Moon.   Thomas Traherne.   GeHe; NAEL-5v1

I saw no Way. The Heavens were stitched.   Emily Dickinson.   BoWoP; TCAPo

I saw nobody coming, so I went instead. (LL)   John Berryman.   LCAP-2; NAAL-2v2; NoAM; PoE; TwCP; VCAP   *Fr.* Dream Songs.

I saw not they were strange, the ways I roam.   After Music.   Josephine Preston Peabody.   TCAPo

I saw old Autumn in the misty morn. Autumn. Thomas Hood. OBEV; OxAEP-2

I saw old Duchesses with their young loves. Vanity. Anna Wickham. FaBoTw

I saw on the slant hill a putrid lamb. For a Lamb. Richard Eberhart. ColAP; OxBSP; RB; SoSe-8

I saw one whom I love more than my life. Noonday Vision, A. Frances Anne [or "Fanny"] Kemble. PoBW

I saw our golden years on a black gale. Sonnet for Christmas. Judith Wright. LW

I saw police biting corktip cigarettes. Mayday. Bill Tremblay. CDa

I saw prophets tearing at their pasted-on beards. What I Saw. Zbigniew Herbert. AF, *tr.* by John Carpenter

I saw red evening through the rain. Robert Louis Stevenson. NOBVV

I saw streaming up out of the sidewalk the homeless women and men. Under Voice, The. Jean Valentine. BodElec; ExTi

I saw, sweet Licia, when the spider ran. Giles Fletcher, the Elder. OxBSo *Fr.* Licia.

I saw that the shanty town had grown over the graves and that the crowd lived among the memorials. Lines for Translation into Any Language. James Fenton. AF

I saw that thieves had burgled as they do. Quatrain. Ilyas Farhat. MAP, *tr.* by John Heath-Stubbs and Salma Khadra Jayyusi

I saw the best minds of my generation. Squeal. Louis Simpson. UnPo

I saw the best minds of my generation destroyed by madness. Allen Ginsberg. HarvBoo; LCAP-2; NAAL-5; NoAM; PmAP; PoM; VCAP *Fr.* Howl.

I Saw the Bird That Dares Behold the Sun. Joachim Du Bellay. Son, *tr.* by Edmund Spenser

I saw the black trees leaning. Trees and Evening Sky. N. Scott Momaday. CDW

I saw the bodies of earth's men. Navigators, The. Walter James Turner. OBMV

I saw the / dead bird on the sidewalk. Maze, The. Joanne Kyger. BB

I saw the early morning mist. Dead Horse, The. Cecília Meireles. TCLAP, *tr.* by James Merrill

I saw the first pear. Orchard. "H. D." APT-1; MoAmPo; OxBA

I saw the garden where my aunt had died. Entertainment of War, The. Roy Fisher. FaBoMo

I saw the islands in a ring all round me. Letter to Pearse Hutchinson. Eiléan Ní Chuilleanáin. FaBoWP

I saw the Man that saw this wondrous sight. (LL) I Saw a Peacock [with a Fiery Tail]. *Unknown.* FaBoCh; OPOU; OTCP; OWoS; OxBSP; OxBoLi; OxNR; RB

I saw the midlands. Kisses in the Train. D. H. Lawrence. MoBrPo

I saw the moon as well. Chiyoni. JDP, *tr.* by Yoel Hoffmann

I Saw the Object. Thomas Watson. Son *Fr.* Tears of Fancy, The.

I saw the old god of war stand in a bog between chasm and rockface. God of War, The. Bertolt Brecht. AF, *tr.* by Michael Hamburger

I saw the ramparts of my native land. Sonnet: Death Warnings. Francisco de Quevedo y Villegas. AWP; OxBEV; WoPoe, *tr.* by John Masefield

I Saw the Red Electric. Joyce Mansour. HAWP, *tr.* by Albert Herzing

I saw the reflection in the mirror. Drunken Americans. John Ashbery. HCAP

I saw the shapes that stood upon the clouds. London Nightfall. John Gould Fletcher. MoAmPo

"I saw the Sibly at Cumæ." Fragment, A. Dante Gabriel Rossetti. PeVV

I saw the sky descending, black and white. Where the Rainbow Ends. Robert Lowell. HCAP; MoAmPo; PoetW

I saw the spiders marching through the air. Mr. Edwards and the Spider. Robert Lowell. CoAP; ColAP; FaBoMo; HarvBoo; HeIP-4; NAAL-2v2; NAAL-5; NOBA; NoP-4; TFi; TwCP

I saw the spires of Oxford. Spires of Oxford, The. Winifred M. Letts. PoRA

I saw the spot where our first parents dwelt. Garden, The. Jones Very. APN-1; OxBA; TAP

I saw the throng, so deeply separate. General Communion, A. Alice Thompson Meynell. NOCV; WPE

I saw the virtues sitting hand in hand. Humility. George Herbert. NOSC

I saw them, caught them in the act. Paulus [or Paulos] Silentiarius. GrAn

I saw these waves. Dread. Frederick D'Aguiar. WaCA

I saw three ships come sailing by. Mother Goose. LB; OxNR

I Saw Three Ships Come Sailing In. *Unknown.* ChrPo

I saw three ships go sailing by. North Ship, The. Philip Larkin. RB

I Saw Two Clouds at Morning. John Gardiner Calkins Brainard. PoToHe

I saw two hares in the corn. Dance, The. Gareth Alban Davies. OBWVE, *tr.* by Gwyn Jones

I saw / wet clothes hanging from a clothes line dripping with. Vision from the Ghetto. Raymond Washington. NBV

I saw where in the shroud did lurk. On an Infant Dying as Soon as Born. Charles Lamb. GTBS-P; OBEV

I saw white pelicans rise. Riding on the Coast Starlight. Ursula K. Le Guin. PoCoUp

I saw with open eyes. Stupidity Street. Ralph Hodgson. MoBrPo; OxBTC

I saw you in Houston, waiting for the verdict. On Visiting the M. D. Anderson. Salma Khadra Jayyusi. MAP, *tr.* by Charles Doria and the author

I saw you naked, gazing past me. One Night When We Paused Half-way. Kate Clanchy. MFPA

I saw you once, Medusa; we were alone. Muse as Medusa, The. May Sarton. HW; NALW

I saw you perform. Count Ossie. Opal Palmer Adisa. WaCA

I saw you smoldering. To an Old Friend. Nadia Hazboun Reimer. PoArWo

I saw you strolling by your solitary. Would You Like to Take a Walk? Harry Warren. ReLy

"I saw you take his kiss!" "Tis true." Coventry Patmore. BoLoP; EnLoPo; NOBVV *Fr.* Angel in the House, The.

I Saw You through My Closed Eye. Joyce Mansour. NAWM-7v2, *tr.* by Serge Gavronsky

I saw your gaping eyes. Renegade. Andrée Chedid. PoArWo, *tr.* by Lucy McNair

I saw your manager fight. He was. Elegy for Lyn James. Leslie Norris. OBWVE; TCAWP

I say. all you young girls waiting to live. Song No. 2. Sonia Sanchez. FFC

I say although the fire were wondrous hot. Ludovico Ariosto. NPeEn *Fr.* Orlando Furioso.

I Say Goodby to Fan An-ch'eng. Shen Yüeh. SuSp, *tr.* by Lenore Mayhew

I say, "Hail!" to the Holy One who appears in the heavens! Holy Priestess of Heaven, The. *Unknown.* HW, *tr.* by Samuel Noah Kramer and Diane Wolkstein

I say hello to the sunshine. Alan Brunton. PeNZ

I say I'll move the mountains. Crazy She Calls Me. Bob Russell. ReLy

I Say, Mr. A. Samuel Allen. SeSe

I say no more for Clavering. Clavering. Edwin Arlington Robinson. OxBA

I say no more.—I care not though thou cease. (LL) Dispute of the Heart and Body of François Villon, The. François Villon. AWP; OBVE, *tr.* by Algernon Charles Swinburne

I say someone in another time will remember us. Sappho. SaLy, *tr.* by Diane Rayor

I say that my sweetly prattling Heliodora will someday. Meleager. HePo *Fr.* Epigrams.

I Say That the Cricket the Scorpion the Grasshopper. Mariella Bettarini. CItWP, *tr.* by Cinzia Sartini Blum and Lara Trubowitz

I say that words are men and when we spell. Anna Hempstead Branch. APT-1; NALW *Fr.* Sonnets from a Lock Box.

I say things to myself. Phraseology. Jayne Cortez. BlSi

I say this evening we'll [or we'd] all get drunk. William Blake. *Fr.* Island in the Moon, An.

I say to the lead. Poem without a Title. Charles Simic. NNaP

I say to you for now, I embrace you brother. (LL) Letter to a Tormented Playwright. Syl Cheney-Coker. HBAPE; PBMAP

I say what Lindbergh's father. Maps for a Son Are Drawn as You Go. Samuel Hazo. GraLe

I say you shall not speak to him of war. (LL) Twelfth Night. Elinor Wylie. ChrPo; SacPr

I, says the buzzard. George Oppen. NNaP *Fr.* Five Poems about Poetry.

I scarce believe [or beleeve] my love to be so pure. Love's Growth. John Donne. ESCV; NOSC; NPeEn

I scarcely know my worthless picture. Any Husband to Many a Wife. Emily Jane Pfeiffer. VWP; ViWPN

I scissor the stem of the red carnation. Salome. Ai. NoAM

I scoop up fine sand with the plastic shovel. On the Anniversary of My Father's Death. Michael Lieberman. BloBone

I scorn the doubts and cares that hurt. Garden Song, A. George R. Sims. NOBVV; OBCoV; OBGa

I scraped off your smile with nails. Capital Punishment. Nina Cassian. PoSu, *tr.* by Nina Cassian

I scream as you bite. Kenneth Rexroth. APSN; APT-2 *Fr.* Love Poems of Marichiko, The.

I Scream You Scream. Don McKay. NOBC

I scrub the long floorboards. Finding a Long Gray Hair. Jane Kenyon. LoL

I sdrive to dddeflect at a blow the blow. César Vallejo. PFTM-1 *Fr.* Trilce.

I'se been upon de karpet. Old Maid's Soliloquy. Maggie Pogue Johnson. CBWP-4

I'se wild Nigger Bill. Wild Negro Bill. *Unknown.* BPo; NAAAL

I / search. Dubbed Out. Jean Binta Breeze. WaCA

I search among the plain and lovely words. Definition. Grace Noll Crowell. PoToHe

I search for not knowing in the middle of what I know best. Evening of the Sixth Day, The. Rose Drachler. APT-2

I search for phrases. Too Marvelous for Words. Johnny Mercer. ReLy

I search the chemistry of specific emotions. At the Electronic Frontier. Miguel Algarin. UnSA

I search the treetops, low-hung branches, for a trace of pink. Palace Song. Wang Chien. CoBCP, *tr. by* Burton Watson

I searched for my Self. Lal Ded [*or* Lalla]. WPoS

I See a Bear. Ted Hughes. NOxBChV

I see a blind man every day. Blind Man, The. Margaret Elizabeth Sangster. PoToHe

I see a chance for peace! What about water? (LL) Sonnet: "Cry, crow." Hayden Carruth. NNaP; Son

I see a farmer walking by himself. Farmer, The. Fredegond Maitland Shove. SacPr

I see a fly. Cold Fly, The. Yang Wan-li. SuSp, *tr. by* Jonathan Chaves

I see a man who is dull. Ancient Song of a Woman of Fez, An. *Unknown.* BoWoP, *tr. by* Willis Barnstone

I see a mild emanation of light. Mozart in a Classroom of Children. Daniel Bachhuber. MiVo

I see a Soldiers service is forgot. Peter Woodhouse. FaBoWar

I see again and again in my eyes. Tendril Love of Africa. Molara Ogundipe-Leslie. HAWP

I see all human wits. Ralph Waldo Emerson. TCAPo *Fr.* Quatrains.

I see as through a skylight in my brain. Persephone. Michael Longley. NPeEn; PBCIP

I see before me now a traveling army halting. Bivouac on a Mountain Side. Walt Whitman. AiP; CBCWP; OxBA

I see before me the gladiator lie. Byron. NOBE *Fr.* Childe Harold's Pilgrimage.

I see bodies in the morning kneel. Shirley Kaufman. BoWoP

I See Chano Pozo. Jayne Cortez. PmAP

I See Chile in My Rearview Mirror. Agha Shahid Ali. NoP-4

I see'd her in de springtime. She Hugged Me and Kissed Me. *Unknown.* BPo

I see during the night guard. Bizerta. George Campbell Hay. NePenScot

I see her against the pearl sky of Dublin. My Mother's Sister. Cecil Day Lewis. OxBTC

I see her close beside me with silent lips sad and tremulous. (LL) Once I Pass'd through a Populous City. Walt Whitman. NAAL-2v1; NAAL-3; NAAL-5; OxBA; RaBo; SAmP

I see her seventeen. Arizona Highways. James Welch. CDW; NoAM

I see her stand with arms a-kimbo. Hersilia. William Johnson Cory. NOBVV

I see her yet, that dark-eyed one. Memory, A. Adah Isaacs Menken. CBWP-1; ViWPN

"I see herrin'"—I hear the glad cry. With the Herring Fishers. Hugh MacDiarmid. CABP

I see him in a sense as strapped to his chair. Francis Webb. BMAP *Fr.* Around Costessey.

I see I've come a pilgrimage. I didn't. *Weepers Tower* in Amsterdam, The. Paul Goodman. VGW

I see in my mind, surrounding God. Vittoria da Colonna, Marchesa di Pescara. WPoS

I see in you the estuary that enlarges and spreads itself. To Old Age. Walt Whitman. Spl

I see in your beautiful face, my lord. Michelangelo Buonarroti. CAGL, *tr. by* James M. Saslow

I see it. Song for the Dead, III. *Unknown.* TTY, *tr. by* Frances S. Herskovits

I see it as it looked one afternoon. Long Island Sound. Emma Lazarus. APN-2; SWaP

I see madmen who. I See Madmen. Tadeusz Rózewicz. PoSu, *tr. by* Adam Czerniawski

I see Mike's painting, called SARDINES. (LL) Why I Am Not a Painter. Frank O'Hara. CoAmPo; HCAP; NOBA; NeAP; NoAM; NoP-4; PoE; PoM; PoPoPo; VCAP

I see my mother waving—her unfussed. Distances. Katherine Gallagher. Prnts

I see roses in December. Crazy in the Heart. Alec Wilder. ReLy

I see that the new will not compare with the old. (LL) Old and New. *Unknown.* AWP; ChiP, *tr. by* Arthur Waley

I see that there it is on the beach. Memorial Service for the Invasion Beach Where the Vacation in the Flesh Is Over. Alan Dugan. TwCP

I see the blue, the green, the golden and the red. Angelus. Kathleen Jessie Raine. BBASP

I see the children running out of school. Poet Laments the Coming of Old Age, The. Dame Edith Sitwell. NAEL-5v2; NAEL-6v2; NoAM

I see the elephants in the yard. Elephants Are in the Yard, The. Indran Amirthanayagam. OpBo

I see the fields the sea. Identities. Paul Eluard. SurPaPo, *tr. by* Mary Ann Caws

I see the Four-fold Man. The Humanity in deadly sleep. William Blake. NOBRP *Fr.* Jerusalem; The Emanation of the Giant Albion.

I see the ginnnnn of resurrection glass to glass! (LL) I Am the Freshly Dead Husband. Kojo Laing. HBAPE; NAfrP

I see the millet combing gold. Midsummer. Alexander L. Posey. APN-2

I See the Moon. *Unknown.* NTCP; OxNR

I see the Sunday sun beating. Memory of Sunday. Mairtin O Direain. ModIr, *tr. by* Patrick Crotty

I see the temple in thy pillar reared. Jacob's Pillow, and Pillar. Henry Vaughan. ChIV-1

I see the thin bell-ringer standing at corners. Jew at Christmas Eve, The. Karl Shapiro. VGW

I see the white / light / And the night / Flies. (LL) Ezra Pound. APT-1; OBVE; VGW; WeW-3 *Fr.* Langue d'Oc.

I see thee ever in my dreams. Karamanian Exile, The. James Clarence Mangan. PeVV

I see thee pine like her in golden story. Coleridge. Theodore Watts-Dunton. GSo; Son

I see them coming up the road. Happy Pair, A. Priscilla Jane Thompson. CBWP-2

I see them crowd on crowd they walk the earth. Dead, The. Jones Very. APN-1; HAP; NOBA; NoP-4; OxBA; SacPr; TAP; TCAPo

I see them standing at the formal gates of their colleges. I Go Back to May 1937. Sharon Olds. BLT; EmeKit; NIL-7

I see them working in old rectories. Country Clergy, The. Ronald Stuart Thomas. GTBS-P; OxBTC; PeECV

I see they worked you over. What you in for? Coming of Age in the County Jail. Carter Revard. VoR

I see thine image through my tears tonight. Elizabeth Barrett Browning. CenSon *Fr.* Sonnets from the Portuguese.

I see trees breaking off their branches. Khairi Mansour. MAP *Fr.* Nightwatch.

I see why the touched needle scents about. John Reynolds. NOEC *Fr.* Death's Vision.

I see you, a child. Album, The. Cecil Day Lewis. EnLoPo; OxBTC

I see you dart into the world. Transformation. Jeni Couzyn. HAWP

I see you every morning with a poet's eyes. Merci Bien, Monsieur. Carlota Caulfield. TANSG, *tr. by* Chris Allen

I see you, Juliet, still, with your straw hat. Wilfrid Scawen Blunt. BoLoP; EnLoPo; OxBTC *Fr.* Love Sonnets of Proteus, The.

I see you, not as you stand before me. Letter to Yeni on Peering into Her Life. Sandra M. Castillo. TouFir

I see you now, my mother and father. Beachy Head. Hilary Davies. Prnts

I see you sitting. Matmiya. Mary Tallmountain. HATNAP; LoL

I see you what you are: you are too proud. William Shakespeare. OxAEP-1 *Fr.* Twelfth Night.

I See Your Face Before Me. Howard Dietz. ReLy

I see your lights! But ours had long died out. (LL) Wilfred Owen. EBNV; PeFWW; PoWW

I seek a form that my style cannot discover. I Seek a Form. "Rubén Dario." TCLAP, *tr. by* Lysander Kemp

I seek about this world unstable. Of the Changes of Life. William Dunbar. WoPoe, *tr. by* Andrew Glaze

I seek for my own use to trace out here. (LL) When I Read the Book. Walt Whitman. NAAL-2v1; NAAL-3

I seek in prayerful words, dear friend. God Bless You. *Unknown.* PoToHe

I seek it in the steamy odor. Prayer to the Muse of Ordinary Life. Kate Daniels. ExTi

I seek mercy / for the women stoned. For All Mary Magdalenes. Desanka Maksimovic. WPOW, *tr. by* Vasa D. Mihailovich

I seem to be the victim of a cruel jest. And Her Mother Came Too. Ivor Novello. OBCoV; ReLy

I seen't dis papuh cup dancin' across the street 2day. Dancin' Our Lives Away. Lorena M. Craighead. InTrad

I send a garland to my love. Lover's Posy, The. Rufinus. AWP, *tr. by* W. H. D. Rouse

I send a message, my worthy chief. Message to a Loved One Dead, A. Josephine D. Henderson Heard. CBWP-4

I send, I send here my supremest kiss. His Tears to Thamesis [*or* Thamasis]. Robert Herrick. NOSC

I send my messages ahead of me. Poet and Person. Denise Levertov. GifTon

I send thee myrrh, not that thou mayest be. Not of Itself but Thee. *Unknown.* AWP, *tr. by* Richard Garnett

I send to thee. (LL) Hafiz [*or* Hafez]. AWP; TAL *Fr.* Odes.

I send you a box. Yakamochi (Otomo no Yakamochi). OHPJ

I send you a lock of hair. Martial. PGA

I send you here a sort of allegory. To — With the Following Poem. Tennyson. NOBRP

I send you here a wreath of blossoms blown. Roses. Pierre de Ronsard. AWP, *tr. by* Andrew Lang

I Send You My Verses. Minuchihiri. ArPe, *tr. by* Omar S. Pound

I sent a letter to my love.   George Barker.   FaBoTw   *Fr.* True Confession of George Barker, The.

I sent a letter to my love.   *Unknown.*   LB

I sent for Radcliffe; was so ill.   Remedy Worse than the Disease, The.   Matthew Prior.   FaBoEE

I Sent Thee Late.   Louis Zukofsky.   APT-2

I sente a ringe, a little bande.   To Helene.   George Darley.   NOBRP

I serve a mistress whiter than snow.   Anthony Munday.   HAP; SCGP   *Fr.* Fedele and Fortunio.

I set aside to tell the restless toil.   George Gascoigne.   FaBoWar   *Fr.* Fruits of War, The.

I set down the emerald lamp.   Gekkutsu-Sei.   ZenPo, *tr. by* Takashi Ikemoto and Lucien Stryk

I set forth hopeful—cotton-blossom Lal.   Lalleswari.   WPOW

I set my bag on the table that is also a toilet. Sit in my chair that is also.   Sleeper.   Amy Fusselman.   HeMarv

I set my table with metaphor.   Passover.   Linda Pastan.   TaR

I set sail.   When I Am with You.   Ghazi Al-Gosaibi.   MAP, *tr. by* Charles Doria and Sharif Elmusa

I set the bowl of raw vegetables on the table.   Before You Leave.   Ai.   GT

I sh'd think 'e'll get right again. (LL)   Collier's Wife, The.   D. H. Lawrence.   FaBoVe; OxBTC

I shadow the pond.   Black Bean Soup.   Lucien Stryk.   BodElec

I shake my hair in the wind of morning.   Triumph of Love.   John Hall Wheelock.   MoAmPo

I shake my robe—and mists disperse, leaving clear autumn sky.   Hsü Chung-hsing.   CoBLCP   *Fr.* At Dawn, Climbing the Heavenly Pillar Peak of Mysterious Mountain.

I shall be careful to say nothing at all.   How She Resolved to Act.   Merrill Moore.   MoAmPo

I shall be found, ac more in Crist. (LL)   All Other Love Is Like the Moon.   *Unknown.*   MiEL; SacPr

I shall be glad to be silent, Mother, and hear you speak.   White Thought, The.   Stevie Smith.   Spl

I shall be gone, and you may whistle for me. (LL)   Oh, Oh, you will be sorry for that word!   Edna St. Vincent Millay.   BoWoP; HeIP-4; NALW

I shall be mad if you get smashed about.   Soldier Addresses his Body, The.   Edgell Rickword.   PeFWW; PoWW

I shall be still stronger.   I Want to Sleep.   Jorge Guillén.   WoPoe, *tr. by* James Wright and James Wright

I shall but love thee better after death. (LL)   Elizabeth Barrett Browning.   AmFaPo; BWW; BoLoP; CTC; CenSon; EBVV; GSo; HeIP-4; ITBLP; InPK-6; MakPoe; NAEL-5v2; NAEL-6v2; NALW; NIL-7; NIP-4; NoP-4; OPOU; OxAEP-2; OxBSo; PoE; PoPoPo; PoRA; PoToHe; Son; TFi; UV; UnPo; VWP; WPE   *Fr.* Sonnets from the Portuguese.

I shall come back to die.   In This Dark House.   Edward Davison.   OBMV

I shall cry God to give me a broken foot.   Flash Crimson.   Carl Sandburg.   MoAmPo

I shall die, but that is all that I shall do for Death.   Conscientious Objector.   Edna St. Vincent Millay.   FaBoWar; WPOW

I shall ebb out with them, who homeward go. (LL)   John Donne.   BASC; FSCP; NOSC   *Fr.* Elegies.

I shall find in paradise that emaciated rose shoot.   Maria Luisa Spaziani.   NeIt   *Fr.* Star of Free Will, The.

I Shall Forget.   "Laurence Hope."   OxBSo

I Shall Forget You Presently, My Dear.   Edna St. Vincent Millay.   APT-1; HeIP-4; TAP

I shall gather myself into myself again.   Crystal Gazer, The.   Sara Teasdale.   MoAmPo

I shall give them all to my elder daughter. (LL)   If I Should Ever by Chance.   Edward Thomas.   FaBoCh; MoBrPo; OBMV; OBWVE

I shall give you five words for your birthday.   Five Words for Joe Dunn on His 22nd Birthday.   Jack Spicer.   PoM

I shall go among red faces and virile voices.   Cattle Show.   Hugh MacDiarmid.   FaBoMo; HAP; MoBrPo; OBMV; OxBEV; OxBTC

I shall go as my father went.   Tenancy, The.   Mary Gilmore.   CBAP

I shall go back again to the bleak shore.   I shall go back.   Edna St. Vincent Millay.   MoAmPo; UnPo

I shall go down.   Félix Lope de Vega Carpio.   HAP, *tr. by* Geoffrey Hill   *Fr.* Pentecost Castle, The.

I shall hate you.   Hatred.   Gwendolyn B. Bennett.   BlSi; RaBo

I shall have had my day. (LL)   Tennyson.   NAEL-5v2; NAEL-6v2; NOBVV   *Fr.* Maud [A Monodrama].

I shall hear that grand Amen. (LL)   Lost Chord, A.   Adelaide Anne Procter.   ITBLP; SacPr; UV; VWP

I shall keep singing!   Emily Dickinson.   APN-2

I shall knock three times at the door.   'Ali Al-Sharqawi.   MAP   *Fr.* Psalm 23 to the Singer's Nectar.

I shall know why—when Time is over.   Emily Dickinson.   NOCV; SAmP

I shall lie hidden in a hut.   Prophecy.   Elinor Wylie.   BoWoP; FaBoWP; ItWoWo; VGW

I shall live to be old, who feared I should die young.   I Shall Live To Be Old.   Sara Teasdale.   APT-1

I shall look at the grass.   Perseverance.   Martin Sorescu.   VCWP, *tr. by* D. J Enright and Joana Russell-Gebbett

I shall look for loving crops from the birth, life, death, immortality, I plant so lovingly now. (LL)   Woman Waits for Me, A.   Walt Whitman.   ErotSp; HeIP-4; NOBA

I shall make a song like your hair.   Secret.   Gwendolyn B. Bennett.   BlSi

I shall make it simple so you understand.   Simple Poem.   Anthony Thwaite.   DiPo

I shall make rings around you.   Fortresses.   Night-Piece.   Joy Davidman.   YaYoPo

I shall marry the very next man who asks me.   (I'll Marry) the Very Next Man.   Sheldon Harnick.   ReLy

I shall never forget his blue eye.   Dylan Thomas.   UV   *Fr.* Parachutist.

I shall never forget you, Broadway.   Broadway.   Carl Sandburg.   AiP

I shall never get you put together entirely.   Colossus, The.   Sylvia Plath.   FaBoWP; HCAP; NALW; NOBA; NoAM; NoP-4; TAP; VCAP; WoPoe

I shall not be myself, death.   Zenith.   Juan Ramón Jiménez.   SpanPo, *tr. by* Kate Flores

I Shall Not Care.   Sara Teasdale.   APT-1; MoAmPo; TCAPo; UnPo

I shall not fail that rendezvous. (LL)   I Have a Rendezvous with Death.   Alan Seeger.   APT-1; AiP; BRP; FaBoWar; TCAPo

I shall not forget it (that evening either).   In the Restaurant.   Aleksandr Aleksandrovich Blok.   TCRP, *tr. by* Geoffrey Thurley

I Shall Not Go to Heaven When I Die.   Helen Waddell.   MLL

I shall not lie to find a lurid rhyme.   Sofiya Parnok.   ARWW, *tr. by* Catriona Kelly

I shall not linger in that draughty square.   Osbert Lancaster.   NOBL; PeLV   *Fr.* Afternoons with Baedeker.

I shall not live in Vain. (LL)   Emily Dickinson.   AH; BRP; PWR; PoToHe

I shall not lose thee though I die. (LL)   Tennyson.   EBVV; FHYEP; HeIP-4; NAEL-6v2   *Fr.* In Memoriam A. H. H.

I Shall Not Pass This Way Again.   *Unknown.*   ChAP

I shall not regard my swelled head as a sign of real glory.   Aimé Césaire.   TTY   *Fr.* Return to My Native Land.

I shall not repeat others' comments about me. (LL)   Wet Casements.   John Ashbery.   NAAL-2v2; PoM

I shall not see thee. Dare I say.   Tennyson.   NAEL-6v2   *Fr.* In Memoriam A. H. H.

I shall not sing a May song.   Crazy Woman, The.   Gwendolyn Brooks.   ItWoWo; NALW

I shall not tell how much I loved him then. (LL)   Sonnet: On the Detection of a False Friend.   Guido Cavalcanti.   AWP; EaItPo, *tr. by* Dante Gabriel Rossetti

I Shall Not Want: In Deserts Wild.   Charles F. Deems.   AH

I shall note first / the ones I loved.   Chronicler, The.   Alexander Bergman.   TrJP

I shall rejoice, and my prediction's true. (LL)   Vote, The.   Ralph Knevet.   FaBoWar; NOSC

I shall rot here, with those whom in their day.   In Death Divided.   Thomas Hardy.   SCGP

I shall say, Lord, "Is it music, is it morning."   Resurgam.   Marjorie Lowry Christie Pickthall.   SacPr; TrCP

I Shall Say What Inordinate Love Is.   Robert Frost.   OxBSP

I shall say what inordinat[e] love is.   Inordinate Love.   *Unknown.*   EBEV; MiEL; OxBSP

I shall see justice done.   Witch.   Patricia Beer.   OxBC

I shall sleep calm beneath its wave! (LL)   Letitia [*or* Laetitia] Elizabeth Landon.   RWP; VWP   *Fr.* Improvisatrice, The.

I shall sleep in white calico.   Song of War.   Kofi Awoonor.   PBMAP; PoetW

I shall slough my self as a snake its skin.   "I."   Louis Golding.   TrJP

I Shall Take You in Rough Weather.   Frank Prewett.   HATNAP

I shall think of you.   Kasa no Iratsume.   ArkPo, *tr. by* Edwin A. Cranston

I shall tune my lute to sing your litanies as the quiet hours pass.   Ode to Africa.   Bernard Dadié.   NegPo, *tr. by* Ellen Conroy Kennedy

I shall vote Centre because.   I Shall Vote Centre.   Roger Woddis.   UV

I shall vote Labour because.   I Shall Vote Labour.   Christopher Logue.   UV

I shall walk down the road.   Death.   Maxwell Bodenheim.   TrJP

I shall weave you a wreath.   Wreath for Africa, A.   Bernard Dadié.   NegPo, *tr. by* Ellen Conroy Kennedy

I Shall Weep.   Peretz Hirshbein.   TrJP, *tr. by* Joseph Leftwich

I shall yet be footloose. (LL)   Broken-Face Gargoyles.   Carl Sandburg.   MoAmPo; OxBA

I shan't be gone long—You come too. (LL)   Pasture, The.   Robert Frost.   APT-1; MoAmPo; NAAL-2v2; NAAL-5; NOBA; OxBA; PoE; SAmP; TLR; TRP; TTTS; WHSW

I shift my pillow. Saiba. JDP, *tr.* by Yoel Hoffmann

I shipped, d'ye see, in a Revenue sloop. Sir William Schwenck Gilbert. NOBL *Fr.* Ruddigore.

I shook myself awake, saw. Freak. Chandrashekhar Patil. OMIP, *tr.* by A. K. Ramanujan

I shoot the hippopotamus. Hippopotamus, The. Joseph Hilaire Pierre Belloc. InPK-6

I shot a rocket in the air. Enough. Tom Masson. OBAL

I shot an arrow into the air. Shot at Random, A. Dominic Bevan Wyndham Lewis. UV

I shot an arrow into the air. Arrow and the Song, The. Henry Wadsworth Longfellow. BRP; ColAP; PWR; PoToHe; TCAPo; UV

I should be able to give up tea, I think. And wine. (LL) Women. Trần Tế Xu'o'ng. EaWin; WoPoe, *tr.* by W. S. Merwin and Nguyen Ngoc Bich

I should be glad I didn't get the clap. Parting Roundel. Jemal Sharah. NOBAu

I should be glad of another death. (LL) Journey of the Magi. T. S. Eliot. ChrPo; FaBoCh; FaBoMo; GI; HAP; HeIP-4; InPK-6; MoAmPo; NAAL-5; NAEL-5v2; NAEL-6v2; NIL-7; NIP-4; NOCV; NoP-4; OBCP; OBMV; OxBTC; PAI; PoE; TAP; TFi; TRP; TwCP

I should be happy with my lot. Nameless Pain. Elizabeth Stoddard. SWaP

I Should Care. Sammy Cahn. ReLy

I should have been too glad, I see. Emily Dickinson. APN-2; NOCV; SacPr

I should have kept right on going. Small Fat Boy Walking Backwards, A. Gerry Murphy. BiHa

I should have seen the sign: "Fresh paint." Fresh Paint. Boris Leonidovich Pasternak. TrJP, *tr.* by Babette Deutsch

I should have thought. At Baia. "H. D." APT-1; ColAP; NAAL-2v2; NOBA; PoBW

I should know what God and man is. (LL) Flower in the Crannied Wall. Tennyson. BBASP; BRP; ITBLP; InPK-6; NAEL-5v2; NAEL-6v2; TFi

'I should like,' said the vase from the china-store. Toys Talk of the World, The. Katharine Pyle. NOxBChV; OBCA

I should like to creep. Mona Lisa, A. Angelina Weld Grimké. APT-1; BlSi

I should like to rise and go. Travel. Robert Louis Stevenson. FaBoCh; OTCP

I should like you all to know. I'm a Gigolo. Cole Porter. OBCoV; ReLy

I should never have taken the trout. (LL) Limerick. Edward Gorey. PeLV; PeLi

I should not feel it to be strange. (LL) Tennyson. EBVV; FHYEP; NAEL-6v2 *Fr.* In Memoriam A. H. H.

I should not have waited. Akazome Emon. OHPJ

I should not presume to express any view. Triangular Legs. Sir Alan Patrick Herbert. NBLV

I should retire at half-past eight? (LL) Grown-up. Edna St. Vincent Millay. NoAM; PAI

I shouldered a kind of manhood. Funeral Rites. Seamus Heaney. BiHa; ModIr; PBCIP; PoetW

I shouldn't write this. No. Idea Vilariño. TANSG, *tr.* by Louise B. Popkin

I shouted at Him. At the Mosque. Chairil Anwar. PoetW, *tr.* by Burton Raffel

I showed her Heights she never saw. Emily Dickinson. PoBW

I shudder thinking. Cold Irish Earth, The. Knute Skinner. InPK-6

I shut down the lawnmower. Leroy Gorman. HA

I shut the door, hoping to drive off sorrow. Written for My Own Amusement. Wang An-shih. CoBCP, *tr.* by Burton Watson

I shut the door on the racket. Shoe Shop. Barton Sutter. SoSe-8

I sicken of myself, my members all are shaking. To Himself. Andreas Gryphius. GePo, *tr.* by George C. Schoolfield

I sigh at day-dawn, and I sigh. Sappho. Christina Georgina Rossetti. VWP

I sigh for the heavenly country. Heavenly City, The. Stevie Smith. FaBoTw

I sigh for the land of the Cypress and Pine. Song—Written at the North. Samuel Henry Dickson. APN-1

I sigh to myself I am traveling far. Recalling When I Was Drunk. Yüan Chên. SuSp, *tr.* by Dell R. Hales

I sike when I singe. Crucifixion, The. *Unknown.* MiEL

I simply wish to die. Sappho. SaLy, *tr.* by Diane Rayor

I sing a song of sixpence, and of rye. Ode. Anthony C. Deane. NOBL

I sing America, in its wild and autochthonous state. Manifesto, A. José Santos Chocano. TCLAP, *tr.* by Andrew Rosing

I sing divine Astræa's praise. Dialogue between two shepherds, Thenot and Piers, in praise of ASTRÆA. Mary Sidney Herbert, Countess of Pembroke. EMWP; NAEL-6v1

I Sing for the Animals. *Teton Sioux Oral Tradition.* TCAPo; TTTS

I sing, I sing, I sing. Incantation Songs of the Klamath Lake People. *Unknown.* APN-2, *tr.* by Albert S. Gatschet

I sing my own true story, tell my travels. Seafarer, The. *Unknown.* NoP-4

I sing of a hero, unsung, unrecorded. Crispus Attucks McCoy. Sterling Allen Brown. BPo

I Sing of a Maiden. *Unknown.* CABP; ChrPo; ChIV-2; EBEV; FaBoCh; InPK-6; MiEL; NAEL-5v1; NAEL-7v1; NOBE; NOCV; NoP-4; PoE; SCGP; SCV; TFi; TOF

I sing of a world reshaped. (LL) I Sing of Change. Niyi Osundare. NAfrP; PBMAP

I sing of Aphrodite, the lover's goddess. *Unknown.* HW, *tr.* by Patricia Monaghan *Fr.* Homeric Hymns.

I sing of brooks, of blossom[e]s, birds, and bowers. Argument of His Book, The. Robert Herrick. AWP; BASC; BeJo; CaPo; CavPo; EBEV; HAP; NAEL-5v1; NAEL-6v1; NAEL-7v1; NOSC; NPeEn; NoP-4; OxAEP-1; PeECV; PoE; PoPoPo; PoRA; SacPr; TFi; TTTS; WoPoe

I Sing of Change. Niyi Osundare. NAfrP; PBMAP

I sing of great hotels and a man. In the foyer. Strand Hotel, Rosslare, The. James Liddy. CIP-2

I sing of myself, a sorrowful woman. Wife's Lament. *Unknown.* PoE, *tr.* by Kemp Malone

I Sing of Olaf Glad and Big. E. E. Cummings. AF; AmFaPo; ColAP; FaBoWar; HeIP-4; NAAL-2v2; NAAL-5; NOBA; NoAM; NoP-4; OBSV; OBWP; PoWW; VGW

I sing of pilchards, caught on a rod. Pilchard-Curing Song, The. Alice Oswald. MFPA

I sing of simple people and the harder virtues, by Associated Stuffed Shirts & Company, Incorporated, 358 West 42d Street, New York, brochure enclosed. Literary. Kenneth Fearing. APT-2

I sing of sweepers, frequent in thy streets. Sweepers, The. William Whitehead. ECEV; NOEC

I sing / of the beauty of Athens. I Sing of Change. Niyi Osundare. NAfrP; PBMAP

I sing of warfare and a man at war. Virgil [*or* Vergil]. NAWM-5v1; NAWM-7v1, *tr.* by Robert Fitzgerald *Fr.* Aeneid [*or* Eneados, *Aeneis*], The.

I sing th' adventures of mine worthy mighty. Poem: "I sing th' adventures of mine worthy wights." Thomas Morton. SCAP

I sing the birth, was born[e] to-night. Hymn[e] on the Nativity [*or* Nativitie] of My Saviour, A. Ben Jonson. BeJo; ChIV-2; ChrPo; SacPr; TrCP

I Sing the Body Electric. Walt Whitman. CTC
   "I have perceiv'd that to be with those I like is enough." SAmP
   "I knew a man, a common farmer, the father of five sons." BLT
   "Male is not less the soul nor more, he too is in his place, The." ErotSp
   "Man's body at auction, A." SAmP
   "This is the female form." ErotSp

I sing the glorious Power with azure eyes. *Unknown.* AWP, *tr.* by Percy Bysshe Shelley *Fr.* Homeric Hymns.

I sing the Man, by Heav'ns peculiar grace. Poem on Elijahs Translation, A. Benjamin Colman. SCAP

I sing the man that never equal knew. Alexandreis. Anne Killigrew. NoP-4

I sing the olive oil, I who lately sang. Year of the Olive Oil, The. Charles North. FTOS

I sing the quality of bamboo. Bamboo. Eric Rolls. NOBAu

I sing the steir, strabush, and strife. William Tennant. NePenScot *Fr.* Papistry Storm'd.

I sing the tree is a heron. Merce of Egypt. Charles Olson. APT-2

I sing thee with the stock-dove's throat. "Michael Field." VWP

I sing this song about myself, full sad. *Unknown. See* I make this song about me full sadly

I sing to a breeze that runs through the rafters. Vox Angelica. Timothy Liu. NeAmPo; WiU

I sing to him that rests below. Tennyson. NAEL-6v2; NAWM-7v2 *Fr.* In Memoriam A. H. H.

I sing *tree*, making green. Last Night's Dream. Denise Levertov. NoAM

I sing what I saw. Gorcheanu: Three Laments, The. Aneirin. WoPoe, *tr.* by Desmond O'Grady

I sink in the falling snow. Monstrance. János Pilinszky. PoSu, *tr.* by Peter Jay

I sink into bed. My Imperialism. Tamura Ryuichi. AF; PFTM-2; VCWP, *tr.* by Christopher Drake

I sit. Everything I Need to Know I Learned in Kindergarten. Martin Jude Farawell. OPRER

I sit alone among dark bamboos. Bamboo Grove. Wang Wei. ChinPo, *tr.* by Yip Wai-lim

I sit alone in the bamboo dark. At a House in the Bamboo Grove. Wang Wei. CrYelRi, *tr.* by Sam Hamill

I sit alone late at night. Extra Joyful Chorus for Those Who Have Read This Far, An. Robert Bly. SPE

I sit alone on the rocks trying to prepare. In the Wilderness. James Simmons. GI

I sit and beat the wizard's magic drum. Wizard's Chant, The. *Unknown.* APN-2, *tr.* by Charles Godfrey Leland and John Dyneley Prince

I Sit and Look Out. Walt Whitman. NAAL-2v1; NAAL-3; OxBA; PAI; SAmP; TAP

I Sit and Sew. Alice Moore Dunbar-Nelson. BlSi; NAAAL; NALW; WPOW

I Sit and Wait for Beauty. Mae V. Cowdery. BlSi

I sit at a gold table with my girl. Robert Lowell. InPK-6 *Fr.* Between the Porch and the Altar.

I sit at home. Kakinomoto no Hitomaro. OHPJ

I sit at my desk. Kenneth Rexroth. APSN; APT-2 *Fr.* Love Poems of Marichiko, The.

I sit at the foot of snow-capped mountains. Keeping Watch. Sojourner Kincaid Rolle. GeoHom

I sit beside my old ship, the timbers rotting. Old Jason, the Argonaut, The. Denis Glover. PeNZ

I sit beside my peaceful hearth. Due of the Dead, The. William Makepeace Thackeray. FaBoWar; OBWP

I sit by the mossy fountain; on the top of the hill of winds. James Macpherson. NOEC; NePenScot *Fr.* Fragments of Ancient Poetry, Collected in the Highlands of Scotland.

I sit by the roadside. Changing the Wheel. Bertolt Brecht. PoSu, *tr.* by Michael Hamburger

I sit by the shed. Winter Billet. Peter Huchel. PoSu, *tr.* by Michael Hamburger

I Sit by the Window. Joseph Brodsky. VCWP, *tr.* by Howard Moss

I sit crotch high. Under the Oak Table. Colleen J. McElroy. GT

I sit down at a table and open a book of poems. Library. Louis Jenkins. RaBo

I sit down beside my brass lamp. Peeling Pippins. Mary Tallmountain. HATNAP

I sit drinking wine and, for a long time, don't notice the dusk. Losing Myself. S. J. Marks. BodElec

I Sit Here. Kumeroa Ngoingoi Pewhairangi. PeNZ, *tr.* by the author

I sit here at your edge, in your embankment's screen. Shepherd-Song. Sigmund von Birken. GePo, *tr.* by George C. Schoolfield

I sit here long, the lamp burns dim. Green Banana Leaves. Yün Shou-p'ing. CoBLCP, *tr.* by Jonathan Chaves

I sit here with affection for the lingering Year. Year Hsin-hai (Fifteen Fifty One), New Year's Eve: Keeping Watch, The. Wen Cheng-ming. CoBLCP, *tr.* by Jonathan Chaves

I sit here with all my words intact. Silence Around an Ancient Stone. Rosario Castellanos. TANSG, *tr.* by Magda Bogin

I sit here with the wind is in my hair. To Helen of Troy (N.Y.). Peter Viereck. WeW-3

I sit in an office at 244 Madison Avenue. Spring Comes to Murray Hill. Ogden Nash. APT-2

I sit in another house whose character is. House Is Old, The. Ron Schreiber. GLP

I sit in front of our Zenith TV, eat. Marlo Thomas in Seven Parts and Epilogue. Jeffery Conway. WiU

I sit in Lees. At 11:40 PM with. Poem for vipers, A. John Weiners. BB

I Sit in My Room. Jean Toomer. GT

I sit in my sorrow a-weary, alone. Window Just Over the Street, The. Alice Cary. PoBW; SWaP

I sit in one of the dives. September 1, 1939. W. H. Auden. AF; HarvBoo; MoBrPo; OxAEP-2; OxBA; PoE

I sit in the top of the wood, my eyes closed. Hawk Roosting. Ted Hughes. GTBS-P; HAP; HeIP-4; OWoS; OxBEV; OxBTC; TwCP; UnPo

I sit, in treatment, at the movies, devoted. Valerio Magrelli. NeIt

I sit musing, ten minutes from the Jap. Letter for Marian, A. Thomas McGrath. VGW

I sit on horseback at Twin Bridges. Wen Cheng-ming. CoBLCP *Fr.* Improvised on Horseback to Say Good-bye to Those Who Are Seeing Me Off.

I sit on the edge. Piano, The. Frank Daley. NOBC

I sit on the lonely headland. On the Headland. Bayard Taylor. CAGL

I sit too still and think about five years. August 1990. C. Mikal Oness. GeoHom

I sit under Rand MacNally's. Westering. Seamus Heaney. HarvBoo

I sit with Joseph Conrad in Monet's garden. Zimmer Imagines Heaven. Paul Zimmer. PBCAP

I sit with my back to the engine, watching. Crossing the Border. Norman MacCaig. HarvBoo

I Sit with My Dolls. *Unknown.* TrJP, *tr.* by Joseph Leftwich

I sit with my wine—there's no singing or dancing. Drinking. Chu Yün-ming. CoBLCP, *tr.* by Jonathan Chaves

I sit within my room and joy to find. Presence, The. Jones Very. HAP

I slap on latex gloves before I put. Towards Curing AIDS. Rafael Campo. BloBone; NeAmPo

I sleep alone. (LL) Moon Has Set, The. Sappho. PGA; WoPoe, *tr.* by Kenneth Rexroth

I sleep alone. *Unknown.* OHMPJ

I sleep but my heart is awake. Bible, O.T. BoWoP; TrJP, *tr.* by Willis Barnstone *Fr.* Song of Solomon, The [*or* The Song of Songs].

I sleep now with the Lord, by the Lord's strength will I rise up. Lady

Katherine Killigrew Wrote This Poem about Her Own Death, The. Katherine Killigrew. EMWP

I slept the sleep of the just. New Life, The. Louise Glück. BodElec

I slide into his life. I Have Taken the Suits and Shoes to Oxfam. Felicity Napier. Prnts

I slouch in bed. James Wright (1927–80). EmeKit *Fr.* Two Hangovers.

I slow down the waterfall to a chandelier. Frozen Rain. Michael Longley. PBCIP

I slowly crack my joints to ready and steady myself. Sharpen my mind on. Mimi Goese. HeMarv

I smashed a hot dog into her face. Hot Dog Poem, The. Jane Barnes. GLP

I smell dry snuffy turf smoke clouding the cottages. Irish Scullery Maid, The. Joyce Herbert. TCAWP

I Smile, but Oh! My Heart Is Breaking. Mary E. Tucker. CBWP-1

I sniff for hot coals. Bridal Rites. Rebecca McClanahan. MPUn

I So Liked Spring. Charlotte Mew. OxAEP-2; OxBEV; OxBTC

I, Solomon, David's son, King of Jerusalem. Henry Howard, Earl of Surrey. ChIV-1 *Fr.* Paraphrase of Part of the Book of Ecclesiates, A.

I sometimes alligators heard. Mattie J. Peterson. VerBaPo *Fr.* Old Homestead, The.

I sometimes hold it half a sin. Tennyson. CAGL; NAEL-6v2; NAWM-7v2; PeECV; TOF *Fr.* In Memoriam A. H. H.

I sometimes sleep with other girls. Cavalier Lyric. James Simmons. UV

I sometimes think that I should like. I Sometimes Think. *Unknown.* EroLit

I sometimes think that never blows so red. Omar Khayyám. CABP; TRP, *tr.* by Edward Fitzgerald *Fr.* Rubáiyát of Omar Khayyám [of Naishápúr], The.

I sought a theme and sought for it in vain. Circus Animals' Desertion, The. W. B. Yeats. FaBoMo; FaBoTw; HarvBoo; MakPoe; NAEL-5v2; NAEL-6v2; NAWM-7v2; NIP-4; NOBE; NOIV; NoAM; NoP-4; OxBTC; PAI; TFi

I sought for Peace, but could not find. Peace. Samuel Speed. SacPr

I sought instruction from my dawning years. Cure for Poetry, A. Annabella Blount. ECWP

I sought my lover at twilight. Tsangyang Gyatso. WoPoe, *tr.* by Brian Cutillo and Rick Fields *Fr.* Love-Poems of the Sixth Dalai Lama.

I sought of bishop and priest and judges. On Christians, Mercy Will Fall. *Unknown.* OBWVE, *tr.* by D. Myrddin Lloyd

I sought to hear the voice of God. Voice of God, The. Louis I. Newman. PoToHe

I sought to share. Passage, The. "Adonis" [*or* "Adunis"]. VCWP, *tr.* by Samuel Hazo

I sowed the seeds of love. Seeds of Love, The. Mrs. Fleetwood Habergham. FaBoCh; OxBoLi

I span and Eve span. Eve-Song. Mary Gilmore. CBAP; LW

I speak, and I don't want to lie. Life Story. Paul Zweig. BodElec

I speak directly. Rifle, The. Tymoteusz Karpowicz. PoSu, *tr.* by Jan Darowski

I speak for Erin. Muse of Amergin, The. *Unknown.* BIrV, *tr.* by John Montague

I speak for the world of scholarship. Happy Arabia. Tom Matthews. PNI

I speak no polite. Turf Song. Sterling Plumpp. GT

I speak now of printers and bookmen. Printers. Denis Glover. PeNZ

I speak of that great house. Beyond the Hunting Woods. Donald Justice. CoAmPo

I speak of that lady I heard last night. Lady's Complaint, The. John Heath-Stubbs. TwCP

I Speak of the City. Octavio Paz. VCWP, *tr.* by Eliot Weinberger

I speak of walls and chains; of the vials. Terms of Appointment. Arthur Rex Dugard Fairburn. PeNZ

I speak this poem now with grave and level voice. Immortal Autumn. Archibald MacLeish. MoAmPo; NAAL-2v2

I speak to my Lord though I am dust and ashes. Oaks and Squirrels. Anne Porter. ChIV-1

I speak to the unbeautiful of this bird. Peacock, The. James Merrill. OWoS

I Spend the Night in a Room by the River. Tu Fu. SuSp, *tr.* by Mark Perlberg

I spent a nicht amang the cognoscenti. I Was Fair Beat. Robert Garioch. OBCoV; OxBTC

I spent a night turning in bed. Whip, The. Robert Creeley. NeAP; PFTM-2; PoE; PoM

I spent my youth in a loony bin. Palette of Grief. Leonid Gubanov. TCRP, *tr.* by Bradley Jordan

I spent the afternoon rummaging through. Black Tulips. Martha Vertreace. IllVoic

I spent the entire day in official details. At the Desk. Theodor Storm. WoPoe, *tr.* by Robert Bly

I spent the entire night leading a blind man. Uncertain Oneiromancy. Denise Levertov. MakPoe

I Spent the Night. Dacia Maraini. CItWP, *tr.* by Cinzia Sartini Blum and Lara Trubowitz

I spied a very small brown duck. Duck-chasing. Galway Kinnell. TwCP; VGW

I spied John Mouldy in his cellar. John Mouldy. Walter De la Mare. RB

I spin through time. Planet Earth Speaks, The. Alma Villanueva. HW

I splashed water on my face. Scholar I. Seamus Deane. NOIV

I spoiled the day. Wasted Day, A. Frances Darwin Cornford. MoBrPo

I sport with you. *Unknown.* CoBCP, *tr. by* Burton Watson *Fr.* Nine Songs.

I spotted these daffs by the lake. Limerick. E. O. Parrott. PeLi

I sprang to the rollocks and Jorrocks and me. How I Brought the Good News from Aix to Ghent (or Vice Versa). R. J. Yeatman. UV

I sprang to the stirrup, and Joris, and he. Robert Browning. EBNV; FHYEP; NAEL-5v2; NAEL-6v2; OBSP; PeVV; UV

I Spread Out unto Thee My Hands. Henry Ainsworth. AH

I Spy the Three-Colored Peach Blossom. Kim Ku. WoPoe, *tr. by* Kevin O'Rourke

I staggered on through darkness. Edgar Lee Masters. APT-1 *Fr.* Spoon River Anthology.

I / stand alone. Another Moment. Sim Kombem. NAfrP

I Stand Alone. Tu Fu. CrYelRi, *tr. by* Sam Hamill

I stand alone in the cold autumn. Mao Tse-tung [*or* Mao Zedong]. WoPoe, *tr. by* David Lattimore

I stand and listen, head bowed. Self-employed. David Ignatow. NNaP

I stand and watch the rain. Rain and the Tyrants. Jules Supervielle. WoPoe, *tr. by* David Gascoyne

I stand at the field's edge. Earth Movers, The. Christopher Cokinos. UrbNat

I stand beside my window in the night. From Soul to Soul. Árpád Tóth. IQMS, *tr. by* Watson Kirkconnell

I Stand Here, Do You Understand. Olav H. Hauge. RaBo, *tr. by* Robert Bly

I stand high in the belfry tower. On the Tower. Annette von Droste-Hülshoff. WPOW, *tr. by* James Edward Tobin

I stand in full armor. Poem. Paul Klee. PFTM-1

I stand in the dark light in the dark street. Birthplace Revisited. Gregory Corso. NeAP; PoM; VGW

I stand in the hall upstairs. Closed Doors. Marie Thorson. PWR

I stand in the kitchen scrubbing. Tonight. Regina DeCormier-Shekejian. SpudSo

I stand like some country crow across the street. Romania, Romania. Gerald Stern. LCAP-2; MiVo

I stand on slenderness all fresh and fair. Cut Flower, A. Karl Shapiro. HAP; WeW-3

I stand on the mark beside the shore. Runaway Slave at Pilgrim's Point, The. Elizabeth Barrett Browning. BrRo; NALW; VWP; ViWPN

I stand to-day on this historic ground. National Cemetery, Beaufort, South Carolina, The. Josephine D. Henderson Heard. CBWP-4

I stand up. (LL) Miss Rosie. Lucille Clifton. BlSi; ESEAA; TwCP

I stand upon a hill and see. Map of the City, A. Thom Gunn. NAEL-5v2; NAEL-6v2; NoP-4; PoE

I stand with standing stones. All the Earth, All the Air. Theodore Roethke. HarvBoo

I stand within the willowing shadows of Memp-ch-ton. On Hearing the Marsh Bird's Water Cry. Duane Niatum. CDW

I star in the loam. Deadsong. Don Domanski. NOBC

I stared at the printed words. Printed Words. Liz Sohappy Bahe. CDW

I start awake at night afraid of death. Sonnet 21. Paul Goodman. VGW

I start with a straight back and two points. Peter Dale. NewEx

I started a fire with Kali's name. Āsutos Deb. SinGod, *tr. by* Rachel Fell McDermott

I started by reading the banner headline. Story of Abraham, The. Alicia Ostriker. InvLi

I Started Early, Took My Dog. Emily Dickinson. *See* By the Sea

I started picking up the stones. Apologia pro Vita Sua. A. R. Ammons. HCAP; NOBA

I started to write a song about love, then I decided, No. Difficult Music, The. Reginald Shepherd. NeAmPo

I Starve My Belly for a Sublime Purpose. Anna Swirszczynska. BLT

I stay clear. I Have No Strength for Mine. Joanne Kyger. PoM

I stayed [*or* staid] the night for shelter at a farm. Robert Frost. APT-1; NOBA; NoAM; PoE *Fr.* Two Witches.

I stayed overnight at a motel by the E3. Gallery, The. Tomas Tranströmer. PFTM-2, *tr. by* Robin Fulton

I step out into the snow, my eyes shut. Summer Again. Yves Bonnefoy. VCWP, *tr. by* Lisa Sapinkopf

I stepped from black to black. Black Power. Raymond R. Patterson. NBV

I stepped from Plank to Plank. Emily Dickinson. NOBA; NOCV; OxBSP; SAmP; TCAPo

I stifled in that room. We Were Sisters Weren't We. Katie Donovan. BiHa

I still am where I was. A fig for thee. (LL) Fig for Thee, Oh! Death, A. Edward Taylor. NAAL-2v1; NAAL-3

I Still Have Everything You Gave Me. Naomi Shihab Nye. ExTi

I still kept thinking that I was rich. Elizaveta Kuzmina-Karavayeva. TCRP

I still remember Conch-Shell Slope, west of the River Tzu. Hsieh Chin. CoBLCP *Fr.* In Grief, Lamenting for My Elder Brother Ts'ang-ch.

I still remember that first day. We got off with our splintered. Murdered Luggage. Jose Angel Figueroa. PueRic

I still remember the time at the mountain hut. Painting of Yams, A. Yün Shou-p'ing. CoBLCP, *tr. by* Jonathan Chaves

I still shall smile and go my careless way. Sonnet. Mamie A. Richardson. LW

I stink to make you bitch. Pathology of Proximity, The. Mark Bibbins. AmPoNex

I stirred wet sand and gathered myself. Seamus Heaney. NoAM *Fr.* Sweeney Redivivus.

I stole forth dimly in the dripping pause. Moon Compasses. Robert Frost. ITBLP

I stole from you, my coy Juventius honey. To Juventius. Catullus. CAGL, *tr. by* Frank O. Copley

I stole through the dungeons, while everyone slept. Alternative Endings to an Unwritten Ballad. Paul Dehn. OBCoV

I stomp about these rooms in an old overcoat. Sketch for an Aesthetic Project. Jay Wright. GT

I stood and leant upon the mast. Voyage, The. Heinrich Heine. AWP, *tr. by* John Todhunter

I stood and watched the still, mysterious Night. Night. Augusta Cooper Bristol. APN-2

I stood as one enchanted. Entangled. Mathilde Blind. VWP

I stood aside to let the cows. Man and Cows. Andrew Young. EBEV

I stood at the back of the shop, my dear. Thomas Hardy. MoBrPo *Fr.* Satires of Circumstance in Fifteen Glimpses.

I stood before it for hours in wintertime. (LL) Hill, A. Anthony Hecht. CoAP; NIL-7; NoP-4; VCAP

I stood beside a hill. February Twilight. Sara Teasdale. OBCA

I stood beside thy lowly grave. Grave of a Poetess, The. Felicia Dorothea Hemans. RWP

I stood by Honor and the Dean. Coventry Patmore. EBVV *Fr.* Angel in the House, The.

I stood by the bars at evening. By the Pasture Bars. George Sands Johnson. PWR

I stood by the unvintageable sea. Vita Nuova. Oscar Wilde. CAGL

I stood in the doorway. Spring Storm. Johanna Rayl. PasH

I Stood in the Maytime Meadows. *Unknown.* TTTS

I stood in the ruins of Dowlais. Idris Davies. AngWePo *Fr.* Gwalia Deserta.

I stood in Venice, on the Bridge of Sighs. Byron. NAEL-5v2; NAEL-6v2 *Fr.* Childe Harold's Pilgrimage.

I Stood on a Tower in the Wet. Tennyson. OxBSP

I stood on the bridge at midnight. Bridge, The. Henry Wadsworth Longfellow. APN-1; ITBLP

I stood still and was a tree amid the wood. Tree, The. Ezra Pound. HarvBoo

I Stood Tip-Toe upon a Little Hill. John Keats. "Here are sweet peas, on tiptoe for a flight." FHYEP

I stood today on a mound of clay. Created Clay. Maimee Lee Brown. PWR

I stood upon a high place. Stephen Crane. APN-2 *Fr.* Black Riders [and Other Lines], The.

I stood with three comrades in Parliament Square. Armistice Day. Charles Causley. NAEL-5v2; NAEL-6v2; NoP-4; OBWP

I stood within the empty House of Youth. Helen Waddell. MLL

I Stood within the Heart of God. William Vaughn Moody. AH *Fr.* Fire-Bringer, The.

I stoompled oud ov a dafern. Wein Geist. Charles Godfrey Leland. APN-2

I stoop to gather a seabird's feather. Feather, The. Vernon Watkins. FaBoTw

I stooped to the silent Earth and lifted a handful of her dust. Handful of Dust, A. James Oppenheim. TrJP

I stop for a short rest at the wine seller's west of the city. Leaving the City. Liu K'o-chuang. CoBCP, *tr. by* Burton Watson

I stop my boat on the pure Ssu. Mooring My Boat on the Ssu River and Watching the Moon. Wen Cheng-ming. CoBLCP, *tr. by* Jonathan Chaves

I stop somewhere waiting for you. (LL) Walt Whitman. AmFaPo; CAGL; ColAP; MoAmPo; NAAL-3; NAAL-5; NAWM-7v2; NOBA; OxBA; SAmP *Fr.* Song of Myself.

I stop to consult my diary and think how queer. Rogation Day: Portrush. James Simmons. PBCIP

I stop to listen. Arizona Zipper. HA

I stop worrying about anything. Old Man in Retirement. Muso Soseki. EaWin, *tr. by* W. S. Merwin

I stopped at her door for a drink of water. Girl by Green River, The. *Unknown.* OHMPC, *tr. by* Kenneth Rexroth

I stopped deep. African in Louisiana. Kojo Gyinaye Kyei. PBA

I stopped home at lunch because I left my cock on the bathroom sink. Trash. Linda Smukler. WiU

I stopped in the open under an apple bough. Field, The. Christopher Pilling. NLP

I stopped in Tupelo, Elvis. Van K. Brock. AllShUp

I stopped the car and stepped out onto gravel. Tracey Herd. NeBl *Fr.* Mystery of the Missing Century, The.

I stopped to pick up the bagel. Bagel, The. David Ignatow. CoAmPo; TwCP

I stopped writing poetry. Bernard Welt. BAP-01

I strayed, all alone, where the Autumn. Rose in October, A. James Whitcomb Riley. OBAL

I strayed along the strand with mussels strewn. Along the Strand. Alfred Mombert. TrJP, *tr.* by Jethro Bithell

I stretch my hand. Hand. Shinkichi Takahashi. ZenPo, *tr.* by Takashi Ikemoto and Lucien Stryk

I stretch out flat to the horizon. Before They Made Things Be Alive They Spoke. Lucario Cuevish. STP, *tr.* by Jerome Rothenberg

I stretched my hand out in front of me, into the darkness. In Darkness. Amir Gilbo'a. MHP, *tr.* by Ruth Finer Mintz

I stretched out. Brotherhood. Thomas Kinsella. HarvBoo

I strolled across. Waking, The. Theodore Roethke. TTTS

I strolled around the zoo. Nikolai Ivanovich Glazkov. TCRP

I strolled upon the Brooklyn Bridge one day. It Was All for Him. Amin Al-Rihani. GraLe

I strove with all, for all were worth my strife. Epitaph for G. B. Shaw. Max Beerbohm. FaBoEE

I strove with none for none was worth my strife. I Strove with None. Edward Morgan Forster. UV

I strove with none, for none was worth my strife. Walter Savage Landor. NOBE; NPeEn; OxBEV; TFi; TRP; UV *Fr.* Last Fruit Off an Old Tree, The.

I struck the board, and cried [*or* cry'd], No more. Collar, The. George Herbert. AWP; BASC; CABP; ClHu; EBEV; FSCP; FaBoVe; GeHe; HAP; HeIP-4; InvLi; MeLP; NAEL-5v2; NAEL-6v1; NAEL-7v1; NIL-7; NIP-4; NOBE; NOCV; NOSC; NPeEn; NoP-4; OBWVE; PBRV; PoE; PoPoPo; PoRA; SCGP; SCV; SacPr; TFi; TOF; WeW-3

I struck tomorrow square in the face. Hidesong. Aig Higo. PBMAP; TTY

I struggled to read Homer in translation. God Shed His Grace. Philip Stephens. AmPoNex

I studied in the hedge school. Herd, The. Peter Fallon. PBCIP

I study out a dark similitude. Swan, The. Theodore Roethke. VGW

I study rocks / strewn into the distance. I Study Rocks. Jeannette Armstrong. ReEnLa

I study the board like the rules of a dead language. Prince. Ann Sansom. NeBl

I study the lives on a leaf: the little. Minimal, The. Theodore Roethke. HCAP; NOBA; NoAM; RB

I Substitute for the Dead Lecturer. Imamu Amiri Baraka. PoE

I subtract the days one by one, seal them. Before Our Encounter. Margherita Guidacci. CItWP, *tr.* by Cinzia Sartini Blum and Lara Trubowitz

I succumbed to all the visions. Nicole Brossard. PFTM-2, *tr.* by Barbara Godard *Fr.* Barbizon, The.

I Suck. Chrystos. WiU

I Suddenly. George Buchanan. PNI

I suddenly have come to love. I Suddenly. George Buchanan. PNI

I suggested the opera because he said he had never been. Ditches. Karen Kipp. BodElec

I summon to the winding ancient stair. Dialogue of Self and Soul, A. W. B. Yeats. FaBoMo; MoBrPo; NAEL-5v2; NAEL-6v2; NoAM; PoE

I summoned my best skill, and toiled, intent. William Wordsworth. NAEL-6v2 *Fr.* Prelude, The; Growth of a Poet's Mind [1850 vers.].

I suppose France this morning is as white as here. Behind the Line. Ivor Gurney. HarvBoo

I suppose I could try if I chose. Limerick. "E. F. C." PeLi

I suppose it hasn't been easy living with me either. Poem in Praise of My Husband (Taos). Diane Di Prima. BB

I suppose it's myself that you're making allusion to. At the "Atlantic" Dinner, December 15, 1874. Oliver Wendell Holmes. OBCoV

I suppose the time will come. Emily Dickinson. FaBoVe

I suppose you just gape and let your gaspings. Ted Hughes. HAP *Fr.* Skylarks.

I surprise girlhood. I Want Aretha to Set This to Music. Sherley Anne Williams. NAAAL

I surprise the women. In the Locker Room. Madeline DeFrees. ExTi

I surrender to *Roget's Pocket Thesaurus*. Written in Blood. Tiffany Midge. ReEnLa

I survived. (LL) Survivor, The. Tadeusz Rózewicz. HP; PoSu, *tr.* by Adam Czerniawski

I suspect he knew that trunks are metaphors. Houdini. Eli W. Mandel. NIP-4; NOBC

I swam the Huron of love, and am not ashamed. Huron, The. Ruth Herschberger. WPE

I swan! it's pleasant now we've beaten. Hospital Soliloquy, A. Rose Terry Cooke. SWaP

I Swear. Bella [*or* Izabella] Akhatovna Akhmadulina. TCRP, *tr.* by Albert C. Todd

I swear by desire. Meleager. PGA

I swear I ain't done what Richard. Say Hello to John. Sherley Anne Williams. BlSi

I sweep the sidewalk, over and over again, in the summer afternoons. Eve in Eden. Manuela Fingueret. MirDau, *tr.* by Roberta Gordenstein

I sweep the street and lift me hat. Old Man at the Crossing, The. Leonard Alfred George Strong. OBMV

I swing the spirit like a child. Imploration for Clear Weather. *Unknown.* APN-2, *tr.* by W. J. Hoffman

I swing / the thin tin. Compass. Elizabeth Alexander. NAPBL

I swore I would go back. O Lyric Love. Winfield Townley Scott. VGW

I swore, love, by your / dominion, to rest. Maccius. GrAn

I swore to you, son of Kronos, never. Strato [*or* Straton]. GrAn

I syng of a mayden that is makeles. I Sing of a Maiden. *Unknown.* ChIV-2; EBEV; FaBoCh; InPK-6; MiEL; NAEL-5v1; NOBE; NOCV; PoE; SCGP; SCV; TFi; TOF

I take as my theme "The Independent Woman." Carolyn Kizer. FFC; VCAP *Fr.* Pro Femina.

I take down the old guitar from the wall. Old Guitar, The. John Hollander. DiPo

I take heart, breaking in. Mud Dauber Wasp, The. Peter Kane Dufault. NoP-4

I take him outside. Speaking. Simon J. Ortiz. NIL-7

I take horse before cockcrow. Visit to the Monastery of Good Omen. Lu Chi. OHMPC, *tr.* by Kenneth Rexroth

I take leave. Rairai. JDP, *tr.* by Yoel Hoffmann

I take my bike. Oregon Landscape with Lost Lover. Olga Broumas. GifTon

I take my endless way. (LL) From Far, from Eve and Morning. A. E. Housman. HAP; MoBrPo; NoP-4

I take my pen in hand. Letter, The. Elizabeth Riddell. LW; NOBAu

I take my son outside. What I Tell Him. Simon J. Ortiz. CDW; ChAP

I take my stand by the Ulster names. Ulster Names. John Hewitt. BiHa

I take my wine jug out among flowers. Drinking Alone with the Moon. Li Po. CrYelRi, *tr.* by Sam Hamill

I take off my shirt, I show you. Taking Off My Clothes. Carolyn Forché. NIL-7; NoAM

I take on / her legacy. Jacqueline Goldberg. MirDau, *tr.* by Joanne Friedman *Fr.* Luba.

I take the clue divine. (LL) Emily Dickinson. APN-2; NAAL-2v1; NAAL-3

I take the pressure of thine hand. (LL) Tennyson. FHYEP; NAEL-6v2; SCV *Fr.* In Memoriam A. H. H.

I take the royal carriage for an evening outing. Lotus Pond, The. Ts'ao P'i. SuSp, *tr.* by Ronald C. Miao

I take the snap from center, fake to the right, fade back. Football. Louis Jenkins. MoASP; RaBo

I take the twist-about, empty street. Rendezvous, The. Bernard Spencer. GTBS-P

I Take Thee Life. Margot Ruddock. OBMV

I take their hands. They. Ronald Stuart Thomas. OxBTC

I Take Two of These Tablets Tonight and in the Morning Go on Living. Denise Riley. Oth *Fr.* Seven Strangely Exciting Lies.

I take up my belly and go. Wanting To. Jan G. Elburg. TuT, *tr.* by Peter Van de Kamp

I take you by the hand. Your eyes. Goodbye to Brigid / An Agnus Dei. Padraic Fiacc. CIP-2

I take you looking at the statue. Statue, The. Kenneth Allott. SPE

I take you with me. Theatre. Remco Campert. TuT, *tr.* by Theo Dorgan

I TAKE your poems in my hand and read them beside the candle;. On Board Ship: Reading Yüan Chên's Poems. Po Chü-i. ChiP, *tr.* by Arthur Waley

I takes and [I] paints. Poem by a Perfectly Furious Academician. Shirley Brooks. NOBVV; PeLV

I takes up for my colored men. Generation Gap, The. Ruby C. Saunders. BlSi

I Talk to My Body. Anna Swirszczynska. BLT

I talk to your photograph each day. If I Had a Talking Picture of You. Ray Henderson. ReLy

I talked one midnight with the jolly ghost. All in a Garden Green. William Ernest Henley. OBMV

I talked to a farmer one day in Iowa. Iowa Farmer. Margaret Walker Alexander. GT

I talked to old Lem. Old Lem. Sterling Allen Brown. APT-2; BPo; TTY

I Taste a Liquor Never Brewed. Emily Dickinson. APN-2; HeIP-4; ITBLP; MoAmPo; NAAL-2v1; NAAL-3; NOBA; NoAM; OxBA; SoSe-8; TAP; TCAPo; TFi; WPE

I taught myself poetry for a few pennies. Coppers. Boris Abramovich Slutsky [*or* Slutskii]. TCRusP, *tr.* by Daniel Weissbort

I taught myself to live simply and wisely. Anna Andreyevna Akhmatova. ItWoWo, *tr.* by Richard McKane

I teach German literature, and this is how it goes. Teaching German Literature. Vincent Buckley. OBCoV

I teach how we cheat the young. 4 Part Geometry Lesson, A. Robin Blaser. NeAP

I tear at my belly. U Tam'si Tchicaya. PBMAP   *Fr.* Le Ventre (1964).

I tell a wanderer's tale, the same. Encounter at St. Martin's. Ken Smith. OPOU

I tell her she has outlived her usefulness. Altar. Marilyn Chin. PoPoPo

I tell it the way it is. Letters from the Poet Who Sleeps in a Chair. Nicanor Parra. AF, *tr.* by Miller Williams

I tell my mother my girlfriend is a good Catholic girl—. Votive Candles. Nick Carbó. NeAmPo

I tell my secret? No indeed, not I. Winter: My Secret. Christina Georgina Rossetti. BrRo; NAEL-5v2; NAEL-6v2; NOBVV; NPeEn; VWP

I tell myself, I'm through with you. Foolin' Myself. Jack Lawrence. ReLy

I Tell of Another Young Death. César Tiempo. TrJP, *tr.* by Donald Devenish Walsh

I tell thee, Dick, where I have been. Sir John Suckling. BASC; BeJo; CaPo; EBEV; EBNV; NAEL-7v1; NoP-4

I tell words that talk in trees, this hill. Pot Shot. Padraic Fallon. CIP-2

I tell ye, Sue, it ain't no use! Goin' Back T'morrer. Hamlin Garland. OBAL

I tell yeh whut! The chankin' Horses Chawin' Hay. Hamlin Garland. OBAL

I tell you, hopeless grief is passionless. Grief. Elizabeth Barrett Browning. HeIP-4; InPK-6; NALW; NOBVV; NPeEn; OBEV; VWP; WPE

I tell you how dat hypocrite do. That Hypocrite. *Unknown.* BPo

I tell you I am angry. Friendship, The. Toi Derricotte. PBCAP

I tell you it was a hard punch to my brain. Edoardo Sanguineti. ItPo, *tr.* by Gayle Ridinger   *Fr.* Reisebilder.

I tell you that I see her still. I Only Am Escaped Alone to Tell Thee. Howard Nemerov. CoAP; HeIP-4; NoAM

I tell you this across the blackened vine. (LL) Edna St. Vincent Millay. HeIP-4; VGW

I tell you what I dreamed last night. Christina Georgina Rossetti. PeVV   *Fr.* Convent Threshold, The.

I tell you (you needn't believe it). Parrhasios. GrAn

I terminated with the color red. Scarlet Skirt. Víctor Hernández Cruz. TouFir

I test my bath before I sit. Samson Agonistes. Ogden Nash. APT-2; OBCoV

I tethered my horse beside the plum blossoms. From Chekiang I Went to Hsin-an and Climbed Even-with-the-Clouds Mountain. . Hsü Wei. CoBLCP, *tr.* by Jonathan Chaves

I' th' isle of Britain, long since famous grown. Satire on Charles II, A. John Wilmot, 2d Earl of Rochester. NOSC; PeLV

I thank all who have loved me in their hearts. Elizabeth Barrett Browning. CenSon   *Fr.* Sonnets from the Portuguese.

I Thank God I'm Free at Las'   *Unknown.* BPo; TAP

(O free at last.) (LL) APN-2

I Thank Life for So Many Gifts. Violeta Parra. TANSG, *tr.* by Bonnie Shepard

I thank the, Lord so dere, that wold vowchsayf. *Unknown.* PoE   *Fr.* Noah.

I thank thee and I praise thee, O thou radiant grace. Thanksgiving. "Yehoash." TrJP, *tr.* by Isidore Goldstick

I thank thee, Father, that the night is near. Night. Jones Very. InvLi

I thank you, dear blessed mother. Mother's Birthday. Lydia Wagenlander. PWR

I thank you for the many steps. Dear Mother. Ebba M. Leaf. PWR

I thank You God for most this amazing. I Thank You God. E. E. Cummings. TAP; TrCP

I thank you, Lord, for having made me Black, I Thank You, Lord. Bernard Dadié. NegPo, *tr.* by Ellen Conroy Kennedy

I that erstwhile the world's sweet air did draw. George Wither. NOSC   *Fr.* Shephe[a]rd's Hunting, The.

I that have been a lover, and could show it. Sonnet to the Noble Lady, the Lady Mary Wroth, A. Ben Jonson. BeJo; NAEL-7v1; NoP-4

I that in heill wes [*or* health was] and gladnes[s] [*or* gladiness]. Lament for the Makaris. William Dunbar. EBEV; HAP; MakPoe; NePenScot; OxBS

I that lived ever about you. English Girl. *Unknown.* OBMV, *tr.* by E. Powys Mathers

I, the bosun's mate, John Reading. Death of the Bosun's Mate. Louis Johnson. PeNZ

I, the genius Severyanin. Epilogue. "Igor Severyanin [*or* Severianin]." TCRP, *tr.* by Bernard Meares

I' the how-dumb-deid o' the cauld hairst nicht. Eemis-Stane, The. Hugh MacDiarmid. NAEL-5v2; NAEL-6v2; NPeEn; NePenScot

I, the marble statue with fiery head, while. Marble Beads. Delmira Agustini. TANSG, *tr.* by Mark McCaffrey

I, the Neighbor Mr. Uskovich, Watch Every Morning Kenji Takezo Hold His Breath. Rick Noguchi. NeAmPo

I, the old woman of Beare. Old Woman of Beare Regrets Lost Youth, The. *Unknown.* OBMV, *tr.* by Frank O'Connor

I, the poet William Yeats. To Be Carved on a Stone at Thoor Ballylee. W. B. Yeats. FaBoEE; NoAM; NoP-4

I, the priest of Rhea, long-haired. Erucius [*or* Erycius] of Cyzicus. GrAn

I the Roses Love in the Gardens of Adonis. Fernando Pessoa. WoPoe, *tr.* by Edwin Honig

I, the Survivor. Bertolt Brecht. HP; PoSu

I, therefore, will begin. Soul of the age! Ben Jonson. NOBE   *Fr.* To the Memory of My Beloved, the Author Mr [*or* Master] William Shakespeare [And What He Hath Left Us].

I thi hovie an thi howd o sleep. Socialist Manifesto for East Balgillo, The. W. N. Herbert. NePenScot

I Think. James Schuyler. TTTS

I think a man's seventy years are few! Seventy Years Are Few. Lu Chih. WoPoe, *tr.* by Bruce Carpenter

I think a time will come when you will understand. For My Father. Paul Potts. FaBoTw

I think about you & it's like having spirits come down on me. Yuwaku. STP

I think all this is somewhere in myself. Room, The. W. S. Merwin. NOBA

I think Archie Shepp played hambone hambone where you been in our. Suite Repose. Carl Hancock Rux. SpirFl

I think at a distance I hear a loud voice. Missionary, The. Mrs. Henry Linden. CBWP-4

I Think Continually of Those Who Were Truly Failures. Joseph Awad. GraLe

I Think Continually of Those Who Were Truly Great. Stephen Spender. HAP; HarvBoo; HeIP-4; MoBrPo; NOBE; NoP-4; OxBTC; PAI; PoRA; RaBo; TFi

(Truly Great, The.) CABP

I think he sits at that strange table. At It. Ronald Stuart Thomas. OxBC

I think he was behind me. Behind Me. Martha Rhodes. ExTi

I think I am becoming. Interior Monologue 666. Tom Marshall. NOBC

I think I came close to being insane a few months ago. Poem. C. K. Williams. BodElec

I think I could turn and live with animals, they are so placid and self-contained. Walt Whitman. HAP; NAWM-7v2; SAmP; WeW-3   *Fr.* Song of Myself.

I think I grow tensions. Flower, The. Robert Creeley. PAI; PmAP

I think I have no other home than this. Old Memories of Earth. Ronald Allison Kells Mason. PeNZ

I think I heard the belle. Old Lady's Lament for Her Youth, The. François Villon. BoLoP, *tr.* by Robert Lowell

I Think I Know No Finer Things than Dogs. Hally Carrington Brent. ITBLP

I think I'll get a paper. Nerves. "Sagittarius." OxBTC

I think I must have lived. Fox, The. Philip Levine. SoSe-8

I think I see her sitting bowed and black. Oriflamme. Jessie Redmond Fauset. BlSi

I think I see my father's sister stand. Elizabeth Barrett Browning. NALW   *Fr.* Aurora Leigh.

I think I should have loved you presently. Edna St. Vincent Millay. APT-1; NAAL-2v2; NAAL-5

I think I smell smoke. Il Janitoro. George Ade. OBAL

I think I was enchanted. Emily Dickinson. APN-2; NALW

I think I was three. Once upon a Seesaw with Charlie Chan. Cyn Zarco. ReBoTo

I think I will not hang myself to-day. (LL) Ballade of Suicide, A. Gilbert Keith Chesterton. NBLV; OBCoV

I think I wrote a poem today but I don't know well. Noon Point. Clark Coolidge. PmAP

I think if you had loved me when I wanted. Success. Rupert Brooke. OxBTC

I think in fours. Thought. Fazil Hüsnü Daglarca. CRP

I think it better that in times like these. On Being Asked for a War Poem. W. B. Yeats. FaBoWar; NIP-4; OBWP; OxAEP-2; PoWW

I think it happened. Anyway. Barbara Jagger. Prnts

I think it is in Virginia, that place. Low Fields and Light. W.S. Merwin. CoAmPo; LCAP-2

I think it mercy if thou wilt forget. (LL) John Donne. BASC; EBEV; FaBoVe; NAEL-5v1; NAEL-6v1; NAEL-7v1; NoP-4; OxAEP-1; SCGP; Son; UnPo   *Fr.* Holy Sonnets.

I think it must be lonely to be God. Gwendolyn Brooks. InvLi; NAAAL   *Fr.* Street in Bronzeville, A.

I Think It Rains. Wole Soyinka. AF

I think it's good the squirrel lives with us. Red Squirrel. Bruce Weigl. BodElec

I think it was Spring—but not certain I am. Epicurean Reminiscences of a Sentimentalist. Thomas Hood. PeLV

I think mice. (Mice). Rose Fyleman. NTCP

I think my friend's mother. Kali. Leslie Simon. HW

I think naught great: I am the highest thing of all. "Angelus Silesius." GePo, *tr. by* George C. Schoolfield *Fr.* Cherubical Wanderer, The.

I think no woman of such skill. Sappho. SaLy, *tr. by* Diane Rayor

I think not on the state, nor am concerned. Upon the Double Murther of King Charles I. Katherine Philips. BASC; NAEL-7v1

I think of a flower that no eye has ever seen. Beauty. Laurence Binyon. MoBrPo

I think of a tiger. The half-light enhances. Other Tiger, The. Jorge Luis Borges. PoetW, *tr. by* Alastair Reid

I think of all the galloping. Johnny's Team. Eugene Field. PWR

I think of all the places I've been. *Unknown.* CoBCP

I think of all the toughs through history. Lines for a Book. Thom Gunn. CABP

I think of all the treasures of the earth. Rachel. Joy Williams. IBA

I think of corner shots, the ball. Day and Night Handball. Stephen Dunn. MoASP

I think of him / Who lives south of the big sea. *Unknown.* BoWoP

I Think of Housman Who Said the Poem Is a Morbid Secretion, like a Pearl. Judith Kroll. UnPo

I think of it with wonder now. Glass, The. Sharon Olds. NIL-7; NIP-4

I think of my wife, and I think of Lot. Marriage Couplet. William Cole. OBAL

I think of Oedipus, old, led by a boy. (LL) Terminal. Thom Gunn. CAGL; OxBEV

I think of our anonymous boys. Nocturnal Visits. Claribel Alegría. TANSG; VCWP, *tr. by* Darwin Flakoll

I think of that meadow off down in Coyne's. Coyne's. John Ennis. PBCIP

I think of the Celts as rather a whining lady. Celts, The. Stevie Smith. NoP-4

I think of the days. Fujiwara no Atsutada. OHPJ

I think of the Martian landscape late delivered. Martian Landscape. Abbie Huston Evans. APT-1

I think of the ones like the poet John Haines. Working in Darkness. Thomas McGrath. BodElec

I think of the razor-sharp knife. Talking of Sharp Things. Frank Mkalawile Chipasula. HBAPE

I think of the sea changing and changing. Marina. O. B. Hardison, Jr. AiP; CRP

I think of thee!—My thoughts do twine and bud. Elizabeth Barrett Browning. CenSon *Fr.* Sonnets from the Portuguese.

I think of things like the shadow of a branch. Shadow of a Branch, The. Edith Marcombe Shiffert. WPE

I think of things we used to do. It's Been So Long. Walter Donaldson. ReLy

I think of those mornings before dawn. I Think of Those Mornings. Morton Marcus. GeoHom

I think of when she comes. Shen Yüeh. CoBCP *Fr.* Six Poems on Remembering.

I think of when she sits. Wang Seng-ta. CoBCP

I think of when she sleeps. Wang Seng-ta. CoBCP

I Think of You as of a Good Life-boat. Emily Hickey. PoBW

I think of you with nothing on. (LL) Celia Celia. Adrian Mitchell. FaBoEE; OPOU

I think, old bone, the world's not with us much. To William Wordsworth from Virginia. Julia Randall. WPE

I think on the whole I would rather read. Frank O'Hara Five, Geoffrey Chaucer Nil. Geoff Hattersley. NeBl

I think once more he seems to die. (LL) Tennyson. EBVV; FHYEP *Fr.* In Memoriam A. H. H.

I Think Over Again My Small Adventures. *Unknown.* WoPoe

I think she sleeps: it must be sleep, when low. George Meredith. NAEL-5v2; NAEL-6v2 *Fr.* Modern Love.

I Think Sometimes. Michael Hartnett. CIP-2

I think sometimes about. Friedrich von Hausen. GePo

I think 'Sorry Missus' was what he said. (LL) Wounds. Michael Longley. ModIr; NPeEn; PBCIP; PNI

I think that God is proud of those who bear. I Think That God is Proud. Grace Noll Crowell. PoToHe

I think that I live in a street. For the Record. George Jonas. MoCV

I think that I shall never read. Poems. Thomas M. [*or* "Tom"] Disch. UV

I Think That I Shall Never See. Jim Heynen. UrbNat

I think that I shall never see. Song of the Open Road. Ogden Nash. APT-2; OBAL

I think that I shall never see / A poem. Trees. Joyce Kilmer. APT-1; BRP; ChAP; ITBLP; TCAPo; UV

I think that look of Christ might seem to say. Meaning of the Look, The. Elizabeth Barrett Browning. SacPr; TrCP

I think that Sadness is an idiot born. Sadness. Mary Elizabeth Coleridge. ViWPN

I think that the Root of the Wind is Water. Emily Dickinson. RB

I think the dead are tender. Shall we kiss?—. She. Theodore Roethke. BoLoP; NIL-7

I think the Hemlock likes to stand. Emily Dickinson. NCAP

I think the loathed minutes one by one. Moments. Ivor Gurney. OxBSP

I think the thing you call Renown. Winthrop Mackworth Praed. OBSV *Fr.* Chaunt of the Brazen Head, The.

I think the train is headed this way. Airports of the World. Eugene Richie. KGB

I think there are most tigers in the wood. (LL) Ceremony. Richard Wilbur. CoAP; NAAL-2v2; NAAL-5; NoAM

I think therefore I am not. Cogito Ergo. Jerzy Ficowski. PoSu, *tr. by* Frank J. Corliss, Jr. and Grazyna Sandel

I think these days of the wind in your hair. Savage Memories. Yehuda Amichai [*or* Amikhai]. FIT, *tr. by* Robert Friend

I think they give us uniforms. Waitresses. Ranice Henderson Crosby. WWork

I think this house's mouth is full of dirt. Independence Day, 1956: A Fairy Tale. James Galvin. PoPoPo

I think this is something you should get clear. *Unknown.* GrAn

I think this night is cold for Hugh; the heaviness of its downpour is a cause. On Maguire's Winter Campaign. Eochaidh Ó Heóghusa. PBRV

"I think," thought Sam Butler. English Liberal. Geoffrey Taylor. FaBoEE

I think to Live—may be a Bliss. Emily Dickinson. SWaP

I think to make love to a nurse would be perfect. Angel. Andrew Elliott. PNI

I think to say this / wrongly. (LL) Whip, The. Robert Creeley. NeAP; PFTM-2; PoE; PoM

I think too often of funeral ceremonies. Night in the Shape of a Bison. Joyce Mansour. SurWo, *tr. by* Mary Beach

I think true love is never blind. True Love. Phoebe Cary. PoToHe

I think very well of Susan but I do not know her name. Gertrude Stein. NoP-4

I think you are ready. (LL) Tract. William Carlos Williams. MoAmPo; NOBA; NoAM; PAI; SAmP; TAP; TwCP; VGW

I think you would like this seaside town—it makes me dream of whales. Anchorage, The. Mark Wunderlich. NeAmPo

I thirst, but not as once I did. William Cowper. TrCP *Fr.* Olney Hymns.

I thirst for God, to Him my soul aspires. Living God, The. Abraham Ibn Ezra. TrJP, *tr. by* Alice Lucas

I thirst for violins, as drunkards thirst. Ideal and Reality. Joseph Campbell. BIrV

I thirst for water; wine is my need no longer. Uri Zvi Greenberg. FIT, *tr. by* Robert Friend

I though from condemnation free. Ralph Erskine. SacPr *Fr.* Believer's Riddle, The.

I Thought About You. Johnny Mercer. ReLy

I thought all your walled cities. Tumbling Dice. Rachel Loden. SwNoth

I thought, and took a street-car back to Harvard Square. (LL) I Walked over the Grave of Henry James. Richard Eberhart. APT-2; VGW

I thought, as I wiped my eyes on the corner of my apron. Ancient Gesture, An. Edna St. Vincent Millay. NALW; NIL-7

I thought he was bankrupt. Max Jacob. PFTM-1 *Fr.* Cock and the Pearl, The.

I thought he was dumb. Tortoise Shout. D. H. Lawrence. NAEL-5v2; NAEL-6v2; PFTM-1

I thought I'd end up a Hippie American Gothic. No, No Nostalgia! Stephanie Brown. BodElec

I thought I saw an angel flying low. Nocturne at Bethesda. Arna Bontemps. ChIV-2; NAAAL

I thought I wanted to wear. My Tattoo. Mark Doty. WiU

I thought I was growing wings. Seeing for a Moment. Denise Levertov. VCAP

I thought I was so tough. Tamer and Hawk. Thom Gunn. FaBoTw; HarvBoo

I thought if only I could marry. Unfair to Women. *Unknown.* OBWVE, *tr. by* Gwyn Jones

I thought it made me look more "working class." Tony Harrison. NAEL-6v2 *Fr.* School of Eloquence, The.

I thought it rained last night yet it's sunny this morning. Staying Overnight at the Temple of the Holy Vulture. Yang Wan-li. SuSp, *tr. by* Sherwin S. S. Fu

I Thought It Was Harry. William Bronk. APSN

I thought it was spring—lazy sun, soft breeze. To the Tune: Bodhisattva's Headdress. Li Ch'ing-chao. CrYelRi, *tr. by* Sam Hamill

I thought it would last my time. Going, Going. Philip Larkin. NoAM; OxAEP-2

I thought love's game was over. Taking a Chance on Love. Ted Fetter. ReLy

I thought my all was given before.   Wretten by Me at the Death of My 4th Sonne and 5th Child Perigrene Payler.   Mary Carey.   EMWP

I thought of eden.   Civilization Aha.   Sipho Sepamla.   PBMAP

I thought of leaving her for a day.   Second Thoughts.   "Michael Field."   LW; ViWPN

I thought of thee—I thought of thee.   Confessional, The.   Nathaniel Parker Willis.   APN-1

I thought of Thee, my partner and my guide.   William Wordsworth.   CenSon   *Fr.* River Duddon [A Series of Sonnets], The.

I thought of Troy, what we had built her for. (LL)   Aeneas at Washington.   Allen Tate.   APT-2; FuPo; NOBA; NoAM; OxBA

I thought once how Theocritus had sung.   Elizabeth Barrett Browning.   BWW; CenSon; EBVV; NOBE; NoP-4; OBEV; OxAEP-2; PoPoPo; WPE   *Fr.* Sonnets from the Portuguese.

I thought Silver must have snaked logs.   Silver.   A. R. Ammons.   NoP-4

I thought so once; but now I know it. (LL)   My Own Epitaph.   John Gay.   FaBoEE; NIL-7; NIP-4; NOEC; NPeEn; OxBEV; PeLV

I thought someone had said Olmsted brought them.   Hollywood Finch, The.   A. V. Christie.   NAPBL

I thought that I was ravished to a height.   Unum est Necessarium.   Agnes Mary Frances Robinson.   VWP

I thought that Love had been a boy.   *Unknown.*   EnLoPo

I thought that you were an anchor in the drift of the world.   World, The.   William Bronk.   APSN

I thought the night without a sound was falling.   William Force Stead.   OBMV   *Fr.* Uriel.

I thought the war was.   In the Casbah.   Salma Khadra Jayyusi.   PoArWo, *tr. by* Charles Doria

I thought thee wondrous when thy soul portrayed.   To Charlotte Cushman.   Eliza Cook.   VWP

I Thought There Were Limits.   Douglas G. Jones.   MoCV

I thought to be for ever separate.   Dante Alighieri.   EaItPo, *tr. by* Dante Gabriel Rossetti

I thought to view the comeliness.   József Gvadányi.   IQMS, *tr. by* Watson Kirkconnell   *Fr.* Village Notary's Journey to Buda, A.

I thought when he hadn't been there for two or three days—.   In the Chung Mode, to the Tune of "P'u T'ien Lo."   *Unknown.*   ColAnChi, *tr. by* Wayne Schlepp

I thought you always knew it well.   One Way of Looking at It.   Arthur Joseph Munby.   NOBVV

'I thought you loved me.'   'No, it was only /fun.' .   In the Orchard.   Muriel Stuart.   EBNV; OxBTC

I thought you were good.   Divorce Song.   *Unknown.*   STP, *tr. by* Carl Cary

I thought you were without genitals, that nothing cracked you open and made you insatiable.   For Sister Sue Ellen and Her Special Messenger.   Toi Derricotte.   ExTi

I threw the inside of my gizzard out, splashing.   Zimmer Drunk and Alone, Dreaming of Old Football Games.   Paul Zimmer.   PBCAP

I throw the line in from this little island.   Lake of the Ten Thousand Mountains, The.   Meng Hao Jan.   EaWin, *tr. by* W. S. Merwin

I thumped on you the best I could.   W. D. Snodgrass.   NoAM   *Fr.* Heart's Needle.

I, thy King, so say! (LL)   Before the Feast of Shushan.   Anne Spencer.   BlSi; NAAAL

I tie eight sticks together.   Cabato.   Ray Gonzalez.   TouFir

I tink I hear my brudder say.   Stars Begin to Fall.   *Unknown.*   SacPr

I, to make myself laugh louder and longer.   Velemir [*or* Viktor Vladimirovich] Khlebnikov.   TCRP   *Fr.* War in a Mousetrap.

I To my Brothers.   Judith Wright.   BMAP   *Fr.* For a Pastoral Family.

I to the hills lift up mine eyes.   Bible, *O.T.*   OBCA   *Fr.* Bay Psalm Book, The.

I to the Hills Will Lift Mine Eyes.   Francis Rous.   AH

I to the Lord from My Distress.   *Unknown.*   AH

I told everyone / your name was Arthur.   Arturo.   Maria Gillan.   UnSA

I told her: the sidewalks are muddy.   Konstantin Konstantinovich Sluchevsky [*or* Sluchevskii].   TCRP

I told my love I told my love.   William Blake.   OxBEV

I told the Sun that I was glad.   Sun, The.   John Drinkwater.   NTCP

I, Too.   Langston Hughes.   APT-2; HCAP; HarvBoo; HeIP-4; MakPoe; NAAAL; NAAL-5; NOxBChV; PoPoPo; SSLK

I Too am changed—I scarce know why.   Ten Years Ago.   Alaric Alexander Watts.   TreFP

I too am waiting.   Pablo.   Dieter Weslowski.   InvLad

I too beneath your moon, almighty Sex.   Edna St. Vincent Millay.   APT-1; NAAL-2v2; NAAL-5; NALW

I, too, bless the cradle that rocked me.   To János Arany in Answer to His Poem "Cosmopolitan Poetry."   Gyula Reviczky.   IQMS, *tr. by* Madeline Mason

I too could give my heart to history.   History.   Carl Dennis.   BAP-97

I, too, dislike it: there are things that are important beyond all this fiddle.   Poetry.   Marianne Craig Moore.   APT-1; AmFaPo; BoWoP; ColAP; FaBoWP; HAP; HeIP-4; MoAmPo; NAAL-2v2; NAAL-5; NALW; NIP-4; NOBA; NoAM; NoP-4; OxBA; PAI; PoE; PoPoPo; TAP; TCAPo; TFi; UnPo

I, too, have been a Wanderer; but, alas!   William Wordsworth.   OxAEP-2   *Fr.* Prelude, The; Growth of a Poet's Mind [1805 vers.].

I too have been in love, and my sleepless.   Boris Leonidovich Pasternak.   TCRP   *Fr.* Poem, A.

I too have encompassed a lot: a mother thrice—.   Elizaveta Kuzmina-Karavayeva.   TCRP   *Fr.* Whit Monday.

I, too, have faked the glamor of gray towers.   Disloyal Lines to an Alumnus.   Edmund Wilson.   OBCoV

I, too, saw God through mud.   Apologia Pro Poemate Meo.   Wilfred Owen.   MoBrPo; NAEL-5v2; NAEL-6v2; PeFWW

I, too, want to be.   Self-Portrait.   Milán Füst.   IQMS, *tr. by* Paul Tabori

I too wanted love pure and simple. (LL)   Each Day.   David Ignatow.   BodElec; NNaP

I, too, was born for happiness.   Philosophy of Life.   Dániel Berzsenyi.   IQMS, *tr. by* Watson Kirkconnell

I too was born out of a lion's mouth.   Let Heroes Account to Love.   Alan Dugan.   NoAM

I took a piece of the rare cloth of Ch'i.   Present from the Emperor's New Concubine, A.   Pan Chieh-yû.   BoWoP; OHMPC; WoPoe, *tr. by* Kenneth Rexroth

I took a shortcut through blood.   Back in the World.   Ai.   BAP-97

I took a walk on the railroad track.   Walk, A.   Raymond Carver.   GM

I took each word he said as gospel truth.   Can't We Be Friends?   Paul James.   ReLy

I took for emblem the upland moors and the rocky.   Llanafan Unrevisited.   T. Harri Jones.   AngWePo

I took her dainty eyes, as well.   Villanelle of His Lady's Treasures.   Ernest Christopher Dowson.   MakPoe

I took him by the arm and said.   F. Mullen.   UV

I took love home with me.   Act #2.   John Weiners.   BB

I took money and bought flowering trees.   Planting Flowers on the Eastern Embankment.   Po Chü-i.   OBGa, *tr. by* Arthur Waley

I took my cat apart.   Secret in the Cat, The.   May Swenson.   PAI

I took my cousin to Prettyboy Dam.   Poems for My Cousin.   Josephine Jacobsen.   APT-2

I took my girl to a fancy ball.   I Had But Fifty Cents.   *Unknown.*   NBLV; WHSW

I took my heart in my hand.   Twice.   Christina Georgina Rossetti.   NOBE; OBEV; TOF; TrCP; VWP

I took my life and threw it on the skip.   Skip, The.   James Fenton.   HarvBoo

I took my oath I would inquire.   Inquest, The.   William Henry Davies.   AngWePo; GTBS-P; NOBE; OxBTC; RB

I took my Power in my Hand.   Emily Dickinson.   ChIV-1; SAmP

I took one Draught of Life.   Emily Dickinson.   APN-2

I took the road from Brighton-town.   Search.   Eleanor Slater.   YaYoPo

I took the scroll: I could not brook.   Lines Written Under a Picture of a Girl Burning a Love-Letter.   Letitia [*or* Laetitia] Elizabeth Landon.   NOBRP

I took the thought.   Carillonneur.   Ricardo M. de Ungria.   ReBoTo

I took up the burden of life anew.   To My Mother.   Mary Weston Fordham.   CBWP-2

I took wild honey from the plants.   Distribution of Poetry.   Jorge de Lima.   PFTM-1

I tossed my friend a wreath of roses, wet.   Gifts.   Mary Elizabeth Coleridge.   VWP

I touch nothing but the heart of things I hold the thread. (LL)   Vigilance.   André Breton.   NAWM-7v2; SurPaPo, *tr. by* Jean-Pierre Cauvin and Mary Ann Caws

I touch you in the night, whose gift was you.   Science of the Night, The.   Stanley Kunitz.   APT-2; ColAP; MoAmPo; TwCP

I touch your hand.   Younger Than Springtime.   Richard Rodgers.   ReLy

I touched the flesh with my eyes.   Fish.   Joe Rosenblatt.   NOBC

I touched up sexy Hermione.   Asclepiades.   GrAn

I—Towards a Definition.   Alice Notley.   ExTi

I towered far, and lo! I stood within.   God-Forgotten.   Thomas Hardy.   InvLi

I train my train into this city of mud and brick and collide.   This Sun.   John Rybicki.   AmPoNex

I trained me a falcon, for more than a year.   *Unknown.*   GePo

I tramped out hundreds of miles in the war.   Ballad of the Shot Heart.   Nikolai Vasil'evich Panchenko.   TCRP, *tr. by* Daniel Weissbort

I Travel Day and Night.   Su Tung-p'o (Su Shih).   CoBCP, *tr. by* Burton Watson

I travel far in a little boat.   Traveling by Boat at Shun-ch'ang.   Hsü Chung-hsing.   CoBLCP, *tr. by* Jonathan Chaves

I travel your body as I would travel the world.   Octavio Paz.   BLPSL, *tr. by* Rene de Costa, Rigas Kappatos and Eleni Paidoussi   *Fr.* Sunstone.

I traveled [*or* travell'd] among unknown men.   William Wordsworth.   AWP; GTBS-P; NAEL-6v2   *Fr.* Lucy.

I traveled to the ocean. Prayer to the Pacific. Leslie Marmon Silko. CDW; NoP-4; PoPoPo; VoR; WeW-3

I Traveled with Them. Don Allen Johnson. AWP, *tr.* by J. B. Trend

I travelled [*or* travel'd] thro' a land of men. Mental Traveller, The. William Blake. ChIV-2; NAEL-5v2; NAEL-6v2; PoE; WoPoe

I travelled [*or* travell'd *or* traveled] on, seeing the hill, where lay. Pilgrimage, The. George Herbert. BASC; ESCV; GeHe; NAEL-5v1; NAEL-6v1; NAEL-7v1; NOSC; PAI; PoE

I travelled the land from Leap to Corbally. Volatile Kerryman, The. Owen Roe O'Sullivan. BIrV, *tr.* by Sean O'Riada

I tried each thing, only some were immortal and free. As One Put Drunk into the Packet-Boat. John Ashbery. HAP; HCAP; VCAP

I tried repeating, which feels now. Foolish Thing. Michael Burkard. BodElec

I tried this play one day. My father leaves his medicines open. I take. Daredevil. Ania Walwicz. BMAP

I Tried to Exchange Two Painting for Some Grain But Failed. Hsü Wei. CoBLCP, *tr.* by Jonathan Chaves

I tried to tell her. Offspring. Naomi Long Madgett. GT; SoSe-8

I tried to tell the doctor. Oh, I'm 10 Months Pregnant. Ntozake Shange. GT

I tried to turn the handle, but. (LL) Lewis Carroll. EBEV; NOBVV; NPeEn *Fr.* Through the Looking-Glass.

I tripped up his heels and he fell on his nose. (LL) Bandy Legs. Mother Goose. OxNR; ReMoGo

I trundle the bodies, on the iron bars. John Berryman. NOBA *Fr.* Homage to Mistress Bradstreet.

I trust every animal. Dogalypse. Andrey [*or* Andrei] Andreievich Voznesensky [*or* Voznesenskii]. CLPP

I trust I have not wasted breath. Tennyson. FHYEP; NAEL-6v2 *Fr.* In Memoriam A. H. H.

I try the dead lighter. Lighter. Sargon Boulus. MAP, *tr.* by Sargon Boulus and Alistair Elliot

I try to be good. Greta's Song. Matthew Graham. Unle

I try to forget, but it is in vain. To the Distant One. Po Chü-i. TAL

I try to hold your face in my mind's million eyes. Bride's Hours, A. Jean Valentine. FaBoWP; MPUn

I try to listen for the abstract shape. Ode to Mozart. Maura Stanton. MiVo

I try to make wishes right. Jacob Nibenegenesabe. WoPoe, *tr.* by Howard Norman *Fr.* Wishing Bone Cycle, The.

I try to tune in, but Europe's blurred voice. Short Wave. Hilary Llewellyn-Williams. TCAWP

I Try to Turn in My Jock. David Hilton. MoASP

I Try to Waken and Greet the World Once Again. James Wright (1927–80). EmeKit *Fr.* Two Hangovers.

I tumbled next to him, his body turned. Razglednica (4). Miklós Radnóti. IQMS, *tr.* by Peter Zollman

I turn out the driveway, point down the street. Artemis in Echo Park. Eloise Klein Healy. GeoHom

I turn the carriage, yoke and set off. *Unknown.* CoBCP

I turn the page and read. At the British Museum. Richard Aldington. MoBrPo

I turn to you high priests. Lament. Tadeusz Rózewicz. PoSu, *tr.* by Magnus J. Krynski

I turn you out of doors. Alain Chartier. BoLoP, *tr.* by Edward Lucie-Smith

I turned and gave my strength to woman. Two Generations. Leonard Alfred George Strong. OBMV

I turned, and saw them whispering about it. (LL) I Bended unto Me. Thomas Edward Brown. NOBVV; NTCP

I turned aside and bowed my head and wept. (LL) Tropics in New York, The. Claude McKay. APT-1; GT; MakPoe; NoAM; TTY

I turned on the TV. Tube Time. Eve Merriam. TLR

I twist the dial and you are everywhere. (LL) Elegy for Elvis. Richard Blessing. AllShUp; SwNoth

I, underground giant, waiting to be fried. Insulted and the Injured, The. Peter Viereck. SpudSo

I undersign'd Lord Kitchener of Karthoum. Proclamation, or Paper Bomb, The. F. W. Reitz. PeSAV, *tr.* by F. W. Reitz

I understand. In the Restaurant. Gerald William Barrax. GT

I understand. Ryoto. JDP, *tr.* by Yoel Hoffmann

I understand Death's contract. Scream, A. Muhammad Al-Faituri [*or* Al-Fituri *or* Al-Fayturi]. MAP, *tr.* by Sargon Boulus and Peter Porter

I understand her well because I too practice love. Etymolgy. Olga Broumas. WiU

I understand now, Tara, I understand. Rāmdulāl Nandī. SinGod, *tr.* by Rachel Fell McDermott

I understand the large hearts of heroes. Walt Whitman. SAmP *Fr.* Song of Myself.

I understand you well enough, John Donne. Letter to John Donne, A. Charles Hubert Sisson. HarvBoo; NOCV

I undress and lie down next to you in bed. On This Side of the River. Stephen Berg. GifTon

I Undressed Myself. Thérèse 'Awwad. PoArWo, *tr.* by Kamal Boullata

I upon the first creation. Christopher Smart. NOEC *Fr.* Hymns for the Amusement of Children.

I urge you. Sappho. SaLy, *tr.* by Diane Rayor

I urge you, milord, not to cherish your robe of golden thread. Robe of Golden Thread, The. Autumn Maid Tu (Tu Ch'iu-niang). ColAnChi, *tr.* by Victor H. Mair

I urgency, I begged. *Give me your dish,* I said, icy. Hélène Cixous. VCAP *Fr.* Vivre L'Orange.

I used the table as a reference and just did things from there. Texas. Mei-Mei Berssenbrugge. PmAP

I used to be / an admissions counselor. Skin Color from the Sun. Daryl Ngee Chinn. LTA

I used to be my mother's baby. I'm Nobody's Baby. Benny Davis. ReLy

I used to dream of Chuang Tzu. Painting of the Butterfly Dream by the Master Artist Li Tsai, A. Chu Yün-ming. CoBLCP, *tr.* by Jonathan Chaves

I used to dream that I would discover. Bill (Original Version). P. G. Wodehouse. ReLy

I used to dream that I would discover. Bill. P. G. Wodehouse. ReLy

I used to fall. My Heart Belongs to Daddy. Cole Porter. OBAL; ReLy

I used to kno when mango ripe. Plenty Time Pass Fast, Fas Dey So. Cheryl Boyce Taylor. WiU

I used to lead a lovely life of sin. Fings Ain't Wot They Used t'Be. Lionel Bart. ReLy

I used to live in a big house by the Church of St. Francis. León. Ernesto Cardenal. TCLAP, *tr.* by Jonathan Cohen

I used to make fun of you when you were a little girl & poor. Song for the Richest Woman in Wrangell. Guxnawu. STP, *tr.* by James Koller

I used to peer inside. Posthuman. Maura Stanton. BodElec

I used to prefer them and now I'm one of them. Older Men. Alfred Corn. GLP

I used to sit under trees and meditate. Buddha. Jack Kerouac. BB

I used to tell you, "Frances, we grow old." Ausonius. NNaP; PGA; WoPoe, *tr.* by Kenneth Rexroth

I used to think all poets were Byronic. Triolet. Wendy Cope. OBCoV

I used to think it might be fun to be. Lucky to Be Me. Leonard Bernstein. ReLy

I used to think that grown-up people chose. Childhood. Frances Darwin Cornford. FaBoWP; KaS; OxBEV; OxBSP; OxBTC

I used to think that immortality. Superman Is Dead. Rafael Campo. ReTh

I used to think. . . number was fixed and still. Anna Hempstead Branch. APT-1 *Fr.* Sonnets from a Lock Box.

I used to visit all the very gay places. Lush Life. Billy Strayhorn. ReLy

I used to walk on solid gr'und. To a Sea Eagle. Hugh MacDiarmid. MoBrPo

I used to walk the morning stream. Brian [*or* Bryan] Merriman [*or* Merryman]. BIrV, *tr.* by Brendan Behan *Fr.* Midnight Court, The.

I used to watch her / pacing. White Candles. BonniLee. GotH

I used to watch the roses loosen. Boy Crazy. Maurya Simon. GeoHom

I Usually Look Around Me. Iman Mirsal. NAfrP, *tr.* by Clarissa C. Burt

I vanish. Shiko. JDP, *tr.* by Yoel Hoffmann

I've a beau, his name is Jim. Laziest Gal in Town, The. Cole Porter. ReLy

I've a head like a concertina, I've a tongue like a buttonstick. Cells. Rudyard Kipling. FaBoWar

I've a mouth like a parrot's cage. Tripoli. Peter A. Sanders. FaBoWar

I've already promised my mouth and belly. (LL) Su Tung-p'o (Su Shih). CoBCP; ColAnChi, *tr.* by Burton Watson *Fr.* Eastern Slope.

I've always been afraid of death by fire. Ten Million Flames of Los Angeles, The. Amy Uyematsu. GeoHom

I've always been going somewhere—Vancouver. Madwoman on the Train, The. Alfred Wellington Purdy. NoAM

I've always hated. I Want to Hear a Yankee Doodle Tune. George M. Cohan. ReLy

I've always known that old age would arrive. Feeling Old Age. Liu Tsung-yüan. SuSp, *tr.* by Jan W. Walls

I've always liked the view from my mother-in-law's house at night. Looking West from Laguna Beach at Night. Charles Wright. MakPoe

I've always loved (your) Grace in 14 lines, sometimes. Birthday Sonnet for Grace. Bernadette Mayer. PmAP

I've always wanted one. Wanting a Mummy. Sandra McPherson. LCAP-2

I've always wanted to play the part. Little Brown Brother. Nick Carbó. AmPoNex; ReBoTo

I've an empty stomach. Ballad of Biddy Early, The. Nancy Willard. FFC

I've been a moonshiner for seventeen long years. Kentucky Moonshiner. *Unknown.* OBAL

I've been a pris'ner, locked in a jail. Over My Shoulder. Harry Woods. ReLy

I've Been Around: It Gets Me Nowhere. Marie Ponsot. ExTi

I've been blue all day, my gal's gone away. Gulf Coast Blues. Clarence Williams. NAAAL

I've been booed in the shower. Singing in the Toyota. Dave Etter. IllVoic

I've been chanting poems for forty years. Chanting Poems. Wang Chiu-ssu. CoBLCP, tr. by Jonathan Chaves

I've been cherishing. Room with a View, A. Noël Coward. PeLV

I've been eating. Minnesota Fats Describes His Youth. Elizabeth Alexander. AmPoNex

I've been given these hot delicious muffins. How Long Does the Curator Dance For? Edwin Torres. HeMarv

I've been giving a lot of thought. Sea Things. Gwendolyn MacEwen. FaBoWP

I've been hunting through woods. It Never Was You. Kurt Weill. ReLy

I've been in an open field. Day in the Life of . . . , A. Conyus. GT

I've been in love for long. In Love For Long. Edwin Muir. BoLoP; MoBrPo

I've been in love. Who hasn't? I went out and got drunk. Philodemus. HePo Fr. Epigrams.

I've been in the storm so long. Been in the Storm So Long. Unknown. NAAAL

I've been loveless all my life. On Love. Hsü Tsai-ssu. CrYelRi; ErotSp, tr. by Sam Hamill

I've been married and married. To Keep My Love Alive. Richard Rodgers. ReLy

I've been named Poosie, and. Confession. Paul Gallico. TriCat

I've been scarred and battered. Still Here. Langston Hughes. SAmP

I've been smoking steadily all morning. Mathios Paskalis among the Roses. George Seferis. PFTM-1; PoetW, tr. by Edmund Keeley and Philip Sherrard

I've Been to a Marvelous Party. Noël Coward. NBLV; ReLy

I've been to Palestine. Nicholas Vachel Lindsay. MoAmPo Fr. Booker Washington Trilogy, The.

I've been trying to fashion a wifely ideal. Plea for Trigamy, A. Sir Owen Seaman. NOBL; PeLV

I've been worried all day long. You Made Me Love You (I Didn't Want to Do It). Joseph McCarthy. ReLy

I've begun to love the cold, the slick, bitter seed. Outlook. Crystal Bacon. UrbNat

I've blown up your chest for thirty minutes. Morning—A Death. Basil T. Paquet. CDa

I've brewed myself a whole bunch of trouble. To the Tune "Moon Over West River." Yang Shen. CoBLCP; ColAnChi, tr. by Jonathan Chaves

I've cleaned house. Saturday Afternoon, When Chores Are Done. Harryette Mullen. ISC

I've combed out my beard and I've found. Limerick. Pauline Phillips. PeLi

I've come a long way. (LL) Poor Crow! Mary Mapes Dodge. OBCA; SWaP

I've come back all skin and bone. Diggins-Oh, The. Unknown. NOBAu

I've come back many times today. Gift from Kenya. May Miller. BlSi

I've come back to my city. These are my own old tears. Leningrad. Osip Emilevich Mandelstam [or Mandelshtam]. AF

I've come back to the country where I was happy. Adult. Linda Gregg. BLT

I've come this far to freedom and I won't turn back. Midway. Naomi Long Madgett. BPo; BlSi

I've come to close your door, my handsome, my darling. Frances Bellerby. FaBoWP

I've come to give you fruit from out of my orchard. Crossed Apple, The. Louise Bogan. HeIP-4; NALW

I've come to tell you of things dear to me. Skin / Meat / BONES. Anne Waldman. PmAP

I've come to the house of the Immortals. At Home in the Summer Mountains. Yu Xuanji. WPoS, tr. by Jane Hirshfield

I've cracked the blue bowl! China Maniacs. May Probyn. VWP

I've cropped the black hair Diego loves. Painting / (Frida Kahlo). Elizabeth Alexander. GT

I've decided to return to the emperor's court. Return of the Proconsul, The. Zbigniew Herbert. PoSu

I've dimmed the lights low. Pleasure. Allison Joseph. PasH

I've discovered a way to stay friends forever. Friendship. Shel [or Shelley] Silverstein. NTCP

I've done my bits of mindless aggro too. Tony Harrison. FaBoVe

I've drawn a salary in the capital for forty years now. Yang Shih-ch'i. CoBLCP Fr. Sent to All My Nephews and Nieces at Tung-ch'eng.

I've Dreamed of You So Much. Robert Desnos. WoPoe, tr. by Michael Benedikt and William Kulik

I've dreamed such dreams of you that you're losing / your reality. I've dreamed such dreams of you. Robert Desnos. MFP, tr. by Martin Sorrell

I've dropped me swag in many camps. Search, The. Charles Shaw. NOBAu

I've eaten handfuls of fire. Back Then. Yusef Komunyakaa. GT

I've expanded like the swollen door in summer. Yom Kippur, Taos, New Mexico. Robin Becker. TaR

I've forgotten. Ryokan. WoPoe, tr. by Burton Watson

I've found out why, that day, that suicide. John Berryman. PoE Fr. Sonnets to Chris.

I've given up wanting. Dīnrām. SinGod, tr. by Rachel Fell McDermott

I've gone and done. (LL) Hay for the Horses. Gary Snyder. BB; CoAmPo; LoL; TRP

I've gone mad drinking nectar. Mahendranāth Bhattācārya. SinGod, tr. by Rachel Fell McDermott

I've got a brand new sweetie. I'll Say She Does. B. G. DeSylva. ReLy

I've got a creed. Spread a Little Happiness. Clifford Grey. ReLy

I've Got a Feelin' You're Foolin' Arthur Freed. ReLy

I've got a Gal in Kalamazoo. Harry Warren. ReLy

I've got a home in a-that Rock. Got a Home in That Rock. Unknown. APN-2

I've got a mule, her name is Sal. Erie Canal, The. William S. Allen. HHAm

I've Got a Pocketful of Dreams. Johnny Burke. ReLy

I've got a stubborn goose whose gut's. Rhyme. Sylvia Plath. BodElec

I've got a taste for trashy thrillers. My Taste for Trash. Chase Twichell. ExTi

I've Got an Apple Ready. John Walsh. NOxBChV

I've Got Five Dollars. Richard Rodgers. ReLy

I've got my chair and a good book and I'm sitting. Homage: Summer/Winter, Shay Creek. Joseph Stroud. GeoHom

I've Got My Love to Keep Me Warm. Irving Berlin. ReLy

I've Got Rings on My Fingers. Maurice Scott. ReLy

I've got some good news, honey. Darktown Strutter's Ball, The. Shelton Brooks. ReLy

I've Got the World on a String. Ted Koehler. ReLy

I've got to keep moving. Hellhound on My Trail. Robert Johnson. APT-2; NAAAL; PFTM-2

I've Got You Under My Skin. Cole Porter. ReLy

I've Got Your Number. Cy Coleman. ReLy

I've Gotten a Rock, I've Gotten a Reel. Susanna Blamire. ECWP

I've gotten used to this window. Glimpse from the Past. Ilse Aichinger. AF, tr. by Allen H. Chappel

I've Grown Accustomed to Her Face. Frederick Loewe. ReLy

I've had a mighty busy day. When the Midnight Choo-Choo Leaves for Alabam' Irving Berlin. ReLy

I've had a million dreams. You Stepped Out of a Dream. Nacio Herb Brown. ReLy

I've had enough. Bridge Poem, The. Kate Rushin. GLP

I've had enough of your baseness, and I haven't killed myself. To the Enemies. Vladimir Holan. AF, tr. by C. G. Hanzlicek

I've Had Many an Aching Pain. John Clare. NOBVV

I've had tangled feelings lately. Breakthrough. Carolyn M. Rodgers. BPo

I've Had the Wagon Hauled Out. Unknown. SuSp, tr. by C. H. Wang

I've heard about Houdini and the rest of them. It's Magic. Sammy Cahn. ReLy

I've heard from strangers you may be living. To My Younger Brother. Tu Fu. CrYelRi, tr. by Sam Hamill

I've heard her thin cry, where the rivers meet. (LL) Two Rivers. Hilary Llewellyn-Williams. AngWePo; TCAWP

I've heard it said about this valley. Owl's Landscape, An. Jon Veinberg. GeoHom

I've heard it sung—it may be true or no. Sebestyén Tinódi. IQMS, tr. by Michael Beevor Fr. Chronicle of Sigismund, The.

I've heard the case for clarity. I know. Giant Killer. George Garrett. CRP

I've heard them lilting at loom and belting. Cecil Day Lewis. NoP-4; OBMV Fr. Two Songs.

'I've hell on the inside as well as the out!' (LL) Devil in Texas, The. Unknown. NBLV; RB

I've hunched so long above this puzzle. Big Jigsaw. Chris Forhan. NAPBL

I've interviewed Leslie Howard. Zip. Richard Rodgers. ReLy

I've jolliest merriment for Saturday:—. Folgore da San Geminiano [or Gimignano]. EaItPo, tr. by Dante Gabriel Rossetti

I've just come up. Naito Joso. TTTS

I've just found joy. Sweet Lorraine. Mitchell Parish. ReLy

I've just had an astounding dream as I lay in the straw. Minstrel's Song. Ted Hughes. OBCP

I've kept a haughty heart thro' grief and mirth. To My Mother. Heinrich Heine. AWP

I've kissed thee, sweetheart, in a dream at least. Sleep. Theophile De Viau. AWP, tr. by Sir Edmund William Gosse

I've known a Heaven, like a Tent. Emily Dickinson. NCAP

I've known; all fading past me into peace. (LL) Falling Asleep. Siegfried Sassoon. MoBrPo; OxBTC

I've known ere now an interfering branch. Axe-Helve, The. Robert Frost. OxBA

I've known fancies turn into dreaming. Describing a Dream for Someone. Wang Seng-ju. ColAnChi, tr. by Anne Birrell

I've known him so long I've almost forgotten the first photo he showed. Man Struck Twenty Times by Lightning, The. Maxine Chernoff. PmAP

I've known rivers. Negro Speaks of Rivers, The. Langston Hughes. APT-2; AiP; BPo; ColAP; HAP; HCAP; HarvBoo; HeIP-4; ISC; NAAAL; NAAL-2v2; NAAL-5; NIL-7; NIP-4; NOBA; NoAM; NoP-4; OBCA; PAI; RaBo; SSLK; TAP; TCAPo; TFi; TTY; WeW-3

I've learnt to laugh now at adversity. Quatrain. Ilyas Farhat. MAP, tr. by John Heath-Stubbs and Salma Khadra Jayyusi

I've learnt to wash in petrol tins, and shave myself in tea. Lament of a Desert Rat. N. J. Trapnell. FaBoWar

I've left my own old home of homes. Flitting, The. John Clare. OxAEP-2

I've left on this dreary boat once too often. Sealink. Brendan Cleary. NeBl

I've lived in the ghetto here for more than a / year. Homesick. Unknown, fr. Terezin Concentration Camp. INSAB

I've long desired dawn. Wishes. Philippe Jaccottet. MFP, tr. by Martin Sorrell

I've lost my Love, I know not where. Madness. Robert Merry. NOBRP

I've lost my rifle and bayonet. Unknown. PoWW

I've lost pal, 'e's the best in all the tahn. It's a Great Big Shame. Edgar Bateman. OBCoV

I've met enough people. Alena Synková. INSAB

I've moved here to the Immortal's place. Staying in the Mountains in Summer. Yü Hsüan-chi. BoWoP, tr. by Geoffrey Waters

I've neither wealth nor power. I'll Get By (As Long As I Have You). Fred E. Ahlert. ReLy

I've never been to Australia. Walking the Places I've Never Been. Yury [or Iurii] Arabov. TCRP, tr. by John High and Katya Olmsted

I've never been to Prague, and the last time. Letter to Jorge Luis Borges: Apropos of the Golem. John Hollander. TaR

I've never been too keen on lions and. At the Zoo. John Davies. AngWePo

I've never bothered with the names of flowers. My Field Guide. Erin Belieu. NAPBL

I've never feared the setting of the Pleiades. I've Never Feared. Antipater of Thessalonica. WoPoe, tr. by Sam Hamill

I've never seen a soul detached from its gender. Horse. Chase Twichell. ExTi

I've no tooth to sing you the song. Pat Cloherty's Version of The Maisie. Richard Murphy. RB

I've not much of my own, lady, mistress, but I. Gifts to a Lady. Antiphilus [or Antiphilos]. GrAn

I've oft been told by learned friars. Argument, An. Thomas Moore. BoLoP; EnLoPo; OxBSP

I've often heard my mother say. Unknown Color, The. Countee Cullen. OBCA

I've often on a Sabbath day. Sabbath Bells. John Clare. FHYEP

I've often wish'd that I could write a book. John Hookham Frere. NOBRP Fr. Prospectus and Specimen of an Intended National Work by William and Robert Whistlecraft . . . Relating to King Arthur and His Round Table.

I've paid thee what I promised; that's not all. To His Peculiar Friend Master Thomas Shapcott, Lawyer. Robert Herrick. NOSC

I've peeled off the shiny green bark. New Bamboo in the North Garden at Ch'ang-ku. Li Ho. SuSp, tr. by Irving Y. Lo

I've plucked every bud hanging over the wall. To the Tune "A Spray of Flowers" (Not Giving in to Old Age). Kuan Han-ch'ing. WoPoe, tr. by Stephen Owen

I've plucked every flower that grows over the wall. In the Southern Mode, to the Tune "A Sprig of Flowers" The Refusal to Get Old. Kuan Han-ch'ing. ColAnChi, tr. by Wayne Schlepp

I've Plucked the Berry. William Motherwell. OxAEP-2

I've positioned myself to relax. Insomnia on a Summer Night. Umberto Saba. AWTN, tr. by Christopher Millis

I've pulled the last of the year's young onions. Eating Alone. Li-Young Lee. NAAL-5; TRP; WeW-3

I've quenched my lamp, I struck it in that start. Pilate's Wife's Dream. Charlotte Brontë. VWP

I've Reached the Land of Corn and Wine. Edgar P. Stites. AH

I've read that Luther said (it's come to me). Author to the Reader, The. Randall Jarrell. OxBC

I've said good-bye many times. To My Mother. Simeon Dumdum. ReBoTo

I've sailed several of the world's oceans. First Canzone. Nikolai Stepanovich Gumilyov [or Gumiliov or Gumilev]. TCRusP, tr. by Mary Jane White

I've seen a Dying Eye. Emily Dickinson. APN-2; BoWoP; NAAL-3; NCAP; NOBA

I've seen Babylon's walls wide enough to take traffic. Temple of Artemis at Ephesos, The. Antipater of Thessalonica. GrAn, tr. by Tony Harrison

I've seen him many times before. Towards Delhi. Kunwar Narain. OMIP, tr. by Vinay Dahrwadker

I've seen one in a fairground. Bearded Woman, by Ribera, The. Paul Muldoon. BiHa

I've seen the famous Rembrandts. You Leave Me Breathless. Ralph Freed. ReLy

I've seen the grey-haired lyrists come down from the hills. Grand Finale. Irving Layton. NOBC

I've seen the lights of gay Broadway. Beale Street Blues. William Christopher Handy. APT-1

I've / seen the Mississippi River. Mississippi Blues. Lamont B. Steptoe. SpirFl

I've seen the moonbeam's shining light. Life. Unknown. PoToHe

I've seen the sea—how could I settle for a river? When We Are Apart. Yuan Chen. CrYelRi, tr. by Sam Hamill

I've seen the smiling of Fortune beguiling. Flowers of the Forest, The. Alison Rutherford Cockburn. ECWP

I've served my country nine and twenty years. Edward Thompson. NOEC Fr. Humble Wish; off Porto-Sancto, March 29, 1779, An.

I've set six stones in a row near the eastern. Ghost of Santo Domingo, The. Suzanne Gardinier. NeAmPo

I've smelled the barracks and live by rules. Continuation of Life. Boris Petrovich Kornilov. TCRP, tr. by Bernard Meares

I've solved the riddles of the planets. Galileo. János Székely. IQMS, tr. by George Gömöri and Adam Makkai

I've stayed in the front yard all my life. Gwendolyn Brooks. ESEAA; NAAAL; NAAL-2v2; NOBA; NOxBChV; NoAM Fr. Street in Bronzeville, A.

I've stitched my dress with continents. Knowledge. Nina Cassian. BoWoP, tr. by Michael Impey and Brian Swann

I've suffered bitterness from tyrant fate. Moth, The. Ahmad al-Safi Al-Najafi. MAP, tr. by John Heath-Stubbs and Salma Khadra Jayyusi

I've taken my fun where I've found it. Ladies, The. Rudyard Kipling. FaBoWar; MoBrPo; NAEL-5v2; NAEL-6v2

I've taken the last drag. City, Evening, and an Old Man: Me, The. "Dhoomil." OMIP; WoPoe, tr. by Vinay Dharwadker

I've talked (remember). Alba. Imamu Amiri Baraka. FTOS

I've Tasted My Blood. Milton Acorn. MoCV; NOBC

I've Thirty Months. John Millington Synge. OBMV

I've thrown away my toys. On the Good Ship Lollipop. Sidney Clare. ReLy

I've Told Ev'ry Little Star. Jerome Kern. ReLy

I've tossed an apple at you; if you can love me. Apple, The. Plato. WeW-3

I've touched each string, each muse I have invoked. Pindaric, to the Athenian Society, A. Elizabeth Singer Rowe. BASC

I've tried the new moon tilted in the air. Freedom of the Moon, The. Robert Frost. APT-1

I've tried to explain that you are my Heaven on earth. Until the Real Thing Comes. Alberta Nichols. ReLy

I've tried to seal it in. Knot, The. Stanley Kunitz. HAP

I've two teenage daughters, a decent. Fear of Shoplifting. Maureen Seaton. FFC

I've used up all my film on bombed hospitals. In Thai Binh (Peace) Province. Denise Levertov. AF

I've ventured it of purpose free. Ulrich von Hutten's Song. Ulrich von Hutten. GePo, tr. by Catherine Winkworth

I've waltzed my friends. Sleepless Night. Léon Damas. NegPo, tr. by Ellen Conroy Kennedy

I've wandered east, I've wandered west. Jeanie Morrison. William Motherwell. TreFP

I've watched thee, Scarab! Yea, an hour in vain. Scarabæus Sisyphus. Mathilde Blind. ViWPN

I've wined and dined on Mulligan stew. Lady Is a Tramp, The. Richard Rodgers. OBAL; ReLy

I've wished ill to the searing warplanes. Jet Planes. Gwyn Williams. TCAWP

I've won (lost) my day. Elegy. Carlos Drummond de Andrade. TCLAP, tr. by Virginia de Araújo

I've written you a song. Blah, Blah, Blah. George Gershwin. OBAL; ReLy

I've yoked together my large silence and my small outcry. And That Is Your Glory. Yehuda Amichai [or Amikhai]. BBASP, tr. by Stephen Mitchell

I verse a settler's tale of olden times. Charles Harpur. CBAP Fr. Creek of the Four Graves, The.

I Vision God. Unknown. NAAAL; TTY

I Visit the Twenty-four Coin-op Church of Elvis. Fleda Brown Jackson. AllShUp

I visited Père Lachaise to look for the remains of Apollinaire. At Apollinaire's Grave. Allen Ginsberg. BB

I vow'd unvarying faith. Coventry Patmore. NOBVV; OxBSP Fr. Angel in the House, The.

I wad ha'e gi'en him my lips tae kiss. Mary's Song. Marion Angus. LW

I wage not any feud with Death. Tennyson. NAEL-6v2 *Fr.* In Memoriam A. H. H.

I wait, dear child, for you to come. You'll Never Know. Ruby Marion Wray. PWR

I wait for her who restores my fingertips. Song of Expectancy. George Hitchcock. SPE

I wait for the mailman. Crystal Chandeliers. David Ignatow. BodElec

I Wait My Lord. *Unknown.* AWP, *tr. by* Helen Waddell *Fr.* Shi King.

I wait to tangle fear around my hand. Night along the Mackinac Bridge. Roberta Hill Whiteman. CDW

I wait, white clouds. Chosui. JDP, *tr. by* Yoel Hoffmann

I wait, with those that rest. Jay Macpherson. NOBC *Fr.* Ark, The.

I waited and worked / To win myself leisure. Koheleth. Louis Untermeyer. ChIV-1; TrJP

I waited eighteen years to become a man. Basket Case. Basil T. Paquet. CDa; FaBoWar

I Waited for Chuang Hsüan-yüan But He Never Came. Mo Shih-lung. CoBLCP, *tr. by* Jonathan Chaves

I waited for my. *Unknown.* OHPJ

I Waited for You Last Night. Zindzi Mandela. HAWP; NAfrP

I waited full two hours, or more. Tryst, The. Mary E. Tucker. CBWP-1

I waited, heavy-hearted; then went on. After the Voices. Victor Hugo. SxFrPo, *tr. by* E. H. Blackmore and A. M. Blackmore

I waited too long. In a Boat Shed. Robert Creeley. InvLad

I wake alone, sighing for Peggy Browne. (LL) Peggy Browne. Turlough Carolan [*or* O'Carolan]. BIrV; OxBEV, *tr. by* Austin Clarke

I wake and feel the fell of dark, not day. Gerard Manley Hopkins. AWTN; CABP; FaBoVe; NAEL-6v2; NPeEn; NoP-4; OxAEP-2; OxBSo; PeVV; TRP

I wake and find. Ome Shushiki. JDP, *tr. by* Yoel Hoffmann

I wake and my bed is gleaming with moonlight. Quiet Night Thoughts. Li Po. EaWin, *tr. by* W. S. Merwin

I wake because the phone is really ringing. Fucking. Frederick Seidel. BodElec

I wake! delusive phantoms hence, away! Reaches Sicily. Mary Robinson. CenSon; RWP

I wake from a nap, light clouds. Waking from a Nap. Ni Tsan. CoBLCP, *tr. by* Jonathan Chaves

I wake from my noon nap. Muso Soseki. EaWin, *tr. by* W. S. Merwin

I wake! I feel the day is near. Chanticleer. Celia Laighton Thaxter. NOxBChV

I wake in the dark and remember. Rain Travel. W. S. Merwin. ColAP

I wake in the morning. Lilith. Suzanne Benton. HW

I Wake Thinking of Myself as a Man. Susan Griffin. GLP

I wake to sleep, and take my waking slow. Waking, The. Theodore Roethke. APT-2; AmFaPo; CRP; CoAP; HAP; HCAP; HeIP-4; ITBLP; InPK-6; MakPoe; MoAmPo; NAAL-2v2; NAAL-5; NIL-7; NIP-4; NOBA; NoAM; NoP-4; PoPoPo; RaBo; TAP; TFi; TwCP; VCAP; WeW-3; WoPoe

I wake to strangled voices. Stepping in the Same River. Karen Chamberlain. GeoH

I wake to the sound of a soft, low patter. Night Rain. Countee Cullen. GT

I wake up. Raul Bopp. TCLAP, *tr. by* Renato Rezende *Fr.* Black Snake.

I wake up. Rokushi. JDP, *tr. by* Yoel Hoffmann

I Wake Up Alone. Li Shang-yin. OHMPC, *tr. by* Kenneth Rexroth

I wake up and say: I'm through. Morning Exercises. Nina Cassian. PoSu, *tr. by* Andrea Deletant and Brenda Walker

I wake up chasing my breath, my. Falso Brilhante. Nathaniel Mackey. NAAAL

I wake up cold, I who. Man With Night Sweats, The. Thom Gunn. CABP; HarvBoo; PoPoPo

I wake up dreaming I'm forty years in. Winged Abyss. Nathaniel Mackey. ESEAA

I wake up growling apples and dirt. Shiner. Maggie Nelson. AmPoNex

I wake up in your bed. I know I have been dreaming. Adrienne Rich. ErotSp; NAAL-2v2; NoAM; TRP *Fr.* Twenty-one Love Poems.

I wake up on my left side. Kukutis's Consciousness Becomes Alienated. Marcelijus Martinaitis. TWW, *tr. by* Laima Sruoginis

I wake up standing before a scene I stood. Phantom Light of All Our Day, The. Nathaniel Mackey. GT

I waked [*or* wak'd], she fled, and day brought back my night. (LL) On His Deceased Wife. John Milton. NPeEn; OBEV; OxBSo; PoE; SCV; SacPr; TFi

I wakened my thoughts from slumber. Sources of My Being, The. Moses Ibn Ezra. TOF, *tr. by* David Goldstein

I wakened on my hot, hard bed. Watch, The. Frances Darwin Cornford. InPK-6; MoBrPo; OxBTC

I wakened, still a child. Life Ahead, The. Philip Levine. NoAM

I Walk a Little Faster. Cy Coleman. ReLy

I walk a road—an ancient, trodden way. Another While. Morris Jacob Rosenfeld. TrJP

I walk about in the night. Magic Song. *Unknown.* APN-2, *tr. by* Henry Rowe Schoolcraft

I walk among dark shapes. Hunting in Twilight. David Scott Ward. AmPoNex

I walk among men with tall bones. Ruth Dallas. PeNZ *Fr.* Letter to a Chinese Poet.

I walk and I wonder. Spring. Isaac Rosenberg. TrJP

I walk and think of various things. Georgy [*or* Georgii] Vladimirovich Ivanov. TCRP

I walk around the city. Infections. Miguel Algarin. PueRic

I walk at dawn across the hollow hills. Poem. Ruthven Todd. SPE

I walk back. Getting the Mail. Galway Kinnell. UnPo

I walk behind you, hand. Days of 1956. Robin Magowan. SPE

I walk beside the prisoners to the road. Randall Jarrell. *See* I walk [*or* walked] beside the prisoners to the road

I walk'd in the lonesome evening. Across the Sea. William Allingham. EnLoPo

I walk down a long / passage way. Poem for museum goers, A. John Weiners. BB

I walk down the garden paths. Patterns. Amy Lowell. APT-1; AWP; AmFaPo; BoWoP; MoAmPo; NoP-4; OxBA; WHSW

I walk in loneliness through the greenwood. *Unknown.* BoWoP

I Walk in the History of My People. Chrystos. UnSA

I Walk in the Old Street. Louis Zukofsky. VGW

I walk into a forest wintery. Winter Forest. Hans Leifhelm. AuPH, *tr. by* Lowell A. Bangerter

I walk into the vineyard at night, into acres of cordoned vines. Revelation in the Mother Lode. George Evans. AF; PmAP

I walk naked and. Alone in Your House. Kim Addonizio. PasH

I walk on meadows run to weed. Magyar Fallow, The. Endre Ady. IQMS, *tr. by* Anton N. Nyerges

I walk on the sea-shore. Voice. Zbigniew Herbert. PoSu, *tr. by* Czeslaw Milosz

I walk on the waste-ground for no good reason. For No Good Reason. Peter Redgrove. PoE

I walk [*or* walked] beside the prisoners to the road. Camp in the Prussian Forest, A. Randall Jarrell. FaBoWar; MoAmPo; OBWP; OxBC; PoWW

I Walk Out into the Country at Night. Lu Yu. OHPC, *tr. by* Kenneth Rexroth

I walk six blocks to the park. Hoarfrost and Fog. Barton Sutter. UrbNat

I walk some hundred paces from the old house. Depths of Fields. Luis Cabalquinto. ReBoTo

I walk the forest in the moonlight. In Front of Good Prince Silence. Endre Ady. IQMS, *tr. by* Alan Dixon

I walk the land of Anahuac which is the land of my dead. Return, The. Rosario Castellanos. TANSG; TCLAP, *tr. by* Magda Bogin

I walk the purple carpet into your eye. Inside Out. Diane Wakoski. CoAP

I walk the streets and though not meanly drest. Poor, The. Jones Very. SacPr

I walk through the long schoolroom questioning. Among School Children. W. B. Yeats. CABP; GTBS-P; HAP; HarvBoo; MoBrPo; NAEL-5v2; NAEL-6v2; NAWM-7v2; NIL-7; NIP-4; NOBE; NPeEn; NoAM; NoP-4; OxBEV; OxBTC; PoE; PoPoPo; SCGP; TFi; TRP

I walk through the polders. Polderland. Hendrik Marsman. TuT, *tr. by* Michael Longley

I walked abroad in [*or* on] a snowy day. Soft Snow. William Blake. SoSe-8

I walked alone and thinking. Sinner's Rue. A. E. Housman. PeVV

I walked along the streets of Hong Kong town. Love Is a Many-Splendored Thing. Paul Francis Webster. ReLy

I walked around in my mother's high heels. Cobwebs. Melinda Goodman. WiU

I walked around New York half-dazed, and what. Mengele Shitting. Jason Sommer. NAPBL

I walked beside the stone. My Grandmother's Burial Ground. Elizabeth Cook-Lynn. HATNAP

I walked down the street. Listeners, The. Louis Simpson. BodElec

I walked entranced / through a land of Morn. Vision of Connaught in the Thirteenth Century, A. James Clarence Mangan. NOIV

I walked, gritting my teeth, past charred. In Those Years. Sergey [*or* Sergei] Sergeievich Narovchatov. TCRusP, *tr. by* Bob Perelman and Shirley Rihner

I Walked in a Desert. Stephen Crane. NAAL-2v2 *Fr.* Black Riders [and Other Lines], The.

I walked into a loge in the Teatro Melisso. Pound at Spoleto. Lawrence Ferlinghetti. PoM

I walked into the room. To My Father. John Berryman. PoPoPo

I walked on the banks of the tincan banana dock. Sunflower Sutra. Allen Ginsberg. CoAP; HCAP; NAAL-2v2; NOBA; NeAP; VCAP

I walked on the edge of the churchyard, my shoes hurt my.   At the Pauwels. Diane Glancy.   CRP

I walked [or walk'd] along a stream for pureness rare.   Fragment, A.   Gervase Markham.   CTC

I walked [or walkt] the other day (to spend my hour).   I Walked [or Walkt] the Other Day to Spend My Hour.   Henry Vaughan.   BASC; ESCV; FSCP; GeHe; NAEL-6v1

I walked out of my dress.   Like the Magic Glow of Paradise.   Clementina Suárez.   TANSG, tr. by Janet N. Gold

I Walked over the Grave of Henry James.   Richard Eberhart.   APT-2; VGW

I walked, regardless of obstacles, toward that day. (LL)   Margarita Iosifovna Aliger.   ItWoWo; TCRP, tr. by Daniel Weissbort

I walked slowly along the river.   One Hundred and Fifty Years.   Jack Davis. BMAP

I Walked [or Walkt] the Other Day to Spend My Hour.   Henry Vaughan. BASC; ESCV; FSCP; GeHe; NAEL-6v1

I walked the two blocks from the subway down.   Going Home Madly.   Brooke Wiese.   UrbNat

I walked through Ballinderry in the spring-time.   Lament for the Death of Thomas Davis.   Sir Samuel Ferguson.   BIrV; NOIV

I walked, when love was gone.   Breath of Air, A.   James Wright (1927–80). NOBA

I walked where in their talking graves.   At the British War Cemetery, Bayeux. Charles Causley.   NAEL-5v2; NAEL-6v2; NoP-4; OBWP; OxBC; PoWW

I walked with him one melancholy night.   Lycidas.   Thomas Bailey Aldrich. TreFP

I walked with you as far as the graineries beside the gates.   Songs for a Three-String Guitar.   Léopold Sédar Senghor.   PBA, tr. by Miriam Koshl

I walked you to the village where the granaries are at the threshold of Night. Léopold Sédar Senghor.   NegPo   Fr. Songs for Signare.

I Wan Bi President.   Ezenwa-Ohaeto.   NAfrP

I wander aimless, to and fro.   Aimless.   Louis Palagyi.   TrJP, tr. by Watson Kirkconnell

I wander all night in my vision.   Walt Whitman.   AWTN; NAAL-2v1; NAAL-3   Fr. Sleepers, The.

I wander by the edge.   He Hears the Cry of the Sedge.   W. B. Yeats.   OxBTC; RB

I wander more and more about the city.   On Death.   Aleksandr Aleksandrovich Blok.   TCRP, tr. by Geoffrey Thurley

I wander through a crowd of women.   At Piccadilly Circus.   Vivian de Sola Pinto.   OBMV

I wander through [or thro'] each chartered [or charter'd] street.   William Blake. AWP; CABP; ClHu; FHYEP; HAP; HeIP-4; InPK-6; NAEL-5v2; NAEL-6v2; NAWM-7v2; NIL-7; NIP-4; NOBE; NOBRP; NOEC; NPeEn; NoP-4; OxAEP-2; OxBEV; PoE; PoPoPo; RB; SCGP; SCV; TFi; TRP; UnPo; WeW-3   Fr. Songs of Experience.

I wandered away from my early childhood, framed by her massive hair. Officials rob.   Material's Daughter.   Aaron Shurin.   FTOS

I wandered forth at night alone.   Lament over the Ruins of the Abbey of Teach Molaga.   James Clarence Mangan.   NOIV, tr. by James Clarence Mangan

I wandered in a suburb of the north.   James Thomson.   NOBVV   Fr. City of Dreadful Night, The.

I wandered lonely as a cloud.   En Famille.   Robert Creeley.   BAP-01

I wandered lonely as a cloud in Foyles.   Upon Finding Dying: An Introduction, by L. E. Sissman, Remaindered at IS.   Louis Edward Sissman.   NoP-4

I wandered lonely by the sea.   Goose-Girl, The.   Edith Nesbit.   VWP

I wandered [or wander'd] lonely as a Cloud.   Daffodils, The.   William Wordsworth.   BRP; ClHu; InPK-6; NAEL-5v2; NAEL-6v2; NOBRP; PoRA; SCGP; SoSe-8; TFi; TTTS; UnPo

I wandered [or / wander'd] today to the hill, Maggie.   When You and I Were Young, Maggie.   George W. Johnson.   TCAPo

I wandered out a while agone.   George Wither.   NOSC   Fr. Fair Virtue, the Mistress of Philarete.

I wandered out through the steeples of rust, the gate that was a broken bed. (LL) Dresden.   Ciaran Carson.   CIP-2; ModIr; NPeEn; PBCIP; PNI

I wandered through the ancient wood.   Cataract Isle, The.   Christopher Pearse Cranch.   APN-1

I wandered through the pills of light.   Molino.   Maggie Nelson.   HeMarv

I Wanna Be Black.   Michelle T. Clinton.   InTrad

I Wanna Be Loved.   Johnny Green.   ReLy

I wanna be the leader.   Leader, The.   Roger McGough.   OPOU

I Wannabe Your Queen.   Susan Swartwout.   SwNoth

I want. (LL)   For W.C.W.   Robert Creeley.   FTOS; LCAP-2

I want a good lover.   What Do You Want?   John Newlove.   NOBC

I want a hero: an uncommon want.   Byron.   NAEL-5v2; NAEL-6v2; PoE   Fr. Don Juan.

I want / a love to hold.   Defense Rests.   Vassar Miller.   MoAmPo

I Want a Tenant; a Satire.   John O'Keefe [or O'Keeffe].   NOEC

I Want Aretha to Set This to Music.   Sherley Anne Williams.   NAAAL

I want him to have another living summer.   14-Year-Old Convalescent Cat in the Winter, A.   Gavin Ewart.   OPOU; OxBSP

I want his doughnut. He was eating that fucking doughnut the first.   Riot at Winchell's.   Bruce Jackson.   AmPoNex

I want, in the shade of a wing.   José Martí.   BLPSL, tr. by Rene de Costa, Rigas Kappatos and Eleni Paidoussi

I want me a home.   Black Woman Throws a Tantrum.   Nayo-Barbara Watkins. NBV

I want men that I can squeeze.   Nobody Makes a Pass at Me.   Harold Rome. ReLy

I want my father to stop sending me down there.   Cellar, The.   Laure-Anne Bosselaar.   SpudSo

I want my funeral to include this detour.   Detour.   Michael Longley.   CIP-2

I want my soul to find its proper body. (LL)   Piano Solo.   Nicanor Parra. PoetW; TCLAP, tr. by William Carlos Williams

I want no paradise only to be.   Kiwi Bird in the Kiwi Tree, The.   Charles Bernstein.   FTOS

I want nothing but your fire-side now.   Hearthstone.   Harold Monro.   OBMV

I want [or wanted] to sniff the glue that holds families together.   Logic in the House of Sawed-off Telescopes.   Jeffrey McDaniel.   AmPoNex; NeAmPo

I want something suited to my special needs.   Needs.   A. R. Ammons.   NIL-7; NIP-4; OBAL

I want that picture, the perfect view.   Immortal Picture, The.   Richard Eberhart. BodElec

I want the phone to ring.   Talkin' Trash.   Elena Georgiou.   WiU

I want the robes, the skins of the game animals, the meat of the game animals. Bring them to me. Let us enjoy ourselves.   *Unknown.*   APN-2   *Fr.* Minnetare Songs.

I want these words / to stand.   Task, The.   Subhash Mukhopadhyay.   OMIP, tr. by Pritish Nandy

I want things.   On the Corner.   Kit Robinson.   FTOS

I want to be.   Last of the Fire Kings, The.   Derek Mahon.   PNI

I want to be a white horse!   Three Presidents.   Robert Bly.   LCAP-2

I Want to Be Bad.   Ray Henderson.   ReLy

I want to be buried in an anonymous crater inside the moon.   Unholy Missions. Bob Kaufman.   TTY

I want to be carried, heavily sedated.   Dream of a Slave.   Gavin Ewart. EmeKit

I Want to Be Happy.   Irving Caesar.   ReLy

I want to be in a garden with my love.   *Unknown.*   BoWoP

I want to be known.   Claim to Fame.   Beau Sia.   HeMarv

I Want to Be Loved.   Endre Ady.   IQMS, tr. by Peter Zollman

I want to be near this mild unforgiving man.   Father.   Paul Zweig.   BodElec

I want to be remembered.   Cover Photograph.   Marilyn Nelson.   InvLi

I want to be simple.   Dark Star, Black Star.   Rikki Ducornet.   SurWo

I want to be with my love in a garden.   *Unknown.*   BoWoP

I want to check.   After the Anti-Semitic Calls on a Local Talk Station.   Lyn Lifshin.   UnSA

I want to clear my head.   Bent Branches.   Amjad Nasir.   MAP, tr. by Charles Doria and May Jayyusi

I want to cry my pain and I am telling you so you will love me and cry for me in a nightfall of nightingales with a dagger, with kisses and with you. Federico García Lorca.   CAGL, tr. by David William Foster   *Fr.* Sonetos del Amor Oscuro [Sonnets of Dark Love].

I Want to Die While You Love Me.   Georgia Douglas Johnson.   APT-1; BlSi; ISC; NAAAL; TCAPo

(And nothing more to give.) (LL)   OxWW

I want to drown in good-salt water.   Miss Millay Says Something Too. Samuel Hoffenstein.   NBLV

I want to enter death.   Desire.   Claribel Alegría.   LoL

"I want to fight you," he said in a Belfast accent.   Experience.   James Simmons.   BIrV

I want to find your texture under water.   Touching You Underwater.   Stephen J. Lyons.   PasH

I want to gather your darkness.   To Drink.   Jane Hirshfield.   PasH

I want to get the screams in here.   Elvis Presley.   Rochelle Nameroff. SwNoth

I want to go on.   First Prelude.   Francis J. Smith.   CRP

I Want to Go to Keta.   Kobena Eyi Acquah.   NAfrP

I Want to Hear a Yankee Doodle Tune.   George M. Cohan.   ReLy

I want to kill myself.   Dezső Kosztolányi.   IQMS, tr. by Peter Zollman   *Fr.* Laments of a Poor Little Child.

I want to know today.   Poem.   Sargon Boulus.   MAP, tr. by Sargon Boulus and Alistair Elliot

I want to lament the princess who was killed.   In Memory, 1978.   Judith Kazantzis.   BrRo

I want to live.   Aleksandr Aleksandrovich Blok.   TCRP

I want to live in the shade of your face.   Tinfoil.   Joyce Mansour.   MFP, tr. by Martin Sorrell

I want to look at what happened. (LL) Ofay-Watcher Looks Back. Mongane Wally Serote. NAfrP; PBMAP

I want to love my real father so he can see me. Range of It, The. Michael Klein. WiU

I Want to Love You Very Much. 'Marnia. LW

I want to make a toast to some victory. Childhood. Hoda Hussein. PoArWo, *tr. by* Cornelia Al-Khaled

I want to make you. Haiku. Sonia Sanchez. ISC

I want to mow while riding. (LL) Needs. A. R. Ammons. NIL-7; NIP-4; OBAL

I want to remember the fallen palm. Oblivion. Ellis Ayitey Komey. PBA; PBMAP

I want to return to the first urges, those urges that seemed so unconscious of their beginnings. To Return to the Urges Unconscious of their Beginnings. Pham Tien Duat. AmFaPo, *tr. by* Kevin Bowen and Ngo Vinh Hai

I Want to Say Your Name. Léopold Sédar Senghor. TTTS, *tr. by* Kenneth Koch

I want to scream into the pink hearing aid nestled in his hairy ear, *Where is your fist?.* Finding His Fist. Patricia Smith. SpirFl

I want to see it face to face. Nothing. Charles Simic. NNaP

I want to see the slim palm-trees. Heritage. Gwendolyn B. Bennett. BlSi; ColAP; NAAAL

I Want to Sleep. Jorge Guillén. WoPoe, *tr. by* James Wright and James Wright

I want to speak with the blood that lies down. James Tipton. GeoH

I want to study philosophy in Paris. Frontier. Oswald de Andrade. TCLAP, *tr. by* Flavia Vidal

I want to take the word back into my body, back. Cajun. Sheryl St. Germain. OPRER

I want to tell jokes. Tenderitis. Maxine Chernoff. IllVoic

I want to tell what happens. Washing Your Hair. Lucia Cordell Getsi. IllVoic

I want to travel the common road. Common Road, The. Silas H. Perkins. ITBLP

I want to understand light years. Brown Rosellen. FFC

I want to wash my father's face. Last Acts. Sharon Olds. NIP-4

I want to write, but out comes foam. Intensity and Height. César Vallejo. PoetW, *tr. by* Clayton Eshleman

I want to write you. Love Poem. Linda Pastan. NIL-7; NIP-4

I want you to have some of what I'm having. Labor Day Picnic Poem. Todd Colby. HeMarv

I Want You to Know. Micere Githae Mugo. HAWP

I wanta say just gotta say something. Beautiful Black Men. Nikki Giovanni. BPo; NAAAL

I wanted a rib sandwich. Rib Sandwich. William J. Harris. UnSA

I wanted a stamp for the parcel of figs. Encounter at the Post Office Counter. Christopher Pilling. NLP

I wanted my name. Poem for Ed "Whitey" Ford, A. Jonathan Holden. MoASP

I wanted so ably. World, The. Robert Creeley. NoP-4; PmAP; VCAP

I wanted the heart to scream. Song of the Burning. David Wojahn. SwNoth

I wanted them over. Say Ja. Tom Mandel. PmAP

I wanted this morning to bring you a gift of roses. Roses of Sa'adi, The. Marceline Desbordes-Valmore. BoWoP, *tr. by* Barbara Howes

I wanted to be a nature poet. "Honeysuckle Was the Saddest Odor of All, I Think." Thadious M. Davis. BlSi

I wanted to be sure to reach you. To the Harbormaster. Frank O'Hara. CRP; CoAP; NAAAL-2v2; PoM; VCAP

I wanted to be touched, so I went walking. Who Owns the Night and Lease Stars. Reginald Shepherd. AmPoNex

I wanted to bring you this Jap iris. For C. Philip Whalen. NeAP; VGW

I Wanted to Dream the Mailman. Vivian Lamarque. CItWP, *tr. by* Cinzia Sartini Blum and Lara Trubowitz

I wanted to feel exalted so I picked up. James [*or* Jim] Harrison. BodElec *Fr.* Letters to Yesenin.

I wanted to go down to where the roots begin. Origins. Eric Ormsby. NoP-4

I wanted to have a wedding. Wedding Party. Allison Joseph. AmPoNex; ExTi; MPUn

I wanted to hear. Static. Mary Barnard. APT-2

I wanted to know my mother when she sat. Leroy. Imamu Amiri Baraka. BPo; PmAP

I wanted to see the self, so I looked at the mulberry. Self and the Mulberry, The. Marvin Bell. BodElec

I wanted to see you, / thighs showing. Leila Miccolis. BoWoP, *tr. by* Willis Barnstone and Nelson Cerqueira

I wanted to start the story. We Are Going to Be Here Now. Primus St. John. GT

I wanted to take a walk. Walking Past Paul Blackburn's Apt. on 7th St. Diane Wakoski. TAP

I wanted to teach him the names of flowers. Michael Longley. ModIr *Fr.* Mayo Monologues.

I wanted to write. For Saundra. Nikki Giovanni. BPo; NAAAL; TTY

I wanted to write you a letter. Letter from a Contract Worker. Antonio Jacinto. PBMAP; PoetW, *tr. by* Margaret Dickinson and Michael Wolfers

I wanted you here in the wards, where I am the doctor! (LL) Variations on a Theme by William Carlos Williams. Kenneth Koch. NBLV; NIL-7; NIP-4; NoAM; PmAP; PoM

I wanted you in the kitchen of my heart. James Tipton. GeoH

"I warn ye all, ye gay ladies." Child Waters. *Unknown.* ESPB; OxBB

I warn you to remain velvet and motionless on whatever. Wildlife. Tracy Philpot. AmPoNex

I was a bad dog and didn't obey. Stay. Ben Sonnenberg. Unle

I was a boy when I heard three red words a thousand Frenchmen. Threes. Carl Sandburg. OxBA

I was a boy when I left home. Homecoming. Ho Ch'e Ch'ang. OHMPC, *tr. by* Kenneth Rexroth

I was a child when first I read your books. To Elizabeth Barrett Browning. Bessie Rayner Parkes. VWP

I was a clockwork doll that night. Clockwork Doll. Dahlia Ravikovitch [*or* Ravikovich]. FIT, *tr. by* Robert Friend

I was a cottage maiden. Cousin Kate. Christina Georgina Rossetti. VWP

I was a diver then. Reprieve, The. Elizabeth Garrett. NeBl

I was a girl waiting by the roadside for my boyfriend to come. Elwha River, The. Gary Snyder. NoAM

I was a humble clerk. African Trader's Complaint, The. Dennis C. Osadebay. PBA

I was a humdrum person. What Is This Thing Called Love? Cole Porter. ReLy

I was a joke at dinners; aye, any would-be wit. Propertius. AWP, *tr. by* Kirby Flower Smith *Fr.* Elegies.

I was a lady of high renown. Jamie Douglas. *Unknown.* ESPB

I was a leather skinned harridan. Granny Crack. James Reaney. NOBC

I was a mere boy in a stone-cutter's shop. Abraham. Delmore Schwartz. ChIV-1; TaR

I was a murderer ninety times a day. (LL) Mary Elizabeth Coleridge. VWP; ViWPN

I was a pawn when we began this. I bowed to your black majesty. Lament of the White Queen. Ann Drysdale. TCAWP

I was a peasant girl from Germany. Edgar Lee Masters. NoAM; OxBA; PAI *Fr.* Spoon River Anthology.

I Was a Phony Baloney! Stephanie Brown. AmPoNex; BodElec

I was a quick-footed, long-eared hare, just snatched from my mother's. Meleager. HePo *Fr.* Epigrams.

I was a real phony baloney. I Was a Phony Baloney! Stephanie Brown. AmPoNex; BodElec

I was a rebel, if you please. Address by an Ex-Confederate Soldier to the Grand Army of the Republic, An. Maurice Thompson. CBCWP

I was a ripe fig. Paranoia. Salwa Al-Neimi. PoArWo, *tr. by* Subhi Hadidi and Nathalie Handal

I was a shepherd to fools. Rudyard Kipling. WoPoe *Fr.* Epitaphs of the War [1914–18].

I was a sorry, sorry. (Baloney.). (LL) I Was a Phony Baloney! Stephanie Brown. AmPoNex; BodElec

"I Was a Stranger and Ye Took Me In." Mary E. Tucker. CBWP-1

I was a stranger in the city. Foggy Day (in London Town), A. George Gershwin. ReLy

I was a stricken deer, that left the herd. William Cowper. NAEL-5v1; NAEL-6v1; NAEL-7v1; PAI *Fr.* Task, The.

I was a voice. (LL) Anna Liffey. Eavan Boland. BodElec; ModIr

I was a week away from the red chip when they outed me. Rounding the Horn. L. S. Asekoff. BAP-97

I was a youth of studious mind. Constance Naden. VWP *Fr.* Evolutional Erotics.

I Was About Three Years of Age. Hanny Michaelis. TuT, *tr. by* Peter Van de Kamp

I was again beside my Love in a dream. Mathilde Blind. ViWPN *Fr.* Love in Exile.

I was alone on a sunny shore. Forest Lake. Edith Södergran. WPoS, *tr. by* Stina Katchadourian

I was already. In China. Terry Wolverton. WiU

I was altered in the placenta. Dead Poet, The. Alfred Wellington Purdy. NOBC

I was always fascinated. Mother, May I? Alma Villanueva. WPOW

I was an Arab. Fantasy, A. Mathilde Blind. PoBW; VWP; ViWPN

I was angry with my friend. William Blake. AWP; FHYEP; HAP; NAEL-5v2; NAEL-6v2; NPeEn; OxAEP-2; OxBEV; RB; SCV; SoSe-8; TFi; WeW-3 *Fr.* Songs of Experience.

I was as dark and slim as a Polynesian girl. Sketch. Cecília Meireles. TCLAP, *tr. by* Luiz Fernández García

I was asking for something specific and perfect for my city. Mannahatta. Walt Whitman. MoAmPo

I was asleep but my heart stayed awake. Song. Bible, *O.T.* WPoS

I was barely in country. December, hot. Surrounding Blues on the Way Down. Bruce Weigl. CDa

I was blue / Just as blue as I could be. Blue Skies. Irving Berlin. ReLy

I was born a foreigner. Minority. Imtiaz Dharker. NeBl

I Was Born Almost Ten Thousand Years Ago. *Unknown.* OBCoV

I Was Born at Birth of Blossoms. Rosalía de Castro. STV, *tr. by* John Frederick Nims

I was born downtown on a wintry day. Recapitulations. Karl Shapiro. TaR

I was born in a dough trough. Kukutis's Fruitless Bread. Marcelijus Martinaitis. TWW, *tr. by* Laima Sruoginis

I was born in a Free City, near the North Sea. Curriculum Vitae. Lisel Mueller. IllVoic

I was born in a time of peace. Ts'ai Yen. BoWoP; WPOW *Fr.* Eighteen Verses Sung to a Tatar Reed Whistle.

I was born in Belfast between the mountain and the gantries. Carrickfergus. Louis MacNeice. NAEL-5v2; NAEL-6v2; NOIV; NoAM; PNI

I was born in Belgium, I am Belgian. Place and Date. Leonard Nolens. TuT, *tr. by* Michael O'Loughlin

I was born in Boston in. American Poem, An. Eileen Myles. WiU

I was born in Bristol, and it is possible. Family Fortunes. Charles Hubert Sisson. OxBC

I was born in Kansas. Sunflower. Mack David. ReLy

I was born in Mississippi;. Poem for Myself (Or Blues for a Mississippi Black Boy), A. Etheridge Knight. PoPoPo

I was born in the Congo. Ego Tripping [(There May Be a Reason Why)]. Nikki Giovanni. RaBo

I was born into this world. Gizan Zenrai. JDP, *tr. by* Yoel Hoffmann

I was born on an Irish sea of eggs and porter. HMS *Glory.* Charles Causley. FaBoWar

I Was Born on the Twenty-First in Spring. Alda Merini. CItWP, *tr. by* Cinzia Sartini Blum and Lara Trubowitz

I was born out of sun-rays. Iris. Jacques Perk. TuT, *tr. by* Peter Van de Kamp

I was born the year of the gray pennies. 1943. Sandra McPherson. FaBoWP

I was born the year of the loon. Chronicle. Mei-Mei Berssenbrugge. FSt; OpBo

I was born to the god's disappointment. Under an Impure Star. Armanda Guiducci. CItWP, *tr. by* Cinzia Sartini Blum and Lara Trubowitz

I was born unto this snowy-red earth. Song Taught to Joseph, The. Ray A. Young Bear. AF

I was born with a song in my tongue. Ars. Marina Ivanovna Tsvetayeva [*or* Tsvetaeva]. BoWoP, *tr. by* Willis Barnstone and Edward Brown

I was born with a stone in my hand. In My Other Life. Shara McCallum. AmPoNex

I was brought up on old Aristotle. Limerick. C. S. Cook. PeLi

I was buried near this dyke [*or* Dike]. Epitaph, An. William Blake. FaBoEE; OBCoV

I was burning incense, paying respects to my mother. Night of the First Full Moon, The. Li K'ai-hsien. CoBLCP, *tr. by* Jonathan Chaves

"I was but [*or* bat] seven year auld [*or* alld]" Laily Worm and the Machrel of the Sea, The. *Unknown.* ESPB; OxBB; SCGP

I was combing some long hair coming out of a tree. In the Forest. Russell Edson. LCAP-2

I was coming back from. Truck, The. John A. Stone. BloBone

I was coming to that. (LL) Welsh Incident. Robert Graves. NOBE; OBSP; OxBEV; OxBTC

I was counting time in the heartbeat of the storm. Hero and Thief. Kofi Anyidoho. PBMAP

I was created for one man alone. Don't Ever Leave Me. Jerome Kern. ReLy

I Was Dancing Alone in Binh Dinh Province. D. F. Brown. CDa

I was dead and I wanted peace. Grammar, A. Andrei Codrescu. SPE

I was descending from the mountains of sleep. Afternoon Sleep. Robert Bly. WoPoe

I was doing nothing in particular. Pain. Charles Simic. BodElec

I was drowsy, but my heart was awake. Listen! Bible, *O.T.* WoPoe, *tr. by* Peter Jay *Fr.* Song of Solomon, The [*or* The Song of Songs].

I was eating a chicken sandwich with mayonnaise. Frenchie. Stephen Dobyns. BodElec

I was eighteen when I came in these gates. Words from Hell. David Helwig. NOBC

I was empty as a new car, and. Reading *Bonjour, Tristesse* at the Florence Crittenden Home for Unwed Mothers. Diane Wakoski. GeoHom

I Was Fair Beat. Robert Garioch. OBCoV; OxBTC

I was familiar with the word. April in Houston. Dolores de Iruretagoyena de Humphrey. ReBoTo

I was far forward on the plain, the burning swamp. Little Girl with Bands on Her Teeth, The. Genevieve Taggard. VGW

I was fishing in the abandoned reservoir. Quinnapoxet. Stanley Kunitz. LoL

I was flying over sydney. Flying. Michael Dransfield. BMAP

I was following a man. Following a Man. John Ash. HarvBoo

I was foretold that on a certain day. Sonnet XX. Louise Labé. BoWoP, *tr. by* Willis Barnstone

I was foretold, your rebel[l] sex. Deposition from Love, A. Thomas Carew. BASC; BeJo; CaPo; CavPo; MeLP

I was four in this photograph fishing. Fifth Grade Autobiography. Rita Dove. ISC; NIL-7; NIP-4

I was glad to sit down. Kinaxixi. Agostinho Neto. PoetW; WoPoe, *tr. by* W. S. Merwin

I was going along a dusty highroad. Mountain Talk. A. R. Ammons. HCAP

I was going thru the big earth. Song about a Dead Person—or Was It a Mole?, A. *Unknown.* STP, *tr. by* Richard Johnny John and Jerome Rothenberg

I was going thru the big smoke. Another Song about That Same Dead Person or Mole—Whichever it Was. *Unknown.* STP, *tr. by* Richard Johnny John and Jerome Rothenberg

I was going to ardently pursue this day. Topophilia. Mary Ruefle. BAP-97

I was going to say something. Ancestor. Thomas Kinsella. BIrV; ModIr; NOIV; NPeEn; OxBEV; PBCIP; PoE

I WAS going to the City to sell the herbs I had plucked. Hermit and Politician. Po Chü-i. ChiP, *tr. by* Arthur Waley

I was going to the river for water. Mirabai [*or* Mira Bai]. WPoS

I was going up to say something. Thomas Kinsella. *See* I was going to say something

I was grown up and ready for Him now. (LL) Day Zimmer Lost Religion, The. Paul Zimmer. InPK-6; PBCAP

I was helping my mother. Fifteen. Patricia Pogson. NLP

I was here first. Daisy, Five, Speaks to Sophia, Two. Ralph Lombreglia. Unle

I was Hermocrateia: Twenty-nine / children I bore. Antipater of Thessalonica. GrAn

I was, I am not; smiled, that since did weep. Epitaph, An. Thomas Heywood. OxBSP

I was ill, lying on my bed of old papers. Secret Garden, The. Rita Dove. NoAM

I was in blossom when I was a child. Ballade. Charles, Duc d' Orléans. WoPoe, *tr. by* Willis Barnstone and Tony Barnstone

I was in deep, through. Arrival. Debra Kang Dean. UrbNat

I was in Hawaii, but the letter. How I Got the Word. Marvin Bell. BodElec

I was in prison in that town. Sebastopol. Ilya [*or* Karl] L'vovich Selvinsky [*or* Sel'vinskii]. TCRP, *tr. by* Daniel Weissbort

I was in the army of the Zanj. First Communiqué from One Returning from the Zanj Revolt. Abd al-Aziz Al-Maqalih. MAP, *tr. by* John Heath-Stubbs and Lena Jayyusi

I was in the bookstore, reading the ends of mysteries. Three Songs. Rachel Wetzsteon. RA

I was in the lane and saw the car pass. and B, A. Charles Hubert Sisson. OxBC

I was innocent of grief. Lament of Mary, The. *Unknown.* IQMS, *tr. by* Adam Makkai

I was invested in mother-earth, the crypt of roots. Geoffrey Hill. NoAM *Fr.* Mercian Hymns

I was just beginning to feel in the mood. Old Husband Suspects Adultery, An. Gavin Ewart. NoAM

I was just turned twenty-one. Edgar Lee Masters. APT-1 *Fr.* Spoon River Anthology.

I was Kallimachos, age five. Lucianus [*or* Lucian]. GrAn

I was kissed once. Kiss, The. Alice Walker. GT

I was late in understanding the meaning of humility, and it's the fault of those who taught me to place it at the other end of pride. You must domesticate the idea of existence in you to understand it. Odysseus Elytis. GiftTon, *tr. by* Olga Broumas *Fr.* Anoint the Ariston.

I was leaning across your chest. Hydromaniac. Rosemary Tonks. EmeKit

I was led into captivity by the bitch business. Money. Charles Hubert Sisson. OxBSP

I was living in New York. Mary's Dream. Van K. Brock. AllShUp; SwNoth

I was looking for the powerful spring grass, how powerful. Sixty-Six Poems for a Blackfoot Bundle. *Unknown.* STP, *tr. by* Jerome Rothenberg

I Was Looking for the University. Clarence Major. GT

I was looking for your hair. A un Desconocido. Lorna Dee Cervantes. TouFir

I was making my way home late one night. Aisling. Paul Muldoon. PNI

I was mindless. Potter's Wheel, The. Calvin Forbes. GT

I was miserable, of course, for I was seventeen. Mingus at the Showplace. William Matthews. SeSe

I was myself blown. For My People. Wendy Rose. CDW

I was naked for the first kiss of my mother. U Tam'si Tchicaya. PBMAP *Fr.* Epitomé (1962).

I was never able to recite a fable. You Were Never Lovelier. Johnny Mercer. ReLy

I was never an ascetic. "Naum Korzhavin." TCRP

I was never in! (LL) Baffled for just a day or two. Emily Dickinson. PAI; PoBW

I was never the light lad. Spawn of Slums, The. James W. Thompson. BPo

I was never the one to spot him walking. Blueberry Man. David Bergman. GLP

I was not a good daughter. Persephone. Kathleen Norris. HW

I was not born from your womb. Angola. Amélia Veiga. HAWP, *tr. by* Julia Kirst

I was not born to Helicon, nor dare. Gratulatory to Mr. Ben Johnson for His Adopting of Him to Be His Son, A. Thomas Randolph. BeJo; NPeEn

I was not chosen to head the dragon list. Tune: "Overtures"—On Myself. Ch'iao Chi. SuSp, *tr. by* Sherwin S. S. Fu

I was not in safety, neither had I rest, neither was I quiet; yet trouble came. (LL) Bible, *O.T.* NPeEn; OBVE; TrJP *Fr.* Job.

I was not; now I am—a few days hence. Mystery, The. Paul Laurence Dunbar. APN-2

I was not sorrowful, I could not weep. Spleen. Ernest Christopher Dowson. MoBrPo; NOBVV

I Was Not There. Karen Gershon. HP

I was not useful? So. Fidelity Rewarded. Dora Greenwell. VWP

I was not—was born—was. Inscribed on a Statue of Hermes. *Unknown.* GrAn, *tr. by* Peter Jay

I was of delicate mind. I stepped aside for my needs. Rudyard Kipling. FaBoEE; FaBoTw; NPeEn; PeFWW *Fr.* Epitaphs of the War [1914–1918].

I was on a white coast once. Canticle. David Shapiro. TTTS

I was on my high / horse then. Thorn Merchant's Mistress, The. Yusef Komunyakaa. RACG

I was on the couch when the jehova's witnesses came. Patrick Pardo. ReBoTo

I was one of maybe 20 people sitting in a dark theater on Fourth Stree. Puffy Jacket. Amy Fusselman. HeMarv

I was one of the saved. As a Child. Robert Bly. InvLad

I was one out of a hundred, out of thousands. When They Robbed Me of My Name. Nora Strejilevich. MirDau, *tr. by* Celeste Kostopulos-Cooperman

I was out in my kayak. Spring Fiord. *Unknown.* STP, *tr. by* Armand Schwerner

I was out in the early evening, taking a walk in the fields to think about this. Strange Fruit. Joy Harjo. SeSe

I was parading the Côte d'Azur. My Father's Geography. Michael S. Weaver. GT; PBCAP

I was passing through the village of mottled bamboo. Woman Tung. Wu Chia-chi. CoBLCP, *tr. by* Jonathan Chaves

I was passionate. Lal Ded [*or* Lalla]. WPoS

I was playing golf the day. Harry Graham. PeLV *Fr.* Some Ruthless Rhymes.

I was playing hopscotch on the slate. Our Sharpeville. Ingrid De Kok. HAWP

I was playing, I suppose. When It Happened. Hilda Schiff. HP

I was promised a horse but what I got instead. Palladas [*or* Pallades]. GrAn

I was pulling veronica out of the lawn when this hornet came. A. R. Ammons. NoAM *Fr.* Sphere.

I was reading about rationalism. Bat, The. Jane Kenyon. LoL

I Was Received in an Early Audience at Heaven-Gate and Then at Noon I Was Summoned to the Yu-shun Gate. In the Evening I Withdrew, and Improvised This Poem. Yang Shih-ch'i. CoBLCP, *tr. by* Jonathan Chaves

I was resting comfortably. Just in Time. Betty Comden. ReLy

I was riding one of the best-loved horses in the world. Out West. Bill Manhire. EmeKit

I was run over by the truth one day. To Whom It May Concern. Adrian Mitchell. FaBoWar; OBWP

I was scared to walk out / with the dough. (LL) Situation. Langston Hughes. APSN; OBAL

I Was Sent For. Lupenga Mphande. NAfrP

I was sent forth from the power. *Unknown.* PFTM-1 *Fr.* Thunder, Perfect Mind, The.

I was sent in to see her. Tear. Thomas Kinsella. ModIr; NOIV; NoP-4; OxBEV

I was sent to fetch an eye. Naked Vision. Gwen Harwood. EmeKit

I was seventy-seven, come August. Little Old Lady in Lavender Silk, The. Dorothy Parker. NBLV

I was sewing a seam one day. Seams. Hazel Hall. APT-1

I was sick. Jesus Was Crucified or: It Must Be Deep. Carolyn M. Rodgers. BlSi

I Was Sick and in Prison. Jones Very. ColAP; NOBA; SacPr

I was sitting behind a somewhat neat old person. Concert. Josephine Miles. NALW

I was sitting in mcsoreley's. outside it was New York and beauti- / fully snowing. E. E. Cummings. NoAM

I was sitting in my study. Papa's Letter. *Unknown.* WeW-3

I was sitting on the roof with my grandmother. Coming of Age. Michael Palma. UnSA

I was sitting there, taking my ease. Limerick. Cyril Ray. PeLi

I Was Sleeping Where the Black Oaks Move. Louise Erdrich. HATNAP; NoP-4; PoPoPo

I was sleepless, I was awake all night. Sleepless. Al-Khansa. BoWoP, *tr. by* Willis Barnstone

I was so assailed by the memory. Quant Souvenir Me Ramentoit. Charles, Duc d' Orléans. WoPoe, *tr. by* Fred Chappell

I was so buoyant. Bella [*or* Izabella] Akhatovna Akhmadulina. TCRusP, *tr. by* Daniel Weissbort

I was so chill, and overworn, and sad. Song. Anna Wickham. MoBrPo

I was so sick last night I. Morning After. Langston Hughes. NAAL-2v2; NBLV; NoAM; OBCoV

I Was Speaking of Oranges to a Lady. José Garcia Villa. WoPoe

I was standing at the pond, in my posh fly fishing class, when a squeal. Mother Nature. Amy Fusselman. HeMarv

I was standing in a crap game doing no harm, Baby! You've Been a Good Old Wagon, but You've Done Broke Down. Ben Harney. OBAL

I was standing in the bedroom. I Don't Remember Christmas. Richard Maltby, Jr. ReLy

I was standing there. Oral Tradition, The. Eavan Boland. PBCIP

I was sticking my hands into his pockets. Inside Father's Pockets. Martha Rhodes. ExTi

I was suffering exile like a rambling. I Was Suffering Exile. Nahabed Kouchag. WoPoe, *tr. by* Desmond O'Grady

I was summoned to the porter's lodge for an overseas call from California. Scrabble. David Starkey. ReTh

I Was Surprised to Find Myself Out Here & Acting like a Crow. *Unknown.* STP, *tr. by* Johnny John and Jerome Rothenberg

I was takin' off my bonnet. Darwinism in the Kitchen. *Unknown.* NBLV

I was talking / to a friend. Eagle in the Land of Oz. Don Receveur. CDa

I was teaching my little sister how to fly when she broke her. Station (2). James Galvin. GifTon

I was that lonely. (LL) Geranium, The. Theodore Roethke. CoAP; EmeKit; UnPo; WeW-3

I was the first fruits of the battle of Missionary Ridge. Edgar Lee Masters. OxBA *Fr.* Spoon River Anthology.

I was the last of my line. Gus Speaks. Maxine W. Kumin. Unle

I was the last passenger of the day. Bus, The. Leonard Cohen. HeIP-4

I was the Moor Moraima. Lovely Young Moor, A. *Unknown.* BoWoP, *tr. by* Willis Barnstone

I was the one who waited in the garden. Resurrection, The. Elizabeth Jennings. HarvBoo

I was the only child of Frances Harris of Virginia. Edgar Lee Masters. NoAM; OxBA; PAI *Fr.* Spoon River Anthology.

I was the patriarch of the shining land. John Sutter. Yvor Winters. MoAmPo; NOBA; NoAM

I was the poetry editor. Poetry Editor. Yevgeny [*or* Evgenii] Mikhailovich Vinokurov. TCRP, *tr. by* Daniel Weissbort

I was the reflection of malevolence. Ugly Heart, The. Martha Anthony. InTrad

I was the rock. Child of Adam. Viola C. White. YaYoPo

I was the staunchest of our fleet. Derelict, The. Rudyard Kipling. NoAM

I was the type who would laugh at romance. It's Love Again. Sam Coslow. ReLy

I was there. Yearning, A. Arapera Hineira Blank. PeNZ, *tr. by* the author

I was thinking about her all the way from Troy. Fortunes of War. Kit Wright. PeLV

I was thinking, Mother, of that poor old horse. Reserved. Walter De la Mare. GTBS-P

I was thirsty. Epigram. Meleager. GrAn, *tr. by* Peter Whigham

I was thrashing on the couch. That Great Wingless Bird. Adrian C. Louis. UnSA

I was three-ish. Right Arm, The. Paul Muldoon. NoAM

I was thrilled when I went to the Zoo. Limerick. Victor Gray. PeLi

I was thy Neighbour once, thou rugged Pile! Elegiac Stanzas Suggested by a Picture of Peele Castle, in a Storm, Painted by Sir George Beaumont. William Wordsworth. GTBS-P; NAEL-5v2; NAEL-6v2; NOBRP; NPeEn; PoE

I was tired of being a woman. Consorting with Angels. Anne Sexton. NALW

I was tired. So I lay down. Mnemonic. Li-Young Lee. UnSA

I was too late for the most important. Longing for Jail, A. Edvard Kocbek. PoSu, *tr. by* Michael Scammell and Veno Taufer

I was twelve, and did not. Lesson on Braces. Valerie Jean. SpirFl

I was upon my way to seek him there. (LL) Henry Wadsworth Longfellow. APN-1; TCAPo Fr. Tales of a Wayside Inn.

I was upon the high and blessed mound. Sonnet: Of the Grave of Selvaggia, on the Monte della Sambuca. Cino da Pistoia. AWP; EaltPo, tr. by Dante Gabriel Rossetti

I Was Very Prolific. Suzanne Wise. AmPoNex

I was walking a mile. Tennyson. EBVV Fr. Maud [A Monodrama].

I was walking along the Sea of Galilee. Walking along the Sea of Galilee. "Dovid Knut." TCRP; TCRusP, tr. by John Glad

I was walking behind Elliot Carter. Poem for Elliot Carter on His 90th Birthday. Alan Dugan. BodElec

I was walking down by the old / Santee. Second Carolina Said-Song. A. R. Ammons. OBAL

I was walking downtown. Man in Black, The. Mark Strand. SPE

I was walking in a government warehouse. Fifteen Million Plastic Bags. Adrian Mitchell. EmeKit; OBSV; OxBTC

I was walking near the hotel in the evening. Southern Dawn. Pier Paolo Pasolini. VCWP, tr. by Norman MacAfee

I was washing my daughter's hair. Name of god, The. Imtiaz Dharker. NeBl

I Was Washing Outside in the Darkness. Osip Emilevich Mandelstam [or Mandelshtam]. AF

I was watching for it, everytime watching, for the neck that was. Untitled. Karen Volkman. AmPoNex

I was Willie Metcalf. Edgar Lee Masters. APT-1 Fr. Spoon River Anthology.

I was with Special Force, blue-X-ing raids. Trial. Ruth Padel. MFPA

I was wrapped in black. Us. Anne Sexton. MPUn

I wash off. (LL) For My Lover, Returning to His Wife. Anne Sexton. HCAP; UnPo; WPE

I Wash the Shirt. Anna Swirszczynska. BLT

I washed a load of clothes. Alone for a Week. Dolores Kendrick. FFC

I wasn't driving. Bus Driver Poem, The. Khaled Mattawa. AmPoNex

I wasn't with you when death came. When Death Came. Adam Zagajewski. VCWP, tr. by Renata Gorcyznski

I Waste Away. Bible, O.T. TrJP Fr. Isaiah.

I waste my teeming age. I do not know. Abishag. Jacob [orJakov] Fichman. TrJP

I wat was mony a weeping e'e. (LL) Jamie Telfer of [or in] the Fair Dodhead. Unknown. ESPB; IBB; OxBB

I watch a man in the schoolyard. Speech Against Stone. Charles Martin. RA

I watch a streak of red that might have issued from Christ's breast. (LL) Soldiers Bathing. Frank Templeton Prince. GTBS-P; MoBrPo; NOCV; OBWP; OxBTC

I watch, and long have watched, with calm regret. William Wordsworth. OxBSo; Son

I watch her in the corner there. Arachne. Rose Terry Cooke. APN-2

I watch her silhouette. Her Back to Me. Ed Stever. PasH

I watch me until I disappear and we. Analogue. Marie Ponsot. CLPP

I watch, O youths, this farmhouse and this place. Unknown. PriapPo, tr. by Richard W. Hooper Fr. Priapus Poems, The.

I watch Tai Chi per / forating my mind. I am the Babe of Joseph Stalin's Daughter. Rochelle Owens. PFTM-2

I watch the Beast as it licks itself. War. André Breton. AF, tr. by Mary Ann Caws

I watch the happier people of the house. Neurasthenia. Agnes Mary Frances Robinson. NOBVV; NPeEn

I watch the Indians dancing to help the young corn at Taos pueblo. The old men squat in a ring. New Mexican Mountain. Robinson Jeffers. NoAM

I watch the limitless distance of autumn. Watching the Distances. Tu Fu. CrYelRi, tr. by Sam Hamill

I watch the sanitary state. Unknown. VerBaPo

I watch them killing my husband. Last Take. Carol Muske. GeoHom

I watch you. Watching You. Simon J. Ortiz. HATNAP

I watched a laughing cloud. Evening. King D. Kuka. VoR

I watched a rosebud very long. Symbols. Christina Georgina Rossetti. NALW

I watched him breathe. (LL) Race, The. Sharon Olds. InvLad; RaBo

I watched its first green push. Tulip. Penny Harter. TWW

I watched little black boys. Nayo-Barbara Watkins. NBV

I watched my mother at the microphone. Nostalgia. Darryl Holmes. InTrad

I watched old squatting chimpanzee: He traced. Sporting Acquaintances. Siegfried Sassoon. OxBSo; OxBTC

I watched the hills drink the last color of light. Thought's End. Léonie Adams. MoAmPo

I watched the Moon around the House. Emily Dickinson. APN-2; NCAP

I watched the seeds come down this afternoon. At a Country Hotel. Howard Nemerov. PoRA

I watched thee when the foe was at our side. Love and Death. Byron. CAGL; EBEV; NOBE

I watched them float up the dark chimney. (LL) Sorrow. D. H. Lawrence. GTBS-P; NPeEn; OBMV

I watched you roll it out. (LL) Bamboo Mat. Yuan Chen. CrYelRi; ErotSp, tr. by Sam Hamill

I watched you walk across the street. Dangerous World, The. Naomi Replansky. PoBW

I watcht as the flung screen door. Envies, The. George Bowering. NOBC

I watered my horse at the Long Wall caves. Song. Susan Ch'en Lin. ColAnChi, tr. by Burton Watson

I wear a cloak of laughter. Cloak of Laughter. Abigail Cresson. PoToHe

I wear a warning bloodcoat. Elba. Gerrit Kouwenaar. PFTM-2, tr. by Peter Nijmeijer

I wear bright colours. Elma Mitchell. NewEx

I wear the scaly skin of frequent fevers. Genius. Margit Szécsi. IQMS, tr. by Agnes Arany-Makkai

I weary of these noisy nights. Away. Max Ehrmann. PoToHe

I weave the night, I cross the weft with stars. In the Flight of the Blue Heron: To Montezuma. Anita Endrezze. CDW

I weave with brightly colored strings. Falling in Love with Love. Richard Rodgers. ReLy

I weep and weep a tear. Tear, The. Martin Sorescu. VCWP, tr. by Seamus Heaney and Joana Russell-Gebbett

I weep, but with no bitterness I weep. Souvenir. Alfred de Musset. AWP, tr. by George Santayana

I weep for Adonais—he is dead! Shelley. EBEV; FHYEP; NAEL-6v2; NOBRP; OxAEP-2; TFi

I weep for Adonis, "The lovely Adonis is dead." Bion. See Wail, wail, Ah for Adonis!

I weigh 486 lbs on Jupiter. Letter to Ron Silliman on the Back of a Map of the Solar System, A. Dennis Schmitz. LCAP-2

I welcome you, silvery moon. Early Graves, The. Friedrich Gottlieb Klopstock. GePo, tr. by J. W. Thomas

I welcomed the Spring in romantic Chungking. Lyric to Spring. Joseph W. Stilwell. OBAL

I well remember how some threescore years. Very Old Man. James Henry. NOBVV; OxBEV

I Wende to Dede. Unknown. HAP; MiEL

I wende to deeth, knight stith in stour. Unknown. OHMEL

I went a-sailing with my deer. Tail of the See, A. Elizabeth T. Corbett. OBCA

I went across the road to the pub; wrote this. (LL) Death of a Poet. Charles Causley. EmeKit; OxBTC

I went away from the lights of Fourteenth Street. Hello, Dolly! Jerry Herman. ReLy

I went back in the alley. Homecoming. Langston Hughes. SAmP; TRP

I went before God, and he said. Love's Compensation. Voltairine de Cleyre. SWaP

I went by this building. Red Flower. Ann Turner. SSCS

I went don the tree-lined street of false gods. Marvels of the City, The. Charles Simic. LCAP-2

I went down by Cascadilla. Cascadilla Falls. A. R. Ammons. NOBA

I went down to Jordan. Singing Hallelujia. Fenton Johnson. NAAAL

I went down to my garden patch. Unknown. TLR

I went down to the railway. Willow Song. Anne Stevenson. NoP-4

I went down to the river. Life Is Fine. Langston Hughes. NBLV; SAmP

I Went Downtown. Unknown. TLR

I went for a walk over the dunes again this morning. Corsons Inlet. A. R. Ammons. CoAP; ColAP; NAAL-2v2; NAAL-5; NOBA; NoAM; NoP-4; PoE; VCAP

I went into a public-'ouse to get a pint o' beer. Tommy. Rudyard Kipling. CABP; EBEV; FaBoWar; MoBrPo; NoP-4; OBWP; OxAEP-2; OxBTC; PeVV; UV

I went into my garden to gather some herbs. Ditty. Sister Bertken [or Bertke]. WPOW, tr. by Jonathan Crewe

I went into my grandmother's garden / And there I found a farden. Swinging. Unknown. OxNR

I went into my grandmother's garden, / And there I found a farthing. Farthing, A. Unknown. OxNR

I went into my mother as. To the Unborn and Waiting Children. Lucille Clifton. InPK-6

I went into the barber's and said, quite calmly. They Don't Understand a Thing. Vladimir Vladimirovich Mayakovsky [or Maiakovskii]. TCRP, tr. by Bernard Meares

I went into the kitchen just now to stir the black beans and rice. Kitchens. Aurora Levins Morales. PueRic

I Went Into the Maverick Bar. Gary Snyder. HCAP; NAAL-2v2; PoE; VCAP

I went into the wood one day. Fairy Story. Stevie Smith. NOxBChV; OBSP

I went my Sunday mornings round. Song. John Clare. NOBVV

I went on Friday afternoons. Au Tombeau de Mon Père. Ronald McCuaig. NOBAu

I Went Out. Velemir [or Viktor Vladimirovich] Khlebnikov. TCRusP, tr. by Kathy Lewis and Bob Perelman

I went out at daybreak and stood on Primrose Hill. Birds Waking. W. S. Merwin. NOBA

I WENT out at the eastern gate. Eastern Gate, The. Unknown. ChiP, tr. by Arthur Waley

I went out in the night. I Went Out. Velemir [or Viktor Vladimirovich] Khlebnikov. TCRusP, tr. by Kathy Lewis and Bob Perelman

I went out in the Spring. Tsurayuki. OHMPJ

I Went Out into the Garden. Moses Ibn Ezra. TrJP, tr. by Solomon Solis-Cohen

I went out of the conf'rence to get a pint of beer. Mary Wilson. UV Fr. Harold Wilson's Selected Poems.

I went out on a frosty morning. Ice Cold. Sean O Riordain. NOIV, tr. by Thomas Kinsella

I went out seeking love. More Stanzas Applied to Spiritual Things. Saint John of the Cross. TOF, tr. by K. Kavanaugh and O. Rodrigues

I went out to the hazel wood. Song of Wandering Aengus, The. W. B. Yeats. ChAP; FaBoCh; MoBrPo; OTCP; PoRA; RaBo; TFi; TTTS

I went to a party. Rose on My Cake, The. Karla Kuskin. TLR

I went to bat for the Lady Chatte. Lass in Wonderland, A. Francis Reginald. MoCV

I went to ch'ch, 'tother night. Sister Johnson's Speech. Maggie Pogue Johnson. CBWP-4

I went to Cuba on a raft I made. Belonging. Rafael Campo. AmPoNex; WiU

I went to Frankfort, and got drunk. Porson's Visit to the Continent. Richard Porson. FaBoEE

I went to Gold Mountain to Visit a Ch'an Master But He Was Not at Home. Mo Shih-lung. CoBLCP, tr. by Jonathan Chaves

I went to Hsun-yang River to see a friend off at night. Song of the P'i-P'a. Po Chü-i. ChinPo, tr. by Yip Wai-lim

I went to London both blithe and gay. Highwayman, The. Unknown. ECEV

I went to ma daddy. Hard Daddy. Langston Hughes. NAAAL

I went to Noke. Unknown. OxNR

I went to play with Billy. He. What Johnny Told Me. John Ciardi. TLR

I went to river last night. Voz de la Gente. Jimmy Santiago Baca. PmAP

I Went to See Irving Babbitt. Richard Eberhart. OBAL

I went to the animal fair. Animal Fair. Unknown. NTCP

I went to the coffeehouse. Cup and Rose. Nizar Qabbani. MAP, tr. by Diana Der Hovanessian and Lena Jayyusi

I went to the dances at Chandlerville. Edgar Lee Masters. HAP; IllVoic; MoAmPo; NOBA; NoAM; OxBA Fr. Spoon River Anthology.

I went to the field to break. Unsteady Yellow. Tess Gallagher. InvLad

I went to the Garden of Love. William Blake. AWP; EnLoPo; FHYEP; HAP; NAEL-5v2; NAEL-6v2; NPeEn; NoP-4; OBGa; OxAEP-2; OxBEV; PoE; PoPoPo; RB; SCGP; TFi; TOF; TRP Fr. Songs of Experience.

I went to the Hotel Broog. Difference of Zoos, A. Gregory Corso. VGW

I went to the toad that lies under the wall. Unknown. OxNR

I went to the wood and got it. Thorn, A. Unknown. ReMoGo

I went to this party and all the ones who had disappeared. Bermuda Triangle. Joel Long. AmPoNex

I went to turn the grass once after one. Tuft of Flowers, The. Robert Frost. APT-1; AWP; MoAmPo; NAAL-2v2; OxBA

I went under cover of night. Nicodemus. Howard Nemerov. GI; TaR

I went up one pair of stairs / Just like me. Just Like Me. Unknown. ReMoGo

I went walking in the Rose Gardens. Washington Park. Gerald Costanzo. UrbNat

I went with the Duchess to tea. Limerick: "I went with the Duchess to tea." Woodrow Wilson. PeLi

I Wept as I Lay Dreaming. Heinrich Heine. AWP, tr. by John Todhunter

"I wept it! Ha ha!" (LL) Crying. Galway Kinnell. ChAP; KaS; NTCP

I were unkind unless that I did shed. Lines on His Companions Who Died in the Northern Seas. Thomas James. NOSC

I whisk the litter from my mother's tomb. Sweeping. Leslie Monsour. FFC

I whispered, 'I am too young." Brown Penny. W. B. Yeats. BoLoP; FaBoCh

I who am dead a thousand years / And wrote this crabbed post-classic screed. To a Poet a Thousand Years Hence. John Heath-Stubbs. OxBC

I who am dead a thousand years / And wrote this sweet archaic song. To a Poet a Thousand Years Hence. James Elroy Flecker. MoBrPo; PoRA

I, who am Nature, the mother of all things, the mistress of all the elements. I who am Nature, mother of all. Lucius Apuleius. HW

I who am the beauty of the green earth and the white moon. Charge of the Goddess, The. Doreen Valiente. HW, tr. by Starhawk

I who by day am function of the light. Epigram. James Vincent Cunningham. VGW

I, who could have been the best of poems. Nikolai Stepanovich Gumilyov [or Gumiliov or Gumilev]. TCRP

I, who cut off my sorrows. Akazome Emon. BoWoP; WPOW

I who employ a poet's tongue. Timid Lover. Countee Cullen. ColAP

I who erewhile the happy Garden sung. John Milton. PeECV Fr. Paradise Regained [or Regain'd].

I who have always believed too much in words. (LL) Fly. W. S. Merwin. ChAP; NNaP; OWoS

I, who in times before, with youthful mind. Miklós Zrínyi. IQMS, tr. by Thomas Kabdebo Fr. Zrinyiad, The.

I, who leapt beneath the Mtskhetian white moon. Lines Written during a Sleepless Night in Tbilisi. Bella [or Izabella] Akhatovna Akhmadulina. ARWW, tr. by Catriona Kelly

I, who used to score five, even nine times. Philodemus. GrAn

I, who used to ward off the starlings and that snatcher. Antipater of Sidon. HePo Fr. Epigrams.

I who wait for myself. Poetry Calendar, A. Chimako Tada. VCWP, tr. by Naoshi Koriyama

I Who Was Born. Adriann Roland Holst. TuT, tr. by Desmond Egan

I, who was lower than any worm. Seven. Natan Zach. FIT, tr. by Robert Friend

I whole in body and in minde. Isabella Whitney. BWW Fr. Manner of Her Will and What She Left to London and to All Those in It, at Her Departing, The.

I will accept thy will to do and be. Bruised Reed Shall He Not Break, A. Christina Georgina Rossetti. OxAEP-2

I will admit freely that it hurt. Small Talk in a Garden. O. B. Hardison, Jr. CRP

I will always be new! (LL) I Am Cherry Alive. Delmore Schwartz. NOxBChV; TTTS

I will arise and go now, and go to Innisfree. Lake-Isle of Innisfree, The. W. B. Yeats. CABP; ChAP; ClHu; HeIP-4; InPK-6; MoBrPo; NAEL-5v2; NAEL-6v2; NOBE; NoAM; NoP-4; OBEV; OxAEP-2; OxBTC; PAI; PoE; PoPoPo; PoRA; TFi; UV

I will arise and go now, and go to Inverness. Cockney of the North, The. Harry Graham. UV

I will be deaf / when my children need my help. (LL) Elena. Pat Mora. NIL-7; UnSA

I will be home in two months and look you in the eyes. (LL) Message. Allen Ginsberg. CoAmPo; NeAP; VGW

I will be in Ostia. Ostia Will Receive You. Friederike Mayröcker. PFTM-2, tr. by Beth Bjorklund

I will be / M o ving in the Street of her. E. E. Cummings. VGW

I will be patient while my Lord. Cinderella. Ruby C. Saunders. BlSi

"I will be sorry for their childishness" (LL) Coventry Patmore. EBEV; EBVV; NOBVV; OBEV; OxAEP-2; PoToHe; SoSe-8 Fr. Unknown Eros, The.

I will be the gladdest thing. Afternoon on a Hill. Edna St. Vincent Millay. APT-1; ChAP; NTCP; OBCA; OxBA; TTTS

I will be true, despite thy scythe and thee. (LL) William Shakespeare. OxAEP-1; Son Fr. Sonnets.

I will be your lover. Bush Speaks, The. Ernest G. Moll. NOBAu

I will be your mouth now, to do your singing. Funeral Plainsong from a Younger Woman to an Older Woman, A. Judy Grahn. GLP

I will begin by mentioning the word. Phase Four. John Berryman. BodElec

I will begin to delineate the green family. Green Family, The. Colleen Thibaudeau. NOBC

I will blame him. After Listening to Jack Teagarden. . . . James McKean. SeSe

I Will Bow and Be Simple. Unknown. TCAPo

I Will Bring You Twin Grays. Marla Big Boy. ReEnLa

I will build a house of rest. House of Rest, The. Julia Ward Howe. SWaP

I will build my fire today. Charm for Lighting the Fire, A. Unknown. NOIV, tr. by Thomas Kinsella

I will build you a house. Tou Wan Speaks to Her Husband Liu Sheng. Rita Dove. ESEAA

I will build you a house of windows to let. Song of a Thousand Empty Hands. Adele Ne Jame. PoArWo

I will call you. My Friend the Wind. King D. Kuka. VoR

I will carry my coat and not put on my belt. Unknown. BoWoP Fr. Tzu Yeh Songs.

I WILL cast out Wisdom and reject Learning. Taoist Song. Hsi K'ang. ChiP, tr. by Arthur Waley

I will choose a place where the snakes feel safe. Ideal Retreat, The. W.S. Merwin and Nguyen Ngoc Bich. EaWin, tr. by W. S. Merwin and Nguyen Ngoc Bich

I will come to you. Yakamochi (Otomo no Yakamochi). OHPJ

I will confesse. Hymne to Love, An. Robert Herrick. NOSC

I will consider the outnumbering dead. Merlin. Geoffrey Hill. InPK-6; TRP

I Will Cut Out the Middle Watch. Hwang Chin-i. WoPoe, *tr.* by John S. Major

I will die in Miami in the sun. Variations on a Text by Vallejo. Donald Justice. NoAM; VCAP

I will die in Paris, on a rainy day. Black Stone Lying on a White Stone. César Vallejo. TCLAP, *tr.* by Robert Bly and John Knoepfle

I will dream it again. (LL) Wormwood. Thomas Kinsella. CIP-2; PBCIP

I will drink to your health, sweet Amy. To Amy. J. Gordon. OBAL

I will duly pass the day O my mother, and duly return to you. (LL) Walt Whitman. NAAL-2v1; NAAL-3

I will enjoy thee now my Celia, come. Thomas Carew. BASC; BeJo; CABP; CaPo; NAEL-5v1; NAEL-6v1; NAEL-7v1; OxAEP-1; PBRV *Fr.* Rapture, A.

I will exchange a city for a sunset. Barter. Marie Blake. PoToHe

I will find that it's still there. (LL) Mementos, 1. W. D. Snodgrass. MoAmPo; NoP-4; UnPo; VCAP

I will follow. (LL) Grandfather. Lance Henson. CDW; HATNAP, *tr.* by Lance Henson

I will give my love an apple without e'er a core. *Unknown.* RB

I will go and plough in the Palace Yard. King's Courtyard, The. *Hungarian Oral Tradition.* IQMS, *tr.* by Dermot Spence

I Will Go Back to the Great Sweet Mother. Algernon Charles Swinburne. NAEL-5v2; NAEL-6v2 *Fr.* Triumph of Time, The.

I will go home to my children. (LL) Fathers and Sons. Tom Leonard. CABP; NePenScot

I Will Go into the Ghetto. Charles Reznikoff. VGW

I will go up the mountain after the Moon. Fannie Stearns Gifford. RACG *Fr.* Songs of Conn the Fool, The.

I will go with the first air of morning. Fishing. Dorothy Wellesley, Duchess of Wellington. OBMV

I will grieve alone. In Response to a Rumor that the Oldest Whorehouse in Wheeling, West Virginia, Has Been Condemned. James Wright (1927–80). CoAP; NNaP; NoAM; VCAP

I will haunt these States. Vow, A. Allen Ginsberg. OBWP

I will have all my beds blown[e] up, not stuft. Ben Jonson. EBEV; OxBEV *Fr.* Alchemist, The.

I will have few cooking-pots. Domestic Economy. Anna Wickham. ItWoWo

I will have to accept women. This Form of Life Needs Sex. Allen Ginsberg. CLPP; NNaP

I will have to ask for my slum location again. When I Lost Slum Life. Sipho Sepamla. PeSAV

I will have to forget. To Ms. Ann. Lucille Clifton. ESEAA

I will have you. (LL) *Unknown.* LB; OxNR

I will have / you meet. Slick. Víctor Hernández Cruz. PueRic

I will hold beauty as a shield against despair. Beauty as a Shield. Elsie Robinson. PoToHe

I will in Cassio's lodging lose this napkin. William Shakespeare. OxAEP-1 *Fr.* Othello.

I will lament and love. (LL) Bitter-Sweet. George Herbert. FHYEP; GeHe; NOBE; OxBSP; PAI

I will leave this old village behind me . . . . Farewell Song. Nikolai Mikhailovich Rubtsov. TCRP, *tr.* by Bradley Jordan and Katya Zubritskaya

I will let loose against you the fleet-footed vines. Rudyard Kipling. NOxBChV *Fr.* Second Jungle Book, The.

I will lift up mine eyes unto the hills. Bible, *O.T.* AWP *Fr.* Psalms.

I Will Live and Survive. Irina Ratushinskaya [*or* Ratushinskaia]. ItGoST, *tr.* by David McDuff

I will live in Ringsend. Ringsend. Oliver St. John Gogarty. OBMV; OxBTC

I Will Look Up. Josephine D. Henderson Heard. CBWP-4

I will look with detachment. On Being Head of the English Department. Pinkie Gordon Lane. BlSi; GT

I will lose you. It is written. Sweater, The. Gregory Orr. TRP

I will make love. *Unknown.* BoWoP

I will make you brooches and toys for your delight. Song of a Traveller, The. Robert Louis Stevenson. EBVV; MoBrPo; OBEV

I will miss you. Do not expect applause. (LL) Johann Joachim Quantz's Five Lessons. William Sydney Graham. EmeKit; FaBoMo; HarvBoo

I will my collection of hats. Exchange of Hats, An. Stanley Moss. BodElec

I will never again. Promise, The. Toi Derricotte. GT

I will never be a hero. Name, A. Aleksandr Samsonovich Ginger. TCRP, *tr.* by Albert C. Todd

I will never be able to stop my tears. On the Death of His Baby Son. Su Tung-p'o (Su Shih). OHPC, *tr.* by Kenneth Rexroth

I will never be this beautiful again. On the Death of Nizar Qabbani. Mohja Kahf. PoArWo

"I will never eate nor drinke," Robin Hood said. Robin Hood's Death. *Unknown.* ESPB

I will no longer kiss. On Himselfe. Robert Herrick. CaPo

I will not, cannot go. (LL) Spellbound. Emily Jane Brontë. NOBE; NOBVV; NPeEn

I Will Not Crush the World's Corolla of Wonders. Lucian Blaga. PFTM-1

I will not die completely, my dear friend! Non Omnis Moriar. Manuel Gutiérrez Nájera. BLPSL, *tr.* by Rene de Costa, Rigas Kappatos and Eleni Paidoussi

I will not die for you. *Unknown.* NOIV

I will not doubt, though all my ships at sea. Faith. Ella Wheeler Wilcox. PoToHe

I Will Not Give Thee All My Heart. Grace Hazard Conkling. LW

I will not go down like an old rag. Worker Dies, A. Clementina Suárez. TANSG, *tr.* by Janet N. Gold

I will not have or value a man. I. Gabriella Sica. CItWP, *tr.* by Cinzia Sartini Blum and Lara Trubowitz

I will not have you think me less. Santob de Carrion. TrJP *Fr.* Consejos y Documentos al Rey Dom Pedro.

I Will Not Let Thee Go. Robert Bridges. EnLoPo

I will not let you say a Woman's part. Woman's Answer, A. Adelaide Anne Procter. VWP

I will not perturbate. To the Dead Cardinal of Westminster. Francis Thompson. PeVV

I will not pity you, nor lend a hand. (LL) James Vincent Cunningham. GrAn; OBVE, *tr.* by James Vincent Cunningham *Fr.* Five Epigrams.

I will not play at tug o' war. Hug o' War. Shel [*or* Shelley] Silverstein. NTCP

I will not shut me from my kind. Tennyson. CABP; FHYEP; NAEL-6v2 *Fr.* In Memoriam A. H. H.

I will not speak. No. Patti Tana. PasH

I Will Not Tell the Secrets. Wilfrid Scawen Blunt. Son *Fr.* Esther [a Young Man's Tragedy].

I will not toy with it nor bend an inch. White City, The. Claude McKay. APT-1; BPo; NoAM; RaBo; TAP

I will not try to reach again. Evenlode, The. Joseph Hilaire Pierre Belloc. OxAEP-2

I will now only believe that he has died. Now I Will Only Believe. B. W. Vilakazi. PeSAV

I will now sing this beautifully. Sappho. SaLy, *tr.* by Diane Rayor

I will obey you to my utmost power. To a Lady, Who Desired Me Not To Be in Love with Her. John, Baron Cutts Cutts. NOSC

I will—of You— (LL) Emily Dickinson. SoSe-8; TCAPo

I will pluck from my tree a cherry-blossom wand. Cherry-Blossom Wand, The. Anna Wickham. MoBrPo

I Will Pronounce Your Name. Léopold Sédar Senghor. PBMAP

I will put Chaos into fourteen lines. Edna St. Vincent Millay. Son

I will read a few of these to see if they exist. Theory of the Flower, The. Michael Palmer. HarvBoo

I will remember. Courage. Boris Leonidovich Pasternak. FaBoWar, *tr.* by *Unknown*

I will rise / from my troth. Wine Bowl. "H. D." NoP-4

I will roar and squander. Folly's Song. Thomas Dekker. NOSC

I will sing a song of battle. Song of Chess, The. Abraham Ibn Ezra. TrJP, *tr.* by Nina Davis Salaman

I will sing, if ye will hearken. Laird o' Logie, The. *Unknown.* ESPB

I will sing in the rising. Song Poem, The. Lenard D. Moore. SpirFl

I will sing no more songs! O'Bruadair. David [*or* Daibhi][*or* Daithi] O'Bruadair [*or* Ó Bruadair]. BIrV, *tr.* by James Stephens

I will sleep. December. Ron Padgett. SPE

I will speak about women of letters, for I'm in the racket. Carolyn Kizer. NALW *Fr.* Pro Femina.

I Will Still Sing. Amelia Blossom Pegram. HAWP

I will stop dreaming now. Success. Cornelius Eady. ISC

I will take that ancestral one. (LL) Two Standards. Elise Paschen. OPRER; ReEnLa

I will teach you my townspeople. Tract. William Carlos Williams. MoAmPo; NOBA; NoAM; PAI; SAmP; TAP; TwCP; VGW

I will teach you to become American, my students. Notes for a Lecture. David Ignatow. NNaP

I will tell a true tale of myself. Seafarer. *Unknown.* PoE, *tr.* by Kemp Malone

I Will Tell You during the Walk. Isabel Meyrelles. SurWo, *tr.* by Guy Ducornet

I will tell you. Maybe. David St. John. GeoHom *Fr.* Of the Remembered.

I will tell you, / The barge she sat in, like a burnisht throne. William Shakespeare. OxBEV *Fr.* Antony and Cleopatra.

I will tell you what he told me. Berryman. W. S. Merwin. GifTon

I will the devil kiss. (LL) Small Fig Tree, A. Donald Hall. ChIV-2; GI

I will throw this bridge across. (LL) This Bridge Across. Christopher Gilbert. ESEAA; GT

I will track you down the years. Quest. Naomi Long Madgett. BPo

I will turn on nothing. Promise. Joe Wenderoth. BodElec

I will walk into some one's dwelling. Love Song. *Unknown.* APN-2, *tr. by* Henry Rowe Schoolcraft

I will walk with a lover of wisdom. Little Elegy. Denis Devlin. ModIr; NOIV

I will whisper your name. Eshu. Adesanya Alakoye. ISC

I Will Write Songs against You. Charles Reznikoff. VGW

I will write you a letter. I Think. James Schuyler. TTTS

I will write you a poem instead of bringing rice. Paying a Sick-call to Yao Ts'un-tao in the Rain. Shen Chou. CoBLCP, *tr. by* Jonathan Chaves

I will you allë swalewë withouten any bot. Dragon Speaks, The. *Unknown.* NPeEn

I, Willie Wastle. *Unknown.* OxNR

I wince in self-revelation. Sincerity. Ágnes Nemes Nagy. VCWP, *tr. by* Hugh Maxton

I winced. Catching fire, I shivered with cold. Marburg. Boris Leonidovich Pasternak. TCRP, *tr. by* Yakov Hornstein

I. WINEMAKING. Elegy. Arthur L. Clements. UnSA

I Winna Let On. James King Annand. NOxBChV

I wish a greater knowledge, then t'attaine. Francis Quarles. PBRV *Fr.* Divine Fancies.

I wish all the / mandragona. Blue Funk. Joel Oppenheimer. NeAP

I wish, God, for some end I do not will. Elizabeth Jennings. PeECV; TOF *Fr.* Sonnets of Michelangelo, The.

I wish I could be. Marichiko. OHMPJ

I wish I could be. Kenneth Rexroth. APSN; APT-2 *Fr.* Love Poems of Marichiko, The.

I wish I could be. Theophanes. GrAn

I wish I could lend a coat. *Var. authors.* AWP *Fr.* Manyo Shu, Part 2 of 4.

I wish I could remember the [*or* that] first day. Christina Georgina Rossetti. BoLoP; LW; OxBSo; Son *Fr.* Monna Innominata.

I wish I could still stay. Peacock Poems: 1, The. Sherley Anne Williams. NAAAL

I Wish I Didn't Love You So. Frank Loesser. ReLy

I wish I had been born beside a river. Upper Canadian, The. James Reaney. NOBC

I wish I had the voice of Homer. Cancer's a Funny Thing. John Burdon Sanderson Haldane. OxBTC

I wish I knew the names of flowers. Naming of Flowers, The. Jennie Osborne. Prnts

I wish I loved the human race. Wishes of an Elderly Man, [Wished at a Garden Party, June 1914]. Sir Walter Alexander Raleigh. FaBoCh; FaBoEE; NBLV; NOBL; OBCoV; PeLV

I wish I owned a Dior dress. Reflections at Dawn. Phyllis McGinley. NBLV; NOBL

I wish I thought *What Jolly Fun*! (LL) Wishes of an Elderly Man, [Wished at a Garden Party, June 1914]. Sir Walter Alexander Raleigh. FaBoCh; FaBoEE; NBLV; NOBL; OBCoV; PeLV

I Wish I Was a Grown up Man. Maggie Pogue Johnson. CBWP-4

I wish I was in de land ob cotton. Dixie [*or* Dixie's Land]. Daniel Decatur Emmett. APN-1; CBCWP; TCAPo

I wish I was where I would be. John Clare. NOBVV

I wish i were. Poem For My Nephew. Nikki Giovanni. NOxBChV

I Wish I Were. *Unknown.* OxBoLi

I wish I were a / Elephantiaphus. I Wish I Were. *Unknown.* OxBoLi

I wish I were a wild beast. Aleksandr Ivanovich Vvedensky [*or* Vvedenskii]. TCRP

I wish I were close. Akahito. OHPJ

I Wish I Were in Love Again. Lorenz Hart. OBCoV
(You don't know that I felt good.) ReLy

I wish I were spring water. Gabriella Sica. CItWP, *tr. by* Cinzia Sartini Blum and Lara Trubowitz *Fr.* Poems for a Little Boy.

I wish I were the wind, and you. *Unknown.* GrAn

I wish I were where Helen lies. Helen of Kirconnell. *Unknown.* AWP; OBEV; OxBEV; SCGP

I wish in the city of your heart. Robley, Jr. Wilson. InvLad

I wish it soon may have a Better. (LL) Verses on the Death of Dr. Swift, D.S.P.D., Occasioned by Reading a Maxim in Rochefoucauld. Jonathan Swift. NAEL-6v1; NAEL-7v1; NOEC

I wish it were over the terrible pain. Introspective. Christina Georgina Rossetti. VWP

I wish she were here. Issa. SoOfWa, *tr. by* Sam Hamill

I wish that all my poems. Untitled. Juan Ramon Jimenez. MiVo, *tr. by* Dennis Maloney

I wish that I could get in line. They Don't Speak English in Paris. Ogden Nash. OBAL

I wish that my room had a floor. Limerick. Frank Gelett Burgess. OBCA; OxIBACP; PeLi

I wish that there were some wonderful place. Land of Beginning Again, The. Louisa Fletcher. ITBLP

I wish that when you died last May. May and Death. Robert Browning. NOBE

I wish the rent. Little Lyric (of Great Importance). Langston Hughes. APT-2; NBLV; OBAL; OBCoV

I wish them cramps. Wishes for Sons. Lucille Clifton. NAAAL

I wish there were a touch of these boats about my life. Boat Poem. Bernard Spencer. EmeKit; FaBoTw; OxBTC

I wish they were / Grass. (LL) Late November in a Field. James Wright (1927–80). NAAL-2v2; NNaP

I wish they would hurry up their trip to Mars. Projection, A. Reed Whittemore. AiP

I wish this body. Tembo. JDP, *tr. by* Yoel Hoffmann

I wish to be a nameless woman. Nameless Woman, A. No Ch'ŏn-myŏng. WoPoe, *tr. by* Ko Won

"I wish to buy a dog," she said. On Buying a Dog. Edgar Klauber. NTCP

I wish to die. Rangai. JDP, *tr. by* Yoel Hoffmann

I wish to God I could forget the Frenchman. French Prisoner, The. János Pilinszky. IQMS, *tr. by* Peter Zollman

I wish to God I never saw you, Mag. Mag. Carl Sandburg. APT-1

I wish to make my sermon brief. Praise of Little Women. Juan Ruiz, Archpriest of Hita. AWP, *tr. by* Henry Wadsworth Longfellow

I wish to make this preaching short. Charms of Small Women. Juan Ruiz, Archpriest of Hita. BLPSL, *tr. by* Rene de Costa, Rigas Kappatos and Eleni Paidoussi

I wish to paint my eyes. *Unknown.* BoWoP

I wish to say something to you, but shame. Sappho. SaLy, *tr. by* Diane Rayor

I wish to state in the first place that. SURcenSURE. Marcel Duchamp. PFTM-1

I wish to submit a memorial expressing my feelings. Submitting a Memorial Requesting Permission to Return Home and Care for My Parents. Yang Chi. CoBLCP, *tr. by* Jonathan Chaves

I wish you Alfred now a good night. To Alfred Gwyer. Joseph Gwyer. VerBaPo

I wish you knew September. If You Knew September. John Nelson. GeoH

I Wish You Love (Que Reste-t-il de Nos Amours?). Charles Trenet. ReLy, *tr. by* Albert A. Beach

I wish you would come. Lady Izumi. BoWoP

I wished to shirk my task one day. Discovery. Benjamin Keech. PoToHe

I with the mind then of a child squandering. On the Shores of Szántód. Ferenc Jankovich. IQMS, *tr. by* Madeline Mason

I with time to life ascend. Musical Pumpkin-Hut. Heinrich Albert. GePo, *tr. by* George C. Schoolfield

I, with whose colors [*or* colours] Myra dressed [*or* dress'd] her head. Fulke Greville, 1st Baron Brooke. HAP; NOBE; NoSic; OBEV *Fr.* Caelica.

I woke as mist licked the pavement. Climbing. C. Mikal Oness. GeoHom

I woke at dawn—and you were lying there. Morn's Recompense. "Clement Andrews." CAGL

I woke at three; for I was bid. Coventry Patmore. PeVV *Fr.* Angel in the House, The.

I woke before the day, when the night bird. Thomas Iron-Eyes. Marnie Walsh. WPOW

I woke before the morning, I was happy all the day. Good Boy, A. Robert Louis Stevenson. PWR

I woke up about 2:30 this morning and thought about Philip's / hat. Philip Whalen's Hat. Joanne Kyger. BB

I woke up and found you above me. Husband and Wife. Edward Hirsch. IllVoic

I woke up in the dark. After *The Little Mariner.* Olga Broumas. BodElec

I woke up singing this morning. It's a Most Unusual Day. Jimmy McHugh. ReLy

I woke up this mornin' Sylvester's Dying Bed. Langston Hughes. NoAM; SAmP; UnPo

I woke up this mornin' Empty Bed Blues. Bessie Smith. APT-2; OBAL; UnPo

I woke up this mornin' with the blues all round my bed. I Got the Blues. *Unknown.* TTY

I Woke up This Morning. Karla Kuskin. TLR

I woke up to the bleating of a lamb. Chriseaster. Molly Peacock. FFC

I woke up with purple hair and Paul. *Rocket to Russia.* Alison Stone. SwNoth

I, Woman. Irma McClaurin. BlSi

I won't be my father's Jack. Other Little Tune, T' Mother Goose. OxNR; ReMoGo

I won't be reconstructed and I don't give a damn. (LL) Rebel, The. Innes Randolph. NBLV; OBAL; OxBoLi

I won't care / if you desert me. *Chinook Oral Tradition.* ErotSp, *tr. by* Sam Hamill

I Won't Dance. Dorothy Fields. ReLy

I won't go in today, I'll stay out today. Untitled. Karen Volkman. NeAmPo

I won't go with you. I want to stay with Grandpa! My Last Afternoon with Uncle Devereux Winslow. Robert Lowell. NAAL-2v2; NoP-4; VGW

I won't kiss your hand, madam. My Romance. Richard Rodgers. ReLy

I won't let even. For Taihei Osho. Muso Soseki. EaWin, *tr.* by W. S. Merwin

I won't say much about it now, except that she got. Reading the Elephant. Andrew Motion. HarvBoo

I Won't Sell His Love. Fadwa Tuqan [or Tuquan]. AF, *tr.* by Mounah Aikhouri

I Won't Send Roses. Jerry Herman. ReLy

I Wonder. Jeannie Kirby. OTCP

I wonder about Rifkah, my grandmother's sister. Oil of Her Hands, The. Mark Nepo. GotH

I wonder about the trees. Sound of Trees, The. Robert Frost. APT-1; NoAM

I wonder as into bed I creep. Sweet Dreams. Ogden Nash. OTCP

I wonder, by my troth, what thou and I. Good-Morrow, The. John Donne. AWP; BASC; BoLoP; CABP; ClHu; EBEV; ESCV; EnLoPo; FHYEP; FSCP; FaBoVe; MeLP; NAEL-5v1; NAEL-6v1; NAEL-7v1; NAWM-5v1; NIL-7; NOSC; NoP-4; OxAEP-1; OxBEV; PoE; PoRA; SCV; SoSe-8; TFi

I wonder do you feel today. Two in the Campagna. Robert Browning. EBEV; EBVV; FHYEP; GTBS-P; NAEL-5v2; NAEL-6v2; NOBE; NOBVV; NPeEn; NoP-4; OxAEP-2; OxBEV; PoE; SCGP; TFi; TOF

I wonder, Duddon, if you still remember. To the River Duddon. Norman Nicholson. NLP; NoP-4

I wonder how King Arthur felt. Limerick. Moss Rich. PeLi

I wonder how many old men last winter. Minneapolis Poem, The. James Wright (1927–80). NoAM; UnPo

I wonder if I could find it. Searching for *Melinda's Magic Moment*. Allison Joseph. NAPBL

I wonder if the elephant. Pete at the Zoo. Gwendolyn Brooks. TLR

I wonder if the sap is stirring yet. First Spring Day, The. Christina Georgina Rossetti. FaBoVe

I wonder is there nowhere a / Do-right man? (LL) Early Evening Quarrel. Langston Hughes. SAmP; UnPo

I wonder poet, can you take it. Muse to an Unknown Poet, The. Paul Potts. FaBoTw

I wonder sometimes if the soldiers lying. Song for the Heroes. Alex Comfort. MoBrPo

I Wonder What Became of Me. Johnny Mercer. ReLy

I wonder what day of the week. Untimely Thought, An. Thomas Bailey Aldrich. PWR

I wonder what eagle did to him. Gaxe. STP

I Wonder What Happened to Him. Noël Coward. ReLy

I wonder what he'll think of me! Soliloquy. Richard Rodgers. ReLy

I wonder what I ought to do today. Anne Hathaway Composes Her 18th Sonnet. Neil Curry. NLP

I Wonder What It Feels Like to Be Drowned? Robert Graves. MoBrPo

I wonder what Spanish poets would say about this. Cicada Blue. Charles Wright. KGB

I wonder what to mean by *sanctuary,* if a real or. Triphammer Bridge. A. R. Ammons. ColAP; NAAL-2v2; NOBA

I wonder what Wright and Baldwin. Mental Terrorism. Kevin Powell. InTrad

I wonder where. Hakuen. JDP, *tr.* by Yoel Hoffmann

I wonder where it is we belong. Should I Stay or Should I Go? Sarah Rosenblatt. AmPoNex

I wonder where julia found that strange, rather common / little boy? (LL) False Security. Sir John Betjeman. NoAM; NoP-4

I wonder whether. Dieback. Elizabeth Dodd. UrbNat

I Wonder Why She Kept on Saying "Si-Si-Si-Si-Senor." Sam M. Lewis. ReLy

I wonder why that scene comes back tonight, Pilate Remembers. William E. Brooks. ChIV-2

I wonder why the grass is green. I Wonder. Jeannie Kirby. OTCP

I wondered always where. Hunchback of Dugbe, The. Wole Soyinka. VCWP

I wondered why the covers felt so cold. Night Snow. Po Chü-i. CoBCP, *tr.* by Burton Watson

I Wonta Thank Ya. Tejumola Ologboni. NBV

I work all day, and get half-drunk at night. Aubade. Philip Larkin. AWTN; BodElec; CABP; NAEL-6v2; NoP-4; PoetW; SoSe-8; TRP

I work and I remember. I conceive. That's All. Lawrence Joseph. GraLe; PBCAP

I work and I remember, that's all. (LL) That's All. Lawrence Joseph. GraLe; PBCAP

I work at night, surrounded by city. Burial in the East. Pablo Neruda. TRP

I work at night, the city all around me. Funeral in the East. Pablo Neruda. TRP, *tr.* by Robert Bly

I work at the Palace Ballroom. Ten Cents a Dance. Richard Rodgers. ReLy

I work for the C.I.A. It's Miller Time. Víctor Hernández Cruz. PueRic; TouFir

I work in the evening, alone and in silence. James Harpur. NewEx

I work nights at the University Bookshop. Thoughts of Jack Kerouac—& Other Things. Peter Olds. PeNZ

I work nights, in the ring of the city. Burial in the East. Pablo Neruda. TRP, *tr.* by Ben Belitt

I work up this mornin' Langston Hughes. *See* I woke up this mornin'

I worked all the winter. Tired as I Can Be. *Unknown.* FaBoVe

I worked for a woman. Madam and Her Madam. Langston Hughes. RACG; SAmP

I Worry. Wendy Cope. HarvBoo

I worry. Lola's Lament. Arthur Miller. Unle

I worship the greatest first. Hippolytus Temporizes. "H. D." APT-1; HarvBoo; RACG

I Worship Thee, O Holy Ghost. William F. Warren. AH

I worshipped—did not "pray" (LL) Emily Dickinson. APN-2; BBASP

I wot a tree XII bowes betake. *Unknown.* MiEL

I would ask of you, my darling. Will You Love Me When I'm Old? *Unknown.* ITBLP

I Would Be Clad in Christ's Skin. *Unknown.* MiEL
(Gold and al this worldës wyn.) NPeEn
(I Would be Clad in Christis Skin.) SacPr

I would be married, but I'd[e] have no wife. On Marriage. Richard Crashaw. FaBoEE

I would be ready, Lord. Ready. Margaret Junkin Preston. PWR

I Would Be True. Howard Arnold Walter. ITBLP; PoToHe

I Would but I Can't. *Unknown.* GrAn, *tr.* by Thomas Meyer

I would choose to be a doorkeeper. Katharine Tynan. SacPr

"I would doubt," said the Bishop of Balham. Limerick. Terence Rattigan. PeLi

I would fain know[e] what she hath deserved. (LL) Lover Showeth How He Is Forsaken of Such as He Sometime Enjoyed, The. Sir Thomas Wyatt. ClHu; EnLoPo; HAP; HeIP-4; InPK-6; MakPoe; NAEL-5v1; NPeEn; NoSic; OxBC; OxBEV; PoE; PoRA; SCGP; SCV; TFi; TRP

I would have been as great as George Eliot. Margaret Fuller Slack. Edgar Lee Masters. APT-1; RACG

I would have been as great as George Eliot. Edgar Lee Masters. APT-1; IllVoic; RACG *Fr.* Spoon River Anthology.

I Would Have Loved You. Fernando Charry Lara. BLPSL, *tr.* by Rene de Costa, Rigas Kappatos and Eleni Paidoussi

I would hear Spanish first. If I Were Rita Hayworth. Patricia Jones. ReTh

I would hold another person in my thoughts. " Eduard Veniaminovich Limonov." TCRP

I Would I Might Forget That I Am I. George Santayana. AWP

I would I were Actaeon, whom Diana did disguise. I Would I Were Actaeon. ------ Bewe. NoSic

I would I were the glow-worm, thou the flower. Mathilde Blind. ViWPN *Fr.* Love in Exile.

I would, if I could. Mother Goose. OxNR

I would immortalize these nymphs: So bright. L'Après-Midi d'un Faune. Stéphane Mallarmé. AWP, *tr.* by Aldous Huxley

I Would It Were Not As It Is. Sir Edward Dyer. SCGP

I would lie low—the ground on which men tread. Earth, The. Jones Very. APN-1; OxBA

I would like all things to be free of me. Proof. Brendan Kennelly. CIP-2; PBCIP

I would like better in the grace to be. Cecco Angiolieri, da Siena. EaItPo, *tr.* by Dante Gabriel Rossetti

I would like for ebony and ivory. Harmony. Andrea M. Wren. InTrad

I would like just to be silent. Jerzy Ficowski. HP

I would like to ask that dumb ox, Thomas. Prospect Park. David Schubert. APT-2

I would like to be that elderly Chinese gentleman. Dreaming in the Shanghai Restaurant. Dennis Joseph Enright. EmeKit

I would like to believe that in the darkness. Burning Bush. Alison Apotheker. PoCoUp

I would like to bury. Anne Sexton. BodElec *Fr.* Furies, The.

I Would Like to Describe. Zbigniew Herbert. PoSu, *tr.* by Czeslaw Milosz

I would like to dive. Diver, The. W. W. Eustace Ross. NOBC

I would like to let things be. Facts of Life, Ballymoney. Eamon Grennan. PBCIP

I would like to tell about an enduring sorrow I have not forgotten. Ode to a Long Sorrow. Ricardo Molinari. TCLAP, *tr.* by Inés Probert

I would like to undo it, to take back. Lament. G. E. Patterson. AmPoNex

I would like to use. Basho. SoOfWa, *tr.* by Sam Hamill

I would like to watch you sleeping. Variation on the Word *Sleep*. Margaret Atwood. AmFaPo; NOBC

I Would Like You for a Comrade.   Edward Abbott Parry.   NOxBChV

I would listen even again to that labouring breath. (LL)   Remorse.   Sir John Betjeman.   MoBrPo; OxBSP

I would live all my life in nonchalance and insouciance.   Introspective Reflection.   Ogden Nash.   NBLV; OBCoV

I would live for a day and a night.   Song-Maker, The.   Anna Wickham.   MoBrPo

I would live in your love as the sea-grasses live in the sea.   I Would Live in Your Love.   Sara Teasdale.   LW

I would make a crown / Of all the cities I have known.   Express.   Vincente Huidobro.   PFTM-1

I would never marry a young girl or an old woman.   Honestus.   GrAn

I would not alter thy cold eyes.   Flos Lunae.   Ernest Christopher Dowson.   OBMV; PeVV

I would not always reason. The straight path.   Conjunction of Jupiter and Venus, The.   William Cullen Bryant.   APN-1

I would not argue with you tonight.   No Argument Tonight.   Tijan M. Sallah.   NAfrP

I would not ask Thee that my days.   Humble Heart, A.   Alfred Norris.   PWR

I would not be the Moon, the sickly thing.   In Dispraise of the Moon.   Mary Elizabeth Coleridge.   PEW; ViWPN

I would not breathe, when blows thy mighty wind.   Spirit, The.   Jones Very.   NCAP

I would not, could I, make thy life as mine.   Vain Wish, A.   Philip Bourke Marston.   GSo

I would not do by thee as thou hast done! (LL)   Lines on Hearing That Lady Byron Was Ill.   Byron.   EBEV; NPeEn; OxAEP-2

I would not go to old Joe's house.   Old Joe Clark.   Unknown.   APN-2

I would not have the risk diminished. (LL)   Map of the City, A.   Thom Gunn.   NAEL-5v2; NAEL-6v2; NoP-4; PoE

I would not leave that land, if I were thou.   To Charles Roux, of Switzerland.   Nathaniel Parker Willis.   APN-1

I Would Not Live Alway.   William Augustus Mühlenberg.   AH

I would not paint—a picture.   Emily Dickinson.   APN-2; NAEL-2v1; NAEL-3; NAEL-5; NOBA; NoP-4; TCAPo; TRP

I Would Not Recommend Love.   Harold Norse.   CLPP

I would not sail again with sheep. (LL)   Sheep.   William Henry Davies.   MoBrPo; NPeEn; RB

I would not the good bishop be. (LL)   Ralph Waldo Emerson.   APN-1; AWP; NAEL-2v1; NAEL-3; NOBA; OxBA; TAP

I would not write a lament for you.   Salt.   Anne Hartigan.   CIP-2

I would prefer.   Counterfeiter, The.   Michael Davitt.   PBCIP, tr. by Philip Casey

I would put on my coat and galoshes. (LL)   White Apples.   Donald Hall.   LoL; TAP

I would rid myself of an old way of life.   Diogenes.   Arthur Rex Dugard Fairburn.   PeNZ

I would set all things whatsoever front to back.   Percy Wyndham Lewis.   CTC Fr. One-Way Song.

I would sleep until the mottled jaguar dawn.   Auditory Hallucinations.   Joyce Mansour.   HAWP, tr. by Carol Cosman

I Would Steal Horses.   Sherman Alexie.   NeAmPo

I would tell a marvelous vision.   Dream of the Cross, The.   Unknown.   EBEV, tr. by Sally Purcell

I would that all men my hard case would know.   Behold the Deeds!   Henry Cuyler Bunner.   NBLV

I would that folk forgot me quite.   Tess's Lament.   Thomas Hardy.   FaBoTw; FaBoVe

I woulde the gift I offer here.   Dedication.   John Greenleaf Whittier.   APN-1; OxBA

I would the God of Love would die.   To His Mistress.   James Shirley.   BeJo

I would to heaven that I were so much clay.   Byron.   CTC; NAEL-5v2; NAEL-6v2; NOBL; OxBEV; OxBSP Fr. Don Juan.

I would wear one by my side. (LL)   Mother Goose.   LB; OxNR; ReMoGo

I would worship if I could.   Great Spaces.   Howard Moss.   TwCP

I Wouldn't.   John Ciardi.   TLR

I wouldn't be bothered with drawers.   Limerick.   Unknown.   PeLi

I wouldn't coax the plant if I were you.   Woman with Flower.   Naomi Long Madgett.   GT

I wouldn't have known if I didn't stay home.   Night in a World, A.   Heather McHugh.   InvLad

I wouldn't know what it's like to be a pawn.   Maurizio Cucchi.   ItPo, tr. by Gayle Ridinger

I wouldn't marry a farmer.   Railroad Man for Me, A.   Unknown.   CA

I wouldn't much object, if I were black.   Negro Cemetery Next to a White One, A.   Howard Nemerov.   OxBSP

I wove myself of many delicious strands.   Einstein's Bathrobe.   Howard Moss.   VCAP

I wove this basket.   Pozo Basket, The.   Glenna Luschei.   GeoHom

I wrap the blue towel.   White Porch, The.   Cathy Song.   NAAL-5; YaYoPo

I, wretched Virtue, sit.   Mnasalcas.   GrAn

I write, erase, rewrite.   Hokushi.   JDP, tr. by Yoel Hoffmann

I Write For.   John Hewitt.   PNI

I write in praise of the solitary act.   Against Coupling.   Fleur Adcock.   EmeKit; NALW

I write my God in blue.   Meta-A and the A of Absolutes.   Jay Wright.   ESEAA; TRP

I write now in English and now in Scots.   Caledonian Antisyzygy, The.   Hugh MacDiarmid.   OxBEV

I write of Jam, a subject stiff.   On Jam.   Joseph Hilaire Pierre Belloc.   NBLV

I Write Poems.   Gloria Fuertes.   WPOW, tr. by Philip Levine

I write the poetry of degenerate youth.   Handicraft—After Marina Tsvetaeva.   Duo Duo (Li Shizheng).   PoetW, tr. by Michelle Yeh

I write this poem.   For Musia's Grandchildren.   Irving Layton.   NOBC

I write to make you suffer.   Anne-Marie Kegels.   BoWoP

I write to you beneath this tent.   Post Card.   Guillaume Apollinaire.   AF; FaBoWar, tr. by Oliver Bernard

I write you from Wordsworth's cottage.   For a Portrait of Annette Vallon.   Andrey [or Andrei] Andreievich Voznesensky [or Voznesenskii].   RusPo, tr. by Robert Arthur Douglas Ford

I wrote a book, thank the Lord.   Fluency.   Adelia Prado.   TCLAP, tr. by Marcia Kirinus

I wrote a panegyric on you—and I'm sorry.   Composing.   "Anvari."   WoPoe, tr. by Dick Davis

I wrote: In the dark cavern of our birth.   Strange Type.   Malcolm Lowry.   NPeEn

I wrote so meagerly to you. But what I couldn't write.   To Friends Behind a Frontier.   Tomas Tranströmer.   WoPoe, tr. by Robin Fulton

I wrote some lines once on a time.   Height of the Ridiculous, The.   Oliver Wendell Holmes.   OBAL; OBCA

I wrote them with my nail on the plaster.   Flowers of Mildew.   Tudor Arghezi.   WoPoe, tr. by Michael Impey and Brian Swann

I wrote this when the sky was still serene.   Prologue.   Mihály Vörösmarty.   IQMS, tr. by Peter Zollman

I wrote to you to say that I'd be there.   One's Correspondence.   Connie Bensley.   OBCoV

I wrote "Who wrote Icon Basilike?" (LL)   On ["Who Wrote Icon Basilike" by Dr.] Christopher Wordsworth, Master of Trinity.   Benjamin Hall Kennedy.   FaBoEE; OBCoV

I wrung my hands under my dark veil.   Anna Andreyevna Akhmatova.   BoLoP; PoetW; RaBo, tr. by Max Hayward and Stanley Kunitz

I wud sooner sleep. (LL)   Old Shepherd's Prayer.   Charlotte Mew.   MoBrPo; OxBTC; WPE

I wuz goin' wif Puddin.   Interlude.   Sibby Anderson-Thompkins.   InTrad

I, YANG TZŪ, hid from life.   Poverty.   Yang Hsiung.   ChiP, tr. by Arthur Waley

I Years had been from Home.   Emily Dickinson.   NOBA; OxBA; PoRA; SAmP

I'yehe! my children.   Unknown.   STP Fr. Ghost-Dance Songs.

I yet SUPERIOR am to you. (LL)   Forsaken Wife, The.   Elizabeth Thomas.   ECWP; LW

I, Yi, Yi, Yi, Yi (I Like You Very Much).   Harry Warren.   ReLy

I Yield Thee Praise.   Philip Jerome Cleveland.   SacPr

I yielded myself to the perfect whole. (LL)   Each and All.   Ralph Waldo Emerson.   APN-1; AWP; ColAP; NAEL-2v1; NAEL-3; NAEL-5; NCAP; NOBA; OxBA; TAP; TCAPo; TreFP

I, you, he, she, we.   Jelaluddin [or Jalal al-Din] Rumi.   LoL

I? / I walk alone.   Soliloquy of the Solipsist.   Sylvia Plath.   HarvBoo

Iago Prytherch his name, though, be it allowed.   Peasant, A.   Ronald Stuart Thomas.   AngWePo; OBWVE; OxBEV

Iambic Feet Considered as Honorable Scars.   William Meredith.   OxBSP

Iambica.   Edmund Spenser.   See Iambicum Trimetrum

Iambically runs. (LL)   On the Imprint of the First English Edition of "The Works of Max Beerbohm."   Max Beerbohm.   InPK-6; OBCoV

Iambicum Trimetrum.   Edmund Spenser.   BoLoP; EBEV; NPeEn; OBEV (Iambica.)   OxBoLi

Ianthe.   Walter Savage Landor.

"From you, Ianthe, little troubles pass."   OBEV; NOBE

"Mild is the parting year, and sweet."   EnLoPo

"Past ruined [or ruin'd] Ilion Helen lives."   AWP; CTC; EnLoPo; HAP; NAEL-5v2; NOBE; NOBRP; NoP-4; NPeEn; OBEV; OxBEV; PoRA; SCGP; TFi; WeW-3

"Proud word you never spoke, but you will speak."   EnLoPo; OBEV

Remain, Ah Not in Youth Alone.   HAP; OBEV

"Well I remember how you smiled."   HAP; NAEL-6v2

"When Helen first saw wrinkles in her face."   EnLoPo

"Ye walls! sole witnesses of happy sighs."   EnLoPo

Ibn Gabirol. Yehuda Amichai [*or* Amikhai]. AF, *tr.* by Assia Gutmann

Icarus. Ronald Bottrall. GTBS-P

Icarus. Valentin Iremonger. BIrV; CIP-2; ModIr

Icarus. *Unknown.* OBEV

Icarus, by *cire* you were *perdu.* Julianus Sees a Bronze Statue of Icarus in a Public Bath. Julianus of Egypt. GrAn, *tr.* by Lee T. Pearcy

Icarus drowning. (LL) William Carlos Williams. LCAP-2; NAAL-2v2; NAAL-5; NoAM   *Fr.* Pictures from Brueghel.

Icarus in November. Alec Brock Stevenson. FuPo

Icarus Schmicarus. Adrian Mitchell. OBCoV

Ice. Walter De la Mare. OTCP

Ice. Alan Gould. NOBAu

Ice. Ágnes Nemes Nagy. IQMS, *tr.* by Ila Egon

Ice. Maureen Seaton. IllVoic

Ice. Stephen Spender. FaBoMo; GTBS-P

Ice, The. Wilfrid Wilson Gibson. OxBTC

Ice age is here, The. Attention. Adrienne Rich. TAP

Ice ages exist, ice ages exist. Alphabet 9, 10. Inger Christensen. PFTM-2, *tr.* by Pierre Joris

Ice and eternity enchain us. (LL) Another Planet. Boris Iulianovich Poplavsky [*or* Poplavskii]. TCRP; TCRusP, *tr.* by Emmett Jarrett and Richard Lourie

Ice and Fires Contend with My Child. Félix Lope de Vega Carpio. SpanPo, *tr.* by W. S. Merwin

Ice and the scotch, the fable, The. Tacit. Thom Ward. AmPoNex

Ice Cold. Seán O Riordain. NOIV, *tr.* by Thomas Kinsella

Ice Eagle, The. Diane Wakoski. PFTM-2

Ice Handler. Carl Sandburg. OxBA

Ice has been cracking all day. Spring. Michael Hogan. InPK-6

Ice honed by wind. Tracking the Siuslaw Man. Jim Barnes. HATNAP

Ice in the school-room, listen. Schooling, A. Seamus Deane. CIP-2; PNI

Ice inside the window seems forever, The. Whistling in January. David J. Rothman. GeoH

Ice of Ladoga, The. Aleksandr Petrovich Mezhirov. TCRP, *tr.* by Deming Brown

Ice on eaves, sparrow melts in my head. Eternity. Shinkichi Takahashi. ZenPo, *tr.* by Takashi Ikemoto and Lucien Stryk

Ice: On the way a miracle: water become bone. Cynewulf. ASW   *Fr.* Riddles (Exeter Book).

Ice plates the tarn in its hollow. Pinder. Mick North. NLP

Ice Skating. Greg Kuzma. InvLad

Ice Storm. Robert Earl Hayden. APT-2; ESEAA

Iceberg: Curious, fair creature came floating on the waves, A. Cynewulf. ASW   *Fr.* Riddles (Exeter Book).

Iced with a vanilla. Meeting of Cultures, A. Donald Davie. OxBC

Icehouse in Summer, The. Howard Nemerov. NoAM

Iceman, The. Gordon Challis. PeNZ

Ich Am of Irlaunde [*or* Irlonde]. *Unknown.* MiEL; NAEL-6v1; NAEL-7v1; NoP-4; NPeEn; OPOU; SCGP

(I am of Irelond.) OHMEL

(Irish Dancer, The.) FaBoCh; NOBE; OBEV

Ich sterbe. . . Life ebbs with an easy flow. End of a War, The. Sir Herbert Read. OBMV; PeFWW

Ich was ein chint so wolgetan. *Unknown.* EroLit, *tr.* by David Parlett   *Fr.* Carmina Burana.

Ich was not yet. Calypso. Ernst Jandl. PFTM-2

Ich Weiss Nicht Was Soll es Bedeuten. Heinrich Heine. AWP, *tr.* by Alexander Macmillan

Ichabod[!]. John Greenleaf Whittier. APN-1; NAAL-2v1; NAAL-3; NAAL-5; NOBA; OxBA; TAP; TCAPo

Ichabod! The Glory Has Departed. Ludwig Uhland. AWP, *tr.* by James Clarence Mangan

Ichot a burde in a bour ase beryl so bright. *Unknown.* MiEL

Ichot a burde in boure bryht. Blow, Northern Wind. *Unknown.* OBEV

Ichthycide. Joe Rosenblatt. NOBC

Icicle the moon drifting through it, An. Matsuo Allard. HA

Icicles, An. *Unknown. See* Riddle: "Lives in winter."

Icicles upon the pane, The. February. Henrietta Cordelia Ray. CBWP-3

Ickle ockle, blue bockle. *Unknown.* OxNR

Iconography of Childhood, The. Sherley Anne Williams.

"Buildings of the, The." GeoHom

"Summer mornings we." GeoHom

"Town less, A." GeoHom

Icons. Miriam Waddington. NOBC

Icos. Charles Tomlinson. GTBS-P

Icy, empty dawn cracks in the fields, The. Pacifists. George Woodcock. NOBC

Icy evil that struck his father down, The. El-Hajj Malik El-Shabazz. Robert Earl Hayden. ESEAA

Icy sun rises silently, The. Quail Sky. Li Ch'ing-chao. OHPC, *tr.* by Kenneth Rexroth

Icy wind bites, An. What Maks Makems. Tom Pickard. Oth

Id. Harry Clifton. PBCIP

ID bracelet I never did give, The. How Near Vietnam Came to Us. Paul Zarzyski. SwNoth

Idaho Russets, Late Beauties of Hebron. Digging Potatoes. Colette Inez. SpudSo

Idanre and Other Poems (1967). Wole Soyinka.

Death in the Dawn. PBMAP

Prisoner. PBMAP

Season. PBMAP

Night. PBMAP; WoPoe

Idbury bells are ringing. Country Thought. Sylvia Townsend Warner. MoBrPo

Idea. Michael Drayton.

"As Love and I, late harboured in one inn." NoSic

"As other men, so I myself can do muse." NOSC; NoSic; Son

Calling to [my] mind[e] since first my love begun. NOBE; SCGP

"Clear Ankor, on whose silver-sanded shore." NOSC

"Deare [*or* Dear], why should you command [*or* commaund] me to my rest." GSo; NOBE; Son

"Evil [*or* Evill] spirit, your beauty, haunts me still, An." NOBE; NoSic

(Farewell to Love.) MakPoe; NOSC

How Many Paltry, Foolish, Painted Things. AEP; EnLoPo; HAP; HeIP-4; NAEL-5v1; NAEL-7v1; NIP-4; NOSC; SCGP

"Into these loves, who but for passion look[e]s." NAEL-5v1; NAEL-6v1; NAEL-7v1; NOSC; NoP-4; SCGP

Like an Adventurous Seafarer Am I. NOSC; Son

"Love, in a humour, played the prodigal." NoSic

(Love's Farewell.) GTBS-P

Methinks I See Some Crooked Mimic Jeer. Son

(Parting, The.) OBEV; SCV

"Since there's no help, Come let us kiss and part." AmFaPo; BASC; CABP; NAEL-5v1; NAEL-6v1; NAEL-7v1; NoP-3; NPeEn; OxBEV; PoPoPo

"There's nothing grieves me, but that age should haste." NOSC

"To nothing fitter can I Thee compare." SCGP; Son

(To the Critic.) NOSC

"Truce, gentle love, a parley now I crave." NoSic

"Whilst thus my pen strives to eternize thee." Son

"Why should your fair eyes with such sovereign grace." SCGP

"You not alone, when you are still alone." OxBSo

"Some, misbelieving and profane in love." AEP

Idea, The. Agnes Mary Frances Robinson. VWP

Idea danced before us as a flag, The. Many Soldiers. Edgar Lee Masters. TCAPo

Idea of a Swimmer. Jean-Richard Bloch. TrJP, *tr.* by "S. P."

Idea of an infinite number of stars brought Newton to his knees, The. Presocratic, Surfing, Breathing Cosmology Blues, The. Christopher Buckley. BodElec

Idea of Ancestry, The. Etheridge Knight. AF; BPo; CoAmPo; ESEAA; ISC; NAAAL; NIP-4; NNaP; PBCAP; RaBo

Idea of Entropy at Maenporth Beach, The. Peter Redgrove. FaBoMo

Idea of Islands, The. Judith Ortiz Cofer. PueRic

Idea of justice may be precious, An. Ode. Frank O'Hara. NeAP

Idea of Love Between Us, The. Kate Light. AmPoNex

Idea of Order at Key West, The. Wallace Stevens. APT-1; AmFaPo; ColAP; HAP; HCAP; HarvBoo; HeIP-4; MakPoe; MoAmPo; NAAL-2v2; NAAL-5; NAWM-7v2; NIL-7; NIP-4; NOBA; NoAM; NoP-4; OxBA; PoE; PoPoPo; SAmP; TAP; TFi

Idea of Russia, The. Viktor Krivulin. TCRusP, *tr.* by Anna Barker and Daniel Weissbort

Idea of Trust, The. Thom Gunn. HarvBoo; NPeEn

Idea's Mirrour. Michael Drayton.

"Golden sun upon his fiery wheels, The." NoSic

Ideal. Padraic Pearse. AWP, *tr.* by Thomas Macdonagh

Ideal, An. Henrietta Cordelia Ray. CBWP-3

Ideal, The. T. R. Hummer. LTA

Ideal and Reality. Joseph Campbell. BIrV

Ideal Angels. John Robert Colombo. MoCV

Ideal Bar, The. Frank O'Hara. BodElec

Ideal General, The. Archilochus. FaBoWar, *tr.* by A. Watson Bain

Ideal Retreat, The. W.S. Merwin and Nguyen Ngoc Bich. EaWin,

Idealism. Ronald Arbuthnott Knox. NBLV; OxBEV

(Limerick: "There once was a man who said 'God.'") NOBL; PeLi

Ideally, you should be in your own.   American Living-room: A Tract, The.   William Meredith.   BodElec

Ideals.   Robert Greene.   PoToHe

Idem the Same.   Gertrude Stein.   *See* Valentine to Sherwood Anderson, A

Identification in Belfast (I.R.A. Bombing).   Robert Lowell.   OxBC

Identities.   Paul Eluard.   SurPaPo, *tr. by* Mary Ann Caws

Identity.   Thomas Bailey Aldrich.   TCAPo

Identity.   Margit Mikes.   IQMS, *tr. by* Suzanne K. Walther

Identity A Poem.   Gertrude Stein.   PFTM-1

Identity Card.   Mahmoud Darwish.   VCWP, *tr. by* Denys Johnson-Davies

Idiocy of the hemp family.   Eros Poesis.   Tatiana Shcherbina.   ItGoST, *tr. by* J. Kates

Idiom of the Hero.   Wallace Stevens.   OxBA

Idiosyncracy / Didn't do much. (LL)   Historical Reflections.   John Hollander.   OBAL; OBCoV

Idiot.   Allen Tate.   FaBoMo

Idiot, The.   Dudley Randall.   BPo; LTA

Idiot, The.   Charles Reznikoff.   APT-2

Idiot-Born, The.   Eliza Cook.   VWP

Idiot Boy, The.   William Wordsworth.   NOBRP; OBNV

Idiot Girl, The.   Mary F. Johnson.   CenSon

Idiot greens the meadows with his eyes, The.   Idiot.   Allen Tate.   FaBoMo

Idiot in the Bath, The.   M. Vasalis.   TuT, *tr. by* Peter Van de Kamp

Idiot me has ended one more day's official grind!   Climbing K'uai Pavilion.   Huang T'ing-chien.   SuSp, *tr. by* Michael E. Workman

Idiotic silence of state holidays, The.   Gratitude.   György Petri.   VCWP, *tr. by* George Gömöri and Clive Wilmer

'Idle as trout in light Colonel Jones.'   Famine Road, The.   Eavan Boland.   FaBoWP

Idle Charon.   Eugene Lee-Hamilton.   NOBVV

Idle Droning.   Po Chü-i.   CoBCP, *tr. by* Burton Watson

Idle, I enjoy only tranquillity.   Replying to Hsi-mei's "Thoughts in Early Autumn."   Lu Kuei Meng.   SuSp, *tr. by* Robin D. S. Yates

Idle poet, here and there, An.   Coventry Patmore.   EnLoPo; GTBS-P; HAP; OxBSP   *Fr.* Angel in the House, The.

Idle Pursuits.   Pope.   ECEV; OBSV   *Fr.* Dunciad, The.

Idle Thoughts.   Lu Yu.   CoBCP, *tr. by* Burton Watson

Idle Verse.   Henry Vaughan.   MiEL

Idle Visitation, An.   Edward Dorn.   NOBA; PmAP   *Fr.* Gunslinger.

Idle Words.   Walter Savage Landor.   OBSV

Idleness.   Lu Yu.   OHPC, *tr. by* Kenneth Rexroth

Idler Listening to Socrates Discussing Philosophy with His Boy-Friends, An.   Edward Cracroft Lefroy.   CAGL

Idler with a wand for a walking stick, An.   Batyushkov.   Osip Emilevich Mandelstam [*or* Mandelshtam].   OBVE

Idlers.   Leonid Nikolaevich Martynov.   TCRP, *tr. by* J. R. Rowland

Idleset: "Ill's the airt o the Word the day."   Thurso Berwick.   OxBS

Idling pivot of the frigate bird, The.   Man o' War Bird.   Derek Walcott.   TTY

Idling through the mean space dozing.   Choice.   A. R. Ammons.   PAI

Idols.   Witter Bynner.   APT-1

Idonean lemur, sport with me.   Invitation.   Orrick Johns.   APT-1

Idyl.   Henrietta Cordelia Ray.   CBWP-3

   Sunrise.   BlSi

   Sunset.   BlSi

Idyl 1.   Theocritus.   WoPoe, *tr. by* William Carlos Williams   *Fr.* Idylls.

Idyl: "And my young sweetheart sat at board with me."   Alfred Mombert.   AWP, *tr. by* Ludwig Lewisohn

Idyl of Harvest Time, An.   John Townsend Trowbridge.   APN-2

Idyl of Spring, An.   Henrietta Cordelia Ray.   CBWP-3

Idyl: "Tiny fish."   John James.   Oth

Idyll.   Samuel Johnson.   *See* Hermit Hoar

Idyll.   Miklós Zrínyi.

   "Early in the spring-time a huntsman full of sorrow."   IQMS, *tr. by* René Bonnerjea

Idyll 29.   Theocritus.   CAGL, *tr. by* W. Douglas P. Hill   *Fr.* Idylls.

Idyll: "He was a selfish shellfish."   Stoddard King.   NBLV

Idyll: "Lord, forgive me if I do not look for you."   Henriqueta Lisboa.   TCLAP, *tr. by* Hélcio Veiga Costa

Idyll of the Rose.   Ausonius.   AWP, *tr. by* John Addington Symonds

Idyll of the South, An.   Albery Allson Whitman.

   "I had a dream: Columbia the Great."   APN-2

Idylls.   Theocritus.

   "And so an easier life our Cyclops drew."   OBVE

Damoetas and Daphnis.   HePo, *tr. by* Barbara Hughes Fowler

Death of Daphnis, The.   AWP, *tr. by* Charles Stuart Calverley

Enchantment, The.   CTC; OBVE, *tr. by* Thomas Creech

Fishermen, The.   AWP; OBVE, *tr. by* Charles Stuart Calverley

"For love there is no other drug, Nicias."   HePo, *tr. by* Barbara Hughes Fowler

Gorgo and Praxinoa.   HePo, *tr. by* Barbara Hughes Fowler

Harvest-Home.   AWP, *tr. by* Charles Stuart Calverley

Herdsmen, The.   AWP, *tr. by* Charles Stuart Calverley

Hylas.   HePo, *tr. by* Barbara Hughes Fowler

Idyl 1.   WoPoe, *tr. by* William Carlos Williams

Idyll 27.   OBVE, *tr. by* Dryden

Idyll 29.   CAGL, *tr. by* W. Douglas P. Hill

Incantation, The.   AWP, *tr. by* Charles Stuart Calverley

Little Heracles.   HePo, *tr. by* Barbara Hughes Fowler

Neteheard.   NoSic; OBVE,

("Sweet is the whispering of that pine tree, goatherd.")   HePo, *tr. by* Barbara Hughes Fowler

("There was a time when Eucritus and I were going.")   HePo, *tr. by* Barbara Hughes Fowler

("Where is my bay? Bring it, Thestylis. Where are my charms?")   HePo, *tr. by* Barbara Hughes Fowler

"Whisper of the wind in, The."   WoPoe, *tr. by* William Carlos Williams

Idylls of the King.   Geoffrey Hill.   NoAM; PoE   *Fr.* Apology for the Revival of Christian Architecture in England, An.

Idylls of the King.   Tennyson.

   Holy Grail, The.

      "When the hermit made an end."   PeVV

   Passing of Arthur, The.   FHYEP; NAEL-5v2; NAEL-6v2

      "And answer made King Arthur, breathing hard."   PeECV

      "Pray for my soul. More things are wrought by prayer."   SacPr

   Prayer: "Pray for my soul. More things are wrought by prayer."   SacPr

      "Then rose the King and moved his host by night."   PeVV

   Pelleas and Ettarre.   NAEL-5v2; NAEL-6v2

Iersche brybour baird, vyle beggar with thy brattis.   William Dunbar.   NePenScot   *Fr.* Flyting of Dunbar and Kennedy, The.

IESU is in my heart, his sacred name.   Iesu.   George Herbert.   SacPr

Iesu, swete son dere!   Our Lady's Song.   *Unknown.*   OBEV

If.   Franklin Pierce Adams.   APT-1; OBAL

If.   Jared Angira.   PBMAP

If.   John Kendrick Bangs.   OBCA

If.   Edward Bond.   HP

If.   Mortimer Collins.   OBCoV

If—.   Rudyard Kipling.   BRP; ChAP; ITBLP; OxBTC; PWR; UV

If.   Patrick Lane.   NOBC

If.   Daria Menicanti.   CItWP, *tr. by* Cinzia Sartini Blum and Lara Trubowitz

If.   Sipho Sepamla.   PeSAV

If.   Robert Penn Warren.   BodElec

If a custom-tailored vet.   Cole Porter.   NBLV   *Fr.* Always True to You in My Fashion.

If a fir tree had a foot or two like a turtle, or a wing.   That Journeys Are Good.   Jelaluddin [*or* Jalal al-Din] Rumi.   RaBo, *tr. by* Robert Bly

If a Fish Fell in a Forest.   John Nelson.   GeoH

If a good man were ever housed in Hell.   Good Man in Hell, The.   Edwin Muir.   MoBrPo

If a large hart: Joyned with a Noble minde.   M. S. Sir Will: Dyer, Kt: Who Put on Immortality Aprill the 29th Anno Domini 1621.   Lady Catherine [*or* Katherine] Dyer.   EMWP

If a Man who Turnips cries.   Turnip Vendor, The.   Samuel Johnson.   OxNR

If a man with a shovel came down the road.   Diggers, The.   W. S. Merwin.   SPE

If a monkey drives a car.   Poems We Can Understand.   Paul Hoover.   PmAP

If a peacock ever passes.   Disillusion for Rubén Darío.   Nancy Morejón.   TCLAP, *tr. by* Kathleen Weaver

If a pig wore a wig.   Christina Georgina Rossetti.   NPeEn

If a Privileged Light.   Gabriella Leto.   CItWP, *tr. by* Cinzia Sartini Blum and Lara Trubowitz

If a song flies to me from the garden.   Tatiana Bek.   ItGoST, *tr. by* Richard McKane

If a straight horizontal thread one meter long falls from a height of one.   1914 Box, The.   Marcel Duchamp.   PFTM-1

If a Suite in Praise of the Yoruba Oracle.   Awotunde Aworinde.

   "Slender as a needle."   PFTM-1

If a swan / sang. (LL)   Swan and Shadow.   John Hollander.   InPK-6; VCAP

If, after I die they should want to write my biography.   If, after I Die.   Fernando Pessoa.   PeSAV, *tr. by* Jonathan Griffin

If after rude and boisterous seas.   Plaudite, or End of Life, The.   Robert Herrick.   CaPo

If, after the bombardment is over.   Discourse on Method, The.   Heberto Padilla.   VCWP

If again in the spring.   Seeing the Plum Blossoms by the River.   Lady Ise.   BoWoP, *tr. by* Etsuko Terasaki

If all be true that I do think. Catch, A. Henry Aldrich. FaBoEE; NOSC; OxBSP

If all happy families are alike. Happy and Unhappy Families 1. Lisel Mueller. ExTi

If all of me is still there. Plenty-hawk. STP

If all our life were one broad glare. Joy of Incompleteness, The. Albert Crowell. PoToHe

If all the answer's to be the Sinai sort. Golden Calf. Norman MacCaig. ChIV-1; OxBS

If all the good people were clever. Good and Clever. Elizabeth Wordsworth. OxBTC

If all the grief and woe and bitterness. Planh for the Young English King. Ezra Pound. APT-1

If all the hearts that shrivelled in their graves. Sándor Petőfi. IQMS, tr. by Peter Zollman Fr. Clouds, The.

If all the lovely melodies. Won't You Dad? Kevin Gilbert. IBA

If all the seas were one sea. Mother Goose. OxNR; ReMoGo

If all the sorrows of this weary earth. Friends. Thomas Curtis Clark. PoToHe

If all the trees in all the woods were men. Cacoëthes Scribendi. Oliver Wendell Holmes. NBLV; OBCoV

If all the world and love were young. Nymph's [or Nimph's] Reply to the Shepherd [or Sheepheard], The. Sir Walter Ralegh. AmFaPo; CTC; ClHu; HAP; HeIP-4; InPK-6; NAEL-5v1; NAEL-6v1; NAEL-7v1; NBLV; NIL-7; NIP-4; NOBE; NPeEn; NoP-4; NoSic; PAI; PoE; PoPoPo; RACG; RB; SCGP; TFi; TRP; WeW-3

If all the world were apple-pie. Mother Goose. ReMoGo

If all the world were cake. To Drink. Philippe Soupault. SurPaPo, tr. by Mary Ann Caws and Patricia Terry

If All the World Were Paper. Unknown. NOSC; NTCP; OBCoV; OxNR; TTTS

(Interrogativa Cantilena.) OxBEV

If all transgressions here should have their pay. Gods Providence. Robert Herrick. SacPr

If all you boast of your great art be true. To Alchemists. Ben Jonson. BASC

If all you need, my sister sweet. Alfred de Musset. WoPoe, tr. by Claire Nicholas White Fr. Night in May, A.

If Amoret, that glorious eye. To Amoret, Walking in a Starry Evening. Henry Vaughan. BeJo

If amorous faith, a heart of guileless ways. Petrarch. AWP Fr. Sonnets to Laura.

If an audience could be arranged. Nizar Qabbani. MAP Fr. Notes on the Book of Defeat.

If an eagle be imprisoned. America. Henry Dumas. ChAP

If an inaudible whistle. What the Dog Perhaps Hears. Lisel Mueller. MiVo

If an unkind word appears. On File. John Kendrick Bangs. PoToHe

If any ask why there's no great She-Poet. Dedication of the Cook. Anna Wickham. MoBrPo; NALW

If Any Be Pleased to Walk into My Poor Garden. Francis Daniel Pastorius. SCAP

If any have a stone to shy. Pebble, The. Elinor Wylie. ChIV-1; MoAmPo

If any his own foolishness might see. Mazzeo di Ricco da Messina. EaItPo, tr. by Dante Gabriel Rossetti

If any little word of mine. Little Word, The. Unknown. PWR

If any man would know the very cause. He Is Out of Heart with His Time. Guerzo di Montecanti. AWP; EaItPo, tr. by Dante Gabriel Rossetti

If any mourn us in the workshop, say. Rudyard Kipling. WoPoe Fr. Epitaphs of the War [1914–1918].

If any one had anything to say. Rustico Di Filippo. EaItPo, tr. by Dante Gabriel Rossetti

If any pleasure can come to a man through recalling. 76. Catullus. NAWM-7v1, tr. by Charles Martin

If any question why we died. Rudyard Kipling. FaBoEE; FaBoTw; HarvBoo; NPeEn; PeFWW; WoPoe Fr. Epitaphs of the War [1914–1918].

If any thing delight me for to print. To God. Robert Herrick. SacPr

If any wench Venus's girdle wear. John Gay. PeLV Fr. Begger's Opera.

If any woman of us all. Magdalen. Harriet Prescott Spofford. SWaP

If anybody comes to I. On Dr. Lettsom. Unknown. FaBoEE

If anyone asks you. Like This. Jelaluddin [or Jalal al-Din] Rumi. ErotSp, tr. by Coleman Barks

If art and industry should doe as much. New English Canaan; Prologue. Thomas Morton. SCAP

If art were a series of arbitrary digs. On Geoffrey Grigson. Cyril Connolly. OBCoV

If as a flower [or flowre] doth spread and die. Employment (1). George Herbert. GeHe

If, as Plato called them, shadows. Boethius at Cavalzero. John Macoubrie. CRP

If as the wind[e]s and waters here below. Storm, The. George Herbert. ESCV

If, as thou say'st, thy love tormenteth thee. Terino da Castel Fiorentino. EaItPo, tr. by Dante Gabriel Rossetti

If, at the pharmacy, I say to the woman. Pharmacy. Aaron Anstett. AmPoNex

If at your coming princes disappear. Comets and Princes. Samuel Johnson. FaBoEE

If aught can teach us aught, Affliction's looks. Sir John Davies. NOBE; WoPoe Fr. Nosce Teipsum.

If aught of oaten stop, or pastoral song. Ode to Evening. William Collins. AWP; CABP; HAP; NAEL-5v1; NAEL-6v1; NAEL-7v1; NOBE; NOEC; OBEV; OxAEP-1; PoE; SCGP; TFi

If aught of simple song have power to touch. Birthday Crown, The. William Alexander, Archbishop of Armagh. SacPr

If Auschwitz had been in Hampshire. If. Edward Bond. HP

If bathing were a virtue, not a lust. Opus 118. Arthur Davison Ficke. APT-1, tr. by Anne Knish

If bees are few. (LL) Emily Dickinson. BoWoP; HeIP-4; NBLV; OBCA; OxBA; TCAPo

If bees stay at home. Unknown. OxNR

If Bethlehem were here today. Christmas Morning. Elizabeth Madox Roberts. MoAmPo

If between basin and range you wake. Waking at the Middle of Nowhere. Reg Saner. PoCoUp

If Birds That neither Sow nor Reap. Roger Williams. AH

If blocked, a fart can kill a man. Nicarchus of Alexandria. GrAn

If boy, or man, or woman steals I hump. Unknown. PriapPo, tr. by Richard W. Hooper Fr. Priapus Poems, The.

If but God wearieth. (LL) Antique Harvesters. John Crowe Ransom. MoAmPo; OxBA

If but some vengeful god would call to me. Hap. Thomas Hardy. AWP; CABP; EBVV; GSo; MoBrPo; NAEL-5v2; NAEL-6v2; NoAM; NoP-4; OxBSo; Son

If by chance, Flaccus, someone could offer me for the asking. Martial. CAGL, tr. by Richard E. Prior Fr. Epigrams.

If by Dull Rhymes Our English Must be Chained. John Keats. CenSon (On the Sonnet.) NIL-7; NIP-4; NoP-4

If by his torturing, savage foes untraced. Captive Escaped in the Wilds of America, The. Addressed to the Hon. Mrs. O'Neill. Charlotte Smith. CenSon; Son

If by mischance the people in the street. George Wither. PBRV Fr. Britain's Remembrancer Canto 4.

'If Candlemas be fine and clear.' At Candlemas. Charles Causley. OBCP

If Chickens Could Talk. Víctor Hernández Cruz. PueRic

If China. Stanislaw Baranczak. AF, tr. by Magnus J. Krynski

If Christmas brought me nothing more. Poem for Christmas, A. C. A. Snodgrass. PoToHe

If Church spire be clëar. Senilio's Weather Saw. Martin Bell. PeLV

If clothed in black you tread the busy town. John Gay. ECEV Fr. Trivia; or, The Art of Walking the Streets of London.

If come into this world again I must. Dew on a Dusty Heart. Jean Starr Untermeyer. MoAmPo

If "compression is the first grace of style." To a Snail. Marianne Craig Moore. APT-1; FaBoMo; FaBoWP; NAAL-2v2; NALW; PoPoPo

If constancy in love, if a brave heart. Petrarch. ErotSp, tr. by Sam Hamill

If Cynthia Be a Queen, a Princess, and Supreme. Sir Walter Ralegh. NoP-4

If Dante mourns, there wheresoe'er he be. Giovanni Boccaccio. AWP; EaItPo, tr. by Dante Gabriel Rossetti Fr. Sonnets.

If design govern in a thing so small. (LL) Design. Robert Frost. APT-1; ColAP; HeIP-4; InPK-6; NAAL-2v2; NAAL-5; NIL-7; NOBA; NoAM; NoP-4; OxBSo; PAI; PoPoPo; RaBo; SAmP; SoSe-8; Son; TAP; TFi; TRP

If doughty [or daughty] deeds my lady please[s]. Robert Graham. GTBS-P; OBEV

If, dumb too long, the drooping Muse hath stayed. To the Earl of Warwick, on the Death of Mr. Addison. Thomas Tickell. NOEC; OxAEP-1

If duty, wife, lead thee to deem. Husband to Wife. John Harington. NoSic

If dying well is courage's great test. For the Athenian Dead at Plataia. Simonides. GrAn, tr. by Peter Jay

If e'er in thy sight I found favour, Apollo. Poet's Prayer, The. Unknown. OBSV

If Each Day Falls. Pablo Neruda. WoPoe, tr. by William O'Daly

If earthward you could wing your flight. England Expects? Sir Owen Seaman. NOBL

If Eve hadn't eaten the apple. Limerick. Wendy Cope. PeLi

If Ever Hapless Woman Had a Cause. Mary Sidney Herbert, Countess of Pembroke. MakPoe; WPE

If ever I go to sea. Me—Pirate. Clive Sansom. OTCP

If ever I had unmoored my dead name. To My Friend (With an Identity Disc). Wilfred Owen. CAGL

If ever I should condescend to prose. Byron. OxBoLi; PeLV Fr. Don Juan.

If Ever I Would Leave You. Frederick Loewe. ReLy

If ever love had force in huma[i]ne bre[a]st? Mary Sidney Wroth, Countess of Montgomery. BASC; BWW *Fr.* Pamphilia to Amphilanthus.

If ever mercy move you murder me. To the Mercy Killers. Dudley Randall. SoSe-8

If ever sonnet held so true a speech. (LL) Sonnet: He Is Past All Help. Cecco Angiolieri, da Siena. AWP; EaItPo, *tr. by* Dante Gabriel Rossetti

If ever there lived a Yankee lad. Darius Green and His Flying-Machine. John Townsend Trowbridge. OBAL; OBCA

If ever there was a beginning. Let There Be Light! D. H. Lawrence. ChIV-1

If ever there was a vehicle for nostalgia. Trains. William Scammell. NLP

If ever two were one, then surely we. To My Dear and Loving Husband. Anne Bradstreet. AmFaPo; BASC; BoWoP; ColAP; ErotSp; HAP; HeIP-4; ITBLP; LW; NAAL-2v1; NAAL-3; NAAL-5; NIL-7; NIP-4; NOBA; NOCV; NOSC; NoP-4; OxBA; OxBEV; OxBSP; OxWW; PEW; PoE; SCAP; SacPr; TAP; TCAPo; TFi; WPE; WeW-3

If ever you go to the North Countree. Edenhall. "Susan Coolidge." OBCA

If ever you should go by chance. How To Tell the Wild Animals. Carolyn Wells. NBLV

If every name is (as the Greek maintains). Golem, The. Jorge Luis Borges. PoetW, *tr. by* John Hollander

If everyone decided to be flowers. Flowers. Leo Vroman. TuT, *tr. by* James Liddy

If everything happens that can't be done. E. E. Cummings. SoSe-8; WeW-3

If evil could be safer, on the whole. (LL) Election Day, 1984. Carolyn Kizer. ExTi; GifTon

If external action is effete. Past Is the Present, The. Marianne Craig Moore. APT-1; NAAL-2v2

If famous Apelles with his hand of art. Pietro Aretino. GS

If fictive music fails your lyre, confess. Richard Wilbur. NBLV *Fr.* Flippancies.

If, finding it, he fails to find / Its master. (LL) Snail, The. Vincent Bourne. NPeEn; OBVE, *tr. by* William Cowper

If, flying south, gas, cylinders, and wings uphold you. Mathematician's Dream, The. Reuel Denney. YaYoPo

If for all the promises you regard so lightly. Horace. STV, *tr. by* John Frederick Nims *Fr.* Odes.

If Fortune Smiles. Rofel G. Brion. ReBoTo

If Fred Astaire had been really smart. Johnny Laces Up His Red Shoes. Cornelius Eady. InvLad

If, friends, you would but now this place accost. Invitation to my Friends at Cambridge, An. Jane Barker. BASC

If from my lips some angry accents fell. Charles Lamb. CenSon

If from the height of that celestial sphere. To Shakespeare. Frances Anne [*or* "Fanny"] Kemble. Son

If from the public way you turn your steps. Michael [A Pastoral Poem]. William Wordsworth. FHYEP; NAEL-5v2; NAEL-6v2; NOBRP; OxAEP-2

If fruits are fed on any beast. Epitaph after Reading Ronsard's Lines from Rabelais. John Millington Synge. FaBoEE

If girls were nice. Rufinus. GrAn

If God as a scribe were to write. They Who Are Poor. Attila József. IQMS, *tr. by* Vernon Watkins

If God compel thee to this destiny. Thought for a Lonely Death-Bed, A. Elizabeth Barrett Browning. ViWPN

If God had a wife, she'd be a doozy. Coward. Maurya Simon. ExTi

If God had stopped work after the fifth day. Imperfect Paradise, The. Linda Pastan. SoSe-8

If God had stopped work after the third day. Linda Pastan. *See* If God had stopped work after the fifth day

If grief for grief can touch thee. Emily Jane Brontë. EnLoPo

If half my heart is here, doctor. Angina Pectoris. Nazim Hikmet. VCWP

If Hart Crane played trumpet. Almost Blue. Mark Doty. SeSe

If hate is painful and if love's a pain. Euenus. GrAn

If he asks about me, trace on the ground. Nocturne and Elegy. Emilio Ballagas. CAGL, *tr. by* Fanny Arango-Ramos and William Keeth

If he but raises his slothfulness' blinds. (LL) Spring Joy Praising God. Catharina Regina von Greiffenberg. AuPH; GePo, *tr. by* George C. Schoolfield

If he could have kept. Sam. Lucille Clifton. UnSA

If he could solve the riddle. Sphinx. Robert Earl Hayden. GT; HCAP

If he did not come apart in her hands, he fell. Diane Di Prima. PFTM-1 *Fr.* Loba.

If He Had. Gary Young.

"Fog descends over the tidal surge and the shallow lagoons." GeoHom

"Owl drifts slowly through the canyon where three flickers worry a pitted oak for grubs, An." GeoHom

If he had only been a more inspiring Leader. On the Death of Ludwig Erhard. Hal Colebatch. NOBAu

If he have feeling, is[,] to cry! (LL) When Lovely Woman. Phoebe Cary. APN-2; UV

If He Let Us Go Now. Shirley Williams. BoWoP

If he turns them, they are purple, black from head to heel. Pathologist. Ellen Dudley. OPRER

If He Walked into My Life. Jerry Herman. ReLy

If he wanted to. (LL) Louise Glück. FaBoWP; NALW *Fr.* Dedication to Hunger.

If he were I, he would do what I did. (LL) Hanging Man, The. Sylvia Plath. HCAP; VCAP

If he would dig it all up again they would not die. (LL) In Nunhead Cemetery. Charlotte Mew. FaBoWP; NoP-4

If heav'n the grateful liberty would give. Choice, The. John Pomfret. NOEC

If Heaven had no love for wine. Drinking Alone in Moonlight. Li Po. TAL

If Heaven has into being deigned to call. Slavery. Hannah More. RWP; WoRP

If heaven were to do again. Peaceful Shepherd, The. Robert Frost. MoAmPo

If Heaven weren't fond of wine. Li Po. SuSp *Fr.* Drinking Alone beneath the Moon.

If Hercules' tall stature might be guessed. On a Good Leg and Foot. William Strode. NOSC

If homely virtues draw from me a tune. Envoy. James Weldon Johnson. SacPr

If honour to an ancient name be due. On the Welsh Language. Katherine Philips. EMWP; NOSC

If Hot Flowers Come to the Street. R. Meenakshi. OMIP; WoPoe, *tr. by* Martha Ann Selby

If I Am Too Brown or Too White for You. Wendy Rose. HATNAP

If I Became a Stone. So Chong-Ju. VCWP, *tr. by* David R. McCann

If I Blindfold You. Marjorie Welish. FTOS

If I but stretch out my hand, someone grips it. I feel this is certain. Unknown World, The. György Sárközi. IQMS, *tr. by* Watson Kirkconnell

If I can let you go as trees let go. May Sarton. PoBW *Fr.* Autumn Sonnets, The.

If I can stop one Heart from breaking. Emily Dickinson. AH; BRP; PWR; PoToHe

If I consider / My body like the fields. Lady Ise. WPOW

If I could be still / there would be a beach. Truro. Rose Solari. AmPoNex

If I Could Be with You. James P. Johnson. ReLy

If I could chop wood. Karate. Stanley Plumly. MoASP

If I could come back from the dead, I would come back. Apple. Susan Stewart. BAP-01

If I could just touch your ankle, he whispers, *there.* Persephone Underground. Rita Dove. FFC

If I could keep my innermost me. Sanctuary, The. Sara Teasdale. APT-1

If I could linger on his lovely chest. Sonnet 13. Louise Labé. BoWoP, *tr. by* Aliki and Willis Barnstone

If I could live to God for just one day. Just One Day. Susan E. Gammons. PWR

If I could only get all of you. Trying Again. Dahlia Ravikovitch [*or* Ravikovich]. VCWP

If I could only hear. Speak to Me. Fanny Carrión de Fierro. TANSG, *tr. by* Sally Cheney Bell

If I could [*or* co'd], I would [*or* wo'd] not so. (LL) Bracelet to Julia, The. Robert Herrick. BASC; OBEV

If I could raise rivers, I'd raise them. Douglas Crase. NAAL-2v2

If I could send him only. Her Reticence. Theodore Roethke. RACG

If I Could Shut the Gate against My Thoughts. *Unknown.* NOCV

If I Could Tell You. W. H. Auden. HarvBoo

If I could track you down to have you taste. Patterns. Roberta Hill Whiteman. HATNAP

If I Could Walk Out into the Cold Country. Elizabeth Brewster. NOBC

If i cud ever write a. To P. J. (2 Yrs Old Who Sed Write a Poem for Me in Portland, Oregon). Sonia Sanchez. CA; OxIBACP

If I'd a sack of florins, and all new. Cecco Angiolieri, da Siena. EaItPo, *tr. by* Dante Gabriel Rossetti

If I'd as much money as I could spend. Chairs to Mend. *Unknown.* LB

If I describe my house. House, The. George Bowering. NOBC

If I desire something, I know it not. Hadewijch II. WPoS

If I did come of set intent. To Archinus. Callimachus. AWP, *tr. by* F. A. Wright

If I die, don't take me to the cemetery. Life-Hook. Juana de Ibarbourou. WPOW, *tr. by* Marti Moody

If I Died Tonight. Idea Vilariño. TANSG, *tr. by* Louise B. Popkin

If I don't drive around the park. Dorothy Parker. APT-1 *Fr.* Some Beautiful Letters.

If I don't go out I'll only mope. Out and Back on the Fifteenth Night of the First Month. Mei Yao Ch'en. CoBCP, *tr. by* Burton Watson

If I don't take anything to the party I'll feel bad. *Unknown.* STP

If I drink water while this doth last. Thomas Love Peacock. NBLV *Fr.* Crotchet Castle.

If I entreat this lady that all grace. Sonnet: To a Friend Who Does Not Pity His Love. Guido Cavalcanti. AWP; EaItPo, *tr. by* Dante Gabriel Rossetti

If I ever read it. (LL) Patch of Old Snow, A. Robert Frost. OxBSP; WeW-3

If I Felt Less. Morris Wintchevsky. TrJP, *tr. by* Joseph Leftwich

If I Forget Thee. Emanuel Litvinoff. TrJP

If I found you wandering round the edge. On Ballycastle Beach. Medbh McGuckian. PBCIP

If I freely may discover. Ben Jonson. BeJo *Fr.* Poetaster, The.

If I gave 5 birds. Red Shirt, The. Philip Levine. BodElec

If I go alone. Rod Willmot. HA

If I grow bitterly. Scrub. Edna St. Vincent Millay. APT-1

If I had a beau. Dashing White Sergeant, The. John Burgoyne. FaBoWar

If I had a donkey that wouldn't go. *Unknown.* OxNR

If I had a Green Automobile. Green Automobile, The. Allen Ginsberg. BB

If I Had a Gun. Gig Ryan. BMAP

If I had a little wife. *Unknown.* OxNR

If I had a nickel. .05. Ishmael Reed. ESEAA

If I had a son! A little child. Barren. "Rachel" [*or* "Rahel"]. TrJP, *tr. by* L. V. Snowman

If I Had a Talking Picture of you. Ray Henderson. ReLy

If I had a trunk like a big elephant. If. John Kendrick Bangs. OBCA

If I had always known what I've learnt. Private Truce. Lőrinc Szabó. IQMS, *tr. by* Peter Zollman

If I had but one year to live. One Year to Live. Mary Davis Reed. PoToHe

If I had chosen thee, thou shouldst have been. Wilfrid Scawen Blunt. GSo; Son *Fr.* Love Sonnets of Proteus, The.

If I had given you that love and care. John Hewitt. PNI *Fr.* Sonnets for Roberta (1954).

If I had known in the morning. Our Own. Margaret Elizabeth Munson Sangster. PoToHe

If I had known this burden on my tongue. Mama. Timothy Liu. WiU

If I Had Made the World. Sarah Morgan Bryan Piatt. NCAP

If I had no memory. Bad Truth. Jane Rohrer. BodElec

If I had [*or* I'd] as much money as I could spend. Mother Goose. OxNR

If I had peace to sit and sing. Singer, The. Anna Wickham. MoBrPo

If I had thought thou couldst have died. To Mary. Charles Wolfe. OBEV

If I Had You. Ted Shapiro. ReLy

If I have faltered more or less. Celestial Surgeon, The. Robert Louis Stevenson. EBVV; MoBrPo; PoToHe

If i have made, my lady, intricate. If I Have Made, My Lady. E. E. Cummings. NOBA; PoRA

If I have sinned in act, I may repent. Hartley Coleridge. CenSon

If I Have to Yield My Bones. Milán Füst. IQMS, *tr. by* Paul Tabori

If I have wronged you Lord forgive me. Migrant's Lament: A Song. Alfred Temba Qabula. PeSAV

If I held back each word, perhaps. Poem. Timothy Liu. AmPoNex

If I journeyed to a suburb of a Sunday. Marbled Chuckle in the Savannahs. Kenward Elmslie. FTOS

If I just had a piano. Testimonial. Langston Hughes. APT-2

If I Knew You and You Knew Me. Nixon Waterman. PoToHe

If I leave all for thee, wilt thou exchange. Elizabeth Barrett Browning. CenSon; Son *Fr.* Sonnets from the Portuguese.

If I lie naked. Confession. Pearl Cleage. ISC

If I, like Solomon. O To Be A Dragon. Marianne Craig Moore. APT-1; CTC; ChIV-1; NAAL-5; NALW

If I live [*or* grow] to be old, for I find I go down. Old Man's Wish, The. Walter Pope. NOSC

If I lived in this place for a thousand years. Cuchulainn. Michael O'Loughlin. BiHa; PBCIP

If I look up from here. When Suzy Was. Kelvin Corcoran. Oth

If I love you. Thread. Catherine Lucy Czerkawska. LW

If I Love You. Frank Prewett. HATNAP

If I love you. To the Oak. "Shu Ting." CarOv, *tr. by* Carolyn Kizer and Y. H. Zhao

If I love you! (LL) Madam and Her Madam. Langston Hughes. RACG; SAmP

If I Loved You. Richard Rodgers. ReLy

If I'm Going to Die I'm going to Have Some Fun. George M. Cohan. ReLy

If I make it over the pass. Hauling Over Wolf Creek Pass in Winter. Walter McDonald. CDa

If I make the lashes dark. Before the World Was Made. W. B. Yeats. GTBS-P

If I may have it, when it's dead. Emily Dickinson. NCAP

If I Might Be an Ox. *Unknown.* RB, *tr. by* Enrico Cerulli (Love Song.) WoPoe

If I might guess, then guess I would. Dorcas. George Macdonald. SacPr

If I might offer. *Unknown.* ArkPo, *tr. by* Helen Craig McCullough

If I might only love my God and die! If Only. Christina Georgina Rossetti. SacPr; TrCP

If I might where I pleased compose my nest. Golden Grove, Carmarthen. Rowland Watkyns. AngWePo

If I must dial a number to call you. Valerio Magrelli. NeIt

If I must die. Kafu. JDP, *tr. by* Yoel Hoffmann

If I must die. Koyo. JDP, *tr. by* Yoel Hoffmann

If I must of my Senses lose. Prayer. Theodore Roethke. TwCP

If I offered up my bell and bones to you, Boy. Amanda. Lisa Glatt. AmPoNex

If I once got free of this net. Mary Hogan's Quatrains. Máire Mhac an tSaoi. ModIr, *tr. by* Patrick Crotty

If I Only Had a Brain (If I Only Had a Heart) (If I Only Had the Nerve). Harold Arlen. ReLy

If I only had time! To Vera, Who Asked a Song. Edith Nesbit. PoBW

If I Only Knew. Nelly Sachs. PoSu, *tr. by* Matthew Mead and Ruth Mead

If I owned all of Alba. Saint Columcille [*or* Columba]. NOIV

If I popped in at Downing Street. Prayer, A. Max Beerbohm. UV

If I profane with my unworthiest hand. William Shakespeare. OxAEP-1; SoSe-8; Son *Fr.* Romeo and Juliet.

If I put my hand into the water. Pigeon Rock: Lebanon. Elmaz Abinader. GraLe

If I remember right, his first letter. Letter, The. Andrew Motion. EmeKit

If I remember you, Oh Jerusalem. Psalms (Chapter 137, Verse 5–6). Manuela Fingueret. MirDau, *tr. by* Roberta Gordenstein

If I said I once loved a girl who stacked. Working Girl. David Marlatt. AmPoNex

If I said, "Little wives." Wives, The. Donald Hall. CoAP

If I shall enterprise to make. Praise of Faith, The. John Hall. ChIV-2

If I shall ever return home. (LL) Another Spring. Tu Fu. BLT; OHPC, *tr. by* Kenneth Rexroth

If I should cast off this tattered coat. Stephen Crane. APN-2 *Fr.* Black Riders [and Other Lines], The.

If I Should Die. Ben King. NBLV; OBAL

If I should die, think only this of me. Rupert Brooke. AmFaPo; CABP; FaBoWar; GSo; HeIP-4; MoBrPo; NAEL-5v2; NAEL-6v2; NOBE; NoP-4; OBEV; OBWP; OxBTC; PeFWW; PoRA; PoWW; Son; TFi; UV *Fr.* 1914.

If I Should Die To-Night. Charles Walter Brown. PWR

If I Should Ever by Chance. Edward Thomas. FaBoCh; MoBrPo; OBMV; OBWVE

If I should go away. Post-Script: for Gweno. Alun Lewis. AngWePo; BoLoP; GTBS-P

If I should learn, in some quite casual way. Edna St. Vincent Millay. APT-1; HeIP-4

If I should lose, think only this of me. Doctor, The. Roger Woddis. UV

If I should now forget, or not remember thee. To Spencer. George Turberville. NoSic

If I should pass the tomb of Jonah. Losers. Carl Sandburg. MoAmPo; NoAM

If I should see your eyes again. Jewels. Sara Teasdale. APT-1

If I should sleep with a lady called death. E. E. Cummings. BoLoP; VGW

If I should suddenly start to sing. Things Are Looking Up. George Gershwin. ReLy

If I should treat my lady with aplomb. Ballad of Fat Margot. Augustus Young. CIP-2

If I singe, ye will me lakke. *Unknown.* MiEL

If I speak always of the dead. Poem. Salah Fa'iq. MAP, *tr. by* Patricia Alanah Byrne and Salma Khadra Jayyusi

If I speek good english. Changed Mind (or the Day I Woke Up). Tejumola Ologboni. NBV

If I Stand in My Window. Lucille Clifton. BPo

If I stretch my neck all the way. Goree. Harriet Jacobs. SpirFl

If I think you'll think I'm brainwashed. Looking Up My Balance. Anselm Berrigan. HeMarv

If I thought I could get away. Kenneth Rexroth. APSN *Fr.* Love Poems of Marichiko, The.

If I told you I used to know the circular truth. Eagles. James Dickey. BodElec

If I told you we could see nail polish stopping. Small Patch of Ice, A. Betsy Sholl. PBCAP

If I use my forbidden hand. Bond, The. Nuala Ni Dhomhnaill. PBCIP, *tr. by* Medbh McGuckian

If I've a taste, it's not alone. Hunger. Arthur Rimbaud. AWP, *tr. by* Louise Varese

If I've been dead for twenty years or so. Abu Sa'id Abul Khayr. WoPoe, *tr. by* Dick Davis *Fr.* Four Poems on Death.

If I Walked Straight Slap. Ivor Gurney. Spl

If I was not myself, I would be somebody else. Somebody Else. Jackie Kay. NeBl

If I was you. (LL) Bad Luck Card. Langston Hughes. NoP-4; SAmP; TRP

If I Went Away. Desmond O'Grady. CIP-2

If I Were a Bell. Frank Loesser. ReLy

If I were a cassowary. Impromptu. Samuel Wilberforce. NBLV; OWoS

If I were a cinnamon peeler. Cinnamon Peeler, The. Michael Ondaatje. NOBC

If I were a man. I Know Exactly the Sort of Woman I'd Like to Fall in Love With. Deryn Rees-Jones. MFPA

If I were a man, I'd have all the moonlight. Woman. Juana de Ibarbourou. TCLAP, tr. by Sophie Cabot Black

If I were a poet / of love, I would make. Antonio Machado Ruiz. ErotSp, tr. by Robert Bly

If I Were a Rich Man. Sheldon Harnick. ReLy

If I were a young animal ready to turn home at dusk. (LL) Hunting Pheasants in a Cornfield. Robert Bly. CoAmPo; TRP

If I were but a bird. Unknown. GePo

If I were called in. Water. Philip Larkin. EmeKit; FaBoMo; OxBSP; PeECV

If I were certain, o my dear companion. If I Were Certain. Faiz Ahmad Faiz. CarOv, tr. by Carolyn Kizer

If I were dead, and in my place. Song to Amoret, A. Henry Vaughan. NAEL-7v1

If I were doing my Laundry I'd wash my dirty Iran. Homework. Allen Ginsberg. NoAM

If I were fierce and bald and short of breath. Base Details. Siegfried Sassoon. FaBoWar; MoBrPo; NPeEn; OxBEV; OxBSP; PeFWW

If I were fire, I'd burn the world away. Sonnet: Of All He Would Do. Cecco Angiolieri, da Siena. AWP; EaItPo, tr. by Dante Gabriel Rossetti

If I were French, I'd write. Breasts. Maxine Chernoff. PmAP; ReTh; SpudSo

If I were from Timbuktu, perhaps. Dark Mirror. Calvin Forbes. GT

If I were God, up in the sky. Child's Thought, A. Bertha Moore. VerBaPo

If I were home right now. Good Friday. Rofel G. Brion. ReBoTo

If I were in China this minute. Foreign Ways. Diana Chang. UnSA

If I were loved, as I desire to be. Tennyson. GSo; OxBSo; Son

If I were only dafter. Witter Bynner. TCAPo Fr. Spectra.

If I were Pablo Neruda. My Name. Daniel Berrigan. AF

If I Were Rita Hayworth. Patricia Jones. ReTh

If I were sitting. Midnight Song. Pinkie Gordon Lane. GT

If I were still that man, worthy to love. Guido Cavalcanti. EaItPo, tr. by Dante Gabriel Rossetti

If I were stone dead and buried under. Felo de Se. Richard Hughes. OBMV

If I were the spreading tide sheets I would overwhelm your insteps. Spray. Biddy Jenkinson. ModIr, tr. by Alex Osborne

If I were the type to play around. Sleigh Ride in July. Jimmy Van Heusen. ReLy

If I were to paint myself for you. Make-Up. Cheryl Clarke. WiU

If I were to tell of our labours, our hard lodging. Aeschylus. FaBoWar, tr. by Louis MacNeice Fr. Agamemnon.

If I were to walk this way. Wood Road, The. Edna St. Vincent Millay. APT-1

If I were to write with my blood. Nok Lady in Terracotta. Ifi Amadiume. HAWP

If I were tortur'd with greensickness. Song. Elizabeth Polwhele. EMWP

If I were used to writing verse. First Attempt in Rhyme, A. Thomas Hood. OBCoV

If I were writing on rock. Mesa Blanca. Víctor Hernández Cruz. PFTM-2

If I when my wife is sleeping. William Carlos Williams. See If when my wife is sleeping

If I Write a Poem. A. Van Jordan. SpirFl

If I Yes. Olga Broumas. GifTon

If / ice shall melt. If Ice. W. W. Eustace Ross. NOBC

If "ifs" and "ans" [or If ifs and ands were pots and pans]. Unknown. LB

If, in a fisherman's hut, you poke. Hand-Rolled Cigarettes. Yevgeny Aleksandrovich Yevtushenko [or Evtushenko]. VCWP

If, in an odd angle of the hutment. Eighth Air Force. Randall Jarrell. NOBA; NoAM; NoP-4; OBWP; PoWW; TRP; VCAP

If in his study he hath so much care. Antiquary. John Donne. EBEV; NOSC

If in my womb and mind You placed. Hymn. Alda Merini. CItWP, tr. by Cinzia Sartini Blum and Lara Trubowitz

If in that Syrian garden, ages slain. Easter Hymn. A. E. Housman. EBEV; GI

If, in the month of dark December. Written After Swimming from Sestos to Abydos. Byron. NAEL-5v2; NAEL-6v2; NBLV; NoP-4

If in the years to come you should recall. Edna St. Vincent Millay. HeIP-4

If in your heart you make. It Depends on You. "Angelus Silesius." EnlH, tr. by Stephen Mitchell

If instead of being this way. Of Another Fashion. Emilio Ballagas. CAGL, tr. by Fanny Arango-Ramos and William Keeth

If intercourse gives you thrombosis. Limerick. Unknown. PeLi

If it ain't simply this, what is it? Keep Talking. Philip Levine. WeW-3

If It Be Destined. Petrarch. AWP, tr. by Edward Fitzgerald Fr. Sonnets to Laura.

If it be event, I go towards and not back. I go tower, not floor. Untitled. Karen Volkman. NAPBL

If it be night then, when the screech-owl's call. Sonnet. Alec Brock Stevenson. FuPo

If It Be True. Esther Johnson. OxBSP

If it but herald death, the vision is divine! (LL) Emily Jane Brontë. NOBE; NoP-4; OBEV Fr. Prisoner, The.

If it chance your eye offend you. A. E. Housman. ChIV-2

If it could weep, it could arise and go. (LL) Grief. Elizabeth Barrett Browning. HeIP-4; InPK-6; NALW; NOBVV; NPeEn; OBEV; VWP; WPE

If it doesn't open up. Naming of Things, The. Bahinabai Chaudhari. OMIP, tr. by Philip Engblomb

If it ever is. Invitation, The. Robert Creeley. FTOS

If it ever occurs to her to be kind to me. Ghazal 25. Mirza Asadullah Khan Ghalib. EaWin, tr. by Aijaz Ahmad and W. S. Merwin

If it form the one landscape that we, the inconstant ones. In Praise of Limestone. W. H. Auden. HAP; HarvBoo; NAEL-5v2; NAEL-6v2; NoAM; NoP-4

If it had been possible. Cesare Greppi. ItPo, tr. by Gayle Ridinger

If it is but sleep. Unknown. ArkPo, tr. by Edwin A. Cranston

If It Is Not My Portion. Rabindranath Tagore. OBMV Fr. Gitanjali.

If it is real the white. Certainty. Octavio Paz. TCLAP, tr. by Charles Tomlinson

If it is true. Georg Heym—The Almost Metaphysical Adventure. Zbigniew Herbert. PoetW, tr. by John Carpenter and Bogdana Carpenter

If it is you, there / in the light boat on the pond. Lady Ise. BoWoP; WoPoe, tr. by Irma Brandeis and Etsuko Terasaki

If it must be; if it must be, O God! David Gray. OxBS Fr. In the Shadows.

If It's Ever Spring Again. Thomas Hardy. OxBTC

If It's Only Rhythm. Dennis Phillips. FTOS Fr. Etudes.

If it's true you made light. Creed. Belkis Cuza Malé. TANSG, tr. by Pamela Carmell

If it's Tuesday. Moulton Transformations. Dixie Salazar. GeoHom

If it were a sea, this immense wind. Maria Luisa Spaziani. NeIt

If it were done when 'tis done, then 'twere well. William Shakespeare. OxAEP-1 Fr. Macbeth.

If it / Were lighter touch. Guarded Wound, The. Adelaide Crapsey. APT-1; WPE

If it were not your face that melts. If It Were Not. Andrea Zanzotto. VCWP, tr. by Ruth Feldman

If it were real / Perhaps I'd understand it. Ono no Komachi. WPOW

If its a spiritual offense does it as wrongdoing take place more in more in the second. Where Leftover Misery Goes. Alice Notley. BAP-01

If, Jerusalem, I Ever Should Forget Thee. Heinrich Heine. TrJP, tr. by Margaret Armour

If Juan Rodriguez is alive today. Disgrace. David Hall. CDa

If just for once for just one day I could be a hippopotamus. If Just For Once. Toon Tellegen. TuT, tr. by Peter Van de Kamp

If life be time that here is spent. Of the Loss of Time. John Hoskyns [or Hoskins]. FaBoEE

If life is but a blot on a dying day. Lamarck. Osip Emilevich Mandelstam [or Mandelshtam]. TCRusP, tr. by John Glad

If Life's a Lousy Picture, Why Not Leave before the End. Roger McGough. OxBTC

If life were never bitter. If. Mortimer Collins. OBCoV

If Light can thus deceive, wherefore not Life? (LL) To Night. Joseph Blanco White. EBEV; GSo; OBEV; OxAEP-2; Son

If, like winds semaphored by a rose. If, like winds. Robert Desnos. MFP, tr. by Martin Sorrell

If Lincoln were to come again to earth. If Lincoln Should Return. Margaret E. Bruner. PoToHe

If livelihood by knowledge were endowed. Sadi [or Saadi or Sa'di]. AWP, tr. by L. Cranmer-Byng Fr. Gulistan, The.

If, Lord, Thy Love for Me Is Strong. Saint Theresa [or Teresa] of Avila. AWP, tr. by Arthur Symons

If love is chaste, what bears adultery? Sonnet. Sibylla Schwarz. GePo, tr. by George C. Schoolfield

If love should count you worthy, and should deign. Decision. Unknown. PoToHe

If love were what the rose is. Match, A. Algernon Charles Swinburne. NOBVV

If Lucy should be dead! (LL) Strange Fits of Passion Have I Known. William Wordsworth. EBEV; NAEL-5v2; NAEL-6v2; NOBE; OBEV; PoE

If lust should chase my soule, made swift by fright. Francis Quarles. ESCV *Fr.* Emblems.

If Luther's day expand to Darwin's year. Herman Melville. APN-2; NCAP; TCAPo *Fr.* Clarel: A Poem and Pilgrimage in the Holy Land.

If maiden is your soul, like Mary undefiled. "Angelus Silesius." GePo, *tr. by* George C. Schoolfield *Fr.* Cherubical Wanderer, The.

If mama / could see. Lucille Clifton. NAAAL

If man could name what he loves. If Man Could Name. Luis Cernuda. BLPSL, *tr. by* Rene de Costa, Rigas Kappatos and Eleni Paidoussi

If Marilyn Monroe. Leo Romero. LTA

If Martin Van Buren ever swam in water. Jackson Mac Low. APSN *Fr.* Presidents of the United States of America, The.

If Mary came would Mary. Penitent Considers Another Coming of Mary, A. Gwendolyn Brooks. NoAM

If meat the gods give, I the steam. Steam in Sacrifice. Robert Herrick. CaPo

If medals were ordained for drinks. To a Boon Companion. Oliver St. John Gogarty. OBMV

If men be judged wise. Epigram. Joseph Solomon Del Medigo. TrJP

If money grew on trees. Annual Returns. Greg Williamson. RA

If more than once, as annals tell. Timoleon. Herman Melville. APN-2

If muscles are the currency of dreams. Lifting. Dorothy Barresi. MoASP

If music [*or* musique] and sweet poetry [*or* poetrie] agree. To His Friend Master R.L., In Praise of Music and Poetry. Richard Barnfield [*or* Barnefield]. Son

If, My Darling. Philip Larkin. EBEV

If my dear love were but the child of state. William Shakespeare. NoSic *Fr.* Sonnets.

If my disciple thou wilt be. Lady Hungerford's Meditacions upon the Beades, The. Anne Dormer, Lady Hungerford. EMWP

If my feet will arrive again, at my home. Lyric in Exile, A. Hussein Elhami. AmFaPo, *tr. by* Shmuel Shoshani

If my imprisonment has no end. From Prison. Todros ben Judah Abulafia. TOF, *tr. by* David Goldstein

If my kisses wrong you, then tit for tat. Strato [*or* Straton]. GrAn

If my lips shred to pieces—oh, courage! Before Easter. Mihály Babits. IQMS, *tr. by* Peter Zollman

If my mother had never been the protected child. House in St. Petersburg. Stanley Burnshaw. WoPoe

If my next wish you cannot guess. (LL) You've Told Me, Maro. Martial. NIL-7; NIP-4, *tr. by* F. Lewis

If my nipples were to drip milk. Sappho. BoWoP

If my parents and your parents. Almost a Love Poem. Yehuda Amichai [*or* Amikhai]. HP, *tr. by* Glenda Abramson

If my poor Harp has ever poured. To the Late William Jerdan. Eliza Cook. VWP

If, my religion safe, I durst embrace. To Sir Henry [*or* Henrie] Savile [upon His Translation of Tacitus]. Ben Jonson. BASC

If my torch goes out it will be dark. Search. Claribel Alegría. BoWoP, *tr. by* Aliki Barnstone and Willis Barnstone

If Myra counts fifteen cows and Alfredo counts nine. Baltazar Beats His Tutor at Scrabble. Belle Waring. ExTi

If Nancy Hanks / Came back as a ghost. Nancy Hanks. Rosemary Benét. NTCP

If Nature Bellows. Mariella Bettarini. CItWP, *tr. by* Cinzia Sartini Blum and Lara Trubowitz

If nature prompts you, or if friends persuade. William Whitehead. OBSV *Fr.* Charge to the Poets, A.

If neither brass, nor marble, can withstand. Power of Time, The. Jonathan Swift. FaBoEE

If night takes the form of a whale and. Isabel Fraire. BoWoP

If nine times you your bridegroom[e] kiss[e]. Tithe [*or* Tythe]: To the Bride, The. Robert Herrick. CaPo

If no love is, O God, what fele I so. Geoffrey Chaucer. AWP *Fr.* Troilus and Criseyde [*or* Criseide].

If no Pain were, how judge we of Pleasure? Limerick. William Bliss. PeLi

If not a so-called Negro bought a bottle. Racist Psychotherapy. Isaac J. Black. NBV

If not enjoyed, it sighing cries, / Heigh ho! (LL) Samuel Daniel. NOBE; OBEV *Fr.* Hymen's Triumph.

If not famous ourselves, oh let us. Vanna White's Bread Pudding. Michael Pettit. ReTh

If not for Uncle Li. X. Daniel Hall. YaYoPo

If not what I want. (LL) I used to tell you, "Frances, we grow old." Ausonius. NNaP; PGA; WoPoe, *tr. by* Kenneth Rexroth

If not you? (LL) Muriel Rukeyser. APSN; APT-2; GLP; LCAP-2; PFTM-2

If Now You Knocked on My Door. Patrizia Cavalli. CItWP, *tr. by* Cinzia Sartini Blum and Lara Trubowitz

If, O Maecenas, versed in lore antique. Horace. OBVE

If, O my Lesbia, I should commit. Second Philosopher's Song. Aldous Leonard Huxley. OBCoV

If of the dead save good nought should be said. William Drummond, of Hawthornden. NOSC

If on your walks you have moved some stones. Word to the Wise, A. Octavio Armand. TCLAP, *tr. by* Carol Maier

If on your way you see. Heart and the Severed Head, The. Rosita Copioli. CItWP, *tr. by* Lara Trubowitz

If once again a flood fell from the spheres. Couplets. Yehuda Amichai [*or* Amikhai]. FIT, *tr. by* Robert Friend

If once he lose his sting, he grows a drone. (LL) Abraham Cowley. BeJo; NOSC *Fr.* Mistress, The.

If One Always Denies. Luciana Notari. CItWP, *tr. by* Cinzia Sartini Blum and Lara Trubowitz

If one could have that little head of hers. Face, A. Robert Browning. CTC

If one revolves a vine-enamored thumb. Images for the Gospel of Christ. Paul Ramsey. CRP

If one should bring me this report. Tennyson. EBVV; FHYEP; NAEL-6v2 *Fr.* In Memoriam A. H. H.

If Only. Herman De Coninck. TuT, *tr. by* Theo Dorgan

If Only. Christina Georgina Rossetti. SacPr; TrCP

If Only. Lina Tibi. PoArWo, *tr. by* Subhi Hadidi and Nathalie Handal

If only a small miracle. Small Miracle, A. Anabel Torres. TANSG, *tr. by* Celeste Kostopulos-Cooperman

If Only for One Night. Gordon Chambers. InTrad

If only God were a violet. If Only. Lina Tibi. PoArWo, *tr. by* Subhi Hadidi and Nathalie Handal

If only I could be, just a little, sick again. If Only. Herman De Coninck. TuT, *tr. by* Theo Dorgan

If only I could forget that Frenchman. French Prisoner, The. János Pilinszky. PoSu, *tr. by* Janos Csokits

If only I might touch Neobule's hand. Archilochus. SaLy, *tr. by* Diane Rayor

If only Life-and-Death. *Unknown.* TAL

If only now you were to emerge from. Lingua Franca. Chris Stroffolino. BodElec

If only she could make herself. Security. Shirley Kaufman. DTA

If only that so many dead lie round. (LL) Church Going. Philip Larkin. CABP; GTBS-P; HarvBoo; HeIP-4; MoBrPo; NAEL-5v2; NAEL-6v2; NIL-7; NIP-4; NoAM; NoP-4; PAI; SCV; SoSe-8; TFi; TwCP; UnPo

If only the bell keeps him alive though that is. Night. Gerald Stern. BodElec

If only the phantom would stop reappearing! Faust. John Ashbery. TwCP

If only, when one heard. *Var. authors.* AWP *Fr.* Kokin Shu.

If orange chiffon sadness. Orange Chiffon. Jayne Cortez. BlSi

If our antagonists take me. [Last Poems]. Osip Emilevich Mandelstam [*or* Mandelshtam]. PFTM-1

If our love were not. Our Love. Xavier Villaurrutia. TCLAP, *tr. by* Michael Surman

If out of a dire suspicion. Robert Penn Warren. NoAM *Fr.* Penological Study: Southern Exposure.

If parting be decreed for the two of us. Parting. Judah Halevi. AWP; TrJP, *tr. by* Nina Davis Salaman

If patience true could termine passions warr. Joshua Sylvester. OxBSo *Fr.* Du Bartas: His Divine Weeks and Works.

If people in this neighborhood get sick. Ballad of the Neighborhood Shaman. Kao Ch'i. CoBLCP, *tr. by* Jonathan Chaves

If Pigs Could Fly. James Reeves. OTCP

If Pliny, Lord High Treasurer of all. Painture [*or* Peinture]. Richard Lovelace. CaPo

If poems are eternal occasions, then. Marginalization of Poetry, The. Bob Perelman. FTOS

If poisonous [*or* poysonous] mineral[l]s, and if that tree. John Donne. BASC; EBEV; FaBoVe; NAEL-5v1; NAEL-6v1; NAEL-7v1; NoP-4; OxAEP-1; SCGP; Son; UnPo *Fr.* Holy Sonnets.

If poor (you say) she drains her husband's purse. Geoffrey Chaucer. OBSV *Fr.* Canterbury Tales, The.

If Praxiteles had been an animator, this form. Louganis. Eloise Klein Healy. WiU

If *puce* were sound not color. First Performance of the Rock 'n Roll Band *Puce Exit.* Kevin Stein. SwNoth

If Pythias has a customer. Poseidippus. PGA

If questioning could make us wise. Because She Would Ask Me Why I Loved Her. Christopher John Brennan. CBAP

If right in front of me. Flowering Quince. Winfield Townley Scott. APT-2

If rightly tuneful bards decide. Amoret. Mark Akenside. OBEV

If Rome so great, and in her wisest age. To Edward Alleyn. Ben Jonson. NOSC

If safety can be had from hollow men. Kate Light. AmPoNex *Fr.* Five Urban Love Songs.

If Sanct Paules day be fair and cleir. *Unknown.* MiEL

If saying No. Solo for Two Voices. Octavio Paz. STV, *tr. by* John Frederick Nims

If she be made of white and red. William Shakespeare. CTC *Fr.* Love's Labour's Lost.

If she be not as kind as fair. Song. William Walsh. NOSC

If she come to it. (LL) Girl, A. "Michael Field." VWP; ViWPN

If she could see it, she would never let him see. (LL) Lovers, The. Dorianne Laux. BodElec; ErotSp

If She Only Had One Minute. Kay Ryan. ExTi

If she should give me all I ask of her. George Henry Boker. APN-2 *Fr.* Sonnets: A Sequence on Profane Love.

If she was beautiful is uncertain the more. Legend of Lilja. Sarah Kirsch. AF, *tr. by* Wayne Kvam

If she whom I love, should love me. (LL) Love's Deity [*or* Deitie]. John Donne. AWP; ESCV; SoSe-8

If she wishes to go I will not forgive her. (LL) River God, The. Stevie Smith. BrRo; FaBoTw; FaBoWP

If Sleep and Death be truly one. Tennyson. PeECV *Fr.* In Memoriam A. H. H.

If snow falls on the far field. Mother's Song. *Unknown.* BoWoP, *tr. by* Willis Barnstone

If so be a toad be laid. Charme, or an Allay for Love, A. Robert Herrick. FaBoCh

If So the Man You Are. Dominic Bevan Wyndham Lewis. OBSV

If solitaries, why so many? Monks. Palladas [*or* Pallades]. GrAn, *tr. by* Peter Jay

If, some morning, you go out. Regarding Music. Siv Cedering. MiVo

If some nosey body asks "well." Poem for a "Divorced" Daughter. Horace Coleman. ISC

If some rejoiced, more did lament. (LL) To the Memory of My Dear and Ever Honored Father Thomas Dudley Esq. Who Deceased July 31, 1653, and of His Age 77. Anne Bradstreet. NAAL-2v1; NAAL-3

If someone barefoot stood in a saloon. Saloon with Birds. Christopher Middleton. HarvBoo

If someone came what would I do. Lazy Cloud's Nest 2. Ali Hsiying. ColAnChi, *tr. by* Jerome P. Seaton

If someone's with her. Poseidippus. GrAn

If someone said, Escape. Longface Mahoney Discusses Heaven. Horace Gregory. VGW

If Someone Tells You It's Not for Sure. Jaime Sabines. PoetW; TCLAP, *tr. by* Philip Levine

If Someone Would Come. Lady Izumi. WoPoe, *tr. by* Steven D. Carter

If Sometimes in the Haunts of Men. Byron. CAGL

If strange things happen where she is. On Portents. Robert Graves. FaBoMo; HarvBoo

If such there were—with *you*, the moral of his strain! (LL) Byron. NAEL-5v2; NAEL-6v2 *Fr.* Childe Harold's Pilgrimage.

If Suddenly a Clod of Earth. Harold Monro. MoBrPo *Fr.* Strange Meetings.

If sunlight fell like snowflakes. Sunflakes. Frank Asch. NTCP

If that a sinner's sighs angels' food. Madrigal. *Unknown.* SacPr

If that exact Appelles now did live. Contemplation on Bassets Down-Hill by the Most Sacred Adorer of the Muses Mrs. A. K., A. Anne Kemp. EMWP

If That—indeed—redeem. (LL) Emily Dickinson. APN-2; NCAP

If that my hand, like yours, dear George, were skilled. To G. H. B. James Bayard Taylor. Son

If the blues would let me. Miss Blues'es Child. Langston Hughes. ChAP; SAmP; TTTS

If the clouds come good, our tobacco will grow. We will be happy. *Unknown.* APN-2 *Fr.* Minnetare Songs.

If the dull substance of my flesh were thought. William Shakespeare. Son *Fr.* Sonnets.

If the egg had one spot of blood on it. White Petticoats. Chana Bloch. MPUn

If the following day is slow to arrive. (LL) Saturday Night in the Village. Giacomo Leopardi. OBVE; WoPoe, *tr. by* Robert Lowell

If the great outside system—species and stars—proceeds. Across Space and Time. Charles Olson. PoM

If the green lizard darts. Eugenio Montale. WoPoe, *tr. by* Dana Gioia *Fr.* Motets, The.

If the heart is a house my parents. Pulse, The. Martha Kapos. Prnts

If the heart of a man is deprest [*or* depressed] with cares. John Gay. EnLoPo; NAEL-5v1; NAEL-6v1 *Fr.* Begger's Opera.

If the hill overlooking our city has always been known as Adam's Grave. W. H. Auden. FaBoMo *Fr.* Horae Canonicae.

If the lady hath any loveliness, let it die. Blackberry Winter. John Crowe Ransom. APT-1; OxBA; PoRA

If the light of the sun, moon, and stars. Robert Frost. Novella Nikolaevna Matveyeva [*or* Matveieva]. TCRP, *tr. by* Deming Brown

If the lost word is lost, if the spent word is spent. T. S. Eliot. UV *Fr.* Ash Wednesday [*or* Ash-Wednesday].

If the man who turnips cries. Ballad. Samuel Johnson. OxAEP-1

If the moon smiled, she would resemble you. Rival, The. Sylvia Plath. PAI

If the muse were mine to tempt it. Colored Soldiers, The. Paul Laurence Dunbar. APN-2; CBCWP; NAAAL

If the oak is out before the ash. *Unknown.* OxNR

If the Owl Calls Again. John Haines. CoAP; GifTon; HeIP-4

(At dusk.) CoAmPo

If the Prophets Broke in. Nelly Sachs. BBASP, *tr. by* Matthew Mead and Ruth Mead

If the quick spirits in your eye. Persuasions to Enjoy. Thomas Carew. BeJo; NOBE

If the red slayer think he slays. Brahma. Ralph Waldo Emerson. APN-1; AWP; ColAP; HAP; NOBA; NoP-4; OBEV; OxBA; PAI; PoE; PoRA; TAP; TCAPo; TFi; UV; UnPo

If the romantic land whose soil I tread. Richard Henry Wilde. APN-1 *Fr.* Hesperia.

If the scorn of your bright eyne. William Shakespeare. CTC *Fr.* As You Like It.

If the Soul Loses Its Gift Then It Loses Ground, If Hell. Amelia Rosselli. CItWP, *tr. by* Cinzia Sartini Blum and Lara Trubowitz

If the Soul was Born with Pinions. Marina Ivanovna Tsvetayeva [*or* Tsvetaeva]. WPoS

If the stars fell; night's nameless dreams. Joseph. Gilbert Keith Chesterton. ChIV-2; ChrPo

If the time ever came. Poem for Ben Barney. Leslie Marmon Silko. CDW; VoR

If the times were good. Issa. EH, *tr. by* Robert Hass

If the Tomb Is Not Oblivion. Manuel González Prada. SpanPo, *tr. by* William M. Davis

If the tombstone placed over me is small to see and close. Leonidas of Tarentum. HePo *Fr.* Epigrams.

If the unfortunate fate engulfing me. Farewell to My Mother. "Plácido." TTY, *tr. by* James Weldon Johnson

If the wild bowler thinks he bowls. Brahma. Andrew Lang. NOBL; PeLV; UV

If the winds of heaven. Henjō Abbot. OHPJ

If the year is meditating a suitable gift. Request to a Year. Judith Wright. CBAP; FaBoWP; ItWoWo; NALW; NoAM; NoP-4

If there are any heavens my mother will (all by herself) have. E. E. Cummings. MoAmPo; NAAL-2v2

If there be a rainbow in the eve. *Unknown.* FaBoVe

If there be any lover in the world, O Moslems, 'tis I. Jelaluddin [*or* Jalal al-Din] Rumi. TOF

If there be any one can take my place. Christina Georgina Rossetti. OxBSo *Fr.* Monna Innominata.

If there be none, never mind it. (LL) Mother Goose. LB; OxNR; ReMoGo

If there be nothing new, but that which is. William Shakespeare. TreFP *Fr.* Sonnets.

If there exists a hell—the case is clear. To Sir Toby. Philip Freneau. NAAL-2v1; NAAL-3; NoP-4; TAP

If there is a god. To the Six Million. Irving Feldman. TaR

If there is a man white as marble. Metaphor as Degeneration. Wallace Stevens. LCAP-2

If there is a Pure Land. Death Sunyata Chant: A Rite for Passing Over. Diane Di Prima. BB

If There Is a Scheme. Charles Reznikoff. WoPoe

If there is any life when death is over. On the Dunes. Sara Teasdale. TCAPo

If there is no connection between the wild. Discoveries, Trade Names, Genitals, and Ancient Instruments. Carl Rakosi. APT-2

If there is only one world, it is this one. Decrescendo. Larry Levis. SwNoth

If there is someone above. Double-face. STP

If There Is Someone Lovelier Than You. Howard Dietz. ReLy

If there is something that takes you. Conjuring Against Alien Spirits. Quincy Troupe. ISC

If there is still some room left in your heart. To a Hooligan Girl. Lajos Kassák. IQMS, *tr. by* Michael Kitka

If there must be a god in the house, must be. Less and Less Human, O Savage Spirit. Wallace Stevens. BBASP; VGW

If there's no Sun, I still can have the Moon. Philosophy. John Kendrick Bangs. PoToHe

If there was a house with three girls in it. Céilí. Ciaran Carson. PBCIP

If there was a world more disturbing than this. Amnesia. Bruce Weigl. CDa

If there were a road to the horizon. Shadow Grammar. Terence Winch. BAP-97

If there were an open way. On One Condition. Charles Madge. SPE

If there were another. Songs of an Other. Robert Duncan. PmAP

If there were any power in human love. Sonnet. Frances Anne [*or* "Fanny"] Kemble. VWP

If there were dreams to sell. Dream-Pedlary. Thomas Lovell Beddoes. HAP; NOBE; OBEV; OxAEP-2

If there were locomotives to ride home on. Connoisseur of Jews, The. Jerome Rothenberg. TaR

If there were nothing in the desert but. Blank to Fill in on the Visa of Pollen. Aimé Césaire. WoPoe, *tr.* by Gregson Davis

If there were, oh! an Hellespont of cream. John Davies of Hereford. NPeEn; OBCoV; Son *Fr.* Scourge of Folly, The.

If there were seven blind men. Essex Hemphill. NAAAL *Fr.* Conditions.

If there were time for everything. Lights at Newport Beach, The. Joe Bolton. AmPoNex

If they are mine or no. (LL) A. E. Housman. GTBS-P; NOBE; NPeEn; NoAM; OxBEV; OxBTC; SCV

If they ask, who here doth lie. Epitaph on Sir Walter Pye. John Hoskyns [*or* Hoskins]. FaBoEE

If they can get across our garden they have eaten it. Negotium Perambulans. Peter Redgrove. OBGa

If they'd had a spark of wit or vision. Florida. Campbell McGrath. NAPBL

If they had cursed the man. Part-Sequence for Change, A. Robert Duncan. VGW

If They Honoured Me, Giving Me Their Gifts. "Michael Field." OBMV

If they say: "you must suffer both torture and burning"—. Mikhail Alekseievich Kuzmin. TCRP

If they show me a stone and I say stone they will say stone. If They Show Me a Stone and I Say Stone. Amir Gilbo'a. MHP, *tr.* by Ruth Finer Mintz

If they true bailiffs be, who for the law maintaining. On Mercenary and Unjust Bailiffs. Henricus Selyns. SCAP

If they would ask me I would say. I Didn't Know About You. Duke Ellington. ReLy

If this brain's over-tempered. I've Tasted My Blood. Milton Acorn. MoCV; NOBC

If this is paradise: trees, beehives. If This Is Paradise. Dorianne Laux. GeoHom

If this is the way it is, we must live through it. If. Robert Penn Warren. BodElec

If this is true. (LL) Lady Izumi. BoWoP; WoPoe, *tr.* by Willis Barnstone

If This Isn't Love. Burton Lane. ReLy

If this night passes. This Night. N. Revathi Devi. OMIP

If this our little life is but a day. Sonnet to Heavenly Beauty, A. Joachim Du Bellay. AWP; CTC, *tr.* by Andrew Lang

If this prime ass is with his brother worms. Monody on Doctor Olmsted. Edgar Allan Poe. TCAPo

If this room is our world, then let. If this Room is Our World. Weldon Kees. AWTN

If this was our battle, if these were our ends. To a President. Witter Bynner. OBAL

If this were a movie, the sound of sizzling would foretell disaster. Schadenfreude. Stephanie Brown. BodElec

If this were a world. *Var. authors.* WoPoe, *tr.* by Helen Craig McCullough *Fr.* Kokin Shu.

If this world's friends might see but once. Seed Growing Secretly, The. Henry Vaughan. ChIV-2; ESCV; GeHe

If those paint sorrow best—who feel it most! (LL) Charlotte Smith. BWW; CenSon

If thou art sleeping, maiden. Song. Gil Vicente. AWP; CTC, *tr.* by Henry Wadsworth Longfellow

If thou be'st ice, I do admire. Miracle, The. Sir John Suckling. CaPo

If thou beest he; but O how fall'n! how chang'd. John Milton. SCV *Fr.* Paradise Lost.

If thou but suffer God to guide thee. Georg Neumark. SacPr, *tr.* by Catherine Winkworth

If thou could'st empty all thy self of self. Indwelling. Thomas Edward Brown. SacPr

If thou didst feed on western plains of yore. To a Goose [*or* Gosse]. Robert Southey. CenSon; NOBL; PeLV; Son

If thou dislik'st the piece thou light'st on first. To the Sour[e] Reader. Robert Herrick. NBLV

If thou dost bid thy friend farewell. Parting. Coventry Patmore. PoToHe

If thou hadst offered, friend, to blessed Mary. Guido Orlandi. EaItPo, *tr.* by Dante Gabriel Rossetti

If thou hast squander'd years to grave a gem. Charge, A. Herbert Trench. OBEV

If thou indeed derive thy light from Heaven. William Wordsworth. TrCP

If thou kiss not me? (LL) Love's Philosophy. Shelley. BoLoP; FHYEP; GTBS-P; OxAEP-2; PoToHe; SCGP

If thou must love me, let it be for nought [*or* naught]. Elizabeth Barrett Browning. BWW; CTC; CenSon; GSo; HeIP-4; LW; OBEV; OxAEP-2; OxBSo; SoSe-8 *Fr.* Sonnets from the Portuguese.

If thou shouldst ever come by choice or chance. Ginevra. Samuel Rogers. OxAEP-2

If Thou Shouldst Return. Clara Ann Thompson. CBWP-2

If thou wilt come and dwell with me at home. Richard Barnfield [*or* Barnefield]. CAGL *Fr.* Affectionate Shepherd [*or* Shephearde], The.

If Thou Wilt Hear. John Grave. AH

If thou wilt let down thy milk to me. (LL) Mother Goose. OxNR; ReMoGo

If thou would'st view fair Melrose aright. Sir Walter Scott. OxAEP-2 *Fr.* Lay of the Last Minstrel, The.

If thou wouldest roses scent. Francis Daniel Pastorius. SCAP

If Thou Wouldst Know. Hayyim Nahman [*or* Khayim Nakhman *or* Chaim Nachman] Bialik. TrJP, *tr.* by Harry H. Fein

If thought can reach to Heaven. Rabbi's Song, The. Rudyard Kipling. ChIV-1

If thus we needs must go. Heart, The. Michael Drayton. NOSC

If thy wife is small bend down to her and. Ian Wedde. PeNZ *Fr.* Earthly: Sonnets for Carlos.

If Time Waits. Fanny Carrión de Fierro. TANSG, *tr.* by Sally Cheney Bell

If tired of trees I seek again mankind. Vantage Point, The. Robert Frost. OxBA

If to be absent were to be. To Lucasta, [on] Going beyond the Seas. Richard Lovelace. BeJo; CaPo; GTBS-P; MeLP; OBEV; OxAEP-1

If to the Pump Room in the morn we go. *Unknown.* NOEC *Fr.* Diseases of Bath; a Satire, The.

If to your ear it wonder bring. Ben Jonson. OxBEV *Fr.* Key Keeper, The.

If true that notion, which but few contest. *Unknown.* FaBoEE

If truth in hearts that perish. A. E. Housman. CAGL

If waker care, if sudden [*or* sodayne] pale colo[u]r. Sir Thomas Wyatt. NoSic

If Washington should come to life and see how matters stand. If Washington Should Come to Life. George M. Cohan. ReLy

If we all knew where. Rainbow, The. Opal Palmer Adisa. GT

If we are dying, let's do it slowly, together. Well-Known Elizabethan Double Entendre, A. Pamela Alexander. YaYoPo

If we are lucky. Starwork. L. S. Asekoff. BodElec

If we are to cross the barriers of snow. Ark for Lawrence Durrell, An. Robert Duncan. RaBo

If we are truly free, and live in a free country. Turning Away from Lies. Robert Bly. LCAP-2

If we, as we are, are dust, and dust, as it will, rises. Snow. Charles Wright. ColAP; LCAP-2

If we be fools of chance, indeed, and tend. Emily Jane Pfeiffer. ViWPN *Fr.* To Nature.

If we but knew what forces helped to mold. Plea for Tolerance. Margaret E. Bruner. PoToHe

If we could know the mystery. Our Task. Henrietta Cordelia Ray. CBWP-3

If we could only push these walls. Maze Without a Minotaur. Dana Gioia. RA

If We Didn't Have to Eat. Nixon Waterman. OBAL

If we don't listen. (LL) Malcolm Spoke / Who Listened? Haki R. Madhubuti. ESEAA; NAAAL

If we eat, we choke. Bread wedges in our throats. Publick Fast on Account of the Afflicted: March 31, 1692. Nicole Cooley. NeAmPo

If we give love and sympathy. Helen King. PoToHe

If we had dope for an excuse, or love. In Memory of My First Chapatis. Diane Di Prima. PoM

If we live all our lives under lies. Cuba Libre. Imamu Amiri Baraka. BB

If we live well, in heaven with Christ our souls shall dwell. (LL) For Soldiers. Humphrey [*or* Humfrey] Gifford. FaBoWar; NoSic

If we meet a gorilla. We Must Be Polite. Carl Sandburg. OxIBACP

If We Must Die. Claude McKay. APT-1; BPo; ColAP; ISC; NAAAL; NAAL-5; NoAM; SSLK; Son; TFi; TTY; UnPo

If we must part. Valediction, A. Ernest Christopher Dowson. BoLoP

If we no old historian's name. Enquiry, The. Katherine Philips. OxBEV

If we talk, we're too tired to make love; if we. Marilyn Hacker. VCAP *Fr.* Taking Notice.

If we tell, gently, gently. Vanity. Birago Diop. PBMAP; WoPoe, *tr.* by Ulli Beier and Gerald Moore

If we those generous sons deservedly praise. Upon My Lord Winchilsea's Converting the Mount in His Garden to a Terrace. Anne Finch, Countess of Winchilsea. OBGa

If we throw our eyes way out to sea. Across the Bay. Naomi Shihab Nye. ExTi

If We Try. George Sands Johnson. PWR

If we've promised them aught, let us keep our promise! (LL) Robert Browning. EBNV; FaBoCh; NOxBChV; OBNV; OBSP; PeLV

If well thou viewst us with no squinted eye. Against a Rich Man Despising Poverty. Phineas Fletcher. NOSC

If what I find now. Resignation. Santob [*or* Shem-Tob] De Carrion. TrJP, *tr.* by George Ticknor

If what the *Curious* have observ'd be true. Cameleon Lover, The. *Unknown.* TCAPo

If, what this said, I dared repeat at last! (LL)   Elizabeth Barrett Browning. CenSon; HAP; OxAEP-2   *Fr.* Sonnets from the Portuguese.

If What we could—were what we would.   Emily Dickinson.   TCAPo

If whatever is, is right.   Pope.   Manuel González Prada.   SpanPo, *tr. by* William M. Davis

If, when a blind moth.   Meteor Showers—Yosemite.   Dixie Salazar.   GeoHom

If when Don Cupid's dart.   Love's Offence.   Sir John Suckling.   CaPo; NOSC

If, when I die, I must be buried, let.   My Grave.   Ella Wheeler Wilcox.   SWaP

If when my wife is sleeping.   Danse Russe.   William Carlos Williams.   AmFaPo; NoP-4

If, when night comes, you bid me go away. (LL)   Michael Drayton.   NOBE; Son   *Fr.* Idea.

If when the sun at noon displays.   Beautiful Mistress, A.   Thomas Carew.   CavPo

If when the wind blows.   Daniel Webster's Horses.   Elizabeth Jane Coatsworth.   MoAmPo; OBCA

If, when you speak, your words are of no worth. (LL)   Sonnet: To Certain Ladies; When Beatrice Was Lamenting Her Father's Death.   Dante Alighieri.   AWP; EaItPo, *tr. by* Dante Gabriel Rossetti

If where we hunt defines us.   After the Noise of Saigon.   Walter McDonald.   OPRER

If, whittler and dumper, gross carver.   Arc Inside and Out, The.   A. R. Ammons.   NoAM; NoP-4

If Winter comes, can Spring be far behind? (LL)   Ode to the West Wind. Shelley.   AWP; CenSon; ClHu; EBEV; FHYEP; GTBS-P; HAP; HeIP-4; MakPoe; NAEL-5v2; NAEL-6v2; NAWM-7v2; NIL-7; NIP-4; NOBE; NOBRP; NPeEn; NoP-4; OBEV; OxAEP-2; OxBEV; OxBSo; PAI; PeECV; PoE; PoPoPo; PoRA; SCGP; TFi; TRP; WeW-3

If wishes were horses.   Mother Goose.   LB; OxNR; ReMoGo

If Wishing for the Mystic Joys of Love.   Thomas Chatterton.   OxBSP

If with the literate, I am.   Dorothy Parker.   APT-1; NALW   *Fr.* Pig's-Eye View of Literature, A.

If within the cruel Southland you have chanced to take a ride.   Jim Crow Cars. Lizelia Augusta Jenkins Moorer.   CBWP-3

If witt may be the Childe of chance and rise.   On the Returne of King Charles 2nd.   Ann Lee.   EMWP

If Women Could Be Fair.   Edward de Vere, 17th Earl of Oxford.   NoSic (Renunciation, A.)   GTBS-P

If words could speak words should have told.   Out There.   Breyten Breytenbach.   VCWP

If worthy to be thine. (LL)   Canzonetta: Of His Lady, and of His Making Her Likeness.   Jacopo da Lentino.   AWP; EaItPo, *tr. by* Dante Gabriel Rossetti

If ye'll only gimme RUM! (LL)   Convicts' Rum Song.   *Unknown.*   FaBoVe; NOBAu

If yet I have not all thy love.   Lovers' Infiniteness[e].   John Donne.   ESCV; MeLP; NOSC

If You.   Robert Creeley.   NOBA; NeAP; NoAM

If you are a gentleman.   Sure Test, A.   *Unknown.*   OxNR; ReMoGo

If you are a revolutionary.   Reactionary Poet, The.   Ishmael Reed.   ESEAA; GT

If you are always kind. (LL)   Mary's Lamb [*or* Mary and Her Lamb].   Sarah Josepha Buell Hale.   BRP; OBCA; OxIBACP; OxNR; SWaP

If you are cold, this poem will not warm you.   This Poem.   Constance Urdang.   PBCAP

If you are living, remember.   Farewell to Maria.   Tadeusz Borowski.   HP, *tr. by* Tadeuszt Pióro

If you are still alive when you read this.   Goodbye.   Bill Knott.   SPE

If you ask me where I am.   If You Ask Me.   Gunnar Ekelof.   PFTM-1

If you ask what my favourite programme is.   Video Box: 25, The.   Edwin Morgan.   EmeKit

If you burn my scorched soul too often, Love, she'll fly.   Meleager.   HePo   *Fr.* Epigrams.

If you came to my secret glade.   If You Came.   Ruth Pitter.   PoBW

If You Can Hear My Hooves.   Harold Littlebird.   VoR

If you can keep your head when all about you.   Recruiting Song.   Michael Foster.   UV

If you can keep your head when all about you.   If—.   Rudyard Kipling.   BRP; ChAP; ITBLP; OxBTC; PWR; UV

If you can see why she feels that she kneels if you can see why he knows that he shows what he bestows.   On Her Way.   Gertrude Stein.   PFTM-1

If you can sleep when those who write about you.   Rewards and Fairies. Roger Woddis.   UV

If you can sniff out danger and keep barking.   Sniff.   Lily Tuck.   Unle

If you can't be free, be a mystery. (LL)   Canary.   Rita Dove.   ESEAA; LoL; SeSe; VCAP

If you come at all.   Yourself and Myself.   *Unknown.*   NOIV, *tr. by* Thomas Kinsella

If you come my way that is.   Poem from Llanybri.   Lynnette Roberts.   AngWePo; TCAWP

If you come to a land with no ancestors.   Riding into California.   Shirley Lim.   GeoHom

If you complain your flames are hot.   To Her Lover's Complaint.   Jane Barker.   NPeEn; OxBSP

If you could come on the late train for.   Young Ionia, The.   John Frederick Nims.   IllVoic

If you could crowd them into forty lines!   Limitations.   Siegfried Sassoon.   MoBrPo

If you could see, fair brother, how dead beat.   Prolonged Sonnet: When the Troops Were Returning from Milan.   Niccolò degli Albizzi.   AWP; EaItPo; OBVE, *tr. by* Dante Gabriel Rossetti

If you could sit with me beside the sea to-day.   Longing.   Paul Laurence Dunbar.   ErotSp

If you could turn graffiti into gold.   *Unknown.*   PriapPo, *tr. by* Richard W. Hooper   *Fr.* Priapus Poems, The.

If you'd died I would've cut off my hair.   *Unknown.*   STP

If you, dear Celia, cannot bear.   Sacrifice: An Epistle to Celia, The.   Mary Leapor.   PEW

If you didn't see the six-legged dog.   Country Fair.   Charles Simic.   EmeKit

If you do love, as well as I.   Thought, The.   Edward Herbert, 1st Baron Herbert of Cherbury.   AngWePo

If you do love me weel, Willie.   Fair Janet.   *Unknown.*   ESPB

If you do not have a towel.   Camp.   Janet Fisher.   MFPA

If you do not shake the bottle.   On Tomato Ketchup.   *Unknown.*   NBLV; Spl

If you doan mind, would you please Mind moving over, *please.*   Gloria. Lincoln Kirstein.   APT-2

If you don't blink, nothing is funny or so.   Evidence.   Joanna Fuhrman.   AmPoNex

If you don't come to the mountains in autumn.   Staying Overnight at Blue Cloud Temple.   Mo Shih-lung.   CoBLCP, *tr. by* Jonathan Chaves

If-you-don't-go-down-with ME! (LL)   Disobedience.   Alan Alexander Milne. NOxBChV; NTCP; OTCP; TLR; UV

If you don't have a woman that lives with you.   Strange Business.   Jelaluddin [*or* Jalal al-Din] Rumi.   LoL, *tr. by* Coleman Barks

If you don't know how, why pretend?   To the Tune "Red Embroidered Shoes." Huang O [*or* Huang Ho].   WPOW

If you don't know the kind of person I am.   Ritual to Read to Each Other, A. William Stafford.   RaBo

If you don't know your place, then I'll tietzsche. (LL)   Limerick: "'If you're aristocratic,' said Nietzsche."   Gerry Hamill.   OBCoV; PeLi

If you don't like my apples.   *Unknown.*   OxBoLi

If you don't put your shoes on before I count fifteen then.   One, Two, Three. Michael Rosen.   OTCP

If you draw a bow, draw the strongest.   Tu Fu.   SuSp   *Fr.* Frontier Songs, First Series.

If you dream of scissors.   Book of Dreams, The.   Richard Garcia.   TouFir

"If you dream," said the eminent Freud.   Limerick.   Russell Miller.   PeLi

If you dropped me on the table.   Cesare Greppi.   ItPo, *tr. by* Gayle Ridinger

If you evah go to Houston.   Midnight Special.   *Unknown.*   APT-1

If you ever find.   Imamu Amiri Baraka.   PFTM-1   *Fr.* Why's / Wise.

If you ever plan to motor west.   (Get Your Kicks On) Route 66!   Bobby Troup. ReLy

If you ever see Pedro.   Poet Pedro Pietri.   Jose Angel Figueroa.   PueRic

If you feel that you're right on your beam ends.   Limerick.   Leslie Johnson. PeLi

If you find for your verse there's no call.   Limerick.   *Unknown.*   PeLi

If you for orders, and a gown design.   John Oldham.   *Fr.* Satyr Address'd to a Friend That Is About to Leave the University, and Come Abroad in the World, A.

If you found my heart's scroll in the dust.   Hayyim Nahman [*or* Khayim Nakhman *or* Chaim Nachman] Bialik.   FIT, *tr. by* Robert Friend

If you go away, / why should I adorn myself?   *Unknown.*   BoWoP

If you had a friend strong, simple, true.   If You Had a Friend.   Robert Lewis. PoToHe

If you had a lot of money.   It Follows.   Ruth Stone.   BodElec

If you had fallen from sleep.   Eurydice.   Luciana Frezza.   CItWP, *tr. by* Cinzia Sartini Blum and Lara Trubowitz

If You Hadn't—But You Did.   Betty Comden.   ReLy

If You Happy Would Be.   Abraham Fernández.   AH

If you have a daughter.   Toishan Song, A.   *Unknown.*   WoPoe, *tr. by* Gary Gach and C. H. Kwock

If you have a tender message.   Before It Is Too Late.   Frank Herbert Sweet. PoToHe

If you have a word of cheer.   Tell Him So.   J. A. Egerton.   PWR

If you have a word of cheer.   Tell Her So.   Mrs. Henry Linden.   CBWP-4

If you have conquered.   Only You.   Fanny Carrión de Fierro.   TANSG, *tr. by* Sally Cheney Bell

If you have forgotten water-lilies floating.   Water-Lilies.   Sara Teasdale. MoAmPo

If you have lost the radio beam, then guide yourself by the sun or the stars. Any Man's Advice to His Son. Kenneth Fearing. IllVoic

If you have no time. Lady Izumi. BoWoP

If you have revisited the town, thin Shade. To a Shade. W. B. Yeats. NAEL-5v2; NAEL-6v2

If you have spoken something beautiful. If You Made Gentler the Churlish World. Max Ehrmann. PoToHe

If you have taken this rubble for my past. Delta. Adrienne Rich. HarvBoo; LoL; NIL-7; NIP-4

If you have tears, prepare to shed them now. William Shakespeare. OxAEP-1 *Fr.* Julius Caesar.

If you haven't made noise enough to warn him, singing, shouting. Meeting a Bear. David Wagoner. HAP; WeW-3

If you hear a song in blue. Prelude to a Kiss. Irving Gordon. ReLy

If You Hear That a Thousand People Love You. Guadalupe de Saavedra. PAI

If you in the village think that my work was a good one. Edgar Lee Masters. APT-1 *Fr.* Spoon River Anthology.

If you insult me in my absence. Apollinarius. GrAn

If You Knew. Robert Desnos. SurPaPo, *tr. by* Mary Ann Caws

If You Knew September. John Nelson. GeoH

If You Knew Susie (Like I Know Susie). Joseph Meyer. ReLy

If You Leave at Daybreak. Félix Lope de Vega Carpio. SpanPo, *tr. by* Kate Flores

If you like I'll take you back. Willingness. Chairil Anwar. PoetW, *tr. by* Burton Raffel

If You Listen. Rosemerry Wahtola Trommer. GeoH

If you live along with all the other people. Worm Either Way. D. H. Lawrence. NoAM

If you'll listen for a moment, I will tell you now, my friends. What We Teach at Claflin. Lizelia Augusta Jenkins Moorer. CBWP-3

If you look for the truth outside yourself. Tung-shan. EnlH

If you love it not, of night. (LL) Out in the Dark. Edward Thomas. GTBS-P; MoBrPo; NOBE; OBWVE; OxBEV; RB

If you love me. Lady Izumi. BoWoP; WoPoe, *tr. by* Willis Barnstone

If you loved me ever so little. Satia Te Sanguine. Algernon Charles Swinburne. PeVV

If You Made Gentler the Churlish World. Max Ehrmann. PoToHe

If you mean to keep this appointment. Instructions for Elijah. Myra Sklarew. CRP

If you melt some lead. Valerio Magrelli. NeIt

If you mice are looking for *food*. Ariston. GrAn

If you / my lover / want to drop a penny from the top of the. 12 second poem. Trasi Johnson. InTrad

If You Need a Reason. Silvia Curbelo. BodElec

If you never do anything for anyone else. Immoral Proposition, The. Robert Creeley. NeAP; PoM

If you never spend your money. Icarus Schmicarus. Adrian Mitchell. OBCoV

If you plow foul furrows filling up fine paper. To The Poets. Ábrahám Barcsay. IQMS, *tr. by* Adam Makkai

If You're Anxious for to Shine in the High Aesthetic Line. Sir William Schwenck Gilbert. NAEL-5v2; NAEL-6v2; NBLV *Fr.* Patience.

"If you're aristocratic," said Nietzsche. Limerick. Gerry Hamill. OBCoV; PeLi

If you're ever in a jam, here I am. Friendship. Cole Porter. ReLy

If you're great enough. Shame on You. Langston Hughes. APT-2

If you're looking for water. Tinker Mather. NewEx

If You're Lost. S. B. Sowbel. SpudSo

If you're not going to sleep. Jelaluddin [*or* Jalal al-Din] Rumi. EaWin, *tr. by* Talat Sait Halman and W. S. Merwin

If you're not home, where. Numbers, Letters. Imamu Amiri Baraka. BPo; NOBA; PFTM-2

If you're one of seven. Seven Deadly Sins. Yusef Komunyakaa. BAP-01

If you're one who keeps a bust made in my likeness. Ovid. RomPo, *tr. by* Peter Green *Fr.* Tristia.

If you're so out of love with happiness. John Oldham. OBSV *Fr.* Satyr Address'd to a Friend That Is About to Leave the University, and Come Abroad in the World, A.

If you really care for me. *Unknown.* BoWoP

If you really imagine wisdom grows with a beard. Lucianus [*or* Lucian]. GrAn

If you really love me honey, hey- yah. *Unknown.* STP *Fr.* Kiowa "49" Songs.

If you refuse me once, and think again. Ditty. Edward Herbert, 1st Baron Herbert of Cherbury. NOSC

If You Saw a Negro Lady. June Jordan. GT

If you saw my little backyard, "Wot a pretty spot!" you'd cry. Cockney's Garden, The. Edgar Bateman. OBGa

If you say, Come back later. Sengai Gibon. JDP, *tr. by* Yoel Hoffmann

If You Say the Right Word, I Can Sing. Meret Oppenheim. SurWo, *tr. by* Catherine Schelbert

If you see me, keep to one side. (LL) Self-Portrait of the Other. Heberto Padilla. TCLAP; VCWP, *tr. by* Andrew Hurley and Alastair Reid

If you see someone beautiful / hammer it out right then. Adaios of Macedon. GrAn

If you seek for Eldorado. (LL) Eldorado. Edgar Allan Poe. APN-1; AWP; ColAP; FaBoCh; NOBA; OxBA; PAI; TAP; TCAPo

If you set out in this world. Seventh, The. Attila József. AF; RB, *tr. by* John Batki

If you sheltered me like a maybug in a cupboard. Listen. Benjamin Péret. SurPaPo, *tr. by* Rachel Stella

If you should come to our silent. Father. John Tripp. TCAWP

If you should look for this place after a handful of lifetimes. Tor House. Robinson Jeffers. APT-1

If you should say to me Don't mention love. Sadi [*or* Saadi *or* Sa'di]. WoPoe, *tr. by* Dick Davis

If you should see a man. Truth, The. Ted Joans. TTY

If you should see unchaste obscenities. *Unknown.* PriapPo, *tr. by* Richard W. Hooper *Fr.* Priapus Poems, The.

If you sneeze on Monday, you sneeze for danger. Sneezing. *Unknown.* ReMoGo

If you start to write a poem. Poem, The. Clementina Suárez. TANSG, *tr. by* Janet N. Gold

If you stay in comfort too long. You Will Forget. Chenjerai Hove. HBAPE; NAfrP

If you still have bacon and eggs for breakfast. If. Sipho Sepamla. PeSAV

If you strike. Genuine Poem, Found on a Blackboard in a Bowling Alley in Story City, Iowa. Ted Kooser. KaS

If you strike a thorn or rose. Keep a-Goin' Frank Lebby Stanton. PWR

If you take the moon in your hands. "H. D." APT-1; BoWoP; FaBoWP *Fr.* Sigil.

If you, that have grown old, were the first dead. New Faces, The. W. B. Yeats. GTBS-P

If You Think Kindly of Me. *Unknown.* CoBCP, *tr. by* Burton Watson

If you think you are beaten, you are. Victor, The. C. W. Longenecker. PWR

If you try to do what's right. Lines Suggested by an Edition of Blake's Poems. Sir Walter Alexander Raleigh. OBCoV

If you upon a woman. Bitter Cup, A. Mihály Vörösmarty. IQMS, *tr. by* Watson Kirkconnell

If you've given your heart away. Ghazal. Mirza Asadullah Khan Ghalib. WoPoe, *tr. by* Frances W. Pritchett

If you've got but fifty cents! (LL) I Had But Fifty Cents. *Unknown.* NBLV; WHSW

If you wander far enough. Oh No. Robert Creeley. HeIP-4; InPK-6

If you want a game to tame you and to take your measure in. Trucker, The. Will Dyson. NOBAu

If you want a thing bad enough. Success. Berton Braley. PoToHe

If you want my apartment, sleep in it. Rent. Jane Cooper. TAP

If you want to die you will have to pay for it. (LL) Charon. Louis MacNeice. FaBoTw; OxBEV; PNI

If you want to get to the heaven. Litany of the Little Bourgeois. Nicanor Parra. TCLAP, *tr. by* James Laughlin

If you want to live, then live . . . . Georgy [*or* Georgii] Vladimirovich Ivanov. TCRP

If you want to make good in a Broadway show. Down by the Erie Canal. George M. Cohan. ReLy

If you watch me. Cleaning Indian Dahl. Jane O. Wayne. InvLad

If You Weep, I Think That. Larry Eigner. FTOS

If you were an owl. That's What We'd Do. Mary Mapes Dodge. OBCA

If you were coming in the Fall. Emily Dickinson. NOBA; OxBA; PoRA; SoSe-8; TCAPo

If you were drowning, I'd come to the rescue. Love Song. Joseph Brodsky. BAP-97

If you were exchanged in the cradle and. Story That Could Be True, A. William Stafford. KaS; NTCP; RaBo

"If you were me . . ." the lad began. Agreement of Predicate Pronouns, The. Thomas M. [*or* "Tom"] Disch. KGB

If you were not what I know you to be. Forbidden Love. Elizabeth Daryush. PoBW

If you were only one inch tall, you'd ride a worm to school. One Inch Tall. Shel [*or* Shelley] Silverstein. OBCA

If you were riding in a coach. Oaths of Friendship. *Unknown.* ChiP, *tr. by* Arthur Waley

If You Were the Only Girl in the World. Clifford Grey. ReLy

If you were to ask me why I dwell among green mountains. Conversations in the Mountains. Li Po. RaBo; TAL, *tr. by* Robert Payne

If you were to squeeze me and wash. Bitter. Ifi Amadiume. HAWP; NAfrP

If you were twenty-seven. Heaven. Philip Levine. LCAP-2

If you will come on such a day. Gardener, The. Sidney Keyes. MoBrPo

If you will tell me why the fen. I May, I Might, I Must. Marianne Craig Moore. AmFaPo; ChAP; FaBoWP; OBAL; OxBSP

If you wish I'll give you. Present, The. Marie Laurencin. CuPo

If you wish in this world to advance. *Thought from* Ruddigore, A. Sir William Schwenck Gilbert. OBCoV

If you wish to move your reader. In Praise of Coldness. Jane Hirshfield. BAP-01

If you wish to pull a cork. Lilliputian's Beer Song. Septimus Winner. OBAL

If you wish to sell your kisses. Balade. Charles, Duc d' Orléans. NAWM-7v1, *tr. by* Sarah Spence

If you wonder why. No Offense. Kevin Young. LTA

If you would give as I do. Mother Lakshmi's Poem. Cassia Berman. HW

If you would give me. Story of Keys, The. Richard Garcia. TouFir

If you would learn. Antiquary, The. Joseph Campbell. OxBTC

If you would only stop to count your blessings. Count Your Blessings. Mrs. Henry Linden. CBWP-4

If you would seek us. William Shakespeare. OxAEP-1 *Fr.* Winter's Tale, The.

If you wound my hide it bleeds to enrich your crops. Words of an Old Woman. Howard Phelps Putnam. APT-2

If your first memory was the arms of your father. Reprieve on the Stoop. Belle Waring. PBCAP

If your friendship to take I must take too your clack. To a Lady, Who Was a Great Talker. Elizabeth Moody. PoBW

If your mother is a Jew, you are a Jew. Meditation in Seven Days, A. Alicia Ostriker. PBCAP; TaR

If your mouth's all set for fig fruit. *Unknown.* PriapPo, tr. by Richard W. Hooper *Fr.* Priapus Poems, The.

IFF. Howard Nemerov. BodElec

Ifor Hael's hall, poorly it looks. Hall of Ifor Hael, The. Evan Evans. OBWVE, *tr. by* Gwyn Williams

Ignoramuses. How to Drink the Sun. Vladimir Alekseievich Soloukhin. TCRusP, *tr. by* Daniel Weissbort

Ignorance, error, cupidity, and sin. To the Reader. Charles Baudelaire. WoPoe, *tr. by* Stanley Kunitz

Ignorance of Death. William Empson. NoAM

Ignorant, in the sense. Death of an Irishwoman. Michael Hartnett. CIP-2; EmeKit; PBCIP

Ignorant man does well to shut his trap, The. Palladas [*or* Pallades]. GrAn

Ignorant of all logic and all law. Palladas [*or* Pallades]. GrAn

Ignorant people so that. Brief Curriculum. Reiner Kunze. PoSu, *tr. by* Michael Hamburger

Ignore dull days; forget the showers. Lesson From a Sundial [Sun-Dial]. *Unknown.* Spl

Ignored what needed to be ignored—though can one? Laureate. Hugh Seidman. BodElec

Ignoring lash and rope. Ox Turned Loose. Muso Soseki. EaWin, *tr. by* W. S. Merwin

Ignotum per Ignotius, or a Furious Hodge-Podge of Nonsense; a Pindaric. *Unknown.* NOEC

Ihesus woundes so wide. Wounds, as Wells of Life, The. *Unknown.* SacPr

Ikebana. Cathy Song. YaYoPo

Ikeja, Friday, Four O'Clock. Wole Soyinka. PoetW

Ikhnaton looked like. Why I Often Allude to Osíris. Ishmael Reed. GT

Ikon. Timothy Liu. ReTh

Ikon: The Harrowing of Hell. Denise Levertov. BodElec

Ikoyi / The moon here. Niyi Osundare. NAfrP *Fr.* Moonsongs.

Il Capriccio Dramatico. Lorenzo Da Ponte.
  To an Artful Theatre Manager. TrJP, *tr. by* John Mazzinghi

Il faut laisser maison, et vergers et jardins. Miklós Radnóti. IQMS, *tr. by* Neville Masterman

Il Janitoro. George Ade. OBAL

Il Pastor Fido. Sir Richard Fanshawe.
  Fall, The. NOSC, *tr. by* Sir Richard Fanshawe
  Golden Age, The. NOSC; OBVE
  (Great Favorit Beheaded, A.) NPeEn; OBVE; OxBEV; WoPoe
  "How I forsook/ Elias and Pisa after, and betook." AWP
  "Learn women all from this housewifery." OBVE
  (Nymph's Song.) OxBSP
  Ode on His Majesty's Proclamation. NOBE
  Of Beauty. BoLoP
  "Our beauty is to us that which to men." OBVE
  Rose, A. OBEV
  (Rose of Life, The.) AWP
  "Well may that kisse be sweet that's giv'n t' a sleek." OBVE

Il Penseroso. John Milton. AWP; BASC; FHYEP; GTBS-P; HAP; NAEL-6v1; NAEL-7v1; NOSC; NoP-4; OBEV; TFi

Il Pleut Doucement sur la Ville. Paul Verlaine. AWP, *tr. by* Ernest Dowson

Ilahi. Pir Sultan Abdal. WoPoe, *tr. by* Murat Nemet-Nejat

Ilaria, thou that wert so fair and dear. Tomb of Ilaria Giunigi, The. Edith Wharton. APN-2

Ildrich mitzdonja—astatootch. Klink—Hratzvenga (Deathwail). Else Von Freytag-Loringhoven. APT-1

Ile Au Haut is way down there in the distance. Chart Indent. Richard Eberhart. BodElec

Ile give thee leave my love, in beauties field. Sir William Alexander, Earl of Stirling. OxBS *Fr.* Aurora.

Iliad. Humbert Wolfe. MoBrPo

Iliad, The. Homer.
  Achilles and Priam. NAWM-7v1, *tr. by* Robert Fagles
  Achilles' Dream. CAGL, *tr. by* Emile Victor Rieu
  Achilles' Lament and the Funeral of Patroclus. CAGL, *tr. by* Emile Victor Rieu
  Achilles Over the Trench. OBVE, *tr. by* Alfred Tennyson, 1st Baron Tennyson
  "Achilles with wild fury in his heart." OBWP, *tr. by* Robert Fitzgerald
  Ajax and his Brother. OBVE, *tr. by* Pope
  "Ajax the swift swerv'd never from the side." OBVE, *tr. by* William Cowper
  "All grave old men, and souldiers they had bene, but for age." OBVE, *tr. by* George Chapman
  "All silent stood; at last stood forth one dolon, that did dare." FaBoWar, *tr. by* George Chapman
  "And as in winter time when Jove his cold-sharpe javelines throwes." NPeEn; OBVE
  "And as when with the West-wind's flawes the sea thrusts up her waves." OBVE, *tr. by* George Chapman
  "And now was Paris come / From his high towres." OBVE, *tr. by* George Chapman
  Andromache's Lamentation. OBVE, *tr. by* William Congreve
  Apollo Defeats Patroclus. OBVE, *tr. by* Christopher Logue
  (Apollo Strikes Patroclus.) NPeEn
  "As when an architect some palace wall." OBVE, *tr. by* William Cowper
  "As when devouring flames some forest seize." OBVE, *tr. by* William Cowper
  "As when of frequent bees." OBVE, *tr. by* George Chapman
  "As when the winds, ascending by degrees." OBVE, *tr. by* Pope
  "At her departure his disdain return'd." OBVE, *tr. by* Dryden
  "Atrides summon'd all to arms, to arms himself dispos'd." FaBoWar, *tr. by* George Chapman
  Battle. OBVE, *tr. by* Alfred Tennyson, 1st Baron Tennyson
  "Big with great purposes and proud, they sat." OBVE, *tr. by* William Cowper
  "Bright-footed Thetis did the sphere aspire." NoSic *tr. by* George Chapman
  "But ere sterne conflict mixt both strengths, faire Paris stept before." OBVE, *tr. by* George Chapman
  "But Jove against the Greeks sent forth his son." FaBoWar, *tr. by* Edward Earl of Derby
  "But now, no longer deaf to honour's call." OBVE, *tr. by* Pope
  "Dardanus . . . was son of Zeus the Lord of the clouds." CAGL, *tr. by* Emile Victor Rieu
  Death of Hector, The. NAWM-7v1, *tr. by* Robert Fagles
  Destruction of the Grecian Fort, The. OBVE, *tr. by* Pope
  Embassy to Achilles, The. NAWM-7v1, *tr. by* Robert Fagles
  "Embodied close, the lab'ring Grecian train." OBVE, *tr. by* Pope
  "Fierce they drove on, impatient to destroy." OBVE, *tr. by* Pope
  "Frail as the leaves that quiver on the sprays." OBVE, *tr. by* Samuel Johnson
  Goddess intervenes between Achilles and Agamemnon, The. OBVE, *tr. by* Dryden
  Greeks Like Clouds, The. OBVE, *tr. by* George Chapman
  Hector Arms. NOSC, *tr. by* George Chapman
  Hector Flees before Achilles. OBVE, *tr. by* Alexander Pope
  Hector Returns to Troy. NAWM-7v1, *tr. by* Robert Fagles
  Hector's Child and the Plume. OBVE, *tr. by* George Chapman
  Hector's Defiance. NOSC, *tr. by* George Chapman
  Helen and the Elders. NPeEn, *tr. by* George Chapman
  Helen's Lamentation. OBVE, *tr. by* William Congreve
  "Here," said the Cloud-gatherer Zeus, "that is a journey you may well postpone."" EroLit, *tr. by* Emile Victor Rieu
  Homer's Gift of Fame. NOSC, *tr. by* George Chapman
  "Host set forth, and pour'd his steel waves far out of the fleet, The." FaBoWar, *tr. by* George Chapman
  Invocation, The: "The Wrath of *Peleus* Son, O Muse, resound." OBVE, *tr. by* John Dryden

"Like Leaves on Trees the Race of Man is found." OBVE, *tr.* by Pope

Neptune Goes to the Greeks. NOSC, *tr.* by George Chapman

Night Piece: the Trojans outside Troy. OBVE, *tr.* by George Chapman

Night Piece: the Trojans outside Troy. OBVE, *tr.* by Alexander Pope

"Nor lingered Paris in the lofty house." OBVE, *tr.* by Tennyson

"Now Here of the Golden Throne, looking out from where she stood on the summit of Olympus, was quick to observe two things." EroLit, *tr.* by Emile Victor Rieu

Old Trojan Chiefs See Helen, The. OBVE, *tr.* by Alexander Pope

Paris and Menelaus. OBVE, *tr.* by Alexander Pope

Patroclus Fights and Dies. NAWM-7v1, *tr.* by Robert Fagles

Patroclus Spears Thestor. OBVE, *tr.* by William Cowper

Priam and Achilles. NOSC, *tr.* by George Chapman

Proposition and Invocation. NOSC, *tr.* by George Chapman

Rage of Achilles, The. NAWM-7v1, *tr.* by Robert Fagles

River Scamander Attacks Achilles. OBVE, *tr.* by Alexander Pope

"Rude Mars had th' ordering of their spirits; of Greeks, the learned Maid." FaBoWar, *tr.* by George Chapman

Sacrifice to Apollo, The. OBVE, *tr.* by John Dryden

Sarpedon's Speech to Glaucus. NPeEn; OBVE, *tr.* by Sir John Denham

Shield of Achilles, The. NOSC, *tr.* by George Chapman

Shield of Achilles, The. NAWM-7v1, *tr.* by Robert Fagles

"So mourn'd Pelides his late loss, so weighty were his moans." FaBoWar, *tr.* by George Chapman

Stones and Snow. OBVE, *tr.* by Pope

"Then Achilles." WoPoe, *tr.* by Christopher Logue

"Then rash Patroclus with new fury glows." FaBoWar, *tr.* by Alexander Pope

"Then tall Hektor of the shining helm answered her: 'All these.' AmFaPo, *tr.* by Richmond Lattimore

"Then to th' extremest heat of fight he did his valour turn." FaBoWar, *tr.* by George Chapman

"This said, divine Talthybius he call'd, and bad him haste." FaBoWar, *tr.* by George Chapman

"Through the host with this the goddess ran." FaBoWar, *tr.* by George Chapman

"Thus Neptune rous'd these men." FaBoWar, *tr.* by George Chapman

Tide of Battle Turns, The. NAWM-7v1, *tr.* by Robert Fagles

"To this, great hector said." FaBoWar, *tr.* by George Chapman

Two Ajaxes Compared to Oxen, The. OBVE, *tr.* by George Chapman

Vulcan Forges the Shield of Achilles. OBVE, *tr.* by Pope

Wasps, The. OBVE, *tr.* by Pope

Watch and the Dogs, The. OBVE, *tr.* by Pope

Wearing Achilles' Armour, Patroclus, along with the Myrmidons, Attacks the Trojans. OBVE, *tr.* by Christopher Logue

"Why dost thou so explore." OBVE, *tr.* by George Chapman

Ilicet. Algernon Charles Swinburne. NOBVV

Ill blows the wind that profits nobody. William Shakespeare. FaBoWar *Fr.* King Henry VI, Pt. III.

Ill fares the land to giddy lust of power. Vanity of National Grandeur, The. John Thelwall. CenSon

Ill fares the land, to hastening ills a prey. Oliver Goldsmith. OBSV; UV *Fr.* Deserted Village, The.

Ill fates pursue me, may I never find. Lady Mary Wortley Montagu. ECEV *Fr.* Town Eclogues.

Ill Government. Robert Herrick. CavPo

Ill Humor. Goethe. STV, *tr.* by John Frederick Nims

Ill lay he long, upon this last return. John Berryman. TAP *Fr.* Dream Songs.

Ill's the airt o the Word the day. Idleset: "Ill's the airt o the Word the day." Thurso Berwick. OxBS

Ill Wind. Ted Koehler. ReLy

Ill Wind, The. Jay Macpherson. MoCV

Ill wind with a Samsonite suitcase, An. Chance. Ai. ExTi

Illa mala rulidala. Mater Dolorosa. Eugene Jolas. APT-2

Ille Terrarum. Robert Louis Stevenson. OxBS

Illegitimate Poem. Vivian Lamarque. CItWP, *tr.* by Cinzia Sartini Blum and Lara Trubowitz

Illegitimate Things. William Carlos Williams. MoAmPo

Illicit Passion. Abena Busia. NAfrP

Illinois Farmer. Carl Sandburg. HHAm

Illiterate, The. William Meredith. NoP-4; OxBSo; VCAP

Illness. Franta Bass. INSAB

Illness. Boris Leonidovich Pasternak.
  "At dusk you appear, a school-girl still." WoPoe, *tr.* by Theodore Weiss

Illness. Po Chü-i. ChiP, *tr.* by Arthur Waley

Illness. David Scott. NLP

Illness and idleness give me much leisure. Illness and Idleness. Po Chü-i. ChiP, *tr.* by Arthur Waley

Illness lingers on and on. Gimei. JDP, *tr.* by Yoel Hoffmann

Illogical logic of life is exactly, The. 1 x 2. Hedva Harechavi. DTA, *tr.* by Miriyam Glazer

Ills of all the human race, The. Misunderstood. Lizelia Augusta Jenkins Moorer. CBWP-3

Illuminated City, The. Felicia Dorothea Hemans. RWP

Illumination. D. F. Brown. CDa

Illumination. Anthony Hecht. ChrPo

Illumination. Jeffrey Wainwright. DiPo

Illumination, The. Stanley Kunitz. TAP

Illuminations. Louise Glück. HarvBoo; NALW

Illuminations. Arthur Rimbaud.
  Chercheuses de Poux, Les. AWP, *tr.* by T. Sturge Moore
  Dawn. TTTS, *tr.* by Enid Rhodes Peschal
  "I embraced the summer dawn." TTTS, *tr.* by Enid Rhodes Peschal
  "When forehead full of torments hot and red." AWP, *tr.* by T. Sturge Moore

Illumined bright now shines the splendid dome. Mary Tighe. NOBRP *Fr.* Psyche.

Illusion. Colleen J. McElroy. ISC

Illusion is one of the flatness: the sky, The. Winter, Never Mind Where. Hyam Plutzik. APT-2

Illusion works impenetrable. Maia. Ralph Waldo Emerson. APN-1

Illusions. Ralph Waldo Emerson. APN-1
  (Motto to "Illusions") NCAP

Illusions. Sally Roberts Jones. AngWePo

Illusions. Tzu Yeh. CrYelRi, *tr.* by Sam Hamill

Illusions she didn't know she had were shattered when. Scholar, The. Vijay Seshadri. KGB

Illusions, The: they fit like an iron lung, and. Memorandum / The Accountant's Notebook. Kathleen Norris. OBAL

Illustration. John Ashbery. NAAL-2v2; NAAL-5

Illustration / is nothing to you without the application, The. To a Steam Roller. Marianne Craig Moore. APT-1; BoWoP; FaBoMo; MoAmPo; OxBA; VGW

Illustration of a Picture. Oliver Wendell Holmes. TreFP

Illustrious Ancestors. Denise Levertov. NAAL-2v2; NOBA; PmAP; TaR; VGW

Illustrious Holland! hard would be his lot. Byron. OBSV *Fr.* English Bards and Scotch Reviewers.

Illustrious monarch of Iberia's soil. Columbus to Ferdinand. Philip Freneau. OBCA

Ilmarinen struck. *Unknown.* WoPoe, *tr.* by Keith Bosley *Fr.* Kalevala, The.

Ilonam Budai leaned out through her window. Ilona Budai, The Cruel Mother. *Hungarian Oral Tradition.* IQMS, *tr.* by Adam Makkai

I'm busy! / I am building. New Heart, The. Semyon [*or* Semion] Isaakovich Kirsanov. CLPP, *tr.* by Anselm Hollo

(Im)c-a-t(mo). E. E. Cummings. HAP

I'm Callicratia / who bore / 29 children. *Unknown.* GrAn

I'm goin' where de Southern crosses top de C. & O. Tin Roof Blues. Sterling Allen Brown. NAAAL

Im Traum sah ich ein Männchen klein und putzig. Heinrich Heine. AWP, *tr.* by Sir Theodore Martin

Image. Thomas Ernest Hulme. InPK-6; NPeEn; OxBTC

Image, The. Roy Fuller. GTBS-P; OxBTC

Image, The. Robert Hass. BLT

Image, The. Richard Hughes. OBMV

Image comes, An. Laser. A. R. Ammons. NAAL-2v2; NOBA; NoAM

Image dance of change, An. Conclusion. Siegfried Sassoon. MoBrPo

Image from Beckett, An. Derek Mahon. ModIr; NPeEn

Image in Lava, The. Felicia Dorothea Hemans. CABP; NOBRP

Image insists, An. Christopher Okigbo. PBMAP *Fr.* Limits (1962).

Image-Maker, The. Oliver St. John Gogarty. OBEV; OBMV; PoRA

Image-Nation 22. Robin Blaser. PFTM-2

Image-Nation (the Poësis). Robin Blaser. PoM

Image-Nation 13 (the Telephone). Robin Blaser. PoM

Image-Nation 3. Robin Blaser. PoM

Image o' God, The. Joe Corrie. ChIV-1; OxBS

Image of City. Lance Henson. VoR

Image of Leda, An. Frank O'Hara. HCAP; LCAP-2

Image of Lethe, An. Coming of War, The; Actaeon. Ezra Pound. PoE

Image of the Engine. George Oppen. APT-2

Image of the Engineer's model, An. Birdland. Allen Fisher. Oth

Image of the frozen lake, The. Luigi Fontanella. NeIt

Image of thee is written in my soul, The. Sonnet 5. Baldomero Garcilaso de la Vega. BLPSL, *tr.* by Rene de Costa, Rigas Kappatos and Eleni Paidoussi

Image / of truth is fire: it mounts, The. Day Without Night. Louise Glück. TaR

Image the images the great games therefore the locked.   Book of Job and a Draft of a Poem to Praise the Paths of the Living, The.   George Oppen. NNaP

Image / the pawnees, The.   Pride, The.   John Newlove.   MoCV; NOBC

(the image) / (the rim) / and going 'round.   Poem for the Sefirot as a Wheel of Light, A.   Naftali Bacharach.   PFTM-1

Image Was of Me Flowing Through You, The.   David Steinberg.   PasH

Imagerie d'Epinal.   Aleksander Wat.   AF

Imageries of dreams reveal a gracious age.   Age of a Dream, The.   Lionel Pigot Johnson.   OBMV

Images.   Richard Aldington.   MoBrPo

Images.   Valery Larbaud.   BLT, tr. by William Jay Smith

Images.   Naomi Long Madgett.   LTA

Images.   Miklós Radnóti.   IQMS, tr. by Peter Zollman

Images.   Richard von Schaukal.   AWP, tr. by Ludwig Lewisohn

Images drip down my back like sweat.   On the Morning of the Third Night above Nisqually.   W. M. Ransom.   CDW

Images for the Gospel of Christ.   Paul Ramsey.   CRP

Images from the Arcadian Dream Garden.   Ian Hamilton Finlay.   "Ruined stone temple by the side of a lake, A."   PFTM-2

Images leap with him from branch to branch.   Poet at Twenty, A.   Donald Hall.   SPE

Images of a faded world possessed me, I cannot flee!   Saul [or Shaul] Tchernichovsky [or Tchernichovsky].   MHP   Fr. To the Sun.

Images of Angels.   Patricia K. Page.   MoCV; NoAM

Images of J—— assail him.   Bus Trip, The.   Joel Oppenheimer.   NeAP

Images of John (1967–92).   Danton R. Remoto.   ReBoTo

Images of San Luis.   Luis Lopez.   GeoH

Images of the San Francisco Disaster.   Larry Kramer.   GeoHom

Images! Venerable as Druidical trees.   George Barker.   FaBoMo   Fr. In Memory of David Archer.

Imaginary Career.   Rainer Maria Rilke.   BBASP, tr. by Stephen Mitchell

Imaginary Dialogue.   Antiphilus [or Antiphilos].   GrAn, tr. by Dudley Fitts

Imaginary Elegies.   Jack Spicer.
   "God must have a big eye to see everything."   NeAP; PmAP
   "God's other eye is good and gold. So bright."   NeAP; PmAP
   "Poetry, almost blind like a camera."   NeAP; PmAP
   "Yes, be like God. I wonder what I thought."   NeAP

Imaginary Elegies, I–IV.   Jack Spicer.   NeAP

Imaginary foes. (LL)   Alley Cat.   Esther Valck Georges.   OTCP; Spl

Imaginary Iceberg, The.   Elizabeth Bishop.   FaBoWP; MoAmPo

Imaginary man, go. Here is your passport.   Instructions for Crossing the Border.   Dan Pagis.   PoSu, tr. by Stephen Mitchell

Imaginary Sonnets.   Eugene Lee-Hamilton.
   "Ay, buzz and buzz away. Dost thou suppose."   Son
   Luther to a Bluebottle Fly.   Son

Imaginary Translation.   Marilyn Hacker.   DiPo

Imaginary tremolo.   Jean-Joseph Rabéarivelo [or Rebéarivelo].   NegPo

Imagination.   Johnny Burke.   ReLy

Imagination.   Margaret Lucas Cavendish, Duchess of Newcastle.   BASC; NOSC

Imagination.   John Davidson.   MoBrPo   Fr. New Year's Eve.

Imagination all walled up.   Crime and Punishment.   János Pilinszky.   IQMS, tr. by Adam Makkai

Imagination and Taste, How Impaired and Restored.   William Wordsworth.   NAEL-6v2   Fr. Prelude, The; Growth of a Poet's Mind [1850 vers.].

Imagination Dead Imagine.   Samuel Beckett.   PFTM-2

Imagination, How Impaired and Restored.   William Wordsworth.   Fr. Prelude, The; Growth of a Poet's Mind [1805 vers.].

Imagination in flight: an improvisational duet.   Harriet Jacobs.   SpirFl

Imagination of Necessity, The.   Andrei Codrescu.   SPE

Imagination that we spurned and crave, The. (LL)   To the One of Fictive Music.   Wallace Stevens.   APT-1; MoAmPo; NoP-4; TCAPo

Imaginative Life, The.   Geoffrey Hill.   NoAM

Imagine.   Andrée Chedid.   HAWP, tr. by Mirène Ghossein and Samuel Hazo

Imagine a Forest.   William Sydney Graham.   HarvBoo

Imagine a forest.   Imagine a Forest.   William Sydney Graham.   HarvBoo

Imagine a girl from Poland.   Polish Girl Standing on a Chair, A.   J. B. Charles.   TuT, tr. by Gregory O'Donoghue

Imagine: A Town.   Daphne Marlatt.   NOBC   Fr. Steveston.

Imagine a town where no one walks the streets.   Hopper's "Nighthawks" (1942).   Ira Sadoff.   PoSol

Imagine a woman who honors the face of the Goddess in her own changing face.   Patricia Lynn Reilly.   HW   Fr. Imagine a Woman.

"Imagine being the first to say: surveillance"   Inventors.   Michael C. Blumenthal.   DiPo; NoAM

Imagine bouncing bumping humping over a cliff.   Drift.   Alberta Turner.   LCAP-2

Imagine corn new-discovered, tassels.   Goddess Corn Finds Her Dress in Disarray, The.   Terese Svoboda.   ExTi

Imagine father that you had a brother were.   Landscape with Next of Kin.   Olga Broumas.   BoWoP; WiU

Imagine hailing a taxi.   Hidden Meaning.   Susan Musgrave.   NIL-7

Imagine it, a Sophocles complete.   Fire at Alexandria, The.   Theodore Weiss.   NoAM; SAmP; TAP

Imagine living in a strange, dark city for twenty years.   Foreign.   Carol Ann Duffy.   HarvBoo

Imagine me elsewhere and kneeling.   Post-Communion Striptease.   Jill Alexander Essbaum.   NAPBL

Imagine or remember how the road at last led us.   Nocturne Militaire.   Thomas McGrath.   AF

Imagine spring's thaw, your brother said.   Heroin.   Bob Hicok.   AmPoNex; BAP-97

Imagine that any mind ever thought a red geranium!   Red Geranium and Godly Mignonette.   D. H. Lawrence.   GTBS-P; NoAM

Imagine that July morning: Cape Henry and Virginia.   Tempest, The.   William Jay Smith.   MoAmPo

Imagine the Angels of Bread.   Martín Espada.   TouFir

Imagine the bridge launched, its one foot.   Bridges.   Leslie Norris.   TCAWP

Imagine / The monk took off.   Masaoka Shiki.   ZenPo, tr. by Takashi Ikemoto and Lucien Stryk

Imagine the ocean.   Imagine.   Andrée Chedid.   HAWP, tr. by Mirène Ghossein and Samuel Hazo

Imagine the sound of words.   Between Language and Desire.   Silvia Curbelo.   TouFir

Imagine the South.   George Woodcock.   MoCV; NOBC

Imagine them as they were first conceived.   Images of Angels.   Patricia K. Page.   MoCV; NoAM

Imagine this: a mighty giant asleep.   Dmitry [or Dmitrii] Aleksandrovich Prigov.   ItGoST, tr. by Robert Reid

Imagine waking.   Agoraphobia.   Linda Pastan.   ExTi

Imagine. You come easily to me.   Genesis.   Ali Smith.   PoBW

Imagining Point Dume.   Diane Wakoski.   GeoHom

Imagining Their Own Hymns.   Brigit Pegeen Kelly.   IllVoic

Imago.   Amy Clampitt.   VCAP

Imani in Sunburst Summer: A Chant.   Askia M. Toure.   SpirFl

Imelda.   Felicia Dorothea Hemans.   RWP

Imitating an Ode by Sapho.   Gertrudis Gomez de Avellaneda.   BLPSL, tr. by Rene de Costa, Rigas Kappatos and Eleni Paidoussi

Imitating the Old Poems.   Pao Chao.   CoBCP, tr. by Burton Watson

Imitating the Old Poems, No. 4.   T'ao Ch'ien [or T'ao Yuan-ming].   CoBCP, tr. by Burton Watson

Imitation.   Joseph Hilaire Pierre Belloc.   OBCoV

Imitation of Boileau.   Yelena [or Elena] Shwarts [or Shvarts].   TCRusP, tr. by Anna Barker and Daniel Weissbort

Imitation of Chaucer.   Pope.   OBCoV

Imitation of Horace, An. Book 1, Satire 9.   Horace.   BASC, tr. by John Oldham
   "As I was walking in the Mall of late."   NPeEn, tr. by John Oldham

Imitation of Julia A. Moore.   "Mark Twain."   OBAL

Imitation of Life.   Michael S. Weaver.   UnSA

Imitation of Martial, Book II Ep, An 105.   "Captain H——"   NOEC

Imitation of Monsieur Beranger.   "Naum Korzhavin."   TCRP, tr. by Albert C. Todd

Imitation of Pope   A Compliment to the Ladies.   William Blake.   OBCoV

Imitation of the Arabic.   Alexander Sergeyevich Pushkin.   CAGL, tr. by Michael Green

Imitation warrior.   Warrior.   Frank Mkalawile Chipasula.   PeSAV

Immaculate Conception.   Louise Erdrich.   BBASP

Immaculate Conception, The.   Paul Eluard.
   "Reciprocal love, the only love that should concern us here, is the love that."   PFTM-1
   32 Positions of Love, The.   PFTM-1

Immaculate Sir Walter Raleigh, The.   Limerick.   T. L. McCarthy.   PeLi

Immaculate white bed. (LL)   Nantucket.   William Carlos Williams.   HAP; HarvBoo; OxBA; TAP; TRP; WeW-3

Immanuel Kant.   Miroslav Holub.   VCWP

Immeasurable haze.   To the Holy Spirit.   Yvor Winters.   MoAmPo; VGW

Immeasurable pain!   Immeasurable Pain.   Po Chü-i.   ChiP, tr. by Arthur Waley

Immeasurable sadness!   Sadness.   Tennyson.   FaBoEE

Immediate Content Recognition.   Diane Ward.   PmAP

Immense architecture / building in air.   Nathaniel Tarn.   APSN

Immense, august, like some Titanic bloom.   Chartres.   Edith Wharton.   APN-2

Immense coldness from the Longobards, An.   Longobards, The.   Zbigniew Herbert.   PoSu, tr. by Czeslaw Milosz

Immense hope, and forbearance, The.   Spring Day.   John Ashbery.   ColAP; NOBA

Immense Hour.   Juan Ramón Jiménez.   SpanPo, *tr.* by Edward F. Gahan.

Immense plain, The.   Ruined City, The.   Pao Chao.   WoPoe, *tr.* by Michael Bullock and C. J. Chen.

Immensity.   Morning.   Giuseppe Ungaretti.   PFTM-1

Immensity cloistered [*or* Immensitie cloysterd] in thy dear[e] womb[e].   John Donne.   ChrPo   *Fr.* Holy Sonnets.

IMMERITO. (LL)   Edmund Spenser.   NAEL-6v1; NAEL-7v1   *Fr.* Shepheardes [*or* Shepeards *or* Shepherd's] Calender, The.

Immigrant.   Fleur Adcock.   OPOU

Immigrant.   Arthur Nortje.   PeSAV

Immigrant, The.   Donald Davidson.   FuPo

Immigrants.   Debra Kang Dean.   NAPBL

Immigrants.   Robert Frost.   AmFaPo

Immigrants.   Pat Mora.   UnSA

Immigrants.   Aurora Levins Morales.   PueRic

Immigrants in Our Own Land.   Jimmy Santiago Baca.   AF; UnSA

Immobile, but fearless.   Hares, The.   Susan Miles.   LW

Immoderate Death that wouldst not once confer.   On the Death of the Lord Treasurer.   *Unknown.*   FaBoEE

Immolated.   Herman Melville.   NCAP

Immoral Proposition, The.   Robert Creeley.   NeAP; PoM

Immorality, An.   Ezra Pound.   MoAmPo; NOBA; OBAL; TCAPo

Immortal.   Mark Van Doren.   MoAmPo

Immortal. And will wash itself of all deaths. (LL)   River.   Ted Hughes.   NAEL-5v2; NAEL-6v2; NoP-4

Immortal as our Soul. (LL)   To My Excellent Lucasia, On Our Friendship.   Katherine Philips.   BASC; LW; MeLP; NALW; NOSC; NPeEn; NoP-4; OxBEV; PBRV; PEW; PoBW; WPE; WPOW

Immortal Autumn.   Archibald MacLeish.   MoAmPo; NAAL-2v2

Immortal babe, who this dear day.   For Christmas Day.   Joseph Hall.   SacPr

Immortal Bard! thou fav'rite of the Nine!   Womans Labour, an epistle, The.   Mary Collier.   PEW

Immortal Hate.   John Milton.   NOBE   *Fr.* Paradise Lost.

Immortal Heat, O let thy greater flame.   Love (2).   George Herbert.   GeHe; Son

Immortal, invisible, God only wise.   Walter Chalmers Smith.   SacPr

Immortal is an ample word.   Emily Dickinson.   NOCV

Immortal Israel.   Judah Halevi.   TrJP, *tr.* by Solomon Solis-Cohen

Immortal Love, author of this great frame.   Love (1).   George Herbert.   GeHe; Son

Immortal Love, Forever Full.   John Greenleaf Whittier.   AH

Immortal Newton never spoke.   On Mr. Nash's Present of His Own Picture at Full Length.   Philip Dormer Stanhope, 4th Earl of Chesterfield.   NOEC

Immortal Part, The.   A. E. Housman.   MoBrPo; SCGP; SoSe-8; UnPo

Immortal Picture, The.   Richard Eberhart.   BodElec

Immortal with his bamboo cane, The.   Cane of Ch'iung Bamboo, The.   Hsü Chung-hsing.   CoBLCP, *tr.* by Jonathan Chaves

Immortality.   "Æ."   AWP; OBMV

Immortality.   "Badawi al-Jabal."   MAP, *tr.* by John Heath-Stubbs and Matthew Sorenson

Immortality.   Samuel Marshak.   RusPo, *tr.* by Robert Arthur Douglas Ford

Immortality.   "Nicolai Maksimovich Minsky."   TrJP, *tr.* by Babette Deutsch

Immortality.   Lizelia Augusta Jenkins Moorer.   CBWP-3

Immortality of Verse the.   Horace.   AWP   *Fr.* Odes.

Immortal[l] clothing I put on.   Transfiguration, The.   Robert Herrick.   CaPo

Immortall love, authour of this great frame.   Love.   George Herbert.   Son

Immortals, The.   Isaac Rosenberg.   FaBoTw; TrJP

Immortals come and assemble, the.   Inscribed on a Wall Painting of Assembled Immortals.   Chao Meng-fu.   CoBLCP, *tr.* by Jonathan Chaves

Immortals don't stay long in the world of men.   Replying to a Poem by a New Graduate Lamenting the Loss of His Wife.   Yü Hsüan-chi.   SuSp, *tr.* by Geoffrey R. Waters

Immutable as my regret. (LL)   Grave of Love, The.   Thomas Love Peacock.   OxAEP-2; OxBSP

Imogene.   Eloise Bibb.   CBWP-4

Impartial Law enrolled a name, The.   My Name and I.   Robert Graves.   NoAM

Impatient as we were for all of them to join us.   Bungalows, The.   John Ashbery.   CoAP

Impatient Heart, The.   Bruce Andrews.   FTOS

Impatient with Desire.   George Granville [*or* Grenville], Baron Lansdowne.   OxBSP

Impediment.   Stephen Dunn.   PoSol

Impenitent, we meet again.   To Levine on the Day of Atonement.   Robert Mezey.   TaR

Imperator Victus.   Hart Crane.   OxBA

Imperceptible / It withers in the world.   Ono no Komachi.   OHPJ

Imperceptively the world became haunted by her white dress.   White Dress, The.   Marya Alexandrovna Zaturenska.   MoAmPo

Impercipient, The.   Thomas Hardy.   EBVV; NAEL-5v2; NAEL-6v2

Imperfect Enjoyment, The.   John Wilmot, 2d Earl of Rochester.   BASC; BoLoP; NAEL-7v1

Imperfect Enjoyment, The.   William Walsh.   NOSC

Imperfect enough once for all at thirty.   Last Things, Black Pines at 4 a.m.   Robert Lowell.   NOBA

Imperfect Is Our Paradise, The.   Joy Katz.   NeAmPo

Imperfect Paradise, The.   Linda Pastan.   SoSe-8
    (If God had stopped work after the third day.)   InvLi

Imperfect Sestina.   Phyllis Webb.   NOBC

Imperial Adam.   Alec Derwent Hope.   BMAP; CBAP; ChIV-1; HAP; HarvBoo; NIP-4; NoAM; NoP-4

Imperial Eloquence.   Samuel Daniel.   *See* Musophilus; or, Defence of All Learning

Imperial host before proud Gloucester lay, The.   Powers of Darkness.   Abraham Cowley.   NOSC

Imperious bath-maid, O why.   *Unknown.*   GrAn

Imperious Fool! think not because you're fair.   To a Proud Beauty.   "Ephelia."   PEW

Imperious Muse, your arrows ever strike.   Japanese Beetles.   X. J. Kennedy.   OBAL

Imperishable creatures.   Furnace, The.   Thomas Kinsella.   BiHa

Impermanence.   Lal Ded [*or* Lalla].   BoWoP

Imperturbable wader, The.   Rondeau Tempo.   Rossana Ombres.   CItWP, *tr.* by Cinzia Sartini Blum and Lara Trubowitz

Impetuous purple success, The.   Painter's Son, The.   Frank O'Hara.   BodElec

Impetus.   Mary Leader.   NAPBL

Implacable angel / Has shot his dart, The.   Epitaph.   Leone da Modena.   TrJP

Implicated generations made, The.   Celtic Cross.   Norman MacCaig.   OxBS

Implications of One Plus One.   Marge Piercy.   PasH

Implicit Faith.   Aubrey Thomas De Vere.   SacPr

Imploration for Clear Weather.   *Unknown.*   APN-2, *tr.* by W. J. Hoffman

Imploring Mecca / to achieve.   Be-Bop Boys.   Langston Hughes.   APSN; APT-2; OBAL

Imponderable the dinosaur.   Hart Crane.   MoAmPo   *Fr.* Bridge, The.

"Important is the nation's health."   Double Standard, The.   Franklin Pierce Adams.   OBAL

Important thing is not, The.   Is.   Patrick Kavanagh.   FaBoTw

Importune me no more! (LL)   When I Was Fair and Young.   Queen of England Elizabeth I.   NIP-4; NoSic; PoRA

Impose the letters CD on a staff.   *Unknown.*   PriapPo, *tr.* by Richard W. Hooper   *Fr.* Priapus Poems, The.

Impossibilities to His Friend.   Robert Herrick.   OxBSP

Impossible, The.   Abdul Wahab [*or* 'Abd al-Wahhab] Al-Bayati [*or* Al-Bayyati].   MAP, *tr.* by Salma Khadra Jayyusi and Christopher Middleton

Impossible, The.   Jane Miller.   BodElec

Impossible, The.   Bruce Weigl.   BodElec

Impossible Pictures, The.   Tom Paulin.   CABP; CIP-2

Impossible Poem, The.   George Oppen.   NNaP   *Fr.* Some San Francisco Poems.

Impossible Tasks.   *Vietnamese Oral Tradition.*   CaDao, *tr.* by John Balaban

Impossible, the way one black walnut, fallen.   Man Who Knew the Words to "Louie, Louie", The.   David Keller.   SwNoth

Impossible to be silent, impossible to speak.   Travel Notes.   John Riley.   Oth

Impossible to call a lamb a lambkin.   Gone Are the Days.   Norman MacCaig.   CABP; OxBC

Impossible to Trust Women.   *Unknown.*   MiEL

Impossible truth: I asked God, The.   Above the Timberline.   Alan Michael Parker.   AmPoNex

Imposture, The.   James Shirley.
    Piping Peace.   NOBE
    "You virgins that did late despair."   NOBE

Impotent Lover, The.   Automedon.   GrAn

Impression.   E. E. Cummings.   MoAmPo; OxBA

Impression de Nuit; London.   Lord Alfred Bruce Douglas.   OBEV

Impression Du Matin.   Oscar Wilde.   EBVV; MoBrPo; NAEL-5v2; NAEL-6v2; NoAM

Impressions.   Lu Yu.   SuSp, *tr.* by Irving Y. Lo

Impressions.   Oscar Wilde.
    (Garden, The.)   PoRA
    Les Silhouettes.   EBVV
    "Sea is flecked with bars of grey, The."   EBVV

Impressions / of Chicago; For Howlin' Wolf.   Quincy Troupe.   NAAAL; NBV

Impressions of Things Encountered.   Ch'en Tzu-ang.
    "As the crescent moon is born from the Western Sea."   SuSp

"Kingfishers nest on South Sea islands." SuSp

"Orchids grow through spring and summer." SuSp

Imprimis—My departed Shade I trust. Mira's Will. Mary Leapor. BWW; ECWP; NOEC; NoP-4; OxBEV; PEW

Imprimis, there's a table blotted. Inventory of the Furniture of a Collegian's Chamber, An. John Winstanley. OBSV

Imprint of Microscopic Life Found in Arctic Stones. Patricia Goedicke. GifTon

Imprisoned. Celia Laighton Thaxter. TCAPo

Imprisoned, The. Robert Fitzgerald. TwCP

Imprisoned Recusant Writes to His Wife, An. Francis Tregian. NoSic

Imprisoned Soul, The. Walt Whitman. *See* Last Invocation, The

Imprisoned Souls. János Arany. IQMS, *tr. by* Peter Zollman

Imprisoned winds slumber within their caves, Th' On the Dark, Still, Dry, Warm Weather Occasionally Happening in the Winter Months. Gilbert White. NOEC

Impromptu. Mary Elizabeth Coleridge. VWP

Impromptu. Benjamin Franklin. NOBL

  (Impromptu.) NOBL

  (Sampson Imitated.) FaBoEE

Impromptu. Frances Anne [*or* "Fanny"] Kemble. APN-1

Impromptu. Pope. *See* Impromptu to Lady Winchelsea

Impromptu. Tu Fu. CrYelRi, *tr. by* Sam Hamill

Impromptu. Samuel Wilberforce. NBLV; OWoS

Impromptu. Wu Wei-yeh. CoBLCP, *tr. by* Jonathan Chaves

Impromptu Inspirations. Yang Wei-chen. CoBLCP, *tr. by* Jonathan Chaves

Impromptu; Late Spring at Pan-shan. Wang An-shih. CoBCP, *tr. by* Burton Watson

Impromptu on a Hangover. P'i Jih-hsiu. CoBCP; ColAnChi, *tr. by* Burton Watson

Impromptu on Charles II. John Wilmot, 2d Earl of Rochester. BASC; FaBoEE; NBLV; NOBL; OBSV; OxAEP-1; PeLV

Impromptu Poems. Li K'ai-hsien. CoBLCP, *tr. by* Jonathan Chaves

Impromptu to Lady Winchelsea. Pope. NAEL-7v1

  (Impromptu.) NoP-4

Improperia. Francis Sparshott. MoCV

Improved Binoculars, The. Irving Layton. NOBC

Improvement, The. John Ashbery. AmFaPo

Improvement too, the idol of the age. William Cowper. OBGa *Fr.* Task, The.

Improvisation for Jerald Bullis, An. A. R. Ammons. BodElec

Improvisation. Alfred Kreymborg. APT-1

Improvisation for Piano. Michael S. Weaver. UnSA

Improvisation for the Stately Dwelling, An. A. R. Ammons. BodElec

Improvisations. Chu Yün-ming. CoBLCP, *tr. by* Jonathan Chaves

Improvisations on a Sentence by Poe. Jack Spicer. APSN

Improvisations on Aesop. Anthony Hecht. OBAL

Improvisatrice, The. Letitia [*or* Laetitia] Elizabeth Landon.

  "Farewell, my lute!—and would that I." RWP; VWP

  "From many a lip came sounds of praise." RWP

  "I am a daughter of that land." RWP

  Introduction. RWP

  Lorenzo. RWP

  Sappho's Song. RWP; VWP

Improvised on Horseback to Say Good-bye to Those Who Are Seeing Me Off. Wen Cheng-ming.

  "All of you are seeing me off, east of the Emperor's city." CoBLCP

  "Beneath the Shrine of the Three Loyal Ones." CoBLCP

  "Floating clouds and worldly affairs." CoBLCP

  "For three years I sadly listened." CoBLCP

  "I remove my court gown and part from the Emperor's precincts." CoBLCP

  "I sit on horseback at Twin Bridges." CoBLCP

  "In the past when I saw friends off." CoBLCP

  "This man of leisure for twenty years." CoBLCP

  "Wine of parting flowed and flowed, The." CoBLCP

  "Wishing to try retirement, I requested release from duty." CoBLCP

Improvised Song of Joy. Takomaq. WoPoe, *tr. by* Knud Rasmussen

Impulse, The. Robert Frost. RaBo; TCAPo *Fr.* Hill Wife, The.

Impulse among us is to throw eyes, The. Dark Underfoot. Thom Ward. AmPoNex

In a back room. Resonance. Christopher Gilbert. ESEAA

In a Bath Teashop. Sir John Betjeman. EnLoPo

In a beaker sits a beetle. Beetle, The. Nikolai Makarovich Oleynikov. TCRP, *tr. by* Anatoly Liberman

In a Bed-Sitter. Hal Porter. NOBAu

In a big wind, in a ruined house. Man: 1961. Pranabendu Dasgupta. OMIP, *tr. by* Buddhadeva Bose

In a "bijou" abode. Noël Coward. *See* I'll sing you a song

In a bitter wind. Buson. SoOfWa, *tr. by* Sam Hamill

In a Blind Garden. David Shapiro. ChIV-1

In a Boat, Getting Up at Night. Su Tung-p'o (Su Shih). SuSp, *tr. by* Irving Y. Lo

In a Boat on a Summer Evening. Lu Yu. CoBCP, *tr. by* Burton Watson

In a Boat on a Summer Evening, I Heard the Cry of a Water Bird. Lu Yu. SuSp, *tr. by* Burton Watson

In a Boat on the Cha River. Chang Yü. CoBLCP, *tr. by* Jonathan Chaves

In a Boat Shed. Robert Creeley. InvLad

In a Book-Box I Found the Lost Manuscript of a Poem Sent to Me by the Late Kao [Ch'i]. Chang Yü. CoBLCP, *tr. by* Jonathan Chaves

In a Book-store. Francis Saltus Saltus.

  "Sad, on Broadway next afternoon." VerBaPo

In a branch of a willow hid. To a Caty-did. Philip Freneau. TAP

In a brief symphony of candied light. (LL) Winnings. Garrett Kaoru Hongo. GeoHom; OpBo

In a Building Named for a Governor. Christopher L. Dornin. CRP

In a Bye-Canal. Herman Melville. APN-2; NCAP

In a Café. Rosemary Dobson. CBAP

In a cafe under a lazy fan. Country Nun. Geoff Page. CBAP

In a Calendar of Saints. Neil Curry. NLP

In a Cathedral City. Thomas Hardy. EnLoPo

In a cavern, in a canyon. Paul Dehn. KaS *Fr.* Rhymes for a Modern Nursery.

In a cavern, in a canyon. Clementine. *Unknown*. KaS

In a certain sense, they are not serious. Robert Pinsky. NoAM *Fr.* Essay on Psychiatrists.

In a chain reaction. Atomic Pantoum. Peter Meinke. WeW-3

In a Chain-Store Cafeteria. Paul Grano. NOBAu

In a Charleston, South Carolina gift store. 1994 Inventory. Toi Derricotte. SpirFl

In a childhood of hats. Hat Lady, The. Linda Pastan. SoSe-8

In a Christian Churchyard. James Thomson. NOBVV

In a Church of Padua. Herman Melville. APN-2

In a Churchyard. Richard Wilbur. HeIP-4

In a circle of thaw. Virginia Brady Young. HA

In a city, Trieste or Udine. Day of My Death, The. Pier Paolo Pasolini. VCWP

In a Classroom. Adrienne Rich. LoL

In a clearing. Traveling Valise. Marjorie Agosin. MirDau, *tr. by* Laura Nakazawa

In a coign of the cliff between lowland and highland. Forsaken Garden, A. Algernon Charles Swinburne. EBEV; GTBS-P; NOBE; NOBVV; NPeEn; NoP-4; OBGa; OxAEP-2; SCGP

In a common pit, without a headstone. Few Autobiographical Facts, A. Anna Barkova. ARWW, *tr. by* Catriona Kelly

In a Convent Garden. Alan Brownjohn. OBGa

In a Copy of More's (or Shaw's or Wells's or Plato's or Anybody's) Utopia. Max Beerbohm. OBCoV

In a Copy of Omar Khayyám. James Russell Lowell. NCAP

In a Corner of the Sky. Federico García Lorca. PFTM-1

In a cottage by the mountain. Aphra Behn. EroLit

In a cottage in Fife. Two Comical Folk. Mother Goose. OxNR; ReMoGo

In a Country Church. Ronald Stuart Thomas. FaBoMo; HarvBoo; TOF

In a Country Museum. Patricia Beer. FaBoWP

In / a / cove. Signs, The. Norman Henry Pritchard, II. NBV

In a dark and trying hour. Cornelius Whur. VerBaPo *Fr.* Unfortunate Gentleman, The.

In a dark bar corner we talk for about an hour. Hangover. Jeffery Conway. WiU

In a dark, dark wood, there was a dark, dark house. Dark House, The. *Unknown*. NTCP

In a dark night, when the light. Dark Night. Saint John of the Cross. WoPoe, *tr. by* Frank Bidart

In a Dark Time. Theodore Roethke. APT-2; HAP; HeIP-4; MoAmPo; NAAL-2v2; NAAL-5; NOBA; NoAM; NoP-4; PeECV; PoE; RaBo; TAP; TFi; VCAP

In a dark time, the eye begins to see. In a Dark Time. Theodore Roethke. APT-2; HAP; HeIP-4; MoAmPo; NAAL-2v2; NAAL-5; NOBA; NoAM; NoP-4; PeECV; PoE; RaBo; TAP; TFi; VCAP

In a darkening house we sat. Sunday the Power Went Off, The. Duncan Bush. TCAWP

In a Day. Li Shang-yin. SuSp, *tr. by* Eugene Eoyang

In a day or two the chairs will fall to pieces. Little House, Big House. Medbh McGuckian. PNI

In a deep sleep. One the Morening the King was Taken Ill my Dreame of Him. Frances Feilding. EMWP

In a desert land, this pearl-studded city. Jaisalmer, 1. Ghulam Mohammed Sheikh. OMIP, *tr. by* Saleem Peeradina

In a diary found beside a skeleton. Oink as Taunt. Roger Fanning. NAPBL

In a dim corner of my room for longer than my fancy thinks. Oscar Wilde. TriCat *Fr.* Sphinx, The.

In a dingy kitchen. Lamentations. Alter Brody. APT-2; TrJP

In a disingenuous letter. Oranges Returned, The. Gilbert Sorrentino. FTOS

In a dismal air; a light of breaking summer. Lament. George Sutherland Fraser. PoWW

In a Double Rainbow. Harold Littlebird. VoR

In a drawer in the kitchen. Letter to a Former Mother Superior. Mary Kay Rummel. SpudSo

In a dream. Issa. EH, *tr. by* Robert Hass

In a Dream. Lu Yu. SuSp, *tr. by* Irving Y. Lo

In a dream he fled the house. Coleridge. Medbh McGuckian. CIP-2

In a dream I bought a. Dream May 18, 1958. Peter Orlovsky. BB

"In a dream I never exactly dreamed." Another Life. Frank Bidart. HCAP; VCAP

In a dream I returned to the river of bees. River of Bees, The. W. S. Merwin. HeIP-4; LCAP-2; VCAP

In a Dream I Traveled among Ten Thousand Acres of Lotuses. Lu Yu. SuSp, *tr. by* Irving Y. Lo

In a dream I wasn't having yet. Night Is out of Sight, The. Pedro Juan Pietri. PueRic

In a dreamlike fall, the long. Apis Mellifica. Roger McDonald. NOBAu

In a drear-nighted December. Stanzas. John Keats. NOBE

In a drugstore north of Ft. Lauderdale. Story I Like to Tell, The. Robin Becker. PBCAP

In a Duplex Near the San Andreas Fault. Dionisio D. Martinez. NoP-4

In a far-away northern county in the placid pastoral region. Ox-Tamer, The. Walt Whitman. RB

In a far off hamlet near the sea. Uranne. Mary Weston Fordham. CBWP-2

In a fashionable suburb of Santa Barbara. In Montecito. Randall Jarrell. CoAP; VGW

In a few moments. Death of a Negro Poet, The. Conrad Kent Rivers. BPo

In a field. Keeping Things Whole. Mark Strand. CoAP; HCAP; HeIP-4; LCAP-2; PoPoPo; TAP; VCAP

In a flowerless country? (LL) Seeing the Returning Geese. Lady Ise. BoWoP; WoPoe, *tr. by* Irma Brandeis and Etsuko Terasaki

In a flurry of zeal. Régime. Karel Soudijn. TuT, *tr. by* Ruth Hooley

In a foreign land in an old foreign house. Before the Map of Russia. "Teffi." TCRP, *tr. by* Albert C. Todd

In a forest of frost, in a dawn of cornflowers. (LL) Poppies in October. Sylvia Plath. FaBoCh; HCAP; LCAP-2; NoAM

In a frith as I con fare fremede. Lady in the Wood, The. *Unknown.* MiEL

In a frosty sunset. Winter: East Anglia. Edmund Charles Blunden. OxBTC

In a Garden. Elizabeth Jennings. NOCV

In a Garden in the Grounds of Coleorton, Leicestershire. William Wordsworth. OBGa

In a garden shady this holy lady. Song for St. Cecilia's Day. W. H. Auden. FaBoTw; TwCP

In a garden shady this holy lady. W. H. Auden. FaBoTw; TwCP *Fr.* Anthem for St. Cecilia's Day.

In a garden shed two tea-chests. Hyperion's Bones. Tracey Herd. NeBl

In a garden that I know. Ownership. Ina Coolbrith. SWaP

In a garden where the whitethorn spreads her leaves. Alba Innominata. *Unknown.* AWP, *tr. by* Ezra Pound

In a Garret. Herman Melville. OBAL

In a gay jar upon his shoulder. Amphora, The. Fyodor [*or* Fiodor] Kuz'mich Sologub. AWP, *tr. by* Babette Deutsch and Avrahm Yarmolinsky

In a glass room. Tale of the Assyrian Statue. Mahmoud Al-Buraikan. MAP, *tr. by* Lena Jayyusi and Naomi Shihab Nye

In a Glass-Window for Inconstancy. Edward Herbert, 1st Baron Herbert of Cherbury. OxBSP

In a Gondola. Robert Browning.
Song: "Moth's kiss, first, The!" BoLoP; OBEV

In a grass hut lodged at the end of the narrow lane. In the Year with the Cyclical Sign *Mou-shen*. T'ao Ch'ien [*or* T'ao Yuan-ming]. CoBCP, *tr. by* Burton Watson

In a greatbig . . . night . . . big . . . night. (LL) Sylvester's Dying Bed. Langston Hughes. NoAM; SAmP; UnPo

In a great steep-banked ravine. Pit of Cologne, The. Boris Abramovich Slutsky [*or* Slutskii]. TCRP, *tr. by* J. R. Rowland

In a green place lanced through. Blue Heron, The. Theodore Goodridge Roberts. NOBC

In a grove most rich of shade. Sir Philip Sidney. NoSic; PBRV *Fr.* Astrophil and Stella.

In a gust of wind the white dew. Bunya no Asayasu. OHPJ

In a heavy light like yellow onions. (LL) Yellow Light. Garrett Kaoru Hongo. GeoHom; OpBo

In a herber [*or* a harbour *or* an arbour] green [*or* grene], asleep [*or* aslepe] whereas [*or* where as *or* where] I lay. Robert Wever. NOBE; OBEV *Fr.* Lusty Juventus.

In a Hercules his shape. (LL) Ben Jonson. NAEL-6v1; NAEL-7v1 *Fr.* Celebration of Charis in Ten Lyric[k] Pieces [*or* Peeces], A.

In a hidden spot on the northern mountain. Yün Shou-p'ing. CoBLCP *Fr.* On the Day of the Mid-Autumn Festival of the Year Ping-yin (1686), Together with Chang Han-chan, Ching-fan, and Ching-t'ien, I Saw the Kuei Blossoms at the Northern Garden of Jade Peak.

In a high wind, on a rock in the back paddock. Laurie Duggan. BMAP *Fr.* Ash Range, The.

In a highly classified report smuggled. Wings. Maureen Seaton. FFC

In a hollow of the forest. Bomber, The. "Brian Vrepont." NOBAu

In a holy place with a god I walk. *Unknown.* NAAL-5 *Fr.* Night Chant, The.

In a home for incurables. Visit, A. Anna Swirszczynska. PoSu

In a Hospital Garden. Randall Jarrell. OBGa

In a hotel in Tashkent. Political Relations. Audre Lorde. GLP

In a Hotel Writing-Room. John Cowper Powys. OxBTC

In a house of empty rooms. Closing, A. May Miller. ISC

In a jail is safe from another thief. (LL) Madman (Prologue), The. Kahlil Gibran. GraLe; TCAPo

In a Japanese Moss Garden. Brad Leithauser. OBGa

In a land named. Fig Curtain of Atherton, The. Michael Spence. PoCoUp

In a land whose novelty was speech. (LL) California Peninsula: El Camino Real. Al Young. GT; GeoHom

In a land whose prosperity constantly grows. Olga Beshenkovskaya [*or* Beshenkovskaia]. TCRP

In a language pile I should like to be starting. Language Pile, The. Donald Berger. NAPBL

In a Late Hour. James McAuley. BMAP

In a Letter to A.R.C. on Her Wishing to Be Called Anna. Matilda Barbara Betham-Edwards. ECWP; PoBW; WoRP

In a liftship near Hue. Him, on the Bicycle. Bruce Weigl. CDa

In a light fantastic round. (LL) John Milton. FaBoCh; NPeEn; OBEV *Fr.* Comus; a Masque Presented at Ludlow Castle.

In a lit-tle bed a wo-man was born, In a. Turkey in the Corn. Woody Guthrie. KaS

In a little house keep I pictures suspended, it is not a fix'd house. My Picture-Gallery. Walt Whitman. NAAL-2v1; NAAL-3

In a London Drawingroom. "George Eliot." NPeEn

In a long forgotten snow. (LL) Song: "Let it be forgotten, as a flower is forgotten." Sara Teasdale. MoAmPo; TCAPo

In a long line from the founding of the race. (LL) Virgil [*or* Vergil]. NAWM-5v1; NAWM-7v1, *tr. by* Robert Fitzgerald *Fr.* Aeneid [*or* Eneados, *Aeneis*], The.

In a long wide veil. Female Figure. Olga Sedakova. ItGoST, *tr. by* Catriona Kelly

In a loose robe of tinsel forth [*or* tynsell foorth] she came. George Chapman. OxAEP-1 *Fr.* Ovid's Banquet of Sense.

In a lost sphere a paradise. Sephirot. Leonor Scliar-Cabral. MirDau, *tr. by* Regina Igel

In a lovely garden, filled with fair and blooming flowers. Mission of the Flowers, The. Frances Ellen Watkins Harper. BlSi

In a Lovely Garden Walking. Ludwig Uhland. AWP, *tr. by* George Macdonald

In a maiden-time professed. Thomas Middleton. OxBSP *Fr.* Witch, The.

In a major vein shooting blood. Thrombosis Trombone. Thomas Lux. BodElec

In a mayonnaise jar I keep the tiny. Conjurer, The. Maura Stanton. YaYoPo

In a meadow. Father Mat. Patrick Kavanagh. CIP-2; ModIr; PoE

In a Meadow. John Swinnerton Phillimore. OBEV

In a mean abode in [*or* on] the Shankill Road. Ballad of William Bloat, The. *Unknown.* NOBL; PeLV

In a melancholly studdy. Robert Wild. PBRV *Fr.* Alas poore Scholler, whither wilt thou goe.

In a mirror of bronze. To the Fortuneteller Hsüeh T'ieh-yai. Hsieh Chin. CoBLCP, *tr. by* Jonathan Chaves

In a Monotonous Dream. Elaine Equi. PmAP

In a month all those frozen waterfalls. Modern Love. Gerald Stern. BodElec

In a Moonlight Wilderness. Samuel Taylor Coleridge. FaBoCh

In a more hostile view, the psychiatrists. Robert Pinsky. HCAP *Fr.* Essay on Psychiatrists.

In a Motel on Lake Erie. James Tate. LCAP-2

In a Motel Room at Dawn. Malena Mörling. AmPoNex

In a Mucker fog. (LL) Kerr's Ass. Patrick Kavanagh. ModIr; NOIV; RB

In a Museum in the Capital. William Stafford. LCAP-2

In a Music-Hall. John Davidson. EBVV

In a myriad arched yurts, the men are drunk. Tune: "As If in a Dream." Nara Singde. ColAnChi, *tr. by* David McCraw

In a Myrtle [*or* Mirtle] Shade. William Blake. ChIV-1

In a narrow road where there was not room to pass. Meeting in the Road. *Unknown.* ChiP, *tr. by* Arthur Waley

In a neighborhood of tinkling jade. Ballad of the Deserted Mansion. Kao Ch'i. CoBLCP, *tr. by* Jonathan Chaves

In a nook. In May. John Millington Synge. MoBrPo

In a Notebook. James Fenton. NPeEn

In a nutshell. (LL) Žito the Magician. Miroslav Holub. PoSu; WoPoe, *tr. by* Ian Milner and George Theiner

In a pack. March 9 1976. Brian Meeks. WaCA

In a package of minutes there is this We. Aspect of Love, Alive in the Ice and Fire, An. Gwendolyn Brooks. BPo; PAI; TAP

In a pan of stars. (LL) Campfire Extinguished. Raymond Roseliep. HA; InPK-6

In a Parlor Containing a Table. Galway Kinnell. NBLV; OxBSP

In a pine tree, / A few yards from my window sill. James Wright (1927–80). EmeKit *Fr.* Two Hangovers.

In a plain pleasant cottage, conveniently neat. Miller, The. John Cunningham. ECEV

In a Plantation. Basil T. Paquet. CDa

In a post-coach and four, with postillions as fine. Priscilla Pointon. ECWP *Fr.* Letter to a Sister, Giving an Account of the Author's Wedding-Day.

In a previous incarnation, I climbed mountains. Death's Boots. Geoff Hattersley. NeBl

In a Prominent Bar in Secaucus [One Day]. X. J. Kennedy. AiP; CoAmPo; NBLV; NIL-7; NIP-4; OBAL; TRP

In A Queen's Domain. Sarah Morgan Bryan Piatt. NCAP

In a quiet water'd land, a land of roses. Dead at Clonmacnois [*or* Clonmacnoise], The. Angus O'Gillan. OBEV; OBMV, *tr. by* Thomas William Hazen Rolleston

In a red winter hat blue. William Carlos Williams. LCAP-2 *Fr.* Pictures from Brueghel.

In a Remote Cloister Bordering the Empyrean. Joel Sloman. VGW

In a Roman tram, where the famous Roman mob. Thief, The. Stanley Kunitz. MoAmPo; VGW

In a Room. William Virgil Davis. YaYoPo

In a room on a shelf away from everything else. I Held His Name. Alberto A. Ríos. NoAM

In a Rose Garden. John Bennett. ITBLP

In a salt ring of moonlight. Moorings. Norman MacCaig. OxBTC

In a Season of Unemployment. Margaret Avison. MoCV; NOBC

In a sense. Life. Artie Gold. NOBC

In a sense a bee may be. Edwin Emanuel Bradford. VerBaPo *Fr.* Tree of Knowledge, The.

In a shack of trimmed fir struts and a mud floor. At Maruža's. Imants Ziedonis. WoPoe, *tr. by* Barry Callaghan

In a shoe box stuffed in an old nylon stocking. Meadow Mouse, The. Theodore Roethke. ChAP; HeIP-4; PAI; RB; TRP

In a slick, black bodysuit Job stood before me. Maya Bejerano. DTA, *tr. by* Tsipi Keller *Fr.* Hymns of Job.

In a slumbir late as I was. In Slumber Late. *Unknown.* SacPr

In a small theodolite of paper. Soluble Noughts and Crosses; or, California, Here I Come. Roger Roughton. SPE

In a solitude of the sea. Convergence of the Twain, The. Thomas Hardy. CABP; FaBoTw; HarvBoo; HeIP-4; InPK-6; MakPoe; MoBrPo; NAEL-5v2; NAEL-6v2; NIL-7; NPeEn; NoAM; NoP-4; OxBEV; OxBTC; PAI; PeVV; PoPoPo; SCGP; TFi

In a spathe of silence. Messenger, The. Frances Horovitz. BrRo

In a spiral of lights. (LL) Banneker. Rita Dove. ESEAA; LCAP-2; NAAL-5; NoAM

In a Spring Grove. William Allingham. OxBSo

In a springtime, before noon, the kitchen door. Till Eulenspiegel. "Eduard Georgievich Bagritzky" [*or* Bagritsky]. TCRP, *tr. by* Vera Dunham

In a stable of boats I lie still. Lifeguard, The. James Dickey. NoP-4; SoSe-8

In a Station of the Metro. Ezra Pound. APT-1; ChAP; ColAP; HAP; HeIP-4; InPK-6; MoAmPo; NAAL-2v2; NAAL-5; NIL-7; NIP-4; NOBA; NPeEn; NoAM; NoP-4; OxBA; PAI; PoE; PoPoPo; TAP; TCAPo; TFi; UnPo; VGW; WeW-3

In a Storm. Antoine-Roger Bolamba. NegPo, *tr. by* Ellen Conroy Kennedy

In a summer [*or* somer] season, when [*or* whan] soft[e] was the sun[ne] [*or* sonne]. William Langland. PoE *Fr.* Vision of Piers Plowman, The.

In a swaying boat drifting along with the stream. Seeking Hsin E in the Western Hills. Meng Hao Jan. SuSp, *tr. by* Daniel Bryant

In a swirl they come forward and bow. Second Song for the Worship of the Goddess at Yu Mountain: "Bidding the Goddess Farewell." Wang Wei. ColAnChi, *tr. by* Stephen Owen

In a Tavern. Louis Jenkins. RaBo

In a tedious evening of trick or treat. To the Death of Mirrors. Nancy Joyce Peters. SurWo

In a terrible fog I once lost my way. Lost. James Godden. OBSP

In a thick stand of trees in a forest. So Terrifyingly Melancholy. Hagiwara Sakutaro. PFTM-1

In a thicket this morning, river-hung, a feed sack. Gathering at the River. Anne Caston. NAPBL

In a thin rain out and across the river / leaving no footprints. (LL) This Version of Love. Dorothy Hewett. BMAP; CBAP

In a thousandth of a second. Asymmetry of the Universe. Fabio Doplicher. NeIt, *tr. by* Stephen Sartarelli

In a throng, / A festal company of Maids and Youths. William Wordsworth. EBEV *Fr.* Prelude, The; Growth of a Poet's Mind [1805 vers.].

In a Time of Pestilence. Thomas Nashe [*or* Nash]. *See* Summer's Last Will and Testament

In a Time of Sickness. Orpingalik. STP, *tr. by* Edward Field

In a tissue-thin monotone of blue-grey buds. Spring Strains. William Carlos Williams. APT-1; TCAPo

In a town with a name as beautiful. Dogknotting in Quezaltenango. Vincent O'Sullivan. PeNZ

In a Train. Robert Bly. InvLad; TTTS

In a tree standing. Saigyo. WoPoe, *tr. by* Donald Keene

In a U-Haul North of Damascus. David Bottoms. ReTh

In a vacant lot behind a body shop. Child in the City, A. Lucien Stryk. UrbNat

In a valley of leafless scrub oaks. On the Road Home. C. G. Hanzlicek. GeoHom

In a valley [*or* the vale *or* the vaile] of this restless [*or* restles] mind. Quia Amore Langueo. *Unknown.* NOBE; NOCV; OBEV, *tr. by* Helen Gardner

In a vase of gold. Irises. "Michael Field." ViWPN

In a villa in a little old Italian town. Mona Lisa. Ray Evans. ReLy

In a Village by the River. Li Po. CrYelRi, *tr. by* Sam Hamill

In a Village by the River. Tu Fu. CrYelRi, *tr. by* Sam Hamill

In a Warm Bath. Carl Rakosi. TAP

In a wee, twee cul-de-sac. Fruit of Knowledge, The. Robert Johnstone. PNI

In a weird, forlorn voice. President Slumming, The. James Tate. OBAL

In a wheat field. Conversation, A. Gisèle Prassinos. PFTM-1

In a while, all the rooms will be sealed. Departure of '82. Sa'di Yusuf. MAP, *tr. by* Lena Jayyusi and Naomi Shihab Nye

In a white gully among fungus red. Native Born. Eve Langley. WPE

In a Wood. Thomas Hardy. PAI

In a wooden barrel. (LL) Salt. Yusef Komunyakaa. OPRER; UnSA

In a wooden room, surrounded by lights and / Faces. Killing, The. George MacBeth [*or* Macbeth]. FaBoMo

In a word of glitter and glow. I See Your Face Before Me. Howard Dietz. ReLy

In a world of souls, I set out to find them. Worldling. Elizabeth Spires. ExTi

In a year the nightingales were said to be so loud. Kingfisher, The. Amy Clampitt. HCAP; OWoS

In / ability to love, The. Ghost Song. Jack Spicer. APSN

In Abyrdeyn he gert a consaill cry. Blind Harry. NePenScot *Fr.* Actis and Deidis of the Illustere and Vailyeand Campioun Schir William Wallace, Knicht of Ellerslie, The.

In Acknowledgment of the Praises of European Writers. Sister Juana Inés de la Cruz. SpanPo, *tr. by* Constance Urdang

In Adam's fall/ We sinned all. *Unknown.* OBCA *Fr.* New England Primer, The.

In Æsop's tales an honest wretch we find. Fable, A. Matthew Prior. NoP-4

In aeternum I was once determed. Sir Thomas Wyatt. NoSic

In Africa. Roy Fuller. PoWW

In Africa, the saying is. No, Women Don't Cry. Opal Palmer Adisa. WaCA

In After Days. Austin Dobson. OBEV

In ages past [animals] lived and died. James Milligan. VerBaPo *Fr.* Science of Geology, The.

In Agypt's land contaygious to the Nile. Pharao's Daughter. Michael Moran. BIrV; ChIV-1

In Air. Peter Clarke. PBA

In air hard as sand. Mary Kinzie. FFC

In Aku Aku is there double. Oh, Noa, Noa! William Cole. NBLV

In al this world nis a murier lyf. *Unknown.* OHMEL

In Alaska an Eskimo girl. Eskimo Girl, The. David Ray. LTA

In all ages, always, everywhere, and everywhere. Yuliya [*or* Iuliia] Vladimirovna Drunina. TCRP

In all dying things. (LL) Saint Rose of Lima. Judith Ortiz Cofer. PueRic; TouFir

In all my Emma's beauties blest.   Translation of a South American Ode.   Oliver Goldsmith.   NOIV

In all my six and fifty years.   Doyu.   JDP, *tr. by* Yoel Hoffmann

In all ten directions of the universe.   Ryokan.   EnlH

In all the country.   Another Spring.   Tu Fu.   CrYelRi, *tr. by* Sam Hamill

In all the Eastern hemisphere.   Fall of J. W. Beane, The.   Oliver Herford.   OBAL

In all the good Greek of Plato.   Survey of Literature.   John Crowe Ransom.   FaBoCh; NBLV; OBAL; TAP; TwCP; VGW

In all the kingdom southward.   Ikkyu Sojun.   JDP, *tr. by* Yoel Hoffmann

In all the land no women found so fair.   (LL)   Beauty of Job's Daughters, The.   Jay Macpherson.   ChIV-1; MoCV; NOBC

In All the Magic of Christmas-Tide.   John Jacob Niles.   AH

In all the old paintings.   Annunciation.   Kay Smith.   NIL-1; NIP-4

In all the space of space.   Chauvinist.   Norman MacCaig.   NPeEn

In all the windows / of stone.   (LL)   Path among the Stones, The.   Galway Kinnell.   NNaP; NOBA

In all the world.   Fujiwara No Toshinari.   OHPJ

In all these rotten shops, in all this broken furniture.   Dancing, The.   Gerald Stern.   LCAP-2; LoL; UnSA

In all those stories the hero.   Heroes.   Robert Creeley.   NOBA; NoP-4

IN) all those who got.   E. E. Cummings.   FaBoEE

In all thy humors, whether grave or mellow.   Temperament.   Martial.   AWP, *tr. by* Joseph Addison

In Allusion to the French Song.   Richard Lovelace.   CaPo

In america.   Bow to Allah.   Brian G. Gilmore.   ISC

In america.   Essex Hemphill.   NAAAL   *Fr.* Conditions.

"In America," began / the lecturer, "everyone must have a."   Student, The.   Marianne Craig Moore.   NAAL-2v2; TwCP

In America, or now this silence between songs.   (LL)   Cures.   David Rivard.   AllShUp; SwNoth

In America, television is a special god.   Television as God.   Tijan M. Sallah.   NAfrP

In America, there is an answer for everything.   Tomorrow, We'll Dance in America.   James Harms.   AmPoNex

In Ampezzo.   Trumbull Stickney.   APN-2; ColAP

In Amsterdam there dwelt a maid.   Fair Maid of Amsterdam, The.   *Unknown.*   OxBoLi; PeLV; RB

In amusements he was so cagey and in his caginess amusing.   On the Death of My Tomcat Murr.   Vladislav Felitsianovich Khodasevich.   TCRusP, *tr. by* Mary Jane White

In an airplane I'm supposed to.   In an Airplane I'm Supposed To.   Sarah Kirsch.   PFTM-2, *tr. by* Wayne Kvam

In an Album.   James Russell Lowell.   OBAL

In an ancient overgrown park.   Duckweed.   Leopold Staff.   PoSu, *tr. by* Adam Czerniawski

In An Artist's Studio.   Christina Georgina Rossetti.   NAEL-5v2; NAEL-6v2; NALW; PAI; ViWPN

(One face looks out from all his canvases.)   NoP-4; PEW; VWP

In an early childhood day.   Too Many Rings Around Rosie.   Irving Caesar.   ReLy

In an elegy for a musician.   Elegy for Bob Marley, An.   William Matthews.   SwNoth

In an Emergency.   (LL)   Emily Dickinson.   APN-2; NAAL-2v1; NAAL-3; NAAL-5; NCAP; NOBA; NoP-4; OxBA; TAP; TCAPo

In an Empty Field at Night.   Gregory Orr.   PAI

In an envelope marked.   Personal.   Langston Hughes.   NOBA

In an eternal night.   (LL)   Algernon Charles Swinburne.   AWP; CABP; HAP; NAEL-5v2; NAEL-6v2; NOBE; NOBVV; NoP-4; OxBEV; PeVV; PoE; PoRA; SCV; TFi

In an exciting world of love-bites, nipple-nipping.   Lovesleep, The.   Gavin Ewart.   OxBC

In an idle hour I thought of former days.   Thinking of the Past.   Po Chü-i.   ChiP, *tr. by* Arthur Waley

In an Indian ditch lies.   World's Last Unnamed Poem, The.   A. K. Redwing.   VoR

In an Iridescent Time.   Ruth Stone.   MoAmPo; NALW; OxWW

In an Irish Churchyard.   "Violet Fane."   VWP

In an old garden-square.   (LL)   "H. D."   APT-1; BoWoP   *Fr.* Tribute to the Angels.

In an orchard a little fountain flows.   Song of the Ill-Married.   *Unknown.*   BoWoP, *tr. by* Patricia Terry

In an orchard soft with rot.   (LL)   Edna St. Vincent Millay.   APT-1; NAAL-2v2; OxBSP

In an uncumbered clime / Minute inductons wake.   (LL)   Coffee.   James Vincent Cunningham.   MoAmPo; VGW

In an upper room at midnight.   Love Feast, The.   W. H. Auden.   OBCoV

In an upstairs room.   John Wills.   HA

In an Urban School.   Toi Derricotte.   PBCAP

In ancient days, when God cast down his gaze.   Words.   Nikolai Stepanovich Gumilyov [*or* Gumiliov *or* Gumilev].   TCRP, *tr. by* Simon Franklin

In ancient times, as story tells.   Baucis and Philemon.   Jonathan Swift.   NOEC

In ancient times, no matter where.   Little Britain.   *Unknown.*   NOEC

In ancient times—'twas no great loss.   On a Nomination to the Legion of Honour.   *Unknown.*   FaBoEE

In and Out.   Jane Kenyon.   LoL   *Fr.* Having It Out With Melancholy.

In and Out of Check Points.   Yip Wai-lim.   OPRER

In and out the bushes, up the ivy.   Chipmunk's Day, The.   Randall Jarrell.   OBCA

In and out the slipping slates.   (LL)   Ireland with Emily.   Sir John Betjeman.   GTBS-P; OxBTC

In Andrea's Garden.   Susan Hampton.   BMAP

In another being, at last.   (LL)   Words for the Wind.   Theodore Roethke.   CoAP; NOBA

In another poem about the vandals, the vandals.   Another Poem about the Vandals.   Alan Michael Parker.   NeAmPo

In Answer of an Elegiacal[l] Letter, Upon the Death of the King of Sweden [from Aurelian Townsend, Inviting Me to Write on That Subject].   Thomas Carew.   BeJo

In Answer to a Question From P. W.   Lew Welch.   BB

In Answer to Their Questions.   Giovanna (Janet) Capone.   UnSA

In Answer to Your Query.   Naomi Lazard.   NBLV

In Antwerp, Bruges, Ostend and Ghent.   Ballade 2.   Eustache Deschamps.   WoPoe, *tr. by* David Curzon and Jeffrey Fiskin

In April.   Richard Kenney.   YaYoPo

In April, in New England, the earth ball yields.   In April.   Richard Kenney.   YaYoPo

In April one seldom feels cheerful.   Waste Land Limericks.   Wendy Cope.   FaBoWP; HarvBoo

In April [*or* Aprill], the koocoo can sing her song by rote.   Koocoo, The.   *Unknown.*   TTTS

In April the carnival came.   Distance Between Zero and One, The.   David Keplinger.   AmPoNex

In April when the flowers spring.   Heinrich von Veldeke.   GePo

In Aprile at the hicht of noon.   On Seein an Aik-Tree Sprent Wi Galls.   Robert Garioch.   OxBS

In Arabia.   Gertrude Gerard.   PeLi

In Arabia's book of fable.   Princess Sabbath.   Heinrich Heine.   TrJP, *tr. by* Charles Godfrey Leland

In Arcadia.   Lawrence Durrell.   MoBrPo

In Arden.   Charles Tomlinson.   OxBC

In Arizona.   Louis Zukofsky.   TRP   *Fr.* 29 Songs.

In Arizona coming across the border with dope in my tires.   Itinerary.   Doug Anderson.   OPRER

In Arizona / (how many years in the mountains).   Louis Zukofsky.   TRP   *Fr.* 29 Songs.

In Armorik, that is called Britayne [*or* Britaine].   Geoffrey Chaucer.   NAEL-5v1; NAEL-6v1   *Fr.* Canterbury Tales, The.

In Artois or Picardy they lie— free of useless fashions.   (LL)   Bohemians, The.   Ivor Gurney.   FaBoWar; PeFWW

In at our windows, blinking, summer peers.   Lines in Honor of Natalya.   Pavel Nikolaevich Vasilyev [*or* Vasil'ev].   TCRP, *tr. by* David Macduff

In Atlanta, Gee A.   (LL)   Slim in Atlanta.   Sterling Allen Brown.   APT-2; NoP-4

In Auckland it was the twelve days' garland.   James Keir Baxter.   HarvBoo   *Fr.* Jerusalem Sonnets.

In August.   Hamlin Garland.   APN-2

In August he boarded the bus / the A.D.O. / for southern Mexico and saw.   Mexican World Mural / 5 x 25.   Juan Felipe Herrera.   TouFir

In August, when the air of love was peeled.   Bible Story.   Charles Causley.   TOF

In autumn.   Absentia Animi.   Gunnar Ekelof.   PFTM-1

In Autumn.   Ma Chih-yüan.   CrYelRi, *tr. by* Sam Hamill

In Autumn.   Charles Hubert Sisson.   PeECV

In autumn moonlight the face turns icy.   Meng Chiao.   SuSp   *Fr.* Autumn Meditations.

"In autumn moonlight, when the white air wan."   Robert Bridges.   GSo

In autumn when the woods are red.   Robert Louis Stevenson.   NOBVV

In back of our town.   Gasco.   Günter Grass.   CLPP, *tr. by* Jerome Rothenberg

In Back of the Real.   Allen Ginsberg.   HeIP-4

In balance with this life, this death.   (LL)   Irish Airman Foresees His Death, An.   W. B. Yeats.   ChAP; FaBoCh; FaBoMo; FaBoWar; GTBS-P; HarvBoo; HeIP-4; MoBrPo; NOBE; NoAM; NoP-4; OBMV; OBWP; PoPoPo; PoWW; SCV; TFi; WeW-3

In Ball's Market after surfing till noon.   Supremes, The.   Mark Jarman.   GeoHom; SwNoth

In Barracks.   Siegfried Sassoon.   FaBoTw

In *Bath* a wanton wife did dwell. *Unknown*. PBRV *Fr.* Wanton Wife of Bath, The.
In Battle. Abu-l-Hasan Ibn Al-Qabturnuh. NAWM-7v1, *tr.* by Lysander Kemp
In Bayreuth once. Mary Desti's Ass. Frank O'Hara. FTOS
In Beatle light. For Craig Who Leapt Off a Cliff in to Hummingbird Light. Diane Wakoski. PmAP
In Beauty May I Walk. *Unknown*. RB, *tr.* by Jerome K. Rothenberg
In bed, asleep, I dream. Leaving the Monastery Early in the Morning. Lu Yu. OHPC, *tr.* by Kenneth Rexroth
In bed, dull man[?]. Upon My Lord Brohall's Wedding. Sir John Suckling. CaPo
In bed I muse on Tenier's [*or* Teniers'] boors. Bench of Boors, The. Herman Melville. APN-2; AWTN; NAAL-2v1; NAAL-3; OBAL; SoSe-8
In Bed this Morning. Teresa Blagg. PasH
In bed we laugh, in bed we cry. Translation of Lines by Benserade. Isaac de Benserade. FaBoEE; WoPoe, *tr.* by Samuel Johnson
In bed with our bodies so completely intertwined. Love Poem, The. Andrew Elliott. PNI
In bed with the stranger who had picked him up. Bride, A. Harry Fainlight. BoLoP
In Belfast, Europe, your man. British Connection, The. Padraic Fiacc. PNI
In Berlin, August 1945: Lehrte Bahnhof. Alun Llywelyn-Williams. OBWVE, *tr.* by Joseph P. Clancy
In Bertram's Garden. Donald Justice. BoLoP; VGW
In Bethlehem. Christus Natus Est. Countee Cullen. ChIV-2; ChrPo
In between. (LL) Advice. Langston Hughes. NBLV; SAmP
In black core of night, it explodes. African Dream. Bob Kaufman. GT
In Blackwater Woods. Mary Oliver. NAAL-5
In Blanco County. Russell T. Fowler. NOBC
In Bloemfontein. Alan Ross. BoLoP
In Blood's Domaine. Robert Duncan. PFTM-2 *Fr.* Passages.
In blossom today, then scattered. Blossoms in the Wind. Takajiro Ohnishi. FaBoWar
In Blue-Stocking Hollow. Donald Davidson. FuPo
In body healthy, and composed in mind. (LL) Mira's Will. Mary Leapor. BWW; ECWP; NOEC; NoP-4; OxBEV; PEW
In bold letters. (LL) Can't Tell. Nellie Wong. ItWoWo; LTA; OpBo
In Bonds. Alice Cary. SWaP
In both I read thy name. (LL) Thine Eyes Still Shined. Ralph Waldo Emerson. ColAP; NOBA
In both stirrups. (LL) Buson. ChAP; EH, *tr.* by Robert Hass
In bounty and peace remain. (LL) Kilcash. *Unknown*. BIrV; OBMV, *tr.* by Frank O'Connor
In bowler hats and Sunday suits. Richard Murphy. NOIV *Fr.* Battle of Aughrim, The.
In boyhood's days we read with keen delight. Christopher Pearse Cranch. APN-1 *Fr.* Seven Wonders of the World.
In Breughel's great picture, The Kermess. William Carlos Williams. *See* In Brueghel's great picture, The Kermess.
In Brief. Angel Cuadra. AF, *tr.* by Katherine Rodriguez Nieto
In bright succession raise, her *Ornament* and *Guard*! (LL) Robert Burns. NOBRP; TreFP
In brilliant gas light. Good Night. William Carlos Williams. SAmP
In Britain's isles, as Heylyn notes. Matthew Prior. NOEC *Fr.* Alma; or, The Progress of the Mind.
In broad daylight. Lament for Kepa Anaha Ehau. Arapeta Awatere. PeNZ, *tr.* by the author
In broad daylight I dream I. Dream at Night, A. Mei Yao Ch'en. BLT; OHPC, *tr.* by Kenneth Rexroth
In Broad Daylight I Dream of My Dead Wife. Mei Yao Ch'en. OHPC, *tr.* by Kenneth Rexroth
In Broken Images. Robert Graves. HarvBoo; NoP-4; TRP
In Brueghel's great picture, The Kermess. Dance, The. William Carlos Williams. APT-1; HAP; HarvBoo; HeIP-4; InPK-6; NAAL-2v2; NAAL-5; NIL-7; NIP-4; NOBA; NoAM; OxBA; PAI; PoE; SAmP; SoSe-8; TAP; TFi
In bubbles to the elbow, on my knees. Story After the Story, The. Marie Ponsot. ExTi
In Buddy's Eyes. Stephen Sondheim. ReLy
In bulging heads that crowd for miles the dazzling south. (LL) April, 1885. Robert Bridges. OxBSP; OxBTC
In bunches bright as marigolds. Duckling, Swan. Jim Elledge. SwNoth
In bygone days, you surely know. Nighingale, The. János Arany. IQMS, *tr.* by Peter Zollman
In Ca Mau. In Ca Mau. Horace Coleman. CDa
In cabinets of amethyst and frost. (LL) Geoffrey Hill. NAEL-5v2; NAEL-6v2; NPeEn; NoAM; PoE *Fr.* Apology for the Revival of Christian Architecture in England, An.
In California. Donald Davie. NoAM
In California. Kathy Fagan. GeoHom

In California. Nov 22, 1988. Ishmael Reed. ESEAA
In California, north of the Golden Gate. Mendocino Rose. Garrett Kaoru Hongo. WeW-3
In California with Neruda. Shirley Lim. GeoHom
In calm and cool and silence, once again. First-Day Thoughts. John Greenleaf Whittier. APN-1; TrCP
In calm of sleep. White Solitude. Leopoldo Lugones. TCLAP, *tr.* by Julie Schumacher
In came her sister. Lady Maisry. *Unknown*. ESPB; OxBB
In Camp. Jibanananda Das. OMIP, *tr.* by Clinton B. Seely
In candent ire the solar splendor flames. Oliver Wendell Holmes. NOBL; OBAL; TCAPo *Fr.* Autocrat of the Breakfast Table, The.
In Carrowdore Churchyard. Derek Mahon. CIP-2; NoP-4; PBCIP; PNI
In Case. James Sherry.
  "What should be the title of a king. Too, how also to include. What happened when." FTOS
In Case of Monsters. Stephen Knight. NeBl
In case you fancy coloring books. My Coloring Book. John Kander. ReLy
In casual simplicity. (LL) Emily Dickinson. APN-2; RB
In catholic school. For Talking. Denise Nico Leto. UnSA
In caves with a single purpose. Fish and Chips on the Merry-Go-Round. K. O. Arvidson. PeNZ
In ceaseless Rosemary. (LL) Emily Dickinson. APN-2; SWaP; TCAPo
In Celebration. Mark Strand. NoAM
In Celebration of My Uterus. Anne Sexton. NALW
In Celebration of Spring. John Balaban. CDa
In Celia's face a question did arise. Lips and Eyes. Giambattista [*or* Giovanni Battista] Marino. OBVE; OxBSP, *tr.* by Thomas Carew
In Cemeteries. Dennis Joseph Enright. OxBC
In Central Park. Moyshe-Leyb [*or* Moishe-Leib *or* Leyb] Halpern. WoPoe, *tr.* by John Hollander
In certain places, still, surprisingly, you come. Footnote on Monasticism, A: Dingle Peninsula. John Montague. BBASP
In chamber low and scored by time. Herman Melville. APN-2 *Fr.* Clarel: A Poem and Pilgrimage in the Holy Land.
In Chandler Country. Dana Gioia. GeoHom
In Chapel. John Pook. AngWePo
In Charon's palm it pay the toll to Death. (LL) Dante Gabriel Rossetti. GSo; NIL-7; Son *Fr.* House of Life, The.
In Cheever Country. Dana Gioia. GM
In Chicago, it is snowing softly. Legend, The. Garrett Kaoru Hongo. LoL; MakPoe; OpBo; TRP
In childhood it's easy to feel. Limerick. Nigel Andrew. PeLi
In childhood, never believed till now. (LL) Snowfall, The. Donald Justice. CRP; VGW
In childhood's sunny day my heart was taught to love. To Whittier. Josephine D. Henderson Heard. CBWP-4
In childhood's unsuspicious hours. Epicurean. William James Linton. EBVV
In China. Cathy Song. NAAL-5
In China. Terry Wolverton. WiU
In China, / even the peasants. Lost Sister. Cathy Song. NoAM
In China swings the mandarin. Encouraging. Attila József. WoPoe, *tr.* by John Batki
In Choker's Lane, the doors appear. Choker's Lane. Kenneth Slessor. BMAP
In Chota Nagpur and Bengal. Tree Marriage. William Meredith. GLP
In Christ Church, Bristol, on Thomas Turner, Twice Master of the Company of Bakers. Francis, Lord Jeffrey Jeffrey. FaBoEE; NBLV
  (Epitaph in Christ Church, Bristol, on Thomas Turner, Twice Master of the Company of Bakers.) OxBoLi
In Christ there is no East or [*or* nor] West. All One in Christ. John Oxenham. SacPr
In Chu hai, dead machine guns lie frozen in the sun. Chrome Babies Eating Chocolate Snowmen in the Moonlight. A. K. Redwing. VoR
In Church. Thomas Hardy. InPK-6; MoBrPo; SCV *Fr.* Satires of Circumstance in Fifteen Glimpses.
In churches, said the Pardoner, when I preach. Geoffrey Chaucer. NAWM-5v1; NAWM-7v1, *tr.* by Theodore Morrison *Fr.* Canterbury Tales, The.
In cinemas we sought. Sing, Brothers, Sing! William Robert Rodgers. MoBrPo
In cities I'm as rare as I'm unwelcome. James Turner. NewEx
In cittie nor on hill, but all the night must sleep alone. (LL) Theocritus. NoSic; OBVE, *tr.* by Unknown *Fr.* Idylls.
In classic beauty, cold, immaculate. Mnemosyne. Madison Cawein. APN-2
In classical environs. Goliardic Song. Anthony Hecht. OBCoV
In climes beyond the solar road. Thomas Gray. OxAEP-1 *Fr.* Progress of Poesy, The.

In cloaks of snow, hairs snow-white, and beaks of blue jade. Egrets. Tu Mu. SuSp

In Cloe's chamber, she and I. Fragment, A. John Bancks. NOEC

In clouds drew on the evening's close. Evening, Gertrude. Anne Batten Cristall. ECWP; RWP

In Cnidus born, the consort I became. By Heraclides. *Unknown.* OBVE, *tr. by* William Cowper

In cock-wattle sunset or grey. Nostalgia. Louis MacNeice. OxAEP-2

In cold grey morning. Prisoner of Los Angeles (2). Wanda Coleman. GeoHom

In Cold Hell, in Thicket. Charles Olson. APT-2; PmAP; PoM

In cold rain at Kao-yu. Mooring at Night at Kao-yu. Wang Shih-chieng. CoBLCP, *tr. by* Jonathan Chaves

In cold stiff soils the bleaters oft complain. John Dyer. ECEV *Fr.* Fleece, The.

In Cold Storm Light. Leslie Marmon Silko. NoAM; VoR

In cold weather on a. At Seven a Son. Elaine Feinstein. HarvBoo

In colour, with their eyelids shut. (LL) Martian Sends a Postcard Home, A. Craig Raine. NAEL-5v2; NAEL-6v2; NPeEn; NoAM; NoP-4

In coming to the feast I found. Horn, The. Léonie Adams. MoAmPo

In Commendation of Music. William Strode. OBEV

In Communication with a UFO. Helen Chasin. YaYoPo

In considering things gastronomic. Limerick. *Unknown.* PeLi

In Consort to Wednesday, Jan. 1st. 1701. Richard Henchman. SCAP

In contact, lo! the flint and steel. Ambrose Bierce. APN-2 *Fr.* Devil's Dictionary, The.

In Containing a Thought Satisfied with Chaste Love. Sister Juana Inés de la Cruz. BLPSL, *tr. by* Rene de Costa, Rigas Kappatos and Eleni Paidoussi

In Contemplation of My Wretched Life. Katherine Parr, Lady Borough. "Christ was obedient unto his father." EMWP

In converse with the mountains, moors, and fens. (LL) Prelude: "Still south I went and west and south again." John Millington Synge. AWP; MoBrPo; OBMV

In Cool, Green Haunts. Mahlon Leonard Fisher. WeW-3

In cool seas of September click the stones. Reculver Bay. Vicki Raymond. NOBAu

In copious gulps of potent ale expires. (LL) Birth of the Squire; an Eclogue, The. John Gay. NAEL-5v1; NAEL-6v1; NOEC

In corridor and cubicle. Spring Song of A Civil Servant. James Keir Baxter. PeLV

In Cosmum. Sir John Davies. NPeEn *Fr.* Epigrams.

In countless upward-striving waves. Nominalist and Realist. Ralph Waldo Emerson. APN-1

In court to serve, decked with fresh array. Courtier's Life, The. Sir Thomas Wyatt. FaBoEE; NoSic

In Creve Coeur, Missouri. Rosanna Warren. PoPoPo

In crisis you may know me. October Poem. Tamura Ryuichi. AF, *tr. by* Christopher Drake

In crisp italic, meticulous and signed. Man Who Wrote Yeats, the Man Who Wrote Mozart, The. Michael Hartnett. ModIr

In crystal. Autumn Rose. Amal Moussa. PoArWo, *tr. by* Khaled Mattawa

In danger of which. Poem: "In danger of which." Ray DiPalma. FTOS

In Dante's Hell. Geoff Page. OBCoV

In dark fens of the Dismal Swamp. Slave in the Dismal Swamp, The. Henry Wadsworth Longfellow. TCAPo

In Darkness. Amir Gilbo'a. MHP, *tr. by* Ruth Finer Mintz

In darkness, crabs are believed to rest. Duressor. Larissa Szporluk. AmPoNex

In Days Gone By. Hera Katene-Horvath. PeNZ

In days, my Lord, when mother Time. Soame Jenyns. OBSV *Fr.* Epistle Written in the Country to the Right Honourable the Lord Lovelace, An.

In days of old beside the Nile. Cleopatterer. P. G. Wodehouse. ReLy

In days of old, certain patriots bold. Independence Day. *Unknown.* VerBaPo

In days of old, / So I've been told. Feast of the Monkeys, The. John Philip Sousa. OBAL

In days of summer let me go. In Ampezzo. Trumbull Stickney. ColAP

In daytime hours. Better Days. Essex Hemphill. CAGL

In dealing with time it is loud. Limerick. V. R. Ormerod. PeLi

In Death Divided. Thomas Hardy. SCGP

In death I know well enough all things end in emptiness. To Show to My Sons. Lu Yu. ColAnChi, *tr. by* Burton Watson

In Death's Field. Al-Khansa. BoWoP, *tr. by* Willis Barnstone

In death's worst hour the works of Christian men? (LL) On the Russian Persecution of the Jews. Algernon Charles Swinburne. OxBSo; Son

In Death Valley. APN-2

In death we will share one coffin. (LL) Married Love. Kuan Tao Shêng. PasH; WoPoe, *tr. by* Chung Ling and Kenneth Rexroth

In Debtor's Yard the stones are hard. Oscar Wilde. NOBVV *Fr.* Ballad of Reading Gaol, The.

In December, snow. Why We Play Basketball. Sherman Alexie. MoASP

In December, when the days draw to be short. Little John Nobody. *Unknown.* OxBoLi

In deep Siberian mines retain. Message to Siberia. Alexander Sergeyevich Pushkin. AWP; TTY

In Defence of Drunkards. Jan Kochanowski. WoPoe, *tr. by* Jerzy Peterkiewicz and Burns Singer

In Defence of Humanism. David Gascoyne. *See* Salvador Dali

In Defence of Metaphysics. Charles Tomlinson. MoBrPo

In Defence of Poetry. Mafika Pascal Gwala. PeSAV

In Defense of Black Poets. Conrad Kent Rivers. BPo

In deference to the cloud parade. Cloud Parade, The. Laura Jensen. LCAP-2

In degenerate times, people love extravagance. To Ch'eng Fei-t'ao. Wu Chia-chi. CoBLCP, *tr. by* Jonathan Chaves

In Derision of a Country Life. Edward Ravenscroft. NOSC

In Desolation. John Beaumont. SacPr

In Despair. Constantine P. Cavafy. CAGL, *tr. by* Edmund Keeley and Philip Sherrard

In despair at not being able to rival the creations of God. Hymn to Her Unknown. Walter James Turner. OBMV

In detention / in concentration camps. Intifada. June Jordan. NAAAL

In die time auf Hilda. War Poem, A. Jennifer Allen. Unle

In dim green depths rot ingot-laden ships. Sunken Gold. Eugene Lee-Hamilton. GSo; NOBVV

In Directions. John Rybicki. AmPoNex

In Dispraise of the Moon. Mary Elizabeth Coleridge. PEW; ViWPN

In Distrust of Merits. Marianne Craig Moore. APT-1; ColAP; MoAmPo; NAAL-2v2; NAAL-5; OBWP; OxBA

In Divés' Dive. Robert Frost. GI; VGW *Fr.* Ten Mills.

In doggerel and stout let me honour this country. Western Landscape. Louis MacNeice. ModIr

In-doors and out,—summer and winter—Mirth. (LL) To the Grasshopper and the Cricket. Leigh Hunt. CenSon; GSo; OxBSo; Son

In dread, all that the clergy teach the young. (LL) Straying Student, The. Austin Clarke. BIrV; CIP-2; ModIr; NOIV; NPeEn

In dream I saw two Jews that met by chance. Moses and Jesus. Israel Zangwill. TrJP

In dream / the beavers come to. Seneca Journal 1: "A Poem of Beavers." Jerome Rothenberg. APSN

In Dream: The Privacy of Sequence. Ray A. Young Bear. CDW

In Dreams. Patricia Pogson. NLP

In / dreams / diving deeper / than my disbelief. Keith Cartwright. AmPoNex

In dreams I crossed a barren land. Ballade of Broken Flutes. Edwin Arlington Robinson. APN-2

In Drear-nighted December. John Keats. PoPoPo

In drugstores across America. Gia. Tracey Herd. MFPA

In Duc Ninh a village of 1,654 households. Two Villages. Grace Paley. FaBoWar

In due course of course you will all be issued with. Henry Reed. NAEL-6v2 *Fr.* Lessons of the War.

In Duffryn Woods. John Stuart Williams. AngWePo

(In each line move the comma to follow the preceding noun, and read it again). (LL) I Saw a Fish-Pond All on Fire. *Unknown.* NOBL; OxNR

In Earliest Spring. William Dean Howells. *See* Earliest Spring

In early days / If kings were made by men. Human Debasement; a Fragment. Edward Rushton. NOEC

In early March, I watch you sleep, your mouth. Sonnet to the Imagination. Robin Becker. BodElec

In early morning twilight, raw and chill. William Allingham. BIrV; NOIV *Fr.* Laurence Bloomfield in Ireland.

In Early Summer Lodging in a Temple to Enjoy the Moonlight. Po Chü-i. ChiP, *tr. by* Arthur Waley

In early summer when the grasses grow. On Reading the Seas and Mountains Classic. J. R. Hightower. ColAnChi

In early summer, with two or three more. In Early Summer Lodging in a Temple to Enjoy the Moonlight. Po Chü-i. ChiP, *tr. by* Arthur Waley

In early youth's unclouded scene. Thirty-eight: Addressed to Mrs H—y. Charlotte Smith. ECWP; NALW; PEW; WPOW

In earth and sky. Chirin. JDP, *tr. by* Yoel Hoffmann

In eastern village and western village. Silkworm Song of Torchlit Fields. Kao Ch'i. CoBLCP; ColAnChi, *tr. by* Jonathan Chaves

In Easton a certain citizen. Tune: "Wu Yeh-erh" Twitting the Teller of Tall Tales. *Unknown.* ColAnChi, *tr. by* James I. Crump

In eaves sole sparrow[e] sit[t]s not more alone. David's Peccavi. Robert Southwell. ChIV-1

In Ecclesiastes I Read. J. P. White. ChIV-1

In Ecclesiastes I read, "That which is far off and exceeding deep." In Ecclesiastes I Read. J. P. White. ChIV-1

In Egypt's sandy silence, all alone. Ozymandias. Horace [or Horatio] Smith. CenSon

In Egypt they worshiped me. I Am the Cat. Leila Usher. ITBLP

In Egypt we had the best time. World War II. Jeni Couzyn. PeSAV

In 8 is alle my love. Unknown. MiEL

In eighteen hundred and eighty nine. Obituary. Conrad Potter Aiken. OBAL

In eighteen hundred and forty-one. Working on the Railway. Unknown. APN-2

In eighteen months she has grown. Nicola. William Scammell. NLP

In 1861, George Hew sailed in a rowboat. Network, The. Arthur Sze. AiP; OpBo

In either hand the hast'ning angel caught. John Milton. OPOU Fr. Paradise Lost.

In either onion broth or bread. (LL) Names of the Hare, The. Unknown. RB; WoPoe, tr. by Seamus Heaney

In elderis dayis, as Esope can declair. Taill of the Foxe, That Begylit the Wolf, in the Schadow of the Mone, The. Robert Henryson. OxBS

In Emily's Manner. Armanda Giuducci. CItWP, tr. by Cinzia Sartini Blum and Lara Trubowitz

In Emmanuel's Land. Anne R. Cousin. SacPr

In Emulation of Mr Cowleys Poem Call'd The Motto. Mary Astell. EMWP; NOSC

In England. Duo Duo (Li Shizheng). PoetW, tr. by Maghiel Van Crevel

In England's green and pleasant Land. (LL) William Blake. AWP; CIHu; FaBoCh; HAP; HeIP-4; NAEL-5v2; NAWM-7v2; NOBRP; NPeEn; OxBEV; PAI; PeECV; PoE; PoRA; SCGP; TFi; WoPoe Fr. Milton.

In English in a Poem. Lynn Emanuel. ExTi

In Eternum. Sir Thomas Wyatt. NOBE

In eternum I was once determed. In Eternum. Sir Thomas Wyatt. NOBE

In ethics class so many years ago. Ethics. Linda Pastan. InPK-6

In Europe, you can't move without going down into history. In the Yukon. Ralph Gustafson. MoCV; NoP-4

In ev'ry race, in ev'ry clime. Lines to a Graduate. Lizelia Augusta Jenkins Moorer. CBWP-3

In ev'ry town where Thamis rolls his tide. Alley; an Imitation of Spenser, The. Pope. NOEC

In even Will Hunter's hands. (LL) Weepies, The. Paul Muldoon. NoAM; PNI

In Evening Air. Theodore Roethke. TAP

In every breast affection fires, there dwells. Anna Seward. CenSon

In every dream thy lovely features rise. Sonnet. William Barnes. BoLoP

In every half-filled glass a river. Drinking Song. Silvia Curbelo. TouFir

In every hotel. Avignon. Remco Campert. PoetW, tr. by Jeffery Paine

In every meanest face I see. Sons of Promise. Thomas Curtis Clark. PoToHe

In every old lady I chance to meet. Old Ladies. Will Allen Dromgoole. WeW-3

In every one be her great glory famed. (LL) Anne Bradstreet. NAAL-5; NALW

In every part of every living thing. Lake Superior. Lorine Niedecker. FaBoWP

In every photo in your album the women workers huddle. What Seeps In. Devorah Amir. DTA, tr. by Miriyam Glazer

In every place, on every shore, I will be waiting for you. Portrait of the Beautiful Unknown Woman. Juan Sánchez Peláez. BLPSL, tr. by Rene de Costa, Rigas Kappatos and Eleni Paidoussi

In every week. (LL) Planter's Daughter, The. Austin Clarke. CIP-2; ModIr; NPeEn; OxBEV; OxBTC

In evil hour, and with unhallow'd voice. William Crowe. NOBRP

In evil hour did Pope's declining age. On the Edition of Mr. Pope's Works with a Commentary and Notes. Thomas Edwards. OxBSo

"In Evil Long I Took Delight." John Newton. SacPr

In evrich mart that stands on British ground. School-Mistress, The. William Shenstone. NOEC

In Exchange for Forty Acres. Bruce Jackson. AmPoNex

In Exile. Emma Lazarus. APN-2

In Extremis. John Updike. OBCoV

In fact, what change? The chimney of the spine. Son Fr. Richard Kenney. Hours of the Day, The.

In fair London city I was born. Deserter, The. Unknown. FaBoWar

In fair Provence, the land of lute and rose. Sestina. Sir Edmund William Gosse. MakPoe

In faith, I do[e] not love thee with mine eyes. William Shakespeare. HeIP-4; OxAEP-1 Fr. Sonnets.

In faith, Squier, thou hast thee wel yquit. Geoffrey Chaucer. NAEL-5v1; NAEL-6v1 Fr. Canterbury Tales, The.

In faith thou shalt haue mine. Robin Hood Rescuing Three Squires. Unknown. ESPB

In fall. Namagusai Tazukuri. JDP, tr. by Yoel Hoffmann

In fall we raked. Winter Before the War, The. Walter McDonald. CDa

In fall, when afternoons begin. Near-Sightedness. Edmond Yi-teh Chang. OpBo

In fallow college days, Tom Harland. Ballad of Lager Bier, The. Edmund Clarence Stedman. OBAL

In far-off England, years ago. Destiny. Eloise Bibb. CBWP-4

In Fargo, North Dakota, a man. To Flood Stage Again. James Wright (1927–80). NOBA

In farming country you are sure to find them. Old Yellow Shop, The. Abbie Huston Evans. APT-1

In fascination of her brightness. (LL) Dome of Sunday, The [or A]. Karl Shapiro. CoAP; MoAmPo; NoAM; OxBA

In Favor of One's Time. Frank O'Hara. NeAP

In fear and trembling, I think I would fulfill my life. Task, A. Czeslaw Milosz. AF, tr. by Czeslaw Milosz

In fear of the rich mouth. Frightened Man, The. Louise Bogan. FaBoWP

In February, digging his garden, planting potatoes. Letters from Yorkshire. Maura Dooley. NeBl

In February I give you gallant sport. Folgore da San Geminiano [or Gimignano]. EaItPo, tr. by Dante Gabriel Rossetti Fr. Sonnets of the Months.

In feeling I was but a child. One Year Ago. Adah Isaacs Menken. CBWP-1

In Ferrara. John Jenkins. BMAP

In Festubert. Edmund Charles Blunden. OBMV

In Fields of Sleepdreaming. Delmira Agustini. TANSG, tr. by Mark McCaffrey

In Fields of Summer. Galway Kinnell. VGW

In fields where roses fade. (LL) With Rue My Heart Is Laden. A. E. Housman. AWP; HAP; HeIP-4; InPK-6; MoBrPo; NAEL-5v2; NAEL-6v2; NoAM; NoP-4; PoE; PoPoPo; TFi; UnPo

In 15 minutes. California Peninsula: El Camino Real. Al Young. GT; GeoHom

In 'Fifty Congress Passed a Bill. Elymas Payson Rogers. CBCWP Fr. Poem on the Fugitive Slave Law, A.

In fifty-nine. Oxford Gardens. Charles McDonald. NLP

In filthy Puerto Rico lives a bird with no. Hayden Carruth. BodElec Fr. Paragraphs.

In fire-script. Thou Shalt Not. Malka Heifetz-Tussman. AWP, tr. by Marcia Falk

In First People's sky there is no moon. Raven/Moon. Anita Endrezze. VoR

In flame and a clamorous breath known to the eye-pecking gulls. (LL) Rudyard Kipling. FaBoEE; PeFWW; PoWW; WoPoe Fr. Epitaphs of the War [1914–1918].

In Flanders Fields the poppies blow. In Flanders Fields. John McCrae. BRP; FaBoWar; ITBLP; NOBC; OBWP; PeFWW; PoWW

(In Flanders Fields.) (LL) ChAP; NoP-4

(In Flanders fields the poppies blow.) NoP-4

In Flaundres whilom was a compaignye. Geoffrey Chaucer. EBNV Fr. Canterbury Tales, The.

In Fla[u]ndres whylom [or whilom] was a compa[ig]nye. Geoffrey Chaucer. FHYEP; NAEL-6v1; NAEL-7v1; NAWM-5v1; PoE Fr. Canterbury Tales, The.

In Flavia's eyes is every grace. On Miss Eleanor Ambrose, a Celebrated Beauty in Dublin. Philip Dormer Stanhope, 4th Earl of Chesterfield. FaBoEE

In flight in escape. Nelly Sachs. BoWoP

In-flight Note. Judith Rodriguez. BMAP

In Flood. Charles Hubert Sisson. HarvBoo

In flowed [or flow'd] at once a gay embroidered [or embroider'd] race. Pope. NOEC Fr. Dunciad, The.

In fond delusion once I left thy side. Sonnet to My Mother, A. Heinrich Heine. TrJP, tr. by Emma Lazarus

In Fond du Lac, Bronxville, Butte, Chicago. Last Year's Discussion: The Nobel Russian. Phyllis McGinley. FaBoEE

In form and feature, face and limb. Twins, The. Henry Sambrooke Leigh. OxIBACP

In former days we'd both agree. Bhartrihari. BoLoP, tr. by John Brough

In former years I passed this city. Sha-ch'eng, "Sand City." Yang Shih-ch'i. CoBLCP, tr. by Jonathan Chaves

In '42 he was conscripted to work on trains. Villanelle from a Sentence in a Poet's Brief Biography. Jacqueline Osherow. ExTi

In Fragments, In Streams. Talvikki Ansel.
    "Along the road, the bright painted crosses." YaYoPo
    "At night, coolness like water lapping." YaYoPo
    "Before first light, we would open the nets." YaYoPo
    "Halley's Comet crossed the jungle sky." YaYoPo
    "Teatro Amazonas, remnant, the." YaYoPo
    "Waking, months after I leave the jungle." YaYoPo

In fragrance. I can / eat as I go. (LL)   Stepping Westward.   Denise Levertov. NALW; VGW

In Francum.   Sir John Davies.   FaBoEE

  (Francus.)   OBCoV

In Freedom's War, of "Thirty Years" and more.   Enfant perdu.   Heinrich Heine.   AWP, *tr. by* Lord Houghton

In from the fields they come.   Harvesters, The.   Mary Gilmore.   NOBAu

In from the night.   Answer Me.   Adah Isaacs Menken.   CBWP-1; PoBW; ViWPN

In Front of a Large Number of People.   John Godfrey.   FTOS

In front of everyone. (LL)   Crows in a Strong Wind.   Cornelius Eady. ESEAA; InvLad

In Front of Good Prince Silence.   Endre Ady.   IQMS, *tr. by* Alan Dixon

In front of Hua-yang cave, autumns pass like sleet.   Drinking at the Cave Mouth.   Tsung Ch'en.   CoBLCP, *tr. by* Jonathan Chaves

In front of me, the palings of a fence.   For Signs.   Thom Gunn.   PoE

In front of my horse's head, I see Red Heart Station.   Red Heart Station.   Yang Shih-ch'i.   CoBLCP, *tr. by* Jonathan Chaves

In front of our mouths, wherever we swim.   Goldfish on the Writing Desk.   Max Brod.   TrJP, *tr. by* Babette Deutsch and Avrahm Yarmolinsky

In front of the City Hotel in Kumasi.   Rock Thrown into the Water Does Not Fear the Cold, A.   Audre Lorde.   NAAL-2v2

In Front of the Mirror.   Vladislav Felitsianovich Khodasevich.   TCRP, *tr. by* Michael Frayn

In front of the throb.   Before John and Maria's Wedding.   Hilda Raz.   ExTi

In front of us the road's turned misty-grey.   Evening Halo of Light, An.   Árpád Tóth.   IQMS, *tr. by* Thomas Kabdebo

In front of you I go.   I Am With You.   Lajos Kassák.   IQMS, *tr. by* Edwin Morgan

In full-blown Dignity, see Wolsey stand.   Samuel Johnson.   OxBEV   *Fr.* Vanity of Human Wishes, The; The Tenth Satire of Juvenal Imitated.

In full glare [*or* flare] I came here, man-tall but thin.   Roundhouse Voices, The.   Dave Jeddie Smith.   NoAM; VCAP

In full voice sent.   Continental Walk.   Allen Fisher.   PFTM-2

In Fury and Terror.   Storm, The.   Elizabeth Jane Coatsworth.   OBCA

In Fuscum.   Sir John Davies.   FaBoEE

In futurity / I prophetic see.   William Blake.   FHYEP; NOBRP   *Fr.* Songs of Experience.

In futurity / I prophetic see.   William Blake.   FHYEP; NOBRP   *Fr.* Songs of Innocence.

In Fuzhou, far away, my wife is watching.   Moonlit Night.   Tu Fu.   WoPoe, *tr. by* Vikram Seth

In Gaetam.   Thomas Bastard.   FaBoEE

In Galilee.   Jessie Mackay.   SacPr

In Gardens in the Rhondda.   Idris Davies.   AngWePo

In gayer hours, when high my fancy ran.   Richard Savage.   NOEC; OBSV   *Fr.* Bastard, The.

In Genesis, Adam's the winner.   Limerick.   Bill Greenwell.   PeLi

In Geneva I pawned my pocket watch and passport.   Sam Truitt.   AmPoNex   *Fr.* Anamorphosis Eisenhower.

In gentle childhood cradle dream I see.   Chord.   Anton Wildgans.   AuPH, *tr. by* Lowell A. Bangerter

In Germany once lived a censor.   Ballad about the German Censor, The.   "David Samuilovich Samoylov" [*or* Samoilov].   TCRP, *tr. by* Lubov Yakovleva

In gestures of invincible desire. (LL)   Sonnet: "Winter deepening, the hay all in, The."   Richard Wilbur.   OxBSo; Son

In ghostlier demarcations, keener sounds. (LL)   Idea of Order at Key West, The.   Wallace Stevens.   APT-1; AmFaPo; ColAP; HAP; HCAP; HarvBoo; HeIP-4; MakPoe; MoAmPo; NAAL-2v2; NAAL-5; NAWM-7v2; NIL-7; NIP-4; NOBA; NoAM; NoP-4; OxBA; PoE; PoPoPo; SAmP; TAP; TFi

In Glasgow, in 'Eighty-four.   In a Music-Hall.   John Davidson.   EBVV

In Glencullen.   John Millington Synge.   OBMV

In God alone my confidence do stay. (LL)   Joachim Du Bellay.   AWP; Son   *Fr.* Visions of Bellay, The.

In God's Eternity.   Hosea, I Ballou.   AH

In gold sandals.   Sappho.   BoWoP

In Golden Gate Park that day.   Lawrence Ferlinghetti.   PmAP; RB

In gonia once which was Pata.   Limerick.   Arthur Shaw.   PeLi

In good King Charles's golden days.   Vicar of Bray, The.   *Unknown.*   NOBE; NOBL; OBSV; OxBEV; OxBoLi

In good old Stalin's early days.   Garland for a Propagandist.   Ted Pauker.   NOBL

In gorgeous reticence. (LL)   Brancusi's Golden Bird.   Mina Loy.   APT-1; HarvBoo

In Gothic times, when feudal laws obtained.   Triumph of Superstition, The.   Raphael and Ianthe.   Anne Batten Cristall.   RWP

In Goya's greatest scenes we seem to see.   Lawrence Ferlinghetti.   HeIP-4; NeAP; NoAM; PmAP; PoM; TAP

In grade school I wondered.   Zimmer in Grade School.   Paul Zimmer.   KaS; PBCAP

In grandfather's house I ran up and down.   Doris Hulme.   NewEx

In graves where drips the winter rain.   *Unknown.*   OBMV, *tr. by* Ernest Rhys   *Fr.* Black Book of Carmarthen, The.

In Greece in 1939, these kids had this little snake trapped in a corner, kicking it and laughing.   Art of the Snake Story, The.   Amy England.   BAP-01

In grey-haired Celia's withered arms.   Paraphrase from the French, A.   Matthew Prior.   OxBoLi; PeLV

In grief and anguish of my heart, my voice I did extend.   Song of Jonah in the Whale's Belly, The.   Michael Drayton.   ChIV-1

In Grief, Lamenting for My Elder Brother Ts'ang-ch.   Hsieh Chin.

"I still remember Conch-Shell Slope, west of the River Tzu."   CoBLCP

In grievous deity my cat.   Startled into Life Like Fire.   Charles Bukowski.   PmAP

In grimy winter dusk / We slowed for a concrete platform.   Stop.   Richard Wilbur.   LCAP-2

In Gurgle Veritas.   Luis H. Francia.   ReBoTo

In haist ga hy thee to sum hoill.   John Rolland.   OxBS   *Fr.* Seven Seages, The.

In happy hours, when the imagination.   Henry Wadsworth Longfellow.   TCAPo   *Fr.* Michael Angelo: A Fragment.

In hard / country.   Hard Country.   Philip Booth.   CoAP

In Hardwood Groves.   Robert Frost.   HAP

In Harlem wandering from street to street. (LL)   Harlem Shadows.   Claude McKay.   APT-1; ColAP; NAAAL; NAAL-5; TCAPo

In harmony.   What Was Not Conceivable.   Fatima Mahmoud.   PoArWo, *tr. by* Khaled Mattawa

In Harmony with Kao "The Second" Ch'i's Poem "On Hearing a P'i-p'a Played Next Door."   Hsü Pen.   CoBLCP, *tr. by* Jonathan Chaves

In Harmony with Nature.   Matthew Arnold.   CABP

In Hässelby.   Evening Walk.   Sonja Åkesson.   WPOW, *tr. by* Joanna Bankier

In haste one evening while making dinner.   Potato.   Jane Kenyon.   SpudSo

In haste poste haste, when first my wandering [*or* wandring] mind[e].   George Gascoigne.   NoSic; Son   *Fr.* Gascoigne's Memories.

In Hayden's Collage.   Michael S. Harper.   ESEAA; NAAAL

In heart's space hath Eros.   Meleager.   GrAn

In hearts all rocky now the late remorse of love. (LL)   Byron.   NAEL-5v2; NAEL-6v2   *Fr.* Childe Harold's Pilgrimage.

In hearts at peace, under an English heaven. (LL)   Rupert Brooke.   AmFaPo; CABP; FaBoWar; GSo; HeIP-4; MoBrPo; NAEL-5v2; NAEL-6v2; NOBE; NoP-4; OBEV; OBWP; OxBTC; PeFWW; PoRA; PoWW; Son; TFi; UV   *Fr.* 1914.

In hearts like thine ne'er may I hold a place.   Answer to ——'s Professions of Affection.   Byron.   OxBSP

In Heaven.   Ssu-k'ung Shu.   SuSp, *tr. by* Irving Y. Lo

In Heaven a spirit doth dwell.   Israfel.   Edgar Allan Poe.   APN-1; AWP; NAAL-2v1; NAAL-3; NOBA; OxBA; PoE; TAP; TCAPo

In heaven-high musings and many.   Euripides.   AWP, *tr. by* A. E. Housman   *Fr.* Alcestis.

In heaven I will find the words not said.   To the Victims of Mauthausen.   Maria Luisa Spaziani.   CltWP, *tr. by* Cinzia Sartini Blum and Lara Trubowitz

In Heaven [*or* Heav'n], their earthy [*or* earthly] bodies left behind. (LL)   To Lucasta, [on] Going beyond the Seas.   Richard Lovelace.   BeJo; CaPo; GTBS-P; MeLP; OBEV; OxAEP-1

In Heaven, Queen Juno saw. She's trapped.   Virgil [*or* Vergil].   EroLit, *tr. by* Kenneth McLeish   *Fr.* Aeneid [*or* Eneados, *Aeneis*], The.

In heaven soaring up, I dropped [*or* dropt] an ear[e].   Edward Taylor.   NAAL-2v1; NAAL-3; OxBA; SCAP   *Fr.* God's Determinations [touching his Elect].

In Heaven / Some little blades of grass.   Stephen Crane.   MoAmPo   *Fr.* Black Riders [and Other Lines], The.

In heaven, too.   Heard in a Violent Ward.   Theodore Roethke.   HCAP

In heavenly realms of hellas dwelt.   E. E. Cummings.   NOBA; OBSV

In heavy drink and in love.   Atlantis.   Slavko Mihalic.   PoSu, *tr. by* Charles Simic

In Heavy Mind.   James Agee.   MoAmPo

In heavy snow.   Kyutaro.   JDP, *tr. by* Yoel Hoffmann

In Hecate's Garden.   Ziporah Hildebrandt.   HW

In hell, maximum use.   Fresco.   Martin Sorescu.   VCWP, *tr. by* D. J Enright and Joana Russell-Gebbett

In Henry Carlile's *Writing 213*.   Martha Silano.   AmPoNex

In her best gingham dress, teased hair.   God of Pepper, The.   Alan Michael Parker.   NeAmPo

In her boudoir, the young lady—unacquainted with grief.   *Unknown.*   OBVE; OxBEV, *tr. by* Arthur Waley

In her clapping hand. (LL)   Mother of the Groom.   Seamus Heaney.   OxBSP; PAI

In her gnarled sleep it.   Cherry Tree, The.   Thom Gunn.   GLP

In her golden chamber. Alice. Isa Blagden. PoBW

In her hand the knife, brisk, brilliant as moon-claw. Cleaning a Fish. Dave Jeddie Smith. NoAM

In her hands she holds. Man She Called Honey, and Married, The. Alberto A. Ríos. ReTh

In her lap woman gathers all labors;. Fragment for the Mother. Mariella Bettarini. CItWP, tr. by Cinzia Sartini Blum and Lara Trubowitz

In her last sickness, my mother took my hand in hers. Kaddish. Charles Reznikoff. TaR

In her old voice the mountains. Marlene Mountain. HA

In Her Only Way. Robert Graves. OxBSP Fr. Three Songs for the Lute.

In her ornate tower by bright moonlight always she thinks of him. Tune: Deva-like Barbarian. Wen T'ing-yün. CoBCP, tr. by Burton Watson

In Her Own Image. Eavan Boland. PBCIP

In her own isle's remotest grove. Temple of Venus, The. Soame Jenyns. NOEC

In Her Praise. Robert Graves. BIrV

In Her Prison. Sarah Morgan Bryan Piatt. NCAP

In her room at the prow of the house. Writer, The. Richard Wilbur. HCAP; NoAM; OxBC; PoPoPo; SoSe-8

In her storefront living room. Palm Reader, The. Nicholas Christopher. NoP-4

In her tomb by the sounding sea. (LL) Annabel Lee. Edgar Allan Poe. AWP; AiP; BRP; ChAP; HeIP-4; ITBLP; NAAL-2v1; NAAL-3; NAAL-5; NCAP; OBCA; OBSP; TCAPo; TFi

In her very name is a ripple of applause. Portrait of Plisetskaya. Andrey [or Andrei] Andreievich Voznesensky [or Voznesenskii]. RusPo, tr. by Robert Arthur Douglas Ford

'In here,' our teacher said. Owl. Ted Walker. NOxBChV

In hermetic enclosure. Jacques Rabémanganjara. NegPo Fr. Lamba.

In Hexameter sings serenely a Harvard Professor. Couplet: February 24, 1847. Henry Wadsworth Longfellow. APN-1

In Heytesbury Wood. Siegfried Sassoon. OBGa

In high school I had a friend. Domingo Limón. Alberto A. Ríos. NAAL-5

In highest way of heav'n the sun did ride. Sir Philip Sidney. Son Fr. Astrophil and Stella.

In him inexplicably mixed appeared. Byron. NOBRP Fr. Lara.

In Him We Live [& Move & Have Our Being]. Jones Very. APN-1; OxBA

In his blue suit, an Oxford Standard Authors. Study in Blue. Evan Jones. NOBAu

In His face they spit their icy scorn. New Negro Sermon. Jacques Roumain. NegPo, tr. by Ellen Conroy Kennedy

In his father's cupped hands. Pheasant Plucker's Son, The. Mick North. NLP

In his father's face flying. Icarus. Ronald Bottrall. GTBS-P

In his low-ceilinged oaken room. Silent Room, The. Kingsley Amis. OxBC

In his malodorous brain what slugs and mire. God. Isaac Rosenberg. OxBEV

In his narrow, gleaming eyes. Leader, The. Yunna Petrovna [or Iunna Pinkhusovna] Moritz [or Morits]. TCRusP, tr. by Daniel Weissbort

In his own age, Democritus could find. Juvenal. BASC, tr. by John Dryden Fr. Satires.

In his portrait of Carlyle, Whistler builds. After Whistler. Stanley Plumly. LCAP-2

In his tall senatorial. Drum; the Narrative of the Demon of Tedworth, The. Dame Edith Sitwell. FaBoTw

In his unsteady box at last into the earth. (LL) Cinquevalli. Edwin Morgan. HarvBoo; NePenScot

In his unweeting way. (LL) New Year's Eve. Thomas Hardy. MoBrPo; NoAM

In his wedding band watching the clouds pass. Alexis Rotella. HA

In his winged collar. Japanese Jokes. Peter Porter. DBCoV

In history's mysteries vast. Limerick. Unknown. PeLi

In holiday gown, and my new-fangled hat. Holiday Gown. John Cunningham. ECEV

In honor of the dumb the blind the deaf. Second Nature. Paul Eluard. SurPaPo, tr. by Samuel Beckett

In Honor of the Sardana and the Tenora. Max Jacob. CuPo

In honour of something or other—poor. Sign Illuminated, A. Roy Fisher. EmeKit

In Honour of St. Alphonsus Rodriguez. Gerard Manley Hopkins. EBEV; OxAEP-2

In Honour of St. David's Day. Unknown. OBWVE

In Honour of Taffy Topaz. Christopher Darlington Morley. WHSW

In Honour of that High and Mighty Princess Queen Elizabeth of Happy Memory. Anne Bradstreet. NAAL-5; NALW

"Here lies the pride of Queens, pattern of Kings." TCAPo

"Here sleeps the Queen, this is the royall bed." OxBEV; TCAPo

In Honour of the Holy Spirit. Hildebert. MLL, tr. by Helen Waddell

In Hospital. James Elroy Flecker. OxBTC

In Hospital. William Ernest Henley.

Before. MoBrPo

"Behold me waiting—waiting for the knife." MoBrPo

"Gaunt brown walls, The." NPeEn

Interior. NPeEn

"Square, squat room (a cellar on promotion), A." NAEL-5v2; NAEL-6v2; NOBVV; NPeEn

Waiting. NAEL-5v2; NAEL-6v2; NOBVV; NPeEn

In Hospital. Frank O'Hara. LCAP-2

In Hospital-land. Gillian Ferguson. MFPA

In Hospital: Poona (1). Alun Lewis. AngWePo; OBWVE; TCAWP

In hospital where windows meet. Lady of Quality, A. Thomas Kinsella. PBCIP

In Hsü-chou, in the District of Ku-fêng. Chu Ch'ên Village. Po Chü-i. ChiP, tr. by Arthur Waley

In Humenne, in this time of drought. Huckster at Noontime. James Ragan. TWW

In Hung-fu Monastery we brush off the dust from purple window gauze. Passing Hung-fu Monastery with Yüan-ming: Inscribed in Jest. Huang T'ing-chien. SuSp, tr. by Michael E. Workman

In idle August, while the sea soft. Derek Walcott. ESEAA; HarvBoo; NoP-4; PoetW Fr. Schooner Flight, The.

In Ignorant Cadence. Maura Stanton. YaYoPo

In Illness, Dismissing My Singing Girl. Ssu-k'ung Shu. ColAnChi, tr. by Burton Watson

(Ten thousand things wound my heart when you're before my eyes.) CoBCP, tr. by Burton Watson

In Illyria, the love-sick Orsino. Limerick. Stanley J. Sharpless. PeLi

In Imitation. Larry Eigner. FTOS

In Imitation of Anacreon. Matthew Prior. FaBoEE; OxBEV

In Imitation of Ancient Songs. Li Po. SuSp, tr. by Joseph J. Lee

In Imitation of Ancient-style Poetry. Pao Chao. SuSp, tr. by Daniel Bryant

In Imitation of Horace. Aphra Behn. NOSC

In Imitation of Hsü Kan. Liu Chün. SuSp, tr. by Jan W. Walls

In Imitation of T'ao P'eng-tse. Wei Ying-wu. SuSp, tr. by Irving Y. Lo

In Imitation of "The King of Huai-nan." Pao Chao. CoBCP, tr. by Burton Watson

In Innocence. James Vincent Cunningham. OxBSP

In innocence I said. In Innocence. James Vincent Cunningham. OxBSP

In innocent slumber—like this. (LL) Sleepy Giant, The. Charles Edward Carryl. NOxBChV; OTCP

In Ireland, we're all of us just. Deadly Seven, The. Sydney Bernard Smith. PeLi

In it there is a dream. Girl's Head, A. Katherine Gallagher. NOBAu

In Italy a man's name, here a woman's. How I Changed My Name, Felice. Felix Stefanile. UnSA

In Italy, where this sort of thing can occur. Hill, A. Anthony Hecht. CoAP; NIL-7; NoP-4; VCAP

In its first dumb form. Susan Howe. FTOS Fr. Secret History of the Dividing Line.

In its going down, the moon. Poem. Robert Hoggra. MoCV

In its streets my visions multiply. Blind City. Mona Saudi. PoArWo, tr. by Kamal Boullata

In Jana's Garden. Joyce Carol Oates. SpudSo

In Japan. Michael Burn. TCAWP

In Japan the poets write to each other. In Japan. Michael Burn. TCAWP

In Jimmy's Garden. Quincy Troupe. GT

In joy, that our lives / are so familiar. (LL) Return of the Native. Imamu Amiri Baraka. APSN; BPo

In joye withouten ende. (LL) Ubi Sunt Qui Ante Nos Fuerunt? Unknown. EBEV; PoE

In joyous Summer, when the exulting earth. Lament of the Forest, The. Thomas Cole. APN-1

In Judgment of the Leaf. Kenneth Patchen. VGW

In July month, ae bonny morn. Robert Fergusson. VGW Fr. Leith Races.

In June. Robert Kelly. FTOS

In June, amid the golden fields. Groundhog, The. Richard Eberhart. APT-2; FaBoMo; MoAmPo; NoAM; PAI; RaBo; TAP; TFi; TRP; UnPo

In June and Gentle Oven. Anne Wilkinson. MoCV; NOBC

In June, examiners. Grand Central Hotel, The. Roy McFadden. PNI

In June I give you a close-wooded fell. Folgore da San Geminiano [or Gimignano]. EaItPo, tr. by Dante Gabriel Rossetti Fr. Sonnets of the Months.

In June the sun is a bonnet of light. Sun. Gary Soto. TRP

In June was a jar had. In June. Robert Kelly. FTOS

In June, which is still June here, but once removed. June: Dutch Harbor. William Meredith. YaYoPo

In just a Country Town. (LL)   Emily Dickinson.   APN-2; SAmP; SoSe-8

In just an instant mist and cloud.   Inscribed on "Drunk in the Autumn Woods." Tao-chi.   CoBLCP, *tr. by* Jonathan Chaves

In Just-.   In Just-spring.   E. E. Cummings.   ChAP; FaBoVe; HarvBoo; HeIP-4; InPK-6; MoAmPo; NAAL-2v2; NAAL-5; NIL-7; NIP-4; NOxBChV; NoP-4; OxIBACP; PoPoPo; SoSe-8; WeW-3

In Kansas.   Carter Revard.   HATNAP

In Kenscoff Market the breeze brought spices.   Kenscoff.   Lorna Goodison.   GT

In Kensington Gardens.   Arthur Symons.   EnLoPo

In Kerry.   John Millington Synge.   MoBrPo

In Kind.   Linda France.   NeBl

In Köhln [Köln], a town of monks and bones.   Cologne.   Samuel Taylor Coleridge.   FaBoEE; NBLV

In La Mancha he mopeth.   Rusty Man, The.   Herman Melville.   NCAP

In labor, as in prayer, fulfilling the same law. (LL)   Dedication: "I would the gift I offer here."   John Greenleaf Whittier.   APN-1; OxBA

In Lady Lusher's drawing-room, where float the strains of Brahms.   Martyred Democrat, The.   C. J. Dennis.   CBAP

In Lakeview Cemetery.   Christian Wiman.   AmPoNex

In lamplight, I open your book, and start to weep.   Lamenting for Kao Ch'ing-ch'iu, Chi-ti.   Chang Yü.   CoBLCP, *tr. by* Jonathan Chaves

In Lamplight, Watching My Wife Preparing a Flower Arrangement—Playfully Inscribing Four Poems.   Ch'ien Ch'ien-i [*or* Ch'ien Ch'ien-yi].   CoBLCP, *tr. by* Jonathan Chaves

In Language.   Eugene Gloria.   OpBo

In Lantana Street's mid-morning.   At the Nature-Strip.   Judith Rodriguez.   CBAP

In Late Spring of the Year *Keng-hsü* (1790), I Stayed at the Sun Family's Gemstone Mountain Villa at West Lake. Before Leaving, I Wrote These Poems as Mementos.   Yüan Mei.   CoBLCP, *tr. by* Jonathan Chaves

In late sun, the beauty of river and hill.   Chüeh-chü.   Tu Fu.   CoBCP, *tr. by* Burton Watson

In late winter.   Bear, The.   Galway Kinnell.   CoAP; MakPoe; NNaP; TAP; TRP; VCAP; VGW

In late years, I love only the stillness.   To Subprefect Chang.   Wang Wei.   SuSp, *tr. by* Irving Y. Lo

In later life, quietude my only care.   Answer to Vice-Prefect Chang.   Wang Wei.   ChinPo, *tr. by* Yip Wai-lim

In length of days and soundness of limb you and I are one.   To Liu Yü-hsi.   Po Chü-i.   ChiP, *tr. by* Arthur Waley

In letters of gold on T'ang's bathtub.   Confucius.   PFTM-1   *Fr.* Great Digest, The.

In Librum.   Sir John Davies.   FaBoEE

In Lidda, in Ramla, in the Galilee.   Here We Will Stay.   Tawfiq Zayyad.   MAP, *tr. by* Charles Doria and Sharif Elmusa

In life and death, O Lord, abide with me! (LL)   Abide With Me.   Henry Francis Lyte.   EBVV; InvLi; NOCV; PWR

In life I stroll the capital city.   Poem in the Form of a Coffin-Puller's Song.   Miu Hsi.   CoBCP, *tr. by* Burton Watson

In life three ghostly friars were we.   Ghosts, The.   Thomas Love Peacock.   OBCoV

In light, and nothing else, awake. (LL)   At the San Francisco Airport.   Yvor Winters.   AiP; HeIP-4; InPK-6; NIL-7; NIP-4; NOBA

In light metal coverings the moon falls on my face.   Remembering the Night Fountains.   I. K. Bonset.   TuT, *tr. by* Desmond Egan

In Line at the Supermarket.   Greg Pape.   PBCAP

In Little Rock the people bear.   Chicago *Defender* Sends a Man to Little Rock, The.   Gwendolyn Brooks.   NAAAL

In little time I stake my claim.   Ann Griffiths.   Sally Roberts Jones.   AngWePo

In living Streams that Spring.   Some Account of Anne Whitehead's Early Experience, as Written by Her Near Thirty Years Ago.   Anne Greenwell.   EMWP

In London city was Bicham born.   Young Beichan.   *Unknown.*   ESPB

In London / every now and then.   Like a Beacon.   Grace Nichols.   OPOU

In London I never know what to be at.   Country and Town.   Charles Morris.   NOEC

In London stands a famous pile.   South Sea Ballad, A.   Edward Ward.   OBCoV

In London there I was bent.   London Lickpenny.   *Unknown.*   OBSV

In London Town.   Mary Elizabeth Coleridge.   VWP

In looking o'er the prospects.   Prospect of the Future, The.   Mrs. Henry Linden.   CBWP-4

In Los Angeles / while the mountains cleared of smog.   Tongue-tied in Black and White.   Michael S. Harper.   ESEAA; HCAP

In Love.   Amanda Dalton.   NeBl   *Fr.* Room of Leaves.

In Love.   David Wevill.   MoCV

In Love For Long.   Edwin Muir.   BoLoP; MoBrPo

In Love In Vain.   Leo Robin.   ReLy

In Love's name you are charged: oh, fly [*or* charged hereby].   Love's Hue and Cry.   James Shirley.   BeJo

In love's name, Your emissary. (LL)   Gift, The.   Louise Glück.   FaBoWP; TaR

In love's rubber armor I come to you.   Love Sonnet.   John Updike.   Son

In love to be sure what disasters we meet.   Lover's Arithmetic, The.   *Unknown.*   OxBoLi; PeLV

In love with mountains, I go out my gate.   Evening View from Grass Hill.   Gensei.   WoPoe, *tr. by* Burton Watson

In Love with Wholes.   Alberta Turner.   LCAP-2

In loving thee thou know'st I am forsworn.   William Shakespeare.   HeIP-4   *Fr.* Sonnets.

In lowly dale, fast by a river's side.   James Thomson.   NOEC   *Fr.* Castle of Indolence, The.

In lurid cartoon colors, the big baby.   Eden.   Emily Grosholz.   FFC; RA

In Magic Words.   Merrill Moore.   Son

In man, ambition is the common'st thing.   Ambition.   Robert Herrick.   CaPo

In man's cannot be right. (LL)   Double Standard, A.   Frances Ellen Watkins Harper.   BlSi; NAAAL; PWR

In Manchester there are a thousand puddles.   Watch Your Step—I'm Drenched.   Adrian Mitchell.   RB

In Manchester today a man was seen.   Here is the News.   Michael Rosen.   OBSP

In many a village churchyard's simple grave.   Obscurity of Woman's Worth.   Caroline Elizabeth Norton.   VWP

In marble walls [*or* halls] as white as milk.   Mother Goose.   OxNR

In March and April, thereabout.   Alison.   *Unknown.*   HAP

In March birds couple, a new birth.   Leaves Come Again, The.   Henry Vaughan.   FaBoEE

In March I give you plenteous fisheries.   Folgore da San Geminiano [*or* Gimignano].   EaItPo, *tr. by* Dante Gabriel Rossetti   *Fr.* Sonnets of the Months.

In March the seed.   Mater Dei.   Padraic Fallon.   NOCV

In Marion, the honey locust trees are falling.   Two Poems about President Harding.   James Wright (1927–80).   CoAP

In martial sports I had my cunning tried.   Sir Philip Sidney.   NAEL-5v1; NAEL-6v1; NAEL-7v1; NoSic   *Fr.* Astrophil and Stella.

In mass graves the bodies of plants.   Mikhail Grobman.   TCRusP, *tr. by* John Glad

In math I was the whiz kid, keeper.   Flash Cards.   Rita Dove.   ESEAA; LoL; PoPoPo

In mathematic[k]s he was greater.   Samuel Butler (1612–80).   NOBL   *Fr.* Hudibras.

In May.   John Millington Synge.   MoBrPo

In May it muryeth when it dawes.   *Unknown.*   MiEL

In May, when sea-winds pierced our solitudes.   Rhodora, The [On Being Asked Whence Is the Flower].   Ralph Waldo Emerson.   APN-1; AWP; AmFaPo; ITBLP; NAAL-2v1; NAAL-3; NAAL-5; NOBA; NoP-4; OxBA; PWR; PoE; TAP; TCAPo; TFi

In McNeil Island Prison for bad checks, my father worked to pay off his debts.   Father and Farther.   Sherman Alexie.   AmPoNex

In me a moonscape of organs.   Scan.   Gillian Ferguson.   NeBl

In me is a little painted square.   Old Age.   Maxwell Bodenheim.   TaR

In Me, Past, Present, Future Meet.   Siegfried Sassoon.   OBEV; OxBSP

In me something glimpsed its occasion.   Passing Through.   Patrick Williams.   PNI

In me the sleeping wound of stupor. (LL)   This time I won't permit the blue.   Patrizia Cavalli.   NeIt; VCWP, *tr. by* Judith Baumel

In me, the sound something numb come alive makes. (LL)   Purr, The.   Molly Peacock.   ExTi; PasH

In me (the worm) clearly.   "H. D."   APT-1   *Fr.* Walls Do Not Fall, The.

In me they dump their cans, their toilet paper.   River's Answer, The.   Ben Howard.   PoCoUp

In meetin' come nex' Sunday. (LL)   James Russell Lowell.   NOBA; OBAL   *Fr.* Biglow Papers, The.

In melancholic fancy.   Hallo My Fancy.   William Cleland.   OxBoLi

In Mem'ry's fairest court a shrine is set.   To Laura.   Henrietta Cordelia Ray.   CBWP-3

In Memorial.   J. Gordon Coogler.   OBAL

In Memoriam.   Bernard Dadié.   NegPo, *tr. by* Ellen Conroy Kennedy

In Memoriam.   W. J. Gruffydd.   OBWVE, *tr. by* R. Gerallt Jones

In Memoriam.   Martin Johnston.   BMAP; NOBAu

In Memoriam.   Michael Longley.   ModIr; PNI

In Memoriam.   M. R. Peacocke.   NLP

In Memoriam.   Léopold Sédar Senghor.   PoetW, *tr. by* Melvin Dixon

In Memoriam.   Léopold Sédar Senghor.   PBMAP

In Memoriam A. H. H.   Tennyson.

  "Again at Christmas did we weave."   EBVV; NAEL-6v2; NAWM-7v2; PeECV

"And all is well, though [*or* tho'] faith and form." NAEL-6v2

"And was the day of my delight." NAEL-6v2

"Be near me when my light is low." CABP; EBVV; HAP; HeIP-4; NAEL-6v2; NAWM-7v2; NOCV; PeECV; SCGP; SCV

By night we lingered [*or* linger'd] on the lawn. EBVV; FHYEP; HAP; NAEL-6v2; NAWM-7v2; PeECV; TOF

  "Till now the doubtful dusk reveal'd." GTBS-P

"Calm is the morn without a sound." EBEV; EBVV; FHYEP; HeIP-4; NAEL-6v2; NAWM-7v2; NOBE; NPeEn; OxBEV; PeECV

"Contemplate all this work of Time." EBVV; NAEL-6v2; NAWM-7v2

"Danube to the Severn gave, The." EBVV; GTBS-P; NAEL-6v2; NAWM-7v2

"Dark house, by which once more I stand." EBEV; EBVV; FHYEP; GTBS-P; HAP; HeIP-4; NAEL-6v2; NAWM-7v2; NOBE; NPeEn; OxBEV; SCGP; SCV; SoSe-8; UnPo

"Dear friend, far off, my lost desire." CAGL; FHYEP; NAEL-6v2

"Dip down upon the northern shore." EBVV; NAEL-6v2

"Doors, where my heart was used to beat." FHYEP; NAEL-6v2; SCV

"Dost thou look back on what hath been." NAEL-6v2

Epilogue.

  "And rise, O moon, from yonder down." NAEL-6v2

  "Today the grave is bright for me." NAWM-7v2

"Fair ship, that from the Italian shore." CAGL; EBVV; NAEL-6v2

"Happy lover who has come, A." NAEL-6v2

"Heart-affluence in discursive talk." NAEL-6v2

"How pure at heart and sound in head." NAEL-6v2

"I cannot see the features right." NAEL-6v2

"I climb the hill: from end to end." EBVV; FHYEP

"I dreamed there would be Spring no more." NOBE

I envy not in any moods. CABP; CAGL; FHYEP; NAEL-6v2; NAWM-7v2

  "I hold it true, whate're befall." UV

"I hear the noise about thy keel." EBVV; NAEL-6v2; NAWM-7v2

"I held it truth, with him who sings." CAGL; EBVV; HeIP-4; NAEL-6v2; NAWM-7v2

"I know that this was Life—the track." CAGL; NAEL-6v2

"I leave thy praises unexpressed." NAEL-6v2

"I passed beside the reverend walls." EBVV; NAEL-6v2

"I shall not see thee. Dare I say." NAEL-6v2

"I sing to him that rests below." NAEL-6v2; NAWM-7v2

"I sometimes hold it half a sin." CAGL; NAEL-6v2; NAWM-7v2; PeECV; TOF

"I trust I have not wasted breath." FHYEP; NAEL-6v2

"I wage not any feud with Death." NAEL-6v2

"I will not shut me from my kind." CABP; FHYEP; NAEL-6v2

"If one should bring me this report." FHYEP; NAEL-6v2

"If Sleep and Death be truly one." PeECV

"In those sad words I took farewell." NAEL-6v2

"Is it, then, regret for buried time." FHYEP

"It is the day when he was born." EBVV; FHYEP; NAEL-6v2

"Lo, as a dove when up she springs." NAEL-6v2

"Love is and was my Lord and King." CAGL; NAEL-6v2; NOBE; NOCV; OBEV; PeECV

"My own dim life should teach me this." FHYEP; NAEL-6v2

"Now fades the last long streak of snow." EBVV; FHYEP; GTBS-P; NAEL-6v2; NOBE; NPeEn

"Now, sometimes in my sorrow shut." CAGL; NAEL-6v2; NAWM-7v2

"O days and hours, your work is this." PeECV

"O living will that shalt endure." EBVV; NAEL-6v2

"O Sorrow, cruel fellowship." HAP; NAEL-6v2; NAWM-7v2

"O Sorrow, wilt thou live with me." NAEL-6v2

"O thou that after toil and storm." PeECV

"O, yet we trust that somehow good." CABP; EBVV; FHYEP; NAEL-6v2; PeECV

"Old warder of these buried bones." NAEL-6v2; PeECV

"Old yew, which graspest at the stones." EBVV; GTBS-P; NAEL-6v2; NAWM-7v2; NOBE; NPeEn; PAI; UnPo

"On that last night before we went." NAEL-6v2

"One writes, that "Other friends remain" NAEL-6v2

"Path by which we twain did go, The." CAGL; EBVV; NAEL-6v2; NAWM-7v2; PeECV; SCV

"Peace; come away: the song of woe." EBVV; FHYEP; NAEL-6v2

Ring Out, Wild Bells. ChrPo; EBVV; FHYEP; NAEL-6v2; NAWM-7v2; OxAEP-2; PeECV; TreFP

"Risest thou thus, dim dawn, again." NAEL-6v2; PeECV

"Risest thou thus, dim dawn, again." EBVV; NAEL-6v2

"Sad Hesper o'er the buried sun." EBVV; NAEL-6v2

"Sleep, kinsman thou to death and trance." NAEL-6v2

"So careful of the type?" but no." EBVV; FHYEP; HAP; NAEL-6v2; NAWM-7v2; NPeEn; TOF

"Still onward winds the dreary way." NAEL-6v2

"Strong Son of God, immortal Love." EBVV; HAP; NAEL-6v2; NAWM-7v2; SacPr; TrCP

"Sweet after showers, ambrosial air." EBVV; NAEL-6v2

"Tears of the widower, when he sees." CAGL; NAEL-6v2

"That each, who seems a separate whole." NAEL-6v2

That which we dare invoke to bless. EBVV; FHYEP; NAEL-6v2; NAWM-7v2; NOCV; SacPr; TOF

"There rolls the deep where grew the tree." HAP; NAEL-6v2; NOBE

"Thou comest, much wept for: such a breeze." EBVV; PeECV

"Thy spirit ere our fatal loss." CAGL

"Thy voice is on the rolling air." EBVV; FHYEP; HeIP-4; NAEL-6v2

"Time draws near the birth of Christ, The." EBVV; FHYEP; NAEL-6v2; NAWM-7v2; NOCV; SoSe-8

"Time draws near the birth of Christ, The." ChrPo; EBVV; NAEL-6v2

"'Tis well, 'tis something; we may stand." EBVV

"To Sleep I give my powers away." NAEL-6v2

"Tonight the winds begin to rise." EBVV; GTBS-P; NAEL-6v2; NAWM-7v2; NOBE; PeECV

"Tonight ungathered let us leave." ChrPo; EBVV; FHYEP; NAEL-6v2

"Unwatched, the garden bough shall sway." EBVV; FHYEP; GTBS-P; OBGa; PeECV; SCV

"We leave the well-beloved place." EBVV; FHYEP; TreFP

"What words are these have fallen from me?" EBEV; NAWM-7v2

"When I contemplate all alone." NAEL-6v2

"When Lazarus left his charnel-cave." EBVV; FHYEP; PeECV; TOF

"When on my bed the moonlight falls." NAEL-6v2; PeECV; SCGP

"When rosy plumelets tuft the larch." FHYEP; NAEL-6v2

"Wild bird, whose warble, liquid sweet." NAEL-6v2

"Wish, that of the living whole, The." EBVV; FHYEP; HAP; NAEL-6v2; NAWM-7v2; SacPr; TOF

"Witch-elms that counterchange the floor." EBVV; NAEL-6v2; OBGa

"With such compelling cause to grieve." EBVV; NAEL-6v2

"With trembling fingers did we weave." EBVV; FHYEP; NAEL-6v2

"Yet if some voice that man could trust." NAEL-6v2

"You say, but with no touch of scorn." NAEL-6v2; NOCV

In Memoriam Akbar Babool. Wopko Jensma. PeSAV

In Memoriam. Alphonse Campbell Fordham. Mary Weston Fordham. CBWP-2

In Memoriam Ben Zwane. Wopko Jensma. PeSAV

In Memoriam Charles Reznikoff. George Oppen. APT-2

In Memoriam [Easter 1915]. Edward Thomas. *See* In Memoriam (Easter, 1915)

In Memoriam (Easter, 1915). Edward Thomas. GTBS-P; NOBE; OBWP; OBWVE; OxBTC; PeFWW; Spl

  (In Memoriam [Easter 1915].) NoP-4

In Memoriam Francis Ledwidge. Seamus Heaney. CIP-2; NoAM

In Memoriam Frederick Douglass. Eloise Bibb. CBWP-4

In Memoriam Frederick Douglass. Henrietta Cordelia Ray. CBWP-3

In Memoriam Gyula Juhász. Sándor Weöres. IQMS, *tr.* by Edwin Morgan

In Memoriam, J.A.R., Drowned, East London. Guy Butler. PeSAV

In Memoriam James Joyce. Hugh MacDiarmid.

  In the Fall.

  "Let the only consistency." FaBoMo

  "We must look at the harebell as if." NAEL-5v2; NAEL-6v2; NoP-4

In Memoriam John Coltrane. Michael Stillman. InPK-6

In Memoriam Krishna Menon. E. J. Thribb. OBCoV

In Memoriam Larry Parnes ("Mr Parnes Shillings and Pence"). E. J. Thribb. OBCoV

In Memoriam: Martin Luther King, Jr. June Jordan. NAAAL

In Memoriam of E. B. Clark. Lizelia Augusta Jenkins Moorer. CBWP-3

In Memoriam Paul Celan. Edward Hirsch. MakPoe

In Memoriam Paul Laurence Dunbar. Henrietta Cordelia Ray. CBWP-3

In Memoriam[, Private D. Sutherland]. Ewart Alan Mackintosh. PoWW

In Memoriam S. L. Akintola. David Knight. MoCV

In Memoriam Salvador Dali. E. J. Thribb. OBCoV

In Memoriam. Susan Eugenia Bennett. Mary Weston Fordham. CBWP-2

In Memoriam the Master—Noel Coward (1900–1973). E. J. Thribb. PeLV

In Memorium: Robert Hayden. Norman J. Loftis. SpirFl

In Memory, 1978. Judith Kazantzis. BrRo

In Memory of a Black Union Leader. Aimé Césaire. VCWP

In Memory of a Friend. George Barker. OxBTC

In Memory of Aaron, Murdered Grandfather. Seymour Mayne. GotH

In Memory of Arthur Clement Williams. Eloise Bibb. CBWP-4

In Memory of Arthur Winslow. Robert Lowell.

Death from Cancer. TwCP
"This Easter, Arthur Winslow, less than dead." TwCP
In Memory of Basil, Marquess of Dufferin and Ava. Sir John Betjeman. OBWP
In Memory of Captain Underwood Who Was Drowned. *Unknown*. FaBoEE
In Memory of David Archer. George Barker.
  "Images! Venerable as Druidical trees." FaBoMo
In Memory of Elizabeth Kearney, Blasket-Islander. Michael Davitt. BiHa, *tr. by the author*
In Memory of Eva Gore-Booth and Con Markievicz. W. B. Yeats. NPeEn; NoAM; OBMV; OxBTC
In Memory of Gerard Dillon. Michael Longley. BiHa; PBCIP
In Memory of H. F. Peter Klappert. YaYoPo
In memory of Harriet Tubman. Harriet Tubman. *Unknown*. HHAm
In Memory of His Father. Publius Papinius Statius. RomPo, *tr. by* W. G. Shepherd *Fr.* Sylvae.
In Memory of Ho Chi-chen. Li Po. CrYelRi, *tr. by* Sam Hamill
In Memory of Idris Davies. John Tripp. AngWePo
In Memory of Izziddin al-Qalaq. Ahmad Dahbur. MAP, *tr. by* Charles Doria and Lena Jayyusi
In Memory of James M. Rathel. Josephine D. Henderson Heard. CBWP-4
In Memory of Jane Fraser [*or* Frazer]. Geoffrey Hill. NAEL-5v2; NAEL-6v2; NIL-7; NoAM; OxBTC
In Memory of John Keats. Yury [*or* Iurii] Mikhailovich Kublanovsky [*or* Kublanovskii]. TCRusP
In Memory of Kathleen. Kenneth Patchen. MoAmPo
In Memory of M. B. Anna Andreyevna Akhmatova. PoetW, *tr. by* Max Hayward and Stanley Kunitz
In Memory of Major Robert Gregory. W. B. Yeats. EBEV; NAEL-6v2; SCGP
In Memory of My Arab Grandmother. Evelyn Arcad Zerbe. WPOW
In Memory of My Dear Grandchild Anne Bradstreet Who Deceased June 20, 1669, Being Three Years and Seven Months Old. Anne Bradstreet. BoWoP; NAAL-2v1; NAAL-3; TrCP
In Memory of My Dear Grandchild Elizabeth Bradstreet Who Deceased August, 1665, Being a Year and Half Old. Anne Bradstreet. BASC; ColAP; NAAL-2v1; NAAL-3; NAAL-5; NOCV; SCAP; WPE
In Memory of My Feelings. Frank O'Hara. APSN; ColAP; HarvBoo; NAAL-2v2; NeAP; PoM
In Memory of My First Chapatis. Diane Di Prima. PoM
In Memory of My Friend the Bassoonist John Lenox. Donald Justice. BodElec
In Memory of My Mother. Patrick Kavanagh. BIrV; CIP-2; NoAM; RaBo
In Memory of Radio. Imamu Amiri Baraka. BB; NAAAL; NAAL-2v2; NeAP; PoM
In Memory of Sigmund Freud. W. H. Auden. HAP; NoAM; OxBA
In Memory of the Boys of Dexter, Kentucky. Joe Bolton. AmPoNex
In Memory of the Funeral Horses. Zoltán Jékely. IQMS, *tr. by* George Gömöri and Adam Makkai
In Memory of the Unknown Poet, Robert Boardman Vaughn. Donald Justice. DiPo; NoAM
In Memory of the Utah Stars. William Matthews. MoASP
In Memory of the Vertuous and Learned Lady Madre de Teresa that Sought an Early Martyrdome. Richard Crashaw.
  "Love thou art absolute, sole Lord." SacPr
In Memory of Titian Tabidze. Yunna Petrovna [*or* Iunna Pinkhusovna] Moritz [*or* Morits]. TCRP, *tr. by* J. R. Rowland
In Memory of W. B. Yeats. W. H. Auden. AmFaPo; HAP; HeIP-4; MakPoe; MoBrPo; NAEL-6v2; NIL-7; NOBE; NPeEn; NoAM; NoP-4; OxAEP-2; OxBTC; PAI; TFi; TRP; UnPo; WeW-3
  "Earth, receive an honoured guest." FaBoTw
In memory we are walking. In Memory We Are Walking. Maria Gillan. UnSA
A Merche, after the first C. *Unknown*. MiEL
In Mercy, Lord, Incline Thine Ear. Isaac M. Wise. AH
In merry Scotland, in merry Scotland. Henry Martyn. *Unknown*. ESPB
In mery May, quhen medis springis. John Barbour. OxBS *Fr.* Buik of Alexander, The.
In Mexico I'll finish the novel I'll write. In Answer to a Question From P. W. Lew Welch. BB
In Mexico, I met myself one day. El Día de los Muertos. Rafael Campo. RA
In Mexico? (LL)   I Am Not a Conspiracy Everything Is Not Paranoid The Drug Enforcement Administration Is Not Everywhere. Susan Musgrave. NIL-7; NoAM
In mid-river we join the ancient force. Baptism. Dale Zieroth. NOBC
In midair, he hesitates at the moment. From Rooftops, Kenji Takezo Throws Himself. Rick Noguchi. NeAmPo
In middle life when the skin slackens. Ambulando. Charles Brasch. PeNZ

In midnight sadness and tobacco fumes. Epistle to Baron Delvig. Oleg Grigorevich Chukhonstev. TCRP, *tr. by* Simon Franklin
In midnight sleep of many a face of anguish. Old War-Dreams. Walt Whitman. OxBSP
In midnights of November. A. E. Housman. PeVV
In Millais' painting, Ophelia dies face up. Bellocq's Ophelia. Natasha Trethewey. NeAmPo
In Minako Wada's House. Brad Leithauser. NoP-4
In Mind. Denise Levertov. NAAL-5; NALW
In mine one [*or* own] monument I lie [*or* lye]. Song. Richard Lovelace. OxBSP
In Missing. Ray A. Young Bear. CDW
In Modern Dress. Craig Raine. NoAM
In mole-blue indolence the sun. Alun Lewis. AngWePo; OBWVE
In moments of anguish. Old Wharf Canto. Jared Angira. NAfrP
In moments of desperation. Moments of Ridicule and Love. Fawaz Turki. GraLe
In Moncur Street. Dorothy Hewett. NOBAu
In Montecito. Randall Jarrell. CoAP; VGW
In Morfudd's Arms. Dafydd [*or* David] ap Gwilym. OBWVE, *tr. by* Rolfe Humphries
In morning light my damson show'd [*or* showed]. Plum Tree by the House, The. Oliver St. John Gogarty. OBEV; PoRA
In mothers womb thy fingers did me mak. Thankful Acknowledgment of God's Providence, A. John Cotton. SCAP
In Mourning for His Dead Wife. P'an Yüeh. OHMPC, *tr. by* Kenneth Rexroth
In mourning for your second son. Consoling Wu Te-cheng on the Death of His Son. Shen Chou. CoBLCP, *tr. by* Jonathan Chaves
In mourning wise since daily I increase. Sir Thomas Wyatt. NoSic
In moving-slow he has no Peer. Sloth, The. Theodore Roethke. ChAP; OBAL; OBCA; OxIBACP; TRP
In Murasaki's time. Tale of Genji. Hugh Seidman. YaYoPo
In musty light, in the thin brown air. In the Basement of the Goodwill Store. Ted Kooser. OPRER
In my bed at night. Bible, *O.T.* *See* By night on my bed I sought him whom my soul loveth
In my begging bowl. Ryokan. WoPoe, *tr. by* Burton Watson
In my beginning is my end. In succession. T. S. Eliot. HAP; VGW *Fr.* Four Quartets.
In my bein' dead. (LL) Wake. Langston Hughes. OBAL; OBCoV
In My Boat, Painting a Picture of Going Home by Boat. Yün Shou-p'ing.
  "Essence of ink, The." CoBLCP
In my boat that goes. Saigyo. AWP
In my breast are stored weapons of every description. Inscribed on My Grass-script Calligraphy Written While Drunk. Lu Yu. SuSp, *tr. by* Irving Y. Lo
In my broken heart's disdain! (LL) Runaway Slave at Pilgrim's Point, The. Elizabeth Barrett Browning. BrRo; NALW; VWP; ViWPN
In my chest a cave. Last Bullet, The. Nidaa Khoury. PoArWo, *tr. by* Roger Tavor and Linda Zisquit
In my childhood trees were green. Autobiography. Louis MacNeice. ModIr; NOIV; NPeEn; PNI; RB
In my country. Jackie Kay. MFPA; NeBl
In My Craft or Sullen Art. Dylan Thomas. AmFaPo; BoLoP; GTBS-P; HAP; HeIP-4; NIL-7; NIP-4; NoAM; NoP-4; OPOU; PAI; PoE; PoPoPo; RaBo; TCAWP; WeW-3; WoPoe
In my dark cell, low prostrate on the ground. Abelard to Eloisa. Judith Madan. RACG
In My Days. Giovanna Pollarolo. TANSG, *tr. by* Marjorie Agosin
In my days it seems like a dream, like fiction. In My Days. Giovanna Pollarolo. TANSG, *tr. by* Marjorie Agosin
In my declining years, in a land beyond the ocean. Joseph Brodsky. TCRusP, *tr. by* Bernard Meares *Fr.* Sonnets on the Statue of Mary, Queen of Scots, in the Luxembourg Gardens, Paris.
In My Dream. A. V. Christie. AmPoNex
In my dream. Author of the Jesus Papers Speaks, The. Anne Sexton. PFTM-2
In my dream, children. Jerusalem. Adrienne Rich. TaR
In my dream dark wings. Bird of Death. Sharon Olinka. TWW
In my dream I take. Kemo Sabe. Diane Glancy. LTA
In my dream I was catching the vanishing shadows. Vanishing Shadows. Konstantin Dmitrievich Balmont. TCRP, *tr. by* April FitzLyon
In my dream of the hydroplane. Sailing to Bien Hoa. Bruce Weigl. CDa
In my dream Pinocchio is six feet tall. Here, I Say. Joanna Fuhrman. AmPoNex
In my dream, sweaters are referred to as "vulvas." Vulva Operetta. Jessica Tarahata Hagedorn. ReBoTo
In my dream you're wearing an old trenchcoat. Tower. Deborah Woodard. CDa

In My Dreams. Stevie Smith. FaBoWP

In my dry cell. Riven Quarry, The. Gloria C. Oden. GT

In my enormous city it is—night. Marina Ivanovna Tsvetayeva [or Tsvetaeva]. OxBEV, tr. by Elaine Feinstein Fr. Insomnia.

In my eye I've no apple; every object. Instrument and Agent. Norman MacCaig. NePenScot

In my family. People in My Family. Grace Paley. TaR

In my family there are two famous paintings. I Tried to Exchange Two Painting for Some Grain But Failed. Hsü Wei. CoBLCP, tr. by Jonathan Chaves

In My Father's House. George Barlow. ESEAA

In My Father's House. Bruce Smith. Address. Son

In my father's house are many cobwebs. Portrait of the Artist as an Old Man. Michael Dransfield. BMAP; CBAP

In my first gentle days. Nicholas Kilmer. PeECV Fr. Petrarch.

In My First Hard Springtime. James Welch. CDW

In my grandmother's house there was always chicken soup. Story About Chicken Soup, A. Louis Simpson. NNaP; PoE; PoWW; TAP; UnSA

In my great loneliness. "Rachel" [or "Rahel"]. FIT, tr. by Robert Friend

In my hand. (LL) Eve. Dorothy Livesay. ItWoWo; NALW

In my hands, in my eyes, and in myself. (LL) Serenity in Stones, The. Simon J. Ortiz. CDW; ColAP

In my hands your. Praise. Anne K. Smith. PasH

In my heart's depth. Akazome Emon. WPOW

In my hidden house. Issa. SoOfWa, tr. by Sam Hamill

In my home town we called them the loonies. Touched. Elizabeth Dodd. AmPoNex

In my hometown, there is rust. Elders Are Gods, The. Tijan M. Sallah. NAfrP

In my house / Mice and fireflies. Issa. ZenPo, tr. by Takashi Ikemoto and Lucien Stryk

In my house we had an elephant named Italy. Autobiography. Robert Viscusi. UnSA

In my idleness. In My Idleness. Lady Izumi. WoPoe, tr. by Steven D. Carter

In my innermost vein I must hide him. Totem, The. Léopold Sédar Senghor. NegPo, tr. by Ellen Conroy Kennedy

In My Labyrinth (The Minotaur's Game). Carlota Caulfield. TANSG, tr. by Chris Allen

In my lady's chamber. (LL) I Have a Gentle Cock [or Gentil Cok]. Unknown. MiEL; NOBE; OPOU; PeLV

In my land there are no distinctions. Poem for the Young White Man Who Asked Me How I, An Intelligent, Well-Read Person Could Believe in the War Between Races. Lorna Dee Cervantes. PBCAP; PoPoPo; WPOW

In my last poem. Erratum. E. J. Thribb. PeLV

In my left pocket a Chickasaw hand. Truth Is, The. Linda Hogan. HATNAP; ItWoWo; LTA

In my life / As in the twilight. Issa. OHPJ

In My Lifetime. James Welch. CDW

In my lonely house, I'm drunk with passion again. (LL) One Night. Constantine P. Cavafy. CAGL; EroLit, tr. by Edmund Keeley and Philip Sherrard

In my medicine cabinet. Jack Kerouac. HA

In my melodious city cupolas burn. Marina Ivanovna Tsvetayeva [or Tsvetaeva]. AF Fr. Cycle Akhmatova, The.

In My Mind. Norman MacCaig. OxBC

In My Mother's Room. Colleen J. McElroy. GT

In my mouth I taste sacrilege. Salomé. Silvia Grénier. SurWo, tr. by Natalie Kenvin

In my narrow room, I throw. Mist. Li Ch'ing-chao. OHPC, tr. by Kenneth Rexroth

In my native province when I was young. From the Tibetan. John Hewitt. PNI

In my neighborhood I saw two swans take a taxi. Swans' Book, The. Víctor Hernández Cruz. PueRic

In My Other Life. Shara McCallum. AmPoNex

In my Park Avenue penthouse. Little Girl from Little Rock. Leo Robin. ReLy

In my remote springtime. (LL) Far Away and Long Ago. "Rubén Dario." PFTM-1; SpanPo, tr. by Denise Levertov

In my room, on the whitewashed wall. Fishing-Tackle, The. Bertolt Brecht. PoSu, tr. by Lee Baxendall

In my rose-wet cave—whatever happens, this is. (LL) Adrienne Rich. EroLit; NALW; NoAM Fr. Twenty-one Love Poems.

In my season as red as the red-breasted. Reality of Autumn, The. Duane Niatum. HATNAP

In my sixty-eighth year drought stopped the song of the rivers. Judith Wright. HarvBoo Fr. Shadow of Fire: Ghazals, The.

In my sleep I was fain of their fellowship, fain. Sidney Lanier. TCAPo Fr. Hymns of the Marshes.

In my solitude, you'll haunt me. Solitude. Duke Ellington. ReLy

In my stars there's three times ten. Antipater of Thessalonica. GrAn

In My Study in Monastery, Rising after a Nap. Huang T'ing-chien. "Peach and plum blossoms, speechless, keep swaying in the wind." SuSp "Short on brains, long on stupidity, the mantis seizes the cicada." SuSp

In my sweet and sad song. Mary Stuart, Queen of Scots. EMWP

In My Thirtieth Year. Archibald MacLeish. See L'An Trentiesme de Mon Eage

In my view. In My View. Tukaram. WoPoe, tr. by Dilip Chitre

In my village, another year has gone floating by. Sitting by Myself. K'ang Hai. CoBLCP, tr. by Jonathan Chaves

In my wicker basket. (LL) Wicker Basket, A. Robert Creeley. HAP; NoAM

In my young days I never. To an Old Tune. Hsin Ch'i-chi. OHMPC, tr. by Kenneth Rexroth

In my youth I lived for a time in the house of some aunts. Tunnel, The. Nicanor Parra. TCLAP, tr. by W. S. Merwin

In my youth's summer I did sing of One. Byron. NOBRP Fr. Childe Harold's Pilgrimage.

In my youth the growls. Tennyson. FaBoEE

In nameless warmth, sun light in every corner. Edgar Bowers. VCAP Fr. Autumn Shade.

In narrow room nature's whole wealth, yea more. John Milton. NOSC Fr. Paradise Lost.

In nature apt to like when I did see. Sir Philip Sidney. NAEL-5v1; NAEL-6v1; NAEL-7v1 Fr. Astrophil and Stella.

In Nature's pieces still I see. Divine Mistress, A. Thomas Carew. BeJo; CavPo

In Nature There Is Neither Right nor Left nor Wrong. Randall Jarrell. OxBC

In "nature" there's no choice. Beyond the End. Denise Levertov. NeAP; VGW

In Neglect. Robert Frost. OxBSP; VGW

In New Jersey Once. Maria Gillan. InvLad

In New Jersey once, marigolds grew wild. In New Jersey Once. Maria Gillan. InvLad

In New Orleans dwelt a young Creole. Limerick. Alben Barkley. PeLi

In New South Wales, as I plainly see. William Forster. CBAP Fr. Devil and the Governor, The.

In New York. Dennis Cooper. ReTh Fr. Some Adventures of John Kennedy Jr.

In / New York. My Father's Girlfriend. E. Ethelbert Miller. SpirFl

In Nick Ray's "Bigger Than Life." 1956. Maxine Scates. PBCAP

In night, when colors [or colours] all to black[e] are cast. Fulke Greville, 1st Baron Brooke. NPeEn; Son Fr. Caelica.

In Nine Sleep Valley. James Merrill. "Geode, the troll's melon." HCAP

In 1985 / the Lone Ranger. Confessions from the Last Cloud. Jose Angel Figueroa. PueRic

In 1915 my grandfather's. Grandfather. Michael S. Harper. ESEAA; LCAP-2; NAAAL; TAP; VCAP

In 1940. Anna Andreyevna Akhmatova. "At the burial of an epoch." FaBoWar; PoetW, tr. by Max Hayward

In 1944. Statistic. Michelle Parkerson. ISC

In 1943 Althea was a welder. Of Althea and Flaxie. Cheryl Clarke. GLP

In 1914 I was young and creative. Jacky Hears the Century Cry. Mudrooroo Narogin. IBA

In 1900. Borinkins in Hawaii. Víctor Hernández Cruz. PueRic

In nineteen hundred they preferred. Upper Family. Maxwell Bodenheim. OBAL

In 1969. Katharyn Howd Machan. SwNoth

In 1910 a royal princess. Osbert Lancaster. NOBL; PeLV Fr. Afternoons with Baedeker.

In 1935 Hitler said / "The Third Reich." Distances. Otto René Castillo. AF, tr. by Margaret Randall

In 1939 the skylark had nothing to say to me. Ninth of July, The. John Hollander. CoAP

In 1937, Robert Johnson. Man Who Beat Hemingway, The. Martín Espada. MoASP

In 1936. Reforma Agraria. Ian Duhig. ModIr

In nineteen years, we have parted, and met. To Hsiao Shih-ying. Hsieh Chin. CoBLCP, tr. by Jonathan Chaves

In no country. No Offence. Dennis Joseph Enright. OxBTC

In No Strange Land. Francis Thompson. See Kingdom of God, The

In no wise is the pillar-of-fire. "H. D." WPoS Fr. Walls Do Not Fall, The.

In North Great George's Street. "Seumas O'Sullivan." BIrV

In North Ward they do many strange dances. Juan Chi. CoBCP Fr. Singing of Thoughts.

In northern climes there liv'd a chief of fame. Otagamiad. Jane Johnston Schoolcraft. SWaP

In Norway land there lived a maid. Grey Selchie of Sule Skerry, The. *Unknown.* OxBB

In Nottamun Town not a soul would look up. Nottamun Town. *Unknown.* OxBoLi

In Nottingham there lives a jolly tanner. Robin Hood and the Tanner. *Unknown.* ESPB

In November: "Hills and leafless forests slowly yield, The." Archibald Lampman. NIL-7

In November, in the days to remember the dead. St. Malachy. Thomas Merton. VGW

In November: "With loitering step and quiet eye." Archibald Lampman. NOBC

In No. 64 Von Tempsky has his picture up. Von Tempsky's Dance. Murray Edmond. PeNZ

In number, weight, and measure, needs not rhyme [*or* rhime]. (LL) On Mr Milton's "Paradise Lost." Andrew Marvell. BASC; CABP; FSCP; NOSC

In Numbers, and but these few. Ode on the Birth of Our Saviour, An. Robert Herrick. ChrPo

In Nunhead Cemetery. Charlotte Mew. FaBoWP; NoP-4

In o'er-strict calyx lingering. To Beethoven. Sidney Lanier. NCAP

In Obitum Ben. Jons. Mildmay Fane, 2d Earl of Westmorland. OxBSP (In Obitum Ben Johnson Poetae Eximii.) NOSC (On Ben Jonson.) BeJo

In October. Claire Malroux. VCWP, *tr. by* Marilyn Hacker

In October marching, taking the sweet air. Towards Lillers. Ivor Gurney. NAEL-5v2; NAEL-6v2; NoP-4

In October of the year. Ox Cart Man. Donald Hall. LCAP-2; LoL

In Ohio. James Wright (1927–80). NNaP

In Ojinaga-across-the-river. West Texas Rain Journal. Candice Favilla. ExTi

In Oklahoma / Bonnie and Josie. Life Is Motion. Wallace Stevens. SAmP

In old age / I'm back. Pond in a Bowl, The. Han Yü. SuSp, *tr. by* Kenneth O. Hanson

In old Barcelona I met sweet Romona. I Wonder Why She Kept on Saying "Si-Si-Si-Si-Senor." Sam M. Lewis. ReLy

In old days those who went to fight. Hearing That His Friend Was Coming Back from the War. Wang Chien. ChiP, *tr. by* Arthur Waley

In old Minako Wada's house. In Minako Wada's House. Brad Leithauser. NoP-4

In old Savannah. Hard-Hearted Hannah (The Vamp of Savannah). Milton Ager. ReLy

In old stories the jungle was busy. Sun-Hunters, The. Mark O'Connor. NOBAu

In olden times we oft have heard. Natal Hunters, The. Allen F. Gardiner. PeSAV

In One Battle. Imamu Amiri Baraka. BPo

In one corner. George Swede. HA

In 100% surefire arsenic. Shake'nbake Ballad. Peter Van Toorn. NOBC

In one late dart. Late Flight of The Love God. Mona Van Duyn. ExTi

In one night. Reply to Suzan Osho's Snow Poem. Muso Soseki. EaWin, *tr. by* W. S. Merwin

In one night fell to the dust. (LL) Li K'ai-hsien. CoBLCP; ColAnChi, *tr. by* Jonathan Chaves *Fr.* Earthquake.

In one of the three pots. Viaticum. Birago Diop. PBMAP

In one of those excursions (may they ne'er). William Wordsworth. NAEL-6v2 *Fr.* Prelude, The; Growth of a Poet's Mind [1850 vers.].

In one of your earlier letters, the one you wrote in response to Song of the. Song of the Andoumboulou: 6. Nathaniel Mackey. FTOS

In only thee, my timid, fleet gazelle. Timid Gazelle, The. Kasmuneh. TrJP

In Orangeburg My Brothers Did. Alfred B. Spellman. BPo

In order to blow what it's like being born. (LL) Lester Leaps In. Al Young. ESEAA; SeSe

In order to perfect all readers. Wall, Cave, and Pillar Statements, after Asôka. Alan Dugan. CoAP

In order to play one needs magic and Rousseau and must remember play. Magic (or Rousseau). Carla Harryman. FTOS

In order to reach you. Reencounter with the Goddess. Olga Nolla. TANSG, *tr. by* Paula Vega

In order to revitalize the roaring of phosphenes. In Order to Speak. Aimé Césaire. VCWP

In order to snuff out two candles. Addition to the Opposition. Aleksandr Yeryomenko [*or* Eremenko]. TCRP, *tr. by* Albert C. Todd

In Order to Speak. Aimé Césaire. VCWP

In Orknay. William Fowler. OxBS (Sonet. In Orknay.) NePenScot

In other arms. (LL) Meleager. BoLoP; GrAn; WoPoe, *tr. by* Peter Whigham

In other days. (LL) Fare Well. Walter De la Mare. GTBS-P; NOBE; NoP-4; OBEV; OxBEV

In other days, I was poor enough to suit. Cold Mountain Poem No. 158. Hanshan. WoPoe, *tr. by* E. Bruce Brooks

In our backyard. Laughing Tomatoes. Francisco Alarcon. OxIBACP

In our backyard, the agama. Mr. Agama. Tijan M. Sallah. NAfrP

In our community everything was kept quiet. Kiss in the Dark, A. Thomas Sayers Ellis. GT

In our content, before the autumn came. Elinor Wylie. NAAL-2v2; NALW *Fr.* One Person.

In our family goodness is a guest. Humans. Attila József. IQMS, *tr. by* Vernon Watkins

In our hands is a fresh yearning for you. Prayer to the New Year, A. Fadwa Tuqan [or Tuquan]. PoArWo, *tr. by* Samira Kawar

In our kitchen. Truth About Karen, The. Kenneth Carroll. ISC

In our midst, on a wooden stick. Tricks. Daniil Kharms. TCRP, *tr. by* Bradley Jordan

In our monotonous sublime. (LL) Waking Early Sunday Morning. Robert Lowell. FaBoMo; HCAP; HarvBoo; NOBA; OxBC; VCAP

In our old shipwrecked days there was an hour. George Meredith. BoLoP; NAEL-6v2; NOBVV *Fr.* Modern Love.

In our place. Relief. Charles Vildrac. PeFWW, *tr. by* Christopher Middleton

In our souls everything. Antonio Machado Ruiz. EnlH

In Our Tenth Year. Simon Armitage. OxBSo

In our time men die before they are dead. Ferry of Lead, The. Iwan [*or* Yvan] Goll. WoPoe, *tr. by* Galway Kinnell

In our town, people live in rows. Fired Pot, The. Anna Wickham. FaBoTw; FaBoWP; LW; NPeEn; OxBTC

In our very own little civil war. Brendan Kennelly. ModIr *Fr.* Cromwell.

In our world it's unusual. Nikolay Novikov. TCRusP, *tr. by* Daniel Weissbort *Fr.* Stone and Sky.

In Oxford there lived a merchant by trade. Crafty Farmer, The. *Unknown.* ESPB

In pain, in poverty, at night. Relentlessly Lovelorn, the Non-Sleeper Whispers and Re-Whispers a Magic Charm Against His Wound's Roar. Stephen Margulies. AWTN

In pain she bore the son who her embrace. Elegy. Moses Ibn Ezra. TrJP, *tr. by* Solomon Solis-Cohen

In painting bamboo, the spirit must be transmitted. Painting of Bamboo by Ni Yün-lin, A. Yang Chi. CoBLCP, *tr. by* Jonathan Chaves

In pairs / as if to illustrate their sisterhood. For the Sisters of the Hôtel Dieu. Abraham Moses Klein. NoP-4

In pale moonlight. Buson. SoOfWa, *tr. by* Sam Hamill

In Parenthesis. David Jones.
"And the deepened stillness as a calm, cast over us." NPeEn
"And the place of their waiting a long burrow." FaBoMo
"And to Private Ball it came as if a rigid beam of great weight." OBWVE
"But sweet sister death has gone debauched today and stalks." NPeEn; OBWP; OxAEP-2; PeFWW
"But why is Father Larkin talking to the dead?" PoE
"Every one of these, stood, separate, upright, above ground." PeECV
Five Unmistakable Marks, The.
"Across upon this undulated board of verdure chequered bright." NoAM
"Gentle slopes are green to remind you, The." NAEL-5v2; NAEL-6v2
King Pellam's Launde.
"So thus he sorrowed till it was day." NoAM
Private John Ball Wounded in the Wood. TCAWP
"This Dai adjusts his slipping shoulder-straps." AngWePo
"You can hear the silence of it." FaBoMo; FaBoWar

In Paris, at the Opera. Arthur Hugh Clough. PeLV *Fr.* Dipsychus [and the Spirit].

In Paris the tower of Saint-Jacques swaying. Vigilance. André Breton. NAWM-7v2; SurPaPo, *tr. by* Jean-Pierre Cauvin and Mary Ann Caws

In Paris with You. James Fenton. NoP-4

In paschall feast, the end of a[u]ncient rite. Of the Blessed Sacrament of the Altar [*or* Aulter]. Robert Southwell. OBEV

In passing with my mind. Right of Way, The. William Carlos Williams. APT-1

In passion-lighted silence, 'tranced and sweet. (LL) Speechless: Upon the Marriage of Two Deaf and Dumb Persons. Philip Bourke Marston. EBVV; OxBSo

In Paths Untrodden. Walt Whitman. APN-1; CAGL; NOBA; OxBA; TCAPo

In peace. Louis Zukofsky. APT-2 *Fr.* A.

In peace, and reck'ns thee her eldest son. (LL) To Sir Henry Vane the Younger. John Milton. PBRV; Son

In peace the aleph. Aleph Poem. Jerome Rothenberg. FTOS

In Peblis town sum tyme, as I heard tell. John, of Stobo Reid. OxBS *Fr.* Thre Prestis of Peblis, The.

In Père La Chaise. Joaquin Miller. APN-2

In Pereira and Armenia rescue workers use listening devices. After the Colombian Earthquake. Maurice Kilwein Guevara. NAPBL

In Perspective. Robert Graves. OxBSP
In Peru, the Quechuans Have a Thousand Words for Potato. Ray Gonzalez. SpudSo
In Peterborough Churchyard. Paulus [or Paulos] Silentiarius. FaBoEE; NOBL
In Petrograd. Yury [or Iurii] Mikhailovich Kublanovsky [or Kublanovskii]. "Armor of the Petrograd oak is rusty, but, The." TCRusP
In Piam Memoriam. Geoffrey Hill. OxBC
In Pilgrim Life Our Rest. Edwin Sandys. AH; ChIV-1
In Pinter's new play that's now running. Limerick. Frank Richards. PeLi
In pinup ruffles now she flaunts. Mundus Muliebris. Mary Evelyn. NOSC
In pious times ere [or e'r] priest-craft did begin. Dryden. BASC; FHYEP; HAP; MakPoe; NAEL-5v1; NAEL-6v1; NAEL-7v1; NOSC; PoE Fr. Absalom and Achitophel.
In Piranesi's rarer prints. Herman Melville. TCAPo Fr. Clarel: A Poem and Pilgrimage in the Holy Land.
In pity for my pain. (LL) Gary Snyder. GeoHom; NOBA Fr. Myths and Texts.
In placid hours well-pleased we dream. Art. Herman Melville. AmFaPo; APN-2; ColAP; NAAL-2v1; NAAL-3; NCAP; NOBA
In Plague Time. Thomas Nashe [or Nash]. See Summer's Last Will and Testament
In plazas calcined pure white, bulls charge. Interludes. Fabio Doplicher. NeIt, tr. by Stephen Sartarelli
In Pleasant Lands Have Fallen the Lines. James Flint. AH
In poems free and helpless and unjust. (LL) Cottage Street, 1953. Richard Wilbur. BodElec; FaBoMo; HCAP; PoPoPo
In Pompano Beach, Florida. Robin Becker. PBCAP
In Port Talbot. John Davies. TCAWP
In Portugal, 1912. Alice Thompson Meynell. NOCV
In Portuguese. Adelia Prado. TCLAP, tr. by Marcia Kirinus
In Prague, or perhaps Budapest. Statues. Lisel Mueller. ExTi
In Prais of Wemen. William Dunbar. NoP-4
In Praise of a Contented Mind. Sir Edward Dyer. See My Mind to Me a Kingdom Is
In Praise of a Girl. Huw Morus. OBWVE, tr. by Gwyn Williams
In Praise of a Gold and Silver Painted Scene of the Buddha Manifestation in the Pure Land of the West, with a Preface. Li Po. WoPoe, tr. by Elling O. Eide
In Praise of a Sword Given Him by His Prince. Colman mac Lenini. WoPoe, tr. by Richard O'Connell
In Praise of Austria. Franz Grillparzer. AuPH, tr. by Lowell A. Bangerter
In Praise of California Wines. Yvor Winters. APT-2
In Praise of Carnations. Wang Chi. SuSp, tr. by Hellmut Wilhelm
In Praise of Ching K'o. Ch'ien T'ao. ColAnChi, tr. by J. R. Hightower
In Praise of Cocoa, Cupid's Nightcap. Stanley J. Sharpless. NBLV; PeLV
In Praise of Coldness. Jane Hirshfield. BAP-01
In Praise of Creation. Elizabeth Jennings. PAI
In Praise of Drainage. Anne Wilson. ECWP Fr. Teisa, a Descriptive Poem of the River Tees, Its Towns and Antiquities.
In Praise of Fidelia. Mildmay Fane, 2d Earl of Westmorland. BeJo; NOSC; OxBSP
In Praise of His Mistress. Thomas Carew. BASC
In Praise of Hope. Abraham Cowley. OxAEP-1
In Praise of Ivy. Unknown. MiEL
In Praise of Krishna. Ruskhan. WoPoe, tr. by Stephen Schaffer and Allen Shapiro
In Praise of Laudanum. William Harrison. NOEC
In Praise of Limestone. W. H. Auden. HAP; HarvBoo; NAEL-5v2; NAEL-6v2; NoAM; NoP-4
In Praise of My Sister. Wislawa Szymborska. PoSu
(My sister does not write poems.) BLT
In Praise of Old Women. Marya Fiamengo. WPOW
In Praise of Owain Gwynedd. Cynddelw Brydydd Mawr. OBWVE, tr. by Joseph P. Clancy
In Praise of Poor Scholars. T'ao Ch'ien [or T'ao Yuan-ming]. SuSp, tr. by Eugene Eoyang
In Praise of Rain. Tu Fu. CrYelRi, tr. by Sam Hamill
In Praise of Self-Deprecation. Wislawa Szymborska. BLT
In Praise of Tenby. Unknown. OBWVE, tr. by Joseph P. Clancy
In Praise of the Body. Anna Hajnal. IQMS, tr. by Kenneth McRobbie
In Praise of the Potato. David Williams. SpudSo
In Praise of the Sun. "A. W." CTC
In Praise of Three Young Men. Lochlann Og O Dalaigh. NOIV
In Praise of War. Bertrans [or Bertran or Bertrand] de Born. NAWM-7v1, tr. by Frederick Goldin
In Praise of Wine. Unknown. MLL, tr. by Helen Waddell
In Praise of Wisdom. Solomon ibn Gabirol. TrJP, tr. by Solomon Solis-Cohen
In Praise of Women. William Dunbar. CABP

In Praise of Women in General. Thomas Randolph. NOSC
In Praise of Zigzags. Jane O. Wayne. InvLad
In print you told the world, the first imprint. Kinda Blue Miles Davis Died Today. Everett Hoagland. BodElec
In Prison. William Morris. FaBoWar; PeVV
In Prison. Michael Smith. PWR
In prison cell I sadly sit—. Last Rhyme and Testament of Tony Lumpkin. Harry Morant. FaBoWar
In prison joys, fettered [or fetter'd] with chains of gold. (LL) Courtier's Life, The. Sir Thomas Wyatt. FaBoEE; NoSic
In prison you put on your clothes. Rehabilitative Report: We Can Still Laugh. Daniel Berrigan. AF
In Procession. Robert Graves. TwCP
In program notes. Program Notes. Ruth Roston. MiVo
In Progress. Christina Georgina Rossetti. BoWoP; NAEL-5v2; NAEL-6v2; WPE
In Protest. Li Ho. SuSp, tr. by Maureen Robertson
In purest song one plays the constant fool. Infirmity. Theodore Roethke. CoAP; NAAL-2v2
In Pusseyville, where pussies live. Cats and Dogs. Howard Moss. OBAL
In Queen St., Cardiff, I halt to watch in a choice. Living in Real Times. Duncan Bush. TCAWP
In Queen Victoria's early days. New Vicar of Bray, The. Colin Ellis. NOBL
In raging winds the crows' cries continue without end. Following the Rhymes of Wang An-shih's Poem "Inscribed on the Wall of the Temple of Western Great Unity." Huang T'ing-chien. SuSp, tr. by Michael E. Workman
In Railway Halls. Stephen Spender. FaBoMo
In rain, two hundred runners streaming. Marathon. John Powell Ward. TCAWP
In Re Conferences. Vladimir Vladimirovich Mayakovsky [or Maiakovskii]. TCRP, tr. by Albert C. Todd
In re Solomon Warshawer. Abraham Moses Klein. MoCV
In reality the barn wasn't clean, ninety men. Trakl. Norman Dubie. BodElec
In Recompense. Eda Lou Walton. LW
In rectangular vertigo the balepress. Making Hay. Philip Hodgins. NOBAu
In red wool jacket and earflaps. Week-End Indian, The. Anita Endrezze. VoR
In Reference to Her Children, 23 June, 1659 [or 1659]. Anne Bradstreet. BoWoP; NAAL-3; TAP
In Remembrance of the Forgotten. "Lu Hsün." SuSp, tr. by William R. Schultz
In Reply to Questions. T'ai-shang. CoBCP, tr. by Burton Watson
In Reply When Lesser Officials of Chung-tu Brought a Pot of Wine and Two Fish to My Inn as Gifts. Li Po. CoBCP, tr. by Burton Watson
In Residence: A Worst Case View. Sean O'Brien. OBCoV
In respect of riches, then, just or unjust. Unrighteous Mammon (Luke 16:9). Ernesto Cardenal. GI, tr. by Robert Pring-Mill
In Respect of the Elderly. Thomas Love Peacock. VoR
In Response to a Rumor that the Oldest Whorehouse in Wheeling, West Virginia, Has Been Condemned. James Wright (1927–80). CoAP; NNaP; NoAM; VCAP
In restaurants we argue. They Eat Out. Margaret Atwood. NoAM
In resurrection, there is confusion. "H. D." APT-1 Fr. Flowering of the Rod, The.
In Retrospect. Richard Kenney. Son Fr. Hours of the Day, The.
In Reverie. Harriet McEwen Kimball. TreFP
In rice fields of Ch'ang-ku, by the fifth month. Ch'ang-ku. Li Ho. SuSp, tr. by Maureen Robertson
In roaring he shall rise and on the surface die. (LL) Kraken, The. Tennyson. NAEL-5v2; NAEL-6v2; NoP-4; PeECV; TOF
In Rome, on Campo dei Fiori. Campo dei Fiori. Czeslaw Milosz. HP
In Romney Marsh. John Davidson. EBVV; OxBTC
In rosy-fingered dawn they go. Jersey Cattle. Ralph Nixon Currey. OxBTC
In rosy morn I saw Aurora red. Shortness of Life. Thomas Fairfax, Baron Fairfax of Cameron. NOSC
In Rough Weather. Paul Lake. RA
In royal Anna's golden days. Given to a Lady Who Asked Me to Write a Poem. Janet Little. ECWP
In Ruin Reconciled. Aubrey Thomas De Vere. BIrV
In ruling well what guerdon? Life runs low. Two Old Kings, The. John Byrne Leicester Warren, 3d Baron De Tabley. OBEV
In run-out ground in coveys. Fringed Gentians. Abbie Huston Evans. APT-1
In Russia fear is dying now. Fear (Extracts). Yevgeny Aleksandrovich Yevtushenko [or Evtushenko]. RusPo, tr. by Robert Arthur Douglas Ford
In Saba, as by one consent. Herman Melville. APN-2 Fr. Clarel: A Poem and Pilgrimage in the Holy Land.
In Sabbath quiet, a street. Grace-Note, The. Denise Levertov. CoAmPo
In sable clad, Urania come, Ode on the Passion. Thomas Warton, the Elder. ChIV-2

In sad and ashy weeds.   Good Shepherd's Sorrow for the Death of His Beloved Son, The.   Anne, Duchess of Arundel Howard.   NOSC

In Saginaw, in Saginaw.   Saginaw Song, The.   Theodore Roethke.   NBLV; RB

In Salem.   Lucille Clifton.   ESEAA; PAI

In Salem Dwelt a Glorious King.   Thomas Traherne.   ChIV-1

In Salem seasick spindrift charis or skips.   Salem.   Robert Lowell.   AiP; Son

In sand.   Poem.   Chimalum Nwankwo.   NAfrP

In Santa Maria del Popolo.   Thom Gunn.   FaBoMo; GTBS-P; HarvBoo; NPeEn; OxBC; PoE

In Santiago.   Félix Lope de Vega Carpio.   WoPoe, *tr.* by W. S. Merwin

In Santiago the green.   In Santiago.   Félix Lope de Vega Carpio.   WoPoe, *tr.* by W. S. Merwin

In Saram.   John Cotton.   SCAP

In Saturn's reign, at Nature's early birth.   Juvenal.   NPeEn; OBSV; OBVE; OxBEV, *tr.* by John Dryden   *Fr.* Satires.

In Scarlet town, where I was born [*or* bound].   Barbara Allen.   *Unknown.* EBNV

In scenes paternal, not beheld through years.   Anna Seward.   NOEC   *Fr.* Eyam.

In schomer, when the leves spryng.   Robin Hood and the Potter.   *Unknown.* ESPB

In School.   Dennis Cooper.   ReTh; WiU   *Fr.* Some Adventures of John Kennedy Jr.

In School-Days.   John Greenleaf Whittier.   OBCA

In School House.   Henry Cuyler Bunner.
    Real Romance, A.   VerBaPo

In school I was taught the names.   Columbus Day.   Jimmie Durham.   HATNAP; LTA

In science today we learned.   Stars.   Nikki Giovanni.   KaS

In Scotland there was a babie born.   Hind Horn.   *Unknown.* ESPB

In Scotland town where I was borned.   Hind Horn.   *Unknown.* ESPB

In sea-cold Lyonesse.   Sunk Lyonesse.   Walter De la Mare.   FaBoCh

In sealed box cars travel.   Still.   Wislawa Szymborska.   AF, *tr.* by Robert A. Maguire

In Search of Aunt Jemima.   Crystal Williams.   AmPoNex

In Search of Solitude.   Chao Yi.   SuSp, *tr.* by Chang Yin-nan

In Search of the Traitor.   Max Jacob.   AF, *tr.* by Michael Brownstein

In search of treasure near the Pyramids.   Stanzas in Bloomsbury.   Richard Howard.   MakPoe

In search of wisdom, far from wit I fly.   Wit and Wisdom.   Ambrose Philips.   OxAEP-1

In Search of Yacove Eved.   Fawaz Turki.   GraLe

In Season.   Lisa Suhair Majaj.   PoArWo

In seasonal rain.   Buson.   SoOfWa, *tr.* by Sam Hamill

In Seclusion.   Tu Fu.   CrYelRi, *tr.* by Sam Hamill

In secreit place, this hyndir [*or* hindir] nycht [*or* nicht].   Man of Valour to His Fair Lady, The.   William Dunbar.   MiEL

In secret, Lois Lane wore coins and jewels.   No, Superman Was Not the Only One.   Katharyn Howd Machan.   ReTh

In secret place where once I stood.   Flesh and the Spirit, The.   Anne Bradstreet.   BASC; ChIV-2; NAAL-2v1; NAAL-3; NOBA; OxBA; OxWW; SCAP; TAP

In secret sorrow, and sad pensiveness. (LL)   Edmund Spenser.   NAEL-5v1; PoE   *Fr.* Amoretti.

In September.   John Ormond.   TCAWP

In September 1939.   Bernard Gutteridge.   PoWW

In September, at falling of the leaf.   The Lady of the Assembly.   OBGa   *Fr.* Assembly of Ladies, The.

In serving, serve.   Jinzu.   ZenPo, *tr.* by Takashi Ikemoto and Lucien Stryk

In seventeen hundred and forty-four.   Kilruddery Hunt, The.   Thomas Mozeen.   BIrV

In seventh grade Larry Saclarides had a gym locker next to mine, and dark skin, and dark hair.   Corporeal.   Robert Ayres.   OPRER

In Shadow.   Hart Crane.   NOBA

In shadows of this willow rests.   Epitaph.   Marie von Ebner-Eschenbach.   AuPH, *tr.* by Lowell A. Bangerter

In *Shall We Dance*, the thirties musical.   Shall We Dance.   Joe Osterhaus.   NAPBL

In shantung suits we whites are cool.   Devil-Dancers, The.   William Plomer.   PeSAV

In Shanty Malone's, hot night one day after.   September 5.   Robert Peterson.   GeoHom

In shaping the snow into blossoms.   "Ping Hsin."   BoWoP; WPOW   *Fr.* Spring Waters.

In Shards the Sylvan Vases Lie.   Herman Melville.   *See* Ravaged Villa, The

In short, my deary, kiss me, and be quiet. (LL)   Summary of Lord Lyttleton's 'Advice to a Lady,' A.   Lady Mary Wortley Montagu.   FaBoEE; OxBEV

In Siberia's wastes.   Siberia.   James Clarence Mangan.   BIrV; NOBVV; NOIV; NPeEn

In Sickness.   Jonathan Swift.   NOEC
    (In Sickness. Written Soon after the Author's Coming to Live in Ireland, upon the Queen's Death, October 1714.)   CABP

In signe of favor stedfast still.   To His Darrest Freind.   John Steward of Baldynneis [*or* Stewart of Baldynnis].   OxBS

In silence / The overloaded canoe leaves our shores.   Exile.   Mbella Sonne Dipoko.   PBMAP

In silent night when rest I took.   Here Follows Some Verses upon the Burning of Our House [July 10th, 1666. Copied Out of a Loose Paper].   Anne Bradstreet.   AiP; BASC; BoWoP; ColAP; EMWP; MakPoe; NAAL-2v1; NAAL-3; NAAL-5; NALW; NOBA; NOSC; NoP-4; OxBA; PEW; SCAP; SacPr; TAP; TCAPo; WPE

In simmer, whan aa sorts foregether.   Embro to the Ploy.   Robert Garioch.   OxBS

In Singapore, in the airport.   Singapore.   Mary Oliver.   NIL-7

In sixth grade Mrs. Walker.   Persimmons.   Li-Young Lee.   NAAL-5; NIL-7; NIP-4; NoP-4; OPRER

In Sleep.   Alice Thompson Meynell.   BrRo

In sleep a King, but waking no such matter. (LL)   William Shakespeare.   CAGL; EBEV; GTBS-P; NAEL-5v1; NAEL-6v1; NOBE; NoSic; OBEV; OxAEP-1; Son; TFi   *Fr.* Sonnets.

In sleep I saw my mother scrubbing stairs.   Mother.   Daphne Rock.   Prnts

In sleep when an old man's body is no longer aware of its boundaries.   Journey through the Moonlight, A.   Russell Edson.   LCAP-2

In Slumber Late.   *Unknown.*   SacPr

In small backyards old men's long underwear.   Patricians, The.   Douglas Dunn.   OxBC

In Snow.   William Allingham.   OxBSo

In sober mornings, do[e] not thou rehe[a]rse.   When He Would Have His Verses Read.   Robert Herrick.   BASC; BeJo; CaPo; CavPo; NOBE; NOSC; SCGP

In soft hanging coils, she embroiders her hair.   Tune: "Southern Song, A."   Wen T'ing-yün.   SuSp, *tr.* by William R. Schultz

In solitude, for company. (LL)   W. H. Auden.   BBASP; TrCP   *Fr.* Horae Canonicae.

In solitude. Without a hand to hold. (LL)   Gwendolyn Brooks.   InvLi; NAAAL   *Fr.* Street in Bronzeville, A.

In somber eyes no tears of grieving.   Silesian Weavers, The.   Heinrich Heine.   NAWM-7v2, *tr.* by Hal Draper

In some cool room in college after.   We Could Have Met.   Lee Cataldi.   BMAP

In some location.   Inventing Fables about the Stone.   Julia Galemire.   MirDau, *tr.* by Roberta Gordenstein

In some of the stores they sell a cheese rinse.   Operators Are Standing By.   John Ashbery.   BodElec

In Some Seer's Cloud Car.   Christopher Middleton.   TwCP

In some small town, one indifferent summer. (LL)   Syringa.   John Ashbery.   APSN; HCAP; NoAM; VCAP

In some unused lagoon, some nameless bay.   Dismantled Ship, The.   Walt Whitman.   OxBA; TCAPo

In Some Way or Other the Lord Will Provide.   Mrs. M. A. W Cook.   AH

In somer when the shawes be sheyne.   May in the Green-Wood.   *Unknown.* OBEV

In somer, when the shawes be sheyne.   Robin Hood and the Monk.   *Unknown.* ESPB; OBNV

In something you have written in school, you say.   Robert Pinsky.   ColAP   *Fr.* Explanation of America, An.

In songs of triumph, to proclaim him mine! (LL)   Phaon Awakes.   Mary Robinson.   CenSon; RWP

In sooth, I know not why I am so sad.   William Shakespeare.   OxAEP-1   *Fr.* Merchant of Venice, The.

In sorrow deepe, I wake, I sleepe with griefe my Hart opprest.   Dittie to the Same Subject, A.   Dame Gertrude More.   EMWP

In Soto's bosom you may find.   Soto, a Character.   Mary Leapor.   ECWP

In South Oregon the Klamath play.   Woyi, The.   Lew Blockcolski.   VoR

In Spanish he whispers there is no time left.   Visitor, The.   Carolyn Forché.   OPOU

In Spanish potato is papa.   La Papa.   Rudolfo Anaya.   SpudSo

In Spanishburg there are boys in tight jeans.   Spitting in the Leaves.   Maggie Anderson.   PBCAP

In Sparkhill buried lies that man of mark.   Local Note.   Arthur Guiterman.   NBLV

In Spayn.   Sir Thomas Wyatt.   NoSic; OPOU; SCGP
    (Tagus fare well that westward with thy strems.)   PBRV

In Spite.   Rufinus.   GrAn, *tr.* by Alan Marshfield

In spite of all.   Her Body Is Private.   Eleanor Wilner.   ExTi

In spite of all the learned have said.   Indian Burying Ground, The.   Philip Freneau.   ColAP; HAP; NAAL-2v1; NAAL-3; NOBA; NoP-4; OxBA; TAP; TCAPo; TFi

In spite of ice, in spite of snow. On Observing a Large Red-Streak Apple. Philip Freneau. NAAL-2v1; NAAL-3

In spite of thee, and by firm faith deserve her. (LL) Thomas Lodge. NoSic; Son *Fr.* Phyllis.

In splintering shallows at the local pool. Swimming Pool Ghost, The. Gillian Ferguson. MFPA

In spotted globes, that have resembled all. Greatness in Little. Richard Leigh. NOSC

In Spring. Ibycus. SaLy, *tr.* by Diane Rayor and Diane J. Rayor

In spring, I dream through dawn. Spring Dreams. Meng Hao Jan. CrYelRi, *tr.* by Sam Hamill

In Spring I look gay. *Unknown.* OxNR

In spring if there are dogs they will bark. Ballade of Sayings. W. S. Merwin. NNaP

In Spring of the Year *Ping-shen*. Ch'ien Ch'ien-i [*or* Ch'ien Ch'ien-yi]. "Pavilions of dance, terraces of song." CoBLCP

"Willow catkins beyond the garden wait for evening tides." CoBLCP

In spring of youth it was my lot. Lake: To———, The. Edgar Allan Poe. APN-1

In spring rain. Issa. EH, *tr.* by Robert Hass

In Spring We Gather Mulberry Leaves. *Unknown.* OHMPC, *tr.* by Kenneth Rexroth

In springtime the violets. Springtime. Nikki Giovanni. TLR

In springtime, when the gardens new are waking. Maidens in Spring. Herbert Strutz. AuPH, *tr.* by Lowell A. Bangerter

In stained barn drenched. Paysagesque. Norman Henry Pritchard, II. GT

In State. Forceythe Willson. APN-2

In steel clouds. Charles Reznikoff. WoPoe

In still transparency, the water pools. Waterfall. Greg Williamson. RA

In stillness, I. Hamon. JDP, *tr.* by Yoel Hoffmann

In stone settlements when the moon is stone. Peter Levi. EBEV; TOF

In Stratis Viarum IV. Arthur Hugh Clough. EBEV

In streets east, streets west, they expound the Buddhist canon. Girl of Mount Hua, The. Han Yü. CoBCP; ColAnChi, *tr.* by Burton Watson

In strenuous hope I wrought. Vesica Piscis. Coventry Patmore. SacPr

In Styria, 'tis the glorious time. Late Autumn in Styria. Hans Kloepfer. AuPH, *tr.* by Lowell A. Bangerter

In subsequent waves. Sleeplessness. Luigi Fontanella. NeIt, *tr.* by W. S. Di Piero

In such a fix to be so fertile. (LL) Ogden Nash. NoP-4; OBAL; SoSe-8; TAP

In such a night, when every louder wind. Nocturnal Reverie, A. Anne Finch, Countess of Winchilsea. BWW; EBEV; ECEV; ECWP; NAEL-5v1; NAEL-6v1; NAEL-7v1; NALW; NOEC; NoP-4; OxAEP-1; OxBEV; PoE; WPE

In sudden flare / Of the mosquito wick. Buson. ZenPo, *tr.* by Takashi Ikemoto and Lucien Stryk

In suits bright as birthday balloons. Learning to Swim. Arlene Naganawa. FSt

In sullen Humour one Day Jove. Mercury and Cupid. Matthew Prior. PeLV

In summer. Lesbian Corn. Elaine Equi. IllVoic

In summer elms are made for me. Dilemma of the Elm. Genevieve Taggard. MoAmPo

In Summer, in the open air. Summer Sabbath. Jessie E. Sampter. TrJP

In summer, like the theaters, I close up. Valerio Magrelli. NeIt

In summer's heat[e] and mid-time of the day. Ovid. BoLoP; CABP; EBEV; NPeEn; NoSic; OBVE; OxAEP-1; OxBEV, *tr.* by Christopher Marlowe *Fr.* Elegies.

In summer's mellow midnight. Emily Jane Brontë. *See* Night Wind, The

In summer the Jews of my childhood sit on chairs. Rue de Rosiers: To My Brother Fred. Liliane Richman. TWW

In summer-time, when all the sky was blue. Song Out of Season, A. May Probyn. VWP

In summer time, when leaves grew green and birds were singing. King Edward the Fourth and a Tanner of Tamworth. *Unknown.* ESPB

In summer time, when leaves grow green and flowers are fresh and gay. Robin Hood and the Curtal Friar. *Unknown.* ESPB

In summer time, when leaves grow green / Down a down a down. Robin Hood and the Tinker. *Unknown.* ESPB

In summer time, when leaves grow green, when they doe grow both green and long. Noble Fisherman; or, Robin Hood's Preferment, The. *Unknown.* ESPB

In summer, when the days were long. Summer Days. Wathen Mark Wilks Call. EBVV

In summertime it was a paradise. Seaside: In and Out of the Season, The. Charles Tennyson Turner. Son

In summertime on Bredon. Bredon Hill. A. E. Housman. EBVV; MoBrPo; NAEL-5v2; NAEL-6v2; OxAEP-2; SoSe-8; UV

In sun or cold the weather picks scarecrow bones clean. Long Blues, The. Calvin C. Hernton. GT

In sunburnt parks where Sundays lie. Cobb Would Have Caught It. Robert Fitzgerald. HAP; TwCP

In superstitious panic. "Nikolai Nikolaevich Morshen." TCRusP, *tr.* by John Glad

In Syros' harbor abandoned merchant ships lay idle. Syros. Tomas Tranströmer. BLT, *tr.* by Leif Sjöberg and May Swenson

In Szetejnie. Czeslaw Milosz. BodElec, *tr.* by Robert Hass

In t' other hundred, o'er yon swarthy moor. Country Curate, The. Henry Taylor. NOEC

In Tagalog Ibon Means Bird. Nick Carbó. AmPoNex

In Teesdale. Andrew Young. OxBSP

In Temptation. Charles Wesley. NOEC

(Jesu, Lover of my Soul.) SacPr

In ten thousand pine trees. Painting of People Strolling through a Pine Forest, A. Hsü Wei. CoBLCP, *tr.* by Jonathan Chaves

In ten years, not once have these colours shown. Queen's Tears. Tony Curtis. TCAWP

In tender May when the sweet laugh of Christ. Puritan, The. Karl Shapiro. MoAmPo

In Tenebris. Thomas Hardy. NOBE

"When the clouds' swoln bosoms echo back the shouts of the many and strong." ChIV-1; NoAM; OxBTC

In Teos and in Samos. Anacreon. Friedrich von Hagedorn. GePo, *tr.* by George C. Schoolfield

In Terezin i the so-called park. Yes, That's the Way Things Are. Miroslav Košek. INSAB

In Thai Binh (Peace) Province. Denise Levertov. AF

In that ago when being was believing. History of Truth, The. W. H. Auden. FaBoMo

In that ancient time—in eternity. Words Spoken by Pasternak during a Bombing. Bella [*or* Izabella] Akhatovna Akhmadulina. BoWoP, *tr.* by Olga Carlisle and Jean Valentine

In that building, long and low. Ropewalk, The. Henry Wadsworth Longfellow. NCAP

In That Corner Where We Slept Together. César Vallejo. WoPoe, *tr.* by Willis Barnstone and Tony Barnstone

In that corner where we slept together. César Vallejo. BLPSL, *tr.* by Rene de Costa, Rigas Kappatos and Eleni Paidoussi

In that country the animals. Animals in That Country, The. Margaret Atwood. NALW; NoAM

In that denoted city of the dead. (LL) Robert Louis Stevenson. NePenScot; PeVV

In that empty house. Clement Hoyt. HA

In that great day / People, in that great day. Judgment Day, The. James Weldon Johnson. APT-1; ChIV-2

In that great day when God's a-going to rain down fire? (LL) Judgment Day, The. James Weldon Johnson. APT-1; ChIV-2

In that hotel my life. Illumination, The. Stanley Kunitz. TAP

In that I have so greatly failed thee, Lord. So Little and So Much. John Oxenham. SacPr

In that I loved you, Love, I worshipped you. To Eros. Wilfred Owen. CAGL

In that instant. Image from Beckett, An. Derek Mahon. ModIr; NPeEn

In that it falls her sacrifice. (LL) Sonnet: "Tell me[e] no more how fair[e] she[e] is." Henry King, Bishop of Chichester. EnLoPo; MeLP; OxBEV

In that land all is and nothing's ought. Neither Here nor There. William Robert Rodgers. MoBrPo

In that land, in that land. Southern Paiute Poetry. *Unknown.* APN-2, *tr.* by John Wesley Powell

In that land we tried to speak. Siren. Anna Semionovna Prismanova. TCRP, *tr.* by Bradley Jordan

In that lightning flash. Clement Hoyt. HA

In that lost Caucasian garden. Naming of the Beasts, The. Francis Sparshott. NOBC

In That Moment When the Body Drowns. Mariella Bettarini. CItWP, *tr.* by Cinzia Sartini Blum and Lara Trubowitz

In that moment you sailed for all of death. Elegy for Your Absence. Eugenio Florit. TCLAP, *tr.* by Hoffman Reynolds Hays

In that novel you bought at the chain, a young woman looks back on her life. Fictions. William Kulik. BodElec

In that November off Tehuantepec. Sea Surface Full of Clouds. Wallace Stevens. APT-1; MoAmPo; VGW

In that, O Queen of queens, thy birth was free. To Our Blessed Lady. Henry Constable. NoSic

In That proud port, which her so goodly graceth. Edmund Spenser. Son *Fr.* Amoretti.

In that same gardin all the goodly flowres. Edmund Spenser. NOBE; NPeEn *Fr.* Faerie Queene, The.

In that shop which deals exclusively in forests sawn into. Wood merchant's parlour, The. Pierre McOrlan. MFP, *tr.* by Martin Sorrell

In that small dark fever of every reawakening. Patrizia Cavalli. ItPo, *tr.* by Gayle Ridinger

In that so sudden summer storm they tried. Summer Storm. Louis Simpson. OxBC; OxBSo

In that state I came return. (LL) Retreat[e], The. Henry Vaughan. AWP; BASC; CABP; ClHu; ESCV; FSCP; GTBS-P; GeHe; HAP; InPK-6; MeLP; NAEL-5v1; NAEL-6v1; NAEL-7v1; NIP-4; NOBE; NOCV; NOSC; NPeEn; NoP-4; OBEV; OBWVE; OxBEV; PBRV; PeECV; PoE; PoRA; SCGP; TFi; TOF

In that this happening. Louis Zukofsky. APT-2 *Fr.* 29 Songs.

In that town I was twenty. Snow there lay. Yunna Petrovna [or Iunna Pinkhusovna] Moritz [or Morits]. TCRP

In that world as it may be, newborn and haunted, what will solitude mean? (LL) Yom Kippur 1984. Adrienne Rich. GLP; NoAM; TaR

In he 50s, we drove each month to my uncle's house. Gambling. Vince Gotera. OpBC

In the Absence of Bliss. Maxine W. Kumin. NoAM; TaR

In the afternoon. (LL) Poem for the Insane, A. John Weiners. NeAP; PmAP; PoM

In the afternoon sun. Beams. Audre Lorde. ESEAA; NoAM

In the afternoon, while the wind. Views from the High Camp. W. S. Merwin. CoAmPo

In the Age of Postcapitalism. Lawrence Joseph. PBCAP

In the Aging City. Fadwa Tuqan [or Tuquan]. MAP, *tr.* by Patricia Alanah Byrne, Salma Khadra Jayyusi and Naomi Shihab Nye

In the air, in the empty air. (LL) War in the Air, The. Howard Nemerov. ColAP; DiPo; VCAP

In the air that limps between seashells. Hot Evening, A. Sa'di Yusuf. MAP, *tr.* by Lena Jayyusi and Naomi Shihab Nye

In the air to aggravate the truly menacing. (LL) Chez Jane. Frank O'Hara. CoAP; ColAP; NOBA; NeAP; NoAM; PoE

In the airconditioned drone. Monsoon Girl. Harry Clifton. BiHa; PBCIP

In the almond—what dwells in the almond? Mandorla. Paul Celan. PoSu, *tr.* by Michael Hamburger

In the Ambulance. Wilfrid Wilson Gibson. FaBoWar

In the America of the dream. Lonesome Dream, The. Lisel Mueller. CoAP

In the Ancient Manner. Chao Meng-fu. CoBLCP, *tr.* by Jonathan Chaves

In the annals saints. Holy Well. Padraic Fallon. BBASP

In the antique forest dreary. Rhyme of the Antique Forest. Henrietta Cordelia Ray. CBWP-3

In the apartment above me. No, No, Nora. Ted Fiorito. ReLy

In the Arab House. Al-Munsif Al-Wahaybi. MAP, *tr.* by Salma Khadra Jayyusi and Naomi Shihab Nye

In the Arab Maghreb. Badr Shakir Al-Sayyab. MAP, *tr.* by Lena Jayyusi and Christopher Middleton

In the arms of the sea. (LL) Response to Rimbaud's Later Manner. Thomas Sturge Moore. CABP; OBMV

In the Ashtray. Vasco [or Vasko] Popa. VCWP, *tr.* by Anne Pennington

In the attention it pays to each detail. Love. Kelly Cherry. CRP

In the autumn-come-winter park. David Kherdian. UrbNat *Fr.* Taking the Soundings on Third Avenue

In the Autumn, on Retreat at a Mountain Temple. Lady Izumi. WPoS (Autumn, On Retreat at a Mountain Temple.) WoPoe

In the Aviary. Gerald Costanzo. UrbNat

In the back bedroom, laughing when you pull. First Time: 1950. Honor Moore. FFC; GLP

In the back of the dark Chinese store. Thrashing Doves, The. Jack Kerouac. PmAP

In the back yard. Ode to Señor Leal's Goat. Gary Soto. OxIBACP

In the Backs. Frances Darwin Cornford. BrRo

In the Backs. James Kenneth Stephen. NOBVV

In the Backyard. Julio Marzán. PueRic

In the backyard of our house on Norwood. Minks, The. Toi Derricotte. UrbNat

In the bad old days a bewigged country Squire. Wigs and Beards. Robert Graves. NOBL

In the Badlands. David Wagoner. UnPo

In the balmy night, in the night. Song of the Silent Night. Aurelio Arturo. BLPSL, *tr.* by Rene de Costa, Rigas Kappatos and Eleni Paidoussi

In the banana zone, in the poinciana tropics. Louvres. Les A. Murray. BMAP

In the Barn. Roger Fanning. OPRER

In the barn the tenant cock. Morning. John Cunningham. NOEC

In the baroque style of coral, India. Coral Reef, The. John Blight. NOBAu

In the Basement of the Goodwill Store. Ted Kooser. OPRER

In the basement of the museum finery is on display; a history of costume. History of Costume, A. Michelle Cliff. OxWW

In the Bathtub, to Mnemosyne. John Wheelwright. APT-2

In the Bavarian steeple, on the hour. Spire, The. Ellen Bryant Voigt. NoAM

In the Bay of Sumi. Toshiyuki. OHPJ

In the beauty shop, the saleswoman dabs. Bergamot. Justin Chin. AmPoNex

In the bed are two, submissive. Strato [or Straton]. CAGL, *tr.* by Byrne Fone

In the beggar's tin. Issa. SoOfWa, *tr.* by Sam Hamill

In the beginnin o aa things the Wurd wis there ense. Bible, *N.T.* FaBoVe *Fr.* St. John.

In the Beginning. Jill Alexander Essbaum. NAPBL

In the Beginning. Sandra Maria Esteves. PueRic

In the Beginning. Shara McCallum. NAPBL

In the Beginning. Howard Nemerov. BodElec

In the Beginning. Valerie Sinason. BrRo

In The Beginning. Dylan Thomas. ChIV-2

In the Beginning. Miriam Therese Winter. HW

In the beginning, at every step, he turned. Karl Shapiro. CRP *Fr.* Adam and Eve.

In the beginning God created the heaven and the earth. Bible, *O.T.* NAWM-5v1 *Fr.* Genesis.

In the beginning God created the heavens and. REcreation. Askhari. InTrad

In the beginning God made thee. Aholibah. Algernon Charles Swinburne. ChIV-1

In the beginning, God, the great schoolmaster. Autograph on the Soul, The. Adah Isaacs Menken. CBWP-1

In the beginning he merely marked. West Coast Indian. George Clutesi. HATNAP

In the beginning I stood by the window. Windows in Providence. Aliki Barnstone. BoWoP

In the beginning Love satisfies us. Love's Maturity. Hadewijch. WPoS, *tr.* by Oliver Davies

In the beginning of old. Ch'u Yüan. WoPoe, *tr.* by Stephen Field *Fr.* Heaven Questions, The.

In the beginning the desert. Desert, The. Al-Munsif Al-Wahaybi. MAP, *tr.* by Salma Khadra Jayyusi and Naomi Shihab Nye

In the beginning, the word. You Bet Your Life. Nancy Vieira Couto. PBCAP

In the beginning there were transports. Genesis. Jules Alan Wein. TrJP

In the beginning was the number cruncher. Computer Aided Design: Creation. Jackie Hardy. NeBl

In the beginning was the sound. In the Beginning. Sandra Maria Esteves. PueRic

In the beginning was the three-pointed star, In The Beginning. Dylan Thomas. ChIV-2

In the Beginning Was the Word. Anna Hempstead Branch. APT-1

In the beginning was the Word. Gail Holst-Warhaft. GI *Fr.* St. John.

In the beginning, / Wisdom. In the Beginning. Miriam Therese Winter. HW

In the Big Rock Candy Mountains. (LL) Big Rock Candy Mountains, The. *Unknown.* FaBoA; NOBA; OBAL; TTTS

In the Bistro. Gwen Harwood. FaBoWP

In the Black Camaro. David Bottoms. ReTh

In the black moon. Song of the Rider. Federico García Lorca. WoPoe, *tr.* by Edwin Honig

In the black winter morning. Bereft. Thomas Hardy. BoLoP; NoAM

In the blackberry. Otogami. ArkPo, *tr.* by Edwin A. Cranston

In the bleak mid-winter. Christina Georgina Rossetti. NOBVV; OxBEV; SacPr; VWP

In the blink of an eye. Snapshots. Sharif Elmusa. GraLe

In the blizzard. From the Spotted Night. Ray A. Young Bear. HATNAP

In the blood, Winnowing. Carl Phillips. WiU

In the Blooming Time o'th' year. Silvio's Complaint: A Song, To a Fine Scotch Tune. Aphra Behn. EMWP

In the blossom-land Japan. Old Song, An. "Yehoash." AWP, *tr.* by Marie Syrkin

In the blue air. Bats. Mary Oliver. HeIP-4

In the blue distance. Nelly Sachs. BoWoP

In the blue-green shadows. On a Landscape by Myself. Yün Shou-p'ing. CoBLCP, *tr.* by Jonathan Chaves

In the blue hubbub of the same-through-wealth sky. Geography. Kenneth Koch. NoAM

In the blue night. Pine Tree Tops. Gary Snyder. NOBA

In the blue velvet gown nobody else could wear. Party She Outdid Herself, The. Craig Arnold. NAPBL

In the Bluemist Motel. Greg Pape. ReTh

In the blurring low-blood-pressure. Judgment, The. Kathleen Spivack. BoWoP

In the boat / Crescent moon's light. Tan Taigi. ZenPo, *tr.* by Takashi Ikemoto and Lucien Stryk

In the Body. Ferreira Gullar. TCLAP, *tr.* by Renato Rezende

In the Bookstore. Allison Joseph. IllVoic

In the Borghese, Caravaggio, painter of boy whores, street punk. Caravaggio: Swirl and Vortex. Larry Levis. GeoHom

In the Borghese Gardens. Charles Tomlinson. OBGa

In the Boston Public Library on Boylston Street, where all the bums come in stinking from the cold. Critic, The. C. K. Williams. OPRER

In the *Boston Sunday Herald* just three lines. To an American Poet Just Dead. Richard Wilbur. HCAP; NBLV

In the bottom of my mind. (LL) Goat Paths, The. James Stephens. AWP; SCGP; UnPo

In the Bottomless Pit. Maksimilian Aleksandrovich Voloshin. TCRP, *tr.* by Yakov Hornstein

In the Bower of Bliss. Edmund Spenser. EBEV *Fr.* Faerie Queene, The.

In the bramble bush shelley slowly eats a lark's heart. Hot Day at the Races. Tom Raworth. SPE

In the Bramble Stream, white stones stick out. In the Mountain. Wang Wei. ChinPo, *tr.* by Yip Wai-lim

In the brave days of old. (LL) Thomas Babington Macaulay, 1st Baron Macaulay. CABP; EBNV; FaBoCh; FaBoWar; OBNV; OBWP; OxAEP-2; TreFP *Fr.* Lays of Ancient Rome.

In the Breeze. Boris Leonidovich Pasternak. TrJP, *tr.* by C. M. Bowra

In the bright bay of your morning, O God. Prayer. Claire Goll. TrJP, *tr.* by Babette Deutsch and Avrahm Yarmolinsky

In the bright broad Swiss glare I stand listening. Recessional. Thomas MacGreevy [or McGreevy]. CIP-2; ModIr

In the brown grasses slanting with the wind. William Ellery Leonard. APT-1 *Fr.* Two Lives.

In the brown water. Pike, The. Amy Lowell. APT-1

In the brutal nights we used to dream. Reveille. Primo Levi. HP, *tr.* by Ruth Feldman

In the bus café drinking tea, I watch. Connection in Bridgend. John Tripp. TCAWP

In the cabin.... Three Dimensions. José Craveirinha. PBMAP

In the cabinet with the lattice. Confession. Susan Hahn. IllVoic

In the Cage. Robert Lowell. NOBA; Son

In the callows of my intern year of. Venipuncture. John Graham-Pole. BloBone

In the Camp There Was One Alive. Randall Jarrell. HP

In the capital Spring comes late. Buying Flowers. Po Chü-i. TAL

In the captured photo album, attic-dusted and insect-infested. Potato Conflicts. Walter Bargen. SpudSo

In the Carolinas. Wallace Stevens. SAmP; VGW

In the Casbah. Salma Khadra Jayyusi. PoArWo, *tr.* by Charles Doria

In the Case of Lobsters. Petra von Morstein. BoWoP, *tr.* by Rosmarie Waldrop

In the casket of the Hours. *Unknown.* TAL *Fr.* Meditations, The.

In the Cathedral. Patricia Beer. OxBC

In the Cathedral Close. Edward Dowden. EBVV

In the cave with a long-ago flare. Painters. Muriel Rukeyser. NAAL-5

In the cedar canoe gliding and paddling. Geese Gone Beyond. Gary Snyder. NoAM

In the Cemetery. Thomas Hardy. InPK-6; Son *Fr.* Satires of Circumstance in Fifteen Glimpses.

In the cemetery of the whales. Cemetery of the Whales, The. Yevgeny Aleksandrovich Yevtushenko [or Evtushenko]. RusPo, *tr.* by Robert Arthur Douglas Ford

In the censer the coals are high. Final Prayer. Enheduanna. BoWoP, *tr.* by Aliki Barnstone and Willis Barnstone

In the center of the bloodvein. My Uncle Is My Honor and a Guest in My House. Etheridge Knight. BodElec

In the centre of the poster, Napoleon. Arthur Rimbaud. OBWP, *tr.* by Robert Lowell *Fr.* Eighteen-Seventy.

In the chamber the lady knows no sadness. Complaint from a Lady's Chamber. Wang Ch'ang-ling. ChinPo, *tr.* by Yip Wai-lim

In the Chariot Drawn by Dragons. Michael Van Walleghen. IllVoic

In the cherry blossom's shade. Issa. EnlH

In the *chih-yüan* period, the being *hsin-mao*. Poem of Prefectural Judge Yang T'ien-jui Righting a Wrong. Chao Meng-fu. CoBLCP, *tr.* by Jonathan Chaves

In the childhood of April, while purple woods. Dead to the Living, The. Edith Nesbit. VWP

In the Children's Hospital. Hugh MacDiarmid. NAEL-5v2; NAEL-6v2; PAI

In the Chung Mode, to the Tune of "P'u T'ien Lo." *Unknown.* ColAnChi, *tr.* by Wayne Schlepp

In the church fallen like dancers. Enfidaville. Keith Douglas. PoWW

In the Church of I AM she hears there is a time to heal. Do What You Can. Lawrence Joseph. PBCAP

In the Church of Marosszentimre. Zoltán Jékely. IQMS, *tr.* by John Gordon Nichols

In the Churchyard. Eleanor Ross Taylor. UnPo

In the Churchyard at Cambridge. Henry Wadsworth Longfellow. TAP

In the citadel of Jade Gate Pass, elm leaves early scatter yellow. Wang Ch'ang-ling. SuSp *Fr.* Following the Army on Campaign.

In the city of St. Francis they have taken down the statue of St. Francis. Afterwards, They Shall Dance. Bob Kaufman. TwCP; VGW

In the City Park. Bulat Shalvovich Okudzhava. TCRP, *tr.* by Deming Brown

In the city, under the saw-toothed leaves of an oak. Rita Dove. NAAL-5 *Fr.* Thomas and Beulah.

In the clear light that confuses everything. Laurel Tree, The. Louis Simpson. NNaP

In the Clear Long After. Olena Kalytiak Davis. NAPBL

In the clear water by the beach. Bianor. GrAn

In the clearing stands. Missionaries in the Jungle. Linda Piper. BlSi

In the close covert of a grove. Geranium, The. Richard Brinsley Sheridan. BoLoP

In the cloud-gray mornings. Hoar-Frost. Amy Lowell. ColAP

In the Cloud of Unknowing. Carol Rumens. DiPo

In the clutter and clatter of the Bronx. Providence Journal V: Israel of Puerto Rico. Michael S. Weaver. SpirFl

In the Coach. Thomas Edward Brown. Conjergal Rights. PeVV

In the coffins. (LL) War. Miguel Hernández. AF; RaBo

In the cold Campèa, where ridges. Campèa. Andrea Zanzotto. VCWP, *tr.* by Ruth Feldman

In the cold change, which time hath wrought on love. Caroline Elizabeth Norton. CenSon

In the cold, cold parlor. First Death in Nova Scotia. Elizabeth Bishop. CoAP; FaBoWP; HarvBoo; LCAP-2; NOBA

In the cold dome of the college observatory. Conjunctions. Eamon Grennan. PBCIP

In the cold I will rise, I will bathe. Lonely Death, The. Adelaide Crapsey. APT-1

In the cold shed sharpening saws. Sixth-Month Song in the Foothills. Gary Snyder. HCAP

In the cold snows of a dream. (LL) W. B. Yeats. BIrV; NOBE; NPeEn; PoE *Fr.* Meditations in Time of Civil War.

In the Coliseum. Henry Wadsworth Longfellow. TCAPo *Fr.* Michael Angelo: A Fragment.

In the coming heat. Frances Densmore. APT-1 *Fr.* Chippewa Music.

In the convent vegetable garden the nuns. In a Convent Garden. Alan Brownjohn. OBGa

In the cool of morning Andrew Jackson came. Twilight on Union Street. Donald Davidson. FuPo

In the cool waters of the river. Woman. Valente Goenha Malangatana. PBA; PBMAP; TTY, *tr.* by Dorothy Guedes and Philippa Rumsey

In the cool waters of the river. Woman. Malangatana Ngwenya. PeSAV, *tr.* by Philippa Rumsey

In the coolness of black suns. Bad Days Will End, The. Penelope Rosemont. SurWo

In the corner of a flower-shop. Twelve. Rossana Ombres. NeIt, *tr.* by Ruth Feldman

In the corner of the living room was an album of unbearable photos. Dead in Frock Coats, The. Carlos Drummond de Andrade. PFTM-1

In the corner where she crouched. On the Threshold. Pierre Reverdy. CuPo

In the Counselor's Waiting Room. Bettie M. Sellers. InPK-6

In the Country. Lu Yu. OHMPC, *tr.* by Kenneth Rexroth

In the Country. Ssu-k'ung Shu. SuSp, *tr.* by Hellmut Wilhelm

In the Country of the Black Pig. Christopher Hope. EmeKit

In the County Tyrone, in [*or* near] the town of Dungannon. Old [*or* Ould] Orange Flute, The. *Unknown.* OBCoV; OxBoLi

In the court of examinations. Spring Vista from the Tower of Illuminated Distance. Li Meng-yang. CoBLCP, *tr.* by Jonathan Chaves

In the courtyard is a marvelous tree. *Unknown.* SuSp

In the Courtyard of the Servants. Ferenc Jankovich. IQMS, *tr.* by Madeline Mason

In the courtyard where the cooing of pigeons. Courtyard, The. Eddy Van Vliet. VCWP, *tr.* by John Van Tiel

In the Covenant's Radiance. Uri Zvi Greenberg. MHP, *tr.* by Ruth Finer Mintz

In the covenant's radiance that moment had come. In the Covenant's Radiance. Uri Zvi Greenberg. MHP, *tr.* by Ruth Finer Mintz

In the cowslip's peeps I lie. Clock-A-Clay. John Clare. EBEV; EBVV; NAEL-5v2; NAEL-6v2

In the cowslips peeps I lye. John Clare. *See* In the cowslip's peeps I lie

In the cream gilded cabin of his steam yacht. Ezra Pound. MoAmPo *Fr.* Hugh Selwyn Mauberley (Life and Contacts).

In the Crevices of Night. Gloria Vando. TouFir

In the cross field. Out West. Gary Snyder. NNaP

In the Cross of Christ I Glory. Sir John Bowring. SacPr

In the curious phenomenon of your occipital horn. (LL)   To a Snail.   Marianne Craig Moore.   APT-1; FaBoMo; FaBoWP; NAAL-2v2; NALW; PoPoPo

In the daily space.   Daily Space.   João Cabral de Melo Neto.   VCWP

In the daisied lap of summer.   Season's Lovers, The.   Miriam Waddington.   MoCV

In the Damp Places.   Nijole Miliauskaite.   VCWP, tr. by Jonas Zdanys

In the Dark.   James Merrill.   LCAP-2

In the dark.   Black Jewel, The.   W. S. Merwin.   LCAP-2

In the dark.   Ken Smith.   See In the dark / each sits alone

In the Dark.   Patrick Williams.   PNI

In the dark and narrow street.   When the Night and Morning Meet.   Dora Greenwell.   EBVV

In the Dark Backward.   Gloria Vando.   TouFir

In the dark blue night.   Mirror, The.   "Shu Ting."   PFTM-2, tr. by Dennis Ding, Fang Dai and Edward Morin

In the Dark Body of Metamorphosis.   Mario Luzi.
   "But then an even greater sense of the inexpressible."   ItPo, tr. by Gayle Ridinger
   "Reflective life separates us from the sources of reflection."   ItPo, tr. by Gayle Ridinger

In the dark / each sits alone.   Train.   Ken Smith.   SPE

In the dark house, the cry of a child.   Teething.   Tom Wayman.   CDa

In the dark lobby.   L. A. Davidson.   HA

In the Dark None Dainty.   Robert Herrick.   CaPo
   (Night hides our thefts; all faults then pardon'd be.)   CavPo

In the dark room, lit only by the stray light.   Why a Boy.   Justin Chin.   WiU

In the dark sky there.   Lyn Hejinian.   FTOS   Fr. Cell, The.

In the dark womb where I began.   C. L. M.   John Masefield.   MoBrPo; OxBTC

In the Dark Word, Khurbn.   Jerome Rothenberg.   TaR

In the Dark World.   Haniel Long.   APT-1

In the darkening church.   Rufus Prays.   Leonard Alfred George Strong.   MoBrPo

In the Darkness of the Other.   Clara Silva.   TANSG, tr. by Celeste Kostopulos-Cooperman

In the dating bar, the potted ferns lean down.   History of Civilization, A.   Albert Goldbarth.   HCAP

In the dawn.   Sakanoe No Korenori.   OHMPJ

In the dawn, although I know.   Fujiwara no Michinobu.   OHPJ

In the dawn-dirty light, in the biggest snow of the year.   Roe-Deer.   Ted Hughes.   NOxBChV; NoAM; OxAEP-2

In the dawning of the day. (LL)   My Delight and Thy Delight.   Robert Bridges.   NOBE; OBEV

In the days before the high tide.   Sea Song, A.   Digby Mackworth Dolben.   EBVV

In the days of Caesar Augustus.   Christmas Day; the Family Sitting.   John Meade Falkner.   ChIV-2; NOCV; OxBTC

In the days of lace-ruffles, perukes and brocade.   Brown Bess.   Rudyard Kipling.   FaBoWar

In the days of mild Jerry Ford.   Limerick.   Unknown.   PeLi

In the days of old.   Thomas Love Peacock.   NOBRP

In the Days of Old Rameses.   Unknown.   OBCoV

In the Days of Rin-Tin-Tin.   Daniel Gerard Hoffman.   ReTh

In the Days of Socrates.   Friedrich Hölderlin.   PFTM-1

In the days of the broken cubes of Picasso.   Cubes.   Langston Hughes.   APT-2

In the days when moles still held their general meetings.   Brief Thoughts on Cats Growing on Trees.   Miroslav Holub.   PoSu, tr. by Ian Milner and Jarmila Milner

In the days when they were first planted before the Calyx Tower.   Willow Branch Song.   Liu Yu Hsi.   SuSp, tr. by Daniel Bryant

In the dead hour of night.   Silent Night, The.   Mrs. Henry Linden.   CBWP-4

In the dead night we walk behind a hearse.   Abel.   John Wheelwright.   ChIV-1

In the dead of the night.   Moon and Spectator, The.   Léonie Adams.   APT-2

In the Dean's porch a nest of clay.   In the Cathedral Close.   Edward Dowden.   EBVV

In the december of my springs.   December of My Springs, The.   Nikki Giovanni.   GT

In the Deep Channel.   William Stafford.   RB

In the Deep Museum.   Anne Sexton.   MoAmPo

In the deep night, that all is well. (LL)   Tennyson.   CAGL; NAEL-6v2; NOBE; NOCV; OBEV; PeECV   Fr. In Memoriam A. H. H.

In the deep silence of nights.   Thought.   Ahmad Nadeem Qasmi.   WoPoe, tr. by Raja Changez Sultan

In the deepest night and a full moon.   Untitled.   Merle Woo.   FSt

In the Defences.   Elizabeth Akers Allen.   SWaP

In the dense scopes.   Figures in an Ancient Ink.   Carl Rakosi.   APT-2

In the Deposits of the Heart.   Anna Cascella.   CltWP, tr. by Cinzia Sartini Blum and Lara Trubowitz

In the depths of the parasol I see the marvelous prostitutes.   Man and Woman Absolutely White, A.   André Breton.   PFTM-1

In the Desert.   Semyon [or Semion] Izrailevich Lipkin.   TCRP, tr. by Albert C. Todd

In the desert.   Desert Has Many Teachings, The.   Mechthild von Magdeburg.   WPoS, tr. by Jane Hirshfield

In the Desert.   Herman Melville.   NCAP

In the Desert.   Dmitry [or Dmitrii] Aleksandrovich Prigov.   ItGoST, tr. by Robert Reid

In the desert of Itabira.   Traveling as a Family.   Carlos Drummond de Andrade.   TCLAP, tr. by Virginia de Araújo

In the deserted village, sunken down.   Deserted Village, The.   "Robin Hyde."   PeNZ; WPE

In the difficulty of what it is to be. (LL)   Wallace Stevens.   ColAP; NOBA   Fr. Notes toward a Supreme Fiction.

In the dimly lit room.   Vision of Your Body.   Daisy Zamora.   LoL, tr. by Dinah Livingston

In the Distance.   Silvio Giussani.   ItPo, tr. by Gayle Ridinger

In the Distress upon Me.   Henry Ainsworth.   AH

In the doll's.   Bob Boldman.   HA

In the Dome Car of the "Canadian."   Sid Marty.   NOBC

In the Doorway.   Robert Browning.   SCGP   Fr. James Lee's Wife.

In the Dordogne.   John Peale Bishop.   APT-1; OBWP; PeFWW; PoWW; VGW

In the downhill of life, when I find I'm declining.   Tomorrow.   John Collins.   GTBS-P

In the Downtown Tombs of long long ago.   Partial Luetic History of an Individual at Risk.   J. M. Regan.   GLP

In the drained fields.   Buson.   EH, tr. by Yoel Hoffmann

In the dream, I am burning the rice.   Offering.   Sharan Strange.   GT

In the dream I became 2 men my age.   (1980).   C. S. Giscombe.   GT

In the dream I enter the house.   Bone-Flower Elegy.   Robert Earl Hayden.   APT-2; NoAM

In the dreamy silence.   Autumn.   Alexander L. Posey.   APN-2

In the dreamy silence after bath.   Mother, The.   Sharon Olds.   PBCAP

In the Dresden Gallery.   Yevgeny [or Evgenii] Mikhailovich Vinokurov.   TCRP, tr. by Albert C. Todd

In the drifting rain the cows in the yard are as black.   Milking before Dawn.   Ruth Dallas.   PeNZ

In the Due Honor of the Author Master Robert Norton.   John Smith.   SCAP

In the Dunes.   Aleksandr Aleksandrovich Blok.   TCRP, tr. by Geoffrey Thurley

In the dungeon-crypts, idly did I stray.   Emily Jane Brontë.   NAEL-6v2; NALW; NOBVV

In the dusk the path.   Lady Izumi.   WPOW

In the dusk the path.   Izumi Shikibu.   OHMPJ

In the Dying Afternoon.   Ramón López Velarde.   BLPSL, tr. by Rene de Costa, Rigas Kappatos and Eleni Paidoussi

In the early days of marriage.   Before these Wars.   Carol Rumens.   Prnts

In the early evening.   Reading by Mechanic Light.   Thomas McGrath.   BodElec; GifTon

In the early evening, as now, a man is bending.   Poem.   Louise Glück.   HCAP

In the early evening, the suspended bowls.   Specter, The.   Anna Andreyevna Akhmatova.   TCRP, tr. by Daniel Weissbort

In the early hours of the next morning dawning.   Unknown.   WoPoe, tr. by David Ferry   Fr. Epic of Gilgamesh, The.

In the early hours / the lovebirds.   Paraguay.   Carl Rakosi.   FTOS

In the early mornings.   May Song.   Félix Lope de Vega Carpio.   SpanPo, tr. by Kate Flores

In the early springtime, after their tea.   En Famille.   Dame Edith Sitwell.   NALW

In the earnest path of duty.   Poem.   Charlotte Forten.   BlSi

In the East.   Georg Trakl.   PeFWW
   (Dark wrath of people, The.)   AF, tr. by Daniel S. Simko

In the East Central State of Nigeria, four years.   Epilogue to Casualties.   John Pepper Clark Bekedermo.   HBAPE

In the East, in the East is my heart.   My Heart Is in the East.   Judah Halevi.   TrJP

In the eastern quarter dawn breaks, the stars flicker pale.   Cock-crow Song.   Unknown.   ChiP, tr. by Arthur Waley

In the ebony of an ancient cupboard. (LL)   My Cousin Agueda [or Agatha].   Ramón López Velarde.   OBVE; TCLAP, tr. by Samuel Beckett

In the Egg.   Günter Grass.   AF

In the eggs.   John Corben.   Spl

In the eggshell after the chick has hatched.   Michael Segers.   HA

In the elbow of a macaroni.   Blue Jeaned Rock Queen in Search of Happiness on a Blind Thursday at 1/3 Speed and Crying, A.   A. K. Redwing.   VoR

In the Elegy Season.   Richard Wilbur.   InPK-6

In the Elementary School Choir. Gregory Djanikian. OPRER; UnSA

In the embankment's mad roar. On the Railway. Aleksandr Aleksandrovich Blok. TCRP, *tr. by* Geoffrey Thurley

In the Emperor's bed. Kikaku. SoOfWa, *tr. by* Sam Hamill

In the empire there is none. Song of Thanks. Martin Joseph Prandstetter. AuPH, *tr. by* Lowell A. Bangerter

In the Emptied Rest Home. Bella [*or* Izabella] Akhatovna Akhmadulina. BoWoP, *tr. by* Olga Carlisle and Jean Valentine

In the empty church. Nicholas Virgilio. HA

In the empty city a morning horn. Tune: "Pale-golden Willows." Chiang K'uei. SuSp, *tr. by* Chiang Yee

In the empty lot—a place. Wild, The. Wendell Berry. VGW

In the empty mountains. Kakinomoto no Hitomaro. OHPJ

In the empty mountains after the new rain. Autumn Twilight in the Mountains. Wang Wei. OHMPC, *tr. by* Kenneth Rexroth

In the encyclopedia. Fact. Kenneth Rexroth. OBAL

In the End. Peter Everwine. NNaP

In the end. Hairbrush, The. Sandra Hochman. YaYoPo

In the end. Dario Villa. ItPo, *tr. by* Gayle Ridinger

In the end. Wakyu. JDP, *tr. by* Yoel Hoffmann

In the end darkness drowned Zenobia. Goodbye, Zenobia. Saniyya Salih. MAP, *tr. by* Patricia Alanah Byrne, Charles Doria and Salma Khadra Jayyusi

In the End Is the Body. Gail Holst-Warhaft. GI

In the End of Days. Bible, *O.T.* TrJP *Fr.* Isaiah.

In the end of the sabbath, as it began to dawn toward the first day of the week. Bible, *N.T.* NAWM-5v1 *Fr.* St. Matthew.

In the end when the doctors circle around. Advantages of Being a World Class Athlete, The. Anthony Lacavaro. MoASP

In the end you are weary of this ancient world. Zone. Guillaume Apollinaire. WoPoe, *tr. by* Samuel Beckett

In the endless night, having deserted me, where have you gone? Tune: "Telling of Innermost Feelings." Ku Hsiung. SuSp, *tr. by* James J. Y. Liu

In the eternal / Light of the spring day. Ki no Tomonori. OHPJ

In the Evening. Anna Andreyevna Akhmatova. TCRP, *tr. by* Daniel Weissbort

In the Evening. Siv Cedering Fox. CA

In the evening. Another Night in the Ruins. Galway Kinnell. CoAP; InvLad

In the evening, an animated salesman, a cartoon version of a man. Persuasion. Patty Seyburn. AmPoNex

In the evening at the palace, she lowers her pearl screen. Complaint Near the Jade Stairs. Hsieh T'iao. CrYelRi, *tr. by* Sam Hamill

In the evening came the order. Susie's Lament for Johnny. Mihály Csokonai Vitéz. IQMS, *tr. by* Anthony Edkins

In the evening dusk when earth. Interpretation of Dinner by the Uninvited Guest, An. Lorna Dee Cervantes. TouFir

In the evening gusts of wind and rain. Tune: "Song of Picking Mulberry." Li Ch'ing-chao. SuSp, *tr. by* Eugene Eoyang

In the Evening I Walk by the River. Ou-yang Hsiu. OHPC, *tr. by* Kenneth Rexroth

In the evening the autumn woods ring. Georg Trakl. *See* At nightfall the autumn woods cry out

In the evening the dusk. Poet Is Dead, The. William Everson. NoAM

In the evening / The mists trail. *Unknown.* TAL

In the evening / The rice leaves in the garden. Minamoto no Tsunenobu. OHPJ

In the Evening the Sky Roams, a Meaager. Amelia Rosselli. CItWP, *tr. by* Cinzia Sartini Blum and Lara Trubowitz

In the Evening, Walking in the Western Fields. Chang Yü. CoBLCP, *tr. by* Jonathan Chaves

In the evening when the light is dim. Valerio Magrelli. NeIt

In the Evening Your Vision Widens. Nelly Sachs. WPoS, *tr. by* Michael Roloff

In the evenings. When did she know, when did she know it. Lucille Clifton. ExTi

In the evil time. A. Velichansky. TCRusP, *tr. by* Daniel Weissbort

In the eye of seafaring man. Winds of Change, The. Charles G. Ballard. VoR

In the Eyes of the Gods. André Breton. WoPoe, *tr. by* Jack Rogow and Bill Zavatsky

In the face before he ran out into the street. (LL) I Found Orpheus Levitating. Nick Carbó. NAPBL; ReBoTo

In the faint blue light. Vincent Buckley. BMAP *Fr.* Stroke.

In the Fall. Hugh MacDiarmid. *Fr.* In Memoriam James Joyce.

In the Falling Deer's Mouth. Michael Levien. PoRA

In the falling snow. Richard Wright. NIL-7

In the far corner. Blackbird, The. Humbert Wolfe. NOxBChV

In the far spaces of eternity. Harmony. Thomas Grant Springer. PoToHe

In the Far West. Cow Boy. Vincente Huidobro. PFTM-1

In the few warm weeks. Christmas Message, A. Gavin Ewart. FaBoMo

In the Field. Richard Wilbur. NAAL-2v2

In the field-furrow. "H. D." APT-1 *Fr.* Tribute to the Angels.

In the Fields. Charlotte Mew. MoBrPo; OxAEP-2

In the fifteenth she was painted. Beatrice. J. Bernlef. TuT, *tr. by* Peter Van de Kamp

In the final hour, dear. "Valery Frantsevich Pereleshin." TCRP

In the final years of the twelfth century. Inferno 1, 32. Jorge Luis Borges. PoetW, *tr. by* Anthony Kerrigan

In the fine land, the west land, the land where I belong. (LL) West Wind, The. John Masefield. CABP; MoBrPo

In the first Autumn night. First Autumn Night. Katie Donovan. BiHa

In the first cage. Aisle of Dogs. Chase Twichell. EmeKit

In the first country. Bright after Dark. Pearse Hutchinson. PBCIP

In the first negative, a shape presages. Sound Waves. Mary Kinzie. FFC

In the first rank of these did Zimri stand. Dryden. HAP *Fr.* Absalom and Achitophel.

In the first ruder age, when love was wild. Love's Force. Thomas Carew. CaPo

In the first taxi he was alone tra-la. Taxis, The. Louis MacNeice. EmeKit; NPeEn; OxBTC; PNI

In the first year of the last disgrace. News of the World II. George Barker. FaBoTw

In the fish shop. Basho. EH, *tr. by* Robert Hass

In the Fist of Your Hatred. Gwendoline C. Konie. HAWP

In the flash of that explosion. Wedding Day at Nagasaki. Rodney Hall. CBAP

In the flatlands. Fall, The. John Kinsella. NeBl

In the Flight of the Blue Heron: To Montezuma. Anita Endrezze. CDW

In the flower of fury, the folded poppy, / Night. (LL) Sentry, The. Alun Lewis. AngWePo; PoWW; TCAWP

In the flower-time of youth. Love of Boys, The. Solon. CAGL, *tr. by* John Addington Symonds

In the Flowering Season. Michael Roberts. FaBoTw

In the Flux. Fadwa Tuqan [*or* Tuquan]. MAP, *tr. by* Patricia Alanah Byrne, Charles Doria and Salma Khadra Jayyusi

In the Fog. Lilian Moore. TLR

In the fog we drift hither. Rain on the River. Lu Yu. OHPC, *tr. by* Kenneth Rexroth

In-the-foot song, drinking cool beatitudes. (LL) Afterwards, They Shall Dance. Bob Kaufman. TwCP; VGW

In the Footsteps of Genghis Khan. Jan Barry. CDa

"In the footsteps of the walking air." Kenneth Patchen. SPE

In the foreign land. With the Crescent Moon, with the Evening Star. Hans Leifhelm. AuPH, *tr. by* Lowell A. Bangerter

In the Forest. Heather Allen. GifTon

In the Forest. George Bowering. NOBC

In the Forest. Russell Edson. LCAP-2

In the forest, in unexplored. Michael Dransfield. CBAP *Fr.* Geography.

In the forest of noyous hevynesse. Lost. Charles, Duc d' Orléans. NPeEn

In the Forest of Vaal. János Vajda. IQMS, *tr. by* Watson Kirkconnell

In the forest overhead. Les Grottes. Gillian Clarke. HarvBoo

In the Forests of Sleep. Habiba Muhammadi. PoArWo, *tr. by* Ibrahim Muhawi

In the Formal Garden. Peter Jones. OBGa

In the forties the populace was sucking on barb. New/Aguas Buenas/Jersey. Víctor Hernández Cruz. TouFir

In the foul rag-and-bone shop of the heart. (LL) Circus Animals' Desertion, The. W. B. Yeats. FaBoMo; FaBoTw; HarvBoo; MakPoe; NAEL-5v2; NAEL-6v2; NAWM-7v2; NIP-4; NOBE; NOIV; NoAM; NoP-4; OxBTC; PAI; TFi

In the frayed apple leaves a grin of copper. Child Is Revenant to the Man, The. Vincent Buckley. BMAP

In the frozen ground under my feet. Wild Hyacinth. Joan I. Siegel. PoCoUp

In the garbage bin. Alexis Rotella. HA

In the garden. Garden. Michael Bullock. OBGa

In the Garden. Edward Dowden. Singer, The. OxBSo

In the Garden. *Unknown.* SoSe-8

In the garden a strange tree grows. *Unknown.* CoBCP

In the Garden at Swainston. Tennyson. OBEV

In the Garden City Café with its murals on the wall. Huxley Hall. Sir John Betjeman. CABP; OBSV

In the garden of dusk. In the Beginning. Shara McCallum. NAPBL

In the Garden of Eden lay Adam. Limerick. *Unknown.* PeLi

In the garden of Shut-Eye Town. (LL) Sugar-Plum Tree, The. Eugene Field. ITBLP; NBLV; OTCP

In the Garden of the Lord. Helen Keller. SacPr

In the Garden of Time and Destiny. Nâbî. WoPoe, *tr.* by Walter Andrews, Najaat Black and Mehmet Kalpakli

In the garden on a summer night. Brazen Image. Anne Hartigan. CIP-2

In the garden pool. O. Mabson Southard. HA

In the garden shed, among flower-pots. Voice. Susan Wicks. MFPA

In the garden there strayed. In the Garden. *Unknown.* SoSe-8

In the Garden: Villa Cleobolus. Lawrence Durrell. OBGa

In the gardens. Flower-sellers, Budapest. Kathleen Jamie. NePenScot

In the gathering dew. Lady Sagami. BoWoP

In the gathering gloom they lie. Terror. "Yehoash." TrJP, *tr.* by Isidore Goldstick

In the ghosts' moonshine. (LL) Thomas Lovell Beddoes. EBEV; NAEL-5v2; TFi *Fr.* Death's Jest Book.

In the Giant's Castle. Ruth Dallas. PeNZ

In the girdered dark. Drink of Milk, A. John Montague. ModIr; PNI

In the glassed-in jazz club acres above. Night above the Town. Thomas Lux. SeSe

In the Gloaming. Charles Stuart Calverley. NOBL; OBCoV; PeLV

In the Gloaming. Jennifer Maiden. BMAP

In the gloom of whiteness. Snow. Edward Thomas. FaBoTw; OPOU

In the Gloom on the Left. Joyce Mansour. PFTM-2, *tr.* by Molly Bendall

In the Gloriovs Epiphanie of Ovr Lord God, A Hymn. Svng as by the Three Kings. Richard Crashaw. FSCP

  (Bright BABE! Whose awfull beautyes make.) FSCP

  (Hymne for the Epiphanie, A; Sung as by the three Kings.) ESCV

In the Gold Mines. B. W. Vilakazi. TTY

In the golden air, the risky autumn. Piazzas. Barbara Guest. NeAP

In the golden olden glory of the days gone by. (LL) Days Gone By, The. James Whitcomb Riley. APN-2; OBCA

In the golden reign of Charlemaign the king. Rhotruda. Frederick Goddard Tuckerman. NCAP

In the golden twilight the rain. Terrace in the Snow, The. Su Tung-p'o (Su Shih). OHPC, *tr.* by Kenneth Rexroth

In the Good Old U.S.A. José Angel Sr. Villalongo. UnSA

In the gorge where bells resound. Return to Wang River. Wang Wei. CrYelRi, *tr.* by Sam Hamill

In the Grass. Josef Weinheber. AuPH, *tr.* by Lowell A. Bangerter

In the grass of the twilight: the seventh day is God. Géza Páskándi. IQMS, *tr.* by Agnes Arany-Makkai *Fr.* Language Memory.

In the Grave No Flower. Edna St. Vincent Millay. NAAL-2v2; NAAL-5

In the Graveyard. Macdonold Clarke. PWR

In the great gardens, after bright spring rain. Dame Edith Sitwell. NOBE; OxBTC *Fr.* Sleeping Beauty, The.

In the Great House, and in the House of Fire. *Unknown.* AWP *Fr.* Book of the Dead.

In the great nave of the church. Musician, The. Philip Dacey. MiVo

In the great night my heart will go out. Owl Woman's Death Song. *Unknown.* BoWoP, *tr.* by Ruth Underhill

In the great white tent lit by floodlight. Mostly Mozart at Planting Fields Arboretum. David Zeiger. MiVo

In the great world—which, being interpreted. Byron. OxBoLi; PeLV *Fr.* Don Juan.

In the green and yellow grass of the broad field. Sabbath Morning. Marcia Falk. TaR

In the green escape of my palace, over a bridge, under a. Etel Adnan. PoArWo *Fr.* There.

In the green fleece shorts is taking off. That Man. Reginald Shepherd. WiU

In the green light of water, like the day. Swans, The. Dame Edith Sitwell. WPE

In the greenest of our valleys. Haunted Palace, The. Edgar Allan Poe. APN-1; NAAL-3; NOBA; OxBA; TAP; TCAPo; TFi

In the Greenhouse. Eugenio Montale. PoetW, *tr.* by Jonathan Galassi

In the greenhouse lives a wren. *Unknown.* OxNR

In the Greenwood. Desmond O'Grady.

  "My darling, my love." CIP-2

In the grey evening. Garden Hose, The. Beatrice Janosco. NTCP

In the grey wastes of dread. Horses on the Camargue. Roy Campbell. GTBS-P

In the Grounds. Douglas Dunn. NoP-4

In the Grove. Rachel Hadas. KGB

In the groves of Africa from their natural wonder. African Elegy, An. Robert Duncan. NoAM

In the grownups' stories for the young. Wolf, The. Unsi Al-Haj [*or* Hajj]. MAP, *tr.* by Sargon Boulus and Alistair Elliot

In the guest room. Alexis Rotella. HA

In the gutter / boys who try. Up-Beat. Langston Hughes. APT-2

In the half-light / And. (LL) Ezra Pound. APT-1; HAP; MoAmPo; NOBA; NoAM; OxBA *Fr.* Cantos.

In the hall of mirrors nobody speaks. Roman Baths at Nîmes, The. Henri Cole. MakPoe

In the hall of The Mountain King. Real Estate. Michael Hannon. GeoHom

In the hallway above the pit of the stairwell. Indictment of Senior Officers. Sharon Olds. PBCAP

In the harbour, in the island, in the Spanish Seas. Trade Winds. John Masefield. FaBoCh; OBMV

In the harvest too. And Then the Water. Milo De Angelis. NeIt, *tr.* by Lawrence Venuti

In the heart of little old New York. Forty-second Street. Harry Warren. ReLy

In the heart of night, in winter, there was this hour. Rain at Night. Jakov [*or* Jacob] Steinberg. FIT, *tr.* by Robert Friend

In the Heart of the Desert. Al-Tirimmah. ArPe, *tr.* by Omar S. Pound

In the heart of the heart. Missing Jew, The. Rodger Kamenetz. TaR

In the heart of the Hills of Life, I know. My Springs. Sidney Lanier. UnPo

In the heart of the Indian territory of Oklahoma. Go For Broke. André Breton. PFTM-1

In the heart of winter and a boy running. (LL) History Lessons. Seamus Deane. BiHa; PBCIP; PNI

In the heat. Bob Boldman. HA

In the heat of noon. Consolation to Empty Pitchers. K. S. Narasimhaswami. OMIP, *tr.* by A. K. Ramanujan

In the Heat of the Morning. Anne Szumigalski. FaBoWP

In the Heat of the Night. Lee Smith. Unle

In the heights of heaven is the throne of your dwelling. Sanctification. Joseph Ibn Abithur. TOF, *tr.* by David Goldstein

In the hellish heat and thick smoke. Food-Factory Kitchen. Vladimir Salimon. TCRP, *tr.* by Vera Dunham

In the heydays of 'forty-five. For George Santayana. Robert Lowell. NAAL-2v2; VGW

In the hickory scent. Smokehouse, The. Yusef Komunyakaa. NoP-4

In the high, high grass of Guinea. Country Graveyard. Charles Pressoir. NegPo, *tr.* by Edna Worthley Underwood

In the high jungle where Assam meets Tibet. Moschus Moschiferus. Alec Derwent Hope. CBAP

In the high seat, before-dawn dark. Why Log Truck Drivers Rise Earlier Than Students of Zen. Gary Snyder. GeoHom; LoL; NNaP

In the high wilderness. Coplas. Antonio Machado. AF, *tr.* by Robert Bly

In the highlands, in the country places. Robert Louis Stevenson. FaBoCh; OBEV; OxBS; SCGP

In the Hills. Wang Wei. TAL

In the hills where the hoop. Death of Crazy Horse, The. Lucille Clifton. ESEAA

In the hole we found beside the road. Construction of the Museum. Michael Palmer. BodElec

In the Holy Nativity of Our Lord God. Richard Crashaw. GeHe; NAEL-6v1; NAEL-7v1

  Shepherds' Hymn, The. NOBE

  (Verses from the Shepherd's Hymn.) OBEV

In the home of mysterious life I lie. Songs of the Sacred Mysteries. *Unknown.* APN-2, *tr.* by Alfred Longley Riggs

In the Home of the Scholar Wu Su-chiang. Wu Tsao. BoWoP; WPOW

In the hometown tonight. Castle in Lynn, A. Linda McCarriston. LoL

In the Hospital Near the End. Sharon Olds. NIP-4

In the hottest time, when all is still and windless. *Unknown.* CoBCP *Fr.* Tzu Yeh Songs.

In the hour between wolf and dog the sacred cow of hardship. Sacred Cow of Hardship, The. Agi Mishol. DTA, *tr.* by Tsipi Keller

In the hour of death, after this life's whim. Dominus Illuminatio Mea. Richard Doddridge Blackmore. OBEV; SacPr

In the hour[e] of my distress[e]. His Litany to the Holy Spirit. Robert Herrick. BASC; BeJo; NOSC; PeECV

In the House Blues. Bessie Smith. NAAAL

In the house east of here lives an old woman. *Unknown.* CoBCP

In the house in Detroit. Sand Nigger. Lawrence Joseph. GraLe; OPRER

In the house of life. (LL) Pax. D. H. Lawrence. EnlH; PeECV; TrCP

In the house of red leaves are the most beautiful dances. House of Red Leaves, The. Liu E. CoBLCP, *tr.* by Jonathan Chaves

In the house of the hangman. Hangman's Love Song, The. Stanley Moss. VGW

In the house of the man with no hands. Probable Cause. Thomas McGrath. GifTon

In the house of those who serve the Muses, a dirge. Sappho. SaLy, *tr.* by Diane Rayor

In the house that has died. Water Song. Michael S. Weaver. ISC

In the house with the tortoise chair. Poem to Ease Birth. *Unknown.* BoWoP; STP, *tr.* by Anselm Hollo

In the huge, rectangular room, the ceiling. My Mother, Who Came from China, Where She Never Saw Snow. Laureen Mar. WPOW
In the huge, wide-open, sleeping eye of the mountain. Bear, The. Ted Hughes. FaBoMo
In the hummingbird house. Hummingbird Light. Diane Wakoski. PmAP
In the hungry kitchen. Kitchen Poem. Francis Scarfe. SPE
In the Huon Valley. James Philip McAuley. CBAP
In the Inner City. Lucille Clifton. HeIP-4; SSCS; UnSA
In the Interest of Possibility. Thom Ward. AmPoNex
In the Jackdaw folder of "Historical Genitalia." Politics of Envy. Duncan Forbes. PeLV
In the Jerusalem Hills. Leah Goldberg. FIT, tr. by Robert Friend
In the Jeta Pavilion of the Setting Sun. Drinking at Night in the Western Pavilion of the Fa-hua Temple. Liu Tsung-yüan. SuSp, tr. by Jan W. Walls
In the Jewish Synagogue at Newport. Emma Lazarus. TaR
In the Jury Room, in Pain. Paul Goodman. BodElec
In the Just Dampened Park. Patrizia Cavalli. CItWP, tr. by Cinzia Sartini Blum and Lara Trubowitz
In the key of life. (LL) Wedding Party. Allison Joseph. AmPoNex; ExTi; MPUn
In the Khamsin. Yitzhak Lamdan.
    "Distant soughing of pine forests caresses my ear, The." MHP
    "How little of God's grace caresses you, Massadah." MHP
    "On roads beyond the camp the Khamsin struck me." MHP
    "Why did Hagar weep over Ishmael when he thirsted." MHP
In the Kifah Street, near the Fadl Mosque. Woman, A. Yasin Taha Hafiz. MAP, tr. by Sharif Elmusa and Christopher Middleton
In the King's Rooms. Timothy Steele. RA
In the Kingdom of Perpetual Repair. Kevin Stein. IllVoic
In the Kitchen. Mary Leapor. ECWP Fr. Crumble Hall.
In the kitchen. Peeling Potatoes. Philip L. Miller. SpudSo
In the kitchen a tanged fetid forest. Cemetery in the Mind, The. Dambudzo Marechera. NAfrP
In the kitchen as the toast browns. At My Father's House. Nancy Travis. ISC
In the Kitchen Before Dinner. Jane Rohrer. BodElec
In the Laboratory. Dan Pagis. PoSu, tr. by Robert Friend
In the laboratory waiting room. Through a Glass Eye, Lightly. Carolyn Kizer. BoWoP
In the Labyrinth of Elements. Duane Niatum. PoCoUp
In the Lake District. Joseph Brodsky. BLT, tr. by George L. Kline
In the lamplight falling. Night. Peter Everwine. NNaP
In the land o' the leal. (LL) Land o' the Leal, The. Carolina Oliphant, Baroness Nairne. GTBS-P; NOBRP; NPeEn; NePenScot; OBEV; OxBEV; OxBS
In the land of dwarfs. Forugh Farrokhzad. BoWoP
In the land of milk and honey. People of Figs. Nidaa Khoury. DTA, tr. by Karen Alkalay-Gut
In the land of Schlaraffenland. Igor Vladimirovich Chinnov. TCRusP, tr. by John Glad
In the land of turkeys in turkey weather. Dance of the Macabre Mice. Wallace Stevens. NOBA; OxBA; PFTM-1
In the language of the spirit. Leap Year. Charles North. FTOS
In the last days. Apocalypse. Francis Ernest Kobina Parkes. PBA
In the last, far field, half-buried in barberry bushes, red-fruited. Dead Horse in Field. Robert Penn Warren. BodElec
In the last light I drove. After Supper. David Keller. SwNoth
In the last low cottage in Blackthorn Lane. Wise-Woman, The. Agnes Mary Frances Robinson. VWP
In the last minutes he said more to her. Seamus Heaney. PNI Fr. Clearances.
In the last storm, when hawks. Epitaph Ending in And, The. William Stafford. LCAP-2
In the late autumn's dusky-golden prime. Vespertilia. Rosamund Marriott Watson. ViWPN
In the laundermat. Sydell Rosenberg. HA
In the Lebanese Mountains. Nadia Tuéni. PoArWo, tr. by Samuel Hazo
In the Lecture Room. James Keir Baxter. PeLV Fr. Cressida.
In the lens of memory, that smudged bungler. Spectral Dues. Pimone Triplett. AmPoNex
In the lethargy which follows the machinations of the. Amelia Rosselli. PFTM-2, tr. by Lawrence R. Smith Fr. Martial Variations.
In the Library. Michael Patrick Hearn. NTCP
In the Library. Hamutal Bar Yosef. DTA, tr. by Shirley Kaufman
In the Life and Death of Rosamel Del Valle. Eunice Odio.
    "It is not true that you are far from 'the light that can find you.'" TANSG, tr. by Arthur Natella
    "It is the dawn." TANSG, tr. by Arthur Natella

In the Line of Duty. Jayne Cortez. SurWo
In the little courtyard, by the side window. Li Ch'ing-chao. SuSp Fr. Tune: "Sand of Silk-washing Stream."
In the little red house by the river. Wilderspin. Mary Elizabeth Coleridge. VWP; ViWPN
In the lives of their friends. (LL) Beware: Do Not Read This Poem. Ishmael Reed. BPo; NIP-4; PAI
In the lobby, three old women, in deep armchairs, sit. Lagoon. Joseph Brodsky. TCRusP, tr. by Daniel Weissbort
In the Local Museum. Walter De la Mare. HAP
In the Locker Room. Madeline DeFrees. ExTi
In the log dugout hidden by osiers. Sighs of the Gunner from Dakar, The. Guillaume Apollinaire. PeFWW, tr. by Anne Hyde Greet
In the long journey out of the self. Journey to the Interior. Theodore Roethke. LCAP-2; TRP; VGW
In the long journey out of the self. Theodore Roethke. DiPo Fr. North American Sequence.
In the long run we must fix our compass. Respected, Feared, and Somehow Loved. Marjorie Welish. PmAP
In the long run you're tired of this ancient world. Zone. Guillaume Apollinaire. CuPo
In the long, sleepless watches of the night. Cross of Snow, The. Henry Wadsworth Longfellow. APN-1; AWTN; ColAP; GSo; HeIP-4; NOBA; NoP-4; OxBA; TAP; TCAPo
In the Longhouse, Oneida Museum. Roberta Hill Whiteman. NoAM
In the Looking Glass. Anna Andreyevna Akhmatova. TCRP, tr. by Daniel Weissbort
In the Lord's eyes. (LL) This Place Rumord to Have Been Sodom. Robert Duncan. CAGL; NOBA; NeAP; PoM
In the Lost Province. Tom Paulin. PBCIP
In the love of home and country and the flag of Uncle Sam. Loyalty to the Flag. Lizelia Augusta Jenkins Moorer. CBWP-3
In the Lungs. Milo De Angelis. NeIt, tr. by Lawrence Venuti
In the Lybian desert I. Modo and Alciphron. Sylvia Townsend Warner. MoBrPo
In the Madison Zoo. Roberta Hill Whiteman. CDW
In the Madonna Dell' Orto. Peter Rafferty. NLP
In the main square of Berdyansk. Sky, The. Vladimir Nikolaevich Kornilov. TCRP, tr. by Daniel Weissbort
In the manger of course were cows and the Child Himself. Pig. Anthony Hecht. OxBC
In the Marble Quarry. James Dickey. NoP-4
In the market, car horns, alarms, the barking of dogs. (LL) Diver for the NYPD Talks to His Girlfriend, A. Richard Garcia. TouFir; UrbNat
In the market, in the cloister—only God I saw. Baba Kuhi of Shiraz. TOF
In the marketplace where St Florian. She Looked At the Sun. Tadeusz Rózewicz. PoSu, tr. by Magnus F. Krynski
In the marriage, not able to anticipate how they would feel. Short Narrative of Hand and Face in Service of PLOT, Entitled, A. Claudia Rankine. NAPBL
In the May breeze. Elegy. M. Safdar Mir. CarOv, tr. by Carolyn Kizer
In the mazes of loitering people, the watchful and furtive. Chance Meetings. Conrad Potter Aiken. TCAPo
In the Meadow There's a Dead Deer. Unknown. CoBCP, tr. by Burton Watson
In the melon-patch / Thief, fox. Tan Taigi. ZenPo, tr. by Takashi Ikemoto and Lucien Stryk
In the Menagerie. Oleg Grigorevich Chukhonstev. TCRP, tr. by Simon Franklin
In the merry month of May. Var. authors. NoSic; OBEV; TTTS Fr. Honourable Entertainment Given to the Queen's Majesty in Progress at Elvetham, 1591, The.
In the mid-1800s. Island of Women, The. June McGlashan. ReEnLa
In the mid-sixties. TV in Black and White. Gary Soto. ReTh
In the middle. Black Love Black Hope. Doughtry Long. SeSe
In the middle / of a dimly lit room. 3rd Untitled Poem. Pedro Juan Pietri. PueRic
In the middle of a tiny spot and nearly bare there is a nice thing to say that. Leave, A. Gertrude Stein. PFTM-1
In the middle of our times. Middle. Jimmie Durham. HATNAP
In the middle of Priest Lake. Madeline DeFrees. ExTi
In the Middle of Reading One More Poem with Brueghel as a Metaphor. Doris Safie. GraLe
In the middle of the day. To B. P. Aleksandr Semionovich Kushner. TCRusP, tr. by Daniel Weissbort
In the middle of the harbour. Derek Walcott. TTY Fr. Sea-Chantey, A.
In the middle of the journey of our life. Dante Alighieri. BiHa, tr. by Seamus Heaney Fr. Divina Commedia.
In the middle of the night. Philodemus. PGA

In the middle of the night he started up. Silver Wedding. Ralph Hodgson. OxBTC

In the middle of the night I slipped away from my husband. Philodemus. HePo *Fr.* Epigrams.

In the middle of the night in the next room. Cell of Himself, The. Arthur Freeman. TwCP

In the middle of the night, when we get up. True Love. Sharon Olds. BodElec

In the middle of the poem my daughter reminds me. Finding What's Lost. Dorianne Laux. GeoHom

In the Middle of the Road. Carlos Drummond de Andrade. BLT; PoetW, *tr. by* Elizabeth Bishop

In the Middle of the Road. Carlos Drummond de Andrade. TCLAP, *tr. by* John Nist

In the middle of the sea. Song. *Unknown.* STP, *tr. by* Jerome Rothenberg

In the middle of the wood I set sail. Amhrán na mBréag. Pearse Hutchinson. PBCIP

In the middle silences of this night's course the blackthorn. David Jones. OxAEP-2 *Fr.* Mabinog's Liturgy.

In the Midst of Life. Tadeusz Rózewicz. PoSu, *tr. by* Adam Czerniawski (It was a voice of another man.) (LL) HP

In the midst of my garden. Palm Tree, The. Abd-ar-Rahman I. AWP, *tr. by* J. B. Trend

In the midst of the Great Sadovaya. Secret Agent, A. Yevgeny [*or* Evgenii] Borisovich Rein. ItGoST, *tr. by* Judith Hemschemeyer

In the midst of this world. Issa. SoOfWa, *tr. by* Sam Hamill

In the Mile End Road. Amy Levy. PEW; RACG; ViWPN

In the mirror. Penny Harter. HA

In the mirror in front of me. Your Body Glistens from the Bath. Charles Rossiter. PasH

In the mirror of the open window the mirror-cloud drifts. Clouds. Sándor Weöres. IQMS, *tr. by* Edwin Morgan

In the Miscroscope. Miroslav Holub. PoSu; WoPoe, *tr. by* Ian Milner and Jarmila Milner

In the Moldavian Steppe. Aleksandr [*or* Viktor Fyodorovich] Vertinsky [*or* Vertinskii]. TCRP, *tr. by* Daniel Weissbort

In the moment before it disappears. (LL) Garden, The. Mark Strand. ColAP; NoAM

In the month of Averil. Cuckoo, The. *Unknown.* FaBoVe

In the month of June the grass grows high. Reading the Book of Hills and Seas. Ch'ien T'ao. ChiP, *tr. by* Arthur Waley

In the Moonlight. Thomas Hardy. NoAM *Fr.* Satires of Circumstance in Fifteen Glimpses.

In the moonlight. Anecdote of the Prince of Peacocks. Wallace Stevens. AWTN

In the Morgue. Israel Zangwill. TrJP

In the Morning. Jayne Cortez. BlSi

In the Morning. Paul Laurence Dunbar. BPo

In the Morning. Steve Kowit. BLT

In the morning and at night. T'ao Ch'ien [*or* T'ao Yuan-ming]. SuSp *Fr.* Seasons Come and Go, The.

In the morning, as he was returning to the city. Donald Hall. GI *Fr.* St. Matthew.

In the morning, before breakfast, I save my own life. Man Saves Own Life. Aaron Anstett. AmPoNex

In the morning he steps out. Crier, The. Philip Kahclamet. STP, *tr. by* Dell Hymes

In the Morning I Look for You. Solomon ibn Gabirol. TOF, *tr. by* David Goldstein

In the Morning I Will Pray. William Henry Furness. AH

In the morning in the blue snow. Annual Gaiety. Wallace Stevens. MoAmPo

In the morning light a line. Morning Light, The. Louis Simpson. NNaP

In the morning of the tribe this name Ancapagari was given to these mountains. Ancapagari. Carolyn Forché. YaYoPo

In the morning or at any time, in the morning. Morning. Duo Duo (Li Shizheng). PoetW, *tr. by* Maghiel Van Crevel

In the morning part. Did John's Music Kill Him? Alfred B. Spellman. NAAAL; SeSe

In the morning she thinks. Learning to Live with the Piano. Ann Lundberg Grunke. MiVo

In the morning sow thy seed, and in the evening withhold not thine hand: for thou knowest not whether shall prosper, either this or that, or whether they both shall be alike good. (LL) Bible, *O.T.* AWP; OBVE *Fr.* Ecclesiastes.

In the morning the bitch whelped. Bitch, The. Sergey [*or* Sergei] Aleksandrovich Yesenin [*or* Essenin]. TCRP, *tr. by* Daniel Weissbort

In the morning, the water fed the sky. Commentary Text Commentary Text Commentary Text. David Shapiro. PmAP

In the morning they build embankments against floods. Wu Chia-chi. CoBLCP *Fr.* Returning to the Alluvial Fields.

In the morning when I leave my hogan. Mother's Lace. Shonto Begay. NOxBChV

In the morning with my staff I sought the topmost crag. On Climbing the Highest Peak of Stone Gate Mountain. Hsieh Ling-yün. ColAnChi, *tr. by* Richard W. Bodman

In the morning with the journey all before us on the road. One Step at a Time. Joseph Morris. ITBLP

In the most inconceivable places. Queen Esther Award, The. Richard Michelson. GotH

In the most obscure of streets in the shadow of architectural ribs, where. Zurich Chronicle February 1916. Tristan Tzara. PFTM-1

In the Mountain. Wang Wei. ChinPo, *tr. by* Yip Wai-lim

In the mountain rain. Death Poems in September. Diane Di Prima. BB

In the mountain temple they beat the Dharma Drum. Dawn at Chiao Mountain, Seeing Off K'un-lun on His Way Back to Ching-k'ou. Wang Shih-chieng. SuSp, *tr. by* Richard John Lynn

In the mountain village. Kanemori. OHMPJ

In the Mountain Village. Wang Hung Kung. OHMPC, *tr. by* Kenneth Rexroth

In the mountain village. Minamoto no Morotada. OHPJ

In the mountain where you are unworshiped. Inanna and Ebih. Enheduanna. BoWoP

In the Mountains. Ssu-k'ung Shu. SuSp, *tr. by* Edward H. Schafer

In the Mountains. Andrey [*or* Andrei] Andreievich Voznesensky [*or* Voznesenskii]. RusPo, *tr. by* Robert Arthur Douglas Ford

In the Mountains. Wang An-shih. SuSp, *tr. by* Jan W. Walls

In the Mountains. Wang Po. CrYelRi, *tr. by* Sam Hamill

In the Mountains as Autumn Begins. Wen T'ing-yün. OHMPC, *tr. by* Kenneth Rexroth

In the Mountains on a Summer Day. Li Po. AWP, *tr. by* Arthur Waley

In the Mountains on a Summer Day. Li Po. TAL

In the Mountains, Parting from Master Ning as I Return to West Bank. Kao Ch'i. CoBLCP, *tr. by* Jonathan Chaves

In the Mourning. Keorapetse Kgositsile. PBMAP *Fr.* Present is a Dangerous Place to Live, The.

In the Mourning Time. Robert Earl Hayden. BPo

In the movie plays. Cup of Coffee, a Sandwich, and You. Joseph Meyer. ReLy

In the MR waiting room, gown pants and booties. MRI. Ron Charach. BloBone

In the mud of the Cambrian main. Ballade of Evolution, A. Grant Allen. EBVV

In the multitude of counsellors. Kyrielle: Party Politics. Frederick Thomas Bennett Macartney. NOBAu

In the Museum. Isabella Gardner. SoSe-8

In the museum of translucent. Exhibits, The. Tracey Herd. MFPA

In the Naked Bed, in Plato's Cave. Delmore Schwartz. APT-2; MoAmPo; NOBA; NoAM; VGW

In the name of Love. (LL) Sirventes. Paul Blackburn. NeAP; PoM

In the name of the God of strangers, we beg you. Damagetus. GrAn

In the name of the people. Matsemela Manaka. PeSAV *Fr.* Pula.

In the nativity of time. Love Made in the First Age[: To Chloris]. Richard Lovelace. BeJo; CaPo; NAEL-5v1; NAEL-6v1; NAEL-7v1

In the Neolithic Age. Rudyard Kipling. NOBVV

In the network, in the ruin. Trope Market. Jackson Mac Low. PmAP

In the New Country. Barbara Ras. OPRER

In the New Sun. Philip Levine. NNaP

"In the New World Happiness Is Allowed." Peter Porter. BMAP

In the new year twelve hundred ninety-one. (LL) Sonnet: Of the 20th of June 1291. Cecco Angiolieri, da Siena. AWP; EaItPo, *tr. by* Dante Gabriel Rossetti

In the next seat the young man from Bangalore sleeps. Carpe Diem: Time Piece. Marilyn Krysl. PuP-23

In the Night. Ch'oe Ch'ung. WoPoe, *tr. by* Jean S. Grigsby

In the Night. Robert Ivanovich Rozhdestvensky [*or* Rozhdestvenskii]. RusPo, *tr. by* Robert Arthur Douglas Ford

In the night. Blues. Sonia Sanchez. GT

In the Night. James Stephens. OBMV

In the Night. *Unknown.* NBLV

In the Night. Ella Wheeler Wilcox. SWaP

In the night, awash with symbols. Night. Duo Duo (Li Shizheng). PoetW, *tr. by* Donald Finkel and Li Guohua

In the night, in the wind, at the edge of the rain. Irises. Li-Young Lee. BLT

In the night of the beginning. Alice Rahon. SurWo, *tr. by* Nancy Deffebach and Vanina Deler

In the Night of the Full Moon. Carl Busse. AWP, *tr. by* Jethro Bithell

In the night she told a story. Story, A. Jean Ingelow. VWP

In the night there are naturally the seven marvels of the world. Sleep Spaces. Robert Desnos. SurPaPo, *tr. by* Mary Ann Caws

In the night there was a murder in the street. Of Autumn. Veronica Porumbacu. BoWoP

In the night / Though we're apart. Haunted Heart. Arthur Schwartz. ReLy

In the Nighttime Someone. Luigi Fontanella. NeIt, *tr. by* Michael Palma

In the Nine Provinces there is not room enough. Vision, A. Ts'ao Chih. ChiP, *tr. by* Arthur Waley

In the 19th Century, clever mediums. Veiled Lady, The. Maura Stanton. BodElec

In the 19th century concert hall. Re-Emergence of the Trombone, The. Fred Muratori. MiVo

In the north birds feather a long wind. Portrait of a Lady Walking. Djuna Barnes. APT-1

In the north there is a lovely woman. Song, A. Li Yen-nien. ColAnChi, *tr. by* Anne Birrell

In the north-west there is a high house. *Unknown.* ChiP *Fr.* Seventeen Old Poems.

In the northern hemisphere. Kangaroo. D. H. Lawrence. EBEV; OxBTC

In the northwest there is a drifting cloud. Ts'ao P'i. SuSp

In the numb, numberless days. Burning, The. N. Scott Momaday. HATNAP

In the Nuptial Chamber. Thomas Hardy. InPK-6 *Fr.* Satires of Circumstance in Fifteen Glimpses.

In the ocean there's a very sad turtle. Jack Kerouac. PoM *Fr.* Mexico City Blues.

In the office is Mrs. Apostolacos; the bus driver is Ray. (LL) Questions, The. Robert Pinsky. ColAP; NoAM

In the offing scatterest foam, thy white sails crowding. (LL) Passer-by, A. Robert Bridges. MoBrPo; OBEV; OxBTC; SCGP

In the old accents I will sing, my Glory, my Delight. Fellowship. "Michael Field." VWP

In the old age black was not counted fair. William Shakespeare. NAEL-6v1; NAEL-7v1; OxAEP-1 *Fr.* Sonnets.

In the old back streets o' Pimlico. Rambling Sailor, The. Charlotte Mew. PoRA

In the Old City. Jacob [*or* Jakov] Fichman. TrJP, *tr. by* Sholom J. Kahn

In the old days (a custom laid aside). Abraham Davenport. John Greenleaf Whittier. NoP-4; TCAPo

'In the old days,' she explained to a grandchild bred in England. Stone of Patience. Mimi Khalvati. MFPA

In the old days when King Arthur ruled the nation. Geoffrey Chaucer. NAWM-7v1, *tr. by* Theodore Morrison *Fr.* Canterbury Tales, The.

In the old days with married women's stockings. Libertine, The. Louis MacNeice. ModLr; NoAM

In the old house. Formal Poem, A. Amal Moussa. PoArWo, *tr. by* Khaled Mattawa

In the Old Neighborhood. Rita Dove. SpirFl

In the old neighborhood, each funeral parlor. Teach Us to Number Our Days. Rita Dove. ESEAA; NoAM

In the old, old days when the West was young. Texas Ranger, The. Margie B. Boswell. AiP

In the old park frozen and alone. Exchange of Feelings. Paul Verlaine. SxFrPo, *tr. by* Martin Sorrell

In the old stone pool. Basho. InPK-6

In the old testament. Bible Study. Gloria C. Oden. ESEAA; GT

In the old time, by the forks of the Santiam. Kalapuya Prophecy, A. *Unknown.* STP, *tr. by* Jarold Ramsey

In the old time women's cunts had teeth in them. How Her Teeth Were Pulled. *Unknown.* STP, *tr. by* Jarold Ramsey

In the old way and raise our heritage. (LL) Poem from Llanybri. Lynnette Roberts. AngWePo; TCAWP

In the one cool room in the house. Andrew Taylor. *See* In the one cool room of the house

In the one cool room of the house. Developing a Wife. Andrew Taylor. CBAP

In the one light on. First Aid at 4 A.M. Christopher Bursk. InPK-6

In the one-two domestic goose one-two one-two step. Henry Beissel. MoCV *Fr.* New Wings for Icarus.

In the open sea. *Unknown.* OHMPJ

In the Operating Room. Alden Nowlan. NOBC

In the Orchard. Henrik Ibsen. AWP, *tr. by* Sir Edmund William Gosse

In the orchard. Plume. Richard Kenney. NoP-4

In the Orchard. Anne Stevenson. ColAP

In the Orchard. Muriel Stuart. EBNV; OxBTC

In the Orchard. Algernon Charles Swinburne. BoLoP

In the orchard grass, through the daisies and clover. Blossom. May Probyn. VWP

In the orchard rooms. Fruit. Philippe Jaccottet. MFP, *tr. by* Martin Sorrell

In the other gardens. Autumn Fires. Robert Louis Stevenson. NOxBChV

In the outer suburbs the coalmen race their carts. Coalmen, The. László Nagy. IQMS, *tr. by* Tony Connor

In the Outhouse. Katherine Pierpoint. MFPA

In the painkilling cold that wrapped. Snow. David Wevill. MoCV

In the painting above your bed a woman pauses. Thirst. Mark Wunderlich. AmPoNex

In the Palace of the President this morning. Easter Sunday, 1985. Charles Martin. RA

In the palace of the Queen Chinee. (LL) Dame Edith Sitwell. NAEL-5v2; NAEL-6v2 *Fr.* Façade.

In The Palace of the slums. Welsh Valley Cinema, 1930s. Dannie Abse. TCAWP

In the Palais Royal Garden. Christopher Pearse Cranch. APN-1

In the pale light of the half moon, she sees him. Somnambulist. Adele Ne Jame. PoArWo

In the pale moonlight. World's First Face, The. W. S. Rendra. WoPoe, *tr. by* Burton Raffel

In the Pantry. Hugh MacDiarmid. NoAM

In the pantry the dear dense cheeses, Cheddars and harsh. O Cheese. Donald Hall. DiPo

In the parched word, unformulated, it shrinks. On the Facets: The Flashing. Coral Bracho. PFTM-2, *tr. by* Thomas Hoeksema

In the Park. Judith Beveridge. BMAP

In the Park. Gwen Harwood. BMAP; CBAP; NIL-7

In the Park. Peter Jones. OBGa

In the park a crow awakes. Kenneth Rexroth. APSN *Fr.* Love Poems of Marichiko, The.

In the parking lot. Cor Van den Heuvel. HA

In the parking lot where the path to the sea begins. Homeless. Michael Hannon. GeoHom

In the parlour of the shanty where the lives have all gone wrong. Will Yer Write It Down for Me? Henry Lawson. CBAP

In the Past. Trumbull Stickney. ColAP; NOBA; OxBA

In the past I brought trouble upon myself when I sought rank and honor. Tune: "Wild Geese Have Come Down; Song of Victory." *Unknown.* SuSp, *tr. by* Sherwin S. S. Fu

In the past the warring nations. Civilisation. János Arany. IQMS, *tr. by* Peter Zollman

In the past when I saw friends off. Wen Cheng-ming. CoBLCP *Fr.* Improvised on Horseback to Say Good-bye to Those Who Are Seeing Me Off.

In the pathway of the sun. Penelope. Dorothy Parker. FaBoWar

In the Paul Guillaume Gallery. Pierre Albert-Birot. CuPo

In the Pauper's Turnip-Field. Herman Melville. OxBSP

In the penetrating damp. Restless Night in Camp, A. Tu Fu. OHPC, *tr. by* Kenneth Rexroth

In the Person of a Lady, to Bajazet, Her Unconstant Gallant. "Ephelia." PEW

In the Person of Womankind [A Song Apologetic]. Ben Jonson. BeJo

In the Person of Womankind (In Defense of Their Inconstancy). Ben Jonson. *See* Another. In Defense of Their Inconstancy [*or* Inconstancie]. A Song

In the "phoenix ranks" I was granted the Purple Robe. Selling My Official Robe. Yang Chi. CoBLCP, *tr. by* Jonathan Chaves

In the photograph he stands alone. Chinese Camp, Kamloops (circa 1883). Andrew Suknaski. NOBC

In the Pines. Bill Monroe. GM

In the place where. Judy Grahn. NALW *Fr.* Edward the Dyke and Other Poems.

In the pleasant pastime of temple viewing. Manners. Edith Marcombe Shiffert. WPE

In the poem about the vandals, the vandals. Vandals, The. Alan Michael Parker. NeAmPo

In the poem that comes just before sleep. Just Before Sleep. Peter Everwine. GeoHom

In the poor man's house. Teiga. SoOfWa, *tr. by* Sam Hamill

In the Poppy Field. James Stephens. PoRA

In the Post Office. Thom Gunn. CAGL

In the postmodern world. Being Sick Together. Elaine Equi. IllVoic

In the Potting Shed. Sir Osbert Sitwell. OBGa

In the Praise of Music. Humphrey [*or* Humfrey] Gifford. NoSic

In the prelight. Monday Morning. Audrey Shafer. BloBone

In the presence of blue, it's the eye. Past Midnight, My Daughter Awakened by Miles Davis' *Kind of Blue.* Kevin Stein. IllVoic

In the Prison Pen. Herman Melville. TAP

In the *Proceedings of the Royal Institute of Anthropophagy.* Perversion, A. Christopher Reid. OBCoV

In the prose version. Helen Paints a Room (1984). John A. Scott. BMAP

In the Public Garden. Marianne Craig Moore. NOBA

In the Public Theater lobby, I wait for Marie. Marilyn Hacker. VCAP *Fr.* Taking Notice.

In the pure light, my tears fall: a poem. (LL) Spring Thoughts Sent to Tzu-an. Yü Hsüan-chi. BoWoP; WoPoe, *tr. by* Geoffrey Waters

In the Purple Bar. Gig Ryan. BMAP

In the purple light, heavy with redwood, the slopes drop seaward. Apology for Bad Dreams. Robinson Jeffers. APT-1; MoAmPo; NOBA; OxBA

In the quarries should you toil. Make Your Mark. David Barker. TreFP

In the quarter of the Negroes. Cultural Exchange. Langston Hughes. BPo

In the Queen Anne's lace a toad. Alexis Rotella. HA

In the Queen's Room. Norman Cameron. OxBTC *Fr.* Three Love Poems.

In the quiet of the morning I heard a knock at my door. Ch'ien T'ao. ChiP

In the railroad yards, leaving the city of darkness. And as for Man. Loren C. Eiseley. GM

In the rain in a yard in Cessnock. Limerick. Ruth Silcock. PeLi

In the rain, the naked old father is dancing, he will get wet. Natural History. Robinson Penn Warren. NAAL-2v2

In the rains of winter the pa children. James Keir Baxter. PeNZ *Fr.* Five Sestinas.

In the ranks of the Austrian you found him. Forced Recruit, The. Elizabeth Barrett Browning. FaBoWar

In the rat race he won by a whisker. Lifelines. Gavin Ewart. SPE

In the Reading-Room of the British Museum. Louise Imogen Guiney. APN-2

In the Realm of Emptiness. (LL) Saying Good-bye to a Singing Girl Who Has Decided to Become a Nun. Mo Shih-lung. CoBLCP; ColAnChi; WoPoe, *tr.* by Jonathan Chaves

In the realms of the good and great. (LL) "Mark Twain." NBLV; OBAL *Fr.* Adventures of Huckleberry Finn, The.

In the rear-view mirror suddenly. Auto Mirror. Adam Zagajewski. BLT

In the rear-view mirrors of the passing cars. (LL) War against the Trees, The. Stanley Kunitz. HAP; PAI

In the Red Book. Kelvin Corcoran. Oth

In the Refectory. Alcuin. MLL, *tr.* by Helen Waddell

In the Refugee Camp. Sharif Elmusa. GraLe

In the region of rain and cloud. Desire's Persistence. Jay Wright. ESEAA

In the Restaurant. Gerald William Barrax. GT

In the Restaurant. Aleksandr Aleksandrovich Blok. TCRP, *tr.* by Geoffrey Thurley

In the Restaurant. Thomas Hardy. MoBrPo *Fr.* Satires of Circumstance in Fifteen Glimpses.

In the Ringwood. Thomas Kinsella. PBCIP

In the ripest days of August, sunflowers. Whisper, The. Eugene Gloria. OpBo

In the river bank, an empty sandpit. Frankfurt. János Pilinszky. PoSu

In the Roman Forum. István Vas. IQMS, *tr.* by Bruce Berlind

In the Room. James Thomson. NOBVV; NePenScot; OxBEV; PeVV

In the Room I. Jacqueline Brown. Prnts

In the Room of the Bride-Elect. Thomas Hardy. InPK-6 *Fr.* Satires of Circumstance in Fifteen Glimpses.

In the room's corner the shadow played its little flute. Flute, The. Sophia De Mello Breyner. VCWP, *tr.* by Ruth Fainlight

In the room the women come and go. Mother Dawning. Janine Canan. HW

In the room where we lie, light. This Close. Dorianne Laux. ExTi

In the Root Cellar. Maxine W. Kumin. FaBoWP

In the rose creeping into the tower of exiles. Winter Day, A. Philip Lamantia. CLPP

In the Royal City spring is almost over. Flower Market, The. Po Chü-i. ChiP, *tr.* by Arthur Waley

In the rubbish dumps, a concrete dam far off in the mountain. (LL) Summer Holiday. Robinson Jeffers. MoAmPo; OxBA

In the Rue Monsieur le Prince. Song for "Buvez les Vins du Postillion"—Advt. Jean Garrigue. TAP

In the rush odour of Danish meadows. Peter Huchel. PoSu

In the sacred city of Benares. (LL) Courtesy, A Trenchant Grace, A. Cyrus Cassells. GT; WiU

In the salt warp / was the plasma. Origins. Carl Rakosi. FTOS

In the same post, the Old Fox receives. Negotiation. Alan Brownjohn. PeLV

In the same way. (LL) Apology. William Carlos Williams. OxBA; SAmP

In the sand I grew, by the rocky sea-wall. Husband's Message, The. *Unknown.* AnOE, *tr.* by Charles W. Kennedy

In the satin shade of an olive tree. Achilles and the Tortoise. Miroslav Holub. PoSu, *tr.* by Stuart Friebert

In the scented bud of the morning—O. Daisies, The. James Stephens. AWP

In the school auditorium. Bully. Martín Espada. LTA

In the schoolyard, in the cloakrooms, the children boasted their scars of dried snot; wrists and knees garnished with impetigo. (LL) Geoffrey Hill. HAP; NAAL-5v2; NAAL-6v2; NPeEn; NoAM; NoP-4; PoE; WoPoe *Fr.* Mercian Hymns.

In the Sea. Brendan Kennelly. BiHa

In the sea. (LL) Little Fish. D. H. Lawrence. OxBTC; RB; Spl; TTTS

In the sea, Biscayne, there prinks. Homunculus et la Belle Étoile. Wallace Stevens. MoAmPo

In the Sea of Tears. Naomi Replansky. BrRo

In the sea, sunset. O. Mabson Southard. HA

In the season of late August star-fall. Amazing Grace in the Back Country. Robert Penn Warren. ColAP

In the season of this ripening. Elemental. Marjorie M. Evasco. ReBoTo

In the Second Month of Summer, Taking My Family to the Villages East of the City. Li K'ai-hsien. CoBLCP, *tr.* by Jonathan Chaves

In the second month, sleeping a lot, all sleepy and dazed. Daytime Dream. Tu Fu. WoPoe, *tr.* by Eva Shan Chou

In the Secret House. Christopher Middleton. FaBoMo

In the Secret House of Night. Jorge Teillier. BLPSL, *tr.* by Rene de Costa, Rigas Kappatos and Eleni Paidoussi

In the secret of night. Liana, The. Gabriela Mistral. BBASP, *tr.* by Doris Dana

In the sedge beyond Chalco. Flowering War, The. *Unknown.* STP, *tr.* by Jerome Rothenberg

In the Seminole darkness of your singing eyes. Poem to a Redskin. Wendy Rose. CDW

In the sequestered court quiet reigns. Tune: "Beating Silk Floss." Li Yü. ColAnChi, *tr.* by Jiaosheng Wang

In the Servants' Quarters. Thomas Hardy. FaBoVe; MoBrPo

In the Service of the Wheel. Hans Faverey. TuT, *tr.* by Peter Van de Kamp

In the Seven Woods. W. B. Yeats. NoAM

In the seventh month, declining is the Fire Star. *Unknown.* ColAnChi, *tr.* by Jeffrey Riegel *Fr.* Classic of Odes.

In the seventh month the Fire-star declines. In the Seventh Month. *Unknown.* SuSp, *tr.* by Irving Y. Lo

In the shabby train no seat is vacant. Refugees, The. Randall Jarrell. MoAmPo

In the shade of a metaphor. Patrizia Cavalli. NeIt

In the shade of a plane tree with our shopping. City Park. Christine Crow. SSCS

In the shade of a wall. New Sweater. Kees Ouwens. TuT, *tr.* by Peter Van de Kamp

In the shadow of a wing. José Martí. TCLAP, *tr.* by Elinore Randall *Fr.* Simple Verses.

In the Shadow of Fire. Frieda Hughes. NeBl

In the Shadows. David Gray.

Sonnet I: "If it must be; if it must be, O God!" OxBS

In the Shadows of the Wu-t'ung Tree. *Unknown.* CrYelRi, *tr.* by Sam Hamill

In the Shakespeare Garden at Northwestern University. Paul Carroll. IllVoic

In the shaking of the sieve, the refuse. Bible, Apocrypha. TrJP *Fr.* Ecclesiasticus.

In the shambles of love, they kill only the best, Jelaluddin [or Jalal al-Din] Rumi. RaBo *Fr.* Four Quatrains.

In the shimmering countries that exude the summer. Manuscript Found in a Book of Joseph Conrad. Jorge Luis Borges. PoetW, *tr.* by Alastair Reid

In the shop in the muceque. Note on a Shop in the Muceque. Geraldo Bessa Victor. PeSAV, *tr.* by Donald Burness

In the shop, she, her mother, and grandmother. Charles Reznikoff. APT-2

In the shower, at the shaving mirror or beach. My Mammogram. J. D. McClatchy. WiU

In the shower naked. Breast Examination. Wanda Coleman. GT

In the Shreve High football stadium. Autumn Begins in Martins Ferry, Ohio. James Wright (1927–80). ColAP; HCAP; HeIP-4; InPK-6; MoASP; NAAL-5; NoAM; VCAP; WeW-3

In the sightless air I dwell. Song of a Spirit. Ann Radcliffe. ECWP; RWP

In the Silence. Stephany Fuller. BPo

In the silence and the gloom. (LL) Aftermath. Henry Wadsworth Longfellow. APN-1; NAAL-2v1; NAAL-3; NOBA; PoPoPo; TAP

In the silence that prolongs the span. Black Jackets. Thom Gunn. HeIP-4; NAEL-5v2; NAEL-6v2; NoP-4; TwCP

In the silences between peals of the bell. Chin Nung. CoBLCP *Fr.* I Have Recently Edited My Unworthy Poems in Four Chapters, Copied Them Out in My Own Hand, and Entrusted Them to My Daughter to Keep. Five Miscellaneous Poems.

In the silent halls of Hades, down the windless halls of Hades. Danaïds, The. Mihály Babits. IQMS, *tr.* by Peter Zollman

In the Silent Night. Isaac Leibush [or Yitskhok Leybush] Peretz [or Perets]. TrJP, *tr.* by Joseph Leftwich

In the Silurian seas! (LL) Lay of the Trilobite. May Kendall. NPeEn; VWP; ViWPN

In the singed breath of London. Liberty and Ten Years of Return. Christopher Howell. CDa

In the sister's garden it is still winter. Family History, The. Nicole Cooley. AmPoNex

In the sixth month, outside the gate. Wen Cheng-ming. CoBLCP *Fr.* Chung-i Temple, The.

In the sixty-eight years. Accounting. Claribel Alegría. TANSG, *tr.* by Darwin Flakoll

In the sixty-three years. Summing Up. Claribel Alegría. LoL

In the sky. Last Hour, The. Tudor Arghezi. WoPoe, *tr.* by Michael Impey and Brian Swann

In the sky. Hameed. Salah Niyazi [*or* Niazi]. MAP, *tr.* by Charles Doria and Lena Jayyusi

In the sky, not a sliver of cloud. On the Night of the Sixteenth of the Eighth Month: Watching the Moon from the Deck of the Ship, Aimo-maru in the Black Water Sea. Liu E. CoBLCP, *tr.* by Jonathan Chaves

In the sky the eagle, there is his place, there far above us. Eagle Above Us, The. *Unknown.* WoPoe, *tr.* by Willard Trask

In the sky the Milky Way turns. Tune: "Southern Song, A." Li Ch'ing-chao. SuSp, *tr.* by Eugene Eoyang

In the sky there is a moon and stars. Proportion. Amy Lowell. BoWoP

In the slight ripple, the fishes dart. In the Slight Ripple, the Mind Perceives the Heart. Delmore Schwartz. APT-2

In the sludge drawer of animals in arms. Rules of Sleep. Howard Moss. VCAP

In the small beauty of the forest. Psalm. George Oppen. APT-2; HarvBoo; NNaP; PFTM-2; WoPoe

In the small old barn. Eternal Landscape, The. Lenard D. Moore. GT

In the small town where the hero was born. Pietà. Wislawa Szymborska. VCWP

In the Smoking-Car. Richard Wilbur. CoAmPo; GM; MoAmPo

In the smoky outhouses of the court of love. Norman Cameron. OxBTC *Fr.* Three Love Poems.

In the Snake Park. William Plomer. OxBTC

In the Snowfall. Gwerfyl Mechain. BoWoP, *tr.* by Willis Barnstone

In the south aisle of the abbey at Hexham. Musician, The. David Wright. NLP

In the South be drooping trees. Confucius. CTC *Fr.* Chou and the South.

In the South be drooping trees. *Unknown.* CTC, *tr.* by Ezra Pound *Fr.* Shi King.

In the south, sleeping against. Legacy. Imamu Amiri Baraka. ColAP; NOBA; NoAM

In the South there is a saying. Why Are Daddies So Mean? Jane Chambers. GLP

In the southern land many birds sing. South, The. Wang Chien. AWP; BLT; ChiP, *tr.* by Arthur Waley

In the Southern Mode, to the Tune "A Sprig of Flowers:" The Refusal to Get Old. Kuan Han-ch'ing. ColAnChi, *tr.* by Wayne Schlepp

In the southern village the boy who minds the ox. Herd-Boy, The. Lu Yu. ChiP, *tr.* by Arthur Waley

In the Spring. Meleager. AWP, *tr.* by Andrew Lang

In the spring, by the big shuck-pile. Burning the Cat. W. S. Merwin. NIP-4

In the Spring Garden. Geoffrey Grigson. OBGa

In the spring ravine. Onoe No Shibafune. OHMPJ

In the Spring the quince and the. Ibycus. PGA; WoPoe, *tr.* by Kenneth Rexroth

In the Spring when the feeling was chronic. You Took Advantage of Me. Richard Rodgers. ReLy

In the spring, when winds blew and farmers were plowing fields. American Spring Song. Sherwood Anderson. APT-1

In the spring woods, how good it is to see. Aspects of the World like Coral Reefs. William Bronk. VGW

In the Springtime I am always. Old Age. Ou-yang Hsiu. OHPC, *tr.* by Kenneth Rexroth

In the square of a lighted window. Observation of a Bee. Leah Goldberg. WPOW, *tr.* by Stephen Mitchell

In the State of "Old Palmetto," from the town of Eutawville. Eutawville Lynching, The. Lizelia Augusta Jenkins Moorer. CBWP-3

In the States. Robert Louis Stevenson. AiP

In the Stealth of Stillness. Thurayya Al-Urayyid. PoArWo, *tr.* by Farouk Mustafa

In the steamer is the trout. Eating Together. Li-Young Lee. IllVoic; InvLad; NAAL-5

In the still-blistering late afternoon. Farmer, The. Ellen Bryant Voigt. WeW-3

In the Still of the Night. Cole Porter. ReLy

In the stillness. Expectant Mother. Penelope Shuttle. BrRo

In the stillness after dawn we two. Equinox 1980. Peter Davison. NoP-4

In the Stopping Train. Donald Davie. NPeEn

In the Storm of Roses. Ingeborg Bachmann. AF, *tr.* by Mark Anderson (Aria 1.) WoPoe

In the Stravinsky book by Lillian Libman. Reading in the Night. Roy Fuller. OxBC

In the Street. Constantine P. Cavafy. CAGL, *tr.* by Edmund Keeley and Philip Sherrard

In the Street. John Shaw Neilson. CBAP

In the street of the sky night walks scattering poems. (LL) Impression. E. E. Cummings. MoAmPo; OxBA

In the street two children sharpen. East Bronx. David Ignatow. CoAmPo

In the streetcar conductor's uniform. Portrait: The Freedom Fighter. George Jonas. NOBC

In the stump of the old tree, where the heart has rotted out. Poem. Hugh Sykes Davies. SPE

In the Style of Han Shan and Shih Te. Wang An-shih.
    "Had I been an ox or horse." SuSp; WoPoe, *tr.* by Jan W. Walls
    "Wind blew, a tile fell from the roof, The." SuSp

In the Suburbs. Louis Simpson. TRP

In the suburbs our lives were separated. Walls, The. Douglas Goetsch. AmPoNex

In the summer months on every crossing to Piraeus. Watching for Dolphins. David Constantine. HarvBoo

In the summer of the first year of Chia-yu (A.D. 1056). Cicada, The. Ou-yang Hsiu. AWP, *tr.* by Arthur Waley

In the summer rain. Buson. EH, *tr.* by Robert Hass

In the sun-drenched. City of Salt, The. Gregory Orr. BodElec

In the sun, it is hot. Office Geraniums. Laura Newburn. UrbNat

In the sun's path. Dawn in the Valley. Fily-Dabo Sissoko. NegPo, *tr.* by Ellen Conroy Kennedy

In the sunny orchard closes. In the Orchard. Henrik Ibsen. AWP, *tr.* by Sir Edmund William Gosse

In the sweet shire of Cardigan. Simon Lee [the Old Huntsman]. William Wordsworth. GTBS-P; NAEL-5v2; NAEL-6v2

In the sweetness of new spring. Spring Song. William of Aquitaine. NAWM-7v1, *tr.* by Peter Dronke

In the swirling waters. Streets. Mudrooroo Narogin. IBA

In the swollen head of the nation. (LL) Robert Duncan. APSN; NNaP *Fr.* Passages.

In the Synagogue. Cynthia Ozick. TaR

In the Tail of the Scorpion. Genevieve Taggard. VGW

In the tall orange marigolds, some bees. August. Pamela Stewart. ExTi

In the tall quiet pines of Washington. For Tom Numkena, Hopi/Spokane. Harold Littlebird. VoR

In the Tank. Thom Gunn. NoAM

In the tattered wallpaper I see a butterfly dying. Poem No. X. Sang Yi. PFTM-1

In the tavern where I slept last night. Dead Eyes. Syl Cheney-Coker. NAfrP

In the teacher's lounge, the tall, pretty. Art. Susan Aizenberg. ExTi

In the temple. Bob Boldman. HA

In the Tenth Month of the Year Jen-tzu (1672) the Imperial Censor Tan Chiang-shang, Mountain Man Wang Shih-ku and I Traveled by Boat to Pi-ling and Moored There. We Lingered Among the Frosty Trees and Red Leaves. Wang Was Entrusted with the Task of P. Yün Shou-p'ing.
    "Scorpion's tails, silver hooks." CoBLCP

In the terrible years of Yezhovism I spent seventeen months standing in. Instead of a Preface. Anna Andreyevna Akhmatova. PFTM-1

In the Theatre. Dannie Abse. BloBone; NoAM; TCAWP

In the thicket's shade. Issa. EH, *tr.* by Robert Hass

In the third-class seat sat the journeying boy. Midnight on the Great Western. Thomas Hardy. NOBE; OxAEP-2; WoPoe

In the third day of May. Boy and the Mantle, The. *Unknown.* ESPB; OxBB

In the third decade of March. Where Art Is a Midwife. Tom Paulin. ModIr; NPeEn

In the Third Month. David Ray. RaBo

In the third month, a sudden flow of blood. Vow, The. Anthony Hecht. CoAmPo; InPK-6; TaR

In the third month her laughter sounds strained. On the Metamorphoses Brought About By Emotion: The Rebellion of the Eyes. Andrey [*or* Andrej] Andreievich Voznesensky [*or* Voznesenskii]. PFTM-2, *tr.* by Anselm Hollo

In the time of old sin without sadness. Variations on [*or* of] an Air: After [Algernon Charles] Swinburne. Gilbert Keith Chesterton. NOBL

In the tombs orgies go on by themselves. Letter to Her Brother. Amelia Rosselli. PFTM-2, *tr.* by Lucia Re and Paul Vangelisti

In the top and front of a bus, eager to meet his fate. Figure of Eight. Louis MacNeice. OxBSP

In the Torrent. Johannes Bobrowski. WoPoe, *tr.* by Mark Rudman

In the Touch of This Bosom There Worketh a Spell. Samuel Taylor Coleridge. RB *Fr.* Christabel.

In the Town. *Unknown.* OBCP, *tr.* by Eleanor Farjeon

In the town dump I find a still-beating heart. George Swede. HA

In the town of Athy one Jeremy Lanigan. Lanigan's Ball. *Unknown.* OxBoLi

In the town of Bardez where Armenians. Dance, The. Siamanto. AF, *tr.* by Peter Balakian

In the town of Odessa. Dvonya. Louis Simpson. NNaP; NOBA

In the town streets. Sparrow. Reginald Gibbons. IllVoic

In the town where every man is king. Josephine Miles. NALW

In the Toy Shop. May Kendall. ViWPN

In the Tradition of Bobbitt. Saundra Sharp. SpirFl

In the Tradition Too. Ras Baraka. InTrad

In the train. Only in Poetry. Ajip Rosidi. WoPoe, tr. by Harry Aveling

In the Train. James Thomson. OBEV

In the tranced dancing of men. (LL) Bear on the Delhi Road, The. Earle Birney. HeIP-4; MoCV; NOBC; NoAM; NoP-4

In the Tree-Top. Lucy Larcom. OBCA

In the Trenches. Richard Aldington. PeFWW

In the tunnel of woods, as the road. Last Things. William Meredith. NoAM

In the twelfth month of this Eighth Year. Bitter Cold, Living in the Village. Po Chü-i. SuSp

In the Twentieth Century. James Philip McAuley. ChIV-2

In the Twenty-Fifth Year of Marriage, It Goes On. Alicia Ostriker. PBCAP

In the twenty-fifth year of my age. Petit Testament. "Ern Malley." BMAP

In the twilight of the nineteenth century. Fin de Siècle. Joe Bolton. AmPoNex

In the twinkling of an eye. Bone Scan. Gwen Harwood. HarvBoo

In the Underworld. Muriel Rukeyser. APSN

In the universal Sun. (LL) To Jane: The Invitation. Shelley. GTBS-P; NAEL-5v2; NAEL-6v2; NPeEn

In the unmade light I can see the world. West Wall. W. S. Merwin. RaBo

In the usual way of the young / we made appointments. I Say Goodby to Fan An-ch'eng. Shen Yüeh. SuSp, tr. by Lenore Mayhew

In the vale of resteles mynde. Unknown. OHMEL

In the vale [or vaile] of restless mind. Quia Amore Langueo. Unknown. NOBE; NOCV, tr. by Helen Gardner

In the Valley. Priscilla Jane Thompson. CBWP-2

In the Valley of Cauteretz. Tennyson. BoLoP; NAEL-5v2; NAEL-6v2; NOBE

In the Valley of the Elwy. Gerard Manley Hopkins. NOBVV; NOCV; OxAEP-2; TOF

In the Valley of the Jerte. Time of Cherries, A. Suzanne Burrows. Prnts

In the valley of the shade of life. Gravedigger, The. Kahlil Gibran. GraLe, tr. by Andrew Ghareeb

In the valley there is an order to these things. Preparations. Tony Curtis. TCAWP

In the valleys of the future we shall walk. Desmond O'Grady. PBCIP Fr. Lines in a Roman Schoolbook.

In the very earliest time. Magic Words. Eskimo Oral Tradition. BLT; RaBo; STP, tr. by Edward Field

In the Very Midst of Life. Martin Luther. GePo, tr. by F. Samuel Janow

In the Vices. Donald Evans. APT-1

In the village churchyard she lies. In the Churchyard at Cambridge. Henry Wadsworth Longfellow. TAP

In the Village of My Forefathers. Vasco [or Vasko] Popa. PoSu, tr. by Anne Pennington Fr. Raw Flesh.

In the village of the dead. Gary Snyder. NOBA; PFTM-2 Fr. Myths and Texts.

In the vine-shadows on the veranda. Sisters, The. Judith Wright. NALW

In the visions of sailors. Between Rivers and Seas. Lance Henson. VoR

In the Waiting Room. Elizabeth Bishop. APT-2; FaBoWP; HeIP-4; LCAP-2; NAAL-2v2; NAAL-5; NALW; NOBA; NoAM; PoE; PoetW; VCAP

In the waiting room of the railway. Hen, The. Christian Morgenstern. RB, tr. by Lore Segal and W. D. Snodgrass

In the waiting room, she releases. First Payment. Jon Mukand. BloBone

In the wake. Gustave Keyser. HA

In the Wake of Home. Adrienne Rich. LCAP-2

In the waking night. Cage, The. David Gascoyne. SPE

In the War they made a celestial cave. Robert Duncan. APSN Fr. Passages.

In the Ward. Robert Lowell. NAAL-2v2

In the watchtower of fantasy. Peregrin, Wandering Hunter of Faces. José María Eguren. TCLAP, tr. by Iver Lofving

In the waters, blue and permanent. (LL) Drowned Children, The. Louise Glück. HCAP; VCAP

In the Way Back. Debra Kang Dean. UnSA

In the way that most of the wind. Wind and Tree. Paul Muldoon. NPeEn

In the Wee Small Hours of the Morning. Bob Hilliard. ReLy

In the welfare waiting room. Institutional Blue. Ann Townsend. NAPBL

In the well-bucket / A morning glory. Chiyojo [or Chiyo or Chiyo-Ni or Kaga no Chiyo or Fukuda Chiyo-Ni]. ZenPo, tr. by Takashi Ikemoto and Lucien Stryk

In the west cloud masses swelled, but even the wind was powerless to breathe. Idlers. Leonid Nikolaevich Martynov. TCRP, tr. by J. R. Rowland

In the west, the weary Day. In Reverie. Harriet McEwen Kimball. TreFP

In the west you're still asleep. You Who Sleep. Philippe Soupault. AF, tr. by Eden Paul

In the white egg. Yannis Ritsos. PFTM-2, tr. by Kostas Myrsiades Fr. 3 x 111 Tristychs.

In the white of my thought. For Robert Desnos. Tristan Tzara. AF

In the white of noon-day's brightness the city seems blotted out. In the Old City. Jacob [or Jakov] Fichman. TrJP, tr. by Sholom J. Kahn

In the white plum blossoms. Buson. EH, tr. by Robert Hass

In the white snowflakes of a blizzard. Dance of the Soul. Vladimir Shchirovsky [or Shchirovskii]. TCRP, tr. by Bradley Jordan

In the wide and rocky pasture where the cedar trees are gray. Connecticut Road Song. Anna Hempstead Branch. TCAPo

In the wild October night-time, when the wind raved round the land. Thomas Hardy. FaBoCh; MoBrPo; OBMV Fr. Dynasts, The.

In the wild soft summer darkness. Summer Night, Riverside. Sara Teasdale. APT-1

In the Wilderness. Robert Graves. ChIV-2; MoBrPo; PeECV

In the Wilderness. James Simmons. GI

In the wilds, a dead doe. Unknown. ChinPo, tr. by Yip Wai-lim

In the Wilds There Is a Dead Doe. Unknown. SuSp, tr. by Wu-Chi Liu

In the willows along the river at Pleasure Bay. At Pleasure Bay. Robert Pinsky. NAAL-5

In the wind that blows. Dead, The. René Arcos. FaBoWar; PeFWW, tr. by Christopher Middleton

In the wind that ripples over them. Last Scene in the First Act. Marge Piercy. NoAM

"In the wind." This is the wind in a field of corn. (LL) Wind. James Fenton. NAEL-5v2; NAEL-6v2

In the window of the drawing-room. Family Photograph, The. Vona Groarke. MFPA

In the Winter. Sir Osbert Sitwell. OBGa

In the winter dusk. Surveillances. Tom Paulin. CIP-2; PNI

In the Winter of My Thirty-eighth Year. W. S. Merwin. NOBA

In the winter river. Prince Shiki. SoOfWa, tr. by Sam Hamill

In the winter stadium, picturing. What You Can't See. Karen Chase. SeSe

In the winter time we go. White Fields. James Stephens. OTCP

In the wintertime. Toe'osh; a Laguna Coyote Story. Leslie Marmon Silko. CDW; NoAM; VoR

In the wintertime my father wears a hat. Clock on Hancock Street. June Jordan. FaBoWP

In the wonder of the Sea. (LL) Sea Gypsy, The. Richard Hovey. BRP; TCAPo

In the wondrous light of a pair of brown eyes. Admiration. Josephine D. Henderson Heard. CBWP-4

In / the / woods. Marlene Mountain. HA

In the Woods. Heinz Piontek. CLPP, tr. by Jerome Rothenberg

In the woods are filaments of light. Signs. Mariana Romo-Carmona. WiU

In the woods I came on an old friend fishing. Finding a Teacher. W. S. Merwin. NNaP

In the woodyard were green and dry. Rick of Green Wood, The. Edward Dorn. NeAP; PmAP; PoM

In the Workhouse. George R. Sims. See Christmas Day in the Workhouse

In the world. (LL) World, The. Robert Creeley. NoP-4; PmAP; VCAP

In the world are distant roads. Wanderer, The. "Andrey Platonov." TCRP, tr. by Albert C. Todd

In the world of friends, in the world of long-distance travel. From the Window of a Plane. Andrey [or Andrei] Andreievich Voznesensky [or Voznesenskii]. TCRusP, tr. by Daniel Weissbort

In the world of the high jump, if something can go wrong. Learning from the Movies. Rachel Wetzsteon. ExTi

In the World's Heart Burns a Torch of Fire. Shin Shalom. MHP, tr. by Ruth Finer Mintz

In the world we've made. Kiev, the Ukraine, Nuclear Accident. David Romtvedt. GifTon

In the worst inn's worst room, with mat half-hung. Pope. NOBE Fr. Epistle III, to Allen Lord Bathurst.

In the yard across the street we saw a snowman holding a garbage can lid smashed into a likeness of the mad English king, George the Third. (LL) You Were Wearing. Kenneth Koch. AiP; CoAP; NIP-4; NNaP; SPE

In the Yard of the Policlinic. Vladimir Holan. AF, tr. by C. G. Hanzlicek

In the Year Chi-hai (1299), While Returning by Way of Purple Fungus Mountain at Springmouth, I Lamented for Lecture Master Chin. Tai Piao-yüan. CoBLCP, tr. by Jonathan Chaves

In the year tan-o. Rhyme-Prose on the Owl. Chia Yi. CoBCP, tr. by Burton Watson

In the Year with the Cyclical Sign Mou-shen. T'ao Ch'ien [or T'ao Yuan-ming]. CoBCP, tr. by Burton Watson

In the years of her age the most beautiful. Petrarch. OBMV Fr. Sonnets to Laura.

In the yellow-cloud dusk, the crows. Crows at Dusk. Li Po. CrYelRi, tr. by Sam Hamill

In the yellow of butter.   Afternoon in Pangasinan with No Electricity, An. Regie Cabico.   ReBoTo

In the yellow pickup.   Weekend Equestrian, The.   Michael S. Weaver.   GT

In the yellow room among the grey furniture I sit sorrowfully.   Corner Boy's Farewell.   Burns Singer.   HarvBoo

In the Yiddish song a goat danced under.   Under Her Crib.   Marcia Pelletiere. OPRER

In the young spring evening.   Sappho.   HW, tr. by Charoula

In the Yukon.   Ralph Gustafson.   MoCV; NoP-4

In the Yukon the other day.   Foundlings in the Yukon.   A. K. Ramanujan. PoetW

In the zócalo.   Three Portraits.   George Hitchcock.   VGW

In the Zoo.   A. K. Ramanujan.   VCWP

In the zoo's glass room, two dozen warblers.   Maintaining the Species. Deborah Burnham.   UrbNat

In Thee! (LL)   Emily Dickinson.   APN-2; EroLit; ErotSp; HeIP-4; NAAL-2v1; NAAL-3; NALW; NIP-4; NOBA; NoAM; OxBA; PoBW; RaBo; TAP; TCAPo; WPE

In their dark, Mexican eyes. (LL)   Sonrisas.   Pat Mora.   NIL-7; NIP-4

In their depths? (LL)   Mona Lisa, A.   Angelina Weld Grimké.   APT-1; BISi

In their direction. (LL)   Death of a Soldier, The.   Wallace Stevens.   APT-1; OBWP; OxBSP; SAmP; SoSe-8

In their house some door is always.   In Their House.   Leah Aini.   DTA, tr. by Miriyam Glazer

In their long hair they lie.   Tombs of the Hetaerae.   Rainer Maria Rilke. PFTM-1

In their own order.   At Nagasaki.   Lucille Clifton.   ESEAA

In their purple hearts. (LL)   Pear Tree.   "H. D."   BoWoP; ColAP; MoAmPo; NOBA; PoE; TCAPo; UnPo

In their religion they are so unev'n.   Daniel Defoe.   OBSV   Fr. True-born Englishman, The.

In their small, queer houses.   Ant-Hills.   "Marian Douglas."   OBCA

In Thelmon's breast contending passions rise.   Thelmon and Carmel: An Irregular Poem.   Anne Batten Cristall.   RWP

In them days / they won't hardly no way to know if.   First Carolina Said-Song. A. R. Ammons.   OBAL

In there these short hairs.   All Shook Up.   Dan Sicoli.   AllShUp; SwNoth

In these all-white courtyards where the south wind blows.   Mad Pomegranate Tree, The.   Odysseus Elytis.   WoPoe, tr. by Edmund Keeley and Philip Sherrard

In these cold evenings, when the rain.   Fear of the Earth.   Alex Comfort. MoBrPo

In these days.   Longing.   Thomas McGrath.   BodElec

In these days, every mother's son or daughter.   In These Days.   Ebenezer Elliott.   Son

IN these deep solitudes and awful cells.   Pope.   NAEL-5v1; NAEL-6v1; NAEL-7v1; RACG

In These Dissenting Times.   Alice Walker.
Women.   WPOW; WWork

In these mountain villages and harbor towns.   Muso Soseki.   EaWin, tr. by W. S. Merwin

In these neat boxes.   New World.   Sally Roberts Jones.   AngWePo

In Thessaly there is a deep-set valley.   Ovid.   NAWM-7v1, tr. by Allen Mandelbaum   Fr. Metamorphoses.

In things a moderation keep[e].   Moderation.   Robert Herrick.   FaBoEE

In this acquiescent world. (LL)   City a Wrecked Ship, The.   Amal Dunqul. MAP; NAfrP, tr. by Sharif Elmusa and Thomas G. Ezzy

In this age of decadence people love antiques.   Collecting Antiques.   Cheng Hsieh.   CoBLCP, tr. by Jonathan Chaves

In this and whatever days to come.   Et Quidquid Aspiciebam Mors Erat. Robert Fitzgerald.   APT-2

In this bath Cypris once was bathed by Love, her son.   Marianus.   GrAn

In this big house.   Saturn.   Günter Grass.   AF

In this blue light.   San Sepolcro.   Jorie Graham.   HCAP; VCAP

In this book I see your face and in your face.   Frontispiece.   May Swenson. CoAP; WPE

In this café they have solved the problem of names.   Martin Johnston.   BMAP Fr. In Transit: A Sonnet Square.

In this chill morning of a wintry spring.   Sonnet Written from an Eastern Apartment in the Bishop's Palace at Lichfield, Which Commands a View of Stowe Valley.   Anna Seward.   RWP

In this city how many masters are clouds.   Amsterdam.   Jean Garrigue.   TAP

In this city where it's perfectly ordinary.   Oh, the Gingkos.   Edward Field. BodElec

In this cloudy sky overhead now.   Cabin in the Sky.   John Latouche.   ReLy

In this cold monument lies one.   Epitaph on M. H., An.   Charles Cotton. EBEV; FaBoEE; NPeEn

In this cold room.   Samuel Hearne in Wintertime.   John Newlove.   NOBC

In This Cool Transparent Spring.   Osip Emilevich Mandelstam [or Mandelshtam].   TCRusP, tr. by John Glad

In this country.   October Falls in Black and White.   Joe Lothamer.   GeoH

In this country I planted not one seed.   Sailing from the United States.   Stanley Moss.   VGW

In this country lightning quickens stone.   Mineral Kingdom.   Jacques Dupin. VCWP, tr. by Paul Auster

In this country you may not.   Small Passing.   Ingrid De Kok.   HAWP

In This Dark House.   Edward Davison.   OBMV

In this dark I rest.   Eye Mask.   Denise Levertov.   BLT

In this day and age Lord.   Loss.   C. K. Williams.   MakPoe

In this deep solitude of wastes more than forlorn.   Solitude.   Andreas Gryphius.   GePo, tr. by George C. Schoolfield

In this delusive world.   Saikaku.   JDP, tr. by Yoel Hoffmann

In this dingy café.   Lola Ridge.   APT-1   Fr. Ghetto, The.

In this dream I walked.   You Can't Escape Your Life Record.   Manila Koordada.   WoPoe

In this earthly configuration.   Concentration Constellation.   Lawson Fusao Inada.   GeoHom

In this factory, here the axe-grinders.   University Curriculum.   William Price Turner.   OxBS

In this garden, after a day of rain.   Where Are You?   Carole Satyamurti. Prnts

In this gay village hangs a wondrous sign.   North Country Village, A. Susanna Blamire.   RWP

In this green month when resurrected flowers.   Memorial Wreath.   Dudley Randall.   CBCWP

In this high pasturage, the Blunden time.   Archaeological Picnic, The.   Sir John Betjeman.   EnLoPo

In this house, she said, in this high second storey.   Under.   Sir John Collings Squire.   FaBoTw

In this house without walls on a hill.   Smile, A.   Tzu Yeh.   CrYelRi; ErotSp, tr. by Sam Hamill

In this image.   MRI of a Poet's Brain.   Vernon Rowe.   BloBone

In this kingdom.   Egg.   Linda Pastan.   InvLad

In this land vague malevolence.   Van Diemen's Land.   Allen Afterman. NOBAu

In this little room.   Slave Cabin, Sotterly Plantation, Maryland, 1989.   Lucille Clifton.   LoL

In this little Urn[e] is laid.   Upon Prue [or Prew], His Maid.   Robert Herrick. BeJo; CaPo; NAEL-5v1; NAEL-6v1; NAEL-7v1; NPeEn; PAI

In this lone, open glade I lie.   Matthew Arnold.   FHYEP; NAEL-6v2

In this meadow starred with spring.   Morning Glory.   Siegfried Sassoon. TrCP

In this meantime the Trachin king sore vexed in his thought.   Ovid.   NoSic, tr. by Arthur Golding   Fr. Metamorphoses.

In this mind.   Nod.   Christopher Davis.   AmPoNex

In this mirror I am enclosed.   Guillaume Apollinaire.   TTTS   Fr. Heart, Crown, and Mirror.

In this moment I am sitting contented and alone.   Handsome Is as Handsome Does.   James Wright (1927–80).   BodElec

In this mountain village.   Issa.   SoOfWa, tr. by Sam Hamill

In this old house. (LL)   Gwendolyn Brooks.   ESEAA; InPK-6; NAAAL; NOBA; NoAM; TAP   Fr. Street in Bronzeville, A.

In this old village now, at night.   Village.   Jean Earle.   AngWePo

In this parable of vengeance.   Impossible Pictures, The.   Tom Paulin.   CABP; CIP-2

In this place an Irishman should feel at home.   November in Boston.   Thomas McCarthy.   BiHa

In this place years ago.   At the Door of the Native Studies Director.   Robert H. Davis.   HATNAP

In this quiet alley, Ch'ien-ming Temple.   Mural, Ch'ien-ming Temple.   Lu Yu. CrYelRi, tr. by Sam Hamill

In this river the heart is like a ruined waterwheel; in whichever direction it turns, there is water before it.   Jelaluddin [or Jalal al-Din] Rumi.   BBASP, tr. by A. J. Arberry

In this road that I must take.   Journey.   Roy Daniells.   MoCV

In this room.   No One.   Lilian Moore.   TLR

In this room, holding hands.   All Day We've Longed for Night.   Sarah Webster Fabio.   BISi

In this season, through the clear tears.   August, on the Rented Farm.   Dave Jeddie Smith.   ColAP

In this short interval to tear.   Ejaculation.   Elinor Wylie.   APT-1

In this short Life.   Emily Dickinson.   SAmP

In this small character is sent.   Upon a Braid of Hair in a Heart.   Henry King, Bishop of Chichester.   EnLoPo

In this small fort, besieged with snow.   Lines Written on a Window at The Leasowes.   William Shenstone.   NPeEn; OxBSP

In this small hut.   Muso Soseki.   EaWin, tr. by W. S. Merwin

In this small Lanthorn would contract her light. (LL)   To the Queen[e], Entertain[e]d at Night by the Countess[e] of Anglesey.   Sir William Davenant [or D'Avenant].   MeLP; NOSC

In this soft age, in my soft.   Rock Climbers, The.   Robert Francis.   MoASP

In this splendor of white sky.   White Claw, The.   Alfonsina Storni.   TCLAP, tr. by Andrew Rosing

In this squalid, dirty dooryard.   Pear Tree, The.   Edna St. Vincent Millay.   MoAmPo

In this stoned and.   Definition of Nature.   Eugene B. Redmond.   NBV

In this the moment of departure.   Departure.   Mai Sayigh.   PoArWo, tr. by Lena Jayyusi and Naomi Shihab Nye

In this Theayter they has plays.   Old Woman, Outside the Abbey Theater, An.   Leonard Alfred George Strong.   MoBrPo

In this vain, busy world, where the good and the gay.   Stanzas.   Mary Robinson.   ECWP; WoRP

In This Way.   Gertrude Stein.   PFTM-1

In this way the day slipped.   Expectation: Night and Day.   Christian Dotremont and Pierre Joris.   MAP, tr. by Diana Der Hovanessian and Lena Jayyusi

In this way the future enters.   Song/for Sanna.   Olga Broumas.   PoBW

In this white room in Mojácar.   Verso Libre.   Nick Carbó.   NAPBL

In this wind, the sharp blue cut of the San Gabriels flattens against the neon east.   Killarney Clary.   GeoHom

In this world.   Issa.   EH, tr. by Robert Hass

In this world.   Flannery O'Connor.   Dorothy Walters.   PoRA

In this world / Even butterflies.   Issa.   ZenPo, tr. by Takashi Ikemoto and Lucien Stryk

In this world, shadows do not speak to us.   Skin.   Anthony Butts.   AmPoNex

In this world, (the *Isle of Dreames*).   White Island.   Robert Herrick.   BeJo; NOSC; TOF

In this year of cataclysm pre-predicted.   Heartease 3.   Lorna Goodison.   WaCA

In this year of executioners' songs.   Let the Midnight Special.   Joseph Bruchac.   GM

In tholde [or th'olde] dayes of the king Arthour.   Geoffrey Chaucer.   FHYEP; NAEL-5v1; NAEL-6v1; NAEL-7v1   Fr. Canterbury Tales, The.

In those days.   David Diop.   See In those days / When civilization kicked us in the face

In those days a decree went out.   Peregrine.   Barton Sutter.   UrbNat

In those days, I couldn't tell if I was strong.   Working Construction.   Eric Chock.   OpBo

In those days, in a place where dentists thrive.   In the Lake District.   Joseph Brodsky.   BLT, tr. by George L. Kline

In those days it was haughty and proud.   Louse.   Wolf Ehrlich [or Erlikh].   TCRP, tr. by Daniel Weissbort

In those days said Hiawatha.   Henry Wadsworth Longfellow.   APN-1   Fr. Song of Hiawatha, The.

In those days the oatfields.   Stacking the Straw.   Amy Clampitt.   VCAP

In those days / When civilization kicked us in the face.   Vultures, The.   David Diop.   PBA; TTY; WoPoe, tr. by Ulli Beier and Gerald Moore

In those far years of inertia.   Aleksandr Aleksandrovich Blok.   TCRP   Fr. Retribution.

In those painful days, we knew.   Yesterday's Illusion or Remembering the Thirties.   Alun Llywelyn-Williams.   OBWVE, tr. by R. Gerallt Jones

In Those Rooms.   Marianne van Hirtum.   SurWo, tr. by Guy Flandre and Peter Wood

In those sad words I took farewell.   Tennyson.   NAEL-6v2   Fr. In Memoriam A. H. H.

In those vast fields of light, ethereal plains.   William Drummond, of Hawthornden.   NOSC   Fr. Hymn of the Fairest Fair, The.

In Those Years.   Sergey [or Sergei] Sergeievich Narovchatov.   TCRusP, tr. by Bob Perelman and Shirley Rihner

In those years, people will say, we lost track.   In Those Years.   Adrienne Rich.   ExTi; LoL

In those years when our sense, desire and wit.   Fulke Greville, 1st Baron Brooke.   NOCV   Fr. Caelica.

In three weeks he will be back down talking.   Called Up: Tinker to Evers to Chance.   Dorothy Barresi.   MoASP

In thrice 10,000 seasons, I will come back to this world.   Domestic Mysticism.   Lucie Brock-Broido.   PoPoPo

In through the porch and up the silent stair.   Old House, The.   Amy Levy.   PEW; VWP; ViWPN

In thy own self's perennial masterdom. (LL)   At Sainte-Marguerite.   Trumbull Stickney.   APN-2; OxBA; TCAPo

In till this tyme that I of tell.   Macbeth.   Andrew of Wyntoun.   OxBS

In Time.   Kathleen Jessie Raine.   WPE

In time all undertakings are made good.   In Time.   Robert Graves.   FaBoEE

In time it came round, the time.   Christmas Ballad.   Saint John of the Cross.   STV, tr. by John Frederick Nims

In Time like Glass.   Walter James Turner.   MoBrPo; OBMV

In Time of Grief.   Lizette Woodworth Reese.   APN-2

In Time of Need.   William Stafford.   UnPo

In Time of Pestilence.   Thomas Nashe [or Nash].   See Summer's Last Will and Testament

In Time of Silver Rain.   Langston Hughes.   SAmP

In Time of "The Breaking of Nations."   Thomas Hardy.   BoLoP; ChIV-1; EBEV; HAP; HarvBoo; MoBrPo; NAEL-5v2; NAEL-6v2; NOBE; NoAM; NoP-4; OBEV; OBWP; OPOU; OxAEP-2; PoWW; RB; TFi; WeW-3

In time of yore when shepherds dwelt.   Olden Love-making.   Nicholas Breton.   NoSic

In time's assembly line.   Assembly Line.   "Shu Ting."   VCWP

In Time's concatenation and.   Robert Penn Warren.   NOBA   Fr. Mortmain.

In time the Princess playing with the child.   Michael Drayton.   ChIV-1   Fr. Moses His Birth and Miracles.

In Time the Strong and Stately Turrets Fall.   Giles Fletcher, the Elder.   EBEV   Fr. Licia.

In time we rode that trail.   Thanksgiving at Snake Butte.   James Welch.   AiP

In Times and Places.   Umberto Piersanti.   NeIt, tr. by Stephen Sartarelli

In times like these, when widows, orphans weep.   To a Friend in Love during the Riots.   William Parsons.   NOEC

In times of stormy weather.   Strange Hurt.   Langston Hughes.   APT-2

In to thir dirk and drublie days.   Meditatioun in Wyntir.   William Dunbar.   NPeEn; OxBS

In Tolouse or Ankara, in Hungary or Scotland.   All.   Antoni Slonimski.   TrJP, tr. by Wanda Dynowska

In Town.   Austin Dobson.   MakPoe

In Transit: A Sonnet Square.   Martin Johnston.
  Café of Situations, The.   BMAP
  Drinking Sappho Brand Ouzo.   BMAP

In Trauma 1, a gay Latino kid.   Rafael Campo.   WiU   Fr. Ten Patients, and Another.

In tropical climes there are certain times of day.   Mad Dogs and Englishmen.   Noël Coward.   NBLV; NOBL; PeLV; ReLy

In troth, I do myself persuade [or perswade].   Love Enthroned.   Richard Lovelace.   CaPo

In Trouble and Shame.   D. H. Lawrence.   OBMV

In truth how glorious was the High Priest.   High Priest, The.   Unknown.   TrJP, tr. by Arthur Davis

In truth it was a landscape wildly gay.   James Kirke Paulding.   APN-1   Fr. Backwoodsman, The.

In truth, O Love, with what a boyish kind.   Sir Philip Sidney.   OxBSo; PoE   Fr. Astrophil and Stella.

In Trying Times.   Heberto Padilla.   AF; PoetW, tr. by Andrew Hurley and Alastair Reid

In Tsegihi.   Arthur Rimbaud.   PFTM-1   Fr. Night Chant, The.

In turns therefrom sipped lovers' wine. (LL)   Under the Waterfall.   Thomas Hardy.   BoLoP; CTC; NAEL-5v2; NAEL-6v2; NoP-4

In twenty minutes he forgot the sirens. (LL)   Sirens, The.   John Streeter Manifold.   MoBrPo; Son

In Two Fields.   Waldo Williams.   OBWVE, tr. by Gwyn Jones

In two large columns on thy motley page.   Verses Addressed to the Imitator of the First Satire of the Second Book of Horace: An Attack on Pope.   Lady Mary Wortley Montagu.   ECEV

In undetected trains we left our land.   Embarkation, 1942.   John Jarmain.   PoWW

In unexperienced infancy.   Shadows in the Water.   Thomas Traherne.   GeHe; HAP; NoP-4; SCGP; WoPoe

In unplowed Maine he sought the lumberers' gang.   Ralph Waldo Emerson.   TAP   Fr. Woodnotes I ("For this present, hard").

In using there are always two.   Song of the Fucked Duck.   Marge Piercy.   BoWoP

In utter chaos no sooner were you born.   Lamenting for My Late Daughter.   Wu Wei-yeh.   CoBLCP, tr. by Jonathan Chaves

In Vain.   Adah Isaacs Menken.   CBWP-1

In vain against the formless wolves of air.   John Gneisenau Neihardt.   APT-1   Fr. Song of the Messiah, The.

In vain by various griefs oppressed.   Swansea Bay.   Julia Ann Hatton.   AngWePo

In vain, dear Madam, yes, in vain you strive.   Epistle to a Lady, An.   Mary Leapor.   BWW; CABP; ECWP; NOEC

In vain, fair sorceress, thy eyes speak charms.   William Habington.   BeJo   Fr. Castara.

In vain her veins incised—jagged boulders.   Spokane Falls.   Phillip [or "Phil"] William George.   VoR

In vain I gather up these stars from the ground.   Meng Chiao.   SuSp   Fr. Apricots Die Young.

In vain I see the morning rise.   Poet's Delay, The.   Henry David Thoreau.   TCAPo

In vain, in vain it is, I find.   Necessity of Fate, The.   Jane Barker.   BWW; EMWP

In vain! In vain! My pleading all in vain! Arria to Poetus. Mary E. Tucker. CBWP-1

In vain, in vain—the all-composing Hour. Pope. EBEV; NoP-4; SCV *Fr.* Dunciad, The.

In vain, or else in vain his wings. (LL) Persuasions to Enjoy. Thomas Carew. BeJo; NOBE

In vain, poor nymph, to please our youthful sight. Elegy, to an Old Beauty, An. Thomas Parnell. ECEV; NOEC

In vain, search in the dust. Milan, August 1943. Salvatore Quasimodo. WoPoe, *tr.* by Peter Russell

In vain the dusky night retires. Hymn. Elizabeth Singer Rowe. ECWP

In vain / They shook their garments. Irony of God. Eva Warner. TrCP

In vain to me the smiling [*or* smileing] Mornings shine. Sonnet [on the Death of Mr. Richard West]. Thomas Gray. CenSon; NOEC; OxBSo; PoE

In vain to woods and deserts I retire. Verses Design'd By Mrs A. Behn to be Sent to a Fair Lady, that Desir'd She Would Absent Herself to Cure Her Love. Left Un. Aphra Behn. PoBW

In vain you boast poetic names of yore. Impromptu to Lady Winchelsea. Pope. NAEL-7v1

In vain your bangles cast. Abiku. Wole Soyinka. PBA; PBMAP; PoetW

In vain[e] fair[e] sorceress[e], thy eyes speak[e] charm[e]s. To a Wanton. William Habington. NOSC

In valleys green and still. A. E. Housman. FaBoTw; SCV

In vaulted place where shadows flit. In a Church of Padua. Herman Melville. APN-2

In Verona, my late cousin Romeo. This Can't Be Love. Richard Rodgers. ReLy

In Vietnam. Militerotics. Chuck Ortleb. GLP

In Vietnam I was always afraid of mines. Mines. Bruce Weigl. CDa

In Vietnam, poets brushed on printed silk. For Mrs. Cam, Whose Name Means "Printed Silk." John Balaban. CDa

In Virgyne the sweltrie sun gan sheene. Excelente Balade of Charitie, An. Thomas Chatterton. EBEV; NOEC; OxAEP-1

In Vorkuta no disciple of the Lord. Vorkuta. Horst Bienek. AF

In Waka Bay when. Akahito. OHMPJ

In *Wakefield* there lives a jolly Pinder. Jolly Pinder of Wakefield, The. *Unknown.* ESPB; PBRV

In Wales there is a borough town. Tale of a Friar and A Shoemaker's Wife, a. Thomas Churchyard. NoSic

In walking naked. (LL) Coat, A. W. B. Yeats. NAEL-5v2; NAEL-6v2; NoAM; OxAEP-2; OxBSP

In wanting to achieve any song. (LL) Minor Bird, A. Robert Frost. APT-1; OWoS; SAmP

In Waste Places. James Stephens. MoBrPo; SCGP

In water-heavy nights behind grandmother's porch. Adolescence—I. Rita Dove. ISC; NAAL-5; NoAM

In water nothing is mean. The fugitive. Patience. Elaine Feinstein. BrRo; FaBoWP

In waters still as a burnished mirror's face. Fishing in the Wei River. Po Chü-i. ChiP, *tr.* by Arthur Waley

In waters where no charts avail. Island, The. Herman Melville. NCAP

In waves of untraveled seas. To a Lady Combing Her Hair. Juan de, Count of Villamediana Tassis y Peralta. BLPSL, *tr.* by Rene de Costa, Rigas Kappatos and Eleni Paidoussi

In waves still as the skillful yachts pass over. (LL) Yachts, The. William Carlos Williams. APT-1; HeIP-4; MoAmPo; NOBA; NoAM; NoP-4; OxBA; PoE; SAmP; TFi

In Wee-John-Boo the bellies of bloodhounds. Orange Jews. Ted Berrigan. SPE

In western skies. Henrietta Cordelia Ray. BlSi *Fr.* Idyl.

In Westminster Abbey. Sir John Betjeman. FaBoWar; HarvBoo; InPK-6; NBLV; NIL-7; NIP-4; NOBL; NoAM; OBSV; OxAEP-2; TOF

In Westminster not long ago. Ratcatcher's Daughter, The. *Unknown.* OxBoLi

In wet May, in the months of change. Exequy, An. Peter Porter. NoAM; NoP-4; OxBC

In what dark silent grove. Cogitabo Pro Peccato Meo. William Habington. ChIV-1

In what dynasty, under what emperor. Against Conscription. Wei Chuang. CrYelRi, *tr.* by Sam Hamill

In what estate so ever I be. *Unknown.* NoP-4; SacPr

In what house, the jade flute that sends these dark notes drifting. Spring Night in Lo-Yang—Hearing a Flute. Li Po. CoBCP; TTTS, *tr.* by Burton Watson

In what language do I pray? Two Voices. Diana Der Hovanessian. TWW

In what place in years to come. Sitting Alone in the Courtyard. Yü Chi. CoBLCP, *tr.* by Jonathan Chaves

In what place is one most free of bonds? To Patriarch Sun at Hua-yang Grotto. Li Te-yü. ColAnChi, *tr.* by Edward H. Schafer

In what recesses of the brain. Memory, a Poem. Laetitia Pilkington. ECWP

In What Region, in What Part of the World. Gutierre de Cetina. SpanPo, *tr.* by Kate Flores

In what rich harmony, what polished lays. John Pierpont. APN-1; TreFP *Fr.* Airs of Palestine.

In what soft language shall my thoughts get free. Upon the Death of Her Husband. Elizabeth Singer Rowe. ECWP

In what torn[e] ship soever I embark[e]. John Donne. BASC; EBEV; ESCV; MeLP; NAEL-5v1; NAEL-6v1; NAEL-7v1; NOSC; NPeeEn; OxAEP-1; PeECV; SacPr

In which being there together is enough. (LL) Final Soliloquy of the Interior Paramour. Wallace Stevens. APT-1; BBASP; ColAP; HAP; HCAP; HarvBoo; LCAP-2

In Which He Rejoices Over Having Discarded Love. Bálint Balassi. IQMS, *tr.* by Joseph Leftwich

In which if they turn and twist, it is neither with volition nor consciousness. (LL) Grave, A. Marianne Craig Moore. APT-1; FaBoWP; HAP; HeIP-4; NAAL-2v2; NOBA; NoAM; NoP-4; PoE; TAP; TFi; TRP; UnPo; WPE; WeW-3

In Which Names. Ilse Aichinger. AF, *tr.* by Allen H. Chappel

In Which Roosevelt Is Compared to Saul. Nicholas Vachel Lindsay. ChIV-1

In Which She Satisfies a Fear with the Rhetoric of Tears. Sister Juana Inés de la Cruz. BoWoP, *tr.* by Aliki and Willis Barnstone

In White. Robert Frost. TRP

In White America. Lucille Clifton. LTA

In white clouds, in green mountains. Taoist Song. Teng Yu-pin. CrYelRi, *tr.* by Sam Hamill

In white pleated trousers, peering through green. Stravinsky in L.A. Elizabeth Alexander. AmPoNex

In white tulips. Raymond Roseliep. HA

In whom the *Lord of Hosts* did pitch his tent! (LL) Anagram. George Herbert. ChIV-2; GeHe

In whose will is our peace? Thou happiness. Epigram. James Vincent Cunningham. VGW

In Wild Iris Time. Jerry Martien. GeoHom

In wind from Asia and a wanton rain. (LL) Way a Ghost Dissolves, The. Richard Hugo. NAAL-2v2; NoAM; NoP-4

In wind or water streame do require to be writ. (LL) Catullus. OBVE; WoPoe, *tr.* by Sir Philip Sidney

In Windsor Castle. Henry Howard, Earl of Surrey. *See* Prison in Windsor Castle

In Winter. Anastasius Grün. AuPH, *tr.* by Lowell A. Bangerter

In winter. (LL) Ode to My Socks. Pablo Neruda. RaBo; TCLAP; TRP, *tr.* by Robert Bly

In winter evenings. March. Rosemerry Wahtola Trommer. GeoH

In winter I get up at night. Bed in Summer. Robert Louis Stevenson. BRP; NBLV; OTCP

In Winter in my Room. Emily Dickinson. APN-2; NAAL-2v1; NAAL-3; NALW; NCAP; NOBA; NoAM; OxBA

In winter in the woods alone. Robert Frost. HeIP-4

In winter it darkens the moment lunch is over. Eclogue IV: Winter. Joseph Brodsky. TCRP, *tr.* by Joseph Brodsky

In winter my loved one retires. Fog Land. Ingeborg Bachmann. WoPoe, *tr.* by Michael Hamburger

In winter on her hearth lighting some coal. Antipater of Thessalonica. GrAn

In winter, sprawled on soft cushions. War Memories. Xenophanes. WoPoe, *tr.* by Theodore Blanchard

In winter, those first mornings after my father died. Pier, The. Garrett Kaoru Hongo. OpBo

In winter, when he was out of work and it was too cold outside to. Shooting Crows. Peter Markus. AmPoNex

In winter, when the fields are white. Lewis Carroll. EBEV; NOBVV; NPeeEn *Fr.* Through the Looking-Glass.

In winter when the rain rain'd cauld. Tak' Your Auld Cloak about Ye. *Unknown.* OxBS

In winter, with dusk enshrouding the town. Rejected Gift, The. Ida G. M. Gerhardt. TuT, *tr.* by Ruth Hooley

In wit, as nature, what affects our hearts. Pope. HAP *Fr.* Essay on Criticism, An.

In with them, and tore down the slaughterhouse [*or* slaughter-house]. (LL) Reuben Bright. Edwin Arlington Robinson. APN-2; MoAmPo; NOBA; Son; TAP

In Worcester, Massachusetts. In the Waiting Room. Elizabeth Bishop. APT-2; FaBoWP; HeIP-4; LCAP-2; NAAL-2v2; NAAL-5; NALW; NOBA; NoAM; PoE; PoetW; VCAP

In Word and Will I am a friend to you. On Himself. William Oldys. FaBoEE

In wrath and grief away the Paynims fly. *Unknown.* OBWP *Fr.* Song of Roland, The.

In Wyoming, at the confluence. Dreaming at the Rexall Drug. Robin Becker. ReTh

In Xanadu did Kubla Khan. Kubla Khan: or, A Vision in a Dream. Samuel Taylor Coleridge. AWP; BRP; CABP; FHYEP; FaBoCh; HAP; HeIP-4; InPK-6; NAEL-5v2; NAEL-6v2; NAWM-7v2; NIL-7; NIP-4; NOBE; NOBRP; NPeEn; NoP-4; OBEV; OBGa; OxAEP-2; OxBEV; PAI; PoE; PoPoPo; PoRA; SCGP; SCV; SoSe-8; TFi; TOF; TRP; WeW-3; WoPoe

In Xóchitl in Cuícatl. Ernesto Cardenal. PFTM-2, tr. by Carlos Altschul and Monique Altschul

In years of old. John Addington Symonds. CAGL Fr. Eudiades.

In years to come, I ask, be kind. Strato [or Straton]. CAGL, tr. by Byrne Fone

In yellow meadows I take no delight. Sir Thomas Browne. FaBoEE

"In yonder fields" (with that directs her eye). William Chamberlayne. NOSC Fr. Pharonnida.

In yonder grave a Druid lies. Ode Occasioned by the Death of Mr. Thomson. William Collins. NOEC; PoE

In Your Absence. Elizabeth Baxter. PoToHe

In your astral palace, I. Hsüeh T'ao. WoPoe, tr. by Jeanne Larsen Fr. Trying on New-Made Clothes: Three Poems.

In Your Bad Dream. Richard Hugo. LCAP-2

In Your Dream after Falling in Love. Richard Hugo. BodElec

In your dream you met Demeter. Demeter. Genevieve Taggard. HW

In your ears my song. You Laughed and Laughed and Laughed. Gabriel Okara. PBA

In Your Honor. Arthur Sze. GifTon

In your honor, a man presents a sea bass. In Your Honor. Arthur Sze. GifTon

In your honor, Lord Priapus. Unknown. PriapPo, tr. by Richard W. Hooper Fr. Priapus Poems, The.

In Your Mind. Carol Ann Duffy. EmeKit

In your mystery. For Larry Levis in Memory. Luis Omar Salinas. GeoHom

In your next letter I wish you'd say. Letter to N.Y. Elizabeth Bishop. TwCP

In your old age. Mourning for the Layman Named Cloud Peak. Muso Soseki. EaWin, tr. by W. S. Merwin

In Your Own Sweet Time. Alane Rollings. IllVoic

In your palm, the ripe weight. (LL) Persimmons. Li-Young Lee. NAAL-5; NIL-7; NIP-4; NoP-4; OPRER

In your panties. Hal Roth. HA

In your presence I rediscovered my name. Your Presence. David Diop. PBA; PBMAP, tr. by Ulli Beier

In your quest or request God is remote. Love Poem. Huda Na'mani. BBASP; MAP, tr. by Samuel Hazo and Lena Jayyusi

In Your Racing Dream. Richard Hugo. BodElec

In your sight. Spinal Cord. 'Aisha Arnaout. PoArWo, tr. by Mona Fayad

In your silence sank as into a deep sea. Dialogue. Leah Goldberg. MHP, tr. by Ruth Finer Mintz

In your twenties you knew with elegiac certainty. Lifetime Devoted to Literature, A. Judith Rodriguez. NOBAu

In Your Version of Heaven I am Younger. Rachel Zucker. BAP-01

In your wide-brimmed, black. Moscow Station, The. Yevgeny [or Evgenii] Borisovich Rein. ItGoST, tr. by Judith Hemschemeyer

In Your Young Dream. Richard Hugo. InPK-6

In youth, gay scenes attract our eyes. Vanity of Existence, The. Philip Freneau. TCAPo

In youth I had nothing. Poem on Returning to Dwell in the Country. T'ao Ch'ien [or T'ao Yuan-ming]. WoPoe, tr. by William Acker

In youth I loved the adventurous race. To Match the Prince of Lang-yeh's Poem in the Old Style. Wang Seng-ta. CoBCP, tr. by Burton Watson

In Youth Is Pleasure. Robert Wever. NOBE; OBEV Fr. Lusty Juventus.

In youth, it was a way I had. Indian Summer. Dorothy Parker. NIL-7; NIP-4

In youth's spring, it was my lot. Edgar Allan Poe. See In spring of youth it was my lot

In youth thou enteredst [or enter'dst] on glass-bottled wall. (LL) To a Cat. John Keats. CenSon; FaBoCh; OxBSo; TriCat

In youth we dream of death. Hardy Perennial. Richard Eberhart. AiP

In yr absence / i. Max Factor Pink. Nigel Roberts. BMAP

In Yüeh Viewing the Past. Li Po. CoBCP, tr. by Burton Watson

In zummer, leate at evenen tide. Rwose in the Dark, The. William Barnes. NOBVV

Ina Unique TracethatRemovesBeforeandAfterLeftandRight. Poem No. V. Sang Yi. PFTM-1

INAMORATAS, with an approbation. Sundays of Satin-Legs Smith, The. Gwendolyn Brooks. NAAAL; SeSe

Inanna and An. Enheduanna. BoWoP

Inanna and Ebih. Enheduanna. BoWoP

Inanna and Enlil. Enheduanna. BoWoP

Inanna and Ishkur. Enheduanna. BoWoP

Inanna and the Anunna. Enheduanna. BoWoP

Inanna and the City of Uruk. Enheduanna. BoWoP

Inanna and the Divine Essences. Enheduanna. BoWoP

Inanna, Astarte, Ishtar and Isis. Prayer of Dedication. Cosi Fabian. HW

Inanna Exalted. Enheduanna.
"O lady of all truths bright light going forth." WPOW

Inanna's Chant. Janine Canan. HW

Inanna spoke. Unknown. WoPoe, tr. by Samuel Noah Kramer and Diane Wolkstein Fr. Cycle of Inanna: The Courtship of Inanna and Dumazi, The.

Inapprehensiveness. Robert Browning. NOBVV

Inattentive, suborned, betrayed, and shiftless. Young Prince of Tyre. "Ern Malley." BMAP

Inauguration. Lorenzo Thomas. NBV

Inauguration Day: January 1953. Robert Lowell. OxBSo

Inauguration of Fukusan Dormitory. Muso Soseki. EaWin, tr. by W. S. Merwin

Inca had three arrows in his hand, The. Inca's Arrows, The. Manuel González Prada. SpanPo, tr. by Kate Flores

Inca's Arrows, The. Manuel González Prada. SpanPo, tr. by Kate Flores

Inca Tupac Upanqui, The. William Hart-Smith. NOBAu

Incantation. Bella [or Izabella] Akhatovna Akhmadulina. TCRP, tr. by Albert C. Todd

Incantation. Zinaida Nikolayevna [or Nikolaevna] Gippius. ARWW, tr. by Catriona Kelly

Incantation. Czeslaw Milosz. VCWP

Incantation. Elinor Wylie. APT-1

Incantation Songs of the Klamath Lake People. Unknown. APN-2, tr. by Albert S. Gatschet

Incantations, The. Theocritus. AWP, tr. by Charles Stuart Calverley Fr. Idylls.

Incantations for Warriors. Alistair Paterson. PeNZ

Incantations of Modoc Conjurers. Unknown. APN-2, tr. by Albert S. Gatschet

Incantations of the Sea: Moando Coast. Mukula Kadima-Nzuji. NAfrP, tr. by Gerald Moore

Incarnate One, The. Edwin Muir. PeECV

Incarnatio Est Maximum Dei Donum [or Donum Dei]. William Alabaster. NoSic

Incarnation, The. William Langland. OBEV Fr. Vision of Piers Plowman, The.

Incarnation, The. Charles Wesley. NOCV

Incarnation and Passion, The. Henry Vaughan. GeHe; SacPr; TrCP

Incarnation Poem. John Leax. TrCP

Incautious—of the Sun. (LL) Emily Dickinson. APN-2; PoE

Incautious young woman named Venn, An. Limerick. Edward Gorey. PeLV; PeLi

Incautious youth, why do'st thou so misplace. To My Young Lover. Jane Barker. BASC; LW

Incendiary. Vernon Scannell. OxBC

Incense, and flesh of swine, and this year's grain. Horace. AWP, tr. by Austin Dobson Fr. Odes.

Incense burned to ash in a bronze bowl. Night Watch. Wang An-shih. CrYelRi, tr. by Sam Hamill

Incense burns to embers in the burner. To the Tune: The Water Clock. Wen T'ing-yün. CrYelRi, tr. by Sam Hamill

Incessant now their hollow sides they pound. Paul Whitehead. ECEV Fr. Gymnasiad, The, or Boxing Match.

Incessantly / A wild gazelle. Gazelle, The. Yasin Taha Hafiz. MAP, tr. by Sharif Elmusa and Christopher Middleton

Inch of nothing for your soul, An. (LL) E. E. Cummings. BoLoP; VGW

Inchcape Rock, The. Robert Southey. EBNV; OBNV; OBSP; OxAEP-2

Inching / From dark to dark. Gyodai. ZenPo, tr. by Takashi Ikemoto and Lucien Stryk

Incidence. Rae Armantrout. FTOS

Incident. Muhammad Al-Faituri [or Al-Fituri or Al-Fayturi]. MAP, tr. by Sargon Boulus and Peter Porter

Incident. Imamu Amiri Baraka. AF; NoAM

Incident. Countee Cullen. APT-2; BPo; ChAP; KaS; NAAAL; NAAL-2v2; NAAL-5; NOxBChV; NTCP; NoAM; NoP-4; OBCA; OxIBACP; PoPoPo; SSLK; VGW

Incident. Eamon Grennan. BiHa

Incident, An. Douglas Le Pan. MoCV; NoP-4

Incident, An. Frederick Tennyson. SacPr

Incident at Imuris. Alberto A. Ríos. NIP-4

Incident in a Rose Garden. Donald Justice. CRP

Incident in the Early Life of Ebenezer Jones, Poet, 1828, An. Sir John Betjeman. NoAM

Incident in Transylvania. Roger McDonald. BMAP

Incident of the French Camp. Robert Browning. OBWP

Incident to murder. (LL) John Berryman. CoAP; HarvBoo Fr. Dream Songs.

Incidents in the Life of My Uncle Arly. Edward Lear. OBCoV; OxBoLi
(O my agèd Uncle Arly!) NOxBChV

Incitement for Rowing to Sailing-place. Alexander MacDonald. NePenScot, tr. by Hugh MacDiarmid *Fr.* Clanranald's Galley.

Incline Thine ear, O God. Therefore, We Thank Thee, God. Reuben Grossman. TrJP, tr. by L. V. Snowman

Inclined House, The. Sabah Al-Kharrat Zwein.
    "I have already lost the style and maze of language." PoArWo, tr. by Kaissar Afif

Inclusiveness. Dante Gabriel Rossetti. NAEL-5v2; NAEL-6v2 *Fr.* House of Life, The.

Incognita. Austin Dobson. EBVV

Incognito Lounge, The. Denis Johnson. ReTh

Incommunicado. Sylvia Plath. BodElec

Incomparable-Verse Valley. Muso Soseki. EaWin, tr. by W. S. Merwin

Incomplete Scenario Involving What the Voice Said. Jane Mead. NAPBL

Incompleteness. Adelaide Anne Procter. TreFP

Incompleteness. Henrietta Cordelia Ray. CBWP-3

Incomprehensible, The. Isaac Watts. SacPr

Inconclusive Evening, An. Frances Bellerby. FaBoTw

Inconstancy. James Harrington. PBRV

Inconstancy's the Greatest of Sins. Edward Herbert, 1st Baron Herbert of Cherbury. OxBSP

Inconstant Dawn, thou tak'st thy time. Meleager. GrAn

Incontestably sang, and the people were beautiful. (LL) Unpredicted, The. John Heath-Stubbs. BoLoP; OxBC

Incontinence. Susan Hahn. IllVoic

Inconvenience, An. John Raven. BPo; CRP

Incorrigible, false coquette. Kiss, The. Francis Saltus Saltus. VerBaPo

Increase his rule by gentlest summer means. (LL) Pray to What Earth Does This Sweet Cold Belong. Henry David Thoreau. NCAP; UnPo

Increasing moonlight drifts across my bed, The. Fredericksburg. Thomas Bailey Aldrich. TCAPo

Incredible splendour—ethereal, delicate! Hayim Lenski. FIT, tr. by Robert Friend

Incredibly bright blue almost white open sky, An. I Just Heard John Buffington Died. Kalamu ya Salaam. SpirFl

Incrusted in his island home that lies beyond the sea. Neutral British Gentleman, The. "Orpheus C. Kerr." OBAL

Indecent Exposure (A True Story). Linwood M. Ross. InTrad

Indeed, good Sir, you're quite mistaken. Verses Designed to Be Sent to Mr. Adams. Elizabeth Frances Amherst. ECWP

Indeed I have sought thee too long, O Apollo. Search for Apollo, A. Agnes Mary Frances Robinson. VWP

Indeed I must confess. Abraham Cowley. BeJo *Fr.* Mistress, The.

Indeed Indeed, I Cannot Tell. Henry David Thoreau. RaBo

Indeed indeed it is growing very sultry. Cubical Domes, The. David Gascoyne. SPE

Indeed, it will soon be over, I shall be done. Intimations of Mortality. Stanley Kunitz. MoAmPo

Indeed, Sir Peter, I could wish, I own. On Clergymen Preaching Politics. John Byrom. ECEV

Indeed, the enemy. *Zuni Oral Tradition.* NAWM-7v2, tr. by Ruth L. Bunzel *Fr.* Scalp Dance, The.

Indeed then, it was your own courage. Anyte [*or* Anytes]. GrAn

Indeed this very love which is my boast. Elizabeth Barrett Browning. CenSon *Fr.* Sonnets from the Portuguese.

Indeed You Came Home Too Late. Gabriella Leto. CItWP, tr. by Cinzia Sartini Blum and Lara Trubowitz

Indefiniteness is an element of the true music. Improvisations on a Sentence by Poe. Jack Spicer. APSN

Independance wid a vengeance. Independance. Louise Bennett. FaBoVe

Independence. Nancy Cato. WPE

Independence. Adebayo Faleti. PBA, tr. by Ulli Beier and Bakare Gbadamosi

Independence Bell—July 4, 1776. *Unknown.* HHAm

Independence Day. William Jay Smith. TwCP

Independence Day. *Unknown.* VerBaPo

Independence Day, 1956: A Fairy Tale. James Galvin. PoPoPo

Independent, The. Phyllis McGinley. FaBoEE

Independent Squire. Samuel Butler (1612–80). NOBE *Fr.* Hudibras.

Independent Study. Paul Beatty. AmPoNex

Index. Paul Violi. PmAP

India. Walter James Turner. MoBrPo

India Guide, The; or, Journal of a Voyage to the East Indies in 1780. Sir George Dallas.
    Miss Emily Brittle Sails for India. NOEC

India that one read about, The. I Wonder What Happened to Him. Noël Coward. ReLy

Indian, The. Eliza Kirkham Mathews. CenSon

Indian at the Burial-Place [*or* Burying-Place] of His Fathers, An. William Cullen Bryant. APN-1

Indian Bagman's Toast. *Unknown.* FaBoVe

Indian Blood. Mary Tallmountain. UnSA

Indian Boarding School: The Runaways. Louise Erdrich. HATNAP; NoAM; UnSA

Indian Burying Ground, The. Philip Freneau. ColAP; HAP; NAAL-2v1; NAAL-3; NOBA; NoP-4; OxBA; TAP; TCAPo; TFi

Indian Car. Catron Grieves. ReTh

Indian Cave Jerry Ramsey Found, The. William Stafford. NoAM

Indian Children Speak. Juanita Bell. PAI

Indian City, The. Felicia Dorothea Hemans. RWP

Indian Convert, The. Philip Freneau. TAP

Indian Corn. William W. Cook.
    "Corn, corn, sweet Indian corn." VerBaPo

Indian Counsel. Edwin Ford Piper. APT-1

Indian Girl. Lenard D. Moore. GT

Indian Girl's Song, The. Shelley. *See* Indian Serenade, The

Indian Gone!, The. Josiah D. Canning. APN-1

Indian Love Song. Lew Blockcolski. VoR

Indian Maid, The; Demararie, Oct. 27, 1781. Edward Thompson. NOEC

Indian Movie, New Jersey. Chitra Divakaruni. NIL-7; UnSA

Indian Names. Lydia Huntley Sigourney. APN-1; ColAP; SWaP

Indian Never Had a Horse, The. Etel Adnan.
    "There is a word that never." PoArWo

Indian Peaks, Colorado. Reg Saner. PoCoUp

Indian Princess, The. Pet Deer, The. James Tate. SPE

Indian Reservation: Caughnawaga. Abraham Moses Klein. NOBC; NoP-4

Indian Rock, Bainbridge Island, Washington. Duane Niatum. CDW

Indian Rope Trick. Geoffrey Holloway. NLP

Indian Ruins Along Rio de Flag. Greg Pape. PBCAP

Indian's Retort, The. Jones Very. NCAP

Indian's Welcome to the Pilgrim Fathers, The. Lydia Huntley Sigourney. TCAPo

Indian Serenade, The. Shelley. AWP; OBEV; RaBo; TTTS; TreFP
    (Indian Girl's Song, The.) NAEL-5v2; NAEL-6v2
    (Lines to an Indian Air.) GTBS-P

Indian Singing in 20th Century America. Gail Tremblay. HATNAP; LTA; ReEnLa

Indian Song: Survival. Leslie Marmon Silko. CDW; VoR

Indian Student; or, Force of Nature, The. Philip Freneau. OxBA

Indian Summer. Olga Fiodorovna Berggolts [*or* Bergholts]. TCRusP, tr. by Daniel Weissbort

Indian Summer. Wilfred Campbell. NOBC

Indian Summer. Cristina Campo. CItWP, tr. by Cinzia Sartini Blum and Lara Trubowitz

Indian Summer. Karen Chamberlain. GeoH

Indian Summer. Emily Dickinson. APN-2; MoAmPo; NAAL-2v1; NAAL-3; NAAL-5; TCAPo

Indian Summer. Hamlin Garland. APN-2

Indian summer. Lorraine Ellis Harr. HA

Indian Summer. William Ellery Leonard. APT-1 *Fr.* Two Lives.

Indian Summer. Dorothy Parker. NIL-7; NIP-4

Indian Summer. Boris Leonidovich Pasternak. RusPo, tr. by Robert Arthur Douglas Ford

Indian Summer. Lizette Woodworth Reese. SWaP

Indian Summer Day on the Prairie, An. Nicholas Vachel Lindsay. IllVoic

Indian summer / Dragonfly shadows seldom. Masaoka Shiki. ZenPo, tr. by Takashi Ikemoto and Lucien Stryk

Indian Summer: Montana, 1956. W. M. Ransom. CDW

Indian upon God, The [*or* An]. W. B. Yeats. MoBrPo

Indian weed [*now*] withered quite, The. Religious Use of [Taking] Tobacco, A. Robert Wisdome. OBCoV; SCGP

Indian, who lived at Muskingum, remote, An. Indian Convert, The. Philip Freneau. TAP

Indian Woman's Death-Song, The. Felicia Dorothea Hemans. PEW

Indians are ignorant of Europe's Coyne yet call it Monéash and notice. Rosmarie Waldrop. PFTM-2 *Fr.* Key into the Language of America, A.

Indians at the Guthrie. Gerald Vizenor. VoR

Indians count of men as dogs, The. Roger Williams. SCAP

Indians have mostly gone, The. Like Ghosts of Eagles. Robert Francis. LCAP-2

Indians in the Woods, The. Janet Lewis. IllVoic

Indians prize not English gold, The. Roger Williams. SCAP

Indians stole fair Annie, The. Fair Annie. *Unknown.* ESPB; OxBB

Indictment of Senior Officers. Sharon Olds. PBCAP

Indies, The. Edouard Glissant.

"Child climbs to the island's highest point, The." NegPo

"O Sun! O age-old labor mutely mixed with ocean." NegPo

"One of them, taking advantage of the crew's momentary carelessness." NegPo

"They fastened a people to merchant ships." NegPo

Indifference. Dmitry [or Dmitrii] Vasil'evich Bobyshev. TCRusP, *tr. by* Daniel Weissbort

Indifference. Dmitry [or Dmitrii] Vasil'evich Bobyshev. TCRP, *tr. by* Albert C. Todd

Indifference. Harry Graham. NBLV

Indifference. Geoffrey Anketell Studdert-Kennedy. TrCP

Indifference, The / of rain. Death. Joe Wenderoth. AmPoNex

Indifferent, The. John Donne. BASC; BoLoP; ESCV; NAEL-5v1; NAEL-6v1; NAEL-7v1; NAWM-5v1; NOSC; SoSe-8

Indifferent as a statue. Similes. Charles Reznikoff. APT-2

Indifferent glimmer of distant stars, The. Garden of Gethsemane, The. Boris Leonidovich Pasternak. GI, *tr. by* Nina Kossman

Indifferent, he condescends to glide. (LL) Swan, The. Rainer Maria Rilke. NAWM-7v2; OWoS, *tr. by* Stephen Mitchell

Indifferent or unaware. (LL) Cortège. Paul Verlaine. AWP; OBVE, *tr. by* Arthur Symons

Indifferent to heaven and hell. (LL) "Michael Field." VWP; ViWPN

Indignant at the fumbling wits, the obscure spite. Paudeen. W. B. Yeats. HAP; OxBSP

Indignation. José Santos Chocano. TCLAP, *tr. by* Andrew Rosing

Indignation Dinner, An. James David Corrothers. NAAAL

Indignation Jones. Edgar Lee Masters. APT-1 *Fr.* Spoon River Anthology.

Indigo. Chitra Divakaruni. OpBo

Indiscriminate Venus grasps at any remedy, The. *Unknown.* CAGL, *tr. by* John Boswell *Fr.* Leiden Manuscript, The.

Individual's Soliloquy, The. Nicanor Parra. PFTM-2, *tr. by* Lawrence Ferlinghetti and Allen Ginsberg

Individualist Speaks, The. Louis MacNeice. OBMV

Indolence. Vernon Watkins. FaBoTw

Indolent Housewife—in Daisies—lain! (LL) Emily Dickinson. HAP; NAAL-2v1; NAAL-3; TCAPo; WeW-3

Indolent vicar of Bray, An. Limerick. Langford Reed. PeLi

Indoor Cat, The. Paul Petrie. PoCoUp

Indoors I sat, with my two sons. Night Song. Lajos Áprily. IQMS, *tr. by* Watson Kirkconnell

Indoors the tang of a tiny oil lamp. Outdoors. House on a Cliff. Louis MacNeice. HarvBoo; ModIr; NOIV; NPeEn

Indra, the Supreme God. *Unknown.* AWP *Fr.* Vedic Hymns.

Induction, The. John Milton. PoE *Fr.* Paradise Lost.

Induction, The. Thomas, 1st Earl of Dorset Sackville. NoSic *Fr.* Induction to "A Mirror for Magistrates."

Induction to "A Mirror for Magistrates." Thomas, 1st Earl of Dorset Sackville. Induction, The. NoSic

("Midnight was come, and every vital thing.") AEP

("'When Fortune frown'd, the feller made my fall'") (LL) AEP

Indulgence. Leopoldo Lugones. TCLAP, *tr. by* Julie Schumacher

Indulgent Nature on each kind bestows. On Dr. Evans Cutting Down a Row of Trees. *Unknown.* FaBoEE

Industrial City. Antigone Kefala. BMAP

Industrial Evils. Joseph Cottle. NOEC *Fr.* Malvern Hills.

Industrious young obstetrician, An. Limerick. Isaac Asimov. PeLi

Industry undressing in front of Agriculture. Eclogue. Michael Hofmann. HarvBoo

Indwelling. Thomas Edward Brown. SacPr

Ineffable, The. Delmira Agustini. TCLAP, *tr. by* Karl Kirchwey

Ineffable, The. Delmira Agustini. TANSG, *tr. by* Mark McCaffrey

Ineffable Dou, The. Sydney Goodsir Smith. OxBS

Inept young person, Miss Muffet, The. Limerick. Dean Walley. PeLi

Inertia. Kirti Chaudhari. WPOW, *tr. by* Leonard Nathan

Inertia. Vivienne Finch. BrRo

Inescapable: to start with the history. Seq. Maggie Hannan. NLP

Iness. (LL) L(a. E. E. Cummings. NIL-7; NIP-4; TRP

Inevitable. Sir John Betjeman. MoBrPo

Inexhaustible. Israel Zangwill. TrJP

Inexorable. William Drummond, of Hawthornden. *See* Madrigal: "Like the Idalian Queen[e]"

Inexorable. William Drummond, of Hawthornden. *See* Madrigal: "My thoughts hold mortal[l] strife."

Inextinguishable Blaze. Charles Wesley. NOEC

(Inextinguishable Blaze.) NOEC

Infancy. Carlos Drummond de Andrade. TCLAP, *tr. by* Elizabeth Bishop

Infancy! fearless, lustful, happy, nestling for delight. William Blake. OxAEP-2 *Fr.* Visions of the Daughters of Albion.

Infant, The. Agnes Strickland. CenSon

Infant Boy at Midcentury. Robert Penn Warren. When the Century Dragged. MoAmPo

Infant Innocence. A. E. Housman. FaBoCh; NOBL; OxBoLi; PeLV; Spl

Infant is white, like down, The. And the youth dark-complexioned, like shingle. A. Velichansky. TCRusP, *tr. by* Daniel Weissbort

Infant Joy. William Blake. FHYEP; NAEL-5v2; OxAEP-2; OxBSP *Fr.* Songs of Innocence.

Infant quirk of a pine, An. Navidad, St. Nicholas Ave. Alfred Corn. NoP-4

Infant Song. Charles Causley. NOxBChV; OxBC

Infant Sorrow. William Blake. FHYEP; NAEL-5v2; NAEL-6v2; OxAEP-2; OxBEV; OxBSP; PoPoPo; RB *Fr.* Songs of Experience.

Infant—wailing in maneless fear, An. Life. Ella Wheeler Wilcox. PoToHe

Infanta Marina. Wallace Stevens. APT-1

Infantry. Alun Lewis. PoWW

Infatuation. Frederick Goddard Tuckerman. NCAP

Infatuation, sadism, lust, avarice. To the Reader. Charles Baudelaire. NAWM-7v2, *tr. by* Robert Lowell

Infections. Miguel Algarin. PueRic

Infelice. Stevie Smith. LW

Infelix. Adah Isaacs Menken. CBWP-1; TCAPo

Infernal. Karen Volkman. BAP-97

Inferno. Dante Alighieri. NAWM-5v1 *Fr.* Divina Commedia.

Inferno. Dante Alighieri. NAWM-7v1, *tr. by* Allen Mandelbaum *Fr.* Divine Comedy, The (Mandelbaum Translation).

Inferno 1, 32. Jorge Luis Borges. PoetW, *tr. by* Anthony Kerrigan

Infidel Reclaimed, The. Edward Young. NOEC *Fr.* Night Thoughts.

Infidelity. Olga Fiodorovna Berggolts [or Bergholts]. BoWoP, *tr. by* Daniel Weissbort

Infidelity. Louis Untermeyer. TrJP

Infinite, The. Giacomo Leopardi. NAWM-7v2, *tr. by* Ottavio M. Casale

Infinite a sudden Guest, The. Emily Dickinson. WPoS

Infinite consanguinity it bears. Hart Crane. AmFaPo; ColAP; OxBA *Fr.* Voyages.

Infinite grief! amazing woe! Look on Him Whom They Pierced, and Mourn. Isaac Watts. NOCV

Infinite in the Skies, The. Alphonse Marie Louis de Lamartine. SxFrPo, *tr. by* E. H. Blackmore and A. M. Blackmore

Infinite peach-blossom shades. Peach Blossoms. Yuan Chen. CrYelRi, *tr. by* Sam Hamill

Infinite task of the human heart, The. (LL) For the One Who Would Take Man's Life in His Hands. Delmore Schwartz. MoAmPo; VGW

Infinite We Count the Dead! The Dance is Almost Finished! Death. Amelia Rosselli. CItWP, *tr. by* Cinzia Sartini Blum and Lara Trubowitz

Infinite weariness comes into the faces of the old tenements, An. Ghetto Twilight. Alter Brody. TaR

L' infinito. Giacomo Leopardi. AWP

Infinity, when all things it beheld. Edward Taylor. HAP; NAAL-2v1; NAAL-3; NOBA; NOSC; OxBA; OxBEV; SCAP; TCAPo *Fr.* God's Determinations [touching his Elect].

Infir Taris. *Unknown.* OxNR

Infirm and aged, doth he sit. Old Year, The. Priscilla Jane Thompson. CBWP-2

Infirmity. Theodore Roethke. CoAP; NAAL-2v2

Inflammable Woman, The. James Keir Baxter. OxBC

Inflation. Nicanor Parra. AF, *tr. by* Miller Williams

Influence. Sarah Knowles Bolton. PWR

Influence of Local Attachment, The. Richard Polwhele. Visit to the Author's Paternal Seat, A. NOEC

Influence of Natural Objects, The. James Simmons. PNI

Influence of Natural Objects [in Calling Forth and Strengthening the Imagination in Boyhood and Early Youth]. William Wordsworth. AWP; OxBEV *Fr.* Prelude, The; Growth of a Poet's Mind [1850 vers.].

Inform the Lakedaimonians, friend—we rest. Simonides. *See* Go tell at Sparta, traveler passing by

Informant, The. Eiléan Ní Chuilleanáin. ModIr

Informer, art thou in the tree. On the Meetings of the Scotch Covenanters. *Unknown.* FaBoEE

Informing a correct compassion, that performs its love, and makes it live. (LL) Correct Compassion, A. James Kirkup. FaBoTw; OxBTC

Ing? Is it possible to mean ing? Ing. Walter Conrad Arensberg. APT-1

Ingathering. Carolyn Kizer. ExTi

Ingenious god was old Zeus, An. Deus "Sex" Machina. Harriet Mandelbaum. PeLi

Ingenious insect, but of ruthless mould. To the Spider. Thomas Russell. CenSon; Son

Ingenuity too astonishing, An. Sun Underfoot among the Sundews, The. Amy Clampitt. NoP-4

Inglorious Milton, The. Francis Letters. NOBAu

Ingmar Bergman's "Seventh Seal." Robert Duncan. PoE

Ingoldsby Legends, The. "Thomas Ingoldsby."
Jackdaw of Rheims, The. EBNV; OBCoV; OBNV; OBSP

Ingrateful[l] Beauty Threatened. Thomas Carew. BeJo; CaPo; MeLP; OBEV
(Ingrateful Beauty Threat'ned.) CavPo
(Ingratefull beauty threatned.) PBRV

Ingratitude, how deadly is thy smart. Sonnet: Ingratitude. Anna Seward. CenSon; ECWP; NOEC

Ingredients of Glass. Margaret Speak. Prnts

Inhale, exhale. Gesshu Soko. JDP, *tr.* by Yoel Hoffmann

Inhaling His Hair. Gillian Ferguson. NeBl

Inheritance, The. Sami Mahdi. MAP, *tr.* by May Jayyusi

Inheritors, The. Gary Geddes. NOBC

Inheritors, The. William Peskett. PNI

Inhuman Henry. A. E. Housman. NBLV

Iniquity of the Fathers upon the Children, The. Christina Georgina Rossetti. FaBoVe

Inis Fal. Egan [*or* Aodhagán] O'Rahilly [*or* O'Reilly *or* Ó Rathaille]. BIrV; OBMV, *tr.* by James Stephens

Inishbofin on a Sunday morning. Seamus Heaney. HarvBoo *Fr.* Seeing Things.

Initial, Dæmonic, and Celestial Love. Ralph Waldo Emerson.
Dæmonic and the Celestial Love, The. APN-1

Initiate, The. W. S. Merwin. NNaP

Initiation. Monifa Atungaye Love. ISC

Initiation. Rainer Maria Rilke. TrJP, *tr.* by C. F. MacIntyre

Initiations. Paul Niger.
"What?/ a rhythm." NegPo

Injian Ocean sets an' smiles, The. For to Admire. Rudyard Kipling. MoBrPo

Injured Maple. Ronald G. Everson. NOBC

Injured Prince Vindicated, or, A Scurrilous and Detracting Pamphlet Answered, An. Elinor James. BASC

Injustice of the Courts. Lizelia Augusta Jenkins Moorer. CBWP-3

Ink ain't spewed from this pen. And Now Yu. David S. Mills. InTrad

Ink bottles and pens. Flute and Wind in the Hermit's Cell. Khalil Hawi. MAP, *tr.* by Sharif Elmusa and Diana Der Hovanessian

Ink runs from the corners of my mouth. Eating Poetry. Mark Strand. NoAM; TAP

Ink-specked sheets feel like cigar leaf;, The. Opening Le Ba Khon's Dictionary. John Balaban. CDa

Inks of all colours are filling my dreams. Dezső Kosztolányi. IQMS, *tr.* by Leslie A. Kery *Fr.* Laments of a Poor Little Child.

Inkstone Inscription for the Blind Scholar Ho Yung-kuang, An. Chin Nung. CoBLCP, *tr.* by Jonathan Chaves

Inky gloss of your mane, The. *Unknown.* GrAn

Inlaid Lute, The. Li Shang-yin. ChinPo, *tr.* by Yip Wai-lim

Inland. Edna St. Vincent Millay. HarvBoo

Inland, / far inland go my thoughts. Song of the Rejected Woman. Kibkarjuk. WPOW, *tr.* by Tom Lowenstein and Knud Rasmussen

Inland far though and away. Salt Longing. Austin Hummell. AmPoNex

Inland, inland, inland, inland. Oxaitoq's Song. *Unknown.* APN-2, *tr.* by Franz Boas

Inland sea—blue as a sapphire—set, An. Opal Sea, The. Ella Higginson. SWaP

Inmate, An. Peter Kocan. NOBAu

Inmates. Maggie Hannan. NLP

Inn at Kirchstetten, The. James Laughlin. PmAP

Inn of Angels, The. Giampiero Neri. ItPo, *tr.* by Gayle Ridinger

Inn That Missed Its Chance, The. Amos Russel Wells. TrCP

Inn moves impressively on the bank of the ancient river, The. To the Innkeeper at Five Rivers, Sun Pen. Chang Yü. CoBLCP, *tr.* by Jonathan Chaves

Inner Bloke. Joanne Limburg. NeBl

Inner greet. Greenberg said it. Columbus. Muriel Rukeyser. AF

Inner Man, The. Charles Simic. OPRER

Inner Part, The. Louis Simpson. RaBo

Inner Realm, The. Priscilla Jane Thompson. CBWP-2

Inner Temple Masque, The. William Browne (1591–1643).
Sirens' Song, The. NOBE; OBEV

Inner Tube. Michael Ondaatje. NoAM

Inner Vision, The. William Wordsworth. *See* Poems Composed or Suggested During a Tour, in the Summer of 1833

Inniskeen Road: July Evening. Patrick Kavanagh. CIP-2; NPeEn; NoAM; OxBSo

Innkeeper's Wife, The. Clive Sansom. OBCP

Innocence. Thom Gunn. HP

Innocence. Patrick Kavanagh. ModIr; RB

Innocence. Wislawa Szymborska. PoSu, *tr.* by Jan Darowski

Innocence. Thomas Traherne. BASC; CABP; ChIV-2; ESCV; MiEL; NOSC

Innocence, The. Robert Creeley. NeAP

Innocence of her, The. Innocent Breasts, The. Joel Oppenheimer. PoM

Innocence of the world. Prikaz. André Salmon. CuPo

Innocence? / In a sense. Life, A. Howard Nemerov. OBCoV

Innocence? Soon as you try putting your finger on it. 1966. David Rivard. PBCAP

Innocency or Not Song X. Gerald Early. BodElec

Innocent, The. Denise Levertov. KaS

Innocent Breasts, The. Joel Oppenheimer. PoM

Innocent bride from the Mission, An. Limerick. *Unknown.* PeLi

Innocent decision: to enjoy. Triple Feature. Denise Levertov. NoP-4

Innocent England. D. H. Lawrence. NPeEn; OBCoV

Innocent Ill, The. Abraham Cowley. BASC

Innocent Landscape. Elinor Wylie. OxBA

Innocent maiden of Gloucester, An. Limerick. *Unknown.* PeLi

Innocent Play. Isaac Watts. NOEC

Innocent's Song. Charles Causley. GTBS-P; OBCP

Innocent Spring, The. Dame Edith Sitwell. NOBE; OxBTC *Fr.* Sleeping Beauty, The.

Innocents have come to make their cast, The. Kites: Ars Poetica. Ben Belitt. APT-2

Innominatus. Sir Walter Scott. OBEV *Fr.* Lay of the Last Minstrel, The.

Inns are not residences. (LL) Silence. Marianne Craig Moore. APT-1; FaBoMo; FaBoWP; HarvBoo; NALW; NOBA; PAI; TRP; WoPoe

Innsbruck, now I must depart. *Unknown.* GePo

Innumerable Christ, The. Hugh MacDiarmid. EBEV; HarvBoo; OxAEP-2; OxBS

Innumerable the images. Documentary Film. "Ern Malley." BMAP

Innumerable worlds! We dream of them. Contemplation of the Heavens. Bill Manhire. PeNZ

Inordinate Love. *Unknown.* EBEV; MiEL; OxBSP

Inpatient. Dolores Kendrick. FFC

Inquest, The. William Henry Davies. AngWePo; GTBS-P; NOBE; OxBTC; RB

Inquietude. Pauli Murray. BlSi

Inquirers, trailing printed liberty. (LL) Scholar II. Seamus Deane. CIP-2; NOIV

Inquiring about the Health of Li Te-hua. Hsü Chung-hsing.
"Who would have thought that a disease of the ordinary world." CoBLCP

Inquisition. Gloria Wade-Gayles. ISC

Inquisition, The. Victor Hugo. SxFrPo, *tr.* by E. H. Blackmore and A. M. Blackmore

Inquisitive Bridegroom, The. William Somervile [*or* Somerville]. ECEV

Inquisitors, The. Robinson Jeffers. MoAmPo

INRI. Melanie Hope. WiU

Insatiable envy. (LL) Love Poem for a Wife, 2. A. K. Ramanujan. OMIP; WoPoe

Insatiable Priest, The. Matthew Prior. OxBSP

Insatiableness. Thomas Traherne. BBASP; NOSC

Inscribed at Summit Temple. Li Po. WoPoe, *tr.* by Elling O. Eide

Inscribed in Melrose Abbey. *Unknown.* FaBoEE

Inscribed on a Landscape by Mi Yüan-hui. Chao Meng-fu. CoBLCP, *tr.* by Jonathan Chaves

Inscribed on a Lichen-Covered Wall in My Hut. Chin Nung.
"Three lines of "clerk script" calligraphy." CoBLCP

Inscribed on a Painting. Cheng Hsieh. SuSp, *tr.* by Irving Y. Lo

Inscribed on a Painting. Hsü Wei. CoBLCP, *tr.* by Jonathan Chaves

Inscribed on a Painting. Ni Tsan. CoBLCP, *tr.* by Jonathan Chaves

Inscribed on a Painting. Shen Chou. SuSp, *tr.* by Daniel Bryant

Inscribed on a Painting. Shen Chou. SuSp, *tr.* by Irving Y. Lo

Inscribed on a Painting. T'ang Yin. CoBLCP, *tr.* by Jonathan Chaves

Inscribed on a Painting. T'ang Yin. SuSp, *tr.* by Chiang Yee

Inscribed on a Painting. Tao-chi. CoBLCP, *tr.* by Jonathan Chaves

Inscribed on a Painting. Yü Chi. CoBLCP, *tr.* by Jonathan Chaves

Inscribed on a Painting. Yün Shou-p'ing. CoBLCP, *tr.* by Jonathan Chaves

Inscribed on a Painting by Shih-ku. Yün Shou-p'ing.
"Through the windy valley." CoBLCP

Inscribed on a Painting: Cultivating Leisure. Wen Cheng-ming.
"Volumes of books, tea and incense." CoBLCP

Inscribed on a Painting of a Cock. T'ang Yin. SuSp, *tr.* by Chiang Yee

Inscribed on a Painting of a Fisherman. T'ang Yin. CoBLCP, *tr.* by Jonathan Chaves

Inscribed on a Painting of a Wu-t'ung Tree by Myself. Tao-chi. CoBLCP, *tr.* by Jonathan Chaves

Inscribed on a Painting of Bamboo. T'ang Yin. CoBLCP, *tr.* by Jonathan Chaves

Inscribed on a Painting of Bamboo. Wu Chen. CoBLCP, *tr.* by Jonathan Chaves

Inscribed on a Painting of Bamboo Presented to Lecturer Ch'en Upon His Departure to Resume His Duties at Nanking. Yang Shih-ch'i.
"Even ordinarily, parting is difficult." CoBLCP

Inscribed on a Painting of Dragons by Ch'en So-weng. Hsieh Chin. CoBLCP, *tr.* by Jonathan Chaves

Inscribed on a Painting of Sailboats on the River—Seeing Off Yen-chi on His Journey to Ch'ang-an. Yün Shou-p'ing. CoBLCP, *tr.* by Jonathan Chaves

Inscribed on a Painting of Windy Bamboo, to Be Presented to Tzu-kan. Hsü Wei. SuSp, *tr.* by Chiang Yee

Inscribed on a Plantain Leaf to Show to a Certain Person. Liu Ling-hsien. CoBCP, *tr.* by Burton Watson

Inscribed on a Scroll "Plum Blossoms by the Water." Huang T'ing-chien. SuSp, *tr.* by Michael E. Workman

Inscribed on a Snowscape. Yün Shou-p'ing. CoBLCP, *tr.* by Jonathan Chaves

Inscribed on a Statue of Hermes. *Unknown.* GrAn, *tr.* by Peter Jay

Inscribed on a Wall Painting of Assembled Immortals. Chao Meng-fu. CoBLCP, *tr.* by Jonathan Chaves

Inscribed on an Album Leaf Painted by Dr. Lin. Pien Kung. CoBLCP, *tr.* by Jonathan Chaves

Inscribed on Byron's Poetic Works. Su Man-shu. SuSp, *tr.* by Wu-Chi Liu

Inscribed on "Drunk in the Autumn Woods." Tao-chi. CoBLCP, *tr.* by Jonathan Chaves

Inscribed on My Grass-script Calligraphy Written While Drunk. Lu Yu. SuSp, *tr.* by Irving Y. Lo

Inscribed on My Ink Landscape Painting. Tao-chi. CoBLCP, *tr.* by Jonathan Chaves

Inscribed on My Large Landscape Hanging Scroll "Listening to a Waterfall." Tao-chi. CoBLCP, *tr.* by Jonathan Chaves

Inscribed on My Little Painting of Plum Blossom and Bamboo. Tao-chi. CoBLCP, *tr.* by Jonathan Chaves

Inscribed on Paintings for the People of Hangchow. Hsü Wei. CoBLCP, *tr.* by Jonathan Chaves

Inscribed on Sun An-chih's "Painting of Pines and Catalpas." Chao Meng-fu. CoBLCP, *tr.* by Jonathan Chaves

Inscribed on the Arbor of the Old Drunkard (Tsui-weng-t'ing) at Ch'u-chou. Ou-yang Hsiu. SuSp, *tr.* by Irving Y. Lo

Inscribed on the Doors of My Bookshelves. Yang Hsün-chi. ColAnChi, *tr.* by John Timothy Wixted

Inscribed on the Fan of a Wealthy Old Man. Shen Chou. SuSp, *tr.* by Irving Y. Lo

Inscribed on the Painting "Meaning of a Poem by Wang Wei." Li Tung-yang. CoBLCP, *tr.* by Jonathan Chaves

Inscribed on the Painting of "Garden for Retirement:" Pavilion of Sincerity, on Rocky Mountain. Chu Yi-tsun. SuSp, *tr.* by Chang Yin-nan

Inscribed on the Painting "Pleasures of the Lute by the River." Lin Hung. SuSp, *tr.* by Irving Y. Lo

Inscribed on the Painting, "River in Autumn." Ni Tsan. CoBLCP, *tr.* by Jonathan Chaves

Inscribed on the Painting, Solitary Crane, in the Collection of Jao Shih-ying. Yü Chi. CoBLCP, *tr.* by Jonathan Chaves

Inscribed on the Painting "Spring Dawn at Peach Blossom Spring" by Scholar Shang Te-fu. Chao Meng-fu. CoBLCP, *tr.* by Jonathan Chaves

Inscribed on the Painting, Stabbing a Tiger, by Chao Tzu-ang, in the Collection of Scholar Yang. Yang Shih-ch'i. CoBLCP, *tr.* by Jonathan Chaves

Inscribed on the Wall at the Temple of the Auspicious Talisman. Tao-chi. CoBLCP, *tr.* by Jonathan Chaves

Inscribed on the Wall of a Rice Cake Shop. Chin Nung. CoBLCP, *tr.* by Jonathan Chaves

Inscribed on the Wall of Hsü Hsüan-Ping's Retreat. Li Po. WoPoe, *tr.* by Elling O. Eide

Inscriptio. Pope. OxBSP

Inscription. William Cowper. OBGa
(Other stones the era tell.) OBGa
(And sweeten my repose.) (LL) OBGa
(Here free from riot's hated noise.) OBGa

Inscription at Mount Vernon. *Unknown.* HHAm

Inscription at Villers-Bretonneux. Geoff Page. NOBAu

Inscription by the Sea, An. Edwin Arlington Robinson. AWP; FaBoEE

Inscription by the Sea, An. *Var. authors.* AWP; FaBoEE *Fr.* Variations of Greek Themes.

Inscription for a Graveyard. Yvor Winters. CRP

Inscription for a Grotto. Mark Akenside. NOEC; OBGa

Inscription for a Headstone. Austin Clarke. BIrV; CIP-2

Inscription for a Mirror in a Deserted Dwelling. William Rose Benét. MoAmPo

Inscription for a Portrait. T'ang Yin. WoPoe, *tr.* by Graham Martin and John A. Scott

Inscription for a Portrait of Dante. Giovanni Boccaccio. AWP; EaItPo, *tr.* by Dante Gabriel Rossetti *Fr.* Sonnets.

Inscription for a Statue of Pan. *Unknown.* GrAn, *tr.* by Dudley Fitts

Inscription for a War. Alec Derwent Hope. BMAP; NoP-4

Inscription for a Wayside Spring. Frances Darwin Cornford. BrRo

Inscription for an Old Bed. William Morris. OBEV

Inscription: "For one long term, or e'er her trial came." George Canning. FaBoEE

Inscription for the Entrance to a Wood. William Cullen Bryant. APN-1; OxBA; TAP

Inscription for the Moss-Hut at Dove Cottage. William Wordsworth. OBGa

Inscription for the Tank. James Wright (1927–80). TwCP

Inscription in a Beautiful Retreat Called Fairy Bower. Hannah More. ECWP; NoP-4

Inscription in Monastic Refectory. Alcuin. MLL, *tr.* by Helen Waddell

Inscription in Osmington Church, Dorset. *Unknown.* NPeEn

Inscription in St Mary Magdalene Church, Milk Street, London. *Unknown.* NPeEn

Inscription on a Statue. Hermocreon. GrAn, *tr.* by Alistair Elliot

Inscription on a Tree atop mount Sacrifice (Ssu Shan) and Sent to Censor Ch'iao. Ch'en Tzu-ang. SuSp, *tr.* by Geoffrey R. Waters

Inscription on the Flyleaf of a Bible. Dannie Abse. TrJP

Inscription on the Liberty Bell. Bible, *O.T.* CA

Inscription on the Tomb[e] of the Lady Mary Wentworth, The. Thomas Carew. *See* Maria Wentworth

Inscription over His Door. Gido. ZenPo, *tr.* by Takashi Ikemoto and Lucien Stryk

Inscription, The: "While yet Rolfe's foot in stirrup stood." Herman Melville. APN-2 *Fr.* Clarel: A Poem and Pilgrimage in the Holy Land.

Inscription: "To them who crossed the flood." Herman Melville. UnPo

Inscription: "Whoe'er thou art whose path, in summer lies." Mark Akenside. NOEC
(Tragedy of a Shepherd.) ECEV

Inscriptions. Adrienne Rich.
History. NIL-7

Inscriptions at the City of Brass. *Unknown.* AWP *Fr.* Thousand and One Nights, The.

Inscriptions on Greek tombstones intrigued him. Ronald Wyn. Robert Bagg. TwCP

Inscrutable question, The. Simon Williams. NewEx

Insect. Sándor Weöres. IQMS, *tr.* by Peter Zollman

Insect Kitchen, The. Nicki Jackowska. BrRo

Insect song. (LL) Issa. BLT; ZenPo, *tr.* by Takashi Ikemoto and Lucien Stryk

Insects. Issa. WoPoe, *tr.* by Robert Bly

Insects. Isidor Schneider. APT-2; TrJP

Insects, The. Nancy Willard. LCAP-2

Insects are neat in death. Bee. Patricia Pogson. NLP

Insects: come, The. (LL) Visit. A. R. Ammons. CoAP; TwCP

Insects on a bough. Issa. EH; NIL-7, *tr.* by Robert Hass

Insects, why cry? Insects. Issa. WoPoe, *tr.* by Robert Bly

Insensibility. Wilfred Owen. FaBoTw; FaBoWar; NoP-4; OBWP; OxAEP-2; OxBTC; PeFWW; PoWW

Inseparable. Philip Bourke Marston. BoLoP

Inseparable from the fire. Coda. William Carlos Williams. NOBA

Insert, The. R. L. Barth. CDa; InPK-6

Inserting the Mirror. Rosmarie Waldrop.
"To explore the nature of rain I opened the door because inside the workings of language clear vision is impossible." PmAP

Inside, The. David Wojahn. YaYoPo

Inside Diameter. Clarence Major. PmAP

Inside Father's Pockets. Martha Rhodes. ExTi

Inside: George Gaines at Graterford Prison, 1981. David Keplinger. AmPoNex

Inside Green Eyes, Black Eyes. Diana Der Hovanessian. TWW

Inside his head he heard the stormy crows. (LL) Brainstorm. Howard Nemerov. HAP; TRP

Inside, it is bare but dimly alive. Thomas Kinsella. CIP-2 *Fr.* Messenger, The.

Inside / (jittery / burned language). Re:searches (Fragments, after Anakreon, for Emily Dickinson). Kathleen Fraser. PmAP

Inside Job, An. Brendan Galvin. PoCoUp

Inside my ears. P Word Poem, The. Leticia R. Benson. InTrad

Inside my eye. Inside Green Eyes, Black Eyes. Diana Der Hovanessian. TWW

Inside my father's close. My Father's Close. *Unknown.* AWP, *tr.* by Dante Gabriel Rossetti

Inside My Zulu Hut. Mbuyiseni Oswald Mtshali. PBMAP

Inside of which careen. Kingdom of Heaven, The. Pattiann Rogers. PoCoUp

Inside or out, the key is pain. It holds. Hospital. Karl Shapiro. VGW

Inside Out. Diane Wakoski. CoAP

Inside the brain they are holding a mass funeral for the dead brain cells. Brain Cells, The. Donald Hall. TAP

Inside, the church lights up today's rain. Fernando Pessoa. PFTM-1 *Fr.* Oblique Rain.

Inside the coconut is Katerina's baby. Coconut for Katerina, A. Sandra McPherson. LCAP-2

Inside the empty chamber of a wave is the same. Not Surfing Some Days. Rick Noguchi. AmPoNex

Inside the Fence: Tule Lake Internment Camp. Kim R. Stafford. GifTon

Inside the Horizon. New Song. Vincente Huidobro. CuPo

Inside the light of a three-way lamp. Fire Burns Low, The. John Leax. TrCP

Inside the lunchroom the travelling nuns wove. Feathered Dances. Kenward Elmslie. PmAP

Inside the mask her eyes are very dark. Face Mask. Patricia Pogson. NLP

Inside the nighttime of the storm. Enormous Hand, The. Jorge de Lima. PFTM-1

Inside the skull the wakeful brain. Camera Obscura, The. John Addington Symonds. NOBVV

Inside the strict pine coffin. Shards. Enid Shomer. TaR

Inside the temple enclosure. Hall of the Guardian God. Muso Soseki. EaWin, *tr. by* W. S. Merwin

Inside the tower not a broken tower two. Image-Nation (the Poësis). Robin Blaser. PoM

Inside the Tulip. George Bowering. MoCV

Inside the veins there are navies setting forth. Waking from Sleep. Robert Bly. NOBA; NoP-4; SPE

Inside the White Star it was warm, tumbled clothes. White Star, The. Minnie Bruce Pratt. ExTi

Inside / The wireless is irritable with static. Dog Fight. Eric Rolls. NOBAu

Inside the Wolf's fang, the mountain of heather. Amulet. Ted Hughes. NOxBChV

Inside this clay jar there are meadows and groves and the One who made them. Kabir. EnIH

Inside those caves, grottos of shame, full of mud, a child is still taking shelter, hopping. Geranium and the Child. Ece Ayhan. PFTM-2, *tr. by* Murat Nemet-Nejat

Inside water, a waterwheel turns. Jelaluddin [*or* Jalal al-Din] Rumi. WoPoe, *tr. by* Coleman Barks and John Moyne

Inside Your Sea My Boat Was Sailing. Patrizia Cavalli. CItWP, *tr. by* Cinzia Sartini Blum and Lara Trubowitz

Insides of Alfred Hitchcock, The. Alejandrino Hufana. ReBoTo

Insincere Wish Addressed to a Beggar, An. Mary Elizabeth Coleridge. NOBVV; NPeEn; PEW; VWP

Insistently through sleep—a tide of voices. Hart Crane. MoAmPo; NOBA; NoAM; OxBA *Fr.* Bridge, The.

Insomnia. Elizabeth Bishop. AWTN

Insomnia. Tristan Corbière. AWTN, *tr. by* Georges Guy and Kenneth Koch

Insomnia. Cornelius Eady. AWTN; ESEAA

Insomnia. Dana Gioia. AWTN

Insomnia. Abu Amir Ibn al-Hammarah. WoPoe, *tr. by* Cola Franzen

Insomnia. Lu Yu. OHMPC, *tr. by* Kenneth Rexroth

Insomnia. Osip Emilevich Mandelstam [*or* Mandelshtam]. TCRusP, *tr. by* John Glad

Insomnia. Debra Nystrom. AWTN

Insomnia. Joyce Carol Oates. AWTN

Insomnia. Wyatt Prunty. RA

Insomnia. Salvatore Quasimodo. AWTN, *tr. by* Allen Mandelbaum

Insomnia. Dante Gabriel Rossetti. AWTN

Insomnia. Tiziano Rossi. ItPo, *tr. by* Gayle Ridinger

Insomnia. Marina Ivanovna Tsvetayeva [*or* Tsvetaeva].
  "Here's another window." AWTN, *tr. by* Elaine Feinstein
  "In my enormous city it is—night." OxBEV, *tr. by* Elaine Feinstein
  "Tonight—I am alone in the night." AWTN, *tr. by* Elaine Feinstein
  "Who sleeps at night? No one is sleeping." AWTN, *tr. by* Elaine Feinstein

Insomnia I. Howard Nemerov. DiPo

Insomnia at the Solstice. Jane Kenyon. AWTN

Insomnia. Homer. Taut Sails. Osip Emilevich Mandelstam [*or* Mandelshtam]. AWTN, *tr. by* Clarence Brown and W. S. Merwin

Insomnia. Homer. Taut sails. Insomnia. Osip Emilevich Mandelstam [*or* Mandelshtam]. TCRusP, *tr. by* John Glad

Insomnia, impalpable Creature! Insomnia. Tristan Corbière. AWTN, *tr. by* Georges Guy and Kenneth Koch

Insomnia Litany. Joan Logghe. OPRER

Insomnia of Tremayne, The. Donald Justice. AWTN

Insomnia on a Summer Night. Umberto Saba. AWTN, *tr. by* Christopher Millis

Insomnia Song. Gregory Orr. AWTN

Insomnia: The Distances. Sydney Lea. RA

Insomnia the Gem of the Ocean. John Updike. NBLV

Insomnia thinks and pronounces syllables. Insomnia. Tiziano Rossi. ItPo, *tr. by* Gayle Ridinger

Insomniac. M. Loncar. AmPoNex

Insomniac. Sylvia Plath. AWTN

Insomniac Poem. Ron Loewinsohn. NeAP

Insomniac Sleeps Well for Once and, The. Hayden Carruth. NNaP

Insomniac trees rattle silken little. Unholy Spring. John Godfrey. FTOS

Inspector Hsü Claims He Has Found the Secret of Youth. T'ang Hsien-tsu. CoBLCP, *tr. by* Jonathan Chaves

Inspiration. Mário de Andrade. TCLAP, *tr. by* Jack E. Tomlins

Inspiration. Robert W. Service. WeW-3

Inspiration. James Tate. BodElec

Inspiration. Henry David Thoreau. APN-1; ColAP; NCAP; NOBA; OxBA

Inspiration, An. Ella Wheeler Wilcox. ITBLP
  (Only One Way.) PWR

Inspirer and hearer of prayer. Hymn. Augustus Montague Toplady. SacPr

Instability. Henrietta Cordelia Ray. CBWP-3

Instance of fore-ordained harmony, An. Igor Vladimirovich Chinnov. TCRusP, *tr. by* John Glad

Instans Tyrannus. Robert Browning. EBEV

Instant Control. Michael Portnoy. HeMarv

Instant he boarded the plane, The. Toad. Shinkichi Takahashi. ZenPo, *tr. by* Takashi Ikemoto and Lucien Stryk

Instead of a Preface. Anna Andreyevna Akhmatova. PFTM-1

Instead of a solemn wedding and marriage-bed. Anyte [*or* Anytes]. GrAn

Instead of an Animal. Leslie Scalapino. PFTM-2

Instead of becoming the empress of joined kingdoms. End of the Game. Artur Miedzyrzecki. PoSu, *tr. by* John Batki and Artur Miedzyrzecki

Instead of bridal bed and holy wedding songs. Anyte [*or* Anytes]. SaLy, *tr. by* Diane Rayor

Instead of Clements' Ferry, it is now Sunset Retreat. (LL) To Clements' Ferry. Josephine D. Henderson Heard. CBWP-4; SWaP

Instead of coin and money. John Skelton. NoSic *Fr.* Elinour Rumming.

Instead of his leash. Karen Alkalay-Gut. DTA *Fr.* Between Bombardments: A Journal.

Instead of icepacks. Dancing in Menopause. Dorothy Perry Thompson. SpirFl

Instead of Lent I have been feasting. God and the Holy Stones. Annie Foster. NLP

Instead of two cats, there weren't any. (LL) Cats of Kilkenny, The. *Unknown.* ChAP; PeLi; ReMoGo

Instinct. Edith Södergran. PFTM-1

Instinct, The. Jack Myers. BodElec

Instinct of Self-Preservation, The. Nanni Balestrini.

"What matters here is (can a fish live)." PFTM-2, *tr. by* Lawrence R. Smith

Instinctive resistance to the perils of sleep. (LL) Gunner, The. Francis Webb. BMAP; CBAP

Institute for Social Change, The. Joshua Clover. AmPoNex

Institution of the dear love of comrades, The. (LL) I Hear It Was Charged against Me. Walt Whitman. APN-1; CAGL; MoAmPo

Institutional Blue. Ann Townsend. NAPBL

Instructed by the fiery dead. (LL) Cross, The. Allen Tate. AWP; ChIV-2; MoAmPo; OxBA

Instructed in love. Ingeborg Bachmann. WPOW *Fr.* Songs in Flight.

Instructed then even by the diety [*or* Dietie]. (LL) Thomas Traherne. BASC; ESCV *Fr.* Third Century, The.

Instructed to speak of God with emphasis. Memorial to a Missionary. Keith Sinclair. PeNZ

Instructing Clarity in a Confusion. Arkadii Dragomoschenko. ItGoST, *tr. by* Elena Balashova and Lyn Hejinian

Instruction, The. Thomas Traherne. BASC

Instruction Manual, The. John Ashbery. HAP; NOBA; NeAP; NoAM; PoM; YaYoPo

Instructions for a Waitress. Yehuda Amichai [*or* Amikhai]. PoSu, *tr. by* Harold Schimmel

Instructions for Building Straw Huts. Yusef Komunyakaa. GT

Instructions for Crossing the Border. Dan Pagis. PoSu, *tr. by* Stephen Mitchell

Instructions for Elijah. Myra Sklarew. CRP

Instructions for Your New Osiris. Lorenzo Thomas. PmAP

Instructions of King Cormac. Cormac, King of Cashel. PoToHe

Instructions of King Cormac, The. *Unknown.*
  "O Cormac, grandson of Conn," said Carbery." BIrV

Instructions on landscaping. Richard Jago. OBGa *Fr.* Edge-Hill.
Instructions, Supposed to Be Written in Paris, for the Mob in England. Mary Alcock. ECWP
Instructions to a Celebrated Laureat. "Peter Pindar."
George III Visits Whitbread's Brewery. NOEC
Instructions to a Seed. David Curzon. GI
Instructions to the Double. Tess Gallagher. FaBoWP
Instructions to the Player. Carl Rakosi. APT-2; MiVo
Instructor said, The. Theme for English B. Langston Hughes. APT-2; ColAP; FaBoA; HCAP; NIL-7; NIP-4; NOBA; NoAM; NoP-4; PoPoPo; SSLK
Instrument. Gerrit Achterberg. TuT, *tr. by* Peter Van de Kamp
Instrument and Agent. Norman MacCaig. NePenScot
Insufficient, like all apologies. Knob Pines. David Swanger. GeoHom
Insular Celts, The. Ciaran Carson. BIrV; CIP-2
Insular firebird, The. Cages, The. James Tate. YaYoPo
Insulin Receptor. H. J. Van Peenen. BloBone
Insult, An. *Unknown.* NOIV
Insult before Gift-Giving. Frank Bolton. STP, *tr. by* Armand Schwerner
Insulted. Priscilla Jane Thompson. CBWP-2
Insulted and the Injured, The. Peter Viereck. SpudSo
Insurance salesman named Flint, An. Limerick. Charles Barsotti. PeLi
Insusceptibles, The. Adrienne Rich. CoAmPo; HeIP-4; Son
Intact. Stephanie Strickland. ExTi
Intact Pitcher. Yolanda Bedregal. TANSG, *tr. by* Carolyne Wright
Integrity. Adrienne Rich. ColAP
Intellect. Ralph Waldo Emerson. APN-1; NoP-4
Intellect of man is forced to choose, The. Choice, The. W. B. Yeats. NoAM; OxBSP; OxBTC
Intellectual, The. Yury [*or* Iurii] Timofeievich Galanskov. TCRusP, *tr. by* Olive Dehn
Intellectual cautious- / ly creeping cat. (LL) Bird-witted. Marianne Craig Moore. APT-1; NAAL-2v2
Intellectual Powers of the Soul, The. John Davies. SacPr
Intelligence of stars, The. (LL) Stanley Kunitz. OPRER; TaR
Intelligence Quotients. Dorothy Perry Thompson. SpirFl
Intelligent Sheepman and the New Cars, The. William Carlos Williams. OBAL
Intemperate torch grazed, The. Night-piece. "Ern Malley." BMAP
Intendant Yao Shan Has Requested Six Poems on Living in the Mountains, The. Yang Shih-ch'i.
White Stone Slope. CoBLCP, *tr. by* Jonathan Chaves
Intended for Sir Isaac Newton. Pope. ECEV; FaBoEE; InPK-6; WeW-3
(Epitaph Intended for Sir Isaac Newton, in Westminster Abbey.) NPeEn; OxBEV
Intense and terrible beauty, how has our race with the frail naked nerves. Gale in April. Robinson Jeffers. MoAmPo
Intensity and Height. César Vallejo. PoetW, *tr. by* Clayton Eshleman
Intensive Care. Carol Muske. PBCAP
Intent ear hears the silence hears silence and then the pen, The. Pen Vine and Scroll. John Taggart. FTOS
Intent to consider. Kit Robinson. FTOS *Fr.* Up Early.
Inter, mitzy, titzy, tool. *Unknown.* FaBoVe; OxNR
Inter-Office Memorandum. Ogden Nash. APT-2
Intercede for us dear saint we beseech thee. Prayer to Saint Grobianus. Roger McGough. NOxBChV
Interchange. Ted Kooser. UrbNat
Intercity Dub. Jane King. WaCA
Intercity, Swansea-London. Jon Dressel. TCAWP
Interest points for. Bleecker Street. Hugh Seidman. BodElec
Interesting case, the progress of a bird. When, An. Will to Will. Keith Waldrop. PmAP
Interesting how we fall in love. Unwritten Law. Louise Glück. BodElec
Interests of a black man in a cellar, The. Black Tambourine. Hart Crane. InPK-6; NoAM; OxBA; OxBSP; TAP
Interface. Gloria Anzaldúa. GLP
Interim. Frank Ormsby. CIP-2
Interior. Padraic Colum. MoBrPo
Interior. William Ernest Henley. NPeEn *Fr.* In Hospital.
Interior. Sir John Collings Squire. OxBSP
Interior at Petworth: From Turner. Rosanna Warren. NoAM
Interior Landscape. Gloria Fuertes. BoWoP, *tr. by* Willis Barnstone
Interior Monologue 666. Tom Marshall. NOBC
Interior Music, The. Patricia Goedicke. MiVo
Interior Scroll. Carolee Schneemann. PFTM-2
Interior (With Jane). Frank O'Hara. LCAP-2

Interlaced Lines for the Same Moment. Ghada El-Shafa'i. PoArWo, *tr. by* Atef Abu-Seif and Nathalie Handal
Interlinked is truth to duty, have you had the precious thought. Duty, or Truth at Work. Lizelia Augusta Jenkins Moorer. CBWP-3
Interlude. Sibby Anderson-Thompkins. InTrad
Interlude. Maya Bejerano. DTA, *tr. by* Tsipi Keller *Fr.* Hymns of Job.
Interlude. Maxwell Bodenheim. APT-1
Interlude. Walter Savage Landor. GTBS-P
Interlude. Keidrych Rhys. AngWePo
Interlude. Dame Edith Sitwell. MoBrPo
Interlude of Joy. George Seferis. PoetW, *tr. by* Edmund Keeley and Philip Sherrard
Interludes. Fabio Doplicher. NeIt, *tr. by* Stephen Sartarelli
Intermission from Friday. Pedro Juan Pietri. PueRic
Intermission from Monday. Pedro Juan Pietri. PueRic
Intermission from Saturday. Pedro Juan Pietri. PueRic
Intermission from Sunday. Pedro Juan Pietri. PueRic
Intermission from Thursday. Pedro Juan Pietri. PueRic
Intermission from Wednesday. Pedro Juan Pietri. PueRic
Intermittent Dream of a Sad Night. Marceline Desbordes-Valmore. WoPoe, *tr. by* Louis Simpson
Internal Migration: On Being on Tour. Alan Dugan. NoAM
International Chainpoem. *Unknown.* SPE
International Conference. Colin Ellis. FaBoEE
International Date Line, Monday/Monday 27:XI:67. Philip Whalen. BB
Interpretation of Dinner by the Uninvited Guest, An. Lorna Dee Cervantes. TouFir
Interracial. Georgia Douglas Johnson. TTY
Interred [*or* Interr'd] beneath this marble stone. Epitaph, An. Matthew Prior. FaBoEE; NAEL-5v1; NAEL-6v1; NAEL-7v1; OBCoV; OBSV
Interrogation. Qasim Haddad. MAP, *tr. by* Lena Jayyusi and Christopher Middleton
Interrogation. Richard Michelson. GotH
Interrogation, The. Li-Young Lee. PoPoPo
Interrogation, The. Edwin Muir. NPeEn; PoWW
Interrogations of the Sparrow. Elizabeth Spires. FFC
Interrogativa Cantilena. *Unknown. See* If All the World Were Paper
Interrogator, The. Elizabeth Jennings. WPE
Interrupt this Ground. (LL) Emily Dickinson. MoAmPo; NAAL-2v1; NAAL-3; OxBA; WoPoe
Interrupted Meditation. Robert Hass. BAP-97
Interrupted Reproof, The. Priscilla Jane Thompson. CBWP-2
Interruption of Flight. Lisa Williams. AmPoNex
Interruption to a Journey. Norman MacCaig. RB
Intersection, The. Charles Bernstein. PFTM-2 *Fr.* Artifice of Absorption.
Intersection in the Sky. Mcavoy Layne. CDa
Interstate 80. Michael Anania. IllVoic
Interstices. William J. Higginson. HA
Interval, An. June 30th. Vera Gherarducci. CItWP
Interview. Manuel Bandeira. TCLAP, *tr. by* Candace Slater
Interview. Sara Henderson Hay. OBCA
Interview, An. K. W. Grandsen. OxBTC
Interview with a Guy Named Fawkes, U.S. Army. Walter McDonald. CDa
Interview with an Alchemist in the New Age. Stephanie Brown. BodElec
Interview with Doctor Drink. James Vincent Cunningham. OxBSP; VGW; WoPoe
Intery, mintery, cutery corn. Mother Goose. FaBoVe; OxNR; ReMoGo
Intifada. June Jordan. NAAAL
Intil the pit-mirk nicht we northwart sail. Arctic Convoy. James King Annand. OxBS
Intimate. Gabriela Mistral. SpanPo, *tr. by* Kate Flores
Intimate Associations. Charles Baudelaire. WoPoe, *tr. by* Robert Bly
Intimate Conversations with God. Kwaja Abdullah Ansari.
"O God, / I have bound myself to you to the exclusion of all else." BBASP, *tr. by* Wheeler M. Thackston
Intimate evenings, times long past, refined to remembrance. Á La Recherche. Miklós Radnóti. IQMS, *tr. by* Peter Zollman
Intimate Letter 1973. Padraic Fiacc. PNI
Intimate Mixture. Elena Georgiou. WiU
Intimate Parnassus. Patrick Kavanagh. MoBrPo
Intimate Supper. Peter Redgrove. FaBoMo; OxBC
Intimates. D. H. Lawrence. BoLoP; NBLV; OxBSP; RaBo
Intimations. Howard Nemerov. BodElec
Intimations of Anxiety. Laila Al-Saih. PoArWo, *tr. by* May Jayyusi and Naomi Shihab Nye
Intimations of Mortality. Stanley Kunitz. MoAmPo
Intimations of an Autobiography. James Tate. NoAM

Into a dark and lonely wood. (LL)   Villain, The.   William Henry Davies. AngWePo; MoBrPo; OxBSP; OxBTC

Into a sweet May morning.   John of Hazelgreen.   *Unknown.*   ESPB

Into a ward of the whitewashed walls.   Somebody's Darling.   Marie La Coste.   UnPo

Into an isle of joy. (LL)   Manhattan.   Richard Rodgers.   OBAL; ReLy

Into azure cloudland searching.   To My Distant Beloved.   Alois Jeitteles.   TrJP, *tr.* by the Reverend Dr. Troutbeck

Into Battle.   Julian Grenfell.   FaBoWar; OBEV; OBMV; OBWP; OxBTC; PeFWW

Into Concrete Mixer Throw.   Barbara Roe.   UV

Into each other's gaze. (LL)   Judas Iscariot.   Stephen Spender.   MoBrPo; NIP-4

Into exile with only a few shirts.   Cloak, The.   Robert Graves.   HarvBoo

Into Her Eyes a Tear Crept.   Gustavo Adolfo Bécquer.   SpanPo, *tr.* by Kate Flores

Into her mother's bedroom to wash the ballooning body.   Jessie Mitchell's Mother.   Gwendolyn Brooks.   BoWoP; ColAP; NALW

Into hey nony nony. (LL)   William Shakespeare.   AWP; CTC; NoSic; PAI; UV   *Fr.* Much Ado about Nothing.

Into his rosy chamber stepped the Sun.   At Sunset.   Henrietta Cordelia Ray.   CBWP-3

Into Mexico.   Mona Van Duyn.   VCAP

Into my bosom and be lost in me. (LL)   Tennyson.   BoLoP; EBEV; EBVV; FHYEP; GTBS-P; NAEL-5v2; NAEL-6v2; NOBE; NPeEn; NoP-4; OxAEP-2; SCGP; SCV; TFi; WoPoe   *Fr.* Princess, The.

Into my empty head there come.   Morning Swim.   Maxine W. Kumin.   WPE

Into my eyes he loving looked.   Mirror, The.   Judah Halevi.   TrJP, *tr.* by Emma Lazarus

Into my heart a seed was cast.   Hunger.   Mikhail Naimy.   GraLe

Into my heart an air that kills.   Yon Far Country.   A. E. Housman.   EBEV; HarvBoo; MoBrPo; NOBE; NOBVV; NPeEn; NoAM; OPOU; OxAEP-2; OxBEV; OxBTC; TFi

Into one of three pots.   Viaticum.   Birago Diop.   NegPo, *tr.* by Ellen Conroy Kennedy

Into ourselves / who   (look).   ,startled. (LL)   Four III.   E. E. Cummings.   FaBoMo; TTTS

Into—Renown! (LL)   Emily Dickinson.   AH; NOCV

Into space-time walks bass strings of charlie mingus.   One for Charlie Mingus.   Quincy Troupe.   SpirFl

Into Suburbia between eight and nine.   Three-handed Fugue.   Phyllis Gotlieb.   NOBC

Into Such Assembly.   Myung Mi Kim.   FSt

Into that dark permanence of ancient forms. (LL)   Like Dolmens Round My Childhood, the Old People.   John Montague.   EBEV; ModIr; NoP-4; PBCIP; PNI

Into that house whose tenants do not love. (LL)   Things, The.   Conrad Potter Aiken.   HAP; WeW-3

Into that peace all history must feed. (LL)   At Vshchizh.   Fyodor [*or* Feodor] Ivanovich Tyutchev.   OBWP; OxBEV; WoPoe, *tr.* by Henry Gifford and Charles Tomlinson

Into that pit.   Burning Shit at An Khe.   Bruce Weigl.   CDa

Into the Ark.   John Blight.   BMAP

Into the atmosphere, out of this world.   Tune: "The Charm of Nien-nu"—Kunlun Mountains.   Mao Tse-tung [*or* Mao Zedong].   SuSp, *tr.* by Eugene Eoyang

Into the Beautiful. (LL)   As imperceptibly as grief.   Emily Dickinson.   APN-2; NAAL-2v1; NOBA; NoP-4; PoE; SoSe-8

Into the blinding sun.   Nicholas Virgilio.   HA; InPK-6

Into the blue river hills.   Sunset from Omaha Hotel Window.   Carl Sandburg.   APT-1; AiP

Into the changes of autumn brush.   To Kill a Deer.   Carol Frost.   MoASP

Into the clouds, and never more return! (LL)   Ode on Indolence.   John Keats.   NAEL-5v2; NAEL-6v2

Into the common bowl.   Salad Days.   Bruce Berger.   SwNoth

Into the darkness and the hush of night.   Night.   Henry Wadsworth Longfellow.   APN-1

Into the Depths.   Adah Isaacs Menken.   CBWP-1

Into the destination of the wind! (LL)   To the Lacedemonians.   Allen Tate.   NAAL-2v2; NoAM

Into the Dusk-Charged Air.   John Ashbery.   APSN

Into the flame Godmother put her hand.   David's Night in Veliès.   James Merrill.   HarvBoo

Into the Foghorn.   Paul Celan.   BBASP, *tr.* by Michael Hamburger

"Into the future. Let what will be, be." (LL)   Acceptance.   Robert Frost.   GSo; OxBA

Into the Glacier.   John Haines.   CoAP

Into the gloom of the deep, dark night.   Engine, The.   Ella Wheeler Wilcox.   APN-2

Into the glories of the [*or* th'] almighty sun. (LL)   On a Drop of Dew.   Andrew Marvell.   BASC; ESCV; FSCP; GeHe; HAP; MeLP; NIL-7; NOSC; SCGP

Into the grave. (LL)   To Blossoms.   Robert Herrick.   BeJo; CaPo; GTBS-P; NAEL-5v1; NAEL-6v1; NOSC; OBEV; SCGP; TreFP

Into the haven where they would be. (LL)   Coventry Patmore.   EBVV; NOBVV   *Fr.* Angel in the House, The.

Into the Hearth They Are Tossing Logs.   Manuel González Prada.   SpanPo, *tr.* by Kate Flores

Into the house.   Lucien Stryk.   IllVoic   *Fr.* Issa: A Suite of Haiku.

Into the last dream of Offa the King. (LL)   Geoffrey Hill.   HAP; NoAM; WoPoe   *Fr.* Mercian Hymns.

Into the Light.   Pattiann Rogers.   PoCoUp

Into the Next One.   Valerie Martínez.   AmPoNex

Into the Park a-maying! (LL)   Sister, Awake!   *Unknown.*   NOBE; OBEV

Into the pause, while peppermints were passed.   Dylan Thomas at Tenby.   Raymond Garlick.   TCAWP

Into the pool of silence our tears made.   Ancient Couple on Lu Mountain, The.   Mark Van Doren.   VGW

Into the quiet of this room.   Room, The.   William Soutar.   EBEV; NePenScot

Into the ragged meadow of my soul. (LL)   If I Have Made, My Lady.   E. E. Cummings.   NOBA; PoRA

Into the Red Velvet.   Joyce Mansour.   SurWo, *tr.* by Guy Flandre and Peter Wood

Into the red velvet of your belly.   Into the Red Velvet.   Joyce Mansour.   SurWo, *tr.* by Guy Flandre and Peter Wood

Into the regions of eternity. (LL)   Praise Ye the Lord, O Celebrate His Fame.   Peleg Folger.   AH; ChIV-1

Into the rescued world newcomer.   Beyond Knowledge.   Alice Thompson Meynell.   ChIV-1

Into the sea at the end of the pier. (LL)   Novelty Shop, The.   Duane Niatum.   CDW; ReTh

Into the Silent Land!   Song of the Silent Land.   Johann Gaudenz von Salis-Seewis.   AWP, *tr.* by Henry Wadsworth Longfellow

Into the silver night.   Revelation.   Sir Edmund William Gosse.   OBEV

Into the sixties.   Don't Cry, Scream.   Haki R. Madhubuti.   SeSe

Into the skies, one summer's day.   Thought, The.   William Brighty Rands.   OBEV

Into the soil a seed is sown.   Mors et Vita.   James Edwin Campbell.   TCAPo

Into the soil of England. (LL)   How Beastly the Bourgeois Is.   D. H. Lawrence.   NAEL-5v2; NAEL-6v2; OBSV; PAI

Into the street the Piper stept.   Robert Browning.   OxAEP-2   *Fr.* Pied Piper of Hamelin, The.

Into the sunshine.   Fountain, The.   James Russell Lowell.   OBCA; TreFP

Into the towering gulfs of air. (LL)   Veni Coronaberis.   Geoffrey Hill.   DiPo; NoP-4

Into the underneath.   Recessional.   Robert Kelly.   FTOS

Into the unknown ocean of the sun at noon. (LL)   Hat Factory, The.   Paul Durcan.   BiHa; ModIr

Into the void behold my shuddering flight,   Anna Hempstead Branch.   NALW   *Fr.* Sonnets from a Lock Box.

Into the woods my Master went.   Ballad of Trees and the Master, A.   Sidney Lanier.   APN-2; ChIV-2; ColAP; ITBLP; NOBA; OxBA; TCAPo

Into these loves, who but for passion look[e]s.   Michael Drayton.   NAEL-5v1; NAEL-6v1; NAEL-7v1; NOSC; Son   *Fr.* Idea.

Into thir inmost bower.   John Milton.   TOF   *Fr.* Paradise Lost.

Into this other world he cannot build without you. (LL)   Thief, The.   Dorianne Laux.   ErotSp; ExTi; PasH

Into this pleasant Shadow all the weak & weary.   William Blake.   NOBRP   *Fr.* Milton.

Into this wild abyss.   John Milton.   NOSC   *Fr.* Paradise Lost.

Into whose ear the deeds are spoken. The only.   History.   Jorie Graham.   HarvBoo

Into windowpanes and lights. (LL)   City, Evening, and an Old Man: Me, The.   "Dhoomil."   OMIP; WoPoe, *tr.* by Vinay Dharwadker

Into your arms I came.   To the Anxious Mother.   Valente Goenha Malangatana.   PBA; PBMAP, *tr.* by Dorothy Guedes and Philippa Rumsey

Into your trunk.   Her Story.   Leah Korican.   HW

Intolerably sad, profound.   Before the Anæsthetic; or, A Real Fright.   Sir John Betjeman.   HarvBoo

Intoothed constrict.   Giant Yellow.   Maggie O'Sullivan.   Oth

Intoxicating draughts he never does drink.   Joseph Gwyer.   VerBaPo   *Fr.* Ode on the Visit of the Shah of Persia.

Intoxication of final loneliness. (LL)   Medlars and Sorb-Apples.   D. H. Lawrence.   FaBoVe; NPeEn; NoAM

Intra-Political.   Margaret Avison.   MoCV

Intrepid Ricardo, The.   Edmund Clerihew Bentley.   OBCoV   *Fr.* Clerihews.

Intricately vast process has produced, The.   Prospero Listens to the Night.   Jack Gilbert.   BodElec

Introduced / to the Upanishads / by T. S. Eliot. Situation. Kaa Naa Subramanyam. OMIP, *tr. by* Kaa Naa Subramanyam

Introduction. Anna Andreyevna Akhmatova. PFTM-1

Introduction. William Blake. *See* Songs of Innocence

Introduction. Letitia [*or* Laetitia] Elizabeth Landon. RWP *Fr.* Improvisatrice, The.

Introduction. James Russell Lowell. *Fr.* Biglow Papers, The.

Introduction. Edgar Allan Poe. *See* Romance

Introduction, The. Louis MacNeice. PNI

Introduction—Childhood and School-Time. William Wordsworth. FHYEP; NAEL-6v2 *Fr.* Prelude, The; Growth of a Poet's Mind [1850 vers.].

Introduction: "Hear the voice of the Bard!" William Blake. ChIV-1; EBEV; FHYEP; HAP; NAEL-5v2; NAEL-6v2; NAWM-7v2; NOBE; NOBRP; NOEC; NPeEn; NoP-4; OxBEV; PoE; RB; TFi *Fr.* Songs of Experience.

Introduction: "I bespeak words." Clere Parsons. FaBoTw

Introduction: "I don't know politics but I know the names." Kamala Das. NALW; WPOW

Introduction: "Joy of the poor knocked on the door, The." Nathan [*or* Natan] Alterman. MHP, *tr. by* Ruth Finer Mintz *Fr.* Joy of the Poor, The.

Introduction: My Themes. Pablo Neruda. GifTon, *tr. by* William O'Daly

Introduction of a refrain, The. 'Twixt Cup and Lip. Mark Hollis. NBLV

Introduction: "Should you ask me, whence these stories?" Henry Wadsworth Longfellow. ColAP; NOBA; PoE *Fr.* Song of Hiawatha, The.

Introduction, The: "Did I, my lines intend for public[k] view." Anne Finch, Countess of Winchilsea. BWW; EMWP; NAEL-5v1; NAEL-6v1; NAEL-7v1; NALW; NoP-4; WPOW

Introduction to a Poem. Nikolai Ivanovich Glazkov. TCRP, *tr. by* Daniel Weissbort

Introduction to a Prayer. Fritzi Harmsen van Beek. WoPoe, *tr. by* Claire Nicholas White and Claire Nicolas White

Introduction to Poetry. Paul Lake. RA

Introduction to the Franklin's Prologue and Tale. Geoffrey Chaucer. NAEL-5v1; NAEL-6v1 *Fr.* Canterbury Tales, The.

Introduction to the Pardoner's Prologue and Tale. Geoffrey Chaucer. *See* Canterbury Tales, The.

Introduction to the Pardoner's Tale. Geoffrey Chaucer. NAWM-7v1, *tr. by* Theodore Morrison *Fr.* Canterbury Tales, The.

Introduction to the Pardoner's Tale. Geoffrey Chaucer. NAEL-6v1; NAEL-7v1 *Fr.* Canterbury Tales, The.

Introduction to the Parson's Tale, The. Geoffrey Chaucer. NAEL-5v1; NAEL-6v1 *Fr.* Canterbury Tales, The.

Introductory Poem to the Penitential Psalms. Sir Thomas Wyatt. SacPr

Introit. Padraic Fiacc. CIP-2

Introit. Paul Murray. BBASP

Introitus. János Pilinszky. IQMS, *tr. by* Ted Hughes

Introspective. Christina Georgina Rossetti. VWP

Introspective Reflection. Ogden Nash. NBLV; OBCoV

Intruder. Alison Bielski. AngWePo

Intruder, The. Delmira Agustini. BLPSL, *tr. by* Rene de Costa, Rigas Kappatos and Eleni Paidoussi

Intruder, The. Carolyn Kizer. BoWoP; InPK-6

Intruder in a Set Scene. Norman MacCaig. NePenScot

Intruder, uprooter. Since Akkad, Since Elam, Since Sumer. Aimé Césaire. WoPoe, *tr. by* Gregson Davis

Intrusion. Denise Levertov. VCAP

Intuition of reciprocal knowledge, An. Nicole Brossard. PFTM-2, *tr. by* Barbara Godard *Fr.* Barbizon, The.

Inundation, The. Howard Sergeant. SPE

Inupiat Christmas Pageant, The. Peggy Shumaker. PBCAP

Invaders, The. Bernard Spencer. FaBoWar

Invaders from Mars. Robert Glück. WiU

Invaders from South of the Border Imperil Native Population. Charles Harper Webb. GeoHom

Invades, and drowns them all in tears. (LL) Foreign Ruler, A. Walter Savage Landor. OBSV; OxBEV

Invalid girl asked, An. Those Who Do Not Dance. Gabriela Mistral. WPoS, *tr. by* Maria Giachetti

Invalid's Song. Harata Tangikuku. PeNZ, *tr. by* Margaret Orbell

Invaluable is the Soto Way. Gasan. ZenPo, *tr. by* Takashi Ikemoto and Lucien Stryk

Invariably when wine redeems the sight. Wine Menagerie, The. Hart Crane. APT-2; NOBA; NoAM; OxBA; VGW

Invasion. Eileen Duggan. PeNZ

Invasion. Anna Enquist. TuT, *tr. by* Peter Van de Kamp

Invasion Exercise on the Poultry Farm. Sir John Betjeman. NOBL

Invasion of Grenada, The. William Daniel Ehrhart. CDa

Invasion Summer. Laurie Lee. OxBSP

Invective against Denise, a Witch. Pierre de Ronsard. WoPoe, *tr. by* Anthony Hecht

Invective against Ibis. Ovid. "While Thracians shal with arrowes war, Iazyges with bowe." OBVE

Inventing a story with grass. Birth, A. James Dickey. NOBA

Inventing Fables about the Stone. Julia Galemire. MirDau, *tr. by* Roberta Gordenstein

Inventing My Parents. Susan Bartels Ludvigson. PoSol

Invention begs from door to door in the indescribable darkness. Kissing Natalia. Eldon Grier. NOBC

Invention of a Garden, The. Jay Wright. GT

Invention of Comics, The. Imamu Amiri Baraka. CRP; GT; NAAAL

Invention of Fire, The. Andrew Taylor. CBAP

Invention of Pittsburgh, The. Maggie Anderson. PBCAP

Invention of White People, The. Leslie Marmon Silko. STP

Inventions. Miroslav Holub. PoSu, *tr. by* George Theiner

Inventions. William Scammell. NLP

Inventors. Michael C. Blumenthal. DiPo; NoAM

Inventory. Günter Eich. AF, *tr. by* David Young

Inventory. Joan Larkin. WiU

Inventory. Dorothy Parker. NBLV

Inventory. Jacques Prévert. STV, *tr. by* John Frederick Nims

Inventory of Places Propitious for Love. Angel González. VCWP, *tr. by* Steven Ford Brown

Inventory of the Furniture of a Collegian's Chamber, An. John Winstanley. OBSV

Inverey cam doun Deeside, whistlin and playin. Baron of Brackley, The. *Unknown.* ESPB

Inversnaid. Gerard Manley Hopkins. FaBoVe; GTBS-P; MoBrPo; NPeEn; NoAM; PeVV; PoRA; RB; SCGP; SacPr; TFi; UnPo

Investigative Poetry. Edward Sanders. "Content of History Will be Poetry, The." PFTM-2

Investment, The. Robert Frost. APT-1; OxBA

Invictus. William Ernest Henley. AmFaPo; BRP; CABP; MoBrPo; NAEL-6v2; NOBE; OBEV; OBMV *Fr.* Echoes.

Invisible ancestors. Letter from Mexico. Homero [*or* Umberto] Aridjis. TCLAP, *tr. by* Eliot Weinberger

Invisible Atoms of the Air, The. Gustavo Adolfo Bécquer. SpanPo, *tr. by* Kate Flores

Invisible Autumn. Joseph Ceravolo. FTOS

Invisible catches and secret hooks, bone. Chastity Belt. Yusef Komunyakaa. KGB

Invisible, chimerical. Riddle. Daryl Hine. NoP-4

Invisible Dreams. Toi Derricotte. PuP-23

Invisible Element, The. István Vas. IQMS, *tr. by* George Szirtes

Invisible Hand. L. S. Asekoff. BodElec

Invisible History. Walta Borawski. GLP

Invisible, indivisible Spirit. "H. D." APT-1; BoWoP *Fr.* Tribute to the Angels.

Invisible is stronger than the visible, The. History of the Invisible. Rodger Kamenetz. TaR

Invisible King, The. Goethe. RaBo, *tr. by* Robert Bly

Invisible Men, The. Nakasuk. RaBo, *tr. by* Edward Field

Invisible Mender, The. Sarah Maguire. MFPA

Invisible Tree. Tamura Ryuichi. WoPoe, *tr. by* Naoshi Koriyama and Edward Lueders

Invisible wall, The. Luis Cernuda. CAGL, *tr. by* Rick Lipinski

Invitation. Marion Angus. LW

Invitation. Orrick Johns. APT-1

Invitation. Myra Cohn Livingston. TLR

Invitation. Grace Nichols. "Come up and see me sometime." EroLit

Invitation. Solomon ibn Gabirol. TrJP, *tr. by* Israel Zangwill

Invitation, The. Robert Creeley. FTOS

Invitation, The. George Herbert. ChIV-1; ESCV

Invitation, The. Robert Herrick. CaPo

Invitation, The. Charles Kingsley. NOBVV

Invitation, The. Goronwy Owen. OBWVE, *tr. by* George Borrow

Invitation, The. Shelley. *See* To Jane: The Invitation

Invitation, The. Leonard Welsted. NOEC

Invitation from a Country Cottage, The. Martha Sansom. ECWP

Invitation into the Country, in Imitation of Horace, An. Jane Colman Turell. "Though my small incomes never can afford." TCAPo

Invitation Standing. Paul Blackburn. VGW

Invitation to a Voyage. Max Jacob. CuPo

Invitation to Brecknock, An. Henry Vaughan. "Since last we met, thou and thy horse, my dear." AngWePo

Invitation to Dalliance. *Unknown.* FaBoEE

Invitation to Hsiao Ch'u-shih. Po Chü-i. ChiP; OBVE, *tr. by* Arthur Waley

Invitation to Juno.   William Empson.   FaBoMo

Invitation to Madison County, An.   Jay Wright.   ESEAA

Invitation to Miss Marianne Moore.   Elizabeth Bishop.   NALW

Invitation to my Friends at Cambridge, An.   Jane Barker.   BASC

Invitation to the Dance.   Apollinaris Sidonius.   AWP, *tr. by* Howard Mumford Jones

Invitation to the Dance.   Pentti Saarikoski.
   "No, Quetzalcoatl, don't come back."   VCWP

Invitation to the Voyage.   Charles Baudelaire.   SxFrPo, *tr. by* James McGowan

Invitation to the Voyage.   Charles Baudelaire.   *See* L'Invitation au Voyage

Invite to Eternity [, An].   John Clare.   NAEL-5v1; NAEL-5v2; NAEL-6v2; NOBVV

Invited guests in silent order sat, Th'   Animal Magnetism; the Pseudo-Philosopher Baffled.   Laurence Hynes Halloran.   NOEC

Invited onto the grounds of the god.   Poetry.   Jane Miller.   GifTon

Invites His Nymph to His Cottage.   Philip Ayres.   EnLoPo

Invites Poets and Historians to Write in Cynthia's Praise.   Philip Ayres.   Son

Inviting a Friend to Supper.   Ben Jonson.   AWP; BASC; BeJo; NAEL-6v1; NAEL-7v1; NOBE; NOSC; NPeEn; NoP-4; OxBoLi; PAI; PBRV; PeLV

Inviting a Tiger for the Weekend.   José Garcia Villa.   WoPoe

Invocation.   Maria Elena Cruz Varela.   VCWP, *tr. by* Mairym Cruz-Bernal

Invocation.   Samuel Hoffenstein.
   "Come, live with me and be my love."   NBLV

Invocation.   Sana'i.   BBASP, *tr. by* Nasrollah Pourjavady and Peter Lamborn Wilson

Invocation.   Shelley.   *See* Song: "Rarely, rarely, comest thou."

Invocation: "Almighty God, who fillest the recesses of the heavens."   Bishop Patrick.   NOIV

Invocation: "American muse, whose strong and diverse heart."   Stephen Vincent Benét.   APT-2   *Fr.* John Brown's Body.

Invocation, An: "Hear, sweet spirit, hear the spell."   Samuel Taylor Coleridge.   PeECV   *Fr.* Remorse.

Invocation, An: "My claw is tired of scribing!"   Saint Columcille [*or* Columba].   NOIV

Invocation and Prelude.   Stefan George.   AWP, *tr. by* Ludwig Lewisohn

Invocation: "Appear, O Mother, was the perpetual cry."   Wilfred Watson.   MoCV

Invocation: "Come down from heaven to meet me when my breath."   Siegfried Sassoon.   MoBrPo

Invocation: "Earth, ocean, air, belovèd brotherhood!"   Shelley.   NAEL-5v2   *Fr.* Alastor; or, The Spirit of Solitude.

Invocation for Storing Corn.   Unknown.   WPoS, *tr. by* Francisco X. Alarcón

Invocation: "I, who in times before, with youthful mind."   Miklós Zrínyi.   IQMS, *tr. by* Thomas Kabdebo   *Fr.* Zrinyiad, The.

Invocation: "It's crazy to think one could describe them."   Robert Pinsky.   NoAM   *Fr.* Essay on Psychiatrists.

Invocation: "Last night my soul departed."   Muireadhach Albanach O'Dalaigh.   NOIV

Invocation: "Let me be buried in the rain."   Helene Johnson.   NAAAL

Invocation: "Maidens young and virgins tender."   Horace.   *See* Odes

Invocation: "O holy Justice! Hiding your puissance."   Benedek Virág.   IQMS, *tr. by* Watson Kirkconnell

Invocation of Death.   Kathleen Jessie Raine.   OxBTC   *Fr.* Two Invocations of Death.

Invocation of Silence.   Richard Flecknoe.   NOSC; OxBSP

Invocation of the Creator.   *Yoruba Oral Tradition.*   BLT, *tr. by* Ulli Beier
   (He is patient, he is not angry.)   BLT, *tr. by* Ulli Beier

Invocation of the Great Bear.   Ingeborg Bachmann.   VCWP, *tr. by* Mark Anderson

Invocation: "Pheobus, arise! / And paint the sable skies."   William Drummond, of Hawthornden.   OBEV
   (Summons to Love.)   GTBS-P

Invocation: "Senator Smoot (Republican, Ut.)."   Ogden Nash.   OBAL

Invocation: "Ten bloody years with this quill lying."   Valentin Iremonger.   BIrV

Invocation, The: "Wrath of *Peleus* Son, O Muse, resound, The."   Homer.   OBVE, *tr. by* John Dryden   *Fr.* Iliad, The.

Invocation: "This August night, raccoons."   Jane Hirshfield.   BodElec; GeoHom

Invocation: "This is for Elsa, also known as Liz."   Marilyn Hacker.   ExTi; PuP-23; WiU

Invocation to Dsilyi N'Eyani.   *Unknown.*   APN-2; TCAPo, *tr. by* Washington Matthews   *Fr.* Mountain Chant, The.

Invocation. To Horror.   Hannah Cowley.   NOBRP

Invocation to Kali, The.   May Sarton.
   "It is time for the invocation."   HW

Invocation to Melancholy, An.   Henry Headly.
   "Child of the potent spell and nimble eye."   ECEV

Invocation to the Conference of the Birds.   Farid-uddin Attar.   BBASP, *tr. by* C.S. Nott

Invocation, To the Genius of Slumber Written Oct. 1787.   Anna Seward.   PEW

Invocation to the Muse.   Richard Hughes.   MoBrPo

Invocation to the Muse.   Henrietta Cordelia Ray.   CBWP-3

Invocation to the Spirit Said to Haunt Wroxall Down.   Mary F. Johnson.   CenSon

Invocation to the U' wannami.   *Unknown.*   APN-2, *tr. by* Matilda Coxe Stevenson

Invocation to Urania.   John Milton.   EBEV; NAEL-5v1; NAEL-6v1; NOSC; TOF   *Fr.* Paradise Lost.

Invocation to Youth.   Laurence Binyon.   OBEV

Invoice, The.   Robert Creeley.   VGW

Invokes Reason.   Mary Robinson.   CenSon; RWP

Involuntary, / I may live on.   Sanjō Emperor.   OHPJ

Involuntary Music.   D. Nurske.   MiVo

Inward. (LL)   Purdah, 1.   Imtiaz Dharker.   NeBl; OMIP

Inward Conversation.   Charles Baudelaire.   InPK-6, *tr. by* Robert Bly

Io and Jove.   Ovid.   NAWM-7v1, *tr. by* Allen Mandelbaum   *Fr.* Metamorphoses.

Io! Paean! Io! sing.   Charles Lamb.   OxAEP-2   *Fr.* Triumph of the Whale, The.

Iolanthe.   Sir William Schwenck Gilbert.
   Nightmare, [A *or* The].   NOBL; OBCoV; OxBoLi; PeLV; PoRA
   "When Britain really ruled the waves."   NAEL-5v2; NAEL-6v2

Iona.   Frederick Tennyson.   SacPr

Iovis XIX: Why That's a Blade Can Float.   Anne Waldman.   PFTM-2

Iowa Blues Bar Spiritual.   Juan Felipe Herrera.   ReTh

Iowa Farmer.   Margaret Walker Alexander.   GT

Iphigenia [*or* Iphigeneia] in Aulis.   Euripides.
   "And Pergamos, / City of the Phrygians."   AWP; OBVE

Iphione.   Thomas Caulfield Irwin.   EnLoPo

Iphis and Ianthe.   Ovid.   NAWM-7v1, *tr. by* Allen Mandelbaum   *Fr.* Metamorphoses.

Ipsey Wipsey spider.   *Unknown.*   OxNR

Ipsissimus.   Eugene Lee-Hamilton.   PeVV

Ipsithilla, my pet, my favorite dish.   Catullus.   WoPoe, *tr. by* Robert Mezey

IpsofactopaperAnswerallquesti.   Headrock.   Brian Coffey.   CIP-2

Iram indeed is gone with all his rose.   Omar Khayyám.   OBVE, *tr. by* Edward Fitzgerald   *Fr.* Rubáiyát of Omar Khayyám [of Naishápúr], The.

Iranian Song.   Velemir [*or* Viktor Vladimirovich] Khlebnikov.   TCRusP, *tr. by* Kathy Lewis and Bob Perelman

Iranian whirling girl, Iranian whirling girl.   Po Chü-i.   ColAnChi, *tr. by* Victor H. Mair

Iranian Whirling Girls.   Po Chü-i.   ColAnChi, *tr. by* Victor H. Mair

Iranian Whirling Girls.   Yüan Chên.   ColAnChi, *tr. by* Victor H. Mair

Irapuato.   Earle Birney.   NIL-7

Ire.   Ronald Stuart Thomas.   OxBSP

Ireland.   John Hewitt.   CIP-2

Ireland.   Paul Muldoon.   PBCIP

Ireland.   Richard Ryan.   CIP-2

Ireland.   Dora Sigerson Shorter.   OBEV

Ireland Never Was Contented.   Walter Savage Landor.   FaBoEE; OxBSP; OxBoLi; PeLV

(Ireland.)   GTBS-P; OBCoV

Ireland 1972.   Paul Durcan.   PBCIP

Ireland with Emily.   Sir John Betjeman.   GTBS-P; OxBTC

Irene loves a man.   One Secret That Has Carried, The.   Jason Shinder.   OPRER

Iris.   Herman Melville.   NCAP

Iris.   Jacques Perk.   TuT, *tr. by* Peter Van de Kamp

Iris.   Muriel Rukeyser.   APSN; ColAP

Iris.   David St. John.   LCAP-2; MakPoe

Iris.   William Carlos Williams.   LCAP-2; WeW-3

Iris, An.   Buson.   EH, *tr. by* Robert Hass

Iris, Her Book.   Oliver Wendell Holmes.   NCAP

Irises.   "Michael Field."   ViWPN

Irises.   Li-Young Lee.   BLT

Irises.   Gustaf Sobin.   APSN

Irish.   Paul Celan.   OBVE, *tr. by* Michael Hamburger

Irish Airman Foresees His Death, An.   W. B. Yeats.   ChAP; FaBoCh; FaBoMo; FaBoWar; GTBS-P; HarvBoo; HeIP-4; MoBrPo; NOBE; NoAM; NoP-4; OBMV; OBWP; PoPoPo; PoWW; SCV; TFi; WeW-3

Irish-American Dignitary.   Austin Clarke.   BIrV

Irish Antiquities.   Thomas Moore.   FaBoEE

Irish Childhood in England: 1951, An.   Eavan Boland.   CIP-2

Irish Cliffs of Moher, The.   Wallace Stevens.   NOBA; RaBo; TOF; VGW

Irish Dancer, The. *Unknown*. FaBoCh; NOBE; OBEV

  (I am of Ireland.) OHMEL

  (Ich am of Irlaunde [*or* Irlonde].) MiEL; NAEL-6v1; NAEL-7v1; NPeEn; OPOU; SCGP

  (Icham of Irlaunde.) NoP-4

Irish Fairy lost her way, An. Irish Fairy, The. Menella Bute Smedley. VWP

Irish for No, The. Ciaran Carson. PNI

Irish have the thickest ankles in the world, The. John Berryman. TAP *Fr.* Dream Songs.

Irish Hierarchy Bans Colour Photography. Paul Durcan. BiHa; PBCIP

Irish lady can say, that to-day is every day, The. Cézanne. Gertrude Stein. TAP

Irish Lake, An. William Robert Rodgers. BIrV

Irish Lamentation, An. Goethe. AWP, *tr.* by James Clarence Mangan

Irish Marriage Night, An. Brian [*or* Bryan] Merriman [*or* Merryman]. BIrV, *tr.* by Frank O'Connor *Fr.* Midnight Court, The.

Irish Patriarch, The. Ruth Pitter. NALW

Irish Picture, An. J. Stanyan Bigg. NOBVV

Irish poets, learn your trade. W. B. Yeats. OxAEP-2 *Fr.* Under Ben Bulben.

Irish Requiem, An. Michael O'Loughlin. PBCIP

Irish Scullery Maid, The. Joyce Herbert. TCAWP

Irish Sheep, The. Job Degenaar. TuT, *tr.* by Aidan Sharkey

Irish Song [Rosie O'Grady]. Noël Coward. NBLV; OBCoV

Irish soul walks away from Paddy's, An. Day Lily and the Fox, The. Emily Hiestand. OPRER

Irishman in Coventry, An. John Hewitt. BIrV; CIP-2; ModIr; PNI

Iroko. Onwuchekwa Jemie. PBMAP

Iron. Walter De la Mare. NOBL

Iron bells toll, The. Van Gogh. David Mitchell. PeNZ

Iron cannons from the Revolution. Ghost music. Common, The. Gail Mazur. UrbNat

Iron chains and silver cangues: crowds of prisoners. Prisons Are Full of Convicts, The. Yang Yi. SuSp, *tr.* by Jonathan Chaves

Iron Heaven. Betti Alver. BoWoP, *tr.* by Willis Barnstone and Felix Oinas

Iron Horse is rusting, The. End of the Line, The. Thomas McGrath. GM

Iron Industry in Birmingham, The. Richard Jago. NOEC *Fr.* Edge-Hill; or, The Rural Prospect Delineated and Moralised.

Iron Lung. Lavinia Greenlaw. MFPA

Iron Lung, The. Stanley Plumly. LCAP-2

Iron Man of the Hoh. Nelson Bentley. GifTon

"Iron Man" sat with gone eyes, The / a witnessing body. Rogue and Jar: 4/27/77. Thulani Davis. SeSe

Iron scallops border the path, barely. Earliest Spring. Denise Levertov. LCAP-2

Iron Spike. Seamus Heaney. BodElec; TRP

Iron thing coming from Pompi, from the round-house. Train, The. *Unknown.* TTY, *tr.* by D. F. van der Merwe

Iron tree blooms. Wakuan-Shitai. ZenPo, *tr.* by Takashi Ikemoto and Lucien Stryk

Ironical Elegy, Composed in Those Terribly Sad Moments When I Cannot Write. Andrey [*or* Andrei] Andreievich Voznesensky [*or* Voznesenskii]. RusPo, *tr.* by Robert Arthur Douglas Ford

Ironing. Nellie Wong. FFC

Ironing Goatskin. Víctor Hernández Cruz. PueRic

Irony. Louis Untermeyer. TrJP

Irony of God. Eva Warner. TrCP

Irradiations. John Gould Fletcher. MoAmPo

  "Trees, like great jade elephants, The." MoAmPo

Irrationale. László Szabédi. IQMS, *tr.* by John Gordon Nichols

Irreconcilable, The. Damaris, Lady Masham. EMWP

Irregular continuity of discrete particles blasted into the atmosphere: writing, The. Radiant. James Sherry. FTOS

Irregular rattle (shutters) and, An. Master of the Golden Glow, The. James Schuyler. FTOS

Irregular Verses. Dorothy Wordsworth. PoBW

Irresolute the down upon your cheek. Martial. RomPo, *tr.* by Peter Whigham

Irresponsive silence of the land, The. Christina Georgina Rossetti. NOBE; OBEV *Fr.* Thread of Life, The.

Irreverent Epistle to Jesus Christ. Romelia Alarcón de Folgar. TANSG, *tr.* by Alison Ridley

IRT at Rush Hour, The. Christopher Millis. GotH

Irving. James Russell Lowell. TAP *Fr.* Fable for Critics, A.

Irving Katzenstein told me a poem once. Beer Bottles. Lindley Williams Hubbell. APT-2

Is. Patrick Kavanagh. FaBoTw

Is a black shambling bear. Earth is a living thing, The. Lucille Clifton. HW

Is a cave, there are bones at the hearth. (LL) Abel's Bride. Denise Levertov. FaBoWP; NALW; VGW

Is a little wind. Four Bird Songs. Simon J. Ortiz. HATNAP

Is a mildewed tent. Under the center pole. Despair. Maxine W. Kumin. FFC

Is a monstrance / the blue dogs bay. Moon Is the Number 18, The. Charles Olson. APT-2; HarvBoo; PFTM-2; PoE

Is a plantigrade-gaited and prowly inquisitor. This Grizzly. Reg Saner. PoCoUp

Is a question of strength. Oppression. Jimmy Santiago Baca. AF

Is a secret one infers. Landscapes with Set-Screws. X. J. Kennedy. UrbNat

Is a short string of beautiful. My Past. Dennis Cooper. GLP

Is a son born into this world of woe? Charles Churchill. OBSV *Fr.* Times, The.

Is a / Spring / Loaded / Sperm. Twin Barrel Bucky: A Kingston 12 Dub, The. Brian Meeks. WaCA

Is a stately thing. (LL) Stranger, The. Jean Garrigue. NOBA; TwCP

Is a strange brooch in this all-hating world. (LL) William Shakespeare. OxAEP-1; WoPoe *Fr.* King Richard III.

Is a trifle too gay. (LL) Don Marquis. APT-1; OBCoV *Fr.* Archy and Mehitabel.

Is About. Allen Ginsberg. BAP-97

Is all laze and boudoir. She reclines, wigless. April. Angela Shaw. NeAmPo

Is all overrun with rue? (LL) Seeds of Love, The. Mrs. Fleetwood Habergham. FaBoCh; OxBoLi

Is all the light of all their day. (LL) Coventry Patmore. EnLoPo; GTBS-P; HAP; OxBSP *Fr.* Angel in the House, The.

Is all the rest I knew! (LL) Emily Dickinson. HAP; WeW-3

Is all this sorrow? I don't know. Yehuda Amichai [*or* Amikhai]. PoSu *Fr.* Laments on the War Dead.

Is *also* Stewart Granger. (LL) Prisoner of Zenda, The. Richard Wilbur. NBLV; OBCoV

Is always acted out. (LL) Caledonia. Colleen J. McElroy. BlSi; NAAAL

Is an assemblage. Le passage (Morbihan). Tony Baker. Oth

Is an astonishingly slim. Chris Wallace-Crabbe. BMAP *Fr.* Bits and Pieces, The.

Is an enchanted thing. Mind Is an Enchanting Thing, The. Marianne Craig Moore. APT-1; HeIP-4; InPK-6; MoAmPo; NAAL-2v2; NAAL-5; NoP-4; OxBA; PoE; WPOW

Is an unnatural act. (LL) Phenomenology of Anger, The. Adrienne Rich. PFTM-2; PoE

Is anything central? One Thing That Can Save America, The. John Ashbery. AiP; FaBoA; NOBA; NoAM; PmAP

Is as a future. (LL) Africa of the Statue, The. Amina Said. HAWP; NAfrP, *tr.* by Eric Sellin

Is as it had not been. (LL) Emily Dickinson. APN-2; TCAPo

Is back upon your mouth these thousand years. (LL) To Jesus on His Birthday. Edna St. Vincent Millay. ChIV-2; HeIP-4; TrCP

Is being bandied like dust. (LL) Lady Ise. BoWoP; WoPoe, *tr.* by Irma Brandeis and Etsuko Terasaki

Is best from age to age. (LL) John Bunyan. EBEV; NOBE; OBEV; SacPr *Fr.* Pilgrim's Progress, The.

Is better for man and for woman than cycles of blossoming Spring. (LL) Magdalen Walks. Oscar Wilde. EBVV; MoBrPo

Is blisse with immortalitie. Her Majestie Resembled to the Crowned Piller. Ye Must Read Upward. George Puttenham. PBRV

Is both stimulating and delightful. (LL) Tame Cat. Ezra Pound. APT-1; OBAL

Is bright as on creation's day. (LL) Goethe. AWP; OBVE *Fr.* Faust.

Is broken, be admitted in. (LL) Shadows in the Water. Thomas Traherne. GeHe; HAP; NoP-4; SCGP; WoPoe

Is buried with the pole. (LL) Astronomy. A. E. Housman. NoP-4; OBWP

Is burning, burning the unbired grain. (LL) Children of Light. Robert Lowell. NAAL-2v2; OxBA

Is burning in their eyes. (LL) Daniel Boone. Stephen Vincent Benét. APT-2; KaS

Is—*Bury me not in a land of slaves!* (LL) Bury Me in a Free Land. Frances Ellen Watkins Harper. BPo; ColAP; ISC; NAAAL; TCAPo

Is but a child's balloon, forgotten after play. (LL) Above the Dock. Thomas Ernest Hulme. FaBoMo; GTBS-P

Is by His hand alone that guides nature and fate. (LL) In Memory of My Dear Grandchild Elizabeth Bradstreet Who Deceased August, 1665, Being a Year and Half Old. Anne Bradstreet. BASC; ColAP; NAAL-2v1; NAAL-3; NAAL-5; NOCV; SCAP; WPE

Is Cathleen, the daughter of Houlihan. (LL) Red Hanrahan's Song about Ireland. W. B. Yeats. FaBoCh; NOIV

Is come, my love is come to me. (LL) Birthday, A. Christina Georgina Rossetti. AWP; CABP; LW; NAEL-5v2; NAEL-6v2; NALW; NOBE; NOBVV; OBEV; PEW; PeVV; PoE; TFi; TTTS; UV; VWP; ViWPN; WPE

Is coming, and makes noise. (LL) Approach of the Storm, The. *Chippewa Oral Tradition.* NAAL-5; OBVE; TTTS, *tr.* by Frances Densmore

Is covered with clouds. (LL) Murasaki Shikibu. BoWoP; OHPJ

Is cruel to thy cruelty. (LL) Limits. Ralph Waldo Emerson. APN-1; OxBSP

Is Culcha Weapon? Brian Meeks. WaCA

Is different now. The body. What's It For. Pamela Stewart. ExTi

Is each neat niplet of her breast. (LL) Upon the Nipples of Julia's Breast. Robert Herrick. CaPo; ErotSp; NAEL-5v1; NAEL-6v1; NAEL-7v1; NOSC; PeLV

Is even more fun than going to San Sebastian, Irún, Hendaye, Biarritz, Bayonne. Having a Coke with You. Frank O'Hara. GLP; VCAP

Is everything made of dry ice? January, Anchorage. Linda McCarriston. UrbNat

Is fair and wise [or bonny and blithe] and good and gay. (LL) Birthdays. Mother Goose. FaBoCh; LB; NBLV; OTCP; OxNR

Is far too good for thee' (LL) Jellon Grame. Unknown. EBEV; ESPB; OxBB

Is gazing at the moon again. Selenologist, The. Bill Manhire. PeNZ

Is getting to be quite a bore. (LL) Limerick: "I wish that my room had a floor." Frank Gelett Burgess. OBCA; OxIBACP; PeLi

Is giv'n thee till the break of day. (LL) William Blake. ChIV-1; EBEV; FHYEP; HAP; NAEL-5v2; NAEL-6v2; NAWM-7v2; NOBE; NOBRP; NOEC; NPeEn; NoP-4; OxBEV; PoE; RB; TFi Fr. Songs of Experience.

Is given in outline and no more. (LL) Tennyson. CAGL; NAEL-6v2; NAWM-7v2; PeECV; TOF Fr. In Memoriam A. H. H.

Is grace delivered. Streetcorner Church. Sharan Strange. InTrad

Is heaven a place where pearly streams. What Is Heaven? Philip James Bailey. PWR

Is hovering in the air, there, in the highest. All the Wide Grin of Him. Eleanor Wilner. ExTi

Is hows to hump a cows. (LL) E. E. Cummings. NOBA; NoAM; OxBA

Is I. (L) Napoleon. Walter De la Mare. FaBoCh; FaBoTw; NOBE; NPeEn; OxBEV; RB; Spl; WoPoe

Is immortal diamond. (LL) That Nature Is a Heraclitean Fire and of the Comfort of the Resurrection. Gerard Manley Hopkins. EnlH; FaBoMo; FaBoVe; GTBS-P; PFTM-1; PoE

Is in love with someone. Someone. Ruth Forman. AmPoNex

Is inverted, slow and gay. (LL) Operation, The. W. D. Snodgrass. InPK-6; TAP

Is it a cuckoo that cries? Yun Sŏndo. WoPoe, tr. by Peter H. Lee Fr. Angler's Calendar, The.

Is it a dream, and nothing more—this faith. Is It a Dream? Geoffrey Anketell Studdert-Kennedy. PoToHe

Is It a Month. John Millington Synge. BIrV

Is it a plane in the sky. Poem. "Paul Dermée." CuPo

Is it a road at the world's edge? (LL) Denise Levertov. CoAmPo; LCAP-2

Is it an idle fantasy. Mist Maiden, The. Henrietta Cordelia Ray. CBWP-3

Is it anxiety, nausea. Self-Portrait of the Other. Heberto Padilla. TCLAP; VCWP, tr. by Andrew Hurley and Alastair Reid

Is it any better in Heaven, my friend Ford. To Ford Madox Ford in Heaven. William Carlos Williams. ColAP; NOBA

Is it as plainly in our living shown. On Seeing Weather-Beaten Trees. Adelaide Crapsey. APT-1

Is it bad to have come here. Gallant Château. Wallace Stevens. MoAmPo

Is it because my hair is golden brown that even when I wear it. Rose of Sharon, A. Myung Mi Kim. FSt

Is It Because of Some Dear Grace. Louis Golding. TrJP

Is it because your sable hair. La Belle Juive. Henry Timrod. APN-2; TCAPo

Is it better to die by the hand of an intimate. Infernal. Karen Volkman. BAP-97

Is it enough? Theodore Roethke. CoAP Fr. Meditations of an Old Woman.

Is it illusion? or does there a spirit from perfecter ages. Arthur Hugh Clough. EBEV; OxAEP-2 Fr. Amours de Voyage.

Is it indeed so? If I lay here dead. Elizabeth Barrett Browning. CenSon Fr. Sonnets from the Portuguese.

Is it ironical, a fool enigma. Dartmoor: Sunset at Chagford. Thomas Edward Brown. NOBVV

Is it just like picking a lock. Bomb Disposal, The. Ciaran Carson. CIP-2

Is it like. Toyokuni. JDP, tr. by Yoel Hoffmann

Is it me the raven calls. Shukabo. JDP, tr. by Yoel Hoffmann

Is it me tossing. Insomnia Song. Gregory Orr. AWTN

Is it merely an image that keeps haunting me? (LL) Gold Glade. Robert Penn Warren. CRP; TRP

Is it my clothes, my way of walking. Disembarking at Quebec. Margaret Atwood. PoE

Is it not fine to fling against loaded dice. Hughie at the Inn. Elinor Wylie. WPE

Is it not fit the mold and frame. Dedication of My First Son, A. Mildmay Fane, 2d Earl of Westmorland. BeJo

Is it not lovely, while the day flows on. By the Swannanoa. William Gilmore Simms. APN-1

Is it not so, my Tory, ultra-Julian? (LL) Byron. CTC; OBSV Fr. Don Juan.

Is it not strange that men can die. Reflection. Walter James Turner. OBMV

Is It Not Strange? Elizabeth Delmore. NLP

Is it not sure a deadly pain. Unknown. EnLoPo

Is it not sweet to die? for, what is death. Death Sweet. Thomas Lovell Beddoes. NOBVV

Is It Nothing to You? May Probyn. OBEV; SacPr

Is it only me? Rochu. JDP, tr. by Yoel Hoffmann

Is it poetry I'm after those moments when. Vocation. Carol Rumens. DiPo

Is It Possible. Sir Thomas Wyatt. See Varium et Mutabile

Is it raining. Mary, can you see? Wildflowers. Richard Howard. NoAM

Is it really a revolution, though? Lunch with Pancho Villa. Paul Muldoon. ModIr

Is it really so very unthinkable. Limerick. Basil Ransome-Davies. PeLi

Is it serious, or funny. B. Larry Eigner. NeAP

Is it the boy in me who's looking out. Boy, The. Marilyn Hacker. ExTi; WiU

Is it the motion of the stabbing knife, and. Stone Wall and Fiesta. János Pilinszky. IQMS, tr. by Adam Makkai

Is it the palm, the cocoa-palm. Palm-Tree, The. John Greenleaf Whittier. NCAP

Is it, then, regret for buried time. Tennyson. FHYEP Fr. In Memoriam A. H. H.

"Is it thou?" "Ay," cries Fra Lippo Lippi. Limerick. Gerard Benson. PeLi

Is it thy will thy image should keep open. William Shakespeare. AWTN; CAGL Fr. Sonnets.

Is it time now to go away? Death of a Vermont Farm Woman. Barbara Howes. MoAmPo

Is it time to change the record? But I'm dreaming again. Sergey Gandlevsky. ItGoST, tr. by Philip Metres

Is it to love, to fix the tender gaze. Describes the Characteristics of Love. Mary Robinson. CenSon; RWP

Is it to me, this sad lamenting strain? Answer to a Love-Letter in Verse, An. Lady Mary Wortley Montagu. ECWP

Is it true that after this life of ours we shall one day be awakened. Resurrection. Vladimir Holan. PoSu

Is it true that black birds infinitely dispersed. To Krishna Haunting the Hills. Andal. BoWoP, tr. by Willis Barnstone

Is It True What They Say about Dixie? Irving Caesar. ReLy

Is it Ulysses that approaches from the east. World as Meditation, The. Wallace Stevens. HeIP-4; LCAP-2

Is It Wise? Stevie Smith. NAEL-5v2; NAEL-6v2

Is it worth while, dear, now. Long Plighted. Thomas Hardy. NOBVV

Is it your command. Lady Ise. OHPJ

Is John Smith within? Mother Goose. OxNR; ReMoGo

Is Joy's insuring quality. (LL) Emily Dickinson. MoAmPo; NIL-7; NIP-4

Is jy klaar. Haanetjie's Morning Dialogue. Essop Patel. PeSAV

Is large, bald, beakless and blind. (LL) Fork. Charles Simic. ChAP; ColAP; HCAP; LCAP-2; PoPoPo; TRP; WeW-3

Is learned. In this poem they're right. Cruelty, the Vandals Say. Alan Michael Parker. NeAmPo

Is less ta'en up wi't. (LL) Empty Vessel. Hugh MacDiarmid. FaBoTw; NPeEn; NePenScot; OxBEV; OxBS

Is Life itself but many ways of thought. Substitution. Anne Spencer. BlSi

Is Life Worth Living? Alfred Austin. PWR

Is like a tin cup toppled in the straw. (LL) Desert of Love, The. János Pilinszky. IQMS; OBVE, tr. by Ted Hughes

Is like swimming alone. Singing Alone. Nancy Cox. MiVo

Is like the brushing together of thin wing-tips of / silver. (LL) Skaters, The. John Gould Fletcher. KaS; MoAmPo

Is Lisle and Lucas slaine? Oh say not soe. On Those Two Unparalleld Friends, Sr: G: Lisle and Sr: C: Lucas, Who Were Shott to Death at Colechester. Hester Lee Pulter. EMWP

Is, Listen, listen, I am a man like you. (LL) Hill Farmer Speaks, The. Ronald Stuart Thomas. GTBS-P; OBWVE

Is love a fancy, or a feeling? No. Hartley Coleridge. CenSon

Is love a light for me? A steady light. Secret Flowers. Katherine Mansfield. LW

Is love so prone to change and rot. Bed of Forget-Me-Nots, A. Christina Georgina Rossetti. VWP

Is made up of reservoirs. Hard Structure of the World, The. Richard Eberhart. NoAM

Is man a. Ryosa. JDP, tr. by Yoel Hoffmann

Is manhood less because man's face is black? Albery Allson Whitman. APN-2 Fr. Twasinta's Seminoles; Or Rape of Florida.

Is master of all I am. (LL) Sphinx, The. Ralph Waldo Emerson. APN-1; NOBA; OxBA; TCAPo

Is memory most of miseries miserable. Memory. Dante Gabriel Rossetti. OxBSP

Is merry glory. Langston Hughes. Gwendolyn Brooks. ColAP

Is more than taper flame or slender lyre. (LL) Many Indeed Must Perish in the Keel. Hugo von Hofmannsthal. AWP; TrJP, *tr. by* Jethro Bithell

Is mother of silences. (LL) Seasons of the Soul. Allen Tate. FuPo; OxBA

Is music is men. Eddie Priest's Barbershop and Notary. Kevin Young. AmPoNex; ISC; SpirFl

Is my black Mother Syama really black? Kamalākānta Bhaṭṭācārya. SinGod, *tr. by* Rachel Fell McDermott

Is my favourite. Who flies. Owl. George MacBeth [*or* Macbeth]. EmeKit

Is my sweet, bonie Lady! (LL) Geordie [An Old Ballad]. *Unknown.* ESPB; OxBB

Is my team plowing? A. E. Housman. EBVV; MoBrPo; NoAM; NoP-4; OBEV

Is nature, which is larger and more still. (LL) Solar Creation. Charles Madge. FaBoMo; OBMV; OxBTC

Is not a cloud at all. (LL) Cloud of Unknowing, The. Christopher Edgar. BAP-01

Is not one of the seven deadly sins. Self-Pity. Philip Hodgins. NOBAu

Is not the woman moulded by your wish. Pastiche. Elinor Wylie. NALW

Is not thilke the mery moneth of May. Edmund Spenser. PBRV *Fr.* Shepheardes [*or* Shepeards *or* Shepherd's] Calender, The.

Is not unlike building a poem: the pure. Building an Outhouse. Ronald Wallace. PBCAP

Is not worth a fly. (LL) Swarm of Bees, A. *Unknown.* LB; OxNR; ReMoGo

Is nothing real but when I was fifteen. Ground Swell. Mark Jarman. GeoHom; MoASP

Is nothing to the Dead. (LL) Emily Dickinson. APN-2; OBWP

Is now as weak as ever. (LL) Time I've Lost in Wooing, The. Thomas Moore. AmFaPo; NAEL-5v2; NAEL-6v2; NOBRP; PeLV

Is of no profit and idly bears the name. (LL) *Unknown.* BoWoP; ChiP

Is of the slightest bondage made aware. (LL) Silken Tent, The. Robert Frost. APT-1; ColAP; InPK-6; NOBA; NoP-4; OxBSo; Son; TAP; TRP; TwCP; WeW-3

Is of your [*or* yowr] maidenhood [*or* maydenhede]. (LL) John Skelton. EBEV; EnLoPo; NOBE; OBEV *Fr.* Garland [*or* Garlande *or* Garlands] of Laurel[l], The.

Is one of liberty. (LL) My Times Are in Thy Hand. Anna L. Waring. PWR; SacPr

Is only a plateful of mince. (LL) Bitcherel. Eleanor Brown. MFPA; NeBl

Is only Monday in the world. (LL) King of the Cats is Dead, The. Peter Porter. EmeKit; NoAM

Is only not to be disgraced. (LL) Northern Suburb, A. John Davidson. NOBVV; NPeEn; NePenScot

Is only stronger far than death. (LL) Incarnation and Passion, The. Henry Vaughan. GeHe; SacPr; TrCP

Is only there. (LL) Peace. George Herbert. AWP; ESCV; GeHe; NOCV; NOSC; TreFP

Is oppression as old as the moss around ponds? World's One Hope, The. Bertolt Brecht. AF

Is peopled with many surfaces. My Rival's House. Liz Lochhead. EmeKit

Is pounding and pounding, and the mouth answering. (LL) Gargoyle. Carl Sandburg. NOBA; NoAM

Is powerless to our Western Cotton! (LL) Haschish, The. John Greenleaf Whittier. APN-1; NCAP; OBAL

Is proud, and makes the breath of glory real! (LL) Sonnet to Lake Leman. Byron. CenSon; Son

Is quicker. (LL) Reflections on Ice-breaking. Ogden Nash. APT-2; AiP; NBLV; OBAL; PeLV

Is / red beans. Energy. Víctor Hernández Cruz. PueRic

Is rounded with a sleep. (LL) William Shakespeare. RB; UV *Fr.* Tempest, The.

Is saved today, tomorrow to be slain. (LL) Dryden. EBNV; NOSC *Fr.* Theodore and Honoria, from [Fables Ancient and Modern from] Boccace.

Is scarcely right; this red should have been much duller. (LL) Vlamertinghe. Edmund Charles Blunden. NoP-4; OBWP; PeFWW

Is scented with White Heliotrope. (LL) White Heliotrope. Arthur Symons. BoLoP; EBEV; NPeEn; PeVV

Is she dead? Confessional. Frank Bidart. GLP

Is she mine,—and for life. Mésalliance, A. May Probyn. NPeEn

Is shut / 22 hours a day and all day Sunday. James Fenton. FaBoMo *Fr.* Exempla.

Is Sin, then, fair? Sting of Death, The. Frederick George Scott. SacPr

Is slender and her red hair lights the wall. (LL) Degrees of Gray in Philipsburg. Richard Hugo. CoAP; NAAL-2v2; NoAM; TRP; VCAP

Is slow. Tedious. Like midnight mass on Christmas Eve. Unlearning English. Michael Melo. ReBoTo

Is so frigid upon the fundament. (LL) Samson Agonistes. Ogden Nash. APT-2; OBCoV

Is something like the rest. Politics of Rich Painters, The. Imamu Amiri Baraka. VGW

Is spread any more. (LL) Mouse, The. Elizabeth Jane Coatsworth. NOxBChV; OBCA

Is sung, but breaks off in the middle. (LL) Samuel Butler (1612–80). BASC; EBEV; NAEL-5v1; NAEL-6v1; NAEL-7v1 *Fr.* Hudibras.

Is't here the fairies haunt the place. On a Nook Called Fairyland. Henrietta Cordelia Ray. CBWP-3

Is taken by surprise. Sometimes the Mind. Jane Mead. NAPBL

Is tell you my mind, Annes Tayliur: Dame. At the Tavern. *Unknown.* MiEL

Is that an attitude for a flower, to stand. Hyacinth. Louise Glück. NoAM

Is that dance slowing in the mind of man. Theodore Roethke. APT-2; MoAmPo; NOBA; NoAM

Is that foolish youth still sawing. Ancient Autumn. Charles Simic. ColAP

Is that not the moon? Narihira (Ariwara no Narihira). WoPoe, *tr. by* F. Vos *Fr.* Ise Monogatari, The.

Is that one day they'll win. My Worst Fear. Cyn Zarco. ReBoTo

Is that the moon, nearing its final quarter. Pogrom. Ed. Hoornik. TuT, *tr. by* Mary E. O'Donnell

Is that the same moon. Narihira (Ariwara no Narihira). ErotSp, *tr. by* Sam Hamill

Is that where it happens? Improvement, The. John Ashbery. AmFaPo

Is that you sistah Harris? Afternoon Gossip, An. Priscilla Jane Thompson. CBWP-2

Is the Ahkond of Swat! (LL) A[h]kond of Swat, The. Edward Lear. FaBoCh; PeLi

Is the alphabet responsible. Learning to Write. Audre Lorde. GT

Is the applause always plausible that applauds the bosses' Tasty 'Tanjarines' of Inhambane, The. José Craveirinha. PeSAV, *tr. by* Michael Wolfers

Is the ball very stupid *ma mignonne*? At the Ball! Charles Henry Webb. OBAL

Is the body's way. Coming. Heather McHugh. EmeKit

Is the clock wound up, is it wound? Insect Kitchen, The. Nicki Jackowska. BrRo

Is the fatherland of men. (LL) Where Are the Men Seized in this Wind of Madness? Alda do Espirito Santo. PBMAP; TTY; WPOW, *tr. by* Alan Ryder

Is the fish ready? You're a tedious while. Edward Ward. NOEC *Fr.* Nuptial Dialogues.

Is the kitchen tap still dripping? Guest. Dennis Joseph Enright. OxBC

Is the man bigger than a fly's wing? what pleasure! Tablet V. Armand Schwerner. PFTM-1

Is the man here, they said. Margaret Atwood. PoetW *Fr.* Four Small Elegies.

Is the Moon Tired? Christina Georgina Rossetti. OTCP

Is the mother of earth, moon, and stars. El Hogarcito de La Madrugada. Anthony R. Vigil. AmPoNex

Is the one gift you cannot give. (LL) At the British War Cemetery, Bayeux. Charles Causley. NAEL-5v2; NAEL-6v2; NoP-4; OBWP; OxBC; PoWW

Is the orange and black / oriole's swinging nest! (LL) Fall 1961. Robert Lowell. OBWP; VGW

Is the poem at the end of the world. (LL) Shapeshifter Poems. Lucille Clifton. BodElec; LoL

Is the pride of thus dying for thee. (LL) Pro Patria Mori. Thomas Moore. GTBS-P; OxAEP-2

Is the reader leaning back and reading there. (LL) House Was Quiet and the World Was Calm, The. Wallace Stevens. AiP; HAP; NoP-4; SAmP; VGW

Is the river a boundary line? In and Out of Check Points. Yip Wai-lim. OPRER

Is the slim curved crook of the moon tonight! (LL) Winter Moon. Langston Hughes. KaS; SAmP

Is the snow on Kurakake mountain. (LL) Snow on Saddle Mountain, The. Miyazawa Kenji. ColAP; NOBA; NoAM; PAI, *tr. by* Gary Snyder

Is the soul solid, like iron? Some Questions You Might Ask. Mary Oliver. ColAP

Is the spirit the true lover of the flesh? Sándor Petőfi. IQMS, *tr. by* Peter Zollman *Fr.* Clouds, The.

Is the struggle and strife. Let the Rest of the World Go By. J. Keirn Brennan. UnPo

Is the sun a miner, a thief, a gambler. June Ghazal. Arthur Sze. GifTon

Is the vision that you have lived here. (LL) More Beautiful Than Your Eyes. Sa'id 'Aql. ErotSp; MAP, *tr. by* Naomi Shihab Nye and Matthew Sorenson

Is the world's wonder. (LL) *Unknown.* FaBoVe; LB

Is then no nook of English ground secure. On the Projected Kendal and Windermere Railway. William Wordsworth. CenSon

Is there a great green commonwealth of Thought. John Masefield. MoBrPo *Fr.* Sonnets.

Is there a hand-rail to the stairs? (LL) Had We Two Met. Walter Savage Landor. FaBoEE; OxBSP

Is there a solitary wretch who hies. On Being Cautioned against Walking on an Headland Overlooking the Sea, because It Was Frequented by a Lunatic. Charlotte Smith. CenSon; ECWP; NPeEn; WoRP

Is there an imagination that sits enthroned. Wallace Stevens. HCAP *Fr.* Auroras of Autumn, The.

Is there any reward? Joseph Hilaire Pierre Belloc. OBCoV

Is there any treasure like the Mother's name? Kalyānkumār Mukhopādhyāy. SinGod, *tr. by* Rachel Fell McDermott

"Is there anybody there?" said the Traveler. Listeners, The. Walter De la Mare. AWP; ClHu; HAP; HeIP-4; InPK-6; MoBrPo; NOBE; NOxBChV; NoAM; NoP-4; OBEV; OBMV; OBSP; OxAEP-2; PoRA; SoSe-8; TFi

Is there anyone around who cannot see. Between the Devil and the Deep Blue Sea. Ted Koehler. ReLy

Is there anything as I can do ashore for you. Valediction (Liverpool Docks), A. John Masefield. OBMV

Is there anything sweeter than this hour? *Unknown, fr.* Egyptian hieroglyphics. EroLit, *tr. by* Joseph Kaster

Is there, for honest Poverty. For A' That and A' That ["Is there, for honest poverty"]. Robert Burns. NAEL-5v2; NAEL-6v2; OxAEP-2; TFi; TreFP; UV

Is, there is not a word of fear. (LL) Death Stands above Me. Walter Savage Landor. NOBE; OxBSP

Is there never a man in all *Scotland*. Johnie Armstrong. *Unknown.* ESPB

Is There No Balm in Christian Lands? *Unknown.* AH

Is there no vision in a lovely place? William Montgomerie. OxBS *Fr.* Kinfauns Castle.

Is there really a new Mr. Nixon. Limerick. T. Griffiths. PeLi

Is there still any shadow there, on the rainwet window of the coffee pot. Memo. Kenneth Fearing. PoE

Is there There in dying. Luis H. Francia. ReBoTo

Is this a fast, to keep. To Keep a True Lent. Robert Herrick. SacPr; TrCP

Is this a holy thing to see. William Blake. FHYEP; NAEL-5v2; NAEL-6v2; NOBRP; NOEC; NoP-4 *Fr.* Songs of Experience.

Is This Africa. Roland Tombekai Dempster. PBA

Is This All That Remains of Love? Yusuf Al-Sa'igh. MAP, *tr. by* Diana Der Hovanessian and Salma Khadra Jayyusi

Is this, baby, what you were born to feel, and do, and be? (LL) American Rhapsody. Kenneth Fearing. APT-2; MoAmPo

Is this darkness the night of Power, or the black falling of your hair? Bibi Hayati. WPoS

Is this happening. Ronald Johnson. FTOS *Fr.* Ark.

Is this my tomb, this humble stone. Charlotte Brontë. VWP

Is this peace? Kayaking through. Peace #3. Alma Villanueva. FFC

Is this rapture that your rums have filled me with. Marie Galante. Guy Tirolien. NegPo, *tr. by* Ellen Conroy Kennedy

Is this, saith one, the Nation that we read. Andrew Marvell. PBRV *Fr.* First Anniversary of the Government under O. C., The.

Is this the little girl I carried? Sunrise, Sunset. Sheldon Harnick. ReLy

Is this the monument of Leonato? William Shakespeare. OxAEP-1 *Fr.* Much Ado about Nothing.

Is this the self I thought I knew, within. Reflections. Vivian Smith. CBAP

Is this the street? Never a sign of life. Stormy Night. William Robert Rodgers. ModIr; PNI

Is this the way my Father. Matin Hymn. Josephine D. Henderson Heard. CBWP-4

Is this—the way? (LL) Emily Dickinson. APN-2; NALW; NOBA; TCAPo

Is this then a touch? . . .quivering me to a new identity. Walt Whitman. CAGL *Fr.* Song of Myself.

Is this, then, the star of freedom? Imprisoned Souls. János Arany. IQMS, *tr. by* Peter Zollman

Is this what you've done to us. Torn Apart. Pam Tjanara-Williams. IBA

Is this where Tasso walked? Old Sant'Onofrio. Pure Dust. Maria Luisa Spaziani. NeIt, *tr. by* Beverly Allen

Is this your special light. Six Nations Museum Onchiota, New York—January. Wendy Rose. HATNAP

Is thy face like thy mother's, my fair child! Byron. NAEL-5v2; NAEL-6v2 *Fr.* Childe Harold's Pilgrimage.

Is thy sun obscured to-day. My Grace Is Sufficient. Josephine D. Henderson Heard. CBWP-4

Is Time? I cannot bite the day to the core. (LL) Glory, The. Edward Thomas. HarvBoo; OxBTC; TOF

Is to become a footnote. My Ambition. James Laughlin. GifTon

Is to leave all, and take the thread of love. Mary Sidney Wroth, Countess of Montgomery. BASC; EMWP *Fr.* Pamphilia to Amphilanthus.

Is too good to be true, in all its definitions. Purple Loosestrife. Ann Townsend. ExTi; NeAmPo

Is too precise in every part. (LL) Delight in Disorder. Robert Herrick. BASC; BeJo; CABP; CaPo; CavPo; ClHu; EBEV; EnLoPo; ErotSp; HAP; HeIP-4; InPK-6; NAEL-5v1; NAEL-6v1; NAEL-7v1; NIL-7; NoP-4; NOBE; NOSC; NPeEn; NoP-4; OBEV; OxAEP-1; OxBEV; PBRV; PeLV; PoE; PoRA; SCGP; TFi; TRP; WeW-3

Is waiting for his Old Dutch? (LL) Fat White Woman Speaks, The. Gilbert Keith Chesterton. OBCoV; UV

Is water deep enough to drown. (LL) Muse of Water, A. Carolyn Kizer. FFC; VCAP

Is what the sea-birds know. (LL) Inscription by the Sea, An. Edwin Arlington Robinson. AWP; FaBoEE

Is what the sea-birds know. (LL) *Var. authors.* AWP; FaBoEE *Fr.* Variations of Greek Themes.

Is what to make of a diminished thing. (LL) Oven Bird, The. Robert Frost. APT-1; AWP; GSo; HeIP-4; NAAL-2v2; NAAL-5; NOBA; NoAM; NoP-4; OWoS; OxBA; PoE; Son; TAP; TCAPo

Is what you first see, stepping off the train. Welcome to Hiroshima. Mary Jo Salter. DiPo; NIL-7; NIP-4; RA

Is where we turned around, surrendered to fate. Delphos, Ohio. Campbell McGrath. NeAmPo

Is wired within for this, in every room. (LL) Elizabeth Daryush. NPeEn; OxBEV; OxBSo

Is without world. Howling of Wolves, The. Ted Hughes. OxBTC

Is won[e] with flesh, not drapery. (LL) Clothes Do but Cheat and Cozen [or Cousen] Us. Robert Herrick. CaPo; ErotSp

Is worth an age without a name. (LL) Thomas Osbert Mordaunt. EBEV; FaBoEE; NOBE *Fr.* Verses Written during the War, 1756–1763.

Is your icebox full of food? Straw Hat in the Rain. Harry Akst. ReLy

Is Your Town Nineveh? Marianne Craig Moore. APT-1

Isaac. Amir Gilbo'a. MHP, *tr. by* Ruth Finer Mintz

Isaac: a Poise. Peter Cole. ChIV-1

Isaac and Archibald. Edwin Arlington Robinson. APT-1; OxBA

Isaac's Marriage. Henry Vaughan. ChIV-1

Isaac Singer (you probably know). Limerick. Peter Brookes. PeLi

Isabel met an enormous bear. Adventures of Isabel. Ogden Nash. ChAP; MoAmPo; NOxBChV; NTCP; OBAL; OBCA; OxIBACP

Isabella; or, The Morning. Sir Charles Hanbury Williams. "Monkey, lap-dog, parrot, and her Grace, The." NOEC

Isabella spits at Spain. Bourbons. Walter Savage Landor. OBSV

Isaiah. Bible, *O.T.*

   All Flesh Is Grass. TrJP

   "Comfort ye, comfort ye my people." OBVE; TrJP

   For Zion's Sake. TrJP

   Hear the Word of the Lord. TrJP

   How Beautiful upon the Mountains. TrJP

   "I am the first and I am the last." InvLi, *tr. by* New Revised Standard Version

   I Waste Away. TrJP

   In the End of Days. TrJP

   Israel, My Servant. TrJP

   Let Me Sing of My Well-beloved. TrJP

   Messiah, The. AWP

   My Thoughts Are Not Your Thoughts. TrJP

   Rod of Jesse, The. AWP; OBVE; TrJP

   Song of the Harlot. TrJP

   Song of the Suffering Servant, The. NAWM-5v1

   Watchman, What of the Night? AWP

   Whom Shall One Teach. TrJP

   "Wildernesse and the solitarie place shall be glad for them, The." OBVE

Isaiah 66.11. Francis Quarles. ChIV-1

Isaiah by Kerosene Lantern Light. Robert Harris. ChIV-1; NOBAu

Isaiah: Chapter 66. David Rosenberg. ChIV-1

Isalutu. Askhari. InTrad

Isandula. Hume Nisbet. FaBoWar

Isatou Died. Lenrie Peters. HBAPE; PBMAP; PoetW

Ise Monogatari, The. Narihira (Ariwara no Narihira).

   Facing His Own Death. WoPoe, *tr. by* F. Vos

   Regretting the Past. WoPoe, *tr. by* F. Vos

Ishmael. Herbert Edward Palmer. OBEV

Ishtar. Judith Wright. NALW; NoAM

Isiah said would be the serpent's meat. (LL) On Falling Asleep by Firelight. William Meredith. ChIV-1; NoAM

Isias my love, with your scented breath. Argentarius. GrAn

Isidor. Louis Simpson. NNaP

Isis (Lady of Petals). Jonathan Cott. HW

Isis Wanderer. Kathleen Jessie Raine. NALW; OxBS

Isla Mujeres. Lorna Dee Cervantes. TouFir

Island. Langston Hughes. APT-2; HCAP *Fr.* Lenox Avenue Mural.

Island, The. Randall Jarrell. HarvBoo

Island, The. Brendan Kennelly. PBCIP

Island, The. Herman Melville. NCAP

Island, The. Ronald Stuart Thomas. InvLi

Island, The. George Woodcock. MoCV

Island and Europe, The. Luis Andrade Silva. NAfrP, *tr. by* Don Burness

Island and the Cattle, The.   Nicholas Moore.   SPE
Island Celebration.   Kenward Elmslie.   FTOS
Island eyes.   23 October 1992.   Virginia Cerenio.   ReBoTo
Island in the Earth.   Sara de Ibáñez.   TCLAP, *tr. by* Inés Probert
Island in the Light.   Sara de Ibáñez.   TCLAP, *tr. by* Inés Probert
Island in the Moon, An.   William Blake.
   Chapter Six.
     Quid the Cynic's Song.   RB
   I say this evening we'll [*or* we'd] all get drunk.
     "Hail Matrimony, made of Love!"   OxBEV
Island Mary.   Lucille Clifton.   NALW
Island of Eternity.   Baisei.   JDP, *tr. by* Yoel Hoffmann
Island of Puerto Rico.   Caribbean Sea.   Gabriela Mistral.   TANSG, *tr. by*
   Maria Jacketti
Island of the Three Marias.   Alberto A. Ríos.   NoAM
Island of Women, The.   June McGlashan.   ReEnLa
Island Waters.   Tony Beyer.   PeNZ
Island within Island.   Henry Dumas.   GT
Island Women of Paris, The.   Rita Dove.   LoL
Islandis.   Víctor Hernández Cruz.   TouFir
Islandman.   Brenda Chamberlain.   AngWePo; OBWVE
Islands.   Nicholas Hasluck.   NOBAu
Islands, The.   "H. D."   MoAmPo; TCAPo
Islands, The.   Robert Earl Hayden.   ESEAA
Islands, The.   Randall Jarrell.   SPE
Islands are green.   Alaskan Fragments June 1981—Summer Solstice.   Wendy
   Rose.   HATNAP
Islands scars of the water.   Aimé Césaire.   PFTM-1   *Fr.* Notebook of a Return
   to the Native Land.
Islands Where I Was Born, The.   Gloria Rawlinson.   PeNZ
Islands which have.   Islands.   Nicholas Hasluck.   NOBAu
Isle! / Island of the syllables of flame!   Song.   Jacques Rabémanganjara.
   NegPo, *tr. by* Ellen Conroy Kennedy
Isle of Portland, The.   A. E. Housman.   MoBrPo
"Isle of the Hares" confessed to me, The.   Saint Margaret's Legend.   Endre
   Ady.   IQMS, *tr. by* Anton N. Nyerges
Isles of Greece, The.   Demetrios Capetanakis.   GTBS-P
Isles of Greece, the isles of Greece!, The.   Byron.   AWP; NOBE; OBEV;
   OxAEP-2   *Fr.* Don Juan.
Ism, The.   Wanda Coleman.   PmAP
Ismailia Eclipse.   Khaled Mattawa.   NAPBL
Isn't It a Pity?   George Gershwin.   ReLy
Isn't It Funny?   Essex Hemphill.   GLP
Isn't it good she asked as.   Rhyme.   James Laughlin.   WeW-3
Isn't it plain the sheets of moss, except that.   Landscape.   Mary Oliver.
   HeIP-4
Isn't it rich?   Send in the Clowns.   Stephen Sondheim.   ReLy
Isn't it strange.   Bag of Tools, A.   R. L. Sharpe.   PoToHe
Isn't it strange some people make.   Some People.   Rachel Lyman Field.
   ChAP; NTCP
Isn't it sweet to hear one's language lift.   Upon Overhearing Tagalog.   Fatima
   Lim-Wilson.   AmPoNex
Isn't it wonderful, when you think.   Wonderful.   Julian S. Cutler.   PWR
Isn't She Not a Bird.   Nina Iskrenko.   PFTM-2, *tr. by* Forrest Gander and Mala
   Kotamraju
Isn't the violet a dear little flower? And the daisy, too.   Lay Preacher Ponders,
   The.   Idris Davies.   OxBTC
Isn't This a Lovely Day (To Be Caught in the Rain?).   Irving Berlin.   ReLy
Isolate.   Clarence Major.   PmAP
Isolate *and*.   Barrett Watten.   FTOS   *Fr.* Progress.
Isolate and full, the moon.   Full Moon.   Tu Fu.   OHPC
Isolation.   Alphonse Marie Louis de Lamartine.   SxFrPo, *tr. by* E. H.
   Blackmore and A. M. Blackmore
Isolation.   Arthur Symons.   OxBSP
Isolation of exile is a gutted, The.   Waiting.   Arthur Nortje.   HBAPE
Isolation: To Marguerite.   Matthew Arnold.   NAEL-6v2   *Fr.* Switzerland.
Israel in ancient days.   William Cowper.   ChIV-2; TrCP   *Fr.* Olney Hymns.
Israel.   Yitzhak Lamdan.   MHP, *tr. by* Ruth Finer Mintz
Israel.   Carl Rakosi.   ChIV-1
Israel.   Israel Zangwill.   TrJP
Israel II.   Charles Reznikoff.   ChIV-1
Israel, My Servant.   Bible, *O.T.*   TrJP   *Fr.* Isaiah.
Israel Revisited.   Luisa Futuransky.   MirDau, *tr. by* Celeste Kostopulos-
   Cooperman
Israel's Duration.   Judah Halevi.   TrJP, *tr. by* Nina Davis Salaman
Israeli Navy, The.   Marvin Bell.   TaR

Israfel.   Edgar Allan Poe.   APN-1; AWP; NAAL-2v1; NAAL-3; NOBA;
   OxBA; PoE; TAP; TCAPo
Isreal I.   Charles Reznikoff.   ChIV-1
Issa: A Suite of Haiku.   Lucien Stryk.
   "After night in."   IllVoic
   "Charcoal fire."   IllVoic
   "Cherry blossoms."   IllVoic
   "Frog and I."   IllVoic
   "Into the house."   IllVoic
   "Morning glory."   IllVoic
   "My empty face."   IllVoic
   "My thinning hair."   IllVoic
   "New Year's Day."   IllVoic
   "Plum in bloom."   IllVoic
   "Snail—baring / Shoulders."   IllVoic
   "Song of skylark."   IllVoic
   "What a moon."   IllVoic
   "Winter moon."   IllVoic
   "Wonderful / Under cherry blossoms."   IllVoic
   "Woodpecker on."   IllVoic
Issei Men: The First Generation.   Rose Furuya Hawkins.   FSt   *Fr.* Proud upon
   an Alien Shore.
Issue for me, The.   Note to My Liberal Feminist Sister, A.   Naana Banyiwa
   Horne.   NAfrP
Issue, with cold feet, jumped in bed with us, An.   All-Night Issue, The.   Jackie
   Warren-Moore.   SpirFl
Issues.   Christine Ama Ata Aidoo.   HAWP
Issues from the hand of God, the simple soul.   Animula.   T. S. Eliot.   CRP
It.   Roger Mitchell.   PoCoUp
It.   Muso Soseki.   EaWin, *tr. by* W. S. Merwin
It.   Gary Snyder.   LCAP-2
It absently through her ring. (LL)   Dacca Gauzes, The.   Agha Shahid Ali.
   NIL-7; NoP-4
It ain't forever, *Gimme!* (LL)   Preference.   Langston Hughes.   APSN; HCAP;
   NOBA
It Ain't Necessarily So.   George Gershwin.   OBAL; ReLy
It ain't so much a question of not knowin' whut to do.   I Cain't Say No.
   Richard Rodgers.   ReLy
It All Depends on How You Look at It.   Miroslav Košek.   INSAB
It All Depends on You.   Ray Henderson.   ReLy
It all returns. (LL)   For Love.   Robert Creeley.   CoAmPo; NOBA; PmAP;
   VCAP
It all wears out. I keep telling myself this, but.   Down by the Station, Early in
   the Morning.   John Ashbery.   HCAP
It Allows a Portrait in Line Scan at Fifteen.   Les A. Murray.   HarvBoo
It always falls most heavily on the person least able to deal with it.   Lonely
   Tylenol.   Sharon Mesmer.   HeMarv
It always felt to me—a wrong.   Emily Dickinson.   ChIV-1
It Amazes Me!   Cy Coleman.   ReLy
It arches like a rainbow.   Bridge Where the Moon Crosses, The.   Muso Soseki.
   EaWin, *tr. by* W. S. Merwin
It Arrives Suddenly and Carries Us Off As Usual.   Marge Piercy.   PasH
It asked a crumb—of Me. (LL)   "Hope" is the thing with feathers.   Emily
   Dickinson.   APN-2; AmFaPo; ChAP; MoAmPo; NOBA; NoP-4; OxBA;
   SAmP; TAP; TCAPo
It asked for bread and butter first.   Perfect Child, The.   Adrian Porter.   NBLV
It baffles the foreigner like an idiom.   Drug Store.   Karl Shapiro.   OxBA;
   TwCP
It be as short as yours. (LL)   Life.   George Herbert.   BASC; ESCV; FSCP;
   GeHe; MeLP; NOSC; NoP-4
It be the last time I'm snuffin' candles in cold dark.   Sadie Snuffs a Candle.
   Dolores Kendrick.   ESEAA
It befell at Martynmas.   Captain Car; or, Edom o Gordon.   *Unknown.*   ESPB
It began as a joke: she did not like to leave the house.   Another Poem about the
   Madness of Women.   Tom Wayman.   NOBC
It began as truth, as fact.   Lawson Fusao Inada.   GeoHom   *Fr.* Legends from
   Camp.
It began in her pram.   Renaming, The.   Valerie Sinason.   BrRo
It began well didn't it, all that euphoria.   Alice's Cat, New Year's Eve 1990.
   Anne Grimes.   Prnts
It began / When God popped His head.   Noah's Ark.   Roger McGough.
   OBSP
It begins again, the nocturnal pulse.   Assassination, The.   Donald Justice.
   VCAP
It begins as a house, an end terrace.   Zoom!   Simon Armitage.   HarvBoo
It begins to tell 'round midnight, 'round midnight.   'Round Midnight.
   Thelonius Monk.   ReLy

It begins with my dog, now dead, who all his long life. Retrieval System, The. Maxine W. Kumin. FaBoWP; InvLad; WeW-3

It begins with one or two soldiers. Truce. Paul Muldoon. FaBoWar; PBCIP; PNI

It Being Forbidden. Martha Rhodes. KGB; NAPBL

It bends the trees and floats them. After Life. Anna Hajnal. IQMS, *tr. by* Jeannette Nichols

It bothers me: the genital smell of the bay. Rondeau at the Train Stop. Erin Belieu. GifTon; NeAmPo

It breaks up green moss ground. Pond in a Basin. Tu Mu. SuSp, *tr. by* Eddie Tsang

It burns in the void. World, The. Kathleen Jessie Raine. OxBTC

It came one day like a thunderbolt. Why Don't I? O. F. Diaz-Duque. ReTh

It came to his palms. Fifty Gunner, The. Frank A. Cross. CDa

It came to mind but by chance, suggested by the. Main Idea, The. Milo De Angelis. ItPo, *tr. by* Gayle Ridinger

It came to pass. "Adonis" [*or* "Adunis"]. PFTM-2, *tr. by* Allen Hibbard and Osama Isber *Fr.* Desire Moving through the Maps of the Material.

It came today to visit. Visitor, The. Jack Prelutsky. OTCP

It Came upon the Midnight Clear. Edmund Hamilton Sears. AH; APN-1; ChrPo; SacPr; TCAPo

(Angels' Song, The.) PWR

It came upon the noontide air. Bishop James A. Shorter. Josephine D. Henderson Heard. CBWP-4

It Can Be Done. *Unknown.* PoToHe

It can kill a man. (LL) Poetry Is a Destructive Force. Wallace Stevens. APT-1; OxBA; RaBo

It can rain, it can snow, it can sleet, it can blow. My Special Friend (Is Back in Town). J. C. Johnson. ReLy

It cannot be. Where is that mighty joy. Temper (2), The. George Herbert. GeHe

It cannot come. Balboa, the Entertainer. Imamu Amiri Baraka. NoAM

It ceased to hurt me, though so slow. Emily Dickinson. SAmP

It chanced his lips did meet her forehead cool. George Meredith. NOBVV *Fr.* Modern Love.

It chaunced me on day beside the shore. Ruines of Time, The. Edmund Spenser. OxAEP-1

It comes as a surprise once more. Autopsy. James L. Foy. BloBone

It comes back. Deceased. Cid Corman. VGW

It comes blundering over the. How Poetry Comes to Me. Gary Snyder. LoL; PoPoPo

It comes from out of the blue. (All of a Sudden) My Heart Sings. Henri Herpin. ReLy

It comes to mind. Likenesses. Norman MacCaig. NePenScot

It comes to this. Revelations. David Meltzer. NeAP

It comes up out of the ocean. August. William Stafford. BodElec

It comes with the force of a body blow. Clair de Lune. Jules Laforgue. WoPoe, *tr. by* William Jay Smith

It contains nothing. Museum Vase. Robert Francis. APT-2

It costs $1.50 for my van to enter. Taos Pueblo Indians: 700 Strong According to Bobby's Last Census. Miguel Algarin. PueRic

It Could Happen to You. Jimmy Van Heusen. ReLy

It could take from Monday to Thursday. World Where News Travelled Slowly, A. Lavinia Greenlaw. MFPA

It Couldn't Be Done. Edgar Albert Guest. BRP; ITBLP

It crawls, the underground snake. Readers of Newspapers. Marina Ivanovna Tsvetayeva [*or* Tsvetaeva]. TCRP, *tr. by* Elaine Feinstein and Angela Livingstone

It creeps up behind you on all fours. Mess With It. Linda France. MFPA

It cried three times. Buson. EH, *tr. by* Robert Hass

It crumbles. Border. Gillian Clarke. HarvBoo

It darted across the pond. Catch, The. Stanley Kunitz. APT-2

It Depends on You. "Angelus Silesius." EnlH, *tr. by* Stephen Mitchell

It descended one schoolday. Eclipse, Kenwick, 1974. Tracy Ryan. NeBl

It descends rapidly under the twistable vine in the sky. Ivano Fermini. ItPo, *tr. by* Gayle Ridinger

It Did. Robert Lowell. NoAM

It did no good to think, or to stop thinking. It did no good. Responsibility. Lisa Lewis. BodElec

It did not condemn. (LL) Emily Dickinson. APN-2; ChIV-1; NAAL-2v1; NAAL-3; NoP-4

It did not last; the Devil howling Ho. Sir John Collings Squire. FaBoEE

It Didn't Begin with Horned Owls Hooting at Noon. Kevin Stein. IllVoic

It didn't matter where we lived. To All Us Sansei Who Wanted to Be Westside. Amy Uyematsu. GeoHom

It didn't require great character at all. Power of Taste, The. Zbigniew Herbert. PoSu; PoetW, *tr. by* John Carpenter and Bogdana Carpenter

It dissipated suspected. Epitaph. Marie-Claire Bancquart. MFP, *tr. by* Martin Sorrell

It dissipates day. Mirror of a Moment, The. Paul Éluard. NAWM-7v2, *tr. by* Lloyd Alexander

It does help to know. Poster. Ferreira Gullar. TCLAP, *tr. by* Renato Rezende

It does not happen. That love, removes. Audubon, Drafted. Imamu Amiri Baraka. TTY

It does not matter. After Theresienstadt. Myra Sklarew. TaR

It doesn't always do to let a mug know everything. Charlie Piecan. L. Murray. OxBoLi

It doesn't do to do much talking. Not Much Talking. *Unknown.* PWR

It doesn't exist, I know, but I love. Buddy Bolden Cylinder, The. William Matthews. SeSe

It doesn't look like a finger it looks like a feather of broken glass. Poem. Hugh Sykes Davies. SPE

It doesn't look like him. Photograph of Survivors. Gail Newman. GotH

It doesn't matter how deep you dig in. Dancing on Beethoven's Birthday. Edith Rylander. MiVo

It doesn't matter if you can't see. Some Kind of Crazy. Major L. Jackson. SpirFl

It doesn't matter / whether / a tree falls. Lyric. Elizabeth Dodd. AmPoNex

It doesn't really matter if I met him in a bar, picked him up or was. Future. Vicki Viidikas. BMAP

It doesn't speak and it isn't schooled. Desire. Molly Peacock. RA

It Don't Mean a Thing (If It Ain't Got That Swing). *Unknown.* NAAAL

It drizzled, but didn't bend. Sultry Night, A. Boris Leonidovich Pasternak. TCRusP, *tr. by* Bogdan Boychuk and Mark Rudman

It Dropped So Low in My Regard. Emily Dickinson. HAP; HeIP-4; InPK-6; OxBA; OxBSP

It ended, and the morrow brought the task. George Meredith. NAEL-6v2 *Fr.* Modern Love.

It faces west, and round the back and sides. Domicilium. Thomas Hardy. OBGa

It faded on the crowing of the cock. William Shakespeare. PeECV; TOF *Fr.* Hamlet.

It falles me here to write of Chastity. Edmund Spenser. NAEL-5v1; NAEL-6v1; NAEL-7v1 *Fr.* Faerie Queene, The.

It feels a shame to be Alive. Emily Dickinson. FaBoWar

It feels good as it is without the giant. Wallace Stevens. ColAP; NOBA *Fr.* Notes toward a Supreme Fiction.

It feels like a bear eating me. Divorce. Adam Koehn. AiP

It feels so good to be by myself. Deceiving Words. Leonor Scliar-Cabral. MirDau, *tr. by* Regina Igel

It feels so neat to be a fish again. Ode on a Bicycle on Halsted Street in a Sudden Summer Thunderstorm. Paul Carroll. IllVoic

It fell about the Lambmass tide. Bonny Lizie Baillie. *Unknown.* ESPB

It fell about the Lammas tide. *Unknown. See* Yt fell abowght the Lamasse tyde

It fell about the Lammas time. Lord Livingston. *Unknown.* ESPB; OxBB

It fell about the Martinmas. Jamie Telfer of [*or* in] the Fair Dodhead. *Unknown.* ESPB; IBB; OxBB

It fell about the Martinmas time. Get Up and Bar the Door. *Unknown.* ESPB; HeIP-4; NePenScot; NoP-4; OxBS

It fell about the Martinmas[s]. Edom o' Gordon. *Unknown.* NePenScot; OxBB

It fell in the ancient periods. Uriel. Ralph Waldo Emerson. APN-1; NAAL-2v1; NAAL-3; NOBA; OxBA

It fell on a day, and a bonnie simmer [*or* bonny summer] day. Bonnie House o' Airlie, The. *Unknown.* ESPB; OBEV; OxBB; OxBS

It Fell on a Summer's [*or* Sommers] Day [*or* Daie]. Thomas Campion. HAP

It fell upon a Wodensday [*or* Wednesday]. Brown Robyn's [*or* Robin's] Confession. *Unknown.* ESPB

It fell upon the Lammas time. Young Ronald. *Unknown.* ESPB

It fell when I was sleeping. In my dream. Land-Mine, The. George MacBeth [*or* Macbeth]. OBWP

It felt like the zero in brook ice. Funeral, The. Norman Dubie. InPK-6; NoAM

It Figures. Ogden Nash. PeLi

It first began when sitting in the huge auditorium. On Having Been an Experimental Sacred Cow for Four Years, and a Token African on Faculty. Kofi Awoonor. HBAPE

It flows through old hushed Egypt and its sands. Nile, The. Leigh Hunt. CenSon; EBEV; GSo; NOBE

It Follows. Ruth Stone. BodElec

It fortifies my soul to know. With Whom Is No Variableness, Neither Shadow of Turning. Arthur Hugh Clough. SacPr

It gets awful lonely. Lonely. Bloke Modisane. PBA

It gets is at night, and from his old nurse, a woman poor, nonpolitical. (LL) Apology for Domitian. Robert Penn Warren. NOBA; PAI

It gives a lovely light! (LL) First Fig. Edna St. Vincent Millay. APT-1; AiP; BRP; ChAP; FaBoWP; NALW; NIL-7; NoAM; NoP-4; TAP

It gives our nights sorrow and pain. Five Hymns to Pain. Nazik Al-Malaika. PoArWo, *tr.* by Husain Haddawy

It gives such divine materials to men, and accepts such leavings from / them at last. (LL) This Compost. Walt Whitman. AWP; MoAmPo; NAAL-2v1; NAAL-3; PFTM-1

It glimmers like a wakeful lake in the dusk narrowing room. Mirror, The. Isaac Rosenberg. NoAM

It Goes against My Interest to Confess It. Gustavo Adolfo Bécquer. SpanPo, *tr.* by Doreen Bell

It goes away from you suddenly, doesn't it surely first? Saturday Night. Clark Coolidge. FTOS

It got me up. Monster, The. Karen L. Mitchell. GT

It got so bad I never saw. Arsonist Tells His Story to the Attorney, The. Charles Rafferty. AmPoNex

It grew in the black mud. Rice. Mary Oliver. PoCoUp

It had been badly shot. Widgeon. Seamus Heaney. NPeEn

It had taken this to notice. Colour of the Old Man's Eyes, The. Judy Gahagan. Prnts

It Had to Be You. Isham Jones. ReLy

It hangs from heaven to earth. Tapestry. Charles Simic. LCAP-2; VCAP

It happened at midnight. Enough Rain for Agnes Walquist. Allen Grossman. BAP-01

It happened before my eyes. Love's Fool. Margit Szécsi. IQMS, *tr.* by Kenneth McRobbie

It happened—I felt it happen. Have You Met Miss Jones? Richard Rodgers. ReLy

It happened in an instant. Blueness of the Day, The. David Mura. OPRER

It happened in Paris. My Night with Frederico García Lorca (As Told by Edouard Roditi). Jaime Manrique. WiU

It Happened in Vallen-Koski. Innokenty Fiodorovich Annensky. TCRP, *tr.* by Daniel Weissbort and Lubov Yakovleva

It happened not far away. Clonfeacle. Paul Muldoon. CIP-2

It happened once upon a time. James Hatley. *Unknown.* ESPB

It happened that a fama was dancing respite and dancing. Normal Behavior of the Famas. Julio Cortázar. TCLAP, *tr.* by Paul Blackburn

It happened that a gentleman dropped his glasses on the. Very Real Story, A. Julio Cortázar. TCLAP, *tr.* by Paul Blackburn

It happens lonely—no one. Moment, The. William Stafford. NNaP

It happens that I am tired of being a man. Walking Around. Pablo Neruda. PoetW, *tr.* by W. S. Merwin *See also* It so happens I am sick of being a man

It happens through the blond window, the trees. Ascension. Denis Devlin. BIrV; ChIV-2

It happens when I've been driving. I Caught a Glimpse. Philip Levine. GeoHom

It happens. Will it go on? Paralytic. Sylvia Plath. FaBoWP

It hardly mattered what time of year. No Tool or Rope or Pail. Bob Arnold. OPRER

It has a head like a cat, feet like a cat. Riddle. *Unknown.* NTCP

It has a hole in it. Not only where I. Surface, The. Jorie Graham. HarvBoo

It has all. From Gloucester Out. Edward Dorn. NOBA; PmAP; PoM

It has all begun with still waters. Maya Bejerano. DTA, *tr.* by Tsipi Keller *Fr.* Hymns of Job.

It has always been King Herod that I feared. Twelfth Night. Elinor Wylie. ChrPo; SacPr

It has been a month since I gave up shaving. House Plants. David McFadden. NOBC

It has been days, and still this wind. State of Fever, A. Sa'di Yusuf. MAP, *tr.* by Lena Jayyusi and Naomi Shihab Nye

It has been long since first my fears grew light. Jakov [*or* Jacob] Steinberg. FIT, *tr.* by Robert Friend

It has been proposed that the stars should be removed from sight. Paavo Haavikko. WoPoe, *tr.* by Anselm Hollo *Fr.* Fifteen Epigrams in Praise of the Tyrant.

It has been raining for three days. Rainy Season. Charles Reznikoff. APT-2

It has been raining now a place where. Rain Downriver. Philip Levine. VCAP

It has done its work—I toss it carelessly to fall where it may. (LL) Spontaneous Me. Walt Whitman. NAAL-2v1; NAAL-3; NAAL-5; OxBA

It has for ages been observed. Vladimir Uflyand [*or* Ufliand]. TCRP; TCRusP, *tr.* by Daniel Weissbort

It has gone with me as with a child. Heinrich von Morungen. GePo

It has happened / and it goes on happening. What Happens. Tadeusz Rózewicz. AF, *tr.* by Robert A. Maguire

It has happened suddenly. Je Suis une Table. Donald Hall. SPE

It has no wings. Loneliness and July Ninth. Claribel Alegría. BoWoP, *tr.* by Aliki and Willis Barnstone

It has rained. Wet. Yusuf Al-Sa'igh. MAP, *tr.* by Diana Der Hovanessian and Salma Khadra Jayyusi

It Has Snowed Repeatedly and We Can Count on a Good Crop of Wheat and Barley. Lu Yu. SuSp, *tr.* by Burton Watson

It has something to do with final words. Gladys Cardiff. ReEnLa

It has stayed stuck in my eyes. Wild Root. Juana de Ibarbourou. TCLAP, *tr.* by Sophie Cabot Black and Maria Negroni

It has taken me. Leaving You. Lily Brett. HP

It Has the Unassuming Face of a Burnt-out Candle. Velemir [*or* Viktor Vladimirovich] Khlebnikov. AF, *tr.* by Paul Schmidt

It has to be a hill. Michael Hartnett. PBCIP *Fr.* Notes on My Contemporaries.

It has to be the end of the day. Surf-casting. W. S. Merwin. NOBA

It has turned cold. Autumn. Wang Wei. OHMPC, *tr.* by Kenneth Rexroth

It hath been said of old that plays are feasts. To the Reader of Master William Davenant's Play [*The Wits*]. Thomas Carew. CaPo

It held its head still. Gray Heron, The. Galway Kinnell. OWoS

It hurries down to wither on the strand. (LL) Memory. Walter Savage Landor. EBEV; NOBVV; NPeEn

It is. Dario Villa. ItPo, *tr.* by Gayle Ridinger

It Is a Beauteous Evening. William Wordsworth. AWP; BRP; CenSon; FHYEP; GSo; GTBS-P; HeIP-4; NAEL-5v2; NAEL-6v2; NIP-4; NOBRP; NoP-4; OxAEP-2; PAI; SCGP; Son; TFi
(Evening on Calais Beach.) OBEV

It is a beautiful summer night. Summer Night. Antonio Machado Ruiz. WoPoe, *tr.* by Willis Barnstone

It is a boring song / but it works every time. (LL) Margaret Atwood. HAP; NIL-7; NIP-4; WeW-3 *Fr.* Songs of the Transformed.

It is a child of a subjected land. To Lord Byron. Gyula Juhász. IQMS, *tr.* by John Gordon Nichols

It is a clearing deep in a forest: overhanging boughs. Johnson's Cabinet Watched by Ants. Robert Bly. NOBA

It is a cold and snowy night. The main street is deserted. Driving to Town Late to Mail a Letter. Robert Bly. HeIP-4; InPK-6; VGW

It is a cramped little state with no foreign policy. Shame. Richard Wilbur. CoAmPo; EmeKit; FaBoMo; OBCoV; OxBC

It is a dreary evening. My Journal. Adelaide Anne Procter. VWP

It is a fearful thing to be. Pope, The. A. E. Housman. NPeEn; OBCoV

It is a fearful thing to fall into the hands of the living God. Hands of God, The. D. H. Lawrence. ChIV-2; InVLi

It is a flower. On this mountainside it is dying. (LL) Flower Herding on Mount Monadnock. Galway Kinnell. HeIP-4; LCAP-2; NOBA; NoAM

It is a funny thing, but true. Folks and Me. Lucile Crites. PWR

It Is a German Honeymoon. Kenneth Rexroth. APT-2

It is a God-damned lie to say that these. Another Epitaph on an Army of Mercenaries. Hugh MacDiarmid. FaBoWar; InPK-6; NAEL-5v2; NAEL-6v2; NoAM; NoP-4; OBWP; RB

It is a great day. (LL) Today Is a Day of Great Joy. Víctor Hernández Cruz. LoL; PueRic; TTY

It is a hive. Inside My Zulu Hut. Mbuyiseni Oswald Mtshali. PBMAP

It is a hollow garden, under the cloud. Winter Swan. Louise Bogan. APT-2; ColAP; OWoS

It is a huge spider, which can no longer move. Spider, The. César Vallejo. RaBo, *tr.* by Robert Bly

It is a human universe: & I. Ted Berrigan. PFTM-2 *Fr.* Sonnets, The.

It is a kind of triage, a setting. Triage. Margot Schilpp. AmPoNex

"It is a kynde knowyng," quod she, "that kenneth in thine herte." William Langland. OxBEV *Fr.* Vision of Piers Plowman, The.

It is a land with neither night nor day. Cobwebs. Christina Georgina Rossetti. CABP; NAEL-5v2; NAEL-6v2; NALW; VWP

It is a lost road into the air. Airstrip in Essex, 1960, An. Donald Hall. LCAP-2

It is a month, and isna mair. White Fisher, The. *Unknown.* ESPB

It is a night of summer: overhead. John Addington Symonds. CAGL *Fr.* Three Visions of Imperial Rome.

It is a pilgrim coming from the East. Pilgrim from the East, The. Gustave Kahn. TrJP, *tr.* by Jethro Bithell

It is a place where poets crowded may feel the heart's decaying. Cowper's Grave. Elizabeth Barrett Browning. OxAEP-2

It is a puzzle for the insane. Different Ones #6—Future Possibilities (An AIDS Soliloquy). Viki Akiwumi. InTrad

It is a simple ritual. My Brother. Patricia Parker. GLP

It Is a Small Plant. William Carlos Williams. ColAP

It is a strange bird. Strange Bird, A. Michael Dransfield. BMAP

It is a stubble field, where a black rain is falling. De Profundis. Georg Trakl. WoPoe, *tr.* by James Wright

It is a sultry day; the sun has drank [*or* drunk]. Summer Wind. William Cullen Bryant. APN-1

It is a terror. Perspectives on the Second World War. Irena Klepfisz. TaR

It is a test you have to pass. Essie Parrish in New York. Elsie Parrish. STP, *tr.* by George Quasha

It is a theatre floating through the clouds. Wallace Stevens. HCAP *Fr.* Auroras of Autumn, The.

It is a thought breaking the granite heart. On the Death of Her Body. James Keir Baxter. PeNZ

It is a very curious fact. Lines for a Worthy Person Who Has Drifted by Accident into a Chelsea Revel. Sir Alan Patrick Herbert. NOBL

It is a warm grey afternoon in August. Out of Control; the Quarry. Christopher Dewdney. NOBC

It is a wicked world of toil without much mirth, and the multitude. Conversation between Two Sisters, One Choosing an Aged Man, and the Other Choosing Youth, A. Angharad Pritchard. EMWP

It is a while when summer is over. Willow Poem. William Carlos Williams. NAAL-2v2

It is a winter afternoon. What We Lost. Eavan Boland. HarvBoo

It is a year of good harvest. Harvesting Wheat for the Public Share. Li Chü. BoWoP

It is a year to-day that thou art gone. (LL) Dante Alighieri. AWP; MiVo, *tr. by* Dante Gabriel Rossetti *Fr.* La Vita Nuova.

It is again. "Stephany." NBV

It is all right. All they do. To the Muse. James Wright (1927–80). NAAL-2v2; NNaP

It is All Souls' Day, then, a reverential day in Portugal. Lisbon. Russell Atkins. GT

It Is Almost Beautiful when fraud and hypocrisy. Senate Hearings. Michael McClure. BB

It is almost time to grow up. Movin' with Nancy. David Trinidad. PmAP

It is always a shock when they take off their caps. Callers. Christine Evans. TCAWP

It is always a temptation to an armed and agile nation. Dane-Geld. Rudyard Kipling. OxBTC

It is always difficult to measure. Our World Is Less Full Now That Mr. Fuller Is Gone. Kalamu ya Salaam. ISC

It is always easy to sentimentalize old lovers. They are distant. To H. N. David Mura. UnSA

It is always embarrassing for a German to order. Harry's Bar Ballad. Giulia Niccolai. CItWP, *tr. by* Cinzia Sartini Blum and Lara Trubowitz

It is always night here. Star & Garter Theater. Dennis Schmitz. LCAP-2

It is an ancestral castle. Life in the Castle. Anne Hébert. BoWoP, *tr. by* Aliki and Willis Barnstone

It is an ancient custom. Ancient Custom, An. Anatoly Steiger. TCRusP, *tr. by* John Glad

It is an ancient Mariner. Samuel Taylor Coleridge. AmFaPo; CABP; EBEV; EBNV; FHYEP; FaBoCh; HAP; HeIP-4; NAEL-6v2; NOBE; NoP-4; OBEV; OBNV; OxAEP-2; OxBEV; PeECV; PoE; PoPoPo; SCGP; TFi; TOF *Fr.* Rime of the Ancient Mariner, The.

It is an antique carcass eaten up by rust. Frisco-City. Blaise Cendrars. BLT, *tr. by* Monique Chefdor

It is an August evening, in Wicklow. Thomas Kinsella. ModIr *Fr.* Messenger, The.

It is an auncient waggonere. Rime of the Auncient Waggonere, The. William Maginn. ClHu

It is an honorable Thought. Emily Dickinson. NOCV

It is an illusion that we were ever alive. Rock, The. Wallace Stevens. APT-1

It is an image of irreversible loss. Sorrow Garden, The. Thomas McCarthy. BiHa

It is as if infancy were the whole of incarnation. Luci Shaw. SacPr

It is as if the birds have segregated you. Hoopoe Bird, The. Saleem Barakat. MAP, *tr. by* Lena Jayyusi and Naomi Shihab Nye

It is as if they are ashamed. Elephants Dying, The. Michael C. Blumenthal. NoAM

It is as old as it thinks itself to be. Parmenides Machine, A. Charles Stein. PFTM-2

It is as true as strange, else trial feigns. John Davies of Hereford. OxBSo *Fr.* Wit's Pilgrimage.

It is Ash Wednesday and Christ is waiting. Campesino's Lament, The. Judith Ortiz Cofer. PueRic; TouFir

It Is at Moments after I Have Dreamed. E. E. Cummings. OxBA

It is at morning, twilight they expire. After Midnight. Charles Vildrac. AWP, *tr. by* Jethro Bithell

It is autumn at the grass hut on Jade Peak. At the Thatched Hall of the Ts'ui Family. Tu Fu. CrYelRi, *tr. by* Sam Hamill

It is because of exile I am here. Tristia. Charles Hubert Sisson. HarvBoo

It is because you were my friend. Mortal Combat. Mary Elizabeth Coleridge. VWP

It is best. At Night. Jane Hirshfield. BodElec

It is best so, sith so it was to be. (LL) Dialogue: Lover and Lady. Ciullo d'Alcamo. AWP; EaItPo, *tr. by* Dante Gabriel Rossetti

It Is Better. Bible, O.T. TrJP *Fr.* Ecclesiastes.

It is better. Abandoning Your Car in a Snowstorm: Rosslyn, Virginia. Michael C. Blumenthal. NoAM

It is better not to go back to the village. Baleful Return. Ramón López Velarde. TCLAP, *tr. by* Victor Tulli

It is blood. It is not hail, battering my temples. July 18, 1936–July 18, 1938. Miguel Hernández. AF, *tr. by* Timothy Baland

It is blue. (LL) Blue Monday. Diane Wakoski. NALW; PmAP

It is building music. (LL) Then. Muriel Rukeyser. GLP; LCAP-2

It is burning ice, it is a cold fire. Amorous Sonnet Defining Love. Francisco de Quevedo y Villegas. BLPSL, *tr. by* Rene de Costa, Rigas Kappatos and Eleni Paidoussi

It is Christmas Day in the workhouse, and the cold, bare walls are bright. Christmas Day in the Workhouse. George R. Sims. EBNV

It is clear that Napoleon's Queen. Limerick. Moss Rich. PeLi

It Is Clear Why the Angels Come No More. Jack Gilbert. YaYoPo

It is cold, bitter as a penny. Who Will Know Us? Gary Soto. GM

It is cold dark midnight, yet listen. Homeless. Adelaide Anne Procter. VWP

It is cold here. Moths, The. W. S. Merwin. HeIP-4

It is colder now. Epistle to Be Left in the Earth. Archibald MacLeish. APT-1; MoAmPo; NOBA

It is common knowledge to every schoolboy and even every Bachelor of Arts. Portrait of the Artist as a Prematurely Old Man. Ogden Nash. APT-2

It is dangerous for a woman to defy the gods. Letter to My Sister. Anne Spencer. BlSi; NAAAL; TCAPo

It is dangerous to leave written that which is badly written. William Carlos Williams. PFTM-2 *Fr.* Paterson.

It Is Dangerous to Read Newspapers. Margaret Atwood. HeIP-4; OBWP

It is dark. Last Bus, The. Mark Strand. TwCP

It is dark, now, and grave. Melting Pot. Michael Echeruo. PBMAP; TTY

It is daybreak everywhere. (LL) Bells of San Blas, The. Henry Wadsworth Longfellow. APN-1; OxBA

It is December. Morning Songs. Robert E. Penn. WiU

It is December in Wicklow. Seamus Heaney. NPeEn; PBCIP; PNI

It Is Deep. Carolyn M. Rodgers. NAAAL; SSLK

It is difficult now to speak of poetry. George Oppen. NNaP *Fr.* Of Being Numerous.

It Is Difficult to Exaggerate the Importance of Mushrooms as Food. Chris Torrance. Oth

It is difficult to keep sane in it. Rain Forest. Eric Rolls. NOBAu

It is difficult to read. The page is dark. Phosphor Reading by His Own Light. Wallace Stevens. APT-1

It is disastrous to be a wounded deer. Hello. Gregory Corso. PoM

It is done! Laus Deo! John Greenleaf Whittier. CBCWP

It is done by us all, as God disposes, from. Excrement Poem, The. Maxine W. Kumin. FaBoWP

It is done in beauty. (LL) *Unknown.* APN-2; TCAPo, *tr. by* Washington Matthews *Fr.* Mountain Chant, The.

It is dusty on the edges. I Still Have Everything You Gave Me. Naomi Shihab Nye. ExTi

It is duty and not hospitality that has diverted the ancient guest. Dream of Mimesis, A. Katherine Lederer. BodElec

It is early dawn. The city forty miles away draws airplanes. Written Forty Miles South of a Spreading City. Robert Bly. NNaP

It is early evening, still, in Honolulu, and in London, now, it must be well past dawn. 4 A.M. Kenneth Fearing. APT-2

It is early morning. Aubade, An. Irving Layton. WoPoe

It is early morning within this room: without. Winter Sunrise. Laurence Binyon. NPeEn

It is early, yet. Grand Canyon, The. James Merrill. TAP

It is earnest. Scenes from the Door. Gertrude Stein. AF

It is easily forgotten; year to. Memorial Day. Michael Anania. NoAM

It is Easter / The last flurries. Three-Card Monte. Malena Mörling. AmPoNex

It is easy enough to be pleasant. Worthwhile. Ella Wheeler Wilcox. PoToHe

It is easy enough to love flowers but these. Giant Decorative Dahlias. Molly Holden. OxBTC

It is easy for the mind. Point and Counter-Point in All Things. Jane Mead. NAPBL

It is easy to be young. (Everybody is). How to Be Old. May Swenson. UnPo

It is easy to proclaim yourself. Marginalization of Poetry, The. Mitch Highfill. HeMarv

It is enough for me. Old Man Told Me. Lance Henson. VoR

It is enough for me by day. Enough. Sara Teasdale. APT-1

It is enough for me to. Bridge, The. Khalil Hawi. MAP, *tr. by* Diana Der Hovanessian and Lena Jayyusi

It is enough! I saw you vanish into air. (LL) Butterfly. D. H. Lawrence. BLT; NoAM; TTTS

It is enough! My feeble sense. Dying Song. Anton Ulrich. GePo, *tr. by* George C. Schoolfield

It is equal to living in a tragic land. Dry Loaf. Wallace Stevens. NOBA; OxBA; PoRA; RaBo

It is essential that Summer be grafted to. Poem for July 4, 1994. Sonia Sanchez. SpirFl

It is essential that the U.S.A. standard of hygiene and inspection. Laurie Duggan. BMAP *Fr.* Three Found Poems.

It is evening before I rise. In Seclusion. Tu Fu. CrYelRi, *tr. by* Sam Hamill

It Is Everywhere. Jean Toomer. GT

It is far from just between us. *Unknown.* NOIV

It is finished. The enormous dust-cloud over Europe. Armistice. Paul Dehn. OxBTC

'It is finished.' The last nail. Tenebrae. David Gascoyne. PeECV

It is first that angle at which you sleep. Milkflowers. Robert Wrigley. PasH

It is fitting that you be here. On Seeing Two Brown Boys in a Catholic Church. Frank Horne. TTY

It is 5:15 A.M. Dear Chris, hello. (LL) Ted Berrigan. FTOS; PFTM-2; PmAP *Fr.* Sonnets, The.

It is for me poetry. Rochelle Owens. PFTM-2 *Fr.* W. C. Fields in French Light.

It is for us to / praise the Lord of all. Kingdom of God, The. Rab. TrJP

It is for you, my mother fair. For You. James Harvey Spencer. PWR

It is forbidden to write about a certain class of violence. With Your Permission. Mario Benedetti. TCLAP, *tr. by* David Arthur McMurray

It is four in the afternoon. Time still for a poem. Public Journal. Phyllis McGinley. NBLV

It is four times as big as the bush! (LL) Limerick: "There was an Old Man who said, 'Hush!'" Edward Lear. KaS; NOBL; OxBoLi; PeLV; PeLi

It is friday / the eagle has flown. Coming of John, The. Amus Mor. SeSe

It is from the ideas of you that you emerge. Correspondences. Robert Duncan. PoM

It is fun to ride the horse. Kenneth Rexroth. NNaP *Fr.* Bestiary, A.

It is ghosts that kill you without a drop of blood. Purple Thought, The. Houda Al-Na'mani. PoArWo, *tr. by* Richard McKane

It is glorious. Old Song of the Musk Ox People. Brian Swann. PoCoUp

It is going to be a splendid summer. Future Work. Fleur Adcock. DiPo

It is going to rain. She Thinks of Her Beloved. Lu Chi. OHMPC, *tr. by* Kenneth Rexroth

It is good in May, in marvelous wet May, to be the chairman of the All-Russian Extraordinary Committee in the city of Odessa. "Eduard Veniaminovich Limonov." TCRusP, *tr. by* William Tjalsma *Fr.* Secret Notebook.

It is growing dark. L. A. Davidson. HA

It is hard as diamonds; it wants to destroy us all. (LL) Unbeliever, The. Elizabeth Bishop. NAAL-2v2; NAAL-5; NoAM

It is hard for those who have never known persecution. T. S. Eliot. SacPr *Fr.* Rock, The.

It is hard going to the door. Door, The. Robert Creeley. NAAL-5; NeAP; NoAM; PoM; VGW

It is hard to beat a good meal. Thomas Kinsella. CIP-2 *Fr.* Technical Supplement, A.

It is hard to become a truly good. Simonides. SaLy, *tr. by* Diane Rayor

It is hard / To make a poem in prison. To Make a Poem in Prison. Etheridge Knight. AF

It is hard to remember parents at their loving. Train Song. Fiona Kidman. PeNZ

It is hard to want a thing you know will hurt another. From a Vacant House. Mark Wunderlich. NeAmPo

It is hardly enough to stir and mix. Secrets of the Landscape, The. Jacob [*or* Jakov] Fichman. FIT, *tr. by* Robert Friend

It is harm to me and anguish. Dirge. Mary Macleod (Màiri Nighean Alasdair Ruaidh). EMWP

It Is Her Cousin's Death. Gail Fox. NOBC

It is her eyes. In Her Own Image. Eavan Boland. PBCIP

It is her right, to bind with warmest ties. Woman's Rights. Rebekah Gumpert Hyneman. SWaP

It is I, O Azure, come from the caves below. Helen. Paul Valéry. WoPoe, *tr. by* Richard Wilbur

It is I who travel in the winds. George Copway's Dream Song. *Unknown.* APN-2, *tr. by* George Copway

It Is Important. Gail Tremblay. WeW-3

It is important to do something meaningless. First Thing. Kit Robinson. FTOS

It is in captivity. Bull, The. William Carlos Williams. TwCP

It is in slow choking. Man, That Is Born of a Woman. Rosanna Warren. ExTi

It Is in Vain, the Sorrow. Paul Fleming. GePo, *tr. by* J. W. Thomas

It is incessantly. Sui Veneris / The Poet of No Return. Ricardo M. de Ungria. ReBoTo

It is indeed like that. Kangyu. JDP, *tr. by* Yoel Hoffmann

It is June, it is June. Andraitx—Pomegranate Flowers. D. H. Lawrence. NoP-4

It is late at night and still I am losing. Robert Frost. GI; VGW *Fr.* Ten Mills.

It is late in the day of the world. Latter Day Lysistrata. Lauris Edmond. PeNZ

It is late in the Winter night. Winter Night. Yüan Mei. OHMPC, *tr. by* Kenneth Rexroth

It is late in the year. Night in the House by the River. Tu Fu. OHPC, *tr. by* Kenneth Rexroth

It is late last night the dog was speaking of you. Donal Og. *Unknown.* RB, *tr. by* Lady Augusta Gregory

It is Leviathan, mountain and world. History. Robert Fitzgerald. APT-2

It is like smoke escaping through a screened. In a Room. William Virgil Davis. YaYoPo

It is like the first and last time I tried a Coleman. Falling in Love at Sixty-Five. Mona Van Duyn. NoP-4

It is likely enough that lions and scorpions. Ante Mortem. Robinson Jeffers. MoAmPo

It is little I repair to the matches of the Southron folk. At Lord's. Francis Thompson. EBVV; OPOU; OxBSP; PeLV

It is made to be rolled down. Poem Like a Grenade, A. John Haines. SPE

It is Margaret you mourn for. (LL) Spring and Fall. Gerard Manley Hopkins. CABP; EBEV; GTBS-P; HAP; HeIP-4; InPK-6; NAEL-5v2; NAEL-6v2; NIL-7; NIP-4; NOBE; NoAM; NoP-4; OPOU; PAI; PeVV; PoE; PoPoPo; RB; SCGP; SCV; TFi; TOF; TRP

It is May on every hand. Bird Song. William Carlos Williams. SAmP

It is midnight. Poem at Thirty. Sonia Sanchez. BPo; BlSi; NAAAL

It is miserable. Líadan and Cuirithir. *Unknown.* NOIV

It is Monday morning. Goldfish Wife, The. Sandra Hochman. UnPo

It Is Monsoon at Last. Basil T. Paquet. CDa

It is morning because the sun has risen. Concerning the Afterlife, the Indians of Central California Had Only the Dimmest Notions. Robert Hass. LoL

It is morning, Chrysilla. Some time ago the clarion cock. Antipater of Thessalonica. GrAn

It is morning, Senlin says, and in the morning. Conrad Potter Aiken. NoAM *Fr.* Senlin; a Biography.

It is most curious to see what a power a few calm words. Arthur Hugh Clough. NPeEn *Fr.* Amours de Voyage.

It is most true that eyes are formed to serve. Sir Philip Sidney. NAEL-5v1; NAEL-6v1; NAEL-7v1; NoSic; Son *Fr.* Astrophil and Stella.

It is much like ocean the way it opens. Open Country. Richard Hugo. LCAP-2

It is my celebration. I Will Still Sing. Amelia Blossom Pegram. HAWP

It is my desire, it is my wish. Elias Lönnrot. PFTM-1 *Fr.* Kalevala, The.

It is my desire moving. "Adonis" [*or* "Adunis"]. PFTM-2, *tr. by* Allen Hibbard and Osama Isber *Fr.* Desire Moving through the Maps of Material.

It is my joy at evening to be gazing. Soul Woven of Shadows. Árpád Tóth. IQMS, *tr. by* Edmund Charles Blunden and John Gordon Nichols

It is my last night in Havana. El Apagón. Sandra M. Castillo. TouFir

It is my nature that makes me love you often. How God Answers the Soul. Mechthild von Magdeburg. WPoS, *tr. by* Oliver Davies

It is my only description. (LL) I Keep to Myself Such Measures. Robert Creeley. NoAM; PmAP

It is myself. To a Dog Injured in the Street. William Carlos Williams. LCAP-2; SAmP

It Is Near Toussaints' Ivor Gurney. PeFWW

It is necessary that things. Anaximander. PGA

It is necessary to wait until the boss's eyes are on you. Notes from a Slave Ship. Edward Field. WWork

It Is New. Al-Hutay'a. ArPe, *tr. by* Omar S. Pound

It is night. Cholera. Nazik Al-Malaika. PoArWo, *tr. by* Husain Haddawy and Nathalie Handal

It is night again. Tzu Yeh. EroLit; WPOW; WoPoe, *tr. by* Chung Ling and Kenneth Rexroth

It is night and the barbarians have not come. Poem Beginning with a Line by Cavafy. Derek Mahon. PNI

It is night for the last time. Letters, The. Louise Glück. HarvBoo

It is night like a red rag. Moment of War, A. Laurie Lee. OBWP

It is night. You are asleep. And beautiful tears. Ted Berrigan. PFTM-2 *Fr.* Sonnets, The.

It is no fault to be deformed. To a Hunchback. Ibn al-Rumi. ArPe, *tr. by* Omar S. Pound

It is no madness to say. "H. D." FaBoMo *Fr.* Flowering of the Rod, The.

It is no vulgar nature I have wived. George Meredith. NAEL-5v2; NAEL-6v2 *Fr.* Modern Love.

It Is Not. Valerie Martínez. TouFir

It is not a range of a mountain. Gertrude Stein. NoP-4

It is not a trip to the Prater or Augarten to play. Waving Her Farewell. Train Station, Vienna XV, 1939. Lisa Ress. GotH

It Is Not Always May. Henry Wadsworth Longfellow. PWR

It is not as though you come. All the Same. Clarence Major. BodElec

It Is Not Beauty I Demand. George Darley. NAEL-6v2
(Loveliness of Love, The.) GTBS-P; OxAEP-2
(Song, A.) NOBRP

It is not, Celia, in our power. To a Lady Asking Him How Long He Would Love Her. Sir George Etherege. OBEV

It is not clear how he entered me. Houdini. Moniza Alvi. EmeKit; MFPA

It is not cosy to live. From the Chinese. Michael Smith. CIP-2; PBCIP

It is not enough to drink. "When the Wild Goose Finds Food He Calls His Comrades"—I Ching. Jan Kemp. PeNZ

It is not far beyond the Village church. Walden. William Ellery Channing. APN-1

It is not far to my place. Visit. A. R. Ammons. CoAP; TwCP

It is not for you, finally, that I write these lines. Madrigal 3. Aurelio Arturo. BLPSL, tr. by Rene de Costa, Rigas Kappatos and Eleni Paidoussi

It is not grief or pain. After Soufrière. "Michael Field." VWP

It is not gunfire I hear but a hunting horn. (LL) Aristocrats. Keith Douglas. FaBoMo; FaBoWar; NAEL-5v2; NAEL-6v2; NoAM; NoP-4; OBWP

It is not happiness. Not the man standing. Ariel Singing. Timothy Liu. NeAmPo

It is not I, ever or now. (LL) Pebble, The. Elinor Wylie. ChIV-1; MoAmPo

It is not—I swear it by every fiery omen to be seen these nights. Readings, Forecasts, Personal Guidance. Kenneth Fearing. MoAmPo

It is not in yr service that I wear myself out. Loba Addresses the Goddess, The / or The Poet as Priestess Addresses the Loba-Goddess. Diane Di Prima. HW; PmAP

It Is Not Just. Shakuntala Hawoldar. HAWP

It is not just that I am looking. It Is Not Just. Shakuntala Hawoldar. HAWP

It is not mine to run, with eager feet. Not Mine. Julia Caroline Ripley Dorr. PWR

It is not now I learn. Song. Louise Bogan. APT-2

It is not right to judge a man. First Impressions. Alfred Grant Walton. PoToHe

It is not safe to know. (LL) Lover and Philosopher. Sir William Davenant [or D'Avenant]. NOBE; OBEV

It is not so much the image of the man. Photograph of Haymaker, 1890. Molly Holden. OxBTC

It is not that the sea lanes. Stone and Fern. Leslie Norris. AngWePo

It is not that there is beginning is there. Work, The. Armand Schwerner. BodElec

It is not / the Afro. I Am Africa. Kimberly Ann Collins. InTrad

It is not the earth that I worship. Earth Song. Thomas Love Peacock. VoR

It is not the moon, I tell you. Mock Orange. Louise Glück. MakPoe; NoAM; PoPoPo; VCAP

It is not true that the shortest path between two points is the. Lover of Blue Writing above the Sea, The. Ghada Al-Samman. PoArWo, tr. by Saad Ahmed and Miriam Cooke

It is not true that you are far from "the light that can find you." Eunice Odio. TANSG, tr. by Arthur Natella Fr. In the Life and Death of Rosamel Del Valle.

It is not what they built. It is what they knocked down. James Fenton. HarvBoo; NAEL-5v2; NAEL-6v2; NPeEn; NoAM

It is not wine that makes me reel / Not juice of grape I crave. Agathias. GrAn

It is nothing to me, the beauty said. Nothing and Something. Frances Ellen Watkins Harper. PWR

It is now nearly forty years, I guess. Mother's Lament, The. Helen Selina Blackwood, Countess of Dufferin. VWP

It is—Occasionally. (LL) Emily Dickinson. NIL-7; NIP-4

It is, of course, the wrong house. Houses of Emily Dickinson, The. Larry Rubin. NIP-4

It is on the Earth that all things transpire. Fish Tea Rice. Linda Gregg. ExTi

It is only a door. (LL) Prospective Immigrants Please Note. Adrienne Rich. AiP; AmFaPo; VGW

It is other people who have separated. Lady Otomo no Sakanoé. TAL

It is out in the flimsy suburbs. Sunday in Glastonbury. Robert Bly. CoAmPo

It is over. What is over? Amen. Christina Georgina Rossetti. WPoS

It is overdue time. Ron Welburn. NBV

It is perfectly natural for the Sun to shine initially in the upper / lefthand corner of the first page of this book. Sun as a Spinning Top (I), The. Francis Ponge. AF, tr. by Serge Gavronsky

It is plain now what you are. Your head has dropped. Harold Monro. PeFWW Fr. Youth in Arms.

It is pleasant in October. Nights in Fresno. Luis Omar Salinas. GeoHom

It is portentous, and a thing of state. Abraham Lincoln Walks at Midnight. Nicholas Vachel Lindsay. APT-1; CBCWP; IllVoic; MoAmPo; NOBA; OxBA; TAP; TCAPo; TFi; VGW

It is possible the heights of this view are a museum. Les A. Murray. BMAP Fr. Sydney Highrise Variations, The.

It is Priapos warns you, god of this harbor. (LL) Priapos of the Harbor. Antipater of Sidon. GrAn; WoPoe, tr. by Dudley Fitts

It is raining softly. Front Window, The. Rae Desmond Jones. BMAP

It Is Raining Today. Sandra Maria Esteves. PueRic

It Is Said by Some Sailors, the Old. Maria Luisa Spaziani. CItWP, tr. by Cinzia Sartini Blum and Lara Trubowitz

It is said he was a relative of Jesus. For Jude's Lebanon. Joseph Awad. GraLe

It is said that a lover seen in dreams. Dreams. Myŏng'ok. WoPoe, tr. by Okhee Yoo and Michael Stephens

It is said that that western land is of Earth the best. Land Called Scotia, The. Saint Donatus. NOIV

It is said there are those who can never be sane. Bill. Peter Kocan. CBAP

It is scribbled along the body. Eighth Sky. Michael Palmer. FTOS

It is senseless for any man. Praise of God. Unknown. NOIV

It is she alone that matters. Bouquet of Belle Scavoir. Wallace Stevens. MoAmPo

It is simply this. Poem for Sophie. David Lampert. GotH

It is so clear. Domino Theory (or Snoop Dogg Rules the World), The. Kenneth Carroll. SpirFl

It is so hard to be earth bound. Ornithology. Laini Mataka. ISC

It is so long gone by, and yet. Reminiscence, A. Amy Levy. VWP

It is so much easier to forget than to have been Mr. Whittier. Mr. Whittier. Winfield Townley Scott. VGW

It is so old, the date is dim. My House Not Made with Hands. Helen Hunt Jackson. SWaP

It is so peaceful on the ceiling! Sleeping on the Ceiling. Elizabeth Bishop. APT-2; OBGa; TTTS

It is so sad. Loneliness, The. John Wieners. PmAP

It is so small a thing. Matthew Arnold. OBEV Fr. Empedocles on Etna.

It is so still in the house. Mother's Song, The. Unknown. OBCP, tr. by Peter Freuchen

It is so thin a splinter of singing. (LL) Splinter. Carl Sandburg. KaS; OBCA; SoSe-8; Spl

It is some time since I have been. Hill, The. Robert Creeley. CRP; RaBo; TRP

It Is Soul Brother Number One, James Brown. David Wojahn. PBCAP Fr. Mystery Train: A Sequence.

It is spring, almost dawn when the crowds gather. Leaving Government Offices. Tu Fu. CrYelRi, tr. by Sam Hamill

It is Spring in the mountains. Written on the Wall at Chang's Hermitage. Tu Fu. EnlH; OHPC, tr. by Kenneth Rexroth

It is Spring on the lake and. Sailing on the Lake to the Ching River. Lu Yu. OHPC, tr. by Kenneth Rexroth

It is spring today. Visitation. Jaime Jacinto. ReBoTo

It is spring when the storks return. Reading. Ruth Stone. ExTi

It is springtime out here in Kansas. Kansas. J. P. Dunn. VerBaPo

It Is Sticky in the Subway. David Schubert. APT-2

It Is Still Early. Elvira Levy. MirDau, tr. by Roberta Gordenstein

It is still I. (LL) For Miriam. Marjorie Oludhe Macgoye. HAWP; WPOW

It is strange to think of the Annas, the Vronskys, the Pierres, all the Tolstoyan lot wiped out. Fate and the Younger Generation. D. H. Lawrence. OxBoLi

It is subtle, and weary, and wide. Doubt, A. Sarah Morgan Bryan Piatt. NCAP

It is such a beautiful day I had to write you a letter. Thoughts of a Young Girl. John Ashbery. CoAmPo; TAP; VGW

It is summer, and we are in a house. Modern Love. Douglas Dunn. NPeEn

It is summer and we sit on the front porch. Gentry, The. Elmaz Abinader. GraLe

It is Sunday. In Memoriam. Léopold Sédar Senghor. PBMAP

It is Sunday afternoon. At the End of the Weekend. Ted Kooser. PBCAP

It is sweet in summer to slake. Asclepiades. PGA

It is talked the warld all over. Sheath and Knife. Unknown. ESPB

It is terrible, I admit that. All for Nothing. Lőrinc Szabó. IQMS, tr. by Edwin Morgan

It is Tet. Night Flare Drop, Tan Son Nhut. Horace Coleman. CDa

It is that hour when listening ones will weep. John Neal. APN-1 Fr. Battle of Niagara, The.

It is the best thing. Pregnancy. Sandra McPherson. BoWoP; LoL

It is the box from which no jack will spring. Funeral, The. Donald Hall. Son

It is the breast I remember seeing. Possible. Ruth L. Schwartz. WiU

It is the cause, it is the cause, my soul [or my soule]. William Shakespeare. EBEV; OxBEV Fr. Othello.

It is the clay that makes the earth stick to his spade. In Nunhead Cemetery. Charlotte Mew. FaBoWP; NoP-4

It is the cry of women, my good Lord. William Shakespeare. OxBEV *Fr.* Macbeth.

It is the dawn. Eunice Odio. TANSG, *tr. by* Arthur Natella *Fr.* In the Life and Death of Rosamel Del Valle.

It is the day of all the year. *Unknown.* OxNR

It is the day when he was born. Tennyson. EBVV; FHYEP; NAEL-6v2 *Fr.* In Memoriam A. H. H.

It is the deep spring of my life, this love for men. Wellspring, The. Sharon Olds. BodElec

It is the evening. Nativity Poem. Louise Glück. GI; HarvBoo

It is the evening hour. To Mary: It Is the Evening Hour. John Clare. BoLoP

It is the fashion now to wave aside. Edna St. Vincent Millay. HeIP-4

It is the first mild day of March. To My Sister. William Wordsworth. MakPoe

It is the football season once more. Autumn. Vernon Scannell. OxBTC

It is the gentle poet's art. Iron. Walter De la Mare. NOBL

It is the grass that moves, not the quails. Quails. Shinkichi Takahashi. ZenPo, *tr. by* Takashi Ikemoto and Lucien Stryk

It is the Harvest Moon! On gilded vanes. Harvest Moon, The. Henry Wadsworth Longfellow. APN-1

It is the heart of the night. Curfew. Teresa de Jesús. AF, *tr. by* Maria Proser

It is the immodesty we bring to these. Huguenot Graveyard at the Heart of the City, The. Eavan Boland. HarvBoo

It is the kindness of the rabbi I remember now, nine months. Grief. Robin Becker. TaR

It is the little girl. Franz Wright. BLT *Fr.* After Picasso.

It is the little stone of unhappiness. What I Have Written I Have Written. Peter Porter. BMAP; NOBAu

It is the middle of October. First Dimension of Skunk, The. Ray A. Young Bear. HATNAP

It is the middle of the night—I cannot sleep. Juan Chi. ColAnChi *Fr.* Songs of My Soul.

It is the miller's daughter. Miller's Daughter, The. Tennyson. OBEV

It is the nature of man that puzzles me. Nature of Man, The. Charles Hubert Sisson. FaBoTw

It is the Negro's tragedy I feel. Negro's Tragedy, The. Claude McKay. BPo

It is the normal excellence, of long accomplishment. (LL) Abnormal Is Not Courage, The. Jack Gilbert. CoAP; YaYoPo

It is the Old Man through the sleeping town. Fall Again, The. Howard Nemerov. CoAmPo

It is the pain, it is the pain, endures. Villanelle. William Empson. EnLoPo; HarvBoo; NoAM; PoE; TRP; UV

It is the past that maketh my despair. Experience Too Late. Letitia [*or* Laetitia] Elizabeth Landon. RWP

It is the picnic with Ruth in the spring. Picnic, The. John Logan. CoAmPo; TRP

It is the roots from all the trees that have died. Across the Swamp. Olav H. Hauge. RaBo; WoPoe, *tr. by* Robert Bly

It is the Sabbath bell, which calls to prayer. House of God, The. Bishop Richard Mant. SacPr

It is the saddest part of a sad story. Wiglaf. Marisa De Los Santos. NAPBL

It is the same each time. Daylight a broad blade. Milagros Mourns the Queen of Scat. Marisa De Los Santos. NAPBL

It Is the Season. Josephine Jacobsen. TAP

It is the silver seeking salvation. Plight, The. James W. Thompson. BPo

It is the sinners' dust-tongued bell claps me to churches. Dylan Thomas. OxBTC

It is the soul that sees; the outward eyes. George Crabbe. OxAEP-1 *Fr.* Lover's Journey, The.

It is the sound of lions lapping. Bush. Josephine Jacobsen. NoP-4

It is the spot I came to seek. Indian at the Burial-Place [*or* Burying-Place] of His Fathers, An. William Cullen Bryant. APN-1

It is the sun's doing. River Song. Roberta Spear. GeoHom

It Is the Third Watch. *Unknown.* WoPoe, *tr. by* Kevin O'Rourke

It is the time of illusion and reality. January 30, 1976: Message to Myself. Bob Kaufman. PFTM-2

It is the time of rain and snow. Lady Izumi. WPOW

It is the time of rain and snow. Izumi Shikibu. OHMPJ

It is the time when. Kenneth Rexroth. APSN *Fr.* Love Poems of Marichiko, The.

It is the way of a pleasant path. Green Frog at Roadstead, Wisconsin. James Schevill. TAP

It is the year's end, the winds are blasting, and I. December 30th. Ivor Gurney. NAEL-5v2; NAEL-6v2

It is their way to find the surface. Poem by the Charles River. Robin Blaser. NeAP

It is this deep blankness is the real thing strange. Let It Go. William Empson. FaBoMo; HarvBoo; NPeEn; OxBEV; OxBSP; OxBTC

It Is This Way with Men. C. K. Williams. RaBo; VCAP

It is three o'clock in the morning. Trials of a Tourist. Anne Tibble. NBLV

It is Thursday, October 23rd. Ocean of the Streams of Story. Primus St. John. GT

It is time for the invocation. May Sarton. HW *Fr.* Invocation to Kali, The.

It is time for the others to come. Magus, The. James Dickey. GI

It is time to be old. Terminus. Ralph Waldo Emerson. APN-1; AWP; NCAP; NOBA; OxBA; TAP; TCAPo

It is time to think. Natalya [*or* Natal'ia] Gorbanevskaya [*or* Gorbanyevskaya *or* Gorbanevskaia]. TCRusP, *tr. by* Daniel Weissbort

It is to be without the staple references of male heterosexual poets. After Hearing Heterosexual Poets in October 1974: What It Seems like to Write a Male Homosexual Love Poem Now. Joseph Cady. CAGL

It is to my people as a gift in their lap. Wulf and Eadwacer: A Woman's Lament. *Unknown.* WoPoe, *tr. by* Jonathan McKeage

It is to thee, my Derest Lord, that I. Sepr. Ye 6th 1666 Thursday a Thanks Geving for the Stoping of the Fire in London. Elizabeth, Viscountess Mordaunt. EMWP

It is tomorrow now. Morning Star. Thomas Hornsby Ferril. VGW

It is too early for white boughs, too late. Mid-March. Lizette Woodworth Reese. SWaP

It is true, as someone has said, that in. Mark Strand. NoP-4 *Fr.* Dark Harbor.

It is true, fellow citizens. Edgar Lee Masters. APT-1 *Fr.* Spoon River Anthology.

It Is True. I Am Not a Poet the Way You Are. Biancamaria Frabotta. CItWP, *tr. by* Cinzia Sartini Blum and Lara Trubowitz

It is true; many cities conserve. More Chagall than Chagall. Luisa Futuransky. MirDau, *tr. by* Celeste Kostopulos-Cooperman

It is true, Martin Heidegger, as you have written. Envelope, The. Maxine W. Kumin. NALW

It is true, modern life is complicated. For the Market. Jane Mayhall. TAP

It is true, that even in the best-run state. Murder of William Remington, The. Howard Nemerov. CoAP

It is true that I held Thero fair. Epigram. Meleager. GrAn, *tr. by* Peter Whigham

It is 12:20 in New York a Friday. Day Lady Died, The. Frank O'Hara. HCAP; LCAP-2; NAAL-2v2; NOBA; NeAP; NoAM; NoP-4; PAI; PFTM-2; PmAP; PoE; PoM; RaBo; SwNoth; TRP; VCAP

It is twelve years since I have been there. Kartúshkiya-Beróza. Alter Brody. TaR

It is twenty years. Piper, The. W. S. Merwin. NAAL-2v2

It is very early now, no light yet, nor. La Brea. Richard Kenney. DiPo

It is waking in the night. Fix. Michael Dransfield. NOBAu

It is well for small birds that can rise up on high. *Unknown.* NOIV

It is well—it is well with the child! (LL) Nativity, A. Rudyard Kipling. ChrPo; GI

It Is Well with My Soul. Horatio G. Spafford. SacPr

It is what he does not know. On a Squirrel Crossing the Road in Autumn, in New England. Richard Eberhart. APT-2; HeIP-4

It is what they do not say. (LL) James Fenton. HarvBoo; NAEL-5v2; NAEL-6v2; NPeEn; NoAM

It is what, to tell the truth, you sometimes feel. History. Kelly Cherry. FFC

It is when gulfs and bays of blood. Punishments. Rafael Alberti. AF, *tr. by* Geoffrey Connell

It is when I hear Mozart. Deafness. Richard Ryan. BIrV; PBCIP

It is windy today. A wall of wind crashes against. Cloudy Day. Jimmy Santiago Baca. LoL

It is wine-harvest, summer, the year's heart. Poem for Maurice O'Shea, A. Geoffrey Lehmann. NOBAu

It is winter again. Stopping to Take Notes. Michael Smith. PBCIP

It is winter and the new year. Mark Strand. UnPo *Fr.* Elegy for My Father.

It Is Winter, I Know. Merrill Moore. MoAmPo

It is winter in California, and outside. California Winter. Karl Shapiro. AiP

It is with the poet as with a guinea worm. To a Friend and Fellow Poet. Hugh MacDiarmid. NePenScot

It is world of the back hune wone it is. Emilio Villa. ItPo *Fr.* Words.

It is worthless to write a line. Chantars No Pot Gaire Valer. Bernard [*or* Bernart] de Ventadour [*or* Ventadorn]. APSN, *tr. by* Paul Blackburn

It is written in the Book of Usable Minutes. Train Rising out of the Sea. John Ashbery. ColAP

It is your last day and hour and you are alone. Who. Edwin Honig. TAP

It is yourself you seek. Man Alone. Louise Bogan. NoP-4

It isn't a game for girls. Reaching Yellow River. Roberta Hill Whiteman. HATNAP

It isn't a very big cake. Poets. Gavin Ewart. PeLV

It isn't any of this. Nanni Cagnone. ItPo, *tr. by* Gayle Ridinger

It isn't Aphrodite, but wild Eros. Alcman. SaLy, *tr. by* Diane Rayor

It isn't as if I never enjoyed good wine. I'm Not Complaining. Philip Schultz. SoSe-8

It isn't raining for me. Robert Loveman. *See* It isn't raining rain to me

It isn't raining rain to me. April Rain. Robert Loveman. TrJP

It isn't that the threat of the bomb is great. Cocoon. Rin Ishigaki. WPOW, *tr. by* Ayusawa Takako

It isn't that you were ignorant. From the Meadow. Peter Everwine. GeoHom

It isn't the body. Inner Man, The. Charles Simic. OPRER

It isn't the thing you do, dear. At Sunset. Margaret Elizabeth Munson Sangster. PWR

It isn't the young men sprawling in chairs I mind. Old Professor, The. John Holmes. APT-2

It isn't winter that brings it. Earth. Margaret Atwood. PoE

It jangles in a mild breeze. Sean Dunne. ModIr *Fr.* Sydney Place.

It Just Doesn't Matter. Rodney M. McNeil. InTrad

It just so happens that I'm tired of being a man. Pablo Neruda. *See* It so happens I am sick of being a man

It keeps eternal whisperings around. On the Sea. John Keats. NoP-4

It later befell in the years that followed. *Unknown.* AnOE, *tr. by* Charles W. Kennedy *Fr.* Beowulf.

It lies—when urged to, it lies. Nanni Cagnone. ItPo, *tr. by* Gayle Ridinger

It lieth, gazing on the midnight sky. On the Medusa of Leonardo da Vinci in the Florentine Gallery. Shelley. GS

It lights up. Chine. JDP, *tr. by* Yoel Hoffmann

It little profits that an idle king. Ulysses. Tennyson. AWP; AmFaPo; CABP; ClHu; EBEV; FHYEP; HAP; HeIP-4; InPK-6; MakPoe; NAEL-5v2; NAEL-6v2; NAWM-7v2; NIL-7; NIP-4; NOBE; NOBVV; NPeEn; NoP-4; OxAEP-2; OxBEV; PoE; PoPoPo; PoRA; SCGP; SCV; SoSe-8; TFi; TRP; UnPo; WeW-3

It looked extremely rocky for the Mudville nine that day. Casey at the Bat. Ernest Lawrence Thayer. ChAP; ITBLP; PoRA

It looks like she's drowning. Gwyneth Lewis. NeBl

It looks to me like a hero's welcome. Anna Akhmatova's Funeral. Martin Mooney. ModIr

It Makes a Change. Mervyn Laurence Peake. OTCP

It matters little where I was born. What Does It Matter? Noah Barker. PWR

It matters not if the pasture is far. Cowherd; a Song, The. Ch'u Kuang-hsi. SuSp, *tr. by* Joseph J. Lee

It may be able for resistance found. (LL) Philip Freneau. NAAL-2v1; NAAL-3 *Fr.* House of Night, The.

It may be that she wields a pen. Note. Mary Abigail Dodge (Gail Hamilton). SWaP

It may be these things never did occur. Kinnereth. "Rachel" [*or* "Rahel"]. TrJP, *tr. by* A. M. Klein

It may be / they dare to. Whitewash. Léon Damas. NegPo, *tr. by* Ellen Conroy Kennedy

It may be true that she has passed her spring. Beauty of Ilona Zrínyi, The. István Gyöngyösi. IQMS, *tr. by* Watson Kirkconnell

It may be when the sunlight strikes the sill. In Your Absence. Elizabeth Baxter. PoToHe

It may happen again—this much. Flight, The. John Haines. SPE

It may indeed be phantasy [*or* fantasy], when I. To Nature. Samuel Taylor Coleridge. OxBSo

It may not always be so; and i say. E. E. Cummings. BoLoP

It may of course be John his father-in-law. Stone Face, The. Harri Webb. AngWePo

It means everything. Sizeline. Felix Mnthali. PeSAV

It midnights, not a moon is out. Midnightmouse, The. Christian Morgenstern. RB, *tr. by* Lore Segal and W. D. Snodgrass

It Might as Well Be Spring. Richard Rodgers. ReLy

It might be any night. These Days. Andrew Motion. DiPo

It might be lonelier. Emily Dickinson. APN-2; SAmP; TCAPo

It might be so. (LL) Slice of Wedding Cake, A. Robert Graves. BoLoP; NAEL-5v2; NAEL-6v2; NOBE; OxBTC

It might give us—what?—some flowers soon? (LL) What Is Poetry. John Ashbery. HarvBoo; LCAP-2

It might have been a neurotic's paradise. Cana. Peter Steele. GI

It Might Have Been Worse. G. J. Russell. PoToHe

It might mean immersion, that sign. Alice Fulton. ExTi

It might seem matter for regret. Lower Life, The. May Kendall. VWP

It mounts at sea, a concave wall. From the Wave. Thom Gunn. NAEL-5v2; NAEL-6v2; NoP-4

It moves out through the room. Polka. Diane Jarvenpa. MiVo

It must acknowledge the spiritual forces which have made it. (LL) When I Buy Pictures. Marianne Craig Moore. APT-1; ColAP; OxBA

It Must Be Abstract. Wallace Stevens. ColAP; NOBA *Fr.* Notes toward a Supreme Fiction.

It must be done, my soul, but 'tis a strange. Meditation, The. John Norris. NOSC

It must be mine! no other heart could prove. Returned Heart, The. Sarah Dixon. ECWP

It must have been a Friday. I could hear. Katherine's Dream. Robert Lowell. CoAmPo

It must have been a single thread of tears. Meng Chiao. SuSp *Fr.* Apricots Die Young.

It must have been 1988. For Whom the Bells Toll and Toll and Toll. John Nelson. GeoH

It must have been one o'clock at night. Comes to Rest. Constantine P. Cavafy. CAGL, *tr. by* Edmund Keeley and Philip Sherrard

It must have been one or one-thirty. To Remain. Constantine P. Cavafy. BoLoP, *tr. by* Stephen Spender and Nikos Stangos

It must've been lousy. (LL) Elizabethans Called It Dying, The. James Schuyler. NeAP; PoM

It nearly cancels my fear of death, my dearest said. Cremation. Robinson Jeffers. BLT

It needn't have ribaldry's taint. Limerick. Don Marquis. PeLi

It neither was the words nor yet the tune. Two Girls Singing. Iain Crichton Smith. NePenScot

It Never Entered My Mind. Richard Rodgers. ReLy

It Never Was You. Kurt Weill. ReLy

It nods and curtseys and recovers. A. E. Housman. NOBVV; OxBEV

It occurred on the evening before Waterloo. Old Sam. Stanley Holloway. OBCoV

It occurred when she crossed the Atlantic. Limerick. *Unknown.* PeLi

It occurs to me now. Lesson, The. Charles Simic. AF; HCAP

It once happened. Issa. EH, *tr. by* Robert Hass

It once might have been, once only. Youth and Art. Robert Browning. CTC; NAEL-5v2; NAEL-6v2; NOBVV; NPeEn

It Out-Herods Herod. Pray You, Avoid It. Anthony Hecht. AF; CoAP; NIP-4; NOBA; NoAM; OxBC

It pales. As if a look. Horae. Robert Fitzgerald. APT-2

It passes, you'll remember, through lead. Passes through. Workmen Photographed inside the Reactor. David Wojahn. IllVoic

It pierces through me. Buson. WoPoe, *tr. by* Tony Barnstone

It piles up, thick and formidable, on the marble terrace. Shadow of Flowers, The. Su Tung-p'o (Su Shih). OHPC, *tr. by* Kenneth Rexroth

It pours. Night Rain. Karen L. Mitchell. GT

It put forth buds at the end of the Nine Splendors. Fragrant Tree, The. Shen Yüeh. SuSp, *tr. by* Richard B. Mather

It puts itself right. (LL) Cat and the Weather. May Swenson. HAP; WeW-3

It puzzles much the sages' brains. On Lord Cobham's Garden. Nathaniel Cotton. OBGa

It raindrops on the cold. Introit. Padraic Fiacc. CIP-2

It rained in my sleep. September. Linda Pastan. InvLad

It rained quite a lot, that spring. You woke in the morning. Metropolitan Nightmare. Stephen Vincent Benét. APT-2

It Rains. Edward Thomas. OxBEV; OxBTC; PoE

It rains above the sea in gentle murmurs. Gray Waves. Leopoldo Lugones. TCLAP, *tr. by* Julie Schumacher

It rains across the country I remember. (LL) Mnemosyne. Trumbull Stickney. APN-2; NOBA; OxBA; TCAPo

It rains on the roofs. Sottoportico San Zaccaria. Kenneth Rexroth. ErotSp

It rattles dully on the roof. Rain. Konstantin Iakovlevich Vanshenkin. TCRusP, *tr. by* Daniel Weissbort

It really irks me to think I'm afraid of heights. Abyss. Diane Di Prima. BB

"It relaxes me," he said. Six Reasons for Drinking. Vernon Scannell. OxBC

It rests me to be among beautiful women. Tame Cat. Ezra Pound. APT-1; OBAL

It rises over the lake, the farms. Kite, The. Mark Strand. ColAP

It rose dark as a stack of peat. Suilven. Andrew Young. OxBS

It's a beautiful day: sunny, crisp, cloudless. Flexible. William Kulik. BodElec

It's a Bit Rich. Max Fatchen. OTCP

It's a Blue World. Robert Wright. ReLy

It's a comfort to me in life's battle. Little Child's Faith, The. Louis E. Thayer. PoToHe

It's a funny thing. Poem for Sigmund. Lorna Crozier. LW

It's a Good Day. Peggy Lee. ReLy

It's a good harvest this year. "Mang Ke." PFTM-2, *tr. by* Nicholas Jose and Wu Baohe *Fr.* Aperhd.

It's a good thing Dad deserted Mom. How I Came to Have a Man's Name. Emma Lee Warrior. HATNAP

It's a grand thing when you're old, love. Life's Golden Sunset. Mrs. Henry Linden. CBWP-4

It's a Great Big Shame. Edgar Bateman. OBCoV

It's a Hard, Hard World for a Man. P. G. Wodehouse. ReLy

It's a hell / creeping back into. Back into the Garden. Sarah Webster Fabio. BlSi

It's a lazy afternoon. Lazy Afternoon. John Latouche. ReLy

It's a lean car. . .a long-legged dog of a car. . .a gray-ghost eagle.   Portrait of a Motorcar.   Carl Sandburg.   APT-1

It's a limited edition given out by the Gideons.   Bill, Posted, A.   Philip Kobylarz.   BAP-97

It's a long time since the dawn chase over shires.   Hunt-Cup, The.   Daniel Tobin.   NAPBL

It's a long walk in the dark.   John's Song.   Joan Aiken.   TLR

It's a long way to Tipperary.   Tipperary.   Desmond O'Grady.   BiHa

It's a Lovely Day Today.   Irving Berlin.   ReLy

It's a Low Down Dirty Shame.   Ollie Shepard.   NAAAL

It's a madman, I said.   Dream.   Nana Issaia.   BoWoP, tr. by Helle Tzaopoulou Barnstone

It's a Most Unusual Day.   Jimmy McHugh.   ReLy

It's a nightmare that horrifies hakes.   Limerick.   Allan M. Laing.   PeLi

It's a Party (1959).   Baron Wormser.   SeSe

It's a pity that Casabianca.   Limerick.   Victor Gray.   PeLi

It's a Queer Time.   Robert Graves.   MoBrPo

It's a question of altitude, or latitude.   Brute Image.   John Ashbery.   NoP-4

It's a real old-fashioned butcher's shop.   Crafty Butcher, The.   Susan Hampton.   BMAP; NOBAu

It's a real rock.   Wobbly Rock.   Lew Welch.   PoM

It's a rheumatic world if you ever stop to listen.   What Happens in Shakzpeare.   Alan Brunton.   PeNZ

It's a sentimental toy for children.   Battery Woman.   Pierre McOrlan.   MFP, tr. by Martin Sorrell

It's a sheroot, that's what.   To Jerusalem, 1990.   Myra Shapiro.   OPRER

It's a sign of the times when even barbers.   Phanias.   GrAn

It's a singular thing that Ned.   Ned.   Eleanor Farjeon.   OTCP

It's a slow, slow process.   On Watching a Caterpillar Become a Butterfly.   Clarence Major.   NAAAL

It's a slow warmth I find once more.   Luigi Fontanella.   NeIt

It's a south wind that drives you back.   Hardon ("Get One Today").   Ian Wedde.   PeNZ

It's a story as famous as the three little pigs.   Going out for Cigarettes.   Billy Collins.   OPRER

It's a strange courage.   El Hombre.   William Carlos Williams.   SAmP

It's a sudden hue.   Resolve.   Leslie Ullman.   ExTi

It's a sunny pleasant anchorage, is Kingdom Come.   Port of Many Ships.   John Masefield.   OBMV

It's a Terrible Thing!   Everett Hoagland.   BPo

It's a thrill to love a boy: even Kronos' son, king of immortals, once longed for Ganymede.   Theognis.   CAGL, tr. by Peter Bing and Rip Cohen   Fr. Second Book of Theognis, The.

It's a Thursday, getting late.   Barbells of the Gods, The.   Mark Cox.   OPRER

It's a town house built between the wars.   Aerial, The.   Robert Minhinnick.   TCAWP

It's a very odd thing.   Miss T.   Walter De la Mare.   NTCP

It's a wandering kind of crazy way I'm taken.   Visiting New York.   Sarah Rosenblatt.   AmPoNex

It's a warm wind, the west wind, full of birds' cries.   West Wind, The.   John Masefield.   CABP; MoBrPo

It's a weary life, it is.   From the Antique.   Christina Georgina Rossetti.   OxBEV; PEW

It's a white nest!   Small Bird's Nest Made of White Reed Fiber, A.   Robert Bly.   NNaP

It's a Woman's World.   Eavan Boland.   CIP-2; ItWoWo

It's a Wonder.   Monique Charbonel.   SurWo, tr. by Myrna Bell Rochester

It's aborbed, perceived, partially picked up. The brighness envelops.   Alicia Kozameh.   MirDau, tr. by David Davis   Fr. Saltos Sobre El Exilio.

It's about style.   Place Where He Arose, The.   George Barlow.   GT

It's after one.   Last Statement.   Vladimir Vladimirovich Mayakovsky [or Maiakovskii].   PBCIP, tr. by Tom Paulin

It's all.   Young Girl Peeling Apples.   Mary Jo Salter.   FFC

It's all Aboard for THIS IS IT. (LL)   P.O.E.   Lincoln Kirstein.   APT-2; PoWW

It's all familiar.   Dream, A.   Bella [or Izabella] Akhatovna Akhmadulina.   BoWoP, tr. by Olga Carlisle and Jean Valentine

It's all go to Claridges, it's all go to the champers.   More Bagpipe Music.   E. O. Parrott.   UV

It's all ordinary experience.   Dream and Poetry.   Hu Shih.   WoPoe, tr. by Kai-yu Hsu

It's all over.   Andrey Dmitrievich Dementyev [or Dement'ev].   TCRP

It's All Right with Me.   Cole Porter.   ReLy

It's All the Same.   Thadious M. Davis.   BlSi

It's all the same to me what time it is.   Paradise Lost, Book IV, lines 639—654.   Leslie Johnson.   UV

It's all the same to morning what it dawns on.   Aubade.   Nuala Ni Dhomhnaill.   BiHa; PBCIP, tr. by Michael Longley

It's all / Too much to bear!   How I Became a Dog.   Vladimir Vladimirovich Mayakovsky [or Maiakovskii].   TCRP, tr. by Bernard Meares

It's all very well for preachin'   Pledge at Spunky Point, The.   John Milton Hay.   OBAL

It's all very well to dream of a dove that saves.   Birdwatchers of America.   Anthony Hecht.   NOBA; NoAM

It's All Yours.   Dorothy Fields.   ReLy

It's almost Biblical driving this midnight burning highway.   Red Velvet Jacket.   Lynda Hull.   ExTi

It's already past one. You'll have gone to bed.   Vladimir Vladimirovich Mayakovsky [or Maiakovskii].   TCRP

It's always.   Dark, The.   Myra Cohn Livingston.   TLR

It's always ourselves we find in the sea. (LL)   Maggie and Milly and Molly and May.   E. E. Cummings.   ChAP; NOBA; NOxBChV; NoAM; RB

It's an awful feeling to watch the moon and stars above.   Shake Down the Stars.   Eddie DeLange.   ReLy

It's an easy game, this reviewin'—the editor sends yer a book.   Ballad of George R. Sims, The.   Sir John Betjeman.   OBCoV; UV

It's an ordinary rock.   From the Wailing Wall.   Enid Shomer.   TaR

It's an overcome sooth for age an' youth.   Robert Louis Stevenson.   NOBVV; OxBEV

It's any kid's most exquisite fantasy.   David Wojahn.   AllShUp; PBCAP   Fr. Mystery Train: A Sequence.

It's as if our heads were on fire, the way.   Kando.   ZenPo, tr. by Takashi Ikemoto and Lucien Stryk

It's autumn in the country I remember.   Mnemosyne.   Trumbull Stickney.   APN-2; NOBA; OxBA; TCAPo

It's awf'lly bad luck on Diana.   Hunter Trials.   Sir John Betjeman.   OBCoV

It's awf'ly nice of all you girls to see me to the train.   So Long, Mary.   George M. Cohan.   ReLy

It's bad luck with a coughing baby.   John Tranter.   CBAP   Fr. Crying in Early Infancy.

It's been a hard winter, but summer is here and the fields.   Tomas Tranströmer.   RaBo   Fr. Standing Up.

It's been a long day's drive through a landscape.   Cinema Point.   Philip Mead.   BMAP

It's been a long time.   Joanne Kyger.   BB

It's been almost thirty-five years.   Valentino's Hair.   Yvonne Sapia.   PeVV; TRP

It's been 50 years since.   My Father's Retirement.   A. Van Jordan.   SpirFl

It's been forever since I returned to walk.   Remembering East Mountain.   Li Po.   CrYelRi, tr. by Sam Hamill

It's been going on a long time.   Way of Life, A.   Howard Nemerov.   NIL-7; NIP-4

It's been like fixing a clock, jamming the wheels.   Making Up for a Soul.   David Wagoner.   VGW

It's been pelting down.   Sheltering Places.   Gerald Dawe.   PNI

It's Been So Long.   Walter Donaldson.   ReLy

It's been so long since I headed for East Mountain.   Thinking of East Mountain.   Li Po.   CoBCP; TTTS, tr. by Burton Watson

It's been this way for some time.   New Jersey Turnpike.   Richard Cumbie.   NBLV

It's been years since we left Ethiopia.   Mother of Andromeda, The.   Julie Fay.   NAPBL

It's best made in dry-fish camp.   How to Make Good Baked Salmon from the River.   Nora Dauenhauer.   ReEnLa

It's best to be best.   Best?   Siv Widerberg.   NTCP, tr. by Verne Moberg

It's better not to live in Moscow.   Dmitry [or Dmitrii] Aleksandrovich Prigov.   ItGoST, tr. by Robert Reid

It's bright the icy foam as it flows.   From Exile.   Dafydd [or David] Benfras.   OBWVE, tr. by Anthony Conran

It's brilliant. It's a tear you can stand a car.   Prince Rupert's Drop, The.   Jane Draycott.   OxBSo

It's cold at last and cautious winds creep.   Grandfather at the Indian Health Clinic.   Elizabeth Cook-Lynn.   HATNAP; UnSA

It's cold, you say, the house.   From a Conversation during Divorce.   Carol Rumens.   EmeKit

It's common to say of bad acting, or family photos like these.   Family Grove.   Albert Goldbarth.   HCAP

It's crazy to think one could describe them.   Robert Pinsky.   NoAM   Fr. Essay on Psychiatrists.

It's dark, almost foggy, the first day.   Runaway.   Honor Moore.   Unle

It's dark . . . / The bastard street lamp's run away.   Drunkard's Nocturnes, A. "Sasha Chorny [or Chiornyi]."   TCRP, tr. by Bernard Meares

It's darker than the dark bottom.   Doing the Reactionary.   Harold Rome.   ReLy

It's daybreak and I wish I could believe.   Paul Celan: A Grave and Mysterious Sentence.   Edward Hirsch.   TaR

It's De-Lovely.   Cole Porter.   ReLy

It's devilishly hot.   Poem Seen in a Motel Fan.   Alberto Blanco.   CLPP, tr. by John Oliver Simon

It's difficult to say what it all meant.   Jack, Afterwards.   Philip Dacey.   ReTh

It's disturbing that it's not a surprise. Undertakers. Robert Johnstone. PNI

It's done phonetically, of course, at great. Francis Ford Coppola and Anthropologist Interpreter Teaching Gartewienna Tribesmen to Sing "Light My Fire," Philippine Jungle, 1978. David Wojahn. ReTh

It's driving into all that goldness makes. California, *She Replied.* Kathy Fagan. GeoHom

It's dull in the huge palace where I live. Warm to the Cuddly-toy Charm of a Koala Bear. Gavin Ewart. EmeKit

It's early morning and across the street. Homage to Sharon Stone. Lynn Emanuel. BodElec

It's early when we set out on the Ch'en-ts'ang Road. Ch'ai-kuan Mountain Pass. Wang Shih-chieng. ColAnChi, *tr. by* Richard John Lynn

It's earthquake weather in California. Earthquake Weather. Janice Gould. GeoHom

It's Easy. Lee Cataldi. BMAP

It's easy for me to believe. On Inheriting Departure. HeidiLynn Nilsson. NeAmPo

It's easy to be witty in French. For the Common Market. Michael Burn. OBCoV

It's easy to invent a Life. Emily Dickinson. APN-2; TCAPo

It's either the Prize or a terminal worry. Memory, A. Heinrich Heine. WoPoe, *tr. by* Francis C. Golffing

It's fading. By an Unknown Poet from Eastern Europe, 1955. György Petri. VCWP, *tr. by* George Gömöri and Clive Wilmer

It's February But. Janet Fisher. MFPA

It's fifty miles to Sittingen's Rocks. Prince Robert. *Unknown.* ESPB; OxBB

It's 5 A.M. I'm wide awake so to your bed I race. Lewis Describes His Day. Merrill Markoe. Unle

It's five o'clock. Someone's taped my name out. Threnody for Sunset. Richard Cecil. BodElec

It's 4 P.M. the day before Christmas and I think of you. Memories of Christmas. Joy Williams. IBA

It's freezing and you try to remember June. Against Numerology. Richard Caddel. Oth

It's Friday night and I've just had. 6/20/97. Harvey Shapiro. KGB

It's from before the spin of human fire. Chambered Nautilus. Linda Hogan. BodElec

It's full as Opera. (LL) Emily Dickinson. APN-2; NCAP; TCAPo

It's fun to take speed. Speed, a Pastoral. John Forbes. BMAP

It's funny, but I don't remember much. Depressive Episode. Janet Holmes. ExTi

It's funny how beetles. Upside Down. Aileen Fisher. OTCP

It's funny to look at a hurrying hound. Hound, The. Kaye Starbird. KaS

It's Gardena, late Saturday afternoon. Winnings. Garrett Kaoru Hongo. GeoHom; OpBo

It's getting dark, little thief of starlight! Tristan Corbière. WoPoe, *tr. by* Randall Jarrell *Fr. Afterwards.*

It's getting / to be a thing. Be You. Norman Jordan. NBV

It's going to be a thick night tonight. Officers' Mess. Gavin Ewart. FaBoWar; OxBTC

It's gonna rain any minute. Good for Nothin' Joe. Ted Koehler. ReLy

It's good, isn't it? Nowadays. John Kander. ReLy

It's good, my child, you often wash your hair. Pope Alexander VI. Geoffrey Lehmann. NOBAu

It's Got to Be Love. Richard Rodgers. ReLy

It's great to be alive, and be. It's Simply Great. Sidney Warren Mase. PoToHe

It's Halloween. Jack Prelutsky. NTCP

It's Hard to Dislike Ewart. Gavin Ewart. OBCoV

It's hard to know if you're alive or dead. It's a Queer Time. Robert Graves. MoBrPo

It's hard to say, John, but I need some money. Imre Madách. IQMS, *tr. by* Iain MacLeod *Fr. Tragedy of Man.*

It's hard to see but think of a sea. Louis Zukofsky. APT-2; VGW

It's hard to tell what bird it is. After Frost. Brian Patten. EBEV

It's hard to understand how one can leave. Stanislav Iurievich Kunyayev [*or* Kuniaev]. TCRP

It's here at last. Eyes in the know. Comet Come. Norman Nicholson. NLP

It's hot, and smoggy as Mars outside. Dennis Cooper. ReTh *Fr. Some Adventures of John Kennedy Jr.*

It's impossible to live. Hierofant. Oswald de Andrade. TCLAP, *tr. by* Flavia Vidal

It's in the Egg. Joe Rosenblatt. NOBC

It's in the featureless. Son et Lumière. Mark Todd. GeoH

It's in the perilous boughs of the tree. Childhood's Retreat. Robert Duncan. NoAM

It's just as well that now you save your breath. (LL) To an American Poet Just Dead. Richard Wilbur. HCAP; NBLV

It's just begun. (LL) To a Child Trapped in a Barber Shop. Philip Levine. InPK-6; NOBA; NoAM; PAI; TAP; VGW

It's just no use. Execution. James A. Randall, Jr. BPo

It's just the little homely things. Little Things. *Unknown.* PoToHe

It's Kind of Lonesome out Tonight. Duke Ellington. ReLy

It's kind of you to let me come alone. Imre Madách. IQMS, *tr. by* Iain MacLeod *Fr. Tragedy of Man.*

It's Lamkin was a mason good. Lamkin. *Unknown.* ESPB; NPeEn; OxBB

It's languor and ecstasy. Paul Verlaine. SxFrPo, *tr. by* Martin Sorrell

It's leaving thee, my bonnie [*or* bony] Mary! (LL) Silver Tassie, The. Robert Burns. NOBE; OBEV; WoPoe

It's like a jungle sometimes, it makes me wonder. Message, The. Grandmaster Flash and the Furious Five. NAAAL

It's like a story. Alive or Not. Alfred Wellington Purdy. NOBC

It's like a tap-dance. Muriel Rukeyser. MakPoe

It's like a terrible dream designed to make you scream. Drama, The. Suliaman El-Hadi. SpirFl

It's like snow. Statue, The. Ivano Fermini. ItPo, *tr. by* Gayle Ridinger

It's like the Light. Emily Dickinson. FaBoVe

It's like the riddle Tolstoy. Slow Dance. David St. John. LCAP-2

It's like the sweet must that wasps. When Slow October Changes Color. Umberto Piersanti. NeIt, *tr. by* Stephen Sartarelli

It's little I care what path I take. Departure. Edna St. Vincent Millay. MoAmPo

It's long way from Keats' Corner to Sandburg Ave. All around the Town. Genevieve Taggard. APT-2

It's Love Again. Sam Coslow. ReLy

It's Magic. Sammy Cahn. ReLy

It's me, Cassandra. Monologue for Cassandra. Wisława Szymborska. PoSu, *tr. by* Grazyna Drabik

It's me—I am a War Eagle! *Unknown.* APN-2 *Fr. War Dance.*

It's me, O passerby, the poplar tree. *Unknown.* PriapPo, *tr. by* Richard W. Hooper *Fr. Priapus Poems, The.*

It's me, the pregnant Puerto Rican girls, short Mexicans. Me and Baby. Ana Castillo. IllVoic

It's midnight in a drizzling fog. North of Santa Monica. Carter Revard. VoR

It's Miller Time. Víctor Hernández Cruz. PueRic; TouFir

It's more than just an easy word for casual good-bye. Aloha Oe. Don Blanding. PoToHe

It's much too cold to travel. Going and Coming of Sequins. Joyce Mansour. PFTM-2, *tr. by* Molly Bendall

"It's my custom," said dear Lady Norris. Limerick. *Unknown.* PeLi

It's my lunch hour, so I go. Step Away from Them, A. Frank O'Hara. CoAmPo; HCAP; NAAL-2v2; VCAP; VGW; WoPoe

It's narrow, narrow, make your bed. Fair Annie. *Unknown.* ESPB

It's natural the Boys should whoop it up for. Moon Landing. W. H. Auden. EmeKit; OxAEP-2

It's nearly ten o'clock in the morning and I have work to do. Walking the Baby to the Liquor Store. Michael Van Walleghen. IllVoic

It's Never Too Late to Fall in Love. Sandy Wilson. ReLy

It's nice that though you are casual about me. Sulpicia. BoWoP

It's night, an extra quilt. Steve Sims. NewEx

It's nightfall and between two grey facades. Souvenir. Paul Van Ostaijen. TuT, *tr. by* Tony Curtis

It's 1982 and 200 years gone by. White Man Problem, The. Jim Everett. IBA

It's no coincidence / this is a used. Tricks with Mirrors. Margaret Atwood. NIP-4

It's no go the merry-go-round [*or* merrygoround], it's no go the rickshaw. Bagpipe Music. Louis MacNeice. CABP; GTBS-P; HarvBoo; MakPoe; NAEL-5v2; NAEL-6v2; NBLV; NOBE; NOBL; NoAM; NoP-4; OBSV; OxBEV; OxBTC; PeLV; RB; TFi; UV

It's no great matter what men deem. Resolution, The. Richard Baxter. SacPoe

It's no great step for a poor man to the grave. Palladas [*or* Pallades]. GrAn

It's no one else's fault, Syama Ma. Dāśarathi Rāy. SinGod, *tr. by* Rachel Fell McDermott

It's no use. Sappho. HW, *tr. by* Mary Barnard

"It's no use," he says, "she's left me." This is after several. In a Tavern. Louis Jenkins. RaBo

It's No Use Raising a Shout. W. H. Auden. OBMV

It's Nostalgia Week at Frank 'n' Helen's. At Frank 'n' Helen's. Constance Urdang. PBCAP

It's not a dress, and he hasn't got the lips. Girl in a Fur-Trimmed Dress. Honor Moore. WiU

It's not always easy. Face the Animal. Jean Follain. BLT, *tr. by* Heather McHugh

It's not as if we never played at cards. Playing at Cards. Belle Randall. CRP

It's not bad news, it's no news at all that this night. City Life. Alvin Greenberg. UrbNat

It's not celestial music it's the girl in the bathroom singing.   Ode on Celestial Music.   Brian Patten.   OxBTC

It's not like anything.   Basho.   EH, tr. by Robert Hass

It's Not Me Shouting at No One.   Lawrence Joseph.   GraLe

It's not much of a choice.   Troth.   Michael Davidson.   FTOS

It's not much of a fall with.   Improvisation for Jerald Bullis, An.   A. R. Ammons.   BodElec

It's not my world, I grant, but I made it.   Ride.   Josephine Miles.   FaBoWP

It's not nature that upholds utility.   Gudo.   ZenPo, tr. by Takashi Ikemoto and Lucien Stryk

It's not only the accumulation of small slights.   Keep Going.   Gail Mazur.   ExTi

It's not Siva.   Rāmprasād Sen.   SinGod, tr. by Rachel Fell McDermott

It's Not so Good to be Born a Girl / Sometimes.   Ntozake Shange.   SSLK

It's not so much the partis pris as.   Philosophical Songs.   Charles North.   KGB

It's not so much what you say.   Tone of Voice, The.   Unknown.   PoToHe

It's not something I like to burden my readers with as a rule.   How Much Is This Poem Going to Cost Me?   Denise Duhamel.   NeAmPo

It's not surprising.   Pan Cogito on Virtue.   Zbigniew Herbert.   PoSu, tr. by Adam Czerniawski

It's not that I don't like the hospital.   Lost in the Hospital.   Rafael Campo.   AmPoNex

It's not that you were present.   Mourning.   Daniel Weissbort.   GI

It's not the year two-thousand, my poor love.   Towards the New Millennium.   Zoltán Jékely.   IQMS, tr. by George Szirtes

It's not too late I suppose.   How to Write Anglo-Welsh Poetry.   John Davies.   AngWePo; TCAWP

It's not when they leave.   Maya Borisova.   TCRusP, tr. by Daniel Weissbort

It's nothing really, and really, it could have been worse, and of course, he's.   Grandfather-in-law.   David Mura.   LoL

It's November the thirty-third.   Ninth Symmetrical Poem.   Michael Palmer.   HarvBoo

It's of a rich squire in Bristol doth dwell.   Squire and Milkmaid; or, Blackberry Fold.   Unknown.   OxBB

It's of a young lord o' the Hielands.   Lizie Lindsay.   Unknown.   ESPB

It's of three rioters I have to tell.   Geoffrey Chaucer.   SCV   Fr. Canterbury Tales, The.

It's off in the distance.   Song of My Song, in Three Parts, A.   Unknown.   STP, tr. by Richard Johnny John and Jerome Rothenberg

It's on this railroad bank I stand.   Careless Love.   Unknown.   UnPo

It's once I courted as pretty a lass.   Unknown.   OxNR

It's Only a Paper Moon.   Harold Arlen.   ReLy

It's only a trickle.   Laocoon / Serpent.   Novica Tadic.   VCWP, tr. by Charles Simic

It's only a week but already you are slipping.   History.   Maura Dooley.   NeBl

It's only at Christmas and New Year.   Fitzroy.   Andrew Taylor.   BMAP

"It's Only Rock and Roll but I Like It:" The Fall of Saigon, 1975.   David Wojahn.   IllVoic; ReTh

It's only the attic I miss.   Anorexic, The.   Ruth Anderson Barnett.   OPRER

It's only whiskey that makes you pity me.   Kagank.   STP

It's over a(see just).   E. E. Cummings.   OxBA; VGW

It's over, love. Look at me pushing fifty now.   Late Night Ode.   Horace.   WiU; WoPoe, tr. by J. D. McClatchy

It's over now; I've known it all.   Emily Jane Brontë.   NOBVV

It's over now, the time for observation, for.   Maurizio Cucchi.   ItPo, tr. by Gayle Ridinger

It's pleasant to board the ferry in the sunscape.   Déjeuner sur l'herbe.   Tu Fu.   BLT; CarOv, tr. by Carolyn Kizer

It's practically impossible.   Guerrilla War.   William Daniel Ehrhart.   CDa

It's probably the year her marriage.   Satin Doll.   David Wojahn.   PBCAP

It's quarter to three.   One for My Baby (And One More for the Road).   Johnny Mercer.   ReLy

"It's queer," she said; "I see the light."   Maid-Servant at the Inn, The.   Dorothy Parker.   ChrPo

It's quiet for me, now that I have buried the child.   Ritual Three.   David Ignatow.   CoAmPo

It's quiet here among the haunted tenses.   Last of England, The.   Peter Porter.   GS

It's quiet in Hell just now, it's very tame.   Lament of an Idle Demon.   Richard Percival Lister.   NOBL

It's quiet in the house so quiet.   Mother's Song.   Unknown.   WoPoe, tr. by Stephen Berg

It's Raining.   Guillaume Apollinaire.   TTTS

It's raining.   Rain, The.   Valerie Patterson Napanangka.   IBA

It's raining . . . don't sleep yet.   Rainy Night.   Juana de Ibarbourou.   TCLAP, tr. by Sophie Cabot Black

It's raining, it's pouring.   Unknown.   OxNR

It's raining stair-rods and chairlegs.   Black Wet, The.   W. N. Herbert.   NeBl

It's really something, the onion.   Onion.   Wislawa Szymborska.   PoSu, tr. by Grazyna Drabik

It's run an' jump an' hop an' skip.   Owdham Footbo'   Ammon Wrigley.   FaBoVe

It's sad that it rains in the Autumn.   Fever Tune.   Karel Van de Woestijne.   TuT, tr. by Tony Curtis

It's sad / To be the Mayor of Jerusalem.   Mayor.   Yehuda Amichai [or Amikhai].   PoSu, tr. by Assia Gutmann

It's said you spoke once and then chose silence.   Refusing the Call.   Enid Shomer.   TaR

It's said you take a long time over a bath.   Lucilius.   GrAn

It's Saturday afternoon at the edge of the world.   Laguna Blues.   Charles Wright.   PoPoPo

It's Saturday night, and I'm feeling reckless.   Saturday Night.   Sir Alan Patrick Herbert.   NBLV

It's 7 A.M. mother, the walking.   Election Day.   R. Zamora-Linmark.   ReBoTo

It's silly to hope for Father's wealth.   Rāmprasād Sen.   SinGod, tr. by Rachel Fell McDermott

It's Simply Great.   Sidney Warren Mase.   PoToHe

It's '66 and Keaton's playing.   Buster's Last Hand.   Jennifer O'Grady.   AmPoNex

It's smoke, the star, a broom.   Smoke.   Rubén Bonitaz Nuño.   STV, tr. by John Frederick Nims

It's / snowing defective.   Self-Pity Is a Kind of Lying, Too.   James Schuyler.   BodElec; PoM

It's snowing hard enough that the taxis aren't running.   Rites of Manhood, The.   Alden Nowlan.   RaBo

It's so dark now.   Tip, The.   Albert Goldbarth.   HCAP

It's so easy.   Buddy Holly Poem, The.   Maurice Kilwein Guevara.   TouFir

It's so hard to say in a son's words.   Prayer to My Mother.   Pier Paolo Pasolini.   VCWP

It's so much easier to get further from home than nearer that all men become travelers.   Vectors: Forty-five Aphorisms and Ten-second Essays.   James Richardson.   BAP-01

It's So Peaceful in the Country.   Alec Wilder.   ReLy

It's so pure in the cemetery.   Not Like That.   Adrienne Rich.   EmeKit

It's soldiers who sing these days. (LL)   White Low Sun, A.   Marina Ivanovna Tsvetayeva [or Tsvetaeva].   AF; PeFWW, tr. by David McDuff

It's Spring Returning, It's Spring and Love.   Unknown.   HAP

It's still a good idea.   To Friends Who Have Also Considered Suicide.   Phyllis Webb.   NOBC

It's still here. It's still here-er. Be ready. Be ready.   Mothering.   Carla Harryman.   FTOS

It's such a / Bore.   Ennui.   Langston Hughes.   OBAL; OBCA

It's such a little thing to weep.   Life's Trades.   Emily Dickinson.   RB; TCAPo

It's Sunday evening. Pomp holds the receipts.   Chopin.   Marilyn Nelson.   RA

It's Sunday, October ninth, and the earth here is barren after harvest.   Gary Young.   GeoHom   Fr. Braver Deeds.

It's sweaty work, the getting ready part.   Early Thoughts of Winter.   Maxine W. Kumin.   ExTi

It's ten. Evening. The room is in half light.   My Sister.   Alfonsina Storni.   BoWoP, tr. by Aliki and Willis Barnstone

It's that hour when I empty my dreams of my existence in order.   Hot and Cold.   Silvio Giussani.   ItPo, tr. by Gayle Ridinger

It's that old devil called love again.   That Old Devil Called Love.   Allan Roberts.   ReLy

It's the anarchy of poverty.   Poor, The.   William Carlos Williams.   MoAmPo

It's the boom of ice.   When She Laughs.   Judith Sornberger.   HW

It's the broken phrases, the fury inside him.   Art Pepper.   Edward Hirsch.   SeSe

It's the ceaseless wind.   Insomnia.   Debra Nystrom.   AWTN

It's the country of childhood.   Jardin des Colombières.   Lauris Edmond.   OBGA

It's the darkest morning of the year.   St. Thomas's Day.   Gillian Clarke.   HarvBoo

It's the Enobarbus Complex.   Unknown.   GrAn

It's the first night, I suppose.   First Night, A.   Peter Kane Dufault.   DiPo; NoP-4

It's the fourteenth of August, and I'm too hot.   Tu Fu.   CarOv, tr. by Carolyn Kizer   Fr. Banishment.

It's the hot air, the dare, the heat of sway.   Blames, for Rane and Diane.   Glenn Sheldon.   MiVo

It's the kind of place where.   American Standard.   David Baratier.   AmPoNex

It's the last snow of the season.   All, the Nothing, The.   Yves Bonnefoy.   VCWP, tr. by Lisa Sapinkopf

It's the long road to Guinea.   Guinea.   Jacques Roumain.   NegPo; TTY, tr. by Langston Hughes

It's the old rule that drunks have to argue.   New Rule, The.   Jelaluddin [or Jalal al-Din] Rumi.   RaBo, tr. by Coleman Barks and Robert Bly

It's the only thing Kenji Takezo does.   Breath He Holds, The.   Rick Noguchi. NeAmPo

It's the poor first light of morning.   Obscure, The.   Norman Dubie.   NoAM

It's the ragged source of memory.   House on Moscow Street, The.   Marilyn Nelson Waniek.   UnSA

It's the same thing with me. (LL)   Mutual Problem.   William Cole.   OBAL; OBCoV

It's the story of a very unfortunate Memphis man.   Hong Kong Blues.   Hoagy Carmichael.   ReLy

It's the story that counts.   Margaret Atwood.   NALW   *Fr.* Circe / Mud Poems.

It's the Talk of the Town.   A. J. Neiburg.   ReLy

It's the torque of a spring Sunday.   Blues in "C."   Ron Overton.   SeSe

It's the wine, this ache, this longing.   Song.   Liu Yung.   CrYelRi, *tr.* by Sam Hamill

It's the world's longest car, I swear.   Longmobile.   Shel [*or* Shelley] Silverstein.   AiP

It's the wrong place and the wrong time.   It's All Right with Me.   Cole Porter. ReLy

It's their otherness I admire.   Can Pigeons Be Heroes?   Ruth L. Schwartz. WiU

It's there, somewhere in the Platonic cold store.   Peter Porter.   OxBSo   *Fr.* Sanitized Sonnets, The.

It's there you'll see confectioners with sugar sticks and dainties.   Galway Races.   *Unknown.*   OxBoLi

It's thirty years ago.   Free Throw.   Mark Kraushaar.   MoASP

It's this crazy weather we've been having.   Crazy Weather.   John Ashbery. ColAP; PoE

It's those helmets we remember.   Trainride, Vienna—Bonn.   Margaret Atwood. LCAP-2

"It's Three No Trumps," the Soldier Said.   Guy Innes.   UV

It's thus he does it of a winter night. (LL)   Old Man's Winter Night, An. Robert Frost.   APT-1; AWP; HAP; MoAMPo; NAAL-2v2; NoAM; OxBA; VGW

It's time I got my valour to grow big. (LL)   Sonnet: Of Becchina in a Rage. Cecco Angiolieri, da Siena.   AWP; EaItPo, *tr.* by Dante Gabriel Rossetti

It's time I told you why.   Hindoo: He Doesn't Hurt a Fly or a Spider Either, The.   A. K. Ramanujan.   OxBC

It's time to end my lonely holiday.   Autumn in New York.   Vernon Duke. ReLy

It's time to get back to the car. Already, at half-past three.   Sunday in Great Tew.   Peter McDonald.   ModIr; PNI

It's time to make love. Douse the glim.   Limerick.   Conrad Potter Aiken. NBLV; PeLi

It's to possess more than the skin.   Cutting the Jewish Bride's Hair.   Ruth Whitman.   TaR

It's to the other man, to Borges, that things happen.   Borges and Myself.   Jorge Luis Borges.   PoetW, *tr.* by Norman Thomas Di Giovanni

It's to you I come in my hours of thirsting, as to.   Life.   Delmira Agustini. TANSG, *tr.* by Mark McCaffrey

It's too dark to see black.   Mother Speaks: The Algiers Motel Incident, Detroit, A.   Michael S. Harper.   BPo; NBV

It's too darn hot.   Too Darn Hot.   Cole Porter.   ReLy

It's too easy.   Malaria.   Paolo Ruffilli.   NeIt, *tr.* by Felix Stefanile

It's too good for them.   Sex and the Over Forties.   Peter Porter.   BMAP

It's too much, B writing to A's wife.   Institute for Social Change, The.   Joshua Clover.   AmPoNex

It's true, I could hold you.   Red River.   Molly Fisk.   PasH

It's true I got caught in / the world.   After Lalon.   Allen Ginsberg.   BB

It's True I Went to the Market.   Mirabai [*or* Mira Bai].   WPoS, *tr.* by Robert Bly

It's true! It's true! The crown has made it clear.   Camelot.   Frederick Loewe. ReLy

It's true, then.   "?!"   "Shu Ting."   CarOv, *tr.* by Carolyn Kizer and Y. H. Zhao

It's 2157. Two adventuring spacemen rocketing home.   Counterfeit Earth!, The. Albert Goldbarth.   ReTh

It's twenty years ago and more.   In Moncur Street.   Dorothy Hewett.   NOBAu

It's up the spout and Charley Wag.   Moral, The.   William Ernest Henley. OxAEP-2

It's useless.   Panorama.   Romelia Alarcón de Folgar.   TANSG, *tr.* by Alison Ridley

It's winter. The city sleeps in its yellow mist.   Capitol, The.   Innokenty Fiodorovich Annensky.   WoPoe, *tr.* by Stephen Berg

It's with glasses.   Pair of Glasses, A.   Savithri Rajeevan.   OMIP, *tr.* by K. Ayyappa Paniker

It's wonderful how I jog.   Animals Are Passing from Our Lives.   Philip Levine.   CoAP; ColAP; NOBA; RaBo; TAP

It's you puts the green sprig in my hatband.   *Unknown.*   WoPoe, *tr.* by Anselm Hollo   *Fr.* Three Gypsy Songs.

It's your best friend's 16th birthday party.   Heavy-Petting Zoo, The.   Clare Pollard.   NeBl

It's your father.   Therapist's Comment, The.   Jenny Hamlett.   Prnts

It sat between my husband and my children.   Seele im Raum.   Randall Jarrell. LCAP-2

It says here.   Adelaide's Lament.   Frank Loesser.   ReLy

It Says, I Did So.   Mary Jo Bang.   KGB

It seconds the crickets of the province.   Rocking Chair, The.   Abraham Moses Klein.   HeIP-4

It seemed a simple case of opulence.   Herod's Palace.   Gwyneth Lewis. HarvBoo

It seemed as if the enormous journey.   Non-Stop.   James Tate.   BodElec

It seemed corrival of the world's great prime.   Fallen Yew, A.   Francis Thompson.   MoBrPo

It seemed that out of battle I escaped.   Strange Meeting.   Wilfred Owen. FaBoMo; FaBoWar; GTBS-P; HarvBoo; HeIP-4; MakPoe; MoBrPo; NAEL-5v2; NAEL-6v2; NOBE; NoAM; NoP-4; OBWP; OxAEP-2; OxBEV; PeFWW; PoE; PoWW; RB; SCV; TCAWP; TFi

It seemed the kind of life we wanted.   Clouds Gathering.   Charles Simic. ColAP

It seemed the obvious place to go, the sea.   Cricketer's Retirement Day, The. Julia Copus.   NeBl

It seemed / the sky was a harbor, into which rode.   Casualty.   Edwin Rolfe. APT-2

It seemed to Pliny, stationed at Misenum.   Pompeii: Plaster Casts.   Peter Scupham.   HarvBoo

It seems a certain time ago: a-maybe.   One Time.   Douglas Livingstone. NoP-4

It seems a day.   Nutting.   William Wordsworth.   NAEL-5v2; NAEL-6v2; NOBRP; RB

It seems a flower, but not a flower.   Flower, A.   Po Chü-i.   TAL

It seems a stage.   Gypsy's Window, The.   Denise Levertov.   CLPP

It seems, for a moment, the river ceases flowing. (LL)   Summer near the River. Carolyn Kizer.   CoAP; VGW

It seems high time / I challenged you to song-contest!   Dispute between Women, A.   *Unknown.*   STP, *tr.* by Tom Lowenstein

It seems I have no tears left. They should have fallen.   Tears.   Edward Thomas.   GTBS-P; NAEL-5v2; NAEL-6v2

It seems I impregnated Marge.   Limerick.   *Unknown.*   PeLi

It seems no day passes now.   Family Procession, A.   John Pepper Clark Bekedermo.   HBAPE

It seems our days are shaped by conflagration.   Fire.   Luis J. Rodriguez. UnSA

It seems that Aphrodite took with joy.   Nossis.   SaLy, *tr.* by Diane Rayor

It Seems That God Bestowed Somehow.   Amanda Benjamin Hall.   AH

It seems to be. (LL)   Twice Times Then Is Now.   Ibn Hazm al-Andalusi. ArPe; OBVE; WoPoe, *tr.* by Omar S. Pound

It seems to be a flower, yet not a flower.   Tune: "Water Dragon's Chang" after Chang Chi-fu's Lyric on the Willow Catkin.   Su Tung-p'o (Su Shih). SuSp, *tr.* by James J. Y. Liu

It seems to be the time of bad gigs.   Written in Bracing, Gray L.A. Rainlight. Al Young.   SpirFl

It seems to me I'm resurrected.   Leonid Nikolaevich Martynov.   TCRP

"It seems to me," said Booker T.   Booker T. and W. E. B.   Dudley Randall. NoAM

It seems wrong that out of this bird.   Blackbird Singing, A.   Ronald Stuart Thomas.   OBWVE

It semes white and is red.   Sacrament of the Altar, The.   *Unknown.*   NoP-4

It shall suffice that they were breathed [*or* breath'd], and died [*or* dyed] for her delight. (LL)   Devotion.   Thomas Campion.   BASC; EBEV; EnLoPo; HAP; NOSC; NoSic; OxAEP-1; PoE

It shames one to look.   Yury [*or* Iurii] Timofeievich Galanskov.   TCRusP, *tr.* by Daniel Weissbort

It shines in the garden.   Garden, The.   Mark Strand.   ColAP; NoAM

It should be in your nature to instantly trivialize anything.   Advice to a Young Philosopher.   Anselm Berrigan.   HeMarv

It should have a woman's name.   Lake in Central Park, The.   Jay Wright. ESEAA; GT

It should have been enough that we were poor.   Sustenance.   Jason Santalucia. SpudSo

It Shouldn't Happen to a Dream.   Don George.   ReLy

It sifts from Leaden Sieves.   Snow, The.   Emily Dickinson.   SoSe-8; WHSW

It silvers the lawn.   Moonlight.   Michael Ryan.   BodElec

It sinks; and I am ready to depart. (LL)   Walter Savage Landor.   NOBE; NPeEn; OxBEV; TFi; TRP; UV   *Fr.* Last Fruit off an Old Tree, The.

It sleeps among the thousand hills.   Unnamed Lake, The.   Frederick George Scott.   NOBC

It slides into a cloud over Point Lobos. (LL)   Phenomena.   Robinson Jeffers. NOBA; OxBA

It smiles to see me.   Lethargy.   Donald Justice.   CRP

It snowed.   Marmalade.   Elizabeth Delmore.   NLP

It snowed so much, a lady loved a gentleman so dearly.   Lady of the Snow,

The. Vivian Lamarque. CItWP, *tr. by* Cinzia Sartini Blum and Lara Trubowitz

It snows and stops, now it is January. Alicia Ostriker. ExTi *Fr.* Mastectomy Poems, The.

It snows on this place. Wednesday at North Hatley. Ralph Gustafson. NOBC

It so happens I am sick of being a man. Walking Around. Pablo Neruda. RaBo; SPE

It so happens I'm tired of just being a man. Walking Around. Pablo Neruda. TCLAP, *tr. by* Ben Belitt

It soars alone. Another Summit. Muso Soseki. EaWin, *tr. by* W. S. Merwin

It sometimes happens. Curse of the Cat Woman. Edward Field. WeW-3

It soothes the savage doubts. Apocalypse. Dennis Joseph Enright. OBSV

It Sounded. Larry Eigner. FTOS

It sounded as if the Streets were running. Storm. Emily Dickinson. NAAL-2v1; NAAL-3; OxBSP

It sounds unconvincing to say "When I was young." In the Winter of My Thirty-eighth Year. W. S. Merwin. NOBA

It stands where northern willows weep. Queen of Prussia's Tomb, The. Felicia Dorothea Hemans. RWP

It Started. Jimmy Santiago Baca. LoL

It started about noon. On top of Mount Batte. Seeing the Eclipse in Maine. Robert Bly. InvLad

It started before Christmas. Now our son. Red Hat, The. Rachel Hadas. RA

It started. First the salts. Geyser, The. Ágnes Nemes Nagy. PoSu, *tr. by* Bruce Berlind

It started with the Greatest Hits album. On the Elvis Mailing List. Neal Bowers. AllShUp; SwNoth

It starts: a white girl in a dark house. Alternatives. Kingsley Amis. OxBC

It starts in the morning. Foreplay. Natasha Josefowitz. PasH

It starts in the park near Brentwood Primary School. Bright Cigar-Shaped Object Hovers over Mount Pleasant, A. John Kinsella. NeBl

It starts in the small hours. An interlude. James Merrill. NoAM *Fr.* Mirabell: Books of Number.

It starts / inevitably / as something. Insomniac. M. Loncar. AmPoNex

It starts on the Lower East Side. Lower East Side: The George Bernstein Story. Edward Field. OBCoV

It starts, somehow, in the hot damp. Barn Fire. Thomas Lux. LCAP-2

It starts with the picture of my grandfather. Cloud Unfolding, The. Ernesto Trejo. LTA

It steals in through her screen. (LL) To the Tune: The Wine Spring: "Eternal autumn rain—evening sounds." Li Hsun. CrYelRi; ErotSp, *tr. by* Sam Hamill

It stifles me—God, must I sit and sew? (LL) I Sit and Sew. Alice Moore Dunbar-Nelson. BlSi; NAAAL; NALW; WPOW

It stood in the sunset sky. Barn and the Down, The. Edward Thomas. OxBEV

It stops the town we come through. Troop Train. Karl Shapiro. APT-2; OxBA

It sushes. Cynthia in the Snow. Gwendolyn Brooks. TLR

It sweeps, as sweeps an army. Scale Force, Cumberland. Letitia [*or* Laetitia] Elizabeth Landon. RWP

It swings upon the leafless tree. Snow-filled Nest, The. Rose Terry Cooke. OBCA

It takes a fast car. Lost Parents. Lawrence Ferlinghetti. PoM; ReTh

It takes a heap o' livin' in a house t' make it home. Home. Edgar Albert Guest. BRP; ITBLP; OBAL; PWR

It takes a long time to hear what the sands. Bones, The. W. S. Merwin. CoAmPo

It takes a mighty fire. H. D. Carberry. CA

It takes a very stupid dolt. *Unknown.* ColAnChi, *tr. by* Jeffrey Riegel *Fr.* Classic of Odes.

It takes all sorts of in- and outdoor schooling. Robert Frost. SoSe-8

It takes life to love Life. (LL) Edgar Lee Masters. HAP; IllVoic; MoAmPo; NOBA; NoAM *Fr.* Spoon River Anthology.

It takes time, and there are setbacks. Difficult Adjustment, A. Lauris Edmond. FaBoWP

It takes time to make. Time to Myself. Paulette Jiles. NOBC

It takes two hands to turn the key. Locking the Church. David Scott. NLP

It Took a Village. Stephanie Brown. AmPoNex

It took generations to mature. Liberace. Jonathan Holden. ReTh

It took me ten days. In the Beginning Was the Word. Anna Hempstead Branch. APT-1

It Took One Hundred Years. Malika O'Lahsen. HAWP; WoPoe, *tr. by* Eric Sellin

It Took TV to Civilize Our Village. Richard Moore. Son *Fr.* Word from the Hills.

It took 27 years to write this poem. Ruth. Colleen J. McElroy. BlSi

It took us both to water the new lawn. Watering the New Lawn. Michael S. Smith. PasH

It took Without to make Within a heaven. Within and Without. Elizabeth Jessup Blake. YaYoPo

It towers. Gem Mountain. Muso Soseki. EaWin, *tr. by* W. S. Merwin

It trails always behind me. Jamaica 1980. Lorna Goodison. GT

It trembled so the wind swept it away. Poplar Leaf, The. George Seferis. PFTM-1

It tried to get from out the cage. Cage, The. James Stephens. OxBEV; OxBTC

It turns out. Little Dantesque. James Galvin. BAP-01

It turns out you can have a daughter selling. Mama Loves Janis Joplin. Richard Speakes. SwNoth

It turns out / You can kill them. Redwings. James Wright (1927–80). NNaP

It Used to Be. Ciaran Carson. *See* Céilí

It used to be at the bottom of the hill. Sea, The. E. A. Markham. EmeKit

It used to be that the rat was a cynic. Rat, The. Karen Kipp. BodElec

It vanished from history, as from legend. (LL) Not Being Oedipus. John Heath-Stubbs. EmeKit; OxBC

It wants to be dark, lavish. Love Poem. Barbara J. Orton. NeAmPo

It wants to be somewhere else. Looking at Henry Moore's Elephant Skull Etchings in Jerusalem during the War. Shirley Kaufman. LCAP-2

It wants to say something. Why the Stone Remains Silent. William Kloefkorn. GifTon

It warms my bones. Uses of Light, The. Gary Snyder. PAI

It was a bad sign I was born under. Judas Goat, The. Susan Musgrave. NOBC

It was a bash! I Heard the Byrd. Oliver Lagrone. SeSe

It was a beauty that I saw. Ben Jonson. BeJo *Fr.* New Inn, The.

It was a bird of Paradise. In London Town. Mary Elizabeth Coleridge. VWP

It was a blue fly with wings of pomegranate gold. Blue Fly. Joaquim Maria Machado de Assis. TTY, *tr. by* Frances Ellen Buckland

It was a Borgia-pot, he told me. Curiosity-Shop, The. Peter Redgrove. OxBC

It was a bow-legged conductor of a Twopenny Bus. (LL) Polly Perkins. *Unknown.* OBCoV; OxBoLi; PeLV

It was a bowl of roses. Bowl of Roses, A. William Ernest Henley. MoBrPo

It was a brave attempt! adventurous he. Launching into Eternity. Isaac Watts. SacPr

It was a bright and cheerful afternoon. Summer and Winter. Shelley. OxAEP-2; SCGP

It was a bright day and all the trees were still. Silence. Walter James Turner. MoBrPo

It was a chilly winter's night. Winter Night, A. William Barnes. NOBE; WoPoe

It was a chosen plot of fertile land. Edmund Spenser. *See* Lo I the man, whose Muse whilome [*or* whylome] did maske

It was a cool evening. Freeman Field. Marilyn Nelson Waniek. ESEAA

It was a damp mild day of clinging mists that we met. Meeting at a Salesyard. John Ennis. CIP-2

It was a dark, dank, dreadful night. Malfeasance, The. Alan Bold. OBSP

It was a day peculiar to this piece of the planet. Scotland. Alastair Reid. NePenScot

It was a dim October day. Thomas Caulfield Irwin. BIrV *Fr.* Swift.

It was a dismal and a fearful night. Abraham Cowley. BeJo; EBEV; NOBE; OBEV; OxAEP-1 *Fr.* On the Death of Mr. William Hervey [*or* Harvey].

It was a dismal day when chilling rain. Greater Gift, The. Margaret E. Bruner. PoToHe

It was a divine hour for the human race. Swan, The. "Rubén Dario." TCLAP, *tr. by* Lysander Kemp

It was a dream and shouldn't I bother about a dream? Songe d'Athalie. Stevie Smith. OxBEV

It was a dream and you were walking through a field of hosannas. Abstract. Sam Hamill. BodElec

It was a dreary morning when the wheels. William Wordsworth. NAEL-6v2 *Fr.* Prelude; Growth of a Poet's Mind [1850 vers.] The.

It was a feather of paint. Allen Curnow. PeNZ *Fr.* Moro Assassinato.

It was a friar of orders gray [*or* grey]. Friar of Orders Gray, The. *Unknown.* NOEC

It Was a Funky Deal. Etheridge Knight. BPo; NBV

It was a gentle air, with turns and pauses. It Was a Gentle Air. "Rubén Dairo." TCLAP, *tr. by* Lysander Kemp

It was a glorious May morning. Victor Garibaldi. Melvin B. Tolson. GT

It was a good day and I was about to do something important. Precision German Craftsmanship. Matthew Rohrer. NAPBL; NeAmPo

It was a good word once, a little sparkler. Protest Poem. Vernon Scannell. OBCoV

It was a graveyard scene. The crescent moon. Great Unaffected Vampires and the Moon. Stevie Smith. NoAM

It was a hand. God looked at it. Hand, The. Ronald Stuart Thomas. NOCV; OxBC

It was a hard thing to undo this knot. At a Welsh Waterfall. Gerard Manley Hopkins. NOBVV

It was a heartfelt game, when it began. Portrait. Judith Wright. OxBSP; SoSe-8

It was a house of female habitation. House of Mercy, A. Stevie Smith. FaBoWP; HarvBoo

It was a kind and northern face. Praise for an Urn. Hart Crane. AWP; HAP; MoAmPo; NOBA; NoAM; OxBA; WeW-3

It was a Knight in Scotland borne. Fair Flower of Northumberland, The. *Unknown.* ESPB; OxBB

It was a lady of the north she lov'd a gentleman. Room for a Jovial Tinker: Old Brass to Mend. *Unknown.* OxBB

It was a little captive cat. Singing Cat, The. Stevie Smith. OxBTC

It Was a Long Time Before. Leslie Marmon Silko. NoAM

It was a long way round from. For Norman Nicholson. David Scott. NLP

It was a lovely night. William Robert Rodgers. PNI *Fr.* Resurrection: An Easter Sequence.

It was a lover and his lass. William Shakespeare. AWP; GTBS-P; NAEL-5v1; NOBE; NoSic; OBEV; RB; SCGP; TFi; TTTS *Fr.* As You Like It.

It was a Maine lobster town. Water. Robert Lowell. HeIP-4; LCAP-2; NOBA; NoP-4; PoE

It was a mighty monarch's child. Mir träumte von einem Königskind. Heinrich Heine. AWP, *tr. by* Richard Garnett

It was a mild spring. Kitchen Beast. Amanda Dalton. NeBl

It was a mother and a maid. Milk White Doe, The. *Unknown.* AWP, *tr. by* Andrew Lang

It was a night of early spring. Wisdom. Sara Teasdale. MoAmPo

It was a night when the planets. Perspective Lovesong. "Ern Malley." BMAP

It was a party; I had on my party dress. Origins. Joan Larkin. WiU

It was a place where apples sprouted teeth. Childhood. Chitra Divakaruni. OpBo

It was a poignant moment. Howl, Howl. Christopher Reid. OBCoV

It was a quiet way—. Emily Dickinson. NCAP

It was a real well, real. Old Wives' Tales. Constance Urdang. PBCAP

It was a rich merchant man. Merchant and the Fidler's Wife, The. *Unknown.* OxBB

It was a school where all the children wore darned worsted. Fond Memory. Eavan Boland. ModIr

It Was a Season Tattooed on the Forehead of the Earth. Venus Khoury-Gata. PoArWo, *tr. by* Lucy McNair

It was a simple world. (LL) Hen Woman. Thomas Kinsella. CIP-2; ModIr; NPeEn; PBCIP

It was a small, private school and the walls told. Elegy for a Professor. Nicholas Samaras. TWW

It was a summer evening. Sentences While Remembering Hiraethog. T. Glynne Davies. OBWVE, *tr. by* R. Gerallt Jones

It was a summer evening. Robert Southey. *See* It was a summer [*or* summer's] evening

It was a summer evening in an Alabama city. René Depestre. NegPo, *tr. by* Ellen Conroy Kennedy *Fr.* Epiphanies of the Voodoo Gods.

It was a summer [*or* summer's] evening. Battle of Blenheim, The. Robert Southey. BRP; FaBoWar; OBWP; TFi

It was a Summer's night, a close warm night. William Wordsworth. MakPoe *Fr.* Prelude, Growth of a Poet's Mind [1805 vers.], The.

It was a tall young oysterman lived by the river-side. Ballad of the Oysterman, The. Oliver Wendell Holmes. TCAPo

It was a testimony. Gregory's House. David Huddle. PBCAP

It was a time, that summer '66. I Wanna Be Black. Michelle T. Clinton. InTrad

It was a time when wise men. Period. Ronald Stuart Thomas. HarvBoo

It was a tortoise aspiring to fly. Improvisations on Aesop. Anthony Hecht. OBAL

It was a trance: Thieves, clowns, and the blind girl. Clamor. Ann Lauterbach. PmAP

It Was a Very Good Year. Ervin Drake. ReLy

It was a vision he had, a candle he lit. Idea of Love between Us, The. Kate Light. AmPoNex

It was a waning crescent. July Dawn. Louise Bogan. AWTN

It was a warm September night. Gettin' Straight. Mcavoy Layne. CDa

It was a way of punishing the house, setting it a blaze. Interior at Petworth: From Turner. Rosanna Warren. NoAM

It was a winter's morning. Harry Graham. UV *Fr.* Battue of Berlin, The.

It was about the deep of night. Ballad of Christmas, A. Walter De la Mare. OBCP

It was after vespers one evening. Low Church. Stanley J. Sharpless. NBLV; OBCoV; PeLV

It was after war; Edward Thomas had fallen at Arras. Mangel-Bury, The. Ivor Gurney. HarvBoo

It was after we laid the infant. Leaf. Cathy Song. ExTi

It was afterwards. Another Love Affair /Another Poem. E. Ethelbert Miller. ISC

It was agreed we would not mount by those. Jacob's Ladder. Donald Davie. OxBSo

It was all different; that, at least, seemed sure. Mutability. W. D. Snodgrass. DiPo

It Was All for Him. Amin Al-Rihani. GraLe

It was all like a childhood picture. Cuckoo. Robert Desnos. PFTM-1

It was all so different from what she'd expected. At Thirty-three. Hans Magnus Enzensberger. VCWP, *tr. by* Hans Magnus Enzensberger and Michael Hamburger

It Was All Very Tidy. Robert Graves. NPeEn; OxBTC; RB

"It was an accident." (LL) Dolls, The. W. B. Yeats. NoAM; PoE

It was an Artless Poster Girl pinned up against my wall. Poster Girl's Defence, The. Carolyn Wells. SWaP

It was an evening in November. Pig, The. *Unknown.* FaBoEE; OBCoV

It was an icy day. Complete Destruction. William Carlos Williams. SAmP

It was announced in the *Daily Times*, the *New Nigerian.* Launching Our Community Developement Fund. Tanure Ojaide. HBAPE

It was April in the year Kuei-mao. Lament of the Lady of Ch'in, The. Wei Chuang. SuSp, *tr. by* Robin D. S. Yates

It was as if. Spring Song. Peter Fallon. CIP-2; PBCIP

It was as if God had taken a pen of fire. American Apocalypse. Edward Hirsch. IllVoic

It was as if the devil of evil had got. García Lorca. Louis Dudek. MoCV; NOBC

It was astonishing to walk into room 233 at the Days Inn. Days Inn. Linda Smukler. WiU

It was at dinner as they sat. Laird of Wariston, The. *Unknown.* ESPB

It was at the Noon Bridge we were drinking—. Tune: "Immortal at the Riverbank." Ch'en Yü-i. ColAnChi, *tr. by* Jiaosheng Wang

It was at the roadside pavilion that we were to bid adieu. Tune: "Bells Ringing in the Rain." Liu Yung. ColAnChi, *tr. by* Jiaosheng Wang

It was at the very date to which we have come. Anniversary, An. Thomas Hardy. OxBTC

It was august, i was inner city. Friendly Town #1. Safiya Henderson-Holmes. UnSA

It was beautiful as God. White Tiger, The. Ronald Stuart Thomas. AngWePo

It was better when we were. For My Mother. Louise Glück. UnPo

It was bleak december just last night or the night. New Philosophy of Composition, or, How to Ignore the Non-Reasoning Creature Capable of *Speeech* Perched Outside Your Bathroom Window, A. Olena Kalytiak Davis. NAPBL

It was booze made my boss talk of Stalin's days. Hospital Gypsy Song. Aleksandr Arkadevich Galich. TCRusP, *tr. by* Gerry Smith

It was born to become the imperial capital. Leningrad. "Naum Korzhavin." TCRP, *tr. by* Albert C. Todd

It was boss cook's fault. He left. Tip, The. Belle Waring. PBCAP

It was but a little thing. Peace-Offering, The. Thomas Hardy. OxBSP

It was by such a state of logical perpendiculars. Thinking the Alps. Michael Davidson. PmAP

It was cold in that room, after the cold hours. My Grandmother Died in the Early Hours of the Morning. T. Harri Jones. AngWePo; TCAWP

It was cold then in the cautious hours. Curtain. Lance Henson. VoR

It was dark and frosty, pain congealed into ice. Deportation. "M. B." TrJP, *tr. by* A. Glanz-Leyeles

It was day. I felt I had to leave the village. I did. Before long. Farmer, The. Kees Ouwens. TuT, *tr. by* Peter Van de Kamp

It was death, and death indeed. (LL) There was a man of double deed. *Unknown.* OxNR; RB

It was deep April, and the morn. "Michael Field." VWP; ViWPN

It was early, early all in the Spring. My Boy Willie. *Unknown.* MakPoe

It was early, early in the spring. Croppy Boy, The. *Unknown.* NOIV; OxBoLi

It was early, early one mornin' Stagolee. *Unknown.* TTY

It was early in the morning. Goodhousekeeping #17. Safiya Henderson-Holmes. ISC

It was early last December. Drunkard and the Pig, The. *Unknown.* OBAL

It was early Sunday mornin. Stagolee. *Unknown.* OxBoLi; TTY

It was Easter as I walked in the public gardens. 1929. W. H. Auden. OxAEP-2

It was easy enough. Circe. "H. D." PoRA

It was $8,000 with a GI loan. Floor Plans. Maxine Scates. PBCAP

It was exactly eleven. Pawiak 1943. Jerzy Ficowski. PoSu, *tr.* by Frank J. Corliss, Jr. and Grazyna Sandel

It was exhausting. To Love a Stranger. Sibby Anderson-Thompkins. InTrad

It was fabulous, what the body told. (LL) What the Body Told. Rafael Campo. AmPoNex; BloBone; NeAmPo; WiU

It was far in the sameness of the wood. Demiurge's Laugh, The. Robert Frost. OxBA

It Was Fever That Made the World. Jim Powell. NIP-4; SwNoth

It was first marching, hardly we had settled yet. First March. Ivor Gurney. OxBEV

It was for this that man came into the world, to fight. Chapter and Verse. Gonzalo Rojas. TCLAP, *tr.* by Christopher Maurer

It was for you that the mountains shook at Sinai. Epitaph. *Unknown.* TrJP

It was for your sake, was it not. Holy Russia. Maksimilian Aleksandrovich Voloshin. TCRP, *tr.* by Bernard Meares

It was general conflagration. (LL) Devil's Thoughts, The. Samuel Taylor Coleridge. OBSV; OxBoLi; PeLV

It was genuine—real fox. Cross Country. Ann Sansom. MFPA

It was good. Love Song, A. Lindiwe Mabuza. HAWP

It was good for the virgin mary. Poem for Unwed Mothers. Nikki Giovanni. OBAL

It was good when you were here. Paul Goodman. BodElec

It was here, in the long red meadow. Two Rivers. Hilary Llewellyn-Williams. AngWePo; TCAWP

It was him, Elvis, sheepishly. Elvis at the End of History. Fleda Brown Jackson. AllShUp

It was his story. It would always be his story. In Memory of the Unknown Poet, Robert Boardman Vaughn. Donald Justice. DiPo; NoAM

It was hot. A size too large. High Holy Days. Jane Shore. NoP-4

It was hot. The forest burnt. Time. Monkey. Vladislav Felitsianovich Khodasevich. TCRusP, *tr.* by Daniel Weissbort

It was iMpossible. 25 Mesostics Re and Not Re Mark Tobey. John Cage. PmAP

It was impossible for one to read. Holy Was Demeter Walking th' Corn Furrow. Edward Sanders. PoM

It was in Abomey that I felt. Dahomey. Audre Lorde. NAAL-2v2

It was in an empty lot. How I Learned English. Gregory Djanikian. UnSA

It was in and about the Martinmas time. Bonny Barbara Allan ("In Scarlet Town where I was born"). *Unknown.* AWP; BoLoP; ESPB; HeIP-4; InPK-6; NAEL-5v1; NAEL-6v1; NAEL-7v1; NePenScot; OxBB; PAI

It was in autumn that I met. Picture, A. Dora Greenwell. EBVV

It was in June the eight and thirtieth day. John Taylor. NOSC *Fr.* Sir Gregory Nonsense's News from No Place.

It was in October the woe began. Fire of Frendraught, The. *Unknown.* ESPB

It was in the month of January the hills. Month of January. Frankie Armstrong. BrRo

It was in the Spring of 1825. Noel Petty. UV

It was in winter. Steeples, spires. Fortunate Traveller, The. Derek Walcott. NoAM

It was insane. I thought it myself. The winter. First Reader Santee Training School, 1873, The. Diane Glancy. LTA

It was Ips, Gips, and Johnson, as I've heard many say. Three Butchers, The. *Unknown.* PeVV

It was just a gas station. It was not spectacular carnage. World, The. Gillian Conoley. BodElec

It was just this summer I began to forgive. I was six, all cow. Martin. Pamela Stewart. ExTi

It was last year. Fox Glove Song. Christina Beer. PeNZ

It was late in the night when the Squire came home. Gipsy Laddie, The. *Unknown.* FaBoCh; OxBoLi

It was late last night when my lord came home. Cyril Connolly. OBCoV *Fr.* Where Engels Fears to Tread.

It was late on a winter's evening. Autobiography. John Burnside. NePenScot

It was late, we. Man and Wife. Mitchell Goodman. VGW

It was like a church to me. Moor, The. Ronald Stuart Thomas. OBWVE

It was like a stream. Mahadevi. WPoS

It was like soul-kissing, the way the words. How I Discovered Poetry. Marilyn Nelson. ExTi

It was lit at the bride's hearth while she played. Take: A Roman Wedding. Alice Fulton. ExTi

It was long since she could sleep in that wooden home of hers. Ballad of the Wondrous Moment. Pavel Grigoryevich Antokolsky. TCRP, *tr.* by Bernard Meares

It was many and many a year ago. Samuel Brown. Phoebe Cary. APN-2; OBAL

It was many and many a year ago. Annabel Lee. Edgar Allan Poe. AWP; AiP; BRP; ChAP; HeIP-4; ITBLP; NAAL-2v1; NAAL-3; NAAL-5; NCAP; OBCA; OBSP; TCAPo; TFi

It was Montmartre. Mam'selle. Edmund Goulding. ReLy

It was Murupaenga who brought me here. Slave Girl's Song. *Unknown.* PeNZ, *tr.* by Margaret Orbell

It was my bridal night I remember. I Remember. Stevie Smith. BoLoP; BoWoP; FaBoWP; InPK-6; NIL-7; OxBC

It was my fate to help Billy Redanz learn how to read. Story of My Life, The. Liz Rosenberg. PBCAP

It was my fifth year to heaven. Christopher Robin Changes Guard with Dylan Thomas. Bill Greenwell. UV

It was (my love told me) my sister. For C., Who Died of Childbirth at the Age of One Year and Eleven Months. Giovanni Raboni. ItPo, *tr.* by Gayle Ridinger

It was my thirtieth year to heaven. Poem in October. Dylan Thomas. AngWePo; NAEL-5v2; NAEL-6v2; NPeEn; NoAM; OxAEP-2; PoRA; RB; SoSe-8; TCAWP; UV

IT was near a thicky shade. Description of the Shepherd and His Wife, The. Robert Greene. NoSic

It was near evening, the room was cold. Oath, The. Allen Tate. FaBoMo; OxBA; VGW

It was near midnight when I entered. Ivan Alekseievich Bunin. TCRP

It was near the Coliseum, RKO, / in the Bronx. Laughing Gas. Ruth Whitman. UnSA

It was nearly seven thousand years ago. Lady of Pazardzik. Starr Goode. HW

It was no vast dynastic fate. Father's Death, A. John Hewitt. PNI

It was not a very formal affair but. Chinese Banquet, A. Kitty Tsui. GLP

It was not always so. The shaping hand. Birth of the Smile, The. Rainer Maria Rilke. EroLit, *tr.* by J. B. Leishman

It was not Death, for I stood up. Emily Dickinson. APN-2; NAAL-2v1; NAAL-3; NAAL-5; NOBA; SAmP; TCAPo

It was not dying: Everybody died. Losses. Randall Jarrell. AmFaPo; HCAP; LCAP-2; OxBA; TAP; UnPo

It was not I who began it. Eve to Her Daughters. Judith Wright. NALW; NoP-4

It was not like your great and gracious ways. Coventry Patmore. NOBE; OBEV *Fr.* Unknown Eros, The.

It was not love. No flowers or ripened figs. Immaculate Conception. Louise Erdrich. BBASP

It was not meant for human eyes. Combat, The. Edwin Muir. MoBrPo; NOBE

It was not our duty to question but to guard. Bread and a Pension. Louis Johnson. PeNZ

It was not that I lost direction. Martha Sansom. ECWP

It was not that you were pure. Possibiliites: Remembering Malcolm X. Haki R. Madhubuti. SpirFl

It was not warm. Innocency or Not Song X. Gerald Early. BodElec

It Was Not You. André Spire. TrJP, *tr.* by Jethro Bithell

It was nothing more than a Neapolitan Christmas creche. The light. Horrible Today, The. Max Jacob. AF, *tr.* by Ron Padgett

It was October once, fragile as. In the Beginning. Jill Alexander Essbaum. NAPBL

It was official, in an American sort of way. Homesteading. Eva Salzman. MFPA

It was on a May, on a midsummer's day. Sir Hugh; or, The Jew's Daughter. *Unknown.* ESPB

It was on a Wednesday night, the moon was shining bright. Jesse James. *Unknown.* UnPo

It was on an evning sae saft and sae clear. Broom of Cowdenknows, The. *Unknown.* ESPB

It was on one Monday morning just about one o'clock. *Titanic,* The. *Unknown.* APT-1

It was on the floor, being X-ed out by her long. Marianne Faithfull's Cigarette. Gerry Gomez Pearlberg. WiU

It was only a small place and they had cheered us too much. St. Aubin d'Aubigne. Paul Dehn. OBWP

It was only a tiny seed. Only a Litlle Thing. M. P. Handy. PoToHe

It was only important. Moss of His Skin, The. Anne Sexton. CoAP; NALW; PAI

It was [only] that snow had fallen! (LL) *Var. authors.* AWP; TAL *Fr.* Manyo Shu, Part 3 of 4.

It was only that the poor. Skibbereen the Famine Pit. John Knoepfle. SpudSo

It was only yesterday. Gone with the Wind. Herb Magidson. ReLy

It was over at Isândula, the bloody work was done. Fight at Rorke's Drift, The. Emily Jane Pfeiffer. ViWPN

It was over here that my love, in his mercy. Michelangelo Buonarroti. CAGL, *tr.* by James M. Saslow

It was over Target Berlin the flak shot up our plane. World War II. Edward Field. GLP

It was perfect. He could do. Other. Ronald Stuart Thomas. AngWePo

It was plain to see the sense of being a woman. Inflammable Woman, The. James Keir Baxter. OxBC

It was pneumonia. Lament of the Virtues and Verses on Account of the Death of Don Guido. Antonio Machado Ruiz. OBVE

It was proper for them, awaking in ordered houses. Apology. Anthony Cronin. CIP-2

It was Puerto Rico waking up inside her. Puerto Rico waking her. Puertoricanness. Aurora Levins Morales. PueRic

It was quiet. The yardman could see. Accordionist, The. Vasily [or Vasilii] Vasilevich Kazin. TCRP, tr. by Daniel Weissbort

It was quite a sight for a boy from Tennessee. Nun in Ninh Hoa, A. Jan Barry. CDa

It was roses, roses, all the way. Patriot, The [An Old Story]. Robert Browning. FHYEP

It was rumored on the block. Figure Motioned with Its Mangled Hand Toward the Wall behind It, The. Kenneth Patchen. APT-2

It was said at the / flirting creekwater's birth. To an Imaginary Father. Wendy Rose. CDW

It was shattered. Battle of Maldon, The. Unknown. ASW; OBWP; tr. by Kevin Crossley-Holland

It was shattered. Unknown. See Was broken. / He bade a warrior abandon his horse

It was Sir Christopher Gardiner. Rhyme of Sir Christopher, The. Henry Wadsworth Longfellow. NCAP

It was six men of Hindostan. Blind Men and the Elephant, The. John Godfrey Saxe. ITBLP; OBCA; OTCP; PoToHe

It was six men of Indostan. John Godfrey Saxe. See It was six men of Hindostan

It was snowing. For the first time, conquered. Victor Hugo. WoPoe, tr. by Louis Simpson Fr. Expiation.

It was solitary and serene. Birds' Refuge, The. Sojourner Kincaid Rolle. GeoHom

It was something to see that their white was different. Holiday in Reality. Wallace Stevens. OxBA

It was spring, saturday. To Hell and Back, with Cake. Safiya Henderson-Holmes. UnSA

It was strange. Taino. Jose Angel Figueroa. PueRic

It was such a pretty little donkey. Donkey, The. Stevie Smith. HarvBoo

It was summer. Summer or Its Ending. Yehuda Amichai [or Amikhai]. PoSu, tr. by Dennis Silk

It was Summer, all the time. When Mark Deloach Ruled the World. Dominique Parker. SpirFl

It was Sunday in the fair ears of my burro. César Vallejo. TCLAP, tr. by Clayton Eshleman

It was taken some time ago. This Is a Photograph of Me. Margaret Atwood. NALW; NoAM; NoP-4

It was the Age of Reason. Swallows and Tortoises. Neil Curry. NLP

It was the arrival of the kings. Adoration of the Magi, The. Christopher Pilling. OBCP

It was the Bastot Maulion. Orthone. Philip Pendleton Cooke. APN-1

It was the colour of incense. Womanhood, The. Elizabeth Garrett. MFPA

It was the day when the sun's rays turned pale with grief for his. Petrarch. NAWM-7v1, tr. by Robert M. Durling Fr. Sonnets to Laura.

It was the dead who groaned within! (LL) Sleeper, The. Edgar Allan Poe. NAAL-2v1; NAAL-3; NCAP; NOBA; OxBA; TAP

It was the first day of the war. Silence. Bella Abramovna Dizhur. ItGoST, tr. by Sarah Bliumis

It was the first gift he ever gave her. Black Lace Fan My Mother Gave Me, The. Eavan Boland. BiHa; HarvBoo; ModIr; NPeEn

It was the flowery season of the year. Luis de Góngora y Argote. SpanPo, tr. by Edward E. Wilson Fr. Solitudes, The.

It was the frog in the well. Marriage of the Frog and the Mouse, The. Unknown. EBEV

It was the frosty early hours when finally. Weakness, The. Bernard O'Donoghue. ModIr; NoP-4

It was the garden of the golden apples. Long Garden, The. Patrick Kavanagh. HarvBoo; OBGa

It was the hour of night, when thus the Son. John Milton. EBEV; PeECV Fr. Paradise Regained [or Regain'd].

It was the middle of the night and I had lived. Mt. Pisgah. James Kimbrell. NAPBL

It was the morning of that blessed day. Petrarch. NAWM-5v1 Fr. Sonnets to Laura.

It was the [or a] worthy Lord of Lorn [or Learne]. Lord of Lorn and the False [or Fals] Steward, The. Unknown. ESPB; OxBB

It was the Rainbow gave thee birth. Kingfisher, The. William Henry Davies. AngWePo; NOBE; OBEV; OBWVE

It was the schooner Hesperus. Wreck of the Hesperus, The. Henry Wadsworth Longfellow. APN-1; BRP; EBNV; OBCA; OBNV; TCAPo; TreFP

It was the season, when through all the land. Henry Wadsworth Longfellow. OxBA Fr. Tales of a Wayside Inn.

It was the Southern drifting over the flats on a hundred low trestles. (The Recent Past). C. S. Giscombe. GT

It was the stage-driver's story, as he stood with his back to the wheelers. Stage-Driver's Story, The. Bret Harte. EBNV

It Was the Time. Joachim Du Bellay. Son, tr. by Edmund Spenser

It was the time before. Tear. Linda Hogan. ExTi

It was the time that Rigby. Rigby. Mark Todd. GeoH

It was the time when, granted from the gods. Virgil [or Vergil]. NAEL-5v1 Fr. Aeneid [or Eneados, Aeneis], The.

It was the time, when rest, soft sliding downe. Joachim Du Bellay. AWP; Son Fr. Visions of Bellay, The.

It was the twilight of the iguana. Some Beasts. Pablo Neruda. TCLAP, tr. by James Wright

It was the west wind caught her up, as. Ring of, The. Charles Olson. NOBA; VGW

It was the wind. Autumn Evening. George Anthony. SPE

It was the winter I had to get away. Men Talk. Stephen P. Dunn. NIP-4

It was the winter wild[e]. John Milton. NOBE; OBEV Fr. On the Morning of Christ's Nativity.

It was the year the Icondic. Ballad of the Icondic. John Ciardi. OBAL

It was their fate to live in a strange time. Juan Lopez and John Ward. Jorge Luis Borges. FaBoWar, tr. by Rodolfo Torragno

It was then night: The sound[e] and quiet sleep [or slepe]. Virgil [or Vergil]. MakPoe, tr. by Henry Howard, Earl of Surrey Fr. Aeneid [or Eneados, Aeneis], The.

It was then that destiny decided to take me by the hand. Destiny. Maria Luisa Spaziani. NeIt, tr. by Beverly Allen

It was three slim does and a ten-tined buck in the bracken lay. Revenge of Hamish, The. Sidney Lanier. APN-2; EBNV; NCAP

It was time when children bound to meet. Switzer's Wife, The. Felicia Dorothea Hemans. RWP

It was too late for Man. Emily Dickinson. BBASP

It was too lonely for her there. Robert Frost. RaBo; TCAPo Fr. Hill Wife, The.

It was too soon. Water and Light. Noah Blaustein. MoASP

It was up there. Accident, An. Frank A. Cross. CDa

It was upon a Cristemesse night. Robert Mannyng [or Manning]. PoE Fr. Handling Sin.

It was upon a Shere [or Scere] Thorsday that vre [or oure] Loverd [or Lord] aros. Judas. Unknown. MiEL; PoE

It was upon the twilight of that day. Samuel Daniel. OBWP Fr. Civil Wars, The.

It was very funny, Grypus. Publius Papinius Statius. RomPo, tr. by W. G. Shepherd Fr. Sylvae.

It was warm in Grandma's kitchen. Throughout this, her second. Diana Helen Melhem. GraLe Fr. Rest in Love.

It was, when scarce had rang the morning bells. Almanack for the Year of Our Lord, 1657, An. Samuel Bradstreet. SCAP

It was when we were living. When My Grandmother Said "Pussy." Carole Bernstein. AmPoNex; UnSA

It was where the wooden bridge. Dora Markus. Eugenio Montale. PoetW, tr. by William Arrowsmith

It was wild. Assassination. Haki R. Madhubuti. GT

It was winter. We Were Three. Claribel Alegría. AF; TCLAP, tr. by Carolyn Forché

It was winter. Boris Leonidovich Pasternak. See All was winter and chill

It was winter and already dusky in town. Rejected Gift, The. Ida G. M. Gerhardt. TuT, tr. by Peter Van de Kamp

It was Winter in Manhattan. Violets for Your Furs. Matt Dennis. ReLy

It was winter. The wind. Christmas Star, The. Boris Leonidovich Pasternak. WoPoe, tr. by Nina Kossman

It was with resolution that she gave up the. Ice Eagle, The. Diane Wakoski. PFTM-2

"It Was Wrong to Do This" Said the Angel. Stephen Crane. PAI Fr. Black Riders [and Other Lines], The.

It was yesterday morning. Little Old Letter. Langston Hughes. SAmP

It was you / I could have crawled. Watching Salmon Jump. Simon J. Ortiz. CDW

It was your birthday, we had drunk and dined. Hug, The. Thom Gunn. HarvBoo; NPeEn

It was your lightness that drew me. Lightness. Meg Bateman. NePenScot

It was your resting-place. (LL) Ah, Are You Digging on My Grave? Thomas Hardy. MoBrPo; NAEL-5v2; NAEL-6v2; PAI

It wasn't by chance that Marpessa preferred Idas over Apollo. Marpessa's Choice. Yannis Ritsos. VCWP, tr. by Edmund Keeley

It wasn't Ernest; it wasn't Scott. Song for the Squeeze-Box. Theodore Roethke. NBLV

It wasn't in my time, or so I suppose.   Responses to Montale.   Brian Turner.   PeNZ

It wasn't on Crete, but in the hills of Berkeley.   Night Blooming Jasmine.   Diane Wakoski.   GeoHom

It wasn't only envy but also a vague desire.   Christmas Story, A.   Alan Shapiro.   TaR

It wasn't our battalion, but we lay alongside it.   Sergeant-Major Money.   Robert Graves.   FaBoWar; OBWP

It wasn't so long ago, I tell you in a stream.   See No Indian, Hear No Indian.   Victoria Lena Manyarrows.   TWW

It Wasn't the Love of Others or Mine.   Gabriella Leto.   CItWP, *tr.* by Cinzia Sartini Blum and Lara Trubowitz

It wasn't the rooster's familiar cry.   Birds That Woke Us: An Urban Pastoral, The.   Jeffrey Harrison.   UrbNat

It waved not through an eastern sky.   Palm-tree, The.   Felicia Dorothea Hemans.   ViWPN

It well bespeaks a man beheaded, quite.   Division of an Estate.   George Moses Horton.   NAAAL

It well may be. I do not think I would. (LL)   "Love is not all: It is not meat nor drink."   Edna St. Vincent Millay.   APT-1; GSo; HAP; HeIP-4; NoAM; OxBA; TAP

It went many years.   Lockless Door, The.   Robert Frost.   NOBA; TCAPo

It were a thing to which one might aspire. (LL)   Sonnet: Of Why He Would Be a Scullion.   Cecco Angiolieri, da Siena.   AWP; EaItPo, *tr.* by Dante Gabriel Rossetti

It were my soul's desire.   Soul's Desire, The.   *Unknown.*   SacPr, *tr.* by Eleanor Hull

It wes upon a Shere [*or* Scere] Thorsday that ure [*or* oure] Louerd [*or* Lord] aros.   Judas Sells His Lord.   *Unknown.*   MiEL

It will be cold, going back. (LL)   Déjeuner sur l'herbe.   Tu Fu.   BLT; CarOv, *tr.* by Carolyn Kizer

It will be cold now in Crete.   Time Zones.   Jane Duran.   MFPA

It will be looked for, book[e], when some but see.   To My Book.   Ben Jonson.   BeJo; FaBoVe; NAEL-5v1; NAEL-6v1; NAEL-7v1

It will be otherwise. (LL)   Otherwise.   Jane Kenyon.   AmFaPo; LoL

It will look as though I am flying into myself. (LL)   Death.   Bill Knott.   PBCAP; SPE

It will make the muslins drop.   May—1941.   Valentine Penrose.   SurPaPo, *tr.* by Mary Ann Caws

It Will Not Apprehend the Object.   Patrizia Cavalli.   CItWP, *tr.* by Cinzia Sartini Blum

It will not be / any more.   No More.   Idea Vilariño.   BLPSL, *tr.* by Rene de Costa, Rigas Kappatos and Eleni Paidoussi

"It will not be long, love, till our wedding day." (LL)   She Moved through the Fair.   Padraic Colum.   BIrV; NOIV

It Will Not Do.   Deryn Rees-Jones.   MFPA

It will not do how stupidly you love her.   It Will Not Do.   Deryn Rees-Jones.   MFPA

It will not hurt me when I am old.   Moonlight.   Sara Teasdale.   VGW

It will not resemble the sea.   New Poem, The.   Charles Wright.   HCAP

It will not shine again.   Emily Jane Brontë.   NOBVV

It will rain tonight.   New Life.   Joseph E. Kariuki.   TTY

It will resound finely.   Frances Densmore.   APT-1   *Fr.* Chippewa Music.

It would be.   Phone Call to Rutherford.   Paul Blackburn.   PFTM-2; PoM

It would be easier.   Albuquerque Graveyard, The.   Jay Wright.   ESEAA

It would be easier if they were on.   Lovers, The.   Geoffrey Holloway.   NLP

It would be nice, I think.   What She Said.   Kallatanar.   WoPoe, *tr.* by A. K. Ramanujan

It would be painful to interfere.   Memo.   Charles G. Ballard.   VoR

It would be very pleasant to die with a wolf woman.   Yoldugu.   STP

It would be worth it to go ninety miles out of your way.   Royal Manor Road.   Gerald Stern.   InvLad

It would be wrong for us. It is not right.   Sappho.   BoWoP

It would have been a dragon, this monstrous jet.   Dragon-Watching in St. Louis.   Carter Revard.   UrbNat

It would have been better than this. (LL)   Waiting for Icarus.   Muriel Rukeyser.   LCAP-2; NNaP

It would have starved a Gnat.   Emily Dickinson.   NCAP

It would have to be a dream.   Twilight Time.   Floyd Skloot.   MiVo

It would melt.   Basho.   ChAP; EH, *tr.* by Robert Hass

It would never be Common—more—I said.   Emily Dickinson.   APN-2

It would never be morning, always evening.   Memory of Brother Michael.   Patrick Kavanagh.   HarvBoo

It would surely be known for years after as the day I shot.   James [*or* Jim] Harrison.   BodElec   *Fr.* Letters to Yesenin.

Italia, Io Ti Saluto!   Christina Georgina Rossetti.   VWP; WPE

Italia! Oh Italia! thou who hast.   Italy.   Vincenzo da Filicaia.   AWP, *tr.* by Byron

Italian.   In Answer to Their Questions.   Giovanna (Janet) Capone.   UnSA

Italian, The.   Mikhail Arkadyevich [*or* Arkad'evich] Svetlov.   TCRP, *tr.* by Daniel Weissbort

Italian dust covers a Libyan.   Antipater of Thessalonica.   GrAn

Italian Eclogues.   Derek Walcott.   BAP-97

Italian Garden, The.   William Carlos Williams.   OBGa

Italian in England, The.   Robert Browning.   OBNV

Italian Marcello, you breathe a much sweeter air.   Elena Ignatova.   ItGoST, *tr.* by Sibelan Forrester   *Fr.* Verses about Music.

Italian Music in Dakota.   Walt Whitman.   APN-1

Italian soldier shook my hand, The.   George Orwell.   OBWP; OxAEP-2

Italians Are Excited, The.   Freda Downie.   EmeKit

Italic.   Roger McGough.   OBCoV

Italics.   Anselm Hollo.   PmAP

Italist Chant.   Rohan B. Preston.   WaCA

Italy.   Vincenzo da Filicaia.   AWP, *tr.* by Byron

Italy.   Edward Coote [*or* Coate] Pinkney.   APN-1

Italy.   Giuseppe Ungaretti.   PeFWW, *tr.* by David McDuff

Italy 1942.   Franco Fortini.   ItPo, *tr.* by Gayle Ridinger

Italy versus England.   Byron.   NOBE   *Fr.* Beppo; a Venetian Story.

Itch, The.   K. Ayyappa Paniker.   OMIP, *tr.* by K. Ayyappa Paniker

Itchin, when I behold thy banks again.   To the River Itchin, near Winton.   William Lisle Bowles.   CenSon; NAEL-6v2; OxBSo

Ité.   Ezra Pound.   HAP; MoAmPo

Item.   E. E. Cummings.   MoAmPo

Items in an envelope. What he'd kept.   Father's Things.   R. V. Bailey.   Prnts

Iterating Sonnet.   Leigh Hunt.   OxBSo

Iteration.   Piera Oppezzo.   CItWP, *tr.* by Cinzia Sartini Blum and Lara Trubowitz

Ithaca-Liverpool.   Gladys Mary Coles.   Prnts

Ithaca: The Palace at Four A.M.   Richard Howard.   Last Words.   DiPo

Ithaka.   Constantine P. Cavafy.   WoPoe, *tr.* by Edmund Keeley and Philip Sherrard

Itherness.   Ellie McDonald.   CABP

Ithin the woodlands, flow'ry gleaded.   My Orcha'd in Linden Lea.   William Barnes.   EBVV; FaBoVe; NOBVV; NPeEn; OxBEV

Itinerary.   Doug Anderson.   OPRER

Itinerary.   Edwin Morgan.   HarvBoo; OBCoV

ITMA.   Roddy Lumsden.   NeBl

"It's a '49," Rhinehardt said, and slammed.   Making Money: Drought Year in Minkler, California.   Gary Soto.   NoAM

It's altogether something else with shrapnel.   Proverbs.   Teresa de Jesús.   AF, *tr.* by Maria Proser

Its apotheosis, at last—the hurricane! (LL)   Air Plant, The.   Hart Crane.   MoAmPo; PAI

Its back was leaves that mimed the leaves in back of us, but.   Station (1).   James Galvin.   GifTon

Its beak is red and it has a battlefield-look.   Valentine Delivered by a Raven.   Tess Gallagher.   ExTi

Its body brevity, and wit its soul. (LL)   What Is an Epigram?   Samuel Taylor Coleridge.   FaBoEE; NIL-7; NIP-4

Its body in a rag-tag army. (LL)   Louis MacNeice.   OBWP; OxAEP-2   *Fr.* Autumn Journal.

"Its claws have struck through the clouds."   Wolfram von Eschenbach.   GePo

Its country and its God! (LL)   Homes of England, The.   Felicia Dorothea Hemans.   NOBRP; PEW; RWP; UV; ViWPN; WPE

Its dark pages. (LL)   To the Reader.   Denise Levertov.   PoM; VGW

Its edges foamed with amethyst and rose.   Great Breath, The.   "Æ."   MoBrPo; OBEV; OBMV

It's 8:54 A.M. in Brooklyn it's the 28th [*or* 26th] of July [and].   Ted Berrigan.   PmAP   *Fr.* Sonnets, The.

Its expanse is gigantic.   Factory, The.   Lajos Kassák.   IQMS, *tr.* by Michael Kitka

Its Explanation found. (LL)   Emily Dickinson.   NAAL-2v1; NAAL-3

Its eyes falling back against the interior of their cylinders, opened—thus laying—.   Forward or Back.   Aaron Shurin.   FTOS

Its former green is blue and thin.   Garden Seat, The.   Thomas Hardy.   HAP; RB

Its gaze filled my abyss, its gaze melted.   Pain.   Enrique Gonzáles Martínez.   TCLAP, *tr.* by Samuel Beckett

Its glory and its kingdom and its power! (LL)   To ———: "Vainly my heart had with thy sorceries striven."   Sarah Helen Whitman.   APN-1; TCAPo

Its grandest lesson: "On! sail on!" (LL)   Columbus.   Joaquin Miller.   APN-2; BRP

Its lettered pleats and crevices.   Letters from the Concertina File 1939–1940.   Sue MacIntyre.   Prnts

Its manure. (LL)   Un-American Investigators.   Langston Hughes.   BPo; HHAm

Its "mild wild head doth lie." (LL)   Sea Unicorns and Land Unicorns. Marianne Craig Moore.   NALW; PFTM-1

Its mother on guard.   Issa.   EH, *tr.* by Robert Hass

It's 1962 March 28th.   Things I Didn't Know I Loved.   Nazim Hikmet.   AF; AmFaPo; VCWP

Its nostrils black, the horse plunges.   Battle.   Aleksandr Petrovich Tkachenko.   ItGoST, *tr.* by Maia Tekses

It's 110 in Atascadero.   Arrangement.   Glenna Luschei.   GeoHom

Its own identity. (LL)   Emily Dickinson.   NAAL-2v1; NAAL-3

Its pale tendrilous horn. (LL)   Cuttings.   Theodore Roethke.   APT-2; HCAP; LCAP-2; NAAL-2v2; NAAL-5; NOBA; NoAM; OBGa; TAP; UnPo

Its pecked-at ripeness that scans you, then moves on. (LL)   Haw Lantern, The.   Seamus Heaney.   HarvBoo; MakPoe; NoAM; PNI

Its pieces flash now in the crown / of the tallest oak. (LL)   Trees, The.   Adrienne Rich.   CoAP; EmeKit; NOBA; WPE

Its Pliancy.   Hans Lodeizen.   TuT, *tr.* by Eamon Grennan

Its presence is not impeded by visible form.   Human Mind, The.   Ai Shih-te.   TrJP, *tr.* by William C. White

Its pristine bloom. (LL)   On Receiving News of the War.   Isaac Rosenberg.   HarvBoo; MoBrPo; OBWP; OxAEP-2; PeFWW; PeSAV; PoWW

Its quick soft silver bell beating, beating.   Auto Wreck.   Karl Shapiro.   APT-2; NIL-7; NIP-4; RB; VGW

Its radiance bursts forth in summer's bright light.   Sunflower.   Kao Ch'i.   SuSp, *tr.* by Irving Y. Lo

Its rails and the Main Chance gone to scrap.   Rights of Way.   Thomas Reiter.   GM

Its rancid saliva can't fill up a shell.   Su Tung-p'o (Su Shih).   SuSp, *tr.* by Irving Y. Lo   *Fr.* Two Poems on Insect Painting by Candidate Yin.

Its retributions work like clockwork.   Under the Eyes.   Tom Paulin.   CIP-2; PNI

Its savage eyes, at whom do they glare?   Su Tung-p'o (Su Shih).   SuSp, *tr.* by Irving Y. Lo   *Fr.* Two Poems on Insect Painting by Candidate Yin.

Its senile pleasure. (LL)   University.   Karl Shapiro.   APT-2; OxBA

Its skirt of rain and wind and snow.   Second Rondeau.   Johann Nikolaus Götz.   GePo, *tr.* by George C. Schoolfield

Its strength, and struck. (LL)   Eight O'Clock.   A. E. Housman.   InPK-6; MoBrPo; NoAM; OxBSP; PAI; PoE; SoSe-8

Its teeth worked doubtfully.   Key, The.   John Ormond.   AngWePo; TCAWP

Its this familiar black line from the tops.   Elaine Randell.   Oth   *Fr.* Snoad Hill Poems, The.

Its trunk as of dead silver cast.   Felled Plane Tree, The.   Anna Hajnal.   BoWoP, *tr.* by William Jay Smith

Its wednesday night baby.   Master Charge Blues.   Nikki Giovanni.   OBAL

Its work is memory.   Pen, The.   Galway Kinnell.   BodElec

Its wrinkled foreskin, twisting open, opens.   Morning Glory.   Howard Moss.   DiPo

Its youth. The sea grows old in it. (LL)   Fish, The.   Marianne Craig Moore.   APT-1; ColAP; FaBoWP; MoAmPo; NAAL-2v2; NoAM; NoP-4; OxBA

Itself, until, at last, the cry concerns no one at all. (LL)   Course of a Particular, The.   Wallace Stevens.   APT-1; HCAP

Itylus.   Algernon Charles Swinburne.   NPeEn; UV

Ivan and the Serf.   "David Samuilovich Samoylov [*or* Samoilov]."   TCRP, *tr.* by Lubov Yakovleva

Ivan, do not kill your son!   Sketches from History.   Sergey [*or* Sergei] Drofenko.   TCRP, *tr.* by Lubov Yakovleva

Ivanovs, The.   Nikolai Alekseievich Zabolotsky [*or* Zabolotskii].   TCRP, *tr.* by Daniel Weissbort

I've heard the[m] lilting at our [*or* the] ewe-milking [*or* yowe-milking *or* yewe-milking].   Flowers of the Forest, The.   Jane [*or* Jean] Elliot.   ECWP; FaBoCh; NePenScot; OxBEV; OxBS; SCGP; WPE

Ivied Tree-Top, An.   *Unknown.*   NOIV

Ivory Tower, The.   Allen Tate.   APT-2

Ivy, chefe of trees it is.   In Praise of Ivy.   *Unknown.*   MiEL

Ivy Compton-Burnett's irritations.   Limerick.   *Unknown.*   PeLi

Ivy Crown, The.   William Carlos Williams.   NAAL-2v2; NoAM

Ivy on my window sill, The.   Last Poem.   Mihály Tompa.   IQMS, *tr.* by Madeline Mason

Ivy ties the cellar door in autumn.   Dreaming of Hair.   Li-Young Lee.   BodElec

I.W. To her unconstant Lover.   Isabella Whitney.   EMWP; PBRV

Iwapele, release me.   Release.   Femi Osofisan.   NAfrP

Izhab-O-Rasai.   N. M. Rashid.   CarVo, *tr.* by Carolyn Kizer

J

J. Alfred Prufrock to.   Said.   George Starbuck.   OBAL

J. C. Lawson / my great-grandfather.   Town History, 1917.   David Huddle.   PBCAP

J Car, The.   Thom Gunn.   MakPoe

J is for Jealousy.   William Henry Davies.   TCAWP

J. M. W. Turner on Switzerland.   Consolations of Art.   Roy Fuller.   OxBC

J o l l y m e r r y.   Computer's First Christmas Card, The.   Edwin Morgan.   NOxBChV; OxBEV

J. S. Mill.   Edmund Clerihew Bentley.   OxBoLi; PeLV   *Fr.* Clerihews.

J's the Jumping Jay-Walker.   Phyllis McGinley.   SSCS   *Fr.* All around the Town.

Ja Nul Homs Pris Ne Ira a Raison.   Richard I, Coeur de Lion.   WoPoe, *tr.* by Frank Templeton Prince

(Coeur de Lion.)   HarvBoo

JA ZZ : (The "Say What?") IS IS JA LIVES.   Imamu Amiri Baraka.   SpirFl

Jabberwocky.   Lewis Carroll.   AmFaPo; BRP; CABP; ChAP; CIHu; EBEV; EBVV; HeIP-4; ITBLP; InPK-6; NAEL-5v2; NAEL-6v2; NBLV; NOBE; NOBL; NOBVV; NOxBChV; NTCP; NoAM; NoP-4; OBSP; OxAEP-2; OxBEV; PeLV; PeVV; PoRA; RB; TFi; TRP; TTTS; UV   *Fr.* Through the Looking-Glass.

Jacaranda.   Roo Borson.   NOBC

Jack.   Louis Golding.   TrJP

Jack.   Charles Henry Ross.   NOxBChV; Spl

Jack, Afterwards.   Philip Dacey.   ReTh

Jack and Dinah Want Freedom.   *Unknown.*   BPo; NAAAL

Jack and Gill [*or* Jill] went up the hill.   Jack and Gill.   Mother Goose.   OxBoLi; OxNR; PeLV

Jack and Gye.   *Unknown.*   OxNR

Jack and His Fiddle.   Mother Goose.   OxNR; ReMoGo

Jack and I got see-double drunk. (LL)   Rank.   Lincoln Kirstein.   FaBoA; OBWP

Jack and Jill.   A. E. Housman.   UV

Jack and Jill went up the hill.   *Unknown.*   OxBEV

Jack and Jill went up the hill / To fetch some heavy water.   Paul Dehn.   ReMoGo   *Fr.* Rhymes for a Modern Nursery.

Jack and Joan they think no ill.   Jack and Joan.   Thomas Campion.   FaBoCh

Jack Barrett went to Quetta.   Story of Uriah, The.   Rudyard Kipling.   NOBVV; OxBEV; PeVV; SCV

Jack be nimble.   Mother Goose.   LB; OxNR; ReMoGo

Jack, dear, at last we are free!—But her mother came to! (LL)   And Her Mother Came Too.   Ivor Novello.   OBCoV; ReLy

"Jack fell as he'd have wished," the Mother said.   Hero, The.   Siegfried Sassoon.   OBWP

Jack finds his wife a perfect beauty. (LL)   Double Transformation, The.   Oliver Goldsmith.   OBCoV; OBNV

Jack Frost.   Celia Laighton Thaxter.   OBCA

Jack Frost.   Fay Zwicky.   BMAP

Jack Giantkiller took and struck.   Driving Cross-Country.   X. J. Kennedy.   TwCP

Jack Gilbert.   Campbell McGrath.   NAPBL

Jack Hall.   Thomas Hood.   NOBRP

Jack hammer! brain chiseller! come out!   Men at Work.   Richard Tipping.   NOBAu

Jack, if you got to be a rounder.   Street Song.   Langston Hughes.   APT-2

Jack-in-the-Box is faithful.   Jack-in-the-Box.   John Mole.   NOxBChV

Jack in the Pulpit.   *Unknown.*   OxNR

Jack Jelf.   *Unknown.*   ReMoGo

Jack Jingle.   *Unknown.*   ReMoGo

Jack Johnson Does the Eagle Rock.   Cornelius Eady.   ESEAA; MoASP

Jack johnson licked.   White Hope.   Ishmael Reed.   ISC

Jack jump over / The candlestick. (LL)   Mother Goose.   LB; OxNR; ReMoGo

Jack London once told the story.   Johnny.   Vladimir Nikolaevich Kornilov.   TCRP, *tr.* by Daniel Weissbort

Jack of the North.   *Unknown.*

"Now for that slawnders sake."   PBRV

Jack's Last Words.   Stephen Kessler.   GeoHom

Jack's Pigeon.   R. F. Langley.   HarvBoo

Jack Satan smelts the dead to make new bullets. (LL)   Ambrose Bierce.   APN-2; OBAL   *Fr.* Devil's Dictionary, The.

Jack Sprat could eat no fat.   Mother Goose.   LB; OxNR; ReMoGo

Jack Sprat's Cat.   *Unknown.*   OxNR

Jack Steeplejack.   Tall Story for Fred Dibnah.   Geoffrey Summerfield.   OTCP

Jack the Giant-Killer.   James Whitcomb Riley.   NOxBChV

Jack the Giant Queller; an Antique History.   Henry Brooke.   NOEC

Jack the Piper.   *Unknown.*   OxNR

Jack Would Speak through the Imperfect Medium of Alice.   Alice Notley.   PmAP

Jack, you are quiet now among the dead.   To John Reed.   Max Eastman.   APT-1

Jackdaw of Rheims, The.   Richard Harris Barham.   CABP

Jackdaw of Rheims, The. "Thomas Ingoldsby." EBNV; OBCoV; OBNV; OBSP *Fr.* Ingoldsby Legends, The.

Jackdaw sat on the Cardinal's chair!, The. Jackdaw of Rheims, The. Richard Harris Barham. CABP

Jackdaw sat on the Cardinal's chair, The. "Thomas Ingoldsby." EBNV; OBCoV; OBNV; OBSP *Fr.* Ingoldsby Legends, The.

Jacket Notes. Ishmael Reed. UnSA

Jacket of Gray, The. Caroline Augusta Ball. CBCWP

Jackey Jackey gallops on a horse like a swallow. Bushranger, A. Kenneth Slessor. CBAP; NOBAu

Jackie. King D. Kuka. VoR

Jackie and I cross-legged. Brown Girl, Blonde Okie. Gary Soto. NOxBChV

Jackie in Cambodia. Catherine Bowman. ReTh

Jacklight. Louise Erdrich. HATNAP; NIL-7; WeW-3

Jackson Pollock had a quaint. Phyllis McGinley. FaBoEE; OBCoV; OBSV *Fr.* Spectator's Guide to Contemporary Art.

Jacky, come give me thy fiddle. Jack and His Fiddle. Mother Goose. OxNR; ReMoGo

Jacky Demonstrates for Land Rights. Mudrooroo Narogin. IBA

Jacky Hears the Century Cry. Mudrooroo Narogin. IBA

Jacky him been sit listening to the wind. Song Circle of Jacky. Mudrooroo Narogin. IBA

Jacky Sings His Songs. Mudrooroo Narogin. IBA

Jacob. Phoebe Cary. APN-2; OBAL

Jacob. George Garrett. CRP

Jacob. Ruth Gilbert. PeNZ *Fr.* Leah.

Jacob. Else Lasker-Schüler. BoWoP, *tr. by* Rosmarie Waldrop

Jacob. Delmore Schwartz. ChIV-1; TaR

Jacob and Esau. Else Lasker-Schüler. BoWoP, *tr. by* Rosmarie Waldrop

Jacob, hear! Richard Beer-Hofmann. TrJP, *tr. by* Ida Bension Wynn *Fr.* Jacob's Dream.

Jacob's Destiny. Richard Beer-Hofmann. TrJP, *tr. by* Ida Bension Wynn *Fr.* Jacob's Dream.

Jacob's Dream. Richard Beer-Hofmann.
  Jacob's Destiny. TrJP, *tr. by* Ida Bension Wynn

Jacob's Ladder. Donald Davie. OxBSo

Jacob's Ladder, The. Denise Levertov. APSN; ChIV-1; NAAL-5; PFTM-2; PoM

Jacob's Pillow, and Pillar. Henry Vaughan. ChIV-1

Jacob Wrestling with the Angel. Jones Very. ChIV-1

Jacobite's Epitaph, A. Thomas Babington Macaulay, 1st Baron Macaulay. NOBE; OBEV
  (Epitaph on a Jacobite.) EBEV; NOBVV; OxAEP-2

Jacobite Toast. John Byrom. FaBoEE
  (Extempore [Verses] Intended to Allay the Violence of Party-Spirit.) NOBL; PeLV
  (God bless the king, God bless our faith's defender.) SacPr

Jacques s'apprête. Luis d'Antin Van Rooten. OBCoV *Fr.* Mots d'Heures: Gousses, Rames.

Jade cave, ten thousand flowering peach trees, A. Painting. Chang Yü. CoBLCP, *tr. by* Jonathan Chaves

Jade dews deeply wilt and wound the maple woods. Tu Fu. SuSp *Fr.* Autumn Thoughts.

Jade faces of the girls on Yueh Stream, The. Girls of Yueh, The. Li Po. TAL

Jade Flower Palace. Tu Fu. ColAnChi, *tr. by* David Lattimore

Jade river: Birds are dazzling white and whiter. Wu-Chuen. Tu Fu. ChinPo, *tr. by* Yip Wai-lim

Jade slipped from my wrist, The. Spaces We Leave Empty. Cathy Song. YaYoPo

Jade Steps Plaint. Hsieh T'iao. SuSp, *tr. by* Ronald C. Miao

Jade trees from the rear courtyard of the empire of Ch'en. Li K'ai-hsien. CoBLCP *Fr.* On Snow.

Jade water runs. Poem Fifty. Nancy Morejón. TANSG, *tr. by* Joy Renjilian-Burgy

Jaffa Gate. Notes in Jerusalem. Nicholas Samaras. TWW

Jaffa, July 1948. Hamutal Bar Yosef. DTA, *tr. by* Shirley Kaufman

Jagged head. King & Queen. John Montague. PBCIP

Jagged mouth. Woodland God. Johannes Bobrowski. WoPoe, *tr. by* Rich Ives

Jaguar's Dream, The. Charles Marie René Leconte de Lisle. WoPoe, *tr. by* James Lasdun

Jah Brown si-down. Ethiopia Unda a Jamaican Mango Tree. Opal Palmer Adisa. WaCA

Jah Music. Lorna Goodison. WaCA

Jah Son / Another Way. Kendel Hippolyte. WaCA

Jahr der Seele, Das. Stefan George.
  "No way too long--no path too steep." AWP

Jaikur and the City. Badr Shakir Al-Sayyab. MAP, *tr. by* Lena Jayyusi and Christopher Middleton

Jail Poems. Bob Kaufman. NAAAL

Jail was the only place for them. Leave to appeal was refused. (LL) Wife Who Smashed Television Gets Jail. Paul Durcan. CABP; CIP-2

Jailbird. Vernon Scannell. OxBC

Jain Bird Hospital in Delhi, The. William Meredith. VCAP

Jair son of Manasseh went and seized the encampments. Thomas Merton. ChIV-1 *Fr.* Geography of Lograire, The.

Jaisalmer, 1. Ghulam Mohammed Sheikh. OMIP, *tr. by* Saleem Peeradina

Jake Balokowsky, my biographer. Posterity. Philip Larkin. OxBC

Jalan Thamrin in Denpasar. Walking down Jalan Thamrin. Robert Francis Brissenden. CBAP

Jalapeña Gypsies. Jay Wright. NBV

Jam Session. Langston Hughes. APT-2

Jam Trap, The. Charles Tomlinson. MoBrPo

Jamaica Market. Agnes Maxwell-Hall. TTY; WHSW

Jamaica 1980. Lorna Goodison. GT

Jamaica, October 18, 1972. Shara McCallum. AmPoNex

Jamaican Bus Ride. Arthur Seymour John Tessimond. OxBTC

Jamal; Nineteen Cows In a Slow Line Walking. Gwendolyn Brooks. ESEAA *Fr.* Children Going Home.

Jamal's Lamentation. Reuben Jackson. GT

James Alan Park / Came naked stark. Thomas Erskine, 1st Baron Erskine. FaBoEE

James Bond Movie, The. May Swenson. FaBoWP

James Brown. Linwood M. Ross. InTrad

James Cagney was the one up both our streets. Continuous. Tony Harrison. NPeEn

James Dean. Rae Desmond Jones. BMAP

James Dean and the Pig. Joseph Like. ReTh

James Grant. *Unknown.* ESPB

James Harris. *Unknown. See* Demon Lover, The

James Harris. *Unknown. See* Carpenter's Wife, The

James Harris (The Daemon Lover). *Unknown.* ESPB

James Hatley. *Unknown.* ESPB

James Hugo Johnston. Maggie Pogue Johnson. CBWP-4

James James. Disobedience. Alan Alexander Milne. NOxBChV; NTCP; OTCP; TLR; UV

James Lee's Wife. Robert Browning.
  Among the Rocks. OxBSP
  In the Doorway. SCGP

James Madison's hand cd lead an ox to water. Jackson Mac Low. APSN *Fr.* Presidents of the United States of America, The.

James Monroe / laid a hand. Jackson Mac Low. APSN *Fr.* Presidents of the United States of America, The.

James Powell on Imagination. Larry Neal. BPo

James went first because James always went first. The year I was six. Licking Wounds. Alice Anderson. AmPoNex

James Wetherell. Edwin Arlington Robinson. MoAmPo

Jameson's Ride. Alfred Austin. UV

Jamie Douglas. *Unknown.* ESPB *See* Waly, Waly [Love Be Bonny]
  (Lord Douglas.) OxBB

Jamie Telfer of [or in] the Fair Dodhead. *Unknown.* ESPB; IBB; OxBB

Jamila. Nazik Al-Mala'ika. WPOW, *tr. by* Kamal Boullata

Jammed into denim, grinning in Polaroid. Ballad of the Bright Angel. Bruce Berger. GeoH

Jan's Birthday. David Lee. GifTon

Jan van Hogspeuw staggers to the door. Card-Players, The. Philip Larkin. BLT; OxBC

Jane. Philip Hammial. BMAP

Jane Austen. Patricia Beer. CABP

Jane Austen at the Window. Patricia Beer. FaBoWP

Jane Doe #2. Rafael Campo. AmPoNex; WiU *Fr.* Ten Patients, and Another.

Jane Hollybrand; or, Virtue Rewarded. Edward Edwin Foot. VerBaPo

Jane, Jane / Tall as a crane. Aubade. Dame Edith Sitwell. BWW; MoBrPo; NALW; NoAM; PoRA

Jane looks down at her organdy skirt. In Bertram's Garden. Donald Justice. BoLoP; VGW

Janet Waking. John Crowe Ransom. APT-1; ColAP; FuPo; InPK-6; MoAmPo; NAAL-2v2; NoAM; PoE; RB; TAP

Jankin. *Unknown. See* Kyrie, So Kyrie

Janna. King D. Kuka. VoR

János Kemény. István Gyöngyösi.
  "Day is done; the twilight grows more dark, The." IQMS, *tr. by* Watson Kirkconnell

Januar: by this fire [or thys fyre] I warme my handes. Labours of the Months. *Unknown.* EBEV

Januaries, Nature greets our eyes. Brazil, January 1, 1502. Elizabeth Bishop. BLT; FaBoWP; NoAM; PoPoPo; PoetW; VCAP

January. Douglas Gibson. OBCP

January. Hoffman Reynolds Hays. SPE

January. John Heath-Stubbs. OBCP

January. Issa. EH, *tr. by* Robert Hass

January. Weldon Kees. CoAP

January. Henrietta Cordelia Ray. CBWP-3

January. Folgore da San Geminiano [*or* Gimignano]. EaItPo, *tr. by* Dante Gabriel Rossetti *Fr.* Sonnets of the Months.

January. William Carlos Williams. MoAmPo

January 1, 1829. Nathaniel Parker Willis. APN-1

January 1st. Anne Sexton. HCAP

January 15 as a National Holiday. Carter Revard. VoR

January 30, 1976: Message to Myself. Bob Kaufman. PFTM-2

January, 1795. Mary Robinson. ECWP; OxBEV; WoRP

January 1939. Ilya Grigoryevich Ehrenburg [*or* Erenburg]. TCRP, *tr. by* Cathy Porter

January 1939. Dylan Thomas. *See* Because the Pleasure-Bird Whistles

January, Anchorage. Linda McCarriston. UrbNat

January and February were never so empty and gray. Spring Will Be a Little Late This Year. Frank Loesser. ReLy

January brings the snow. Garden Year, The. Sara Coleridge. ChAP; OTCP

JANUARY FIRST. Bob Boldman. HA

January first isn't New Year's. Happy New Year, Anyway. Joanna Cole. NTCP

January in Kyoto. Nishiwaki Junzaburo. WoPoe

January Morning. William Carlos Williams. APT-1

January night, A. Moonlight. Significant Fevers. Alison Fell. BrRo

January 1965, Looking on. Kenneth Irby. FTOS

January of a Gnat, The. Carl Rakosi. APT-2; FTOS

January Ovaries. Susan Hahn. ExTi

January played. One Year. N. M. Bodecker. TLR

"January wraps up the wound of his arm." Charles Henri Ford. SPE

Janus. Laurence Perrine. InPK-6

Janus am I; oldest of potentates. Poet's Calendar, The. Henry Wadsworth Longfellow. APN-1

Janus, old man. January in Kyoto. Nishiwaki Junzaburo. WoPoe

Japan. Maxine Chernoff. PmAP

    Amble. PmAP

    Black. PmAP

Japanese Archery. Aleksander Wat. TOF, *tr. by* Richard Lourie

Japanese Beetles. X. J. Kennedy. OBAL

Japanese City. Kenward Elmslie. PmAP

Japanese Figures 1. *Unknown.* EaWin, *tr. by* W. S. Merwin

Japanese Figures 2. *Unknown.* EaWin, *tr. by* W. S. Merwin

Japanese Jokes. Peter Porter. OBCoV

Japanese paragraph, The. Annotations Tropes and Lacunae of the Itoku Master. Ray DiPalma. FTOS

Japanese Presentation I and II. Joan Retallack. FTOS

Japanese Print. Austin Clarke. NOIV

Japanese restaurant is good in autumn—in dank weather—the hot napkins, the warm sake, The. " Eduard Veniaminovich Limonov." TCRusP, *tr. by* William Tjalsma *Fr.* Secret Notebook.

Japanese soldier, A. Narrow Road to the Deep North, The. Paul Muldoon. HarvBoo

Jar containing vermilion, The. Forgive Me. Shakti Chattopadhyay. OMIP, *tr. by* Prithvindra Chakravarty

Jar of cider and my pipe, A. Sluggard, The. William Henry Davies. OBMV

Jardin des Colombières. Lauris Edmond. OBGa

Jarrangulli. Roland Robinson. NOxBChV

Jars of octopus, The. Basho. EH, *tr. by* Robert Hass

Jasbo Brown. DuBose Heyward. SeSe

Jasmine. Claude McKay. APT-1; GT

Jasmine. E. Ethelbert Miller. GT

Jasmine blinker of your breath, The. Ideal Bar, The. Frank O'Hara. BodElec

Jason. Anthony Hecht. ColAP

Jason—sham—too. (LL) Emily Dickinson. NOBA; TCAPo

Jaunty crop-haired graying, The. Poem about People. Robert Pinsky. VCAP

Jaunty traveller that comes to peer, The. Llyn y Gadair. T. H. Parry-Williams. OBWVE, *tr. by* Anthony Conran

Jay a-Pass'd. William Barnes. NOBVV

Jay: I've one mouth but many voices. Cynewulf. ASW *Fr.* Riddles (Exeter Book).

Jaya / Don't wake up Hara's wife. Harināth Majumdār. SinGod, *tr. by* Rachel Fell McDermott

Jaya, tell him that Uma will not be sent. Kamalākānta Bhattācārya. SinGod, *tr. by* Rachel Fell McDermott

Jays, The. John Heath-Stubbs. NOxBChV

Jazz. Angela Ball. BAP-01

Jazz as Was. Al Young. ESEAA

Jazz at the Intergalactic Nightclub. Michael McClure. SeSe

Jazz Band. Frank Marshall Davis. SeSe

Jazz Band in a Parisian Cabaret. Langston Hughes. MoAmPo

Jazz Dancer. Cornelius Eady. SeSe

Jazz Fan Looks Back. Jayne Cortez. ESEAA

Jazz Fantasia. Carl Sandburg. AiP; MoAmPo

Jazz of This Hotel, The. Nicholas Vachel Lindsay. SeSe

Jazz Station. Michael S. Harper. NoAM

Jazzonia. Langston Hughes. ColAP

    (O, silver tree!) NAAAL

Je ne veux de personne aupres de ma tristesse. Henri De Regnier. AWP, *tr. by* Seumas O'Sullivan

Je Suis une Table. Donald Hall. SPE

Je T'Adore. Thomas Kinsella. NoAM

Jealosie. John Donne. ESCV *Fr.* Elegies.

Jealous Adam. Itsik [*or* Itzik *or* Itzig] Manger. TrJP, *tr. by* Jacob Sonntag

Jealous girls these sometimes were. How Marigolds Came Yellow. Robert Herrick. TTTS

Jealousy. Mei-Mei Berssenbrugge. OpBo; PmAP

Jealousy. Mary Elizabeth Coleridge. EnLoPo; LW; WPE

Jealousy. Esther Johnson. OxBSP

    (O shield me from his rage, celestial Powers!) LW

    (On Jealousy.) LW

Jean. Robert Burns. *See* Of A' the Airts [the Wind Can Blaw]

Jean-Baptiste Chardin. Self-Portrait on a Summer Evening. Eavan Boland. NPeEn

Jean, death comes close to us all. Child Bearers, The. Anne Sexton. BoWoP

Jean Rhys. William Scammell. NLP

Jean Richepin's Song. Herbert Trench. OBMV

Jeane Dixon's America. Gerald Costanzo. ReTh

Jeanie Morrison. William Motherwell. TreFP

Jeanie with the Light Brown Hair. Stephen Collins Foster. APN-2

Jeanne Duval's Confession. Yusef Komunyakaa. BAP-97

Jeanne was holed up (pitch darkness; bread and water). Victor Hugo. SxFrPo, *tr. by* E. H. Blackmore and A. M. Blackmore

Jeannette. Otto Julius Bierbaum. AWP, *tr. by* Jethro Bithell

Jeare your Benefactress, that's but Just. To; Oxon. Marey Waller. EMWP

Jeep Driver, The. Martín Espada. PueRic

Jeepers Creepers. Johnny Mercer. ReLy

Jeepney. Gemino H. Abad. ReBoTo

Jeepneyfying. Noel Mateo. ReBoTo

Jeffers Country. Sherod Santos. GeoHom

Jefferson Company, The. Clarence Major. BodElec

Jeffrey Lee Pierce is dead, at age 37, Salt Lake City, Utah. Jeffrey Lee Pierce. Campbell McGrath. NAPBL

Jehovah evokes the promised signs. Tovu-Vavohu. Manuela Fingueret. MirDau, *tr. by* Roberta Gordenstein

Jehovah, God, Who Dwelt of Old. Lewis R. Amis. AH

Jehovah, Lord and Majesty. Conrad Weiser. AH, *tr. by* Sheema Z. Buehne

Jehovah Our Righteousness. William Cowper. NOCV *Fr.* Olney Hymns.

Jellicle Cats are black and white. Song of the Jellicles, The. T. S. Eliot. FaBoCh

Jellon Grame. *Unknown.* EBEV; ESPB; OxBB

Jellyfish, A. Marianne Craig Moore. OxBSP

    (Jelly-Fish, A.) ChAP

Jellyfish Eggs. Gregory Orfalea. GraLe

Jemima. Mother Goose. *See* There Was a Little Girl

Jemmy Ball, a lucky digger. Moggy's Wedding. Charles Robert Thatcher. NOBAu

Jennie McGrew. Edgar Lee Masters. RACG

Jennifer Gentle and Rosemary. *Unknown.* *See* Riddles Wisely Expounded

Jenny come ower the hill. Doors of Sleep, The. Marion Angus. NePenScot

Jenny come tie my. Bonny Cravet, The. Mother Goose. OxNR

Jenny hit me when we met. Jenny Hit Me. John Clarke. UV

Jenny in Love. Dolores Kendrick. ESEAA

Jenny in sleep. Dolores Kendrick. ESEAA

Jenny kissed [*or* kiss'd] me! (LL) Rondeau: "Jenny kissed [*or* kiss'd] me when we met." Leigh Hunt. CABP; NBLV; NIL-7; NTCP; OBEV; OxAEP-2; OxBEV; PeLV; PoRA

Jenny Nettles. *Unknown.* NePenScot

Jenny out from Hwome. William Barnes. SCGP

Jenny Wren. William Henry Davies. MoBrPo

Jenny Wren. Walter De la Mare. OWoS

Jenny Wren. Mother Goose. OxNR; ReMoGo

Jenny Wren fell sick. Ungrateful Jenny. Mother Goose. OxNR

Jephtha's Daughter. Byron. ChIV-1

Jephthah's Daughter. "Yehoash." TrJP, tr. by Alter Brody

Jerboa, The. Marianne Craig Moore. NALW

Jeremiah. Bible, O.T.
  As Fowlers Lie in Wait. TrJP
  But Fear Thou Not, O Jacob. TrJP
  Cry of the Daughter of My People, The. TrJP
  Cursed Be the Day. TrJP
  "For Thus saith The Lord to the men of Judah and Jerusalem." OBVE
  O Lord, Thou Hast Enticed Me. TrJP
  Oh That I Were in the Wilderness. TrJP

Jeremiah. Stefan Zweig. TrJP, tr. by Eden and Cedar Paul

Jeremiah, blow the fire. Unknown. OxNR

Jeremiah Obadiah, puff, puff, puff. Jeremiah Obadiah. Unknown. OTCP

Jeremie .17. Bible, Apocrypha. ChIV-1

Jerking and twitching as he walks. Mightier than the Pen. Kingsley Amis. OBCoV

Jerome in His Study. Clark Coolidge. FTOS

Jerry Hall / He is so small. Mother Goose. OxNR; ReMoGo

JERRY'S HOME TOLD YOU not to move the couch, hurt hip *leg tonight* why. Hannah Weiner. PFTM-2 *Fr.* Clairvoyant Journal.

Jerry's Plains, 1848. Geoff Page. BMAP

Jersey Cattle. Ralph Nixon Currey. OxBTC

Jersey Rain. Robert Pinsky. BAP-01

Jerusalem. William Blake. See Milton

Jerusalem. Sara Riwka Erlich. MirDau, tr. by J. M. Deisler and Auristela Xavier

Jerusalem. James Fenton. HarvBoo

Jerusalem. Jacob [or Jakov] Fichman. FIT, tr. by Robert Friend

Jerusalem. Manuela Fingueret. MirDau, tr. by Roberta Gordenstein

Jerusalem. Uri Zvi Greenberg.
  Jerusalem the Dismembered. TrJP, tr. by Charles A. Cowen

Jerusalem. Judah Halevi. TOF, tr. by David Goldstein

Jerusalem. David Morley. NLP

Jerusalem. Adrienne Rich. TaR

Jerusalem. David Rokeah [or Rokeakh]. MHP, tr. by Ruth Finer Mintz

Jerusalem a child reborn every day. Jerusalem. Sara Riwka Erlich. MirDau, tr. by J. M. Deisler and Auristela Xavier

Jerusalem, a Whirling Glass. Luisa Futuransky. MirDau, tr. by Celeste Kostopulos-Cooperman

Jerusalem and the Hour. Rashid Husain [or Hussein]. MAP, tr. by Lena Jayyusi and Peter Porter

Jerusalem! Cry of the hungry heart, oblivion's. Jerusalem. Jacob [orJakov] Fichman. FIT, tr. by Robert Friend

Jerusalem Delivered. Torquato Tasso.
  "Who first of Christian warriors now did chance." FaBoWar, tr. by G. Grinnell-Milne

Jerusalem, I am a pilgrim. Olga Klein Weisz. MirDau, tr. by Leslie MacIntosh

Jerusalem, My Happy Home. Unknown. PoE

Jerusalem roses are complicated. Jerusalem, a Whirling Glass. Luisa Futuransky. MirDau, tr. by Celeste Kostopulos-Cooperman

Jerusalem sits on her mountains, a woman. Bride, The. Alicia Ostriker. TaR

Jerusalem Song. Lisa Suhair Majaj. PoArWo

Jerusalem Sonnets. James Keir Baxter.
  "Bees that have been hiving above the church pond, The." PeNZ
  "Brother Ass, Brother Ass, you are full of fancies." HarvBoo
  "Colin, you can tell my words are crippled now." HarvBoo; PeNZ
  "I am dying now because I do not die." HarvBoo
  "In Auckland it was the twelve days' garland." HarvBoo
  ("Small gray cloudy louse that nests in my beard, The.") NoP-4; PeNZ
  "Yesterday I planted garlic." PeNZ

Jerusalem the Dismembered. Uri Zvi Greenberg. TrJP, tr. by Charles A. Cowen *Fr.* Jerusalem.

Jerusalem; The Emanation of the Giant Albion. William Blake.
  Epigraph. Spl
  Fields from Islington to Marybone, The. OBNV
  "Hampstead Highgate Finchley Hendon Muswell hill: Rage loud." NOBRP
  "I see the Four-fold Man. The Humanity in deadly sleep." NOBRP
  Prelude: "England! awake! awake! awake!" FHYEP; NoP-4

Jerusalem, Timeless. Luisa Futuransky. MirDau, tr. by Celeste Kostopulos-Cooperman

Jerusalem, ungoverned city. Stratis the Sailor by the Dead Sea. George Seferis. WoPoe, tr. by Rex Warner

Jervis Bay, The. Michael Thwaites.
  "On either side the *Jervis Bay* the convoy was dipping." FaBoWar

Jesse James. William Rose Benét. MoAmPo

Jesse James. Unknown. APN-2; UnPo

Jesse James was a lad who [or that] killed many a man. Jesse James. Unknown. APN-2

Jesse James was a two-gun man. Jesse James. William Rose Benét. MoAmPo

Jessie Mitchell's Mother. Gwendolyn Brooks. BoWoP; ColAP; NALW

Jest, The. Austin Clarke. BIrV

Jest 'fore Christmas. Eugene Field. ChrPo

Jester walked in the garden, The. Cap and Bells, The. W. B. Yeats. MoBrPo; NoAM; RB

Jesu. George Herbert. MeLP
  (Iesu.) GeHe

Jesu! bless our slender Boat. William Wordsworth. SacPr *Fr.* Memorials of a Tour of the Continent; 1820.

Jesu Christ, my Leman Swete. Unknown. SacPr

Jesu, Come on Board. Johann C. Pyrlaeus. AH, tr. by Sheema Z. Buehne

Jesu Crist, heovene king. Unknown. MiEL

Jesu Crist, myn leman swete. Jesu Christ, my Leman Swete. Unknown. SacPr

Jesu, for thy muchele might. Unknown. MiEL

JESU is in my heart, his sacred name. Jesu. George Herbert. MeLP

Jesu our raunsoun. William Herebert. MiEL

Jesu, sweete sone dear. Virgin's Song, The. Unknown. NOBE

Jesu that is most of might. Unknown. MiEL

Jesu, thie love within mee is soe maine. William Alabaster. ESCV *Fr.* Divine Meditations.

JESU, thy love within me is so main. Divine Sonnet, A. William Alabaster. NoSic

Jesu, to Thee My Heart I Bow. Nikolaus [or Nicolaus] Ludwig, Graf von Zinzendorf. AH, tr. by John Wesley

Jesus. Francis Lauderdale Adams. OxBS

Jesus. James Philip McAuley. CBAP; ChIV-2

Jesus. Novica Tadic. VCWP, tr. by Charles Simic

Jesus a Child His Course Begun. Margaret Fuller. AH

Jesus and His Mother. Thom Gunn. OxBC

Jesus Asleep. Anne Sexton. PFTM-2

Jesus before Pilate. René Daumal. GI, tr. by Katharine Washburn

Jesus Bids Man Remember. Unknown. MiEL

Jesus calls us! O'er the tumult. Cecil Frances Alexander. SacPr

Jesus Dies. Anne Sexton. PFTM-2; RACG

Jesus, Enthroned and Glorified. Zachary Eddy. AH

Jesús, Estrella, Esperanza, Mercy. Middle Passage. Robert Earl Hayden. APT-2; BPo; ColAP; NAAL-5; NoAM; TRP; VCAP

Jesus got up one day a little later than usual. Goodtime Jesus. James Tate. LCAP-2

Jesus had gone far up the dark slope, when he looked back. Quetzalcoatl Looks Down on Mexico. D. H. Lawrence. PeECV

Jesus I am resting, resting. Jean Sophia Pigott. SacPr

Jesus, I Come to Thee. Nathan S. S. Beman. AH

Jesus, I Live to Thee. Henry Harbaugh. AH

Jesus, in Sickness and in Pain. Thomas H. Gallaudet. AH

Jesus Is Condemned to Death. Pamela Mordecai. WaCA

Jesus, Keep Me Near the Cross. Fanny Crosby. AH

Jesus Loves Me, This I Know. Anna Bartlett Warner. AH

Jesus, Master, O Discover. Unknown. AH

Jesus, Merciful and Mild! Thomas Hastings. AH

Jesus' mother never had no man. Conception. Waring Cuney. APT-2

Jesus, my Light. They Shall Look on Him. "Michael Field." VWP

Jesus Never Sleeps. David Graham. SwNoth

Jesus Praying. Hartley Coleridge. ChIV-2

Jesus Reproaches His People. Unknown. MiEL

Jesus Saviour, Pilot Me. Edward Hopper. AH

Jesus shall reign where'er the sun. Isaac Watts. SacPr

Jesus, Shepherd of Thy Sheep. George Washington Bethune. AH

Jesus slept as still as a toy. Jesus Asleep. Anne Sexton. PFTM-2

Jesus Spreads His Banner o'er Us. Roswell Park. AH

Jesus Suckles. Anne Sexton. PFTM-2

Jesus, the very thought of thee With sweetness fills my breast. Unknown. SacPr, tr. by Edward Caswell

Jesus, These Eyes Have Never Seen. Ray Palmer. AH; SacPr

Jesus, they run into millions. (LL) Soldiers. Unknown. FaBoEE; FaBoWar

Jesus, Thou Divine Companion. Henry Van Dyke. AH

Jesus, Thou Joy of Loving Hearts. Bernard of Clairvaux. SacPr, tr. by Ray Palmer

Jesus, thy blood and righteousness.   Nikolaus [*or* Nicolaus] Ludwig, Graf von Zinzendorf.   SacPr, *tr. by* John Wesley

Jesus to Those Who Pass By.   *Unknown.*   MiEL
(Ye That Pasen by the Weye.)   NAEL-7v1

Jesus Unborn.   Anne Sexton.   PFTM-2

Jesus Was Crucified or: It Must Be Deep.   Carolyn M. Rodgers.   BlSi

Jesus Wept.   William Michael Rossetti.   CenSon

Jesus! What a friend for sinners!   J. Wilbur Chapman.   SacPr

Jesus, where'er thy people meet.   William Cowper.   SacPr   *Fr.* Olney Hymns.

Jet Planes.   Gwyn Williams.   TCAWP

Jet Ring Sent, A.   John Donne.   OxBSP

Jet Set Melodrama.   Michael Brownstein.   FTOS

Jets.   Christopher Meredith.   AngWePo

Jetty, The.   Elaine Randell.   Oth   *Fr.* Snoad Hill Poems, The.

Jetty with its old wormeaten planks, The.   Re-encounter.   Joaquim Paço D'Arcos.   PeSAV, *tr. by* Roy Campbell

Jew.   James A., Jr. Randall.   BPo

Jew, The.   Isaac Rosenberg.   ChIV-1; MoBrPo

Jew answers every question with another question, The.   Edmond Jabès.   PFTM-2, *tr. by* Rosmarie Waldrop   *Fr.* Book of Questions, The.

Jew at Christmas Eve, The.   Karl Shapiro.   VGW

Jew's hands, translucent in the dusk, The.   Spinoza.   Jorge Luis Borges.   TCLAP, *tr. by* Richard Howard and César Rennert

Jew Walks in Westminster Abbey, A.   Aubrey Hodes.   TrJP

Jewel, The.   James Wright (1927–80).   CoAP; NAAL-2v2

Jewel Cliff.   Muso Soseki.   EaWin, *tr. by* W. S. Merwin

Jewel Field.   Muso Soseki.   EaWin, *tr. by* W. S. Merwin

Jewel of the almost islands and the isles.   Catullus.   *See* Apple of islands, Sirmio, & bright peninsulas, set

Jewel of the secret treasury, The.   Hafiz [*or* Hafez].   AWP   *Fr.* Odes.

Jewel Stairs' Grievance, The.   Li Po.   NOBA; OBVE, *tr. by* Ezra Pound

Jewelled steps are already quite white with dew, The.   Jewel Stairs' Grievance, The.   Li Po.   NOBA; OBVE, *tr. by* Ezra Pound

Jewels.   Sara Teasdale.   APT-1

Jewels, The.   Charles Baudelaire.   BoLoP, *tr. by* Roy Campbell

Jewels wherever we look.   *Unknown.*   GifTon, *tr. by* David Ray

Jewish.   Harvey M. Plotnick.   OPRER

Jewish Arabic Liturgies.   *Unknown.*   TrJP, *tr. by* Hartwig Hirschfeld

Jewish Bride, The.   Paul Durcan.   BiHa

Jewish Cemetery at Newport, The.   Henry Wadsworth Longfellow.   APN-1; ChIV-1; ColAP; FaBoA; HAP; HeIP-4; NAAL-5; NCAP; NOBA; NoP-4; OxBA; PoPoPo; TAP; TCAPo

Jewish Cemetery at Olsany, Kafka's Grave, April, Sunny Weather, The.   Miroslav Holub.   PoSu

Jewish Cemetery in Guanabacoa, The.   Ruth Behar.   MirDau

Jewish Conscript, The.   Florence Kiper Frank.   TrJP

Jewish King Lear is getting ready, The.   Adler.   Gerald Stern.   TaR

Jewish May, The.   Morris Jacob Rosenfeld.   TrJP, *tr. by* Helena Frank and Rose Pastor Stokes

Jewish Poet Counsels a King, A.   Santob de Carrion.   TrJP   *Fr.* Consejos y Documentos al Rey Dom Pedro.

Jewish Singles Event, The.   Stewart Florsheim.   GotH; UnSA

Jews at Haifa.   Randall Jarrell.   MoAmPo

Jews in Babylonia.   Charles Reznikoff.

I.   FTOS

Jews in Hell.   Tom Mandel.   PmAP

Jews in the Land of Israel.   Yehuda Amichai [*or* Amikhai].   PoSu, *tr. by* Warren Bargad

Jews, like their neighbors the Pheonicians and the Arabs.   Mannus the Pompeiian to a Greek.   Kahlil Gibran.   GraLe

Jews Speak in Heaven, The.   Gary Catalano.   NOBAu

Jews That We Are, The.   Richard Michelson.   GotH

Jezebel to the Eunuchs.   Eleanor Brown.   MFPA

Jezrael.   Avraham Shlonsky.   MHP, *tr. by* Ruth Finer Mintz

Jhesu, since thou me made and bought.   Prayer to Jesus 1.   Richard Rolle of Hampole.   SacPr

Jig fades to silence, except it doesn't, The. (LL)   Notations of Ten Summer Minutes.   Norman MacCaig.   EmeKit; NPeEn

Jig! Let's dance, A!   Streets 1.   Paul Verlaine.   SxFrPo, *tr. by* Martin Sorrell

Jig Tune: Not for Love.   Thomas McGrath.   VGW

Jigsaw Puzzle.   Russell Hoban.   NTCP

Jihad.   Thelma Seto.   TWW

Jill, A Pindaric Ode.   Elizabeth Thomas.
"Nine times the sun his yearly course had run."   ECWP

Jill's Death.   George Buchanan.   PNI

Jilted Nymph, The.   Thomas Campbell.   EnLoPo

Jilted Queen, The.   Virgil [*or* Vergil].   NAEL-7v1, *tr. by* Henry Howard, Earl of Surrey   *Fr.* Aeneid [*or* Eneados, *Aeneis*], The.

Jim.   Joseph Hilaire Pierre Belloc.   *See* Jim Who Ran Away from His Nurse, and Was Eaten by a Lion

Jim Bludso of the Prairie Belle.   John Milton Hay.   APN-2

Jim Crack Corn; or The Blue Tali Fly.   *Unknown.*   APN-2
(Ole massa an' dat blue tail fly.) (LL)   APN-2

Jim Crow Car.   Langston Hughes.   GM

Jim Crow Cars.   Lizelia Augusta Jenkins Moorer.   CBWP-3

Jim Desterland.   Hyam Plutzik.   RB; VGW

Jim Dumps was a most unfriendly man.   Force.   *Unknown.*   OBCoV   *Fr.* Advertising Rhymes.

Jim, give me your paw! For luck!   To Kachalov's Dog.   Sergey [*or* Sergei] Aleksandrovich Yesenin [*or* Essenin].   TCRP, *tr. by* Daniel Weissbort

Jim Hall's guitar walking around.   From Rich Uneasy America to My Friend Christopher Logue.   Adrian Mitchell.   SeSe

Jim Jackson caught a cold.   If I'm Going to Die I'm going to Have Some Fun.   George M. Cohan.   ReLy

Jim Jones.   *Unknown.*   CBAP

Jim O'Shea was cast away upon an Indian isle.   I've Got Rings on My Fingers.   Maurice Scott.   ReLy

Jim Who Ran Away from His Nurse, and Was Eaten by a Lion.   Joseph Hilaire Pierre Belloc.   EBNV; NOxBChV; OBSP; OxAEP-2
(Jim.)   NoAM; PeLV

Jimeen Connor, the butcher, is coming round.   Brendan Kennelly.   ModIr   *Fr.* Cromwell.

Jimi and Tony.   Mark Doty.   WiU   *Fr.* Atlantis.

Jiminy Whillikers / Admiral Samuel.   Monarch of the Sea.   George Starbuck.   OBAL

Jimmy C.   Courthouse Graffiti for Two Voices.   Martín Espada.   InvLad

Jimmy Jet and His TV Set.   Shel [*or* Shelley] Silverstein.   OBCA; OBCoV

Jimmy's Enlisted; or, The Recruited Collier.   *Unknown.*   EBEV

Jimmy the Mowdy.   Greedy Tom.   *Unknown.*   OxNR

Jimmy was soldier brave and bold.   K-K-K-Katy.   Geoffrey O'Hara.   ReLy

Jinan means eternal waiting.   Descent of Abu Nuwas.   Hasab al-Shaikh Ja'far.   MAP, *tr. by* Diana Der Hovanessian and Salma Khadra Jayyusi

Jingle Bells.   James S. Pierpont.   TCAPo

Jingle bells! jingle, bells!   *Unknown.*   OxNR

Jingle in a broken tongue, A. (LL)   Poet, The.   Paul Laurence Dunbar.   BPo; NAAAL; TCAPo

Jingling her moon of parchment.   Preciosa and the Wind.   Federico García Lorca.   STV, *tr. by* John Frederick Nims

Jinny.   *Unknown.*   NOSC

Jinny the Just.   Matthew Prior.   NOBE; NOEC; OBEV

Jist Ti Let Yi No.   Tom Leonard.   NePenScot

Jo Jo, My Child.   *Unknown.*   TrJP, *tr. by* Immanuel Olsvanger

Joal.   Léopold Sédar Senghor.   NegPo, *tr. by* Ellen Conroy Kennedy

Joan Miró.   Ruthven Todd.   SPE

Joan of Arc.   Benjamin Péret.   PFTM-1

Joan of Arc in Rheims.   Felicia Dorothea Hemans.   RWP; ViWPN

Joan's one-eighth. I'm a quarter.   Two Standards.   Elise Paschen.   OPRER; ReEnLa

João young like us.   Poem of João, The.   Noémia da Sousa.   PeSAV, *tr. by* Margaret Dickinson

Job.   Bible, *O.T.*   NAWM-5v1
"As a servant earnestly desireth the shadow, and as an hireling looketh for the reward of his work."   AWTN, *tr. by* King James Version
(Job's Entreaty.)   AWP
Job Cries Out.   OBVE
(Job's Curse.)   AWP
Let the Day Perish [Wherein I Was Born].   NPeEn; OBVE; TrJP
Moreover the Lord answered Job, and said.   OBVE
Leviathan.   OBVE
"Gird up thy loins now like a man."   AWP
Out of the Whirlwind.   AWP
Not Flesh of Brass.   TrJP
"Then Job spoke and cursed his day and chanted and said."   WoPoe, *tr. by* R. P. Scheindlin
Then the Lord Answered.   AWP
"Knowest thou the time when the wild goates of the rocke bring forth?"   OBVE
"Then the Lord answered Job out of the whirlwind, and sayd."   AWP; OBVE; WoPoe
"Then the Lord answered Job out of the whirlwind."   InvLi, *tr. by* New Revised Standard Version
"Wing of the ostrich rejoiceth, The."   OWoS

Job.   Elizabeth Sewell.   ChIV-1

Job 18, 2.   José Emilio Pacheco.   TCLAP, *tr. by* Alastair Reid

Job Davies, eighty-five. Lore. Ronald Stuart Thomas. NoP-4; OxBC; RB

Job: I was cast onto a new life cycle. Maya Bejerano. DTA, *tr.* by Tsipi Keller *Fr.* Hymns of Job.

Job in certain lives has been to find **A**, The. Spell, The. Molly Peacock. FFC

Job Militant. Francis Quarles.
    Meditatio Tertia Decima. ChIV-1

Job. I. John Hall. ChIV-1

Job's Curse. Bible, *O.T. See* Job

Job's Epitaph. Joshua Sylvester. ChIV-1

Job's Wife. Shirley Kaufman. DTA

Job sat in a corner of the dump eating asparagus. Cæsura. John Ashbery. ChIV-1

Job-seeker, this time hoping. Mr. Bezuidenthout's Dogs. Musaemura Bonus Zimunya. NAfrP

Job the Father. Richard Shelton. PBCAP

Jock o' the Side. *Unknown.* ESPB; IBB; OxBB

Jock of Hazeldean. Sir Walter Scott. GTBS-P; NAEL-5v2; NAEL-6v2; NOBRP; OxBS

Jock the Leg and the Merry Merchant. *Unknown.* ESPB

Jocular Lines to Plotius Grypus. Publius Papinius Statius. RomPo, *tr. by* W. G. Shepherd *Fr.* Sylvae.

Jocund his Muse was; but his Life was chast. (LL) Pillar of Fame, The. Robert Herrick. BeJo; CaPo; NIP-4

Jocund his muse was, but his life was chaste. (LL) To His Book's End. Robert Herrick. CaPo; NAEL-5v1

Joe. Emily Pauline Johnson. SWaP

Joe and Ned. Susanna Blamire. *See* Wey, Ned, Man!

Joe Gargery's Epitaph on His Father. Charles Dickens. FaBoVe *Fr.* Great Expectations.

Joe Hill. Alfred Hayes. UnPo

Joe insisted that life is extreme. Conversation in Woodside. Kim Addonizio. GeoHom

Joe's Luck. Albert Brodrick. PeSAV

Jog On, jog on, the footpath way. William Shakespeare. FaBoCh; NoSic *Fr.* Winter's Tale, The.

Jogger on Riverside Drive, 5:00 A.M., The. Agha Shahid Ali. MoASP

Johann Joachim Quantz's Five Lessons. William Sydney Graham. EmeKit; FaBoMo; HarvBoo

Johannes Agricola in Meditation. Robert Browning. SacPr; TOF

Johannes Milton, Senex. Robert Bridges. PeECV

John. Ebenezer Elliott. Son

John. Jones Very. ChIV-2

John 1:1 and 14. Gail Holst-Warhaft. GI *Fr.* St. John.

John 1:14 (1964). Jorge Luis Borges. GI

John 1:14 (1969). Jorge Luis Borges. GI, *tr. by* Norman Thomas Di Giovanni

John 1:14; And the Word became flesh and dwelt among us. Jorge Luis Borges. GI *Fr.* St. John.

John 2:1–12; On the third day there was a marriage. Rainer Maria Rilke. GI *Fr.* St. John.

John 3:1–15; Now there was a man. Howard Nemerov. GI *Fr.* St. John.

John 3; But Men Loved Darknesse Rather than Light. Bible, *N.T..* ChIV-2, *tr. by* Richard Crashaw *Fr.* St. John.

John 11:30–44; Now Jesus had not yet come to the village. Rainer Maria Rilke. GI *Fr.* St. John.

John 12:24–25; Truly, truly, I say to you. Pier Paolo Pasolini. GI *Fr.* St. John.

John 13:21–30; When Jesus had thus said, he was troubled. Nina Kossman. GI *Fr.* St. John.

John 14:1–2. Mary Elizabeth Fullerton. GI *Fr.* St. John.

John 20:11–18; But Mary stood weeping outside the tomb. Rainer Maria Rilke. GI *Fr.* St. John.

John Adams knew the hand. Jackson Mac Low. APSN *Fr.* Presidents of the United States of America, The.

John Adams lies here, of the parish of Southwell. On a Carrier Who Died of Drunkenness. Byron. NBLV

John and Anne. William Meredith. BodElec

John Anderson, my jo, John, / I wonder what ye mean. Robert Burns. FaBoVe; OxBS

John Anderson my jo, John / When we were first acquent. Robert Burns. AWP; BoLoP; GTBS-P; HeIP-4; InPK-6; NOBE; NOBRP; NOEC; NePenScot; OBEV; OxBEV; PAI; PoE; PoToHe; TFi; TRP; TreFP; WoPoe

John Armstrongs last good night. *Unknown. See* Johnie Armstrong

John Barley-Corn, My Foe. Charles Follen Adams. OBAL

John Barleycorn [a Ballad]. Robert Burns. FaBoCh; RB

John Berryman asked me to write a poem about roosters. Poem with Capital Letters, A. Jane Cooper. FaBoWP

John Berryman Listening to Robert Johnson's "King of the Delta Blues," January 1972. David Wojahn. SeSe

John Bird, a laborer, lies here. Epitaph. Sylvia Townsend Warner. MoBrPo

John Brown. Nicholas Vachel Lindsay. MoAmPo *Fr.* Booker Washington Trilogy, The.

John Brown, glowing far and down. Smell of Coal Smoke, The. Les A. Murray. NOBAu

John Brown's Body. Stephen Vincent Benét.
    Congressmen Came Out to See Bull Run, The. CBCWP
    "He was a farmer, he didn't think much of towns." AiP
    Invocation: "American muse, whose strong and diverse heart.". APT-2
    "John Brown's body lies a-mouldering in the grave." APT-2
    John Brown's Prayer. CBCWP
    Love Came by from the Riversmoke. MoAmPo
    Song of the Riders. MoAmPo

John Brown's body lies a-mouldering in the grave. John Brown's Body. Henry Howard Brownell. HHAm

John Bun. *Unknown.* NBLV

John Burns of Gettysburg. Bret Harte. CBCWP

John Cabot, out of Wilma, once a Wycliffe. Riot. Gwendolyn Brooks. BPo; NAAAL; NALW; NBV; SSLK; TAP

John Chapman. Richard Wilbur. OxBC

John Charles Fremont waited for Jupiter. Jupiter at Beer Springs. Thomas Hornsby Ferril. YaYoPo

John Coltrane. Alfred B. Spellman. SeSe

John Cook had a little grey mare. Mother Goose. OxNR

John Donne. James Simmons. CIP-2

John Dory. *Unknown.* ESPB

John Evereldown. Edwin Arlington Robinson. APN-2; NCAP; OxBA
    (Where are you going tonight, tonight.) ColAP

John Fane Dingle. Glaucopis. Richard Hughes. OBMV

John, founder of towns, - dweller in none;. Bread-Word Giver. John Wheelwright. ChIV-2

John Gilbert Was a Bushranger. *Unknown.* NOBAu

John Gorham. Edwin Arlington Robinson. MoAmPo

John had. Happiness. Alan Alexander Milne. AmFaPo; NOxBChV

John Hancock. Lee Bennett Hopkins. HHAm

John Hardy. *Unknown.* APN-2

John Harralson, John Harralson, you are a wretched creature. Two Appeals to John Harralson, Agent. *Unknown.* OBAL

John he comes to my house. For Jan, with Love. David Lee. GifTon

John Henry. *Unknown.* NOBA; OxBoLi
    (John Henry tol' his cap'n.) TCAPo
    (When John Henry was a little babe [*or* fellow].) BPo; NAAAL
    (When John Henry was a little boy.) HHAm

John Henry tol' his cap'n. *Unknown. See* John Henry was a lil [*or* little] baby

John Henry was a lil [*or* little] baby. John Henry. *Unknown.* NOBA; OxBoLi

John in Prison. Sydney E. Jerrold. SacPr

John. In the sound of that rebellious word. John. Ebenezer Elliott. Son

John-John. Thomas Macdonagh. AWP

John Keats. Byron. FaBoEE; UV

John Keats rose at dawn. Nick Enright. PeLi

John Kinsella's Lament for Mrs. Mary Moore. W. B. Yeats. RB

John Knox. Iain Crichton Smith. OxBS

John Landless Leads the Caravan. Iwan [*or* Yvan] Goll. TrJP

John, look what Mis' Nelson give me. Easter Bonnet, The. Clara Ann Thompson. CBWP-2

John Marr. Herman Melville.
    "Since as in night's deck-watch ye show." APN-2

John Masefield Relates the Story of Tom, Tom, the Piper's Son. Louis Untermeyer. MoAmPo *Fr.* Mother Goose Up-to-Date.

John Maydew or The Allotment. Charles Tomlinson. OBGa

John Milton and My Father. Patricia Beer. HarvBoo

John Mouldy. Walter De la Mare. RB

John Muir on Mt. Ritter. Gary Snyder. NOBA *Fr.* Myths and Texts.

John of Hazelgreen. *Unknown.* ESPB

John of Tours. *Unknown.* AWP, *tr. by* Dante Gabriel Rossetti

John Peel. John Woodcock Graves. OxBoLi

John Percy / Said to his nursy. John Percy. John Bingham Morton. UV

John Quincy Adam's right hand. Jackson Mac Low. APSN *Fr.* Presidents of the United States of America, The.

John Quincy Adams. Rosemary Benét. OBCA

John Rabbit, by Dame Eagle chased. Eagle and the Beetle, The. Jean de La Fontaine. OBVE, *tr. by* Elizur Wright

John Reed's Monologue. Yevgeny Aleksandrovich Yevtushenko [*or* Evtushenko]. RusPo, *tr. by* Robert Arthur Douglas Ford

John Rogers' Exhortation to His Children. *Unknown.* OBCA *Fr.* New England Primer, The.

John's efforts to extract a thorn / failed miserably. Ammianus. GrAn

John's Song. Joan Aiken. TLR

John Smith and His Son, John Smith. Wallace Stevens. TLR

John Smith, fellow fine. *Unknown.* OxNR

John Smith of His Friend Master John Taylor. John Smith. SCAP

John spared his patient labouring ox. Adaios of Macedon. GrAn

John Stuart Mill. Edmund Clerihew Bentley. OxBoLi; PeLV *Fr.* Clerihews.

John Sutter. Yvor Winters. MoAmPo; NOBA; NoAM

John Thomson and the Turk. *Unknown.* ESPB

John, Tom, and James. Charles Henry Ross. NBLV

John was a bad boy, and beat a poor cat. John, Tom, and James. Charles Henry Ross. NBLV

John while swimming in the ocean. Brats. X. J. Kennedy. NBLV

John Winthrop, "Reasons to be Considered for . . . the Intended Plantation in New England," 1629. Nicole Cooley. NeAmPo

John, you were figuring in the gay career. To John Lamb, Esq.: Of the South-Sea House. Charles Lamb. Son

Johnie Armstrang. *Unknown.* ESPB; IBB; OxBB

(John Armstrongs last good night.) PBRV

Johnie Blunt. Robert Burns. OxBB

Johnie Cock. *Unknown.* ESPB

(Johnie o' Cocklesmuir.) OxBB

Johnie Scot. *Unknown.* ESPB

Johnna at the Windmill. Diane Glancy. CRP

Johnnie Cope. Adam Skirving. NePenScot; OxBS

Johnnie Crack and Flossie Snail. Dylan Thomas. OTCP *Fr.* Under Milk Wood.

Johnnie get your gun, get your gun, get your gun. Over There. George M. Cohan. FaBoA; ReLy

Johnnie Norrie. *Unknown.* OxNR

Johnny. Vladimir Nikolaevich Kornilov. TCRP, *tr.* by Daniel Weissbort

Johnny and Jane and Jack and Lou. Children's Ball-Bouncing Song. *Unknown.* NOBAu

Johnny Armstrong killed a calf. *Unknown.* OxNR

Johnny B. Goode. James Seay. SwNoth

Johnny Cock, in a May morning. Johnie Cock. *Unknown.* ESPB

Johnny come down de hollow. *Unknown.* APN-2

Johnny could only sing one note. Johnny One-Note. Lorenz Hart. ReLy

Johnny Crow's Garden. L. Leslie Brooke. NOxBChV

Johnny Dow [*or* Doo]. *Unknown.* FaBoEE

Johnny Guitar is watching Duncan Renaldo. Kinescope. Dionisio D. Martinez. TouFir

Johnny, I Hardly Knew Ye. *Unknown.* BIrV; FaBoWar; NPeEn; OxBoLi

Johnny Laces Up His Red Shoes. Cornelius Eady. InvLad

Johnny One-Note. Lorenz Hart. ReLy

Johnny's into England gane. McNaughtan. *Unknown.* OxBB

Johnny's Pet Superstition. Clara Ann Thompson. CBWP-2

Johnny's Team. Eugene Field. PWR

Johnny's the Lad I Love. *Unknown.* OxBoLi

Johnny shall have a new bonnet. Mother Goose. OxNR; ReMoGo

Johnny, the kitchen sink has been clogged for days, some utensil probably fell down there. What the Living Do. Marie Howe. ExTi

Johnny was bashful and shy. You'd Be Surprised. Irving Berlin. ReLy

Johnny Weissmuller Dead in Acapulco. Clive James. NOBAu

Johnson's Cabinet Watched by Ants. Robert Bly. NOBA

Johny Faa. *Unknown.* OxBB

Johny he has risen up i' the morn. Johnie Cock. *Unknown.* ESPB

Join Me in Celebrating. James Simmons. PNI

Join with the noble-hearted. Distich. Shuraikh. TrJP

Joining Sir Ulick's at the river's bend. William Allingham. NOIV *Fr.* Laurence Bloomfield in Ireland.

Joining the Army: A Song. Wang Ts'an. SuSp, *tr.* by Ronald C. Miao

Joint is Jumpin', The. J. C. Johnson. ReLy

Jojopan. Art Goodtimes. GeoH

Joke, A. Aleksander Wat. BLT

Joke's on me!, The. (LL) Sarah. Delmore Schwartz. ChIV-1; TaR

Joke the size of a small moon headed, A. For Stuart Porter, Who Asked for a Poem That Would Not Depress Him Further. Jeffrey Skinner. PBCAP

Jolly Beggar, The. James V, King of Scotland. OxBB

Jolly Beggars, The. Robert Burns.

Drinking Song. NPeEn; NePenScot; PoE

"I am a Bard of no regard." PoE

I Once Was a Maid. NBLV; OxBoLi

("I once was a maid, though I cannot tell when.") RACG

"Poor Merry-andrew, in the [*or* a] neuk." OBCoV

"So sung the BARD—and Nansie's waws." PoE

("Who have character to lose.") (LL) NBLV

Jolly Fat Widows, The. Julia Fields. GT

Jolly Good Ale and Old. William Stevenson. OBEV *Fr.* Gammer Gurton's Needle.

Jolly good, I said. (LL) I Saw a Jolly Hunter. Charles Causley. EBNV; NOxBChV; OPOU

Jolly Jankin. *Unknown.* See Kyrie, So Kyrie

Jolly Jugger, The. *Unknown.* EBEV; NPeEn

Jolly Pinder of Wakefield, The. *Unknown.* ESPB; PBRV

Jolly Shepherd, The. *Unknown.* NOBE

Jolly young fellow from Yuma, A. Limerick. Ogden Nash. PeLi

Jolly Young Waterman, The. Charles Dibdin. NOEC; OxAEP-1

Jonah. Bible, *O.T.*

Jonah's Prayer. TrJP

Jonah. Randall Jarrell. ChIV-1

Jonah and the Whale. Gareth Owen. OBSP

Jonah and the Whale. *Unknown.* NPeEn *Fr.* Patience.

Jonah had his whale but we had sedans. Big Cars. Jane Flanders. PBCAP

Jonah's Prayer. Mihály Babits. IQMS, *tr.* by Peter Zollman

Jonah's Prayer. Bible, *O.T.* TrJP *Fr.* Jonah.

Jonah was an immigrant, so runs the Bible tale. Darky Sunday School. *Unknown.* OxBoLi

Jonah wept within the whale. To a Song of Sappho Discovered in Egypt. Leonora Speyer. APT-1

Jonathan. "Rachel" [*or* "Rahel"]. TrJP, *tr.* by L. V. Snowman

Jonathan Houghton. Edgar Lee Masters. OxBA *Fr.* Spoon River Anthology.

Jonathan Swift Somers. Edgar Lee Masters. OBAL *Fr.* Spoon River Anthology.

Jone o' Grinfilt. Joseph Lees. NOBRP

Joni Mitchell. Joseph Hutchison. SwNoth

Joplin's voice, edged like a crack. People Are Dropping Out of Our Lives. Albert Goldbarth. SwNoth

Jordan (1). George Herbert. BASC; FHYEP; FSCP; GeHe; HAP; MeLP; NAEL-5v1; NAEL-6v1; NAEL-7v1; NOCV; NOSC; NoP-4; OxBEV; PeECV; PoE; TFi; TrCP; WoPoe

Jordan (2). George Herbert. BASC; CABP; ESCV; FSCP; GeHe; NAEL-5v1; NAEL-6v1; NAEL-7v1; NOSC; OBWVE; PBRV; SacPr

Joseph. Gilbert Keith Chesterton. ChIV-2; ChrPo

Joseph. Timothy Steele. RA

Joseph, being seventeen years old, was feeding the flock with his brethren. Bible, *O.T.* NAWM-5v1 *Fr.* Genesis.

Joseph Come Back as the Dusk. Franz Wright. LCAP-2

Joseph Conrad. Malcolm Lowry. CLPP

(But words beyond the life of ships dream on.) (LL) CLPP

Joseph, I afraid of stars. Holy Night. Lucille Clifton. NALW

Joseph in Carcere. Sir Francis Hubert. ChIV-1 *Fr.* Egypt's Favorite.

Joseph Joseph breathed slower. Then. Lawrence Joseph. GraLe; PBCAP

Joseph's Coat. George Herbert. ChIV-1; GeHe

Joseph's Suspicion. Rainer Maria Rilke. TrCP

Joseph was an old man. Cherry-Tree Carol, The. *Unknown.* ChrPo; EBEV; ESPB; HeIP-4; MakPoe; OxBB; OxBoLi; PeECV; SCGP; TFi

Joseph, you are crying, but you have cried enough! Song for Joseph. *Unknown.* PeNZ, *tr.* by Margaret Orbell

Josephine Josephine. (LL) So Many Feathers. Jayne Cortez. BISi; ISC

Joshu exclaimed, "Dog's no Buddha." Ichigen. ZenPo, *tr.* by Takashi Ikemoto and Lucien Stryk

Joshu's "Oak in the courtyard." Eian. ZenPo, *tr.* by Takashi Ikemoto and Lucien Stryk

Joshu's "Oak in the courtyard." Monju-Shindo. ZenPo, *tr.* by Takashi Ikemoto and Lucien Stryk

Joshu's word—Nothingness. Kuchu. ZenPo, *tr.* by Takashi Ikemoto and Lucien Stryk

Joshua. X. J. Kennedy. ChIV-1

Joshua at Schechem. Charles Reznikoff. ChIV-1

Joshua Fit de Battle of Jericho [*or ob* Jerico]. *Unknown.* APN-2; BPo; NOBA; TAP

Joshua Reynolds. Oliver Goldsmith. *See* Retaliation

Journal. Amy Fusselman. HeMarv

Journal. Gayl Jones.

3-31-70. BISi

Journal of Society, The. Godfrey Turner. NOBL; PeLV

Journal of the Laguna de San Ignacio. Nathaniel Tarn. APSN

Journal of the Plague Years, A. Walter Holland. CAGL

Journalist, The. Cornelius Mathews. APN-1 *Fr.* Poems on Man in His Various Aspects under the American Republic.

Journalist's Convention 1987. Esther Iverem. InTrad

Journalists. Rudyard Kipling. HarvBoo *Fr.* Epitaphs of the War [1914–1918].

Journals, The. Gaylord Brewer. AmPoNex

Journey. Breyten Breytenbach. AF, *tr.* by Denis Hirson

Journey. Elizabeth Cook-Lynn. HATNAP

Journey. Roy Daniells. MoCV

Journey. Rodney Hall. NOBAu

Journey. Judith Nicholls. OBSP

Journey. Vasco [*or* Vasko] Popa. PoSu *Fr.* Besieged Serenity.

Journey. Cathy Song. ExTi

Journey, A. Edward Field. BLT

Journey, The. Igor Bobrowsky. CDa

Journey, The. Eavan Boland. BiHa

Journey, The. Emmy Bridgwater. SurWo

Journey, The. Chikamatsu Monzaemon. WoPoe, *tr.* by Donald Keene *Fr.* Love Suicides at Sonezaki, The.

Journey, The. Franz Wright. LCAP-2

Journey, The. James Wright (1927–80). NAAL-5; NoAM; PoE

Journey and Observations of a Countryman, The. John Hawthorn. Deathbed, A. NOEC

Journey, and the struggles of the moon, The. (LL) Ajanta. Muriel Rukeyser. APT-2; MoAmPo; NNaP

Journey Away, A. Carl Rakosi. PFTM-1

Journey Back to Christmas. Gwen Dunn. OBCP

Journey in the Orient. Maria Luisa Spaziani. BoWoP, *tr.* by Ruth Feldman

Journey in Winter. Goethe.
Three Stanzas. WoPoe, *tr.* by James Wright

Journey it went. (LL) John Keats. NAAL-5v2; NAEL-6v2 *Fr.* Sleep and Poetry.

Journey, 1966. Anselm Hollo. PmAP

Journey North. Tu Fu. ColAnChi; SuSp, *tr.* by Hugh M. Stimson

Journey North, The. Tu Fu. CrYelRi, *tr.* by Sam Hamill

Journey of a Doe. Chava Pinchas-Cohen. DTA, *tr.* by Miriyam Glazer

Journey of no return, A. Kyoshu. JDP, *tr.* by Yoel Hoffmann

Journey of the Magi. T. S. Eliot. ChrPo; FaBoCh; FaBoMo; GI; HAP; HeIP-4; InPK-6; MoAmPo; NAAL-5; NAEL-5v2; NAEL-6v2; NIL-7; NIP-4; NOCV; NoP-4; OBCP; OBMV; OxBTC; PAI; PoE; TAP; TFi; TRP; TwCP

Journey of the Shadow, The. Nada El-Hage. PoArWo, *tr.* by Nathalie El-Hani

Journey Onwards, The. Thomas Moore. GTBS-P; OxAEP-2

Journey Out. Rachel Hadas. RA

Journey Renewed. William Wordsworth. CenSon *Fr.* River Duddon [A Series of Sonnets], The.

Journey's End. Humbert Wolfe. TrJP

Journey's end / Still alive. Basho. ZenPo, *tr.* by Takashi Ikemoto and Lucien Stryk

Journey: The North Coast. Robert Gray. BMAP

Journey through Hell. Nicanor Parra. WoPoe, *tr.* by Miller Williams

Journey through the Moonlight, A. Russell Edson. LCAP-2

Journey to a Village. Wang Yü-ch'eng. CoBCP, *tr.* by Burton Watson

Journey to Hell, A; or, A Visit Paid to the Devil. Edward Ward.
Parish Poor-Officers, The. NOEC

Journey to Mount Tamalipais. Etel Adnan.
"Sometimes, they open a new highway, and let it roll, open wide." GraLe

Journey to the Interior. Theodore Roethke. DiPo; LCAP-2; TRP; VGW *Fr.* North American Sequence.

Journey to the Interior. William Jay Smith. DiPo

Journey to the Place of Ghosts. Jay Wright. GT; VCAP

Journey west, The. Baiseki. JDP, *tr.* by Yoel Hoffmann

Journeying by Stream: Following Chin-chu Torrent I Cross the Mountains. Hsieh Ling-yün. SuSp, *tr.* by Francis Westbrook

Journeying to Hsiang-yi. Ch'en Yü-i. SuSp, *tr.* by Irving Y. Lo

Journeying to the Village. Wang Yü-ch'eng. SuSp, *tr.* by Irving Y. Lo

Journeys. Meg Campbell. PeNZ

Journeys, The. Edward Kamau Brathwaite. HarvBoo

Jove descends in sleet and snow. Storm, The. Alcaeus [*or* Alkaios]. AWP, *tr.* by John Hermann Merivale

Jove, for Europa[e]s love took[e] shape of bull. Barnabe Barnes. OxBSo *Fr.* Parthenophil and Parthenophe.

Jove send me never such afternoon[e]s as this. (LL) Ovid. BoLoP; CABP; EBEV; NPeEn; NoSic; OBVE; OxAEP-1; OxBEV, *tr.* by Christopher Marlowe *Fr.* Elegies.

Jove wields the lightning, Neptune's trident-lord. *Unknown.* PriapPo, *tr.* by Richard W. Hooper *Fr.* Priapus Poems, The.

Jove would leap down to surfeit here. (LL) John Lyly. NOBE; NoSic *Fr.* Alexander and Campaspe.

Jove, you hold Dodona sacred. *Unknown.* PriapPo, *tr.* by Richard W. Hooper *Fr.* Priapus Poems, The.

Jovencita across the street sinks into the dark mouth of her bus, Una. As the Beer Trucks Eclipse the Light of Morning. Anthony R. Vigil. AmPoNex

Joy. Gavin Bantock. OxBTC

Joy. Thomas Centolella. GifTon

Joy. Sydney Owenson, Lady Morgan. NOBRP

Joy. Susan Wicks. MFPA

Joy—a beginning. Anguish, ardor. Relearning the Alphabet. Denise Levertov. NOBA

Joy a fix'd state—a tenure, not a start! Joy. Sydney Owenson, Lady Morgan. NOBRP

Joy! a heart so overflowing. Bernard [*or* Bernart] de Ventadour [*or* Ventadorn]. STV

Joy Addict, The. James Harms. NAPBL; NeAmPo

Joy and anger are not caused by outside things. Miscellaneous Feelings in the Sui Garden. Yüan Mei. CoBLCP; ColAnChi, *tr.* by Jonathan Chaves

Joy and Peace in Believing. William Cowper. NOCV *Fr.* Olney Hymns.

Joy and Pleasure. William Henry Davies. OBMV

Joy and Temperance. *Unknown.* SoSe-8

Joy, did I [*or* I did] lock thee up; but some bad man. Bunch of Grapes, The. George Herbert. ChIV-1; ESCV; GeHe; NAEL-5v1; NAEL-6v1; NAEL-7v1; NOSC; TOF

Joy-fulfiller / fruit provider / many-skilled cook of the whole year. On the Fruit-Providing Autumn Season. Catharina Regina von Greiffenberg. WPoS, *tr.* by Michael Hamburger

Joy has round eyes and terror has. In the City Park. Bulat Shalvovich Okudzhava. TCRP, *tr.* by Deming Brown

Joy in this meeting grieves our two white heads. Tu Fu. CarOv, *tr.* by Carolyn Kizer *Fr.* Banishment.

Joy is a trick in the air. Birth-Dues. Robinson Jeffers. MoAmPo

Joy Island. Marianne Vitale. HeMarv

Joy May Kill. Michelangelo Buonarroti. AWP, *tr.* by John Addington Symonds

Joy Mountain. Muso Soseki. EaWin, *tr.* by W. S. Merwin

Joy of Church Fellowship Rightly Attended, The. Edward Taylor. NAAL-2v1; NAAL-3; OxBA; SCAP *Fr.* God's Determinations [touching his Elect].

Joy of dewdrops, The. Koraku. JDP, *tr.* by Yoel Hoffmann

Joy of Incompleteness, The. Albert Crowell. PoToHe

Joy of Knowledge. Isidor Schneider. TrJP

Joy of Life. Moses Ibn Ezra. TrJP, *tr.* by Solomon Solis-Cohen *Fr.* Book of Tarshish, The.

Joy of living. Seigan Soi. JDP, *tr.* by Yoel Hoffmann

Joy of my life, full oft for loving you. Edmund Spenser. HeIP-4 *Fr.* Amoretti.

Joy of My Life! While Left Me Here. Henry Vaughan. BASC; GeHe

Joy of the Poor, The. Nathan [*or* Natan] Alterman.
Convert Comes to the City, A. MHP, *tr.* by Ruth Finer Mintz
Introduction: "Joy of the poor knocked on the door, The.". MHP, *tr.* by Ruth Finer Mintz
Song to the Wife of His Youth, The. MHP, *tr.* by Ruth Finer Mintz

Joy of the poor knocked on the door, The. Nathan [*or* Natan] Alterman. MHP, *tr.* by Ruth Finer Mintz *Fr.* Joy of the Poor, The.

Joy of Union, The. Yang Fang. CoBCP, *tr.* by Burton Watson

Joy, Shipmate, Joy! Walt Whitman. MoAmPo; TAP

Joy Sonnet in a Random Universe. Helen Chasin. NIL-7

Joy to the bridegroom and the bride. Milkmaid's Epithalamium, The. Thomas Randolph. BoLoP

Joy to the World. Isaac Watts. SacPr

Joyce was afraid of thunder. Volcano. Derek Walcott. OxBC

Joyful Noise, A. Donald Finkel. CoAP

Joyful Sound It Is, A. George Strebeck. AH

Joyfully, Joyfully Onward I Move. William Hunter. AH

Joyless / what I have done. Liadan Laments Cuirithir. *Unknown.* BIrV, *tr.* by John Montague

Joyous birds, hid under greenewood shade, The. Torquato Tasso. OBVE *Fr.* Godfrey of Bulloigne; or, The Recoverie of Jerusalem [Gerusalemme Liberata].

Joyous, who can help but sing? Bitter Harvest. Tzu Yeh. CrYelRi, *tr.* by Sam Hamill

Joys of the Country: Seven Poems. Wang Wei.
"Lush, lush, fragrant grasses in autumn green." CoBCP

Joze was born in the village of Loski Potok. Yugoslav Story. Susan Hampton. BMAP

Juan and Haïidée. Byron. EBNV *Fr.* Don Juan.

Juan de Juni the priest said. Aodh Ruadh O'Domhnaill. Thomas MacGreevy [*or* McGreevy]. CIP-2; OBMV

Juan in England. Byron. FaBoVe *Fr.* Don Juan.

Juan Lopez and John Ward. Jorge Luis Borges. FaBoWar, *tr.* by Rodolfo Torragno

Juan's Puberty. Byron. NPeEn *Fr.* Don Juan.

Juan's Song. Louise Bogan. NoP-4

Juana. Felicia Dorothea Hemans. RWP

Juana. Alfred de Musset. AWP, *tr.* by Andrew Lang

Jubilate Agno. Christopher Smart.
"For the word of God is a sword on my side—no matter what other weapon a stick or a straw." BBASP
Fragment A.
"Let Anaiah bless with the Dragon-fly, who sails over the pond by the wood-side and feedeth on the cresses." FaBoVe
Fragment B.
"For I will consider my Cat Jeoffry." CABP; ChAP; CTC; FaBoCh; HAP; HeIP-4; NAEL-5v1; NAEL-6v1; NAEL-7v1; NOEC; NPeEn; NoP-4; OBWVE; OxAEP-1; OxBEV; PAI; PoE; PoPoPo; RB; SCV; TRP; TTTS; TriCat; WeW-3
"For man is between the pinchers while his soul is shaping and purifying." ChIV-1
"For the doubling of flowers is the improvement of the gard'ner's talent." ChIV-2; NOEC; NPeEn
"For the spiritual musick is as follows." NOEC
"Let Ephah rejoice with Buprestis, the Lord endue us with temperance and humanity, till every cow have her mate!" NOEC
"Let Peter rejoice with the Moon Fish who keeps up the life in the waters by night." ChIV-2
"Let Shobi rejoice with the Kastrel—blessed be the name JESUS in falconry and in the MALL." NOEC
My Cat Jeoffry. CABP; CTC; FaBoCh; HAP; HeIP-4; NAEL-5v1; NAEL-6v1; NAEL-7v1; NOEC; NPeEn; NoP-4; OBWVE; OxAEP-1; PAI; PoE; PoPoPo; RB; SCV; TRP; TTTS; TriCat; WeW-3
Fragment C.
"For I prophesy that they will understand the blessing and virtue of the rain." ECEV
"For I prophesy that we shall have our horns again." ChIV-1
Jubilate Matteo. Gavin Ewart. UV
Jubilation T. Cornpone. Johnny Mercer. OBAL; OBCoV
Jubilee. Sabah As-Sabah. InTrad
Juce of lekes with gotes galle. Unknown. MiEL
Judaeus Errans. Louis Golding. TrJP
Judah in Exile Wanders. George Sandys. AH; ChIV-1
Judas. Vassar Miller. ChIV-2; MoAmPo
Judas. Unknown. ESPB; MiEL; PoE
(It wes upon a shere thorsday that our lord aros.) NAEL-6v1
Judas and Jesus. Endre Ady. IQMS, tr. by Peter Zollman
Judas and the Profiteer. Sir Osbert Sitwell. FaBoWar
Judas descended to this lower Hell. Judas and the Profiteer. Sir Osbert Sitwell. FaBoWar
Judas Goat, The. Susan Musgrave. NOBC
Judas Iscariot. Stephen Spender. MoBrPo; NIP-4
Judas Iscariot / sat in the upper. Judas Iscariot. Ronald Allison Kells Mason. PeNZ; SacPr
Judas Maccabeus. Bible, Apocrypha. TrJP Fr. First Maccabees.
Judas' Reproach. Nina Kossman. GI
Judas says the dead man's alibi had collapsed and. Alibi of a Dead Man. Giovanni Raboni. ItPo, tr. by Gayle Ridinger
Judas Sells His Lord. Unknown. MiEL
Judas Touch, The. David Malouf. BMAP
Judas? You want Judas? Look. Woodcarver of Stendal, The. Sheenagh Pugh. TCAWP
Judenrein. This Is the Map. Rodger Kamenetz. TaR
Judge, The. Yaroslav [or Iaroslav] Vasilevich Smelyakov [orSmeliakov]. TCRP, tr. by Simon Franklin and Albert C. Todd
Judge eternal, throned in splendours. Henry Scott Holland. SacPr
Judge Gives Negro 90 Days in County Jail. (LL) Ballad of the Landlord. Langston Hughes. HCAP; NAAAL; NOBA
Judge Gorba. "Mikhail Semionovich Golodny [or." Golodnyi]. TCRP, tr. by Simon Franklin
Judge, judge, tell the judge. Unknown. OxBoLi
Judge Me, O God. Joel Barlow. AH
Judge Not. Josephine D. Henderson Heard. CBWP-4
Judge Not. Theodore Roethke. ChIV-2; GI
Judge not a Princess' worth impeached hereby. Michael Drayton. NoSic Fr. England's Heroical Epistles.
Judge not, that you be not judged. Theodore Roethke. GI Fr. St. Matthew.
Judge Not the Preacher; for He is Thy Judge. George Herbert. OxAEP-1
Judge not; the workings of his brain. Adelaide Anne Procter. SacPr
Judge of an abnormal stone. Narrator, The. Milo De Angelis. NeIt, tr. by Lawrence Venuti
Judge Somers. Edgar Lee Masters. FaBoEE; OBSV Fr. Spoon River Anthology.
Judge tenderly—of Me! (LL) This Is My Letter to the World. Emily Dickinson. APN-2; HeIP-4; NAAL-2v1; NAAL-3; NALW; NOBA; NoAM; OxBA; OxWW; SAmP; SCV; TAP; TCAPo; WPE
Judge with the Sore Rump, The. St. George Tucker. OBAL

Judged by my goddess' doom to endless pain. William Percy. Son Fr. Coelia.
Judged by the Company One Keeps. Unknown. NBLV
Judgement. Ciaran Carson. PBCIP
Judgement. George Herbert. ESCV; GeHe
Judgement Day. Odia Ofeimun. HBAPE
Judgement of God, The. William Morris. PeVV
Judgement of Tiresias, The. Hildebrand Jacob. NOEC
Judges. Bible, O.T.
Song of Deborah, The. AWP; BoWoP
"Blessed above women/ shall Jael the wife of Heber the Kenite be." WPOW
(Then Sang Deborah and Barak.) TrJP
Judges, who rule the world by laws. Psalm 58. Isaac Watts. NoP-4
Judging Distances. Henry Reed. BoLoP; GTBS-P; NAEL-6v2; NIL-7; NIP-4; NOBE; NPeEn; NoP-4; OxBEV; PoWW Fr. Lessons of the War.
Judgment. Eleanor Wilner. ExTi
Judgment, The. Kathleen Spivack. BoWoP
Judgment Day. Robert Garioch. OBVE
Judgment Day. Ronald Stuart Thomas. CRP
Judgment Day, The. James Weldon Johnson. APT-1; ChIV-2
Judgment in Heaven, A. Francis Thompson.
Epilogue: "Heaven, which man's generations draws.". MoBrPo
Judgment of Paris, The. W. S. Merwin. NAAL-2v2; NNaP
Judgment of Paris, The. Ralph Schomberg. TrJP
Judicious Observation of That Dreadful Comet, A. Ichabod Wiswall. SCAP
Judith. Lascelles Abercrombie.
Song: "Balkis was in her marble town.". MoBrPo
Judith. Eloise Bibb. CBWP-4
Judith. Bible, Apocrypha.
"Begin unto my God with timbrels." TrJP
With Timbrels. TrJP
Judith. Gertrud Kolmar. AF, tr. by David Kipp
Judith. Félix Lope de Vega Carpio. WoPoe, tr. by Brian Soper
(On the Triumph of Judith.) SpanPo
Judith. Adah Isaacs Menken. APN-2; CBWP-1; SWaP; ViWPN
Judith dances on my wall. Dance She Does, The. Harryette Mullen. ISC
Judith of Bethulia. John Crowe Ransom. APT-1; FaBoMo; NOBA; NoAM
Judith Recalls Holofernes. Maura Stanton. YaYoPo
Judy likens the day with Elly. Girls Sitting Together Like Dolls. Christiania Whitehead. NeBl
Judy-One. Haki R. Madhubuti. TAP
Judy Sugden! Judy, I made you caper. Barnsley and District. Donald Davie. NoAM; OxBC
Judy Travaillo Variations, The. Michael Anania. IllVoic
Jug of water in the hand, and on, A. Dawn. "Rachel" [or "Rahel"]. TrJP, tr. by A. M. Klein
Jugged Hare. Jean Earle. TCAWP
Juggler. Richard Wilbur. TAP
Juggler and the baron's daughter, The. Unknown. NoSic
Juggy's Christening. Unknown. NOEC
Jugs, The. Paul Celan. HP; OBVE, tr. by Christopher Middleton
Jugurtha. Henry Wadsworth Longfellow. TCAPo
JuJu. Askia Muhammad Touré. SeSe
Juke Box Love Song. Langston Hughes. NAAAL; SAmP; TTTS
Jukebox Saturday Night. Paul McGrane. ReLy
Jules Pascin. Mina Loy. HarvBoo
Julia Disdainful: Or, The Frozen Zone. Robert Herrick. See Frozen Zone; or, Julia Disdainful, The
Julia, how Irishly you sacrifice. Reproach to Julia. Robert Graves. FaBoEE
Julia, I bring. Ring Presented to Julia, A. Robert Herrick. PeLV
Julia, if I chance to die. His Request to Julia. Robert Herrick. BeJo; CaPo; CavPo; NOSC
Julia's Petticoat. Robert Herrick. BeJo; CaPo
(Upon Julia's Petticoat.) CavPo
Julia, when thy Herrick dies. To Julia. Robert Herrick. CaPo; NOSC
Julian and Maddalo; A Conversation. Shelley. FHYEP
"I rode one evening with Count Maddalo." NPeEn
Julian and Mia. Estrellitas. Carlos Cumpian. IllVoic
Juliana. Cynewulf.
"I have great need that the Saint grant help." AnOE
Julianus Sees a Bronze Statue of Icarus in a Public Bath. Julianus of Egypt. GrAn, tr. by Lee T. Pearcy
Julianus Sees a Magistrate's Axe. Julianus of Egypt. GrAn, tr. by Lee T. Pearcy
Julianus Sees the Chair of the Sophist Craterus. Julianus of Egypt. GrAn, tr. by Lee T. Pearcy

Juliet. Joseph Hilaire Pierre Belloc. BoLoP; EnLoPo

Juliet's Garden. Charles Tomlinson. OBGa

Juliet was next me and I do not know. (LL) Juliet. Joseph Hilaire Pierre Belloc. BoLoP; EnLoPo

Julius Caesar. William Shakespeare.

    Antony's Oration [over Caesar's Body]. MakPoe; OxAEP-1; OxBEV

    "How died my master, Strato?" OxAEP-1

    "If you have tears, prepare to shed them now." OxAEP-1

    "O mighty Cæsar! dost thou lie so low?" OxAEP-1

    "O, pardon me, thou bleeding piece of earth." OxAEP-1

    "Since Cassius first did whet me against Cæsar." OxAEP-1

    "There is a tide in the affairs of men." ITBLP

    "Who ever knew the heavens menace so?" OxAEP-1

Julius Caesar. *Unknown.* InPK-6

Julius Caesar and the Honey-Bee. Charles Tennyson Turner. OxBSo

July. Daniel Gray-Kontar. SpirFl

July. Julio Herrera y Reissig. TCLAP, *tr.* by Andrew Rosing

July. Marion Lomax. NeBl

July. Alexander L. Posey. APN-2

July. Henrietta Cordelia Ray. CBWP-3

July. Folgore da San Geminiano [*or* Gimignano]. EaItPo, *tr.* by Dante Gabriel Rossetti *Fr.* Sonnets of the Months.

July. Sonia Sanchez. GT

July. Margit Szécsi. IQMS, *tr.* by Agnes Arany-Makkai

July 4, 1984: For Buck. June Jordan. NoAM

July 18, 1936–July 18, 1938. Miguel Hernández. AF, *tr.* by Timothy Baland

July 27. Norman Jordan. NBV

July Dawn. Louise Bogan. AWTN

July Has Come for the Dead. Milo De Angelis. ItPo, *tr.* by Gayle Ridinger

July in Indiana. Robert Fitzgerald. AiP

July in Washington. Robert Lowell. LCAP-2; NAAL-2v2

July 1914. Anna Andreyevna Akhmatova. PeFWW; WPOW

July the first, of a morning clear, one thousand six hundred and ninety. Boyne Water, The. *Unknown.* NOIV

Jumbled in the Common Box. W. H. Auden. PoRA

Jumblies, The. Edward Lear. CABP; EBEV; NAEL-5v2; NAEL-6v2; NOxBChV; OxBoLi; PeLV; PeVV; PoRA; TFi; UV

Jump back, honey, jump back. (LL) Negro Love Song, A. Paul Laurence Dunbar. APN-2; ColAP; NAAAL; SSLK

Jump Black Honey Jump Black. Malkia Amala Cyril. InTrad

Jump Cabling. Linda Pastan. InPK-6

Jump for Joy. Sid Kuller. ReLy

Jump he went over. (LL) Mother Goose. LB; OxNR; ReMoGo

Jump-Rope Rhyme. *Unknown.* NTCP

Jump Shooter, The. Dennis Trudell. MoASP

Jump stone hand leaf shadow sun. Robert Duncan. APSN; VGW *Fr.* Passages.

Jump stop shake. (LL) Blackberry Sweet. Dudley Randall. HAP; ISC; KaS; SoSe-8; WeW-3

Jumping Joan. Mother Goose. *See* Little Jumping Joan

Jumping out of the straw. Supposed Dancer, The. Roy Fisher. HarvBoo

Juncos. William Stafford. OWoS

June. William Cullen Bryant. TreFP

June. Elaine Feinstein. BrRo

June. Mary Weston Fordham. CBWP-2

June. Francis Ledwidge. BIrV; NOIV

June. Henrietta Cordelia Ray. CBWP-3

June. Folgore da San Geminiano [*or* Gimignano]. EaItPo, *tr.* by Dante Gabriel Rossetti *Fr.* Sonnets of the Months.

June. Edmund Spenser. AEP *Fr.* Shepheardes [*or* Shepeards *or* Shepherd's] Calender, The.

June 10. Magdalena de Rodriguez. WPOW, *tr.* by Nina Serrano

June 30th. Vera Gherarducci. CItWP

June at Truro Beach the joyous bathers. Kite-Flying. Christopher Gilbert. GT

June Bracken and Heather. Tennyson. EnLoPo

June, but the morning's cold, the wind. Porth Cwyfan. Roland Mathias. AngWePo; TCAWP

June: Dutch Harbor. William Meredith. YaYoPo

June Fugue. Thomas William Shapcott. NOBAu

June Ghazal. Arthur Sze. GifTon

June heat exiles our real needs, the. Without Villages. Ray Gonzalez. TouFir

June in her eyes, in her heart *January.* (LL) Spring, The. Thomas Carew. BeJo; CaPo; CavPo; NoP-4; PBRV; PoE

June Is Bustin' Out All Over. Richard Rodgers. ReLy

June means weddings in everyone's lexicon. Here Usually Comes the Bride. Ogden Nash. NIL-7

June, 1915. Charlotte Mew. OxAEP-2

June rain / hollyhocks turning. Basho. ZenPo, *tr.* by Takashi Ikemoto and Lucien Stryk

June sun in an orchard. My Mother's Burial. Sean O Riordain. ModIr, *tr.* by Patrick Crotty

Juneteenth. Marilyn Nelson. ExTi

Jungle, The. Diane Di Prima. PoM

Jungle, The. Alun Lewis. AngWePo; OBWVE

    "Grey monkeys gibber, ignorant and wise." FaBoWar

Jungle Book. Tom Raworth. PFTM-2

Jungle Book, The. Rudyard Kipling.

    Kaa's Hunting.

        ("This is the way of the Monkey-kind!") (LL) OBCoV

Jungle Café, The. Gary Soto. NoAM

Jungle Husband, The. Stevie Smith. FaBoWP; HarvBoo; NBLV; NIL-7; NIP-4; RB

Jungle Music. Warren Woessner. MiVo; SwNoth

Jungle Night. "K." FaBoWar

Jungle night—it rains and rains, roofs leak, A. Jungle Night, A. Nguyễn Chí Thiên. VCWP, *tr.* by Huynh Sanh Thông

Jungle Warfare. Jack Spicer. APSN

Jungles. Kamal Sabti.

    "What remains in the hands." MAP

Junior Addict. Langston Hughes. BPo

Junior High Dance. Allison Joseph. UnSA

Juniper. Abbie Huston Evans. APT-1

Juniper. Robert Francis. VGW

Juniper, aspen, blue spruce, just thawing snow. Call of Nature, The. Tony Harrison. NoAM

Juniper Moon Pulls at My Bones, The. Earle Thompson. HATNAP

Junk. Richard Wilbur. HAP; WeW-3

    (From my neighbor's ashcan.) NoP-4

Junk Man passed the house today, The. Ol' Clothes. *Unknown.* PoToHe

Junkies loved Charles Parker and the sports, The. Historiography. Lorenzo Thomas. SeSe

Junkyard dog, The. Nicholas Virgilio. HA

Juno still jealous[e] of her husband Jove. Mary Sidney Wroth, Countess of Montgomery. OxBSo *Fr.* Pamphilia to Amphilanthus.

Jupiter and Mercury. David Garrick. ECEV

Jupiter and Ten. James Thomas Fields. OBAL

Jupiter at Beer Springs. Thomas Hornsby Ferril. YaYoPo

Just. Judith Johnson Sherwin. TAP

Just a few of us here at midday. My Train. Barbara Ras. NAPBL

Just a few years ago, when everything was permanent. Tesoro. Valerie Martínez. TouFir

Just a Gigolo. Julius Brammer. ReLy, *tr.* by Irving Caesar and Leonello Casucci

Just a herd of Negroes. Share-Croppers. Langston Hughes. SAmP

Just a line to remind my friends that after much trouble. Dear Folks. Patrick Kavanagh. FaBoTw

Just a little party, nothing swank. Her Retirement. Anne Rouse. NeBl

Just a little white with the dust. (LL) Break of Day in the Trenches. Isaac Rosenberg. CABP; FaBoMo; GTBS-P; HarvBoo; MoBrPo; NAEL-5v2; NAEL-6v2; NIL-7; NOBE; NPeEn; NoAM; NoP-4; OBWP; OxAEP-2; OxBEV; PeFWW; PoWW; TFi

Just a Product of a Certain Situation. Steve Griffiths. AngWePo

Just a Smack at Auden. William Empson. MoBrPo; OBCoV; PeLV; UnPo

Just above where my house sits on the slope. Thomas Müntzer. Jeffrey Wainwright. HarvBoo

Just across the street from the Instituto Dante Allighieri. And Yet I Know. James Wright (1927–80). BodElec

Just after Michael's Death, the Game of Pool. Richard Tipping. BMAP

Just after Noon with Fierce Shears. Tram Combs. TwCP

Just an hour before the hump of last night, when—not with an old. Their Hats Is Always White. Jim Elledge. SwNoth

Just an instant the sun hung. Williamsbridge. Jana Beranová. TuT, *tr.* by Aidan Sharkey

Just an Old Sweet Song. Donagh MacDonagh. CIP-2

Just an old woman, my pet, that wishes you well. (LL) Tall Girl, The. John Crowe Ransom. OxBSo; Son

Just and fit actions, Ptolemy (he saith). Lucan. OBVE, *tr.* by Ben Jonson *Fr.* Pharsalia.

Just Another Gig. Baron James Ashanti. SeSe

Just are the ways of God. John Milton. InvLi *Fr.* Samson Agonistes.

Just as a child, already by sleep possessed. Welcome to Thomas Mann. Attila József. IQMS, *tr.* by Vernon Watkins

Just as fear never kills.　This Strange Calculation of Roots.　Edouard J. Maunick.　NegPo, *tr. by* Teo Savory

Just as he gets a beard.　Statilius Flaccus.　GrAn

Just as He spoke it from his Hands.　Emily Dickinson.　APN-2

Just as I Am.　Charlotte Elliott.　SacPr

Just as I joy at noble autumn.　To the Tune "Partridge Sky."　Yang Shen.　CoBLCP, *tr. by* Jonathan Chaves

Just as my fingers on these keys.　Peter Quince at the Clavier.　Wallace Stevens.　APT-1; HeIP-4; InPK-6; MoAmPo; NAAL-5; NAWM-7v2; NOBA; NoAM; NoP-4; OxBA; PAI; PoE; SAmP; TAP; TCAPo; TFi; TwCP

Just as she was about to turn on the lights. (LL)　Old Couple.　Charles Simic.　HCAP; PoPoPo

Just as soon as the average type.　Salute, Friends!　Vladimir Salimon.　TCRP, *tr. by* Albert C. Todd

Just as sun.　This River.　Annette Allen.　MPUn

Just as that monkey would, poor Polly, have done for you. (LL)　Poor Poll.　Robert Bridges.　EBEV; OxBTC; OxBoLi

Just as the shady grove delights all with its whispering breezes.　Anna Dering on Bartolomeo Silva, Doctor of Turin.　Anne Lok [*or* Locke].　EMWP

Just as the signal tower lights flash.　Night at an Airport.　David Ignatow.　NNaP

Just as the twilight's holy hour.　To an Infant.　Mary Weston Fordham.　CBWP-2

Just as the watchman in the wine fields.　Just as The Watchman.　Rainer Maria Rilke.　BBASP, *tr. by* Robert Bly

Just as the white ibis runs.　Eye of Creation, The.　Angelina Muñiz Huberman.　MirDau, *tr. by* Aurora Camacho

Just as the Winged Energy of Delight.　Rainer Maria Rilke.　RaBo

Just as Thou Art.　Russell Sturgis Cook.　AH

Just as we were amazed to learn.　Psychopathology of Everyday Life, The.　William Matthews.　NIP-4

Just as you think you've gained great wealth.　Caroline Gilman.　SWaP　*Fr.* Oracles for Youth.

Just as you walk out of the Japanese garden.　Carp.　Dionisio D. Martinez.　TouFir

Just back from a beach of sand and shells.　Old Lobsterman, The.　John Townsend Trowbridge.　APN-2

Just Because I Am.　Malkia Amala Cyril.　InTrad

Just because I forget.　Letter for Duncan.　Larry Eigner.　FTOS; PoM

Just because it perished? (LL)　Passer Mortuus Est.　Edna St. Vincent Millay.　FaBoWP; MoAmPo; OxBA

Just because of you.　*Unknown.*　ArkPo, *tr. by* Helen Craig McCullough

Just because there is music.　Maybe I'm Amazed.　Jim Carroll.　PmAP

Just before dawn.　Alan Pizzarelli.　HA

Just before Sleep.　Peter Everwine.　GeoHom

Just before the storm.　Alan Pizzarelli.　HA

Just before the tunnel, the train.　City Animals.　Chase Twichell.　UrbNat

Just beyond the gate.　Issa.　SoOfWa, *tr. by* Sam Hamill

Just broke from school, pert, impudent, and raw.　Soame Jenyns.　ECEV; OBSV　*Fr.* Modern Fine Gentleman, The.

Just by being / I'm here.　Issa.　ZenPo, *tr. by* Takashi Ikemoto and Lucien Stryk

Just call it a personal favor for you. (LL)　On Covering the Bones of Chang Chin, the Hired Man.　Liu Tsung-yüan.　SuSp; WoPoe, *tr. by* Jan W. Walls

Just came home from a disturbing appointment with my new primary.　Ticker.　Amy Fusselman.　HeMarv

Just controls their operations: The Napoleon of Crime! (LL)　Macavity: The Mystery Cat.　T. S. Eliot.　ChAP; NBLV; NOBL; OBCA; OxIBACP; PeLV; PoRA; RB; UV

Just days after the vet came.　Healing the Mare.　Linda McCarriston.　LoL

Just don't get caught. I won't exact a tithe.　*Unknown.*　PriapPo, *tr. by* Richard W. Hooper　*Fr.* Priapus Poems, The.

Just drop a tear for the Croppy Boy. (LL)　Croppy Boy, The.　*Unknown.*　NOIV; OxBoLi

Just enough of rain.　Haiku.　Richard Wright.　APT-2

Just Folks.　Edgar Albert Guest.　ITBLP

Just for a handful of silver he left us.　Lost Leader, The.　Robert Browning.　FHYEP; NAEL-5v2; NAEL-6v2; PWR; SCGP

Just for a space that I met her.　Incognita.　Austin Dobson.　EBVV

Just for the sake of recovering.　Loch Thom.　William Sydney Graham.　NePenScot

Just for to-Day.　Ernest R. Wilberforce.　PWR

Just for Today.　Ervin Drake.　ReLy

Just four miles to go and the frontier ahead.　German Frontier at Basel: 1942 and 1992, The.　Hilda Schiff.　HP

Just Friends.　Robert Creeley.　NeAP

Just Friends.　John Klenner.　ReLy

Just give me a minute to get myself.　So You Want to Hear the Blues.　Grace Bauer.　MiVo

Just God! and these are they.　Clerical Oppressors.　John Greenleaf Whittier.　NAAL-2v1

Just half our three score years and ten.　Martial.　RomPo, *tr. by* Peter Whigham

Just have snow / to wear too. (LL)　Self-Pity Is a Kind of Lying, Too.　James Schuyler.　BodElec; PoM

Just How Crazy Brenda Is.　Melinda Goodman.　GLP

Just How It Happened.　Priscilla Jane Thompson.　CBWP-2

Just in Time.　Betty Comden.　ReLy

Just last friday.　Jamal's Lamentation.　Reuben Jackson.　GT

Just life and death make up our worldly state.　Quatrain.　Ilyas Farhat.　MAP, *tr. by* John Heath-Stubbs and Salma Khadra Jayyusi

Just Like Me.　*Unknown.*　ReMoGo

Just like that. When he brings the new bike home.　Bicycle Rider, The.　Thomas William Shapcott.　CBAP

Just Like the Legend.　Léon Damas.　PFTM-1

Just like the time he first set off for school. (LL)　Written in a Carefree Mood.　Lu Yu.　CoBCP; ColAnChi, *tr. by* Burton Watson

Just like unto a nest of boxes round.　Of Many Worlds in This World.　Margaret Lucas Cavendish, Duchess of Newcastle.　NOSC; NPeEn

Just locking up—to Die. (LL)　Emily Dickinson.　HAP; NIL-7

Just look at them, the shameless well-to-do.　Palladas [*or* Pallades].　GrAn

Just look, Manetto, at that wry-mouth'd minx.　Sonnet: Of an Ill-Favored Lady.　Guido Cavalcanti.　AWP; EaItPo, *tr. by* Dante Gabriel Rossetti

Just look, 'tis a quarter past six, love.　Coming Woman, The.　Mary Weston Fordham.　CBWP-2; SWaP

Just lost, when I was saved!　Called Back.　Emily Dickinson.　MoAmPo; NOBA; NOCV

Just man followed then his angel guide, The.　Lot's Wife.　Anna Andreyevna Akhmatova.　BoWoP, *tr. by* Richard Wilbur

Just missed him! (LL)　On a Squirrel Crossing the Road in Autumn, in New England.　Richard Eberhart.　APT-2; HeIP-4

Just my luck. I gave up smoking last month.　Luck.　Marc J. Straus.　BloBone

Just now I found a young boy.　Catullus.　EroLit, *tr. by* Peter Whigham

Just now / Out of the strange.　Warning, The.　Adelaide Crapsey.　APT-1; Spl; TCAPo; WPE

Just now the lilac is in bloom.　Old Vicarage, Grantchester, The.　Rupert Brooke.　MoBrPo; NoP-4; OxBTC; PoRA

Just off his motorbike.　Going to Mass after Fifteen Years.　Maxine Scates.　PBCAP

Just off the highway to Rochester, Minnesota.　Blessing, A.　James Wright (1927–80).　AmFaPo; InPK-6; NAAL-2v2; NOBA; NoAM; PoE; RaBo; TRP; TwCP; VCAP

Just off the Santa Monica Pier.　Dolphin, The.　Maurya Simon.　GeoHom

Just once before I die.　Lower East Side Poem, A.　Miguel Piñero.　PueRic

Just One Day.　Susan E. Gammons.　PWR

Just one hundred poems in this little book.　Reading the Poetry Collection of Lü Fang-ch'ing.　Chang Yü.　CoBLCP, *tr. by* Jonathan Chaves

Just One of Those Things.　Cole Porter.　APT-1; ReLy

Just past sunset.　Bob Boldman.　HA

Just quartering a Tree. (LL)　Thunder-Storm, A.　Emily Dickinson.　APN-2; HAP; NAAL-2v1; NCAP; NIL-7; WeW-3

Just say, "He's out."　Absence.　Shinkichi Takahashi.　ZenPo, *tr. by* Takashi Ikemoto and Lucien Stryk

Just short of the pass—juniper and spruce.　Beyond Freedom.　Michael Hannon.　GeoHom

Just sitting around smoking, drinking and telling stories.　And with March a Decade in Bolinas.　Joanne Kyger.　BLT

Just so long and long enough. (LL)　E. E. Cummings.　NOBA; OxBA; TAP; VGW

Just-So Stories.　Rudyard Kipling.
　　How the Camel Got His Hump.
　　　　"Camel's hump is an ugly lump, The."　NOxBChV
　　　　Hump, The.　NOxBChV
　　Merrow Down.　NOxBChV

Just stand aside and watch yourself go by.　Watch Yourself Go By.　Strickland W. Gillilan.　PoToHe

Just the lessons given you now.　Maxims in Rhyme for the Young.　J. Clark.　PWR

Just the luck of the draw.　Our 17th Street Years.　Bruce Weigl.　BodElec

Just the Two of Us.　Kate Jennings.　BMAP

Just the Two of Us.　Taeko Tomioka.　WPOW

Just then, forgetful of the strict command.　Homer.　OBVE　*Fr.* Odyssey.

Just there, in a corner of the whin-field.　Our Lady of Ardboe.　Paul Muldoon.　BiHa; PBCIP

Just this one day in all the year.　Skeleton in the Cupboard, The.　Dora Sigerson Shorter.　VWP

Just to Be Needed.　Mary Eversley.　PoToHe

Just to keep her from the foggy, foggy dew. (LL)   Foggy, Foggy Dew, The. *Unknown.* OxBoLi; PeLV

Just to say the word.   Issa.   SoOfWa, *tr. by* Sam Hamill

Just too late to save the stamp. (LL)   Waste.   Harry Graham.   OBCoV; UV

Just us / In our little house.   Kenneth Rexroth.   APSN   *Fr.* Love Poems of Marichiko, The.

Just Walk on, Condemned to Die.   Miklós Radnóti.   IQMS, *tr. by* Zsuzsanna Ozsváth and Frederick Turner

Just Walking Around.   John Ashbery.   NAAL-2v2

Just when hope withers, a reprieve is granted.   Exit.   Rita Dove.   ExTi

Just when I thought there wasn't room enough.   My Philosophy of Life.   John Ashbery.   BodElec

Just when our drawing-rooms begin to blaze.   William Cowper.   NOEC; NPeEn; NoP-4   *Fr.* Task, The.

Just when the sermon.   Prince Shiki.   SoOfWa, *tr. by* Sam Hamill

Just when Thou wilt, O Master, call!   Just When Thou Wilt.   Frances Ridley Havergal.   VWP

Just when you thought it safe enough.   Androgyny.   Steve [*or* Stephen] Orlen.   OPRER

Just who was Miss Mary Mack.   On Sidewalks, on Streetcorners, as Girls.   Allison Joseph.   IllVoic

Just Word Wranglin'   John Nelson.   GeoH

Justice.   Agathias.   GrAn, *tr. by* Peter Whigham

Justice.   George Chapman.   NOSC   *Fr.* Euthymiae Raptus; or, The Teares of Peace.

Justice.   Langston Hughes.   BPo

Justice.   Ben Marcus.   HeMarv

Justice.   Petra von Morstein.   BoWoP, *tr. by* Rosmarie Waldrop

Justice Arnett.   Edgar Lee Masters.   APT-1   *Fr.* Spoon River Anthology.

Justice Denied in Massachusetts.   Edna St. Vincent Millay.   AiP; MoAmPo

Justice is Done.   Oumar Ba.   PBMAP

Justice of Men! I Go in Search of You.   Rosalía de Castro.   SpanPo, *tr. by* Edwin Morgan

Justice of the Peace, The.   Joseph Hilaire Pierre Belloc.   NOBVV; OBSV

Justice of the Peace, The.   Alison Luterman.   MPUn

Justice to Scotland.   *Unknown.*   NBLV

Justification.   William Strode.   NOSC

Justified—through Calvaries of Love. (LL)   Renunciation.   Emily Dickinson.   APN-2; MoAmPo; NAAL-2v1; NAAL-3; NOBA

Justify all those renowned generations.   Renowned Generations, The.   W. B. Yeats.   OxBoLi

Justiniano Lamé Has Been Killed.   Jimmie Durham.   HATNAP

Justly might Female *Tortoises* complain.   Oppian.   NPeEn, *tr. by* William Diaper   *Fr.* Halieutica.

Justus Quidem Tu Es, Domine.   Gerard Manley Hopkins.   *See* Thou Art Indeed Just, Lord

K

K for the Klondyke, a country of gold.   Joseph Hilaire Pierre Belloc.   NoAM   *Fr.* Moral Alphabet, A.

K k k k k.   Marlene Mountain.   HA

K-K-K-Katy.   Geoffrey O'Hara.   ReLy

Ka 'Ba.   Imamu Amiri Baraka.   BPo; ISC; NBV; PmAP; TAP

Ka Waiapo Lani.   Queen Lili'u-o-ka-lani.   SWaP

Kaa's Hunting.   Rudyard Kipling.   *Fr.* Jungle Book, The.

Kabul town's by Kabul river.   Ford o' Kabul River.   Rudyard Kipling.   FaBoTw; PeVV

Kaddish.   Allen Ginsberg.   HCAP; NAAL-2v2; NOBA; NeAP; PmAP; PoM IV.   BB

Kaddish.   David Ignatow.   RaBo; TaR

Kaddish.   Levi-Yitzhok [*or* Levi-Isaac] of Berditchev.   TrJP, *tr. by* Joseph Leftwich

Kaddish.   Charles Reznikoff.   TaR

Kadia the Young Mother Speaks.   Jessie E. Sampter.   TrJP

Kagwa hunted the lion.   Huntsman, The.   Edward Lowbury.   OBSP

Kalahari Bushman fires flowing.   Firebowl.   Sydney Clouts.   PeSAV

Kalaloch.   Carolyn Forché.   NoAM; YaYoPo

Kalapuya Prophecy, A.   *Unknown.*   STP, *tr. by* Jarold Ramsey

Kaleidoscope.   Maria Elena Cruz Varela.   VCWP, *tr. by* Mairym Cruz-Bernal

Kaleidoscope.   G. K. Page.   NoAM

Kaleidoscope, A.   Sunfish Races.   James Preston.   InPK-6

Kaleidoscope, The.   Douglas Dunn.   OxBSo

Kalevala, The.   Elias Lönnrot.   "It is my desire, it is my wish."   PFTM-1

Kalevala, The.   *Unknown.*   Fire.   WoPoe, *tr. by* Keith Bosley

Kali.   Lucille Clifton.   HW; NAAL

Kali.   Elsa Cross.   TANSG, *tr. by* Patricia Dubrava

Kali.   Ziporah Hildebrandt.   HW

Kali.   Leslie Simon.   HW

Kali / Is everything You do misleading?   Kamalākānta Bhattācārya.   SinGod, *tr. by* Rachel Fell McDermott

Kali, Ma.   Rāmprasād Sen.   SinGod, *tr. by* Rachel Fell McDermott

Kali / my toes strike lightning.   Kali.   Ziporah Hildebrandt.   HW

Kali / Today in the dark grove.   Kamalākānta Bhattācārya.   SinGod, *tr. by* Rachel Fell McDermott

Kali, what family are You from?   Kamalākānta Bhattācārya.   SinGod, *tr. by* Rachel Fell McDermott

Kali, you have removed all my difficulties.   Kamalākānta Bhattācārya.   SinGod, *tr. by* Rachel Fell McDermott

Kallignotos swore to Ionis—no one.   Callimachus.   GrAn

Kallirrhoê: A Dedication.   Agathias.   GrAn, *tr. by* Dudley Fitts

Kallistion the wife of Kritias.   Callimachus.   GrAn

Kallo dedicated her portrait in the house of golden.   Nossis.   SaLy, *tr. by* Diane Rayor

Kalmyk poppies, horde of pan-Mongol tulips.   A. Velichansky.   TCRusP, *tr. by* Daniel Weissbort

Kangaroo.   D. H. Lawrence.   EBEV; OxBTC

Kangaroo, The.   Barron Field.   NOBAu

Kangaroo, The.   Pansy Rose Napaljarri.   IBA

Kangaroo is standing up, and dwindling like a plant, A.   Dusk, The.   Robert Gray.   BMAP

Kangaroo, Kangaroo!   Kangaroo, The.   Barron Field.   NOBAu

Kanheri Caves.   Dom Moraes.   NoP-4

Kannon's tiled temple.   Basho.   SoOfWa, *tr. by* Sam Hamill

Kansas.   J. P. Dunn.   VerBaPo

Kansas City.   Oscar Hammerstein, II.   OBAL

Kansas City Kitty.   Edgar Leslie.   ReLy

Kanteletar, The.   *Unknown.*   Lullabies, 2:174.   WoPoe, *tr. by* Keith Bosley

Kanyariri, Village of Toil.   Village, The.   Marina Gashe.   HAWP; PBA

Karamanian Exile, The.   James Clarence Mangan.   PeVV

Karanje Village.   Alun Lewis.   TCAWP

Karate.   Stanley Plumly.   MoASP

Karazah to Karl.   Adah Isaacs Menken.   CBWP-1

Karen, comrade and sister poet, sends me this news article.   Whenever You're Cornered, the Only Way Out Is to Fight.   Merle Woo.   FSt

Karl Marx Died 1883 Aged 65.   Antonio Cisneros.   TCLAP, *tr. by* Maureen Ahern and David Tipton

Karma.   Edwin Arlington Robinson.   APT-1; HeIP-4; MoAmPo; TrCP

Karshish, the picker-up of learning's crumbs.   Epistle Containing the Strange Medical Experience of Karshish, the Arab Physician, An.   Robert Browning.   ChIV-2; NAEL-5v2; NAEL-6v2

Kartúshkiya-Beróza.   Alter Brody.   TaR

Kashmir shrinks into my mailbox.   Postcard from Kashmir.   Agha Shahid Ali.   NIL-7

Kaspar Is Dead.   Hans [*or* Jean] Arp.   PFTM-1

Kassacks.   Annette M'Baye d'Erneville.   HAWP, *tr. by* Brian Baer

Kassak.   Birago Diop.   NegPo, *tr. by* Ellen Conroy Kennedy

"Kat" can play ball, Man, The.   Funky Football.   Ruby C. Saunders.   BlSi

Katemir's muse, next the world's cant immured.   Lomonosov.   Anna Semionovna Prismanova.   ARWW, *tr. by* Catriona Kelly

Kathaleen Ny-Houlahan [*or* Kathleen-Ni-Houlahan].   William Heffernan.   NOIV, *tr. by* James Clarence Mangan

Katharine Jaffray.   *Unknown.*   ESPB

Käthe Kollwitz.   Muriel Rukeyser.   NALW

Katherine is warm.   Why?   Melba Joyce Boyd.   BlSi

Katherine Jaffray.   *Unknown.*   OxBB

Katherine's Dream.   Robert Lowell.   CoAmPo

Katherine's Hair.   David Marlatt.   AmPoNex

Katie Casey was base-ball mad.   Take Me Out to the Ball Game.   Jack Norworth.   TCAPo

Katie Kádár.   *Hungarian Oral Tradition.*   IQMS, *tr. by* Adam Makkai

Katie's Words.   Lawrence Raab.   Unle

Katie Went to Haiti.   Cole Porter.   ReLy

Katisje's Patchwork Dress.   Pauline Smith.   PeSAV

Katori Maru, October 1920.   James Masao Mitsui.   OpBo

Katrina on the Porch.   Alice Cary.   APN-2

Katsu!   Kogetsu Sogan.   JDP, *tr. by* Yoel Hoffmann

Katsu!   Yoso Soi.   JDP, *tr. by* Yoel Hoffmann

Katya's proud she has a much-admired husband.   Party on Women's Day, A.   Olesya [*or* Olesia] Nikolayeva [*or* Nikolaeva].   ItGoST, *tr. by* Paul Graves and Carol Ueland

Katydids.   Amy Lowell.   APT-1

Katyn Forest.   Steven Sherrill.   BAP-97

Katzenjammer Kids, The.   James Reaney.   MoCV

Kaunas 1941.   Johannes Bobrowski.   AF

Kavikanthabharana.   Kshemendra.
   "Poet should learn with his eyes, A."   EaWin; WoPoe, *tr.* by J. Moussaieff Masson and W. S. Merwin

Kaya-Magan am I! the first person.   Kaya-Magan, The.   Léopold Sédar Senghor.   PFTM-1

Kayenta Times Yet Dreaming On.   Nia Francisco.   HATNAP

Ke-Mo Village Girl.   *Vietnamese Oral Tradition.*   CaDao, *tr.* by John Balaban

Keats.   Henry Wadsworth Longfellow.   Son; TAP

Keekin' Glass, The.   Robert Burns.   FaBoEE

Keen as the blade of the guillotine, grey as its steel.   Execution of Madame du Barry, The.   J. J. Bray.   NOBAu

Keen, Fitful Gusts are Whisp'ring.   John Keats.   CenSon; Son

Keen stars were twinkling, The.   To Jane.   Shelley.   NAEL-6v2

Keener tempests come, The: and fuming dun.   James Thomson.   EBEV   *Fr.* Seasons, The.

Keep a-Goin'   Frank Lebby Stanton.   PWR

Keep a Hand on Your Dream.   X. J. Kennedy.   CA

Keep a red heart of memories.   Haze.   Carl Sandburg.   TCAPo

Keep away from asps and toads.   *Unknown.*   GrAn

Keep back the one word more.   Reserve.   Lizette Woodworth Reese.   SWaP

Keep bees and.   Advice to the Young.   Miriam Waddington.   NIP-4; NOBC

Keep Going.   Gail Mazur.   ExTi

Keep in God's way; keep pace with evry hour.   To Be Engraven on a Dial.   Samuel Sewall.   SCAP

Keep in the heart the journal nature keeps.   Conrad Potter Aiken.   OxBA   *Fr.* Preludes for Memnon; or, Preludes to Attitude.

Keep It Dark.   *Unknown.*   PBA, *tr.* by Hugh Tracey

Keep it simple / Don't make too much of love.   Keep It Simple.   Jay Livingston.   ReLy

Keep love for youth, and violets for the spring.   Autumn Violets.   Christina Georgina Rossetti.   ViWPN

Keep Me Still, for I Do Not Want to Dream.   Larry Eigner.   NeAP

Keep Not Thou Silence.   Bible, *O.T.*   TrJP   *Fr.* Psalms.

Keep off your thoughts from things that are past and done.   Resignation.   Po Chü-i.   ChiP, *tr.* by Arthur Waley

Keep on walkin and walkin   talkin to mysel.   Hard Road Blues.   *Unknown.*   FaBoVe

Keep pushing—'tis wiser than sitting aside.   Never Say Fail.   *Unknown.*   PWR

Keep Talking.   Philip Levine.   WeW-3

Keep the commandments, Trapp, and go no further.   Abel Evans.   FaBoEE

Keep the dream alive and growing always.   Song.   Edwin Rolfe.   TrJP

Keep the Season.   James McAuley.   BMAP

Keep their feet, mount their tails, and away! (LL)   Appeal to Cats in the Business of Love, An.   Thomas Flatman.   EnLoPo; HAP; OBCoV

"Keep this for me."   Faith.   *Unknown.*   PoToHe

Keep thou.   Anguish.   Adelaide Crapsey.   APT-1

Keep to yourself your kisses.   Taisigh Agat Fein Do Phog.   *Unknown.*   BIrV, *tr.* by Maire Cruise O'Brien

Keep walking, though there's no place to get to.   Jelaluddin [*or* Jalal al-Din] Rumi.   LoL

Keep watch over the orchard, attentive Priapus!   *Unknown.*   PriapPo, *tr.* by Richard W. Hooper   *Fr.* Priapus Poems, The.

Keep Ye Holy Sabbath Rest.   *Unknown.*   TrJP, *tr.* by Herbert Loewe

Keep your kiss to yourself.   *Unknown.*   NOIV

Keep your whiskers crisp and clean.   King of Cats Sends a Postcard to His Wife, The.   Nancy Willard.   OBCA; OxIBACP

Keeper.   Esther Iverem.   GT

Keeper of the Midnight Gate, The.   George Mackay Brown.   OxBC

Keeper who worked at the zoo, A.   Limerick.   Frank Richards.   PeLi

Keepin' Out of Mischief Now.   Andy Razaf.   ReLy

Keeping Christmas.   Eleanor Farjeon.   OBCP

Keeping Going.   Seamus Heaney.   ModIr

Keeping Hair.   Ramona Wilson.   VoR

Keeping their difficult balance. (LL)   Love Calls Us to the Things of This World.   Richard Wilbur.   AmFaPo; HAP; HeIP-4; MoAmPo; NAAL-5; NIL-7; NIP-4; NoAM; PoE; PoRA; TAP; TFi; UnPo; VCAP; VGW

Keeping Things Whole.   Mark Strand.   CoAP; HCAP; HeIP-4; LCAP-2; PoPoPo; TAP; VCAP

Keeping Track.   Maurya Simon.   GeoHom

Keeping Track of the Serpents.   Víctor Hernández Cruz.   TouFir

Keeping Watch.   Sojourner Kincaid Rolle.   GeoHom

Kehama's Curse.   Robert Southey.   NOBRP   *Fr.* Curse of Kehama, The.

Keine Kadish wird man sagen. (LL)   Louis Zukofsky.   PFTM-1; TaR   *Fr.* "Poem Beginning, The."

Keine Lazarovitch, 1870–1959.   Irving Layton.   NIP-4

Kelly.   Rafael Campo.   WiU   *Fr.* Ten Patients, and Another.

Kelly on a Mountain.   Man from Strathbogie, The.   Olive Mary Finnin.   NOBAu

Kelly's kept an unlicensed bull, well away.   Outlaw, The.   Seamus Heaney.   NIL-7; OxBC

Kelly sharpened is powerful, asexual and yawns.   Anorexia.   Jennifer Maiden.   BMAP

Kellyburnbraes.   Robert Burns.   OxBB

Kelp.   Nora Dauenhauer.   HATNAP

Kemo Sabe.   Diane Glancy.   LTA

Kemp Owyne.   Alice Cary.   ESPB

Kemp Owyne.   *Unknown.*   ESPB
   (Kempion.)   OxBB

Ken.   Charlotte Mew.   VWP

Kendall Gulls.   Ricardo Pau-Llosa.   UrbNat

Keng-tzu (1180), First Month, Fifth Day, Dawn: Crossing by the Ta-kao Ferry.   Yang Wan-li.   CoBCP, *tr.* by Burton Watson

Kenji Takezo Becomes Water.   Rick Noguchi.   NeAmPo

Kenji Takezo does not have the gift of vision.   Really Long Ride, The.   Rick Noguchi.   NeAmPo

Kenji Takezo feels everybody.   Turn of Privacy, The.   Rick Noguchi.   AmPoNex; NeAmPo

Kenless Strand, The.   Sydney Goodsir Smith.   WoPoe

Kenscoff.   Lorna Goodison.   GT

Kensington Gardens.   Muriel Spark.   OBGa

Kentucky.   M. Loncar.   NAPBL

Kentucky Belle.   Constance Fenimore Woolson.   CBCWP

Kentucky Moonshiner.   *Unknown.*   OBAL

Kentucky Mountain Farm.   Robert Penn Warren.
   History among the Rocks.   CBCWP; MoAmPo

Kentucky water, clear springs: a boy fleeing.   Swimmers, The.   Allen Tate.   APT-2; FuPo; MoAmPo; NOBA; NoAM

Kenyatta Listening to Mozart.   Imamu Amiri Baraka.   PmAP

Kepe well X, and flee fro VII.   Ten Commandments, Seven Deadly Sins, and Five Wits.   *Unknown.*   FaBoEE; MiEL

Kept.   Louise Bogan.   APT-2

Kept Waiting in the Boat at Chiu-K'ou Ten Days by an Adverse Wind.   Po Chü-i.   ChiP, *tr.* by Arthur Waley

Kéramos.   Henry Wadsworth Longfellow.   APN-1

Kerensky.   Lola Ridge.   APT-1

Kerf, The.   Sam Truitt.   AmPoNex   *Fr.* Anamorphosis Eisenhower.

Kerosene.   Chase Twichell.   ExTi

Kerouac and.   Future Martyr of Supersonic Waves.   Juan Felipe Herrera.   TouFir

Kerr's Ass.   Patrick Kavanagh.   ModIr; NOIV; RB

Ketjak.   Ron Silliman.
   "Revolving door."   PFTM-2

Kettle Rooted to the Void.   Anabel Torres.   TANSG, *tr.* by Celeste Kostopulos-Cooperman

Kettle sang the boy to a half-sleep, The.   Halibut Cove Harvest.   Kenneth Leslie.   NOBC

Kevin and Nicole.   Amanda Nazario.   HeMarv

Kevin of the N.E. Crew.   Elizabeth Alexander.   FFC

Kew.   Erasmus Darwin.   OBGa   *Fr.* Botanic Garden, The.

Key, The.   Richard Jones.   GifTon

Key, The.   John Ormond.   AngWePo; TCAWP

Key, The.   Peter Scupham.   HarvBoo

Key, A. The door. Open.   Tom.   James Schuyler.   GLP

Key and the Tree, The.   Alessandro Ceni.   ItPo, *tr.* by Gayle Ridinger

Key into the Language of America, A.   Rosmarie Waldrop.
   Chapter XXIII: Of Marriage.   PFTM-2
   Chapter XXIV: Concerning Their Coyne.   PFTM-2

Key is always nomadic, The.   Role Reversal.   Maria Luisa Spaziani.   CItWP, *tr.* by Cinzia Sartini Blum and Lara Trubowitz

Key Keeper, The.   Ben Jonson.
   Song: "If to your ear it wonder bring."   OxBEV

Key: nnnn N N gahn.   13th Horse Song of Frank Mitchell, The.   María Sabina.   PFTM-1

Key of the kingdom, The.   *Unknown.*   *See* This Is the Key

Key to Dreams.   Georg Nikolic.   IllVoic

Keys.   Barbara J. Garshman.   PasH

Keys lids acid and speed. (LL)   Street Song.   Thom Gunn.   HeIP-4; OxBC

Keys please.   In This Way.   Gertrude Stein.   PFTM-1

Keys that open doors, The.   Thorny Gaps Suddenly Moving.   Fatma Kandil.   PoArWo, *tr.* by Khaled Mattawa

Keys turning.   Liberator, The.   Emily Holmes Coleman.   SPE

Khaldeyev, Naldeyev, and Peppermaldeyev. Daniil Kharms. TCRP

Khalida / Sadness around which. Mirror to Khalida, A. "Adonis" [or "Adunis"]. MAP, tr. by John Heath-Stubbs and Lena Jayyusi

Khalil the Heretic. Kahlil Gibran.
    "From the grasp of Pharaoh." GraLe, tr. by Suheil B. Bushrui

Khikhimora. Nikolai Ivanovich Glazkov. TCRP, tr. by Daniel Weissbort

Khobayza. Zulaykha Abu-Risha. PoArWo, tr. by Clarissa C. Burt and Nathalie Handal

Khrushchev is coming on the right day! Poem. Frank O'Hara. NeAP; PoM

Khurbn. Jerome Rothenberg.
    Dibbukim (Dibbiks). PFTM-2
    Dos Geshray (The Scream). FTOS; PFTM-2
    Dos Oysleydikn (The Emptying). PFTM-2

Ki-u-nad'-dis-si's Song. Unknown. APN-2, tr. by Stephen Powers Fr. Sacred Songs of the Konkau.

Kiacatoo. Kevin Gilbert. IBA

Kiche Manitou. Nathaniel Mackey. FTOS

Kick a Little Stone. Dorothy Aldis. TLR

Kick at the rock, Sam Johnson, break your bones. Epistemology. Richard Wilbur. CRP; NOBA; NoAM; OxBSP

Kick outer the Litany. (LL) Edmund Clerihew Bentley. NOBL; OBCoV Fr. Clerihews.

Kicking his mother until she let go of his soul. Mundus et Infans. W. H. Auden. MoBrPo; NoAM

Kid, The. Ai. GT; NoAM

Kid kid kid kootje. Scaring Hens. Peter Finch. Oth

Kid Stuff. Frank Horne. NOxBChV

Kid was already noxious carrion, The. Song at the End of a Meal. John Hollander. TaR

Kidnap Poem. Nikki Giovanni. BPo; TAP

Kidnapped. Rudyard Kipling. Fr. Plain Tales from the Hills.

Kidnappers. Iris Clayton. IBA

Kids! Lee Adams. ReLy

Kids and her, The. 2 Months Rent Due and 1 Bag of Rice. Luci Beach. ReEnLa

Kids are good at this, The. Their nimble fingers. Origami. Greg Williamson. NAPBL

Kids / I don't know what's wrong with these kids today! Kids! Lee Adams. ReLy

'Kids make a home,' he said, the family man. Family Man, The. Bruce Dawe. BMAP

Kids on Television Imagine Me, The. Jordan Davis. HeMarv

Kids shoot out of the car roaring. St Bees in Winter. William Scammell. NLP

Kiev, the Ukraine, Nuclear Accident. David Romtvedt. GifTon

Kilaben Bay Song. Unknown. NOBAu, tr. by Perce Haslam

Kilbarchan now may say alas! Life and Death of [Habbie Simson] the Piper of Kilbarchan, The. Robert Sempill. OxBS

Kilcash. Unknown. BIrV; OBMV, tr. by Frank O'Connor

Kilfenora Teaboy, The. Paul Durcan. PBCIP

Kilimanjaro. Hélène d'Oettingen. CuPo

Kill, The. Carl Phillips. WiU

Kill me not every [or ev'ry] day. Affliction. George Herbert. NOSC

Kill me with spite; yet we must not be foes. (LL) William Shakespeare. HeIP-4; OxAEP-1; SCGP Fr. Sonnets.

Kill That Crowing Cock. Unknown. OHMPC, tr. by Kenneth Rexroth

Kill yourselves with knives and poisoned gas. Strangers Are We All upon the Earth. Franz Werfel. TrJP, tr. by Edith Abercrombie Snow

Killdeer, The. Larry Gates. HA

Killed. Lee Ranaldo. HeMarv

Killed at the Ford. Henry Wadsworth Longfellow. CBCWP

Killed / by a white woman. Clay. Imamu Amiri Baraka. ESEAA

Killed by an omnibus—why not? On a Man Run over by an Omnibus. Henry Luttrell. FaBoEE

Killed by the Elevator, C—e Factory, Dundee. Nelly's Lament for the Pirnhouse Cat. Ellen Johnston. VWP

Killer, The. A'yunini. STP, tr. by Jerome Rothenberg

Killer, The. Judith Wright. BMAP

Killer Blues. Calvin Forbes. IllVoic

Killers, The. Leonard Cohen. NOBC

Killers said. Synagogue in Prague. Alan Sillitoe. HP

Killing, The. George MacBeth [or Macbeth]. FaBoMo

Killing, The. Edwin Muir. GI

Killing Memory. Haki R. Madhubuti. IllVoic

Killing No Murder. Sylvia Townsend Warner. MoBrPo

Killing of the Birds, The. Shirley Williams. BoWoP

Kilmeny. James Hogg. OBEV; OxAEP-2 Fr. Queen's Wake, The.

Kiln-charred children in the yard, The. Sculpture Garden. Austin Hummell. AmPoNex

Kilroy. Peter Viereck. MoAmPo
    (Kilroy Was Here.) PoRA

Kilroy is gone. Kilroy. Eugene McCarthy. AiP

Kilruddery Hunt, The. Thomas Mozeen. BIrV

Kiltartan Legend. Padraic Fallon. ModIr; NOIV

Kim. Rudyard Kipling.
    Prodigal Son, The. NoAM

Kim-San. Steve Denning. CDa

Kimchee in Worcester (Mass.). Alfred Corn. WiU

Kimono, The. James Merrill. ColAP

Kin. Ruth Forman. AmPoNex

Kin. Michael S. Harper. LCAP-2

Kinaxixi. Agostinho Neto. PoetW; WoPoe, tr. by W. S. Merwin

Kind-, The. James Laughlin. CDa

Kind, almost courtly, a "good listener," he kept lovers. One-Page Novel. David Gewanter. NAPBL

Kind Are Her Answers. Thomas Campion. BoLoP
    (Kinde are her answeres.) OxBEV

Kind are my stars indeed but that so late. To Mrs B. from a Lady Who Had a Desire to See Her, and Who Complains on the Ingratitude of Her Fugitive Lover. Unknown. EMWP

Kind gentlemen, will you be patient awhile? Robin Hood's Birth, Breeding, Valor, and Marriage. Unknown. ESPB

Kind lovers, love on. John Crowne. OxBSP Fr. Calisto.

Kind o'er the kinderbank leans my Myfanwy. Myfanwy. Sir John Betjeman. BoLoP

Kind of Act Of, The. Robert Creeley. NeAP

Kind of change came in my fate, A. Byron. NOBE Fr. Prisoner of Chillon, The.

Kind of Culture, A. Mihály Babits. IQMS, tr. by Peter Zollman

Kind of empty in the way it sees everything, the earth gets to its feet. For John Clare. John Ashbery. HarvBoo

Kind of Loss, A. Ingeborg Bachmann. PoetW, tr. by Mark Anderson

Kind of rain we knew is a thing of the past, The. Kinsale. Derek Mahon. BiHa

Kind pity [or Kinde pitty] chokes my spleen[e]; brave scorn forbids. John Donne. BASC; EBEV; ESCV; FHYEP; FSCP; MeLP; NAEL-5v1; NAEL-6v1; NAEL-7v1; NoP-4; OxAEP-1; SacPr Fr. Satires.

Kind Words Can Never Die. Abby Hutchinson. AH

Kinda Blue Miles Davis Died Today. Everett Hoagland. BodElec

Kindely is now my coming. Unknown. MiEL

Kindertotenlieder. Timothy Liu. NeAmPo

Kindertotenlieder. Michael Longley. CIP-2

Kindle the Taper. Emma Lazarus. AH

Kindly Deed, A. Priscilla Jane Thompson. CBWP-2

Kindly I envy thy song's [or songs] perfection. To Mr. R. W. John Donne. ESCV

Kindly Neighbor, The. Edgar Albert Guest. PoToHe

Kindly people of Vancouver, B.C., The. Parable of the Boy and the Polar Bear. Roger Fanning. NAPBL

Kindly Vision. Otto Julius Bierbaum. AWP, tr. by Jethro Bithell

Kindly watcher by my bed, lift no voice in prayer. Music. George Du Maurier. OBEV

Kindly word and a tender tone, A. Gentle Word, A. Unknown. PoToHe

Kindness. Thomas Sturge Moore. OBMV

Kindness. Sylvia Plath. FaBoWP

Kindness. Mary E. Tucker. CBWP-1

Kindness and Generosity. Tiruvalluvar. WoPoe, tr. by Emmons E. White Fr. Kural, The.

Kindness glides about my house. Kindness. Sylvia Plath. FaBoWP

Kindness to Animals. Laura Elizabeth Richards. NTCP

Kindness to Animals. Unknown. WHSW

Kinds of Shel-fish. William Wood. SCAP

Kinescope. Dionisio D. Martinez. TouFir

Kinfauns Castle. William Montgomerie.
    "Is there no vision in a lovely place?" OxBS

King, The. Skipwith Cannell. APT-1

King, The. Rudyard Kipling. CABP

King and No King, A. Robert Herrick. PBRV

King & Queen. John Montague. PBCIP

King and Queen of the Pelicans we. Pelican Chorus, The. Edward Lear. OBSP

King: April 4, 1968. Gerald William Barrax. ESEAA; GT

King Arthur. Dryden.
    Song of Venus. OxBoLi

King Arthur. Mother Goose. LB; OxNR

King Arthur and King Cornwall. *Unknown*. ESPB

King Arthur made new knights to fill the gap. Tennyson. NAEL-5v2; NAEL-6v2 *Fr.* Idylls of the King.

King Arthur's Waes-hael. Robert Stephen Hawker. OBEV

King asked, The. King's Breakfast, The. Alan Alexander Milne. UV

King Balak sat on his gaudy throne. Balaam. Charles Causley. EBNV

King Berdok. *Unknown*. OxBS

King Billy. Edwin Morgan. NePenScot; NoP-4

King Billy on the Walls. Sheenagh Pugh. AngWePo

King but an' his nobles a', The. Brown Robin. *Unknown*. ESPB; OxBB

King by whose rich grace His servants be, The. Dante Alighieri. EaItPo, *tr. by* Dante Gabriel Rossetti

King Ch'in rides a tiger to roam the Eight Poles. King Ch'in Drinks Wine. Li Ho. ChinPo, *tr. by* Yip Wai-lim

King Charles the First. *Unknown*. FaBoCh; OxNR

King Charles the First walked and talked. *Unknown*. OxNR

King Christian. Johannes Evald. AWP, *tr. by* Henry Wadsworth Longfellow

King Cobra as Political Assassin, The. Ray A. Young Bear. HATNAP

King David. Stephen Vincent Benét. ChIV-1

King David and King Solomon. Authorship. James Ball Naylor. NBLV

King David Dances. John Berryman. ChIV-1; OxBC; OxBSP

King Don Luis. O. V. de L. Milosz. WoPoe, *tr. by* John Peck

King Duffus. Sylvia Townsend Warner. FaBoWP

King Easter has courted her for her gowd. Fause Foodrage. *Unknown*. ESPB

King Edward scales the hills of Wales. Bards of Wales, The. János Arany. IQMS, *tr. by* Peter Zollman

King Edward the Fourth and a Tanner of Tamworth. *Unknown*. ESPB

King Enjoys His Own Again, The. Martin Parker. FaBoCh; OxBoLi

(Upon Defacing of Whitehall.) NOSC; PBRV

(What *Booker* doth prognosticate.) PBRV

King Estmere. *Unknown*. ESPB; OBNV; OxBB

King for the night! the rabbi cried. Bar Mitzvah, The. Philip Schultz. TaR

King George V. Charles W. Hayward. NOBAu

King Harald's Trance. George Meredith. EBNV; PeVV

King has written a braid letter, The. Lord Derwentwater. *Unknown*. ESPB

King he hath been a prisoner, The. Willie o Winsbury. *Unknown*. ESPB

King he reigns on a throne of gold, The. Leveller, The. "Barry Cornwall." OxAEP-2

King [he] sits in Dumferline [*or* Dumferling] town [*or* toune], The. Sir Patrick Spens [*or* Spence]. *Unknown*. AWP; ClHu; EBEV; ESPB; FaBoCh; HAP; InPK-6; MakPoe; NAEL-5v1; NAEL-6v1; NAEL-7v1; NIP-4; NOBE; NPeEn; NePenScot; OBEV; OBSP; OxBB; OxBEV; OxBS; PoE; RB; SCGP; TFi; UnPo; WeW-3

King Henry. *Unknown*. ESPB; OxBB

King Henry IV, Pt. I. William Shakespeare. NAEL-5v1

"I have learn'd." OxAEP-1

"My liege, I did deny no prisoners." FaBoWar

"O, Harry! thou hast robb'd me of my youth." OxAEP-1

"So shaken as we are, so wan with care." OxAEP-1

King Henry IV, Pt. II. William Shakespeare.

"But wherefore did he take away the crown?" OxAEP-1

"How many thousand of my poorest subjects." AWTN

"This new and gorgeous garment, majesty." OxAEP-1

King Henry V. William Shakespeare.

"Doth Fortune play the huswife with me now?" FaBoWar

"Fortune is Bardolph's foe, and frowns on him." FaBoWar

Henry V at the Siege of Harfleur. OxAEP-1

"How yet resolves the Governor of the town?" FaBoWar

"King is full of grace and fair regard, The." OxAEP-1

Muse of Fire, A. OxAEP-1; SCV

"Now entertain conjecture of a time." EBEV; FaBoWar; OxAEP-1; RB

"O! that we now had here." FaBoWar; OxAEP-1

(Speech before Harfleur, The.) ITBLP

"Thus far, with rough and all-unable pen." CTC

"Thus with imagin'd wing our swift scene flies." EBEV; OxAEP-1

"We are but warriors for the working-day." FaBoWar

"We few, we happy few, we band of brothers." UnPo

Yon Island Carrions Desperate of Their Bones. RB

King Henry VI, Pt. I. William Shakespeare.

King Is Dead, A. OxAEP-1

King Henry VI, Pt. III. William Shakespeare.

"Great lords, wise men ne'er sit and wail their loss." FaBoWar

"Ill blows the wind that profits nobody." FaBoWar

"Owl shriek'd at thy birth, an evil sign, The." OxAEP-1

King Henry VIII. John Fletcher.

Music. FaBoCh; NOSC

(Orpheus.) OBEV

(Sweet Music's Power.) NOBE

King Henry Fifth's Conquest of France. *Unknown*. ESPB

King Henry the Eighth was a Tudor. Limerick. Kirkham Talbot. PeLi

King Honour's Eldest Son. Elinor Wylie. SacPr

King I saw who walked a cloth of gold, The. Cloth of Gold. Francis Reginald. MoCV

King in Thule, The. Goethe. STV, *tr. by* John Frederick Nims

King Is Dead, A. William Shakespeare. OxAEP-1 *Fr.* King Henry VI, Pt. I.

King is full of grace and fair regard, The. William Shakespeare. OxAEP-1 *Fr.* King Henry V.

King is Quair, The. James I, King of Scotland. EBEV *Fr.* Kingis Quair, The.

King is thinking Tricia's got nice tits, The. Nixon Names Elvis Honorary Federal Narcotics Agent at Oval Office Ceremony, 1973. David Wojahn. AllShUp

King James and Brown. *Unknown*. ESPB

King Jamie hath made a vow. Flodden Field. *Unknown*. ESPB

King John. William Shakespeare.

"Must you with hot irons burn out both mine eyes?" OxAEP-1

"This England never did, nor never shall." OxAEP-1

King John and the Bishop. *Unknown*. ESPB

King Kong Meets Wallace Stevens. Michael Ondaatje. NIL-7

King Lear. Peter Huchel. PoSu, *tr. by* Michael Hamburger

King Lear. William Shakespeare.

Blow, Winds. OxAEP-1

"Come on, sir; he[e]re's the place: stand still." OxAEP-1; OxBEV

"He wakes; speak to him." SCV

"Here is the place, my lord; good my lord, enter." OxAEP-1

"Howl, howl, howl! O! you are men of stones." OxAEP-1

"I prithee, daughter, do not make me mad." OxAEP-1

"O my dear father! Restoration, hang." OxAEP-1

"Please you, draw near.—Louder the music there!" EBEV

King Lear Bewildered. Patricia Storace. FFC

King lear in a mr. whippy van. Revisionism. Joanne Burns. BMAP

King Lot's Envoys. Drummond Allison. OxBSP

King Louis gave lessons in Class. Limerick. *Unknown*. PeLi

King Louis on his bridge is he. Le Père Sévère. *Unknown*. AWP, *tr. by* Andrew Lang

King luikit owre his castle wa', The. Sir Colin. *Unknown*. OxBB

King Mark, Tristram, and Palamede. Algernon Charles Swinburne. EBNV *Fr.* Tristram of Lyonesse.

King Matthias in Gömör. János Garay. IQMS, *tr. by* James Turner

King Midas. Howard Moss. CoAP; TAP

King Midas. Ovid. CTC, *tr. by* Arthur Golding *Fr.* Metamorphoses.

King must rule kingdom. Cities are seen from afar. Maxims (Cotton MS.). *Unknown*. AnOE, *tr. by* Charles W. Kennedy

King of Brentford's Testament *abr, The*. William Makepeace Thackeray. OBNV

King of Cats Sends a Postcard to His Wife, The. Nancy Willard. OBCA; OxIBACP

King of Ch'in rides out on his tiger and roams to the Eight Bounds, The. King of Ch'in Drinks Wine, The. Li Ho. WoPoe, *tr. by* A. C. Graham

King of China's Daughter, The. Dame Edith Sitwell. FaBoMo; MoBrPo

King of Comforts! King of life! Praise. Henry Vaughan. ESCV

King of France, the king of France / with forty thousand men, The. Mother Goose. OxNR

King of France went up the hill, The. Mother Goose. *See* King of France, the king of France / with forty thousand men, The

King of Glory [*or* Glorie], King of Peace / I will love thee. Praise (2). George Herbert. ChIV-1; ESCV

King of Glory [*or* Glorie], King of Peace / With the one make war[re] to cease. L'Envoy. George Herbert. BASC; ESCV

King of Glory sends his Son, The. Miracles at the Birth of Christ. Isaac Watts. NOCV

King of honour, louder than of England, The. Lament for the Country Soldiers. Les A. Murray. BMAP

King of Huai-nan, The. In Imitation of "The King of Huai-nan." Pao Chao. CoBCP, *tr. by* Burton Watson

King of Huainan, The. Magic Cinnabar. Pao Chao. ColAnChi, *tr. by* Anne Birrell

King of Ireland's Cairn, The. "Ethna Carbery." WPE

King of Mercy, King of Love. Begging. Henry Vaughan. ESCV

King of Oo-Rinktum-Jing, The. James Whitcomb Riley. NOxBChV

King of Owls, The. Louise Erdrich. NoAM

King of rock 'n' roll, The. Painkillers. Thom Gunn. AllShUp; SwNoth

King of Spain. Tiger, The. Marie Laurencin. CuPo

King of the Beasts, deep in the wood, The. Lion and the Echo, The. Brian Patten. OBSP

King of the Castle. *Unknown.* OxNR

King of the Cats is Dead, The. Peter Porter. EmeKit; NoAM

King of the gods once loved a Trojan boy, The. Ovid. CAGL, *tr. by* Rolfe Humphries *Fr.* Metamorphoses.

King of the Hobbledygoblins, The. Laura Elizabeth Richards. OBCA

King of the Mountains is on his way to Hara's abode, The. Kamalākānta Bhattācārya. SinGod, *tr. by* Rachel Fell McDermott

King of the perennial holly-groves, the riven sandstone. Geoffrey Hill. HAP; NPeEn; NoAM; WoPoe *Fr.* Mercian Hymns.

King of Thulé, The. Goethe. AWP, *tr. by* James Clarence Mangan

King of waters, the sea shouldering whale, The. Sea's Abundant Progeny, The. William Wood. NOSC; SCAP

King of Yellow Butterflies, The. Nicholas Vachel Lindsay. OBCA

King of Yvetot, The. Pierre Jean de Béranger. AWP, *tr. by* William Toynbee

King Oliver of New Orleans. Satchmo. Melvin B. Tolson. BPo; NAAAL

King, once summoned his favorites, A. King's Favorites, The. Priscilla Jane Thompson. CBWP-2

King Orfeo. *Unknown.* ESPB; OxBB; OxBoLi

King Pellam's Launde. David Jones. *Fr.* In Parenthesis.

"King Rear was foorish man his girls make crazy." Girdle round the Earth, A. Anthony Thwaite. PeLV

King Richard II. William Shakespeare.

    "Draw near, / And list what with our council we have done." OxAEP-1

    Let's Talk of Graves.

        Death of Kings, The. TRP

    Richard 2. OBGa

    ("This royal throne of kings, this scepter'd isle.") UV

    ("This royall Throne of Kings, this sceptred Isle.") OxBEV

King Richard III. William Shakespeare.

    Hate the Idle Pleasures. PoE

    "I have been studying how I may compare." OxAEP-1; WoPoe

    Methought That I Had Broken from the Tower. RB

    "Now is the winter of our discontent." OxBEV

    "Where is the duke my father with his power?" OxAEP-1

    "Why looks your Grace so heavily today?" OxAEP-1

King Richard hearing of the pranks. King's Disguise, and Friendship with Robin Hood, The. *Unknown.* ESPB

King Richard, in one of his rages. Limerick. Amanda Benjamin Hall. PeLi

King's Breakfast, The. Alan Alexander Milne. UV

King's College Chapel. Charles Causley. PeECV; TOF

King's Courtyard, The. *Hungarian Oral Tradition.* IQMS, *tr. by* Dermot Spence

King's Daughter / Wouldst thou be all fair. Everymaid. John Oxenham. TrCP

King's Disguise, The. John Cleveland. BASC

King's Disguise, and Friendship with Robin Hood, The. *Unknown.* ESPB

King's Dochter Lady Jean, The. *Unknown.* ESPB

King's fame lives. Go now, deny his tierce, The. (LL) Epigram. To the Household. 1630, An. Ben Jonson. BeJo; Son

King's Favorites, The. Priscilla Jane Thompson. CBWP-2

King's Last Farewell to the World, The. *Unknown.* BASC

King's poet was his captain of horse in the wars, The. Mount Badon. Charles Williams. FaBoTw

King's Son, The. Thomas Boyd. OBMV

King's young dochter was sitting in her window, The. King's Dochter Lady Jean, The. *Unknown.* ESPB

King Saul and I. Yehuda Amichai [*or* Amikhai]. PoSu, *tr. by* Assia Gutmann

King Saul was disconcerted. David and Goliath. Priscilla Jane Thompson. CBWP-2

King sent for his wise men all, The. W. James Reeves. NOxBChV; NTCP

King Shall Reign in Righteousness, A. Sebastian Streeter. AH

King sits in Dumferling town, The. *Unknown. See* King [he] sits in Dumferline [*or* Dumferling] town [*or* toune], The.

King Solomon, before his palace gate. Henry Wadsworth Longfellow. APN-1; TCAPo *Fr.* Tales of a Wayside Inn.

King Solomon's Camel is a hypocritical creature. King Solomon's Camel. Natan Zach. PoSu, *tr. by* Jon Silkin

King Solomon's Magnetic Quiz. John Wieners. FTOS

King Solomon Vistas. Ian Wedde. PeNZ

King Star trails nine lesser stars, The. King Star, The. *Vietnamese Oral Tradition.* CaDao, *tr. by* John Balaban

King then left his coach, The. Homer. NOSC, *tr. by* George Chapman *Fr.* Iliad, The.

King, this is Mihyar, A. Mihyar, A King! "Adonis" [*or* "Adunis"]. MAP, *tr. by* John Heath-Stubbs and Lena Jayyusi

King to Oxford sent a troop of horse, The. Epigram. Sir William Browne (1692–1774). FaBoEE; OxBEV

King Tut in America. Kwadwo Opoku-Agyemang. NAfrP

King upon whose bosom let me lie, The. (LL) Torso / Passages 18, The. Robert Duncan. CAGL; HarvBoo; PmAP

King William's Dispatch to Queen Augusta. Coventry Patmore. FaBoEE

Kingcups. Sacheverell Sitwell. MoBrPo

Kingdom. Leopold Staff. PoSu, *tr. by* Adam Czerniawski

Kingdom, The. Barry Silesky. IllVoic

Kingdom Coming. Henry Clay Work. APN-2

Kingdom of God, The. Rab. TrJP

Kingdom of God, The. Francis Thompson. GTBS-P; NOCV; SacPr
   (In No Strange Land.) HAP; ITBLP; MoBrPo; NOBE; OBEV; TrCP

Kingdom of Heaven. Léonie Adams. MoAmPo

Kingdom of Heaven, The. Pattiann Rogers. PoCoUp

Kingdom of Heaven Compared to a Grain of Mustard-Seed, The. Henry Vaughan. ChIV-2

Kingdom of heaven is likened unto a man which sowed good seed in his field, The. Bible, *N.T.* InPK-6 *Fr.* St. Matthew.

Kingdoms fall in sequence, like the waves on the shore, The. Sparrow's Skull, The. Ruth Pitter. FaBoWP

Kinge Arthur lives in merry Carleile. Marriage of Sir Gawain, The. *Unknown.* ESPB

Kinged. Shalin Hai-Jew. UnSA

Kinges baneres beth forth ilad, The. *Unknown.* MiEL

Kingfisher. Norman MacCaig. NoP-4

Kingfisher, The. Amy Clampitt. HCAP; OWoS

Kingfisher, The. William Henry Davies. AngWePo; NOBE; OBEV; OBWVE

Kingfisher, The. John Heath-Stubbs. NOxBChV

Kingfisher, The. John Lloyd. AngWePo

Kingfisher, The. Mary Oliver. BLT

Kingfisher blue along a tangled bank. Poem to the Tune "Riverbank Willows." Yü Hsüan-chi. BoWoP, *tr. by* Geoffrey Waters

Kingfisher Flat. William Everson. PoM

Kingfisher green lines the deserted shore. Composed on the Theme "Willows by the Riverside." Yü Hsüan-chi. SuSp; WPOW, *tr. by* Jan W. Walls

Kingfisher is a glorious thing, The. Kingfisher, The. John Lloyd. AngWePo

Kingfisher rises out of the black wave, The. Kingfisher, The. Mary Oliver. BLT

Kingfisher's Boxing Gloves, The. James Fenton. NoAM

Kingfishers, The. Charles Olson. APSN; HarvBoo; NAAL-2v2; NOBA; NeAP; PoM; VCAP

Kingfishers frolic among the orchid blossoms. Poem on the Wandering Immortal. Kuo P'o. CoBCP; ColAnChi, *tr. by* Burton Watson

Kingfishers nest on South Sea islands. Ch'en Tzu-ang. SuSp *Fr.* Impressions of Things Encountered.

Kingfishers sport among orchids and begonias. Kuo P'o. ChinPo, *tr. by* Yip Wai-lim

Kingis Quair, The. James I, King of Scotland.

    "Heigh in the hevynnis figure circulere." NePenScot

    King is Quair, The. EBEV

    ("Now was there made fast by the touris wall.") OBGa

Kingly lyon, and the strong arm'd beare, The. William Wood. SCAP

Kings, The. Louise Imogen Guiney. SacPr

Kings and Stars. John Erskine. TrCP

Kings Came Riding. Charles Williams. OBCP

Kings cast wreaths at your feet and fall upon their faces. At Your Feet, Jerusalem. Uri Zvi Greenberg. MHP, *tr. by* Ruth Finer Mintz

Kings do not touch doors. Pleasures of the Door, The. Francis Ponge. WoPoe, *tr. by* Raymond Federman

Kings don't touch doors. Delights of the Door, The. Francis Ponge. RaBo, *tr. by* Robert Bly

Kings go by with jeweled crowns, The. John Masefield. MoBrPo *Fr.* Lollingdon Downs.

Kings / like golden gleams. History Lesson, A. Miroslav Holub. PoSu; RB, *tr. by* George Theiner

Kings of Peru were the Incas, The. Limerick. *Unknown.* PeLi

Kings of the sea, The. (LL) Matthew Arnold. EBEV; FHYEP; FaBoCh; NAEL-5v2; NAEL-6v2; OBNV; OBSP

Kings passed in the dark barge, which Merlin dreamed. (LL) Hospital Barge at Cérisy. Wilfred Owen. HarvBoo; RB; TCAWP

Kings shall go, so will their pretty queens, The. Eternity. Kabir. WoPoe, *tr. by* Arvind Krishna Mehrotra

Kings who have died. Guillaume Apollinaire. TTTS *Fr.* Heart, Crown, and Mirror.

Kinigar. Archie Weller. IBA

Kinky. Denise Duhamel. AmPoNex

Kinky young girl from Uttoxeter, A. Limerick. Herbert Kretzmer. PeLi

Kinloch Ainort. Sorley MacLean (Somhairle MacGill-Eain). HarvBoo

Kinmont Willie. *Unknown.* ESPB; IBB; OxBB

Kinnereth. "Rachel" [*or* "Rahel"]. TrJP, *tr. by* A. M. Klein

Kinsale. Derek Mahon. BiHa

Kinshasa, Lumbumbasha. Bajji. Rashidah Ismaili. HAWP

Kinshasa, we feel, is not the place to reach. Flight of the White South Africans, The. Christopher Hope. PeSAV

Kinsman of Death, The. Endre Ady. IQMS, *tr. by* Peter Zollman

Kinu the milkman's alley. Flute-music. Rabindranath Tagore. OMIP, *tr. by* William Radice

Kiowa "49" Songs. *Unknown.*
   "I don't care if you're married, I'll still get you." STP
   "If you really love me honey, hey- yah." STP
   "She said she don't love me anymore because I drink whiskey." STP
   "You know that I love you, sweetheart, but every time I come around." STP

Kirk Lonegren's Home Movie Taking Place Just North of Prince George, with Sound. Sharon Thesen. NOBC

KIRK OF ULPHA to the pilgrim's eye, The. William Wordsworth. CenSon *Fr.* River Duddon [A Series of Sonnets], The.

Kirk's Alarm, The. Robert Burns. OxBoLi

Kirkwall Auction Mart. David Scott. NLP

Kirkyaird by the Sea, The. Douglas Young.
   "Steekit, consecrat, fou o fire but fuel." OBVE

Kirkyard. George Mackay Brown. NPeEn; NePenScot

Kirsten. Ted Berrigan. TTTS

Kisimiso. Musaemura Bonus Zimunya. HBAPE; NAfrP

Kiss. Susan Aizenberg. ExTi

Kiss. Emanuel Carnevali. APT-2

Kiss, A. Mary E. Tucker. CBWP-1

Kiss, The. Angela Ball. ExTi

Kiss, The. Charlotte Dacre. CABP; NOBRP

Kiss, The. Marie Howe. ExTi

Kiss, The. Thomas Moore. EnLoPo; NOBRP

Kiss, The. Edith Nesbit. LW

Kiss, The. Coventry Patmore. BoLoP; EnLoPo; NOBVV *Fr.* Angel in the House, The.

Kiss, The. Plato. STV, *tr. by* John Frederick Nims

Kiss, The. Dante Gabriel Rossetti. NOBVV; Son *Fr.* House of Life, The.

Kiss, The. Francis Saltus Saltus. VerBaPo

Kiss, The. Alice Walker. GT

Kiss from her, A! Her mouth, coming even close to your own, how. Kiss from Her, A. Rufinus. STV, *tr. by* John Frederick Nims

Kiss I begged; but, smiling, she, A. Weeping and Kissing. Sir Edward Sherburne. NOSC

Kiss I didn't give you, The. Time. Dulce Maria Loynaz. TANSG, *tr. by* Alan West

Kiss in the Dark, A. Thomas Sayers Ellis. GT

Kiss in the Rain, A. Samuel Minturn Peck. OBAL

Kiss in the Ring. *Unknown.* OxBoLi

Kiss me. Way April Leads to Autumn, The. Lynne Yamaguchi Fletcher. FSt

Kiss me again, and kiss me still, and kiss. Louise Labé. EroLit, *tr. by* Frances Webb

Kiss me again, re-kiss and kiss me whole. Sonnet 18. Louise Labé. WPOW

Kiss me and hug me. *Unknown.* BoWoP

Kiss me then, my merry May. *Unknown.* AWP

Kiss my grey hair, oh, my love. Healing. Abraham Reisen. TrJP, *tr. by* Joseph Leftwich

Kiss my lips. She did. Gertrude Stein. APT-1; PFTM-1; PoBW *Fr.* Lifting Belly.

Kiss my mother left here when she died, The. (LL) Elizabeth Barrett Browning. CenSon; EBVV; HAP; OxBSo *Fr.* Sonnets from the Portuguese.

Kiss of Caiaphas, The. (LL) Oscar Wilde. NPeEn; OxBEV *Fr.* Ballad of Reading Gaol, The.

Kiss that's on thy lip impressed, The. Duet. Lady Caroline Lamb. RWP

Kiss, The 1656. To Mrs. C. Thomas Shipman. NOSC

Kiss Tomorrow Goodbye. Marjorie Welish. FTOS

Kiss A? Pray tell me, what is in a kiss. Kiss, A. Mary E. Tucker. CBWP-1

Kiss[e], A. Robert Herrick. CaPo

Kiss[e] me, sweet: The wary [*or* warie] Lover. Ben Jonson. BeJo; EroLit; NOSC, *tr. by* Ben Jonson *Fr.* Volpone.

Kisses. Giancarlo Majorino. ItPo, *tr. by* Gayle Ridinger

Kisses. William Strode. FaBoEE; NOSC

Kisses, The. "Johannes Secundus." EroLit, *tr. by* Wayland Young *Fr.* Basia.

Kisses and embraces disgusted her. Gustave Thibon, How Simone Weil Appeared to Me/ 3. Stephanie Strickland. ExTi

Kisses Desired. William Drummond, of Hawthornden. EnLoPo

Kisses in the Train. D. H. Lawrence. MoBrPo

Kisses Loathesome. Robert Herrick. CaPo; OxBSP
   (I abhor the slimy kiss.) CavPo
   (Kisses Loathsome.) CavPo

Kisses upon the doors! The houses fall. Poeta Fui. Julia Budenz. FFC

Kissie Lee. Margaret Abigail Walker. BlSi; NALW

Kissing. Edward Herbert, 1st Baron Herbert of Cherbury. EnLoPo; NOSC

Kissing Agathon, I found. Sokrates to Agathon. Plato. GrAn, *tr. by* Peter Jay

Kissing and Bussing. Robert Herrick. BeJo

Kissing Helena. Plato. OBVE, *tr. by* Percy Bysshe Shelley

Kissing Hippomenes, I crave. Epigram. Paulus [*or* Paulos] Silentiarius. GrAn, *tr. by* Andrew Miller

Kissing Natalia. Eldon Grier. NOBC

Kissing Ramén. Michael Lassell. WiU

Kissing Stieglitz Goodbye. Gerald Stern. LCAP-2

Kissing, still unable to speak. (LL) All Legendary Obstacles. John Montague. BIrV; CIP-2; NOIV; PBCIP; PNI

Kitchen. Laura Jensen. LCAP-2

Kitchen Beast. Amanda Dalton. NeBl

Kitchen Door Blues. Tennessee Williams. OBAL

Kitchen Poem. Francis Scarfe. SPE

Kitchen's old-fashioned planter's clock portrays, The. Nightfishing. Gjertrud Schnackenberg. WeW-3

Kitchenette Building. Gwendolyn Brooks. BPo; FaBoWP; GT; NAAAL; NAAL-2v2; NAAL-5; NoP-4; PoE; PoPoPo; UnPo *Fr.* Street in Bronzeville, A.

Kitchens. Aurora Levins Morales. PueRic

Kitchie-Boy, The. *Unknown.* ESPB

Kite. Laura Jensen. LCAP-2

Kite, A. Hsü Wei. CoBLCP, *tr. by* Jonathan Chaves

Kite, The. Aleksandr Aleksandrovich Blok. PeFWW, *tr. by* David McDuff

Kite, The. Aleksandr Aleksandrovich Blok. FaBoWar, *tr. by* Frances Cornford, Esther Polinowsky Salaman and Esther P. Salamon

Kite, The. Adelaide O'Keeffe. NOxBChV

Kite, The. Mark Strand. ColAP

Kite, completed thus, is borne along, The. Samuel Bowden. NOEC *Fr.* Paper Kite, The.

Kite-Flying. Christopher Gilbert. GT

Kite-Flying. Sarah Kirsch.
   Call. PFTM-2, *tr. by* Wayne Kvam
   Mornings. PFTM-2, *tr. by* Wayne Kvam
   Renting a Room. PFTM-2, *tr. by* Wayne Kvam

Kite Is a Victim, A. Leonard Cohen. NOBC

Kite Poem. James Merrill. TwCP

Kite / Summon not me to enter: there's no doubt. For a Lady's Summons of Non-Entry. William Drummond, of Hawthornden. NOSC

Kites: Ars Poetica. Ben Belitt. APT-2

Kites at the Washington Monument. Greg Williamson. NAPBL

Kites shriek / Together—. Issa. ZenPo, *tr. by* Takashi Ikemoto and Lucien Stryk

Kith. Marion Lomax. NeBl

Kithairon sang of cunning Kronos. Korinna [*or* Corinna]. BoWoP

Kitten and [the] Falling Leaves, The. William Wordsworth.
   Kitten at Play, The. ChAP

Kitten can, A. Where Knock Is Open Wide. Theodore Roethke. HAP; VGW

Kitten, writes the mousy boy in his neat. In-flight Note. Judith Rodriguez. BMAP

Kitty-Cat Bird, The. Theodore Roethke. OBAL

Kitty's Atalantis for the year 1766. *Unknown.*
   "What's that in which good housewives take delight." EroLit

Kitzbuhl Church. Karen Alkalay-Gut. DTA

Kiwi Bird in the Kiwi Tree, The. Charles Bernstein. FTOS

Kleptomaniac. Polly Clark. NeBl

Kleptomaniac, The. Roger McGough. NOxBChV

Kleson's goat snorted all night through the dark. Erucius [*or* Erycius] of Cyzicus. GrAn

Klink—Hratzvenga (Deathwail). Else Von Freytag-Loringhoven. APT-1

Klockius so deeply hath sworn[e], ne'er more to come. Klockius. John Donne. PeLV

Klupzy Girl, The. Charles Bernstein. PmAP

Klytemnestra. Emily Jane Pfeiffer. ViWPN

Knave of darkness, limber in the leaves, The. Death for the Dark Stranger. Thomas McGrath. VGW

Knedneuch land. In the Pantry. Hugh MacDiarmid. NoAM

Knee, The. Ciaran Carson. PNI

Knee, The. Christian Morgenstern. RB, *tr.* by Lore Segal and W. D. Snodgrass

Kneel, and let us pray for the departed. Lost Property. Elizabeth Garrett. MFPA

Kneel, and thank Heaven they are not yours. (LL) William Gifford. Walter Savage Landor. FaBoEE; GTBS-P

Kneeling. Gertrude Stein. PFTM-1

Kneeling down to Look [*or* Peer] into a Culvert. Robert Bly. NoAM

Kneeling / in this store window. Smash Your Fist. Anabel Torres. TANSG, *tr.* by Celeste Kostopulos-Cooperman

Knees of a Natural Man. Henry Dumas. GT

Knees on off fists and hello lute's. armillaria mellea. Tony Baker. Oth

Knell, The. Muhammad Al-Faituri [*or* Al-Fituri *or* Al-Fayturi]. TTY, *tr.* by Samir M. Zoghby

Knell for the onset! (LL) Pibroch of Donuil Dhu. Sir Walter Scott. FaBoCh; OxBS

Knew her themselves, through all her veils [*or* vailes]. (LL) Ingrateful[l] Beauty Threatened. Thomas Carew. BeJo; CaPo; MeLP; OBEV

Knicht had two sons o sma fame, A. Sir Lionel. *Unknown.* ESPB

Knickerbocker Knockabout. Clyde Watson. NOxBChV

Knife. Gloria Vando. TouFir

Knife, The. Keith Douglas. NoAM

Knife, The. Milton Kaplan. TrJP

Knife All Blade, A. João Cabral de Melo Neto. VCWP, *tr.* by Galway Kinnell

Knife blade of cold air keeps prying, A. Upstate. Derek Walcott. GT; OPRER

Knife like a precious bond, The. Journey. Rodney Hall. NOBAu

Knife reduces a polished oval, The. Anne Cluysenaar. Prnts *Fr.* Poems of Memory.

Knife's edge, moon's edge, water's edge. Edge. Robert David Fitzgerald. CBAP

Knife That Is All Blade, The. Joao Cabral de Melo Neto. "Like a bullet." TCLAP, *tr.* by Elizabeth Gordon

Knife-thrower's wife stands, The. Knife-Thrower's Wife, The. Mekeel McBride. OPRER

Knife was much sharper than I thought, The. Accuser, The. Shirley Kaufman. GifTon

Knifing deep. Anita Virgil. HA

Knight and the Lady, The. William Cornish. NOBE

(You and I and Amyas.) NoSic

Knight and the Shepherd's Daughter, The. *Unknown.* ESPB

(Shepherd's Dochter, The.) OxBB

(There was a shepherd's dochter.) NoP-4

Knight, Death, and the Devil, The. Randall Jarrell. GS; WeW-3

Knight Errant, The. Louise Imogen Guiney. RACG

Donatello's Saint George.

"Oh, give my youth, my faith, my sword." TCAPo

Knight Fallen on Evil Days, The. Elinor Wylie. MoAmPo

Knight in the Wood, The. John Byrne Leicester Warren, 3d Baron De Tabley. NOBVV; PeVV

Knight of Liddesdale, The. *Unknown.* ESPB

Knight of My Maiden Love. Priscilla Jane Thompson. CBWP-2

Knight of "silver tongue" and stately grace, A. Wendell Phillips. Henrietta Cordelia Ray. CBWP-3

Knight of the Burning Pestle, The. Francis Beaumont.

"Nose, nose, jolly red nose." FaBoCh; OxNR

Knight of the Grail, The. *Unknown. See* Corpus Christi Carol, The

Knight [*or* Knyght] ther[e] was, and that a worthy man, A. Geoffrey Chaucer. UV *Fr.* Canterbury Tales, The.

Knight's Ghost, The. *Unknown.* ESPB

Knight's Interruption of the Monk's Tale, The. Geoffrey Chaucer. NAWM-5v1, *tr.* by Theodore Morrison *Fr.* Canterbury Tales, The.

Knight's Prayer, The. *Unknown.* InvLi

Knight's Tale, The. Geoffrey Chaucer. *Fr.* Canterbury Tales, The.

Knight's Tomb, The. Samuel Taylor Coleridge. FaBoCh; NPeEn; RB

Knight stands in the stable-door, The. Young Johnstone. *Unknown.* ESPB

Knight went down to the river's rim, A. Ballad. Gerda Mayer. OBSP

Knight who came was Launcelot at good need, The. (LL) Defense of Guenevere, The. William Morris. NAEL-5v2; NAEL-6v2

Knight with starry shield, The. Sir Roland; A Fragment. Robert Merry. NOEC

Knighthood, The. Geoffrey Chaucer. UV *Fr.* Canterbury Tales, The.

Knights of the Joyous Venture, The. Rudyard Kipling. *Fr.* Puck of Pook's Hill.

Knitted Things. Karla Kuskin.

"There was a witch who knitted things." KaS

Knitting. Mary E. Tucker. CBWP-1

Knob Pines. David Swanger. GeoHom

Knock at a star with my exalted head. (LL) Bad Season Makes the Poet Sad, The. Robert Herrick. BASC; BeJo; CaPo; CavPo; NAEL-5v1; NAEL-6v1; NAEL-7v1; SCGP

Knock at the doorie. *Unknown.* OxNR

Knock the zoo out of your eye, the sand dollar with dried. American Avalon. Connie Deanovich. AmPoNex

Knocker, A. Zbigniew Herbert. PoSu, *tr.* by Czeslaw Milosz

Knocking Around. John Ashbery. NoAM

Knocking Donkey Fleas off a Poet from the Southside of Chi. Haki R. Madhubuti. SeSe

Knocking on the door. Mimi Khalvati. Prnts *Fr.* Entries on Light.

Knole. Charles Hubert Sisson. NOCV

Knot. Susan Wicks. EmeKit

Knot, The. Vinda Karandikar. OMIP, *tr.* by Vinay Dharwadker

Knot, The. Stanley Kunitz. HAP

Knot, The. Henry Vaughan. BASC

Knot Hole Gang, The. Brendan Galvin. MoASP

Know, The. Christine Qunta. NAfrP

Know Celia, (since thou art so proud,). Ingrateful[l] Beauty Threatened. Thomas Carew. BeJo; CaPo; MeLP; OBEV

Know er thou knitte; prove er thou preise it. *Unknown.* MiEL

Know him for a white man. Passing into Storm. Patrick Lane. NOBC

Know'st thou the land which lovers ought to choose? Italy. Edward Coote [*or* Coate] Pinkney. APN-1

Know, that I would accounted be. To Ireland in the Coming Times. W. B. Yeats. NOIV; NoAM

Know that more than white is missing. (LL) Lessons from a Mirror. Thylias Moss. ESEAA; LTA

Know that one soldier has not died in vain. (LL) Karl Shapiro. HAP; OBWP; OxBA

Know then, I was born in a strange country. To My People. Edwin Seaver. TrJP

Know then, the only joy of an anchor—to be strong. Anchor, The. John Blight. BMAP

Know then thyself, presume not God to scan. Pope. ECEV; FHYEP; NAEL-5v1; NAEL-6v1; NAEL-7v1; NOEC; PAI; SacPr; TFi *Fr.* Essay on Man, An.

Know then / Toward summer when the sun is in Hyades. Ezra Pound. OBVE

Know this wind as. Prophetissa. Diane Di Prima. PFTM-2

Know Thyself. Kenneth Burke. OBAL

Know Thyself. Pope. *See* Essay on Man, An

Know 'tis but a loom of land. Land, Ho! Thomas Edward Brown. SacPr

Know what I'll promise you? Song. *Unknown.* STP, *tr.* by Jerome Rothenberg

Know what I'm like? Some captain moors his ship. Ausiàs March. STV

Know ye the man whom God has blessed. Lines to the Hon. George L. Knox. Eloise Bibb. CBWP-4

Know you fair[e], on what you look[e]? On Mr. G. Herberts Booke, The Temple. Richard Crashaw. ESCV; GeHe

Know you that land where forest shadows fold. Mignon. Goethe. WoPoe, *tr.* by Anthony Hecht

Know Yourself. John Arbuthnot. ECEV

Knowes what was first, and what shall be the end. (LL) Fulke Greville, 1st Baron Brooke. NOSC; NoSic *Fr.* Caelica.

Knowest thou the time when the wild goates of the rocke bring forth? Bible, *O.T.* OBVE *Fr.* Job.

Knowing. Mary Coghill. BrRo

Knowing, The. Sharon Olds. PasH

Knowing I Live in a Dark Age. Milton Acorn. NOBC

Knowing I would never be. Stilt-walker. Susan Wicks. Prnts

Knowing Love in Herself. Hadewijch. WPoS, *tr.* by Oliver Davies

Knowing nothing shuts the iron gates; the new love opens them. Knowing Nothing Shuts the Iron Gates. Kabir. RaBo, *tr.* by Robert Bly

Knowing the volume of our trade in kisses. (LL) 5. Catullus. NAWM-7v1; WoPoe, *tr.* by Charles Martin

Knowing those cared for whom they love. (LL) Due of the Dead, The. William Makepeace Thackeray. FaBoWar; OBWP

Knowingness. John Hughes. PNI

Knowledge. Louise Bogan. APT-2

Knowledge. Nina Cassian. BoWoP, *tr.* by Michael Impey and Brian Swann

Knowledge. John Greenleaf Whittier. PoToHe

Knowledge, Acquaintance, Resort, Favour, with Grace. John Skelton. CABP

Knowledge after Death. Henry Charles Beeching. SacPr

Knowledge, I know, is sure, of gradual thought. Young Knowledge. "Robin Hyde." PeNZ

Knowledge is an old error remembering its youth. Aphorisms. Francis Picabia. SurPaPo, *tr.* by Marcel Jean

Knowledge not of sorrow, you were, The. Discrete Series. George Oppen. APT-2; PFTM-1

Knowledge of God.   John Frederick Nims.   InvLi

Knowledge of Light, The.   Henry Rago.   VGW

Knowledgeable Child, The.   Leonard Alfred George Strong.   OBMV

Knowlt Hoheimer.   Edgar Lee Masters.   OxBA   *Fr.* Spoon River Anthology.

Known to the boys in his Latin class as "Sir."   Mysteries of Caesar, The.   Anthony Hecht.   NoP-4

Knows as I make for her white side, shivering. (LL)   Hooters.   Meic Stephens.   AngWePo; TCAWP

Knows for certain who salvaged that load. (LL)   Ship of Death, A.   Seamus Heaney.   NAEL-6v2; NoP-4

Knows the new maid steals, and forgives her. (LL)   Difference between Pepsi and Coke, The.   David Lehman.   PmAP; ReTh

Knoxville, Tennessee.   Nikki Giovanni.   BPo; BlSi; OxIBACP

Ko-Ishin-Mit Goes Fishing.   George Clutesi.   HATNAP

Ko-jin goes west from Ko-kaku-ro [or Ko-keku-to].   Separation on the River Kiang.   Li Po.   UnPo, *tr. by* Ezra Pound

Köcsey.   Ferenc Kölcsey.   IQMS, *tr. by* Watson Kirkconnell

Koel (Rainbird) and Effigy.   Unknown.   NOBAu, *tr. by* Mungayana Nundhirribala

Koheleth.   Louis Untermeyer.   ChIV-1; TrJP

Kojo: I Am A Black.   Gwendolyn Brooks.   ESEAA   *Fr.* Children Going Home.

Kokin Shu.   *Var. authors.*
  "Although it is not plainly visible to the eye."   AWP
  "Beloved person must I think, The."   AWP; TAL
  "Did I ever think."   AWP
  "Hoping all the time."   AWP
  "If only, when one heard."   AWP
  "If this were a world."   WoPoe, *tr. by* Helen Craig McCullough
  "My love / Is like the grasses."   AWP
  "O Cuckoo."   AWP
  "Since I heard."   AWP
  "Thing which fades, A."   AWP; BoWoP
  "Though you made me think."   WoPoe, *tr. by* Helen Craig McCullough
  "When the dawn comes."   AWP

Koko Taylor sang.   Blues at 1.   Dorothy Perry Thompson.   SpirFl

Kol Nidra.   Joseph Leiser.   TrJP

Kommunalka. Rider-rider-rider. Along a wall / crawls a spider.   Communal Krakovyak.   Vladimir Druk.   TCRP, *tr. by* Albert C. Todd

Komsomol Song.   Iosif Pavlovich Utkin.   TCRP, *tr. by* Lubov Yakovleva

Kong Breaks a Leg at the William Morris Agency.   William Trowbridge.   ReTh

Koocoo, The.   Unknown.   TTTS

Kookaburra.   Frieda Hughes.   NeBl

"Kookoorookoo! kookoorookoo!" / Crows the cock before the morn.   Christina Georgina Rossetti.   FaBoVe

Kopis'taya.   Paula Gunn Allen.   HATNAP

Kora in Hell.   William Carlos Williams.
  "Pathology literally speaking is a flower garden."   TCAPo
  "Some fools once were listening to a poet reading his poem."   TCAPo
  "There is neither beginning nor end to the imagination."   CLPP
  "There's force to this cold sun, makes beard stubble stand shinily."   TCAPo
  "Why go further? One might conceivably rectify the rhythm."   TCAPo

Kore.   Robert Creeley.   NAAL-5; RaBo

Kore in Hades.   Kathleen Jessie Raine.   NALW

Korean Figures.   Unknown.   EaWin, *tr. by* W. S. Merwin

Korean Mums.   James Schuyler.   PmAP; VCAP

Korf invents some jokes of a new sort.   Delayed Action.   Christian Morgenstern.   RB, *tr. by* Lore Segal and W. D. Snodgrass

Korf receives one day from the coppers.   Summons.   Christian Morgenstern.   WoPoe, *tr. by* David R. Slavitt

Korf, whom worry easily attacks.   Anxiety for the Future.   Christian Morgenstern.   WoPoe, *tr. by* William DeWitt Snodgrass

Kőrös was our river, we would go, The.   Black Kőrös.   József Erdélyi.   IQMS, *tr. by* Alan Dixon

Korosta Katzina Song.   Koianimptiwa.   AWP, *tr. by* Natalie Curtis Burlin

Koskiusko.   Samuel Taylor Coleridge.   OxBSo   *Fr.* Effusions.

Kosmos.   Julia Ward Howe.   ColAP

Kou-chien, king of Yüeh, came back from the broken land of Wu.   In Yüeh Viewing the Past.   Li Po.   CoBCP, *tr. by* Burton Watson

Kouretes hid the goddess's, The.   Korinna [or Corinna].   SaLy, *tr. by* Diane Rayor

Kraken, The.   Tennyson.   NAEL-5v2; NAEL-6v2; NoP-4; PeECV; TOF

Kral Majales.   Allen Ginsberg.   PFTM-2; PoM
  (And the Communists have nothing to offer but fat cheeks and.)   BB

Krantor.   Theaitetus.   GrAn, *tr. by* Dennis Schmitz

Kreutzer Sonata.   Ted Hughes.   FaBoMo

Kreutzer Sonata, A.   "Sasha Chorny" [or Chiornyi].   TCRP, *tr. by* Bernard Meares

Krĭk'ĭt.   Marlene Mountain.   HA

Krishna played on the charmingly juicy flute.   Song, The.   Balakrishna Sama.   PoetW

Krismas Dinnah.   Maggie Pogue Johnson.   CBWP-4

Kropotkin Poems, The.   Phyllis Webb.
  "Syllables disintegrate ingrate alphabets."   NOBC

Kruger sets his feet.   Brass Knuckles.   Stuart Dybek.   PBCAP

Ku Feng (After the Style of Ancient Poems).   Li Po.   ChinPo, *tr. by* Yip Wai-lim

Ku Klux.   Langston Hughes.   BPo

Ku Li.   "Robin Hyde."   PeNZ

Ku-ring-gai Rock Carvings.   David Campbell.
  Lovers, The.   BMAP

Kŭ' siut Song.   Unknown.   APN-2, *tr. by* Franz Boas

Ku'u Pua I Paoakalani.   Queen Lili'u-o-ka-lani.   SWaP

Kuan-kuan call the ospreys.   Unknown.   ColAnChi, *tr. by* Jeffrey Riegel   *Fr.* Classic of Odes.

Kuan-kuan, the ospreys.   Unknown.   ChinPo, *tr. by* Yip Wai-lim

Kubla Khan: or, A Vision in a Dream.   Samuel Taylor Coleridge.   AWP; BRP; CABP; FHYEP; FaBoCh; HAP; HeIP-4; InPK-6; NAEL-5v2; NAEL-6v2; NAWM-7v2; NIL-7; NIP-4; NOBE; NOBRP; NPeEn; NoP-4; OBEV; OBGa; OxAEP-2; OxBEV; PAI; PoE; PoPoPo; PoRA; SCGP; SCV; SoSe-8; TFi; TOF; TRP; WeW-3; WoPoe

Kudzu Spreads Till It Darkens the Brier, The.   Unknown.   CoBCP, *tr. by* Burton Watson

Kukutis broke into song: How fortunate I am.   Kukutis's Song.   Marcelijus Martinaitis.   TWW, *tr. by* Laima Sruoginis

Kukutis Describes His Hut.   Marcelijus Martinaitis.   TWW, *tr. by* Laima Sruoginis

Kukutis in the Reich's Guard House.   Marcelijus Martinaitis.   TWW, *tr. by* Laima Sruoginis

Kukutis, Kukutis, you good soul.   Kukutis's Lament under the Heavens.   Marcelijus Martinaitis.   TWW, *tr. by* Laima Sruoginis

Kukutis's Consciousness Becomes Alienated.   Marcelijus Martinaitis.   TWW, *tr. by* Laima Sruoginis

Kukutis's Fruitless Bread.   Marcelijus Martinaitis.   TWW, *tr. by* Laima Sruoginis

Kukutis's Lament under the Heavens.   Marcelijus Martinaitis.   TWW, *tr. by* Laima Sruoginis

Kukutis's Sermon to the Pigs.   Marcelijus Martinaitis.   TWW, *tr. by* Laima Sruoginis

Kukutis's Sinful Spirit.   Marcelijus Martinaitis.   TWW, *tr. by* Laima Sruoginis

Kukutis's Song.   Marcelijus Martinaitis.   TWW, *tr. by* Laima Sruoginis

Kukutis's Swallow's Hymn.   Marcelijus Martinaitis.   TWW, *tr. by* Laima Sruoginis

Kukutis's Trip on the Samogitian Highway.   Marcelijus Martinaitis.   TWW, *tr. by* Laima Sruoginis

Kulakundalini, Goddess Full of Brahman, Tara.   Rāmprasād Sen.   SinGod, *tr. by* Rachel Fell McDermott

Kumara / Nich, nich, pasalam, bada.   Bald Mountain Zaum-Poems.   Unknown.   PFTM-1

Kumquat for John Keats, A.   Tony Harrison.   NoP-4

Kumuhea the night-caterpillar loves the woman.   Woman Who Married a Caterpillar, The.   Unknown.   WoPoe, *tr. by* Armand Schwerner

Kun-shih, my pride, my son.   Boasting of My Son.   Li Shang-yin.   ColAnChi, *tr. by* James J. Y. Liu

Kundiman.   Bataan Faigao.   ReBoTo

Kundry was Wagner's creation. And they brought Tefnut back, from her wilderness.   Structure of Rime XVIII.   Robert Duncan.   FTOS

Kung walked / by the dynastic temple.   Ezra Pound.   APT-1; FaBoMo; PoE   *Fr.* Cantos.

Kupris bears trophies away.   Sophocles.   CTC   *Fr.* Women of Trachis.

Kural, The.   Tiruvalluvar.
  Gift of Children, The.   WoPoe, *tr. by* Emmons E. White
  Kindness and Generosity.   WoPoe, *tr. by* Emmons E. White
  Learning.   WoPoe, *tr. by* Emmons E. White

Kurt, last night Dwight Evans put it all.   Fifth Inning, The.   Donald Hall.   MoASP

Kurt, terror is merely the thesis.   Eighth Inning, The.   Donald Hall.   MoASP

Kwaakwaa.   Gynae One.   Christine Ama Ata Aidoo.   HAWP

Kwakwha. / Askwali.   Parallax.   Arthur Sze.   GifTon

Kwela for Tomorrow.   Rui Knopfli.   PeSAV, *tr. by* the author

KYE HO! Wonderful!   Kambala.   WPoS

KYE HO! Wonderful!   Dakini Lion-Face.   WPoS

Kylemore Castle.   Richard Murphy.   ModIr   *Fr.* Price of Stone, The.

Kyoto Garden, A.   Dennis Joseph Enright.   OBGa

Kypris and Nereids, let that brother.   Sappho.   SaLy, *tr. by* Diane Rayor

Kypris keeps this spot. Anyte [*or* Anytes]. PGA

Kypris / May she find you very bitter. Sappho. SaLy, *tr. by* Diane Rayor

Kypros! Andromache's Wedding. Sappho. BoWoP, *tr. by* Willis Barnstone

Kyrie. Ellen Bryant Voigt.
"All ears, nose, tongue and gut." ExTi

Kyrie, So Kyrie. *Unknown.* MiEL
(Jankin.) NOBE
(Jolly Jankin.) OxBoLi; PeLV; PoE

Kyrielle. May Probyn. VWP

L

L(a. E. E. Cummings. NIL-7; NIP-4; TRP

L.A. spring, our boulevard of flowering jaca. Blue Kashmir, '74. Carol Muske. PuP-23

L'Agulhas, a Walk. Wilma Stockenström. PeSAV, *tr. by* Rosa Keet

L'Allée. Paul Verlaine. *See* Dans l'Allée

L'Allegro. John Milton. AWP; BASC; FHYEP; GTBS-P; HAP; NAEL-6v1; NAEL-7v1; NOSC; NoP-4; OBEV; PBRV; PoPoPo; TFi

L'amiral cherche une maison à louer. Richard Huelsenbeck. PFTM-1

L'Amitié et l'Amour. John Swanwick [*or* Swanick] Drennan. BIrV

L'Amitie: To Mrs. Mary [*or* M.] Awbrey. Katherine Philips. NIL-7; NOSC

L'amour. Chanson. Ernst Jandl. PFTM-2

L'An Trentiesme de Mon Eage. Archibald MacLeish. NOBA
(In My Thirtieth Year.) MoAmPo

L'Après-Midi d'un Faune. Stéphane Mallarmé. AWP, *tr. by* Aldous Huxley

L'Arc Musical (1970). U Tam'si Tchicaya.
Epitaph. PBMAP

L. E. L.'s Last Question. Elizabeth Barrett Browning. VWP

L'Embarquement pour Cythère. John Streeter Manifold. CBAP

L'Enfant Glacé. Harry Graham. NBLV; OBCoV; PeLV

L'Envoi. Rudyard Kipling. BRP; PWR
(When Earth's Last Picture Is Painted.) UV

L'Envoi. Edwin Arlington Robinson. ITBLP; TrCP

L'Envoi: "What is the moral? Who rides may read." Rudyard Kipling. MoBrPo

L'Envoy. George Herbert. BASC; ESCV

L'Homme Moyen Sensuel. Ezra Pound. OBSV

L'indifférent. "Michael Field." ViWPN

L'Invitation au Voyage. Charles Baudelaire. WoPoe, *tr. by* Richard Wilbur
(Invitation to the Voyage.) NAWM-7v2

L M F B R. Gary Snyder. PoM

"L" may stand for fifty, Lais. Myrinos. GrAn

L'Orangerie. Frank Ormsby. ModIr *Fr.* Paris Honeymoon, A.

L.R.D.G. J. G. Meddemmen. FaBoWar

L Y L Y T. David Meltzer. PFTM-2 *Fr.* Hero / Lil.

La balala ika. Balalaïka. Pierre Albert-Birot. CuPo

La Bella Bona-Roba. Richard Lovelace. BeJo; CaPo; EBEV; NOSC; OxBEV

La Belle Confidente. Thomas Stanley. MeLP

La Belle Dame sans Merci [A Ballad]. John Keats. AWP; BRP; CABP; ClHu; FHYEP; FaBoCh; GTBS-P; HAP; HeIP-4; NAEL-5v2; NAEL-6v2; NAWM-7v2; NOBE; NOBRP; NPeEn; NoP-4; OBEV; OBSP; OxAEP-2; OxBEV; PAI; PoE; PoPoPo; PoRA; RB; SCGP; SCV; SoSe-8; TFi; TRP; UV; UnPo; WoPoe

La Belle Juive. Henry Timrod. APN-2; TCAPo

La Berline Arrêtée dans la Nuit. O. V. de L. Milosz. GifTon, *tr. by* Kenneth Rexroth

La Bodega Sold Dreams. Miguel Piñero. PueRic

La Brea. Richard Kenney. DiPo

La Chute. Charles Olson. InPK-6; PAI

La Corona. John Donne. ChIV-2; ESCV; Son *Fr.* Holy Sonnets.

La Corona. John Donne. *See also* Holy Sonnets

La Crosse at Ninety Miles an Hour. Richard Eberhart. APT-2

La Fabrique de Tabac (Tobacco Harvest). Beverly Matherne. TWW

La Fayette. Samuel Taylor Coleridge. CenSon *Fr.* Effusions.

La Figlia Che Piange. T. S. Eliot. APT-1; FaBoTw; HarvBoo; HeIP-4; OxBEV; OxBTC; TCAPo; UnPo; VGW

La Fontaine de Vaucluse. Marilyn Hacker.
"Azure striation swirls beyond the stones." Son
"We may be learning how to tell the truth." Son

La Gialletta Gallante, or the Sunburned Exotic Beauty. Edward Herbert, 1st Baron Herbert of Cherbury. NOSC

La Gioconda; Leonardo Da Vinci, the Louvre. "Michael Field." CABP; PeVV; ViWPN

La Gorgue. Ivor Gurney. OxBEV

La Guardia, the Story. Jane Mead. BodElec

La, La, La! Thomas M. [*or* "Tom"] Disch. NBLV

La, la, la. To live with, to be like, to be. Hymn to Yellow. Genevieve Taggard. APT-2

La Llorona. Juan Delgado. GeoHom

La Madonna dell' Acqua. John Ruskin. NOBVV

La Máquina a Houston. Edward Dorn. PoM

La Mélinite: Moulin-Rouge. Arthur Symons. PeVV

La Migra. Pat Mora. NIL-7; UnSA

La Milarosa. Víctor Hernández Cruz. TouFir

La muerte es una tormenta. La tormenta. Martín Espada. PueRic

La narrativa says you must paint a flower. Untitled (April '91). Michael Palmer. BodElec

La Naval De Manila: Selim Sot as a Modern Political Observer. Eric Gamalinda. ReBoTo

La Nuit Blanche. Rudyard Kipling. MoBrPo; UV

La Papa. Rudolfo Anaya. SpudSo

La Pathétique. Lily Brett. HP

La Plata, Missouri: Clear November Night. Jim Barnes. HATNAP

"La Pologne? La Pologne? It's very cold over there, isn't it?" the lady. Words. Wislawa Szymborska. PoSu, *tr. by* Krystof Zarzecki

La Préface. Charles Olson. APT-2; PFTM-2; PoM

La Promessa Sposa. Walter Savage Landor. NOBVV

La Puente. Elsa Rediva E'der. ReBoTo

La Quinque Rue. Edmund Charles Blunden. PeFWW

La Selva. Cid Corman. VGW

La Sombra of Who I Am. Michaela Raen. PoArWo

La tormenta. Martín Espada. PueRic

La Tormenta. Geraldine Monk. Oth

La Vita Nuova. Dante Alighieri.
"All my thoughts always speak to me of love." AWP; EaItPo, *tr. by* Dante Gabriel Rossetti
"All ye that pass along Love's trodden way." AWP; EaItPo, *tr. by* Dante Gabriel Rossetti
"At whiles (yea oftentimes) I muse over." AWP; EaItPo, *tr. by* Dante Gabriel Rossetti
"Beyond the sphere which spreads to widest space." AWP; CTC; EaItPo, *tr. by* Dante Gabriel Rossetti
"Canst thou indeed be he that still would sing." AWP; EaItPo, *tr. by* Dante Gabriel Rossetti
"Day agone, as I rode sullenly, A." AWP; EaItPo, *tr. by* Dante Gabriel Rossetti
"Death, alway cruel, Pity's foe in chief." AWP; EaItPo, *tr. by* Dante Gabriel Rossetti
"Even as the others mock, thou mockest me." AWP; EaItPo, *tr. by* Dante Gabriel Rossetti
"Eyes that weep for pity of the heart, The." AWP
"For certain he hath seen all perfectness." AWP; EaItPo, *tr. by* Dante Gabriel Rossetti
"Gentle thought there is will often start, A." AWP; EaItPo, *tr. by* Dante Gabriel Rossetti
"I felt a spirit of love begin to stir." AWP; EaItPo, *tr. by* Dante Gabriel Rossetti
"Ladies that have intelligence in love." AWP; EaItPo, *tr. by* Dante Gabriel Rossetti
"Love and the gentle heart are one same thing." AWP; EaItPo, *tr. by* Dante Gabriel Rossetti
"Love and the gentle heart are one thing." NAWM-7v1, *tr. by* Dino Cervigni and Edward Vasta
"Love hath so long possessed me for his own." AWP; EaItPo, *tr. by* Dante Gabriel Rossetti
"Love's pallor and the semblance of deep ruth." AWP; EaItPo, *tr. by* Dante Gabriel Rossetti
"Mine eyes beheld the blessed pity spring." AWP; EaItPo, *tr. by* Dante Gabriel Rossetti
"My lady carries love within her eyes." AWP; EaItPo, *tr. by* Dante Gabriel Rossetti
"My lady looks so gentle and so pure." AWP; EaItPo, *tr. by* Dante Gabriel Rossetti
"Song, 'tis my will that thou do seek out Love." AWP; EaItPo, *tr. by* Dante Gabriel Rossetti
"Stay now with me, and listen to my sighs." AWP; EaItPo, *tr. by* Dante Gabriel Rossetti
"That lady of all gentle memories." AWP; MiVo, *tr. by* Dante Gabriel Rossetti
"That she hath gone to Heaven suddenly." CTC
"Thoughts are broken in my memory, The." AWP; EaItPo, *tr. by* Dante Gabriel Rossetti
"To every heart which the sweet pain doth move." AWP; EaItPo, *tr. by* Dante Gabriel Rossetti

"Very bitter weeping that ye made, The." AWP; EaItPo, *tr. by* Dante Gabriel Rossetti

"Very pitiful lady, very young, A." AWP; CTC; EaItPo, *tr. by* Dante Gabriel Rossetti

"Weep, Lovers, with Love's very self doth weep." AWP; EaItPo, *tr. by* Dante Gabriel Rossetti

"Whatever while the thought comes over me." AWP; EaItPo, *tr. by* Dante Gabriel Rossetti

"Woe's me! by dint of all these sighs that come." AWP; EaItPo, *tr. by* Dante Gabriel Rossetti

"Ye pilgrim-folk, advancing pensively." AWP; CTC; EaItPo, *tr. by* Dante Gabriel Rossetti

"You that thus wear a modest countenance." AWP; EaItPo, *tr. by* Dante Gabriel Rossetti

La Vita Nuova. Weldon Kees. VGW

Lab Lines. Robert Hugh Benson. Unle

Laban, I curse you for this trick you played! Ruth Gilbert. PeNZ *Fr.* Leah.

Labane. Annette M'Baye d'Erneville. HAWP, *tr. by* Brian Baer

Labasheedy (The Silken Bed). Nuala Ni Dhomhnaill. CABP; CIP-2, *tr. by the author*

Label, the labor, the color, the shade, The. The shirt. (LL) Shirt. Robert Pinsky. ColAP; HarvBoo; NAAL-5

Labor and Rest. Dinah Maria Mulock. TreFP

Labor Day. Louise Glück. NIL-7; NoAM

Labor Day Picnic Poem. Todd Colby. HeMarv

Labor raises honest sweat. Dignity of Labor, The. Robert Bersohn. NBLV

Laboratory Poem. James Merrill. InPK-6; TwCP

Laboratory (Ancien Régime), The. Robert Browning. NAEL-5v2; NAEL-6v2; OBEV

Laborer, The. Richard Dehmel. AWP, *tr. by* Jethro Bithell

Laborer, The. José-Maria de Heredia. AWP, *tr. by* Wilfrid Thorley

Laborers, The. Jones Very. SacPr

Laborers of Christ! Arise. Lydia Huntley Sigourney. AH

Laboring and Heavy Laden. Jeremiah Eames Rankin. AH

Laborious, stumpy, droopy, askew. Complete Semen Study. Michael Ryan. BodElec

Labors of Hercules, The. Marianne Craig Moore. OxBA

Labour. Kristina Rungano. HAWP

Labour and Delivery. Ron Charach. BloBone

Labourer, The. Iolo Goch. OBWVE, *tr. by* Gwyn Williams

Labourer's Wife, A. John Davidson. EBVV *Fr.* To the Street Piano.

Labouring man, that tills the fertile soil, The. Pains and Gains. Edward de Vere, 17th Earl of Oxford. NoSic

Labouring poor, in spite of double pay, The. Daniel Defoe. NOBL *Fr.* True-born Englishman, The.

Labours of the Months. *Unknown.* EBEV

Laburnum. Paula Meehan. ModIr

Labyrinth. Jaime Torres Bodet. TCLAP, *tr. by* Sonja Karsen

Labyrinth, The. Jorge Luis Borges. PoetW; WoPoe, *tr. by* John Updike

Labyrinth, The. Edwin Muir. MoBrPo

Labyrinth of byways, A. Forever Parted: Graveyard. Gu Cheng. VCWP, *tr. by* Jerome P. Seaton

Lacedemonian Instruction. William Blake. WoPoe

Lachesis. Victor James Daley. CBAP

Lachin y Gair. Byron. NePenScot; OxBS

Lachrimae; or Seven Tears Figured in Seven Passionate Pavans. Geoffrey Hill.
    Lachrimae Amantis. NOCV; OxBSo; WoPoe, *tr. by* Geoffrey Hill
    Lachrimae Verae. NAEL-5v2; NAEL-6v2; NoAM
    Masque of Blackness, The. NoAM

Lack of Balance but not Fatal, A. Jackson Mac Low. FTOS

Lackawanna. Galway Kinnell. GM

Lackawanna Elegy. Iwan [or Yvann] Goll. AF, *tr. by* Galway Kinnell

Lackblockblackb. Ian Hamilton Finlay. TRP

Lacking grace / beauty. Capito. GrAn

Lacking my love, I go from place to place. Edmund Spenser. NoSic *Fr.* Amoretti.

Lacking rich acres, thick grape-crops. Apollonides. GrAn

Laconic as anglers and, like them, submissive. At the Ferry. U. A. Fanthorpe. FaBoWP

Lacquer dust and powdered bone and red cinnabar grains. Arrowhead from the Ancient Battlefield of Ch'ang-p'ing, An. Li Ho. FaBoWar, *tr. by* A. C. Graham

Lacrimae Rerum. Patricia Goedicke. ExTi

Lacrimas or There Is a Need to Scream. K. Curtis Lyle. NBV

Lacy mobile changing lazily, A. Watching a Cloud. Dannie Abse. OxBC

Lad came to the door at night, The. True Lover, The. A. E. Housman. EBNV

Lad, come kiss me. Invitation. Marion Angus. LW

Lad, glancing like a virgin. Anacreon. SaLy, *tr. by* Diane Rayor

Lad I lo'e dearly, Tam Glen, The. (LL) Tam Glen. Robert Burns. AWP; OxBS

Lad of Athens, faithful be. Emily Dickinson. FaBoEE

Lad of the brainier kind, A. Limerick. Hymie Sneak. PeLi

Ladder stretching up to heaven, A. Hymn to Holy Women, A. Notker Balbulus. NAWM-7v1, *tr. by* Peter Dronke

Ladders. Elizabeth Alexander. FFC

Ladie [*or* Lady], that in the prime of earliest youth. Sonnet 9. John Milton. OxBSo

Ladie stude in her bour-door, The. Young Hunting. *Unknown.* ESPB

Ladies, The. Rudyard Kipling. FaBoWar; MoBrPo; NAEL-5v2; NAEL-6v2

Ladies and gentlemen. Complaint on the Oblivion of the Dead. Jules Laforgue. WoPoe, *tr. by* William Jay Smith

Ladies and gentlemen. I Move the Meeting Be Adjourned. Nicanor Parra. TCLAP, *tr. by* Allen Ginsberg

Ladies and gentlemen, allow me to introduce to you Breyten Breytenbach. Threat of the Sick. Breyten Breytenbach. PoetW, *tr. by* Denis Hirson

Ladies and gentlemen come to supper. Hot Boiled Beans. *Unknown.* ReMoGo

Ladies and gentlemen, that is the end of the programme. Epilogue to a Poetry Reading. M. K. Joseph. PeNZ

Ladies and gentlemen, this is High Wood. High Wood. Philip Johnstone. FaBoWar

Ladies and gentlemen this little girl. E. E. Cummings. PoE

Ladies bow, and partners set, The. Soliloquy of a Maiden Aunt. Dollie Radford. NOBVV; OxBEV

Ladies Defence or, the Bride-Woman's Counsellor Answered, The. Mary Lee, Lady Chudleigh.
    "Unhappy they, who by their duty led." PEW

Ladies' Home Journal, The. Sandra M. Gilbert. NIP-4
    (Sonnet.) NIL-7

Ladies, I crave your indulgence for. Young Laundryman, The. William Carlos Williams. SAmP

Ladies, I do here present you. Present to a Lady, A. *Unknown.* PeLV

Ladies, I do here present you. Hannah Wolley. EMWP *Fr.* Queen-Like Closet, The.

Ladies of St. James's, The. Austin Dobson. PoRA

Ladies of the morning gauze their mouths, The. Canonical Hours. William Dickey. CoAP

Ladies Prayer to Cupid, A. Thomas Carew. *See* Lady's Prayer to Cupid, A

Ladies that guild the glittering noon. General Eclipse, The. John Cleveland. BASC

Ladies that have intelligence in love. Dante Alighieri. AWP; EaItPo, *tr. by* Dante Gabriel Rossetti *Fr.* La Vita Nuova.

Ladies, though to your conquering eyes. Sir George Etherege. OxBSP *Fr.* Comical Revenge, The.

Ladies, to this advice give heed. Maxim Revised, A. *Unknown.* NBLV

Ladies Who Lunch, The. Stephen Sondheim. PoE

Ladies Who Sing with a Band, The. George Marion, Jr. ReLy

Ladies, you see time flieth. *Unknown.* NoSic

Lads in their hundreds to Ludlow come in for the fair, The. Lads in Their Hundreds, The. A. E. Housman. MoBrPo; OxBTC

Lads of the Village, The. Stevie Smith. OxBSP

Lads of Wamphray, The. *Unknown.* ESPB; IBB

Lads that will die in their glory and never be old, The. (LL) Lads in Their Hundreds, The. A. E. Housman. MoBrPo; OxBTC

Lady, A. Amy Lowell. MoAmPo; TCAPo

Lady A. L., My Asylum [in a Great Extremity], The. Richard Lovelace. CaPo
    (Lady A. L, The.) CavPo
    (With that delight the royal captive's brought.) CavPo

Lady, accept this garland. Dancing Girl. Walther [*or* Walter] von der Vogelweide. NAWM-7v1, *tr. by* Peter Dronke

Lady Alice was sitting in her bower-window. Lady Alice. *Unknown.* ESPB

Lady and the Bear, The. Theodore Roethke. ChAP; NBLV

Lady and the Doctor, The. Helen Leigh. WoRP

Lady and the Magpie, The. *Unknown.* ChiP, *tr. by* Arthur Waley

Lady asks me, A / I speak in season. Ezra Pound. APT-1 *Fr.* Cantos.

Lady at the Castle, The. John Hollander. NoAM

Lady, / baby. *Unknown.* OxNR

Lady came to a Bear by a Stream, A. Lady and the Bear, The. Theodore Roethke. ChAP; NBLV

Lady Charlotte Guest. Goronva Camlan. AngWePo

Lady Cicely Wemyss. James I, King of England. NOSC

Lady Comes to an Inn, A. Elizabeth Jane Coatsworth. MoAmPo

Lady Diamond. *Unknown.* ESPB

Lady Elspat. *Unknown.* ESPB

Lady Erskine sits in her chamber. Child Owlet. *Unknown.* ESPB

Lady Fortune is both friend and foe, The. Fortune. *Unknown*. HeIP-4

Lady Freedom among Us. Rita Dove. LoL

Lady from near Rising Sun, A. It Figures. Ogden Nash. PeLi

Lady from Vanity Fair, A. Limerick. W. F. N. Watson. PeLi

Lady Hsi. Wang Wei. CoBCP, *tr. by* Burton Watson

Lady Hungerford's Meditacions upon the Beades, The. Anne Dormer, Lady Hungerford. EMWP

Lady I Know, A. Countee Cullen. *See* Four Epitaphs

Lady! I would that verse of mine. Stanzas. Edgar Allan Poe. NCAP

Lady in Kicking Horse Reservoir, The. Richard Hugo. CoAP; LCAP-2; NAAL-2v2; NoAM; NoP-4; VCAP

Lady in Red, The. Allie Wruber. ReLy

Lady in the Pink Mustang, The. Louise Erdrich. HATNAP; OPRER; ReTh

Lady in the unbecoming bonnet, The. All Hallow. Josephine Miles. APT-2

Lady in the White Dress, Whom I Helped into the Omnibus, The. Nathaniel Parker Willis. APN-1

Lady in the Wood, The. *Unknown*. MiEL

Lady in whom love is manifest, A. Guido Cavalcanti. EaItPo, *tr. by* Dante Gabriel Rossetti

Lady Is a Tramp, The. Richard Rodgers. OBAL; ReLy

Lady is smarter than a gentleman, maybe, A. Trial and Error. Phyllis McGinley. PeLV

Lady Isabel. *Unknown*. ESPB

Lady Isabel and the Elf-Knight. *Unknown*. ESPB

Lady Jane. Sir Arthur Thomas Quiller-Couch. PeLV

Lady Jane; a Humorous Novel in Rhyme, The. Nathaniel Parker Willis. OBAL

Lady Katherine Killigrew Wrote This Poem about Her Own Death, The. Katherine Killigrew. EMWP

Lady known as Paris, A. Last Time I Saw Paris, The. Jerome Kern. ReLy

Lady, Lady, I saw your face. Lady, Lady. Anne Spencer. BlSi; NAAAL

Lady, lady should you meet. Dorothy Parker. LW *Fr.* Some Beautiful Letters.

Lady Laments for Her Lost Lover, by Similitude of a Falcon, A. *Unknown*. AWP; EaItPo, *tr. by* Dante Gabriel Rossetti

Lady, last Saturday. I Like the Likes of You. Vernon Duke. ReLy

Lady Lazarus. Sylvia Plath. AmFaPo; ChIV-2; CoAmPo; FaBoWP; HCAP; HarvBoo; NAAL-2v2; NALW-5; NALW; NIL-7; NIP-4; NOBA; NoAM; NoP-4; OxWW; PoPoPo; PoetW; TAP; TRP; VCAP; VGW

Lady Lost. John Crowe Ransom. MoAmPo

(This morning, flew up the lane.) NoP-4; UnPo

Lady Love. Paul Éluard. OBVE; SurPaPo; WoPoe, *tr. by* Samuel Beckett

Lady, lovely lady. Vain and Careless. Robert Graves. NOxBChV

Lady loves her will, The. (LL) Mother Goose. FaBoCh; OxNR; ReMoGo

Lady Lowbodice. *Unknown*. PeLV; PeLi

Lady Macbeth. Nikolai Nikolaevich Ushakov. TCRP, *tr. by* Daniel Weissbort

Lady Maisdry was a lady fair. Lord Ingram and Chiel Wyet. *Unknown*. ESPB

Lady Maisry. *Unknown*. ESPB; OxBB

Lady Maisry. *Unknown*. *See also* Lord Ingram and Chiel Wyet

Lady Maisry lives intill a bower. Thomas o Yonderdale. *Unknown*. ESPB

Lady Margaret sat in her bower-door. Prince Heathen. *Unknown*. ESPB

Lady Margaret sat in her bowry all alone. Sweet William's Ghost. *Unknown*. AWP; ESPB

Lady Margaret sits in her bower door. Hind Etin. *Unknown*. ESPB

Lady Margery May sits in her bower. Prince Heathen. *Unknown*. ESPB

Lady *Mary Villers* lyes, The. Thomas Carew. *See* Lady Mary Villiers lies, The

Lady Mary Villiers lies, The. Epitaph on the Lady Mary Villiers. Thomas Carew. BeJo; CaPo; FaBoEE; NOBE; OBEV

Lady Moon, Lady Moon, where are you roving? Lady Moon. Richard Monckton, 1st Baron Houghton Milnes. NOxBChV

Lady Murasaki says. Murasaki Shikibu. BoWoP *Fr.* Tale of Genji, The.

Lady, my wedded thought. Bonaggiunta Urbiciani. EaItPo, *tr. by* Dante Gabriel Rossetti

Lady never shakes free the ashes, The. Sonia at 32. Morrie Warshawski. GotH

Lady of all powers. From The Hymn to Inanna. Enheduanna. WPoS

Lady of all the essences, full light. Inanna and the Divine Essences. Enheduanna. BoWoP

Lady of Arngosk, The. *Unknown*. ESPB

Lady of Chaos. 'Ali Ja'far Al-Allaq. MAP, *tr. by* Sharif Elmusa and Thomas G. Ezzy

Lady of dusk-wood fastnesses. First Praise. William Carlos Williams. VGW

Lady of features cherubic, A. Limerick. *Unknown*. PeLi

Lady of Heaven and earth, and therewithal. His Mother's Service to Our Lady. François Villon. AWP; CTC, *tr. by* Dante Gabriel Rossetti

Lady of Heaven, the mother glorified. Fra Guittone d'Arezzo. EaItPo, *tr. by* Dante Gabriel Rossetti

Lady of High Degree, A. *Unknown*. AWP, *tr. by* Andrew Lang

Lady of Largest Heart. Enheduanna. HW, *tr. by* Betty De Shong Meador

Lady of Miracles. Nina Cassian. WPOW, *tr. by* Laura Schiff

Lady of Pazardzik. Starr Goode. HW

Lady of Petals, / gone into Underworld. Isis (Lady of Petals). Jonathan Cott. HW

Lady of Quality, A. Thomas Kinsella. PBCIP

Lady of Shalott, The. Tennyson. FHYEP; NAEL-5v2; NAEL-6v2; NOBE; NOBRP; NoP-4; OBEV; OBNV; OBSP; OxAEP-2; PoE; TFi; TOF

Lady of shrouding hair. *Unknown*. NOIV

Lady of the bright coils and curlings. Eire. David [*or* Daibhi][*or* Daithi] O'Bruadair [*or* Ó Bruadair]. BIrV, *tr. by* Austin Clarke

Lady of the Ferry Inn. Gwerful Mechain. BoWoP, *tr. by* Willis Barnstone

Lady of the house is on her benders, The. Five Domestic Interiors. Vernon Scannell. OxBC

Lady of the Lake, The. Sir Walter Scott.
  (Ballad: Alice Brand.) OxAEP-2
  (Boat Song.) OxAEP-2
  Chase, The. NePenScot
  Coronach.
  Flowers and Trees. OxAEP-2
  (Harp of the North, Farewell!) OxAEP-2
  "Now, yield thee, or by Him who made." OxBS
  Soldier Rest! [Thy Warfare O'er.] AWP; NOBE; PoRA

Lady of the Lambs, The. Alice Thompson Meynell. *See* Shepherdress, The

Lady of the Last Time, The. Vivian Lamarque. CItWP, *tr. by* Cinzia Sartini Blum and Lara Trubowitz

Lady of the legless world I have. Notes after Blacking Out. Gregory Corso. NeAP

Lady of the Manor, The. George Crabbe. NOBE *Fr.* Parish Register, The.

Lady of the Morning, The. *Unknown*. HW, *tr. by* Samuel Noah Kramer and Diane Wolkstein

Lady of the Night star-breathed. Night-Blooming Jasmine, The. Audre Lorde. ColAP

Lady of the Pearls, The. Alexandre Dumas.
  "We set out yesterday upon a winter drive." TTY

Lady of the Snow, The. Vivian Lamarque. CItWP, *tr. by* Cinzia Sartini Blum and Lara Trubowitz

Lady of the White Castle, The. Endre Ady. IQMS, *tr. by* Dermot Spence and Paul Tabori

Lady of the winds. Palm Tree, A. Rosario Castellanos. TCLAP, *tr. by* Myralyn F. Allgood

Lady of Trees, The. Mary Elizabeth Coleridge. VWP

Lady on climbing Mount Shasta, A. Limerick. *Unknown*. PeLi

Lady on Streetcar. Sandro Penna. STV, *tr. by* John Frederick Nims

Lady Picking Flowers, A. Shen Chou. CoBLCP, *tr. by* Jonathan Chaves

Lady Poets with Foot Notes, The. Ernest Hemingway. IllVoic

Lady Poverty was fair, The. Lady Poverty, The. Alice Thompson Meynell. NOBVV; OBMV; PeVV

Lady Queen Anne she sits in the sun. *Unknown*. OxNR

Lady Ralegh's Lament. Robert Lowell. OxBSP

Lady "Rogue" Singleton. Stevie Smith. FaBoWP; OPOU; OxBSP

Lady's Boogie. Langston Hughes. APT-2

Lady's Complaint, The. John Heath-Stubbs. TwCP

Lady's Days. Larry Neal. NBV; SeSe

Lady's Diary, The. Charles Dibdin. NOEC

Lady's Dressing Room, The. Jonathan Swift. NAEL-7v1

Lady's Farewell, The. Nuño Fernández Torneol. WoPoe, *tr. by* Yvor Winters

Lady's in Love with You, The. Burton Lane. ReLy

Lady's love is gained, A. Price of Disrespect, The. Lizelia Augusta Jenkins Moorer. CBWP-3

Lady's-Maid's Song, The. John Hollander. TwCP

Lady's Prayer to Cupid, A. Thomas Carew. CaPo
  (Ladies Prayer to Cupid, A.) OBVE

Lady's Resolve, The. Lady Mary Wortley Montagu. BoWoP; OxBSP
  (Resolve, The.) ECWP

Lady's Third Song, The. W. B. Yeats. FaBoTw

Lady's Way. Reuben Jackson. GT

Lady Selecting Her Christmas Cards. Phyllis McGinley. ChrPo

Lady Sings, The. John Milton. *See* Comus; a Masque Presented at Ludlow Castle

Lady stands in her bower door, The. Twa Magicians, The. *Unknown*. ESPB; OxBB

Lady Stood, A. Dietmar, von Aist [*or* Eist]. AWP, *tr. by* Jethro Bithell

Lady Stood Alone, A. Dietmar, von Aist [*or* Eist]. AuPH, *tr. by* Lowell A. Bangerter

Lady Stood Alone, A. Dietmar, von Aist [or Eist]. GePo, tr. by J. W. Thomas

Lady T-rc——l's Ring. *Unknown.* NOBRP

Lady Tactics. Anne Waldman. PoM

Lady, take this garland. Walther [or Walter] von der Vogelweide. GePo

Lady, tell me, will you, pray. Found—Who Lost? Mary E. Tucker. CBWP-1

Lady that hast my heart within thy hand. Hafiz [or Hafez]. AWP *Fr.* Odes.

Lady That in the Prime. John Milton. *See* Sonnet 9: "Ladie [or Lady], that in the prime of earliest youth."

Lady, the shepherds have all gone. Ya Se Van Los Pastores. Dudley Fitts. APT-2

Lady there was in Antigua, A. Limerick. *Unknown.* PeLi

Lady, this alabaster. Soap. M. R. Peacocke. NLP

Lady, this is my sonnet to your eyes. (LL) George Meredith. CABP; HAP; NoP-4 *Fr.* Modern Love.

Lady, those cherries plenty. *Unknown.* NoSic

Lady, thy face is very beautiful. Letitia [or Laetitia] Elizabeth Landon. NOBRP

Lady walked by the ocean strand, The. Strand-Thistle. Gustav Falke. AWP, tr. by Jethro Bithell

Lady walked down a roadbed, A. Gentle Heart: Two, A. Judith Johnson Sherwin. BoWoP

Lady, we would behold thee moving bright. To Christina Rossetti. "Michael Field." VWP

Lady weare those bayes, you may. Eleanora Wyatt Finch. EMWP

Lady weeps at a dark window, A. Moonless Night. Louise Glück. AWTN

Lady / when ya purple heels hit concrete. You So Woman. Ruth Forman. SpirFl

Lady Who Ascends into the Heavens, The. *Unknown.* HW, tr. by Samuel Noah Kramer and Diane Wolkstein

Lady Who Offers Her Looking-Glass to Venus, The. Matthew Prior. FaBoEE; NOEC; NPeEn; OBEV; OxBEV; OxBSP

(Farewell, A: "Venus, take my votive glass.") AWP

Lady who rules Fort Montgomery, A. Limerick. Morris Gilbert Bishop. PeLi

Lady, who signs herself "Vexed," A. Limerick. Edward Gorey. OBAL; PeLi

Lady, whom my beloved loves so well! Petition, A. Frances Anne [or "Fanny"] Kemble. LW

Lady with a Falcon on Her Fist, A. Richard Lovelace. CaPo

Lady, with all the pains that I can take. Ciuncio Fiorentino. EaItPo, tr. by Dante Gabriel Rossetti

Lady with the Unicorn, The. Vernon Watkins. TwCP

Lady with thine eyes of beauty. Valentine, The. Mary Weston Fordham. CBWP-2

Lady, you think too much of speeds. Statistics. Stephen Spender. MoBrPo

Lady, you think you spite me. *Unknown.* NoSic

Ladybird. *Unknown.* FaBoVe

Ladybird, Ladybird fly away home. Mother Goose. FaBoVe; LB; OxNR; ReMoGo

Ladybug. Raymond Souster. MoCV

Lady's "Yes," The. Elizabeth Barrett Browning. ViWPN

Laertes. Homer. ModIr, tr. by Michael Longley *Fr.* Odyssey.

Lafayette. Dolley Madison. AiP

Lago Maggiore. Thomas Cole. APN-1

Lagoon. Joseph Brodsky. TCRusP, tr. by Daniel Weissbort

Lagoonal Calendar. Aimé Césaire. VCWP

Lagoons, Hanlan's Point. Raymond Souster. NOBC

Lagos you are dirty. Lagos. Rashidah Ismaili. HAWP

Laguna Blues. Charles Wright. PoPoPo

Laguna man said. Wind and Glacier Voices. Simon J. Ortiz. HATNAP

Lai. May Probyn. VWP

Laid in my quiet bed, in study as I were. Laid in My Quiet Bed. Henry Howard, Earl of Surrey. CABP

Laid like weights on the table. (LL) Garden, The. Louise Glück. HCAP; NAAL-2v2; VCAP

Laid many heavy loads on thee! (LL) On Sir John Vanbrugh [Architect]. Abel Evans. FaBoEE; NPeEn

Laid Off. Francis Webb. BMAP

Laid out for dead, let thy last kindness be. To Robin Redbreast. Robert Herrick. PoE

Laid with papyrus to catch fire. Martial. FaBoEE

Laila Boasting. Laila Akhyaliyya. BoWoP, tr. by Willis Barnstone

Laily Worm and the Machrel of the Sea, The. *Unknown.* ESPB; OxBB; SCGP

Laïque, says the Frenchman to the Frenchman, and the. Like. Robert Desnos. MFP, tr. by Martin Sorrell

Lair, The. Rachel Hadas. FFC

Laird, a lord, A. *Unknown.* OxNR

Laird o' Cockpen, The. Carolina Oliphant, Baroness Nairne. NOBRP; NPeEn; OxBEV; WPE

Laird o Drum, The. *Unknown.* ESPB

Laird o' Logie, The. *Unknown.* ESPB

Laird o' Ochiltree Wa's, The. *Unknown.* OxBB

Laird of Bristol's daughter was in the woods walking, The. Captain Wedderburn's Courtship. *Unknown.* ESPB

Laird of Leys is on to Edinbrugh [or Edinburgh], The. Baron o [or of] Leys, The. *Unknown.* ESPB; OxBB

Laird of Wariston, The. *Unknown.* ESPB

Lais. "H. D." MoAmPo

Lais, courtesan of Corinth, why has. Lais. Elaine Feinstein. FaBoWP

Lais' Mirror. Julianus of Egypt. GrAn, tr. by Robin Skelton

Lais' Mirror. *Unknown.* GrAn, tr. by Peter Jay

Lais now old, that erst attempting lass. *Unknown, after the Greek of* Plato. FaBoEE

Lais to Aphrodite. Edwin Arlington Robinson. FaBoEE

Lais to Aphrodite. *Var. authors.* FaBoEE *Fr.* Variations of Greek Themes.

Lais, who was a lovely flower. Pompeius. GrAn

Lak of Stedfastnesse. Geoffrey Chaucer. AWP; MiEL

Lake. Octavio Paz. TCLAP, tr. by Rachel Benson

Lake. Ronald Albert Simpson. CBAP

Lake, A. Thomas Lovell Beddoes. NOBVV; NPeEn *Fr.* Last Man, The.

Lake, The. Ted Hughes. FaBoTw

Lake, The. Alphonse Marie Louis de Lamartine. NAWM-7v2, tr. by Andrea Moorhead

Lake, The. Alphonse Marie Louis de Lamartine. SxFrPo, tr. by E. H. Blackmore and A. M. Blackmore

Lake, The. Geoffrey O'Brien. KGB

Lake, The. Gertrude Pape. SurWo, tr. by Her de Vries

Lake, The. Edgar Allan Poe. *See* Lake: To———, The

Lake, The. James Stephens. MoBrPo

Lake Balaton. Ágnes Nemes Nagy. IQMS, tr. by Hugh Maxton

Lake Baskunchak. Andrey Alekseievich Amalrik. TCRP; TCRusP, tr. by John Glad

Lake Drummond Dream. Dave Jeddie Smith. VCAP

Lake Has Swallowed the Whole Sky, The. Silvia Curbelo. TouFir

Lake in Central Park, The. Jay Wright. ESEAA; GT

Lake / Is a river curled and asleep like a snake, A. Lake, A. Thomas Lovell Beddoes. NOBVV

Lake is blue with morning; and the sky, The. Morning on the Shore. Wilfred Campbell. NOBC

Lake is deserted now, The. Dispossessed, The. Thomas Kinsella. NOCV

Lake is sharp along the shore, The. Lakeshore. Francis Reginald Scott. MoCV; NOBC

Lake Isle, The. Ezra Pound. OBCoV; OxBSP

Lake-Isle of Innisfree, The. W. B. Yeats. CABP; ChAP; ClHu; HeIP-4; InPK-6; MoBrPo; NAEL-5v2; NAEL-6v2; NOBE; NoAM; NoP-4; OBEV; OxAEP-2; OxBTC; PAI; PoE; PoPoPo; PoRA; TFi; UV

Lake Leman woos me with its crystal face. Byron. NAEL-5v2; NAEL-6v2; NOBRP *Fr.* Childe Harold's Pilgrimage.

Lake lies blind and glinting in the sun, The. Virginia Lake. James Keir Baxter. PeNZ

Lake Morning in Autumn. Douglas Livingstone. NoP-4

Lake Murry. Pinkie Gordon Lane. GT

Lake of Gaube, The. Algernon Charles Swinburne. CABP; NAEL-5v2; NAEL-6v2

Lake of night is still in the valley, The. Pine, The. Saunders Lewis. OBWVE, tr. by Gwyn Morgan

Lake of the Ten Thousand Mountains, The. Meng Hao Jan. EaWin, tr. by W. S. Merwin

Lake of the Woods, The. Richard Ryan. PBCIP

Lake of Zurich, The. Friedrich Gottlieb Klopstock. GePo, tr. by George C. Schoolfield

Lake Song. Jean Starr Untermeyer. TrJP

Lake Success. Robert Conquest. OxBC

Lake sunken among, A. Woman Skating. Margaret Atwood. FaBoWP

Lake Superior. Lorine Niedecker. FaBoWP

Lake; or, Modern Improvement in Landscape, The. Anna Seward. OBGa

Lake: To———, The. Edgar Allan Poe. APN-1

(In youth's spring, it was my lot.) NAAL-2v1; NAAL-3

(Lake, The.) NAAL-2v1; NAAL-3

Lake was covered all over, The. Dorothy Wordsworth. KaS

Lake was filled with distinguished fish, The. Twilight Polka Dots. Barbara Guest. PmAP

Lakefront, Cleveland. Russell Atkins. GT

Lakes. David Donnell. NoAM

Lakes, The. David Wright. NLP

Lakeshore. Francis Reginald Scott. MoCV; NOBC

Lakeside. Edmund Wilson. OBCoV *Fr.* Easy Exercises in the Use of Difficult Words.

Lakeside Identification, A. Robert Pinsky. *See* Essay on Psychiatrists

Lakeside Incident. Robin Skelton. NOBC

Lakeward. Trumbull Stickney. APN-2

Lakota Sister / Cherokee Mother. Victoria Lena Manyarrows. UnSA

Lakshmi. Padraic Fallon. NOIV

Lalai (Dreamtime). Sam Woolagoodjah. NOBAu

Lalla Rookh. Thomas Moore.
    "Fly to the desert, fly with me." BIrV
    "Oh! ever thus from childhood's hour." UV

Lama of Outer Mongolia, A. Limerick. Ogden Nash. PeLi

Lamarck. Osip Emilevich Mandelstam [*or* Mandelshtam]. TCRusP, *tr. by* John Glad

Lamb. Michael Dennis Browne. RaBo

Lamb, The. William Blake. ChIV-2; FHYEP; FaBoCh; HeIP-4; ITBLP; NAEL-5v2; NAEL-6v2; NAWM-7v2; NIL-7; NIP-4; NOBRP; NOEC; NoP-4; OxAEP-2; PAI; PoE; PoPoPo; SoSe-8; TFi; TRP; TrCP; UnPo *Fr.* Songs of Innocence.

Lamb and the Wolves, The. Ignacy Krasicki. WoPoe, *tr. by* Jerzy Peterkiewicz and Burns Singer

Lamb could not get born, A. Ice wind. February 17th. Ted Hughes. NPeEn

Lamb of the shepherds, Child, how still you lie. (LL) Holy Innocents, The. Robert Lowell. CoAmPo; MoAmPo; OBCP; OxBC

Lamba. Jacques Rabémanganjara.
    "In hermetic enclosure." NegPo

Lambent cobblestones refract the blue, The. Next to the *Café Chaos.* Olga Broumas. BodElec

Lambeth Lyric. Lionel Pigot Johnson. NOBVV

Lambeth Walk. Noel Gay. ReLy

Lambeth you've never seen. Lambeth Walk. Noel Gay. ReLy

Lambs that learn to walk in snow. First Sight. Philip Larkin. NTCP

Lame Beggar, A. John Donne. NoSic; PeLV

Lame Boy Returns, The. Juan Delgado. TouFir

Lament. Liu Chi-hsün. WoPoe, *tr. by* Tony Barnstone and Chou Ping

Lament. Máire Mhac an tSaoi. ModIr, *tr. by* Patrick Crotty

Lament. G. E. Patterson. AmPoNex

Lament, A: "O world! O life! O time!" Shelley. GTBS-P; NOBE; PoRA
    (O World, O Life, O Time.) NAEL-5v2; NAEL-6v2

Lament after Her Husband Bishr's Murder. Al-Khirniq. BoWoP, *tr. by* Willis Barnstone

Lament at Night. H. Leivick [*or* Leyvick]. AWTN, *tr. by* Marie Syrkin

Lament Beginning w/a Line after Cavafy. Eric Gamalinda. ReBoTo

Lament: "Blue, so blue that eye of sky." Jacques Rabémanganjara. NegPo, *tr. by* Ellen Conroy Kennedy

Lament: "Cheek by cheek on our pillow[s]." *Unknown.* ErotSp, *tr. by* Sam Hamill
    (Elegy.) CrYelRi

Lament for a Brother. Al-Khansa. ArPe, *tr. by* Omar S. Pound

Lament for a Courtesan. Li Ho. CrYelRi, *tr. by* Sam Hamill

Lament for a Cricket Eleven. Kenneth Allott. OxBTC

Lament for a Dialect. Mary Duroux. IBA

Lament for a Husband. *Unknown.* BoWoP, *tr. by* Don Laycock

Lament for a Leg. John Ormond. AngWePo; NoP-4; OBWVE

Lament for Adonis. Bion. AWP
    (I weep for Adonis, "The lovely Adonis is dead") HePo, *tr. by* Barbara Hughes Fowler

Lament for an Arab Encampment. Abid ibn al-Abras. ArPe, *tr. by* Omar S. Pound

Lament for Aquileia Destroyed, and Never to be Built Again. Paulinus of Aquileia. MLL, *tr. by* Helen Waddell

Lament for Art O Laoghaire, The. Eibhlin Dubh O'Connell.
    "My steadfast love!" NOIV

Lament for Arthur O'Leary, The. *Unknown.*
    "My love forever!" BIrV

Lament for Banba. Egan [*or* Aodhagán] O'Rahilly [*or* O'Reilly *or* Ó Rathaille]. AWP, *tr. by* James Clarence Mangan

Lament for Bion. Moschus. AWP
    (Sing me "Woe," you glades and Dorian water.) HePo, *tr. by* Barbara Hughes Fowler

Lament for Ch'en T'ao. Tu Fu. CrYelRi, *tr. by* Sam Hamill

Lament for Chaucer. Thomas Hoccleve [*or* Occleve]. OBEV *Fr.* De Regimine Principum.

Lament for Culloden. Robert Burns. FaBoWar; GTBS-P; OBEV

Lament for Damon. John Milton. MLL, *tr. by* Helen Waddell

Lament for Evolution. Joy Davidman. YaYoPo

Lament for Fearghal Ruadh. Tadhg Og O'Huiginn. NOIV

Lament for Five Sons Lost in a Plague. Abu Dhu'ayb al-Hudhali. ArPe; WoPoe, *tr. by* Omar S. Pound

Lament for Flodden, The. Jane [*or* Jean] Elliot. *See* Flowers of the Forest, The

Lament for Fortune's Frailty, A. Chiu Tsz-Yung and Cecil Clement. ColAnChi, *tr. by* Cecil Clementi *Fr.* Cantonese Love-Songs.

Lament for Hathimoda, Abbess of Gandesheim. *Unknown.* MLL, *tr. by* Helen Waddell

Lament for Hsieh T'iao. Shen Yüeh. SuSp, *tr. by* Lenore Mayhew

Lament for Ignacio Sánchez Mejías. Federico García Lorca. NAWM-7v2, *tr. by* J. L. Gili and Stephen Spender

Lament for Ignacio Sánchez Mejías. Federico García Lorca. OBVE, *tr. by* Arthur Lloyd

Lament for Ignacio Sanchez Mejias. Federico García Lorca.
    Absence of the Soul. WoPoe, *tr. by* Alan S. Trueblood
    "At five in the afternoon." WoPoe, *tr. by* Alan S. Trueblood
    Goring and the Death, The. WoPoe, *tr. by* Alan S. Trueblood

Lament for Kepa Anaha Ehau. Arapeta Awatere. PeNZ, *tr. by* the author

Lament for Lleucu Llwyd. Llywelyn Goch ap Meurig Hen. OBWVE, *tr. by* Joseph P. Clancy

Lament for Llywelyn ap Gruffudd. Gruffudd ab yr Ynad Coch. OBWVE, *tr. by* Joseph P. Clancy

Lament for Lu Yin. Meng Chiao. SuSp, *tr. by* Stephen Owen

Lament for MacGregor of Glenstrae. Mrs. MacGregor, of Glenstrae. NePenScot, *tr. by* Iain Crichton Smith

Lament for Myself, A. Yün Shou-p'ing.
    "As old age approaches." CoBLCP

Lament for Our Lady's Shrine at Walsingham, A. *Unknown.* NPeEn; NoP-4; PBRV
    (In the wrackes of walsingam.) PBRV
    (In the wracks of Walshingham.) NoP-4
    (Ruins of Walsingham, The.) NoSic
    (Walsingam oh farewell.) (LL) PBRV

Lament for Pasiphaë. Robert Graves. FaBoTw

Lament for Passenger Pigeons. Judith Wright. HarvBoo

Lament for Philip Larkin, A. Joseph Awad. GraLe

Lament for Prince Chagoo. *Unknown.* WoPoe, *tr. by* Jean S. Grigsby

Lament for Siôn y Glyn. Lewis Glyn Cothi. OBWVE, *tr. by* Joseph P. Clancy

Lament for Tadhg Cronin's Children. Aodhagán O Rathaille. ModIr; PBCIP; RB; WoPoe, *tr. by* Michael Hartnett

Lament for Tawhiao. *Unknown.* PeNZ, *tr. by* Margaret Orbell

Lament for Te Heuheu Herea. Te Heuheu Tukino. PeNZ, *tr. by* Margaret Orbell

Lament for Te Iwi—ika. *Unknown.* PeNZ, *tr. by* Margaret Orbell

Lament for the Country Soldiers. Les A. Murray. BMAP

Lament for the Cuckoo. Alcuin. NAWM-5v1

Lament for the Death of a Bullfighter. Joshua Beckman. AmPoNex

Lament for the Death of Eoghan Ruadh O'Neill. Thomas Osborne Davis. NOIV

Lament for the Death of Guillén Peraza. *Unknown.* WoPoe, *tr. by* W. S. Merwin

Lament for the Death of Thomas Davis. Sir Samuel Ferguson. BIrV; NOIV

Lament for the Dorsets. Alfred Wellington Purdy. NoAM

Lament for the Drowned Country. Mary Durack. NOBAu

Lament for the Evanescence of Life, A. Yamanoé [*or* Yamanoué] no Okura. WoPoe, *tr. by* Helen Craig McCullough

Lament for the Graham. Henry the Minstrel. OxBS

Lament for the Great Music. Hugh MacDiarmid.
    "Yet there is no great problem in the world today." OxBTC

Lament: "For the green turtle with her pulsing burden." Gillian Clarke. HarvBoo; TCAWP

Lament for the Makaris. William Dunbar. EBEV; HAP; MakPoe; NePenScot; OxBS
    (I that in heill was and gladness.) NoP-4
    (Lament for the Makars, The.) OxBEV
    (Lament for the Makers.) OBEV; SCGP
    (Lament: When He Wes Sek.) NPeEn
    (Timor Mortis Conturbat Me.) NOBE

Lament for the Makers: "No call upon anyone but the timber drifting in the waves." Jack Spicer. FTOS

Lament for the O'Neills. John Montague. CIP-2

Lament for the People of Lung. P'i Jih-hsiu. SuSp, *tr. by* William H. Nienhauser

Lament for the Poets: 1916. Francis Ledwidge. AWP

Lament for the State of the Country, A. Iain Lom. NePenScot, *tr. by* Meg Bateman

Lament for the Two Brothers Slain by Each Other's Hand. Aeschylus. AWP *Fr.* Seven against Thebes, The.

Lament for the Willows outside the City Walls, A. Yün Shou-p'ing. CoBLCP, tr. by Jonathan Chaves

Lament for Thomas MacDonagh. Francis Ledwidge. BIrV (Thomas MacDonagh.) NOIV

Lament for Troy. Hugh, Primate of Orleans. MLL, tr. by Helen Waddell

Lament for Urien, The. Unknown. OBMV, tr. by Ernest Rhys Fr. Red Book of Hergest, The.

Lament for Ying, A. Ch'u Yüan. SuSp, tr. by Wu-Chi Liu

Lament: "Gizzard and some ruby inner parts, A." Margaret Avison. HAP

Lament: "Hills are white with snow, The." Cho Wen-chun. CrYelRi, tr. by Sam Hamill

Lament: "I cried on my mother's breast, cried sore." Cathal Ó Searcaigh. ModIr, tr. by Seamus Heaney

Lament: "I turn to you high priests." Tadeusz Rózewicz. PoSu, tr. by Magnus J. Krynski

Lament: "In a dismal air; a light of breaking summer." George Sutherland Fraser. PoWW

Lament in Good Weather. Lucia Maria Perillo. ExTi

Lament, lament, Sir Isaac Heard. Epitaph on Tuft-Hunter. Thomas Moore. FaBoEE

Lament: "Late autumn, a brief shower." Liu Yung. CrYelRi, tr. by Sam Hamill

Lament: "My man is a bone ringèd with weed." Brenda Chamberlain. WPE; WPOW

Lament of a Desert Rat. N. J. Trapnell. FaBoWar

Lament of a Man for His Son. Unknown. AWP, tr. by Mary Austin

Lament of a Soldier's Wife. Kao Ch'i. SuSp, tr. by Irving Y. Lo

Lament of a Subwayite. Eugene O'Neill. UV

Lament of a Woman Acorn-gatherer. P'i Jih-hsiu. SuSp, tr. by William H. Nienhauser

Lament of an Idle Demon. Richard Percival Lister. NOBL

Lament of Edward Blastock, The. Dame Edith Sitwell. OBMV

Lament of Gilgamesh for Enkidu, The. Unknown. CAGL, tr. by N. K. Sandars Fr. Epic of Gilgamesh, The.

Lament of Hsi-chün. Hsi-chün. BoWoP, tr. by Arthur Waley

Lament of Hsi-Chün. Unknown. ChiP, tr. by Arthur Waley

Lament of Maev Leith-Dherg, The. Unknown. OBWP, tr. by Thomas W. H. Rolleston

Lament of Mary, The. Unknown. IQMS, tr. by Michael Beevor

Lament of Mary, The. Unknown. IQMS, tr. by Adam Makkai

Lament of Mary, The. Unknown. IQMS, tr. by Watson Kirkconnell

Lament of Swordy Well, The. John Clare. FaBoVe

Lament of the Border Widow, The. Unknown. OxBB

Lament of the Captive, The. Richard Henry Wilde. APN-1; ColAP; TCAPo

Lament of the Drums (1964). Christopher Okigbo.
"Lion-hearted cedar forest, gonads for our thunder." PBMAP

Lament of the Farm Wife of Wu. Su Tung-p'o (Su Shih). CoBCP; ColAnChi, tr. by Burton Watson

Lament of the Flowers, The. Jones Very. APN-1; ColAP; NOBA; OxBA

Lament of the Flutes. Christopher Okigbo. PBA

Lament of the Forest, The. Thomas Cole. APN-1

Lament of the Frontier Guard. Li Po. OBVE; OBWP; VGW, tr. by Ezra Pound

Lament of the Frontier Guard. Rihaku. APT-1; NPeEn, tr. by Ezra Pound

Lament of the Lady of Ch'in, The. Wei Chuang. SuSp, tr. by Robin D. S. Yates

Lament of the Unmarried Girl, The. Brian [or Bryan] Merriman [or Merryman]. OBVE, tr. by Frank O'Connor Fr. Midnight Court, The.

Lament of the Virgin. Unknown. NAWM-7v1
(Of all women that ever were born.) NAWM-7v1

Lament of the Virtues and Verses on Account of the Death of Don Guido. Antonio Machado Ruiz. OBVE

Lament of the White Queen. Ann Drysdale. TCAWP

Lament: "Oh, everything is far." Rainer Maria Rilke. TrJP, tr. by C. F. MacIntyre

Lament over the Ruins of the Abbey of Teach Molaga. James Clarence Mangan. NOIV, tr. by James Clarence Mangan

Lament: "Sleep and death, the dusky eagles." Georg Trakl. PeFWW, tr. by Michael Hamburger

Lament: "Someone is dead." Anne Sexton. CoAmPo; WPE

Lament: "Spell, treasure-bearing spell, prop up the sky standing above." Unknown. PeNZ, tr. by Margaret Orbell

Lament: "Those we love die like birds." Mai Sayigh. MAP, tr. by Charles Doria and Salma Khadra Jayyusi

Lament: "Ways of heaven are mysterious, The." T'ao Ch'ien [or T'ao Yuan-ming]. CrYelRi, tr. by Sam Hamill

Lament: "We who are left, how shall we look again." Wilfrid Wilson Gibson. OxBTC

Lament: "What face, in the water." William Carlos Williams. VGW

Lament: When He Wes Sek. William Dunbar. See Lament for the Makaris

Lament: "Young men of the world, The." Francis Stewart [or "Frank"] Flint. PeFWW

Lament: "Your dying was a difficult enterprise." Thom Gunn. CAGL; GLP

Lamentation. Bible, O.T. TrJP Fr. Ezekiel.

Lamentation, The. John Marckant. AH; SacPr

Lamentation, The. Ts'ai Yen. SuSp, tr. by Yi-T'ung Wang

Lamentation after Jeremiah to Exorcise High Rental / High Rise Building Scheduled for Construction with Public Funds. Diana Helen Melhem. GraLe

Lamentation during His Most Painful Illness. Simon Dach. GePo, tr. by Ingrid Waløe-Engel

Lamentation for Celin, The. Unknown. AWP, tr. by John Gibson Lockhart

Lamentation of Queen Elizabeth, A. Sir Thomas More. NoSic

Lamentation of the Old Pensioner, The. W. B. Yeats. HAP; InPK-6; NoAM; PeVV; TRP; WeW-3

Lamentation on My Dear Son Simon, A. John Saffin. SCAP

Lamentation on Ninety-Mile Beach. Barry Mitcalfe. PeNZ

Lamentations. Bible, O.T.
Affliction. TrJP
Desolation in Zion. TrJP
"How doth the city sit solitary that was full of people." WoPoe, tr. by Susan Stewart
"I have been brought into darkness." WoPoe, tr. by Susan Stewart
Misery of Jerusalem, The. AWP
"Scribes have cast the blame, The." WoPoe, tr. by Susan Stewart

Lamentations. Alter Brody. APT-2; TrJP

Lamentations. Norman Dubie. NoAM

Lamentations. Louise Glück. BoWoP; HCAP; VCAP

Lamentations. Siegfried Sassoon. OBSV; OxAEP-2; PeFWW

Lamentations of Jeremy, for the Most Part According to Tremeullius. John Donne.

Lamentations of the Bronze Camels. Li Ho. SuSp, tr. by Irving Y. Lo

Lamentations of the Fallen Angels. Unknown. AnOE, tr. by Charles W. Kennedy Fr. Christ and Satan.

Lamenting for Kao Ch'ing-ch'iu, Chi-ti. Chang Yü. CoBLCP, tr. by Jonathan Chaves

Lamenting for My Late Daughter. Wu Wei-yeh. CoBLCP, tr. by Jonathan Chaves

Lamenting for My Wife. Wang Shih-chieng. CoBLCP, tr. by Jonathan Chaves

Lamenting Noble Scholar Chu. Ni Tsan. CoBLCP, tr. by Jonathan Chaves

Lamenting Tauba. Laila Akhyaliyya. BoWoP, tr. by Willis Barnstone

Lamenting the Civil War. Muso Soseki. EaWin, tr. by W. S. Merwin

Lamenting the Dead. P'an Yüeh. CoBCP, tr. by Burton Watson

Lamenting the Inevitable. Alicia Ostriker. UnSA

Lamenting the Taoist Wei Kung-yüan. Chao Meng-fu. CoBLCP, tr. by Jonathan Chaves

Lamenting thru gipsies his fast suicide. (LL) Political Poem. Imamu Amiri Baraka. AF; CoAP; NAAL-2v2; NoAM; PmAP

Lamenting Yang Ch'uan. "Lu Hsün." SuSp, tr. by William R. Schultz

Laments, The. Jan Kochanowski.
I'd Buy You, Wisdom. WoPoe, tr. by Stanislaw Barańczak and Seamus Heaney
Where Is That Gate for Grief. WoPoe, tr. by Stanislaw Barańczak and Seamus Heaney

Laments Her Early Misfortunes. Mary Robinson. CenSon; RWP

Laments of a Poor Little Child. Dezső Kosztolányi.
"Dear mum's old picture." IQMS, tr. by Peter Zollman
"I want to kill myself." IQMS, tr. by Peter Zollman
"Inks of all colours are filling my dreams." IQMS, tr. by Leslie A. Kery
"Like someone who has fallen between the rails." IQMS, tr. by Egon F. Kunz

Laments of a Sad Man. Dezső Kosztolányi.
"I am an entry in all kinds of books." IQMS, tr. by Leslie A. Kery

Laments of the Gorges. Meng Chiao.
"Edges of the gorges hack up sun and moon, The." SuSp
"Owls mimic human speech." SuSp

Laments on the War Dead. Yehuda Amichai [or Amikhai].
"Is all this sorrow? I don't know." PoSu

Laments the Volatility of Phaon. Mary Robinson. CenSon; RWP

Lamia. John Keats. FHYEP; NAEL-6v2
"Upon a time, before the faery broods." NOBRP

Lamisca, who breathed her last in lamentable pangs of labor. Dioscorides. HePo Fr. Epigrams.

Lamium. Louise Glück. HarvBoo

Lamkin. Unknown. ESPB; NPeEn; OxBB

Lamp, The. Charles Whitehead. OBEV

Lamp are you, above all stars of night, A. Pole Star, The. Coslett Coslett. OBWVE, *tr. by* Kenneth Hurlstone Jackson

Lamp burns blue, everyone asleep, The. Sharing Lodging with Hsieh Shih-hou. Mei Yao Ch'en. CoBCP; ColAnChi, *tr. by* Burton Watson

Lamp lit, A. Roberto Juarroz. VCWP *Fr.* Third Vertical Poetry.

Lamp must be replenish'd [*or* replenished], but even then, The. Byron. NAEL-5v2; NAEL-6v2; NOBRP

Lamp[e], The. Henry Vaughan. ChIV-2; ESCV

Lamper, The. Maggie Hannan. NLP

Lamplight from our kitchen window-pane. Again. Glyn Jones. OBWVE; TCAWP

Lamplighter, The. "Seumas O'Sullivan." BIrV

Lamplighter, The. Robert Louis Stevenson. EBVV; ITBLP; NePenScot

Lamplighter, if you can't set two equally. Rufinus. HePo, *tr. by* Barbara Hughes Fowler

Lamprey, glowing with uncommon fires, The. William Diaper. ECEV; OBVE *Fr.* Halieutica.

Lampriskos, the dear Muses allow you. Schoolmaster, The. Herodas. HePo, *tr. by* Barbara Hughes Fowler

Lamps Are Burning, The. Charles Reznikoff. TrJP

Lamps now glitter down the street, The. Armies in the Fire. Robert Louis Stevenson. EBVV

Lana Turner has collapsed! Poem. Frank O'Hara. CLPP; FTOS; PmAP; VGW

Lancashire Winter. Tony Connor. OxBTC

Lance Corporal Purdue Grace, U. S. M. C. Bryan Alec Floyd. CDa

Lancer. A. E. Housman. MoBrPo; OBWP

Lancet, The. Denis Devlin. NOIV

Land. Carroll Arnett. VoR

Land, The. Rudyard Kipling. MoBrPo

Land, The. Victoria Mary Sackville-West. OBGa

Land and Sea Tales. Rudyard Kipling.
　Hour of the Angel, The. OxBSo
　"How do we know, by the bank-high river." OxBTC
　Last Lap, The. OxBTC
　Nurses, The. NoAM
　"Sooner or late—in earnest or in jest." OxBSo

Land Army Photographs. Tony Curtis. TCAWP

Land at the World's End, The. Brian Swann. PoCoUp

Land Beneath the Sea, The. Thomas Jeffrey Llewelyn Prichard.
　"What can you see in yonder bay." AngWePo

Land between us, The. Honesty-Stones. J. S. Harry. NOBAu

Land breaks yellow south below, pale squares. View from Cortona, A. Richard Hugo. AF

Land Called Scotia, The. Saint Donatus. NOIV

Land Dirge, A. John Webster. *See* White Devil, The

Land floats by under us, The. Love Making. James Tate. SPE

Land here, little birdie, come across the green woods! Rare Is the Wheat-Field in Which There's No Blemish. *Hungarian Oral Tradition.* IQMS, *tr. by* Adam Makkai

Land, Ho! Thomas Edward Brown. SacPr

Land is cold and its men gather earth for no reason, The. Woman's Song, A. Colleen J. McElroy. BISi

Land Is Gone, The. *Unknown.* PeNZ, *tr. by* Margaret Orbell

Land is lonely now: Anathema, The. Robert Stephen Hawker. EBVV *Fr.* Quest of the Sangraal, The.

Land Laws, The. Merimeri Penfold. PeNZ, *tr. by* Margaret Orbell

Land lies in water; it is shadowed green. Map, The. Elizabeth Bishop. APT-2; ColAP; NOBA

Land Love. Douglas Dunn. NePenScot

Land-Mine, The. George MacBeth [*or* Macbeth]. OBWP

Land not mine, still, A. Anna Andreyevna Akhmatova. WPoS

Land o'Lakes, Wisconsin: Vajrayana Seminary. Allen Ginsberg. BBASP

Land o' the Leal, The. Carolina Oliphant, Baroness Nairne. GTBS-P; NOBRP; NPeEn; NePenScot; OBEV; OxBEV; OxBS

Land of Beginning Again, The. Louisa Fletcher. ITBLP

Land of blue skies, and sunlight, A. Limerick. Ruth Silcock. PeLi

Land of Cokaygne, The. *Unknown.* NOIV

Land of Cotton. Gilbert Sorrentino. FTOS

Land of Counterpane, The. Robert Louis Stevenson. ChAP; EBEV; NBLV; NTCP; PWR; TLR; WHSW

Land of fandangoes. Spanish Jake. Irving Caesar. ReLy

Land of Heart's Desire, The. W. B. Yeats.
　(Fairy Song.) MoBrPo
　Wind Blows out of the Gates of the Day, The. RB

Land of Indolence, The. James Thomson. NOEC *Fr.* Castle of Indolence, The.

Land of leaning ice, A. North Labrador. Hart Crane. FaBoMo

Land of Lincoln. Angela Sorby. AmPoNex

Land of Little Sticks, 1945. James Tate. BodElec; LCAP-2

Land of Mirrors, The. Amira El-Zein. PoArWo, *tr. by* Husain Haddawy

Land of Mountains, Riverland. Paula von Preradovic. AuPH, *tr. by* Lowell A. Bangerter

Land of Nod, The. Robert Louis Stevenson. PWR

Land of old codgers after the summer, A. Autumn. Maurice Gilliams. TuT, *tr. by* Sean Dunne

Land of our fathers where at eventide. Intermittent Dream of a Sad Night. Marceline Desbordes-Valmore. WoPoe, *tr. by* Louis Simpson

Land of Pharoah. Whichway. Ron Welburn. NBV

Land of Song. Nigel Jenkins. AngWePo

Land of spices; something understood, The. (LL) Prayer (1): "Prayer the Church's banquet, Angels' age." George Herbert. AngWePo; BASC; EBEV; ESCV; GSo; GeHe; NAEL-5v1; NAEL-6v1; NOBE; NOSC; NoP-4; OBWVE; OxAEP-1; OxBSo; PeECV; PoE; PoPoPo; TFi; TOF

Land of Story-Books, The. Robert Louis Stevenson. ChAP; ITBLP; NePenScot; PWR

Land of the Ching tribes is not my home, The. Wang Ts'an. SuSp *Fr.* Seven Poems of Lament.

Land of the ding-dong doorbell and trim hedges. Costa Geriatrica. Stanley J. Sharpless. PeLV

Land's end. And sound and river come. Point, The. Robert Earl Hayden. ESEAA

Land Stretching Up to the Sky, A. Nada El-Hage. PoArWo, *tr. by* Nathalie El-Hani

Land up here hasn't been worked in years, The. Eternity's Woods. Paul Zweig. BodElec

Land was ours before we were the land's, The. Gift Outright, The. Robert Frost. AiP; ColAP; FaBoA; HHAm; HarvBoo; MoAmPo; NAAL-2v2; NAAL-5; NOBA; NoAM; NoP-4; OxBA; PoPoPo; TFi; TRP

Land was theirs after we were the land's, The. Big Rock-Candy Mountain, The. Louis Edward Sissman. GM

Land was there before us, The. Inauguration. Lorenzo Thomas. NBV

Land was white, The. *Unknown.* FaBoVe; OxNR

Land Where the Good Songs Go, The. P. G. Wodehouse. ReLy

Land Which No Mortal May Know, The. Bernard Barton. PWR

Landcrab I. Margaret Atwood. LCAP-2; NIP-4

Landcrab II. Margaret Atwood. NIP-4

Landfall. Randolph Stow. BMAP

Landfall, The. John Blight. BMAP

Landfall in Unknown Seas. Allen Curnow. NoP-4

Landfill. Michael S. Harper. LCAP-2

Landing Area. J. H. Prynne. PFTM-2

Landing of Rochambeau, The. Michael Davidson. FTOS

Landing of the Pilgrim Fathers [in New England], The. Felicia Dorothea Hemans. BRP; HHAm; ITBLP; NAEL-6v2; NoP-4; WPE

Landing on the Moon. Odia Ofeimun. EmeKit

Landing on the Moon. May Swenson. TAP

Landlady, The. Margaret Atwood. NALW

Landlady in Bangkok, The. Karen Swenson. GifTon

Landlord is wringing our lives dry, The. (LL) Drinking Art, The. Robert Minhinnick. AngWePo; TCAWP

Landlord, landlord. Ballad of the Landlord. Langston Hughes. HCAP; NAAAL; NOBA

Landlord's coat is tulip red, The. Wild Sports of the West. John Montague. CABP

Landlord's Tale: Paul Revere's Ride, The. Henry Wadsworth Longfellow. *See* Tales of a Wayside Inn

Landmarch by camel and shipsail we take. Cargoes of the Radanites. Harry Alan Potamkin. TrJP

Lands around my dwelling, The. Improvised Song of Joy. Takomaq. WoPoe, *tr. by* Knud Rasmussen

Lands which leap very high. On the Islands of All Winds. Aimé Césaire. VCWP

Landscape. David Gascoyne. FaBoMo

Landscape. Johanna Kruit. TuT, *tr. by* Micheal O'Siadhail

Landscape. Maria Manuela Margarido. HAWP, *tr. by* Julia Kirst

Landscape. Hendrik Marsman. TuT, *tr. by* Michael Longley

Landscape. Eve Merriam. KaS

Landscape. Mary Oliver. HeIP-4

Landscape. Octavio Paz. OBVE, *tr. by* Charles Tomlinson

Landscape. Hannie Rouweler. TuT, *tr. by* Aidan Sharkey

Landscape. Paul Van Ostaijen. TuT, *tr. by* Tony Curtis

Landscape. Yün Shou-p'ing.
　"Brush in rocks, draw a stream." CoBLCP

Landscape, A.   Margaret Lucas Cavendish, Duchess of Newcastle.   NOSC

Landscape, The.   George Daniel.   NOSC

Landscape, The.   Richard Payne Knight.
   "Oft when I've seen some lonely mansion stand."   OBGa

Landscape as it stood, The.   Landscape.   Hannie Rouweler.   TuT, tr. by Aidan Sharkey

Landscape beyond Warsaw.   Peter Huchel.   PoSu
   (March strikes the ice of the sky.)   AF, tr. by Daniel S. Simko

Landscape Described, A.   William Cowper.   NAEL-5v1; NAEL-6v1; NAEL-7v1   Fr. Task, The.

Landscape / full of holes, A.   Loose Woman Poem.   Sharon Thesen.   NOBC

Landscape Gardeners, The.   Geoffrey Grigson.   OBGa

Landscape Heard, A.   Filippo Tommaso Marinetti.   PFTM-1

Landscape I.   Charles Madge.   See Poem: "Character of a landscape stands always in a mysterious relation, The."

Landscape in Late Autumn.   Ferdinand von Saar.   AuPH, tr. by Lowell A. Bangerter

Landscape near an Aerodrome, The.   Stephen Spender.   MoBrPo; NoAM; OxBTC

Landscape of return is drawn, A.   Mercedes Roffé.   TANSG, tr. by Kathryn Kopple

Landscape of return is sketched, A.   Scene of Return is Sketched, A.   Mercedes Roffé.   MirDau

Landscape of the Capibaribe River.   João Cabral de Melo Neto.   VCWP, tr. by Richard Zenith

Landscape Painted on a Fan—Echoing a Poem by Wen Cheng-ming, A.   Chu Yün-ming.   CoBLCP, tr. by Jonathan Chaves

Landscape Painting.   Diane Glancy.   TWW

Landscape (the landscape!) again: Gloucester, The.   Librarian, The.   Charles Olson.   PmAP

Landscape with Boat.   Wallace Stevens.   APT-1

Landscape with Figures.   Frank Ormsby.   PBCIP

Landscape with Leaves and Figure.   Olga Broumas.   BoWoP

Landscape with Little Figures.   Donald Justice.   LCAP-2

Landscape with Next of Kin.   Olga Broumas.   BoWoP; WiU

Landscape with Nymphs and Satyrs.   Norman Henry Pritchard, II.   GT

Landscape with One Figure.   Douglas Dunn.   NePenScot

Landscape with Saxophonist.   Thylias Moss.   ESEAA

Landscape with the Fall of Icarus.   William Carlos Williams.   LCAP-2; NAAL-2v2; NAAL-5; NoAM   Fr. Pictures from Brueghel.

Landscape with Yellow Birds.   Shuntaro Tanikawa.   PoetW, tr. by Harold Wright

Landscapepeople.   John Ashbery.   HCAP

Landscapes.   T. S. Eliot.   RB
   Cape Ann.   NAEL-5v2; NAEL-6v2; NoAM
   "Children's voices in the orchard."   FaBoCh; GTBS-P; NoAM; WeW-3
   "Do not suddenly break the branch, or."   FaBoCh; NOCV; PeECV
   "Here the crow starves, here the patient stag."   NAEL-5v2; NAEL-6v2
   New Hampshire.   FaBoCh; GTBS-P; NoAM; WeW-3
   "O quick quick quick, quick hear the song sparrow."   NAEL-5v2; NoAM
   Rannoch, by Glencoe.   NAEL-5v2; NAEL-6v2
   "Red river, red river."   FaBoA; InPK-6
   Usk.   FaBoCh; NOCV; PeECV
   Virginia.   FaBoA; InPK-6

Landscapes.   Duriel Harris.   SpirFl

Landscapes.   Pauline Kaldas.   PoArWo

Landscapes.   Heberto Padilla.   VCWP

Landscapes with Set-Screws.   X. J. Kennedy.   UrbNat

Landwind: a gale at dawn scooping down from the hills.   Gale at Dawn.   William Everson.   APT-2

Lang Johnny More.   Unknown.   ESPB

Lang Mountain Monastery.   Yang Yi.   SuSp, tr. by Jonathan Chaves

Langston.   Frederick D'Aguiar.   Oth

Langston Blues.   Dudley Randall.   SeSe

Langston Hughes.   Lew Blockcolski.   VoR

Langston Hughes.   Gwendolyn Brooks.   ColAP

Langston Hughes.   Kevin Young.   NeAmPo

Language.   Marjorie Agosin.   TANSG, tr. by Cola Franzen

Language.   Jennifer Maiden.   BMAP

Language.   Marc Matthews.   WaCA

Language.   Nizar Qabbani.   MAP, tr. by Diana Der Hovanessian and Lena Jayyusi

Language.   Jack Spicer.
   Thing Language.   APSN

Language, The.   Robert Creeley.   PmAP; TAP
   (Locate I / love you somewhere in.)   FTOS

Language, The / created the landscape.   In a Monotonous Dream.   Elaine Equi.   PmAP

Language Difficulty.   Ann Drysdale.   TCAWP

Language Event Two.   Robert Desnos.   PFTM-1

Language has not the power to speak what love indites.   Fragment.   John Clare.   FaBoEE; OxBSP

Language is only an instrument for the attainment of science.   Taxonomy.   Joy Katz.   NeAmPo

Language is the first perversion of the senses.   Genesis.   Brian Higgins.   FaBoTw

Language Issue, The.   Nuala Ni Dhomhnaill.   ModIr; NPeEn, tr. by Paul Muldoon

Language Memory.   Géza Páskándi.
   "Close your eyes over my sins."   IQMS, tr. by Agnes Arany-Makkai
   "I have killed a virgin by being born."   IQMS, tr. by Agnes Arany-Makkai
   "In the grass of the twilight: the seventh day is God."   IQMS, tr. by Agnes Arany-Makkai
   "Mother of God, you tired Mary."   IQMS, tr. by Agnes Arany-Makkai
   "My shirt got torn to rags."   IQMS, tr. by Agnes Arany-Makkai
   "You don't even have any sins!"   IQMS, tr. by Agnes Arany-Makkai

Language Mesh.   Paul Celan.   VCWP, tr. by Michael Hamburger

Language of Fossils, The.   Anita Endrezze.   HATNAP

Language of Great-Aunts, The.   Alberto A. Ríos.   UnSA

Language of Love.   Rae Armantrout.   PmAP

Language of the Brag, The.   Sharon Olds.   MakPoe; PBCAP

Language of the Dead, The.   Thomas McGrath.   BodElec

Language of Weather, The.   Ray A. Young Bear.   HATNAP

Language Pile, The.   Donald Berger.   NAPBL

Language sovereign secret incompatible submerged in the universal wound.   Mohammed Dib.   PFTM-2, tr. by Carol Lettieri and Paul Vangelisti   Fr. Formulaires.

Language that but sparely floo'ers, The.   Hugh MacDiarmid.   NePenScot   Fr. Drunk Man Looks at the Thistle, A.

Languages.   Carl Sandburg.   APT-1; ColAP

Langue d'Oc.   Ezra Pound.
   Alba ("When the nightingale to his mate").   APT-1; OBVE; VGW; WeW-3

Languid African nights.   Nights.   Alda Lara.   HAWP, tr. by Julia Kirst

Languid, and sad, and slow, from day to day.   Languid, and sad, and slow.   William Lisle Bowles.   CenSon; NAEL-6v2

Languid lady next appears in state, The.   Edward Young.   NPeEn   Fr. Love of Fame, the Universal Passion.

Languid, lethargic, listless and slow.   Complacent Tortoise, The.   Brian Patten.   OBSP

Langwell.   Kingsley Amis.   NOBL; OxBC   Fr. Evans Country, The.

Lanigan's Ball.   Unknown.   OxBoLi

Lank poverty, dank poverty.   Tin Wash Dish, The.   Les A. Murray.   BMAP

Lanky hank of a she in the inn over there, The.   Glass of Beer, A.   James Stephens.   InPK-6; NBLV; OBCoV; OBMV; OxBEV; OxBS; OxBTC; RB

Lantern-ceiling and quiet, A.   Presbyterian Study.   Tom Paulin.   PBCIP

Lantern out of Doors, The.   Gerard Manley Hopkins.   SacPr; TrCP

Lantern sways from the Banner Pole, A.   Pole at the Village Pagoda, The.   Vietnamese Oral Tradition.   CaDao, tr. by John Balaban

Lanterns—swinging slowly in narrow arcs. (LL)   Art of Measuring Light, The.   Ellen Hinsey.   AmPoNex; YaYoPo

Lanval.   Marie de France.   NAEL-7v1

Lanza 51.   Filippo Scarlatti.   CAGL, tr. by James J. Wilhelm

Lao Figures.   Unknown.   EaWin, tr. by W. S. Merwin

Lao Tzŭ.   Po Chü-i.   ChiP, tr. by Arthur Waley

Laocoön.   Virgil [or Vergil].   OBVE, tr. by Henry Howard, Earl of Surrey   Fr. Aeneid [or Eneados, Aeneis], The.

Laocoon/Serpent.   Novica Tadic.   VCWP, tr. by Charles Simic

Laocöon! thou great embodiment.   Josiah Gilbert Holland.   APN-1   Fr. Marble Prophecy, The.

Lap dog in a cloth-wrapped box.   Lap Dog.   Shinkichi Takahashi.   ZenPo, tr. by Takashi Ikemoto and Lucien Stryk

Lapiade, Opus 3.   Ödön Palasovszky.   IQMS, tr. by Kenneth McRobbie

Lapis Lazuli.   W. B. Yeats.   CABP; EnIH; FaBoMo; FaBoTw; HeIP-4; NAEL-5v2; NAEL-6v2; NAWM-7v2; NOBE; NoAM; NoP-4; TFi

Laplander's Song to His Mistress, A.   Elizabeth Singer Rowe.   ECWP

Lapping of lake water, The.   Lake Song.   Jean Starr Untermeyer.   TrJP

Lapping of waters / thick, upon razorblade.   Marsden Hartley.   APT-1

Laprairie Hunger Strike.   Ronald G. Everson.   MoCV

Lapse of time and rivers is the same, The.   Comparison, A.   William Cowper.   OxBSP

Lapsus Linguae.   Keith Preston.   NBLV; OBAL; OBCoV

Lara.   Byron.
   Serfs are glad through Lara's wide domain, The.
   "In him inexplicably mixed appeared."   NOBRP

Large Bad Picture. Elizabeth Bishop. OxBC

Large glooms were gathered in the mighty fane. James Thomson. EBEV *Fr.* City of Dreadful Night, The.

Large Grieving Women. Slavko Mihalic. PoSu, *tr. by* Charles Simic

Large-headed beauty, head so alluring, The. *Unknown.* ColAnChi, *tr. by* Jeffrey Riegel *Fr.* Classic of Odes.

Large, low, whirring block of perfectly white, perfectly flat marble, on chrome legs. Hospital. Charles North. FTOS

Large plate from the eighteenth century, The. Solitude. Michael Cuddihy. GifTon

Large Red Man Reading. Wallace Stevens. APT-1; HAP; LCAP-2

Large Room with Wood Floor. Clarence Major. GT

Large slug slides, A. Ransetsu. SoOfWa, *tr. by* Sam Hamill

Large transparent baby like a skeleton in a red tree, A. Visible Baby, The. Peter Redgrove. EmeKit

Large, yellow sky. A mountain ridge. Pinetree. Ágnes Nemes Nagy. PoSu, *tr. by* Bruce Berlind

Large yellow wings, black-fringed, The. Butterfly on Rock. Irving Layton. NOBC; NoAM

Larger. John Wills. HA

Largest stock of armaments allows me, The. Civilian. Josephine Miles. WPE

Largo. Paul Celan. PoSu, *tr. by* Michael Hamburger

Largo. Deryn Rees-Jones. TCAWP

Lariat snaps; the cowboy rolls, The. Closing of the Rodeo, The. William Jay Smith. AiP; TwCP

Lark. Tom Earley. AngWePo

Lark, The. Mother's Mark. Jana Beranová. TuT, *tr. by* Aidan Sharkey

Lark, The. Bernard [*or* Bernart] de Ventadour [*or* Ventadorn]. CTC

Lark, The. *Unknown.* NOSC; OWoS

Lark begins to go up, The. Ted Hughes. HAP *Fr.* Skylarks.

Lark drives invisible pistons in the air. Movements. Norman MacCaig. OxBC

Lark Now Leaves His Watery [*or* Wat'ry] Nest. Sir William Davenant [*or* D'Avenant]. OxBEV; OxBSP; PoRA; TFi

(Aubade: "Lark now leaves his watery [*or* wat'ry] nest, The.") NOBE; OBEV

(Song: "Lark now leaves his wat'ry [*or* watery] nest, The.") AWP; MeLP; NOSC

Lark's Nest, A. Christopher Smart. *See* Hymns for the Amusement of Children

Larkin. Gibbons Ruark. DiPo

Larkin Automatic Car Wash, The. Gavin Ewart. NoAM

Larousse Gastronomique. Anne Stevenson. PeLV

Lars Porsena of Clusium. Thomas Babington Macaulay, 1st Baron Macaulay. CABP; EBNV; FaBoCh; FaBoWar; OBNV; OBWP; OxAEP-2 *Fr.* Lays of Ancient Rome.

L'Art, 1910. Ezra Pound. HeIP-4; OxBA; TCAPo

Larva, The. Tadeusz Różewicz. PoSu, *tr. by* Magnus F. Krynski

Las calles lloran / Streets Are Crying. Francisco Alarcon. GeoHom

Las casitas near the gray cannery. Freeway 280. Lorna Dee Cervantes. NoAM; WeW-3

Las Flores para una Niña Negra. Demetrice A. Worley. SpirFl

'Las, how long shall I. John Lyly. NoSic *Fr.* Midas.

Las Magdalenas. Judith Ortiz Cofer. TouFir

Las manos abiertas de Mongo. Dándole la mano a Mongo. Martín Espada. SeSe

Las Marías, our Indian mothers, have. Marías, Old Indian Mothers. Rigoberto González. GeoHom

Las! Mort Qui T'a Fait Si Hardie. Charles, Duc d' Orléans. WoPoe, *tr. by* Fred Chappell

Las, Où Est Maintenant Ce Mespris de Fortune. Joachim Du Bellay. WoPoe, *tr. by* Fred Beake

Las Trampas U.S.A. Charles Tomlinson. TwCP

Lascars, The. Peter Thomas. AngWePo

Laser. A. R. Ammons. NAAL-2v2; NOBA; NoAM

Lash like mine no honest man shall dread, A. Pope. NPeEn *Fr.* Epistle to Dr. Arbuthnot.

Lashed to the wheel of night. Paris. Ingeborg Bachmann. VCWP, *tr. by* Mark Anderson

Lasithi: notable for windmills. Summits are. Lasithi. David Constantine. HarvBoo

Lass A-Laundering. *Unknown.* STV, *tr. by* John Frederick Nims

Lass from Bally-na-Lee, The. Anthony [*or* Antoine] Raftery [*or* Raifteiri]. BIrV, *tr. by* Desmond O'Grady

Lass in the Female Factory, The. *Unknown.* NOBAu

Lass in Wonderland, A. Francis Reginald. MoCV

Lass of Aughrim, The. Paul Muldoon. NoAM; PBCIP

Lass of curvacious physique, A. Limerick. Douglas Catley. PeLi

Lass of Patie's Mill, The. Allan Ramsay. OxAEP-1

Lass of Roch Royal, The. *Unknown.* ESPB

Lass of the Hill, The. Mary Jones. ECWP

Lass, when they talk of love, laugh in their face. Love. Francis Jammes. AWP, *tr. by* Jethro Bithell

Lass with a Lump of Land. Allan Ramsay. NOEC; OxBEV

Lasses, like nuts at bottom brown. Epigram. Allan Ramsay. FaBoEE

Lassie, can ye say. For a Wife in Jizzen. Douglas Young. OxBS

Lassie, What Mair Wad You Hae? Heinrich Heine. OxBS, *tr. by* Alexander Gray

Lassie, with the lips sae rosy. Mädchen mit dem rothen Mündchen. Heinrich Heine. AWP, *tr. by* Sir Theodore Martin

Last Acts. Sharon Olds. NIP-4

Last Affair: Bessie's Blues Song. Michael S. Harper. ESEAA; HCAP; LCAP-2

Last All Saints' holy-day, even now gone by. Sonnet: Of Beatrice de' Portinari, on All Saints' Day. Dante Alighieri. AWP; EaItPo, *tr. by* Dante Gabriel Rossetti

Last and greatest herald of Heaven's King, The. Saint John Baptist. William Drummond, of Hawthornden. GTBS-P; NOBE; OBEV; OxAEP-1; TrCP

Last and greatest Herauld of Heavens King, The. For the Baptiste. William Drummond, of Hawthornden. NPeEn; OxBEV; PBRV

Last and the first tree, The. (LL) Children Playing Checkers at the Edge of the Forest. Adrienne Rich. LCAP-2; WeW-3

Last Apple, The. Carol Coiffait. Prnts

Last at Lucy's, The. John Tripp. TCAWP

Last Banquet of Antony and Cleopatra, The. Felicia Dorothea Hemans. RWP

Last Battle and Death of Chingis Khan, The. *Unknown.* WoPoe, *tr. by* Paul Kahn *Fr.* Secret History of the Mongols, The.

Last bell is ringing, The. Czech Dream. Lee Harwood. Oth

Last Bison, The. Charles Mair.

Song: "Hear me, ye smokeless skies and grass-green earth." NOBC

Last bridge I won't. Marina Ivanovna Tsvetayeva [*or* Tsvetaeva]. EroLit, *tr. by* Elaine Feinstein *Fr.* Poem of the End.

Last Buccaneer, The. Charles Kingsley. EBVV

(Last Buccanier, The.) PeVV

Last Bullet, The. Nidaa Khoury. PoArWo, *tr. by* Roger Tavor and Linda Zisquit

Last Bus, The. Mark Strand. TwCP

Last Call. Silvia Curbelo. TouFir

Last carpenter feelie pocket guru. Twenties 27. Jackson Mac Low. PmAP

Last Chance, The. Andrew Lang. NOBVV

Last Chance for the Tarzan Holler. Thylias Moss. ExTi

Last Chantey, The. Rudyard Kipling. FaBoCh; MoBrPo

Last Chapter, The. Walter De la Mare. MoBrPo

Last Child. X. J. Kennedy. OxBSP

Last chord of a *bolero*, The. (LL) Two Guitars. Víctor Hernández Cruz. PueRic; TouFir

Last Christmas, when Puss was in Boots. Limerick. Gina Berkeley. PeLi

Last Confession, A. W. B. Yeats. BoLoP; HAP; NIP-4

Last Conqueror, The. James Shirley. GTBS-P

Last Cry of the Damp Fly, The. Dennis Lee. NTCP

Last Day. Martinus Nijhoff. TuT, *tr. by* Desmond Egan

Last Day, The. Kevin Hart. BMAP

Last Day, The. George Seferis. PoetW, *tr. by* Edmund Keeley and Philip Sherrard

"Day was cloudy, The. No one could come to a decision." AF

Last Day and the First, The. Theodore Weiss. TwCP; VGW

Last day in the month of March. Child Is Not a Knife, A. Göran Sonnevi. PFTM-2, *tr. by* Rika Lesser

Last Day of the Year, The. Su Tung-p'o (Su Shih). OHPC, *tr. by* Kenneth Rexroth

Last Day of the Year (New Year's Eve), The. Annette von Droste-Hülshoff. BoWoP, *tr. by* Willis Barnstone

Last Day of the Year; or, New Year's Eve, The. Mrs. Henry Linden. CBWP-4

Last day of your sweet companionship, The. Les Dizains. Maurice Scève. WoPoe, *tr. by* Phillip Lopate

Last Daybreak Song. *Unknown.* APN-2, *tr. by* Washington Matthews *Fr.* Mountain Chant, The.

Last Days at Teddington. Thom Gunn. OBGa

Last Days of Alice. Allen Tate. APT-2; FuPo; NAAL-2v2; NOBA; OxBA; UnPo

Last Days of Home. Dulce Maria Loynaz.

"I have slept and I awaken . . . Or I haven't awakened." TANSG, *tr. by* Alan West

Last days of November, and everything so green, The! Volunteer's Thanksgiving, The. Lucy Larcom. OBCA

Last days of the summer: bright and clear, The. Harvest Gathering. Phoebe Cary. SWaP

Last decent man alive, The. Across to the Peloponnese. James Welch. CDW

Last Defile, The. Amy Carmichael. TrCP

Last Drink, A. *Unknown.* MiEL

Last Drunkard, The. William Bingham Tappan.
"He stood, the last—the last of all." VerBaPo

Last enchanted white deer come to drink, The. (LL) Sanctuary. Donald Davidson. APT-1; FuPo

Last eve I passed beside of a blacksmith's door. Anvil—God's Word, The. John Clifford. PoToHe

Last Evening. Rainer Maria Rilke. OBWP

Last Evening, The. Rainer Maria Rilke. FaBoWar, *tr. by* Carlyle Ferren MacIntyre and C. F. MacIntyre

Last Farewell to Kukutis. Marcelijus Martinaitis. TWW, *tr. by* Laima Sruoginis

Last Farewell to the Hills. Duncan Ban MacIntyre.
On Ben Dorain.
To the Air of a Pibroch. NePenScot, *tr. by* Iain Crichton Smith

Last fart, A. Kyo'on. JDP, *tr. by* Yoel Hoffmann

Last, for December, houses on the plain. Folgore da San Geminiano [*or* Gimignano]. EaItPo, *tr. by* Dante Gabriel Rossetti *Fr.* Sonnets of the Months.

Last Friday, in the big light of last Friday night. Reality Is an Activity of the Most August Imagination. Wallace Stevens. APT-1; NoAM

Last Fruit off an Old Tree, The. Walter Savage Landor.
(Dying Speech of an Old Philosopher.) FaBoEE; GTBS-P; NOBVV; NoP-4
(Finis.) OBEV
"I strove with none, for none was worth my strife." NOBE; NPeEn; OxBEV; TFi; TRP; UV
(On His Seventy-Fifth Birthday.) AWP; EBEV; OxAEP-2; SCGP

Last Fullblood, The. Frank Doolan. IBA

Last Galway Hooker, The. Richard Murphy. PBCIP

Last Giustiniani, The. Edith Wharton. APN-2

Last Gods. Galway Kinnell. PasH; RaBo

Last Good War—and Afterward, The. Isabel Joshlin Glaser. HHAm

Last Hellos, The. Les A. Murray. HarvBoo

Last Hill in a Vista. Louise Bogan. FaBoWP

Last Hour, The. Tudor Arghezi. WoPoe, *tr. by* Michael Impey and Brian Swann

Last Hymn. Philip Paul Bliss. SacPr

Last I heard of Paul Hanson he was dead, The. Four Dead Sons. James Wright (1927–80). BodElec

Last Instructions. Garth Tate. ISC

Last Instructions to a Painter, The. Andrew Marvell.
"After two sittings, now our Lady State." OBSV
Charles II. OBSV
"Paint Castlemaine in colours that will hold." OBSV

Last Invocation, The. Walt Whitman. MoAmPo; OxBA
(Imprisoned Soul, The.) OBEV

Last Journey. Enrique Gonzáles Martínez. TCLAP, *tr. by* Samuel Beckett

Last Journey. John Montague. CIP-2; ModIr; PBCIP; PNI

Last Journey, The. Leonidas of Tarentum. AWP, *tr. by* Charles Merivale

Last Judgment. John Gould Fletcher. AWP

Last Judgment, The. *Unknown.* AnOE, *tr. by* Charles W. Kennedy *Fr.* Christ 3.

Last July 4th, like every July 4th for four years. Triple Trouble. Assotto Saint. GLP

Last land rights' demonstration is over, The. Jacky Demonstrates for Land Rights. Mudrooroo Narogin. IBA

Last Lap, The. Rudyard Kipling. OxBTC *Fr.* Land and Sea Tales.

Last Lauch. Douglas Young. NBLV; OxBS

Last Leaf, The. Oliver Wendell Holmes. BRP; ITBLP; NAAL-2v1; NAAL-3; PWR; TCAPo

Last Lesson of the Afternoon. D. H. Lawrence. NoAM

Last Letter. Gerald William Barrax. ESEAA

Last Letter, The. Bertus Aafjes. TuT, *tr. by* Tony Curtis

Last Letter to Pablo. Pat Lowther. NOBC

Last Lie, The. Bruce Weigl. AF

Last Light. Robert Kelly. VGW

Last light falls across your pictured face, The. Letter, A. Sophie Jewett. PoBW

Last light muffles itself in cloud and goes, The. Mise en Scène. Robert Fitzgerald. VGW

Last Lines. X. J. Kennedy. OBAL

Last Lines on a Wrestler. X. J. Kennedy. CRP

Last Link, The. Iris Clayton. IBA

Last Look at La Plata, Missouri. Jim Barnes. CDW

Last Look at the Mutineers, A. Matthew Rohrer. AmPoNex

Last Look in the Sambre Canal, A. John Bensko. YaYoPo

Last Love. Fyodor [*or* Feodor] Ivanovich Tyutchev. BoLoP; WoPoe, *tr. by* Vladimir Vladimirovich Nabokov

Last Love. Nikolai Alekseievich Zabolotsky [*or* Zabolotskii]. TCRP, *tr. by* Daniel Weissbort

Last Man, The. Thomas Lovell Beddoes.
Crocodile, A. NOBVV; NPeEn; OxBEV; RB
Lake, A. NPeEn

Last Man, The. Thomas Campbell. NOBRP

Last Man, The. Thom Gunn. OxAEP-2 *Fr.* Misanthropos.

Last meal together, Leeds, the Queen's Hotel. Queen's English, The. Tony Harrison. DiPo

Last Meeting. Robert Penn Warren. DiPo

Last Merchant, The. Wolf Ehrlich [*or* Erlikh]. TCRP, *tr. by* Daniel Weissbort

Last Month. John Ashbery. CoAP

Last month of the year, grass roots taste sweet. Li Ho. SuSp *Fr.* About Horse.

Last Night. David Ignatow. VGW

Last Night. Antonio Machado Ruiz. RaBo, *tr. by* Robert Bly

Last night. Hazel Tells LaVerne. Katharyn Howd Machan. ReTh

Last night. Loving Again. Gloria Wade-Gayles. ISC

Last Night, The. Alfred Austin. PeVV

Last night a few years ago my sister. Sky. James Harms. NAPBL

Last night a plum branch blossomed by my door. (LL) Rebirth. Man Giac. EaWin; WoPoe, *tr. by* W. S. Merwin and Nguyen Ngoc Bich

Last night, ah, yesternight, betwixt her lips and mine. Non Sum Qualis Eram Bonae sub Regno Cynarae. Ernest Christopher Dowson. AWP; BoLoP; CABP; ClHu; EBVV; EnLoPo; GTBS-P; HAP; HeIP-4; MoBrPo; NOBE; NoP-4; OBEV; OBMV; PeVV; PoRA; TFi; UnPo

Last night along the river banks. Boats Are Afloat, The. Chu Hsi. OHPC, *tr. by* Kenneth Rexroth

Last night, among his fellow roughs. Private of the Buffs; or, The British Soldier in China. Sir Francis Hastings Doyle. FaBoWar; OBEV

Last night as I lay beside you all the desire had gone out of me. House. Murray Edmond. PeNZ

Last night, as I was sleeping. Last Night. Antonio Machado Ruiz. RaBo, *tr. by* Robert Bly

Last night at black midnight I woke with a cry. Ghosts of the Buffaloes, The. Nicholas Vachel Lindsay. MoAmPo

Last night at midnight. Tune: The Taoist Priestess. Wei Chuang. CoBCP, *tr. by* Burton Watson

Last night at midnight. Wen T'ing-yün. CoBCP

Last Night at the Flamingo. John Iozia. CAGL

Last night, before I came to bear. Angel, The. James Wright (1927–80). YaYoPo

Last night blonde spitfire Angie Dickinson beat steel-eyed. Brute Strength. Wanda Coleman. PmAP

Last night, dead drunk, I dawdled. Tune: "Airing Inmost Feelings." Li Ch'ing-chao. ColAnChi, *tr. by* Jiaosheng Wang

Last night for the first time since you were dead. To L. H. B. Katherine Mansfield. FaBoWar

Last night his clumsy love. Music. David Huddle. MiVo

Last night I did not fight for sleep. In Hospital: Poona (1). Alun Lewis. AngWePo; OBWVE; TCAWP

Last night, I dreamed of America. More. Ai. GT

"Last night I dreamed we parted once again." Frederick Goddard Tuckerman. GSo

Last night I dreamed you drank coffee. One More Sign. Roberta Hill Whiteman. HATNAP

Last night I dreamt in Chinese. Modern Secrets. Shirley Lim. OPOU; UnSA

Last night I flew a helicopter. Short Story. Maura Stanton. BodElec

Last night I heard your long-drawn sighs. Seeing the Beloved in a Dream. Shen Yüeh. ColAnChi, *tr. by* Richard Mather

Last night, I heard your mother. Apology to Andrew. Richard Jones. AWTN

Last night I saw the savage world. Song for a Birth or a Death. Elizabeth Jennings. EBEV; HarvBoo

Last night I saw your corpse. Joyce Mansour. BoWoP; HAWP, *tr. by* Willis Barnstone

Last night I slew my wife. Harry Graham. PeLV *Fr.* Some Ruthless Rhymes.

Last night I spent beside my lover. Fêng Mêng-lung. ColAnChi, *tr. by* Richard W. Bodman *Fr.* Mountain Songs.

Last night I spoke to a dead woman with green face. Last Night. David Ignatow. VGW

Last night I started out happy. That Old Feeling. Sammy Fain. ReLy

Last night I supped on lobster; it nearly drove me mad. Dream, The. *Unknown.* OxBoLi

Last night I talked to a woman. Dance Pianist, The. Angela Ball. ExTi

Last night I tell you, I do not lie. Osip Emilevich Mandelstam [*or* Mandelshtam]. TCRP

Last night I was reading the Chronicle of the Three Kingdoms. Tune: "Trimming the Silver Lamp." Fan Chung-yen. ColAnChi, *tr. by* J. R. Hightower

Last night I watched my brothers play. Brothers, The. Edwin Muir. GTBS-P; HeIP-4

Last night in a dream I returned to my old home. *Unknown.* CoBCP

Last Night in Calcutta. Allen Ginsberg. FTOS; NoAM

Last night in dream so clear I saw her. To the Tune "Child at Play." Yang Shen. CoBLCP, *tr. by* Jonathan Chaves

Last night in Fall River in Lafayette Park. How It Will Always Seem. David Rivard. PBCAP

Last night in Havana. Richard Blanco. NAPBL

Last night in La Plata an avalanche of stars. La Plata, Missouri: Clear November Night. Jim Barnes. HATNAP

Last night in stomped. Dardanelles 1916. Padraic Fallon. CIP-2

Last night in swirling colour we danced again. Dermot Bolger. BiHa *Fr.* Stardust Sequence, The.

Last night in the open shippen. Christmas Day. Andrew Young. OBCP

Last night it was already half past eleven. Do You Wonder Why I Am Sleepy. James Purdy. CAGL

Last night, just as the tints of autumn's sky. Fruit-Gift, The. John Greenleaf Whittier. TCAPo

Last night my kisses drowned in the softness of black hair. Black Hair. *Unknown.* EroLit

Last night my soul departed. Invocation. Muireadhach Albanach O'Dalaigh. NOIV

Last night my soul witihin a dream. Tune: "Gazing at the South." Li Yü. SuSp, *tr. by* Daniel Bryant

Last Night of the Third Month, The. Chia Tao. CoBCP, *tr. by* Burton Watson

Last night returning from my twilight walk. Ballad of Past Meridian, A. George Meredith. PeVV

Last Night's Dream. Denise Levertov. NoAM

Last night's planets and stars, last night's wind. Li Shang-yin. CoBCP

Last night's stars, last night's winds. Without Title (1). Li Shang-yin. ChinPo, *tr. by* Yip Wai-lim

Last night, scattering rains, sudden winds. Tune: "Dream Song." Li Ch'ing-chao. ChinPo, *tr. by* Yip Wai-lim

Last Night that She Lived, The. Emily Dickinson. BoWoP; HeIP-4; NAAL-2v1; NAAL-3; OxBA

Last night the cherry-apple. Inscription for a Portrait. T'ang Yin. WoPoe, *tr. by* Graham Martin and John A. Scott

Last night the rainbow. Moon Shadow. George Bowering. MoCV

Last night the stars seemed not themselves. Atomic Psalm. Maurya Simon. GifTon

Last night there was rain with a soughing wind. Tune: "The Crow's Nocturnal Cry." Li Yü. ColAnChi, *tr. by* Jiaosheng Wang

Last night thin rain, gusty wind. Li Ch'ing-chao. BoWoP

Last night thou didst invite me home to eat[e]. Upon Showbread [*or* Shewbread]: Epigram. Robert Herrick. CaPo

Last night watching the Pleiades. Gary Snyder. HAP; VGW; WeW-3 *Fr.* Four Poems for Robin.

Last night we had a thunderstorm in style. Robert Louis Stevenson. NOBVV; NPeEn

Last night we sailed, my love and I. Barcarolle. May Probyn. VWP

Last night we sat with the stereopticon. Readings of History. Adrienne Rich. CoAmPo

Last night went walking with a woman that I know. Trap Door. Vítězslav Nezval. PFTM-1

Last night when the yellow moon. Wadasa Nakamoon, Vietnam Memorial. Ray A. Young Bear. CDa; HATNAP

Last Night When We Were Young. Harold Arlen. ReLy

Last night, while I lay thinking here. Whatif. Shel [*or* Shelley] Silverstein. OTCP

Last night with hair unbrushed. *Unknown.* ChinPo, *tr. by* Yip Wai-lim

Last night without sight of you my brain was ablaze. Sadi [*or* Saadi *or* Sa'di]. WoPoe, *tr. by* Basil Bunting

Last night you were a river. Conquest. Pauli Murray. GT

Last night your ghost walked in at two. Deadman's Shoes. Kate Clanchy. MFPA

Last o' the Tinkler, The. Violet Jacob. OxBS

Last of April, The. John Clare. CenSon

Last of England, The. Peter Porter. GS

Last of England, The! O'er the sea, my dear. Last of England, The. Ford Madox Brown. GS

Last of His Tribe. Oodgeroo of the tribe Noonuccal (Kath Walker). BMAP

Last of His Tribe, The. Henry Clarence Kendall. CBAP

Last of the Courtyard, The. Emily Grosholz. FFC

Last of the Fire Kings, The. Derek Mahon. PNI

Last of the Poet's Car. Tony Connor. OxBTC

Last of the Princes, The. A. K. Ramanujan. OxBC

Last of the shadows may close my eyes. Love Constant beyond Death. Francisco de Quevedo y Villegas. WoPoe, *tr. by* W. S. Merwin

Last of the wheat is drought-bruised, bending, The. Walking Fields at Night South of Hampton, Iowa. Steve Gehrke. AmPoNex

Last of thy unhappy mother's verse, The. (LL) On the Death of My First and Dearest Child[e], Hector Philip[p]s. Katherine Philips. NAEL-6v1; NAEL-7v1

Last One, The. W. S. Merwin. LCAP-2; NoAM; VGW

  (Well they'd made up their minds to be everywhere because.) ChAP

Last one, The / to die here. Nelly Sachs. BoWoP

Last Ones, The. "Robin Hyde." PeNZ

Last Ones, The. Dan Pagis. PoSu

Last Oracle from Delphi. *Unknown.* WoPoe, *tr. by* Katherine Washburn

Last Page of the Civil War. Vladimir Vladimirovich Mayakovsky [*or* Maiakovskii]. RusPo, *tr. by* Robert Arthur Douglas Ford

Last pale rank of poplar-trees, The. Aubade Triste. Agnes Mary Frances Robinson. NOBVV

Last peach in the water—full of fish and eyes, The. (LL) Leaving, The. Brigit Pegeen Kelly. IllVoic; YaYoPo

Last Performance, The. May Kendall. ViWPN

Last Picnic, The. Stanley Kunitz. AF

Last Platform, The. Yury [*or* Iurii] Timofeievich Galanskov. TCRusP, *tr. by* Olive Dehn

Last Poem. Margaret Atwood. LCAP-2

Last Poem. Robert Desnos. AmFaPo, *tr. by* X. J. Kennedy

Last Poem. Charles Donnelly. BIrV

  (Poem: "Between rebellion as a private study and the public.") CIP-2

Last Poem. Po Chü-i. ChiP, *tr. by* Arthur Waley

Last Poem. Mihály Tompa. IQMS, *tr. by* Madeline Mason

Last Poem. Hugo Williams. NPeEn

Last Poem, The. Jiri Orten. AF, *tr. by* Lyn Coffin

Last Poem: Goodbye to My Garden. Yuan Mei. GifTon, *tr. by* Jerome P. Seaton

Last Poems. Osip Emilevich Mandelstam [*or* Mandelshtam]. PFTM-1

Last pose flickered, failed, The. Rain after a Vaudeville Show. Stephen Vincent Benét. MoAmPo

Last quatrain, The. (LL) Bronzeville Mother Loiters in Mississippi, A. Meanwhile, a Mississippi Mother Burns Bacon. Gwendolyn Brooks. ESEAA; IllVoic

Last Quatrain of the Ballad of Emmett Till, The. Gwendolyn Brooks. ESEAA; LCAP-2; NAAL-5; WPE

Last Refuge, The. Augustus Young. BIrV

Last Republicans, The. Austin Clarke. CIP-2

Last Rhyme and Testament of Tony Lumpkin. Harry Morant. FaBoWar

Last Ride Together, The. Robert Browning. BoLoP; EroLit; FHYEP; ITBLP; NAEL-5v2; NAEL-6v2; OBEV; UnPo

Last Ride Together (from Her Point of View), The. James Kenneth Stephen. UnPo

Last Rites. Christina Georgina Rossetti. FaBoVe; NPeEn

Last river leaves for desolation, The. Last River, The. Iwan [*or* Yvan] Goll. AF, *tr. by* Galway Kinnell

Last Rose of Summer, The. Thomas Moore. *See* 'Tis the Last Rose of Summer

Last Round, The. Anna Wickham. MoBrPo

Last Sark, The. Ellen Johnston. NePenScot

Last Scene in the First Act. Marge Piercy. NoAM

Last screech owl cry. Foster Jewell. HA

Last settlement scraggled out with a barbed wire fence, The. Flight in the Desert, The. William Everson. ChIV-2; VGW

Last Snow. Andrew Young. OxBTC

Last Solo: Charlie Parker, Hotel Stanhope, March 12, 1955. David Jauss. MiVo

Last Song of Sappho, The. Felicia Dorothea Hemans. VWP

Last Song of the Exploding Stick. *Unknown.* APN-2, *tr. by* Washington Matthews *Fr.* Mountain Chant, The.

Last Songs. Galway Kinnell. PAI; VCAP

Last Spell Cast, The. Michael Brownstein. FTOS

Last Statement. Vladimir Vladimirovich Mayakovsky [*or* Maiakovskii]. PBCIP, *tr. by* Tom Paulin

Last Statement for a Last Oracle. Alan Dugan. NoAM

Last Still Days in a Bunker, The. Walter McDonald. AF

Last Stop. George Seferis. AF

Last Stroll: Homage to Pascoli, The. Edoardo Sanguineti. PFTM-2, *tr. by* Richard Collins

Last summer. Eleanor Schick. CA

Last summer, in the blue heat.   La Vita Nuova.   Weldon Kees.   VGW

Last sunbeam, The.   Dirge for Two Veterans.   Walt Whitman.   APN-1; BLT; CBCWP; MoAmPo

Last Sunday was a fine day.   Being a Good *Americani*.   Fawaz Turki.   GraLe

Last Supper, The.   Jacques Prévert.   CLPP, *tr.* by Lawrence Ferlinghetti

Last suppers, I fancy, are always wide-screen.   Gwyneth Lewis.   NeBl

Last Survivor's Speech, The.   *Unknown*.   NAEL-5v1   *Fr.* Beowulf.

Last Take.   Carol Muske.   GeoHom

Last Testaments.   Lorna Crozier.
   "Before she walked into the river."   LW

Last, the very last, The.   Butterfly, The.   Pavel Friedmann.   INSAB

Last thin acre of stalks that stood, The.   Immortal.   Mark Van Doren.   MoAmPo

Last Things.   William Meredith.   NoAM

Last Things, Black Pines at 4 A.M.   Robert Lowell.   NOBA

Last things / the turning leaves slip in the wind.   Vincent O'Sullivan.   PeNZ   *Fr.* Brother Jonathan, Brother Kafka.

Last time around the forest floor.   Rainier.   Jim Tollerud.   VoR

Last time he saw her he did not know that it was the, The.   Lady of the Last Time, The.   Vivian Lamarque.   CItWP, *tr.* by Cinzia Sartini Blum and Lara Trubowitz

Last time I gave my body up, The.   Kill, The.   Carl Phillips.   WiU

Last time I saw Donald Armstrong, The.   Performance, The.   James Dickey.   CoAP; CoAmPo; FaBoWar; PoE

Last Time I Saw Paris, The.   Jerome Kern.   ReLy

Last time I slept with the Queen, The.   Limerick.   Dylan Thomas.   PeLi

Last time, I think.   Issa.   EH, *tr.* by Robert Hass

Last time i was home, The.   Mothers.   Nikki Giovanni.   UnPo

Last time it was shearwaters, The.   Feeding Frenzies.   C. G. Hanzlicek.   GeoHom

Last time the curtain arises, The.   Last Performance, The.   May Kendall.   ViWPN

Last Train, The.   Linda Pastan.   GM

Last trainees are climbing the diving tower, The.   Naval Trainees Learn How to Jump Overboard, The.   David Wagoner.   VCAP

Last Trains, The.   C. G. Hanzlicek.   GM

Last Trams.   Kenneth Slessor.   BMAP

Last truck gone, The. (LL)   Gary Snyder.   NOBA; PFTM-2   *Fr.* Myths and Texts.

Last twist of the knife, The. (LL)   Rhapsody on a Windy Night.   T. S. Eliot.   HeIP-4; PoE

Last two Februarys have passed, The.   St. Bridget's Cross.   Anne Hartigan.   CIP-2

Last Utterance of the Delphic Oracle, The.   *Unknown*.   OBVE, *tr.* by Kenneth Rexroth

Last Vision of Eoghan Rua Ó Súilleabháin, The.   Michael Hartnett.   PBCIP

Last Visit.   Robert Finch.   NOBC

Last Waltz in Santiago.   Ariel Dorfman.   AF, *tr.* by Ariel Dorfman

Last War, The.   Kingsley Amis.   OBSV; OxBC

Last war was my favourite picture story, The.   In September 1939.   Bernard Gutteridge.   PoWW

Last week a half-crazed Mormon woman in blue-white.   Pharaoh's Palace.   David Wojahn.   AllShUp

Last week / our telephone pole sprouted.   Letter from Turtle Beach.   Susan K. C. Lee.   FSt

Last Will and Testament.   Hans Magnus Enzensberger.   PoSu

Last Will and Testament.   Géza Páskándi.   IQMS, *tr.* by John Gordon Nichols

Last Will and Testament, A.   John Winstanley.   FaBoVe; OBSV

Last Wish, The.   "Owen Meredith."   OxBSP

Last Wolf, The.   Mary Tallmountain.   ReEnLa
   (Last wolf hurried toward me, The.)   LoL; UnSA

Last Word, A.   Ernest Christopher Dowson.   GSo; MoBrPo

Last Word, The.   Matthew Arnold.   NOBE; SCGP

Last Word, The.   Imamu Amiri Baraka.   UnSA

Last Word, The.   Peter Davison.   InPK-6

Last Word of a Bluebird, The.   Robert Frost.   NOxBChV; OxIBACP

Last word, the last hasty swallow, The.   Professional Poet.   Bogomil Gjuzel.   CarOv, *tr.* by Carolyn Kizer

Last Words.   Emily Jane Brontë.   WPE

Last Words.   John Hollander.   OBAL

Last Words.   Richard Howard.   DiPo   *Fr.* Ithaca: The Palace at Four A.M.

Last Words.   James Merrill.   TAP

Last Words, The.   Maurice Maeterlinck.   AWP, *tr.* by Frederick York Powell

Last Words before Winter.   Louis Untermeyer.   MoAmPo

Last Words, 1968.   Lance Henson.   CDW

Last Words of Don Henriquez, The.   Zalman Schneour.   TrJP, *tr.* by Joseph Leftwich

Last Words of My English Grandmother, The.   William Carlos Williams.   APT-1; RB; RaBo; SAmP

Last Words of the Prophet.   *Unknown*.   APN-2, *tr.* by Washington Matthews   *Fr.* Mountain Chant, The.

Last Words on Greece.   Byron.   CAGL

Last World, A.   John Ashbery.   PoM

Last year among the flowers I saw you off.   To Send to Li Tan and Yüan Hsi.   Wei Ying-wu.   CoBCP, *tr.* by Burton Watson

Last year at the Feast of Lanterns.   Lost.   Chu Shu-chen.   BoWoP; OHMPC, *tr.* by Kenneth Rexroth

Last year fighting at the source of the Sang-kan.   Fighting South of the Wall.   Li Po.   WoPoe, *tr.* by Elling O. Eide

Last year I lost an.   Poem on Losing One's Teeth.   Han Yü.   GifTon; SuSp, *tr.* by Kenneth O. Hanson

Last year I rejoined the Emperor by this road.   Tu Fu.   CarOv, *tr.* by Carolyn Kizer   *Fr.* Adviser to the Court.

Last year I used to ride the J CHURCH Line.   J Car, The.   Thom Gunn.   MakPoe

Last year in a lovely temple in Hirosawa.   Hakugai.   ZenPo, *tr.* by Takashi Ikemoto and Lucien Stryk

Last year in the spring when the birds were calling.   *Unknown*.   CoBCP

Last year, Orlando.   Political Orlando, The.   George MacBeth [*or* Macbeth].   NOBL

Last year's decencies.   Odysseus.   Padraic Fallon.   CIP-2

Last Year's Discussion: The Nobel Russian.   Phyllis McGinley.   FaBoEE

Last year the magnolias flared.   On Commonwealth Avenue and Brattle Street.   Diana Der Hovanessian.   UrbNat

Last year we fought.   They Fought South of the Walls.   Li Po.   SuSp, *tr.* by Joseph J. Lee

Last year we fought by the springs of Sankan river.   Fighting on the South Frontier.   Li Po.   TAL

Last year we parted as the flowers began to bloom.   Lady Picking Flowers, A.   Shen Chou.   CoBLCP, *tr.* by Jonathan Chaves

Last year when I accompanied you.   To a Traveler.   Su Tung-p'o (Su Shih).   OHPC, *tr.* by Kenneth Rexroth

Lastly, Marvelous, I wanted to be rich.   E-Mail.   Reetika Vazirani.   NAPBL

Lastly, with friends t' enjoy our day[e]s. (LL)   Four[e] Things Make Us Happy Here.   Robert Herrick.   CaPo; Spl

Lastness.   Galway Kinnell.   NNaP
   "Black bear sits alone, A."   RaBo

Laszlo.   Frieda Hughes.   NeBl

Lat never a man a wooing wend.   King Henry.   *Unknown*.   ESPB; OxBB

Lat take a cat, and fostre him wel[l] with milk.   Geoffrey Chaucer.   TriCat   *Fr.* Canterbury Tales, The.

Late.   Benjamin Paul Blood.   APN-2

Late.   Louise Bogan.   APT-2; VGW

Late Afternoon.   Molly Fisk.   PasH

Late Afternoon at the Arboretum.   Kelly Cherry.   SwNoth

Late Afternoon, Late in the Twentieth Century.   Jeffrey Skinner.   PBCAP

Late afternoon rain of a postponed summer.   Dusk: July.   Marilyn Hacker.   FFC

Late Apostasy, A.   V. Penelope Pelizzon.   AmPoNex

Late April and you are three; today.   W. D. Snodgrass.   VCAP   *Fr.* Heart's Needle.

Late April. Taking stock.   Generalities.   Robert Conquest.   OxBC

Late Arrivals.   Sybil Kollar.   FFC

Late arrivals at Mass, in lace.   Sunday.   Mário de Andrade.   TCLAP, *tr.* by Jack E. Tomlins

Late at een, drinkin' the wine.   Dowie Houms o' Yarrow, The.   *Unknown*.   OBEV; OxBS

Late at Night.   William Stafford.   NNaP

"Late at night I stood on a battlement."   Der von Kürenberg.   GePo

Late at night, listening to the winter rain.   Ryokan.   AWTN, *tr.* by John Stevens   *Fr.* Winter.

Late at night, when you're so lonely.   Pure Loneliness, The.   Michael Ryan.   BodElec

Late Aubade, A.   Richard Wilbur.   PAI; SòSe-8

Late August.   Alexis Rotella.   HA

Late August, given heavy rain and sun.   Blackberry-Picking.   Seamus Heaney.   ChAP

Late August on the Lido.   John Hollander.   YaYoPo

Late August, say the records, when the gowk-storm.   Chartres of Gowrie, The.   Don Paterson.   NePenScot

Late Author: Snapshot in the Rain, The.   Dan Pagis.   FIT, *tr.* by Robert Friend

Late autumn.   Cor Van den Heuvel.   HA

Late autumn, a brief shower.   Lament.   Liu Yung.   CrYelRi, *tr.* by Sam Hamill

Late Autumn in Styria.   Hans Kloepfer.   AuPH, *tr.* by Lowell A. Bangerter

Late autumn strips the distant hills.   To a Friend.   Li Po.   CrYelRi, *tr.* by Sam Hamill

Late Bloomer at the Front of My Garden. Li Po. ColAnChi, *tr.* by Elling O. Eide

Late-blooming cherry. Hyakka. JDP, *tr.* by Yoel Hoffmann

Late-born and woman-souled I dare not hope. Echoes. Emma Lazarus. APN-2; GSo

Late-born daughters of famous fathers, The. Late-Born Daughters, The. Lisel Mueller. ExTi

Late Bus (After a Series of Hold-Ups). Russell Atkins. LTA

Late butterflies gliding through the air. Timothy Liu. NeAmPo

Late day flames. Evening Song. Ralph J. Mills, Jr. IllVoic

Late December noon, near freezing. Parthenon at Nashville, The. Joe Bolton. AmPoNex

Late evening cow, The. Buson. SoOfWa, *tr.* by Sam Hamill

Late evening finally comes. Yakamochi (Otomo no Yakamochi). ErotSp, *tr.* by Sam Hamill

Late evening, July, and no one at home. California Twilight. Charles Wright. GeoHom

Late Express, The. Barbara Giles. OTCP

Late Flight of the Love God. Mona Van Duyn. ExTi

Late for Breakfast. Mary Dawson. TLR

Late Friday / we watched Eddie blow the blues. With Thanks to Eddie Shaw. Janet Lowe. PasH

Late Ghazal. Adrienne Rich. HarvBoo

Late Gothic. Phyllis Gotlieb. NOBC

Late Hour, The. Mark Strand. AWTN; HCAP

Late in an evening as I walk'd alone. Complaint of Thames 1647 When the Best of Kings Was Imprisoned by the Worst of Rebels at Holmbie, The. Hester Lee Pulter. EMWP

Late in an evening forth as I went. Archie o Cawfield. *Unknown.* ESPB

Late in Fall. Ramona Wilson. VoR

Late in Han. Tune: "Happily Flitting Oriole." Wu Li. ColAnChi, *tr.* by Jonathan Chaves

Late in life, I care for ease alone. Reply to a Magistrate. Wang Wei. CrYelRi, *tr.* by Sam Hamill

Late in November. Thaw, The. Marianne Wolfe. GifTon

Late in the afternoon the light. Crepuscular. Richard Howard. TwCP

Late in the day, the sun. Midsummer. Sherod Santos. GeoHom

Late in the evening. Alan Pizzarelli. HA

Late in the evening when the children are at play. Little Brown Jacks Nyimbung. Rex Marshall. IBA

Late in the Forest I Did Cupid See. Mary Sidney Wroth, Countess of Montgomery. NPeEn; OxBSo; PBRV *Fr.* Pamphilia to Amphilanthus.

Late in the morning, on the side balcony. Breakfast on the Balcony. Yevgeny [*or* Evgenii] Borisovich Rein. TCRusP, *tr.* by Daniel Weissbort

Late in the season the world digs in, the fat blossoms. Over and Over Stitch. Jorie Graham. HCAP; VCAP

Late in the Year K'uei-yu (1333), Staying at the Temple of the Upper Regions. Yü Chi. CoBLCP, *tr.* by Jonathan Chaves

Late Indian summer's. Sun Bu-er. WPoS; WoPoe, *tr.* by Jane Hirshfield

Late, just past midnight. Off from Swing Shift. Garrett Kaoru Hongo. GeoHom; ReTh

Late Lamented Fame of the Giant City of New York. Bertolt Brecht. "Who is there still remembers." FaBoA, *tr.* by Frank Jellinek

Late Lark, A. William Ernest Henley. *See* Echoes

Late lark twitters from the quiet skies, A. William Ernest Henley. MoBrPo; NOBE; OBEV *Fr.* Echoes.

Late Last Night. Arthur Gregor. VGW

Late, Last Rook, The. Ralph Hodgson. MoBrPo

Late, late in a gloamin' Kilmeny came hame! (LL) James Hogg. OBEV; OxAEP-2 *Fr.* Queen's Wake, The.

Late, late, so late! and dark the night and chill! Tennyson. SacPr

Late lies the wintry sun a-bed. Winter Time [*or* Winter-Time]. Robert Louis Stevenson. EBVV; MoBrPo

Late Light. Edmund Charles Blunden. EnLoPo

Late light allows us to begin. 59th Light Poem: for La Monte Young and Marian Zazeela—6 November 1982. Jackson Mac Low. PmAP

Late Lights in Minnesota. Ted Kooser. BLT

Late March mist is an angry Cerberus, The. Persephone, 1978. Thomas McCarthy. ModIr

Late Mr Charles Lynch Digresses, The. Paul Durcan. ModIr

Late Night Ode. Horace. WiU; WoPoe, *tr.* by J. D. McClatchy

Late night over the Neva. Over the Neva. Wilgelm Aleksandrovich Zorgenfrey [*or* Zorgenfrei]. TCRP, *tr.* by Sophie Lund

Late Night Radio. Geoff Page. BMAP

Late Night Radio. Aleda Shirley. ExTi

Late night, with my bundle of new straws. Burden of Decision, The. Peter Everwine. NNaP

Late nights without hope. Nights without Hope (Rebetiko Song). Yannis Papaionnou. WoPoe, *tr.* by Gail Holst-Warhaft

Late November. Sherod Santos. Son

Late November in a Field. James Wright (1927–80). NAAL-2v2; NNaP

Late November on our way to work. I Learn a Lesson about Our Society. Janice Gould. GeoHom

Late October Camping in the Sawtooths. Gary Snyder. BLT

Late October sun. White Earth. Gerald Vizenor. HATNAP

Late one night I hear his breath. Coltrane and My Father. Ralph Sneeden. SeSe

Late Passenger, The. Clive Staples Lewis. TrCP

Late repentance, and the long despair, The. To George Sand on her Interview with Elizabeth Barrett Browning. Isa Blagden. VWP

Late Rising on Spring Days. Wei Chuang. CoBCP, *tr.* by Burton Watson

Late Round. Kim Addonizio. MoASP

Late Sabbath afternoon, remembering. Home for Winter. Marcia Falk. TaR

Late Show, The. Rachel Wetzsteon. NeAmPo

Late Singer, The. William Carlos Williams. SAmP

Late singer of a sunless day. Linnet in November, The. Francis Turner Palgrave. EBVV

Late Sir John Ogilvy, The. William McGonagall. VerBaPo

Late snowfall. Lorraine Ellis Harr. HA

Late Sonnet. Hayden Carruth. Son

Late Spring. Fan Ch'eng-ta. SuSp, *tr.* by Irving Y. Lo *Fr.* Seasonal Poems on Fields and Gardens.

Late Spring. Robert Hass. BLT

Late Spring. Tzu Yeh. CrYelRi, *tr.* by Sam Hamill

Late Spring. Yüan Chên. SuSp, *tr.* by Dell R. Hales

Late spring has snatched away the blossoms. Impromptu; Late Spring at Pan-shan. Wang An-shih. CoBCP, *tr.* by Burton Watson

Late spring / Paling rose. Sodo. ZenPo, *tr.* by Takashi Ikemoto and Lucien Stryk

Late Spring—Traveling through the Mountains. Chu Yün-ming. CoBLCP, *tr.* by Jonathan Chaves

Late Summer. Ruth L. Schwartz. AmPoNex

Late summer, and at midnight. Guttural Muse, The. Seamus Heaney. HarvBoo; NOIV

Late Summer Litany. Julie Moulds. AmPoNex

Late Summer News. Dorothy Barresi. SwNoth

Late summer rain crashes, The. La Fabrique de Tabac (Tobacco Harvest). Beverly Matherne. TWW

Late summers, early autumns, you can see something that binds. Adrienne Rich. NAAL-5 *Fr.* Atlas of the Difficult World, An.

Late sun, the stream and the hills; the beauty. Quatrain. Tu Fu. SuSp, *tr.* by Jerome Seaton

Late that summer. Surrendered Names. Gerald Vizenor. HATNAP

Late Twentieth-Century Prayer, A. Ernest Sandeen. WeW-3

Late 20th Century: Spring. Jerry Martien. GeoHom

Late Victorian Girl, The. Bill Manhire. PeNZ

Late Wasp, The. Edwin Muir. HarvBoo

Late, when it returns from the city wall. Crow Cries at Night, The. Po Chü-i. SuSp, *tr.* by Irving Y. Lo

Late Winter. James McAuley. BMAP

Late winter. Ice cold and drained of color. GWB in the Rain, The. Mary Stewart Hammond. KGB

Late Winter in Menard County. John Knoepfle. IllVoic

Late Wisdom. George Crabbe. OBEV *Fr.* Reflections.

Late Words for My Sister. Robin Becker. ExTi

Lately, alas, I knew a gentle boy. Sympathy. Henry David Thoreau. CAGL

Lately I saw a sight most quaint. "Gross, Coarse, Hideous" (Police Description of My Pictures). D. H. Lawrence. FaBoEE

Lately, I think of my love for you and the rose. Rose Growing into the House, The. Gibbons Ruark. InPK-6

Lately, I've become accustomed to the way. Preface to a Twenty Volume Suicide Note. Imamu Amiri Baraka. AmFaPo; BB; ESEAA; NAAAL; PoM; TTY

Lately I've become religious about atoms. Metamorpho I. Joe Rosenblatt. MoCV

Lately I've felt a grave concern. Beatrice [*or* Beatriz *or* Beatriz], Countess de Die [*or* Dia]. BoWoP

Lately my neighbor wheezes. Running. Leslie Ullman. PBCAP

Lately on yonder swelling bush. Budd, The. Edmund Waller. PBRV

Later, a cormorant. Cormorant. Peter Preece. AngWePo

Later, back in my cell, back in the thick stench. Between the Lines. Michael Hamburger. HP

Later he must have watched. Swimming in the Flood. John Burnside. EmeKit

Later Life: A Double Sonnet of Sonnets. Christina Georgina Rossetti. "Something this foggy day, a something which." NAEL-5v2; NAEL-6v2 (Sonnet 26.) VWP

This Life Is Full of Numbness. Son

To Love and to Remember. Son

"Tread softly! all the earth is holy ground." WPoS

Later, on the Neckar's oil-slick banks. On Finding a Swastika Carved on a Tree in the Hills above Heidelberg. Kevin Prufer. AmPoNex

Later Still. Philip Levine. ColAP

Later, the firecat closed his bright eyes / And slept. (LL) Earthy Anecdote. Wallace Stevens. RB; SAmP

Latest Decalogue, The. Arthur Hugh Clough. CABP; ChIV-1; EBEV; EBVV; FaBoEE; GTBS-P; HAP; NAEL-5v2; NAEL-6v2; NOBE; NOBVV; NPeEn; NoP-4; OBSV; OxBEV; PAI; PeECV; SCGP; SacPr; TFi; WeW-3; WoPoe

Latet Anguis. William Cornish. OBEV

Lathe we were at, The. Metal-work. David Morley. NLP

Latin and Soul for Joe Bataan. Víctor Hernández Cruz. PueRic

Latin Lesson, The. Eavan Boland. ModIr

Latin Music in New York. Jessica Tarahata Hagedorn. PmAP

Latin Night at the Pawnshop. Martín Espada. TRP

Latitudes of Home, The. Alistair Elliot. OxBSo

Latrine in a Suburb of Smyrna, A. Agathias. GrAn, tr. by Guy Davenport

Latter-day Geography Lesson. Ronald Allison Kells Mason. PeNZ

Latter Day Lysistrata. Lauris Edmond. PeNZ

Latter Day Psalms. Cliff Ashby. NOCV

Latter-Day Warnings. Oliver Wendell Holmes. NCAP

Latter rain, it falls in anxious haste, The. Latter Rain, The. Jones Very. APN-1; OxBA; TCAPo

Lattice at / of (Com)pare (Dis)pair. Tina Darragh. FTOS

Lattice at "Split." Tina Darragh. FTOS

Latvian Autumn, The. Johannes Bobrowski. PoSu

Latvian Songs. Johannes Bobrowski. AF

Laudanum. Unknown. NOEC

Laudare. Constance Carrier. APT-2

Lauds. W. H. Auden. BBASP; TrCP Fr. Horae Canonicae.

Lauds. John Berryman. HAP

Laugh aloud, then pass by, with a kind. Nossis. GrAn

Laugh and Be Merry. John Masefield. MoBrPo

Laugh, and the world laughs with you. Solitude. Ella Wheeler Wilcox. BRP; PWR; SWaP; TCAPo

Laugh is just like sunshine, A. Sunshine and Music. Unknown. PoToHe

Laugh on, laugh on at all the dreams. I Believe. Saul [or Shaul] Tchernichowsky [or Tchernichovsky]. TrJP, tr. by Reginald V. Feldman

Laughed every goblin. Christina Georgina Rossetti. BrRo Fr. Goblin Market.

Laughing All the Way. Liz Cashdan. Prnts

Laughing, before the lamps, we pour each other. Year I-mao (Fifteen Fifty Five), New Year's Eve, The. Wen Cheng-ming. CoBLCP, tr. by Jonathan Chaves

Laughing eyes followed. Asante Sana, Te Te. Thadious M. Davis. BlSi

Laughing Gas. Ruth Whitman. UnSA

Laughing Hyena, after [or by] Hokusai, The. Dennis Joseph Enright. TwCP

Laughing, merry, childish voices, woke us in their eager glee. Christmas, South, 1866. Mary E. Tucker. CBWP-1

Laughing Moon, The. Moniza Alvi. MFPA

Laughing Mountain. Muso Soseki. EaWin, tr. by W. S. Merwin

Laughing softly. Anita Virgil. HA

Laughing Song. William Blake. See Songs of Innocence

Laughing through clouds, his milk-teeth still unshed. Rudyard Kipling. PoWW Fr. Epitaphs of the War [1914–1918].

Laughing Tomatoes. Francisco Alarcon. OxIBACP

Laughing, with a TV's blue-static figures. When Loneliness Is a Man. Yusef Komunyakaa. AWTN

Laughing youngsters, the. Spring Song. Federico García Lorca. SpanPo, tr. by Rachel Benson and Robert O'Brien

Laughter. Wislawa Szymborska. PoSu, tr. by Magnus F. Krynski

Laughter of a Faun, The. Novella Nikolaevna Matveyeva [or Matveieva]. TCRP, tr. by Deming Brown

Laughter out of dead bellies. (LL) Ezra Pound. HarvBoo; HeIP-4; MoAmPo; NOBE; NPeEn; OBWP; PoE; PoWW; TRP; VGW Fr. Hugh Selwyn Mauberley (Life and Contacts).

Laughter pours from a thousand homes, as the water clock drips and drips. Sentiments on New Year's Eve in the Year Kuei-ssu. Huang Ching-jen. SuSp, tr. by Chang Yin-nan

Launch, The. Alice Thompson Meynell. PeVV; WPE

Launch into writing and you launch into the unnamed future, with language as a cutting edge. Provisionally. Ken Edwards. Oth

Launch thy bark, mariner. Mariner's Hymn. Caroline Anne Bowles Southey. TreFP

Launching into Eternity. Isaac Watts. SacPr

Launching Our Community Developement Fund. Tanure Ojaide. HBAPE

Laundress, The. Velemir [or Viktor Vladimirovich] Khlebnikov. Burning Field, The. TCRusP, tr. by Kathy Lewis and Bob Perelman

Laundress, The. Thomas Kinsella. HarvBoo

Laundry. Bruce Smith. Son

Laundry so near the ocean bothered Frank. Duo-Tang. Kenward Elmslie. FTOS

Laura. Thomas Campion. See Observations in the Art of English Poesie

Laura. Johnny Mercer. ReLy

Laura. Robert Tofte.
Unto Thy Favor. Son
When She Was Born. Son

Laura to Petrarch. Mary Robinson. CenSon

Laura was lightsome, gay, and free from guile. Caroline Elizabeth Norton. VWP Fr. Marriage and Love.

Laureate. Hugh Seidman. BodElec

Laureate, The. William Edmonstoune [or Edmondstoune] Aytoun. UV

Laureate, The. Robert Graves. BIrV; FaBoTw; OBSV

Laurel Axe, The. Geoffrey Hill. NAEL-5v2; NAEL-6v2; NPeEn; NoAM; PoE Fr. Apology for the Revival of Christian Architecture in England, An.

Laurel in bloom. John Wills. HA

Laurel of Liberty, The. A Poem. Robert Merry.
"Genius, or Muse, whate'er thou art! whose thrill." NOBRP

Laurel Street, 1950. Dorothy Perry Thompson. SpirFl

Laurel Tree, The. Louis Simpson. NNaP

Laurence Bloomfield in Ireland. William Allingham.
Eviction, The. BIrV; NOIV
Lord Crashton: The Absentee Landlord. NOIV

Laurentia. Medbh McGuckian. BiHa

Laurentian Shield. Francis Reginald Scott. NOBC

Laus Deo. Roland Mathias. AngWePo Fr. Tide-Reach.

Laus Deo! John Greenleaf Whittier. CBCWP

Laus Mariae. Sidney Lanier. Son

Laus Virginitatis. Arthur Symons. EnLoPo

Lausanne: In Gibbon's Old Garden: 11–12 P.M. Thomas Hardy. FaBoTw

Lavatory Attendant, The. Wendy Cope. UV

Lavender Woman, The. Lizette Woodworth Reese. APN-2

Lavinia is polite, but not profane. Edward Young. ECEV Fr. Satires.

Law. Tiziano Rossi. ItPo, tr. by Gayle Ridinger

Law, The. Samuel Butler. NBLV

Law, The. Abraham Ibn Ezra. TrJP, tr. by Alice Lucas

Law, The. Ella Wheeler Wilcox. PWR

Law against Lovers, The. Sir William Davenant [or D'Avenant].
(Viola's Song.) NOSC
Wake All the Dead. FaBoCh; HAP; SCGP

Law can take a purse in open court, The. Law, The. Samuel Butler (1612–80). NBLV

Law comes sirening across the town, The. (LL) Third Sermon on the Warpland, The. Gwendolyn Brooks. BPo; SeSe

Law Given at Sinai, The. Isaac Watts. ChIV-1

Law makes long spokes of the short stakes of men. Legal Fiction. William Empson. FaBoMo; HarvBoo; NoAM; NoP-4

Law of God be to thee thy rest, The. Unknown. MiEL

Law should have ear-plugs, not bandaged eyes, The. Nicarchus of Alexandria. GrAn

Law That Says, The. Sipho Sepamla. AF

Law was ever above kings, The. Morgan Llwyd. AngWePo Fr. Charles, the Last King of Britain.

Law which (as they say) Priapus coined, The. Unknown. PriapPo, tr. by Richard W. Hooper Fr. Priapus Poems, The.

Law, which each citizen knows well. Boris Abramovich Slutsky [or Slutskii]. TCRusP, tr. by Daniel Weissbort

Lawd, Dese Colored Chillum. Ruby C. Saunders. BlSi; LTA

Lawd Zambesi! For Singing in Good Mood. Lebert Bethune. GT

Lawde and Prayse Made for Our Sovereigne Lord the Kyng, A. John Skelton.
"Rose both white and Rede, The." PBRV

Lawn as white as driven snow. William Shakespeare. NPeEn; NoSic Fr. Winter's Tale, The.

Lawn of Excluded Middle. Rosmarie Waldrop. FTOS

Lawn Roller, The. Robert Layzer. OBGa

Lawn Sprinkler, The. Queen Lili'u-o-ka-lani. WoPoe, tr. by Alfons L. Korn and Mary Kawena Pukui

Lawns darken, evening broods in the black, The. Tennyson. Alan Ansen. CoAP

Lawrence and Edison in New Jersey: 1923. Linda Bierds. ExTi

Lawrence here for ever blames. D. H. Lawrence and James Joyce. Humbert Wolfe. FaBoEE

Lawrence—not the bearded one—the one. Any Complaints? Vernon Scannell. OxBTC

Lawrence of virtuous [or vertuous] Father virtuous [or vertuous] Son. To Mr. Lawrence. John Milton. AWP; GTBS-P; OBEV; PoE

Laws are the secret avengers, The. Avengers, The. Edwin Markham. MoAmPo

Laws of blind unrest, not art, The. Prayer. Kathleen Jessie Raine. BBASP

Laws of God, the Laws of Man, The. A. E. Housman. CAGL; MoBrPo; NOBVV; NPeEn; OBSV
  (Laws of God, The.) OxBoLi

Lawyer and the critic but behold, The. Byron. NePenScot Fr. Don Juan.

Lawyer had a legal mouse, A. Legal Mouse, A. Lizelia Augusta Jenkins Moorer. CBWP-3

Lawyers. Unknown. OBCoV

Lawyers, Bob, know too much, The. Lawyers Know Too Much, The. Carl Sandburg. PoE

Lawyers Know Too Much, The. Carl Sandburg. PoE

Lawyers may revere that tree, The. Epigram on a Lawyer's Desiring One of the Tribe to Look with Respect to a Gibbet. Robert Fergusson. OxBS

Lawyers themselves uphold the commonweal. Lawyers. Unknown. OBCoV

Lay a garland on my hearse. Francis Beaumont. AWP; HAP; NOBE; OBEV; SCGP Fr. Maid's Tragedy, The.

Lay aside phrases; speak as in the night. This Is Not Death. Humbert Wolfe. MoBrPo

Lay down, boys, and take a little nap / Lay down, boys, and take a little nap. Cumberland Gap. Unknown. APN-2

Lay down the red carpet—My dowry is death. (LL) Streets of Laredo, The. Louis MacNeice. FaBoWar; OBWP

Lay down their life; they do not hate. (LL) At a Calvary near the Ancre. Wilfred Owen. ChIV-2; GI

Lay down these words. Riprap. Gary Snyder. HCAP; NAAL-2v2; NAAL-5; NOBA; NeAP; NoAM; PmAP; PoM; PoPoPo; VCAP

Lay me in yon place, lad. Last o' the Tinkler, The. Violet Jacob. OxBS

Lay me on an anvil, O God. Prayers of Steel. Carl Sandburg. MoAmPo; SSCS; TrCP

Lay neither the scrawny. Rufinus. GrAn

Lay of a Golden Goose, The. Louisa May Alcott. SWaP

Lay of an Irish Harp, or Metrical Fragments, The. Sydney Owenson, Lady Morgan.
  Fragment 10. The Boudoir. RWP
  Fragment 19. L'Amant Mutin. RWP
  Fragment 35. The Irish Jig. RWP

Lay of Finn, The. Unknown. AnOE, tr. by Charles W. Kennedy Fr. Beowulf.

Lay of Ike, The. John Berryman. LCAP-2 Fr. Dream Songs.

Lay of King Saint Ladislas, The. Unknown. IQMS, tr. by Anthony Edkins

Lay of the Captive Count, The. Goethe. AWP, tr. by James Clarence Mangan

Lay of the Honeysuckle, The. Marie de France. WPE, tr. by Robin Johnson

Lay of the Lash, The. Unknown. FaBoWar

Lay of the Last Minstrel, The. Sir Walter Scott.
  "Breathes there the [or a] Man with soul so dead." ITBLP; NePenScot; OxBEV; OxBS; SoSe-8; TFi
  (Innominatus.) OBEV
  Love. OxAEP-2
  Melrose Abbey. OxAEP-2
  Minstrel, The. OxAEP-2
  (Nature's Sympathy with the Poet.) OxAEP-2
  "O Caledonia! stern and wild." NePenScot
  "O [or Oh] listen, listen, ladies gay!" GTBS-P
  (Patriotism.) NOBE; OxAEP-2
  (Poet, The.) TreFP
  Rosabelle. GTBS-P

Lay of the Rover. Aimé Césaire. WoPoe, tr. by Gregson Davis

Lay of the Trilobite. May Kendall. NPeEn; VWP; ViWPN

Lay [or Short Lay] of Sigurd, The. Unknown. AWP, tr. by Eirikr Magnusson and William Morris Fr. Elder Edda, The.

Lay Preacher Ponders, The. Idris Davies. OxBTC

Lay these words into the dead man's grave. In Memoriam Paul Celan. Edward Hirsch. MakPoe

Lay to Eliza, The. Edmund Spenser. NOBE Fr. Shepheardes [or Shepeards or Shepherd's] Calender, The.

Lay wreaths upon the stone. Wreaths. Requiescat. Haim [or Chaim or Khayim] Guri [or Gouri]. MHP, tr. by Ruth Finer Mintz

Lay Your Arms Aside. Pierce Ferriter. BIrV, tr. by Eiléan Ní Chuilleanáin

Lay your head in my lap. Olga Popova. ItGoST, tr. by J. Kates

Lay your head on a block of butter and chop. Lakshminkara. WPoS

Lay your sleeping head, my love. Lullaby. W. H. Auden. GLP; HAP; HarvBoo; NAEL-5v2; NAEL-6v2; NOBE; NoAM; NoP-4; OxAEP-2; OxBEV; OxBTC; PoE; TFi; UnPo; WeW-3

Lay your weapons down, young lady. Piaras Feiritear. NOIV

Layer by layer, the dust of bitterness. Bangla Desh: 2. Faiz Ahmad Faiz. CarOv, tr. by Carolyn Kizer

Layer on layer of hemp leaves, jute leaves shining. Tune: Sand of Silk-washing Stream. Su Tung-p'o (Su Shih). CoBCP, tr. by Burton Watson Fr. Along the Road to Stone Lake.

Layers, The. Stanley Kunitz. BodElec

Laying the pen aside, when he had signed. Faustus. Alec Derwent Hope. NOBAu

Lays of Ancient Rome. Thomas Babington Macaulay, 1st Baron Macaulay.
  Horatius [or Horatius at the Bridge]. CABP; EBNV; FaBoCh; FaBoWar; OBNV; OBWP; OxAEP-2
    "But hark! the cry is Astur." OBWP
    "Then out spake brave Horatius." CABP; TreFP

Lazarus. James Keir Baxter. HarvBoo

Lazarus. Ron Koertge. OPRER

Lazarus. Ágnes Nemes Nagy. IQMS, tr. by Adam Makkai

Lazarus. Ágnes Nemes Nagy. IQMS, tr. by Hugh Maxton

Lazarus. Ágnes Nemes Nagy. IQMS, tr. by Ila Egon

Lazarus. Ágnes Nemes Nagy. PoSu, tr. by Frederic Will

Lazarus / don't come forth from the grave. Anti-Lazarus, The. Nicanor Parra. GI, tr. by Edith Grossman

Lazarus, kindling at the breath of pain. Second Life of Lazarus, The. Gwen Harwood. CBAP

Lazarus' Sister. Elaine Feinstein. HarvBoo

Laziest Gal in Town, The. Cole Porter. ReLy

Lazily I stir a white feather fan. In the Mountains on a Summer Day. Li Po. TAL

Lazy. Lu Yu. OHMPC, tr. by Kenneth Rexroth

Lazy Afternoon. John Latouche. ReLy

Lazy are slaughtered, the. Measures Taken, The. Erich Fried. WoPoe, tr. by Michael Hamburger

Lazy-bones, lazy-bones, wake up and peep! Nonsense Verses. Charles Lamb. OBCoV

Lazy Cloud's Nest 1. Ali Hsiying. ColAnChi, tr. by Jerome P. Seaton

Lazy Cloud's Nest 2. Ali Hsiying. ColAnChi, tr. by Jerome P. Seaton

Lazy deuks that sit i' the coal-neuks. Unknown. OxNR

Lazy dog (a bomb containing ten), The. John Cage. APSN Fr. Diary: How to Improve the World (You Will Only Make Matters Worse).

Lazy flowers brew honey for the bees. Love Song. Hu Chih-yu. CrYelRi, tr. by Sam Hamill

Lazy Man, The. Unknown. WoPoe, tr. by Ulli Beier and Bakare Gbadamosi

Lazy Man's Song. Po Chü-i. ChiP; OBVE, tr. by Arthur Waley

Lazy Marcus once dreamed. Lucilius. GrAn

Lazy People, The. Shel [or Shelley] Silverstein. NTCP

Lazy Pussy, The. Palmer Cox. OBCA; OxIBACP

Lazy River. Hoagy Carmichael. ReLy

Lazy Thought, A. Eve Merriam. SSCS

Lazy Witch. Myra Cohn Livingston. NOxBChV

LD Ansure, The. Lady Dorothy Shirley. EMWP

Le Balcon. Charles Baudelaire. AWP, tr. by Lord Alfred Bruce Douglas

Le Chariot. John Wieners. VGW

Le Diner. Arthur Hugh Clough. OBCoV; OBSV Fr. Spectator ab Extra.

Le Jazz Hot. Anselm Hollo. PoM; SeSe

Le Livre. Stéphane Mallarmé.
  "End / conscience." PFTM-1

Le Livre Est sur la Table. John Ashbery. SPE

Le Loupgarou. Derek Walcott. OxBSo

Le Monocle de Mon Oncle. Wallace Stevens. TCAPo

Le Mort. Howard Buck. YaYoPo

Le passage (Morbihan). Tony Baker. Oth

Le Père Sévère. Unknown. AWP, tr. by Andrew Lang

Le Rêve. Edgar Bowers. CoAmPo

Le Roy, you're earning too much money now. (LL) Elizabeth Bishop. FaBoVe; FaBoWP Fr. Songs for a Colored Singer.

Le Tombeau de Pierre Falcon. James Reaney. MoCV

Le Ventre (1964). U Tam'si Tchicaya.
  "Congo is myself (Lumumba), The." PBMAP

Le Ventre (1964). U Tam'si Tchicaya.
  "I tear at my belly." PBMAP

Leaba Shíoda. Nuala Ni Dhomhnaill. CABP

Lead. Ambrose Bierce. APN-2; OBAL Fr. Devil's Dictionary, The.

Lead & zinc company, The. Holes Commence Falling. David Huddle. PBCAP

Lead disc composed of black stuff for marking, A. Damocharis of Kos. GrAn

Lead gently, Lord, and slow. Hymn, A. Paul Laurence Dunbar. SacPr

Lead, Kindly Light, amid the encircling gloom.   Pillar of the Cloud, The.   John Henry, Cardinal Newman.   ChIV-1; InvLi; NPeEn; SacPr

Lead me away with my eyes blindfolded.   From "The Blue Notebook" No. 12.   Daniil Kharms.   TCRP, tr. by Bradley Jordan

Lead me home. (LL)   Take My Hand, Precious Lord.   Thomas A. Dorsey.   APT-2; ISC

Lead me, Sicilian Maids, to haunted bowers.   Her Confirmed Despair.   Mary Robinson.   CenSon; RWP

Lead my pony.   Basho.   SoOfWa, tr. by Sam Hamill

Lead On, O King Eternal.   Ernest W. Shurtleff.   AH

Lead the black bull to slaughter, with the boar.   Upon Master Walter Montagu's Return from Travel.   Thomas Carew.   CaPo

Lead us, Evolution, lead us.   Evolutionary Hymn.   Clive Staples Lewis.   NOBL

Lead Us, O Father, in the Paths of Peace.   William Henry Burleigh.   AH

Leadbelly.   Cornelius Eady.   ESEAA

Leadbelly Gives an Autograph.   Imamu Amiri Baraka.   PmAP

Leaden Echo and the Golden Echo, The.   Gerard Manley Hopkins.   GTBS-P; MoBrPo; NOBVV; OBMV

Leaden-eyed, the.   Nicholas Vachel Lindsay.   FaBoEE; OxBSP; PoE; RB; TCAPo

Leaden eyelids of wan twilight close, The.   George Henry Boker.   APN-2   Fr. Sonnets: A Sequence on Profane Love.

Leader.   Bruce Bennett.   InPK-6

Leader, The.   J. P. Clark Bekederemo.   PBMAP

Leader, The.   Dorothy Livesay.   MoCV

Leader, The.   Roger McGough.   OPOU

Leader, The.   Yunna Petrovna [or Iunna Pinkhusovna] Moritz [or Morits].   TCRusP, tr. by Daniel Weissbort

Leaders of the Crowd, The.   W. B. Yeats.   EBEV; MoBrPo; OxAEP-2

Leading him in.   Alexis Rotella.   HA

Leading liot act to foriage is activity.   On Autumn Lake.   John Ashbery.   LCAP-2

Leading to the underworld. (LL)   Tu Do Street.   Yusef Komunyakaa.   LTA; SwNoth

Leaf.   Cathy Song.   ExTi

Leaf, A.   Ludwig Uhland.   AWP, tr. by John S. Dwight

Leaf falls softly at my feet, A.   Leaf, A.   Ludwig Uhland.   AWP, tr. by John S. Dwight

Leaf floats in endless space, A.   Seeking a Mooring.   Wang Wei.   BoWoP; WPOW

Leaf for Hand in Hand, A.   Walt Whitman.   APN-1

Leaf from freedom's golden chaplet fair, A.   To My Father.   Henrietta Cordelia Ray.   BlSi; CBWP-3; Son

Leaf from the Devil's Jest-Book, A.   Edwin Markham.   APN-2

Leaf knows sorrow in this time of thorns, The.   Anglo-American Chainpoem.   Unknown.   SPE

Leaf of a light boat, A.   Tune: "Joy of Eternal Union"—Passing the Seven-league Shallows.   Su Tung-p'o (Su Shih).   SuSp, tr. by Irving Y. Lo

Leaf / Of the yam.   Kikaku.   ZenPo, tr. by Takashi Ikemoto and Lucien Stryk

Leaf-picking, The.   Frédéric Mistral.   AWP, tr. by Harriet Waters Preston

Leaf this boat, its light sail rolled, A.   Tune: "Prelude to Allure Goddesses."   Liu Yung.   SuSp, tr. by Jerome P. Seaton

Leaf-Treader, A.   Robert Frost.   MoAmPo

Leaf, treeless, A.   Paul Celan.   PoSu

Leaf, Treeless for Bertolt Brecht, A.   Paul Celan.   AF, tr. by Michael Hamburger

Leaf will wrinkle to decay, The.   Crest Jewel, The.   James Stephens.   MoBrPo

Leafage of years is brown, your hair is not brown, The. (LL)   Your Hand Full of Hours.   Paul Celan.   OBVE; PoetW, tr. by Michael Hamburger

Leafbud straggles forth, The.   Upper Broadway.   Adrienne Rich.   HCAP; ItWoWo

Leaf[e] gold, Lord of thy golden wedge o'erlaid.   Edward Taylor.   NAAL-2v1; NAAL-3; NAAL-5   Fr. Preparatory Meditations before My Approach to the Lord's Supper.

Leafless are the trees; their purple branches.   Golden Mile-Stone, The.   Henry Wadsworth Longfellow.   NCAP

Leafless buoyancy.   Sukhanovo.   Natalya [or Natal'ia] Gorbanevskaya [or Gorbanyevskaya or Gorbanevskaia].   AF, tr. by Daniel Weissbort

Leafshade stirring on lichened bark.   Culture and Anarchy.   Adrienne Rich.   NALW

Leafy the boughs—they also hide big fruit. (LL)   Do Not Expect Again a Phoenix Hour.   Cecil Day Lewis.   FaBoMo; MoBrPo; NoAM; OxBTC; PoRA

Leafy-with-love banks and the green waters of the canal.   Canal Bank Walk.   Patrick Kavanagh.   CIP-2; FaBoTw; MoBrPo; NoAM; NoP-4

Leaguered in fire.   Autumn Sunset, An.   Edith Wharton.   APN-2

Leah.   Ruth Gilbert.
   Jacob.   PeNZ

Leak in the Dike, The.   Phoebe Cary.   ITBLP

Leaking Roof.   Gahlia Gwangwa'a.   NAfrP

Leaks on the Chinese carpet. (LL)   Alligator Bride, The.   Donald Hall.   CoAmPo; SPE

Lean Gaius, Who Was Thinner than a Straw.   Lucilius.   GrAn; OBVE; WoPoe, tr. by Peter Porter

Lean is the ghost of Molly Means. (LL)   Molly Means.   Margaret Abigail Walker.   BlSi; NALW

Lean Street.   George Sutherland Fraser.   OxBS

Lean-to of tin.   Robert Spiess.   HA

Lean way out, y'all said.   Y'All Are Bird Dogs, Aren't You?   Mark Richard.   Unle

Leander's Return.   Christopher Marlowe.   EBNV   Fr. Hero and Leander.

Leander Stormbound.   Sydney Goodsir Smith.   OxBS

Leane, The.   William Barnes.   EBVV

Leaning against the golden undertow.   Kenneth Slessor.   CBAP   Fr. Out of Time.

Leaning against the—Sun. (LL)   I Taste a Liquor Never Brewed.   Emily Dickinson.   APN-2; HeIP-4; ITBLP; MoAmPo; NAAL-2v1; NAAL-3; NOBA; NoAM; OxBA; SoSe-8; TAP; TCAPo; TFi; WPE

Leaning all by himself.   Dry Tree.   Muso Soseki.   EaWin, tr. by W. S. Merwin

Leaning into the afternoons I cast my sad nets.   Leaning into the Afternoons.   Pablo Neruda.   TCLAP, tr. by W. S. Merwin

Leaning into the handlebars.   Man in Novosibirsk.   H. L. Hix.   SpudSo

Leaning into you now, my dark head.   Retired Greyhound, II.   Natalie Kusz.   Unle

Leaning on a lamp.   Leaning on a Lamppost.   Noel Gay.   ReLy

Leaning / on the parapet.   My Father Spoke with Swans.   Patrick Galvin.   BiHa

Leaning over the wall at Trafalgar Square.   Cosmos in London.   Arthur Nortje.   HBAPE; PeSAV

Leans listening on the gate, in all respect. (LL)   Middle of the World.   D. H. Lawrence.   HAP; NoAM; WoPoe

Leap, The.   James Dickey.   NIL-7; NIP-4

Leap before You Look.   W. H. Auden.   NoAM

Leap-Centuries.   Paul Celan.   OBVE, tr. by Michael Hamburger

Leap in the Dark.   Roberta Hill Whiteman.   WPOW

Leap into the light, ye living Forms!   Cornelius Mathews.   APN-1   Fr. Poems on Man in His Various Aspects under the American Republic.

Leap of the salmon, The.   Shannon Estuary Welcoming the Fish, The.   Nuala Ni Dhomhnaill.   CIP-2, tr. by the author

Leap out, chill water, over reeds and brakes.   River God, The.   Sacheverell Sitwell.   MoBrPo

Leap, plashless as they swim. (LL)   Emily Dickinson.   APN-2; AmFaPo; ColAP; HeIP-4; ITBLP; MoAmPo; NAAL-2v1; NAAL-3; NAAL-5; NAWM-7v2; NCAP; NOBA; NTCP; NoAM; NoP-4; OBAL; OBCA; OxBA; PoRA; SAmP; TFi

Leap then, down on the line that draws to the earth's deep, heavy center. (LL)   Kangaroo.   D. H. Lawrence.   EBEV; OxBTC

Leap Yeah Party, De.   Maggie Pogue Johnson.   CBWP-4

Leap Year.   Charles North.   FTOS

Leaped at the caribou.   Ho Ho Ho Caribou.   Joseph Ceravolo.   PmAP

Leaping Fire, The.   John Montague.
   Little Flower's Disciple, The.   CIP-2

Leaping from the eucalyptus branch, the wild desert pigs.   Border, The.   Joanna Rawson.   AmPoNex

Leaping into the Gulf.   Patricia Beer.   OxBC

Leaping Laughers, The.   George Barker.   OBMV

Leaping trout sees, The.   Onitsura.   SoOfWa, tr. by Sam Hamill

Lear.   William Carlos Williams.   NAAL-2v2; NAAL-5; NOBA

Learn, flowers, from me, what parts we play.   Luis de Góngora y Argote.   SpanPo; WoPoe, tr. by Roy Campbell   Fr. Spectre of the Rose, The.

Learn from me, Son of Kunti! also this.   Unknown.   TOF   Fr. Bhagavad-Gita, The.

Learn, lads and lasses, of my garden.   Francis Daniel Pastorius.   SCAP

Learn now, dear Prince! how, if thy soul be set.   Unknown.   TAL   Fr. Bhagavad-Gita, The.

Learn the rhythm which binds all men. (LL)   Archilochus.   AmFaPo; PGA, tr. by Kenneth Rexroth

Learn. The winter trees.   Winter Trees.   Ágnes Nemes Nagy.   IQMS, tr. by Hugh Maxton

Learn to conform the order of our lives. (LL)   William Cullen Bryant.   APN-1; TAP

Learn to Count.   Unknown.   NAAAL

Learn to labor and to wait. (LL)   Henry Wadsworth Longfellow.   APN-1; AmFaPo; BRP; ITBLP; NAAL-2v1; NAAL-3; NAAL-5; OBCA; PWR; TAP; TCAPo

Learn to live, and live and learn.   Saturday Review, The.   Dora Greenwell.   EBVV

Learn to mak your bed, Annie. Fair Annie. *Unknown.* OxBB

Learn to speak this little word. No! Eliza Cook. PoToHe

Learn to wait—life's hardest lesson. Learn to Wait. *Unknown.* PoToHe

Learn women all from this housewifery. Sir Richard Fanshawe. OBVE *Fr.* Il Pastor Fido.

Learned and a happy ignorance, A. Eden. Thomas Traherne. ChIV-1; ESCV; GeHe

Learned, full of inward pride, The. Two Monkeys, The. John Gay. OBCoV

Learned Man [Came to Me Once], A. Stephen Crane. MoAmPo *Fr.* Black Riders [and Other Lines], The.

Learned Mistress, A. *Unknown.* OBMV, *tr. by* Frank O'Connor

Learned Wife, The. Juvenal. BASC, *tr. by* John Dryden *Fr.* Satires.

Learning. Michael Casey. YaYoPo

Learning. Tiruvalluvar. WoPoe, *tr. by* Emmons E. White *Fr.* Kural, The.

Learning by Doing. Howard Nemerov. HAP; TwCP; WeW-3

Learning Experience. Marge Piercy. NoAM

Learning from the Movies. Rachel Wetzsteon. ExTi

Learning from the tale of Admetos, my friend, love the brave. Praxilla. SaLy, *tr. by* Diane Rayor

Learning ("So Learned Men in Controversies Spend"). George Chapman. NOSC *Fr.* Euthymiae Raptus; or, The Teares of Peace.

Learning the Language. Brewster Ghiselin. APT-2

Learning the Spells; a Diptych. Anita Endrezze. CDW

Learning the Trees. Howard Nemerov. VCAP

Learning the War. Wendy Wilder Larsen. OPRER

Learning to Count. Sara Berkeley. BiHa

Learning to Laugh. Allison Joseph. PasH

Learning to Live with the Piano. Ann Lundberg Grunke. MiVo

Learning to Love America. Shirley Lim. GeoHom

Learning to love differently is hard. To Have without Holding. Marge Piercy. NIL-7; NIP-4

Learning to Read. Frances Ellen Watkins Harper. BlSi; NAAAL; NALW

Learning to Smile. Art Goodtimes. GeoH

Learning to Speak. Peter Everwine. NNaP

Learning to Swim. Arlene Naganawa. FSt

Learning to Swim at Forty-Five. Colleen J. McElroy. GT

Learning to Walk Alone. Judith Ortiz Cofer. PueRic

Learning to Write. Audre Lorde. GT

Learning Window. James Longenbach. NAPBL

Learnng the Ropes. Custer Street. Evanston, 1949. Lisa Ress. GotH

Leasowes: Or, A Poetical Description of the Late Mr. Shenstone's Rural Retirement, The. Joseph Giles.
"Here circling trees, which form a shade." OBGa

Least, the meanest, The. Least, The. Roy Fisher. HarvBoo

Least the world, flesh[e], yea Devil[l] put[t] thee out. (LL) John Donne. BASC; FSCP; NAEL-5v1; NAEL-6v1; NAEL-7v1; NOSC; PBRV; Son *Fr.* Holy Sonnets.

Leather-black waters. (LL) Philip Larkin. NPeEn; RB *Fr.* Livings.

Leather: I travel by foot, trample the ground. Cynewulf. ASW *Fr.* Riddles (Exeter Book).

Leave, A. Gertrude Stein. PFTM-1

Leave go my hands, let me catch breath and see. In the Orchard. Algernon Charles Swinburne. BoLoP

Leave Helen to her lover. Draw away. White Isle of Leuce, The. Sir Herbert Read. FaBoTw

Leave him alone, sweet enemy. Lonely Traveller, The. Kwesi Brew. PBA; TTY

Leave him: he's quiet enough: and what matter. Here Lies a Prisoner. Charlotte Mew. MoBrPo

Leave in Mid-Winter. John Short. FaBoWar

Leave It to Me Blues. Joel Oppenheimer. VGW

Leave Krete and come to this holy temple. Sappho. BoWoP

Leave, leave, thy gadding thoughts. Henry Vaughan. SacPr *Fr.* Search, The.

Leave me, all sweet refrains my lip hath made. Sonnet. Luis de Camões [or Camõens]. AWP, *tr. by* Richard Garnett

Leave me alone! my mirth would make you weep. (LL) Solo. Mary Elizabeth Coleridge. VWP; ViWPN

Leave me alone! my tears would make you laugh. Solo. Mary Elizabeth Coleridge. VWP; ViWPN

Leave me but love and sherry. (LL) Loose Saraband, A. Richard Lovelace. BeJo; CaPo

Leave me, love, and never come back. Love Turned the Light Out. John Latouche. ReLy

Leave me, my love, it's time to part. Farewell. Ibrahim Naji. MAP, *tr. by* Issa Boullata and John Heath-Stubbs

Leave Me O Love. Sir Philip Sidney. AEP; GSo; HeIP-4; NIP-4; NOBE; NPeEn; OxAEP-1; PoE; SacPr; Son; TFi

Leave me: oh! leave me. Dying. Adah Isaacs Menken. CBWP-1

Leave me to the night. Voice, A. Lina Tibi. PoArWo, *tr. by* Subhi Hadidi and Nathalie Handal

Leave my tomb. Employ your pick. Saint Gregory of Nazianzus. GrAn

Leave off, good Beroe, now. To an Old Gentlewoman That Painted Her Face. George Turberville. OxBSP

Leave-Taking. Frank Gelett Burgess. OBCoV

Leave-Taking, A. Arno Holz. AWP, *tr. by* Jethro Bithell

Leave-taking, A. Algernon Charles Swinburne. NOBE; NOBVV; OxBEV

Leave the bars lying in the grass. Fall. Robert Francis. VGW

Leave the rags, you tiny lusts. Asclepiades. GrAn

Leave the window open. Death Song. *Unknown.* BoWoP, *tr. by* Reza Baraheni and Zahra-Soltan Shokoohtaezeh

Leave the Word Alone. Edward Marshall. NeAP

Leave Them Alone. Patrick Kavanagh. OxBSP

Leave them to the *black* folks! (LL) Hiccups. Léon Damas. NegPo; PFTM-1, *tr. by* Ellen Conroy Kennedy

Leave thine own home, O youth, seek distant shores! Encouragement to Exile. Petronius Arbiter. AWP, *tr. by* Howard Mumford Jones

Leave this gaudy gilded stage. Song. John Wilmot, 2d Earl of Rochester. OxBSP

Leave what is white for whiter use. Stone for A Statue. Sarah Morgan Bryan Piatt. NCAP

Leave what you die for and be safe to die. (LL) Teasers, The. William Empson. HarvBoo; OxBTC

Leaves. Frank Asch. NTCP

Leaves. Countee Cullen. GT

Leaves. William Henry Davies. MoBrPo

Leaves. "Michael Field." VWP

Leaves. Sam Hamod. GraLe; UnSA

Leaves. Ted Hughes. OxBC

Leaves. Frederic Manning. NOBAu

Leaves. Lloyd Schwartz. UrbNat

Leaves a-Vallen. William Barnes. NOBVV; NPeEn

Leaves and flowers are never rated the same. For Lotus Flower. Li Shang-yin. SuSp, *tr. by* Eugene Eoyang

Leaves are fading and falling, The. November. Alice Cary. OBCA

Leaves are sere, The. November. Henrietta Cordelia Ray. CBWP-3

Leaves are storm-rattled jester's bells, The. King Lear Bewildered. Patricia Storace. FFC

Leaves blowing into a sentence. Bob Boldman. HA

Leaves Come Again, The. Henry Vaughan. FaBoEE

Leaves Compared with Flowers. Robert Frost. NOBA

Leaves fall, fall as if from far away, The. Autumn. Rainer Maria Rilke. TrJP, *tr. by* C. F. MacIntyre

Leaves fall, slanting sun lights the river. Tune: Palace of Night Revels. Chou Pang-yen. CoBCP, *tr. by* Burton Watson

Leaves fall turning to the ground. Han Yü. CoBCP; WoPoe, *tr. by* Burton Watson *Fr.* Autumn Thoughts.

Leaves floated down picturesquely, The. Words. "David Samuilovich Samoylov" [*or* "Samoilov"]. TCRP, *tr. by* Lubov Yakovleva

Leaves from eternity are simple things. Eternity of Nature, The. John Clare. EBEV

Leaves have a sense of, The. Elegy. Lewis Warsh. BodElec

Leaves have their time to fall. Hour of Death, The. Felicia Dorothea Hemans. NOBRP

Leaves her all wild, sad, weeping, and forlorn. (LL) Morning, Rosamonde. Anne Batten Cristall. ECWP; RWP

Leaves like Fish. Gladys Cardiff. CDW

Leaves looked in at the window, The. House across the Way, The. Ralph Hodgson. FaBoTw

Leaves moil in the yard. Clement Hoyt. HA

Leaves / Murmuring by myriads in the shimmering trees. From My Diary, July 1914. Wilfred Owen. FaBoMo; MoBrPo

Leaves must be green in Spring. (LL) Malvern Hill. Herman Melville. APN-2; CBCWP; ColAP; TAP

Leaves never fall. Chori. JDP, *tr. by* Yoel Hoffmann

Leaves of a Dream Are the Leaves of an Onion, The. Arthur Sze. OpBo

Leaves of Grass (1855). Walt Whitman. *See* Boston Ballad [1854], A

Leaves of Grass (1855). Walt Whitman. *See* Europe, the 72d and 73d Year of These States

Leaves of Grass (1855). Walt Whitman. APN-1

Leaves of Grass (1855). Walt Whitman. *See* Song of Myself

Leaves of Grass (1855). Walt Whitman. *See* Song for Occupations, A

Leaves of Heaven, The. Edward Sanders. RaBo

Leaves of Hypnos. René Char.
"Poet, conserver of the infinite faces of the living, The." PFTM-1

Leaves of Hypnos No. 128. René Char. AF, *tr. by* Cid Corman

Leaves of words. Jomei. JDP, *tr. by* Yoel Hoffmann

Leaves should be lush and the petals frail, The. (LL) Tune: "As in a Dream; a Song." Li Ch'ing-chao. BoWoP; SuSp, *tr.* by Eugene Eoyang

Leaves some trout. Buson. EH, *tr.* by Robert Hass

Leaves, that whisper, whisper ever. Rosabel. Angelina Weld Grimké. PoBW

Leaves though thick are falling; one by one, The. Autumn Leaves. Jones Very. APN-1

Leaves were already on the trees, the fruit blossoms, The. With Janice. Kenneth Koch. PmAP

Leaves will fall again sometime and fill, The. Sunday Morning Apples. Hart Crane. HarvBoo

Leaves without Trees. Yehuda Amichai [or Amikhai]. MHP, *tr.* by Ruth Finer Mintz

Leavetaking. Gunnar Ekelof. PFTM-2, *tr.* by Muriel Rukeyser and Leif Sjöberg *Fr.* Mölna Elegy.

Leavetaking. Veronica Rospigliosi. Prnts

Leaving. Rae Armantrout. FTOS

Leaving. Pamela Brown. BMAP

Leaving. T. Crunk. YaYoPo

Leaving. Tiziano Rossi. ItPo, *tr.* by Gayle Ridinger

Leaving. Cathy Song. NoAM

Leaving. Richard Wilbur. HarvBoo

Leaving, The. Brigit Pegeen Kelly. IllVoic; YaYoPo

Leaving a world too old to name. For Fawzi in Jerusalem. Samuel Hazo. GraLe

Leaving again in rags. (LL) George Oppen. APSN; NNaP *Fr.* Some San Francisco Poems.

Leaving all his wisdom standing. Hots, The. Michael Sharkey. NOBAu

Leaving all the morning glories closed. Elizabeth Searle Lamb. HA

Leaving Barra. Louis MacNeice. EBEV

Leaving behind for ever the thundering Aegean. Plato. GrAn *Fr.* Two Poems on the Eretrians Taken Prisoner by the Persians.

Leaving behind us the alien, foreign city of Dublin. Going Home to Mayo, Winter, 1949. Paul Durcan. CIP-2; PBCIP

Leaving Ch'in-chou. Tu Fu. CrYelRi, *tr.* by Sam Hamill

Leaving Crete, come visit again our temple. Sappho. STV; WeW-3

Leaving Eden. Nadya Aisenberg. OPRER

Leaving Eden. Ralph Dickey. ESEAA

Leaving for the Front. Alfred Lichtenstein. PeFWW, *tr.* by Patrick Bridgwater

Leaving Forever. Denise Levertov. InPK-6

Leaving Government Offices. Tu Fu. CrYelRi, *tr.* by Sam Hamill

Leaving Home. Sarah Rosenblatt. AmPoNex

Leaving Mother, 1954. John Graham-Pole. BloBone

Leaving my footprints. From My Hut in Miura. Muso Soseki. EaWin, *tr.* by W. S. Merwin

Leaving my house in the morning. Mikhail Alekseievich Kuzmin. CAGL, *tr.* by Michael Green

Leaving my loneliness inside her. George Swede. HA

Leaving Port Authority for the St. Regis Rezz. Wendy Rose. HATNAP

Leaving Rattle Bar. Clark Coolidge. FTOS

Leaving San Francisco. Marilyn Chin. GeoHom

Leaving Something Behind. David Wagoner. CoAP

Leaving Syracuse. Al Young. ESEAA

Leaving the Atocha Station. John Ashbery. PmAP

Leaving the audience by the quiet corridors. Tu Fu. CarOv, *tr.* by Carolyn Kizer *Fr.* Adviser to the Court.

Leaving the Boys Behind. Rufinus. GrAn, *tr.* by Alan Marshfield

Leaving the City. Liu K'o-chuang. CoBCP, *tr.* by Burton Watson

Leaving the city where new houses, new inhabitants, / and the newly rich reign. Seven Beginnings. Olesya [or Olesia] Nikolayeva [or Nikolaeva]. TCRP, *tr.* by Vera Dunham

Leaving the Country. Wyn Cooper. OPRER

Leaving the door of the whitewashed house ajar. Couple Waiting, A. Matthew Sweeney. BiHa

Leaving the Monastery Early in the Morning. Lu Yu. OHPC, *tr.* by Kenneth Rexroth

Leaving the Motel. W. D. Snodgrass. NIL-7; NIP-4

Leaving the Old Gods. Janet McAdams. OPRER

Leaving the [streams] of Ocean. Korinna [or Corinna]. SaLy, *tr.* by Diane Rayor

Leaving the Village. *Vietnamese Oral Tradition.* CaDao, *tr.* by John Balaban

Leaving the white glow of filling stations. Strand at Lough Beg, The. Seamus Heaney. CIP-2; NPeEn; NoAM; OBWP

Leaving thine outgrown shell by life's unresting sea! (LL) Oliver Wendell Holmes. APN-1; ColAP; ITBLP; NAAL-3; NCAP; NOBA; NoP-4; TCAPo; TFi *Fr.* Autocrat of the Breakfast Table, The.

Leaving West Archery Hall at Dusk. Hsieh Ling-yün. SuSp, *tr.* by Francis Westbrook

Leaving You. Lily Brett. HP

Leaving you. Courtesy, a Trenchant Grace, A. Cyrus Cassells. GT; WiU

Leaving Yuba City. Chitra Divakaruni. GeoHom

Lebanon. Frank O'Hara. CAGL

Lebanon, land of our birth and hopefully of our dying. Eugene Paul Nasser. GraLe *Fr.* East Utica.

Lebensraum. Thom Gunn. PAI

Lecherous young Lilliputian, A. Limerick. C. Vita-Finzi. PeLi

Lecture #1. Brenda Coultas. HeMarv

Lecture Hall. Patrick Kavanagh. FaBoTw

Lecture on Nothing. John Cage. FTOS; PFTM-2

Lecture upon the Shadow, A. John Donne. AWP; ESCV; NAEL-5v1; NAEL-6v1; NAEL-7v1; NoSic; SCGP; UnPo

Lectured by Pa and Ma o'er night. Lady's Diary, The. Charles Dibdin. NOEC

Lecturer's impartial prose, The. James Keir Baxter. PeLV *Fr.* Cressida.

Lectures on Love, The. Edward Hirsch. PuP-23

Led by a blind and teachit by a bairn. (LL) Fra Bank to Bank, Fra Wood to Wood I Rin. Mark Alexander Boyd. OxBEV; Son

Led by the pow'r [or powre] of grief[e], to wailings [or waylings] brought. Mary Sidney Wroth, Countess of Montgomery. PEW *Fr.* Pamphilia to Amphilanthus.

Leda. "Rubén Dario." SpanPo, *tr.* by Doreen Bell

Leda. "H. D." NAAL-2v2

Leda. Rainer Maria Rilke. RaBo, *tr.* by Robert Bly

Leda and the Swan. Oliver St. John Gogarty. EBNV; HAP

Leda and the Swan. W. B. Yeats. CABP; ClHu; EBEV; EroLit; GSo; GTBS-P; HAP; HarvBoo; HeIP-4; InPK-6; MoBrPo; NAEL-5v2; NAEL-6v2; NAWM-7v2; NIL-7; NIP-4; NOBE; NPeEn; NoAM; NoP-4; OWoS; OxAEP-2; OxBEV; OxBSo; PAI; PoE; PoPoPo; SCV; SoSe-8; Son; TFi; TRP; WeW-3

Leda in Stratford, Ont. Anne Wilkinson. MoCV

Leda's Sister and the Geese. Katharyn Machan Aal. SoSe-8

Leda's Version. James [or Jim] Harrison. NIP-4

Lede guiterriste was a craftie ladde, The. Probatioun Officeres Tale, The. Gerard Benson. NBLV

Lee in the Mountains. Donald Davidson. CBCWP; FuPo

Lee Morgan. David Henderson. SeSe

Lee's Lunch / Spaghetti. Brilliant Sad Sun. William Carlos Williams. HarvBoo

Lee to the Rear. John Randolph Thompson. CBCWP

Leesome Brand. *Unknown.* ESPB

Leeward of the house is nothing but the tip. Lilacs. David Biespiel. AmPoNex

Leezie Lindsay. *Unknown.* FaBoCh

Left All Alone Again Blues. Anne Caldwell. ReLy

Left Bank Jazz Society, The. Michael S. Weaver. UnSA

Left but this. (LL) Victims, The. Sharon Olds. NIL-7; SoSe-8

Left by his friend to breakfast alone on the white. Edward Lear. W. H. Auden. OxAEP-2; OxBSo

Left Eye of Odin, The. Regina DeCormier-Shekejian. TWW

Left for us to assume what purpose. Skiddaw House. David Scott. NLP

Left hand leading a yellow hound. Tune: "A Riverside Town." Su Tung-p'o (Su Shih). ColAnChi, *tr.* by Jiaosheng Wang

Left her / beneath. (LL) Death Camp. Irena Klepfisz. GLP; TaR

Left in the field / among big-bellied ewes. Naayawva Taawi. Wendy Rose. UnSA

Left leg flung out, head cocked to the right. Poet. Karl Shapiro. MoAmPo; NoAM

Left like an unknown's breath on mirrors. Lawrence Durrell. MoBrPo *Fr.* Eight Aspects of Melissa.

Left on the beach. Akiko Yosano. OHMPJ

Left Rites. Hylda Sims. Prnts

Left side of her world is gone, The. Strokes. William Stafford. CoAmPo

Left the Old Year lost to all. (LL) Old Year, The. John Clare. NOBVV; OBCP

Left to the wind. Alexis Rotella. HA

Left-wing young lady from Wick, A. Limerick. Gerry Hamill. PeLi

Leftover Blessings. Julia Kasdorf. PBCAP

Leg, The. Karl Shapiro. HAP; MoAmPo; UnPo; WeW-3

Leg in a Plaster Cast, A. Muriel Rukeyser. MoAmPo

Leg over leg. Mother Goose. LB; OxNR; ReMoGo

Legacies. Emily Grosholz. FFC

Legacies. Léon Laleau. NegPo, *tr.* by Ellen Conroy Kennedy *Fr.* Black Music.

Legacies. Heberto Padilla. TCLAP, *tr.* by Andrew Hurley and Alastair Reid

Legacy. Imamu Amiri Baraka. ColAP; NOBA; NoAM

Legacy. Siobhan Campbell. MFPA

Legacy. Maurice Kenny. HATNAP

Legacy. Joan Larkin. WiU

Legacy. Stephanie Sugioka. FSt

Legacy, The. Bible, *O.T.* TrJP *Fr.* Proverbs.

Legacy, The. Heinrich von Morungen. GePo, *tr. by* F. C. Nicholson

Legacy of a Brother. Renaldo Fernandez. NBV

Legal Fiction. William Empson. FaBoMo; HarvBoo; NoAM; NoP-4

Legal Mouse, A. Lizelia Augusta Jenkins Moorer. CBWP-3

Legend. W. H. Auden. CAGL

Legend. Charles Causley. TOF

Legend. Hart Crane. OxBA

Legend. Anne Ethuin. SurWo, *tr. by* Guy Ducornet

Legend. Louise Glück. TaR

Legend. Judith Wright. NOBAu; RB

Legend, A. Adelaide Anne Procter. SacPr

Legend, The. Garrett Kaoru Hongo. LoL; MakPoe; OpBo; TRP

Legend is whispered, The. Shapeshifter Poems. Lucille Clifton. BodElec; LoL

Legend lives on from the Chippewa on down, The. Wreck of the Edmund Fitzgerald, The. Gordon Lightfoot. NoP-4

Legend of Britomartis, or of Chastitie, The. Edmund Spenser. NAEL-5v1; NAEL-6v1; NAEL-7v1 *Fr.* Faerie Queene, The.

Legend of Captain Jones, The. David Lloyd.
("Roses and tulips Flora gathers here.") AngWePo

Legend of Good Women, The. Geoffrey Chaucer.
"And as for me, though that I konne [*or* can] but [*or* my wit be] lyte." HeIP-4

Balade: "Hide [*or* Hyd], Absalon, thy gilte tresses clere." AWP; EBEV; HAP; NOBE; OBEV; SCGP

Ballade: "Hide, Absalom, thy gilte tresses clear." WoPoe, *tr. by* Burton Raffel and Selden Rodman

Legend of Hell, The. C. D. Wright. LCAP-2

Legend of Home, The. Lawson Fusao Inada. GeoHom *Fr.* Legends from Camp.

Legend of Lilja. Sarah Kirsch. AF, *tr. by* Wayne Kvam

Legend of Provence, A. Adelaide Anne Procter. VWP

Legend of the Albino Farm. Erin Belieu. NeAmPo

Legend of the Crossing-Sweeper. May Kendall. VWP

Legend of the Hive, A. Robert Stephen Hawker. EBVV

Legend of the Knight of the Red Crosse, or of Holinesse, The. Edmund Spenser. FHYEP; NAEL-5v1; NAEL-7v1 *Fr.* Faerie Queene, The.

Legend of the Northland, A. Phoebe Cary. OBCA; OBSP

Legend of Versailles, A. Melvin B. Tolson. BPo; NAAAL

Legendary. James McAuley. BMAP

Legendary, as prophesied. (LL) Back on Times Square, Dreaming of Times Square. Allen Ginsberg. CLPP; PoE

Legendary life of a long-ago tribe, The. Dirge for a Hidden Art. Mary Duroux. IBA

Legendary muscle that wants and grieves, The. Hearts, The. Robert Pinsky. VCAP

Legends from Camp. Lawson Fusao Inada.
"F.B.I. swooped in early, The." GeoHom
"It began as truth, as fact." GeoHom
Legend of Home, The. GeoHom

Legion Club, The. Jonathan Swift.
"As I strole the city, oft I." BIrV

Legion hall in Atherton contains, The. By-Products. Baron Wormser. ReTh

"Legion" to "Lent" for "R." Tina Darragh. FTOS

Legree's big house was white and green. Nicholas Vachel Lindsay. TAP *Fr.* Booker Washington Trilogy, The.

Legs, The. Robert Graves. PeLV; RB

Legs of the elk punctured the snow's crust, The. To Christ Our Lord. Galway Kinnell. HeIP-4; TwCP

Lehayyim, my brethren, Lehayyim, I say. Simhat Torah. Judah Leib Gordon. TrJP, *tr. by* Helena Frank and Alice Lucas

Lehmann does well with Largactil. Laprairie Hunger Strike. Ronald G. Everson. MoCV

Leiden Manuscript, The. *Unknown.*
Wise Rejoice with Ganymede, The. CAGL, *tr. by* John Boswell

Leisure. William Henry Davies. AWP; AngWePo; MoBrPo; NOBE; OBEV; OBMV; PoRA; TFi

Leisurely Stroll, A. Hsü Pen.
"Mountain of green trees and orioles everywhere!" CoBLCP

Leisurely talk in low voices. Tune: "*Wu-t'ung* Leaves"—Written in Jest at a Banquet. Lu Chih. SuSp, *tr. by* Hellmut Wilhelm

Leith police dismisseth us, The. *Unknown.* OxNR

Leith Races. Robert Fergusson.
My Winsome Dear. VGW

L. E. L. Christina Georgina Rossetti. VWP

Lela's Charms. Lizelia Augusta Jenkins Moorer. CBWP-3

"Lem" cuts a figure eight around "le ma" and "le me." "Legion" to "Lent" for "R." Tina Darragh. FTOS

Lemme be wid Casey Jones. Odyssey of Big Boy. Sterling Allen Brown. NAAAL

Lemmings die every year. Over the cliff. Lemmings. Patricia Beer. CABP

Lemon and Rosemary. Veronica Forrest-Thomson. Oth

Lemon, Hot Water and a Blood Clot. Dacia Maraini. CItWP, *tr. by* Cinzia Sartini Blum and Lara Trubowitz

Lemon-house was being over-, The. In the Greenhouse. Eugenio Montale. PoetW, *tr. by* Jonathan Galassi

Lemon Pie. Edgar Albert Guest. OBAL

Lemon rind rubbed on the rim. Espresso. Carol Lee Saffoti. UnSA

Lemon Trees, The. Eugenio Montale. PoetW; WoPoe, *tr. by* William Arrowsmith

Lemon Trees, The. Eugenio Montale. PFTM-1

Lemonade Stand. Myra Cohn Livingston. TLR

Lena Lovelace. Melvin B. Tolson. GT

Lenaia. Susan M. Whitmore. AmPoNex

Lend me a battle of unavoidable suggestions. Emilio Villa. ItPo, *tr. by* Gayle Ridinger *Fr.* Words.

Lend me, a little while, the key. Pedlar, The. Charlotte Mew. NOxBChV

Lend me cruel light. To an Angry God. X. J. Kennedy. CRP

Lend me your arm. Little Song of the Maimed. Benjamin Péret. OBWP; PeFWW, *tr. by* David Gascoyne

Lend me your precious toys. To W. S.—On His Wonderful Toys. Walter Davies. NOxBChV

Lend my thy mare to ride a mile. Money and the Mare. *Unknown.* ReMoGo

Length of Days. Horatius Bonar. PWR

Length of Life, The. Amos Russel Wells. PWR

Lengthening Days. *Unknown.* ReMoGo

Lenin. Nikolai Alekseievich Klyuev [*or* Kliuev *or* Klyuev].
"Lenin has the spirit of an Old Believer." TCRP

Lenin. Dorothy Wellesley, Duchess of Wellington.
"So I came down the steps to Lenin." OBMV

Leningrad. "Naum Korzhavin." TCRP, *tr. by* Albert C. Todd

Leningrad. Osip Emilevich Mandelstam [*or* Mandelshtam]. TCRusP, *tr. by* John Glad

Leningrad. Osip Emilevich Mandelstam [*or* Mandelshtam]. AF
(I returned to my city, familiar as tears.) TCRP, *tr. by* Bernard Meares

Leningrad Cemetery, Winter of 1941. Sharon Olds. NIL-7; NIP-4

Leningrad stairwell, A. Sergey Stratanovsky. ItGoST, *tr. by* J. Kates

Lennox Island. David McFadden. NOBC

Lenore. Edgar Allan Poe. APN-1; TCAPo

Lenox Avenue / by daylight. Dive. Langston Hughes. APT-2

Lenox Avenue Mural. Langston Hughes.
"Between two rivers, / North of the park." APT-2; HCAP
Comment on Curb. APSN; APT-2
(Dream Deferred.) InPK-6; SoSe-8
Good Morning. APSN; APT-2
Harlem. APSN; APT-2; AiP; GLP; GT; HCAP; HeIP-4; NAAAL; NoP-4; RaBo; SAmP; SSLK
(Harlem (A Dream Deferred).) NIL-7; NIP-4
Island. APT-2; HCAP
Letter. APT-2; PoE
Same in Blues. APSN; APT-2; SSLK

Lens. Anne Wilkinson. MoCV; NOBC

Lens of crystal whose transparence calms, A. Self-Portrait. Elinor Wylie. APT-1

Lent. William Robert Rodgers. ModIr; PNI

Lent in a Year of War. Thomas Merton. SPE

Lenten Is [*or* Ys] Come [with Love to Toune]. *Unknown.* HAP; MiEL
(Lenten is come with love to towne.) EBEV
(Lenten is comen wyth love to toun.) OHMEL
(Spring-Tide.) OBEV

Lentinus! thou dost nought but fume, and fret. Martial. OBVE

León. Ernesto Cardenal. TCLAP, *tr. by* Jonathan Cohen

Leon, A? No. Chippewa Love Song. *Unknown.* BoWoP, *tr. by* Frances Densmore

Leona, dear, twelve months ago. Eloise Bibb. CBWP-4

Leonard. Jeffrey McDaniel. AmPoNex

Leonardo's "Mona Lisa." Edward Dowden. GSo

Leonardo's Secret. Robert Bly. NNaP

Leopard in Eden, The. Gail White. FFC

Leopard Lives in a Muu Tree, A. Jonathan Kariara. PBMAP

Leopard Skin. Douglas Stewart. NOBAu

Lepanto. Gilbert Keith Chesterton. EBNV; FaBoWar; MoBrPo; OBMV; OBNV; RB

Leper, The. Algernon Charles Swinburne. NOBVV; OxBEV

Leper-House and the Impenitents, The. James Thomson. NePenScot *Fr.* Castle of Indolence, The.

Leper opens the hydrant, drinks water, A. Nowadays. Tushar Roy. WoPoe, *tr. by* Ron D. K. Banerjee

Lepers Cry. Peter Orlovsky. GLP

Lepidoptery. James Sherry. FTOS

Leron-leron sinta, umakyat sa papaya. When the Grain Is Golden and the Wind Is Chilly, Then It Is the Time to Harvest. Nick Carbó. NeAmPo

Leroy. Imamu Amiri Baraka. BPo; PmAP

Les Anges Sont Blancs. George Seferis. PFTM-1
  (Like a sailor in the ship's rigging he slid over the tropic of Cancer and the / tropic of Capricorn.) PFTM-1

Les Ballons. Oscar Wilde. NOBVV

Les Congés du Lépreux. Jean Bodel. WoPoe, *tr. by* Frank Templeton Prince

Les Demoiselles de Sauve. John Gray. NOBVV; PeVV

Les Estreines. Matthew Prior. OxBSP

Les Fils (Sons). Beverly Matherne. TWW

Les Grottes. Gillian Clarke. HarvBoo

Les Hiboux. Charles Baudelaire. AWP, *tr. by* Arthur Symons

Les Luths. Frank O'Hara. NOBA; NoAM

Les Manèges de la Mer (1964). Edouard J. Maunick.
  "Further off is the measured force the word of the sea." PBMAP
  "I love to encounter you in strange cities." PBMAP

Les Millwin. Ezra Pound. APT-1; OBCoV

Les Planches-en-Montagnes. Michael Roberts. OBMV

Les Racines Congolaises (1968). Jean-Baptiste Tati-Loutard.
  Noonday in Immaturity. PBMAP

Les Silhouettes. Oscar Wilde. EBVV *Fr.* Impressions.

Les Sylphides. Louis MacNeice. BoLoP *Fr.* Novelettes.

Lesbia. Catullus. EroLit, *tr. by* Peter Whigham

Lesbia. William Congreve. OxBSP

Lesbia, Caelius—yes, our darling. 58. Catullus. NAWM-7v1, *tr. by* Charles Martin

Lesbia hurls abuse at me in front of her husband. 83. Catullus. NAWM-7v1, *tr. by* Charles Martin

Lesbia, let us live only for loving. 5. Catullus. NAWM-7v1; WoPoe, *tr. by* Charles Martin

Lesbia / live with me. Catullus. EroLit *Fr.* Carmina.

Lesbia Railing. Catullus. AWP, *tr. by* Jonathan Swift *Fr.* Carmina.

Lesbia's sparrow! Catullus. EroLit, *tr. by* Peter Whigham

Lesbian Corn. Elaine Equi. IllVoic

Lesbian girl of Khartoum, A. Limerick. *Unknown.* NOBL; PeLV

Lesbian youths are all abroad today, The. Erinna's Spinning. Margaret Junkin Preston. SWaP

Lesbos. Lawrence Durrell. EBEV

Lesley Gore got her rival good. Answer Song. David Trinidad. WiU

Less and Less Human, O Savage Spirit. Wallace Stevens. BBASP; VGW

Less how to spell it. (LL) Surgery. Kenneth Pitchford. CAGL; GLP

Less Nonsense. Sir Alan Patrick Herbert. OxBTC

Less said about Edward's slut the better, The. Bliss. George Johnston. NOBC

Less said the better. Missing. John Pudney. OxBTC

Less than a golden one it cannot be. (LL) Abraham Cowley. NOSC; OxAEP-1 *Fr.* Sylva.

Less than total is a bucketful of radiant toys. (LL) Cut the Grass. A. R. Ammons. HAP; TAP; WeW-3

Less to improve her body than to trick. Winter Swim. Pimone Triplett. NAPBL

Less we paid, the more we climbed, The. Tendrils. Cheap Seats, the Cincinnati Gardens, Professional Basketball, 1959. William Matthews. MoASP

Less[e] loss[e] to let her go[e]. (LL) Robert Southwell. ChIV-2; NoSic

Lesser proof than old Voltaire's, yet greater, A. Orange Buds by Mail from Florida. Walt Whitman. NAAL-2v1; NAAL-3

Lesson. Barbara Winder. MiVo

Lesson, A. William Wordsworth. GTBS-P
  (Small Celandine, The.) NPeEn

Lesson, The. Miroslav Holub. PoSu, *tr. by* Ian Milner and Jarmila Milner

Lesson, The. Robert Lowell. LCAP-2

Lesson, The. Edward Lucie-Smith. OxBTC; TwCP

Lesson, The. Charles Simic. AF; HCAP

Lesson 3. Helmut Heissenbüttel. PFTM-2, *tr. by* Pierre Joris *Fr.* Textbook 10.

Lesson for Mamma, A. Sydney Dayre. OBCA

Lesson from a Sundial [Sun-Dial]. *Unknown.* Spl

Lesson from the Cockerel. Maggie O'Sullivan. Oth

Lesson in a Picture, A. Sarah Morgan Bryan Piatt. NCAP

Lesson in Anatomy, A. Liz Rosenberg. NIL-7

Lesson in Love, A. Philip Hobsbaum. OxBTC

Lesson in Natural History, A. Vyacheslav Kupriyanov [*or* Kuprianov]. TCRusP, *tr. by* Pamela Davidson

Lesson in Observation, A. Dan Pagis. AF, *tr. by* Stephen Mitchell

Lesson in Translation, A. Gabriel Preil. FIT, *tr. by* Robert Friend

Lesson of Night, A. Charles Ghigna. MiVo

Lesson of Silence, A. Tymoteusz Karpowicz. PoSu, *tr. by* Czeslaw Milosz

Lesson of the Sugarcane, The. Judith Ortiz Cofer. TouFir

Lesson of the Teeth, The. Judith Ortiz Cofer. TouFir

Lesson of the Water Mill, The. Sarah Doudney. PoToHe

Lesson on Braces. Valerie Jean. SpirFl

Lessons. Jan Barry. CDa

Lessons. Cleopatra Mathis.
  Given What Manages. ExTi

Lessons. Graham Thomas. AngWePo

Lessons from a Mirror. Thylias Moss. ESEAA; LTA

Lessons in History. Robert Penn Warren. BodElec

Lessons in Parsing. Rashid Husain [*or* Hussein]. MAP

Lessons of Nature, The. William Drummond, of Hawthornden. *See* Book, The

Lessons of the War. Henry Reed. HeIP-4; OBWP
  Judging Distances. BoLoP; GTBS-P; NAEL-6v2; NIL-7; NIP-4; NOBE; NPeEn; NoP-4; OxBEV; PoWW
  Naming of Parts. AmFaPo; FaBoWar; MoBrPo; NAEL-6v2; NOBE; NoP-4; OxBEV; OxBTC; PAI; PoPoPo; PoRA; RaBo; SoSe-8; TFi; UV; UnPo
  Unarmed Combat. NAEL-6v2

Lest her own captive else should her subdue. (LL) On the Welsh Language. Katherine Philips. EMWP; NOSC

Lest I forget. Lost Friend, The. Marjorie Lowry Christie Pickthall. PoBW

Lest it may more quarrels breed. Twelve Articles. Jonathan Swift. NBLV; OBCoV

Lest men suspect your tale to be untrue. Devil's Advice to Story-Tellers, The. Robert Graves. NAEL-5v2; NAEL-6v2; NoAM

Lest one touch of this heart convey its grief. (LL) Elizabeth Barrett Browning. BWW; BrRo; CABP; CenSon; VWP *Fr.* Sonnets from the Portuguese.

Lest Poets paint each Jewish saint. Battles of Joshua. *Unknown.* VerBaPo

Lest the fair cheeks begin their shrivelling. Homework. Mona Van Duyn. FFC; VCAP

Lest thou forget in the years between. Lest Thou Forget. William Leroy Stidger. PoToHe

Lestenyt, lordynges, both elde and yinge. Of a Rose, a Lovely Rose. *Unknown.* OBEV

Lester Leaps In. Al Young. ESEAA; SeSe

Let *a* be taken as. Project of Linear Inquiry, The. Michael Palmer. PmAP

Let age approve of youth, and death complete the same! (LL) Robert Browning. NAEL-5v2; NAEL-6v2

Let Age no longer toil with feeble strife. John Langhorne. NOEC *Fr.* Country Justice, The.

Let all chaste matrons, when they chance to see. Upon a Young Mother of Many Children. Robert Herrick. CaPo

Let All Created Things. Artis Seagrave. AH

Let all mortal flesh keep silence, And with fear and trembling stand. *Unknown.* SacPr, *tr. by* Gerard Moultrie

Let all the family gather. Light Another Candle. Miriam Chaikin. NTCP

Let all the little poets be gathered together in classes. To School! Stevie Smith. FaBoEE

Let all the multitudes of light. F. B. MacNutt. SacPr

Let all the nation judge it. (LL) Thomas D'Urfey [*or* Durfey]. FaBoCh; OxBoLi *Fr.* Fool's Preferment, A.

Let all the world in ev'ry corner sing / *My God and King*. Antiphon. George Herbert. PeECV

Let America Be America Again. Langston Hughes. AF; AiP

Let Anaiah bless with the Dragon-fly, who sails over the pond by the wood-side and feedeth on the cresses. Christopher Smart. FaBoVe *Fr.* Jubilate Agno.

Let any thief whom we carelessly suffer to pass. *Unknown.* PriapPo, *tr. by* Richard W. Hooper *Fr.* Priapus Poems, The.

Let Aphrodite herself. Manifesto. Agathias. GrAn, *tr. by* Dudley Fitts

Let Archimedes loud his glasses' glory roar. Her Eyes. Daniel Casper von Lohenstein. GePo, *tr. by* George C. Schoolfield

Let baths and wine-butts be November's due. Folgore da San Geminiano [*or* Gimignano]. EaItPo, *tr. by* Dante Gabriel Rossetti *Fr.* Sonnets of the Months.

Let beasts whine at your grave my father. In Memoriam Gyula Juhász. Sándor Weöres. IQMS, *tr. by* Edwin Morgan

Let but the son of earth. Ages of Man, The. Abraham Ibn Ezra. TrJP, tr. by Nina Davis Salaman

Let but thy voice engender with the string. Upon Her Voice. Robert Herrick. CaPo

Let by Rain. Edward Taylor. See Address to the Soul Occasioned by a Rain, An

Let Christian Hearts Rejoice Today. Unknown. AH, tr. by Francis X. Curley

Let clownish Cymon, in fond rustic strains. St. Anthony and His Pig; a Cantata. Frederick Forrest. NOEC

Let dainty wits cry on the sisters nine. Sir Philip Sidney. NoSic; Son Fr. Astrophil and Stella.

Let dirty streets be paved with flow'ry green. Unknown. NOEC Fr. Comparison, The.

Let each fair maid, who fears to be disgraced. Soame Jenyns. ECEV Fr. Art of Dancing, The.

Let each man first seek out his proper totem. Joyful Noise, A. Donald Finkel. CoAP

Let each man hope / and believe / what he can. (LL) Darwin. Lorine Niedecker. APSN; APT-2

Let earth and heaven combine. Charles Wesley. NPeEn

Let 'em censure: what care I? In Imitation of Anacreon. Matthew Prior. FaBoEE; OxBEV

Let Ephah rejoice with Buprestis, the Lord endue us with temperance and humanity, till every cow have her mate! Christopher Smart. NOEC Fr. Jubilate Agno.

Let Evening Come. Jane Kenyon. MakPoe

Let every prudish reader use his feet. Martial. RomPo, tr. by Anthony Reid

Let folly praise that fancy loves, I praise and love that child. Child My Choice, A. Robert Southwell. SacPr

Let fools great Cupid's yoke disdain. Song: The Willing Prisoner to His Mistress. Thomas Carew. CaPo

Let foreign [or forrain] nations of their language boast. Son[ne], The. George Herbert. AngWePo; GeHe; PeECV

Let Friday be your highest hunting-tide,—. Folgore da San Geminiano [or Gimignano]. EaItPo, tr. by Dante Gabriel Rossetti

Let gleaming motes of hayseed in the barn. Moments of Summer. Rachel Hadas. RA

Let go of the present and death. Once Again. Liz Sohappy Bahe. CDW

Let Go the Whore of Babylon. Miles Coverdale. ChIV-2

Let Grace conduct thee to the paths of peace. Francis Quarles. ESCV Fr. Emblems.

Let her be courtesan, scholar or saint. Beirut. Nadia Tuéni. PoArWo

Let her lie naked here, my hand resting. News of the World III. George Barker. FaBoTw

Let her who walks in Paphos. Lais. "H. D." MoAmPo

Let Heroes Account to Love. Alan Dugan. NoAM

Let him answer as he will. Companion, The. Edwin Arlington Robinson. NoAM

Let Him have his sleep! (LL) Sister Juana Inés de la Cruz. WPoS; WoPoe, tr. by Alan S. Trueblood Fr. Fifth Villancico, in Alternating Voices, Written for the Feast of the Nativity in Puebla, 1689, The.

Let him have his spats and cane. (LL) Sporting Beasley. Sterling Allen Brown. APT-2; NAAAL

Let Him Return. Leona Hill. PoToHe

Let him that will, ascend the tottering seat. Seneca. OBVE, tr. by Sir Matthew Hale Fr. Thyestes.

Let him who may. To Be Recited to Flossie on Her Birthday. William Carlos Williams. VGW

Let Him with Kisses of His Mouth. Unknown. AH; ChIV-1

Let Horace blush, and Virgil too. (LL) Epitaph for One Who Would Not Be Buried in Westminster Abbey. Pope. FaBoEE; NPeEn

Let it all be seen in your light, blushing drops. (LL) Trickle Drops. Walt Whitman. APN-1; NAAL-2v1; NAAL-3; NAAL-5

Let It Be. Musaemura Bonus Zimunya. NAfrP

Let it be alleys. Let it be a hall. Lovely Love, A. Gwendolyn Brooks. BPo; NAAAL

Let it be forgotten, as a flower is forgotten. Song. Sara Teasdale. MoAmPo; TCAPo

Let it be known that. Let It Be Known. Joette Harland-Watts. InTrad

Let it be Sabbath, Sabbath! Eternal Sabbath. Isaac Leibush [or Yitskhok Leybush] Peretz [or Perets]. TrJP, tr. by Joseph Leftwich

Let it disturb no more at first. Fountain. Elizabeth Jennings. WPE

Let it end here where the blueprint. Making Chicago. Dennis Schmitz. IllVoic; LCAP-2

Let It Go. William Empson. FaBoMo; HarvBoo; NPeEn; OxBEV; OxBSP; OxBTC

Let it live and grow. (LL) Love Letters. Josephine D. Henderson Heard. CBWP-4; SWaP

Let it no longer be a forlorn[e] hope. On the Baptized Ethiopian. Richard Crashaw. ChIV-2; FaBoEE, tr. by Richard Crashaw

Let it not come near me, let it not. Fragment for the Dark. Elizabeth Jennings. FaBoWP

Let it not come unto you, all ye that pass by. Bible, O.T. TrJP Fr. Lamentations.

Let it not your wonder move. Ben Jonson. NAEL-6v1; NAEL-7v1; NOSC Fr. Celebration of Charis in Ten Lyric[k] Pieces [or Peeces], A.

Let it rain and thunder! Who Cares? George Gershwin. ReLy

Let It Snow. David J. Rothman. GeoH

Let It Snow! Let It Snow! Let It Snow! Jule Styne. ReLy

Let kings command, and do[e] the best they may. Power in the People, The. Robert Herrick. BASC; CaPo

Let love come under your roof. Carol for Advent. John Heath-Stubbs. OxBC

Let man's soul[e] be a sphe[a]re, and then, in this. Good Friday [or Goodfriday], 1613. Riding Westward. John Donne. BASC; BBASP; ChIV-2; ESCV; FSCP; MeLP; NAEL-5v1; NAEL-6v1; NAEL-7v1; NOCV; NOSC; NoP-4; PBRV; PeECV; PoE; SacPr; TFi

Let Man toil to win his living. Song for the Workers, A. Eliza Cook. VWP

Let Mary Live long. Loyal English Man's Wish for the Preservation of the King and Queen, The. Anne Morcott. EMWP

Let me alone, alas, and drive him back to London. (LL) Thyrsis, Sleep'st Thou? Unknown. NoSic; OxBSP

Let Me Be a Giver. Mary Carolyn Davies. PoToHe

Let me be a little kinder, let me be a little blinder. (My Daily Creed). Unknown. PWR

Let me be at the castle. Psalm Concerning the Castle. Denise Levertov. TwCP; WPE

Let me be buried as flesh, not burned, I say. Earth Buried. Kenneth Mackenzie. CBAP

Let me be buried in the rain. Invocation. Helene Johnson. NAAAL

Let Me Be Held When the Longing Comes. Stephany Fuller. BPo

Let me be my own fool. Counterpoint, A. Robert Creeley. NeAP

Let me be the great nail holding a skyscraper through blue nights into / white stars. (LL) Prayers of Steel. Carl Sandburg. MoAmPo; SSCS; TrCP

Let me be to Thee as the circling bird. Gerard Manley Hopkins. SacPr

Let me borrow her corpse a little. Death of a Grandmother. Harvey Shapiro. TaR

Let me but do my work from day to day. Work. Henry Van Dyke. SacPr

Let me call a ghost. Song of Three Smiles. W. S. Merwin. CoAP; NOBA; VGW

Let Me Call You Sweetheart. Beth Slater Whitson. TCAPo

Let me confess. I'm sick of these sestinas. My Confessional Sestina. Dana Gioia. RA

Let me confess that we two must be twain. William Shakespeare. HeIP-4 Fr. Sonnets.

Let Me Die a Youngman's Death. Roger McGough. PeLV

Let me die in the Spring, said a sweet young girl. Time to Die, The. Matilda Caroline Edwards. PWR

Let me die on the prairie! and o'er my rude grave. Let Me Die on the Prairie. Fanny Crosby. SWaP

Let me do to you what they do. Knot. Susan Wicks. EmeKit

Let Me Enjoy. Thomas Hardy. AWP; NoAM

Let me feed full, till that I fart, say[e]s Jill. (LL) Upon Jack and Jill: Epigram. Robert Herrick. CaPo; NAEL-5v1; NAEL-6v1; NAEL-7v1

Let me find Roland, I won't stop till I kill him! (LL) Unknown. NAWM-5v1; NAWM-7v1, tr. by Frederick Goldin Fr. Song of Roland, The.

Let me find time. Two African Breasts. Nizar Qabbani. MAP, tr. by Diana Der Hovanessian and Lena Jayyusi

Let Me Gallop, Let Me Go. Unknown. SuSp, tr. by C. H. Wang

Let me gather from the Earth, one full grown fragrant flower. Let Me Gather from the Earth. Margaret Fuller. TCAPo

Let me give something!—as the years unfold. Frederick Goddard Tuckerman. APN-2 Fr. Sonnets.

Let me give something!—though my spring be done. Frederick Goddard Tuckerman. APN-2 Fr. Sonnets.

Let me go forth, and share. Ode in May. Sir William Watson. OBEV

Let Me Go Warm. Luis de Góngora y Argote. AWP, tr. by Henry Wadsworth Longfellow

Let Me Go Where Saints Are Going. Lewis Hartsough. AH

Let me hide myself in thee. (LL) Rock of Ages. Augustus Montague Toplady. NOCV; SCGP; SacPr

Let Me In. Judith Baumel. TaR

Let me know something when I'm dead. (LL) Things That Matter, The. Edith Nesbit. OxBTC; VWP

Let me lament the exodus of so many men from their. Iwan [or Yvan] Goll. PeFWW, tr. by Patrick Bridgwater Fr. Requiem for the Dead of Europe.

Let me lay it to you gently, Mr. Gone! Ray Bremser. NeAP Fr. Poem of Holy Madness.

Let me make the songs for the people. Songs for the People. Frances Ellen Watkins Harper. NAAAL; PWR

Let me move slowly through the street. Crowded Street, The. William Cullen Bryant. NCAP

Let me never have her father. Prayer to Be with Mercurial Women. Roddy Lumsden. NeBl

Let me never know myself apart from the living God! (LL) Hands of God, The. D. H. Lawrence. ChIV-2; InvLi

Let me not die for ever, when I'm gone. Wish, A. Frances Anne [*or* "Fanny"] Kemble. WPE

Let me not live, if I not love. On Himselfe. Robert Herrick. CaPo

Let me not love thee, if I love thee not. (LL) Affliction (1). George Herbert. BASC; ESCV; FHYEP; FSCP; GeHe; MeLP; NAEL-5v1; NAEL-6v1; NAEL-7v1; NOBE; NOSC; NoP-4

Let me not thirst with this Hock at my Lip. Emily Dickinson. WPoS

Let me obtain forgiveness of thee, Samson. John Milton. EBEV *Fr.* Samson Agonistes.

Let me open mama your 3 corner box. Blues for Franks Wooten. Tom Weatherly. NBV

Let me out in the dark, let me go, let me go! (LL) Divorce. Anna Wickham. MoBrPo; NALW

Let me pour [*or* powre] forth. Valediction: of Weeping, A. John Donne. BASC; ESCV; FHYEP; FSCP; HAP; HeIP-4; MeLP; NAEL-5v1; NAEL-6v1; NAEL-7v1; NOSC; NoP-4; PoE; SCGP; WeW-3

Let me recall my Fathers' (names). Sacrifice of Isaac, The. Rabbi Ephraim ben Jacob. NAWM-7v1, *tr. by* Judah Goldin

Let me see you. Mirabai [*or* Mira Bai]. BoWoP, *tr. by* Willis Barnstone and Usha Nilsson

Let Me Sing and I'm Happy. Irving Berlin. ReLy

Let Me Sing of My Well-beloved. Bible, *O.T.* TrJP *Fr.* Isaiah.

Let me sleep this night away. Upon Himselfe Being Buried. Robert Herrick. PBRV

Let me speak one word, muzzle. Farewell, The. Rosario Castellanos. TANSG, *tr. by* Magda Bogin

Let me strap / the baby in the seat. If He Let Us Go Now. Shirley Williams. BoWoP

Let me take this other glove off. In Westminster Abbey. Sir John Betjeman. FaBoWar; HarvBoo; InPK-6; NBLV; NIL-7; NIP-4; NOBL; NoAM; OBSV; OxAEP-2; TOF

Let me tell you a little story. Miss Gee. W. H. Auden. EBNV; OxBTC; UV

Let me tell you a little story / About Miss Edith Gee. Moral Tale, A. Roger Woddis. UV

Let me tell You a thing or two, Tara. Rāmprasād Sen. SinGod, *tr. by* Rachel Fell McDermott

Let me tell you the story of how I began. Song: Lift-Boy. Robert Graves. OxAEP-2

Let me thy Angell bee, bee thou my Lord. (LL) Edward Taylor. NOSC; OxBA; TAP; TCAPo *Fr.* Preparatory Meditations before My Approach to the Lord's Supper.

Let me today do something that will take. Morning Prayer, A. Ella Wheeler Wilcox. PoToHe

Let mee thinke no more on thee. Nicholas Breton. NPeEn *Fr.* Solemne Long Enduring Passion, A.

Let Mine Eyes See Thee. Saint Theresa [*or* Teresa] of Avila. AWP, *tr. by* Arthur Symons

Let Mother Earth now deck herself in flowers. Sir Philip Sidney. OxAEP-1, *tr. by* Robert Hass *Fr.* Arcadia.

Let my first Knowing be of thee. Emily Dickinson. TCAPo

Let my fond lips but drink thy golden wine. Go into the Highways and Hedges, and Compel Them to Come In. Aleister Crowley. CAGL

Let My People Go. Noémia da Sousa. HAWP, *tr. by* Jacques-Noël Gouat

Let My People Go. *Unknown.* APN-2

Let my people go! (LL) Go Down, Moses. *Unknown.* BPo; NAAAL; NoP-4

Let my sweet song be pleasing unto Thee. Love Song. Judah Halevi. TrJP, *tr. by* Nina Davis Salaman

Let my words. Prayer. Joseph Bruchac. UnSA

Let No Charitable Hope. Elinor Wylie. APT-1; ColAP; MoAmPo; NAAL-2v2; NALW; OxBA; OxBSP; VGW

Let no girl wait on you on that day when you bind your wild. Alchemy of Day, The. Anne Hébert. BoWoP, *tr. by* A. Poulin, Jr.

Let no man boste of cunning nor vertu. Like a Midsummer Rose. John Lydgate. SacPr

Let no man deem that he is free! (LL) Storm Cone, The. Rudyard Kipling. NoAM; OxBTC

Let no one impute to self-pity or censure. Poem of the Gifts. Jorge Luis Borges. TCLAP, *tr. by* Ben Belitt

Let no one say the past is dead. Past, The. Oodgeroo of the tribe Noonuccal (Kath Walker). IBA

Let no tempest subside no rock stagger. In Memory of a Black Union Leader. Aimé Césaire. VCWP

Let no word with its thinking threat. A La Une. Marie Ponsot. CLPP

Let Noah build an ark out of the old lady's shoe and. Anne Sexton. NALW *Fr.* O Ye Tongues.

Let none look at *me*! (LL) Mother and Poet. Elizabeth Barrett Browning. NAEL-5v2; NAEL-6v2; NALW; VWP; ViWPN

Let not a star suspect the mystery! Embalmment. "Michael Field." VWP

Let not Death boast his conquering power. On Eleanor Freeman, Who Died 1650, Aged 21. *Unknown.* OBEV

Let not his humble vesture make thee blind. Poor Scholar, The. Abraham Ibn-Chasdai. TrJP, *tr. by* J. Chotzner

Let not my titles, crowns, and worldly honors. (To the Virgin). Maria De' Medici. WPoS, *tr. by* Laura Anna Stortoni

Let not our naive labours have been in vain! (LL) Disused Shed in Co. Wexford, A. Derek Mahon. BiHa; CABP; CIP-2; EmeKit; ModIr; NOIV; NPeEn; NoP-4; OxBC; PBCIP; PNI

Let not the inhabitants of Hell despair. Cecco Angiolieri, da Siena. EaItPo, *tr. by* Dante Gabriel Rossetti

Let not the rugged brow the rhymes accuse. Mary Tighe. NoP-4; RWP *Fr.* Psyche.

Let not the sluggish sleep. Song. William Byrd. OxBSP; SacPr

Let not the title of my verse offend. Natural Child, The. Helen Leigh. ECWP; WoRP

Let not this plunder be misconstrued. Dennis Brutus. EroLit

Let not thy beauty make thee proud. Aurelian Townshend [*or* Townsend]. NOSC

Let not young souls be smothered out before. Leaden-eyed, The. Nicholas Vachel Lindsay. FaBoEE; OxBSP; PoE; RB; TCAPo

Let not your heart be troubled. Mary Elizabeth Fullerton. GI *Fr.* St. John.

Let nothing disturb thee. (Lines Written on a Bookmark Found in Her Breviary). Teresa de Cepeda Y Ahumada. WPoS, *tr. by* Henry Wadsworth Longfellow

Let nothing disturb thee. Lines Written in Her Breviary. Saint Theresa [*or* Teresa] of Avila. AWP, *tr. by* Henry Wadsworth Longfellow

Let now thy power be great O Lord. Numeri XIII. John Hall. ChIV-1

Let Observation, Shuddering the While. F. Mullen. UV

Let Observation with extensive View. Samuel Johnson. CABP; EBEV; ECEV; MakPoe; NAEL-6v1; NAEL-7v1; NOEC; NoP-4; OxAEP-1; OxBEV; TFi; UV; WoPoe *Fr.* Vanity of Human Wishes; The Tenth Satire of Juvenal Imitated, The.

Let oken club now strike, and poast of might. Seneca. OBVE *Fr.* Hercules Furens.

Let other mount aloft, let other sore. Seneca. OBVE *Fr.* Hercules Oetaeus.

Let other people come as streams. Dew. Charles Reznikoff. VGW

Let other poets raise a fracas. Scotch Drink. Robert Burns. ChIV-1

Let others cope with governing. Roistering I'll Chaff. Luis de Góngora y Argote. SpanPo, *tr. by* William M. Davis

Let others creep by timid steps, and slow. Pope. ECEV *Fr.* Dunciad, The.

Let others draw from smiling skies their theme. Philip Freneau. NAAL-2v1; NAAL-3 *Fr.* House of Night, The.

Let others from the town retire. Nonpareil. Matthew Prior. EnLoPo

Let others hail the holidays with laughter. Ausiàs March. STV

Let others pile their yellow ingots high. Pastoral Elegy, A. Tibullus. AWP, *tr. by* Sir Charles Abraham Elton

Let others pray for the passenger pigeon. Elegy for the Giant Tortoises. Margaret Atwood. BoWoP

Let others probe the mystery if they can. Right Thing, The. Theodore Roethke. PeECV

Let others sing of knights and paladins [*or* palladines]. Samuel Daniel. NAEL-7v1; NOBE; NoSic; OBEV; SCGP *Fr.* To Delia.

Let others write of battles fought. True Heroism. *Unknown.* ITBLP

Let passion's swelling tide my senses drown! Ibnu 'l-Farid. TOF

Let Peter rejoice with the Moon Fish who keeps up the life in the waters by night. Christopher Smart. ChIV-2 *Fr.* Jubilate Agno.

Let poetry be like a key. Ars Poetica. Vincente Huidobro. PFTM-1; TCLAP, *tr. by* David Guss

Let poets praise the blossom of wild Spring. Spring in London. John Bingham Morton. OBCoV

Let poets praise the softer winds of spring. John Bingham Morton. FaBoEE

Let rigid Cato read these lines of mine. (LL) When He Would Have His Verses Read. Robert Herrick. BASC; BeJo; CaPo; CavPo; NOBE; NOSC; SCGP

Let's be brave when the laughter dies. Let's Be Brave. Edgar Albert Guest. ITBLP

Let's be girls, Ma. Najrul Islām. SinGod, *tr. by* Rachel Fell McDermott

Let's Be Merry. Christina Georgina Rossetti. TLR *Fr.* Sing-Song.

Let's Begin. Otto Harbach. ReLy

Let's build a ferry boat. Sile Na gCioch. Pat Parnell. HW

Let's build bridges here and there. Interracial. Georgia Douglas Johnson. TTY

Let's call him *Jim Crow*. Reconsideration of the Blackbird, A. Thylias Moss. ESEAA

Let's Call it the / Collective Consciousness (We've Got). John Cage. APSN *Fr.* Diary: How to Improve the World (You Will Only Make Matters Worse).

Let's Call the Whole Thing Off. George Gershwin. ReLy

Let's contend no more, Love. Woman's Last Word, A. Robert Browning. NAEL-5v2; NAEL-6v2; RACG

Let's count the bodies over again. Counting Small-Boned Bodies. Robert Bly. CDa; SPE

Let's Do It. Noël Coward. ReLy

"Mr. Irving Berlin." UV

Let's Do It, Let's Fall in Love. Cole Porter. OBAL; PeLV; ReLy; UV

Let's dress up in grown-up clothes. Let's Dress Up. Mary Ann Hoberman. TLR

Let's drink up: with wine, what original. Hedylos. GrAn

Let's enjoy, while the season invites us. Lorenzo Da Ponte. TrJP, *tr. by* Natalie MacFarren *Fr.* Don Giovanni.

Let's enter the literary scene. Limerick. *Unknown.* PeLi

Let's Face the Music and Dance. Irving Berlin. ReLy

Let's Fall in Love. Ted Koehler. ReLy

Let's forget the many troubles. Let's Forget. Charles L. H. Wagner. PoToHe

Let's get Away from It All. Matt Dennis. ReLy

Let's get our dreams unstuck. Cape of Good Hope, The. Jean Cocteau. CuPo

Let's go back to the rooms where we once walked. Sister. Magali Alabaú. TANSG, *tr. by* Mary Jane Treacy

Let's go—much as that dog goes. Overland to the Islands. Denise Levertov. PmAP; UnPo

Let's go rolling, rolling. Getting Dirty. Dorthi Charles. TLR

Let's go see Old Abe. Lincoln Monument: Washington. Langston Hughes. CBCWP

Let's go to the wood, says this pig. *Unknown.* OxNR

Let's go up to the hillside today. Play Song. Peter Clarke. PBA

Let's have a look at another five. (LL) Robert Frost. GI; VGW *Fr.* Ten Mills.

Let's Have Another Cup of Coffee. Irving Berlin. ReLy

Let's have less nonsense from the friends of Joe. Less Nonsense. Sir Alan Patrick Herbert. OxBTC

Let's hear it for Dwayne Coburn, who was small. Body Bags. R. S. Gwynn. RA

Let's Hear It for Goliath. Jon Dressel. AngWePo; TCAWP

Let's hear the music first and foremost. Art of Poetry, The. Paul Verlaine. SxFrPo, *tr. by* Martin Sorrell

Let's Live Cheerfully. Shinkichi Takahashi. ZenPo, *tr. by* Takashi Ikemoto and Lucien Stryk

Let's look for the kids. One Two or Three. Philippe Soupault. SurPaPo, *tr. by* Mary Ann Caws and Patricia Terry

Let's make a bureaucracy. On The Empress's Mind. John Ashbery. RACG

Let's meet on the road to Morocco. Road to Morocco, The. Jimmy Van Heusen. ReLy

Let's not fool ourselves. Sentences. Nicanor Parra. AF, *tr. by* Miller Williams

Let's not have tea. White wine. Artemis. Olga Broumas. YaYoPo

Let's Not Talk about Love. Cole Porter. ReLy

Let's not use eyes anymore. Dialogue—2 Dollmakers. Gregory Corso. NeAP

Let's play *La Migra*. La Migra. Pat Mora. NIL-7; UnSA

Let's put aside. Gaelic Is Alive. Aonghas Macneacail. NePenScot

Let's Put Out the Lights and Go to Sleep. Herman Hupfeld. ReLy

Let's radio opinions, koorie side effects in death. No Grudge. Lionel Fogarty. BMAP

Let's Say. Bob Perelman. PmAP

Let's say it was Jesus. Who is Jesus? Why should Jesus be the name. Visions of Jesus. Jerome Rothenberg. APSN

Let's say you are a man (some of you are). Allegorical Matters. Stephen Dobyns. BodElec

Let's see first afros I saw were on these girls from. Southern University, 1962. Kevin Young. SpirFl

Let's spit the two of us let's spit. Poem to Shout in the Ruins. Louis Aragon. PFTM-1

Let's start from Zeus. Strato [*or* Straton]. GrAn

Let's step on daddy's head shout. Step on His Head. James Laughlin. VGW

Let's sup before we go. (LL) Mother Goose. LB; OxBoLi; OxNR

Let's Take a Walk around the Block. Harold Arlen. ReLy

Let's take / The duckweed way. Issa. ZenPo, *tr. by* Takashi Ikemoto and Lucien Stryk

Let's Talk of Graves. William Shakespeare. *Fr.* King Richard II.

Let's talk of graves, of worms, and epitaphs. William Shakespeare. TRP *Fr.* King Richard II.

Let's talk to the swallows visiting us in summer. Talk to the Peach Tree. Sipho Sepamla. PBMAP

Let's to the Prado and make the most of time. (LL) How It Strikes a Contemporary. Robert Browning. CTC; GTBS-P; NPeEn

Let's try another hand, let's redo the count. Edoardo Cacciatore. ItPo, *tr. by* Gayle Ridinger *Fr.* Full Powers: Five Warning Signs.

Let's try the present hour. Francis Picabia. PFTM-1 *Fr.* Eunuch Unique.

Let's write a poem about lazy people. Lazy People, The. Shel [*or* Shelley] Silverstein. NTCP

Let sailors watch the waning Pleiades. Edward Cracroft Lefroy. AWP *Fr.* Echoes from Theocritus.

Let school-masters puzzle their brain. Oliver Goldsmith. BIrV; NOIV *Fr.* She Stoops to Conquer.

Let Shobi rejoice with the Kastrel—blessed be the name Jesus in falconry and in the Mall. Christopher Smart. NOEC *Fr.* Jubilate Agno.

Let sleep take her, let sleep take her, let sleep. Fourth Song the Night Nurse Sang. Robert Duncan. VGW

Let Sol his annual journeys run. Hint from Voiture. William Shenstone. EnLoPo

Let some sad trumpeter stand. Back on Times Square, Dreaming of Times Square. Allen Ginsberg. CLPP; PoE

Let Sporus tremble—"What? That thing of silk." Pope. AWP; NOBE; OBSV; OxBEV; SCV *Fr.* Epistle to Dr. Arbuthnot.

Let the ascetics sing of the garden of Paradise. Mirza Asadullah Khan Ghalib. EnIH

Let the bells ring, and let the boys sing. John Fletcher. SCGP *Fr.* Spanish Curate, The.

Let the bird of loudest [*or* lowdest] lay. Phoenix and the Turtle, The. William Shakespeare. NOBE; NoSic; OBEV; OxAEP-1; OxBEV; PeECV; SCGP

Let the boy try along this bayonet-blade. Arms and the Boy. Wilfred Owen. HAP; MoBrPo; OxBEV; OxBSP; PoE; WeW-3

Let the crocus air invoke spring. Crocus Air. Winfield Townley Scott. APT-2

Let the crows go by hawking their caw and caw. River Roads. Carl Sandburg. VGW

Let the cruel spring begin, Sweeney. Epithalamion. Nancy Schoenberger. SwNoth

Let the damned ride their earwigs to Hell, but let me not join them. Rock Pilgrim. Herbert Edward Palmer. OxBTC

Let the day perish, wherein I was borne, and the night in which it was said, There is a man-childe conceived. Bible, *O.T.* NPeEn; OBVE; TrJP *Fr.* Job.

Let the Deep Organ Swell. Constantine Pise. AH

Let the eugenist reach for his gun! Limerick. Stanley J. Sharpless. PeLi

Let the first syllable of PEnelope be followed by the first of DIdo, the first of CAnus by that of REmus. *Unknown.* EroLit

Let the flowers make a journey. Anne Sexton. BoWoP; BodElec *Fr.* Furies, The.

Let the form be a garden in wild wilderness. This Poem. Barbara Leslie Jordan. ExTi

Let the four-clustered ivy flourish about you, Anacreon. Antipater of Sidon. HePo *Fr.* Epigrams.

Let the greater praise belong. (LL) Lament for the Death of Thomas Davis. Sir Samuel Ferguson. BIrV; NOIV

Let the harp be mute for ever. Lady Caroline Lamb. RWP *Fr.* Fugitive Pieces and Reminiscences of Lord Byron with Some Original Poetry, Letters and Recollections of Lady Caroline Lamb, ed. I. Nathan.

Let the light of late afternoon. Let Evening Come. Jane Kenyon. MakPoe

Let the lover be disgraceful, crazy. Jelaluddin [*or* Jalal al-Din] Rumi. RaBo *Fr.* Three Quatrains.

Let the male Poets their male Phoebus choose [*or* chuse]. To the Excellent Orinda. "Philo-Philippa." BASC

Let the memorial hill remember, instead of me. Yehuda Amichai [*or* Amikhai]. PoSu *Fr.* Patriotic Songs.

Let the Midnight Special. Joseph Bruchac. GM

Let the night keep. Night. William Rose Benét. MoAmPo

Let the only consistency. Hugh MacDiarmid. FaBoMo *Fr.* In Memoriam James Joyce.

Let the rain kiss you. April Rain Song. Langston Hughes. NOxBChV; NTCP; OBCA; OxIBACP

Let the rain plunge radiant. Way Through, The. Denise Levertov. NeAP; PoM

Let the Rest of the World Go By. J. Keirn Brennan. UnPo

Let the rest play step. Alice. Noy Holland. Unle

Let the snake wait under. Sort of a Song, A. William Carlos Williams. APT-1; NAAL-2v2; OxBSP; TAP; WoPoe

Let the speckled hens praise her. Speckled Hen's Morning Song to Biddy Early, The. Nancy Willard. FFC

Let the storm wash the plates. (LL)   Strawberries.   Edwin Morgan.   BoLoP; NoP-4

Let the superstitious wife.   Another.   Robert Herrick.   BeJo

Let the tale's sailor from a Christian voyage.   Dylan Thomas.   FaBoMo   *Fr.* Altarwise by Owl-Light.

Let the wind blow, for many a man shall die. (LL)   Nostalgia.   Karl Shapiro.   CoAP; TrJP; TwCP

Let the words be shed like amber.   Let the Words.   Boris Leonidovich Pasternak.   TCRusP, *tr. by* Bogdan Boychuk and Bob Perelman

Let the words of my mouth, and the meditation of my heart, be acceptable in thy sight, O Lord, my strength, and my redeemer. (LL)   Bible, *O.T.*   AWP; NAWM-5v1   *Fr.* Psalms.

Let the world's sharpness, like a clasping knife.   Elizabeth Barrett Browning.   CenSon; NOBVV; OxBEV   *Fr.* Sonnets from the Portuguese.

Let the young people.   Soldiers.   Sutardji Calzoum Bachri.   WoPoe, *tr. by* Harry Aveling

Let them be! Get out!   Imre Madách.   IQMS, *tr. by* Iain MacLeod   *Fr.* Tragedy of Man.

Let them bestow on every airt[h] a limb.   On Himself, upon Hearing What Was His Sentence.   James Graham, Marquess of Montrose.   NOSC; NPeEn; NePenScot

Let them bloom or.   Rekisen.   JDP, *tr. by* Yoel Hoffmann

Let them bury your big eyes.   Edna St. Vincent Millay.   APT-1; MoAmPo; OxBA; PoRA   *Fr.* Memorial to D. C.

Let Them Call It Jazz.   Stewart Brown.   WaCA

Let Them Choose Paths.   Odia Ofeimun.   HBAPE

Let them count scalps under the barroom wall.   Lying in a Yuma Saloon.   Jim Barnes.   CDW

Let them identify you to the future in these songs. (LL)   Spirit Whose Work Is Done.   Walt Whitman.   CBCWP; NAAL-2v1; NAAL-3

Let them lie perilous and beautiful. (LL)   Equilibrists, The.   John Crowe Ransom.   APT-1; FuPo; HAP; NAAL-2v2; NOBA; NoAM; OxBA; TAP

Let them lie—their day is over.   Refrigerium.   Frederick Goddard Tuckerman.   TCAPo

Let them say to my lover.   Amor Mysticus.   Sister Marcela de Carpio de San Felix.   AWP, *tr. by* John Hay

Let there be commerce between us. (LL)   Pact, A.   Ezra Pound.   APT-1; ColAP; NAAL-2v2; NAAL-5; NOBA; NoAM; OxBA; PAI; TAP

Let there be laid, when I am dead.   Posthumous Coquetry.   Théophile Gautier.   AWP; PeVV, *tr. by* Arthur Symons

Let there be life, said God. And what He wrought.   Power and the Glory, The.   Siegfried Sassoon.   OBMV

Let There Be Light.   William M. Vories.   AH

Let There Be Light!   D. H. Lawrence.   ChIV-1

"Let there be light!" said God, and there was light!   Byron.   OBWP   *Fr.* Don Juan.

Let there be treaties, bridges.   Against Extremity.   Charles Tomlinson.   HarvBoo

Let there be within these phantom walls.   Dream House.   Catherine Parmenter Newell.   PoToHe

Let this life of worry.   Palladas [*or* Pallades].   PGA

Let those toil for gold who please.   Solitude: An Ode.   James Grainger.   ECEV

Let those who are in favour with their stars.   William Shakespeare.   FaBoWar; OxAEP-1; SCGP   *Fr.* Sonnets.

Let those with cost deck their ill-fashioned clay.   To ———.   Thomas Rymer.   OxBSP

Let thy kind hand exalt it to my brow. (LL)   Necessity of Fate, The.   Jane Barker.   BWW; EMWP

Let Thy Kingdom.   *Unknown.*   AH

Let thy tears, Le Vayer, let them flow.   To Monsieur de la Mothe le Vayer.   Molière.   AWP, *tr. by* Austin Dobson

Let Tyrants Shake Their Iron Rod.   William Billings.   AH; TCAPo

Let uh revolution come.   U Name This One.   Carolyn M. Rodgers.   BlSi

Let us abandon then our gardens and go home.   Justice Denied in Massachusetts.   Edna St. Vincent Millay.   AiP; MoAmPo

Let us await the great American novel!   Critical Observations.   Archibald MacLeish.   OBAL

Let us be guests in one another's house.   Any Wife or Husband.   Carol Haynes.   ITBLP

Let Us Be Midwives!   Kurihara Sadako.   ItWoWo, *tr. by* Richard H. Minear

Let us be still.   To Usward.   Gwendolyn B. Bennett.   BlSi

Let us be tender to each other, dear.   Beggar Love.   Adriann Roland Holst.   TuT, *tr. by* Desmond Egan

Let us begin and carry up this corpse.   Grammarian's Funeral, A.   Robert Browning.   NAEL-5v2; NAEL-6v2; NOBVV; PeECV

Let us begin to understand the argument.   Ivory Tower, The.   Allen Tate.   APT-2

Let Us Believe.   Hildegarde Flanner.   WPE

Let Us Break Bread Together.   *Unknown.*   AH

Let us bribe the Moon God.   Prince Yuhara.   OHMPJ

Let us bring out those heavy dice.   Birth.   Gabriela Melinescu.   BoWoP

Let us call her footnote, oddity, heart tug.   Woman Who Died in Line, The.   Patricia Smith.   SpirFl

Let us celebrate the single-cloaked beings.   Psalm to the Creatures.   Gwilym R. Jones.   OBWVE, *tr. by* Joseph P. Clancy

Let Us Cheer the Weary Traveler.   *Unknown.*   AH

Let Us Consider Where the Great Men Are.   Delmore Schwartz.   MoAmPo   *Fr.* Shenandoah.

Let us describe how they went. It was a very windy night and the road.   Let Us Describe.   Gertrude Stein.   PFTM-1

Let us do, or die! (LL)   Robert Bruce's March to Bannockburn.   Robert Burns.   NAEL-5v2; NAEL-6v2; OxBS

Let Us Drink.   Alcaeus [*or* Alkaios].   AWP, *tr. by* John Hermann Merivale

Let us drink and be merry, dance, joke, and rejoice [*or* rejoyce].   Careless Gallant, The.   Thomas Jordan.   HAP; OxBoLi

Let us each day enure our selves to dye.   Blessednesse of Faithfull Soules by Death, The.   William Drummond, of Hawthornden.   SacPr

Let us effect a moratorium on things.   Scalpel in Hand.   Marjorie Welish.   FTOS

Let us forgive Ty Kendricks.   Southern Cop.   Sterling Allen Brown.   SoSe-8

Let us gather hand in hand.   Medieval Poem of the Nativity, A.   *Unknown.*   TrCP

Let us give thanks to God above.   Thanksgiving.   Lizelia Augusta Jenkins Moorer.   CBWP-3

Let us give up our trips.   Direction.   Barbara Guest.   WPE

Let us go hence, my songs; she will not hear.   Leave-taking, A.   Algernon Charles Swinburne.   NOBE; NOBVV; OxBEV

Let us go hence: the night is now at hand.   Last Word, A.   Ernest Christopher Dowson.   GSo; MoBrPo

Let us go into the temple.   Nossis.   PGA

Let us go on then.   Free Radicals.   James Sherry.   FTOS

Let us go then, you and I.   T. S. Eliot.   APT-1; AWP; AmFaPo; ClHu; ColAP; EBEV; HAP; HarvBoo; HeIP-4; InPK-6; MakPoe; MoAmPo; NAAL-2v2; NAAL-5; NAEL-5v2; NAEL-6v2; NAWM-7v2; NIL-7; NOBA; NOBE; NPeEn; NoAM; NoP-4; OxAEP-2; OxBEV; OxBTC; PoE; PoPoPo; PoRA; SoSe-8; TAP; TCAPo; TFi; TRP; TwCP; WeW-3; WoPoe

Let us go to the temple.   Nossis.   GrAn

Let us have a rest about the sunset.   To the Poets.   *Unknown.*   PeNZ

Let us have deities, he said, but not as indulgence.   Near House, The.   Mark Van Doren.   APT-2

Let Us Have Peace.   Nancy Byrd Turner.   PoToHe

Let us have winter loving that the heart.   Winter Love.   Elizabeth Jennings.   BoLoP

Let us honour if we can.   W. H. Auden.   PeLV   *Fr.* Shorts [1927–1932].

Let us, however, recover the Sceptre.   "H. D."   HarvBoo   *Fr.* Walls Do Not Fall, The.

Let us leave talking of angelic hosts.   Elinor Wylie.   OxBA   *Fr.* One Person.

Let Us Love as We Choose: Water.   Mariella Bettarini.   CItWP, *tr. by* Cinzia Sartini Blum and Lara Trubowitz

Let us move the stone gentleman to the toadstool wood.   Stone Gentleman, The.   James Reeves.   OxBSP

Let us not speak, for the love we bear one another.   In a Bath Teashop.   Sir John Betjeman.   EnLoPo

Let us now praise famous men.   Bible, Apocrypha.   OBVE; TrJP   *Fr.* Ecclesiasticus.

Let us pause to consider the English.   England Expects.   Ogden Nash.   PeLV

Let us pledge allegiance to the flag.   Let Us Pledge.   Wendell Berry.   PoCoUp

Let us praise our Maker, with true passion extol Him.   Anthem.   W. H. Auden.   NOCV

Let us preserve.   Three Written Poems, Unconnected.   Marianne Vitale.   HeMarv

Let us rejoice on our cots, for His nocturnal miracles.   Lauds.   John Berryman.   HAP

Let us say good-bye.   Bags Packed and We Expected This.   Ramona Wilson.   VoR

Let us say I was sitting in this place.   Kitzbuhl Church.   Karen Alkalay-Gut.   DTA

Let us see, is this real.   Pawnee War-Song.   *Unknown.*   APN-2, *tr. by* Daniel Garrison Brinton

Let us sing of Federation.   Federation.   W. T. Goodge.   NOBAu

Let us sing the sacred songs. (LL)   Carriers of the Dream Wheel.   N. Scott Momaday.   CDW; ColAP

Let us sleep now. (LL)   Strange Meeting.   Wilfred Owen.   FaBoMo; FaBoWar; GTBS-P; HarvBoo; HeIP-4; MakPoe; MoBrPo; NAEL-5v2; NAEL-6v2; NOBE; NoAM; NoP-4; OBWP; OxAEP-2; OxBEV; PeFWW; PoE; PoWW; RB; SCV; TCAWP; TFi

Let us sleep together here tonight.   Kenneth Rexroth.   APSN   *Fr.* Love Poems of Marichiko, The.

Let Us Strive to Do Something.   Mrs. Henry Linden.   CBWP-4

Let us suppose it a California day. Founding of Yuba City, The. Chitra Divakaruni. GeoHom

Let us synge unto the Lorde, for he is become glorious. Bible, *O.T.* OBVE *Fr.* Exodus.

Let us take to our heart a lesson, no braver lesson can be. Tapestry Weaver, The. Anson G. Chester. ITBLP

Let us thank Almighty God. Creatrix. Anna Wickham. MoBrPo

Let us two a burden try. (LL) Robin Hood. John Keats. AWP; SCGP

Let us use it while [*or* whilst] we may. Sir Richard Fanshawe. BoLoP *Fr.* Il Pastor Fido.

Let us walk in the white snow. Velvet Shoes. Elinor Wylie. MoAmPo; PAI; WHSW

Let us walk with this cone of light. Clair de Lune. Gwen Harwood. BMAP

Let us wash each other's body. Rufinus. GrAn

Let who so lyst with mighty mace to raygne. Seneca. OBVE, *tr. by* Jasper Heywood *Fr.* Thyestes.

Let who will think[e] us dead, or wish our death. (LL) Ben Jonson. NAEL-6v1; NAEL-7v1 *Fr.* Celebration of Charis in Ten Lyric[k] Pieces [*or* Peeces], A.

Let Wisdom Wear the Crown: Hymn for Gaia. Elsa Gidlow. HW

Let wits contest. Posy [*or* Posie], The. George Herbert. ChIV-1; NOSC

Let Words and Sense be set by thee. (LL) To Mr. Henry Lawes, Who Had Then Newly Set a Song of Mine in the Year 1635. Edmund Waller. BeJo; CTC

Let you drag me here, without demurring. To Belinda. Goethe. STV, *tr. by* John Frederick Nims

Let your eyes look at old people. In Respect of the Elderly. Thomas Love Peacock. VoR

Let your permanency under the brilliance of the stars be long. Jaime Saenz. BLPSL, *tr. by* Rene de Costa, Rigas Kappatos and Eleni Paidoussi

Let your wandering fingers. Sand Seer, The. Niyi Osundare. PBMAP

Let Zeus Record. "H. D."
     "Stars wheel in purple, yours is not so rare." APT-1; MoAmPo; NOBA; TAP

Lethargic vs violence as alternatives of each other for los americanos, The. Anecdotes of the Late War. Charles Olson. CBCWP

Lethargy. Donald Justice. CRP

Lethargy of evil in her eyes, The. Dying Viper, A. "Michael Field." CABP

Lethe. Mary Barnard. APT-2

Lethe. "H. D." APT-1; FaBoWP; MoAmPo; PoRA; TCAPo; VGW

Lethe had passed those lips, and he knew all. (LL) George Meredith. NAEL-6v2; NoP-4 *Fr.* Modern Love.

Let[t] folly praise that fancy [*or* phancy] loves, I praise and love that Child[e]. Child[e] My Choice [*or* Choyse], A. Robert Southwell. OxBEV; PeECV

Letter. Yehuda Amichai [*or* Amikhai]. VCWP

Letter. Alexander Bergman. TrJP

Letter. William Daniel Ehrhart. CDa

Letter. Janet Frame. PeNZ

Letter. Keith Gilyard. SpirFl

Letter. Sam Hamod. GraLe

Letter. Sue Hubbard. Prnts

Letter. Langston Hughes. PoE

Letter. Langston Hughes. APT-2; PoE *Fr.* Lenox Avenue Mural.

Letter. Dhabya Khamees. PoArWo, *tr. by* Clarissa C. Burt

Letter. W. S. Merwin. HAP

Letter. Leonard Nathan. PBCAP

Letter. Sarah Ruden. AmPoNex

Letter. Mark Strand. NoAM

Letter. Margit Szécsi. IQMS, *tr. by* Kenneth McRobbie

Letter. Iosif Pavlovich Utkin. TCRP, *tr. by* Lubov Yakovleva

Letter, A. Ralph Waldo Emerson. OxBA

Letter, A. Anthony Hecht. OxBC

Letter, A. Sophie Jewett. PoBW

Letter, A. Viktor Aleksandrovich Sosnora. ItGoST, *tr. by* Maia Tekses

Letter, The. W. H. Auden. FaBoTw; NoAM

Letter, The. Patricia Beer. OxBC

Letter, The. John Blight. CBAP

Letter, The. Amy Lowell. NALW; PoBW

Letter, The. Morton Marcus. GeoHom

Letter, The. Andrew Motion. EmeKit

Letter, The. Po Chü-i. ChiP, *tr. by* Arthur Waley

Letter, The. Elizabeth Riddell. LW; NOBAu

Letter, The. Tennyson. TTTS

Letter 1. George Crabbe. CABP *Fr.* Borough, The.

Letter 1. Thomas Moore. NOBRP *Fr.* Fudge Family in Paris, The.

Letter 3. Charles Olson. APT-2; PmAP *Fr.* Maximus Poems, The.

Letter V. William Sydney Graham. OxBTC

Letter 5. Michael Palmer. FTOS *Fr.* Letters to Zanzotto.

Letter VI. William Sydney Graham. FaBoMo

Letter, A ("This kind o' sogerin' ain't a mite like our October trainin."). James Russell Lowell. OxBA *Fr.* Biglow Papers, The.

Letter, A ("Thrash away, you'll hev to rattle."). James Russell Lowell. OxBA *Fr.* Biglow Papers, The.

Letter about Horror, A. Milán Füst. IQMS, *tr. by* Jess Perlman

Letter: Blues. Elizabeth Alexander. RA

Letter Following. Aidan Carl Mathews. PBCIP

Letter for All-Hallows (1949), A. Peter Kane Dufault. NoP-4

Letter for Duncan. Larry Eigner. FTOS; PoM

Letter for Marian, A. Thomas McGrath. VGW

Letter from a Black Soldier. Bill Anderson. VGW

Letter from a Captain in Country Quarters to his Corinna in Town, A. Isaac Hawkins Browne. ECEV

Letter from a Contract Worker. Antonio Jacinto. PBMAP; PoetW, *tr. by* Margaret Dickinson and Michael Wolfers

Letter from a Coward to a Hero. Robert Penn Warren. MoAmPo

Letter from a Girl to Her Own Old Age, A. Alice Thompson Meynell. MoBrPo; VWP

Letter, from a Lady in London to a Lady at Lausanne, A. Winthrop Mackworth Praed. *See* Talented Man, The

Letter from An Hoc (4), by a Seedbed. R. L. Barth. CDa

Letter from an Island. John Malcolm Brinnin. TAP

Letter from Aragon, A. John Cornford. OBWP

Letter from Artemisa in the Town, to Chloe [*or* Cloe], in the Country, A. John Wilmot, 2d Earl of Rochester. NPeEn; PoE

Letter from Berlin, A. Jon Stallworthy. OBWP; OxBC

Letter from Brazil, A. Louis Simpson. BodElec

Letter from Brooklyn, A. Derek Walcott. OxBTC

Letter from Chicago. May Sarton. NALW

Letter from Ephesus. Rufinus. GrAn, *tr. by* Alan Marshfield

Letter from Home. G. E. Patterson. AmPoNex

Letter from Home in Spanish. Judith Ortiz Cofer. ExTi

Letter from Italy [to the Right Honourable Charles Lord Halifax], A. Joseph Addison. NOEC

Letter from Li Po, A. Conrad Potter Aiken.
     "Winds of doctrine blow both ways at once, The." VGW

Letter from Mexico. Homero [*or* Umberto] Aridjis. TCLAP, *tr. by* Eliot Weinberger

Letter from Mr Crashaw to the Countess of Denbigh, against Irresolution and Delay in Matters of Religion, A. Richard Crashaw. *See* To the Noblest and Best of Ladies, the Countess of Denbigh

Letter from my brother, A. Surroundings. Joseph A. Soldati. CDa

Letter from my love today, A! Ballad of Hell, A. John Davidson. MoBrPo

Letter from my mother was waiting, A. Poem in Which I Refuse Contemplation. Rita Dove. NAAL-5

Letter from Phillis Wheatley, A. Robert Earl Hayden. ESEAA; NAAAL; NoAM

Letter from Pretoria Central Prison. Arthur Nortje. HBAPE

Letter from the Caribbean, A. Barbara Howes. CoAP; UnPo

Letter from the Coast, A. Mark Doty. HarvBoo

Letter from the Pygmies, A. Theodore Weiss. VGW

Letter from Turtle Beach. Susan K. C. Lee. FSt

Letter from Underground. Ronald G. Everson. MoCV

Letter Home from Brooklyn. Enid Shomer. UrbNat

Letter lies unanswered, thus free of lies, The. Correspondence. Henri Coulette. DiPo

Letter like pink thrift breaks up the rock-slate, A. Nevrazumitelny. Wendy Mulford. Oth

Letter of a Mother. Robert Penn Warren. MoAmPo

Letter of Advice, A. Winthrop Mackworth Praed. NOBL; OxBoLi; PeLV

Letter of the 26th June. Philippe Jaccottet. MFP, *tr. by* Martin Sorrell

Letter Sent by the Mayor and Inhabitants of the, A. *Unknown.*
     "O thow archbishop and metropolitan." NOIV

Letter Six—The Pious Editors' Creed. James Russell Lowell. APN-1; NCAP *Fr.* Biglow Papers, The.

Letter Smuggled in a Fish. Yuan Chen. CrYelRi, *tr. by* Sam Hamill

Letter to a Bedouin Informer. Khalifa Al-Wuqayyan. MAP, *tr. by* John Heath-Stubbs and Lena Jayyusi

Letter to a Benedictine Monk. Marilyn Nelson Waniek. GT

Letter to a Boy at School. Anna Wickham. NOxBChV

Letter to a Chinese Poet. Ruth Dallas.
     Autumn Wind. PeNZ
     Clouds on the Sea. PeNZ

Letter to a Cretan Flute-Maker. Justin Vitiello. UnSA

Letter to a Dead Father. Richard Shelton. PBCAP

Letter to a Former Mother Superior. Mary Kay Rummel. SpudSo

Letter to a Friend. Marjorie Oludhe Macgoye. HAWP

Letter to a Friend. Jon Stallworthy. NoAM

Letter to a Friend. Robert Penn Warren. MoAmPo

Letter to a Friend: Who Is Nancy Daum? James Schuyler. PmAP

Letter to a Lady in London, A. Esther Lewis.
   "You midst gay crowds reside, I, hid in shades." ECWP

Letter to a Poet. Robert Hass. YaYoPo

Letter to a Roving Poet. Amadou Lamine Sall. NAfrP

Letter to a Sister, Giving an Account of the Author's Wedding-Day. Priscilla Pointon.
   "In a post-coach and four, with postillions as fine." ECWP

Letter to a Son, A. Charles Mungoshi. PeSAV

Letter to a Tormented Playwright. Syl Cheney-Coker. HBAPE; PBMAP

Letter to Alex Comfort. Dannie Abse. FaBoTw; TwCP

Letter to an American Visitor. Alex Comfort. FaBoWar; OxBTC

Letter to an Exile. Claribel Alegría. TANSG, tr. by Louise B. Popkin

Letter to an Imaginary Friend. Thomas McGrath.
  Part One.
   "And I hear the pad of feet to the union hall." NNaP
   "From here it is necessary to ship all bodies east." GifTon
   "We go out in the stony midnight." NNaP
  Part Two.
   "Begun before Easter." NNaP
  Part Three.
   "And we, of the damned poor, trot our frost-furred horses." GifTon
   "Evening—another evening—and the lights flare." NNaP
   "Windless city built on decaying granite, loose ends." NNaP

Letter to Anne Ridler. George Sutherland Fraser. OxBS

Letter to Be Disguised as a Gas Bill. Marge Piercy. WPE

Letter to Bee. Emily Dickinson. SAmP; TLR; TTTS

Letter to Bell from Missoula. Richard Hugo. NNaP

Letter to Ben Jonson, A. Francis Beaumont. BeJo

Letter to Birch from Deer Lodge. Richard Hugo. BodElec

Letter to Blessing from Missoula. Richard Hugo. BodElec

Letter to Breyten Breytenbach from Hong Kong. C. J. Driver. PeSAV

Letter to Carlos Pellicer. Eunice Odio. TCLAP, tr. by Martha Collins

Letter to Daddy, A. Unknown, fr. Terezin Concentration Camp. INSAB

Letter to Daphnis, A. Anne Finch, Countess of Winchilsea. EMWP; EnLoPo; LW; MakPoe; NALW; PEW
  (Letter to Daphnis, April 2, 1685, A.) NOSC

Letter to Derek Mahon. Michael Longley. CIP-2
  (To Derek Mahon.) CABP

Letter to E. Franklin Frazier. Imamu Amiri Baraka. BPo

Letter to Einstein Beginning Dear Albert. Paul Hoover. IllVoic

Letter to El Flaco on His Birthday. Richard Blanco. NAPBL

Letter to Ellen Conroy Kennedy. Edouard J. Maunick. NegPo, tr. by Ellen Conroy Kennedy

Letter to Eve. Alan Dugan. YaYoPo

Letter to Friends East and West. Albert Goldbarth. IllVoic

Letter to Gale from Ovando. Richard Hugo. BodElec

Letter to Goldbarth from Big Fork. Richard Hugo. BodElec

Letter to Haislip from Hot Springs. Richard Hugo. BodElec

Letter to Her Brother. Amelia Rosselli. PFTM-2, tr. by Lucia Re and Paul Vangelisti

Letter to Her Father, A. Inib-sarri. BoWoP, tr. by Willis Barnstone

Letter to Her Husband, Absent upon Public[k] Employment, A. Anne Bradstreet. HAP; HeIP-4; NAAL-2v1; NAAL-3; NAAL-5; NALW; NoP-4; PEW; PoPoPo; SCAP

Letter to Her Mother, A. Eristi-Aya. BoWoP, tr. by Willis Barnstone

Letter to Hill from St. Ignatius. Richard Hugo. BodElec

Letter to His Friend Isaac, A. Judah Halevi. TrJP, tr. by Emma Lazarus

Letter to Hugo from Later. Jane Hirshfield. GeoHom

Letter to Ibrahim. Khaled Mattawa. AmPoNex

Letter to Jeanne (at Tassajara). Diane Di Prima. BB

Letter to John Donne, A. Charles Hubert Sisson. HarvBoo; NOCV

Letter to John Dryden, A. James Philip McAuley.
  "Dear John, whoever now takes pen to write." CBAP

Letter to Jorge Luis Borges: Apropos of the Golem. John Hollander. TaR

Letter to Julia, in Rhyme. Henry Luttrell.
  "Have you not seen (you must remember)." NOBRP
  "London, within thy ample verge." NOBRP

Letter to Lady Margaret Cavendish Holles-Harley, When a Child, A. Matthew Prior. See Letter to the Honourable Lady Miss Margaret Cavendish Holles-Harley, A

Letter to Levertov from Butte. Richard Hugo. NNaP

Letter to Libbey from St. Regis. Richard Hugo. BodElec

Letter to Logan from Milltown. Richard Hugo. NNaP

Letter to Lord Byron. W. H. Auden.
  "England, my England—you have been my tutrix." OBSV
  "I like your muse because she's gay and witty." NOBL
  "Ottava Rima would, I know, be proper." NOBL
  "Thought of writing came to me today, The." NOBL
  "You lived and moved among the best society." OBSV

Letter to Mantsch from Havre. Richard Hugo. MoASP

Letter to Maria Gisborne. Shelley.
  To Maria Gisborne in England, from Italy. NOBE
  "You are now / In London, that great sea." EBEV

Letter to Miguel Otero Silva, in Caracas. Pablo Neruda. AF, tr. by Robert Bly

Letter to Miss E. B. at Bath. Mary Savage. ECWP

Letter to Miss E. B. on Marriage. Mary Savage.

Letter to My Daughter at the End of Her Second Year. Donald Finkel. CoAP

Letter to My Father on the Other Side. Jack Marshall. GraLe

Letter to My Love—All Alone, Past 12, in the Dumps, A. "The Amorous Lady." ECWP

Letter to My Mother. Suzanne Gardinier. NeAmPo

Letter to My Mother. Sergey [or Sergei] Aleksandrovich Yesenin [or Essenin]. RusPo, tr. by Robert Arthur Douglas Ford

Letter to My Mother. Sergey [or Sergei] Aleksandrovich Yesenin [or Essenin]. TCRP, tr. by Geoffrey Thurley

Letter to My Mother, A. Eva Johnson. IBA

Letter to My Sister. Anne Spencer. BlSi; NAAL; TCAPo

Letter to My Spouse. Miklós Radnóti. IQMS, tr. by Peter Zollman

Letter to My Wife. Miklós Radnóti. AF

Letter to N.Y. Elizabeth Bishop. TwCP

Letter to Oberg from Pony. Richard Hugo. BodElec

Letter to Pearse Hutchinson. Eiléan Ní Chuilleanáin. FaBoWP

Letter to Peter Levi, A. Elizabeth Jennings. OxAEP-2

Letter to Reed from Lolo. Richard Hugo. NNaP

Letter to Robert Fergusson. Alexander Scott. OxBS

Letter to Robert Frost, A. Robert Silliman Hillyer. MoAmPo

Letter to Ron Silliman on the Back of a Map of the Solar System, A. Dennis Schmitz. LCAP-2

Letter to Russel Barron. Robert Gibb. SwNoth

Letter to Scanlon from Whitehall. Richard Hugo. NNaP

Letter to the Academy. Langston Hughes. AF

Letter to the Actor Charles Laughton Concerning the Work on the Play "The Life of Galileo." Bertolt Brecht. PoSu, tr. by Michael Hamburger

Letter to the Countess of Denbigh. Richard Crashaw. See To the Noblest and Best of Ladies, the Countess of Denbigh

Letter to the Front. Muriel Rukeyser.
  "Even during war, moments of delicate peace." TrJP
  To be a Jew in the Twentieth Century. NALW; TaR; TrJP

Letter to the Honourable Lady Miss Margaret Cavendish Holles-Harley, A. Matthew Prior. NOEC; NoAM; OxBC; OxBSP
  (Letter to Lady Margaret Cavendish Holles-Harley, When a Child, A.) NOBE; OBEV

Letter to the Immigration Officer. Jan Kemp. PeNZ

Letter to the Survivors. Charles E. Butler. YaYoPo

Letter to Three Irish Poets, A. Michael Longley. BIrV

Letter to Wagoner from Port Townsend. Richard Hugo. NNaP

Letter to Welch from Browning. Richard Hugo. NNaP

Letter to William Carlos Williams, A. Kenneth Rexroth. NNaP

Letter to William Carlos Williams, A. George Young. BloBone

Letter to Yeni on Peering into Her Life. Sandra M. Castillo. TouFir

Letter to Youki. Robert Desnos. AF, tr. by Carolyn Forché

Letter Written on a Ferry While Crossing Long Island Sound. Anne Sexton. CoAP; NAAL-2v2; TwCP

Letters. Ralph Waldo Emerson. OxBSP

Letters, The. Louise Glück. HarvBoo

Letters and Other Worlds. Michael Ondaatje. NOBC; NoAM; NoP-4

Letters at School, The. Mary Mapes Dodge. OBCA

Letters Come to Prison. Shahid. GLP

Letters from a Father. Mona Van Duyn. NoP-4

Letters from a Man in Solitary. Nazim Hikmet. AF

Letters from a Married Man. Don Mager.
  "Beloved, / What does it take to put a house in order?" GLP

Letters from a New England Negro. Sherley Anne Williams. ESEAA

Letters from an Exile. Valerie Duff. OPRER

Letters from Baron Von Hügel to a Niece. David Scott. NLP

Letters from Chankiri Prison. Nazim Hikmet. PFTM-1

Letters from Home. Elmaz Abinader. GraLe; PoArWo

Letters from Poston Relocation Camp (1942–45). David Mura. LTA

Letters from School, The. Juan Delgado. TouFir

Letters from the Concertina File 1939–1940. Sue MacIntyre. Prnts

Letters from the Front.   Michael Klein.   WiU

Letters from the Ming Dynasty.   Joseph Brodsky.   PoetW; TCRP, *tr. by* Derek Walcott

Letters from the North Star.   Kevin Young.   NeAmPo

Letters from the Poet Who Sleeps in a Chair.   Nicanor Parra.   AF, *tr. by* Miller Williams

Letters from Yorkshire.   Maura Dooley.   NeBl

Letters in the Family.   Adrienne Rich.   NIL-7

Letters of the Jews as strict as flames, The.   Alphabet, The.   Karl Shapiro.   APT-2; NoAM; TaR

Letters [*or* Notes] Found near a Suicide.   Frank Horne.
   To "Chick."   BPo
   To James.   BPo
   To Mother.   BPo
   To You.   BPo

Letters she left to clutter up the desk.   Gesture by a Lady with an Assumed Name, A.   James Wright (1927–80).   CoAmPo

Letters to a Young Poet.   Adrienne Rich.   ExTi

Letters to an Unknown Woman.   Nicanor Parra.   BLPSL, *tr. by* Rene de Costa, Rigas Kappatos and Eleni Paidoussi

Letters to Lebanon.   Ben Bennani.   GraLe

Letters to Live Poets.   Bruce Beaver.   CBAP
   ("Room by room like a shabby genteel boarding house, age.") (LL)   BMAP
   "Three images of dying stick in my mind like morbid transfers."   NOBAu

Letters to Martha.   Dennis Brutus.   PeSAV

Letters to Walt Whitman.   Ronald Johnson.   VGW

Letters to Yesenin.   James [*or* Jim] Harrison.
   "I am four years older than you but scarcely an unwobbling."   BodElec
   "I don't have any medals. I feel their lack."   BodElec
   "I wanted to feel exalted so I picked up."   BodElec
   "It would surely be known for years after as the day I shot."   BodElec
   "Lustra. Officially the cold comes from Manitoba."   BodElec
   "This matted and glossy photo of Yesenin."   BodElec
   "What if I own more paper clips than I'll ever use in this."   BodElec

Letters to Zanzotto.   Michael Palmer.
   "Desired, the snow falls upward."   FTOS

Lettie Walker was 71.   Older American, The.   Cheryl Clarke.   GLP

Letting.   Gary Hotham.   HA

Letting down the isinglass curtains.   Parent.   Josephine Miles.   NALW

Letting Go.   Daryl Hine.   NoP-4

Letting his wisdom be the whole of love.   World and the Child, The.   James Merrill.   MakPoe

Letting in the Jungle.   Rudyard Kipling.   *Fr.* Second Jungle Book, The.

Letting midnight / out on bail.   Jam Session.   Langston Hughes.   APT-2

Letting My Feelings Out.   Yü Hsüan-chi.   BoWoP, *tr. by* Geoffrey Waters

Letting my tongue.   Michael McClintock.   HA

Letting the Beat Go.   Robert Duncan.   FTOS

Letting us know for certain you didn't want that kind of Jew.   Fairy Straighttalk.   Carl Morse.   GLP

Lettre Sende by on Yonge Woman to A-noder, Whiche Aforetyme Were Felowes To-geder, A.   *Unknown.*   EMWP

Lettuce devours its leaves, The.   Passage.   Penelope Rosemont.   SurWo

Letty's Globe.   Charles Tennyson Turner.   NOBVV; NPeEn; OBEV; OxBEV; OxBSo; PeVV

Levantine, A.   William Plomer.   OBMV

Levedy Fortune is bothe frend and fo, The.   *Unknown.*   MiEL

Levedy, ic thonke thee.   Thanks and a Plea to Mary.   *Unknown.*   FaBoVe; MiEL

Levee: Letter to No One, The.   Lorna Dee Cervantes.   TouFir

Level fields expand into lakes.   Inscribed on the Painting "Meaning of a Poem by Wang Wei."   Li Tung-yang.   CoBLCP, *tr. by* Jonathan Chaves

Level forest stretching far and wide, A.   Wu Chen.   CoBLCP

Levelled Churchyard, The.   Thomas Hardy.   NOBL

Leveller, The.   "Barry Cornwall."   OxAEP-2

Leveller, The.   Robert Graves.   FaBoWar

Leveller's Rant, The.   Alexander Brome.   BASC

Leviathan.   Bible, *O.T.*   OBVE   *Fr.* Job.

Leviathan.   Jay Macpherson.   MoCV

Leviathan.   W. S. Merwin.   ChIV-1; CoAmPo; NOBA; NoAM

Leviathan.   Peter Quennell.
   "Music met Leviathan returning, A."   MoBrPo

Levis Exsurgit Zephirus.   *Unknown.*   WoPoe, *tr. by* David Ferry   *Fr.* Cambridge Songs.

Levite and His Concubine at Gibeah, The.   Paul Durcan.   ModIr

Leviticus (Chapter 7, Verse 2–5).   Manuela Fingueret.   MirDau, *tr. by* Roberta Gordenstein

Levivot.   Saul [*or* Shaul] Tchernichowsky [*or* Tchernichovsky].   MHP, *tr. by* Ruth Finer Mintz

Lewesdon Hill.   William Crowe.
   "Up to thy summit, Lewesdon, to the brow."   NOEC

Lewis Describes His Day.   Merrill Markoe.   Unle

Lewis Mumford.   George Buchanan.   PNI

Lexically.   Ken Edwards.   Oth   *Fr.* 3600 Weekends.

Li Fu-Jên.   Emperor Wu of Han [*or* Wu Ti *or* Ou-ty *or* Liu Ch'e *or* Liu Ch'u].   ChiP, *tr. by* Arthur Waley

Li Po.   Undressing for Li Po.   Carl Phillips.   WiU

Li Po drowned when he stepped into a pond.   Li Pos of the Polis.   Simeon Dumdum.   ReBoTo

Li Po on board, ready to push off.   Presented to Wang Lun.   Li Po.   CoBCP, *tr. by* Burton Watson

Li Po's poetry: no match anywhere.   Spring Day: Thinking of Li Po.   Tu Fu.   ChinPo, *tr. by* Yip Wai-lim

Li Pos of the Polis.   Simeon Dumdum.   ReBoTo

Li Sao.   Ch'u Yüan.
   "Oftentimes, I grew dejected and sobbed."   SuSp
   Yüan, Ch'ü   SuSp

Liadain.   *Unknown.*   WPOW, *tr. by* Frank O'Connor

Líadan and Cuirithir.   *Unknown.*   NOIV

Liadan Laments Cuirithir.   *Unknown.*   BIrV, *tr. by* John Montague

Liam.   Mary Jo Salter.   ExTi

Liana, The.   Gabriela Mistral.   BBASP, *tr. by* Doris Dana

Lianas in bright bloom hang from mahogany shade.   Jaguar's Dream, The.   Charles Marie René Leconte de Lisle.   WoPoe, *tr. by* James Lasdun

Liar, The.   Imamu Amiri Baraka.   NOBA

'Lias! 'Lias! Bless de Lawd!   In the Morning.   Paul Laurence Dunbar.   BPo

Lib. 2. Metrum 5.   Boethius.   NOSC; OBVE; PAI, *tr. by* Henry Vaughan   *Fr.* Consolation of Philosophy, The ("De Consolacione Philosophie").

Libation.   Palorine Williams.   Prnts

Libation Bearers, The.   Aeschylus.   NAWM-5v1

Libation. / Hey sisters, we the color of our men.   Ceremony.   Jewel C. Latimore.   BlSi

Libationer Hu Became Ill from Eating Sunflowers. These Poems Are Playfully Presented to Him and Are Also Intended to Thank Him for the Vegetables He Sent Me.   Yang Shih-ch'i.
   "After the rain, the vegetables from your garden."   CoBLCP

Libations.   Ferenc Kölcsey.   IQMS, *tr. by* Adam Makkai

Liber doth vaunt how chastely he hath liv'd.   In Librum.   Sir John Davies.   FaBoEE

Libera nos, Domine—Deliver Us, O Lord.   Philip Freneau.   OxBEV

Liberace.   Jonathan Holden.   ReTh

Liberal, or Innocent by Definition.   James Philip McAuley.   NOBAu

Liberation.   Abena Busia.   HAWP; PoetW

Liberation.   Ruth Stone.   BoWoP

Liberation / Poem.   Sonia Sanchez.   NBV

Liberator, The.   Emily Holmes Coleman.   SPE

Liberia? / No micro-footnote in a bunioned book.   Melvin B. Tolson.   UnPo   *Fr.* Libretto for the Republic of Liberia.

Libertine, The.   Louis MacNeice.   ModIr; NoAM

Liberty.   Paul Éluard.
   "On my school notebooks."   TTTS

Liberty.   Emile Ologoudou.   PBMAP

Liberty, The.   Sarah Fyge Egerton.   EMWP

Liberty and Peace.   Phillis Wheatley.   AiP
   "Lo! Freedom comes. Th' prescient Muse foretold."   BlSi

Liberty and Ten Years of Return.   Christopher Howell.   CDa

Liberty [*or* Libertie], that we[e]'ll enjoy tonight, The. (LL)   Inviting a Friend to Supper.   Ben Jonson.   AWP; BASC; BeJo; NAEL-6v1; NAEL-7v1; NOBE; NOSC; NPeEn; NoP-4; OxBoLi; PAI; PBRV; PeLV

Liberty to be defended on.   Poem in Defense of Children.   Joel Oppenheimer.   CDa

Liberty to M. le Diplomate.   Sydney Thompson Dobell.   OxBSo

Libido.   Larissa Szporluk.   AmPoNex

Libido portion goes haywire, The.   Century of Hands.   Michael Davidson.   FTOS

Libra, September.   John Taylor.   NOSC

Librarian, The.   Charles Olson.   PmAP

Library.   Louis Jenkins.   RaBo

Library, The.   Aidan Carl Mathews.   CIP-2

Library, The.   Timothy Steele.   RA

Library book, The.   Gary Hotham.   HA

Library closing.   Sydell Rosenberg.   HA

Library in a Garden, A.   Richard Le Gallienne.   OBGa

Libretto for the Republic of Liberia.   Melvin B. Tolson.

On the Founding of Liberia. UnPo

Ti. APT-2

Libyan / Egyptian Acrobats / Israeli Air Circus. Sam Hamod. GraLe

Lice, The. Mei Yao Ch'en. CrYelRi, *tr.* by Sam Hamill

Lice-Seekers. Arthur Rimbaud. SxFrPo, *tr.* by Martin Sorrell

Licentious Person, A. John Donne. PeLV

Lich Gate, The. Clayton Eshleman. PmAP

Licia. Giles Fletcher, the Elder.

"Are those two stars, her eyes, my life's light gone." Son

"First did I fear, when first my love began." Son

"I saw, sweet Licia, when the spider ran." OxBSo

In Time the Strong and Stately Turrets Fall. EBEV

("Sad, all alone, not long I musing sat.") Son

Licking Wounds. Alice Anderson. AmPoNex

Licorice Chronicles. Ted Greenwald.

"Coordinating cities gulls still gull, and, arms binged with wine, as wine." FTOS

Licorice Fields at Pontefract, The. Sir John Betjeman. CABP

Lid of the Chevy trunk couldn't close, The. First TV in a Mennonite Family. Julia Kasdorf. AmPoNex

Liddell and Scott. Thomas Hardy. OBCoV; OxBoLi; PeLV

Liddesdale Crosiers hae ridden a race, The. Death of Parcy Reed, The. *Unknown.* ESPB

Lidice sounds like marriage bells in June. Lidice. Ernst Waldinger. FaBoWar, *tr.* by *Unknown*

Lie, The. Rudyard Kipling. NOBL *Fr.* Naulahka, The.

Lie, The. Sir Walter Ralegh. CTC; EBEV; HAP; NAEL-5v1; NAEL-6v1; NAEL-7v1; NOBE; NPeEn; NoSic; OxBEV; RB; SCGP; SCV; TFi

(Go, soul, the body's guest.) NoP-4; PoPoPo

(Goe soule the bodies guest.) PBRV

Lie, The. Sir Walter Alexander Raleigh. SacPr

Lie back, daughter, let your head. First Lesson. Philip Booth. TwCP

Lie down beside me if it's good for you. Coming Downtown. Marilyn Hacker. PoBW

Lie down in sleep but suddenly. Insomnia. Joyce Carol Oates. AWTN

Lie down with us and wait. (LL) Gathering Mushrooms. Paul Muldoon. BiHa; CIP-2; HarvBoo; ModIr; NoP-4; PBCIP; PNI

Lie for lie! (LL) Goddess, The. Denise Levertov. NALW; NOBA; NeAP; PoM

Lie still, my newly married wife. Griesly Wife, The. John Streeter Manifold. MoBrPo

Lie still now. This Room and Everything in It. Li-Young Lee. IllVoic; NAAL-5; OpBo

Lie, that we come from water, A. Landcrab I. Margaret Atwood. LCAP-2; NIP-4

Lie where you fell and longed. Letter V. William Sydney Graham. OxBTC

Lie you must, and not with me. (LL) When the Eye of Day Is Shut. A. E. Housman. NOBVV; NPeEn

Liebhartstal. Josef Weinheber. AuPH, *tr.* by Lowell A. Bangerter

Lieh Mountain. Wang Shih-chieng. SuSp, *tr.* by Richard John Lynn

Lien-ch'ang Palace was overgrown with bamboo. On Lien-ch'ang Palace. Yüan Chên. SuSp, *tr.* by Angela Jung Palandri

Lies. Christopher Bursk. CDa

Lies. Martha Collins. ExTi; PuP-23

Lies a dead deer on younder plain. Ezra Pound. APSN

Lies I could tell, The. White Lies. Natasha Trethewey. TWW

Lies in flawed words and stubborn sounds. (LL) Poems of Our Climate, The. Wallace Stevens. APT-1; NoP-4; OxBA; SoSe-8; TwCP

Lies in the full, soft rain. (LL) "Michael Field." VWP; ViWPN

Lies like a rod of rippled jade. (LL) Symphony in Yellow. Oscar Wilde. EBVV; MoBrPo; NOBVV; NoAM; OPOU; OxBSP

Lies lost in a strength of jasmine down a summer beach. (LL) Málaga. Pearse Hutchinson. BIrV; ModIr; PBCIP

Lies rusting, mouldering. (LL) Dismantled Ship, The. Walt Whitman. OxBA; TCAPo

Lieth there so cold? [*or* cold!] (LL) What the Bullet Sang. Bret Harte. APN-2; OBEV

Lieutenant, The. Konstantin Mikhailovich Simonov. TCRP, *tr.* by Lubov Yakovleva

Lieutenant Gilbert took us down the hill. P.O.W.s. R. L. Barth. CDa

Life. Delmira Agustini. TANSG, *tr.* by Mark McCaffrey

Life. Francis Bacon. *See* Life of Man, The

Life. Anna Laetitia Barbauld. GTBS-P; NAEL-6v2; NoP-4; OBEV; OxAEP-1; PWR

Life. Anna Laetitia Barbauld.

Life's "Good-Morning" TreFP

Life. "Sasha Chorny" [*or* "Chiornyi"]. TCRP, *tr.* by Bernard Meares

Life. Ralph Waldo Emerson.

"Him strong Genius urged to roam." TCAPo

Life. Artie Gold. NOBC

Life. George Herbert. BASC; ESCV; FSCP; GeHe; MeLP; NOSC; NoP-4

Life. Henrietta Cordelia Ray. CBWP-3

Life. Grace Treasone. InPK-6

Life. Mary E. Tucker. CBWP-1

Life. *Unknown.* PoToHe

Life. Edith Wharton. APN-2

Life. Ella Wheeler Wilcox. PoToHe

Life, A. Janet Fisher. MFPA

Life, A. Howard Nemerov. OBCoV

Life, A. Sylvia Plath. NOBA

Life, The. James Wright. LCAP-2

Life: a cloud crossing the peak. Mumon Gensen. ZenPo, *tr.* by Takashi Ikemoto and Lucien Stryk

Life Ahead, The. Philip Levine. NoAM

Life ain't never been promised to nobody. For Aunt Cathy. Kevin Powell. InTrad

Life and Character of Dean Swift, The. Jonathan Swift.

"Day will come, when't shall be said, The." NOIV

Life and Death. Walter James Turner. FaBoTw

Life and Death of Edward II, The. Sir Francis Hubert.

"This highest scholar in the school of sin." NOSC

Life and Death of [Habbie Simson] the Piper of Kilbarchan, The. Robert Sempill. NPeEn; OxBS

Life and Death of Jason, The. William Morris.

Garden by the Sea, A. NOBE

(Nymph's Song to Hylas, The.) OBEV

Life and Genuine Character of Dr Swift, The. Jonathan Swift.

From The Life and Character of Dean Swift. NOBL

Life and Impellance. William Frederick Stevenson. NOBVV

Life and Lucubrations of Crispinus Scriblerus, The. James Woodhouse. NOEC

Life and the Universe show spontaneity. Positivists, The. Mortimer Collins. EBVV

Life, are you keeping something in reserve? Gift, The. Amado Nervo. TCLAP, *tr.* by Sue Standing

Life as a Book That Has Been Put Down. John Ashbery. FTOS

Life / At fifteen. For a Black Child. David Diop. NegPo, *tr.* by Ellen Conroy Kennedy

Life at last I know is terrible. What Is Terrible. Roy Fuller. PoWW

Life at Richkings. Frances Seymour, Countess of Hertford. ECWP

Life at the Capital. Li Ho. CrYelRi, *tr.* by Sam Hamill

Life at War. Denise Levertov. VGW

Life brings everything, time's length can shift. Plato the Younger. GrAn

Life calls us, and we go, massing our courage. Karolina Pavlova. ARWW, *tr.* by Catriona Kelly

Life can hold such lovely things! Thank You, God. Nina Stiles. PoToHe

Life contracts and death is expected. Death of a Soldier, The. Wallace Stevens. APT-1; OBWP; OxBSP; SAmP; SoSe-8

Life-cutting axe. Tanko (d. 1735). JDP, *tr.* by Yoel Hoffmann

Life Cycle of Common Man. Howard Nemerov. NBLV

Life death does end and each day dies with sleep. (LL) No Worst, There Is None. Pitched Past Pitch of Grief. Gerard Manley Hopkins. EBVV; FaBoMo; GTBS-P; HeIP-4; MoBrPo; NAEL-5v2; NAEL-6v2; NOBE; NOBVV; NoAM; OxAEP-2; PeVV; PoE; TFi; WoPoe

Life Doesn't Frighten Me. Maya Angelou. ChAP

Life Draws a Tree. Roberto Juarroz. TCLAP, *tr.* by W. S. Merwin

Life flows to death as rivers to the sea. Epigram. James Vincent Cunningham. APT-2; VGW

Life for a Life. Mary E. Tucker. CBWP-1

Life-Force, afflicted with doubt, The. Limerick. Thomas Thorneley. PeLi

Life Forms. Robin Becker. BodElec

Life, friends, is boring. We must not say so. John Berryman. ColAP; HAP; HCAP; HarvBoo; HeIP-4; NAAL-2v2; NOBA; NoAM; NoP-4; PoetW; TAP; TRP; TwCP; VCAP *Fr.* Dream Songs.

Life Goes On. Karen Alkalay-Gut. GotH

Life grows so clear, beneath the dreaming lamp. Vision of Niamh, The. Eva Gore-Booth. PoBW

Life has conquered, the wind has blown away. Hope. *Unknown.* CIP-2, *tr.* by Frank O'Connor

Life has dark secrets; and the hearts are few. Letitia [*or* Laetitia] Elizabeth Landon. VWP *Fr.* Fragments.

Life has just begun. 'S Wonderful. George Gershwin. ReLy

Life has loveliness to sell. Barter. Sara Teasdale. ITBLP; SoSe-8

Life holds no sweeter thing than this—to teach. Life-Hook. Juana de Ibarbourou. WPOW, *tr.* by Marti Moody

Life-Hook. Juana de Ibarbourou. TCLAP, tr. by Sophie Cabot Black and Maria Negroni

Life-Hook. Juana de Ibarbourou. WPOW, tr. by Marti Moody

Life, hope, they conquer death, generally, always. After the Convention. Robert Lowell. NoAM

Life! I know not what thou art. Life. Anna Laetitia Barbauld. GTBS-P; NAEL-6v2; NoP-4; OBEV; OxAEP-1; PWR

Life I Led, The. Nikki Giovanni. GT

Life impaled him high on a cliff. Biography of an Agnostic. Louis Ginsberg. TrJP

Life in a day: he took his girl to the ballet. Louis MacNeice. BoLoP Fr. Novelettes.

Life in a Love. Robert Browning. FHYEP

Life in Death. Ellice Hopkins. PeVV

Life-in-Love. Dante Gabriel Rossetti. HAP Fr. House of Life, The.

Life in the Boondocks. A. R. Ammons. HAP

Life in the Castle. Anne Hébert. BoWoP, tr. by Aliki and Willis Barnstone

Life in the City: In Memoriam Edward Gibbon. Philip Whalen. PoM

Life in this world. Basho. EH, tr. by Robert Hass

Life in this world. Iio Sogi. SoOfWa, tr. by Sam Hamill

Life Is a Dream. Pedro Calderón de la Barca. NAWM-5v1
 "We live, while we see the sun." AWP

Life is a game with a glorious prize. Playing the Game. Unknown. PWR

Life is a glass wherein we dimly see. Life's Boundary. Henrietta Cordelia Ray. CBWP-3

Life is a jest; and all things show it. My Own Epitaph. John Gay. FaBoEE; NIL-7; NIP-4; NOEC; NPeEn; OxBEV; PeLV

Life Is a Killer. John Giorno. PmAP

Life is a long discovery, isn't it? Discovery. Joseph Hilaire Pierre Belloc. OxBSP

Life Is a Platform. Peter Levi.
 "Smoke when the sun fell and when it rose." FaBoTw

Life is a Shylock; always it demands. Law, The. Ella Wheeler Wilcox. PWR

Life Is a Song, Let's Sing It Together. Fred E. Ahlert. ReLy

Life is an ever-rolling wheel. Mumon Gensen. JDP, tr. by Yoel Hoffmann

Life Is Fine. Langston Hughes. NBLV; SAmP

Life is full of mirth and pleasure. Adieu. Mary E. Tucker. CBWP-1

Life is (I think) a blunder and a shame. (LL) William Ernest Henley. NAEL-5v2; NAEL-6v2; NOBVV; NPeEn Fr. In Hospital.

Life is in the rice-field, wealth in the wheat. Grace before Meat. Robert David Fitzgerald. NOBAu

Life is inadequate, but there are many real. Independence Day. William Jay Smith. TwCP

Life Is Just a Bowl of Cherries. Ray Henderson. ReLy

Life Is Life. Robert Walker. IBA

Life is like a cloud of mist. Mumon Gensen. JDP, tr. by Yoel Hoffmann

Life is like a jagged tooth. Life. Grace Treasone. InPK-6

Life Is Long. Unknown. OHMPC, tr. by Kenneth Rexroth

Life is Long, the. John Harington. ChIV-2

Life is lovely in seclusion. Retirement. Yuan Chen. CrYelRi, tr. by Sam Hamill

Life is made. Veronique Tadjo. NAfrP, tr. by Faustine Boateng Gyima

Life is made up of vanities—so small. Stern Truth. Letitia [or Laetitia] Elizabeth Landon. VWP

Life Is Motion. Wallace Stevens. SAmP

Life is never meaningless: there is always food. Dog Kibble: A Villanelle. Charles Baxter. Unle

Life is not a highway strewn with flowers. April Showers. Louis Silvers. ReLy

Life is not a horse with a winner's garland. Look Sheila Seeing You've Asked Me. Vincent O'Sullivan. PeNZ

Life is not made for meetings. Presented to Wei Pa, Gentleman in Retirement. Tu Fu. CoBCP, tr. by Burton Watson

Life is nothing but time. Gloria Gervitz. MirDau, tr. by Stephen Tapscott

Life . . . is remembering waking up. Sandro Penna. CAGL, tr. by John McRae

Life is sad and so slow and so cold. Limerick. Gavin Ewart. PeLi

Life is simple and gay. For the Moment. Pierre Reverdy. TTTS, tr. by Ron Padgett

Life is slow, but it seems exciting. In Buddy's Eyes. Stephen Sondheim. ReLy

Life is such a great adventure. Hundred Years from Today, A. Victor Young. ReLy

Life Is the Body's [or Bodies] Light. Robert Herrick. BeJo; CavPo

Life it asks of us is a dog's life, The. (LL) Victor Dog, The. James Merrill. NoAM; NoP-4

Life keeps me alive: all its tubes. Life Supports. William Bronk. APSN

Life lasts the course of a kiss. Aleksandr Makarov [or Makarov-Krotkov]. TCRP

"Life! length of life!" for this, with earnest cries. Juvenal. OBVE Fr. Satires.

Life, like a marble block, is given to all. Life. Edith Wharton. APN-2

Life like the periodical not yet. James Merrill. HCAP Fr. Book of Ephraim, The.

Life, looking out attentive from the eyes of the doe. (LL) Buck in the Snow, The. Edna St. Vincent Millay. ColAP; NALW; NoP-4

Life Mask. Charles Brasch. PeNZ

Life Model. Maggie Hannan. NeBl

Life of a Dead Dog. David Avidan. FIT, tr. by Robert Friend

Life of a Nun. Pope. ECEV Fr. Eloisa to Abelard.

Life of a Salesman. Emily Grosholz. RA

Life of Ages, Richly Poured. Samuel Johnson. AH

Life of an Echo, The. Judith Ortiz Cofer. PueRic

Life of Art, The. Denise Levertov. BodElec

Life of Hubert, The. Thomas Cole. NOEC

Life of Ideas, The. Chris Wallace-Crabbe. OBGa

Life of Intimate Fleeing, A. Robert Kelly. FTOS

Life of Life. Shelley. NOBE; PoE Fr. Prometheus Unbound [A Lyrical Drama in Four Acts].

Life of Lincoln West, The. Gwendolyn Brooks. NoAM

Life of Man, The. Francis Bacon. NoSic
 (Life.) GTBS-P; OxAEP-1

Life of Man, The. Barnabe Barnes. EBEV Fr. Divine Century of Spiritual Sonnets, A.

Life of my life, take not so soon thy flight. To His Dying Brother, Master William Herrick. Robert Herrick. CaPo; CavPo; NOSC

Life of sabbaths here beneath!, A. Thomas Traherne. ESCV Fr. Third Century, The.

Life of significant soil, The. (LL) T. S. Eliot. AiP; NoP-4; OxBA Fr. Four Quartets.

Life of St Sava, The. Vasco [or Vasko] Popa. PoSu, tr. by Anne Pennington Fr. St Sava's Spring.

Life of the Blessed, The. Luís De León. AWP, tr. by William Cullen Bryant

Life of the Body, The. Diane Bonds. PoSol

Life of the nameless foetus, The. Birthmarks. Rajani Parulekar. OMIP, tr. by Vinay Dharwadker

Life of the roebuck was mine, The. To Lady Elizabeth Foster, from Georgiana, Duchess of Devonshire, When She Was Apprehensive of Losing Her Eyesight–1796. Georgiana Cavendish, Duchess of Devonshire. PoBW

Life of This World. Unknown.
 "Life of this world, woe betide thee!" MLL

Life of wealth does not appeal to me at all, A. Room in Bloomsbury, A. Sandy Wilson. ReLy

Life of writing, unless wondrous short, A. William Whitehead. ECEV Fr. Charge to the Poets, A.

Life of yon trim Shakspere [or Shakespeare] on the tree?, The. (LL) Mocking Bird, The. Sidney Lanier. APN-2; TCAPo

Life on Earth. Frank O'Hara.
 "Shine, 'O world! don't weary the gulping Pole." UnPo

Life owes me nothing. Let the years. Life Owes Me Nothing. Unknown. PoToHe

Life Plastic. "Michael Field." VWP

Life pours out images, the accidental. Rokeby Venus, The. Robert Conquest. GS

Life (priest and poet say) is but a dream. Dragon-Fly, The. Walter Savage Landor. OBEV

Life roars on, of course. Longing. Femi Osofisan. NAfrP

Life's a Funny Proposition after All. George M. Cohan. ReLy

Life's a game. I Know That You Know. Anne Caldwell. ReLy

Life's a performance. Either join in. Palladas [or Pallades]. GrAn

Life's an empty thing. Me and My Girl. Noel Gay. ReLy

Life's an ocean crossing where winds howl. Palladas [or Pallades]. GrAn

Life's as we / Find it—death too. Daie-Soko. ZenPo, tr. by Takashi Ikemoto and Lucien Stryk

Life's Boundary. Henrietta Cordelia Ray. CBWP-3

Life's Circumnavigators. William Robert Rodgers. GTBS-P

Life's dreary for me. Body and Soul. Edward Heyman. ReLy

Life's Golden Sunset. Mrs. Henry Linden. CBWP-4

Life's "Good-Morning." Anna Laetitia Barbauld. TreFP Fr. Life.

Life's Journey. Ella Wheeler Wilcox. PWR

Life's Made up of Little Things. Mary R. Hartman. PoToHe

Life's Mirror. "Madeline Bridges." PWR

Life's Morning. Howell Elvet [or Elfed] Lewis. OBWVE, tr. by H. Idris Bell

Life's Parallels, A. Christina Georgina Rossetti. NAEL-5v2; NAEL-6v2

Life's pathway to me is dreary. Opium-Eater, The. Mary E. Tucker. CBWP-1

Life's Progress. Anne Finch, Countess of Winchilsea. ECWP

Life's smallest miseries are, perhaps, its worst. Small Miseries. Letitia [or Laetitia] Elizabeth Landon. VWP

Life's sorrows and regrets—who can escape them? Tune: Song of Tzu-yeh. Li Yü. CoBCP, tr. by Burton Watson

Life's spent guarding, A. What there is to guard. August the First: The Watchman Speaks. Marjorie Oludhe Macgoye. HBAPE

Life's stormy surge had scarcely touched. Grafted Bud, The. Mary Weston Fordham. CBWP-2

Life's Trades. Emily Dickinson. RB; TCAPo

Life's Will. Abu al-Qasim Al-Shabbi. MAP, tr. by Sargon Boulus and Christopher Middleton

Life's wisdom is best found in living drunk. Wisdom of Life, The. "Al-Akhtal al-Saghir." MAP, tr. by Issa Boullata and Thomas G. Ezzy

Life-Saving Medal. Philippe Soupault. PFTM-1

Life Sentence. János Pilinszky. IQMS, tr. by Peter Jay

Life should be a humane. Lebensraum. Thom Gunn. PAI

Life sometimes held such sweetness for him. My Grandfather and His Apple-Tree. John Ormond. AngWePo; TCAWP

Life Story. Taeko Tomioka. WPOW, tr. by Harry Guest, Lynn Guest and Kajima Shozo

Life Story. Unknown. OBSP

Life Story. Tennessee Williams. GLP

Life Story. Paul Zweig. BodElec

Life Supports. William Bronk. APSN

Life that dies and that subsists. Interview. Manuel Bandeira. TCLAP, tr. by Candace Slater

Life the hound. Hound, The. Robert Francis. SoSe-8

Life, the story goes. Anna Liffey. Eavan Boland. BodElec; ModIr

Life today is hectic. What's Going to Happen to the Tots? Noël Coward. NBLV

Life up to now had been no mistake. Elvis Acts as His Own Pallbearer. Fleda Brown Jackson. AllShUp

Life was a song. You Were Meant for Me. Arthur Freed. ReLy

Life was back lanes, therefore out of bounds. Alan Wearne. BMAP Fr. Nightmarkets, The.

Life was so peaceful at the drive-in. Arthur Murray Taught Me Dancing in a Hurry. Johnny Mercer. ReLy

Life we find is nevermore. Deception. Josephine D. Henderson Heard. CBWP-4

Life! We've been long together. Anna Laetitia Barbauld. TreFP Fr. Life.

Life which now I lead is as a perfect death, The. Love Is Life and Death. Georg Rudolph Weckherlin. GePo, tr. by George C. Schoolfield

Life whirls past like drunken wildfire. (LL) Winter Dawn. Tu Fu. BLT; OHPC, tr. by Kenneth Rexroth

Life will keep hammering the grass blades into the ground. Force. Derek Walcott. OxBC

Life with the graveyard. (LL) Familial. Jacques Prévert. CLPP; FaBoWar, tr. by Lawrence Ferlinghetti

Life Withdrawn, The. Luís De León. SpanPo, tr. by Edwin Morgan

Life without Passion, The. William Shakespeare. See Sonnets

Life yet of his lines shall never out, The. (LL) Upon the Lines and Life of the Famous Scenic Poet, Master William Shakespeare. Hugh Holland. AngWePo; OBWVE

Life You Have, The. Yona Volach. DTA, tr. by Miriyam Glazer

Lifeguard, The. James Dickey. NoP-4; SoSe-8

Lifeless plains at the foot of. Wanderings on a Heavenly Body. László Kálnoky. IQMS, tr. by Kenneth McRobbie and Zita McRobbie

Lifeless solitude—an angry waste, A. On the Telescopic Moon. John Swanwick [or Swanick] Drennan. BIrV

Lifeless son—the mother's agony, The. Three Marys at Castle Howard, in 1812 and 1837, The. Ebenezer Elliott. SacPr

Lifeline. Vijay Seshadri. BAP-97

Lifelines. Gavin Ewart. SPE

Lifelong. Sharon Olds. ExTi

Lifelong farewell. Idea Vilariño. TANSG, tr. by Louise B. Popkin

Lifers file into the hall, The. In the Cage. Robert Lowell. NOBA; Son

Lifes. Achy Obejas. WiU

Lifetime. Narayan Surve. OMIP, tr. by Vinay Dharwadker

Lifetime Devoted to Literature, A. Judith Rodriguez. NOBAu

Lifetime mirrored: Chang and Eng, A. Siamese Twins in Love. Susan Swartwout. ReTh

Lifetime's teaching grammar come to this, A. Palladas [or Pallades]. GrAn

Lift Every [or Ev'ry] Voice and Sing. James Weldon Johnson. APT-1; ISC; TCAPo

    (Lift Ev're Voice and Sing.) NAAAL

Lift latch, step in, be welcome, Sir. Luncheon, A. Max Beerbohm. NOBL; OBSV; OxBTC; PeLV

Lift Me Higher. Mary E. Tucker. CBWP-1

Lift up thine eyes, sweet Psyche! What is she. Psyche, before the Tribunal of Venus. Nathaniel Parker Willis. APN-1

Lift up, ye poor! your everlasting prayer! Poor of London, The. William Forster. CBAP

Lift Up Your Heads, Rejoice! Thomas Toke Lynch. TrCP

Lift your arms to the stars. Love and Liberation. John Hall Wheelock. MoAmPo

Lift your feet and you sink deeper in the mud! Ruinous Rains. Fu Hsien. CoBCP, tr. by Burton Watson

Lift your flowers. Chicory and Daisies. William Carlos Williams. APT-1

Lift Your Glad Voices in Triumph on High. Henry Ware, Jr. AH

Lift your heads, all you peoples, to the wet heat rising in the airshaft. Praise Psalm of the City-Dweller. April Bernard. NIL-7

Lifted by a little breeze. Lucilius. GrAn

Lifted by its tufts. Shroud, The. Galway Kinnell. LCAP-2

Lifting. Dorothy Barresi. MoASP

Lifting, The. Sharon Olds. NIL-7

Lifting Belly. Gertrude Stein.
    "Kiss my lips. She did." APT-1; PFTM-1; PoBW
    "Lifting belly. Are you. Lifting." OxWW

Lifting, both hands pulling whitely. Grandpa's .45. W. M. Ransom. CDW

Lifting his slowly trickling jaws. Tête-à-Tête. Edwin Honig. NoAM

Lifting Illegal Nets by Flashlight. James Wright. NNaP

Lifting my fingers. Frozen Hands. Joseph Bruchac. CDW

Lifts up his voice and shouts: "Strike! you are warriors!" AOI. (LL) Unknown. NAWM-5v1; NAWM-7v1, tr. by Frederick Goldin Fr. Song of Roland, The.

Light. Marianne Boruch. PoSol

Light. Fireflies. Paul Fleischman. NOxBChV

Light. Richard Kenney. Son

Light. Peter Markus. AmPoNex

Light. John Milton. See Paradise Lost

Light. Martinus Nijhoff. TuT, tr. by Desmond Egan

Light. Michael Ondaatje. NIP-4

Light. Diane Wakoski. OPOU

Light, The. Nude by Edward Hopper, A. Lisel Mueller. PoSol

Light, The. Martinus Nijhoff. WoPoe, tr. by Raphael Rudnik

Light across the courtyard. Saint's Bridge. Lola Ridge. WPE

Light after darkness, gain after loss. Afterwards. Frances Ridley Havergal. SacPr

Light along the hills in the morning, The. Notice What This Poem Is Not Doing. William Stafford. LCAP-2

Light and air, The? They are mountain-perfect, here in Taos, near. Hopi Prophet Chooses a Pop. Heid E. Erdrich. AmPoNex

Light and dry. Locust Wood Mallet for Papermaking, A. Lin Pu. ColAnChi, tr. by Paul Hansen

Light and joyous figure, one that seems, A. Dancing Girl, The. Letitia [or Laetitia] Elizabeth Landon. CenSon

Light and Rejoicing to Israel. Unknown. TrJP, tr. by Israel Abrahams

Light and Shadow. Hugh MacDiarmid. HarvBoo

Light Another Candle. Miriam Chaikin. NTCP

Light at Equinox. Léonie Adams. ColAP

Light-Bearer of Liberty, The. J. W. Scholl.
    "Gooing babies, helpless pygmies." VerBaPo

Light beats upon me, The. Mid-day. "H. D." APT-1; NAAL-5

Light became her grace and dwelt among, The. Ballatetta. Ezra Pound. VGW

Light begins. Snow begins. Un Extraño. Tess Gallagher. ExTi

Light Breaks Where No Sun Shines. Dylan Thomas. FaBoMo; MoBrPo; OxAEP-2; OxBEV; OxBTC

Light breeze rustles the reeds, A. Night Thoughts While Travelling. Tu Fu. OHPC, tr. by Kenneth Rexroth

Light brush of dawn, A. Louise Herlin. MFP, tr. by Martin Sorrell

Light do I see within my Lady's eyes. Ballata 5. Guido Cavalcanti. CTC, tr. by Ezra Pound

Light drifts from the stalled. Out of My Own Pocket. Martha Collins. ExTi

Light drizzle falling off, A. Taking a Captive / 1984. Barney Bush. HATNAP

Light exists in Spring, A. Emily Dickinson. APN-2; BoWoP; ITBLP; NCAP; NOBA; OxBA

Light Exists in The Fire, The. "Angelus Silesius." GePo, tr. by George C. Schoolfield Fr. Cherubical Wanderer, The.

Light Falls Obliquely. Eric Gamalinda. ReBoTo

Light-fingered Dio takes after the God of Thieves. Lucilius. GrAn

Light flows our war of mocking words, and yet. Buried Life, The. Matthew Arnold. FHYEP; NAEL-5v2; NAEL-6v2

Light foot hears you and the brightness begins, The. Poem Beginning with a Line by Pindar, A. Robert Duncan. NNaP; NeAP; PmAP; PoM; VCAP

Light from the planet Venus, soon to set. Evening-Star. Louise Bogan. APT-2

Light from the street lamp shines, The. Night. Justin Chin. AmPoNex

Light Furs, Fat Horses. Po Chü-i. CoBCP, tr. by Burton Watson

Light, God's white light breaks and must bedizen, The. Light, The. Martinus Nijhoff. WoPoe, tr. by Raphael Rudnik

Light, God's white light, breaks up into colours. Light. Martinus Nijhoff. TuT, tr. by Desmond Egan

Light going out in the forehead, A. Swimming by Night. James Merrill. ColAP; HarvBoo; VGW

Light growth of green dreams drying, A. (LL) Losing Track. Denise Levertov. HeIP-4; NOBA; PoE; PoM

Light-hearted I walked into the valley wood. Conversion. Thomas Ernest Hulme. FaBoMo; OxBSP

Light here has begun to pass and as it passes, The. Art of Measuring Light, The. Ellen Hinsey. AmPoNex; YaYoPo

Light hosann'd in the mirrors. Timing. Anne Rouse. NeBl

Light Hotel. Peter Redgrove. PoE

Light I don't have slanting through broken walls. Air. John Godfrey. FTOS

Light in Darkness. Mary E. Tucker. CBWP-1

Light, in light breezes and a favoring sun. Watching Tennis. John Heath-Stubbs. OxBSo; Son

Light in One's Blood, The. Gemino H. Abad. ReBoTo

Light in the moon the only light is on Sunday, A. Gertrude Stein. TCAPo Fr. Rooms.

Light in the skull of the bird, The. Nathaniel Tarn. APSN Fr. Lyrics for the Bride of God.

Light in the Window, The. C. L. Erickson. PWR

Light in the window seemed perpetual, The. Room above the Square, The. Stephen Spender. NOBE

Light into the olive entered. After Greece. James Merrill. CoAmPo; ColAP; NOBA; TRP

Light Invested. Carlos A. Angeles. ReBoTo

Light is around the petals, and behind them. Looking at Some Flowers. Robert Bly. NOBA

Light is burning late, A. Herbert Street Revisited. John Montague. CIP-2; ModIr; PBCIP; PNI

Light is laying waste the heavens. Native Stone. Octavio Paz. TCLAP, tr. by Muriel Rukeyser

Light is on my body also, The. Lilith. Linda Gregg. WPOW

Light is the inside, The. Girl Powdering Her Neck. Cathy Song. NoP-4

Light-Keeper, The. Robert Louis Stevenson. NePenScot
"Brilliant kernel of the night, The." EBVV

Light Listened. Theodore Roethke. MoAmPo

Light looks from a dazzled leaf. Dazzle. Dorothy Roberts. NOBC

Light. Love. Freedom. Like a Blessing. Stanley Crouch. GT

Light mist girdles the mountain. Inscribed on a Painting. T'ang Yin. SuSp, tr. by Chiang Yee

Light mist, then dense fog. Li Ch'ing-chao. BoWoP; OHMPC

Light, my light, who commanded, Disappear! Hayim Lenski. FIT, tr. by Robert Friend

Light of awakening, The. Moon Mountain. Muso Soseki. EaWin, tr. by W. S. Merwin

Light of evening, Lissadell, The. In Memory of Eva Gore-Booth and Con Markievicz. W. B. Yeats. NPeEn; NoAM; OBMV; OxBTC

Light of joy there, there is something to be said. Hafiz [or Hafez]. WoPoe, tr. by Basil Bunting

Light of Other Days, The. Thomas Moore. See Oft In the Stilly Night

Light of our cigarettes, The. Pastel: Masks and Faces. Arthur Symons. NOBVV

Light of Our Souls. Kata Szidónia Petröczy [or Petröczi]. IQMS, tr. by Marie B. Jaffe

Light of our souls, to you we call. Light of Our Souls. Kata Szidónia Petröczy [or Petröczi]. IQMS, tr. by Marie B. Jaffe

Light of the moon. Buson. EH, tr. by Robert Hass

Light of the silver torch that has no smoke. In the Night. Ch'oe Ch'ung. WoPoe, tr. by Jean S. Grigsby

Light on his pins. Roethke Plain. John Malcolm Brinnin. TAP

Light on his thigh was like, The. King of the Cats is Dead, The. Peter Porter. EmeKit; NoAM

Light / on my mother's tongue. Lucille Clifton. ESEAA

Light or Sheade. William Barnes. NOBVV

Light painted the sky, some months ago, The. Painting the Eaves. Tony Towle. PmAP

Light passes, The. Evening. "H. D." APT-1; FaBoMo; HarvBoo; VGW; WPE

Light projected lifetimes ago. Telescope. Sydney Lea. RA

Light pulling away from trees, The. Distance. Peter Everwine. GeoHom; NNaP

Light rain doesn't slick the road. Tu Fu. SuSp Fr. Rain, Four Poems.

Light rain makes me long for you, The. San Diego (On a rainy day). Lamea Abbas Amara. PoArWo, tr. by Nathalie Handal and Mike Maggio

Light rain settles this white dust. White Dress. Yuan Chen. CrYelRi, tr. by Sam Hamill

Light Reading. Vassar Miller. FFC

Light river wind, A. Robert Spiess. HA

Light's glittering morn bedecks the sky. Hymn for Easter Morn. John Mason Neale. TrCP

Light's Reading, The. Alan Williamson. PoSol

Light's rosary, blood-bright spheres. Ribes rubrum. Elizabeth Garrett. NeBl

Light screams, it backs me up, The. Noise Will Start Tomorrow, The. Jeanne Megnen. SurWo, tr. by Guy Ducornet

Light Shining out of Darkness. William Cowper. CABP; EBEV; ECEV; FHYEP; FaBoCh; NOBE; NOCV; NOEC; NPeEn; OxBEV; PWR; SacPr; TFi; TOF Fr. Olney Hymns.

Light silently shifts even as three kittens leap, The. Patio. Manuel A. Viray. ReBoTo

Light Sleep. Hazel Hall. APT-1

Light slides through lace panels on the window, The. Family Photos: Black and White: 1960. Virginia Cerenio. FSt

Light splashed this morning. Round, The. Stanley Kunitz. BodElec

Light-spring, oh sun, in light our wedding joys immure. Daniel Casper von Lohenstein. GePo Fr. Arminius.

Light stands over me, The. Descartes at Daybreak. Aidan Carl Mathews. CIP-2

Light starts in a promising street, The. Capriccio of Roman Ruins and Sculpture with Figures, A. J. D. McClatchy. GS

"The light that cannot fade." William Daniel Ehrhart. CDa

Light That Failed, The. Rudyard Kipling.
Heriot's Ford. PoRA
"What's that that hirples at my side?" PoRA

Light that shone when Hope was born, The. (LL) Tennyson. EBVV; FHYEP; NAEL-6v2 Fr. In Memoriam A. H. H.

Light the first light of evening, as in a room. Final Soliloquy of the Interior Paramour. Wallace Stevens. APT-1; BBASP; ColAP; HAP; HCAP; HarvBoo; LCAP-2

("The Light They Make."). Debra Bruce.
Sonnet 2: "Deep in her seventh month, my sister dozes." FFCI
Sonnet 4: "Wet streets, black trees, a gold leaf smacked." FFC

Light Throws Shadows. Drahomira Vandas. SurWo, tr. by Guy Ducornet

Light up thy halls! 'Tis closing day. F. de Samara to A. G. A. Emily Jane Brontë. NALW

Light was out; the sky was down, The. Gnostic Prelude. James McAuley. BMAP

Light weed, whose poisoned scent with sickly power. Poppy, The. Sarah Hamilton. CenSon

Light white, a disgrace, an ink spot, a rosy charm, A. Gertrude Stein. TTTS Fr. Tender Buttons.

Light-Winged Smoke, Icarian Bird. Henry David Thoreau. APN-1; ColAP; NOBA; TAP; TCAPo Fr. Walden.

Light winter rain. Buson. SoOfWa, tr. by Sam Hamill

Light Woman's Song, The. Judith Johnson Sherwin. TAP

Light Years and the Love Lost in the Oleanders. Alane Rollings. WeW-3

Light You Give Off, The. Jelaluddin [or Jalal al-Din] Rumi. RaBo, tr. by Coleman Barks and John Moyne

Light young man lay with a lighter woman, A. On Tom Holland and Nell Cotton. Unknown. FaBoEE

Lighted brazier. Winter. Ngo Chi Lan. EaWin, tr. by W. S. Merwin and Nguyen Ngoc Bich

Lighten up. Prayer. Lucille Clifton. NAAAL

Lightening, The. Gabriella Sica. CItWP, tr. by Cinzia Sartini Blum and Lara Trubowitz

Lightenings. Seamus Heaney.
"Annals say: when the monks of Clonmacnoise, The." EmeKit; ModIr; NPeEn
"Boat that did not rock or wobble once, A." ModIr

Lighter. Sargon Boulus. MAP, tr. by Sargon Boulus and Alistair Elliot

Lightheartedly breathing of the silvery winter. Hero. Yevgeny [or Evgenii] Aronovich Dolmatovsky [or Dolmatovskii]. TCRP, tr. by Daniel Weissbort

Lightheartedly Take from the Palms of My Hands. Osip Emilevich Mandelstam [or Mandelshtam]. WoPoe, tr. by James Greene

Lighthouse. Novella Nikolaevna Matveyeva [or Matveieva]. TCRP, tr. by Deming Brown

Lighthouse. Gerard Woodward. EmeKit

Lighthouse as an image, The. February: Pemaquid Point. Ira Sadoff. PoSol

Lighthouse in the Night. Alfonsina Storni. BoWoP, tr. by Aliki and Willis Barnstone

Lighthouse invites the storm and lights it, The. Malcolm Lowry. NOBC *Fr.* Roar of the Sea and the Darkness, The.

Lighthouse of Alexandria, The. Mercedes Roffé. TANSG, *tr.* by Kathryn Kopple

Lighthouses. Dorothy Wellesley, Duchess of Wellington. WPE

Lighting a Fire. X. J. Kennedy. NOxBChV

Lighting her thin French cigarette. Bathing Girls, The. Tracey Herd. NeBl

Lighting one candle. Buson. EH, *tr.* by Robert Hass

Lighting the lantern. Buson. EH, *tr.* by Robert Hass

Lighting up, lest all our hearts should break. Words for Jazz Perhaps. Michael Longley. SeSe

Lightly a slight shadow floats on the March snows. Hayim Lenski. FIT, *tr.* by Robert Friend

Lightly Bound. Stevie Smith. NALW

Lightly forsaking / the Spring mist as it rises. Seeing the Returning Geese. Lady Ise. BoWoP; WoPoe, *tr.* by Irma Brandeis and Etsuko Terasaki

Lightly, gently, earth. (LL) Francis Beaumont. AWP; HAP; NOBE; OBEV; SCGP *Fr.* Maid's Tragedy, The.

Lightly he laughed, as one that read my thought. Tennyson. OBGa *Fr.* Gardener's Daughter, The.

Lightly, lightly o'er [*or* ore] the dead. (LL) Upon a Maid[e]. Robert Herrick. CaPo; FaBoCh; FaBoEE; OxBoLi

Lightly she lifts the large, pure, luminous shell. Imprisoned. Celia Laighton Thaxter. TCAPo

Lightly she turns back her long red sleeves. Kuan Han-ch'ing. SuSp *Fr.* Tune: "Green Jade Flute."

Lightly stepped a yellow star. Emily Dickinson. MoAmPo; OxBA; SAmP

Lightness. Meg Bateman. NePenScot

Lightning. Basho. EH, *tr.* by Robert Hass

Lightning. Witter Bynner. APT-1

Lightning. D. H. Lawrence. MoBrPo

Lightning. Haniel Long. APT-1

Lightning, The. Judah Al-Harizi. BLT, *tr.* by T. Carmi

Lightning and the gale!, The. (LL) Old Ironsides. Oliver Wendell Holmes. APN-1; AiP; BRP; NAAL-2v1; NAAL-3; NCAP; PWR; TAP; TCAPo; TFi

Lightning and thunder, The. Baby-Sermon, A. George Macdonald. NOxBChV; Spl

Lightning bug has wings of gold, The. Bugs. *Unknown.* HHAm

Lightning flash. Basho. EH, *tr.* by Robert Hass

Lightning flash, A. Buson. SoOfWa, *tr.* by Sam Hamill

Lightning flashes, The! Haiku. Basho. SoSe-8, *tr.* by Earl Miner

Lightning flickers. Amano Hachiro. JDP, *tr.* by Yoel Hoffmann

Lightning gleam, A. Haiku. Basho. SoSe-8, *tr.* by Harold G. Henderson

Lightning-gleam, A. Basho. TAL

Lightning hits the roof. Woman to Man. Ai. NoAM

Lightning in the clouds! Basho. WeW-3

Lightning is a yellow Fork, The. Emily Dickinson. InPK-6; NCAP

Lightning is angry in the night. Michael Is Afraid of the Storm. Gwendolyn Brooks. NOxBChV; OxIBACP

Lightning / is the future brightening. Mabrak. "Bongo Jerry." WaCA

Lightning Rod Salesman, The. M. L. Hester. CRP

Lightning's shaft, but dazzles to destroy!, The. (LL) Dreams of a Rival. Mary Robinson. CenSon; RWP

Lightning scratched our sugar maple, blood. Injured Maple. Ronald G. Everson. NOBC

Lights. Ernesto Cardenal. TCLAP, *tr.* by Jonathan Cohen

Lights are bright. I Wonder What Became of Me. Johnny Mercer. ReLy

Lights are burning / In quiet rooms. Bus Stop. Donald Justice. LCAP-2

Lights are going out, The. Buson. EH, *tr.* by Robert Hass

Lights are going out, The. Larry Gates. HA

Lights are out in the street, and a cool wind swings, The. Aubade. Rosamund Marriott Watson. ViWPN

Lights at Newport Beach, The. Joe Bolton. AmPoNex

Lights dimmed, the scraper scraped, and I could feel. Surgical Moves. Rachel Wetzsteon. AmPoNex; ExTi

Lights extinguished, by the hearth I leant, The. Legend of Provence, A. Adelaide Anne Procter. VWP

Lights from the Cambucí district on nights of crime. Nocturne. Mário de Andrade. TCLAP, *tr.* by Jack E. Tomlins

Lights from the parlour and kitchen shone out, The. Escape at Bedtime. Robert Louis Stevenson. OTCP

Lights in the Sky Are Stars, The. Kenneth Rexroth. Heart of Herakles, The. BLT

Lights in the theater fail, The. The long racks. Dancer's Life, A. Donald Justice. LCAP-2

Lights. Not the histrionic reds and golds. Port Phillip Night. Francis Webb. BMAP

Lights of London, The. Louise Imogen Guiney. APN-2

Lights of the city come on for further exploits, The. (LL) Rain is Falling, The. Homero [*or* Umberto] Aridjis. STV; TCLAP, *tr.* by John Frederick Nims

Lights off, the clock glowing 2:10, The. Soup, The. Gary Soto. NoP-4

Lights on the shore. Planting. Okogbule Wonodi. PBMAP

Lights out. How to Meditate. Jack Kerouac. BB; PoM

Lights out. Edward Thomas. HarvBoo; NOBE; OxAEP-2; PoWW; WoPoe

Lights out. Shades up. Girl in a Nightgown. Wallace Stevens. AmFaPo; OxBA

Lights shining above the Neva. Yury [*or* Iurii] Konstantinovich Terapiano. TCRP

Ligurra's fearful I'll contrive. Martial. RomPo, *tr.* by Peter Whigham

Like. Robert Desnos. MFP, *tr.* by Martin Sorrell

Like a Beacon. Grace Nichols. OPOU

Like a Blessing. Stanley Crouch. GT

Like a bolt of silk, the rippled course of this southern river. Evening Scene at Twin Forests. Chin Nung. CoBLCP, *tr.* by Jonathan Chaves

Like a bullet. Joao Cabral de Melo Neto. TCLAP, *tr.* by Elizabeth Gordon *Fr.* Knife That Is All Blade, The.

Like a bullet. Knife All Blade, A. João Cabral de Melo Neto. VCWP, *tr.* by Galway Kinnell

Like a Bulrush. Marianne Craig Moore. APT-1

Like a bulwark against fate. At Rest in the Blast. Marianne Craig Moore. MoAmPo

Like a caravan of nursing camels with humps in the sky. Jezrael. Avraham Shlonsky. MHP, *tr.* by Ruth Finer Mintz

Like a child's cut-out, she holds her weight. Dark Horse. Phillis Levin. FFC

Like a cloud the feathered albatross. Haka: The Feathered Albatross. Muru Walters. PeNZ, *tr.* by the author

Like a convalescent, I took the hand. Seamus Heaney. NAEL-5v2; NAEL-6v2; NoAM; TOF *Fr.* Station Island.

Like a dead man's grave. (LL) Brave New World. Archibald MacLeish. NOBA; OxBA

Like a deserted beach. Man Closing Up, The. Donald Justice. CoAP

Like a disk, a trembling coin spinning on its own diameter. Edoardo Sanguineti. ItPo, *tr.* by Gayle Ridinger *Fr.* Scartabello.

Like a Dog. Mihály Babits. IQMS, *tr.* by Peter Zollman

Like a dog howling endlessly. Idea Vilariño. TANSG, *tr.* by Louise B. Popkin

Like a dog in his lowly corner. Like a Dog. Mihály Babits. IQMS, *tr.* by Peter Zollman

Like a dragged gem, floating. Night of Fathers. Valerie Martínez. TouFir

Like a dragon you have filled the land. Inanna and An. Enheduanna. BoWoP

Like a drop of water is my heart. Youth and Maidenhood. Sarah Williams. LW

Like a drummer's brush. Rain. Emanuel DiPasquale. InPK-6; KaS

Like a drunk treading on his trouser cuffs. Convalescing in London. Thomas [*or* "Tom"] M. Disch. RA

Like a fastball, or a perfect pass. (LL) Dennis Cooper. ReTh; WiU *Fr.* Some Adventures of John Kennedy Jr.

Like a fawn from the arrow, startled and wild. Eliza Harris. Frances Ellen Watkins Harper. NAAAL

Like a fine *what* shirt I put it on. House beside the Sea, The. Rachel Hadas. FFC

Like a Fire in a Fire. Mary Jo Bang. NAPBL

Like a first coat of whitewash when it's wet. Twelfth Morning; or What You Will. Elizabeth Bishop. APT-2

Like a flash of light that bewitches the word. Desert 1. Monica Mansour [*or* Mansur]. MirDau, *tr.* by Celeste Kostopulos-Cooperman

Like a flight of arrows the wind. Stormy Night in Autumn. Chu Shu-chen. BoWoP; OHPC, *tr.* by Kenneth Rexroth

Like a Floating Jasmine. Idea Vilariño. TANSG, *tr.* by Louise B. Popkin

Like a Flower. Fily-Dabo Sissoko. NegPo, *tr.* by Ellen Conroy Kennedy

Like a funeral bell. (LL) Afternoon in February. Henry Wadsworth Longfellow. APN-1; ColAP

Like a gaunt, scraggly pine. Lincoln. John Gould Fletcher. CBCWP; MoAmPo

Like a gondola of green scented fruits. Images. Richard Aldington. MoBrPo

Like a grey wall around Europe. Iwan [*or* Yvan] Goll. PeFWW, *tr.* by Patrick Bridgwater *Fr.* Requiem for the Dead of Europe.

Like a handful of leaves. Cesare Greppi. ItPo, *tr.* by Gayle Ridinger

Like a hidden spring. My Love-Song. Else Lasker-Schüler. TrJP, *tr.* by Jethro Bithell

Like a hot stone your cock weighs on mine, young man. Long Lines: Youth and Age. Paul Goodman. GLP

Like a hound with nose to the trail. Michaelmas. Norman Nicholson. MoBrPo

Like a huntsman after weary chase. Edmund Spenser. HeIP-4; NAEL-5v1; PoE; Son *Fr.* Amoretti.

Like a kinsman. Tollund Man, The. Hugo Claus. PFTM-2, *tr.* by Theo Hermans

Like a lit-up Christmas Tree. Lover and the Syringa-Bush, The. Herman Melville. OBAL

Like a lizard in the sun, though not scuttling. Laureate, The. Robert Graves. BIrV; FaBoTw; OBSV

Like a love-letter, full of sweet surprise. (LL) Still-Life. Elizabeth Daryush. FaBoWP; NPeEn; OxBEV; WPE

Like a mad lion, like a wild bull. Race, The. Nuala Ni Dhomhnaill. CIP-2; PBCIP, *tr.* by Michael Hartnett

Like a madwoman and almost alone. Interior Landscape. Gloria Fuertes. BoWoP, *tr.* by Willis Barnstone

Like a mauve carnation puckered up and dim. Sonnet to the Asshole. Paul Verlaine. CAGL, *tr.* by Alan Stone

Like a Midsummer Rose. John Lydgate. SacPr

Like a minaret. Abode of Arrival. Ahmed Taha. NAfrP, *tr.* by Clarissa C. Burt

Like a miracle song. Another Me. Api. OMIP, *tr.* by A. K. Ramanujan

Like a model's smile. (LL) Mantle. William Heyen. MoASP; ReTh

Like a mountain bristled. CXXX. Pita Amor. TANSG, *tr.* by Shaun Griffin and Emma Sepúlveda-Pulvirenti

Like a mountain whirlwind. Sappho. BoWoP

Like a Mourningless Child. Kenneth Patchen. MoAmPo

Like a painting it is set before one. View from the Window, The. Ronald Stuart Thomas. NoP-4

"Like a plum!" Lawrence says. "Frieda in anger." Lawrence and Edison in New Jersey: 1923. Linda Bierds. ExTi

Like a poisonous snake in my blood. Love. Samar Sen. WoPoe, *tr.* by Pritish Nandy

Like a poor buffoon, of his deformity. Horn of Roland, The. Marina Ivanovna Tsvetayeva [*or* Tsvetaeva]. TCRusP, *tr.* by William Tjalsma

Like a pot turned on the straw. How Is He Coming Then. Lucille Clifton. NALW

Like a prowling wolf, I padded from door to door. Return, The. Evan J. Thomas. AngWePo

Like a rainstorm, he said, the braided colors. Worsening Situation. John Ashbery. NOBA

Like a ravaged sea / this bed. Lady Ise. BoWoP

Like a relative. Tollund Man. Hugo Claus. TuT, *tr.* by Peter Van de Kamp

Like a relentless milkman up the stairs. (LL) Living in Sin. Adrienne Rich. NIL-7; NIP-4; NoP-4; SoSe-8; TAP; UnPo

Like a rich man who's made a galley-slave. (LL) Sonnet: He Argues His Case with Death. Cecco Angiolieri, da Siena. AWP; EaItPo, *tr.* by Dante Gabriel Rossetti

Like a river glorious. Perfect Peace. Frances Ridley Havergal. SacPr

Like a river she was. Memory, The. Robert Creeley. VGW

Like a root growing. (LL) Eleven. Archibald MacLeish. HAP; WeW-3

Like a rope that has been snapped. Irrationale. László Szabédi. IQMS, *tr.* by John Gordon Nichols

Like a round loaf, that's how small you were. To the Newborn. Judit Tóth. WPOW, *tr.* by Laura Schiff

Like a rubber tire another. Strong Winds below the Canyons. Larry Kramer. GeoHom

Like a ruddy child you fall asleep in september. Aleksey [*or* Aleksei] Petrovich Tsvetkov. TCRusP

Like a seesaw, like a rainbow, the colored. Patrizia Vicinelli. ItPo, *tr.* by Gayle Ridinger   *Fr.* Foundations of Being, The.

Like a skein of loose silk blown against a wall. Garden, The. Ezra Pound. APT-1; AWP; HeIP-4; MoAmPo; NIL-7; NIP-4; OxBSP; TwCP

Like a small gray / coffee-pot. Gray Squirrel, The. Humbert Wolfe. MoBrPo

Like a soldier from Anders's army. Natalya [*or* Natal'ia] Gorbanevskaya [*or* Gorbanyevskaya *or* Gorbanevskaia]. TCRP

Like a soldier's ribbon on a tunic tacked. (LL) Pathology of Colours. Dannie Abse. BloBone; NIP-4; NoAM; TCAWP

Like a spear thrust deep within my heart. Developers, The. W. Les Russell. IBA

Like a sprinter in a long-awaited race. If Only for One Night. Gordon Chambers. InTrad

Like a sweet apple reddening on the high. Sappho. BoWoP

Like a sweet orange sucked by a boy. Creation. Ifi Amadiume. HAWP

Like a thick horse's mane. Marina Ivanovna Tsvetayeva [*or* Tsvetaeva]. WoPoe, *tr.* by David McDuff   *Fr.* Poem of the End.

Like a veiled dream thy memory comes. To a Loved One of Other Days. Matilda Caroline Edwards. PWR

Like a wave crest. Uda Emperor. OHPJ

Like a white candle through a shuttered hand. (LL) Sisters, The. Roy Campbell. BoLoP; FaBoTw; NoP-4; OBMV

Like a woman you've longed to make love to, and finally did. Pennsylvania Winter Indian 1974. Harold Littlebird. VoR

Like a worm I writhe in your tight fist. In the Fist of Your Hatred. Gwendoline C. Konie. HAWP

Like a wounded bear. Dark Blue Hussars. Nikolai Nikolaievich Aseyev [*or* Aseiev]. TCRP, *tr.* by Daniel Weissbort and Lubov Yakovleva

Like Achilles you had a goddess for mother. On Looking into E. V. Rieu's Homer. Patrick Kavanagh. NOIV

Like air on skin, coolness of yachts at mooring. Yachts on the Nile. Bernard Spencer. NoAM

Like all fools, I believed. You Are Too Beautiful. Richard Rodgers. ReLy

Like all guests my son got in the way. Speaking of Gabriel. Rosario Castellanos. TANSG, *tr.* by Magda Bogin

Like all other impropagandula? (LL) Conrad Potter Aiken. OBAL; OBCoV

Like all the apes in the neighborhood. Ready. Dan Pagis. FIT, *tr.* by Robert Friend

Like an accident or an insistence, without model or precedent. Earliest Known Representation of a Storm in Western Art, The. Lavinia Greenlaw. MFPA

Like an Adventurous Seafarer Am I. Michael Drayton. NOSC; Son   *Fr.* Idea.

Like an adversity. (LL) Emily Dickinson. NCAP; OxBSP

Like an Animal. Jimmy Santiago Baca. AF

Like an arrow shot / To Death from Birth. Wine. Micah Joseph Lebensohn. TrJP, *tr.* by A. M. Klein

Like an elephant. Mahadevi. WoPoe, *tr.* by A. K. Ramanujan

Like an enfranchised bird, who wildly springs. Sonnet 007. Caroline Elizabeth Norton. CenSon; VWP

Like an extinguished star. Abandonment. Al-Zahra Al-Mansouri. PoArWo, *tr.* by Richard McKane and Tahia Abdel Nasser

Like an imperialist, it has changed the landscape forever. (LL) Purple Loosestrife. Ann Townsend. ExTi; NeAmPo

Like an object whose loss has begun to be felt. Lost and Found and Lost Again. John Ashbery. BodElec

Like an old stone tree. (LL) Moss of His Skin, The. Anne Sexton. CoAP; NALW; PAI

Like an old, wrecked sponge-diver leaking. Sometimes Feel. Pearse Hutchinson. ModIr

Like an otter, but warm. Pastoral. Rita Dove. NAAAL

Like an ox streaming saliva, yoked to the plough. Like an ox. Jules Supervielle. MFP, *tr.* by Martin Sorrell

Like Ana. Nina Cassian. PoSu, *tr.* by Nina Cassian

Like Ankle-Rings, This Music. Gunnar Ekelof. PFTM-1

Like any seagull in old tales I left . . . alone . . . while friends clung to. Veins All Dried Up. Fatma Kandil. PoArWo, *tr.* by Khaled Mattawa

Like as a huntsman after weary chase. Edmund Spenser. *See* Like a huntsman after weary chase

Like as a ship, that through the ocean wide. Edmund Spenser. NAEL-5v1; PoE   *Fr.* Amoretti.

Like as the armèd knight. Ballad Which Anne Askew Made and Sang When She Was in Newgate, The. Anne Askew. CABP; EMWP; NoSic; WPE

Like as the culver on the bared bough. Edmund Spenser. PoE   *Fr.* Amoretti.

Like as the damask[e] rose you see. Simon Wastell. FaBoCh   *Fr.* Microbiblion.

Like as the fountain[e] of all light created. Incarnatio Est Maximum Dei Donum [*or* Donum Dei]. William Alabaster. NoSic

Like as the waves make towards the pebbled shore. William Shakespeare. CABP; EBEV; NAEL-7v1; NIP-4; NOBE; NoSic; OxAEP-1; OxBSo; PoRA; SCGP; Son; TFi; TreFP; UnPo   *Fr.* Sonnets.

Like as, to make our appetites more keen. William Shakespeare. SCGP   *Fr.* Sonnets.

Like ashes, like oceans swarming. Dead Gallop. Pablo Neruda. TCLAP, *tr.* by John Felstiner

Like Attracts Like. Emmett Williams. WeW-3

Like bees after being out in the world, gathering and sucking up their lot. Sadness of Memory, The. Barbara Ras. NAPBL

Like bodiless water passing in a sigh. Fog. Louise Imogen Guiney. APN-2

Like butterflies but lately come. Beautiful Creatures Brief as These. Douglas G. Jones. MoCV

Like callow birds left desert to the skies. (LL) Elizabeth Barrett Browning. BWW; CenSon   *Fr.* Sonnets from the Portuguese.

Like cancer cells, ivy, arthritis. Carol Rumens. NewEx

Like clouds that sail in summer skies. Like Clouds. Sándor Petőfi. IQMS, *tr.* by George F. Cushing

Like Coleridge, I waltz. Under the Ice. Stewart Conn. NePenScot

Like costumes grandsires wore. (LL) Emily Dickinson. NOBA; SoSe-8

Like Crusoe with the bootless gold we stand. Experience. Edith Wharton. APN-2

Like cutting the dry rot out of a potato. Dark Conclusions. Ruth Stone. BoWoP

Like death-row prisoners, they have till the morning stars to live. Mayakovsky. Mikhail Valentinovich Kulchitsky [*or* Kulchitskii]. TCRP, *tr.* by Bradley Jordan

Like Deity—to keep. (LL) Emily Dickinson. APN-2; NALW

Like dewdrops. Senryu. JDP, *tr. by* Yoel Hoffmann

Like dives in the deeps of hell. Save the Boys. Frances Ellen Watkins Harper. PWR

Like Dolmens round My Childhood, the Old People. John Montague. EBEV; ModIr; NoP-4; PBCIP; PNI

Like dry wood in a burning fire. Michelangelo Buonarroti. CAGL, *tr. by* James M. Saslow

Like empty beer cans, like empty. Ernesto Cardenal. TCLAP, *tr. by* Thomas Merton *Fr.* Gethsemani, KY.

Like Etna's dread volcano see the ample forge. Anchorsmiths, The. Charles Dibdin. NOEC

Like Father. Herbert Williams. AngWePo

Like foxgloves in the school of the grass moon. Flower Master, The. Medbh McGuckian. ModIr; PNI

Like fragments of an uncompleted world. Sierras. Joaquin Miller. APN-2

Like full, plump. Soko. JDP, *tr. by* Yoel Hoffmann

Like Galen even him. Elegy for Aisha. Abdul Wahab [*or* 'Abd al-Wahhab] Al-Bayati [*or* Al-Bayyati]. MAP, *tr. by* Sargon Boulus and Christopher Middleton

Like garden gods—and not so decent either. (LL) Byron. NOBL; PeLV *Fr.* Don Juan.

Like Ghosts of Eagles. Robert Francis. LCAP-2

Like giant with a dwarf who thwarts him. Lóci Becomes a Giant. Lőrinc Szabó. IQMS, *tr. by* Egon F. Kunz

Like God. Lynn Emanuel. PuP-23

Like good unprocessed. Spiritual: "How did you feel when you come out the wilderness?" William W. Cook. SpirFl

Like Grandpa Paul / The water is all of my mind. Louis Zukofsky. ChIV-1 *Fr.* A.

Like gript stick. Sermon, The. Richard Hughes. OBMV

Like Groping Fingers. Abraham Sutskever [*or* Sutzkever]. TrJP, *tr. by* Joseph Leftwich

Like ground that's been walked over, it echoes. Valerio Magrelli. ItPo, *tr. by* Gayle Ridinger

Like Grumbling Roman Plebs. Osip Emilevich Mandelstam [*or* Mandelshtam]. TCRusP, *tr. by* John Glad

Like Gulliver in Brobdingnag. György Sárközi. IQMS, *tr. by* Roy Fuller

Like Gulliver pulling a hundred ships. Nina Cassian. BoWoP

Like Hebe, ever fair and young. (LL) Evan Lloyd. AngWePo; OBWVE *Fr.* Powers of the Pen, The.

Like Her Body the World. Martha Collins. ExTi

Like hibiscus. Like a Flower. Fily-Dabo Sissoko. NegPo, *tr. by* Ellen Conroy Kennedy

Like his own sweat or the insults of the sea. (LL) Second Voyage, The. Eiléan Ní Chuilleanáin. EmeKit; ModIr; NPeEn

Like hooved up ground / thats what. (LL) Hermit Cackleberry Brown, on Human Vanity, The. Jonathan Williams. OBAL; PoM

Like ice in storage. Sentoku. JDP, *tr. by* Yoel Hoffmann

Like it used to be, not even the future. (LL) Ö. Rita Dove. HCAP; WeW-3

Like John on Patmos, brooding on the Four. Commination, A. Alec Derwent Hope. ChIV-2

Like Jonah in the green belly of the whale. Emily Carr. Wilfred Watson. MoCV; NOBC

Like killer kings on an Etruscan cup. (LL) Beyond the Alps. Robert Lowell. LCAP-2; NOBA

Like Leaves on Trees the Race of Man is found. Homer. OBVE, *tr. by* Alexander Pope *Fr.* Iliad, The.

Like liquid gold the wheat-field lies. Dakota Wheat-Field, A. Hamlin Garland. OBCA

Like Lise, moreover, my mother was white. Black Man's Son, The. Oswald Durand. TTY

Like lust in the chill of the grave. (LL) Hamatreya. Ralph Waldo Emerson. APN-1; NAAL-3; NCAP

Like Mandelstam's swallow. Irina Ratushinskaya [*or* Ratushinskaia]. ItGoST, *tr. by* David McDuff

Like many a one, when you had gold. Old Story, The. Argentarius. AWP, *tr. by* E. A. Robinson

Like many a one, when you had gold. *Var. authors.* AWP *Fr.* Variations of Greek Themes.

Like many of us, born too late. Shut In. Robert B. Shaw. SoSe-8

Like medals given the brave. (LL) Field Hospital, The. Paul Muldoon. CIP-2; PNI

Like Memory, Caverns. Elizabeth Dodd. AmPoNex

Like men riding. Nelly Trim. Sylvia Townsend Warner. MoBrPo

Like Michinoku. Minamoto no Tōru. OHPJ

Like misty moonlight. Issa. SoOfWa, *tr. by* Sam Hamill

Like music come back to life. Small Variation. Octavio Paz. VCWP, *tr. by* Mark Strand

Like Musical Instruments. Tom Clark. PmAP; TRP (Poem.) CoAmPo

Like my mother, and my grandmother too. Heaven. Chairil Anwar. PoetW, *tr. by* Burton Raffel

Like my own boke. (LL) Off the Back of a Lorry. Tom Paulin. ModIr; PBCIP

Like nervous birds in the sky. (LL) Enemy Dead, The. Bernard Gutteridge. FaBoWar; PoWW

Like Noah's Weary Dove. William Augustus Mühlenberg. AH

Like nomads we came. Claiming the Dust. Jean Janzen. GeoHom

Like nothing else in Tennessee. (LL) Anecdote of the Jar. Wallace Stevens. ColAP; FaBoA; HCAP; HeIP-4; InPK-6; MoAmPo; NAAL-2v2; NAAL-5; NAWM-7v2; NIL-7; NOBA; NoAM; NoP-4; OxBA; OxBSP; PAI; PoPoPo; SAmP; TAP; TCAPo; TFi; UnPo

Like Odysseus under the ram. Archilochus. OBVE

Like oil lamps, we put them out the back. Emigrant Irish, The. Eavan Boland. AmFaPo; EmeKit

Like old women knitting, breathless / to tell their tales. (LL) Necessities of Life. Adrienne Rich. HCAP; NOBA

Like one of those old sulphur matches. Spanish Dancer. Oliver Reynolds. TCAWP

Like one of yours, ye multitudinous ocean. (LL) Walt Whitman. NAAL-2v1; NAAL-3 *Fr.* Fancies at Navesink.

Like One Who. Ágnes Nemes Nagy. VCWP, *tr. by* Hugh Maxton

Like one who brings an important letter to the counter after office hours: the counter is already closed. When Evil-Doing Comes Like Falling Rain. Bertolt Brecht. AF, *tr. by* John Willett

Like one who brought news from far. Like One Who. Ágnes Nemes Nagy. VCWP, *tr. by* Hugh Maxton

Like one who in [*or* who'in] her third widowhood [*or* widdowhood] doth profess[e]. To Mr. Roland Woodward. John Donne. ESCV

Like other things. Girl in the Kitchen. "Vaidehi." OMIP, *tr. by* A. K. Ramanujan

Like others I get drunk in my blood. Road to Exile Thinking of Vallejo, The. Syl Cheney-Coker. PBMAP

Like Our Bodies' Imprint. Yehuda Amichai [*or* Amikhai]. AF, *tr. by* Assia Gutmann

Like Oxford colledg[e] bells, to supp. (LL) On Westwall Downes [*or* On Westwell Downs]. William Strode. NOSC; NPeEn

Like pain of fire runs down my body my love to you, my dear! *Unknown.* APN-2, *tr. by* Franz Boas *Fr.* Songs of the Kwakiutl Indians.

Like Pornography. Rob MacKenzie. Oth

Like priceless treasures sinking in the sand. (LL) America. Claude McKay. NAAAL; NAAL-5; NIL-7; NIP-4; NoAM; TAP; TTY

Like, pussy cat, pussy cat, where is you was? Cool Cat. Michael Myer. TriCat

Like rain falling. Camel, The. Al-Munsif Al-Wahaybi. MAP, *tr. by* Salma Khadra Jayyusi and Naomi Shihab Nye

Like Rain it sounded till it curved. Emily Dickinson. NCAP; RB

Like Raquel. Maria Arrillaga. TANSG

Like shabby ghosts down dried-up river beds. Prisoners of War. John Jarmain. FaBoWar

Like shifting forms in the world. Lu Chi. WoPoe, *tr. by* Tony Barnstone and Chou Ping *Fr.* Art of Writing, The.

Like silver dew are the tears of love. Epitaph. Alfred Edgar Coppard. OBMV

Like Sister and Brother. Enrique Gonzáles Martínez. TCLAP, *tr. by* Nancy Christoph

Like some ill-fated butterfly, the literalists. John Hollander. VCAP *Fr.* Powers of Thirteen.

Like some seraglio of an Eastern king. Curtain, The. Darl Macleod Boyle. YaYoPo

Like some winter animal the moon licks the salt of your hand. Salt Lake, The. Iwan [*or* Yvan] Goll. WoPoe, *tr. by* George Hitchcock

Like Someone in Love. Jimmy Van Heusen. ReLy

Like someone newly dead. Familiar. Maria Luisa B. Aguilar-Cariño. ReBoTo

Like someone who has fallen between the rails. Dezső Kosztolányi. IQMS, *tr. by* Egon F. Kunz *Fr.* Laments of a Poor Little Child.

Like something broken of wing. Chamber Music. Carl Phillips. NAPBL

Like South Sea stock, expressions rise and fall. James Bramston. NOEC *Fr.* Art of Politics, The.

Like tall men with a battering-plank—the colt. Letter from Underground. Ronald G. Everson. MoCV

Like tender branches. (LL) Compromise. Akhtar-ul-Iman. OMIP; WoPoe, *tr. by* Vinay Dharwadker and C. M. Naim

Like that dying woman in Mexico. If. Patrick Lane. NOBC

Like that man who kicks off his shoes. Idea Vilariño. TANSG, *tr. by* Louise B. Popkin

Like the beat beat beat of the tom-tom. Night and Day. Cole Porter. ReLy

Like the briliance of an eye in darkness. Your Anger. Paz Molina. TANSG, *tr. by* Steven F. White

Like the buffalo. To You. Elolongue Epanya Yondo. NegPo, *tr. by* Ellen Conroy Kennedy

Like the cadence of an old love song. Child Life. Mary E. Tucker. CBWP-1

Like the Chinese, I too am going to. Maurizio Cucchi. ItPo, *tr. by* Gayle Ridinger

Like the city skyline they. Commuters. Betsy Hearne. SSCS

Like the crash of the thunder. Zionist Marching Song. Naphtali Herz Imber. TrJP, *tr. by* Israel Zangwill

Like the dark germs across the filter clean. Loss. Charles Madge. FaBoMo

Like the eyes of a mild savior. (LL) Blue Booby, The. James Tate. NoAM; SPE

Like the Eyes of Wolves. Nachum Yud. TrJP, *tr. by* Joseph Leftwich

Like the fey goose-girl in the enchanted wood. Horror. Henry Treece. SPE

Like the fish of the bright and twittering fin. Song from *Mardi*. Herman Melville. APN-2

Like the foghorn that's all lung. Syrinx. Amy Clampitt. NoP-4

Like the golden scale that emerges. Personae Separatae. Eugenio Montale. AF, *tr. by* William Arrowsmith

Like the honeycomb dropping honey. Hildegard von Bingen. WPOW

Like the Idalian Queen[e]. Madrigal. William Drummond, of Hawthornden. NOSC; SCGP

Like the inflatable palm tree I gave to my lover. In Pompano Beach, Florida. Robin Becker. PBCAP

Like the inside of a picnic box. Mount Fuji. Kaneko Mitsuharu. WoPoe, *tr. by* James Kirkup and Akiko Takemoto

Like the last Gazette, or the last Address. (LL) Pope. ECEV; OBSV *Fr.* Epilogue to the Satires, in Two Dialogues.

Like the leaves already blazing and falling farther north. (LL) Children Walking Home from School through Good Neighborhood. Donald Justice. DiPo; NIL-7; NIP-4

Like the Magic Glow of Paradise. Clementina Suárez. TANSG, *tr. by* Janet N. Gold

Like the roofs of buildings. Zombie Jet. Connie Deanovich. AmPoNex

Like the rose I am laughing with all my body, not only with. Jelaluddin [*or* Jalal al-Din] Rumi. BBASP, *tr. by* A. J. Arberry

Like the small sound. How It Comes. Dorothy Barresi. SwNoth

Like the stalks of wheat in the fields. Heinrich Heine. TrJP *Fr.* North Sea, The.

Like the steps of footsore armies. Waiting for Death. Mordecai Gebirtig. TrJP, *tr. by* Joseph Leftwich

Like the sun, blowing out these evil stars. (LL) Love Poem for My Country, A. Frank Mkalawile Chipasula. HBAPE; NAfrP

Like the sweet-apple. Sappho. EroLit, *tr. by* Josephine Balmer

Like the sweet apple which reddens upon the topmost bough. One Girl. Sappho. AWP, *tr. by* Dante Gabriel Rossetti

Like the swell of Summer's ocean. (LL) Stanzas for Music. Byron. AWP; GTBS-P; HAP; NAEL-5v2; NAEL-6v2; PoRA

Like the tides' flood. *Unknown.* OHMPJ

Like the tides I rise and fall. Patricia Bishop. NewEx

Like the Touch of Rain. Edward Thomas. BoLoP; EnLoPo

Like the Trails of Ndakinna. Cheryl Savageau. TWW

Like the undulant lark. Where the Light. Giuseppe Ungaretti. WoPoe, *tr. by* Denis Devlin

Like the vain curlings of the watery [*or* wat'ry] maze. First Anniversary of the Government under His Highness the Lord Protector, 1655, The. Andrew Marvell. BASC

Like the very gods in my sight is he who. Sappho. NAWM-7v1; WPOW, *tr. by* Richmond Lattimore

Like the water's outflow, the dream continues to bleed. Friends. May Muzaffar. PoArWo, *tr. by* Tahia Abdel Nasser

Like the waters. (LL) Old Men Admiring Themselves in the Water, The. W. B. Yeats. FaBoCh; KaS

Like the White. Qasim Haddad. MAP, *tr. by* Charles Doria and Sharif Elmusa

Like the wild organs of the winter storm. In the East. Georg Trakl. PeFWW

Like thee I once have stemm'd the sea of life. Epitaph, An. James Beattie. OBEV

Like they had never been. (LL) Tryst [*or* Trysting Place], The. William Soutar. EBEV; NPeEn; NePenScot; OxBS

Like This. Lajos Kassák. IQMS, *tr. by* Edwin Morgan

Like This. Carol Muske. ExTi

Like This. Jelaluddin [*or* Jalal al-Din] Rumi. ErotSp, *tr. by* Coleman Barks

Like this before you, just as I am. Like This before You. Yocheved Bat-Miriam. MHP, *tr. by* Ruth Finer Mintz

Like this one. (LL) Flower, The. Robert Creeley. PAI; PmAP

Like this stone of. I Am a Creature. Giuseppe Ungaretti. PeFWW, *tr. by* David McDuff

Like This Together. Adrienne Rich. VGW

Like this. . . You wouldn't hang me? I thought not. (LL) How Annandale Went Out. Edwin Arlington Robinson. APT-1; GSo; MoAmPo; NOBA; NoAM; SoSe-8

Like those boats which are returning. Saigyo. AWP

Like those flailing flames. Ted Hughes. HAP *Fr.* Skylarks.

Like those jars that women put out to catch the dew of night. Gabriela Mistral. WPoS *Fr.* Prayer.

Like Those Sick Folks. Sir Philip Sidney. OxBSP *Fr.* Arcadia.

Like thousands, I took just pride and more than just. Reading Myself. Robert Lowell. HCAP; NAAL-2v2; TAP; VCAP

Like Thousands of Others. Aleksandr Petrovich Tkachenko. ItGoST, *tr. by* Maia Tekses

Like tiny golden. Akiko Yosano. OHMPJ

Like to a baker's oven is the grave. In Christ Church, Bristol, on Thomas Turner, Twice Master of the Company of Bakers. Francis Jeffrey, Lord Jeffrey. FaBoEE; NBLV

LIKE to a ring without a finger. *Unknown.* NoSic

Like to the Arctic Needle. Francis Quarles. EBEV; NOCV *Fr.* Emblems.

Like to the clear [*or* cleere] in highest sphere [*or* spheare]. Thomas Lodge. GTBS-P; OBEV *Fr.* Rosalynde; or Euphues' Golden Legacy.

Like to the damaske rose you see. Francis Quarles. NOSC *Fr.* Argalus and Parthenia.

Like to the falling of a star. Sic Vita. Henry King, Bishop of Chichester. BASC; NOBE; NOSC; OxBSP; PAI; SCGP

Like to the Grass That's Green Today. Peter Bulkeley, the Younger. AH

Like to the Indians, scorched with the sun[ne]. Mary Sidney Wroth, Countess of Montgomery. BASC; EMWP; NOSC *Fr.* Pamphilia to Amphilanthus.

Like to the marigold, I blushing close. Edward Taylor. ChIV-2; SCAP *Fr.* Preparatory Meditations before My Approach to the Lord's Supper.

Like to the sentinel stars, I watch all night. To Lucasta. Richard Lovelace. NOSC

Like to thee [*or* the], faire cruell [*or* cruel] May. (LL) Song: "Shephard loveth thow me vell?" Jean Passerat. NPeEn; OBVE, *tr. by* William, of Hawthornden Drummond

Like to these unme[a]surable montains [*or* mountayns]. Jacopo Sannazaro. PoE

Like toenails, clipped them like ends of / split hair. (LL) Hypocrite Women. Denise Levertov. NALW; PoM

Like Trains of Cars on Tracks of Plush. Bee, The. Emily Dickinson. MoAmPo

Like / treasure hidden in the ground. Mahadevi. WPOW

Like tree shadows into the polished windscreen. (LL) From the Frontier of Writing. Seamus Heaney. CABP; ModIr; PoPoPo; PoetW

Like truthles[s] dream[e]s, so are my joys expired. Farewell to the Court. Sir Walter Ralegh. NoSic

Like trying to blow a feather. Mouth to Mouth. Steve Gehrke. AmPoNex

Like two proud armies marching in the field. Your Beauty and My Reason. *Unknown.* NoSic

Like unto Them That Dream. Bible, *O.T.* TrJP *Fr.* Psalms.

Like us he had his. Ulumbo, a Cat. Rutger Kopland. VCWP, *tr. by* James Brockway

Like vapour, the titanic scheme. Ultima Ratio. Friedrich Georg Jünger. WoPoe, *tr. by* Les A. Murray

Like voices on the gale. (LL) Stanzas: "Black absence hides upon the past." John Clare. EnLoPo; NOBVV

Like wanderers in elevated meekness. In the Desert. Semyon [*or* Semion] Izrailevich Lipkin. TCRP, *tr. by* Albert C. Todd

Like Water down a Slope. Zalman Schneour. TrJP, *tr. by* Harry H. Fein

Like we call it / home. (LL) In the Inner City. Lucille Clifton. HeIP-4; SSCS; UnSA

Like wet cornstarch, I slide. Refugee Ship. Lorna Dee Cervantes. PoPoPo

Like widow'd turtle still her loss complain. (LL) To His Lute. William Drummond, of Hawthornden. GTBS-P; NOSC; SCGP; Son

Like wings in waiting on the darkling lake. (LL) This Unimportant Morning. Lawrence Durrell. BoLoP; OxBTC

Like winter fog, the coal dust climbs her stockings. Vespertilio. Linda Bierds. ExTi

Like wolf—and black bull or goblin hound. Charlotte Brontë. VWP

Like Yellowstone National Park. (LL) Further Notice. Philip Whalen. PoM; VGW

Like yours may sweeten and perfume my death. (LL) Contemplation upon Flowers, A. Henry King, Bishop of Chichester. MeLP; OBEV; SCGP

Likelihood is, The. Children. Bill Manhire. PeNZ

Likelihood of Snow, The / The Danger of Fire. Gerald Dawe. PNI

Likely. Lisa Coffman. AmPoNex

Likely as not a ruined head gasket. George Oppen. APT-2

Likeness, A. Robert Browning. CTC

Likeness, The. Arthur Gregor. VGW

Likeness has made them animal and shy. Twins, The. Karl Shapiro. MoAmPo; TrJP

Likenesses. Norman MacCaig. NePenScot

LIKES to a hermit poor in place obscure. Sir Walter Ralegh. NoSic

Lil' Pito. Sandra Maria Esteves. PueRic

Lila's Potatoes. Leland Bardwell. SpudSo

Lilac. Mary Ellen Solt. NIL-7

Lilac by the Museum on St. Wenceslas Square, The. Vitĕzslau Nezval. AF, tr. by Ewald Osers

Lilac Ice Cream. "Igor Severyanin" [or "Severianin"]. TCRP, tr. by Bernard Meares

Lilac ribbon is unbound, A. Country of No Lack. Jean Starr Untermeyer. MoAmPo

Lilacs. David Biespiel. AmPoNex

Lilacs. Karl Kraus. AuPH, tr. by Lowell A. Bangerter

Lilacs. Amy Lowell. APT-1; MoAmPo; OxBA; PoRA

Lilacs and the Roses, The. Louis Aragon. OBWP, tr. by Louis MacNeice

Lilacs are in bloom, The. Late Afternoon at the Arboretum. Kelly Cherry. SwNoth

Lilacs blowing across his face glad he brought you. (LL) Tennis Court Oath, The. John Ashbery. NoAM; TAP

Lilacs in NYC. Mark Doty. WiU

Lilacs lift in generous bloom, The. At Home from Church. Sarah Orne Jewett. APN-2

Lilacs wither in the Carolinas, The. In the Carolinas. Wallace Stevens. SAmP; VGW

Lilatu Laili. Amin Al-Rihani. GraLe

Lili Brik, stretched on a bridge. Mayakovsky in Paris. Andrey [or Andrei] Andreievich Voznesensky [or Voznesenskii]. TCRusP, tr. by Daniel Weissbort

Lilian's Second Letter. Bessie Rayner Parkes. VWP Fr. Summer Sketches.

Lilies. Mary Oliver. BBASP

Lilies, The. Richard Emil Braun. NoAM

Lilies are white. Unknown. LB; OxNR

Lilies, are you come! Tiger-Lilies. "Michael Field." ViWPN

Lilies clustered fair and tall, The. Alone. Celia Laighton Thaxter. TCAPo

Lilies for the Prophet. Nazik Al-Mala'ika. MAP

Lilies of his love appear, The. (LL) Revival, The. Henry Vaughan. InvLi; NOCV

Lilies of the Field. Anne Rouse. MFPA; NeBl

Lilies of the Valley. Jon Silkin. NoAM

Lilies swinging censers fair. Easter Carol. Henrietta Cordelia Ray. CBWP-3

Lilies that fester smell far worse than weeds. (LL) William Shakespeare. NAEL-5v1; NAEL-6v1; NAEL-7v1; NIL-7; NOBE; NoSic; OBEV; OxAEP-1; OxBEV; OxBSo; PoE; SCGP; SCV; Son; TRP; WoPoe Fr. Sonnets.

Lilith. Suzanne Benton. HW

Lilith. Linda Gregg. WPOW

Lilith, Adam's First Companion. Elina Wechsler. MirDau, tr. by Darrell Lockhart

Lilith and the Doctor. Kathleen Norris. HW

Lilith is our daughter. Medusa and Perseus III: Lilith. Pat Parnell. HW

Lilli Burlero [A New Song]. Thomas Wharton, 1st Marquess of Wharton. BASC; NOIV; OxBoLi

Lilliputian Ode on Their Majesties' Accession, A. Henry Carey. FaBoVe; NOEC; NPeEn; OBCoV

Lilliputian's Beer Song. Septimus Winner. OBAL

Lily. Nicholas Virgilio. HA

Lily, The. William Blake. FHYEP; NOBRP Fr. Songs of Experience.

Lily, The. Vadim Sergeievich Shefner. TCRP, tr. by Albert C. Todd

Lily Adair. Thomas Holley Chivers. APN-1; OBAL

Lily Events. Unknown. PFTM-1

Lily in a Crystal, The. Robert Herrick. BeJo; NAEL-5v1; NAEL-6v1; NOSC; SCGP

Lily on liquid roses floating. Champagne Rosée. John Kenyon. OBEV

Lily Pond. Vicki Feaver. EmeKit

Limb of forests rises up, The. Yvonne Caroutch. BoWoP

Limblike to his own snout, projecting there. On a Chaplain's Nose. Francisco de Quevedo y Villegas. WoPoe, tr. by Roy Campbell

Limbo. Seamus Heaney. CIP-2; NoAM; OxBC

Limbo Dancer, The. Josephine Jacobsen. FFC

Limejuice Tub, The. Unknown. NOBAu

Limeraiku. Ted Pauker. NOBL; PeLi

Limerick: "According to old Sigmund Freud." Unknown. PeLi

Limerick: "'Active balls?' said an old man of Stoneham." C. D. Cudmore. PeLi

Limerick: "After lunch the old Duchess of Teck." Unknown. PeLi

Limerick: "Albert Einstein's the man we must credit." Stanley J. Sharpless. PeLi

Limerick: "All his life, Mr. George Bernard Shaw." Audrey Herbert. PeLi

Limerick: "Amoeba named Sam, and his brother, An." Unknown. PeLi

Limerick: "Amorous maiden antique, An." Unknown. PeLi

Limerick: "Ancient biologist, Heine, An." Carol Rumens. PeLi

Limerick: "Angry young husband called Bicket, An." John Galsworthy. PeLi

Limerick: "Angst, poetry, urbanized fret." Sydney Bernard Smith. PeLi

Limerick: "Ankle's chief end is exposiery, The." Anthony Euwer. PeLi

Limerick: "April. Bad month. Visit spa." Stanley J. Sharpless. PeLi

Limerick: "Archimedes, the early truth-seeker." Stanley J. Sharpless. PeLi

Limerick: "Argentine gaucho named Bruno, An." Unknown. NOBL

Limerick: "Arnolfinis both sat to Van Eyck." Sir Robert Witt. PeLi

Limerick: "Artist who lived in St. Ives, An." A. G. Prys-Jones. PeLi

Limerick: "Artist who lived near Montmartre, An." Sir John Waller. PeLi

Limerick: "As dull as the life of the cloister." Unknown. PeLi

Limerick: "As he filled up his order book pp." Unknown. PeLi

Limerick: "As Mozart composed a sonata." Unknown. PeLi

Limerick: "As played by the phantoms of Shrule." Tony Butler. PeLi

Limerick: "As the elevator car left our floor." Unknown. PeLi

Limerick: "As the natives got ready to serve." Ed Cunningham. PeLi

Limerick: "As the poets have mournfully sung." W. H. Auden. PeLi (Aesthetic Point of View, The.) NBLV; OBAL

Limerick: "As the poets have mournfully sung." W. H. Auden. PeLi Fr. Shorts [1948–1957].

Limerick: "As tourists inspected the apse." Edward Gorey. PeLV; PeLi

Limerick: "Ascetic art student named Josh, An." D. H. Cudmore. PeLi

Limerick: "Astute Melanesians on Munda." Unknown. PeLi

Limerick: "At Harvard a randy old Dean." Unknown. PeLi

Limerick: "At last I've seduced the au pair." Cyril Ray. PeLi

Limerick: "At spirit séances in Queen's." Morris Gilbert Bishop. PeLi

Limerick: "At the orgy I humped twenty-two." Unknown. PeLi

Limerick: "Authoress, armed with a skewer, An." Unknown. PeLi

Limerick: "Babe, with a cry brief and dismal, The." Edward Gorey. OBAL; PeLi

Limerick: "Ballistical student named Raffity, A." D. H. Cudmore. PeLi

Limerick: "Bashful young fellow of Brighton, A." E. O. Parrott. PeLi

Limerick: "Bather whose clothing was strewed, A." Unknown. PeLi

Limerick: "Bells from the steeple resound, The." John Stanley. PeLi

Limerick: "Big cities are reeking with grief." Unknown. PeLi

Limerick: "Binary mathematician, A." Unknown. PeLi

Limerick: "Boadicea often would goad." Douglas Catley. PeLi

Limerick: "Boastful young fellow of Neath, A." Frank Richards. PeLi

Limerick: "Book and a jug and a dame, A." Unknown. PeLi

Limerick: "Both Keats and Boccaccio tell a." Joyce Johnson. PeLi

Limerick: "Bottle of perfume that Willie sent, The [or A]." Unknown. PeLi

Limerick: "Breasts of a barmaid of Crale, The." Unknown. NOBL

Limerick: "Brickie who had a fine tool, A." E. O. Parrott. PeLi

Limerick: "Budding young playwright named Coward, A." Doris Pulsford. PeLi

Limerick: "Business-like harlot named Draper, A." Unknown. PeLi

Limerick: "By Loch Ness they can toss, like confetti." Bill Greenwell. PeLi

Limerick: "Calculus fit to compute on, A." Gina Berkeley. PeLi

Limerick: "Candid Professor confesses, A." Thomas Thorneley. PeLi

Limerick: "Canner, Exceedingly Canny, A." Carolyn Wells. PeLi

Limerick: "Careless explorer named Blake, A." Ogden Nash. PeLi

Limerick: "Careless old cook of Salt Ash, A." Unknown. PeLi

Limerick: "Carpenter living in Crewe, A." E. O. Parrott. PeLi

Limerick: "Cassandra declining to follow." Basil Ransome-Davies. PeLi

Limerick: "Certain young chap named Bill Beebee, A." Unknown. PeLi

Limerick: "Certain young gourmet of Crediton, A." Charles Cuthbert Inge. PeLi

Limerick: "Certain young man of Hilgay, A." Ida Thurtle. PeLi

Limerick: "Certain young pate who was addle, A." Arthur Shaw. PeLi

Limerick: "Certain young sheik I'm not namin', A." Unknown. PeLi

Limerick: "Chap was so pose that was adi, A." Arthur Shaw. PeLi

Limerick: "Charlotte Brontë said, 'Wow, sister! What a man!'" Victor Gray. NOBL; PeLi

Limerick: "Chief Stewardess on a Boeing, The." Paul Alexander. PeLi

Limerick: "Cleric once heard with dismay, A." Joan Dare. PeLi

Limerick: "Come and see our French goods—you can try 'em." Unknown. PeLi

Limerick: "'Come now,' said Bell, 'this is choice.'" Frank Richards. PeLi

Limerick: "Come to Noah's for wine and strong waters." Unknown. PeLi

Limerick: "Comely young widow named Ransom, A." Unknown. PeLi

Limerick: "Complacent old Don of Divinity, A." Unknown. PeLi

Limerick: "Conception, an Archbishop said, The." "L. E. J." PeLi
Limerick: "Concerning the bees and the flowers." Unknown. PeLi
Limerick: "Concert conductor in Rio, A." Unknown. PeLi
Limerick: "Conclusion I reach at the Tate, The." "Tallis." PeLi
Limerick: "Connoisseurs of coition aver." Unknown. PeLi
Limerick: "Consider the Emperor Nero." Unknown. PeLi
Limerick: "Consider the lowering Lynx." Langford Reed. PeLi
Limerick: "Consistent disciples of Marx." A. Cinna. PeLi
Limerick: "Couple from old Aberystwyth, A." Stuart Woods. PeLi
Limerick: "Couple there was in Blefuscu, A." W. F. N. Watson. PeLi
Limerick: "Couturier from Haverford West, A." E. O. Parrott. PeLi
Limerick: "Creature of charm is the gerbil, A." Unknown. PeLi
Limerick: "Cried the maid: 'You must marry me, Hume!'" P. W. R. Foot. PeLi
Limerick: "Crusader's wife slipped from the garrison, A." Ogden Nash. PeLi
Limerick: "Cryptic philosopher, Kant, The." "E. F. C." PeLi
Limerick: "Cute secretary, none cuter, A." Ogden Nash. PeLi
Limerick: "Cynic says: Now that we know, A." Thomas Thorneley. PeLi
Limerick: "Cynical sage with a kink, A." Hassall Pitman. PeLi
Limerick: "Dad waited while Mum bought the ham." Coral E. Copping. PeLi
Limerick: "Daring young lady of Guam, A." Unknown. PeLi
Limerick: "Dear Albert, of Saxe-Coburg-Gotha." W. F. N. Watson. PeLi
Limerick: "Dear Sir, You're quite wrong about me." M. Trench. PeLi
Limerick: "Decrepit old gas man named Peter, A." Unknown. SoSe-8
Limerick: "Democracy works (entre nous)." W. Stewart. PeLi
Limerick: "Desperate spinster of Clare, A." Unknown. PeLi
Limerick: "Devil's no longer a myth, The." "Little Billee." PeLi
Limerick: "Devil, who plays a deep part, The." "Little Billee." PeLi
Limerick: "Dickensian borough of Coketown, The." Martin Fagg. PeLi
Limerick: "Did Ophelia ask Hamlet to bed?" A. Cinna. PeLi
Limerick: "Divine by the name of McWhinners, A." Unknown. PeLi
Limerick: "Don't thee think, Zurrr, I be zo amazin.'" Elizabeth H. Lister. PeLi
Limerick: "Don't think it will fall to your lot." Leslie Johnson. PeLi
Limerick: "Dowager Duchess of Spout, The." Edward Gorey. PeLV; PeLi
Limerick: "Dr. Johnson, when sober or pissed." A. Cinna. PeLi
Limerick: "Each Lon was a notable man." L. G. Udall. PeLi
Limerick: "Each night father fills me with dread." Edward Gorey. PeLi
Limerick: "Earnest young leftie named Tariq." Bernard Levin. PeLi
Limerick: "Elderly bride of Port Jervis, An." Ogden Nash. PeLi
Limerick: "Emperor Marcus Aurelius, The." "Yorick." PeLi
Limerick: "English professor named Brooks, An." D. H. Cudmore. PeLi
Limerick: "Enjoyment of sex, although great, The." Unknown. PeLi
Limerick: "Epicure, Dining at Crewe, An." Unknown. NTCP; PeLi; PeLV (Waiter, Please.) NBLV
Limerick: "Ethnologists up with the Sioux." Unknown. PeLi
Limerick: "Evangelical vicar in want." Ronald Arbuthnott Knox. PeLi
Limerick: "Example of Kant's sterling wit, An." Victor Gray. PeLi
Limerick: "Exposing his plate to the air." Joyce Johnson. PeLi
Limerick: "Exquisite bartender at Sweeney's, The." Unknown. PeLi
Limerick: "Fabulous Wizard of Oz, The." Unknown. PeLi
Limerick: "Fact of the matter is, Jack, The." John Stanley. PeLi
Limerick: "Famed big-hitter in cricket, A." Douglas Catley. PeLi
Limerick: "Famous philosopher, Kant, The." C. S. Cook. PeLi
Limerick: "Famous theatrical actress, A." Unknown. PeLi
Limerick: "Far beyond all the girls of Pirelli." I. D. M. Morley. PeLi
Limerick: "Fascist, erect and irate, A." Thomas Thorneley. PeLi
Limerick: "Fat-tailed Dwarf Lemur, in bed, A." Gerry Hamill. PeLi
Limerick: "Fellow from far Erewhon, A." W. F. N. Watson. PeLi
Limerick: "Fellow who fucked but as few can, A." Unknown. PeLi
Limerick: "Feminine mouth in Utopia, The." W. F. N. Watson. PeLi
Limerick: "Fencing instructor named Fisk, A." Unknown. PeLi
Limerick: "Few people could hope to compare." J. Endersby. PeLi
Limerick: "Few things to desire can so prod us." W. F. N. Watson. PeLi
Limerick: "Figure is not anatomical, The." Thomas Thorneley. PeLi
Limerick: "Filthy young fellow called Lawrence, A." Bill Greenwell. PeLi
Limerick: "Finding God's taboos totalitarian." Basil Ransome-Davies. PeLi
Limerick: "First chap to fuck little Sophie, The." Victor Gray. PeLi
Limerick: "Flighty young lady from Loddon, A." Ida Thurtle. PeLi
Limerick: "For his Campbell's Soup screen-prints, society's." Bill Greenwell. PeLi
Limerick: "For hours my wife says 'Goodbye.'" Frank Gelett Burgess. PeLi
Limerick: "'For the tenth time, dull Daphnis,' said Chloe." Unknown. PeLi
Limerick: "For Travelers Going Sidereal." Robert Frost. OBAL; PeLi
Limerick: "For Widower—wanted, house-keeper." Unknown. PeLi
Limerick: "French are a race among races, The." Unknown. PeLi

Limerick: "French poodle espied in the hall, A." Unknown. PeLi
Limerick: "From the bathing machine came a din." Edward Gorey. OBAL; OBCoV; PeLi
Limerick: "From the crypt of the church of St. Giles." Unknown. PeLi
Limerick: "From the elephant paddock one day." Frank Richards. PeLi
Limerick: "From the west to the fabulous east." Unknown. PeLi
Limerick: "G. B. Shaw wrote to Yeats: 'P'raps it's mad of me.'" W. A. Rathkey. PeLi
Limerick: "G'uggery G'uggery Nunc." Sir John Betjeman. PeLi
Limerick: "Gamekeeper of Lady Chatterley, The." Gerry Hamill. PeLi
Limerick: "Gay soccer spectator from Wix, A." Cyril Mountjoy. PeLi
Limerick: "General once lived named de Gaulle, A." Paul Bristow. PeLi
Limerick: "George Stephenson said: 'These repairs.'" Frank Richards. PeLi
Limerick: "George Washington said to his dad." Frank Richards. PeLi
Limerick: "Giraffes, yes, even the strongest." Frank Davies. PeLi
Limerick: "Girl who was touring Zambesi, A." Unknown. PeLi
Limerick: "'Given faith,' sighed the vicar of Deneham." Unknown. PeLi
Limerick: "Glib little beer-buff from Troon, A." Bill Greenwell. PeLi
Limerick: "God brought perfect man to fruition." Douglas Catley. PeLi
Limerick: "God's plan made a hopeful beginning." Unknown. PeLi
Limerick: "Goddess capricious is Fame, A." Langford Reed. PeLi
Limerick: "Goliath was known for ferocity." Frank Richards. PeLi
Limerick: "Good mechanics are all of one mind." Douglas Catley. PeLi
Limerick: "Great-grandfather at Waterloo." Frank Richards. PeLi
Limerick: "Handsome young monk in a wood, A." Unknown. PeLi
Limerick: "Having rid Hamelin town of its vermin." Ted Thompson. PeLi
Limerick: "Headstrong young lady of Ealing, A." Edward Gorey. PeLi
Limerick: "Heart of O'Leary, S.J., The." David Phillips. PeLi
Limerick: "Henley's a special regatta." Jim Anthony. PeLi
Limerick: "Her husband was hors de combat." C. Vita-Finzi. PeLi
Limerick: "Her limp lover Maud couldn't pardon." Kit Wright. PeLi
Limerick: "Herder who hailed from Terre Haute, A." Unknown. PeLi
Limerick: "Hibiscus is flaming and frillier." Ruth Silcock. PeLi
Limerick: "Highly bored damsel called Brown, A." Unknown. PeLi
Limerick: "His sister named [or called] Lucy O'Finner." Lewis Carroll. PeLi
Limerick: "Honourable Winifred Wemyss, The." Unknown. PeLi
Limerick: "Hoover, in grim silence, sat, The." David Woodsford. PeLi
Limerick: "Hopeful old fellow called Rousseau, A." John Fay. PeLi
Limerick: "Horsewoman of charm at Uttoxeter, A." R. D. Condon. PeLi
Limerick: "'How much,' sighed the gentle Narcissus." Stephen Sylvester. PeLi
Limerick: "How often and often I wish." Frances Darwin Cornford. PeLi
Limerick: "How Socratic is Somerset Maugham!" R. B. S. Instone. PeLi
Limerick: "How varied the family Sen!" Roy Fuller. PeLi
Limerick: "Husband who lived in Tiberias, A." Unknown. PeLi
Limerick: "I admire your felicitous phrasing." A. M. Sayers. PeLi
Limerick: "I, Caesar, when I learned of the fame." Unknown. PeLi
Limerick: "I consider I really am through." Elizabeth H. Lister. PeLi
Limerick: "I fear, Mr. Lear, you're a clot." Eric Swainson. PeLi
Limerick: "'I have heard,' said a maid from Montclair." Morris Gilbert Bishop. PeLi
Limerick: "I haven't a clue where I've been." Sydney Bernard Smith. PeLi
Limerick: "I'm getting deep lines on my forehead." Ron Rubin. PeLi
Limerick: "'I'm glad pigs can't fly,' said young Sellers." Ron Rubin. PeLi
Limerick: "I'm in love with a girl from Uttoxeter." Gerard Benson. PeLi
Limerick: "'I must leave here,' said Lady De Vere." Unknown. PeLi
Limerick: "I once had a cat called Maria." Paul Griffin. PeLi
Limerick: "I once knew a spinster of Staines." Plaiwon. PeLi
Limerick: "I once took my girl to Southend." Veronica Nicolson. PeLi
Limerick: "I sat next to the Duchess at tea." Unknown. SoSe-8
Limerick: "I spotted these daffs by the lake." E. O. Parrott. PeLi
Limerick: "I suppose I could try if I chose." "E. F. C." PeLi
Limerick: "I've combed out my beard and I've found." Pauline Phillips. PeLi
Limerick: "I was brought up on old Aristotle." C. S. Cook. PeLi
Limerick: "I was sitting there, taking my ease." Cyril Ray. PeLi
Limerick: "I was thrilled when I went to the Zoo." Victor Gray. PeLi
Limerick: "I went with the Duchess to tea." Woodrow Wilson. PeLi
Limerick: "I wish that my room had a floor." Frank Gelett Burgess. OBCA; OxIBACP; PeLi
Limerick: "I wonder how King Arthur felt." Moss Rich. PeLi
Limerick: "'I would doubt,' said the Bishop of Balham." Terence Rattigan. PeLi
Limerick: "I wouldn't be bothered with drawers." Unknown. PeLi
Limerick: "If Eve hadn't eaten the apple." Wendy Cope. PeLi
Limerick: "If intercourse gives you thrombosis." Unknown. PeLi
Limerick: "If no Pain were, how judge we of Pleasure?" William Bliss. PeLi

Limerick: "'If you dream,' said the eminent Freud." Russell Miller. PeLi

Limerick: "If you feel that you're right on your beam ends." Leslie Johnson. PeLi

Limerick: "If you find for your verse there's no call." *Unknown*. PeLi

Limerick: "'If you're aristocratic,' said Nietzsche." Gerry Hamill. OBCoV; PeLi

Limerick: "Immaculate Sir Walter Raleigh, The." T. L. McCarthy. PeLi

Limerick: "In childhood it's easy to feel." Nigel Andrew. PeLi

Limerick: "In considering things gastronomic." *Unknown*. PeLi

Limerick: "In dealing with time it is found." V. R. Ormerod. PeLi

Limerick: "In Genesis, Adam's the winner." Bill Greenwell. PeLi

Limerick: "In gonia once which was Pata." Arthur Shaw. PeLi

Limerick: "In history's mysteries vast." *Unknown*. PeLi

Limerick: "In Illyria, the love-sick Orsino." Stanley J. Sharpless. PeLi

Limerick: "In New Orleans dwelt a young Creole." Alben Barkley. PeLi

Limerick: "In Pinter's new play that's now running." Frank Richards. PeLi

Limerick: "In the days of mild Jerry Ford." *Unknown*. PeLi

Limerick: "In the Garden of Eden lay Adam." *Unknown*. PeLi

Limerick: "In the rain in a yard in Cessnock." Ruth Silcock. PeLi

Limerick: "Incautious young woman named Venn, An." Edward Gorey. PeLV; PeLi

Limerick: "Indolent vicar of Bray, An." Langford Reed. PeLi

Limerick: "Industrious young obstetrician, An." Isaac Asimov. PeLi

Limerick: "Inept young person, Miss Muffet, The." Dean Walley. PeLi

Limerick: "Innocent bride from the Mission, An." *Unknown*. PeLi

Limerick: "Innocent maiden of Gloucester, An." *Unknown*. PeLi

Limerick: "Insurance salesman named Flint, An." Charles Barsotti. PeLi

Limerick: "Is it really so very unthinkable." Basil Ransome-Davies. PeLi

Limerick: "'Is it thou?' 'Ay,' cries Fra Lippo Lippi." Gerard Benson. PeLi

Limerick: "Is there really a new Mr. Nixon." T. Griffiths. PeLi

Limerick: "Isaac Singer (you probably know)." Peter Brookes. PeLi

Limerick: "It is clear that Napoleon's Queen." Moss Rich. PeLi

Limerick: "It needn't have ribaldry's taint." Don Marquis. PeLi

Limerick: "It occurred when she crossed the Atlantic." *Unknown*. PeLi

Limerick: "It's a nightmare that horrifies hakes." Allan M. Laing. PeLi

Limerick: "It's a pity that Casabianca." Victor Gray. PeLi

Limerick: "'It's my custom,' said dear Lady Norris." *Unknown*. PeLi

Limerick: "It's time to make love. Douse the glim." Conrad Potter Aiken. NBLV; PeLi; PeLV

Limerick: "It seems I impregnated Marge." *Unknown*. PeLi

Limerick: "Ivy Compton-Burnett's irritations." *Unknown*. PeLi

Limerick: "Jolly young fellow from Yuma, A." Ogden Nash. PeLi

Limerick: "Keeper who worked at the zoo, A." Frank Richards. PeLi

Limerick: "King Henry the Eighth was a Tudor." Kirkham Talbot. PeLi

Limerick: "King Louis gave lessons in Class." *Unknown*. PeLi

Limerick: "King Richard, in one of his rages." Amanda Benjamin Hall. PeLi

Limerick: "Kings of Peru were the Incas, The." *Unknown*. PeLi

Limerick: "Kinky young girl from Uttoxeter, A." Herbert Kretzmer. PeLi

Limerick: "Lad of the brainier kind, A." Hymie Sneak. PeLi

Limerick: "Lady from Vanity Fair, A." W. F. N. Watson. PeLi

Limerick: "Lady of features cherubic, A." *Unknown*. PeLi

Limerick: "Lady on climbing Mount Shasta, A." *Unknown*. PeLi

Limerick: "Lady there was in Antigua, A." *Unknown*. PeLi

Limerick: "Lady who rules Fort Montgomery, A." Morris Gilbert Bishop. PeLi

Limerick: "Lady, who signs herself 'Vexed,' A." Edward Gorey. OBAL; PeLi

Limerick: "Lama of Outer Mongolia, A." Ogden Nash. PeLi

Limerick: "Land of blue skies, and sunlight, A." Ruth Silcock. PeLi

Limerick: "Lass of curvacious physique, A." Douglas Catley. PeLi

Limerick: "Last Christmas, when Puss was in Boots." Gina Berkeley. PeLi

Limerick: "Last time I slept with the Queen, The." Dylan Thomas. PeLi

Limerick: "Lecherous young Lilliputian, A." C. Vita-Finzi. PeLi

Limerick: "Left-wing young lady from Wick, A." Gerry Hamill. PeLi

Limerick: "Lesbian girl of Khartoum, A." *Unknown*. NOBL; PeLV

Limerick: "Let's enter the literary scene." *Unknown*. PeLi

Limerick: "Let the eugenist reach for his gun!" Stanley J. Sharpless. PeLi

Limerick: "Life-Force, afflicted with doubt, The." Thomas Thorneley. PeLi

Limerick: "Life is sad and so slow and so cold." Gavin Ewart. PeLi

Limerick: "Limerick Is Furtive and Mean, The." Morris Gilbert Bishop. NBLV; PeLi

Limerick: "Limerick lacks the precision, The." *Unknown*. PeLi

Limerick: "Limerick packs laughs anatomical, The." *Unknown*. PeLi

Limerick: "Limerick realm now prepares, The." *Unknown*. PeLi

Limerick: "Limerick's birth is unclear, The." *Unknown*. PeLi

Limerick: "Limerick's callous and crude, The." *Unknown*. PeLi

Limerick: "Lisping young lady called Beth, A." *Unknown*. PeLi

Limerick: "Lissom psychotic named Jane, A." *Unknown*. PeLi

Limerick: "Lonely old maid named Loretta, A." *Unknown*. PeLi

Limerick: "Lonely young fellow of Eton, A." *Unknown*. PeLi

Limerick: "Lord, since it's hard to explain." J. E. Press. PeLi

Limerick: "Maiden at college called Breeze, A." Mrs. Mercy Warren. PeLi

Limerick: "Man called Andronicus (Titus), A." Paul Wigmore. PeLi

Limerick: "Man from Maputo and so on, A." J. H. Lee. PeLi

Limerick: "Man from the *Washington Post*, A." Anthony Burgess. PeLi

Limerick: "Man hired by John Smith and Co., A." "Mark Twain." InPK-6; PeLi

Limerick: "Man in the Land of the Houyhnhnms, A." W. S. Brownlie. PeLi

Limerick: "Man who had lately declared, A." Thomas Thorneley. PeLi

Limerick: "Man who was asked out to dinner, A." Spike Milligan. PeLi

Limerick: "Marconi, whose ardour was tireless." Stanley J. Sharpless. PeLi

Limerick: "Marquis de Sade and Genet, The." W. H. Auden. PeLi

Limerick: "Meanwhile, back home at the ranch." Victor Gray. PeLi

Limerick: "Mechanical marvel was Bill, A." *Unknown*. PeLi

Limerick: "Menagerie came to Cape Race, A." *Unknown*. PeLi

Limerick: "Millionaire, filled with elation, A." Thomas Thorneley. PeLi

Limerick: "Minister up in Vermont, A." *Unknown*. PeLi

Limerick: "Miranda, remember that Inn?" John Stanley. PeLi

Limerick: "Mr. Wells of the big cerebellum." H. G. Wells. PeLi

Limerick: "Modern composer called Cage, A." Peter Alexander. PeLi

Limerick: "Modern young curate called Hyde, A." D. W. Pain. PeLi

Limerick: "Modest young maiden of Rennes, A." A. C. Cossins. PeLi

Limerick: "Monkey exclaimed with great glee, A." Frank Richards. PeLi

Limerick: "Monsieur Gauguin? 'E's gone to Tahiti." Stanley J. Sharpless. PeLi

Limerick: "Mordant and decadent Youth, A." Thomas Thorneley. PeLi

Limerick: "Mosquito was heard to complain, A." *Unknown*. PeLi

Limerick: "Most women get married, 'tis true." Barney Blackley. PeLi

Limerick: "Mr. Alan Jay Lerner (with by-play)." J. A. Lindon. PeLi

Limerick: "Mr Lear, I'm the Akond of Swat." Ethel Talbot Scheffauer. PeLi

Limerick: "Mr. Rochester's wife's pyromania." Gina Berkeley. PeLi

Limerick: "Mrs. Whitehouse, mixed bathing at Deal." T. L. McCarthy. PeLi

Limerick: "Much-worried mother once said, A." *Unknown*. PeLi

Limerick: "Musical maiden from Frome, A." Cyril Bibby. PeLi

Limerick: "My beard's overcrowded. Now that." Richard Unwin. PeLi

Limerick: "My demands upon life are quite modest." Robert Conquest. PeLi

Limerick: "My purpose was purely corrective." Leslie Johnson. PeLi

Limerick: "Naïve young lady of Bude, A." C. Chevallier. PeLi

Limerick: "Naïve young lady of Cork, A." Reg Yearley. PeLi

Limerick: "Near-sighted fellow named Walter, A." *Unknown*. PeLi

Limerick: "New cinematic emporium, The." *Unknown*. PeLi

Limerick: "Nice pot of gold that was mari, A." Arthur Shaw. PeLi

Limerick: "Night's bible-black darkness prevails." V. R. Ormerod. PeLi

Limerick: "Ninety summers—and never a platitude." Stanley J. Sharpless. PeLi

Limerick: "No, listen, there's this albatross." Bill Greenwell. PeLi

Limerick: "'No more mistresses,' King Edward said." Frank Richards. PeLi

Limerick: "No Portuguese Lady is Nautical." Sydney Hoffman. PeLi

Limerick: "None could better our sex limousine." *Unknown*. PeLi

Limerick: "Not that it always transpired." Cyril Ray. PeLi

Limerick: "Novelist, flushed with success, A." Thomas Thorneley. PeLi

Limerick: "Novelist of the Absurd, A." Ogden Nash. PeLi

Limerick: "O Great Queen Whom I idolize." Jeffery Littman. PeLi

Limerick: "O, I yearn to go back to the Cam!" E. O. Parrott. PeLi

Limerick: "O sage of the stage, Shaw of Shaws!" Harold Ellis. PeLi

Limerick: "Oedipus said to the Sphinx." Victor Gray. PeLi

Limerick: "Of a sudden, the great prima donna." *Unknown*. PeLi

Limerick: "Of all God's jokes none is bluer." A. Cinna. PeLi

Limerick: "Of attractions the Sabines ain't stinted." D. W. Barker. PeLi

Limerick: "Of my husband I do not ask much." *Unknown*. PeLi

Limerick: "'Oh, halt!' cried Virginia, 'Enough!'" Otto Watteau. PeLi

Limerick: "Old archaeologist, Throstle, An." *Unknown*. PeLi

Limerick: "Old Danish jester named Yorick, An." Ogden Nash. PeLi

Limerick: "Old East End worker called Jock, An." Victor Gray. NOBL

Limerick: "Old gourmet who's grown somewhat stout, An." "Yorick." PeLi

Limerick: "Old Indian chief, Running B'ar, An." Mary Rita Hurley. PeLi

Limerick: "Old poet called Omar cried: 'Now,' An." "J. E. C." PeLi

Limerick: "Old Woman who lived in the Shoe, The." Joyce Johnson. PeLi

Limerick: "On a date with a charming young bird." *Unknown*. PeLi

Limerick: "On an outing with seventeen Czechs." *Unknown*. PeLi

Limerick: "On May Day, the girls of Penzance." *Unknown*. PeLi

Limerick: "On Saturn the sexes are three." *Unknown*. PeLi

Limerick: "'On the beach,' said John sadly, 'there's such.'" Isaac Asimov. PeLi

Limerick: "On the chest of a barmaid in Sale." *Unknown*. PeLi

Limerick: "One-day-old baby in Wallabout, A." Morris Gilbert Bishop. PeLi

Limerick: "One midnight, old D. G. Rossetti." Victor Gray. PeLi

Limerick: "One morning old Wilfrid Scawen Blunt." Victor Gray. NOBL

Limerick: "One morning the Monarch said: 'When.'" D. W. Barker. PeLi

Limerick: "Orgy was held on the lawn, The." *Unknown*. PeLi

Limerick: "Othello loved Desdemona." A. Cinna. PeLi

Limerick: "Our existence would be that much grimmer ex-." Robert Conquest. PeLi

Limerick: "Our novels get longa and longa." H. G. Wells. PeLi

Limerick: "Painter, encumbered with cash, A." Thomas Thorneley. PeLi

Limerick: "Pansy who lived in Khartoum, A." *Unknown*. PeLi

Limerick: "Patriot living at Ewell, A." Langford Reed. PeLi

Limerick: "People the Churches love best, The." Patrick Braybrook. PeLi

Limerick: "Philosopher Berkeley once said, The." P. W. R. Foot. PeLi

Limerick: "Platinum blonde, Goldilocks, A." Fiona Pitt-Kethley. PeLi

Limerick: "Plumber from Lowater Creek, A." *Unknown*. PeLi

Limerick: "Poet from Cheltenham Spa, A." Betty Morris. PeLi

Limerick: "Policeman from Nottingham Junction, A." *Unknown*. PeLi

Limerick: "'Political women,' thought Yeats." R. K. R. Thornton. PeLi

Limerick: "Poor Ophelia sighed: 'I deplore.'" Frank Richards. PeLi

Limerick: "Pop's tops!" Bill Greenwell. PeLi

Limerick: "Postmaster-General cried: 'Arsehole!', The." Victor Gray. PeLi

Limerick: "Precede us, O Lord, with Thy Grace." Frank R. McManus. PeLi

Limerick: "Prince Charles in his Welsh principality." Bernard Levin. PeLi

Limerick: "'Princess,' said the Frog, 'Do not wince.'" Gina Berkeley. PeLi

Limerick: "Professor of Ethical Culture, A." *Unknown*. PeLi

Limerick: "Prostitute living in London, A." Douglas Catley. PeLi

Limerick: "Prudish old lady called Muir, A." *Unknown*. PeLi

Limerick: "Psychiatrist fellow from Rye, A." Stephen Cass. PeLi

Limerick: "Psychic researcher's elation, A." Cyril Mountjoy. PeLi

Limerick: "Publisher went off to France, A." *Unknown*. PeLi

Limerick: "Pulmonary tuberculosis." L. G. Udall. PeLi

Limerick: "Pushing young man in Patchogue, A." Morris Gilbert Bishop. PeLi

Limerick: "Quadratic function, ambitious, A." Leo Moser. PeLi

Limerick: "Quirky old gent, name of Freud, A." Martin Fagg. PeLi

Limerick: "Quoth a cow in the marshes of Glynne." Conrad Potter Aiken. PeLi

Limerick: "Randy young girl called Miranda, A." Peter Alexander. PeLi

Limerick: "Rapist, who reeked of cheap booze, A." *Unknown*. PeLi

Limerick: "Rascal far gone in treachery, A." *Unknown*. PeLi

Limerick: "Rather extreme vegetarian, A." "Sagittarius." PeLi

Limerick: "Reason we're asked to endure, The." Bill Greenwell. PeLi

Limerick: "Rebuke by the Bishop of London, A." Victor Gray. PeLi

Limerick: "Remarkable race are the Persians, A." *Unknown*. PeLi

Limerick: "Remember when you are bemusing." Cyril Hughes. PeLi

Limerick: "Retired Civil Servant from Gateley, A." Ida Thurtle. PeLi

Limerick: "Revelations—we've come to the lewd." *Unknown*. PeLi

Limerick: "Reverend Henry Ward Beecher, The." Oliver Wendell Holmes. PeLi

Limerick: "Reverend Mr. Uprightly, The." *Unknown*. PeLi

Limerick: "Riverrun where can you guess?" *Unknown*. PeLi

Limerick: "Ronald Reagan screamed out in dismay." Frank Richards. PeLi

Limerick: "Rose gives a tremulous glance, The." Anne Norris. PeLi

Limerick: "Round-bottomed babe from Mobile, A." *Unknown*. PeLi

Limerick: "Rupert Murdoch, with glee, shouted: 'What.'" Frank Richards. PeLi

Limerick: "Said a boastful young student from Hayes." Frank Richards. PeLi

Limerick: "Said a diffident lady named Drood." *Unknown*. PeLi

Limerick: "Said a dreadfully literate cat." Conrad Potter Aiken. PeLi

Limerick: "Said a fair-headed maiden of Klondike." Langford Reed. PeLi

Limerick: "Said a famous old writer called Fender." Victor Gray. PeLi

Limerick: "Said a fervent young lady of Hammels." Morris Gilbert Bishop. PeLi

Limerick: "Said a foolish young lady of Wales." Langford Reed. PeLi

Limerick: "Said a girl in green Mansfield Park." E. O. Parrott. PeLi

Limerick: "Said a gloomy young fellow called Fart." Victor Gray. PeLi

Limerick: "Said a God-fearing lady called Whitehouse." Roger Woddis. PeLi

Limerick: "Said a herring one day to a sole." Stanley J. Sharpless. PeLi

Limerick: "Said a luscious young lady called Wade." *Unknown*. PeLi

Limerick: "Said a Marxist who stood on the pier." W. H. G. Price. PeLi

Limerick: "Said a medical student, unmanned." Allan M. Laing. PeLi

Limerick: "Said a parson, addressing his flock." W. J. Strachan. PeLi

Limerick: "Said a practical thinker: 'One should.'" Frank Watson. PeLi

Limerick: "Said a pupil of Einstein: 'It's rotten.'" C. F. Best. PeLi

Limerick: "Said a Tripper: 'O joy, to have found.'" Thomas Thorneley. PeLi

Limerick: "Said a wife to her husband near Scole." Ida Thurtle. PeLi

Limerick: "Said an ape as he swung by his tail." *Unknown*. PeLi

Limerick: "Said an elderly Bishop called Greville." "Little Billee." PeLi

Limerick: "Said an eminent, erudite ermine." *Unknown*. PeLi

Limerick: "Said an erudite sinologue: 'How.'" R. J. P. Hewison. OBCoV; PeLi

Limerick: "Said Arnold to Arthur Hugh Clough." Victor Gray. PeLi

Limerick: "Said Freud: 'I've discovered the Id.'" Frank Richards. PeLi

Limerick: "Said Isolde to Tristan: 'How curious!'" Conrad Potter Aiken. PeLi

Limerick: "Said Marlowe: 'Bay City's a drag.'" Peter Alexander. PeLi

Limerick: "Said Mars when entangled with Venus." Mary Holtby. PeLi

Limerick: "Said Miss Farrow, on one of her larks." *Unknown*. PeLi

Limerick: "Said Nelson at his most la-di-da-di." A. Cinna. PeLi

Limerick: "Said Old Father William: 'I'm humble.'" Conrad Potter Aiken. PeLi

Limerick: "Said Old Nick: 'Mister Lewis and me.'" M. Cassell. PeLi

Limerick: "Said Orville to Wilbur 'Hold tight!'" Stanley J. Sharpless. PeLi

Limerick: "Said Paisley: 'I've given up hope.'" Frank Richards. PeLi

Limerick: "Said philosopher-physicist Jeans." R. C. Owen. PeLi

Limerick: "Said Plato: 'The things that we feel.'" Basil Ransome-Davies. PeLi

Limerick: "Said Powell: 'Don't call me insane.'" Roger Woddis. PeLi

Limerick: "Said Queen Isabella of Spain." *Unknown*. PeLi

Limerick: "Said Tebbitt: 'I don't understand 'em.'" Gerry Hamill. PeLi

Limerick: "Said Tennyson: 'Yes, *Locksley Hall*'s." Victor Gray. PeLi

Limerick: "Said the boy driving home towards Clere." Ida Thurtle. PeLi

Limerick: "Said the Chinese philosopher, Lin." Len. PeLi

Limerick: "Said the Duchess of Alba to Goya." *Unknown*. PeLi

Limerick: "Said the famous philosopher, Russell." Victor Gray. PeLi

Limerick: "Said the mythical King of Algiers." *Unknown*. PeLi

Limerick: "Said the newly-weds staying near Kitely." *Unknown*. PeLi

Limerick: "Said the Queen to her favourite ghillie." A. Cinna. PeLi

Limerick: "Said the Stoic, tormented by gout." Thomas Thorneley. PeLi

Limerick: "Said the vet as he looked at my pet." Frank Richards. PeLi

Limerick: "Said Wellington: 'What's the location.'" Frank Richards. PeLi

Limerick: "Said Wilbur Wright, 'Oh, this is grand.'" Frank Richards. PeLi

Limerick: "Said Wittgenstein: 'Don't be misled!'" Peter Alexander. PeLi

Limerick: "Salopian student of Greek, A." Martin Fagg. PeLi

Limerick: "Salvation lassie named Claire, A." *Unknown*. PeLi

Limerick: "Sardines seem to get out of hand." Leslie Johnson. PeLi

Limerick: "Scion of Boston society, A." Conrad Potter Aiken. PeLi

Limerick: "Scribe, to the vulgar inclined, A." Douglas Catley. PeLi

Limerick: "Sculptor remarked: 'I'm afraid,' A." *Unknown*. PeLi

Limerick: "Señorita who strolled on the Corso, A." *Unknown*. PeLi

Limerick: "Sensitive girl called O'Neill, A." *Unknown*. PeLi

Limerick: "Serious young lady from Welwyn, A." C. Armstrong Gibbs. PeLi

Limerick: "Sermon our Pastor, Rt. Rev., The." *Unknown*. PeLi

Limerick: "Sexy young student once toyed, A." Richard Taylor. PeLi

Limerick: "She was caught, a young girl of Uttoxeter." Tim Hopkins. PeLi

Limerick: "Shed a tear for the WREN named McGinnis." *Unknown*. PeLi

Limerick: "Shelley's death—was it really his wish." Bill Greenwell. PeLi

Limerick: "Shepherd who lived up in Gwent, A." E. O. Parrott. PeLi

Limerick: "Shiftless young fellow of Kent, A." *Unknown*. PeLi

Limerick: "Sighed a dear little shipboard divinity." Conrad Potter Aiken. OBAL; PeLi

Limerick: "Sigmund Freud says that one who reflects." Peter Alexander. PeLi

Limerick: "Sign your name in the book. It's just ink." Sydney Bernard Smith. PeLi

Limerick: "Simple living was clearly the nub." Joyce Johnson. PeLi

Limerick: "Since my overdraft threatens to be." S. Tonkin. PeLi

Limerick: "Sir John Shagbag (Conservative, Nore)." Victor Gray. PeLi

Limerick: "Sky's are a pitiful lot, The." Bob Scott. PeLi

Limerick: "Slow-footed stockman called Beales, A." Cyril Mountjoy. PeLi

Limerick: "Smile on the famed Mona Lisa, The." Stanley J. Sharpless. PeLi

Limerick: "So obese is my cousin from Hendon." A. H. Baynes. PeLi

Limerick: "Solipsist with triplets said: 'Though,' A." Lupellus. PeLi

Limerick: "Some Harvard men, stalwart and hairy." Edward Gorey. OBAL; OBCoV

Limerick: "Some lives are so odd—you agree?" *Unknown*. PeLi

Limerick: "Some people may think I'm a bit la-di." C. Vita-Finzi. PeLi

Limerick: "Sometimes there are airs grave and gentle." *Unknown*. PeLi

Limerick: "Southern hill-billy named Hollis, A." *Unknown*. PeLi

Limerick: "Staid schizophrenic named Struther, A." *Unknown*. NIP-4

Limerick: "'Strip,' Leofric said, 'and you'll find.'"   Harry Thomas.   PeLi

Limerick: "Student from Pembroke once said, A."   Andrew Stoker.   PeLi

Limerick: "Student of nuclear fission, A."   W. Bernard Wake.   PeLi

Limerick: "T. S. Eliot is quite at a loss."   W. H. Auden.   PeLi

Limerick: "Taxi-cab whore out at Iver, A."   Victor Gray.   NOBL; PeLi

Limerick: "Teacher of tots at Uttoxeter, A."   Kate McPower.   PeLi

Limerick: "Texan Rhodes Scholar named Fred, A."   Lyndon T. Mole.   PeLi

Limerick: "That fine English poet, John Donne."   Wendy Cope.   PeLi

Limerick: "That smasher of shams, Bernard Shaw."   Frank Buckland.   PeLi

Limerick: "Then scorn not the limerick either."   Robert Conquest.   PeLi

Limerick: "Ther once was this ladye from Tyre."   Tim Hopkins.   PeLi

Limerick: "There is a creature called God."   Dante Gabriel Rossetti.   PeLi

Limerick: "There is an old he-wolf named Gambart."   Dante Gabriel Rossetti. FaBoEE; PeLi

Limerick: "There isn't a shadow of doubt."   *Unknown.*   PeLi

Limerick: "There once was a bard of Hong Kong."   Gerard Benson.   OBCoV

Limerick: "There once was a couple named Mound."   *Unknown.*   PeLi

Limerick: "There once was a doctor who said."   Towanbucket.   PeLi

Limerick: "There once was a fellow called Hyde."   E. J. Jackson.   PeLi

Limerick: "There once was a Fellow of Trinity."   *Unknown.*   PeLi

Limerick: "There once was a Fellow of Wadham / Who approved of the doings of Sodom."   *Unknown.*   PeLi

Limerick: "There once was a flock of wild geese."   B. Semeonoff.   PeLi

Limerick: "There once was a girl from St. Paul."   *Unknown.*   NIP-4

Limerick: "There once was a judge of Assize."   *Unknown.*   PeLi

Limerick: "There once was a lady called Lily."   *Unknown.*   PeLi

Limerick: "There once was a lass of Shalott."   Mary Holtby.   PeLi

Limerick: "There once was a man [*or* There was a young man] who said, 'Damn!'"   Maurice Evan Hare.   NOBL; OxBoLi; PeLi; PeLV

Limerick: "There once was a man who said 'God.'"   Ronald Arbuthnott Knox. *See* Idealism

Limerick: "There once was a monarch of Spain."   *Unknown.*   PeLi

Limerick: "There once was a painter named Scott."   Dante Gabriel Rossetti. PeLi

Limerick: "There once was a person of Chiswick."   J. M. Ross.   PeLi

Limerick: "There once was a plesiosaurus."   *Unknown.*   PeLi

Limerick: "There once was a Scot who said: 'Evil.'"   "H. M."   PeLi

Limerick: "There once was a sculptor named Phidias."   *Unknown.*   PeLi

Limerick: "There once was a vicar of Ryhill."   *Unknown.*   PeLi

Limerick: "There once was a wicked young minister."   Conrad Potter Aiken. OBAL; PeLi

Limerick: "There once was a wise politician."   A. M. Sayers.   PeLi

Limerick: "There once was a writer called James."   R. K. R. Thornton.   PeLi

Limerick: "There once was an artist called Pat."   Margaret Galbreath.   PeLi

Limerick: "There once was an eccentric of Metz."   Leslie Johnson.   PeLi

Limerick: "There once was an eccentric old boffin."   *Unknown.*   PeLi

Limerick: "There once was an old man of Lyme."   Edward Lear.   OxBoLi

Limerick: "There once was a monarch called Harry."   Mary Holtby.   PeLi

Limerick: "There once were two Babes in the Wood."   Roger Woddis.   PeLi

Limerick: "There's a combative artist named Whistler."   Dante Gabriel Rossetti. FaBoEE; PeLi

Limerick: "There's a fortunate priest of St. Paul's."   Douglas Catley.   PeLi

Limerick: "There's a notable family named Stein."   *Unknown.*   NOBL

Limerick: "There's a Portuguese person named Howell."   Dante Gabriel Rossetti.   PeLi

Limerick: "There's a publishing party named Ellis."   Dante Gabriel Rossetti. PeLi

Limerick: "There's a sensitive type in Tom's River."   *Unknown.*   PeLi

Limerick: "There's a slow tolling bell in the dark."   Gavin Ewart.   PeLi

Limerick: "There's a tiresome young man of Bay Shore."   Morris Gilbert Bishop.   PeLi

Limerick: "There's a very prim girl called McDrood."   *Unknown.*   PeLi

Limerick: "There's a wonderful family called Stein."   *Unknown.*   PeLi

Limerick: "There's an emerald frog down the loo."   Ruth Silcock.   PeLi

Limerick: "There was a collection of schemers."   Basil Ransome-Davies.   PeLi

Limerick: "There was a crusader of Parma."   *Unknown.*   PeLi

Limerick: "There was a faith-healer of Deal."   *Unknown.*   PeLi

Limerick: "There was a fat lady of Clyde."   *Unknown.*   PeLi

Limerick: "There was a French bard who said: 'Hell!'"   Towanbucket.   PeLi

Limerick: "There was a good Canon of Durham."   William Ralph Inge.   PeLi

Limerick: "There was a great German Grammarian."   Thomas Thorneley. PeLi

Limerick: "There was a great Marxist called Lenin."   Ted Pauker.   PeLi

Limerick: "There was a kind lady called Gregory."   James Joyce.   FaBoEE; PeLi

Limerick: "There was a rash fellow called Weir."   *Unknown.*   PeLi

Limerick: "There was a sick man of Tobago."   *Unknown.*   PeLi

Limerick: "There was a small boy of Quebec."   Rudyard Kipling.   PeLi

Limerick: "There was a trombonist called Herb."   Ron Rubin.   PeLi

Limerick: "There was a wee lassie of Ulva."   David Fisher.   PeLi

Limerick: "There was a young artist called Saint."   *Unknown.*   PeLi

Limerick: "There was a young boy, Jack Horner."   Fiona Pitt-Kethley.   PeLi

Limerick: "There was a young bride named McWing."   *Unknown.*   PeLi

Limerick: "There was a young critic of King's."   Arthur Clement Hilton.   PeLi

Limerick: "There was a young curate called Lloyd."   Duncan Campbell McGregor.   PeLi

Limerick: "There was a young curate of Hants."   Edmund George Valpy Knox. PeLi

Limerick: "There was a young curate of Kew."   *Unknown.*   PeLi

Limerick: "There was a young curate of Salisbury."   *Unknown.*   PeLi

Limerick: "There was a young faggot called Willy."   Kenneth Petchenik.   PeLi

Limerick: "There was a young fellow called Baker."   *Unknown.*   PeLi

Limerick: "There was a young fellow called Bliss."   *Unknown.*   PeLi

Limerick: "There was a young fellow called Cager."   *Unknown.*   PeLi

Limerick: "There was a young fellow called Chubb."   *Unknown.*   PeLi

Limerick: "There was a young fellow called Clyde."   *Unknown.*   PeLi

Limerick: "There was a young fellow called Crouch."   Victor Gray.   NOBL; PeLi

Limerick: "There was a young fellow called Hall."   *Unknown.*   PeLi

Limerick: "There was a young fellow called Lancelot."   *Unknown.*   PeLi

Limerick: "There was a young fellow called Price."   *Unknown.*   PeLi

Limerick: "There was a young fellow called Shit."   Victor Gray.   PeLi

Limerick: "There was a young fellow called Wyatt."   *Unknown.*   PeLi

Limerick: "There was a young fellow from Tyne."   *Unknown.*   PeLi

Limerick: "There was a young fellow named Fisher."   *Unknown.*   PeLi

Limerick: "There was a young fellow named Fonda."   Ogden Nash.   PeLi

Limerick: "There was a young fellow named Menzies."   *Unknown.*   PeLi

Limerick: "There was a young fellow named Skinner."   Norman Douglas. PeLi

Limerick: "There was a young fellow named Sydney."   Don Marquis.   PeLi

Limerick: "There was a young fellow of Burma."   Aldous Leonard Huxley. PeLi

Limerick: "There was a young Fellow of Caius."   *Unknown.*   NOBL

Limerick: "There was a young fellow of Ceuta."   *Unknown.*   PeLi

Limerick: "There was a young Fellow of King's."   *Unknown.*   NOBL

Limerick: "There was a young fellow of Lyme."   *Unknown.*   PeLi

Limerick: "There was a young fellow of Perth."   *Unknown.*   PeLi

Limerick: "There was a young fellow of Trinity."   *Unknown.*   PeLi

Limerick: "There was a young Fellow of Wadham."   *Unknown.*   NOBL; PeLi

Limerick: "There was a young genius of Queens."   Arthur Clement Hilton. PeLi

Limerick: "There was a young girl called Bianca."   *Unknown.*   PeLi

Limerick: "There was a young girl from a Mission."   A. H. Baynes.   PeLi

Limerick: "There was a young girl from Uttoxeter / Who kept hens, but refused to have cocks. It a."   Alastair Chambre.   PeLi

Limerick: "There was a young girl from Uttoxeter / Who made passing oarsmen gape through locks at her."   L. W. Bailey.   PeLi

Limerick: "There was a young girl from Uttoxeter / Who one dreary night had a fox at her."   George Cowley.   PeLi

Limerick: "There was a young girl from Uttoxeter / Who out on a date with two Jocks at a."   Bob Scott.   PeLi

Limerick: "There was a young girl from Uttoxeter / Who sported a tight-fitting baroque sweater."   Stanley J. Sharpless.   PeLi

Limerick: "There was a young girl of Aberystwyth."   Algernon Charles Swinburne.   PeLi

Limerick: "There was a young girl of Australia."   *Unknown.*   PeLi

Limerick: "There was a young girl of Bahari."   R. P. M. Lehmann.   PeLi

Limerick: "There was a young girl of Cape Cod."   *Unknown.*   PeLi

Limerick: "There was a young girl of Darjeeling."   *Unknown.*   PeLi

Limerick: "There was a young girl of East Anglia."   Aldous Leonard Huxley. PeLi

Limerick: "There was a young girl of La Plata."   *Unknown.*   PeLi

Limerick: "There was a Young Girl of Majorca."   Edward Lear.   PeLi

Limerick: "There was a young girl of Mauritius."   Victor Gray.   PeLi

Limerick: "There was a young girl of old Natchez."   Ogden Nash.   PeLi

Limerick: "There was a young girl of Penzance."   *Unknown.*   PeLi

Limerick: "There was a young girl of Shanghai."   Bertrand Arthur William Russell, 3d Earl Russell.   PeLi

Limerick: "There was a young girl of Siam."   *Unknown.*   PeLi

Limerick: "There was a young girl of St. Cyr."   *Unknown.*   PeLi

Limerick: "There was a young girl of Tralee."   *Unknown.*   PeLi

Limerick: "There was a young girl of Trebarwith."   R. J. P. Hewison.   PeLi

Limerick: "There was a young girl of Uttoxeter / Who noticed that men waved their cocks at her."   D. Kartun.   PeLi

Limerick: "There was a young girl of Uttoxeter / Who worked nine to five as a choc-setter." Stanley J. Sharpless. PeLi

Limerick: "There was a young girl whose frigidity." *Unknown.* PeLi

Limerick: "There was a young girl with a hernia." Heywood Broun. PeLi

Limerick: "There was a young gourmand of John's." Arthur Clement Hilton. PeLi

Limerick: "There was a young Jap on a syndicate." *Unknown.* PeLi

Limerick: "There was a young Japanese geisha." Ron Rubin. PeLi

Limerick: "There was a young lady at court." D. H. Cudmore. PeLi

Limerick: "There was a young lady called Alice." *Unknown.* PeLi

Limerick: "There was a young lady called Clarice." H. A. C. Evans. PeLi

Limerick: "There was a young lady called Etta." *Unknown.* PeLi

Limerick: "There was a young lady called Flynn." *Unknown.* PeLi

Limerick: "There was a young lady called Gloria." *Unknown.* PeLi

Limerick: "There was a young lady called Harris." Ogden Nash. PeLi

Limerick: "There was a young lady called Hilda." *Unknown.* PeLi

Limerick: "There was a young lady called Kate." *Unknown.* PeLi

Limerick: "There was a young lady called Maud." *Unknown.* PeLi

Limerick: "There was a young lady called Muffet." *Unknown.* PeLi

Limerick: "There was a young lady called Smith." *Unknown.* PeLi

Limerick: "There was a young lady called Starky." *Unknown.* PeLi

Limerick: "There was a young lady from Pecking." *Unknown.* PeLi

Limerick: "There was a young lady from Ulva." Russell Lucas. PeLi

Limerick: "There was a young lady named Kent." *Unknown.* PeLi

Limerick: "There was a young lady named [*or* called] Bright." Arthur Buller. NOBL; OxBoLi; PeLV; PeLi

Limerick: "There was a young lady of Aenos." *Unknown.* PeLi

Limerick: "There was a young lady of Brabant." *Unknown.* PeLi

Limerick: "There was a young lady of Chichester." *Unknown.* PeLi

Limerick: "There was a young lady of Chiswick." *Unknown.* PeLi

Limerick: "There was a young lady of Ealing." *Unknown.* PeLi

Limerick: "There was a young lady of Ealing / And her lover before her was kneeling." Isaac Asimov. PeLi

Limerick: "There was a young lady of fashion." *Unknown.* PeLi

Limerick: "There was a young lady of Florence." *Unknown.* PeLi

Limerick: "There was a young lady of Joppa." *Unknown.* PeLi

Limerick: "There was a young lady of Kew." *Unknown.* PeLV

Limerick: "There was a young lady of Leicester." Alan Clark. PeLi

Limerick: "There was a young lady of Limerick." Andrew Lang. PeLi

Limerick: "There was a young lady of Louth." Norman Douglas. PeLi

Limerick: "There was a young lady of Lundy." W. F. N. Watson. PeLi

Limerick: "There was a young lady of Nantes." S. Littman. PeLi

Limerick: "There was a young lady of Nîmes." "Little Billee." PeLi

Limerick: "There was a Young Lady of Norway, / Who casually sat in a doorway." Edward Lear. PeLi

(There Was a Young Lady of Norway.) EBEV

Limerick: "There was a young lady of Norway / Who hung by her toes in a doorway." Algernon Charles Swinburne. PeLi

Limerick: "There was a young lady of Riga." Cosmo Monkhouse. NIL-7; PeLi

Limerick: "There was a young lady of Ryde, / Who ate some green apples and died." *Unknown.* PeLi

Limerick: "There was a young lady of Ryde / Who was carried too far by the tide." *Unknown.* PeLi

Limerick: "There was a young lady of Ryde / Whose shoe-strings were seldom untied." Edward Lear. OxBoLi; PeLV; PeLi

Limerick: "There was a young lady of Rye." *Unknown.* PeLi

Limerick: "There was a young lady of Slough." *Unknown.* PeLi

Limerick: "There was a young lady of Spain." *Unknown.* PeLi

Limerick: "There was a young lady of station." Lewis Carroll. PeLi

Limerick: "There was a young lady of Sweden." Edward Lear. EBEV; PeVV

Limerick: "There was a young lady of Tottenham." *Unknown.* PeLi; WeW-3

Limerick: "There was a young lady of Trent." *Unknown.* PeLi

Limerick: "There was a young lady of Ulva / Who drunkenly said: 'What a hulva.'" Bill Greenwell. PeLi

Limerick: "There was a young lady of Ulva / Who kept a pet bee in her hand-bag." T. Johnston. PeLi

Limerick: "There was a young lady of Ulva / Who said: 'I have granted a culver.'" T. Griffiths. PeLi

Limerick: "There was a young lady of Ulva / Who was famed far and wide for her vulva." Gavin Ewart. PeLi

Limerick: "There was a young lady of Ulva / Whose boy-friend said: 'Look, I will pulver.'" Stanley J. Sharpless. PeLi

Limerick: "There was a young lady of Ulva / Whose sexual feelings were null. Va." Barbara E. Goff. PeLi

Limerick: "There was a young lady of Wantage." *Unknown.* PeLi

Limerick: "There was a young lady of Where?" *Unknown.* PeLi

Limerick: "There was a young lady of Whitby." Lewis Carroll. PeLi

Limerick: "There was a young lady . . . tut, tut!" Stanley J. Sharpless. PeLi

Limerick: "There was a Young Lady whose chin." Edward Lear. PeLi

Limerick: "There was a young lady whose eyes." Edward Lear. EBEV; NOBVV

Limerick: "There was a young lass of Pitlochry." *Unknown.* PeLi

Limerick: "There was a young lawyer called Rex." *Unknown.* PeLi

Limerick: "There was a young maid of Peru." Isaac Asimov. PeLi

Limerick: "There was a young maid who said, 'Why.'" *Unknown.* SoSe-8

Limerick: "There was a young maiden from Multerry." *Unknown.* PeLi

Limerick: "There was a young maiden of Devon." *Unknown.* PeLi

Limerick: "There was a young man from Darjeeling." *Unknown.* PeLi

Limerick: "There was a young man named Racine." *Unknown.* PeLi

Limerick: "There was a young man of Australia." *Unknown.* PeLi

Limerick: "There was a young man of Belgrade." Isaac Asimov. PeLi

Limerick: "There was a young man of Calcutta." *Unknown.* PeLi

Limerick: "There was a young man of Cape Horn." Algernon Charles Swinburne. PeLi

Limerick: "There was a young man of Cape Race." *Unknown.* PeLi

Limerick: "There was a young man of Devizes." Archibald Marshall. PeLi

Limerick: "There was a young man of Dumfries." *Unknown.* PeLi

Limerick: "There was a young man of Ghent." *Unknown.* PeLi

Limerick: "There was a young man of Japan." *Unknown.* PeLi

Limerick: "There was a young man of Madras." *Unknown.* PeLi

Limerick: "There was a young man of Montrose." Arnold Bennett. OxBoLi; PeLi

Limerick: "There was a young man of Nepal." *Unknown.* PeLi

Limerick: "There was a young man of Newcastle." Terence Melican. PeLi

Limerick: "There was a young man of Ostend." E. O. Parrott. PeLi

Limerick: "There was a young man of Porthcawl." A. G. Prys-Jones. PeLi

Limerick: "There was a young man of St John's." *Unknown.* PeLV

Limerick: "There was a young man of Wood's Hole." *Unknown.* PeLi

Limerick: "There was a young man so benighted." Frances Parkinson Keyes. PeLi

Limerick: "There was a young man who said: 'Ayer.'" *Unknown.* PeLi

Limerick: "There was a young monarch called Ed." *Unknown.* PeLi

Limerick: "There was a young monk from Siberia." *Unknown.* PeLi

Limerick: "There was a young outlaw named Hood." E. O. Parrott. PeLi

Limerick: "There was a young peasant named Gorse." *Unknown.* PeLi

Limerick: "There was a young person called Tate." Carolyn Wells. PeLi

Limerick: "There was a young person of Leigh." Basil Ransome-Davies. PeLi

Limerick: "There was a young person of Smyrna." Edward Lear. OxBoLi; PeLV

Limerick: "There was a young plumber of Leigh." *Unknown.* PeLi

Limerick: "There was a young poet of Kew." *Unknown.* PeLi

Limerick: "There was a young poet of Thusis." *Unknown.* OxBoLi; PeLi

Limerick: "There was a young priest of Dun Laoghaire." *Unknown.* PeLi

Limerick: "There was a young princess, Snow-White." Gerard Benson. PeLi

Limerick: "There was a young student called Fred." V. R. Ormerod. PeLi

Limerick: "There was a young student called Jones." *Unknown.* PeLi

Limerick: "There was a young student of John's." *Unknown.* PeLi

Limerick: "There was a young woman called Myrtle." *Unknown.* PeLi

Limerick: "There was a young woman called Starky." *Unknown.* NOBL

Limerick: "There was a young woman named Plunnery." Edward Gorey. OBAL

Limerick: "There was a young woman of Dee." *Unknown.* PeLi

Limerick: "There was a young woman who said." Frances Darwin Cornford. PeLi

Limerick: "There was an archdeacon who said." *Unknown.* OBCoV; OxBoLi

Limerick: "There was an old Bey of Calcutta." *Unknown.* PeLi

Limerick: "There was an old cynic who said." Allan M. Laing. PeLi

Limerick: "There was an old dame of Toulouse." A. M. Sayers. PeLi

Limerick: "There was an old Doctor called Coué." Bob Scott. PeLi

Limerick: "There was an old drunk called Hieronymus." Ron Rubin. PeLi

Limerick: "There was an old drunkard of Devon." Ron Rubin. PeLi

Limerick: "There was an old fellow named Hewing." *Unknown.* PeLi

Limerick: "There was an old fellow of Fife." *Unknown.* PeLi

Limerick: "There was an old fellow of Kaber." Philip Larkin. OBCoV

Limerick: "There was an old fellow of Trinity." Arthur Clement Hilton. PeLi

Limerick: "There was an old gossip called Baird." Ogden Nash. PeLi

Limerick: "There was an old housewife of Staines." E. O. Parrott. PeLi

Limerick: "There was an old lady of Leicester." Ian T. MacKenzie. PeLi

Limerick: "There was an old madam called Rainey." *Unknown.* PeLi

Limerick: "There was an old maid of Duluth." *Unknown.* PeLi

Limerick: "There was an old man called Dupree." "R. I." PeLi

Limerick: "There was an Old Man in a boat."   Edward Lear.   EBEV; OBCoV

Limerick: "There was an Old Man in a tree."   Edward Lear.   CABP; NoP-4; PeLi

Limerick: "There was an old man in a trunk."   Ogden Nash.   PeLi

Limerick: "There was an old man of Bengal."   "F. Anstey."   PeLi

Limerick: "There was an old man of Boulogne."   *Unknown.*   OxBoLi; PeLi; PeLV

Limerick: "There was an old man of Cape Horn."   Edward Lear.   EBEV; PeLi

Limerick: "There was an old man of Dunblane."   Edward Lear.   EBEV

Limerick: "There was an old man of Dundee."   *Unknown.*   PeLi

Limerick: "There was an old man of Ibreem."   Edward Lear.   EBEV

Limerick: "There was an old man of Kamschatka."   Edward Lear.   NOBL

Limerick: "There was an old man of Khartoum."   William Ralph Inge.   NOBL; OxBoLi; PeLi

Limerick: "There was an old man of Lugano."   Victor Gray.   PeLi

Limerick: "There was an old man of [*or* from] Peru / Who dreamt [*or* dreamed] he was eating his shoe."   *Unknown.*   KaS; SoSe-8

  (Old Man from Peru, An.)   NTCP

Limerick: "There was an old man of the Cape."   Robert Louis Stevenson.   PeLi

Limerick: "There was an old man of the coast."   Edward Lear.   PeLi

Limerick: "There was an old man of Thermopylae."   Edward Lear.   EBEV; NOBL; OxAEP-2; PeLi

Limerick: "There was an old man of Whitehaven."   Edward Lear.   EBEV; NPeEn; OxAEP-2

Limerick: "There was an old man on some rocks."   Edward Lear.   NOBVV; OxBEV; PeLi

Limerick: "There was an old man on the Border."   Edward Lear.   EBEV

Limerick: "There was an Old Man on whose nose."   Edward Lear.   PeLi

Limerick: "There was an old man who averred."   *Unknown.*   PeLi

Limerick: "There was an old man who said: 'How.'"   Edward Lear.   PeLi

Limerick: "There was an Old Man who said, 'Hush!'"   Edward Lear.   KaS; NOBL; OxBoLi; PeLV; PeLi

Limerick: "There was an Old Man who said: 'Well!'"   Edward Lear.   PeLi

Limerick: "There was an old man who screamed out."   Edward Lear.   EBEV; NOBVV; NPeEn; OxAEP-2; OxBEV

Limerick: "There was an Old Man who supposed."   Edward Lear.   NAEL-5v2; NAEL-6v2; NOBVV; NoP-4; PeLi

Limerick: "There was an Old Man with a Beard / Who said: 'I demand to be feared.'"   Roger Woddis.   PeLi

Limerick: "There was an old Member called Bevan."   Barbara Leigh.   PeLi

Limerick: "There was an old mickey called Cassidy."   Conrad Potter Aiken.   PeLi

Limerick: "There was an old miser at [*or* of] Reading."   *Unknown.*   PeLi

Limerick: "There was an old person of Basing."   Edward Lear.   EBEV; NPeEn; OBCoV; OxAEP-2; PAI; PeLi

Limerick: "There was an old person of Bow."   Edward Lear.   EBEV; OxAEP-2

Limerick: "There was an Old Person of Cromer."   Edward Lear.   PeLi

Limerick: "There was an Old Person of Fratton."   *Unknown.*   PeLi

Limerick: "There was an Old Person of Hurst."   Edward Lear.   PeLi

Limerick: "There was an old person of Persia."   William Plomer.   PeLi

Limerick: "There was an old person of Skye."   Edward Lear.   KaS

Limerick: "There was an old person of Slough."   George Robey.   PeLi

Limerick: "There was an old sage of New Delhi."   Joyce Parr.   PeLi

Limerick: "There was an old Scot called McTavish."   *Unknown.*   PeLi

Limerick: "There was an old Welshman called Morgan."   Ron Rubin.   PeLi

Limerick: "There was an Old Woman of Gloster."   *Unknown.*   PeLi

Limerick: "There was an Old Woman of Lynn."   *Unknown.*   PeLi

Limerick: "There was once a young man of Oporta."   Lewis Carroll.   PeLi

Limerick: "There we was, and wanting our tea."   "P. E. A."   PeLi

Limerick: "There were once two young people of taste."   Monica Curtis.   PeLi

Limerick: "These days, the ubiquitous db."   A. P. Cox.   PeLi

Limerick: "They say that I was in my youth."   *Unknown.*   PeLi

Limerick: "Thomas Hobbes of Malmesbury thought."   Peter Alexander.   PeLi

Limerick: "Though clerical errors are fun."   *Unknown.*   PeLi

Limerick: "Though his plan, when he gave her a buzz."   *Unknown.*   PeLi

Limerick: "Though Sir James (God's-a-Formula) Jeans."   R. J. P. Hewison.   PeLi

Limerick: "Though the limerick can not be deaded."   *Unknown.*   PeLi

Limerick: "Though your dreams may seem normal and right."   J. C. B. Date.   PeLi

Limerick: "Three Aldis, not one of them dim."   Joyce Johnson.   PeLi

Limerick: "Three scribblers whose names end in Bert."   C. Vita-Finzi.   PeLi

Limerick: "Three wonderful people called Ley."   Tim Hopkins.   PeLi

Limerick: "Three wonderful people called Wick."   A. M. Sayers.   PeLi

Limerick: "Throughout the whole world, experts say."   *Unknown.*   PeLi

Limerick: "Thus spake an old Chinese mandarin."   *Unknown.*   PeLi

Limerick: "'Tis strange how the newspapers honour."   Eugene Field.   PeLi

Limerick: "To Algebra God is inclined."   J. C. B. Date.   PeLi

Limerick: "To avoid matrimonial disasters."   Martin Fagg.   PeLi

Limerick: "To her friends, said the Bright one, in chatter."   Arthur Buller.   PeLi

Limerick: "To her gardener, a lady named Liliom."   *Unknown.*   PeLi

Limerick: "To his bride said a numbskull named Clarence."   *Unknown.*   PeLi

Limerick: "To his club-footed child said Lord Stipple."   Edward Gorey.   OBCoV; PeLi

Limerick: "To his Queen said the circumspect Burleigh."   A. Cinna.   PeLi

Limerick: "To his wife said the lynx-eyed detective."   Langford Reed.   PeLi

Limerick: "Tone-deaf old person of Tring, A."   *Unknown.*   PeLi

Limerick: "Toper who spies in the distance, A."   Leslie Johnson.   PeLi

Limerick: "Traveller to Timbuktu, A."   *Unknown.*   PeLi

Limerick: "Trouble with General Sherman, The."   Basil Ransome-Davies.   PeLi

Limerick: "Truth about truth is elusive, The."   *Unknown.*   PeLi

Limerick: "Try our Rubber Girl-Friend (air-inflatable)."   *Unknown.*   PeLi

Limerick: "Tutor who tooted a flute, A."   Carolyn Wells.   PeLi; SoSe-8

Limerick: "Two earnest young fellows named Wright."   Basil Ransome-Davies.   PeLi

Limerick: "Two middle-aged ladies from Fordham."   *Unknown.*   PeLi

Limerick: "Two playwrights called Beaumont and Fletcher."   Fiona Pitt-Kethley.   PeLi

Limerick: "Two she-camels spied on a goat."   *Unknown.*   PeLi

Limerick: "Undressing a maiden called Sue."   Brian Allgar.   PeLi

Limerick: "Unfortunate lad from Madrid, An."   *Unknown.*   PeLi

Limerick: "United States Constitution, The."   Peter Alexander.   PeLi

Limerick: "Unperson from West Oceania, An."   C. Vita-Finzi.   PeLi

Limerick: "Unpopular man of Cologne, An."   *Unknown.*   PeLi

Limerick: "Up the street sex is sold by the piece."   *Unknown.*   PeLi

Limerick: "Vain old Professor of Greek, A."   Ron Rubin.   PeLi

Limerick: "Van Gogh, feeling devil-may-care."   "Pibwob."   PeLi

Limerick: "Very apt question struck me, A."   Sydney Bernard Smith.   PeLi

Limerick: "Vice most obscene and unsavoury, A."   *Unknown.*   NOBL; PeLV

Limerick: "Victoria said: 'We've no quarrel.'"   Frank Richards.   PeLi

Limerick: "Victoria was bitterly short."   Cyril Mountjoy.   PeLi

Limerick: "Victorian gent said: 'This dance,' A."   Frank Richards.   PeLi

Limerick: "Viscount Stansgate, or Wedgwood, or Benn."   Tim Hopkins.   PeLi

Limerick: "Wanting children a couple once sat."   G. W. Hanney.   PeLi

Limerick: "Wanton young lady of Wimley, A."   *Unknown.*   PeLi

Limerick: "Watt's dream was the cream of steam engines."   Bill Greenwell.   PeLi

Limerick: "We all place a great deal of reliance."   *Unknown.*   PeLi

Limerick: "'We're not amused,' said Victoria."   Stanley J. Sharpless.   PeLi

Limerick: "We've got a new maid called Chrysanthemum."   *Unknown.*   PeLi

Limerick: "We've socially-conscious biography."   *Unknown.*   PeLi

Limerick: "Wee Jamie, a canny young Scot."   Joyce Johnson.   PeLi

Limerick: "Well-buggered boy named Delpasse, A."   *Unknown.*   PeLi

Limerick: "Well, I took your advice, Doc,' said Knopp."   *Unknown.*   PeLi

Limerick: "Well, if it's a sin to like Guinness."   Cyril Ray.   PeLi

Limerick: "Well, it's partly the shape of the thing."   *Unknown.*   KaS; SoSe-8

Limerick: "'What have I done?' said Christine."   *Unknown.*   PeLi

Limerick: "What led to the crassness of Custer."   Bill Greenwell.   PeLi

Limerick: "What! Parted! Not even a kiss?"   "X. A. M."   PeLi

Limerick: "'What's the matter, old chap?' 'Well, I came.'"   Joyce Johnson.   PeLi

Limerick: "When a feverish groom in Armenia."   Morris Gilbert Bishop.   PeLi

Limerick: "When a friend said to Leda: 'Come on.'"   Peter Alexander.   PeLi

Limerick: "When a friend told a typist called Eve."   Gordon Harper.   PeLi

Limerick: "When a man's too old even to toss off, he."   Robert Conquest.   PeLi

Limerick: "When an amorous youth from Atlantis."   C. Vita-Finzi.   PeLi

Limerick: "When an obstinate fellow of Fife."   Allan M. Laing.   PeLi

Limerick: "When approached by a person from Porlock."   Richard Leighton Greene.   PeLi

Limerick: "When Gauguin was visiting Fiji."   Victor Gray.   NOBL

Limerick: "When he raped a young maid in a train."   *Unknown.*   PeLi

Limerick: "When I sit in the Churchyard at Stoke."   A. M. Sayers.   PeLi

Limerick: "When I thought of this Duchess affair."   *Unknown.*   PeLi

Limerick: "When Ireland was bloody and leaderless."   Gina Berkeley.   PeLi

Limerick: "When Jael crept in to see Sisera."   Bill Greenwell.   PeLi

Limerick: "When Keats was at work on *Endymion*."   Victor Gray.   PeLi

Limerick: "When Lazarus came back from the dead."   *Unknown.*   PeLi

Limerick: "When our dean took a pious young spinster."   Victor Gray.   NOBL; PeLi

Limerick: "When Pegotty found Barkis was willing."   Douglas Catley.   PeLi

Limerick: "When the census man called upon Gail." George McWilliam. PeLi

Limerick: "When the judge with his wife having sport." *Unknown*. PeLi

Limerick: "When the Prince, who was terribly smit." Joyce Johnson. PeLi

Limerick: "When your capitalist boss takes his toll." Dominic Fitzpatrick. PeLi

Limerick: "Whenever he got in a fury, a." *Unknown*. PeLi

Limerick: "While Dubliner leopold bloom sought solace." Gerard Benson. PeLi

Limerick: "While Titian was grinding rose madder." *Unknown*. NOBL

Limerick: "While visiting Arundel Castle." Victor Gray. NOBL

Limerick: "Whilst Titian was mixing rose madder." *Unknown*. PeLi

Limerick: "Widow (conscious that time's on the wing)." Stanley J. Sharpless. PeLi

Limerick: "Wily Napoleon Bonaparte, The." Douglas Catley. PeLi

Limerick: "Wily old writer called Maugham, A." Martin Fagg. PeLi

Limerick: "Winter is here with his grouch." *Unknown*. PeLi

Limerick: "Wonderful bird is the pelican, A." Dixon Lanier Merritt. PeLi

Limerick: "Yogi from far-off Beirut, A." *Unknown*. PeLi

Limerick: "Young bride and groom of Australia, A." *Unknown*. PeLi

Limerick: "Young couple who lived at 'The Laurels,' A." W. F. N. Watson. PeLi

Limerick: "Young engine-driver called Hunt, A." Victor Gray. NOBL

Limerick: "Young girl of English nativity, A." *Unknown*. PeLi

Limerick: "Young girl who was no good at tennis, A." *Unknown*. PeLi

Limerick: "Young Irish servant in Drogheda, A." *Unknown*. PeLi

Limerick: "Young Joseph's new coat was real nice." Cyril Mountjoy. PeLi

Limerick: "Young lady, whose life-style the malicious, A." Gavin Ewart. PeLi

Limerick: "Young man by a girl was desired, A." *Unknown*. PeLi

Limerick: "Young man who lived at Holme Hale, A." Ida Thurtle. PeLi

Limerick: "Young man with passions quite gingery, A." *Unknown*. PeLi

Limerick: "Young men who frequent picture palaces." *Unknown*. PeLV

Limerick: "Young Oedipus learned from the Sphinx." Basil Ransome-Davies. PeLi

Limerick: "Young things who frequent picture-palaces, The." Philip Heseltine. NOBL; PeLi
    (Picture-Palaces.) OBCoV

Limerick: "Youth and a maiden from Costessey, A." S. C. Turner. PeLi

Limerick issued from Lear, The. J. A. Lindon. PeLi

Limerick Train. Brendan Kennelly. PBCIP

Limericks and Puns. *Unknown*. PeLi

Limestone pavement, The. Maen Madoc. Chris Torrance. AngWePo

Limit. Diane Ward. FTOS

Limitation, / limp, / simply. (LL) Little Tumescence, A. Jonathan Williams. NeAP; PoM

Limitations. Henrietta Cordelia Ray. CBWP-3

Limitations. Siegfried Sassoon. MoBrPo

Limited. Carl Sandburg. HAP; MoAmPo; OxBA

Limited Liability. John Ashbery. BodElec

Limits. Jorge Luis Borges. PoetW, *tr. by* Alastair Reid

Limits. Ralph Waldo Emerson. APN-1; OxBSP

Limits (1962). Christopher Okigbo.
    "Banks of reed." PBMAP
    "For he was a shrub among the poplars." PBMAP
    "Image insists, An." PBMAP
    "Suddenly becoming talkative." PBMAP

Limits of Desire, The. Linda Gregg. ExTi

Limits of Submission, The. Faarah Nuur. TTY, *tr. by* B. W. Andrejewski and I. M. Lewis

Limits (or Good-byes). Jorge Luis Borges. PoetW; TCLAP, *tr. by* Alan Dugan

Limpid river / rippling in dawn light. Inscribed on a Landscape by Mi Yüan-hui. Chao Meng-fu. CoBLCP, *tr. by* Jonathan Chaves

Limping past the Guthrie theater. Indians at the Guthrie. Gerald Vizenor. VoR

Limpopo. Walter Battiss. PeSAV

Limpopo and Tugela churned. Scorpion, The. William Plomer. OBMV; PeSAV

Lincoln. John Gould Fletcher. CBCWP; MoAmPo

Lincoln. Henrietta Cordelia Ray. CBWP-3

Lincoln. Delmore Schwartz. APT-2

Lincoln Bedroom, The. Donald Berger. NAPBL

Lincoln Monument: Washington. Langston Hughes. CBCWP

Lincoln's Grave. Maurice Thompson. CBCWP

Lincoln, the Man of the People. Edwin Markham. MoAmPo

Lincoln was sixty years old when the doctor told him he only had forty more years to live. Diagnosis, The. James Tate. BAP-01

Lincolnshire Poacher, The. *Unknown*. OxBoLi; PeLV

Linda. Jack Lawrence. ReLy

Linda, Linda, slender and pretty. Linda. John Fuller. PeLV

Linden blossomed, the nightingale sang, The. Farewell. Heinrich Heine. AWP, *tr. by* John Todhunter

Lindie, chile, fo' Lawd sake, tell me. After the Quarrel. Priscilla Jane Thompson. CBWP-2

Line. Milo De Angelis. NeIt, *tr. by* Lawrence Venuti

Line Drive. Arthur Ginsberg. BloBone

Line Drive Caught by the Grace of God. Linda Gregerson. ExTi; MoASP

Line from St. David's, A. Ronald Stuart Thomas. AngWePo

Line-Gang, The. Robert Frost. OxBSP

Line in long array where they wind betwixt green islands, A. Cavalry Crossing a Ford. Walt Whitman. AiP; CBCWP; HeIP-4; InPK-6; NAAL-2v1; NAAL-3; NAAL-5; NoAM; OxBA; PAI; SAmP; TAP; TCAPo; TFi; TRP; UnPo

Line Like. Nelly Sachs. BoWoP, *tr. by* Michael Hamburger

Line of a Poem. Zali Gurevitch. FIT, *tr. by* Robert Friend

Line of martins, A. Martins. Mike Jenkins. AngWePo

Line through the hold in the dank, The. Bellrope. Robert Morgan. BLT

Line Up. Forrest Hamer. OPRER

Lineage. Margaret Abigail Walker. BlSi; ItWoWo; NALW; OxWW; WWork

Lineage. Daisy Zamora. LoL, *tr. by* Margaret Randall

Lineaments of a plummet-measured face, The. (LL) Statues, The. W. B. Yeats. NoAM; WeW-3

Lineaments of Gratified Desire, The. (LL) William Blake. ErotSp; FaBoEE; NoP-4; OxBEV; WoPoe *Fr.* Several Questions Answered.

Lined coat, warm cap and easy felt slippers. Ease. Po Chü-i. Spl, *tr. by* Arthur Waley

Linen Industry, The. Michael Longley. CIP-2; ModIr; NoP-4; PBCIP; PNI

Linen Weaver, The. *Unknown*. NOEC

Linen Workers, The. Michael Longley. BiHa; CIP-2; ModIr; NPeEn *Fr.* Wreaths.

Lines: "From fair Jamaica's fertile plains." "Ada" (Sara Louisa Forten). BlSi
    (Lines Suggested on Reading "An Appeal to Christian Women of the South," by A. E. Grimke.) NAAAL
    (My spirit leaps in joyousness tow'rd thine.) NAAAL

Lines. Ina Coolbrith. SWaP

Lines. Frances Anne [*or* "Fanny"] Kemble. VWP

Lines. Sara Teasdale. APT-1

Lines. Henry Timrod. *See* Ode: "Sleep sweetly in your humble graves."

Lines Written a Few Miles above Tintern Abbey. William Wordsworth. *See* Lines Composed a Few Miles above Tintern Abbey on Revisiting the Banks of the Wye during a Tour, July 13, 1798

Lines about a Little Boy. Aleksandr Petrovich Mezhirov. TCRP, *tr. by* Deming Brown

Lines among the Leaves. Eliza Cook.
    "Varied theme it utters, A." VerBaPo

Lines are cast and the nets are set and waiting, The. *Unknown*. PGA

Lines are straight and swift between the stars, The. Stars at Tallapoosa. Wallace Stevens. WoPoe

Lines: "At the Portals of the Future." Frances Ellen Watkins Harper. APN-2

Lines by a Lady on the Loss of Her Trunk. Richard Brinsley Sheridan. OBCoV

Lines Composed a Few Miles above Tintern Abbey on Revisiting the Banks of the Wye during a Tour, July 13, 1798. William Wordsworth. AmFaPo; CABP; FHYEP; HeIP-4; NAEL-6v2; NAWM-7v2; NIL-7; NPeEn; NoP-4; OxAEP-2; OxBEV; PoPoPo; SCGP; TFi

Lines: Composed at the Old Temples of Maralipoor. Charles Timothy Brooks. APN-1

Lines Composed in a Wood on a Windy Day. Anne Brontë. EBVV
    (My soul is awakened, my spirit is soaring.) VWP

Lines Contributed to Goldsmith's "The Traveller." Samuel Johnson. NPeEn

Lines Contributed to Hawkesworth's "The Rival." Samuel Johnson. NPeEn

Lines Descriptive of Thomson's Island. Benjamin Lynde. SCAP

Lines for a Book. Thom Gunn. CABP

Lines for a Painter. Anthony Cronin. PBCIP

Lines for a Tomb. Donald Davidson. FuPo

Lines for a Worthy Person Who Has Drifted by Accident into a Chelsea Revel. Sir Alan Patrick Herbert. NOBL

Lines for an Interment. Archibald MacLeish. NOBA

Lines for an Old Man. T. S. Eliot. FaBoTw; RB; RaBo

Lines for Cuscuscaraway and Mirza Murad Ali Beg. T. S. Eliot. NBLV; OBAL; OBCoV; PeLV; UV *Fr.* Five-Finger Exercises.

Lines for Marking Time. Roberta Hill Whiteman. BoWoP; CDW

Lines for Roethke Twenty Years after His Death. Duane Niatum. HATNAP

Lines for Translation into Any Language. James Fenton. AF

Lines from Love Letters. *Unknown*. OBEV

Lines from Love Letters, I. *Unknown.* OBEV

Lines from the Testament. Pier Paolo Pasolini. VCWP, *tr. by* Norman MacAfee

Lines: "Gather the sacred dust." Abram Joseph Ryan. APN-2

Lines: "Here often, when a child, I lay reclined." Tennyson. PAI

Lines I fashioned yesterday, The. Sacrifice. Gyula Illyés. IQMS, *tr. by* Marie B. Jaffe

Lines: I Praise God's Mankind in an Old Woman. Wilfred Watson. NOBC

Lines in a Roman Schoolbook. Desmond O'Grady.
 "In the valleys of the future we shall walk." PBCIP
 "This introspective exile here today." PBCIP

Lines in Dejection. Jean Valentine. YaYoPo

Lines in Honor of Natalya. Pavel Nikolaevich Vasilyev [*or* Vasil'ev]. TCRP, *tr. by* David Macduff

Lines in Praise of a Self-Chiming Clock. Hsüan-yeh. ColAnChi, *tr. by* Jonathan D. Spence

Lines in Prison. Anne Askew. *See* Ballad Which Anne Askew Made and Sang When She Was in Newgate, The

Lines in the Corner of a Manuscript. *Unknown.* FaBoVe

Lines Left at Mr Theodore Hook's House in June, 1834. "Thomas Ingoldsby." OBCoV

Lines Lost among Trees. Billy Collins. BAP-97

Lines Occasioned by the Burning of Some Letters. Sarah Dixon. ECWP; NOEC

Lines of Life. Letitia [*or* Laetitia] Elizabeth Landon. NOBRP; NPeEn

Lines of the Hand, The. Julio Cortázar. TCLAP, *tr. by* Paul Blackburn and Pal Blackburn

Lines of this new song are nothing, The. Louis Zukofsky. APT-2; VGW

Lines of your arteries, The. Robert. Wendy Rose. HATNAP

Lines on a Boer War Pin-up Girl Seen in the Falcon Hotel, Bude. Christopher Hope. PeSAV

Lines on a Dead Girl. Priscilla Jane Thompson. CBWP-2

Lines on a Platonic Friendship. Daryl Hine. IllVoic

Lines on a Purple Cap Received as a Present from My Brother. George Alsop. SCAP

Lines on a Van's Dereliction. Douglas Houston. TCAWP

Lines on a Young Lady's Photograph Album. Philip Larkin. EnLoPo; HAP

Lines on Cambridge of 1830. Tennyson. OxBSo

Lines on Carmen Sylva. Emma Lazarus. TrJP

Lines on Hearing That Lady Byron Was Ill. Byron. EBEV; NPeEn; OxAEP-2

Lines on Hearing the Organ. Charles Stuart Calverley. NOBL

Lines on His Companions Who Died in the Northern Seas. Thomas James. NOSC

Lines on Nonsense. Eliza Lee Cabot Follen. SWaP

Lines on Roger Hilton's Watch. William Sydney Graham. NPeEn

Lines on the Award "Pipe Man of the Year" to Magnus Magnusson. E. J. Thribb. OBCoV

Lines on the Death of the Rev. S. K. Talmage. Mary E. Tucker. CBWP-1

Lines on the Hundredth Anniversary of the Birth of W. Somerset Maugham. E. J. Thribb. PeLV

Lines on the Mermaid Tavern. John Keats. FHYEP; PoRA; SCGP
 (Mermaid Tavern, The.) GTBS-P

Lines on the Return to Britain of Billy Graham. E. J. Thribb. PeLV

Lines on the Tombs in Westminster. Francis Beaumont. NOBE; OBEV; SCGP *Fr.* On the Tombs in Westminster Abbey.

Lines on Thomas Warton's Poems. Samuel Johnson. FaBoEE
 (Lines Written in Ridicule of Certain Poems.) SCGP

Lines: "Other day I was loving a sweet little fruitpie-and-cream, The." Gavin Ewart. SPE

Lines Printed under the Engraved Portrait of Milton [In Tonson's Folio of the "Paradise Lost"]. Dryden. InPK-6; OxAEP-1
 (Epigram on Milton.) NAEL-6v1; NAEL-7v1

Lines: "Repressive desublimation." David Bromige. FTOS

Lines Rhymed in a Letter from Oxford. John Keats. *See* On Oxford

Lines Rhymed in a Letter Received (by J. H. R[eynolds]) from Oxford. John Keats. *See* On Oxford

Lines Scribbled on an Envelope. Madeleine L'Engle. SacPr

Lines Started outside Filene's Basement. James R. Scrimgeour. OPRER

Lines Suggested by an Edition of Blake's Poems. Sir Walter Alexander Raleigh. OBCoV

Lines Suggested by Hearing Music on the Boston Common at Night. Thomas Cole. APN-1

Lines / Suggested by the Song of a Nightingale. Eliza Cook. VWP

Lines Suggested on Reading "An Appeal to Christian Women of the South," by A. E. Grimke. "Ada" (Sarah Louisa Forten). *See* Lines

Lines through these words, The. Michael Palmer. PFTM-2 *Fr.* Sun.

Lines to———. Mary Weston Fordham. CBWP-2

Lines to a Don. Joseph Hilaire Pierre Belloc. MoBrPo; OBSV

Lines to a Graduate. Lizelia Augusta Jenkins Moorer. CBWP-3

Lines to a Movement in Mozart's E-Flat Symphony. Thomas Hardy. NoAM

Lines to a Nasturtium. Anne Spencer. APT-1

Lines to a Reviewer. Shelley. OxBSP

Lines to a World-famous Poet Who Failed to Complete a World-famous Poem; or, Come Clean, Mr. Guest! Ogden Nash. OBAL

Lines: To a Young Gentleman of Surpassing Beauty. Ellen Johnston. VWP

Lines to Accompany Flowers for Eve. Carolyn Kizer. BoWoP

Lines to an Indian Air. Shelley. *See* Indian Serenade, The

Lines to an Old Dress. Mary E. Tucker. CBWP-1

Lines to an Old School-House. Priscilla Jane Thompson. CBWP-2

Lines to Ellen, the Factory Girl. Ellen Johnston. VWP

Lines to Emma. Priscilla Jane Thompson. CBWP-2

Lines to Florence. Mary Weston Fordham. CBWP-2

Lines to Mr Hodgson. Byron. OBCoV
 (Lisbon Packet, The.) NBLV

Lines to Mother. Rose M. Stein. PWR

Lines to Mrs. Isabel Peace. Mary Weston Fordham. CBWP-2

Lines to Mrs. M. C. Turner. Eloise Bibb. CBWP-4

Lines to My Father. Sam Hamod. GraLe

Lines to Ralph Hodgson Esqre. T. S. Eliot. NBLV; OBAL; PeLV *Fr.* Five-Finger Exercises.

Lines to the Black Oak. Oliver La Grone. NBV

Lines to the Hon. George L. Knox. Eloise Bibb. CBWP-4

Lines: "When the lamp is shattered [*or* shatter'd]." Shelley. NAEL-5v2; OBEV; OxBEV
 (Flight of Love, The.) GTBS-P

Lines: "When youthful faith hath fled." John Gibson Lockhart. OBEV

Lines Where Beauty Lingers. Franklin Pierce Adams. OBAL

Lines Written at Bridgewater, 27 July 1797. John Thelwall.
 "Day of my double birth, if such the year." NOEC

Lines Written at Night during Insomnia. Alexander Sergeyevich Pushkin. AWTN, *tr. by* D. M. Thomas

Lines Written beneath a Picture. Byron. OxBSP

Lines Written during a Period of Insanity. William Cowper. EBEV; HAP; NOEC; NPeEn; NoP-4
 (Lines Written under the Influence of Delerium.) ChIV-1

Lines Written during a Sleepless Night in Tbilisi. Bella [*or* Izabella] Akhatovna Akhmadulina. ARWW, *tr. by* Catriona Kelly

Lines Written for a Friend on the Death of His Brother, Caused by a Railway Train Running over Him Whilst He Was in a State of Inebriation. James Henry Powell. VerBaPo

Lines Written for Allen Tate on His Sixtieth Anniversary. Donald Davidson. FuPo

Lines Written for Gene Kelly to Dance To. Carl Sandburg. AiP

Lines Written Immediately after Parting from a Lady. Sir Samuel Egerton Brydges. NOEC

Lines Written in Boston on a Beautiful Autumnal Day. Margaret Fuller. SWaP

Lines Written in Early Spring. William Wordsworth. FHYEP; NAEL-5v2; NAEL-6v2; NOBRP; PAI; SacPr
 (Written in Early Spring.) GTBS-P

Lines Written in Her Breviary. Saint Theresa [*or* Teresa] of Avila. AWP, *tr. by* Henry Wadsworth Longfellow
 (Bookmark.) CTC; WPOW

Lines Written in Kensington Gardens. Matthew Arnold. FHYEP; NAEL-6v2; OBGa

Lines Written in Ridicule of Certain Poems. Samuel Johnson. *See* Lines on Thomas Warton's Poems

Lines Written in the Bay of Lerici. Shelley. NAEL-6v2
 (Bright wanderer, fair coquette of heaven.) NAEL-5v2

Lines Written in the Church Yard of Richmond, Yorkshire. Herbert Knowles. SacPr

Lines Written in the Dog-Days. William Woty. NOEC

Lines Written in Windsor Forest. Pope. EBEV
 (Hymn Written in Windsor Forest, A.) NOEC; OxBSP

(Lines Written on a Bookmark Found in Her Breviary). Teresa de Cepeda Y Ahumada. WPoS, *tr. by* Henry Wadsworth Longfellow

Lines Written on a Farewell View of the Franconia Mountains at Twilight. Henrietta Cordelia Ray. CBWP-3

Lines Written on a Seat on the Grand Canal, Dublin. Patrick Kavanagh. BIrV; NOIV

Lines Written on a Very Boisterous Day in May, 1844. John Clare. OxBSP

Lines Written on a Window at The Leasowes. William Shenstone. NPeEn; OxBSP

Lines Written on New Year's Day—In the Manner of Liu Hou-ts'un [Liu K'o-chuang (1187–1269)]. Wen Cheng-ming.
 "There was no reason to expect sadness." CoBLCP

Lines, Written on Seeing My Husband's Picture, Painted When He Was Young: "Those are the features, those the smiles." Anna Sawyer. ECWP; LW

Lines Written to Console Those Ladies Distressed by the Lines "Men Never Make Passes, etc." Ogden Nash. PeLV

Lines Written under a Picture of a Girl Burning a Love-Letter. Letitia [or Laetitia] Elizabeth Landon. NOBRP

Lines Written under the Influence of Delerium. William Cowper. See Lines Written during a Period of Insanity

Lines Written under the Portrait of Robert Fergussson, the Poet, in a Copy of That Author's Works Presented to a Young Lady in Edinburgh, March 19th, 1787. Robert Burns. NePenScot

Lines Written upon a Window-Shutter at Weston. William Cowper. NOEC

Lingam and the Yoni, The. Alec Derwent Hope. NoAM

Lingard and the Stars. Edwin Arlington Robinson. OxBSo

Linger not, stranger; shed no tear. Inscription for a War. Alec Derwent Hope. BMAP; NoP-4

Lingerie shopping with Mom, I braced myself. Eve's Striptease. Julia Kasdorf. NeAmPo

Lingering clouds, rolling, rolling, The. Flood. Ch'ien T'ao. ChiP, tr. by Arthur Waley

Lingering fade the rays of daylight, and the listening air is chilly. Philip and Mildred. Adelaide Anne Procter. VWP

Lingering sun: rivers and mountains brighten. Wu-Chueh. Tu Fu. ChinPo, tr. by Yip Wai-lim

Lingua Franca. Chris Stroffolino. BodElec

Linguist parrot flicked his flowery wings, The. Crinagoras. GrAn

Linked-Verse Sequence throughout the Town, The. Mukai Kyorai. "Each year it is but a peck of rice." WoPoe, tr. by Earl Miner

Linked Verses. Vietnamese Oral Tradition. CaDao, tr. by John Balaban

Linnet, The. Robert Bridges. See I Heard a Linnet Courting

Linnet in November, The. Francis Turner Palgrave. EBVV

Linnet in the rocky dells, The. Emily Jane Brontë. See Song: "Linnet in the rocky dells, The."

Linnet who had lost her way, A. Tenebris Interlucentem. James Elroy Flecker. MoBrPo

Linnets. Larry Levis. LCAP-2

Linstead Market. Unknown. FaBoVe

Lint. Rita Dove. TRP

Lintie in a Cage. Alice V. Stuart. OxBS

Lion, The. Joseph Hilaire Pierre Belloc. MoBrPo; NBLV; WHSW

Lion, The. Ogden Nash. TLR; WHSW

Lion, The. Walter James Turner. MoBrPo

Lion, The. István Vas. IQMS, tr. by Peter Zollman

Lion and Albert, The. Marriott Edgar. OBNV

Lion and his shadow the lioness, The. Girl with Pitcher. Ruth Dallas. PeNZ

Lion and lioness are intractable, The. Letter to Eve. Alan Dugan. YaYoPo

Lion and the Echo, The. Brian Patten. OBSP

Lion and the unicorn, The. Mother Goose. OxBoLi

Lion and his tamer, The. Crunch, The. Gerda Mayer. OBSP

Lion dishonoured bids death come, The. Reversionary. Stevie Smith. FaBoEE

Lion for Real, The. Allen Ginsberg. EmeKit; GLP; HCAP; RB

Lion, he prowleth far and near, The. Hunters, The. Ruth Temple Lindsay. SacPr

Lion-hearted cedar forest, gonads for our thunder. Christopher Okigbo. PBMAP Fr. Lament of the Drums (1964).

Lion Hunts. Patricia Beer. OxBTC

Lion is never a lion in a royal hunt, A. Lion Hunts. Patricia Beer. OxBTC

Lion is the [or a] beast to fight, The. Sage Counsel. Sir Arthur Thomas Quiller-Couch. NBLV

Lion Lion. Tom Raworth. PFTM-2

Lion Named Passion, A. John Hollander. NoAM

Lion of Judah, The. Jan Emmens. WoPoe, tr. by Adrienne Rich

Lion of the stars is losing power, The. Lion, The. István Vas. IQMS, tr. by Peter Zollman

Lion of waking roars, The. In the Forests of Sleep. Habiba Muhammadi. PoArWo, tr. by Ibrahim Muhawi

Lion over the Tomb of Leonidas, The. Unknown. AWP, tr. by Walter Leaf

Lion remembers the forest, The. Captivity. Amy Levy. ViWPN

Lion's Bride, The. Gwen Harwood. BoWoP

Lion's Skeleton, The. Charles Tennyson Turner. NOBVV

Lion tamers wrestle with the lions in a cage, The. Apex. Nate Salsbury. NBLV

Lion, the Lion, he dwells in the waste, The. Lion, The. Joseph Hilaire Pierre Belloc. MoBrPo; NBLV; WHSW

Lionel, do you remember "Dark Shadows." After the Children Have Gone to Bed. Nicholas Samaras. TWW

Lions of fire, The. Kenneth Patchen. APT-2; VGW

Lions of the hill are gone, The. Deirdre's [or Deidre's] Lament for the Sons of Usnach. Unknown. NOIV, tr. by Sir Samuel Ferguson

Lions who ate the Christians on the sands of the arena, The. Sunt Leones. Stevie Smith. NoAM

Lip. James Vincent Cunningham. OBAL Fr. Five Epigrams.

Lip was a man who used his head. James Vincent Cunningham. OBAL Fr. Five Epigrams.

Lip which had once been stolid, now moving, A. Divine Love. Michael Benedikt. CoAP; CoAmPo

Lipman and Cohen, butchers, Hercules Lane. At the Jaffé Memorial Fountain, Botanic Gardens. Frank Ormsby. CIP-2

Lips. Lance Larsen. AmPoNex

Lips and Eyes. Giambattista [or Giovanni Battista] Marino. OBVE; OxBSP, tr. by Thomas Carew

Lips and tongue. Hand of Solo, A. Thomas Kinsella. CIP-2; NOIV

Lips of that Evangelist, The. (LL) Tennyson. EBVV; FHYEP; PeECV; TOF Fr. In Memoriam A. H. H.

Lips of the dead once thoughtlessly. Yehuda Amichai [or Amikhai]. FIT, tr. by Robert Friend

Lips of the one I love are my perpetual pleasure, The. Lord Be Praised, The. Hafiz [or Hafez]. BoLoP, tr. by Peter Avery and John Heath-Stubbs

Lips pressed against my heart. (LL) Evening Song. Jean Toomer. APT-2; BPo; GT

Lips That Touch Liquor. George W. Young. NBLV

Lips to the already dead Ayler. Migration of Drummond's Organs (After Death), The. Norman Weinstein. WaCA

Lips Tongueless[e]. Robert Herrick. CaPo

Lipsticktion. Edwin Torres. HeMarv

Liquidation. Leah Aini. DTA, tr. by Miriyam Glazer

Liquidity's a mystery; it's very rarely seen. Accounting Cat, The. John Clarke. UV

Liquor, wages, automobiles, women, dope. Elegy for Llywelyn Humphries. Meic Stephens. TCAWP

Lisa, Leona, Loretta? Salt. Yusef Komunyakaa. OPRER; UnSA

Lisbon. Russell Atkins. GT

Lisbon Packet, The. Byron. See Lines to Mr Hodgson

Lispeth. Rudyard Kipling. Fr. Plain Tales from the Hills.

Lisping young lady called Beth, A. Limerick. Unknown. PeLi

Lissom psychotic named Jane, A. Limerick. Unknown. PeLi

List, I hear the church bells ring. Church Bells, The. Mrs. Henry Linden. CBWP-4

List! list! the sleigh bells peal across the snow. December. Henrietta Cordelia Ray. CBWP-3

List of the Delusions of the Insane, A / What They Are Afraid Of. David Antin. APSN

List the harp in window wailing. Aeolian Harp, The. Herman Melville. NCAP

List to me while I tell you. Spaniard That Blighted My Life, The. Billy Merson. OBCoV

List to the sad wind, drearily moaning. Autumn. Priscilla Jane Thompson. CBWP-2

List while the poet trolls. Rival Curates, The. Sir William Schwenck Gilbert. PeLV

Listed into the cause of sin. True Use of Music, The. Charles Wesley. SacPr

Listen. Marylin Butler. CDa

Listen. Jessica Tarahata Hagedorn. WPOW

Listen. Vladimir Vladimirovich Mayakovsky [or Maiakovskii]. PFTM-1

Listen. Spectacular. Lilian Moore. KaS

Listen. Benjamin Péret. SurPaPo, tr. by Rachel Stella

Listen. Iain Crichton Smith. HarvBoo

Listen. Yeshe Tsogyel. WPoS

Listen! Vladimir Vladimirovich Mayakovsky [or Maiakovskii]. CLPP, tr. by Maria Enzensberger

Listen! Lilian Moore. NTCP

Listen! To Olga. Alena Synková. INSAB

Listen / All creeping things. Issa. ZenPo, tr. by Takashi Ikemoto and Lucien Stryk

Listen, and when thy hand this paper presses. Letter from a Girl to Her Own Old Age, A. Alice Thompson Meynell. MoBrPo; VWP

Listen awhile ye nations, and be dumb. (LL) Great Spirits Now on Earth. John Keats. CenSon; Son

Listen, Big Boy! Button Up Your Overcoat. Ray Henderson. ReLy

Listen but once to the words written out by my hand. Short Summary. Louise Bogan. APT-2

Listen Carefully. Philip Levine. EmeKit

Listen Children. Lucille Clifton. ISC; NOxBChV; OxIBACP

Listen, comrades of the flaming centuries. Listen Comrades. David Diop. NegPo, tr. by Ellen Conroy Kennedy

Listen comrades of the struggling centuries. David Diop. *See* Listen, comrades of the flaming centuries

Listen, for example, to the thudding of the winter stream. Inconclusive Evening, An. Frances Bellerby. FaBoTw

Listen, good people, and you shall hear. W. H. Auden. OBNV *Fr.* Six Commissioned Texts.

Listen! Hear how I dreamed a great dream. Dream of the Rood, The. *Unknown.* NePenScot, *tr. by* Robert Crawford

Listen—help me! Ears. Sonja Åkesson. WPOW, *tr. by* Joanna Bankier

Listen here, Joe. Without Benefit of Declaration. Langston Hughes. TTY

Listen, I stole Wagner's. "New World" Interview. Bruce Sweet. MiVo

Listen! I've a big surprise! Invitation. Myra Cohn Livingston. TLR

Listen! I will describe the best of dreams. Dream of the Rood, The. *Unknown.* ASW, *tr. by* Kevin Crossley-Holland

Listen, / if stars are lit. Listen! Vladimir Vladimirovich Mayakovsky [*or* Maiakovskii]. CLPP, *tr. by* Maria Enzensberger

Listen—listen. Richard Ntiru. EroLit *Fr.* Rhythm of the Pestle.

Listen. Listen here, all about birds and beasts. Talking about Birds. *Vietnamese Oral Tradition.* CaDao, *tr. by* John Balaban

Listen! Listen to shopkeepers talking. Shopkeepers at the Party Meeting. Thomas McCarthy. BiHa

Listen! / Listen to the witch! Listen! Lilian Moore. NTCP

Listen, lively lordings all. Rising in the North, The. *Unknown.* ESPB

Listen, Lord—[a Prayer]. James Weldon Johnson. BPo

Listen more often. Breaths. Birago Diop. TTY, *tr. by* Anne Atik

Listen Mr Oxford Don. John Agard. NPeEn; Oth

Listen my children, and you shall hear. Henry Wadsworth Longfellow. AiP; BRP; EBNV; FaBoTw; HHAm; ITBLP; OBAL; OBCA; OBNV; PWR; TCAPo; TFi *Fr.* Tales of a Wayside Inn.

Listen, my dearest, once this flesh of mine. Two Hearts Divided. R. Williams Parry. OBWVE, *tr. by* Joseph P. Clancy

Listen, my friend, this road is the heart opening. Heat of Midnight Tears, The. Mirabai [*or* Mira Bai]. WPoS, *tr. by* Robert Bly

Listen natives of a dry place. Old Boast, The. W. S. Merwin. NOBA

Listen, nephew / When I opened the cantina. Tale of Sunlight, The. Gary Soto. NoAM

Listen not to the rain piercing the woods, pelting the leaves! Tune: "Calming Windswept Waves." Su Tung-p'o (Su Shih). ColAnChi, *tr. by* Jiaosheng Wang

Listen! Now I have come to step over your soul. Sacred Formula to Destroy Life. *Unknown.* PAI, *tr. by* James Mooney

Listen, now, verse should be as natural. Poetry for Supper. Ronald Stuart Thomas. OxBC

Listen old man listen. Sweat-House Ritual No. 1. *Unknown.* STP, *tr. by* Alia Fletcher, Francis La Flesche and Jerome Rothenberg

Listen. Put on Morning. William Sydney Graham. FaBoTw

Listen, Sanoe. Sanoe. Queen Lili'u-o-ka-lani. SWaP

Listen sweet Dove unto my song. Whitsunday. George Herbert. GeHe

Listen! The fame of Danish kings. *Unknown.* ASW

Listen, the hay-bells tinkle as the cart. Holy Innocents, The. Robert Lowell. CoAmPo; MoAmPo; OBCP; OxBC

Listen: the laureled poets. Lemon Trees, The. Eugenio Montale. PoetW; WoPoe, *tr. by* William Arrowsmith

Listen! The night-raven's song. Nicarchus of Alexandria. GrAn

Listen; the poets laureate. Lemon Trees, The. Eugenio Montale. PFTM-1

Listen: there was a goat's head hanging by ropes in a tree. Brigit Pegeen Kelly. ExTi; IllVoic *Fr.* Southern Review, the.

Listen. This is the Noise of Myth. Eavan Boland. ModIr

Listen to me and you shall hear. World Is Turned Upside Down, The. *Unknown.* NOSC

Listen to me, as when ye heard our father. Canadian Boat Song. John Galt. FaBoCh; OBEV

Listen to my tale of woe. Oh, Lady, Be Good! George Gershwin. ReLy

Listen to the coal. In Memoriam John Coltrane. Michael Stillman. InPK-6

Listen to the Mocking Bird. Septimus Winner. TCAPo

Listen to the phone calls they do not. Metaphor as Illness. Chuck Ortleb. GLP

Listen to the Rock Island train. Riding the Rock Island through Kansas. Dave Etter. GM

Listen to the sea. Guillaume Apollinaire. PFTM-1 *Fr.* Victoire.

Listen to the Sound of My Horn. Rita Dove. SeSe

Listen to the story of Willie the Weeper. Willie the Weeper. *Unknown.* OBAL

Listen to the tale. Slim Greer. Sterling Allen Brown. NAAAL

Listen to Things. Spirits. Birago Diop. NegPo, *tr. by* Ellen Conroy Kennedy

Listen, / when i found there was no safety. To My Friend, Jerina. Lucille Clifton. ESEAA

Listen. . . / With faint dry sound. November Night. Adelaide Crapsey. APT-1; PAI; Spl; TCAPo

Listen, you rhythm rounders. Truckin' Ted Koehler. ReLy

Listen! you shouldn't be so hopelessly severe. Plot with Bitterness. Vadim Gabrielevich Shershenevich. TCRP, *tr. by* Daniel Weissbort

Listenen to Big Black at S. F. State. Sonia Sanchez. BPo

Listener's Guide to the Birds, A. Elwyn Brooks White. OWoS

Listeners, The. Walter De la Mare. AWP; ClHu; HAP; HeIP-4; InPK-6; MoBrPo; NOBE; NOxBChV; NoAM; NoP-4; OBEV; OBMV; OBSP; OxAEP-2; PoRA; SoSe-8; TFi

Listeners, The. Louis Simpson. BodElec

Listenin' to that. Trio. Kimberly Ann Collins. InTrad

Listening. Aileen Fisher. NTCP

Listening. Rod Willmot. HA

Listening closely to the noises of the earth. Hospital, The. Sofiya [*or* Sofiia] Iul'evna Preygel [*or* Preigel']. TCRP, *tr. by* Bradley Jordan

Listening for the sound. Nocturne. Pinkie Gordon Lane. BlSi

Listening in heaven. (LL) To Mark Anthony in Heaven. William Carlos Williams. NOBA; SAmP; TCAPo

Listening, listening; it is never still. Märchen, The. Randall Jarrell. HarvBoo

Listening Macaws, The. Hazel Hall. APT-1

Listening Nydia. Henrietta Cordelia Ray. CBWP-3

Listening to a Cricket in the Wainscoting. Robert Bly. InvLad

Listening to a Flute at Night near the City Wall. Li Yi. CrYelRi, *tr. by* Sam Hamill

Listening to a Flute in Yellow Crane Pavilion. Li Po. CrYelRi, *tr. by* Sam Hamill

Listening to a Flute on a Spring Night in Lo-yang. Li Po. CrYelRi, *tr. by* Sam Hamill

Listening to a Monk from Shu Playing the Lute. Li Po. WoPoe, *tr. by* Vikram Seth

Listening to a Monk from Shu Playing the Lute. Li Po. SuSp, *tr. by* Joseph J. Lee

Listening to a Monk Play the Reed Pipes. Hsüeh T'ao. ColAnChi, *tr. by* Jeanne Larsen

Listening to a Wanderer's "Water Melody." Wang Ch'ang-ling. SuSp, *tr. by* Joseph J. Lee

Listening to a White Man Play the Blues. Silvia Curbelo. TouFir

Listening to Aunt Sue's stories. (LL) Aunt Sue's Stories. Langston Hughes. APT-2; SAmP

Listening to Collared Doves. Edith Jay Scovell. HarvBoo

Listening to Dvorak's Serenade in E. Colette Inez. MiVo

Listening to Gibbons at Rock-Pool Creek. Shen Yüeh. ColAnChi, *tr. by* Richard W. Bodman

Listening to Grownups Quarreling. Ruth Whitman. NTCP

(Standing in the hall against the.) KaS

Listening to Mozart at Meadow Brook. Patricia Hooper. MiVo

Listening to that lonesome whistle blow. (LL) Globe in North Carolina, The. Derek Mahon. BiHa; PBCIP

Listening to the Köln Concert. Robert Bly. RaBo

Listening to the Lute Played by Monk Chun from Shu. Li Po. ChinPo, *tr. by* Yip Wai-lim

Listening to the moon. Buson. EH; NIL-7, *tr. by* Robert Hass

Listening to the newsreel today. Newscast. Jared Angira. NAfrP

Listening to the plovers. Buson. EH, *tr. by* Robert Hass

Listening to the Rain. K'ang Hai. CoBLCP, *tr. by* Jonathan Chaves

Listening-to-the-Rain Studio. Chu Yi-tsun. SuSp, *tr. by* Chang Yin-nan

Listening to the River. Su Tung-p'o (Su Shih). TAL

Listening to the Washblock in the Moonlight. Liu Ch'ang-ch'ing. SuSp, *tr. by* Dell R. Hales

Listless. Tu Fu. CrYelRi, *tr. by* Sam Hamill

Listless beauty of the hour, The. History. D. H. Lawrence. RaBo

Listless dingo whelps—lolled by the door, The. Gularwundul's Wish. Kevin Gilbert. IBA

Listless he eyes the palisades. In the Prison Pen. Herman Melville. TAP

Listless the silent ladies sit. Music. William Bell Scott. NOBVV

Listn the male chauvinist in mi dad. Girls Can We Educate We Dads? James Berry. NOxBChV

Lists became shorter, The. Making Lists. Gladys Cardiff. HATNAP

Lit-elle messe, moffette. Luis d'Antin Van Rooten. OBCoV *Fr.* Mots d'Heures: Gousses, Rames.

Litanies of Julia Pastrana (1832–1860), The. Thomas William Shapcott. CBAP; NOBAu

Litany. Carolyn Creedon. BodElec

Litany. Elise Paschen. FFC

Litany, A. John Donne.

   Father, The. NOCV

   Holy Ghost, The. NOCV

   Son, The. NOCV

Litany, A. Frank O'Hara. BodElec

Litany, A. Gregory Orr. BodElec

Litany, A: "Ring out your bells." Sir Philip Sidney. *See* Dirge: "Ring out your bells [*or belles*], let mourning shows [*or shewes*] be spread."

Litany, The. Dana Gioia. BAP-97

Litany for Dictatorships. Stephen Vincent Benét. OxBA

Litany for Survival, A. Audre Lorde. NAAAL

Litany: "From a ruler that's a curse." Charles Cotton. OBSV

Litany in Time of Plague, A. Thomas Nashe [*or* Nash]. *See* Summer's Last Will and Testament

Litany: "My sweet, beloved companion." Margit Kaffka. IQMS, *tr. by* Paul Tabori

Litany of [*or at*] Atlanta, A. William Edward Burghardt DuBois. APT-1; TCAPo

Litany of Sleep. Tristan Corbière.
"You who snore with your sleeping wife so near." OBVE

Litany of the Dark People, The. Countee Cullen. ChIV-2

Litany of the Little Bourgeois. Nicanor Parra. TCLAP, *tr. by* James Laughlin

Litany of the Rooms of the Dead. Franz Werfel. TrJP, *tr. by* Edith Abercrombie Snow

Litany to Our Lady. Eugene O'Curry. HW

Litany to Satan. Charles Baudelaire. AWP, *tr. by* James Elroy Flecker

Litany to the Holy Spirit. Robert Herrick. *See* His Litany to the Holy Spirit

Literally thin-skinned, I suppose, my face. Weathering. Fleur Adcock. DiPo

Literary. Kenneth Fearing. APT-2

Literary Dinner, A. Vladimir Vladimirovich Nabokov. OBAL; PeLV

Literary Excellence. Robert Harris. BMAP

Literary Importation. Philip Freneau. TAP

Literary Reminiscences. Thomas Hood. OxBSo

Literature and Action. Goronva Camlan. AngWePo

Literature: The God, Its Ritual. Merrill Moore. FuPo

Lithuania. Myra Sklarew.
"At three-thirty in the morning in America." TaR

Lithuania, after Fifty-Two Years. Czeslaw Milosz.
Goddess, A. BodElec
Who? BodElec

Lithuanian Grandmother. Merra Young-Prottengeier. GotH

Litrajure of Everyday Life, The. Michael C. Blumenthal. NoAM

Little. Dorothy Aldis. NTCP; WHSW

Little ash, a painted rose, a name, A. After a Death. Charles Tomlinson. HarvBoo

Little Aster. Gottfried Benn. PFTM-1

Little babe, while burns the west. Jean Ingelow. VWP

Little Ballad of the Three Rivers. Federico García Lorca. BLPSL, *tr. by* Rene de Costa, Rigas Kappatos and Eleni Paidoussi

Little, barb'rous, cruel fly! Walsingham; or, The Pupil of Nature. Mary Robinson. RWP

Little Beauty That I Was Allowed, The. Elinor Wylie. Son *Fr.* One Person.

Little before midnight down by the docks, A. In the Eyes of the Gods. André Breton. WoPoe, *tr. by* Jack Rogow and Bill Zavatsky

Little Belgian Orphan, A. Amanda Ros. VerBaPo

Little Bell. Mary E. Tucker. CBWP-1

Little Benny sat one evening. Misplaced Sympathy. Charles Follen Adams. OBAL

Little Betty Blue. Betty Blue. Mother Goose. OxNR; ReMoGo

Little Betty Pringle [*or* Winckle] she had a pig. Betty Pringle's Pig. Mother Goose. OxNR

Little Billee. William Makepeace Thackeray. FaBoCh; NOBL; OxAEP-2 (Three Sailors, The.) OxBB

Little Billy Breek. *Unknown.* OxNR

Little Birch Tree, The. Stepan Petrovich Shchipachov [*or* Shchipachiov]. TCRP, *tr. by* Daniel Weissbort

Little Bird, The. Mother Goose. OxNR; ReMoGo

Little Bird, The. *Unknown.* PBA, *tr. by* Rolf Italiander

Little bird, The. *Unknown.* NOIV, *tr. by* Thomas Kinsella *Fr.* Four Glosses.

Little bird, a tender bird, A. Siren Bird, The. Henrietta Cordelia Ray. CBWP-3

Little bird flew through the dell, A. Autumn Song. Johann Ludwig Tieck. AWP, *tr. by* James Clarence Mangan

Little bird of paradise. *Unknown.* OxNR

Little bird with tuneful throat. My Canary. Josephine D. Henderson Heard. CBWP-4

Little Birds. Jacob Sternberg. TrJP, *tr. by* Joseph Leftwich

Little Birds Are Playing. Lewis Carroll. OWoS

Little birds aren't on rollers, The. Joan of Arc. Benjamin Péret. PFTM-1

Little birds in a row. Little Birds. Jacob Sternberg. TrJP, *tr. by* Joseph Leftwich

Little Birds of the Night. Stephen Crane. APN-2

Little birds sit in their nest and beg, The. Little Birds, The. *Unknown.* NTCP

Little birds warble their song in the tree, The. Bird Song, The. Mrs. Henry Linden. CBWP-4

Little Bit in Love, A. Betty Comden. ReLy

Little Bit Independent, A. Edgar Leslie. ReLy

Little bit, more or less each day, A. Beethoven's Sixth Symphony. Steve Benson. FTOS

Little Bit Off, A. Richard Maltby, Jr. ReLy

Little Black Boy, The. William Blake. AWP; AmFaPo; CABP; ChAP; FHYEP; HeIP-4; NAEL-5v2; NAEL-6v2; NAWM-7v2; NOBRP; NOEC; NoP-4; OBEV; PeECV; PoE; PoPoPo; SCGP; TFi *Fr.* Songs of Innocence.

Little Black Boy's Prayer, A. Guy Tirolien. NegPo, *tr. by* Ellen Conroy Kennedy

Little Black Bug. Margaret Wise Brown. NTCP

Little black dog ran round the house, The. *Unknown.* OxNR

Little Black Rose. *Unknown.* NOIV, *tr. by* Thomas Kinsella

Little Black Rose shall be red at last!, The. Song: Little Black Rose, The. Aubrey Thomas De Vere. BIrV

Little black thing among the snow, A. William Blake. FHYEP; NAEL-5v2; NAEL-6v2; NAWM-7v2; NOEC; RB *Fr.* Songs of Experience.

Little Black Train Is A-Comin' *Unknown.* GM

Little blessed Earth that turns, The. O Earth, Turn! George Johnston. MoCV

Little blood, more or less, he said, A. Great and Strong. Miroslav Holub. RB, *tr. by* George Theiner

Little Blue Ben, who lives in the glen. Little Blue Ben. *Unknown.* OxNR

Little Blue Betty lived in a den. Little Blue Betty. *Unknown.* OxNR

Little Bo-Peep has lost her sheep. Little Bo-Peep. Mother Goose. WHSW

Little boat floats by the dock, The. Inscribed on a Painting. Tao-chi. CoBLCP, *tr. by* Jonathan Chaves

Little boat on the great river, A. Crossing the Yellow River. Wang Wei. CrYelRi, *tr. by* Sam Hamill

Little boat, tied up at the dock, The. Painting a Picture, the Tranquil Boat—Sent to Ko Ju-ching. Wen Cheng-ming. CoBLCP, *tr. by* Jonathan Chaves

Little boat—untie the line. To the Tune, "Ch'ing-p'ing Yüeh." Yang Shen. CoBLCP, *tr. by* Jonathan Chaves

Little boat with stubby oars, and West Lake's good, A. Tune: "Song of Picking Mulberry"—Recollections of West Lake. Ou-yang Hsiu. SuSp, *tr. by* Jerome P. Seaton

Little boats were patchwork on the bay, The. Three Years from Sorrento. Dorothy Belle Flanagan. YaYoPo

Little Bob Robin. Bob Robin. Mother Goose. OxNR

Little Bobby Snooks was fond of his books. Bobby Snooks. *Unknown.* ReMoGo

Little bones of. Poem. Michael O'Brien. KGB

Little book—no, I don't begrudge you—you're off to the City. Ovid. RomPo, *tr. by* Peter Green *Fr.* Tristia.

Little Books / Indians. Hannah Weiner.
Little Books 137 Silence Mar 22 79. FTOS

Little Box from Olinalá. Gabriela Mistral. TANSG, *tr. by* Maria Jacketti

Little boy, The. Junior Addict. Langston Hughes. BPo

Little boy, A / Was wild about. Gimme a Little Kiss (Will Ya, Huh?). Jack Smith. ReLy

Little Boy Blue. Eugene Field. BRP; ChAP; ITBLP; OBAL; OBCA; SoSe-8

Little Boy Blue, come blow [*up*] your horn[!]. Mother Goose. OxNR

Little Boy Found, The. William Blake. FHYEP; NoP-4 *Fr.* Songs of Innocence.

Little boy, laid sick and low, A. Dying Child's Request, The. Hannah Flagg Gould. OBCA

Little boy lived on the outskirts of Kolpino, A. Lines about a Little Boy. Aleksandr Petrovich Mezhirov. TCRP, *tr. by* Deming Brown

Little Boy Lost. Stevie Smith. FaBoTw

Little Boy Lost, A. William Blake. FHYEP; PeECV *Fr.* Songs of Experience.

Little Boy Lost, The. William Blake. FHYEP *Fr.* Songs of Innocence.

Little Boy, to show his might and power, The. Metamorphosis, The. Sir John Suckling. CaPo; FaBoEE

Little boy was looking for his voice, The. Little Mute Boy, The. Federico García Lorca. RB

Little boy went into a barn, A. Boy in the Barn, The. *Unknown.* ReMoGo

Little Britain. *Unknown.* NOEC

Little Brother, The. James Reeves. OxBTC

Little Brown Baby. Paul Laurence Dunbar. APN-2; NAAAL; NoP-4

Little Brown Brother. Nick Carbó. AmPoNex; ReBoTo

Little Brown Jacks Nyimbung. Rex Marshall. IBA

Little Brown Jug. Joseph E. Winner. OBAL

Little Brown Seed, The. Harriett Mulford Lothrop. PWR

Little buoy said, "Mother, deer," A. Misspelled Tail, A. Elizabeth T. Corbett. OBCA

Little by Little. *Unknown.* PWR

Little by little it becomes clear to me. Unusual Autumn, An. Dahlia Ravikovitch [*or* Ravikovich]. DTA, *tr.* by Chana Bloch

Little by little, wean yourself. Jelaluddin [*or* Jalal al-Din] Rumi. BLT

Little Cape Cod Landscape. Charles North. FTOS

Little cares that fretted me, The. Out in the Fields [with God]. Elizabeth Barrett Browning. ITBLP

Little Carol of the Virgin, A. Félix Lope de Vega Carpio. SpanPo, *tr.* by Denise Levertov

Little cart jolting and banging through the yellow haze of dusk, The. Little Cart, The. Ch'en Tzu-lung. ChiP, *tr.* by Arthur Waley

Little caterpillar creeps, The. Cocoon. David McCord. OBCA

Little Cavalier, A. Lucy Larcom. SWaP

Little Chap Who Follows Me, The. *Unknown.* PoToHe

Little Child's Faith, The. Louis E. Thayer. PoToHe

Little child sat on the floor, A. Where Do School Days End? Josephine D. Henderson Heard. CBWP-4

Little child she, half defiant came, A. Augusta Davies Webster. VWP *Fr.* Mother and Daughter.

Little children, never give. Kindness to Animals. *Unknown.* WHSW

Little children you will all go. Song of Man Chipping an Arrowhead. W. S. Merwin. InPK-6

Little churches wake up in the half light, The. Nuns Go Walking. Aldo Palazzeschi. PFTM-1

Little Citizen, Little Survivor. Hayden Carruth. OPRER

Little City. Robert Horan. YaYoPo

Little Clan, The. Frederick Robert Higgins. OBMV

Little Cloth, The. Hilary Llewellyn-Williams. TCAWP

Little cock sparrow sat on a green tree, A. Boy and the Sparrow. Mother Goose. OxNR; ReMoGo

Little cousin is dead, by foul subtraction, The. Dead Boy. John Crowe Ransom. FaBoMo; FuPo; HarvBoo; NoAM; NoP-4; OxBA; PoE; TwCP

Little cramped words scrawling all over the paper. Letter, The. Amy Lowell. NALW; PoBW

Little creatures, everywhere! (LL) Little Things. James Stephens. MoBrPo; PoRA

Little Crisis Framed in My Window. Christopher Davis. AmPoNex

Little crystal globe. Earth. Jules Supervielle. MFP, *tr.* by Martin Sorrell

Little cullud boys / with fears. Tag. Langston Hughes. APT-2

Little Dance outside the Ruins of Unreason. Carl Phillips. NAPBL

Little Dancers, The. Laurence Binyon. MoBrPo; OxBTC

Little Dantesque. James Galvin. BAP-01

Little Death. Gwyn Thomas. OBWVE, *tr.* by Joseph P. Clancy

Little Demon, The. Zinaida Nikolayevna [*or* Nikolaevna] Gippius. TCRP, *tr.* by Lubov Yakovleva

Little Dicky Dilver. *Unknown.* OxNR

Little Dog that wags his tail, A. Emily Dickinson. NOxBChV

Little drink enjoyed in the east of town, A. Evening Stroll. Ema Saiko. WoPoe, *tr.* by Conrad Totman

Little drum. Bonguemba. Antoine-Roger Bolamba. NegPo, *tr.* by Ellen Conroy Kennedy

Little East of Jordan, A. Emily Dickinson. ChIV-1; NoP-4

Little Elegy. Denis Devlin. ModIr; NOIV

Little Elegy. X. J. Kennedy. CoAP; CoAmPo

Little Elf, The. John Kendrick Bangs. NTCP; OBCA

Little Ellie sits alone. Romance of the Swan's Nest, The. Elizabeth Barrett Browning. VWP

Little Exercise. Elizabeth Bishop. CoAP; ColAP; MoAmPo

(Little Exercise at 4. A.M.) UnPo

Little Falls. Robert Hogg. MoCV

Little Fay's Thanksgiving. Henrietta Cordelia Ray. CBWP-3

Little fevered island, blued to closing. Foundered Star. Jane Miller. ExTi

Little finger on the right, The. (LL) One, Two, Three, Four, Five! *Unknown.* LB; OxNR

Little Fish. D. H. Lawrence. OxBTC; RB; Spl; TTTS

Little fishes in a brook. *Unknown.* OxNR

Little flame mouths. Dragon Night. Jane Yolen. OTCP

Little fleece of my flesh. Close to Me. Gabriela Mistral. TCLAP, *tr.* by Doris Dana

Little flocks of peaceful clouds. Black Cloud, The. William Henry Davies. RB

Little Flower's Disciple, The. John Montague. CIP-2 *Fr.* Leaping Fire, The.

Little Fly. William Blake. NAEL-5v2; NAEL-6v2; NBLV *Fr.* Songs of Experience.

Little fogs were gathered in every hollow. Country Wedding, The. Thomas Hardy. UnPo

Little Fred. *Unknown.* ReMoGo

Little French Lawyer, The. John Fletcher.

Song in the Wood. NOSC

Little Friend. *Unknown.* WoPoe

Little Furnace. Brenda Hillman. BodElec

Little garden, A. Garden, The. Franta Bass. INSAB

Little General Monk. *Unknown.* OxNR

Little Gidding. T. S. Eliot. CABP; FaBoMo; FaBoTw; GTBS-P; NAEL-5v2; NAEL-6v2; NAWM-7v2; NOBA; NOBE; NoAM; OxAEP-2; OxBTC; PeECV; TAP; TFi *Fr.* Four Quartets.

Little Giffen. Francis Orrery [*or* Orray] Ticknor. CBCWP

Little girl. Another Rhythm. Akasha (Gloria) Hull. ISC

Little Girl. Vivian Lamarque. CItWP, *tr.* by Cinzia Sartini Blum and Lara Trubowitz

Little Girl. Mother Goose. OxNR

(Little Girl and Queen.) ReMoGo

Little Girl and Queen. Mother Goose. *See* Little Girl

Little Girl, Be Careful What You Say. Carl Sandburg. NOxBChV

Little Girl Blue. Lorenz Hart. APT-2

(Sit there and count your fingers.) ReLy

Little girl called Silé Javotte. Christmas 1970. Spike Milligan. OBCP

Little girl dressed, The. Celebration. Ray A. Young Bear. CDW

Little Girl Found, The. William Blake. FHYEP; NOBRP *Fr.* Songs of Experience.

Little Girl Found, The. William Blake. FHYEP; NOBRP *Fr.* Songs of Innocence.

Little girl from Little Rock. Leo Robin. ReLy

Little girl I was, The. Laughter. Wislawa Szymborska. PoSu, *tr.* by Magnus F. Krynski

Little girl is shy, The. Dream Come True. Molly Peacock. RA

Little girl, little girl, / Where have you been? Little Girl. Mother Goose. OxNR

Little Girl Lost, The. William Blake. FHYEP; NOBRP *Fr.* Songs of Experience.

Little Girl Lost, The. William Blake. FHYEP; NOBRP *Fr.* Songs of Innocence.

Little Girl, My String Bean, My Lovely Woman. Anne Sexton. NAAL-5

Little Girl of the Black Forest. Lise Deharme. SurWo, *tr.* by Franklin Rosemont

Little girl riding the fallen tree like a spindly horse, The. Light Hotel. Peter Redgrove. PoE

Little Girl's Dream World, A. Della Burt. BlSi

Little girl saw her first troop parade and asked, "What are those?", The. Carl Sandburg. HHAm *Fr.* People, Yes, The.

Little girl that a good family adopted, taken, The. Daughter. Olesya [*or* Olesia] Nikolayeva [*or* Nikolaeva]. ItGoST, *tr.* by Paul Graves and Carol Ueland

Little girl under a peach tree, A. Peach, The. Shinkichi Takahashi. ZenPo, *tr.* by Takashi Ikemoto and Lucien Stryk

Little Girl Wakes Early. Robert Penn Warren. PoE

Little girl was traveling unattached, as they say, The. Travelers. Josephine Miles. KaS

Little Girl with Bands on Her Teeth, The. Genevieve Taggard. VGW

Little girl with scarlet enameled fingernails, A. Melodic Trains. John Ashbery. GM; NoP-4

Little girl won't eat her sandwich, The. Blasting from Heaven. Philip Levine. CoAP

Little Girls. Laurence Alma-Tadema. WHSW

Little Girls Posing All Dressed Up. Clarence Major. BodElec

Little Good Fellows, The. Herman Melville. NCAP

Little green involute fronds of fern at creekside. Interrupted Meditation. Robert Hass. BAP-97

Little grey hill-glade, close-turfed, withdrawn, A. Marsyas. G. D. Roberts. NoP-4

Little group above the foreign wood, A. (LL) Byrnies, The. Thom Gunn. NoAM; OxBTC

Little Hans. Steve McCaffery. FTOS

Little has come down to me in tears. Pattern, The. Paula Meehan. ModIr

Little head, and no eyes. (LL) Tongs. Mother Goose. LB; OxNR; ReMoGo

Little Hearts, where light-wing'd Passion raignes, The. Fulke Greville, 1st Baron Brooke. PBRV *Fr.* Cælica.

Little hedge-row birds, The. Old Man Travelling [Animal Tranquillity and Decay, a Sketch]. William Wordsworth. FaBoCh; NPeEn; OBWP

Little hedgerow birds, The. Animal Tranquillity and Decay. William Wordsworth. OxBEV

Little Heracles. Theocritus. HePo, *tr.* by Barbara Hughes Fowler *Fr.* Idylls.

Little hiders hide in the hills and groves. Refuting the "Invitation to Hiding." Wang K'ang-chü. CoBCP, *tr.* by Burton Watson

Little hints of reality march across the back. Backing into the Future. Dick Gallup. BAP-97

Little hollows in the pavements shine, The. Dream of Sappho, A. Ella Higginson. SWaP

Little horses fleeing, The. Rondeau of the Little Horses. Manuel Bandeira. TCLAP, *tr.* by Candace Slater

Little hours: two lovers herd upstairs, The. Almost Aubade. Marilyn Hacker. NoAM

Little House, Big House. Medbh McGuckian. PNI

Little house there stood within a glen, A. John Hawthorn. NOEC *Fr.* Journey and Observations of a Countryman, The.

Little Hundred. *Unknown.* OxNR

Little Hunger. Richard Murphy. BIrV

Little I ask; my wants are few. Oliver Wendell Holmes. APN-1; OxBA; PWR *Fr.* Autocrat of the Breakfast Table, The.

Little Infinite Poem. Federico García Lorca. RaBo, *tr.* by Robert Bly

Little ink more or less!, A. Stephen Crane. APN-2 *Fr.* War Is Kind.

Little interrogation of the sky, A. Concerning Paradise. Christopher Buckley. GeoHom

Little Invitation in a Hushed Voice. Tess Gallagher. PasH

Little island whispered over his shoulder. Wound, A. Brendan Kennelly. BiHa

Little Jack Dandy-prat. *Unknown.* OxNR

Little Jack Horner / Sat in a corner. Mother Goose. LB; OxNR; ReMoGo; SoSe-8

Little Jack Jelf. Jack Jelf. *Unknown.* ReMoGo

Little Jack Jingle. Jack Jingle. *Unknown.* ReMoGo

Little Jack Sprat / Once had a pig. *Unknown.* OxNR

Little Jenny Wren. *Unknown.* ReMoGo

Little Jesus came to town, The. Christmas Folk-Song, A. Lizette Woodworth Reese. OBCA; TrCP

Little Jew lived in a little straw hut, A. Biography. Abraham Moses Klein. TrJP

Little Jo wakes me up. Bill Griffiths. Oth *Fr.* Building: The New London Hospital.

Little Jock Elliot. *Unknown.* IBB

Little joe gould has lost his teeth and doesn't know where. E. E. Cummings. NoAM

Little John a Begging. *Unknown.* ESPB

Little John Jiggy Jag. *Unknown.* OxNR

Little John Nobody. *Unknown.* OxBoLi

Little Johnny wants to play. (LL) *Unknown.* OxNR; ReMoGo

Little Josie buried under the bright moon. Half-Caste Girl. Judith Wright. NALW

Little Jumping Joan. Mother Goose. NTCP; ReMoGo

   (Jumping Joan.) OxNR

Little King Boggen. *Unknown.* ReMoGo

Little King Pippin. Mother Goose. OxNR

Little Kingdom I Possess, A. Louisa May Alcott. AH

Little lad, little lad. *Unknown.* OxNR

Little lady coyly shy. Caprichosa. Angelina Weld Grimké. PoBW

Little lady lairdie, The. *Unknown.* OxNR

Little Lady of Ch'ing-ch'i, The. *Unknown.* ChiP, *tr.* by Arthur Waley

Little Lamb, A. *Unknown.* OBCoV

Little Lamb God bless thee! (LL) William Blake. ChIV-2; FHYEP; FaBoCh; HeIP-4; ITBLP; NAEL-5v2; NAEL-6v2; NAWM-7v2; NIL-7; NIP-4; NOBRP; NOEC; NoP-4; OxAEP-2; PAI; PoE; PoPoPo; SoSe-8; TFi; TRP; TrCP; UnPo *Fr.* Songs of Innocence.

Little Lamb, who made thee? William Blake. ChIV-2; FHYEP; FaBoCh; HeIP-4; ITBLP; NAEL-5v2; NAEL-6v2; NAWM-7v2; NIL-7; NIP-4; NOBRP; NOEC; NoP-4; OxAEP-2; PAI; PoE; PoPoPo; SoSe-8; TFi; TRP; TrCP; UnPo *Fr.* Songs of Innocence.

Little Landscape, A. Chu Yün-ming. CoBLCP, *tr.* by Jonathan Chaves

Little Landscape by Chao Ch'ien-li, A. Yü Chi. CoBLCP, *tr.* by Jonathan Chaves

Little Landscape by Yen Wen-kuei, A. Yü Chi. CoBLCP, *tr.* by Jonathan Chaves

Little Language, A. Robert Duncan. PoM *Fr.* Dante.

Little late rain, A. Sarah's Choice. Eleanor Wilner. TaR

Little learning is a dangerous [*or* dang'rous] thing, A. Pope. HAP; NOBE; OxBEV *Fr.* Essay on Criticism, An.

Little less returned for him each spring, A. Anglais Mort à Florence. Wallace Stevens. SAmP

Little Libbie. Julia A. Moore.

   "One morning in April, a short time ago." VerBaPo

Little light is going by, A. Firefly. Elizabeth Madox Roberts. NTCP

Little Lost Pup. Arthur Guiterman. ITBLP

Little Love-God, The. Meleager. AWP, *tr.* by Walter Headlam

Little lute, when I am gone. Richard Corbet [*or* Corbett]. FaBoEE

Little Lyric (of Great Importance). Langston Hughes. APT-2; NBLV; OBAL; OBCoV

Little Madness in the Spring, A. Emily Dickinson. AmFaPo; TAP; TCAPo

Little Maid, The. Anna Maria Wells. OBCA

Little maid, pretty maid, / Whither goest thou? Mother Goose. OxNR; ReMoGo

Little Man, The. Hughes Mearns. NOxBChV

   (Antigonish.) BRP; NBLV

   (As I was walking up the stair.) NOxBChV

Little man in coal pit. Putting on Nightgown. *Unknown.* OxNR

Little man, whom I love so much. Ode to Chaplin. Zoltán Jékely. IQMS, *tr.* by Joseph Leftwich

Little marsh-plant, yellow green, A. Sundew, The. Algernon Charles Swinburne. PeVV

Little Mary Bell had a fairy in a nut. Long John Brown & Little Mary Bell. William Blake. ECEV; RB

Little Millwins attend the Russian Ballet, The. Les Millwin. Ezra Pound. APT-1; OBCoV

Little Miss Muffet. W. S. Brownlee. PeLi

Little Miss Muffet discovered a tuffet. Embarrassing Episode of Little Miss Muffet, The. Guy Wetmore Carryl. OBCA

Little Miss Muffet / Sat on a tuffet. Miss Muffet. Mother Goose. LB; OxNR; ReMoGo

Little monkey goes like a donkey that means to say, A. Gertrude Stein. TTTS *Fr.* Tender Buttons.

Little months little smokes. Comrade. Philippe Soupault. PFTM-1

Little Moppet, The. Mother Goose. OxNR; ReMoGo

Little More Cider, A. *Unknown.* KaS

Little more kindness and a little less creed, A. World Needs, The. *Unknown.* PoToHe

Little more of his love, A. (LL) From Father to Son. Emyr Humphreys. AngWePo; OBWVE; TCAWP

Little More Traveling Music, A. Al Young. NBV

Little moth round candle turning, The. Similie. Charlotte Dacre. NOBRP

Little Mother. Guido Gezelle. TuT, *tr.* by Mary E. O'Donnell

Little moths are creeping, The. Interior. Padraic Colum. MoBrPo

Little Mouse, The. Miroslav Košek. INSAB

Little Mouse, The. *Unknown.* ReMoGo

Little Musgrave and Lady Barnard. *Unknown.* ESPB; OxBB

Little Mute Boy, The. Federico García Lorca. RB

Little Nancy [*or* Nanny] Etticoat. Candle, A. Mother Goose. LB; OxNR; ReMoGo

Little nearer please, A. And a little nearer. Photograph and White Tulips. Dannie Abse. TCAWP

Little nearer, this time, A. After the Second Operation. Patricia Goedicke. TAP

Little Night, A. Douglas Oliver. Oth

Little night: when you. Little Night. Paul Celan. VCWP, *tr.* by Michael Hamburger

Little noises of the house, The. During a Bombardment by V-Weapons. Roy Fuller. OxBSP

Little Ode for X. Maura Stanton. IllVoic

Little Ode to Melancholy. Ricardo Molinari. TCLAP, *tr.* by Inés Probert

Little of distinction, guide-books had said. Little of Distinction. Ruth Bidgood. TCAWP

Little of myself do I remember. Patrizia Cavalli. NeIt

Little old-fashioned girl, The. At Grandfather's. Clara Doty Bates. OBCA

Little Old Lady in Lavender Silk, The. Dorothy Parker. NBLV

Little Old Letter. Langston Hughes. SAmP

Little old man of Derby, A. *Unknown.* OxNR; ReMoGo

Little one, go to sleep. Sleep soundly. Lullaby. *Vietnamese Oral Tradition.* CaDao, *tr.* by John Balaban

Little one sleeps in its cradle, The. Walt Whitman. ColAP; SAmP *Fr.* Song of Myself.

Little Ones' A. B. C., The. Noël Coward.

   "A. Stands for Absolutely Anything." NBLV

Little onion lay by the fireplace, A. Song. Nicholas Moore. SPE

Little onward lend thy guiding hand, A. John Milton. BASC; FHYEP; NAEL-6v1; OxAEP-1; WoPoe *Fr.* Samson Agonistes.

Little Orphant Annie's come to our house to stay. Little Orphant Annie. James Whitcomb Riley. APN-2; BRP; ChAP; ITBLP; NBLV; OBAL; OBCA; OxIBACP; TCAPo

Little Overture. David Barber. AmPoNex

Little owl flew through the night, The. On the Adequacy of Landscape. Wallace Stevens. SAmP

Little painted lady with your lovely clothes. Glad Rag Doll. Dan Dougherty. ReLy

Little, passionately, not at all, A? Villanelle of Marguerites. Ernest Christopher Dowson. MoBrPo

Little path dotted with red. Tune: "Treading on Grass." Yen Shu. SuSp, *tr. by* James J. Y. Liu

Little Peach, The. Eugene Field. OBAL

Little Peach Blossoms in the Garden. Li Shang-yin. SuSp, *tr. by* Eugene Eoyang

Little People. Isaac Leibush [*or* Yitskhok Leybush] Peretz [*or* Perets]. TrJP, *tr. by* Joseph Leftwich

Little picks of the roosters, The. Ballad of Black Grief. Federico García Lorca. STV, *tr. by* John Frederick Nims

Little Pig. *Unknown.* OxNR

Little Poem. Max Jacob. CuPo

Little Poll Parrot. *Unknown.* OxNR

Little Polly Flinders. Mother Goose. LB; OxNR; ReMoGo

Little poppies, little hell flames. Poppies in July. Sylvia Plath. FaBoWP; LCAP-2; RB

Little pretty Nancy girl. *Unknown.* OxNR

Little priest of Felton, The. Priest of Felton. *Unknown.* OxNR

Little ragged girl, our ball-boy, A. Game at Salzburg, A. Randall Jarrell. NoAM

Little Random Creatures, The. *Unknown.* STP, *tr. by* Armand Schwerner

Little Red Riding Hood. Ania Walwicz. BMAP

Little Red Riding Hood and the Wolf. Gillie Bolton. Prnts

Little red wagon for d black bureaucrat, A. Catechism of d Neoamerican Hoodoo Church. Ishmael Reed. NBV

Little Research in Snow, A. Gabriel Preil. FIT, *tr. by* Robert Friend

Little Road—not made of Man, A. Emily Dickinson. SWaP

Little Road says, Go, The. House and the Road, The. Josephine Preston Peabody. ITBLP

Little roads to happiness, they are not hard to find, The. Little Roads to Happiness. Wilhelmina Stitch. PoToHe

Little robin grieves, The. When the Snow Is on the Ground. *Unknown.* ReMoGo

Little Robin Redbreast / Came to visit me. Visitor. *Unknown.* OxNR

Little Robin Redbreast / Sat upon a rail. Niddle Noddle. Mother Goose. OxNR

Little Robin Redbreast sat upon a tree. Catch. Mother Goose. LB; OxNR

Little room, depressing, old, A. Tailor, The. "S. Ansky." TrJP, *tr. by* Joseph Leftwich

Little Rose. *Unknown.* TreFP

Little rose bloomed in the way, A. Rose by the Wayside, The. D. A. Drown. TreFP

Little Ruth. Yehuda Amichai [*or* Amikhai]. VCWP, *tr. by* Benjamin Harshav

Little Saint best fits a little Shrine, A. Ternarie of Littles, upon a Pipkin of Jellie [*or* Jelly] Sent to a Lady, A. Robert Herrick. BeJo; FaBoCh

Little Shoes That Died, The. Mary Gilmore. NOBAu

Little Shon a [*or* Johnny] Morgan, shentleman [*or* gentleman] of Wales. Shon a Morgan. *Unknown.* OxNR

Little Shrub Growing By, A. Ben Jonson. BeJo

Little Sleep's-Head Sprouting Hair in the Moonlight. Galway Kinnell. LCAP-2

Little sleeping and much grieving—the traveller. On the Way to Hangchow: Anchored on the River at Night. Po Chü-i. ChiP, *tr. by* Arthur Waley

Little snow blew in where we stood, A. Shift. Aaron Anstett. AmPoNex

Little snow people are hurrying down, The. Putting the World to Bed. Esther W. Buxton. NOxBChV

Little Song. Langston Hughes. TLR

Little song, A! Why is it so. Little Song, A. Marie von Ebner-Eschenbach. AuPH, *tr. by* Lowell A. Bangerter

Little Song of Life, A. Lizette Woodworth Reese. OBCA

Little Song of the Maimed. Benjamin Péret. OBWP; PeFWW, *tr. by* David Gascoyne

Little soul so sleek and smiling. Animula, Vagula, Blandula. Stevie Smith. OBVE

Little sparrows, The. Pastoral. William Carlos Williams. SAmP; TwCP

Little state-funded barrack, A. It Started. Jimmy Santiago Baca. LoL

Little stream used to cross my land, A. Su Tung-p'o (Su Shih). CoBCP; ColAnChi, *tr. by* Burton Watson *Fr.* Eastern Slope.

Little Sunlight, A. Shinkichi Takahashi. ZenPo, *tr. by* Takashi Ikemoto and Lucien Stryk

Little sycamore, The. Love Song. *Unknown.* TTY, *tr. by* J. E. Manchip White

Little sycamore she planted, The. *Unknown, fr. Egyptian hieroglyphics.* ErotSp, *tr. by* Sam Hamill

Little sympathy, who kicks beneath my ribs. Eighteenth-Century Medical Illustration: The Infant in Its Little Room. Ann Townsend. AmPoNex

Little Tales. Zakiyya Malallah. PoArWo, *tr. by* Wen Chin Ouyang

Little Tee-wee. *Unknown.* OxNR

Little Testament. Eugenio Montale. PoetW, *tr. by* Robert Lowell

Little Things. John Orrick. PoToHe

Little Things. James Stephens. MoBrPo; PoRA

Little Things. *Unknown.* PoToHe

Little Things, The. Elizabeth Isler. PoToHe

Little Things in Life, The. Irving Berlin. ReLy

Little things that no one needs. Bric-à-Brac. Dorothy Parker. APT-1

Little things, that run, and quail. Little Things. James Stephens. MoBrPo; PoRA

Little think'st thou, poor [*or* poore] flower. Blossom [*or* Blossome], The. John Donne. AWP; ESCV; MeLP; NAEL-5v1; NAEL-6v1; NAEL-7v1; SCGP; UnPo

Little thinkest thou, poor ant, who there. Ant, The. Richard Flecknoe. NOSC

Little thinks, in the field, yon red-cloaked clown. Each and All. Ralph Waldo Emerson. APN-1; AWP; ColAP; NAAL-2v1; NAAL-3; NAAL-5; NCAP; NOBA; OxBA; TAP; TCAPo; TreFP

Little time for laughter, A. After. Philip Bourke Marston. NOBVV

Little Tin Box. Sheldon Harnick. ReLy

Little toe, big toe, three toes between. Close Quarters. John Banister Tabb. OBAL

Little toe is attractive, The. Time of Man, The. Phyllis Webb. MoCV

Little Tokyo bar. Iowa Blues Bar Spiritual. Juan Felipe Herrera. ReTh

Little Tom Tittlemouse / Lived in a bell-house. *Unknown.* OxNR

Little Tommy [*or* Tom] Tucker. Tommy Tucker. Mother Goose. LB; OxNR; ReMoGo

Little Tommy Tacket. *Unknown.* OxNR

Little Tommy Tittlemouse / Lived in a little house. Tommy Tittlemouse. Mother Goose. OxNR; ReMoGo

Little too abstract, a little too wise, A. Return. Robinson Jeffers. HarvBoo

Little Tooth, A. Thomas Lux. BodElec

Little toy dog is covered with dust, The. Little Boy Blue. Eugene Field. BRP; ChAP; ITBLP; OBAL; OBCA; SoSe-8

Little Travel Story, A. David Oliveira. GeoHom

Little tree / little silent Christmas tree. E. E. Cummings. NTCP; OBCP

Little trotty hetty coat. Riddle. *Unknown.* FaBoVe

Little Trotty Wagtail. John Clare. NOxBChV; RB; SCGP; UnPo

Little Tumescence, A. Jonathan Williams. NeAP; PoM

Little Turtle, The. Nicholas Vachel Lindsay. NOxBChV; NTCP; OBAL; OBCA; OBSP; OxIBACP

Little Vagabond, The. William Blake. FHYEP; NBLV; OBSV *Fr.* Songs of Experience.

Little verses seek their meal, The. Salon de Vers. Orrick Johns. APT-1

Little Village, A. Mei Yao Ch'en. SuSp, *tr. by* Jonathan Chaves

Little wanderer, hie thee home. (LL) William Blake. FHYEP; NOBRP *Fr.* Songs of Innocence.

Little water, A. It would lie on the thick dust, gleaming. (LL) Water. Leslie Norris. AngWePo; OBWVE

Little While, A. Sara Teasdale. APT-1

Little while, a little while, A. Emily Jane Brontë. VWP

Little while spring will claim its own, A. My Heart Has Known Its Winter. Arna Bontemps. GT

Little while, that in me sings no more, A. (LL) Sonnet: "What lips my lips have kissed, and where, and why." Edna St. Vincent Millay. APT-1; BoLoP; HeIP-4; MakPoe; MoAmPo; NAAL-2v2; NIP-4; OPOU; Son

Little while when I am gone, A. Little While, A. Sara Teasdale. APT-1

Little white clouds are racing over the sky, The. Magdalen Walks. Oscar Wilde. EBVV; MoBrPo

Little White Lies. Walter Donaldson. ReLy

Little white mermaidens live in the sea, The. Mermaidens, The. Laura Elizabeth Richards. OBCA

Little White Rose, The. Hugh MacDiarmid. NePenScot

Little wild bird sometimes at my ear, A. Ballata: Of True and False Singing. *Unknown.* AWP; EaItPo, *tr. by* Dante Gabriel Rossetti

Little wild birds have come flying, The. Love-Song. *Unknown.* AWP, *tr. by* W. R. S. Ralston

Little Woman with Medusa Eyes, A. Dacia Maraini. CItWP, *tr. by* Cinzia Sartini Blum and Lara Trubowitz

Little Word, The. *Unknown.* PWR

(Good Creed, A.) PoToHe

Little Words. Benjamin Keech. PoToHe

Little work, a little play, A. *Unknown.* PoToHe

Little Wren, A. Priscilla Jane Thompson. CBWP-2

Liturgy for Lilith. Cosi Fabian. HW

Liu Ch'e. Ezra Pound. APT-1; OBVE; VGW

Liv lying on the floor looking at. Short Narrative of Breasts and Wombs in Service of Plot Entitled, A. Claudia Rankine. BAP-01

Live at Club Mozambique. Charles Simic. BodElec

Live / Bird Which. Larry Eigner. FTOS

Live Blindly and upon the Hour. Trumbull Stickney. APN-2; TCAPo; WoPoe

Live, Evil Veil. John Wheelwright. ChIV-1

Live fish—someone's New Year's gift to me. On New Year's Day of the Year Kuei-ssu (1533), Releasing Live Creatures. Wang T'ing-hsiang. CoBLCP, tr. by Jonathan Chaves

Live for tonight, and then the lights come. (LL) Gods at Three A.M., The. Reginald Shepherd. NeAmPo; WiU

Live fowl squatting on the grapefruit and bananas, The. Jamaican Bus Ride. Arthur Seymour John Tessimond. OxBTC

Live in these conquering leaves; live all the same. Richard Crashaw. OxAEP-1 *Fr.* Flaming Heart, The.

Live, lads, and I will die. (LL) Carpenter's Son, The. A. E. Housman. ChIV-2; MoBrPo; OxAEP-2; UV

Live large, man, and dream small. (LL) Lore. Ronald Stuart Thomas. NoP-4; OxBC; RB

"Live like the wind," he said, "unfettered." Wind Bloweth Where It Listeth, The. Countee Cullen. GT

Live, live with me, and thou shalt see. To Phyllis to Love and Live with Him. Robert Herrick. CaPo

Live Oak, with Moss. Walt Whitman. NAAL-5

Live so that you. Certain Maxims of Archy. Don Marquis. OBAL

Live storm went through last night, The. Glad at the Cold (1955). Alan Dugan. NoAM

Live While You Live. Philip Doddridge. SacPr

Lived to see you throwing. Hesitate to Call. Louise Glück. LW

Lived unwedded. (LL) Edgar Lee Masters. APT-1; IllVoic *Fr.* Spoon River Anthology.

Livelier than elsewhere, Stella's image see. (LL) Sir Philip Sidney. GSo; NAEL-5v1; NAEL-6v1; NAEL-7v1; NoSic; OxAEP-1; OxBSo; PoE; PoRA; SCGP; SCV; Son; TFi *Fr.* Astrophil and Stella.

Lively lark stretched forth her wing, The. Edward de Vere, 17th Earl of Oxford. NoSic

Lives. Derek Mahon. EmeKit; ModIr; PBCIP

Lives and Times of John Keats, Percy Bysshe Shelley, and George Gordon Noel, Lord Byron, The. Dorothy Parker. APT-1; NALW *Fr.* Pig's-Eye View of Literature, A.

Lives and times of Oedipus and Elektra, The. This One's on Me. Phyllis Gotlieb. MoCV; NOBC

Lives in eternity's sun rise. (LL) William Blake. AWP; AmFaPo; EBEV; EnlH; FaBoEE; NOBE; NoP-4; OxBSP; RB; SCGP; SoSe-8; Spl *Fr.* Several Questions Answered.

Lives in winter. Riddle. *Unknown.* NTCP

Lives of Alchemists, The. Charles Simic. KGB

Lives of many men are, The. To Wei Pa, a Retired Scholar. Tu Fu. OHPC, tr. by Kenneth Rexroth

Lives of my mother fit in one name, The. Lifes. Achy Obejas. WiU

Lives of the Great Composers. Dana Gioia. RA

Lives of the Heart, The. Jane Hirshfield. ExTi

Lives of the Saints. Debora Greger.
  "Notre Dame, Sainte Chapelle, Sacré Coeur by foot." NoP-4

Lives there on Earth to whom I am unknown. Gilbert West. ECEV *Fr.* Triumphs of the Gout, The.

Livid lightnings flashed in the clouds, The. Stephen Crane. InvLi *Fr.* Black Riders [and Other Lines], The.

Livid sky on London, A. Old Song, The. Gilbert Keith Chesterton. FaBoTw

Living. Denise Levertov. BLT; OPOU; VGW; WPE

Living. Jaime Torres Bodet. TCLAP, tr. by Sonja Karsen

Living, The. Robert Pinsky. NoAM

Living alone in a sad-looking house. Jerry's Plains, 1848. Geoff Page. BMAP

Living Alone with Jesus. Maxine W. Kumin. UnSA

Living along the path. North Corridor. Michael Collier. GM

Living and dying. (LL) Grammarian's Funeral, A. Robert Browning. NAEL-5v2; NAEL-6v2; NOBVV; PeECV

Living and Dying. Manuel González Prada. SpanPo, tr. by Kate Flores

Living and Dying Prayer for the Holiest Believer in the World, A. Augustus Montague Toplady. *See* Rock of Ages

Living between heaven and earth. Tune: "A Sprig of Flowers"—Written for My "Ugly Studio." Chung Ssu-ch'eng. SuSp, tr. by Sherwin S. S. Fu

Living by the Red River. James Wright (1927–80). NNaP

Living by your words. Rituals, Yours—and Mine. Kimberly M. Blaeser. ReEnLa

Living for you is easy living. Easy Living. Ralph Rainger. ReLy

Living God, The. Abraham Ibn Ezra. TrJP, tr. by Alice Lucas

Living God, The. Daniel ben Judah. TrJP, tr. by Israel Zangwill

Living God O magnify and bless, The. Living God, The. Daniel ben Judah. TrJP, tr. by Israel Zangwill

Living Heaven thy prayers respect, The. Spiritual Laws. Ralph Waldo Emerson. APN-1

Living in a Riverside Village—Miscellaneous Impressions. Yang Chi. CoBLCP, tr. by Jonathan Chaves

Living in a wide landscape are the flowers. Desert Flowers. Keith Douglas. FaBoTw; HarvBoo; NPeEn

Living in at Least Two Worlds. C. L. Rawlins. OPRER

Living in Cheston. Cynthia Rylant. HHAm *Fr.* Soda Jerk.

Living in Exile at Ch'ien-nan. Huang T'ing-chien. SuSp, tr. by Michael E. Workman

Living in Master Fang's Garden. Yang Chi. CoBLCP, tr. by Jonathan Chaves

Living in Real Times. Duncan Bush. TCAWP

Living in Retirement at Te-ch'ing. Chao Meng-fu. CoBLCP, tr. by Jonathan Chaves

Living in retirement beyond the World. Valley Wind, The. Lu Yün. ChiP, tr. by Arthur Waley

Living in Sin. Adrienne Rich. NIL-7; NIP-4; NoP-4; SoSe-8; TAP; UnPo

Living in the Country at Kou-ch'ü in Autumn—Miscellaneous Impressions. Yang Chi. CoBLCP, tr. by Jonathan Chaves

Living in the earth-deposits of our history. Power. Adrienne Rich. ColAP; NALW; NIL-7; TAP

Living in the La Brea Tar Pits. Nancy Vieira Couto. PBCAP

Living in the Mountains. Tai Shu-lun. SuSp, tr. by William H. Nienhauser

Living in the Summer Mountains. Yü Hsüan-chi. WoPoe, tr. by Chung Ling and Kenneth Rexroth

Living in the Woods. Wang Chiu-ssu.
  "I love the serenity of living in the woods." CoBLCP

Living in this room, / in this house, in these people, in this moment. (LL) Dying with the Wrong Name. Sam Hamod. GraLe; UnSA

Living is no laughing matter. On Living. Nazim Hikmet. PoetW, tr. by Randy Blasing and Mutlu Konuk

Living Juliet, The. William Shakespeare. PAI *Fr.* Romeo and Juliet.

Living long is containing. Rosina Alcona to Julius Brenzaida. Judith Wright. NALW

Living man is blind and drinks his drop, A. W. B. Yeats. RaBo *Fr.* Dialogue of Self and Soul, A.

Living Memory. Adrienne Rich. TRP

Living mother-of-pearl of a salmon, The. Hazel Stick for Catherine Ann, A. Seamus Heaney. NoAM

Living Near the Plaza of Thieves. Leslie Ullman. PBCAP

Living or having lived. Flush / a Play. Leslie Scalapino. PmAP

Living paradise of flowers, land of honey. Merioneth. John Machreth Rees. OBWVE, tr. by Kenneth Hurlstone Jackson

Living quality of, The. William Carlos Williams. NoAM *Fr.* Pictures from Brueghel.

Living Quetzalcoatl, The. D. H. Lawrence. OWoS

Living's getting harder day by day. My Village Home. Lu Yu. CoBCP, tr. by Burton Watson

Living secluded. Cloud Mountain. Muso Soseki. EaWin, tr. by W. S. Merwin

Living someplace else is wrong. Spring Offensive of the Snail, The. Marge Piercy. TAP

Living Space. Imtiaz Dharker. NeBl

Living Temple, The. Oliver Wendell Holmes. APN-1 *Fr.* Autocrat of the Breakfast Table, The.

Living Tenderly. May Swenson. OBCA

Living Together. Jean Valentine. LCAP-2

Livings. Philip Larkin.
  Seventy Feet Down. NPeEn; RB

Liza! call dat chile. Meal Time. Maggie Pogue Johnson. CBWP-4

Liza, go steep your long white hands. Spring Pastoral. Elinor Wylie. TCAPo

Lizard. D. H. Lawrence. RB

Lizard, The. Alphonse Marie Louis de Lamartine. SxFrPo, tr. by E. H. Blackmore and A. M. Blackmore

Lizard, The. Hilda Morley. PmAP

Lizard, The. Rona Murray. NOBC

Lizard, The. Lydia Pender. NOxBChV

Lizard, The. Theodore Roethke. NOxBChV

Lizard inching, A. Elizabeth Searle Lamb. HA

Lizard on the wall, engrossed, The. Possibility, The. James Fenton. HarvBoo

Lizard ran out on a rock and looked up, listening, A. Lizard. D. H. Lawrence. RB

Lizard's heart throbs, The. Lizard, The. Hilda Morley. PmAP

Lizards and Snakes. Anthony Hecht. FaBoMo; TwCP

Lizards in Sardinia. Eamon Grennan. BiHa

Lizie Lindsay. *Unknown.* ESPB
  (Donald of the Isles.) OxBB

Lizzie. Cheryl Burke. WiU

Lizzie. Nancy Vieira Couto. PBCAP

Llama, The. Joseph Hilaire Pierre Belloc. FaBoCh

Llanafan Unrevisited. T. Harri Jones. AngWePo

Llangollen Vale. Anna Seward.
To Time Past. RWP

Llanrhaeadr Ym Mochnant. Ronald Stuart Thomas. AngWePo

Lloyd George and Woodrow Wilson and Clemenceau. Legend of Versailles, A. Melvin B. Tolson. BPo; NAAAL

Llyn y Gadair. T. H. Parry-Williams. OBWVE, tr. by Anthony Conran

Lo! above the mournful chanting. Kol Nidra. Joseph Leiser. TrJP

Lo! an old song, yellow with centuries! Love, Weeping, Laid This Song. Lizette Woodworth Reese. APN-2

Lo! as a careful housewife runs to catch. William Shakespeare. SCGP Fr. Sonnets.

Lo, as a dove when up she springs. Tennyson. NAEL-6v2 Fr. In Memoriam A. H. H.

Lo as I pause in the alien vale of the airport. Twenty-third Flight. Earle Birney. HeIP-4; OxBC

Lo! As the Potter Mouldeth. Unknown. TrJP, tr. by Elsie Davis

Lo, between the Myrtles Standing. Ann Griffiths. OBWVE, tr. by H. Idris Bell

Lo, Collin, here the place whose pleasaunt syte. Edmund Spenser. AEP Fr. Shepheardes [or Shepeards or Shepherd's] Calender, The.

Lo! Death has reared himself a throne. City in the Sea, The. Edgar Allan Poe. APN-1; NAAL-2v1; NAAL-3; NCAP; NOBA; NoP-4; OxBA; PoE; SCV; TAP; TCAPo; TFi; TRP

Lo, Della Crusca! In his closet pent. William Gifford. NOBRP Fr. Baviad, The.

Lo! down yon steep of vales proud Deva borne. Speech of the Nymph. Anna Seward. NOBRP

Lo! dreary Winter, howling o'er the waste. To———. Ann Yearsley. CenSon

Lo, for I to myself am unknown, now in God's name what must I do? Jelaluddin [or Jalal al-Din] Rumi. TOF

Lo! Freedom comes. Th' prescient Muse foretold. Phillis Wheatley. BlSi Fr. Liberty and Peace.

Lo, haply walking in some clattering street. Haunted Streets. Mathilde Blind. ViWPN

Lo here hath been dawning. Morning. Thomas Carlyle. PWR

Lo here I am lord, whither wilt thou send me? To Christ. William Alabaster. NoSic; OxBSo

Lo here I sit at Holyhead. Holyhead. September 25, 1727. Jonathan Swift. BIrV; NOIV

Lo, here the state of every mortal wight. Respice Finem. Thomas Proctor. NoSic

Lo here, within the waters liquid womb. Thomas Traherne. ChIV-1 Fr. Meditations on the Six Days of the Creation.

Lo, How a Rose E'er Blooming. Unknown. ChrPo

Lo, how a rose is growing. Unknown. GePo

Lo how the sailor in a stormy night. Sonnet: on Loss. Sir Robert Aytoun [or Ayton]. NOSC

Lo! Hymen passes through th' admiring crowds. Epithalamium. Unknown. ECWP

Lo! I am come to autumn. Gold Leaves. Gilbert Keith Chesterton. OxBTC

Lo! I am she who makes the wheel to turn. Guido Cavalcanti. EaItPo, tr. by Dante Gabriel Rossetti

Lo, I Am Stricken Dumb. Unknown. TrJP, tr. by Theodor H. Gaster Fr. Dead Sea Scrolls, The.

Lo! I have learned of the loveliest of lands. Unknown. AnOE Fr. Phoenix, The.

Lo I the man, whose Muse whilome [or whylome] did maske. Edmund Spenser. FHYEP; NAEL-5v1; NAEL-6v1; NAEL-7v1 Fr. Faerie Queene, The.

Lo! I will tell the dearest of dreams. Dream of the Rood, A. Cynewulf. AnOE, tr. by Charles W. Kennedy

Lo-Imi, Lo-Imi! T. Carmi. MHP, tr. by Ruth Finer Mintz Fr. René's Songs.

Lo! in the painted oriel of the West. Evening Star, The. Henry Wadsworth Longfellow. APN-1

Lo it is dawn, so rise and let us part. Veiled Land. Kahlil Gibran. MAP, tr. by Michael Beard and Adnan Haydar

Lo, Lord, Thou ridest! Hurricane, The. Hart Crane. MoAmPo; OxBA; TrCP

Lo, my good son, lo, my dear son, hey. I Chant of the "Miracle Stag" (Shamanistic Version). Hungarian Oral Tradition. IQMS, tr. by Adam Makkai

Lo, my loved is dying, and the call. "Michael Field." VWP; ViWPN

Lo now he shineth yonder. Epitaph on Prince Henry. Hugh Holland. FaBoEE

Lo! now with red rent cloak and bonnet black. George Crabbe. EBEV Fr. Parish Register, The.

'Lo, on her dying couch, the sufferer lies. Jane Alice Sargant. CenSon

Lo! sun and moon, these minister for aye. Israel's Duration. Judah Halevi. TrJP, tr. by Nina Davis Salaman

Lo! the glorious dawn is breaking. Easter Morn. Josephine D. Henderson Heard. CBWP-4

Lo, the unbounded sea. Ship Starting, The. Walt Whitman. TCAPo

Lo, thou, my Love, art fair. Christ to His Spouse [or The Beloved to the Spouse]. William Baldwin. NOCV

Lo, thus, as prostrate, "In the dust I write." James Thomson. OxBS Fr. City of Dreadful Night, The.

Lo thus in breife (most sacred Majestye). To Queen Elizabeth. Jane Seager. EMWP

Lo! 'tis a gala night. Conqueror Worm, The. Edgar Allan Poe. APN-1; AWP; NCAP; NOBA; TCAPo

Lo, What Enraptured Songs of Praise. Sebastian Streeter. AH

Lo! what [or quhat] it is to love [or lufe]. Rondel of Luve [or Love], A. Alexander Scott. BoLoP; OBEV; OxBEV; OxBS

Lo, where envy and where lies. Written on the Walls of His Dungeon. Luís De León. TrJP, tr. by Thomas Walsh

Lo, where he shineth yonder. Hugh Holland. See Lo now he shineth yonder

Lo, where left 'mid the sheaves, cut down by the iron-fanged reaper. On a Forsaken Lark's Nest. Mathilde Blind. VWP; ViWPN

Lo! where the four mimosas blend their shade. For an Epitaph at Fiesole. Walter Savage Landor. FaBoEE

Lo! where the rosy-bosomed [or bosom'd] Hours. Ode on the Spring. Thomas Gray. GTBS-P; NOEC

Lo, where with flowery head and hair all brightsome. Unknown. NoSic

Lo, Who Could Stand. Unknown. TrJP, tr. by Israel Zangwill

Lo worms enjoy the seat of bliss. Epitaph. Robert Burns. FaBoEE

Lo-yang. Emperor Chien Wen-Ti. AWP; ChiP, tr. by Arthur Waley

Lo! ye children of men and the mother. Unknown. APN-2 Fr. Generation of the Seeds, or the Origin of Corn, The.

Lo Yu Park. Tu Fu. CarOv, tr. by Carolyn Kizer

Loaded like spoons. Slaveship. Lucille Clifton. ESEAA

Loaded with mail of linked lies. Basil Bunting. FaBoWar Fr. Briggflatts [An Autobiography].

Loads of trash and we light the match. Landfill. Michael S. Harper. LCAP-2

Loadstone beckons to the long needle, The. Joy of Union, The. Yang Fang. CoBCP, tr. by Burton Watson

Lob's Courtship. Elizabeth Hands. ECWP

Loba. Diane Di Prima.
"If he did not come apart in her hands, he fell." PFTM-1
("O lost moon sisters / crescent in hair.") BB

Loba Addresses the Goddess, The / or The Poet as Priestess Addresses the Loba-Goddess. Diane Di Prima. HW; PmAP

Loba as Eve. Diane Di Prima. HW

Loba's acid breast. San Fransisco. Miguel Algarin. PmAP

Lobbed ball plops, then dribbles to the cup, The. Ford Madox Ford. Robert Lowell. OxBC; TwCP

Lobe of opalescent glass. Heredom. Kenneth Irby. FTOS

Lobengula: Having a son at 38. Nikky Finney. SpirFl

Lobo. Charles Lillard. NOBC

Lobster. Anne Sexton. ChAP

Lobster, The. Lorine Niedecker. APT-2

Lobster Quadrille, A. Lewis Carroll. NoAM; OxAEP-2; UV Fr. Alice's Adventures in Wonderland.

Lobsterpot labyrinths wait. A porridge. Lobsterpot Labyrinths. Daniel Gerard Hoffman. YaYoPo

Lobsters in the Brain Coral. Laurence Lieberman. IllVoic

Lobsters in the Window. W. D. Snodgrass. TAP; TRP

Local groceries are all out of broccoli, The. Against Broccoli. Roy Blount, Jr. NBLV; OBAL

Local I'll bright my tale on, how. Children of Greenock, The. William Sydney Graham. FaBoTw

Local Note. Arthur Guiterman. NBLV

Local peddler of geographies, The. Executive Geochrone. Daniel Anderson. AmPoNex

Local Poet, A. John Hewitt. ModIr; PNI

Local row, A. Gods make their own importance. (LL) Epic: "I have lived in important places, times." Patrick Kavanagh. BIrV; CABP; CIP-2; HarvBoo; MakPoe; ModIr; NOIV; NPeEn; NoP-4; OxBSo

Locale. Penelope Shuttle. BrRo

Locate I / love you somewhere in. Language, The. Robert Creeley. PmAP; TAP

Loch Ness Monster's Song, The. Edwin Morgan. NePenScot; OPOU

Loch Thom. William Sydney Graham. NePenScot

Lochiel's Warning. Thomas Campbell.
"Lochiel, Lochiel! beware of the day." NePenScot
Wizard. NePenScot

Lochinvar. Sir Walter Scott. EBNV; NAEL-6v2; NOBE; NePenScot; OxAEP-2; OxBS; PoRA; TFi *Fr.* Marmion.

Lochmaben Harper, The. *Unknown.* ESPB; OxBB

Lochside silverschistsand disturbed-to-black-below distributed. Colin Simms. Oth *Fr.* Shots at Otters.

Lóci Becomes a Giant. Lőrinc Szabó. IQMS, *tr. by* Egon F. Kunz

Lock and Key. *Unknown.* ReMoGo

Lock me up. I am a. No Immunity. Dolores de Iruretagoyena de Humphrey. ReBoTo

Lock the dairy door. *Unknown.* OxNR

Lock the door, Lariston, lion of Liddesdale. Lock the Door, Lariston. James Hogg. IBB; OxBS

Lock the Place in Your Heart. Zindzi Mandela. HAWP

Locke sank into a swoon. Fragments. W. B. Yeats. NoAM

Locked arm in arm they cross the way. Tableau. Countee Cullen. NAAAL

Locked House, A. W. D. Snodgrass. VCAP

Locked in bathrooms for hours. Hully Gully. Rita Dove. SwNoth

Locked into rooms, alone. (LL) Triolet against Sisters. Phyllis McGinley. KaS; OBCA; OxIBACP

Locked up in mother's chamber. (LL) Yankee Doodle. Richard Shuckburg. OBAL; OxNR

Locked up until next season's harvest. Death of the Farm Workers' Cat. Rigoberto González. AmPoNex

Locker Room Etiquette. Craig Arnold. MoASP

Locket, The. John Montague. BiHa; PBCIP

Locking the Church. David Scott. NLP

Lockless Door, The. Robert Frost. NOBA; TCAPo

Locks. Kenneth Koch. CoAP

Locksley Hall. Tennyson. EBEV; NAEL-5v2; NAEL-6v2

Loco. Jane Holland. MFPA

Locomotive, The. Christopher Pearse Cranch. APN-1; GM *Fr.* Seven Wonders of the World.

Locomotives' Graveyard, The. Yaroslav [*or* Iaroslav] Vasilevich Smelyakov [*or* Smeliakov]. TCRP, *tr. by* Simon Franklin

Locus, The. Cid Corman. VGW

Locust. Father Lullabies the Unborn. Sharif Elmusa. GraLe

Locust, The. *Unknown.* RB, *tr. by* A. Marre and Willard R. Trask (Coyote and the Locust, The.) AWP

Locust, locust, playing a flute. Coyote and the Locust, The. *Unknown.* AWP

Locust Shell. Jody Gladding. YaYoPo

Locust Swarm, The. Hsu Chao. OHPC, *tr. by* Kenneth Rexroth

Locust thought, The. Locust Shell. Jody Gladding. YaYoPo

Locust Tree in Flower, The. William Carlos Williams. Spl; TTTS (Among.) PFTM-1

Locust Wood Mallet for Papermaking, A. Lin Pu. ColAnChi, *tr. by* Paul Hansen

Locusts a-wing, multiply. Ezra Pound. APSN

Locusts laid their eggs in the corpse. Locust Swarm, The. Hsu Chao. OHPC, *tr. by* Kenneth Rexroth

Locusts, or Appolyonists, The. Phineas Fletcher. "Say Muses, say; who now in those rich fields." ChIV-1

Sin, Despair, and Lucifer. NOSC

Lodestoned salmon, hurtling, The. Weir Bridge. Padraic Fallon. CIP-2

Lodgepole Pine: the wonderful reproductive. Gary Snyder. NOBA *Fr.* Myths and Texts.

Lodging-House Fuchsias, The. Thomas Hardy. OxBSP (Mrs. Master's fuchsias hung.) OBGa

Lodging House in Town, A. Muso Soseki. EaWin, *tr. by* W. S. Merwin

Lodging with the Old Man of the Stream. Po Chü-i. AWP; BLT; ChiP, *tr. by* Arthur Waley

Loe! formest of a rout that followd him. Virgil [*or* Vergil]. OBVE, *tr. by* Henry Howard, Earl of Surrey *Fr.* Aeneid [*or* Eneados, *Aeneis*], The.

Loew's Bridge: A Broadway Idyl. Mary E. Tucker. "Men swell the current,—many of them wear." SWaP

Loft. Michael Dransfield. CBAP

Lofty railings, taxus hedges. Prologue to the Book "Anatol." Hugo von Hofmannsthal. AuPH, *tr. by* Lowell A. Bangerter

Lofty trees of the south, The. *Unknown.* ColAnChi, *tr. by* Jeffrey Riegel *Fr.* Classic of Odes.

Lofty trees, ten thousand or more trunks. Enjoying Coolness. Wang Wei. SuSp, *tr. by* Hugh M. Stimson

Lofty worth and lovely excellence, The. Mazzeo di Ricco da Messina. EaItPo, *tr. by* Dante Gabriel Rossetti

Log. David Bromige. FTOS

Log, The. Camp Fire. Alfonsina Storni. TANSG, *tr. by* Mark McCaffrey

Log Jam, The. William Henry Drummond. NOBC

Log of Pi, The. Marc J. Straus. BloBone

Logan Braes. John Mayne. OxBS

Logbook of a Lost Caravan. Gyula Illyés. PFTM-1

Logging. Gary Snyder. *Fr.* Myths and Texts.

Logging Trestle. Mary Barnard. APT-2

Logic does well at school. Scholars. Walter De la Mare. NoAM

Logic in the House of Sawed-Off Telescopes. Jeffrey McDaniel. AmPoNex; NeAmPo

Logic is logic. That's all I say. (LL) Oliver Wendell Holmes. APN-1; BRP; ITBLP; NAAL-3; NOBA; OBAL; OBCA; OxBA; PoRA; TAP; TCAPo; TFi *Fr.* Autocrat of the Breakfast Table, The.

Logical Positivist, The. David Bromige. FTOS

Logical principle is said to be an empty, A. Michael Palmer. HarvBoo *Fr.* Series.

Logs, at the door, by the fence; broadcast over the paddock. Blanche Edith Baughan. PeNZ *Fr.* Bush Section, A.

Lois at the Hair Salon. Lesley Dauer. AmPoNex

Loitered, you might say. On the Conditions of Place. Michael Anania. IllVoic

Loitering with a vacant eye. A. E. Housman. SoSe-8

Loíza Aldea. Víctor Hernández Cruz. PueRic

Lok and bowe downe thyne eare o Lorde. Songe Made by Her Majestie and Songe before Her at Her Cominge from White Hall to Powles through Fleete Streete in Anno Domini 1588, A. Queen of England Elizabeth I. EMWP

Loke that none of you departe. The Peniarth Poet. AngWePo *Fr.* Drinking Song, A.

Loki tongue does not lend itself, The. Word from the Loki, A. Maurice Riordan. ModIr

Lola's Lament. Arthur Miller. Unle

Lola the Elder. AKA. Bruce Andrews. PFTM-2

Lolita. Vladimir Vladimirovich Nabokov. "Wanted, wanted: Dolores Haze." APT-2

Lollies Noir. Dorothy Porter. BMAP

Lollingdon Downs. John Masefield. Choice, The. MoBrPo Night on the Downland. MoBrPo Sonnet: "Here in the self is all that men can know." AWP

Lollipop Lady. John Agard. OTCP

Lollipops of the Pomeranian Baroque. James Fenton. PeLV

Lollocks. Robert Graves. RB

Lomonosov. Anna Semionovna Prismanova. ARWW, *tr. by* Catriona Kelly

London. William Blake. AWP; CABP; ClHu; FHYEP; HAP; HeIP-4; InPK-6; NAEL-5v2; NAEL-6v2; NAWM-7v2; NIL-7; NIP-4; NOBE; NOBRP; NOEC; NPeEn; NoP-4; OxAEP-2; OxBEV; PoE; PoPoPo; RB; SCGP; SCV; TFi; TRP; UnPo; WeW-3 *Fr.* Songs of Experience.

London. John Davidson. NOBE

London. Daniel Defoe. NOEC *Fr.* Reformation of Manners.

London. John Oldham. NOSC *Fr.* Satyr, A.

London. J. R. Rowland. CBAP

London: A Poem in Imitation of the Third Satire of Juvenal. Samuel Johnson. Poverty in London. NOEC; NPeEn; OBSV; OxAEP-1 "Tho' grief and fondness in my breast rebel." NPeEn

London after the Great Fire, 1666. Dryden. *See* Annus Mirabilis

London Airport. Christopher Logue. OPOU

London Bells ("Gay go up and gay go down.") *Unknown.* OxBoLi; PeLV ([And] here comes a chopper to chop off your head.) (LL) LB; OxNR (Say the bells at St. Paul's.) (LL) PoRA

London Bells ("Two sticks and an apple.") *Unknown.* OPOU

London Bridge is broken down. London Bridge. Mother Goose. FaBoVe; LB; NPeEn; OxBoLi; OxNR; ReMoGo

London Bridge was built. Stranger than the Worst. Babette Deutsch. WPE

London Despair. Frances Darwin Cornford. OBMV

London 1802. William Wordsworth. AWP; HAP; HeIP-4; NAEL-5v2; NAEL-6v2; NIL-7; NIP-4; NOBRP; OxAEP-2; PoRA; SCGP; Son; TFi; UV (England, 1802, II.) OBEV (Milton! thou shouldst be living at this hour.) NoP-4 (Same, The [London, MDCCII].) GTBS-P

London Fete, A. Coventry Patmore. EBVV; HAP; PeVV

London, Greater London (After *Satire III*). John Holloway. WoPoe

London in July. Amy Levy. PoBW

London is full of chickens, on electric spits. Peter Porter. OxBTC *Fr.* Annotations of Auschwitz.

London is painted round them: burly railings. Street Performers, 1851. Terence Tiller. GTBS-P

London: John Lane, the Bodley Head. On the Imprint of the First English Edition of "The Works of Max Beerbohm." Max Beerbohm. InPK-6; OBCoV

London Lickpenny. *Unknown.* OBSV

London, MDCCCII.   William Wordsworth.   *See* Written in London, September, 1802

London Nightfall.   John Gould Fletcher.   MoAmPo

London Pavement Artist.   James Schevill.   TAP

London Plane-Tree, A.   Amy Levy.   PEW; ViWPN

London Poets.   Amy Levy.   ViWPN
   (They trod the streets and squares where now I tread.)   PEW

London Pride has been handed down to us.   London Pride.   Noël Coward.   ReLy

London Rain.   Louis MacNeice.   NoP-4

London Rurality.   George Colman, the Younger.
   "Peace to each swain, who rural rapture owns."   OBGa

London's Resurrection.   Simon Ford.
   "Hail, glorious day; mayst thou be writ in gold."   NOSC

London's Summer Morning.   Mary Robinson.   ECWP; RWP; WoRP

London Snow.   Robert Bridges.   EBEV; EBVV; GTBS-P; MoBrPo; NOBE; NOBVV; NoAM; OxAEP-2; OxBTC; TFi

London Spring.   Antoni Slonimski.   TrJP, *tr. by* Frances Notley

London Subverted by the Furies.   Abraham Cowley.   NOSC

London, thou art of townes.   To the City of London [*or* In Honour of the City of London].   William Dunbar.   EBEV; OBEV

London, thou art the flour [*or* flower] of Cities all. (LL)   To the City of London [*or* In Honour of the City of London].   William Dunbar.   EBEV; OBEV

London Welsh v. Bridgend.   John Powell Ward.   TCAWP

London, within thy ample verge.   Henry Luttrell.   NOBRP   *Fr.* Letter to Julia, in Rhyme.

Londonderry Air, The.   Nicolas Bentley.   OBCoV

Lone and forgotten / Through a long sleeping.   Lonely, The.   "Æ"   AWP

Lone and level sands stretch far away, The. (LL)   Ozymandias.   Shelley.   AWP; BRP; CABP; CenSon; ChAP; ClHu; FaBoCh; GSo; GTBS-P; HAP; HeIP-4; InPK-6; MakPoe; NAEL-5v2; NAEL-6v2; NIL-7; NIP-4; NOBE; NPeEn; NoP-4; OPOU; OxBEV; OxBSo; PAI; PoE; PoPoPo; PoRA; RB; SCGP; SCV; SoSe-8; Son; TFi; UV

Lone Bather.   Abraham Moses Klein.   HeIP-4

Lone boat, a sliver of moon facing the maple woods, A.   Listening to a Wanderer's "Water Melody."   Wang Ch'ang-ling.   SuSp, *tr. by* Joseph J. Lee

Lone Buck.   *Unknown.*   WoPoe, *tr. by* Andrew Schelling   *Fr.* Gathasaptasati, The.

Lone Dog.   Irene McLeod.   NOxBChV

Lone drake, upended, The.   Mary Barnard.   APT-2

Lone figure is waving, A.   Postcard from North Antrim, A.   Seamus Heaney.   PBCIP; PNI

Lone, lone, and lone I stand.   Myall in Prison, The.   Mary Gilmore.   CBAP

Lone monk, A.   Tamashichi.   JDP, *tr. by* Yoel Hoffmann

Lone paulownia leaf, A.   Gohei.   JDP, *tr. by* Yoel Hoffmann

Lone Performer, The.   Velemir [*or* Viktor Vladimirovich] Khlebnikov.   TCRP, *tr. by* Gary Kern

Lone red-winged blackbird.   Nicholas Virgilio.   HA

Lone temple bell tolls at dusk, A.   Returning Late to Lu-men Shan.   Meng Hao Jan.   CrYelRi, *tr. by* Sam Hamill

Lone tern turns in the blowsy wind, A.   Because You Mentioned the Spiritual Life.   Stephen Dunn.   BodElec

Lone Theudotos placed this gift beneath the mountain.   Anyte [*or* Anytes].   SaLy, *tr. by* Diane Rayor

Lone Wild Fowl, The.   H. R. MacFayden.   AH

Lone Wild Goose.   Tu Fu.   CrYelRi, *tr. by* Sam Hamill

Lone Wild Goose, A.   Lu Kuei Meng.   SuSp, *tr. by* Robin D. S. Yates

Loneliness.   Ivan Alekseievich Bunin.   TCRP, *tr. by* Yakov Hornstein

Loneliness.   Antonio Cisneros.
   Hampton Court.   TCLAP, *tr. by* William Rowe
   Paris Cinquième.   TCLAP, *tr. by* Maureen Ahern and David Tipton

Loneliness.   Robert Frost.   VGW   *Fr.* Hill Wife, The.

Loneliness.   Dhabya Khamees.   PoArWo, *tr. by* Clarissa C. Burt

Loneliness.   Amjad Nasir.   BBASP; MAP, *tr. by* Charles Doria and May Jayyusi

Loneliness.   Tu Fu.   OHPC, *tr. by* Kenneth Rexroth

Loneliness.   Franz Werfel.   TrJP, *tr. by* Edith Abercrombie Snow

Loneliness, A.   Haki R. Madhubuti.   GT

Loneliness, The.   John Wieners.   PmAP

Loneliness and July Ninth.   Claribel Alegría.   BoWoP, *tr. by* Aliki and Willis Barnstone

Loneliness chases me.   Aleksandr Petrovich Mezhirov.   TCRP

Loneliness comes out of his mattress face.   Elegy for 6 So Far.   Gig Ryan.   BMAP

Loneliness leapt in the mirrors, but all week.   Departure's Girl-friend.   W. S. Merwin.   CoAmPo

Loneliness of Lincoln, The.   X. J. Kennedy.   HHAm

Loneliness One dare not sound, The.   Emily Dickinson.   TCAPo

Loneliness without rest!   Ballad of One Doomed to Die.   Federico García Lorca.   AWTN, *tr. by* Langston Hughes

Lonely.   Bloke Modisane.   PBA

Lonely.   André Spire.   AWP; TrJP, *tr. by* Jethro Bithell

Lonely, The.   "Æ"   AWP

Lonely Affair, A.   Reuben Jackson.   GT

Lonely and dreary was the day.   Heart's Ease.   Mary E. Tucker.   CBWP-1

Lonely and the feckless end, The. (LL)   Late Hour, The.   Mark Strand.   AWTN; HCAP

Lonely Beauty.   Samuel Daniel.   CTC   *Fr.* Complaint of Rosamond, The.

Lonely Coed, A.   Billy Strayhorn.   ReLy

Lonely courtyard, / once more slanting wind, misty rain.   Tune: "Charm of Nien-nu, The."   Li Ch'ing-chao.   SuSp, *tr. by* Eugene Eoyang

Lonely Death, The.   Adelaide Crapsey.   APT-1

Lonely, desolate, the new literary scene.   Hesitation.   "Lu Hsün."   SuSp; WoPoe, *tr. by* William R. Schultz

Lonely Dog, The.   Margaret E. Bruner.   PoToHe

Lonely Eagles.   Marilyn Nelson Waniek.   ESEAA

Lonely Farmer, The.   Ronald Stuart Thomas.   NoP-4

Lonely Heart, The.   John Hewitt.   *Fr.* Freehold.

Lonely Hearts.   Wendy Cope.   OBCoV

Lonely I am. There wove me the destiny spinning.   Sad Ode.   Alma Johanna Koenig.   AuPH, *tr. by* Lowell A. Bangerter

Lonely in the Regent Palace.   Flight from Bootle, The.   Sir John Betjeman.   PeLV

Lonely Isle, The.   Claudian.   AWP, *tr. by* Howard Mumford Jones

Lonely Lady, The.   Charlotte Brontë.   VWP

Lonely Land, The.   Arthur James Marshall Smith.   NOBC

Lonely Love.   Edmund Charles Blunden.   OxBTC

Lonely Man, The.   Randall Jarrell.   OxBC

Lonely man, The.   Gas.   Sidney Wade.   PoSol

Lonely man, his head among the stars, A.   Merlin.   Thomas Caldecot Chubb.   YaYoPo

Lonely man—leads a dog's life, A.   Life of a Dead Dog.   David Avidan.   FIT, *tr. by* Robert Friend

Lonely Masquerader.   Velemir [*or* Viktor Vladimirovich] Khlebnikov.   TCRusP, *tr. by* Kathy Lewis and Bob Perelman

Lonely moon loiters above the village, The.   Sailing at Dusk from T'u-sung.   Wu Wei-yeh.   SuSp, *tr. by* Chang Yin-nan

Lonely Mother, The.   Fenton Johnson.   NAAAL

Lonely Night.   P. C. Boutens.   TuT, *tr. by* Tony Curtis

Lonely Night in Early Autumn.   Po Chü-i.   TAL

Lonely old maid named Loretta, A.   Limerick.   *Unknown.*   PeLi

Lonely pond in age-old stillness sleeps, A.   Basho.   AWP

Lonely Road.   Peter Abrahams.   PBA

Lonely rock above a midnight plain, A.   Te Whetu Plains.   Edward Tregear.   PeNZ, *tr. by* Alan Myers

Lonely, save for a few faint stars, the sky.   Little Dancers, The.   Laurence Binyon.   MoBrPo; OxBTC

Lonely Settler, The.   Oliver Goldsmith, the Younger.   NOBC   *Fr.* Rising Village, The.

Lonely silence.   Basho.   SoOfWa, *tr. by* Sam Hamill

Lonely Street, The.   William Carlos Williams.   APT-1; TwCP

Lonely stretch, in the bind of poor fishing and drouth, A.   Daydreaming on the Trail.   Miyazawa Kenji.   PFTM-1

Lonely task it is to plow, A.   Plowing: A Memory.   Hamlin Garland.   ChAP

Lonely the Sea-Bird Lies at Her Rest.   W. B. Yeats.   RB

Lonely Tower, The.   Tom Paulin.   ModIr

Lonely Town.   Betty Comden.   ReLy

Lonely Traveller, The.   Kwesi Brew.   PBA; TTY

Lonely trembling soul can ache, The.   José Martí.   TCLAP, *tr. by* Elinore Randall   *Fr.* Simple Verses.

Lonely Tylenol.   Peter Gizzi.   ReTh

Lonely Tylenol.   Sharon Mesmer.   HeMarv

Lonely wanderer, wounded with iron, A.   Cynewulf.   AnOE, *tr. by* Charles W. Kennedy   *Fr.* Riddles (Exeter Book).

Lonely way, and as I went my eyes, A.   Two Infinities.   Edward Dowden.   GSo

Lonely Wife, The.   Li Po.   NIL-7, *tr. by* Amy Lowell

Lonely Woman.   Jayne Cortez.   NBV

Lonely Woman's Room, The.   Ahmad 'Abd al-Mu'ti Hijazi.   MAP, *tr. by* Sargon Boulus and Peter Porter

Lonely World.   Mrs. Henry Linden.   CBWP-4

Lonely young fellow of Eton, A.   Limerick.   *Unknown.*   PeLi

Lonesome Boy Blues.   Kenneth Patchen.   APT-2

Lonesome Dream, The.   Lisel Mueller.   CoAP

Lonesome Valley.   *Unknown.*   APN-2

Lonesome Water. Roy Helton. APT-1; MoAmPo

Long after Heine. Gwen Harwood. HarvBoo

Long after hours. (LL) Hamlet. Ciaran Carson. FaBoVe; ModIr; PNI

Long after it was heard no more. (LL) Solitary Reaper, The. William Wordsworth. AWP; CABP; ClHu; FHYEP; FaBoCh; HAP; HeIP-4; NAEL-5v2; NAEL-6v2; NOBE; NOBRP; NoP-4; OBEV; OxAEP-2; OxBEV; PAI; PoPoPo; PoRA; SCGP; SCV; SoSe-8; TFi; UnPo; WeW-3

Long after life has fled. (LL) Lines of Life. Letitia [or Laetitia] Elizabeth Landon. NOBRP; NPeEn

Long after rainfall, Sorceress Hills grow dark. Clear after Rain. Tu Fu. CrYelRi, tr. by Sam Hamill

Long after the time we were supposed to arrive. 20th Century, The. Lesley Dauer. NAPBL

Long after you have swung back. Losing Track. Denise Levertov. HeIP-4; NOBA; PoE; PoM

Long Afternoon, The. Louis Simpson. BodElec

Long afterward, Oedipus, old and blinded, walked the. Myth. Muriel Rukeyser. APT-2; FaBoWP; NAAL-5; NALW; NIL-7; NNaP

Long afterwards. Judgment of Paris, The. W. S. Merwin. NAAL-2v2; NNaP

Long ago a brown alighted story was told. Remember Something Like This. Lionel Fogarty. BMAP

Long Ago (And Far Away). George Gershwin. ReLy

Long ago and far away I met the right love. There's a Man in My Life. George Marion, Jr. ReLy

Long ago, at fourteen or fifteen. Juan Chi. CoBCP Fr. Singing of Thoughts.

Long ago at the end of Deborah's song. His Mother. Haim [or Chaim or Khayim] Guri [or Gouri]. MHP, tr. by Ruth Finer Mintz

Long ago her mother. What the Informant Said to Franz Boas in 1920. Unknown. STP, tr. by Armand Schwerner

Long ago, his skin itches as men enter his pores. Mudrooroo Narogin. BMAP Fr. Song Cycle of Jacky, The.

Long ago I learned how to sleep. Wind Song. Carl Sandburg. MoAmPo

Long Ago I Lived in the Country. Su Tung-p'o (Su Shih). CoBCP, tr. by Burton Watson

Long ago I made that journey, fall rain coming down lightly. I Had Occasion to Tell a Visitor about an Old Trip I Took. Lu Yu. WoPoe, tr. by Burton Watson

Long ago in a poultry yard. Lay of a Golden Goose, The. Louisa May Alcott. SWaP

Long ago, in Kentucky, I, a boy stood. Robert Penn Warren. FuPo; NAAL-5 Fr. Audubon: A Vision.

Long ago my heart and mind. My Ideal. Newell Chase. ReLy

Long-ago, still guiltless generations, The. New Stars, The. Martinus Nijhoff. WoPoe, tr. by Raphael Rudnik

Long ago sweet songs were sung. For a Birthday. Sophie Jewett. PoBW

Long ago the ancient flutes sang. Secret Melodies. Debra Taub. SurWo

Long ago there was a mighty snake, and beings evil to men. Unknown. APN-2 Fr. Walam Olum; or, Red Score [of the Lenâpé], The [or The Wallam Olum; The Red Score or Painted History of the Lenni Lenape].

Long ago there was an immortal man. Juan Chi. SuSp Fr. Poems Expressing My Feelings.

Long ago to a white-haired gentleman. Hat Given to the Poet by Li Chien, The. Po Chü-i. ChiP, tr. by Arthur Waley

Long ago, when we were children. Strawberry Picking. Alexander the Wild. NAWM-7v1, tr. by Peter Dronke

Long ago when you wanted to marry me. To the Singing Girl Named Luu. Nguyễn Khuyến. WoPoe, tr. by Nguyen Ngoc Bich

Long ago you were perhaps. To the Waters of the Chia-ling. Yüan Chên. SuSp, tr. by William H. Nienhauser

Long and Lazy [or Lazie]. Robert Herrick. FaBoEE

Long as I can call to mind. Childish Game, A. Reinmar von Hagenau. AWP, tr. by Jethro Bithell

Long as the Darkening Cloud Abode. George Richards. AH

Long autumn grass under my body, The. Field Manoeuvres. Richard Aldington. PeFWW

Long Barren. Christina Georgina Rossetti. TrCP; ViWPN

Long-Barrow Princess 2. Elizaveta Kuzmina-Karavayeva. ARWW, tr. by Catriona Kelly

Long before I hear it, Naples bright. Napoli Again. Richard Hugo. AF; LCAP-2

Long before morning glories perched upon opening day. Hometown. Salih Michael Fisher. CAGL

Long before the adult flora of. Grace of Animals, The. Richard Harteis. GLP

Long before the father died. Himself. Peter Fallon. PBCIP

Long before the Spaniards came. Cuando el tecolote canta, el Indio muere. Consuelo de Aerenlund. OPRER

Long before the wars. Queen Hera. Burleigh Mutén. HW

Long black night, The. Dusk in My Backyard. Keith Wilson. BLT

Long Blues, The. Calvin C. Hernton. GT

Long body of the water fills its hollow, The. Staring at the Sea on the Day of the Death of Another. May Swenson. APT-2

Long bound in ice and horrid hills of snow. After a Storm, Going a Hawking. George Daniel. NOSC

Long Branch Song, A. Robert Pinsky. NoP-4

Long closed door, oh open it again, The. Love Song. Judah Al-Harizi. TrJP, tr. by Emma Lazarus

Long Coats with Deep Pockets. Sean Thomas Dougherty. AmPoNex

Long conversations. Basho. SoOfWa, tr. by Sam Hamill

Long day of pining, A. To the Tune: Drunk in Flower Shadows. Li Ch'ing-chao. CrYelRi, tr. by Sam Hamill

Long desired, the dead return. Jay Macpherson. NOBC Fr. Way Down, The.

Long desired, the journey is begun. The suppliants. Landscapeople. John Ashbery. HCAP

Long did I toil and knew no earthly rest. At Home. John Quarles. SacPr

Long Distance. Maurice Kilwein Guevara. TouFir

Long Distance. Laila Halaby. PoArWo

Long Distance. Tony Harrison. NAEL-5v2; NAEL-6v2 Fr. School of Eloquence, The.

Long Distance. Dana Naone. CDW

Long Distance. Aleda Shirley. ExTi

Long Distance. Max Winter. NeAmPo

Long-Distance Call to Gregg, Who Lived with AIDS as Long as He Could. Alfred Corn. WiU

Long Distance Moan. Blind Lemon Jefferson. APT-2

Long Division; a Tribal History. Wendy Rose. OPRER

Long Enough. Long Enough. Muriel Rukeyser. NAAL-5

Long-expected one and twenty. Short Song of Congratulation [or To a Young Heir], A. Samuel Johnson. EBEV; HAP; InPK-6; NAEL-6v1; NOBE; NOEC; NPeEn; OBCoV; OBSV; OxAEP-1; OxBEV; PeLV; PoE; TFi; UnPo; WoPoe

Long farewell to all you universe-swivelling optics, A. Philip of Thessalonica. GrAn

Long-felt desires, hopes as long as vain. Long-Felt Desires. Louise Labé. WoPoe, tr. by Annie Finch

Long Feud. Louis Untermeyer. MoAmPo

Long Finish. Paul Muldoon. HarvBoo

Long for home and hate your homeland. Long for Home. Moyshe-Leyb [or Moishe-Leib or Leyb] Halpern. WoPoe, tr. by Meyer Schapiro

Long fragrant leash of steam, A. Toast to the Cook, A. Bernard Cooper. Unle

Long Garden, The. Patrick Kavanagh. HarvBoo; OBGa

Long Gone. Sterling Allen Brown. APT-2; BPo; NAAAL

Long gone the smoke-and-pepper childhood smell. Sarabande on Attaining the Age of Seventy-Seven. Anthony Hecht. BAP-01

Long goodbyes, the whistles in the dark, The. Eugenio Montale. WoPoe, tr. by Dana Gioia Fr. Motets, The.

Long green grasses of my island, The. Socope. Maria Manuela Margarido. HAWP, tr. by Julia Kirst

Long had I grieved at what I deemed abuse. Resignation. Paul Laurence Dunbar. SacPr

Long Hair. Gary Snyder. NOBA

Long hair, and curls woven not by Nature but by Art. Strato [or Straton]. CAGL, tr. by Daryl Hine

Long hair, endless curls trained by the devoted. Epigram. Strato [or Straton]. GrAn, tr. by Teddy Hogge

Long-haired preachers come out every [or ev'ry] night. Preacher and the Slave, The. Joe Hill. APT-1

Long Handscroll of Bamboo by Wang Meng-tuan, The. Li Tung-yang. CoBLCP, tr. by Jonathan Chaves

Long Harbour, The. Mary Ursula Bethell. PeNZ

Long hard journey, A. Buson. SoOfWa, tr. by Sam Hamill

Long hast thou, friend! been absent from thy soil. Mr. Pope's Welcome from Greece. John Gay. EBEV; OxAEP-1; OxBoLi

Long have I framed weak phantasies of Thee. Agnosto Theo [To an Unknown God]. Thomas Hardy. InvLi

Long have I looked for my lost child. Lost Child, The. James Reaney. NOBC

Long have I lov'd this bonny Lasse. Thomas Deloney. PBRV

Long have I yearned and sought for beauty. I Sit and Wait for Beauty. Mae V. Cowdery. BlSi

Long Hill, The. Sara Teasdale. MoAmPo; TCAPo

Long hoe, long hoe, handle of white wood. Tu Fu. CoBCP Fr. Seven Songs Written during the Ch'ien-yüan Era.

Long I followed [or follow'd] happy guides. Forerunners. Ralph Waldo Emerson. APN-1; OBEV; OxBA

Long I Thought That Knowledge Alone Would Suffice. Walt Whitman. NOBA

Long in thy shackles [or shackels], liberty. To Lucasta, from Prison. Richard Lovelace. BASC; BeJo; CaPo; CavPo

Long is the night. Curriculum Vitae. Ingeborg Bachmann. BoWoP; PFTM-2, tr. by Jerome Rothenberg

Long Island Sound. Emma Lazarus. APN-2; SWaP

Long Island sound, the pitiless clamor, The. Penitential Cries of Jupiter Hammond, The. Gary Smith. GT

Long Island Springs. Howard Moss. UnPo

Long John Brown & Little Mary Bell. William Blake. ECEV; RB

Long-Legged Fly. W. B. Yeats. FaBoMo; FaBoTw; NAEL-5v2; NAEL-6v2; NOBE; NPeEn; NoAM; NoP-4; PAI; PoE

Long legs, crooked thighs. Tongs. Mother Goose. LB; OxNR; ReMoGo

Long Lifetime, A. Kenneth Rexroth. BLT

Long line of bohunks and hunyaks: we settled in podunk, A. thirteen consonants. D. A. Powell. AmPoNex

Long line of web, A. J. W. Hackett. HA

Long Lines. Paul Goodman. VGW

Long lines, clean and syllabic as knotted bamboo. / Yes! (LL) Poetics against the Angel of Death. Phyllis Webb. MoCV; NOBC

Long Lines: Youth and Age. Paul Goodman. GLP

Long live the people! How they lived! and boiled. Part II. Elizabeth Barrett Browning. PEW

Long Live the Potato: Viva la Papa! Angela de Hoyos. SpudSo

Long Live the Weeds. Theodore Roethke. NOBA; NoAM

Long live the weeds and the wilderness yet. (LL) Inversnaid. Gerard Manley Hopkins. FaBoVe; GTBS-P; MoBrPo; NPeEn; NoAM; PeVV; PoRA; RB; SCGP; SacPr; TFi; UnPo

Long long ago when the world was a wild place. Bedtime Story. George MacBeth [or Macbeth]. EmeKit; SoSe-8

Long, long between your hands you held the warrior's black face. Léopold Sédar Senghor. NegPo Fr. Songs for Signare.

Long, long river, The. Boncho. OHPJ

Long love that in my thought doth harbo[u]r, The. Sir Thomas Wyatt. GSo; NAEL-5v1; NAEL-6v1; NAEL-7v1

(Long Love, The.) SCGP

(Longe love, that in my thought doeth harbar, The.) OxBEV

(Lover for Shamefastness Hideth His Desire within His Faithful Heart, The.) Son

(Sonnet: "The long love.") AEP

Long low sweeping ground, The. Aboriginal Reserve. Jack Davis. IBA

Long lustrous tiger, the flowered leopard, The. Felines. Daria Menicanti. CItWP, tr. by Cinzia Sartini Blum and Lara Trubowitz

Long-Man. Grace Nichols. Oth

Long may our hearts, Nealce, guard that night. Petronius Arbiter. RomPo, tr. by J. P. Sullivan

Long Melancholy Tune, A. Li Ch'ing-chao. ColAnChi, tr. by Jiaosheng Wang

Long Nature travailed, till at last she bore. Nature's Travail. Unknown. AWP, tr. by Goldwin Smith

Long neglect has worn away. Emily Jane Brontë. NOBVV; NoP-4; PoE

Long night, The. Martin Shea. HA

Long night drags on and on—, The. In the Ancient Manner. Chao Meng-fu. CoBLCP, tr. by Jonathan Chaves

Long night is deep, deep as water, The. Sleepless. Ch'in Kuan. CrYelRi, tr. by Sam Hamill

Long night of linden trees, your honey hands. Figurehead, The. Maria Luisa Spaziani. NeIt, tr. by Beverly Allen

Long night, the short sleep, and La Gorgue to wander, The. La Gorgue. Ivor Gurney. OxBEV

Long night: unable to sleep. Unknown. ChinPo, tr. by Yip Wai-lim

Long nights when he neglects me—where's he gone? Tune: Telling of Innermost Feelings. Ku Hsiung. CoBCP, tr. by Burton Watson

Long Nook. John Wieners. FTOS

Long over whatever edge. Edge, The. Robert Creeley. FTOS

Long past midnight I sit here. Forsaken. Zalman Schneour. TrJP, tr. by Joseph Leftwich

Long, perfect loveliness of sow, The. (LL) Saint Francis and the Sow. Galway Kinnell. AmFaPo; ChAP; InPK-6; NAAL-5; RB

Long Person. Gladys Cardiff. CDW

Long Picnic, The. Russell Edson. LCAP-2

Long Plighted. Thomas Hardy. NOBVV

Long rain falls on the empty forest. Smoke rises, The. After Long Rain. Wang Wei. TAL

Long rains, The. Basho. EH, tr. by Robert Hass

Long Reality, The. Haki R. Madhubuti. NAAAL

Long River, The. Donald Hall. CoAmPo; LCAP-2

Long road and a village, A. Holy Family. Muriel Rukeyser. ChIV-2; MoAmPo

Long rolling, The. Main-Deep, The. James Stephens. MoBrPo; OBMV; UnPo

Long sea, how short-lasting, The. There Is No Land Yet. Laura Riding Jackson. ChIV-1

Long Shadow of Lincoln: A Litany, The. Carl Sandburg. CBCWP

Long shadows. Gem Forest. Muso Soseki. EaWin, tr. by W. S. Merwin

Long Sigh: Written When Spending the Night at Green Mountain Store. Lu Yu. CoBCP, tr. by Burton Watson

Long since I'd ceased to care. Parrot, The. Wilfrid Wilson Gibson. OBMV

Long slick black feller. Riddle. Unknown. FaBoVe

Long sobs of, The. Autumn Song. Paul Verlaine. SxFrPo, tr. by Martin Sorrell

Long steel grass. Dame Edith Sitwell. NAEL-5v2; NAEL-6v2 Fr. Façade.

Long-Suffering of God. Christopher Smart. NOCV Fr. Hymns for the Amusement of Children.

Long summer day. Michael McClintock. HA

Long summer rains / Barley's tasteless. Mokusetsu. ZenPo, tr. by Takashi Ikemoto and Lucien Stryk

Long-tailed pig, A. Mother Goose. OxNR

Long Tale, A. Lewis Carroll. NoAM; OBCoV Fr. Alice's Adventures in Wonderland.

Long the flimsy skirts. Wang Chien. SuSp Fr. Palace Poems.

Long the loose wits of a degenerate age. Verses to Mr. Richardson on His History of Sir Charles Grandison. Anna Williams. ECWP

Long they pine in weary woe, the nobles of our land. Kathaleen Ny-Houlahan [or Kathleen-Ni-Houlahan]. William Heffernan. NOIV, tr. by James Clarence Mangan

Long thin window to the stars holds up the tenement, The. Hotel de L'Etoile. Matthew Rohrer. AmPoNex

Long Time a Child. Hartley Coleridge. CenSon; NPeEn; OxBSo; Son ("Long time a child, and still a child, when years.") GSo

Long Time Ago. Leslie Marmon Silko. NoAM

LONG time ago, A. Ch'ien T'ao. ChiP

Long time ago, A. T'ao Ch'ien [or T'ao Yuan-ming]. FaBoCh

Long time ago, A / A million years B.C. Pennies from Heaven. Johnny Burke. ReLy

Long time ago, I think, A. Hypothesis. Ted Olson. YaYoPo

Long time ago / in the beginning. Invention of White People, The. Leslie Marmon Silko. STP

Long Time Back, A. Unknown. EaWin; WoPoe, tr. by J. Moussaieff Masson and W. S. Merwin

Long time had Israel been disus'd from rest. Foreigners, The. John Tutchin. BASC

Long time hath Christ, long time I must confess. Of the Reed That the Jews Set in Our Saviour's Hand. William Alabaster. NPeEn; NoSic

Long time have human ignorance and guilt. William Wordsworth. NAEL-6v2 Fr. Prelude, The; Growth of a Poet's Mind [1850 vers.].

Long time he lay upon the sunny hill. Childhood. Edwin Muir. HeIP-4; NPeEn; NePenScot; NoP-4

Long time in one place and I always think of moving, A. Cold Night. Ch'en Shih-tao. CoBCP, tr. by Burton Watson

Long time in some forgotten churchyard earth of Warwickshire. Who Were before Me. John Drinkwater. OBMV

Long time Plain Dealing in the haughty town. Plain Dealing's Downfall. Unknown. OBSV

Long time's gone, A. On a Phrase from Southern Ohio. James Wright. LTA

Long time since the last scream cut short, A. Rathlin. Derek Mahon. ModIr

Long time yet, because you're strong as a mule, A. (LL) George. Dudley Randall. BPo; CoAmPo; NoAM

Long Tom. Wilfrid Wilson Gibson. OxBTC

Long Track Blues. Sterling Allen Brown. GM

Long Voyage, The. Malcolm Cowley. SoSe-8

Long war had ended, The. Next War, The. Sir Osbert Sitwell. PoWW

Long was Society o'er-run. Hannah More. PEW Fr. Bas Bleu; Or, Conversation, The.

Long was the night of error, nor dispelled. William Mason. OBGa Fr. English Garden, The.

Long Way after Ronsard, A. James Simmons. PBCIP

Long way from the whorehouse. Solo: The Good Blues. Dolores Kendrick. FFC

Long Way outside Yellowstone, A. Thomas McGrath. VGW

Long ways, A. Remembrance of a Color inside a Forest, A. Ray A. Young Bear. CDW

Long wedge of geese, A. Robert Spiess. HA

Long white banners flutter on the breeze, The. White Banners. Sung Sammun. WoPoe, tr. by Jean S. Grigsby

Long White Seam, The. Jean Ingelow. NOBVV; OxBEV

Long wind coming from beyond the horizon. Commandeering the Wind. Su Shun-ch'in. SuSp, tr. by Irving Y. Lo

Long Wind, the Dawn Wind. Ezra Pound. APT-1

Long wintry months are past; the Moon that now. Charlotte Smith. *Fr.* Emigrants, The.

Long Woman Bathing, The. Maurice Kilwein Guevara. TouFir

Long years ago I wandered here. On Recrossing the Rocky Mountains after Many Years. John Charles Frémont. AiP

Long years ago the envoy of Han departed. Tune: "Pacifying the Western Barbarians." Wen T'ing-yün. SuSp, *tr. by* William R. Schultz

Long years have passed since first a merry child. To One Who Sleepeth. Mary E. Tucker. CBWP-1

Long years of pleasant friendship may be broken. True to the Best. Benjamin Keech. PoToHe

Long[e] love that in my thought do[e]th [*or* I] harbour [*or* harber *or* harbar], The. Petrarch. NPeEn, *tr. by* Sir Thomas Wyatt *Fr.* Sonnets to Laura.

Longer we are together, The. Ripening. Wendell Berry. RaBo

Longest and much the dearest. Book Review. Russell Davies. FaBoEE

Longest night, The. David Lloyd. HA

Longest train I ever saw, The. In the Pines. Bill Monroe. GM

Longest winter night, The. Bankoku. JDP, *tr. by* Yoel Hoffmann

Longface Mahoney Discusses Heaven. Horace Gregory. VGW

Longfellow. Henrietta Cordelia Ray. CBWP-3

Longfellow's Visit to Venice. Sir John Betjeman. NOBL; OBCoV

Longing. Matthew Arnold. SoSe-8

Longing. Ina Coolbrith. SWaP

Longing. Paul Laurence Dunbar. ErotSp

Longing. Judah Halevi. TrJP, *tr. by* Nina Davis Salaman

Longing. George Herbert. ESCV; UV
(With sick and famish eyes.) FSCP

Longing. Thomas McGrath. BodElec

Longing. Femi Osofisan. NAfrP

Longing. Lilly Sauter. AuPH, *tr. by* Lowell A. Bangerter

Longing, a Documentary. Anne Carson. BAP-01

Longing achieves nothing. Gamelia. Susan M. Whitmore. AmPoNex

Longing for Death. "Novalis." WoPoe, *tr. by* Dick Higgins *Fr.* Hymns to the Night.

Longing for Eternal Life, The. Liz Rosenberg. PBCAP

Longing for His Son, Furuhi. Yamanoé [*or* Yamanoué] no Okura. WoPoe, *tr. by* Helen Craig McCullough

Longing for Jail, A. Edvard Kocbek. PoSu, *tr. by* Michael Scammell and Veno Taufer

Longing for Jerusalem. Judah Halevi. TrJP, *tr. by* Emma Lazarus

Longing for someone in Ch'ang-an. Longing for Someone. Li Po. CrYelRi; ErotSp, *tr. by* Sam Hamill

Longing, I watch out the open window. Song. Tzu Yeh. CrYelRi, *tr. by* Sam Hamill

Longing in My Heart. Wei Ying-wu. SuSp, *tr. by* Irving Y. Lo

Longingly homeward the crane out of regions afar is returning. Szondi. Ferenc Kölcsey. IQMS, *tr. by* Watson Kirkconnell

Longmobile. Shel [*or* Shelley] Silverstein. AiP

Longobards, The. Zbigniew Herbert. PoSu, *tr. by* Czeslaw Milosz

Longon lights are far abeam, The. Old Australian Ways. Andrew Barton Paterson. NOBAu

Longshore Intellectual. Sean Lucy. CIP-2

Lonnie up and moved away. Teed Off. John Nelson. GeoH

Loo! loo! Lulu! lulu! Loo! loo! loot! loot! Rudyard Kipling. UV *Fr.* Loot.

Loo-wit. Wendy Rose. HATNAP

Loofah blooms and, The. Masaoka Shiki. JDP, *tr. by* Yoel Hoffmann

Loofah water. Masaoka Shiki. JDP, *tr. by* Yoel Hoffmann

Look. Belle Waring. ExTi

Look, The. Elizabeth Barrett Browning. TrCP

Look, The. Sara Teasdale. APT-1; LW

Look, a mirage, like a round rim, a strange. Horizon. David Emrys James. WoPoe, *tr. by* Anthony Conran

Look after in the street. (LL) Martha Blake. Austin Clarke. ModIr; OxBEV

Look, among the boughs. Those stars are men. Star-Tribes, The. *Aborigine Oral Tradition.* NOBAu, *tr. by* Fred Biggs

Look and remember. Look upon this sky. Travelogue for Exiles. Karl Shapiro. MoAmPo; TrJP

Look as they rise, rise. Song of the Pleiades. *Unknown.* TCAPo

Look at all these waves. Mahendranāth Bhattācārya. SinGod, *tr. by* Rachel Fell McDermott

Look at him, over there. Disillusion. Maureen Burge. BrRo

Look at him there in his stovepipe hat. American Primitive. William Jay Smith. InPK-6; MoAmPo; OxBSP; PAI; RaBo; TwCP

Look at how upset you've got me. *Unknown.* PriapPo, *tr. by* Richard W. Hooper *Fr.* Priapus Poems, The.

Look at it, the season's shifting. On Opening. Mark Wunderlich. NAPBL

Look at Jonah embarking from Joppa, deterred by. Tom Fool at Jamaica. Marianne Craig Moore. APT-1

Look at Me. Kim Ly Bui-Burton. PasH

Look at me / I'm as helpless as a kitten up a tree. Misty. Erroll Garner. ReLy

Look at me now, mother. Amanda Dalton. NeBl *Fr.* Room of Leaves.

Look at my continent containing. Human Geography. Gloria Fuertes. BoWoP, *tr. by* Willis Barnstone

Look at my knees. I Wonder What It Feels Like to Be Drowned? Robert Graves. MoBrPo

Look at Peter: sad and glum. Young Pete. Mihály Vörösmarty. IQMS, *tr. by* Yakov Hornstein

Look at That Gal. Julian Bond. TTY

Look at that girl in blouse and patterned skirt. Deception. Kim Sujang. WoPoe, *tr. by* Kevin O'Rourke

Look at the horned goat of Dionysus. Anyte [*or* Anytes]. GrAn

Look at the ripe wheat. Grainfield. Ibn 'Iyad. WoPoe, *tr. by* Cola Franzen

Look at the sky: two doves are chasing. Impossible Tasks. *Vietnamese Oral Tradition.* CaDao, *tr. by* John Balaban

Look at the stars! look, look up at the skies! Starlight Night, The. Gerard Manley Hopkins. GTBS-P; MoBrPo; NAEL-5v2; NAEL-6v2; PoE

Look at the valleys down there in the darkness. Angry Summer 20, The. Idris Davies. TCAWP

Look at these most wretched remains of a man. Philip of Thessalonica. GrAn

Look at this Champagne factory. New Guide, A. Kenneth Koch. BodElec

Look at this, golden-horned moon. Argentarius. GrAn

Look at this keepsake. Kasa no Iratsume. ArkPo, *tr. by* Edwin A. Cranston

Look at yourself. Glad to Be Unhappy. Lorenz Hart. ReLy

Look Away child. Susan Cavin. GLP

Look away! Look away! Look away! Dixie Land. (LL) Dixie [*or* Dixie's Land]. Daniel Decatur Emmett. APN-1; CBCWP; TCAPo

Look Back into the Future. Andrey [*or* Andrei] Andreievich Voznesensky [*or* Voznesenskii]. PFTM-2, *tr. by* Anselm Hollo

Look back with longing eyes and know that I will follow. Flight, The. Sara Teasdale. LW

Look between the bow and the bowstring, beneath. Backgrounds to Italian Paintings: Fifteenth Century. Anne Ridler. WPE

Look'd up in perfect silence at the stars. (LL) When I Heard the Learn'd Astronomer. Walt Whitman. BRP; ChAP; ColAP; HAP; MoAmPo; NAAL-2v1; NAAL-3; NAAL-5; NoP-4; OxBA; PAI; PoPoPo; SoSe-8; TAP; WeW-3

Look, Delia, how we [e]steem the half-blown rose. Samuel Daniel. NoSic; SCGP *Fr.* To Delia.

Look down. Heavier now. Onus of observable spectrums. Fait Accompli. Anne Waldman. BodElec

Look First at the Air and Its Black Element Which Never Stops. Roberto Juarroz. TCLAP, *tr. by* W. S. Merwin

Look for color everywhere. (LL) Today's News. Elizabeth Alexander. ISC; InTrad

Look for the address. Survival 1. Chiqui Vicioso. TANSG, *tr. by* Emma Jane Robinett

Look for the Silver Lining. B. G. DeSylva. ReLy; TCAPo

Look for You Yesterday, Here You Come Today. LeRoi Jones. SSLK

Look for your other half. Antonio Machado Ruiz. RaBo *Fr.* Moral Proverbs and Folk Songs.

Look! From my window there's a view. There Is. Louis Simpson. CoAmPo

Look he trusts again It's good. Warning. Tadeusz Rózewicz. PoSu, *tr. by* Magnus F. Krynski

Look Here. Pamela Alexander. ExTi

Look here. Rāmprasād Sen. SinGod, *tr. by* Rachel Fell McDermott

Look: Here our bodies lie in a long, long line. But We Shall Bloom. Haim [*or* Chaim *or* Khayim] Guri [*or* Gouri]. TrJP, *tr. by* David Kuselewitz

Look here, Petah! whut's dis here. Examination, The. Priscilla Jane Thompson. CBWP-2

Look here, upon this picture, and on this. William Shakespeare. OxAEP-1 *Fr.* Hamlet.

Look how handsome I am. Hymn of the Patriotic War Veterans. Benjamin Péret. AF, *tr. by* Keith Hollaman

Look How Rich We Are Together. Micere Githae Mugo. HAWP

Look! how the clouds are flying south! Snow-Man, The. "Marian Douglas." OBCA

Look how the lark soars upward and is gone. False Poets and True. Thomas Hood. CenSon

Look how the table's becoming. Trompe l'oeil. Tracy Ryan. NeBl

Look how we're wedded. New Song of Solomon. Cyrus Cassells. WiU

Look how yon lecher's legs are worn away. Epigram. John Taylor. NOSC

Look, I don't speak the language. Message about the Times. Remco Campert. TuT, *tr. by* Theo Dorgan

Look, I don't speak the language. Sign of the Times. Remco Campert. TuT, *tr. by* Desmond Egan

Look / I was lifted up. Thomas Kinsella. ModIr *Fr.* One.

Look in my face; my name is Might-have-been. Dante Gabriel Rossetti. EBVV; GSo; GTBS-P; NAEL-5v2; NAEL-6v2; NoP-4 *Fr.* House of Life, The.

Look in the dark alcove under the stairs. Under the Stairs. Frank Ormsby. PBCIP

Look, in the Labyrinth of Memory. Delmore Schwartz. TrJP

Look in the Past, A. Jared Angira. PBMAP

Look in thy glass and tell the face thou viewest. William Shakespeare. NAEL-5v1; NAEL-6v1; NAEL-7v1; NoP-4; SCGP *Fr.* Sonnets.

Look into thought and say what thou dost see. Diving. Charlotte Brontë. PEW

Look! It is there! (LL) Not Marble nor the Gilded Monuments. Archibald MacLeish. BoLoP; PoRA; TwCP

"Look! It's a wedding!" At the ice cream shop's. What Do Women Want? Mary Jo Salter. FFC; RA

Look it's clear. Michael McClintock. HA

Look it up. There Is No Word for Sex in Taglog. Noel Mateo. ReBoTo

Look, life has been constructed this way to make sure. Paavo Haavikko. WoPoe, *tr. by* Anselm Hollo *Fr.* Fifteen Epigrams in Praise of the Tyrant.

Look, Loig, behind. Only Jealousy of Emer, The. *Unknown.* BIrV, *tr. by* John Montague

Look, look at yourself in the mirror. Glance. Belkis Cuza Malé. TANSG, *tr. by* Pamela Carmell

Look Look! / Look at the back. Song in the Symbol, The. Grandfather Koori. IBA

Look, look! rejoice and wonder! Return of Astraea, The. Ben Jonson. NOBE

Look lovelier still compared to the angry children. (LL) Cythera. David Ferry. DiPo; GS

Look. New sprouts push through the fields. Prayer on the Threshold of Tomorrow. Vahan Tekeyan. AF, *tr. by* Diana Der Hovanessian and Marzbed Margossian

Look, No Hands. Pearse Hutchinson. PBCIP

Look north if you like. Map Reading. Raymond Garlick. AngWePo

Look not in my eyes, for fear. A. E. Housman. CAGL

Look not on the infinite wave. Dame Edith Sitwell. BWW *Fr.* Sleeping Beauty, The.

Look not thou on beauty's charming. Sir Walter Scott. NAEL-6v2; NOBE; NPeEn; OBEV; OxAEP-2; OxBEV; OxBS; WoPoe *Fr.* Bride of Lammermoor, The.

Look, / O heartless ones. We Have Even Lost Our Tongues! Ifi Amadiume. HAWP

Look of day with last night's rid of moths, The. (LL) Nothing So Far. Laura Riding Jackson. APT-2; ColAP

Look of love alarms, The. William Blake. WoPoe *Fr.* Several Questions Answered.

Look of shock on an old friend's face after years of not meeting, The. Karl Shapiro. BodElec *Fr.* Bourgeois Poet, The.

Look of sympathy, the gentle word, The. These Are Not Lost. Richard Metcalf. PoToHe

Look off, of thee, what is it like, The. Emily Dickinson. InvLi

Look off, dear Love, across the sallow sand. Evening Song. Sidney Lanier. UnPo

Look on Him Whom They Pierced, and Mourn. Isaac Watts. NOCV

Look on that form, once fit for the sculptor! Working and Waiting. Adah Isaacs Menken. CBWP-1

Look—on the topmost branches of the world. Sunday Evening in the Common. John Hall Wheelock. MoAmPo

Look on these waters, with how soft a kiss. Aestuary, An. George Croly. NOBRP

Look on this statue, traveller; look well. Theocritus. GrAn

Look once more ere we leave this specular Mount. John Milton. NOSC; PeECV *Fr.* Paradise Regained [*or* Regain'd].

Look one way and the sun is going down. Mockingbird, The. Randall Jarrell. OWoS

Look, our Spaniard's yawning. Antonio Machado Ruiz. STV

Look out how you use proud words. Primer Lesson. Carl Sandburg. MoAmPo

Look out there. *Unknown.* NOIV

Look out upon the stars, my love. Serenade. Edward Coote [*or* Coate] Pinkney. APN-1

Look: rat has skin. Rat, The. *Unknown.* WoPoe, *tr. by* John S. Major

Look round, brown moon, brown bird, as you rise to fly. God Is Good. It Is a Beautiful Night. Wallace Stevens. APT-1; SAmP

Look round our world; behold the chain of love. Pope. FHYEP *Fr.* Essay on Man, An.

Look round: You see a little supper room. De Cœnatione Micae. Martial. FaBoCh; RomPo, *tr. by* Robert Louis Stevenson

Look! she said you can see. Kris Hemensley. BMAP *Fr.* Mile from Poetry, A.

Look Sheila Seeing You've Asked Me. Vincent O'Sullivan. PeNZ

Look sour, and hum a tune—as you may now. (LL) Epistle to Miss [*or* Miss Teresa] Blount, on Her Leaving the Town after the Coronation. Pope. BoLoP; EBEV; FHYEP; NAEL-5v1; NAEL-6v1; NAEL-7v1; NOBE; NOEC

Look straight ahead. What's there? Bassui Tokusho. JDP, *tr. by* Yoel Hoffmann

Look, stranger, on this island now. On This Island. W. H. Auden. HarvBoo; NAEL-5v2; NAEL-6v2; OxBEV; PoE

Look that is that uninvited. Vasco [*or* Vasko] Popa. PoSu *Fr.* Far within Us.

Look! The air shudders when you breathe it in. Paul Engle. OxBSo

Look the builders of ruins are working. November 1936. Paul Éluard. AF, *tr. by* Gilbert Bowen

Look. The land ends up. Some Grand River Blues. Daniel David Moses. HATNAP

Look: the lute sounds in the girl's arms. Lute, The. Judah Al-Harizi. BLT, *tr. by* T. Carmi

"Look," the ocean said (it was tumbled, like our sheets), "look in my eyes." (LL) Crystal Lithium, The. James Schuyler. PmAP; PoM; VCAP

Look: the sun has spread its wings. Sun, The. Judah Al-Harizi. BLT, *tr. by* T. Carmi

Look, the trees / are turning / their own bodies. In Blackwater Woods. Mary Oliver. NAAL-5

Look there at the star! Shepherd's Song at Christmas. Langston Hughes. ChrPo

Look / There / The smiling infant. Cold. Brian Coffey. CIP-2

Look there! What a wheaten. Hill Field, The. Donald Davie. NPeEn

Look, this string of words. So Be It. Ruth Stone. ExTi

Look thy last on all things shitty. Shitty. Kingsley Amis. OxBC

Look to the Mountain. Simon J. Ortiz. PoCoUp

Look to this day! Salutation to the Dawn. Kalidasa. PoToHe

Look up, and swear by the slain of the War that you'll never forget! (LL) Aftermath. Siegfried Sassoon. MoBrPo; PoWW; TrJP

Look—up and tangle. Life Model. Maggie Hannan. NeBl

Look up, dear one, nor be cast down. Truth. Josephine D. Henderson Heard. CBWP-4

Look up. . . From bleakening hills. Snow. Adelaide Crapsey. APT-1

Look upon me. Nag Hammadi Library. HW *Fr.* Thunder: Perfect Mind, The.

Look wha' happen las' week at de Oval! Edward Kamau Brathwaite. FaBoVe *Fr.* Rites.

Look what I did for you. (LL) Emptying Town. Nick Flynn. AmPoNex; NAPBL

Look what's come to light. Mikhail Aizenberg. ItGoST, *tr. by* J. Kates

Look where she sits in languid loveliness. On a Beautiful Woman. Mary Russell Mitford. CenSon

Look where the Great Bear glows: he beats his son to teach him silence. Winegrower, The. Milán Füst. IQMS, *tr. by* Jess Perlman

Look, ye saints! The sight is glorious. Second Advent, The. Thomas Kelly. SacPr

Look, You Have Cast Out Love! Rudyard Kipling. OxBSP *Fr.* Plain Tales from the Hills.

Looka here. (LL) Song No. 3: "Cain't nobody tell me any different." Sonia Sanchez. FFC; NOxBChV

Look[e] Home. Robert Southwell. ESCV; NOCV; NoSic

Looked after him thro' happy tears. (LL) Athenian Garden, An. Trumbull Stickney. APN-2; NoP-4

Looking. Robert Kelly. FTOS

Looking as I've looked before, straight down the heart. Stranger, The. Adrienne Rich. NNaP

Looking at a Dead Wren in My Hand. Robert Bly. NNaP

Looking at a Dry Canadian Thistle Brought In from the Snow. Robert Bly. NNaP

Looking at Each Other. Muriel Rukeyser. GLP; NNaP

Looking at Henry Moore's Elephant Skull Etchings in Jerusalem during the War. Shirley Kaufman. LCAP-2

Looking at Her. Alan Brownjohn. OxBSo

Looking at Mount T'ai. Tu Fu. CrYelRi, *tr. by* Sam Hamill

Looking at Mount T'ai-Shan. Tu Fu. ChinPo, *tr. by* Yip Wai-lim

Looking at My Knife-hilt Ring, a Song. Liu Yu Hsi. SuSp, *tr. by* Daniel Bryant

Looking at New-Fallen Snow from a Train. Robert Bly. GM

Looking at Pictures to Be Put Away. Gary Snyder. NNaP

Looking at Some Flowers. Robert Bly. NOBA

Looking at the clouds. Inscribed on a Painting. Shen Chou. SuSp, *tr. by* Irving Y. Lo

Looking at the Moon. Vivian Lamarque. CItWP, *tr. by* Cinzia Sartini Blum and Lara Trubowitz

Looking at the post love world. Immediate Content Recognition. Diane Ward. PmAP

Looking Back. Joanna Kadi. PoArWo

Looking back at the valley. Bako. JDP, *tr.* by Yoel Hoffmann

Looking back in my mind I can see. Elementary Scene, The. Randall Jarrell. PoE

Looking back, the language scribbles. Rereading Old Writing. David Ferry. DiPo

Looking Before and After. Carter Revard. HATNAP

Looking Both Ways before Crossing. John Woods. CoAmPo

Looking Deep. Magdalena Gomez. PueRic

Looking deeper. John Wills. HA

Looking down into my father's / dead face. Good Night, Willie Lee, I'll See You in the Morning. Alice Walker. WeW-3

Looking down on the open-cast pit. Truant, A. Mike Jenkins. TCAWP

Looking for a Country under Its Original Name. Colleen J. McElroy. BlSi

Looking for a Recluse but Failing to Find Him. Chia Tao. CoBCP; ColAnChi, *tr.* by Burton Watson

Looking for a shrine that would not fall. Aristophanes. Plato. GrAn, *tr.* by Peter Jay

Looking for Indians. Cheryl Savageau. TWW

Looking for love, she read cookbooks. Woman Who Loved to Cook, The. Erica Jong. TAP

Looking for Lu Hung-chien but Failing to Find Him. Chiao-jan. CoBCP, *tr.* by Burton Watson

Looking for Master Yung Ts'un near His Hermitage. Li Po. CrYelRi, *tr.* by Sam Hamill

Looking for Mountain Beavers. David Wagoner. VGW

Looking for Mushrooms at Sunrise. W. S. Merwin. NOBA

Looking for Poetry. Carlos Drummond de Andrade. ChAP, *tr.* by Mark Strand

Looking for something I had lost. 1st Untitled Poem. Pedro Juan Pietri. PueRic

Looking for something in the Sunday paper. Sunday News, The. Dana Gioia. WeW-3

Looking for the Melungeon. Dave Jeddie Smith. HCAP

Looking for Trouble. Roque Dalton. TCLAP, *tr.* by Richard Schaaf

Looking for you and me, my dear, looking for you and me. (LL) W. H. Auden. AmFaPo; HP; OxAEP-2 *Fr.* Ten Songs.

Looking for your light. For the Lord of Caves. Allama Prabhu. PFTM-1

Looking Forward. Robert Louis Stevenson. NBLV

Looking from the Pavilion over the Lake. Su Tung-p'o (Su Shih). OHPC, *tr.* by Kenneth Rexroth

Looking-Glass, A. Thomas Carew. CaPo

Looking-Glass, The. Rudyard Kipling. FaBoTw; OBMV

Looking-Glass for Men and Maids, A. *Unknown.* BASC

Looking-Glass for Smokers, A. Lawrence Spooner. On Giving Up Smoking. NOEC

Looking in a Mirror the Day before the Advent of Autumn. Li Yi. SuSp, *tr.* by William H. Nienhauser

Looking in the Lake. Po Chü-i. TAL

Looking into a Face. Robert Bly. NOBA

Looking into History. Richard Wilbur. VCAP; VGW

Looking into my daughter's eyes I read. For My Daughter. Weldon Kees. CoAP; OxBSo

Looking into the blue. Horizon Blues. David Henderson. GT

Looking North. Pamela Gillilan. Prnts

Looking out from death you will always see. Looking Out from Death. Duo Duo (Li Shizheng). AF, *tr.* by Gregory Lee

Looking Out in All Directions. *Vietnamese Oral Tradition.* CaDao, *tr.* by John Balaban

Looking Out to Sea Again on the Uptown Express. Sanford Fraser. UrbNat

Looking over my shoulder. Allen Ginsberg. NIL-7

Looking thru the commercial. Loneliness, A. Haki R. Madhubuti. GT

Looking to the sea, it is a line. Innocence, The. Robert Creeley. NeAP

Looking toward the west where the sun sinks away. In Praise of a Gold and Silver Painted Scene of the Buddha Manifestation in the Pure Land of the West, with a Preface. Li Po. WoPoe, *tr.* by Elling O. Eide

Looking Up. Sujata Bhatt. EmeKit

Looking up at the sky. Looking Out in All Directions. *Vietnamese Oral Tradition.* CaDao, *tr.* by John Balaban

Looking up at the stars, I know quite well. More Loving One, The. W. H. Auden. TOF

Looking up: blue sky's end. Orchid Pavilion. Wang Hsi-chih. ChinPo, *tr.* by Yip Wai-lim

Looking Up My Balance. Anselm Berrigan. HeMarv

Looking up to the wide sky where the white sun rushes on. (LL) Seven Songs Written while Living at T'ung-ku in 759. Tu Fu. ColAnChi; SuSp, *tr.* by Geoffrey Waters and Goeffrey Waters

Looking West from Laguna Beach at Night. Charles Wright. MakPoe

Looks like what drives me crazy. Evil. Langston Hughes. APT-2

Looks not unnavigable to me. (LL) Narrow Sea, The. Robert Graves. FaBoEE; FaBoMo

Looks that weren't. Homage to a Bellhop. Yusef Komunyakaa. BodElec

Loom of Time, The. *Unknown.* ITBLP

Looming and almost molten and slowly moving its gold down hill. Sirmione. James Wright. BodElec

Looming bastion fringed with fire, A. (LL) Tennyson. EBVV; GTBS-P; NAEL-6v2; NAWM-7v2; NOBE; PeECV *Fr.* In Memoriam A. H. H.

Looming up. Strange Peak. Muso Soseki. EaWin, *tr.* by W. S. Merwin

Loon, A. Frances Densmore. APT-1 *Fr.* Chippewa Music.

Loon, The. Michael S. Harper. ESEAA

Loon Call, A. Richard Eberhart. ColAP

Loon / I thought it was, A. My Love Has Departed. *Chippewa Oral Tradition.* NAAL-5, *tr.* by Frances Densmore

Loon I Thought It Was, A. *Unknown.* OBVE, *tr.* by Frances Densmore

Loon's Egg, The. Peter Dale Scott. MoCV

Loon's long night call, A. Three Seasons. Francis Sparshott. NOBC

Loon upon the Lake, The. *Ojibwa Oral Tradition.* APN-2; OWoS, *tr.* by Charles Fenno Hoffman

Loon? No, A. Chippewa Love Song. *Unknown.* BoWoP, *tr.* by Frances Densmore

Loons Mating. David Wagoner. BLT

Loop Canal, The. Nikolai Alekseievich Zabolotsky [*or* Zabolotskii]. TCRusP, *tr.* by Denis Johnson and Kathy Lewis

Loop, Fleck, Sound *and So On.* Marianne Vitale. HeMarv

Loop of rusty cable incises, The. "Luckies." Reginald Gibbons. IllVoic

Loop-the-Loop in Prospect Park (1905). Gerry Gomez Pearlberg. WiU

Loopy Dupes. Andrew Crozier. Oth

Loose as clouds, the curled hair. Tune: "Sheep on Mountain Slope"—Boudoir Thoughts. *Unknown.* SuSp, *tr.* by Hellmut Wilhelm

Loose hands and part: I am not she you sought. Renunciation. Lizette Woodworth Reese. TCAPo

Loose heady laughter shook the humid night. Jasbo Brown. DuBose Heyward. SeSe

Loose in the brush pines. Tango. Ntozake Shange. GT

Loose Saraband, A. Richard Lovelace. BeJo; CaPo

Loose Shoes. Charles Bernstein. FTOS

Loose to the wind her golden tresses streamed. Petrarch. CenSon; RWP, *tr.* by Charlotte Smith *Fr.* Sonnets to Laura.

Loose Woman. X. J. Kennedy. WeW-3

Loose Woman Poem. Sharon Thesen. NOBC

Loose Women. Sandra Cisneros. IllVoic

Loosed from its bonds my spirit fled away. Dream, or the Type of the Rising Sun, A. Jean Adams. ECWP; NOEC

Loosed from Winter's prison. *Unknown.* TAL

Loosing their feverish clutch. His Friend's Last Battle. Theodore Nicholl. AngWePo

Loot. Rudyard Kipling.
    "Loo! loo! Lulu! lulu! Loo! loo! Loot! loot!" UV

Loot the legions sent embraced these three, The. Victor, The. Lajos Áprily. IQMS, *tr.* by Watson Kirkconnell

Looters, The. Robert Minhinnick. TCAWP

Lop-sided from a shrapnel wound. Arthur. Geoffrey Adkins. FaBoWar

Lopped tree in time may grow again, The. Times Go by Turns. Richard Verstegan [*or* Verstegen]. SacPr

Loppèd tree in time may grow again [*or* againe *or* agayne], The. Times [*or* Tymes] Go[e] By Turn[e]s. Robert Southwell. ChIV-1; NoSic

Lorca Variations (XXVIII), The. Jerome Rothenberg. PFTM-2

Lord. Prayer for Marilyn Monroe. Ernesto Cardenal. TCLAP, *tr.* by Robert Pring-Mill

Lord. Troparion. Kassiane. WPoS, *tr.* by Liana Sakelliou

Lord. Awakening, The. Alejandra Piznarnick. TCLAP, *tr.* by Frank Graziano and María Rosa Fort

Lord! Executioner of Flowers. Muhammad Al-Maghut. PFTM-2, *tr.* by May Jayyusi and Naomi Shihab Nye

Lord, all I am and hope to be. Offering, An. Eloise Bibb. CBWP-4

Lord among the Clouds, The. *Unknown.* CoBCP, *tr.* by Burton Watson *Fr.* Nine Songs, The.

Lord Apollo, who has never died, The. Many Are Called. Edwin Arlington Robinson. GI; OxBA

Lord Arnold delicately sought to name. Edward Edwin Foot. VerBaPo

Lord, art thou at the table head above. Edward Taylor. ChIV-1; OxBA; TCAPo *Fr.* Preparatory Meditations before My Approach to the Lord's Supper.

Lord, at This Closing Hour. Eleazar Thompson Fitch. AH

Lord, at thy voice, my heart for fear hath trembled. Song of the Faithful, A. Michael Drayton. ChIV-1

Lord Barrenstock. Stevie Smith. NALW; NBLV; OBSV

Lord Be Praised, The. Hafiz [*or* Hafez]. BoLoP, *tr. by* Peter Avery and John Heath-Stubbs

"Lord, being dark," I said, "I cannot bear." Shroud of Color, The. Countee Cullen. NAAAL

Lord Bless Africa. Enoch Sontonga. PeSAV, *tr. by* D. D. T. Jabava

Lord, bless us Hungarians. National Anthem. Ferenc Kölcsey. IQMS, *tr. by* Earl M. Herrick, Watson Kirkconnell and Adam Makkai

Lord, blow the Coal: Thy Love Enflame in mee. (LL) Edward Taylor. NOCV; SCAP *Fr.* Preparatory Meditations before My Approach to the Lord's Supper.

Lord, but *how* much beauty was there / Back in 1955! (LL) Betjeman, 1984. Charles Causley. NOBL; OxBTC; PeLV; UV

Lord, by thy sweet and saving sign. Howres for the Hours of Matines, The. Richard Crashaw. PeECV

"Lord Byron" was an Englishman. Sketch of Lord Byron's Life. Julia A. Moore. OBAL

Lord, can a crumb of dust the earth outweigh. Edward Taylor. NAAL-2v1; NAAL-3; NAAL-5; TCAPo *Fr.* Preparatory Meditations before My Approach to the Lord's Supper.

Lord Chancellors were cheap as sprats. Gilbertian Cats. Sir William Schwenck Gilbert. TriCat

Lord Christ, we pray thy mercy on our table spread. In the Refectory. Alcuin. MLL, *tr. by* Helen Waddell

Lord Clive. Edmund Clerihew Bentley. NOBL; PeLV *Fr.* Clerihews.

Lord, come away! Hymn for Advent. Jeremy Taylor. SacPr

Lord, confound this surly sister. Curse, The. John Millington Synge. FaBoEE; NOIV; OBCoV

Lord Coningsby's Epitaph. Pope. FaBoEE

Lord Cozens Hardy. Sir John Betjeman. OxBTC

Lord Crashton: The Absentee Landlord. William Allingham. NOIV *Fr.* Laurence Bloomfield in Ireland.

Lord, Dear God! to Thy Attending. Heinrich Otto. AH, *tr. by* Sheema Z. Buehne

Lord decided suddenly, The. Tale of the Cyclopses, The. Nikolai Ivanovich Glazkov. TCRP, *tr. by* Daniel Weissbort

Lord Delamere. *Unknown.* ESPB

Lord, Deliver, Thou Canst Save. Eliza Lee Cabot Follen. AH

Lord Derwentwater. *Unknown.* ESPB

Lord Descended from Above, The. Majesty of God, The. Thomas Sternhold. AH

Lord Douglas. *Unknown.* *See* Jamie Douglas

Lord Douglas. *Unknown.* *See* Waly, Waly [Love Be Bonny]

Lord Elderley, Lord Borrowmere, Lord Sickert and Lord Camp. Noël Coward. OBCoV

Lord Erlinton had ae daughter. Erlinton. *Unknown.* ESPB

Lord Finchley. Joseph Hilaire Pierre Belloc. FaBoEE; NBLV; NOBL; NoAM; OxAEP-2; OxBoLi; PeLV

Lord Finchley tried to mend the Electric Light. Lord Finchley. Joseph Hilaire Pierre Belloc. FaBoEE; NBLV; NOBL; NoAM; OxAEP-2; OxBoLi; PeLV

Lord Fluting Dreams of America on the Eve of His Departure from Liverpool. Paul Zimmer. VGW

Lord, for to-morrow and its needs. Just for To-Day. Ernest R. Wilberforce. PWR

Lord, forgive me if I do not look for you. Idyll. Henriqueta Lisboa. TCLAP, *tr. by* Hélcio Veiga Costa

Lord / forgive me / if I twist the sunset. Hungry Black Child, The. Adam David Miller. NBV

Lord Galloway. Robert Burns. OxBoLi *Fr.* Epigrams on Lord Galloway.

Lord, give me Love! give me the silent bliss. Love, Death, and Art. Agnes Mary Frances Robinson. VWP

Lord, give me vision that shall see. Beyond the Profit of Today. *Unknown.* PoToHe

Lord God, forgive white Europe! Léopold Sédar Senghor. TTY *Fr.* Prayer for Peace.

Lord God of Heaven, who only are. Prayer of Nehemiah, The. George Wither. ChIV-1

Lord God of Hosts. Shepherd Knapp. AH

Lord God of trajectory and blast. Norman Corwin. TrJP *Fr.* On a Note of Triumph.

Lord God's jealous of yourself and me, The. (LL) Dread. John Millington Synge. BoLoP; MoBrPo; OxBSP

Lord God said to Wu Yang, The. Summons of the Soul, The. Ch'u Yüan. WoPoe, *tr. by* David Hawkes

Lord God! this was a stone. Stone, The. Thomas Vaughan. OBWVE

Lord Gorbals. Harry Graham. PeLV

Lord, Grant Us Calm. Christina Georgina Rossetti. SacPr

Lord Harry has written a novel. Novel of High Life, A. Thomas Haynes Bayly. OxAEP-2

Lord Has a Child, The. Langston Hughes. AH

Lord has shown me, The. Prayer in Four Verses. Pak Mokwŏl. WoPoe, *tr. by* Kim Chong-gil

Lord, have mercy on us! (LL) Thomas Nashe [*or* Nash]. EBEV; HAP; HeIP-4; NPeEn; NoP-4; NoSic; OxBEV; TFi; TRP *Fr.* Summer's Last Will and Testament.

Lord, he thought he'd make a man. Dese Bones Gwine to Rise Again. *Unknown.* OxBoLi

Lord, hear my prayer when trouble glooms. Lord, Hear My Prayer. John Clare. BBASP; ChIV-1; NOCV; TrCP

Lord Heygate. Joseph Hilaire Pierre Belloc. OBCoV; OxBoLi

Lord Hippo. Joseph Hilaire Pierre Belloc. NoAM

Lord, how can man preach thy eternal[l] word? Windows, The. George Herbert. BASC; ESCV; GeHe; MeLP; NAEL-5v1; NAEL-6v1; NAEL-7v1; NOCV; NoP-4; PeECV; PoE; TrCP

Lord Hsieh's youngest, his favorite child. Airing Painful Memories. Yüan Chên. CoBCP, *tr. by* Burton Watson

Lord, I also want to meet you, see. Second Coming. Adam Small. PeSAV, *tr. by* Carról Lasker

Lord I am here, O give me thy commission. (LL) To Christ. William Alabaster. NoSic; OxBSo

Lord, I am lonely. Stranger in This Land, A. Cliff Ashby. NOCV

Lord I am not entirely selfish. Prayer. Gavin Ewart. OxBC

Lord, I Am Thine. Samuel Davies. AH

Lord, I confesse, that Thou alone art able. To His Saviour. Robert Herrick. SacPr

Lord I know, and I know you know I know. Margin Prayer from an Ancient Psalter. Ian Duhig. EmeKit; NeBl

Lord, I Know Thy Grace Is Nigh Me. Hervey Doddridge Ganse. AH

Lord, I'm done for: now Margot. Rondeau. Vincent Voiture. WoPoe, *tr. by* William Jay Smith

Lord, I'm tired. Little Black Boy's Prayer, A. Guy Tirolien. NegPo, *tr. by* Ellen Conroy Kennedy

Lord, I remember, and am sore amazed. Hymn of Weeping. Amittai ben Shefatiah. TrJP, *tr. by* Nina Davis Salaman

Lord I Sleep and I Sleep. David Shapiro. ChIV-1

Lord, I Want to Be a Christian. *Unknown.* AH

Lord, if I loved her, count it not my shame. (LL) Of the Gentle Heart. Guido Guinicelli. AWP; CTC; EaItPo; OBVE, *tr. by* Dante Gabriel Rossetti

Lord, in my silence how do I despise. Frailty. George Herbert. NOCV

Lord in the matter of your ninety-second element. To Whom It May Concern. Judith Johnson Sherwin. YaYoPo

Lord, in Thy Presence Here. Jesse L. Holman. AH

Lord Ingram and Chiel Wyet. *Unknown.* ESPB
(Lady Maisry.) OxBB

Lord into His Garden Comes, The. *Unknown.* AH

Lord Is King, The. *Unknown.* TrJP, *tr. by* Solomon Solis-Cohen

Lord is my herd, nae want sal fa' me, The. Bible, *O.T.* *See* Lord is my shepherd; I shall not want, The

Lord is my Shepherd, I have all I need, The. 23rd Psalm, The. Bobby McFerrin. HW

Lord is my shepherd, I shall not, The. Neo-Thomist Poem. Ernest Hemingway. OBAL

Lord is my shepherd; I shall not want, The. Bible, *O.T.* AWP; NAWM-5v1; NIL-7; NIP-4; TFi; TrJP *Fr.* Psalms.

Lord is my shepherd, I shall not want, The. Bible, *O.T.* InvLi, *New Revised Standard Version* *Fr.* Psalms.

Lord: it is time. The summer was immense. Autumn Day. Rainer Maria Rilke. WoPoe, *tr. by* John Felsteiner

Lord: it is time. The summer was so grand. Autumn Day. Rainer Maria Rilke. AuPH, *tr. by* Lowell A. Bangerter

Lord, it is time. The summer was too long. Autumn Day. Rainer Maria Rilke. TrJP

Lord Jesus, at the end of this book which I offer you. Léopold Sédar Senghor. NegPo *Fr.* Prayer for Peace.

Lord Jesus Christ, in whose hand is the breath. *Unknown.* MLL

Lord Jesus Christ, We Humbly Pray. Henry Eyster Jacobs. AH

Lord Jesus, who would think that I am Thine? Christina Georgina Rossetti. NOBVV

Lord Jesus! with what sweetness and delights. Ascension-Day. Henry Vaughan. ESCV

Lord, knights, and squires, the num'rous band. To a Child of Quality of Five Years Old, the Author Supposed Forty. Matthew Prior. NOEC

Lord! Lead the Way the Saviour Went. William Croswell. AH

Lord, let me make this rule. School Days. Maltbie Davenport Babcock. PWR

Lord let me suffer much. Prayer That Will Be Answered, A. Anna Kamienska. BLT, *tr. by* Stanislaw Baranczak

Lord, let thy mercy come. (LL) Lamentation, The. John Marckant. AH; SacPr

Lord Livingston. *Unknown.* ESPB; OxBB

Lord, Lord, an East Virginia man. (LL) John Henry. *Unknown.* NOBA; OxBoLi

Lord Lovel he stands at his stable-door. Lord Lovel. *Unknown.* ESPB

Lord Lovel he stood at his castle gate. Lord Lovel. *Unknown.* ESPB

Lord Lovell he stood at his own front door. Tale of Lord Lovell, The. *Unknown.* NOBL; PeLV

Lord Lucky. Joseph Hilaire Pierre Belloc. NBLV

Lord Lundy. Joseph Hilaire Pierre Belloc. OBSV; OxBoLi; PeLV

Lord Lundy from his earliest years. Lord Lundy. Joseph Hilaire Pierre Belloc. OBSV; OxBoLi; PeLV

Lord, make me an instrument of Thy Peace. Prayer of St. Francis of Assisi for Peace. Saint Francis of Assisi. PoToHe

Lord, make me coy and tender to offend. Unkindness. George Herbert. NOSC

Lord, Make Me to Know Mine End. Bible, *O.T.* TrJP *Fr.* Psalms.

Lord, make me worthy of this number. To Anne Frank. Rosita Kalina. MirDau, *tr. by* Roberta Gordenstein

Lord, Many Times. Richard Chenevix Trench. SacPr

Lord, Many Times Thou Pleased Art. George Wither. AH

Lord Maxwell has te'n his last good-night. (LL) Lord Maxwell's Last Goodnight. *Unknown.* ESPB; OxBB

Lord Maxwell's Last Goodnight. *Unknown.* ESPB; OxBB

Lord, may there be no moment in her life. Prayer of Any Husband. Mazie V. Caruthers. PoToHe

Lord, mine eye offended. Matthew V. 29-30. Derek Mahon. CIP-2

Lord, My Weak Thought in Vain Would Climb. Ray Palmer. AH

Lord of All Being, Throned Afar. Oliver Wendell Holmes. AH *Fr.* Professor at the Breakfast Table, The.

Lord of all worlds, let thanks and praise. John Quincy Adams. SacPr

Lord of Each Soul. Paul Engle. AH

Lord of Gododdin will be praised in song, A. Aneirin. NePenScot, *tr. by* Joseph P. Clancy *Fr.* Gododdin, The.

Lord of Heaven and Earth has made a feast, The. On a Feast. Francis Quarles. ChIV-2

Lord of Hosts, and God of Israel! Prayer of Hezekiah, The. George Wither. ChIV-1

Lord of Life, All Praise Excelling. Clement Clarke Moore. AH

Lord of Lorn and the False [*or* Fals] Steward, The. *Unknown.* ESPB; OxBB

Lord of My Heart's Elation. Bliss Carman. AH; NOBC

Lord of my love, to whom in vassalage. William Shakespeare. HeIP-4 *Fr.* Sonnets.

Lord of Nature. Leonid Nikolaevich Martynov. TCRP, *tr. by* J. R. Rowland

Lord of Rosslyn's daughter gaed through the wud her lane, The. Captain Wedderburn's Courtship. *Unknown.* ESPB

Lord of the Isle, The. Stefan George. AWP, *tr. by* Ludwig Lewisohn

Lord of the River. *Unknown.* CoBCP, *tr. by* Burton Watson *Fr.* Nine Songs.

Lord of the River Hsiang. Ch'u Yüan. SuSp, *tr. by* Wu-Chi Liu

Lord of the Throne. Al-Tirimmah. ArPe, *tr. by* Omar S. Pound

Lord of the Winds. Mary Elizabeth Coleridge. SacPr

Lord of the World. *Unknown.* TrJP, *tr. by* D. A. de Sola

Lord of the Worlds Below! James Freeman. AH

Lord of them that hurt his Saints, doth say, The. Mary Mollineux. EMWP, *tr. by* Henry Mollineux

Lord Our God Alone Is Strong, The. Caleb T. Winchester. AH

Lord over all! whose power the sceptre swayed. Lord of the World. *Unknown.* TrJP, *tr. by* D. A. de Sola

Lord, pity such sinners. Monday afternoon. Devotional Sonnet, A. Timothy Steele. CRP

Lord Quicksilver, god of erections, come down. To Hermes. Alfred Corn. CAGL; WiU

Lord Rameses of Egypt sighed. Birthright. John Drinkwater. OxBTC

Lord Randal[l]. *Unknown.* AWP; EBEV; EBNV; ESPB; HAP; HeIP-4; NoP-4; OxBB; OxBEV; OxBS; PAI; PoPoPo; SCGP; TFi; TRP; WeW-3

Lord, receive my prayer / Sweet as incense smoke. Evening Prayer. Thomas Merton. ChIV-1

Lord, Remember Me! *Unknown.* APN-2

Lord's Arrival, The. Endre Ady. IQMS, *tr. by* Anton N. Nyerges

Lord's lost Him His mockingbird. Mourning Poem for the Queen of Sunday. Robert Earl Hayden. HCAP; NAAAL; NoAM; NoP-4; PoPoPo

Lord's my shepherd, I'll not want, The. Bible, *O.T.* *See* Lord is my shepherd; I shall not want, The

Lord's name be praised, The. Litanies of Julia Pastrana (1832–1860), The. Thomas William Shapcott. CBAP; NOBAu

Lord's Prayer. D. H. Lawrence. PeECV

(For thine is the kingdom / the power.) GI

Lord's Prayer. Nicanor Parra. GI, *tr. by* Miller Williams

Lord's Prayer, The. Massillon Coicou. NegPo, *tr. by* Ellen Conroy Kennedy

Lord said unto Jonah: "Rise, go down," The. Book of Jonah, The. Mihály Babits. IQMS, *tr. by* István Tótfalusi

Lord Saltoun and Auchanachie. *Unknown.* ESPB

Lord, shall I find it in Thy Holy Church. Truth. Claude McKay. BPo

Lord she's gone done left me done packed / up and split. Feeling Fucked / Up. Etheridge Knight. GT; NNaP; PBCAP; RaBo

Lord, since it's hard to explain. Limerick. J. E. Press. PeLi

Lord speaks, The / this way. Isaiah: Chapter 66. David Rosenberg. ChIV-1

Lord, stand up for the Soviets. Prayer: "Lord, stand up for the Soviets." Nikolai Ivanovich Glazkov. TCRP, *tr. by* Daniel Weissbort

Lord Stanhope hit upon a novel plan. Thomas Baker. VerBaPo *Fr.* Steam Engine; or, The Power of the Flame, The.

Lord summons Elijah-like, The. On Elijah's Chariot. Endre Ady. IQMS, *tr. by* Anton N. Nyerges

Lord, surely you took the position designed to infuriate. Strength. Helen Chasin. YaYoPo

Lord Tennyson and Lord Melchett. D. H. Lawrence. FaBoEE

Lord, the Roman hyacinths are blooming in bowls and. Song for Simeon, A. T. S. Eliot. ChIV-2; NOCV

Lord, the snowful sky. Sailor's Carol. Charles Causley. OBPC; PeECV

Lord, Thine humble servants hear. Hymn for Atonement Day. Judah Halevi. TrJP, *tr. by* Solomon Solis-Cohen

Lord, this woman who fell into many sins. Kassia. BoWoP

Lord Thomas and Fair Annet. *Unknown.* ESPB; NPeEn

Lord Thomas and Lady Margaret. *Unknown.* ESPB

Lord Thomas is to the hunting gone. Lord Thomas and Lady Margaret. *Unknown.* ESPB

Lord Thomas Stuart. *Unknown.* ESPB

Lord, thou hast been our dwelling place in all generations. Bible, *O.T.* AWP *Fr.* Psalms.

Lord, Thou hast crushed Thy tender ones, o'erthrown. Messina, 1908. Alice Thompson Meynell. SacPr

Lord, Thou hast given me a cell. Thanksgiving to God for His House, A. Robert Herrick. BASC; BeJo; CavPo; HAP; NOSC; PeECV; PoRA; TrCP

Lord, Thou hast made this world below the shadow of a dream. McAndrew's Hymn. Rudyard Kipling. OxBTC

Lord, Thou Hast Promised. Samuel K. Cox. AH

Lord thou hast told us that there be. God's Two Dwellings. Thomas Washbourne. SacPr

Lord, Thou who art like the sea. Night Prayer of Glückel of Hameln, The. Edouard Roditi. CRP

Lord 'tis midnight. Three Phases of Africa. Francis Ernest Kobina Parkes. PBA

Lord to me a shepherd is, The. Bible, *O.T.* *See* Lord is my shepherd; I shall not want, The

Lord to me [*or* mee] a shepherd is, The. Bible, *O.T.* OBCA; TCAPo *Fr.* Bay Psalm Book, The.

Lord to your honour. Prayer to God. Esther Kello. EMWP

Lord Ullin's Daughter. Thomas Campbell. GTBS-P; NOBRP

Lord, very fair my lot and beautiful my story. Very Fair My Lot. Jacob David Kamzon. TrJP, *tr. by* Sholom J. Kahn

Lord Walter's Wife. Elizabeth Barrett Browning. HAP; NPeEn

('But why do you go?' said the lady, while both sat under the yew.) VWP

Lord wants me to go to Florida, The. Pentecost. Gwyneth Lewis. MFPA

Lord! what a busy [*or* busie], restles[s] thing. Pursuit[e], The. Henry Vaughan. AngWePo; GeHe; NOSC; SacPr; TrCP

Lord! what a goodly thing is want of shirts. John Cleveland. OBSV *Fr.* Rebel Scot, The.

Lord, / What a menagerie! Noah's Prayer. Carmen Bernos de Gasztold. TrCP, *tr. by* Rumer Godden

Lord, what am I, that, with unceasing care. To-Morrow. Félix Lope de Vega Carpio. AWP, *tr. by* Henry Wadsworth Longfellow

Lord, what am I? A worm, dust, vapour, nothing! Anthem for the Cathedral of Exeter. Joseph Hall. SacPr

Lord, what are the sins. In a U-Haul North of Damascus. David Bottoms. ReTh

Lord, What Is Man? Carl Rakosi. FTOS

Lord, what is man? why should he cost[e] thee [*or* you]. C[h]aritas Nimia; or, The Dear[e] Bargain. Richard Crashaw. ESCV; NOCV; NOSC

Lord, what these weders ar cold. *Unknown.* NAEL-5v1; NAEL-7v1

Lord, when I look at lovely things which pass. In the Fields. Charlotte Mew. MoBrPo; OxAEP-2

Lord, when the clock strikes. Reader, The. Thomas Merton. CRP

Lord, when the meadow has gone cold. Rooks, The. Arthur Rimbaud. FaBoWar, *tr. by* Norman Cameron

Lord, when the sense of Thy sweet grace. Song. Richard Crashaw. InvLi

Lord, when the wise men came from far[r]. Hymn. Sidney Godolphin. BeJo; HAP; MeLP; NOCV; NPeEn; PeECV; SacPr

Lord, when they kill me, let the job be thorough. Merthyr. Glyn Jones. AngWePo

Lord! when thou didst thy self undress. Incarnation and Passion, The. Henry Vaughan. GeHe; SacPr; TrCP

Lord, when will it be? Takahashi Mutsuo. PFTM-2, tr. by Hiroaki Sato Fr. Self-Portraits.

Lord, Where Shall I Find Thee? Judah Halevi. TrJP, tr. by Nina Davis Salaman

Lord, who createdst man in wealth and store. Easter Wings. George Herbert. AngWePo; BASC; CABP; ChIV-1; ESCV; FHYEP; FSCP; GeHe; HAP; HeIP-4; InPK-6; MakPoe; MeLP; NAEL-5v1; NAEL-6v1; NAEL-7v1; NIL-7; NIP-4; NOSC; NoP-4; PAI; PBRV; PoE; PoPoPo; SacPr; TFi; TOF; TRP; TrCP; WeW-3; WoPoe

Lord, who hast formed me out of mud. Trinity Sunday. George Herbert. OxBSP

Lord, who hast made me free. G.W. Briggs. SacPr

Lord, Who's the Happy Man. Nahum Tate. AH

Lord / whose face is this. Riddle. Gharib Nawaz. BBASP, tr. by Nasrollah Pourjavady and Peter Lamborn Wilson

Lord Will Happiness Divine, The. William Cowper. NOCV Fr. Olney Hymns.

Lord William; or, Lord Lundy. Unknown. ESPB

Lord with glowing heart I'd praise thee. Francis Scott Key. SacPr

Lord with thine Altars Fire, mine Inward man. Edward Taylor. TCAPo Fr. Preparatory Meditations before My Approach to the Lord's Supper.

Lord, with what care hast thou begirt us round! Sin (1). George Herbert. GeHe; OxAEP-1

Lord, with what glory [or glorie] wast thou served [or serv'd] of old. Sion. George Herbert. ChIV-1; ESCV

Lord, within thy fold I be. Hymn. Priscilla Jane Thompson. CBWP-2

Lord, you are my lover. How the Soul Speaks to God. Mechthild von Magdeburg. WPoS, tr. by Oliver Davies

Lord, You Have Ripped Away. Antonio Machado Ruiz. GI, tr. by Robert Bly

Lord, You may not recognize me. Gift, The. Louise Glück. FaBoWP; TaR

Lord! You Saved Me from Ur-Germany as I Fled. Uri Zvi Greenberg. MHP, tr. by Ruth Finer Mintz

Lord, you visited Paris on the day of your birth. Paris in the Snow. Léopold Sédar Senghor. PBA, tr. by Ulli Beier

Lorde is my shepherde; therefore can I lack nothing, The. Bible, O.T. See Lord is my shepherd; I shall not want, The.

Lordinges, listen, and hold you still. Durham Field. Unknown. ESPB

"Lording[e]s," quod he, "in chirches whan I preche." Geoffrey Chaucer. FHYEP; NAEL-6v1; NAWM-5v1; PoE Fr. Canterbury Tales, The.

Lordly and Isolate Satyrs, The. Charles Olson. CoAP; NeAP; PoM

Lordly Hudson, The. Paul Goodman. APT-2; CoAP; VGW

Lords do crave all, The. Postscript to Verses on the History of France, A. Unknown. NOIV

Lords have been made whose hired robes have hidden. On the Relinquishment of a Title. Geoffrey Grigson. FaBoEE

Lords, knights, and squires, the numerous band. To a Child of Quality [Five Years Old, the Author Supposed Forty]. Matthew Prior. NOBE; NOEC; OBEV; OxBEV

Lords of life, the lords of life, The. Experience. Ralph Waldo Emerson. APN-1; TAP; TCAPo

Lore. Ronald Stuart Thomas. NoP-4; OxBC; RB

Lorelei. Heinrich Heine. TrJP

Lorenzo. Letitia [or Laetitia] Elizabeth Landon. RWP Fr. Improvisatrice, The.

Lorenzo! Such the glories of the world! Edward Young. NOEC Fr. Night Thoughts.

Lorine, Lorine. For Lorine Niedecker in Heaven. Ralph J. Mills, Jr. IllVoic

Lorry made the windows shake, A. James Keir Baxter. PeLV Fr. Cressida.

Los Angeles. James Harms. GeoHom

Los Angeles after the Rain. Dana Gioia. UrbNat

Los Angeles Nocturne. Xavier Villaurrutia. TCLAP, tr. by Rachel Benson

Los Angeles, the Angels. James Harms. NeAmPo; PuP-23

Los árboles son poetas / Trees Are Poets. Francisco Alarcon. GeoHom

Los Mineros. Edward Dorn. PoM

Los Olivos. Michael Lieberman. BloBone

"Lose and love" is love's first art. Song by the Shore, A. Richard Hovey. APN-2

Loser, The. Adrienne Rich. RACG

Losers. Carl Sandburg. MoAmPo; NoAM

Losing a Language. W. S. Merwin. NoP-4

Losing a Slave-Girl. Po Chü-i. AWP, tr. by Arthur Waley
  (Around my courtyard the little wall is low.) ChiP, tr. by Arthur Waley

Losing altitude, you can see below you the flames. Death of Thomas Merton. Harry Clifton. PBCIP

Losing My Mind. Stephen Sondheim. ReLy

Losing My Sight. Lisel Mueller. ExTi

Losing Myself. S. J. Marks. BodElec

Losing myself in the swaying gray. Ecologue. Eugenio Montale. WoPoe, tr. by William Arrowsmith

Losing the Marbles. James Merrill. DiPo

Losing Track. Denise Levertov. HeIP-4; NOBA; PoE; PoM

Loss. Judith Herzberg. TuT, tr. by Joan McBreen

Loss. Charles Madge. FaBoMo

Loss. C. K. Williams. MakPoe

Loss. Yevgeny Aleksandrovich Yevtushenko [or Evtushenko]. TCRP, tr. by James Reagan and Yevgeny Yevtushenko

Loss is an unintentional decline in or disappearance of. Definitions for Mendy. David Antin. APSN

Loss of an Oil Tanker. Charles Causley. OxBC

Loss of our learning brought darkness, weakness and woe. Epigram. Unknown. NOIV, tr. by Thomas Kinsella

Loss of something ever felt I, A. Emily Dickinson. ChIV-2; NALW; NCAP

Loss of the Royal George. William Cowper. See On the Loss of the Royal George

Loss[e] in Delay[e]. Robert Southwell. NoSic

Losses. Randall Jarrell. AmFaPo; HCAP; LCAP-2; OxBA; TAP; UnPo

Lost. W. H. Auden. FaBoEE Fr. Shorts I.

Lost. Chu Shu-chen. BoWoP; OHMPC, tr. by Kenneth Rexroth

Lost. James Godden. OBSP

Lost. Orkhan Muyassar. BBASP; MAP, tr. by Samuel Hazo and Lena Jayyusi

Lost. Charles, Duc d' Orléans. NPeEn

Lost. Richard Henry Stoddard. TreFP

(Never Again.) PWR

Lost, The. Jones Very. APN-1; NOBA; NoP-4

Lost Acres. Robert Graves. NoAM

Lost and bewildered in the thickening mist. On the Great Fog in London, December 1762. James Eyre Weeks. NOEC

Lost and Found. Maxine Chernoff. PmAP

Lost and Found. Jane Griffiths. NeBl

Lost and Found. George Macdonald. SacPr

Lost and Found and Lost Again. John Ashbery. BodElec

Lost Angel, The. Philip Levine. NOBA

Lost Baby Poem, The. Lucille Clifton. AmFaPo; BlSi; ESEAA; ISC; WPE

Lost Bee, The. Phillis Levin. RA

Lost behind the Back of God. Gyula Juhász. IQMS, tr. by Adam Makkai

Lost Bird. Chenjerai Hove. HBAPE

Lost Body. Terry Ehret. GifTon

Lost Bride, The. Antiphanes. GrAn, tr. by Dudley Fitts

Lost Caress, The. Alfonsina Storni. BLPSL, tr. by Rene de Costa, Rigas Kappatos and Eleni Paidoussi

Lost Child, The. James Reaney. NOBC

Lost Children, The. Randall Jarrell. CoAP; TAP

Lost Chord, A. Adelaide Anne Procter. ITBLP; SacPr; UV; VWP
  (Lost Chord, The.) BRP

Lost Chord, The. Dominic Bevan Wyndham Lewis. UV

Lost City. Harold Farmer. PeSAV

Lost Continent, The. Jenny Joseph. BrRo

Lost! Cupid! / One lost Cupid! Meleager. GrAn

Lost Daughter. Magdalena Gomez. PueRic

Lost days of my life until to-day, The. Dante Gabriel Rossetti. SacPr Fr. House of Life, The.

Lost Desire. Meleager. AWP, tr. by William M. Hardinge

Lost for a Rose's Sake. Unknown. AWP, tr. by Andrew Lang

Lost Friend, The. Marjorie Lowry Christie Pickthall. PoBW

Lost from an airy. Mac Wellman. HeMarv Fr. Rat Minaret: Miniaturist-Divan, The.

Lost Fugue for Chet. Lynda Hull. SeSe

Lost Heifer, The. Austin Clarke. BIrV; ModIr; WoPoe

Lost Horizon. Hsi-chün. ColAnChi, tr. by Anne Birrell

Lost Horseman, The. Endre Ady. IQMS, tr. by Anton N. Nyerges

Lost Illusions. Georgia Douglas Johnson. NAAAL

Lost in bamboo. Issa. ZenPo, tr. by Takashi Ikemoto and Lucien Stryk

Lost in contemplation. Jean Daive. MFP, tr. by Martin Sorrell

Lost in glass gullies, searching for a suitcase. Hotel Marine. David Campbell. BMAP

Lost in God, in Godhead found. (LL) Ralph Waldo Emerson. APN-1; TCAPo

Lost in Heaven. Robert Frost. MoAmPo

Lost in the Desert. Clarence Major. FTOS

Lost in the ground. (LL) Miners. Wilfred Owen. MoBrPo; NOBE; OBWVE; OxAEP-2; PeFWW

Lost in the heart's worship and the body's sleep. (LL) Love-Poem: "Yours is the face that the earth turns to me." Kathleen Jessie Raine. LW; MoBrPo

Lost in the Hospital. Rafael Campo. AmPoNex

Lost in the Stars. Kurt Weill. ReLy

Lost in the vastness of the void Pacific. Homecoming. Karl Shapiro. APT-2

Lost in Translation. James Merrill. HCAP; LCAP-2; NAAL-2v2; NoAM; NoP-4; VCAP *Fr.* Book of Ephraim, The.

Lost in wonder, love, and praise! (LL) Love Divine, All Loves Excelling. Charles Wesley. NOCV; SacPr

Lost Jewel, A. Robert Graves. EnLoPo

Lost Jewel, The. Julia Ward Howe. SWaP *Fr.* Lyrics of the Street.

Lost Lady, The. Sir William Berkeley.
    Song: "Where did you borrow that last sigh." OxBSP

Lost Lane. Dorothy Wellesley, Duchess of Wellington. WPE

Lost Leader, The. Robert Browning. FHYEP; NAEL-5v2; NAEL-6v2; PWR; SCGP

Lost Light, The. Emily Jane Pfeiffer. VWP

Lost! lost! lost! Anne Boleyn. Eloise Bibb. CBWP-4

Lost—lost—lost! Into the Depths. Adah Isaacs Menken. CBWP-1

Lost! lost! lost! Advertisement of a Lost Day. Lydia Huntley Sigourney. TreFP

Lost, lost too soon in yonder house or hall. (LL) Pope. NAEL-6v1; NAEL-7v1 *Fr.* Dunciad, The.

Lost Love. Dick Allen. NIP-4

Lost Love. Robert Graves. AWP; FaBoCh; MoBrPo

Lost Lover, The. Delariviere Manley.
    Prologue [Spoken by Mr. Horden]: "First Adventurer for her fame I stand, The." EMWP

Lost manor where I walk continually. Pier-Glass, The. Robert Graves. NoAM

Lost Mistress, The. Robert Browning. BoLoP; NOBE; OBEV

Lost Mohican Visits Hell's Kitchen, A. A. K. Redwing. VoR

Lost Name Woman. Shirley Lim. UnSA

Lost Occasion, The. John Greenleaf Whittier. NOBA

Lost on a fog-bound spit of sand. W. H. Auden. FaBoEE *Fr.* Shorts I.

Lost on Both Sides. Dante Gabriel Rossetti. NoP-4 *Fr.* House of Life, The.

Lost Opportunities. Henrietta Cordelia Ray. CBWP-3

Lost Orchard, The. Edgar Lee Masters. ColAP

Lost Parasol, The. Sándor Weöres.
    "Where metalled road invades light thinning air." OBVE

Lost Parents. Lawrence Ferlinghetti. PoM; ReTh

Lost Pilot, The. James Tate. CoAP; EmeKit; NoAM; OBWP; TwCP; UnPo

Lost Plaza Is Everywhere, The. Rafael Campo. AmPoNex

Lost Pleiad, The. Felicia Dorothea Hemans. NOBRP

Lost Pleiad, The. William Gilmore Simms. APN-1

Lost Property. Elizabeth Garrett. MFPA

Lost Seed. Patrick Williams. PNI

Lost Shoe, The. *Unknown.* ReMoGo

Lost Sister. Cathy Song. NAAL-5; NOAM

Lost Son, The. Theodore Roethke. APT-2; HAP; HCAP; NAAL-2v2; NoP-4; TRP; VGW
    Flight, The. RB

Lost Songs. Vladimir Alekseievich Soloukhin. TCRP, *tr.* by Daniel Weissbort

Lost Soul, A. Jay Macpherson. NOBC; NoP-4

Lost Teddy Bear, The. Maggie Pogue Johnson. CBWP-4

Lost: The Original, Its Reason and Its Rhyme. Translation. Rika Lesser. KGB

Lost to one another, the living and the dead, these ten years. Tune: "River Town." Su Tung-p'o (Su Shih). ColAnChi, *tr.* by J. R. Hightower

Lost to the world; lost to my selfe; alone. On Himselfe. Robert Herrick. NPeEn

Lost to the world; lost to myself; alone. On Himself. Robert Herrick. BeJo

Lost Tradition, A. John Montague. CIP-2; PBCIP

Lost Tribe, The. Ruth Pitter. WPOW

Lost Wife, The. Sean Dunne. ModIr *Fr.* Sydney Place.

Lost Women, The. Lucille Clifton. BodElec

Lost Wood, The. Renée Weiss. PoCoUp

Lost Word of Jesus, A. Henry Van Dyke. TrCP

Lot. David Helwig. NIP-4

Lot and His Daughters I. Alec Derwent Hope. ChIV-1

Lot and His Daughters II. Alec Derwent Hope. ChIV-1

Lot and his two daughters and their sons: A man sat sozzled with his two wives. Cynewulf. ASW *Fr.* Riddles (Exeter Book).

Lot of love along the way, A. (LL) Day, A. William Leroy Stidger. PoToHe; SoSe-8

Lot of love is chosen, The. I learnt that much. Chosen. W. B. Yeats. BoLoP

Lot of Night Music, A. Anthony Hecht. OxBC

Lot of the old folks here—all that's left, A. Reflections in a Slum. Hugh MacDiarmid. FaBoTw

Lot's Wife. Anna Andreyevna Akhmatova. BoWoP, *tr.* by Richard Wilbur

Lot's Wife. Abraham Cowley. NPeEn *Fr.* Davideis.

Lotos-Eaters, The. Tennyson. *See* Lotus-Eaters, The

Lotos Eating. Mortimer Collins. NOBVV

Lots of stripes. Automatic Text for Anne Ethuin. Elisabeth Lenk. SurWo, *tr.* by Gisela Baumhauer and Greta Wenziger

Lots of truisms don't have to be repeated. Anatomy of Happiness, The. Ogden Nash. TAP

Lotus. Hsü Wei. SuSp, *tr.* by Irving Y. Lo
    "Fifth day of the fifth month." CoBLCP

Lotus-Eaters, The. Tennyson. SCGP
    (Choric Song.) HeIP-4
    (Song of the Lotus-Eaters.) NOBE; OBEV

Lotus-flower doth languish, The. Die Lotusblume ängstigt. Heinrich Heine. AWP, *tr.* by James Thomson

Lotus-gatherer's Song. Po Chü-i. SuSp, *tr.* by Irving Y. Lo

Lotus-Gathering Boat. Hsüeh T'ao. ColAnChi, *tr.* by Jeanne Larsen

Lotus-laden. Lotus-Gathering Boat. Hsüeh T'ao. ColAnChi, *tr.* by Jeanne Larsen

Lotus Lake. Ts'ao P'i. CoBCP, *tr.* by Burton Watson

Lotus Lover, The. Tzu Yeh. CrYelRi, *tr.* by Sam Hamill

Lotus Pond, The. Ts'ao P'i. SuSp, *tr.* by Ronald C. Miao

Lotus seeds. Sosen. JDP, *tr.* by Yoel Hoffmann

Lotus seeds in ten. Donsui. JDP, *tr.* by Yoel Hoffmann

Lotuses have withered, they put up no umbrellas to the rain. Presented to Liu Ching-wen. Su Tung-p'o (Su Shih). CoBCP, *tr.* by Burton Watson

Lotuses on the Crooked Pond. Lu Chao-lin. SuSp, *tr.* by Paul W. Kroll

Loud complaints being made, in these quick-reading times. Announcement of a New Grand Acceleration Company for the Promotion of the Speed of Literature. Thomas Moore. OBCoV

Loud in my ear: screams. Tōge Sankichi. PFTM-2, *tr.* by Richard H. Minear *Fr.* Poems of the Atomic Bomb.

Loud, louder still, resounds the thundering peal. Thunder Storm. Mary F. Johnson. CenSon

Loud midnight-soothing melancholy bird. Edward Moxon. CenSon

Loud Report through Lybian Cities goes, The. Virgil [*or* Vergil]. NPeEn; OBVE, *tr.* by John Dryden *Fr.* Aeneid [*or* Eneados, *Aeneis*], The.

Loud roars the wind that shakes this wall. Joanna Baillie. ECWP *Fr.* Night Scenes of Other Times.

Loud talk in the overlighted house. Ends. Robert Frost. TRP

Loud the storm is howling. Song of the Dogs, The. Sándor Petőfi. IQMS, *tr.* by George Sutherland Fraser

Loud the storm is howling. Song of the Wolves, The. Sándor Petőfi. IQMS, *tr.* by George Sutherland Fraser

Loud thunder. Muso Soseki. EaWin, *tr.* by W. S. Merwin

Loud Thundering Storm. *Unknown.*
    "Proud Queen of the Earth Gods, Supreme among the Heaven Gods." HW, *tr.* by Samuel Noah Kramer and Diane Wolkstein

Loud were they, loud, as they rode o'er the hill. Charms for a Sudden Stitch. *Unknown.* AnOE, *tr.* by Charles W. Kennedy

Loud wind. Leroy Gorman. HA

Loudens the sea-wind, downward plunge the bows. To D'Annunzio: Lines from the Sea. Robert Malise Bowyer Nichols. OBMV

Louder than gulls the little children scream. Beach, The. Robert Graves. OxBSP

Loudon Hill; or, Drumclog. *Unknown.* ESPB

Louerd, thu clepedest me. *Unknown.* MiEL

Louganis. Eloise Klein Healy. WiU

Lough Derg. Denis Devlin. BIrV; CIP-2

Louie the Tailor. Gary Pacernick [*or* Pacernik]. GotH

Louis Armstrong. Ernst Moerman. SeSe

Louis B. Russell. Bruce Guernsey. InPK-6

Louis, Louis, Louis, Louis. For Louis Armstrong, a Ju-Ju. Sarah Webster Fabio. SeSe

Louisa's Wedding. Tracy Philpot. AmPoNex

Louise. Richard A. Whiting. ReLy

Louise, have you forgotten yet. Old Loves. Henry Murger. AWP, *tr.* by Andrew Lang

Louise in Love. Mary Jo Bang. NAPBL

Louise on the Door-Step. Charles MacKay. EBVV

Louise peered into the corner of the cabinet. Dog Bark, The. Mary Jo Bang. NAPBL

Louisiana. Steve Crow. HATNAP

Louisiana Perch. Ron Padgett. FTOS

Louisville Lou (The Vampin' Lady). Milton Ager. ReLy

Lounge in the shade of the luxuriant laurel's. Anyte [or Anytes]. BoWoP

Lourenço Marques. Charles Eglington. PeSAV

Louse. Wolf Ehrlich [or Erlikh]. TCRP, tr. by Daniel Weissbort

Louse Hunting. Isaac Rosenberg. EBEV; FaBoWar; NAEL-5v2; NAEL-6v2; NoAM; NoP-4; OxAEP-2; OxBEV; OxBTC; PeFWW

Lousy in Center Field. James Tate. MoASP

"Lousyana was my home. So scram!" (LL) Melvin B. Tolson. BPo; NAAAL; TTY Fr. Harlem Gallery.

Louvres. Les A. Murray. BMAP

Love. Anna Andreyevna Akhmatova. TCRP, tr. by Daniel Weissbort

Love. Al-Abbas ibn al-Ahnaf. ArPe, tr. by Omar S. Pound

Love. "Angelus Silesius." GePo, tr. by George C. Schoolfield Fr. Cherubical Wanderer, The.

Love. Henry Baker. NOEC

Love. Robert Browning. EnLoPo Fr. Earth's Immortalities.

Love. Samuel Butler. TreFP

Love. Kelly Cherry. CRP

Love. Samuel Taylor Coleridge. GTBS-P; OBEV

Love. Abraham Cowley. AWP; BeJo; OBVE

Love. Roy Croft. ITBLP

(Why Do I Love You?) PoToHe

Love. Kahlil Gibran. GraLe

Love. Joan Gordon. Prnts

Love. George Granville [or Grenville], Baron Lansdowne. BoLoP

Love. George Herbert. ESCV; PeECV; Son

Love. Immanuel di Roma. TrJP, tr. by J. Chotzner

Love. Francis Jammes. AWP, tr. by Jethro Bithell

Love. Juan Ramón Jiménez. SpanPo, tr. by Angel Flores

Love. Hugh MacDiarmid. PoE

Love. George Peele. NOBE

Love. Samuele Romanelli. TrJP, tr. by A. B. Rhine

Love. Sappho. tr. by William Ellery Leonard

Love. Sir Walter Scott. OxAEP-2 Fr. Lay of the Last Minstrel, The.

Love. Samar Sen. WoPoe, tr. by Pritish Nandy

Love. William Shakespeare. See Merchant of Venice, The

Love. Otto Stoessl. AuPH, tr. by Lowell A. Bangerter

Love. Torquato Tasso. AWP, tr. by John Hermann Merivale

Love. Thomas Traherne. GeHe

Love ("Love is a funny thing.") Unknown. TTY

Love. Unknown. BlrV, tr. by John Montague

Love ("There's the wonderful love of a beautiful maid.") Unknown. SoSe-8

Love. Elolongue Epanya Yondo. NegPo, tr. by Ellen Conroy Kennedy

Love (3). George Herbert. AWP; BASC; BBASP; CABP; ChIV-2; ClHu; EBEV; ESCV; EnlH; FHYEP; FSCP; FaBoVe; GeHe; HeIP-4; InPK-6; InvLi; MeLP; NAEL-5v1; NAEL-6v1; NAEL-7v1; NOBE; NOCV; NOSC; NPeEn; NoP-4; OBEV; OBWVE; OxAEP-1; OxBEV; PBRV; PoPoPo; SCV; TFi; TOF; TrCP; WeW-3

Love a child is ever crying [or criing]. Mary Sidney Wroth, Countess of Montgomery. BASC; LW; NAEL-6v1; NAEL-7v1; NOSC; NoP-4; OxBEV Fr. Pamphilia to Amphilanthus.

Love / a Many Splintered Thing. Kevin Powell. InTrad

Love a woman? You're [or Y'are] an ass. Song. John Wilmot, 2d Earl of Rochester. NBLV; NOBL; NOSC; PeLV; WoPoe

Love Affair, A. Arnold Bennett. OxBTC

Love Affair 36. Jennifer Rankin. BMAP

Love: "Afternoon is offered to us, The." Oscar Cerruto. BLPSL, tr. by Rene de Costa, Rigas Kappatos and Eleni Paidoussi

Love Again. Philip Larkin. PoetW

Love, again sweetly streaming down. Alcman. SaLy, tr. by Diane Rayor

Love always repairs to the noble heart. Love and Nobility. Guido Guinicelli. NAWM-7v1, tr. by James J. Wilhelm

Love among Lepers. Richard Ronan. BodElec

Love among the Ruins. Robert Browning. FHYEP; HAP; NAEL-5v2; NAEL-6v2; NOBE; OBEV; SCGP

Love and Age. Thomas Love Peacock. NOBVV; OBEV Fr. Gryll Grange.

Love and Death. Byron. CAGL; EBEV; NOBE

Love and Death. Catullus. AWP, tr. by H.W. Garrod Fr. Carmina.

Love and Death: A Symphony. John Addington Symonds. CAGL "Thou dost establish—and our hearts receive." CAGL

Love and Debt Alike Troublesome. Sir John Suckling. CavPo

Love and Discipline. Henry Vaughan. GeHe; SacPr

Love and Folly. Jean de La Fontaine. AWP, tr. by William Cullen Bryant

Love and forgetting might have carried them. Two Look at Two. Robert Frost. MoAmPo

Love and Friendship. Emily Jane Brontë. EBVV; InPK-6; LW; PoBW

Love and Honour. Joseph Hilaire Pierre Belloc. SacPr

Love and Jealousy. William Walsh. BoLoP

Love and Knowledge. Robert Penn Warren. NAAL-5 Fr. Audubon: A Vision.

Love and Language. Louisa S. Guggenberger. NOBVV

Love and Liberation. John Hall Wheelock. MoAmPo

Love and Libery—A Cantata. Robert Burns. See Jolly Beggars, The

Love and Life. John Wilmot, 2d Earl of Rochester. BoLoP; EnLoPo; HAP; NOBE; NPeEn; OBEV; OxBEV

(Love and Life: A Song.) NOSC

Love and Life. Grace Buchanan Sherwood. NoP-4

Love and Life: A Song. John Wilmot, 2d Earl of Rochester. See Love And Life

Love and Life of Women, The. Night Café. Gottfried Benn. PFTM-1

Love and Lust. Isaac Rosenberg. TrJP

Love and Marriage. Sammy Cahn. ReLy

Love and Nobility. Guido Guinicelli. NAWM-7v1, tr. by James J. Wilhelm

Love and Poetry. Dante Alighieri. NAWM-7v1, tr. by James J. Wilhelm

Love and Sleep. Algernon Charles Swinburne. BoLoP; GSo; OxBSo

Love and thank you all for the best performance by a male. (LL) Up. Bill Kushner. GLP; ReTh

Love and the gentle heart are one same thing. Dante Alighieri. AWP; EaItPo, tr. by Dante Gabriel Rossetti Fr. La Vita Nuova.

Love and the gentle heart are one thing. Dante Alighieri. NAWM-7v1, tr. by Dino Cervigni and Edward Vasta Fr. La Vita Nuova.

Love, and the Gout invade the idle Brain. Remedia Amoris. Elizabeth Thomas. LW

Love and the Lady Lagia, Guido and I. Sonnet: On the Detection of a False Friend. Guido Cavalcanti. AWP; EaItPo, tr. by Dante Gabriel Rossetti

Love, and the thoughts that yearn for human kind. (LL) Samuel Taylor Coleridge. FHYEP; OBWP

Love at First Sight. Christopher Marlowe. NOBE Fr. Hero and Leander.

"Love at first sight," some say, misnaming. At First Sight. Robert Graves. FaBoEE; OxBSP

Love at Large. Coventry Patmore. EBVV; NOBVV Fr. Angel in the House, The.

Love at Sea. Algernon Charles Swinburne. AWP

Love at the closing of our days. Last Love. Fyodor [or Feodor] Ivanovich Tyutchev. BoLoP; WoPoe, tr. by Vladimir Vladimirovich Nabokov

Love at the Door. Meleager. AWP, tr. by John Addington Symonds

Love at the lips was touch. To Earthward. Robert Frost. APT-1; MoAmPo; NOBA; NoAM; NoP-4; OxBA; RaBo; TAP; TRP

Love, Attributed City. Nancy Morejón. TCLAP, tr. by Kathleen Weaver

Love bade me welcome: yet my soul drew back. Love (3). George Herbert. AWP; BASC; BBASP; CABP; ChIV-2; ClHu; EBEV; ESCV; EnlH; FHYEP; FSCP; FaBoVe; GeHe; HeIP-4; InPK-6; InvLi; MeLP; NAEL-5v1; NAEL-6v1; NAEL-7v1; NOBE; NOCV; NOSC; NPeEn; NoP-4; OBEV; OBWVE; OxAEP-1; OxBEV; PBRV; PoPoPo; SCV; TFi; TOF; TrCP; WeW-3

Love before Dinner. Alfred A. Yuson. ReBoTo

Love between women. Ordinary, as Love. Susan Griffin. GifTon

Love beyond Death. Francisco de Quevedo y Villegas. BLPSL, tr. by Rene de Costa, Rigas Kappatos and Eleni Paidoussi

Love Birds. Paul Henry. TCAWP

Love Bit, The. Joel Oppenheimer. PoM

Love—bittersweet, irrepressible. Sappho. BoWoP

Love, brave vertue's younger brother. Love's Horoscope. Richard Crashaw. MeLP

Love brought by night a vision to my bed. Lost Desire. Meleager. AWP, tr. by William M. Hardinge

Love brought me to a silent Grove. Upon Love. Robert Herrick. BeJo

Love built a stately house; where Fortune came. World, The. George Herbert. GeHe; NOSC

Love buries itself in me, up to the hilt. (LL) Renewal, A. James Merrill. OxBSP; VCAP

Love Burned Out the Light. Hala Mohammad. PoArWo, tr. by Cornelia Al-Khaled

Love, by sure proof I may call thee unkind. Sir Philip Sidney. Son Fr. Astrophil and Stella.

Love Calls Us to the Things of This World. Richard Wilbur. AmFaPo; HAP; HeIP-4; MoAmPo; NAAL-5; NIL-7; NIP-4; NoAM; PoE; PoRA; TAP; TFi; UnPo; VCAP; VGW

Love came along and said, "I know." Limits of Desire, The. Linda Gregg. ExTi

Love Came By from the Riversmoke. Stephen Vincent Benét. MoAmPo Fr. John Brown's Body.

Love can be a blessing. In Love In Vain. Leo Robin. ReLy

Love can be a moment's madness. Love. Hugh Martin. ReLy

Love cast! Meleager. GrAn

Love Charm, The. *Unknown.* STP, *tr.* by Jerome Rothenberg

Love-Charm Song. *Chippewa Oral Tradition.* NAAL-5

Love-Charms. Thomas Campion. *See* Thrice Toss[e] These Oaken Ashes in the Air [*or* Ayre]

Love Child—a Black Aesthetic. Everett Hoagland. BPo

Love comes along like a popular song. I Found a Million Dollar Baby (In a Five and Ten Cent Store) Harry Warren. ReLy

Love Constant beyond Death. Francisco de Quevedo y Villegas. WoPoe, *tr.* by W. S. Merwin

Love Constant beyond Death. Francisco de Quevedo y Villegas. AmFaPo, *tr.* by Willis Barnstone

Love Constraining to Obedience. William Cowper. NOCV *Fr.* Olney Hymns.

Love: "Dark falls on this mid-western town." Eavan Boland. HarvBoo

Love, Death, and Art. Agnes Mary Frances Robinson. VWP

Love delivers to me its sweetest thoughts. Petrarch. ErotSp, *tr.* by Sam Hamill

Love Deposed. Thomas Stanley. NOSC

Love. Desire is stronger than age. (LL) Antipater of Sidon. GrAn; PGA

Love Divine, All Loves Excelling. Charles Wesley. NOCV; SacPr

Love Dream Verse. Gabriella Leto. CItWP, *tr.* by Cinzia Sartini Blum and Lara Trubowitz

Love, drunk the other day, knocked at my breast. Dual, The. Richard Lovelace. CaPo

Love Enthroned. Richard Lovelace. CaPo

Love Equals Swift and Slow. Henry David Thoreau. TCAPo

Love essential unto youth. Ninety. Mary Elizabeth Fullerton. CBAP

Love Feast, The. W. H. Auden. OBCoV

Love fed Heliodora's fingernail and made. Meleager. HePo *Fr.* Epigrams.

Love Flows from God. Mechthild von Magdeburg. WPOW, *tr.* by Lucy Menzies

Love flows not from my liver but her living. George Chapman. OxBSo; Son *Fr.* Coronet for His Mistress Philosophy, A.

Love for a Hand. Karl Shapiro. CoAP

Love for Enjoying. James Shirley. BeJo

Love for Sale. Cole Porter. ReLy

Love: "Fragile as a spider's web." May Sarton. PoBW

Love from a Foreign City. Lavinia Greenlaw. EmeKit; MFPA

Love Ghost. Mimi Goese. HeMarv

Love, give me leave to serve thee, and be wise. Elegy, An. Thomas Randolph. BeJo; NOSC

Love gives away again to Fear. (LL) Master and Guest. Mary Elizabeth Coleridge. VWP; ViWPN

Love God and keep his commandments. (LL) Edgar Lee Masters. APT-1; IllVoic *Fr.* Spoon River Anthology.

Love-goddess, saviour / Of the sea-wrecked. *Unknown.* GrAn

Love grows alone (though my brain for counsel harrow). He Loves in Vain. Christian Hofmann von Hofmannswaldau. GePo, *tr.* by George C. Schoolfield

Love Guards [*or* Guides] the Roses of Thy Lips. Thomas Lodge. NoSic; Son *Fr.* Phyllis.

Love had socked me. Ridin' High. Cole Porter. ReLy

Love Has Eyes. William Forster. CBAP

Love has fooled us. Easy Come, Easy Go. Edward Heyman. ReLy

Love has found its awakening. (LL) This Morning. Kristina Rungano. HAWP; NAfrP

Love has found out how to mix. Asclepiades. GrAn; PGA

Love has its secrets, joy has its revealings. Love Secret, The. *Unknown.* AWP, *tr.* by Wilfrid Scawen Blunt

Love has made me tender. Never Swat a Fly. Ray Henderson. ReLy

Love has never read the Ave Maria. Love. Immanuel di Roma. TrJP, *tr.* by J. Chotzner

Love has pierced my heart with its flame. Alcuin. EroLit, *tr.* by John Boswell

Love has seven names. Hadewijch. BoWoP; WoPoe, *tr.* by Willis Barnstone and Elene Kolb

Love has subjugated me. Hadewijch. WPoS

Love hath so long possessed me for his own. Dante Alighieri. AWP; EaItPo, *tr.* by Dante Gabriel Rossetti *Fr.* La Vita Nuova.

Love, he is nearer (though the moralist). Love's Varlets. Francis Thompson. SacPr

Love he to morrow, who lov'd never. *Unknown.* OBVE *Fr.* Vigil of Venus, The.

Love held a harp between his hands, and, lo! Love's Music. Philip Bourke Marston. GSo

Love her he doesn't but the thought he puts. John Berryman. FaBoMo *Fr.* Dream Songs.

Love Her, Mind. Rāmprasād Sen. SinGod, *tr.* by Rachel Fell McDermott

Love, hide me in your breast. Ship of Love, The. Salma Khadra Jayyusi. MAP, *tr.* by Charles Doria and the author

Love holds my thoughts and feelings. Continues in the Same State of Feeling. Francisco de Quevedo y Villegas. BLPSL, *tr.* by Rene de Costa, Rigas Kappatos and Eleni Paidoussi

Love, how thou'rt tired out with rhyme! Margaret Lucas Cavendish, Duchess of Newcastle. EnLoPo

Love, I am sick for thee, sick with an absolute grief. Grief of Love, The. *Unknown.* AWP, *tr.* by Wilfrid Scawen Blunt

Love, I demand to have my lady in fee. Lapo Gianni. EaItPo, *tr.* by Dante Gabriel Rossetti

Love, I, in mine, celebrate the love-choir. (LL) Ovid in the Third Reich. Geoffrey Hill. CABP; FaBoMo; HP; HarvBoo; NPeEn; NoAM; OxBEV

Love I love whose lips I love, A. Accomplices, The. Conrad Potter Aiken. NOBA

Love, I think, is a disease. Maghnas O Domhnaill. NOIV

Love, if I could give you the eternal summer sun. Beijing Spring. Marilyn Chin. ExTi

Love: if I die don't take me to the cemetery. Life-Hook. Juana de Ibarbourou. TCLAP, *tr.* by Sophie Cabot Black and Maria Negroni

Love If This Is Love. Dacia Maraini. CItWP, *tr.* by Cinzia Sartini Blum and Lara Trubowitz

Love in a bungalow high on a hill. Cottage for Sale, A. Larry Conley. ReLy

Love, in a humour, played the prodigal. Michael Drayton. NoSic *Fr.* Idea.

Love in a Life. Robert Browning. FHYEP; NOBE; NOBVV; NPeEn; OxBEV

Love in a Village. Isaac Bickerstaffe.
"There was a jolly miller once." LB; OxNR

Love in a Warm Room in Winter. James Wright. OBAL

Love in America. Marianne Craig Moore. AiP; NIL-7

Love in Exile. Mathilde Blind.
"I charge you, O winds of the West, O." TrJP
"I was again beside my Love in a dream." ViWPN
"I would I were the glow-worm, thou the flower." ViWPN
"Thou walkest with me as the spirit-light." ViWPN

Love in fantastic [*or* fantastique] triumph sat [*or* sate *or* satt]. Aphra Behn. BASC; NALW; NOBE; NOSC; NPeEn; NoP-4; OBEV; OxAEP-1; OxBEV; PEW; WPE; WeW-3 *Fr.* Abdelazer.

Love in her sunny eyes does basking play. Abraham Cowley. MeLP *Fr.* Mistress, The.

Love in Labrador. Carl Sandburg. VGW

Love in May. Jean Passerat. AWP, *tr.* by Andrew Lang

Love in Mayfair. May Probyn. VWP

Love in my bosom[e] like a bee. Thomas Lodge. NOBE; NoSic; OBEV *Fr.* Rosalynde; or Euphues' Golden Legacy.

Love in silence shall. Meleager. GrAn

Love in the Classroom. Al Zolynas. BLT; LTA

Love in the peaceful u.s.a. Love U.S.A. Kathleen Spivack. BoWoP; LW

Love in the Valley. George Meredith. EBVV; NOBE; OBEV

Love in the Weather's Bells. Jay Wright. ESEAA

Love in Vain. Robert Johnson. UnPo

Love is a circle that doth restless[e] move. Love What It Is. Robert Herrick. FaBoEE

Love is a funny thing. Love. *Unknown.* TTY

Love is a green girl. Song. Michael Stillman. TLR

Love is a hovering, a deafening. Rear Window. Angela Shaw. NeAmPo

Love Is a Keeper of Swans. Humbert Wolfe. MoBrPo

Love Is a Many-Splendored Thing. Paul Francis Webster. ReLy

Love is a place. E. E. Cummings. FaBoEE

Love Is a Random Thing. George, Jr. Marion. ReLy

Love is a region full of fires. Description of Love, A. Sir John Beaumont. NOSC

Love is a secret feeding fire that gives all creatures. *Unknown.* OxBSP

Love Is a Sickness. Samuel Daniel. NOBE; OBEV *Fr.* Hymen's Triumph.

Love is a strange and powerful thing. Darn That Dream. Eddie DeLange. ReLy

Love is a twelve o'clock notion. Morning After, The. Dory Langdon Previn. ReLy

Love is a twin to death; it makes my senses dead. "Angelus Silesius." GePo, *tr.* by George C. Schoolfield *Fr.* Cherubical Wanderer, The.

Love is a universal migraine. Symptoms of Love. Robert Graves. BoLoP

Love is and was my Lord and King. Tennyson. CAGL; NAEL-6v2; NOBE; NOCV; OBEV; PeECV *Fr.* In Memoriam A. H. H.

Love is begot by fancy, bred. Love. George Granville [*or* Grenville], Baron Lansdowne. BoLoP

Love is best. (LL) Love among the Ruins. Robert Browning. FHYEP; HAP; NAEL-5v2; NAEL-6v2; NOBE; OBEV; SCGP

Love Is Enough. William Morris.
"Love is enough: though the World be a-waning." OBEV

Love is false, that he loves me is a lie.   Love Is False.   Kim Sang-yong.   WoPoe, *tr.* by Chung Chong-wha

Love is foolish which studies the skin.   Wrinkling Together.   Leo Vroman.   TuT, *tr.* by Anne Kennedy

Love Is Here to Stay.   George Gershwin.   ReLy

Love Is Just around the Corner.   Leo Robin.   ReLy

Love Is Kind.   Benjamin Keech.   PoToHe

Love Is Life.   Richard Rolle of Hampole.   SacPr

Love Is Life and Death.   Georg Rudolph Weckherlin.   GePo, *tr.* by George C. Schoolfield

Love is life that lasteth ay, ther it in Crist is fest.   Love Is Life.   Richard Rolle of Hampole.   SacPr

Love is like butter, Evans mused, and stuck.   Kingsley Amis.   NOBL   *Fr.* Evans Country, The.

Love is like the wild rose-briar.   Love and Friendship.   Emily Jane Brontë.   EBVV; InPK-6; LW; PoBW

Love is lovelier.   Second Time Around, The.   Jimmy Van Heusen.   ReLy

Love is no more.   Amor Vincit Omnia.   Edgar Bowers.   VCAP

Love Is Not.   Argentarius.   GrAn, *tr.* by Fleur Adcock

Love is not all: it is not meat nor drink.   Edna St. Vincent Millay.   APT-1; GSo; HAP; HeIP-4; NoAM; OxBA; Son; TAP

Love is not just a function of the eyes.   Love Is Not.   Argentarius.   GrAn, *tr.* by Fleur Adcock

Love is not will, it is fate.   Love Is Not Will but Destiny.   Juan de Tassis y Peralta, Count of Villamediana.   BLPSL, *tr.* by Rene de Costa, Rigas Kappatos and Eleni Paidoussi

Love is round like a seed or an egg.   Love Is Round.   Alicia Galaz Vivar.   TANSG, *tr.* by Oliver Welden

Love is soft, love is swete, love is goed sware.   Love Is Weal, Love Is Wo.   *Unknown.*   MiEL

Love Is Sweeping the Country.   George Gershwin.   ReLy

Love Is That Orbit.   George Henry Boker.   Son

Love is the blossom where there blows.   Giles Fletcher, the Younger.   OBEV   *Fr.* Christ's Victory and Triumph.

Love is the center and circumference.   What Love Is.   Ella Wheeler Wilcox.   PWR

Love is the end. (LL)   Resurgam.   Marjorie Lowry Christie Pickthall.   SacPr; TrCP

Love is the lesson which the Lord us taught. (LL)   Edmund Spenser.   ChIV-2; HAP; NAEL-5v1; NOCV; NoSic; PoE; SacPr; Son   *Fr.* Amoretti.

Love is the peace, whereto all thoughts do[e] strive.   Fulke Greville, 1st Baron Brooke.   NPeEn; NoSic   *Fr.* Caelica.

Love is the plant of peace and most precious of virtues.   William Langland.   NOBE   *Fr.* Vision of Piers Plowman, The.

(Love Is) The Tender Trap.   Sammy Cahn.   ReLy

Love Is the Thing.   Victor Young.   ReLy

Love is the whole and more than all. (LL)   My Father Moved through Dooms of Love.   E. E. Cummings.   ColAP; HAP; NAAL-2v2; NAAL-5; NOBA; NoAM; NoP-4; OxBA; TAP; UnPo; WoPoe

Love is too great a happiness.   Love.   Samuel Butler.   TreFP

Love is too young to know what conscience is.   William Shakespeare.   EBEV; HeIP-4; NoSic; OxAEP-1; PoE   *Fr.* Sonnets.

Love is unjust: justice is loveless. (LL)   Jacob.   Delmore Schwartz.   ChIV-1; TaR

Love Is Weal, Love Is Wo.   *Unknown.*   MiEL

Love is what lacks then: but what does it mean to you?   Remonstrance, A.   James Kenneth Stephen.   NOBVV

Love, it is night. The orb of day.   Passionate Professor, The.   Bert Leston Taylor.   NBLV

Love, it was good to talk to you tonight.   Rondeau after a Transatlantic Telephone Call.   Marilyn Hacker.   ColAP; NoAM

Love itself shall slumber on. (LL)   To ———: "Music, when soft voices die."   Shelley.   AWP; FHYEP; GTBS-P; HeIP-4; NAEL-5v2; NAEL-6v2; NOBE; OBEV; OxAEP-2; OxBEV; OxBSP; TFi

Love Lament.   *Vietnamese Oral Tradition.*   CaDao, *tr.* by John Balaban

Love leave to urge, thou know'st thou hast the hand.   Mary Sidney Wroth, Countess of Montgomery.   BASC; Son   *Fr.* Pamphilia to Amphilanthus.

Love-Lesson, A.   Clément Marot.   AWP, *tr.* by Leigh Hunt

Love Letter.   Carole C. Gregory Clemmons.   BlSi

Love Letter.   Sylvia Plath.   LW; NOBA

Love Letter.   Katayoon Zandvakili.   AmPoNex

Love-letter, A.   Mary E. Tucker.   CBWP-1

Love-Letter-Burning.   Daniel Hall.   NoP-4

Love Letter to Elizabeth Thatcher, A.   Thomas Thatcher.   SCAP

Love Letters.   Josephine D. Henderson Heard.   CBWP-4; SWaP

Love Letters.   Lotte Kramer.   Prnts

Love Letters of the Dead.   Douglas Street.   FaBoWar

Love Letters to Her Who Lives [Alas!] Away.   Nell Altizer.
   Sonnet 2: "My own heart let me have. More pity on."   FFC

Love like a jugler, comes to play his prize [*or* prise].   Mary Sidney Wroth, Countess of Montgomery.   EMWP   *Fr.* Pamphilia to Amphilanthus.

Love, like a mountain-wind upon an oak.   Love.   Sappho.   AWP, *tr.* by William Ellery Leonard

Love long dormant showing itself.   Palais des Arts.   Louise Glück.   VCAP

Love-lorn Maid, at some far distant time, A.   William Wordsworth.   CenSon   *Fr.* River Duddon [A Series of Sonnets], The.

Love-lorn microbe met by chance, A.   Microbe's Serenade, The.   George Ade.   OBAL

Love, love, a lily's my care.   Words for the Wind.   Theodore Roethke.   CoAP; NOBA

Love: "Love can be a moment's madness."   Hugh Martin.   ReLy

Love, love, love, love.   That's My Weakness Now.   Sam H. Stept.   ReLy

Love, love today, my dear.   Song.   Charlotte Mew.   MoBrPo

Love ("Love was before the light began").   *Unknown.*   AWP   *Fr.* Thousand and One Nights, The.

Love, love! What nonsense it is.   Natalya [*or* Natal'ia] Gorbanevskaya [*or* Gorbanyevskaya *or* Gorbanevskaia].   WPOW

Love, love, what wilt thou with this heart of mine?   Rondel.   Jean Froissart.   AWP, *tr.* by Henry Wadsworth Longfellow

Love Made in the First Age[: To Chloris].   Richard Lovelace.   BeJo; CaPo; NAEL-5v1; NAEL-6v1; NAEL-7v1

Love Making.   James Tate.   SPE

Love Me.   Amal Moussa.   PoArWo, *tr.* by Khaled Mattawa

Love Me!   Stevie Smith.   OxBSP

Love me broughte.   Christ's Love-Song.   *Unknown.*   MiEL

"Love me, for I love you"—and answer me.   Christina Georgina Rossetti.   OxBSo; Son   *Fr.* Monna Innominata.

Love me in another's body. (LL)   Before Your Waking.   Anna Gréki.   HAWP; WPOW, *tr.* by Anita Barrows

Love Me Little, Love Me Long.   Robert Herrick.   CaPo; SCGP

Love me, Love me, I cried to the rocks and the trees.   Love Me!   Stevie Smith.   OxBSP

Love me no more, now let the god depart.   Edna St. Vincent Millay.   HeIP-4

Love Me, O Love.   Sir Philip Sidney.   HeIP-4

Love Me or Leave Me.   Walter Donaldson.   ReLy

Love me, Sweet, with all thou art.   Man's Requirements, A.   Elizabeth Barrett Browning.   RACG; ViWPN

Love me with the left hand.   Light Woman's Song, The.   Judith Johnson Sherwin.   TAP

Love Medicine, A.   Louise Erdrich.   HATNAP

Love mocks us all. Then cast aside.   Horace.   AWP, *tr.* by Austin Dobson   *Fr.* Odes.

Love much. Earth has enough of bitter in it.   Ella Wheeler Wilcox.   PoToHe

Love Necessitates.   Eugene B. Redmond.   ISC

Love Nest, The.   Louis A. Hirsch.   ReLy

Love never asks what right and wrong may be.   On Love of the Homeland.   Ernst Waldinger.   AuPH, *tr.* by George C. Schoolfield

Love not a loveliness too much.   Ownership.   Lizette Woodworth Reese.   MoAmPo

Love Notes.   Jennifer Strauss.   BMAP

Love now no fire hath left him.   Out of the Italain.   Giambattista [*or* Giovanni Battista] Marino.   OBVE, *tr.* by Richard Crashaw

Love of a woman, The.   Air.   Robert Creeley.   VCAP; VGW

Love of Boys, The.   Solon.   CAGL, *tr.* by John Addington Symonds

Love of Christ, The.   John Austin.   SacPr

Love of Fame, the Universal Passion.   Edward Young.   OBSV
   "Languid lady next appears in state, The."   NPeEn

Love of God, unutterable and perfect, The.   Dante Alighieri.   EnlH   *Fr.* Divina Commedia.

Love of Hell, The.   Abraham Burstein.   TrJP

Love of King David and Fair Bethsabe.   George Peele.   See David and [Fair] Bethsabe

Love of my heart, living death, I await in vain your written word and I think with the dying flower, that if I live without myself I want to lose you.   Federico García Lorca.   CAGL, *tr.* by David William Foster   *Fr.* Sonetos del Amor Oscuro [Sonnets of Dark Love].

Love of my life came not, The.   Deep-Sea Pearl, The.   Edith Matilda Thomas.   PoBW

Love of Nature, The.   Mark Akenside.   NOEC   *Fr.* Pleasure of Imagination, The.

Love of Our Country, The.   Evan Evans.
   "Whatever clime we travel or explore."   AngWePo

Love of the Quartz Pebble, The.   Vasco [*or* Vasko] Popa.   PoSu, *tr.* by Anne Pennington   *Fr.* Quartz Pebble, The.

Love, of this clearest, frailest Glass.   In a Glass-Window for Inconstancy.   Edward Herbert, 1st Baron Herbert of Cherbury.   OxBSP

Love of women leaves me cold; desire, The.   *Unknown.*   CAGL, *tr.* by Daryl Hine

Love, oh love, oh careless love.   Careless Love.   *Unknown.*   UnPo

Love on a day (wise poets tell). How Violets Came Blue. Robert Herrick. BeJo; CaPo; TTTS

Love on the Farm. D. H. Lawrence. CABP; MoBrPo; NAEL-5v2; NAEL-6v2; NoAM; NoP-4; SCGP

Love (1). George Herbert. GeHe; Son

Love only reading unto me this art. (LL) Sir Philip Sidney. NAEL-7v1; NoSic *Fr.* Astrophil and Stella.

Love opened a vista rare with stars. Love's Vista. Henrietta Cordelia Ray. CBWP-3

Love or Fame. Caroline Lindsay. VWP

Love plays a lute, and Thought an organ grand. Two Musicians, The. Henrietta Cordelia Ray. CBWP-3

Love Poem. Roque Dalton. AF, *tr. by* Richard Schaaf

Love-Poem. Fêng Mêng-lung. ChiP, *tr. by* Arthur Waley

Love Poem. John Forbes. BMAP

Love Poem. Denise Levertov. NIL-7

Love Poem. Audre Lorde. GLP; NoAM; PoBW

Love Poem. Barbara J. Orton. NeAmPo

Love Poem. Linda Pastan. NIL-7; NIP-4

Love Poem. Norman Henry Pritchard, II. GT

Love Poem, A. John Ashbery. HCAP

Love Poem, A. Vagura. WoPoe, *tr. by* Peter Dent and Edwin Gerow

Love Poem, A. Vidya. WoPoe, *tr. by* Peter Dent and Edwin Gerow

Love Poem, The. Andrew Elliott. PNI

Love Poem for a Wife, 2. A. K. Ramanujan. OMIP; WoPoe

Love Poem for My Country, A. Frank Mkalawile Chipasula. HBAPE; NAfrP

Love Poem for Three for Kaye & Me. Gregory Corso. PmAP

Love Poem: "In your quest or request God is remote." Huda Na'mani. BBASP; MAP, *tr. by* Samuel Hazo and Lena Jayyusi

Love Poem: "My clumsiest dear, whose hands shipwreck vases." John Frederick Nims. IllVoic; InPK-6

Love Poem: "Olfactory paradise." E. K. Caldwell. PasH

Love Poem: "Rain smell comes with the wind." Leslie Marmon Silko. UnPo; VoR

Love Poems. Jack Spicer.
    "Sable arrested a fine comb." FTOS

Love Poems of Marichiko, The. Kenneth Rexroth.
    "As I came from the." APSN
    "As the wheel follows the hoof." APSN
    "Chilled through, I wake up." APT-2
    "Come to me, as you come." APSN
    "Did you take me because you loved me?" APSN; APT-2
    "Every morning, I." APSN; APT-2
    "Fires / Burn in my heart." APSN
    "Frost covers the reeds of the marsh." APSN
    "Half in a dream." APSN; APT-2
    "How long, long ago." APSN
    "How many lives ago." APSN; APT-2
    "I am sad this morning." APSN
    "I cannot forget." APSN; APT-2
    "I hate this shadow of a ghost." APT-2
    "I hold your head tight between." APSN; APT-2
    "I pass the day tense, day-." APSN
    "I scream as you bite." APSN; APT-2
    "I sit at my desk." APSN; APT-2
    "I wish I could be." APSN; APT-2
    "If I thought I could get away." APSN
    "In the park a crow awakes." APSN
    "It is the time when." APSN
    "Just us. / In our little house." APSN
    "Let us sleep together here tonight." APSN
    "Lying in the meadow, open to you." APSN
    "Night is too long to the sleepless, The." APT-2
    "Night without end. Loneliness." APSN; APT-2
    "Now the fireflies of our youth." APSN
    "Oh the anguish of these secret meetings." APSN; APT-2
    "On the bridges / And along the banks." APSN
    "Once I shone afar like a." APSN
    "Scorched with love, the cicada." APSN
    "Some day in six inches of." APSN; APT-2
    "Spring is early this year." APSN
    "This flesh you have loved." APSN; APT-2
    "Two flowers in a letter." APSN
    "Uguisu sing in the blossoming trees." APT-2
    "Uguisu sleeps in the bamboo grove, The." APSN
    "Who is there? Me." APSN

    "Without me you can only." APSN; APT-2
    "You ask me what I thought about." APSN; APT-2
    "You wake me, / Part my thighs, and kiss me." APSN
    "Your tongue thrums and moves." APSN; APT-2

Love-Poems of the Sixth Dalai Lama. Tsangyang Gyatso.
    "I sought my lover at twilight." WoPoe, *tr. by* Brian Cutillo and Rick Fields
    "Lover met by chance on the road." WoPoe, *tr. by* Brian Cutillo and Rick Fields
    "White teeth smiling." WoPoe, *tr. by* Brian Cutillo and Rick Fields
    "Wild horses running in the hills." WoPoe, *tr. by* Brian Cutillo and Rick Fields

Love poured her beauty into my warm veins. (LL) Fragment of a Sonnet. Pierre de Ronsard. AWP; OBVE, *tr. by* Keats

Love-prone Asclepias with eyes like a summer's day. Meleager. HePo *Fr.* Epigrams.

Love, Reason, Hate, did once bespeak. Barley-Break , A. Sir John Suckling. BASC; CaPo; CavPo

Love Redeemed. "William Baylebridge."
    "Quiet moon, immaculate of face, The." CBAP

Love Rejected. Lucille Clifton. BPo

Love Returned. Bayard Taylor. CAGL

Love rises up some days. "Michael Field." VWP

Love's a baby dat grows up wild. Dat's Love (Habanera). Georges Bizet. ReLy

Love's Advocate. Phoebe Hesketh. LW

Love's Alchemy [*or* Alchemie]. John Donne. BASC; ESCV; NAEL-5v1; NAEL-6v1; NAEL-7v1; NoP-4; PoE

Love's an headstrong wild desire. Love. Henry Baker. NOEC

Love's Clock. Sir John Suckling. CaPo; NOSC

Love's Compensation. Voltairine de Cleyre. SWaP

Love's Constancy. Hadewijch. WPoS, *tr. by* Oliver Davies

Love's Cure. Francis Beaumont.
    Song: "Turn, turn thy beauteous face away." NOSC

Love's Deity [*or* Deitie]. John Donne. AWP; ESCV; SoSe-8

Love's domain, supernal Zion. Kingsley Amis. NOBL *Fr.* Evans Country, The.

Love's Emblem. John Clare. NIL-7; NIP-4

Love's Emblems. John Fletcher. BoLoP; NOBE; NOSC *Fr.* Tragedy of Valentinian, The.

Love's Ending. *Unknown.* NoSic

Love's Entreaty. Michelangelo Buonarroti. AWP, *tr. by* John Addington Symonds

Love's Epitaph. William Cavendish, Duke of Newcastle. OxBSP

Love's Farewell. Michael Drayton. GTBS-P *Fr.* Idea.

Love's Farewell. Edmund Waller. OxBSo

Love's Fidelity. Petrarch. AWP; HAP; NoSic; OxBSo, *tr. by* Henry Howard, Earl of Surrey *Fr.* Sonnets to Laura.

Love's Flight. Else Lasker-Schüler. TrJP, *tr. by* Jethro Bithell

Love's Fool. Margit Szécsi. IQMS, *tr. by* Kenneth McRobbie

Love's Force. Thomas Carew. CaPo

Love's Glory. Fulke Greville, 1st Baron Brooke. Son *Fr.* Caelica.

Love's Growth. John Donne. ESCV; NOSC; NPeEn
    (I scarce beleeve my love to be so pure.) PBRV
    (I scarce believe my love to be so pure.) NoP-4

Love's Guerdons. Edith Nesbit. NOBVV

Love's hidden pearl is shining yet. Hafiz [*or* Hafez]. TOF

Love's Horoscope. Richard Crashaw. MeLP

Love's Hue and Cry. James Shirley. BeJo

Love's in the daily doings. Here. Glenna Luschei. GeoHom

Love's Innocence. Thomas Stanley. BeJo

Love's Justification. Michelangelo Buonarroti. AWP; OBVE, *tr. by* William Wordsworth
    (To the Marchesana of Pescara.) CTC

Love's Labour's Lost. William Shakespeare.
    Blossom, The. OBEV
    Heavenly Rhetoric, The. Son
    (Hiems.) AWP; FaBoCh; InPK-6; NOBE; NoSic; PoRA
    "Holla, Approach." NPeEn
    "If she be made of white and red." CTC
    (Love's Perjuries.) GTBS-P
    "O! And I forsooth in love!" OBCoV
    ('On a day—alack the day!') AEP
    Spring. HAP; InPK-6; NAEL-5v1; NAEL-6v1; NBLV; NIL-7; NIP-4; NOBE; NoSic; OBEV; PAI; PoRA; SCGP; TFi; UnPo
    (When Daisies Pied.) NoP-4
    ("When Dasies pied, and Violets blew.") OxBEV

Winter. ClHu; GTBS-P; HAP; MakPoe; NAEL-5v1; NAEL-6v1; NIL-7; NIP-4; NoP-4; OBEV; OxBEV; PAI; SCGP; TFi; TRP; UnPo; WeW-3

Love's Last Lesson. Letitia [or Laetitia] Elizabeth Landon. RWP

Love's Last Resource. Sadi [or Saadi or Sa'di]. AWP, tr. by L. Cranmer-Byng Fr. Gulistan, The.

Love's Martyrs. John Ford. NOBE; NOSC Fr. Broken Heart, The.

Love's martyrs must be ever, ever dying. (LL) John Ford. NOBE; NOSC Fr. Broken Heart, The.

Love's Matrimony. William Cavendish, Duke of Newcastle. NOSC

Love's Maturity. Hadewijch. WPoS, tr. by Oliver Davies

Love's memories haunt my footsteps still. John Clare. NOBVV

Love's Mirror. Constance Naden. VWP; ViWPN

Love's Mourner. Augusta Davies Webster. VWP; ViWPN Fr. Mother and Daughter.

Love's multitudinous boneyard. Jack Kerouac. NeAP Fr. Mexico City Blues.

Love's Music. Philip Bourke Marston. GSo

Love's Mystery. Joseph Beaumont. NOSC

Love's night and a lamp. Meleager. BoLoP; GrAn; WoPoe, tr. by Peter Whigham

Love's Not Time's Fool. William Shakespeare. See Sonnets

Love's Offence. Sir John Suckling. CaPo; NOSC

Love's Omnipresence. Joshua Sylvester. See "Were I as Base as Is the Lowly Plain."

Love's Pains. John Clare. NOBVV

Love's pallor and the semblance of deep ruth. Dante Alighieri. AWP; EaItPo, tr. by Dante Gabriel Rossetti Fr. La Vita Nuova.

Love's Parallel. Elizabeth Garrett. MFPA

Love's Perjuries. William Shakespeare. See Love's Labour's Lost

Love's Philosophy. Shelley. BoLoP; FHYEP; GTBS-P; OxAEP-2; PoToHe; SCGP

Love's Progress. John Donne. BASC Fr. Elegies.

Love's Remorse. Edwin Muir. OxBTC

Love's Resume. Heinrich Heine. See Rose, die Lilie, die Taube, die Sonne, Die

Love's Résumé. Heinrich Heine. TrJP, tr. by J. F. C.

Love's Secret. William Blake. EnLoPo; ITBLP; NOBE; NPeEn; OxBEV; SCGP
  (Never Pain to Tell Thy Love.) NAEL-5v2; NAEL-6v2

Love's Siege. Sir John Suckling. CaPo; NPeEn
  ('Tis now, since I sate down before.) CavPo

Love's Sun. William Cavendish, Duke of Newcastle. NOSC

Love's the boy stood on the burning deck. Casabianca. Elizabeth Bishop. FaBoWP; NIL-7; OxBSP; WoPoe

Love's thrice a robber, however you take it. On Love. Diophanes of Myrina. WoPoe, tr. by Dudley Fitts

Love's Triumph must be Honour's Funeral. (LL) Loving and Beloved. Sir John Suckling. BeJo; CaPo; CavPo; NAEL-5v1; NAEL-6v1; NAEL-7v1

Love's Varlets. Francis Thompson. SacPr

Love's Vista. Henrietta Cordelia Ray. CBWP-3

Love's Votary. George Augustus Simcox. NOBVV

Love's Witness. Aphra Behn. BoWoP; LW

Love's worshipers alone can know. Love and Folly. Jean de La Fontaine. AWP, tr. by William Cullen Bryant

Love Says. Daria Menicanti. CItWP, tr. by Cinzia Sartini Blum and Lara Trubowitz

Love Secret, The. Unknown. AWP, tr. by Wilfrid Scawen Blunt

Love seeketh not Itself to please. William Blake. EnLoPo; FHYEP; NAEL-5v2; NAEL-6v1; NOBE; NPeEn; NoP-4; OxAEP-2; OxBEV; OxBSP; PoE; RB; SCGP; SCV; TFi Fr. Songs of Experience.

Love Serviceable. Coventry Patmore. EnLoPo Fr. Angel in the House, The.

Love set them going, our mothers. Sunday. Achy Obejas. WiU

Love set you going like a fat gold watch. Morning Song. Sylvia Plath. BoWoP; ColAP; HCAP; HarvBoo; HeIP-4; InPK-6; ItWoWo; LCAP-2; NAAL-2v2; NAAL-5; NIL-7; NIP-4; NOBA; NoP-4; PoPoPo; VCAP

Love shook my senses. Sappho. SaLy, tr. by Diane Rayor

Love, since it is thy will that I return. Dante Alighieri. EaItPo, tr. by Dante Gabriel Rossetti

Love Sleeping. Plato. AWP; FaBoEE, tr. by Thomas Stanley

Love so alike, that none do slacken, none can die. (LL) Good-Morrow, The. John Donne. AWP; BASC; BoLoP; CaPo; ClHu; EBEV; ESCV; EnLoPo; FHYEP; FSCP; FaBoVe; MeLP; NAEL-5v1; NAEL-6v1; NAEL-7v1; NAWM-5v1; NIL-7; NOSC; NoP-4; OxAEP-1; OxBEV; PoE; PoRA; SCV; SoSe-8; TFi

Love Song. Rofel G. Brion. ReBoTo

Love Song. Joseph Brodsky. BAP-97

Love Song. Jaufré Rudel. NAWM-7v1, tr. by Roy Rosenstein and George Wolf

Love-Song. Else Lasker-Schüler. TrJP, tr. by Jethro Bithell

Love Song. Marilyn Nelson. ExTi

Love Song. Unknown. BoWoP, tr. by Reza Baraheni and Zahra-Soltan Shokoohtaezeh

Love Song. Unknown. BoWoP; WoPoe, tr. by Ulli Beier and H. Gaden

Love Song. Unknown. See If I Might Be an Ox

Love Song, A. Lindiwe Mabuza. HAWP

Love-song: "Beautiful, delicate bright gazelle, The." Walter James Turner. OBMV

Love Song: "Beautiful is she, this woman." Unknown. AWP, tr. by Constance Lindsay Skinner Fr. Three Songs from the Haida.

Love Song: "By the fierce flames of love I'm in a sad taking." Royall Tyler. TAP

Love Song: "Clouds circle the moon." Ma Chih-yüan. CrYelRi, tr. by Sam Hamill

Love Song: "Come to me in the night—we shall sleep closely together [or Let us sleep entwined]." Else Lasker-Schüler. BoWoP; TrJP

Love Song: "Do not love me, my friend." Flavien Ranaivo. PBA
  (Common Lover's Song, The.) NegPo, tr. by Ellen Conroy Kennedy
  (Do not love me, cousin.) NegPo, tr. by Ellen Conroy Kennedy

Love Song: "Early I rose." Unknown. AWP, tr. by Mary Austin

Love Song: "Fondling and snuggling." Kuan Yün-shih. CrYelRi, tr. by Sam Hamill

Love Song for Chrysokomos (Goldenlocks). Angelo [or Andrea] Poliziano. CAGL, tr. by James J. Wilhelm Fr. Greek Epigrams.

Love Song for Difficult Times. Maria Elena Cruz Varela. VCWP, tr. by Mairym Cruz-Bernal

Love Song for Marcus, A. Pacifico Massimi. CAGL, tr. by James J. Wilhelm Fr. Hecateleguim.

Love Song: "For what as easy." W. H. Auden. PeLV Fr. Five Songs.

Love Song for Words. Nazik Al-Mala'ika. MAP, tr. by Christopher Middleton and Matthew Sorenson

Love Song: I and Thou. Alan Dugan. AmFaPo; InPK-6; NoAM

Love Song: "I love you, I love you, is my song." Pablo Neruda. ErotSp; GifTon, tr. by William O'Daly

Love Song: "I passed by the house of the young man who loves me." Unknown. TTY, tr. by J. E. Manchip White

Love Song: "I will walk into some one's dwelling." Unknown. APN-2, tr. by Henry Rowe Schoolcraft

Love Song: "Lazy flowers brew honey for the bees." Hu Chih-yu. CrYelRi, tr. by Sam Hamill

Love Song: "Let my sweet song be pleasing unto Thee." Judah Halevi. TrJP, tr. by Nina Davis Salaman

Love Song: "Like pain of fire runs down my body my love to you, my dear!" Unknown. APN-2, tr. by Franz Boas Fr. Songs of the Kwakiutl Indians.

Love Song: "Little sycamore, The." Unknown. TTY, tr. by J. E. Manchip White

Love-Song: "Little wild birds have come flying, The." Unknown. AWP, tr. by W. R. S. Ralston

Love Song: "Long closed door, oh open it again, The." Judah Al-Harizi. TrJP, tr. by Emma Lazarus

Love Song: "My boat sails downstream." Unknown. TTY, tr. by J. E. Manchip White

Love Song: "My love is a lotus blossom." Unknown. TTY, tr. by J. E. Manchip White

Love Song: "My loved one is unique, without a peer." Unknown. TTY, tr. by J. E. Manchip White

Love Song of Audrey. Jim Shepard. Unle

Love Song of J. Alfred Prufrock, The. T. S. Eliot. APT-1; AWP; AmFaPo; ClHu; ColAP; EBEV; HAP; HarvBoo; HeIP-4; InPK-6; MakPoe; MoAmPo; NAAL-2v2; NAAL-5; NAEL-5v2; NAEL-6v2; NAWM-7v2; NIL-7; NOBA; NOBE; NPeEn; NoAM; NoP-4; OxAEP-2; OxBEV; OxBTC; PoE; PoPoPo; PoRA; SoSe-8; TAP; TCAPo; TFi; TRP; TwCP; WeW-3; WoPoe

Love Song of J. Alfred Prufrock, The. J. Walker. PeLi

Love Song of Tommo Frogley. Roger Crawford. UV

Love Song: "On the hill tops I visit the snares." Unknown. PeNZ, tr. by Margaret Orbell

Love Song: "One with eyes the fairest." Euripides. AWP Fr. Cyclops, The.

Love Song: "Orioles and orioles." Ch'iao Chi. CrYelRi, tr. by Sam Hamill

Love Song: "Out of the blackthorn hedges." Ivor Gurney. EnLoPo

Love Song: "See'st thou o'er my shoulders falling." Judah Halevi. TrJP, tr. by Emma Lazarus

Love Song: "She is a reed swaying in blue." Earle Thompson. HATNAP

Love Song: "Sweep the house clean." William Carlos Williams. MoAmPo; SAmP

Love Song: "That haughty tyranny of thine." Luís De León. TrJP, tr. by Thomas Walsh

Love Song: "There is a strong wall about me to protect me." Mary Carolyn Davies. LW

Love Song: "Though to think / Rejoiceth me." Margot Ruddock. OBMV

Love Song: "Tiny children." Yityangu Ejong. CBAP, *tr.* by Frank Wordick

Love Song to Eohippus. Peter Viereck. MoAmPo

Love Song to King Shu-Suen. Kubatum. WPOW, *tr.* by Thorkild Jacobsen

Love Song to the Foal-Hide Flask. Mihály Csokonai Vitéz. IQMS, *tr.* by Thomas Kabdebo and Valerie Becker Makkai

Love Song: "You've got nice knees." Gavin Ewart. OxBTC

Love Song: "Your handkerchief should be blue." *Unknown.* BoWoP, *tr.* by Reza Baraheni and Zahra-Soltan Shokoohtaezeh

Love Songs. Mina Loy. VGW; WPE

Love-songs, at Once Tender and Informative. Samuel Hoffenstein. OBAL "Your little hands." NBLV; OBCoV; TrJP

Love Songs in Age. Philip Larkin. OxBEV

Love Songs of Corca Bascinn. James Liddy. History. CIP-2

Love Sonnet. John Updike. Son

Love Sonnet, A. George Wither. *See* I Loved a Lass

Love Sonnets. Zora Cross. CBAP

Love Sonnets of Proteus, The. Wilfrid Scawen Blunt. As to His Choice of Her. GSo; Son Depreciating Her Beauty. OBMV Farewell to Juliet. "I see you, Juliet, still, with your straw hat." BoLoP; EnLoPo; OxBTC St. Valentine's Day. EnLoPo Woman with a Past, A. Son

Love steals unheeded o'er the tranquil mind. Tyranny of Love, The. Mary Robinson. CenSon; RWP

Love steered my course, while yet the sun rode high. Giovanni Boccaccio. AWP; EaItPo, *tr.* by Dante Gabriel Rossetti *Fr.* Sonnets.

Love still a boy, and oft a wanton is. Sir Philip Sidney. Son *Fr.* Astrophil and Stella.

Love still has something of the sea. Song. Sir Charles Sedley. NOBE; OxAEP-1; OxBEV

Love Story, A. Robert Graves. FaBoTw; NAEL-5v2; NAEL-6v2

Love struck into his life. Dove-Breeder, The. Ted Hughes. PAI

Love Suicides at Sonezaki, The. Chikamatsu Monzaemon. Journey, The. WoPoe, *tr.* by Donald Keene

Love supreme, a love supreme, A. (LL) Dear John, Dear Coltrane. Michael S. Harper. ISC; NAAL-5; NIL-7; NIP-4; VCAP

Love, take off your bandana. Sunken Road, Antietam 1980, The. Gregory Orfalea. GraLe

Love taking leave, my heart then leaveth me. Maestro Migliore. EaItPo, *tr.* by Dante Gabriel Rossetti

Love-Talker, The. "Ethna Carbery." WPE

Love that a reign of terror struck dumb. Poem for a New Year. Rachel Wetzsteon. NeAmPo

Love that breeds, The. Unbosoming. "Michael Field." VWP

Love, That Doth Reign and Live Within My Thought. Henry Howard, Earl of Surrey. GSo; NAEL-6v1; NAEL-7v1; NoP-4

Love, That Doth Reign [or Raine] and Live Within My Thought. Petrarch. HeIP-4; NAEL-5v1; OBVE, *tr.* by Henry Howard, Earl of Surrey *Fr.* Sonnets to Laura.

Love, that drained her, drained him she'd loved, though each. Turtle Dove, The. Geoffrey Hill. FaBoTw; OxBEV

Love that is alone with love. Love and Language. Louisa S. Guggenberger. NOBVV

Love that is hoarded, moulds at last. Song. Harold C. Sandall. PoToHe

Love that is not pardoned, A. Doors. Tom Clark. CoAmPo

Love That's Pure, Itself Disdaining. Johann A. Gruber. AH, *tr.* by Sheema Z. Buehne

Love the drill, confound the dentist. Saint's Logic. Linda Gregerson. ExTi

Love, the great master of true eloquence. Love. Torquato Tasso. AWP, *tr.* by John Hermann Merivale

Love, the Light-Giver [or To Tommaso de' Cavalieri]. Michelangelo Buonarroti. AWP, *tr.* by John Addington Symonds

Love the Wild Swan. Robinson Jeffers. APT-1; MoAmPo; NoAM; Son

Love thee? Yes, I'm sure I love thee. City by the Sea, The. Josephine D. Henderson Heard. CBWP-4

Love, thou art absolute sole lord. Richard Crashaw. BASC; EBEV; ESCV; FSCP; GeHe; HAP; MeLP; NOBE; NoP-4; NOSC; OBEV; OxBEV *Fr.* Hymn to the Name and Hono[u]r of the Admirable Saint[e] Teresa, A.

Love thou art absolute, sole Lord. Richard Crashaw. SacPr *Fr.* In Memory of the Vertuous and Learned Lady Madre de Teresa that Sought an Early Martyrdome.

Love thou saist. John Milton. TOF *Fr.* Paradise Lost.

Love thy God and love Him only. Reality. Sir Aubrey De Vere. SacPr

Love Thy Neighbor. Harry Revel. ReLy

Love Thy Neighbour. D. H. Lawrence. ChIV-2

Love, to give law unto his subject hearts. Sir Thomas Wyatt. ChIV-1 *Fr.* Penitential Psalms.

Love to gyve law unto his subject hertes. Introductory Poem to the Penitential Psalms. Sir Thomas Wyatt. SacPr

Love to Hermes, Aphrodite the friend, The. (LL) To the Fair Clarinda [or Clorinda], Who Made Love to Me, Imagined [or Imagin'd] More Than Woman. Aphra Behn. BASC; CABP; EMWP; NALW; NIL-7; NoP-4; PEW; PoBW

Love, Today My Lip. Cristina Campo. CItWP, *tr.* by Cinzia Sartini Blum and Lara Trubowitz

Love Triumphant. Dryden. "As, when some treasurer lays down the stick." NOSC Prologue to "Love Triumphant." OxBoLi

Love tunes my Heart just to my strings. (LL) Love. Abraham Cowley. AWP; BeJo; OBVE

Love Turned the Light Out. John Latouche. ReLy

Love, 20c the First Quarter Mile. Kenneth Fearing. HAP; WoPoe

Love twists. Pressures, The. Imamu Amiri Baraka. BPo

Love (2). George Herbert. GeHe; Son

Love U.S.A. Kathleen Spivack. BoWoP; LW

Love Undeclared. *Unknown.* MiEL

Love Unexpressed. Constance Fenimore Woolson. APN-2

Love Unfeigned. Geoffrey Chaucer. NOBE; OBEV *Fr.* Troilus and Criseyde [or Criseide].

Love unreturn[e]d, howe'er [how ere] the flame. Constancy[e]. Sidney Godolphin. BeJo; NOSC

Love versus Learning. Constance Naden. VWP; ViWPN

Love was alone with love. And there was nothing I could do about it. Love was. Matter. Carla Harryman. FTOS

Love was before the light began. *Unknown.* AWP *Fr.* Thousand and One Nights, The.

Love was late in coming, and coming. "Rachel" [or "Rahel"]. FIT, *tr.* by Robert Friend

Love, we curve downwards, we are set to night. After Midsummer. Edith Jay Scovell. OxBTC

Love we thought would never stop, The. Ending. Gavin Ewart. NBLV; OxBSP; SoSe-8

Love, Weeping, Laid This Song. Lizette Woodworth Reese. APN-2

Love What and thou? A vain thought. Mary Sidney Wroth, Countess of Montgomery. NAEL-5v1; NAEL-6v1; NAEL-7v1; NoP-4 *Fr.* Urania.

Love What It Is. Robert Herrick. FaBoEE

Love Which Frees. Gloria Fuertes. WPOW, *tr.* by Philip Levine

Love Who Will, for I'll Love None. William Browne. NOSC

Love, Whose Month Was Ever May. Ulrich von Liechtenstein. AWP, *tr.* by Jethro Bithell

Love, Why Don't You Come. *Unknown.* WoPoe, *tr.* by Kevin O'Rourke

Love will expire; the gay, the happy dream. Procrastination. George Crabbe. NOBRP

Love Will Find Out the Way. *Unknown.* FaBoCh; OBEV (Great Adventure, The.) GTBS-P (He will find out his way.) (LL) GTBS-P

Love will not have me cry. Canzonetta: He Will Neither Boast nor Lament to His Lady. Jacopo da Lentino. AWP, *tr.* by Dante Gabriel Rossetti

Love winged my hopes and taught me how to fly. Icarus. *Unknown.* OBEV

Love without Hope is like Breath without Air. To Colinda. Elizabeth Thomas. LW

Love wooing Honour, Honour's love did win. Love and Honour. Joseph Hilaire Pierre Belloc. SacPr

Love you alone have been with us. Jelaluddin [or Jalal al-Din] Rumi. EaWin, *tr.* by Talat Sait Halman and W. S. Merwin

Love you dare but look I find, To. To Cleon's Eyes. Martha Sansom. ECWP

Love, you have struck me straight, my Lord! Resolution. Charles Leo O'Donnell. SacPr

Love, You've Been a Villain. James Robinson Planché. NOBL

Love, you were dying and one came and drew. Picture, A. "Michael Field." VWP

Love Your Enemy. Yusef Iman. BPo; GI; TTY

"Love, / your mother" / Which is Naomi. (LL) Kaddish. Allen Ginsberg. HCAP; NAAL-2v2; NOBA; NeAP; PmAP; PoM

Love-Poem: "Yours is the face that the earth turns to me." Kathleen Jessie Raine. LW; MoBrPo

Love? Too dangerous. Fourth Wish. Alberta Turner. LCAP-2

Love? We should smother it. Ruth Miller. LW *Fr.* Aspects of Love.

Loved by thee. (LL) Woman's Last Word, A. Robert Browning. NAEL-5v2; NAEL-6v2; RACG

Loved of My Soul. Israel Najara. TrJP, *tr.* by Nina Davis Salaman

Loved, on a sudden thou didst come to me. "Michael Field." VWP; ViWPN

Loved Once. Elizabeth Barrett Browning. ViWPN

Loved One, The.   Evelyn Waugh.
  "They told me, Francis Hinsley, they told me you were hung."   OBCoV
Loved [or Lov'd] I not Hono[u]r more. (LL)   To Lucasta, [on] Going to the
  War[re]s.   Richard Lovelace.   AWP; BASC; BeJo; CABP; CaPo; CavPo;
  ClHu; EnLoPo; FaBoWar; GTBS-P; HAP; InPK-6; MeLP; NAEL-5v1;
  NAEL-6v1; NAEL-7v1; NIL-7; NIP-4; NOBE; NOSC; NPeEn; NoP-4;
  OBEV; OBWP; OxAEP-1; OxBEV; OxBSP; PAI; PBRV; PoE; PoPoPo;
  PoRA; SCGP; SCV; TFi; UV; WeW-3
Loved stream, that meanders along.   Sir John Carr.   NOEC   Fr. Derwent; an
  Ode.
Loveless and sleepless the sea. (LL)   Silence Wager Stories.   Susan Howe.
  BodElec; FTOS
Loveliest flowers, though crooked in their border.   Gardener.   Robert Graves.
  OBGa
Loveliest girl in Vienna, The.   Alma.   Tom Lehrer.   NBLV
Loveliest of Pies.   Peter De Vries.   OBAL
Loveliest of trees, the cherry now.   A. E. Housman.   AWP; ChAP; ClHu; HAP;
  InPK-6; MakPoe; MoBrPo; NAEL-6v2; NoAM; NoP-4; OxBTC; PoE;
  PoPoPo; RB; SCGP; SoSe-8; TFi; WeW-3
Loveliest of what I leave.   Adonis, Dying.   Praxilla.   WPOW, tr. by Richard
  Lattimore
Lovelight.   Gysbert Japicx.   WoPoe, tr. by Rod Jellema
Loveliness.   Christopher Smart.   NOCV   Fr. Hymns for the Amusement of
  Children.
Loveliness beyond words.   Bihari.   ErotSp, tr. by Sam Hamill
Loveliness of Love, The.   George Darley.   See It Is Not Beauty I Demand
Lovely.   Erin Belieu.   ExTi
Lovely! all the essential parts.   These Purists.   William Carlos Williams.
  OBAL
Lovely cherries on the tree.   Adjectives.   Moishe Nadir.   TrJP, tr. by Joseph
  Leftwich
Lovely Childhood.   Gottfried Benn.   PFTM-1
Lovely companionship of school, lovely those days.   Thoughts on
  Schoolchildren.   Ahmad Shauqi.   MAP, tr. by M. Mustafa Badawi and
  John Heath-Stubbs
Lovely courier of the sky.   Anacreon's Dove.   Samuel Johnson.   AWP
Lovely Étan, The.   Unknown.   NOIV
Lovely fairy! Charming sprite!   Ode Composed in Sleep, An.   Judith Madan.
  ECWP
Lovely grapes and apples.   Tabernacle Thought, A.   Israel Zangwill.   TrJP
Lovely hill-torrents are.   Song.   Walter James Turner.   MoBrPo
Lovely interlude.   I'm in the Mood for Love.   Dorothy Fields.   ReLy
Lovely Is the Modest Girl.   Unknown.   SuSp, tr. by Wu-Chi Liu
Lovely Lady.   Tu Fu.   CoBCP, tr. by Burton Watson
Lovely, lasting peace of mind!   Hymn to Contentment, A.   Thomas Parnell.
  NOEC
Lovely Leda.   Yaroslav [or Iaroslav] Vasilevich Smelyakov [or Smeliakov].
  TCRP, tr. by Simon Franklin and Albert C. Todd
Lovely Love, A.   Gwendolyn Brooks.   BPo; NAAAL
Lovely Maya, Hermes' mother.   Barnabe Barnes.   NoSic   Fr. Parthenophil and
  Parthenophe.
Lovely Monster.   Joyce Mansour.   SurWo, tr. by Guy Flandre and Peter Wood
Lovely Morning Thought.   Arthur Rimbaud.   SxFrPo, tr. by Martin Sorrell
Lovely Pamela, who found.   Epitaph on a Party Girl.   Richard Usborne.
  FaBoEE; OBCoV
Lovely Rose Is Sprung, A.   Unknown.   AWP, tr. by Margarete Münsterberg
Lovely Shall Be Choosers, The.   Robert Frost.   MoAmPo; NOBA; OxBA; PoE
Lovely spot which thou dost see, The.   Upon a Mole in Celia's Bosom.
  Thomas Carew.   BeJo
Lovely Spring breeze has come, The.   Spring Day on West Lake.   Ou-yang
  Hsiu.   OHPC, tr. by Kenneth Rexroth
Lovely spring night, A.   Basho.   SoOfWa, tr. by Sam Hamill
Lovely Stuff.   Diane Ward.   PmAP
Lovely to be.   Bouquet of Objects, A.   Elaine Equi.   PmAP
Lovely to Look At.   Dorothy Fields.   ReLy
Lovely viper, haste not on.   Song of the Cannibals, A.   Anne Finch, Countess
  of Winchilsea.   PoE
Lovely was the night in May.   Postillion, The.   Nikolaus Lenau.   AuPH, tr. by
  Winthrop H. Root
Lovely whore though.   Cathleen.   Unknown.   BIrV, tr. by Thomas MacIntyre
Lovely world of cottages.   Victory at Guernica, The.   Paul Eluard.   SurPaPo,
  tr. by Mary Ann Caws
Lovely Young Moor, A.   Unknown.   BoWoP, tr. by Willis Barnstone
Lovepoem Writing Me.   Madeline J. Tiger.   MiVo
Lover, The.   Coventry Patmore.   OxAEP-2   Fr. Angel in the House, The.
Lover and Philosopher.   Sir William Davenant [or D'Avenant].   NOBE; OBEV
  (Philosopher and the Lover; To a Mistress Dying, The.)   NPeEn
  (To a Mistress Dying.)   SacPr
Lover and the Syringa-Bush, The.   Herman Melville.   OBAL

Lover, Come Back to Me!   Sigmund Romberg.   ReLy
Lover Compareth Himself to the Painful Falconer, The.   Unknown.   NoSic
Lover Complaineth the Unkindness of His Love, The.   Sir Thomas Wyatt.   See
  My Lute, Awake!
Lover Digresses, The.   Luis Cernuda.   CAGL, tr. by Rick Lipinski
Lover for Shamefastness Hideth His Desire within His Faithful Heart.   Petrarch.
  NPeEn, tr. by Sir Thomas Wyatt   Fr. Sonnets to Laura.
Lover in Winter Plaineth for the Spring, The.   Unknown.   See Western Wind
Lover is a slender, glowing urn, A.   Fantastic Simile, A.   Thomas Lovell
  Beddoes.   Son
Lover Man.   James Cushing.   SeSe
Lover met by chance on the road.   Tsangyang Gyatso.   WoPoe, tr. by Brian
  Cutillo and Rick Fields   Fr. Love-Poems of the Sixth Dalai Lama.
Lover Mourns for the Loss of Love, The.   W. B. Yeats.   WeW-3
Lover of Blue Writing above the Sea, The.   Ghada Al-Samman.   PoArWo, tr.
  by Saad Ahmed and Miriam Cooke
Lover of Love.   Hagiwara Sakutaro.   PFTM-1
Lover of Mountains.   Muso Soseki.   EaWin, tr. by W. S. Merwin
Lover of Rain in an Inkwell, The.   Ghada Al-Samman.   PoArWo, tr. by Miriam
  Cooke and Richard McKane
Lover's Appeal, The.   Sir Thomas Wyatt.   EnLoPo; GTBS-P; NAEL-5v1;
  NoSic; SCGP
  (And wilt thou leave me thus?)   NAEL-6v1; NAEL-7v1
Lover's Arithmetic, The.   Unknown.   OxBoLi; PeLV
Lover's Confession, A.   Charles, Duc d' Orléans.   See My Ghostly Fader
Lover's death, how regular, The.   Stark Major.   Hart Crane.   FuPo
Lover's Farewell, The.   George Moses Horton.   NAAAL
Lover's Journey, The.   George Crabbe.
  "It is the soul that sees; the outward eyes."   OxAEP-1
Lover's Leap; a Tale, The.   Andrew Macdonald.   NOEC
Lover's Lullaby, A.   George Gascoigne.   See Lullaby [or Lullabie] of a Lover,
  The
Lover's Meeting.   Ray Mathew.   CBAP
Lover's Melancholy, The.   John Ford.
  Dawn.   OBEV
Lover's Plea, A.   Thomas Campion.   See Shall I Come, Sweet Love
Lover's Posy, The.   Rufinus.   AWP, tr. by W. H. D. Rouse
Lover's Prize, A.   Beatrice [or Beatritz or Beatriz], Countess de Die [or Dia].
  EroLit; NAWM-7v1, tr. by Peter Dronke
Lover's Progress, The.   John Fletcher.
  Dead Host's Welcome, The.   OxAEP-1
Lover's quarrel will never rest his roots, A. (LL)   Cosmos in London.   Arthur
  Nortje.   HBAPE; PeSAV
Lover's Question, A.   James Baldwin.   GLP
Lover's Reply to Good Advice.   Richard Hughes.   MoBrPo
Lover's Resolution, A.   George Wither.   See Fair Virtue, the Mistress of
  Philarete
Lover's Return.   Langston Hughes.   SAmP
Lover's Return on a Bicycle, The.   J. Gordon Coogler.
  "Her charming steel-horse could not miss."   VerBaPo
Lover Showeth How He Is Forsaken of Such as He Sometime Enjoyed, The.
  Sir Thomas Wyatt.   ClHu; EnLoPo; HAP; HeIP-4; InPK-6; MakPoe;
  NAEL-5v1; NPeEn; NoSic; OxBC; OxBEV; PoE; PoRA; SCGP; SCV; TFi;
  TRP
  (Remembrance.)   BoLoP; NOBE; WoPoe
  (They fle from me that sometyme did me seke.)   PBRV
  (They Flee from Me.)   NAEL-6v1; NAEL-7v1; NIL-7; NoP-4; PoPoPo
  (They Flee from Me, That Sometime Did Me Seek.)   CABP
  (They flee from me, that sometime me did seek.)   WoPoe
  (Vixi Puellis Nuper Idoneus.)   OBEV
Lover that Durst Not Speak to His M[istress], A.   James Shirley.   NOSC
Lover; a Ballad, The.   Lady Mary Wortley Montagu.   ECWP; NAEL-5v1;
  NAEL-6v1; NAEL-7v1; NoP-4; OxBEV; PEW
Lover to His Lady, The.   Plato.   CTC; FaBoEE; NoSic, tr. by George
  Turberville
Lover under Suspicion.   Ádám Pálóczi Horváth.   IQMS, tr. by John Gordon
  Nichols
Lover, upon an Accident Necessitating His Departure, Consults with Reason, A.
  Thomas Carew.   CaPo
Lover, Whose Mistress Feared a Mouse, Declareth That He Would Become a
  Cat if He Might Have His Desire, The.   George Turberville.   TriCat
Loverd, thou clepedest me.   Wait a Little!   Unknown.   NOCV
Lovers.   Witter Bynner.   APT-1
Lovers.   "Michael Field."   PoBW; ViWPN
Lovers, The.   David Campbell.   BMAP   Fr. Ku-ring-gai Rock Carvings.
Lovers, The.   Geoffrey Holloway.   NLP
Lovers, The.   Dorianne Laux.   BodElec; ErotSp
Lovers, The.   William Robert Rodgers.   BIrV; OxBSP; PNI

Lovers, The. Jaime Sabines. TCLAP, *tr.* by Claudine-Marie D'Angelo

Lovers, The. William Jay Smith. MoAmPo

Lovers, The. Marya Alexandrovna Zaturenska. MoAmPo

Lovers become quiet. Lovers, The. Jaime Sabines. TCLAP, *tr.* by Claudine-Marie D'Angelo

Lovers, continual lovers, only repay me. (LL) City of Orgies. Walt Whitman. APN-1; CAGL; ErotSp

Lovers depend on moonlight. It All Depends on You. Ray Henderson. ReLy

Lovers' Duet. Wendy Lee. PasH

Lovers, fresh plighting lovers in our age. Lovers. "Michael Field." PoBW; ViWPN

Lovers How They Come and Part. Robert Herrick. OxBSP; OxBoLi

Lovers in ladies' magazines. Song. Thomas McGrath. VGW

Lovers in the act dispense. Thieves, The. Robert Graves. BoLoP; GTBS-P

Lovers in the rain and flowers in the stall. Another Song about Paris. Dave Frishberg. ReLy

Lovers in Winter. Robert Graves. FaBoEE

Lovers' Infiniteness[e]. John Donne. ESCV; MeLP; NOSC

Lover's Lament *or* The Willows by the Water Side, A. *Unknown.* AWP, *tr.* by H. J. Spinden

Lovers may find similitudes. Cascade, The. Edgell Rickword. FaBoTw

Lovers of Achilles, The. Sophocles.
    "This disease is an evil bound upon the day." EroLit, *tr.* by Anne Carson

Lovers of the Poor, The. Gwendolyn Brooks. ESEAA; IllVoic; LCAP-2; LTA; NAAL-2v2; NOBA; NoAM
    (Arrive. The Ladies from the Ladies' Betterment League.) NAAAL; SSLK

Lovers' Song. Kofi Awoonor. PBMAP *Fr.* Three Poems from Rediscovery (1964).

Lovers who are young indeed, and wish to know the sort of life. Love, You've Been a Villain. James Robinson Planché. NOBL

Lovers whose lifted hands are candles in winter. For a Child Expected. Anne Ridler. SacPr

Loves and sorrows of those who lose an orchard. Lost Orchard, The. Edgar Lee Masters. ColAP

Loves Lives beyond the Tomb. John Clare. FHYEP
    (Song: Love Lives beyond the Tomb.) NoP-4

Loves of the Fishes, The. Oppian. NPeEn *Fr.* Halieutica.

Loves of the Plants, The. Erasmus Darwin. *Fr.* Botanic Garden, The.

Loves of the Puppets. Richard Wilbur. OxBC

Loves of the Tortoise, The. Oppian. NPeEn, *tr.* by William Diaper *Fr.* Halieutica.

Loves that ended long ago. Streets. Henrik Nordbrandt. VCWP, *tr.* by Henrik Norbrandt and Alexander Taylor

Loves Victory. Aurelian Townshend [*or* Townsend]. MeLP

Lovesickness: A Medieval Text. Jack Coulehan. BloBone

Lovesickness is like a creditor. Tune: "Clear River, a Prelude"—Lovesickness. Hsü Tsai-ssu. SuSp, *tr.* by Sherwin S. S. Fu

Lovesickness— / What is the cure? Ma Chih-yüan. SuSp *Fr.* Tune: "Song of Shou-yang."

Lovesight. Dante Gabriel Rossetti. EBVV; GTBS-P; NAEL-5v2; NAEL-6v2 *Fr.* House of Life, The.

Lovesleep, The. Gavin Ewart. OxBC

Lovest Thou Me? William Cowper. ChIV-2 *Fr.* Olney Hymns.

Lovey Joe, a boy I know, an expert judge of gals. Magnolia. Ray Henderson. ReLy

Loving Again. Gloria Wade-Gayles. ISC

Loving along Western Rivers. Stephen J. Lyons. PasH

Loving and Beloved. Sir John Suckling. BeJo; CaPo; CavPo; NAEL-5v1; NAEL-6v1; NAEL-7v1

Loving and Liking [Irregular Verses Addressed to a Child]. Dorothy Wordsworth. SacPr; WoRP

Loving another, yet she married my father. Generations. Rachel [*or* Rokhl] Korn. CarOv, *tr.* by Carolyn Kizer

Loving in truth, and fain[e] in verse my love to show. Sir Philip Sidney. AWP; CABP; EBEV; HAP; NAEL-5v1; NAEL-6v1; NAEL-7v1; NPeEn; NoP-4; NoSic; OxAEP-1; OxBSo; PoE; SCGP; Son; TFi *Fr.* Astrophil and Stella.

Loving Mad Tom ("From the hag[g] and hungry [*or* hungrie] goblin.") *Unknown. See* Tom o' Bedlam's Song

Loving Mad Tom ("I'll bark against the Dog-star.") *Unknown.* NOSC

Loving old priceless things. Layman Makusho. ZenPo, *tr.* by Takashi Ikemoto and Lucien Stryk

Loving the rituals that keep men close. Palladas [*or* Pallades]. OBVE

Loving You. Frances Horovitz. LW

Loving you less than life, a little less. Edna St. Vincent Millay. NAAL-2v2

Loving you was all that really mattered. Where Are You? Harold Adamson. ReLy

Lovingly I turn me down. After Mass. "Michael Field." WPE

Low-Anchored Cloud. Henry David Thoreau. NCAP *Fr.* Week on the Concord and Merrimack Rivers, A.

Low and mournful be the strain. Ralph Waldo Emerson. APN-1; CBCWP

Low Barometer. Robert Bridges. CABP; NOCV; NoAM; SCGP

Low beating of the tom-toms, The. Danse Africaine. Langston Hughes. NAAAL

Low Bridge, Everybody Down. William S. Allen. *See* Erie Canal, The

Low Church. Stanley J. Sharpless. NBLV; OBCoV; PeLV

Low clouds yellow in a mist wind. First Movement. Padraic Fiacc. PNI

Low Fields and Light. W. S. Merwin. CoAmPo; LCAP-2

Low hang the eaves of the thatched hut. Tune: "Pure Serene Music" Rural Life. Hsin Ch'i-chi. ColAnChi, *tr.* by Jiaosheng Wang

Low huts, groans muffled. Thieves, The. Celia Gilbert. ChIV-1

Low in the eastern sky. To the Maiden in the East. Henry David Thoreau. OxBA

Low in the grave he lay—Jesus, my Saviour. Up from the Grave He Arose. Robert Lowry. SacPr

Low in thy grave with thee. David's Lament for Jonathan. Peter Abelard. NAWM-5v1

Low-Level Cross-Country. Howard Nemerov. GM

Low murmurs creep along the woody vale. Written at Bignor Park in Sussex, in August, 1799. Charlotte Smith. CenSon

Low river flows like smoked glass, The. Prayer for My Son. James Applewhite. BLT

Low sandy beach and the thin scrub pine, The. Cape Cod. George Santayana. APN-2

Low temple keeps its gods in the dark, A. Low Temple, A. Jejuri Arun Kolatkar. EmeKit

Low tide. Anita Virgil. HA

Low Tide on Grand Pré. Bliss Carman. NOBC

Low to High. Langston Hughes. APT-2

Low to the water's edge. Elegy on a Young Airedale Bitch Lost Two Years Since in the Salt-Marsh. Yvor Winters. APT-2

Low Trick, A. Frank Gelett Burgess. OBCA

Low Volume. Reiner Kunze. PoSu, *tr.* by Michael Hamburger

Low winter moon. Ruth Yarrow. HA

Low ye hills in ocean lie. My Heart Is in Merioneth. *Unknown.* OBWVE, *tr.* by Richard Llwyd

Lowell. James Russell Lowell. NOBA; OxBA; TAP; TCAPo *Fr.* Fable for Critics, A.

Lower East Side Poem, A. Miguel Piñero. PueRic

Lower East Side: The George Bernstein Story. Edward Field. OBCoV

Lower leaves of the trees, The. Sone Yoshitada. AmFaPo; OHMPJ, *tr.* by Kenneth Rexroth

Lower Life, The. May Kendall. VWP

Lower New York. George Cabot Lodge. APN-2

Lower the Standard: That's My Motto. Karl Shapiro. NoAM

Lower them and dream of home. (LL) Still Night Thoughts. Li Po. CoBCP; ColAnChi; TTTS, *tr.* by Burton Watson

Lowery Cot. Leonard Alfred George Strong. MoBrPo

Lowest circle of hell, The. Contrary to prevailing opinion it is inhabited. What Mr. Cogito Thinks about Hell. Zbigniew Herbert. VCWP; WoPoe, *tr.* by John Carpenter and Bogdana Carpenter

Lowest Place, The. Christina Georgina Rossetti. NOBVV

Lowest Trees Have Tops, The. Sir Edward Dyer. NoSic; OxBSP; RB
    (Modest Love, A.) SCGP

Lowlands. William Reed Huntington. APN-2

Lowlands. *Unknown.* OxBoLi

Lowlands o' [*or* of] Holland, The. *Unknown.* OxBB

Lowliest duties on herself [*or* itself] did lay, The. (LL) London 1802. William Wordsworth. AWP; HAP; HeIP-4; NAEL-5v2; NAEL-6v2; NIL-7; NIP-4; NOBRP; OxAEP-2; PoRA; SCGP; Son; TFi; UV

Loyal English Man's Wish for the Preserving of the King and Queen, The. Anne Morcott. EMWP

Loyal Housewife. Daisy Zamora. LoL, *tr.* by Margaret Randall

Loyal subject, thou, to that bright Queen, A. To W. L. G. on Reading His "Chosen Queen." Charlotte Forten. BlSi

Loyalty. Harvey Shapiro. TaR

Loyalty to the Flag. Lizelia Augusta Jenkins Moorer. CBWP-3

Lu Chi speaks of the heavenly arrow. Meditation on the Wen Fu. Eleanor Wilner. GifTon

Lu-lung Village, Autumn. Hsu Hsuan. CrYelRi, *tr.* by Sam Hamill

Lu wine like amber. In Reply When Lesser Officials of Chung-tu Brought a Pot of Wine and Two Fish to My Inn as Gifts. Li Po. CoBCP, *tr.* by Burton Watson

Luanda, you are like a white seagull. We Shall Return, Luanda. Ngudia Wendel. PBMAP

Luba. Jacqueline Goldberg.
    "I take on / her legacy." MirDau, *tr.* by Joanne Friedman

"Luba / conversation." MirDau, *tr.* by Joanne Friedman

"She does not speak." MirDau, *tr.* by Joanne Friedman

Lubin. *Unknown.* FaBoVe

Luca Signorelli to His Son. Eugene Lee-Hamilton. PeVV

Lucan's Pharsalia Book 1. Christopher Marlowe.

"This said, the restles generall through the darke." PBRV

Lucasia, Rosania and Orinda Parting at a Fountain, July 1663. Katherine Philips. EMWP; PEW

Lucasia's and Orinda's Name. (LL) Friendship in Emblem[e], or the Seal[e], to my dearest Lucasia. Katherine Philips. CABP; EMWP; PBRV

Lucasta, frown and let me die. To Lucasta: Her Reserved Looks. Richard Lovelace. CaPo

Lucasta Replies to Lovelace. Gilbert Keith Chesterton. UV

Lucasta's Fan[ne], with a Looking-Glass[e] in It. Richard Lovelace. CaPo

(Estrich, thou feather'd fool and easy prey.) CavPo

(Lucasta's Fan.) CavPo

Lucasta's World. Richard Lovelace. BeJo; CaPo

Lucent dew congeals into frost, The. Juan Chi. ColAnChi *Fr.* Songs of My Soul.

Lucent lake was lit with sheen, The. Thought of Lake Ontario, A. Henrietta Cordelia Ray. CBWP-3

Lucifer in Starlight. George Meredith. AWP; CABP; ChIV-1; EBVV; GSo; HAP; InPK-6; NAEL-5v2; NAEL-6v2; NOBE; NOBVV; NoP-4; OBEV; OxBEV; OxBSo; PoE; SCGP; Son; TFi; UnPo

Lucifer in the Train. Adrienne Rich. GM

Lucina, Care. Perses. GrAn

Lucinda Matlock. Edgar Lee Masters. HAP; IllVoic; MoAmPo; NOBA; NoAM; OxBA *Fr.* Spoon River Anthology.

Lucindy, who you 'spose I seed. Common Occurrence, A. Priscilla Jane Thompson. CBWP-2

Lucio. Frisbees on Light. Giulia Niccolai. CItWP, *tr.* by Cinzia Sartini Blum and Lara Trubowitz

Luck. Wilfrid Wilson Gibson. OBMV

Luck. Langston Hughes. APT-2; SAmP

Luck. Marc J. Straus. BloBone

Luck, Be a Lady. Frank Loesser. APT-2; ReLy

Luck has no songs, luck has no thoughts, luck has nothing. Pain. Edith Södergran. WPOW, *tr.* by Jaakko A. Ahokas

Luck is yours that you can talk about, The. Love Poem, A. Vidya. WoPoe, *tr.* by Peter Dent and Edwin Gerow

Luck of Edenhall, The. Ludwig Uhland. AWP, *tr.* by Henry Wadsworth Longfellow

Luck to the craft that bears this name of mine. To a Cape Ann Schooner. John Greenleaf Whittier. OxBSo

Luck, we've had it; our character the public's. It Did. Robert Lowell. NoAM

Luckies. Reginald Gibbons. IllVoic

Luckily for us. (LL) Humming-Bird. D. H. Lawrence. NoAM; OWoS; OxBEV; RB

Luckily my lover put out the fire in my stern. (LL) Fêng Mêng-lung. ColAnChi; WoPoe, *tr.* by Richard W. Bodman *Fr.* Mountain Songs.

Lucky 7. Katharine Harer. MiVo

Lucky Chance, The. Aphra Behn.

("O Love! that stronger art than wine.") LW

Song: "Oh! Love, that stronger art than wine." WPE; WPOW

Lucky Eugene. Michael Foley. PNI

Lucky Life. Gerald Stern. BodElec

"Dear waves, what will you do for me this year?" InvLad

Lucky life isn't one long string of horrors. Gerald Stern. BodElec

Lucky magpie, holy bird, what hateful lies you tell! Lady and the Magpie, The. *Unknown.* ChiP, *tr.* by Arthur Waley

Lucky Marriage, The. Thomas Blackburn. GTBS-P

Lucky my ears 'pop' at the hilltop. Ron Silliman. FTOS *Fr.* Hidden.

Lucky One, The. Reginald Shepherd. GT

Lucky ones with their shadows, The. (LL) Last One, The. W. S. Merwin. LCAP-2; NoAM; VGW

Lucky shepherd, if only on the hill. Crinagoras. GrAn

Lucky Spence's Last Advice. Allan Ramsay. NePenScot

Lucky Strikes. Ron Padgett. FTOS

Lucky the husband. Mabel Kelly. Turlough Carolan [or O'Carolan]. BIrV; CIP-2; OxBEV, *tr.* by Austin Clarke

Lucky to Be Me. Leonard Bernstein. ReLy

Lucky with day approaching, with leaning dawn. (LL) Wanderer, The. W. H. Auden. HarvBoo; NoAM; RB; WeW-3; WoPoe

Lucrece and Nara. Laura Riding Jackson. APT-2

Lucrece's Death. William Shakespeare. NoSic *Fr.* Rape of Lucrece, The.

Lucretius could not credit centaurs. Invitation to Juno. William Empson. FaBoMo

Lucretius felt the change of the world in his time, the great republic riding to the height. Prescription of Painful Ends. Robinson Jeffers. APT-1; MoAmPo; OxBA

Lucretius knew. De Natura Rerum. Yves Bonnefoy. VCWP, *tr.* by Lisa Sapinkopf

Lucretius versus the Lake Poets. Robert Frost. OBCoV

Lucy. William Wordsworth. FHYEP; NOBE; OBEV; SCGP; TFi

I Travelled among Unknown Men. AWP; GTBS-P; NAEL-6v2

Lucy. EBEV; NAEL-5v2; NOBE; NOBRP; OBEV; PoE

She dwelt among the untrodden ways. AWP; BoLoP; EnLoPo; GTBS-P; HAP; HeIP-4; NAEL-6v2; NIL-7; NIP-4; NPeEn; OxAEP-2; OxBSP; PAI; PWR; UV; UnPo; WeW-3

(Song.) NOBRP

Three Years She Grew. GTBS-P; HAP; NAEL-6v2

Lucy Ashton's Song. Sir Walter Scott. NAEL-6v2; NOBE; NPeEn; OBEV; OxAEP-2; OxBEV; OxBS; WoPoe *Fr.* Bride of Lammermoor, The.

Lucy goes down the celestial escalator in light. Lucy Taking Birth. Diana Scott. BrRo

Lucy Gray; or, Solitude. William Wordsworth. NAEL-5v2; NAEL-6v2; NOBRP; OxAEP-2

Lucy Lipschutz, Lucy Lipschutz. Girl Refugee, The. Matilde Salganicoff. MirDau, *tr.* by Celeste Kostopulos-Cooperman

Lucy Locket lost her pocket. Mother Goose. LB; OxBoLi; OxNR; ReMoGo

Lucy's Bones. Christine Evans. TCAWP

Lucy's Letter. James Berry. FaBoVe

Lucy Taking Birth. Diana Scott. BrRo

Lucy, you brightness[e] of our sphere [or spheare], who are. To Lucy, Countess[e] of Bedford, with Mr. Donnes Satire's [or Satyres]. Ben Jonson. BeJo; NAEL-6v1; NAEL-7v1

Lud! what a group the motley scene discloses! Oliver Goldsmith. OBSV *Fr.* Epilogue to "The Sister."

Lufthansa. John Tranter. BMAP; NOBAu

Lug us back lifeward—bone by infant bone. (LL) Hart Crane. NAAL-2v2; OxBA *Fr.* Bridge, The.

Lugs Benedict on the Coast, 1934. Tom Rea. GifTon

Lui et Elle. D. H. Lawrence. NoAM

Luini in porcelain! Ezra Pound. TCAPo *Fr.* Hugh Selwyn Mauberley (Life and Contacts).

Luis de Camões. Roy Campbell. FaBoTw; OxAEP-2

Luke 1:26–38; In the sixth month the angel Gabriel. Anna Kamienska. GI *Fr.* St. Luke.

Luke 1:39–56; In those days Mary arose. Rainer Maria Rilke. GI *Fr.* St. Luke.

Luke 2:8–20; And in that region there were shepherds. Bertolt Brecht. GI *Fr.* St. Luke.

Luke 2:1–7; In those days a decree went out from Caesar Augustus. Louise Glück. GI *Fr.* St. Luke.

Luke 2:21–40; And at the end of eight days, when he was circumcised. T. S. Eliot. GI *Fr.* St. Luke.

Luke 5:1–11; While the people pressed upon him. Czeslaw Milosz. GI *Fr.* St. Luke.

Luke 6:25. Francis Quarles. ChIV-2

Luke 6:39. William Carlos Williams. GI *Fr.* St. Matthew; He also told them a parable.

Luke 7; She Began to Wash His Feet with Teares and Wipe Them with the Haires of Her Head. Bible, *N.T.* NOSC; SacPr, *tr.* by Richard Crashaw *Fr.* St. Luke.

Luke 10. Richard Crashaw. SacPr

Luke 10:25–37; And behold, a lawyer. Stephen Mitchell. GI *Fr.* St. Luke.

Luke 10:38–42; Now as they went on their way. Anna Kamienska. GI *Fr.* St. Luke.

Luke 11: Blessed Be the Paps Which Thou Hast Sucked. Richard Crashaw. NAEL-7v1

Luke 15:11–19; And he said, "There was a man." Rainer Maria Rilke. GI *Fr.* St. Luke.

Luke 15:20–32; And he arose and came. Edwin Arlington Robinson. GI *Fr.* St. Luke.

Luke 16:19–26; "There was a rich man." Robert Frost. GI *Fr.* St. Luke.

Luke 16:1–9; He also said to the disciples. Ernesto Cardenal. GI *Fr.* St. Luke.

Luke XXIII. Jorge Luis Borges. GI, *tr.* by David Curzon

(Gentile or Hebrew or simply a man.) GI, *tr.* by David Curzon

(To sin, to the blood-stained gamble.) (LL) GI, *tr.* by David Curzon

Luke 23:26–38; And as they led him away. W. H. Auden. GI *Fr.* St. Luke.

Luke 23:39–43; One of the criminals. Jorge Luis Borges. GI *Fr.* St. Luke.

Luke 24:13–32; That very day two of them. Eric Pankey. GI *Fr.* St. Luke.

Luke 24:36–49; As they were saying this, Jesus. Alec Derwent Hope. GI *Fr.* St. Luke.

Luke Havergal. Edwin Arlington Robinson. APN-2; AWP; MoAmPo; NAAL-2v2; NAAL-5; NOBA; NoAM; TCAPo; TFi; UnPo

Luke Preach-Ill admires what we laymen can mean. Insatiable Priest, The. Matthew Prior. OxBSP

Lulee, lullay. Lullaby. Janet Lewis. NOCV

Lulla, la lulla, lulla lullaby. Lulla, My Sweet Little Baby. William Byrd. ChIV-2

Lulla, My Sweet Little Baby. William Byrd. ChIV-2

Lullabies, 2:174. *Unknown.* WoPoe, *tr. by* Keith Bosley *Fr.* Kanteletar, The.

Lullaby. William Barnes. SCGP

Lullaby. Breyten Breytenbach. VCWP, *tr. by* Breyten Breytenbach

Lullaby. Debra Gregerman. AmPoNex

Lullaby. Jon Mukand. BloBone

Lullaby. Joan Murray. YaYoPo

Lullaby. *Vietnamese Oral Tradition.* CaDao, *tr. by* John Balaban

Lullaby. Elolongue Epanya Yondo. NegPo, *tr. by* Ellen Conroy Kennedy

Lullaby, A. Lewis Carroll. *See* Alice's Adventures in Wonderland

Lullaby, A: "For wars his life and half a world away." Randall Jarrell. HCAP; OxBC

Lullaby: "Beloved, may your sleep be sound." W. B. Yeats. BoLoP; FaBoTw; OBMV

Lullaby: "Big as a down duvet the night." Molly Peacock. PasH

Lullaby: "But who killed Johannes, mama . . . ?" Jeremy Cronin. PeSAV

Lullaby: "Din of work is subdued, The." W. H. Auden. FaBoMo; GLP; NoAM

Lullaby for Ann-Lucian. Calvin Forbes. NBV

Lullaby for Mirjam. Richard Beer-Hofmann. AuPH, *tr. by* Naemah Beer-Hofmann

Lullaby for My Dead Child. Denise Jallais. BoWoP, *tr. by* Maxine W. Kumin and Judith Kumin

Lullaby for Rachael. James Simmons. PNI

Lullaby for Suzanne. Michael Stillman. TLR

Lullaby for the Hungry. Muhammad Mahdi Al-Jawahiri. MAP, *tr. by* Issa Boullata and John Heath-Stubbs

Lullaby: "Grown still loud voices of the day." Ferdinand von Saar. AuPH, *tr. by* Lowell A. Bangerter

Lullaby: "Hush, lullay." Léonie Adams. MoAmPo

Lullaby: "Hush ye, hush ye! honey, darlin'." Clara Ann Thompson. CBWP-2

Lullaby: "Lay your sleeping head, my love." W. H. Auden. GLP; HAP; HarvBoo; NAEL-5v2; NAEL-6v2; NOBE; NoAM; NoP-4; OxAEP-2; OxBEV; OxBTC; PoE; TFi; UnPo; WeW-3

   (Song XI: "Lay your sleeping head, my love") EnLoPo

Lullaby: "Lulee, lullay." Janet Lewis. NOCV

Lullaby, lullaby. / It is daybreak. Lullaby. *Unknown.* APN-2, *tr. by* Washington Matthews *Fr.* Mountain Chant, The.

Lullaby: "Lullee, lullay." Janet Lewis. CRP; NOCV

Lullaby: "Nocturnal, my panther, has eyes that spark, The." Tuvia Rivner. MHP, *tr. by* Ruth Finer Mintz

Lullaby: "O! hush thee, my darling, sleep soundly my son." *Unknown.* TrJP, *tr. by* Alice Lucas

Lullaby, O, lullaby! Thomas Hood. NBLV   *Fr.* Domestic Poems.

Lullaby of Birdland. George David Weiss. ReLy

Lullaby of Broadway. Harry Warren. ReLy

Lullaby of Donald Gorm, by his Nurse. *Unknown.* EMWP

Lullaby of the Onion. Miguel Hernández. AF, *tr. by* Robert Bly

Lullaby [*or* Lullabie] of a Lover, The. George Gascoigne. EBEV; HAP; NAEL-5v1; NAEL-6v1; SCGP

   (Gascoigne's Lullaby [*or* Lullabie].) NoP-4; NoSic

   (Lover's Lullaby, A.) OBEV

   (Sing lullaby, as women do.) NoP-4

Lullaby "Purple." Eve Merriam. NOxBChV

Lullaby: "Puva, puva, puva." *Unknown.* TTTS, *tr. by* Natalie Curtis

Lullaby: "Say to me: out there are only streets, and cars." Constance Merritt. AmPoNex

Lullaby: "Sky is letting its blue eyes close, The." Attila József. IQMS, *tr. by* Vernon Watkins

Lullaby: "Sleep and rain, two gangsters." Alan Michael Parker. AmPoNex

Lullaby: "Sleep, baby, sleep." *Unknown.* NOBE, *tr. by* Geoffrey Bownas

   (Nurse's Song) OTCP

Lullaby: "Sleep, my little baby, sleep." Samuel Hoffenstein. TrJP

Lullaby: "Someone would like to have you for her child." *Unknown.* TTTS; WoPoe, *tr. by* Kwabenia Nketia

Lullaby: "Though the world has slipped and gone." Dame Edith Sitwell. NALW

Lullaby Town. John Irving Diller. ITBLP

Lullaby: "Upon my lap my sovereign sits." Richard Verstegan [*or* Verstegen]. OBEV; SCGP

   (Our Lady's Lullaby.) SacPr

Lullaby: "You are safe / You are lying in a hammock." Alpay Ulku. AmPoNex

Lullabye for a Butch. Melinda Goodman. WiU

Lullay, by-by, lullay. (LL) Thys Endris Nyght. *Unknown.* EBEV; NOCV

Lullay, Lullay, Like a Child. John Skelton. NAEL-6v1; NAEL-7v1; NoSic; SCGP   *Fr.* Garland [*or* Garlande *or* Garlands] of Laurel[l], The.

Lullay, lullay, litel child, child reste thee a throwe. *Unknown.* MiEL

Lullay, lullay, litel child, why wepest thu so sore? *Unknown.* MiEL

Lullay, lullay, lully, lullay / The faucon hath born my make away. *Unknown. See* He bare him [*or* hym] up, he bare him [*or* hym] down

Lulled, at silence, the spent attack. Baggot Street Deserta. Thomas Kinsella. CIP-2; NoAM

Lulled by rumble, babble, beep. Manhattan Lullaby. Norma Farber. SSCS; TLR

Lullee, lullay. Lullaby. Janet Lewis. CRP; NOCV

Lulling me to sleep. Michael Dudley. HA

Lulls swears he is all heart, but you'll suppose. Upon Lulls. Robert Herrick. CaPo

Lully, Lulla. *Unknown.* TTTS

Lully, lullay, lully, lullay. Corpus Christi Carol, The. *Unknown.* MiEL; NAEL-5v1; NOBE; SCV

Lulu's Back in Town. Harry Warren. ReLy

Lumber of a London-going dray, The. Incident in the Early Life of Ebenezer Jones, Poet, 1828, An. Sir John Betjeman. NoAM

Lumbering tractor rolls its panting round, The. Agricultural Show, Flemington, Victoria, The. Suzanne Gardinier. CBAP

Lumbers the wain; and day fades out like smoke. (LL) Potato Harvest, The. Sir Charles G. D. Roberts. NIL-7; NOBC

Lumberyard, The. Ruth Herschberger. WPE

Lumens. Olga Broumas. ExTi

Luminous, The. Barbara Guest. PoM

Luminous blaze! Ode on Gas, An. *Unknown.* OBAL

Luminous cows, mysterious cows. Cows of Heaven, The. Saleem Barakat. MAP, *tr. by* Lena Jayyusi and Naomi Shihab Nye

Luminous, tranquil eyes. Madrigal 1. Gutierre de Cetina. BLPSL, *tr. by* Rene de Costa, Rigas Kappatos and Eleni Paidoussi

Luminous winds flicker in the moonrise. *Unknown.* SuSp *Fr.* Tzu-yeh Songs of the Four Seasons.

Luminously indiscreet; / Complete; continuous." (LL) Sermon on the Warpland, The. Gwendolyn Brooks. BPo; NOBA

Lumpish trollop!, The. Pastoral. Dominic Bevan Wyndham Lewis. UV

Lunar Baedeker. Mina Loy. APT-1; VGW

Lunar Eclipse. Harry Mathews. CoBCP, *tr. by* Burton Watson

Lunar Eclipse. Mei Yao Ch'en. CoBCP, *tr. by* Burton Watson

Lunar Eclipse. Tracy Ryan. NeBl

Lunar eclipse, and your solos spread, A. Blues Villanelle for Sonny Criss. Sascha Feinstein. AmPoNex

Lunar Frost. Mary Kinzie. IllVoic

Lunar Games, The. Eeva-Liisa Manner. WPOW, *tr. by* Jaakko A. Ahokas

Lunar Paraphrase. Wallace Stevens. SAmP

Lunatic of Lindley Meadow, The. August Kleinzahler. PmAP

Lunatic, the lover, and the poet, The. William Shakespeare. CTC *Fr.* Midsummer Night's Dream, A.

Lunatics. Bella [*or* Izabella] Akhatovna Akhmadulina. TCRusP, *tr. by* Daniel Weissbort

Lunch and Afterwards. Dannie Abse. BloBone

Lunch at the Coq d'Or. Peter Davison. TwCP

Lunch at The Mars. Question of Vitamins, A. Ron Charach. BloBone

Lunch in Nablus City Park. Naomi Shihab Nye. GraLe

Lunch with Girl Scouts. Sharon Bryan. ReTh

Lunch with Pancho Villa. Paul Muldoon. ModIr

Luncheon, A. Max Beerbohm. NOBL; OBSV; OxBTC; PeLV

   (Luncheon (Thomas Hardy Entertains the Prince of Wales), A.) UV

Luncheon on the Grass. Carl Phillips. AmFaPo

Lundys Letter, The. Gerald Dawe. BiHa

Lung Massif stands tens of thousands of feet. Lament for the People of Lung. P'i Jih-hsiu. SuSp, *tr. by* William H. Nienhauser

Lungi Crossing. Iyamide Hazeley. NAfrP

Lungs draw in the air and rattle it out again, The. Remorse. Sir John Betjeman. MoBrPo; OxBSP

Lungs of the wrinkled gray-eyed man, The. Refugee. Laila Halaby. PoArWo

Lurching from gloomy limousines we slip. My Father's Funeral. Karl Shapiro. TaR

Lure, 1963. Denise Riley. Oth

Lure of the night's dædalian sea-born breath. On an Æolian Harp. George Cabot Lodge. APN-2

Lurking under the maple trees. Jewish Cemetery at Olsany, Kafka's Grave, April, Sunny Weather, The. Miroslav Holub. PoSu

Luscious lobster, with the crabfish raw, The.   Kinds of Shel-fish.   William Wood.   SCAP

Lush grow the leaves on green stems.   In Praise of Carnations.   Wang Chi.   SuSp, *tr. by* Hellmut Wilhelm

Lush Life.   Billy Strayhorn.   ReLy

Lush, lush, fragrant grasses in autumn green.   Wang Wei.   CoBCP   *Fr.* Joys of the Country: Seven Poems.

Lusiads, The.   Luis de Camões [*or* Camões].   OBVE, *tr. by* Sir Richard Fanshawe

"Battle's uncertain work begins; and move."   FaBoWar, *tr. by* Richard Burton

"Feats of Arms, and famed heroick Host, The."   FaBoWar, *tr. by* Richard Burton

"Rev'rend Father stood inculcating, The."   PeSAV

"With glad reception our Commander meets."   FaBoWar, *tr. by* Richard Burton

Lusitanian Song.   János Vajda.   IQMS, *tr. by* Jean Overton Fuller

Lusitanian Variant, The.   H. C. ten Berge.

Dança Mortal.   TuT

Duel.   TuT

"Fortunes in knee breeches."   TuT

Luss! be for ever sunk beneath.   Mercury; on Losing My Pocket Milton at Luss near Ben Lomond, and Other Mountains.   Robert Andrews.   NOEC

Lust.   Star Black.   KGB

Lust in the long run spins a kingdom of lull.   Spider of Doubt.   Pimone Triplett.   AmPoNex

Lust it comes out, that gluttony went in. (LL)   On Gut.   Ben Jonson.   NPeEn; NoP-4; PoPoPo

Lust of the Eyes, The.   Elizabeth Siddal.   VWP

Lust's too genteel to let the weather in.   In a Bed-Sitter.   Hal Porter.   NOBAu

Lustra.   Christopher Okigbo.   PBMAP   *Fr.* Heavensgate (1961).

Lustra.   Ezra Pound.

Further Instructions.   TwCP

Rest, The.   MoAmPo; NOBA; NoAM; OxBA

Lustra. Officially the cold comes from Manitoba.   James [*or* Jim] Harrison.   BodElec   *Fr.* Letters to Yesenin.

Lusty Juventus.   Charles Madge.   FaBoMo

Lusty Juventus.   Robert Wever.

In Youth Is Pleasure.   NOBE; OBEV

(Of Youth He Singeth.)   NPeEn

Lusty May.   *Unknown.*   OBEV

(Four May Poems.)   OxBS

Lusty wench as nimble as an eel, A.   Epigram.   John Taylor.   NOSC

Lute, The.   Judah Al-Harizi.   BLT, *tr. by* T. Carmi

Lute, companion of my calamity.   Sonnet 12.   Louise Labé.   BoWoP, *tr. by* Aliki and Willis Barnstone

Lute Music.   Kenneth Rexroth.   TAP

Lute of Afric's Tribe, The.   Albery Allson Whitman.   APN-2

Lute Player, The.   Li Ho.   CrYelRi, *tr. by* Sam Hamill

Lute Song, The.   Kung Tzu-chen.   SuSp, *tr. by* An-yan Tang

Lute trills the most wondrous melodies, The.   Singing Lute, The.   Ibn Arfa' Ra'suh.   NAWM-7v1, *tr. by* James T. Monroe

Lutel wot it any mon.   *Unknown.*   MiEL

"Luteous" to "Lymph" for "F."   Tina Darragh.   FTOS

Luther.   W. H. Auden.   PAI

Luther, they say, was unwise; he didn't see how things were going.   Arthur Hugh Clough.   FaBoVe   *Fr.* Amours de Voyage.

Luther to a Bluebottle Fly.   Eugene Lee-Hamilton.   Son   *Fr.* Imaginary Sonnets.

Lutheran, Popish, Calvinistic, all of these confessions three.   Faith.   Friedrich von Logau.   GePo, *tr. by* George C. Schoolfield

Luttrell.   Richard Murphy.   PBCIP   *Fr.* Battle of Aughrim, The.

Luttrell, Master of Luttrellstown.   Richard Murphy.   PBCIP   *Fr.* Battle of Aughrim, The.

Luvin' wumman is a licht, A.   Love.   Hugh MacDiarmid.   PoE

Lux Est Umbra Dei.   John Addington Symonds.   GSo

Lux in Tenebris.   Katharine Tynan.   SacPr

Luxembourg Garden.   Michael S. Weaver.   GT

Luxembourg 1939.   Léopold Sédar Senghor.   PBMAP

Luxuriant, clustered round your cottage door! (LL)   Jasmine.   Claude McKay.   APT-1; GT

Luxurious Man, to bring his Vice in use.   Mower against Gardens, The.   Andrew Marvell.   BASC; CABP; EBEV; ESCV; NAEL-5v1; NAEL-6v1; NAEL-7v1; NIL-7; NOSC; NPeEn; NoP-4; OBGa; OxAEP-1; PBRV; PoE

Luxurious room, evening.—A large lighted chandelier.   Open French win.   They Are Coming.   Filippo Tommaso Marinetti.   PFTM-1

Luxury.   Yehuda Amichai [*or* Amikhai].   PoSu, *tr. by* Assia Gutmann

Luxury.   Donald Justice.   HeIP-4

Luxury, then, is a way of.   Political Poem.   Imamu Amiri Baraka.   AF; CoAP; NAAL-2v2; NoAM; PmAP

Luzumiyya.   Abdul Wahab [*or* 'Abd al-Wahhab] Al-Bayati [*or* Al-Bayyati].   MAP, *tr. by* Salma Khadra Jayyusi and Christopher Middleton

Luzzato.   Charles Reznikoff.   BBASP

Lwonesomeness.   William Barnes.   NOBVV; OxBEV

Lybica.   Jane Seager.   EMWP

Lyce.   William Walsh.   BoLoP

Lychee, The.   Wang I.   FaBoCh, *tr. by* Arthur Waley

Lychee-tree, The.   Wang I.   ChiP, *tr. by* Arthur Waley

Lychees.   Medbh McGuckian.   PBCIP

Lycidas.   Thomas Bailey Aldrich.   TreFP

Lycidas.   John Milton.   AWP; AmFaPo; BASC; CABP; ClHu; EBEV; FHYEP; GTBS-P; HAP; MakPoe; NAEL-6v1; NAEL-7v1; NIL-7; NOBE; NOSC; NPeEn; NoP-4; OBEV; OxAEP-1; OxBEV; PAI; PBRV; PoPoPo; SCGP; TFi; UnPo

"Return Alpheus, the dread voice is past."   PeECV

Lycidas and Moeris.   Virgil [*or* Vergil].   AWP, *tr. by* John Dryden   *Fr.* Eclogues.

Lycidas, in this valley have you maybe seen.   Titus Calpurnius Siculus.   RomPo, *tr. by* Guy Lee   *Fr.* Eclogues.

Lycoris darling, once I burned for you.   Martial.   BoLoP

Lydia, in Heavens Name.   Horace.   OBVE, *tr. by* Sir Richard Fanshawe   *Fr.* Odes.

Lydia is as wide and slack.   Martial.   RomPo, *tr. by* Olive Pitt-Kethley

Lydia, oh, Lydia.   Lydia, the Tattooed Lady.   Harold Arlen.   ReLy

Lydia Pinkham.   *Unknown.*   OBCoV

Lydia's Phantasmagoria.   Gloria Vando.   TouFir

Lydia, the Tattooed Lady.   Harold Arlen.   ReLy

Lydstep Caverns.   Sir Lewis Morris.

"Here in these fretted caverns whence the sea."   AngWePo

Lyell's Hypothesis Again.   Kenneth Rexroth.   APSN; APT-2

Lyf So Short, The.   Palladas [*or* Pallades].   GrAn, *tr. by* Dudley Fitts

Lying.   Richard Wilbur.   DiPo; HCAP; MakPoe; PeVV

Lying above.   Air.   Charlotte Gardelle.   CuPo

Lying amber of the histories, The. (LL)   Lullaby, A: "For wars his life and half a world away."   Randall Jarrell.   HCAP; OxBC

Lying apart now, each in a separate bed.   One Flesh.   Elizabeth Jennings.   FaBoWP; LW; NoP-4; OxAEP-2; OxBTC; Prnts

Lying asleep between the strokes of night.   Love And Sleep.   Algernon Charles Swinburne.   BoLoP; GSo; OxBSo

Lying at Leisure during Rain.   Kao Ch'i.   CoBLCP, *tr. by* Jonathan Chaves

Lying Awake.   Thomas Hardy.   FaBoVe; NPeEn

Lying Awake.   W. D. Snodgrass.   MoAmPo

Lying close to your heart-beat, my lips.   Fleur Adcock.   PeNZ   *Fr.* Night-Piece.

Lying disconsolate in new spring white wadded robes.   Spring Rain.   Li Shang-yin.   CoBCP, *tr. by* Burton Watson

Lying Down.   *Unknown.*   STP, *tr. by* Franz Boas

Lying down alone.   Lady Izumi.   ArkPo, *tr. by* Earl Miner

Lying down I lift my legs.   Troubles with the Soul at Morning Calisthenics.   Anna Swirszczynska.   BLT

Lying down in the frugality of sleep. (LL)   Märchenbilder.   John Ashbery.   LCAP-2; NOBA

Lying full length.   George Oppen.   APSN; NNaP   *Fr.* Some San Francisco Poems.

Lying here alone.   Lady Izumi.   WeW-3

Lying here quietly beside you.   Quietly.   Kenneth Rexroth.   ErotSp

Lying in a cold hell.   Nuclear Winter, The.   W. Les Russell.   IBA

Lying in a Hammock at William Duffy's Farm in Pine Island, Minnesota.   James Wright.   CoAmPo; ColAP; HAP; HCAP; MakPoe; NOBA; TRP; VCAP

Lying in a Yuma Saloon.   Jim Barnes.   CDW

Lying in Bed.   Amaru.   WoPoe, *tr. by* Henry Heifetz

Lying in bed in the dark, I hear the bray.   Weather Ear.   Norman Nicholson.   OxBSP

Lying in bed late, you read to me.   Anniversary.   Judith Ortiz Cofer.   PueRic; TouFir

Lying in Bed on a Summer Morning.   Carl Rakosi.   APT-2

Lying in bed turned away from each other, holding their.   Lying in Bed.   Amaru.   WoPoe, *tr. by* Henry Heifetz

Lying in Small Pieces.   Carol Bell.   GeoH

Lying in the Grass.   Sir Edmund William Gosse.   EBVV

Lying in the meadow, open to you.   Kenneth Rexroth.   APSN   *Fr.* Love Poems of Marichiko, The.

Lying in the wet grass.   Alexis Rotella.   HA

Lying in their lowly state.   Rispond Miser, The.   Robert MacKay (Rob Donn Macaoidh).   NePenScot, *tr. by* Derick Thomson

Lying is an occupation.   Song, A.   Laetitia Pilkington.   PEW; WPE
Lying just under potation.   American Heritage Potato, The.   Jim Barnes.   SpudSo
Lying like broken sticks among the stones.   (LL)   Wiltshire Downs.   Andrew Young.   GTBS-P; OxBTC
Lying on my pillow, I am startled to see.   New Year's Day—Following the Rhymes of Inspector Luan-chiang.   Pien Kung.   CoBLCP, *tr.* by Jonathan Chaves
Lying opposite the sun.   Months of Love, The.   Jack Marshall.   GraLe
Lying so primly propped.   (LL)   Bells for John Whiteside's Daughter.   John Crowe Ransom.   APT-1; ColAP; FuPo; HAP; HarvBo; HeIP-4; InPK-6; MakPoe; MoAmPo; NAAL-2v2; NIL-7; NIP-4; NOBA; NoAM; NoP-4; OxBA; PAI; PoE; RB; TAP; TFi; UnPo; VGW; WeW-3
Lying under the olive tree[s], O world, O death?   (LL)   Ultima Ratio Regum.   Stephen Spender.   FaBoWar; OBWP; PoWW
Lying under the stars.   Kenneth Rexroth.   BLT   *Fr.* Lights in the Sky Are Stars, The.
Lyk as the dum.   Solsequium, The.   Alexander Montgomerie.   OxBS
Lyke as a huntsman after weary chace.   Edmund Spenser.   *See* Like a huntsman after weary chase
Lyke as a ship that through the ocean wyde.   Edmund Spenser.   *See* Like as a ship, that through the ocean wide
Lyke as the armed knyght.   Anne Askew.   *See* Like as the armèd knight
Lyke as the Culver on the barèd bough.   Edmund Spenser.   *See* Like as the culver on the bared bough
Lyke-Wake Dirge, The [*or* A].   *Unknown.*   EMWP; FaBoCh; HAP; NOBE; NPeEn; OBEV; OxBEV; PeECV; TFi; WeW-3; WoPoe
  (This as night, this ae night.)   NoP-4; SacPr
Lyke-Wake Song, A.   Algernon Charles Swinburne.   PAI
Lyle Donaghy, Poet, 1902–1949.   George Buchanan.   PNI
Lynch—strip of unplowed land.   "Luteous" to "Lymph" for "F."   Tina Darragh.   FTOS
Lynched / the lakes.   Our Earth Will Not Die.   Niyi Osundare.   HBAPE
Lynching.   Lizelia Augusta Jenkins Moorer.   CBWP-3
Lynching, The.   Claude McKay.   APT-1; ColAP; GT; NAAL-5
  (His spirit is smoke ascended to high heaven.)   TCAPo
Lynching, The.   Thylias Moss.   GT
Lynching and Burning.   Primus St. John.   ISC
Lynmouth Widow, A.   Amelia Josephine Burr.   LW
Lynn Schmidt says.   Epiphany.   Pem Kremer.   HW
Lynx, The.   Charles Edward Eaton.   DiPo
Lynx-eyed, cat-quiet, sleepy mild.   Tintype of a Private in the Fifteenth Georgia Infantry.   Paul Horgan.   CBCWP
Lyra Apostolica.   John Keble.
  United States.   SacPr
Lyra Innocentium.   John Keble.   SacPr   *Fr.* Waterfall, The.
Lyre neglected, and the tuneful lay, The.   To Lysander.   Judith Madan.   ECWP
Lyre of the sonnet, that fully [*or* full] many a time.   Written December 1790.   Anna Seward.   CenSon; Son
Lyric Afterwards, A.   Tom Paulin.   PNI
Lyric by Nine.   *Unknown.*   SPE
Lyric elixir of death, A.   Poe.   Mina Loy.   APT-1
Lyric: "Embodiment of what, The."   Arthur Gregor.   TAP
Lyric in Exile, A.   Hussein Elhami.   AmFaPo, *tr.* by Shmuel Shoshani
Lyric: "It doesn't matter / whether / a tree falls."   Elizabeth Dodd.   AmPoNex
Lyric on the Lyric, A.   Lizette Woodworth Reese.   APN-2
Lyric Poem.   Semyon [*or* Semion] Isaakovich Kirsanov.   TCRP, *tr.* by April FitzLyon
Lyric Poet's Epilogue, The.   Mihály Babits.   IQMS, *tr.* by Peter Zollman
Lyric to Mirth, A.   Robert Herrick.   CaPo
Lyric to Spring.   Joseph W. Stilwell.   OBAL
Lyric to the Tune "Immortal by the River."   Li Ch'ing-chao.   WoPoe, *tr.* by Julie Landau
Lyrical Letter to the Other Woman.   Alfonsina Storni.   TCLAP, *tr.* by Dana Stangel
Lyric[k] for Legacies.   Robert Herrick.   BeJo
Lyrics.   James Agee.   MoAmPo
  "Not met and marred with the year's whole turn of grief."   APT-2
Lyrics for the Bride of God.   Nathaniel Tarn.
  Section: America (2): Seen as a Bird.   APSN
  (Section: America: Seen as a Bird.)   PFTM-2
Lyrics of the Street.   Julia Ward Howe.
  Lost Jewel, The.   SWaP
  Outside the Party.   SWaP
  Soul-Hunter, The.   SWaP
  Street Yarn.   SWaP
Lyrics shimmy like.   Ron Welburn.   NBV

Lyrics to the Tune "Fairy Grotto."   Su Tung-p'o (Su Shih).   WoPoe, *tr.* by Greg Whincup
Lyrics to the Tune "The Charms of Niennu": At the Red Cliff I Ponder Over Antiquity.   Su Tung-p'o (Su Shih).   WoPoe, *tr.* by David Lattimore
Lysidice dedicated to you, Cypris.   Asclepiades.   HePo   *Fr.* Epigrams.
Lysidice, I'm anxious to find out the meaning.   Antipater of Sidon.   GrAn
Lysidike dedicates.   Kenneth Rexroth.   NNaP; PGA
Lysimachus' cushion caught Antiochus' eye.   Lucilius.   GrAn
Lysistrata.   Aristophanes.   NAWM-5v1; NAWM-7v1, *tr.* by B. B. Rogers
  How the Women Will Stop War.   FaBoWar
Lyth and listen, gentlemen.   Robin Hood and the Beggar, II.   *Unknown.*   ESPB
Lythe and listin, gentilmen.   *Unknown.*   ESPB; NAEL-6v1; OxBB   *Fr.* Gest of Robyn Hode.
LZ Gator Body Collector, The.   Michael Casey.   YaYoPo

M

M'Fingal.   John Trul.
  Town-Meeting, A.M., The.   TCAPo
M. François le Vaillant Recalls His Travels to the Interior Parts of Africa.   Patrick Cullinan.   PeSAV
M is for Marx.   Cyril Connolly.   OBCoV   *Fr.* Where Engels Fears to Tread.
M. l'Epicier in his white hat.   Soissons.   Keith Douglas.   NoAM
M. le professeur in prominent senility.   My Neighbor in the Mirror.   Louise Glück.   Son
M. [*or* Mr.] Crashaw's Answer for Hope.   Richard Crashaw.   NOSC
  (Answer for Hope.)   MeLP
  (On Hope.)   NOBE
M. S. Sir Will: Dyer, Kt: Who Put on Immortality Aprill the 29th Anno Domini 1621.   Lady Catherine [*or* Katherine] Dyer.   EMWP
M., Singing.   Louise Bogan.   ColAP; NoAM
Ma.   Paul Muldoon.   PNI
Ma, are you really dead?   Mahendranāth Bhattācārya.   SinGod, *tr.* by Rachel Fell McDermott
Ma, Hara's Beloved, Tara.   Nīlmani Pātunī.   SinGod, *tr.* by Rachel Fell McDermott
Ma / I never saw you.   I Never Saw You.   Jyoti Lanjewar.   OMIP, *tr.* by Vinay Dharwadker
Ma, I've drunk Your poisoned nectar.   Dīnrām.   SinGod, *tr.* by Rachel Fell McDermott
Ma, if You wore a Benarasi sari.   Mā Bāsantī Cakrabarttī.   SinGod, *tr.* by Rachel Fell McDermott
Ma'ii was trotting along like he's always done.   Coyote, Skunk, and the Prairie Dogs.   *Navajo Oral Tradition.*   NAAL-5
Ma lass by munelicht fesht me frae the fail.   Deean Tractorman, Deleerit, The.   Edith Anne Robertson.   OxBS
Ma Ma Ma Malcolm.   I Remember Malcolm.   Ras Baraka.   InTrad
Ma mammy bot me oot a shop.   Telling Part, The.   Jackie Kay.   Prnts
Ma man's a gypsy.   Gypsy Man.   Langston Hughes.   NAAAL
Ma, my heart must be made of rice straw.   Nellie Wong.   UnSA   *Fr.* Heart of Rice Straw, A.
Ma people, come an get ready.   In Memoriam Ben Zwane.   Wopko Jensma.   PeSAV
Ma Rainey.   Sterling Allen Brown.   APT-2
  (When Ma Rainey.)   ISC; NAAAL
Ma Ramon.   R. Erica Doyle.   BAP-01
Ma Ramon would fall upon the floor.   Ma Ramon.   R. Erica Doyle.   BAP-01
Ma, the mail train is leaving now.   Kalyānkumār Mukhopādhyāy.   SinGod, *tr.* by Rachel Fell McDermott
Ma-wei.   Yüan Mei.   CoBLCP, *tr.* by Jonathan Chaves
Ma, You are Brahmani in the world of Brahma.   Śāradā Bhāndārī.   SinGod, *tr.* by Rachel Fell McDermott
Ma, You're inside me.   Rāmprasād Sen.   SinGod, *tr.* by Rachel Fell McDermott
Mabel Kelly.   Turlough Carolan [*or* O'Carolan].   BIrV; CIP-2; OxBEV, *tr.* by Austin Clarke
Mabel was married last week.   Emily Writes Such a Good Letter.   Stevie Smith.   OBCoV
Mabel Woo.   Belle Randall.   CRP   *Fr.* Hundred Ways of Playing Solitaire, A.
Mabinog's Liturgy.   David Jones.
  "In the middle silences of this night's course the blackthorn."   OxAEP-2
Mabrak.   "Bongo Jerry."   WaCA
Mac Flecknoe [*or,* A Satire upon the True-Blue Protestant Poet T. S.].   Dryden.   BASC; CABP; FHYEP; HAP; NAEL-5v1; NAEL-6v1; NAEL-7v1; NoP-4; OBSV; OxAEP-1; OxBoLi; PeLV; PoE; TFi
  Crown Prince of Dullness, The.   NOBE; OBCoV; OxBEV; SCV
  ("Thou last great prophet of tautology.")   (LL)   NOSC

Macadam, gun-grey as the tunny's belt. Hart Crane. MoAmPo *Fr.* Bridge, The.

Macavity's a Mystery Cat: he's called the Hidden Paw. Macavity: The Mystery Cat. T. S. Eliot. ChAP; NBLV; NOBL; OBCA; OxIBACP; PeLV; PoRA; RB; UV

Macavity: The Mystery Cat. T. S. Eliot. ChAP; NBLV; NOBL; OBCA; OxIBACP; PeLV; PoRA; RB; UV

Macaw preens upon a branch outspread, A. Decoration. Louise Bogan. MoAmPo

Macbeth. Andrew of Wyntoun. OxBS

Macbeth. William Shakespeare.
    "Glamis thou art, andd Cawdor; and shalt be." OxAEP-1
    ("Hang out our banners on the outward walls.") EBEV; OxAEP-1
    "I have done the deed. Didst thou not hear a noise?" EBEV; OxAEP-1
    ("If it were done when 'tis done, then 'twere well.") UnPo
    "If it were done when 'tis done, then 'twere well." OxAEP-1
    "It is the cry of women, my good Lord." OxBEV
    Macbeth Does Murder Sleep. EBEV; OxAEP-1
    "Now o'er the one half-world." OxAEP-1
    "Scale of dragon, tooth of wolf." UV
    "Seyton!—I am sick at heart." OxAEP-1
    "She should have died hereafter." SoSe-8
    Thrice the Brinded Cat Hath Mewed. RB
    Tomorrow, and Tomorrow, and Tomorrow. SoSe-8
    Vaulting Ambition. OxAEP-1
    "What bloody man is that? He can report." FaBoWar

Macduff. Charles Tomlinson. OxBC

MacGregor's Gathering. Sir Walter Scott. OxBS

Machberoth. Immanuel di Roma. TrJP, *tr. by* J. Chotzner

Macheath and Polly. John Gay. *See* Begger's Opera

Machete. Rikki Ducornet. SurWo

Machine-gun bullets, The. Mexico, August 20, 1940. Ai. NoAM

Machine gunner aims, A. El Alamein. Steve Crow. HATNAP

Machines waited for me, The. "Antler." CLPP *Fr.* Factory.

Machynlleth. Allen Fisher. Oth *Fr.* Emergent Manner.

Mackerel-man drives down the street, The. Pretty Ambition, A. Mary Eleanor Wilkins Freeman. OBCA

Mackerel sky. *Unknown.* OxNR

Mackintosh— / And that / (Said John) / Is / That. (LL) Happiness. Alan Alexander Milne. AmFaPo; NOxBChV

Macrinus against Trees. "Michael Field." WPE

Macrocarpas. Michael Jackson. PeNZ

Macumba Word. Aimé Césaire. PFTM-1

Mad, The. Robert Pinsky. NoAM *Fr.* Essay on Psychiatrists.

Mad about the Boy. Noël Coward. ReLy

Mad angel hammered with raging might, A. Memories of a Summer Night. Endre Ady. IQMS, *tr. by* Peter Zollman

Mad are predators, The. Too often lately they harbour against us. A novel heresy exculpates all maimed souls. Abjure it! I am the King of Mercia, and I know. Geoffrey Hill. NoP-4 *Fr.* Mercian Hymns.

Mad as the Mist and Snow. W. B. Yeats. RaBo

Mad barber wants to cut my hair, The. Theology. Sherman Alexie. NeAmPo

Mad daddy like mule. Enclosure. Christopher Gilbert. SwNoth

Mad Dogs and Englishmen. Noël Coward. NBLV; NOBL; PeLV; ReLy

Mad Farmer, Flying the Flag of Rough Branch, Secedes from the Union, The. Wendell Berry. PoCoUp

Mad Fight Song for William S. Carpenter, 1966, A. James Wright. NoAM

Mad flight of a butterfly, The. Nazi Song. Paul Éluard. AF, *tr. by* Lloyd Alexander

Mad Gardener's Song, The. Lewis Carroll. WoPoe *Fr.* Sylvie and Bruno.

Mad girl, The. Buson. EH, *tr. by* Robert Hass

Mad girl with the staring eyes and long white fingers, The. Cassandra. Robinson Jeffers. APT-1; HeIP-4

Mad Hatter's Song, The. Lewis Carroll. NOBL; UV *Fr.* Alice's Adventures in Wonderland.

Mad is mad. Mad Talk. Karel Appel. PFTM-2

Mad is the poet men call Kit. Christopher Smart. Stanley Shaw. UV

Mad Maid's Song, The. Robert Herrick. AWP; CaPo; EnLoPo; OBEV; RACG

Mad monsters of no kind? (LL) Hide and Seek. Robert Graves. KaS; NTCP

Mad Murray Kadish. Boots and Saddles. Louis Simpson. BodElec

Mad Negro Soldier Confined at Munich, A. Robert Lowell. FaBoMo; OxBC

Mad old maid of Amherst, The. Emily Dickinson. Yury [*or* Iurii] Ivask. TCRusP, *tr. by* William Tjalsma

Mad Patsy said, he said to me. In the Poppy Field. James Stephens. PoRA

Mad Poem Addressed to My Nephews and Nieces, A. Po Chü-i. ChiP, *tr. by* Arthur Waley

Mad Pomegranate Tree, The. Odysseus Elytis. WoPoe, *tr. by* Edmund Keeley and Philip Sherrard

Mad Potter, The. John Hollander. ColAP; VCAP

Mad Queen Aeronautical Corporation . . Cyclone. 3030. Telephone Directory. Harry Crosby. SPE

Mad Scene, The. James Merrill. CoAP; NOBA; PoE; TAP

Mad sculptor in our park, A. Helen. Peter Meinke. PBCAP

Mad Soldier, The. Edward Wyndham Tennant. FaBoWar

Mad Song. William Blake. NAEL-5v2; NAEL-6v2; NOEC; PoE

Mad Song. Denise Levertov. TAP

Mad Sonnet 1. Michael McClure. PoM

Mad Sonnet: Fame. Michael McClure. BB

Mad Sonnet: Grace. Michael McClure. BB

Mad Talk. Karel Appel. PFTM-2

Mad to be had, to be felt and smelled. My lips. W. H. Auden. EroLit *Fr.* Platonic Blow, The.

Mad Tom's Song. *Unknown. See* Tom o' Bedlam's Song

Mad Wolf in Lunar Web, Mad Crow on the Beach. Mac Wellman. FTOS

Mad Woman. Su'ad al-Mubarak Al-Sabah. MAP; PoArWo, *tr. by* John Heath-Stubbs and May Jayyusi

Mad Woman of Punnet's Town, The. Leonard Alfred George Strong. MoBrPo

Mad Yak, The. Gregory Corso. BB; PFTM-2; PmAP

Madalena. Maria Eugénia Lima. HAWP, *tr. by* Julia Kirst

Madam and Her Madam. Langston Hughes. RACG; SAmP

Madam and the Census Man. Langston Hughes. SAmP

Madam and the Minister. Langston Hughes. NOBA

Madam and the Rent Man. Langston Hughes. SAmP

Madam and the Wrong Visitor. Langston Hughes. SAmP

Madam, / I cannot but congratulate. Advice to Virgins. Katherine Philips. EMWP

MADAM, / I hope you'll think it's true. Strephon to Celia. Mary Leapor. ECWP; RACG

Madam Life. William Ernest Henley. *See* Madam Life's a Piece in Bloom

Madam Life's A Piece in Bloom. William Ernest Henley. EBVV; NAEL-5v2; NAEL-6v2; OxBEV; PeVV
    (Madam Life.) MoBrPo
    (To W. R.) NOBVV; NPeEn

Madam Mouse Trots. Dame Edith Sitwell. FaBoCh

Madam! permit a Muse, that has been long. To Madam Bhen. "Ephelia." EMWP

Madam, / Reason is our soul's left hand, Faith her right. To the Countess of Bedford. John Donne. NOSC

Madam's Calling Cards. Langston Hughes. SAmP

Madam's Past History. Langston Hughes. HHAm; NoAM; SAmP

Madam, the Lady Valeria is come to visit you. William Shakespeare. OxAEP-1 *Fr.* Coriolanus.

Madam to a Young Courtesan, The. Sarangapani. WoPoe, *tr. by* V. Narayana Rao, A. K. Ramanujan and David Shulman

Madam to you. (LL) Madam's Past History. Langston Hughes. HHAm; NoAM; SAmP

Madam, twice through the Muses' Grove I walked. Upon Mrs. Anne Bradstreet, Her Poems, Etc. John Rogers. SCAP

Madam, / Were you but only great, there are some men. To the Excellent Pattern of Beauty and Virtue, Lady Elizabeth, Countess of Ormonde. James Shirley. BeJo

Madam would speak with me. So, now it comes. George Meredith. NOBVV; NPeEn; OxBEV *Fr.* Modern Love.

Madam / You were the very Magazine of rich. On my honorable Grandmother, Elizabeth Countess of Shrewbury. Lady Jane Cavendish. EMWP

Madam, your beauty and your lovely parts. Platonic Love. Edward Herbert, 1st Baron Herbert of Cherbury. NOSC

Madam, your humble servant, Samuel Sewall. (LL) Samuel Sewall. Anthony Hecht. NBLV; PeLV; PoRA; TwCP

Madame Butterfly. David Moolten. BloBone

Madame d'Albert's Laugh. Clément Marot. AWP, *tr. by* Leigh Hunt

Madame Eglantine. Geoffrey Chaucer. *See* Canterbury Tales, The

Madam[e], had all antiquity [*or* antiquitie] been lost. To Mary, Lady Wroth. Ben Jonson. NOSC

Madame Maynard of the hard pebble. Stranded in My Ontario. Ronald G. Everson. NOBC

Madame, withouten Many Wordes. Sir Thomas Wyatt. EnLoPo; NAEL-5v1; NAEL-6v1; NAEL-7v1; NoP-4; NoSic; OBVE; OxBSP

Madame X. Margherita Guidacci. CItWP, *tr. by* Cinzia Sartini Blum and Lara Trubowitz

Madame, ye be[e]n of al[le] beaute[e] shryne *or* shryne [*or* shrine]. To Rosamounde. Geoffrey Chaucer. PoE

Madarika. Vince Gotera. OpBo; ReBoTo

Madboy's Song. Muriel Rukeyser. MoAmPo; TrJP

Mädchen mit dem rothen Mündchen. Heinrich Heine. AWP, *tr. by* Sir Theodore Martin

Madding moon, A. Niyi Osundare. HBAPE *Fr.* Moonsongs.

Made hair? The girls here. Naola Beauty Academy, New Orleans, Louisiana, 1943. Natasha Trethewey. NeAmPo; SpirFl

Made him take up his shirt, lay down his sword. (LL) Upon Pagget. Robert Herrick. CaPo; FaBoCh

Made in Sweden: carts are my trade. (LL) Carriage from Sweden, A. Marianne Craig Moore. HAP; TwCP

Made it for ever after red. (LL) How Roses Came Red. Robert Herrick. CaPo; SoSe-8

Made me dance with you. Latin Music in New York. Jessica Tarahata Hagedorn. PmAP

Made Out of Links. Hilda Morley. PmAP

Made Shine. Josephine Miles. NoAM

Made to Order Smile, The. Paul Laurence Dunbar. GT

Madeleine in Church. Charlotte Mew. VWP

"Find rest in Him! One knows the parsons' tags." ChIV-2

"How old was Mary out of whom you cast." MoBrPo

Madeline, a Domestic Tale. Felicia Dorothea Hemans. RWP

Madem you say I am sad I ansure noe. Upon the LD Saying KT Could Be Sad in Her Company. Katherine Thimelby Aston. EMWP

Madge Wildfire's [Death] Song. Sir Walter Scott. *See* Heart of Midlothian, The

Madge Wildfire Sings. Sir Walter Scott. *See* Heart of Midlothian, The

Meditation on the Nativity. Sidney Godolphin. *See* Hymn: "Lord, when the wise men came from far[r]"

Madly Singing in the Mountains. Po Chü-i. BLT; ChiP; WoPoe, *tr. by* Arthur Waley

Madman, The. Tu Fu. CrYelRi, *tr. by* Sam Hamill

Madman (Prologue), The. Kahlil Gibran. GraLe; TCAPo

Madman's Song. Elinor Wylie. MoAmPo; PoRA

Madman saith He said so: it is strange, The. (LL) Epistle Containing the Strange Medical Experience of Karshish, the Arab Physician, An. Robert Browning. ChIV-2; NAEL-5v2; NAEL-6v2

Madness. John Armstrong. NOEC *Fr.* Art of Preserving Health, The.

Madness. Robert Merry. NOBRP

Madness. Sachiko Yoshihara. BoWoP, *tr. by* James Kirkup and Shozo Tokunaga

Madness . . . madness. Five Nights of Bleeding. Linton Kwesi Johnson. WaCA

Madness of King Goll, The. W. B. Yeats. NAEL-5v2; NAEL-6v2

Madness of Love, The. Hadewijch. WPoS, *tr. by* Oliver Davies

Madness, the way they gallop off to foreign shores! Tanzan. ZenPo, *tr. by* Takashi Ikemoto and Lucien Stryk

Madonna of the Angels in the skies. Song to the Virgin Mary. András Vásárhelyi. IQMS, *tr. by* René Bonnerjea

Madonna of the Evening Flowers. Amy Lowell. NAAL-5; NALW

Madonna of the Peaches. Joan Logghe. HW

Madras, / 1965, and rain. Some Indian Uses of History on a Rainy Day. A. K. Ramanujan. OxBC

Madre Sofía. Alberto A. Ríos. NAAL-5; NoAM

Madrid. Frank O'Hara. FTOS

Madrid. Jay Wright. ESEAA

Madrid—1937. Langston Hughes. AF

Madrid, 1937. Octavio Paz. BLPSL, *tr. by* Rene de Costa, Rigas Kappatos and Eleni Paidoussi *Fr.* Sunstone.

Madrigal. Edmund Bolton. SacPr

Madrigal. Charles Cotton. FaBoEE

Madrigal. Nicolás Guillén. CLPP, *tr. by* Kenneth Rexroth

Madrigal. Giovanni Raboni. ItPo, *tr. by* Gayle Ridinger

At the Moated Grange. William Shakespeare. *See* Measure for Measure

Madrigal. William Shakespeare. *See* Measure for Measure

Madrigal. William Shakespeare. *See* Merchant of Venice, The

Madrigal. Sir Philip Sidney. NoSic *Fr.* Arcadia.

Madrigal. Thomas Weelkes. *See* Fara Diddle Dyno

Madrigal, A. *Var. authors.* GTBS-P *Fr.* Passionate Pilgrim, The.

Madrigal 1. Gutierre de Cetina. BLPSL, *tr. by* Rene de Costa, Rigas Kappatos and Eleni Paidoussi

Madrigal 3. Aurelio Arturo. BLPSL, *tr. by* Rene de Costa, Rigas Kappatos and Eleni Paidoussi

Madrigal: "Ah! silly soul, what wilt thou say." William Drummond, of Hawthornden. SacPr

Madrigal: "Astrea in this time." William Drummond, of Hawthornden. NOSC *Fr.* Urania, or Spiritual Poems.

Madrigal: "Ay me, alas, heigh ho, heigh ho!" Thomas Weelkes. FaBoCh; NPeEn; OxBoLi

Madrigal: "Daedal of my death, A." William Drummond, of Hawthornden. NOSC

Madrigal: Eyes of Clear Serenity. Gutierre de Cetina. SpanPo, *tr. by* Kate Flores

Madrigal: "How the tenor warbles in April!" Mary Leader. NAPBL

Madrigal: "If that a sinner's sighs be angels' food." *Unknown.* SacPr

Madrigal: "Like the Idalian Queen[e]." William Drummond, of Hawthornden. NOSC; OBAL; PeLV; SCGP

(Inexorable.) NOBE; OBEV

Madrigal: "My Love in her attire doth show her wit." *Unknown.* BoLoP; GTBS-P; HeIP-4; NAEL-5v1; NAEL-6v1; NIP-4; NOBE; OBEV; OxBSP; TFi

Madrigal: "My mistress frowns when she should play." John Hilton. OxBoLi

Madrigal: "My mistress is as fair as fine." Thomas Ravenscroft. OxBoLi

Madrigal: "My thoughts hold mortal[l] strife." William Drummond, of Hawthornden. GTBS-P; NOSC; OxBSP

(Inexorable.) NOBE; OBEV

Madrigal: "Since Bonny-boots was dead, that so divinely." *Unknown. See* Since Bonny-Boots Was Dead

Madrigal: "This life, which seems so fair." William Drummond, of Hawthornden. NOSC

Madrigal: "This world a hunting is." William Drummond, of Hawthornden. OxBSP

Madrigal: "Unhappie [*or* Unhappy] Light." William Drummond, of Hawthornden. NOSC

Madrigal: "Your love is dead, lady, your love is dead." Ronald Stuart Thomas. BoLoP; EnLoPo

Madwoman at Rodmell. Michele Roberts. BrRo

Madwoman in the Park, The. Dame Edith Sitwell. PFTM-1

Madwoman of Cork, The. Patrick Galvin. BiHa

Madwoman on the Train, The. Alfred Wellington Purdy. NoAM

Madwomen of the Plaza de Mayo, The. Eli W. Mandel. NOBC

Mae Marsh, Motion Picture Actress. Nicholas Vachel Lindsay.

"Arts are old, old as the stones, The." APT-1

"She is madonna in an art." APT-1

Mae West Chats It Up with Bessie Smith. Colleen J. McElroy. BAP-01

Mæcenas, you, beneath the myrtle shade. To Mæcenas. Phillis Wheatley. NAAAL; NAAL-5

Mæg ic be me sylfum so???ogied wrecan. *Unknown.* CABP *Fr.* Seafarer (c. 10th century), The.

Maen Madoc. Chris Torrance. AngWePo

Maesia's Song. Robert Greene. CTC; UnPo *Fr.* Farewell to Folly.

Mafioso. Sandra M. Gilbert. UnSA

Mag. Carl Sandburg. APT-1

Mag Uidhir's Winter Campaign. Eochadh [*or* Eochy] O'Hussey [*or* O'Heughusa]. NOIV

Magalu. Helene Johnson. APT-2; BlSi

Magdalen. Amy Levy. VWP; ViWPN

Magdalen. Harriet Prescott Spofford. SWaP

Magdalen at Michael's gate. At Glastonbury. Henry Kingsley. PoRA

Magdalen Walks. Oscar Wilde. EBVV; MoBrPo

Magdalene. Marina Ivanovna Tsvetayeva [*or* Tsvetaeva]. GI, *tr. by* Michael M. Naydan

Magdalene at Michael's gate. Henry Kingsley. SacPr

Magdalene (I). Boris Leonidovich Pasternak. GI, *tr. by* Nina Kossman

Maggid. Marge Piercy. TaR

Maggie. Duane Niatum. HATNAP

Maggie and Milly and Molly and May. E. E. Cummings. ChAP; NOBA; NOxBChV; NoAM; RB

Maggie Lauder. Francis Sempill. NePenScot; OxBS

Maggot Song. *Unknown.* NOBAu

Magi. Sylvia Plath. GI

Magi, The. Jeffrey Fiskin. GI

Magi, The. Louise Glück. GI; HarvBoo

Magi, The. Ramon Guthrie. GI; PoE

Magi, The. W. B. Yeats. ChIV-2; GI; HAP; HarvBoo; InPK-6; NPeEn; NoAM; OxAEP-2; PoE; TRP; TrCP

Magi in Europe, The. Khalil Hawi. MAP, *tr. by* Diana Der Hovanessian and Lena Jayyusi

Magic. Aimé Césaire. NegPo, *tr. by* Clayton Eshleman and Denis Kelly

Magic. Ovid. AWP, *tr. by* William Shakespeare *Fr.* Metamorphoses.

Magic. William Shakespeare. AWP; EBEV; OxAEP-1; SCV *Fr.* Tempest, The.

Magic. Walter James Turner. OBGa

Magic and mystery, spells Circæan. Thomas Love Peacock. NOBRP *Fr.* Rhododaphne.

Magic Apple Tree, The. Elaine Feinstein. BrRo; HarvBoo

Magic Carpet, The. Maurice Kilwein Guevara. TouFir

Magic Cinnabar. Pao Chao. ColAnChi, *tr. by* Anne Birrell

Magic City Monastery. Wang Yang-ming. CrYelRi, *tr. by* Sam Hamill

Magic Composer. Gilbert Sorrentino. FTOS

Magic dance, The. After the Ball. Imamu Amiri Baraka. NAAL-2v2

Magic Formula. *Unknown.* CA

Magic Fox. James Welch. CDW; HATNAP; NoAM

Magic Glass, The. Felicia Dorothea Hemans. NOBRP

Magic Mist, A. Owen Roe O'Sullivan. NOIV, *tr. by* Thomas Kinsella

Magic mists twirl around the sky. Inscribed on a Painting. Yün Shou-p'ing. CoBLCP, *tr. by* Jonathan Chaves

Magic / my man. Black Magic. Sonia Sanchez. BPo

Magic of the day is the morning, The. Ballad of the Morning Streets. Imamu Amiri Baraka. TTTS

Magic (or Rousseau). Carla Harryman. FTOS

Magic Song. *Unknown.* APN-2, *tr. by* Henry Rowe Schoolcraft

Magic Wood, The. Henry Treece. SPE

(Wood is full of shining eyes, The.) SPE

Magic Words. *Eskimo Oral Tradition.* BLT, *tr. by* Edward Field

Magic Words. *Unknown.* RaBo; STP, *tr. by* Edward Field

Magic Words for Hunting Caribou. *Unknown.* STP, *tr. by* Johnny John and Jerome Rothenberg

Magic Words for Hunting Seal. *Unknown.* STP, *tr. by* Edward Field

Magic Words to Feel Better. Nakasuk. STP, *tr. by* Jerome Rothenberg

Magical Devices. Clara Silva. TANSG, *tr. by* Celeste Kostopulos-Cooperman

Magical Mouse, The. Kenneth Patchen. KaS

Magistrate. Chŏng Ch'ŏl. WoPoe, *tr. by* Graeme Wilson

Magna Est Veritas. Coventry Patmore. GTBS-P; HAP; NOBE; NOBVV; NPeEn; OBEV; OxBEV; OxBSP *Fr.* Unknown Eros, The.

Magna Est Veritas. Stevie Smith. NPeEn; OxBC; OxBEV

Magnet. Valerie Worth. KaS

Magnet, The. Thomas Stanley. NOBE

Magnet, The. Ruth Stone. MoAmPo

Magnetic Fields, The. André Breton.

"Factory." PFTM-1

"Great legend of the railways and reservoirs, the weariness of carriage, The." PFTM-1

Magnetic Mountain, The. Cecil Day Lewis.

Nearing Again the Legendary Isle. FaBoTw; MoBrPo

Tempt Me No More. MoBrPo; OBMV

Magnificat. Michele Roberts. BrRo; PoBW

Magnificat, The. Bible, *N.T.* BoWoP *Fr.* St. Luke.

Magnificat! Michael S. Glaser. OPRER

Magnificence. John Skelton.

"Stow, birde, stow, stow!" NoSic

"Unto this process briefly compiled." NoSic

Magnificence. James Wright. BodElec

Magnificent Bull, The. *Dinka Oral Tradition.* TTTS

Magnificent! Magnificent! Fumon. ZenPo, *tr. by* Takashi Ikemoto and Lucien Stryk

Magnificent Peak. Muso Soseki. EaWin, *tr. by* W. S. Merwin

Magnificent Tomorrows. Haki R. Madhubuti. SpirFl

Magnolia. Mary Weston Fordham. CBWP-2

Magnolia. Ray Henderson. ReLy

Magnolia bloom can sex the air. Likely. Lisa Coffman. AmPoNex

Magnolia oars; a boat of spice-wood. River Song. Li Po. ChinPo, *tr. by* Yip Wai-lim

Magnum Vectigal Parsimonia. George Gascoigne. NoSic

Magpie. Alan Michael Parker. AmPoNex

Magpie and Pines. Louis Johnson. PeNZ

Magpie, magpie, flutter and flee. *Unknown.* OxNR

Magpie's Shadow, The. Yvor Winters. APT-2

Magpies. *Unknown.* OWoS

Magpies, The. Denis Glover. PeNZ

Magpies in Picardy. T. P. Cameron Wilson. FaBoWar

Magryme, The. William Dunbar. FaBoVe

Maguire is not afraid of death, the Church will light him a candle. Patrick Kavanagh. CIP-2 *Fr.* Great Hunger, The.

Magus, The. James Dickey. GI

Magwere, Who Waits Wondering. Kingsley Fairbridge. PeSAV

Magyar Fallow, The. Endre Ady. IQMS, *tr. by* Anton N. Nyerges

Magyar Messiahs, The. Endre Ady. IQMS, *tr. by* Anton N. Nyerges

Magyar Scene through Magyar Eyes, A. Gyula Juhász. IQMS, *tr. by* Godfrey Turton

Magyars, they say, are not fit for the art of dancing. Dance of the Magyars, The. Ádám Pálóczi Horváth. IQMS, *tr. by* John Gordon Nichols

Mahabharata, The. *Unknown.*

Sâvitrî; or, Love and Death. TAL

Mahler. Jonathan Williams.

"Pan's / spring rain." VGW

Symphony No. 3, in D Minor. VGW

Mahogany men. Uncles. Nikky Finney. ISC

Mahogany Ship, The. Judith Rodriguez. BMAP

Mahogany Tree, The. William Makepeace Thackeray. ChrPo

Mahratta Ghats, The. Alun Lewis. AngWePo; OBWVE; PoWW; TCAWP

Maia. Ralph Waldo Emerson. APN-1

Maid, The. Nathan [*or* Natan] Alterman. MHP, *tr. by* Ruth Finer Mintz

Maid and the Palmer, The. *Unknown.* ESPB

Maid comes into the hall, The. Lunar Eclipse. Harry Mathews. CoBCP, *tr. by* Burton Watson

Maid comes into the hall, The. Lunar Eclipse. Mei Yao Ch'en. CoBCP, *tr. by* Burton Watson

Maid Freed from the Gallows, The. *Unknown.* AWP; ESPB

Maid Maia shook her head, here is, The. *Unknown.* WoPoe, *tr. by* Padraic Fallon *Fr.* Homeric Hymns.

Maid Marian. Thomas Love Peacock.

Over, Over. OxAEP-2

Robin Hood and the Grey Friars. OxAEP-2

Maid Mars Me, A. *Unknown.* MiEL

Maid of Athens, Ere We Part. Byron. EBEV

(Song.) FHYEP

Maid of dark eyes, that glow with shy sweet fire. Rondels. Aleister Crowley. CAGL

Maid of Ehrenthal, The. Henrietta Cordelia Ray. CBWP-3

Maid of Kent, A. *Unknown.* OxBoLi

Maid of Neidpath, The. Thomas Campbell. GTBS-P

Maid of Neidpath, The. Sir Walter Scott. GTBS-P

Maid of Orleans, The. Johann Christoph Friedrich von Schiller. AWP, *tr. by* James Clarence Mangan

Maid of the Moor; or, The Water-Fiends, The. George Colman, the Younger.

"Cold blows the blast—the night's obscure." NOEC

Maid's Complaint for Want of a Dil Doul, The. *Unknown.* EroLit

Maid's Husband, The. Henry Carey. ECEV

Maid's Lament, The. Walter Savage Landor. OBEV; TreFP *Fr.* Citation and Examination of William Shakespeare, The.

Maid's Tragedy, The. Francis Beaumont.

Aspatia's Song. AWP; HAP; NOBE; OBEV; SCGP

Bridal Song: "Cynthia, to thy power." OBEV

(Song: "Hold back thy hours, dark night, till we have done.") OxBSP

Maid-Servant at the Inn, The. Dorothy Parker. ChrPo

Maid she[e] went to the well to wash[e], The. Maid and the Palmer, The. *Unknown.* ESPB

Maid, where's my lawrel? Oh my rageing soul! Theocritus. CTC; OBVE *Fr.* Idylls.

Maid Who Becomes a Bear sought the gods and found them. *Unknown.* APN-2, *tr. by* Washington Matthews *Fr.* Mountain Chant, The.

Maid Who Becomes a Bear walks far around, The. *Unknown.* APN-2, *tr. by* Washington Matthews *Fr.* Mountain Chant, The.

Maiden, The. Peter Hille. AWP, *tr. by* Jethro Bithell

Maiden and River. Mary Weston Fordham. CBWP-2

Maiden at college called Breeze, A. Limerick. Mrs. Mercy Warren. PeLi

Maiden Castle. Dorothy Wellesley, Duchess of Wellington. PoBW

Maiden caught me in the wild, The. Crystal Cabinet, The. William Blake. FaBoCh; NPeEn; PAI

Maiden in the Moor [*or* Mor], A. *Unknown.* MiEL

(Maiden in the morë lay.) NPeEn

Maiden Lies in Her Chamber, A. Heinrich Heine. AWP, *tr. by* Louis Untermeyer

Maiden moder milde. *Unknown.* MiEL

Maiden Name. Philip Larkin. GTBS-P

Maiden, not to be greeted unbenignly. (LL) Hendecasyllabics. Tennyson. EBEV; NOBL; PeLV

Maiden's Plight, The. Brian [*or* Bryan] Merriman [*or* Merryman]. BIrV, *tr. by* Frank O'Connor *Fr.* Midnight Court, The.

Maiden, there is something more. To Hersa. Forceythe Willson. APN-2

Maiden There Lived, A. *Unknown.* NOBL; PeLV

Maiden, thou wert thoughtless once. Fragment, A. Anne Brontë. VWP

Maiden to the Delphic temple came, A. Love or Fame. Caroline Lindsay. VWP

Maiden wept and, as a comforter, A. Passion and Love. Paul Laurence Dunbar. ErotSp

Maidenhair. "Michael Field." OxBSo

Maidenhead. "Ephelia." WPE

(At your entreaty, I at last have writ.) PEW

(Maidenhead Written at the Request of a Friend.) NOSC; PEW

Maidens Blush, The. Joshua Sylvester.

"But, fair Iëmpsar (wife of Potiphar)." ChIV-1

Maidens in Spring. Herbert Strutz. AuPH, *tr. by* Lowell A. Bangerter

Maidens, kilt your skirts and go. Celia's Home-Coming. Agnes Mary Frances Robinson. OBEV; VWP

Maidens of London's Brave Adventures, or, a Boon Voyage Intended for the Sea, The. Laurence Price. NOSC

Maidens who this bursting [*or* burning] May. Young Man's Song, A. William Bell. FaBoTw

Maides to bed, and cover coale. Belmans Song, A. Thomas Ravenscroft. NPeEn; PBRV

Maids, not to you my mind doth change. "Michael Field." VWP; ViWPN

Maids to bed and cover coal. Bellman's Song, The. *Unknown.* EBEV; SCGP

Mail. Sarah Kirsch. AF, *tr. by* Wayne Kvam

Mail from Right Here, The. Brendan Galvin. PoCoUp

Mail Has Come, The. Mary E. Tucker. CBWP-1

Mail King. Paul B. Janeczko. HHAm

Mail on the counter. Rod Willmot. HA

Mail Order Catalogs. William Matthews. ReTh

Mailman passes by, The. I'm Gonna Sit Right Down and Write Myself a Letter. Fred E. Ahlert. ReLy

Maim[e]'d Debauchee, The. John Wilmot, 2d Earl of Rochester. *See* Disabled Debauchee, The

Main bridge of Constitution, The. Matthew XXV:30. Jorge Luis Borges. GI, *tr. by* David Curzon

Main cook lies sick on a banquette, and his assistant, The. Restaurant. Maxine Hong Kingston. OpBo

Main-Deep, The. James Stephens. MoBrPo; OBMV; UnPo

Main Idea, The. Milo De Angelis. ItPo, *tr. by* Gayle Ridinger

Main Street. "Demyan [*or* Dem'ian] Bedny [*or* Bednyi]." TCRP, *tr. by* Daniel Weissbort and Lubov Yakovleva

Main Temple Street, Puri. Jayanta Mahapatra. VCWP

Maine Lake at Night. Harry Morris. CRP

Maine Vastly Covered with Much Snow. John Tagliabue. InPK-6

Mainly I was led to them, the casinos of aluminium. Painting Mount Taranaki. David Eggleton. PeNZ

Maintaining the Species. Deborah Burnham. UrbNat

Maintrunk Country Roadsong. Sam Hunt. PeNZ

Maisie. James Merrill. HeIP-4

Maison Aragon. Tristan Tzara. PFTM-1

Majeski Plays the Saxophone. Martín Espada. SeSe

Majestic and brilliant. Forever Martial. *Unknown.* WoPoe, *tr. by* John S. Major

Majestic, from the most distant time. From the Most Distant Time. Emperor Wu of Han [*or* Wu Ti *or* Ou-ty *or* Liu Ch'e *or* Liu Ch'u]. OHMPC, *tr. by* Kenneth Rexroth

Majestic Valley. Chu Yi-tsun. SuSp, *tr. by* Chang Yin-nan

Majesty of God, The. Thomas Sternhold. AH

Major abstraction is the idea of man, The. Wallace Stevens. NOBA *Fr.* Notes toward a Supreme Fiction.

Major Bowes' Diary. Imamu Amiri Baraka. NAAL-2v2

Major Macroo. Stevie Smith. NBLV

Makar, The. William Soutar. OxBS

Make a Miracle. Frank Loesser. ReLy

Make a most infernal clatter, here the dinner comes! (LL) Going In to Dinner. Edward Richard Burton Shanks. OBMV; OxBTC

Make a wide dreaming pansy of an old pond in the night. (LL) Nocturne in a Deserted Brickyard. Carl Sandburg. APT-1; MoAmPo

Make a wish, Tom, make a wish. (LL) Drifters. Bruce Dawe. BMAP; CBAP; NoAM

Make all your sorrow neat. Young Wife, The. Derek Walcott. DiPo

Make Believe. Jerome Kern. ReLy

Make Believe. Gerda Mayer. Prnts

Make Bright the Arrows. Edna St. Vincent Millay. ChIV-1

Make clay ascend more quick than light. (LL) Ascension Hymn. Henry Vaughan. ESCV; GeHe; NOSC; TrCP

Make company break. Thomas Tusser. NoSic *Fr.* Five Hundred Points of Good Husbandry.

Make friendship with the stars. Stars, The. Lydia Huntley Sigourney. ColAP; TCAPo

Make haste away, and let one be. To His Book[e]. Robert Herrick. NOSC

Make haste slowly, my friend, make haste slowly. József Kiss. IQMS, *tr. by* Anthony Edkins *Fr.* About My Grandfather.

Make Ifa. Jayne Cortez. SurWo

Make me a bowl, a mighty bowl. Cup, The. John Oldham. AWP

Make me a captive, Lord. Christian Freedom. George Matheson. SacPr

Make me a grave where'er you will. Bury Me in a Free Land. Frances Ellen Watkins Harper. BPo; ColAP; ISC; NAAAL; TCAPo

Make me a heaven, and make me there. Eye, The. Robert Herrick. CaPo

Make Me Loathe Earthly Likings. *Unknown.* SacPr

Make me, O Lord, thy spin[n]ing wheel[e] comple[a]te. Huswifery. Edward Taylor. ColAP; ITBLP; InvLi; NAAL-2v1; NAAL-3; NAAL-5; NIP-4; NOBA; NOBE; OxBA; SCAP; SacPr; TAP; TCAPo; TFi

Make me too brave to lie or be unkind. Prayer for Every Day, A. Mary Carolyn Davies. PoToHe

Make men beleeve no Paradice. (LL) To Cynthia, on Concealment of Her Beauty. Sir Francis Kynaston. MeLP; NOBE

Make miniatures of the once-monstrous theme. Short History of British India, A. Geoffrey Hill. OxBC

Make my grave shape of heart so like a flower be free aired. Snail Poem. Peter Orlovsky. BB

Make my heart as powerful as your own. Lead me to conquer. *Unknown.* APN-2 *Fr.* Minnetare Songs.

Make new friends, but keep the old. New Friends and Old Friends. Joseph Parry. ITBLP; PoToHe

Make no mistake: if He rose at all. Seven Stanzas at Easter. John Updike. TrCP

Make no mistake; there will be no forgiveness. Easter Hymn. Alec Derwent Hope. ChIV-2; GI

Make no sound, do not speak. Reading. Jean-Joseph Rabéarivelo [*or* Rebéarivelo]. NegPo, *tr. by* Ellen Conroy Kennedy

Make one place ev'rywhere. (LL) Temper (1), The. George Herbert. ESCV; GeHe; NOCV

Make over the alleys and gardens to birdsong. Before. Sean O'Brien. EmeKit

Make pleasing music, and not wild uproar. (LL) 'How Many Bards Gild the Lapses of Time!' John Keats. CenSon; OxAEP-2

Make quiet, so quiet, your awesome bearing. *Unknown.* ColAnChi, *tr. by* Jeffrey Riegel *Fr.* Classic of Odes.

Make Someone Happy. Adolph Green. ReLy

Make sure that they are thoroughly cremated. (LL) Shipment to Maidanek. Ephim G. Fogel. OBWP; TrJP

Make the Bed. Stephen Cushman. AWTN

Make the Bedlamp Tipsy with Oil. Philodemus. WoPoe, *tr. by* James Laughlin

Make the greate God thy Fort, and dwell. Psalme 91. Bible, *O.T.* NPeEn, *tr. by* Thomas Carew

Make the Man Love Me. Dorothy Fields. ReLy

Make the rhyme you're reading now. (LL) Do It Yourself. Joan Aiken. KaS; NOxBChV

Make there my tomb, beneath the lime-tree's shade. By the Same. Charlotte Smith. CenSon; RWP

Make three fourths of a cross, and a circle complete. *Unknown.* OxNR

Make thyself known, Sibyl, or let despair. Leonardo's "Mona Lisa." Edward Dowden. GSo

Make-Up. Cheryl Clarke. WiU

Make-Up. Maurice Kilwein Guevara. TouFir

Make us Thy mountaineers. Last Defile, The. Amy Carmichael. TrCP

Make way, make way. Stream's Song, The. Lascelles Abercrombie. OBMV

Make way, make way, give leave to rove. Little Good Fellows, The. Herman Melville. NCAP

Make we mery bothe more and lasse. *Unknown.* MiEL

Make we myrie bothe more and lasse. *Unknown. See* Make we mery bothe more and lasse

Make with the Feet. Harold Adamson. ReLy

Make Ye a Joyful Sounding Noise. *Unknown.* AH

Make Your Body a Heart. Rosita Copioli. CItWP, *tr. by* Cinzia Sartini Blum and Lara Trubowitz

Make Your Mark. David Barker. TreFP

Make Your Radiant Twining Curls. Mohammed Iqbal. WoPoe, *tr. by* Frances W. Pritchett

Make yourself pure before you purify others. Tune: "As in a Dream; a Song." Su Tung-p'o (Su Shih). SuSp, *tr. by* Irving Y. Lo

Make/n My Music. Angela Jackson. SeSe

Maker-of-Sevens in the scheme of things. Wife-Woman, The. Anne Spencer. NAAAL

Maker on High, The. Saint Columba. NePenScot, *tr. by* Edwin Morgan

Makers, The. Howard Nemerov. DiPo

Makes him to his own blood strange. (LL) Intellect. Ralph Waldo Emerson. APN-1; NoP-4

Makes lime for Mammon's tower. (LL) Ravaged Villa, The. Herman Melville. APN-2; CTC; NOBA; TCAPo

Makes the eye happy. Buson. EH, *tr. by* Robert Hass

Makes Time so vicious in his reaping. (LL) For a Dead Lady. Edwin

Arlington Robinson.   APT-1; HeIP-4; MoAmPo; NOBA; NoAM; OxBA; PoRA; TCAPo; TFi

Makes You Go Oohhh!   Kalamu ya Salaam.   SpirFl   *Fr.* New Orleans Haiku.

Makhno's Philosophers.   John Streeter Manifold.   CBAP; NOBAu

Makin' Jump Shots.   Michael S. Harper.   ISC; MoASP; PoE

Makin' Whoopee.   Walter Donaldson.   OBCoV
   (Ev'rytime I hear that march from Lohengrin.)   ReLy

Making a Door.   Dennis Schmitz.   LCAP-2

Making a Fist.   Naomi Shihab Nye.   GraLe

Making Babies.   Hilary Llewellyn-Williams.   TCAWP

Making Camp.   David Wagoner.   PoCoUp; VCAP

Making Chicago.   Dennis Schmitz.   IllVoic; LCAP-2

Making Contact.   John Streeter Manifold.   CBAP

Making Conversation.   Maggie Hannan.   MFPA

Making Ends Meet.   Thomas Sayers Ellis.   InTrad

Making Feet and Hands.   Benjamin Péret.   SPE, *tr. by* David Gascoyne

Making for Planet Alice.   Deryn Rees-Jones.   MFPA

Making Fun of the Well at the Inn below the Mountain.   Chu Yün-ming.   CoBLCP, *tr. by* Jonathan Chaves

Making Hay.   Philip Hodgins.   NOBAu

Making It.   Magdalena Gomez.   PueRic

Making It New.   Elmaz Abinader.   GraLe

Making It Stick.   Lawson Fusao Inada.   BAP-97

Making Lists.   Gladys Cardiff.   HATNAP

Making love and omelettes.   Pfarr-Schmerz (Village-Anguish).   Veronica Forrest-Thomson.   HarvBoo

Making love down through the centuries.   Here Today.   Andrew Elliott.   PNI

Making love for ten thousand years on a rockledge.   David Campbell.   BMAP   *Fr.* Ku-ring-gai Rock Carvings.

Making Love, Killing Time.   Anne Ridler.   SacPr

Making Love to Myself.   James L. White.   GLP

Making Money: Drought Year in Minkler, California.   Gary Soto.   NoAM

Making of a Servant, The.   J. J. R. Jolobe.   PeSAV

Making of Color, The.   Hugh Seidman.   YaYoPo

Making of Eve, The.   Julia Copus.   NeBl

Making of the Cross, The.   William Everson.   VGW

Making of the Drum, The.   Edward Kamau Brathwaite.   EmeKit

Making Old Bones.   Alberta Turner.   LCAP-2

Making Our Clowns Martyrs.   Jack A. Mapanje.   HBAPE; NAfrP

Making our pillows either down, or dust. (LL)   Death.   George Herbert.   ESCV; FSCP; GeHe; NAEL-5v1; NAEL-6v1; NAEL-7v1; NoP-4

Making Poems; on the road in Minneapolis.   Sekou Sundiata.   SpirFl

Making Poetry.   Anne Stevenson.   DiPo

Making the batter understand too late. (LL)   Pitcher, The.   Robert Francis.   MoASP; OxBSP; RaBo; WeW-3

Making the Children Behave.   William Daniel Ehrhart.   CDa

Making the green one red. (LL)   William Shakespeare.   EBEV; OxAEP-1   *Fr.* Macbeth.

Making the Jam without You.   Maxine W. Kumin.   NALW

Making the Move.   Paul Muldoon.   NoAM

Making the woods reëcho with his song. (LL)   Fair Morning, The.   Jones Very.   GSo; NOBA

Making tracks.   Aleksandr Aleksandrovich Blok.   WoPoe, *tr. by* Anselm Hollo   *Fr.* Twelve, The.

Making Up for a Soul.   David Wagoner.   VGW

Makings of Happiness, The.   Ronald Wallace.   PBCAP

Makpelah.   Anna Hajnal.   IQMS, *tr. by* Kenneth McRobbie

Mal'Occhio.   Jennifer Martelli.   OPRER

Malacoda.   Samuel Beckett.   CIP-2

Malady of Love Is Nerves, The.   Petronius Arbiter.   AWP, *tr. by* Howard Mumford Jones

Málaga.   Pearse Hutchinson.   BIrV; ModIr; PBCIP

Malaria.   Paolo Ruffilli.   NeIt, *tr. by* Felix Stefanile

Malay Figures.   *Unknown.*   EaWin, *tr. by* W. S. Merwin

Malcolm.   Lucille Clifton.   NAAAL

Malcolm.   Welton Smith.   BPo

Malcolm Is 'bout More than Wearing a Cap.   Michael Warr.   UnSA

Malcolm Lowry.   Epitaph.   Malcolm Lowry.   OBCoV

Malcolm Mooney's Land.   William Sydney Graham.   NPeEn; NePenScot

Malcolm Spoke / Who Listened?   Haki R. Madhubuti.   ESEAA; NAAAL

Malcolm X.   Gwendolyn Brooks.   IllVoic; TTY
   (Original.)   NAAAL

Malcolm X—an Autobiography.   Larry Neal.   BPo

Maldive Shark, The.   Herman Melville.   APN-2; ColAP; NAAL-2v1; NAAL-3; NCAP; NOBA; NoP-4; OxBA; PAI; PoE; RB; TAP; TCAPo

Maldoror.   Comte de Lautréamont.

"I am filthy. Lice gnaw me. Swine, when they look at me, vomit. The scabs."   PFTM-1

Male, The.   Carla Harryman.   PmAP

Male child—ox abandoned to the vultures!, A.   War Song of the Basotho, A.   *Unknown.*   PeSAV, *tr. by* Daniel P. Kunene

Male Grownups.   Hoda Hussein.   PoArWo, *tr. by* Cornelia Al-Khaled

Male is not less the soul nor more, he too is in his place, The.   Walt Whitman.   ErotSp   *Fr.* I Sing the Body Electric.

Male Nipples.   Brenda Hillman.   ExTi

Male Rage Poem.   Pier Giorgio Di Cicco.   NOBC

Malediction.   *Unknown.*   WoPoe, *tr. by* Arthur Waley

Malediction upon Myself.   Elinor Wylie.   ColAP

Malefic Return, The.   Ramón López Velarde.   OBVE, *tr. by* Samuel Beckett

Malepractice and maleabsence issue is loneliness & limiting to-.   Men and Birth: the Unexplainable.   Haki R. Madhubuti.   RaBo

Malest Cornifici Tuo Catullo.   Allen Ginsberg.   BB; NeAP

Malfeasance, The.   Alan Bold.   OBSP

Malibú, El.   Richard Blanco.   AmPoNex

Malice of Innocence, The.   Denise Levertov.   BodElec; NNaP

Malicious insect, little vengeful bee.   To an Angry Bee.   John Clare.   CenSon

Malignant gnomes who write reviews in Rhodes, The.   Prologue to the Aetia.   Callimachus.   WoPoe, *tr. by* Stanley Lombardo and Diane Rayor

Malignant planets! do ye still combine.   Sow of Feeling, The.   Robert Fergusson.   NOEC

Malines.   James Kenneth Stephen.   OBCoV

Malines.   Paul Verlaine.   SxFrPo, *tr. by* Martin Sorrell

Mallard Nests, The.   *Hungarian Oral Tradition.*   IQMS, *tr. by* Watson Kirkconnell

Mallard nests among the reeds, The.   Mallard Nests, The.   *Hungarian Oral Tradition.*   IQMS, *tr. by* Watson Kirkconnell

Malleus Maleficarum 4.   Maureen Seaton.   ExTi

Malta.   John Forbes.   NOBAu

Maltese Dog, A.   Tymnes.   FaBoCh; FaBoEE; Spl; WoPoe, *tr. by* Edmund Charles Blunden   *Fr.* Epigrams.

Malvern at a Distance.   John Keble.   OxBSo

Malvern Hill.   Herman Melville.   APN-2; CBCWP; ColAP; TAP

Malvern Hills.   Joseph Cottle.
   Industrial Evils.   NOEC

Malvern Water, says Dr. John Wall.   Malvern Waters.   *Unknown.*   FaBoEE

Malvern Waters.   *Unknown.*   FaBoEE

Malvolio in San Francisco.   Jack Gilbert.   YaYoPo

Mam'selle.   Edmund Goulding.   ReLy

Mama.   Claire Kageyama.   UnSA

Mama.   Timothy Liu.   WiU

Mama.   Rohan B. Preston.   AmPoNex

Mama and Daughter.   Langston Hughes.   UnPo

Mama, Come Back.   Nellie Wong.   UnSA

Mama Dot.   Frederick D'Aguiar.   Oth

Mama Dot Warns against an Easter Rising.   Frederick D'Aguiar.   Oth

Mama / eats death / tastes like fish.   Monogram 4.   Martina Werner.   BoWoP, *tr. by* Rosmarie Waldrop

Mamá Go see for yourself.   Tomás.   Luis Lopez.   GeoH

Mama / I wish I were silver.   Silly Song.   Federico García Lorca.   TTTS, *tr. by* M. D. Herter Norton

Mama Loves Janis Joplin.   Richard Speakes.   SwNoth

Mama Mary's counting them.   Birds on a Powerline.   Herbert Asquith.   NAAAL

Mama, / papa, / and us.   Inconvenience, An.   John Raven.   BPo; CRP

Mama, please brush off my coat.   Mama and Daughter.   Langston Hughes.   UnPo

Mame.   Jerry Herman.   ReLy

Mame was singing.   Queen of the Blues.   Gwendolyn Brooks.   NALW; SeSe

Mamie.   Carl Sandburg.   APT-1

Mamie beat her head against the bars of a little Indiana town and.   Mamie.   Carl Sandburg.   APT-1

Mamma!   Frank Horne.   BPo

Mamma Goes Where Papa Goes.   Jack Yellen.   ReLy

Mamma! mamma! two eaglets cried.   Taking Time to Grow.   Mary Mapes Dodge.   SWaP

Mammals.   Lesley Dauer.   NAPBL

Mammals cling so! It must come.   Vigil.   Blair Gibb.   Prnts

Mammon Marriage.   George Macdonald.   BoLoP; EBVV; SacPr

Mammoth morning moved grey flanks and groaned, A.   Walking Wounded.   Vernon Scannell.   OBWP

Mammy mine / Your little rollin' stone that rolled away.   Rock-a-Bye Your Baby with a Dixie Melody.   Jean Schwartz.   ReLy

Mams, pig-sick of oilstains in the wash, The.   Breaking the Chain.   Tony Harrison.   UV

Man. Sir John Davies. *Fr.* Nosce Teipsum.

Man. Oscar Hahn. TCLAP, *tr.* by Sandy McKinney

Man. George Herbert. BASC; ESCV; FSCP; GeHe; NAEL-5v1; NAEL-6v1; NAEL-7v1; NoP-4

Man. Christopher Southgate. NewEx

Man. Archana Varma. OMIP, *tr.* by Aruna Sitesh

Man. Henry Vaughan. ESCV; GeHe; MeLP; NOBE; NOCV; OBEV; SCGP

Man. Humbert Wolfe. MoBrPo

Man, A. Nicanor Parra. VCWP, *tr.* by W. S. Merwin

Man, The. Man and Woman Go through the Cancer Ward. Gottfried Benn. PFTM-1

Man, The. Robert Creeley. OBAL

Man, A. I think it is a man. My Dream about the Poet. Lucille Clifton. TRP

Man, a man, a kingdom for a man!, A. John Marston. NoSic *Fr.* Satires.

Man, A / Who sleeps by the window was. Tale of Bananas, A. Víctor Hernández Cruz. PueRic

Man, a Woman, A. Vincent Buckley. BMAP

Man, a woman, an old man. They are in a hut. The man holds a news-, A. Hair Tonic. Gisèle Prassinos. PFTM-1

Man Adrift on a Slim Spar, A. Stephen Crane. APN-2; NAAL-2v2

Man against the Sky, The. Edwin Arlington Robinson. OxBA; TCAPo

Man Alone. Louise Bogan. NoP-4

Man alone at the third-floor window, The. West Strand Visions. James Simmons. ModIr; PBCIP

Man and a Woman, A. Juan Gelman. BLPSL, *tr.* by Rene de Costa, Rigas Kappatos and Eleni Paidoussi

Man and a woman recite their dreams, A. Tracing of an Evening. David Shapiro. PmAP

Man and Bat. D. H. Lawrence. RB

Man and Beast. Léopold Sédar Senghor. PFTM-1

Man and Cows. Andrew Young. EBEV

Man and Dog. Edward Thomas. PeFWW

Man and God Distinguished. Michael Echeruo. PBMAP

Man and His Image, The. Jean de La Fontaine. OBVE, *tr.* by Elizur Wright

Man and the Tree, The. Philip Mead. NOBAu

Man and the Weasel, The. Phaedrus. AWP, *tr.* by Christopher Smart

Man and Wife. Mitchell Goodman. VGW

Man and Wife. Robert Lowell. BoLoP; CoAmPo; ColAP; NAAL-2v2; VCAP

Man and Woman. Robert Conquest. OxBTC

Man and woman, a. Woman's Dream, The. Frances Horovitz. BrRo

Man and Woman Absolutely White, A. André Breton. PFTM-1

Man and Woman Go through the Cancer Ward. Gottfried Benn. PFTM-1

Man and woman lie on a white bed, A. Happiness. Louise Glück. HarvBoo

Man and woman walking, A. Feather, The. Lilian Bowes-Lyon. LW

Man at leisure. Cassia flowers fall. Bird-Singing Stream. Wang Wei. ChinPo, *tr.* by Yip Wai-lim

Man at the moment of departure, turning, A. Ritual of Departure. Thomas Kinsella. CIP-2

Man Awakened by a Song above His Roof, The. Tomas Tranströmer. SPE, *tr.* by Robert Bly

(Morning, May rain. The city is silent still.) SPE, *tr.* by Robert Bly

Man Be Merie as Bryd on Berie. *Unknown.* SacPr

Man beats his wife on the mountainside, A. Mines in Sepia Tint, The. Steve Griffiths. TCAWP

Man behind you spoke to the tracery, The. Walkways, The. John Ashbery. BodElec

Man bent over his guitar, The. Wallace Stevens. NoAM; RaBo *Fr.* Man with the Blue Guitar, The.

Man, bewar of thine wowing. *Unknown.* MiEL

Man blew away, A. Blizzard, The. Roger McDonald. NOBAu

Man-brained and man-handed ground-ape, physically, The. Original Sin. Robinson Jeffers. MoAmPo

Man called Andronicus (Titus), A. Limerick. Paul Wigmore. PeLi

Man Can Complain, Can't He?, A. Ogden Nash. NBLV

Man Cannot Name Himself. Luci Shaw. TrCP

Man carries a skull of red yarn, A. In an Empty Field at Night. Gregory Orr. PAI

Man Carrying Bale. Harold Monro. MoBrPo

Man Closing Up, The. Donald Justice. CoAP

Man comes last: he's got to. Gregorio Scalise. ItPo, *tr.* by Gayle Ridinger

Man Condemned to Death, The. Jean Genet. CAGL, *tr.* by David Fisher and Guy Wernham

Man, could you in yourself the vermin all behold. "Angelus Silesius." GePo, *tr.* by George C. Schoolfield *Fr.* Cherubical Wanderer, The.

Man dear, did you never hear of buxom Molly Bloom at all. Post Ulixem Scriptum. James Joyce. OBCoV

Man, dream[e] no more of curious mysteries. Fulke Greville, 1st Baron Brooke. NOSC; NoSic *Fr.* Caelica.

Man Escaped, A. Lewis Warsh. BodElec

Man-Fate, The. William Everson. NoAM

Man Feared that He Might Find an Assassin, A. Stephen Crane. APN-2; NAAL-2v2; NoP-4 *Fr.* Black Riders [and Other Lines], The.

Man feels humiliated, A. Instinct, The. Jack Myers. BodElec

Man filled grain, A. Tattered Sack, The. Devara Dasimayya. WoPoe, *tr.* by A. K. Ramanujan

Man Flammonde, from God knows where, The. Flammonde. Edwin Arlington Robinson. NoAM

Man flees suffocation. René Char. AF

Man! Foolish Man! On Exodus 3:14: "I am that I am." Matthew Prior. ChIV-1; NOCV

Man fools about with self-analysis. Collective Portrait, The. Robert Finch. MoCV

Man, for whom everything is past. Remembrance of Five Loaves. Mikhail Pozdnyayev [*or* Pozdniaev]. TCRP, *tr.* by Vladimir Lunis and Albert C. Todd

Man Frail, and God Eternal. Isaac Watts. ECEV; InvLi; NPeEn; NOCV; OBVE; OxBEV; PWR; SacPr; TOF

(Our God, Our Help.) NoP-4

Man from Changi, The. Graeme Hetherington. NOBAu

Man from Maputo and so on, A. Limerick. J. H. Lee. PeLi

Man from Snowy River, The. Andrew Barton Paterson. CBAP

Man from Strathbogie, The. Olive Mary Finnin. NOBAu

Man from the Death Institute. Novica Tadic. VCWP, *tr.* by Charles Simic

Man from the *Washington Post*, A. Limerick. Anthony Burgess. PeLi

Man from Washington, The. James Welch. CDW; HATNAP; NoAM; PoPoPo; RaBo

Man git his feet set in a sticky mudbank, A. Riverbank Blues. Sterling Allen Brown. MakPoe

Man goes down the street, A. Song of the Alpine Hunter. Paul Van Ostaijen. TuT, *tr.* by Theo Dorgan

Man grows old and indolent, A. (LL) But I Am Growing Old and Indolent. Robinson Jeffers. APT-1; ColAP; NOBA; TAP

Man had just married an automobile, A. Automobile, The. Russell Edson. LCAP-2; RaBo

Man half Alan and half Uncle Arnold, A. Impetus. Mary Leader. NAPBL

Man has been in the VAH Library all day long, A. Simon J. Ortiz. NAAL-5 *Fr.* Poems from the Veterans Hospital.

Man has been standing, A. Tunnel, The. Mark Strand. HeIP-4; TwCP

Man has created death. (LL) Death. W. B. Yeats. OxAEP-2; OxBSP

Man has forgot his Origin; in vain. Origin of Man, I, The. Jones Very. APN-1

Man has found no comfort in the grave, The. (LL) Man Who Dreamed of Faeryland, The. W. B. Yeats. NAEL-5v2; NAEL-6v2; NoAM

Man has no roots, A. T'ao Ch'ien [*or* T'ao Yuan-ming]. SuSp

Man has nought so much his own. Bonds of Friendship, The. Simon Dach. GePo, *tr.* by Ingrid Waløe-Engel

Man hath a weary pilgrimage. Remembrance. Robert Southey. TreFP

Man He Killed, The. Thomas Hardy. ChAP; FaBoWar; HAP; HarvBoo; HeIP-4; MoBrPo; NIP-4; OBWP; PAI; RB; TFi; WeW-3

Man held his hands to his heart as he danced, The. Of the Ever-Changing Agitation in the Air. Jorie Graham. ExTi

Man hired by John Smith and Co., A. Limerick. "Mark Twain." InPK-6; PeLi

Man, The. His Bowl. His Raspberries. Claudia Rankine. GT

Man, husband existence: ne'er launch on the sea. Epitaph of Cleonicus. Theocritus. FaBoEE, *tr.* by Charles Stuart Calverley

Man I had a love for, The. Old Woman's Lamentations, An. François Villon. MoBrPo; OBMV, *tr.* by J. M. Synge

Man I Love, The. George Gershwin. ReLy

Man I Love and I Have a Typical Evening the Night Richard M. Nixon Dies, The. Jim Elledge. ReTh

Man I Love and I Shop at Jewel, The. Jim Elledge. IllVoic; ReTh

Man I love cooks me potatoes, The. Potatoes. Daisy Rhau. SpudSo

Man I married twice, The. Reject Jell-o. Lucille Day. MPUn

Man I saw in the forest, The. Dream 2: Brian the Still-Hunter. Margaret Atwood. BoWoP

Man, if I said once, "I know." Islands, The. Randall Jarrell. SPE

Man, if you God as balm, as light, and sweetness take. "Angelus Silesius." GePo, *tr.* by George C. Schoolfield *Fr.* Cherubical Wanderer, The.

Man, if you're dead, why are you leading. Sonny's Purple Heart. Adrian C. Louis. ReTh

Man, if your heart is gold, and if your soul is pure. "Angelus Silesius." GePo, *tr.* by George C. Schoolfield *Fr.* Cherubical Wanderer, The.

Man Impregnated. Moniza Alvi. NeBl

Man in a restaurant shook hands with someone, A. Considering How Exaggerated Music Is. Leslie Scalapino. FTOS

Man in a Shell, The. Angela Ball. ExTi

Man in Black, The.   Mark Strand.   SPE

Man in Blue, A.   James Schuyler.   FTOS; PmAP

Man in California says he understands me, A.   Long Distance.   Aleda Shirley.   ExTi

Man in Hangchou Spread Word that I Had Died. Chen-chü Heard of This and Was Upset, So I Have Written This to Send Him, A.   Ni Tsan.   CoBLCP, *tr. by* Jonathan Chaves

Man in His Life, A.   Yehuda Amichai [*or* Amikhai].   VCWP, *tr. by* Benjamin Harshav

Man in his life has no time to have, A.   Man in His Life, A.   Yehuda Amichai [*or* Amikhai].   VCWP, *tr. by* Benjamin Harshav

Man in his secret shrine.   Hymn in Columbus Circle.   Stephen Vincent Benét.   OBAL

Man in Love, A.   Lady Mary Wortley Montagu.   LW

Man in Novosibirsk.   H. L. Hix.   SpudSo

Man in Our Town.   *Unknown.*   ReMoGo

Man in righteousness arrayed, The.   Horace.   *See* Virtue, dear friends, needs no "defense."

Man in righteousness arrayed [*or* array'd], The.   To Sally.   John Quincy Adams.   APN-1; AWP; OBAL

Man in terror of impotence, A.   Ninth Symphony of Beethoven Understood at Last as a Sexual Message, The.   Adrienne Rich.   PFTM-2; TAP

Man in the black suit delivers a eulogy, The.   Eulogy, The.   Carol Muske.   PBCAP

Man in the clot of colors—which are people, A.   La Guardia, the Story.   Jane Mead.   BodElec

Man in the feed store called them mountain beavers, The.   Looking for Mountain Beavers.   David Wagoner.   VGW

Man in the Honeysuckle, The.   David Campbell.   BMAP

Man in the Land of the Houyhnhnms, A.   Limerick.   W. S. Brownlie.   PeLi

Man in the Middle of the Street.   Petronius Arbiter.   WoPoe, *tr. by* Tim Reynolds

Man in the Moon.   Linda Hogan.   HATNAP

Man in the Moon ("The Man in the moon drinks claret.").   *Unknown.*   OxNR

Man in the Moon ("The Man in the moon was caught in a trap.").   *Unknown.*   OxNR

Man in the Moon ("The Man in the moon came tumbling down.").   *Unknown.*   OxBoLi; ReMoGo

Man in the Moon ("Mon in the mone stond and strit.").   *Unknown.*   MiEL

Man in the Moon, The.   Alvin Greenberg.   OPRER

Man in the moon, The.   *Unknown.*   LB; OxBoLi; OxNR

Man in the Moon, The ("The Man in the Moon, as he sails the sky.").   *Unknown.*   OTCP

Man in the Moon, as he sails the sky, The.   Man in the Moon, The.   *Unknown.*   OTCP

Man in the moon came tumbling down.   Man in the Moon.   *Unknown.*   OxBoLi; ReMoGo

Man in the moon drinks claret / But he is a dull jack-a-dandy, The.   Man in the Moon.   *Unknown.*   OxNR

Man in the Moon looked out of the moon, The.   Bedtime.   *Unknown.*   ReMoGo

Man in the Moon Stayed up Too Late, The.   John Ronald Reuel Tolkien.   OBSP

Man in the moon was caught in a trap, The.   Man in the Moon.   *Unknown.*   OxNR

Man in the mune, The / is making shune.   *Unknown.*   OxNR

Man in the next office, The.   Hubris.   Mary Karr.   NIL-7

Man in the red scarf comes—from five split places, The.   Raspberry in the Pudding, The.   Philip O'Connor.   SPE

Man in the Street.   Robert Penn Warren.   OBAL

Man in the street is fed, The.   Carl Sandburg.   OxBA

Man in the Tree, The.   Mark Strand.   SPE

Man in the Valley of Women, A.   Chris Greenhalgh.   NeBl

Man in the white room next door wrote this, I think: wrote this thinking I wanted to read it, The.   For the Reader (Blank Book).   Laura Mullen.   ExTi

Man in the White Suit, The.   Nick Drake.   NeBl

Man in the wilderness asked [of] me [*or* said to me], The [*or* A].   Mother Goose.   FaBoCh; LB; OxNR; ReMoGo; Spl

Man into a Churchyard.   Bernard Gutteridge.   SPE

Man, introverted man, having crossed.   Science.   Robinson Jeffers.   OxBA

Man Is a Spirit.   Stevie Smith.   OxBC

Man Is a Weaver.   Moses Ibn Ezra.   TrJP, *tr. by* Emma Lazarus

Man is approaching, A.   Man Went to See the Doltons, A.   Giovanna Pollarolo.   TANSG, *tr. by* Marjorie Agosin

Man is bending his wife, A.   Conjugal.   Russell Edson.   PmAP

Man is blest which can indure, The.   Verses Written by a Gentlewoman upon the Jaylors Conversion.   Anne Dowriche.   EMWP

Man Is Born in Tao.   Chuang Tzu.   BLT, *tr. by* Thomas Merton

Man is Buddha.   Ryushi.   JDP, *tr. by* Yoel Hoffmann

Man Is Dead, A.   Claire Gebeyli.   PoArWo, *tr. by* Mona Takyeddine Amyuni

Man is dear to man: the poorest poor.   William Wordsworth.   PoToHe

Man is following me, A.   Jennifer Rankin.   BMAP

Man Is in Pain.   Philip Lamantia.   NeAP

Man is leaning on a cold iron rail, A.   Man Who Loved Islands, The.   Derek Walcott.   BodElec; NoAM

Man is lonely: the moon shines all the brighter.   Chiu Tsz-Yung and Cecil Clement.   ColAnChi, *tr. by* Cecil Clementi   *Fr.* Cantonese Love-Songs.

Man is no microcosm, and they detract.   Habitation, The.   Ralph Knevet.   NOSC

Man is permitted much.   Elements, The.   John Henry, Cardinal Newman.   SacPr

Man is pictured in the photo—, A.   My Photograph.   Vadim Konstantinovich Strelchenko.   TCRP, *tr. by* Lubov Yakovleva

Man is shut in.   Man-today.   Andrée Chedid.   HAWP, *tr. by* Mirène Ghossein and Samuel Hazo

Man is still alive, The.   Amnesty.   "Ivan Venediktovich Elagin."   TCRP; TCRusP, *tr. by* Bertram D. Wolfe

Man Is the Highest Thing.   "Angelus Silesius."   GePo, *tr. by* George C. Schoolfield   *Fr.* Cherubical Wanderer, The.

Man is the judgment of the world. (LL)   Variations.   Randall Jarrell.   VGW; WoPoe

Man Is What He Wills to Be.   Mrs. Henry Linden.   CBWP-4

Man knocked three times, A.   Madam and the Wrong Visitor.   Langston Hughes.   SAmP

Man knows not love—such love as woman feels.   Woman's Love.   *Unknown.*   TreFP

Man know[e]s where first he ships himself[e], but he.   Man's Dying-Place Uncertain.   Robert Herrick.   CaPo

Man Leavens the Batch.   Mildmay Fane, 2d Earl of Westmorland.   BeJo

Man letters the sign for his grocery in Arabic and English, A.   Steps.   Naomi Shihab Nye.   ExTi

Man, like others, formed by God, A.   Saxons of Flint, The.   *Unknown.*   OBWVE, *tr. by* Mary C. Llewelyn

Man lives his life in a dust bowl.   Han-shan.   SuSp

Man lives in the wide world, A.   Aleksandr Petrovich Mezhirov.   TCRP

Man looking into the sea.   Grave, A.   Marianne Craig Moore.   APT-1; FaBoWP; HAP; HeIP-4; NAAL-2v2; NOBA; NoAM; NoP-4; PoE; TAP; TFi; TRP; UnPo; WPE; WeW-3

Man Lost by a River, A.   Michael C. Blumenthal.   RaBo

Man Lying in a Hallway.   Huw Jones.   TCAWP

Man Lying on a Wall.   Michael Longley.   ModIr; NPeEn; PNI

Man may longe lyves wene.   *Unknown.*   *See* Man meye longe him lives wene

Man may make a Remark, A.   Emily Dickinson.   SAmP

Man May Tear a Jewel, A.   Bhartrihari.   WoPoe, *tr. by* Barbara Stoler Miller

Man Meeting Himself.   Howard Sergeant.   SPE

Man Meets a Woman in the Street, A.   Randall Jarrell.   NoP-4

Man, mek me tell yu, dat was a fete.   Dance Hall.   Geoffrey Philp.   WaCA

Man meye longe him lives wene.   *Unknown.*   MiEL

Man-Moth, The.   Elizabeth Bishop.   APT-2; MoAmPo; NALW; NOBA; NoAM

Man must tempt his heart with fancy, A.   World of Fancy.   Sami Mahdi.   MAP, *tr. by* May Jayyusi

Man Named Troy, A.   Reginald Shepherd.   IllVoic

Man never knows precisely what is right.   Essay on Man.   *Unknown.*   PoToHe

Man: 1961.   Pranabendu Dasgupta.   OMIP, *tr. by* Buddhadeva Bose

Man o' War Bird.   Derek Walcott.   TTY

Man, obsessed by people, A.   Man Rises from the Cave of Hira', A.   Al-Munsif Al-Wahaybi.   MAP, *tr. by* Salma Khadra Jayyusi and Naomi Shihab Nye

Man of Bombay, The.   *Unknown.*   ReMoGo

Man of bone confirms his throne, The.   New Ancient of Days, The.   Herman Melville.   OBAL

Man of God is drunken without wine, The.   Jelaluddin [*or* Jalal al-Din] Rumi.   TAL   *Fr.* Dīvāni Shamsi Tabrīz.

Man of Green Hill.   Song of the Man of Green Hill, The.   Kao Ch'i.   CoBLCP; ColAnChi, *tr. by* Jonathan Chaves

Man of independent means, A.   No Occupation.   George Rostrevor Hamilton.   FaBoEE

Man of Law's Epilogue, The.   Geoffrey Chaucer.   NAEL-7v1   *Fr.* Canterbury Tales, The.

Man of Life Upright, The.   Thomas Campion.   NoSic; PoRA

Man of marble holds the throne, A.   Roman Stage, The.   Lionel Pigot Johnson.   NOBVV

Man of numbers, The.   Numerology.   Jerome Rothenberg.   FTOS

Man of Taste, The.   James Bramston.
    "Whoe'er he be that to a taste aspires."   NOEC

Man of the House, The. David Wagoner. NoAM

Man of the Stone City. Mahmoud Al-Buraikan. MAP, *tr. by* Lena Jayyusi and Naomi Shihab Nye

Man of Thessaly, [The]. *Unknown. See* Alexander's Song

Man of Tyre, The. D. H. Lawrence. TOF

Man of Valour to His Fair Lady, The. William Dunbar. MiEL

Man-of-War Hawk, The. Herman Melville. APN-2; OWoS

Man of Words, A. *Unknown.* OTCP

Man on a Fire Escape. Edward Hirsch. UrbNat

Man on his own in a car, A. Meditation on the A30. Sir John Betjeman. RB

Man on the Bed, The. Debora Greger. PoSol

Man on the Dump, The. Wallace Stevens. APT-1; HAP; NAWM-7v2; NoAM

Man on the Edge. Heberto Padilla. VCWP

Man on the Flying Trapeze, The. *Unknown.* OxBoLi

Man on the Hotel Room Bed, The. Galway Kinnell. VCAP

Man on the Tower, The. Charles Rafferty. AmPoNex

Man once married who hunts wife once more, A. *Unknown.* GrAn

Man—pitiful insect. Ch'i-yü-ko. *Unknown.* CoBCP, *tr. by* Burton Watson

Man Proposes, God Disposes. Bachner. INSAB

Man pulling radishes, The. Issa. EH; EnlH

Man Rapes 25 in fight. Up, Up, Home & Away. John Forbes. NOBAu

Man Rises from the Cave of Hira', A. Al-Munsif Al-Wahaybi. MAP, *tr. by* Salma Khadra Jayyusi and Naomi Shihab Nye

Man Root, The. Kazuko Shiraishi. PFTM-2, *tr. by* Ikuko Atsumi and Kenneth Rexroth

Man's a Man for A' That, A. Robert Burns. *See* For A' That and A' That ["Is there, for honest poverty"]

Man's a poor deluded bubble. Song. Robert Dodsley. OxBSP

Man's [a] Sliding Mood, A. Mary Elizabeth Fullerton. CBAP; NOBAu

Man's and woman's bodies lay without souls. Childish Prank, A. Ted Hughes. CABP; NPeEn; OxBC

Man's body at auction, A. Walt Whitman. SAmP, *Fr.* I Sing the Body Electric.

Man's Civil[l] War[re]. Robert Southwell. NoSic

Man's Country. Daryl Hine. IllVoic

Man's Days. Eden Phillpotts. OBEV; OxBTC

Man's dead, The. Edward Hopper Retrospective, The. Tony Quagliano. PoSol

Man's Dying-Place Uncertain. Robert Herrick. CaPo

Man's end. Hamei. JDP, *tr. by* Yoel Hoffmann

Man's got a heart, A. Reviewing the Situation. Lionel Bart. ReLy

Man's Life. Inscription in Osmington Church, Dorset. *Unknown.* NPeEn

Man's life is a hundred years' constant vexation, A. Sent to Recluse Ch'eng. Wang Chi. SuSp, *tr. by* Hellmut Wilhelm

Man's life is death. Yet Christ endured to live. Wednesday in Holy Week. Christina Georgina Rossetti. TrCP

Man's life is laid in the loom of time. Loom of Time, The. *Unknown.* ITBLP

Man's life is like a Sparrow, mighty King! William Wordsworth. OWoS *Fr.* Ecclesiastical Sonnets.

Man's life is warm, glad, sad, 'twixt loves and graves. Leigh Hunt. NPeEn *Fr.* Fish, the Man, and the Spirit, The.

Man's life is well compared to a feast. Comparison of the Life of Man, A. Richard Barnfield [*or* Barnefield]. NoSic; OxBSP

Man's life's tragedy: his mother's womb. De Morte. Sir Henry Wotton. BASC; NOSC; OxBSP

Man's makeshift days would flash past at the best. Antiphanes. GrAn

Man's Mortality. Simon Wastell. FaBoCh *Fr.* Microbiblion.

Man's mother is very sick, A. Man, A. Nicanor Parra. VCWP, *tr. by* W. S. Merwin

Man's Natural Infirmity. John Day. InvLi

Man's own resinous heart has fed. (LL) W. B. Yeats. FaBoTw; HAP; NOBE; PoE *Fr.* Resurrection, The.

Man's Requirements, A. Elizabeth Barrett Browning. RACG; ViWPN

Man's Song, about His Daughter, A. *Unknown.* STP, *tr. by* Armand Schwerner

Man's witness to himself. (LL) Hiroshima. "Agyeya." OMIP; WoPoe, *tr. by* Agyeya and Leonard Nathan

Man's years fall short of a hundred. *Unknown.* CoBCP

Man said, The. Historic Moment, An. William J. Harris. KaS

Man said to the universe, A. Stephen Crane. APN-2; BRP; FaBoEE; NAAL-2v2; OBAL; OBSV; TAP; TCAPo; WeW-3 *Fr.* War Is Kind.

Man said unto his Angel, A. Kings, The. Louise Imogen Guiney. SacPr

Man sat in the felon's tank, alone, A. In the Tank. Thom Gunn. NoAM

Man sat staring at a doll's house, A. Doll's House, A. Kit Wright. EmeKit

Man Saves Own Life. Aaron Anstett. AmPoNex

Man, seated high on Learning's awful throne. Women of the Future. Mary Scott. ECWP

Man Seeking Experience Enquires His Way of a Drop of Water, The. Ted Hughes. OxAEP-2

Man sees a tiny couple in the distance, and thinks they might be his mother and father, A. Optical Prodigal, The. Russell Edson. PmAP

Man sees the stars. Man and God Distinguished. Michael Echeruo. PBMAP

Man She Called Honey, and Married, The. Alberto A. Ríos. ReTh

Man shot himself, A. Leader. Bruce Bennett. InPK-6

Man should have no thought for property, A. Property. Robert Garioch. FaBoWar

Man should hold in very dear esteem, A. Masolino da Todi. EaItPo, *tr. by* Dante Gabriel Rossetti

Man sits in a timelessness, The. Rescue, The. Robert Creeley. CRP; VCAP

Man Splitting Wood in the Daybreak, The. Galway Kinnell. VCAP

Man, standing in the shadows of a, A. For H. W. Fuller. Carolyn M. Rodgers. BPo

Man staring at a small lake sees, A. Fishing in Winter. Ralph Burns. MoASP

Man still light of foot, but ageing, took, A. Thinking of Mr. D. Thomas Kinsella. NoAM

Man stole fire, and Zeus created flame. Pallades [*or* Pallades]. GrAn

Man stood in the laurel tree, A. Things. Louis Simpson. OxBC

Man Struck Twenty Times by Lightning, The. Maxine Chernoff. PmAP

Man That Got Away, The. Harold Arlen. ReLy

Man that had six mortal wounds, a man, A. Cuchulain Comforted. W. B. Yeats. TOF

Man that hath a handsome wife, The. Things Forbidden. *Unknown.* NoSic

Man that hath great griefs I pity not, The. Pain. Thomas Edward Brown. SacPr

Man, That Is Born of a Woman. Rosanna Warren. ExTi

Man, that is borne of a woman is of a few dayes, and full of trouble. Bible, *O.T.* OBVE *Fr.* Job.

Man that mates wi' Poverty, The. Comfort in Puirtith. Helen B. Cruickshank. OxBS

Man that never will declare his thought, The. Sadi [*or* Saadi *or* Sa'di]. AWP, *tr. by* L. Cranmer-Byng *Fr.* Gulistan, The.

Man that sees by chance his picture made, A. Robert Bridges. NoAM *Fr.* Growth of Love, The.

Man, the egregious egoist. Cold-blooded Creatures. Elinor Wylie. OxBSP

Man the hare has met, The. Names of the Hare, The. *Unknown.* RB; WoPoe, *tr. by* Seamus Heaney

Man the Monarch. Mary Leapor. ECWP

Man. The Woman, The. Hans [*or* Jean] Arp. PFTM-1

Man Then Suddenly Stops Moving, A. Alberto A. Ríos. NoAM

Man (they say), A. Paulus [*or* Paulos] Silentiarius. GrAn

Man Thinking about Woman. Haki R. Madhubuti. PAI

Man throws ten thousand shovels of grael at a window screen, A. El periférico, or Sleep. Joshua Clover. NeAmPo

Man-thunder, woman-lightning. Opus 17. Witter Bynner. APT-1, *tr. by* Emanuel Morgan

Man-today. Andrée Chedid. HAWP, *tr. by* Mirène Ghossein and Samuel Hazo

Man too bad you don't notice that my eyes. Mississippi. Aimé Césaire. NegPo, *tr. by* Clayton Eshleman and Denis Kelly

Man traveled in Europe among Fauves, A. Night Shadows. William Carpenter. PoSol

Man United. *Unknown.* FaBoVe

Man unto His Fellow Man. Norman Corwin. TrJP *Fr.* On a Note of Triumph.

Man upon mold, whatsoever thou be. Money Is What Matters. *Unknown.* MiEL

Man Upright, The. Thomas Macdonagh. BIrV

Man walks a dusty road, A. Olmos. Dennis Nurkse. OPRER

Man walks beside them, A. White Oxen. Louis Simpson. NoAM

Man Walks By with a Loaf of Bread on His Shoulder, A. César Vallejo. PoetW; TCLAP, *tr. by* Clayton Eshleman

Man walks calmly on his legs in the grass, A. We Shall Overcome. Breyten Breytenbach. PeSAV, *tr. by* Ernst Van Heerden

Man walks into a room, A. There is a corpse on the floor. Gorg, a Detective Story. B. P. Nichol. NOBC

Man walks on the bridge and gives away the change in his, A. Sri Sri. OMIP *Fr.* Some People Laugh, Some People Cry.

Man walks towards town, A. Late Hour, The. Mark Strand. AWTN; HCAP

Man wants but little here below. Wants of Man, The. John Quincy Adams. APN-1; OBAL

Man was made of social earth. Ralph Waldo Emerson. APN-1 *Fr.* Initial, Dæmonic, and Celestial Love.

Man Was Made to Mourn, a Dirge. Robert Burns. TreFP

Man was sitting underneath a tree, A. Seumas Beg. James Stephens. OxBTC

Man watches a woman disrobe in a window, A.　Voyeur.　David Moolten. BloBone

Man Watching, The.　Rainer Maria Rilke.　RaBo, *tr. by* Robert Bly

Man waxy— he jogs along the fields, The.　Arthur Rimbaud.　OBWP, *tr. by* Robert Lowell　*Fr.* Eighteen-Seventy.

Man went a-hunting at Reigate, A.　*Unknown.*　ReMoGo

Man went forth one day at eve, A.　Tragedy.　"Æ"　MoBrPo

Man Went to See the Doltons, A.　Giovanna Pollarolo.　TANSG, *tr. by* Marjorie Agosin

Man, what is hope? . . . a horrifying whore.　On Hope.　Sándor Petőfi.　IQMS, *tr. by* Peter Zollman

Man White, Brown Girl and All That Jazz / Upon the Occasion of His Marriage. Gloria C. Oden.　GT

Man Who Beat Hemingway, The.　Martín Espada.　MoASP

Man Who Became Old, The.　Alberto A. Ríos.　NoAM

Man who buries his house in the sand, The.　Houses.　Agha Shahid Ali. NIP-4

Man Who Came to the Last Floor, The.　Víctor Hernández Cruz.　PueRic

Man who changed the paths of earth and sea, The.　Thermopylai.　Parmenion of Macedon.　GrAn, *tr. by* Peter Jay

Man Who Closed Shop, The.　Stephen Dunn.　NIP-4

Man who doesn't love boys and single-foot horses and dogs, his heart will never know pleasure, The.　Theognis.　CAGL, *tr. by* Peter Bing and Rip Cohen *Fr.* Second Book of Theognis, The.

Man Who Dreamed of Faeryland, The.　W. B. Yeats.　NAEL-5v2; NAEL-6v2; NoAM

　(He stood among a crowd at Drumahair.)　NoP-4

Man who feels not, more or less, somewhat, The.　Sonnet: Of Love in Men and Devils.　Cecco Angiolieri, da Siena.　AWP; EaItPo, *tr. by* Dante Gabriel Rossetti

Man who feels the dear disease, The.　Man in Love, A.　Lady Mary Wortley Montagu.　LW

Man Who Feigns Deafness, The.　Nguyễn Khuyến.　WoPoe, *tr. by* Nguyen Ngoc Bich

Man who fiercest charged in fight, The.　Stonewall Jackson.　Herman Melville. NCAP

Man Who Finds That His Son Has Become a Thief, The.　Raymond Souster. NOBC

Man who first built up with good strong words, The.　Antipater of Thessalonica.　GrAn

Man who fixed his eyes, A.　Sentences after *Defence of Poetry.*　Paul Goodman.　BodElec

Man who had fallen among thieves, A.　E. E. Cummings.　ChIV-2; HAP; NOBA; NoAM; OxBA; TAP

Man who had lately declared, A.　Limerick.　Thomas Thorneley.　PeLi

Man, who had no rivals in the love, A.　Man and His Image, The.　Jean de La Fontaine.　OBVE, *tr. by* Elizur Wright

Man who, having collapsed, rises, takes steps, is insane.　Forced March. Miklós Radnóti.　AF

Man who in his life trusts in this world, A.　Epitaph.　*Unknown.*　TrJP

Man Who Invented Pain, The.　Craig Raine.　EmeKit

Man who is very angry, A.　9th Untitled Poem.　Pedro Juan Pietri.　PueRic

Man who keeps a diary, pays, A.　Writing.　William Allingham.　NOBVV

Man Who Killed Himself to Avoid August, The.　Maureen Seaton.　ExTi

Man Who Knew the Words to "Louie, Louie," The.　David Keller.　SwNoth

Man who lies on his back under huge trees, The.　Breathing Space July. Tomas Tranströmer.　RB, *tr. by* Robert Bly

Man who lives for only making money, The.　Nice Work if You Can Get It. George Gershwin.　ReLy

Man who lost both legs, A.　Monologue at the Chinook Bar and Grill.　Tess Gallagher.　BodElec

Man Who Loved Flamenco, The.　Joseph Awad.　GraLe

Man Who Loved Islands, The.　Derek Walcott.　BodElec; NoAM

Man Who Loved White Chocolate, The.　Robert Kelly.　PFTM-2

Man who loves hiking, A.　Hiking.　Joseph Bruchac.　CDW

Man who loves me, A.　Troubadour Love.　Olga Nolla.　TANSG, *tr. by* Paula Vega

Man who loves *rancheras* holds out his hand, The.　Turns at the Dance.　Diana García.　TouFir

Man Who Makes Brooms, The.　Naomi Shihab Nye.　LoL

Man Who Married Magdalene, The.　Anthony Hecht.　ChIV-2; PeLV

Man Who Married Magdalene, The.　Louis Simpson.　NoAM; TAP

Man who misses the fun, The.　It Can Be Done.　*Unknown.*　PoToHe

Man Who Offers Me His Chest, The.　Hala Mohammad.　PoArWo, *tr. by* Cornelia Al-Khaled

Man, who once against thee fought, The. (LL)　Reprisal[l], The.　George Herbert.　ESCV; GeHe

Man Who Reads Homer, A.　Nishiwaki Junzaburo.　WoPoe, *tr. by* Masaya Saito

Man Who Sang the Sillies, The.　John Ciardi.　OBCA

Man who seemed, A.　Regulation equipment.　Joyce Mansour.　MFP, *tr. by* Martin Sorrell

Man who sold his lawn to standard oil, The.　War against the Trees, The. Stanley Kunitz.　HAP; PAI

Man who stood beside me, The.　Sweet Will.　Philip Levine.　LCAP-2; VCAP

Man who thinks God is too kind, The.　God Correctly Understood.　J. Gordon Coogler.　VerBaPo

Man Who Thinks He Can, The.　Walter D. Wintle.　ITBLP

Man Who Tried to Rape You, The.　Erin Belieu.　AmPoNex

Man who wants no children, The.　Five Smooth Stones.　Deborah Digges. ExTi

Man who was asked out to dinner, A.　Limerick.　Spike Milligan.　PeLi

Man Who Went Absent from the Native Literature, The.　Anthony Cronin. CIP-2

Man Who Wrote Yeats, the Man Who Wrote Mozart, The.　Michael Hartnett. ModIr

Man whose height his fear improved he, The.　Medgar Evers.　Gwendolyn Brooks.　ESEAA; NoP-4

Man will keep a horse for prestige, A.　Gateposts.　Medbh McGuckian. BiHa; MakPoe; ModIr; PBCIP

Man will put a large-headed nail, The.　Of Green Steps and Laundry.　Ralph Gustafson.　NoP-4

Man with a Hole in His Face, The.　Jack Coulehan.　BloBone

Man with a scythe: the torrent of his swing.　Gardens No Emblems.　Donald Davie.　OBGa

Man with a thousand hearts, The.　Image-Nation 13 (the Telephone).　Robin Blaser.　PoM

Man with his lion under the shed of wars, The.　Song of the Borderguard, The. Robert Duncan.　NeAP; PoM

Man with laughing eyes stopped smiling, The.　Arabic.　Naomi Shihab Nye. PoArWo

Man with Long Legs, The.　Dacia Maraini.　CItWP, *tr. by* Cinzia Sartini Blum and Lara Trubowitz

Man With Night Sweats, The.　Thom Gunn.　CABP; HarvBoo; PoPoPo

Man with No Family to Take Leave of, The.　Tu Fu.　CoBCP, *tr. by* Burton Watson

Man with One Small Hand.　Patricia K. Page.　MoCV

Man with the big mouth, The.　And Again.　Alison Fell.　LW

Man with the Blue Guitar, The.　Wallace Stevens.

　"I cannot bring a world quite round."　RaBo

　"Man bent over his guitar, The."　NoAM; RaBo

Man with the camera comes, The.　Reservation Special.　Lew Blockcolski. VoR

Man with the green cigarette strolls down the path.　Jungle Night.　"K." FaBoWar

Man with the Hoe, The.　Edwin Markham.　APN-2; BRP; GS; MoAmPo; TCAPo; TFi

Man with the red hat, The.　Glazunoviana.　John Ashbery.　LCAP-2; VCAP

Man with the Saxophone, The.　Ai.　SeSe

Man with the Wooden Leg, The.　Katherine Mansfield.　FaBoWar

Man with Three Friends, The.　Dora Greenwell.　SacPr

Man with wrinkly lips, The.　Amiti´ Amoureuse.　Gregorio Scalise.　ItPo, *tr. by* Gayle Ridinger

Man without a Middle, The.　Angela Sorby.　AmPoNex

Man without Sense of Direction.　John Crowe Ransom.　OxBA

Man you / are / a liar.　Insult before Gift-Giving.　Frank Bolton.　STP, *tr. by* Armand Schwerner

Man, you funny thing.　I Wanna Be Loved.　Johnny Green.　ReLy

Man, you know, assured and kind, The.　Almost Human.　Cecil Day Lewis. NoAM

Man, you too, aren't you, one of these rough followers of the criminal?　In the Servants' Quarters.　Thomas Hardy.　FaBoVe; MoBrPo

Managed as they say about such men.　Peter Porter.　PeLV　*Fr.* Nine Points of the Law.

Management is pleased to announce, The.　Jazz at the Intergalactic Nightclub. Michael McClure.　SeSe

Manager lady of this, The.　Incognito Lounge, The.　Denis Johnson.　ReTh

Managing the house is a big problem.　Rāmprasād Sen.　SinGod, *tr. by* Rachel Fell McDermott

Mañana (Is Soon Enough for Me).　Peggy Lee.　ReLy

Manchán's Prayer.　Saint Manchán.　NOIV

Manchester by Night.　Mathilde Blind.　ViWPN

Maniple's Tale, The.　Geoffrey Chaucer.　*Fr.* Canterbury Tales, The.

Mandalay.　Rudyard Kipling.　BRP; HarvBoo; MoBrPo; NOBE; NPeEn; OxAEP-2

Mandan Chief, The.　Fanny Crosby.　SWaP

Mandarin Duck Lake is at Chia-ho.　Ni Tsan Poem Following Rhyme-Words of Wu Chen.　Wu Chen.　CoBLCP, *tr. by* Jonathan Chaves

Mandarin Who Couldn't Do Anything, The. *Vietnamese Oral Tradition.* CaDao, *tr. by* John Balaban

Mandarins Got Their Raise, The. Tu Mo. WoPoe, *tr. by* Nguyen Ngoc Bich

Mandoline. Paul Verlaine. AWP; OBMV, *tr. by* Arthur Symons

Mandorla. Paul Celan. PoSu, *tr. by* Michael Hamburger

Mandrake Hert, The. Sydney Goodsir Smith. OxBS

Mandrakes for Supper. James Keir Baxter. OxBC

Maner of Her Wyll, & What She Left to London, And to All Those in It, The. Isabella Whitney. *See* Manner of Her Will and What She Left to London and to All Those in It, at Her Departing, The

Manfred. Byron. NAEL-5v2; NAEL-6v2; NOBRP

  "Stars are forth, the moon above the tops, The." AmFaPo; TreFP

  "We are the fools of time and terror: Days." AmFaPo

Mangel-Bury, The. Ivor Gurney. HarvBoo

Mango, A. Joyce Mansour. SurWo, *tr. by* Mary Beach

Mango on the Mango Tree, The. Robert Penn Warren. NoAM *Fr.* Mexico Is a Foreign Country: Four Studies in Naturalism.

Mango Poem. Regie Cabico. WiU

Mangoes. Richard Tipping. NOBAu

Mangoes are not cigarettes. Mangoes. Richard Tipping. NOBAu

Mangosteens. Daniel Hall. NoP-4

Mangrove. John Blight. NOBAu

Manhattan. Hoffman Reynolds Hays. SPE

Manhattan. Osbert Lancaster. NOBL; PeLV *Fr.* Afternoons with Baedeker.

Manhattan. Richard Rodgers. OBAL; ReLy

Manhattan, a small hotel. Thursday. Miklós Radnóti. IQMS, *tr. by* John Wain

Manhattan dance Latin. Side 12. Víctor Hernández Cruz. PueRic

Manhattan faces and eyes forever for me. (LL) Give Me the Splendid Silent Sun. Walt Whitman. CBCWP; HAP; MoAmPo; NOBA

Manhattan / I'm up a tree. Down in the Depths. Cole Porter. ReLy

Manhattan is really as grand as it's painted. Moon about Town. Dana Suesse. ReLy

Manhattan Lullaby. Norma Farber. SSCS; TLR

Manhattan Lullaby. Rachel Lyman Field. HHAm; TLR

Manhattan Madness. Irving Berlin. ReLy

Manhattan, Manhattan. Manhattan Madness. Irving Berlin. ReLy

Manhattan Pastures. Sandra Hochman. YaYoPo

Manhole Covers. Karl Shapiro. NoAM

Mani-Mani Gatha. Jackson Mac Low. PFTM-1

Maniac, The. Mary Bryan. CenSon

Maniac, The. Agnes Strickland. CenSon

Maniac's Song, The. Ann Taylor. NOBRP

Manic: A Conversation with Jimi Hendrix. Tim Seibles. OPRER

Manic-depressive Lincoln, national hero! Lincoln. Delmore Schwartz. APT-2

Manichaeans, The. Gary Snyder. VGW

Manichean Geography I. Tom Paulin. PNI

Manicheans did no idols make, The. Fulke Greville, 1st Baron Brooke. NOCV; SacPr *Fr.* Caelica.

Manifest, The. Olga Nolla. TANSG, *tr. by* Paula Vega

Manifest Destiny. Anita Endrezze. CDW

Manifest Destiny. Suheir Hammad. PoArWo

Manifest Destiny. Pearse Hutchinson. CIP-2

Manifesto. Agathias. GrAn, *tr. by* Dudley Fitts

Manifesto. Peter E. Murphy. UrbNat

Manifesto, A. José Santos Chocano. TCLAP, *tr. by* Andrew Rosing

Manifesto of Futurism, The. Filippo Tommaso Marinetti.

  "We had stayed up all night, my friends and I, under hanging mosque lamps." PFTM-1

Manifesto of Surrealism (1924). André Breton.

  Three Excerpts. PFTM-1

Manifesto of the Presidents of the Terrestrial Globe. Velemir [*or* Viktor Vladimirovich] Khlebnikov. TCRP, *tr. by* Gary Kern

Manifesto on Ars Poetica. Frank Mkalawile Chipasula. HBAPE; NAfrP

Manila Bay. Eugene Fitch Ware. OBCoV

Manila is full of the black ruins of my life. Lament Beginning w/a Line after Cavafy. Eric Gamalinda. ReBoTo

Manila Paper. Cyn Zarco. ReBoTo

Mankind on a little globe. Twenty Billion Light Years of Loneliness. Shuntaro Tanikawa. PoetW, *tr. by* Harold Wright

Mankind should hope. Mary Savage. ECWP; LW *Fr.* Letter to Miss E. B. on Marriage.

Manless Society, The. Pierre Unik. SPE, *tr. by* David Gascoyne

Manly Ferry. John Philip. NOBAu

Manly Love. Donald Malloch. CAGL

Manly Sports. Marion Bernstein. NePenScot

Manna. Jared Angira. PBMAP

Manna. Joseph Stroud. GeoHom

Manna. James Tate. GM

Mannahatta. Walt Whitman. MoAmPo

Mannequins. Daniel Mark Epstein. ReTh

Manner of Her Will and What She Left to London and to All Those in It, at Her Departing, The. Isabella Whitney. NoSic

  "And now let mee dispose such things." BWW

  "And (though I am perswade) that I." BWW

  "For Women shall you Taylors have." BWW

  "I whole in body and in minde." BWW

  "Now for the people in thee left." BWW

  "Now London have I (for thy sake)." BWW

  "Now when thy folke are fed and clad." BWW

  "Rejoice in God that I am gon." BWW

  "Yf they that keepe what I you leave." BWW

Manner of the World Nowadays, The. John Skelton.

  "So many cloisters closed." PeECV

Mannerly Margery Mylk and Ale. John Skelton. NAEL-5v1

  (Ay, beshrew you! by my fay.) NoP-4

  (Mannerly Margery Milk and Ale.) NAEL-6v1; NAEL-7v1; NoP-4

Manners. Pamela Alexander. ExTi

Manners. Elizabeth Bishop. NOxBChV; OxBC; RB

Manners. Howard Nemerov. NBLV

Manners. Edith Marcombe Shiffert. WPE

Manners in the dining-room. *Unknown.* OxNR

Manners may prevail. (LL) Emily Dickinson. ChIV-1; SoSe-8

Mannus the Pompeiian to a Greek. Kahlil Gibran. GraLe

Manon Lescaut. Yaroslav [*or* Iaroslav] Vasilevich Smelyakov [*or* Smeliakov]. TCRP, *tr. by* Simon Franklin

Manon Reassures Her Lover. Martha Elizabeth. PasH

Manong Chito Tells Manong Ben about His Dream over Breakfast at the Manilatown Cafe. Vince Gotera. ReBoTo

Manong with a Thousand Tribal Visions, The. Al Robles. ReBoTo

Manor Garden, The. Sylvia Plath. FaBoWP; HarvBoo; LCAP-2

Manora. Pimone Triplett. NAPBL

Manos Karastefanís. James Merrill. TAP

Mans Fall, and Recovery. Henry Vaughan. ESCV

Mans Knowledge, Ignorance in the Misteries of God. William Drummond, of Hawthornden. SacPr

Mans restlesse soule hath restlesse eyes and ears. Roger Williams. SCAP

Manservants on the last trains. North to Milwaukee. Gerald Vizenor. VoR

Mansion. A. R. Ammons. AmFaPo

Mansion is full of spiders, The. Pick up. Soon. Pamela Alexander. ExTi

Mansize. Maura Dooley. NeBl

Mantanza to Welcome Spring. Jimmy Santiago Baca. PmAP

Mantatee Horde, The. Mtutuzeli Matshoba. PeSAV

Mantis. David McCord. OBAL

Mantis. Ruth Miller. PeSAV

Mantle. William Heyen. MoASP; ReTh

Mantle ran so hard, they said. Mantle. William Heyen. MoASP; ReTh

Mantova. James Wright. NNaP

  (First Days, The.) TRP

Mantreya Upanishad, The. *Unknown.* *Fr.* Upanishads, The.

Manual System. Carl Sandburg. APT-1

Manuel. Rafael Campo. WiU *Fr.* Ten Patients, and Another.

Manuelzinho. Elizabeth Bishop. FaBoWP

Manuscript. Angelina Muñiz Huberman. MirDau, *tr. by* Aurora Camacho

Manuscript Found in a Book of Joseph Conrad. Jorge Luis Borges. PoetW, *tr. by* Alastair Reid

Manuscript in a Bottle. Pablo Antonio Cuadra. TCLAP, *tr. by* Ann McCarthy de Zavala and Grace Schulman

Manuscript in a Bottle. Pablo Antonio Cuadra. BLPSL, *tr. by* Rene de Costa, Rigas Kappatos and Eleni Paidoussi

Manuscript with Illumination. Robert Fitzgerald. APT-2

Many a lip is gaping for drink. Eliza Cook. VerBaPo *Fr.* Song of the Sea Weed.

Many a long, long year ago. Alarmed Skipper, The. James Thomas Fields. NBLV

Many a man gets bewitched by the elves. Heinrich von Morungen. GePo

Many a miner has gone. Anne Sexton. BodElec *Fr.* Furies, The.

Many a New Day. Richard Rodgers. ReLy

Many a poet in his lay. May. Dafydd [*or* David] ap Gwilym. CABP

Many a soldier's kiss dwells on these bearded lips. (LL) Wound-Dresser, The. Walt Whitman. APN-1; CBCWP; ColAP; NAAL-2v1; NAAL-3; NAAL-5; NOBA; OBWP; TAP; TCAPo

Many a summer is dead and buried, A. Spirits Everywhere. Ludwig Uhland. AWP, *tr. by* James Clarence Mangan

Many a swan-white breast. (LL) Dead at Clonmacnois [*or* Clonmacnoise], The. Angus O'Gillan. OBEV; OBMV, *tr. by* Thomas William Hazen Rolleston

Many a year has fled away. My Old Palette. Christopher Pearse Cranch. APN-1

Many American flags, The. Grand Entry, The. Gary Snyder. NoAM

Many and many a happy year. (LL) Tennyson. GTBS-P; NOBVV; PeECV

Many and More. Maya Angelou. LW

Many Are Called. Edwin Arlington Robinson. GI; OxBA

Many are making love. Privilege of Being. Robert Hass. NIP-4

Many are the hills. Written after Climbing Kaguyama to Survey the Land. Emperor Jomei. WoPoe, *tr. by* Helen Craig McCullough

Many are thy tones, O Ocean. Sea Cadences. Henrietta Cordelia Ray. CBWP-3

Many as noticed by the one, The. De Imagine Mundi. John Ashbery. FaBoMo

Many builders there have been. Love Nest, The. Louis A. Hirsch. ReLy

Many centuries ago, on a road to Athens, two poets met. Two Poems, The. Kahlil Gibran. GraLe

Many-colored sandal, A. Sappho. SaLy, *tr. by* Diane Rayor

Many colors will take you to themselves. Never Seek to Tell Thy Love. John Ashbery. HCAP

Many creatures don't have one. Penelope Shuttle. NewEx

Many desperate arms about us and the things we know. (LL) Character of Love Seen as a Search for the Lost, The. Kenneth Patchen. CLPP; VGW

Many Die Here. Gayl Jones. BlSi

Many fair hours have been buried here. Millinery District: "Many fair hours have been buried here." Charles Reznikoff. APT-2

Many find Quintia stunning. I find her attractive. 86. Catullus. NAWM-7v1, *tr. by* Charles Martin

Many folks are in a snit. Freud's Butcher. Charles Bernstein. BodElec

Many girls I've met. Maybe This Is Love. Ray Henderson. ReLy

Many-headed Hydra, or the people, The. Common People, The. Rowland Watkyns. AngWePo; BASC

Many in aftertimes will say of you. Christina Georgina Rossetti. CABP; MakPoe; OxBSo *Fr.* Monna Innominata.

Many Indeed Must Perish in the Keel. Hugo von Hofmannsthal. AWP; TrJP, *tr. by* Jethro Bithell

Many ingenious lovely things are gone. W. B. Yeats. BIrV; PoE *Fr.* Nineteen Hundred and Nineteen.

Many long years ago, I loved a youth. Blight of Love, The. Mary E. Tucker. CBWP-1

Many-maned scud-thumper, tub. Winter Ocean. John Updike. InPK-6; PAI

Many, many things. Basho. TAL

Many men with lofty aims. Folks Who Live on the Hill, The. Jerome Kern. ReLy

Many, monstrous, tumbled, dun-gray boulders, The. You Were Broken. Giuseppe Ungaretti. STV, *tr. by* John Frederick Nims

Many nights on the road. Basho. EH, *tr. by* Robert Hass

Many people have been frighted & died in cemeteries. My Gang. Jack Kerouac. PoM

Many people have gathered together. Foot Race Song. *Unknown.* OBVE, *tr. by* Frank Russell

Many policemen wear upon their shoulders. Sergeant Brown's Parrot. Kit Wright. OPOU

Many red devils ran from my heart. Stephen Crane. TAP *Fr.* Black Riders [and Other Lines], The.

Many Said. Kakkai Patiniyar Naccellaiyar. WoPoe, *tr. by* George L. III Hart

Many say Japan has neither a poetics nor a language in which poetry can be written. Fujii Sadakazu. PFTM-2, *tr. by* Christopher Drake *Fr.* Where Is Japanese Poetry?

Many sewing days ago. Listening Macaws, The. Hazel Hall. APT-1

Many shapes of wings. Environs. Larry Eigner. FTOS; NeAP

Many ships have asked for sanctuary. Free Harbor. Su'ad al-Mubarak Al-Sabah. MAP, *tr. by* John Heath-Stubbs and May Jayyusi

Many ships that left our country, The. Exiles, The. Iain Crichton Smith. HarvBoo; NePenScot

Many Soldiers. Edgar Lee Masters. TCAPo

Many strange mountains in Shu and Han. Imitating the Old Poems. Pao Chao. CoBCP, *tr. by* Burton Watson

Many there are, praisers of Poverty. Giotto di Bondone. EaItPo, *tr. by* Dante Gabriel Rossetti

Many Things. Oliver Wendell Holmes. PoToHe

Many things befell me as I followed Buddha. Ensetsu. JDP, *tr. by* Yoel Hoffmann

Many things have come and gone. Breezing Dawn of the New Day, The. Mongane Wally Serote. PeSAV

Many things I might have said today. Aprons of Silence. Carl Sandburg. NOBA

Many things to absorb I teach to help you become eleve of mine. To a Western Boy. Walt Whitman. APN-1

Many Thousand Gone. *Unknown. See* No More Auction Block

Many times the mountains have turned from green to yellow. Muso Soseki. ZenPo, *tr. by* Takashi Ikemoto and Lucien Stryk

Many Wagons Ago. John Ashbery. HCAP

Many weary weeks divide me. Ship's Cook, a Captive Sings, The. Hugo von Hofmannsthal. TrJP, *tr. by* Charles Wharton Stork

Many Will Love You. Mathilde Blind. ViWPN

Many will love you; you were made for love. Many Will Love You. Mathilde Blind. ViWPN

Many winters have gone by. Dora Markus and Her Actors. Gregorio Scalise. ItPo, *tr. by* Gayle Ridinger

Many without Elegy. William Sydney Graham. OxBS

Many Workmen. Stephen Crane. TAP *Fr.* Black Riders [and Other Lines], The.

Many Worlds Are Walked Once. Kojo Laing. HBAPE

Many years and many days ago. Manon Lescaut. Yaroslav [*or* Iaroslav] Vasilevich Smelyakov [*or* Smeliakov]. TCRP, *tr. by* Simon Franklin

Many years, and one of them a little harder. Eugenio Montale. WoPoe, *tr. by* Dana Gioia *Fr.* Motets, The.

Many years from now, when I am a little heap of silenced dust, play. To the Children. Gabriela Mistral. SpanPo, *tr. by* Kate Flores

Many years have passed, mica. Accomplices. Bei Dao. AF, *tr. by* Bonnie S. McDougall

Manyo Shu, Part 1 of 4. *Var. authors.*
"Because he is young." AWP
"By way of pretext." AWP
"Dress that my brother has put on is thin, The." AWP
"For my sister's sake." AWP

Manyo Shu, Part 2 of 4. *Var. authors.*
"How will you manage." AWP
"I am of this world." BoWoP
"I wish I could lend a coat." AWP
("In the sea of ivy clothed Iwami.") OHPJ, *tr. by* Kenneth Rexroth
"May the men who are born." AWP; TAL
("May those who are born after me.") OHPJ, *tr. by* Kenneth Rexroth
"Men of valor, The." AWP; TAL

Manyo Shu, Part 3 of 4. *Var. authors.*
"He is coming, my long-desired lord." AWP, *tr. by* Lafcadio Hearn
"My heart, thinking." AWP
"O boy cutting grass." AWP
"O pine-tree standing." AWP; TAL
"On the moor of Kasuga." AWP
"On the shore of Nawa." AWP
("Over the Spring fields.") OHMPJ, *tr. by* Kenneth Rexroth
"Plum-blossom, The." AWP; TAL
"Shall we make love." AWP

Manyo Shu, Part 4 of 4. *Var. authors.*
"Thousand years, you said, A." BoLoP
"Unknown love / Is as bitter a thing." AWP
("Unknown love / is bitter.") BoWoP, *tr. by* Willis Barnstone
"What am I to do with my sister?" AWP
"When evening comes." AWP
("When she was still alive.") OHPJ, *tr. by* Kenneth Rexroth

Manzanita, The. Yvor Winters. VGW

Manzini; Escape Artist. Gwendolyn MacEwen. NOBC

Mao Yen-shou, your painter's brush seems to move the gods. Wang Chao-chün. Li Shang-yin. SuSp, *tr. by* Irving Y. Lo

Map. Linda Hogan. ExTi

Map. Raymond Radiguet. CuPo

Map. Martin Sorescu. VCWP, *tr. by* Michael Longley and Russell-Gebbett

Map, The. Elizabeth Bishop. APT-2; ColAP; NOBA

Map, The. Gary Soto. NoAM

Map Burnt Through. Joanna Rawson. AmPoNex

Map of Montana in Italy, A. Richard Hugo. LCAP-2

Map of My Country, A. John Holmes. AiP
(Map of my native country is all edges, A.) CA

Map of Places, The. Laura Riding Jackson. APT-2

Map of the City, A. Thom Gunn. NAEL-5v2; NAEL-6v2; NoP-4; PoE

Map of the Western Part of the County of Essex in England, A. Denise Levertov. CoAP; NAAL-2v2
(Something forgotten twenty years: though my fathers.) CoAmPo

Map of the Winter Sky, The. Margherita Guidacci. CItWP, *tr. by* Cinzia Sartini Blum and Lara Trubowitz

Map of the World, The. Anna Couani. BMAP

Map of the world is felt from the inside, The. Rough around the. Map of the World, The. Anna Couani. BMAP

Map of Verona, A. Henry Reed. HarvBoo

Map Reading. Raymond Garlick. AngWePo

Map Room, The. Joshua Clover. BAP-97; NeAmPo

Map shows me where it is you are. I, The. Gloria C. Oden. *See* Map shows me where it is you are, The

Map the dominie had tacked up, The. St Kilda. Neil Curry. NLP

Maple. Bill Griffiths. Oth *Fr.* Building: The New London Hospital.

Maple and Sumach. Cecil Day Lewis. FaBoMo; Son

Maple and the Pine, The. Robert Garioch. NPeEn

Maple Bridge Night Mooring. Chang Chi. ColAnChi, *tr. by* Gary Snyder

Maple Leaf. "Shu Ting." VCWP

Maple leaves fill the emerald mountain. Boiling Falls. Liu E. CoBLCP, *tr. by* Jonathan Chaves

Maple Tree, The. John Clare. OxBSo

Maple with its tassel[l] flowers of green, The. Maple Tree, The. John Clare. OxBSo

Mapooram. *Aborigine Oral Tradition.* NOBAu, *tr. by* Fred Biggs

Maps. Bruce Guernsey. IllVoic

Maps for a Son Are Drawn as You Go. Samuel Hazo. GraLe

Maps, his father said, are history. Winners. Katherine Frost. Prnts

Maquillage. Arthur Symons. OxBSP

Mar 7 Signal. Hannah Weiner. PFTM-2 *Fr.* Clairvoyant Journal.

Marated Bastilled age, A. Boris Nartsissov. TCRusP, *tr. by* John Glad

Marathon. Cyrus Cassells. WiU

Marathon. Louise Glück.
    Song of Obstacles. LW

Marathon. John Powell Ward. TCAWP

Marban, a Hermit Speaks. *Unknown.* BIrV; CIP-2, *tr. by* Michael Hartnett

Marble. Zulaykha Abu-Risha. PoArWo, *tr. by* Clarissa C. Burt

Marble Beads. Delmira Agustini. TANSG, *tr. by* Mark McCaffrey

Marble Floor. Karol Wojtyla. CRP

"Marble I thought thee, and brickwork I find thee!" the Tourist may answer. (LL) Arthur Hugh Clough. EBVV; FaBoVe; OxAEP-2 *Fr.* Amours de Voyage.

Marble mausoleum solemnly holds the rich, A. Quatrains. Salah Jahin. TTY, *tr. by* Samir M. Zoghby

Marble on the milk of this night. Marble. Zulaykha Abu-Risha. PoArWo, *tr. by* Clarissa C. Burt

Marble one so warmed would speak, A. (LL) To a Fair Lady Playing with a Snake. Edmund Waller. CABP; EBEV; NOSC; PoE

Marble Prophecy, The. Josiah Gilbert Holland.
    "Laocöon! thou great embodiment." APN-1

Marble surfaces. Joanne Burns. BMAP

Marble-Top. Elwyn Brooks White. OBAL

Marbled Chuckle in the Savannahs. Kenward Elmslie. FTOS

Marblehead's a rocky place. Royall Tyler. NAAL-3 *Fr.* Contrast, The.

Marburg. Boris Leonidovich Pasternak. TCRP, *tr. by* Yakov Hornstein

March. Elizabeth Jane Coatsworth. Spl

March. Jane Cooper.
    "Cousin, it's of you I always dream." FaBoWP
    El Sueño de la Razón. FaBoWP

March. Daryl Hine.
    "Once when I was coming from art class they surprised me." GLP

March. A. E. Housman. FaBoCh

March. Henrietta Cordelia Ray. CBWP-3

March. Folgore da San Geminiano [or Gimignano]. EaItPo, *tr. by* Dante Gabriel Rossetti *Fr.* Sonnets of the Months.

March. Rosemerry Wahtola Trommer. GeoH

March. Marina Ivanovna Tsvetayeva [or Tsvetaeva].
    "O what tears in eyes now." TCRP
    "They took quickly, they took hugely." AF, *tr. by* Elaine Feinstein; TCRP

March 1, The. Robert Lowell. HCAP; PoPoPo; PoetW

March 4th Anno 1698/9; a Charracteristicall Satyre. John Saffin. SCAP

March 9 1976. Brian Meeks. WaCA

March beyond green outskirts. Girls' School. Alan Moore. BiHa

March comes, / and Eastern bluebird shows himself. This Year's Drive to Appomattox. Eleanor Ross Taylor. CBCWP

March Day in London, A. Amy Levy. VWP

March Elegy. Arkadii Dragomoschenko. ItGoST, *tr. by* Elena Balashova and Lyn Hejinian

March Evening. Leonard Alfred George Strong. MoBrPo

March Hares. Andrew Young. SAmP

March has come to the bridge head. Poem by the Bridge at Ten-shin. Li Po. OBVE, *tr. by* Ezra Pound

March in the Ranks Hard-Prest, and the Road Unknown, A. Walt Whitman. CBCWP; NAAL-2v1; NAAL-3; OxBA; PAI

March in Transylvania. Lajos Áprily. IQMS, *tr. by* Adam Makkai

March into Virginia, The. Herman Melville. HAP; NAAL-2v1; NCAP; PoE; TAP

March Journal. Charles Wright. LCAP-2

March, march, head erect. Mother Goose. OxNR

March Night. Herbert Strutz. AuPH, *tr. by* Lowell A. Bangerter

March 1979 and I am watching Nazis. Jews That We Are, The. Richard Michelson. GotH

March, now, and almost the season. Small Girl Brings an Injured Bird into the Surgery, A. Michael O'Reilly. BloBone

March of the Cordilleras, The. Raúl Zurita. TCLAP, *tr. by* Jack Schmitt

March of the Rebel Angels. John Milton. TreFP *Fr.* Paradise Lost.

March of the Women, The. Cicely Hamilton. BrRo

March Snow. Don McKay. NOBC

March . . . Someone has walked across the snow. Vacancy in the Park. Wallace Stevens. LCAP-2; SAmP

March strikes the ice of the sky. Peter Huchel. *See* March with its sharp pick

March strongly forth, my Muse, whilst yet the temperate air. Michael Drayton. NOSC *Fr.* Polyolbion.

3-31-70. Gayl Jones. BlSi *Fr.* Journal.

March toward the Front, The. Odysseus Elytis. AF

March went out like a lion. June Is Bustin' Out All Over. Richard Rodgers. ReLy

March wind blows the garden gate. Riding the Lion, Riding the Lamb. Karen Chamberlain. GeoH

March winds and April showers. *Unknown.* LB; OxNR; ReMoGo

March with its sharp pick. Landscape beyond Warsaw. Peter Huchel. PoSu

Marchant was ther with a forked berd, A. Geoffrey Chaucer. CTC *Fr.* Canterbury Tales, The.

Marché aux Oiseaux. Richard Wilbur. OWoS

Marche Funèbre. Gunnar Ekelof. PFTM-2, *tr. by* Muriel Rukeyser and Leif Sjöberg *Fr.* Mölna Elegy.

Märchen, The. Randall Jarrell. HarvBoo

Märchenbilder. John Ashbery. LCAP-2; NOBA

Marching. Isaac Rosenberg. PeFWW

Marching armies of the past, The. Confederate Memorial Day. *Unknown.* CBCWP

Marching Still. Minna Irving. CBCWP

Marching through Georgia. Henry Clay Work. APN-2; CBCWP

Marcia and I went over the curve. Millions of Strawberries. Genevieve Taggard. NOxBChV

Marco Bozzaris. Fitz-Greene Halleck.
    "At midnight, in his guarded tent." APN-1

Marco Polo. Marvin Bell. BodElec

Marconi's Cottage. Medbh McGuckian. ModIr

Marconi, whose ardour was tireless. Limerick. Stanley J. Sharpless. PeLi

Marcus Antoninus Cui Cognomen Erat Aurelius. Burns Singer. OxBS

Marcus Aurelius. Dezső Kosztolányi. IQMS, *tr. by* Earl M. Herrick

Marcus Aurelius. Charles Hubert Sisson. OxBC

Marcus Curtius. Oliver St. John Gogarty. OBMV

Marcus in the armed hoplites' race. Lucilius. GrAn

Mardi Gras Premortem. Ann Townsend. NeAmPo

Mare, The. Vernon Watkins. OBWVE

Mare lies down in the grass where the nest of the skylark is hidden, The. Mare, The. Vernon Watkins. OBWVE

Mare Nostrum. Joel Oppenheimer. NeAP

Mare's skeleton in the clearing: another sign of life, The. Adrienne Rich. FaBoWP *Fr.* Shooting Script.

Mares of the Camargue, The. Frédéric Mistral. AWP, *tr. by* George Meredith *Fr.* Mirèio.

Marfa Lights, The. W. S. Merwin. BodElec

Marg'ret of humbler stature by the head. Charles Cotton. BoLoP; EnLoPo *Fr.* Resolution in Four Sonnets, of a Poetical Question Put to Me by a Friend, Concerning Four Rural Sisters.

Margaret Are You Drug. George Starbuck. InPK-6

Márgarét, áre you gríeving. Spring and Fall. Gerard Manley Hopkins. CABP; EBEV; GTBS-P; HAP; HeIP-4; InPK-6; NAEL-5v2; NAEL-6v2; NIL-7; NIP-4; NOBE; NoAM; NoP-4; OPOU; PAI; PeVV; PoE; PoPoPo; RB; SCGP; SCV; TFi; TOF; TRP

Margaret Fuller Slack. Edgar Lee Masters. APT-1; RACG

Margaret Fuller Slack. Edgar Lee Masters. APT-1; IllVoic; RACG *Fr.* Spoon River Anthology.

Margaret Grady—I fear she will burn. Witch, The. Katharine Tynan. NOBVV

Margaret / Haskell Indian School. Carolyn Marie Dunn. ReEnLa

Margaret Morse. From the Green Book of Yfan. Rolfe Humphries. APT-2

Margaret wrote a letter. Dusty Miller, The. *Unknown.* ReMoGo

Margarita, A. (LL) Of Time and the Line. Charles Bernstein. NIL-7; PFTM-2; PmAP; ReTh

Margarita first possest [*or* possessed]. Chronicle; a Ballad, The. Abraham Cowley. OxAEP-1

Margaritæ Sorori [I. M.]. William Ernest Henley. MoBrPo; NOBE; OBEV *Fr.* Echoes.

Margery Mutton-pie. Mother Goose. OxNR

Margin Prayer from an Ancient Psalter. Ian Duhig. EmeKit; NeBl

Marginalia. Stephanie Brown. AmPoNex

Marginalization of Poetry, The. Mitch Highfill. HeMarv

Marginalization of Poetry, The. Bob Perelman. FTOS

Marguerite. "Rubén Dario." SpanPo, *tr. by* Anita Volland

Maria! Maria! Maria! Vladimir Vladimirovich Mayakovsky [*or* Maiakovskii]. TCRP *Fr.* Cloud in Trousers, The.

Maria, she said. No city river. Scuba Diver Recovers the Body of a Drowned Child, The. Gerald William Barrax. GT; NBV

Maria to Henric. *Unknown.* EMWP

Maria Wentworth. Thomas Carew. CaPo; MeLP; NPeEn; PeECV

(And here the precious dust is laid;) CavPo

(Epitaph for Maria Wentworth.) BeJo

(Inscription on the Tomb of the Lady Mary Wentworth, The.) CavPo; SCGP

Mariachi beckon, their guitars, The. On Plaza Garibaldi. Nellie Wong. OpBo

Mariam. Lady Elizabeth Carey. WPE

Marian Hymn. Christiania Whitehead. NeBl

Mariana. R. F. Langley. HarvBoo

Mariana. Tennyson. AWP; FHYEP; NAEL-5v2; NAEL-6v2; NOBE; NOBRP; OBEV; OxAEP-2; PeVV; PoE; SCGP; TFi; UnPo

(With blackest moss the flower-plots.) NoP-4

Mariana II. Maria Arrillaga. TANSG

Marianne Faithfull's Cigarette. Gerry Gomez Pearlberg. WiU

Marías, Old Indian Mothers. Rigoberto González. GeoHom

Maridunum. Douglas Phillips. AngWePo

Marie antoinette, The / slice. After / the Moratorium Reading. Nigel Roberts. NOBAu

Marie Farrar, born in April. Concerning the Infanticide, Marie Farrar. Bertolt Brecht. WoPoe, *tr. by* Hoffman Reynolds Hays

Marie Galante. Guy Tirolien. NegPo, *tr. by* Ellen Conroy Kennedy

Marie Hamilton's to the kirk gane. Queen's Marie, The. *Unknown.* OBEV

Marie Lucille. Gwendolyn Brooks. TLR

Marie moder, wel thee be! *Unknown.* OHMEL

Marie [*or* Mary] Magdalens Complaint at Christs Death. Robert Southwell. ChIV-2; ESCV

Marigold, The. George Wither. NOSC; SacPr *Fr.* Collection of Emblemes, Ancient and Moderne, A.

Marigold nowhere turns from the sun, The. To Henry Darnley, King of Scots. George Buchanan. NePenScot, *tr. by* Robert Crawford

Marijuana joints make circles. Round Irving High School. Cheryl Boyce Taylor. WiU

Marikudo in Kalibo, 1979. Dominador I. Ilio. ReBoTo

Marilyn. Ōoka Mokoto. PFTM-2, *tr. by* Thomas Fitzimmons

Marilyn Climbs Out of the Pool. Tracey Herd. NeBl

Marilyn Monroe Indian. Leo Romero. ReTh

Marin. Philip Booth. AiP

Marina. T. S. Eliot. APT-1; CABP; FaBoMo; GTBS-P; HeIP-4; NAEL-5v2; NAEL-6v2; NOBE; NOCV; NPeEn; OxBEV; PoE; TOF

Marina. O. B. Hardison, Jr. AiP; CRP

Marina. Eugenio Montejo. BLPSL, *tr. by* Rene de Costa, Rigas Kappatos and Eleni Paidoussi

Marine Aquarium, The. Louis Dudek. MoCV *Fr.* Atlantis.

Mariner's Hymn. Caroline Anne Bowles Southey. TreFP

Mariner's Ideal Epitaph. Juan Ramón Jiménez. SpanPo, *tr. by* Kate Flores

Mariner that on smooth waves doth glide, The. Anne Bradstreet. WPOW *Fr.* Contemplations.

Marines look vernal, The. Sound Bite. Frederick D'Aguiar. Oth

Marisel. Juan Gonzalo Rose. BLPSL, *tr. by* Rene de Costa, Rigas Kappatos and Eleni Paidoussi

Maritae Suae. William Philpot. OBEV

Marital quarrels are not poetic. Temptation. Salwa Al-Neimi. PoArWo, *tr. by* Subhi Hadidi and Nathalie Handal

Maritime. Reginald Shepherd. AmPoNex

Maritime Ode. Fernando Pessoa.

"Ah, pirates, pirates, pirates!" PFTM-1

Maritime Pastoral. Ted Benttinen. PoCoUp

Maritimes. Penelope Shuttle. BrRo

Mark. John Tranter. NoAM

Mark, The. Robert Dana. OPRER

Mark 5:21–43; And when Jesus had crossed. Czeslaw Milosz. GI *Fr.* St. Mark.

Mark 14:26–42; And when they had sung. Boris Leonidovich Pasternak. GI *Fr.* St. Mark.

Mark 16:19–20; So then the Lord Jesus, after. A. E. Housman. GI

Mark finished it himself, choosing midnight. Mark. John Tranter. NoAM

Mark how the bashful morn in vain. Boldness[e] in Love. Thomas Carew. CaPo

Mark how this polished [*or* polish'd] Eastern sheet. Fancy, A. Thomas Carew. BeJo; NOSC

Mark, how yond eddy steals away. To My Mistress Sitting by a River's Side; an Eddy. Thomas Carew. BeJo; CaPo

Mark is a fag scratched in blue ink. Geometry Class. Mark Bibbins. AmPoNex; WiU

Mark Stern. Frederick Feirstein. RA

Mark Stern Wakes Up. Frederick Feirstein. RA

Mark Twain said he wouldn't want to be a boy again. Origins, Divergences. Cynthia Ozick. TaR

Mark, when the Evening's cooler wings. To Amoret, of the Difference 'twixt Him and Other Lovers, and What True Love Is. Henry Vaughan. BeJo

Mark where the pressing wind shoots javelin-like. George Meredith. EnLoPo; NAEL-6v2; NOBE; OBEV; SCGP *Fr.* Modern Love.

Mark yon round parson, fat and sleek. Robert Lloyd. ECEV; OBSV *Fr.* Familiar Epistle to J. B. Esq, A.

Mark you how the peacock's eye. Peacock's Eye, The. Gerard Manley Hopkins. OWoS

Mark you the floor[e]? that square and speckled stone. Church-Floor[e], The. George Herbert. EBEV; ESCV; MeLP; NOSC; PeECV

Mark[e] but this flea, and mark[e] in this. Flea, The. John Donne. AmFaPo; BASC; BoLoP; EBEV; ESCV; FSCP; InPK-6; NAEL-5v1; NAEL-6v1; NAEL-7v1; NBLV; NIL-7; NIP-4; NoP-4; NoSic; OxAEP-1; PAI; PoE; SCV; TFi

Marke how this polist Easterne sheet. Thomas Carew. *See* Mark how this polished [*or* polish'd] Eastern sheet

Marked by no fence. Jackson Mac Low. APSN *Fr.* Presidents of the United States of America, The.

Marked Ones, The. Gyula Illyés. IQMS, *tr. by* John Brander and John Wilkinson

Marked with D. Tony Harrison. NAEL-5v2; NAEL-6v2 *Fr.* School of Eloquence, The.

Marked you, by yon thatched farm that skirts the down—. Village Maid, The. Mary F. Johnson. CenSon

Marker at Auschwitz, The. Rational Man. Muriel Rukeyser. AF

Marker slants, flowerless, day's almost done, The. John Berryman. HCAP; PoPoPo; VCAP *Fr.* Dream Songs.

Marketwoman of Luanda. Maria Eugénia Lima. HAWP, *tr. by* Julia Kirst

Marking of Folders. Anne Anderton. UV

Marking Time. Peter Steele. NOBAu

Markings on a shitter wall. Legacy of a Brother. Renaldo Fernandez. NBV

Marks. Linda Pastan. NIL-7; NIP-4

Marks the English Left on the Map. Peter Finch. Oth

Marl white road, the Dorée rushing cool, The. Tales of the Islands. Derek Walcott. OxBTC

Marlburyes Fate. Benjamin Tompson. SCAP

Marlene Dietrich is singing a lament. Blue Angel, The. Allen Ginsberg. BB

Marlo Thomas in Seven Parts and Epilogue. Jeffery Conway. WiU

Marm Grayson's Guests. Mary Eleanor Wilkins Freeman. OBCA

Marmalade. Elizabeth Delmore. NLP

Marmion. Sir Walter Scott.

"Along the bridge Lord Marmion rode." FaBoWar

Fitz-Eustace's Song. GTBS-P

"Heap on more wood!—the wind is chill." ChrPo; OBCP

Lochinvar. EBNV; NAEL-6v2; NOBE; NePenScot; OxAEP-2; OxBS; PoRA; TFi

(Marmion.) TreFP

Nelson, Pitt, Fox. OBEV

("O, Young Lochinvar is come out of the west.") ChAP

(Song.) NOBRP

"To mute and to material things." OBEV

"Where shall the lover rest." GTBS-P

(Young Lochinvar.) OBNV

Marooned in it, stealthy as fishes, we may even be dead. (LL) Mess Deck. Alan Ross. FaBoWar; PoWW

Marpessa's Choice. Yannis Ritsos. VCWP, *tr. by* Edmund Keeley

Marquis de Sade, The. André Breton. WoPoe, *tr. by* Jack Rogow and Bill Zavatsky

Marquis de Sade and Genet, The. Limerick. W. H. Auden. PeLi

Marquis de Sade has gone back inside the erupting volcano, The. Marquis de Sade, The. André Breton. WoPoe, *tr. by* Jack Rogow and Bill Zavatsky

Marriage. William Blake. OxBoLi; PeLV

Marriage. Stephanie Brown. BodElec

Marriage. Austin Clarke. BIrV; GTBS-P

Marriage. Mary Elizabeth Coleridge. LW; NALW; PEW; PoBW; VWP; ViWPN

Marriage. Gregory Corso. CoAP; NeAP; NoP-4; OBAL; PeLV; PmAP; TAP; TRP

Marriage. Mary Weston Fordham. CBWP-2

Marriage. Amy Gerstler. PmAP

Marriage. Marianne Craig Moore. APT-1; ColAP; NALW; NOBA

Marriage. Mary Ellen Solt. BoWoP

Marriage. Walter James Turner. NOBAu

Marriage, A. Michael C. Blumenthal. PoPoPo

Marriage, A. Robert Creeley. NeAP; RaBo
(First retainer, The.) PoPoPo

Marriage, A. Ronald Stuart Thomas. TCAWP

Marriage, The. Anne Stevenson. NALW

Marriage, The. Mark Strand. NoAM; SPE

Marriage, The. Anna Wickham. ItWoWo

Marriage à la Mode. Dryden.
(Song: "Whilst Alexis lay pressed.") BoLoP
(Song: "Why should a foolish marriage vow.") AWP
"Whil'st Alexis lay prest [or press'd]." NPeEn; PeLV
"Why should a foolish marriage vow." NAEL-5v1; NAEL-6v1; NAEL-7v1; NIL-7; NIP-4

Marriage and Love. Caroline Elizabeth Norton.
"Laura was lightsome, gay, and free from guile." VWP

Marriage and Money. Sir Charles Sedley. OBSV   Fr. Happy Pair, The.

Marriage betwixt Scrape, Monarch of the Maunders, and Blobberlips, Queen of the Gypsies, A. Alexander Pennecuik.
"Below fair Peebles, on the river's side." NOEC

Marriage Couplet. William Cole. OBAL

Marriage has gone the way of God! (LL) Ballad of Religion and Marriage, A. Amy Levy. NPeEn; VWP; ViWPN

Marriage in Eden, The. William Williams. OBWVE, tr. by Gwyn Jones and Lewis Saunders   Fr. View of Christ's Kingdom, A.

Marriage in the Nineties, A. Alfred Corn. WiU

Marriage is a going forth. Marriage Song for Many Voices. Jennifer Weinblatt. MPUn

Marriage is a lovely thing. Christine de Pisan. WPOW, tr. by Joanna Bankier

Marriage is not / a house or even a tent. Habitation. Margaret Atwood. BoWoP; FaBoWP; WeW-3

Marriage of a Virgin, The. Dylan Thomas. ChIV-2

Marriage of Death, The. László Szabédi. IQMS, tr. by John Gordon Nichols

Marriage of Heaven and Hell, The. William Blake. NAEL-5v2; NAEL-6v2; NOBRP
Memorable Fancy, A. NAEL-6v2
Proverbs of Hell.
Pride of the Peacock, The. RaBo
Song of Liberty, A. NAEL-6v2

Marriage of Hector and Andromache, The. Sappho. OBVE, tr. by Guy Davenport

Marriage of Sir Gawain, The. Unknown. ESPB

Marriage of Sorts, A. Pamela Alexander. YaYoPo

Marriage of St. Katharine, by the same; in the Hospital of St. John at Bruges. Dante Gabriel Rossetti. CenSon

Marriage of the Frog and the Mouse, The. Unknown. EBEV

Marriage Prospect, A. William Hurrell Mallock. NOBVV

Marriage Ring, The. George Crabbe. BoLoP; EnLoPo; OBEV; OxBEV
(His Late Wife's Wedding-Ring.) NOBE

Marriage Song. Judah Halevi. TrJP, tr. by Alice Lucas

Marriage Song for Many Voices. Jennifer Weinblatt. MPUn

Marriage Vow. Mrs. Henry Linden. CBWP-4

Marriage Vow, The. Letitia [or Laetitia] Elizabeth Landon. VWP

Marriage, which might have been a mateship sweet. Elizabeth Wolstenholme-Elmy. BrRo   Fr. Woman Free.

Married life for a poor man. Cillactor. GrAn

Married Love. Kuan Tao Shêng. PasH; WoPoe, tr. by Chung Ling and Kenneth Rexroth

Married Love. Liz Rosenberg. NIL-7

Married Love. Sherod Santos. Son

Married Lover, The. Coventry Patmore. OBEV; OxAEP-2; SacPr   Fr. Angel in the House, The.

Married man comes nearest to the dead, A. Samuel Butler. FaBoEE

Married, poor soul! your empire's over. Jane West. ECWP   Fr. To a Friend on her Marriage.

Married State, A. Katherine Philips. BASC; NAEL-7v1

Married state affords but little ease, A. Married State, A. Katherine Philips. BASC; NAEL-7v1

Married to a Soldier. John Clare. SCGP

Marrow, The. Theodore Roethke. PeECV

Marrow of My Bone. Mari E. Evans. BPo

Marrow of time; eternity in brief. Church Festivals. Christopher Harvey. NOSC

Marrows. Louis Johnson. PeNZ

Marry. Linda Smukler. WiU

Marrying Again. Mei Yao Ch'en. CoBCP; ColAnChi, tr. by Burton Watson

Marrying left your maiden name disused. Maiden Name. Philip Larkin. GTBS-P

Marrying Maiden, The. Unknown. PFTM-1   Fr. I Ching, The.

Marrying the Hangman. Margaret Atwood. NOBC

Mars and Venus. Rachel Hadas. GS

Mars, brilliant lord of the sky's fifth sphere. To Mars, a Prayer for Peace. Janus Pannonius. IQMS, tr. by Anthony Barrett

Mars is braw in crammasy. Bonnie Broukit Bairn, The. Hugh MacDiarmid. FaBoCh; FaBoVe; HAP; HarvBoo; NePenScot

Marsh marigold. Robert Spiess. HA

Marsh, New Year's Day, The. Peter Everwine. NNaP

Marsh's Plants Bewilder, The. Unknown. WoPoe, tr. by Barbara Hughes Fowler

Marsh Song—At Sunset. Sidney Lanier. NOBA; TCAPo   Fr. Hymns of the Marshes.

Marshes, The. Jane Mayhall. TAP

Marshes of Glynn, The. Sidney Lanier. NOBA; OxBA; TCAPo   Fr. Hymns of the Marshes.

Marshland merges with a tarry sea. Candle at Canterbury, A. Tessa Rose Chester. MFPA

Marshlands. Emily Pauline Johnson. NOBC; SWaP

Marsilion sees his people's martyrdom. Unknown. NAWM-5v1; NAWM-7v1, tr. by Frederick Goldin   Fr. Song of Roland, The.

Marston. Stephen Spender. FaBoTw

Marsyas. G. D. Roberts. NoP-4

Marta we found the little box. Protect Me, My Talisman. Milo De Angelis. NeIt, tr. by Lawrence Venuti

Martha. Walter De la Mare. MoBrPo

Martha and Mary. Gabriela Mistral. GI, tr. by Doris Dana

Martha Blake. Austin Clarke. ModIr; OxBEV

Martha Blake at Fifty-one. Austin Clarke. CIP-2; ModIr; NOIV; NPeEn

Martial. Thom Gunn. OBGa, tr. by Peter Porter

Martial Cadenza. Wallace Stevens. OxBA; VGW

Martial. Epigram XLVII, Book X. Ben Jonson. FaBoEE; OBVE

Martial [or Marshall or My Friend], the thing[e]s that do [or for to] attain [or attayne]. Happy Life, The. Martial. NOBE; NoSic; OBVE, tr. by Henry Howard, Earl of Surrey

Martial Variations. Amelia Rosselli.
"In the lethargy which follows the machinations of the." PFTM-2, tr. by Lawrence R. Smith

Martian Landscape. Abbie Huston Evans. APT-1

Martian Sends a Postcard Home, A. Craig Raine. NAEL-5v2; NAEL-6v2; NPeEn; NoAM; NoP-4

Martin. Pamela Stewart. ExTi

Martin and My Father. David Hernandez. UnSA

Martin Buber in the Pub. Max Harris. NOBAu

Martin Luther King. Aileen Fisher. HHAm

Martin's Blues. Michael S. Harper. HCAP; NAAL-5

Martin was too peaceful for me. Martin and My Father. David Hernandez. UnSA

Martins. Mike Jenkins. AngWePo

Marty's Mother. Stephen Kessler. GeoHom

Marty was the first holy man I knew. Tishah B'Ov / 1952. David Meltzer. TaR

Martyr. Mary Elizabeth Fullerton. CBAP

Martyr, The. Herman Melville. CBCWP; ColAP; NCAP; TAP; TCAPo

Martyr, The. Ibrahim Tuqan. MAP, tr. by John Heath-Stubbs and Lena Jayyusi

Martyr of Antioch, The. Henry Hart Milman.
"For thou didst die for me, O Son of God!" SacPr

Martyr Poets—did not tell, The. Emily Dickinson. APN-2

Martyr's Death, A. Menahem ben Jacob. TrJP

Martyr wears a crown, The. Be He Ezra Pound, Kennedy, or King. Belle Randall. GifTon

Martyrdom. Yolanda Bedregal. TANSG, tr. by Carolyne Wright

Martyrdom. "Rufus Learsi." TrJP

Martyrdom of Brébeuf and Lalemant, 16 March 1649, The. Edwin John Pratt. NOBC   Fr. Brébeuf and His Brethren.

Martyrdom of Saint Sebastian, The.   Eugenio Florit.   TCLAP, *tr. by* Peter Fortunato

Martyrdom of St. Theresa, The.   Alec Derwent Hope.   CBAP

Martyrdom of Two Pagans.   Philip Whalen.   NeAP

Martyred Democrat, The.   C. J. Dennis.   CBAP

Martyred Earth, The.   Ewart Milne.   BIrV

Martyred Tamarind, The.   Alberto Ferreira Gomes.   NAfrP, *tr. by* Gerald M. Moser

Martyrology 7, The.   B. P. Nichol.
  Hill Songs of Saint Orm, The.   PFTM-2
  Monotones.   PFTM-2
  Scraptures: 17th Sequence.   PFTM-2

Martyrs, The.   Jay Macpherson.   MoCV

Maru Mori brought me.   Ode to My Socks.   Pablo Neruda.   AmFaPo, *tr. by* Stephen Mitchell

Maru Mori brought me.   Ode to My Socks.   Pablo Neruda.   RaBo; TCLAP; TRP, *tr. by* Robert Bly

Marvel, A.   Carolyn Wells.   OBCA

Marvel, The.   Keith Douglas.   RB

Marvel No More.   Sir Thomas Wyatt.   SCGP

Marvel of Marvels.   Christina Georgina Rossetti.   NOBE

Marvel [*or* Marvaill] no more although [*or* all tho].   Marvel No More.   Sir Thomas Wyatt.   SCGP

Marvell! I think you'd neither seen nor smelt.   Hibernia.   Stuart Howard-Jones.   NOBL

Marvellous Grass.   Nuala Ni Dhomhnaill.   PBCIP, *tr. by* Michael Hartnett

Marvellous Martin.   Charles Harpur.   CBAP

Marvellously elate.   Jacopo da Lentino.   EaItPo, *tr. by* Dante Gabriel Rossetti

Marvelous Beast.   Patti Tana.   PasH

Marvelous four-cylindered beast.   Mechanical Cow, The.   Robley Wilson, Jr.   PBCAP

Marvelous is this wall-stone—but the fates broke.   Ruin, The.   *Unknown.*   NAWM-7v1, *tr. by* Lee Patterson

Marvelous Land of Indefinitions, The.   Lorenzo Thomas.   PmAP

Marvelous thing I have mused in my mind, A.   Mirabile Misterium.   *Unknown.*   SacPr

Marvels of the City, The.   Charles Simic.   LCAP-2

Marx the Sign Painter.   Edgar Lee Masters.   NoAM; TAP   *Fr.* New Spoon River, The.

Marxist to Liberals, A.   David Lindley.   NLP

Mary.   Philip Appleman.   GI

Mary.   Bertolt Brecht.   GI

Mary.   John Clare.   *See* To Mary: "It Is the Evening Hour."

Mary.   Lucille Clifton.   BBASP

Mary and Gabriel.   Rupert Brooke.   ChIV-2

Mary and *mare*, anagrammatized.   Epigram, a Supposed Construction.   John Taylor.   NOSC

Mary and the Bramble.   Lascelles Abercrombie.   OBMV

Mary at Peace with the Risen Lord.   Rainer Maria Rilke.   GI

Mary at the Feet of Christ.   Felicia Dorothea Hemans.   CenSon

Mary Celeste.   Judith Nicholls.   OBSP

Mary Desti's Ass.   Frank O'Hara.   FTOS

Mary had a little lamb.   Mary's Lamb [*or* Mary and Her Lamb].   Sarah Josepha Buell Hale.   BRP; OBCA; OxIBACP; OxNR; SWaP

Mary had a little lamb.   *Unknown.*   LB

Mary had a little lamb.   Little Lamb, A.   *Unknown.*   OBCoV

Mary had a pretty bird.   Mary's Canary.   *Unknown.*   ReMoGo

Mary Hamilton ("O Mary Hamilton to the kirk is gane.").   *Unknown.*   NOBE; OxBB

Mary Hamilton ("There were ladies, they lived in a bower.").   *Unknown. See* Mary [*or* Marie] Hamilton

Mary Hamilton ("Word's gane to the kitchen.").   *Unknown.*   ESPB; NePenScot; NoP-4; SCGP

Mary has a thingamajig clamped on her ears.   Manual System.   Carl Sandburg.   APT-1

Mary Hogan's Quatrains.   Máire Mhac an tSaoi.   ModIr, *tr. by* Patrick Crotty

Mary! I want a lyre with other strings.   To Mary Unwin.   William Cowper.   CenSon; GTBS-P; OBEV

Mary laid her Child among.   Carol.   Norman Nicholson.   OBCP

Mary Lifted from the Dead.   William Alfred.   AH

Mary Magdalen.   Kahlil Gibran.   GraLe

Mary Magdalene.   Saunders Lewis.   OBWVE, *tr. by* Gwyn Morgan

Mary Magdalene (I).   Boris Leonidovich Pasternak.   AF, *tr. by* Lydia Pasternak Slater

Mary Magdalene, that easy woman.   Lent.   William Robert Rodgers.   ModIr; PNI

Mary Martin, leader of the Lost Boys.   Peter Pan in North America.   Robin Becker.   ReTh

Mary, Mary, quite contrary.   Mother Goose.   LB; OxNR; ReMoGo

Mary mild, good maiden.   Saint Columcille [*or* Columba].   NOIV

Mary Morelle Show, The.   Denise Nico Leto.   UnSA

Mary Morison.   Robert Burns.   GTBS-P; NePenScot; OBEV; OxBS
  (Song: Mary Morison.)   AWP

Mary mother, dost thou sleep?   Mary's Dream.   *Unknown.*   OBWVE, *tr. by* C. C. Bell

Mary [*or* Marie] Hamilton.   *Unknown.*   ESPB
  (Mary Hamilton.)   NoP-4

Mary [*or* Marie] Magdalene.   George Herbert.   ESCV; SacPr

Mary Pickford, doll divine.   To Mary Pickford—Moving Picture Actress.   Nicholas Vachel Lindsay.   IllVoic

Mary, pray for Paris.   Sister Mary Madeleva.   CRP   *Fr.* Of Mary.

Mary prevents the day; she rose to weep.   Gardener, The.   Rowland Watkyns.   NOSC

Mary rose up, as one in sleep might rise.   Jesus Wept.   William Michael Rossetti.   CenSon

Mary's a Grand Old Name.   George M. Cohan.   ReLy

Mary's Canary.   *Unknown.*   ReMoGo

Mary's Dream.   Van K. Brock.   AllShUp; SwNoth

Mary's Dream.   Lucille Clifton.   NALW

Mary's Dream.   *Unknown.*   OBWVE, *tr. by* C. C. Bell

Mary's Lamb [*or* Mary and Her Lamb].   Sarah Josepha Buell Hale.   BRP; OBCA; OxIBACP; OxNR; SWaP

Mary's Plea.   Daisy Utemorrah.   IBA

Mary's poem vision.   Gold on Oak Leaves Said Young.   George Oppen.   BodElec

Mary's Song.   Marion Angus.   LW

Mary's Song.   Charles Causley.   OBCP

Mary's Song.   Sylvia Plath.   ChIV-2; FaBoMo; FaBoWP

Mary's Visitation.   Rainer Maria Rilke.   GI

Mary sat musing on the lamp-flame at the table.   Death of the Hired Man, The.   Robert Frost.   APT-1; HeIP-4; MoAmPo; NAAL-2v2; NAAL-5; NoP-4; OxBA; SAmP; TCAPo

Mary Smith had a college education.   Personality.   Jimmy Van Heusen.   ReLy

Mary stood in the kitchen.   Ballad of the Bread Man.   Charles Causley.   RB

Mary Stuart.   Edwin Muir.   RB

Mary Suffers with Her Son.   *Unknown.*   MiEL

Mary, the Blessed Virgins name.   Profit and Loss: An Elegy upon the Decease of Mrs. Mary Gerrish.   John Danforth.   SCAP

Mary the Cook-Maid's Letter to Dr. Sheridan.   Jonathan Swift.   NPeEn; OxBoLi; PeLV

Mary, the Mother of Jesus.   Ada Belle Gardner.   PWR

Mary, the Scots are sots in any case.   Joseph Brodsky.   TCRusP, *tr. by* Bernard Meares   *Fr.* Sonnets on the Statue of Mary, Queen of Scots, in the Luxembourg Gardens, Paris.

Mary Trevellyn to Miss Roper.   Arthur Hugh Clough.   FaBoVe   *Fr.* Amours de Voyage.

Mary Warren's Sampler.   Nicole Cooley.   NeAmPo

Mary was Mother of the Lord.   Hymn of the Magdalen.   Marbod of Rennes.   MLL, *tr. by* Helen Waddell

Mary Weeps for Her Child.   *Unknown.*   OxBoLi

Mary, will you ever grow?   Water, blessed by bishops.   Song for Healing.   Roberta Hill Whiteman.   CDW

Mary, your great.   Jesus Suckles.   Anne Sexton.   PFTM-2

Marye, maide, milde and fre.   Song to Mary, A.   William of Shoreham.   MiEL

Maryland.   James Ryder Randall.   *See* My Maryland

Maryland Virginia Caroline.   Emblems.   Allen Tate.   AWP; VGW

Mas-Soñer / Restaurat—Any.   House, The.   Robert Creeley.   FTOS

Masaccio's *Expulsion from Paradise*.   Julia Copus.   MFPA

Masai warrior is not, The.   Outbreak.   Bill Anderson.   VGW

Mashed potatoes cannot hurt you, darling.   Giving Potatoes.   Adrian Mitchell.   NBLV; RB

Mask.   Sapardi Djoko Damono.   WoPoe, *tr. by* John H. McGlynn

Mask.   Stephen Spender.   MoBrPo

Mask, A.   John Milton.   OxAEP-1   *Fr.* Comus; a Masque Presented at Ludlow Castle.

Mask, The.   Elizabeth Barrett Browning.   VWP

Mask, The.   Patty L. Harjo.   VoR

Mask, The.   Laura Riding Jackson.   HarvBoo

Mask, The.   Irma McClaurin.   BlSi

Mask for Lydia, A.   Thomas Randolph.   BeJo

Mask-Maker.   Michael Jackson.   PeNZ

Mask of Anger, A.   Lyn Hejinian.   FTOS

Mask of Evil, The.   Bertolt Brecht.   PoSu; WoPoe, *tr. by* Hoffman Reynolds Hays

Mask of Gaiety, The.   Letitia [*or* Laetitia] Elizabeth Landon.   VWP

Mask [*or* Masque] of Anarchy, The. Shelley. FHYEP; OBSV; OxAEP-2; RB; SCV

"As I lay asleep in Italy." NPeEn; WoPoe

Maske of Cupid, The. Edmund Spenser. NAEL-6v1; NAEL-7v1 *Fr.* Faerie Queene, The.

Masks! O Masks! Prayer to the Masks. Léopold Sédar Senghor. NegPo, *tr. by* Ellen Conroy Kennedy

Mason, The. Aloysius Bertrand. BLT, *tr. by* E. D. Hartley

Mason Abraham Knupfer is singing, trowel in hand, scaffolded, The. Mason, The. Aloysius Bertrand. BLT, *tr. by* E. D. Hartley

Mason's finger, The. Buson. EH, *tr. by* Robert Hass

Mason's Trick. James Hayford. InPK-6

Masons, cart drivers and occasional fishermen. Havana Harbor. Nancy Morejón. TANSG, *tr. by* Joy Renjilian-Burgy

Masons, when they start upon a building. Scaffolding. Seamus Heaney. ChAP

Masque of Blackness, The. Geoffrey Hill. NoAM *Fr.* Lachrimae; or Seven Tears Figured in Seven Passionate Pavans.

Masque of Christmas, The. Ben Jonson. ChrPo; OxBoLi

Masque of Queens, The. Ben Jonson.

"Help, help all tongues to celebrate this wonder." NOSC

Witches' Charms, The.

(Witches' Charm.) FaBoCh

(Witches' Chasm.) RB

Masque of the Inner Temple and Gray's Inne, The. Francis Beaumont.

Fourth Song, The. NOSC

(Song for a Dance.) FaBoCh

Masque of the Middle Temple and Lincoln's Inn, The. George Chapman.

Bridal Song: "Now sleep, bind fast the flood of air." OxBSP

Masque of the Virtues against Love. Mary Monck. ECWP; NOEC

Masquerade. Carolyn M. Rodgers. BlSi

Masquerading. May Probyn. NPeEn; VWP

Mass. César Vallejo. TCLAP, *tr. by* Clayton Eshleman *Fr.* Spain, Take This Cup from Me.

Mass at Dawn. Roy Campbell. OxAEP-2

Mass Graves. Charles Reznikoff.

("Jews from Holland, France, and Hungary, and later from.") HP

Mass hysteria, wave after breaking wave. Willowware Cup. James Merrill. VCAP

Mass Is Over, The. Sara Berkeley. PBCIP

Mass is over, they have gone in peace, The. Mass Is Over, The. Sara Berkeley. PBCIP

Mass of ledged rock, A. Winter Nocturne: The Hospital. Alter Brody. APT-2

Massacre, October '66. Wole Soyinka. AF; PBMAP

Massacre of the Boys. Tadeusz Rózewicz. AF; GI; HP

(Children cried "Mummy!," The) AF; GI

(Massacre of the Boys.) AF; GI; HP

(With no star in its crown.) (LL) AF; HP

Massacre of the Innocents. Alec Derwent Hope. GI

Massacre of the Innocents, The. Giambattista [*or* Giovanni Battista] Marino.

"Yet on the other side, faine would he start." OBVE

Massacre Sandhill. Grandfather Koori. IBA

Massacres. Charles Reznikoff. APSN

Massenet. Antony Butts. OBCoV

Masses. César Vallejo. RB, *tr. by* Robert Bly *Fr.* España, Aparta de me Este Caliz.

Masses, The. Cornelius Mathews. APN-1 *Fr.* Poems on Man in His Various Aspects under the American Republic.

Masses of flowers and plants envelop the riverbanks. Tu Fu. SuSp *Fr.* Strolling along the Riverbank, Looking for Flowers.

Masses of mountain peaks. T'ung Pass. Chang Yang-hao. WoPoe, *tr. by* Sam Hamill

Masseuse, The. Olga Broumas. WiU

Massive engines lift beautifully from the deck. Teeth Mother Naked at Last, The. Robert Bly. NNaP

Massive hills, numberless valleys, all point to Ching-men. Thoughts on Historical Sites: Wang Chao-chün. Tu Fu. SuSp, *tr. by* Irving Lo

Massive rains darken the marshes and slopes. Dreaming of Master Chung-lu. K'ang Hai. CoBLCP, *tr. by* Jonathan Chaves

Massive rock head but the guy's eyes dart. O Pioneers! Jane Miller. GifTon

Mast Year, The. Medbh McGuckian. CIP-2

Mastectomy. Wanda Coleman. NAAAL

Mastectomy Poems, The. Alicia Ostriker.

Bridge, The. ExTi

Healing. ExTi

Wintering. ExTi

Master. Brendan Kennelly. BiHa

Master, The. Bryn Griffiths. TCAWP

Master, The. Edwin Arlington Robinson. CBCWP; MoAmPo

Master—. Her Habit. Lucie Brock-Broido. ExTi

Master and Guest. Mary Elizabeth Coleridge. VWP; ViWPN

Master and Man. Mother Goose. OxNR; ReMoGo

Master and Man. Sir Henry John Newbolt. OxBTC

Master and the Dog, The. Ignacy Krasicki. WoPoe, *tr. by* Jerzy Peterkiewicz and Burns Singer

Master and the slave go hand in hand, The. Sonnet. Edwin Arlington Robinson. APN-2

Master Bertuccio, you are called to account. Rustico Di Filippo. EaItPo, *tr. by* Dante Gabriel Rossetti

Master Brunetto, this my little maid. Sonnet: To Brunetto Latini. Dante Alighieri. AWP; EaItPo, *tr. by* Dante Gabriel Rossetti

Master Carpenter, The. G. Shankara Kurup. OMIP, *tr. by* K. M. George

Master Charge Blues. Nikki Giovanni. OBAL

Master Chia. Li Shang-yin. ColAnChi, *tr. by* James J. Y. Liu

Master dragon-tamer has fled the world, The. Li Ho. SuSp *Fr.* About Horse.

Master Francesco, I have come to thee. Petrarch. Giosuè Carducci. AWP, *tr. by* William Dudley Foulke

Master I have, and I am his man. Master and Man. Mother Goose. OxNR; ReMoGo

Master Jen has long been famous. Thanking Doctor Jen. Li K'ai-hsien. CoBLCP; ColAnChi, *tr. by* Jonathan Chaves

Master Joshu and the dog. Soen. ZenPo, *tr. by* Takashi Ikemoto and Lucien Stryk

Master Liu Painted a Portrait of Me in My Old Age and Asked Me to Write a Poem about the Picture. Yang Wan-li. SuSp, *tr. by* Jonathan Chaves

Master Mo Tzu and Master Lao Tzu. Inspector Hsü Claims He Has Found the Secret of Youth. T'ang Hsien-tsu. CoBLCP, *tr. by* Jonathan Chaves

Master, No Offering. Edwin Pond Parker. AH

Master of Auschwitz, angel of death. For the Bones of Josef Mengele, Disinterred June 1985. Robert Bringhurst. NIP-4

Master of beauty, craftsman of the snowflake. John Berryman. InvLi; PAI; UnPo *Fr.* Eleven Addresses to the Lord.

Master of blood I am yours. Nocturnal Heart. Anne-Marie Kegels. BoWoP

Master of the Golden Glow, The. James Schuyler. FTOS

Master of *The Monarch of the Glen*, The. Unsagacious Animal, An. David Gascoyne. PeLV

Master only left old Mistus. Frances Ellen Watkins Harper. SWaP *Fr.* Aunt Chloe.

Master Shih's medical fame, because of Master Ch'en. Sent to the Master Physician, "Almond Orchard" Shih. Li K'ai-hsien. CoBLCP; ColAnChi, *tr. by* Jonathan Chaves

Master-songs are ended, and the man, The. Walt Whitman. Edwin Arlington Robinson. APN-2; NCAP; OxBA; TCAPo

Master stood upon the mount, and taught, The. Progress. Matthew Arnold. ChIV-2

Master, the swabber, the boatswain and I, The. William Shakespeare. NOBL; OxBSP *Fr.* Tempest, The.

Master, the tempest is raging. Peace Be Still. *Unknown.* NAAAL

Master, they say that when I seem. Prayer. Clive Staples Lewis. SacPr; TrCP

Master Tung-p'o, in raising children, was afraid of their being clever. Rebuttal of Tung-p'o's Poem on "Bathing the Infant," A. Ch'ien Ch'ien-i [*or* Ch'ien Ch'ien-yi]. SuSp, *tr. by* Irving Y. Lo

Master—you were having your veins cleaned out of Me—. Prescient. Lucie Brock-Broido. ExTi

Masters, The. Gillian Conoley. BodElec

Masters, The. Francis Saltus Saltus.

"Come! show your jolly tricks, and be possessed." VerBaPo

Masters, be kind to the old house that must fall. Rockland. Julia Randall. WPE

Masters go abrod to vew the towne, The. Ludovico Ariosto. OxBEV, *tr. by* John Harington *Fr.* Orlando Furioso.

Masters, in this Hall. French Noel. William Morris. ChrPo

Masters of Taoist Arts, The. (LL) Slowly, Slowly Poem, The. Yüan Hung-tao. CoBLCP; ColAnChi, *tr. by* Jonathan Chaves

Masters, the mock orange is blooming in Syracuse without scent, having been bred. Of Distress Being Humiliated by the Classical Chinese Poets. Hayden Carruth. WoPoe

Masts at Dawn. Robert Penn Warren. NAAL-2v2; NoP-4; VCAP

Mat to Weave, A. U Tam'si Tchicaya. NegPo, *tr. by* Ellen Conroy Kennedy

(He came to deliver the secret of the sun.) PBMAP

Matadors, The. Josephine Jacobsen. TAP

Match, A. Algernon Charles Swinburne. NOBVV

Match, The. Andrew Marvell. EBEV

Match, The. Henry Vaughan. ESCV

Match-bark of the younger dog sets fire to, The. Table-Birds. Kenneth Mackenzie. BMAP; NOBAu

Match Me Such Marvel. William Basil Tickell Jones. UV

Match me such marvel save in college port. Match Me Such Marvel. William Basil Tickell Jones. UV

Match me such marvel save in Eastern clime. John William Burgon. UV *Fr.* Petra.

Match with the Moon, A. Dante Gabriel Rossetti. NOBVV; NPeEn; OxBEV

Matches among other things that were not allowed. Burnt Child, The. W. S. Merwin. NoAM

Matching a Poem by Secretary Kuo, No. 1. T'ao Ch'ien [*or* T'ao Yuan-ming]. CoBCP, *tr. by* Burton Watson

Matching Flowers. Kate Foley. Prnts

Matching the wine in my veins. (LL) Stripper, The. Anita Endrezze. CDW; ReTh

Matchmaker. Sheldon Harnick. ReLy

Matchmaker, matchmaker, make me a match. Matchmaker. Sheldon Harnick. ReLy

Mater Dei. Padraic Fallon. NOCV

Mater Dolorosa. William Barnes. NOBE; OBEV

Mater Dolorosa. Eugene Jolas. APT-2

Material's Daughter. Aaron Shurin. FTOS

Materialism. C. E. M. Joad. PeLi

Materialism. Lőrinc Szabó. IQMS, *tr. by* Laurence James

Maternal Despotism; or, The Rights of Infants. Richard Graves. NOEC

Maternal Earth stirs redly from beneath. Roy Campbell. MoBrPo *Fr.* Flaming Terrapin, The.

Maternity. Alice Thompson Meynell. OxBSP; PEW; VWP

Maternity Gown. David Holbrook. OxBTC

Matey. Patrick MacGill. PoWW

Mathematician's Dream, The. Reuel Denney. YaYoPo

Mathematicians take a huge area like a whole world. To Myself. Abba Kovner. AF, *tr. by* Shirley Kaufman

Mathenge. Marjorie Oludhe Macgoye. HBAPE

Mathilde in Normandy. Adrienne Rich. YaYoPo

Mathios Paskalis among the Roses. George Seferis. PFTM-1; PoetW, *tr. by* Edmund Keeley and Philip Sherrard

Mathmid, The. Hayyim Nahman [*or* Khayim Nakhman *or* Chaim Nachman] Bialik. AWP, *tr. by* Maurice Samuel

Matière de Bretagne. Paul Celan. WoPoe, *tr. by* Margaret Guillemin and Katherine Washburn

Matière de Bretagne. Paul Celan. VCWP, *tr. by* Michael Hamburger

Matilda. Joseph Hilaire Pierre Belloc. FaBoCh; NOBE

Matilda, and the House, were Burned. (LL) Matilda. Joseph Hilaire Pierre Belloc. FaBoCh; NOBE

Matilda Maud Mackenzie frankly hadn't any chin. How a Girl Was Too Reckless of Grammar [by Far]. Guy Wetmore Carryl. OBAL

Matilda told such Dreadful Lies. Matilda. Joseph Hilaire Pierre Belloc. FaBoCh; NOBE

Matilde, sleeping / that feverish sleep, a day or a year. Final. Pablo Neruda. WoPoe, *tr. by* Ben Belitt

Matin Hymn. Josephine D. Henderson Heard. CBWP-4

Matin Song. Thomas Heywood. *See* Rape of Lucrece, The

Matinee. Susan Clements. UnSA

Matinée Idylls. Molly Bendall. AmPoNex

Matinees. James Merrill. HCAP; NOBA

Mating. Yang Wei-chen. ColAnChi, *tr. by* John Timothy Wixted

Mating the Goats. Aliki Barnstone. BoWoP

Matins. Louise Glück. InvLi

Matins. George Herbert. *See* Mattens

Matins. Denise Levertov. FaBoWP; NOBA; NoAM

Matins. Molly Peacock. ExTi

Matins and Lauds. Marie Ponsot. CLPP

Matins: James Brown and His Famous Flames Tour the South, 1958. David Wojahn. PBCAP *Fr.* Mystery Train: A Sequence.

Matins [*or* Mattens], or Morning Prayer. Robert Herrick. BASC; CaPo

Matisse: Blue Nude, 1952. Dionisio D. Martinez. TouFir

Matisse: "The Red Studio." W. D. Snodgrass. GS

Matmiya. Mary Tallmountain. HATNAP; LoL

Matrimony. John Williams. NOEC

Matrix. Dorothy Wellesley, Duchess of Wellington.
"Spiritual, the carnal, are one, The." OBMV

Matsushima. Gochikubo. JDP, *tr. by* Yoel Hoffmann

Matsushima. Isaibo. JDP, *tr. by* Yoel Hoffmann

Matt Casey formed a social club that beat the town for style. Band Played On, The. John F. Palmer. OBAL

Matt the Gooseherd. Mihály Fazekas.
"But good Sir, look here"—said he." IQMS, *tr. by* Thomas Kabdebo

Mattens. George Herbert. ESCV
(Matins.) SCGP

Matter. Carla Harryman. FTOS

Matter of Control, A. Diana García. TouFir

Matter of Division, A. Frankie Paino. AmPoNex

Matter / of fact. Catherine Walsh. Oth *Fr.* Pitch.

Matter? More than anything else. For Gil and Other Incurables. Renée Weiss. BodElec

Matters of Policy. Charles Bernstein. FTOS

Matthew 1:18–25: Now the birth of Jesus Christ took place. Philip Appleman. GI *Fr.* St. Matthew.

Matthew 2:1–12; Now when Jesus was born. T. S. Eliot. GI *Fr.* St. Matthew.

Matthew 2:16–18; Then Herod, when he saw. Julia Hartwig. GI *Fr.* St. Matthew.

Matthew 4:1–11; Then Jesus was led up by the spirit. Czeslaw Milosz. GI *Fr.* St. Matthew.

Matthew 5:1–12; Seeing the crowds, he went up on the mountain. Jorge Luis Borges. GI *Fr.* St. Matthew.

Matthew 5:13; You are the salt of the earth. Gail Holst-Warhaft. GI *Fr.* St. Matthew.

Matthew 5:27–30; You have heard that it was said. Gail Holst-Warhaft. GI *Fr.* St. Matthew.

Matthew V. 29–30. Derek Mahon. CIP-2

Matthew 5:38–48; "You have heard that it was said, 'An eye.'" Jacob Glatstein [*or* Glatsteyn]. GI *Fr.* St. Matthew.

Matthew 6:7–15; "And in praying do not heap up empty." D. H. Lawrence. GI *Fr.* St. Matthew.

Matthew 7:1–2; "Judge not, that you be not." Theodore Roethke. GI *Fr.* St. Matthew.

Matthew 8:20; And Jesus said to him. Karl Kirchwey. GI *Fr.* St. Matthew.

Matthew 8:28–34; And when he came to the other side. Richard Wilbur. GI *Fr.* St. Matthew.

Matthew 9.12. Francis Quarles. ChIV-2

Matthew 10:1. Philip Larkin. GI *Fr.* St. Matthew.

Matthew 13:1–9; That same day Jesus. Stephen Mitchell. GI *Fr.* St. Matthew.

Matthew 19:16–24; And behold, one came up to him. Anna Kamienska. GI *Fr.* St. Matthew.

Matthew 21:1–11. Boris Leonidovich Pasternak. GI *Fr.* St. Matthew.

Matthew 21:18–22; In the morning. Donald Hall. GI *Fr.* St. Matthew.

Matthew 22:1–14; And again Jesus spoke to them. Edwin Arlington Robinson. GI *Fr.* St. Matthew.

Matthew 22:15–22; Then the Pharisees went and. Desanka Maksimovic. GI *Fr.* St. Matthew.

Matthew 24:15–31. W. B. Yeats. GI *Fr.* St. Matthew.

Matthew 25:14–30; "For it will be as when a man." Jorge Luis Borges. GI *Fr.* St. Matthew.

Matthew XXV:30. Jorge Luis Borges. GI, *tr. by* David Curzon

Matthew 26:17–29. Rainer Maria Rilke. GI *Fr.* St. Matthew.

Matthew 26:47–56; While he was still speaking, Judas came. Boris Leonidovich Pasternak. GI *Fr.* St. Matthew.

Matthew 27:3–10; When Judas, his betrayer, saw. Zbigniew Herbert. GI *Fr.* St. Matthew.

Matthew 27:11–24; Now Jesus stood before. René Daumal. GI *Fr.* St. Matthew.

Matthew 27:45–56; Now from the sixth hour there was darkness. Ted Hughes. GI *Fr.* St. Matthew.

Matthew 27:57–61; When it was evening, there came a rich man. Rainer Maria Rilke. GI *Fr.* St. Matthew.

Matthew 28:1–6; Now after the sabbath. Czeslaw Milosz. GI *Fr.* St. Matthew.

Matthew 28:16–20; Now the eleven disciples went to Galilee. W. B. Yeats. GI *Fr.* St. Matthew.

Matthew and Mark and Luke and holy John. Epi-strauss-ium. Arthur Hugh Clough. NAEL-5v2; NAEL-6v2

Matthew, and Mark, and Luke, and John. N. T. Charles Wesley. ChIV-2

Matthew, Mark, Luke and John. *Unknown.* OxNR

Matthew, Mark, Luke, and John / Bless the bed that I lie on. Before Sleeping. *Unknown.* FaBoCh; OxNR

Matthew, Mark, Luke and John, / Hold the horse till I leap on. Matthew, Mark, Luke and John. *Unknown.* OxNR

Matthew X. 28. Roger Wolcott. SCAP

Matthias' Demented Scholar. Endre Ady. IQMS, *tr. by* Anton N. Nyerges

Mattie dear. When in Rome. Mari E. Evans. ESEAA; SoSe-8

Mattress loved the explicit, The. She would find. Peridot. Rebecca Reynolds. AmPoNex

Mauberly (1920). Ezra Pound. *Fr.* Hugh Selwyn Mauberley (Life and Contacts).

Maud [A Monodrama].   Tennyson.
 "Ah, what shall I be at fifty."   NAEL-5v2; NAEL-6v2
 ("As he glowed like a ruddy shield on the Lion's breast.") (LL)   OBWP
 "Birds in the high Hall-garden."   NAEL-5v2; NAEL-6v2; PeVV
 "Catch not my breath, O clamorous heart."   NAEL-5v2; NAEL-6v2
 Come into the Garden, Maud.   EBVV; FHYEP; NOBE; NOBVV; OxAEP-2;
   OxBEV; PoE; UV; WoPoe
 "Go not, happy day."   EBVV
 "I have led her home, my love, my only friend."   EBVV; NAEL-5v2; NAEL-
   6v2; NOBVV
 "I have played with her when a child."   NAEL-6v2
 "I was walking a mile."   EBVV
 (Maud.)   OBGa
 "Maud has a garden of roses."   FHYEP
 "O let the solid ground."   NAEL-5v2; NAEL-6v2; NOBVV
 "O [or Oh] that 'twere possible."   BoLoP; NAEL-5v2; NAEL-6v2; NOBE;
   NOBVV; OBEV; PoE
 "Perhaps the smile and tender tone."   NAEL-6v2
 "She came to the village church."   EBVV; NAEL-5v2; NAEL-6v2
 (Song.)   AWP
Maud Fitzgerald.   Unknown.   PeLi
Maud has a garden of roses.   Tennyson.   FHYEP   Fr. Maud [A Monodrama].
Maud Muller.   John Greenleaf Whittier.   APN-1; BRP; TAP; TreFP
Maud Muller, all that summer day.   Mrs. Judge Jenkins[; Being the Only
   Genuine Sequel to "Maud Muller"].   Bret Harte.   APN-2
Maud Stevens received her first tattoo in 1904.   Book of Human Anomalies,
   The.   Albert Goldbarth.   OPRER
Maud went to college.   Gwendolyn Brooks.   ESEAA; InPK-6; NAAAL;
   NOBA; NoAM; TAP   Fr. Street in Bronzeville, A.
Maude Clare.   Christina Georgina Rossetti.   EBVV; ViWPN
Maugre thee my love shall stay. (LL)   Marie [or Mary] Magdalens Complaint
   at Christs Death.   Robert Southwell.   ChIV-2; ESCV
Maui.   Meg Campbell.   PeNZ
Maui's Fish.   Blanche Edith Baughan.
 "Toward the dawn."   PeNZ
Maunder's Praise of His Strowling Mort, The.   Unknown.   OxBoLi; PeLV
Maunding Soldier; or, The Fruits of Warre Is Beggery, The.   Martin Parker.
   FaBoWar
Maundy Thursday.   Jenő Dsida.   IQMS, tr. by George Gömöri and Clive
   Wilmer
Maundy Thursday.   Wilfred Owen.   NPeEn; OxBSo
Maura.   Thomas Lynch.   EmeKit
Maureen Dean, wearing persimmon summer silk.   On the Watergate Women.
   Robin Morgan.   GLP
Maureen in England, Joseph in Guelph.   Wishbone, The.   Paul Muldoon.
   CIP-2; PBCIP
Maurice was in an Exhibition Hall.   Austin Clarke.   PoE   Fr. Mnemosyne Lay
   in Dust.
Maurus.   Palladas [or Pallades].   GrAn, tr. by Tony Harrison
Mauve and printed silk go well, The.   Culture Nervous.   Ricardo M. de
   Ungria.   ReBoTo
Mauve summer rain, The.   Dame Edith Sitwell.   BWW   Fr. Sleeping Beauty,
   The.
Mavis.   James King Annand.   NOxBChV
Mavis, mavis.   Mavis.   James King Annand.   NOxBChV
Maw Broon Visits a Therapist.   Jackie Kay.   MFPA
Mawu of the Waters.   Abena Busia.   HAWP; NAfrP
Max Factor Pink.   Nigel Roberts.   BMAP
Max Jacob at Saint Benoît.   Rosanna Warren.   OPRER
Max's Lecture on Canine Buddhism.   Amy Gerstler.   Unle
Max Schmitt in a Single Scull.   Richmond Lattimore.   AiP
Max Who Caught a Car.   Ron Carlson.   Unle
Maxfield Parrish.   Eileen Myles.   WiU
Maxie Allen.   Gwendolyn Brooks.   NAAL-2v2
Maxim Gun, The.   Joseph Hilaire Pierre Belloc.   FaBoWar   Fr. Modern
   Traveller, The.
Maxim Revised, A.   Unknown.   NBLV
Maxims (Cotton MS.).   Unknown.   AnOE, tr. by Charles W. Kennedy
Maxims (Exeter Book).   Unknown.   AnOE
Maxims in Rhyme for the Young.   J. Clark.   PWR
Maximus.   D. H. Lawrence.   BLT; TOF
Maximus from Dogtown-II.   Charles Olson.   PFTM-2   Fr. Maximus Poems,
   The.
Maximus Poems, The.   Charles Olson.
 "Added to / making a Republic."   PFTM-2
 "Boats' lights in the dawn going so swiftly the, The."   BodElec
 Celestial Evening, October 1967.   NAAL-5; PoM

 ("Chockablock Once a man was traveling through the woods, and.")   FTOS
 Cole's Island.   PoM
 "Colored pictures."   NoAM
 I, Maximus of Gloucester, to You ("By ear, she sd.").   NeAP
 I, Maximus of Gloucester, to You ("Off-shore, by islands hidden in the
   blood.").   NOBA; NoAM; PmAP; PoM
 Letter 3.   APT-2; PmAP
 Maximus from Dogtown-II.   PFTM-2
 Maximus, to Gloucester, Letter 2.   NoAM
 Maximus, to Gloucester, Letter 27.   NOBA; PoE
 Maximus, to Gloucester, Sunday, July 19.   NAAL-2v2; TRP
 Maximus, to Himself.   APT-2; NAAL-5; NOBA; NeAP; PmAP; PoE; PoM;
   VGW
 Ocean, The.   APT-2
 Poem 143.   APSN; ColAP
 "Sea—turn yr Back on, The."   PFTM-2
 Songs of Maximus.   NeAP
  All / wrong.   NoAM
  "Colored pictures / of all things to eat: dirty."   NeAP; NoAM
 Telesphere, The.   BodElec
Maximus, to Gloucester, Letter 2.   Charles Olson.   NoAM   Fr. Maximus
   Poems, The.
Maximus, to Gloucester, Letter 27.   Charles Olson.   NOBA; PoE   Fr.
   Maximus Poems, The.
Maximus, to Gloucester, Sunday, July 19.   Charles Olson.   NAAL-2v2; TRP
   Fr. Maximus Poems, The.
Maximus, to Himself.   Charles Olson.   APT-2; NAAL-5; NOBA; NeAP;
   PmAP; PoE; PoM; VGW   Fr. Maximus Poems, The.
May.   W. H. Auden.   EBEV
May.   Dafydd [or David] ap Gwilym.   CABP
May.   Edward Hovell-Thurlow, 2d Baron Thurlow.   OBEV
May.   Mrs. Henry Linden.   CBWP-4
May.   John Shaw Neilson.   NOBAu
May.   Henrietta Cordelia Ray.   CBWP-3
May.   Christina Georgina Rossetti.   NOBVV; NPeEn; OxBEV
May.   Folgore da San Geminiano [or Gimignano].   EaItPo, tr. by Dante Gabriel
   Rossetti   Fr. Sonnets of the Months.
May.   Edmund Spenser.   PBRV   Fr. Shepheardes [or Shepeards or
   Shepherd's] Calender, The.
May.   John Updike.   OBCA   Fr. Child's Calendar, A.
May 24, 1980.   Joseph Brodsky.   TCRP, tr. by Joseph Brodsky
May—1941.   Valentine Penrose.   SurPaPo, tr. by Mary Ann Caws
May 1968.   Sharon Olds.   NIP-4
May 1970.   Stephen Berg.   CDa
May all comers wax poetic.   Unknown.   PriapPo, tr. by Richard W. Hooper
   Fr. Priapus Poems, The.
May All Earth Be Clothed in Light.   George Hitchcock.   VGW
May all that dread the cruel feind of night.   Warning to Travailers Seeking
   Accomodations at Mr. Devills Inn.   Sarah Kemble Knight.   SCAP
May all the deities keep me from chewing like you.   Unknown.   PriapPo, tr. by
   Richard W. Hooper   Fr. Priapus Poems, The.
May all your tears, wanderer.   Song of the Wanderer.   Wang T'ing-hsiang.
   CoBLCP, tr. by Jonathan Chaves
May and Death.   Robert Browning.   NOBE
May, and the wall was warm again. For miles.   Winter's Cold.   William Robert
   Rodgers.   EnLoPo
May at his peril[l] further go. (LL)   Superliminare.   George Herbert.   ESCV;
   NOSC
May be opened for inspection. (LL)   Epitaph for a Postal Clerk.   X. J.
   Kennedy.   NIL-7; NIP-4
May be refin'd, and join th'angelic train. (LL)   On Being Brought from Africa
   to America.   Phillis Wheatley.   NAAL-2v1; NAAL-3; NAAL-5; NALW;
   NOBA; NOEC; OxBEV; RWP; SacPr; TAP; TTY; WPE
May! be thou never graced with birds that sing.   [Epitaph] In Obitum M. S., X°
   Maij [or Maii], 1614.   William Browne.   FaBoEE; NOBE; OBEV
May blaze the virtue [or vertue] of their sires. (LL)   Nuptiall Song, or
   Epithalamie, on Sir Clipseby Crew and His Lady, A.   Robert Herrick.
   BeJo; CaPo
May Collin.   Lady Isabel and the Elf-Knight.   Unknown.   ESPB
May Colven [or May Colvin].   Unknown.   OxBB
May come up with bird-din.   Nuts in May.   Louis MacNeice.   MoBrPo
May crown Thy Feet, that could not crown Thy Head. (LL)   Coronet, The.
   Andrew Marvell.   BASC; ESCV; FHYEP; FSCP; GeHe; MeLP; NAEL-
   5v1; NAEL-6v1; NAEL-7v1; NOCV; NOSC; NoP-4; PBRV; PoE; SCGP;
   SacPr; TOF
May-Day.   Aaron Hill.   NOEC
May Day Rounds: Renfrew County.   Joan Finnigan.
 "Stoop on the log-house is brown with sweet rain-rot, The."   WPE

May 15th. Raymond Souster. MoCV

May filter in my daily songs. (LL)   As I Sit Writing Here.   Walt Whitman. NAAL-2v1; NAAL-3

May find you planting lentils on my grave. (LL)   Prodigal Son, The.   Edwin Arlington Robinson.   GI; MoAmPo

May God be praised for woman.   On Woman.   W. B. Yeats.   ChIV-1

May God bless your home.   Marriage Vow.   Mrs. Henry Linden.   CBWP-4

May God Go with You, Son.   C. Wright.   FaBoWar

May God grant me the memory to recall my life.   Sergey [or Sergei] Gondlevsky [or Gondlevskii].   TCRP

May God save, protect we pray.   National Folk Hymn.   Karl Kraus.   AuPH, tr. by Lowell A. Bangerter

"May Grace be with you all" said the bishop.   Unknown.   GrAn

May has come out from the showers.   Jewish May, The.   Morris Jacob Rosenfeld.   TrJP, tr. by Helena Frank and Rose Pastor Stokes

May have killed the cat; more likely.   Curiosity.   Alastair Reid.   SoSe-8

May he fall in with beasts that scatter fire.   Ballad against the Enemies of France.   François Villon.   AWP, tr. by Algernon Charles Swinburne

May he lose his way on the cold sea.   Archilochus.   OBVE; WoPoe, tr. by Guy Davenport

May he that bade me trust him, but did not come.   Malediction.   Unknown.   WoPoe, tr. by Arthur Waley

May he who brings / Flowers tonight.   Kikaku.   ZenPo, tr. by Takashi Ikemoto and Lucien Stryk

May his Counsels Sweet uphold you.   God Be with You.   Unknown.   PoToHe

May I ask you a question? Narrows, The.   Anne Rouse.   MFPA

May I come in? May I come in?   Jean-Joseph Rabéarivelo [or Rebéarivelo].   NegPo

May i feel said he.   E. E. Cummings.   BoLoP; HeIP-4; NBLV; NOBE; OBCoV; PeLV; PoPoPo

May I for my own self song's truth reckon.   Seafarer, The.   Ezra Pound.   APT-1; CTC; FaBoTw; HeIP-4; NoP-4; OxBA; TCAPo; WoPoe

May I for my own self song's truth reckon.   Unknown.   CABP

May I forever a Muse.   Vow.   John Updike.   PeLV

May I, goldencrowned Aphrodite.   Sappho.   SaLy, tr. by Diane Rayor

May I learn the shape of that hurt.   For the D.   Anthony McNeill.   WaCA

May I say, "It is Nestus Gurley." (LL)   Nestus Gurley.   Randall Jarrell.   HeIP-4; TwCP

May I with Mary choose the better part.   Mary English.   EMWP

May in the Green-Wood.   Unknown.   OBEV

May is a pious fraud of the almanac.   James Russell Lowell.   APN-1; TCAPo   Fr. Under the Willows.

May is Mary's month, and I.   May Magnificat, The.   Gerard Manley Hopkins.   PeECV

May is the moneth maist amene.   Of May.   Alexander Scott.   OxBS

May Isis Heal Me.   Unknown.   HW

May Isis heal me as she healed her son Horus.   May Isis Heal Me.   Unknown.   HW

May It Be.   Boris Leonidovich Pasternak.   TrJP, tr. by C. M. Bowra

May–June, 1940.   Robinson Jeffers.   MoAmPo

May Levine.   Susan Fromberg Schaeffer.   TaR

May look to heaven as I depart. (LL)   To the Fringed Gentian.   William Cullen Bryant.   APN-1; AWP; TAP

May Magnificat, The.   Gerard Manley Hopkins.   PeECV

May Margret stood in her bower door.   Hind Etin.   Unknown.   ESPB; OxBB

May Morn.   Michael McClure.   SPE

May Morning.   George Buchanan.   PBRV

May my heart always be open to little.   E. E. Cummings.   OxBSP

May never hope to have her company. (LL)   Dante Alighieri.   AWP; EaItPo, tr. by Dante Gabriel Rossetti   Fr. La Vita Nuova.

May, 1945.   Peter Porter.   HP; OxBC

May no man slepe in youre halle.   Unknown.   MiEL

May not have been in vain. (LL)   David Gascoyne.   ChIV-2; NoP-4; OBWP; PeECV   Fr. Miserere.

May nothing evil cross this door.   Prayer for This House.   Louis Untermeyer.   PoToHe

May nothing I own be stolen or concealed.   For the Theft of Cattle.   Unknown.   ASW, tr. by Kevin Crossley-Holland

May one who fought in honor for the South.   Maurice Thompson.   CBCWP

May Ours Not Be.   Funso Aiyejina.   NAfrP

May ours not be like the story.   May Ours Not Be.   Funso Aiyejina.   NAfrP

May peace be established throughout the land.   Te Atairangikaahu.   Kingi M. Ihaka.   PeNZ, tr. by Kingi M. Ihaka

May-Pole, The.   Robert Herrick.   CavPo

May poverty, without offence, approach.   Nicholas James.   NOEC   Fr. Complaints of Poverty, The.

May Queen, The.   Tennyson.   TreFP

May! queen of blossoms.   May.   Edward Hovell-Thurlow, 2d Baron Thurlow.   OBEV

May rain.   Rod Willmot.   HA

May rains.   Buson.   EH, tr. by Robert Hass

May rains!   Sanpu.   TTTS

May's Invocation after a Tardy Spring.   Henrietta Cordelia Ray.   CBWP-3

May say Alas but cannot help or pardon. (LL)   Spain 1937.   W. H. Auden.   AF; NAEL-5v2; NAEL-6v2; NoP-4; OBWP

May say their lords have built, but thy lord dwells. (LL)   Ben Jonson.   AWP; BASC; BeJo; CABP; NAEL-6v1; NAEL-7v1; NOSC; NoP-4; OxBEV; PBRV; TFi

May see the spinning is all done. (LL)   Year's Spinning, A.   Elizabeth Barrett Browning.   NAEL-5v2; NAEL-6v2

May seven tears in every week.   Wish, A.   John Millington Synge.   FaBoEE

May Song.   Goethe.   STV, tr. by John Frederick Nims

May Song.   Félix Lope de Vega Carpio.   SpanPo, tr. by Kate Flores

May sun—whom, The.   Tulip Bed, The.   William Carlos Williams.   OBGa

May supple-footed theatre-growing ivy.   Erucius [or Erycius] of Cyzicus.   GrAn

May that vast motive wash and wash our own. (LL)   On the Marginal Way.   Richard Wilbur.   CoAP; NOBA

May the Babylonish curse.   Farewell to Tobacco, A.   Charles Lamb.   OxBoLi

May the hide of the earth split beneath my feet.   Death and Rebirth.   Jean-Baptiste Tati-Loutard.   PBMAP

May the Lord bless you and keep you.   Blessing Attributed to Saint Clare, The.   Clare of Assisi.   BBASP, tr. by Regis J. Armstrong

May the maiden.   Song for "The Jacquerie."   Sidney Lanier.   NCAP

May the man who gained my trust yet did not come.   Ryojin Hisho.   BoWoP

May the man who has cruelly murdered his sire.   Horace.   NBLV, tr. by Roswell Martin Field   Fr. Epodes.

May the men who are born.   Var. authors.   AWP; TAL   Fr. Manyo Shu, Part 2 of 4.

May the Saddest Memory.   Birthday Wishes to a Husband.   Lizelia Augusta Jenkins Moorer.   CBWP-3

May the smell of thyme and lavender accompany us on our journey.   On Pilgrimage.   Czeslaw Milosz.   AmFaPo, tr. by Robert Hass

May the soil cover / your interred corpse.   Ammianus.   GrAn

May the whole world judge me! But the dark laughter of a faun.   Laughter of a Faun, The.   Novella Nikolaevna Matveyeva [or Matveieva].   TCRP, tr. by Deming Brown

May the will come from Thee.   Annul Wars.   Rabbi Nahman [or Nachman] of Bratzlav.   TrJP, tr. by Jacob Sloan

May the wind blows sweetness.   Unknown.   WoPoe, tr. by Raimundo Panikkar   Fr. Vedic Hymns.

May the youths love me for my words and songs.   Fragment 17.   Anacreon.   CAGL, tr. by Eugene O'Connor

May there always be sun!   Kostya [or Kostia] Barannikov.   TCRP

May they come, may they come.   Song of the Highest Tower.   Arthur Rimbaud.   AWP, tr. by Edgell Rickword

May they stumble [or wander]; stage by stage.   Travel[l]er's Curse after Misdirection[, The].   Robert Graves.   MoBrPo; NBLV; OBCoV

May those who are born after me.   Var. authors.   See May the men who are born

May toss[e] him to my breast. (LL)   Pulley, The.   George Herbert.   AWP; BASC; BBASP; ChIV-1; FHYEP; FSCP; GeHe; HAP; HeIP-4; InPK-6; InvLi; NAEL-5v1; NAEL-6v1; NAEL-7v1; NOBE; NOCV; NOSC; NoP-4; OBEV; OxAEP-1; PAI; SCGP; TFi

May Tree, The.   Jean Earle.   TCAWP

May very well cost you your life. (LL)   Poem about My Rights.   June Jordan.   GLP; ISC; NAAAL; NoAM

May we now venture to be kind. (LL)   Exit.   Edwin Arlington Robinson.   MoAmPo; OxBSP

May winds and sorrows.   Sappho.   SaLy, tr. by Diane Rayor

May with its light behaving.   May.   W. H. Auden.   EBEV

May yet outlast the pageant and the dream. (LL)   Sonnet: "Record is nothing, and the hero great."   John Byrne Leicester Warren, 3d Baron de Tabley.   EBVV; OxBSo

May you be reborn in the supreme lotus, the realm of truth.   Mourning My Son.   Yüan Chên.   SuSp, tr. by Angela Jung Palandri

May you drink beer, or that adult' rate wine.   William Habington.   BeJo   Fr. Castara.

May you live forever. In that eternity.   Curse on Herod, A.   Amy Witting.   ChIV-2; NOBAu

May you not be long on the way! (LL)   Thoughts of a Young Girl.   John Ashbery.   CoAmPo; TAP; VGW

May you rejoice, Paeon lord, who rule.   Women at the Temple.   Herodas.   HePo, tr. by Barbara Hughes Fowler

May / You rest in peace.   Monologue with Commentary.   Andrey [or Andrei] Andreievich Voznesensky [or Voznesenskii].   RusPo, tr. by Robert Arthur Douglas Ford

May you sleep on the breast of a tender companion. Sappho. SaLy, *tr.* by Diane Rayor

May your journey, Uaithne, be in the name of the Holy Spirit. Fionnghuala Ínghean Uí Domhnaill Bhriain (O'Brien). EMWP

Maya to Herself and Then to Her Gardener. Reetika Vazirani. NAPBL

Mayakovsky. Mikhail Valentinovich Kulchitsky [*or* Kulchitskii]. TCRP, *tr.* by Bradley Jordan

Mayakovsky in Paris. Andrey [*or* Andrei] Andreievich Voznesensky [*or* Voznesenskii]. TCRusP, *tr.* by Bradley Jordan

Mayakovsky's hat worn by a horse. (LL) Answer to Voznesenko and Evtushenko. Frank O'Hara. LCAP-2; NNaP; PoM

Mayakovsky's Suicide Note. Vladimir Vladimirovich Mayakovsky [*or* Maiakovskii]. TCRP

(She love me, loves me not.) PFTM-1

Mayan Glyphs Unread, The. William Bronk. APSN

Maybe all I saw was the mirror. Vision. Delmira Augustini. WPOW, *tr.* by Marti Moody

Maybe because I was married and felt secure and dead. Visiting My Gravesite: Talbott Churchyard, West Virginia. Irene McKinney. PBCAP

Maybe I knew it wouldn't last long that night, that the joys of us. Different Strokes Bar, San Francisco, The. Forrest Hamer. GeoHom

Maybe I'm a king. (LL) Story That Could Be True, A. William Stafford. KaS; NTCP; RaBo

Maybe I'm Amazed. Jim Carroll. PmAP

Maybe I'm old-fashioned. When I Fall in Love. Edward Heyman. ReLy

Maybe I'm seven in the open field—. Sudden Journey. Tess Gallagher. NIL-7; NIP-4

Maybe I'm sick, I've been shivering. Chill, A. Bella [*or* Izabella] Akhatovna Akhmadulina. TCRusP, *tr.* by Kathy Lewis and Bob Perelman

Maybe I Should Change My Ways. Duke Ellington. ReLy

Maybe I should go back to the white leather. Desnos Reading the Palms of Men on Their Way to the Gas Chambers. Stephen Berg. GotH; TaR

Maybe I should have saved those leftover dreams. Here's That Rainy Day. Johnny Burke. ReLy

Maybe if you saw Hiroshima. Maybe Then. Idea Vilariño. TANSG, *tr.* by Louise B. Popkin

Maybe it happens this way. How Little We Know. Johnny Mercer. ReLy

Maybe it is the shyness of the pride. Surge, The. Molly Peacock. PasH

Maybe it's not the city you thought. Like This. Carol Muske. ExTi

Maybe it's the time I spend in high school classrooms. Why I Forgive My Younger Self Her Transgressions. Ruth L. Schwartz. NeAmPo

Maybe it was the music. This Heart of Mine. Harry Warren. ReLy

Maybe morning lightens over. For My Grandmother, Bridget Halpin. Michael Hartnett. BIrV; ModIr; PBCIP

Maybe she does her homework. In Praise of Zigzags. Jane O. Wayne. InvLad

Maybe the street is tired of being a street. New Year. Naomi Shihab Nye. LoL

Maybe the sun gave me the pow'r. Almost Like Being in Love. Frederick Loewe. ReLy

Maybe the winds die down tomorrow. Balitaw. Bataan Faigao. ReBoTo

Maybe Then. Idea Vilariño. TANSG, *tr.* by Louise B. Popkin

Maybe there is an evening meant. Runt of a Dream, A. Arthur Rimbaud. WoPoe, *tr.* by Denis Goacher

Maybe there's a God Around. Aleksandr Ivanovich Vvedensky [*or* Vvedenskii]. TCRP, *tr.* by Bradley Jordan

Maybe This Is Love. Ray Henderson. ReLy

Maybe we are the same darkness the same words. Gloria Gervitz. MirDau, *tr.* by Stephen Tapscott *Fr.* Yiskor.

Maybe what Thomas means when he says grace. Reading Aquinas. Michael Heffernan. WeW-3

Maybe when her eye first gave her trouble, but when I did not yet know. Contemporary American Poetry. Alan Feldman. BAP-01

Maybe you escaped from the marsh. Bullfrog. Brendan Galvin. PoCoUp

Maybe you ranted in the grove. Ezry. Archibald MacLeish. NOBA

Maybe Zizi is right. Venice Beach: Brief Song. Dorothy Barresi. SeSe; SwNoth

Maybrick trial is over now, there's been a lot of jaw, The. Penal Servitude for Mrs. Maybrick. *Unknown.* OxBoLi

Mayday. Bill Tremblay. CDa

Mayden in the moor lay—. *Unknown.* OHMEL

Mayfly. Louis MacNeice. ModIr

Mayo Monologues. Michael Longley.

Self-Heal. ModIr

Mayombe-bombe-mayombé! Sensemayá. Nicolás Guillén. PFTM-1

Mayor. Yehuda Amichai [*or* Amikhai]. PoSu, *tr.* by Assia Gutmann

Mayor couldn't be here, but he sends his grand whereases, The. State Poetry Day. Ronald Wallace. PBCAP

Mayor of Scuttleton, The. Mary Mapes Dodge. SWaP

Maypole, The. Robert Herrick. BeJo

Maypole is up, The. Maypole, The. Robert Herrick. BeJo

Mayst [*or* may'st] find thy darling in an urn. (LL) Epitaph on the Lady Mary Villiers. Thomas Carew. BeJo; CaPo; FaBoEE; NOBE; OBEV

Mayst thou die desp'rate in some dirty pool. Adieu to My Landlady, An. George Farewell. NOEC

Maytide's evenen wer a-dyen, A. Light or Sheade. William Barnes. NOBVV

Maytime. *Unknown.* AWP, *tr.* by L. Cranmer-Byng *Fr.* Shi King.

Maytime, loveliest season. Sadness in Spring. *Unknown.* OBWVE, *tr.* by Gwyn Jones

Mazatlan: Sea. Robert Creeley. APSN

Maze, The. Joanne Kyger. BB

Maze is round and blue and green, The. Marriage of Sorts, A. Pamela Alexander. YaYoPo

Maze of Blood, A. N. C. G. Mathema. PeSAV

Maze without a Minotaur. Dana Gioia. RA

Mazeppa. Byron.

"Bring forth the horse!" The horse was brought." TreFP

Mazing around my mind like moths at a shaded candle. Ghosts. Robert Bridges. OxBEV

Mbaye Dyôb! I want to say your name and your honor. Taga for Mbaye Dyôb. Léopold Sédar Senghor. PFTM-1

Mbuyazi (Henry Francis Fynn). *Unknown.* PeSAV

Mbuyazi of the Bay! Mbuyazi (Henry Francis Fynn). *Unknown.* PeSAV

McAndrew's Hymn. Rudyard Kipling. OxBTC

McDermott's War Song. G. W. Hunt.

"Dogs of war are loose and the rugged russian bear, The." FaBoWar

McDonald's, New Hartford, NY. Valerie Worth. AiP

McLean's Welcome. James Hogg. OxBS

McNaughtan. *Unknown.* OxBB

Me. Chairil Anwar. PoetW, *tr.* by Burton Raffel

Me. Lady Ukon. WoPoe, *tr.* by Howard S. Levy

Me an my captain don't agree. me and My Captain. *Unknown.* NAAAL

Me and Baby. Ana Castillo. IllVoic

Me and Marlene sit tight in her truck. Our Lady of the Laundromat. Belle Waring. PBCAP

Me and my brother would jump off the porch. Pushing. Christopher Gilbert. LTA; SoSe-8

Me and My Captain. *Unknown.* NAAAL

Me and My Girl. Noel Gay. ReLy

Me and Russia. Velemir [*or* Viktor Vladimirovich] Khlebnikov. TCRusP, *tr.* by Kathy Lewis and Bob Perelman

Me and the Devil Blues. Robert Johnson. APT-2

Me at the Bottom of the Sea. Alfonsina Storni. TCLAP, *tr.* by Andrew Rosing

Me back to my mountain and far, far, west. (LL) August on Sourdough, a Visit from Dick Brewer. Gary Snyder. LoL; NAAL-5

Me best of all, Maude Clare. (LL) Maude Clare. Christina Georgina Rossetti. EBVV; ViWPN

Me clairvoyant. Gilbert Keith Chesterton. NOBL; UV *Fr.* Variations on an Air Composed on Having to Appear in a Pageant as Old King Cole.

Me, Colored. Peter Abrahams. PBA *Fr.* Tell Freedom.

Me—come! My dazzled face. Emily Dickinson. APN-2

Me! dutiful son going back to South Wales, this time afraid. Down the M4. Dannie Abse. OxBC

Me, for example. Say Girls in Shoe Ads: "I Go for a Man Who's Tall!" Robley Wilson, Jr. PBCAP

Me from Myself—to banish. Emily Dickinson. NALW; TCAPo; TRP

Me go to Morant Bay. Morant Bay. *Unknown.* FaBoVe

Me good friend Beverley. Beverley's Saga. Grace Nichols. WaCA

Me happy, night, night full of brightness. Ezra Pound. VGW *Fr.* Homage to Sextus Propertius.

Me! he says, hand on his chest. Myself I Sing. George Oppen. FTOS

Me, I like to putz in the kitchen and regard. Breeze in Translation. Belle Waring. PBCAP

Me I will throw away. Self-slaved, The. Patrick Kavanagh. MoBrPo

Me Imperturbe. Walt Whitman. NOBA

Me Lord? can'st Thou mispend. Phineas Fletcher. TOF *Fr.* Divine Wooer, The.

Me lover gone a Colon Bay. Colon Bay. *Unknown.* FaBoVe

"Me loving subjects," sez she. Queen's After-Dinner Speech, The. William Percy French. OBCoV

Me lusteth [*or* list] [*or* lenger] rotten bough[e]s to climb [*or* clymbe]. (LL) Sonnet: "Farewell, Love." Sir Thomas Wyatt. GSo; NAEL-5v1; NAEL-6v1; NAEL-7v1; NoSic; OxBSo; SCGP

Me miserable! which way shall I fly. John Milton. PoE *Fr.* Paradise Lost.

Me 'n' Dunbar. James David Corrothers. NAAAL

Me not no Oxford don. Listen Mr Oxford Don. John Agard. NPeEn; Oth

Me—of Me? (LL)   Emily Dickinson.   NALW; TCAPo; TRP

Me on the floor / lizard on the wall.   Next Page.   Atmanam.   OMIP, tr. by A. K. Ramanujan

Me one, way out in the crowd.   Valley Prince.   Mervyn Morris.   WaCA

Me—Pirate.   Clive Sansom.   OTCP

Me she hated.   Stepmother.   Dinah Livingstone.   Prnts

Me so oft my fancy drew.   Choice, The.   George Wither.   OBEV

Me the youngest of the Lumière brothers.   How Old Is the Old Mole?   Marie-Dominique Massoni.   SurWo, tr. by Myrna Bell Rochester

Me thinks I heare some Cavillers object.   John Taylor.   PBRV   Fr. Comparison betwixt a Whore and a Booke, A.

Me thinks I see our mighty monarch stand.   Unknown.   OBSV   Fr. Royal Angler, The.

Me thinks [or Methinks], I see, with what a busie [or busy] hast[e].   On Zacheus [or Zacchaeus].   Francis Quarles.   HAP

Me thought I passed through th' Idalian groves.   Author's Dream to the Lady Mary, the Countess Dowager of Pembroke, The.   Aemilia Bassano Lanyer.   BASC

Me to strike for your life's blood, and you to strike for mine. (LL)   D. G. C. to J. A.   Emily Jane Brontë.   BrRo; EnLoPo

Me up at does.   E. E. Cummings.   OxBSP; WeW-3

Me when she ironed clothes. (LL)   Deep-Sea Bathing (Inna Reggae Dancehall).   Rohan B. Preston.   AmPoNex; WaCA

Me? / I never could keep my edges and kitchen.   For Sistuhs Wearin' Straight Hair.   Carolyn M. Rodgers.   NAAAL

Mea Shearim.   Tamara Kamenszain.   MirDau, tr. by Roberta Gordenstein

Meadow, The.   Peter Fallon.   PBCIP

Meadow and the mountain with desire, The.   Attraction.   Ella Wheeler Wilcox.   LW

Meadow brown; across the yonder edge, A.   Joe.   Emily Pauline Johnson.   SWaP

Meadow Bug.   Rossana Ombres.   NeIt, tr. by Ruth Feldman

Meadow is venomous but pleasant in autumn, The.   Meadow Saffron.   Guillaume Apollinaire.   WoPoe, tr. by Robert Mezey

Meadow Mouse, The.   Theodore Roethke.   ChAP; HeIP-4; PAI; RB; TRP

Meadow Saffron.   Guillaume Apollinaire.   WoPoe, tr. by Robert Mezey

Meadows again!, The. (LL)   Old Song.   Edward Fitzgerald.   OBEV; OxAEP-2

Meadowsweet.   Rolf Jacobsen.   WoPoe, tr. by Roger Greenwald

Meadowsweet, those dizzying flowers.   Meadowsweet.   Rolf Jacobsen.   WoPoe, tr. by Roger Greenwald

Meal for the Monks, A.   Wang Wei.   CrYelRi, tr. by Sam Hamill

Meal of words made by a moth, A.   Cynewulf.   WoPoe, tr. by Edwin Morgan   Fr. Riddles (Exeter Book)

Meal Time.   Maggie Pogue Johnson.   CBWP-4

Mean Drunk Poem.   Sharon Thesen.   NOBC

Mean mean mean to be free. (LL)   Runagate Runagate.   Robert Earl Hayden.   APT-2; BPo; ESEAA; GM; LCAP-2; NAAAL; SSLK

Mean old Hermon.   Lucilius.   GrAn

Mean to Me.   Fred E. Ahlert.   ReLy

Meandering abroad in the Lincolnshire meadows day.   George Barker.   SPE   Fr. Calamiterror.

Meandering River.   Tu Fu.

  "Returning from court day after day, I pawn my spring clothes."   SuSp

  "Single petal swirling diminishes the spring, A."   SuSp

Meandering River Poems, The.   Tu Fu.

  Drinking There Alone.   CarOv, tr. by Carolyn Kizer

  Drinking with Friends.   CarOv, tr. by Carolyn Kizer

  I Go Too.   CarOv, tr. by Carolyn Kizer

  Rain There.   CarOv, tr. by Carolyn Kizer

  Spring Goes.   CarOv, tr. by Carolyn Kizer

Meanest trick I ever knew, The.   Low Trick, A.   Frank Gelett Burgess.   OBCA

Meanin' of captivity!, The. (LL)   Half-Ballad of Waterval.   Rudyard Kipling.   FaBoWar; PeSAV

Meaning a context or vision to confer with this which could be a book.   Approximately.   Diane Ward.   FTOS

Meaning of a Letter, The.   Unknown.   PoToHe

Meaning of Africa, The.   Abioseh Nicol.   PBA

Meaning of Simplicity, The.   Yannis Ritsos.   PFTM-2, tr. by Kimon Friar

Meaning of the Look, The.   Elizabeth Barrett Browning.   SacPr; TrCP

Meaning: this world holds every sort of weather. (LL)   Pelicans.   Judith Wright.   BMAP; OWoS

Means.   Dennis Phillips.

  "Hounds are either the work of wind, The."   FTOS

Means only those who broke—in life—thy peace. (LL)   Timber, The.   Henry Vaughan.   GeHe; OBEV

Means to Attain the Happy Life, The.   Martial.   See Happy Life, The

Meantime from an adjoining chamber came.   Philip Freneau.   NAAL-3   Fr. House of Night, The.

Meanwhile, back home at the ranch.   Limerick.   Victor Gray.   PeLi

Meanwhile, in Rwanda.   Patricia Smith.   SpirFl

Meanwhile [or Mean while] the Adversary of God and Man.   John Milton.   EBEV; OBNV   Fr. Paradise Lost.

Meanwhile the cars continued in a persistent flow down.   C. D. Wright.   ExTi   Fr. Deepstep Come Shining.

Meanwhile the heinous [or hainous] and despiteful [or despightfull] act.   John Milton.   FHYEP   Fr. Paradise Lost.

Meanwhile the Troops beneath Patroclus' Care.   Homer.   OBEV, tr. by Alexander Pope   Fr. Iliad, The.

Meanwhile the Turtle.   Ann Lauterbach.   ExTi

Meanwhile the two men pressed on where the pathway led.   Virgil [or Vergil].   NAWM-5v1; NAWM-7v1, tr. by Robert Fitzgerald   Fr. Aeneid [or Eneados, Aeneis], The.

Meanwhile with Vine there, Clarel stood.   Herman Melville.   APN-2   Fr. Clarel: A Poem and Pilgrimage in the Holy Land.

Measure.   Robert Hass.   YaYoPo

Measure, The.   Patrick Lane.   NOBC

Measure for Measure.   Sipho Sepamla.   AF; PeSAV

Measure for Measure.   William Shakespeare.

  "Ay[e], but to die, and go we know not where."   RB

  (At the Moated Grange.)   NOBE

  (Madrigal.)   GTBS-P

  Take, O Take Those Lips Away.   AWP; EBEV; EnLoPo; NoSic; OBEV; SCGP; TFi

  ("Take, oh take those lips away.")   OxBEV

  "What saies my brother?"   OxBEV

Measure me for a burial.   Dimensions.   Laura Riding Jackson.   FuPo

Measure's inherent.   Parade.   Robert Creeley.   BodElec

Measured blood beats out the year's delay, The.   Simple Autumnal.   Louise Bogan.   MoAmPo; Son

Measured rise. (LL)   Diver, The.   Robert Earl Hayden.   BPo; MoASP

Measurements.   Louisa Sarah Bevington.   VWP

Measures Taken, The.   Erich Fried.   WoPoe, tr. by Michael Hamburger

Meat ants, meat-coloured, greet each other.   Anguish of Ants, The.   David Campbell.   BMAP

Mechanical Cow, The.   Robley, Jr. Wilson.   PBCAP

Mechanical digger wrecks the drill, A.   At a Potato Digging.   Seamus Heaney.   CIP-2

Mechanical marvel was Bill, A.   Limerick.   Unknown.   PeLi

Mechanism.   A. R. Ammons.   HAP

Med Building.   Gerald McCarthy.   CDa   Fr. War Story.

Meda Songs.   Unknown.   APN-2, tr. by Henry Rowe Schoolcraft

Medal [or Medall], The.   Dryden.

  Vox Populi.   NOBE

Medallion.   Sylvia Plath.   HeIP-4

Medallion, The.   Herman Melville.   APN-2   Fr. Clarel: A Poem and Pilgrimage in the Holy Land.

Medea.   Euripides.

  Chorus: "Sweet are the ways of death to weary feet."   OBEV, tr. by John Byrne Leicester Warren, Lord de Tabley

Medea.   Euripides.   NAWM-5v1

Medea.   Seneca.

  Deaths of Orphues and Hercules, The.   OBVE

  Medea's Frenzy.   OBVE, tr. by John Studley

Medea in Athens.   Augusta Davies Webster.

  "Dead is he? Yes, your stranger guest said dead."   ViWPN

  "Oh smooth adder / who with fanged kisses changedst my natural blood."   BrRo

Medea's Frenzy.   Seneca.   OBVE, tr. by John Studley   Fr. Medea.

Medea's Incantation.   Ovid.   OBVE, tr. by Arthur Golding   Fr. Metamorphoses.

Medea Speaks.   Z Budapest.

  "Medea speaks: / This is God, children, listen up well. The."   HW

Medgar Evers.   Gwendolyn Brooks.   ESEAA; NoP-4

Medical Science.   Robin Becker.   PBCAP

Medical Student Learns Love and Death, A.   Rafael Campo.   WiU   Fr. Song for My Lover.

Medicina pro morbo caduco et le fevre.   Unknown.   MiEL

Medicine.   Alice Walker.   PAI

Medicine.   Wang Shih-chieng.   ColAnChi, tr. by Richard John Lynn

Medicine Bearer.   Gail Tremblay.   HATNAP

Medicine Song of an Indian Lover.   Unknown.   APN-2, tr. by Charles Fenno Hoffman

Medicine Songs.   Unknown.   APN-2, tr. by Francis La Flesche

Medieval Norman Song.   Unknown.   AWP, tr. by John Addington Symonds

Medieval Poem of the Nativity, A. *Unknown.* TrCP

Medieval town, with frieze, The. What Is Poetry. John Ashbery. HarvBoo; LCAP-2

Mediocrity in Love Rejected. Thomas Carew. BeJo; NoP-4

Meditate, O mind, on the mystery of Kali. My blissful Mother exists fully through every creature! Lex Hixon. HW

Meditate on Kali! Why be anxious? Rāmprasād Sen. SinGod, *tr. by* Rachel Fell McDermott

Meditating at midnight. Zhou Xuanjing. WPoS

Meditating on Star Light while Traveling Highway. Anita Endrezze. HATNAP

Meditating on the Start of a New Era. Yo Inlŏ. WoPoe, *tr. by* Jean S. Grigsby

Meditatio. Ezra Pound. FaBoCh; OBAL

Meditatio Septima. Francis Quarles. ChIV-1

Meditatio Tertia Decima. Francis Quarles. ChIV-1 *Fr.* Job Militant.

Meditation. Charles Baudelaire. InPK-6, *tr. by* Robert Lowell

Meditation. Palladas [*or* Pallades]. GrAn, *tr. by* Dudley Fitts

Meditation, The. John Norris. NOSC

Meditation 8. Philip Pain. NOBA; NOSC; OxBSP

Meditation 8 (First Series). Edward Taylor. ChIV-2; ColAP; NAAL-2v1; NAAL-3; NAAL-5; NOBA; NoP-4; OxBA; SCAP; TAP *Fr.* Preparatory Meditations before My Approach to the Lord's Supper.

Meditation 10. Philip Pain. NOBA

Meditation 16 (First Series). Edward Taylor. NAAL-2v1; NAAL-3; NAAL-5 *Fr.* Preparatory Meditations before My Approach to the Lord's Supper.

Meditation 22 (First Series). Edward Taylor. NAAL-2v1; NAAL-3; NAAL-5; TCAPo *Fr.* Preparatory Meditations before My Approach to the Lord's Supper.

Meditation 26. Edward Taylor. NAAL-2v1; NAAL-3 *Fr.* Preparatory Meditations before My Approach to the Lord's Supper.

Meditation 38. Edward Taylor. NAAL-2v1; NAAL-3; NOBA; OxBA *Fr.* Preparatory Meditations before My Approach to the Lord's Supper.

Meditation 42 (First Series). Edward Taylor. NAAL-2v1; NAAL-3; NAAL-5 *Fr.* Preparatory Meditations before My Approach to the Lord's Supper.

Meditation 62. Philip Pain. NOBA

Meditation 150 (Second Series). Edward Taylor. ColAP; SCAP *Fr.* Preparatory Meditations before My Approach to the Lord's Supper.

Meditation among Trees. Marbod of Rennes. MLL, *tr. by* Helen Waddell

Meditation at Kew. Anna Wickham. FaBoTw; MoBrPo; NALW

Meditation at Lagunitas. Robert Hass. AmFaPo; ColAP; GeoHom; MakPoe; NoP-4; VCAP

Meditation at Oyster River. Theodore Roethke. MoAmPo *Fr.* North American Sequence.

Meditation Brought About by George Bogin's Translation of Jules Supervielle's Poem "The Sea." Michael Burkard. BodElec

Meditation by the Xerox Machine. Doris Safie. GraLe; PoArWo

Meditation. Can. 1.3. Thy Good Ointment. Edward Taylor. TCAPo *Fr.* Preparatory Meditations before My Approach to the Lord's Supper.

Meditation. Cant.6.11. Edward Taylor. OxBEV *Fr.* Preparatory Meditations before My Approach to the Lord's Supper.

Meditation Celestial and Terrestrial. Wallace Stevens. APT-1

Meditation. Col. 1.18. He is the Head of the Body. Edward Taylor. *Fr.* Preparatory Meditations before My Approach to the Lord's Supper.

Meditation Eight. Edward Taylor. ChIV-2; NAAL-3

Meditation, Followed by Excellent Advice. Eratosthenes. GrAn, *tr. by* Dudley Fitts

Meditation for Christmas, A. Selwyn Image. OBEV

Meditation for His Mistress[e], A. Robert Herrick. CaPo; NOBE; NOSC; OBEV

Meditation for this Day. Antonio Machado Ruiz. CLPP, *tr. by* Kenneth Rexroth

Meditation Hall. Liu Tsung-yüan. SuSp, *tr. by* Jan W. Walls

Meditation. Heb. 13. 10. Wee have an Altar. Edward Taylor. ChIV-2; NOSC; TCAPo *Fr.* Preparatory Meditations before My Approach to the Lord's Supper.

Meditation in Loudoun County. Thomas Bolt. YaYoPo

Meditation in Seven Days, A. Alicia Ostriker. PBCAP; TaR
   "If your mother is a Jew, you are a Jew." TaR

Meditation. Joh. 15.5. Without me yee can do nothing. Edward Taylor. TCAPo *Fr.* Preparatory Meditations before My Approach to the Lord's Supper.

Meditation. Mal. 4.2. With Healing in His Wings. Edward Taylor. *Fr.* Preparatory Meditations before My Approach to the Lord's Supper.

Meditation. Numb. 28.4.9. One Lamb shalt thou offer in the Morning, and the other at Even. And on the Sabbath day two Lambs etc. Edward Taylor. ChIV-1; TCAPo *Fr.* Preparatory Meditations before My Approach to the Lord's Supper.

Meditation of a Mariner. Dorothy Auchterlonie. CBAP

Meditation on a Bone. Alec Derwent Hope. NoAM; WoPoe

Meditation on a News Item. John Updike. PeLV

Meditation on Communion with God. Judah Halevi. TrJP, *tr. by* Solomon Solis-Cohen

Meditation on Gal. 3.16. And to thy Seed Which is Christ. Edward Taylor. *Fr.* Preparatory Meditations before My Approach to the Lord's Supper.

Meditation on Rhode Island Coal, A. William Cullen Bryant. TAP
   (I sat beside the glowing grate, fresh heaped.) NCAP

Meditation on Statistical Method. James Vincent Cunningham. CoAP; VGW

Meditation on the A30. Sir John Betjeman. RB

Meditation on the Feminine Nature of Shekinah, A. Ann Gottlieb. HW

Meditation on the Threshold. Rosario Castellanos. TANSG, *tr. by* Magda Bogin

Meditation on the Wen Fu. Eleanor Wilner. GifTon

Meditation on Yellow. Olive Senior. WaCA

Meditation. Phil. 3 Ult. Our Vile Bodie. Edward Taylor. *Fr.* Preparatory Meditations before My Approach to the Lord's Supper.

Meditation Rock, The. Mo Shih-lung. CoBLCP, *tr. by* Jonathan Chaves

Meditation. Rom. 9.5. God blessed forever. Edward Taylor. TCAPo *Fr.* Preparatory Meditations before My Approach to the Lord's Supper.

Meditation. Zech. 9.11. The Pit wherein is no water. Edward Taylor. *Fr.* Preparatory Meditations before My Approach to the Lord's Supper.

Meditations. Margaret Fuller. SWaP

Meditations. Solomon ibn Gabirol. TrJP, *tr. by* Emma Lazarus

Meditations, The. *Unknown.*
   "In the casket of the Hours." TAL

Meditations and Maxims. Margherita Guidacci.
   "First to feast is love, The. On the scraps of love the fever feasts." CItWP, *tr. by* Cinzia Sartini Blum and Lara Trubowitz
   "Tiny dew reinvigorates the tiny grass, The." CItWP, *tr. by* Cinzia Sartini Blum and Lara Trubowitz

Meditations for August 1, 1666. Philip Pain. SCAP

Meditations for July 25, 1666. Philip Pain. SCAP

Meditations for July 26, 1666. Philip Pain. NOBA; SCAP

Meditations for July 19, 1666. Philip Pain. SCAP

Meditations in an Emergency. Frank O'Hara. PmAP; TAP; VCAP

Meditations in Time of Civil War. W. B. Yeats.
   Ancestral Houses. OBGa
   Road at My Door, The. BIrV; NOBE; NPeEn; PoE
   Stare's Nest by My Window, The. BIrV; GTBS-P; NOBE

Meditations of a Parrot. John Ashbery. TTTS

Meditations of an Old Woman. Theodore Roethke.
   First Meditation. LCAP-2; NOBA
   I'm Here. CoAP
   What Can I Tell My Bones? NOBA

Meditations of Man's Mortalitie; or, A Way to True Blessedness. Alice Sutcliffe.
   Of our losse by Adam, and our gayne by Christ.
   "God by his Wisdome, and all seeing Pow'r." EMWP

Meditations of Mr. Cogito on Redemption. Zbigniew Herbert. GI, *tr. by* John Carpenter

Meditations on Persecution. Mary Mollineux. EMWP

Meditations on Stevie. Gordon Chambers. InTrad

Meditations on the Moon. Paula Gunn Allen. HATNAP

Meditations on the Sepulchre in the Garden. Philip Doddridge. NOCV; NOEC; OBGa

Meditations on the Six Days of the Creation. Thomas Traherne.
   Third Day. ChIV-1

Meditatioun in Wyntir. William Dunbar. NPeEn; OxBS

Mediterranean, The. Allen Tate. APT-2; FaBoMo; FuPo; HAP; MoAmPo; VGW; WoPoe

Medium, The. Elaine Feinstein. BrRo

Medlars and Sorb-Apples. D. H. Lawrence. FaBoVe; NPeEn; NoAM

Medley of Southern and Northern Tunes—Scenic Tour of West Lake. Kuan Yün-shih.
   "Don't say: How can Phoenix Hill." SuSp, *tr. by* Richard John Lynn
   "Excited woodwinds, staccato strings in noisy clamor." SuSp, *tr. by* Richard John Lynn
   "Fresh breezes waft across march orchid fragrance as." SuSp, *tr. by* Richard John Lynn
   "Here you can find joy in cloudy weather or bright, day or night." SuSp, *tr. by* Richard John Lynn
   "How crowded and bustling it is over there." SuSp, *tr. by* Richard John Lynn
   "How is it that." SuSp, *tr. by* Richard John Lynn
   "Now I see lotus-pickers singing the lotus-pickers' song." SuSp, *tr. by* Richard John Lynn
   "Tier upon tier of storied buildings, decorated pavilions." SuSp, *tr. by* Richard John Lynn
   Tune: "Butterflies." SuSp, *tr. by* Richard John Lynn

Tune: "Chilly East Wind." SuSp, *tr. by* Richard John Lynn

Tune: "Coda." SuSp, *tr. by* Richard John Lynn

Tune: "Going Up Small Pavilion." SuSp, *tr. by* Richard John Lynn

Tune: "Happy Events Approaching." SuSp, *tr. by* Richard John Lynn

Tune: "Moth Fluttering against Lamp." SuSp, *tr. by* Richard John Lynn

Tune: "Pomegranate Blossoms." SuSp, *tr. by* Richard John Lynn

Tune: "Squabbling Quails." SuSp, *tr. by* Richard John Lynn

"Unportrayable on the light silk of a small fan." SuSp, *tr. by* Richard John Lynn

Medoro's Inscription Book XXIII. Ludovico Ariosto. NOBRP, *tr. by* William Parsons *Fr.* Orlando Furioso.

Medrano Academy. Blaise Cendrars. CuPo

Medusa. Louise Bogan. APT-2; AWP; BoWoP; MoAmPo; NALW; NoAM; NoP-4; PAI; WPE

Medusa. Amy Clampitt. VCAP

Medusa. Vincent O'Sullivan. PAI

Medusa. Sylvia Plath. NALW

Medusa and Perseus III: Lilith. Pat Parnell. HW

Mee thinks mount Aetna with his force is closed in my brest. (LL) Ovid. CTC; OBVE, *tr. by* Arthur Golding *Fr.* Metamorphoses.

Meek and the Proud, The. Abraham Ibn-Chasdai. TrJP, *tr. by* J. Chotzner

Meek dew shone, the grass lay prostrate, The. Tree, The. Ilya Grigoryevich Ehrenburg [*or* Erenburg]. TrJP, *tr. by* Babette Deutsch

Meek Francis lies here, friend, without stop or stay. Epitaph. Matthew Prior. FaBoEE

Meek Friend! I have been traversing the steep. Written at the Hotwells, near Bristol. Charles Lloyd. CenSon

Meek Shall Disinherit the Earth, The. Horace Gregory. APT-2 *Fr.* Chorus for Survival.

Meek twilight! soften the declining day. Helen Maria Williams. CenSon *Fr.* Poems.

Meet Me in St. Louis, Louis. Andrew B. Sterling. OBAL

Meet Me in the Green Glen. John Clare. SCGP

Meet me there. (LL) Perhaps It's as You Say. Peter Everwine. GeoHom; NNaP

Meet me tonight. Jackie. King D. Kuka. VoR

Meet-on-the-Road. *Unknown.* TTTS

("Now pray, where are you going, child?") OBSP; OTCP

Meet Rabbi Shatz in his correct black homburg. Tales of Shatz. Dannie Abse. OxBC

Meet the Beat of My Heart. Harry Revel. ReLy

Meet the Supremes. David Trinidad. SwNoth

Meet was at "The Cock and Pye," The. John Masefield. OxBTC *Fr.* Reynard the Fox.

Meeting. George Crabbe. OBEV

Meeting. László Kálnoky. IQMS, *tr. by* Kenneth McRobbie and Zita McRobbie

Meeting, The. Louise Bogan. NoAM

Meeting, The. Nicki Jackowska. BrRo

Meeting, The. Isabel Ecclestone MacKay. PoBW

Meeting, The. Katherine Mansfield. LW

Meeting, The. Harriet Monroe. IllVoic

Meeting, The. Muriel Rukeyser. MoAmPo; TrJP

Meeting, The. Ramona Wilson. VoR

Meeting a Bear. David Wagoner. HAP; WeW-3

Meeting a lovely boy face to face. Strato [*or* Straton]. GrAn

Meeting after Separation. Marula. BoWoP, *tr. by* Tambimuttu and G. V. Vaiyda

Meeting and Passing. Robert Frost. OxBA; OxBSo

Meeting at a Salesyard. John Ennis. CIP-2

Meeting at Night. Robert Browning. AWP; BRP; BoLoP; FHYEP; FaBoVe; HeIP-4; ITBLP; NAEL-5v2; NAEL-6v2; NOBE; NOBVV; OBEV; OPOU; OxBEV; OxBSP; PAI; PeVV; PoRA; SCGP; SCV; SoSe-8; TFi; UnPo

(Grey sea and the long black land, The.) CABP

Meeting Bida. Fily-Dabo Sissoko. NegPo, *tr. by* Ellen Conroy Kennedy

Meeting by chance and speaking. Judas Touch, The. David Malouf. BMAP

Meeting Gaylen's 5th Grade Class. Miguel Algarin. PueRic

Meeting-House Hill. Amy Lowell. APT-1; ColAP; MoAmPo; OxBA; PoRA; TCAPo

Meeting-house is not what it used to be, The. Elegy in a Presbyterian Burying-Ground. Robert Noble Denison Wilson. BIrV

Meeting in the Road. *Unknown.* ChiP, *tr. by* Arthur Waley

Meeting is hard. Harder, separation. Without Title (2). Li Shang-yin. ChinPo, *tr. by* Yip Wai-lim

Meeting Mescalito at Oak Hill Cemetery. Lorna Dee Cervantes. PBCAP

Meeting My Fellow Countryman, Yü Wu-chung. Yang Chi. CoBLCP, *tr. by* Jonathan Chaves

Meeting My Former Self. Norman Cameron. NePenScot

Meeting my former self in a nostalgia. Meeting My Former Self. Norman Cameron. NePenScot

Meeting of Cultures, A. Donald Davie. OxBC

Meeting of Friends, A. Phillis Levin. RA

Meeting of the Bards, The. Written for an Eisteddford, or Meeting of Welsh Bards, Held in London, 22 May 1822. Felicia Dorothea Hemans. RWP *Fr.* Siege of Valencia, The.

Meeting of the Waters, The. Thomas Moore. NOIV; OxBoLi

Meeting Place. Pauline Hawkesworth. Prnts

Meeting Point. Louis MacNeice. ModIr; NPeEn; PNI

Meeting the Angel. Susan Aizenberg. ExTi

Meeting the British. Paul Muldoon. BiHa; CIP-2; EmeKit; NoAM; NoP-4; PNI

Meeting, the Departure, The. Goethe. STV, *tr. by* John Frederick Nims

Meeting the Gulf, hosannas silently below. (LL) Hart Crane. GM; MoAmPo; NAAL-5; NOBA; OxBA *Fr.* Bridge, The.

Meeting the Herdsmen. Mei Yao Ch'en. SuSp, *tr. by* Jonathan Chaves

Meeting the Mountains. Gary Snyder. NoAM; TAP

Meeting Together of Poles & Latitudes: In Prospect. Margaret Avison. NOBC

Meeting Trappers on the Road in Heavy Snow. Li K'ai-hsien. CoBLCP, *tr. by* Jonathan Chaves

Meeting when all the world was in the bud. Loves of the Puppets. Richard Wilbur. OxBC

Meeting with Time, slack thing, said I. Time. George Herbert. NAEL-5v1; NAEL-6v1; NAEL-7v1

Meeting with Vilakazi, the Great Zulu Poet, A. Raymond Mazisi Kunene. PeSAV, *tr. by* the author

Meetings. Paul Éluard. AF, *tr. by* Lloyd Alexander

Meetings meetings meetings. Yuh Lookin Good. Carolyn M. Rodgers. BPo

Meets our bouquet of death—and turns sharp right. (LL) Unseen Fire. Ralph Nixon Currey. OBWP; OxBTC; PoWW

Meg Merrilies [*or* Merrilees]. John Keats. FaBoCh; NOxBChV

(Old Meg.) FHYEP; ITBLP

Megaceph, chosen to serve the State. Ambrose Bierce. APN-2; OBAL *Fr.* Devil's Dictionary, The.

Mehinaku Girl in Seclusion, A. Cathy Song. OpBo

Mehitabel S Extensive Past. Don Marquis. TriCat

Mehitabel the cat claims that. Mehitabel S Extensive Past. Don Marquis. TriCat

Mein Breast, mein Corset und mein Legs. Pallades [*or* Pallades]. GrAn

Mein Herz, Mein Herz Ist Traurig. Heinrich Heine. AWP, *tr. by* James Thomson

Mein Kind, wir waren Kinder. Heinrich Heine. AWP; OBVE; TrJP, *tr. by* Elizabeth Barrett Browning

Mein Liebchen, wir sassen zusammen. Heinrich Heine. AWP, *tr. by* James Thomson

Mek me tell you wha me Mudder do. Wha Me Mudder Do. Grace Nichols. NOxBChV

Melancholic. Li Ho. CrYelRi; ErotSp, *tr. by* Sam Hamill

Melancholy. "Rubén Darío." SpanPo, *tr. by* Anita Volland

Melancholy. John Fletcher. GTBS-P; OBEV *Fr.* Nice Valor, The.

Melancholy. David Keller. UrbNat

Melancholy. Thomas Middleton. NOSC

Melancholy Conceit. Samuel Rowlands. *See* Melancholy Knight, The

Melancholy days are come, the saddest of the year, The. Death of the Flowers, The. William Cullen Bryant. OBCA; TreFP

Melancholy days come once a year, The. View on Death, A. Roy W. Watson. PWR

Melancholy days have come, The. Autumn Leaves. Charles Henry Webb. OBAL

Melancholy face Charles Carville had, A. Charles Carville's Eyes. Edwin Arlington Robinson. OxBA; TAP

Melancholy inside Families. Pablo Neruda. RaBo

Melancholy Knight, The. Samuel Rowlands.

Sir Eglamour. FaBoCh

Melancholy Lay, A. Marjory Fleming. FaBoCh; NBLV

Melancholy remembrances and vesperal. (LL) Church of a Dream, The. Lionel Pigot Johnson. CABP; OBMV

Melancholy Year [Is Dead with Rain], The. Trumbull Stickney. APN-2

Melanie. Nathaniel Parker Willis.

"Calm and lovely paradise, A." APN-1

Melanin. J. H. Prynne. PFTM-2

Melbourne or the Bush. Philip Mead. BMAP

Melchizedek. John Henry, Cardinal Newman. SacPr

Meleager. Ovid. CTC, *tr. by* Arthur Golding *Fr.* Metamorphoses.

Meleager. Ovid. NOBRP, *tr. by* John Herman Merivale *Fr.* Metamorphoses.

Melinna herself is re-created: notice the face. Nossis. SaLy, *tr. by* Diane Rayor

Melinna herself! It *is*—see how kindly. Nossis. GrAn

Melissa means honeybee; yes, you're true. Argentarius. GrAn

Melissa where is the golden. In Spite. Rufinus. GrAn, *tr. by* Alan Marshfield

Melissias. Rufinus. GrAn, *tr. by* Alan Marshfield

Melissias denies her love, but her body screams. Rufinus. HePo, *tr. by* Barbara Hughes Fowler

Melissias denies she's in love. Melissias. Rufinus. GrAn, *tr. by* Alan Marshfield

Mellifluous as bees, these brittle men. On First Looking in on Blodgett's Keats's "Chapman's Homer." George Starbuck. OBAL

Mellisandra. Harriet Rose. BrRo

Mellow as the glory roses. (LL) Gloire de Dijon. D. H. Lawrence. EnLoPo; NoAM; PAI

Mellow moon hangs golden in the sky, The. October. Henrietta Cordelia Ray. CBWP-3

Mellow on Morphine. Dana Shuster. FaBoWar

Mellow on morphine, he smiles and floats. Mellow on Morphine. Dana Shuster. FaBoWar

Mellow year is hasting to its close, The. Hartley Coleridge. CenSon *Fr.* Sonnets to the Seasons.

Melodic Trains. John Ashbery. GM; NoP-4

Melodies bring memories. Georgia on My Mind. Hoagy Carmichael. ReLy

Melon Girl. Mei Yao Ch'en. OHPC, *tr. by* Kenneth Rexroth

Melon Grower, The. Alice Oswald. MFPA

Melon / How well. Ransetsu. ZenPo, *tr. by* Takashi Ikemoto and Lucien Stryk

Melon / In morning dew. Basho. ZenPo, *tr. by* Takashi Ikemoto and Lucien Stryk

Melpomene (at whose mischeifous tove). Carmen Elegiacum. Thomas Morton. SCAP

Melrose Abbey. Sir Walter Scott. OxAEP-2 *Fr.* Lay of the Last Minstrel, The.

Melt me. Amanda Nazario. HeMarv

Melting icicle, a leaking tap, A. During an Illness. Vladimir Holan. WoPoe, *tr. by* Ian Milner and Jarmila Milner

Melting in thin mist and heavy clouds. Li Ch'ing-chao. BoWoP

Melting melodious words to lutes of amber. (LL) Upon Julia's Voice. Robert Herrick. InPK-6; NOBE; NPeEn; SoSe-8

Melting Milk. Bill Berkson. PmAP

Melting Pot. Michael Echeruo. PBMAP; TTY

Melting Pot, The. Dudley Randall. BPo; NBV

Melting snows, The. Kenju. JDP, *tr. by* Yoel Hoffmann

Mem'ries light the corners of my mind. Way We Were, The. Alan Bergman. ReLy

Member of the modern great, A. Epigram. John Cunningham. FaBoEE

Members of the Orchestra, The. Kevin Hart. NOBAu

Memento. Stephen Spender. HP

Memento for Mortality, A. Francis Beaumont. *See* On the Tombs in Westminster Abbey

Memento Mori. Billy Collins. EmeKit

Memento of Roads. Nathan [*or* Natan] Alterman. MHP, *tr. by* Ruth Finer Mintz

Mementos, 1. W. D. Snodgrass. MoAmPo; NoP-4; UnPo; VCAP

Memling. Roland Mathias. AngWePo

Memo. Charles G. Ballard. VoR

Memo. Kenneth Fearing. PoE

Memo. Leslie Ullman. YaYoPo

Memo from the Desk of X. Donald Justice. TwCP

Memo to Auden. Anne Rouse. MFPA

Memo to J. C. Maureen Watson. IBA

Memo: you have only 16 lifetimes. More than 9 Lives. Bruce Beaver. BMAP

Memoir. Honor Moore. GLP

Memoirs. Aleksandr Semionovich Kushner. ItGoST, *tr. by* Paul Graves and Carol Ueland

Memoirs in Oxford. Frank Templeton Prince. "Somewhere in Mauriac a girl." PeSAV

Memoirs of a Turcoman Diplomat. Denis Devlin. Oteli Asia Palas, Inc. ModIr; NOIV

Memoirs of a Velvet Urinal. Michael Dransfield. BMAP

Memoirs of the World. Thom Gunn. *Fr.* Misanthropos.

Memorabilia. Robert Browning. FHYEP; NAEL-5v2; NAEL-6v2; NOBVV; NPeEn; NoP-4; OxBEV; PoE; PoPoPo; RB

Memorable Fancy, A. William Blake. NAEL-6v2 *Fr.* Marriage of Heaven and Hell, The.

Memoranda. William Dickey. YaYoPo

Memoranda for Rosario. Maria Elena Caballero-Robb. ReBoTo

Memorandum. Yunna Petrovna [*or* Iunna Pinkhusovna] Moritz [*or* Morits]. TCRusP, *tr. by* Daniel Weissbort

Memorandum of Martha Moulsworth Widdowe, The. Martha Dorsett Prynne. EMWP

Memorandum of Martha Moulsworth, Widow, The. Martha Moulsworth. NAEL-7v1

Memorandum / The Accountant's Notebook. Kathleen Norris. OBAL

Memoriae Matris Sacrum. George Herbert. "Ah Mater, quo te deplorem fonte? Dolores." PBRV

Memoriae Positum R. G. Shaw. James Russell Lowell. CBCWP

Memorial. Marjorie Agosin. TANSG, *tr. by* Celeste Kostopulos-Cooperman

Memorial. Mihály Babits. IQMS, *tr. by* Peter Zollman

Memorial. Robert Pinsky. HCAP

Memorial. Sonia Sanchez. BlSi

Memorial Couplets for the Dying Ego. George Barker. EBEV

Memorial Day. Michael Anania. NoAM

Memorial Day. Clara Ann Thompson. CBWP-2

Memorial Day: a collaboration. Ted Barrigan. "& Now the book is closed." SPE

Memorial for the City. W. H. Auden. "Alone in a room Pope Gregory whispered his name." SacPr

Memorial for Trane. Sam Greenlee. SeSe

Memorial Fountain, The. Roy Fisher. NPeEn

Memorial of Mary, The. Felicia Dorothea Hemans. CenSon

Memorial on the Slain at Chickamauga. Herman Melville. CBCWP

Memorial Pillar, The. Felicia Dorothea Hemans. RWP

Memorial Poem. Roy Fuller. OxBSP

Memorial Rain. Archibald MacLeish. MoAmPo; OBWP

Memorial Service for the Invasion Beach Where the Vacation in the Flesh Is Over. Alan Dugan. TwCP

(I see that there it is on the beach. It is.) AF

Memorial Tablet. Siegfried Sassoon. PoWW

Memorial to a Missionary. Keith Sinclair. PeNZ

Memorial to D. C. Edna St. Vincent Millay. Elegy: "Let them bury your big eyes." APT-1; MoAmPo; OxBA; PoRA "O, loveliest throat of all sweet throats." OxBA

Memorial Verses. Matthew Arnold. CABP; NAEL-5v2; NAEL-6v2

Memorial Wreath. Dudley Randall. CBCWP

Memorials, The. Ernst Waldinger. AuPH, *tr. by* Lowell A. Bangerter

Memorials of a Tour in Italy, 1837. William Wordsworth. ("Eternal Lord! eased of a cumbrous load.") SacPr

Memorials of a Tour of the Continent; 1820. William Wordsworth. Column Intended by Buonaparte for a Triumphal Edifice in Milan, Now Lying by the Way-Side in the Simplon Pass, The. OxBSo Hymn for the Boatmen, as They Approach the Rapids under the Castle of Heidelberg. SacPr ("O Life! without thy chequered scene.") SacPr

Memories. Charles Bernstein. BodElec

Memories, The. Storing Memories. Belinda Zubicueta Carmona. TANSG, *tr. by* Celeste Kostopulos-Cooperman

Memories of a Lost War. Louis Simpson. OBWP; VGW

Memories of a Summer Night. Endre Ady. IQMS, *tr. by* Peter Zollman

Memories of Childhood. Sir John Carr. NOEC *Fr.* Derwent; an Ode.

Memories of Chinatown. Roy McFadden. Bigamy. PNI

Memories of Christmas. Joy Williams. IBA

Memories of Marriage. Enrique Lihn. TCLAP, *tr. by* John Felstiner

Memories of Mess Duty and the War. Christopher Howell. CDa

Memories of Mudland-Meadow. István Sinka. IQMS, *tr. by* Adam Makkai

Memories of My Father. Galway Kinnell. "When I come back to my father's house." RaBo

Memories of past struggles were expelled by fear. Catius As Conius Silius Italicus. RomPo, *tr. by* Marcus Wilson *Fr.* Punica, The.

Memories of President Lincoln. Walt Whitman. Hush'd be the Camps To-Day. SAmP O Captain! My Captain! APN-1; BRP; CBCWP; ChAP; FaBoCh; HHAm; InPK-6; MakPoe; MoAmPo; OBCA; SAmP; TAP; TCAPo; TFi When Lilacs Last in the Dooryard Bloom'd. APN-1; AWP; CBCWP; ColAP; HAP; MoAmPo; NAAL-2v1; NAAL-3; NAAL-5; NCAP; NIL-7; NOBA; NoP-4; OxBA; PAI; PoPoPo; PoRA; SAmP; TAP; TCAPo; TFi "And I saw askant the armies." FaBoWar Carol of Death, The. SCV

Memories of the Village School. Al-Tijani Yusuf Bashir. MAP, *tr. by* Issa Boullata and John Heath-Stubbs

Memories of Verdun. Alan Dugan. OxBSP; RB

Memories of West Street and Lepke. Robert Lowell. AF; EmeKit; NAAL-2v2; NAAL-5; NOBA; NoAM; PoE; VCAP

Memories of You. Andy Razaf. ReLy

Memoriter. Charles Spear. PeNZ

Memory. Thomas Bailey Aldrich. TCAPo

Memory. Margaret Walker Alexander. GT

Memory. Anne Brontë. EBVV

Memory. William Browne. OBEV *Fr.* Britannia's Pastorals.

Memory. Robert Burns. MoASP

Memory. Roque Dalton. BLPSL, *tr.* by Rene de Costa, Rigas Kappatos and Eleni Paidoussi

Memory. Ralph Waldo Emerson. APN-1; TCAPo *Fr.* Quatrains.

Memory. Federico García Lorca. PFTM-1

Memory. Oliver Goldsmith. *See* Captivity, The

Memory. Nikolai Stepanovich Gumilyov [*or* Gumiliov *or* Gumilev]. TCRP, *tr.* by Yakov Hornstein

Memory. Michael Hamburger. OxBTC

Memory. Walter Savage Landor. EBEV; NOBVV; NPeEn

Memory. Dante Gabriel Rossetti. OxBSP

Memory. Erik Johann Stagnelius. AWP, *tr.* by Sir Edmund William Gosse

Memory. W. B. Yeats. BIrV; PoE

Memory, A. Marceline Desbordes-Valmore. WoPoe, *tr.* by Louis Simpson

Memory, A. Heinrich Heine. WoPoe, *tr.* by Francis W. Golffing

Memory, A. Adah Isaacs Menken. CBWP-1; ViWPN

Memory, A. Leonard Alfred George Strong. NOBL

Memory, A. Yi Chŏngbo. WoPoe, *tr.* by Kevin O'Rourke

Memory, The. Robert Creeley. VGW

Memory 1. George Seferis. PoetW, *tr.* by Edmund Keeley and Philip Sherrard

Memory 2. George Seferis. PoetW, *tr.* by Edmund Keeley and Philip Sherrard

Memory, a Poem. Laetitia Pilkington. ECWP

Memory at Last. Wislawa Szymborska. PoSu, *tr.* by Magnus F. Krynski

Memory at last has what it sought. Memory at Last. Wislawa Szymborska. PoSu, *tr.* by Magnus F. Krynski

Memory cannot make your song everlasting. Ars Poetica. Sándor Weöres. IQMS, *tr.* by Edwin Morgan

Memory, committed to the page, had broke. (LL) Passage. Hart Crane. NOBA; PoE

Memory draws me towards death. (LL) Dream at Night, A. Mei Yao Ch'en. BLT; OHPC, *tr.* by Kenneth Rexroth

Memory: farfields of morning. Persephone. Robert Duncan. NOBA

Memory feeds us on a prison diet. Mandrakes for Supper. James Keir Baxter. OxBC

Memory, flowering prison. Prison, The. Maria Luisa Spaziani. CItWP, *tr.* by Cinzia Sartini Blum and Lara Trubowitz

Memory Gardens. Robert Creeley. FTOS

Memory Gardens. Allen Ginsberg. NNaP

Memory has power as real as thine. (LL) Emily Jane Brontë. FaBoCh; NOBVV; NPeEn

Memory hasn't a chord of what the family lost. Stones Speak of an Earthless Sky. Duane Niatum. PoCoUp

Memory, hither come. Song. William Blake. NAEL-5v2; NAEL-6v2

Memory in sea-green with sea-weed grain. Oracle of the Drowned, The. Douglas Oliver. Oth

Memory is as narrow. Angel's Flight. Maxine Scates. PBCAP

Memory is what has died. Past Perfect. Linda Gregg. BodElec

Memory lifts her smoky mirror: 1943. Adrienne Rich. NoP-4 *Fr.* Eastern War Time.

Memory, like a piece of beautiful and imprecise canvas. Memorial. Marjorie Agosin. TANSG, *tr.* by Celeste Kostopulos-Cooperman

Memory, magnesium flare, you single. Circus at the Barber's Shop. Kendrick Smithyman. PeNZ

Memory of a Dream from the Year 1963. Tadeusz Rózewicz. PoSu

Memory of Brother Michael. Patrick Kavanagh. HarvBoo

Memory of childhood, of stooping, The. For the Dead. Kevin Prufer. AmPoNex

Memory of Elena, The. Carolyn Forché. LoL; NoAM

Memory of Hills. Rex Ingamells.
   "There are rock-rooted ranges to dominate." CBAP

Memory of Holland. Hendrik Marsman. TuT, *tr.* by Michael Longley

Memory of my dead, black hole through everything / gaping on the Sea of Vertigos. Persephone That Is to Say Double Issue. René Daumal. PFTM-1

Memory of My Father. Patrick Kavanagh. RB

Memory of My Private Childhood. Eunice Odio. TCLAP, *tr.* by Suzanne Jill Levine

Memory of poisoned honey. (LL) *Unknown.* PGA; WoPoe, *tr.* by Kenneth Rexroth *Fr.* Carmina Burana.

Memory of Quiet. Rosalie Moore. APT-2

Memory of Sunday. Mairtin O Direain. ModIr, *tr.* by Patrick Crotty

Memory of the past grows paler with each day. A. Velichansky. TCRusP, *tr.* by Daniel Weissbort

Memory of Wilmington. Galway Kinnell. OPRER

Memory of your profile on the pillow, The. (LL) Profile on the Pillow, The. Dudley Randall. BPo; TAP

Memory pales in the face of the moon. On Leaving Baltimore. Duane Niatum. CDW

Memory's branch quivers. Postcard from Trakl. John Yau. OpBo

Memory's Usefulness. Maria Luisa Spaziani. CItWP, *tr.* by Cinzia Sartini Blum and Lara Trubowitz

Memory's Wedge. Ray DiPalma. PmAP

Memory says: Want to do right? Don't count on me. Adrienne Rich. TaR *Fr.* Eastern War Time.

Memory Sire, The. Barney Bush. HATNAP

Memory System, A. *Unknown.* PWR

Memphis Blues. Sterling Allen Brown. APT-2; NAAAL

Memres of Alfred Stoker. Christopher Reid.
   "Firs / born Xmas day." FaBoVe

Men. Dorothy Parker. APT-1

Men, The. E. Ethelbert Miller. UnSA

Men, a word of wisdom. Give. Bernard [*or* Bernart] de Ventadour [*or* Ventadorn]. STV

Men and beasts of the zodiac, The. Winter Dawn. Tu Fu. BLT; OHPC, *tr.* by Kenneth Rexroth

Men and Birth: the Unexplainable. Haki R. Madhubuti. RaBo

Men and women have meaning only as man and woman. Men and Women Have Meaning Only as Man and Woman. Joan Murray. YaYoPo

Men are ashamed to eat shepherd's-purse. Eating Shepherd's-purse. Mei Yao Ch'en. SuSp, *tr.* by Jonathan Chaves

Men Are Children of This World. Moses Ibn Ezra. TrJP, *tr.* by Solomon Solis-Cohen

Men Are Coming Back!, The. Barry Cole. OxBTC

Men are drawn to my ass by. Being Aware. Dennis Cooper. GLP; PmAP

Men are running across a field. Letter. Mark Strand. NoAM

Men are what they are, and what they do. Intimate Parnassus. Patrick Kavanagh. MoBrPo

Men are what they do, women are what they are. In Nature There Is Neither Right nor Left nor Wrong. Randall Jarrell. OxBC

Men at Forty. Donald Justice. NoAM; VCAP

Men at Work. Richard Tipping. NOBAu

Men, brother men, that after us yet live. Epitaph in Form of a Ballad, The. François Villon. CTC, *tr.* by Algernon Charles Swinburne

Men call you fair [*or* fayre], and you do[e] credit it. Edmund Spenser. AWP; NAEL-5v1; Son *Fr.* Amoretti.

Men cannot guess the things they do. Little Things, The. Elizabeth Isler. PoToHe

Men choose a crystal goblet filled with wine. God's Ways, Not Our Ways. Henrietta Cordelia Ray. CBWP-3

Men claim the easiest spots. Fishing the White Water. Audre Lorde. GT

Men clothe him with their praise. (LL) West Country, The. Alice Cary. APN-2; SWaP

Men eat of it and die. (LL) Emily Dickinson. SAmP; TAP

Men Fade Like Rocks. Walter James Turner. OBMV

Men flirt in the silvered mirror, eyelids, shadow-. Other Side, The. Minnie Bruce Pratt. WiU

Men Folks ob Today, De. Maggie Pogue Johnson. CBWP-4

Men gave it different names: there were many words. Letter to the Survivors. Charles E. Butler. YaYoPo

Men go to women mutely for their peace. Everyday Alchemy. Genevieve Taggard. APT-2

Men grew sae cauld, maids sae unkind. Blind Boy's Pranks, The. William Thom. OBEV

Men grow with all that grows. Pablo Neruda. GifTon, *tr.* by William O'Daly

Men have made them gods of love. Pain. "Æ" MoBrPo

Men heard this roar of parleying starlings, saw. February Afternoon. Edward Thomas. NoAM; PeFWW; PoWW

Men hope to last a hundred years. To an Old Tune. Lu Kuei Meng. OHMPC, *tr.* by Kenneth Rexroth

Men, if you love us, play no more. In the Person of Womankind [A Song Apologetic]. Ben Jonson. BeJo

Men Improve with the Years. W. B. Yeats. OxAEP-2

Men in overalls the same color as earth rise from a ditch. Outskirts. Tomas Tranströmer. BLT, *tr.* by Robert Bly

Men in the market pride themselves on their knowledge and craft, The. Ch'en Tzu-ang. ColAnChi, *tr.* by Victor H. Mair *Fr.* Poems of Reflection on the Vicissitudes of Life.

Men keep searching the room, The. Fire in Early Morning. Christiane Jacox Kyle. YaYoPo

Men laughed and baaed like sheep, The. Memories of Verdun. Alan Dugan. OxBSP; RB

Men lean toward the wood. Lynching and Burning. Primus St. John. ISC

Men leave the car, The. Lorine Niedecker. APT-2

Men led me to him, blindfold and alone. (LL) Rudyard Kipling. FaBoEE; FaBoTw; HarvBoo; NPeEn; PeFWW; WoPoe *Fr.* Epitaphs of the War [1914–1918].

Men love papers, The. They love to sign them, file them and. Larry Mitchell. GLP

Men Loved Wholly beyond Wisdom. Louise Bogan. APT-2; ColAP; VGW

Men Made Out of Words. Wallace Stevens. APT-1; NOBA; OxBSP; TAP; VGW

Men May Talk of Country-Christmasses. Philip Massinger. OBCP

Men, The / occupying bedrooms and unemployment lines, on corners, in bars. Empty Warriors. Haki R. Madhubuti. RaBo

Men of a hundred thousand, a million summers away?, The. (LL) Dawn, The. Tennyson. NAEL-5v2; NAEL-6v2

Men of Dawn, The. Efraín Huerta. TCLAP, *tr. by* Todd Dampier

Men of England, wherefore plough. Song to the Men of England. Shelley. CABP; NAEL-6v2; PAI

Men of Old, The. Richard Monckton, 1st Baron Houghton Milnes. OBEV; TreFP

Men of old time, The. (LL) *Var. authors.* AWP; TAL *Fr.* Manyo Shu, Part 3 of 4.

Men of science are a brilliant clan, The. Too Close for Comfort. Jerry Bock. ReLy

Men of the Rocks. Joseph Gordon MacLeod. OxBS

Men of thought! be up, and stirring. Clear the Way. Charles MacKay. TreFP

Men of valor, The. *Var. authors.* AWP; TAL *Fr.* Manyo Shu, Part 2 of 4.

Men of wealthy Sestos, every year, The. Christopher Marlowe. AEP *Fr.* Hero and Leander.

Men openly call you the enemy, call you the swine. Take Down the Fiddle, Karl! John Shaw Neilson. CBAP

Men prefer an island. Other. Dorothy Livesay. NIL-7

Men rent me on rode. Jesus Bids Man Remember. *Unknown.* MiEL

Men rigged my chamfered oak. William Scammell. NewEx

Men Roofing. Eamon Grennan. PBCIP

Men's bodies resinous with sweat. Woodcutting. Gleb Iakovlevich Gorbovsky [*or* Gorbovskii]. TCRP, *tr. by* Lubov Yakovleva

Men's hearts love gold and jade. Lodging with the Old Man of the Stream. Po Chü-i. AWP; BLT; ChiP, *tr. by* Arthur Waley

Men's loving is a false affection. *Unknown.* NOIV

Men's Room in the College Chapel, The. W. D. Snodgrass. MoAmPo

Men's Vices. Joyce Mansour. NAWM-7v2, *tr. by* Serge Gavronsky

Men's Voices. Inger Christensen. BoWoP, *tr. by* Nadia Christensen

Men Say They Know Many Things. Henry David Thoreau. NAAL-3

Men say they know things. Men Say They Know Many Things. Henry David Thoreau. NAAL-3

Men seldom make passes. Dorothy Parker. APT-1; NALW; OBAL *Fr.* Some Beautiful Letters.

Men share perceptions. Switch Blade; or, John's Other Wife, The. Jonathan Williams. NeAP

Men sleep. The cassia blossoms fall. Bird and Waterfall Music. Wang Wei. OHMPC

Men, some to bus'ness, some to pleasure take. Pope. NPeEn; OBSV; OxBEV *Fr.* Epistle [II,] to a Lady[: Of the Characters of Women].

Men speak lightly of frustration. Cormorant. Lucien Stryk. IllVoic

Men spread disease among the faggots, one of the things they, The. Larry Mitchell. GLP

Men stare at me more than at women. William Oxley. NewEx

Men still make steel in the hellish mill. Why We Are Forgiven. Bruce Weigl. BodElec

Men swell the current,—many of them wear. Mary E. Tucker. SWaP *Fr.* Loew's Bridge: A Broadway Idyl.

Men Talk. Stephen P. Dunn. NIP-4

Men talking. Eclogue. George Oppen. APT-2; FTOS

Men that are safe, and sure, in all they do[e]. Ben Jonson. BASC; BeJo

Men That Once Were, The. Owen Gruffydd.
  "Old, old / To live on, wretched to behold." OBWVE

Men that worked for England, The. Elegy in a Country Churchyard. Gilbert Keith Chesterton. FaBoWar; MoBrPo; OBWP; OxBSP

Men truck I-45 up and down Oklahoma. White Roses. David Biespiel. AmPoNex

Men turn to rocks. Answer to Herrick, An. Harry Gilonis. Oth

Men went to Catraeth, keen their war-band. Aneirin. OBWVE *Fr.* Gododdin, The.

Men went to Catraeth. The luxury liner. Elegy for the Welsh Dead, in the Falkland Islands, 1982. Anthony Conran. TCAWP

Men went to Gododdin, laughter-loving. Aneirin. OBWP *Fr.* Gododdin, The.

Men Who Come Behind, The. Henry Lawson. NOBAu

Men Who March Away. Thomas Hardy. OBWP; PoWW

Men with much toil, and time, and pain. Female Wits: A Song by a Lady of Quality, The. *Unknown.* NOSC

Men with picked voices chant the names. Overture to a Dance of Locomotives. William Carlos Williams. GM

Men with the heads of eagles. Margaret Atwood. NoAM *Fr.* Circe / Mud Poems.

Men without rank, excrement spatulas. Guchu. ZenPo, *tr. by* Takashi Ikemoto and Lucien Stryk

Men wore human skins, The. Skin. Linda Hogan. ReEnLa

Men working on the building going up here have got these great, The. Sanctity, The. C. K. Williams. BodElec

Men would never have come to need an attic. W. H. Auden. OxBTC *Fr.* Thanksgiving for a Habitat.

Men would often go hunting rabbits, The. Hunting Rabbits. Peter Skrzynecki. BMAP

Mena, deena, deina, duss. *Unknown.* LB

Menace of the Flower, The. Alfonso Reyes. TCLAP, *tr. by* Samuel Beckett

Menace of the Sick. Breyten Breytenbach. PeSAV, *tr. by* Stephen Gray

Menacing machine turns on and off, The. Terror Conduction. Philip Lamantia. NeAP

Menage, The. Carl Rakosi. FTOS

Ménage à Trois. Howard Moss. VCAP

Menagerie came to Cape Race, A. Limerick. *Unknown.* PeLi

Menaka says, Hey listen, Mountain King. Śāradā Bhāndārī. SinGod, *tr. by* Rachel Fell McDermott

Menaphon. Robert Greene.
  ("For beautie, wit, and matchlesse dignitie / yeeld to *Samela*.") (LL) PBRV
  ("Like to *Diana* in her Summer weede.") PBRV
  (*Samela*.) NOBE; OBEV
  (Sephestia's Lullaby.) NOBE; OBEV
  Sephestia's Song to Her Child[e]. NoSic; OxAEP-1
  (Weep Not My Wanton.) SCGP
  "Weep[e] not, my wanton, smile upon my knee." NoSic; OxAEP-1

Mendacity. Alfred Edgar Coppard. OBMV

Mending Sump. Kenneth Koch. InPK-6; NeAP; NoAM

Mending Wall. Robert Frost. APT-1; BRP; ChAP; ClHu; HAP; HarvBoo; HeIP-4; ITBLP; MoAmPo; NAAL-2v2; NAAL-5; NOBA; NoAM; NoP-4; OxBA; PAI; PoE; PoPoPo; SAmP; SCV; SoSe-8; TAP; TCAPo; TFi; VGW; WeW-3

Mendocino Rose. Garrett Kaoru Hongo. WeW-3

Mene Tekel. Frigyes Karinthy. IQMS, *tr. by* Aaron Kramer

Mengele Shitting. Jason Sommer. NAPBL

Mennonites. Julia Kasdorf. NeAmPo; PBCAP

Menodotis. Leonidas of Alexandria. AWP, *tr. by* Richard Garnett

Menoitas of Lyktos. Callimachus. GrAn

Menses. Edna St. Vincent Millay. APT-1; RACG

Menshikov. Yaroslav [*or* Iaroslav] Vasilevich Smelyakov [*or* Smeliakov]. TCRP, *tr. by* Lubov Yakovleva

Menstrual cramps. Michael Dudley. HA

Mental Cases. Wilfred Owen. FaBoMo; NoAM; PeFWW

Mental Hospital Garden, The. William Carlos Williams.

Mental hospital my shadow stays outside. George Swede. HA

Mental Terrorism. Kevin Powell. InTrad

Mental Traveller, The. William Blake. ChIV-2; NAEL-5v2; NAEL-6v2; PoE; WoPoe

Mental Traveller's Landfall, The. Chris Wallace-Crabbe. BMAP

Mentorides, please tell us who. Antipater of Thessalonica. GrAn

Mentors. Gwendolyn Brooks. ESEAA

Meop. Albert Goldbarth. IllVoic

Mer-Man, and Marstig's Daughter, The. *Unknown.* AWP, *tr. by* Robert Jamieson

Merce of Egypt. Charles Olson. APT-2

Merced. Adrienne Rich. NOBA

Mercenary Soldier, The. *Unknown.*
  "No money yet, why then let's terrify with swords." FaBoWar

Merchant and the Fidler's Wife, The. *Unknown.* OxBB

Merchant Marine. Josephine Miles. TAP; VGW

Merchant of Death. Ramabai Espinet. WaCA

Merchant of Venice, The. William Shakespeare.
  All That Glisters Is Not Gold. CTC
  (Casket Song, A.) NAEL-5v1; NoSic; SCGP; TFi
  Fire Seven Times Tried This, The. CTC
  "Go, draw aside the curtain, and discover." OxAEP-1
  "How sweet the moonlight sleeps upon this bank!" TreFP
  "In sooth, I know not why I am so sad." OxAEP-1
  (Love.) OBEV
  (Madrigal.) GTBS-P

Moonlight. OxAEP-1

(Song.) CTC

(Tell Me Where Is Fancy Bred.) NAEL-6v1

"Then must the Jew be mercifull." OxBEV

Merchant's boat is piled high with goods, The. Ballad of the Merchant. Hsü Pen. CoBLCP, tr. by Jonathan Chaves

Merchant's Joy, The. Chang Yü. CoBLCP; ColAnChi, tr. by Jonathan Chaves

Merchant's Joy, The. Lu Yu. CoBCP; ColAnChi, tr. by Burton Watson

Merchant, to secure his treasure, The. Ode. Matthew Prior. AWP; EnLoPo; GTBS-P; NOEC; NPeEn; PoRA

Merchants from Cathay. William Rose Benét. MoAmPo

Merchants have multiplied more than the stars of heaven. Executive's Death, The. Robert Bly. CoAP

Merchants of London, The. Mother Goose. OxNR; ReMoGo

Merci Bien, Monsieur. Carlota Caulfield. TANSG, tr. by Chris Allen

Mercian Hymns. Geoffrey Hill.

"And it seemed, while we waited, he began to walk towards us." NoAM; NoP-4

"Brooding on the eightieth letter of *Fors Clavigera*." HAP; PoE

"Clash of salutation. As keels thrust into shingle. Ambassadors, pilgrims. What is carried over? The Frankish gift, two-edged, regaled with slaughter." NoAM; NoP-4

"Cohorts of charabancs fanfared Offa's province and his concern, negotiating the by-ways from Teme to Trent. Their windshields signalled with plumes of steam. Twilight menaced the land." OxBEV

"Coins handsome as Nero's; of good substance and." FaBoMo; HAP; NoAM

"Dismissing reports and men, he put pressure on the." HAP

"Gasholders, russet among fields. Milldams, marpools that lay unstirring. Eel-swarms. Coagulations of frogs; once, with branches and half-bricks, he battered a ditchful; then sidled away from the stillness and silence." HAP; NPeEn; NoAM; NoP-4

"He adored the desk, its brown-oak inlaid with ebony, assorted prize pens, the seals of gold and base metal into which he had sunk his name." HAP; NoAM; NoP-4

"I was invested in mother-earth, the crypt of roots." NoAM

"King of the perennial holly-groves, the riven sandstone." HAP; NPeEn; NoAM; WoPoe

"Mad are predators, The. Too often lately they harbour against us. A novel heresy exculpates all maimed souls. Abjure it! I am the King of Mercia, and I know." NoP-4

"Not strangeness, but strange likeness. Obstinate." HAP; NoAM; WoPoe

"'Now when King Offa was alive and dead,' they were." NPeEn

"On the morning of the crowning we chorused our." HAP

"Pet-name, a common name, A. Best-selling brand, curt." NoAM; WoPoe

"Princes of Mercia were badger and raven, The. Thrall to their freedom, I dug and hoarded. Orchards fruited above clefts. I drank from honeycombs of chill sandstone." HAP; NAEL-5v2; NAEL-6v2; NPeEn; NoAM; NoP-4; PoE; WoPoe

"Processes of generation; deeds of settlement." NoP-4

"So much for the elves' wergild, the true governance." NoAM; WoPoe

"Strange church smelled a bit 'high,' of censers, The." EmeKit; PoE

"Their spades grafted through the variably-resistant soil." EmeKit; PoE

"Trim the lamp; polish the lens; draw, one by one, rare." FaBoMo

"We ran across the meadow scabbed with cow-dung, past." HAP

Mercies of the Year, The. John Danforth. SCAP

Merciful Shore, The. Maria Luisa Spaziani. NeIt, tr. by Beverly Allen

Merciles[s] Beaute [or Beautée or Beauty]. Geoffrey Chaucer. BoLoP; CTC; EBEV; EnLoPo; HAP; NAEL-5v1; NAEL-6v1; SCGP

"Youre yen two will slay me suddenly." BoLoP; NAEL-5v1; NAEL-6v1; SCGP

Mercury and Cupid. Matthew Prior. PeLV

Mercury Bay Eclogue. M. K. Joseph. PeNZ

Mercury; on Losing My Pocket Milton at Luss near Ben Lomond, and Other Mountains. Robert Andrews. NOEC

Mercury's Song [to Phaedra]. Dryden. *See* Amphitryon

Mercury shew'd Apollo, Bartas Book. Nathaniel Ward. SCAP

Mercutio Describes Queen Mab. William Shakespeare. RB *Fr.* Romeo and Juliet.

Mercutio's Queen Mab Speech. William Shakespeare. *Fr.* Romeo and Juliet.

Mercy. Andrew Lansdown. NOBAu

Mercy. Roddy Lumsden. NeBl

Mercy. *Unknown.* SacPr

Mercy. Bruce Weigl. CDa

Mercy abid and loke all day. *Unknown.* MiEL

Mercy Flight. Anselm Berrigan. HeMarv

Mercy is whiter than laundry. Angels in Winter. Nancy Willard. ColAP; LCAP-2

Mercy Replies to Justice. Giles Fletcher, the Younger. SacPr *Fr.* Christ's Victory and Triumph.

Mercy Tempering Justice. Francis Quarles. SacPr

Mere ants and gnats and trivia with stings. Palladas [or Pallades]. GrAn

Mere Pleasure of Flying, The. Jane Duran. MFPA

Merely the landscape of a vanished whim. Versailles. Adrienne Rich. OBGa

Merely to know. On the Spirit of the Heart as Moon-Disk. Kojijū. WPoS; WoPoe, tr. by Edwin A. Cranston

'Mergency Man, The. John Millington Synge. NPeEn

'Merica Fst Fd. Thom Tammaro. ReTh

Meridian. Amy Clampitt. NIL-7

Merie sungen the muneches binnen Ely. *Unknown.* PoE *Fr.* Canute at Ely.

Merioneth. John Machreth Rees. OBWVE, tr. by Kenneth Hurlstone Jackson

Merits of Writers. Ferenc Kazinczy. IQMS, tr. by Watson Kirkconnell

Merk. Eileen Myles. WiU

Merl. Jean Toomer. GT

Merle; Uncle Seagram. Gwendolyn Brooks. ESEAA *Fr.* Children Going Home.

Merlin. Thomas Caldecot Chubb. YaYoPo

Merlin. Ralph Waldo Emerson. APN-1; NAAL-2v1; NAAL-3; NOBA
Merlin I. NCAP; OxBA

Merlin. Geoffrey Hill. InPK-6; TRP

Merlin. Edwin Muir. FaBoTw; NePenScot; OxBS; RB

Merlin and the Gleam. Tennyson. FHYEP

Merlin and the Snake's Egg. Leslie Norris. OBSP

Merlin I. Ralph Waldo Emerson. NCAP; OxBA *Fr.* Merlin.

Merlin, they say, an English prophet borne. Caelica, XXIII. Fulke Greville, 1st Baron Brooke. WoPoe

Merlins Prophecy. William Blake. WoPoe

Mermaid, The. Ben King. OBAL

Mermaid, The. Ogden Nash. Spl

Mermaid, The. *Unknown.* ESPB

Mermaid dives deep, A. Mermaid Knows, A. Irene Young. HW

Mermaid Knows, A. Irene Young. HW

Mermaid's / privacy, The. (LL) Necromance. Rae Armantrout. FTOS; PmAP

Mermaid's Song. James C. McCullagh. PoCoUp

Mermaid Tank, The. Stephen Knight. NeBl

Mermaid Tavern, The. John Keats. *See* Lines on the Mermaid Tavern

Mermaiden, A. Thomas Hennell. FaBoTw

Mermaidens, The. Laura Elizabeth Richards. OBCA

Mermaidens' Vesper-Hymn, The. George Darley. NAEL-5v2; NAEL-6v2; NPeEn *Fr.* Syren Songs.

Merman, The. Tennyson. UV

Merops. Ralph Waldo Emerson. APN-1; OxBA

Merrily, Merrily we welcome in the Year. (LL) William Blake. FHYEP; FaBoCh; NOxBChV; TTTS *Fr.* Songs of Innocence.

Merrily swinging on brier and weed. Robert of Lincoln. William Cullen Bryant. OBCA

Merritt Parkway. Denise Levertov. NeAP; PoM

Merrow Down. Rudyard Kipling. NOxBChV *Fr.* Just-So Stories.

MERRY CHR / YSANTHEMUM. (LL) Computer's First Christmas Card, The. Edwin Morgan. NOxBChV; OxBEV

Merry Country Lad, The. Nicholas Breton. NoSic *Fr.* Passionate Shepherd, The.

Merry Cuckoo, The. Edmund Spenser. OWoS

Merry Cuckow, messenger of Spring, The. Merry Cuckoo, The. Edmund Spenser. OWoS

Merry-Go-Round. Langston Hughes. AmFaPo; PAI; SAmP

Merry-go-round. James Philip McAuley. CBAP

Merry-go-round, The. Michael McClintock. HA

Merry-go-round, The. Rainer Maria Rilke. WeW-3, tr. by C. F. MacIntyre

Merry mate amongst the rest, of cloisterers thus told, A. William Warner. NoSic *Fr.* Albion's England.

Merry, merry bells of Yule, The. (LL) Tennyson. EBVV; FHYEP; NAEL-6v2; NAWM-7v2; NOCV; SoSe-8 *Fr.* In Memoriam A. H. H.

Merry, Merry Is My Lord. *Unknown.* CoBCP, tr. by Burton Watson

Merry Merry Sparrow! William Blake. FHYEP *Fr.* Songs of Innocence.

Merry month of May, sunny skies of blue. I've Got the World on a String. Ted Koehler. ReLy

Merry [or Merrie] world did on a day, The. Quip, The. George Herbert. BASC; GeHe; NOSC; OxAEP-1; OxBEV

Merry [or Mirry] Margaret. John Skelton. EBVV; EnLoPo; NAEL-5v1; NAEL-6v1; NBLV; NOBE; NoP-4; NoSic; OBEV; OxBEV; PeLV; PoE; PoRA; SCGP; SCV; TFi *Fr.* Garland [or Garlande or Garlands] of Laurel[l], The.

Merry the green, the green hill shall be merry. Another Song. Donald Justice. CoAmPo; VGW

Merry Window, The.   Francis Scarfe.   SPE

Merthyr.   Glyn Jones.   AngWePo

Mertill though my heart should break.   To Mertill Who Desired Her to Speak to Clorinda of His Love.   Elizabeth Taylor.   EMWP

Meru.   W. B. Yeats.   GSo; NoAM; OxBSo; PoPoPo

Mervell nothyng, Joseph, that Mary be with chyld.   *Unknown.*   SacPr

Mery it is in May morning.   *Unknown.*   MiEL

Mery it was in grene forest.   Adam Bell, Clim of the Clough, and William of Cloudesly.   *Unknown.*   ESPB

Mesa Blanca.   Víctor Hernández Cruz.   PFTM-2

Mésalliance, A.   May Probyn.   NPeEn

Mescaline.   Allen Ginsberg.   PFTM-2

Meseemeth I heard cry and groan.   Complaint of the Fair Armoress [*or* Armouress], The.   François Villon.   AWP; CTC; OBVE, *tr. by* Algernon Charles Swinburne

Meshes.   Elizabeth Robinson.   AmPoNex

Mesmeric hunter of the unseen.   General Strike.   Nancy Joyce Peters.   SurWo

Mesnevi.   Sadi [*or* Saadi *or* Sa'di].   AWP, *tr. by* L. Cranmer-Byng   *Fr.* Gulistan, The.

Mesopotamia.   Rudyard Kipling.   HarvBoo; PoWW
   (Mesopotamia 1917.)   FaBoWar

Mess Boy, The.   Sydney Wilmer.   CAGL

Mess Deck.   Alan Ross.   FaBoWar; PoWW

Mess with It.   Linda France.   MFPA

Message.   Rosario Ferré.   TANSG

Message.   Allen Ginsberg.   CoAmPo; NeAP; VGW

Message.   Renata Pallottini.   WPOW, *tr. by* Carlos Altschul and Monique Altschul

Message, A.   Fleur Adcock.   DiPo

Message, The.   Mathilde Blind.   ViWPN

Message, The.   John Donne.   MeLP

Message, The.   Grandmaster Flash and the Furious Five.   NAAAL

Message, The.   Michael Heffernan.   RACG

Message, The.   Heinrich Heine.   AWP, *tr. by* Kate Freiligrath Kroeker

Message, The.   Jacques Prévert.   WeW-3, *tr. by* John Frederick Nims

Message about the Times.   Remco Campert.   TuT, *tr. by* Theo Dorgan

Message Clear.   Edwin Morgan.   NePenScot

Message for Langston, A.   "Kush."   NBV

Message from a Cross.   Max Harris.   NOBAu

Message from her set his brain aflame, A.   George Meredith.   NOBVV   *Fr.* Modern Love.

Message from Home.   Kathleen Jessie Raine.   WPE

Message from Ohanapecosh Glacier.   W. M. Ransom.   CDW; GifTon

Message from Outside.   Gary Snyder.   BodElec

Message in the Bottle, The.   Frigyes Karinthy.   IQMS, *tr. by* Paul Tabori

Message of King Sakis and the Legend of the Twelve Dreams He Had in One Night, The.   *Unknown.*   WoPoe, *tr. by* Charles Simic

Message of the Rain, The.   Norman H. Russell.   ChAP

Message on Cape Cod, The.   Michael S. Weaver.   GT; PBCAP

Message that St. Francis preached to the birds, The.   St. Francis and the Nun.   Carl Dennis.   KGB

Message to a Loved One Dead, A.   Josephine D. Henderson Heard.   CBWP-4

Message to Siberia.   Alexander Sergeyevich Pushkin.   AWP; TTY, *tr. by* Max Eastman

Message, we conclude, is inevitable, The.   Bachelors, The.   Edward Cortez Garrett.   ReBoTo

Messages.   Naana Banyiwa Horne.   NAfrP

Messages.   Jack A. Mapanje.   HBAPE

Messalonghi. January 22, 1824. On This Day I Complete My Thirty-sixth Year.   Byron.   *See* On This Day I Complete My Thirty-sixth Year

Messe of Nonsense, A.   *Unknown.*   NOSC

Messenger, The.   Frances Horovitz.   BrRo

Messenger, The.   Thomas Kinsella.
   "Inside, it is bare but dimly alive."   CIP-2
   "It is an August evening, in Wicklow."   ModIr

Messenger, The.   Jean Valentine.   LCAP-2

Messenger came in the night, The.   "Rachel" [*or* "Rahel"].   FIT, *tr. by* Robert Friend

Messenger from Rome.   Defence of Poetry, A.   Giolla Brighde Mac Con Midhe.   NOIV

Messenger, hear what I say.   Reinmar der Alte.   GePo

Messenger of Sympathy and Love.   Meaning of a Letter, The.   *Unknown.* PoToHe

Messengers.   Louise Glück.   ColAP; HCAP; VCAP

Messengers, The.   Steve Chimombo.   HBAPE

Messengers, The.   Robert Creeley.   NAAL-5

Messengers, The.   Henrietta Cordelia Ray.   CBWP-3

Messerschmidts still tear one's heart, The.   Hospital.   Boris Abramovich Slutsky [*or* Slutskii].   TCRP, *tr. by* J. R. Rowland

Messiah, The.   Bible, *O.T.*   AWP   *Fr.* Isaiah.

Messiah, The.   John Milton.   PeECV   *Fr.* Paradise Regained [*or* Regain'd].

Messiah, The.   Virgil [*or* Vergil].   AWP   *Fr.* Eclogues.

Messiah: A Sacred Eclogue in Imitation of Virgil's Pollio.   Pope.   ChIV-1
   "Rise, crowned with light, imperial Salem, rise!"   SacPr

Messina, 1908.   Alice Thompson Meynell.   SacPr

Messmates.   Sir Henry John Newbolt.   EBVV; PeVV

Met, hesitated, left double footsteps, then walked on. (LL)   Return to Cardiff. Dannie Abse.   AngWePo; TCAWP

Met Noel at Cheshire Street.   Bill Griffiths.   Oth   *Fr.* Building: The New London Hospital.

Meta-A and the A of Absolutes.   Jay Wright.   ESEAA; TRP

Metal Coughdrops.   Tristan Tzara.   PFTM-1

Metal Denser Than, and Liquid, A.   John Peck.   BAP-01

Metal I, the soul the hearth, the blaze that warms, The.   "Angelus Silesius." GePo, *tr. by* George C. Schoolfield   *Fr.* Cherubical Wanderer, The.

Metal smokestack, The.   Exercise No. 2.   William Carlos Williams.   SAmP

Metal-work.   David Morley.   NLP

Metallic mammal, A. Nocturnal.   Moon.   Nicolás Guillén.   PFTM-1

Metamorpho I.   Joe Rosenblatt.   MoCV

Metamorphoses.   Roy Fuller.   OxBTC

Metamorphoses.   Howard Nemerov.   HCAP

Metamorphoses.   Ovid.
   Acteon.   CTC, *tr. by* Arthur Golding
   "And from the Citie Tegea there came the Paragone."   OBVE
   Apollo and Daphne.   NAWM-7v1, *tr. by* Allen Mandelbaum
   Apollo and Hyacinthus.   CAGL, *tr. by* Rolfe Humphries
   Arethusa Saved.   WoPoe, *tr. by* Thom Gunn
   Baucis and Philemon.   NOSC, *tr. by* John Dryden
   Ceres and Proserpina.   NAWM-7v1, *tr. by* Allen Mandelbaum
   Ceyx and Alcyone.   NoSic, *tr. by* Arthur Golding
   Conclusion.   CTC; OBVE, *tr. by* Arthur Golding
   Cyclops.   CTC; OBVE, *tr. by* Arthur Golding
   Daedalus.   CTC; OBVE, *tr. by* Arthur Golding
   Daphne and Apollo.   NOEC, *tr. by* Matthew Prior
   Daphne and Apollo.   NPeEn; OBVE, *tr. by* Arthur Golding
   Death of Orpheus, The.   WoPoe, *tr. by* Charles Boer
   Deucalion and Pyrrha, sole survivors of the Flood, renew Creation by casting stones behind them.   NPeEn, *tr. by* John Dryden
   Europa and Jove.   NAWM-7v1, *tr. by* Allen Mandelbaum
   "Floods, by nature enemies to land, The."   OBVE
   Golden Age, The.   NAEL-5v1; NAEL-6v1; NAEL-7v1, *tr. by* Arthur Golding
   Io and Jove.   NAWM-7v1, *tr. by* Allen Mandelbaum
   Iphis and Ianthe.   NAWM-7v1, *tr. by* Allen Mandelbaum
   King Midas.   CTC, *tr. by* Arthur Golding
   Magic.   AWP, *tr. by* William Shakespeare
   "Before the Moone should cirlcewise close both hir hornes in one." NPeEn, *tr. by* Arthur Golding
   Medea's Incantation.   OBVE, *tr. by* Arthur Golding
   Meleager.   CTC, *tr. by* Arthur Golding
   Meleager.   NOBRP, *tr. by* John Herman Merivale
   "Moysting Ayre was whist: no leafe ye could have moving sene, The." OxBEV, *tr. by* Arthur Golding
   "My intention is to tell of bodies changed."   NAWM-5v1
   Myrrha and Cinyras.   NAWM-7v1, *tr. by* Allen Mandelbaum
   "Near the Cymmerians, in his dark abode."   OBVE
   "Neare Enna walles there standes a Lake Pergusa is the name."   OBVE
   "Northern breath, that freezes floods, he binds, The."   OBVE
   "Not Pallas, not ev'n Spleen it self could blame."   OBVE
   "Now whyle Hippomenes / Debates theis things."   OBVE
   Of the Pythagorean Philosophy.   OBVE, *tr. by* John Dryden
   "Time was, when we were sow'd, and just began."   NPeEn, *tr. by* John Dryden
   "Persephone ate seven pomegranate seeds. So What? I'll tell you what." ModIr, *tr. by* Ciaran Carson
   Philemon and Baucis.   CTC, *tr. by* Arthur Golding
   "Then Lelex rose, an old experienced man."   AWP; OBVE
   Prologue.   NAWM-7v1, *tr. by* Allen Mandelbaum
   Proserpine and Dis.   NPeEn, *tr. by* Arthur Golding
   Pygmalion.   NAWM-7v1, *tr. by* Allen Mandelbaum
   "Seeing as the father saw the rosy morn."   OBVE
   "So, when she saw Narcissus wandering through the lonely countryside, Echo fell in love with him, and followed secretly in his steps."   EroLit, *tr. by* Mary M. Innes
   "Stones (a miracle to mortal view), The."   OBVE

"There was a man here, Samian born, but he." NAWM-5v1

"To thee obeyeth all the East as far as Ganges goes." OBVE

Venus and Adonis. NAWM-7v1, *tr.* by Allen Mandelbaum

Zeus and Ganymede. CAGL, *tr.* by Rolfe Humphries

Metamorphoses. Yevgeny Aleksandrovich Yevtushenko [*or* Evtushenko]. TCRP, *tr.* by Arthur Boyars and Simon Franklin

Metamorphoses. Nikolai Alekseievich Zabolotsky [*or* Zabolotskii]. TCRusP, *tr.* by John Glad

Metamorphoses of M. John Peale Bishop. APT-1

Metamorphosis. Peter Porter. OxBTC

Metamorphosis. Wallace Stevens. InPK-6; VGW

Metamorphosis, The. Sir John Suckling. CaPo; FaBoEE

Metamorphosis of Pigmalions Image, The. John Marston. "*Pigmalion,* whose hie love-hating minde." PBRV

Metaphor as Degeneration. Wallace Stevens. LCAP-2

Metaphor as Illness. Chuck Ortleb. GLP

Metaphor here is the pool, regular, The. Freestyle, on the First of Tishri. Enid Shomer. TaR

Metaphor of Grass in California. Charles Martin. RA

Metaphors. Sylvia Plath. HeIP-4; InPK-6; SoSe-8

Metaphors of a Magnifico. Wallace Stevens. TCAPo

Metaphysical Amorist, The. James Vincent Cunningham. VGW

Metaphysical Paintings, The. John Perreault. SPE

Metaphysical Sectarian, The. Samuel Butler. MeLP; PeLV *Fr.* Hudibras.

Metaphysical Sonnet. Charles Lloyd. CenSon

Metempsychosis. Kenneth Slessor. NOBAu

Meteor. Alan Pizzarelli. HA

Meteor. Larissa Szporluk. BAP-01

Meteor of the war, The. (LL) Portent, The. Herman Melville. APN-2; CBCWP; ColAP; InPK-6; NAAL-2v1; NAAL-3; NCAP; NOBA; NoP-4; OBWP; OxBA; PoE; TAP; TCAPo

Meteor's arc of quiet; a voiceless rain, The. Faint Music. Walter De la Mare. FaBoCh

Meteor Showers—Yosemite. Dixie Salazar. GeoHom

Meteorology. Linda France. MFPA

Methinks all things have travelled since you shined. On the Sun Coming Out in the Afternoon. Henry David Thoreau. OxBSP

Methinks already, from this chymick flame. Dryden. FaBoCh *Fr.* Annus Mirabilis.

Methinks, dear Tom, I see thee stand demure. To the Revd. Mr. ——— on His Drinking Sea-Water. John Winstanley. NOEC

Methinks How Dainty Sweet It Were. Charles Lamb. Son

Methinks I See Some Crooked Mimic Jeer. Michael Drayton. Son *Fr.* Idea.

Methinks I see with what a busy haste. On Zacchaeus [*or* Zacheus]. Francis Quarles. NOSC; OxBSP

Methinks I spy Almighty holding in. Edward Taylor. HAP *Fr.* Preparatory Meditations before My Approach to the Lord's Supper.

Methinks it is good to be here. Lines Written in the Church Yard of Richmond, Yorkshire. Herbert Knowles. SacPr

Methinks it is no journey. (LL) Tom o' Bedlam. *Unknown.* FaBoCh; PoRA

Methinks, 'tis strange you can't afford. Forsaken Wife, The. Elizabeth Thomas. ECWP; LW

Methinks 'twere no unprecedented feat. William Wordsworth. CenSon *Fr.* River Duddon [A Series of Sonnets], The.

Metho Drinker. Judith Wright. BMAP

Method, The. J. D. McClatchy. MakPoe

Methodist, The. Thomas Chatterton. ECEV

Methodist, The. Evan Lloyd.
  Religion and the Lower Classes. NOEC
  "Sons of War sometimes are known, The." OBSV

Methodology. Bruce Andrews. FTOS

Methought a sweet sound from the street uprose. Street Music. Elizabeth Akers Allen. SWaP

Methought I lived in the icy times forlorn. Great Britain through the Ice: Or, Premature Patriotism. Charles Tennyson Turner. OxBSo; Son

Methought I saw (as I did dream[e] in bed). Vision, The. Robert Herrick. CaPo

Methought I Saw My Late Espousèd Saint. John Milton. *See* On His Deceased Wife

Methought I saw the footsteps of a throne. William Wordsworth. CenSon

Methought I saw the grave where Laura lay. Sir Walter Ralegh. NAEL-5v1; NoSic; SCGP; Son *Fr.* Commendatory Verses to Edmund Spenser's Fairy Queen.

Methought, one night, I saw, in trance sublime. Vision of Sunday in Heaven, A. Victor James Daley. ChIV-2

Methought [*or* Mee thought] I saw my late espoused saint. On His Deceased Wife. John Milton. NPeEn; OBEV; OxBSo; PoE; SCV; SacPr; TFi

Methought That I Had Broken from the Tower. William Shakespeare. RB *Fr.* King Richard III.

Meticulous, past midnight in clear rime. Hart Crane. ColAP; NAAL-2v2; NAAL-5; PoE *Fr.* Voyages.

Metonymy as an Approach to a Real World. William Bronk. APSN; VGW

Metre Colombian, The. *Unknown.* UV

Metric Figure. William Carlos Williams. MoAmPo

Metrical Feet. Samuel Taylor Coleridge. FHYEP; NIL-7; NIP-4

Metrical Translation of the Song of Macgregor Na Ruara. Anne Grant. RWP

Metrics. Rhina P. Espaillat. FFC

Metropolitan / Museum of / Art, The. Miss Pimberton Of. Siv Cedering Fox. PBCAP

Metropolitan Nightmare. Stephen Vincent Benét. APT-2

Metropolitan Railway, The. Sir John Betjeman. EBEV; OxAEP-2; OxBTC

Metrum Parhemiacum Tragicum. Eugenius Vulgarius. FaBoWar, *tr.* by Helen Waddell

Mewl. Zulaykha Abu-Risha. PoArWo, *tr.* by Clarissa C. Burt

Mews Flat Mona. William Plomer. FaBoTw

Mexican Fire Breather, A. Juan Delgado. TouFir

Mexican Loneliness. Jack Kerouac. CLPP

Mexican World Mural / 5 x 25. Juan Felipe Herrera. TouFir

Mexicans Begin Jogging. Gary Soto. LTA

Mexico. Robert Lowell.
  "Difficulties, the impossibilities, The." HCAP
  "South of Boston, south of Washington." HCAP

Mexico, August 20, 1940. Ai. NoAM

Mexico City Blues. Jack Kerouac.
  "Big Engines, The." NeAP
  ("Charley Parker Looked like Buddha.") BB
  "Essence of Existence, The." NeAP
  "Glenn Miller and I were heroes." NeAP
  "Got up and dressed up." NeAP; PmAP
  "I keep falling in love." PmAP
  "In the ocean there's a very sad turtle." PoM
  "Love's multitudinous boneyard." NeAP
  "Nobody knows the other side." NeAP; PmAP
  "Old Man Mose." NeAP
  "Only awake to Universal Mind." NeAP
  "Praised be man, he is existing in milk." NeAP; PmAP
  "Saints, I give myself up to thee." NeAP
  "Void that's highly embraceable, The." NeAP
  "Wheel of the quivering Meat, The." NeAP; PFTM-2; PmAP; PoM

Mexico Is a Foreign Country: Four Studies in Naturalism. Robert Penn Warren.
  Mango on the Mango Tree, The. NoAM

Mexico needs mahogany. El Paso Monologue. Ishmael Reed. SpirFl

Mexico, 1940. Ai. NoAM

Mezuzah. Alan Shapiro. TaR

Mezzo Cammin. Henry Wadsworth Longfellow. APN-1; GSo; NAAL-2v1; NAAL-3; NCAP; PoE; TAP; TCAPo
  (Written at Boppard on the Rhine, August 25, 1842, just before.) ColAP

Mezzo Forte. William Carlos Williams. SAmP

Mi Abuelo. Alberto A. Ríos. NIL-7; PoPoPo

Mi revalueshanary Fren. Linton Kwesi Johnson. Oth

Mi revalueshanary fren is nat di same agen. Mi Revalueshanary Fren. Linton Kwesi Johnson. Oth

Mi Tío Baca el Poeta de Socorro. Jimmy Santiago Baca. PmAP

Mia Carlotta. Thomas Augustin Daly. NBLV

Miami Beach. Howard Moss. BodElec

Miami lights beckon. Journalist's Convention 1987. Esther Iverem. InTrad

Mica flask moves layout hasty. Tab, The. Clark Coolidge. FTOS

Mica, if you peel carefully. Earth Angel. Jeffrey Skinner. PBCAP

Micah. Bible, *O.T.*
  "But in the last days it shall come to pass." FaBoWar, *tr.* by King James Version
  Woe Is Me! TrJP

Mice. Rose Fyleman. NTCP

Mice come first, The. In our bedroom. Virus². Jackie Kay. MFPA

Mice in the eaves, and breathe well my dear. Chess Piece Cornered. John Kinsella. BMAP

Mice in the Hay. Leslie Norris. NOxBChV; OBCP

Michael [A Pastoral Poem]. William Wordsworth. FHYEP; NAEL-5v2; NAEL-6v2; NOBRP; OxAEP-2

Michael Angelo: A Fragment. Henry Wadsworth Longfellow.
  In the Coliseum. TCAPo
  Monologue: The Last Judgment.

Michael Applebaum became. Only Applebaum Can Make a Tree. Joanne Hart. MiVo

Michael didn't want to go. After the Prom. Lisa D. Chavez. AmPoNex

Michael Is Afraid of the Storm. Gwendolyn Brooks. NOxBChV; OxIBACP

Michael Masse. Sam Witt. NeAmPo

Michael Robartes Bids His Beloved Be at Peace. W. B. Yeats. NoAM

Michael Row the Boat Ashore. *Unknown*. APN-2

  (Then you'll hear the horn they blow.) TCAPo

Michael's Dream. Mark Doty. WiU *Fr.* Atlantis.

Michael sets before Adam in vision what shall happ'n till the Flood. John Milton. NPeEn *Fr.* Paradise Lost.

Michael writes to tell me his dream. Mark Doty. WiU *Fr.* Atlantis.

Michaelmas. Veronica Forrest-Thomson. HarvBoo

Michaelmas. Norman Nicholson. MoBrPo

Michal her modest flames sought to conceal. Abraham Cowley. ChIV-1 *Fr.* Davideis.

Micheál Mac Liammóir. Paul Durcan. PBCIP

Mick whore, Grandma Maloney, The. Grandmothers in Green and Orange. Frank R. Maloney. GifTon

Mickey says hey / you guys, go throw. Third Shift. Anthony Walton. NAPBL

Micki, / The message on your new machine. Answering Machine Message. Sari Friedman. GotH

Micmac woman's body has been disinterred and her, The. Report on Her Remains. Daniel David Moses. HATNAP

Microbe's Serenade, The. George Ade. OBAL

Microbiblion. Simon Wastell.

  ("Like as the Damaske Rose you see.") SacPr

Man's Mortality. FaBoCh

Microcosmos. Susan Miles. OxBTC

Micrographic Manuscript, Miniature (1). Esther Ettinger. DTA, *tr. by* Mariana Barr

Micrographic Manuscript, Miniature (2). Esther Ettinger. DTA, *tr. by* Mariana Barr

Microscope. Gwyn Thomas. OBWVE, *tr. by* Joseph P. Clancy

Microscope in Winter, The. Sandra McPherson. LCAP-2; VCAP

Microscope revealed a world of miracles, The. Genealogy of Crosses, The. Andrey [*or* Andrei] Andreievich Voznesensky [*or* Voznesenskii]. PFTM-2, *tr. by* Richard McKane

Mid-August at Sourdough Mountain Lookout. Gary Snyder. ColAP; HAP; InPK-6; LoL; NoP-4; TAP; VCAP

Mid-Autumn Moon. Su Tung-p'o (Su Shih). CoBCP; GifTon, *tr. by* Burton Watson

Mid-Channel. Gwen Harwood. BMAP

Mid-Country Blow. Theodore Roethke. HarvBoo

Mid-day. "H. D." APT-1; NAAL-5

Mid-Day Moon, The. John Banister Tabb. APN-2

Mid-day moon lights up the rocky sky, The. Pastoral in Posters, A. Carolyn Wells. SWaP

Mid-February in America. Cold everywhere but Florida. Patricia Jones. ReTh *Fr.* Billie Holiday Chronicles, The.

Mid-March. Lizette Woodworth Reese. SWaP

Mid-noon is past;—upon the sultry mead. William Wordsworth. CenSon *Fr.* River Duddon [A Series of Sonnets], The.

Mid-Ocean. Emily Jane Pfeiffer. ViWPN

Mid-October, Massachusetts. We drive. Incident. Eamon Grennan. BiHa

'Mid pleasures and palaces though we may roam. Henry Cuyler Bunner. OBAL *Fr.* Home.

'Mid pleasures and palaces though we may roam. John Howard Payne. APN-1; BRP; TCAPo *Fr.* Clari, the Maid of Milan.

Mid-Term Break. Seamus Heaney. AmFaPo; NIL-7; PoPoPo

'Mid the half-lit air, and the lonely place. In the Graveyard. Macdonald Clarke. PWR

'Mid the thick covert of that woodland shade. Mary Tighe. NOBRP *Fr.* Psyche.

Mid-West, The. *Unknown*. OBCoV

Mid western mountains far away. Patterdale. Isabella Lickbarrow. RWP

Mid Winter. Hubert Witheford. PeNZ, *tr. by* Sam Karetu

Mid-Year Report: For Haruko. June Jordan. ReTh

Midafternoon in Norfolk. At the Swings. Henry Taylor. MPUn

Midas. John Lyly.

  Daphne. NoSic

  "'Las, how long shall I." NoSic

  (Pan's Song.) OxAEP-1

  Pan's Syrinx. NPeEn; NoSic; SCGP

  Song of Apollo. NoSic

Midas, they say, possessed the art of old. Epigram. "Peter Pindar." NIL-7; NIP-4

Midcentury Love Letter. Phyllis McGinley. LW

Middelerd for mon wes mad. *Unknown*. MiEL

Midden-Battle between Lady Scotstarvit and the Mistress of Newbarns, The. William Drummond, of Hawthornden. NePenScot, *tr. by* Allan H. MacLaine

Midden of rotting bodies of men, A. Corpses in the Wood. Ernst Toller. TrJP, *tr. by* E. Ellis Roberts

Middle. Jimmie Durham. HATNAP

Middle Age. Patricia Beer. FaBoWP; HarvBoo

Middle Age. Robert Lowell. PAI

Middle Age. Arlene L. Mandell. PasH

Middle Age. Luis Omar Salinas. GeoHom

Middle age—I grow somewhat fond of the way. At My Country Home in Chung-nan. Wang Wei. CoBCP, *tr. by* Burton Watson

Middle-Aged, The. Adrienne Rich. HCAP; PoPoPo

Middle aged / couple playing. 40. Love. Roger McGough. OBCoV

Middle-aged life is merry, and I love to lead it. Peekaboo, I Almost See You. Ogden Nash. PeLV

Middle-aged white man in a beat-up blue Pinto, The. Lucky One, The. Reginald Shepherd. GT

Middle Ages Draw Near!, The. Zalman Schneour. MHP, *tr. by* Ruth Finer Mintz

Middle Ages draw near, The. Do you hear, sensitive man, do you feel. Middle Ages Draw Near!, The. Zalman Schneour. MHP, *tr. by* Ruth Finer Mintz

Middle-Class Blues. Hans Magnus Enzensberger. VCWP, *tr. by* Hans Magnus Enzensberger and Michael Hamburger

Middle East, The. Nadia Hazboun Reimer. PoArWo

Middle-elderly have wrinkled necks, The. Sonnet from Below the Age Gap. Keith Sinclair. PeNZ

Middle Manager in Paradise, The. Michael Foley. PNI

Middle of a War, The. Roy Fuller. OBWP; PoWW

Middle of life's journey; I, The. Dante Alighieri. STV *Fr.* Divina Commedia.

Middle of May, when the iris blows. Iris. Muriel Rukeyser. APSN; ColAP

Middle of the Way. Galway Kinnell.

  "Coals go out, The." RaBo

Middle of the World. D. H. Lawrence. HAP; NoAM; WoPoe

Middle Passage. Sonya Brooks. InTrad

Middle Passage. Robert Earl Hayden. APT-2; BPo; ColAP; NAAL-5; NoAM; TRP; VCAP

  (Sails flashing to the wind like weapons.) NAAAL

Middle Passage and After, The. Larry Neal. NBV

Middle Years, The. Anthony Cronin. CIP-2

Middleaged Man, The. Louis Simpson. BodElec; NNaP

Middleness of the Road, The. Robert Frost. NOBA

Middlesex. Sir John Betjeman. OxBTC

Midfield. Basho. EH, *tr. by* Robert Hass

Midges. "Owen Meredith."

  "She is talking aesthetics, the dear clever creature." VerBaPo

Midgiegooroo. Archie Weller. IBA

Midland. Mark Van Doren. APT-2

Midlife. Robin Becker. BodElec

Midlife. Joseph Millar. OPRER

Midnight. Mary Ursula Bethell. PeNZ

Midnight. Louisa Sarah Bevington. PEW

Midnight. Jacob [*or* Jakov] Fichman. MHP, *tr. by* Ruth Finer Mintz

Midnight. Andreas Gryphius. GePo, *tr. by* George C. Schoolfield

Midnight. Vincente Huidobro. CuPo

Midnight. Jên Jui. WoPoe, *tr. by* Chung Ling and Kenneth Rexroth

Midnight. Alison Kolodinsky. PasH

Midnight. Gabriela Mistral. BoWoP, *tr. by* David Garrison

Midnight. Michael Roberts. OBMV

Midnight. Henry Vaughan. ChIV-2; ESCV

Midnight at Baiae. John Addington Symonds. CAGL *Fr.* Three Visions of Imperial Rome.

Midnight cities cower underfoot, The. Demons of the Cities, The. Georg Heym. WoPoe, *tr. by* Peter Viereck

Midnight Court, The. Brian [*or* Bryan] Merriman [*or* Merryman]. NOIV

  Country's Crisis, The. BIrV, *tr. by* David Marcus

  Husband's Lament, The. OBVE, *tr. by* Frank O'Connor

  Irish Marriage Night, An. BIrV, *tr. by* Frank O'Connor

  Lament of the Unmarried Girl, The. OBVE, *tr. by* Frank O'Connor

  Maiden's Plight, The. BIrV, *tr. by* Frank O'Connor

  Now God Stand Up for Bastards. BIrV, *tr. by* Arland Ussher

  Old Man's Tale, The. BIrV, *tr. by* David Marcus

  Solution, The. BIrV, *tr. by* Arland Ussher

  Walk. BIrV, *tr. by* Brendan Behan

Midnight Diner by Edward Hopper, A. David Ray. PoSol

Midnight Elegy. Léopold Sédar Senghor. NegPo, *tr.* by Ellen Conroy Kennedy

Midnight Flowers. Eavan Boland. ModIr

Midnight frost. Basho. EH, *tr.* by Robert Hass

Midnight Harvest, A. Rosamund Marriott Watson. ViWPN

Midnight has come, and the great Christ Church Bell. W. B. Yeats. OxAEP-2 *Fr.* Vision, A.

Midnight: I still haven't gotten to sleep. At Night, Hearing Someone Singing in the House Next Door. Mei Yao Ch'en. CoBCP, *tr.* by Burton Watson

Midnight in the Assyrian camp! No sound. Rebekah Gumpert Hyneman. SWaP *Fr.* Female Scriptural Characters.

Midnight Lamentation. Harold Monro. OxBTC

"When you and I go down." OBMV

Midnight. No waves. On the Treasury of the True Dharma Eye. Dogen. EnlH

Midnight on Front Street. Roberta Hill Whiteman. CDW

Midnight on the Great Western. Thomas Hardy. NOBE; OxAEP-2; WoPoe

Midnight or after, and the little lights. Train. Donald Justice. GM

Midnight Prayer. Hayyim Nahman [*or* Khayim Nakhman *or* Chaim Nachman] Bialik. TrJP, *tr.* by Helena Frank

Midnight Ramble, The. Charles Woodward. NOEC

Midnight Reports. Lynda Hull. SwNoth

Midnight Rocker, Tiananmen Square, May 27, 1989. Edith Rylander. MiVo

Midnight Run. Jonathan Johnson. AmPoNex

Midnight Saving Time. Adrien Stoutenburg. AWTN

Midnight Show. Karl Shapiro. OxBA

Midnight Skaters, The. Edmund Charles Blunden. FaBoTw; GTBS-P; MoBrPo; NOBE; NPeEn; PeFWW; WoPoe

Midnight Snack, The. James Merrill. OxBSo *Fr.* Five Old Favorites.

Midnight Song. Pinkie Gordon Lane. GT

Midnight Songs. *Unknown.*

"Morning's sun." ColAnChi, *tr.* by Jeanne Larsen

"My perfume?" ColAnChi, *tr.* by Jeanne Larsen

"Night after night, I do not." ColAnChi, *tr.* by Jeanne Larsen

"Night so." ColAnChi, *tr.* by Jeanne Larsen

"Seize the moment!—" ColAnChi, *tr.* by Jeanne Larsen

"So soon. Today, love, we." ColAnChi, *tr.* by Jeanne Larsen

"Sun sinks low, The. I." ColAnChi, *tr.* by Jeanne Larsen

"Through the front gate." ColAnChi, *tr.* by Jeanne Larsen

"When I started wanting." ColAnChi, *tr.* by Jeanne Larsen

Midnight sound / Leap up. Masaoka Shiki. ZenPo, *tr.* by Takashi Ikemoto and Lucien Stryk

Midnight Special. Kenneth Patchen. VGW

Midnight Special. *Unknown.* APT-1

Midnight storm. Trees walking off across the fields in fury. Light. Michael Ondaatje. NIP-4

Midnight Sun. Johnny Mercer. APT-2; ReLy

Midnight sun with phantom glare, The. Russian Student's Tale, The. Mathilde Blind. VWP

Midnight Supper. Ruth L. Schwartz. NeAmPo

Midnight Tennis Match, The. Thomas Lux. MoASP

Midnight. The flowing water of Hu T'o River. Midnight. Jên Jui. WoPoe, *tr.* by Chung Ling and Kenneth Rexroth

Midnight. The wind yawing nor-east. Haddock Fishermen. George Mackay Brown. NoP-4

Midnight the years last day the last. New Year's Eve, 1938. John Frederick Nims. ChrPo

Midnight Thought, A [on the Death of Mrs. *E. H.* and Her Little Daughter]. Elizabeth Thomas. NOSC

Midnight Trolleybus. Bulat Shalvovich Okudzhava. TCRP, *tr.* by Albert C. Todd

Midnight Vapor Light Breakdown. Betsy Sholl. LTA

Midnight Velada, The. María Sabina.

"Ah, Jesu Kri." PFTM-2, *tr.* by Henry Munn

"I am the woman of the great expanse of the water." PFTM-1

Midnight Vigil. Fran Haraway. HHAm

Midnight wakes into noon. Dream Cloud. Lindiwe Mabuza. HAWP

Midnight / You heavy laden, it's midnight. Street of Dreams. Victor Young. ReLy

Midnightmouse, The. Christian Morgenstern. RB, *tr.* by Lore Segal and W. D. Snodgrass

Midnights of consciousness, still, and even. Endsight. Michael Dransfield. BMAP

Midrashim: Proverbs 6:6. David Curzon. *See* Proverbs 6:6

Midst all the dark and knotty snares, Neither Durst Any Man from That Day Ask Him Any More Questions. Richard Crashaw. ChIV-2

'Midst dreary labyrinths of mental night? (LL) Invokes Reason. Mary Robinson. CenSon; RWP

Midst the fair range of buildings which, new-reared. George Keate. NOEC *Fr.* Burlesque Ode, on the Author's Clearing a New House of Some Workmen, A.

Midstream. Dennis Joseph Enright. OxBC

Midstream. Mao Tse-tung [*or* Mao Zedong]. MoCV, *tr.* by Earle Birney

Midstream they met. Challenger and champion. Swans, The. Clifford Dyment. TCAWP

Midsummer. William Cullen Bryant. GSo

Midsummer. Nicholas Christopher. UrbNat

Midsummer. Patricia Cumming. WWork

Midsummer. Alexander L. Posey. APN-2

Midsummer. Sherod Santos. GeoHom

Midsummer. James Scully. TwCP

Midsummer. Derek Walcott.

"Camps hold [*or* held] their distance—[of] brown chestnuts and grey smoke, The." PoetW

"Certain things here are quietly American." NAEL-5v2; NAEL-6v2; NoP-4

"Chicago's avenues, as white as Poland." UrbNat

Gauguin. NoAM

"Oak inns creak in their joints as light declines, The." NoAM

"Rest, Christ! from tireless war. See, it's midsummer." TOF

Midsummer Night's Dream, A. William Shakespeare.

Asleep, My Love? CTC

Bottom's Song. CTC

Fairies' Lullaby, The. NOBE; NoSic; PoRA; SCGP

(Fairy Blessing, The.) OxBoLi

(Fairy Land, 1.) OBEV

(Fairy Land, 2.) OBEV

(Fairy Song ("Over hill, over dale").) NOBE

Flower of This Purple Dye. CTC

Now the Hungry Lion. CTC

"Ousel cock, so black of hue, The." NoSic

Through the Forest Have I Gone. CTC

Through the House. CTC

"Tis strange my Theseus, that these lovers speake of." OxBEV

Up and Down. CTC

Yet but Three? CTC

Midsummer stretches before me with a cat's yawn. Port of Spain. Derek Walcott. NoAM

Midsummer, Tobago. Derek Walcott. MakPoe; OPOU; VCWP

Midway. Robert Desnos. PFTM-1

Midway. Naomi Long Madgett. BPo; BlSi

Midway between Mecca and Medina. To a Hero Dead at al-Safra. Hind bint Uthatha. WPOW, *tr.* by Bridget Connelly and Deirdre Lashgari

Midway in life, attuned to Buddhism. Villa at the Foot of Mount Chungnan. Wang Wei. ChinPo, *tr.* by Yip Wai-lim

Midway in our life's journey, I went astray. Dante Alighieri. NAWM-5v1 *Fr.* Divina Commedia.

Midway the hill of science, after steep. To Mr. S. T. Coleridge. Anna Laetitia Barbauld. CABP; NOEC; NoP-4; WoRP

Midway to birth, you are your own. Child of Our Bodies. Samuel Hazo. GraLe

Midwest, Midcentury. Sharyn Jeanne Skeeter. ISC

Midwest Town. Ruth Delong Peterson. CA

Midwife. Judith Kazantzis. Prnts

Midwife puts a rag in the dead woman's hand, The. Obedience of the Corpse. C. D. Wright. LCAP-2

Midwife's Invocation, A. *Unknown.* WPoS, *tr.* by Michael Coe and Whittaker Gordon

Midwife's Story; Two, A. Anne Szumigalski. NOBC

Midwinter. Margaret E. Bruner. PoToHe

Midwinter spring is its own season. T. S. Eliot. CABP; FaBoMo; FaBoTw; GTBS-P; NAEL-5v2; NAEL-6v2; NAWM-7v2; NOBA; NOBE; NoAM; OxAEP-2; OxBTC; PeECV; TAP; TFi *Fr.* Four Quartets.

Midwives, The. Celia Gilbert. ChIV-1

Midwives all were scarecrows, The. Almanac, 1939, An. Kevin Young. AmPoNex

Might and Right. Clarence Day. NBLV

Might have been. Certainly these ashes might have been pleasures. This Place Rumord to Have Been Sodom. Robert Duncan. CAGL; NOBA; NeAP; PoM

Might have known it. Song. *Unknown.* STP, *tr.* by Jerome Rothenberg

Might I, if you can find it, be given. Saint Nicholas. Marianne Craig Moore. WPE

Might Is Right. Israel Zangwill. TrJP

Might live invisible and dim. (LL) Henry Vaughan. BASC; ChIV-2; EBEV; ESCV; GeHe; MeLP; NAEL-5v1; NAEL-7v1; NOBE; NOCV; OBEV; OBWVE; OxAEP-1; OxBEV; SCGP; TFi; TOF

Might of this pagoda seems to erupt upwards, The. On Climbing the Pagoda of the Temple of Gracious Benevolence with Kao Shih and Hsüeh Chü. Ts'en Shen. SuSp, *tr. by* Daniel Bryant

Might rise from where they slept and go away. (LL) Sheaves, The. Edwin Arlington Robinson. APT-1; AWP; HAP; MoAmPo; NOBA; NoAM; OxBA; SoSe-8; TAP

Might speak them. Then we heard them, every word. (LL) Charles Carville's Eyes. Edwin Arlington Robinson. OxBA; TAP

Might there have been an echo of self. Music's Wife. Joel Long. AmPoNex

Mightier than the Pen. Kingsley Amis. OBCoV

Mightier than the sword thou art. Pen, The. Mary Weston Fordham. CBWP-2

Mighty bell is six o'clock, A. Six to Six. *Unknown.* PBA, *tr. by* A. C. Jordan

Mighty creature is the germ, A. Germ, The. Ogden Nash. APT-2; RB

Mighty empty alien stones of the waterless desert. In the Desert. Dmitry [*or* Dmitrii] Aleksandrovich Prigov. ItGoST, *tr. by* Robert Reid

Mighty Fortress Is Our God, A. Frederic Henry Hedge. AWP; GePo; PWR; SacPr

   (Feste Burg Ist Unser Gott, Ein.) CTC, *tr. by* M. Woolsey Stryker

Mighty gladness by the third fulfill'd, The. (LL) Sonnet: He Speaks of a Third Love of His. Guido Cavalcanti. AWP; EaItPo, *tr. by* Dante Gabriel Rossetti

Mighty God, even the Lord, hath spoken, The. Bible, *O.T.* BrRo   *Fr.* Psalms.

Mighty growth, A! The county side. Old Oak Tree at Hatfield Broadoak, The. Frederick Locker-Lampson. OxAEP-2

Mighty junction of star with star, A. Ode on Slate, The. Osip Emilevich Mandelstam [*or* Mandelshtam]. WoPoe, *tr. by* Bernard Meares

Mighty Lord Is Money, A. Francisco de Quevedo y Villegas. SpanPo, *tr. by* William M. Davis

Mighty love's consuming fire. Shy Request. Mihály Csokonai Vitéz. IQMS, *tr. by* Adam Makkai and Ena Roberts

Mighty Mary, hear me. Muireadhach Albanach O'Dalaigh. NOIV

Mighty Mother, and her son who brings, The. Pope. OxAEP-1   *Fr.* Dunciad, The.

Mighty Ocean, The. Ilya [*or* Karl] L'vovich Selvinsky [*or* Sel'vinskii]. TCRP, *tr. by* Daniel Weissbort

Mighty One, before Whose Face. William Cullen Bryant. AH

Mighty Orion conquered. Korinna [*or* Corinna]. SaLy, *tr. by* Diane Rayor

Mighty, praised beyond compare. Rock of My Salvation. Mordecai ben Isaac. TrJP, *tr. by* Solomon Solis-Cohen

Mighty river flowing dark and deep, The. James Thomson. EBVV   *Fr.* City of Dreadful Night, The.

Mighty Runner, A. Edwin Arlington Robinson. OBAL

Mighty Runner, A. *Var. authors.* OBAL   *Fr.* Variations of Greek Themes.

Mighty Tropicale Orchestra, The. Sean Harvey. SeSe

Mighty wave rush'd o'er him as he spoke, A. Homer. OBVE   *Fr.* Odyssey.

Mighty you are, dark mouth. Dejection. Georg Trakl. PeFWW, *tr. by* Michael Hamburger

Mignon. Goethe. WoPoe, *tr. by* Anthony Hecht

Mignon. Henrietta Cordelia Ray. CBWP-3

Mignon Aspiring to Heaven. Goethe. TreFP

Migraine. Gillian Clarke. Prnts   *Fr.* Glass.

Migrant's Lament: A Song. Alfred Temba Qabula. PeSAV

Migrant tribe of spiders, A. Encampment at Morning, An. W. S. Merwin. GifTon

Migrants by Night. W. S. Merwin. BodElec

Migration. Jane Griffiths. NeBl

Migration. Pinkie Gordon Lane. BlSi

Migration of Drummond's Organs (After Death), The. Norman Weinstein. WaCA

Migratory Bird. Chenjerai Hove. HBAPE

Migratory bird flew with mirth. Lost Bird. Chenjerai Hove. HBAPE

Mih Feel It. Ahdri Zhina Mandiela. WaCA

Mihyar, a King! "Adonis" [*or* "Adunis"]. MAP, *tr. by* John Heath-Stubbs and Lena Jayyusi

Mika / But I will not allow you. Sappho. SaLy, *tr. by* Diane Rayor

Mike Howe's head with frozen frown. Hobart Town, Van Diemen's Land (11th June, 1837). Hal Porter. NOBAu

Milagros Mourns the Queen of Scat. Marisa de Los Santos. NAPBL

Milan, August 1943. Salvatore Quasimodo. WoPoe, *tr. by* Peter Russell

Mild and peaceful spring glow, Cold Food Day. Li Ch'ing-chao. SuSp   *Fr.* Tune: "Sand of Silk-washing Stream."

Mild and slow and young. Girl Help. Janet Lewis. APT-2; HeIP-4; InPK-6

Mild Citizen. Glyn Maxwell. HarvBoo

Mild is the parting year, and sweet. Walter Savage Landor. EnLoPo   *Fr.* Ianthe.

Mild, of sweet / countenance. Paulus [*or* Paulos] Silentiarius. GrAn

Mild Splendor of the various-vested Night! Samuel Taylor Coleridge. CenSon   *Fr.* Effusions.

Mild the mist upon the hill. Emily Jane Brontë. NOBVV

Mild Was the Air. Rosalía de Castro. NAWM-7v2, *tr. by* S. Griswold Morley

Mildred, if you take the trouble to send me what I want. Katherine Killigrew. EMWP

Mildred's Doves. Henrietta Cordelia Ray. CBWP-3

Mile an' a Bittock, A. Robert Louis Stevenson. NOBVV; OxBEV

Mile and mile and mile; but no one would gather. Sea, The. Francis Webb. CBAP

Mile at sea, Cake Rock, against the blue, A. Iron Man of the Hoh. Nelson Bentley. GifTon

Mile behind is Gloucester town, A. William Vaughn Moody. APN-2; NOBA; OxBA; TCAPo

Mile from Poetry, A. Kris Hemensley.
  "Look! she said you can see." BMAP
  "My poem's in the oven where it." BMAP
  "Place was famed for, The." BMAP
  "Poem by John Thorpe, A." BMAP

Mile Hill. Dennis Schmitz. LCAP-2

Mile more down the flat fast road, the homestead, A. Robert Pinsky. NAAL-2v2   *Fr.* Explanation of America, An.

Mile out in the marshes, under a sky, A. Town Dump, The. Howard Nemerov. NIL-7

Milena Jesenká. Edward Hirsch. BodElec

"Miles," and "John Alden" were Synonym. (LL) Emily Dickinson. APN-2; NCAP

Miles of frost / On the lake. Buson. ZenPo, *tr. by* Takashi Ikemoto and Lucien Stryk

Miles of pram in the wind and Pam in the gorse track. Potpourri from a Surrey Garden. Sir John Betjeman. NOBL; NPeEn

Miles Standish. Henry Wadsworth Longfellow.   *Fr.* Courtship of Miles Standish, The.

Milestone: The Birth of an Ancestor. Eugene B. Redmond. SpirFl

Militance of a Photograph in the Passbook of a Bantu under Detention, The. Michael S. Harper. VCAP

Militaris Cantio. *Unknown.* IQMS, *tr. by* Matthew Mead

Military Ball, A. Frank O'Hara. BodElec

Military Creed, The. Ernest Crosby. FaBoWar

Military Harpist, The. Ruth Pitter. FaBoTw; NALW

Military-Industrial Complex, The. Robley Wilson, Jr. PBCAP

Military Life, The. Harold Rome. ReLy

Militerotics. Chuck Ortleb. GLP

Militia, The. Dryden. OBSV   *Fr.* Cymon and Iphigenia.

Milk. Eileen Myles. KGB

Milk. Maurice Riordan. ModIr

Milk and honey. Salt. Viktor Fiodorovich Bokov. TCRP, *tr. by* Bernard Meares

Milk for the Cat. Harold Monro. MoBrPo; OBMV

Milk Maid, The. Mother Goose. LB; OxNR; ReMoGo

Milk White Doe, The. *Unknown.* AWP, *tr. by* Andrew Lang

Milk-white hair-lace wound up all her hairs, A. Woman Drest by Age, A. Margaret Lucas Cavendish, Duchess of Newcastle. PEW

Milk white Hind, immortal and unchang'd, A. Dryden. UV   *Fr.* Hind and the Panther, The.

Milk[e] all the way. (LL) To the Infant Martyrs. Richard Crashaw. ChIV-2; GeHe; NAEL-5v1; NAEL-6v1; NAEL-7v1; OxBSP; PAI

Milkers lace their boots up at the farms, The. (LL) Cock-Crow. Edward Thomas. GTBS-P; MoBrPo; NPeEn; OxBSP; RB

Milkfish. Eugene Gloria. OpBo

Milkflowers. Robert Wrigley. PasH

Milking before Dawn. Ruth Dallas. PeNZ

Milking Time. Elizabeth Madox Roberts. OBCA

Milkmaid. Laurie Lee. BoLoP; FaBoTw

Milkmaid's Epithalamium, The. Thomas Randolph. BoLoP

Milkman and His Son, The. Thomas Lux. LCAP-2

Milkman, Keep Those Bottles Quiet! Gene De Paul. ReLy

Milkweed. Philip Levine. LCAP-2

Milkweed. James Wright. ColAP; LCAP-2; NOBA; RaBo

Milkweed and Monarch. Paul Muldoon. NoP-4; PoetW

Milky Way, The. At the Nachi Kannon Hall. Muso Soseki. EaWin, *tr. by* W. S. Merwin

Milky Way above, The. Fire Island. May Swenson. TAP

Milky Way / Milky Way. Tune: Flirtatious Laughter. Wei Ying-wu. CoBCP, *tr. by* Burton Watson

Milky Way's silver river, The. Song of the Waterfall at Mount Lu. Yang Wei-chen. CoBLCP, *tr. by* Jonathan Chaves

Mill, A. William Allingham. FaBoEE; OxBSP

Mill, The.   Edwin Arlington Robinson.   APT-1; HAP; NAAL-2v2; NoAM; NoP-4; PAI; WeW-3
  (Miller's Wife, The.)   TAP
Mill-Pond, The.   Edward Thomas.   RB
Milla.   *Unknown.*   NOSC
Milla, the glory of whose beauteous rays.   Milla.   *Unknown.*   NOSC
Mille e tre.   Paul Verlaine.   CAGL, *tr.* by Alan Stone
Millefiori.   Lavinia Greenlaw.   MFPA
Millennial Polka.   Alicia Ostriker.   ExTi
Millennium.   Patricia Beer.   HarvBoo
"Millennium," yes; "pandemonium!"   Hometown Piece for Messrs. Alston and Reese.   Marianne Craig Moore.   OBAL
Miller, The.   John Cunningham.   ECEV
Miller's daughter, The.   Spinning Song.   Dame Edith Sitwell.   MoBrPo
Miller's Daughter, The.   Tennyson.   OBEV
Miller's mill-dog lay at the mill-door, The.   Bingo.   *Unknown.*   TTTS
Miller's [*or* Milleres] Tale, The.   Geoffrey Chaucer.   NAEL-6v1; NAEL-7v1; NAWM-5v1; OxBoLi; PeLV   *Fr.* Canterbury Tales, The.
Miller's Prologue, The.   Geoffrey Chaucer.   NAEL-6v1; NAEL-7v1; NAWM-5v1   *Fr.* Canterbury Tales, The.
Miller's Tale, The.   Geoffrey Chaucer.   NAWM-5v1; NAWM-7v1, *tr.* by Theodore Morrison   *Fr.* Canterbury Tales, The.
Miller's Wife, The.   Edwin Arlington Robinson.   *See* Mill, The
Miller's wife had waited long, The.   Mill, The.   Edwin Arlington Robinson.   APT-1; HAP; NAAL-2v2; NoAM; NoP-4; PAI; WeW-3
Millery, millery, dustipole.   *Unknown.*   OxNR
Millets in full rows.   *Unknown.*   ChinPo, *tr.* by Yip Wai-lim
Millie's Date.   Dannie Abse.   BloBone
Millinery District: "Clouds, piled in rows like merchandise, The."   Charles Reznikoff.   APT-2
Millinery District: "Many fair hours have been buried here."   Charles Reznikoff.   APT-2
Million, The.   Peter Redgrove.   OxBC
Million billion trillion stars, A. (LL)   E. E. Cummings.   ChIV-2; HAP; NOBA; NoAM; OxBA; TAP
Million butterflies rose up from South America, A.   Annual Legend.   Winfield Townley Scott.   CoAP
Million million spermatozoa, A.   Fifth Philosopher's Song.   Aldous Leonard Huxley.   OBCoV
Millionaire, filled with elation, A.   Limerick.   Thomas Thorneley.   PeLi
Millions of stars playing tag in the skies.   It Shouldn't Happen to a Dream.   Don George.   ReLy
Millions of Strawberries.   Genevieve Taggard.   NOxBChV
Milltown Union Bar, The.   Richard Hugo.   NoAM
Milne's Bar.   Norman MacCaig.   FaBoTw
Milo's from home; and, Milo being gone.   Epigram.   Martial.   OBVE, *tr.* by Elijah Fenton
Milord I thanke you hartely.   Thursday before New Yeares Day (Being on the Satterdy) the Maide, by Councell of On, She Trustid Well, Excussid Herself on This Wise to Milord, The.   Marie Collyn.   EMWP
Milton.   William Blake.
  And Did Those Feet in Ancient Time.   AWP; ClHu; FaBoCh; HAP; HeIP-4; NAEL-5v2; NAWM-7v2; NOBRP; NPeEn; OxBEV; PAI; PeECV; PoE; PoRA; SCGP; TFi; WoPoe
  "But the Wine-press of Los is eastward of Golgonooza, before the Seat."   NOBRP
  "But turning toward Ololon in terrible majesty Milton."   OxAEP-2
  "Daughters of Beulah! Muses who inspire the Poets Song."   PeECV
  "Into this pleasant Shadow all the weak & weary."   NOBRP
  (Jerusalem.)   FHYEP; NOBE; NOCV; OBEV; OxAEP-2; RB; UV
  (And Did Those Feet.)   ChIV-1; NoP-4
  (Preface.)   CABP
  "There is a place where Contrarities are equally True."   NOBRP
  (Vision of Beulah, The ("Thou hearest the nightingale begin the song of spring").)   NOBE
  Wine-Press of Los, The.   EBEV
Milton.   William Blake.
  "And every Space that a Man views around his dwelling-place."   BLT
Milton.   Henry Wadsworth Longfellow.   AWP; GSo; TAP
Milton.   Edwin Muir.   OxBSo
Milton.   Henrietta Cordelia Ray.   BlSi; CBWP-3
Milton.   John Banister Tabb.   APN-2
Milton.   London 1802.   William Wordsworth.   AWP; HAP; HeIP-4; NAEL-5v2; NIP-4; NOBRP; OxAEP-2; PoRA; SCGP; Son; TFi; UV
Milton [Alcaics].   Tennyson.   PeECV
Milton by Firelight.   Gary Snyder.   CoAP; NAAL-2v2
  (O Hell, what do mine eyes.)   BB; CoAmPo
Milton, his face set fair for Paradise.   Milton.   Edwin Muir.   OxBSo

Milton: On the Busts of Milton, in Youth and Age.   William Lisle Bowles.   Son
Milton's the prince of poets—so we say.   Byron.   NOBL   *Fr.* Don Juan.
Milton, the airport driver, retired now.   Becoming Milton.   Coleman Barks.   RaBo
Milton! thou shouldst be living at this hour.   London, 1802.   William Wordsworth.   NAEL-6v2; NIL-7
Milton was not my father's favourite poet.   John Milton and My Father.   Patricia Beer.   HarvBoo
Mimesis.   Elizabeth Garrett.   MFPA
Mimetic.   Ann Lauterbach.   PmAP
Mimic Muse, The.   Samuel Hoffenstein.
  "With rue my heart is laden."   NBLV
Mimikòs.   Luigi Fontanella.   NeIt, *tr.* by Michael Palma
Mimnermus in Church.   William Johnson Cory.   NOBE; OBEV
Mimshi Maiden, The.   Hugh Raymond McCrae.   NOBAu
Mina Bell's Cows.   Wesley McNair.   TRP
Mind.   Jorie Graham.   HCAP
Mind.   Richard Wilbur.   HCAP; OxBSP; SoSe-8; VCAP
Mind and environment—you have quieted both.   Yang Chi.   CoBLCP, *tr.* by Jonathan Chaves   *Fr.* Thinking of My Friends at Kou-jung Subprefecture.
Mind, and some thin longing that ensnared it, The.   Skull.   Edward Weismiller.   YaYoPo
Mind at peace, cassia flowers fall.   Birdsong Brook.   Wang Wei.   SuSp, *tr.* by Irving Y. Lo
Mind, The / becomes an / oil-slicked pool.   Doper's Dream.   Don Receveur.   CDa
Mind-Body Problem.   Katha Pollitt.   KGB
Mind content both crown and kingdom is, A. (LL)   Robert Greene.   CTC; UnPo   *Fr.* Farewell to Folly.
Mind, don't be duped by others' sneers.   Rāmprasād Sen.   SinGod, *tr.* by Rachel Fell McDermott
Mind has shown itself at times, The.   Hart Crane.   APT-2; NOBA; NoAM
Mind, how do you think you'll find Her?   Rāmprasād Sen.   SinGod, *tr.* by Rachel Fell McDermott
Mind, I'm talking to you.   Rāmkumār Nandī Majumdār.   SinGod, *tr.* by Rachel Fell McDermott
Mind in its [*or* the] purest play is like some bat.   Mind.   Richard Wilbur.   HCAP; OxBSP; SoSe-8; VCAP
Mind Is an Ancient and Famous Capital, The.   Delmore Schwartz.   APT-2; NoAM; TAP
Mind Is an Enchanting Thing, The.   Marianne Craig Moore.   APT-1; HeIP-4; InPK-6; MoAmPo; NAAL-2v2; NAAL-5; NoP-4; OxBA; PoE; WPOW
Mind is his Wife, The. / So be it. (LL)   Prayer for the Great Family.   Gary Snyder.   HAP; WeW-3
Mind is not, The.   Perishing Bird, The.   Douglas G. Jones.   MoCV
Mind, let's go to an estate that's decent.   Rāmdulāl Nandī.   SinGod, *tr.* by Rachel Fell McDermott
Mind of Absolute Trust, The.   Seng-ts'an.   EnlH, *tr.* by Stephen Mitchell
Mind of man is this world's true dimension, The.   Fulke Greville, 1st Baron Brooke.   NOSC   *Fr.* Treaty of Human Learning, A.
Mind of the people is like mud, The.   Talking with Soldiers.   Walter James Turner.   MoBrPo
Mind Pictures.   Beatrice Hastings.   PeSAV
Mind-Reader, The.   Richard Wilbur.   LCAP-2; NAAL-2v2; NoAM
  "What should I tell them?"   CRP
Mind Reborn in Streatham Common, A.   Richard Percival Lister.   OBCoV
Mind returns to it always, The.   Paul Blackburn.   APSN   *Fr.* Selection of Heaven, The.
Mind's circle increases death, The.   Still without Life.   Rosalie Moore.   YaYoPo
Mind's disguise is permanence, The.   Mind's Disguise, The.   Rosalie Moore.   APT-2; YaYoPo
Mind's Disguise, The.   Rosalie Moore.   APT-2; YaYoPo
Mind's eye aches from Henry James, The.   Satie, at the End of Term.   Simon Curtis.   NOBL; PeLV
Mind's immortal, but the man is dead, The. (LL)   Time and the Garden.   Yvor Winters.   APT-2; HarvBoo; MoAmPo; NoAM; VGW
Mind's Liberty, The.   William Henry Davies.   MoBrPo
Mind set free in the Dharma-realm.   Ryushu Shutaku.   ZenPo, *tr.* by Takashi Ikemoto and Lucien Stryk
Mind to taste, the nerve to feel!, The. (LL)   Departed Youth.   Hannah Cowley.   CABP; ECWP
Mind, why this separation from the Mother's feet?   Rāmprasād Sen.   SinGod, *tr.* by Rachel Fell McDermott
Mind, with its own eyes and ears, The.   Mind's Liberty, The.   William Henry Davies.   MoBrPo
Mind, you're still not rid of your illusions.   Rāmprasād Sen.   SinGod, *tr.* by Rachel Fell McDermott

Minde through thee divines on endlesse things, The. Thomas Lodge. PBRV *Fr.* Scillaes Metamorphosis.

Minding Ruth. Aidan Carl Mathews. BiHa; CIP-2; PBCIP

Minding You. Catherine Byron. Prnts

Minds awake in bodies that were asleep. Pandora and the Moon. Merrill Moore. MoAmPo

Mine. Mary E. Tucker. CBWP-1

Mine angry and defrauded young? (LL) Rudyard Kipling. FaBoEE; FaBoWar; NBLV; OPOU; PoWW; WoPoe *Fr.* Epitaphs of the War [1914–1918].

Mine are the night and morning. Song of Nature. Ralph Waldo Emerson. APN-1

Mine arms embrace my God, yet I. Ralph Erskine. SacPr *Fr.* Believer's Riddle, The.

Mine be a cot beside the [*or* a] hill. Wish, A. Samuel Rogers. GTBS-P; NOBE; OBEV; OxAEP-2

Mine be the strength of spirit fierce and free. Tennyson. CenSon

Mine be thy love and thy love's use their treasure. (LL) William Shakespeare. CAGL; HeIP-4; NAEL-5v1; NAEL-6v1; NAEL-7v1; NoP-4; NoSic; OxAEP-1 *Fr.* Sonnets.

Mine—by the Right of the White Election! Emily Dickinson. APN-2; NAAL-2v1; NAAL-3; NALW; NoP-4; WPoS

Mine Enemy is growing old. Emily Dickinson. RaBo

Mine eye and heart are at a mortal war. William Shakespeare. HeIP-4 *Fr.* Sonnets.

Mine eyes beheld the blessed pity spring. Dante Alighieri. AWP; EaItPo, *tr.* by Dante Gabriel Rossetti *Fr.* La Vita Nuova.

Mine eyes have seen the glory of the coming of the Lord. Battle Hymn [*or* Battle-Hymn] of the Republic, The. Julia Ward Howe. AH; APN-1; BRP; CBCWP; HHAm; NOBA; NOCV; OBWP; PWR; SCV; SWaP; TAP; TCAPo; TFi; WPE

Mine eyes, like clouds, were drizzling rain. Rainbow; or Curious Covenant, The. Robert Herrick. ChIV-1

Mine high estate, power and auctority. Sir Thomas More. NoSic

Mine is the ungloved. John Mole. NewEx

Mine—long as Ages steal! (LL) Emily Dickinson. APN-2; NAAL-2v1; NAAL-3; NALW; NoP-4; WPoS

Mine, O thou lord of life, send my roots rain. (LL) Thou Art Indeed Just, Lord. Gerard Manley Hopkins. AWP; EBVV; GTBS-P; HAP; InPK-6; InvLi; MoBrPo; NAEL-5v2; NAEL-6v2; NOBE; NOBVV; NoAM; NoP-4; PAI; PeECV; SCGP; SacPr; TFi; TOF; UnPo

Mine only died. (LL) [Epitaph] In Obitum M. S., X° Maij [*or* Maii], 1614. William Browne (1591–1643). FaBoEE; NOBE; OBEV

Mine [*or* Myne] own[e] John Poyntz, since [*or* sins] ye delight to know. Sir Thomas Wyatt. NPeEn; NoSic; OBSV; OBVE; SCGP *Fr.* Satires.

Mine Own John Poins. Sir Thomas Wyatt. *See* Satires

Mine own John Poins, since ye delight to know. Sir Thomas Wyatt. *See* Mine [*or* Myne] own[e] John Poyntz, since [*or* sins] ye delight to know

Mine was a midwest home—you can keep your world. One Home. William Stafford. CoAP; VGW

Mine was a trading family. Inscribed on the Doors of My Bookshelves. Yang Hsün-chi. ColAnChi, *tr.* by John Timothy Wixted

Mine with inner, weather. (LL) Tree at My Window. Robert Frost. APT-1; MoAmPo; NoAM; OxBA; TAP

Miner rapes, The. Time Is Running Out. Oodgeroo of the tribe Noonuccal (Kath Walker). IBA

Miner's Ballad, The. Lewis Morris. AngWePo

Miner's Helmet, The. George MacBeth [*or* Macbeth]. OxBTC

Miner thus through perils digs his way, The. Thomas Yalden. ECEV *Fr.* To Sir Humphry Mackworth.

Mineral Kingdom. Jacques Dupin. VCWP, *tr.* by Paul Auster

Minerals of Cornwall, Stones of Cornwall. Peter Redgrove. FaBoMo

Miners. Branko Miljkovic. WoPoe, *tr.* by Charles Simic

Miners. Wilfred Owen. MoBrPo; NOBE; OBWVE; OxAEP-2; PeFWW

Miners. James Wright. CoAmPo

Miners' Wives. Joe Corrie. OxBS

Minerva Jones. Edgar Lee Masters. APT-1; IllVoic *Fr.* Spoon River Anthology.

Mines. Bruce Weigl. CDa

Mines in Sepia Tint, The. Steve Griffiths. TCAWP

Ming will be over to make way for the Ch'ing, The. Barbarian Suite. Marilyn Chin. OpBo

Mingled. Langston Hughes. *See* Mingled / breath and smell

Mingled / breath and smell. Subway Rush Hour. Langston Hughes. InPK-6

Mingled the moonlight with daylight—the last in the narrowing west. Thomas Hardy. Walter De la Mare. NoAM

Mingled Yarns. X. J. Kennedy. OBCA

Mingling my prayer. Saigyo. AWP

Mingling with the holiday crowd. Fish 2. Fidelito Cortes. ReBoTo

Mingus at the Showplace. William Matthews. SeSe

Mingus Speaks: Found Poems. George Barlow. ISC

Miniature. Eden Phillpotts. OxBSP

Miniature. Yannis Ritsos. VCWP, *tr.* by Edmund Keeley

Miniature Dialogue. Edmund Wilson. OBCoV

Miniature in brass-rimmed frame, A. Cromwell: The Last Portrait. David Lindley. NLP

Miniaturist, The. Maurice Kilwein Guevara. AmPoNex; TouFir

Minimal, The. Theodore Roethke. HCAP; NOBA; NoAM; RB

Minister, The. Fenton Johnson. APT-1

Minister has all his notes in place, The. Richard Heller. FaBoWar

Minister's enunciations cut like knives, The. Prophecy, The. Robert Wrigley. SwNoth

Minister said it wad [*or* wald] dee, The. Last Lauch. Douglas Young. NBLV; OxBS

Minister up in Vermont, A. Limerick. *Unknown.* PeLi

Ministers are rehabilitated. Nothing-Never. János Székely. IQMS, *tr.* by George Gömöri

Miniver Cheevy. Edwin Arlington Robinson. APT-1; AWP; ChAP; ClHu; FaBoCh; HeIP-4; MoAmPo; NAAL-2v2; NAAL-5; NBLV; NOBA; NoAM; NoP-4; OBSV; OxBA; PAI; PeLV; PoRA; RaBo; SCV; SoSe-8; TAP; TCAPo; TFi

Miniver Cheevy, Jr. David Fisher Parry. NBLV

Minks, The. Toi Derricotte. UrbNat

Minneapolis Poem, The. James Wright. NoAM; UnPo

Minnelied. W. H. Auden. CAGL *Fr.* Three Posthumous Poems.

Minnesota Fats Describes His Youth. Elizabeth Alexander. AmPoNex

Minnetare Songs. *Unknown.*

   "Bring them to me. Bring them to me. Bring them to me." APN-2

   "Make my heart as powerful as your own. Lead me to conquer." APN-2

   "My child, I do this for you. I give this to you." APN-2

   New Moon Ceremonies.

     "Buffalo are coming, The. We will feed and feast. We wish to be fortunate and we expect it." APN-2

     "I want the robes, the skins of the game animals, the meat of the game animals. Bring them to me. Let us enjoy ourselves." APN-2

     "If the clouds come good, our tobacco will grow. We will be happy." APN-2

     "Spring from the earth, food for our children. Give us good health. Let us grow up, and become ripe." APN-2

   Song of the Bald Eagle. APN-2

   Song of the Bear. APN-2

   Song of the Elk. APN-2

   Song of the Gun. APN-2

   Song of the Pheasant. APN-2

   Song of the Weasel. APN-2

   Song of the White Man. APN-2

Minnie and Mrs. Hoyne. Kenneth Fearing. PoRA

Minnie and Winnie. Tennyson. TTTS

Minnie had a house. Housing Poem, The. Dian Million. ReEnLa

Minnie, I canna caa my wheel. Douglas Young. OBVE

Minnie, the Moocher. Cab Calloway. ReLy

Minor Bird, A. Robert Frost. APT-1; OWoS; SAmP

Minor Elegy. Henriqueta Lisboa. BoWoP, *tr.* by Willis Barnstone and Nelson Cerqueira

Minor Elegy, A. "Igor Severyanin" [*or* "Severianin"]. TCRP, *tr.* by Bernard Meares

Minor Figure. Mary Ruefle. ExTi

Minor Poet, A. Amy Levy. VWP

Minor Van Gogh (He Speaks), A. Alicia Ostriker. RACG

Minority. Imtiaz Dharker. NeBl

Minotaur at Supper: Spare the Noritake and the Spode, The. D. A. Powell. WiU

Minotaur Next Door, The. Greg Pape. PBCAP

Minotaur Poems. Eli W. Mandel.

   "My father was always out in the garage." MoCV

Minott, Lee, Willard, Hosmer, Meriam, Flint. Hamatreya. Ralph Waldo Emerson. APN-1; NAAL-3; NCAP

Minstrel. Michael Dransfield. BMAP

Minstrel, The. James Beattie.

   Youth of a Poet, The. NOEC

Minstrel, The. Goethe. AWP, *tr.* by James Clarence Mangan

Minstrel, The. Sir Walter Scott. OxAEP-2 *Fr.* Lay of the Last Minstrel, The.

Minstrel austere, I honour you with gloom. Berzsenyi. Árpád Tóth. IQMS, *tr.* by Watson Kirkconnell

Minstrel Boy, The. Sir Thomas More. ChAP; FaBoWar; OxAEP-2

Minstrel Boy to the war is gone, The. Minstrel Boy, The. Sir Thomas More. ChAP; FaBoWar; OxAEP-2

Minstrel Man. Langston Hughes. AmFaPo
Minstrel's Last Lay, The. John Barth. OBAL
Minstrel's Song. Thomas Chatterton. HAP; NOBE; SCGP *Fr.* Aella; a Tragycal Enterlude.
Minstrel's Song. Ted Hughes. OBCP
Mint bed is in, The / bloom: lavender haze. Sunday. James Schuyler. TTTS
Minted flesh of leaves, The. Town Garden, A. Tony Lucas. OBGa
Minute ago I came from the well, A. Woman, The. Kristina Rungano. HAWP
Minute before Meeting, The. Thomas Hardy. OxBSo
Minute flowers harden. Depend. Lilies of the Valley. Jon Silkin. NoAM
Minute I heard my first love story, The. Jelaluddin [*or* Jalal al-Din] Rumi. LoL
Minute of Consciousness, The. Imamu Amiri Baraka. APSN
Minutes grow tedious, Time too slowly moves. Maria to Henric. *Unknown.* EMWP
Minutes of Gold. *Unknown.* PoToHe
Minutes of Hasiba, The. Holger Teschke. FaBoWar, *tr. by* Margitt Lehbert
Minutiae 3. P. F. Widdows. FaBoWar
Mips and ma the mooly moo. Theodore Roethke. NBLV; RB *Fr.* Praise to the End!
Mir träumte von einem Königskind. Heinrich Heine. AWP, *tr. by* Richard Garnett
Mir träumte wieder der alte Traum. Heinrich Heine. AWP, *tr. by* James Thomson
Mira, as they dear Edward's senses grow. Ann Yearsley. ECWP *Fr.* To Mira, On the Care of her Infant.
Mira is dancing with bells tied on her ankles. Mirabai [*or* Mira Bai]. BoWoP
Mira's Picture, a Pastoral. Mary Leapor.
  Portrait of the Artist, A. ECWP
Mira's Will. Mary Leapor. BWW; ECWP; NOEC; NoP-4; OxBEV; PEW
Mira to Octavia. Mary Leapor. ECWP
Mirabeau Bridge. Guillaume Apollinaire. WoPoe, *tr. by* Richard Wilbur
Mirabeau Bridge, The. Guillaume Apollinaire. BoLoP; OBVE
Mirabell: Books of Number. James Merrill.
  "It starts in the small hours. An interlude." NoAM
  "World was everything that was the case?, The." HCAP
Mirabile Misterium. *Unknown.* SacPr
Miracle. Wen Yi-tuo *or* Wen I-to. PFTM-1
Miracle, The. Walter De la Mare. UnPo
Miracle, The. Boris Leonidovich Pasternak. GI, *tr. by* Nina Kossman
Miracle, The. Sir John Suckling. CaPo
Miracle, The. George Young. BloBone
Miracle Glass Co. Charles Simic. MakPoe
Miracle Indeed, A. Swami Purohit. OBMV
Miracle Mart. Wislawa Szymborska. PoSu, *tr. by* Adam Czerniawski
Miracle mongers. Bedwetters. Hair-shirted wonder workers. Shirkers of the soggy soggy earth. Saints. Amy Gerstler. ExTi
Miracle of the children the brilliant. Exodus. George Oppen. ChIV-1
Miracle of the world, I never will deny. Henry Constable. SCGP *Fr.* Diana.
Miracle seekers bring offerings of money, candy, and teddy bears. Earthly Light. Marcia Southwick. PuP-23
Miracle, this massive, drab constant of experience. (LL) Constant, The. A. R. Ammons. HAP; WeW-3
Miracle Workers. Oleg Khlebnikov.
  "From three sources, / vital sources flowing in dull shades of red." TCRP
Miracles. Conrad Potter Aiken. MoAmPo; TCAPo
Miracles. Arna Bontemps. NAAAL
Miracles. Carol Muske. ExTi
Miracles. Julia Randall. CRP
Miracles. Walt Whitman. SAmP
Miracles at the Birth of Christ. Isaac Watts. NOCV
Miraculous Dawn. R. Williams Parry. OBWVE, *tr. by* Joseph P. Clancy
Miraculous Grass. Nuala Ni Dhomhnaill. ModIr, *tr. by* Seamus Heaney
MIRACULOUS love's wounding! *Unknown.* NoSic
Miraculous Marriage of Zarife Dominquez. Patricia Dubrava. MPUn
Miraculous Ship, The. Delmira Agustini. TCLAP, *tr. by* Karl Kirchwey
Miraculous Weapons, The. Aimé Césaire. PFTM-1
Mirage. R. P. Blackmur. APT-2
Mirage. Christina Georgina Rossetti. BoLoP; PoRA
Mirage has offered its solace to my heart, A. Dark Mirage. "Badawi al-Jabal." MAP, *tr. by* Christopher Tingley and Richard Wilbur
Miranda. W. H. Auden. NPeEn; NoAM *Fr.* Sea and the Mirror, The.
Miranda, remember that Inn? Limerick. John Stanley. PeLi
Mirèio. Frédéric Mistral.
  Mares of the Camargue, The. AWP, *tr. by* George Meredith
Miriam. Marjorie Agosin. MirDau, *tr. by* Monica Bruno Galmozzi

Miriam and Horlick spend a great deal of time putting off going to bed. Goodnight. Stevie Smith. FaBoWP
Miriam's Song. Eleanor Wilner. TaR
Mirkayan, don't show your love, simply relish. Do Not Show Your Love. Sa'id 'Aql. MAP, *tr. by* Naomi Shihab Nye and Matthew Sorenson
Mirra Lokhvitskaia's ashes are now entombed. Prologue. "Igor Severyanin [*or* Severianin]." TCRP, *tr. by* Bernard Meares
Mirror. James Merrill. CoAP
Mirror. Sylvia Plath. FaBoWP; HAP; NIL-7; NIP-4; PAI
Mirror. Chimako Tada. BoWoP
Mirror, A. Jean Follain. BLT
Mirror, The. Dafydd [*or* David] ap Gwilym. WoPoe, *tr. by* Daniel Huws
Mirror, The. Michael Davitt. BiHa; CIP-2; PBCIP, *tr. by* Paul Muldoon
Mirror, The. Robert Graves. NOxBChV
Mirror, The. Judah Halevi. TrJP, *tr. by* Emma Lazarus
Mirror, The. Boris Leonidovich Pasternak. TCRusP, *tr. by* Bogdan Boychuk and Mark Rudman
Mirror, The. Wanted. Mercedes Roffé. TANSG, *tr. by* Kathryn Kopple
Mirror, The. Isaac Rosenberg. NoAM
Mirror, The. "Shu Ting." PFTM-2, *tr. by* Dennis Ding, Fang Dai and Edward Morin
Mirror copies everything it sees, A. Reflections on Mirrors. Elder Olson. CRP
Mirror for Detractors, A. Esther Lewis. ECWP
Mirror for the Twentieth Century, A. "Adonis" [*or* "Adunis"]. AF, *tr. by* Abdullah Al-Udhari
Mirror in February. Thomas Kinsella. CIP-2; GTBS-P; MakPoe; NoAM
Mirror in the Deserted Hall, The. Felicia Dorothea Hemans. NOBRP
Mirror in Which Two Are Seen as One, The. Adrienne Rich. NAAL-2v2; NNaP
Mirror Lake's waters are moon-clear. Li Po. CrYelRi; ErotSp, *tr. by* Sam Hamill *Fr.* Women of Yueh.
Mirror of a Day Chiming Marigold, The. Diane Wakoski. NALW
Mirror of a Moment, The. Paul Éluard. NAWM-7v2, *tr. by* Lloyd Alexander
Mirror of emptiness. Lake, The. Gertrude Pape. SurWo, *tr. by* Her de Vries
Mirror of Matsuyama, The. Sharon Hashimoto. OpBo
Mirror of men's eyes delights me less, The. Laus Virginitatis. Arthur Symons. EnLoPo
Mirror of poets, mirror of our age. Upon Ben Johnson [*or* Jonson]. Edmund Waller. BeJo; NOSC
Mirror of the pond gleams, The. Thoughts while Reading. Chu Hsi. OHPC, *tr. by* Kenneth Rexroth
Mirror Perilous, The. Alan Dugan. TwCP
Mirror. Roll away. Underneath (7). Jorie Graham. BodElec
Mirror to Khalida, A. "Adonis" [*or* "Adunis"]. MAP, *tr. by* John Heath-Stubbs and Lena Jayyusi
Mirrored. Giancarlo Majorino. ItPo, *tr. by* Gayle Ridinger
Mirrored by stream / Swallow darts—. Saimaro. ZenPo, *tr. by* Takashi Ikemoto and Lucien Stryk
Mirrored by the spring. O. Mabson Southard. HA
Mirrors. Sarah Arvio. KGB *Fr.* Visits from the Seventh.
Mirrors. Marta Kornblith. MirDau, *tr. by* Roberta Gordenstein
Mirrors. Fu'ad [*or* Fuad] Rifqa [*or* Rifka]. MAP, *tr. by* Sargon Boulus and Samuel Hazo
Mirrors at 4 A.M. Charles Simic. AWTN
Mirrors in the Room. Rodney M. McNeil. InTrad
Mirrors, The! Amelia Rosselli. CItWP, *tr. by* Cinzia Sartini Blum and Lara Trubowitz
Mirrors, without Song. Keorapetse Kgositsile. PBMAP *Fr.* Present Is a Dangerous Place to Live, The.
Mirth and Melancholy. Margaret Lucas Cavendish, Duchess of Newcastle. WPE
Mirth, Spring, to linger in a garden fair. Hafiz [*or* Hafez]. TAL *Fr.* Odes.
Mirth with thee I mean to live. (LL) John Milton. AWP; BASC; FHYEP; GTBS-P; HAP; NAEL-6v1; NAEL-7v1; NOSC; NoP-4; OBEV; PBRV; PoPoPo; TFi
Mis Mai. Dafydd [*or* David] ap Gwilym.
  "Duw gwyddiad mai da y gweddai." CABP
Misanthropos. Thom Gunn.
  Elegy on the Dust. NoAM
  Last Man, The. OxAEP-2
  Memoirs of the World.
  "Serving man, A. Curled my hair." OxBC
Misapprehension. Paul Laurence Dunbar. BPo
Miscarriage. Joseph P. Clancy. AngWePo
Miscellaneous Feelings. T'ang Yin.
  "Galloping around, north and south." CoBLCP

Miscellaneous Feelings at West Lake. Ch'ien Ch'ien-i [*or* Ch'ien Ch'ien-yi]. CoBLCP, *tr. by* Jonathan Chaves

Miscellaneous Feelings in the Sui Garden. Yüan Mei. CoBLCP; ColAnChi, *tr. by* Jonathan Chaves

Miscellaneous Impressions of T'an-chou. Yang Chi.
"Up at the prow, I wash my mouth, dripping water on my robe." CoBLCP

Miscellaneous Poem on Rural Life. Liu Yin. ColAnChi, *tr. by* John Timothy Wixted

Miscellaneous Poems on Growing Old. Yüan Mei. CoBLCP, *tr. by* Jonathan Chaves

Miscellaneous Poems on Lake Biwa. Liu Ya-tzu.
"Beyond the stream at Seta stretches an endless view." SuSp
"By Flower-and-Moon Pavilion, I stay my carriage." SuSp
"Cataracts flying down a thousand fathoms roll up a raging billow." SuSp

Miscellaneous Poems on Living in the Woods—In the Manner of Han Shan. Wang Chiu-ssu.
"Total failure—Master Han Shan, A." CoBLCP

Miscellaneous Poems on Spirit-Valley Temple. Wang T'ing-hsiang. CoBLCP, *tr. by* Jonathan Chaves

Miscellaneous Poems Written in My Studio on an Autumn Day. Chu Yünming. CoBLCP, *tr. by* Jonathan Chaves

Miscellaneous Poems Written in the Snow. Wang T'ing-hsiang. CoBLCP, *tr. by* Jonathan Chaves

Miscellaneous Poems Written While in Jail. Ch'ien Ch'ien-i [*or* Ch'ien Ch'ien-yi]. CoBLCP, *tr. by* Jonathan Chaves

Miscellaneous Words on the Lake. Tsung Ch'en. CoBLCP, *tr. by* Jonathan Chaves

Miscellanies of the Year Chi-hai. Kung Tzu-chen. SuSp, *tr. by* Irving Y. Lo

Mischievous Raven, The. *Unknown.* OxNR
(Farmer and the Raven, The.) ReMoGo

Misconception, A. James Russell Lowell. OBAL

Misconceptions. Robert Browning. OBEV

Misconstrued, The. Bruce Berger. GeoH

Mise en Scène. Robert Fitzgerald. VGW

Miser. Elizabeth Garrett. NeBl

Miser and the Mouse, The. Lucilius. GrAn

Miserable change now at my end, The. William Shakespeare. EBEV *Fr.* Antony and Cleopatra.

Miserable Estate of the World before the Incarnation of God. William Drummond, of Hawthornden. SacPr

Miserable I lie in desire. Archilochus. SaLy, *tr. by* Diane Rayor

Miserere. David Gascoyne.
Ecce Homo. ChIV-2; NoP-4; OBWP; PeECV
Ex Nihilo. GTBS-P
"Whose is this horrifying face." ChIV-2; NoP-4; OBWP; PeECV

Miserere, My Maker. *Unknown.* NOCV

Misericordia! James Lipton. NBLV

"Miseries of Courtiers" by Æneas Sylvius Ricolomini, The. Alexander Barclay. *Fr.* Eclogues.

Miserimus. Adah Isaacs Menken. CBWP-1

"Miserrimus!" and neither name nor date. Gravestone upon the Floor in the Cloisters of Worcester Cathedral, A. William Wordsworth. SacPr

Misery. Andreas Gryphius. WoPoe, *tr. by* Christopher Benfey

Misery and Splendor. Robert Hass. VCAP

Misery of Jerusalem, The. Bible, *O.T.* AWP *Fr.* Lamentations.

Misfortune sometimes is a prize. Wooden Leg. James McIntyre. VerBaPo

Misfortunes, insults—nothing ever rankled. Farewell to Autumn. Oleg Grigorevich Chukhonstev. TCRP, *tr. by* Simon Franklin

Misfortunes of Elphin, The. Thomas Love Peacock.
War Song of Dinas Vawr, The. AWP; CABP; FaBoCh; FaBoWar; HAP; NAEL-5v2; NAEL-6v2; NOBE; NOBRP; NPeEn; OxAEP-2

Misgivings. Herman Melville. APN-2; NAAL-2v1; NAAL-3; NCAP; NOBA; OxBA; TCAPo

Misguided Angels. Gale Renée Walden. ReTh

Mishipasinghan, Lumchipamudana, Etc. Albert Goldbarth. SpudSo

Mishka. John Gray. NOBVV

Misplaced Sympathy. Charles Follen Adams. OBAL

Misplacing—Mistaking. On Sir Nathaniel Wraxall the Historian. George Colman, the Younger. FaBoEE

Misremembered Lyric, A. Denise Riley. NPeEn; Oth

Misremembered lyric: a soft catch of its song, A. Misremembered Lyric, A. Denise Riley. NPeEn; Oth

Miss Bailey's Ghost. George Colman, the Younger. OxBoLi

Miss Betty's Singing-Bird. John Winstanley. NOEC

Miss Bitter. N. M. Bodecker. NTCP

Miss Blues'es Child. Langston Hughes. ChAP; SAmP; TTTS

Miss Buss and Miss Beale. *Unknown.* FaBoEE; OBCoV
(Two Headmistresses.) OBCoV

Miss Carney handed us out blank paper and marla. Model School, Inchicore. Thomas Kinsella. CIP-2

Miss Cho Composes in the Cafeteria. James Tate. WeW-3

Miss Clement's Second Grade. Maryfrances Cusumano Wagner. UnSA

Miss Dinah when she goes to church. Little More Cider, A. *Unknown.* KaS

Miss Edith's Modest Request. Bret Harte. NOxBChV

Miss Emily Brittle Sails for India. Sir George Dallas. NOEC *Fr.* India Guide; or, Journal of a Voyage to the East Indies in 1780, The.

Miss F[——]ny M[——]t[——]y to Miss P[——]y B[——]s. Fanny [*or* Frances] Macartney Greville. ECWP

Miss Flora McFlimsey, of Madison Square. Nothing to Wear. William Allen Butler. OBAL

Miss Florence Jackson. David Huddle. PBCAP

Miss Foggerty's Cake. *Unknown.* NBLV

Miss Gee. W. H. Auden. EBNV; OxBTC; UV

Miss Grant. Freda Downie. FaBoWP

Miss Havisham. Olga Orozco. TCLAP, *tr. by* Stephen Tapscott

Miss Havisham's Letter. Julia Copus. MFPA

Miss Helen Slingsby was my maiden aunt. Aunt Helen. T. S. Eliot. NPeEn; OBAL

Miss Ivy, tell me supmn. Wha Fe Call I' Valerie Bloom. FaBoVe

Miss J. Hunter Dunn, Miss J. Hunter Dunn. Subaltern's Love-Song, A. Sir John Betjeman. BoLoP; HAP; NOBL; NoAM; OxAEP-2; OxBTC; TwCP

Miss Kilmansegg and Her Precious Leg. Thomas Hood.
Her Accident. EBVV
Her Christening. NOBVV
Her Death. NOBVV
Her Education. EBVV
Her Precious Leg. NOBVV
Miss Kilmansegg's Birth. OBCoV; OxBoLi; PeLV

Miss Lavender. Jon Stallworthy. OxBC

Miss Loo. Walter De la Mare. OxBTC

Miss Marnell. Austin Clarke. OxBEV

Miss Mary Mack. Lisa Buscani. AmPoNex

Miss Millay Says Something Too. Samuel Hoffenstein. NBLV

Miss Muffet. Mother Goose. LB; OxNR; ReMoGo

Miss Muffett in a runaway ugly machine. I mean. Like that. (LL) W. W. Imamu Amiri Baraka. HeIP-4; NOBA; PAI

Miss Nancy Ellicott. Cousin Nancy. T. S. Eliot. OBAL; OxBSP

Miss One, Two, and Three. *Unknown.* OxNR

Miss Otis Regrets. Cole Porter. ReLy

Miss Otis regrets she's unable to lunch today. Miss Otis Regrets. Cole Porter. ReLy

Miss Pimberton Of. Siv Cedering Fox. PBCAP

Miss R. looks at the mantel-piece, which must mean something. (LL) Evening in the Sanitarium. Louise Bogan. FaBoWP; NALW; NIL-7; TwCP

Miss Rafferty wore taffeta. Private Dining Room, The. Ogden Nash. OBCoV

Miss Riley stands above me, fading fast. Bailey Gatzert: The First Grade, 1945. Lonny Kaneko. LTA

Miss Rosie. Lucille Clifton. BlSi; ESEAA; TwCP

Miss Rosie Mae. Miss Rosie Mae Watches Elvis Presley on The Ed Sullivan Show. Herbert Martin. AllShUp

Miss Rosie Mae Watches Elvis Presley on The Ed Sullivan Show. Herbert Martin. AllShUp

Miss T. Walter De la Mare. NTCP

Miss Tristram's *poulet* ended thus: "Nota bene." Mr. Placid's Flirtation. Frederick Locker-Lampson. PeVV

Miss Twye. Gavin Ewart. NOBL

Miss Universe, for Thy Name's Sake, Amen. (LL) Boom! Howard Nemerov. NBLV; NIL-7; NIP-4

Miss Wilson's eyes, opaque. Public School No. 18: Paterson, New Jersey. Maria Gillan. UnSA

Miss You. David Cory. ITBLP

Miss You. *Unknown.* PoToHe

Miss you, miss you, miss you. Miss You. David Cory. ITBLP

Missing. Moniza Alvi. NeBl

Missing. W. H. Auden. OxBTC

Missing. Tracey Herd. MFPA

Missing. John Pudney. OxBTC

Missing, The. Thom Gunn. CAGL; NoP-4

Missing, The. Yannis Ritsos. AF, *tr. by* Edmund Keeley

Missing: A Dog's Doggerel. Mary Morris. Unle

Missing a kick. Jack Kerouac. HA

Missing All—prevented Me, The. Emily Dickinson. APN-2

Missing—Believed Drowned. Michael Greening. FaBoWar

Missing Dates. William Empson. HAP; HarvBoo; MakPoe; MoBrPo; NOBE; NPeEn; NoAM; OxBEV; PoE; UnPo

Missing France. Jules Supervielle. MFP, *tr.* by Martin Sorrell

Missing from the map, the abandoned roads. Old Roads. Eiléan Ní Chuilleanáin. CIP-2

Missing head tells yet of the sacred day, The. Victory of Samothrace, The. "Rubén Dario." GS, *tr.* by Unknown

Missing Jew, The. Rodger Kamenetz. TaR

Missing Link. Sean Lucy. BiHa

Missing My Daughter. Stephen Spender. GTBS-P

Missing Patriarch, The. Michael S. Weaver. PBCAP

Missing so much and so much? (LL) To a Fat Lady Seen from the Train. Frances Darwin Cornford. FaBoWP; MoBrPo; OBMV; OxBEV; UV; WeW-3

Missing the noise of the sea at night. Nocturnal. John Haines. GifTon

Missing the Sea. Derek Walcott. OxBEV

Missing You. "Shu Ting." CarOv; VCWP, *tr.* by Carolyn Kizer and Y. H. Zhao

Mission of the Flowers, The. Frances Ellen Watkins Harper. BlSi

Mission Poem. Tarin Towers. AmPoNex; PuP-23

Mission Work-Boat. Unknown. NOBAu, *tr.* by Mungayana Nundhirribala

Missionaries in the Jungle. Linda Piper. BlSi

Missionary, The. Mrs. Henry Linden. CBWP-4

Mississippi. Aimé Césaire. NegPo, *tr.* by Clayton Eshleman and Denis Kelly

Mississippi. Milán Füst. IQMS, *tr.* by István Tótfalusi

Mississippi. E. Ethelbert Miller. GT

Mississippi Blues. Lamont B. Steptoe. SpirFl

Mississippi China woman, / why do you wear blue jeans in the city? Lost Name Woman. Shirley Lim. UnSA

Mississippi steamed in July. Civil Rights. Ira Sadoff. LTA

Missoula Softball Tournament. Richard Hugo. MoASP

Missouri Sequence. Brian Coffey.
Nightfall, Midwinter, Missouri. CIP-2

Misspelled Tail, A. Elizabeth T. Corbett. OBCA

Misspelt scrawl, upon the wall, The. In an Album. James Russell Lowell. OBAL

Mist. Bob Boldman. HA

Mist. Eugen Gomringer. PFTM-2, *tr.* by Jerome Rothenberg

Mist. Li Ch'ing-chao. OHPC, *tr.* by Kenneth Rexroth

Mist. Henry David Thoreau. *See* Week on the Concord and Merrimack Rivers, A

Mist, The. Unknown. ReMoGo

Mist clears and the cavities, The. Derry Morning. Derek Mahon. NOIV

Mist floats on the Spring meadow. Yakamochi (Otomo no Yakamochi). OHPJ

Mist hangs of late, A. Different. Marga Kool. TuT, *tr.* by Joan McBreen

Mist in the Meadows. John Clare. NPeEn

Mist in the palace willows, The. Echoing Old Man Mu's Poem, "Inscribed on Shen Lang-ch'ien's Little Landscape, Autumn Willows at Stone Cliff." Wang Shih-chieng. CoBLCP, *tr.* by Jonathan Chaves

Mist is thick. On the wide river, the water-plants float smoothly, The. Lonely Wife, The. Li Po. NIL-7, *tr.* by Amy Lowell

Mist Maiden, The. Henrietta Cordelia Ray. CBWP-3

Mist of pain has covered my dour old heart, A. Valentine Browne. Egan [or Aodhagán] O'Rahilly [or O'Reilly or Ó Rathaille]. NOIV, *tr.* by Thomas Kinsella

Mist rauk is hanging, The. Song. John Clare. NOBVV

Mist where Genesis begins, The. (LL) To the Man after the Harrow. Patrick Kavanagh. CIP-2; GTBS-P; ModIr

Mistake, A. Aleksandr Arkadevich Galich. TCRP, *tr.* by Albert C. Todd

Mistake, The. Sami Mahdi. MAP, *tr.* by May Jayyusi

Mistake, The. Theodore Roethke. OBCoV *Fr.* Three Epigrams.

Mistaken. Mary Elizabeth Coleridge. PoBW

Mistaken bird, a whither hast thou strayed? Elegy on a Young Thrush Which Escaped from the Writer's Hand. Helen Maria Williams. ECWP

Mistaken fair, lay Sherlock by. Verses Written in a Lady's Sherlock "Upon Death." Philip Dormer Stanhope, 4th Earl of Chesterfield. EBEV

Mistaken Identity. Lewis Warsh. BodElec

Mistakes. Ella Wheeler Wilcox. PoToHe

Mr. and Mrs. Vite's Journey. Unknown. NOBL

Mr. Aplinio Morales has reported this. Incident at Imuris. Alberto A. Ríos. NIP-4

Mr. Artesian's Conscientiousness. Ogden Nash. NBLV

Mister Backlash, Mister Backlash. Backlash Blues, The. Langston Hughes. BPo

Mr Bones: there is. (LL) John Berryman. BoLoP; ColAP; EmeKit; HAP; HCAP; NoP-4; OBAL; VCAP *Fr.* Dream Songs.

Mr. Brodsky. Charles Tomlinson. NoAM; OxBC
(I had heard.) NoP-4

Mr Cromek to Mr Stothard. William Blake. FaBoEE

Mister Death. (LL) Portrait. E. E. Cummings. HeIP-4; InPK-6; NAAL-2v2; NIP-4; NOBA; OxBSP; PoE; RB; TAP; VGW

Mister East gave a feast. Winds, The. Unknown. ReMoGo

Mr. Edwards and the Spider. Robert Lowell. CoAP; ColAP; FaBoMo; HarvBoo; HeIP-4; NAAL-2v2; NAAL-5; NOBA; NoP-4; TFi; TwCP

Mister Five by Five. Don Raye. ReLy

Mr Flood's Party. Edwin Arlington Robinson. APT-1; AWP; AmFaPo; ClHu; ColAP; EBNV; HAP; HeIP-4; MoAmPo; NAAL-2v2; NAAL-5; NIL-7; NIP-4; NOBA; NoAM; NoP-4; OxBA; PoE; PoRA; SoSe-8; TAP; TCAPo; TFi; TRP; UnPo; WeW-3

Mr. 'Gator. N. M. Bodecker. NTCP

Mr. Hansen, the cop at the campus gate. Officers. Josephine Miles. FaBoWP

Mr. Ibister. Unknown. OxNR

Mr. Irving Berlin. Noël Coward. UV *Fr.* Let's Do It.

Mister Johnson. Ben Harney. OBAL

Mr. Leach made a speech. Forensic Jocularities. Sir George Rose. OxBoLi

Mr. Lizard Is Crying. Federico García Lorca. TTTS, *tr.* by William Bryant Logan

Mr. MacCall at Cleveland Hall. James Thomson. NOBVV

Mr Mistoffelees. T. S. Eliot. NOxBChV

Mr. Murple's got a dog that's long. Noctambule. George Johnston. MoCV

Mr. Pope. Allen Tate. APT-2; ColAP; FuPo; NOBA; NoAM; TwCP; VGW

Mister Shylock was stingy. I've Got Five Dollars. Richard Rodgers. ReLy

Mister Snow. Richard Rodgers. ReLy

Mr T. / bareheaded. Artist, The. William Carlos Williams. LCAP-2; PAI; RB; SAmP

Mr u will not be missed. E. E. Cummings. FaBoEE; OBCoV; VGW

Mr. Wells of the big cerebellum. Limerick. H. G. Wells. PeLi

Mister Williams / lets youn me move. Uncle Iv Surveys His Domain from His Rocker. Jonathan Williams. NBLV; OBAL

Mister Winkler Winkler oh. Devil and the Princess. Unknown. FaBoVe

Mr. Z. M. Carl Holman. SoSe-8

Mistletoe. Mary E. Tucker. CBWP-1

Mistral blows, the plane leaves, The. On the Eve of the Plebiscite. Kenneth Rexroth. NNaP

Mistress, The. Joan Barton. OxBTC

Mistress, The. Abraham Cowley.
Against Fruition. BeJo; NOSC
Against Hope. MeLP; NOSC
Change, The. MeLP
(On Hope.) CABP; NOBE
(Platonic Love.) NoP-4
Platonic[k] Love. BeJo
Spring, The. BeJo; HAP; MeLP; OxAEP-1
Welcome, The. BoLoP
Wish, The. BASC; NOBE; NOSC; NoP-4; OBEV; OxAEP-1; PBRV
Written in Juice of Lem[m]on. CABP

Mistress, The. Pamela Gillilan. Prnts

Mistress, The. John Wilmot, 2d Earl of Rochester. *See* Mistress: A Song, The

Mistress: A Song, The. John Wilmot, 2d Earl of Rochester. EBEV; NOBE; NOSC; NPeEn
(Mistress, The.) OxAEP-1

Mistress Agnes in the streamlet. Mistress Agnes. János Arany. IQMS, *tr.* by William N. Loew

Mrs. Alfred Uruguay. Wallace Stevens. TwCP

Mistress, Behold, in This True-Speaking Glass. Barnabe Barnes. Son *Fr.* Parthenophil and Parthenophe.

Mrs. Bubb was gay and free, fair, fat and forty-three. One Horse Chay, The. Unknown. OxBoLi

Mrs. Chub was rich and portly. Jupiter and Ten. James Thomas Fields. OBAL

Mrs. Coley's three-flat brick. Gwendolyn Brooks. NAAAL; NAAL-2v2; NOBA; NoAM *Fr.* Street in Bronzeville, A

Mrs. Evans fach, you want butter again. Angry Summer, The. Idris Davies. AngWePo

Mrs. Gabrielle Giovanitti comes along Peoria Street every morning. Onion Days. Carl Sandburg. IllVoic

Mrs. Judge Jenkins[; Being the Only Genuine Sequel to "Maud Muller"]. Bret Harte. APN-2

Mrs. Loewinsohn etc. Ron Loewinsohn. NeAP

Mrs. Lorris, Who Died of Being Clean. Barbara Giles. OTCP

Mrs. Macintosh. Rodney Hall. CBAP

Mistress Margaret Hussey. John Skelton. *See* Garland [or Garlande or Garlands] of Laurel[l], The

Mrs. Marmaduke Moore, at the age of ten. Seven Spiritual Ages of Mrs. Marmaduke Moore, The. Ogden Nash. MoAmPo

Mistress Mary is dead and gone! (LL)   Telling the Bees.   John Greenleaf Whittier.   APN-1; AWP; ColAP; NOBA; NoP-4; TAP; TCAPo

Mrs. Mason bought a basin.   Mrs. Mason's Basin.   *Unknown*.   OxNR

Mrs. Mason's Basin.   *Unknown*.   OxNR

Mrs Masters's fuchsias hung.   Lodging-House Fuchsias, The.   Thomas Hardy.   OxBSP

Mrs. Noah in the Ark.   Ballad of Mrs. Noah, The.   Robert Duncan.   NOBA; NoAM

Mistress of all my senses can invite.   To Caelia.   Richard Duke.   NOSC

Mistress of My Own Being.   Ifi Amadiume.   HAWP

Mrs. Peck-Pigeon.   Eleanor Farjeon.   NTCP

Mrs. Severin.   Winfield Townley Scott.   InPK-6

Mrs Simpkins.   Stevie Smith.   OBCoV

Mrs. Snow.   Donald Justice.   NoP-4

Mistress to the Spirit of Her Lover, The.   Charlotte Dacre.   RWP

Mrs. Trollope in America.   Helen Smith Bevington.   NBLV; OBAL

Mists are brooding on the fields, The.   Autumn Song.   József Bajza.   IQMS, *tr. by* Watson Kirkconnell

Mists disappear, the water, The.   Morning.   Judith Herzberg.   TuT, *tr. by* Joan McBreen

Mists over the River.   William Carlos Williams.   ColAP

Mists rise over, The.   Akahito.   OHPJ

Misty.   Erroll Garner.   ReLy

Misty brown of my mourning flees, The.   Adam, Where Art Thou?   Endre Ady.   IQMS, *tr. by* Anton N. Nyerges

Misty grasses.   Buson.   EH, *tr. by* Robert Hass

Misty mountains tell me the secrets you hold, of men.   Errol West.   IBA

Misty rain.   Basho.   EH, *tr. by* Robert Hass

Misty waves in the distance.   Springtime South of the Yangtze.   K'o Chun.   CrYelRi, *tr. by* Sam Hamill

Misunderstood.   Lizelia Augusta Jenkins Moorer.   CBWP-3

Mitayo, The.   Manuel González Prada.   SpanPo, *tr. by* Kate Flores

Mitching.   Michael Smith.   CIP-2

Mite, The.   Boynton, Jr. Merrill.   CRP

Mither's Lament, The.   Sydney Goodsir Smith.   OxBS

Mithras, God of the morning, our trumpets waken the Wall!   Rudyard Kipling.   NoAM   *Fr.* Puck of Pook's Hill.

Mithridates.   Ralph Waldo Emerson.   APN-1; NCAP

Mithridates, he died old. (LL)   Terence, This Is Stupid Stuff.   A. E. Housman.   CABP; HeIP-4; InPK-6; NAEL-5v2; NAEL-6v2; NoAM; NoP-4; TFi

Mitten Song, The.   Marie Louise Allen.   NTCP

Mix a Pancake.   Christina Georgina Rossetti.   NTCP   *Fr.* Sing-Song.

Mixed Emotions.   Huang Ching-jen.   SuSp, *tr. by* Chang Yin-nan

Mixed Feelings.   John Ashbery.   HAP; WeW-3

Mixed Marriage.   Diana Der Hovanessian.   TWW

Mixed Marriage.   Joan Logghe.   MPUn

Mixed Marriage, The.   Paul Muldoon.   PNI

Mixed Sketches.   Haki R. Madhubuti.   BPo; TAP

Mixed with morning dew? (LL)   Isatou Died.   Lenrie Peters.   HBAPE; PBMAP; PoetW

Mixed with quartz grains, rose and amethyst. (LL)   Sandpiper.   Elizabeth Bishop.   APT-2; AiP; HeIP-4; OWoS; RB; TOF

Mixer, The.   Louis MacNeice.   FaBoTw

Mixing fresher Air. (LL)   Storm.   Emily Dickinson.   NAAL-2v1; NAAL-3; OxBSP

Mixtures of this garden, The.   In the Garden: Villa Cleobolus.   Lawrence Durrell.   OBGa

Miz Rosa Rides the Bus.   Angela Jackson.   IllVoic

Mm / I'm a little bit in love.   Little Bit in Love, A.   Betty Comden.   ReLy

Mmenson.   Edward Kamau Brathwaite.   OPOU

Mnasylla, the daughter you lament.   Perses.   GrAn

Mnemonic.   Li-Young Lee.   UnSA

Mnemosyne.   Madison Cawein.   APN-2

Mnemosyne.   Trumbull Stickney.   APN-2; NOBA; OxBA; TCAPo

Mnemosyne Lay in Dust.   Austin Clarke.

"Maurice was in an Exhibition Hall."   PoE

"One night he heard heart-breaking sound."   CIP-2

"Past the house where he was got."   PoE

Mob, The.   Mcavoy Layne.   CDa

Mob of dressing-tables is grazing, A.   Duchesses.   David Campbell.   NOBAu

Mob—the crowd—the mass—will arrive then, The. (LL)   I Am the People, the Mob.   Carl Sandburg.   IllVoic; OxBA; TAP

Mobile, The.   Sean Dunne.   ModIr   *Fr.* Sydney Place.

Mobile, immaculate and austere.   Pastoral, A.   Geoffrey Hill.   NPeEn

Möbius Strip-Tease.   Alec Derwent Hope.   OBCoV

Moby Dick.   Herman Melville.

"Ribs and terrors in the whale, The."   APN-2; ChIV-1

Moby grape jam on the stereo.   Some Sixties.   Ray Gonzalez.   MiVo

Mock Charon, A.   Richard Lovelace.   CaPo

Mock Invocation to Genius, A.   William Woty.

"I now solicit not the Muses nine."   NOEC

Mock On, Mock On, Voltaire, Rousseau.   William Blake.   ChIV-1; HAP; NAEL-5v2; NAEL-6v2; NAWM-7v2; NPeEn; NoP-4; OxBSP; PeECV; PoE; SCGP; TFi

(Scoffers, The.)   UnPo

Mock Orange.   Louise Glück.   MakPoe; NoAM; PoPoPo; VCAP

Mock Song, A.   Richard Lovelace.   BeJo; CaPo

Mock up again, summer, the sooty altars.   Spectacular Blossom.   Allen Curnow.   PeNZ

Mocking-Bird, The.   Joseph Rodman Drake.   APN-1

Mocking-Bird, The.   Richard Hovey.   APN-2

Mocking Bird, The.   Sidney Lanier.   APN-2; TCAPo

Mocking-bird on a branch, A.   Wyncote, Pennsylvania: A Gloss.   Thomas Kinsella.   NOIV

Mocking-Bird's Song, The.   *Unknown*.   APN-2, *tr. by* Alice C. Fletcher

Mocking Fairy, The.   Walter De la Mare.   MoBrPo

Mockingbird, The.   Charles Bukowski.   PmAP

Mockingbird, The.   Randall Jarrell.   OWoS

Mockingbird, knowing he owned the tree, The.   Bluejay and the Mockingbird, The.   Howard Nemerov.   BodElec

Mockingbird leans, A.   Letter to a Poet.   Robert Hass.   YaYoPo

Mockingbird Month.   Mona Van Duyn.   OWoS

Mode of France, The.   *Unknown*.   PBRV

Model, The.   May Probyn.   VWP

Model Children of the Regime, The.   Nguyễn Chí Thiện.   VCWP, *tr. by* Huynh Sanh Thông

Model Church, The.   John H. Yates.   PWR

Model School, Inchicore.   Thomas Kinsella.   CIP-2

Model yachts contend in seas sheltered, The.   Conservatory Pond, Central Park, New York, New York.   Joel Brouwer.   AmPoNex

Models.   Howard Nemerov.   AF

Moder Phoebe.   *Unknown*.   FaBoVe

Moderation.   Robert Herrick.   FaBoEE

Moderation.   Christopher Smart.   NOCV   *Fr.* Hymns for the Amusement of Children.

Moderato.   Susan Wicks.   MFPA

Modern circus, The.   Pierre McOrlan.   MFP, *tr. by* Martin Sorrell

Modern composer called Cage, A.   Limerick.   Peter Alexander.   PeLi

Modern Craft.   Hart Crane.   CAGL

Modern Critics.   Samuel Taylor Coleridge.   FaBoEE

Modern delinquents.   Vices of the Modern World.   Nicanor Parra.   CLPP, *tr. by* Jorge Elliott

Modern English.   Jeffery Conway.   WiU

Modern Female Fashions.   Mary Robinson.   NOBRP

Modern Fine Gentleman, The.   Soame Jenyns.

"Just broke from school, pert, impudent, and raw."   ECEV; OBSV

Modern Fine Lady, The.   Soame Jenyns.   NOEC

"But soon th'endearments of a husband cloy."   ECEV

"For love no time has she, or inclination."   OBSV

Modern Hiawatha, The.   George A. Strong.   OBCoV; PeLV; UV   *Fr.* Song of Milkanwatha, The.

Modern Love.   Douglas Dunn.   NPeEn

Modern Love.   John Keats.   SCGP

Modern Love.   George Meredith.

"Along the garden terrace, under which."   NOBVV

"At dinner, she is hostess, I am host."   NAEL-6v2; NOBVV; NPeEn; PoE; Son

"He felt the wild beast in him betweenwhiles."   NOBVV

"He found her by the ocean's moaning verge."   NAEL-6v2; NoP-4

"I am to follow her. There is much grace."   NAEL-5v2; NAEL-6v2; NOBVV

"I play for Seasons; not Eternities!"   SCGP

"I think she sleeps: it must be sleep, when low."   NAEL-5v2; NAEL-6v2

"In our old shipwrecked days there was an hour."   BoLoP; NAEL-6v2; NOBVV

"It chanced his lips did meet her forehead cool."   NOBVV

"It ended, and the morrow brought the task."   NAEL-6v2

"It is no vulgar nature I have wived."   NAEL-5v2; NAEL-6v2

"Madam would speak with me. So, now it comes."   NOBVV; NPeEn; OxBEV

"Mark where the pressing wind shoots javelin-like."   EnLoPo; NAEL-6v2; NOBE; OBEV; SCGP

"Message from her set his brain aflame, A."   NOBVV

"My lady unto Madam makes her bow."   NOBVV

"She issues radiant from her dressing-room."   NOBVV

Sonnet 29: "Am I failing? For no longer can I cast." SCGP

"Their sense is with their senses all mixed in." NAEL-5v2; NAEL-6v2; NoP-4; SCGP

"This golden head has wit in it. I live." NOBVV

"This was the woman; what now of the man?" NAEL-6v2; Son

"'Tis Christmas weather, and a country house." NAEL-5v2; NAEL-6v2; NOBVV

"We saw the swallows gathering in the sky." EnLoPo; GTBS-P; NOBE; NOBVV; OxBEV

"We three are on the cedar-shadowed lawn." NOBVV

"What are we first? First, animals; and next." CABP; HAP; NoP-4

"You like not that French novel? Tell me why." NOBVV

Modern Love. Anne Ridler. SacPr

Modern Love. Gerald Stern. BodElec

Modern Love Songs. *Unknown.* TTY, *tr.* by B. W. Andrejewski and I. M. Lewis

Modern Major-General, The. Sir William Schwenck Gilbert. *See* Pirates of Penzance, The

Modern malady of love is nerves, The. Nerves. Arthur Symons. CABP; FaBoTw

Modern Male Fashions. Mary Robinson. NOBRP

Modern Man I sing, The. (LL) One's-Self I Sing. Walt Whitman. ColAP; NOBA; OxBA; TCAPo

Modern Manners. Mary Alcock. ECWP

Modern Mother, The. Alice Thompson Meynell. VWP

Modern on the Surface. Nia Francisco. HATNAP

Modern Poet, The. Mary Davys.

"Behind the moth-eaten curtain, 'stead of press." ECWP

Modern Science has destroyed his reputation. Hyena, The. Cees Buddingh' TuT, *tr.* by John Hughes

Modern Secrets. Shirley Lim. OPOU; UnSA

Modern Times. Nicanor Parra. AF, *tr.* by Miller Williams

Modern Traveller, The. Joseph Hilaire Pierre Belloc.

Maxim Gun, The. FaBoWar

Modern World, The. Colin Ellis. FaBoEE

Modern young curate called Hyde, A. Limerick. D. W. Pain. PeLi

Modes of Vallejo Street, San Diego, Los Angeles, The. Hugh Seidman. UnPo

Modest chair people painted grey. People. Hans [or Jean] Arp. PFTM-1

Modest Love, A. Sir Edward Dyer. *See* Lowest Trees Have Tops, The

Modest Proposal, A. Ted Hughes. CABP

Modest rose puts forth a thorn, The. William Blake. FHYEP; NOBRP *Fr.* Songs of Experience.

Modest sinner stood behind, The. Navigation. Ralph Knevet. NOSC

Modest young maiden of Rennes, A. Limerick. A. C. Cossins. PeLi

Modesty. Aaron Hill. OxBSP

Modo and Alciphron. Sylvia Townsend Warner. MoBrPo

Modris. Peter Thabit Jones. AngWePo

Modris sits on the warm doorstep. Modris. Peter Thabit Jones. AngWePo

Moggy's Wedding. Charles Robert Thatcher. NOBAu

Mohács. Károly Kisfaludy.

"Sighing, O greet you and mourn you, O meadow of burial, Mohács." IQMS, *tr.* by Watson Kirkconnell

Mohawk lover who told her he stripped all his clothes, The. Deer Cloud. Susan Clements. UnSA

Mohini Chatterjee. W. B. Yeats. NoAM

Moi-Même. Carmen Bruna. SurWo, *tr.* by Natalie Kenvin

Moiré. Michael McClure. SPE

(The Chanting in Tibet Has Not Ceased— / It Is As Immortal As Meat.) SPE

Moishele, Moishele / Moses Maimonides. Double Dactyls. Eric Salzman. OBCoV

Moist, moist, / the heat leaking through the hinges. Anne Sexton. BodElec *Fr.* Furies, The.

Moist Moon People. Carl Sandburg. MoAmPo

Moist the jade dew that borders the flowers. Thinking of My Family on an Autumn Day. Yang Wen-li. WoPoe, *tr.* by Nancy Hodes and Tung Yuan-fang

Mokau roars, Tamaki roars. Lament for Tawhiao. *Unknown.* PeNZ, *tr.* by Margaret Orbell

Mokuboji Temple. Issa. ZenPo, *tr.* by Takashi Ikemoto and Lucien Stryk

Molasses River. Richard Kendall Munkittrick. OBCA

Moldering Hulk, The. Antonio Machado Ruiz. SpanPo, *tr.* by Kate Flores

Mole, The. Al-Muntafil. RaBo, *tr.* by Robert Bly

Mole, The. Nathan [or Natan] Alterman. FIT, *tr.* by Robert Friend

Mole, The. Christine D'Haen. TuT, *tr.* by Dennis O'Driscoll

Mole and the Eagle, The. Sarah Josepha Buell Hale. OBCA

Mole Catcher. Edmund Charles Blunden. OBMV

Mole is blind, and under ground, The. Mole and the Eagle, The. Sarah Josepha Buell Hale. OBCA

Mole makes his pole redhot. Alonzo Gonzales. STP

Mole who knows. Back to Base. Jenny Joseph. BrRo

Molino. Maggie Nelson. HeMarv

Moll-in-the-wad and I fell out. *Unknown.* OxNR

Molly Means. Margaret Abigail Walker. BlSi; NALW

Molly Mog [or The Fair Maid of the Inn]. John Gay. OBCoV

Molly Moor. George Farewell. NOEC

Molly, my sister and I fell out. Coffee and Tea. *Unknown.* ReMoGo

Molly O'Rourke Cleary Explains. Patricia Cleary Miller. SpudSo

Molly Pitcher. Laura Elizabeth Richards. HHAm

Mölna Elegy. Gunnar Ekelof.

Leavetaking. PFTM-2, *tr.* by Muriel Rukeyser and Leif Sjöberg

Marche Funèbre. PFTM-2, *tr.* by Muriel Rukeyser and Leif Sjöberg

Moly. Thom Gunn. CABP; HAP; NPeEn; NoAM

Mom and Dad Getting Older. Sarah Rosenblatt. AmPoNex

Mom and Dad have abandoned the family home and retired to Palm. Empress of Sighs. Beth Lisick. AmPoNex

Mom Did Marilyn, Dad Did Fred. Jack Myers. ReTh

Mom is smart. Fēng Mēng-lung. ColAnChí; WoPoe, *tr.* by Richard W. Bodman *Fr.* Mountain Songs.

Mom's in the kitchen telling stories. Vesta's Father. Julia Kasdorf. PBCAP

Mom says getting to the new home is a snap. Empress of Sighs. Beth Lisick. BAP-97

Moment. Hildegarde Flanner. APT-2

Moment. C. G. Hanzlicek. GeoHom

Moment, A. Mary Elizabeth Coleridge. LW; PEW

Moment, The. William Stafford. NNaP

Moment, The. Lőrinc Szabó. IQMS, *tr.* by Watson Kirkconnell *Fr.* Cricket Music.

Moment ago the shrill flute whistled in the bridal chamber, A. Philip of Thessalonica. GrAn

Moment and for ever, A. (LL) Félix Lope de Vega Carpio. HAP; WoPoe, *tr.* by Geoffrey Hill *Fr.* Pentecost Castle, The.

Moment comes to me, A. This Bridge Across. Christopher Gilbert. ESEAA; GT

Moment in the box of jade, A. Bob Boldman. HA

Moment of desire, The! the moment of desire! the virgin. William Blake. ErotSp; OxBEV *Fr.* Visions of the Daughters of Albion.

Moment of Eschatological Doubt, A. Stanley J. Sharpless. PeLV

Moment of Mourning, A. Donia El-Amal Ismail. PoArWo

Moment of My Father's Death, The. Sharon Olds. NIP-4

Moment of Truth. Rowley Habib. PeNZ

Moment of Waking, The. John Tranter. BMAP

Moment of War, A. Laurie Lee. OBWP

Moment Please, A. Samuel Allen. PAI; SSLK

Moment's memory to that laurelled head, A. (LL) Coole Park, 1929. W. B. Yeats. CABP; OBMV

Moment the wild swallows like a flight, A. Thunderstorm, A. Archibald Lampman. NOBC

Moment to / moment the / body seems. Time. Robert Creeley. LCAP-2

Moment yellow, just as four years later when, A. Lyn Hejinian. PmAP *Fr.* My Life.

Moments. Ivor Gurney. OxBSP

Moments. Marcel Schwob. TrJP, *tr.* by William Brown Meloney

Moments of Fulfillment—Writing Down Miscellaneous. Yüan Mei. CoBLCP, *tr.* by Jonathan Chaves

Moments of Ridicule and Love. Fawaz Turki. GraLe

Moments of Summer. Rachel Hadas. RA

Moments pass, The. Moment. C. G. Hanzlicek. GeoHom

Moments that hands without a vine . . . laughter. Ivano Fermini. ItPo, *tr.* by Gayle Ridinger

Momentum and wash of the undefined. Platonic Subject. Ann Lauterbach. PmAP

Momma a carrot grows underground. Potlicker Blues. Calvin Forbes. GT

Momma had words for us. Momma Sayings. Harryette Mullen. ISC; ItWoWo

Momma is a big-boned, Nordic looking. For the White Lady Holding Me. Crystal Williams. AmPoNex

Momma Momma Momma. Getting Down to Get Over. June Jordan. TAP

Momma Sayings. Harryette Mullen. ISC; ItWoWo

Momma told me to write to you today. Letter to Daddy, A. *Unknown, fr. Terezin Concentration Camp.* INSAB

Mommy. Jill Ciment. Unle

Mommy, take me home. I'm a changed boy! Ontogeny. Jarold Ramsey. NIP-4

Momus' Song to Mars. Dryden. OxBSP *Fr.* Secular Masque, The.

Mon in the mone stond and strit. Man in the Moon. *Unknown.* MiEL

Mona Lisa. Ray Evans. ReLy

Mona Lisa. Walter Pater. OBMV

Mona Lisa. Edith Wharton. GS

Mona Lisa, A. Angelina Weld Grimké. APT-1; BlSi

Mona Lisa Tea Towel, The. Nigel Roberts. BMAP

Monadnoc. Ralph Waldo Emerson.
  "Every morn I lift my head." APN-1

Monangamba. Antonio Jacinto. TTY

Monarch of Gods and Dæmons, and all Spirits. Shelley. NAEL-5v2; NAEL-6v2; NOBRP

Monarch of Han, he doted on beauty, yearned for a bewitching temptress. Song of Lasting Regret, The. Po Chü-i. ColAnChi, *tr. by* Paul W. Kroll

Monarch of the Sea. George Starbuck. OBAL

Monarche, The. Sir David Lindsay [*or* Lyndsay].
  After the Flood. ChIV-1; OxBS

Monarchs of Parque Tranquilidad. Robin Becker. UrbNat

Monarchs Steering. Shirley Lim. GeoHom

Monasteries Lift Gold Domes, The. Yocheved Bat-Miriam. FIT, *tr. by* Robert Friend

Monastery. Yevgeny [*or* Evgenii] Borisovich Rein. TCRusP, *tr. by* Daniel Weissbort

Monastery, The. Pure Sound Pavilion of the Riverside Temple, The. Muso Soseki. EaWin, *tr. by* W. S. Merwin

Monastic Poems: Four Glosses. *Unknown.* *See* Four Glosses

Mond ist aufgegangen, Der. Heinrich Heine. AWP, *tr. by* James Thomson

Monday. Romelia Alarcón de Folgar. TANSG, *tr. by* Alison Ridley

Monday. Week in the Life of the Ethnically Indeterminate, A. Elena Georgiou. WiU

Monday. Vijaya Mukhopadhyay. OMIP, *tr. by* Vijaya Mukhopadhyay, Sunil B. Ray and Carolyne Wright

Monday a boy who cannot lift. Space. Maura Stanton. OPRER

Monday evening, E. 22nd. Lilacs in NYC. Mark Doty. WiU

Monday has the long face. Monday. Romelia Alarcón de Folgar. TANSG, *tr. by* Alison Ridley

Monday I found a boot. Beachcomber. George Mackay Brown. OxBC

Monday, Monday. David Trinidad. SwNoth

Monday Morning. Audrey Shafer. BloBone

Monday morning broke. Rub a Dub Style inna Regent Park. Lillian Allen. WaCA

Monday Night at Pedro's. Sandra M. Castillo. TouFir

Monday night was for doing the brasses. Portrait in a Brass Gong. Mick North. NLP

Monday rue Christine. Guillaume Apollinaire. CuPo

Monday's child is fair of face. Birthdays. Mother Goose. FaBoCh; LB; NBLV; OTCP; OxNR

Mondays are meshed with Tuesdays. Too Many Names. Pablo Neruda. VCWP, *tr. by* Alastair Reid

Mondays my aunt awoke with the first cockcrow, in the orange dawn. Those Rainy Mornings. Frank Mkalawile Chipasula. HBAPE

Monet: "Les Nymphéas." W. D. Snodgrass. CoAP; CoAmPo

Monet never knew. Monet's Lilies Shuddering. Lawrence Ferlinghetti. PmAP

Monet Refuses the Operation. Lisel Mueller. IllVoic

Monet's Lilies Shuddering. Lawrence Ferlinghetti. PmAP

Monet's "Waterlilies." Robert Earl Hayden. AmFaPo; GT

Monet tires of painting lilies. From Where I Stand. Elena Georgiou. WiU

Money. Richard Armour. NBLV

Money. William Henry Davies. OBEV; OBMV

Money. Philip Larkin. NPeEn

Money. Howard Nemerov. OxBC; VCAP; WeW-3

Money. Bob Perelman. FTOS

Money. Charles Hubert Sisson. OxBSP

Money and the Mare. *Unknown.* ReMoGo

Money burns the pocket, pocket hurts. Seventh Street. Jean Toomer. APT-2; NAAL-2v2

Money Gets the Mastery [*or* Masterie]. Robert Herrick. CaPo

Money Is What Matters. *Unknown.* MiEL

Money Isn't Everything! Oscar Hammerstein, II. OBAL

Money Makes the Mirth. Robert Herrick. CaPo

Money men collect in high rise, The. Thumbing Old Magazines. Gerald Vizenor. VoR

Money, Money. *Unknown.* CABP; MiEL

Money, money, now hay goode day! Money, Money. *Unknown.* CABP; MiEL

Money Song, The. Harold Rome. ReLy

Money thou ow'st me; prithee fix a day. Upon Bunce: Epigram. Robert Herrick. CaPo

Mongo's open hands. Shaking Hands with Mongo. Martín Espada. SeSe

Mongoloid boy is astounded, The. In the Dome Car of the "Canadian." Sid Marty. NOBC

Mongoloid Child Handling Shells on the Beach, A. Richard Snyder. InPK-6; NIL-7

Monitors. Geoffrey Holloway. NLP

Monk. John Taggart. FTOS; PFTM-2

Monk, The. Thomas Kinsella. BBASP

Monk and the Peasant, The. Margaret E. Bruner. PoToHe

Monk Arnulphus uncorked his ink, The. Court Historian, The. George Walter Thornbury. PeVV

Monk at the Five Spot. Crepuscule with Nellie. Charles Simic. SeSe

Monk Chun of Shu with a Green Brocade Lute. Listening to the Lute Played by Monk Chun from Shu. Li Po. ChinPo, *tr. by* Yip Wai-lim

Monk from Shu, carrying a precious lute. Listening to a Monk from Shu Playing the Lute. Li Po. SuSp, *tr. by* Joseph J. Lee

Monk from Shu with his green lute-case walked, The. Listening to a Monk from Shu Playing the Lute. Li Po. WoPoe, *tr. by* Vikram Seth

Monk in the Kitchen, The. Anna Hempstead Branch. APT-1; MoAmPo

Monk of Auspicious Fortune Monastery Asking Me to Name a Pavilion, A. Su Tung-p'o (Su Shih). SuSp, *tr. by* Chiang Yee

Monk of Casal-Maggiore (The Sicilian's Tale), The. Henry Wadsworth Longfellow. OxBA *Fr.* Tales of a Wayside Inn.

Monk's dissonant hat. Bandstand. Michael S. Harper. SeSe

Monk's Dream. Dave Etter. SeSe

Monk's robe hangs in a cloister in the hills, A. Paying a Visit to Monk Yung's Cloister. Meng Hao Jan. SuSp, *tr. by* Joseph J. Lee

Monk sat in his den, The. Weak Monk, The. Stevie Smith. BoWoP; FaBoTw

Monk sips morning tea, A. Basho. EH, *tr. by* Robert Hass

Monk, step further off. *Unknown.* NOIV

Monk ther was, a fair for the maistrye [*or* maistrie], A. Geoffrey Chaucer. OBCoV *Fr.* Canterbury Tales, The.

Monk was preaching: strong his earnest word, The. Legend, A. Adelaide Anne Procter. SacPr

Monkey. Vladislav Felitsianovich Khodasevich. TCRusP, *tr. by* Daniel Weissbort

Monkey. Vladislav Felitsianovich Khodasevich. TCRP, *tr. by* Michael Frayn

Monkey. Bruce Weigl. CDa

Monkey and the Lion, The. Signifying Monkey, The. *Unknown.* NAAAL

Monkey cries accompany the dawn. Crossing the Mountain, I Follow the Chin-chu River. Hsieh Ling-yün. CrYelRi, *tr. by* Sam Hamill

Monkey-eaters. Takahashi Mutsuo. PFTM-2, *tr. by* Hiroaki Sato

Monkey exclaimed with great glee, A. Limerick. Frank Richards. PeLi

Monkey, lap-dog, parrot, and her Grace, The. Sir Charles Hanbury Williams. NOEC *Fr.* Isabella; or, The Morning.

Monkey's Pride. John Forbes. BMAP

Monkeyland. Sándor Weöres. IQMS; RB; WoPoe, *tr. by* Edwin Morgan

Monkeys. Padraic Colum. OxBTC

Monkeys, The. Marianne Craig Moore. APT-1; NOBA; OxBA

Monkeys at the laboratory. Do Not Put Dead Monkeys in the Freezer. Martín Espada. TouFir

Monkeys cry: dawn, they know. From Chin-Chu Creek, Past the Ridge, along the Stream. Hsieh Ling-yün. ChinPo, *tr. by* Yip Wai-lim

Monkeys on Mt. Hiei. Edith Marcombe Shiffert. WPE

Monkeys winked too much and were afraid of snakes, The. Monkeys, The. Marianne Craig Moore. OxBA

Monkeys' world the world we face, The. (LL) Monkeyland. Sándor Weöres. IQMS; RB; WoPoe, *tr. by* Edwin Morgan

Monks. Palladas [*or* Palladus]. GrAn, *tr. by* Peter Jay

Monks recite the sutras in honor of the Founder. Face to Face with My Lover on Daito's Anniversary. Ikkyu Sojun. ErotSp, *tr. by* Sam Hamill

Monmouth. Dryden. NPeEn *Fr.* Absalom and Achitophel.

Monna Innominata. Christina Georgina Rossetti. BWW
  "Come back to me, who wait and watch for you." OxBSo
  "I dream of you to wake: would that I might." OxBSo
  "I, if I perish, perish"—Esther spake." OxBSo
  "I loved you first: but afterwards your love." OxBSo
  "I wish I could remember the [*or* that] first day." BoLoP; LW; OxBSo; Son
  "If there be any one can take my place." OxBSo
  "Love me, for I love you"—and answer me." OxBSo; Son
  "Many in aftertimes will say of you." CABP; MakPoe; OxBSo
  "O my heart's heart, and you who are to me." OxBSo
  "Thinking of you, and all that was, and all." OxBSo
  "Time flies, hope flags, life plies a wearied wing." OxBSo
  "Trust me, I have not earned your dear rebuke." OxBSo
  "Youth gone, and beauty gone if ever there." GSo; OxBSo; Son

Monodrama. Bill Knott. BodElec

Monody. Herman Melville. APN-2; NAAL-2v1; NAAL-3; NoP-4; OxBSP; PoE; PoPoPo; TCAPo

Monody on Doctor Olmsted. Edgar Allan Poe. TCAPo

Monogamy. Gerald Louis Gould.
  "You were young—but that was scarcely to your credit." OxBTC

Monogram 4. Martina Werner. BoWoP, *tr. by* Rosmarie Waldrop

Monogram 23. Martina Werner. BoWoP, *tr. by* Rosmarie Waldrop

Monogram 29. Martina Werner. BoWoP, *tr. by* Rosmarie Waldrop

Monologue. Gottfried Benn. AF, *tr. by* Christopher Middleton

Monologue. Hone Tuwhare. PeNZ

Monologue at the Chinook Bar and Grill. Tess Gallagher. BodElec

Monologue for Cassandra. Wislawa Szymborska. PoSu, *tr. by* Grazyna Drabik

Monologue in a Rand Hospital. William Elijah Hunter. PeSAV

Monologue of a Blue Fox. Yevgeny Aleksandrovich Yevtushenko [*or* Evtushenko]. TCRP, *tr. by* Albert C. Todd and John Updike

Monologue of a Dying Beast. Mark Ameen. GLP

Monologue of the Falconer's Wife. Colette Inez. PuP-23

Monologue of the Magdalene. John Peck. HarvBoo

Monologue: The Last Judgment. Henry Wadsworth Longfellow. *Fr.* Michael Angelo: A Fragment.

Monologue with Commentary. Andrey [*or* Andrei] Andreievich Voznesensky [*or* Voznesenskii]. RusPo, *tr. by* Robert Arthur Douglas Ford

Monotomy. Gabriella Sica. CItWP, *tr. by* Cinzia Sartini Blum and Lara Trubowitz

Monotones. B. P. Nichol. FTOS; PFTM-2 *Fr.* Martyrology 7, The.

Monotonies of my retinas. Processions, The. Mário de Andrade. TCLAP, *tr. by* Jack E. Tomlins

Monotony Song, The. Theodore Roethke. ChAP

Monsieur Étienne de Silhouette. Some Frenchmen. John Updike. NBLV

Monsieur Ezra Pound croit que. Another Canto. John Bingham Morton. UV

Monsieur Gaston. Abraham Moses Klein. MoCV

Monsieur Gauguin? 'E's gone to Tahiti. Limerick. Stanley J. Sharpless. PeLi

Monsieur, your ribcage. Man without a Middle, The. Angela Sorby. AmPoNex

Monsoon Day Fable, A. Jayanta Mahapatra. VCWP

Monsoon Girl. Harry Clifton. BiHa; PBCIP

Monster, The. Karen L. Mitchell. GT

Monster, in a course of vice grown old, A. Monument, The. Samuel Wesley. OxBSP

Monster's Dream, The. William Reichard. AmPoNex

Monstrance. János Pilinszky. PoSu, *tr. by* Peter Jay

Monstrous Pictures of Whales. Dennis Schmitz. GeoHom

Mont Blanc. Shelley. NAEL-5v2; NAEL-6v2; NIP-4; NOBRP; NoP-4

Montague Michael. *Unknown.* OTCP

Montalbert. Charlotte Smith.
  On Passing Over a Dreary Tract of Country, and Near the Ruins of a Deserted Chapel, during a Tempest. BoWoP; WPE

Montana Pastoral. James Vincent Cunningham. APT-2; MoAmPo; VGW

Monterey. David Schubert. APT-2

Monterrey Sun. Alfonso Reyes. TCLAP, *tr. by* Samuel Beckett

Montezuma. Diane Di Prima. BB

Month gone and the day coming up like a bad cold, The. Saturday 6 A.M. Charles Wright. GeoHom

Month of January. Frankie Armstrong. BrRo

Month of plants and of honey. Alexander MacDonald. NePenScot, *tr. by* Derick Thomson *Fr.* Song of Summer.

Month of rain ends. Tanka. Lenard D. Moore. SpirFl

Month of roses. And my rhymes. Spring. "Rubén Darío." SpanPo, *tr. by* Anita Volland

Month of roses. My poems. Springtime. "Rubén Darío." TCLAP, *tr. by* Lysander Kemp

Month of the drowned dog, The. After long rain the land. November. Ted Hughes. GTBS-P

Month or twain to live on honeycomb, A. Before Parting. Algernon Charles Swinburne. NOBVV

Month she died, The. Ein Leben. Dan Pagis. FIT, *tr. by* Robert Friend

Month-Verses. Ludwig Goldscheider. AuPH, *tr. by* Lowell A. Bangerter

Months, The. *Unknown.* MiEL

Months and years have flown. Passing through Ch'ien-hsi, Third Month, 405. T'ao Ch'ien [*or* T'ao Yuan-ming]. CrYelRi, *tr. by* Sam Hamill

Months Go By, The. *Unknown.* OHMPC, *tr. by* Kenneth Rexroth

Months go by like water in a waterfall, The. Months Go By, The. *Unknown.* OHMPC, *tr. by* Kenneth Rexroth

Months of Love, The. Jack Marshall. GraLe

Months of the Year, The. Richard Grafton. MiEL

Montreal. Abraham Moses Klein. MoCV

Montrose to His Mistress. James Graham, Marquess of Montrose. *See* My Dear and Only Love

Monument, A. Vladislav Felitsianovich Khodasevich. TCRusP, *tr. by* John Glad

Monument, A. Charles Madge. FaBoMo

Monument, The. Elizabeth Bishop. HCAP; NOBA; NoAM; TRP

Monument, The. Vladislav Felitsianovich Khodasevich. TCRP, *tr. by* Michael Frayn

Monument, The. Yaroslav [*or* Iaroslav] Vasilevich Smelyakov [*or* Smeliakov]. TCRP, *tr. by* Simon Franklin

Monument, The. Samuel Wesley. OxBSP

Monument of Cleita, The. Edward Cracroft Lefroy. AWP *Fr.* Echoes from Theocritus.

Monument to Birds (Max Ernst). Luiza Neto Jorge. SurWo, *tr. by* Jean R. Longland

Monumental Memorial of Marine Mercy, A. Richard Steere. SCAP; TCAPo

Monuments, The. John Ash. EmeKit

Monuments for a Friendly Girl at a Tenth Grade Party. William Stafford. NoAM

Monuments of Hiroshima, The. Dennis Joseph Enright. OxBSP

Monumentum Aere, Etc. Ezra Pound. NOBA

Mony ane talks o the grass, the grass. Willie and Earl Richard's Daughter. *Unknown.* ESPB

Mony klyf he overclambe in contrayes straunge. *Unknown.* FaBoVe *Fr.* Sir Gawain and the Green Knight.

Moo! Robert Silliman Hillyer. OBAL

Moochie. Eloise Greenfield. NTCP

Moochkap. Boris Leonidovich Pasternak. TCRusP, *tr. by* Bogdan Boychuk and Mark Rudman

Mood Apart, A. Robert Frost. OxBSP

Mood comes on—I want to cross Hsi-ling, The. Tao-chi. CoBLCP

Mood Indigo. William Matthews. WeW-3

Mood of Vichy, The. Hildebert. MLL, *tr. by* Helen Waddell

Moods. Leyb [*or* Leib] Kvitko [*or* Kwitko]. TrJP, *tr. by* Joseph Leftwich

Moods. Sara Teasdale. APT-1

Moods, The. W. B. Yeats. CTC

Moody child and wildly wise, A. Motto to "The Poet." Ralph Waldo Emerson. NCAP

Mooimeisjes. Perceval Gibbon. PeSAV

Mooly cow, mooly cow, home from the wood. Cow-Boy's Song, The. Anna Maria Wells. OBCA; OxIBACP

Mooly cow only said, "Moo-o-o!", The. (LL) Cow-Boy's Song, The. Anna Maria Wells. OBCA; OxIBACP

Moon. Nathan [*or* Natan] Alterman. FIT, *tr. by* Robert Friend

Moon. Nathan [*or* Natan] Alterman. MHP, *tr. by* Ruth Finer Mintz

Moon. Nicolás Guillén. PFTM-1

Moon. Frances Horovitz. BrRo

Moon. Peggy Lyles. HA

Moon. Giovanni Raboni. ItPo, *tr. by* Gayle Ridinger

Moon. Henry Rowe. OBEV

Moon. Shinkichi Takahashi. ZenPo, *tr. by* Takashi Ikemoto and Lucien Stryk

Moon, The. Abraham a Santa Clara. AuPH, *tr. by* George C. Schoolfield

Moon, The. Witter Bynner. APT-1

Moon, The. (LL) Niagara. Adelaide Crapsey. APT-1; PAI

Moon, The. Robert Creeley. VGW

Moon, The. William Henry Davies. MoBrPo

Moon, The. Robert Duncan. APSN *Fr.* Passages.

Moon, The. Gunnar Ekelof. AWTN, *tr. by* Robert Bly

Moon, The. Hsüeh T'ao. SuSp, *tr. by* Eric W. Johnson

Moon, The. Hans Just. AuPH, *tr. by* Lowell A. Bangerter

Moon, The. Shelley. *See* Waning Moon, The

Moon, The. Martha Silano. AmPoNex

Moon, The. Robert Louis Stevenson. PWR; TLR

Moon, The. *Unknown.* FaBoVe

Moon, a ring of crimson snapped in two, The. Long-Barrow Princess 2. Elizaveta Kuzmina-Karavayeva. ARWW, *tr. by* Catriona Kelly

Moon, a sweeping scimitar, dipped in the stormy straits, The. Winged Man. Stephen Vincent Benét. MoAmPo

Moon about Town. Dana Suesse. ReLy

Moon above the milky field, The. Night-Piece. Léonie Adams. MoAmPo

Moon and a Cloud, The. William Henry Davies. RB

Moon and Candle-light. William Renton. NOBVV

Moon and clouds are the same. Wu-Men. EnlH

Moon and Farmstead. Sándor Weöres. IQMS, *tr. by* Edwin Morgan

Moon and Hare. Shinkichi Takahashi. ZenPo, *tr. by* Takashi Ikemoto and Lucien Stryk

Moon and seven Pleiades have set, The. Alone. Sappho. AWP, *tr. by* William Ellery Leonard

Moon and Spectator, The. Léonie Adams. APT-2

Moon and the flowers, The. Issa. EH; NIL-7, *tr. by* Robert Hass

Moon and the Night and the Men, The. John Berryman. CoAP; VCAP; VGW

Moon and the Nightingale, The. John Milton. *See* Paradise Lost

Moon and the Pleiades have set, The. Sappho. SaLy, *tr. by* Diane Rayor

Moon and the Salt Flats, The. Mary Di Michele. NOBC

Moon and the Yew Tree, The. Sylvia Plath. BBASP; CoAP; FaBoMo; FaBoWP; VGW; WPE; WPOW

Moon / Another hour has come through the opening. Sentry. Dennis Saleh. GeoHom

Moon appears from the mouth of the sheer bluff, The. Aboard a Boat at Night, Drinking with My Wife. Mei Yao Ch'en. CoBCP, *tr. by* Burton Watson

Moon at dawn, The. John Wills. HA

Moon at Sea. Nikolai Stepanovich Gumilyov [*or* Gumiliov *or* Gumilev]. TCRusP, *tr. by* Mary Jane White

Moon at the full. Europe has burst its banks. Inundation, The. Howard Sergeant. SPE

Moon at the window. Rosamond Haas. HA

Moon at Three A.M. Lance Henson. CDW

Moon became mired on our bed, The. Ana Istarú. TANSG, *tr. by* Mary Jane Treacy

Moon behind High Tranquil Leaves, The. Robert Malise Bowyer Nichols. OBMV

Moon blackens, geese fly high. Lu Lun. SuSp *Fr.* Frontier Songs.

Moon-Bone Song [*or* Cycle]. *Aborigine Oral Tradition.* CBAP, *tr. by* R. M. Berndt

Moon Bound. Raymond Washington. NBV

Moon Came Late, The. Mary Mapes Dodge. SWaP

Moon came late to a lonesome bog, The. Moon Came Late, The. Mary Mapes Dodge. SWaP

Moon comes from the blue sky, The. Moon in a Winecup, The. Shen Chou. CoBLCP, *tr. by* Jonathan Chaves

Moon Compasses. Robert Frost. ITBLP

Moon cuts through, The. Somewhere near Phu Bai. Yusef Komunyakaa. CDa

Moon departs, The. Kato. JDP, *tr. by* Yoel Hoffmann

Moon does shine as bright as day. (LL) Namby-Pamby. A Panegyric on the New Versification, Address'd to A——— P———, Esq. Henry Carey. NOEC; NPeEn; OBSV; UV

Moon drops one or two feathers into the field, The. Beginning. James Wright. ColAP; VCAP

Moon Eclipse Exorcism. *Unknown.* STP; WoPoe, *tr. by* Armand Schwerner

Moon Fable. Otto Stoessl. AuPH, *tr. by* Lowell A. Bangerter

Moon fades into dawn. J. W. Hackett. HA

Moon falls in shape of little metal plates against my face. Remembrance of the Founts of Night. Theo Van Doesburg. PFTM-1

Moon Festival. Tu Fu. OHPC, *tr. by* Kenneth Rexroth

Moon Fishing. Lisel Mueller. CoAP

Moon flashes in Her blessed face, The. Mahārāja Rāmkrsna Rāy. SinGod, *tr. by* Rachel Fell McDermott

Moon, Flowers, Man. Su Tung-p'o (Su Shih). OHPC, *tr. by* Kenneth Rexroth

Moon Folly. Fannie Stearns Gifford. RACG *Fr.* Songs of Conn the Fool, The.

Moon had risen an hour or more, The. Crescent Moon. William Renton. NOBVV

Moon hangs on a clouded sky, The. Clouded Sky. Miklós Radnóti. GifTon; HP, *tr. by* Stephen Berg, S. J. Marks, F. J. Marks and Steven Polgar

Moon has a face like the clock in the hall, The. Moon, The. Robert Louis Stevenson. PWR; TLR

Moon has a halo, there will be wind, The. I Remember the Blue River. Mei Yao Ch'en. OHPC, *tr. by* Kenneth Rexroth

Moon has already left the cliffs, The. Moon at Sea. Nikolai Stepanovich Gumilyov [*or* Gumiliov *or* Gumilev]. TCRusP, *tr. by* Mary Jane White

Moon has fallen on her back, The. Night-Piece. Frances Horovitz. LW

Moon has gone to her rest, The. Nocturne. Wilfrid Scawen Blunt. OBMV

Moon Has Set, The. Sappho. WoPoe, *tr. by* Jim Powell

Moon Has Set, The. Sappho. PGA; WoPoe, *tr. by* Kenneth Rexroth

Moon-Hops. Ted Hughes. CABP

Moon hung low 'mid clouds enshrined, The. Fading Skiff, The. Henrietta Cordelia Ray. CBWP-3

Moon in a barrel. Mabutsu. JDP, *tr. by* Yoel Hoffmann

Moon in a blue sky, morning loneliness, the need to have children. Blue Sky in Morning. Rob MacKenzie. Oth

Moon in a Winecup, The. Shen Chou. CoBLCP, *tr. by* Jonathan Chaves

Moon in her new era, The. CXLII. Pita Amor. TANSG, *tr. by* Shaun Griffin and Emma Sepúlveda-Pulvirenti

Moon, in her pride, once glanced aside, The. Moon Sings, The. *Unknown.* OxBoLi

Moon in midsky, high. Buson. SoOfWa, *tr. by* Sam Hamill

Moon in the bureau mirror, The. Insomnia. Elizabeth Bishop. AWTN

Moon in the pond, The. Missing France. Jules Supervielle. MFP, *tr. by* Martin Sorrell

Moon in the sky, floating overhead. On My Pneumonia. Mihály Csokonai Vitéz. IQMS, *tr. by* Joseph Leftwich

Moon in your eyes is best, The. Tracking Rabbits: Night. Jim Barnes. CDW

Moon in Your Hands, The. "H. D." APT-1; BoWoP; FaBoWP *Fr.* Sigil.

Moon is a poor woman, The. Sidney Keyes. NoP-4; OBWP *Fr.* Foreign Gate, The.

Moon is a sow, The. Song for Ishtar. Denise Levertov. NALW; NoAM; PoM

Moon is a white sliver, The. I Am Singing Now. Luci Tapahonso. UnSA

Moon is able to command the valley tonight, The. Moist Moon People. Carl Sandburg. MoAmPo

Moon Is Always Female, The. Marge Piercy. NoAM

Moon is an exile, The. Niyi Osundare. HBAPE *Fr.* Moonsongs.

Moon is an ivory tusk in the Utah sky, The. Moon and the Salt Flats, The. Mary Di Michele. NOBC

Moon is at her full, and, riding high, The. Tides, The. William Cullen Bryant. TAP

Moon is cold over the sand-dunes, The. Shore Grass. Amy Lowell. APT-1

Moon is coming up the blue sky, The. Wine Cup and Bright Moon. Shen Chou. SuSp, *tr. by* Irving Y. Lo

Moon is distant from the Sea, The. Emily Dickinson. TCAPo

Moon is eaten and renewed, The. Lunar Games, The. Eeva-Liisa Manner. WPOW, *tr. by* Jaakko A. Ahokas

Moon is full, The. Bob Marley's Dead. Rachel Manley. WaCA

Moon is full, The. *Unknown.* OHMPJ

Moon is fully risen, The. Mond ist aufgegangen, Der. Heinrich Heine. AWP, *tr. by* James Thomson

Moon is not green cheese, The. Night Light. Nancy Willard. LCAP-2

Moon is one, The. Teaching Numbers. Gary Soto. NOxBChV

Moon is out this morning, The. P. M. T. Dorothy Porter. BMAP

Moon Is Rising, The. *Unknown.* TAL

Moon is sick, The. Panic of Birds, The. Olena Kalytiak Davis. AmPoNex

Moon is singing eloquently, The. Sea Song. Luis Omar Salinas. GeoHom

Moon is so high it is, The. I Walk Out into the Country at Night. Lu Yu. OHPC, *tr. by* Kenneth Rexroth

Moon is the companion, The. To the Tune "The Southerner." Yang Shen. CoBLCP, *tr. by* Jonathan Chaves

Moon is the mother of pathos and pity, The. Lunar Paraphrase. Wallace Stevens. SAmP

Moon Is the Number 18, The. Charles Olson. APT-2; HarvBoo; PFTM-2; PoE

Moon is tied to a few strings, The. Cardplayers, The. Jack Spicer. APSN

Moon Is to Blood. Richard Duerden. NeAP

Moon Landing. W. H. Auden. EmeKit; OxAEP-2

Moon leaks out, The. Tanko. JDP, *tr. by* Yoel Hoffmann

Moon/light quarter/back sack. Samuel F. Reynolds. SpirFl

Moon-like Is All Other Love. *Unknown.* NOCV, *tr. by* Donald Davie

Moon lives in all the alone places, The. Meditations on the Moon. Paula Gunn Allen. HATNAP

Moon makes a sign, The. Another wave comes in. Beach, Later. Dennis Saleh. GeoHom

Moon-Man. Dorothy Hewett. CBAP

Moon, moon / Mak' me a pair o'shoon. *Unknown.* OxNR

Moon Mountain. Muso Soseki. EaWin, *tr. by* W. S. Merwin

Moon moves up the outback ridge and they turn chewing. Flying Kangaroos. Coral Hull. PoCoUp

Moon must freeze up there at night. Moon Fable. Otto Stoessl. AuPH, *tr. by* Lowell A. Bangerter

Moon nails a long horn, The. Second Anniversary. Federico García Lorca. SpanPo, *tr. by* Rachel Benson and Robert O'Brien

Moon, neither full nor crescent, leans, The. Expatriates. Sharif Elmusa. GraLe

Moon never lets me down, The. Notes on a Moonwatcher. Kenneth Gangemi. PoCoUp

Moon now from old Avon's stream, The. Rural Lyre, The. Ann Yearsley. RWP

Moon of Huckleberries. Phillip [*or* "Phil"] William George. VoR

Moon of Id came, The. Nur, Empress Jahan. BoWoP, *tr. by* Willis Barnstone

Moon of Mobile, The. Thomas Holley Chivers. OBAL

Moon on the Cold Flood Festival. Tu Fu. CrYelRi, *tr. by* Sam Hamill

Moon on the one hand, the dawn on the other, The. Early Morning, The. Joseph Hilaire Pierre Belloc. OxBSP; Spl; TLR

Moon over Mountain Pass. Li Po. SuSp, *tr. by* Joseph J. Lee

Moon over Prague. Vitězslav Nezval. AF, *tr. by* Ewald Osers

Moon over the Mountain Pass, The. Li Po. TAL

Moon passes her hands softly over my eyes. Moon, The. Gunnar Ekelof. AWTN, *tr. by* Robert Bly

Moon penny bright as silver. Moon, The. *Unknown.* FaBoVe

Moon plays horn, leaning on the shoulder of the dark universe, The. Bird. Joy Harjo. SeSe

Moon, plum blossoms. Issa. EH, *tr. by* Robert Hass

Moon Poem. Max Jacob. AF, *tr. by* Michael Brownstein

Moon Poems. John Wieners. VGW

Moon, Rain, Riverbank. Tu Fu. CrYelRi, *tr. by* Sam Hamill

Moon rattles like a fragment of angry candy. (LL) Cambridge ladies who live in furnished souls, The. E. E. Cummings. HeIP-4; MakPoe; NAAL-2v2; NOBA; NoAM; NoP-4; OBAL; OxBA; PAI; TAP; TCAPo

Moon Rises, The. Federico García Lorca. TTTS, *tr. by* William Bryant Logan

Moon rises, a vengeance on anguish, The. Sleepwalkers. Bella [*or* Izabella] Akhatovna Akhmadulina. BoWoP, *tr. by* Barbara Einzig

Moon rises as Shizu rises from her couch, The. Earth Quake. Ruth Stone. ExTi

Moon rises over White Heron Island, The. Farewell to Yin Shu. Li Po. CrYelRi, *tr. by* Sam Hamill

Moon River. Johnny Mercer. ReLy

Moon River. Joe Wenderoth. NAPBL

Moon River / Wider than a mile. Moon River. Johnny Mercer. ReLy

Moon rolls over the roof and falls behind, The. Continuum. Allen Curnow. HarvBoo

Moon rows burning, The. Nocturn. Herman Van den Bergh. TuT

Moon's a devil jester, The. Traveler, The. Nicholas Vachel Lindsay. MoAmPo

Moon's a little arch, The. Classic Case, A. Gilbert Sorrentino. NeAP

Moon's a path, The. Hansel, Gretel and Ruby Redlips. Anita Endrezze. HATNAP

Moon's Bed, the Bride's Bed, The. W. S. Rendra. WoPoe, *tr. by* Burton Raffel

Moon's brightness turns a freezing blue, The. Hayim Lenski. FIT, *tr. by* Robert Friend

Moon's Cadaver, The. Clara Silva. TANSG, *tr. by* Celeste Kostopulos-Cooperman

Moon's dropped child!, The. (LL) Fame. Charlotte Mew. BrRo; HarvBoo; InPK-6; NPeEn; VWP

Moon's Ending. Sara Teasdale. APT-1

Moon's glow by seven fold multiplied, turned red. After Reading St. John the Divine. Gene Derwood. WPE

Moon's left town. Moon's clean gone. (LL) Arizona Nature Myth. James Michie. FaBoA; NOBL

Moon's my constant mistress, The. Tom o' Bedlam. *Unknown.* FaBoCh; PoRA

Moon's on the lake, and the mist's on the brae, The. MacGregor's Gathering. Sir Walter Scott. OxBS

Moon's the North Wind's Cooky, The. Nicholas Vachel Lindsay. OBCA; OxIBACP

Moon's the same old moon, The. Bunan. ZenPo, *tr. by* Takashi Ikemoto and Lucien Stryk

Moon's up-riding makes a line, The. Night Scenes. Robert Duncan. VGW

Moon Sails Out, The. Federico García Lorca. AmFaPo, *tr. by* Robert Bly

Moon set, a crow caws. Maple Bridge Night Mooring. Chang Chi. ColAnChi, *tr. by* Gary Snyder

Moon sets, The. A crow caws. Night at Anchor by Maple Bridge. Chang Chi. OHMPC, *tr. by* Kenneth Rexroth

Moon setting, crows cawing, frost filling the sky. Tying Up for the Night at Maple River Bridge. Chang Chi. CoBCP, *tr. by* Burton Watson

Moon Shadow. George Bowering. MoCV

Moon-Shadows. Adelaide Crapsey. APT-1

Moon Shatters on Alabama Avenue, The. Martín Espada. PueRic

Moon shines bright, The. *Unknown.* OxNR

Moon shines on valley. *Unknown.* WoPoe, *tr. by* Anselm Hollo *Fr.* Three Gypsy Songs.

Moon shines while billions. Moon. Shinkichi Takahashi. ZenPo, *tr. by* Takashi Ikemoto and Lucien Stryk

Moon Sings, The. *Unknown.* OxBoLi

Moon Sings to the Stream, The. Leah Goldberg. MHP, *tr. by* Ruth Finer Mintz *Fr.* Songs of the Stream.

Moon Song. Chuba Nweke. PBA

Moon, Sun, Sleep, Birds, Live. Kenneth Patchen. WeW-3

Moon-talk. Edgell Rickword. OxBSo

Moon that nights will through your window glow, The. Moon, The. Hans Just. AuPH, *tr. by* Lowell A. Bangerter

Moon, that peeped as she came up, The. Nailsworth Hill. William Henry Davies. OTCP

Moon, the dried weeds, The. William Carlos Williams. APT-1

Moon: the lighted hall of a bell. Personal Atlas. Rosalie Moore. YaYoPo

Moon, the year is over. Remembering Leopardi's Moon. Giacomo Leopardi. WoPoe, *tr. by* Stephen Berg

Moon; then turns about, and earthward, too, is clear, The. (LL) On the Ineffable Inspiration of the Holy Spirit. Catharina Regina von Greiffenberg. WPoS; WoPoe, *tr. by* Michael Hamburger

Moon, they say, called Mantis, The. How Death Came. *Unknown.* TTY, *tr. by* W. H. I. Bleek

Moon this evening, The. Saiokuken Socho. SoOfWa, *tr. by* Sam Hamill

Moon through total darkness hurrying, The. Demons. Alexander Sergeyevich Pushkin. WoPoe, *tr. by* D. M. Thomas

Moon tonight, The. Issa. EH, *tr. by* Robert Hass

Moon Tree Cliff. Muso Soseki. EaWin, *tr. by* W. S. Merwin

Moon trees keep growing and growing, The. Moon Tree Cliff. Muso Soseki. EaWin, *tr. by* W. S. Merwin

Moon upon her fluent Route, The. Emily Dickinson. APN-2

Moon was a thick slab of yellow cheese between thin slices of toasted clouds, The. Sam Jackson. Frank Marshall Davis. APT-2

Moon Was Gliding the River, The. Juan Ramón Jiménez. SpanPo, *tr. by* Eloise Roach

Moon was like a full cup tonight, The. Cows at Night, The. Hayden Carruth. GifTon

Moon Winx Motel. Emily Hiestand. ReTh

Moon Winx with its neon eyes and sly smile, The. Moon Winx Motel. Emily Hiestand. ReTh

Moon, worn thin to the width of a quill. Moon's Ending. Sara Teasdale. APT-1

Moon you could hang a coat on, A. Sean Dunne. ModIr *Fr.* Sydney Place.

Moonburn. Laura H. Kennedy. PasH

Moondown: crows caw. Frost, a skyful. Night-Mooring at Maple Bridge. Chang Chi. ChinPo, *tr. by* Yip Wai-lim

Mooni. Henry Clarence Kendall. OBEV

Moonily. (LL) Thomas Lovell Beddoes. FaBoCh; WoPoe *Fr.* Death's Jest Book.

Moonless darkness stands between. Gerard Manley Hopkins. OBCP

Moonless Night. Louise Glück. AWTN

Moonlight. Kim Caldwell. ReEnLa

Moonlight. Walter De la Mare. EnLoPo

Moonlight. Kim Sujang. WoPoe, *tr. by* Kevin O'Rourke

Moonlight. Michael Ryan. BodElec

Moonlight. William Shakespeare. OxAEP-1 *Fr.* Merchant of Venice, The.

Moonlight. Jacques Tahureau. AWP, *tr. by* Andrew Lang

Moonlight. Sara Teasdale. VGW

Moonlight. Paul Verlaine. NAWM-7v2, *tr. by* Carlyle Ferren MacIntyre

Moonlight and Gas. Constance Naden. VWP; ViWPN

Moonlight Bay. Wu Chen. CoBLCP, *tr. by* Jonathan Chaves

Moonlight Becomes You. Johnny Burke. ReLy

Moonlight Cocktail. Kim Gannon. ReLy

Moonlight, harsh and clear, floods the high pavilion. Small Garden, The. Cheng Hsieh. SuSp, *tr. by* Wu-Chi Liu

Moonlight in front of my bed. Still Night Thoughts. Li Po. CoBCP; ColAnChi; TTTS, *tr. by* Burton Watson

Moonlight in the kitchen is a sign of God. Anne Carson. BodElec *Fr.* Truth about God, The.

Moonlight in Vermont. John Blackburn. ReLy

Moonlight is good, good for solitary sitting, The. Pine Sounds. Po Chü-i. CoBCP, *tr. by* Burton Watson

Moonlight Night. Tu Fu. CoBCP, *tr. by* Burton Watson

Moonlight of a former time, The. Tune: "Dim Fragrance"—Plum Blossoms. Chiang K'uei. SuSp, *tr. by* An-yan Tang

Moonlight on stubbleshining. Nocturne. Yvor Winters. APT-2

Moonlight / On Swanee's muddy shore. Rockin' Chair. Hoagy Carmichael. ReLy

Moonlight pearls on my breast like solder. She Speaks to Her Husband, Asleep. Robert Schultz. AWTN

Moonlight Ride, A. Harriet Hamilton King. VWP

Moonlight ripples, ripples, The. Moonlight Bay. Wu Chen. CoBLCP, *tr. by* Jonathan Chaves

Moonlight shines cold on white bones, The. (LL) Travelling Northward. Tu Fu. BLT; OHPC, *tr. by* Kenneth Rexroth

Moonlight shines on the lotus pond. Moonlight. Kim Sujang. WoPoe, *tr. by* Kevin O'Rourke

Moonlight slanting. Basho. EH, *tr. by* Robert Hass

Moonlight through my gauze curtains. Skein, The. Carolyn Kizer. VGW

Moonlight washes the west side of the house. Winter Verse for His Sister. William Meredith. TAP

Moonlit Apples. John Drinkwater. OBMV; OxBTC; PoRA

Moonlit Night. Tu Fu. ChinPo, *tr. by* Yip Wai-lim

Moonlit Night. Tu Fu. WoPoe, *tr. by* Vikram Seth

Moonlit Night. Tu Fu. CrYelRi, *tr.* by Sam Hamill

Moonlit Night at Fragrant Mountain Temple. Wang Shih-chieng. SuSp, *tr.* by Richard John Lynn

Moonlit night / By melon flowers. Kaya Shirao. ZenPo, *tr.* by Takashi Ikemoto and Lucien Stryk

Moonlit sleet. David Lloyd. HA

Moonmoth and grasshopper that flee our page. Name for All, A. Hart Crane. VGW

Moonrise. Gerard Manley Hopkins. MoBrPo; NOBVV; RB

Moonrise in the Rockies. Ella Higginson. SWaP

Moonrise over Battlefield. Edgell Rickword. PoWW

Moonrise white cat eating the cardinal. Scott Montgomery. HA

Moons. Peter Fallon. BiHa

Moonset. Sir Henry John Newbolt. EBVV

Moonshine. Walter De la Mare. OBCoV

Moonshine Sonata. John Tranter. KGB

Moonshot, A. Giant Rocket. Wes Magee. NOxBChV

Moonshot Sonnet. Mary Ellen Solt. BoWoP

Moonsnow '77. Michael Hartnett. ModIr

Moonsongs. Niyi Osundare.
"Frantic as a prentice poet." HBAPE
"Ikoyi / The moon here." NAfrP
"Madding moon, A." HBAPE
"Moon is an exile, The." HBAPE
"We called the statue." HBAPE

Moonstones. David Trinidad. WiU

Moonstruck. Hugh MacDiarmid. NAEL-5v2; NAEL-6v2

Moor, The. Ralph Hodgson. MoBrPo

Moor, The. Ronald Stuart Thomas. OBWVE

Moor Girl's Well, The. Rosamund Marriott Watson. ViWPN

Moor / Point my horse. Basho. ZenPo, *tr.* by Takashi Ikemoto and Lucien Stryk

Moored boat, A. Buson. EH, *tr.* by Robert Hass

Moored for the Night at the Lan-chi Riverside Courier Station. Yang Wan-li. GifTon, *tr.* by Paul Hansen

Moorer Denies Holyfield in Twelve. Olena Kalytiak Davis. AmPoNex; MoASP

Moorhen. William Logan. DiPo

Mooring at Hsia-k'ou at Night. Li Meng-yang. CoBLCP, *tr.* by Jonathan Chaves

Mooring at K'ou-ch'üeh—Sent to Dr. Lin. Pien Kung. CoBLCP, *tr.* by Jonathan Chaves

Mooring at Night at Kao-yu. Wang Shih-chieng. CoBLCP, *tr.* by Jonathan Chaves

Mooring at Night at the River Mouth, I Heard a Flute—Sent to My Elder Brother Hsi-ch'iao. Wang Shih-chieng. CoBLCP, *tr.* by Jonathan Chaves

Mooring at River Ch'in-Huai. Tu Mu. ChinPo, *tr.* by Yip Wai-lim

Mooring in the Rain at Sung-ling. Chin Nung. CoBLCP, *tr.* by Jonathan Chaves

Mooring My Boat on the Ssu River and Watching the Moon. Wen Cheng-ming. CoBLCP, *tr.* by Jonathan Chaves

Mooring Our Boat at Tan-yang Harbor. Kao Ch'i. CoBLCP, *tr.* by Jonathan Chaves

Moorings. Norman MacCaig. OxBTC

Moorland blazing and a bomber's moon, The. Dornier, The. Gladys Mary Coles. TCAWP

Moorland fires are gathered up, The. Tune: "Big String of Words, A"—The Great Wall. Na-lan Hsing-te. SuSp, *tr.* by Lenore Mayhew

Moose, The. Elizabeth Bishop. DiPo; FaBoWP; NAAL-2v2; NAAL-5; NALW

Moose has lost his way, A. Duluth, Minnesota. Connie Wanek. UrbNat

Moose in the Morning, Northern Maine. Mona Van Duyn. ColAP

Moose's heart, The. Fire Barns. Jordan Davis. HeMarv

Mop-eyed I am, as some have said. Upon Himself. Robert Herrick. OxBSP

Moraine Lake. Brian Henry. PoCoUp

Moral, The. William Ernest Henley. OxAEP-2

Moral Alphabet, A. Joseph Hilaire Pierre Belloc.
"A stands for Archibald who told no lies." NoAM
"B stands for Bear. When bears are seen." NoAM
"Dreadful Dinotherium he, The." NOBL
"E stands for egg." NoAM
"K for the Klondyke, a country of gold." NoAM
"R the reviewer, reviewing my book." NoAM

Moral climbs whose name should be a wreath, A. (LL) Mr. Pope. Allen Tate. APT-2; ColAP; FuPo; NOBA; NoAM; TwCP; VGW

Moral is—Take care how you light, The. (LL) Darius Green and His Flying-Machine. John Townsend Trowbridge. OBAL; OBCA

Moral Poem, A. James Vincent Cunningham. VGW

Moral Proverbs and Folk Songs. Antonio Machado Ruiz.
"But look in your mirror for the other one." RaBo
"Don't trace out your profile." RaBo
"Look for your other half." RaBo
"Narcissism / is an ugly fault." RaBo

Moral Tale, A. Roger Woddis. UV

Moral Tetrastich, A. Sir William Jones. *See* Epigram: "On parent knees, a naked new-born child."

Morality Play: Preface, A. George Oppen. APSN; NNaP *Fr.* Some San Francisco Poems.

Morality, thou deadly bane. Robert Burns. OBSV *Fr.* Dedication to G**** H******* Esq, A.

Morant Bay. *Unknown.* FaBoVe

Morbid. Nancy Eimers. ExTi

Mordant and decadent Youth, A. Limerick. Thomas Thorneley. PeLi

More. Ai. GT

More. Gertrude Stein. TCAPo *Fr.* Tender Buttons.

More a Man Has the More a Man Wants, The. Paul Muldoon. ModIr

More Abandoned, the More Divine, The. "Angelus Silesius." GePo, *tr.* by George C. Schoolfield *Fr.* Cherubical Wanderer, The.

More about God (But with Some Reservations). Victor Hugo. SxFrPo, *tr.* by E. H. Blackmore and A. M. Blackmore

More amorous than Solomon. (LL) Worm Fed on the Heart of Corinth, A. Isaac Rosenberg. NPeEn; PeFWW; PoWW

More Ancient Mariner, A. Bliss Carman. OBAL

More and More. Margaret Atwood. LW

More and more lately, as, not even minding the slippages yet, the aches / and sad softenings. Repression. C. K. Williams. NoP-4

More Bagpipe Music. E. O. Parrott. UV

More Ballads! here's a spick and span new Supplication. Free Parliament Litany, A. *Unknown.* OxBoLi

More beautiful and soft than any moth. Landscape near an Aerodrome, The. Stephen Spender. MoBrPo; NoAM; OxBTC

More beautiful than any gift you gave. Token, The. Frank Templeton Prince. FaBoTw; OxBTC

More Beautiful than Your Eyes. Sa'id 'Aql. ErotSp; MAP, *tr.* by Naomi Shihab Nye and Matthew Sorenson

More bitter is our weeping. Magyar Messiahs, The. Endre Ady. IQMS, *tr.* by Anton N. Nyerges

More brave than me: more blond than you. (LL) I Sing of Olaf Glad and Big. E. E. Cummings. AF; AmFaPo; ColAP; FaBoWar; HeIP-4; NAAL-2v2; NAAL-5; NOBA; NoAM; NoP-4; OBSV; OBWP; PoWW; VGW

More bright and large than this. (LL) Answer to Another Persuading a Lady to Marriage, An. Katherine Philips. HAP; WeW-3

More Care for the Neck than for the Intellect. J. Gordon Coogler. VerBaPo

More Chagall than Chagall. Luisa Futuransky. MirDau, *tr.* by Celeste Kostopulos-Cooperman

More dear, both for themselves and for thy sake! (LL) William Wordsworth. AmFaPo; CABP; FHYEP; HeIP-4; NAEL-6v2; NAWM-7v2; NIL-7; NPeEn; NoP-4; OxAEP-2; OxBEV; PoPoPo; TFi

More delicate than the historians' are the map-makers' colors. (LL) Map, The. Elizabeth Bishop. APT-2; ColAP; NOBA

More discontents I never had. Discontents in Devon. Robert Herrick. BeJo; CaPo; OxBSP

More domestic than elegant, leaves and pigeons. Urban Pastoral. Babette Deutsch. MakPoe

More for asparagus than asparagus does. Angry with China. Douglas Messerli. FTOS

More Foreign Cities. Charles Tomlinson. HarvBoo

More gaily, dance. Quick-Step. Robert Creeley. VGW

More geese than swans now live, more fools than wise. (LL) Silver Swan, The. Orlando Gibbons. FaBoCh; HAP; HeIP-4; NAEL-5v1; NAEL-6v1; OPOU; OWoS; OxBSP; PAI

More grotesque than a row of laundromats. Novelty Shop, The. Duane Niatum. CDW; ReTh

More had she spoke, but yawn'd—All nature nods. Pope. FHYEP *Fr.* Dunciad, The.

More hard than any ghost there is or any man there was! (LL) Looking Glass, The. Rudyard Kipling. FaBoTw; OBMV

More harmless vanity?, A. (LL) On an Infant Dying as Soon as Born. Charles Lamb. GTBS-P; OBEV

More haughty than the rest, the wolfish race. Dryden. NOSC *Fr.* Hind and the Panther, The.

More hopeless the more comforting, The. Autumn. Yunna Petrovna [*or* Iunna Pinkhusovna] Moritz [*or* Morits]. TCRP, *tr.* by J. R. Rowl and Odile Taliani

More I'm with you, the more I can see, The. Everything I Have Is Yours. Burton Lane. ReLy

More I read the papers, The. Love Is Here to Stay. George Gershwin. ReLy

More I've viewed this world, the more I've found, The. Fancy. Thomas Moore. CenSon

More I wonder, The. Observation, An. Kay Sage. SurWo

More intricate. William J. Higginson. HA

More It Snows, The. Alan Alexander Milne. NTCP

More Joy in Heaven. Howard Nemerov. NoAM

More kicks than pence. To Hell with Commonsense. Patrick Kavanagh. FaBoTw

More Light! More Light! Anthony Hecht. AF; CoAP; CoAmPo; EmeKit; HAP; HP; NOBA; NoAM; NoP-4; OBWP; RB; TaR; TwCP; UnPo; VCAP; VGW

More like a stock than like a vine. (LL) Vine, The. Robert Herrick. BeJo; CaPo; EroLit; NAEL-5v2; NAEL-6v1; NAEL-7v1

More liked by her, or loved by me. (LL) To the Most Fair and Lovely Mistress Anne Soame, Now Lady Abdie. Robert Herrick. CaPo; NOBE; NOSC

More Love. *Unknown.* AH

More love or more disdain I crave. Against Indifference. Charles Webbe. OBEV

More Love to Thee, O Christ. Elizabeth Payson Prentiss. AH

More Lovely than Antiquity. Witter Bynner. NoP-4

More Loving One, The. W. H. Auden. TOF

More luck to honest poverty. For A' That and A' That. Shirley Brooks. UV

More man / Than myth, more myth. Tambourine Tommy. Thomas Sayers Ellis. NAPBL

More memories than if I'd lived a thousand years! Spleen LXXVI. Charles Baudelaire. SxFrPo, *tr. by* James McGowan

More of a Corpse than a Woman. Muriel Rukeyser. NALW

More often than not he stops at the headrig to light. Cauliflowers. Paul Muldoon. ModIr

More Poem. Dennis Scott. WaCA

More Power. Egan [*or* Aodhagán] O'Rahilly [*or* O'Reilly *or* Ó Rathaille]. BIrV, *tr. by* John Montague

More powerful than the government. Giles Goodland. NewEx

More Rain. Ben Scammell. NLP

More Reformation. Daniel Defoe.
"To sin's a vice in nature, and we find." OBSV

More rich than Cleopatra's tomb. (LL) Amber Bead, The. Robert Herrick. BeJo; CaPo

More songs. birds follow the sun. Lady's Days. Larry Neal. SeSe

More sound in France—that, too, he secret keeps. (LL) Private, A. Edward Thomas. GTBS-P; PeFWW; TCAWP

More Stanzas Applied to Spiritual Things. Saint John of the Cross. TOF, *tr. by* K. Kavanaugh and O. Rodrigues

More Strong than Time. Victor Hugo. AWP, *tr. by* Andrew Lang

More surprising than a moving statue. Apparition, The. Bernard O'Donoghue. NoP-4

More than a brother to me, Jonathan. Peter Abelard. EroLit, *tr. by* John Boswell

More than a King's my Word does rule to day. Elizabeth Tipper. EMWP; NOSC *Fr.* Pilgrim's Viaticum; or, The Destitute, but Not Forlorn.

More than anything else. I Cherish That Love. Kabir. WoPoe, *tr. by* Pritish Nandy

More than anything, I wanted Charlie. David Trinidad. WiU *Fr.* Eighteen to Twenty-One.

More than Apollo's golden lyre. Meleager. GrAn

More than eager to rid himself of a father. Studies in Desire. Pimone Triplett. AmPoNex

More than ever I want to see. Basho. EH, *tr. by* Robert Hass

More than Morgan, I desire to eat people. Morgan. John Blight. CBAP

More than most fair [*or* fayre], full of the living fire [*or* fyre]. Edmund Spenser. OxBSo; PoE; Son *Fr.* Amoretti.

More than Most People. Eldon Grier. MoCV

More than my brothers are to me. (LL) Tennyson. CAGL; EBVV; NAEL-6v2 *Fr.* In Memoriam A. H. H.

More than 9 Lives. Bruce Beaver. BMAP

More than novelty crooked its finger—silent, austere. Melissa Green. DiPo

More than polished stone. I Am Root. Claribel Alegría. PoetW; VCWP, *tr. by* Carolyn Forché

More than Suspect. André Breton. AF, *tr. by* Mary Ann Caws

More than the color. *Unknown.* ArkPo, *tr. by* Helen Craig McCullough

More than the gems / locked away and treasured. Sent from the Capital to Her Elder Daughter. Lady Otomo no Sakanoé. BoWoP; WPOW, *tr. by* Geoffrey Bownas

More than the Grave is closed to me. Emily Dickinson. APN-2

More than the shortest distance. Barbed Wire Fence Meditates upon the Goldfinch, A. Don McKay. NOBC

More than They that Watch for the Morning. May Probyn. VWP

More than thirty years have rushed. On His Thirty-Third Birthday. Ch'ang Kuo Fan. OHMPC, *tr. by* Kenneth Rexroth

More than thyself to love thy neighbor. (LL) Latest Decalogue, The. Arthur Hugh Clough. CABP; ChIV-1; EBEV; EBVV; FaBoEE; GTBS-P; HAP; NAEL-5v2; NAEL-6v2; NOBE; NOBVV; NPeEn; NoP-4; OBSV; OxBEV; PAI; PeECV; SCGP; SacPr; TFi; WeW-3; WoPoe

More than You Know. Vincent Youmans. ReLy

More then most faire, full of the living fire. Edmund Spenser. *See* More than most fair [*or* fayre], full of the living fire [*or* fyre]

More times than you'll wake. (LL) Letter for Duncan. Larry Eigner. FTOS; PoM

More touching is the deathbed than the bier! (LL) Old Ruralities: A Regret. Charles Tennyson Turner. EBVV; Son

More Trouble with the Obvious. Michael Van Walleghen. IllVoic

More we live, more brief appear, The. River of Life, The. Thomas Campbell. GTBS-P

More whyght thou art than primrose leaf my Lady Galatee. Ovid. CTC; OBVE, *tr. by* Arthur Golding *Fr.* Metamorphoses.

More worthy I to be belov'd of thee. (LL) William Shakespeare. OxAEP-1; SCGP *Fr.* Sonnets.

More ye desire her, the sooner ye miss, The. How to Obtain Her. *Unknown.* NoSic

Moreover the Lord answered Job, and said. Bible, *O.T.* OBVE *Fr.* Job.

Moreover, there with them appear. Michael Wigglesworth. *See* Thus everyone before the throne

Moreton Bay. *Unknown.* CBAP

Morgan. John Blight. CBAP

Morgan's curls are matted. Henry Morgan's March on Panama. A. G. Prys-Jones. AngWePo

Morgan's father will be mailed to her. Complete with Starry Night and Bourbon Shots. Albert Goldbarth. BAP-97

Morituri Salutamus. Henry Wadsworth Longfellow.
"For age is opportunity no less." PoToHe

Morn. Josephine D. Henderson Heard. CBWP-4

Morn hath risen clear and bright, The. Expulsion of Hagar, The. Eloise Bibb. CBWP-4

Morn on her rosy couch awoke. Poetry. Lydia Huntley Sigourney. SWaP

Morn's Recompense. "Clement Andrews." CAGL

Morning. Joanna Baillie. ECWP *Fr.* Winter Day, A.

Morning. Louisa Sarah Bevington. PEW

Morning. William Blake. FaBoCh; WoPoe

Morning. Louise Bogan. APT-2

Morning. William Browne. NOSC *Fr.* Britannia's Pastorals.

Morning. Thomas Carlyle. PWR

Morning. Chu Shu-chen. BoWoP, *tr. by* Kenneth Rexroth
(I get up. I am sick of.) BLT; OHPC, *tr. by* Kenneth Rexroth

Morning. Jeni Couzyn. HAWP

Morning. John Cunningham. NOEC

Morning. Emily Dickinson. OBCA

Morning. Duo Duo (Li Shizheng). PoetW, *tr. by* Maghiel Van Crevel

Morning. Judith Herzberg. TuT, *tr. by* Joan McBreen

Morning. Vincente Huidobro. CuPo

Morning. Glyn Jones. AngWePo

Morning. Pauline Kaldas. PoArWo

Morning. Sami Mahdi. MAP, *tr. by* May Jayyusi

Morning. Gabriela Mistral. TANSG, *tr. by* Maria Jacketti

Morning. Mary Oliver. NIL-7

Morning. Arthur Rimbaud. SxFrPo, *tr. by* Martin Sorrell

Morning. Giuseppe Ungaretti. PFTM-1

Morning. *Unknown.* NOEC

Morning. Wang Wei. TAL

Morning, A. Mark Strand. HCAP

Morning: a polished knifeblade. Jelaluddin [*or* Jalal al-Din] Rumi. EnlH

Morning After. Langston Hughes. NAAL-2v2; NBLV; NoAM; OBCoV

Morning After, The. Dory Langdon Previn. ReLy

Morning After, The. Johari M. Rashad. PasH

Morning After, The. Dorothy Wellesley, Duchess of Wellington. OBMV

Morning after is the first day, The. (LL) Apple Blossom. Louis MacNeice. PeECV; RB

Morning after My Death, The. Larry Levis. OPRER

Morning after the night, The. Raymond of the Rooftops. Paul Durcan. EmeKit

Morning after the storm, townsmen found, The. After the Storm. Henri Faust. YaYoPo

Morning after Woe, The. Emily Dickinson. TCAPo

Morning after. . . Love, The. Kattie M. Cumbo. BlSi

Morning again, nothing has to be done. Second Poem. Peter Orlovsky. NeAP

Morning among the Hills. James Gates Percival. TreFP

Morning and evening. Christina Georgina Rossetti. EBEV; NAEL-5v2;

NAEL-6v2; NALW; NOBVV; NOxBChV; OBNV; OxAEP-2; OxBEV; VWP; ViWPN

Morning and Evening. Antoni Slonimski. TrJP, *tr.* by Watson Kirkconnell

Morning and Evening Calm. James Keir Baxter. HarvBoo

Morning and evening calm: the Lord has spoken. Morning and Evening Calm. James Keir Baxter. HarvBoo

Morning and evening, drunk and singing. For Kuo Hsiang. Yü Hsüan-chi. BoWoP, *tr.* by Geoffrey Waters

Morning and evening, sleep she drove away. Leonidas of Tarentum. AWP, *tr.* by Andrew Lang *Fr.* Epigrams.

Morning and Evening Star. Plato. *See* To Stella

Morning and night I bring. Cottage Song. John Drinkwater. UV

Morning and night I found. Same Cottage—But Another Song, of Another Season. Max Beerbohm. UV

Morning, and streaks of heavenly blue. London Spring. Antoni Slonimski. TrJP, *tr.* by Frances Notley

Morning, and the poet up again and out and about. Poet's Day, The. Richard Weber. CIP-2

Morning and the snow might fall forever. Going to Remake This World. James Welch. CDW

Morning at nine, seven ultra-masculine men. In Your Bad Dream. Richard Hugo. LCAP-2

Morning at Point Dume. May Swenson. DiPo

Morning at the Window. T. S. Eliot. AWP; OxBEV; TCAPo

Morning Athletes. Marge Piercy. MoASP

Morning Baking, The. Carolyn Forché. LoL

Morning bath. Anita Virgil. HA

Morning Becomes Electric. Bruce Dawe. BMAP

Morning: blue, cold, and still. January. Weldon Kees. CoAP

Morning breaks like a pomegranate, The. Wedding Morn. D. H. Lawrence. MoBrPo

Morning breeze. Buson. EH, *tr.* by Robert Hass

Morning Bright, with Rosy Light, The. Thomas O. Summers. AH

Morning broke like an egg. Eggs. Susan Wood. SoSe-8

Morning / broods. Strawberrying. Maurice Kenny. HATNAP

Morning brought strong rain. Harlem Haiku: A Scrapbook. Jabari Asim. InTrad

Morning Call. Richard Murphy. BiHa; ModIr

Morning Chamber Orchestra near Piney Crick, Wyoming, 7 A.M., The. William Borden. MiVo

Morning Coffee. György Petri. VCWP, *tr.* by George Gömöri and Clive Wilmer

Morning comes, and thickening clouds prevail, The. Clouded Morning, The. Jones Very. GSo; NOBA

Morning comes; not slow, with reddening gold, The. Frederick Goddard Tuckerman. APN-2 *Fr.* Sonnets.

Morning comes to consciousness, The. T. S. Eliot. TCAPo *Fr.* Preludes (I–IV).

Morning dawned full darkly, The. William Edmonstoune [*or* Edmondstoune] Aytoun. NePenScot *Fr.* Execution of Montrose, The.

Morning dawning stems that core. Shields Strong, Nulla Nullas Alive. Lionel Fogarty. IBA

Morning drum-call on my eager ear, The. Robert Louis Stevenson. NOBVV

Morning Exercises. Nina Cassian. PoSu, *tr.* by Andrea Deletant and Brenda Walker

Morning finds the self-sequestr'd man, The. William Cowper. *See* I was a stricken deer, that left the herd

Morning fog. Gary Hotham. HA

Morning frost cocoons my car. Gurney Tears. Audrey Shafer. BloBone

Morning frost / Mount Fuji. Tantan. ZenPo, *tr.* by Takashi Ikemoto and Lucien Stryk

Morning glories, The. Basho. SoOfWa, *tr.* by Sam Hamill

Morning glory. Gengen'ichi. JDP, *tr.* by Yoel Hoffmann

Morning Glory. Howard Moss. DiPo

Morning Glory. Ruth Pitter. FaBoWP

Morning Glory. Siegfried Sassoon. TrCP

Morning glory. Lucien Stryk. IllVoic *Fr.* Issa: A Suite of Haiku.

Morning glory, A. Teishi. JDP, *tr.* by Yoel Hoffmann

Morning glory!, The. Chiyojo [*or* Chiyo *or* Chiyo-Ni *or* Kaga no Chiyo *or* Fukuda Chiyo-Ni]. WPoS

Morning-Glory, The. Raymond Roseliep. HA

Morning-Glory, The. *Unknown.* AWP, *tr.* by Helen Waddell *Fr.* Shi King.

Morning-Glory, The. Sarah Helen Whitman. ColAP

Morning glory also, The. Basho. EH, *tr.* by Robert Hass

Morning glory / So pure. Kakei. ZenPo, *tr.* by Takashi Ikemoto and Lucien Stryk

Morning. Good luck! Among the houses! Gray Morning. Aleksandr Aleksandrovich Blok. TCRP, *tr.* by Geoffrey Thurley

Morning Harvest. Gerald Stern. LCAP-2

Morning has its flat first light, its blaze, The. New. Jennifer Maiden. BMAP

Morning he had gone. My Face Is My Own, I Thought. Tom Raworth. SPE

Morning Hours. Rossana Ombres. NeIt *Fr.* Excursion to Ravenna of a Young Girl with Her Parents.

Morning Hymn. Joseph Beaumont. SacPr

Morning Hymn. John Keble. NOCV

Morning Hymn. Thomas Ken. NOSC; SacPr

Morning Hymn. Charles Wesley. NPeEn; TOF

Morning I asked you to marry me, The. Marry. Linda Smukler. WiU

Morning, if this late withered light can claim. Zonnebeke Road, The. Edmund Charles Blunden. OBWP; PeFWW

Morning in My City. Avraham Shlonsky. MHP, *tr.* by Ruth Finer Mintz

Morning in Norfolk. George Barker. HarvBoo

Morning in the Hills. Bliss Carman. NOBC

Morning in the Hospital Solarium. Sylvia Plath. BodElec

Morning in the Islands. John Hollander. ColAP

Morning is lost in a maze. We're OK. Gloria Fuertes. WPOW, *tr.* by Philip Levine

Morning Jitters. John Ashbery. FTOS

Morning Light, The. Louis Simpson. NNaP

Morning Light at Wanship, Utah. Dave Jeddie Smith. BodElec

Morning light creaks down again!, The. (LL) Aubade: "Jane, Jane, / Tall as a crane." Dame Edith Sitwell. BWW; MoBrPo; NALW; NoAM; PoRA

Morning Light Is Breaking, The. Samuel Francis Smith. AH

Morning Light Song. Philip Lamantia. NeAP

Morning Love Song. Marge Piercy. PasH

Morning, May rain. Man Awakened by a Song above His Roof, The. Tomas Tranströmer. SPE, *tr.* by Robert Bly

Morning, May rain. The city is silent still. Tomas Tranströmer. *See* Morning, May rain

Morning muezzin in orange and a mosquito. Clark Coolidge. FTOS *Fr.* At Egypt.

Morning, Noon and Night. Mark Strand. BAP-97

Morning of buttered toast. Not-Yet. Jane Hirshfield. ExTi

Morning of Drunkenness. Arthur Rimbaud. SxFrPo, *tr.* by Martin Sorrell

Morning of Every Sin, The. Maysoun Saqr Al-Qasimi.

    "I'm not sleeping now." PoArWo, *tr.* by Subhi Hadidi

    "Salty like my seashores." PoArWo, *tr.* by Subhi Hadidi

    "Voice is never enough, The." PoArWo, *tr.* by Subhi Hadidi

Morning of our rest has come, The. Poor Man's Sunday Walk, The. Charles MacKay. EBVV

Morning of Sinhala New Year I went to the market, The. Sinhala New Year 1975. Anne Ranasinghe. GotH

Morning, on a beach. A man & woman sitting by fire. Moon Is to Blood. Richard Duerden. NeAP

Morning on the Shore. Wilfred Campbell. NOBC

Morning ought not. Pas de Deux for Lovers. Michael Dransfield. CBAP

Morning-Piece; or, An Hymn for the Hay-Makers, A. Christopher Smart. NOEC

    (Brisk chaunticleer his mattins had begun.) NPeEn

Morning Prayer. *Unknown.* PoToHe

Morning Prayer, A. Ella Wheeler Wilcox. PoToHe

Morning Quatrains, The. Charles Cotton. NOSC; PeECV

Morning quiet. Gary Hotham. HA

Morning rain, evening rain, little plums turned yellow. Feeling Sorry for Myself. Lu Yu. CoBCP, *tr.* by Burton Watson

Morning rain of Wei city wets the white dust, The. Song for Wei City, A. Wang Wei. TAL

Morning Roar of the City, The. Slavko Mihalic. PoSu, *tr.* by Charles Simic

Morning, Rosamonde. Anne Batten Cristall. ECWP; RWP

Morning's at seven. Pippa Passes, but I Can't Get around This Truck. Margaret Blaker. NBLV

Morning's sun. *Unknown.* ColAnChi, *tr.* by Jeanne Larsen *Fr.* Midnight Songs.

Morning seems to have no light to spare. Edward Hopper's Seven A.M. John Hollander. PoSol

Morning service! parson preaches. House of God, The. Alec Derwent Hope. OxBC

Morning sky glitters, The. De Civitate Hominum. Thomas MacGreevy [*or* McGreevy]. CIP-2

Morning Snowfield. Reg Saner. PoCoUp

Morning Song. Conrad Potter Aiken. NoAM *Fr.* Senlin; a Biography.

Morning Song. Afanasi Afanasievich Fet [*or* Foeth]. AWP, *tr.* by Max Eastman

Morning Song. Sylvia Plath. BoWoP; ColAP; HCAP; HarvBoo; HeIP-4; InPK-6; ItWoWo; LCAP-2; NAAL-2v2; NAAL-5; NIL-7; NIP-4; NOBA; NoP-4; PoPoPo; VCAP

Morning Song. Solomon ibn Gabirol. TrJP, *tr.* by Nina Davis Salaman

Morning Song in the Jungle. Rudyard Kipling. NoAM *Fr.* Second Jungle Book, The.

Morning Song of Senlin. Conrad Potter Aiken. *See* Senlin; a Biography

Morning Songs. Robert E. Penn. WiU

Morning Space. Louise Herlin. MFP, *tr.* by Martin Sorrell

Morning space expands the building's. Morning Space. Louise Herlin. MFP, *tr.* by Martin Sorrell

Morning spent itself, The. Street Fair: The Quartet. Marvin Bell. BodElec

Morning spent looking for my calendar. Losing the Marbles. James Merrill. DiPo

Morning Splendour of the Tisza, The. György Bessenyei. IQMS, *tr.* by Gavin Ewart

Morning spreads over. May All Earth Be Clothed in Light. George Hitchcock. VGW

Morning Star. Thomas Hornsby Ferril. VGW

Morning star goes under cover, The. Der von Kürenberg. GePo

Morning Star, O Cheering Sight! *Unknown.* AH

Morning stretched calm, beautiful, and warm, The. Doctor's Journal Entry for August 6, 1945, A. Vikram Seth. OMIP

Morning Sun. Francisco Alarcon. OxIBACP

Morning Sun. Louis MacNeice. MoBrPo; TwCP

Morning sun, The. Poem for Myself and Mei: Abortion. Leslie Marmon Silko. VoR

Morning sun outside D'Agostino's, a young man bends. Beatrix Gates. WiU *Fr.* Triptych.

Morning Sun Shines, The. Emperor Wu of Liang. OHMPC, *tr.* by Kenneth Rexroth

Morning Swim. Maxine W. Kumin. WPE

Morning swoops down on her with words, chews. Learning Window. James Longenbach. NAPBL

Morning that I first loved you, The. New Clouds, The. William Carlos Williams. HarvBoo

Morning Thesis. Christiania Whitehead. NeBl

Morning they set out from home, The. I Was Not There. Karen Gershon. HP

Morning They Shot Tony Lopez, Barber and Pusher Who Went Too Far, 1958, The. Gary Soto. PBCAP

Morning to Remember; or, E Pluribus Unum, A. Edward Dorn. NoAM

Morning traffic murmurs like an ocean. West Willow. Reginald Shepherd. AmPoNex; IllVoic

Morning trickles over the bruised vegetables. Manless Society, The. Pierre Unik. SPE, *tr.* by David Gascoyne

Morning. / Two sparrows sit on the tin roof. Finding the Way Back. Gerald McCarthy. CDa

Morning uptown, quiet on the street. Song Form. Imamu Amiri Baraka. ChAP; TTTS

Morning Vigil. Phillip [*or* 'Phil'] William George. VoR

Morning Walk in Autumn to South Valley Passing an Abandoned Village. Liu Tsung-yüan. ChinPo, *tr.* by Yip Wai-lim

Morning-Watch, The. Henry Vaughan. AngWePo; BASC; ESCV; GeHe; NOSC; PeECV

Morning Watch, The. Jones Very. APN-1

Morning when the things again come back, The. Thanks to the Things. Rutger Kopland. VCWP, *tr.* by James Brockway

Morning Work. D. H. Lawrence. MoBrPo

Morning—A Death. Basil T. Paquet. CDa

Mornings. Sarah Kirsch. PFTM-2, *tr.* by Wayne Kvam *Fr.* Kite-Flying.

Mornings are his, The. Waterwings. Cathy Song. NoAM

Mornings / before the sun's liquid. Lagoons, Hanlan's Point. Raymond Souster. NOBC

Mornings / I got up early. Way It Was, The. Lucille Clifton. WPE

Mornings I see the Wu Mountain recumbent. At the Heng-ts'ui Pavilion of Fa-hui Monastery. Su Tung-p'o (Su Shih). SuSp, *tr.* by Irving Y. Lo

Mornings run their course, clear and deserted, The. Grappa in September. Cesare Pavese. RaBo, *tr.* by William Arrowsmith

Mornings the sparrow twitters seeking food. Han Yü. SuSp

Mornings up before the rooster calls. Autumn Thoughts. Lu Yu. CoBCP, *tr.* by Burton Watson

Morns are meeker than they were, The. Emily Dickinson. ChAP; OBCA; SAmP

Moro Assassinato. Allen Curnow.
Urban Guerrilla, An. PeNZ

Moroccans with the carpets, The. Patrizia Cavalli. NeIt; VCWP, *tr.* by Kenneth Koch

Moroni is a foreigner. Moroni on the Mormon Temple / Angel on the Wall. Eloise Klein Healy. GeoHom

Moroni on the Mormon Temple / Angel on the Wall. Eloise Klein Healy. GeoHom

Morphemes in section. Morphemics. Jack Spicer. PmAP

Morphemics. Jack Spicer. PmAP

Morpheus, the humble god, that dwells. Song, A. Sir John Denham. NOSC

Morrigan, The. *Unknown.* BIrV, *tr.* by Thomas Kinsella

Morrow every listen. Colloam. P. Inman. FTOS

Mors et Vita. James Edwin Campbell. TCAPo

Morse. Les A. Murray. NoP-4

Morse Lesson. Joy Corfield. FaBoWar

Morsel. Ali Sardar Jafri. OMIP, *tr.* by Kathleen Grant Jaeger

Morsels of my lifework: the story of a professional party hostess. Sonnet. D. A. Powell. NeAmPo

Mort aux Chats. Peter Porter. OxBC

Mortal Combat. Mary Elizabeth Coleridge. VWP

Mortal flesh is full of grief. Vanity of the World, The. Siôn Cent. OBWVE, *tr.* by Joseph P. Clancy

Mortal Lease, The. Edith Wharton. LW

Mortal mixed of middle clay. Guy. Ralph Waldo Emerson. NOBA

Mortal my mate, bearing my rock-a-heart. To His Watch. Gerard Manley Hopkins. MoBrPo

Mortal never won to view thee. Hafiz [*or* Hafez]. TOF

Mortal Practice. Gabriel Zaid. TCLAP, *tr.* by Mónica Hernández-Cancio

Mortal, Sneer Not at the Devil. Heinrich Heine. TrJP, *tr.* by Emma Lazarus *Fr.* Homeward Bound.

Mortal though I bé, was ephemeral, if but a moment. From the Greek. Ptolemy. GrAn, *tr.* by Robert Bridges

Mortality [*or* Mortalitie], behold and fear[e]! Francis Beaumont. NOBE; OBEV; SCGP *Fr.* On the Tombs in Westminster Abbey.

Mortars are / the devil coughing. Remembrance of Things Past. Horace Coleman. CDa

Morte d'Arthur. Tennyson.
Epic, The [Morte d'Arthur]. NAEL-5v2; NAEL-6v2
"Here ended Hall, and our last light, that long." NAEL-5v2
"Then loudly cried the bold Sir Bedivere." TOF
"So all day long the noise of battle rolled." EBNV; NIP-4; NOBVV; OBNV; OxAEP-2

Mortification. George Herbert. ESCV; FSCP; GeHe; NOSC

Mortified Genius, The. James Graeme. NOEC

Mortmain. Robert Penn Warren.
After Night Flight Son Reaches Bedside of Already Unconscious Father, Whose Right Hand Lifts in a Spasmodic Gesture, as Though Trying to Make Contact: 1955. NOBA

Morwenna, Julie, don't forget me, Kate. (LL) New Diary, A. Dannie Abse. AngWePo; NoAM

Moschus Moschiferus. Alec Derwent Hope. CBAP

Moscow. December. Nineteen fifty-one. Simple Man, A. Nikolai Ivanovich Glazkov. TCRP, *tr.* by Daniel Weissbort

Moscow / like a Christmas-tree. Capitals. Raymond Garlick. AngWePo

"Moscow" Pool. Pyotr Vegin. TCRusP, *tr.* by Daniel Weissbort

Moscow Station, The. Yevgeny [*or* Evgenii] Borisovich Rein. ItGoST, *tr.* by Judith Hemschemeyer

Moscow: Summer '86. Yevgeny [*or* Evgenii] Bunimovich. TCRP, *tr.* by Bradley Jordan and Albert C. Todd

Mosel, The. Caroline Clive. PoBW

Moses. Amir Gilbo'a. MHP, *tr.* by Ruth Finer Mintz

Moses. Isaac Rosenberg.
"Fine! Fine!" PeFWW

Moses. Sydney Tremayne. OxBS

Moses. *Unknown.* OxNR

Moses: A Story of the Nile. Frances Ellen Watkins Harper.
Death of Moses, The.
"Oh never on that mountain." TCAPo

Moses and Jesus. Israel Zangwill. TrJP

Moses and the Princess. Peter Dickinson. NOxBChV

Moses, from whose loins I sprung. Jew, The. Isaac Rosenberg. ChIV-1; MoBrPo

Moses His Birth and Miracles. Michael Drayton.
"In time the Princess playing with the child." ChIV-1

Moses in Infancy. Jones Very. ChIV-1

"Moses" of Michael Angelo, The. Robert Browning. GS

Moses, who spake with God as with his friend. Death of Moses, The. "George Eliot." ChIV-1

Mosques into snow-palaces; banks, bagnios. City under Snow. Gwyn Williams. AngWePo

Mosquito, The. D. H. Lawrence. NPeEn; RB
(Mosquito Knows, The.) FaBoEE; OxBTC

Mosquito, The. Dan Pagis. FIT, *tr.* by Robert Friend

Mosquito at my ear. Issa. ChAP; EH, *tr.* by Robert Hass

Mosquito Kingdom. Ernesto Cardenal. VCWP, *tr.* by Donald D. Walsh

Mosquito Knows, The. D. H. Lawrence. *See* Mosquito, The

Mosquito lives, The. Mosquito, The. Dan Pagis. FIT, *tr. by* Robert Friend

Mosquito, may you fly, a swift courier for me. Meleager. HePo *Fr.* Epigrams.

Mosquito was heard to complain, A. Limerick. *Unknown.* PeLi

Mosquitoes. P'i Jih-hsiu. SuSp, *tr. by* William H. Nienhauser

Mosquitoes. Franz Wright. LCAP-2

Mosquitoes, shameless and shrill of voice, sucking the blood. Meleager. HePo *Fr.* Epigrams.

Moss below the Stairs. Kao Ch'i. CoBLCP, *tr. by* Jonathan Chaves

Moss-covered bucket that hangs in the well, The. (LL) Old Oaken Bucket, The. Samuel Woodworth. BRP; TCAPo

Moss covered paths between scarlet peonies. Visit to the Hermit Ts'ui. Ch'ien Ch'i. OHMPC, *tr. by* Kenneth Rexroth

Moss covers his stone bed fresh. Weeping for the Zen Master Po-yen. Chia Tao. SuSp, *tr. by* Stephen Owen

Moss-Gathering. Theodore Roethke. BLT; VGW

Moss in the gratings / of a sewer vent. January 1965, Looking On. Kenneth Irby. FTOS

Moss of His Skin, The. Anne Sexton. CoAP; NALW; PAI

Mossbawn. Seamus Heaney. CIP-2; HarvBoo; PNI

   Mossbawn Sunlight. BIrV

   Seed Cutters, The. PNI

   (Sunlight.) ModIr

Most Alluring Clouds That Mount the Sky, The. William Wordsworth. NOBVV

Most Americans like kids. On What the Army Does with Heads. Michael Casey. YaYoPo

Most Ancient Names of Fire, The. Roberto Sosa. ErotSp, *tr. by* Jo Anne Engelbert

Most at home with what is Real. (LL) Doggerel by a Senior Citizen. W. H. Auden. NBLV; NOBL

Most Beautiful, The. Guido Gozzano. TTTS, *tr. by* Victoria Pesce

Most Beautiful Girl in the World, The. Richard Rodgers. OBAL; ReLy

Most beautiful of things I leave is sunlight. Praxilla. BoWoP

Most beautiful! the red-flowering eucalyptus. Torso, The / Passages 18. Robert Duncan. CAGL; HarvBoo; PmAP

Most Beautiful Woman at My Highschool Reunion, The. Ellen Marie Bissert. GLP

Most Beds Are Beds. Sylvia Plath. ChAP *Fr.* Bed Book, The.

Most brightly of all burned the hair of my evening loved one. Night Ray. Paul Celan. AF, *tr. by* Michael Hamburger

Most charming sir, most learned young master. Letter to Carlos Pellicer. Eunice Odio. TCLAP, *tr. by* Martha Collins

Most days, this wild weather. Blondie. Jean Earle. TCAWP

Most Excellent Song Which Was Solomon's, The. Michael Drayton. "By night within my bed, I roamed here and there." ChIV-1

Most explicit— / the sense of trap. Age. Robert Creeley. PmAP

Most glorious Lord of life, that on this day. Edmund Spenser. *See* Amoretti

Most Gracious Queen, we thee implore. On Queen Caroline. *Unknown.* FaBoEE

Most gunmen. Cowboy Sayings. *Unknown.* CA

Most happy letters framed by skilfull trade. Edmund Spenser. NAEL-5v1 *Fr.* Amoretti.

Most high, all powerful, good Lord. Canticle of the Creatures. Saint Francis of Assisi. WoPoe, *tr. by* James Schuyler

Most High, all-powerful, good Lord. Canticle of the Brother Sun, The. Saint Francis of Assisi. BBASP, *tr. by* Regis J. Armstrong and Ignatius C. Brady

Most high, all-powerful sweet Lord. Canticle of the Sun. Saint Francis of Assisi. EnlH, *tr. by* Stephen Mitchell

Most high Lord. Cantico del Sole. Saint Francis of Assisi. CTC, *tr. by* Ezra Pound

Most Holy Night, that still dost keep. Night, The. Joseph Hilaire Pierre Belloc. OBEV

Most holy Satyr. Holy Satyr. "H. D." MoAmPo

Most honoured Hera, who descends from heaven. Nossis. GrAn

Most I riden by Ribbesdale. *Unknown.* MiEL

Most is your name the name of this dark stone. Rainy Mountain Cemetery. N. Scott Momaday. CDW; HATNAP

Most learned Father Grimold. With His Book, of Gardening. Walafrid Strabo. WoPoe, *tr. by* Tim Reynolds

Most likely whatever glimpse we caught. Letter to Russel Barron. Robert Gibb. SwNoth

Most lovely dark, my Æthiopia born. Most Lovely Shade. Dame Edith Sitwell. FaBoTw; GTBS-P

Most Lovely Shade. Dame Edith Sitwell. FaBoTw; GTBS-P

Most Men Know Love. Henry Timrod. Son

Most modern nature lovers have a personal scale of values that tells them. William Wordsworth. Gavin Ewart. NoAM

Most mornings I get away, slip out. Run before Dawn. William Stafford. MoASP

Most mornings we go running side by side. Morning Athletes. Marge Piercy. MoASP

Most near, most dear, most loved and most far. Sonnet to My Mother. George Barker. OxBSo; RaBo

Most noble empress, you have heard of me? William Shakespeare. OxAEP-1 *Fr.* Antony and Cleopatra.

Most, O maid's child, thy choice and worthy the winning. (LL) Spring. Gerard Manley Hopkins. EBVV; GSo; HAP; MoBrPo; NAEL-5v2; NAEL-6v2; NOBE; NOBVV; NoAM; OBMV; RB; TFi; TrCP

Most of his friends, as expected. As Expected. Thom Gunn. GLP

Most of It, The. Robert Frost. APT-1; BLT; HAP; NAAL-2v2; NoP-4; TOF; TRP; WeW-3

Most of my days are passed away, yet my heart is still impure. Worthless Heart, The. Immanuel di Roma. TrJP

Most of our bodies will melt. Lucy's Bones. Christine Evans. TCAWP

Most people don't know. Woman Who Raised Dogs, The. Lisa D. Chavez. AmPoNex

Most people expect their sons to be clever. Bathing the Infant. Su Tung-p'o (Su Shih). SuSp, *tr. by* Irving Y. Lo

Most people in the world stumble. Conversation Overheard. Quincy Troupe. NAAAL

Most poets to a muse that is stone-deaf cry. On the Oxford Book of Victorian Verse. Hugh MacDiarmid. MoBrPo

Most popular "act" in, The. Black Boys Play the Classics. Toi Derricotte. ExTi; SpirFl

Most precious treasure is never fully known, The. Bubbles on the Water. Yang Wan-li. SuSp, *tr. by* Jonathan Chaves

Most prolific seem to be imports, The. Water: City Wildlife and Greenery. Alfred Corn. UrbNat

Most Quietly at Times. Cäsar Flaischlen. AWP, *tr. by* Jethro Bithell

Most reverend Father, I have borne all wrong. Two Souls. Marjorie Lowry Christie Pickthall. NOBC

Most sacred fire, that burnest mightily. Edmund Spenser. NAEL-6v1; NAEL-7v1 *Fr.* Faerie Queene, The.

Most Saturday afternoons. Weepies, The. Paul Muldoon. NoAM; PNI

Most simple things repel. Mac Wellman. HeMarv *Fr.* Rat Minaret: Miniaturist-Divan, The.

Most Sweet It Is with Unuplifted Eyes. William Wordsworth. CenSon *Fr.* Poems Composed or Suggested During a Tour, in the Summer of 1833.

Most terrible was our hero in battle blows. From the Irish. James Simmons. ModIr; PBCIP; PNI

Most that can be said, The. Parade's End. Barbara Guest. PoM

Most, The / Revolutionary act. Revolutionary. Willie Perdomo. InTrad

Most truly hono[u]red, and as truly dear. To Her Father, with Some Verses. Anne Bradstreet. NAAL-3; NAAL-5; NALW

Most Unbelievable Part, The. Marjorie Agosin. TANSG, *tr. by* Cola Franzen

Most unexpectedly it happens, just. Victor Record Catalog. David Schubert. APT-2

Most Unloving One, The. Samuel Daniel. OBEV *Fr.* To Delia.

Most unusual thing I ever stole, The? A snowman. Stealing. Carol Ann Duffy. EmeKit

Most Vital Thing in Life, The. Grenville Kleiser. PoToHe; SoSe-8

Most weeds, whilst young. Francis Daniel Pastorius. SCAP

Most Welshmen are worthless. Case History. Dannie Abse. TCAWP

Most who die, the more we live, The. (LL) What If a Much of a Which of a Wind. E. E. Cummings. HarvBoo; MoAmPo; NAAL-2v2; NAAL-5; NOBA; OxBA; PoRA

Most women get married, 'tis true. Limerick. Barney Blackley. PeLi

Most wounds can Time repair. At Ease. Walter De la Mare. GTBS-P

Mostly it happens in the first year. Non-Accidental Injury Slides. Geoffrey Holloway. NLP

Mostly Mick Jagger. Catie Rosemurgy. BAP-97

Mostly Mozart at Planting Fields Arboretum. David Zeiger. MiVo

Mostly, the men. Western Trail Cook, 1880. Sharyn Jeanne Skeeter. ISC

Mostly we occupy ocular zones, clinging. How the Rainbow Works. Al Young. ESEAA

Mostly, we try to keep it from happening. Guardian Life. Michael Klein. WiU

Mot eran dous miei cossir. Arnaut Daniel. AWP, *tr. by* Harriet Waters Preston

Mote it is to trouble the mind's eye, A. William Shakespeare. OxAEP-1 *Fr.* Hamlet.

Motel pool wasn't flat as safety, The. Tides, The. Michael Klein. WiU

Motel Story. Maggie Nelson. AmPoNex

Motet: "Stranger here, as all my fathers were, A." John Amner. OxBSP

Motets, The. Eugenio Montale.

"Black and white, The." WoPoe, *tr.* by Dana Gioia
"Far away, still I was with you." WoPoe, *tr.* by Dana Gioia
"Frost on the windowpanes; the sick." WoPoe, *tr.* by Dana Gioia
"Here is the sign: it trembles." WoPoe, *tr.* by Dana Gioia
"I had almost lost." WoPoe, *tr.* by Dana Gioia
"If the green lizard darts." WoPoe, *tr.* by Dana Gioia
"Long goodbyes, the whistles in the dark, The." WoPoe, *tr.* by Dana Gioia
"Many years, and one of them a little harder." WoPoe, *tr.* by Dana Gioia
"You know this: I must lose you again and cannot." WoPoe, *tr.* by Dana Gioia
Motetti. Eugenio Montale. *See* Motets, The
Moth. Lance Henson. VoR
Moth, A. Henry Bellyse Baildon. NOBVV
Moth, The. Ahmad al-Safi Al-Najafi. MAP, *tr.* by John Heath-Stubbs and Salma Khadra Jayyusi
Moth, The. Vernon Scannell. OxBC
Moth ate a word, A. To me it seemed. Cynewulf. AnOE *Fr.* Riddles (Exeter Book).
Moth ate words; a marvellous event, A. *Unknown.* NoP-4
Moth belated,—sun and zephyr-kist, A. To a Moth that Drinketh of the Ripe October. Emily Jane Pfeiffer. ViWPN
Moth flew a bee-line, The. Mothy Monologue. Ralph Gustafson. NOBC
Moth-force a small town always has. Strength of Fields, The. James Dickey. VCAP
Moth has got into it, The. Moth, The. Vernon Scannell. OxBC
Moth house is taking over, Sir Footfall. Mac Wellman. HeMarv *Fr.* Rat Minaret: Miniaturist-Divan, The.
Moth, I thought, munching a word, A. Cynewulf. OPOU, *tr.* by Gerard Benson *Fr.* Riddles (Exeter Book).
Moth's kiss, first, The! Robert Browning. BoLoP; OBEV *Fr.* In a Gondola.
Moth-Terror. Benjamin De Casseres. TrJP
Moth under the eaves, The. Prelude to Winter. William Carlos Williams. SAmP
Mother. Max Ehrmann. PoToHe
Mother. Willem Elsschot. TuT, *tr.* by Peter Van de Kamp
Mother. Hermann Hagedorn. PoToHe
Mother. Josephine D. Henderson Heard. CBWP-4
Mother. Vladimir Holan. PoSu, *tr.* by Ian Milner and Jarmila Milner
Mother. Attila József. IQMS, *tr.* by Vernon Watkins
Mother. P. Lankesh. OMIP, *tr.* by A. K. Ramanujan
Mother. Nancy Morejón. TANSG, *tr.* by Joy Renjilian-Burgy
Mother. Nancy Morejón. TCLAP, *tr.* by Kathleen Weaver
Mother. Kiyoko Nagase. BoWoP
Mother. Beryl Philp-Carmichael (Yungha-Dhu). IBA
Mother. Hettye Rayburn Ramsey. PWR
Mother. Poem for a Militant. Jorge Rebelo. PBMAP
Mother. Daphne Rock. Prnts
Mother. Kristina Rungano. HAWP
Mother. River. Shuntaro Tanikawa. VCWP, *tr.* by Harold Wright
Mother. Isobel Thrilling. Prnts
Mother. *Unknown.* PoToHe
Mother, The. Gwendolyn Brooks. ESEAA; ISC; IllVoic; NAAAL; NAAL-5; NALW; PoPoPo *Fr.* Street in Bronzeville, A.
Mother, The. Caroline Clive. VWP
Mother, The. Nikolai Ivanovich Dementyev [*or* Dement'ev]. TCRP, *tr.* by Max Hayward and Lubov Yakovleva
Mother, The. Catulle Mendès. TrJP, *tr.* by W. J. Robertson
Mother, The. Sharon Olds. PBCAP
Mother, The. Dora Sigerson Shorter. VWP
Mother, a mother was born, A. (LL) Maternity. Alice Thompson Meynell. OxBSP; PEW; VWP
Mother and child! whose blending tears. Memorial Pillar, The. Felicia Dorothea Hemans. RWP
Mother and Daughter. Augusta Davies Webster.
"Her father lessons me I at times am hard." ViWPN
"Little child she, half defiant came, A." VWP
Love's Mourner. VWP; ViWPN
"She will not have it that my day wanes low." OxBSo; ViWPN
"Since first my little one lay on my breast." VWP; ViWPN
"Sometimes, as young things will, she vexes me." ViWPN
"That she is beautiful is not delight." ViWPN
"That some day death who has us all for jest." VWP
"There's one I miss. A little questioning maid." VWP; ViWPN
Mother and father are in heaven— / Amen. Chronica. Else Lasker-Schüler. PFTM-1
Mother and I. Shinkichi Takahashi. ZenPo, *tr.* by Takashi Ikemoto and Lucien Stryk

Mother and listener she is, but she does not listen. Question, The. Muriel Rukeyser. WPOW
Mother and Poet. Elizabeth Barrett Browning. NAEL-5v2; NAEL-6v2; NALW; VWP; ViWPN
Mother and Son. Alden Nowlan. RaBo
Mother and Son. Allen Tate. MoAmPo
Mother Asks What I'm Put To. Julia Alvarez. Son *Fr.* 33.
Mother at Shannon, waving to her young, A. Throwing the Beads. Sean Dunne. BiHa
Mother, blood irises unfold. Santorini Daughter. Julie Fay. NAPBL
Mother called to her own son, The. Boy Changed into a Stag Clamours at the Gate of Secrets, The. Ferenc Juhász. IQMS, *tr.* by David Wevill
Mother Cat. John Montague. NOIV
Mother Corn Assumes Leadership. *Unknown.* Fr. Hako, The.
Mother Country, The. Benjamin Franklin. AiP
Mother Dark. Francesca Yetunde Pereira. PBA
Mother darling, I cannot work the loom. Sappho. BoWoP
Mother Dawning. Janine Canan. HW
Mother dear, may I go downtown. Ballad of Birmingham. Dudley Randall. BPo; HeIP-4; ISC; InPK-6; NIL-7; NIP-4; NoAM; NoP-4; SoSe-8
Mother, Dear Mother. Elma Mitchell. Prnts
Mother Dear, O! Pray for Me. *Unknown.* AH
Mother / Deer / Lady. Harold Littlebird. VoR
Mother Dies. Saitō Mokichi.
"From far off I have brought medicines, she watches me because I am her son." WoPoe, *tr.* by Hiroaki Sato and Burton Watson
Mother does knitting, The. Familial. Jacques Prévert. CLPP; FaBoWar, *tr.* by Lawrence Ferlinghetti
Mother Doesn't Want a Dog. Judith Viorst. NBLV
Mother, don't, please don't. To Mother. S. Usha. OMIP, *tr.* by A. K. Ramanujan
Mother Doorstep. Victor James Daley. NOBAu
Mother: Dorcas Good, The. Nicole Cooley. NeAmPo
Mother Earth: Her Whales. Gary Snyder. LCAP-2
Mother eats seaweed and plum pickles. Pearls. Lee Ann Roripaugh. AmPoNex
Mother Egret. *Vietnamese Oral Tradition.* CaDao, *tr.* by John Balaban
Mother fetched the fruit from the mango grove. Mango Poem. Regie Cabico. WiU
Mother, for months a mist has been before me. Light in Darkness. Mary E. Tucker. CBWP-1
Mother Goblin's Lullaby. Jack Prelutsky. NOxBChV
Mother Goose's Garland. Archibald MacLeish. OBAL
Mother Goose Up-to-Date. Louis Untermeyer.
Archibald MacLeish Suspends the Five Little Pigs. MoAmPo
(Edgar A. Guest Considers "The Old Woman Who Lived in a Shoe" and the Good Old Verities at the Same Time.) OBAL
(Edgar A. Guest Syndicates the Old Woman Who Lived in a Shoe.) MoAmPo
Edna St. Vincent Millay Exhorts Little Boy Blue. MoAmPo
John Masefield Relates the Story of Tom, Tom, the Piper's Son. MoAmPo
Walter de la Mare Tells the Listener about Jack and Jill. MoAmPo
Mother has brought me a lavender tree. (LL) Love from a Foreign City. Lavinia Greenlaw. EmeKit; MFPA
Mother has lupus. Dear World. Paula Gunn Allen. HATNAP
Mother Hubbard's Tale. Edmund Spenser.
Fox and the Ape Go to Court, The. NoSic
Mother, I am eighteen this year. Cherished Daughter, The. *Unknown.* WoPoe, *tr.* by Nguyen Ngoc Bich
Mother, I am mothering you now. I'm My Own Mother, Now. Stella P. Chipasula. HAWP
Mother, I bow to gold. Mighty Lord Is Money, A. Francisco de Quevedo y Villegas. SpanPo, *tr.* by William M. Davis
Mother, I Cannot Mind My Wheel. Walter Savage Landor. AWP; BoLoP; NAEL-5v2; NAEL-6v2; NOBE; OBEV; OBVE
Mother, I'll / tell you. Let me tell you it's. Persephone, to Demeter. Marilyn Krysl. HW
Mother, I long to get married. Whistle, Daughter, Whistle. *Unknown.* OxNR; ReMoGo
Mother, I love you so. Human Affection. Stevie Smith. NALW
Mother I never knew. Issa. EH, *tr.* by Robert Hass
Mother, I want to go. *Unknown.* BoWoP
Mother, I weep. Issa. SoOfWa, *tr.* by Sam Hamill
Mother, / If I am where I am. From an Asylum; Kathy Chattle to Her Mother, Ruth Arbeiter. Anne Stevenson. BrRo
Mother in gladness, Mother in sorrow. W. Dayton Wedgefarth. PoToHe
Mother-in-Law Is Cruel. Cheng Hsieh. CoBLCP, *tr.* by Jonathan Chaves
Mother-in-Law of the Marquis de Sade, The. Jennifer Maiden. NOBAu

Mother, is this the darkness of the end. For "Our Lady of the Rocks." Dante Gabriel Rossetti. EBEV

Mother, it pains me that I must confide. Winter Offerings. Frank Ormsby. PNI

Mother Lakshmi's Poem. Cassia Berman. HW

Mother Land / Long lain asleep. Mother Dark. Francesca Yetunde Pereira. PBA

Mother, let me go! (LL) Frosty Night, A. Robert Graves. MoBrPo; OxBTC

Mother lies in travail bed, The. Newly Dead and Newly Born. Eliza Ogilvy. VWP

Mother Love. Rita Dove.
    Demeter Mourning. NAAAL
    Demeter's Prayer to Hades. NAAAL
    History. NAAAL
    Persephone Abducted. NAAAL
    Statistic: The Witness. NAAAL2

Mother Love. Elaine Feinstein. HarvBoo

Mother Love. Stevie Smith. Spl

Mother love is a mighty benefaction. Mother Love. Stevie Smith. Spl

Mother loves me loves me not. Veno Taufer. WoPoe, tr. by Milne Holton Fr. Prayers and Games of the Water People, The.

Mother, make me Your treasurer. Rāmprasād Sen. SinGod, tr. by Rachel Fell McDermott

Mother, May I Go Out to Swim? Unknown. OxNR

Mother, May I? Alma Villanueva. WPOW

Mother, Mother, Are You All There? Felicia Lamport. NBLV

Mother, Mother, my Dear Mother. Katie Kádár. Hungarian Oral Tradition. IQMS, tr. by Adam Makkai

Mother Mother shave me. Song. Unknown. BoWoP, tr. by Ulli Beier

Mother, mother, what illbred aunt. Disquieting Muses, The. Sylvia Plath. NALW

Mother, mother, / Why is it not you? One Who Struggles, The. Ernst Toller. TrJP, tr. by E. Ellis Roberts

Mother Nature. Amy Fusselman. HeMarv

Mother Nature, how fair has your invention's grace. Lake of Zurich, The. Friedrich Gottlieb Klopstock. GePo, tr. by George C. Schoolfield

Mother, never mourn'. (LL) Mater Dolorosa. William Barnes. NOBE; OBEV

Mother Night. James Weldon Johnson. Son

Mother of Andromeda, The. Julie Fay. NAPBL

Mother of fictions. Prayer to Eve, A. Kathleen Norris. HW

Mother of God, The. W. B. Yeats. BBASP; ChIV-2; ChrPo
    (Three-fold terror of love, The.) GI

Mother of God, everyone is invited. Congress of the Insomniacs, The. Charles Simic. EmeKit

Mother of God! no lady thou. Our Lady. Mary Elizabeth Coleridge. OBEV; OBMV; ViWPN; WPE

Mother of God! Our Lady! For Eleanor and Bill Monahan. William Carlos Williams. CRP; VGW

Mother of God that's Lady of the Heavens. Prayer of the Old Woman. François Villon. MoBrPo; PeECV, tr. by J. M. Synge

Mother of God, you tired Mary. Géza Páskándi. IQMS, tr. by Agnes Arany-Makkai Fr. Language Memory.

Mother of gods. Meleager. GrAn

Mother of heaven, regina of the clouds. Le Monocle de Mon Oncle. Wallace Stevens. TCAPo

Mother of Hermes! and still youthful Maia! Fragment of an Ode to Maia Written on May Day, 1818. John Keats. OBEV

Mother of Judas, The. Yevgeny [or Evgenii] Mikhailovich Vinokurov. GI, tr. by Anthony Rudolf

Mother of King Matthias, The. János Arany. IQMS, tr. by Neville Masterman

Mother of memories! O mistress-queen! Le Balcon. Charles Baudelaire. AWP, tr. by Lord Alfred Bruce Douglas

Mother of my birth, for how long were we together. Kaddish. David Ignatow. RaBo; TaR

Mother of Nothing. Naomi Shihab Nye. GraLe

Mother of our own dear mother, good old grandam, wake and smile! Grandmother, The. Victor Hugo. TreFP

Mother of salt and slate. Salmon, The. Duane Niatum. PoCoUp

Mother of the concierge and the concierge will let everything, The. Monday rue Christine. Guillaume Apollinaire. CuPo

Mother of the Groom. Seamus Heaney. OxBSP; PAI

Mother of the muses, we are taught, The. Memory. Walter Savage Landor. EBEV; NOBVV; NPeEn

Mother of the Universe. Yoko Ono. HW

Mother of Us All, The. Gertrude Stein.
    Concluding Aria. PFTM-2

Mother of us all, The. Unknown. HW, tr. by Charles Boer Fr. Homeric Hymns.

Mother, oh mother! where shall we hide us? Others. James Reeves. Spl

Mother: / Only hours after your death. Another Poem to My Mother. Clementina Suárez. TANSG, tr. by Janet N. Gold

Mother Poem. Joel Oppenheimer. PoM

Mother Ruin. Linda Gregerson. ExTi

Mother's Birthday. Lydia Wagenlander. PWR

Mother's Charge, The. Charlotte Perkins Stetson Gilman. SWaP

Mother's Choice, The. Unknown. OxBoLi

Mother's dance blossomed in beauty at last. My Mother Dances a Ballad. István Sinka. IQMS, tr. by Adam Makkai

Mother's Day. Edwin Becker. PWR

Mother's Day. Steve Hassett. CDa

Mother's Day. Daisy Zamora. LoL, tr. by Margaret Randall

Mother's dream, A. Nocturne. Alaide Foppa. TANSG, tr. by Celeste Kostopulos-Cooperman

Mother's face looked tired and worn, The. Skeptic, The. Clara Ann Thompson. CBWP-2

Mother's father. Big Zeb Johnson. Everett Hoagland. GT

Mother's Habits. Nikki Giovanni. BlSi

Mother's Hands. W. Dayton Wedgefarth. PoToHe

Mother's Inheritance. Fawziyya Abu Khalid. WPOW, tr. by Kamal Boullata

Mother's Joy, A. Ruth Fortney Maxwell. PWR

Mother's Lace. Shonto Begay. NOxBChV

Mother's Lament, The. Helen Selina Blackwood, Countess of Dufferin. VWP

Mother's Lament, The. Mary E. Tucker. CBWP-1

Mother's Love, A. Josephine D. Henderson Heard. CBWP-4

Mother's Love, A. Ellen Johnston. VWP

Mother's Malison; or, Clyde's Water, The. Unknown. ESPB

Mother's Mark. Jana Beranová. TuT, tr. by Aidan Sharkey

Mother's Nerves. X. J. Kennedy. ChAP

Mother's Past. Reed Whittemore. BodElec

Mother's past is full of old cars with very large fenders. Mother's Past. Reed Whittemore. BodElec

Mother's Recall. Mary Weston Fordham. CBWP-2

Mother's Room. Nicky Rice. Prnts

Mother's Song ("It's quiet in the house so quiet."). Unknown. WoPoe, tr. by Stephen Berg

Mother's Song ("If snow falls on the far field."). Unknown. BoWoP, tr. by Willis Barnstone

Mother's Song, The. Unknown. OBCP, tr. by Peter Freuchen

Mother's Song to a Baby. Unknown. OxIBACP

Mother Sabbath. Nikolai Alekseievich Klyuyev [or Kliuev or Klyuev]. TCRusP, tr. by John Glad

Mother said: Come now, say your prayers, The. Lord's Prayer, The. Massillon Coicou. NegPo, tr. by Ellen Conroy Kennedy

Mother said if I wore this hat. My Hat. Stevie Smith. BrRo

Mother said thirty years ago. Miss Florence Jackson. David Huddle. PBCAP

Mother said to call her if the H bomb exploded. Belief. Josephine Miles. FaBoWP; NoAM; TAP

Mother Sarah's Lullaby. Itsik [or Itzik or Itzig] Manger. TrJP, tr. by Jacob Sonntag

Mother sat / with hunger on her hands. Child's Parliament. Chenjerai Hove. HBAPE

Mother shake the cherry-tree. Let's Be Merry. Christina Georgina Rossetti. TLR9 Fr. Sing-Song.

Mother Speaks: The Algiers Motel Incident, Detroit, A. Michael S. Harper. BPo; NBV

Mother, the Nurse, and the Fairy, The. John Gay. PeLV Fr. Fables.

Mother then must suck the hoe. (LL) Bible, N.T. ChIV-2; NOSC, tr. by Richard Crashaw Fr. St. Luke.

Mother, they say we never really leave you. Skin. Sari Friedman. GotH

Mother throws her voice in loops, The. Two Couples. Debra Bruce. FFC

Mother to Her Waking Infant, A. Joanna Baillie. ECWP; NOEC; NoP-4; WoRP
    (Now in thy dazzled half-oped eye.) CABP

Mother to Son. Langston Hughes. AmFaPo; ChAP; ISC; NAAAL; NAAL-2v2; NAAL-5; NTCP; OBCA; OxIBACP; SAmP; TTY; WoPoe

Mother Tongue. Rebecca Seiferle. ExTi

Mother Tongue. Jon Stallworthy. NoAM

Mother, unroll the bolts and name. Naming the Fabrics. Julia Alvarez. FFC

Mother used to tell us about a white forest in Russia. Suspicion. Alejandra Piznarnick. TANSG, tr. by Susan Bassnett

Mother wanted the dowry of rice. Arranged Marriage, The. Vietnamese Oral Tradition. CaDao, tr. by John Balaban

Mother was a crack of light. Three Floors. Stanley Kunitz. LoL

Mother Wept. Joseph Skipsey. EBVV

Mother, what trick of light. Mirror of Matsuyama, The. Sharon Hashimoto. OpBo

Mother, while you were at the shops. Snowman, The. Roger McGough. OTCP

Mother, who read and thought and poured herself into me. Arioso Dolente. Anne Stevenson. Prnts

Mother with Child. Lenore Keeshig-Tobias. FFC

Mother with the life-giving power now comes. *Unknown.* APN-2 *Fr.* Hako, The.

Mother wrote to say: "Stay / in Europe. Soak up as much beauty as you." John Cage. APSN *Fr.* Diary: How to Improve the World (You Will Only Make Matters Worse).

Mother, / You did not leave me an inheritance of necklaces for a wedding. Mother's Inheritance. Fawziyya Abu Khalid. WPOW, *tr. by* Kamal Boullata

Mother, you know there is a place somewhere called Paris. Right Meaning, The. César Vallejo. RaBo, *tr. by* Robert Bly

Mother / You're always finding ways to amuse Yourself. Kamalākānta Bhattācārya. SinGod, *tr. by* Rachel Fell McDermott

Motherhood. Mathilde Blind. ViWPN *Fr.* Ascent of Man, The.

Motherhood. Rita Dove. NAAAL

Motherhood. May Swenson. CoAP; NoP-4

Motherhood is so final, Nita. Mariana II. Maria Arrillaga. TANSG

Mothering. Carla Harryman. FTOS

Mothers. Nikki Giovanni. UnPo

Mothers. Francis Saltus Saltus. VerBaPo

Mothers and Daughters. David Campbell. BMAP

Mothers are hardest to forgive. Adversary, The. Phyllis McGinley. FaBoEE; OBCA; OxBSP; SoSe-8

Mothers / cranking the machine. Greater Friendship Baptist Church, The. Carole C. Gregory Clemmons. BlSi

Mothers, Daughters. Shirley Kaufman. BoWoP

Mothers of America / let your kids go to the movies! Ave Maria. Frank O'Hara. CLPP; HCAP; HarvBoo; MakPoe; NAAL-2v2; NNaP; NoP-4; PmAP; PoM; PoPoPo; VCAP

Mothers of Sons. Lesley Saunders. BrRo

Mothers, / That hope of yours, your joyful burden. To the Mothers. Ernst Toller. TrJP, *tr. by* E. Ellis Roberts

Motho Ke Motho Ka Batho Babang (A Person Is a Person because of Other People). Jeremy Cronin. AF

Moths. Adam Zagajewski. BLT, *tr. by* Renata Gorcyznski

Moths, The. Michael Jackson. PeNZ

Moths, The. W. S. Merwin. HeIP-4

Moths, The. Sean O Riordain. NOIV, *tr. by* Thomas Kinsella

Moths watched us through. Moths. Adam Zagajewski. BLT, *tr. by* Renata Gorcyznski

Mothy Monologue. Ralph Gustafson. NOBC

Motion guided a lotion, A. Lack of Balance but Not Fatal, A. Jackson Mac Low. FTOS

Motion of gathering loops of water, The. Glass Bubbles, The. Samuel Greenberg. APT-1

Motion of the Cypher. Ray DiPalma. FTOS

Motion Pictures: 4. Barbara Guest. BodElec

Motion Pictures: 15. Barbara Guest. BodElec

Motion's Holdings. A. R. Ammons. NoAM

Motion's the dead giveaway. Viable. A. R. Ammons. TAP

Motionless Clouds. T'ao Ch'ien [*or* T'ao Yuan-ming]. CoBCP, *tr. by* Burton Watson

Motionless Faces. Carlos Drummond de Andrade. PFTM-1

Motionless—His sons. Death Bed. Thomas Kinsella. CIP-2; PBCIP

Motionless sat the shadow at the helm. Thomas Westwood. PeVV *Fr.* Quest of the Sancgreall, The.

Motionless under the moon-beam. Calvary. W. B. Yeats. PeECV

Motions and means, on land and sea at war. Steamboats, Viaducts, and Railways. William Wordsworth. CenSon; NAEL-5v2; NAEL-6v2

Motions and Means, on land and sea at war. William Wordsworth. NAEL-5v2 *Fr.* Poems Composed or Suggested during a Tour, in the Summer of 1833.

Motive. Reginald Shepherd. NeAmPo

Motive for Mayhem, A. Abigail Child. FTOS

Motive for Metaphor, The. Wallace Stevens. APT-1; MoAmPo

Motley. Peter Davison. NBLV

Motley. Walter De la Mare. PoWW

Motley's the Only Wear. William Shakespeare. OBCoV *Fr.* As You Like It.

Motor Bus. Alfred Denis Godley. NOBL

(On the Motor Bus.) NBLV

Motor Oil Queen. Cheryl Burke. WiU

Motor stops, the boat thuds mud—the river's bed, The. After the Flood. John Foulcher. NOBAu

Motorcycle roaring in the distance, A. Aunt Toni's Heart. Rafael Campo. RA

Motorcycle Ward. David Moolten. BloBone

Motorcyclists, The. James Tate. NoAM; ReTh

Mots d'Heures: Gousses, Rames. Luis d'Antin Van Rooten.

"Jacques s'apprête." OBCoV

"Lit-elle messe, moffette." OBCoV

"Polis poutre catalane." OBCoV

"Pousse y gâte, pousse y gâte." OBCoV

Mottled hands cupped deep. Hands in the Motion of Prayer. Sojourner Kincaid Rolle. GeoHom

Motto. Yüan Mei. WoPoe, *tr. by* Jerome P. Seaton

Motto, The. Abraham Cowley. BeJo; NOSC

Motto for a Sun Dial. James Vincent Cunningham. *See* Epigram: "I who by day am function of the light."

Motto for a Sundial. *Unknown.* FaBoEE

Motto to "Illusions." Ralph Waldo Emerson. *See* Illusions

Motto to "Nature." Ralph Waldo Emerson. *See* Nature [1836]

Motto to "The Poet." Ralph Waldo Emerson. NCAP

Mould of Castile. Jack R. Clemo. NOCV

Moules à la Marinière. Elizabeth Garrett. MFPA

Moulton Transformations. Dixie Salazar. GeoHom

Mound, The. Thomas Hardy. OxBTC

Mound of dung. (LL) Muliebrity. Sujata Bhatt. FSt; HarvBoo

Mounds from the yolk. (LL) Abiku. Wole Soyinka. PBA; PBMAP; PoetW

Mounds of Human Heads. Osip Emilevich Mandelstam [*or* Mandelshtam]. WoPoe, *tr. by* Mark Rudman

Mounds of Human Heads Are Wandering into the Distance. Osip Emilevich Mandelstam [*or* Mandelshtam]. AF

Mounds of human heads recede in mist. Mounds of Human Heads. Osip Emilevich Mandelstam [*or* Mandelshtam]. WoPoe, *tr. by* Mark Rudman

Mount, The. Léonie Adams. MoAmPo

Mount Ararat. Louise Glück. ColAP

Mount Auburn! loveliest city of the dead. Richard Henry Wilde. APN-1 *Fr.* Hesperia.

Mount Badon. Charles Williams. FaBoTw

Mount Bromley Hymn. John Peck. PoCoUp

Mount Chung-Nan. Wang Wei. ChinPo, *tr. by* Yip Wai-lim

Mount Eagle. John Montague. BiHa

Mount Fuji. Kaneko Mitsuharu. WoPoe, *tr. by* James Kirkup and Akiko Takemoto

Mount Kearsarge. Donald Hall. LoL

Mount. Leave your living to the wise. Where the Sun Ends. Peter Davison. ChIV-1

Mount Lykaion. Trumbull Stickney. OxBA; Son *Fr.* Sonnets from Greece.

Mount Melleray. Sean O Riordain. ModIr, *tr. by* Patrick Crotty

Mount of Olives. Henry Vaughan. ESCV; GeHe

Mount of Olives, The. Shirley Kaufman. DTA

Mount of the Muses, The. Robert Herrick. CaPo

Mount rides into the seething alcove. (LL) Women of Rubens, The. Wislawa Szymborska. PoSu; VCWP

Mount Shasta. John Rollin Ridge. APN-2

Mount Sumeru—my fist! Kiko. ZenPo, *tr. by* Takashi Ikemoto and Lucien Stryk

Mount T'ai is one tall mountain rising. Song of Mount T'ai. Lu Chi. CrYelRi, *tr. by* Sam Hamill

Mount T'ai P'ing. Ch'ien Ch'i. OHMPC, *tr. by* Kenneth Rexroth

Mount Wu Is High. Lu Chao-lin. SuSp, *tr. by* Robin D. S. Yates

Mountain, The. Louise Glück. NoAM

Mountain, The. Mikhail Yuryevich Lermontov. AWP, *tr. by* Max Eastman

Mountain, The. W. S. Merwin. VGW

Mountain, The. Jones Very. NCAP

Mountain after mountain / Fold by fold. Tune: "Remembering the Lady of Ch'in—At the Mouth of Dragon Pool." Na-lan Hsing-te. SuSp, *tr. by* Lenore Mayhew

Mountain Afterglow, The. James Laughlin. VGW

Mountain and lake. I Ching. Diane Di Prima. SeSe

Mountain—Buddha's body, The. Layman Sotoba. ZenPo, *tr. by* Takashi Ikemoto and Lucien Stryk

Mountain Building. Víctor Hernández Cruz. PueRic

Mountain Cemetery, The. Edgar Bowers. CoAmPo

Mountain Chant, The. *Unknown.*

First Daylight Song. APN-2, *tr. by* Washington Matthews

First Song of the Exploding Stick. APN-2, *tr. by* Washington Matthews

First Song of the Thunder. APN-2; TCAPo, *tr. by* Washington Matthews

Invocation to Dsilyi N'Eyani. APN-2; TCAPo, *tr. by* Washington Matthews

Last Daybreak Song. APN-2, *tr. by* Washington Matthews

Last Song of the Exploding Stick.   APN-2, *tr. by* Washington Matthews
Last Words of the Prophet.   APN-2, *tr. by* Washington Matthews
One of the Awl Songs.   APN-2, *tr. by* Washington Matthews
Sixth Song of the Holy Young Men.   APN-2, *tr. by* Washington Matthews
(Song of Sequence.)   TCAPo
Song of the Prophet.   APN-2, *tr. by* Washington Matthews
Song of the Rising Sun Dance.   APN-2, *tr. by* Washington Matthews
Twelfth Song of the Holy Young Men.   APN-2, *tr. by* Washington Matthews
Twelfth Song of the Thunder.   APN-2; AWP, *tr. by* Washington Matthews
Mountain colors, whether near or far.   Distant Mountains.   Ou-yang Hsiu.
   CoBCP, *tr. by* Burton Watson
Mountain Corral.   Helen Sorrells.   WPE
Mountain cuckoo, The.   Buson.   EH, *tr. by* Robert Hass
Mountain cuckoo, The.   Issa.   EH, *tr. by* Robert Hass
Mountain Drinking Song.   Li Po.   CrYelRi, *tr. by* Sam Hamill
Mountain, Fire, Thornbush.   Harvey Shapiro.   VGW
Mountain Forest.   "Aleksandr Borisovich Kusikov."   TCRP, *tr. by* Albert C.
   Todd
Mountain Greenery.   Richard Rodgers.   OBAL; ReLy
Mountain in Labor, The.   Aesop.   AWP, *tr. by* William Ellery Leonard
Mountain is the father of the clouds, The.   Painting in the Style of Secretary
   Kao, A.   Yün Shou-p'ing.   CoBLCP, *tr. by* Jonathan Chaves
Mountain Lion.   D. H. Lawrence.   FaBoVe; OxBTC; RB
Mountain Living.   Han-shan Te-ch'ing.
   "Through a few splinters of."   WoPoe, *tr. by* James M. Cryer
Mountain looks gaunt, The.   Tune: "Celebration in the Eastern Plain"—
   Replying to a Lyric Song by the Senior Poet Ma Chih-yüan.   *Unknown.*
   SuSp, *tr. by* Sherwin S. S. Fu
Mountain mist / Torches dropped.   Kaya Shirao.   ZenPo, *tr. by* Takashi
   Ikemoto and Lucien Stryk
Mountain moon shines on a cloudless sky, The.   Written at Mauve Garden: Pine
   Wind Terrace.   Chu Yi-tsun.   SuSp, *tr. by* Chang Yin-nan
Mountain Mountainous in Parturition, A.   Voltaire.   WoPoe, *tr. by* Robert
   Fitzgerald
Mountain of books half-finished, A.   Surf.   Kiyoko Nagase.   ItWoWo, *tr. by*
   Kijima Hajime
Mountain of green trees and orioles everywhere!   Hsü Pen.   CoBLCP   *Fr.*
   Leisurely Stroll, A.
Mountain of yellow gold is no treasure at all, A. (LL)   On the Hall of Precious
   Virtue.   Yang Shih-ch'i.   CoBLCP; ColAnChi, *tr. by* Jonathan Chaves
Mountain our life is, overlooking, A.   Abyss of Death, The.   Ma'ruf Al-Rasafi.
   MAP, *tr. by* Issa Boullata and Christopher Middleton
Mountain over Aberdare, The.   Alun Lewis.   AngWePo; TCAWP
Mountain pony's coat, A. (LL)   Windharp.   John Montague.   CIP-2; PNI
Mountain range, The.   Temple of Eternal Light.   Muso Soseki.   EaWin, *tr. by*
   W. S. Merwin
Mountain Residence of Secretary Cheng Ching-ssu, The.   Hsü Pen.   CoBLCP,
   tr. by Jonathan Chaves
Mountain Retreat of a Recluse, The.   Chang Yü.   CoBLCP, *tr. by* Jonathan
   Chaves
Mountain road ends here, The.   Lyell's Hypothesis Again.   Kenneth Rexroth.
   APSN; APT-2
Mountain road is steep, the stone steps are dangerous, The.   Spring Thoughts
   Sent to Tzu-an.   Yü Hsüan-chi.   BoWoP; WoPoe, *tr. by* Geoffrey Waters
Mountain's a palace, A.   Written in the Mountains.   Kuan Hsiu.   WoPoe, *tr.
   by* Jerome P. Seaton
Mountain's giddy height I sought, A.   Lay of the Trilobite.   May Kendall.
   NPeEn; VWP; ViWPN
Mountain's green and shining, The.   Summer Solstice.   Alan Garner.
   NOxBChV
Mountain Sanctuaries.   Felicia Dorothea Hemans.   CenSon
Mountain shadow.   Foster Jewell.   HA
Mountain sheep are sweeter, The.   Thomas Love Peacock.   AWP; CABP;
   FaBoCh; FaBoWar; HAP; NAEL-5v2; NAEL-6v2; NOBE; NOBRP;
   NPeEn; OxAEP-2   *Fr.* Misfortunes of Elphin, The.
Mountain snow.   Seasons in Santa Fe.   Gerald Vizenor.   HATNAP
Mountain Songs.   Fêng Mêng-lung.
   Feeling the Itch.   ColAnChi; WoPoe, *tr. by* Richard W. Bodman
   Fooling Mom.   ColAnChi, *tr. by* Richard W. Bodman
   My Old Man's Small.   ColAnChi; WoPoe, *tr. by* Richard W. Bodman
   No Old Lady.   ColAnChi, *tr. by* Richard W. Bodman
   Smart.   ColAnChi; WoPoe, *tr. by* Richard W. Bodman
Mountain Spirit, The.   *Unknown.*   CoBCP, *tr. by* Burton Watson   *Fr.* Nine
   Songs.
Mountain Spring, A.   Ch'u Ch'uang I.   OHMPC, *tr. by* Kenneth Rexroth
Mountain Stream, The.   John Ceiriog Hughes.   OBWVE, *tr. by* Kenneth
   Hurlstone Jackson
Mountain stream in wild bamboo, A.   On Chung Mountain.   Wang An-shih.
   CrYelRi, *tr. by* Sam Hamill

Mountain Study.   Peter Van Toorn.   NOBC
Mountain Talk.   A. R. Ammons.   HCAP
Mountain teeth, tips of anemious rippled stone.   On the Subject of Waves.
   Eldon Grier.   MoCV
Mountain temple.   Horoku.   JDP, *tr. by* Yoel Hoffmann
Mountain temple dim and far away, its back against the setting sun, A.   Tune:
   "Sand of Silk-washing Stream."   Wang Kuo-wei.   SuSp, *tr. by* Ching-i Tu
Mountain Tops.   Lizelia Augusta Jenkins Moorer.   CBWP-3
Mountain Town—Mexico.   Eldon Grier.   NOBC
Mountain was in great distress and loud, A.   Mountain in Labor, The.   Aesop.
   AWP, *tr. by* William Ellery Leonard
Mountain / Whose woman have you brought home to our mountain city?
   Rasikcandra Rāy.   SinGod, *tr. by* Rachel Fell McDermott
Mountain Wind, A.   "Æ"   AWP
Mountaineer, The.   Robert Nathan.   TrJP
Mountains.   Gaylord Brewer.   AmPoNex
Mountains.   Alice Oswald.   MFPA
Mountains and cold places on the earth.   Cloud Factory, The.   John Haines.
   SPE
Mountains and rivers lie in the opening sun.   Spring.   Tu Fu.   TAL
Mountains and Rivers without End: The Market.   Gary Snyder.
   Earrings Dangling and Miles of Desert.   APSN
   Hump-Backed Flute Player, the.   APSN; PFTM-2
Mountains and seas.   Whip-the-World.   Hugh MacDiarmid.   FaBoVe
Mountains, and the lonely death at last, The.   To a Traveler.   Lionel Pigot
   Johnson.   MoBrPo
Mountains Are a Lonely Folk, The.   Hamlin Garland.   ITBLP
Mountains are moving, rivers.   Redwoods, The.   Louis Simpson.   CoAP
Mountains bare next the southwest, The. (LL)   Sir David Lindsay [*or* Lyndsay].
   ChIV-1; OxBS   *Fr.* Monarche, The.
Mountains beyond the city fade to nothingness, The.   Bamboo Branch Song of
   Han-chia.   Wang Shih-chieng.   CoBLCP, *tr. by* Jonathan Chaves
Mountains by the seaside—sharp pointed swords.   Poem to Send to Friends in
   the Capital, A.   Liu Tsung-yüan.   CoBCP, *tr. by* Burton Watson
Mountains cannot block this dreamlike song, The.   Hearing a Flute on the River
   Chi.   Wen Cheng-ming.   CoBLCP, *tr. by* Jonathan Chaves
Mountains crackle, The.   Her Garden.   Meena Alexander.   OMIP
Mountains grow—unnoticed, The.   Emily Dickinson.   MoAmPo; SWaP
Mountains have changed to buildings, The.   Mountain Building.   Víctor
   Hernández Cruz.   PueRic
Mountains loom upon the path we take.   Song to the Mountains.   *Unknown.*
   AWP, *tr. by* Alice C. Fletcher
Mountains of California: Part 1, The.   Al Young.   GeoHom
Mountains of California: Part 2, The.   Al Young.   GeoHom
Mountains of Mourne, The.   William Percy French.   OBCoV
Mountains of the bed are high, The.   Fever.   Sean O Riordain.   ModIr, *tr. by*
   Patrick Crotty
Mountains of Yoshino / Shedding petals.   Buson.   ZenPo, *tr. by* Takashi
   Ikemoto and Lucien Stryk
Mountains on all sides.   Suzan Osho's Visit.   Muso Soseki.   EaWin, *tr. by* W.
   S. Merwin
Mountains on the screen shimmer in the golden dawn, The.   Deva-like
   Barbarian.   Wen T'ing-yün.   ColAnChi, *tr. by* Lois Fusek
Mountains ring, the wild wind comes, The.   Wild Wind.   Li Meng-yang.
   CoBLCP, *tr. by* Jonathan Chaves
Mountains rubbed by light clouds.   Tune: "Courtyard Full of Fragrance."
   Ch'in Kuan.   SuSp, *tr. by* James J. Y. Liu
Mountains shine through forest breaks, bamboo hides the wall.   Tune: Partridge
   Sky.   Su Tung-p'o (Su Shih).   CoBCP, *tr. by* Burton Watson
Mountains surround the ancient kingdom in a massive circle.   Chin-ling.   Liu
   Yu Hsi.   SuSp, *tr. by* Paul Kroll
Mountains that hung midair.   Haunts of the Mirage.   Bruce Berger.   GeoH
Mountains that I like, The.   Homeward Bound.   Ezekiel Mphahlele.   AF
Mountains they are silent folk, The.   Mountains Are a Lonely Folk, The.
   Hamlin Garland.   ITBLP
Mountains they knew, and jungle, the sun, the stars.   At Tikal.   William Bronk.
   APSN
Mountains vanish.   Night.   Gabriela Mistral.   TANSG, *tr. by* Maria Jacketti
Mountains wreathed in wisps of light cloud.   Tune: "Perfumed Garden."   Ch'in
   Kuan.   ColAnChi, *tr. by* Jiaosheng Wang
Mountaintops emerge and then vanish.   Hui-chu Temple, Mount K'un.   Wang
   An-shih.   CrYelRi, *tr. by* Sam Hamill
Mounted horse will stop, The.   Pegasus.   Varlam Tikhonovich Shalamov.
   TCRP, *tr. by* Bradley Jordan
Mounted Umbrella, A.   Gertrude Stein.   TCAPo   *Fr.* Tender Buttons.
Mounting on high I begin to realize the smallness of Man's.   Climbing the
   Ling-ying Terrace and Looking North.   Po Chü-i.   BLT; ChiP, *tr. by*
   Arthur Waley

Mounts through all the spires of form. (LL) Nature [1836]. Ralph Waldo Emerson. APN-1; AWP

Mourn for the living through the livelong night. (LL) Consolations of Philosophy. Derek Mahon. BIrV; CIP-2; HarvBoo

Mourn for Yourself. Geoffrey Keating. BIrV, *tr. by* Sean Lucy

Mourn, hapless Caledonia, mourn. Tears of Scotland, The. Tobias Smollett. ECEV; NOEC

Mourn, mourn, ye Muses, all your loss deplore. On the Death of the Late Earl of Rochester. Aphra Behn. BASC; EMWP; NoP-4

Mourn Not for Adonais. Shelley. NOBE *Fr.* Adonais; An Elegy on the Death of John Keats.

Mourn not, friends, mourn not, bereaved. Lines on the Death of the Rev. S. K. Talmage. Mary E. Tucker. CBWP-1

Mourned by scholars who dream of the ghosts of Greek boys. (LL) Funeral, The. Stephen Spender. MoBrPo; NoAM

Mournful gift is mine, oh friends!, A. Second Sight. Felicia Dorothea Hemans. RWP

Mourning. Daniel Weissbort. GI

Mourning Bride, The. William Congreve.
    Music. OxAEP-1

Mourning cloak, A. John Wills. HA

Mourning for Hokuju Rosen. Buson. EH, *tr. by* Robert Hass

Mourning for Lü Hui-chiu. Yün Shou-p'ing.
    "Facing you, on the wall, across from your bed." CoBLCP

Mourning for My Son Jun-erh. Cheng Hsieh. CoBLCP, *tr. by* Jonathan Chaves

Mourning for My Wife. Mei Yao Ch'en. SuSp, *tr. by* Jonathan Chaves

Mourning for the Layman Named Cloud Peak. Muso Soseki. EaWin, *tr. by* W. S. Merwin

Mourning for Yin Yao. Wang Wei. CrYelRi, *tr. by* Sam Hamill

Mourning Letter from Paris, A. Conrad Kent Rivers. BPo

Mourning Letter, March 29 1963. Edward Dorn. CoAmPo

Mourning My Son. Yüan Chên. SuSp, *tr. by* Angela Jung Palandri

Mourning Pablo Neruda. Robert Bly. LCAP-2

Mourning Picture. Adrienne Rich. CoAP

Mourning Poem for the Queen of Sunday. Robert Earl Hayden. HCAP; NAAAL; NoAM; NoP-4; PoPoPo

Mourning Princess Asuka. Kakinomoto no Hitomaro. WoPoe, *tr. by* Helen Craig McCullough

Mourning Song. Robert Pearl. STP, *tr. by* Armand Schwerner

Mourning Songs of Greece. *Unknown.*
    "Close by the shore, the shore." WoPoe, *tr. by* Konstantinos Lardas
    "I beg you, beg you, mother." WoPoe, *tr. by* Konstantinos Lardas
    "My little ship, three-masted." WoPoe, *tr. by* Konstantinos Lardas

Mourning the Death, by Hemorrhage, of a Child from Honai. Basil T. Paquet. CDa

Mourning Women. Mathilde Blind. ViWPN

Mouse, The. Elizabeth Jane Coatsworth. NOxBChV; OBCA

Mouse, The. Jean Garrigue. TwCP

Mouse, The. Laura Elizabeth Richards. OBCA

Mouse and the Cake, The. Eliza Cook. VWP

Mouse-brown foal that fain had fed, The. Foal, The. William Renton. NOBVV

Mouse crawled through it, The. Hole. Leonard Nathan. PBCAP

Mouse Dinner. Aileen Fisher. TLR, *tr. by* Aileen Fisher

Mouse Dinners. Russell Edson. SoSe-8
    (Woman was cooking a mouse for her husband's dinner, A.) SoSe-8

Mouse doesn't dine, A. Mouse Dinner. Aileen Fisher. TLR, *tr. by* Aileen Fisher

Mouse found a beautiful piece of plum-cake, A. Mouse and the Cake, The. Eliza Cook. VWP

Mouse in Her Room, A. *Unknown.* TLR

Mouse in her room woke Miss Dowd, A. Mouse in Her Room, A. *Unknown.* TLR

Mouse in the Wainscot, The. Ian Serraillier. OTCP

Mouse's Lullaby, The. Palmer Cox. NOxBChV; OBCA; OxIBACP; TLR

Mouse's Nest. John Clare. InPK-6; NAEL-5v2; NAEL-6v2; NPeEn; PAI; RB

Mouse's Petition, The. Anna Laetitia Barbauld. ECWP

Mouse Whose Name Is Time, The. Robert Francis. TLR

Mousemeal. Howard Nemerov. TwCP

Mouse's Tale, The. Lewis Carroll. *See* Alice's Adventures in Wonderland

Mousetrap, The. Callimachus. HePo, *tr. by* Barbara Hughes Fowler

Mousie sat upon a shelf, A. Little Mouse, The. Miroslav Košek. INSAB

Mousōnios built this solid, windproof mansion, and built it well. House in Byzantium, A. Agathias. GrAn, *tr. by* Fleur Adcock

Mouth, The. Ciaran Carson. ModIr; PNI

Mouth, A. Can blow or breathe. Cardinal Ideograms. May Swenson. NoP-4; OBCA; OxIBACP

Mouth and the Ears, The. Shem-Tob ben Joseph Palquera. TrJP, *tr. by* J. Chotzner

Mouth in the hidden mirror. Into the Foghorn. Paul Celan. BBASP, *tr. by* Michael Hamburger

Mouth like old silk soft with use, A. Levantine, A. William Plomer. OBMV

Mouth of the Hudson, The. Robert Lowell. AiP; VCAP

Mouth of the Wen River—240 feet wide, The. On Board a Boat at Chi-ning. Yüan Hung-tao. CoBLCP, *tr. by* Jonathan Chaves

Mouth should allow itself to open and shut, The. Preliminary Studies for the Frankfurt Readings 1984. Ernst Jandl. PFTM-2, *tr. by* Jerome Rothenberg

Mouth that gave me your voice, The. Suicide. Lina Tibi. PoArWo, *tr. by* Subhi Hadidi and Nathalie Handal

Mouth to begin with—lightly pursed, The. Three Amoretti. Rick Barot. NeAmPo

Mouth to Mouth. Steve Gehrke. AmPoNex

Mouth to mouth joined we lie, her naked breasts. Tantalos. Paulus [*or* Paulos] Silentiarius. WoPoe, *tr. by* Dudley Fitts

Mouthful of language to swallow, A. Peaches. Donald Hall. NoP-4

Mouvance. Sue Standing. UrbNat

Move. Lucille Clifton. MakPoe; NAAAL

Move, and then / stop. (LL) Turn, The. Robert Creeley. FTOS; LCAP-2

Move him into the sun. Futility. Wilfred Owen. FaBoMo; GTBS-P; HarvBoo; MoBrPo; NAEL-5v2; NAEL-6v2; NPeEn; NoAM; NoP-4; OBWP; PAI; PeFWW; RB; TCAWP

Move over, ham. Hiding Place. Richard Armour. NIL-7; NIP-4

Move to New York. Things to Do in Valley of the Dolls (The Movie). David Trinidad. WiU

Moved. (LL) Unconscious Came a Beauty. May Swenson. APT-2; VCAP

Moved on. None heeded, and few heard. (LL) Cassandra. Edwin Arlington Robinson. APT-1; NoAM; OxBA

Movement. Andrée Chedid. HAWP, *tr. by* Mirène Ghossein and Samuel Hazo

Movement. Blanca Wiethüchter. TANSG, *tr. by* Shaun Griffin and Emma Sepúlveda-Pulvirenti

Movement. Nikolai Alekseievich Zabolotsky [*or* Zabolotskii]. TCRP, *tr. by* Daniel Weissbort

Movement of Fish, The. James Dickey. VGW

Movement Song. Audre Lorde. VCAP

Movements. Norman MacCaig. OxBC

Moves small beyond it. (LL) Door, The. Robert Creeley. NAAL-5; NeAP; NoAM; PoM; VGW

Moves the calm spirit, but disturbs it not. (LL) Ocean, The. Moschus. AWP; OBVE

Movie, The. Steve Denning. CDa

Movie Actors Scribbling Letters Very Fast in Crucial Scenes. Jean Garrigue. TAP

Movie-Going. John Hollander. CoAP

Movie House. John Updike. PeLV

Movie of Robert, A. Bresson's Movies. Robert Creeley. NoP-4; PmAP

Movies are badder. Saturday Afternoon at the Movies. John Logan. NNaP

Movies you wouldn't let them see when they were young. (LL) Ave Maria. Frank O'Hara. CLPP; HCAP; HarvBoo; MakPoe; NAAL-2v2; NNaP; NoP-4; PmAP; PoM; PoPoPo; VCAP

Movin' with Nancy. David Trinidad. PmAP

Moving. Sam Hamod.
    "So we move now." GraLe; UnSA

Moving. Martin Shea. HA

Moving along Main St. One Day. Bobbi Sykes. BMAP; IBA

Moving and moaning. To Michal. Lucille Clifton. ExTi

Moving and St Rage. Kathy Fagan. ExTi

Moving at summer's pace. (LL) Cut Grass. Philip Larkin. NoAM; OxBC; RB

Moving deep. "Stephany." NBV

Moving / Deep into mist. Sampu. ZenPo, *tr. by* Takashi Ikemoto and Lucien Stryk

Moving Finger writes; and, having writ, The. 71. Edward Fitzgerald. CABP

Moving Finger writes; and, having writ, The. Omar Khayyám. TRP, *tr. by* Edward Fitzgerald *Fr.* Rubáiyát of Omar Khayyám [of Naishápúr], The.

Moving from Cheer to Joy, from Joy to All. Next Day. Randall Jarrell. AmFaPo; HAP; HCAP; HarvBoo; NAAL-2v2; NoAM; NoP-4; VCAP; WeW-3

Moving from the bus at the Loop it's possible suddenly. Seeing St. James's. Ray Mathew. NOBAu

Moving House. Ch'ien T'ao. ChiP, *tr. by* Arthur Waley

Moving House, No. 1. T'ao Ch'ien [*or* T'ao Yuan-ming]. CoBCP, *tr. by* Burton Watson

Moving House, No. 2. T'ao Ch'ien [*or* T'ao Yuan-ming]. CoBCP, *tr. by* Burton Watson

Moving In. May Sarton. APT-2

Moving like women: Justice, Truth, such figures. (LL)   Another September. Thomas Kinsella.   BIrV; CABP; CIP-2; HarvBoo; NoP-4

Moving Object.   Jean Day.   FTOS

Moving on or going back to where you came from.   Procession at Candlemas, A.   Amy Clampitt.   FaBoWP; HCAP; PoPoPo

Moving out.   Thing Poem.   Petra von Morstein.   BoWoP, *tr. by* Rosmarie Waldrop

Moving over the hills, crossing the irrigation.   George Oppen.   APSN; NNaP *Fr.* Some San Francisco Poems.

Moving shadows, The.   Virgil Hutton.   InPK-6

Moving sun-shapes on the spray, The.   Going and Staying.   Thomas Hardy. NoAM

Moving through the silent crowd.   Unemployed.   Stephen Spender.   NOBE

Moving up! (LL)   One Day.   Bobbi Sykes.   BMAP; IBA

Moving van zooms, A.   Alan Pizzarelli.   HA

Moviola.   Elena Clementelli.   CItWP, *tr. by* Cinzia Sartini Blum and Lara Trubowitz

Mower against Gardens, The.   Andrew Marvell.   BASC; CABP; EBEV; ESCV; NAEL-5v1; NAEL-6v1; NAEL-7v1; NIL-7; NOSC; NPeEn; NoP-4; OBGa; OxAEP-1; PBRV; PoE

Mower's Song, The.   Andrew Marvell.   BASC; ESCV; NAEL-5v1; NAEL-6v1; NAEL-7v1; NOSC

Mower to the Glowworms [*or* Glow-Worms *or* Glo-Worms], The.   Andrew Marvell.   AWP; BASC; ESCV; EnLoPo; FHYEP; FSCP; GeHe; NAEL-5v1; NAEL-6v1; NAEL-7v1; NOBE; NPeEn; NoP-4; OxBoLi; PBRV; PeLV; SCGP; TFi

Mowers: An Anticipation of the Cholera, 1848, The.   Charles MacKay.   EBVV

Mowgli's Song against People.   Rudyard Kipling.   NOxBChV   *Fr.* Second Jungle Book, The.

Mowing.   Stuart Dybek.   UrbNat

Mowing.   Robert Frost.   APT-1; ColAP; HarvBoo; ITBLP; NAAL-2v2; NAAL-5; NOBA; OxBA; TRP; VGW

Mowing, The.   Sir Charles G. D. Roberts.   NOBC

Mown Lawn, A.   Lydia Davis.   BAP-01

Mown under / like a corpse / or a loose seed. (LL)   Freeway 280.   Lorna Dee Cervantes.   NoAM; WeW-3

Moysting Ayre was whist: no leafe ye could have moving sene, The.   Ovid.   OxBEV, *tr. by* Arthur Golding   *Fr.* Metamorphoses.

Mozart.   Eugenie Fink.   AuPH, *tr. by* Lowell A. Bangerter

Mozart.   John Heath-Stubbs.   EBEV

Mozart and I are leaving Salzburg.   Departure.   Bulat Shalvovich Okudzhava. ItGoST, *tr. by* Ronnie Apter and Mark Herman

Mozart in a Classroom of Children.   Daniel Bachhuber.   MiVo

Mozart in Heaven.   Manuel Bandeira.   TCLAP, *tr. by* Dudley Poore

Mozart, 1935.   Wallace Stevens.   MiVo

Mozart or Beethoven, he asked by his five-foot wall.   To Answer Your Question.   Bruce Berger.   MiVo

Mozart, Piano Concerto No. 20 in D Minor, K.466.   Ernst Waldinger.   AuPH, *tr. by* Lowell A. Bangerter

Mozart's Death.   Richard Foerster.   MiVo

Mr. Agama.   Tijan M. Sallah.   NAfrP

Mr. Alan Jay Lerner (with by-play).   Limerick.   J. A. Lindon.   PeLi

Mr and Mrs Scotland Are Dead.   Kathleen Jamie.   EmeKit

Mr. Beringer, whose son.   Seven Laments for the War-Dead.   Yehuda Amichai [*or* Amikhai].   PoetW, *tr. by* Chana Bloch

Mr. Bezuidenthout's Dogs.   Musaemura Bonus Zimunya.   NAfrP

Mr. Bidery's Spidery Garden.   David McCord.   OTCP

Mr. Billings of Louisville.   Eugene Field.   NBLV

Mr Bleaney.   Philip Larkin.   NPeEn; OxBC; OxBEV; PoE; PoPoPo; TRP; UV

Mr. Cogito and the Imagination.   Zbigniew Herbert.   PoetW, *tr. by* John Carpenter and Bogdana Carpenter

Mr. Cogito Meditates on Suffering.   Zbigniew Herbert.   VCWP, *tr. by* John Carpenter

Mr. Cogito never trusted.   Mr. Cogito and the Imagination.   Zbigniew Herbert. PoetW, *tr. by* John Carpenter and Bogdana Carpenter

Mr. Cogito Tells about the Temptation of Spinoza.   Zbigniew Herbert.   GI, *tr. by* John Carpenter

Mr. Cooper.   Anthony Thwaite.   OxBTC

Mr. Cromek [*or* On Cromek].   William Blake.   FaBoEE

Mr. Dooms would meet us across the Bay Bridge at a restaurant that featured "Dancing Waters."   Killarney Clary.   GeoHom

Mr. Edward Fordham.   Mary Weston Fordham.   CBWP-2

Mr. Eliot Pastor of the Church of Christ at Roxbury.   Edward Johnson.   SCAP

Mr. Frost Goes South to Boston.   Firman Houghton.   UV

Mr. Heath-Stubbs as you must understand.   Epitaph.   John Heath-Stubbs. OxBTC

Mr. Housman's Message.   Ezra Pound.   FaBoEE

Mr. Hughes.   David Campbell.   CBAP

Mr. Irving Berlin.   Noël Coward.   ReLy

Mr Jones.   Harry Graham.   PeLV; UV   *Fr.* Some Ruthless Rhymes.

Mr Jones as the Transported Poet.   T. Harri Jones.   TCAWP

Mr Khalvati? Larger than life he was.   Coma.   Mimi Khalvati.   Prnts

Mr L'Estrange's Verses in the Prison at Lynn.   Sir Roger L'Estrange.   NOSC

Mr Lear, I'm the Akond of Swat.   Limerick.   Ethel Talbot Scheffauer.   PeLi

Mr. McGregor's Garden.   Medbh McGuckian.   CIP-2; PNI

Mr. Molony's Account of the Crystal Palace.   William Makepeace Thackeray. PeVV

Mr. Nabokov's Memory.   Thomas McCarthy.   ModIr

Mr. Nixon.   Ezra Pound.   MoAmPo   *Fr.* Hugh Selwyn Mauberley (Life and Contacts).

Mr Nobody.   *Unknown.*   ITBLP
(I know a funny little man.)   ChAP

Mr. Placid's Flirtation.   Frederick Locker-Lampson.   PeVV

Mr. Pope's Welcome from Greece.   John Gay.   EBEV; OxAEP-1; OxBoLi

Mr. Rochester's wife's pyromania.   Limerick.   Gina Berkeley.   PeLi

Mr. Rockefeller's Hat.   Helen Smith Bevington.   OBAL

Mr. Slatter.   N. M. Bodecker.   TLR

Mr. Strugnell.   Wendy Cope.   UV

Mr. Sung's old house collapses.   Passing Mr. Sung's Old House.   Tu Fu. CrYelRi, *tr. by* Sam Hamill

Mr Teller the Piano Teacher.   Jane Duran.   MFPA

Mr. Teodoro Luna in his later years had taken to kissing.   Teodoro Luna's Two Kisses.   Alberto A. Ríos.   PoPoPo

Mr. Thomas Shepeard.   Edward Johnson.   SCAP

Mr. Tom Narrow.   James Reeves.   OBSP

Mr. Ward of Anagrams Thus.   Nathaniel Ward.   SCAP

Mr. Wells.   Elizabeth Madox Roberts.   KaS

Mr. White Discoverer.   Amelia Blossom Pegram.   HAWP

Mr. Whittier.   Winfield Townley Scott.   VGW

Mr. "X," may we ask you a question?   Little Tin Box.   Sheldon Harnick. ReLy

MRI.   Ron Charach.   BloBone

MRI of a Poet's Brain.   Vernon Rowe.   BloBone

Mririda.   Mririda n'Ait Attik.   WPOW, *tr. by* René Euloge, Daniel Halpern and Paula Paley

Mrs. Albion You've Got a Lovely Daughter.   Adrian Henri.   OxBTC

Mrs. Benjamin Pantier.   Edgar Lee Masters.   APT-1   *Fr.* Spoon River Anthology.

Mrs. Biswas Breaks Her Connection with Another Relative.   Reetika Vazirani. AmPoNex

Mrs. Biswas Goes through a Photo Album.   Reetika Vazirani.   AmPoNex

Mrs. Biswas of Maryland on the Phone.   Reetika Vazirani.   AmPoNex

Mrs. Busk.   Sir Osbert Sitwell.   OxBTC

Mrs. Conti was the first.   First, The.   Grace Cavalieri.   UnSA

Mrs. Davis' younger son was home.   For Tony, Embarking in Spring.   Haniel Long.   APT-1

Mrs. E. Cohrs Brown.   Mary Weston Fordham.   CBWP-2

Mrs. Eden in Town for the Day.   Richard Howard.   KGB

Mrs. Evans Fach, You Want Butter Again.   Idris Davies.   *See* Angry Summer, The

Mrs. Frye and the Pencilsharpener.   Bill Knott.   BodElec

Mrs. Hopley, on Seeing Her Children Say Goodnight to Their Father.   Gerard Manley Hopkins.   FaBoEE

Mrs. Johnson Objects.   Clara Ann Thompson.   BlSi; CBWP-2

Mrs. Josiah Harris.   Letters from a New England Negro.   Sherley Anne Williams.   ESEAA

Mrs. Kriss Kringle.   Edith Matilda Thomas.   OBCA

Mrs. Louise B. Weston.   Mary Weston Fordham.   CBWP-2

Mrs. Mary Furman Weston Byrd.   Mary Weston Fordham.   CBWP-2

Mrs. Meyers.   Edgar Lee Masters.   APT-1; IllVoic   *Fr.* Spoon River Anthology.

Mrs. Myrick's Lecture.   Mary E. Tucker.   CBWP-1

Mrs. Nelson thinks there's no one left.   Lois at the Hair Salon.   Lesley Dauer. AmPoNex

Mrs Nightingale.   Martin Fagg.   UV

Mrs. Rebecca Weston.   Mary Weston Fordham.   CBWP-2

Mrs. Sadie Grindstaff, Weaver and Factotum.   Jonathan Williams.   OBAL

Mrs. Small.   Gwendolyn Brooks.   GT; ItWoWo

Mrs Thimelby, on the Death of Her Only Child.   Gertrude Aston Thimelby. EMWP

Mrs. Whitehouse, mixed bathing at Deal.   Limerick.   T. L. McCarthy.   PeLi

Mrs Worthingtion.   Noël Coward.
"Regarding yours, dear Mrs Worthington."   ReLy; UV

Mt. Pisgah.   James Kimbrell.   NAPBL

Mu.   Melvin B. Tolson.   APT-2; PFTM-1   *Fr.* Harlem Gallery.

Mu'allaqat, The.   *Var. authors.*

Abla.   AWP, *tr.* by E. Powys Mathers

"Have the poets left a single spot for a patch to be sewn?"   TTY

Ode: "Weep, ah weep love's losing, love's with its dwelling place."   AWP; TAL, *tr.* by Wilfrid Scawen Blunt and Lady Anne Blunt

Pour Us Wine.   AWP, *tr.* by E. Powys Mathers

"Tent marks in Mínan are worn away, The."   WoPoe, *tr.* by Michael Sells

Mu-Lan.   *Unknown.*   WoPoe, *tr.* by Hans H. Frankel

Much Ado about Nothing.   William Shakespeare.

Balthasar's Song.   AWP; CTC; NoSic; PAI; UV

Epitaph: "Done to death by slanderous tongues."   CTC

"Is this the monument of Leonato?"   OxAEP-1

"O! good my lord, tax not so bad a voice."   OxAEP-1

"Pardon, goddess of the night."   NoSic

(Song: "Pardon, goddess of the night.")   CTC

Much Ado about Nothing in the City.   *Unknown.*   UV

Much as a man who takes delight in dreaming.   Ausiàs March.   STV

Much as he left it when he went from us.   Why He Was There.   Edwin Arlington Robinson.   APT-1; NOBA; OxBSo

Much did I rage when young.   Youth and Age.   W. B. Yeats.   FaBoEE

Much-discerning public hold, A.   La Nuit Blanche.   Rudyard Kipling.   MoBrPo

Much Distressed.   *Unknown.*   CBAP

Much earlier than most he found.   Childhood of a Spy.   Dick Davis.   DiPo

Much had transpired in the phantom realm.   Louise in Love.   Mary Jo Bang.   NAPBL

Much happens when we're not there.   Window-Blind.   Denise Levertov.   LCAP-2

Much has been said of the.   Three Songs.   Rachel Wetzsteon.   RA

Much have I labored, much read o'er.   Alas for Youth.   Firdowsi.   AWP, *tr.* by R. A. Nicholson

Much have I travell'd [*or* travelled *or* traveled] in the realms of gold.   On First Looking into Chapman's Homer.   John Keats.   BRP; CABP; CenSon; ClHu; FHYEP; FaBoCh; GSo; GTBS-P; HAP; HeIP-4; InPK-6; NAEL-5v2; NAEL-6v2; NAWM-7v2; NIL-7; NIP-4; NOBE; NOBRP; NPeEn; NoP-4; OBAL; OBEV; OPOU; OxAEP-2; OxBEV; OxBSo; PoE; PoPoPo; SCGP; SoSe-8; Son; TFi; TRP; UV; WoPoe

Much have I travell'd in those realms of old.   On First Looking into Krafft-Ebing's *Psychopathosexualis* [*or* Psychopathia Sexualis].   Oliver St. John Gogarty.   UV

Much Madness is divinest Sense.   Much Madness Is Divinest Sense.   Emily Dickinson.   APN-2; BoWoP; HeIP-4; NAAL-2v1; NAAL-3; NALW; NAWM-7v2; NCAP; NOBA; NoAM; NoP-4; OPOU; OxBA; PoPoPo; RaBo; SAmP; SoSe-8; TCAPo; TFi; TRP; WPE

Much melting, and crows close to home.   Seasonal.   Karen Volkman.   AmPoNex

Much of what moves us is wrong, our hearts.   Patsy Cline.   Richard Speakes.   SwNoth

Much spoke he of the myrtle and the yew.   Philip Freneau.   NAAL-2v1; NAAL-3   *Fr.* House of Night, The.

Much suspected by me.   Written with a Diamond on Her Window at Woodstock.   Queen of England Elizabeth I.   PEW; WPE

Much Too Close.   Amaru.   WoPoe, *tr.* by Peter Dent

Much too close to bear his eyes.   Much Too Close.   Amaru.   WoPoe, *tr.* by Peter Dent

Much wine had passed, with grave discourse.   Ramble in St. James's Park, A.   John Wilmot, 2d Earl of Rochester.   BASC; PeLV

Much wonder I—here long low-laid.   Bedridden Peasant, The.   Thomas Hardy.   InvLi

Much-worried mother once said, A.   Limerick.   *Unknown.*   PeLi

Mud.   Mark Bibbins.   WiU

Mud.   Polly Chase Boyden.   NTCP

Mud.   George Kalamaras.   BAP-97

Mud.   Enrique Lihn.   TCLAP, *tr.* by John Felstiner

Mud Dauber Wasp, The.   Peter Kane Dufault.   NoP-4

Mud-Flat.   Willem Jan Otten.   TuT, *tr.* by Seán Lysaght

Mud-Flat.   Willem Jan Otten.   TuT, *tr.* by Peter Van de Kamp

Mud on the first day (night, rather.   Ted Berrigan.   BodElec

Mud Season.   Mark Todd.   GeoH

Mud turkle settin' on de end of a log.   Turtle's Song, The.   *Unknown.*   BPo

Mud, unending malice. All other source gives way at last.   Mud.   Enrique Lihn.   TCLAP, *tr.* by John Felstiner

Mud Vision, The.   Seamus Heaney.   PBCIP

Mud Water Shango.   [Tom] Weatherly.   GT; NBV; SeSe

Muddling up the wooden stairs one night, in my socks.   Spiders.   David Wevill.   MoCV

Muddy Kid Comes Home.   Sandra Cisneros.   FFC

Muddy Waters and the Chicago Blues.   Cornelius Eady.   ESEAA

Muddy-wheeled cart goes lurching, A.   Plain, The.   Sándor Weöres.   BLT

Mudfish are the lowest of all fish.   Chiang Lin-chi Treats Me to Mudfish.   Mei Yao Ch'en.   SuSp, *tr.* by Jonathan Chaves

Muezzin voices break the night, The.   Twenty-Five Laments for Iraq.   Robert Minhinnick.   HarvBoo

Mufaddaliyat, The.   *Var. authors.*   AWP, *tr.* by Sir Charles Lyall

Muffled Cry, A.   Marjorie Oludhe Macgoye.   HAWP

Mufti and their spiritual jurisdictions, The.   Fulke Greville, 1st Baron Brooke.   NOSC   *Fr.* Mustapha.

Mugging.   Allen Ginsberg.   NoAM

"Tonite I walked out of my red apartment door on East tenth street's dusk."   HCAP

Mugoku Osho's Snow Poem.   Muso Soseki.   EaWin, *tr.* by W. S. Merwin

Mugwort recall.   Charm of the Nine Healing Herbs.   *Unknown.*   WoPoe, *tr.* by David Cloutier

Muhammad. (LL)   Narrative: Ali.   Elizabeth Alexander.   ESEAA; MoASP

Muhammad wheels us through.   Enduring Witness, the Mosques of Kattankudi.   Peter Michelson.   OPRER

Muhammedan Call to Prayer.   Bilal.   TTY, *tr.* by Raoul Abdul

Mujer.   William Carlos Williams.   SAmP

Mujin Flowers Blossom on the Rolling Graves, The.   Juan Chi.   WoPoe, *tr.* by Graham Hartill and Wu Fusheng

Mulatto.   Langston Hughes.   NAAL-2v2; NAAL-5

Mulatto Lullaby.   Ralph Dickey.   ESEAA

Mulberries at the roadside break into bud.   Tune: "Partridge Sky" for a Friend.   Hsin Ch'i-chi.   ColAnChi, *tr.* by Jiaosheng Wang

Mulberry Bush, The.   *Unknown.*   LB

Mulberry by the Path.   *Unknown.*   SuSp; WoPoe, *tr.* by Hans H. Frankel

Mulberry Garden, The.   Sir Charles Sedley.

Child and Maiden.   GTBS-P

(To Chloris.)   OBEV

Mulberry up the Lane.   *Unknown.*   ColAnChi, *tr.* by Anne Birrell

Mulch.   Adam David Miller.   NBV

Mulciber.   John Milton.   NOSC   *Fr.* Paradise Lost.

Mule, The.   Merrill Boynton, Jr.   CRP

Mule kicked out in the trees, A. An Early.   Poem.   Norman Dubie.   BodElec

Mule Team and Poster.   Donald Justice.   VCAP

Mule that lived on the road, The.   Young Wife's Lament.   Brigit Pegeen Kelly.   IllVoic

Mules.   Paul Muldoon.   HarvBoo

Muliebrity.   Sujata Bhatt.   FSt; HarvBoo

Mullabinda.   David Rowbotham.   CBAP

Mullein.   Anita Virgil.   HA

Multi-colored chart without a boundary, A.   Missing You.   "Shu Ting."   CarOv; VCWP, *tr.* by Carolyn Kizer and Y. H. Zhao

Multipara: Gravida 5.   Marie Ponsot.   CLPP; VGW

Multiple Assaults.   Letta Neely.   WiU

Multiple generations of the same race on two continents are.   Multiple Assaults.   Letta Neely.   WiU

Multiples in the looks of fright.   Movement.   Blanca Wiethüchter.   TANSG, *tr.* by Shaun Griffin and Emma Sepúlveda-Pulvirenti

Multiplication is vexation.   Arithmetic.   *Unknown.*   ReMoGo

Multum Dilexit.   Hartley Coleridge.   SacPr

Multum vigilavi, laboravi, presto multis fui.   Genus Infoelix Vitae.   Queen of England Elizabeth I.   EMWP

Mum.   Kevin Gilbert.   IBA

Mum, I'll be a fireman!   Ambition, The.   Robert Harris.   BMAP

Mum, you would have loved the way you went!   Going.   Bruce Dawe.   BMAP

Mumbling.   Enrique Banchs.   BLPSL, *tr.* by Rene de Costa, Rigas Kappatos and Eleni Paidoussi

Mumbo . . . Jumbo . . . will . . . hoo-doo . . . you. (LL)   Congo, The.   Nicholas Vachel Lindsay.   APT-1; MoAmPo; NOBA; OxBA; PoRA; TAP

Mummer.   Jack Spicer.   APSN

Mummies.   Nicanor Parra.   TCLAP, *tr.* by Thomas Merton

Mummy Invokes His Soul, The.   "Michael Field."   NPeEn; OxBSo; VWP

Mummy is singing at breakfast and dancing! / So big! (LL)   Eskimo Occasion.   Judith Rodriguez.   CBAP; FaBoWP; ItWoWo; NOBAu

Mumpaty, mumpaty, mump. (LL)   Roger and Dolly.   Henry Carey.   NOEC; OxNR

Munching a plum on.   To a Poor Old Woman.   William Carlos Williams.   BLT; ColAP; OBAL; TAP; TTTS

Mundaka Upanishad.   *Unknown.*   *Fr.* Upanishads, The.

Mundus et Infans.   W. H. Auden.   MoBrPo; NoAM

Mundus Muliebris.   Mary Evelyn.   NOSC

Mundus Qualis.   Joshua Sylvester.   FaBoEE

Mundy, McCall, and Browne, and Saul.   God of the Flies.   John Rimington.   FaBoWar

Mune Rune.   Helen Adam.   APT-2

Munelicht is my knowledge o' mysel', The. Spur of Love, The. Hugh MacDiarmid. OxBEV

Municipal Gallery Revisited, The. W. B. Yeats. GTBS-P; OxBTC

Municipal Gum. Oodgeroo of the tribe Noonuccal (Kath Walker). IBA

Munition Wages. Madeline Ida Bedford. FaBoWar

Muppim and Huppim! Strike blows on your drums! Dance of Despair, The. Hayyim Nahman [or Khayim Nakhman or Chaim Nachman] Bialik. TrJP, tr. by A. M. Klein

Mural, Ch'ien-ming Temple. Lu Yu. CrYelRi, tr. by Sam Hamill

Murder. Yury [or Iurii] Timofeievich Galanskov. TCRusP, tr. by Olive Dehn

Murder. Lucy Grealy. KGB

Murder, He Says. Frank Loesser. ReLy

Murder in the Cathedral. T. S. Eliot.
Chorus: "We do not wish anything to happen." OxBTC
Chorus: "We have not been happy, my Lord, we have not been too happy." OxBTC

Murder Machine 43. Kurt Schwitters. PFTM-1

Murder of William Remington, The. Howard Nemerov. CoAP

Murder One. Allen Fisher. Oth Fr. Emergent Manner.

Murder's not my forte. Eugenio Montale. ItPo, tr. by Gayle Ridinger

Murdered himself, to show some manful deed. (LL) Sardanapalus. Henry Howard, Earl of Surrey. NAEL-6v1; NAEL-7v1; NoSic

Murdered, I went, risen. Life, The. James Wright. LCAP-2

Murdered Luggage. Jose Angel Figueroa. PueRic

Murderer, The. Christopher Davis. OPRER

Murderer, The. Stevie Smith. FaBoWP; OxBSP

Murderer and Sarapis, The. Palladas [or Pallades]. GrAn; WoPoe, tr. by Tony Harrison

Murderer's little daughter, The. Sympathetic Portrait of a Child. William Carlos Williams. APT-1

Murderer spread his palliasse, A. Murderer and Sarapis, The. Palladas [or Pallades]. GrAn; WoPoe, tr. by Tony Harrison

Murderers, The. Paul Van Ostaijen. PFTM-1

Murge with your white stones and green olives. Second Image Sequence. Umberto Piersanti. NeIt, tr. by Stephen Sartarelli

Murillo's Magdalen. William Ellery Channing. APN-1

Murk was the night: nor star, nor moon. Young Man Naughty's Adventure. Charlotte Brontë. VWP

Murky water of the North-Sea. North-Sea, The. Albert Verwey. TuT, tr. by Tony Curtis

Murmur. Esther Iverem. GT

Murmur. Adelia Prado. TANSG, tr. by Ellen Watson

Murmur of a Bee, The. Emily Dickinson. MoAmPo

Murmur of the city sounded on, The. Day-dream, A. Mary Elizabeth Coleridge. VWP

Murmur of the mourning ghost, The. Sydney Thompson Dobell. OBEV Fr. Nuptial Eve, A.

Murmuring. Kofi Anyidoho. NAfrP

Murmuring, in her sleep as it seemed, the ancient slogan / Noblesse oblige. (LL) Belief. Josephine Miles. FaBoWP; NoAM; TAP

Murmuring of Bees, has ceased, The. Emily Dickinson. APN-2

Murmurings in a Field Hospital. Carl Sandburg. IllVoic

Murphy's Law. Alan Jenkins. OxBSo

Murry, on finding le Bon Dieu. On Reading "God." Gilbert Keith Chesterton. OBCoV

Muscat Pruning. William Everson. APT-2

Muse. Sophia de Mello Breyner. VCWP, tr. by Ruth Fainlight

Muse, The. Anna Andreyevna Akhmatova. WoPoe, tr. by Stanley Burnshaw

Muse, The. Anna Andreyevna Akhmatova. PoetW; TCRP, tr. by Max Hayward and Stanley Kunitz

Muse, The. Abraham Cowley. CABP; PBRV

Muse, The. Alfred de Musset. WoPoe, tr. by Claire Nicholas White Fr. Night in May, A.

Muse, The. Ovid. NAWM-7v1, tr. by Allen Mandelbaum Fr. Metamorphoses.

Muse, The. Eleanor Wilner. GifTon

Muse and Poet. Robert Bridges. OBMV

Muse as Medusa, The. May Sarton. HW; NALW

Muse, disgusted at an age and clime, The. On the Prospect of Planting Arts and Learning in America. George Berkeley. AiP; NOEC; OxBEV

Muse forgot, and thou beloved [or belov'd] no more!, The. (LL) Pope. ECEV; NOBE; NOEC; OBEV; SCGP

Muse in Late November. Jonathan Henderson Brooks. ChIV-1

Muse in the New World, The. Walt Whitman. MoAmPo Fr. Song of the Exposition.

Muse Is Always the Other Woman, The. Constance Urdang. PBCAP

Muse, June, Related. Brian Coffey.
"Blooms such as wither at finger-touch." BIrV

Muse! Lament away, complain away. Reader of Poetry, The. Ilya [or Karl] L'vovich Selvinsky [or Sel'vinskii]. TCRP, tr. by Daniel Weissbort

Muse of Amergin, The. Unknown. BIrV, tr. by John Montague

Muse of Fire, A. William Shakespeare. OxAEP-1; SCV Fr. King Henry V.

Muse of Poetry came down one day, The. In Memoriam Paul Laurence Dunbar. Henrietta Cordelia Ray. CBWP-3

Muse of Water, A. Carolyn Kizer. FFC; VCAP

Muse's Favor, The. Priscilla Jane Thompson. CBWP-2

Muse, sing the stir that happy Whitbread made. "Peter Pindar." NOEC Fr. Instructions to a Celebrated Laureat.

Muse teach me the song. Muse. Sophia De Mello Breyner. VCWP, tr. by Ruth Fainlight

Muse to an Unknown Poet, The. Paul Potts. FaBoTw

Musée des Beaux Arts. W. H. Auden. CABP; ClHu; GS; GTBS-P; HAP; HeIP-4; InPK-6; NAEL-5v2; NAEL-6v2; NIL-7; NOBE; NPeEn; NoAM; NoP-4; OxAEP-2; PoE; PoPoPo; PoRA; RaBo; SCV; SoSe-8; TFi; TRP; TrCP; TwCP

Muses are turned gossips; they have lost, The. Washing-Day. Anna Laetitia Barbauld. ECWP; PEW; WoRP

Muses Elizium, The. Michael Prayton.
"Paradice on earth is found, A." PBRV

Muses' Elysium X, The. Michael Drayton.
"Satyr O never ask how I came to this place." AEP

Muses' evening, as their morning-star[re], The. (LL) To Lucy, Countess[e] of Bedford, with Mr. Donnes Satire's [or Satyres]. Ben Jonson. BeJo; NAEL-6v1; NAEL-7v1

Muses' fairest light in no dark time, The. On Ben Jonson. Sidney Godolphin. BeJo

Muses' friend The (grey-eyed Aurora), yet. William Browne. NOSC Fr. Britannia's Pastorals.

Muses' garden, with pedantic weeds, The. Thomas Carew. NOBE Fr. Elegy upon the Death of the Dean of [St.] Paul's, Dr. John Donne, An.

Muses, help me; sorrow swarmeth. Shepherd's Sorrow, Being Disdained in Love, The. Thomas Lodge. NoSic

Muses that fame's loose feathers beautify. George Chapman. OxBSo Fr. Coronet for His Mistress Philosophy, A.

Museum. Joe Wenderoth. BodElec

Museum, The. Wislawa Szymborska. PoSu, tr. by Magnus F. Krynski

Museum Attendant, The. Archibald MacLeish. See Empire Builders

Museum of Man. Earle Birney. OxBC

Museum of the Second Creation, The. Sandra McPherson. LCAP-2

Museum Piece. Richard Wilbur. FaBoMo; InPK-6; NIL-7; NIP-4; TAP; TRP (Good grey guardians of art, The.) CoAmPo

Museum Vase. Robert Francis. APT-2

Museums. Louis MacNeice. MoBrPo

Museums and stockmarkets protect me, The. Four Stanzas Written in Anxiety. George Jonas. MoCV

Museums offer us, running from among the buses. Museums. Louis MacNeice. MoBrPo

Mushroom. Shinkichi Takahashi. ZenPo, tr. by Takashi Ikemoto and Lucien Stryk

Mushroom Gatherer Deep in the Mountains among the White Clouds, A. Hsü Wei. CoBLCP, tr. by Jonathan Chaves

Mushroom Gatherers, The. Donald Davie. OxBEV

Mushroom, Soft Ear, Old Memory. Bring the North. William Stafford. LCAP-2

Mushrooms. Moira Clark. Prnts

Mushrooms. Yury [or Iurii] Kuznetsov. TCRP, tr. by Lubov Yakovleva

Mushrooms. Sylvia Plath. FaBoWP; RB; WPOW

Mushrooms grew near the tree. Peter Rabbit. Sandra McPherson. LCAP-2

Music. Eugenio de Andrade. VCWP, tr. by Alexis Levitin

Music. Bible, Apocrypha. TrJP Fr. Ecclesiasticus.

Music. Madison Cawein. APN-2

Music. William Congreve. OxAEP-1 Fr. Mourning Bride, The.

Music. Abraham Cowley. See Davideis

Music. Christopher Pearse Cranch. APN-1

Music. George du Maurier. OBEV

Music. Alice Moore Dunbar-Nelson. BlSi

Music. John Fletcher. FaBoCh; NOSC Fr. King Henry VIII.

Music. Josephine D. Henderson Heard. CBWP-4

Music. Robert Herrick. CaPo

Music. David Huddle. MiVo

Music. Natasha Josefowitz. PasH

Music. Vladislav Felitsianovich Khodasevich. TCRusP, tr. by Daniel Weissbort

Music. Wilfred Owen. CAGL

Music. Rohan B. Preston. WaCA

Music. William Bell Scott. NOBVV

Music. Henry David Thoreau. APN-1

Music, A. Wendell Berry. VGW

Music and Poetry of the Indians. *Unknown.* APN-2, *tr. by* John Tanner

Music Appreciation. Floyd Skloot. MiVo

Music divides the evening. Tu Do Street. Yusef Komunyakaa. LTA; SwNoth

Music first and foremost of all! Art Poétique. Paul Verlaine. AWP, *tr. by* Arthur Symons

Music for a while. Song at Night. Norman Nicholson. FaBoTw

Music for Brass. Günter Grass. AF, *tr. by* Christopher Middleton

Music for Homemade Instruments. Harryette Mullen. BAP-01

Music for the Cows. Jim Johnson. MiVo

Music for This Time. Ernst Waldinger. AuPH, *tr. by* Lowell A. Bangerter

Music had the heat of blood, The. During Music. Arthur Symons. NOBVV

Music has charms to soothe a savage breast. William Congreve. OxAEP-1 *Fr.* Mourning Bride, The.

Music I Heard. Conrad Potter Aiken. AWP; NOBA; OxBA; PoRA *Fr.* Discordants.

Music I heard with you was more than music. Conrad Potter Aiken. AWP; NOBA; OxBA; PoRA *Fr.* Discordants.

Music in an Empty House. Hugh Sykes Davies. SPE

Music in Camp. John Reuben Thompson. CBCWP

Music in the Age of Iron. Alberto Blanco. CLPP, *tr. by* Julian Palley

Music in the granite hill. (LL) Men Loved Wholly beyond Wisdom. Louise Bogan. APT-2; ColAP; VGW

Music in the Meadow. Alice Wirth Gray. MiVo

Music in the piano stool. That vase, The. (LL) Home Is So Sad. Philip Larkin. InPK-6; OxBSP; PoetW

Music is played, The. Play. Celebration. Joseph Ceravolo. FTOS

Music is your mistress. For duke ellington. Reuben Jackson. ESEAA

Music it was I heard, and music too. Lines Suggested by Hearing Music on the Boston Common at Night. Thomas Cole. APN-1

Music, *jazz,* comes in, The. (LL) Reuben, Reuben. Michael S. Harper. LoL; PoE

Music Like Water, The. Jane Hirshfield. PasH

Music! Lilting, soft and languorous. Music. Alice Moore Dunbar-Nelson. BlSi

Music, Maestro, Please! Herb Magidson. ReLy

Music met Leviathan returning, A. Peter Quennell. MoBrPo *Fr.* Leviathan.

Music Mother. Naomi Feigelson Chase. MiVo

Music of a Tree, The. Walter James Turner. MoBrPo

Music of Colours: The Blossom Scattered. Vernon Watkins. AngWePo

Music of Colours—White Blossom. Vernon Watkins. AngWePo; TCAWP

Music of Forefended Spheres, The. Coventry Patmore. NPeEn *Fr.* Victories of Love, The.

Music of His Steps, The. Samuel Wakefield. AH

Music of Spheres. Jean Follain. BLT

Music of the Altai Mountains. Kelvin Corcoran. Oth

Music of the Spheres. Anthony Barnett. Oth

Music of Words, The. Lu Chi. WoPoe, *tr. by* Tony Barnstone and Chou Ping *Fr.* Art of Writing, The.

Music on the Water. George Johnston. MoCV

Music's Wife. Joel Long. AmPoNex

Music seemed to be so reminiscent, The. My Old Flame. Sam Coslow. ReLy

Music: Sexual misery is wearing you out. Ceriserie. Joshua Clover. BAP-01

Music Swims Back to Me. Anne Sexton. ColAP; MiVo; VCAP

Music That Makes Me Dance. Jule Styne. ReLy

Music, thou queen of souls, get up and string. Song. Thomas Randolph. OxBSP

Music, thou soul of heaven, care-charming spell. Music. Robert Herrick. CaPo

Music was going on, The. At the Fillmore. Philip Levine. NNaP

Music, when soft voices die. To ———. Shelley. AWP; FHYEP; GTBS-P; HeIP-4; NAEL-5v2; NAEL-6v2; NOBE; OBEV; OxAEP-2; OxBEV; OxBSP; TFi

Musica. Philip Dacey. MiVo

Musica No. 3. Richard Duerden. NeAP

Musical Instrument, A. Elizabeth Barrett Browning. CABP; EBVV; NAEL-5v2; NAEL-6v2; NPeEn; NoP-4; OBEV; PEW; PoE; PoPoPo; VWP; ViWPN; WPE

Musical Lion, The. Oliver Herford. OBCA

Musical maiden from Frome, A. Limerick. Cyril Bibby. PeLi

Musical man is walking along the shore, A. Telemachus with a Transistor. Ruth Dallas. PeNZ

Musical Monkey, The. John Mole. OBCoV *Fr.* Penny Toys.

Musical monkey is dressed like a flunkey, The. John Mole. OBCoV *Fr.* Penny Toys.

Musical Orchard, The. Douglas Dunn. FaBoMo

Musical Pumpkin-Hut. Heinrich Albert. GePo, *tr. by* George C. Schoolfield

Musical Saw. David Kresh. MiVo

Musical Strife; in a Pastoral Dialogue, The. Ben Jonson. BeJo

Musical Wine-Jar, A. Hedylos. GrAn, *tr. by* William Moebius

Musicall Consort, A. Thomas Churchyard. "That humor now, declines for age drawes on." PBRV

Musician. Louise Bogan. APT-2

Musician, The. Philip Dacey. MiVo

Musician, The. Martinus Nijhoff. TuT, *tr. by* Desmond Egan

Musician, The. David Wright. NLP

Musician Talks about "Process," The. Rita Dove. ESEAA

Musicians gone. Amateur Drummer. Roberta Gould. MiVo

Musicians wrestle everywhere. Emily Dickinson. APN-2

Music[k]'s Duel[l]. Richard Crashaw. GeHe; NAEL-7v1; NPeEn

Music[k], thou queen of heaven, care-charming spell. To Music: A Song. Robert Herrick. CaPo

Musidora's Vision. Henrietta Cordelia Ray. CBWP-3

Musing on roses and revolutions. Roses and Revolutions. Dudley Randall. BPo; CoAmPo; TAP

Musings. William Barnes. HAP; NOBE

Musk-ox smells, The. Long River, The. Donald Hall. CoAmPo; LCAP-2

Musketaquid. Ralph Waldo Emerson. APN-1

Muskrats rose from the marsh. After the Storm. Edmond Yi-teh Chang. OpBo

Musophilus; or, Defence of All Learning. Samuel Daniel. "Behold how every man, drawn with delight." NoSic

(Heavenly Eloquence.) NOBE

(Imperial Eloquence.) NAEL-7v1

Poet and Critic. NoSic; PBRV

Poetry in England. NoSic

"Power above powers, O heavenly Eloquence." NoSic

"Sacred Religion, mother of form and fear." NoSic

Stonehenge. NPeEn

"Where wil you have your vertuous names safe laid." NPeEn

Muspilli. *Unknown.* GePo, *tr. by* Carroll Hightower

Mussel Rock / Lowtide—Santa Cruz, California 1959. Jeff Tagami. OpBo

Musselburgh Field. *Unknown.* ESPB

Must all successful rebels grow. 1912–1952, Full Cycle. Peter Viereck. OBAL

Must Be Freed. Lizelia Augusta Jenkins Moorer. CBWP-3

Must bear alone the weary strife. (LL) On the Death of Anne Brontë. Charlotte Brontë. VWP; WPE

Must both remain as strangers still to you. (LL) Yourself. Jones Very. APN-1; NOBA; OxBA; Son

Must come upon you unmotivated as a poem. Hour of the Siesta, The. Judith Ortiz Cofer. PueRic

Must fall. (LL) Power of Taste, The. Zbigniew Herbert. PoSu; PoetW, *tr. by* John Carpenter and Bogdana Carpenter

Must fall aswoon, feeling all life grow weak. (LL) Dante Alighieri. AWP; EaItPo, *tr. by* Dante Gabriel Rossetti *Fr.* La Vita Nuova.

Must hapless man, in ignorance sedate. Juvenal. AWP, *tr. by* Samuel Johnson *Fr.* Satires.

Must I *always* be stuck in the audience at these poetry-readings, never. Juvenal. RomPo, *tr. by* Peter Green *Fr.* Satires.

Must I die now? Is this a part of life? (LL) Cut Flower, A. Karl Shapiro. HAP; WeW-3

Must I lament the time that's gone because I've been cast aside? Ch'ien Ch'ien-i [*or* Ch'ien Ch'ien-yi]. SuSp *Fr.* Willow Branch Songs.

Must I live here, with Scripture on my walls. Bed-Sitting Room, The. William Henry Davies. TCAWP

Must I then see, alas! eternal night. Elegy over a Tomb. Edward Herbert, 1st Baron Herbert of Cherbury. MeLP; NOBE; OBEV; OBWVE

Must learn in life to die [*or* dy] like thee. (LL) Richard Crashaw. BASC; FSCP; NOBE; NoP-4; OBEV

Must pine neglected and alone. (LL) Captive Dove, The. Anne Brontë. EBVV; VWP

Must plough the wave no more. (LL) On the Loss of the *Royal George.* William Cowper. EBEV; NOBE

Must quiet a heart accused by its own fear. (LL) At Cooloolah. Judith Wright. BMAP; HarvBoo

Must soon partake his grave. (LL) Epitaph on a Hare. William Cowper. HAP; NOEC; NoP-4; PoPoPo

Must then my crimes become thy scandal too? To Antenor. Katherine Philips. EMWP

Must we part, Von Hügel, though much alike. W. B. Yeats. OBMV *Fr.* Vacillation.

Must you alone then, happy flowers.   To a Nosegay in Pancharilla's Breast.   Soame Jenyns.   ECEV

Must you dance ev'ry dance.   Change Partners.   Irving Berlin.   ReLy

Must you deny me a bite of your raisin? (LL)   Brief Autumnal.   *Unknown.*   GrAn; PAI; WeW-3, *tr. by* Dudley Fitts

Must you have a part in everything? (LL)   Smell.   William Carlos Williams.   MoAmPo; RaBo; TAP

Must you leave, John Holmes, with the prayers and psalms.   Somewhere in Africa.   Anne Sexton.   NALW

Must you with hot irons burn out both mine eyes?   William Shakespeare.   OxAEP-1   *Fr.* King John.

Mustacheless Bard, A.   J. Gordon Coogler.   OBAL

Mustapha.   Fulke Greville, 1st Baron Brooke.
  (Chorus of Priests.)   NoSic; OxAEP-1
  Chorus Primus of Bashaws or Cadis.   NOSC
  Chorus Sacerdotum.   HAP; NAEL-5v1; NAEL-6v1; NAEL-7v1; NOBE; OxBEV
  (From Mustapha.)   NoP-4
  ("O wearisome condition of humanity!")   NoP-4
  "O[h] wearisome condition of humanity."   HAP; NAEL-5v1; NAEL-6v1; NAEL-7v1; NOBE; OxBEV

Musty shed.   Rod Willmot.   HA

Mutability.   Rachel Hadas.   ExTi

Mutability.   Shelley.   NAEL-5v2; NAEL-6v2; NoP-4

Mutability.   W. D. Snodgrass.   DiPo

Mutability.   William Wordsworth.   CenSon; EBEV; HeIP-4; InPK-6; NAEL-6v2; NOBE; NoP-4; OBEV   *Fr.* Ecclesiastical Sonnets.

Mutability Checkers.   Randolph Healy.   Oth

Mutability Claims to Rule the World.   Edmund Spenser.   NoSic   *Fr.* Faerie Queene, The.

Mutable Earth.   Louise Glück.   BodElec

Mutation.   William Cullen Bryant.   NCAP

Mutations.   Robert Fitzgerald.   APT-2

Mutations of the Phoenix.   Sir Herbert Read.
  "Phoenix, bird of terrible pride."   FaBoTw

Mute as it is, the river.   River Song.   Ben Howard.   PoCoUp

Mute is thy wild harp, now, O Bard sublime!   To the Shade of Burns.   Charlotte Smith.   NoP-4

Mute Prophets.   Nicholas Samaras.   OPRER

Mute Swan, The.   Constance Merritt.   AmPoNex

Mute Swans.   Neil Curry.   NLP

Mute the tongue, and closed the eye. (LL)   Three Roses, The.   Walter Savage Landor.   NAEL-5v2; NAEL-6v2

Mute was the marble.   Heirs of Stalin, The.   Yevgeny Aleksandrovich Yevtushenko [*or* Evtushenko].   TCRP, *tr. by* George Reavey

Muted Music.   Robert Penn Warren.   APT-2

Muted Screen of Graham Greene, The.   Phyllis McGinley.   FaBoEE

Muted Tones.   Paul Verlaine.   SxFrPo, *tr. by* Martin Sorrell

Mutes, The.   Denise Levertov.   ErotSp; NALW; NOBA

Mutineer's Ballad, The.   Peter Kocan.   NOBAu

Muttering thunder.   Robert Spiess.   HA

Mutterings over the Crib of a Deaf Child.   James Wright.   LCAP-2

Mutton Bird Man.   Rhyll McMaster.   NOBAu

Mutton birds! I like 'em I'll eat 'em any way.   Ode to Salted Mutton Birds.   Jim Everett.   IBA

Mutual Congratulations of the Poets Anna Seward and Hayley, The.   Richard Porson.   FaBoEE; OBSV

Mutual Problem.   William Cole.   OBAL; OBCoV

Mutual Subjection.   Christopher Smart.   NOCV   *Fr.* Hymns for the Amusement of Children.

Muu's Way; or Pictures from the Uterine World.   *Unknown.*   STP, *tr. by* Jerome Rothenberg

Muvver was barfin' 'er biby one night, A.   Dahn the Plug'ole.   *Unknown.*   RB, *tr. by* Robert Bly

My Acts.   William Meredith.   VCAP   *Fr.* Consequences.

My adored statue.   Arid Husband, The.   E. L. T. Mesens.   SPE

My Africa.   Michael Dei-Anang.   PBA

My age fallen away like white swaddling.   Age.   Philip Larkin.   OxBEV

My age is three hundred and seventy-two.   Sleepy Giant, The.   Charles Edward Carryl.   NOxBChV; OTCP

My aged friend, Miss Wilkinson.   Bards, The.   Walter De la Mare.   NOBL

My Alba.   Allen Ginsberg.   CLPP; NOBA

My Ambition.   James Laughlin.   GifTon

My ancestor was called on to go out.   Wind at Your Door, The.   Robert David Fitzgerald.   NOBAu

My ancestors weren't hippies, cotton.   Botanical Fanaticism.   Thylias Moss.   TRP

My Androgynous Years.   James Harms.   NeAmPo

My angel!   Holiday Present.   Ilya Abu Madi.   GraLe, *tr. by* George Dimitri Selim

My Angel Sister, though thy lovely form.   On a Lock of Miss Sarah Seward's Hair Who Died in Her Twentieth Year.   Anna Seward.   CenSon

My Angeline.   Harry Bache Smith.   NBLV

My answer would have to be music.   Medium, The.   Elaine Feinstein.   BrRo

My apparition rose from the fall of lead.   Civilian and Soldier.   Wole Soyinka.   AF; PBMAP; PoetW

My apple-tree, my willow.   Yunna Petrovna [*or* Iunna Pinkhusovna] Moritz [*or* Morits].   ItGoST, *tr. by* Daniel Weissbort

My ardours for emprize nigh lost.   On an Invitation to the United States.   Thomas Hardy.   AWP; AiP; FaBoA

My Arima mountains closer.   Forever Arima.   Cheryl Boyce Taylor.   WiU

My Arkansas.   Maya Angelou.   BlSi; NAAAL

My arm for a pillow.   Buson.   EH, *tr. by* Robert Hass

My arm sweeps down.   Gesture.   Donald Finkel.   InPK-6

My arms are given.   Absolution.   Diane Ward.   FTOS

My arms are round you, and I lean.   To the Oaks of Glencree.   John Millington Synge.   MoBrPo; NOIV

My arms have mutinied against me—brutes!   Wild with All Regrets.   Wilfred Owen.   SCGP

My arms smell good.   Think.   Please Forward.   James Welch.   CDW

My ash spear is my barley bread.   Archilochus.   GrAn

My aspens dear, whose airy cages quelled.   Binsey Poplars (Felled 1879).   Gerard Manley Hopkins.   EBVV; NAEL-5v2; NAEL-6v2; NoAM; PAI; RB

My Atthis, although our dear Anaktoria.   Sappho.   BoWoP

My attire is noiseless when I tread the earth.   Cynewulf.   AnOE, *tr. by* Charles W. Kennedy   *Fr.* Riddles (Exeter Book).

My Aunt.   Oliver Wendell Holmes.   TAP

My Aunt and the Sun.   Michael Burkard.   BodElec

My Aunt Jane.   *Unknown.*   FaBoVe

My Aunt Jane she took me in.   My Aunt Jane.   *Unknown.*   FaBoVe

My Aunt Maria.   Mary Morelle Show, The.   Denise Nico Leto.   UnSA

My aunt! my dear unmarried aunt!   My Aunt.   Oliver Wendell Holmes.   TAP

My aunt she died a month ago.   Death of My Aunt.   *Unknown.*   OxBoLi

My aunt was an herb doctor, one-eyed with crooked yellow teeth.   To-ta Ti-om.   Peter Blue Cloud.   HATNAP

My aunts washed dishes while the uncles.   Paper Matches.   Paulette Jiles.   NIL-7; NIP-4; NOBC

My baby contemplates the toy catalog.   20 July 1994.   Virginia Cerenio.   ReBoTo

My baby is sleeping overhead.   Dream Maiden, A.   Harriet Hamilton King.   VWP

My Baby Just Cares for Me.   Walter Donaldson.   ReLy

My baby / loves flowers.   William J. Harris.   NBV

My bakelite mantel set pulled him in.   Whatever Happened to Conway Twitty?   Tim Thorne.   BMAP

My bands of silk and miniver.   Full Moon.   Elinor Wylie.   NALW; NoP-4

My Baptismal Birthday [*or* Birth-Day].   Samuel Taylor Coleridge.   ChIV-2; NOCV

My bar is somewhat further down the street. (LL)   Third Avenue in Sunlight.   Anthony Hecht.   CoAP; VCAP

My beak is bent downward, I burrow below.   Cynewulf.   AnOE   *Fr.* Riddles (Exeter Book).

My beard's overcrowded. Now that.   Limerick.   Richard Unwin.   PeLi

My beautiful bird in the eternal the downspouts call you but don't think about.   Pale Blue Line in a Forced Episode, I Cut a Hole in the Flag of the Republic.   Simone Yoyotte.   SurWo, *tr. by* Myrna Bell Rochester

My beautiful one gave it to me when we parted.   Feelings Wakened by a Mirror.   Po Chü-i.   CoBCP, *tr. by* Burton Watson

My beautiful picture of pirates and treasure.   Jigsaw Puzzle.   Russell Hoban.   NTCP

My beautiful trembler! how wildly she shrinks!   Ellen Learning to Walk.   Frances Sargent Osgood.   ColAP

My beauty is not wine to me.   *Unknown.*   AWP   *Fr.* Thousand and One Nights, The.

My bed concealed by a folding screen.   Lying at Leisure during Rain.   Kao Ch'i.   CoBLCP, *tr. by* Jonathan Chaves

My Bed Is a Boat.   Robert Louis Stevenson.   PWR; PeVV

My bed is like a little boat.   My Bed Is a Boat.   Robert Louis Stevenson.   PWR; PeVV

My bed is unmade: sheets on the floor.   Death Is Sitting at the Foot of My Bed.   Oscar Hahn.   TCLAP, *tr. by* Sandy McKinney

My bed was soft, the early night was bliss.   Petronius Arbiter.   RomPo, *tr. by* J. P. Sullivan

My Beloved.   Christine Busta.   AuPH, *tr. by* Lowell A. Bangerter

My Belovèd Compares Herself to a Pint of Stout.   Paul Durcan.   EmeKit

My beloved hath a vineyard.   Vineyard of My Beloved, The.   Priscilla Jane Thompson.   CBWP-2

My Beloved Is Mine, and I Am His; He Feedeth among the Lillies.   Francis Quarles.   MeLP; NOBE   *Fr.* Emblems.

My belovèd is the summer. Vastly sails he.   My Beloved.   Christine Busta.   AuPH, *tr. by* Lowell A. Bangerter

My beloved little billiard balls.   Poem to Some of my Recent Poems.   James Tate.   NoAM

My beloved spake, and said unto me.   Bible, *O.T.*   OPOU   *Fr.* Song of Solomon, The [*or* The Song of Songs].

My beloved was laundering.   Yevgeny [*or* Evgenii] Mikhailovich Vinokurov.   TCRP

My Ben.   Robert Herrick.   BASC

My best belovit brother of the band.   To R. Hudson.   Alexander Montgomerie.   OxBS

My biggest worry is this.   In a Time of Sickness.   Orpingalik.   STP, *tr. by* Edward Field

My biological clock is ticking.   In the Heat of the Night.   Lee Smith.   Unle

My Birds.   Solomon Mutswairo.   PeSAV, *tr. by* Donald E. Herdeck and Solomon Mutswairo

My Birthday.   George Crabbe.   OxBSP

My black cat doesn't know.   Savoir Faire.   Claribel Alegría.   VCWP

My black face fades.   Facing It.   Yusef Komunyakaa.   AmFaPo; ESEAA; NAAAL; PoPoPo; TRP

My black hair tangled.   Lady Izumi.   ErotSp, *tr. by* Sam Hamill

My black hills have never seen the sun rising.   Shancoduff.   Patrick Kavanagh.   BIrV; CIP-2; FaBoTw; HarvBoo; WoPoe

My Blackness Is the Beauty of This Land.   Lance Jeffers.   ISC

My Blessed Lord, how doth my Beautious Spouse.   Edward Taylor.   ColAP; SCAP   *Fr.* Preparatory Meditations before My Approach to the Lord's Supper.

My Blessed Lord, that Golden Linck that joyns.   Edward Taylor.   TCAPo   *Fr.* Preparatory Meditations before My Approach to the Lord's Supper.

My blissful Mother exists fully through every creature!   Lex Hixon.   HW

My Blood Brother.   Frank Mkalawile Chipasula.   HBAPE

My blood sits upright in a chair.   Blood.   Franz Wright.   LCAP-2

My blood so red.   Call, The.   *Unknown.*   OBEV

My Blue Heaven.   Walter Donaldson.   ReLy

My blueveined child. (LL)   Flower Given to My Daughter, A.   James Joyce.   OBMV; RB; RaBo

My boat goes west, yours east.   Farewell.   Ch'ao Li-houa [*or* Chao Li-hua].   BoWoP

My Boat Moored on a River.   Yen Yü.   SuSp, *tr. by* Irving Y. Lo

My boat sails downstream.   Love Song.   *Unknown.*   TTY, *tr. by* J. E. Manchip White

My Body.   Joan Larkin.   WiU

My body a rounded stone.   Living Tenderly.   May Swenson.   OBCA

My body being dead, my limbs [*or* lims] unknown.   Preparative, The.   Thomas Traherne.   BASC; ESCV; GeHe

My body had no entrance, and the black.   Maria [*or* Mariia] Mikhailovna Shkapskaya [*or* Shkapskaia].   TCRP

My body in its autumn.   Ra-in.   JDP, *tr. by* Yoel Hoffmann

My body is a mystery.   Instinct.   Edith Södergran.   PFTM-1

My body is a torn mattress.   Would You Wear My Eyes?   Bob Kaufman.   GT

My body is a white thing in the sun, now.   Morning after My Death, The.   Larry Levis.   OPRER

My body is like / a field wasted by winter.   On Seeing the Field Being Singed.   Lady Ise.   BoWoP, *tr. by* Etsuko Terasaki

My body is opaque to the soul.   Prayer.   Jean Toomer.   NAAAL

My body is weary to death of my mischievous brain.   Nebuchadnezzar.   Elinor Wylie.   ChIV-1; MoAmPo

My body knows it will never bear children.   Waiting.   Jane Cooper.   TAP

My body leaves you drop by drop.   Absence.   Gabriela Mistral.   SpanPo, *tr. by* Kate Flores

My body opens over San Francisco like the day.   Splittings.   Adrienne Rich.   HarvBoo

My body resting in a haunt of mine.   Ubaldo di Marco.   EaItPo, *tr. by* Dante Gabriel Rossetti

My body, useless.   Seisa.   JDP, *tr. by* Yoel Hoffmann

My body, you are an animal.   I Talk to My Body.   Anna Swirszczynska.   BLT

My Bohemia.   Arthur Rimbaud.   SxFrPo, *tr. by* Martin Sorrell

My Bomb.   Beckian Fritz Goldberg.   ExTi

My bones are weary and life is nothing worth. (LL)   To Dante Alighieri: He Conceives of Some Compensation in Death.   Cino da Pistoia.   AWP; EaItPo, *tr. by* Dante Gabriel Rossetti

My bones turn to dark emeralds. (LL)   Jewel, The.   James Wright.   CoAP; NAAL-2v2

My books, my sword, the wind-swept curtain.   Remembering My Late Wife.   Chu Yün-ming.   CoBLCP, *tr. by* Jonathan Chaves

My boss did not like me.   Boss, The.   Boris Abramovich Slutsky [*or* Slutskii].   TCRP, *tr. by* J. R. Rowland

My boy was scarcely ten years auld.   Leesome Brand.   *Unknown.*   ESPB

My boy, what do you think that I can tell you?   Oom Gert's Story.   C. Louis Leipoldt.   PeSAV, *tr. by* C. J. D. Harvey

My Boy Willie.   *Unknown.*   MakPoe

My brain burns with hate of you.   Paradox.   Anna Wickham.   LW

My brain dried like spread turf, my stomach.   Seamus Heaney.   CIP-2   *Fr.* Station Island.

My brain is like the ravaged shores—the sand.   At Night.   Frances Darwin Cornford.   MoBrPo

My brethren all attend.   Zealous Puritan, The.   *Unknown.*   NOSC

My brethren, you see with your own eyes what we are.   Funeral Oration.   *Unknown.*   IQMS, *tr. by* Alan Jenkins

"My bride is not coming, alas!" says the groom.   Thomas Hardy.   MoBrPo   *Fr.* Satires of Circumstance in Fifteen Glimpses.

My bright and beauteous Bride. (LL)   Love.   Samuel Taylor Coleridge.   GTBS-P; OBEV

My Broken Heart.   Fanny Howe.   ExTi

My Brother.   Hendrik de Vries.   TuT, *tr. by* Peter Van de Kamp

My Brother.   Mikhail Naimy.   GraLe, *tr. by* Sharif Elmusa and Gregory Orfalea

My Brother.   Patricia Parker.   GLP

My brother and I.   Miriam.   Marjorie Agosin.   MirDau, *tr. by* Monica Bruno Galmozzi

My brother Cain, the wounded, liked to sit.   Abel.   Demetrios Capetanakis.   GTBS-P

My brother comes home from work.   You Can Have It.   Philip Levine.   AmFaPo; NoP-4; VCAP

My Brother Dear.   Ferdinand Raimund.   AuPH, *tr. by* Lowell A. Bangerter

My brother dear, dear as can be.   My Brother Dear.   Ferdinand Raimund.   AuPH, *tr. by* Lowell A. Bangerter

My brother, good morning: my sister, good night. (LL)   Early Morning, The.   Joseph Hilaire Pierre Belloc.   OxBSP; Spl; TLR

My brother has on / a thin robe.   Lady Otomo no Sakanoé.   BoWoP

My brother is skull and skeleton now.   Epitaph.   William Montgomerie.   OxBS

My brother Jamie lost me all.   Mary Stuart.   Edwin Muir.   RB

My Brother, My Sister.   Jack Davis.   IBA

My brother's done for, by all human law.   János Arany.   IQMS, *tr. by* Watson Kirkconnell   *Fr.* Toldi.

My brother, / staggering amidst the shiny glass mountains of the North Pole.   Hymn of Love, The.   György Sárközi.   IQMS, *tr. by* Adam Makkai

My brother thought they were freaks.   Everly Brothers, The.   Floyd Skloot.   SwNoth

My brother was afraid, even as a boy, of going blind—so deeply.   How Some of It Happened.   Marie Howe.   ExTi

My brother was not a camel driver.   On Her Brother.   Al-Khansa.   BoWoP, *tr. by* Willis Barnstone

My brother you flash your teeth in response to every hypocrisy.   Renegade, The.   David Diop.   PBMAP

My brother, you suffered.   My Brother.   Hendrik de Vries.   TuT, *tr. by* Peter Van de Kamp

My Brothers.   Haki R. Madhubuti.   ISC

My Brothers.   Anna Walters.   VoR

My brothers are big, so much bigger than I.   T. Carmi.   MHP, *tr. by* Ruth Finer Mintz   *Fr.* René's Songs.

My brothers i will not tell you.   My Brothers.   Haki R. Madhubuti.   ISC

My Brothers Make a Lantern.   David Scott Ward.   AmPoNex

My brothers playing on the green. (LL)   Brothers, The.   Edwin Muir.   GTBS-P; HeIP-4

My brothers, you would have me give a toast.   Polish Eagle, The.   Kornel Ujejski.   MLL, *tr. by* Helen Waddell

My Buddy.   Richard Hugo.   SeSe

My bull is white like silver fish in the river.   Magnificent Bull, The.   *Dinka Oral Tradition.*   TTTS

My Burned Suit.   Ilyas Farhat.   MAP, *tr. by* John Heath-Stubbs and Salma Khadra Jayyusi

My camel kneels at Ibn Marwan's door.   Camel.   Laila Akhyaliyya.   BoWoP, *tr. by* Willis Barnstone

My Camping Ground.   Morris Jacob Rosenfeld.   TrJP, *tr. by* Aaron Kramer

My Canary.   Josephine D. Henderson Heard.   CBWP-4

My candle burned alone in an immense valley.   Valley Candle.   Wallace Stevens.   SAmP

My candle burns a flame of jade.   Meditating on the Start of a New Era.   Yo Inlŏ.   WoPoe, *tr. by* Jean S. Grigsby

My candle burns at both ends.   First Fig.   Edna St. Vincent Millay.   APT-1; AiP; BRP; ChAP; FaBoWP; NALW; NIL-7; NoAM; NoP-4; TAP

My candle burns up lank and fair.   Resurrection.   Margiad Evans.   OBWVE

My Care. Peter Fallon. CIP-2

My carefree Namesake, this the art. Martial. RomPo, *tr.* by Peter Whigham

My Careful Life. Frank Ormsby. PBCIP

My careful life says: "No surrender." My Careful Life. Frank Ormsby. PBCIP

My cares comen ever anew. *Unknown.* MiEL

My Carol. Mildmay Fane, 2d Earl of Westmorland. BeJo

My case is this. Sir John Davies. NoSic *Fr.* Gulling[e] Sonnets, The.

My cassia boat, adrift and free. Fishing Rod, The. Shen Yüeh. SuSp, *tr.* by Richard B. Mather

My cat. Issa. EH, *tr.* by Robert Hass

My Cat and I. Roger McGough. OxBTC

My Cat Jeoffry. Christopher Smart. CABP; CTC; FaBoCh; HAP; HeIP-4; NAEL-5v1; NAEL-6v1; NAEL-7v1; NOEC; NPeEn; NoP-4; OBWVE; OxAEP-1; PAI; PoE; PoPoPo; RB; SCV; TRP; TTTS; TriCat; WeW-3 *Fr.* Jubilate Agno.

My ceramic lake in dawn, water settled clear. Han Yü. CoBCP *Fr.* Pond in a Jardiniere, A.

My Chakabuku Mama: A Comic Tale. Jewelle Gomez. BAP-01; GLP

My cheap toy lamp. Child's Song. Robert Lowell. RB

My cheeks still feel their breath: how can it be. On the Transitory. Hugo von Hofmannsthal. WoPoe, *tr.* by Naomi Replansky

My child and I hold hands on the way to school. September, the First Day of School. Howard Nemerov. OxBC

My child, I do this for you. I give this to you. *Unknown.* APN-2 *Fr.* Minnetare Songs.

My child is lying on my knees. Father's Hymn for the Mother to Sing. George Macdonald. SacPr

My child, my child, thou leav'st me! I shall hear. Madeline, a Domestic Tale. Felicia Dorothea Hemans. RWP

My child, my sister. L'Invitation au Voyage. Charles Baudelaire. WoPoe, *tr.* by Richard Wilbur

My child never played the piano. Moderato. Susan Wicks. MFPA

My child perished like the sky when it broke. Kū' siut Song. *Unknown.* APN-2, *tr.* by Franz Boas

My child, the Duck-billed Plat-y-pus. Platypus, The. Oliver Herford. PeLV

My child, we were two children. Mein Kind, wir waren Kinder. Heinrich Heine. AWP; OBVE; TrJP, *tr.* by Elizabeth Barrett Browning

My childhood all a myth. Myth, The. Edwin Muir. HarvBoo

My childhood are remembrances of a court in Seville. Portrait. Antonio Machado Ruiz. SpanPo, *tr.* by Doreen Bell

My Childhood-Home I See Again. Abraham Lincoln. APN-1

My Childhood in Another Part of the World. Rafael Campo. NeAmPo

My childhood is a long way off. Tourist. Muhammad Al-Maghut. MAP, *tr.* by John Heath-Stubbs and May Jayyusi

My childhood is a sphere. Childhood. Thomas Traherne. SacPr

My childhood is all memories of a patio in Sevilla. Portrait. Antonio Machado Ruiz. RaBo; STV; WoPoe, *tr.* by Robert Bly

My childhood's trees stand rejoicing around me: O human! Homecoming. Edith Södergran. WPoS

My Childhood Trees. Edith Södergran. WoPoe, *tr.* by Stina Katchadourian

My childhood trees stand tall in the grass. My Childhood Trees. Edith Södergran. WoPoe, *tr.* by Stina Katchadourian

My children! speak not ill of one another. To Poets. Walter Savage Landor. FaBoEE

My children tug at my coat and ask. Returning Home. Tu Mu. SuSp, *tr.* by John M. Ortinau

My children, when at first I liked the whites. *Unknown.* APN-2, *tr.* by James Mooney *Fr.* Ghost-Dance Songs.

My Chinese uncle, gouty, deaf, half-blinded. Grotesques. Robert Graves. OBCoV

My Christ, by Thee. (LL) Thanksgiving to God for His House, A. Robert Herrick. BASC; BeJo; CavPo; HAP; NOSC; PeECV; PoRA; TrCP

My Christmas; Mum's Christmas. Sarah Forsyth. OBCP

My chums will burn their Indian weeds. Smith of Maudlin. George Walter Thornbury. PeVV

My City. James Weldon Johnson. NAAAL

My city slept. Beginning of a Long Poem on Why I Burned the City, The. Lawrence Benford. TTY

My claw is tired of scribing! Invocation. Saint Columcille [or Columba]. NOIV

My clear windowpane moon. (LL) Love Song. Pablo Neruda. ErotSp; GifTon, *tr.* by William O'Daly

My Close-Committee. Mildmay Fane, 2d Earl of Westmorland. BeJo

My Cloth of Gold. Ina Coolbrith. SWaP

My clothes are standing up without me. When You Wish upon a Star That Turns into a Plane. James Harms. SwNoth

My clumsiest dear, whose hands shipwreck vases. Love Poem. John Frederick Nims. IllVoic; InPK-6

My clumsy poem on the inn-wall none cared to see. Poem on the Wall, The. Po Chü-i. ChiP, *tr.* by Arthur Waley

My cock's great size results in one delight. *Unknown.* PriapPo, *tr.* by Richard W. Hooper *Fr.* Priapus Poems, The.

My Cockroach Lover. Martín Espada. UrbNat

My Cocoon tightens—Colors tease. Emily Dickinson. APN-2; NAAL-2v1; NAAL-3

My colleague knows by heart the morbid verse. Lunch and Afterwards. Dannie Abse. BloBone

My colored child / hood wuz mostly music. Make/n My Music. Angela Jackson. SeSe

My Coloring Book. John Kander. ReLy

My comforts drop and melt away like snow. Answer, The. George Herbert. FaBoVe; NPeEn

My companion in the skies. Fufu. JDP, *tr.* by Yoel Hoffmann

My company. (LL) Hellhound on My Trail. Robert Johnson. APT-2; NAAAL; PFTM-2

My Company. Sir Herbert Read. PoWW

My comrade is in the final agony before death. Yona [or Iona] Degen. TCRP

My Confessional Sestina. Dana Gioia. RA

My conscience has given me several twitches. To My Cousin Mary, for Mending My Tobacco Pouch. Francis Scott Key. OBAL

My contemplation dazzles in the End. Anticipation, The. Thomas Traherne. BASC

My contemporary. He died, not I. To a Poet. Ágnes Nemes Nagy. PoSu, *tr.* by Bruce Berlind

My cottage door opens on the water. At Home. Wang An-shih. CrYelRi, *tr.* by Sam Hamill

My cotton shirts float on the line. Women, The. Cyrus Cassells. UnSA

My Country. Olga Fiodorovna Berggolts [or Bergholts]. TCRP, *tr.* by Daniel Weissbort

My Country. Jaime Torres Bodet. TCLAP, *tr.* by Sonja Karsen

My Country. Elolongue Epanya Yondo. NegPo, *tr.* by Ellen Conroy Kennedy

My Country Audit. Mildmay Fane, 2d Earl of Westmorland. BeJo; NOSC

My country is an asylum where madmen. Dead Erect, The. Malika O'Lahsen. HAWP

My country is handed over from one tyrant. From Exile to Exile. 'Abd-Allah Al-Baraduni. MAP, *tr.* by Sharif Elmusa and Diana Der Hovanessian

My country is not a country. Envoi. Eli W. Mandel. NOBC

My country need not change her gown. Union. Emily Dickinson. FaBoA

My country now is like a barge. Richard II Forty. Louis Aragon. WoPoe, *tr.* by Peter Dale

My country, / t'is of thee / I sing. Lover's Question, A. James Baldwin. GLP

My country, that nobly could dare. For the Fourth of July. Eliza Lee Cabot Follen. SWaP

My country, 'tis of thee. America. Samuel Francis Smith. AiP; HHAm; TCAPo

My Country, to Thy Shore. Theodore Chickering Williams. AH

My Country Weeps. Andreas Gryphius. WoPoe, *tr.* by John Peck

My country, what road do you take? Lusitanian Song. János Vajda. IQMS, *tr.* by Jean Overton Fuller

My countrymen have now become too base. April 1962. Paul Goodman. VGW

My Cousin Abe, Paul Antschel and Paul Celan. Jacqueline Osherow. TaR

My Cousin Agueda [or Agatha]. Ramón López Velarde. OBVE; TCLAP, *tr.* by Samuel Beckett

My Cousin German Came from France. *Unknown.* FaBoCh

My Creed. Alice Cary. TreFP

My Creed. Samuel Ellsworth Kiser. PoToHe

My crown desired, my true love and joy. Love Letter to Elizabeth Thatcher, A. Thomas Thatcher. SCAP

My curse be on the day when first I saw. Sonnet: To the Lady Pietra degli Scrovigni. Dante Alighieri. AWP; EaltPo, *tr.* by Dante Gabriel Rossetti

My Cutey's Due at Two-to-Two Today. Leo Robin. ReLy

My cuticles are a mess. Oh honey, by the way. Motorcyclists, The. James Tate. NoAM; ReTh

My Dad. Beryl Philp-Carmichael (Yungha-Dhu). IBA

My Dad. Laura Whipple. CA

My dad cracks a joke and two men laugh. Show Biz Parties. Elizabeth Claman. OPRER

My dad had done the same. (LL) Epitaph on a Pessimist. Thomas Hardy. FaBoEE; TRP

My Dad was worried about his brother. Lucilius. GrAn

My dad works late in a coffee shop. My Dad. Laura Whipple. CA

My Dada. Judith Kazantzis. Prnts

My daddy has paid the rent. Good Times. Lucille Clifton. BPo; HHAm; PAI; SoSe-8; TAP; TRP; TwCP

My daddy played the market. January 1st. Anne Sexton. HCAP

My daddy rides me piggy-back. Piggy-back. Langston Hughes. TLR

My daddy said, "My son, my son." Bad Report—Good Manners. Spike Milligan. NOxBChV

My Daddy, Whenever He Went Some Place. David Huddle. PBCAP

My daily affairs are quite ordinary. Layman P'ang. EnlH

My Daily Creed. *Unknown.* PWR

My dame hath a lame tame crane. *Unknown.* OxNR

My Damon was the first to wake. Meeting. George Crabbe. OBEV

My Dance. Blaise Cendrars. CuPo

My Dancing Day. *Unknown.* OxBoLi

"To-morrow shall be my dancing day." ChrPo

My dancing is, in my opinion, good. Of Dancing. Alan Brownjohn. FaBoMo

My Daphne's hair is twisted gold. John Lyly. NoSic *Fr.* Midas.

My dark and sultry / love. (LL) Invention of Comics, The. Imamu Amiri Baraka. CRP; GT; NAAAL

My Dark Fathers. Brendan Kennelly. BIrV; CIP-2; PBCIP

My Dark Night Has Come Round Again. *Unknown.* WoPoe, *tr. by* Seamus Heaney *Fr.* Sweeney Astray.

My Dark Rosaleen! (LL) Dark Rosaleen. Owen Roe MacWard. AWP; BIrV; NOIV; OBEV; OxAEP-2, *tr. by* James Clarence Mangan

My darkling child the stars have obeyed. George Barker. TwCP *Fr.* To My Son.

My darling, all around us people clamor. Love Is the Thing. Victor Young. ReLy

My darling lady readers. Mystery Corset, The. André Breton. PFTM-1

My darling little Lou how I love you. Guillaume Apollinaire. PFTM-1 *Fr.* Poems for Lou.

My darling makes me mother to their youth. (LL) Augusta Davies Webster. VWP; ViWPN *Fr.* Mother and Daughter.

My Darling, My Darling. Frank Loesser. ReLy

My darling, my love. Desmond O'Grady. CIP-2 *Fr.* In the Greenwood.

My darling's features, painted by the light. George Henry Boker. APN-2 *Fr.* Sonnets: A Sequence on Profane Love.

My darling, that you loved me? (LL) James Vincent Cunningham. APT-2; NoAM

My darling, thou wilt never know. On the Death of Emily Jane Brontë. Charlotte Brontë. VWP

My darling, we sat together. Mein Liebchen, wir sassen zusammen. Heinrich Heine. AWP, *tr. by* James Thomson

My darling, you know how much I like to see the light on a. Black Hairs, The. Heinz Pasman. RaBo, *tr. by* Robert Bly

My darlings, do you hear me? Trim the fires! (LL) My Lighthouses. Helen Hunt Jackson. APN-2; ColAP

My Darlings' Shoes. *Unknown.* TreFP

My daughter. (LL) Marina. T. S. Eliot. APT-1; CABP; FaBoMo; GTBS-P; HeIP-4; NAEL-5v2; NAEL-6v2; NOBE; NOCV; NPeEn; OxBEV; PoE; TOF

My daughter. Dime after Dime. Mary Weems. SpirFl

My daughter, all is not vanity. Nathan [*or* Natan] Alterman. MHP, *tr. by* Ruth Finer Mintz *Fr.* Joy of the Poor, The.

My daughter, at eleven. Little Girl, My String Bean, My Lovely Woman. Anne Sexton. NAAL-5

My daughter came home from school one day. Battle, Over and Over Again, The. Safiya Henderson-Holmes. UnSA

My daughter has a birthmark hidden under her left arm. Hunger and Imagination. Teresa Whitman. MiVo

My daughter of the Mabinogion name. Rhiannon. T. Harri Jones. AngWePo

My daughter plays on the floor. Spelling. Margaret Atwood. NALW; NoAM

My daughter's dear child here I hold on my lap. After the Inscription on a Greek Stele of a Woman Holding Her Grandchild on Her Knees. *Unknown.* GrAn, *tr. by* Stephen Spender

My daughter spreads her legs. After Reading *Mickey in the Night Kitchen* for the Third Time before Bed. Rita Dove. LoL; ReTh

My day in the hills. Sound of Music, The. Richard Rodgers. ReLy

My daydreams lie buried in autumn leaves. September in the Rain. Harry Warren. ReLy

My Days Are Gliding Swiftly By. David Nelson. AH

My Days Overgrown. Joseph Miezan Bognini. PBMAP *Fr.* Ce Dur Appel de l'Espoir (1960).

My days were a thing for me to live. For One Who Gayly Sowed His Oats. Countee Cullen. APT-2

My Dead. "Rachel" [*or* "Rahel"]. FIT, *tr. by* Robert Friend

My dead brother. Nicholas Virgilio. HA

My dead friend's face as well. (LL) Requiem: "Pour out your light, O stars." Ivor Gurney. FaBoEE; FaBoTw

My dead Love came to me, and said. Apparition, The. Stephen Phillips.

OBEV

My dead piled up, thick, fragrant, on the fire escape. Autumn Leaves. Marilyn Chin. PoPoPo

My Dear and Only Love. James Graham, Marquess of Montrose. BeJo; OxBEV

My dear and only Love, I pray. James Graham, Marquess of Montrose. BeJo; OxBEV

My dear Brother, with courage bear the crosse. Sonnet sent to Blackness to Mr. John Welsch, by the Lady Culross, A. Elizabeth Melville, Lady Culross. EMWP

My dear child, my darling daughter. Dear Child, My Darling Daughter. *Hungarian Oral Tradition.* IQMS, *tr. by* Anthony Edkins

My dear deaf father, how I loved him then. Sir John Betjeman. OxBTC *Fr.* Summoned by Bells.

My dear, do you remember that country. Remember That Country. Jean Garrigue. VGW

My Dear Editor Manchette. Quote Me Wrong Again and I'll Slit the Throat of Your Pet Iguana. David St. John. RACG

"My dear fellow!" said the great poet. Fiction: A Message. Gavin Ewart. OxBC

My Dear Little Fellow. László Mécs. IQMS, *tr. by* Watson Kirkconnell

My dear Maria, my long absent friend. Epistle, An. Elizabeth Hands. PoBW

My dear, my dear, I know. To a Young Girl. W. B. Yeats. EBEV

My dear Odysseus. Letter to an Exile. Claribel Alegría. TANSG, *tr. by* Louise B. Popkin

My dear old village. Issa. SoOfWa, *tr. by* Sam Hamill

My Dear One is mine as mirrors are lonely. W. H. Auden. NPeEn; NoAM *Fr.* Sea and the Mirror, The.

My dear Orange brothers, have you heard of the news. Orange Lily, The. *Unknown.* NOIV

My dear son I am well thanks be to God. Home News. Ahmed Tidjani-Cissé. NAfrP; PBMAP

My Dear Son John's deceas'd ah! gone from hence. Brief Elegie on My Dear Son John, A. John Saffin. SCAP

My dear Telemachus, / The Trojan War. Odysseus to Telemachus. Joseph Brodsky. BLT; PAI, *tr. by* George L. Kline

My dear! this morning we will take a ride. Tête à Tête; or, Fashionable Pair: an Eclogue, The. Ann Murry. ECWP

My dear, / Today a letter from Berlin. Letter from Berlin, A. Jon Stallworthy. OBWP; OxBC

My dear, you would not believe the weather here. Belvedere Marittimo. Greg Williamson. AmPoNex; NeAmPo

My deare, my dearest dust; I come, I come. (LL) Lady Catherine [*or* Katherine] Dyer. BoLoP; EnLoPo *Fr.* Sir William Dyer, Knight.

My dearest Boy, / Since time begun. To a School-Boy at Eton, Yes and No. Mary Savage. ECWP

My dearest consort, my more loved heart. Dying Husband's Farewell, The. Phineas Fletcher. SacPr

My dearest dust, could not thy hasty day. Lady Catherine [*or* Katherine] Dyer. BoLoP; EnLoPo *Fr.* Sir William Dyer, Knight.

My dearest Father! As I write today. Farmer's Son Writes from the City, A. Herbert Strutz. AuPH, *tr. by* Lowell A. Bangerter

My dearest friend is struck, and I must stern beware. He Loves. David Schirmer. GePo, *tr. by* George C. Schoolfield

My dearest rival, lest [*or* least] our love. Sir John Suckling. BeJo; MeLP

My dearest, to let you or the world know. Forfeiture, The. Henry King, Bishop of Chichester. NOSC

My dearest, you may pray now it is Lent. To My Daughter Catherine on Ashwednesday 1645, Finding Her Weeping at Prayers, Because I Would Not Consent to Her Fasting. Katherine Thimelby Aston. EMWP

My Death. Carl Zuckmayer. TrJP, *tr. by* E. B. Ashton

My death grazes just out of sight. Sister Death. Penny Harter. TWW

My death was arranged by special plans in Heaven. New England Bachelor, A. Richard Eberhart. MoAmPo; NoAM

My debt to you, Belovèd. Debts. Jessie Belle Rittenhouse. TCAPo

My deere doghter Venus, quod Saturne. Geoffrey Chaucer. NPeEn *Fr.* Canterbury Tales, The.

My Delight and Thy Delight. Robert Bridges. NOBE; OBEV

My demands upon life are quite modest. Limerick. Robert Conquest. PeLi

My desire for revenge, the bitterness. Till Death Do Us Part. Leila Miccolis. BoWoP, *tr. by* Willis Barnstone and Nelson Cerqueira

My desire is. Clarity. 'Enayat Jaber. PoArWo, *tr. by* Wen Chin Ouyang

My Detacted Villa. Li Shan-fu. SuSp, *tr. by* Edward H. Schafer

My deth I love, my lif ich hate. Cleric Courts His Lady, A. *Unknown.* MiEL

My disaffected gaze falls on the city. Côte de Liesse. Daryl Hine. NoP-4

My Dog. John Kendrick Bangs. ITBLP

My Dog. Marchette Chute. WHSW

My Dog. Emily Lewis. OTCP

My dog came through the pinewoods dragging a dead fox. Wings. Mary Oliver. PoCoUp

My dog lay dead five days without a grave. Pardon, The. Richard Wilbur. NIL-7; NOBA; NoAM; PAI

My dog's assumed my alter ego. Strange Case, The. Michael Ondaatje. EmeKit

My dog went mad and bit my hand. D Is for Dog. William Henry Davies. OxBSP

My dolour is ane cup. Ressaif My Saul. R. Crombie Saunders. OxBS

My Dolphin, you only guide me by surprise. Dolphin. Robert Lowell. NOBA; NoAM; VCAP

My donkey stops. At Her Grave. Kuthaiyir. ArPe, *tr. by* Omar S. Pound

My Dove, My Beautiful One. James Joyce. ChIV-1

My Downfall. Dioscorides. GrAn, *tr. by* Peter Whigham

My downfall: those pink articulate lips. My Downfall. Dioscorides. GrAn, *tr. by* Peter Whigham

My Dream. Lew Blockcolski. VoR

My Dream. Christina Georgina Rossetti. BrRo; VWP; ViWPN

My dream a drink with Lonnie Johnson we discuss the code. Ted Berrigan. NoAM *Fr.* Sonnets, The.

My Dream about the Cows. Lucille Clifton. TRP

My Dream about the Poet. Lucille Clifton. TRP

My dream is the dream of a pond. Gifts. "Shu Ting." VCWP

My dream of America. Chinese Hot Pot. Wing Tek Lum. UnSA

My Dreams. Charlotte Brontë. *See* "Again I find myself alone."

My dreams are of a field afar. A. E. Housman. PeVV

My Dreams, My Works, Must Wait Till after Hell. Gwendolyn Brooks. IllVoic; NoP-4 *Fr.* Gay Chaps at the Bar.

My Drinking Song. Richard Dehmel. AWP, *tr. by* Ludwig Lewisohn

My driver's license is lapsing and so I appear. Vision Test, The. Mona Van Duyn. FFC

My drum, hollowed out thru the thin slit. La Chute. Charles Olson. InPK-6; PAI

My dugout canoe goes. Paddling Song. *Unknown.* PBA, *tr. by* Max Exner

My Dusty Kinsfolk. John Ormond. TCAWP

My dusty kinsfolk in the hill. My Dusty Kinsfolk. John Ormond. TCAWP

My duties took me to a spot by the sea. Bald Mountain. Wang An-shih. ColAnChi, *tr. by* Victor H. Mair

My eager waiting heart can bear no more. He Comes Not To-night. Josephine D. Henderson Heard. CBWP-4

My ear perceives no paltry difference. Blood and Gold. Endre Ady. IQMS, *tr. by* Watson Kirkconnell

My earliest flame, to whom I owe. Letter from a Captain in Country Quarters to His Corinna in Town, A. Isaac Hawkins Browne. ECEV

My early Mistress, now my ancient Muse. Preface to *The Progress of Learning.* Sir John Denham. NOSC; OxBSP

My Easter Dove. Henrietta Cordelia Ray. CBWP-3

My ecstasy is that I have met you. Sa'id 'Aql. MAP *Fr.* Book of Roses, The.

My elder, / Born into death like a message into a bottle. To My Brother Hanson. W. S. Merwin. NAAL-2v2

My elder sister stays by my side. Happy about Being Old. Yüan Mei. CoBLCP, *tr. by* Jonathan Chaves

My eldest sister arrived home that morning. Cuba. Paul Muldoon. CIP-2; ModIr; PNI

My embarrassment at his nakedness. Pool, The. Robert Creeley. CoAP

My emblem is an arrow. John Fairfax. NewEx

My empire of flamboyans. Areyto. Víctor Hernández Cruz. PmAP

My empty face. Lucien Stryk. IllVoic *Fr.* Issa: A Suite of Haiku.

My Enemies. Sophie Hannah. HarvBoo

My enemies, polished inside their caskets. My Enemies. Sophie Hannah. HarvBoo

My enemy came nigh. Hate. James Stephens. MoBrPo

My enemy had bidden me as guest. Compassionate Fool, The. Norman Cameron. GTBS-P; OxBSP; OxBTC; RB

My English Teacher. Chava Pinchas-Cohen. DTA, *tr. by* Miriyam Glazer

My English teacher is a journalist. My English Teacher. Chava Pinchas-Cohen. DTA, *tr. by* Miriyam Glazer

My entire life / has been spent / in refugee camps. Wired In. Lamont B. Steptoe. UnSA

My Epitaph. H. J. Daniel. FaBoEE

My Epitaph. David Gray. EBVV

My epitaph write on your heart. Love's Epitaph. William Cavendish, Duke of Newcastle. OxBSP

My Erotic Double. John Ashbery. LCAP-2; PoE; VCAP

My errors my loves my unlucky star. Sonnet. Luis de Camões [*or* Camõens]. WoPoe, *tr. by* David Wevill

My Estate. John Norris. NOSC

My Exorcist Mother. Patricia Adelman. Prnts

My eye cried and woke me. Night, The. Al-Khansa. BoWoP, *tr. by* Willis Barnstone

My eye descending from the Hill, surveys. Sir John Denham. OxAEP-1; OxBEV *Fr.* Cooper's Hill.

My eye is not on Calvary. Calvary. Sorley MacLean (Somhairle MacGill-Eain). NePenScot

My eyelids red and heavy are. Poor Scholar of the 'Forties, A. Padraic Colum. NOIV

My eyes already touch the sunny hill. Walk, A. Rainer Maria Rilke. RaBo, *tr. by* Robert Bly

My eyes are dim, my hands are clumsy. Getting on Horseback. Yü Chi. CoBLCP, *tr. by* Jonathan Chaves

My eyes are full of rivers and trees tonight. After a Train Journey. May Sarton. GM

My eyes are on a butterfly. Who Are You? "Adonis" [*or* "Adunis"]. MAP, *tr. by* John Heath-Stubbs and Lena Jayyusi

My eyes are the enemy's eyes. Enemy's Eyes, The. Emma Lee Warrior. HATNAP

My eyes are thirsty. Mirabai [*or* Mira Bai]. BoWoP

My eyes can be closed by the last shadow. Love beyond Death. Francisco de Quevedo y Villegas. BLPSL, *tr. by* Rene de Costa, Rigas Kappatos and Eleni Paidoussi

My eyes catch ruddy necks. Marching. Isaac Rosenberg. PeFWW

My eyes eavesdrop on their lashes! Eichu. ZenPo, *tr. by* Takashi Ikemoto and Lucien Stryk

My eyes fly out of the window. Passing through Rajasthan. Umashankar Joshi. OMIP, *tr. by* Niranjan Bhagat

My Eyes Have Seen and Chosen. Meinloh von Sevelingen. GePo, *tr. by* J. W. Thomas

My eyes, peasant woman milking the light. True Man, A. Attila József. IQMS, *tr. by* Edwin Morgan

My eyes wax and wane. 13 June 1994. Virginia Cerenio. ReBoTo

My face is grass. Legacy. Maurice Kenny. HATNAP

My Face Is My Own, I Thought. Tom Raworth. SPE

My faint spirit was sitting in the light. From the Arabic: An Imitation. Shelley. OBEV

My fair-haired child dancing in the dunes. Poem for Melissa. Nuala Ni Dhomhnaill. BiHa

My Fair Lady. *Unknown.* EnLoPo
  (Under the Leaves Green.) OxBoLi

My fairest child, I have no song to give you. Farewell, A. Charles Kingsley. EBVV

My faith / is a great weight. Small Wire. Anne Sexton. InvLi

My Faith Looks Up to Thee. Ray Palmer. AH; SacPr

My faithful friend, if you can see. Impossibilities to His Friend. Robert Herrick. OxBSP

My Faithful Mother Tongue. Czeslaw Milosz. VCWP

My falling tears wet the double gates. (LL) Old Poem. *Unknown.* AWP; BoWoP, *tr. by* Arthur Waley

My family asleep. Leroy Gorman. HA

My family complains like cackling geese. Borrowing Rice from Ju-hui. Mei Yao Ch'en. SuSp, *tr. by* Jonathan Chaves

My family has married me. Song of Sorrow. *Unknown.* CoBCP, *tr. by* Burton Watson

My family married me off. Lament. Liu Chi-hsün. WoPoe, *tr. by* Tony Barnstone and Chou Ping

My family married me to a lost horizon. Lost Horizon. Hsi-chün. ColAnChi, *tr. by* Anne Birrell

My family tree is mist and darkness. Family History. Irving Feldman. VCAP

My fan is preaching abstinence but I want a miracle. Lullaby. Debra Gregerman. AmPoNex

My fancy fled to the South again. (LL) Daisy, The. Tennyson. EnLoPo; NOBVV

My Fate. Anne Wharton. EMWP

My Father. Manuela Fingueret. MirDau, *tr. by* Roberta Gordenstein

My Father. Felix Mnthali. PBMAP

My Father / Against the victories of age. Plaisir d'Amour. Patrick Galvin. BiHa

My father always wanted me to draw roses. Bo Tree. Patricia Pogson. Prnts

My father and I have no place to go. Thoreau. Timothy Liu. AmPoNex; GifTon; OPRER

My Father and Me Making Dresses: Together. D. A. Powell. WiU

My father and mother left me a good living. Han-shan. CoBCP, *tr. by* Burton Watson

My father and mother, my brother and sister. Sightseers, The. Paul Muldoon. BiHa; CIP-2

My father and mother (what ails 'em?) Rural Lass, The. Catherine Jemmat. ECWP; NOEC

My father and my mother never quarreled. Because. James Philip McAuley. BMAP; CBAP; NOBAu

My Father and the Fig Tree. Naomi Shihab Nye. GraLe
  (My Father and the Figtree.) UnSA
My Father arranges the window like a stage. Diane Arbus, New York. Nicole
  Cooley. AmPoNex
My father asks me how I stand it all. Parents. Vincent Buckley. CBAP
My father at the dictionary-stand. Supernatural Love. Gjertrud
  Schnackenberg. DiPo; MakPoe; NoAM; NoP-4; VCAP
My father at the front window. Upturn. Anne-Marie Fyfe. Prnts
My Father at the North Street Boarding House. James Kimbrell. AmPoNex
My father bequeathed me no wide estates. Heirloom. Abraham Moses Klein.
  NIL-7; NOBC; TrJP
My Father Breaks the Neighbor's Nose. Hayan Charara. AmPoNex
My father brought that dog home. Bony. Simon J. Ortiz. CDW
My father brought the emigrant bundle. Europe and America. David Ignatow.
  NNaP; UnPo
My father came in the darkness. Hyena. Unknown. TTY, tr. by George
  Economou
My father came today: an awaited visit. Ithaca–Liverpool. Gladys Mary
  Coles. Prnts
My father could go down a mountain faster than I. That Dark Other Mountain.
  Robert Francis. CRP
My Father, Counting Sheep. Kate Foley. Prnts
My Father Died. Mother Goose. OxNR
My father died a month ago. Bequests. Unknown. OxNR
My father died near evening, having spent. Truth, The. Frankie Paino.
  AmPoNex
My father died nine months before. Birth of a Son. Sam Hunt. PeNZ
My father died of a heart attack / during an afternoon nap. Upkeep. Miriam
  Goodman. UnSA
My Father Died This Spring. Joanne Kyger. PoM
My father dies and is buried in his Brooks Brothers suit. Halfway through the
  Book I'm Writing. Lynn Emanuel. ExTi
My father entered the kingdom of roots. 1933. Philip Levine. LCAP-2
My father fought their war four years or so. Yehuda Amichai [or Amikhai].
  FIT, tr. by Robert Friend
My father found it after the war. House on Buder Street, The. Gary Gildner.
  TAP
My father, gasping, in his white calked shoes. Course, The. Robert Huff.
  CoAP
My father got on his horse and went to the field. Infancy. Carlos Drummond
  de Andrade. TCLAP, tr. by Elizabeth Bishop
My father had a glass eye. My Father's Eye. Eléni Vakaló. BoWoP, tr. by
  Kimon Friar
My father had a lot of friendly enemies. Father-Sequence. Luigi Fontanella.
  NeIt, tr. by Michael Palma
My father he died, but I can't tell you how. My Father Died. Mother Goose.
  OxNR
My father, he was a mountaineer. Ballad of William Sycamore, The. Stephen
  Vincent Benét. MoAmPo; PoRA
My father, his mouth full of nails. Nails. Gary Gildner. PBCAP; TAP
My father, in a 1956 gray suit. Dance of the Letters. Vince Gotera. OpBo
My Father in the Night Commanding No. Louis Simpson. CoAP; CoAmPo;
  HeIP-4; NOBA; NoAM; PAI; TAP; TwCP; VGW
My father in the snowy window, face incandescent. Riding the Empire Builder,
  1948. David Wojahn. GM
My father is a chocolate hoarder. It is a family joke. Souvenirs. Elizabeth
  Rosner. GotH
My father is a hand-/ some guy. Daddy Poem, A. William J. Harris. NBV
My father is clearing the first Party shrine. Party Shrine. Thomas McCarthy.
  BiHa
My father is dead and there is nothing left. Not Saying Much. Linda Gregg.
  AiP
My father is deceas'd. Come, Gaveston. Christopher Marlowe. CAGL Fr.
  Edward the Second.
My father is looking at the end of his life. Journey. Cathy Song. ExTi
My father is sleeping. His noble face. Distant Footsteps, The. César Vallejo.
  RaBo, tr. by John Knoepfle and James Wright
My father is standing on a railroad platform. Departure. Louise Glück. GM
My father is telling me the story of Samuel. Calling, A. W. S. Merwin.
  BodElec
My Father is watching over his mosque, silently. Lines to My Father. Sam
  Hamod. GraLe
My Father, it is surely a blue place. Gwendolyn Brooks. ChAP Fr. Street in
  Bronzeville, A.
My father knew the weight of words. In Season. Lisa Suhair Majaj.
  PoArWo
My father laughing over the morning paper. Reading before We Read,
  Horoscope and Weather. Wyatt Prunty. RA

My father left his English home. Song of the Bounder, The. Edgar Wallace.
  PeSAV
My father left me three acres of land. Sing Ivy. Unknown. OxNR
My father, let no similes eclipse. In Memoriam. Michael Longley. ModIr;
  PNI
My father limps on the leg that healed short. Hook. Floyd Skloot. MoASP
My father, listening. Exiles. Diana Der Hovanessian. OPRER
My father, looking for trouble, would find it. Man of the House, The. David
  Wagoner. NoAM
My father made a synagogue of a boat. Two Fishermen. Stanley Moss.
  CoAP
My Father Makes a Lightbox for Vivienne Westwood. Nicolette Golding.
  Prnts
My Father Moved through Dooms of Love. E. E. Cummings. ColAP; HAP;
  NAAL-2v2; NAAL-5; NOBA; NoAM; NoP-4; OxBA; TAP; UnPo; WoPoe
My father once broke a man's hand. Winter Stars. Larry Levis. GeoHom
My father once told me that as a boy. Site of My Grandfather's House, The.
  Dominador I. Ilio. ReBoTo
My father paces the upstairs hall. Spree. Maxine W. Kumin. NoAM
My Father Paints the Summer. Richard Wilbur. NOBA
My father played the melodion. Patrick Kavanagh. RB Fr. Christmas
  Childhood, A.
My father recommended safety. Belonging to a New Family. Mohammad
  Bennis. MAP; NAfrP, tr. by Charles Doria and Sharif Elmusa
My Father Recounts a Story from His Youth. Kevin Prufer. AmPoNex
My father remembered what it was to be small. In the Giant's Castle. Ruth
  Dallas. PeNZ
My Father's Angels. Ger Killeen. AmPoNex
My Father's Back. Edward Hirsch. VCAP
My father's back. Secret Love. Milton Kessler. UnSA
My father's body was a globe of fear. Letters and Other Worlds. Michael
  Ondaatje. NOBC; NoAM; NoP-4
My father's brother has a farm in the forest. Meditation among Trees.
  Marbod of Rennes. MLL, tr. by Helen Waddell
My Father's Close. Unknown. AWP, tr. by Dante Gabriel Rossetti
My Father's Clothes. Pascale Petit. Prnts
My father's Country. Joyce Lee. NOBAu
My Father's Death. Constance Urdang. PBCAP
My Father's Dream. Sargon Boulus. MAP, tr. by Sargon Boulus and Alistair
  Elliot
My Father's Dreams. Cynthia Fuller. Prnts
My Father's Eye. Eléni Vakaló. BoWoP, tr. by Kimon Friar
My father's eyes were blue. To Human Skin. Cheryl Savageau. TWW
My father's father came. Legend. Louise Glück. TaR
My Father's Fights. Stuart Dybek. PBCAP
My Father's First Baseball Game. Michael S. Weaver. PBCAP
My father's friend came once to tea. Recollection, A. Frances Darwin
  Cornford. FaBoWP
My Father's Funeral. Karl Shapiro. TaR
My Father's Garden. David Wagoner. DiPo; NIL-7; NIP-4
My Father's Geography. Michael S. Weaver. GT; PBCAP
My Father's Girlfriend. E. Ethelbert Miller. SpirFl
My Father's Hands. Jeni Couzyn. PeSAV
My father's heart is on television. Medical Science. Robin Becker. PBCAP
My Father's Heroes. Allison Joseph. NeAmPo; SeSe
My Father's House. Sam Cornish. AllShUp
My Father's House. Calvin Forbes. ESEAA
My Father's Loveletters. Yusef Komunyakaa. ISC; PoPoPo
My Father's Martial Art. Stephen Shu Ning Liu. InPK-6
My Father's Neck. Robert Bly. BodElec
My father's parents sold fish. Erdywurble. Carole Satyamurti. Prnts
My Father's Pornography. David Wojahn. ReTh
My Father's Retirement. A. Van Jordan. SpirFl
My Father's Shadow. Dorothy Nimmo. Prnts
My Father's Singing. Marc J. Sheehan. MiVo
My Father's Song. Simon J. Ortiz. HATNAP; NIL-7
My Father's Story. Priscilla Jane Thompson. CBWP-2
My Father's Wedding. Robert Bly. NoAM; RaBo
My Father's Whistle. Len Roberts. MiVo
My father's white uncle became. Todd. Stewart Conn. NePenScot
My father's womb. Wardrobes. Nicolette Golding. Prnts
My Father's Words. Lucy Hamilton. Prnts
My Father's Workshop. Anna Swir. GifTon, tr. by Czeslaw Milosz and
  Leonard Nathan
My father said I could not do it. Leaving, The. Brigit Pegeen Kelly. IllVoic;
  YaYoPo
My father sang for himself. His Father, Singing. Leslie Norris. TCAWP

My father sat in his chair recovering. Ted Hughes. FaBoWar

My father saw it back in 1910. Halley's Comet. Norman Nicholson. NoP-4

My Father Scything. Sam Hunt. PeNZ

My father sits at the kitchen table. Snow. Regina DeCormier-Shekejian. TWW

My father sits in his chair and snores. Sleeping Father. David Chin. InvLad

My father sits quietly in his brown Naugahyde chair watching / TV with the remote control. Portrait of Assimilation. Chrystos. UnSA

My Father Spoke with Swans. Patrick Galvin. BiHa

My father stands in the picture. Family Album. Amos Neufeld. GotH

My father stands next to my mother. Cuban-American Gothic. Virgil Suárez. AmPoNex

My father taught me to measure. Numbers. Allison Joseph. NeAmPo

My father—that kind smiling hero—went. After the Battle. Victor Hugo. SxFrPo, *tr. by* E. H. Blackmore and A. M. Blackmore

My father the hawk. Latvian Songs. Johannes Bobrowski. AF

My father, the least happy. Cage, The. John Montague. CIP-2; PNI

My Father Today. Sam Hunt. PeNZ

My Father Travels. Dilip Chitre. OMIP; WoPoe

My father travels on the late evening train. My Father Travels. Dilip Chitre. OMIP; WoPoe

My father used to say. Silence. Marianne Craig Moore. APT-1; FaBoMo; FaBoWP; HarvBoo; NALW; NOBA; PAI; TRP; WoPoe

My father was a Cornish customs officer. Naturalised. Cyril Hodges. AngWePo

My father was a dictator. Revolution. Brian G. Gilmore. SpirFl

My father was a Frenchman. *Unknown.* OxNR

My father was a semipro pitcher in the city. Pitching the Potatoes. Martín Espada. SpudSo

My father was a servant-boy. Mixed Marriage, The. Paul Muldoon. PNI

My father was a Toltec. Toltec, The. Ana Castillo. IllVoic

My father was always out in the garage. Eli W. Mandel. MoCV *Fr.* Minotaur Poems.

My father was an enormous man. Sticks. Thomas Sayers Ellis. NAPBL

My father was four years at their war. Yehuda Amichai [*or* Amikhai]. MHP *Fr.* Here We Loved.

My father was six-fingered. Across the canvas, stretched tight, Bruni taught him to guide the soft brush. Dactyls. Vladislav Felitsianovich Khodasevich. TCRusP, *tr. by* Mary Jane White

My father was sixty when I was born. My Father Scything. Sam Hunt. PeNZ

My Father Went to Funerals. Howard Nelson. RaBo

My father! when I saw thee last. To Father. Mary E. Tucker. CBWP-1

My father, who loves my mother. Names the Dead Speak. Sharon Kessler. GotH

My father, who works with stone. Story of How a Wall Stands, A. Simon J. Ortiz. HATNAP

My Father with Cigarette Twelve Years before the Nazis Could Break His Heart. Philip Levine. TaR

My father with great sadness used to say. Plowman of Rákos under the Turks. Károly Kisfaludy. IQMS, *tr. by* Watson Kirkconnell

My father wore it working coal at Shotts. Miner's Helmet, The. George MacBeth [*or* Macbeth]. OxBTC

My father worked with a horse-plough. Follower. Seamus Heaney. CABP; PNI

My Father Writing Joe Hamrah in a Blackout. Gregory Orfalea. GraLe

My father yelled, "Turn that damn thing down!" Jungle Music. Warren Woessner. MiVo; SwNoth

My father, you say. Reply. Reiner Kunze. PoSu, *tr. by* Ewald Osers

My fault, my greatest fault. Child Scribbles, The. Nizar Qabbani. MAP, *tr. by* Diana Der Hovanessian and Lena Jayyusi

My Favorite Monk Is. Connie Deanovich. AmPoNex

My Favorite Things. Richard Rodgers. ReLy

My favourite view of people. Fish Shop Windows. Geoffrey Dutton. NOBAu

My feet are elms, roots in the earth. They Tell Me I Am Lost. Maurice Kenny. HATNAP

My feet mark the passage of time. Waiting. Donald Woods. CAGL

My feet shall tread no more thy mossy side. To the Wissahiccon. Frances Anne [*or* "Fanny"] Kemble. APN-1

My feet taste funny. Why I Didn't Go to Delphi. James Welch. CDW

My feet they are sore, and my limbs they are weary. Orphan Child, The. Charlotte Brontë. VWP

My feet were nourished on her breasts all night. (LL) George Meredith. NAEL-5v2; NAEL-6v2; NOBVV *Fr.* Modern Love.

My female friends, whose tender hearts. Jonathan Swift. NOBL *Fr.* Verses on the Death of Dr. Swift, D.S.P.D.

My fever's over 98 point 6, and still. Belated Lament. Attila József. IQMS, *tr. by* John P. Sadler

My Field Guide. Erin Belieu. NAPBL

My fifteen year old. Some Tentative Definitions 7. Kwame Dawes. WaCA

My fiftieth year had come and gone. W. B. Yeats. RaBo *Fr.* Vacillation.

My Fifty-Plus Years Celebrate Spring. Luis Omar Salinas. GeoHom

My fighting days are done. Mnasalcas. GrAn

My Final Agonies. Benjamin Péret. PFTM-1

My final words are these. Kogaku Soko. JDP, *tr. by* Yoel Hoffmann

My fine web sparkles. Christmas Spider, The. Michael Richards. Spl

My fingers. Message in the Bottle, The. Frigyes Karinthy. IQMS, *tr. by* Paul Tabori

My Fingers. Mary O'Neill. KaS

My fingers are antennae. My Fingers. Mary O'Neill. KaS

My first, as thy name is Joseph, labour so in knowledge to increase. Sarah Goodhue. EMWP

My first big love was cosmically correct. My Chakabuku Mama: A Comic Tale. Jewelle Gomez. BAP-01; GLP

My First Forty Years. Kevin Ireland. PeNZ

My first is in life (not contained within heart). Riddle-Me-Ree. Liz Lochhead. OPOU

My first itch. Itch, The. K. Ayyappa Paniker. OMIP, *tr. by* K. Ayyappa Paniker

My first love sighed for brooches. Prices. Louis Ginsberg. TrJP

My First Riot: Bronx, NYC. Safiya Henderson-Holmes. UnSA

My first thought was, he lied in every word. Childe Roland to the Dark Tower Came. Robert Browning. NAEL-5v2; NAEL-6v2; NAWM-7v2; NOBVV; NoP-4; OBNV; PeVV; PoE; PoPoPo

My first week in Cambridge a car full of white boys. Boston Year. Elizabeth Alexander. GT; OPRER

My fishing boat sails the river. I love spring in the mountains. Song of Peach Tree Spring. Wang Wei. WoPoe, *tr. by* Willis Barnstone, Tony Barnstone and Xu Haixin

My fixed abode is Glen Bolcain. Suibne Geilt. NOIV

My flag is blue and sprouts a fish rampant, locked in and let loose by two bracelets. Flag, The. Pablo Neruda. PoetW, *tr. by* Nathaniel Tarn

My Flesh in Its Sweat. Giancarlo Majorino. ItPo, *tr. by* Gayle Ridinger

My flesh is at a distance from me. Virgin, The. Laura Riding Jackson. ChIV-2

My flower. (LL) Joyce Mansour. BoWoP; HAWP, *tr. by* Willis Barnstone

My flowery and green age was passing away. Petrarch. BIrV; OBMV; OxBEV; WoPoe, *tr. by* John Millington Synge and J. M. Synge *Fr.* Sonnets to Laura.

My Flute. Herbert Krohn. CDa

My Fly. C. K. Williams. AmFaPo

My foamlesss heart, the bloodleap at my wrist. (LL) Rattler, Alert. Brewster Ghiselin. HAP; WeW-3

My foe outstretched [*or* outstretch'd] beneath the tree. (LL) William Blake. AWP; FHYEP; HAP; NAEL-5v2; NAEL-6v2; NPeEn; OxAEP-2; OxBEV; RB; SCV; SoSe-8; TFi; WeW-3 *Fr.* Songs of Experience.

My folk, now answere me. Jesus Reproaches His People. *Unknown.* MiEL

My folk, what habbe I do thee? *etc.* (LL) My Folk, What Have I Done Thee? William Herebert. MiEL; SacPr

My Folk, What Have I Done Thee? William Herebert. MiEL; SacPr

My folks could beg or borrow. (LL) Saturday's Child. Countee Cullen. NAAAL; PAI

My food was pallid till I heard it ring. King Midas. Howard Moss. CoAP; TAP

My Foolish Heart. Ned Washington. ReLy

My foolish heart keeps beckoning to me. Quatrain. Ilyas Farhat. MAP, *tr. by* John Heath-Stubbs and Salma Khadra Jayyusi

My footsteps in this street. Here. Octavio Paz. STV

My foundling, my fondling, my frolic first-footer. Blason, A. Alec Derwent Hope. NOBAu

My four and forty years. Wakyu. JDP, *tr. by* Yoel Hoffmann

My fourthe housbonde was a revelour. Geoffrey Chaucer. NPeEn *Fr.* Canterbury Tales, The.

My frame hath often trembled with delight. William Wordsworth. CenSon *Fr.* River Duddon [A Series of Sonnets], The.

My frame of nature is a ruffled sea. Hurry of the Spirits, in a Fever and Nervous Disorders, The. Isaac Watts. NOEC

My freehold of thanksgiving. (LL) My Triumph. John Greenleaf Whittier. APN-1; NOBA

My Friend. David St. John. BodElec

My friend, a man I love as wholly. My Friend. David St. John. BodElec

My friend conceived the soul hereafter dwells. Aspiration. Edward William Thomson. SacPr

My friend from Asia has powers and magic, he plucks a blue leaf from the young blue-gum. Credo. Robinson Jeffers. MoAmPo

My friend, hold back your heart from enemies. Hafiz [*or* Hafez]. WoPoe, *tr. by* Dick Davis *Fr.* Three Poems on Friendship.

My friend, I went to the market and bought the Dark One. It's True I Went to the Market. Mirabai [or Mira Bai]. WPoS, tr. by Robert Bly

My friend: / In what language shall we begin our conversation? Brief Letter to Donald Walsh (in memoriam). Angel Cuadra. AF, tr. by Katherine Rodriguez Nieto

My friend is always doing good. Faith and Works. Muriel Spark. OxBSP

My friend is dwelling in the eastern mountain. To Tan Ch'iu. Li Po. TAL

My friend is lodging high in the Eastern Range. To Tan-Ch'iu. Li Po. AWP; ChiP, tr. by Arthur Waley

My friend, judge not me. Epitaph. Unknown. NOSC

My friend, limb-loosening. Archilochus. SaLy, tr. by Diane Rayor

My friend! Miserable grass. Letter to a Bedouin Informer. Khalifa Al-Wugayyan. MAP, tr. by John Heath-Stubbs and Lena Jayyusi

My friend must be a Bird. Emily Dickinson. TAP

My friend, my friend. Black Man, The. Sergey [or Sergei] Aleksandrovich Yesenin [or Essenin]. TCRP, tr. by Geoffrey Thurley

My friend Priapus with myself shall rise? (LL) Quaerè. George Farewell. NOEC; NPeEn; OBCoV

My Friend's Dog. Meret Oppenheim. SurPaPo, tr. by Catherine Schelbert

My friend's knife by my side. On the Gift of a Knife. Muireadhach Albanach O'Dalaigh. NOIV

My friend's sweet love came into town. Song to Hymen: 1942. Anthony Richardson. PoWW

My friend said, Let's go down to the river. Bright Light of Responsibility, The. Jennifer L. Knox. BAP-97

My friend says I was not a good son. Yesterday. W. S. Merwin. LCAP-2; RaBo

My friend, speak always once, but listen twice. Mouth and the Ears, The. Shem-Tob ben Joseph Palquera. TrJP, tr. by J. Chotzner

My friend the blue paisley shirt is always assured. Blue Paisley Shirt, The. Thomas William Shapcott. BMAP

My Friend the Cuckold. Morris Gilbert Bishop. OBCoV

My Friend, the Things That Do Attain. Martial. See Happy Life, The

My Friend the Wind. King D. Kuka. VoR

My friend, this body is His lute. He tightens the strings and plays its songs. Kabir. EnlH

My friend, thou sorrowest for thy golden prime. Return of Youth, The. William Cullen Bryant. TreFP

My friend tree. Lorine Niedecker. APT-2

My friend wears boots to sleep. Following Her to Sleep. Jeffrey McDaniel. NeAmPo

My friend, your face. Who Is My Brother? Pinkie Gordon Lane. BlSi

My Friendly People. Frank Mkalawile Chipasula. HBAPE

My Friends. Mikhail Kuz'mich Lukonin. TCRP, tr. by Albert C. Todd

My Friends. Boris Abramovich Slutsky [or Slutskii]. TCRusP, tr. by Daniel Weissbort

My friends are borne to one another. Martin Buber in the Pub. Max Harris. NOBAu

My Friends Are Little Lamps to Me. Elizabeth Whittemore. PoToHe

My friends are real, though very few. (LL) Money. William Henry Davies. OBEV; OBMV

My friends hunted in packs, had themselves photographed. Ancient Evenings. Michael Hofmann. EmeKit

My friends, I love your fame; I joy to raise. Joel Barlow. See Too much of Europe, here transplanted o'er

My friends in tanks were burnt. My Friends. Boris Abramovich Slutsky [or Slutskii]. TCRusP, tr. by Daniel Weissbort

My friends, my sweet barbarians. Breakfast for Barbarians, A. Gwendolyn MacEwen. NOBC

My friends who knew me. Wait Till You See Her. Richard Rodgers. ReLy

My frowning students carve. E. S. L. Charles Martin. RA

My funeral-shaft, and marble shapes that dwell. Baucis. Erinna. AWP, tr. by Richard Garnett

My Funny Valentine. Chris Greenhalgh. NeBl

My Funny Valentine. Richard Rodgers. ReLy

My Future Just Passed. George, Jr. Marion. ReLy

My Galley. Petrarch. NAEL-5v1

My Galley. Petrarch. See also Sonnets to Laura

My Galley. Sir Thomas Wyatt. See "My galley charged with forgetfulness."

My galley charged with forgetfulness. Sir Thomas Wyatt. GSo
   (My Galley.) NAEL-7v1
   (Sonnet.) AEP

My galley [or galy] charged with forgetfulness. Petrarch. HAP; OBVE; OxBEV; SCGP; Son; WeW-3, tr. by Sir Thomas Wyatt Fr. Sonnets to Laura.

My Gang. Jack Kerouac. PoM

My garage is a structure of excessive plainness. Detail. Mary Ursula Bethell. PeNZ

My Garden. Thomas Edward Brown. InPK-6; OBEV; OBGa; UV

My Garden. P. R. Hines. UV

My Garden. J. A. Lindon. InPK-6

My Garden, My Daylight. Jorie Graham. HCAP

My Gartmore friends a blessing on ye. Epistle to Her Friends at Gartmore. Susanna Blamire. ECWP

My Gauri / You've come home! Kamalākānta Bhattācārya. SinGod, tr. by Rachel Fell McDermott

My generation is dying, after long lives. Judith Wright. HarvBoo Fr. Shadow of Fire: Ghazals, The.

My generous muse, assistance lend. Favourite Swain, The. Elizabeth Hands. WoRP

My gentle father. Feliks Skrzynecki. Peter Skrzynecki. CBAP

My gentle friend! I hold no creed so false. Retirement. Henry Timrod. APN-2

My Ghostly Fader. Charles, Duc d' Orléans. BoLoP
   (Lover's Confession, A.) NOBE
   (My gostly fader, I me confesse.) OHMEL
   (My Gostly Fader, I Me Confesse.) EnLoPo; MiEL

My Ghostly Father, I me confess. My Ghostly Fader. Charles, Duc d'Orléans. BoLoP

My girl got me two weeks after she saw. Spoon River Sadie Louise. Anne Lamott. Unle

My girl is waiting for me. Kakinomoto no Hitomaro. OHPJ

My girl, thou gazest much. Lover to His Lady, The. Plato. CTC; FaBoEE; NoSic, tr. by George Turberville

My girlfriend's eyes are nothing like the Sun. I Never Saw a Goddess Go. Austin Hummell. AmPoNex

My Girlfriends. Erich Fried. AF, tr. by Georg Rapp

My glad feet shod with the glittering steel. Skater, The. Sir Charles G. D. Roberts. NOBC

My glass shall not persuade me I am old. William Shakespeare. Son Fr. Sonnets.

My glittering sky, high, clear, profound. Lovers, The. Marya Alexandrovna Zaturenska. MoAmPo

My Gloriana. Bessie. Alvin Aubert. SeSe

My glory, honor, all depend. Gentleman, The. Menahem ben Judah Lonzano. TrJP, tr. by A. B. Rhine

My God. Solomon ibn Gabirol. TrJP, tr. by Alice Lucas Fr. Royal Crown, The.

My God, a verse is not a crown. Quidditie [or Quiddity], The. George Herbert. GeHe; NOSC

My God and King! to thee. Anguish. Henry Vaughan. OxAEP-1

My God, how gracious art thou! I had slipt. Relapse, The. Henry Vaughan. ESCV; TrCP

My God, how perfect are thy ways! William Cowper. NOCV Fr. Olney Hymns.

My God, how wonderful Thou art. Frederick William Faber. SacPr

My God, I heard this day. Man. George Herbert. BASC; ESCV; FSCP; GeHe; NAEL-5v1; NAEL-6v1; NAEL-7v1; NoP-4

My God, I know that those who plead. Solomon ibn Gabirol. TrJP, tr. by Alice Lucas Fr. Royal Crown, The.

My God, I'm wounded by my sin. To God: an Anthem, Sung in the Chapel at White-Hall, before the King. Robert Herrick. ChIV-1

My God, I mean my sinful heart. (LL) Dwelling-Place, The. Henry Vaughan. GeHe; MeLP; NOSC; PeECV

My God, I Thank Thee. Andrews Norton. AH

My God, I thank Thee who hast made. Thankfulness. Adelaide Anne Procter. SacPr

My God, if writings may. Obedience. George Herbert. ESCV; GeHe

My God in Heaven Said to Me. Fenton Johnson. NAAAL

My God most glad to look, most prone to hear [or heere]. Bible, O.T. See Give ear to my prayer, O God

My God, my God, have mercy on my sin. Ash Wednesday. Christina Georgina Rossetti. TrCP

My God, my God, what queer corner am I in? In the Deep Museum. Anne Sexton. MoAmPo

My God, prepare me for that hour. Written a Few Hours before the Birth of a Child. Jane Cave. ECWP

My God shall raise me up, I trust. (LL) Even Such Is Time. Sir Walter Ralegh. HAP; OxBSP; PoRA; RB; TFi

My God, sometimes I cannot pray. Unuttered Prayer. Josephine D. Henderson Heard. CBWP-4

My God, than they? (LL) Ice Storm. Robert Earl Hayden. APT-2; ESEAA

My God, thou that didst dye for me. Dedication, The. Henry Vaughan. ESCV

My God! till I receiv'd thy stroke. William Cowper. ChIV-1 Fr. Olney Hymns.

My God to thee I dedicate. Short Oblation of This Smal Work by the Writer

Gatherer Thereof to Our Most Sweet and Merciful God, A.   Dame Gertrude More.   EMWP

My God, what a dream I had.   Us Two.   Nina Cassian.   PoSu, *tr.* by Nina Cassian

My God, when I walk [*or* walke] in those groves.   Religion.   Henry Vaughan.   ESCV; NOCV; OxAEP-1; PeECV; TOF

My God, where is that ancient heat towards Thee.   Sonnet.   George Herbert.   ESCV; GeHe; NOSC

My God, Why Are You Crying?   Molly Peacock.   PasH

My God would give a Sun-shine after raine. (LL)   Shower [*or* Showre], The.   Henry Vaughan.   ESCV; GeHe

My godmother invited my cousin.   My Cousin Agueda [*or* Agatha].   Ramón López Velarde.   OBVE; TCLAP, *tr.* by Samuel Beckett

My gold star mother.   Nicholas Virgilio.   HA

My Goodness.   God Gave Us Trees to Cut Down.   W. Les Russell.   IBA

My gostly fader, I me confesse.   Charles, Duc d'Orléans.   *See* My Ghostly Father, I me confess

My Grace Is Sufficient.   Josephine D. Henderson Heard.   CBWP-4

My gracious Lord, I would thee glory doe.   Edward Taylor.   SCAP   *Fr.* Preparatory Meditations before My Approach to the Lord's Supper.

My Grandfather Always Promised Us.   Liam Rector.   UrbNat

My Grandfather and His Apple-Tree.   John Ormond.   AngWePo; TCAWP

My grandfather, dead long before I was born.   Charles Reznikoff.   APT-2

My grandfather died one morning in dampness.   Him, His Place.   Liam Rector.   BodElec

My grandfather had the right-hand side of his seat inscribed.   Exhorting Myself.   Ssu-k'ung Shu.   SuSp, *tr.* by Hellmut Wilhelm

My grandfather placed wood.   Mythology.   Earle Thompson.   HATNAP

My grandfather's clock was too large for the shelf.   Grandfather's Clock.   Henry Clay Work.   ITBLP

My Grandfather's Hat.   Judith Ortiz Cofer.   TouFir

My grandfather's painted grandfather.   Cracked Portraits.   Agha Shahid Ali.   OpBo

My Grandfather's Poems.   Edward Hirsch.   TaR

My grandfather said to me.   Manners.   Elizabeth Bishop.   NOxBChV; OxBC; RB

My grandfather used to pray.   Wicked Neighbor, The.   "Zelda."   WPOW, *tr.* by Hannah Hoffman

My Grandfather Walks in the Woods.   Marilyn Nelson Waniek.   ESEAA

My grandma thinks only of me.   Grandmother.   Fily-Dabo Sissoko.   NegPo, *tr.* by Ellen Conroy Kennedy

My Grandmama / dont believe they walked in space.   It's All the Same.   Thadious M. Davis.   BlSi

My Grandmother.   Elizabeth Jennings.   HarvBoo; NoP-4

My Grandmother.   Karl Shapiro.   TaR; VGW

My Grandmother Died in the Early Hours of the Morning.   T. Harri Jones.   AngWePo; TCAWP

My grandmother grew tiny grapes and tiger-lilies.   Her Garden.   Freda Downie.   FaBoWP

My grandmother had a house. My father bought it.   Family Tree, The.   Catalina Cariaga.   ReBoTo

My grandmother had a small shelf of books.   Footbinding.   Patricia Beer.   NoP-4

My grandmother had braids.   Keeping Hair.   Ramona Wilson.   VoR

My grandmother is waiting for me to come home.   Gwendolyn Brooks.   ESEAA   *Fr.* Children Going Home.

My grandmother Lola, with her beautiful sagging face and her fine.   1930.   Aurora Levins Morales.   PueRic

My grandmother moves to my mind in context of sorrow.   My Grandmother.   Karl Shapiro.   VGW

My grandmother / rakes up chicken shit / mixed with mud / to feed her roses.   Upside Down Basket, The.   Alan Chong Lau.   UnSA

My grandmother's.   Door.   Valerie Worth.   CA

My Grandmother's Burial Ground.   Elizabeth Cook-Lynn.   HATNAP

My Grandmother's Funeral.   Thomas Lux.   WeW-3

My Grandmother's Ghost.   James Wright.   Son

My Grandmother's Love Letters.   Hart Crane.   InPK-6; NOBA; NoAM; NoP-4

My Grandmother said, "Now isn't it queer."   Wonders of Nature.   *Unknown.*   OTCP

My grandmother sent me a new-fashioned three-cornered cambric country-cut handkerchief.   *Unknown.*   OxNR

My grandmother taught me the delicate trick.   Blowing Eggs.   Anne Caston.   NAPBL

My grandmother was insane.   Genesis.   K. Satchidanandan.   OMIP, *tr.* by K. Satchidanandan

My grandmothers were strong.   Lineage.   Margaret Abigail Walker.   BlSi; ItWoWo; NALW; OxWW; WWork

My Grandpa lives in a wonderful house.   Painted Ceiling, The.   Amy Lowell.   OBAL

My grandparents lived to a great age in the cold.   Cold.   Dorothy Roberts.   NOBC

My granny used to say that if a shadow.   August the First: The Shadow. Patel Speaks.   Marjorie Oludhe Macgoye.   HBAPE

My Grave.   Ella Wheeler Wilcox.   SWaP

My great God, You been a tenderness to me.   Black Mother Praying.   Owen Dodson.   ISC

My great-grandfather hunted elephants.   Ballad of Hunters, A.   C. J. Driver.   PeSAV

My great-grandfather spoke to Edmund Burke.   Seven Sages, The.   W. B. Yeats.   NOIV

My Great Great Etc. Uncle Patrick Henry.   James Tate.   OBAL

My great wars close.   Treaties.   A. R. Ammons.   HCAP

My greater longings; Love only to you, this last-year date. (LL)   December 30th.   Ivor Gurney.   NAEL-5v2; NAEL-6v2

My Greatgreatuncle the Archbishop.   Ruth Whitman.   TaR

My green leaves are more beautiful.   Leaves.   Frank Asch.   NTCP

My Greenhouse.   Edwin Morgan.   OBGa

My grey-eyed father kept pigs on his farm.   Pigs, The.   Geoffrey Lehmann.   CBAP

My grief on the men of the stories.   Era's End.   Mairtin O Direain.   ModIr, *tr.* by Patrick Crotty

My grief on the ocean.   *Unknown.*   NOIV

My Grief on the Sea.   Biddy Cussrooee.   OBEV, *tr.* by Douglas Hyde

My grief, quoth I, is called Ignorance.   Rachel Speght.   NAEL-7v1   *Fr.* Dream[e], The [*or* A].

My groom, I fear, has grown.   We Are Easily Reduced.   HeidiLynn Nilsson.   NeAmPo

My Ground.   Marie Luise Kaschnitz.   PFTM-2, *tr.* by Lisel Mueller

My gudame wes a gay wif, bot scho wes ryght gend.   Ballad of Kynd Kittok, The.   William Dunbar.   OxBoLi; PeLV

My guest! I have not led you thro'   Interlude.   Walter Savage Landor.   GTBS-P

My gun shines in the misty air.   Picket before Bull Run, The.   John Day.   TreFP

My hair barely covered my forehead.   Song of Ch'ang-Kan (Yueh-Fu), The.   Li Po.   ChinPo, *tr.* by Yip Wai-lim

My hair, Delphic laurel. (LL)   Horace.   CTC; WoPoe, *tr.* by Ezra Pound   *Fr.* Odes.

My hair has dried.   Self Dirge.   Wendy Rose.   CDW

My hair is springy like the forest grasses.   Black Woman.   Naomi Long Madgett.   BlSi; GT; ISC

My hair's falling fast.   Afternoon.   Shinkichi Takahashi.   ZenPo, *tr.* by Takashi Ikemoto and Lucien Stryk

My hair's tightly plaited.   I've Got an Apple Ready.   John Walsh.   NOxBChV

My Hairt Is Heich Aboif.   *Unknown.*   OxBS

My half-sister comes to me to be painted.   Sitting, The.   Medbh McGuckian.   CABP; ModIr; PNI

My hand.   Comparison of Hands One Day Late Summer El Sobrante.   Wendy Rose.   HATNAP

My Hand Is Lady Mori's Hand.   Ikkyu Sojun.   ErotSp, *tr.* by Sam Hamill

My hand is lonely for your clasping, dear.   You and I.   Henry Alford.   ITBLP

My hand is up. It goes up to my father's dark coat.   Atavistic: Traces after the Rain.   Juan Felipe Herrera.   TouFir

My hand is weak and delicate.   Your Hand in Mine.   Alaide Foppa.   TANSG, *tr.* by Celeste Kostopulos-Cooperman

My hand is weary with [*or* has a pain from] writing.   St. Columcille the Scribe.   Saint Columcille [*or* Columba].   BIrV

My hand moved furiously.   Short Poem.   Kenneth Carroll.   SpirFl

My hand moves out.   John Wills.   HA

My hand within you.   Arms and the Woman.   Dorothy Livesay.   PoBW

My hands.   Touch.   Octavio Paz.   BoLoP, *tr.* by Charles Tomlinson

My hands are murder-red. Many a plump head.   Strawberrying.   May Swenson.   VCAP

My hands are smooth, the grooves.   Workaholic.   Nadia Hazboun Reimer.   PoArWo

My hands are withered.   *Unknown.*   NOIV

My hands are wrinkled from the cold.   Pale Ant.   Ellease Southerland.   GT

My hands bones were life-sized, my feet bones.   Lecture #1.   Brenda Coultas.   HeMarv

My hands creep forward on the hot sand.   Sand.   Nina Cassian.   PoSu, *tr.* by Nina Cassian and Naomi Lazard

My hands did numb to beauty.   I Held a Shelley Manuscript.   Gregory Corso.   BB; PmAP; VGW

My hands have not touched water since your hands,—.   Carrier Letter.   Hart Crane.   BoLoP

My hands here, gentle, where her breasts begin.   No Continuing City.   Michael Longley.   PNI

My hands ooze over you.   Portraits of a Moment.   Keith Gilyard.   SpirFl

My hands released at last, the cliff soars. Kanemitsu-Kogun. ZenPo, tr. by Takashi Ikemoto and Lucien Stryk

My hands shook as I bargained for passage. Oedipus. David Ignatow. PAI

My hands turn to claws, tear. Bedouin Eyes. Dima Hilal. PoArWo

My handsewn leather schoolbag. Forty years. Schoolbag, The. Seamus Heaney. BiHa

My Handy Man. Andy Razaf. ReLy

My Handy Man Ain't Handy No More. Andy Razaf. ReLy

My harbouring arms. (LL) Midsummer, Tobago. Derek Walcott. MakPoe; OPOU; VCWP

My Harry was a gallant gay. Highland Harry Back Again. Robert Burns. EBEV

My hasty pen, about to write unkind. Another Letter to a Friend. Mary Mollineux. PoBW

My Hat. Stevie Smith. BrRo

My hated birthday is here, and I must go. Sulpicia. BoWoP

My head and my shoulders, and my book. Kenneth Rexroth. NNaP

My head and shoulders, and my book. Signature of All Things, The. Kenneth Rexroth. APSN; APT-2; NNaP; TRP

My head felt stabbed. I Would Not Recommend Love. Harold Norse. CLPP

My head filled with TV images. Looking for Indians. Cheryl Savageau. TWW

My Head Is Immense. Charles Nokan. PBMAP

My head is unhappy. Poem in Time of Winter. Ray Mathew. NOBAu; OBCoV

My head, my heart, mine Eyes, my life, nay more. Letter to Her Husband, Absent upon Public[k] Employment, A. Anne Bradstreet. HAP; HeIP-4; NAAL-2v1; NAAL-3; NAAL-5; NALW; SCAP

My head on moss reclining. Song, A. Unknown. NOEC

My head's a dark lantern with shattered panes. Stylized Donkey, A. "Sasha Chorny" [or "Chiornyi"]. TCRP, tr. by Bernard Meares

My head's too full of memories for my own good. Spoon Maker's Daughter, The. Susan Utting. Prnts

My head so big. Narrative: Ali. Elizabeth Alexander. ESEAA; MoASP

My head was flame, from steps elated, free. Resurrection. Karl Kraus. AuPH, tr. by Lowell A. Bangerter

My headlights raise them up: a dash. Census of Animal Bodies: Driving Home. Madeline DeFrees. UrbNat

My Heart. Laura Kasischke. AmPoNex

My heart aches and a drowsy numbness pains. John Keats. AWP; AmFaPo; BRP; CABP; CIHu; EBEV; GTBS-P; HAP; HeIP-4; NAEL-5v2; NAEL-6v2; NAWM-7v2; NIL-7; NOBE; NOBRP; NPeEn; NoP-4; OBEV; OWoS; OxBEV; PoE; PoPoPo; PoRA; RB; SCGP; SoSe-8; TFi; TOF; UnPo

My Heart and I. Elizabeth Barrett Browning. VWP

My heart and my body want to separate. Friedrich von Hausen. GePo

My heart beating, my blood running. Time's Dedication. Delmore Schwartz. VGW

My Heart Belongs to Daddy. Cole Porter. OBAL; ReLy

My heart broke for you. When I Died on My Birthday. Kate Clark Spencer. Unle

My heart broke loose on the wind. (LL) Poetry. Pablo Neruda. PoetW; VCWP, tr. by Alastair Reid

My heart did heave, and there came forth, O God! Affliction (3). George Herbert. NOSC

My heart doth in the Lord rejoice [or rejoiceth in the Lord], that living Lord of might. Bible, O.T. AWP Fr. First Samuel.

My heart emptied. Saigyo. OHMPJ

My Heart, Faithful. Ramón López Velarde. BLPSL, tr. by Rene de Costa, Rigas Kappatos and Eleni Paidoussi

My heart, faithful, has earned itself the shadow. My Heart, Faithful. Ramón López Velarde. BLPSL, tr. by Rene de Costa, Rigas Kappatos and Eleni Paidoussi

My heart fell dead before. (LL) All in green went my love riding. E. E. Cummings. HeIP-4; NoAM; NoP-4; OxBA; PAI; PoRA

My heart gives you love. (LL) Dirge for Two Veterans. Walt Whitman. APN-1; BLT; CBCWP; MoAmPo

My heart grows sick before the wide-spread death. Grave-Yard, The. Jones Very. NOBA

My heart has grown rich with the passing of years. Solitary, The. Sara Teasdale. MoAmPo

My Heart Has Known its Winter. Arna Bontemps. GT

My heart has made its mind up. Valentine. Wendy Cope. NoP-4

My heart has thank'd thee, Bowles! for those soft strains. Samuel Taylor Coleridge. Son Fr. Effusions.

My Heart, How Very Hard It's Grown. Cotton Mather. AH

My heart, I cannot still it. Auspex. James Russell Lowell. TAP

My Heart, I Want to Ask You. Friedrich Halm. AuPH, tr. by Lowell A. Bangerter

My heart, I want to ask you. My Heart, I Want to Ask You. Friedrich Halm. AuPH, tr. by Lowell A. Bangerter

My heart / in / another. (LL) Where Have You Gone? Mari E. Evans. BPo; TTY

My heart is. Black Heart as Ever Green, The. Carolyn M. Rodgers. IllVoic

My heart is a-breaking, dear Tittie. Tam Glen. Robert Burns. AWP; OxBS

My Heart Is a Hobo. Johnny Burke. ReLy

My heart is an oil lamp. Rapier of Treason, A. Unknown. BoWoP, tr. by Willis Barnstone

My heart is broken (oh my God). Contrition. Ralph Knevet. ChIV-2

My heart is capable of every form. Ibn al-Arabi. TOF

My heart is crusty. Love Ghost. Mimi Goese. HeMarv

My heart is empty. All the fountains that should run. Naked Seed, The. Clive Staples Lewis. TrCP

My Heart Is High Above. Alexander Scott. OBEV

My Heart Is in Merioneth. Unknown. OBWVE, tr. by Richard Llwyd

My Heart Is in the East. Judah Halevi. TrJP

My heart is in woe. Downfall of the Gael, The. Fearflatha O'Gnive [or O'Gnimh]. AWP, tr. by Sir Samuel Ferguson

My heart is just as heavy. Grief. Unknown. OBWVE, tr. by Aneirin Talfan Davies

My Heart Is Lame. Charlotte Mew. BWW

My heart is lighter than the poll. New-slain Knight, The. Unknown. ESPB

My heart is like a singing bird. Birthday, A. Christina Georgina Rossetti. AWP; CABP; LW; NAEL-5v2; NAEL-6v2; NALW; NOBE; NOBVV; OBEV; PEW; PeVV; PoE; TFi; TTTS; UV; VWP; ViWPN; WPE

My heart is like one asked to dine. Unexpected Pleasure, An. Unknown. UV

My heart is like the failing hearth. Letitia [or Laetitia] Elizabeth Landon. NOBRP Fr. Golden Violet, The.

My heart is not of wax; nor may it one compare. She Boasts Her Constancy. Johann Rist. GePo, tr. by George C. Schoolfield

My heart is on my fist. Tomb of the Kings, The. Anne Hébert. BoWoP, tr. by Aliki and Willis Barnstone

My heart is set upon a lusty pin. Queen Elizabeth of York. WPE

My heart is very faint and low. Dying Child, The. Mary Howitt. VWP

My heart leaps up when I behold. Song to Be Sung by the Father of Infant Female Children. Ogden Nash. MoAmPo

My Heart Leaps Up When I Behold. William Wordsworth. ChAP (Rainbow, The.) OBEV

My heart, like a bird ahover joyously. Voyage to Cythera, A. Charles Baudelaire. WoPoe, tr. by Frederick Morgan

My heart like an upside down flame. Guillaume Apollinaire. TTTS, tr. by Roger Shattuck Fr. Heart, Crown, and Mirror.

My heart, my dove, my snail, my sail, my. Song. Cynthia Zarin. NIL-7; NoP-4

My heart, my heart is mournful. Mein Herz, Mein Herz Ist Traurig. Heinrich Heine. AWP, tr. by James Thomson

My heart's cloth I shall spread before the Savior's feet. Yelena [or Elena] Shwarts [or Shvarts]. TCRusP, tr. by Anna Barker and Daniel Weissbort

My heart's friend, will you tell me who this mischievous youngster is? Dancing-Girl's Song. Kshetrayya. BoWoP, tr. by R. Appalaswamy and Tambimuttu

My Heart's in the Highlands. Robert Burns. ITBLP (Farewell to the Highlands.) NePenScot (Farewell to the Highlands, farewell to the North.) AWP; ChAP (My heart's in the Highlands, my heart is not here.) ChAP

My heart's in the kitchen, my heart is not here. Maria Jane Jewsbury. VWP

My heart's on my fist. Tomb of the Kings, The. Anne Hébert. WoPoe, tr. by A. Poulin, Jr.

My heart's own darling's face. (LL) Es Stehen Unbeweglich. Heinrich Heine. AWP, tr. by James Thomson

My heart's so heavy with a hundred things. Sonnet: In Absence from Becchina. Cecco Angiolieri, da Siena. AWP; EaItPo, tr. by Dante Gabriel Rossetti

My heart's true bride has slept two thousand years. Tomb of Hegeso, The. Mihály Babits. IQMS, tr. by Watson Kirkconnell

My heart serene. Hakujubo. JDP, tr. by Yoel Hoffmann

My heart still feels the weight of that remember'd chain. (LL) Sonnet 007: "Like an enfranchised bird, who wildly springs." Caroline Elizabeth Norton. CenSon; VWP

My heart still hovering round about you. Epigram. Robert Nugent. NOEC

My heart stirs quietly now to think. Hermit's Song, A. Unknown. BIrV, tr. by James Simmons

My Heart Stood Still. Richard Rodgers. ReLy

My heart tells me. Zaragoza Clubs. SWaP, tr. by Luis A. Torres Fr. Héroes del Cinco de Mayo.

My heart, thinking / "How beautiful he is." Lady Otomo no Sakanoé. AWP

My Heart Thinks as the Sun Comes Up. Solomon ibn Gabirol. WoPoe, tr. by Peter Cole

My heart was heavy, for its trust had been. Forgiveness. John Greenleaf Whittier. GSo; TrCP

My heart was like a bird that fluttered joyously. Voyage to Cythera, A. Charles Baudelaire. SxFrPo, *tr. by* James McGowan

My heart was split, and a flower. *Unknown.* EnlH *Fr.* Odes of Solomon, The.

My heid did yak yester nicht. Magryme, The. William Dunbar. FaBoVe

My height: just av'rage. It Amazes Me! Cy Coleman. ReLy

My help, my hope, my strength shall be. Law, The. Abraham Ibn Ezra. TrJP, *tr. by* Alice Lucas

My helpless paradox—because. (LL) Reading a Medal. Terence Tiller. FaBoTw; GTBS-P

My Heritage. Adah Isaacs Menken. CBWP-1

My high hand makes fine patterns. Reason. Philippe Jaccottet. MFP, *tr. by* Martin Sorrell

My highway is unfeatured air. Hymn of the Earth. William Ellery Channing. APN-1

My hoary locks I dye with care. Self-Defense. Santob [*or* Shem-Tob] de Carrion. TrJP, *tr. by* George Ticknor

My home (did you know?)—my home. Mariella Bettarini. CItWP, *tr. by* Cinzia Sartini Blum and Lara Trubowitz *Fr.* Poet's Home, The.

My home is the mountain. Akhtar Amiri. WPOW *Fr.* I Am a Woman.

My home over there, my home over there. That Mountain Far Away. *Unknown.* CA, *tr. by* Herbert Joseph Spinden

My home was at Cold Mountain from the start. Gary Snyder. EnlH

My home? I'm stopping near the town. Stopping Wine. T'ao Ch'ien [*or* T'ao Yuan-ming]. CoBCP, *tr. by* Burton Watson

My homeland is in your eyes, my duty on your lips. Circe. Gabriel Zaid. TCLAP, *tr. by* Andrew Rosing

My homestead lies beside a clear stream. Homestead. Tu Fu. CrYelRi, *tr. by* Sam Hamill

My Honeyed Languor. "Eduard Georgievich Bagritzky" [*or* "Bagritsky"]. TrJP, *tr. by* Babette Deutsch

My hope and treasure lies above. (LL) Here Follows Some Verses upon the Burning of Our House [July 10th, 1666. Copied Out of a Loose Paper]. Anne Bradstreet. AiP; BASC; BoWoP; ColAP; EMWP; MakPoe; NAAL-2v1; NAAL-3; NAAL-5; NALW; NOBA; NOSC; NoP-4; OxBA; PEW; SCAP; SacPr; TAP; WPE

My Hope Is in God. *Unknown.* SacPr

My hope is on what is to come. Anthem for Doomed Youth. Raymond Garlick. AngWePo

My Hope, My Love. *Unknown.* BIrV, *tr. by* Edward Walsh

My horse has wings. Ride, The. Lucinda Roy. GT

My horse threads a mountain trail through bamboos just yellowing. Journey to a Village. Wang Yü-ch'eng. CoBCP, *tr. by* Burton Watson

My horse threads the mountain path as chrysanthemums begin to yellow. Journeying to the Village. Wang Yü-ch'eng. SuSp, *tr. by* Irving Y. Lo

My horse whose tail is like a trailing black cloud. (LL) War God's Horse Song, The. *Unknown.* RB; TTTS, *tr. by* Louis Watchman

My hotel room's small. 63rd and broadway. Reuben Jackson. ESEAA

My hour draws near and I am still alive. Seisetsu Shucho. JDP, *tr. by* Yoel Hoffmann

My hour switched on the cameras take. Voice of America, 1961, The. James Liddy. CIP-2

My House. Robert Adamson. BMAP; CBAP

My House. George Bruce. OxBS

My house gutted. Hokushi. ZenPo, *tr. by* Takashi Ikemoto and Lucien Stryk

My house, I say. But hark to the sunny doves. Robert Louis Stevenson. NOBVV; NPeEn; OxBEV

My House Is Bugged. Mafika Pascal Gwala. PeSAV

My house is empty but for a pair of boots. Flooded Valley, The. Roland Mathias. AngWePo

My house is granite. My House. George Bruce. OxBS

My house is not quiet, I am not loud. Cynewulf. AnOE, *tr. by* Charles W. Kennedy *Fr.* Riddles (Exeter Book).

My house is poor; those that I love have left me. Winter Night. Po Chü-i. ChiP, *tr. by* Arthur Waley

My house lies west of Thousand Mile Bridge. Madman, The. Tu Fu. CrYelRi, *tr. by* Sam Hamill

My House Not Made with Hands. Helen Hunt Jackson. SWaP

My house was a house of winds. Wind. Dana Levin. AmPoNex

My hovering[e] thought[e]s would fly to heaven. Man's Civil[l] War[re]. Robert Southwell. NoSic

My humble Muse sad, and in lonely state. To His Excellency Joseph Dudley. John Saffin. SCAP

My husband. My Husband, before Leaving. *Unknown.* EaWin; WoPoe, *tr. by* J. Moussaieff Masson and W. S. Merwin

My Husband, before Leaving. *Unknown.* EaWin; WoPoe, *tr. by* J. Moussaieff Masson and W. S. Merwin

My husband gives me an A. Marks. Linda Pastan. NIL-7; NIP-4

My husband had a knack of knowing things. Message, The. Michael Heffernan. RACG

My husband made me juice. Two Men, Two Grapefruits. Donna Masini. KGB

My husband never desired the official seal of a marquis. Lament of a Soldier's Wife. Kao Ch'i. SuSp, *tr. by* Irving Y. Lo

My husband, our opened home has broken my heart. Slighted Wife, The. Aaron Hodza. PeSAV, *tr. by* George Fortune

My Husband's Birthday. Josephine D. Henderson Heard. CBWP-4

My husband with no band. Mixed Marriage. Joan Logghe. MPUn

My Hut. Wu Chia-chi. CoBLCP, *tr. by* Jonathan Chaves

My hut / Thatched. Issa. ZenPo, *tr. by* Takashi Ikemoto and Lucien Stryk

My Iambic Pentameter Lines. Robert Crawford. InPK-6

My ice skates on a wall. Cold Lost Marbles. William S. Burroughs. BB

My Ideal. Newell Chase. ReLy

My idleness curdles. Ted Hughes. HAP *Fr.* Skylarks.

My Imperialism. Tamura Ryuichi. AF; PFTM-2; VCWP, *tr. by* Christopher Drake

My Indian Grandmother Speaks to Animals. John E. Smelcer. PoCoUp

My Infelice's face, her brow, her eye. Portrait, A. Thomas Dekker. OxAEP-1

My Infundibuliform Hat. Charles Follen Adams. OBAL

My Inmost Hope. Sarah Copia Sullam. TrJP

My insatiable memory is like. Olga Fiodorovna Berggolts [*or* Bergholts]. TCRusP, *tr. by* Daniel Weissbort

My intention is to tell of bodies changed. Ovid. NAWM-5v1 *Fr.* Metamorphoses.

My intimate companion. Who can keep a blazing fire tied in a cotton cloth? Lex Hixon. HW

My Jacket Old. Herman Melville. TCAPo

My joke and me. (LL) Sphinx. Robert Earl Hayden. GT; HCAP

My Journal. Adelaide Anne Procter. VWP

My Joy, My Jockey, My Gabriel. George Barker. MoBrPo *Fr.* First Cycle of Love Poems.

My Joy, my Life, my Crown! True Hymn, A. George Herbert. GeHe; NOCV

My joys to weep, and now my griefs to sing. (LL) Joseph's Coat. George Herbert. ChIV-1; GeHe

My kingdom for a horse! Kingdom. Leopold Staff. PoSu, *tr. by* Adam Czerniawski

My kite is three feet broad, and six feet long. Kite, The. Adelaide O'Keeffe. NOxBChV

My Kitten. Mother Goose. OxNR; ReMoGo

My Knicks Are Going to Beat Your Spurs—NBA Souvenir Bracelet 1999 for My Long Distance Love. Catherine Bowman. MoASP

My Lady Carenza of the lovely body. *Unknown.* BoWoP

My lady carries love within her eyes. Dante Alighieri. AWP; EaItPo, *tr. by* Dante Gabriel Rossetti *Fr.* La Vita Nuova.

My Lady Carries Stones. Nick Piombino. FTOS

My lady / fair with / soft. Token, A. Robert Creeley. VGW

My Lady Greensleeves. *Unknown.* OxAEP-1

(New Courtly Sonet, [*or* Sonnet] of the Lady Greensleeves, A.) NPeEn; NoSic; PBRV

My Lady Is a Pretty One. *Unknown.* OxBoLi

My lady looks so gentle and so pure. Dante Alighieri. AWP; EaItPo, *tr. by* Dante Gabriel Rossetti *Fr.* La Vita Nuova.

My lady love. Tea Making. Antoinette Scudder. PoBW

My Lady mine, I send. Canzonetta: Of His Lady, and of His Making Her Likeness. Jacopo da Lentino. AWP; EaItPo, *tr. by* Dante Gabriel Rossetti

My Lady Pity, for the help she brings. (LL) Dante Alighieri. AWP; EaItPo, *tr. by* Dante Gabriel Rossetti *Fr.* La Vita Nuova.

My lady pleases me and I please her. Robert Bridges. Son *Fr.* Growth of Love, The.

My Lady's face it is they worship there. Sonetto XXXV: To Guido Orlando. Guido Cavalcanti. CTC, *tr. by* Ezra Pound

My Lady's Grave. Emily Jane Brontë. *See* Song: "Linnet in the rocky dells, The."

My lady's presence makes the roses red. Henry Constable. NIL-7; NIP-4; OBGa *Fr.* Diana.

My Lady's Tears. *Unknown.* *See* I Saw My Lady Weep

My Lady, the Amazement of the Land, the Lone Star. Lady Who Ascends into the Heavens, The. *Unknown.* HW, *tr. by* Samuel Noah Kramer and Diane Wolkstein

My lady, thy delightful high command. Pannuccio dal Bagno Pisano. EaItPo, *tr. by* Dante Gabriel Rossetti

My lady unto Madam makes her bow. George Meredith. NOBVV *Fr.* Modern Love.

My lady walks her morning round. Henchman, The. John Greenleaf Whittier. OBEV

My lady woke upon a morning fair. On His Lady's Waking. Pierre de Ronsard. AWP, *tr.* by Andrew Lang

My Lai / Remuera / Ponsonby. David Mitchell. PeNZ

My lamp and life, both shall in Thee abide. (LL) Morning-Watch, The. Henry Vaughan. AngWePo; BASC; ESCV; GeHe; NOSC; PeECV

My land is bare of chattering folk. Sanctuary. Dorothy Parker. NBLV

My land, my love, sleep well. (LL) Nightsong: City. Dennis Brutus. HBAPE; PBMAP; PoetW; WoPoe

My Last Afternoon with Uncle Devereux Winslow. Robert Lowell. NAAL-2v2; NoP-4; VGW

My Last Dance. Julia Ward Howe. APN-1

My Last Duchess. Robert Browning. AWP; AmFaPo; CABP; ClHu; EBNV; EBVV; FHYEP; GTBS-P; HAP; HeIP-4; ITBLP; InPK-6; MakPoe; NAEL-5v2; NAWM-7v2; NIL-7; NIP-4; NOBE; NOBVV; NPeEn; NoP-4; OxBEV; PAI; PeVV; PoE; PoPoPo; SCGP; SCV; SoSe-8; TFi; TRP

My Last Name. Nicolás Guillén. TCLAP, *tr.* by Robert Marquez and David Arthur McMurray

My last night in California. California. David St. John. SwNoth

My Last Tooth. *Unknown.* VerBaPo

My Latest Sun Is Sinking Fast. Jefferson Haskell. AH

My latest thought brick for an abundant supply for home and clothes. Bill Griffiths. Oth *Fr.* Building: The New London Hospital.

My leafless maple tree, your icy coating. Sergey [*or* Sergei] Aleksandrovich Yesenin [*or* Essenin]. TCRP

My Least Skirtable Deficiency. HeidiLynn Nilsson. NeAmPo

My leg stiffens. The crutch that holds me has become my aromatic rosary. Weaning of Furniture-Nutrition. Juan Felipe Herrera. BodElec

My legs are long. To Trace from Hebrew. Ece Ayhan. PFTM-2, *tr.* by Murat Nemet-Nejat

My Legs Señor. William S. Burroughs. BB

My legs shimmer like fish. Bathroom. Elaine Feinstein. HarvBoo

My legs swollen from pressing pedals. I'm a Worker. Jayne Cortez. NBV

My Lesbia let us love and live. Catullus. *See* Lesbia / live with me

My Lessons in the Jail. Miriam Waddington. MoCV

My letters! all dead paper, mute and white. Elizabeth Barrett Browning. CenSon; HAP; OxAEP-2 *Fr.* Sonnets from the Portuguese.

My Lief Is Faren in Londe. *Unknown.* NAEL-5v1; NAEL-6v1; NAEL-7v1

My liege, I did deny no prisoners. William Shakespeare. FaBoWar *Fr.* King Henry IV, Pt. I.

My life. Hanri. JDP, *tr.* by Yoel Hoffmann

My Life. Lyn Hejinian.

"Moment yellow, just as four years later when, A." PmAP

"Tree rows in orchards are capable of patterns. What, The." FTOS

My life. My Life by Water. Lorine Niedecker. APT-2

My Life. Mark Strand. NoAM

My Life. Joe Wenderoth. BodElec; NAPBL

My life becomes too hard, so I go away. Asylum. Herman Fong. BAP-97

My Life by Water. Lorine Niedecker. APT-2

My Life Closed Twice. Emily Dickinson. APN-2; BoLoP; BoWoP; HeIP-4; LW; MoAmPo; NAAL-2v1; NAAL-3; NIP-4; NOBA; NoAM; OxBA; OxBSP; SAmP; SCV; SacPr; TCAPo; TFi

(My Life Closed Twice Before Its Close.) ColAP

My life had taken the form of a small square. Small Square, The. Sophia de Mello Breyner. VCWP, *tr.* by Ruth Fainlight

My life had taken the shape of the small square. Small Square, The. Sophia de Mello Breyner Andresen. WPOW, *tr.* by Alexis Levitin

My Life Has Been the Poem I Would Have Writ. Henry David Thoreau. APN-1; NCAP; TCAPo

My Life in Yonago. Sharon Mesmer. HeMarv

My Life Is a———. Frederick Locker-Lampson. OBCoV

My life is bitter with thy love; thine eyes. Anactoria. Algernon Charles Swinburne. RACG

My life is done, yet all remains. Robert the Bruce. Edwin Muir. OxBS

My life is engraved on my poems. Of Myself. Leah Goldberg. BoWoP, *tr.* by Ramah Commanday

My life is hung up. Lorine Niedecker. APT-2

My life is like the summer rose. Lament of the Captive, The. Richard Henry Wilde. APN-1; ColAP; TCAPo

My life is measur'd by this glass[e], this glass[e]. On an Hour[e]-Glass[e]. John Hall. MeLP

My Life, my Strength, my Joy, my All. (LL) Hymn to My God in a Night of My Late Sickness[e], A. Sir Henry Wotton. MeLP; NOSC

My life's a maze of seeming traps. Ralph Erskine. SacPr *Fr.* Believer's Riddle, The.

My life's a pleasure and a pain. Ralph Erskine. SacPr *Fr.* Believer's Riddle, The.

My life's blossom might have bloomed on all sides. Edgar Lee Masters. APT-1 *Fr.* Spoon River Anthology.

My life seems dull and flat. Epitaph on a Pet Cat. Joachim Du Bellay. TriCat, *tr.* by Ralph Nixon Currey

My Life, the Quality of Which. Etheridge Knight. NNaP

My life—to Discontent a prey. Rhymes (?). Henry Sambrooke Leigh. NOBL

My life was. Tokugen. JDP, *tr.* by Yoel Hoffmann

My life was never so precious. Inscription for the Tank. James Wright. TwCP

My Life with Horses. Polly Clark. NeBl

My life, your light green eyes. Last Words. James Merrill. TAP

My light will tip tankards of fire in the sky. Constant Labor, A. James W. Thompson. BPo

My Lighthouses. Helen Hunt Jackson. APN-2; ColAP

My lips are sweet, inspired with Stella's kiss. (LL) Sir Philip Sidney. NAEL-5v1; NAEL-6v1; NAEL-7v1; NoSic; Son *Fr.* Astrophil and Stella.

My lips came with a caravan of slaves. History of My Face. Khaled Mattawa. AmPoNex

My lips from this day forgot how to smile. Auguste Lacaussade. TTY *Fr.* Les Salaziennes.

My little Ben, whilst thou art young. To His Son Bennet. John Hoskyns [*or* Hoskins]. FaBoEE

My little boat emerges at Heng-t'ang. Late Spring—Traveling through the Mountains. Chu Yün-ming. CoBLCP, *tr.* by Jonathan Chaves

My little book, as o'er thy page so white. Written in a Blank-Paper Book Given to the Author by a Friend. Mary Russell Mitford. PoBW

My little box. Little Box From Olinalá. Gabriela Mistral. TANSG, *tr.* by Maria Jacketti

My little boy Kun-shih. Poem for My Little Boy. Li Shang-yin. CoBCP, *tr.* by Burton Watson

My little breath, under the willows by the water-side we used to sit. Lover's Lament *or* The Willows by the Water Side, A. *Unknown.* AWP, *tr.* by H. J. Spinden

My Little Dreams. Georgia Douglas Johnson. BlSi; NAAAL

My Little Girl Went to the Sea. Federico García Lorca. SpanPo, *tr.* by Rachel Benson and Robert O'Brien

My little lord, methinks 'tis strange. Prognostication on Will Laud, Late Archbishop of Canterbury, A. *Unknown.* OxBoLi

My Little Maid. *Unknown.* ReMoGo

My little old man and I fell out. Quarrel, The. Mother Goose. OxNR; ReMoGo

My Little Pretty Mopsy. *Unknown.* MiEL

My little ship, three-masted. *Unknown.* WoPoe, *tr.* by Konstantinos Lardas *Fr.* Mourning Songs of Greece.

My Little Sister. Abba Kovner.

"Far, far." HP, *tr.* by Shirley Kaufman

My little sister likes to try my shoes. Poem for My Sister. Liz Lochhead. ItWoWo

My little son enters. Transformations. Tadeusz Rózewicz. ChAP, *tr.* by Czeslaw Milosz

My little son, I have cast you out. Choosing a Name. Anne Ridler. NOBE

My little son, laughing, singing. Poem. Thomas McGrath. GifTon

My little son, when you could command marvels. Geoffrey Hill. NoAM *Fr.* Funeral Music.

My little son, who looked from thoughtful eyes. Coventry Patmore. EBEV; EBVV; NOBVV; OBEV; OxAEP-2; PoToHe; SoSe-8 *Fr.* Unknown Eros, The.

My lizard, my lively writher. Wish for a Young Wife. Theodore Roethke. NAAL-2v2; NAAL-5; NoAM; NoP-4; OxBSP; TAP

My Loneliness. Thérèse 'Awwad. Po ArWo, *tr.* by Kamal Boullata

My long poem, the 'Eternal Grief,' is a beautiful and moving work. Fifteenth Volume, The. Po Chü-i. ChiP, *tr.* by Arthur Waley

My long scythe whispered and left the hay to make. (LL) Mowing. Robert Frost. APT-1; ColAP; HarvBoo; ITBLP; NAAL-2v2; NAAL-5; NOBA; OxBA; TRP; VGW

My long two-pointed ladder's sticking through a tree. After Apple-Picking. Robert Frost. APT-1; MoAmPo; NAAL-2v2; NAAL-5; NOBA; NoAM; OxBA; PAI; PoE; SAmP; SoSe-8; TAP; TCAPo; TFi; TRP; UnPo

My lord and my God, I have hoped in Thee. Mary Stuart, Queen of Scots. NePenScot, *tr.* by Agnes Strickland

My lord, as I was sewing in my closet. William Shakespeare. OxAEP-1 *Fr.* Hamlet.

My Lord, fallen, sin-stained. Sticheron for Matins, Wednesday of Holy Week. Kassia. WPOW, *tr.* by Patrick Diehl

My lord, hearing lately of your opulence in promises and your house. Epistle to a Patron, An. Frank Templeton Prince. HarvBoo; OxBEV

My Lord, I'm coming from the war. Prayer after War. Endre Ady. IQMS, *tr.* by Anton N. Nyerges

My Lord, I take the liberty of submitting a case. Rhyfel y Sais Bach. John Stuart Williams. TCAWP

My Lord / if I worship Thee from fear of Hell. Rabi'a al-Adawiyya. WPOW

My Lord Is Full of Delight. *Unknown.* TAL

My Lord recalls Ferrara? How walls. Nikolaus Mardruz to his Master Ferdinand, Count of Tyrol, 1565. Richard Howard. NoP-4

My Lord's Gone to Service. *Unknown.* CoBCP, *tr. by* Burton Watson

My lord said to my lady. Lamkin. *Unknown.* ESPB

My Lord Tomnoddy. Robert Barnabas Brough. PeLV

My Lord, What a Mornin' *Unknown.* NoP-4

My Lord, What a Morning. Waring Cuney. TTY

My lords, here's something marvelous. Butcher of Abbeville, The. *Unknown.* NAWM-7v1, *tr. by* Ned Dubin

My lords, if you have time to spare. Three Hunchbacks, The. *Unknown.* NAWM-7v1, *tr. by* Ned Dubin

My Lost Brother. Ben Scammell. NLP

My Lost Youth. Henry Wadsworth Longfellow. APN-1; AWP; ITBLP; NAAL-2v1; NAAL-3; NOBA; OBEV; OxBA; PoRA; TAP; TCAPo; TFi

My lov'd [*or* loved], my honor'd [*or* honored], much respected friend. Robert Burns. NOBRP; TreFP

My Love. "Sasha Chorny" [*or* "Chiornyi"]. TCRP, *tr. by* Bernard Meares

My Love. *Unknown.* ReMoGo

My love and I asked little of the world. Right to Love, The. Gene Lees. ReLy

My love and I for kisses played [*or* play'd]. Kisses. William Strode. FaBoEE; NOSC

My love came back to me. All Souls' Night. Frances Darwin Cornford. EnLoPo; OxBSP; OxBTC

My love dwelt in a northern land. Romance. Andrew Lang. NePenScot

My Love Eats an Apple. Ralph Gustafson. MoCV

My Love For You. *Unknown.* Spl

My love forever! *Unknown.* BIrV *Fr.* Lament for Arthur O'Leary, The.

My love has built a bonny ship, and set her on the sea. Lowlands o' [*or of*] Holland, The. *Unknown.* OxBB

My Love Has Departed. *Chippewa Oral Tradition.* NAAL-5, *tr. by* Frances Densmore

My Love Has Departed. Frances Densmore. APT-1 *Fr.* Chippewa Music.

My love has gone down to his garden. Bible, *O.T.* BoWoP *Fr.* Song of Solomon, The [*or* The Song of Songs].

My love has left me has gone from me. Souvenirs. Dudley Randall. BPo

My love he built me a bonnie bower. Lament of the Border Widow, The. *Unknown.* OxBB

My love hot on your scent on the cusp of winter. (LL) Adrienne Rich. LW; NIL-7 *Fr.* Contradictions: Tracking Poems.

My Love I Gave for Hate. *Unknown.* BIrV, *tr. by* George Hay

My love I give to you a threefold thing. James Reaney. MoCV *Fr.* Suit of Nettles, A.

My Love, I Speak to You of a Love. Leila Ferraz. SurWo, *tr. by* Jean R. Longland

My love, if I die and you don't. Pablo Neruda. TCLAP, *tr. by* Stephen Tapscott

My love, if I write a song for you. Sonnet. Veronica Forrest-Thomson. HarvBoo

My Love in her attire doth show her wit. Madrigal. *Unknown.* BoLoP; GTBS-P; HeIP-4; NAEL-5v1; NAEL-6v1; NIP-4; NOBE; OBEV; OxBSP; TFi

My love is a lotus blossom. Love Song. *Unknown.* TTY, *tr. by* J. E. Manchip White

My love is as a fever [*or* feaver], longing still. William Shakespeare. EBEV; NAEL-5v1; NAEL-6v1; NAEL-7v1; OxAEP-1 *Fr.* Sonnets.

My love is falle upon a may. *Unknown.* MiEL

My love is in my house. Mirabai [*or* Mira Bai]. BoWoP, *tr. by* Willis Barnstone and Usha Nilsson

My Love is Like a Lily. Kim Ly Bui-Burton. PasH

My Love is Like a Myrtle. Moses Ibn Ezra. TrJP, *tr. by* Solomon Solis-Cohen

My love is like Mies van der Rohe's. Dea ex Machina. John Updike. UV

My love / Is like the grasses. Ono no Yoshiki. TAL

My love / Is like the grasses. Ono No Yoshiki. AWP *Fr.* Kokin Shu.

My love is like to ice, and I to fire. Edmund Spenser. PAI *Fr.* Amoretti.

My love is living. South of the Great Sea. *Unknown.* ChiP, *tr. by* Arthur Waley

My love is no short year's sentence. Love. *Unknown.* BIrV, *tr. by* John Montague

My love is o' comely height, an' straïght. White an' Blue. William Barnes. GTBS-P

My Love is of a birth as rare. Definition of Love, The. Andrew Marvell. BASC; BoLoP; EBEV; ESCV; FHYEP; FSCP; GeHe; ITBLP; MeLP; NAEL-5v1; NAEL-6v1; NAEL-7v1; NOBE; NOSC; NPeEn; NoP-4; OBEV; OxBEV; PBRV; SCGP; TFi; UnPo

My Love Is Past. Thomas Watson. NoSic

(Ye captive soules of blindfold Cyprians boate.) NPeEn

My love is sick—she has begun to turn. Craig Arnold. NAPBL

My love is strengthen'd, though more weak in seeming. William Shakespeare. AWP; OBEV *Fr.* Sonnets.

My love is white and ruddy. Bible, *O.T.* BoWoP *Fr.* Song of Solomon, The [*or* The Song of Songs].

My Love Is Young. Earle Birney. NOBC

My love lies underground. Hymn to Priapus. D. H. Lawrence. OBMV; PoE; SCGP

My love looks like a girl to-night. Bride, The. D. H. Lawrence. NoAM; OxBTC

My love must be a kind of blind love. I Only Have Eyes for You. Harry Warren. ReLy

My love, my lord. Verses Expressing the Feelings of a Lover. Sister Juana Inés de la Cruz. SpanPo, *tr. by* Samuel Beckett

My Love, my Love, it was a day in June. Sinfonia Eroica. Amy Levy. ViWPN

My love of you was life and not a breath. (LL) Christina Georgina Rossetti. CABP; MakPoe; OxBSo *Fr.* Monna Innominata.

My Love's Dark Place Is Fragrant Like Narcissus. Ikkyu Sojun. ErotSp, *tr. by* Sam Hamill

My love's eyes are red as the sargasso. Talking Fish, The. Ruth Stone. BoWoP

My love's manners in bed. Way, The. Robert Creeley. BoLoP; NeAP

My love sent me a chicken without e'er a bone. *Unknown.* OxNR

My love shall in my verse ever live young. (LL) William Shakespeare. AWP; EBEV; HeIP-4; NAEL-5v1; NAEL-6v1; NAEL-7v1; NoSic; OxAEP-1; PoE; SCGP *Fr.* Sonnets.

My love she is a gentlewoman. Auld Matrons. *Unknown.* ESPB

My Love-Song. Else Lasker-Schüler. TrJP, *tr. by* Jethro Bithell

My love, the tragic night was crying with sobs. Intruder, The. Delmira Agustini. BLPSL, *tr. by* Rene de Costa, Rigas Kappatos and Eleni Paidoussi

My love, this is the bitterest, that thou. Any Wife to Any Husband. Robert Browning. RACG

My love / thy hair is one kingdom. E. E. Cummings. VGW

My love was walking in the sun. Shallow-Water Warning. Helen Adam. APT-2

My Love When This Is Past. Stephany Fuller. BPo

My love will come. Yevgeny Aleksandrovich Yevtushenko [*or* Evtushenko]. TCRP

My love, you are timely come, let me lie by your heart. Door and the Window, The. Henry Reed. HarvBoo

My Love? alas! I must not call you Mine. To J. G. on the News of His Marriage. "Ephelia." LW

My loved one is unique, without a peer. Love Song. *Unknown.* TTY, *tr. by* J. E. Manchip White

My loved ones drift into nothingness. Fuselage Installation. Juan Felipe Herrera. BodElec

My lovely, sweet Ipsithilla. Catullus. ErotSp, *tr. by* Sam Hamill

My lover capable of terrible lies. What She Said. Kaccipettu Nannakaiyar. BoWoP; WPOW, *tr. by* A. K. Ramanujan

My lover is a lotus blossom. *Unknown, fr. Egyptian hieroglyphics.* ErotSp, *tr. by* Sam Hamill

My lover is asleep. Peaceful Sunday. Charlotte Gardelle. CuPo

My Lover Will Soon Be Here. *Unknown.* OHMPC, *tr. by* Kenneth Rexroth

My lovers aren't members of the gentry. Mille e tre. Paul Verlaine. CAGL, *tr. by* Alan Stone

My Loves. Julián de Casal. BLPSL, *tr. by* Rene de Costa, Rigas Kappatos and Eleni Paidoussi

My loving frende, amorous Bune. Lettre Sende by on Yonge Woman to A-noder, Whiche Aforetyme Were Felowes To-geder, A. *Unknown.* EMWP

My Lute, Awake! Sir Thomas Wyatt. BoLoP; NAEL-5v1; NAEL-6v1; NAEL-7v1; NOBE; NoP-4; NoSic; OBEV; SCGP; TFi; WoPoe

(Lover Complaineth the Unkindness of His Love, The.) EBEV; HAP

(My lute, awake! perfourme the last.) NPeEn; OxBEV; PBRV

My lute, awake! Perform the last. My Lute, Awake! Sir Thomas Wyatt. BoLoP; NAEL-5v1; NAEL-6v1; NAEL-7v1; NOBE; NoP-4; NoSic; OBEV; SCGP; TFi; WoPoe

My lute, be as thou wast [*or* wert] when thou didst grow. To His Lute. William Drummond, of Hawthornden. GTBS-P; NOSC; SCGP; Son

My lute be still for I have done. (LL) My Lute, Awake! Sir Thomas Wyatt. BoLoP; NAEL-5v1; NAEL-6v1; NAEL-7v1; NOBE; NoP-4; NoSic; OBEV; SCGP; TFi; WoPoe

My luve [*or* love] is like a red, red rose. Robert Burns. *See* O my love's [*or* luve's *or* love is *or* luve is] like a red, red rose

My luve she lives in Lincolnshire. Alison and Willie. *Unknown.* ESPB

My lyfe shall everlastingly bee lengthened still by fame. (LL) Ovid. CTC; OBVE, *tr. by* Arthur Golding *Fr.* Metamorphoses.

My LYRE! oh, let thy soothing power. To My Lyre. Eliza Cook. VWP

My madness is dear to me. Mad Song. Denise Levertov. TAP

My maid Mary, / She minds the dairy. Mother Goose. OxNR; ReMoGo

My Maker shunneth me. Spiritual Isolation. Isaac Rosenberg. TrJP

My Mall, I mark that when you mean to prove me. Author to His Wife, of a Woman's Eloquence, The. Sir John Harington [or Harrington]. BoLoP

My mama done tol' me. Blues in the Night. Johnny Mercer. APT-2; ReLy

My Mama Moved among the Days. Lucille Clifton. BlSi; ItWoWo

My Mamma is a mean old sing. Insulted. Priscilla Jane Thompson. CBWP-2

My Mammogram. J. D. McClatchy. WiU

My man don't love me. Fine and Mellow. Billie Holiday. NAAAL

My man is a bone ringèd with weed. Lament. Brenda Chamberlain. WPE; WPOW

My man loved me so much. So Long. Jayne Cortez. BoWoP; LW

My Man o' War. Spencer Williams. ReLy

My Man Pa Replies. Li Ho. CoBCP; ColAnChi, tr. by Burton Watson

My man took off yesterday. Wanna Be White. Charmaine Papertalk-Green. IBA

My man, Willard Franklin 'The Bunny' Goodjarrah. Story of Frankie. . . My Man, The. Archie Weller. BMAP

My Mary. John Clare. NOBRP

My Mary. William Cowper. See To Mary

My Maryland. James Ryder Randall. CBCWP

(Maryland.) APN-2

My Masters. Sandor Csoori. VCWP, tr. by Len Roberts

My masters twain made me a bed. Said the Canoe. Isabella Valancy Crawford. NOBC

My Meat and Drink. Jones Very. InvLi

My meditation turns to thinking. Sonnet. Giorgio Baffo. EroLit, tr. by Wayland Young

My Melancholy Baby. Ernie Burnett. ReLy

My Memory. Monica Mansour [or Mansur]. MirDau, tr. by Maria Xirinachs

My memory disrobes at night. My Memory. Monica Mansour [or Mansur]. MirDau, tr. by Maria Xirinachs

My memory is. Charles Olson. PFTM-2

My memory is short, and braine is dry. Anne Bradstreet. TCAPo Fr. Four Ages of Man, The.

My Message. Cecil Rajendra. PoetW

My Metaphors are but dull Tacklings tag'd. Edward Taylor. TCAPo Fr. Preparatory Meditations before My Approach to the Lord's Supper.

My microscopic cushion shows its claws. (LL) Microscope in Winter, The. Sandra McPherson. LCAP-2; VCAP

"My milk-white doo," said the young man. Young Man and the Young Nun, The. Albert D. Mackie. OxBS

My mill grinds pepper and spice. Unknown. OxNR

My Mind. Rāmprasād Sen. SinGod, tr. by Rachel Fell McDermott

My mind i th' mines of rich Philosophy. On My Lord Bacon. John Danforth. SCAP

My mind is dazzled. Shrine Priestess of Ise. ArkPo, tr. by Robert H. Brower and Earl Miner

My mind is intact, but the shapes. Riddle in the Garden. Robert Penn Warren. NoAM

My mind is sad and weary thinking how. Odell. James Stephens. MoBrPo

My mind is stuffed with tablecloths. Poland / 1931 "The Wedding." Jerome Rothenberg. PoM

My mind is worn out, my features grown sharp and gaunt. Sitting at Night with My Nephew Who Has Just Come from Afar. Su Tung-p'o (Su Shih). TAL

My mind lets go a thousand things. Memory. Thomas Bailey Aldrich. TCAPo

My Mind, my helmsman. Rāmprasād Sen. SinGod, tr. by Rachel Fell McDermott

My mind [or minde or mynde] to me a kingdom [or kyngdome] is. My Mind to Me a Kingdom Is. Sir Edward Dyer. NOBE; SCGP

My mind takes a leap. Cor Van den Heuvel. HA

My Mind to Me a Kingdom Is. Sir Edward Dyer. NOBE; SCGP

(In Praise of a Contented Mind.) NAEL-5v1; NAEL-6v1; NoSic

(Sweet and pleasant Sonnet, entitled: My mind to me a kingdom is, A.) BASC

My mind to me mangles iron. An error is mirror to the truth. Stephen Rodefer. PmAP Fr. Plane Debris.

My mind was once the true survey. Mower's Song, The. Andrew Marvell. BASC; ESCV; NAEL-5v1; NAEL-6v1; NAEL-7v1; NOSC

My mirror is always a little taller than I am. Mirror. Chimako Tada. BoWoP

My mission was to sell pottery from booth 109. Tradition and Change. Nora Naranjo-Morse. ReTh

My Mistress. Unknown. NOSC; OBCoV

My mistress' eyes are nothing like the sun. William Shakespeare. AWP; BoLoP; CABP; EBEV; HAP; HeIP-4; inPK-6; NAEL-5v1; NAEL-6v1; NAEL-7v1; NIL-7; NIP-4; NoSic; OxAEP-1; OxBEV; PAI; PoE; PoPoPo; SoSe-8; Son; TFi; WeW-3 Fr. Sonnets.

My mistress frowns when she should play. Madrigal. John Hilton. OxBoLi

My mistress in a hive of bees. Unknown. EroLit

My mistress is as fair as fine. Madrigal. Thomas Ravenscroft. OxBoLi

My mistress loves no woodcocks. My Mistress. Unknown. NOSC; OBCoV

My moccasins are black obsidian. Song of the Black Bear, The. Unknown. RaBo

My Mocking Bird. Josephine D. Henderson Heard. CBWP-4

My monument is done, my task is ended. Epilogue. Miklós Zrínyi. IQMS, tr. by Michael Hatwell

My morning porridge. Kusamaru. JDP, tr. by Yoel Hoffmann

My most distinguished guest and learnèd friend. Edna St. Vincent Millay. VGW

My most respected. At the Top of My Voice. Vladimir Vladimirovich Mayakovsky [or Maiakovskii]. TCRP, tr. by Max Hayward and George Reavey

My most respected / comrades of posterity! Vladimir Vladimirovich Mayakovsky [or Maiakovskii]. AF Fr. At the Top of My Voice.

My mother. That Jewish Crusader. Diana Anhalt. MirDau

My mother. My Mother's Friend. Lily Brett. HP

My Mother. Virginia Cerenio. ReBoTo

My Mother. Mother. P. Lankesh. OMIP, tr. by A. K. Ramanujan

My Mother. Claude McKay. GT

My Mother. Claude McKay. NAAAL

My Mother. Robert Mezey. TaR

My Mother. Gabriela Mistral. TANSG, tr. by Maria Jacketti

My Mother. William Bell Scott. GSo

My Mother. Jane Taylor. ITBLP

My Mother. John Wieners. BB

My Mother. John Wieners. GLP; PmAP

My mother always said. Sappho. BoWoP

My mother and I debate. Black Walnut Tree, The. Mary Oliver. MakPoe

My Mother and I Had a Discussion One Day. Denise Sweet. ReEnLa

My mother and your mother. Unknown. OxNR

My mother asks if I read about the sculptor. Caged Stone. Martha Vertreace. IllVoic

My mother bids me bind my hair. Pastoral Song, A. Anne Hunter. ECWP

My mother bore me. Foolish Child. Unknown. PBA, tr. by J. B. Danquah

My mother bore me in the southern wild. William Blake. AWP; AmFaPo; CABP; ChAP; FHYEP; HeIP-4; NAEL-5v2; NAEL-6v2; NAWM-7v2; NOBRP; NOEC; NoP-4; OBEV; PeECV; PoE; PoPoPo; SCGP; TFi Fr. Songs of Innocence.

My mother, born Jewish. I Never Knew I Was Jewish. Irene Reti. GotH

My mother came to me. Vision. Steve Barney. IBA

My Mother Cunning, yet Innocent. Gloria Vando. TouFir

My Mother Dances a Ballad. István Sinka. IQMS, tr. by Adam Makkai

My mother did not have a garden. Mother. Nancy Morejón. TANSG, tr. by Joy Renjilian-Burgy

My mother died when I was already old. Moviola. Elena Clementelli. CItWP, tr. by Cinzia Sartini Blum and Lara Trubowitz

My mother disappeared in a shoddy. Cold River. Joan Larkin. WiU

My Mother Dressed for the Wedding. Stevie Krayer. Prnts

My mother drives the goat. Pictures. Sarah Kirsch. AF, tr. by Wayne Kvam

My mother even hated. 1956, the Year My Sister, Using Her Ill Health Once Again, Blackmailed My Parents into an Accordion. Susan Firer. MiVo

My mother gave me a bitter tongue. Rhyme of My Inheritance. Joan Larkin. GLP

My mother gave me the prayer to Saint Theresa. What Every Woman Should Carry. Maura Dooley. NeBl

My mother groaned! [or groan'd!, or groand!] my father wept. William Blake. FHYEP; NAEL-5v2; NAEL-6v2; OxAEP-2; OxBEV; OxBSP; PoPoPo; RB Fr. Songs of Experience.

My mother had no patio garden. Mother. Nancy Morejón. TCLAP, tr. by Kathleen Weaver

My mother had two faces and a frying pot. From the House of Yemanjá. Audre Lorde. NALW; NoAM; NoP-4

My Mother Has Forgotten My Name. Neeltje Maria Min. TuT, tr. by Peter Van de Kamp

My mother hated gesturing. My speech. Handnotes. Lyn Moir. Prnts

My mother hates the sea. Sea Chanty. Gregory Corso. BB

My mother held me by my hand. Dead Child Speaks, A. Nelly Sachs. HP; PoSu

My mother hides within folded hands. Making It New. Elmaz Abinader. GraLe

My mother, I cannot endure. Mother. Willem Elsschot. TuT, tr. by Peter Van de Kamp

My Mother, If She Had Won Free Dance Lessons. Cornelius Eady. ISC

My mother / In her youth it was a great. Sappho. SaLy, tr. by Diane Rayor

My Mother in Old Age. Eric Ormsby. NIP-4

My Mother in Three Acts. Jane Cooper. ExTi

My mother is a. Natural High. Jean Binta Breeze. Prnts

My Mother Is a God Fearing Woman. Cornelius Eady. ISC

My mother is a whore without a dagger. Already Night, Already Day. Hedva Harechavi. DTA, *tr.* by Miriyam Glazer

My mother is concerned that I haven't met a nice boy to settle down with. Ex-Boyfriends Named Michael. Justin Chin. WiU

My mother lay on her side to birth me. Coyotismo. Janice Gould. ReEnLa

My mother left me at the foot of the fence. Abandoned, The. Nathan [*or* Natan] Alterman. MHP, *tr.* by Ruth Finer Mintz

My mother lies spread-eagle upon the bed. In My Mother's Room. Colleen J. McElroy. GT

My Mother, Life. John Godfrey. FTOS

My mother lives here, I am told. Searching. Cathy Grindrod. Prnts

My mother lives in a house. My House. Robert Adamson. BMAP; CBAP

My mother made Big Macs and beds. Making Ends Meet. Thomas Sayers Ellis. InTrad

My mother never forgave my father. Portrait, The. Stanley Kunitz. InvLad; RaBo

My mother never heard of Freud. Nomenclature. Alan Dugan. BodElec

My mother never taught me sweeping. How I Learned to Sweep. Julia Alvarez. FFC; RA

My mother of the blue / Anglo-Saxon eyes. Eyes, the Blood, The. David Meltzer. PoM

My Mother Once Told Me. Yehuda Amichai [*or* Amikhai]. WoPoe, *tr.* by Benjamin Harshav and Barbara Harshav

My mother once watched. San Francisco Sunrise. Diane Ackerman. UrbNat

My mother opened her eyes wide. Lesson of the Sugarcane, The. Judith Ortiz Cofer. TouFir

My mother peers. 1973. Reuben Jackson. GT

My mother phoning from far off. Breathing Exercises. Leonard Nathan. PBCAP

My Mother Pieced Quilts. Teresa Palma Acosta. WPOW

My mother—preferring the strange to the tame. Intruder, The. Carolyn Kizer. BoWoP; InPK-6

My mother, red-haired. At the Powwow. Cheryl Savageau. TWW

My Mother's Burial. Sean O Riordain. ModIr, *tr.* by Patrick Crotty

My Mother's Clothes. Pascale Petit. Prnts

My Mother's Council house is occupied. Ornaments. Frank Ormsby. CIP-2

My Mother's Friend. Lily Brett. HP

My Mother's Hands. *Unknown.* ITBLP

My mother's insomnia over at last. Chain, The. Maxine W. Kumin. TaR

My mother's lamp once out. Scenes of Childhood. James Merrill. CoAP

My Mother's Lips. C. K. Williams. EmeKit

My mother's maids [*or* maydes] when they did sew [*or* sowe] and spin [*or* spynne]. Sir Thomas Wyatt. NoSic *Fr.* Satires.

My mother's mother died. From My Mother's Home. Leah Goldberg. FIT, *tr.* by Robert Friend

My mother's name was Mary. Mary's a Grand Old Name. George M. Cohan. ReLy

My mother's old leather handbag. Handbag. Ruth Fainlight. OPOU

My mother's phantom hovers here. Behind Bars, Sel. Fadwa Tuqan [*or* Tuquan]. AF, *tr.* by Hatem Hussaini

My Mother's Sabbath Days. Irena Klepfisz. TaR

My Mother's Sister. Cecil Day Lewis. OxBTC

My mother's uncle was physician to the Persian Shah. Eternal Present, The. Gabriel Preil. FIT, *tr.* by Robert Friend

My Mother's Voice. Mary E. Tucker. CBWP-1

My mother's voice scrapes the ocean floor. Dream of Birth, The. Judith Ortiz Cofer. PueRic

My Mother's Young Sister. Roy McFadden. PNI

My Mother Said. *Unknown. See* Gypsies in the Wood

My mother said, "If just once more." Mother's Nerves. X. J. Kennedy. ChAP

My mother said later that, to the shovel operators, we must have looked like. Visiting the Site of One of the First Churches My Grandfather Pastored. T. Crunk. YaYoPo

My mother said, / [that] I never should. Gypsies in the Wood. *Unknown.* OxBSP; OxBoLi; OxNR

My mother saw the green tree toad. Lorine Niedecker. VGW

My mother sent us to the school. Shoemakker, The. *Unknown.* FaBoVe

My mother sliced the south for us. Lullaby for Ann-Lucian. Calvin Forbes. NBV

My Mother Spinning. Peter Olds. PeNZ

My mother tells me she dreamed. Soloing. Philip Levine. OPRER

My mother, the sage of Aliceville, Alabama. Annie Pearl Smith Discovers Moonlight. Patricia Smith. GT

My mother took me because she couldn't. Madre Sofía. Alberto A. Ríos. NAAL-5; NoAM

My mother took us, when we went walking. Dell, The. Gavin Ewart. OxBC

My mother used to say "Bury me with a band." Bury Me with a Band. Ofelia Zepeda. ReEnLa

My mother used to work for me. Patches. Thomas Russell Shelton. PWR

My mother was a Florentine. Elizabeth Barrett Browning. NALW *Fr.* Aurora Leigh.

My mother was a romantic girl. Papa Love Baby. Stevie Smith. NALW

My mother was an ill woman. Death of Lord Warriston, The. *Unknown.* OxBB

My mother was my midwife. Midwife. Judith Kazantzis. Prnts

My mother was one of the great mothers. Second Elegy. Aida Cartagena de Portalatin. TANSG, *tr.* by Emma Jane Robinett

My mother was some witch or slut. Sans Culotte. Pavel Grigoryevich Antokolsky. TCRP, *tr.* by Bernard Meares

My mother was taken up to heaven in a pink cloud. Ordinary People in the Last Days. Jay Macpherson. PAI

My mother was very small. My Mother. Gabriela Mistral. TANSG, *tr.* by Maria Jacketti

My mother watches videos. Video Mama. Jack Ridl. SwNoth

My mother wept loudly. Austin Clarke. CIP-2 *Fr.* Tiresias.

My mother, when young, scrubbed laundry in a tub. In an Iridescent Time. Ruth Stone. MoAmPo; NALW; OxWW

My Mother, Who Came from China, Where She Never Saw Snow. Laureen Mar. WPOW

My mother, who has a hide. Hide of My Mother, The. Edward Dorn. NeAP

My Mother! With the angels now. Mrs. Louise B. Weston. Mary Weston Fordham. CBWP-2

My Mother Would Be a Falconress. Robert Duncan. FTOS; GLP; PAI; PoM; RaBo; WoPoe

My mother would drift away. (LL) Great Blue Heron, The. Carolyn Kizer. CoAP; InvLad; WPE

My mother writes from Trenton. My Mother. Robert Mezey. TaR

My mouth doth water, and my breast doth swell. Sir Philip Sidney. NAEL-5v1; NAEL-6v1; NAEL-7v1; Son *Fr.* Astrophil and Stella.

My mouth hovers across your breasts. Adrienne Rich. LW; NIL-7 *Fr.* Contradictions: Tracking Poems.

My mouth is on fire. Let it burn. (LL) Billie in Silk. Angela Jackson. ReTh; SeSe

My mouth, steer our lost bodies carefully downward. (LL) E. E. Cummings. PoE; VGW

My movable empire between Athens and Megara. Damastes (Also Known as Procrustes) Speaks. Zbigniew Herbert. PoSu, *tr.* by John Carpenter

My murderer is no thief. "Ivan Venediktovich Elagin." TCRusP, *tr.* by John Glad

My Muse. Eugenio Montale. ItPo, *tr.* by Gayle Ridinger

My muse bad[e], *Bedford* write, and that was she. (LL) On Lucy, Countess[e] of Bedford. Ben Jonson. BASC; BeJo; NAEL-7v1; NOSC

My muse came up from the creek. Virginian Arcady. Anne Rouse. NeBl

My Muse had slept, and none had known my mind. (LL) Samuel Daniel. NOBE; OBEV *Fr.* To Delia.

My muse in meads has spent her many hours. To Mistress Katherine Bradshaw, the Lovely, That Crowned Him with Laurel. Robert Herrick. CaPo

My muse is distant: one could say. My Muse. Eugenio Montale. ItPo, *tr.* by Gayle Ridinger

My muse is in the sulks to-day. Knitting. Mary E. Tucker. CBWP-1

My muse now hap[p]y, lay thy self to rest. Mary Sidney Wroth, Countess of Montgomery. BASC; NAEL-7v1 *Fr.* Pamphilia to Amphilanthus.

My Muse Sits Forlorn. Stevie Smith. BWW

My Muse, the Whore. Linda France. NeBl

My Muse, though airy, glides softly along. Song of the Pen, The. Judah Al-Harizi. TrJP, *tr.* by J. Chotzner

My muse was imprisoned once. I Can No Longer Care for the Dying. Brenda J. Moossy. PoArWo

My Muse what ails this ardour. Sir Philip Sidney. *Fr.* Arcadia.

My Muse will now by chymistry draw forth. To the Learned and Reverend Mr. Cotton Mather, on His Excellent Magnalia. Grindall Rawson. SCAP

My naked simple life was I. My Spirit. Thomas Traherne. GeHe

My Name. Daniel Berrigan. AF

My Name and I. Robert Graves. NoAM

My name is Antigone: I was buried alive. Opprobium. Rosario Ferré. TANSG

My name is David Lowston, I did seal, I did seal. David Lowston. *Unknown.* PeNZ

My Name Is Dimitri. John Ashbery. BodElec

My name is Edgar Poe and I was born. On the Edge. Philip Levine. CoAP; TAP

My name is Eteocles. The sea seduced me from my farm. Isidorus. GrAn

My name is Fermin. Tobera. Jeff Tagami. OpBo

My name is Frank Taylor, a bachelor I am. Starving to Death on a Government Claim. *Unknown.* OBAL

My name is George Nathaniel Curzon. *Var. authors.* FaBoEE; NOBL; OBCoV; PeLV *Fr.* Balliol Rhymes.

My name is Henri. Listen. It's morning. Work Song. Mark Levine. AmPoNex

My name is "I am living." I Have Bowed before the Sun. Anna Walters. WPOW

My name is James A. Wright, and I was born. At the Executed Murderer's Grave. James Wright. HCAP; VCAP

My Name Is Jesus. D. H. Lawrence. PeECV

My name is Jesus, I am Mary's son. My Name Is Jesus. D. H. Lawrence. PeECV

My name is Jew. Permanent Delegate, The. Yuri Suhl. PAI, *tr. by* Walter Lowenfels and Max Rosenfeld

My name is Johnson. Madam's Past History. Langston Hughes. HHAm; NoAM; SAmP

My name is O'Kelly, I've heard the Revelly. Shillin' a Day. Rudyard Kipling. NoAM

My name is Parrot, a bird [or byrd] of paradise. John Skelton. NoSic; OxBoLi *Fr.* Speak [or Speke], Parrot.

My name is Rusty. Rusty. Gordon Lish. Unle

My name is Saartjie Baartman and I come from Kat Rivier. Hottentot Venus. Stephen Gray. PeSAV

My Name Is Shlomit. Schlomit Baytelman. MirDau, *tr. by* Elizabeth Horan

My name is Shlomit. I was born in Afula, in Galilee. My Name Is Shlomit. Schlomit Baytelman. MirDau, *tr. by* Elizabeth Horan

My name is Solomon Levi. Old Cracked Tune, An. Stanley Kunitz. LoL; TaR

My name is Stanford Barnes, I come from Nobleville town. State of Arkansas, The. *Unknown.* APN-2

My name—my country—what are they to thee? No Matter. Paulus [or Paulos] Silentiarius. AWP, *tr. by* William Cowper

My name's James, enlightenment's my game. Hi. William Kulik. BodElec

My name's Philip Marlowe, the chivalrous shamus. Raymond Chandler: The Big Sleep. Basil Ransome-Davies. OBCoV

My name's Polly Parker I come o'er. Collier Lass, The. Frankie Armstrong. BrRo

My name skimmed by the. Name, The. Mariella Bettarini. CItWP, *tr. by* Cinzia Sartini Blum and Lara Trubowitz

My name was Pnytagoras; I died by drowning. Argentarius. GrAn

My name? Where am I coming from? Where am I going? A fusillade of question marks. (LL) Belfast Confetti. Ciaran Carson. BiHa; CIP-2; NPeEn; PNI

My native clay. Growing in Grace. Jack R. Clemo. NOCV

My Native Costume. Martín Espada. TouFir

My native land is up there. At Gold Hill Monastery. Su Tung-p'o (Su Shih). OHPC, *tr. by* Kenneth Rexroth

My nature singing in me is your nature singing. Singing & Doubling Together. A. R. Ammons. NAAL-2v2; NoAM

My Neighbor. Roque Dalton. AF, *tr. by* Richard Schaaf

My neighbor, a scientist and art-collector, telephones me in a. Burning of Paper instead of Children, The. Adrienne Rich. HarvBoo; LCAP-2; NAAL-2v2; VCAP

My neighbor brings me bottom fish. My Garden, My Daylight. Jorie Graham. HCAP

My neighbor Hunks's house and mine. Near Neighbors. Martial. AWP, *tr. by* Jonathan Swift

My Neighbor in the Mirror. Louise Glück. Son

My neighbor runs to me with. In the Country. Lu Yu. OHMPC, *tr. by* Kenneth Rexroth

My neighbor's almost ex-husband, an auto salesman with a different car. Late Summer Litany. Julie Moulds. AmPoNex

My neighbor's boy has lifted his father's shotgun and stolen. Snowy Egret. Bruce Weigl. UrbNat

My Neighbor's Child Cries in the Middle of the Night. Kung Tzu-chen. SuSp, *tr. by* Wu-Chi Liu

My Neighbor's Reply. *Unknown.* PoToHe

My neighbor's rooster hops the stick i throw. Marlene Mountain. HA

My Neighbor's Roses. Abraham L. Gruber. PoToHe

My neighbor's willow sways its frail. Willow, The. Tu Fu. OHPC, *tr. by* Kenneth Rexroth

My neighbor to the East has. Rain in the Aspens. Su Tung-p'o (Su Shih). OHPC, *tr. by* Kenneth Rexroth

My Neighbor to the South, the Office Clerk Hsiao, Came in the Evening to Say Good-bye. Harry Mathews. CoBCP, *tr. by* Burton Watson

My Neighborhood. Stuart Dybek. PBCAP

My neighbors on the right. Next Door. Mei Yao Ch'en. OHPC, *tr. by* Kenneth Rexroth

My neighbour, Mrs Fanshaw, is portly-plump and gay. Stately as a Galleon. Joyce Grenfell. OBCoV

My nephew, who is six years old, is called 'Tortoise." Children. Po Chü-i. ChiP, *tr. by* Arthur Waley

My New Angels. Sinéad Morrissey. MFPA

My new grad-school roommates and I are attending. Dear Derrida. David Kirby. BAP-01

My new neighbors keep asking, are you. Settled In. Michael David Madonick. IllVoic

My new Province is a land of bamboo-groves. Eating Bamboo-Shoots. Po Chü-i. ChiP; OBVE, *tr. by* Arthur Waley

My New Rabbit. Elizabeth Gould. OTCP

My newly rented home commands a view of the temple hall. Solitary Falcon above the Buddha Hall of the Monastery of Universal Purity, A. Mei Yao Ch'en. SuSp; WoPoe, *tr. by* Jonathan Chaves

My next bite is my last. On the Venom Farm. Ruth Padel. EmeKit

My night awake. Muriel Rukeyser. AWTN *Fr.* Speed of Darkness, The.

My Night with Federico García Lorca (As Told by Edouard Roditi). Jaime Manrique. WiU

My Nightingale. Boris Petrovich Kornilov. TCRP, *tr. by* Bernard Meares

My noble, lovely, little Peggy. Letter to the Honourable Lady Miss Margaret Cavendish Holles-Harley, A. Matthew Prior. NOEC; NoAM; OxBC; OxBSP

My noontime nap. Issa. SoOfWa, *tr. by* Sam Hamill

My normal dwelling is the lungs of swine. Autobiography of a Lungworm. Roy Fuller. NoAM; OxBC

My northern pines are good enough for me. Boston. Edwin Arlington Robinson. APN-2

My nose cuts the air. Life-Saving Medal. Philippe Soupault. PFTM-1

My nosegays are for Captives. Emily Dickinson. NCAP

My November Guest. Robert Frost. OxBA

My Number. Sandra Alcosser. ExTi

My number is small. A hundred pounds of water. My Number. Sandra Alcosser. ExTi

My Observation at Sea. Mildmay Fane, 2d Earl of Westmorland. BeJo

My obsession. (LL) Documentary. Claribel Alegría. LoL; VCWP

My old body. Kiba. JDP, *tr. by* Yoel Hoffmann

My Old Cat. Hal Summers. OxBTC

(My old cat is dead.) KaS

My old companion! and my friend! To My Worthy Friend, Mr. James Bayley. Nicholas Noyes. SCAP

My old desire to live in the Southern Village. Moving House. Ch'ien T'ao. ChiP, *tr. by* Arthur Waley

My old druid, winter. Heart. Dieter Weslowski. InvLad

My Old Flame. Sam Coslow. ReLy

My old flame, my wife! Old Flame, The. Robert Lowell. BoLoP; NOBA; NoAM; PAI

My old friend, going west, bids farewell at Yellow Crane Terrace. Seeing Meng Hao-jan Off to Kuang-ling. Li Po. SuSp, *tr. by* Paul W. Kroll

My old friend prepares chicken and millet. Stopping at a Friend's Farm. Meng Hao Jan. SuSp, *tr. by* Daniel Bryant

My old friend takes leave of the west at Yellow Crane Tower. At Yellow Crane Tower Taking Leave of Meng Hao-jan. Li Po. CoBCP, *tr. by* Burton Watson

My old friend takes off from the Yellow Crane Tower. To See Meng Hao-Jan Off to Yang-Chou. Li Po. ChinPo, *tr. by* Yip Wai-lim

My Old Kentucky Home[, Good Night!]. Stephen Collins Foster. APN-2

(My Old Kentucky Home.) FaBoA

My old lady died. Kitchen Door Blues. Tennessee Williams. OBAL

My Old Letters. Horatius Bonar.

"Evening brings all home, The. For that we wait." SacPr

My Old Man. Charles Bukowski. PmAP

My old man's a white old man. Cross. Langston Hughes. ColAP; GT; HarvBoo; NoP-4; SAmP; SoSe-8; TAP

My old man's ears. Buson. EH, *tr. by* Robert Hass

My Old Man's Small. Fêng Mêng-lung. ColAnChi; WoPoe, *tr. by* Richard W. Bodman *Fr.* Mountain Songs.

My old man's small, shriveled and shrunk. Fêng Mêng-lung. ColAnChi; WoPoe, *tr. by* Richard W. Bodman *Fr.* Mountain Songs.

My old men are dying. Boris Abramovich Slutsky [or Slutskii]. TCRusP, *tr. by* Daniel Weissbort

My old Mistiss promise me. Promises of Freedom. *Unknown.* BPo

My Old Palette. Christopher Pearse Cranch. APN-1

My Old Straw Hat. Eliza Cook. BrRo

My old thighs / How thin. Shiseki. ZenPo, *tr. by* Takashi Ikemoto and Lucien Stryk

My old time daddy. Lover's Return. Langston Hughes. SAmP

My old village lies. Issa. SoOfWa, *tr. by* Sam Hamill

My old Welsh neighbor over the way. Robin, The. John Greenleaf Whittier. OWoS

My ole man took me to the fulton fish market. Knees of a Natural Man. Henry Dumas. GT

My ole Mistiss promise me. Promises of Freedom. *Unknown.* NAAAL

My once dear love; hapless that I no more. Surrender, The. Henry King, Bishop of Chichester. BoLoP; EBEV; NOSC

My One. Heather McHugh. BAP-01

My one blood-uncle laughs. Three Men in a Tent. Marilyn Nelson Waniek. ESEAA

My one puny hut leads right off to the slopes. Distant View from a Grass Hill. Gensei. WoPoe, tr. by Burton Watson

My one wish. Kibai. JDP, tr. by Yoel Hoffmann

My only hope against. Naito Meisetsu. JDP, tr. by Yoel Hoffmann

My only love was dead. (LL) In the Mile End Road. Amy Levy. PEW; RACG; ViWPN

My only son, more God's than mine. Jesus and His Mother. Thom Gunn. OxBC

My Opinion. Charles Sackville, 6th Earl of Dorset. BASC

My Orcha'd in Linden Lea. William Barnes. EBVV; FaBoVe; NOBVV; NPeEn; OxBEV

My outspread hands. Hands. Rin Ishigaki. WoPoe, tr. by Naoshi Koriyama and Edward Lueders

My own Araminta, say 'No!' (LL) Letter of Advice, A. Winthrop Mackworth Praed. NOBL; OxBoLi; PeLV

My own Beloved, who hast lifted me. Elizabeth Barrett Browning. CenSon Fr. Sonnets from the Portuguese.

My own dark head (my own, my own). *Unknown.* NOIV

My own darling. Eibhlin Dubh O'Connell. WoPoe, tr. by Patrick Galvin Fr. Death of Art O'Leary, The.

My own dim life should teach me this. Tennyson. FHYEP; NAEL-6v2 Fr. In Memoriam A. H. H.

My Own Epitaph. Mary Chandler. ECWP

My Own Epitaph. John Gay. FaBoEE; NIL-7; NIP-4; NOEC; NPeEn; OxBEV; PeLV

(Life is a jest.) CABP

My Own Fate. Lionel Pigot Johnson. SacPr

My own flesh and blood. Sophocles. NAWM-5v1

My own heart let me have. More pity on. Nell Altizer. FFC Fr. ("Love Letters to Her Who Lives [Alas!] Away.")

My Own Heart Let Me More Have Pity On. Gerard Manley Hopkins. FaBoMo; MoBrPo; NOBVV; NoP-4; TOF

My own in a foreign land. Jewish Conscript, The. Florence Kiper Frank. TrJP

My Own Little Piece of Hollywood. James Harms. AmPoNex

My own Maria!—Ah my own—my own! Maniac, The. Mary Bryan. CenSon

My own mind is very hard to me. Carrying My Mind Around. *Tlingit Oral Tradition.* TCAPo

My own wish. Yoel Hoffman. JDP, tr. by Yoel Hoffmann

My Ox Duke. John Dyer. NOEC; NPeEn

My Packard Bell was set up in the vacant lot near the stump. Campaign, The. Josephine Miles. WPE

My pain[e], still smothered [or smother'd] in my grieved bre[a]st. Mary Sidney Wroth, Countess of Montgomery. NAEL-6v1; NAEL-7v1; NOSC; PEW Fr. Pamphilia to Amphilanthus.

My papa knows you, and he says you're a man who makes reading for / books. Miss Edith's Modest Request. Bret Harte. NOxBChV

My Papa's Waltz. Theodore Roethke. APT-2; AmFaPo; ClHu; ColAP; HAP; HCAP; HeIP-4; InPK-6; LCAP-2; NAAL-2v2; NAAL-5; NBLV; NIL-7; NIP-4; NOBA; NOxBChV; NoAM; NoP-4; PAI; PoE; PoPoPo; RaBo; TAP; TFi; TRP; VGW

(Whisky on your breath, The.) ChAP

My Parents. Stephen Spender. HarvBoo

My parents felt those rumblings. Hongo Store 29 Miles Volcano Hilo, Hawaii, The. Garrett Kaoru Hongo. PoPoPo

My parents had teased that if I ever caught a fish I'd take it to bed. James McMichael. GeoHom Fr. Each in a Place Apart.

My Parents, Know It Well. Carlos German Belli. TCLAP, tr. by Maureen Ahern and David Tipton

My parents' papers lie pound me. Protected Species. Susan Wicks. MFPA

My parents were fish. Digging in the Streets of Gold. Barry Seiler. UnSA

My parents were married the year. 1945. Leslie Ullman. ExTi

My Paris is a land where twilight days. Paris. Arthur Symons. NOBVV

My passion is as mustard strong. New Song of New Similies, A. John Gay. NOBL

My passion is full of seeds issuing secretly from heraclitus and nietzsche. "Adonis" [or "Adunis"]. PFTM-2, tr. by Allen Hibbard and Osama Isber Fr. Desire Moving through the Maps of the Material.

My passion is like turbulence at the head of waters. *Unknown.* BoWoP

My Past. Dennis Cooper. GLP

My patent pardouns ye may see. Sir David Lindsay [or Lyndsay]. OBSV Fr. Ane Satire [or Satyre] of the Three [or Thrie] Estaitis.

My patron has truly opened up my eyes. What Really Goes on in the College of Cardinals. *Unknown.* CAGL, tr. by James J. Wilhelm

My Peggy is a young thing. Allan Ramsay. OxBS; SCGP Fr. Gentle Shepherd, The.

My Pen. Tom Pickard. Oth

My Pen. Sir Thomas Wyatt. SCGP

My pen, take pain a little space. My Pen. Sir Thomas Wyatt. SCGP

My pensive Public, wherefore look you sad? Playhouse Musings. James Smith. OxAEP-2

My pensive Sara! thy soft cheek reclined [or reclin'd]. Samuel Taylor Coleridge. FHYEP; NAEL-5v2; NAEL-6v2; NOBRP; NPeEn Fr. Effusions.

My People. Langston Hughes. APT-2; NOxBChV

My People. Else Lasker-Schüler. See Rock Crumbles, The

My People. Else Lasker-Schüler. WPOW, tr. by Michael Hamburger

My People Are Destroyed for Lack of Knowledge. Jones Very. ChIV-1

My people have married me. Lament of Hsi-chün. Hsi-chün. BoWoP; ChiP, tr. by Arthur Waley

My people? Who are they? Who Are My People? Rosa Zagnoni Marinoni. PoToHe

My perennial nest. (LL) Emily Dickinson. HeIP-4; PoBW

My perfume? *Unknown.* ColAnChi, tr. by Jeanne Larsen Fr. Midnight Songs.

My period had come for Prayer. Emily Dickinson. APN-2; BBASP

My Philosophy of Life. John Ashbery. BodElec

My Photograph. Vadim Konstantinovich Strelchenko. TCRP, tr. by Lubov Yakovleva

My photograph already looks historic. Middle of a War, The. Roy Fuller. OBWP; PoWW

My Picture-Gallery. Walt Whitman. NAAL-2v1; NAAL-3

My Picture Left in Scotland. Ben Jonson. BeJo; NAEL-5v1; NAEL-6v1; NAEL-7v1; NPeEn

(I now thinke, Love is rather deafe, then blind.) PBRV

My pictures blacken in their frames. Death of the Day. Walter Savage Landor. NoP-4

My place is on Cold Mountain. Han-shan. GifTon, tr. by Red Pine

My "place of clear water." Anahorish. Seamus Heaney. HarvBoo; PBCIP

My Plan. Marchette Chute. WHSW

My plate's empty. (LL) Mother Goose. LB; OxNR; ReMoGo

My Playmate. Mary I. Osborn. OTCP

My Playmate. John Greenleaf Whittier. APN-1; NOBA

My pleasant home! where erst when sad and faint. Charles Lloyd. CenSon

My Poem. Nikki Giovanni. BPo; NBV

My poem's in the oven where it. Kris Hemensley. BMAP Fr. Mile from Poetry, A.

My poem would eat nothing. Poem You Asked For, The. Larry Levis. PBCAP

My poet, thou canst touch on all the notes. Elizabeth Barrett Browning. BrRo; CenSon Fr. Sonnets from the Portuguese.

My Poetry. Lajos Kassák. IQMS, tr. by Adam Makkai

My poetry, an imperfect metaphor of life! (LL) On Being a Poet in Sierra Leone. Syl Cheney-Coker. HBAPE; PBMAP

My poetry is exacting a confession. Manifesto on Ars Poetica. Frank Mkalawile Chipasula. HBAPE; NAfrP

My poetry will not be. Sandro Penna. CAGL, tr. by John McRae

My Poker Girl. Tom Masson. OBAL

My poor body is alas unworthy. Ch'in Chia's Wife's Reply. Ch'in Chia. BoWoP; ChiP, tr. by Arthur Waley

My poor expecting Heart beats for thy Breast. To My Heavenly Charmer. Martha Sansom. LW

My Portion. Dániel Berzsenyi. IQMS, tr. by Peter Zollman

My Portion is Defeat—today. Emily Dickinson. APN-2; FaBoWar; OBWP

My Portrait. Moyshe-Leyb [or Moishe-Leib or Leyb] Halpern. TrJP, tr. by Joseph Leftwich

My precious heart, my handsome soldier son. To My Soldier Son. Zseni Várnai. IQMS, tr. by Peter Zollman

My precious life I spent considering. Sadi [or Saadi or Sa'di]. AWP, tr. by L. Cranmer-Byng Fr. Gulistan, The.

My Pretty Rose-Tree. William Blake. BoLoP; FHYEP; NAEL-5v2; NAEL-6v2; NOBRP Fr. Songs of Experience.

My prime of youth is but a frost of cares. Tichborne's Elegy. Chidiock Tichborne [or Tichbourne]. AmFaPo; HAP; HeIP-4; NoP-4; NoSic; PoPoPo; TFi

My puberty tree swayed big, saw-edged leaves. Puberty Tree, The. D. M. Thomas. TOF

My pulse beats fire—my pericranium glows. William Tennant. NePenScot *Fr.* Anster Fair.

My pulses rushed, and, quick, to saddle! Meeting, the Departure, The. Goethe. STV, *tr. by* John Frederick Nims

My purple petunias. (LL) Revolutionary Petunias. Alice Walker. BlSi; NIL-7

My purpose is to tell my own true tale. Seafarer, The. *Unknown.* EBEV, *tr. by* John Wain

My purpose was purely corrective. Limerick. Leslie Johnson. PeLi

My Purse. *Unknown.* EBEV

My Queen her sceptre did lay down. Regina. Mary Elizabeth Coleridge. NALW; PoBW

My Queen, the air has burst in flame. Hackney Coach, The. Endre Ady. IQMS, *tr. by* Anton N. Nyerges

My quiet kin, must I affront you. Preliminary to Classroom Lecture. Josephine Miles. NoAM

My quiet prison guards, much tried. My beloved. Pictures of the Jews. Haim [*or* Chaim *or* Khayim] Guri [*or* Gouri]. MHP, *tr. by* Ruth Finer Mintz

My quietness has a man in it, he is transparent. In Memory of My Feelings. Frank O'Hara. APSN; ColAP; HarvBoo; NAAL-2v2; NeAP; PoM

My quill is charged with fire. Song of Hate. Jacob ben David Frances. TrJP, *tr. by* A. B. Rhine

My quirt dangles freely. Departing in Early Morning. Tu Mu. CrYelRi, *tr. by* Sam Hamill

My Ratclif [*or* Ratcliffe], when the retchlesse [*or* retchless *or* rechless] youth offendes. Exhortation to Learn of Others' Trouble. Henry Howard, Earl of Surrey. FaBoEE

My reckless race is run, green youth and pride be past, Gloze upon This Text, *Dominus iis opus habet*, A. George Gascoigne. ChIV-2

My reflection. Ray A. Young Bear. STP

My relatives are dead. As for my friends. Silence. René Maran. NegPo, *tr. by* Ellen Conroy Kennedy

My Religion. Anne Carson. BodElec *Fr.* Truth about God, The.

My religion makes no sense. Anne Carson. BodElec *Fr.* Truth about God, The.

My rent His Son should pay if I believed. (LL) My Country Audit. Mildmay Fane, 2d Earl of Westmorland. BeJo; NOSC

My report is not of schools. Return from Luluabourg. Michael Jackson. PeNZ

My Revolution. Rosario Morales. PueRic

My revolution is not starched and ironed. My Revolution. Rosario Morales. PueRic

My Rich Uncle, Whom I Only Met Three Times. Marge Piercy. UnSA

My rifle cocked, in savage calm. Hunter's Song at Nightfall, The. Goethe. STV, *tr. by* John Frederick Nims

My Right Hand Don't Leave Me No More. Carter Revard. HATNAP

My Rights. "Susan Coolidge." SWaP

My Ringless Fingers on the Steering Wheel Tell the Story. Laura Boss. UnSA

My Rival. Rudyard Kipling. OxBTC

My Rival's House. Liz Lochhead. EmeKit

My rod is made of fine bamboo. Angling. *Unknown.* WoPoe, *tr. by* Nguyen Ngoc Bich

My Romance. Richard Rodgers. ReLy

My Room. Marceline Desbordes-Valmore. WoPoe, *tr. by* Edmund Charles Blunden

My Room at Aunt Eura's, 1937. Wilma Elizabeth McDaniel. GeoHom

My room has two doors. Window, The. Kay Sage. SurWo

My room is blue, the carpet's blue. Blue Room, The. Richard Edwards [*or* Edwardes]. Spl

My room is so small. Leah Goldberg. BoWoP *Fr.* Nameless Journey.

My room's a square and candle-lighted boat. Country Bedroom, The. Frances Darwin Cornford. MoBrPo

My room's bigger than a coffin. On Saint-Urbain Street. Milton Acorn. NOBC

My Russia, mine! Yury [*or* Iurii] Mikhailovich Kublanovsky [*or* Kublanovskij]. TCRP

My Sad Captains. Thom Gunn. FaBoMo; NAEL-5v2; NAEL-6v2; NPeEn; NoAM; NoP-4; PoPoPo

My Sad Self. Allen Ginsberg. UnPo; VCAP

My Sadness Sits around Me. June Jordan. BPo

My Saigon daughter I saw only once. Black Soldier Remembers, A. Horace Coleman. CDa

My sails by tempest riven. Kenless Strand, The. Sydney Goodsir Smith. WoPoe

My Savior, let me hear Thy voice tonight. I'll Follow Thee. Clara Ann Thompson. CBWP-2

My sculptor husband, when he *was* mine, possessed. Bride of Quietness, The. Kelly Cherry. FFC

My second daughter, I loved her so much! Seeing Flowers I Remember My Late Daughter, Shu. Kao Ch'i. CoBLCP, *tr. by* Jonathan Chaves

My Second Marriage to My First Husband. Alice Fulton. EmeKit

My secrets cry aloud. Open House. Theodore Roethke. NOBA; NoAM

My self to die, and prove mine owne. (LL) Garden, The. James Shirley. BeJo; NOSC

(My selves dissolving, old whore petticoats)——— / To Paradise. (LL) Fever 103°. Sylvia Plath. FaBoWP; NOBA; NoAM; VCAP; VGW

My servant wakes at break of dawn. Rough Ridge. Yüan Mei. CoBLCP, *tr. by* Jonathan Chaves

My Servant Wakes Me. Po Chü-i. ChiP, *tr. by* Arthur Waley

My servant wakes me: "Master, it is broad day." My Servant Wakes Me. Po Chü-i. ChiP, *tr. by* Arthur Waley

My seven sons came back from Indonesia. Homecoming. Peter Viereck. CoAP

My seventy years—a withered. Daibai. JDP, *tr. by* Yoel Hoffmann

My Shadow. W. Hodgson Burnett. UV

My Shadow. Robert Louis Stevenson. ChAP; ITBLP; OTCP; PWR; UV

My Shadow's Stature. John James Piatt. APN-2

My shag-hair Cyclops, come, lets ply. John Lyly. EBEV *Fr.* Sapho and Phao.

My shame in this world. Shokei. JDP, *tr. by* Yoel Hoffmann

My shattered phancy stole away from mee. Edward Taylor. NOSC; SCAP *Fr.* Preparatory Meditations before My Approach to the Lord's Supper.

My Sheep Are Thoughts. Sir Philip Sidney. NoSic *Fr.* Arcadia.

My sheep are thoughts, which I both guide and serve. Sir Philip Sidney. NoSic *Fr.* Arcadia.

My Shepherd. Heather McHugh. Unle

My Shepherd Is the Living Lord. Thomas Sternhold. AH

My Shifting ground from season. Blue Crest of Fondness. Unsi Al-Haj [*or* Hajj]. MAP, *tr. by* Sargon Boulus and Alistair Elliot

My Shining Archipelago. Talvikki Ansel. NeAmPo

My Shining Hour. Johnny Mercer. ReLy

My Ship. Kurt Weill. ReLy

My Ship Does Not Need a Helmsman. Alan Chong Lau. OpBo

My ship has sails that are made of silk. My Ship. Kurt Weill. ReLy

My ship is sinking. Sunken Ship, The. Salma Khadra Jayyusi. PoArWo, *tr. by* Suneet Chopra

My ship laden with forgetfulness passes through a harsh sea, at. Petrarch. NAWM-7v1, *tr. by* Robert M. Durling *Fr.* Sonnets to Laura.

My shirt got torn to rags. Géza Páskándi. IQMS, *tr. by* Agnes Arany-Makkai *Fr.* Language Memory.

My shirt is a token and symbol. Shirt. Carl Sandburg. CA

My Shoes. Charles Simic. CoAP; EmeKit; HCAP; VCAP

My shoes are almost dead. Caesar. W. S. Merwin. LCAP-2

My shoes are red. Red. Jean Yamasaki Toyama. FSt

My shoes. / I have just taken them off. 17. IV. 71. Paul Blackburn. PoM

My shoulders prick, as though they were half-fledged. (LL) Field-Glasses. Andrew Young. GTBS-P; RB

My shrink told me it was unnatural to be. Invisible History. Walta Borawski. GLP

My sickness lingers; I part from this world. Yayu. JDP, *tr. by* Yoel Hoffmann

My silks and fine array. Song. William Blake. RACG; SCGP

My sin! my sin, my God, these cursed dregs. Edward Taylor. SCAP; TCAPo *Fr.* Preparatory Meditations before My Approach to the Lord's Supper.

My sins in their completeness. Mael Isu O Brolchain. NOIV

My Sister. Muhammad Al-Ghuzzi. MAP, *tr. by* John Heath-Stubbs and May Jayyusi

My Sister. Sisters. Wendy Cope. ItWoWo

My Sister. Abba Kovner. TOF, *tr. by* T. Carmi

My Sister. Alfonsina Storni. BoWoP, *tr. by* Aliki and Willis Barnstone

My sister and I used to play this game called Red Hot. Red Hot. Laurie Anderson. OxWW

My sister, between us lie. To Rose. Roberta Hill. ReEnLa

My sister comes from. Student, The. Shauqi Abi Shaqra. MAP, *tr. by* Sargon Boulus and Peter Porter

My sister comes, quietly. Blanco. Gary Soto. GeoHom

My sister doesn't write poems. In Praise of My Sister. Wislawa Szymborska. PoSu

My sister got me the script. I couldn't. Sanctuary. Norman Dubie. BodElec

My sister in her well-tailored silk blouse hands me. Photos, The. Diane Wakoski. NIP-4

My Sister Laura. Spike Milligan. NTCP

My sister Laura's bigger than me. My Sister Laura. Spike Milligan. NTCP

My sister loved milkweed, flower and plant. Weed, The. Genevieve Taggard. APT-2

My sister, my child. Invitation to the Voyage. Charles Baudelaire. SxFrPo, *tr. by* James McGowan

My sister! my sweet sister! if a name. Epistle to Augusta. Byron. FHYEP

My sister rises from our bed hours before dawn. Listen Carefully. Philip Levine. EmeKit

My sister rubs the doll's face in mud. Kid, The. Ai. GT; NoAM

My Sister's Letter. Bogomil Gjuzel. CarOv, *tr. by* Carolyn Kizer

My Sister's Sleep. Dante Gabriel Rossetti. NAEL-5v2; NAEL-6v2

My sister singing the Kyrie. Near Burning. Kathleen Peirce. PBCAP

My Sister, the Empress. Ileana Malancioui. ItWoWo, *tr. by* Dan Dutescu

My Sisters, O My Sisters. May Sarton. NALW

My six and seventy years are through. Yakuo Tokuken. JDP, *tr. by* Yoel Hoffmann

My skin is pumiced to a fault. Fado Singer. Wole Soyinka. HBAPE

My skin is white, but my name is foreign, a dark inflection. Jewish. Harvey M. Plotnick. OPRER

My skin shimmers with all the colours. Charles Hadfield. NewEx

My skinny horse. Shrine of General Pien, The. Chu Yün-ming. CoBLCP, *tr. by* Jonathan Chaves

My small, my beautiful land, all of a summer. All of a Summer. Jakov [*or* Jacob] Steinberg. FIT, *tr. by* Robert Friend

My smile mocked your speed. Lame Boy Returns, The. Juan Delgado. TouFir

My Sodger Laddie. *Unknown.* FaBoWar

My softness heaves its spiral canopy. Snail. Elisabeth Eybers. PeSAV, *tr. by* Elisabeth Eybers

My Son. Yehuda Amichai [*or* Amikhai]. WoPoe, *tr. by* Benjamin Harshav and Barbara Harshav

My Son. Ruth Stone. WPE

My Son and I. Rosemary Norman. BrRo

My son and I kiss the same woman goodbye. Lies. Christopher Bursk. CDa

My son, come pierce my soul with a sword. Ballad of the Scarecrow Christ. Elder Olson. ChIV-2

My Son, Forsake Your Art. Mahon O'Heffernan. BIrV, *tr. by* Maire Cruise O'Brien

My son had a hard time learning the concept of shadow. At first, to him. Shadow. Josip Novakovich. BAP-97

My son invites me to witness with him. Mousemeal. Howard Nemerov. TwCP

My Son, My Executioner. Donald Hall. LoL; TRP

"My son my son" the Blakean figure mourns and affirms. Brian Coffey. BiHa *Fr.* Advent.

My Son's One-Year Test: Improvised. Wen Cheng-ming. "Smiling, we set the testing tray before the hall." CoBLCP

"My son," / she says. HomeMade Smiles. Jose Angel Figueroa. PueRic

My Son Shows Me a Photograph of Michael Jordan Performing a Slam Dunk. Louis Phillips. ReTh

My son Siôn of Anglesey, I am without flattery. To Siôn Lloyd: the Mother's Advice to Her Heir. Catherin Owen Llwyd. EMWP

My son smells of peace when I lean over him. Two Songs of Peace. Yehuda Amichai [*or* Amikhai]. AF, *tr. by* Assia Gutmann

My son squats in the snow in his blue snowsuit. Illuminations. Louise Glück. HarvBoo; NALW

My son swings from black railings. Sean Dunne. ModIr *Fr.* Sydney Place.

My son tells his aunt. San Diego Poem, A. Simon J. Ortiz. CDW

My son was killed while laughing at some jest. I would I knew. Rudyard Kipling. FaBoEE; NPeEn; PeFWW *Fr.* Epitaphs of the War [1914–1918].

My son wears a nappy. My Son and I. Rosemary Norman. BrRo

My son, where is your soul? And If the Angel Should Ask. Hayyim Nahman [*or* Khaim Nakhman *or* Chaim Nachman] Bialik. MHP, *tr. by* Ruth Finer Mintz

My son, you are a sweet bitter shadow. On Your Twenty-First Birthday. Joan Austin Geier. FFC

My son, you loved telling the story of Prince Nata. T'ang Hsien-tsu. CoBLCP; ColAnChi, *tr. by* Jonathan Chaves *Fr.* Twenty-two Quatrains on Receiving the Obituary Notice for my Son Shih-Chü.

My Song. King D. Kuka. VoR

My Song to the Jewish People. Leib Olitski. TrJP, *tr. by* Jacob Sonntag

My song today is the storm-cock's song. Storm-Cock's Song, The. Hugh MacDiarmid. OxBTC

My Songs Are Poisoned. Heinrich Heine. AWP, *tr. by* Louis Untermeyer

My Sons. Ron Loewinsohn. NeAP

My sorrow, deep sorrow, incessant returning. Metrical Translation of the Song of Macgregor Na Ruara. Anne Grant. RWP

My sorrow, Donncha, my thousand-cherished. Padraig O Heigeartaigh. NOIV

My sorrow that I am not by the little dún. Starling Lake, The. "Seumas O'Sullivan." AWP

My sorrow, when she's here with me. My November Guest. Robert Frost. OxBA

My soul, be not disturbed. Address to My Soul. Elinor Wylie. AWP; OxBA

My Soul before Thee Prostrate Lies. C. F. Richter. AH, *tr. by* John Wesley

My soul, calm sister, towards thy brow, whereon scarce grieves. Sigh. Stéphane Mallarmé. AWP, *tr. by* Arthur Symons

My Soul Counselled Me. Kahlil Gibran. "My soul spoke unto me and counselled me." GraLe, *tr. by* Andrew Ghareeb

My soul doth magnify the Lord. Song of the Virgin Mary, The. Miles Coverdale. ChIV-2

My soul doth pant towards thee. Prayer, A. Jeremy Taylor. SacPr

My soul, dread not the pestilence that hags. Preparations for Victory. Edmund Charles Blunden. PeFWW

My soul from a mother's old Arm-chair. (LL) Old Arm-Chair, The. Eliza Cook. BrRo; InPK-6; VWP

My soul from the nethermost Hell! (LL) Wilderspin. Mary Elizabeth Coleridge. VWP; ViWPN

My soul grieved seven times: the first time when it tried to attain. Seven Stages, The. Kahlil Gibran. BBASP, *tr. by* Michael Beard and Adnan Haydar

My soul has grown deep like the rivers. (LL) Negro Speaks of Rivers, The. Langston Hughes. APT-2; AiP; BPo; ColAP; HAP; HCAP; HarvBoo; HeIP-4; ISC; NAAAL; NAAL-2v2; NAAL-5; NIL-7; NIP-4; NOBA; NoAM; NoP-4; OBCA; PAI; RaBo; SSLK; TAP; TCAPo; TFi; TTY; WeW-3

My Soul in the Bundle of Life. *Unknown.* TrJP, *tr. by* E. Margaret Rowley *Fr.* Dead Sea Scrolls, The.

My soul is a castle, ancient, known to be haunted. Lady of the White Castle, The. Endre Ady. IQMS, *tr. by* Dermot Spence and Paul Tabori

My soul is a dark ploughed field. Broken Field, The. Sara Teasdale. APT-1

My soul is awakened, my spirit is soaring. Lines Composed in a Wood on a Windy Day. Anne Brontë. EBVV

My soul is clanging like a cimbalom gone mad. Reply to Petőfi. János Arany. IQMS, *tr. by* Madeline Mason

My soul is an enchanted boat. Shelley. FHYEP *Fr.* Prometheus Unbound [A Lyrical Drama in Four Acts].

My soul is hard as stone. I slept with the wind. Crust on Fresh Snow. Rolf Jacobsen. WoPoe, *tr. by* Olav Grinde

My soul is like the oar that momently. Struggle. Sidney Lanier. OxBA

My Soul is like to a little painful Bee. Spiritual Meditation upon a Bee, A. Amey Hayward. EMWP

My soul is not at rest. There comes a strange. Nathan Brown. SacPr

My soul is the veil of his love. Hafiz [*or* Hafez]. TOF

My soul looked down from a vague height, with Death. Show, The. Wilfred Owen. MoBrPo; OBWVE; OxBEV; OxBTC; PeFWW

My soul looks over the courtyard. Early in the Morning. Jules Supervielle. MFP, *tr. by* Martin Sorrell

My soul magnifies the Lord. Bible, *N.T.* BoWoP *Fr.* St. Luke.

My soul, oh keep it by Thy Word. (LL) Three Enemies, The. Christina Georgina Rossetti. SacPr; TrCP

My soul parted from me last night. Elegy on Mael Mhedha, His Wife. Muireadhach Albanach Ó Dálaigh. NePenScot, *tr. by* Thomas Owen Clancy

My soul's an atom in the world of mind. Metaphysical Sonnet. Charles Lloyd. CenSon

My Soul's Wardrobe. Sharon Dolin. PoCoUp

My soul shall spurn them evermore. (LL) Holy Office, The. James Joyce. FaBoTw; NoAM; OxBTC

My Soul Sinks. Hayyim Nahman [*or* Khaim Nakhman *or* Chaim Nachman] Bialik. FIT, *tr. by* Robert Friend

My soul, sit thou a patient looker-on. Epigram. Francis Quarles. NOBE; PoToHe

My soul spoke unto me and counselled me. Kahlil Gibran. GraLe, *tr. by* Andrew Ghareeb *Fr.* My Soul Counselled Me.

My soul stands at the window of my room. Nostalgia. Karl Shapiro. CoAP; TrJP; TwCP

My soul surcharged with grief now loud complains. Sonnet. Rachel [*or* Rahel] Morpurgo. TrJP, *tr. by* Nina Davis Salaman

My Soul, there is a country [*or* countrie]. Peace. Henry Vaughan. AWP; EBEV; ESCV; FSCP; FaBoCh; GeHe; HAP; NOBE; NOCV; OBEV; OxAEP-1; OxBEV; PoE; SCGP; TFi; TOF; TrCP; WeW-3

My Soul Thirsteth for God. William Cowper. TrCP *Fr.* Olney Hymns.

My soul . . . , turn we to survey. Oliver Goldsmith. FHYEP *Fr.* Travel[l]er; or, A Prospect of Society, The.

My soul was mantled with dark shadows born. Despondency and Aspiration. Felicia Dorothea Hemans. RWP

My Soul, Weigh Not Thy Life. Leonard Swain. AH

My soul, what's lighter than a feather? Wind. Francis Quarles. FaBoEE

My Soul Would Fain Indulge a Hope. Joseph Steward. AH

My soul would sing of metamorphoses. Ovid. NAWM-7v1, *tr. by* Allen Mandelbaum *Fr.* Metamorphoses.

My soule a world is by Contraccion. William Alabaster. ESCV *Fr.* Divine Meditations.

My soul[e] I'll [*or* Ile] pour[e] into thee. (LL)   Night-Piece, to Julia, The. Robert Herrick.   BeJo; CaPo; NAEL-5v1; NAEL-6v1; NAEL-7v1; NOSC; OBEV; PoE; PoRA; SCGP; TFi

My Soule is like a Bird; my Flesh, the Cage.   Francis Quarles.   ESCV   *Fr.* Emblems.

My spading fork turning the earth turns.   Earthworm.   Robert Francis.   APT-2

My Spanish isn't enough.   Elena.   Pat Mora.   NIL-7; UnSA

My Special Friend (Is Back in Town).   J. C. Johnson.   ReLy

My Special Madness.   Rikki Ducornet.   SurWo

My specialty is living said.   E. E. Cummings.   NOBA

My Spirit.   Thomas Traherne.   GeHe

My spirit and flesh, parting now.   At the End.   Richard Ryan.   PBCIP

My spirit is too weak—mortality.   On Seeing the Elgin Marbles.   John Keats.   CenSon; GSo; NAEL-5v2; NAEL-6v2; NIL-7; NIP-4

My spirit leans in joyousness tow'rd thine.   Lines.   "Ada" (Sarah Louisa Forten).   BlSi

My spirit leans in joyousness tow'rd thine.   "Ada" (Sarah Louisa Forten).   *See* My spirit leans in joyousness tow'rd thine

My Spirit Longeth for Thee.   John Byrom.   NOBE; SacPr   (Desiderium.)   OxAEP-1

My spirit loves with thine in peace to dwell. (LL)   Prayer, The.   Jones Very.   APN-1; OxBA; TrCP

My Spirit's Complement.   Henrietta Cordelia Ray.   CBWP-3   (Thy life hath touched the edges of my life.)   TCAPo

My Spirit Will Not Haunt the Mound.   Thomas Hardy.   FaBoVe; MoBrPo

My spotless love hovers, with purest wings.   Samuel Daniel.   OBEV   *Fr.* To Delia.

My spouse, Chunaychunay.   *Unknown.*   BoWoP

My spring is just this.   Issa.   SoOfWa, *tr. by* Sam Hamill

My Spring Thing.   Everett Hoagland.   BPo

My Springs.   Sidney Lanier.   UnPo

My star, start-gazing?—If only I could be.   Aster.   Plato.   GrAn, *tr. by* Peter Jay

My Stars.   Abraham Ibn Ezra.   WoPoe, *tr. by* Robert Mezey

My steadfast love!   Eibhlin Dubh O'Connell.   NOIV   *Fr.* Lament for Art O Laoghaire, The.

My Stearine Candles.   James Henry.   NOBVV

My steps along this street.   Here.   Octavio Paz.   TCLAP, *tr. by* Charles Tomlinson

My steps lead me to a junction of three roads.   Juan Chi.   ColAnChi   *Fr.* Songs of My Soul.

My stick fingers click with a snicker.   Player Piano.   John Updike.   WeW-3

My stock has gone down and my tailor has sent.   Companion's Progress, A.   Paul Laurence Dunbar.   GT

My stock lies dead, and no increase.   Grace.   George Herbert.   ChIV-1; GeHe

My stomach is of many minds.   Stomach.   Kathleen Norris.   OBAL

My Story.   Carla Harryman.   PmAP

My story is much too sad to be told.   Cole Porter.   *See* Until the day

My story would have been longer. (LL)   Mother Goose.   OxNR; ReMoGo; Spl

My story would have been longer. (LL)   There Was a King.   *Unknown.*   NBLV; OxBoLi

My Strawberry.   Helen Hunt Jackson.   SWaP

My straying thoughts, reduced stay.   Song.   Anne Collins.   WPE

My student says he wrote a poem.   Office Hour.   Carol Lem.   GeoHom

My students look at me expectantly.   Mountain, The.   Louise Glück.   NoAM

My summer robes.   Basho.   EH, *tr. by* Robert Hass

My sunlight came pre-packaged.   Nomen.   Naomi Long Madgett.   BlSi

My supermarket is bigger than your supermarket. That's.   Supermarket.   Peter Meinke.   PBCAP

My sweet, beloved companion.   Litany.   Margit Kaffka.   IQMS, *tr. by* Paul Tabori

My sweet did sweetly sleep.   Stolen Pleasure.   William Drummond, of Hawthornden.   EnLoPo

My sweet-faced, tattle-tale brother was born blind.   Twins, The.   Mona Van Duyn.   VCAP

My Sweet Gazelle!   Immanuel di Roma.   TrJP

My sweet old etcetera.   E. E. Cummings.   HeIP-4; OBAL; OBWP; OxBA; PAI; PeFWW

My sweetest Elpis.   Letter from Ephesos.   Rufinus.   GrAn, *tr. by* Alan Marshfield

My Sweetest Lesbia.   Catullus.   NAEL-6v1; NAEL-7v1; NPeEn; NoP-4, *tr. by* Thomas Campion

My sweetest Lesbia, let us live and love.   Catullus.   *See* Lesbia / live with me

My Sweetest Lesbia [Let Us Live and Love].   Catullus.   *See* Carmina

My Sweetheart's Dainty Lips.   Judah Halevi.   TrJP, *tr. by* Emma Lazarus

My swirling wants. Your frozen lips.   Valediction Forbidding Mourning, A.   Adrienne Rich.   NAAL-2v2; NAAL-5; NoAM; NoP-4

My sword at my waist, I climb a high tower.   Li Po.   ColAnChi, *tr. by* Victor H. Mair   *Fr.* Poems in an Old Style.

My sword I shook.   Sword, The.   Abu Bakr.   TTY, *tr. by* A. J. Arberry

My sword leans against the sky.   Shumpo Soki.   JDP, *tr. by* Yoel Hoffmann

My symptoms have become bizarre. As the silver liquid is drained from my.   Dear, I Love.   Todd Colby.   HeMarv

My tailor is against parting.   Against Parting.   Natan Zach.   HP; PoSu

My Task.   Maude Louise Ray.   PWR

My Taste for Trash.   Chase Twichell.   ExTi

My taste in women, Flaccus? Give me one.   Martial.   RomPo, *tr. by* Peter Whigham

My Tattoo.   Mark Doty.   WiU

My tea is nearly ready and the sun has left the sky.   Lamplighter, The.   Robert Louis Stevenson.   EBVV; ITBLP; NePenScot

My teachers are dead men. I was too young.   Autopsy.   Arthur Nortje.   HBAPE

My tedious travels and oft-varying fate. (LL)   Michael Drayton.   NOSC; Son   *Fr.* Idea.

My temples throb, my pulses boil.   To Minerva.   Thomas Hood.   NBLV; NOBL; OxBoLi; PeLV

My Tenth Birthday.   Robert Adamson.   BMAP

My thatched hut.   Muso Soseki.   EaWin, *tr. by* W. S. Merwin

My thatched hut's plenty.   Reclusive.   Wang Fan-chih.   CrYelRi, *tr. by* Sam Hamill

My thinning hair.   Lucien Stryk.   IllVoic   *Fr.* Issa: A Suite of Haiku.

My Thirty Years.   Juan Fransico Manzano.   TTY, *tr. by* Oliver Cobarn and Ursula Lehrburger

My thought awaked me with Thy Name.   Meditation on Communion with God.   Judah Halevi.   TrJP, *tr. by* Solomon Solis-Cohen

My thought is caught in the eyes of love.   Entanglement.   Francis Sparshott.   MoCV

My Thought Was on a Maid So Bright.   *Unknown.*   MiEL

My thoughts are as a garden-plot, that knows.   Thy Garden.   Don Allen Johnson.   AWP, *tr. by* Dulcie L. Smith

My Thoughts Are Not Your Thoughts.   Bible, *O.T.*   TrJP   *Fr.* Isaiah.

My thoughts are perfumed when toward you they turn.   Autumn Verses.   "Rubén Dario."   SpanPo, *tr. by* Kate Flores

My thoughts are with a boat.   Kakinomoto no Hitomaro.   TAL

My Thoughts Do Harbour.   William Shakespeare.   CTC   *Fr.* Two Gentlemen of Verona, The.

My thoughts go back to a heavenly dance.   Song Is Ended (But the Melody Lingers On), The.   Irving Berlin.   ReLy

My thoughts hold mortal[l] strife.   Madrigal.   William Drummond, of Hawthornden.   GTBS-P; NOSC; OxBSP

My thoughts impelled me to the resting-place.   Elegy.   Moses Ibn Ezra.   TrJP, *tr. by* Emma Lazarus

My thoughts, like sailors becalmed in Cape Town harbor.   Sailor's Harbor.   Henry Reed.   MoBrPo

My thoughts, my grief! are without strength.   Poem Written in Time of Trouble by an Irish Priest Who Had Taken Orders in France, A.   *Unknown.*   OBMV, *tr. by* Lady Augusta Gregory

My thoughts the guests, which would thereon have fed. (LL)   Edmund Spenser.   NIP-4; OxBSo   *Fr.* Amoretti.

My Thread.   Dovid [*or* David] Hofshteyn [*or* Hofstein].   TrJP, *tr. by* Joseph Leftwich

My three sisters are sitting.   Women.   Adrienne Rich.   TRP

My Three Wives.   *Unknown, after* Etienne Pasquier.   FaBoEE

My throats / a hungry saxophone.   Ohnedaruth.   Angela Jackson.   SeSe

My tidings for you: the stag bells.   Summer Is Gone.   *Unknown.*   FaBoCh, *tr. by* Kuno Meyer

My time he said was not my own.   Private but Sulphurous.   Tom Matthews.   PNI

My Times Are in Thy Hand.   Anna L. Waring.   PWR; SacPr

My Toilette, Patches, all the World, Adieu! (LL)   Lady Mary Wortley Montagu.   BWW; ECWP; NOEC; WPE   *Fr.* Six Town Eclogues.

My tongue is a pink fire.   Word Is an Egg, The.   Niyi Osundare.   NAfrP

My Tongue Paints a Path.   Eugene B. Redmond.   ISC

My tongue paints a path of fire.   My Tongue Paints a Path.   Eugene B. Redmond.   ISC

My tongue-tied Muse in manners holds her still.   William Shakespeare.   Son   *Fr.* Sonnets.

My towers at last!   Herman Melville.   Conrad Potter Aiken.   NoAM; TAP

My towers at last! these rovings end.   Return of the Sire de Nesle A.D. 16, The.   Herman Melville.   NOBA

My townspeople, beyond in the great world.   Gulls.   William Carlos Williams.   OxBA

My trade takes me frequently into decaying houses.   From a Museum Man's Album.   John Hewitt.   OxBTC

My Train.   Barbara Ras.   NAPBL

My traveling provisions are short, and won't see me through. Sufi Quatrain. Rabi'a bint Isma'il of Syria. WPOW, *tr. by* Deirdre Lashgari

My treadmill memory draws from you yet. (LL) Crystals like Blood. Hugh MacDiarmid. HAP; HarvBoo; RB

My Treasure. John Oxenham. SacPr

My trewest tresowre sa trayturly was taken. Song of the Passion, A. Richard Rolle of Hampole. SacPr

My Triumph. John Greenleaf Whittier. APN-1; NOBA

My Triumph lasted till the Drums. Emily Dickinson. APN-2; OBWP

My Trouble. Diane Wakoski. NALW

My trouble / is that I have the spirit of Gertrude Stein. My Trouble. Diane Wakoski. NALW

My true love breathed her latest breath. Murderer, The. Stevie Smith. FaBoWP; OxBSP

My True Love Hath My Heart. Naomi Mitchison. LW

My true love hath my heart and I have hers. Strugnell's Bargain. Wendy Cope. UV

My True Love Hath My Heart and I Have His. Mary Elizabeth Coleridge. BoLoP

My true love hath my heart [*or* hart], and I have his. Sir Philip Sidney. BoLoP; NPeEn; NoSic; OxBEV; PoE; SCGP; TFi; UV *Fr.* Arcadia.

My True Love Hath My Heart and I Have His. Patricia Stockbridge. UV

My true love makes me happy. Beatrice [*or* Beatriz *or* Beatriz], Countess de Die [*or* Dia]. WPOW

My TV Came Down with a Chill. Willard R. Espy. TLR

My twentieth summer I got a job in Door Locks. Assembler. Debra Allbery. PBCAP

My twin brother swears that at age thirteen. Old Testament, The. Philip Levine. TaR

My twin, the nameless one, wild in the woods. John Berryman. HarvBoo *Fr.* Dream Songs.

My Uma has come! Kamalākānta Bhattācārya. SinGod, *tr. by* Rachel Fell McDermott

My uncle, a craftsman of hammers and wood. Willy Lyons. James Wright. . HCAP; NNaP; PoE

My uncle always insisted. Always Throw the First Punch. Miguel Algarin. PueRic

My Uncle in Treblinka. Marie Syrkin. GotH

My uncle is buried at Sheik Bad'r. Luxury. Yehuda Amichai [*or* Amikhai]. PoSu, *tr. by* Assia Gutmann

My Uncle Is My Honor and a Guest in My House. Etheridge Knight. BodElec

My uncle likes me too much. Gwendolyn Brooks. ESEAA *Fr.* Children Going Home.

My uncle, man of science in Berlin. My Uncle in Treblinka. Marie Syrkin. GotH

My Uncle Mohammed at Mecca, 1981. Naomi Shihab Nye. GraLe

My Uncle Paul of Pimlico. Mervyn Laurence Peake. OTCP

My uncle said, "This is Elijah's wine." On the Eve of the Warsaw Uprising. Robin Becker. TaR

My uncle sleeps in the image of death. Lawrence Durrell. FaBoMo *Fr.* Death of General Uncebunke; a Biography in Little, The.

My uncle was Sabbath crazed. Ichthycide. Joe Rosenblatt. NOBC

My Valentine to you. (LL) Valentine. Ernest Hemingway. IllVoic; OBAL

My village / Dragonflies. Buson. ZenPo, *tr. by* Takashi Ikemoto and Lucien Stryk

My Village Home. Lu Yu. CoBCP, *tr. by* Burton Watson

My virgin womb ha'e met. (LL) O Wha's the Bride? Hugh MacDiarmid. GTBS-P; OxBEV; RaBo

My Voice. Rafael Campo. AmPoNex

My Voice. Oscar Wilde. EBVV

My voice drifts to the ceiling, like a stream of incense, filling. I'll Never Know No Sunday in This Weekday Room. Sabah As-Sabah. InTrad

My voice is sweeter than the lute. Siren, The. "Violet Fane." VWP

My voice is the measure of my life. Revolution of the Aged, The. Njabulo S. Ndebele. PeSAV

My voice is thin I stand in the shower what's that I ask. Shower, The. Linda Smukler. GLP

My Voice Not Being Proud. Louise Bogan. APT-2

My voice rings down through thousands of years. Sappho's Reply. Rita Mae Brown. OxWW

My voice to thee it self extreamly strayning. Bible, *O.T.* PBRV, *tr. by* Mary Sidney Herbert, Countess of Pembroke *Fr.* Psalms.

My Vorarlberg. Natalie Beer. AuPH, *tr. by* Lowell A. Bangerter

My Wage. Jessie Belle Rittenhouse. PoToHe

My waiting time is over. I absolve you. Family Secrets. Sharon Kessler. GotH

My walls outside must have some flowers. Truly Great. William Henry Davies. OBMV

My wardrobe door will not stay closed these days. Presence, The. Medbh McGuckian. PNI

My way is from woe to wonder. Near-Johannesburg Boy, The. Gwendolyn Brooks. ESEAA; IllVoic

My way is in the sand flowing. Samuel Beckett. ModIr; NOIV

My wearied bark, O let it now be crowned! To Crown[e] It. Robert Herrick. CaPo

My weary bosom fill. (LL) "Michael Field." VWP; ViWPN

My weary eyes shall close like folding flowers in sleep. (LL) Columbine, The. Jones Very. ColAP; GSo; NOBA

My wedding-ring lies in a basket. Wedding-Ring. Denise Levertov. NIL-7

My wee wee man was clean awa'. (LL) Wee Wee Man, The. *Unknown*. EBEV; ESPB; FaBoCh; OxBB

My well-beloved was stripped. Knowing my whim. Jewels, The. Charles Baudelaire. BoLoP, *tr. by* Roy Campbell

My Welsh Home. John Morgan. AngWePo

My whining lover, what needs all. Against Absence. Sir John Suckling. CaPo; CavPo

My whiskey is / a tough way of life. Drink. William Carlos Williams. OxBA

My white canoe, like the silvery air. Camp of Souls, The. Isabella Valancy Crawford. NOBC

My white coat waits in the corner. Talking to the Family. John A. Stone. BloBone

My white hair of thirty thousand feet. Li Po. SuSp *Fr.* Songs of Ch'iu-p'u.

My whole eye was sunset red. Eye and Tooth. Robert Lowell. NAAL-2v2

My whole family has died. All That Really Happens. Joe Wenderoth. BodElec

My whole life has led me here. Woolworth's. Donald Hall. OBCoV

My whole life long I've sharpened my sword. Dairin Soto. JDP, *tr. by* Yoel Hoffmann

My whole life long? (LL) Night Song at Amalfi. Sara Teasdale. APT-1; MakPoe; MoAmPo

My Wicked Uncle. Derek Mahon. OxBC

My Wicked Wicked Ways. Sandra Cisneros. ItWoWo

My Wife. Nikolai Ivanovich Glazkov. TCRP, *tr. by* Daniel Weissbort

My Wife and Children. Jaan Kaplinski. BLT

My wife and children were waiting for ice cream. My Wife and Children. Jaan Kaplinski. BLT

My wife and I have asked a crowd of craps. Vers de Société. Philip Larkin. PeLV

My wife and I lived all alone. Ballad of the Despairing Husband. Robert Creeley. NeAP; OBAL; RaBo

My wife and I lived [*or* live] all alone. Little Brown Jug. Joseph E. Winner. OBAL

My wife broke a dollar tube of perfume. Problem, The. Paul Blackburn. NeAP

My Wife Complains I Pray No More. Al-Ifriqi al-Mutayyam. ArPe, *tr. by* Omar S. Pound

My wife has left me. The child. Specimen. Christopher Pilling. NLP

My wife is always knitting, knitting. Stitches. Shinkichi Takahashi. ZenPo, *tr. by* Takashi Ikemoto and Lucien Stryk

My wife is ill! Thomas Jefferson. Lorine Niedecker. HarvBoo

My wife is left-handed. For Hettie. Imamu Amiri Baraka. GT; NOBA; NeAP

My Wife Is My Shirt. Stephen Tropp. InPK-6

My wife still asleep. Gary Hotham. HA

My wife went away, left me. Katda. STP

My wife whose hair is a brush fire. Free Union. André Breton. PFTM-1; TTTS

My wife with eyes that are the equal of water and air and earth and fire. (LL) Free Union. André Breton. PFTM-1; TTTS

My wife with the hair of a wood fire. André Breton. *See* My wife whose hair is a brush fire

My window, barely attached by its butterfly hinge. Matinée Idylls. Molly Bendall. AmPoNex

My window, framed in pear-tree bloom. Villeggiature. Edith Nesbit. LW; NOBVV; PEW

My window looks upon a world grown gray. Midwinter. Margaret E. Bruner. PoToHe

My window shook all night in Camden Town. Responsibilities. Anthony Cronin. PBCIP

My window, window. Window, The. Enrique Gonzáles Martínez. TCLAP, *tr. by* Elizabeth Gordon

My windows now are giant drops of dew. Bright Day, A. William Henry Davies. OBWVE

My windows open to the autumn night. Cadgwith. Lionel Pigot Johnson.

My wine you drink, my bread you snap. (LL)   This Bread I Break.   Dylan Thomas.   ChIV-2; FaBoTw; GI; TRP

My Winsome Dear.   Robert Fergusson.   VGW   *Fr.* Leith Races.

My Winter Past.   Eldon Grier.   NOBC

My Wish for My Land.   Randolph Stow.   NOBAu

My wish for my land is that ladies be beautiful.   My Wish for My Land.   Randolph Stow.   NOBAu

My wish for you / that God should make your love.   Rabi'a of Balkh.   WPOW, *tr. by* Deirdre Lashgari

My wives do not write.   Memory.   Michael Hamburger.   OxBTC

My Woman's Transperance.   Amina Said.   HAWP; NAfrP, *tr. by* Eric Sellin

My woman says she'd rather have me.   Catullus.   ErotSp, *tr. by* Sam Hamill

My woman says there is no one whom she'd rather marry.   70.   Catullus.   NAWM-7v1, *tr. by* Charles Martin

My wont is not to write in verse.   Imprisoned Recusant Writes to His Wife, An.   Francis Tregian.   NoSic

My words are the poor footmen of your pride.   Full Orchestra.   Kenneth Slessor.   OxBSo

My work done, I lean on the window-sill.   Charles Reznikoff.   APT-2

My work is done.   Angel.   John Henry, Cardinal Newman.   SacPr

My world has been laid low, and the wind blows.   Quatrain without Sparrows, Helpful Bells or Hope.   Thomas McCarthy.   PBCIP

My worries: several strands of white hair.   Written upon Returning to the Mountains.   Ku K'uang.   SuSp, *tr. by* Irving Y. Lo

My Worst Fear.   Cyn Zarco.   ReBoTo

My Worst Nightmare.   Kate Light.   AmPoNex

My worst nightmare was to be the couple.   My Worst Nightmare.   Kate Light.   AmPoNex

My worthy [*or* woorthy] Lord, I pray you wonder not.   Gascoigne's Woodmanship.   George Gascoigne.   NoSic

My years on earth were short, but long for me.   On a Shipmate, Pero Moniz, Dying at Sea.   Luis de Camões [*or* Camões].   OxBEV; PeSAV; WoPoe, *tr. by* Roy Campbell

My yellow mou'd mistress, I bid you adieu.   My Sodger Laddie.   *Unknown.*   FaBoWar

My Yellow Straw Hat.   Lessie Jones Little.   TLR

My yesterday was dream, tomorrow earth.   He Points Out the Brevity of Life, Unthinking and Suffering, Surprised by Death.   Francisco de Quevedo y Villegas.   WoPoe, *tr. by* Willis Barnstone

My young love said to me, "My brothers won't mind."   She Moved through the Fair.   Padraic Colum.   BIrV; NOIV

My Young Mother.   Jane Cooper.   FaBoWP

My young son claimed total recall from the sperm last bathnight, which stopped me like a clock.   First Second, The.   Ian Duhig.   NeBl

My Younger Brother.   Igor Shklyarevsky [*or* Shkliarevskii].   TCRP, *tr. by* Lubov Yakovleva

My youth? I hear it mostly in the long, volleying.   Poet at Seventeen, The.   Larry Levis.   GeoHom

My zenith was luckily happier than my night.   Heinrich Heine.   WoPoe, *tr. by* Robert Lowell   *Fr.* Dying in Paris.

Myall in Prison, The.   Mary Gilmore.   CBAP

Mycilla dyes her locks, 'tis said.   On an Old Woman.   Lucilius.   AWP, *tr. by* William Cowper

Myfanwy.   Sir John Betjeman.   BoLoP

Myn owne John poyntz sins ye delight to know.   Sir Thomas Wyatt.   *See* Satires

Mynstrelle's Songe ("O! synge untoe mie roundelaie").   Thomas Chatterton.   *See* Aella; a Tragycal Enterlude

Mynstrelles Songe: "Angelles bee wrogte to bee of neidher kynde."   Thomas Chatterton.   EnLoPo   *Fr.* Aella; a Tragycal Enterlude.

Myopia.   Biancamaria Frabotta.   CItWP, *tr. by* Cinzia Sartini Blum and Lara Trubowitz

Myra.   Fulke Greville, 1st Baron Brooke.   HAP; NOBE; NoSic; OBEV   *Fr.* Caelica.

Myriad cicadas seethe and buzz in the setting sun.   Fan Ch'eng-ta.   SuSp, *tr. by* Irving Y. Lo   *Fr.* Seasonal Poems on Fields and Gardens.

Myriad differences resolved by sitting, all doors opened, The.   Reizan.   ZenPo, *tr. by* Takashi Ikemoto and Lucien Stryk

Myriad times, Ptolemy, your father, myriad times.   Antipater of Sidon.   HePo   *Fr.* Epigrams.

Myrie a tyme I telle in May.   *Unknown.*   OHMEL

Myrrha and Cinyras.   Ovid.   NAWM-7v1, *tr. by* Allen Mandelbaum   *Fr.* Metamorphoses.

Myrtle.   John Ashbery.   NAAL-5

Myrtle.   Ted Kooser.   InvLad

Myrtle bush grew shady, The.   Jealousy.   Mary Elizabeth Coleridge.   EnLoPo; LW; WPE

Myrtle for Two.   Horace.   NBLV, *tr. by* George F. Whicher   *Fr.* Odes.

Mysel I will cast in. (LL)   Lady Maisry.   *Unknown.*   ESPB; OxBB

Myself.   Adah Isaacs Menken.   CBWP-1; ViWPN

Myself.   *Unknown.*   PWR

Myself am Hang the buccaneer.   Flying Fish, The.   John Gray.   NOBVV

Myself and Curtis Dean are seniors together.   Double Date.   Lincoln Kirstein.   PeLV

Myself I Sing.   George Oppen.   FTOS

Myself in the Disguise of an Ancient Queen.   Takahashi Mutsuo.   PFTM-2, *tr. by* Hiroaki Sato   *Fr.* Self-Portraits.

Myself outside at night.   Moonsnow '77.   Michael Hartnett.   ModIr

Myself, Rousseau, a Few Others.   William Meredith.   YaYoPo

Myself unholy, from myself unholy.   Gerard Manley Hopkins.   SacPr

Myself unto myself will give.   Holy Office, The.   James Joyce.   FaBoTw; NoAM; OxBTC

Myself when young did eagerly frequent.   27.   Edward Fitzgerald.   CABP

Myself when young did eagerly frequent.   Omar Khayyám.   TRP, *tr. by* Edward Fitzgerald   *Fr.* Rubáiyát of Omar Khayyám [of Naishápúr], The.

Myself with a Glory Hole.   Takahashi Mutsuo.   PFTM-2, *tr. by* Hiroaki Sato   *Fr.* Self-Portraits.

Myselves / The grievers.   Ceremony after a Fire Raid.   Dylan Thomas.   AF

Mysteries, The.   "H. D."   APT-1

Mysteries, The.   Brenda Hillman.   ExTi

Mysteries of Caesar, The.   Anthony Hecht.   NoP-4

Mysteries of Life.   Mary E. Tucker.   CBWP-1

Mysteries of Small Houses.   Alice Notley.   ExTi

Mysteries of Udolpho, The.   Ann Radcliffe.
    Butterfly to His Love, The.   RWP

Mysteries Remain, The.   "H. D."   NOBA; TAP; VGW; WPOW

Mysteries Revealed after Death.   John Reynolds.   NOEC   *Fr.* Death's Vision.

Mysterious, Ancient World of Mine.   Sergey [*or* Sergei] Aleksandrovich Yesenin [*or* Essenin].   TCRusP, *tr. by* Nigel Stott

Mysterious Cat, The.   Nicholas Vachel Lindsay.   OBCA

Mysterious East.   William Cole.   OBAL

Mysterious Night! when our first parent knew.   To Night.   Joseph Blanco White.   EBEV; GSo; OBEV; OxAEP-2; Son

Mysterious night, when the first man but knew.   Joseph Blanco White.   *See* Mysterious Night! when our first parent knew

Mysterious Nothing! how shall I define.   Sonnet to Nothing.   Thomas Beck.   NOBRP

Mysterious Presence! Source of All.   Seth Curtis Beach.   AH

Mysterious shapes, with wands of joy and pain.   Dreams.   Helen Hunt Jackson.   APN-2

Mysterious things within you, The.   Ahmad al-Mushari Al-'Udwani.   BBASP; MAP, *tr. by* Charles Doria and Hilary Kilpatrick   *Fr.* Signs.

Mysterious valley fountain, The.   Gem Creek.   Muso Soseki.   EaWin, *tr. by* W. S. Merwin

Mystery.   Langston Hughes.   APT-2

Mystery.   Octavio Paz.   TCLAP, *tr. by* Muriel Rukeyser

Mystery.   Lizette Woodworth Reese.   SWaP

Mystery.   "Yehoash."   TrJP, *tr. by* Marie Syrkin

Mystery, The.   Jeni Couzyn.   HAWP

Mystery, The.   Paul Laurence Dunbar.   APN-2

Mystery, The.   Ralph Hodgson.   InvLi; MoBrPo

Mystery, The.   Sara Teasdale.   PasH

'Mystery Boy' Looks for Kin in Nashville.   Robert Earl Hayden.   LCAP-2; NoAM; NoP-4; PoE

Mystery Corset, The.   André Breton.   PFTM-1

Mystery: God, Man's Life, born into man.   Virgin and Child, by Hans Memmeling; in the Academy of Bruges, A.   Dante Gabriel Rossetti.   CenSon

Mystery: Katharine, the bride of Christ.   Marriage of St. Katharine, by the same; in the Hospital of St. John at Bruges.   Dante Gabriel Rossetti.   CenSon

Mystery of Emily Dickinson, The.   Marvin Bell.   InvLad

Mystery of Life, The.   John Gambold.   NOEC

Mystery of Profession great, The.   Anne Docwra.   EMWP

Mystery of the Charity of Charles Péguy, The.   Geoffrey Hill.
    "Dear lords of life, stump-toothed, with ragged breath."   DiPo
    "Violent contrariety of men and days; calm."   FaBoWar

Mystery of the Missing Century, The.   Tracey Herd.
    "I stopped the car and stepped out onto gravel."   NeBl
    "We are sailing on a charming bay."   NeBl

Mystery of the Three Horns, The.   Jules Laforgue.   WoPoe, *tr. by* William Jay Smith

Mystery Story.   Howard Nemerov.   NBLV

Mystery Train: A Sequence.   David Wojahn.
    Assassination of John Lennon as Depicted by the Madame Tussaud Wax Museum, Niagara Falls, Ontario, 1987, The.   PBCAP
    At Graceland with a Six Year Old, 1985.   AllShUp; PBCAP

Buddy Holly Watching *Rebel without a Cause*, Lubbock, Texas, 1956. PBCAP

Colorizing: Turner Broadcasting Enterprises, Computer Graphics Division, Burbank, California, 1987. PBCAP

Custom Job: Hank Williams, Jr., and the Death Car, 1958. PBCAP

Fab Four Tour Deutschland: Hamburg, 1961. PBCAP

Homage: Light from the Hall. PBCAP

Matins: James Brown and His Famous Flames Tour the South, 1958. PBCAP

"Mystery Train" Janis Joplin Leaves Port Arthur for Points West, 1964. GM; PBCAP

Tattoo, Corazon: Ritchie Valens, 1959. PBCAP

Trashmen Shaking Hands with Hubert Humphrey at the Opening of Apache Plaza Shopping Center, Suburban Minneapolis, August 1963, The. PBCAP

Woody Guthrie Visited by Bob Dylan: Brooklyn State Hospital, New York, 1961. PBCAP; SwNoth

Mystic. D. H. Lawrence. BLT; PAI

Mystic and Cavalier. Lionel Pigot Johnson. MoBrPo

Mystic Drum, The. Gabriel Okara. TTY

Mystic in the morning, half asleep, A. Bachelor. William Meredith. NoAM

Mystic Magi, The. Robert Stephen Hawker. OBCP

Mystical Chorus. Goethe. WoPoe, *tr. by* Louis MacNeice *Fr.* Faust.

Mystical strains unheard. Clymène, A. Paul Verlaine. AWP, *tr. by* Arthur Symons

Myth. Muriel Rukeyser. APT-2; FaBoWP; NAAL-5; NALW; NIL-7; NNaP

Myth, The. Edwin Muir. HarvBoo

Myth lilies. A smog-edge sky blurs his eyes. Crow's Way. Duane Niatum. CDW

Myth of the Blaze. George Oppen. PFTM-2

Myth on Mediterranean Beach: Aphrodite as Logos. Robert Penn Warren. HAP

Mythic Fragment. Louise Glück. NoAM

Mythical Founding of Buenos Aires, The. Jorge Luis Borges. TCLAP, *tr. by* Alastair Reid

Mythical Journey, The. Edwin Muir. NoAM; OxBS

Mythistorima. George Seferis.

    Bottle in the Sea. WoPoe, *tr. by* Edmund Keeley and Philip Sherrard

Mythological Sonnets. Roy Fuller.

    There Actually Stood. Son

    Well Now, the Virgin. Son

Mythology. Lawrence Durrell. OxBTC

Mythology. Marilyn Hacker. NoAM; ReTh

Mythology. Earle Thompson. HATNAP

Myths and Texts. Gary Snyder.

    Burning. NeAP; PoM

      John Muir on Mt. Ritter. NOBA

      Second Shaman Song. NOBA; NeAP; PoM

      Text, The. NAAL-2v2

    Hunting.

      First Shaman Song. NOBA; PFTM-2

      This Poem Is for Bear. NOBA; PFTM-2

      This Poem Is for Deer. GeoHom; NOBA

    Logging.

      "Lodgepole Pine: the wonderful reproductive." NOBA

Myths of separation from the Earth, The. Friedrich Hölderlin. WoPoe, *tr. by* David Rattray *Fr.* Seasons, The.

Myxomatosis. Philip Larkin. NoAM

N

N i'm waitin for the light to turn green. Green Boots n Lil Honeys. Ruth Forman. SpirFl

N. N. Tries to Remember the Words of a Prayer. Stanislaw Baranczak. GI, *tr. by* Kevin Windle

N T. Charles Wesley. ChIV-2

N.V., my girlfriend then, who laughed nonstop. Memoirs. Aleksandr Semionovich Kushner. ItGoST, *tr. by* Paul Graves and Carol Ueland

Naaman's Song. Rudyard Kipling. ChIV-1

Naayawwa Taawi. Wendy Rose. UnSA

Nabara, The. Cecil Day Lewis. EBNV; OBNV

Naches River. Just below the falls. Woman Bathing. Raymond Carver. PasH

Nadar. Richard Howard. GS

Nadine held my hand when we were kids. Miss Mary Mack. Lisa Buscani. AmPoNex

Nae man wha loves the lawland tongue. Makar, The. William Soutar. OxBS

Nae sign o' thow yet. Ay, that's me, John Watt o' Dockenhill. Dockens afore his Peers. Charles Murray. NePenScot

Nagasaki. Harry Warren. ReLy

Nagging reminders: the black ghost-melancholy vision. Ovid. RomPo, *tr. by* Peter Green *Fr.* Tristia.

Nahum 2.10. Francis Quarles. ChIV-1

Naiad changes / Quick as these. (LL) Gardener Janus Catches a Naiad. Dame Edith Sitwell. MoBrPo; OBGa

Nail, The. Vasco [*or* Vasko] Popa. PoSu *Fr.* Games.

Nail scratching at the glass, The. Crossroads, The. Maria Luisa Spaziani. CItWP, *tr. by* Cinzia Sartini Blum and Lara Trubowitz

Nàile from Iona, Nàile from above. Lullaby of Donald Gorm, by his Nurse. *Unknown*. EMWP

Nailed eagles beryl alter vasish. Hill Figures. Maggie O'Sullivan. Oth

Nailed like illegible bronze on the futureless future. (LL) Fishnet. Robert Lowell. HCAP; PoetW; VCAP

Nails. Gary Gildner. PBCAP; TAP

Nailsworth Hill. William Henry Davies. OTCP

Naima. Edward Kamau Brathwaite. WoPoe

Naïve young lady of Bude, A. Limerick. C. Chevallier. PeLi

Naïve young lady of Cork, A. Limerick. Reg Yearley. PeLi

Naked. Issa. EH, *tr. by* Robert Hass

Naked among the Trees. Norman Cameron. OxBEV

Naked and knowing my heart my love had left on. Jewels, The. Charles Baudelaire. BoLoP

Naked and the Nude, The. Robert Graves. SoSe-8

Naked as from the earth we came. Submission to Afflictive Providences. Isaac Watts. NOCV

Naked blond head. Peace. Jonetta Barras. ISC

Naked body maybe, A. Nudity. Gabriella Sica. CItWP, *tr. by* Cinzia Sartini Blum and Lara Trubowitz

Naked clarity. Tennis. Pierre Drieu la Rochelle. CuPo

Naked earth is warm with Spring, The. Into Battle. Julian Grenfell. FaBoWar; OBEV; OBMV; OBWP; OxBTC; PeFWW

Naked Face. Yannis Ritsos. PFTM-2, *tr. by* Kimon Friar

Naked Face, The. Andrée Chedid. HAWP, *tr. by* Mirène Ghossein and Samuel Hazo

Naked Girl and Mirror. Judith Wright. NALW

Naked Girl Swimming, A. Arthur Rex Dugard Fairburn. PeNZ

Naked, he lies in the blinded room. Soledad. Robert Earl Hayden. APT-2; NAAAL

Naked house, a naked moor, A. House Beautiful, The. Robert Louis Stevenson. NOBE

Naked I came, naked I leave the scene. James Vincent Cunningham. APT-2; OBAL; TRP; WoPoe *Fr.* Five Epigrams.

Naked I came when I began to be. Nudus Redibo. Thomas Flatman. OxBSP

Naked / I float among the wreckage with steel mustaches. Joyce Mansour. SurPaPo, *tr. by* Mary Ann Caws *Fr.* Pericoloso Sporgersi.

Naked I saw thee. Ideal. Padraic Pearse. AWP, *tr. by* Thomas Macdonagh

Naked I saw thee. Renunciation. Padraic Pearse. NOIV, *tr. by* the author

Naked I Saw You. Padraic Pearse. WoPoe, *tr. by* Desmond O'Grady

Naked is the earth. Poem. Antonio Machado Ruiz. AWP; WoPoe, *tr. by* John Dos Passos

Naked Jaina monk, A. Pleasure. A. K. Ramanujan. PoetW; VCWP

Naked Land, The. Kenneth Patchen. SPE

Naked out of the dark we came. Kenneth Rexroth. FaBoEE

Naked Seed, The. Clive Staples Lewis. TrCP

Naked she lay, clasped in my longing arms. Imperfect Enjoyment, The. John Wilmot, 2d Earl of Rochester. BASC; BoLoP; NAEL-7v1

Naked sun—a yellow sun—, A. Omen. Birago Diop. NegPo, *tr. by* Ellen Conroy Kennedy

Naked to the naked moon. (LL) In Bertram's Garden. Donald Justice. BoLoP; VGW

Naked Truth, The. Marianne van Hirtum. SurWo, *tr. by* Myrna Bell Rochester

Naked truth: that's not her, The. Naked Truth, The. Marianne van Hirtum. SurWo, *tr. by* Myrna Bell Rochester

Naked Vision. Gwen Harwood. EmeKit

Naked warmth of you is still, The. Philodemus. GrAn

Naked without either cover or dress. Pen, The. Solomon ibn Gabirol. WoPoe, *tr. by* Peter Cole

Naked woman and a dead dwarf, A. Stephen Crane. APN-2

Naked woman at the window, The. Untitled (February 2000). Michael Palmer. BAP-01

Naked woman, black woman. Black Woman. Léopold Sédar Senghor. TTY, *tr. by* Anne Atik

Namaqualand after Rain. William Plomer. PeSAV

Namby-Pamby. A Panegyric on the New Versification, Address'd to A———— P————, Esq. Henry Carey. NOEC; NPeEn; OBSV; UV

Namby-Pamby; or, A Panegyric on the New Versification. Henry Carey. NOEC; OBSV

Name. Alan Davies.
  "Personality syndrome, The." FTOS

Name, A. Aleksandr Samsonovich Ginger. TCRP, *tr.* by Albert C. Todd

Name, A. Linda Pastan. TaR

Name, The. Mariella Bettarini. CItWP, *tr.* by Cinzia Sartini Blum and Lara Trubowitz

Name, The. Shrine. Octavio Paz. EroLit

Name Alissa, The. In Which Names. Ilse Aichinger. AF, *tr.* by Allen H. Chappel

Name confronts you, The. Shap. Mick North. NLP

Name for All, A. Hart Crane. VGW

Name Giveaway. Phillip [*or* "Phil"] William George. VoR

Name in a footnote. Faceless name. Crispus Attucks. Robert Earl Hayden. ESEAA

Name in block letters *None that signifie.* Form of Epitaph, A. Laurence Whistler. GTBS-P

Name is hard, The. On the 25th Anniversary of the Liberation of Auschwitz. Eli W. Mandel. NOBC

Name not to be worn out with the years, A. (LL) Ezra Pound. APT-1; HAP; NOBA; OBVE; OxBA; WoPoe *Fr.* Homage to Sextus Propertius.

Name of god, The. Imtiaz Dharker. NeBl

Name—of it—is "Autumn," The. Emily Dickinson. NCAP

Name of Jesus, The. John Newton. ECEV; NOEC; SacPr

Name of my heroine, simply "Rose." Tale of a Pony, The. Bret Harte. OBNV

Name of the product I tested is "Life," The. Consumer's Report, A. Peter Porter. EmeKit; NOBL

Name of this poem is, The. Cameo No. II. June Jordan. BPo

Name only once. America. Kofi Awoonor. HBAPE

Name's another thing, A. My Shepherd. Heather McHugh. Unle

Name the Oldest Member of Your Family. Kalamu ya Salaam. OPRER

Name was curiously given, The. Zalman. Seymour Mayne. GotH

Named and unnamed and renamed. Leaving Eden. Ralph Dickey. ESEAA

Named from the Bible. Rachel. Bobbi Sykes. IBA

Nameless Doon [*or* Dun], The. William Larminie. BIrV

Nameless Epitaph, A. Matthew Arnold. FaBoEE

Nameless Journey. Leah Goldberg.
  "My room is so small." BoWoP

Nameless Love, The. John Henry Mackay. CAGL, *tr.* by Hubert Kennedy

Nameless One, A. Margaret Avison. HeIP-4; NOBC

Nameless One, The. James Clarence Mangan. BIrV; NOIV; OBEV

Nameless Ones, The. Conrad Potter Aiken. OxBA

Nameless Pain. Elizabeth Stoddard. SWaP

Nameless Spirit. Gustavo Adolfo Bécquer. NAWM-7v2, *tr.* by Bruce Phenix

Nameless Thing. Robert Penn Warren. BodElec

Nameless / Weed quickening. Chiun. ZenPo, *tr.* by Takashi Ikemoto and Lucien Stryk

Nameless Woman, A. No Ch'ŏn-myŏng. WoPoe, *tr.* by Ko Won

Names. Medora C. Addison. YaYoPo

Names. Gerald Dawe. PNI

Names. Robert Earl Hayden. GT

Names. William Matthews. PoCoUp

Names. Jelaluddin [*or* Jalal al-Din] Rumi. RaBo

Names, The. Robert Browning. OxBSo

Names and sorrows. D. Rubin Green. CAGL

Names creeping out everywhere, The. (LL) Lying Awake. Thomas Hardy. FaBoVe; NPeEn

Names flow from her mouth as so many hearty allies. Rival, A. Rachel Wetzsteon. NeAmPo

Names for everything I touch. Hollow Thesaurus, The. Roger McDonald. BMAP; CBAP

Names in Monterchi: To Rachel. James Wright. NNaP

Names of Georgian Women, The. Bella [*or* Izabella] Akhatovna Akhmadulina. BoWoP, *tr.* by Olga Carlisle and Stanley Noyes

Names of Horses. Donald Hall. AmFaPo; HAP; InPK-6; SoSe-8; TRP

Names of the dead, The. Eric Amann. HA

Names of the dead, The. Remembrance Day. Ida G. M. Gerhardt. TuT, *tr.* by Robert Greacen

Names of the fallen, The. Remembrance Day. Ida G. M. Gerhardt. TuT, *tr.* by Michael Longley

Names of the Hare, The. *Unknown.* RB; WoPoe, *tr.* by Seamus Heaney

Names of the Humble, The. Les A. Murray. CBAP

Names of things—sparks!, The. Resigning from a Job in a Defense Industry. Sandra McPherson. LCAP-2

Names, Places, Streets, Faces: The Universe in Flame. Octavio Paz. *Fr.* Sunstone.

Names. / She and my uncles looked for names. Number Our Days. Norbert Hirschhorn. BloBone

Names the Dead Speak. Sharon Kessler. GotH

Names will change. Election Time. Lamont B. Steptoe. UnSA

Namesake. Imtiaz Dharker. NeBl

Naming Day, A. Odia Ofeimun. HBAPE; PBMAP

Naming of Cats, The. T. S. Eliot. NBLV

Naming of Cats is a difficult matter. Naming of Cats, The. T. S. Eliot. NBLV

Naming of Flowers, The. Jennie Osborne. Prnts

Naming of Parts. Henry Reed. AmFaPo; FaBoWar; MoBrPo; NAEL-6v2; NOBE; NoP-4; OxBEV; OxBTC; PAI; PoPoPo; PoRA; RaBo; SoSe-8; TFi; UV; UnPo *Fr.* Lessons of the War.

Naming of the Beasts, The. Francis Sparshott. NOBC

Naming of Things, The. Bahinabai Chaudhari. OMIP, *tr.* by Philip Engblomb

Naming Power. Wendy Rose. OxWW

Naming's over. Day is done. (LL) Adam's Task. John Hollander. NIL-7; NIP-4; NoP-4; WoPoe

Naming Souls. Uri Zvi Greenberg. PeFWW, *tr.* by Jon Silkin and Exra Spicehandler

Naming the Animals. Anthony Hecht. ChIV-1

Naming the Animals. Lisel Mueller. IllVoic

Naming the Fabrics. Julia Alvarez. FFC

Naming the Living God. Kathleen Norris. InvLi

Nancy Dawson. *Unknown.* ReMoGo

Nancy Hanks. Rosemary Benét. NTCP

Nane of them durst cum neir his Hald. (LL) Johnie Armstrang. *Unknown.* ESPB; IBB; OxBB

Nani. Alberto A. Ríos. MakPoe; SoSe-8; UnSA

Nanny Tanya. Yevgeny [*or* Evgenii] Borisovich Rein. ItGoST, *tr.* by Judith Hemschemeyer

Nansen. Gary Snyder. BB

Nantucket. William Carlos Williams.
  HAP; HarvBoo; OxBA; TAP; TRP; WeW-3

Naola Beauty Academy, New Orleans, Louisiana, 1943. Natasha Trethewey. NeAmPo; SpirFl

Naomi. Gwendolyn Brooks. NAAL-2v2

Naomi and Ruth. Bible, *O.T.* TrJP *Fr.* Ruth.

Napa, California. Ana Castillo. WPOW

Napoleon. Walter De la Mare. FaBoCh; FaBoTw; NOBE; NPeEn; OxBEV; RB; Spl; WoPoe

Napoleon. Miroslav Holub. ChAP; PoSu, *tr.* by Kaca Plakova

Napoleon. William Makepeace Thackeray. FaBoWar

Napoleon. P. G. Wodehouse. ReLy

Napoleon after Sedan. Arthur Rimbaud. OBWP, *tr.* by Robert Lowell *Fr.* Eighteen-Seventy.

Napoleon was a young guy. Napoleon. P. G. Wodehouse. ReLy

Napoli Again. Richard Hugo. AF; LCAP-2

Napolo has spoken: Death. Messengers, The. Steve Chimombo. HBAPE

Napped half the day. Issa. EH, *tr.* by Robert Hass

Napping at midday. Issa. EH, *tr.* by Robert Hass

Nappy Edges. Ntozake Shange. NAAAL

Nappy Edges (A Cross Country Sojourn). Ntozake Shange. BlSi

Narcissa. Gwendolyn Brooks. NTCP

Narcissi look up like children, quickly and whitely, The. (LL) Among the Narcissi. Sylvia Plath. FaBoMo; RB; SCV

Narcissism / is an ugly fault. Antonio Machado Ruiz. RaBo *Fr.* Moral Proverbs and Folk Songs.

Narcissist's eye is blue, fringed with white and covered, The. Eye, The. Michael Benedikt. CoAmPo

Narcissus. Gerda Mayer. LW

Narcissus. Paul Valéry. AWP, *tr.* by Joseph T. Shipley

Narcissus Learning the Words to This Song. Reginald Shepherd. WiU

Narcissus to Echo. Edgar Bogardus. YaYoPo

Narcolepsy. Maureen Owen. TTTS

Narration. George Seferis. PoetW, *tr.* by Edmund Keeley and Philip Sherrard

Narrative. Russell Atkins. GT

Narrative. Elisabeth Eybers. PeSAV, *tr.* by the author

Narrative: Ali. Elizabeth Alexander. ESEAA; MoASP

Narrative Charm for Ibbotroyd. Maggie O'Sullivan. Oth; PFTM-2

Narrative of the Life and Times of John Coltrane: Played by Himself, A. Michael S. Harper. SeSe

Narrative of the Life of Frederick Douglass, an American Slave. Frederick Douglass.
  Parody, A. NAAL-2v1; NAAL-3; NAWM-7v2

Narrator, The. Milo De Angelis. NeIt, *tr.* by Lawrence Venuti

Narrator of folktales was boasting, A. Atomic Fairy Tale. Yury [*or* Iurii] Kuznetsov. TCRP, *tr.* by Anatoly Liberman

NARRATOR: Suddenly someone wakes me. Still half-asleep, I see standing in front. Douglas Messerli. FTOS *Fr.* Along Without: A Fiction in Film for Poetry.

Narrow black veins on the map, The. Highway Poems. Lisel Mueller. IllVoic

Narrow Fellow in the Grass, A. Emily Dickinson. *See* Snake, The

Narrow for love that must be fitted in. Sophie Hannah. NewEx

Narrow Path, The. Norman Henry Pritchard, II. GT

Narrow Road to the Deep North, The. Paul Muldoon. HarvBoo

Narrow Sea, The. Robert Graves. FaBoEE; FaBoMo

Narrowing of knowledge to one window to a door, A. Elegy for William Soutar. William Montgomerie. OxBS

Narrowing sea embraces it forever, The. Urumbula Song, The. *Unknown.* CBAP, *tr. by* T. G. H. Strehlow

Narrows, The. Anne Rouse. MFPA

Narrows of Birth, The. William Everson. PoM

Nasal whine of power whips a new universe. Hart Crane. MoAmPo *Fr.* Bridge, The.

Nasica raped the doctor's pretty lad. Martial. CAGL, *tr. by* Brian Hill *Fr.* Epigrams.

Naskeag. Alfred Corn. VCAP

Nasturtium Scanned. Judith Rodriguez. BMAP

Nasty snake once bit a Cappadocian, A. Demodocus. GrAn

Nasty surprise in a sandwich, A. God, a Poem. James Fenton. DiPo; NoAM; NoP-4; OBCoV

Nat Love: Black Cowboy. Lee Bennett Hopkins. HHAm

Natal Address to My Child, March 19th 1844, A. Eliza Ogilvy. VWP

Natal Hunters, The. Allen F. Gardiner. PeSAV

Natalie gets discovered in her pit by an old, drunken transient. Connie Deanovich. ReTh *Fr.* Ephemera Today on "All My Children."

Natalya Nikolayevna Goncharova. Don Coles. NOBC

Nathan, no thought today. Bratzlav Rabbi to His Scribe, The. Jacob Glatstein [*or* Glatsteyn]. TrJP, *tr. by* Jacob Sloan

Nathaniel, born Hathorne, you who set. Secret, The. Suzanne Noguere. FFC

Nathaniel Lee to Sir Roger L'Estrange. Nathaniel Lee. FaBoEE

Nathaniel to Ruth. Emily Jane Pfeiffer. ViWPN

Nation Is Like Ouselves, The. Imamu Amiri Baraka. PmAP

Nation is ruined, but mountains and rivers remain, The. Spring View. Tu Fu. ColAnChi, *tr. by* Gary Snyder

Nation of hayricks spotting the green solace, A. Airman Who Flew Over Shakespeare's England, The. Hyam Plutzik. APT-2

Nation of trees, drab green and desolate gray, A. Australia. Alec Derwent Hope. NoAM

Nation Once Again, A. Thomas Osborne Davis. NOIV

Nation shattered, hills and streams remain, The. Spring Prospect. Tu Fu. CoBCP, *tr. by* Burton Watson

Nation true to honor's cause, The. On the Great Western Canal of the State of New York. Philip Freneau. APN-1

Nation Wrapped in Stone, A. Roberta Hill Whiteman. BoWoP; CDW

National Anthem. Ferenc Kölcsey. IQMS, *tr. by* Earl M. Herrick, Watson Kirkconnell and Adam Makkai

National Bird. N. Pichamurti. OMIP, *tr. by* Rajagopal Parthasarathy

National Cemetery, Beaufort, South Carolina, The. Josephine D. Henderson Heard. CBWP-4

National Cold Storage Company. Harvey Shapiro. VGW; WoPoe

National Federation is a grand and glorious band, The. All We Ask Is Justice. Mrs. Henry Linden. CBWP-4

National Folk Hymn. Karl Kraus. AuPH, *tr. by* Lowell A. Bangerter

National Hero, The. Gojko Djogo. AF, *tr. by* Michael March

National Painting, The. Joseph Rodman Drake. GS

National Painting [*or* Paintings], The. Fitz-Greene Halleck. APN-1 *Fr.* Croaker Papers, The.

National Police Headquarters. Nicolás Guillén. PFTM-1 *Fr.* Daily Daily, The.

National Song. Sándor Petőfi. IQMS, *tr. by* Adam Makkai

National Thoughts. Yehuda Amichai [*or* Amikhai]. PFTM-2, *tr. by* Stephen Mitchell

National Trust. Tony Harrison. HarvBoo; NAEL-5v2; NAEL-6v2 *Fr.* School of Eloquence, The.

National Winter Garden. Hart Crane. NAAL-2v2; OxBA *Fr.* Bridge, The.

Nationality. Mary Gilmore. CBAP

Nations die. Japanese Figures 1. *Unknown.* EaWin, *tr. by* W. S. Merwin

Nations That Long in Darkness Walked. John Barnard. AH

Native. Rae Armantrout. PFTM-2

Native, The. W. S. Merwin. PoRA

Native Born. Eve Langley. WPE

Native Moments. Walt Whitman. OxBA

Native's Letter. Arthur Nortje. HBAPE; PeSAV

Native Stone. Octavio Paz. TCLAP, *tr. by* Muriel Rukeyser

Natives, The. David Mura. CDa; WeW-3

Natives are restless tonight, The. Drummer, The. Philip Dacey. MiVo

Natives camped on the hatches, who sang through the, The. Calenture, The. Randolph Stow. BMAP

Natives of America, The. Ann Plato. BlSi; TCAPo

Nativities. U. A. Fanthorpe. NoP-4

Nativity. Gladys May Casely Hayford. PBA; TTY

Nativity. James Montgomery. NOCV
(Good Tidings of Great Joy to All People.) SacPr

Nativity. Craig Powell. NOBAu

Nativity, A. Rudyard Kipling. ChrPo; GI

Nativity, The. Mary Weston Fordham. CBWP-2

Nativity, The. Clive Staples Lewis. ChIV-2; TrCP

Nativity, The. Henry Vaughan. ChrPo

Nativity Chant, The. Sir Walter Scott. FaBoCh *Fr.* Guy Mannering.

Nativity of Christ[e], The. Robert Southwell. OxBEV

Nativity of Our Lord and Saviour Jesus Christ, The. Christopher Smart. ChrPo; NOCV; NPeEn; OxBEV; SacPr *Fr.* Hymns and Spiritual Songs for the Fasts and Festivals of the Church of England.

Nativity of St. John the Baptist, The. Christopher Smart. ChIV-2 *Fr.* Hymns and Spiritual Songs for the Fasts and Festivals of the Church of England.

Nativity [*or* Nativitie]. John Donne. ChrPo *Fr.* Holy Sonnets.

Nativity Poem. Louise Glück. GI; HarvBoo

Natura Naturans. Arthur Hugh Clough. HAP; NOBVV

Natural affinity. (LL) Queen of Hearts, The. Christina Georgina Rossetti. NPeEn; PeVV

Natural Child, The. Helen Leigh. ECWP; WoRP

Natural demeanor warm and soft. Tune: "Rapt with Wine, Loudly Singing; Joy in Spring's Coming." Kuan Yün-shih. ColAnChi; SuSp, *tr. by* Richard John Lynn

Natural Disaster. David Swanger. GeoHom

Natural High. Jean Binta Breeze. Prnts

Natural History. Richard Howard. TAP

Natural History. Harold Monro.
"Vixen woman, The." OBMV

Natural History. Mother Goose. *See* What Are Folks Made Of

Natural History. Giampiero Neri. ItPo, *tr. by* Gayle Ridinger

Natural History. Robert Penn Warren. NAAL-2v2

Natural Selection. Constance Naden. VWP *Fr.* Evolutional Erotics.

Natural silence of a tree, The. Fortune. Charles Madge. FaBoMo

Natural Son. Richard Murphy. ModIr *Fr.* Price of Stone, The.

Natural thirst that never can be quenched. Dante Alighieri. NAWM-7v1, *tr. by* Allen Mandelbaum *Fr.* Divine Comedy, The.

Natural world is a spiritual house, where the pillars, that are alive, The. Intimate Associations. Charles Baudelaire. WoPoe, *tr. by* Robert Bly

Naturalised. Cyril Hodges. AngWePo

Naturalist's Summer-Evening Walk, The. Gilbert White. NOEC

Naturally. Audre Lorde. BlSi; ISC

Naturally the Foundation Will Bear Your Expenses. Philip Larkin. PeLV

Nature. Henry Wadsworth Longfellow. ITBLP; TAP

Nature. Edmund Spenser. AEP *Fr.* Faerie Queene, The.

Nature. Henry David Thoreau. AiP

Nature. Jones Very. ColAP

Nature. Alfred de Vigny. AWP, *tr. by* Margaret Jourdain

Nature and Art. Goethe. STV, *tr. by* John Frederick Nims

Nature and Nature's Laws lay hid in Night. Intended for Sir Isaac Newton. Pope. ECEV; FaBoEE; InPK-6; WeW-3

Nature Be Damned. Anne Wilkinson. NOBC

Nature causes brass to oxidize. X-Ray. Else Von Freytag-Loringhoven. SurPaPo

Nature centres into balls. Circles. Ralph Waldo Emerson. APN-1; TCAPo

Nature, creations law, is judged [*or* judg'd] by sense. Upon Love Fondly Refused [*or* Refus'd] for Conscience's Sake. Thomas Randolph. BeJo

Nature [1844]. Ralph Waldo Emerson. APN-1

Nature [1836]. Ralph Waldo Emerson. APN-1; AWP
(Motto to "Nature.") NCAP

Nature had long a treasure made. Match, The. Andrew Marvell. EBEV

Nature had made them hide in crevices. New Hampshire, February. Richard Eberhart. TwCP

Nature herself doth Scotchmen beasts confess. John Cleveland. OBSV *Fr.* Rebel Scot, The.

Nature in her wisdom has formed the human head. Four Heads & How to Do Them. John Forbes. CBAP

Nature is a temple, where the living. Correspondences. Charles Baudelaire. SxFrPo, *tr. by* James McGowan

Nature is a temple whose living colonnades. Correspondences. Charles Baudelaire. NAWM-7v2, *tr. by* Richard Wilbur

Nature is only for the smug or the empty. Dapper Street. J. C. Bloem. TuT, *tr. by* Desmond Egan

Nature is rising from the dead. Epigram on the First of April. John Winstanley. NOEC

Nature is so near: the rooks in the college garden. Oxford. W. H. Auden. OxAEP-2

Nature Morte. Joseph Brodsky. TCRP, *tr. by* George L. Kline

Nature Morte. Louis MacNeice. NoAM

Nature of a river is to run, The. Rivers. Homero [*or* Umberto] Aridjis. PoCoUp, *tr. by* George McWhirter

Nature of Braille, The. Anthony Butts. AmPoNex

Nature of Man, The. Charles Hubert Sisson. FaBoTw

Nature of Suffering, The. Amy Gerstler. ExTi

Nature of the Siren, The. Cynewulf. WoPoe, *tr. by* Richard Wilbur

Nature of Things, The. Kathleen Ossip. BAP-01

Nature Poem. Adrian Mitchell. Spl

Nature Poetry. Meg Kearney. UrbNat

Nature requires five; custom gives seven. Hours of Sleep. *Unknown.* NBLV

Nature's Cook. Margaret Lucas Cavendish, Duchess of Newcastle. BWW

Nature's decorations glisten. Christopher Smart. OBCP *Fr.* Hymns and Spiritual Songs for the Fasts and Festivals of the Church of England.

Nature's first green is gold. Nothing Gold Can Stay. Robert Frost. APT-1; ColAP; MoAmPo; NAAL-2v2; NAAL-5; NOBA; PAI; SoSe-8; TAP; VGW

Nature's lay idiot [*or* ideot], I taught thee to love. John Donne. BASC; NoP-4; OxAEP-1; PeLV *Fr.* Elegies.

Nature's Lineaments. Robert Graves. FaBoTw; RB

Nature's Minor Chords. Henrietta Cordelia Ray. CBWP-3

Nature's Reply to Mutability. Edmund Spenser. MakPoe; NOBE *Fr.* Faerie Queene, The.

Nature's Sympathy with the Poet. Sir Walter Scott. OxAEP-2 *Fr.* Lay of the Last Minstrel, The.

Nature's Travail. *Unknown.* AWP, *tr. by* Goldwin Smith

Nature's Uplifting. Henrietta Cordelia Ray. CBWP-3

Nature selects the longest way. Northern Suburb, A. John Davidson. NOBVV; NPeEn; NePenScot

Nature—sometimes sears a Sapling. Emily Dickinson. NAAL-2v1; NAAL-3

Nature Study. Craig Raine. NoAM

Nature Study. Trevor Winkfield. KGB

Nature that day a woman was in weakness. Storm in Summer, A. Wilfrid Scawen Blunt. FaBoTw

Nature, That Washed [*or* Washt] Her Hands in Milk[e]. Sir Walter Ralegh. NAEL-6v1; NAEL-7v1; NoP-4

(Shuts up the story of our days.) (LL) NoP-4

Nature—the Gentlest Mother is. Emily Dickinson. EnlH

Nature Was Caught in the Nets of Your Life. Paul Éluard. NAWM-7v2, *tr. by* Lloyd Alexander

Nature, which is the vast creation's soul. To Mr. Henry Lawes. Katherine Philips. NoP-4; WPE

Nature withheld Cassandra in the skies. Fragment of a Sonnet. Pierre de Ronsard. AWP; OBVE, *tr. by* Keats

Natus de Muliere, Brevi Vivens. Emilio Villa. ItPo, *tr. by* Gayle Ridinger

Natzweiler. Rutger Kopland. VCWP, *tr. by* James Brockway

Naught in the world keeps an immortal stay. Juvencus. MLL

Naught's a naught. Learn to Count. *Unknown.* NAAAL

Naughty Boy. Robert Creeley. HeIP-4; NOBA; NoAM

Naughty Paughty Jack-a-Dandy. Namby-Pamby; or, A Panegyric on the New Versification. Henry Carey. NOEC; OBSV

Naughty Preposition, The. Morris Gilbert Bishop. NBLV; PeLV

Naulahka, The. Rudyard Kipling.
  Lie, The. NOBL

Nautical Ballad, A. Charles Edward Carryl. *See* Davy and the Goblin

Nautilus Island's hermit. Skunk Hour. Robert Lowell. CoAP; CoAmPo; ColAP; EmeKit; FaBoMo; HAP; HCAP; HarvBoo; HeIP-4; InPK-6; LCAP-2; MoAmPo; NAAL-2v2; NAAL-5; NIL-7; NIP-4; NOBA; NoAM; NoP-4; OxBC; PAI; PoE; PoPoPo; PoetW; SCV; TAP; TFi; TRP; VCAP

Nauty Pauty Jack-a-Dandy. *Unknown.* OxNR

Nauvoo. Bayard Taylor. OBAL

Naval Base (Part III), The. Jeremy Cronin. AF

Naval Trainees Learn How to Jump Overboard, The. David Wagoner. VCAP

Navidad, St. Nicholas Ave. Alfred Corn. NoP-4

Navies fed to the fish in the dark / Unbridled waters. (LL) Beasts. Richard Wilbur. LCAP-2; TwCP

Navigation. Ralph Knevet. NOSC

Navigation. Ronald Stuart Thomas. HarvBoo

Navigation's gone haywire. Who's to blame? Shipwreck Poem. Karen Volkman. NeAmPo

Navigators, The. Walter James Turner. OBMV

Navy near-black cut in with lemon, fruity bright lime green. Lure, 1963. Denise Riley. Oth

Nay, be content—our door that opens wide. Fall. George Cabot Lodge. APN-2

Nay, but I fancy somehow, year by year. Robert Louis Stevenson. OxBSo

Nay, but of such an one. *Unknown.* TOF *Fr.* Bhagavad-Gita, The.

Nay, *Clytus*, you that cou'd advise. Nathaniel Lee. FaBoWar *Fr.* Rival Queens; or, Alexander the Great, The.

Nay, Death, thou art a shadow! Even as light. Lux Est Umbra Dei. John Addington Symonds. GSo

Nay, do not dream, designer dark. Death's Valley. Walt Whitman. GS

Nay do not smile: my lips shall rather dwell. One Desiring Me to Read, but Slept It Out, Wakening. George Daniel. OxBSP

Nay, Doll, quoth Roger, now you're caught. Dol and Roger. Laetitia Pilkington. PEW

Nay fie, Platonics, still adoring. Epithalamy. Alexander Brome. NOSC

Nay, he could sail a yacht both nigh and large. Cabin-Boy, The. George, 2d Duke of Buckingham Villiers. NOSC

Nay, if there's room for poets in this world. Fifth Book. Elizabeth Barrett Browning. PEW

Nay, if you threaten, all is over. Sydney Owenson, Lady Morgan. RWP *Fr.* Lay of an Irish Harp, or Metrical Fragments, The.

Nay! Ivy, nay! Holly and Ivy. *Unknown.* NPeEn

Nay, lady, one frown is enough. To Helen in a Huff. Nathaniel Parker Willis. OBAL

Nay, lady, sit; if I but wave this wand. John Milton. OxAEP-1 *Fr.* Comus; a Masque Presented at Ludlow Castle.

Nay, let me own it is but vain regret. Continuity of Life. William Bell Scott. OxBSo

Nay, Margaret, thou trickster. Tricky Margaret. Mary Macleod (Màiri Nighean Alasdair Ruaidh). EMWP

Nay, prethee [*or* prithee] dear, draw nigher. Loose Saraband, A. Richard Lovelace. BeJo; CaPo

Nay, prithee tell me, Love, when I behold. Transfiguration of Beauty, The. Michelangelo Buonarroti. AWP, *tr. by* John Addington Symonds

Nay, rush not: time serves: we are going, / Gentlemen. (LL) Ancient to Ancients, An. Thomas Hardy. GTBS-P; OxBTC; SCGP

Nay, Xanthias, feel unashamed. Horace. AWP, *tr. by* Franklin P. Adams *Fr.* Odes.

Nazareth. Rosario Castellanos. GI, *tr. by* Magda Bogin

Nazi Song. Paul Éluard. AF, *tr. by* Lloyd Alexander

Nazis. Ira Sadoff. LTA; OPRER

"Ne crede colori," the Poet erst sang. Prejudice against Colour. Langham Dale. PeSAV

Ne'er fail in old Scotland! (LL) John Barleycorn [a Ballad]. Robert Burns. FaBoCh; RB

Ne'er fash your *thumb* what *gods* decree. Horace. NPeEn, *tr. by* Robert Fergusson

Ne'er tear-filled glance read as significant. Toward Eternal Peace. Karl Kraus. AuPH, *tr. by* Lowell A. Bangerter

Ne'er to be found again[e]. (LL) To Daffodils [*or* Daffadills]. Robert Herrick. AWP; BASC; BeJo; CaPo; FaBoCh; GTBS-P; NOBE; NOSC; NoP-4; OBEV; OxAEP-1; PoRA; SCGP; TFi; TTTS; TreFP; UnPo

Ne hath my soule but fyr and yse. *Unknown.* OHMEL

Ne Me Tangito. Charlotte Mew. VWP

Ne'r may Prophetique *Daphne* crown my Brow. (LL) Welcome to Sack, The. Robert Herrick. BeJo; CaPo

Neaera when I'm there is adamant. James Vincent Cunningham. OBVE

Near. William Stafford. CoAmPo

Near a Waterfall at Ryumon. Lady Ise. BoWoP, *tr. by* Etsuko Terasaki

Near a window. Will-o'-Wisp. Nancy Morejón. TANSG, *tr. by* Joy Renjilian-Burgy

Near an Old Prison. Frances Darwin Cornford. OBMV

Near, and more near, without sight or sound. Anniversaries. May Probyn. VWP

Near are we, Lord. Tenebrae. Paul Celan. PoetW, *tr. by* John Felstiner

Near blackened alcoves. Railway Allotments. M. R. Peacocke. OBGa

Near Burning. Kathleen Peirce. PBCAP

Near Cedar on Lake Street, where the used cars live. (LL) Poet's Final Instructions, The. John Berryman. Son; VGW

Near Damascus. W. S. Di Piero. ChIV-2

Near dawn our old live oak sagged over. Hurricane. John Balaban. UrbNat

Near high tide. Nightfishing. Charles McDonald. NLP

Near House, The. Mark Van Doren. APT-2

Near-Johannesburg Boy, The. Gwendolyn Brooks. ESEAA; IllVoic

Near Kitami Station on the Odakyū Line. Itō Hiromi. PFTM-2, *tr. by* Leith Morton

Near Lanivet, 1872. Thomas Hardy. AWP; NoAM

Near Martinpuich that night of hell. Leveller, The. Robert Graves. FaBoWar

Near Moscow living, I, this winter. On Early Trains. Boris Leonidovich Pasternak. TCRP, *tr. by* George Reavey

Near mud-tide mangrove swamps, under the drilling sun. Along the Mekong. John Balaban. CDa

Near Neighbors. Martial. AWP, *tr. by* Jonathan Swift

Near-neighboured by a blandly boisterous Dean. Blues at Lord's, The. Siegfried Sassoon. PeLV

Near Perigord. Ezra Pound. APT-1; FaBoMo

Near Rhydcymerau. Rhydcymerau. David Gwenallt Jones. OBWVE, *tr. by* Anthony Conran

Near Roscoe and Coldwater. Amy Uyematsu. OpBo

Near Rose's Chop Suey and Jinosuke's grocery. Argument: On 1942, An. David Mura. PoPoPo

Near San Ardo the grasses tremble. Our Life in California. Gary Young. GeoHom

Near Sheridan. Robin Becker. PoCoUp

Near Shinobazu Pond. Shinkichi Takahashi. ZenPo, *tr. by* Takashi Ikemoto and Lucien Stryk

Near-sighted fellow named Walter, A. Limerick. *Unknown.* PeLi

Near-Sightedness. Edmond Yi-teh Chang. OpBo

Near Speech, The. Mark McMorris. AmPoNex

Near the campus, every night. Cockroaches of Liberation. Martín Espada. TouFir

Near the celebrated Lido where the breeze is fresh and free. Longfellow's Visit to Venice. Sir John Betjeman. NOBL; OBCoV

Near the City of Petersburg. V. N. and C. I., The. Maggie Pogue Johnson. CBWP-4

Near the curving harbor where pine trees father. Heart's Ease. Paul Hoover. PmAP

Near the Cymmerians, in his dark abode. Ovid. OBVE *Fr.* Metamorphoses.

Near the Desert Test Sites. Sherod Santos. GeoHom

Near the dry river's water-mark we found. Note Left in Jimmy Leonard's Shack, A. James Wright. HCAP; NoP-4

Near the East Gate. *Unknown.* SuSp, *tr. by* Heng Kuan

Near the end of an extremely important discourse. Discourse on Peace, The. Jacques Prévert. CLPP, *tr. by* Lawrence Ferlinghetti

Near the headwaters of the longest river. Banished Gods, The. Derek Mahon. OxBC

Near the Mill. Hayim Lenski. FIT, *tr. by* Robert Friend

Near the Mississippi. Steve Gehrke. AmPoNex

Near the mountain's summit, when the bells. Fox, The. R. Williams Parry. OBWVE, *tr. by* Gwyn Williams

Near the Ocean. Robert Lowell. NOBA

Near the rim of Hsi-sai Mountain, white egrets fly. Chang Chih-ho. SuSp *Fr.* Fisherman's Songs.

Near the School for Handicapped Children. Thomas William Shapcott. CBAP

Near the shrine, humped back. Clay Image. Shinkichi Takahashi. ZenPo, *tr. by* Takashi Ikemoto and Lucien Stryk

Near the Vipsanian columns where the aqueduct. Martial. OBVE; OxBEV, *tr. by* Peter Porter

Near the Wall of a House. Yehuda Amichai [*or* Amikhai]. BBASP; PFTM-2, *tr. by* Chana Bloch

Near the wall of a house painted. Near the Wall of a House. Yehuda Amichai [*or* Amikhai]. BBASP; PFTM-2, *tr. by* Chana Bloch

Near Twelve Mile Point. Lance Henson. HATNAP

Near where I lived there was a fenced schoolyard. Where Blind Sorrow Is Taught to See. Suzanne Gardinier. AmPoNex

Near yonder copse, where once the garden smiled. Oliver Goldsmith. TreFP *Fr.* Deserted Village, The.

Nearby creatures of the air. Antonio Porta. ItPo, *tr. by* Gayle Ridinger *Fr.* Essences.

Neare Enna walles there standes a Lake Pergusa is the name. Ovid. OBVE *Fr.* Metamorphoses.

Nearer. Judith Herzberg. BoWoP, *tr. by* Shirley Kaufman

Nearer her they get, The. (LL) Emily Dickinson. NAAL-2v1; NAAL-3; NCAP

Nearer Home. Phoebe Cary. PWR; SacPr
(One Sweetly Solemn Thought.) AH

Nearer, My God, to Thee. Sarah Flower Adams. InvLi; SacPr; TCAPo

Nearer to Thee! (LL) Nearer, My God, to Thee. Sarah Flower Adams. InvLi; SacPr; TCAPo

Nearest Dream recedes—unrealized, The. Emily Dickinson. APN-2

Nearing Again the Legendary Isle. Cecil Day Lewis. FaBoTw; MoBrPo *Fr.* Magnetic Mountain, The.

Nearing La Guaira. Derek Walcott. TTY

Nearing Long Moons. J. L. Jacobs. AmPoNex

Nearing the mountain. Foster Jewell. HA

Nearing the Snow-Line. Oliver Wendell Holmes. APN-1

Nearly a hundred when she died. Grandmother, a Caribbean Indian, Described by My Father. Yvonne Sapia. NIL-7; UnSA

Nearly a twelvemonth we had laboured to complete our house. Visitation. John Dronsfield. PeSAV

Nearly Circle. Heather Ramsdell. AmPoNex

Nearly midnight. Windows open. Summertime. Through Time's Segments. István Vas. IQMS, *tr. by* Daniel Gerard Hoffman

Nearly Nowhere. Catherine Walsh. Oth

Nearly right, The. To the Tune of The Coventry Carol. Stevie Smith. FaBoTw; WoPoe

Nearness. David Lindley. NLP

Nearness of You, The. Ned Washington. ReLy

Nearness to Tremendousness, A. Emily Dickinson. TCAPo

Nearsighted child has taken off her glasses, The. Country Stars. William Meredith. VCAP

Neat greens of Monument Hill, The. Plumburst. John Kinsella. NeBl

Neath blue-bell or streamer. Edgar Allan Poe. OxBA *Fr.* Al Aaraaf.

Neatly pressed / dressed / crowds. Requiem. Bobbi Sykes. IBA

Nebraska. Barbara Guest. FTOS

Nebuchadnezzar. Elinor Wylie. ChIV-1; MoAmPo

Nebuchadnezzar's Dream. John Keats. ChIV-1

Nebuchadnezzar's Kingdom-Come. David Rowbotham. ChIV-1; NOBAu

Necessarie Praier in Meeter against Vices, A. Frances Manners, Lady Abergavenny Nevill. EMWP

Necessary Dirge, A. Ogden Nash. APT-2

Necessitarian's Epitaph, A. Thomas Hardy. FaBoEE

Necessitie and Benefit of Affliction, The. Anne Lok [*or* Locke]. EMWP

Necessities. Mei Yao Ch'en. CrYelRi, *tr. by* Sam Hamill

Necessities of Life. Adrienne Rich. HCAP; NOBA

Necessity. Harry Graham. PeLV *Fr.* Some Ruthless Rhymes.

Necessity. Langston Hughes. APSN; NOBA; RaBo

Necessity. Burton Lane. ReLy

Necessity of Fate, The. Jane Barker. BWW; EMWP

Nechama. Shirley Kaufman. LCAP-2

Necklace of flame, little dropped hearts. Tattoos. Charles Wright. BodElec; HCAP

Necklace of human bones. Regalia in Immediate Demand! Philip Whalen. BB

Neckties. Liz Lochhead. NePenScot; OBCoV

Necrological. John Crowe Ransom. FuPo

Necromance. Rae Armantrout. FTOS; PmAP

Necromancy. Rikki Ducornet. SurWo

Necromancy: The Last Days of Brian Jones, 1968. David Wojahn. SwNoth

Necropolis of Pantàlica. Insomnia. Salvatore Quasimodo. AWTN, *tr. by* Allen Mandelbaum

Nectar of Ápan, The. Enrique Gonzáles Martínez. TCLAP, *tr. by* Elizabeth Gordon

Ned. Eleanor Farjeon. OTCP

Ned knew I was short of tobacco one day. Ned's Delicate Way. Henry Lawson. CBAP

Ned's Delicate Way. Henry Lawson. CBAP

Ned Vaughan. Walter De la Mare. FaBoEE

Need, The. Sewing a Dress. Lorine Niedecker. APT-2

Need for Armor, A. Eileen Stratidakis. PasH

Need for Attention, The. William Wadsworth. KGB

Need for Censorship, The. Reiner Kunze. PoSu, *tr. by* Michael Hamburger

Need for Shoes, The. Molly Bendall. InvLad

Need from excess—excess from folly growing. Epigram. Samuel Bishop. NOEC

Need I that you exist and show youself any more than in these songs. (LL) Not Heaving from My Ribb'd Breast Only. Walt Whitman. APN-1; CAGL

Need Increasing Itself by Rounds. Kathleen Peirce. PBCAP

Need Is Our Name. Luci Shaw. TrCP

Need of Being Versed in Country Things, The. Robert Frost. APT-1; NOBA; NoAM; OxBA; SAmP; TCAPo; TRP; UnPo

Need of Loving. Strickland W. Gillilan. PoToHe

Need the warld ken? (LL) Comin[g] thro' [*or* through] the Rye. Robert Burns. FaBoVe; OxAEP-2; OxBS

Need to explore, The. Explorers as Seen by the Natives. Doug Fetherling. NOBC

Need to Win, The. Chuang Tzu. BLT, *tr. by* Thomas Merton

Needing someone. Discover Me. Opal Palmer Adisa. GT

Needle and Thread. Pan Chao. WPOW; WoPoe, *tr. by* Richard Mather and Rob Swigart

Needle and Thread. Pan Zhao. WPoS, *tr. by* Richard Mather

Needle and thread, A. (LL) Mother Goose. NTCP; OxNR; ReMoGo

Needle growing in ancient basalt. Mac Wellman. HeMarv *Fr.* Rat Minaret: Miniaturist-Divan, The.

Needled by death for change, for simple change. Vegetable Garden, The. Wyatt Prunty. OBGa

Needles. Lucia Maria Perillo. IllVoic

Needles and pins, needles and pins. Proverb. *Unknown.* ReMoGo

Needles of the lofty pine, The. *Unknown.* GrAn

Needless to catalogue heroes. No Man Knows War. Edwin Rolfe. TrJP

Needlework. Mimi Khalvati. MFPA

Needling / threading nighttime sewing machine. What Were You Patching? Ruth Lisa Schechter. UnSA

Needs. A. R. Ammons. NIL-7; NIP-4; OBAL

Needy knife-grinder! whither are you going? Friend of Humanity and the Knife Grinder, The. George Canning. OBCoV; UV

Needy were lined up by order of famine, The. Offended, The. Anne Hébert. BoWoP, *tr. by* Willis Barnstone

Negev. David Rokeah [*or* Rokeakh]. MHP, *tr. by* Ruth Finer Mintz

Neglected for days, for weeks. Potatoes. Eamon Grennan. SpudSo

Neglected Muse! of this our western clime. James Kirke Paulding. APN-1 *Fr.* Backwoodsman, The.

Neglected Wife, The. Yi Talch'ung. WoPoe, *tr. by* Jean S. Grigsby

Neglectful Edward. Robert Graves. MoBrPo

Neglecting thy derision. (LL) To Fortune. Robert Herrick. CavPo; OxBSP

Negotiation. Alan Brownjohn. PeLV

Negotiations. Ray Catina. CDa

Negotiations with a Volcano. Naomi Shihab Nye. GraLe

Negotium Perambulans. Peter Redgrove. OBGa

Negritude. James A. Emanuel. BPo

Negro, The. James A. Emanuel. InPK-6

Negro Ballot, The. Lizelia Augusta Jenkins Moorer. CBWP-3

Negro blood flowing on his brown. Amelia Rosselli. ItPo, *tr. by* Gayle Ridinger

Negro Boy, The. David Samwell. AngWePo

Negro Boy's Tale, The. Amelia Alderson Opie. RWP

Negro Cemetery next to a White One, A. Howard Nemerov. OxBSP

Negro Girl, The. Mary Robinson. RWP

Negro Has a Chance, The. Maggie Pogue Johnson. CBWP-4

Negro Heroines. Lizelia Augusta Jenkins Moorer. CBWP-3

Negro Love Song, A. Paul Laurence Dunbar. APN-2; ColAP; NAAAL; SSLK

Negro Mask. Léopold Sédar Senghor. NegPo, *tr. by* Ellen Conroy Kennedy

Negro peddler of revolt. Jacques Roumain. NegPo *Fr.* Ebony Wood.

Negro's Complaint, The. William Cowper. CABP

Negro's Tragedy, The. Claude McKay. BPo

Negro Schools, The. Lizelia Augusta Jenkins Moorer. CBWP-3

Negro Sermon—Simon Legree, A. Nicholas Vachel Lindsay. *See* Booker Washington Trilogy, The

Negro Servant. Langston Hughes. VGW

Negro Soldier's Civil War Chant. *Unknown.* BPo

(Black Soldier's Civil War Chant.) TAP

Negro Speaks of Rivers, The. Langston Hughes. APT-2; AiP; BPo; ColAP; HAP; HCAP; HarvBoo; HeIP-4; ISC; NAAAL; NAAL-2v2; NAAL-5; NIL-7; NIP-4; NOBA; NoAM; NoP-4; OBCA; PAI; RaBo; SSLK; TAP; TCAPo; TFi; TTY; WeW-3

Negro Spiritual. Claude McKay. APT-1

Negro sprouts from the pavement like an asparagus, A. Stumpfoot on 42nd Street. Louis Simpson. NNaP; UnPo; VGW

Negro Tramp. David Diop. NegPo, *tr. by* Ellen Conroy Kennedy

Negro, The / With the trumpet at his lips. Trumpet Player. Langston Hughes. NAAL-2v2; TTY

Negro Woman, A. William Carlos Williams. SAmP

Negroes, labouring, The. Guadalupe, W.I. Nicolás Guillén. TTY, *tr. by* Anselm Hollo

Negrosaurus wrecks. (LL) Theory on Extinction or What Happened to the Dinosaurs? Kenneth Carroll. AmPoNex; SpirFl

NEHI Strawberry Down-and-Away. Luis Lopez. GeoH

Neighbor. Langston Hughes. APSN; PFTM-1

Neighbor. Richard Hugo. GifTon

Neighbor. Bahiyyih Maroon. SpirFl

Neighbor's Elm, The. Robert Ayres. UrbNat

Neighborhood House, The. Jay Wright. NBV

Neighborhood of my youth. Trip through the Mind Jail, A. Raul Salinas. FaBoA

Neighboring Storms. Greg Williamson. AmPoNex

Neighbors. James Tate. LCAP-2

Neighbour's Pear Tree. Tony Curtis. AngWePo

Neighbours. Gillian Clarke. TCAWP

Neil Diamond. Poet Sings His Painting, The. Lloyd Richardson. WaCA

Neither a lender nor a borrower be. Postmodern: A Definition. Joseph Like. ReTh

Neither can you crack a nut. (LL) Fable: "Mountain and the squirrel, The." Ralph Waldo Emerson. APN-1; NBLV; OBAL; OBCA; OxIBACP; TFi

Neither childhood / nor future. Confession. George Oppen. HarvBoo

Neither cloud nor rain casts. Logging Trestle. Mary Barnard. APT-2

Neither Durst Any Man from That Day Ask Him Any More Questions. Richard Crashaw. ChIV-2

Neither father nor lover. (LL) Elegy for Jane. Theodore Roethke. APT-2; CoAP; ColAP; HAP; HCAP; InPK-6; MoAmPo; NoP-4; PAI; PoE; PoPoPo; TAP; TFi; TRP; TwCP; WeW-3

Neither had said they were going to climb to it. Source, The. David Wagoner. VCAP

Neither Here nor There. William Robert Rodgers. MoBrPo

Neither in idleness consume thy days. Walter Savage Landor. FaBoEE

Neither Innocence or Experience. Dambudzo Marechera. NAfrP

Neither is simple. Talent and Friendship. Thomas Kinsella. HarvBoo

Neither leaving, nor wishing that they were staying. Key, The. Peter Scupham. HarvBoo

Neither of them was better than the other. From Plane to Plane. Robert Frost. MoAmPo

Neither on horseback nor seated. Walt Whitman at Bear Mountain. Louis Simpson. CoAmPo; TRP

Neither our vices nor our virtues. Poetry, a Natural Thing. Robert Duncan. NOBA; NoAM; PmAP; TRP

Neither out Far Nor in Deep. Robert Frost. APT-1; HAP; NAAL-2v2; NOBA; NoAM; NoP-4; TAP; TRP; WeW-3; WoPoe

Neither Poverty nor Riches. Bible, *O.T.* TrJP *Fr.* Proverbs.

Neither Shadow of Turning. Jack R. Clemo. NOCV

Neither the interminable patches of land. Like This. Lajos Kassák. IQMS, *tr. by* Edwin Morgan

Neither the mailboxes nor the windows would tell me. Morbid. Nancy Eimers. ExTi

Neither the paths determine, nor the goal. Command, The. Avraham Huss. MHP, *tr. by* Ruth Finer Mintz

Neither war, nor cyclones, nor earthquakes. Antipater of Thessalonica. GrAn; PGA

Neither will I put myself forward as others may do. Eternal Masculine. William Rose Benét. AWP; MoAmPo

Neither wish death, nor fear his might. (LL) Happy Life, The. Martial. NOBE; NoSic; OBVE, *tr. by* Henry Howard, Earl of Surrey

Neither your hard crystal silence of solid rock. Nocturnal Sea. Xavier Villaurrutia. CAGL, *tr. by* Fanny Arango-Ramos and William Keeth

Nel mezzo dle camino I found myself. Circle Jerk. Andrei Codrescu. PmAP

Nell. Rodney Jones. IllVoic

Nell. Raymond Knister. NOBC *Fr.* Row of Stalls, A.

Nellie Gives into Blanche. Leslie Simon. FFC

Nellie named her Blanche for white and French. two. Nellie Gives into Blanche. Leslie Simon. FFC

Nellie Rakerfield. Raymond Knister. NOBC *Fr.* Row of Stalls, A.

Nelly Kelly loved baseball games. Take Me Out to the Ball Game. Jack Norworth. OBAL

Nelly's Lament for the Pirnhouse Cat. Ellen Johnston. VWP

Nelly Trim. Sylvia Townsend Warner. MoBrPo

Nelson, Pitt, Fox. Sir Walter Scott. OBEV *Fr.* Marmion.

Nemea. Lawrence Durrell. FaBoTw; GTBS-P

Nemesis. Ralph Waldo Emerson. NOBA

Nemoroso. Baldomero Garcilaso de la Vega. BLPSL, *tr. by* Rene de Costa, Rigas Kappatos and Eleni Paidoussi

Neo-Classical Urn, The. Robert Lowell. NAAL-2v2

Neo-Thomist Poem. Ernest Hemingway. OBAL

Neocolonialism. Felix Mnthali. PeSAV

Neon sign blinked red, A. Something Old, Something New. Carl H. Greene. NBV

Neon Signs. Langston Hughes. APSN

(Wonder Bar.) PFTM-1

Neon stripes tighten my wall. Zebra Goes Wild Where the Sidewalk Ends, The. Henry Dumas. GT

Neonbright orange. Robben Island Sequence. Dennis Brutus. HBAPE

Nepenthe. George Darley.

Hundred-gated Thebes. NOBE

(Hundred-sunned Phenix.) OWoS

"Hurry me Nymphs! O, hurry me." NPeEn

"O blest unfabled incense tree." BIrV; FaBoCh; OBEV

(Phoenix, The.) NOBE

Nepenthe. Charlotte Smith. NoP-4

Nephelidia. Algernon Charles Swinburne. PeVV *Fr.* Heptalogia, The.

Nephew, I must to Scotland. Thou stay'st here. Christopher Marlowe. CAGL *Fr.* Edward the Second.

Neptune Goes to the Greeks. Homer. NOSC, *tr.* by George Chapman *Fr.* Iliad, The.

Neptune—Polka. Dame Edith Sitwell. NOBE

Nero. Shuntaro Tanikawa. PoetW, *tr.* by Harold Wright

Nero / Another summer is coming soon. Nero. Shuntaro Tanikawa. PoetW, *tr.* by Harold Wright

Nero commanded; but withdrew his eyes. Cruelties. Robert Herrick. CavPo

Nero, thus much for tidings in thine ear. Guido Cavalcanti. EaItPo, *tr.* by Dante Gabriel Rossetti

Nerve pivots and that space, A. Finite Intuition. Milo de Angelis. NeIt, *tr.* by Lawrence Venuti

Nerves. "Sagittarius." OxBTC

Nerves. Arthur Symons. CABP; FaBoTw

Nerves. Anne Waldman. BodElec

Nerves, blind attraction to. Nerves. Anne Waldman. BodElec

Nervous Prostration. Anna Wickham. FaBoWP

Nervy with neons, the main drag. At Barstow. Charles Tomlinson. NoAM; TwCP

Nest. Amanda Dalton. NeBl *Fr.* Room of Leaves.

Nest, The. Carol Moldaw. UrbNat

Nest, The. Andrew Young. Spl

Nest for Everyone, A. Roberta Spear. GeoHom

Nest in a Wall, A. Richard Murphy. BiHa; CIP-2

Nest of Hats, A. Annie Foster. NLP

Nesting among Clouds. Yang Chi. CoBLCP, *tr.* by Jonathan Chaves

Nesting of Layer Protocols. Kit Robinson. FTOS

Nestle-down Cottage. Mary Weston Fordham. CBWP-2

Nests in Elms. "Michael Field." VWP

Nests of golden porridge shattered in the silky-oak trees. Equanimity. Les A. Murray. NOBAu

Nestus Gurley. Randall Jarrell. HeIP-4; TwCP

Net, The. Fleur Adcock. PeNZ

Net, The. William Robert Rodgers. BoLoP; CIP-2; ModIr; PNI

Net, The. Edith Södergran. WoPoe, *tr.* by David McDuff

Net and the Sword, The. Douglas Le Pan. NOBC

Net Breaker, The. Brewster Ghiselin. APT-2

Net of Moon, The. *Unknown.* STP, *tr.* by Jerome Rothenberg

Net of Place, The. Paul Blackburn. PFTM-2; PmAP

Neteheard. Theocritus. NoSic; OBVE, *tr.* by *Unknown Fr.* Idylls.

Netley Abbey. William Lisle Bowles. Son

Netley Abbey; Midnight. William Sotheby. NOEC

Nets are real—heroin (sniffed) clears them, The. For Artaud. Michael McClure. NeAP

Nettle. *Unknown.* WoPoe, *tr.* by Siv Cedering Fox *Fr.* Two Swedish Riddles.

Nettles, The. Thomas Hardy. OxBSP

Nettles in May. Euros Bowen. OBWVE, *tr.* by the author

Network, The. Arthur Sze. AiP; OpBo

Network of the Imaginary Mother, The. Robin Morgan. "As it was in the beginning." HW

Neurasthenia. Agnes Mary Frances Robinson. NOBVV; NPeEn

Neuroanatomy Summer. Marc J. Straus. BloBone

Neutral British Gentleman, The. "Orpheus C. Kerr." OBAL

Neutral Tones. Thomas Hardy. CABP; EBVV; HAP; HeIP-4; InPK-6; MoBrPo; NAEL-5v2; NAEL-6v2; NOBVV; NPeEn; NoAM; TFi; UnPo

Neutrality. Sidney Keyes. MoBrPo

Neutrality Loathsome. Robert Herrick. ChIV-1

Never. George Reavey. BIrV

Never a careworn wife but shows. Wives in the Sere. Thomas Hardy. NOBE; NOBVV

Never a day, never a day passes. Europe's Prisoners. Sidney Keyes. PoWW

Never a ploughman. Never a one. (LL) Ha'nacker Mill. Joseph Hilaire Pierre Belloc. MoBrPo; OxBTC; RB

Never able to enter. Farmers. Kathleen Peirce. PBCAP

Never afraid of those huge creatures. Horseback. Carolyn Kizer. MoASP

Never Again. Noël Coward. ReLy

Never Again. Jaroslav Seifert. AF, *tr.* by Ewald Osers

Never Again. Richard Henry Stoddard. PWR

(Lost.) TreFP

Never again another garden like. Sándor Weöres. IQMS, *tr.* by Bruce Berlind and Mária Kőrösy

Never again, Orpheus. Antipater of Sidon. GrAn; OBVE; PGA, *tr.* by Kenneth Rexroth

Never again rising at dawn. Cock, A. Anyte [*or* Anytes]. GrAn, *tr.* by Sally Purcell

Never Again the Same. James Tate. BodElec

Never Again Would Birds' Song Be the Same. Robert Frost. APT-1; HAP; InPK-6; NIP-4; NoAM; NoP-4; OWoS; SoSe-8; Son; VGW

Never Apologize; Never Explain. Philip Whalen. BB

Never argue with your heart. Why Shouldn't It Happen to Us? Alberta Nichols. ReLy

Never ask me whose. (LL) Is my team plowing? A. E. Housman. EBVV; MoBrPo; NoAM; OBEV

Never ask of money spent. Robert Frost. FaBoCh; OBAL *Fr.* Ten Mills.

Never before without a ring. My Ringless Fingers on the Steering Wheel Tell the Story. Laura Boss. UnSA

Never believe all you hear. Kenneth Rexroth. NNaP *Fr.* Bestiary, A.

Never, believe me, / Appear the Immortals. Visit of the Gods, The. Samuel Taylor Coleridge. OBVE

Never between the branches has the sky. Brilliant Sky. Jean Joubert. GifTon, *tr.* by Denise Levertov

Never Blood So Red. Grandfather Koori. IBA

Never blood / So red so red. Never Blood So Red. Grandfather Koori. IBA

Never closer the whole rest of our lives. (LL) Seamus Heaney. BLT; PNI *Fr.* Clearances.

Never comes now the through-and-through clear. Not-Returning, The. Ivor Gurney. HarvBoo

Never could carry a tune. Zing! Went the Strings of My Heart. James F. Hanley. ReLy

Never-Dead, The. Anna Couani. BMAP

Never did I learn to share. Expanding. To My Twin Sister Who Died at Birth. Kathleene West. GifTon

Never Eat Oranges! John Nelson. GeoH

Never for us those dreams aforetime shown. Of the Earth, Earthy. Rosamund Marriott Watson. ViWPN

Never—forever! (LL) Old Clock on the Stairs, The. Henry Wadsworth Longfellow. PWR; TreFP

Never forget / We walk on hell. Issa. ZenPo, *tr.* by Takashi Ikemoto and Lucien Stryk

Never forgetting him that kept coming constantly so near. (LL) World as Meditation, The. Wallace Stevens. HeIP-4; LCAP-2

Never Give a Bum an Even Break. James Welch. NoAM

Never Give All the Heart. W. B. Yeats. BoLoP

Never giving thought to fame. On Entering His Coffin. Baiho. ZenPo, *tr.* by Takashi Ikemoto and Lucien Stryk

Never Gonna Dance. Dorothy Fields. ReLy

Never has such turmoil. Turmoil, The. Sorley MacLean (Somhairle MacGill-Eain). HarvBoo

Never in all my life have I seen. Rat, O Rat. Christopher Logue. EmeKit

Never Land. Yusef Komunyakaa. ReTh

Never Let Me Go. Jay Livingston. ReLy

Never love with all your heart. Song in Spite of Myself. Countee Cullen. ISC

Never mind how or why. White. Grace Nichols. Oth

Never mind the fantasy about the tweezers and the tongue. Skin. Brian Henry. AmPoNex

Never more will the wind. "H. D." CTC *Fr.* Hymen.

Never, my partridge, O patient heart. Partridge. Agathias. GrAn, *tr.* by Guy Davenport

Never, never may the fruit be plucked from the bough. Edna St. Vincent Millay. APT-1; NAAL-2v2; OxBSP

Never on this side of the grave again. Life's Parallels, A. Christina Georgina Rossetti. NAEL-5v2; NAEL-6v2

Never Pain to Tell Thy Love. William Blake. *See* Love's Secret

Never Pharaoh's Night. In the Desert. Herman Melville. NCAP

Never presume that in this marble stable. Brass Horse, The. Drummond Allison. FaBoTw

Never saw him. Negro, The. James A. Emanuel. InPK-6

Never saw you look. Easter Parade. Irving Berlin. ReLy

Never Say Fail. *Unknown.* PWR

Never seek [*or* pain] to tell thy love. Love's Secret. William Blake. EnLoPo; ITBLP; NOBE; NPeEn; OxBEV; SCGP

Never Seek to Tell Thy Love. John Ashbery. HCAP

Never shall a young man. For Anne Gregory. W. B. Yeats. NAEL-5v2; NAEL-6v2; OxAEP-2

Never Shall I Forget. Elie Wiesel. HP

Never shall I forget that night. Never Shall I Forget. Elie Wiesel. HP

Never since a child. You're Lucky to Me. Eubie Blake. ReLy

Never so bare and naked was church-stone. Cecco Angiolieri, da Siena. EaItPo, *tr.* by Dante Gabriel Rossetti

Never such innocence again. (LL) MCMXIV. Philip Larkin. EBEV; FaBoWar; HarvBoo; NAEL-5v2; NAEL-6v2; NoAM; NoP-4; OBWP; OxAEP-2

Never Such Love. Robert Graves. BoLoP

Never Swat a Fly. Ray Henderson. ReLy

Never take her away. Song. Vinícius de Moraes. WoPoe, *tr.* by Richard Wilbur

Never talk down to a glowworm. Glowworm. David McCord. NTCP

Never Tell. *Unknown.* OBWVE, *tr.* by Anthony Conran

Never tell me that not one star of all. Star in a Stoneboat, A. Robert Frost. APT-1

Never the loaves and fishes multiplied. Christ Seen by Flemish Painters. Elizabeth Jennings. HarvBoo

Never the Time and the Place. Robert Browning. EnLoPo

Never the tramp of foot or horse. Farewell to Anactoria. Sappho. AWP, *tr.* by Allen Tate

Never think she loves him wholly. Appraisal. Sara Teasdale. MoAmPo

Never think you fortune can bear the sway. On Fortune. Queen of England Elizabeth I. WPE

Never to be lonely like that. Face to Face. Adrienne Rich. NAAL-2v2; NoAM

Never Too Late. Robert Greene. Palmer's Ode, The. CTC; NoSic; SCGP

Never Too Late. John Taggart. FTOS

Never too many fish in a swift creek, Jelaluddin [*or* Jalal al-Din] Rumi. RaBo *Fr.* Three Quatrains.

Never touched a drop last night. That Face. Ralph Blane. ReLy

Never treat others with scorn. Love Thy Neighbor. Harry Revel. ReLy

Never turns him to the bride. (LL) When I Watch the Living Meet. A. E. Housman. HarvBoo; MoBrPo; NOBVV; NPeEn; NoP-4; SCGP

Never until the mankind making. Refusal to Mourn the Death, by Fire, of a Child in London, A. Dylan Thomas. AF; EBEV; FaBoMo; FaBoWar; GTBS-P; HarvBoo; HeIP-4; MoBrPo; NOBE; NoAM; NoP-4; OBWVE; OxAEP-2; OxBTC; PAI; PoE; PoWW; TFi; TwCP; UnPo

Never wake up in a million years. (LL) First Night, A. Peter Kane Dufault. DiPo; NoP-4

Never yet or good that did not soothe. Bonaggiunta Urbiciani. EaItPo, *tr.* by Dante Gabriel Rossetti

Never weather-beaten sail[e] more willing bent to shore. O Come Quickly! Thomas Campion. NOBE; NPeEn; OBEV; OxAEP-1; OxBSP

Never—yes, never—before these months just passed. Acquaintance with Time in Early Autumn. Robert Penn Warren. NAAL-5

Never yet could I endure. "Archpoet," The. EroLit, *tr.* by Helen Waddell *Fr.* Confession, The.

Nevertheless. Marianne Craig Moore. HarvBoo; NAAL-2v2; NoP-4; OxBA; SoSe-8

Nevertheless (I'm in Love with You). Harry Ruby. ReLy

Nevertheless I prefer. Nineteen Sixty Eight. Petra von Morstein. BoWoP, *tr.* by Rosmarie Waldrop

Nevertheless the Moon. Muriel Rukeyser. AWTN

Nevrazumitelny. Wendy Mulford. Oth

New. Jennifer Maiden. BMAP

New Age, The. Stevie Smith. NAEL-5v2; NAEL-6v2

New/Aguas Buenas/Jersey. Víctor Hernández Cruz. TouFir

New air has come around us. Dakota: October, 1822, Hunkpapa Warrior. Rod Taylor. WeW-3

New Ancient of Days, The. Herman Melville. OBAL

New Apartment. Linda Hogan. HATNAP; UnSA

New Approach Needed. Kingsley Amis. NoAM; OxBTC

New Arrival. Kenneth Mackenzie. *See* Hospital—Retrospections, The

New Baby, The. Fred Emerson Brooks. VerBaPo

New Bamboo in the North Garden at Ch'ang-ku. Li Ho. SuSp, *tr.* by Irving Y. Lo

New Bath Guide, The. Christopher Anstey. "Hearken, Lady Betty, hearken." NOEC "This morning, dear mother, as soon as 'twas light." ECEV

New Birth, The. Jones Very. APN-1; NCAP; NOBA; SacPr

New book—the making and breaking of me—ringing out from the Tower of the Supreme Hour!, A. Supreme Hour, The. Viktor Aleksandrovich Sosnora. ItGoST, *tr.* by F. D. Reeve

New books of poetry will be written. Coronal, A. William Carlos Williams. TCAPo

New-Born Baby's Song, The. Frances Darwin Cornford. NIL-7

New-born moon gives little light, The. To the Tune "New Moon." Yang Shen. CoBLCP, *tr.* by Jonathan Chaves

New Boy, The. Peter E. Murphy. OPRER

New Brooms, The. Odia Ofeimun. NAfrP

New Canaans Genius; Epilogus. Thomas Morton. SCAP

New Cantata, A. Clara Reeve. ECWP

New cinematic emporium, The. Limerick. *Unknown.* PeLi

New Clouds, The. William Carlos Williams. HarvBoo

New Colossus, The. Emma Lazarus. APN-2; AiP; AmFaPo; CA; FaBoA; GS; GSo; HHAm; NIL-7; NoP-4; SWaP; Son; TCAPo; WPE

New-Comer, A. Herman Melville. *Fr.* Clarel: A Poem and Pilgrimage in the Holy Land.

New Comers. Melinda Goodman. WiU

New Constructions. John Ashbery. KGB

New Corn. Ch'ien T'ao. ChiP, *tr.* by Arthur Waley

New-Courtier, The. Alexander Brome. BASC

New Courtly Sonet [*or* Sonnet], of the Lady Greensleeves, A. *Unknown.* NPeEn; NoSic; PBRV *See also* Greensleeves (My Lady Greensleeves.) OxAEP-1

New Crops for a Free Man. Ai. BodElec

New Cup and Saucer, A. Gertrude Stein. TTTS *Fr.* Tender Buttons.

New Dawn, The. Mafika Pascal Gwala. PeSAV

New Day. Naomi Long Madgett. BlSi

New day cancels dread, The. Psalm: The New Day. Mark Jarman. AWTN

New Days for Old, Old Days for New. Philip Levine. TaR

New decade, the teacher cried, A. My Mother's Young Sister. Roy McFadden. PNI

New Delhi, 1974. Vinay Dharwadker. OMIP

New Diary, A. Dannie Abse. AngWePo; NoAM

New Dodo is finished, The. O! come to my nest. (LL) Thomas Lovell Beddoes. NOBVV; OxBEV *Fr.* Death's Jest Book.

New Dog. Mark Doty. WiU *Fr.* Atlantis.

New doth the sun appear. Change Should Breed Change. William Drummond, of Hawthornden. OBEV

New Dream (Wuski A-Baw-Tan), A. Jennifer Pierce Eyen. ReEnLa

New Dub, A. "Mbala." WaCA

New earth mother. Archie Weller. IBA

New Emigration, The. Kay Boyle. WPE

New England. Edwin Arlington Robinson. HeIP-4; MoAmPo; NAAL-2v2; NOBA; OxBA; PoPoPo; TAP

New England Bachelor, A. Richard Eberhart. MoAmPo; NoAM

New-England Boy's Song about Thanksgiving Day, The. Lydia Maria Child. *See* Thanksgiving Day

New England first a wilderness was found. America. Phillis Wheatley. TCAPo

New England Primer, The. *Unknown.* ABC, An. OBCA (Alphabet.) OxIBACP John Rogers' Exhortation to His Children. OBCA

New England Wind. Eileen Myles. PmAP

New-England's Crisis. Benjamin Tompson. SCAP

New English Canaan; Prologue. Thomas Morton. SCAP

New Faces, The. W. B. Yeats. GTBS-P

New falconer. Invocation. Sana'i. BBASP, *tr.* by Nasrollah Pourjavady and Peter Lamborn Wilson

New Fashions. George Moses Horton. OBAL

New flood came, transcending Ipoly's banks. Lőrinc Szabó. IQMS, *tr.* by Watson Kirkconnell *Fr.* Cricket Music.

New foal, The. Issa. EH, *tr.* by Robert Hass

New follies spring; and now we must be taught. Picturesque; a Fragment. John Aikin. NOEC

New, fresh again, the first sunny breeze. Again! Ferdinand von Saar. AuPH, *tr.* by Lowell A. Bangerter

New Friends and Old Friends. Joseph Parry. ITBLP; PoToHe

New from Ethiopia and the Sudan, The. John Pepper Clark Bekedermo. HBAPE

New Ghost, The. Fredegond Maitland Shove. SacPr

New ghosts weep over lost battles. Facing the Snow. Tu Fu. CrYelRi, *tr.* by Sam Hamill

New Guide, A. Kenneth Koch. BodElec

New Guinea. James Philip McAuley. NOCV

New Guinea Time. Louis Johnson. PeNZ

New Hampshire. T. S. Eliot. FaBoCh; GTBS-P; NoAM; WeW-3 *Fr.* Landscapes.

New Hampshire. Donald Hall. LCAP-2

New Hampshire, February. Richard Eberhart. TwCP

New Heart, The. Semyon [*or* Semion] Isaakovich Kirsanov. CLPP, *tr.* by Anselm Hollo

New Heaven, New War[re]. Robert Southwell. ChIV-2; ESCV; NOBE; NoP-4 (Come to your heaven, you heavenly choirs.) NoP-4 (This little Babe so few dayes olde.) NPeEn

New Heavens for Old. Amy Lowell. APT-1

New Holland is a barren place, in it there grows no grain. Lowlands of Holland, The. *Unknown.* OxBB

New House, The. Edward Thomas. EBEV; MoBrPo; NOBE; OBEV; OBWVE

New houses grasp our hillside. Andante. Gwen Harwood. HarvBoo

New hunt, A / the morning bent. Clark Coolidge. APSN *Fr.* At Egypt.

New Illiterate Lay-Teachers, The. Rowland Watkyns. BASC

New Incidents in the Life of Shelley. Robert Johnstone. "Not from our dreams, not from our daft cadres." PNI

New Indian Medicine. Emma Lee Warrior. HATNAP
New Inn, The. Ben Jonson.
　"It was a beauty that I saw." BeJo
　(Vision of Beauty, A.) BASC; NOSC
New Jersey Boys. Robert Coles. BloBone
New Jersey Turnpike. Richard Cumbie. NBLV
And Did Those Feet. William Blake. *See* Milton
New Jerusalem, The. Allan M. Laing. UV
New Jerusalem, The. *Unknown. See* Hierusalem
New Jewish Hospital at Hamburg, The. Heinrich Heine. TrJP, *tr.* by Charles Godfrey Leland
New Knighthood, The. Rudyard Kipling. UV
New knowledge of reality, A. (LL) Not Ideas about the Thing but the Thing Itself. Wallace Stevens. APT-1; HAP; HCAP; LCAP-2; PFTM-2; SAmP; TAP
New laugh, The. Woman Dragged by Welsh Corgis. Joan Retallack. FTOS
New Leaf, A [*or* The]. Helen Field Fischer. PoToHe
New Life. Joseph E. Kariuki. TTY
New Life, The. Louise Glück. BodElec
New Light, A. William Hawkins. MoCV
New light gives new directions, Fortunes new. Christopher Marlowe. NoSic; PBRV *Fr.* Hero and Leander.
New Lines for Cuscuscaraway and Mirza Murad Ali Beg. Louis Simpson. OBAL
New Litany, Occasioned by an Invitation to a Wedding, A. Elizabeth Thomas. ECWP
New Little Boy, The. Harry Behn. TLR
New little boy moved in next door, A. New Little Boy, The. Harry Behn. TLR
New London, The. Dryden. FaBoCh *Fr.* Annus Mirabilis.
New Love and the Gentle Heart. Dante Alighieri. RaBo
New love and the gentle heart are the same thing. New Love and the Gentle Heart. Dante Alighieri. RaBo
New Man, The. Jones Very. APN-1; NOBA; TCAPo
New man flies in from Manchester, A. New Poet Arrives, A. Gavin Ewart. OxBTC
New Mexican Mountain. Robinson Jeffers. NoAM
New Mistress, The. A. E. Housman. MoBrPo
New Miz Praise de Lawd, The. Nicole Breedlove. InTrad
New Monthly Magazine, 44 286–8. Letitia [*or* Laetitia] Elizabeth Landon. Stanzas on the Death of Mrs Hemans. VWP
New Moon. Tu Fu. ChinPo, *tr.* by Yip Wai-lim
New Moon. Tu Fu. OHPC, *tr.* by Kenneth Rexroth
New Moon, The. William Gilmore Simms. APN-1
New Moon, The. *Unknown.* WoPoe, *tr.* by Siv Cedering Fox *Fr.* Two Swedish Riddles.
New Moon Ceremonies. *Unknown. Fr.* Minnetare Songs.
New moon hangs like an ivory bugle, The. Penny Whistle, The. Edward Thomas. MoBrPo
New moon has come up and the autumn dew is light, A. Song of Autumn Night. Wang Ya. SuSp, *tr.* by Irving Y. Lo
New moon! New king! Marriage of Death, The. László Szabédi. IQMS, *tr.* by John Gordon Nichols
New moon stirs pangs of love, The. First Love. Vidyapati. ErotSp, *tr.* by Sam Hamill
New Morality. George Canning.
　"From mental mists to purge a nation's eyes." NOEC
New Mother. Sharon Olds. PasH
New-mown hay smell and wind of the plain made her a woman whose. Population Drifts. Carl Sandburg. OxBA
New Mr Barnsley Something, The. Geoff Hattersley. NeBl
New Music. Gwen Harwood. CBAP
New Music, A. Haniel Long. APT-1
New Negro Sermon. Jacques Roumain. NegPo, *tr.* by Ellen Conroy Kennedy
New Netherland, 1654. Grace Schulman. OPRER
New Night Thoughts on Death; a Parody. William Whitehead. NOEC
New Noah, The. "Adonis" [*or* "Adunis"]. AF, *tr.* by Abdullah Al-Udhari
New Organ, The. Josephine D. Henderson Heard. CBWP-4
New Orleans. Joy Harjo. HATNAP
New Orleans Haiku. Kalamu ya Salaam.
　All Nite Long. SpirFl
　Everywhere You Eat. SpirFl
　French Quarter Intimacies. SpirFl
　Funeraled Fare Well. SpirFl
　Height, Breadth, Depth. SpirFl
　Makes You Go Oohhh! SpirFl
　New Orleans Rainbow. SpirFl
　Our Natures Rise. SpirFl
　Quarter Moon Rise. SpirFl
　Round Midnight, Place de Congo. SpirFl
　Secondline Send Off. SpirFl
　Spice of Life, The. SpirFl
　Spiritual Geography. SpirFl
　St. Louis Cemetery Crypt. SpirFl
　Sunrise on the River. SpirFl
　Til Death Do Us Part. SpirFl
New Orleans Rainbow. Kalamu ya Salaam. SpirFl *Fr.* New Orleans Haiku.
New Our Father, The. Priscilla Baird Hinckley. HW
New peach blossoms are glowing, The. Flying Petals. Hsiao Kang. OHMPC, *tr.* by Kenneth Rexroth
New Periods—of Pain. (LL) Pain Has an Element of Blank. Emily Dickinson. APN-2; ColAP; HeIP-4; MoAmPo; NAAL-2v1; NAAL-3; SWaP; TCAPo
New Philosophy of Composition, or, How to Ignore the Non-Reasoning Creature Capable of *Speeech* Perched outside Your Bathroom Window, A. Olena Kalytiak Davis. NAPBL
New Poem, A. Robert Duncan. NNaP; PoM
　(New Poem (for Jack Spicer), A.) FTOS
New Poem, The. Charles Wright. HCAP
New Poet Arrives, A. Gavin Ewart. OxBTC
New Presbyter is but old Priest writ[t] large. (LL) On the New Forcers of Conscience under the Long Parliament. John Milton. BASC; NAEL-5v1; NAEL-6v1; NOSC; PBRV; Son
New Prince, New Pomp[e]. Robert Southwell. ChrPo; ESCV; NOBE; NOCV; NoSic; SacPr; TrCP
New Realism. Joseph Ceravolo. PmAP
New Reality Is Better than a New Movie!, A. Imamu Amiri Baraka. NoAM
New Release, A. Alice Fulton. AllShUp
New ridge spreads underneath, A. Volcanoes, often. Wandering Curves. Keith Waldrop. PmAP
New River Head, a Fragment, The. E. Dower. NOEC
New Rock n Roll, The. Brendan Cleary. NeBl
New Rule, The. Jelaluddin [*or* Jalal al-Din] Rumi. RaBo, *tr.* by Coleman Barks and Robert Bly
New salem in patches of snow. Late Winter in Menard County. John Knoepfle. IllVoic
New sensation, A. "H. D." APT-1 *Fr.* Tribute to the Angels.
"New Sensibility" or not, The. Wordsworths: William and Dorothy, The. Thomas Lux. BodElec
New Sentience, The. Alan Davies. FTOS
New Sermons and Preachings of the Christ of Elqui (1979). Nicanor Parra.
　"Who are my friends / the sick / the weak / the poor in spirit." GI
New Shoes. John Agard. OTCP
New shoes, new shoes. Choosing Shoes. Ffrida Wolfe. ChAP
New-slain Knight, The. *Unknown.* ESPB
New snow covers everything, The. Possibility. Charles Coe. UrbNat
New Song. Vincente Huidobro. CuPo
New Song, A. Seamus Heaney. CABP; CIP-2; FaBoTw
New Song of New Similies, A. John Gay. NOBL
New Song of Solomon. Cyrus Cassells. WiU
New Song of Wood's Halfpence, A. Jonathan Swift. OxBoLi
New Song on the Birth of the Prince of Wales, A. John Harkness. NOBVV
New songs of Praise to Christ our King. (LL) Once More, Our God, Vouchsafe to Shine! Samuel Sewall. AH; SacPr
New splendour to the dead. (LL) To Stella. Plato. EnLoPo; FaBoEE; OBVE
New Spoon River, The. Edgar Lee Masters.
　Marx the Sign Painter. NoAM; TAP
　Unknown Soldiers. NoAM; TAP
New Spring, A. Albert D. Mackie. OxBS
New Stanzas to Augusta. Joseph Brodsky.
　"September came on Tuesday." WoPoe, *tr.* by George L. Kline
New Stars, The. Martinus Nijhoff. WoPoe, *tr.* by Raphael Rudnik
New stirrings converge in the mist. Anti-mnemonic self-vaccination. Joyce Mansour. MFP, *tr.* by Martin Sorrell
New Storefront. Russell Atkins. GT
New Strain. George Starbuck. TwCP
New Style, The. David [*or* Daibhi][*or* Daithi] O'Bruadair [*or* Ó Bruadair]. BIrV, *tr.* by John Montague
New styles of architecture, a change of heart. (LL) Petition. W. H. Auden. NAEL-5v2; NAEL-6v2; Son
New Suit, The. Nidia Sanabria de Romero. ChAP, *tr.* by Arnaldo D. Larrosa and Naomi Shihab Nye
New Sweater. Kees Ouwens. TuT, *tr.* by Peter Van de Kamp
New Tarantella. Paul Griffin. UV
New Tenants, The. Edwin Arlington Robinson. NoAM

New Testament, The. Who Will Throw the First Stone? Clara Silva. TANSG, *tr. by* Celeste Kostopulos-Cooperman

New Thatched Hall, A. Po Chü-i. CoBCP, *tr. by* Burton Watson

New thatched hall, five spans by three, A. New Thatched Hall, A. Po Chü-i. CoBCP, *tr. by* Burton Watson

New things succeed, as former things grow old. (LL) Ceremonies for Candlemas[se] Eve. Robert Herrick. BeJo; CaPo

New ties, fifteen each, ten. Ties. Raymond Souster. MoCV

New Time. Leslie Scalapino.
  "There's still on the rim of night (having been in it) which is (in night)." ExTi

New Toy, The. Thomas Hardy. ChAP

New True Anthem, The. Kevin Gilbert. IBA

New Verses for June 7, 1951. Jan Hanlo. TuT, *tr. by* Eamon Grennan

New Vestments, The. Edward Lear. NOBVV

New Vicar of Bray, The. Colin Ellis. NOBL

New volcano has erupted, A. Crusoe in England. Elizabeth Bishop. APT-2; EmeKit; FaBoVe; HCAP; PoPoPo; RACG

New Wife, The. Ng Shao. OHMPC, *tr. by* Kenneth Rexroth

New Wife, The. Wang Chien. BLT
  (I sent some first for sister-in-law to try.) (LL) CoBCP, *tr. by* Burton Watson
  (On the third day she went down to the kitchen.) BLT

New Windows. Claudia Rankine. GT

New Wings for Icarus. Henry Beissel.
  "In the one-two domestic goose one-two one-two step." MoCV

New Words. Coleman Barks.
  "So it is." CRP

New World. Sally Roberts Jones. AngWePo

New World. Derek Walcott. OxBC

New World, The. Imamu Amiri Baraka. NoAM; NoP-4; PmAP

New World, The. Valerie Martínez. TouFir

New World, The. Jones Very. APN-1

New World A-Comin' Edward Kamau Brathwaite. NoP-4 *Fr.* Arrivants: A New World Trilogy, The.

"New World" Interview. Bruce Sweet. MiVo

New World Symphony, A. Kit Wright. NBLV; PeLV

New Year. Philip Larkin. ChrPo

New Year. Naomi Shihab Nye. LoL

New Year. Christopher Smart. ChrPo *Fr.* Hymns and Spiritual Songs for the Fasts and Festivals of the Church of England.

New Year. Stephen Spender. AWP

New year. Yasuharau Teishitsu. JDP, *tr. by* Yoel Hoffmann

New Year, The. Horatio Nelson Powers. PoToHe

New Year, The. Ryu'u. JDP, *tr. by* Yoel Hoffmann

New Year, The. Mark Strand. UnPo *Fr.* Elegy for My Father.

New Year, The. *Unknown. See* New Year Carol, A

New Year, The. Nathaniel Parker Willis. TreFP

New year arrived, The. Issa. SoOfWa, *tr. by* Sam Hamill

New-year bells are wrangling with the snow, The. (LL) Year's End. Richard Wilbur. CoAP; HeIP-4; NAAL-2v2

New Year Carol, A. *Unknown.* OxBoLi
  (New Year, The.) OBCP

New year, forth looking out of Janus' gate. Edmund Spenser. NoSic *Fr.* Amoretti.

New Year Greeting, A. W. H. Auden. HarvBoo

New year has dawned and we meet it with gladness, The. New Year's Morning; or, the First Day of the Year. Mrs. Henry Linden. CBWP-4

New Year Letter. W. H. Auden.
  ("Long time since it seems today, A.") FaBoA

New Year Letter. Edward Kamau Brathwaite. GT

New Year March: A Declaration, The. Yuly [*or* Iulii] Markovich Daniel. TCRP, *tr. by* Arthur Boyars and David Burg

New Year on Dartmoor. Sylvia Plath. FaBoWP

New Year's. Charles Reznikoff. TaR; VGW

New Year's Blizzard, The. Su Tung-p'o (Su Shih). CoBCP, *tr. by* Burton Watson

New Year's dawn. Wagin. JDP, *tr. by* Yoel Hoffmann

New Year's Day. Issa. EH, *tr. by* Robert Hass

New Year's Day. Robert Lowell. ChrPo; CoAmPo; TRP

New Year's Day. Lucien Stryk. IllVoic *Fr.* Issa: A Suite of Haiku.

New Year's Day—Following the Rhymes of Inspector Luan-chiang. Pien Kung. CoBLCP, *tr. by* Jonathan Chaves

New Year's Eve. Boethius. MLL, *tr. by* Helen Waddell *Fr.* Consolation of Philosophy, The ("De Consolacione Philosophie").

New Year's Eve. John Davidson.
  Imagination. MoBrPo

New Year's Eve. Lavinia Greenlaw. MFPA

New Year's Eve. Thomas Hardy. MoBrPo; NoAM

New Year's Eve. D. H. Lawrence. BoLoP

New Year's Eve. Liu E. CoBLCP, *tr. by* Jonathan Chaves

New Year's Eve. Su Tung-p'o (Su Shih). CoBCP, *tr. by* Burton Watson

New Year's Eve. Wen Cheng-ming. CoBLCP, *tr. by* Jonathan Chaves

New Year's Eve. Yang Wen-li. WoPoe, *tr. by* Nancy Hodes and Tung Yuan-fang

New Year's Eve at the Home of Tu Wei. Tu Fu. CrYelRi, *tr. by* Sam Hamill

New Year's Eve Blizzard, The. Su Tung-p'o (Su Shih). CoBCP, *tr. by* Burton Watson

New Year's Eve 1917. Karl Kraus. AuPH, *tr. by* Lowell A. Bangerter

New Year's Eve, 1938. John Frederick Nims. ChrPo

New Year's Eve Poem 1965. Peter Levi. OxAEP-2

New Year's first poem. Buson. SoOfWa, *tr. by* Sam Hamill

New Year's Gift, A. William Cartwright. BeJo

New Year's holiday. Spring Wind on the Riverbank at Kema. Buson. EH, *tr. by* Robert Hass

New Year's Letter in Warsaw, A. Andrey [*or* Andrei] Andreievich Voznesensky [*or* Voznesenskii]. TCRusP, *tr. by* Daniel Weissbort

New Year's Morning. Elmaz Abinader. PoArWo

New Year's morning. Issa. EH, *tr. by* Robert Hass

New Year's Morning; or, the First Day of the Year. Mrs. Henry Linden. CBWP-4

New-Year's [*or* New-Yeares] Gift Sent to Sir Simeon Steward, A. Robert Herrick. CaPo

New Year's [*or* Year] Song. Ted Hughes. OBCP

New Year's Poem. Margaret Avison. NOBC

New Year's Sacrifice: To Lucinda, A. Thomas Carew. CaPo

New Year's Season and Its Poetasters, The. Trần Tế Xu'o'ng. WoPoe, *tr. by* Nguyen Ngoc Bich

New Year's Gift, A. William Cartwright. OxAEP-1

New Yeir Gift to the Quene Mary, quhen scho come first Hame, 1562, Ane. Alexander Scott.
  "Welcum, illustrat Ladye, and oure Quene!" NePenScot

New York. "Æ" OBMV

New York. Steven Blevins. PoCoUp

New York. Federico García Lorca. RaBo, *tr. by* Robert Bly

New York. Marianne Craig Moore. NAAL-2v2

New York. Léopold Sédar Senghor. *See* To New York

New York Airport at Night. Andrey [*or* Andrei] Andreievich Voznesensky [*or* Voznesenskii]. TCRP, *tr. by* William Jay Smith

New York! At first I was bewildered by your beauty. To New York. Léopold Sédar Senghor. PoetW; WoPoe, *tr. by* Melvin Dixon

New York! At first I was confused by your beauty, by those great golden long-legged girls. To New York. Léopold Sédar Senghor. PBA

New York! At first I was confused by your beauty, those tall long-legged golden girls. Léopold Sédar Senghor. *See* New York! At first I was confused by your beauty, by those great golden long-legged girls

New York City. Michael Castro. UrbNat

New York City. Helen Waddell. MLL

New York City fails to be spectacular from my teacher's car. Short History of Autumn, A. Anselm Berrigan. HeMarv

New York City 1970. Audre Lorde. NBV

New York Elegy. Yevgeny Aleksandrovich Yevtushenko [*or* Evtushenko]. TCRP, *tr. by* Albert C. Todd and John Updike

New York Face, A. Edwin Denby. APT-2

New York. Five A.M. Man with the Saxophone, The. Ai. SeSe

New York has had it, newsmen all proclaim. New York Sonnet. Judith Rodriguez. NOBAu

New York is a wonderful town. Who Knows? Harold Rome. ReLy

New York is the Old Country to me. Old Countries. Aurora Levins Morales. PueRic

New York Minute. Joe Osterhaus. AmPoNex

New York, New York. Adolph Green. ReLy

New York Newsday: Truth, Justice and Vomit. Paul Beatty. InTrad

New York Notebooks, The. Howard Moss. BodElec

New York's lovely weather / hurts my forehead. Bean Spasms. Ted Berrigan. PmAP; SPE

New York Sonnet. Judith Rodriguez. NOBAu

New York Spring. Linda France. MFPA

New Zealand. James Keir Baxter. NoP-4

Newark Abbey. Thomas Love Peacock. NOBE

Newark Public Library Reading Room, The. Sotère Torregian. NBV

Newborn, diaper-clad, same as a child. Star Child. Thomas Sayers Ellis. NeAmPo

Newborn Lover. Vivian Lamarque. CItWP, *tr. by* Cinzia Sartini Blum and Lara Trubowitz

Newborn, on the naked sand. Song for the Newborn. *Unknown.* WPE, *tr. by* Mary Austin

Newcombe at the Croydon Gallery. Arthur Nortje. HBAPE

Newcomer's Wife, The. Thomas Hardy. BoLoP; OxBTC

Newcomers on the hill have cut the trees. Broken View, A. Robert Francis. APT-2

Newer headstones tense against the cold, The. Churchyard under Snow. David Scott. NLP

Newgate's Garland. John Gay. ECEV; PeLV

Newly Dead and Newly Born. Eliza Ogilvy. VWP

Newly Discovered "Homeric" Hymn, A. Charles Olson. NeAP; NoAM; PoM

Newly shaven, your eyes only slightly bloodshot. Desires. Connie Bensley. FaBoWP

Newly Wed Girl, The. *Unknown.* WoPoe, *tr. by* David Ray *Fr.* Gathasaptasati, The.

Newly wed girl, pregnant already, The. *Unknown.* WoPoe, *tr. by* David Ray *Fr.* Gathasaptasati, The.

Newlyweds, The. John Updike. OBCoV

News. Lorine Niedecker. PFTM-1

News. Thomas Traherne. NOBE; OBEV *Fr.* Third Century, The.

News, The. Tuini Ngawai. PeNZ, *tr. by* Kumeroa Ngoingoi Pewhairangi

News, The. John Godfrey Saxe. NBLV

News bulletin from Keith Lampe. Joanne Kyger. BB

News for the Delphic Oracle. W. B. Yeats. FaBoMo; NoAM

News from a foreign [*or* forein *or* forrein] country came. Thomas Traherne. NOBE; OBEV *Fr.* Third Century, The.

News from a Pacified Area. James Keir Baxter. OxBC

News from Norwood. Christopher Middleton. FaBoMo

News, Indeed, The!—pray do you call it news. News, The. John Godfrey Saxe. NBLV

News Item. Dorothy Parker. APT-1; NALW; OBAL *Fr.* Some Beautiful Letters.

News of a Baby. Elizabeth Riddell. ItWoWo

News of My Mother. Jean-Baptiste Tati-Loutard. PBMAP *Fr.* Poèmes de la Mer (1968).

News of the Changes. Bryan Aspden. AngWePo

News of the Occluded Cyclone. Alice Fulton. WeW-3

News of the palace. Lady Ise. BoWoP

News of the Phoenix. Arthur James Marshall Smith. MoCV

News of the World II. George Barker. FaBoTw

News of the World III. George Barker. FaBoTw

News of us spreads like a storm. Pounding Rain. Jackie Kay. MFPA; PoBW

News of Your Death. Callimachus. WoPoe, *tr. by* Stanley Lombardo and Diane Rayor

News peels off my arms and legs in a wind that doesn't quite hurt, The. What Say. John Godfrey. FTOS

News Report. David Ignatow. TwCP

News Update. John Balaban. AF; CDa

News which might well reach you, The / before this letter? (LL) Ellen West. Frank Bidart. NAAL-2v2; RACG

Newscast. Jared Angira. NAfrP

Newscast, The. Ian Hamilton. FaBoWar; NPeEn

Newspaper, A. Stephen Crane. APN-2; NAAL-2v2 *Fr.* War Is Kind.

Newspaper, The. Penina Moise. SWaP

Newspaper appears in the morning, The. Elegy. Khalifa Al-Wugayyan. MAP, *tr. by* John Heath-Stubbs and Lena Jayyusi

Newspaper, glanced at by chance, A. It has something to do with final words. Gladys Cardiff. ReEnLa

Newspaper is a collection of half injustices, A. Stephen Crane. APN-2; NAAL-2v2 *Fr.* War Is Kind.

Newspapers rise high in the air over Maryland. At a March against the Vietnam War. Robert Bly. SPE

Newsreel. Cecil Day Lewis. MoBrPo

Newsreel. Adrienne Rich. FaBoWP; HCAP *Fr.* Shooting Script.

Newsvendor with his hut and crutch, The. Imprisoned, The. Robert Fitzgerald. TwCP

Newton's Descent. Irene Plazewska. SurWo

Newton's Statue. William Wordsworth. HAP *Fr.* Prelude; Growth of a Poet's Mind [1850 vers.], The.

Next, bidding all draw near on bended knees. Pope. ECEV; OBSV *Fr.* Dunciad, The.

Next came one / Who mourn'd in earnest, when the Captive Ark. John Milton. EBEV *Fr.* Paradise Lost.

Next Day. Randall Jarrell. AmFaPo; HAP; HCAP; HarvBoo; NAAL-2v2; NoAM; NoP-4; VCAP; WeW-3

Next day, the deadlock broke. (LL) What the Moon Saw. Nicholas Vachel Lindsay. FaBoEE; OxBSP

Next Day the Fog Was Even Worse, The. Yüan Mei. CoBLCP, *tr. by* Jonathan Chaves

Next day they rambled round the town, and swore. James Bisset. NOEC *Fr.* Ramble of the Gods through Birmingham.

Next died the Lady, who yon Hall possess'd. George Crabbe. NOBE *Fr.* Parish Register, The.

Next Door. Laini Mataka. ISC

Next Door. Mei Yao Ch'en. OHPC, *tr. by* Kenneth Rexroth

Next door a woman is hanging. Clean Sheets. Lisa D. Chavez. AmPoNex

Next, for October, to some sheltered coign. Folgore da San Geminiano [*or* Gimignano]. EaItPo, *tr. by* Dante Gabriel Rossetti *Fr.* Sonnets of the Months.

Next Heaven [*or* Heav'n] my vows to thee (O sacred Muse!). Upon the Saying That My Verses Were Made by Another. Anne Killigrew. BASC; CABP; EMWP; NALW; PEW; WPE

Next him Jack Squire through his own tear-drops sploshes. Roy Campbell. OxBTC *Fr.* Georgiad, The.

Next, in a low-browed cave, a little hell. William Thompson. ECEV *Fr.* Sickness.

Next is your lot, fair, to be numbered one. To His Kinswoman, Mrs. Penelope Wheeler. Robert Herrick. CaPo

Next Morning. *Unknown.* WoPoe, *tr. by* Andrew Schelling

Next Page. Atmanam. OMIP, *tr. by* A. K. Ramanujan

Next, Please. Philip Larkin. CABP; HarvBoo; MoBrPo

Next Poem, The. Dana Gioia. DiPo; NoP-4

Next summer she'll be too old for naps. Balance. James Harris. PasH

Next they invented alphabets. Cabalistic Rabbis, The. Rosita Kalina. MirDau, *tr. by* Roberta Gordenstein

Next they leave it leagues behind, The. (LL) Anno 1829. Heinrich Heine. AWP; OBVE, *tr. by* Charles Stuart Calverley

Next thing, I wake up in a swaying bunk. Journey: the North Coast. Robert Gray. BMAP

Next time my mother comes to visit, The. Libation. Palorine Williams. Prnts

Next time 1930 rolls around. (LL) This One's on Me. Phyllis Gotlieb. MoCV; NOBC

Next time she came when the moon was windblown. Night Visit. Adriann Roland Holst. TuT, *tr. by* Paula Meehan

Next time you walk by my place. Look Here. Pamela Alexander. ExTi

Next to my office where I edit poems ("Can poems be edited?") there is the Chicago Models Club. Editing *Poetry.* Karl Shapiro. IllVoic

Next to my own skin, her pearls. My mistress. Warming Her Pearls. Carol Ann Duffy. MakPoe; NePenScot; NoP-4; PoBW

Next to of course god america i. E. E. Cummings. FaBoA; InPK-6; NAAL-2v2; NAAL-5; NBLV; NoP-4; OBWP; OxBA; PAI; PoWW; RaBo; TAP; TFi; VGW

Next to the *Café Chaos.* Olga Broumas. BodElec

Next to the fair ascent our steps we traced. Samuel Boyse. OBGa *Fr.* Triumphs of Nature, The.

Next to the fresh grave of my beloved grandmother. Ireland 1972. Paul Durcan. PBCIP

Next to the white window. Jan Freeman. OxWW *Fr.* Autumn Sequence.

Next to the wine. Claustrophobia. Sean O Riordain. ModIr, *tr. by* Patrick Crotty

Next to Tut. Jon Veinberg. GeoHom

Next Two Tablets, The. Armand Schwerner. BodElec

Next unto God, to whom I owe. To Retiredness. Mildmay Fane, 2d Earl of Westmorland. BeJo; NOSC

Next War, The. Wilfred Owen. Son

Next War, The. Sir Osbert Sitwell. PoWW

Next Year. Nora Perry. PoToHe

Next Year, in Jerusalem. Shirley Kaufman. UnSA

"Next year, next year," we say. Next Year. Nora Perry. PoToHe

Next year the grave grass will cover us. Street Corner College. Kenneth Patchen. APT-2; CLPP; MoAmPo

Next year we are to bring the soldiers home. Homage to a Government. Philip Larkin. EBEV; NoAM; OxBEV

Ngaa. . . now then. Paddy Biran's Song. Paddy Biran. CBAP, *tr. by* R. M. W. Dixon

Ngarnbarndtar. W. Les Russell. IBA

Ngoh m' sick gong tong hwa. Going Home. Wing Tek Lum. UnSA

Ngungalari. Archie Weller. RACG

Ni Tsan Poem Following Rhyme-Words of Wu Chen. Wu Chen. CoBLCP, *tr. by* Jonathan Chaves

Niagara. Adelaide Crapsey. APT-1; PAI

Niagara. Joseph Rodman Drake. APN-1

Niagara or Vesuvius is deferred. (LL) George Meredith. NOBVV; NPeEn; OxBEV *Fr.* Modern Love.

Nialls' cottage had one, The. Hearth Song. John Montague. PNI

Nibble, nibble, little sheep. Sheep. Samuel Hoffenstein. TrJP
Nicander, ooh, your leg's got hairs! Epigram. Alcaeus [or Alkaios]. GrAn, *tr. by Tony Harrison*
Nicaragua Water Fire. Gioconda Belli. TANSG, *tr. by Steven F. White*
Nicaraguan Triptych. "Rubén Dario." TCLAP, *tr. by Lysander Kemp*
Nice pot of gold that was mari, A. Limerick. Arthur Shaw. PeLi
Nice Thing about Counting Stars, The. Dwight Okita. UnSA
Nice Valor, The. John Fletcher.
    Melancholy. GTBS-P; OBEV
Nice Work if You Can Get It. George Gershwin. ReLy
Nicest child I ever knew, The. Charles Augustus Fortescue. Joseph Hilaire Pierre Belloc. NoAM
Nicest Phantasies Are Shared, The. Brian Coffey. CIP-2
Nicetes begins with gentle declamation. Automedon. GrAn
Nichita Stanescu. Brian Turner. PeNZ
Nicholas Ned. Laura Elizabeth Richards. NTCP
Nicholas the ridiculous: you will always be 27 and impossible. No more expectations. D. A. Powell. NeAmPo
Nick and the Candlestick. Sylvia Plath. CoAP; LCAP-2; NALW
Nicodemus. Howard Nemerov. GI; TaR
Nicola. William Scammell. NLP
Nicolas Guillen brought me your letter, written. Letter to Miguel Otero Silva, in Caracas. Pablo Neruda. AF, *tr. by Robert Bly*
Niconoë has just inched past her prime. Nicarchus of Alexandria. GrAn
Niddle Noddle. Mother Goose. OxNR
Nietzsche is pietsche. Graffiti. Alice Archer Sewall James. NBLV
Nietzsche Possessed. Brooks Haxton. Unle
Nievie nievie nick nack. *Unknown.* OxNR
Nigeria in the Year 1999. Catherine Obianuju Acholonu. HBAPE
Nigeria of the Seventies. Molara Ogundipe-Leslie. HAWP
Nigga Section, The. Welton Smith. BPo
Nigger. Sonia Sanchez. BPo
Nigger. Karl Shapiro. OxBA
Nigger and Some Poofters, A. Nigel Roberts. BMAP
Nigger / Can you kill. True Import of Present Dialogue: Black vs. Negro, The. Nikki Giovanni. BPo
Nigger in a Photograph, The. Ece Ayhan. PFTM-2, *tr. by Murat Nemet-Nejat*
Nigger-Lover is a song, spat out. Song. Cornelius Eady. ESEAA; GT
Nigger-Reecan Blues. Willie Perdomo. InTrad
Nigger's Leap, New England. Judith Wright. NOBAu
Nigger Sweat. Edward Baugh. EmeKit; WaCA
Night. Marjorie Agosin. ExTi
Night. William Rose Benét. MoAmPo
Night. Hayyim Nahman [or Khayim Nakhman or Chaim Nachman] Bialik. AWP, *tr. by Maurice Samuel*
Night. William Blake. FHYEP; ITBLP; OBEV *Fr.* Songs of Innocence.
Night. Louise Bogan. APT-2; NoP-4; UnPo
Night. Augusta Cooper Bristol. APN-2
Night. Anne Brontë. VWP
Night. Longing, a Documentary. Anne Carson. BAP-01
Night. Justin Chin. AmPoNex
Night. Hartley Coleridge. OxBSo
Night. Henri De Regnier. AWP, *tr. by* "Seumas O'Sullivan"
Night. Mary Dorcey. PoBW
Night. Paul Laurence Dunbar. InvLi
Night. Duo Duo (Li Shizheng). PoetW, *tr. by Donald Finkel and Li Guohua*
Night. Peter Everwine. NNaP
Night. Herman von Gilm zu Rosenegg. AuPH, *tr. by Lowell A. Bangerter*
Night. Josephine D. Henderson Heard. CBWP-4
Night. Hermann Hesse. AWP, *tr. by Ludwig Lewisohn*
Night. Robinson Jeffers. AWP; ColAP; MoAmPo; NOBA; OxBA
Night. Etheridge Knight. *See* Night music slanted
Night. Henry Wadsworth Longfellow. APN-1
Night. Richard Lovelace. CaPo
Night. Gabriela Mistral. TANSG, *tr. by Maria Jacketti*
Night. Gabriela Mistral. WoPoe, *tr. by Alice Jane McVan*
Night. Boris Leonidovich Pasternak. TCRP, *tr. by Edwin Morgan*
Night. Ann Radcliffe. CenSon; NOBRP; WPE
Night. Shelley. *See* To Night
Night. Maurya Simon. InvLad
Night. Solomon ibn Gabirol. TrJP, *tr. by Emma Lazarus*
Night. Wole Soyinka. PBMAP; WoPoe *Fr.* Idanre and Other Poems (1967).
Night. Gerald Stern. BodElec
Night. S. D. R. Sutu. TTY, *tr. by Jack Cope and Dan Kunene*
Night. Sara Teasdale. NOxBChV

Night. Georg Trakl. PeFWW, *tr. by R. S. Furness, David McDuff and Jon Silkin*
Night. Tu Fu. SuSp, *tr. by Jan W. Walls*
Night. Jones Very. InvLi
Night, The. Al-Khansa. BoWoP, *tr. by Willis Barnstone*
Night, The. Joseph Hilaire Pierre Belloc. OBEV
Night, The. Myra Cohn Livingston. TLR
Night, The. Henry Vaughan. BASC; ChIV-2; EBEV; ESCV; GeHe; MeLP; NAEL-5v1; NAEL-7v1; NOBE; NOCV; OBEV; OBWVE; OxAEP-1; OxBEV; SCGP; TFi; TOF
Night II (Enion's Lament). William Blake. PoE *Fr.* Vala; or The Four Zoas.
Night VIII (The Eternal Man). William Blake. PoE *Fr.* Vala; or The Four Zoas.
Night a Sailor Came to Me in a Dream, The. Diane Wakoski. TAP; VGW
Night: A Street. Aleksandr Aleksandrovich Blok. TCRusP, *tr. by Denis Johnson and Kathy Lewis*
Night: a street, a streetlight; drugstore. Night: A Street. Aleksandr Aleksandrovich Blok. TCRusP, *tr. by Denis Johnson and Kathy Lewis*
Night above the Town. Thomas Lux. SeSe
Night after Bushfire. Judith Wright. BMAP
Night after night from my small bed. Hooters. Meic Stephens. AngWePo; TCAWP
Night after night from our camp on Sugar Loaf Hill. Influence of Natural Objects, The. James Simmons. PNI
Night after night, I do not. *Unknown.* ColAnChi, *tr. by Jeanne Larsen* *Fr.* Midnight Songs.
Night after night, it was very nearly enough. Whippoorwill in the Woods, A. Amy Clampitt. OWoS
Night again. Again the grim sky closes. Night over Birkenau. Tadeusz Borowski. HP, *tr. by Tadeusz Pióro*
Night Alone, The. Meleager. AWTN, *tr. by Dudley Fitts*
Night along the Mackinac Bridge. Roberta Hill Whiteman. CDW
Night; an Epistle to Robert Lloyd. Charles Churchill.
    "Spectators only on this bustling stage." OBSV
Night and a starless sky. Shipwreck. Mary Weston Fordham. CBWP-2
Night, and beneath star-blazoned summer skies. South, The. Emma Lazarus. APN-2; ColAP
Night and Day. Michael Drayton. NOBE; Son *Fr.* Idea.
Night and Day. Cole Porter. ReLy
Night and day arrive, and day after day goes by. For My Son Noah, Ten Years Old. Robert Bly. LoL; RaBo
Night and day under the rind of me. Parodies of Cole Porter's "Night and Day." Ring Lardner. OBAL
Night and Death. Joseph Blanco White. *See* To Night
Night and evening, morning, every day. Recommendation. Andrey [or Andrei] Andreievich Voznesensky [or Voznesenskii]. RusPo, *tr. by Robert Arthur Douglas Ford*
Night. And I am drinking smoky black tea from China. Gabriel Preil. FIT, *tr. by Robert Friend*
Night / and in the warm blackness. Upon Your Leaving. Etheridge Knight. NNaP
Night, and its muffled creakings, as the wheels. Shako, The. Robert Lowell. Son
Night and mist, what bones you have eaten. Leonidas of Tarentum. GrAn
Night and Morning. Austin Clarke. CIP-2
Night and Morning. *Unknown.* OBWVE, *tr. by R. S. Thomas*
Night and Night's longing. Meleager. GrAn
Night, and on all sides only the folding quiet. Night. S. D. R. Sutu. TTY, *tr. by Jack Cope and Dan Kunene*
Night and Sleep. Coventry Patmore. EBVV
Night and Sleep. Jelaluddin [or Jalal al-Din] Rumi. WoPoe, *tr. by Robert Bly*
Night and the distant rumbling; for the train. Last Evening, The. Rainer Maria Rilke. FaBoWar, *tr. by Carlyle Ferren MacIntyre and C. F. MacIntyre*
Night, and the heavens beam serene with peace. Night. Solomon ibn Gabirol. TrJP, *tr. by Emma Lazarus*
Night, / And the yellow pleasure of candlelight. Song of the Rain. Hugh Raymond McCrae. CBAP
Night and we heard heavy and cadenced hoofbeats. Return, The. John Peale Bishop. APT-1; OxBA
Night arches England, and the winds are still. Peace. Walter De la Mare. MoBrPo
Night at an Airport. David Ignatow. NNaP
Night at Anchor by Maple Bridge. Chang Chi. OHMPC, *tr. by Kenneth Rexroth*
Night at Dunkirk. Louis Aragon. FaBoWar, *tr. by Malcolm Cowley and Rolfe Humphries*
Night attendant, a B.U. sophomore, The. Waking in the Blue. Robert Lowell. AmFaPo; CoAP; HCAP; MoAmPo; UnPo

Night Beach.   Vic Coccimiglio.   InvLad

Night before Christmas, The.   Clement Clarke Moore.   *See* Visit from St Nicholas, A

Night before Larry Was Stretched, The.   *Unknown.*   BIrV; NOBL; NOIV; OxBoLi

Night before my uncle Carter got shot, The.   Support Your Local Police Dog.   Carter Revard.   VoR

Night before the First Day of School, The.   E. Ethelbert Miller.   SpirFl

Night before the Soviets, The.   Velemir [*or* Viktor Vladimirovich] Khlebnikov.   "She came and spoke low."   TCRP

Night before they meant to pluck his eyes, The.   Among Philistines.   R. S. Gwynn.   RA

Night begins to gather between her breasts.   George Swede.   HA

Night Bird, The.   Larry Kramer.   GeoHom

Night-bird sight.   Summer.   Luciana Frezza.   CItWP, *tr. by* Cinzia Sartini Blum and Lara Trubowitz

Night-Blooming Cereus, The.   Robert Earl Hayden.   APT-2; ESEAA

Night-Blooming Flowers.   Felicia Dorothea Hemans.   NOBRP

Night Blooming Jasmine.   Diane Wakoski.   GeoHom

Night-Blooming Jasmine, The.   Audre Lorde.   ColAP

Night by nightfall more benighted.   Garcia Lorca Murdered in Granada.   John Streeter Manifold.   CBAP

Night by the Sea, A.   Heinrich Heine.   AWP, *tr. by* Howard Mumford Jones   *Fr.* North Sea, The.

Night Café.   Gottfried Benn.   PFTM-1

Night Call.   George Young.   BloBone

Night Came in the Drowsy Living Room, The.   Delmira Agustini.   BLPSL, *tr. by* Rene de Costa, Rigas Kappatos and Eleni Paidoussi

Night came in the drowsy living room, The.   Night Came in the Drowsy Living Room, The.   Delmira Agustini.   BLPSL, *tr. by* Rene de Costa, Rigas Kappatos and Eleni Paidoussi

Night Chant, The.   Arthur Rimbaud.   "In Tsegíhi."   PFTM-1

Night Chant, The.   *Unknown.*   APN-2, *tr. by* Washington Matthews;   NAAL-5

Night Chill.   Li Shang-yin.   SuSp, *tr. by* Eugene Eoyang

Night Clouds.   Amy Lowell.   MoAmPo

Night clouds scumble overhead, some.   Night in San Francisco.   Carolyn Miller.   UrbNat

Night Club.   Louis MacNeice.   OxBSP   *Fr.* Entered in the Minutes.

Night Club.   Francis Reginald Scott.   NOBC

Night Coach.   Phillis Levin.   RA

Night comes.   Gary Hotham.   HA

Night comes and, drowsy with drink, I'm slow to shed my.   Tune: Telling of Innermost Feelings.   Li Ch'ing-chao.   CoBCP, *tr. by* Burton Watson

Night comes and extinguishes the numbers and the year.   Jaan Kaplinski.   ErotSp

Night comes so people can sleep like fish.   Jelaluddin [*or* Jalal al-Din] Rumi.   WoPoe, *tr. by* Coleman Barks and John Moyne

Night covers the pond with its wing.   Pond, The.   Louise Glück.   ColAP

Night creeps in, The.   Twilight.   Ch'en Yün.   WoPoe, *tr. by* Henry Hart

Night, The / creeps in.   Night, The.   Myra Cohn Livingston.   TLR

Night Cries, Wakari Hospital.   Charles Brasch.   Winter Anemones.   PeNZ

Night Crow.   Theodore Roethke.   InPK-6; NAAL-5; OxBSP; VGW

Night Dances, The.   Sylvia Plath.   AmFaPo; LCAP-2

Night darkens the middle of the road.   Asphalt.   Chimalum Nwankwo.   NAfrP

Night, Death, Mississippi.   Robert Earl Hayden.   LCAP-2; VCAP; VGW (Quavering cry, A. Screech-owl?)   ColAP; NoP-4; PoPoPo

Night deepens.   Buson.   EH, *tr. by* Robert Hass

Night departs, a black bull, The.   Vigil.   Juan Ramón Jiménez.   SpanPo, *tr. by* Willis Barnstone

Night Don Juan came to pay his fees, The.   Don Juan in Hell.   Charles Baudelaire.   AWP, *tr. by* James Elroy Flecker

Night draws with the setting sun, The.   Nomads, The.   Laury Wells.   IBA

Night-dreams trace on Memory's wall.   Ralph Waldo Emerson.   APN-1; TCAPo   *Fr.* Quatrains.

Night Dust-off.   Basil T. Paquet.   CDa

Night Duty in the Palace, Dreaming of a Hsien-yu Temple.   Po Chü-i.   CrYelRi, *tr. by* Sam Hamill

Night falls on single vision zombies everywhere.   Ken Edwards.   Oth   *Fr.* Five Nocturnes, after Derek Jarman.

Night Fear.   Don Receveur.   CDa

Night feast at the Tsos.   Tu Fu.   ChinPo, *tr. by* Yip Wai-lim

Night Feeding.   Muriel Rukeyser.   NoP-4; WPE

Night fell, but you never came back. (LL)   They Fought South of the Wall.   *Unknown.*   CoBCP; ColAnChi, *tr. by* Burton Watson

Night Fishing.   Caroline Price.   Prnts

Night Flare Drop, Tan Son Nhut.   Horace Coleman.   CDa

Night Flight.   Marion Alexopoulos.   NOBAu

Night Flight: New York.   Muriel Rukeyser.   "Believe that we bloom upon this stalk of time."   YaYoPo

Night Flower.   Geoffrey Lehmann.   NOBAu

Night Flute, The.   Beryle Williams.   MiVo

Night for menace with weary eyes. (LL)   Trenches, The.   Frederic Manning.   NOBAu; PoWW

Night forked stigmata.   Different Horizon.   Aimé Césaire.   VCWP

Night found me so flushed with wine.   Tune: "Telling of Innermost Feelings."   Li Ch'ing-chao.   SuSp, *tr. by* Eugene Eoyang

Night from a railroad car window.   Window.   Carl Sandburg.   APT-1

Night frost / Pulsing wings.   Iio Sogi.   ZenPo, *tr. by* Takashi Ikemoto and Lucien Stryk

Night full of talking that hurts, A.   Jelaluddin [*or* Jalal al-Din] Rumi.   RaBo; WoPoe, *tr. by* Coleman Barks and John Moyne   *Fr.* Three Quatrains.

Night Fun.   Judith Viorst.   TLR

Night Funeral in Harlem.   Langston Hughes.   APT-2

Night Game, The.   Robert Pinsky.   TaR

Night Gives Old Woman the Word.   Gail Tremblay.   HATNAP; ItWoWo

Night had passed away among the hills, A.   Morning among the Hills.   James Gates Percival.   TreFP

Night Hair.   Raquel Chalfi.   DTA, *tr. by* Karen Alkalay-Gut

Night Has a Thousand Eyes, The.   Francis William Bourdillon.   BRP; BoLoP; OBEV; OxBSP; PoToHe

Night has come. Let us go then, Goddess of my dreams.   Egyptian Serenade.   'Ali Mahmud Taha.   MAP, *tr. by* Issa Boullata and Thomas G. Ezzy

Night has come on like a woman sleeping, The.   Moon Poems.   John Wieners.   VGW

Night he died, earth's images all came, The.   Poet.   Peter Viereck.   MoAmPo

Night here, the owners asleep upstairs.   Up Late.   Arthur Nortje.   PBMAP

Night Herons.   Gary Snyder.   GeoHom

Night herons nest in the cypress.   Night Herons.   Gary Snyder.   GeoHom

Night hides our thefts; all faults then pardoned be.   In the Dark None Dainty.   Robert Herrick.   CaPo

Night hung o'er Virginia's forest wild, The.   Capt. Smith and Pocahontas.   Eloise Bibb.   CBWP-4

Night I fell in love with you I lost my watch, The.   Perfect Timing.   Sarah Maguire.   LW

Night, I Know All about You.   Yolanda Bedregal.   TANSG, *tr. by* Carolyne Wright

Night I made love to you, The.   Illegitimate Poem.   Vivian Lamarque.   CItWP, *tr. by* Cinzia Sartini Blum and Lara Trubowitz

Night I Met Marilyn, The.   Chris Greenhalgh.   NeBl

Night I met Marilyn it was raining, The.   Night I Met Marilyn, The.   Chris Greenhalgh.   NeBl

Night I understood, The.   Retsuzan.   JDP, *tr. by* Yoel Hoffmann

Night I woke to find the sheets wet from you, The.   Bruise of This, The.   Mark Wunderlich.   NeAmPo

Night in a Room by the River.   Tu Fu.   AWTN; CrYelRi, *tr. by* Sam Hamill

Night in a Village, A.   Ivan Savvich Nikitin.   AWP, *tr. by* P. E. Matheson

Night in a World, A.   Heather McHugh.   InvLad

Night in Elphin goes slow, The.   Author of this is Ossian, The.   *Unknown.*   NePenScot, *tr. by* Derick Thomson

Night in Hell.   Arthur Rimbaud.   SxFrPo, *tr. by* Martin Sorrell

Night in Kolozsvár.   Lajos Áprily.   IQMS, *tr. by* Watson Kirkconnell

Night in May, A.   Alfred de Musset.   Muse, The.   WoPoe, *tr. by* Claire Nicholas White   Poet, The ("Do you believe that I am like the autumn wind.").   WoPoe, *tr. by* Claire Nicholas White   Poet, The ("If all you need, my sister sweet.").   WoPoe, *tr. by* Claire Nicholas White

Night in Nigeria.   Ellease Southerland.   GT

Night in Odessa, A.   Louis Simpson.   NNaP

Night in San Francisco.   Carolyn Miller.   UrbNat

Night in soft slumbers rolled gently away, The.   Miss F[——]ny M[——]t[——]ly to Miss P[——]y B[——]s.   Fanny [*or* Frances] Macartney Greville.   ECWP

Night in the basement of a concrete structure now in ruins.   Let Us Be Midwives!   Kurihara Sadako.   ItWoWo, *tr. by* Richard H. Minear

Night in the bloodstained snow: the wind is chill.   Hialmar Speaks to the Raven.   Charles Marie René Leconte de Lisle.   AWP, *tr. by* James Elroy Flecker

Night in the Forest.   Galway Kinnell.   TAP

Night in the Ghetto.   *Unknown, fr. Terezin Concentration Camp.*   INSAB

Night in the House by the River.   Tu Fu.   OHPC, *tr. by* Kenneth Rexroth

"Night" in the Medici Chapel.   Michelangelo Buonarroti.   WoPoe, *tr. by* William Jay Smith

Night in the Shape of a Bison.   Joyce Mansour.   SurWo, *tr. by* Mary Beach

Night in the sky.   Paris Is Paris Again.   Frederick Loewe.   ReLy

Night in the Trench, A.   Velemir [or Viktor Vladimirovich] Khlebnikov.   "Clan of stony desert women, A."   TCRP

"Night in the Tropics" (1858–59?).   Michael Waters.   MiVo

Night in the Villa by the River.   Tu Fu.   TAL

Night is a cup of evil, The. A watchman's stinging.   Black Cup, The.   César Vallejo.   WoPoe, tr. by Willis Barnstone and Tony Barnstone

Night is a ship of mother-of-pearl and gold.   Nocturne of Hope.   Yolanda Bedregal.   TANSG, tr. by Carolyne Wright

Night is bait, The.   Tercios del Muerte.   Gerry Gordon.   MiVo

Night is beautiful, The.   My People.   Langston Hughes.   APT-2; NOxBChV

Night is bitter, The.   Man That Got Away, The.   Harold Arlen.   ReLy

Night is calm, the cygnet's down, The.   On a Calm Summer's Night.   John Nicholson.   EnLoPo

Night is cold and frosty, The.   Winter Night, A.   Priscilla Jane Thompson.   CBWP-2

Night is come, like to the day, The.   Sir Thomas Browne.   SacPr   Fr. Religio Medici.

Night is come. The land is wrapt in sleep, The. (LL)   Robert Bridges.   GTBS-P; OBMV

Night is covered with signs. The body and face of man, The.   Akiba.   Muriel Rukeyser.   TaR

Night is dark, the.   Yury [or Iurii] Timofeievich Galanskov.   TCRP

Night is dark, the wind has dashed, The.   Midnight Prayer.   Hayyim Nahman [or Khayim Nakhman or Chaim Nachman] Bialik.   TrJP, tr. by Helena Frank

Night is darkening round me, The.   Spellbound.   Emily Jane Brontë.   NOBE; NOBVV; NPeEn

Night is dewy as a maiden's mouth, The.   Summer's Night, A.   Paul Laurence Dunbar.   APN-2

Night is everywhere.   Cuba.   Sandra M. Castillo.   TouFir

Night Is Freezing Fast, The.   A. E. Housman.   OxBSP

Night is full of storm clouds, The.   Freezing Night.   T'ao Hung Ching.   OHMPC, tr. by Kenneth Rexroth

Night is long, she cannot sleep, The.   Song of Tzu-yeh.   Unknown.   SuSp, tr. by Ronald C. Miao

Night is my sister, and how deep in love.   Edna St. Vincent Millay.   HAP; OxBSo

Night Is Near [or Neir] Gone, The.   Alexander Montgomerie.   OBEV; OxBS

Night is o'er England, and the winds are still.   Peace.   Walter De la Mare.   MoBrPo

Night is on the downland, on the lonely moorland.   John Masefield.   MoBrPo   Fr. Lollingdon Downs.

Night Is out of Sight, The.   Pedro Juan Pietri.   PueRic

Night is quiet. All creatures are resting.   Spring Night at Bamboo Pavillion, Presenting a Poem to Subprefect Qian about His Staying for Good in Blue Field Mountains.   Wang Wei.   WoPoe, tr. by Willis Barnstone, Tony Barnstone and Xu Haixin

Night is too long to the sleepless, The.   Kenneth Rexroth.   APT-2   Fr. Love Poems of Marichiko, The.

Night Is Young and You're So Beautiful, The.   Dana Suesse.   ReLy

Night John Henry is born an ax, The.   Melvin B. Tolson.   BPo; NAAAL; TTY   Fr. Harlem Gallery.

Night Journey.   Alfred Noyes.   SacPr

Night Journey.   Theodore Roethke.   AmFaPo; GM; KaS

Night Journey of a River, The.   William Cullen Bryant.   APN-1

Night Las Vegas caught fire, The.   Case, The.   Hoffman Reynolds Hays.   SPE

Night Letter.   Stanley Kunitz.   AF

Night licks the backyard with its reptile tongue.   Clockface.   Rhyll McMaster.   BMAP

Night-life. Letters, journals, bourbon.   Origins and History of Consciousness.   Adrienne Rich.   NIP-4

Night Light.   Nancy Willard.   LCAP-2

Night, lighter than day! Night, more than brilliant night.   On the Birth of Jesus.   Andreas Gryphius.   GePo, tr. by George C. Schoolfield

Night Litany.   Ezra Pound.   TCAPo

Night! loathed [or loathèd] jailor of the locked-up [or lock'd up] sun.   Night.   Richard Lovelace.   CaPo

Night long and wintry / the Pleiades half set.   Asclepiades.   GrAn

Night long, knocking on barn boards, the scuffling mare moves.   Postcard from the Coast.   Katrina Roberts.   NAPBL

Night Mail, The.   W. H. Auden.   OxBTC

Night Mail North, The.   Henry Cholmondeley-Pennell.   EBVV

Night makes no difference 'twixt the Priest and Clerk.   No Difference in the Dark [or i'th'dark].   Robert Herrick.   CaPo

Night Marauders.   Gerry Bostock.   IBA

Night Meeting.   Thomas McGrath.   BodElec

Night Mirror, The.   John Hollander.   VCAP

Night-Mooring at Maple Bridge.   Chang Chi.   ChinPo, tr. by Yip Wai-lim

Night Music.   Linda Gregg.   BLT

Night music slanted.   Cell Song.   Etheridge Knight.   NNaP

Night of Death, The.   Frances Ellen Watkins Harper.   PWR

Night of Fathers.   Valerie Martínez.   TouFir

Night of gentle thunder fells a thousand catkins, A.   Spring Rain.   Ch'in Kuan.   SuSp, tr. by Stephen West

Night of Hell.   Arthur Rimbaud.   "Decidedly we are out of the world. No longer any sound."   AWTN, tr. by Louise Varese

Night of iron wheels and rain, A.   Red Flag, The.   Michael Jackson.   PeNZ

Night of love, A.   Second Madrigal, The.   Anna Swirszczynska.   BLT

Night of My Blood (1971).   Kofi Awoonor.   At the Gates.   PBMAP; VCWP

Night of my cousin's wedding, The.   Anne Sexton.   NAAL-5   Fr. Death of the Fathers, The.

Night of my first cell meeting it was pouring rain, The.   Looking for Trouble.   Roque Dalton.   TCLAP, tr. by Richard Schaaf

Night of nations. On a death-dense bassoon.   Prayer for the Great Lunatic.   László Mécs.   IQMS, tr. by Paul Tabori

Night of our parting in the red tower is enough for sorrow, The.   Tune: "Deva-like Barbarian."   Wei Chuang.   SuSp, tr. by Lois M. Fusek

Night of Sine.   Léopold Sédar Senghor.   PBA, tr. by Ellen Conroy Kennedy   (Woman, rest on my brow your balsam hands, your hands gentler than / fur.)   PBMAP   (Woman, rest your balsam hands upon my brow.)   NegPo, tr. by Ellen Conroy Kennedy

Night of Sleepless Love.   Federico García Lorca.   CAGL, tr. by David William Foster   Fr. Sonetos del Amor Oscuro [Sonnets of Dark Love].

Night of Souls.   Ann Stanford.   WPE

Night of the day, The.   Lunar Frost.   Mary Kinzie.   IllVoic

Night of the eclipse we're parallel, The.   Total Eclipse.   Michael J. Rosen.   DiPo

Night of the Fifteenth, Second Month.   Yüan Mei.   CoBLCP, tr. by Jonathan Chaves

Night of the First Full Moon, The.   Li K'ai-hsien.   CoBLCP, tr. by Jonathan Chaves

Night of the Fourteenth.   Ho Ching-ming.   CoBLCP, tr. by Jonathan Chaves

Night of the Fourth: A Recollection, The.   Victor Hugo.   SxFrPo, tr. by E. H. Blackmore and A. M. Blackmore

Night of the Seventeenth, The.   Li K'ai-hsien.   CoBLCP, tr. by Jonathan Chaves

Night of the Shirts, The.   W. S. Merwin.   VCAP

Night of the wedding she got into bed.   No Balls at All.   Unknown.   FaBoWar

Night of Trafalgar, The.   Thomas Hardy.   FaBoCh; MoBrPo; OBMV   Fr. Dynasts, The.

Night of utter silences, A.   Shadows.   "Yehoash."   TrJP, tr. by Elias Lieberman

Night on earth and sky.   Terrible Thought, A.   Eliezer Steinbarg.   TrJP, tr. by Joseph Leftwich

Night on high the two of us in full moon, I began to cry and you were laughing, The.   Federico García Lorca.   CAGL, tr. by David William Foster   Fr. Sonetos del Amor Oscuro [Sonnets of Dark Love].

Night on the Boulevard.   Lőrinc Szabó.   IQMS, tr. by Laurence James

Night on the Downland.   John Masefield.   MoBrPo   Fr. Lollingdon Downs.

Night on the Great River.   Meng Hao Jan.   OHMPC, tr. by Kenneth Rexroth

Night on the Kho Bha Dinh.   Steve Denning.   CDa

Night on the shores, your voice is no stranger.   Song of Job, A.   Khalil Touma.   MAP, tr. by Samuel Hazo and Lena Jayyusi

Night opens like an almond.   Yvonne Caroutch.   BoWoP

Night Operations, Coastal Command RAF.   Howard Nemerov.   AF

Night Ottawa brought down the budget, The.   Spleen.   August Kleinzahler.   PmAP

Night, our [or the] black summer, simplifies her smells.   Nights in the Gardens of Port of Spain.   Derek Walcott.   NAEL-5v2; NAEL-6v2; OxBC; PoetW

Night Out, A.   Douglas Houston.   TCAWP

Night over Birkenau.   Tadeusz Borowski.   HP, tr. by Tadeuszt Pióro

Night over Georgia; mist across the heights.   Ode on the Hills of Georgia.   Alexander Sergeyevich Pushkin.   WoPoe, tr. by Peter Viereck

Night passes on, and the bright day appears.   Unknown.   NAWM-7v1, tr. by Frederick Goldin   Fr. Song of Roland, The.

Night Patrol.   William Daniel Ehrhart.   CDa

Night Patrol, The.   Arthur Graeme West.   FaBoWar

Night Person, The.   Richard Frost.   AWTN

Night Picnic.   Charles Simic.   BAP-01

Night-Piece.   Léonie Adams.   MoAmPo

Night-Piece.   Fleur Adcock.   Before Sleep.   PeNZ

Night-Piece.   Joy Davidman.   YaYoPo

Night Piece. "Ern Malley." BMAP

Night-Piece. Frances Horovitz. LW

Night Piece. John Streeter Manifold. MoBrPo

Night-Piece, The. Virgil [or Vergil]. MakPoe, tr. by Henry Howard, Earl of Surrey Fr. Aeneid [or Eneados, Aeneis], The.

Night Piece on Death. Thomas Parnell. NOEC

"How deep yon azure dyes the sky!" OxAEP-1

Night-Piece; or, Modern Philosophy, A. Christopher Smart. NOEC

Night Piece: the Trojans outside Troy. Homer. OBVE, tr. by George Chapman Fr. Iliad, The.

Night Piece: the Trojans outside Troy. Homer. OBVE, tr. by Alexander Pope Fr. Iliad, The.

Night-Piece, to Julia, The. Robert Herrick. BeJo; CaPo; NAEL-5v1; NAEL-6v1; NAEL-7v1; NOSC; OBEV; PoE; PoRA; SCGP; TFi

(Her eyes the glowworm lend thee.) NoP-4

Night Prayer, A. Alcuin. MLL, tr. by Helen Waddell

Night Prayer of Glückel of Hameln, The. Edouard Roditi. CRP

Night Raid. Desmond Hawkins. PoWW

Night Rain. J. P. Clark Bekedermo. PBMAP Fr. Reed in the Tide, A.

Night Rain. Countee Cullen. GT

Night Rain. Karen L. Mitchell. GT

Night Rain: A Wall Collapses—Sent To My Neighbors. Yang Shih-ch'i. CoBLCP; ColAnChi, tr. by Jonathan Chaves

Night Rain beneath the City Walls of P'i-chou. Yang Shih-ch'i. CoBLCP, tr. by Jonathan Chaves

Night Rains: A Letter to Go North. Li Shang-yin. ChinPo, tr. by Yip Wai-lim

Night Ray. Paul Celan. AF, tr. by Michael Hamburger

Night: reading Meng Chiao's poems. Reading the Poetry of Meng Chiao: Two Poems. Su Tung-p'o (Su Shih). ColAnChi; WoPoe, tr. by Burton Watson

Night rests like a ball of fur on my tongue. (LL) Adolescence—II. Rita Dove. AWTN; HCAP; ISC; NAAL-5; NoAM; PoPoPo; VCAP

Night's best of all. Night brings delight. Propertius. EroLit, tr. by Kenneth McLeish Fr. Elegies.

Night's bible-black darkness prevails. Limerick. V. R. Ormerod. PeLi

Night's Delights. Kaspar Stieler. GePo, tr. by Ingrid Waløe-Engel

Night's drifts, The. Winter Daybreak above Vence, A. James Wright. LCAP-2; VCAP

Night's Fall. William Sydney Graham. WoPoe

Night's first sweet silence fell, and on my bed. Malady of Love Is Nerves, The. Petronius Arbiter. AWP, tr. by Howard Mumford Jones

Night's moonlight lake was neither water nor air. (LL) Reality Is an Activity of the Most August Imagination. Wallace Stevens. APT-1; NoAM

Night sank upon the dusky beach, and on the purple sea. Thomas Babington Macaulay, 1st Baron Macaulay. PeVV Fr. Armada, The.

Night, say all, was made for rest, The. Upon Visiting His Lady by Moonlight. "A. W." CTC

Night Scenes. Robert Duncan. VGW

Night Scenes of Other Times. Joanna Baillie.

Ghost of Edward. ECWP

Night sea quickens, The. On the shoal or rock. Lighthouses. Dorothy Wellesley, Duchess of Wellington. WPE

Night Serene, The. Luís De León. TrJP, tr. by Thomas Walsh

Night: Setting out from Shih-Kuan Pavilion. Hsieh Ling-yün. ChinPo, tr. by Yip Wai-lim

Night Shadows. William Carpenter. PoSol

Night Shift, after Drinking Dinner, Container Corporation of America, 1972. Kevin Stein. IllVoic

Night sighs, The. Surrogate Mothers. Andrea M. Wren. InTrad

Night Sky. Louise Erdrich. HATNAP

Night Sky, The. Sean Dunne. ModIr Fr. Sydney Place.

Night Sky, The. G. D. Roberts. GSo

Night-sky bird's world. Myth of the Blaze. George Oppen. PFTM-2

Night Sky Hiss. Jonathan Griffin. Oth

Night sky is only a sort of carbon paper, The. Insomniac. Sylvia Plath. AWTN

Night, sleep, death and the stars. (LL) Clear Midnight, A. Walt Whitman. AWTN; HAP; OxBSP; SAmP; Spl

Night sleeps, but the chill, The. Harp of David, The. Jacob Cohen. TrJP, tr. by Sholom J. Kahn

Night Snow. Po Chü-i. CoBCP, tr. by Burton Watson

Night snow / Neighbor's cock. Kagami Shiko. ZenPo, tr. by Takashi Ikemoto and Lucien Stryk

Night so. Unknown. ColAnChi, tr. by Jeanne Larsen Fr. Midnight Songs.

Night Song. Lajos Áprily. IQMS, tr. by Watson Kirkconnell

Night Song at Amalfi. Sara Teasdale. APT-1; MakPoe; MoAmPo

Night Song for a Child. Charles Williams. OBEV

Night Song for a Woman. Alfred Wellington Purdy. NOBC

Night Song for Two Mystics. Paul Blackburn. NeAP

Night Song of the Los Angeles Basin. Gary Snyder. UrbNat

Night Song of the Personal Shadow. György Petri. VCWP, tr. by George Gömöri and Clive Wilmer

Night Sowing. David Campbell. CBAP

Night splintered into stars, The. Ashes. Alejandra Pizarnik. TCLAP, tr. by Frank Graziano and María Rosa Fort

Night stirs the trees. By Achmelvich Bridge. Norman MacCaig. OxBS

Night, street, a lamp, a chemist's window. Aleksandr Aleksandrovich Blok. OBVE Fr. Dances of Death.

Night. Summer Meteors. A Comet. James Thomson. NPeEn Fr. Seasons, The.

Night Sweat. Robert Lowell. HarvBoo; NAAL-2v2; TAP; VGW

Night sweat: my temperature spikes to 102. December 27, 1966. Louis Edward Sissman. DiPo

Night sweet are you. Litany, A. Frank O'Hara. BodElec

Night takes feelings to the window. Birds Leaving. Johanna Kruit. TuT, tr. by Medbh McGuckian

Night Talk in a Dream Chamber. Ikkyu Sojun. ErotSp, tr. by Sam Hamill

Night that cuts between you and you, A. People at Night. Denise Levertov. CLPP

Night that has no star lit up by God, The. New World, The. Jones Very. APN-1

Night the Eighth: Camerados. Bayard Taylor. APN-2 Fr. Echo Club, The.

Night, The Porch, The. Mark Strand. KGB

Night, the rain, who could forget, The? In the Street. John Shaw Neilson. CBAP

Night the Second: All or Nothing. Bayard Taylor. APN-2 Fr. Echo Club, The.

Night the Sixth: Hadramaut. Bayard Taylor. APN-2 Fr. Echo Club, The.

Night, the starless[e] night of passion, The. William Alabaster. ESCV Fr. Divine Meditations.

Night, the street, the lamp, the drugstore, The. Aleksandr Aleksandrovich Blok. TCRP Fr. Dances of Death.

Night Things. Greg Kuzma. InvLad

Night Thoughts. Heinrich Heine. WoPoe, tr. by Mark Rudman

Night Thoughts. Lu Yu. OHPC; WoPoe, tr. by Kenneth Rexroth

Night-Thoughts. Solomon ibn Gabirol. TrJP, tr. by Emma Lazarus

Night Thoughts. Edward Young.

"Bell strikes one: we take no note of time." ECEV

Consolation, The. NOEC

Infidel Reclaimed, The. NOEC

"Lorenzo! Such the glories of the world!" NOEC

"There's naught (thou say'st) but one eternal flux." NOEC

"Tired nature's sweet restorer, balmy Sleep!" NOEC; OxAEP-1

"What am I? and from whence?—I nothing know." SacPr

Night Thoughts aboard a Boat. Tu Fu. SuSp, tr. by James J. Y. Liu and Irving Y. Lo

Night Thoughts: Baby & Demon. Gwen Harwood. CBAP

Night Thoughts Concerning a Dream. Daniel Casper von Lohenstein. GePo, tr. by George C. Schoolfield

Night Thoughts While Travelling. Tu Fu. CrYelRi, tr. by Sam Hamill

Night Thoughts While Travelling. Tu Fu. OHPC, tr. by Kenneth Rexroth

Night-Time: Starting to Write. Bernard Spencer. AWTN

Night Train. Robert Francis. GM

Night train passes, A. Eric Amann. HA

Night trembles in the black storm, The. Rain, The. Muhammad al-Mahdi Al-Majdhub. MAP, tr. by Matthew Sorenson

Night tumbles into town, bruised. Night Tumbles into Town by Rail. Kim Roberts. AmPoNex

Night universe scallop-edged with his faces—, A. Some Metaphysics of Junior Wells. Sandra McPherson. SeSe

Night Up in the Tower. Tu Fu. ChinPo, tr. by Yip Wai-lim

Night usually computes itself in stars. News of the Occluded Cyclone. Alice Fulton. WeW-3

Night / Virgins. Sappho. SaLy, tr. by Diane Rayor

Night Vision. Lucille Clifton. BodElec; GifTon; UnSA

Night Visit. Adriann Roland Holst. TuT, tr. by Paula Meehan

Night Visitor, A. Robert Greene. NoSic

Night Waitress. Lynda Hull. SwNoth

Night Walk. Max Fatchen. OTCP

Night Walk Through the Burg. Hans Just. AuPH, tr. by Lowell A. Bangerter

Night Walking. Robert Penn Warren. BodElec

Night was coming very fast, The. Hens, The. Elizabeth Madox Roberts. OBCA

Night was dark, the rain came down, The. Over the Top with Pershing. Zelda Sayre Fitzgerald. AiP

Night Was Growing Cold, The. Unknown. WHSW

Night was growing old, The. In the Night. Unknown. NBLV

Night was stormy and dark, the town was shut up in sleep, The. Speculators, The. William Makepeace Thackeray. OBCoV; OBSV

Night was winter in his roughest mood, The. William Cowper. FHYEP *Fr.* Task, The.

Night wasn't over / when the moon stood beside my bed. Prison Daybreak, A. Faiz Ahmad Faiz. AF, *tr. by* Agha Shahid Ali

Night Watch. Wang An-shih. CrYelRi, *tr. by* Sam Hamill

Night Watch in the Laboratory. Ann Townsend. NAPBL

Night Watchman of Pont-au-Change, The. Robert Desnos. AF, *tr. by* Carolyn Forché

Night-watchmen think of dawn and things auroral. Blindman's Buff. Peter Viereck. MoAmPo

Night We Called It a Day, The. Tom Adair. ReLy

Night we stayed at Summit Temple, The. Inscribed at Summit Temple. Li Po. WoPoe, *tr. by* Elling O. Eide

Night we went to see the Brisbane River, The. Profiles of My Father. Rhyll McMaster. CBAP

Night we were to meet in the hotel, The. Song for the Lost Private. Bruce Weigl. CDa

Night, welcome art thou to my mind destrest. Mary Sidney Wroth, Countess of Montgomery. NoP-4 *Fr.* Pamphilia to Amphilanthus.

Night when she first gave birth, The. Mary. Bertolt Brecht. GI

Night Will Never Stay, The. Eleanor Farjeon. NTCP

Night Wind, The. Emily Jane Brontë. EBVV; NAEL-5v2; NAEL-6v2; NALW; NIL-7
(In summer's mellow midnight.) VWP

Night-wind shook the tapestry round an ancient palace-room, The. Juana. Felicia Dorothea Hemans. RWP

Night Winds. Adelaide Crapsey. APT-1; TCAPo

Night winds! Dark mountainous skies. Daniil Leonidovich Andreyev [*or* Andreiev]. TCRP *Fr.* Russian Gods, The.

Night with a Friend, A. Li Po. CoBCP, *tr. by* Burton Watson

Night with Hamlet, A. Vladimir Holan.
"When passing from nature to being." PFTM-2, *tr. by* Clayton Eshleman, Frantisek Galan and Michael Heim

Night without end. I cannot sleep. Night Without End. *Unknown.* OHMPC, *tr. by* Kenneth Rexroth

Night without end. Loneliness. Kenneth Rexroth. APSN; APT-2 *Fr.* Love Poems of Marichiko, The.

Night Without Stars, A. Nancy Eimers. ExTi

Night Words. Isabel Meyrelles. SurWo, *tr. by* Jean R. Longland

Night wounded, The. Roça. Maria Manuela Margarido. HAWP, *tr. by* Julia Kirst

Nightfall. Walter Davies. OBWVE; WoPoe, *tr. by* Anthony Conran

Nightfall. "Michael Field." VWP

Nightfall. Gwen Harwood. BMAP

Nightfall. Alexander L. Posey. APN-2

Nightfall. Charles Hanson Towne. PoToHe

Nightfall. *Unknown.* OHMPC, *tr. by* Kenneth Rexroth

Nightfall. Clouds scatter and vanish. Turning Year, The. Su Tung-p'o (Su Shih). OHPC, *tr. by* Kenneth Rexroth

Nightfall . . . grass on the back. Landscape. Maria Manuela Margarido. HAWP, *tr. by* Julia Kirst

Nightfall. He jumped over the hedge. Nightfall. *Unknown.* OHMPC, *tr. by* Kenneth Rexroth

Nightfall. I return from a. Homecoming—Late at Night. Tu Fu. OHPC, *tr. by* Kenneth Rexroth

Nightfall, Midwinter, Missouri. Brian Coffey. CIP-2 *Fr.* Missouri Sequence.

Nightfall of nations brilliant after war. (LL) Troop Train. Karl Shapiro. APT-2; OxBA

Nightfall. The Coolness of My Watered Garden. Juan Ramón Jiménez. SpanPo, *tr. by* Eloise Roach

Nightfall: the town's chromatic nocturne wakes. Game of Chess, A. Gwen Harwood. MakPoe

Nightfishing. Charles McDonald. NLP

Nightfishing. Gjertrud Schnackenberg. WeW-3

Nighthawks. Samuel Yellen. PoSol

Nighthawks circle / through the midwestern elms. For a Winnebago Brave. Joseph Bruchac. CDW

Nightingale. Christian Carstairs. ECWP

Nightingale, The. Mark Akenside. OBEV

Nightingale, The. János Arany. IQMS, *tr. by* Peter Zollman

Nightingale, The. John Clare. EBVV

Nightingale, The. Samuel Taylor Coleridge. FHYEP

Nightingale, The. Marie de France. BoWoP, *tr. by* Patricia Terry

Nightingale, The. Sir Philip Sidney. NAEL-6v1; NAEL-7v1; NoP-4; SCGP
(Philomela.) OxAEP-1

Nightingale, The. William Strode. OBVE

Nightingale, The. *Var. authors. See* Passionate Pilgrim, The

Nightingale as soone as Aprill bringeth, The. Nightingale, The. Sir Philip Sidney. NAEL-6v1; NAEL-7v1; NoP-4; SCGP

Nightingale has a lyre of gold, The. William Ernest Henley. MoBrPo *Fr.* Echoes.

Nightingale / My clogs. Boncho. ZenPo, *tr. by* Takashi Ikemoto and Lucien Stryk

Nightingale near the House, The. Harold Monro. MoBrPo

Nightingale of Uncle Yair, The. Devorah Amir. DTA, *tr. by* Linda Zisquit

Nightingale / Rarely seen. Takai Kito. ZenPo, *tr. by* Takashi Ikemoto and Lucien Stryk

Nightingale's Nest, The. John Clare. NPeEn

Nightingale's song / this morning. Issa. ZenPo, *tr. by* Takashi Ikemoto and Lucien Stryk

Nightingale Sang in Berkeley Square, A. Manning Sherwin. ReLy

Nightingales. Robert Bridges. MoBrPo; NOBE; OBEV; OBMV; SCGP; TFi; UnPo

Nightingales. Mikhail Aleksandrovich Dudin. TCRP, *tr. by* Albert C. Todd

Nightingales, The. Harri Webb. AngWePo; TCAWP

Nightingales, the nightingales!, The. (LL) Bianca Among the Nightingales. Elizabeth Barrett Browning. BrRo; GTBS-P

Nightingales' tongues, your majesty? Figgie Hobbin. Charles Causley. NOxBChV

Nightingales warbled without. In the Garden at Swainston. Tennyson. OBEV

Nightline: An Interview with the General. Ronald Wallace. PBCAP

Nightlong waiting and listening, being schooled. Owl. Robert Mezey. AWTN

Nightly News, The. Daniel Anderson. AmPoNex

Nightly the watchman's rattle startles my sleep. Ch'ien Ch'ien-i [*or* Ch'ien Ch'ien-yi]. SuSp *Fr.* Poems Written in Prison.

Nightly tormented by returning doubt. Struggle, The. René François Armand Sully-Prudhomme. AWP, *tr. by* Arthur O'Shaughnessy

Nightmare. Erasmus Darwin. NOEC *Fr.* Botanic Garden, The.

Nightmare. James A. Emanuel. BPo

Nightmare. Isabella Gardner. CoAP

Nightmare. Matilde Salganicoff. MirDau, *tr. by* Celeste Kostopulos-Cooperman

Nightmare, A. Christina Georgina Rossetti. EroLit

Nightmare, The. Wang Yen-Shou. ChiP, *tr. by* Arthur Waley

Nightmare 1. Abdul Maqsoud Abdul Karim. NAfrP, *tr. by* Clarissa C. Burt

Nightmare 3. Abdul Maqsoud Abdul Karim. NAfrP, *tr. by* Clarissa C. Burt

Nightmare, [A *or* The]. Sir William Schwenck Gilbert. NOBL; OBCoV; OxBoLi; PeLV; PoRA *Fr.* Iolanthe.

Nightmare at Noon. Stephen Vincent Benét. OxBA

Nightmare Begins Responsibility. Michael S. Harper. ESEAA; GT; HCAP; LCAP-2; LoL; PoPoPo; TAP; VCAP

Nightmare Boogie. Langston Hughes. APSN; APT-2

Nightmare leaves fatigue. Louis MacNeice. BIrV; CIP-2; ModIr; PNI *Fr.* Autumn Journal.

Nightmare Number Three. Stephen Vincent Benét. MoAmPo

Nightmare of beasthood, snorting, how to wake. Moly. Thom Gunn. CABP; HAP; NPeEn; NoAM

Nightmare shower room. My tormentor leers, The. Days of 1941 and '44. James Merrill. GLP

Nightmarkets, The. Alan Wearne.
Terri. BMAP
Elise. BMAP
Division of O'Dowd, The. BMAP

Nightpiece. Judith Johnson Sherwin. YaYoPo

Nights. Lyn Hejinian. BAP-01

Nights. Alda Lara. HAWP, *tr. by* Julia Kirst

Nights After Rain When the Moon. Kwŏn Homun. WoPoe, *tr. by* Kevin O'Rourke

Nights along the River. Charles Sullivan. AiP

Nights bring you the fever. Prometheus. Jenny Mastoraki. BoWoP, *tr. by* Nikos Germanakos

Nights grow short. Kafu. JDP, *tr. by* Yoel Hoffmann

Nights in Fresno. Luis Omar Salinas. GeoHom

Nights in Nha Trang. Jan Barry. CDa

Nights in the Gardens of Port of Spain. Derek Walcott. NAEL-5v2; NAEL-6v2; NoP-4; OxBC; PoetW

Nights like this: on the cold apple-bough. Adrienne Rich. HarvBoo *Fr.* Not Somewhere Else, But Here.

Nights of 1964–1966: The Old Reliable. Marilyn Hacker. RA; VCAP

Nights steps from the forest there. Night. Herman von Gilm zu Rosenegg. AuPH, *tr. by* Lowell A. Bangerter

Nights, the house grows larger, open. Retired Greyhound, I. Natalie Kusz. Unle

Nights when I lie. To The Barbarian. Else Lasker-Schüler. PFTM-1

Nights Without Hope (Rebetiko Song). Yannis Papaionnou. WoPoe, tr. by Gail Holst-Warhaft

Nightsong. Frank Mkalawile Chipasula. Dusk. HBAPE

Nightsong. Thamnaret. WoPoe, tr. by Ronald Perry

Nightsong: City. Dennis Brutus. HBAPE; PBMAP; PoetW; WoPoe

Nightsweats. Richard Tayson. AmPoNex; WiU

Nighttime. René Crevel. CAGL, tr. by Michael Taylor

Nighttime am a fallin' Put Your Arms Around Me, Honey. Junie McCree. ReLy

Nighttime. The faithful prison guard. Bedtime Story. Lou Lipsitz. VGW

Nighttrains. Jayne Cortez. PFTM-2

Nightwalker. Thomas Kinsella.
"Foot of the tower. An angle where the darkness, The." PBCIP
"I must lie down with them all soon and sleep." BIrV

Nightwatch. Khairi Mansour.
"I see trees breaking off their branches." MAP

Nightwatcher: / Fast falls the night unfurling its vile veil. Frank Mkalawile Chipasula. HBAPE Fr. Nightsong.

Nightwatchman. Deborah Randall. NeBl

Nightwind sings and rustles through the reeds, The. Nocturne in G Minor. Karl Gustav Vollmoeller. AWP, tr. by Ludwig Lewisohn

Nihilist as Hero, The. Robert Lowell. VCAP

Nijinksy's Dog. Susan Hahn. IllVoic

Nikarete's face, sweetly moistened. Asclepiades. GrAn

Nike. Ernest Bryll. FaBoWar, tr. by Czeslaw Milosz

Nike of Samothrace. Wingless Victory, The. Hervey Allen. YaYoPo

Nikki-Rosa. Nikki Giovanni. BlSi; HeIP-4; PAI; TAP
(Childhood remembrances are always a drag.) FaBoA; GT; ISC; NAAAL; SSLK; UnSA

Nikolaus Mardruz to his Master Ferdinand, Count of Tyrol, 1565. Richard Howard. NoP-4

Nile, The. Leigh Hunt. CenSon; EBEV; GSo; NOBE

Nile the Hermit. Unknown. GrAn, tr. by Guy Davenport

Nima, The. Jorge Isaacs. TrJP, tr. by Alice Jane McVan

Nimble cat and lazy maid, A. On Maids and Cats. Henricus Selyns. SCAP

Nimble sigh, on thy warm wings. To Amoret. Henry Vaughan. EnLoPo

Nimble swan plays in the river pool, The. Presented as a Farewell to Secretary Fu. Pao Chao. SuSp, tr. by Daniel Bryant

Nimbus. Douglas Le Pan. MoCV

Nimium Fortunatus. Robert Bridges. MoBrPo

Nimmers, The. John Byrom. OxAEP-1

Nimrod gazed across the plain. Tower of Babel, The. Laurance Wieder. ChIV-1

Nina. Noël Coward. ReLy

Nina got out. Bruce and Nina. Clarence Major. BodElec

Nina Simone. Lance Jeffers. SeSe

Nine adulteries, 12 liaisons, 64 fornications and something approaching a rape. Temperaments, The. Ezra Pound. BoLoP; NOBA; NoAM; OBCoV; PAI

Nine birds(rising / through a gold moment)climb. E. E. Cummings. UnPo

Nine delightful birthmarks. Mikhail Alekseievich Kuzmin. CAGL, tr. by Simon Karlinsky

Nine dragons—how fluent their undulations! Apotheosis. Wu Yun. ColAnChi, tr. by Edward H. Schafer

Nine humors split and woven, The. Hsüeh T'ao. WoPoe, tr. by Jeanne Larsen Fr. Trying on New-Made Clothes: Three Poems.

999 Call. Elizabeth Bartlett. FaBoWP

999 Smiles. Atukwei Okai. PBMAP

Nine hundred thousand prisoners of war. To Her of Whom They Dream. Paul Éluard. AF, tr. by Lloyd Alexander

Nine Little Goblins, The. James Whitcomb Riley. NOxBChV; OBCA

Nine Lyric Poets, The. Unknown. GrAn, tr. by Peter Jay

Nine miles from here. Miklós Radnóti. See I fell next to him. His body rolled over

Nine-month moon. Kisei. JDP, tr. by Yoel Hoffmann

Nine months I waited in the dark beneath. Pro Sua Vita. Robert Penn Warren. MoAmPo

Nine Nectarines and Other Porcelain. Marianne Craig Moore. OxBA

9 o'clock. The bells come floating in. Journey, The. Franz Wright. LCAP-2

Nine of Clubs, Cleveland, Ohio. Dorothy Barresi. SwNoth

9.1.59: II. Pablo Picasso. CLPP, tr. by Paul Blackburn

9.1.59: VI. Pablo Picasso. CLPP, tr. by Paul Blackburn

Nine Poems for the Unborn Child. Muriel Rukeyser.
They Came to Me and Said, "There Is a Child" Son

Nine Points of the Law. Peter Porter.
"Managed as they say about such men." PeLV

Nine Songs. Ch'u Yüan. CoBCP, tr. by Burton Watson

Nine Songs. Unknown.
Lord of the River. CoBCP, tr. by Burton Watson
Mountain Spirit, The. CoBCP, tr. by Burton Watson
Those Who Died for Their Country. CoBCP, tr. by Burton Watson
Lord among the Clouds, The. CoBCP, tr. by Burton Watson

Nine souls more went in her: the long-boat still. Byron. OxBEV Fr. Don Juan.

Nine swallows sat on a telephone wire. Swallows, The. Elizabeth Jane Coatsworth. TLR

9. The Riding Crop. Lu Chi. WoPoe, tr. by Tony Barnstone and Chou Ping Fr. Art of Writing, The.

9000 Jackals Swimming to Boston. "Lucebert." PFTM-2, tr. by Peter Nijmeijer

Nine Times. James Michie. DiPo

Nine Times a Night. Unknown. EroLit

Nine times out of ten. Airs and Graces. Peter Fallon. PBCIP

Nine times the sun his yearly course had run. Elizabeth Thomas. ECWP Fr. Jill, A Pindaric Ode.

Nine white chickens come. Black November Turkey, A. Richard Wilbur. LCAP-2; NAAL-2v2; OWoS

Nine years and three days later I drop to the earth. Blind-Sided. Rick Mulkey. AmPoNex

Nineteen. Elizabeth Alexander. GT; InTrad; PoPoPo

1918–1941. Robert David Fitzgerald. CBAP

1980. Wayne Koestenbaum. WiU Fr. Erotic Collectibles.

1980. Abraham Sutskever [or Sutzkever]. HP, tr. by Cynthia Ozick Fr. Poems from a Diary.

(1980). C. S. Giscombe. GT

1980–1990: A Poet's Personal Review. Asha Bandele. InTrad

1981 and. Adupe. Jayne Cortez. ESEAA

1915. Anna Andreyevna Akhmatova. WoPoe, tr. by Stephen Berg

1915. Roger McDonald. NOBAu

1915: A Pre-Raphaelite Ending, London. Richard Howard. RACG

1951. Frank O'Hara. LCAP-2

1956. Thomas Kinsella. ModIr Fr. Anniversaries.

1956. Maxine Scates. PBCAP

1956, The Year My Sister, Using Her Ill Health Once Again, Blackmailed My Parents into an Accordion. Susan Firer. MiVo

1953 Re-entry. Time Presses Me. Lee Ranaldo. HeMarv

194 . . . . Mikhail Valentinovich Kulchitsky [or Kulchitskii]. TCRP, tr. by Daniel Weissbort

1940. Bertolt Brecht. HP, tr. by John Willet

1945. Ed Leeflang. TuT, tr. by Peter Van de Kamp

1945. Sir Herbert Read. OxBTC

1945. Leslie Ullman. ExTi

1941. Robert Garioch. FaBoWar

1946, 1957. J. D. McClatchy. WiU Fr. First Steps.

1943. Sandra McPherson. FaBoWP

1914. Rupert Brooke.
Dead, The ("These hearts were woven"). PeFWW; SoSe-8
Peace. NPeEn; OBWP
Safety. EnLoPo
Soldier, The. AmFaPo; CABP; FaBoWar; GSo; HeIP-4; MoBrPo; NAEL-5v2; NAEL-6v2; NOBE; NoP-4; OBEV; OBWP; OxBTC; PeFWW; PoRA; PoWW; Son; TFi; UV

1914. Max Jacob. PFTM-1

MCMXIV. Philip Larkin. EBEV; FaBoWar; HarvBoo; NAEL-5v2; NAEL-6v2; NoAM; NoP-4; OBWP; OxAEP-2

1914 Box, The. Marcel Duchamp. PFTM-1

Nineteen Hundred and Nineteen. W. B. Yeats.
"Many ingenious lovely things are gone." BIrV; PoE
"Some moralist or mythological poet." PoE

19 January 1944. Salvatore Quasimodo. AF, tr. by Jack Bevan

1919. Donald Revell. BodElec

1994 Inventory. Toi Derricotte. SpirFl

1992. Wayne Koestenbaum. WiU Fr. Erotic Collectibles.

1905. David Ignatow. TaR

1904. Frederick Morgan. WeW-3

Nineteen Old Poems, The. Unknown.
"Green, green riverside grass." ColAnChi, tr. by Anne Birrell

Nineteen Old Poems of the Han. Mei Sheng. CoBCP, tr. by Burton Watson

(1978, Remembering 1962). C. S. Giscombe. GT

1974. Abraham Sutskever [or Sutzkever]. BBASP, tr. by Cynthia Ozick Fr. Poems from a Diary.

1974: My Story in a Late Style of Fire. Larry Levis. BodElec
1974—The Sounds. Christina Beer. PeNZ
1971. J. D. McClatchy. WiU Fr. First Steps.
1977. Wayne Koestenbaum. WiU Fr. Erotic Collectibles.
1973. Marilyn Hacker. GLP
1973. Reuben Jackson. GT
1916 Seen from 1921. Edmund Charles Blunden. NoP-4; PeFWW
Nineteen Sixty Eight. Petra von Morstein. BoWoP, tr. by Rosemarie Waldrop
1965. Frankie Paino. AmPoNex
1967, Detroit. My grandfather watches. Time, Temperature. Jim Daniels. LTA
1966. David Rivard. PBCAP
(1962 At the Edge of Town). C. S. Giscombe. GT
1930. Aurora Levins Morales. PueRic
1935. Stephen Vincent Benét. MoAmPo
1933. Kenneth Fearing. APT-2
1933. Philip Levine. LCAP-2
1912–1952, Full Cycle. Peter Viereck. OBAL
1928 film star's breasts, The. Caught. Carole Bernstein. AmPoNex
1925. Edwin Honig. NoAM Fr. To Restore a Dead Child.
1929. W. H. Auden. OxAEP-2
1926. Weldon Kees. CoAP
Nineteenth Century and After, The. W. B. Yeats. FaBoEE
Ninety. Mary Elizabeth Fullerton. CBAP
Ninety-Mile, The. Laurie Duggan. BMAP Fr. Ash Range, The.
Ninety-Nine. Elizabeth Godley. NOxBChV
99. Fanny [or Frances] Macartney Greville. CABP Fr. Caelica.
90 North. Randall Jarrell. CoAP; HarvBoo; NAAL-2v2; NOBA; NoAM; TAP; VCAP
Ninety percent of the mass of the Universe. Certainty Before Lunch. John Berryman. LCAP-2; OxBC
Ninety summers—and never a platitude. Limerick. Stanley J. Sharpless. PeLi
Nineveh, Tyre. Memphis Blues. Sterling Allen Brown. APT-2; NAAAL
Ninguna / No. Frontera / Border. Francisco Alarcon. GeoHom
Ninny's Tomb. Patricia Beer. HarvBoo
Ninth Canticle, The. George Wither. ChIV-1
Ninth Elegy: Fort Capuzzo. Hamish Henderson. FaBoWar
Ninth Evening Voluntary. William Wordsworth. SacPr
9th July, 1932. Mary Ursula Bethell. PeNZ
Ninth of July, The. John Hollander. CoAP
Ninth of Av. Myra Sklarew. CRP
Ninth Symmetrical Poem. Michael Palmer. HarvBoo
Ninth Symphony of Beethoven Understood at Last as a Sexual Message, The. Adrienne Rich. PFTM-2; TAP
9th Untitled Poem. Pedro Juan Pietri. PueRic
Ninth Vertical Poetry. Roberto Juarroz.
    "To die, but far away." VCWP
Niobe. Henrietta Cordelia Ray. CBWP-3
Niobe. Unknown. GrAn, tr. by Peter Jay
Niobe is very old now. Bus Ride. Kate Daniels. PBCAP
Niobe lives in the desert, too. Ethiopia. Kate Daniels. PBCAP
Niobe on Phrygian sands. Wish, The. Thomas Stanley. AWP
Nip in the blossom[e] all our hopes and thee. (LL) Picture of Little T. C. in a Prospect of Flowers, The. Andrew Marvell. BASC; ESCV; FSCP; GeHe; MeLP; NAEL-5v1; NAEL-6v1; NAEL-7v1; NOBE; NoP-4; OBEV; OxAEP-1; PoE; SCGP; TFi
Nipping chill, the frost killed spring. Meng Chiao. SuSp Fr. Apricots Die Young.
Nirvâna. Sidney Lanier. NCAP
Nirvana. James Tate. BodElec
Nirvana. Rosamund Marriott Watson. VWP
Nirvana. John Hall Wheelock. MoAmPo
Nisei Daughter: The Second Generation. Rose Furuya Hawkins. FSt Fr. Proud Upon an Alien Shore.
Nisei Picnic: From an Album, A. David Mura. LoL
Nisei: Second Generation Japanese-American. James Masao Mitsui. GifTon; OpBo
—NIVERSITY of Gottingen. (LL) George Canning. NOEC; OBCoV Fr. Rovers, The.
Nixon Names Elvis Honorary Federal Narcotics Agent at Oval Office Ceremony, 1973. David Wojahn. AllShUp
Nizam the pederast, whose delight in boys. Surprise, Surprise. Unknown. EroLit, tr. by Derek Parker
'Nkongane. W. C. Scully. PeSAV
No. Mark Doty. EmeKit
No. Patti Tana. PasH

No. Treasure, The. U Tam'si Tchicaya. PFTM-2, tr. by Pierre Joris
No. Idea Vilariño. TANSG, tr. by Louise B. Popkin
No! Eliza Cook. PoToHe
No! Thomas Hood. OBCoV
No! Growing, The. Mongane Wally Serote. PBMAP
No. 5, Judith. Rebekah Gumpert Hyneman. SWaP Fr. Female Scriptural Characters.
No airy stretch of sky to rest my eyes on. Non Te Rapiet Quisquam de Manua Mea. Sydney E. Jerrold. SacPr
No alien dust covers your tomb. Simonides. GrAn
No altarpiece includes the painter. No Altarpiece. J. Kates. GI
No ancestral bones of ours. Visit to the Village, A. Michael Smith. PBCIP
No angel has descended here. Visitation, The. Jan Owen. NOBAu
No animals will live. Ritual Murder. Aig Higo. PBMAP
No answers. Only questions. (LL) In the Absence of Bliss. Maxine W. Kumin. NoAM; TaR
No argument, no anger, no remorse. Robert Graves. OxBTC Fr. Three Songs for the Lute.
No Argument Tonight. Tijan M. Sallah. NAfrP
No Balls at All. Unknown. FaBoWar
No barometer but yellow. One, The. James Dickey. BodElec
No bells rang in her house. The silver plate. Miss Marnell. Austin Clarke. OxBEV
No belly / no cry. (LL) Starry Night, The. Anne Sexton. ColAP; NAAL-5; NoAM; PoE; VCAP
No better fate is given than to die in Rome. Aleksandr Semionovich Kushner. TCRP
No better lost than any other woman. Canzone. Marilyn Hacker. NoAM
No Bharatpur Bird Sanctuary in India, or Pantanal. Faithful Daughter Dreams of Spring Break While Installing a Bird Feeder for Her Mother by a Window in the Courtyard of Safe Harbour, The. Vivian Shipley. ExTi
No bird-song floated down the hill. River Path, The. John Greenleaf Whittier. TreFP
No bitterness: our ancestors did it. Ave Caesar. Robinson Jeffers. NOBA; NoAM; OxBA; OxBSP
No black and swirling cloak, no faceless grin. Waiting for the Post. Dorothy Auchterlonie. CBAP
No Bloody Matter 43 42. Michael Haslam. Oth Fr. Continual Song.
No Bobolink—reverse His Singing. Emily Dickinson. SWaP
No Boundaries. Liz Rosenberg. InvLad
No branch nor the last grass. Fossil. E. D. Blodgett. NOBC
No breath of air to break the wave. Byron. NOBRP
No bridge. Buson. EH, tr. by Robert Hass
No Brigadier throughout the Year. Emily Dickinson. OWoS
No burning leaf; prithee, let no bird call. (LL) God's World. Edna St. Vincent Millay. APT-1; ITBLP; MoAmPo; TrCP
No call upon anyone but the timber drifting in the waves. Lament for the Makers. Jack Spicer. FTOS
No Categories! Stevie Smith. NoP-4
No Change of Place. W. H. Auden. OxBTC
No changes of support—only. Last Month. John Ashbery. CoAP
No charm can stay, no medicine can assuage. Walter Savage Landor. FaBoEE
No Child. Padraic Colum. OBMV
No city in the spacious universe. Daniel Defoe. NOEC Fr. Reformation of Manners.
No Classes! Ella Wheeler Wilcox. APN-2; SWaP
No cloud, no relique of the sunken day. Samuel Taylor Coleridge. FHYEP
No cloud or rain all night long. Wang Ping. KGB Fr. Rain, Clouds, Eight Thousand Miles of Roads.
No Cold Approach. Unknown. EBEV
No combat did he unleash, as panting. Portrait of José Cemí. José Lezama Lima. TCLAP, tr. by Gregory Rabassa
No Coming to God without Christ. Robert Herrick. OxBSP; SacPr
No concurrence of bone. (LL) T. S. Eliot. NAEL-5v2; NAEL-6v2 Fr. Landscapes.
No connection. The train would be six hours. Maundy Thursday. Jenő Dsida. IQMS, tr. by George Gömöri and Clive Wilmer
No Consolation. Norman MacCaig. HarvBoo
No Continuing City. Michael Longley. PNI
No cotton picking that day. California Entertainment, 1936. Wilma Elizabeth McDaniel. GeoHom
No! Cover not the fault. The wise revere. Frederick Goddard Tuckerman. TCAPo Fr. Sonnets.
No Coward's Song. James Elroy Flecker. OxBSP
No Coward soul is Mine. Emily Jane Brontë. BWW; BrRo; EBVV; InvLi; NAEL-6v2; NALW; OxAEP-2; TRP; TrCP; WPoS
    ('No Coward Soul Is Mine') CABP; NoP-4; PEW; PoPoPo; VWP

No crooked leg, no bleared eye.   Written in Her French Psalter.   Queen of England Elizabeth I.   WPE
No crosswords ever.   No Words Empty.   Beau Sia.   HeMarv
No danger that worms will attack; thrill them to death.   Sounds.   John Cage.   PFTM-2   *Fr.* Song Books.
No day was sad as the day Sakhr.   On Her Brother Sakhr.   Al-Khansa.   BoWoP, *tr. by* Willis Barnstone
No days that dawn can match for her.   Rachel.   Lizette Woodworth Reese.   TCAPo
No Deal.   Lee Ranaldo.   HeMarv
No deed of mine shall shame thee, gentle name. (LL)   Family Name, The.   Charles Lamb.   CenSon; Son
No Delicacies.   Ingeborg Bachmann.   PoSu, *tr. by* Mark Anderson
No Deposit.   Earle Thompson.   HATNAP
No Deposit Returns.   Carlos Cumpian.   ReTh
No Derry slubberdegullion with college airs.   Untitled.   Ian Duhig.   NeBl
No detail here, nothing but you.   Unbroken gaze.   Glance in White Space.   Clark Coolidge.   FTOS
No Dice.   Annie Foster.   NLP
No Difference in the Dark [*or* i'th'dark].   Robert Herrick.   CaPo
No dignity without chromium.   Ballad of Faith.   William Carlos Williams.   OBAL
No disrespect, mi boss.   Nigger Sweat.   Edward Baugh.   EmeKit; WaCA
No doubt about it.   Issa.   EH, *tr. by* Robert Hass
No doubt I need a year of hallucinating.   Confessions.   Iman Mirsal.   NAfrP, *tr. by* Clarissa C. Burt
No doubt in the mind of Brébeuf that this was the last.   Edwin John Pratt.   NOBC   *Fr.* Brébeuf and His Brethren.
No doubt: the sun.   Monterrey Sun.   Alfonso Reyes.   TCLAP, *tr. by* Samuel Beckett
No doubt this way is best.   No Use.   W. D. Snodgrass.   BoLoP
No doubt to-morrow I will hide.   At Mass.   Nicholas Vachel Lindsay.   VGW
No doubts defend? (LL)   Time Passing, Beloved.   Donald Davie.   BoLoP; HarvBoo; NoP-4
No Dream.   Maria [*or* Mariia] Mikhaylovna Shkapskaya [*or* Shkapskaia].   ARWW, *tr. by* Catriona Kelly
No dream of mortal joy.   Love and Lust.   Isaac Rosenberg.   TrJP
No dreamer, but thy dream. (LL)   Prayer: "Master, they say that when I seem."   Clive Staples Lewis.   SacPr; TrCP
No dust have I to cover me.   Inscription by the Sea, An.   Glaukos.   AWP; FaBoEE *tr. by* Edwin Arlington Robinson
No dust speck anywhere.   Shofu.   ZenPo, *tr. by* Takashi Ikemoto and Lucien Stryk
No ears could hear then the mutter of the Milky Way.   Prophecy.   Eileen Duggan.   PeNZ
No earthbound morning is this.   Cemetery at Petit Saconnex, The.   Deema K. Shehabi.   PoArWo
No Easy Harbour.   Anne Hartigan.   CIP-2
No easy thing to bear, the weight of sweetness.   Weight of Sweetness, The.   Li-Young Lee.   RaBo
No end in sight to the days of my wandering.   Written on the Thirtieth Day, Ninth Month, Second Year of the Ta-li Reign [767].   Tu Fu.   SuSp, *tr. by* Irving Y. Lo
No End of No-Story.   George Macdonald.   NOBVV
No End Point.   Muso Soseki.   EaWin, *tr. by* W. S. Merwin
No faculty not ill at ease.   After a Long Illness.   Robert Duncan.   PFTM-2
No "fan is in his hand" for these.   Threshing Machine, The.   Alice Thompson Meynell.   WPE
No fear of losing my sanity.   Jolanda Insana.   CItWP, *tr. by* Cinzia Sartini Blum and Lara Trubowitz   *Fr.* Colic Passion, The.
No ferns, but.   Solitude of Glass, The.   Yvor Winters.   APT-2
No fiction was it of the antique age.   William Wordsworth.   CenSon; OxBSo   *Fr.* River Duddon [A Series of Sonnets], The.
No fields but are his own. (LL)   W. H. Auden.   OxBTC; PAI; SoSe-8   *Fr.* Five Songs.
No finer gift could come to man.   Tiruvalluvar.   WoPoe, *tr. by* Emmons E. White   *Fr.* Kural, The.
No first-class war can now be fought.   Civil Defense.   Kenneth Burke.   OBAL
No flowers! / Let's blame the god in charge of flowers.   Poem on Drinking Wine with the Degree-Holder Ku.   Ch'ien Ch'ien-i [*or* Ch'ien Ch'ien-yi].   CoBLCP, *tr. by* Jonathan Chaves
No flowers now to wear at.   Waning of the Harvest Moon, The.   John Wieners.   PmAP
No flowers will live in my room.   Nikolai Stepanovich Gumilyov [*or* Gumiliov *or* Gumilev].   TCRP
No fool, the God of Salt, beloved by all.   No Fool, the God of Salt.   Alan Michael Parker.   NeAmPo
No foot of man, commend thyself to God! (LL)   Sonnet—Silence.   Edgar Allan Poe.   ColAP; NOBA; TCAPo

No, for I'll save it! Seven years since.   Apparent Failure.   Robert Browning.   NAEL-5v2; NAEL-6v2; NOBE
No foreign sky protected me.   Requiem.   Anna Andreyevna Akhmatova.   AF; PoetW; TCRP; WoPoe, *tr. by* Max Hayward and Stanley Kunitz
No form at all—it's impossible to imagine its being.   Lyn Hejinian.   FTOS   *Fr.* Oxota: A Short Russian Novel.
No Foundation.   John Hollander.   OBAL; OBCoV
No fragrance yet the fold.   Harry Guest.   NewEx
No Friend Like Music.   Daniel Whitehead Hicky.   PoToHe
No funeral gloom, my dears, when I am gone.   William Allingham.   NOBVV; OxBEV
No future hope no fear for evermore. (LL)   Cobwebs.   Christina Georgina Rossetti.   CABP; NAEL-5v2; NAEL-6v2; NALW; VWP
No Gain.   Muso Soseki.   EaWin, *tr. by* W. S. Merwin
No, go back into your exile, go back quick.   After Wiriyamu Village Massacre by Protuguese.   Jack A. Mapanje.   PeSAV
No, Go On.   Maura Dooley.   LW
No God.   Dennis Cooper.   PmAP
No God but me thou shalt adore.   Fourfold Exercise for the Believer in His Lodging on Earth, A.   Ralph Erskine.   SacPr
No gorgeous coat has he.   My Mocking Bird.   Josephine D. Henderson Heard.   CBWP-4
No great house is finer.   Ivied Tree-Top, An.   *Unknown.*   NOIV
No Great Matter.   David Lawson.   VGW
No Grudge.   Lionel Fogarty.   BMAP
No Hands.   Gillian Clarke.   TCAWP
No haste but good, where wisdome makes the waye.   George Gascoigne.   NoSic; Son   *Fr.* Gascoigne's Memories.
No Hatchet Job.   Luz Maria Umpierre.   PueRic
No hawk hangs over in this air.   Snow Storm, The.   Edna St. Vincent Millay.   NAAL-2v2
No, He is too quick. We never.   Getting Inside the Miracle.   Luci Shaw.   TrCP
"No!" He Said.   Wole Soyinka.   HBAPE
No head-ropes or dung.   Lament for an Arab Encampment.   Abid ibn al-Abras.   ArPe, *tr. by* Omar S. Pound
No Help.   Sarah Morgan Bryan Piatt.   NCAP
No help I'll call till I'm put in the narrow coffin.   Egan [*or* Aodhagán] O'Rahilly [*or* O'Reilly *or* Ó Rathaille].   NOIV
No hesitation.   Mourning Letter, March 29 1963.   Edward Dorn.   CoAmPo
No hoof, no foot, no wheel.   To a Coal Miner in Madrid, New Mexico.   Luis Lopez.   GeoH
No house of stone.   Elements, The.   William Henry Davies.   MoBrPo
No human face is.   Brown Curtain, The.   Alberto Giacometti.   SurPaPo, *tr. by* Mary Ann Caws
No hungr[y] hawke poore patridge to devoure.   Mr. Thomas Shepeard.   Edward Johnson.   SCAP
No, I Am Not as Others Are.   François Villon.   AWP, *tr. by* Arthur Symons
No, / I cannot / turn from love.   To Turn from Love.   Sarah Webster Fabio.   BlSi
No! I don't begrudge en his life.   Bachelor, The.   William Barnes.   PeVV
No, I don't love you.   Anti-Love Poems.   Elizabeth Brewster.   NOBC
No, I have not been cheated by life.   Aleksandr Trifonovich Tvardovsky [*or* Tvardovskii].   TCRP
No, I have tempered haste.   Mount, The.   Léonie Adams.   MoAmPo
No—I'll endure ten thousand deaths.   Chaste Florimel.   Matthew Prior.   BoLoP
No, I'll not, carrion, comfort you.   Comfort.   Sonnet 5.   Nell Altizer.   FFC
No, I'm not going to.   De Souza Prabhu.   Eunice De Souza.   FaBoVe
No: I'm unmoved: nor can thy charming muse.   Reply to Mr.——, The.   Elizabeth Singer Rowe.   BASC
No Images.   Waring Cuney.   APT-2; NIP-4; SSLK; TTY
No imagination to forestall woe. (LL)   Charleston in the Eighteen-Sixties.   Adrienne Rich.   CoAP; NAAL-2v2
No Immunity.   Dolores de Iruretagoyena de Humphrey.   ReBoTo
No, in the New World, happiness is enforced.   In the New World Happiness is Allowed.   Peter Porter.   BMAP
No inheritance.   Old Man To-The-Point.   Muso Soseki.   EaWin, *tr. by* W. S. Merwin
No interval of manner.   George Oppen.   HarvBoo
No, it does not happen.   Snakes.   A. K. Ramanujan.   NoP-4
No, it is not only the date clusters.   Middle East, The.   Nadia Hazboun Reimer.   PoArWo
No, it is not too soon.   Forest Trees of the Sea.   *Unknown.*   WoPoe, *tr. by* Alfons L. Korn and Mary Kawena Pukui
No, it is not wise. (LL)   Is It Wise?   Stevie Smith.   NAEL-5v2; NAEL-6v2
No, it's an impudent falsehood. Men did not.   On a Vulgar Error.   Clive Staples Lewis.   OxBTC
No! It's revenge for my donkey's pain. (LL)   Song of the Crow Pecking at My

Scarred Donkey. Wang Yü-ch'eng. SuSp; WoPoe, *tr. by* Jonathan Chaves

No, it was only a touch of dysentery, he said. He was doing fine. Taking of the Koppie, The. Uys Krige. FaBoWar; PeSAV

No it wasn't. Nothingmas Day. Adrian Mitchell. NOxBChV

No kings be crowned [*or* crown'd], but they some covenants make. (LL) Sir Philip Sidney. NAEL-5v1; NAEL-6v1; NAEL-7v1; OxAEP-1 *Fr.* Astrophil and Stella.

No Labor-Saving Machine. Walt Whitman. APN-1

No lake is so still but that it has its wave. *Unknown.* Spl

No leaf-shaking blast of winds. Simonides. SaLy, *tr. by* Diane Rayor

No—Leave my heart to rest, if rest it may. No—Leave My Heart to Rest. Thomas Moore. CenSon

No Less than Prisoners. Frederick Thomas Bennett Macartney. CBAP

No, let it stay. It speaks but truth. First Grey Hair, The. Mary E. Tucker. CBWP-1

No Letter. Mary E. Tucker. CBWP-1

No, Liberty! People, he must not die! Set Him Apart! Victor Hugo. SxFrPo, *tr. by* E. H. Blackmore and A. M. Blackmore

No light to guide but the moon's pallid ray. Henry More. NOSC *Fr.* Psychozoia, or, the Life of the Soul.

No limbo this week. Or next. Now it turns out. Limbo Dancer, The. Josephine Jacobsen. FFC

No, listen, there's this albatross. Limerick. Bill Greenwell. PeLi

No Loathsomnesse in Love. Robert Herrick. BeJo

No Lock against Lechery. Robert Herrick. CaPo

No longer are the forests green. Storms. Steel Usurps the Forests; Silence Dethrones Dialogue. Bible, Apocrypha. HBAPE

No longer, as before, plying with whirring wings. Anyte [*or* Anytes]. SaLy, *tr. by* Diane Rayor

No longer, as before, will you wake at dawn and flap. Anyte [*or* Anytes]. HePo *Fr.* Epigrams.

No longer can I tar[r]ly. (LL) Aucthour Maketh Her Wyll and Testament, The. Isabella Whitney. BWW; EMWP; NoP-4

No longer, cricket, sitting. Mnasalcas. GrAn

No longer eating meat or dairy products or refined sugar. Acupuncture and Cleansing at 48. Len Roberts. BodElec

No longer for me is there anything late. All is late. Tomorrow the Past Comes. Ion Caraion. AF, *tr. by* Marguerite Dorian

No longer mourn for me when I am dead. William Shakespeare. AWP; EBEV; HAP; HeIP-4; NAEL-5v1; NAEL-6v1; NAEL-7v1; NoSic; OxAEP-1; PAI; PoRA; SCGP; Son; TFi *Fr.* Sonnets.

No longer, O honeytongued, holyvoiced maidens. Alcman. SaLy, *tr. by* Diane Rayor

No longer shall I exult in the floating seas and arch. Anyte [*or* Anytes]. HePo *Fr.* Epigrams.

No longer throne of a goddess to whom we pray. Full Moon. Robert Earl Hayden. BPo; GT

No longer to lie reading *Tess of the d'Urbervilles*. Lesson, The. Robert Lowell. LCAP-2

No longer torn by what she knows. Poor Relation, The. Edwin Arlington Robinson. APT-1

No longer truth, though shown in verse, disdain. George Crabbe. OxAEP-1 *Fr.* Village, The.

No longer will I fling up my neck, exulting. Anyte [*or* Anytes]. SaLy, *tr. by* Diane Rayor

No longer with us, you are that man I once feared. Absence. Jaime Jacinto. ReBoTo

No louder now than falling leaves. (LL) Hillcrest. Edwin Arlington Robinson. APT-1; OxBA

No love deserves the death it has. Phonemics. Jack Spicer. PmAP

No, Love Is Not Dead. Robert Desnos. WoPoe, *tr. by* Bill Zavatsky

No, Love Is Not Dead. Robert Desnos. SurPaPo, *tr. by* Mary Ann Caws

No, love is not dead in this heart and these eyes and this mouth which announced the beginning of this burial. No, Love Is Not Dead. Robert Desnos. SurPaPo, *tr. by* Mary Ann Caws

No Love, No Nothin' Harry Warren. ReLy

No lovelier city than all of this. Toast. Thomas McCarthy. PBCIP

No lover saith, I love, nor any other. Paradox, The. John Donne. NOSC

'No' Madonnas, The. Gwyneth Lewis. TCAWP

No man can bid a fool or sage. Power of Thought, The. Süsskind von Trimberg. TrJP

No man can print a kiss: lines may deceive. (LL) Fulke Greville, 1st Baron Brooke. HAP; NOBE; NoSic; OBEV *Fr.* Caelica.

No man can serve two masters. Bible, *N.T.* OBVE *Fr.* St. Matthew.

No man could have been more unfaithful. Turkish Carpet, The. Paul Durcan. CIP-2

No man could think base thoughts who / looked on her. (LL) Sonnet: He Will Praise His Lady. Guido Guinicelli. AWP; EaItPo, *tr. by* Dante Gabriel Rossetti

No man,if men are gods; but if gods must. E. E. Cummings. VGW

No man knows. When A Woman Gets Blue. Norman Jordan. ISC; NBV

No Man Knows War. Edwin Rolfe. TrJP

No man may mount upon a golden stair. Dino Compagni. EaItPo, *tr. by* Dante Gabriel Rossetti

No man outlives the grief of war. Permanence of the Young Men, The. William Soutar. OxBS

No man's trust let woman claim. Roman Earl, The. *Unknown.* OBVE, *tr. by* Douglas Hyde

No Man's Wood. William Henry Davies. OBGa

No man takes the farm. John Masefield. UV

No Marvel Is It. Bernard [*or* Bernart] de Ventadour [*or* Ventadorn]. AWP, *tr. by* Harriet Waters Preston

No Matter. Paulus [*or* Paulos] Silentiarius. AWP, *tr. by* William Cowper (Epitaph, An: "My name—my country—what are they to thee.") FaBoEE; OBVE

No matter by what hand or trick. (LL) Sonnet: "Of thee, kind boy, I ask no red and white." Sir John Suckling. BASC; BeJo; CaPo; CavPo; MeLP; NOSC; NoP-4; OxBoLi

No matter how I concealed them, even the. Osip Emilevich Mandelstam [*or* Mandelshtam]. PFTM-1 *Fr.* Tristia.

No matter how I shout—there's no reply. Vladimir Aleksandrovich Smolensky [*or* Smolenskii]. TCRP

No matter how loudly I call you the sound of your name. Poem for Guatemala. June Jordan. NAAAL

No matter how much more waiting I'll have to do. Vladimir Vladimirovich Mayakovsky [*or* Maiakovskii]. TCRP *Fr.* Pro Eto.

No matter how small. Smalltown Memorials. Geoff Page. BMAP

No matter how thunderous the chorus. True Descenders. James Kimbrell. AmPoNex; NAPBL

No matter what I say. Eel-Grass. Edna St. Vincent Millay. APT-1

No matter what life you lead. Snow White and the Seven Dwarfs. Anne Sexton. HCAP; PoPoPo

No matter what you did to her, she said. Yeah Yeah Yeah. Roddy Lumsden. NeBl

No matter where I turn, she is there. Rita Dove. NAAAL *Fr.* Mother Love.

No matter where we go, we always arrive too late. No Matter Where We Go. Henrik Nordbrandt. VCWP, *tr. by* Henrik Norbrandt and Alexander Taylor

No McTavish. Genealogical Reflection. Ogden Nash. OBAL

No Mean City. Patrick MacDonogh. BIrV; OxBSP

No memory is here of things once done. Mood of Vichy, The. Hildebert. MLL, *tr. by* Helen Waddell

No mind, no Buddha. Shozan. ZenPo, *tr. by* Takashi Ikemoto and Lucien Stryk

No mind, no Buddha, no being. Tekkan. ZenPo, *tr. by* Takashi Ikemoto and Lucien Stryk

No mind, no Buddhas, no live beings. Chifu. ZenPo, *tr. by* Takashi Ikemoto and Lucien Stryk

No mistakes made here. Broken and Beirut. Suheir Hammad. PoArWo

No mo meetings. Listenen to Big Black at S. F. State. Sonia Sanchez. BPo

No money for lunch so I rode an elevator to the top of the ONB. Vision (2). Sherman Alexie. UnSA

No money to bury him. Ballad of the Man Who's Gone. Langston Hughes. SAmP

No money yet, why then let's terrify with swords. *Unknown.* FaBoWar *Fr.* Mercenary Soldier, The.

No monument stands over Babii Yar. Babii Yar. Yevgeny Aleksandrovich Yevtushenko [*or* Evtushenko]. HP; TCRP; VCWP, *tr. by* George Reavey

No monuments or landmarks guide the stranger. Country without a Mythology, A. Douglas Le Pan. MoCV; NOBC

No Moon. Nancy Eimers. ExTi

No Moon at All. Redd Evans. ReLy

No moon, no chance to meet. Ono no Komachi. WPOW

No More. Idea Vilariño. BLPSL, *tr. by* Rene de Costa, Rigas Kappatos and Eleni Paidoussi

No more alone sleeping, no more alone waking. Marriage. Mary Elizabeth Coleridge. LW; NALW; PEW; PoBW; VWP; ViWPN

No more, America, in mournful strain. Phillis Wheatley. WPOW *Fr.* To the Right Honourable William, Earl of Dartmouth.

No More Auction Block. *Unknown.* BPo; ISC; NAAAL; RaBo (Many Thousand Gone.) APN-2; TCAPo

No more be grieved at that which thou hast done. William Shakespeare. HeIP-4; NAEL-5v1; NAEL-6v1; NAEL-7v1; NoSic; OxAEP-1; PoE; SCGP; UnPo *Fr.* Sonnets.

No More Beneath the Oppressive Hand. *Unknown.* AH

No More Boomerang. Oodgeroo of the tribe Noonuccal (Kath Walker). BMAP

No More Booze. *Unknown.* OBAL

No more by cold philosophy confined. Sir Samuel Egerton Brydges. CenSon

No More Crying Out.   Giuseppe Ungaretti.   PeFWW, tr. by Jon Silkin

No more dying. (LL)   Ode to Joy.   Frank O'Hara.   GLP; NeAP; PmAP

No more for sin's dark stain the debt of death to pay. (LL)   Garden, The.   Jones Very.   APN-1; OxBA; TAP

No more head shaving.   Chitsu.   ZenPo, tr. by Takashi Ikemoto and Lucien Stryk

No more I seek, the prize is found.   Harbor, The.   William Ellery Channing.   APN-1

No more in any house can I be at peace.   Dream, A.   Charles Williams.   OBEV

No more in delightful chase through buoyant seas.   On a Dolphin.   Anyte [or Anytes].   GrAn, tr. by John Heath-Stubbs and Carol A. Whiteside

No more let Greece her bolder fables tell.   Ben Jonson.   BeJo

No More Lewd Lays.   Barnabe Barnes.   Son   Fr. Divine Century of Spiritual Sonnets, A.

No More Love Poems #1.   Ntozake Shange.   BlSi   Fr. For Colored Girls Who Have Considered Suicide When the Rainbow Is Enuf.

"No more mistresses," King Edward said.   Limerick.   Frank Richards.   PeLi

No more, my dear, no more these counsels try.   Sir Philip Sidney.   SCGP   Fr. Astrophil and Stella.

No more, my Stella, to the sighing shades.   To Stella.   Hester Mulso.   ECWP

No more my visionary soul shall dwell.   Pantisocracy.   Samuel Taylor Coleridge.   CenSon

No more ne will I wicked be.   Unknown.   MiEL

No more, no more Jewish townships in Poland.   Elegy.   Antoni Slonimski.   HP, tr. by Isaac Komen

No more, no more, / We are already pined [pin'd].   Riddle.   Alexander Brome.   NOSC

No more, O my spirit.   Euripides.   AWP   Fr. Hippolytus.

No more of I and thou.   Hitler Speaks.   Helen Waddell.   MLL

No more of talk where God or Angel Guest.   John Milton.   FHYEP; NAEL-5v1; NAEL-6v1; NAWM-5v1; NAWM-7v1; OxBEV; TOF   Fr. Paradise Lost.

No more of your titled acquaintances boast.   Toadeater, The.   Robert Burns.   FaBoEE

No more—Oh, never more! (LL)   Lament, A: "O world! O life! O time!"   Shelley.   GTBS-P; NOBE; PoRA

No more poem! he raged, eye red.   More Poem.   Dennis Scott.   WaCA

No more post-stops on the road.   Following the Rhymes of Yang T'ing-ho's Poem, "On the Road Back, Accompanying the Imperial Retinue on a Visit to the Tombs of Former Emperors."   Li Tung-yang.   CoBLCP, tr. by Jonathan Chaves

No more shall I, since I am driven hence.   To Larr [or Lar].   Robert Herrick.   CaPo

No more shall walls, no more shall walls confine.   Hosanna.   Thomas Traherne.   ChIV-2

No more than one memory allowed.   No More Than One Allowed.   Duo Duo (Li Shizheng).   PoetW, tr. by Maghiel Van Crevel

No more the English girls may go.   High Germany.   Edward Richard Burton Shanks.   OBMV

No more the highschool land.   Canada: Case History: 1973.   Earle Birney.   PeLV

No more the scarlet maples flash and burn.   December.   Christopher Pearse Cranch.   APN-1; TCAPo

No More Unto My Thoughts Appear.   Sidney Godolphin.   BeJo

No more walks in the wood.   Old-Fashioned Song, An.   John Hollander.   NoP-4

No more with overflowing light.   For a Dead Lady.   Edwin Arlington Robinson.   APT-1; HeIP-4; MoAmPo; NOBA; NoAM; OxBA; PoRA; TCAPo; TFi

No more you weave, Persephone.   To Persephone.   Harold Vinal.   YaYoPo

No mortal man beneath the sky.   Epitaph for George Moore.   Thomas Hardy.   FaBoEE

No mortal thing enthralled these longing eyes.   Celestial Love.   Michelangelo Buonarroti.   AWP, tr. by John Addington Symonds

No mountain and no forest, land nor sea.   To Arno of Salzburg.   Alcuin.   MLL, tr. by Helen Waddell

No mountains or ocean, but we had orchards.   Produce.   Debra Allbery.   PBCAP

No Music.   Richard Chess.   TaR

No, my body is neither a pelican nor a water lily.   "Adonis" [or "Adunis"].   PFTM-2, tr. by Allen Hibbard and Osama Isber   Fr. Desire Moving Through the Maps of the Material.

No namable danger to the season.   Notes: From the Wait.   Rachel Tzvia Back.   DTA

No need to cling.   Naito Joso.   ZenPo, tr. by Takashi Ikemoto and Lucien Stryk

No need to go.   Jefferson Company, The.   Clarence Major.   BodElec

No need to grieve that they have scattered in the eastern wind. (LL)   To a Pyrotechnist.   Chao Meng-fu.   CoBLCP; ColAnChi, tr. by Jonathan Chaves

No never again without sense.   Now Melanctha Had neither Home, nor Regular Occupation. Life Was Just Beginning for Her.   Piera Oppezzo.   CItWP, tr. by Cinzia Sartini Blum and Lara Trubowitz

No new delights to our desire.   Singers to Come.   Alice Thompson Meynell.   WPE

No new poems his brush will trace.   On Hearing Someone Sing a Poem by Yüan Chên.   Po Chü-i.   ChiP, tr. by Arthur Waley

No New Thing.   Vincent Buckley.   CBAP

No news of navies burnt at seas.   New-Year's [or New-Yeares] Gift Sent to Sir Simeon Steward, A.   Robert Herrick.   CaPo

No Newspapers.   Mary Elizabeth Coleridge.   NPeEn

No, no, fair heretic[k], it needs must be.   Sir John Suckling.   BeJo; CaPo   Fr. Aglaura.

No, no; for my virginity.   True Maid, A.   Matthew Prior.   FaBoEE; NAEL-5v1; NAEL-6v1; NAEL-7v1; NIP-4; NOEC; NPeEn; PeLV

No, no! Go from me. I have left her lately.   Virginal, A.   Ezra Pound.   ColAP; MoAmPo; NAAL-2v2; NIL-7; NIP-4; NOBA; OxBA; Son; TAP; TCAPo

No, no, go not to Lethe, neither twist.   Ode on Melancholy.   John Keats.   CABP; FHYEP; HAP; InPK-6; NAEL-5v2; NAEL-6v2; NAWM-7v2; NIL-7; NOBE; NPeEn; NoP-4; OBEV; OxAEP-2; OxBEV; PoE; PoRA; SCGP; TFi

No, no, it cannot be; for who e'er set.   Beauty and Denial.   William Cartwright.   BeJo

No, No, Nanette.   K. Schippers.   TuT, tr. by Dennis O'Driscoll

No, no, no, I know I was not important as I moved.   Come Dance with Kitty Stobling.   Patrick Kavanagh.   HarvBoo; NPeEn; NoAM

No, no, no, no, my dear, let be. (LL)   Sir Philip Sidney.   HAP; NAEL-5v1; NAEL-6v1; NAEL-7v1; NoP-4; NoSic   Fr. Astrophil and Stella.

No, no, no, she tells me. Why bring it back?   Argument: on 1942, An.   David Mura.   LoL

No, No, Nora.   Ted Fiorito.   ReLy

No, No Nostalgia!   Stephanie Brown.   BodElec

No no: they definitely were.   Testimony.   Dan Pagis.   PoSu, tr. by Stephen Mitchell

No. No. They were certainly.   Evidence.   Dan Pagis.   FIT, tr. by Robert Friend

No, not earth, nor a stone slab.   Glaukos.   GrAn

No, not tonight.   In Teesdale.   Andrew Young.   OxBSP

No, not under the vault of alien skies.   Requiem.   Anna Andreyevna Akhmatova.   NAWM-7v2, tr. by Judith Hemschemeyer

No, not under the vault of another sky.   Anna Andreyevna Akhmatova.   BoWoP, tr. by Richard McKane

No, not writers for Heaven's sake. That bunch of slobbers.   Brothers and Sisters.   Michael Foley.   PNI

No oasis anymore; and beauty.   Beach.   Tiziano Rossi.   ItPo, tr. by Gayle Ridinger

No Obligation.   Victoria Mary Sackville-West.   PoBW

No occasion to. (LL)   British Journalist, The.   Humbert Wolfe.   FaBoEE; OBCoV; OxBEV; OxBTC

No Occupation.   George Rostrevor Hamilton.   FaBoEE

No Offence.   Dennis Joseph Enright.   OxBTC

No Offense.   Kevin Young.   LTA

No Old Lady.   Fêng Mêng-lung.   ColAnChi, tr. by Richard W. Bodman   Fr. Mountain Songs.

No one.   Poem Arrested at Daybreak.   Julia de Burgos.   TANSG, tr. by Heather Rosario Sievert

No One.   Lilian Moore.   TLR

No one believes in the calm.   Belief.   Philip Levine.   ColAP

No one belongs to the path.   Strangers.   Huda Ablan.   PoArWo, tr. by Nathalie Handal and Ibrahim Muhawi

No one calls me that here. No one.   Tísica.   Diana García.   TouFir

No one calls you beautiful.   Adolescence.   Allison Joseph.   AmPoNex

No one can hurt me. They've tried to kill me.   Alone.   Anna Andreyevna Akhmatova.   BoWoP; GifTon, tr. by Stephen Berg

No one ever came out of there.   Why?   Wassily Kandinsky [or Kandinskii].   TCRP, tr. by Albert C. Todd

No one ever walking this our only earth, various, very clouded.   He Had a Quality of Growth.   Muriel Rukeyser.   NNaP

No one forgives you for what.   Dear Ez.   Christopher Pilling.   NLP

No-one has ever seen me. And the seasons.   Memorial.   Mihály Babits.   IQMS, tr. by Peter Zollman

No one has sung "Let the world know!"   Antiphonal Hymn in Praise of Inanna.   Enheduanna.   BoWoP

No one has yet looked at. (LL)   Beach Glass.   Amy Clampitt.   FaBoWP; NoAM; NoP-4; VCAP

No One Heard Him Call.   Dorothy Aldis.   TLR

No one hears her.   Whippoorwill Calls, The.   Beverly McLoughland.   HHAm

No one in the Arrowhead Pub believed.   Man on the Tower, The.   Charles Rafferty.   AmPoNex

No One in the Wide Wilderness of the Wood.   Fernando Pessoa. WoPoe, tr. by Katherine Washburn

No one invited me.   Tune: "Magnolia Blossoms, Abbreviated." Chu Tun-ju. SuSp, tr. by James J. Y. Liu

No one kneads us again out of earth and clay. Psalm. Paul Celan. PoSu; PoetW, tr. by John Felstiner

No one kneads us anew from earth and clay. Psalm. Paul Celan. WoPoe, tr. by Margaret Guillemin and Katherine Washburn

No one knows how long he's been there. River Bidgee. Iris Clayton. IBA

No one knows how old this tree is, standing before the mountain. Song of the Old Oak. Chang Yü. CoBLCP, tr. by Jonathan Chaves

No one knows the way out of his mother. String. Dennis Schmitz. LCAP-2

No one knows what you mean. (LL) Nails. Gary Gildner. PBCAP; TAP

No one knows where the undertaker lives. Owl In Daytime, The. Thylias Moss. GT

No one knows why he came, or why he turned away, and did not climb the hill. (LL) Snowbanks North of the House. Robert Bly. AiP; BodElec; LCAP-2; RaBo

No one lives past a hundred. Wang Fan-chih. SuSp

No one moulds us again out of earth and clay. Psalm. Paul Celan. BBASP; HP; OBVE, tr. by Michael Hamburger

No one needs to ask. Reinmar der Alte. GePo

No one, not even Cambridge, was to blame. A. E. Housman. W. H. Auden. OxAEP-2

No one, not even God, can put back a leaf on to a tree. Fatality. D. H. Lawrence. PeECV

No one notices what I am doing by the border fence. Jaffa, July 1948. Hamutal Bar Yosef. DTA, tr. by Shirley Kaufman

No one really dies in the myths. Singers Change, The Music Goes On, The. Linda Gregg. BAP-01

No one. Red notes sounding in a grey trolley town. (LL) Boston Year. Elizabeth Alexander. GT; OPRER

No One Remembers. Léon Damas. SurPaPo, tr. by Mary Ann Caws

No One Remembers [Abandoning] the Village of White Fir. Duane Niatum. CDW

No one remembers ever having seen. No One Remembers. Léon Damas. SurPaPo, tr. by Mary Ann Caws

No one's dancing here tonight. Dance, The. Daniel Halpern. ChAP

No one's fated or doomed to love anyone. Adrienne Rich. PoBW Fr. Twenty-one Love Poems.

No one's going to read. Dance for Militant Dilettantes, A. Al Young. NBV

No one sees me. Fathoms up. Angel. Ruth Padel. MFPA

No One So Much As You. Edward Thomas. TCAWP

No one speaks a word. (LL) Off from Swing Shift. Garrett Kaoru Hongo. GeoHom; ReTh

No one spoke. Ōshima Ryōta. OHPJ; TTTS

No One to Guide Us. Charmaine Papertalk-Green. IBA

No one understands the Windigo, his voice like. Windigo. Paulette Jiles. NOBC

No one waits down below, as when we were young. Anatoly [or Anatoli] Sergeievich Shteiger. TCRP

No one walks when the guardian drum sounds. Thinking of My Brothers on a Moonlit Night. Tu Fu. TAL

No one wanted to dance with us. Junior High Dance. Allison Joseph. UnSA

No one will laugh, I guess. (LL) Michael Is Afraid of the Storm. Gwendolyn Brooks. NOxBChV; OxIBACP

No One Will Put the Cid up. Only a Small Girl Addresses Him and That to Tell Him to Go Away. The Cid Finds He Has to Make Camp Outside of Town, on the Sand of the Riverbank. Unknown. WoPoe, tr. by Paul Blackburn Fr. Poem of the Cid, The.

No Ordinary Sun. Hone Tuwhare. PeNZ

No ornaments but the double bed and open. Outer Banks, The. Emily Grosholz. RA

No Other Choice. Tobias Hume. EBEV; NOBE

No other man has come down that way with his foot so big. Hallelujah Terrible. Matthew Lippman. BAP-97

No other man, unless it was Doc Hill. Edgar Lee Masters. APT-1; IllVoic Fr. Spoon River Anthology.

No other woman can truthfully say she was cherished. 87. Catullus. NAWM-7v1, tr. by Charles Martin

No Pardon. Friedrich Hölderlin. WoPoe, tr. by Vyt Bakaitis

No part left out. (LL) Lady Izumi. EnlH; WPoS

No part of her will fade. African Queen. Willem M. Roggeman. TuT, tr. by Gabriel Rosenstock

No Passenger was known to flee. Emily Dickinson. SAmP

No pavement chalks the plain with memories. Beginning the Year at Rosebud, S. D. Roberta Hill Whiteman. CDW

No peace or quiet in the countryside. Farewell of an Old Man. Tu Fu. SuSp, tr. by Michael E. Workman

No peacocks will strut in my yard. Estate. Agi Mishol. DTA, tr. by Tsipi Keller

No pets in the projects. Owl and the Lightning, The. Martín Espada. TouFir; UrbNat

No place I love to visit more. Thoughts. Amanda Ros. VerBaPo

No place is extreme. Nanni Cagnone. ItPo, tr. by Gayle Ridinger

No Place Is Here or There. Oscar Hahn. BLPSL, tr. by Rene de Costa, Rigas Kappatos and Eleni Paidoussi

No Place Like Home. Llawdden. OBWVE, tr. by Gwyn Jones

No place seemed farther than your death. And I Am Old to Know. Pauline Hanson. TAP

No place to go, no reason to remain. (LL) Coming to This. Mark Strand. HCAP; VCAP

No planet revolves around the Sun. Law. Tiziano Rossi. ItPo, tr. by Gayle Ridinger

No Platonic [or Platonique] Love. William Cartwright. BeJo; NOSC

No pleasant fruit or blossom gaily smiled. Philip Freneau. NAAL-3 Fr. House of Night, The.

No, please don't. On Thinking of Photographing My Fantasies. Nellie Wong. OpBo

No poem you send. Buson. TAL

No poet's calling were we granted. Old Derzhavin. "David Samuilovich Samoylov [or Samoilov]." TCRP, tr. by Lubov Yakovleva

No poetry before ours. Filippo Tommaso Marinetti. PFTM-1 Fr. Zang Tumb Tuuum.

No point in crying justice. Prescription. Donald Woods. CAGL

No point in leaving you a long list. What I Leave to My Son. Du Tũ' Lê. WoPoe, tr. by Nguyen Ngoc Bich

No point mortgages wilt in daynights. Mac Wellman. HeMarv Fr. Rat Minaret: Miniaturist-Divan, The.

No point now my friend in telling. Heemi. Hone Tuwhare. PeNZ

No poisoned image yours against the sky. Hemlock at Sunset, A. Alec Brock Stevenson. FuPo

No population, roofs that move. Unusual View of the Town. J. P. Ward. AngWePo

No porter guards the passage of your door. Dryden. EBEV Fr. To My Honoured [or Honour'd] Kinsman, John Driden [of Chesterton in the County of Huntingdon, Esquire].

No Portuguese Lady is Nautical. Limerick. Sydney Hoffman. PeLi

No Possum, No Sop, No Taters. Wallace Stevens. HCAP; OxBA; TAP; VGW

No praying allowed, no sneezing. Warnings. Nicanor Parra. AF, tr. by Miller Williams

No Precedent. Muso Soseki. EaWin, tr. by W. S. Merwin

No priests. No tiring-women. If you please. Jezebel to the Eunuchs. Eleanor Brown. MFPA

No private grudge they need, no personal spite. Modern Critics. Samuel Taylor Coleridge. FaBoEE

No! put the work down! No, not another stitch! Unfinished Sewing, The. Evdokiya Rostopchina. ARWW, tr. by Catriona Kelly

No, Quetzalcoatl, don't come back. Pentti Saarikoski. VCWP Fr. Invitation to the Dance.

No Rack can torture me. Emily Dickinson. NALW; TCAPo

No rain, and yet my saddle is damp. Fog at Liang-hsiang. Yüan Mei. CoBLCP, tr. by Jonathan Chaves

No record tells of lance opposed to lance. William Wordsworth. CenSon Fr. River Duddon [A Series of Sonnets], The.

No red ammo spells a tin sign screwed. Steve's Commando Paintball, San Adriano, California. Joel Brouwer. AmPoNex

No Remedy. Drummond Allison. OxBTC

No rest! No rest on this bleak earth for me. Crazed. Mary E. Tucker. CBWP-1; RACG

No rice—In that hour. Basho. TAL

No riches from his scanty store. Song, A. Helen Maria Williams. WoRP

No ring, no Wedding. Unknown. BASC

No Road. Philip Larkin. EBEV; MoBrPo; OxAEP-2

No room at the crowded inn for you. And why? To the Virgin Mary. Andreas Gryphius. WoPoe, tr. by Christopher Benfey

No room for mourning: he's gone out. William Wordsworth. Sidney Keyes. OxBTC

No room in the inn, of course. What the Donkey Saw. U. A. Fanthorpe. OBCP

No rooster wakes them. A donkey brays. In the Madison Zoo. Roberta Hill Whiteman. CDW

No round-shouldered pitchers here, no stewards. Cana Revisited. Seamus Heaney. FaBoMo

No runner clears the final fence. Unfinished Race, The. Norman Cameron. OxBS; OxBSo

"No," said Charles Peace. Edmund Clerihew Bentley. NOBL Fr. Clerihews.

No Second Troy. W. B. Yeats. EnLoPo; GTBS-P; HarvBoo; NAEL-5v2; NAEL-6v2; NOBE; NoAM; OxAEP-2; OxBTC; TFi; WeW-3

No, señora rodriguez. Ancestral Messengers/Composition 13. Ntozake Shange. GT

No shadow on soft-fallen snow. (LL) Hospital Evening. Gwen Harwood. EmeKit; FaBoWP

No sharp edges to this poet, who strolls. Contemporary Poet, A. Steve Wilson. AmPoNex

No, she's brushing a boy's hair. (LL) Facing It. Yusef Komunyakaa. AmFaPo; ESEAA; NAAAL; PoPoPo; TRP

No ship of all that under sail or steam. Immigrants. Robert Frost. AmFaPo

No Shoes No Shirt No Service. Gary Snyder. BB

No Shop Does the Bird Use. Elizabeth Jane Coatsworth. OBCA; OxIBACP

No sickness worse than secret love. Unknown. NOIV

No sign. Basho. JDP, tr. by Yoel Hoffmann

No sign is made while empires pass. Continuity. "Æ." MoBrPo

No Sign of Blood. Faiz Ahmad Faiz. AF, tr. by Naomi Lazard

No Sign of Life. Jorge Teillier. TCLAP, tr. by Carolyne Wright

No sign of men on the empty mountain. Deer Park. Wang Wei. CrYelRi, tr. by Sam Hamill

No Simple Explanations. Jayne Cortez. GT

No single bone in my body is holy. Shumpo Soki. JDP, tr. by Yoel Hoffmann

No Single Thing Abides. Lucretius. AWP, tr. by W. H. Mallock Fr. De Rerum Natura (On the Nature of Things).

"No, sir," said General Sherman. Edmund Clerihew Bentley. NOBL; OBCoV Fr. Clerihews.

No situation presents itself. Every Time We Say Goodbye. James Cushing. SeSe

No sky and no earth at all. Hashin. NIL-7, tr. by Daniel C. Buchanan

No sleep for twelve days. What Happened to a Young man in a Place Where He Turned to Water. Unknown. STP, tr. by Anselm Hollo

No sleep. The sultriness pervades the air. House-Top, The. Herman Melville. APN-2; CBCWP; NAAL-2v1; NAAL-3; NCAP; NOBA; TCAPo

No sleep tonight. Summary. Sonia Sanchez. BPo

No sleeping wind will bear my head. Hourglass Lying Down. Alice Rahon. SurWo, tr. by Nancy Deffebach and Vanina Deler

No son. No moon. Veil. János Pilinszky. IQMS, tr. by Peter Jay

No sooner come [or came] but gone, and fallen [or fall'n] asleep. On My Dear Grandchild Simon Bradstreet, [Who Died on 16th November, 1669, Being But a Month and One Day Old]. Anne Bradstreet. NAAL-2v1; NAAL-3; SCAP

No sooner had they carried their martinis. Drinks in the Town Square. Rachel Wetzsteon. AmPoNex; NeAmPo

No Sorry. Catherine Bowman. BAP-97

No sound. Devil's Destroying Angel Exploded, The. Tom Pickard. Oth

No sound is dissonant which tells of Life. (LL) This Lime-Tree Bower My Prison. Samuel Taylor Coleridge. FHYEP; HeIP-4; NAEL-5v2; NAEL-6v2; OBGa; OxAEP-2; PoE; TOF

No sound of any storm that shakes. Hillcrest. Edwin Arlington Robinson. APT-1; OxBA

No specious splendour of this stone. Cornelian, The. Byron. CAGL; TreFP

No Speech from the Scaffold. Thom Gunn. WoO5

No spinsterlollypop for me—yes—we have. Dozen Cocktails—Please, A. Else Von Freytag-Loringhoven. APT-1

No spot of earth where men have so fiercely for ages of time. Antrim. Robinson Jeffers. BIrV; NOBA; VGW

No spring, nor summer beauty hath such grace. John Donne. BASC; FSCP; NOSC Fr. Elegies.

No square poet's job. (LL) Haiku: "Eastern guard tower." Etheridge Knight. BPo; ESEAA; TAP

No stab thy soul[e] can kill. (LL) Lie, The. Sir Walter Ralegh. CTC; EBEV; HAP; NAEL-5v1; NAEL-6v1; NAEL-7v1; NOBE; NPeEn; NoSic; OxBEV; RB; SCGP; SCV; TFi

No Stars Her Eyes. Thomas Lodge. Son Fr. Phyllis.

No Stewart art thou, Galloway. On Lord Galloway. Robert Burns. FaBoEE

No stir in the air, no stir in the sea. Inchcape Rock, The. Robert Southey. EBNV; OBNV; OBSP; OxAEP-2

No Story So Divine. Samuel Crossman. SacPr

No strength of Nature can suffice. William Cowper. NOCV Fr. Olney Hymns.

No sun—no moon! No! Thomas Hood. OBCoV

No sunrise here three layers of green. Illumination. D. F. Brown. CDa

No, Superman Was Not the Only One. Katharyn Howd Machan. ReTh

No surely, now it cannot be pride. (LL) Tennyson. EBVV; NAEL-5v2; NAEL-6v2 Fr. Maud [A Monodrama].

No Swan So Fine. Marianne Craig Moore. NALW; OxBA; UnPo
(No water so still as the.) NoP-4

No talent. Issa. EH, tr. by Robert Hass

No, Thank You, John. Christina Georgina Rossetti. NAEL-5v2; NAEL-6v2

No Thanks, No. 70. E. E. Cummings. PFTM-1

No, the human heart. Ki no Tsurayuki. OHPJ

No, the serpent did not. Theology. Ted Hughes. FaBoMo; NAEL-5v2; NoAM; NoP-4; PAI

No Theory. David Ignatow. NNaP; RaBo

No thief will ever steal thereof, God wot. (LL) Sonnet: He Jests Concerning His Poverty. Bartolomeo di Sant' Angelo. AWP; EaItPo, tr. by Dante Gabriel Rossetti

No thing existed, nor did nothing exist. Unknown. WoPoe, tr. by Frederick Morgan Fr. Vedic Hymns.

No thing is great on this side of the grave. Heaviness May Endure for a Night, But Joy Cometh in the Morning. Christina Georgina Rossetti. SacPr

No thing / no-thing. Cathexis. Frederick Bryant, Jr. NBV

No! those days are gone away. Robin Hood. John Keats. AWP; SCGP

No; thou'rt a fool, I'll swear, if e'er thou grant. Abraham Cowley. BeJo; NOSC Fr. Mistress, The.

No, throwing yourself under a train like Tolstoy's Anna. Meditation on the Threshold. Rosario Castellanos. TANSG, tr. by Magda Bogin

No thunder blasts Jove's plant, nor can. Occasioned by Seeing a Walk of Bay Trees. Mildmay Fane, 2d Earl of Westmorland. BeJo; NOSC; OxBSP

No thyng is to man so dere. Praise of Women. Robert Mannyng [or Manning]. OBEV

No ticket could touch. (LL) Soul Music. Baron Wormser. LTA; SwNoth

No time ago / or else a life. E. E. Cummings. OxBSP

No, Time, thou shalt not boast that I do change. William Shakespeare. OxAEP-1; Son Fr. Sonnets.

No, 'tis in vain to seek for bliss. Felicity. Isaac Watts. SacPr

No Title. David Schubert. APT-2

No tongue but bumbles, has. Mac Wellman. HeMarv Fr. Rat Minaret: Miniaturist-Divan, The.

No Tool or Rope or Pail. Bob Arnold. OPRER

No touch, but forever and ever this. (LL) At Baia. "H. D." APT-1; ColAP; NAAL-2v2; NOBA; PoBW

No towers tremble now at the blast of my sighs. De Profundis. László Kálnoky. IQMS, tr. by Edwin Morgan

No townsman, Perikles, will blame us for groaning. Archilochus. SaLy, tr. by Diane Rayor

No trace anywhere of life, you say, pah, no difficulty there. Imagination Dead Imagine. Samuel Beckett. PFTM-2

No trace is left upon the vulgar mind. Charles Tennyson Turner. CenSon

No Transport. Tony Lopez. Oth

No Trespassing (Private Beach). Katayoon Zandvakili. AmPoNex

No tricks / nothing doing. Tune: "Greeting the Immortal Guest." Yün-k'an Tzu. SuSp, tr. by Jerome P. Seaton

No Use. W. D. Snodgrass. BoLoP

No use in my going. Blue Monday. Langston Hughes. SAmP

No use to aim that sextant now. Song. Reuel Denney. YaYoPo

No village dames and maidens now are seen. Samuel Jackson Pratt. OBGa Fr. Cottage Pictures.

No walk today;—November's breathings toss. Thomas Doubleday. CenSon

No walls confine! Can nothing hold my mind? Insatiableness. Thomas Traherne. BBASP; NOSC

No water is still, on top. Movement of Fish, The. James Dickey. VGW

No water so still as the / dead fountains of Versailles. No swan. No Swan So Fine. Marianne Craig Moore. NALW; OxBA; UnPo

No waters breed or break. (LL) Next, Please. Philip Larkin. CABP; HarvBoo; MoBrPo

No Way Back to the Past. Allen Ginsberg. BodElec

No way too long—no path too steep. Stefan George. AWP Fr. Das Jahr der Seele.

No, we'll be wits, and then men must be fools. (LL) Emulation, The. Sarah Fyge Egerton. CABP; ECWP; NOEC; PEW

No weather is ill. Unknown. FaBoVe

No West Indians that I could see at my grandfather's funeral. (1962 At the Edge of Town). C. S. Giscombe. GT

No whimsy of the purse is here. Inscription for the Moss-Hut at Dove Cottage. William Wordsworth. OBGa

No. Who can bear it. Only someone. Demeter, Waiting. Rita Dove. BodElec

No winter shall abate the spring's increase. (LL) Love's Growth. John Donne. ESCV; NOSC; NPeEn

No woman's pleasure did I feel. Evidence at the Witch Trials. James Keir Baxter. OxBC

No woman yet has understood. It's a Hard, Hard World for a Man. P. G. Wodehouse. ReLy

No, Women Don't Cry. Opal Palmer Adisa. WaCA

No wonder I'm a poet. Manila Paper. Cyn Zarco. ReBoTo

No wonder I slipped, being soaked. Dionysius. GrAn

No Word. Tu Fu. SuSp, tr. by Eugene Eoyang

No-Word Hut. Muso Soseki. EaWin, tr. by W. S. Merwin

No Words Empty. Beau Sia. HeMarv

No words, no tears can mend. (LL) Father and Child. Gwen Harwood. CBAP; WPE

No, worldling, no, 'tis not thy gold. Second Rapture, The. Thomas Carew. BASC; CaPo

No Worst, There Is None. Pitched Past Pitch of Grief. Gerard Manley Hopkins. EBVV; FaBoMo; GSo; GTBS-P; HeIP-4; MoBrPo; NAEL-5v2; NAEL-6v2; NOBE; NOBVV; NoAM; NoP-4; OxAEP-2; PeVV; PoE; PoPoPo; TFi; WoPoe

No written word has ever explained this mystery. (LL) To the Monk Wu-hsia on the Occasion of His Editing the Lotus Sutra. Mo Shih-lung. CoBLCP; ColAnChi, tr. by Jonathan Chaves

No' yirdit thaim. (LL) Eemis-Stane, The. Hugh MacDiarmid. NAEL-5v2; NAEL-6v2; NPeEn; NePenScot

No, you never will bind him. God (3). Marina Ivanovna Tsvetayeva [or Tsvetaeva]. WPoS, tr. by Paul Graves

Noah. Gerda Mayer. OTCP

Noah. James Reeves. OTCP

Noah. Margit Szécsi. IQMS, tr. by Agnes Arany-Makkai

Noah. Unknown.
   "I thank the, Lord so dere, that wold vowchsayf." PoE

Noah, looking out of the safe Ark. Flood, The. Patricia Beer. HarvBoo

Noah's Ark. Roger McGough. OBSP

Noah's Ark. Marguerite Young. WPE

Noah's Flood. Caedmon. AnOE, tr. by C. W. Kennedy Fr. Genesis.

Noah's Flood. Michael Drayton.
   "By this the sun had sucked up the vast deep." NOSC
   "Hundred years the Ark in the building was, A." ChIV-1

Noah's Flood. Unknown.
   "Noye, to me thou arte full able." InvLi

Noah's Prayer. Carmen Bernos de Gasztold. TrCP, tr. by Rumer Godden

Noah's Raven. W. S. Merwin. ChIV-1; HCAP

Noah was an Admiral. Noah. James Reeves. OTCP

Nobel prize, The. Noble Funerals Arranged. Piet Hein. WoPoe, tr. by Martin Allwood

Nobility. Oumar Ba. PBMAP

Noble ambition spans the four seas, A. T'ao Ch'ien [or T'ao Yuan-ming]. SuSP

Noble Balm, The. Ben Jonson. See Ode, An: "High-spirited friend, / I send not balms, nor corsives to your wound."

Noble Fisherman; or, Robin Hood's Preferment, The. Unknown. ESPB

Noble Funerals Arranged. Piet Hein. WoPoe, tr. by Martin Allwood

Noble gods at the board. Herman Melville. TCAPo Fr. Clarel: A Poem and Pilgrimage in the Holy Land.

Noble hart, that harbours vertuous [or virtuous] thought, The. Edmund Spenser. FHYEP; NoSic Fr. Faerie Queene, The.

Noble horse with courage in his eye, The. Aristocrats. Keith Douglas. FaBoMo; FaBoWar; NAEL-5v2; NAEL-6v2; NoAM; NoP-4; OBWP

Noble King of Brentford, The. King of Brentford's Testament, The. William Makepeace Thackeray. OBNV

Noble lady from the province: sitting together. In the Dying Afternoon. Ramón López Velarde. BLPSL, tr. by Rene de Costa, Rigas Kappatos and Eleni Paidoussi

Noble Nature, The. Ben Jonson. GTBS-P; TreFP Fr. To the Immortal[l] Memory [or Memorie] and Friendship of That Noble Pair[e], Sir Lucius Cary and Sir H. [or Henry] Morison.

Noble range it was, of many a rood, A. Leigh Hunt. OBGa Fr. Story of Rimini, The.

Noble Ritter Hugo, Der. Ballad by Hans Breitmann. Charles Godfrey Leland. APN-2; NOBL; TCAPo

Noble Scholar Playing the Lute, A. Yang Chi. CoBLCP, tr. by Jonathan Chaves

Noble sighed ceaselessly in restless slumber, The. Unknown. EroLit Fr. Sir Gawain and the Green Knight.

Noble Sisters. Christina Georgina Rossetti. VWP

Noble Six Hundred! (LL) Tennyson. BRP; CABP; ChAP; FHYEP; FaBoWar; NAEL-5v2; NAEL-6v2; NOBVV; NoP-4; OBWP; OxAEP-2; OxBEV; PeVV; TFi; UV

Nobles and heralds, by your leave. On Himself. Matthew Prior. FaBoEE

Noblest bodies are but gilded clay. Samuel Harding. NOSC

Noblest Charis, you that are. Ben Jonson. NAEL-6v1 Fr. Celebration of Charis in Ten Lyric[k] Pieces [or Peeces], A.

Noblest of men, woo't die? William Shakespeare. OxAEP-1 Fr. Antony and Cleopatra.

Nobly Born, The. Frances Ellen Watkins Harper. PWR

Nobly, nobly Cape Saint Vincent to the North-west died away. Home-Thoughts, from the Sea. Robert Browning. NAEL-5v2; NAEL-6v2; SCGP

Nobly, the great priest. Buson. SoOfWa, tr. by Sam Hamill

Nobody. Robert Graves. HarvBoo

Nobody. Shel [or Shelley] Silverstein. OTCP

Nobody. Novica Tadic. VCWP, tr. by Charles Simic

Nobody, ancient mischief, nobody. Nobody. Robert Graves. HarvBoo

Nobody asked you, sir, she said. (LL) Milk Maid, The. Mother Goose. LB; OxNR; ReMoGo

Nobody but Lester let Lester leap. Lester Leaps In. Al Young. ESEAA; SeSe

Nobody can please her except God. Mrs. Biswas Breaks Her Connection with Another Relative. Reetika Vazirani. AmPoNex

Nobody comes up from the sea as late as this. You Will Know When You Get There. Allen Curnow. EmeKit; NoP-4; PeNZ

Nobody does any waiting. Jackson Mac Low. FTOS Fr. Pronouns, The—A Collection of 40 Dances—For the Dancers.

Nobody else can have as much fun as. Twenty Grand (Saturday Night on the Block), The. Naomi Long Madgett. NBV

Nobody has ever offered. Personal Footnote, A. Gavin Ewart. FaBoWar

Nobody heard him, the dead man. Not Waving But Drowning. Stevie Smith. AmFaPo; CABP; EmeKit; FaBoWP; GTBS-P; HAP; HarvBoo; HeIP-4; MakPoe; NAEL-5v2; NAEL-6v2; NALW; NOBE; NPeEn; NoAM; NoP-4; OxAEP-2; OxBEV; OxBTC; PoE; PoPoPo; TFi; UV; WeW-3

Nobody Here But Us. Richard Garcia. OPRER; TouFir

Nobody. I, myself. Lemon and Rosemary. Veronica Forrest-Thomson. Oth

Nobody in the lane, and nothing, nothing but blackberries. Blackberrying. Sylvia Plath. HAP; HCAP; NAAL-2v2; NAAL-5; NOBA; NoAM; PoPoPo

Nobody in the widow's household. Passing Through. Stanley Kunitz. BodElec; LoL

Nobody is ever missing. (LL) John Berryman. HAP; HCAP; HarvBoo; NAAL-5; NoP-4; PoE; VCAP Fr. Dream Songs.

Nobody knew, not even you. Secret Love. Sammy Fain. ReLy

Nobody knew when it would start again. Schizophrenic. Patricia K. Page. HeIP-4

Nobody knocks at my door. Nobody comes to hit me. Invocation. Maria Elena Cruz Varela. VCWP, tr. by Mairym Cruz-Bernal

Nobody Knows de Trouble I've Seen. Unknown. AH
   (Nobody Knows de Trouble I've Had.) TCAPo
   (Nobody Knows the Trouble I've Had.) APN-2
   (Oh, Nobody knows the trouble I've seen.) SacPr

Nobody knows the other side. Jack Kerouac. NeAP; PmAP Fr. Mexico City Blues.

Nobody knows the world but me. Professor Noctutus. George Macdonald. NOBVV

Nobody knows what I feel about Freddy. Freddy. Stevie Smith. LW

Nobody knows what love is anymore. For a Masseuse and Prostitute. Kenneth Rexroth. NNaP

Nobody knows what's growing in Bridget. Bulge, The. George Johnston. MoCV

Nobody lies in this earth. Cemetery in Pernambuco. João Cabral de Melo Neto. TCLAP, tr. by Jane Cooper

Nobody loses all the time. E. E. Cummings. NAAL-2v2; NBLV; NOBA; RB; TwCP

Nobody loves me. Nobody. Shel [or Shelley] Silverstein. OTCP

Nobody Makes a Pass at Me. Harold Rome. ReLy

Nobody mentioned war. Malcolm. Lucille Clifton. NAAAL

Nobody noogers the shaff of a sloo. On a Flimmering Floom You Shall Ride. Carl Sandburg. APT-1; OBAL

Nobody, not even the rain, has such small hands. (LL) Somewhere i have never travelled, gladly beyond. E. E. Cummings. BoLoP; MoAmPo; NAAL-2v2; NAAL-5; NoP-4; TwCP; VGW

Nobody on earth has a book of matches. Race of the Kingfishers. Ray A. Young Bear. HATNAP

Nobody planted roses, he recalls. Summertime and the Living. Robert Earl Hayden. TwCP

Nobody put their hand out. All Clear. Roger Woddis. PeLV

Nobody read him, the poor sod. Not Wavell but Browning. Gavin Ewart. UV

Nobody Riding the Roads Today. June Jordan. BPo; NoAM

Nobody's Heart. Richard Rodgers. ReLy

Nobody's heart belongs to me. Nobody's Heart. Richard Rodgers. ReLy

Nobody's Hell. Douglas Goetsch. AmPoNex

Nobody's serious when they're seventeen. Romance. Arthur Rimbaud. AmFaPo, tr. by Paul Schmidt

Nobody said Apples for nearly a minute. Political Intelligence. Arthur James Marshall Smith. SPE

Nobody says: Ah, that is the place. Places. Thomas Hardy. HarvBoo

Nobody Sleeps. Stanley Plumly. BodElec

Nobody stuffs the world in at your eyes. Snow. Margaret Avison. NOBC

Nobody told the flowers to come up nobody. Ikkyu Sojun. WoPoe, *tr. by* Stephen Berg *Fr.* Four Poems.

Nobody understands so let the Rabbi. Prayer. Stephen Berg. TaR

Nobody waits at the foot of the stairs any more. Anatoly Steiger. TCRusP, *tr. by* Paul Schmidt

Nobody wants it to rain at a wedding. Vows. Shirley Kaufman. TaR

Nobody will open the door for you. Blanca Varela. BoWoP

Nocht o' Mortal Sicht. Bessie J. B. Macarthur. OxBS

Noctambule. George Johnston. MoCV

Nocturn: "Moon rows burning, The." Herman Van den Bergh. TuT

Nocturnal. Romelia Alarcón de Folgar. TANSG, *tr. by* Alison Ridley

Nocturnal. John Haines. GifTon

Nocturnal Garden. Nikolai Alekseievich Zabolotsky [*or* Zabolotskii]. TCRusP, *tr. by* Kathy Lewis and Bob Perelman

Nocturnal Heart. Anne-Marie Kegels. BoWoP

Nocturnal honey that glides down from the flanks, The. White on White. Maria Luisa Spaziani. NeIt, *tr. by* Beverly Allen

Nocturnal Landscape. Anton Schnack. PeFWW, *tr. by* Christopher Middleton

Nocturnal, my panther, has eyes that spark, The. Lullaby. Tuvia Rivner. MHP, *tr. by* Ruth Finer Mintz

Nocturnal Reverie, A. Anne Finch, Countess of Winchilsea. BWW; EBEV; ECEV; ECWP; NAEL-5v1; NAEL-6v1; NAEL-7v1; NALW; NOEC; NoP-4; OxAEP-1; OxBEV; PoE; WPE

Nocturnal Sea. Xavier Villaurrutia. CAGL, *tr. by* Fanny Arango-Ramos and William Keeth

Nocturnal Sketch, A. Thomas Hood. PeLV

Nocturnal Sounds. Kattie M. Cumbo. BlSi

Nocturnal Visits. Claribel Alegría. TANSG; VCWP, *tr. by* Darwin Flakoll

Nocturnal water, primaeval silences. Useless Day. Rosario Castellanos. WPOW, *tr. by* Maureen Ahern

Nocturnal, you sword-fight. Luis Cernuda. CAGL, *tr. by* Rick Lipinski

Nocturnal[l] upon Saint Lucy's [*or* S. Lucy's *or* S. Lucies] Day, Being the Shortest Day, A. John Donne. BASC; CABP; EBEV; ESCV; FHYEP; MeLP; NAEL-5v1; NAEL-6v1; NAEL-7v1; NOBE; NOSC; NoP-4; OxAEP-1; PoE; SCGP; TFi

(Tis the yeares midnight, and it is the dayes.) NPeEn; OxBEV; PBRV

Nocturne. Mário de Andrade. TCLAP, *tr. by* Jack E. Tomlins

Nocturne. David Barber. AmPoNex

Nocturne. "Rubén Darío." TCLAP, *tr. by* Lysander Kemp

Nocturne. "Rubén Darío." SpanPo, *tr. by* Kate Flores

Nocturne. Angie Estes. GeoHom

Nocturne. Alaide Foppa. TANSG, *tr. by* Celeste Kostopulos-Cooperman

Nocturne. James McAuley. BMAP

Nocturne. John Crowe Ransom. APT-1

Nocturne. Xavier Villaurrutia. TCLAP, *tr. by* Xavier Leroux

Nocturne. Ellen Bryant Voigt. UrbNat

Nocturne and Elegy. Emilio Ballagas. CAGL, *tr. by* Fanny Arango-Ramos and William Keeth

Nocturne at Bethesda. Arna Bontemps. ChIV-2; NAAAL

Nocturne at Danieli's, A. Sir Owen Seaman. UV

Nocturne, Aubade, and Vesper: "To call it a wet dream would be too barren." James Wright (1927–80). BodElec

Nocturne by Ben Shahn. Ronald Stuart Thomas. OxAEP-2

Nocturne (I Accompanied You). Léopold Sédar Senghor. WoPoe, *tr. by* Melvin Dixon

Nocturne in a Deserted Brickyard. Carl Sandburg. APT-1; MoAmPo

Nocturne in G Minor. Karl Gustav Vollmoeller. AWP, *tr. by* Ludwig Lewisohn

Nocturne in the Women's Prison. Maria Beneyto. WPOW, *tr. by* Catherine Rodriguez-Nieto

Nocturne: "Listening for the sound." Pinkie Gordon Lane. BlSi

Nocturne Militaire. Thomas McGrath. AF

Nocturne: "Moon has gone to her rest, The." Wilfrid Scawen Blunt. OBMV

Nocturne: "Moonlight on stubbleshining." Yvor Winters. APT-2

Nocturne: My Sister Life. Erin Belieu. NeAmPo

Nocturne of Hope. Yolanda Bedregal. TANSG, *tr. by* Carolyne Wright

Nocturne of the Self-evident Presence. Thomas MacGreevy [*or* McGreevy]. BIrV; CIP-2

Nocturne of the Statue. Xavier Villaurrutia. TCLAP, *tr. by* Dana Stangel

Nocturne of the Wharves. Arna Bontemps. BPo; ColAP; GT

Nocturne: "One night / One night full of perfumes, music of wings and murmurs." José Asunción Silva. BLPSL, *tr. by* Rene de Costa, Rigas Kappatos and Eleni Paidoussi

Nocturne (She Flies She Flies). Léopold Sédar Senghor. WoPoe, *tr. by* John Reed and Olive Wake

Nocturne: The Eternal. Xavier Villaurrutia. GifTon, *tr. by* Eliot Weinberger

Nocturne: "To the interior, limbs folded." Valerie Martínez. TouFir

Nocturne: "Topple the house down, wind." Lizette Woodworth Reese. PoBW

Nocturne: "Wildness of haggard flights." Roussan Camille. TTY, *tr. by* Seth L. Wolitz

Nocturnes: "He closed the deal on the night. A real." Dionisio D. Martinez. TouFir

Nocturno de Washington. Pablo Medina. BodElec

Nod. Christopher Davis. AmPoNex

Nod. Walter De la Mare. MoBrPo; OxBTC

Nodding, its great head rattling like a gourd. Original Sin. Robert Penn Warren. NOCV; TAP

Nodding Off. Kao Ch'i. CoBLCP, *tr. by* Jonathan Chaves

No[e] marvel [*or* mervaile] that I grieve, who like want see. (LL) Mary Sidney Wroth, Countess of Montgomery. BASC; EMWP; NOSC *Fr.* Pamphilia to Amphilanthus.

Noe more unto my thoughts appeare. Song. Sidney Godolphin. MeLP

Noël. Joseph Hilaire Pierre Belloc. UV

Noel; Christmas Eve, 1913. Robert Bridges. ChrPo; NOCV; OBCP; SacPr

Not JFK, not MLK. My Father's Heroes. Allison Joseph. NeAmPo

Noise. Ferreira Gullar. TCLAP, *tr. by* Renato Rezende

Noise began in my belly, The. For Carlos Charles Bucillio. Alice Sadongei. HATNAP

Noise dies down. I have appeared, The. Hamlet. Boris Leonidovich Pasternak. TCRP

Noise Grimaced. Larry Eigner. NeAP

Noise of hammers once I heard. Hammers, The. Ralph Hodgson. MoBrPo; NOBE; OxBTC

Noise of the Village, The. *Unknown.* OBVE, *tr. by* Frances Densmore

Noise of water teased his literal ear[s], The. Persistent Explorer. John Crowe Ransom. OxBA

Noise outside. Spring. Pinkie Gordon Lane. GT

Noise suffocates the song, The. Ultrasound. Maria Luisa Spaziani. CItWP, *tr. by* Cinzia Sartini Blum and Lara Trubowitz

Noise That Time Makes, The. Merrill Moore. MoAmPo

(Noise Time makes in passing by, The.) FuPo

Noise Will Start Tomorrow, The. Jeanne Megnen. SurWo, *tr. by* Guy Ducornet

Noiseless at first, a spray. Rainbow Over the Seine, A. Mary Jo Salter. ExTi

Noiselessly / in the blue of night this heart of mine. Beggar, The. Muhammad Al-Ghuzzi. MAP, *tr. by* John Heath-Stubbs and May Jayyusi

Noiselessly, the mountain stream. Sketch of Mount Chung, A. Wang An-shih. SuSp, *tr. by* Jan W. Walls

Noises at night never struck us at all. Reading Milosz. Lev Vladimir Loseff [*or* Losev]. TCRP, *tr. by* G. S. Smith

Noises of the harbour die, the smoke is petrified, The. Statue, The. John Fuller. NOBE

Noisy politicians confuse the world. Rhyming with a Friend. Yü Hsüan-chi. BoWoP, *tr. by* Geoffrey Waters

Noisy urchins scampered round, The. Much Distressed. *Unknown.* CBAP

Nok Lady in Terracotta. Ifi Amadiume. HAWP

Nokes went, he thought, to Styles's wife to bed. Case to the Civilians, A. *Unknown.* FaBoEE

Nokh Aushvits (After Auschwitz). Jerome Rothenberg. TaR

Noli Me Tangere. Jan Polkowski. AF, *tr. by* Michael March

Nomad, A. Jean Daive. MFP, *tr. by* Martin Sorrell

Nomad Exquisite. Wallace Stevens. APT-1; ColAP

Nomad of the Sky, The. Anna Cascella. CItWP, *tr. by* Cinzia Sartini Blum and Lara Trubowitz

Nomads, The. Laury Wells. IBA

Nomen. Naomi Long Madgett. BlSi

Nomenclature. Alan Dugan. BodElec

Nomenclaturik. Harry Hearson. OBCoV

Nominalist and Realist. Ralph Waldo Emerson. APN-1

Nomine Domini / Theotocopoulos. High Renaissance. George Starbuck. NBLV; OBAL

Non-Accidental Injury Slides. Geoffrey Holloway. NLP

Non Amo Te. Thomas [*or* "Tom"] Brown. *See* Doctor Fell

Non-Combatant, The. Sir Henry John Newbolt. FaBoWar

Non Dolet. Oliver St. John Gogarty. OBMV

Non-Emigrant, The. Lotte Kramer. Prnts

Non-native plantings stuck into lawns. Cougar. Brendan Galvin. UrbNat

Non Nobis. Henry Cust. OBEV

Non Omnis Moriar. Manuel Gutiérrez Nájera. BLPSL, *tr. by* Rene de Costa, Rigas Kappatos and Eleni Paidoussi

Non Omnis Moriar. Allen Tate. FuPo

Non Pax—Expectatio. Francis Thompson. OxBSo

Non Piangere, Liù. Peter Porter. OxBC

Non Piu Leggevano. Árpád Tóth. IQMS, *tr. by* Jess Perlman

Non Que Je Veuille Ôter la Liberté. Pernette De [*or* Du] Guillet. WPOW, *tr. by* Raymond Oliver

Non-sense. *Unknown.* NPeEn
  (Oh That My Lungs.) NOBL
Non Sequitur. Margot Schilpp. AmPoNex
Non-Stop. James Tate. BodElec
Non Sum Qualis Eram Bonae sub Regno Cynarae. Ernest Christopher Dowson. AWP; BoLoP; CABP; ClHu; EBVV; EnLoPo; GTBS-P; HAP; HeIP-4; MoBrPo; NOBE; NoP-4; OBEV; OBMV; PeVV; PoRA; TFi; UnPo
  (Cynara.) NAEL-5v2; NAEL-6v2
Non Te Rapiet Quisquam de Manua Mea. Sydney E. Jerrold. SacPr
Non Ti Fidar. Louis Zukofsky. VGW
Nondescript, The. Peter Scupham. HarvBoo
Nondescript express in from the South, A. Gare du Midi. W. H. Auden. OxBSP
None. Duo Duo (Li Shizheng). PoetW, *tr. by* Maghiel Van Crevel
None. Josephine Miles. VGW
None are like you, Shulamite. (LL) Hebrew of Your Poets, Zion, The. Charles Reznikoff. APT-2; ChIV-1; VGW
None but a Muse in love, can tell. On Fruition. Sir Charles Sedley. NOSC
None but my Lely [*or* Lilly] ever drew a mind[e]. (LL) To My Worthy Friend Mr. Peter Lely [*or* Lilly]. Richard Lovelace. BASC; CaPo; CavPo; GS; NOSC
None can experience stint. Emily Dickinson. NCAP
None could better our sex limousine. Limerick. *Unknown.* PeLi
None ever was in love with me but grief. My True Love Hath My Heart and I Have His. Mary Elizabeth Coleridge. BoLoP
None Is Happy. Hartmann von Aue. AWP, *tr. by* Jethro Bithell
None is like Jeshurun's God. Charles Wesley. NoP-4
None is, slight things do lightly please. (LL) His Grange, or Private Wealth. Robert Herrick. BASC; BeJo; CaPo; CavPo
None'll come, and then a lot'll. (LL) On Tomato Ketchup. *Unknown.* NBLV; Spl
None of it true; for Christ's sake, spill the ink. "Robin Hyde." PeNZ *Fr.* Houses, The.
None of the Other Birds. Stevie Smith. BWW
None of the songs myself and can't pronounce them, these are my greatest hits. (LL) Map Room, The. Joshua Clover. BAP-97; NeAmPo
None of them come! (LL) Dame Edith Sitwell. BoWoP; FaBoMo; FaBoWP; MoBrPo; NALW; OBCoV; OxBTC *Fr.* Façade.
None of this makes any sense. Ghost-Who-Walks, The. Colleen J. McElroy. GT
None of this world do I care for. When He Met Julia, He Greeted Her Thus. Bálint Balassi. IQMS, *tr. by* Adam Makkai
None of us are the Waltons, Ricki Lake said that. Tricks for the Barmaid. Roddy Lumsden. NeBl
None of us remembers these, the days. Summer 1983. Mary Jo Salter. RA
None of your business. (LL) Jesus Dies. Anne Sexton. PFTM-2; RACG
None shall gainsay me. I will lie on the floor. Gloriana Dying. Sylvia Townsend Warner. FaBoWP
None with swift feet. (LL) Dance Figure. Ezra Pound. HeIP-4; MoAmPo
Nonflying Weather. Robert Ivanovich Rozhdestvensky [*or* Rozhdestvenskii]. TCRP, *tr. by* Albert C. Todd
Nonpareil. Matthew Prior. EnLoPo
Nonplussed. Ken Bolton. BMAP
Nonsense. Thomas Moore. FaBoEE
Nonsense. *Unknown.* EBEV
Nonsense [*or* Nonsence]. Richard Corbet [*or* Corbett]. FaBoVe
Nonsense Rhyme, A. James Whitcomb Riley. NOxBChV
Nonsense Song, A. Stephen Vincent Benét. OBAL
  (Sad Song, A.) NOxBChV
Nonsense Verses. Charles Lamb. OBCoV
Nook. George Barlow. GT
Noon. John Clare. OxAEP-2
Noon. Thomas Hornsby Ferril. APT-2
Noon. "Michael Field." NOBVV
Noon. Issa. EH, *tr. by* Robert Hass
Noon. Robinson Jeffers. MoAmPo
Noon. Perry Oldham. CDa
Noon. A stale Saturday. The hills. What Could Happen. Dorianne Laux. BodElec; GeoHom
Noon heat in the yard, The. Hen Woman. Thomas Kinsella. CIP-2; ModIr; NPeEn; PBCIP
Noon in the intermountain plain. Headwaters. N. Scott Momaday. NoP-4
Noon is beautiful: the perfect wheel, The. Elegy. Yvor Winters. VGW
Noon is half the passion of light. Noon. Thomas Hornsby Ferril. APT-2
Noon. Lysander. Anne Batten Cristall. RWP
Noon Office. James Schuyler. BodElec
Noon Point. Clark Coolidge. PmAP
Noon's Dream-Song. Eugene Lee-Hamilton. NOBVV

Noon sun beats down the leaf; the noon. Grapes Making. Léonie Adams. APT-2; UnPo
Noon. The luminous tide. Ballydavid Pier. Thomas Kinsella. BIrV
Noon. 12:45 already. Maya Bejerano. DTA, *tr. by* Tsipi Keller *Fr.* Hymns of Job.
Noon Walk on the Asylum Lawn. Anne Sexton. OBGa
Noonday Axeman. Les A. Murray. NoP-4
Noonday in Immaturity. Jean-Baptiste Tati-Loutard. PBMAP *Fr.* Les Racines Congolaises (1968).
Noonday Rest. Mathilde Blind. ViWPN
Noonday square, The. Plane leaves, dust. Max Jacob at Saint Benoît. Rosanna Warren. OPRER
Noonday Vision, A. Frances Anne [*or* "Fanny"] Kemble. PoBW
Nooo! / me nah call him. Wasting Time. Opal Palmer. FaBoVe
Nor a thorn nor a threat stain her beauty bright. (LL) William Blake. FHYEP; NOBRP *Fr.* Songs of Experience.
Nor all earth's flowers, how fair. (LL) Slim Cunning Hands. Walter De la Mare. FaBoEE; NIL-7; NIP-4; WeW-3
Nor all that glisters, gold[!]. (LL) Ode on the Death of a Favourite [*or* Favorite] Cat, Drowned in a Tub [*or* Bowl] of Gold Fishes. Thomas Gray. ClHu; EBEV; ECEV; FHYEP; NAEL-5v1; NAEL-6v1; NAEL-7v1; NBLV; NOBE; NOBL; NOEC; OBCoV; OxBEV; PoE; TFi
Nor antlers through the thickness of his curls. (LL) Arms and the Boy. Wilfred Owen. HAP; MoBrPo; OxBEV; OxBSP; PoE; WeW-3
Nor any road is mine that leads to rest. (LL) Sonnet: In Absence from Becchina. Cecco Angiolieri, da Siena. AWP; EaItPo, *tr. by* Dante Gabriel Rossetti
Nor blame my weakness, till like me ye love! (LL) Tyranny of Love, The. Mary Robinson. CenSon; RWP
Nor, by God, shall we neglect. Diogenes Laertius. GrAn
Nor can I for my soul delight. Soame Jenyns. ECEV *Fr.* Epistle Written in the Country to the Right Honourable the Lord Lovelace, An.
Nor dare we think on what we are. (LL) Stanzas for Music. Byron. NAEL-5v2; OxBSP
Nor delayed the wingèd saint. John Milton. NOSC *Fr.* Paradise Lost.
Nor did the peach complain. (LL) Blue-Fly, The. Robert Graves. NAEL-5v2; NAEL-6v2; NoAM
Nor dread nor hope attend. Death. W. B. Yeats. OxAEP-2; OxBSP
Nor ever chast[e], except you ravish me[e]. (LL) John Donne. BASC; CABP; ClHu; EBEV; FHYEP; FSCP; GSo; HAP; HeIP-4; InPK-6; InvLi; MeLP; NAEL-5v1; NAEL-6v1; NAEL-7v1; NIL-7; NIP-4; NOBE; NOSC; NPeEn; NoP-4; OxAEP-1; OxBSo; PAI; PBRV; PeECV; PoE; PoPoPo; SacPr; SoSe-8; Son; TFi; TOF; TrCP *Fr.* Holy Sonnets.
Nor ever did a wise one. (LL) Impromptu on Charles II. John Wilmot, 2d Earl of Rochester. BASC; FaBoEE; NBLV; NOBL; OBSV; OxAEP-1; PeLV; SCGP; WoPoe
Nor exults he nor complains he; silent bears whate'er befalls him. Ever Watchful. Ta' Abbata Sharra. AWP, *tr. by* W. G. Palgrave
Nor fear the God whom priests and kings have made. (LL) To the Poor. Anna Laetitia Barbauld. ECWP; NoP-4
Nor fear thy latest day, nor wish therefore. (LL) Martial. Epigram XLVII, Book X. Ben Jonson. FaBoEE; OBVE
Nor find one jewel but the blazing log. (LL) To Mrs. Will H. Low. Robert Louis Stevenson. NOBVV; NPeEn
Nor God, nor man, the image thou dost see. Hildebert. MLL
Nor Hammond's love nor Shenstone's was sincere. Elegy. John, Lord Dreghorn Maclaurin. NOEC
Nor happiness, nor majesty, nor fame. Sonnet: Political Greatness. Shelley. CenSon
Nor has my father nor his father / nor any grandmothers. I Have Not Signed a Treaty with the United States Government. Chrystos. UnSA
Nor heed my craft or art. (LL) In My Craft or Sullen Art. Dylan Thomas. AmFaPo; BoLoP; GTBS-P; HAP; HeIP-4; NIL-7; NIP-4; NoAM; NoP-4; OPOU; PAI; PoE; PoPoPo; RaBo; TCAWP; WeW-3; WoPoe
Nor home, but Thee. (LL) Christina Georgina Rossetti. InvLi; SacPr
Nor human. (LL) My Imperialism. Tamura Ryuichi. AF; PFTM-2; VCWP, *tr. by* Christopher Drake
Nor knows he makes the shadow, he pursues! (LL) Constancy to an Ideal Object. Samuel Taylor Coleridge. NAEL-5v2; NAEL-6v2; NOBRP
Nor let his eye see sin[ne], but through my tears. (LL) Hymn: "Drop, drop, slow tears, and bathe those beauteous feet." Phineas Fletcher. OxBSP; SacPr
Nor lingered Paris in the lofty house. Homer. OBVE *Fr.* Iliad, The.
Nor long the Trench or lofty Walls oppose. Homer. OBVE, *tr. by* Alexander Pope *Fr.* Iliad, The.
Nor look'd I back, till to a far off wood. Philip Freneau. TCAPo *Fr.* House of Night, The.
Nor moon. Fragment. Adelaide Crapsey. APT-1
Nor Pirate, though a Prince he be. (LL) Upon Kind[e] and True Love. Aurelian Townshend [*or* Townsend]. MeLP; NOSC

Nor poverty the mind appall. (LL) William Blake. FHYEP; NAEL-5v2; NAEL-6v2; NOBRP; NOEC; NoP-4 *Fr.* Songs of Experience.

Nor practising virtue nor committing crime. Epitaph. Geoffrey Taylor. FaBoEE

Nor riches to the virtues of my love. George Chapman. OxBSo *Fr.* Coronet for His Mistress Philosophy, A.

Nor seek[e] him so[e] given [*or* giv'n] to flying. (LL) Mary Sidney Wroth, Countess of Montgomery. BASC; LW; NAEL-6v1; NAEL-7v1; NOSC; NoP-4; OxBEV *Fr.* Pamphilia to Amphilanthus.

Nor shall you for your fields neglect your stock. Young Stock. Victoria Mary Sackville-West. OxBTC

Nor should this, perchance. William Wordsworth. OxAEP-2 *Fr.* Prelude, The; Growth of a Poet's Mind [1805 vers.].

Nor skin nor hide nor fleece. Lethe. "H. D." APT-1; FaBoWP; MoAmPo; PoRA; TCAPo; VGW

Nor strange it is, to us who walk in bonds. Frederick Goddard Tuckerman. APN-2; TCAPo *Fr.* Sonnets.

Nor success make proud. (LL) Rock and Hawk. Robinson Jeffers. APT-1; ColAP; NOBA; NoAM; OxBA

Nor taste that bliss, which Phaon did not share. (LL) Foresees her Death. Mary Robinson. CenSon; RWP

Nor the full moon more quick to chill. (LL) Voices from the Other World. James Merrill. TwCP; VCAP

Nor the lion's growl. (LL) William Blake. FHYEP; NOBRP *Fr.* Songs of Experience.

Nor the songs. (LL) Euripides. AWP; OBVE *Fr.* Iphigenia [*or* Iphigeneia] in Aulis.

Nor thirteen pence a day. (LL) Grenadier. A. E. Housman. OBMV; OBWP

Nor truth nor good did they know. Gloss. Padraic Fiacc. CIP-2; PNI

Nor used this complaint, nor have thought the day to be so long. (LL) Constant Penelope Sends to Thee. *Unknown.* EnLoPo; NAEL-5v1; NPeEn; NoSic, *tr. by* Ovid

Nor vaunt the balm, to heal a lover's wound. (LL) Contemns Philosophy. Mary Robinson. CenSon; RWP

Nor what God blessed once, prove accurst [*or* accursed]. (LL) Apparent Failure. Robert Browning. NAEL-5v2; NAEL-6v2; NOBE

Nor what he is, nor whither he's to go. (LL) Seneca. BASC; OBVE, *tr. by* Abraham Cowley *Fr.* Thyestes.

Nor will the search be hard or long. Epistle to the President of the Scottish Society of Antiquaries: On Being Chosen a Correspondent Member. Alexander Geddes. OxBS

Nor with the muse's laurel unbestowed. (LL) Sonnet: To the River Lodon. Thomas Warton, the Younger. CenSon; NOEC; OxBSo

Nor would I indulge my passion. (LL) To a Lady in a Garden. Edmund Waller. BeJo; NPeEn

Nor yet do I, your knowing lover. Portrait. John Lyle Donaghy. BIrV

Norbert Dentressangle Van, The. Sophie Hannah. HarvBoo

Norfolk sprang [*or* sprung] thee, Lambeth holds thee dead. Epitaph for [*or* on] Thomas Clere. Henry Howard, Earl of Surrey. NoSic; OxBSo

Norma. Sonia Sanchez. UnSA

Normal Behavior of the Famas. Julio Cortázar. TCLAP, *tr. by* Paul Blackburn

Normal Madness. George Santayana.
  "When I discover that the substance of the beautiful is a certain rhythm." TCAPo

North. Lance Henson. HATNAP

North. Roger Mitchell. PoCoUp

North. Tony Towle. PmAP

North, The. Barry McKinnon. NOBC

North, The. Stephen Spender. *See* Polar Exploration

North American Death Song. Anne Hunter. ECWP

North American Sequence. Theodore Roethke.
  Far Field, The. ColAP; NAAL-2v2; NoAM
  Journey to the Interior. DiPo
  Meditation at Oyster River. MoAmPo
  Rose, The. NOBA; TRP

North American Time. Adrienne Rich.
  "Suppose you want to write." LoL

North and South. Linda France. NeBl

North and south of my cottage, spring waters everywhere. Guest Arrives, A. Tu Fu. ColAnChi, *tr. by* Victor H. Mair

North-born horses do not think of Yueh in the south. Ku Feng (After the Style of Ancient Poems). Li Po. ChinPo, *tr. by* Yip Wai-lim

North Corridor. Michael Collier. GM

North Country. Kenneth Slessor. CBAP

North-country maid up to London had stray'd, A. Oak and the Ash, The. *Unknown.* FaBoCh

North Country Village, A. Susanna Blamire. RWP

North Dakota, North Light. N. Scott Momaday. HATNAP

North-East. *Unknown.* WoPoe, *tr. by* Seamus Heaney

North-east wind did briskly blow, The. James Grainger. ECEV; VerBaPo *Fr.* Bryan and Pereene.

North Express. Joyce Mansour. WPOW, *tr. by* the author

North Haven. Elizabeth Bishop. HCAP; PAI

North Labrador. Hart Crane. FaBoMo

North of my grandfathers house. North. Lance Henson. HATNAP

North of my lodge, south of my lodge, spring rivers all. Guest Arrives, A. Tu Fu. CoBCP, *tr. by* Burton Watson

North of our science, east of the hashish dream. Inglorious Milton, The. Francis Letters. NOBAu

North of Santa Monica. Carter Revard. VoR

North Philadelphia, Trenton, and New York. Richmond Lattimore. APT-2

North Sea. Jeffery Day. PoWW

North Sea. Duo Duo (Li Shizheng). PFTM-2, *tr. by* Tony Barnstone and Newton Liu

North Sea, The. Heinrich Heine.
  Epilog: "Like the ears of wheat in a wheat-field growing." AWP, *tr. by* Louis Untermeyer
  Epilogue: "Like the stalks of wheat in the fields." TrJP
  Evening Twilight. AWP, *tr. by* John Todhunter
  Night by the Sea, A. AWP, *tr. by* Howard Mumford Jones

North-Sea, The. Albert Verwey. TuT, *tr. by* Tony Curtis

North Ship, The. Philip Larkin. RB

North Star. L. S. Asekoff. BodElec

North Star, The. John Morris-Jones. OBWVE, *tr. by* Anthony Conran

North: the watered-down sun. Ideal, The. T. R. Hummer. LTA

North to Milwaukee. Gerald Vizenor. VoR

North Wales girl was once my passion, A. Two-Faced Too. *Unknown.* OBWVE, *tr. by* Glyn Jones

North we climb the T'ai-hang Mountains. Song on Enduring the Cold. Ts'ao Ts'ao. CoBCP; ColAnChi, *tr. by* Burton Watson

North Wind, The. Frederick van Eeden. TuT, *tr. by* Michael Longley

North wind blows, cracking the earth, The. New Year's Eve. Liu E. CoBLCP, *tr. by* Jonathan Chaves

North wind doth blow, The. Mother Goose. OxNR; ReMoGo

North wind heard is heard always, A. Reverberation. Maurice Kenny. HATNAP

North Wind sighed, The. Ice. Walter De la Mare. OTCP

North wind whirls low. Song of the White Snow: Saying Farewell to Supervisor Wu Returning to the Capital. Ts'en Shen. SuSp, *tr. by* C. H. Wang

Northboun' Lucy Ariel Williams Holloway. BlSi

Northeast wind was the wind off the lake, The. Cook County. Archibald MacLeish. IllVoic

Northern breath, that freezes floods, he binds, The. Ovid. OBVE *Fr.* Metamorphoses.

Northern Cobbler, The. Tennyson. EBEV

Northern Farmer: New Style. Tennyson. NAEL-5v2; NAEL-6v2; OBCoV; OxAEP-2; PeVV

Northern har, A. *Unknown.* FaBoVe

Northern Ireland: Two Comments. Seamus Deane. CIP-2

Northern landscape. (LL) Last Journey. John Montague. CIP-2; ModIr; PBCIP; PNI

Northern landscape, / Thousand miles around covered by ice. Tune: "Spring in Ch'in's Garden." Mao Tse-tung [*or* Mao Zedong]. SuSp, *tr. by* Eugene Eoyang

Northern pair, we waive the name, A. Power of Innocence, The. "C. G. H." NOEC

Northern Pike. James Wright (1927–80). NAAL-2v2

Northern snows invade the city. Facing the Snow. Tu Fu. CrYelRi, *tr. by* Sam Hamill

Northern Spring, A. Frank Ormsby.
  Apples, Normandy, 1944. PNI
  Soldier Bathing. PNI
  "Some of us stayed forever, under the lough." CIP-2

Northern Suburb, A. John Davidson. NOBVV; NPeEn; NePenScot

Northern Vigil, A. Bliss Carman. OBEV

Northern Wind / sweeping down from the Sahara. Exile in Nigeria. Ezekiel Mphahlele. PBA

Northhanger Ridge. Charles Wright. HCAP

Northland in Cold, The. Li Ho. CoBCP, *tr. by* Burton Watson

Northumberland Betray[e]d by Douglas [*or* Dowglas]. *Unknown.* ESPB; OxBB

Northward beyond the Lapps to the world's end, the frozen. Juvenal. CAGL, *tr. by* Peter Green *Fr.* Satires.

Northward bound / the ice mumbled. Drumlin Prayer. Tom MacIntyre. CIP-2

Northward I came, and knocked in the coated wall.   Rodez.   Donald Davie.   HarvBoo

Northwest the tall tower stands.   *Unknown.*   CoBCP

North. . . Wind. . . eats. . . again! (LL)   Moon's the North Wind's Cooky, The.   Nicholas Vachel Lindsay.   OBCA; OxIBACP

Nosce Teipsum.   Sir John Davies.   NoSic
   Affliction.   NOBE; WoPoe
   Man.
      "I know my soul hath power to know all things."   OBEV
   Reasons drawn from Divinity.   SacPr
   (Soul and the Body, The.)   CTC; NOBE

Nose.   Ambrose Bierce.   APN-2; OBAL   *Fr.* Devil's Dictionary, The.

Nose, The.   Iain Crichton Smith.   OBSP; RB

Nose, The.   Ruth Stone.   InvLad

Nose, nose, jolly red nose.   Francis Beaumont.   FaBoCh; OxNR   *Fr.* Knight of the Burning Pestle, The.

Nose of the pick-up lifted, The.   Scattering Ashes.   David Scott.   NLP

Nose only above water.   Sandra: At the Beaver Trap.   Michael S. Harper.   NoAM

Nose went away by itself, The.   Nose, The.   Iain Crichton Smith.   OBSP; RB

Nosegay.   Elizabeth Jane Coatsworth.   OBCA

Nosegay, A.   John Reynolds.   OBEV

Nostalgia.   Stephen Berg.   OPRER

Nostalgia.   Christopher Buckley.   SeSe

Nostalgia.   Darryl Holmes.   InTrad

Nostalgia.   Louis MacNeice.   OxAEP-2

Nostalgia.   Lajos Áprily.   IQMS, *tr. by* Watson Kirkconnell

Nostalgia.   Charles Rossiter.   PasH

Nostalgia.   Robert Ivanovich Rozhdestvensky [*or* Rozhdestvenskii].   TCRusP, *tr. by* Daniel Weissbort

Nostalgia.   Karl Shapiro.   CoAP; TrJP; TwCP

Nostalgia and Complaint of the Grandparents.   Donald Justice.   LCAP-2; NoAM

Nostalgic Song for My Beloved.   Adolf Wolfli.   PFTM-1

Noster was a ship of swank, The.   E. E. Cummings.   OBCoV

Nostoi.   Rodolfo Di Biasio.   NeIt, *tr. by* Stephen Sartarelli

Nostradamus Predicts the Destruction of Chicago.   Maureen Seaton.   IllVoic

Not.   Mona Lisa Tea Towel, The.   Nigel Roberts.   BMAP

Not a breath of air.   Marjory Bates Pratt.   HA

Not a Cage.   Joan Retallack.   FTOS

Not a Care in the World.   Vernon Duke.   ReLy

Not a day goes by without someone borrowing books from me.   Li K'ai-hsien.   CoBLCP   *Fr.* Early Summer: At the Riverside, Seeing Off Li Chiu-ho as He Returns to Yeh with the Books I Lent Him.

Not a drum was heard, not a funeral note.   Burial of Sir John Moore [*after* [*or* at] Corunna], The.   Charles Wolfe.   FaBoWar; GTBS-P; NOBE; NOBRP; OBEV; OBWP; OxAEP-2; OxBEV; PWR; PoRA; TFi; TreFP; UV

Not a head stands out.   Post.   Pierre Reverdy.   CuPo

Not a Herod's oath that cannot change. (LL)   Mind Is an Enchanting Thing, The.   Marianne Craig Moore.   APT-1; HeIP-4; InPK-6; MoAmPo; NAAL-2v1; NAAL-5; NoP-4; OxBA; PoE; WPOW

Not a leaf stirring.   Buson.   EH, *tr. by* Robert Hass

Not a line of her writing have I.   Thoughts of Phena.   Thomas Hardy.   EBVV; HarvBoo; NOBVV; NPeEn; NoP-4; OxBTC

Not a mote in the light above.   Tsugen Jakurei.   ZenPo, *tr. by* Takashi Ikemoto and Lucien Stryk

Not a one out of place. (LL)   Naola Beauty Academy, New Orleans, Louisiana, 1943.   Natasha Trethewey.   NeAmPo; SpirFl

Not a poem on your absence.   Speaking Your Name.   Alejandra Piznarnick.   TANSG, *tr. by* Susan Bassnett

Not a pretty tree.   Shagbark.   Faye George.   PoCoUp

Not a prophet, he says of himself.   Witness, The.   Rose Drachler.   TaR

Not a shank of the long lane upwards.   Brechfa Chapel.   Roland Mathias.   AngWePo

Not a *sous* had he got,—not a guinea or note.   Not a Sous Had He Got.   "Thomas Ingoldsby."   UV

Not a thing could I see.   Frustrated.   May Probyn.   VWP

Not a tree but the tree.   There Is Only One of Everything.   Margaret Atwood.   NOBC

Not a Very Cheerful Song, I'm Afraid.   Adrian Mitchell.   OTCP

Not a word, not a word, not a word. (LL)   Crucifixion.   *Unknown.*   BPo; TAP

Not a word, or to the knowing.   Ecstatic Longing.   Goethe.   STV, *tr. by* John Frederick Nims

Not About Death.   Bulat Shalvovich Okudzhava.   RusPo, *tr. by* Robert Arthur Douglas Ford

Not Adlestrop.   Dannie Abse.   AngWePo; NoAM

Not all of them were human.   Village Tudda, The.   Kenneth Patchen.   VGW

Not All, Only a Few, Return As the Rose or the Tulip.   Mirza Asadullah Khan Ghalib.   WoPoe, *tr. by* Adrienne Rich

Not all pale Hecate's direful charms.   Lines Occasioned by the Burning of Some Letters.   Sarah Dixon.   ECWP; NOEC

Not all that tempts one's wand'ring eyes.   Fred.   Ian Duhig.   NeBl

Not all these legends, I suppose.   Popular Mythologies.   Vernon Scannell.   OBCoV

Not all thy flushing suns are set.   Ode to Master Endymion Porter, upon His Brother's Death, An.   Robert Herrick.   CaPo

Not Alone for Mighty Empire.   William Pierson Merrill.   AH

Not alone you came, boy, no.   Heir, The.   Joseph Georg Oberkofler.   AuPH, *tr. by* Lowell A. Bangerter

Not alwayes give a melting kiss.   "Johannes Secundus."   OBVE   *Fr.* Basia.

Not always as the whirlwind's rush.   Call of the Christian, The.   John Greenleaf Whittier.   NOCV

Not always should the tear's ambrosial dew.   Samuel Taylor Coleridge.   CenSon   *Fr.* Effusions.

Not an editorial-writer, bereaved with bartlett.   Portrait of the Poet as Landscape.   Abraham Moses Klein.   NOBC; NoAM

Not an epilogue, but everything coming to an end.   Anatoly Steiger.   TCRusP, *tr. by* Paul Schmidt

Not   and tries   less   once   tries   tries   AH, GOD. (LL)   Falling.   James Dickey.   LCAP-2; NoAM

Not any higher stands the Grave.   Emily Dickinson.   SAmP

Not apocalypse. (LL)   Note on the Iliad.   Raymond Garlick.   AngWePo; TCAWP

Not as a bird with twelve black wings and en eye.   Meeting the Angel.   Susan Aizenberg.   ExTi

Not, as it used to be, round.   Poison, The.   Hans Magnus Enzensberger.   VCWP, *tr. by* Hans Magnus Enzensberger and Michael Hamburger

Not as she is, but as she fills his dream. (LL)   In An Artist's Studio.   Christina Georgina Rossetti.   NAEL-5v2; NAEL-6v2; NALW; PAI; ViWPN

Not as the thirsty soyle desires soft showres.   Francis Quarles.   ESCV   *Fr.* Emblems.

Not as we are but as we must appear.   Geoffrey Hill.   NoAM   *Fr.* Funeral Music.

Not as Wont.   Joseph Skipsey.   NOBVV

Not at Home.   Robert Graves.   CABP

Not at Home to Callers.   Tree in Winter.   Emily Dickinson.   NOxBChV

Not at [the] first sight, nor with a dribbed shot.   Sir Philip Sidney.   NAEL-5v1; NAEL-6v1; NAEL-7v1   *Fr.* Astrophil and Stella.

Not because of his eyes.   Turtle, The.   William Carlos Williams.   EmeKit; RaBo; SAmP

Not because of victories.   Te Deum.   Charles Reznikoff.   ChIV-1; TrJP

Not because of you, not because of me, just that.   Natalya [*or* Natal'ia] Gorbanevskaya [*or* Gorbanyevskaya *or* Gorbanevskaia].   BoWoP

Not because you suck / off a sugar-cane.   Distaste.   Ammianus.   GrAn, *tr. by* Peter Jay

Not Being Oedipus.   John Heath-Stubbs.   EmeKit; OxBC

Not blinking or resting, as if never to alight. (LL)   From the Childhood of Jesus.   Robert Pinsky.   EmeKit; HarvBoo

Not British; certainly.   Expatriates.   Ronald Stuart Thomas.   AngWePo

Not / But near another you have a timid.   Anacreon.   SaLy, *tr. by* Diane Rayor

Not but they die, the teasers and the dreams.   Teasers, The.   William Empson.   HarvBoo; OxBTC

Not by lost killers stranded.   Biggest Killing, The.   Edward Dorn.   VGW

Not by the railing tongues of angry men.   Slavery.   Jones Very.   NCAP

Not by wayout hairdos, bulbous Afro blowouts and certainly.   Only in This Way.   Margaret Goss Burroughs.   BlSi

Not Caesar's deeds, nor all his honours won.   To Clement Edmonds, on His *Caesar's Commentaries* Observed, and Translated.   Ben Jonson.   NOSC

Not caring to observe the Wind.   Of Loving at First Sight.   Edmund Waller.   NOSC

Not, Celia, that I juster am.   Song to Celia.   Sir Charles Sedley.   GTBS-P; OxBEV

Not cherry blossoms.   Buson.   SoOfWa, *tr. by* Sam Hamill

Not comin' back tonight, matey.   Matey.   Patrick MacGill.   PoWW

Not Dead, but Sleeping.   Clara Ann Thompson.   CBWP-2

Not Dead Yet.   Allen Ginsberg.   BodElec

Not die of famine, amid dreams of gold. (LL)   Theocritus.   AWP; OBVE, *tr. by* Charles Stuart Calverley   *Fr.* Idylls.

Not direction—"every step and arrival." (LL)   Overland to the Islands.   Denise Levertov.   PmAP; UnPo

Not easy to state the change you made.   Love Letter.   Sylvia Plath.   LW; NOBA

Not enough.   Field Trip.   Kevin Young.   GT

Not even.   Albert Speer.   W. D. Snodgrass.   NoAM

Not even a shadow in a mirror. (LL)   Sorrow.   Mei Yao Ch'en.   OHPC; WoPoe, *tr. by* Kenneth Rexroth

Not even an hour. (LL)   Sent from the Capital to Her Elder Daughter.   Lady Otomo no Sakanoé.   BoWoP; WPOW, *tr. by* Geoffrey Bownas

Not even death could make these men alike.   Cemetery in Punta Arenas.   Enrique Lihn.   TCLAP; VCWP, *tr. by* David Unger

Not even for a moment.   Seiju.   JDP, *tr. by* Yoel Hoffmann

Not even Hercules saw in the yard of the Hesperides' land.   About a Transdanurban Almond Tree.   Janus Pannonius.   IQMS, *tr. by* Adam Makkai

Not even I—would undo me so! (LL)   Going, The.   Thomas Hardy.   EBEV; HarvBoo; NOBE; OxAEP-2; PAI; SCGP; UnPo

Not even in death can I.   Archias of Byzantium.   GrAn

Not even in dreams / Can I meet him anymore.   Lady Ise.   WPOW, *tr. by* Donald Keene

Not Even Mythology.   Yannis Ritsos.   AF, *tr. by* Edmund Keeley

Not even the cops who can do anything could do this.   Laundry.   Bruce Smith.   Son

Not even the lame grass can answer this *what is this.*   Meanwhile the Turtle.   Ann Lauterbach.   ExTi

Not ever to sit down, a part of one another.   Van Gogh's The Potato Eaters.   Peter Cooley.   SpudSo

Not Every Day Fit for Verse.   Robert Herrick.   BeJo; PoRA

Not every man has gentians in his house.   Bavarian Gentians.   D. H. Lawrence.   CABP; FaBoCh; FaBoMo; GTBS-P; HAP; HarvBoo; InPK-6; NAEL-5v2; NAEL-6v2; NOBE; NPeEn; NoAM; NoP-4; OxBEV; PAI; PoE; PoPoPo; TFi; TTTS

Not every man knows what he shall sing at the end.   End, The.   Mark Strand.   TRP

Not everyone is so skilled.   Anorexia.   Alice Jones.   BloBone

Not excluding mr u. (LL)   E. E. Cummings.   FaBoEE; OBCoV; VGW

Not Falling.   Lynne McMahon.   ExTi

Not falling, not ignoring.   Nan-o-myo.   ZenPo, *tr. by* Takashi Ikemoto and Lucien Stryk

Not Flesh of Brass.   Bible, *O.T.*   TrJP   *Fr.* Job.

Not for a long time now has anyone waited for me.   Leah Goldberg.   FIT, *tr. by* Robert Friend

Not for a moment shall I allow.   Cyclus.   Toeti Herarty.   WoPoe, *tr. by* Harry Aveling

Not for all of beauty.   Commentary Applied to Spiritual Things.   Saint John of the Cross.   TOF, *tr. by* K. Kavanaugh and O. Rodrigues

Not for me! (LL)   Bat.   D. H. Lawrence.   GTBS-P; HAP

Not for me the general renowned nor the well-groomed lady.   Ideal General, The.   Archilochus.   FaBoWar, *tr. by* A. Watson Bain

Not for nothing did we read the theologians.   Mikhail Alekseievich Kuzmin.   CAGL, *tr. by* Michael Green

Not for That City.   Charlotte Mew.   ChIV-2; HarvBoo; MoBrPo; VWP

Not for the Imperial City am I bound.   Tune: "Partridge Sky" At Po-shan Monastery.   Hsin Ch'i-chi.   ColAnChi, *tr. by* Jiaosheng Wang

Not for the promise of the laboured field.   Ode to the Poppy.   Henrietta O'Neill.   ECWP; WPE

Not for these lovely blooms that prank your chambers did I come.   Indeed. Rendezvous.   Edna St. Vincent Millay.   APT-1; NALW

Not for thy gothic trumpet's martial rage.   To Boccaccio.   Thomas Russell.   OxBSo

Not for us alone did the god, Nicias.   Theocritus.   HePo, *tr. by* Barbara Hughes Fowler   *Fr.* Idylls.

Not for you would the winds.   Kerensky.   Lola Ridge.   APT-1

Not forgetting Ko-jen, that.   More Foreign Cities.   Charles Tomlinson.   HarvBoo

Not Fortune's worshipper, nor Fashion's fool.   Pope.   NOBE   *Fr.* Epistle to Dr. Arbuthnot.

Not-France.   Carla Harryman.   PFTM-2

Not free from faults, nor yet too vain to mend. (LL)   Pope.   NAEL-5v1; NAEL-6v1; NAEL-7v1; TFi

Not from cupped hands. It isn't the same at all. (LL)   Aubade: "It's all the same to morning what it dawns on."   Nuala Ni Dhomhnaill.   BiHa; PBCIP, *tr. by* Michael Longley

Not from old age our death will come.   Semyon [*or* Semion] Petrovich Gudzenko.   TCRP

Not from our dreams, not from our daft cadres.   Robert Johnstone.   PNI   *Fr.* New Incidents in the Life of Shelley.

Not from successful love alone.   Halcyon Days.   Walt Whitman.   OxBA

Not from that / could you get it.   City, The.   Robert Creeley.   LCAP-2

Not from the stars do I my judgement pluck.   William Shakespeare.   Son   *Fr.* Sonnets.

Not from Titania's Court do I.   Hob Gobbling's Song.   James Russell Lowell.   OBCA

Not furred nor wet, the pointing words yet make.   Beaver Pond.   Anne Marriott.   NOBC

Not great truths do I ask you.   Words to My Mother.   Alfonsina Storni.   TANSG, *tr. by* Mark McCaffrey

Not having grasped the phrase: darkmotherscream. (LL)   Darkmotherscream. Andrey [*or* Andrei] Andreievich Voznesensky [*or* Voznesenskii].   RaBo; TCRP, *tr. by* Robert Bly and Vera Dunham

Not heart, not soul, and not their joined intent.   Communiqués from Yalta, The.   R. P. Blackmur.   APT-2

Not Heat Flames Up and Consumes.   Walt Whitman.   APN-1

Not Heaving from My Ribb'd Breast Only.   Walt Whitman.   APN-1; CAGL

Not hell but a street, not.   209 Canal.   Richard Howard.   TAP

Not *Here Orinda lies, but Here she lives.* (LL)   Wiston Vault.   Katherine Philips.   BASC; NOSC

Not Hers who brings it nightly to my Ear. (LL)   John Milton.   OxBEV; TOF   *Fr.* Paradise Lost.

Not honey, / not the plunder of the bee.   Fragment 113.   "H. D."   APT-1; NAAL-2v2

Not hurled precipitous from steep to steep.   William Wordsworth.   CenSon   *Fr.* River Duddon [A Series of Sonnets], The.

Not I.   Robert Louis Stevenson.   NOBL

Not, I'll not, carrion comfort, Despair, not feast on thee.   Carrion Comfort. Gerard Manley Hopkins.   BBASP; GSo; HeIP-4; MakPoe; NAEL-5v2; NoAM; PoE; Son; TFi; TOF

Not I, not I, but the wind that blows through me!   Song of a Man Who Has Come Through.   D. H. Lawrence.   FaBoMo; GTBS-P; HarvBoo; OxBTC; PeFWW; PoE; RaBo; TRP

Not Ideas about the Thing but the Thing Itself.   Wallace Stevens.   APT-1; HAP; HCAP; LCAP-2; PFTM-2; SAmP; TAP

Not idly hast thou builded on a rock.   To Peter, Bishop of Poitiers, Who Withstood William of Aquitaine and Died in Exile.   Hildebert.   MLL, *tr. by* Helen Waddell

Not in a silver casket cool with pearls.   Edna St. Vincent Millay.   VGW

Not in envy, ire, or grief.   Farewell to the Muse, A.   Maria Jane Jewsbury.   VWP

Not in my saddle, but above it.   Indian Summer: Montana, 1956.   W. M. Ransom.   CDW

Not in our time, O Lord.   "H. D."   NOBA   *Fr.* Tribute to the Angels.

Not in rich furniture, or fine array.   H[oly] Communion, The.   George Herbert.   ChIV-1; ESCV

Not in sleep I saw it, but in daylight.   Kindly Vision.   Otto Julius Bierbaum.   AWP, *tr. by* Jethro Bithell

Not in sunk Spain's prolonged death agony.   To the Hungarian Nation.   Matthew Arnold.   OxBSo

Not in the chimney, but in the gas-pipes.   Mikhail Aizenberg.   ItGoST, *tr. by* J. Kates

Not in the city, Philoterus.   Nicaenetus.   GrAn

Not in the crises of events.   Coventry Patmore.   EBEV; OxBSP   *Fr.* Angel in the House, The.

Not in the poet is the poem or.   George Barker.   OxAEP-2; OxBSP

Not in the sky.   Lost Pleiad, The.   William Gilmore Simms.   APN-1

Not in the street and not in the square.   Sequel to "A Reminiscence," The.   Amy Levy.   VWP

Not in the world of light alone.   Oliver Wendell Holmes.   APN-1   *Fr.* Autocrat of the Breakfast Table, The.

Not in this way, I said, dragging the little pink blanket along the bottom. Sentimental Suffering of the Oyester of Smoke.   Rossana Ombres.   CItWP, *tr. by* Cinzia Sartini Blum and Lara Trubowitz

Not in thy body is thy life at all.   Dante Gabriel Rossetti.   HAP   *Fr.* House of Life, The.

Not in vain I vow to be faithful.   Mole, The.   Nathan [*or* Natan] Alterman.   FIT, *tr. by* Robert Friend

Not just folklore, or.   Fast Ball.   Jonathan Williams.   NeAP

Not just the body—be it.   Abundance.   Carl Phillips.   PuP-23

Not just the temples, lifting.   Waiting for the Fire.   Philip Appleman.   CDa

Not Just Yet.   Carter Revard.   VoR

Not knowing.   Issa.   EH, *tr. by* Robert Hass

Not Knowing.   Gary Soto.   NoP-4

Not knowing where he was or how he got there.   Bewilderment at the Entrance of the Fat Boy into Eden, A.   Daryl Hine.   NOBC

Not leaving your.   For Gen the New Head Priest of Erin-ji.   Muso Soseki.   EaWin, *tr. by* W. S. Merwin

Not less because in purple I descended.   Tea at the Palaz of Hoon.   Wallace Stevens.   APT-1; AmFaPo; FaBoMo; WoPoe

Not less nor more, but even that word alone. (LL)   Dante Gabriel Rossetti. GSo; NAEL-5v2; NAEL-6v2   *Fr.* House of Life, The.

Not less nor more than five and forty years ago.   In Heytesbury Wood.   Siegfried Sassoon.   OBGa

Not lichen, not yet here when this began.   Beggar Outside Cape Town Station, A.   Sarah Ruden.   AmPoNex

Not like a sock. The one.   Mary Maher.   NewEx

Not like flowers in the city.   Free Verse.   Charles Reznikoff.   APT-2

Not Like That.   Adrienne Rich.   EmeKit

Not like the brazen giant of Greek fame.   New Colossus, The.   Emma Lazarus.

APN-2; AiP; AmFaPo; CA; FaBoA; GS; GSo; HHAm; NIL-7; NoP-4; SWaP; Son; TCAPo; WPE

Not like the cypress. Yehuda Amichai [or Amikhai]. FIT, tr. by Robert Friend

Not like the white filmstars, all rib. Indian Movie, New Jersey. Chitra Divakaruni. NIL-7; UnSA

Not long ago, I studied medicine. What the Body Told. Rafael Campo. AmPoNex; BloBone; NeAmPo; WiU

Not loved enough, nor yet quite lost. Suniti Namjoshi. NewEx

Not-loving. Sylvia Kantaris. LW

Not magnitude, not lavishness. Greek Architecture. Herman Melville. NoP-4

Not many moonlit nights. Reading Seferis. Sam Hamill. GifTon

Not Marble nor the Gilded Monuments. Archibald MacLeish. BoLoP; PoRA; TwCP

Not Marble, Nor the Gilded Monuments. William Shakespeare. See Sonnets

Not marching [now] in the fields of T[h]rasimene. Christopher Marlowe. NAEL-5v1; NAEL-7v1

Not Martha nor Diana—only a woman. On Vermeer's "Young Woman with a Water Jug" (1658) in the Metropolitan Museum. Helen Pinkerton. FFC

Not Me. Shel [or Shelley] Silverstein. KaS; NTCP

Not met and marred with the year's whole turn of grief. James Agee. APT-2 Fr. Lyrics.

Not Mine. Julia Caroline Ripley Dorr. PWR

Not Mine. Adolph Green. ReLy

Not mine own fears nor the prophetic soul. William Shakespeare. AWP; CTC; EBEV; HAP; NAEL-5v1; NAEL-6v1; NAEL-7v1; NoSic; OxAEP-1; SCGP Fr. Sonnets.

Not Mine the Years Time Took Away. Andreas Gryphius. WoPoe, tr. by John Peck

Not more of light I ask, O God. Understanding. Unknown. PoToHe

Not much more than being. Louis Zukofsky. APT-2; PoE Fr. 29 Poems.

Not Much Singing. Charles Bukowski. BodElec

Not Much Talking. Unknown. PWR

Not My Best Side. U. A. Fanthorpe. EmeKit; FaBoWP

Not my hands but green across you now. Lady in Kicking Horse Reservoir, The. Richard Hugo. CoAP; LCAP-2; NAAL-2v2; NoAM; NoP-4; VCAP

Not no socialism/communism classical, but some power to the people jazz. Daniel Gray-Kontar. SpirFl

Not of All My Eyes See. Gerard Manley Hopkins. OxBSP

Not of father nor of mother. Song of Blodeuwedd, The. Unknown. NoP-4; WoPoe, tr. by Robert Graves

Not of Gennesareth, but Thames! (LL) Kingdom of God, The. Francis Thompson. GTBS-P; NOCV; SacPr

Not of Itself but Thee. Unknown. AWP, tr. by Richard Garnett

Not of Itself, but Thee. Unknown. GrAn, tr. by Dudley Fitts

Not of itself [or it selfe] but thee. (LL) Song: To Celia. Ben Jonson. AWP; AmFaPo; BeJo; ClHu; NAEL-5v1; NAEL-6v1; NAEL-7v1; NOSC; OxAEP-1; OxBEV; PoE; SoSe-8; UV

Not of ourselves are we free. Heritage. Mary Gilmore. CBAP

Not of the princes and prelates with periwigged charioteers. Consecration, A. John Masefield. MoBrPo

Not of the wealthy, Coral Gables class. House Sparrows. Anthony Hecht. OWoS

Not often con brio, but andante, andante. Stanley Matthews. Alan Ross. OxBTC

Not one of them has seen! (LL) Blind Men and the Elephant, The. John Godfrey Saxe. ITBLP; OBCA; OTCP; PoToHe

Not one poem about an animal, she said. Florida. Dannie Abse. OxBC

Not only her stone face, laid back staring in the ferns. Pygmalion's Image. Eiléan Ní Chuilleanáin. MakPoe

Not only how far away, but the way that you say it. Henry Reed. BoLoP; GTBS-P; NAEL-6v2; NIL-7; NIP-4; NOBE; NPeEn; NoP-4; OxBEV; PoWW Fr. Lessons of the War.

Not Only in the Six-Day War. Charles Fishman. GotH

Not only marble, but the plastic toys. Wendy Cope. NIL-7

Not only the rape. Objection Overruled. Jackie Hardy. NeBl

Not Only Where God's Free Winds Blow. Shepherd Knapp. AH

Not only with no sense of shame. Tennyson. FaBoEE

Not oriental Indus' crystal streams. Lady Cicely Wemyss. James I, King of England. NOSC

Not Palaces. Stephen Spender. FaBoMo; MoBrPo; NoAM

Not Pallas, not ev'n Spleen it self could blame. Ovid. OBVE Fr. Metamorphoses.

Not past conceiving but past care. (LL) Distant Fury of Battle, The. Geoffrey Hill. FaBoWar; NoP-4

Not probable—The barest Chance. Emily Dickinson. TCAPo

Not public like mountains' but private like companions'. (LL) On a Painting

by Patient B of the Independence State Hospital for the Insane. Donald Justice. CoAP; CoAmPo; NoAM

Not quite dark yet. Buson. EH, tr. by Robert Hass

Not quite remembering, not quite. Marina Ivanovna Tsvetayeva [or Tsvetaeva]. TCRP Fr. Poem of the End.

Not realizing. Six Feet Under. Janet Campbell Hale. VoR

Not recognize a sister? (LL) Eel, The. Eugenio Montale. STV; WeW-3

Not reigns of kings now vanished. Picture, A. Aleksandr Semionovich Kushner. TCRusP, tr. by Daniel Weissbort

Not-Returning, The. Ivor Gurney. HarvBoo

Not "Revelation" 'tis, that waits. Emily Dickinson. EnlH

Not rose of death. Rose in the Afternoon. Jenny Joseph. BrRo

Not Saying Much. Linda Gregg. AiP

Not seeing. Anita Virgil. HA

Not Seeing Is Believing. Paul Petrie. TAP

Not Sense. Gail Tremblay. WeW-3

Not serious about drugs. Angel. John Forbes. NOBAu

Not, Silence, for thine idleness I raise. To Silence. Alice Thompson Meynell. VWP

Not Singing. Kate Daniels. PBCAP

Not slowly wrought, nor treasured for their form. Snowflakes. Howard Nemerov. HCAP

Not so dear was Lyde to the Clarian poet, not so truly. Ovid. RomPo, tr. by Peter Green Fr. Tristia.

Not-so-good Earth, The. Bruce Dawe. CBAP

Not so long ago, the world was complete. Georgy [or Georgii] Vladimirovich Ivanov. TCRusP, tr. by Daniel Weissbort

Not so that Pair whose youthful spirits dance. William Wordsworth. CenSon Fr. River Duddon [A Series of Sonnets], The.

Not so with me as with the little page. Ausiàs March. STV

Not sobered up from my muddy Kao-yang drunk. Yang Shih-ch'i. CoBLCP Fr. Hsi-li Echoed My Poems, and I Respond to Him, Using the Same Rhymes—Also Sent to Tsung-lien.

Not sometimes, but to him that heeds the whole. Frederick Goddard Tuckerman. TCAPo Fr. Sonnets.

Not Somewhere Else, But Here. Adrienne Rich.
   Amends. HarvBoo
   To the Days. AmFaPo; LoL
   What Kind of Times Are These. ExTi; LoL

Not speaking. Alexis Rotella. HA

Not Spring's. Arbutus. Adelaide Crapsey. APT-1

Not starting from the top. Turvy-Topsy. Paul Groves. TCAWP

Not stitched to air or water but to both. Definition of a Waterfall. John Ormond. AngWePo

Not strangeness, but strange likeness. Obstinate. Geoffrey Hill. HAP; NoAM; WoPoe Fr. Mercian Hymns.

Not such a sad story: the woman wakes to an observation. Residue. Paula McLain. AmPoNex

Not Such Your Burden. Agathias. AWP, tr. by William M. Hardinge

Not Surfing Some Days. Rick Noguchi. AmPoNex

Not taking the scarf from her head. Death. Peter France. TCRusP, tr. by Gennady Aygi

Not that by this disdain. Repulse, The. Thomas Stanley. BeJo; MeLP

Not That Far. May Miller. BlSi

Not that he promised not to windowshop. One Man's Wife. Philip Booth. VGW

Not that her blooms are marked with beauty's hue. To Mr. Gray. Thomas Warton, the Younger. Son

Not that I cared about the other women. Colder. Erica Jong. LW

Not that I'm a Punchinello. I Hear Music. Burton Lane. ReLy

Not that I wish to take the liberty. Non Que Je Veuille Ôter la Liberté. Pernette De [or Du] Guillet. WPOW, tr. by Raymond Oliver

Not that in colour it was like thy hair. Bracelet, The. John Donne. NoSic

Not that it always transpired. Limerick. Cyril Ray. PeLi

Not that the earth is changing, O my God! On Refusal of Aid between Nations. Dante Gabriel Rossetti. EBEV; OxAEP-2; SCGP

Not that the Pines were darker there. Long Voyage, The. Malcolm Cowley. SoSe-8

Not that the tree in my garden does not bloom. Harp Song. Lu Yu. CoBCP, tr. by Burton Watson

Not that they die but that they die like sheep. (LL) Leaden-eyed, The. Nicholas Vachel Lindsay. FaBoEE; OxBSP; PoE; RB; TCAPo

Not that thy fair hand. Cloris' Charms Dissolved by Eudora. Anne Killigrew. BASC

Not that we are not all. To a Man Dying on His Feet. William Carlos Williams. APT-1

Not that we are weary. In the Trenches. Richard Aldington. PeFWW

Not the beautiful youth with features of bloom & brightness. Beauty. Walt Whitman. WeW-3

Not the dead today shall praise you, God! Of Those Who Go, Not to Return. Benyamin [or Benjamin] Galai. MHP, tr. by Ruth Finer Mintz

Not the dumb earth, wherein they set their graves. (LL) Cassandra. Louise Bogan. APT-2; HAP; MoAmPo; NALW; VGW

Not the epithet. Lovely. Erin Belieu. ExTi

Not the five feet of water to your chin. Epitaph. Charles Reznikoff. APT-2

Not the heat flames up and consumes. Live Oak, with Moss. Walt Whitman. NAAL-5

Not the numbers but the sound. Death March. Charles Fishman. CDa

Not the poor singer of an empty day. (LL) William Morris. AWP; EBVV; NAEL-5v2; NAEL-6v2 Fr. Earthly Paradise, The.

Not the profound dark. Oblique Prayer. Denise Levertov. SacPr

Not the sharp torture of the critic's pen. To an Author who Loved Truth More than Fame. Bessie Rayner Parkes. VWP

Not the shouted poetry. Monkey's Pride. John Forbes. BMAP

Not the songs that nobly tell. Stanzas on the Psalms. Thomas Warton, the Elder. ChIV-1

Not the train my grandfather escaped. Train Passage. Karen Propp. GotH

Not the wild olive, not the fatal stones. Euphorion. GrAn

Not the wooden spoon. El Zapato. Richard Garcia. TouFir

Not them, O no, but you in them I love. (LL) Sir Philip Sidney. NAEL-5v1; NAEL-6v1; NAEL-7v1; PoE Fr. Astrophil and Stella.

Not There. Tess Gallagher. NIP-4

Not these cut heads posed in a breathless room. Flower Poem. Alec Derwent Hope. BMAP

Not these tall towers of no song. Hart Crane. Paul Engle. YaYoPo

Not They Who Soar! Paul Laurence Dunbar. NAAAL

Not this human sadness. Basho. EH, tr. by Robert Hass

Not this room. Denials. Eric Gamalinda. ReBoTo

Not this. / What then? Ron Silliman. PmAP Fr. Tjanting.

Not this with Cataracts and Creeks. (LL) Waterfall [or Water-Fall], The. Henry Vaughan. AngWePo; ESCV; GeHe; MeLP; NAEL-5v1; NAEL-6v1; NAEL-7v1; NOBE; NOCV; NOSC; OBWVE; OxAEP-1; SacPr

Not thither, Caesar, yet. Katherine Philips. NOSC Fr. Corneille's Pompey.

Not those patient men who knocked and were unheeded. 1918–1941. Robert David Fitzgerald. CBAP

Not three years since—and now he asks my name! Model, The. May Probyn. VWP

Not to be believed, this blunt savage wind. Papermill. Joseph Kalar. APT-2

Not to be bound with ore-nice Pedantry. (LL) Claspe, The. Margaret Lucas Cavendish, Duchess of Newcastle. BWW; PBRV

Not to believe the phoebes wept. (LL) Need of Being Versed in Country Things, The. Robert Frost. APT-1; NOBA; NoAM; OxBA; SAmP; TCAPo; TRP; UnPo

Not to die, as in cold-hands dead. Drink and Agriculture. Dave Etter. IllVoic

Not to do but work. Sum of Life, The. Ben King. CTC

Not to Keep. Robert Frost. OxBA

Not to know vice at all, and keep[e] true state. Epode. Ben Jonson. BeJo

Not to lose the feel of the mountains. Double-headed Snake, The. John Newlove. MoCV

Not To Love. Robert Herrick. CaPo

Not to say what everyone else was saying. Different. Clere Parsons. FaBoTw

Not to sigh and to be tender. Aphra Behn. BoWoP

Not to the butcher did he pass. Old Ox, The. George Rostrevor Hamilton. FaBoEE

Not to the swift, the race. Reliance. Henry Van Dyke. ITBLP

Not to touch, she said to me, anything sticky. Nightpiece. Judith Johnson Sherwin. YaYoPo

Not to Us, Not unto Us, Lord. Unknown. AH

Not to you / Unborn generations. Sentiments for a Dedication. Archibald MacLeish. APT-1

Not too far north from where I write set dawn. Hint for the Incomplete Angler. Kendrick Smithyman. PeNZ

(Not too far past) may to their wits be brought. (LL) Michael Drayton. NOSC; NoSic; Son Fr. Idea.

Not Translation, Not Poetry. Daryl Ngee Chinn. LTA

Not twenty miles from where I work. Getting to Sleep in New Jersey. John A. Stone. BloBone

Not Ulysses, no, nor any other man. Sonnet 1. Louise Labé. BoWoP, tr. by Willis Barnstone

Not until. Paul Celan. AmFaPo, tr. by Michael Hamburger Fr. Zeitgehoft.

Not until my father had led her into the paddock. Nell. Rodney Jones. IllVoic

Not unto thee—oh! not to thee! (LL) Woman and Fame. Felicia Dorothea Hemans. VWP; ViWPN

Not unto us, O Lord. Non Nobis. Henry Cust. OBEV

Not upon earth, as you suppose. Tu Non Se' in Terra, Si Come Tu Credi. Kathleen Jessie Raine. WPE

Not utter, not. Male Nipples. Brenda Hillman. ExTi

Not very anxious. Issa. EH, tr. by Robert Hass

Not very long ago. Orange Poem, The. George MacBeth [or Macbeth]. OBCoV

Not waking, in my dreams, my dreams. Infidelity. Olga Fiodorovna Berggolts [or Bergholts]. BoWoP, tr. by Daniel Weissbort

Not Wavell but Browning. Gavin Ewart. UV

Not Waving But Drowning. Stevie Smith. AmFaPo; CABP; EmeKit; FaBoWP; GTBS-P; HAP; HarvBoo; HeIP-4; MakPoe; NAEL-5v2; NAEL-6v2; NALW; NOBE; NPeEn; NoAM; NoP-4; OxAEP-2; OxBEV; OxBTC; PoE; PoPoPo; TFi; UV; WeW-3

Not wept for and not buried in this tomb. Philip at Kynoskephalai. Alcaeus [or Alkaios]. GrAn, tr. by Alistair Elliot

Not what my hands have done. Horatius Bonar. SacPr

Not when leaves are brown and sere. When I Would Die. Josephine D. Henderson Heard. CBWP-4

NOT, where the stairway turns in the dark. Jennie McGrew. Edgar Lee Masters. RACG

Not while, but long after he had told me. Each Bird Walking. Tess Gallagher. FaBoWP

Not wide but a wing. Table, The. Ray DiPalma. FTOS

Not winds to voyagers at sea. Resurrection, The. Abraham Cowley. ChIV-2

Not with a bang but a whimper. (LL) Hollow Men, The. T. S. Eliot. APT-1; MoAmPo; NAAL-2v2; NAAL-5; OBMV

Not with more glories, in th'ethereal plain. Pope. EBEV; EBNV; ECEV; NOBE; NOEC; OxAEP-1 Fr. Rape of the Lock, The; an Heroi-Comical Poem.

Not with public words can his greatness. Elegy for Jim Larkin. Patrick Kavanagh. ModIr

Not with snow only, east of Buchenwald. (LL) Letter from Berlin, A. Jon Stallworthy. OBWP; OxBC

Not Without Hope Pulsing My Breast. Saint John of the Cross. SpanPo, tr. by James Edward Tobin

Not without hope we suffer and we mourn. (LL) Elegiac Stanzas Suggested by a Picture of Peele Castle, in a Storm, Painted by Sir George Beaumont. William Wordsworth. GTBS-P; NAEL-5v2; NAEL-6v2; NOBRP; NPeEn; PoE

Not wooing, no longer shall wooing, voice that has outgrown it, Rainer Maria Rilke. EnlH Fr. Duino Elegies.

Not Wordsworth's genius, Pestalozzi's love. Sonnet 14. Amos Bronson Alcott. APN-1

Not working, not breathing. Autumn. Bella [or Izabella] Akhatovna Akhmadulina. BoWoP, tr. by Barbara Einzig

Not Yet. William Cullen Bryant. NCAP

Not Yet. Mary Elizabeth Coleridge. PoBW

Not-Yet. Jane Hirshfield. ExTi

Not Yet. Lawrence Joseph. GraLe

Not yet become a Buddha. Issa. EH, tr. by Robert Hass

Not yet dead, not yet alone. Osip Emilevich Mandelstam [or Mandelshtam]. OBVE

Not yet does parting summer gentle the Sun's steeds. Titus Calpurnius Siculus. RomPo, tr. by Guy Lee Fr. Eclogues.

Not yet in sight. 'Twere well to step aside. At the Polo-Ground. Sir Samuel Ferguson. NOIV

Not yet, not yet. Tree, The. Joel Sloman. VGW

Not yet will those measureless fields be green again. Cenotaph, The. Charlotte Mew. OxAEP-2; WPE

Not you, lean quarterlies and swarthy periodicals. To the Film Industry in Crisis. Frank O'Hara. NOBA; OBAL

Not you, not you, not you, not you, not you, not you. (LL) To a Waterfowl. Donald Hall. BodElec; OBAL

Not young and not renewable, but man. (LL) Mirror in February. Thomas Kinsella. CIP-2; GTBS-P; MakPoe; NoAM

Not your winged lust but his must now change suit. William Empson. UV Fr. Death of the King's Canary, The.

Nota: man is the intelligence of his soil. Comedian as the Letter C, The. Wallace Stevens. OxBA; TCAPo

Notable Dinner, A. Lizelia Augusta Jenkins Moorer. CBWP-3

Notations of Ten Summer Minutes. Norman MacCaig. EmeKit; NPeEn

Note. Mary Abigail Dodge (Gail Hamilton). SWaP

Note. Dimitris Tsaloumas. BMAP

Note, The. Melvin B. Tolson. GT

Note Delivered by Female Impersonator. Heather McHugh. RACG

Note Folded Thirteen Ways. Richard Garcia. TouFir

Note is sad, yet musick for a king, The. (LL) Sion. George Herbert. ChIV-1; ESCV

Note Left in Jimmy Leonard's Shack, A. James Wright (1927–80). HCAP; NoP-4

Note of a trumpet was eating the heart of a thunderbolt, The. Sons d'un Cornet, Li. Unknown. WoPoe, tr. by Willard Trask

Note of Thanks, A. Wyatt Prunty. RA

Note old chestnut tie in foreground. Tie, The. William Heyen. GM

Note on a Shop in the Muceque. Geraldo Bessa Victor. PeSAV, tr. by Donald Burness

Note on Commercial Theatre. Langston Hughes. NAAL-5

  (Notes on the Broadway Theatre.) SSLK

  (You've done taken my blues and gone.) SSLK

Note on Local Flora. William Empson. EBEV; FaBoMo; OxAEP-2; OxBEV

Note on my Son's Face, A. Toi Derricotte. ISC

Note on Propertius I.5. Fleur Adcock. BoLoP; PeNZ

Note on the Iliad. Raymond Garlick. AngWePo; TCAWP

Note on the L and N. Richmond Lattimore. GM

Note on the Latin Gerunds, A. Richard Porson. FaBoEE

Note on Wyatt, A. Kingsley Amis. WeW-3

Note, Passed to Superman. Lucille Clifton. ReTh

Note that the fire. Fire Poem, The. Theodore Enslin. CRP

Note the stump, a peach tree. We had to cut it down. Places and Ways to Live. Richard Hugo. NIP-4

Note this survivor, bearing the mark of the violator. Swedenborg's Skull. Vernon Watkins. FaBoTw

Note to My Liberal Feminist Sister, A. Naana Banyiwa Horne. NAfrP

Note to Olga (1966), A. Denise Levertov. NALW

Note to the Ophthalmologist. Dolores Kendrick. FFC

Note to Tony Towle (After WS), A. Charles North. FTOS; PmAP

Notebook, Two. Edmond Jabès. AF, tr. by Rosmarie Waldrop

Notebook of a Return to the Native Land. Aimé Césaire.

  "Islands scars of the water." PFTM-1

Noted outside the window: a fly, the sun on his back. Cold Fly. Yang Wan-li. CoBCP, tr. by Burton Watson

Notes. Friend, A. Paul Klee. PFTM-1

Notes. Friedrich Wilhelm Nietzsche. WoPoe, tr. by Ivor Armstrong Richards Fr. Zarathustra.

Notes About My Face. Michael Burkard. BAP-01

Notes after Blacking Out. Gregory Corso. NeAP

Notes at Edge. Judith Wright.

  Brevity. HarvBoo

Notes for a Lecture. David Ignatow. NNaP

Notes for a Poem from the Middle Passage of Years. Lamont B. Steptoe. SpirFl

Notes for a Poem on Being Asian American. Dwight Okita. NIL-7; UnSA

Notes for a Revised Sonnet. "Edward Pygge." OBCoV

Notes for a Sermon on the Mount. Nin Andrews. BAP-01

Notes for a Sonnet. "Edward Pygge." OBCoV

Notes for a Southern Road Map. Phyllis McGinley. NBLV

Notes for Echo Lake 3. Michael Palmer. PmAP

Notes for My Son. Alex Comfort. MoBrPo Fr. Song of Lazarus, The.

Notes for the Legend of Salad Woman. Michael Ondaatje. NoAM

Notes for the Park Keeper. Peter Bland. OBGa

Notes From a Chinese Love Manual. Sarah Gorham.

  White Tiger Leaps, The. FFC

Notes from a Nonexistent Himalayan Expedition. Wislawa Szymborska. AmFaPo, tr. by Stanislaw Baranczak and Clare Cavanagh

Notes from a Slave Ship. Edward Field. WWork

Notes from an Analyst's Couch. Anita Endrezze. CDW

Notes from the Childhood and the Girlhood. Gwendolyn Brooks. LCAP-2

  Ballad of Late Annie, The. ColAP

  "Do Not Be Afraid of No." ColAP

  Old Relative. ColAP

  Parents: People Like Our Marriage Maxie and Andrew, The. ColAP

  "Pygmies Are Pygmies Still, Though Percht on Alps" ColAP

  Sunday Chicken. ColAP

  Throwing Out the Flowers. ColAP

Notes from the Defense of Colin Ferguson. Sekou Sundiata. ESEAA

Notes from the house of the dead. Aleksandr Soprovsky [or Soprovskii]. TCRP Fr. Two Poems.

Notes: From the Wait. Rachel Tzvia Back. DTA

Notes from Underground: W. H. Auden on the Lexington Avenue IRT. Grace Schulman. ExTi

Notes in Jerusalem. Nicholas Samaras. TWW

Notes Made in the Piazza San Marco. May Swenson. CoAP

Notes on a Moonwatcher. Kenneth Gangemi. PoCoUp

Notes on a Visit to Le Tuc d'Audoubert. Clayton Eshleman. PmAP

Notes on My Contemporaries. Michael Hartnett.

  Person as Dreamer: We Talk about the Future, The. PBCIP

Notes on the Art of Memory. Diane Di Prima. SeSe

Notes on the Book of Defeat. Nizar Qabbani.

  "If an audience could be arranged." MAP

Notes on the Broadway Theatre. Langston Hughes. See Note on Commercial Theatre

Notes on the Impossible. Leonid Lavrov.

  "Farewell, I say, farewell to the incomplete." TCRP

Notes on the Peanut. June Jordan. NoAM

Notes on the tuned frame of strings. Sub Contra. Louise Bogan. APT-2

Notes to the Reader. Robert Bringhurst. NOBC

Notes toward a Supreme Fiction. Wallace Stevens. APT-1

  It Must Be Abstract.

    "Begin, ephebe, by perceiving the idea." ColAP; NOBA

    "First idea was not our own, The. Adam." ColAP; NOBA

    "It feels good as it is without the giant." ColAP; NOBA

    "Major abstraction is the idea of man, The." NOBA

    "Soldier, there is a war between the mind." ColAP; NoAM

  To Henry Church. ColAP; NOBA

Notes towards a Poem That Can Never Be Written. Margaret Atwood. NOBC

Nothin' be as terrible. Jenny in Sleep. Dolores Kendrick. ESEAA

Nothing. Cheryl Clarke. PoBW

Nothing. Julia de Burgos. BoWoP, tr. by Aliki and Willis Barnstone

Nothing. Linda Hogan. ExTi

Nothing. Charles Simic. NNaP

Nothing. Burns Singer. OxBS

Nothing about that life. Little Dance Outside the Ruins of Unreason. Carl Phillips. NAPBL

Nothing about the first abandonment. Belongings. Catherine Davis. FFC

Nothing ades to Loves fond fire. Song. Elizabeth Wilmot, Countess of Rochester. EMWP; LW

Nothing agrees that's great or generous. (LL) Giovanni Boccaccio. AWP; EaItPo, tr. by Dante Gabriel Rossetti Fr. Sonnets.

Nothing, and is nowhere, and is endless. (LL) High Windows. Philip Larkin. FaBoMo; HarvBoo; NAEL-5v2; NAEL-6v2; NoAM; PoPoPo; PoetW

Nothing and Something. Frances Ellen Watkins Harper. PWR

Nothing at All. Ivor Armstrong Richards. CRP

Nothing behind the door, behind the curtain. To Open. Antonio Porta. PFTM-2, tr. by Paul Vangelisti

Nothing but a hovel now. Ruin, The. Dafydd [or David] ap Gwilym. OBWVE, tr. by Rolfe Humphries

Nothing but a little bit of flesh on her—. Fearless One. Genrik Veniaminovich Sapgir. TCRP, tr. by Albert C. Todd

Nothing but a man. Nadia Tuéni. BoWoP

Nothing but a plain black boy. (LL) Gwendolyn Brooks. ESEAA; NOBA; NoAM Fr. Street in Bronzeville, A.

Nothing but a resonance. Voice, The. May Muzaffar. PoArWo, tr. by Tahia Abdel Nasser

Nothing but anniversaries, anniversaries . . . . Konstantin Konstantinovich Sluchevsky [or Sluchevskii]. TCRP

Nothing but Bad News. Jennifer Richter. MoASP

Nothing but Death. Pablo Neruda. SPE, tr. by Robert Bly

  (Only Death.) PFTM-1

"Nothing but heather!"—How marvellously descriptive! And incomplete! (LL) Scotland Small? Hugh MacDiarmid. NePenScot; RB

Nothing but laughter, nothing. Glycon. PGA

Nothing can be done about the rain in your meal. Same Corpse, The. Kojo Laing. HBAPE

Nothing can console me. You may bring silk. Rita Dove. NAAAL Fr. Mother Love.

Nothing can satisfy. (LL) Hamlen Brook. Richard Wilbur. HarvBoo; VCAP; WeW-3

Nothing can soak. Ode to Brother Joe. Anthony McNeill. WaCA

Nothing comforts me, not Gloria Swanson. Ikon. Timothy Liu. ReTh

Nothing could make me sooner to confess[e]. John Donne. ESCV Fr. Of the Progres[se] of the Soule; the Second Anniversarie.

Nothing Could Take Away the Bear-King's Image. Ray A. Young Bear. HATNAP

Nothing derivative here. Litrajure of Everyday Life, The. Michael C. Blumenthal. NoAM

Nothing escapes. Turbulence and Tongue. Anthony Barnett. Oth

Nothing escapes him; he escapes us all. (LL) Grandfather. Derek Mahon. OxBC; OxBSo

Nothing Ever Changes My Love for You. Marvin Fisher. ReLy

Nothing first-hand. I'm not your Saul. No burst. Knowledge of God. John Frederick Nims. InvLi

Nothing for a dirty man. All That Is Lovely in Men. Robert Creeley. RaBo

Nothing for sale in / Stupidity Street. (LL) Stupidity Street. Ralph Hodgson. MoBrPo; OxBTC

Nothing Gold Can Stay. Robert Frost. APT-1; ColAP; MoAmPo; NAAL-2v2; NAAL-5; NOBA; PAI; SoSe-8; TAP; VGW

Nothing grows in vain. Use plants to heal. Creed of Mr. Nicholas Culpeper. Patricia Beer. OxBC

Nothing Happened. Belle Waring. PBCAP

Nothing has to be ugly. Luck of the dumb. To We Who Were Saved by the Stars. Lorna Dee Cervantes. TouFir

Nothing he had done before. Architect. Adrienne Rich. BAP-01

Nothing hurts but the foot is insistent. Democracy. Suzanne Gardinier. NeAmPo

Nothing I wouldn't do for the woman I sleep with. Nothing. Cheryl Clarke. PoBW

Nothing in Heaven Functions as It Ought. X. J. Kennedy. Son

Nothing in my body escapes me. Song of a Prisoner. Jack Spicer. APSN

Nothing in our lives to stop us. Following the Rhymes of Kao Chi-ti's Poem: "We Had Planned to Travel to Cloud Cliff But Couldn't Because of Rain." Hsü Pen. CoBLCP, tr. by Jonathan Chaves

Nothing in That Drawer. Ron Padgett. PmAP

Nothing in the air to call me here. What You Find in the Woods. James Longenbach. NAPBL

Nothing in the cry. Basho. SoOfWa, tr. by Sam Hamill

Nothing in this bright region melts or shifts. From the Highest Camp. Thom Gunn. Son; TwCP

Nothing is better, I well think. Leper, The. Algernon Charles Swinburne. NOBVV; OxBEV

Nothing is certain, only the certain spring. (LL) Laurence Binyon. GTBS-P; NOBE; NPeEn; OxBTC Fr. Burning of the Leaves, The.

Nothing is changed: against the dining-room windows. Guest, The. Anna Andreyevna Akhmatova. ErotSp, tr. by Max Hayward and Stanley Kunitz

Nothing is deeper. Short Song. T. Carmi. WoPoe, tr. by Grace Schulman

Nothing Is Enough. Laurence Binyon. MoBrPo

Nothing Is Lost. Anne Ridler. WPE

Nothing is more cruel than to see. Poem. Salah Fa'iq. MAP, tr. by Patricia Alanah Byrne and Salma Khadra Jayyusi

Nothing is new: we walk where others went. Nothing New. Robert Herrick. CaPo

Nothing is plumb, level or square. Love Song: I and Thou. Alan Dugan. AmFaPo; InPK-6; NoAM

Nothing is sacred now but Villany. (LL) Pope. NOBE; NPeEn; OBSV Fr. Epilogue to the Satires, in Two Dialogues.

Nothing is so beautiful as Spring—. Spring. Gerard Manley Hopkins. EBVV; GSo; HAP; MoBrPo; NAEL-5v2; NAEL-6v2; NOBE; NOBVV; NoAM; OBMV; RB; TFi; TrCP

Nothing is sweeter than love. Nossis. PGA

Nothing is sweeter than love, all other blessings. Nossis. GrAn

Nothing is sweeter than love, all other riches. Nossis. SaLy, tr. by Diane Rayor

Nothing is unexpected or sworn impossible. Archilochus. SaLy, tr. by Diane Rayor

Nothing like her ever came his way before. Semi-Skilled Lover. Maureen Duffy. LW

Nothing, like something, happens anywhere. (LL) I Remember, I Remember. Philip Larkin. HarvBoo; NOBL

Nothing longed for. Yoketsu. ZenPo, tr. by Takashi Ikemoto and Lucien Stryk

Nothing more hesitant. Garden Note II, March. Janet Lewis. APT-2

Nothing move thee. Poem. Saint Theresa [or Teresa] of Avila. CRP; WoPoe, tr. by Yvor Winters

"Nothing much here!" they say. With careless glance. Auction Sale— Household Furnishings. Adele DeLeeuw. PoToHe

Nothing nastier than a white person! Great Palaces of Versailles, The. Rita Dove. ESEAA; NoAM

Nothing-Never. János Székely. IQMS, tr. by George Gömöri

Nothing New. Robert Herrick. CaPo

Nothing New. Ella Wheeler Wilcox. APN-2

Nothing New Beneath the Sun. George M. Cohan. ReLy

Nothing, nothing at all. Shell. Shinkichi Takahashi. ZenPo, tr. by Takashi Ikemoto and Lucien Stryk

Nothing now to mark the spot. Rachel Lyman Field. OBCA Fr. Circus Garland, A.

Nothing of All That. Jan G. Elburg. TuT, tr. by Pat Boran

Nothing of it? (LL) Fury of Overshoes. Anne Sexton. LCAP-2; NIP-4

Nothing [or Nothin'] very bad hapen to me lately. John Berryman. LCAP-2; NAAL-2v2; NoAM; PoE; TwCP; VCAP Fr. Dream Songs.

Nothing out of which to create a new, A. None. Josephine Miles. VGW

Nothing pleases me anymore. No Delicacies. Ingeborg Bachmann. PoSu, tr. by Mark Anderson

Nothing recognizable exists here. Farasa. Nicholas Samaras. TWW

Nothing resting in its own completeness. Incompleteness. Adelaide Anne Procter. TreFP

Nothing's sadder than my sister's grave. Mount Ararat. Louise Glück. ColAP

Nothing's so dainty sweet as lovely melancholy. (LL) John Fletcher. GTBS-P; OBEV Fr. Nice Valor, The.

Nothing Sacred. Roger Woddis. NOBL

Nothing sings in our bodies. Nothing. Linda Hogan. ExTi

Nothing So Far. Laura Riding Jackson. APT-2; ColAP

Nothing so sharply reminds a man he is mortal. Departure in the Dark. Cecil Day Lewis. TwCP

Nothing so true as what you once let fall. Epistle [II,] to a Lady[: Of the Characters of Women]. Pope. NAEL-5v1; NAEL-6v1; NAEL-7v1; NOEC

Nothing so true as what you once let fall. Pope. NAEL-5v1; NOEC

Nothing That Is, The. Ralph Angel. BodElec

Nothing that is not there and the nothing that is. (LL) Snow Man, The. Wallace Stevens. APT-1; AmFaPo; ColAP; EnlH; HAP; HCAP; HarvBoo; HeIP-4; NAAL-2v2; NoAM; NAAL-5; NoAM; NoP-4; PAI; PoE; PoPoPo; SoSe-8; TCAPo; TRP; WeW-3

Nothing that is said or done. At First. Charles Hubert Sisson. OxBC

Nothing that is shall perish utterly. Dedication. Henry Wadsworth Longfellow. TCAPo

Nothing that you say, The. (LL) Félix Lope de Vega Carpio. HAP; OxBEV; WoPoe, tr. by Geoffrey Hill Fr. Pentecost Castle, The.

Nothing: the nothing for which there's no reward. (LL) Thinking of the Lost World. Randall Jarrell. NAAL-5; NOBA; NoAM

Nothing there? nothing up the sky alive. John Berryman. BoLoP Fr. Sonnets to Chris.

Nothing, this foam, this virgin verse. Toast. Stéphane Mallarmé. SxFrPo, tr. by E. H. Blackmore and A. M. Blackmore

Nothing! thou elder brother ev'n [or even] to shade. Upon Nothing. John Wilmot, 2d Earl of Rochester. NOSC; OBSV; OxAEP-1; OxBEV

Nothing to Be Said. Philip Larkin. OxBTC

Nothing to be said about it, and everything. Dying. Robert Pinsky. HCAP; VCAP

Nothing to bury but dead. (LL) Pessimist, The. Ben King. NBLV; OBAL

Nothing to do but work. Pessimist, The. Ben King. NBLV; OBAL

Nothing to Fear. Kingsley Amis. OxBC

Nothing to Wear. William Allen Butler. OBAL

Nothing was foreseen. Prologue to a Time That Is Not Itself. Eunice Odio. TCLAP, tr. by Martha Collins

Nothing Whatsoever. Fujiwara no Yasusue. WoPoe, tr. by Donald Keene

Nothing will ease the pain to come. Annuciation, The. Elizabeth Jennings. ChrPo

Nothing will keep. Personal Letter No. 3. Sonia Sanchez. ESEAA; SSLK

Nothing would sleep in that cellar, dank as a ditch. Root Cellar. Theodore Roethke. ColAP; HarvBoo; HeIP-4; InPK-6; NoP-4; PAI; VCAP

Nothing you could know, or name, or say. Peppergrass. Stanley Plumly. LCAP-2

Nothing you tell me nothing. Gloria Gervitz. MirDau, tr. by Stephen Tapscott Fr. Yiskor.

Nothingmas Day. Adrian Mitchell. NOxBChV

Nothingness, for the, The. Paul Celan. PoSu

Notice. Steve Kowit. BLT

Notice. Robert Lowell. NoAM

Notice the convulsed orange inch of moon. E. E. Cummings. VGW

Notice What This Poem Is Not Doing. William Stafford. LCAP-2

Notice with what careful nonchalance. Portrait. Hyam Plutzik. TaR

Notice yourself ever. As in life you don't. (LL) Misremembered Lyric, A. Denise Riley. NPeEn; Oth

Noticing from what they talk about, and how they stand, or walk. Remembering Lunch. Douglas Dunn. OxBC

Notion of Grace, A. Brenda J. Moossy. PoArWo

Notre Dame. Osip Emilevich Mandelstam [or Mandelshtam]. TCRusP, tr. by John Glad

Notre Dame. Osip Emilevich Mandelstam [or Mandelshtam]. OBVE, tr. by James Greene

Notre Dame, Sainte Chapelle, Sacré Coeur by foot—. Debora Greger. NoP-4 Fr. Lives of the Saints.

Not[t] ceasing offrings to love while I Live. (LL) Mary Sidney Wroth, Countess of Montgomery. BASC; EMWP; NOSC Fr. Pamphilia to Amphilanthus.

Nottamun Town. Unknown. OxBoLi

Nought can anoy them. (LL) Bible, O.T. BASC; PBRV, tr. by Mary Sidney Herbert, Countess of Pembroke Fr. Psalms.

Nought is there under heav'ns wide hollownesse. Edmund Spenser. FHYEP Fr. Faerie Queene, The.

Nought loves another as itself. William Blake. FHYEP; PeECV Fr. Songs of Experience.

Nought may endure but Mutability. (LL) Mutability. Shelley. NAEL-5v2; NAEL-6v2

Nought to me! So I choose to say. "Michael Field." PoBW

Nought vnder heauen so strongly doth allure. Edmund Spenser. NoSic *Fr.* Faerie Queene, The.

Nouns of Assemblage. Stephen Dobyns. BodElec

Nov 22, 1988. Ishmael Reed. ESEAA

Nova. Robinson Jeffers. HAP

Novel, The. Richard Jones. GifTon

Novel of High Life, A. Thomas Haynes Bayly. OxAEP-2

Novel's end. Rod Willmot. HA

Novelettes. Louis MacNeice.
    Les Sylphides. BoLoP

Novelist, flushed with success, A. Limerick. Thomas Thorneley. PeLi

Novelist of the Absurd, A. Limerick. Ogden Nash. PeLi

Novelist Speaks, The. Ann Lauterbach. KGB

Novelle; My Grandmother Is Waiting For Me To Come Home. Gwendolyn Brooks. ESEAA *Fr.* Children Going Home.

Novelty Shop, The. Duane Niatum. CDW; ReTh

Novelty today, tomorrow a ruin from the past, buried and, A. I Speak of the City. Octavio Paz. VCWP, *tr. by* Eliot Weinberger

November. Margaret Atwood. NOBC

November. William Cullen Bryant. APN-1; GSo; Son; TreFP

November. Alice Cary. OBCA

November. Hartley Coleridge. CenSon *Fr.* Sonnets to the Seasons.

November. Frederick William Harvey. OxBTC

November. William Dean Howells. APN-2

November. Ted Hughes. GTBS-P

November. John Keble. OBEV *Fr.* Forest Leaves in Autumn.

November. Lucy Larcom.
    "This is the month sunrise skies." TCAPo

November. Henrietta Cordelia Ray. CBWP-3

November. Folgore da San Geminiano [*or* Gimignano]. EaItPo, *tr. by* Dante Gabriel Rossetti *Fr.* Sonnets of the Months.

November. Frederick Goddard Tuckerman. NOBA

November 22, 1983. Sherman Alexie. ReTh

November 1936. Paul Éluard. AF, *tr. by* Gilbert Bowen

November and Aunt Jemima. Thylias Moss. TRP

November Blue. Alice Thompson Meynell. MoBrPo

November Cotton Flower. Jean Toomer. ColAP; NoAM; UnPo

November, 1806. William Wordsworth. OBWP

November evening. Cor Van den Heuvel. HA

November evening. John Wills. HA

November Harvest. Anita Endrezze. HATNAP

November in Boston. Thomas McCarthy. BiHa

November Landscape, A. Sarah Helen Whitman. ColAP

November light drains fast; the shadowed street. Guys. Sheenagh Pugh. TCAWP

November Night. Adelaide Crapsey. APT-1; PAI; Spl; TCAPo

November rips gold foil from the oak ridges. Damon's Lament for His Clorenda, Yorkshire, 1654. Lupercio Leonardo de Argensola. WoPoe, *tr. by* Geoffrey Hill

November '63: eight months in London. Immigrant. Fleur Adcock. OPOU

November Sunday Morning. Alvin Feinman. CoAP

November Surf. Robinson Jeffers. NAAL-2v2; OxBA

November the 1st. Gold leaves. Autumn. Charles Wright. GeoHom

November through a Giant Copper Beech. Edwin Honig. NoAM

November Woods. S. J. Marks. BodElec

Novgorod: Coming of the Saints. Johannes Bobrowski. WoPoe, *tr. by* John Peck

Novice was sitting on a cornice, A. Illustration. John Ashbery. NAAL-2v2; NAAL-5

Novice when I came beneath thy gaze, A. Stanzas Concerning Love. Stefan George. AWP, *tr. by* Ludwig Lewisohn

Now. Sarah Knowles Bolton. PWR

Now. Robert Browning. OxBSo

Now. Christopher Gilbert. GT

Now. Thomas Ken. SacPr

Now. William Stafford. NNaP

Now. *Unknown.* PWR

Now after David had lived seventy years. Death of David, The. Hayyim Nahman [*or* Khayim Nakhman *or* Chaim Nachman] Bialik. TrJP, *tr. by* Herbert Danby

Now after the sabbath. Czeslaw Milosz. GI *Fr.* St. Matthew.

Now again the world is shaken. Foundation. Henry Van Dyke. SacPr

Now Ain't That Love? Carolyn M. Rodgers. BPo

Now, alas, it is too late. Samuel Hoffenstein. OBCoV *Fr.* Songs of Fairly Utter Despair.

Now all day long the man who is not dead. Mother and Son. Allen Tate. MoAmPo

Now all our hurries that hung up on hooks. War-Time. William Robert Rodgers. OxBSP

Now all that scintillation is a chore. Untrimming the Tree. John N. Morris. ChrPo

Now all that sound of laughter, sound of singing. Rosalía de Castro. BoWoP; STV

Now all the dogs with folded paws. Suburban Song. Elizabeth Riddell. CBAP; NOBAu

Now all the truth is out. To a Friend Whose Work Has Come to Nothing. W. B. Yeats. AWP; InPK-6; MoBrPo; OBMV; OxAEP-2; WoPoe

Now all the world she knew was dead. Sir John Betjeman. OxAEP-2 *Fr.* House of Rest.

Now am I haunted by that taste! that sound! (LL) George Meredith. BoLoP; NAEL-6v2; NOBVV *Fr.* Modern Love.

Now and Again: An Autobiography of Basket. Angie Estes. ExTi

Now and Then. Robert Peterson. GeoHom

Now and then a lost sea gull flutters into. Sea We Read About, The. Philip Levine. GeoHom

Now and then I find myself. Now and Then. Robert Peterson. GeoHom

Now and then there will arise. Song. *Unknown.* OBVE, *tr. by* Frances Densmore

Now are our prayers divided, now. At the "Ye That Do Truly." Charles Williams. NOCV

Now as a spirit. Hokusai. JDP, *tr. by* Yoel Hoffmann

Now as at all times I can see in the mind's eye. Magi, The. W. B. Yeats. ChIV-2; GI; HAP; HarvBoo; InPK-6; NPeEn; NoAM; OxAEP-2; PoE; TRP; TrCP

Now / As day breaks, light. Novgorod: Coming of the Saints. Johannes Bobrowski. WoPoe, *tr. by* John Peck

Now as I was young and easy under the apple boughs. Fern Hill. Dylan Thomas. AmFaPo; AngWePo; CABP; ChAP; ClHu; GTBS-P; HAP; HarvBoo; HeIP-4; InPK-6; MoBrPo; NAEL-5v2; NAEL-6v2; NIL-7; NIP-4; NOBE; NoAM; NoP-4; OBWVE; OxBTC; PAI; PoE; PoPoPo; PoRA; SoSe-8; TCAWP; TFi; TRP; TwCP

Now as I watch the progress of the plague. Missing, The. Thom Gunn. CAGL; NoP-4

Now as the golden. Sunday Morning in Old San Juan. Julio Marzán. PueRic

Now / As the sad rain. From the Threshold to the Sky. Muhammad Al-Maghut. MAP, *tr. by* John Heath-Stubbs and May Jayyusi

Now, as the stars unfleece themselves. Night. Maurya Simon. InvLad

Now as the train bears west. Night Journey. Theodore Roethke. AmFaPo; GM; KaS

Now as they went on their way. Anna Kamienska. GI *Fr.* St. Luke.

Now as we cross this white page together. Escape, The. William Stafford. NNaP

Now, at a particular spot on the radio dial, "—in this corner, wearing purple trunks." Reception Good. Kenneth Fearing. APT-2

Now, at last, even Nikifor's a suitor. Vladimir Uflyand [*or* Ufliand]. TCRusP, *tr. by* Daniel Weissbort

Now, / At the third hour of the twentieth century. Tattoo, The. Muhammad Al-Maghut. MAP, *tr. by* John Heath-Stubbs and May Jayyusi

Now at the turn of the year this coil of clay. Mad Potter, The. John Hollander. ColAP; VCAP

Now banished art, but yet alas how shall? (LL) Sir Philip Sidney. NAEL-5v1; NAEL-6v1; NAEL-7v1 *Fr.* Astrophil and Stella.

Now Be the Gospel Banner. Thomas Hastings. AH

Now, because of you, symmetry and asymmetry interest me *equally.* Outsider: Minnie Evans. Sandra McPherson. ExTi

Now beginneth Glutton [*or* biginneth Glotoun] for to go to shrift[e]. William Langland. PoE *Fr.* Vision of Piers Plowman, The.

Now Behold the Saviour Pleading. John Leland. AH

Now Bekotsidi, that am I. For them I make. Song of Bekotsidi, The. *Unknown.* OBVE, *tr. by* Washington Matthews

Now bernes, buirdes, bolde and blithe. *Unknown.* MiEL

Now bold Robin Hood to the north would go. Robin Hood and the Scotchman. *Unknown.* ESPB

Now, brighter than the host that all night long. Daybreak. Richard Henry Dana. APN-1

Now burst above the city's cold twilight. Six o'Clock. Trumbull Stickney. APN-2; OxBA

Now, by one year, time and our frailty have. Elegy on D. D. Sidney Godolphin. BeJo

Now calumnies arise, and black reproach. Mary Latter. ECWP *Fr.* Soliloquies on Temporal Indigence.

Now came still evening [*or* Ev'ning] on, and twilight gray [*or* grey]. John Milton. NOBE *Fr.* Paradise Lost.

Now can you see the monument? It is of wood. Monument, The. Elizabeth Bishop. HCAP; NOBA; NoAM; TRP

Now children may. John Updike. OBCA *Fr.* Child's Calendar, A.

Now close your eyes. Wedding Reception. Melinda Goodman. GLP

Now coldness comes sifting down, layer after layer. Flute Notes from a Reedy Pond. Sylvia Plath. FaBoMo

Now comes the Course-of-things, shaped like an Ox. Sidney Lanier. TCAPo *Fr.* Clover.

Now comes the evening of the mind. Evening of the Mind, The. Donald Justice. VCAP

Now comes the good rain farmers pray for(and). E. E. Cummings. NoAM

Now comes the happy morning long desired. James Hurdis. ECEV *Fr.* Village Curate, The.

Now cometh alle ye that ben ibroght. Boethius. OBMV; SacPr, *tr. by* John Walton *Fr.* Consolation of Philosophy, The ("De Consolacione Philosophie").

Now crowds on crowds around the goddess press. Pope. NAEL-6v1; NAEL-7v1 *Fr.* Dunciad, The.

Now cumis aige quhair yewth hes bene. William Dunbar. SacPr

Now Cunningham, who rhymed by fits and starts. Terse Elegy for J.V. Cunningham. X. J. Kennedy. DiPo

Now Curll his shop from rubbish drains. Jonathan Swift. PeLV *Fr.* Verses on the Death of Dr. Swift, D.S.P.D.

Now Cynthia shone serene, and ev'ry star. Daventry Wonder, The. "Agricola." NOEC

Now, damn you, you're stiff, uptight—. Private Poem. Strato [*or* Straton]. GrAn, *tr. by* Teddy Hogge

Now Daphne—daughter of the river-god. Ovid. NAWM-7v1, *tr. by* Allen Mandelbaum *Fr.* Metamorphoses.

Now day and night sit balanced. Peter Blue Cloud. ChAP *Fr.* Within the Seasons.

Now did you mark a falcon. Noble Sisters. Christina Georgina Rossetti. VWP

Now didn't Suzdal and Moscow. Holy Russia. Maksimilian Aleksandrovich Voloshin. TCRusP, *tr. by* Bob Perelman

Now do our eyes behold. Aeschylus. AWP *Fr.* Seven against Thebes, The.

Now, do you doubt that your Bird was true? (LL) Emily Dickinson. APN-2; ChIV-2; NoP-4; TCAPo

Now each creature joys the other. Ode. Samuel Daniel. NoSic

Now Endymion dedicates / his cold bed's failure to the moon. Isidorus. GrAn

Now Energy's bound to diminish. Ether Insatiable. May Kendall. CABP

Now entertain conjecture of a time. William Shakespeare. EBEV; FaBoWar; OxAEP-1; RB *Fr.* King Henry V.

Now Ev'ning fades! her pensive step retires. Night. Ann Radcliffe. NOBRP; WPE

Now Evening Puts Amen to Day. Paul Horgan. AH

Now every day the bracken browner grows. September. Mary Elizabeth Coleridge. ViWPN

Now every man at my request. *Unknown.* OBCP

Now every thing that shadowy thought. In Festubert. Edmund Charles Blunden. OBMV

Now Fade the Rose and Lily-Flower. *Unknown.* NOCV, *tr. by* Brian Stone

Now fades the last long streak of snow. Tennyson. EBVV; FHYEP; GTBS-P; NAEL-6v2; NOBE; NPeEn *Fr.* In Memoriam A. H. H.

Now faintly the falling sun. Chengtu. Tu Fu. TAL

Now, Fanny, 'tis too bad, you teazèn maïd! Bit o' Sly Coorten, A. William Barnes. PeLV

Now farewell World, in which is not my treasure. Farewell to the World, A. Michael Wigglesworth. SacPr

Now fetch me out the Turkish concubines. Christopher Marlowe. FaBoWar *Fr.* Tamburlaine the Great, Part 2.

Now, fie on foolish love! It not befits. Fie on Love. James Shirley. OxBSP

Now *Fight Cancer* is there. (LL) Sunny Prestatyn. Philip Larkin. NoAM; OBCoV

Now first, as I shut the door. New House, The. Edward Thomas. EBEV; MoBrPo; NOBE; OBEV; OBWVE

Now first of all he means the night. Song for the Middle of the Night, A. James Wright (1927–80). WeW-3

Now for I see the fields in flower. From the Provençal of William of Poitiers. William of Aquitaine. MLL, *tr. by* Helen Waddell

Now for my story. For many years. Delirium. Norman J. Loftis. SpirFl

Now for that slawnders sake. *Unknown.* PBRV *Fr.* Jack of the North.

Now for the long years when I could not love you. In Recompense. Eda Lou Walton. LW

Now for the opening of the Truth, which is our strength and stay. Some More Scruples Clear'd. Elizabeth Hincks. EMWP

Now for the people in thee left. Isabella Whitney. BWW *Fr.* Manner of Her Will and What She Left to London and to All Those in It, at Her Departing, The.

Now from each van. John Philips. NOEC *Fr.* Blenheim.

Now from Labor and from Care. Thomas Hastings. AH

Now from Leander's place she rose, and found. Christopher Marlowe. EBEV *Fr.* Hero and Leander.

Now from the marshlands under the mist-mountains. *Unknown.* OPOU, *tr. by* Gerald Benson *Fr.* Beowulf.

Now Front to Front the hostile Armies stand. Homer. OBVE, *tr. by* Alexander Pope *Fr.* Iliad, The.

Now gently winding up the fair ascent. Homer. OBVE *Fr.* Odyssey.

Now, George the third rules not alone. On the Conflagrations at Washington. Philip Freneau. APN-1

Now get thee back, retreat, depart, O Serpent. *Unknown.* AWP *Fr.* Book of the Dead.

Now gie me back my milkin' stool. Sonsy Milkmaid, The. Emily Jane Pfeiffer. ViWPN

Now Glutton begins to go to shrift. William Langland. NAEL-6v1; NAEL-7v1 *Fr.* Vision of Piers Plowman, The.

Now Go'th Sun Under Wood. *Unknown.* *See* Now Goeth [*or* goth *or* goothe] Sun [*or* Sonne *or* Sunne] under Wood

Now, God be thanked Who has matched us with His hour. Rupert Brooke. NPeEn; OBWP *Fr.* 1914.

Now God is truly naught, and if He aught may be. "Angelus Silesius." GePo, *tr. by* George C. Schoolfield *Fr.* Cherubical Wanderer, The.

Now God preserve, as you well do deserve. Masque of Christmas, The. Ben Jonson. ChrPo; OxBoLi

Now God Stand Up for Bastards. Brian [*or* Bryan] Merriman [*or* Merryman]. BIrV, *tr. by* Arland Ussher *Fr.* Midnight Court, The.

Now Goeth [*or* goth *or* goothe] Sun [*or* Sonne *or* Sunne] under Wood. *Unknown.* MiEL; NoP-4; OHMEL

(Calvary.) NAWM-7v1

(Sunset on Calvary.) NAEL-5v1; NAEL-6v1; NAEL-7v1

Now Good-night. Good Night. Eleanor Farjeon. NOxBChV; OTCP

Now gowans sprout, an' lavrocks sing. Ode to Mr. F— [*or* Mr. Forbes]. Allan Ramsay. NOEC; OBVE

Now graceful truce suspends the burning war. Joel Barlow. APN-1 *Fr.* Columbiad, The.

Now grapes are plush upon the vines. Contrary Theses (I). Wallace Stevens. OxBA; SAmP

Now Great and Awesome in My Heart. Francisco de Quevedo y Villegas. SpanPo, *tr. by* William M. Davis

Now green the larch; the hedges green. Spring Comes to the Suburbs. Phyllis McGinley. APT-2

Now grimy April comes again. For City Spring. Stephen Vincent Benét. NBLV

Now had th' Almighty Father from above. John Milton. NIL-7; NIP-4 *Fr.* Paradise Lost.

Now hand in hand, you little maidens, walk. Spring. André Spire. AWP, *tr. by* Jethro Bithell

Now hands to seedsheet, boys! Sower's Song, The. Thomas Carlyle. SCGP

Now hardly here and there a hackney-coach. Description of the Morning, A. Jonathan Swift. EBEV; ECEV; HAP; HeIP-4; NIL-7; NOBE; NOEC; NoP-4; OxAEP-1; OxBEV; PAI; PoPoPo; SoSe-8; TFi

Now has ended the battle of Saul. Saul. Nathan [*or* Natan] Alterman. TrJP, *tr. by* Dov Vardi

Now has the wind a sound. Wind. Lizette Woodworth Reese. APT-1

Now haste, my Muse, pursue thy destined way. Soame Jenyns. ECEV *Fr.* Art of Dancing, The.

Now hath my life across a stormy sea. On the Brink of Death. Michelangelo Buonarroti. AWP, *tr. by* John Addington Symonds

Now haud your tongue, baith wife and carle. Sir Walter Scott. OxBB *Fr.* Antiquary, The.

Now have I brought a woork to end which neither Joves fierce [*or* feerce] wrath. Ovid. CTC; OBVE, *tr. by* Arthur Golding *Fr.* Metamorphoses.

Now Have I Fed and Eaten Up the Rose. Gottfried Keller. WoPoe, *tr. by* James Joyce

Now he comes! will he come? alas, no, no! (LL) Seafarer, The. Henry Howard, Earl of Surrey. NPeEn; NoSic; SCGP

Now he has seen the girl Hsiang-Hsiang. Chinese Ballad. Mao Tse-tung [*or* Mao Zedong]. OxBEV, *tr. by* William Empson

Now, he recalls the lamentable wail. John Pierpont. APN-1 *Fr.* Airs of Palestine.

Now heaven be thanked. I am out of love again! Freedom. "Jan Struther." LW

Now Heaven conduct thee with a parent's love! (LL) To Mr. S. T. Coleridge. Anna Laetitia Barbauld. CABP; NOEC; NoP-4; WoRP

Now Help Us, Lord. *Unknown.* AH

Now Here of the Golden Throne, looking out from where she stood on the summit of Olympus, was quick to observe two things. Homer. EroLit, *tr. by* Emile Victor Rieu *Fr.* Iliad, The.

Now here's a story 'bout Minnie, the Moocher. Minnie, the Moocher. Cab Calloway. ReLy

Now high and low, where leaves renew. Autet e bas. Arnaut Daniel. CTC, *tr. by* Ezra Pound

Now his nose's bridge is broken, one eye.   On Hurricane Jackson.   Alan Dugan.   CoAP; PAI; TRP

Now holde [*or* hoold] your[e] pees, my tale I wol beginne [*or* biginne *or* bigynne].   (LL)   Geoffrey Chaucer.   FHYEP; NAEL-6v1; NAWM-5v1; PoE   *Fr.* Canterbury Tales, The.

Now hollow fires burn out to black.   A. E. Housman.   NOBVV

Now homing tradesmen scatter through the streets.   Place Pigalle.   Richard Wilbur.   HeIP-4

Now I am dry bones and my face a stony skull staring in yellow surprise at the / sun sun. . . .   (LL)   Between the World and Me.   Richard Wright.   ISC; PAI

Now I am glad to be one whom people ignore.   At a Reception.   Karen Gershon.   LW

Now I am like a seaweed.   Reborn.   Edison Mpina.   NAfrP

Now I am slow and placid, fond of sun.   With Child.   Genevieve Taggard.   MoAmPo

Now I believe tradition, which doth call.   Upon the Author. By a Known Friend.   Benjamin Woodbridge.   SCAP

Now I can tell you. Hearing the shrill leaves.   Thrasher in the Willow by the Lake, The.   Robert Pack.   ColAP

Now I do believe that he has died.   Now I Do Believe.   B. W. Vilakazi.   PeSAV, *tr. by* Cherie Maclean

Now I don't have to leave this place not for anybody.   Free Abandonment Blues, The.   Jean Valentine.   BodElec

Now I feel safe.   Red Bird.   Gerald Stern.   UrbNat

Now I find myself dried.   Psalm 2.   Mahmoud Darwish.   AF, *tr. by* Denys Johnson-Davies

Now, I gain the Mountain's Brow.   John Dyer.   NPeEn   *Fr.* Grongar Hill.

Now I go down here and bring up a moon.   Auctioneer.   Carl Sandburg.   NOxBChV

Now I have forgotten how to breathe and cry.   To My Daughter.   Vadim Leonidovich Andreyev [*or* Andreiev].   TCRP, *tr. by* Belinda Brindle

Now I have found thee, I will ever more.   William Alabaster.   ESCV; NoSic   *Fr.* Divine Meditations.

Now I have known, O Lord.   Al-Junaid.   TOF

Now I Have Nothing.   Stella Benson.   LW; OxBTC

Now I have Vallejo with me on the desk, his troubled words, and.   End of Communism, The.   Rodney Jones.   IllVoic

Now I invest the world.   What is Beautiful.   Jay Wright.   GT

Now I know that merchants are the happiest of men.   (LL)   Merchant's Joy, The.   Lu Yu.   CoBCP; ColAnChi, *tr. by* Burton Watson

Now I know there are bored, beautiful people everywhere.   Nine of Clubs, Cleveland, Ohio.   Dorothy Barresi.   SwNoth

Now I know they're all the same. A standing cock.   Linda France.   MFPA   *Fr.* On the Game.

Now I Lay Me Down to Take My Sleep.   *Unknown.*   OxNR

Now I'll see whether Siva.   Raghunāth Dās.   SinGod, *tr. by* Rachel Fell McDermott

Now I may wither into the truth.   (LL)   Coming of Wisdom with Time, The.   W. B. Yeats.   FaBoEE; HarvBoo; PAI; SoSe-8

Now I must betray myself.   Prothalamion.   Delmore Schwartz.   OxBA

Now I out walking.   Away!   Robert Frost.   NOBA

Now I pray the man who may love this lay.   Cynewulf.   AnOE   *Fr.* Fates of the Apostles.

Now I Prize Yellow Strawberries.   José Garcia Villa.   WoPoe

Now I realize that I love you.   Italy 1942.   Franco Fortini.   ItPo, *tr. by* Gayle Ridinger

Now I remember: in our town the druggist.   Serving with Gideon.   William Stafford.   LCAP-2

Now I say in structuring the simple slips a seems.   Essay on Concrete, An.   Douglas Messerli.   FTOS

Now I see her face.   Basho.   SoOfWa, *tr. by* Sam Hamill

Now I see its whiteness.   Dead Butterfly, The.   Denise Levertov.   NoP-4

Now I see lotus-pickers singing the lotus-pickers' song.   Kuan Yün-shih.   SuSp, *tr. by* Richard John Lynn   *Fr.* Medley of Southern and Northern Tunes—Scenic Tour of West Lake.

Now I see them sitting me before a mirror.   Sonnet.   Michael Palmer.   HarvBoo; MakPoe

Now I see you.   Grandfather.   Joseph Stroud.   GeoHom

Now I think I hear the laments.   François Villon.   NAWM-7v1, *tr. by* Galway Kinnell   *Fr.* Testament, The.

Now I understand how.   Ryuho.   JDP, *tr. by* Yoel Hoffmann

Now I Want All My Letters White Again.   Cristina Campo.   CItWP, *tr. by* Cinzia Sartini Blum and Lara Trubowitz

Now I was thinking of those bacteria.   Analogy.   János Székely.   IQMS, *tr. by* George Gömöri

Now I will ask for one true word beyond.   Grandfather and Grandmother in Love.   David Mura.   TRP

Now I will do nothing but listen.   Walt Whitman.   SAmP   *Fr.* Song of Myself.

Now I will do to you what you came here for me to do.   (LL)   Prayer to the Sockeye Salmon.   *Unknown.*   WPoS; WoPoe, *tr. by* Jane Hirshfield

Now I will fashion the tale of a fish.   *Unknown.*   AnOE   *Fr.* Physiologus.

Now I will make fat puddings.   Advent.   Anne Hartigan.   CIP-2

Now I Will Only Believe.   B. W. Vilakazi.   PeSAV

Now ice-covered.   Geraldine Clinton Little.   HA

Now ich see blostme springe.   Of Jesu Christ I Sing.   *Unknown.*   PoE

Now if ever it is time to cleanse Helicon.   Ezra Pound.   VGW   *Fr.* Homage to Sextus Propertius.

Now if'n yous go on a motor trip.   Spuds.   Brian Daldorph.   SpudSo

Now if the dull and thankless heart declare.   Malediction Upon Myself.   Elinor Wylie.   ColAP

Now in a thought, now in a shadowed word.   L'Envoi.   Edwin Arlington Robinson.   ITBLP; TrCP

Now in an hour you have me, tight, and loose me.   Fool, The.   Kenneth Mackenzie.   BMAP

Now in more subtle wreaths I will entwine.   Thomas Carew.   EroLit   *Fr.* Rapture, A.

Now in my / heart I / see clearly.   Sappho.   BoWoP, *tr. by* Willis Barnstone

Now in my middle years I glean.   Serene Words.   Gabriela Mistral.   SpanPo, *tr. by* Muriel Kittel

Now in my Samarkand of blue enamels.   Journey in the Orient.   Maria Luisa Spaziani.   BoWoP, *tr. by* Ruth Feldman

Now in the dawn before it dies, the eagle swings.   Story of a Well-made Shield, The.   N. Scott Momaday.   CDW; HATNAP

Now in the Golden Stag's mossy courtyard, where.   Death of Shakespeare, The.   Gyula Juhász.   IQMS, *tr. by* John Gordon Nichols

Now in the jasmine arbour.   Happiness.   Mihály Csokonai Vitéz.   IQMS, *tr. by* Paul Tabori

Now in the palace gardens warm with age.   Trumbull Stickney.   APN-2   *Fr.* Eride.

Now in the patron's mansion see the wight.   Richard Savage.   OBSV   *Fr.* Progress of a Divine, The.

Now in the suburbs and the falling light.   Father and Son.   Stanley Kunitz.   AF; TaR; TwCP, *tr. by* Jack Bevan

Now in this fest, this holy fest.   Nunc Puer Nobis Natus Est.   James Ryman.   SacPr

Now in this mirthfull tyme of May.   Four May Poems, II.   *Unknown.*   OxBS

Now in this while gan Daedalus a wearinesse to take.   Ovid.   CTC; OBVE, *tr. by* Arthur Golding   *Fr.* Metamorphoses.

Now in thy dazzling half-oped eye.   Mother to Her Waking Infant, A.   Joanna Baillie.   ECWP; NOEC; NoP-4; WoRP

Now incense fills the air.   After Yeats.   Allen Ginsberg.   FTOS

Now, innocent, within the deep.   M., Singing.   Louise Bogan.   ColAP; NoAM

Now is a ship / which captain am.   E. E. Cummings.   EmeKit; Spl

Now is it most like as if on ocean.   Cynewulf.   AnOE   *Fr.* Christ 2.

Now is it? You'll remember Mercury.   (LL)   First Men on Mercury, The.   Edwin Morgan.   NePenScot; PeLV

Now is Jonas the Jwe jugged to drowne.   *Unknown.*   NPeEn   *Fr.* Patience.

Now is the globe shrunk tight.   Snowdrop.   Ted Hughes.   FaBoMo; HarvBoo

Now is the hour when, swinging in the breeze.   Harmonie du Soir.   Charles Baudelaire.   AWP, *tr. by* Lord Alfred Bruce Douglas

Now Is the Month of Maying.   *Unknown.*   EBEV; NoSic

Now is the time for mirth.   To Live Merrily, and To Trust to Good Verses.   Robert Herrick.   AWP; BASC; BeJo; CaPo; CavPo; NOSC

Now is the time for the burning of the leaves.   Laurence Binyon.   GTBS-P; NOBE; NPeEn; OxBTC   *Fr.* Burning of the Leaves, The.

Now is the time of year when bees are wild.   Equinox.   Elizabeth Alexander.   ExTi

Now is the time when the great urban heart.   City Christmas.   Phyllis McGinley.   ChrPo; OBCoV

Now is the winter of our discontent.   William Shakespeare.   OxBEV; PoE   *Fr.* King Richard III.

Now is the world withdrawn all.   Carol.   Howard Nemerov.   TrCP

Now isn't it time.   Birthday Cake.   Paul Goodman.   BodElec

Now Israel May Say, and That Truly.   William Whittingham.   AH

Now it begins. The sun plunges down.   Season of Locking-In, The.   Christiane Jacox Kyle.   YaYoPo

Now it belongs not to my care.   Richard Baxter.   NOSC

Now it grows dark.   Hymn to Night.   Melville Cane.   MoAmPo

Now it is almost night, from the bronzey soft sky.   Storm in the Black Forest.   D. H. Lawrence.   FaBoVe

Now it is autumn and the falling fruit.   Ship of Death, The.   D. H. Lawrence.   FaBoTw; GTBS-P; MoBrPo; NAEL-5v2; NAEL-6v2; NoAM; NoP-4; OxAEP-2; OxBEV

Now it is fifteen years you have lain in the meadow.   Lines for an Interment.   Archibald MacLeish.   NOBA

Now it is late winter.   Two Spring Charms.   *Unknown.*   WoPoe, *tr. by* James Wright

Now it is midsummer and the long sun shines. For Hokey and Henrietta. Norman Nicholson. NoP-4

Now it is nearly time when, quivering on its stem. Harmony of Evening, The. Charles Baudelaire. SxFrPo, *tr. by* James McGowan

Now it is only hours before you wake. Letter to My Daughter at the End of Her Second Year. Donald Finkel. CoAP

Now it is over, the midnight funeral that parts. On the New Year. Christopher Okigbo. PoetW

Now it is winter and the fallen snow. Los Mineros. Edward Dorn. PoM

Now it only feels good when it bleeds. (LL) Logic in the House of Sawed-Off Telescopes. Jeffrey McDaniel. AmPoNex; NeAmPo

Now it reveals its hidden side. Ryokan. JDP, *tr. by* Yoel Hoffmann

Now it's a way of remembering, dark by dark, the rows. No Moon. Nancy Eimers. ExTi

Now it's eight o'clock. (LL) Willie Winkie. William Miller. OxBEV; ReMoGo

Now it's in all the novels, what's pornography to do? Peter Porter. OBCoV *Fr.* Sanitized Sonnets, The.

Now it's time for me to go to my society. Zuni Dancers. Eric Mottram. Oth

Now it so happened she came. That Black Girl Fulô. Jorge de Lima. TCLAP, *tr. by* Elizabeth Gordon

Now it was that the Morrigan settled in bird shape. Morrigan, The. *Unknown.* BIrV, *tr. by* Thomas Kinsella

Now Jesus had not yet come to the village. Rainer Maria Rilke. GI *Fr.* St. John.

Now Jesus stood before the governor. René Daumal. GI *Fr.* St. Matthew.

Now Johnson would go up to join the [great] simulacra of men. Robert Duncan. APSN; NNaP *Fr.* Passages.

Now, Joy is born of parents poor. Joy and Pleasure. William Henry Davies. OBMV

Now kept it flat, and raked the walks and shrubs. (LL) Frederick Goddard Tuckerman. APN-2; NoP-4; TCAPo *Fr.* Sonnets.

Now late. Scholar Recruit. Pao Chao. FaBoWar, *tr. by* Arthur Waley

Now leading to the empty room of night. (LL) House-wreckers, The. Charles Reznikoff. APT-2; KaS

Now leave the check-reins slack. To the Man after the Harrow. Patrick Kavanagh. CIP-2; GTBS-P; ModIr

Now let me come unto that stately tree. Aemilia Bassano Lanyer. MakPoe *Fr.* Description of Cooke-ham [*or* Cookham], The.

Now let my habitude be where the vine. Donald Davidson. FuPo *Fr.* Hermitage.

Now let my pen been choakt with gall. Epitaph, uppon Cassandra Mac Willms Wife to Sr Thomas Ridgway Earle of London Derry by ye Lady A. S., An. Lady Anne Harris Southwell. EMWP

Now Let Our Hearts Their Glory Wake. Elizabeth Scott. AH

Now let the cycle sweep us here and there. "H. D." APT-1; VGW *Fr.* Sigil.

Now let the legless boy show the great lady. In the Children's Hospital. Hugh MacDiarmid. NAEL-5v2; NAEL-6v2; PAI

Now let us unto some fair Medow goe. Margaret Maule, Countess of Panmure. EMWP

Now let[t] your constancy your hono[u]r prove. (LL) Mary Sidney Wroth, Countess of Montgomery. BASC; NAEL-7v1 *Fr.* Pamphilia to Amphilanthus.

Now Liddesdale [*or* Liddisdale] has ridden a raid. Jock o' the Side. *Unknown.* ESPB; IBB; OxBB

Now Liddesdale [*or* Liddisdale] has lain long [*or* layen lang] in. Dick o' the Cow. *Unknown.* ESPB; IBB; OxBB

Now life in the houses of flesh help us. Hymn for Seedtime and a Safe Harvest (Arval Hymn). *Unknown.* WoPoe, *tr. by* Janet Lembke

Now light the candles; one; two; there's a moth. Repression of War Experience. Siegfried Sassoon. AF; NoAM; PeFWW; PoE

Now lighted windows climb the dark. Manhattan Lullaby. Rachel Lyman Field. HHAm; TLR

Now like the Lady of Shalott. Before the Mirror. Elizabeth Stoddard. SWaP

Now list and lithe, you gentlemen. Northumberland Betray[e]d by Douglas [*or* Dowglas]. *Unknown.* ESPB; OxBB

Now list you, lithe you, gentlemen. Robin Hood and Queen Katherine. *Unknown.* ESPB

Now Listen! Vladimir Vladimirovich Mayakovsky [*or* Maiakovskii]. TCRP, *tr. by* Bernard Meares

Now listen, honey, 'bout a new dance craze. Walkin' the Dog. Shelton Brooks. ReLy

Now, listen. / I want you new girls, every morning. To the Virgins, to Make the Most of Time. Gavin Ewart. OBCoV

Now listen to boasting which leaves the heart dazed. Al-Samau'al ibn Adiya. TrJP *Fr.* Are We Not the People.

Now London have I (for thy sake). Isabella Whitney. BWW *Fr.* Manner of Her Will and What She Left to London and to All Those in It, at Her Departing, The.

Now look, you see, it's this way like. Road to Hogan's Gap, The. Andrew Barton Paterson. CBAP

Now Lord, or never, they'l[l] believe [*or* beleeve] on Thee. On the Miracle of Loaves. Richard Crashaw. OxBSP

Now lufferis cummis with larges lowd. Petition of the Gray Horse, Auld Dunbar, The. William Dunbar. OxBS

Now manhood and garbroyls I chaunt, and martial horror. Virgil [*or* Vergil]. BIrV; OBVE *Fr.* Aeneid [*or* Eneados, Aeneis], The.

Now may we turn aside and dry our tears. Inis Fal. Egan [*or* Aodhagán] O'Rahilly [*or* O'Reilly *or* Ó Rathaille]. BIrV; OBMV, *tr. by* James Stephens

Now Melanctha Had neither Home, nor Regular Occupation. Life Was Just Beginning for Her. Piera Oppezzo. CItWP, *tr. by* Cinzia Sartini Blum and Lara Trubowitz

Now mirk December's dowie face. Daft Days, The. Robert Fergusson. CABP; NOEC; NPeEn; OxAEP-1; OxBEV

Now Miss Sarah, if you please. I'll See You Again. Noël Coward. ReLy

Now more and more on my concern with the lifted waves of genius gaining. On the Ocean Floor. Hugh MacDiarmid. FaBoMo; HAP

Now Morn her rosie steps in th' Eastern Clime. John Milton. NAEL-5v1 *Fr.* Paradise Lost.

Now must all satisfaction. Certain Mercies. Robert Graves. GTBS-P

Now must I mend my manners. Marbod of Rennes. MLL

Now must I these three praise. Friends. W. B. Yeats. NoAM

Now my charms are all o'erthrown. William Shakespeare. CTC *Fr.* Tempest, The.

Now my fine friend, he said, you Pardoner. Geoffrey Chaucer. NAWM-7v1, *tr. by* Theodore Morrison *Fr.* Canterbury Tales, The.

Now my heart turns to and fro. Queen Hatshepsut. WPOW *Fr.* Obelisk Inscriptions.

Now My Life Has Gained Some Meaning. Walther [*or* Walter] von der Vogelweide. GePo, *tr. by* J. W. Thomas

Now my right hand. "H. D." APT-1; NAAL-5 *Fr.* Walls Do Not Fall, The.

Now, My Usefullness Over. Edwin Honig. NoAM

Now near the end of the middle stretch of road. Jersey Rain. Robert Pinsky. BAP-01

Now new old first day jump. (LL) Robert Duncan. APSN; VGW *Fr.* Passages.

Now new-vamped silks the mercer's window shows. Description of Spring in London, A. *Unknown.* NOEC

Now, now's the time so oft by Truth. Epithalamy to Sir Thomas Southwell and His Lady, An. Robert Herrick. CaPo

Now o'er the one half-world. William Shakespeare. OxAEP-1 *Fr.* Macbeth.

Now, o'er the tessellated pavement strew. Previous to her Interview with Phaon. Mary Robinson. CenSon; RWP

Now of that vision I, bereaven. Francis Thompson. MoBrPo *Fr.* Grace of the Way.

Now of the hue of ashes are the Whites. Guido Orlandi. EaItPo, *tr. by* Dante Gabriel Rossetti

Now of wemen this I say for me. In Praise of Women. William Dunbar. CABP; NoP-4

Now on the first day of Unleavened Bread the disciples came to Jesus. Rainer Maria Rilke. GI *Fr.* St. Matthew.

Now on their coasts our conquering navy rides. Dryden. OxAEP-1 *Fr.* Annus Mirabilis.

Now once more gray mottled buckeye branches. Andree Rexroth. Kenneth Rexroth. APT-2

Now only praise makes me cry. Paul Goodman. BodElec *Fr.* Sentences for Matthew Ready, Series 2.

Now or Never. "Astra." BrRo

Now or Never. Judith Moffett. Son

Now ore the sea from her old Love comes she. Christopher Marlowe. PBRV *Fr.* Ovids Elegies Book 1.

Now our boys have such toys. Toys. Gemino H. Abad. ReBoTo

Now, Parrot, my sweet bird, speak our yet once again. John Skelton. NoSic *Fr.* Speak [*or* Speke], Parrot.

Now Phillipa Is Gone. Anne Ridler. FaBoTw

Now piece by piece we slip away. Sergey [*or* Sergei] Aleksandrovich Yesenin [*or* Essenin]. TCRP

Now polish the crucible. "H. D." NALW *Fr.* Tribute to the Angels.

Now ponder well, you parents dear. Babes in the Wood, The. *Unknown.* OBNV; OxAEP-1

Now Pontius Pilate is to judge the cause. Emilia [*or* Aemelia] Lanier [*or* Lanyer]. EMWP; NAEL-6v1; NALW; NOSC *Fr.* Salve Deus Rex Judaeorum.

"Now, pray, where are you going, child?" said Meet-on-the-Road. Meet-on-the-Road. *Unknown.* TTTS

Now Precedent Songs, Farewell. Walt Whitman. NAAL-3

Now rede me, dear mither, a sonsy rede. Mer-Man, and Marstig's Daughter, The. *Unknown.* AWP, *tr. by* Robert Jamieson

Now rest for evermore, my weary heart! A Sè Stesso. Giacomo Leopardi. AWP

Now rides this renk thurgh the ryalme of Logres. *Unknown.* NPeEn *Fr.* Sir Gawain and the Green Knight.

Now Robin Hood, Will Scadlock and Little John. Robin Hood and the Prince of Aragon. *Unknown.* ESPB

Now, rocking horse! rocking horse! where shall we go? Through Nurseryland. *Unknown.* OTCP

Now Roland feels that he is at death's door. *Unknown.* FaBoWar, *tr. by* Dorothy Leigh Sayers *Fr.* Song of Roland, The.

Now, round my favored grot let roses rise. Phaon Awakes. Mary Robinson. CenSon; RWP

Now's the time for mirth and play. Christopher Smart. NOEC *Fr.* Hymns for the Amusement of Children.

Now seals the fair creation from my sight. (LL) To S. M., a Young African Painter, on Seeing His Works. Phillis Wheatley. BlSi; MakPoe; NAAL-2v1; NAAL-3; NAAL-5

Now secretness dies of the open. For the Nightly Ascent of the Hunter Orion over a Forest Clearing. James Dickey. TwCP

Now, Serena, be not coy. To His Love When He Had Obtained Her. Sir Walter Ralegh. NoSic

Now shall I walk. Best Friend, The. William Henry Davies. OBMV

Now shall the praises of the Lord be sung. First Song of Moses, The. George Wither. ChIV-1

Now she guards her chalice in a temple of fear. Ted Berrigan. BodElec

Now She Is like the White Tree-Rose. Cecil Day Lewis. FaBoTw; MoBrPo *Fr.* From Feathers to Iron.

Now She Is Unadorned. Milo De Angelis. NeIt, *tr. by* Lawrence Venuti

Now she's ninety I walk through the local park. Winter Visit, A. Dannie Abse. NoAM

Now shout into my dream. These trumpets snored. Farewell in a Dream. Stephen Spender. MoBrPo

Now show thy joy, frolic in Angels' sight. Leviathan. Jay Macpherson. MoCV

Now side by side, with like unweary'd care. Homer. OBVE, *tr. by* Alexander Pope *Fr.* Iliad, The.

Now since the members of the world we view. Lucretius. OBVE *Fr.* De Rerum Natura (On the Nature of Things).

Now Sing We, as We Were Wont. John Skelton. SCGP

Now sinks another day to rest. Bull, The. Victoria Mary Sackville-West. WPE

Now sitting, I think, 'twixt thee and me! (LL) Jock o' the Side. *Unknown.* ESPB; IBB; OxBB

Now skrinketh rose and lilie-flour. *Unknown.* MiEL

Now sleep, bind fast the flood of air. George Chapman. OxBSP *Fr.* Masque of the Middle Temple and Lincoln's Inn, The.

Now Sleep My Little Child So Dear. Casper Kriebel. AH, *tr. by* Sheema Z. Buehne

Now sleeps the crimson petal, now the white. Tennyson. BoLoP; EBEV; EBVV; FHYEP; GTBS-P; NAEL-5v2; NAEL-6v2; NIL-7; NOBE; NPeEn; NoP-4; OxAEP-2; SCGP; SCV; TFi; WoPoe *Fr.* Princess, The.

Now slowly winding from the mountain's head. John Jones. AngWePo *Fr.* Holywell.

Now Snow Descends. Jean Garrigue. WPE

Now so many people that are in this place. Thank You: A Poem in Seventeen Parts. *Unknown.* STP, *tr. by* Richard Johnny John and Jerome Rothenberg

Now, sometimes in my sorrow shut. Tennyson. CAGL; NAEL-6v2; NAWM-7v2 *Fr.* In Memoriam A. H. H.

Now spring has come. Bainen. JDP, *tr. by* Yoel Hoffmann

Now spring has come. Primavera. Antonio Machado Ruiz. WoPoe, *tr. by* Samuel Menashe

Now Spring returning beckons the little boats. Priapos of the Harbor. Antipater of Sidon. GrAn; WoPoe, *tr. by* Dudley Fitts

Now springes the spray. *Unknown.* MiEL; PoE

Now stamp the Lord's Prayer on a grain of rice. Dylan Thomas. FaBoMo *Fr.* Altarwise by Owl-Light.

Now stands our love on that still verge of day. James Agee. APT-2 *Fr.* Sonnets.

Now stir the fire, and close the shutters fast. William Cowper. ECEV *Fr.* Task, The.

Now stoops the sun, and dies day's cheerful light. Charles Montague Doughty. FaBoTw *Fr.* Dawn in Britain, The.

Now stop you noses, Readers, all and come. Dryden. AWP *Fr.* Absalom and Achitophel, Part 2.

Now sulkies come haunting softwheeled down the. Ghost at Anlaby, The. Randolph Stow. NOBAu

Now sunk the sun, now twilight sunk, and night. Rhapsody, Written at the Lakes in Westmorland, A. John Brown. NOEC

Now supposing the French or the Neopolitan soldier. Arthur Hugh Clough. PeLV *Fr.* Amours de Voyage.

Now take my word for jewel in the open light. (LL) Coal. Audre Lorde. BlSi; ESEAA; NAAL-5; NALW; NBV; NoAM; VCAP

Now take your fill of love and glee. Double Ballad of Good Counsel, A. François Villon. AWP, *tr. by* Algernon Charles Swinburne

Now tell me, my merry woodman. Estray, The. Forceythe Willson. APN-2

Now tell me where my easy rider gone. Easy Rider Blues. Blind Lemon Jefferson. GM

Now Thank We All Our God. Martin Rinckhart [*or* Rinkhart]. GePo; SacPr, *tr. by* Catherine Winkworth

Now that all your distance surrounds me. Distance. Andrea Zanzotto. VCWP, *tr. by* Ruth Feldman

Now that Fate is dead and gone. Song. Dame Edith Sitwell. MoBrPo

Now that father's leaves are falling. Acorn Speaks, The. Theo Sontrop. TuT, *tr. by* Theo Dorgan

Now that he's free, relatively, often he shuffles. Holiday, The. Hans Magnus Enzensberger. VCWP, *tr. by* Hans Magnus Enzensberger and Michael Hamburger

Now that high, oft-affronted bosom heaves. To the Lady Portrayed by Margaret Dumont. John Hollander. OBAL

Now that his name has turned to elegy. Photo of My Father in a Snowbound Train. David Wojahn. GM

Now that I am fifty-six. Rondel. Muriel Rukeyser. NoP-4

Now That I Am Forever with Child. Audre Lorde. NAAAL; NALW

Now that I am old I get up very early. Growing Old (1). Yüan Mei. WoPoe, *tr. by* Arthur Waley

Now That I Have Grown Up, Mother. Clementina Suárez. TANSG, *tr. by* Janet N. Gold

Now that I have seen Tor House. Tor House. William Everson. APT-2

Now that I have your face by heart, I look. Song for the Last Act. Louise Bogan. NoP-4; UnPo; WPE

Now that I have your hand, let me persuade you. One Last Word. John Glassco. NOBC

Now that I have your heart by heart, I see. (LL) Song for the Last Act. Louise Bogan. NoP-4; UnPo; WPE

Now that I know. Knowledge. Louise Bogan. APT-2

Now that I know so much, I know better. Lion of Judah, The. Jan Emmens. WoPoe, *tr. by* Adrienne Rich

Now that I, tying thy glass mask tightly. Laboratory, The (Ancien Régime). Robert Browning. NAEL-5v2; NAEL-6v2; OBEV

Now that I've kicked in thirty-two. For My Birthday. Attila József. IQMS, *tr. by* Adam Makkai

Now that I've nearly done my days. Things That Matter, The. Edith Nesbit. OxBTC; VWP

Now that I've wasted. My Alba. Allen Ginsberg. CLPP; NOBA

Now that my seagoing self-possession wavers. Autobiography. Charles Causley. Son

Now that my storehouse. Masahide. JDP, *tr. by* Yoel Hoffmann

Now that night is creeping. Evensong. Clive Staples Lewis. TrCP

Now that of absence the most irksome night. Sir Philip Sidney. NAEL-5v1; NAEL-6v1; NAEL-7v1 *Fr.* Astrophil and Stella.

Now that poor, wayward Jane is big with child. Repentance. Louis Untermeyer. NBLV

Now that sea's over that island. Basil Bunting. HarvBoo

Now that spring's returned, I like to get up early. Early Rising. Tu Fu. CrYelRi, *tr. by* Sam Hamill

Now that the April of your Youth. Edward Herbert, 1st Baron Herbert of Cherbury. OxAEP-1

Now that the barbarians have got as far as Picra. Translation. Roy Fuller. NOBE; OxBTC

Now that the city with its masonries. At Villequier. Victor Hugo. SxFrPo, *tr. by* E. H. Blackmore and A. M. Blackmore

Now that the day is done. Centaur Song. "H. D." VGW

Now that the fragrance. *Unknown.* ArkPo, *tr. by* Robert H. Brower and Earl Miner

Now that the hearth [*or* harth] is crowned [*or* crown'd] with smiling fire. Ode. To Sir William Sydney, on His Birthday. Ben Jonson. BeJo

Now that the men have gone off to the choleric wars. Stay Behind, The. Andrew Elliott. PNI

Now that the midd day heate doth scorch my shame. William Alabaster. ESCV *Fr.* Divine Meditations.

Now that the owl-light—in the time between. Owl. John Hollander. OWoS

Now, that the public sorrow doth subside. To the Pious Memory of C. W. Esquire. Henry Vaughan. PeECV

Now that the sunset of hope for my life. Now that the Sunset of Hope. Rosalía de Castro. SpanPo, *tr. by* Kate Flores

Now that the time has come wherein. Advice from Poor Robin's Almanack. *Unknown.* OBCP

Now that the time seems all mine. Patrizia Cavalli. NeIt; VCWP, tr. by Judith Baumel.

Now THAT the triumphant march has entered the last street. Come Thunder. Christopher Okigbo. HBAPE

Now that the war is over. Downed Black Pilot Learns How to Fly, A. Horace Coleman. CDa

Now that the Winter's gone, the earth hath lost. Spring, The. Thomas Carew. BeJo; CaPo; CavPo; NoP-4; PBRV; PoE

Now that the world is all in a maze. Unconcerned, The. Thomas Flatman. FaBoCh

Now that the young buds are tipped with a falling sun. Early Spring. Sidney Keyes. MoBrPo

Now that these wings to speed my wish ascend. Philosophic Flight, The. Giordano Bruno. AWP, tr. by John Addington Symonds

Now that war is in the air, e'en the parson in his lair. W. T. Stead. FaBoWar Fr. War against War in South Africa.

Now that we are close. From This Moment On. Cole Porter. ReLy

Now that we have had the rice and flowers. Shuffle Off to Buffalo. Harry Warren. ReLy

Now that we move and we breathe apart. You Have to Strike Back. Kate Lilley. BMAP

Now that we're almost settled in our house. In Memory of Major Robert Gregory. W. B. Yeats. EBEV; NAEL-6v2; SCGP

Now that we're alone we can talk prince man to man. Elegy of Fortinbras. Zbigniew Herbert. PoSu; VCWP; WoPoe, tr. by Czeslaw Milosz

Now that we're okay, I guess we should finish. As Always. James Harms. NAPBL

Now that we've come to the end. Avenue, The. Paul Muldoon. PBCIP

Now that we've done our best and worst, and parted. Busy Heart, The. Rupert Brooke. MoBrPo

Now that we've finally arrived here. Breaking the Rock Down. Ralph Angel. BodElec

Now that ye be assemblld heer. Lady Margaret Howard. EMWP

Now that you lie. Before Sleep. Anne Ridler. SacPr

Now That Your Eyes Are Shut. Elinor Wylie. APT-1

Now that your nebula, O noble Count, sheds. Luis de Góngora y Argote. SpanPo, tr. by Frances Fletcher Fr. Fable of Polyphemus and Galatea.

Now that your sons are dust. (LL) Father of Women, A [Ad Sororem E. B.]. Alice Thompson Meynell. BrRo; NALW; WPE

Now that your surgery's. Plunder. Debra Bruce. IllVoic

Now the air is visible again, floating. In a Motel Room at Dawn. Malena Mörling. AmPoNex

Now the archbishop comes to Lawrence. Toque de queda: Curfew in Lawrence. Martín Espada. PueRic

Now the bat circles on the breeze of eve. Sonnet. Ann Radcliffe. CenSon; WPE

Now the birds begin to crow. It is time for them to crow. Blues for the Lonely. Jeremy Robson. SeSe

Now the birth of Jesus Christ took place in this way. Philip Appleman. GI Fr. St. Matthew.

Now the bitter pangs of hope deferred. Mail Has Come, The. Mary E. Tucker. CBWP-1

Now the bright crocus flames, and now. In the Spring. Meleager. AWP, tr. by Andrew Lang

Now the children of the future tried to come to terms. Children of the Future. Jalauddin Mansur Nuriddin. SpirFl

Now the crops grow green and the fields flourish with life. Request for Meat and Drink. Sedulius Scottus. NOIV

Now the crossing, now the crossing! Aleksandr Trifonovich Tvardovsky [or Tvardovskii]. TCRP, tr. by April FitzLyon Fr. Vasily Tyorkin.

Now the day is over. Hymn. Sabine Baring-Gould. SacPr; WHSW

Now the declining sun 'gan downwards bend. Nightingale, The. William Strode. OBVE

Now the dreary winter's over. Spring Song. Nahum. TrJP, tr. by Emma Lazarus

Now the eyes of my eyes are opened. (LL) I Thank You God. E. E. Cummings. TAP; TrCP

Now the fireflies of our youth. Kenneth Rexroth. APSN Fr. Love Poems of Marichiko, The.

Now the golden looks are spent. Rounds and Garlands Done, The. Léonie Adams. APT-2

Now the green plane-tree hides the lovers, hides the lovers'/ rites. Thallus. GrAn

Now the heart sings with all its thousand voices. Gateway, The. Alec Derwent Hope. BoLoP

Now the Holy Lamp of Love. Patrick MacDonogh. BIrV

Now the Hungry Lion Roars. William Shakespeare. CTC Fr. Midsummer Night's Dream, A.

Now the ice lays its smooth claws on the sill. Scotland's Winter. Edwin Muir. NePenScot; OxBS; OxBTC

Now the late fruits are in. For a Wine Festival. Vernon Watkins. OxBTC

Now the leaves are still. O. Mabson Southard. HA

Now the light o' the west is a-turn'd to gloom. Evenen in the Village. William Barnes. EBVV

Now the lotuses in the imperial lake. Wang Ch'ing-hui. BoWoP

Now the lovely autumn morning breathes its freshness in earth's face. Run to Death. Amy Levy. ViWPN

Now the midwinter grind. Middle Age. Robert Lowell. PAI

Now the moon is rising. Song. Antonio Machado Ruiz. SpanPo, tr. by Kate Flores

Now the parade is coming! Triumphal March. "Rubén Dario." SpanPo, tr. by Charles Guenther

Now the People Have the Light. Charles G. Ballard. VoR

Now the potato plants are flowering. They've lit up their streets. Gaslight. Rolf Jacobsen. WoPoe, tr. by Roger Greenwald

Now the pumpkin is ripe. Letter to a Son, A. Charles Mungoshi. PeSAV

Now the rain is falling, freshly, in the intervals between sunlight. Spring Rain. Robert Hass. BodElec

Now! The Red Tobacco has come to strike your soul. Unknown. STP Fr. Run toward the Nightland.

Now the rich cherry, whose sleek wood. Country Summer. Léonie Adams. MoAmPo

Now the river is rich, but her voice is low. River in March, The. Ted Hughes. OxBC

Now the seasons are closing their files. Year's End. Ted Kooser. PBCAP

Now the shadows flee and vanish. Hymn. William Williams. AngWePo

Now the shiades o' the elems da stratch muore an muore. Evening, and Maidens. William Barnes. OBEV

Now the spade. Rod Willmot. HA

Now the splendor of the Patriarch's Garden. For Myo's Departure for Anzen-ji. Muso Soseki. EaWin, tr. by W. S. Merwin

Now the stars flush with joy. Song to the Mother of the World. Suzanne Ironbiter. HW

Now the summer air exerts its syrupy drag on the half-dark. Archive of Confessions, a Genealogy of Confessions, An. Joshua Clover. NeAmPo

Now the sun's gane out o' sight. Up in the Air. Allan Ramsay. NOEC; OxBEV

Now the swing is still. Nicholas Virgilio. HA; KaS

Now the table is set, a covenant to endure. Elf Shots. Peter Riley. Oth

Now the thing the Negro has GOT to do—. View from the Corner. Samuel Allen. SSLK

Now the thinkers our old ones remember. Dance of the Rain Gods. Unknown. STP, tr. by Anselm Hollo

Now the trouble with SETting down a: written calypso. Calypsomania. Anthony Brode. PeLV

Now the Two Are One. Frederick D'Aguiar. WaCA Fr. GDR.

Now the white violet blooms and narcissus that loves. Meleager. HePo Fr. Epigrams.

Now the winds are all composure. Christopher Smart. NOCV; NOEC Fr. Hymns and Spiritual Songs for the Fasts and Festivals of the Church of England.

Now the wings of our thoughts belong to one angel. Angel on the Beach, An. Hamutal Bar Yosef. DTA, tr. by Shirley Kaufman

Now Thebes stood in good estate, now Cadmus might thou say. Ovid. CTC, tr. by Arthur Golding Fr. Metamorphoses.

Now then. Setsudo. JDP, tr. by Yoel Hoffmann

Now then, take your seats! for Glasgow and the North. Night Mail North, The. Henry Cholmondeley-Pennell. EBVV

Now then, what are you up to, Dai? Kingsley Amis. NOBL; OxBC Fr. Evans Country, The.

Now there are no bonds except the flesh; listen. Manzini; Escape Artist. Gwendolyn MacEwen. NOBC

Now there comes / The Christmas rose. New Year's [or Year] Song. Ted Hughes. OBCP

Now there is none of the living who can remember. Epitaph for a Concord Boy. Stanley Young. ChAP

Now there'll be a new mantra, Mother. Najrul Islām. SinGod, tr. by Rachel Fell McDermott

Now there's many fool things a woman will do. Gold Tooth Blues. Tennessee Williams. OBAL

Now there was a man of the Pharisees, named Nicode'mus. Howard Nemerov. GI Fr. St. John.

"Now therefore go," He said, "and I will be with thy mouth." (LL) Spit. C. K. Williams. GotH; TaR

Now these four things, if thou. Francesco da Barberino. EaItPo, tr. by Dante Gabriel Rossetti

Now they are married Nature breathes once more. (LL) Summer Storm. Louis Simpson. OxBC; OxBSo

Now they are old, on dull mornings. May Tree, The. Jean Earle. TCAWP

Now they have two cars to clean. Do It Yrself. Larry Eigner. NeAP; PoM

Now they're pillaging the last coast. Vandals, The. Jenny Mastoraki. BoWoP, tr. by Nikos Germanakos.

Now thin mists temper the slow-ripening beams. Garden in September, The. Robert Bridges. OBGa

Now, thirty years on, I shift. Headmaster. John Tripp. AngWePo

Now this bloody war is over. Song. George Barker. PeLV

Now, this is it, the toilsome journey's end. Imre Madách. IQMS, tr. by Iain MacLeod Fr. Tragedy of Man.

Now this is my first counsel. Unknown. AWP Fr. Elder Edda, The.

Now this particular girl. Spinster. Sylvia Plath. FaBoWP; LW; SoSe-8

Now thise foweles syngen and maken her blisse. Unknown. OHMEL

Now thou art dead, no eye shall ever see. Upon His Spaniel[l] Tracie [or Tracy]. Robert Herrick. BeJo

Now thou hast lov'd me one whole day. Woman's Constancy. John Donne. ESCV; NBLV; NOSC

Now thou hast seen my heart. Was it too near? Confessional, The. Frederick William Faber. CenSon

Now through Night's Caressing Grip. W. H. Auden. PoRA

Now Time's Andromeda on this rock rude. Andromeda. Gerard Manley Hopkins. EBEV; FaBoMo; OxAEP-2; SCGP

Now to a softer theme descends my muse. Stephen Duck. OBGa Fr. On Richmond Park.

Now to Aurora, borne by dappled steeds. Walter Savage Landor. NOBRP Fr. Gebir.

Now to be clean he must abandon himself. Swan Bathing, The. Ruth Pitter. MoBrPo

Now to depart from all this complication. Departure of the Prodigal Son, The. Rainer Maria Rilke. GI

Now to dispose the dead, the care remains. Homer. OBVE, tr. by Alexander Pope Fr. Odyssey.

Now to Great Britain we must make our way. Of England, and of Its Marvels. Fazio degli Uberti. AWP, tr. by Dante Gabriel Rossetti

Now to meet only in dreams. Yakamochi (Otomo no Yakamochi). OHPJ

Now, to tense stillness as the door is slammed. Their Thoughts Cling to Everything They See on the Way. Allen Afterman. NOBAu

Now to the author of Toldi my spirit flies through space. To János Arany. Sándor Petőfi. IQMS, tr. by Madeline Mason

Now toils the Heroe; trees on trees o'erthrown. Homer. OBVE Fr. Odyssey.

Now touch the air softly. Pavane for the Nursery, A. William Jay Smith. MoAmPo

Now trouble comes between the forest's selves. Russian New Year. Bill Berkson. PmAP

Now twenty springs had clothed the park with green. Toilette, The. John Gay. ECEV

Now upon this piteous year. Stranger, The. Jean Garrigue. NOBA; TwCP

Now van to van the foremost squadrons meet. Dryden. OBWP Fr. Annus Mirabilis.

Now—wagon full of thunder. Wagon Full of Thunder. Louis Oliver. HATNAP

Now war and vengeance claim. Firdowsi. TAL Fr. Shahnamah, The.

Now war is all the world about. Sir Richard Fanshawe. NOBE Fr. Il Pastor Fido.

Now was there maid fast by the towris wall. James I, King of Scotland. EBEV Fr. Kingis Quair, The.

Now watch this autumn that arrives. Song at the Beginning of Autumn. Elizabeth Jennings. OxBTC

Now we are back to normal, now the mind is. Louis MacNeice. OxAEP-2 Fr. Autumn Journal.

Now we are leaving. Issa. SoOfWa, tr. by Sam Hamill

Now we enter a strange world, where the Hessian Christmas. After the Industrial Revolution, All Things Happen at Once. Robert Bly. CoAP; CoAmPo

Now we flourish / as others have / before. Unknown. GrAn

Now we have heard stories of high valor. Unknown. CABP

Now we hear the tamarack fall. Coming Out on Solid Ground After the Ice Age. Gary Paul Nabhan. PoCoUp

Now we must come to the net. Coming to the net. Brian G. Gilmore. SpirFl

Now we must part, from all things run. Emigrants. Berthold Viertel. AuPH, tr. by Lowell A. Bangerter

Now we must praise the Guardian of Heaven. Cædmon's Hymn. Caedmon. ASW, tr. by Kevin Crossley-Holland

Now we're met, my brethren Benchers. Humours of the King's Bench Prison, a Ballad, The. Leonard Howard. NOEC

Now we should praise Heaven-kingdom's guard. Hymn. Caedmon. PAI, tr. by D. K. Fry

Now weary labourers perceivem well pleased. Joanna Baillie. ECWP Fr. Summer Day, A.

Now Welcom[e], Somer [or Summer]. Geoffrey Chaucer. HAP Fr. Parlement of Foules, The.

Now westward Sol had spent the richest beam[e]s. Music[k]'s Duel[l]. Richard Crashaw. GeHe; NAEL-7v1; NPeEn

Now what do you think. Unknown. OxNR

Now what have I to live for. (LL) Long Time Back, A. Unknown. EaWin; WoPoe, tr. by J. Moussaieff Masson and W. S. Merwin

Now what my mother told me one day as we sat at dinner together. Walt Whitman. BLT Fr. Sleepers, The.

Now what will we do for timber. Cill Chais. Unknown. NOIV, tr. by Thomas Kinsella

Now, when he and I meet, after all these years. Bitch. Carolyn Kizer. GifTon

Now when I have thrust my body. To Forget Me. Theodore Weiss. CoAP

Now when I walk around at lunchtime. Personal Poem. Frank O'Hara. CLPP; PmAP

Now, when it flowereth. Rinaldo D'Aquino. EaItPo, tr. by Dante Gabriel Rossetti

'Now when King Offa was alive and dead', they were. Geoffrey Hill. NPeEn Fr. Mercian Hymns.

Now, when the cheerless empire of the sky. James Thomson. OxBA Fr. Seasons, The.

Now when the solemn Rites of Pray'r were past. Homer. OBVE, tr. by John Dryden Fr. Iliad, The.

Now when thy folke are fed and clad. Isabella Whitney. BWW Fr. Manner of Her Will and What She Left to London and to All Those in It, at Her Departing, The.

Now, whether it were by peculiar grace. William Wordsworth. UV Fr. Resolution and Independence.

Now which is wrong or right? Too glib we talk. Falkland at Newbury, 1643. Hugh Conway. EBVV

Now, while amid those dainty downs and dales. To His Pandora, from England. Alexander Craig. Son

Now, while thou hast the wondrous power of word. Sadi [or Saadi or Sa'di]. AWP, tr. by L. Cranmer-Byng Fr. Gulistan, The.

Now Whitehall's in the grave. Mock Song, A. Richard Lovelace. BeJo; CaPo

Now whyle Hippomenes / Debates theis things. Ovid. OBVE Fr. Metamorphoses.

Now will I a lover be. Combat, The. Thomas Stanley. AWP

Now will I open unto thee—whose heart. Unknown. TAL Fr. Bhagavad-Gita, The.

Now will we plunge into the frigid dark. Autumn Song. Charles Baudelaire. SxFrPo, tr. by James McGowan

Now wilt me take for Jesus' sake. Prayer, A. Katharine Tynan. SacPr

Now wind torments the field. February: Thinking of Flowers. Jane Kenyon. LoL

Now winedrinkers, this way to an airy shrine. Musical Wine-Jar, A. Hedylos. GrAn, tr. by William Moebius

Now winter downs the dying of the year. Year's End. Richard Wilbur. CoAP; HeIP-4; NAAL-2v2

Now Winter Nights. Robert Hass. BodElec

Now Winter Nights Enlarge. Thomas Campion. EBEV; NAEL-7v1; NPeEn; NoP-4; OxAEP-1; OxBEV; NOSC; PBRV

Now Winter's winds are banished from the sky. Spring. Meleager. AWP, tr. by William M. Hardinge

Now with the moon the day-star Lucifer. Folgore da San Geminiano [or Gimignano]. EaItPo, tr. by Dante Gabriel Rossetti

Now / with your head thrown back. I Tell of Another Young Death. César Tiempo. TrJP, tr. by Donald Devenish Walsh

Now, with your palms on the blades of my shoulders. Dead Still. Andrey [or Andrei] Andreievich Voznesensky [or Voznesenskii]. BoLoP; PasH, tr. by Richard Wilbur

Now wither all earth's gallantries! Autumn. Mihály Tompa. IQMS, tr. by Watson Kirkconnell

Now wolde I fayne sum merthis [or faine some merthes] mak[e]. A. Godwin. MiEL; OxBoLi

Now won't you listen, honey, while I say. After You've Gone. J. Turner Layton. ReLy

Now would to God swift ships had ne'er been made! Sopolis. Callimachus. AWP, tr. by William M. Hardinge

Now, yield thee, or by Him who made. Sir Walter Scott. OxBS Fr. Lady of the Lake, The.

Now, yields you, with some sighs, our explanation. (LL) To R. B. Gerard Manley Hopkins. GTBS-P; OxAEP-2

Now you are standing face to face with the clear light. Prayer for the Little Daughter between Death and Burial. Diana Scott. BrRo

Now you aren't here I find. Mansize. Maura Dooley. NeBl

Now you can see him, exactly as he came. Herakles. Parrhasios. GrAn, tr. by Peter Jay

Now, you great stanza, you heroic mould. Single Sonnet. Louise Bogan. Son

Now You Have Burned. John Thompson. NOBC

Now you have come. Foot-Washing, The. A. R. Ammons. ChIV-2

Now you have freely given me leave to love. To a Lady That Desired I Would Love Her. Thomas Carew. BASC; BeJo; CaPo; CavPo; MeLP; SCGP

Now you have stabbed her good. Kreutzer Sonata. Ted Hughes. FaBoMo

Now you hear what the house has to say. Insomnia. Dana Gioia. AWTN

Now you lean across the table, fingers. Malleus Maleficarum 4. Maureen Seaton. ExTi

Now you lie—a grape-offering. Moiro. GrAn

Now you look down. The waters of childhood are there. (LL) Where Are the Waters of Childhood? Mark Strand. EmeKit; HCAP; LCAP-2; VCAP; WeW-3

Now you love me. Divorce Song. Unknown. STP, tr. by Carl Cary

Now you may rest forever. To Himself. Giacomo Leopardi. NAWM-7v2, tr. by Ottavio M. Casale

Now You're Content. André Spire. TrJP, tr. by Stanley Burnshaw

Now you take ol Rufus. He beat drums. For Freckle-Faced Gerald. Etheridge Knight. BPo; ESEAA

Now you think that is right, sah? Talk the truth. Carpenter's Complaint, The. Edward Baugh. OBCoV

Now you've learned not to let your eyes. Battle Lines. John C. Schafer. CDa

Now your grave is sinking. Rainbow-Colored Whale, The. Ferenc Juhász. WoPoe, tr. by David Wevill

Nowadays. John Kander. ReLy

Nowadays. Tushar Roy. WoPoe, tr. by Ron D. K. Banerjee

Nowadays the mess is everywhere. Survivors, The. Daryl Hine. TwCP

Nowe, Parott, my swete byrde, speke owte yet ons agayn. John Skelton. See Now, Parrot, my sweet bird, speak our yet once again

Nowel, el, el, el, el! Unknown. OHMEL

Nowell sing we, both all and some. Nowell Sing We. Unknown. ChrPo

Nowhere else but on the mouth. How He Should Like to Be Kissed. Paul Fleming. GePo, tr. by Harold B. Segel

Nowhere in this world have I a home. Basho 3. Cees Nooteboom. TuT, tr. by Michael O'Loughlin

Nowhere, not among the warriors at their festival. Atimantiyar. WPOW, tr. by A. K. Ramanujan

Nowhere, nowhere is there any trace of blood. No Sign of Blood. Faiz Ahmad Faiz. AF, tr. by Naomi Lazard

Nox Nocti Indicat Scientiam. William Habington. BASC; BeJo; MeLP; NOBE; NPeEn; OBEV; OxBEV; SCGP Fr. Castara.

Nox was lit by lux of Luna, The. Carmen Possum. Unknown. NBLV

Noye, to me thou arte full able. Unknown. InvLi Fr. Noah's Flood.

Nozizwe. Raymond Mazisi Kunene. PeSAV, tr. by the author

Ntabuu / Ntabuu Selina and. Sisters, The. Alexis De Veaux. GLP

Ntozake Shange's Broadway opening. Broadway Opening. Miguel Algarin. PueRic

Nu-plastik Fanfare Red. Judith Rodriguez. BMAP

Nu thu, unsely body, upon here list. Unknown. MiEL

Nub. Chris Wallace-Crabbe. BMAP

Nuchal, a Fragment. Thomas Kinsella. PBCIP

Nuchika torichibi, in Orok, small dream. The newspaper clipping where. Fujii Sadakazu. PFTM-2, tr. by Christopher Drake Fr. Where is Japanese Poetry?

Nuclear ecstasy on the picket line. Cheap Replicas of the Eiffel Tower. Elton Glaser. PBCAP

Nuclear Umbrella. Heberto Padilla. AF, tr. by Alastair Reid

Nuclear Winter. Thomas McGrath. GifTon

Nuclear Winter, The. W. Les Russell. IBA

Nude by Edward Hopper, A. Lisel Mueller. PoSol

Nude Descending a Staircase. X. J. Kennedy. CoAmPo; NIP-4; OxBSP

Nude in a Fountain. Norman MacCaig. OxBS

Nude Swim, The. Anne Sexton. WPE

Nude Woman Spotted in Cappuccino Cup as Advertising Dollar co-opts another life. Bahiyyih Maroon. SpirFl

Nudes—stark and glistening. Louse Hunting. Isaac Rosenberg. EBEV; FaBoWar; NAEL-5v2; NAEL-6v2; NoAM; NoP-4; OxAEP-2; OxBEV; OxBTC; PeFWW

Nudities. André Spire. AWP, tr. by Jethro Bithell

Nudities. André Spire. TrJP, tr. by Stanley Burnshaw

Nudity. Gabriella Sica. CItWP, tr. by Cinzia Sartini Blum and Lara Trubowitz

Nudo de Claridad. Miguel Algarin. PmAP

Nudus Redibo. Thomas Flatman. OxBSP

Nuit Blanche: North End. Conrad Potter Aiken. OxBA

Nulla Fides. Patrick Carey [or Cary]. SCGP
    (For God's sake marcke that Fly.) OxBEV

Nullarbor. William Hart-Smith. BMAP

Nullo. Jean Toomer. APT-2

Number of positions to take with respect to the present, A. Form of Chiasmus; The Chiasmus of Forms, The. Michael Davidson. PmAP

Number One / I slouch in bed. Two Hangovers. James Wright (1927–80). LCAP-2

Number one is a good clean number, The. Million, The. Peter Redgrove. OxBC

Number Our Days. Norbert Hirschhorn. BloBone

Number, Weight, and Measure. Abraham Cowley. NOSC Fr. Davideis.

Numbers. Bible, O.T.
    Balaam's Blessing. OBVE, tr. by William Tyndale
    Blessing of the Priests. TrJP
    "Lorde blesse the and kepe the, The." OBVE, tr. by William Tyndale
    Song of the Well. TrJP

Numbers. Allison Joseph. NeAmPo

Numbers in ass, The. Strato [or Straton]. GrAn

Numbers, Letters. Imamu Amiri Baraka. BPo; NOBA; PFTM-2

Numbly dont get there. (LL) Jack Kerouac. NeAP; PmAP Fr. Mexico City Blues.

Numeri XIII. John Hall. ChIV-1

Numerology. Jerome Rothenberg. FTOS

Numerous host of dreaming saints succeed, A. Dryden. NOBE; OBSV Fr. Absalom and Achitophel.

Numinous, The. William Heyen. GotH

Nun, The. Edward Moore. ECEV

Nun in Ninh Hoa, A. Jan Barry. CDa

Nun's Priest's Prologue, The. Geoffrey Chaucer. FHYEP Fr. Canterbury Tales, The.

Nun's Priest's Tale, The. Geoffrey Chaucer. NAWM-5v1, tr. by Theodore Morrison Fr. Canterbury Tales, The.

Nun's Priest's Tale, The. Geoffrey Chaucer. FHYEP; NAEL-6v1; NAWM-5v1 Fr. Canterbury Tales, The.

Nun Takes the Veil, A. Bernard O'Donoghue. ModIr

Nunc Puer Nobis Natus Est. James Ryman. SacPr

Nunc Viridant Segetes. Sedulius Scottus. BIrV; NAWM-5v1, tr. by Helen Waddell

Nungesser und Coli Sind Verreckt. Benjamin Péret. AF, tr. by Keith Hollaman

Nunnery, The. Anna Williams. ECWP

Nuns at Eve. John Malcolm Brinnin. TwCP

Nuns Fret Not at Their Convent's Narrow Room. William Wordsworth. See Sonnet: "Nuns fret not at their convent's narrow room."

Nuns Go Walking. Aldo Palazzeschi. PFTM-1

Nuns, his nieces, bring the priest in the next. Far Cry after a Close Call, A. Richard Howard. UnPo

Nuns in the Wind. Muriel Rukeyser. NNaP

Nuns of Childhood: Two Views, The. Maxine W. Kumin. FFC

Nuptial Dialogues. Edward Ward.
    Dialogue between a Squeamish Cotting Mechanic and His Sluttish Wife, in the Kitchen. NOEC

Nuptial Eve, A. Sydney Thompson Dobell.
    Ballad of Keith of Ravelston, The. OBEV

Nuptial Sleep. Dante Gabriel Rossetti. EBVV; NAEL-5v2; NAEL-6v2; NOBVV Fr. House of Life, The.

Nuptial Song. John Byrne Leicester Warren, 3d Baron De Tabley. GTBS-P; PeVV

Nuptial Song. Henricus Selyns. See O Christmas Night

Nuptiall Song, or Epithalamie, on Sir Clipseby Crew and His Lady, A. Robert Herrick. BeJo; CaPo

Nuptials of Attila, The. George Meredith.
    "Square along the couch, and stark." PeVV

Nuremberg. Kenneth Slessor. BMAP

Nurse a terror theory back. Principles, When I Felt Them. Prageeta Sharma. HeMarv

Nurse believed the sick man slept, The. Charlotte Brontë. NOBVV

Nurse carried him up the stair, The. At Thomas Hardy's Birthplace, 1953. James Wright (1927–80). CoAmPo

Nurse grits her teeth, stubs out the cigarette, The. (LL) David Wojahn. PBCAP; SwNoth Fr. Mystery Train: A Sequence.

Nurse's Dole in the Medea, The. Byron. OBVE

Nurse's Lament, The. Mary Elizabeth Coleridge. NOBVV; OxBSP

Nurse's Song. William Blake. FHYEP Fr. Songs of Experience.

Nurse's Song. William Blake. AWP; FHYEP; NAEL-5v2; NAEL-6v2; PeLV; RACG; SCGP Fr. Songs of Innocence.

Nurse was in a hospital, A. Syllabling. Sean O Riordain. ModIr, tr. by Patrick Crotty

Nursed on the blood of your inheritance. (LL) America, I Do Not Call Your Name Without Hope. Pablo Neruda. AF; TCLAP, tr. by Robert Bly

Nursery Rhyme. Kenneth Burke. OBAL

Nursery Rhyme. Gavin Ewart. UV

Nursery Rhyme. Kit Robinson. FTOS

Nursery Rhyme. May Sarton. NOxBChV

Nursery Rhyme in Eight Strophes. Rossana Ombres. CItWP, *tr. by* Cinzia Sartini Blum and Lara Trubowitz

Nursery Rhyme of Innocence and Experience. Charles Causley. NOxBChV

Nursery Song. Anna Wickham. NOxBChV

Nursery Vignette. Edmund Wilson. OBCoV *Fr.* Easy Exercises in the Use of Difficult Words.

Nurses, The. Rudyard Kipling. NoAM *Fr.* Land and Sea Tales.

Nurse's Song. *Unknown. See* Lullaby: "Sleep, baby, sleep."

Nursing her child. Issa. EH, *tr. by* Robert Hass

Nursing the Sunburn. Judith Vollmer. SwNoth

Nursing your nerves / to rest, I've roused my own; well. Afterwake, The. Adrienne Rich. NOBA

Nut-brown Maid, The. *Unknown.* NoSic; OBEV

Nut-brown maid of Grasmere plays, The. Eclogue: Clerk of the Weather. William Scammell. NLP

Nut Tree, A. Mother Goose. OxBoLi; OxNR; TTTS

Nut Tree, A. *Unknown.* TTTS

Nuthatch. David Wagoner. OWoS

Nuts an' May. *Unknown.* LB

Nuts in May. Louis MacNeice. MoBrPo

Nutting. John Clare. CenSon

Nutting. William Wordsworth. NAEL-5v2; NAEL-6v2; NOBRP; RB

NW5 and N6. Sir John Betjeman. SCV

Nwinnng buht nawuNNN baheegwinnng. (LL) 12th Horse Song of Frank Mitchell (Blue), The. Frank Mitchell. APSN; STP, *tr. by* Jerome Rothenberg

Nyanu was appointed. Early Losses: a Requiem. Alice Walker. BlSi

Nymph and shepherd raise electric tridents. Chances "R." Allen Ginsberg. CAGL; HCAP

Nymph Complaining for the Death of Her Faun [*or* Fawn], The. Andrew Marvell. BASC; ESCV; GeHe; HeIP-4; NAEL-5v1; NAEL-6v1; NAEL-7v1; RACG

"With sweetest milk and sugar first." FaBoCh

Nymph died more quick, and the shepherd more slow, The. (LL) Dryden. NPeEn; PeLV *Fr.* Marriage à la Mode.

Nymph Fanarett, supposed to be. Penance, A. Francis Daniel Pastorius. NOSC

Nymph in vain bestows her pains, The. Song, A. Anne Finch, Countess of Winchilsea. OxBSP

Nymph of the Fountain to Charlotte, The. Anne Grant. PoBW

Nymph of the garden where all beauties be. Sir Philip Sidney. PoE *Fr.* Astrophil and Stella.

Nymph's [*or* Nimphs] Reply to the Shepherd [*or* Sheepheard], The. Sir Walter Ralegh. AEP; AmFaPo; CABP; CTC; ClHu; HAP; HeIP-4; InPK-6; NAEL-5v1; NAEL-6v1; NAEL-7v1; NBLV; NIL-7; NIP-4; NOBE; NPeEn; NoP-4; NoSic; PAI; PoE; PoPoPo; RACG; RB; SCGP; TFi; TRP; UV; WeW-3

(Her Reply.) BoLoP; OBEV

Nymph's Passion, A. Ben Jonson. BeJo

(Nymph's Secret, A.) OBEV

Nymph's Song. Sir Richard Fanshawe. *See* Il Pastor Fido

Nymph's Song to Hylas, The. William Morris. *See* Life and Death of Jason, The

Nymph turnd home, The. He fell to felling downe. Homer. OBVE *Fr.* Odyssey.

Nymphs and Shepherds dance no more. John Milton. OxBEV *Fr.* Arcades.

Nymphs of the surface, whom Hermokreon gave. Hermocreon. GrAn

Nymphs of water, daughters of Doros. Leonidas of Tarentum. GrAn

Nyooz. belt up. (LL) Tom Leonard. NPeEn; NePenScot *Fr.* Unrelated Incidents.

O

Ö. Rita Dove. HCAP; WeW-3

O a gallant set were they. Huguenot, A. Mary Elizabeth Coleridge. SacPr

O a year from tomorrow I left my own people. Clonmel Jail. *Unknown.* BIrV, *tr. by* Valentin Iremonger

O Abishag, my little serving-maid. Abishag. André Spire. TrJP, *tr. by* Emanuel Eisenberg

O Alison Gross, that lives in yon tower [*or* tow'r]. Alison [*or* Allison] Gross. *Unknown.* ESPB; FaBoCh; OxBB

O All Down within the Pretty Meadow. Kenneth Patchen. HAP; WeW-3

O all the problems other people face. Alcoholic. John Berryman. BodElec; NOCV

O all ye nations of the Lord. Thomas Norton. SacPr

O all you lands, the treasures of your joy. Bible, *O.T.* CABP, *tr. by* Mary Sidney Herbert, Countess of Pembroke *Fr.* Psalms.

O all you little blackey tops. Scaring Crows. *Unknown.* OxNR

O all your ages at the mercy of my loves. John Berryman. NOBA *Fr.* Homage to Mistress Bradstreet.

O Alma Magna Mater, deathless the living death of pride. (LL) Sonnet on Famous and Familiar Sonnets and Experiences. Delmore Schwartz. Son; TRP

O amiable prospect! New Lines for Cuscuscaraway and Mirza Murad Ali Beg. Louis Simpson. OBAL

O an old King in a story. After W. B. Yeats. Gilbert Keith Chesterton. NOBL

O! And I forsooth in love! William Shakespeare. OBCoV *Fr.* Love's Labour's Lost.

O anti-verdurous phallic were't not for your pouring height. Ode to Coit Tower. Gregory Corso. CLPP

O antique city on St. Lawrence shore. Quebec. Henrietta Cordelia Ray. CBWP-3

O! Are Ye Sleepin [*or* Sleeping], Maggie? Robert Tannahill. OxBS

O Aridon, bring back my wealth. Fate of Vultures, The. Tanure Ojaide. NAfrP

O Art, high gift of Heaven! how oft defamed. Art. Washington Allston. APN-1

O Artemis and your virgin girls. Telesilla. BoWoP

O Artemis of Delos and lovely Ortygia. Nossis. SaLy, *tr. by* Diane Rayor

O Autumn! how I love thy pensive air. Written in Autumn. Mary Tighe. CenSon; OxBSo

O Autumn, laden with fruit, and stained. To Autumn. William Blake. NAEL-5v2; NAEL-6v2

O autumn winds. Issa. SoOfWa, *tr. by* Sam Hamill

O autumn winds. Prince Shiki. SoOfWa, *tr. by* Sam Hamill

O Baba! Look at this Cadak tree. Dīnrām. SinGod, *tr. by* Rachel Fell McDermott

O barbarous Corsica, locked in by crags. Seneca. RomPo, *tr. by* J. P. Sullivan

O bards! weak heritors of passion and of pain! Miserimus. Adah Isaacs Menken. CBWP-1

O, Be Not Too Hasty, My Dearest. "Orpheus C. Kerr." OBAL

O be swift. Helmsman, The. "H. D." OxBA

O! bear me witness, night. William Shakespeare. OxAEP-1 *Fr.* Antony and Cleopatra.

O beauteous God! uncircumscribed treasure. Prayer, A. Jeremy Taylor. SacPr

O beautiful. Boat, A. Richard Brautigan. KaS

O beautiful adolescent, O young man. Lanza 51. Filippo Scarlatti. CAGL, *tr. by* James J. Wilhelm

O beautiful for spacious skies. America the Beautiful. Katharine Lee Bates. APN-2; FaBoA; HHAm; TAP

O Beautiful, My Country. Frederick Lucian Hosmer. AH

O beech, unbind your yellow leaf, for deep. Ghostly Tree. Léonie Adams. APT-2; MoAmPo

O beloved of my twenty-seven senses, I. Anna Blume. Kurt Schwitters. NAWM-7v2, *tr. by* David Britt

O benign Jesu, my sovereign Lord and King. John Skelton. SCGP *Fr.* To the Second Person.

O Bessie Bell and Mary Gray. Bessy [*or* Bessie] Bell and Mary Gray. *Unknown.* ESPB; OxBB

O Best of All Nights, Return and Return Again. James Laughlin. GifTon

O Bicci, pretty son of who knows whom. Dante Alighieri. EaItPo, *tr. by* Dante Gabriel Rossetti

O Billie, billie, bonny billie. Battle of Bothwell Bridge, The. *Unknown.* OxBB

O bird crying on the acacia tree, alike are our sorrows. Andalusian Exile, An. Ahmad Shauqi. BBASP; MAP, *tr. by* M. Mustafa Badawi and John Heath-Stubbs

O Bird, So Lovely. Louis Golding. TrJP

O Black and Unknown Bards. James Weldon Johnson. APT-1; BPo; ColAP; HeIP-4; NAAAL; TCAPo; TTY; UnPo

O black winter of savage death. On a Young Wife. Julianus of Egypt. GrAn, *tr. by* Willis Barnstone

O blazing Sun, how happy you are there. Sonnet 22. Louise Labé. BoWoP, *tr. by* Willis Barnstone

O blessed body [*or* bodie]! Whither art thou thrown? Sepulchre. George Herbert. ESCV; MiEL

O blessed breeding sun! draw from the earth. William Shakespeare. OxAEP-1 *Fr.* Timon of Athens.

O Blessed man, that in th'advice. Bible, *O.T.* SCAP *Fr.* Bay Psalm Book, The.

O blessed Solitude. (LL) Woman Alone, A. Denise Levertov. BodElec; WPOW

O Blest Estate, Blest from Above. George Sandys. AH

O blest unfabled incense tree. George Darley. BIrV; FaBoCh; OBEV *Fr.* Nepenthe.

O blithe New-comer! I have heard. To the Cuckoo. William Wordsworth. GTBS-P; NOBRP; UV

O blonde thing! (LL) Sylvia's Death. Anne Sexton. LCAP-2; NAAL-2v2; NAAL-5; NALW

O Bois de Boulogne, don't you remember. Bois de Boulogne. Ahmad Shauqi. MAP, *tr.* by M. Mustafa Badawi and John Heath-Stubbs

O-Bon: Dance for the Dead. Garrett Kaoru Hongo. LoL

O Bonny Baby Livingston. Bonny Baby Livingston. *Unknown.* ESPB

O born in days when wits were fresh and clear. Matthew Arnold. OxBEV *Fr.* Scholar Gypsy, The.

O, born in luckless hour, with every muse. To the Editor of Mr. Pope's Works. Thomas Edwards. Son

O Boston, though thou now art grown. Of Boston in New England. William Bradford. SCAP

O boy cutting grass. *Var. authors.* AWP *Fr.* Manyo Shu, Part 3 of 4.

O boys, O strong of heart in vain. Virgil [*or* Vergil]. MLL *Fr.* Aeneid [*or* Eneados, *Aeneis*], The.

O breake my hart quoth he, O breake and dye. Michael Drayton. CAGL *Fr.* Piers Gaveston.

O brothers mine, take care! Take care! White Witch, The. James Weldon Johnson. APT-1

O brothers, why do you talk. Mahadevi. WPOW, *tr.* by A. K. Ramanujan

O'Bruadair. David [*or* Daibhi][*or* Daithi] O'Bruadair [*or* Ó Bruadair]. BIrV, *tr.* by James Stephens

O, but how white is white, white from shadows come. Music of Colours: The Blossom Scattered. Vernon Watkins. AngWePo

O but Log was too heavy to dance it. (LL) Masque of Christmas, The. Ben Jonson. ChrPo; OxBoLi

O but the wind is keen. My Cloth of Gold. Ina Coolbrith. SWaP

O but there is wisdom. Consolation. W. B. Yeats. OxBSP

O but we talked at large before. Sixteen Dead Men. W. B. Yeats. OBWP

O by the by / has anybody seen. E. E. Cummings. OxBA

O Caledonia! stern and wild. Sir Walter Scott. NePenScot *Fr.* Lay of the Last Minstrel, The.

O Calendar of the Century. Melvin B. Tolson. APT-2 *Fr.* Libretto for the Republic of Liberia.

O cam ye in by the House o Rodes. John Thomson and the Turk. *Unknown.* ESPB

O camp of flowers, with poplars girdled round. Memory. Erik Johann Stagnelius. AWP, *tr.* by Sir Edmund William Gosse

O Captain! My Captain! Walt Whitman. APN-1; BRP; CBCWP; ChAP; FaBoCh; HHAm; InPK-6; MakPoe; MoAmPo; OBCA; SAmP; TAP; TCAPo; TFi *Fr.* Memories of President Lincoln.

O Carib Isle! Hart Crane. APT-2; NoAM; PFTM-1; VGW

O casket of sweet sounds, wherein there lieth. To a Piano. Mary Elizabeth Coleridge. OxBSo

O chansons foregoing. Epilogue. Ezra Pound. OxBA

O Chatterton, how very sad thy fate! To Chatterton. John Keats. CenSon

O Cheese. Donald Hall. DiPo

O chief director of the growing race. Ad Quintilianum. Martial. RomPo, *tr.* by Robert Louis Stevenson

O Child, Do Not Fear the Dark and Sleep's Dark Possession. Delmore Schwartz. NOxBChV

O Child of Lowly Manger Birth. Ferdinand Q. Blanchard. AH

O child's tremble. Forming Child Poems. Simon J. Ortiz. CDW

O child, when you go down to sleep and sleep's secession. O Child, Do Not Fear the Dark and Sleep's Dark Possession. Delmore Schwartz. NOxBChV

O Children, Would You Cherish? Christopher Dock. AH, *tr.* by Samuel W. Pennypacker

O Christ of Bethlehem. H. Glenn Lanier. AH

O Christ of God! whose life and death. Vesta. John Greenleaf Whittier. SacPr

O Christ, our hope, our heart's desire, Redepntion's only spring! *Unknown.* SacPr, *tr.* by John Chandler

O Christ, receive these souls in thy Mother's house. Hibernicus Exul. MLL

O Christ, who in Gethsemane. Prayer. Henrietta Cordelia Ray. CBWP-3

O Christmas Night. Henricus Selyns. AH, *tr.* by Howard Murphy (Nuptial Song.) SCAP

O city metropole, isle riverain! Montreal. Abraham Moses Klein. MoCV

O city of the world, with sacred splendor blest. Longing for Jerusalem. Judah Halevi. TrJP, *tr.* by Emma Lazarus

O clemens! O pia! O dolcis! / Maria! (LL) For Eleanor and Bill Monahan. William Carlos Williams. CRP; VGW

O'clock. Fanny Howe.
   "Set golden butter out in a dish." FTOS

O close of night, I would have you linger. Song, A. "Adonis" [*or* "Adunis"]. MAP, *tr.* by John Heath-Stubbs and Lena Jayyusi

O, close your pale legs! Valery [*or* Valerii] Yakovlevich [*or* Iakovlevich] Bryusov [*or* Briusov]. TCRP

O cloud that wants to be the sky's arrow. Rosario Castellanos. BoWoP, *tr.* by Willis Barnstone

O Come, All Ye Faithful. *Unknown.* SacPr, *tr.* by Frederick Oakeley

O come and take thou me / Beneath thy wing. Beneath Thy Wing. Hayyim Nahman [*or* Khayim Nakhman *or* Chaim Nachman] Bialik. TrJP, *tr.* by Helena Frank

O come, let us sing unto the Lord. Bible, *O.T.* AWP *Fr.* Psalms.

O come, O come, Emmanuel. *Unknown.* SacPr, *tr.* by John Mason Neale

O Come Quickly! Thomas Campion. NOBE; NPeEn; OBEV; OxAEP-1; OxBSP

O come, soft rest of cares, come Night. Christopher Marlowe. NOBE; OBEV *Fr.* Hero and Leander.

O come to me in my dreams love! Lines to———. Mary Weston Fordham. CBWP-2

O Come to My Heart, Lord Jesus. Emily E. S. Elliott. SacPr

O come with me, thus ran the song. Emily Jane Brontë. NOBVV

O commemorate me where there is water. Lines Written on a Seat on the Grand Canal, Dublin. Patrick Kavanagh. BIrV; NOIV

O Constellations of the early night. Constellations, The. William Cullen Bryant. APN-1

O cord of life! Princess Shokushi. ArkPo, *tr.* by Robert H. Brower and Earl Miner

"O Cormac, grandson of Conn," said Carbery. *Unknown.* BIrV *Fr.* Instructions of King Cormac, The.

O Could I Find from Day to Day. Benjamin Cleavland. AH

O could I flow like thee, and make thy stream. Sir John Denham. NPeEn *Fr.* Cooper's Hill.

"O could I love!" and stops, God writeth, "Loved" (LL) True Hymn, A. George Herbert. GeHe; NOCV

O! could my sweet plaint lull to rest. Nightingale. Christian Carstairs. ECWP

O courteous Christkind guest, most gracious host. To a Crucifix. Anna Wickham. MoBrPo

O Courtesy, O Harborage Most Sweet. Luís De León. SpanPo, *tr.* by Brenda M. Sackett

O cricket, from your cheery cry. Basho. AWP, *tr.* by Curtis Hidden Page

O crimson blood. Hildegard von Bingen. WPOW, *tr.* by Patrick Diehl

O crownless soul of Ishmael! Hemlock in the Furrows. Adah Isaacs Menken. CBWP-1

O cruel Death, give three things back. Three Things. W. B. Yeats. OBMV

O cruel Love! on thee I lay. John Lyly. NoSic *Fr.* Sapho and Phao.

O Cuckoo. *Var. authors.* AWP *Fr.* Kokin Shu.

O Cuckoo! shall I call thee Bird. To the Cuckoo. F. H. Townsend. UV

O Cuckoo! shall I call thee Bird. Examination Question. *Unknown.* OBCoV

O cuckoo that sang to us and art fled. Lament for the Cuckoo. Alcuin. NAWM-5v1

O Daedalus, Fly Away Home. Robert Earl Hayden. HAP; NAAAL

O David, highest in the list. Christopher Smart. NOEC; NPeEn; OxBEV *Fr.* Song to David, A.

O David, if I had. That Harp You Play So Well. Marianne Craig Moore. MoAmPo

O Day! he cannot die. Death Scene, A. Emily Jane Brontë. OxAEP-2

O Day most calm, most bright. Sunday. George Herbert. GeHe; PeECV; TrCP

O Day of God, Draw Nigh. Robert Balgarnie Young Scott. AH

O Day of Light and Gladness. Frederick Lucian Hosmer. AH

O Day of Rest and Gladness. Christopher Wordsworth. SacPr

O days and hours, your work is this. Tennyson. PeECV *Fr.* In Memoriam A. H. H.

O' de wurl' ain't flat! Northboun' Lucy Ariel Williams Holloway. BlSi

O dea certe! (LL) Edmund Spenser. NAEL-5v1; NAEL-6v1; OBEV *Fr.* Shepheardes [*or* Shepeards *or* Shepherd's] Calender, The.

O dear! How disgusting is life! Edward Lear. NOxBChV

O dear! I cannot choose but write. Eve. Oliver Herford. OBAL

O dearest, canst thou tell me why. Warum sind denn die Rosen so blass. Heinrich Heine. AWP, *tr.* by Richard Garnett

O Dearest Dread, most glorious King. Prayer unto Christ the Judge of the World, A. Michael Wigglesworth. SCAP

O Death. Bible, Apocrypha. TrJP *Fr.* Ecclesiasticus.

O Death in Life, the days that are no more! (LL) Tennyson. AWP; CABP; EBVV; GTBS-P; HAP; NAEL-5v2; NAEL-6v2; NIL-7; NIP-4; NOBE; NoP-4; OxAEP-2; OxBEV; PoE; PoPoPo; SCGP; TFi; TreFP; UnPo *Fr.* Princess, The.

O Death, Rock Me Asleep. George Boleyn. WPE (Death.) SCGP

O death, thy certainty is such. Henry Luttrell. FaBoEE

O Death! where is thy Sting? (LL) Ode: The Dying Christian to His Soul. Pope. ChIV-2; SacPr

O Death! Why dost thou steal the great. In Memoriam Frederick Douglass. Eloise Bibb. CBWP-4

O deep, creating Light. Gordon Bottomley. MoBrPo Fr. Suilven and the Eagle.

O Deep of Heaven, 'tis thou alone art boundless. Night Sky, The. G. D. Roberts. GSo

O Deep River, O Dark Stream. Deep River. Eugène Marais. PeSAV, tr. by Hugh Finn

O depth sufficient to desire. Adam's Song to Heaven. Edgar Bowers. CoAmPo

O Did you ever hear of the brave Earl Brand. Earl Brand. Unknown. OxBB

O Dieu, Purifiez nos coeurs! Night Litany. Ezra Pound. TCAPo

O, dim, forsaken mirror! Mirror in the Deserted Hall, The. Felicia Dorothea Hemans. NOBRP

O Dirty Bird Yr Gizzard's Too Big & Full of Sand. James Koller. PoM

O distant, distant; deep unapproachable; receive always. Distant, The. Yannis Ritsos. VCWP, tr. by Edmund Keeley

O Divine Mother. Prayer to the Divine Mother, A. Andrew Harvey. HW

O do, Lord, remember me! Lord, Remember Me! Unknown. APN-2

O do not grieve, Dear Heart, nor shed a tear. Margaret Lucas Cavendish, Duchess of Newcastle. EnLoPo

O do support him, do support the land! In Praise of Austria. Franz Grillparzer. AuPH, tr. by Lowell A. Bangerter

O do you in fedora or trenchcoat bear record. Fragmented Address to the FBI. Diane Di Prima. BB

O don't, don't ever ask me for alms. Death and the Plowman. Sidney Keyes. OxBTC

O Donald! Ye Are Just the Man. Susanna Blamire. LW

O Donal[l] Oge, if you go across the sea. Donal[l] Oge [or Og]: Grief of a Girl's Heart. Unknown. RB, tr. by Augusta, Lady Gregory

O dream from the blackness. Sappho. BoWoP

O Dream, where art thou now? Emily Jane Brontë. NOBVV

O Dreams, O Destinations. Cecil Day Lewis.
"To travel like a bird, lightly to view." GTBS-P

O dull cold northern sky. Robert Louis Stevenson. EBVV

O Earl Rothes, an thou wert mine. Earl Rothes. Unknown. ESPB

O early one morning I walked out like Agag. Streets of Laredo, The. Louis MacNeice. FaBoWar; OBWP

O Earnest Be. Unknown. AH

O Earth, adore creative power. Creation. Mary Weston Fordham. CBWP-2

O Earth, lie heavily upon her eyes. Rest. Christina Georgina Rossetti. GSo; NOBE; OBEV

O Earth, My Mother! Not Upon Thy Breast. Mary Elizabeth Coleridge. ViWPN

O Earth, Turn! George Johnston. MoCV

O Earth, unhappy planet born to die. Edna St. Vincent Millay. HeIP-4 Fr. Epitaph for the Race of Man.

O English mother, in the ruddy glow. In Snow. William Allingham. OxBSo

O Englishwoman on the Pincian. Thomas Edward Brown. NOBVV Fr. Roman Women.

O'er a dark field I held my dubious way. Philip Freneau. TCAPo Fr. House of Night, The.

O'er a small suburban borough. Domineering Eagle and the Inventive Bratling, The. Guy Wetmore Carryl. OBAL

O'er all miracles preceding / His inestimable death. (LL) Christopher Smart. NOCV; NOEC Fr. Hymns and Spiritual Songs for the Fasts and Festivals of the Church of England.

O'er all the hill-tops. Goethe. AWP, tr. by Robert Bly Fr. Wanderer's Night-Songs.

O'er Continent and Ocean. John Haynes Holmes. AH

O'er English dust. A broken heart lies here. (LL) Jacobite's Epitaph, A. Thomas Babington Macaulay, 1st Baron Macaulay. NOBE; OBEV

O'er Esthwaite's lake, serene and still. On Esthwaite Water. Isabella Lickbarrow. RWP

O'er me, alas! thou dost to much prevail. Anne Finch, Countess of Winchilsea. ECWP; NPeEn Fr. Spleen, a Pindaric Poem, The.

O'er the dim breast of ocean's wave. Night. Ann Radcliffe. CenSon

O'er the glad waters of the dark blue sea. Byron. Fr. Corsair, The.

O'er the hills far away, at the birth of the morn. O'er the Hills. Francis Hopkinson. TCAPo

O'er the land of the free, and the home of the brave. (LL) Star-Spangled Banner, The. Francis Scott Key. AiP; HHAm; TAP; UV

O'er the men of Ethiopia she would pour her cornucopia. Husband and Heathen. Sam Walter Foss. OBAL

O'er the Muir Amang the Heather. Jean Glover. RACG

O'er the round throat her little head. Harebell and Pansy. Laurence Binyon. CABP

O'er the rugged mountain's brow. Harry Graham. PeLV Fr. Some Ruthless Rhymes.

O'er the tall cliff that bounds the billowy main. Bids Farewell to Lesbos. Mary Robinson. CenSon; RWP

O'er the warm kettles, and the savoury streams. Mary Leapor. ECWP Fr. Crumble Hall.

O'er this huge town, rife with intestine wars. Manchester by Night. Mathilde Blind. ViWPN

O'er twilight fields the autumnal gossamer? (LL) William Wordsworth. CenSon; OxBSo Fr. River Duddon [A Series of Sonnets], The.

O'er Waiting Harp-Strings of the Mind. Mary Baker Eddy. AH

O'erladen with sad musings, till the tear. Charles Tennyson Turner. CenSon

O Eros of the mountains, of the earth. Eros. "Michael Field." VWP

O Eros, silently smiling one, hear me. Hymn to Eros. Denise Levertov. LW

O'erwhelm'd with sorrow, and sustaining long. Verses Intended to Have Been Prefixed to the Novel of Emmeline, but Then Suppressed. Charlotte Smith. BWW

O Eternal, in thy majesty ride. Jewish Arabic Liturgies. Unknown. TrJP, tr. by Hartwig Hirschfeld

O Eve. That rubricose ball is no apple. Plump fist rubbing rub. O Eve. Rosemary C. Hildebrandt. PuP-23

O, ever dear! thy precious, vital powers. Sonnet 31. Anna Seward. PoBW

O everie living warldly wight. Of Gods Omnipotencie. Alexander Hume. NOCV

O everlasting Kingdom of the Scepter. Unknown. AWP Fr. Book of the Dead.

O evil Angel, set me free! (LL) Clever Woman, A. Mary Elizabeth Coleridge. BrRo; VWP; ViWPN

O excellent sovereigne, most semely to see. Unknown. MiEL

O eye, weep for a rider. Rain to the Tribe. Al-Khansa. BoWoP, tr. by Willis Barnstone and Tony Nawfal

O eyes clear with beauty, O tender gaze. Sonnet 11. Louise Labé. BoWoP, tr. by Willis Barnstone

O faithful eyes, day after day as I see and know you—unswerving faithful and beautiful—going about your ordinary work unnoticed. Edward Carpenter. CAGL Fr. Towards Democracy.

O faithless world, and thy more faithless part. Poem Written by Sir Henry Wotton, in His Youth, A. Sir Henry Wotton. NoSic

O false and treacherous Probability. Fulke Greville, 1st Baron Brooke. SacPr Fr. Caelica.

O famished Prodigal, in vain. Echo. John Banister Tabb. APN-2

O fan of white silk. Fan-Piece, for Her Imperial Lord. Ezra Pound. APT-1

O far-off rose of long ago. Far-Off Rose, A. Josephine Preston Peabody. TCAPo

O! farewell, my country—my kindred—my lover. Exile of Erin, The. Unknown. NOBAu

O farther, farther, farther sail! (LL) Walt Whitman. APN-1; NAAL-2v1; NCAP

O Father, give the spirit power to climb. Boethius. MLL Fr. Consolation of Philosophy, The ("De Consolacione Philosophie").

"O Father, I acknowledge, " Job replied. George Sandys. ChIV-1 Fr. Paraphrase Upon Job, A.

O favorable spirit, propitious guest. John Milton. NOCV Fr. Paradise Lost.

O finicky cat. Richard Wright. APT-2

O first created and creating source. Ode to the Sea. Howard Baker. OxBA

O Flame of Living Love. Saint John of the Cross. AWP, tr. by Arthur Symons

O flea! whatever you do. Issa. EH, tr. by Robert Hass

O fleece, billowing even down the neck! Head of Hair. Charles Baudelaire. SxFrPo, tr. by James McGowan

O fleece, that down the neck waves to the nape! Her Hair. Charles Baudelaire. NAWM-7v2, tr. by Doreen Bell

O Florida, Venereal Soil. Wallace Stevens. TCAPo

O flower fawn. Five Flower World Variations. Unknown. STP, tr. by Jerome Rothenberg

O flowers of Mekhmekh, give us peace! Unknown. BoWoP

O Flowery Mountain slopes. On the Slope of Hua Mountain. Unknown. WoPoe, tr. by Chung Ling and Kenneth Rexroth

O fly away home fly away. (LL) O Daedalus, Fly Away Home. Robert Earl Hayden. HAP; NAAAL

O foolish tears, go back! In Vain. Adah Isaacs Menken. CBWP-1

O foolish wisdom sought in books! Longing. Ina Coolbrith. SWaP

O foot, O leg, O thighs for which I rightly died. Philodemus. HePo Fr. Epigrams.

O for a ferryman to steer my yearning. Home-Sickness. Hedwig Lachmann. TrJP, tr. by Jethro Bithell

O for a muse of fire, a sack of dough. Sonnet with a Different Letter at the End of Every Line. George Starbuck. OBAL

O for a Muse of fire, that would ascend. William Shakespeare. OxAEP-1; SCV *Fr.* King Henry V.

O for a toe, such as the funeral pyre. Sir Thomas Browne. FaBoEE

O for doors to be open and an invite with gilded edges. W. H. Auden. PeLV *Fr.* Twelve Songs.

O, for my sake do you with Fortune chide. William Shakespeare. OxAEP-1 *Fr.* Sonnets.

O for our upland meads. Shepherd and Shepherdess. Thomas Hennell. FaBoTw

O for ten years, that I may overwhelm. John Keats. NAEL-5v2; NAEL-6v2 *Fr.* Sleep and Poetry.

O for that warning voice which he who saw. John Milton. NAEL-5v1; NAWM-7v1; OxAEP-1 *Fr.* Paradise Lost.

O for the Happy Hour. George Washington Bethune. AH

O for the Wings of a Dove. Euripides. AWP, *tr. by* Gilbert Murray *Fr.* Hippolytus.

O Fortune. *Unknown.* MLL *Fr.* Carmina Burana.

O fountain of Bandusia. Horace. AWP, *tr. by* Eugene Field *Fr.* Odes.

O Frail Adam. Epitaph for Mr. Moses Levy. *Unknown.* TrJP

O Friend! I know not which way I must look. Written in London, September, 1802. William Wordsworth. GTBS-P; SacPr

O friend, understand: the body. Mirabai [*or* Mira Bai]. WPoS

O friends, I am mad. Mirabai [*or* Mira Bai]. WPoS

O friends on this Path. Mirabai [*or* Mira Bai]. WPoS

O, from [*or* O! From] what power hast thou this powerful might. William Shakespeare. OxAEP-1; SCGP *Fr.* Sonnets.

O furrowed plaintive face. Hurrier, The. Harold Monro. MoBrPo

O Future bards. Prophecy, A. Allen Ginsberg. TAP

O gay thrush! (LL) Basil Bunting. HarvBoo; WoPoe

O generation of the thoroughly smug / and thoroughly uncomfortable. Salutation. Ezra Pound. HeIP-4; MoAmPo; NOBA; OxBA; TAP; VGW

O gentle, gentle land. Night Sowing. David Campbell. CBAP

O Gentle Ships. Meleager. AWP, *tr. by* Andrew Lang

O gentle Sleep, come, wave thine opiate wing. On Dreams, October 15, 1782. Sir Samuel Egerton Brydges. CenSon; Son

O gentle Sleep! do they belong to thee. To Sleep. William Wordsworth. Son

O give me a home where the buffalo roam. *Unknown.* *See* Oh give me a home where the buffalo roam

O give thanks unto the Lord; for he is good: because his mercy endureth for ever. Bible, *O.T.* TrJP *Fr.* Psalms.

O give thanks unto the Lord; for he is good [*or* gracious]: for his mercy endureth for ever. Bible, *O.T.* AWP *Fr.* Psalms.

O Give yee thanks unto the Lord. Bible, *O.T.* SCAP *Fr.* Bay Psalm Book, The.

O Glorious Christ of God; I live. Cotton Mather. SCAP

O glorious dump, how shall I sing your praise! Dump, The. Yelena [*or* Elena] Shwarts [*or* Shvarts]. ItGoST, *tr. by* Catriona Kelly and Michael Molnar

O God. Else Lasker-Schüler. BBASP, *tr. by* Robert P. Newton

O God, above the Drifting Years. John Wright Buckham. AH

O God, Accept the Sacred Hour. Samuel Gilman. AH

O God, for as much as without Thee. Ronald Arbuthnott Knox. PeLi

O God, Great Father, Lord, and King. E. Embree Hoss. AH

O God, I Cried, No Dark Disguise. Edna St. Vincent Millay. AH

O God, / I have bound myself to you to the exclusion of all else. Kwaja Abdullah Ansari. BBASP, *tr. by* Wheeler M. Thackston *Fr.* Intimate Conversations with God.

O God, in the dream the terrible horse began. Dream, The. Louise Bogan. InPK-6; MoAmPo; NALW; NoAM

O God, in Whom the Flow of Days. Donald Campbell Babcock. AH

O God, in Whose Great Purpose. James G. Gilkey. AH

O God, my dream! I dreamed that you were dead. On the Threshold. Amy Levy. LW; NOBVV

O God! O Montreal! Samuel Butler (1835–1902). OBSV; OxBoLi; PeLV

O God, O Venus, O Mercury, patron of thieves. Lake Isle, The. Ezra Pound. OBCoV; OxBSP

O God of Hosts, thine Ear incline. Hymn. *Unknown.* NOBRP

O God of love unbounded! Lord supreme! Prayer to God. "Placido." TTY, *tr. by* Raoul Abdul

O God of Mercy. God of Mercy. Kadya Molodovsky [*or* Molodowsky]. WPOW, *tr. by* Irving Howe

O God of My Salvation, Hear. Joel Barlow. AH

O god of spring forgive me. Pete Winslow. CLPP

O God of Stars and Distant Space. John Franzen. AH

O God of Youth. Bates G. Burt. AH

O God, our loving Father, help us. Christmas Prayer, A. Robert Louis Stevenson. TrCP

O God, Send Men. Elizabeth Burrowes. AH

O God that art the only hope of the world. Prayer of the Venerable Bede, The. Venerable Bede. MLL, *tr. by* Helen Waddell

O God, though Countless Worlds of Light. James D. Knowles. AH

O God, when You send for me, let it be. Prayer to Go to Paradise with the Asses. Francis Jammes. AWP, *tr. by* Jethro Bithell

O God, where do they tend—these struggling aims? Robert Browning. SacPr *Fr.* Pauline [*or* Pauline; A Fragment of a Confession].

O God Whose Presence Glows in All. Nathaniel Langdon Frothingham. AH

O God! whose thunder shakes the sky. Resignation. Thomas Chatterton. TrCP

O God, why hast thou thus. Bible, *O.T.* BASC; NOCV, *tr. by* Mary Sidney Herbert, Countess of Pembroke *Fr.* Psalms.

O Goddess! hear these tuneless numbers, wrung. Ode to Psyche. John Keats. FHYEP; NAEL-5v2; NAEL-6v2; NOBE; NOBRP; NoP-4; OBEV; OxAEP-2; PoE; TFi; TOF

O Gods, it is terrible to be buried this way. Shades of the Newly Buried Complain to the Gods, The. *Unknown.* WoPoe, *tr. by* John S. Major

O gold, a deep contempt for you I own. Quatrain. Ilyas Farhat. MAP, *tr. by* John Heath-Stubbs and Salma Khadra Jayyusi

O golden child the world will kill and eat. (LL) Mary's Song. Sylvia Plath. ChIV-2; FaBoMo; FaBoWP

O Golden Fleece she is where she lies tonight. George Barker. MoBrPo *Fr.* Secular Elegies.

O golden-tongued Romance with serene lute! On Sitting Down to Read "King Lear" Once Again. John Keats. CABP; EBEV; GSo; NAEL-5v2; NAEL-6v2; NoP-4; PoPoPo

O Gongyla, my darling rose. Sappho. BoWoP, *tr. by* Willis Barnstone

O good Lord Judge, and sweet Lord Judge. Maid Freed from the Gallows, The. *Unknown.* AWP; ESPB

O! good my lord, tax not so bad a voice. William Shakespeare. OxAEP-1 *Fr.* Much Ado about Nothing.

O good sun. *Unknown.* AWP, *tr. by* Constance Lindsay Skinner *Fr.* Three Songs from the Haida.

O goodly golden chaine, wherewith yfere. Edmund Spenser. FHYEP *Fr.* Faerie Queene, The.

O Gracious Father of Mankind. Henry Hallam Tweedy. AH

O Gracious Jesus, Blessed Lord! Andrew Fowler. AH

O grandest of the Angels, and most wise. Litany to Satan. Charles Baudelaire. AWP, *tr. by* James Elroy Flecker

O grant me darkness! Let no gleam. But in that Sleep of Death what Dreams may Come? Mary Elizabeth Coleridge. VWP

O grant that like to Peter I. John Keats. ChIV-2 *Fr.* Three Undated Fragments.

O grasses wet with dew, yellow fallen leaves. Glimpse, A. Frances Darwin Cornford. OBMV

O Great Buddha. Kikaku. SoOfWa, *tr. by* Sam Hamill

O Great Mary. Litany to Our Lady. Eugene O'Curry. HW

O Great Queen Whom I idolize. Limerick. Jeffery Littman. PeLi

O great tone-master! low thy massive head. Beethoven. Henrietta Cordelia Ray. CBWP-3

O green, beneath which all of them shall drown! (LL) Kenneth Koch. NNaP; NeAP

O' gude Braid Claith. (LL) Braid Claith. Robert Fergusson. NOEC; OxBEV; OxBS

O guide my judgment and my taste. Christopher Smart. ChIV-1; NOCV *Fr.* Hymns for the Amusement of Children.

O had I known that it ends like this. Boris Leonidovich Pasternak. TCRP

O Hada Cibernetica. Carlos German Belli.
  "Why have they moved me." TCLAP, *tr. by* Maureen Ahern and David Tipton

O Hand of Fire / gatherest. (LL) Hart Crane. MoAmPo; NAAL-5; OxBA *Fr.* Bridge, The.

O handsome chestnut eyes, evasive gaze. Sonnet 2. Louise Labé. BoWoP, *tr. by* Willis Barnstone

O happy hour. *Unknown.* MLL *Fr.* Carmina Burana.

O happy [*or* happie] dames, that may embrace. Seafarer, The. Henry Howard, Earl of Surrey. NPeEn; NoSic; SCGP

O Happy people, where good princes reign. Guillaume de Salluste Du Bartas. NoSic, *tr. by* Joshua Sylvester *Fr.* Divine Weeks and Works, The.

O happy Thames, that didst my Stella bear. Sir Philip Sidney. OxAEP-1 *Fr.* Astrophil and Stella.

O happy Tithon! if thou know'st thy harp. Sir William Alexander, Earl of Stirling. OBEV *Fr.* Aurora.

O Hark to the Herald. Eleazar ben Kalir. TrJP, *tr. by* Israel Zangwill

O Harry Heine, curses be. Translator to Translated. Ezra Pound. FaBoEE

O, Harry! thou hast robb'd me of my youth. William Shakespeare. OxAEP-1 *Fr.* King Henry IV, Pt. I.

O hatefull hellish snake, what furie furst. Edmund Spenser. NAEL-6v1; NAEL-7v1 *Fr.* Faerie Queene, The.

O have ye na heard o' the fause Sakelde? Kinmont Willie. *Unknown.* ESPB; IBB; OxBB

O, have you seen the leper healed. Healing of the Leper, The. Vernon Watkins. FaBoTw

O have you seen the Stratton flood. Stratton Water. Dante Gabriel Rossetti. OxBB

O he is a rest that requires. Anna Trapnell. PBRV *Fr.* Cry of a Stone, The.

O, he who flashed above the moon afar. "Georgy [*or* Georgii] Avdeievich Rayevsky [*or* Raevskii]." TCRP

O Hear My Prayer, Lord. John Craig. AH

O hear the message of the warning voice. To Austria. Erika Mitterer. AuPH, *tr. by* Lowell A. Bangerter

O heard ye of a silly Harper. Lochmaben Harper, The. *Unknown.* OxBB

O heard ye of Sir James the Rose. Sir James the Rose. *Unknown.* ESPB

O hearken and hear, and I will you tell. Friar in the Well. *Unknown.* ESPB

O heart green acre sown with salt. Upward Look, An. James Merrill. PoPoPo

O heart, small urn. "H. D." APT-1 *Fr.* Walls Do Not Fall, The.

O Heart! the equal poise of love's both parts. Richard Crashaw. GeHe *Fr.* Flaming Heart, The.

O Heaven Indulge. Stephen Tilden. AH

O heavenly color, London town. November Blue. Alice Thompson Meynell. MoBrPo

O Heavens! *Unknown.* ChinPo, *tr. by* Yip Wai-lim

O Heavens! O Earth! heer I must pause a space. Sir William Mure. PBRV *Fr.* Cry of Blood, and of a Broken Covenant, The.

O Heavy Step of Slow Monotony. Ernst Toller. TrJP, *tr. by* Ashley Dukes

O Hector, thou wert rooted in my heart. Homer. OBVE, *tr. by* William Congreve *Fr.* Iliad, The.

O Hell-born Tyranny! how blest the land. To Tyranny. John Thelwall. CenSon

O Hell, what do mine eyes. Gary Snyder. *See* Oh hell, what do mine eyes

O help us, Lord! Each hour of need. Henry Hart Milman. SacPr

O helpless few in my country. Ezra Pound. MoAmPo; NOBA; NoAM; OxBA *Fr.* Lustra.

O here it is! And there it is! Mervyn Laurence Peake. NOxBChV

"O Hero, Hero!" thus he cried full oft. Christopher Marlowe. EroLit *Fr.* Hero and Leander.

O Hesperus! thou bringest all good things. Byron. AWP *Fr.* Don Juan.

O hideous little bat, the size of snot. Fly, The. Karl Shapiro. NoAM; SoSe-8

O Holy City Seen of John. Walter Russell Bowie. AH

O Holy Ghost. Stephen Langton. MLL

O Holy Ghost, O faithful Paraclete. For Whitsuntide. Hildebert. MLL, *tr. by* Helen Waddell

O Holy Ghost, whose temple I. John Donne. NOCV *Fr.* Litany, A.

O Holy, Holy, Holy, Lord. James Wallis Eastburn. AH

O holy Justice! Hiding your puissance. Invocation. Benedek Virág. IQMS, *tr. by* Watson Kirkconnell

O Holy Mother, thou who still dost send. At the Tomb of Rachel. "Yehoash." TrJP, *tr. by* Isidore Goldstick

O holy talk show host. Wish Foundation, The. Carol Muske. PBCAP

O holy virgin! clad in purest white. To Morning. William Blake. OxAEP-2

O Holy Water. Margot Ruddock. OBMV

O / Holy / Wood. Sister Mary Madeleva. CRP

O Honored Hera, who often descending from heaven. Nossis. SaLy, *tr. by* Diane Rayor

O Hope! thou soother sweet of human woes! To Hope. Charlotte Smith. RWP

O house, o sloping field, o poplar trees whose tall arms salute. Elaine Randell. Oth *Fr.* Snoad Hill Poems, The.

O! How can Love exulting Reason quell! Contemns its Power. Mary Robinson. CenSon

O how canst thou renounce the boundless store. James Beattie. NOEC *Fr.* Minstrel, The.

O, how I faint when I of you do write. William Shakespeare. CAGL; OxAEP-1 *Fr.* Sonnets.

O how much I would like—. Osip Emilevich Mandelstam [*or* Mandelshtam]. PFTM-1

O how my mind. Confusion. Christopher Hervey. UV

O! How shall I picture, in delicate strain. Sir George Dallas. NOEC *Fr.* India Guide, The; or, Journal of a Voyage to the East Indies in 1780.

O, how sick and weary I. In a Myrtle [*or* Mirtle] Shade. William Blake. ChIV-1

O how that glittering taketh me! (LL) Upon Julia's Clothes. Robert Herrick. AWP; BASC; BeJo; CABP; CaPo; CavPo; ClHu; EBEV; EnLoPo; GTBS-P; HAP; HeIP-4; NAEL-5v1; NAEL-6v1; NAEL-7v1; NBLV; NIL-7; NIP-4; NOBE; NOSC; NoP-4; OBEV; OxAEP-1; OxBEV; OxBSP; PAI; PeLV; PoE; PoPoPo; SCGP; TFi; TPTP; TTTS; UV; WeW-3; WoPoe

O hundred-towered Prague. City With Towers. Vítězslau Nezval. PFTM-1

O, hungry heart. Heart-Hungry. Josephine D. Henderson Heard. CBWP-4

O! hush thee, my darling, sleep soundly my son. Lullaby. *Unknown.* TrJP, *tr. by* Alice Lucas

O'Hussey's Ode to the Maguire. Eochadh [*or* Eochy] O'Hussey [*or* O'Heughusa]. CABP; NOIV, *tr. by* James Clarence Mangan (Ode to the Maguire.) BIrV

O hydrangea. Bairyu. JDP, *tr. by* Yoel Hoffmann

O! I could laugh to hear the midnight wind. Charles Lamb. CenSon

O! I do love thee, meek Simplicity! Samuel Taylor Coleridge. CenSon *Fr.* Sonnets Attempted in the Manner of Contemporary Writers.

O I forbid you, maidens a' [*or* all]. Tam Lin. *Unknown.* ESPB; NOBE; OBEV; OBNV; OxBB; OxBS

O ha'e Silence left. (LL) Hugh MacDiarmid. NAEL-5v2; NAEL-6v2 *Fr.* Drunk Man Looks at the Thistle, A.

O I had a future. I Had a Future. Patrick Kavanagh. BIrV; NoAM

O, I hae come from far away. Witch's Ballad, The. William Bell Scott. NOBVV; OBEV; PeVV; RACG

O I hae tint my rosy cheek. *Unknown.* FaBoVe

O, I have been wounded. Battle of Inverlochy, The. *Unknown.* EMWP

O I'm a jolly old cowboy. *Unknown.* CA

O I'm a professional. Sung in a Graveyard. Anna Wickham. ItWoWo

O I'm off to Hullaboola where the climate's never cooler. Folk Song. Bruce Beaver. OBCoV

O, I remember you. Removal of Our Village, KwaBhanya, The. Mbuyiseni Oswald Mtshali. PeSAV, *tr. by* the author

O I repented, wore my pious cloak. Sadi [*or* Saadi *or* Sa'di]. WoPoe, *tr. by* Dick Davis

O, I wad like to ken—to the beggar-wife says I. Spaewife, The. Robert Louis Stevenson. OxBS

O I went into the stable. Our Goodman. *Unknown.* ESPB

O I will sing to you a sang. Clerk's Twa Sons o Owsenford, The. *Unknown.* ESPB

O, I yearn to go back to the Cam! Limerick. E. O. Parrott. PeLi

O Ihu, lett me neuer forgett thy byttur passion. For Thy Sake Let the World Call Me Fool. *Unknown.* SacPr

O Immaculate Virgin. Conversation of a Private and the Virgin. Nikolai Ivanovich Glazkov. TCRP, *tr. by* Daniel Weissbort

O, insatiable monster! Could'st thou not. Requiem. Mary Weston Fordham. CBWP-2

O interminable desires, O futile hope. Sonnet 3. Louise Labé. BoWoP, *tr. by* Willis Barnstone

O is it Love or is it Fame. Oh, Is It Love? Amy Levy. ViWPN

O Isis, Mother of God, to thee I pray! Prayer to Isis. Christina Walsh. BrRo

O islets green, Nature's immortal gems. Hymn to the Thousand Islands. Henrietta Cordelia Ray. CBWP-3

O it fell out upon a day. Laird o Drum, The. *Unknown.* ESPB

O, it is hard to work for God. Right Must Win, The. Frederick William Faber. PWR

O! it is pleasant, with a heart at ease. Fancy in Nubibus. Samuel Taylor Coleridge. CenSon

O it's best to be a total boor. David [*or* Daibhi][*or* Daithi] O'Bruadair [*or* Ó Bruadair]. NOIV

O it's up in the Highlands, and along the sweet Tay. Bonnie James Campbell. *Unknown.* ESPB

O Italy, I see the lonely towers. To Italy. Giacomo Leopardi. AWP, *tr. by* Romilda Rendel

O Jean, my Jean, when the bell ca's the congregation. Tam i' the Kirk. Violet Jacob. NePenScot

O Jellon Grame sat in Silver Wood. Jellon Grame. *Unknown.* EBEV; ESPB; OxBB

O Jenny dear, lay by your pride. O Jenny Dear. Susanna Blamire. ECWP

O Jenny, don't sobby! vor I shall be true. Zong, A. William Barnes. BoLoP

O Jesus Christ, True Light of Day. John F. Ernst. AH

O Jesus, drink of me. (LL) Better Resurrection, A. Christina Georgina Rossetti. NOBVV; VWP; ViWPN

O Jesus, Hasbrouck, am I drunk or dead? (LL) Hasbrouck and the Rose. Howard Phelps Putnam. APT-2; OxBA

O Jesus, My Savior, I Know Thou Art Mine. Caleb J. Taylor. AH

O Johney was as brave a knight. Johnie Scot. *Unknown.* ESPB

O Jolly brick, with kindly wrinkled face. Holland Brick, A. Wallace Bruce. VerBaPo

O, Jordan bank was a great old bank! One More River. *Unknown.* APN-2

O joy of creation. What the Bullet Sang. Bret Harte. APN-2; OBEV

O joy, too high for my low style to show. Sir Philip Sidney. NAEL-5v1; NAEL-6v1; NAEL-7v1; OxAEP-1 *Fr.* Astrophil and Stella.

O keen pellucid air! nothing can lurk. Brilliant Day, A. Charles Tennyson Turner. NOBVV

O Keeper of the Sacred Key. Forceythe Willson. APN-2

O Kentucky! my parents were driving. Poem of the Forty-eight States, A. Kenneth Koch. NNaP; OBAL

O King, give Angilbert thy rest. Epitaph. Angilbert. MLL, *tr. by* Helen Waddell

O King, I know you gave me poison. Mirabai [*or* Mira Bai]. WPOW, *tr. by* Usha Nilsson

O King of Saints, We Give Thee Praise and Glory. Mary A. Thomson. AH

O King of terrors. To Death. Anne Finch, Countess of Winchilsea. NoP-4

O King of the Friday. *Unknown*. BIrV

O king, whose greatness none can comprehend. William Drummond, of Hawthornden. SacPr *Fr.* Hymn to the Fairest Fair, A.

O kiss, which dost those ruddy gems impart. Sir Philip Sidney. NAEL-5v1; NAEL-6v1; NAEL-7v1; OxBSo; Son *Fr.* Astrophil and Stella.

O knit me, that am crumbled dust! the heape. Distraction. Henry Vaughan. GeHe

O Lady amorous, / Merciless lady. Canzonetta: A Bitter Song to His Lady. Pier Moronelli da Fiorenza. AWP; EaItPo; OBVE, *tr. by* Dante Gabriel Rossetti

O lady full of guile. Geoffrey Keating. NOIV

O lady of all truths bright light going forth. Enheduanna. WPOW *Fr.* Inanna Exalted.

O Lady, rock never your young son young. Young Hunting. *Unknown*. ESPB; OxBB

O ladyis fair of Troy and Grece, attend. Robert Henryson. NPeEn *Fr.* Testament of Cresseid, The.

O Lamb Give Me My Salt. *Unknown*. PBA, *tr. by* Dennis C. Osadebay

O land of elegance, where every grace. Farewell to France. Sarah Hamilton. CenSon

O lapwing, thou fliest around the heath. O Lapwing! William Blake. FaBoEE

O, Lay Thy Hand in Mine, Dear! Gerald Massey. EBVV

O leafy yellowness you create for me. October. Patrick Kavanagh. CIP-2; GTBS-P

O'Leary was a poet—for a while. Shadrach O'Leary. Edwin Arlington Robinson. APT-1

O leave me easy, leave me alone. (LL) Libertine, The. Louis MacNeice. ModIr; NoAM

O Leerie, see a little child and nod to him to-night! (LL) Lamplighter, The. Robert Louis Stevenson. EBVV; ITBLP; NePenScot

O! Lest the world should task you to recite. William Shakespeare. OxAEP-1 *Fr.* Sonnets.

O let him whose sorrow. H. S. Oswald. SacPr, *tr. by* F. E. Cox

O let me be in loving nice. Punctilio. Mary Elizabeth Coleridge. OBEV; PoBW

O let me, Lady, silence calumny. Protestation. Bertrans [*or* Bertran *or* Bertrand] de Born. WoPoe, *tr. by* John Peale Bishop

O let me soar on steadfast wing. Prayer. Dennis Brutus. AF

O let the solid ground. Tennyson. NAEL-5v2; NAEL-6v2; NOBVV *Fr.* Maud [A Monodrama].

O lett it be for ever told. Jane Hawkins. EMWP

O Liberty, God-gifted. To the Bartholdi Statue. Ambrose Bierce. APN-2

O Life That Maketh All Things New. Samuel Longfellow. AH

O life! what letts thee from a quicke decease? I Dye Alive. Robert Southwell. SacPr

O Life, who art thou that with scarcely scanned. Life Plastic. "Michael Field." VWP

O Light Invisible, we praise Thee! T. S. Eliot. SacPr *Fr.* Rock, The.

O Light, 'tis I, who from death's other shores. Helen. Paul Valéry. OBVE

O lips full of lust and of laughter. Algernon Charles Swinburne. UV *Fr.* Dolores.

O, listen for a moment, lads, and hear me tell my tale. Jim Jones. *Unknown*. CBAP

O listen, gude peopell, to my tale. Laird o' Logie, The. *Unknown*. ESPB

O little broken doll, dropped in the well. Broken Doll, The. Nuala Ni Dhomhnaill. BiHa; ModIr, *tr. by* John Montague

O Little Brother. Tree. Zulaykha Abu-Risha. PoArWo, *tr. by* Clarissa C. Burt

O little friend, your nose is ready; you sniff. Dog. Harold Monro. MoBrPo

O little Land of lapping seas. Promised Land, The. Jessie E. Sampter. TrJP

O little mouse, so frightened of each sound. O Pity Our Small Size. Benjamin Rosenbaum. TrJP

O little one, this longing is the pits. Marilyn Hacker. EmeKit

O Little Town of Bethlehem. Phillips Brooks. AH; APN-2; ChrPo; SacPr; TCAPo

O Living Always, Always Dying. Walt Whitman. NOBA

O Living Flame of Love. Saint John of the Cross. SpanPo, *tr. by* Stephen Stepanchev

O living will that shalt endure. Tennyson. EBVV; NAEL-6v2 *Fr.* In Memoriam A. H. H.

O lonely workman, standing there. Thomas Hardy. NoAM *Fr.* Satires of Circumstance in Fifteen Glimpses.

O look not, lady, with disdain! Tooth, The. Rebekah Carmichael. ECWP

O Lord All-Merciful, be merciful to me. (LL) Before the Beginning. Christina Georgina Rossetti. InvLi; SacPr

O Lord, Almighty God. *Unknown*. AH

O Lord, Bow Down Thine Ear. Thomas Prince. AH

O Lord, Help Me to Live Through This Night. Osip Emilevich Mandelstam [*or* Mandelshtam]. WoPoe, *tr. by* Clarence Brown and W. S. Merwin

O Lord, How Lovely Is the Place. *Unknown*. AH

O Lord I shall be whole in deed. Jeremie .17. Bible, Apocrypha. ChIV-1

O, Lord / If in life eternal. "Ping Hsin." WPOW *Fr.* Spring Waters.

O Lord in me there lieth nought. Bible, *O.T.* PEW, *tr. by* Mary Sidney Herbert, Countess of Pembroke *Fr.* Psalms.

O Lord, in your courtesy. Praise of Diseases. Jacopone da Todi. WoPoe, *tr. by* L. R. Lind

O Lord my God, make thou my hart repentant for to be. Necessarie Praier in Meeter Against Vices, A. Frances Manners, Lady Abergavenny Nevill. EMWP

O Lord! my heart is sick. Eternity of God, The. Frederick William Faber. SacPr

O Lord my sinne doth over-charge thy brest. Sinnes Heavie Loade. Robert Southwell. ESCV

O Lord of Life. Washington Gladden. AH

O Lord of Light! A Mystic Sage Returns to Realms of Eternity! Askia Muhammad Touré. SeSe; SpirFl

O Lord, our God, Thy mighty hand. Peace Hymn of the Republic. Henry Van Dyke. AH

O Lord our Lord, how excellent is thy name in all the earth! Bible, *O.T.* AWP; NAWM-5v1 *Fr.* Psalms.

O Lord, our Sovereign. Bible, *O.T.* InvLi, *tr. by* New Revised Standard Version *Fr.* Psalms.

O Lord, praise be. Giotto. Rafael Alberti. WoPoe, *tr. by* Carolyn Tipton

O Lord, Save We Beseech Thee. *Unknown*. TrJP

O Lord, since we have feasted thus. Robert Burns. FaBoEE *Fr.* Graces————at the Globe Tavern.

O Lord, sir, let me live, or let me see my death! William Shakespeare. OxAEP-1 *Fr.* All's Well That Ends Well.

O Lord, That Art My God and King. John Craig. AH

O Lord, the hard-won miles. Prayer, A: "O Lord, the hard-won miles." Paul Laurence Dunbar. SacPr

O Lord, Thou Hast Been to the Land. *Unknown*. AH

O Lord, Thou Hast Enticed Me. Bible, *O.T.* TrJP *Fr.* Jeremiah.

O Lord thou seest my wrongs abound. Ode XV. Thomas Stanley. ChIV-1

O Lord, turn not away thy face. Lamentation, The. John Marckant. AH; SacPr

O Lord two things I thee require. Proverb, XXX. John Hall. ChIV-1

O Lord, we come this morning. Listen, Lord—[a Prayer]. James Weldon Johnson. BPo

O Lord, with whom subduer Love. Anacreon. SaLy, *tr. by* Diane Rayor

O Lord, you know my inmost hope and thought. My Inmost Hope. Sarah Copia Sullam. TrJP

O love, be fed with apples while you may. Sick Love. Robert Graves. BoLoP; EBEV; GTBS-P; HAP; HarvBoo; NOBE; NPeEn; OxAEP-2

O Love Divine, That Stooped to Share. Oliver Wendell Holmes. AH *Fr.* Professor at the Breakfast Table, The.

O Love, how thou art tired out with rhyme! Of the Theme of Love. Margaret Lucas Cavendish, Duchess of Newcastle. OxBSP

O love, I never, never thought. Cancion. Juan II, of Castile. AWP, *tr. by* George Ticknor

O Love in Me. Robert Graves. *See* Sick Love

O, love, in your sweet name enough. Anne Finch (b. 1908). FaBoTw *Fr.* Essay on Marriage.

O Love, Love, Love! O withering might! Fatima. Tennyson. UnPo

O Love, O thou that, for my fealty. Sonnet: To Love, In Great Bitterness. Cino da Pistoia. AWP, *tr. by* Dante Gabriel Rossetti

O Love of God, how strong and true. Hymn. Horatius Bonar. SacPr

O Love That Lights the Eastern Sky. Louis FitzGerald Benson. AH

O Love! that stronger art than wine. Aphra Behn. *See* Oh! Love, that stronger art than wine

O Love That Wilt Not Let Me Go. George Matheson. SacPr

O love, the interest itself in thoughtless heaven. Prologue. W. H. Auden. EBEV; FaBoMo

O love, what hours were thine and mine. Daisy, The. Tennyson. EnLoPo; NOBVV

"O love, / where are you / leading / me now?" (LL) Kore. Robert Creeley. NAAL-5; RaBo

O Love, who all this while hast urged me on. Canzone: To Love and to His Lady. Guido Delle Colonne. AWP; EaItPo, *tr. by* Dante Gabriel Rossetti

O loveliest daughter of Hsieh. Elegy. Yuan Chen. CrYelRi; ErotSp, *tr. by* Sam Hamill

O, loveliest throat of all sweet throats. Edna St. Vincent Millay. OxBA *Fr.* Memorial to D. C.

O lovely age of gold! Torquato Tasso. AWP; OBVE, *tr. by* Leigh Hunt *Fr.* Aminta.

O lovely April, rich and bright. Song. Gustave Kahn. TrJP, *tr. by* Ludwig Lewisohn

O lovely Galatea, sweeter than. Luis de Góngora y Argote. SpanPo, *tr. by* Frances Fletcher *Fr.* Fable of Polyphemus and Galatea.

O lovely maiden, thou hast drawn my heart. Unhappy Lover, The. Judah Al-Harizi. TrJP, *tr. by* J. Chotzner

O lovely thing. Bible, *O.T.* PEW, *tr. by* Mary Sidney Herbert, Countess of Pembroke *Fr.* Psalms.

O luely, luely cam she in. Tryst [*or* Trysting Place], The. William Soutar. EBEV; NPeEn; NePenScot; OxBS

O Lusty May, with Flora queen! Lusty May. *Unknown.* OBEV

O luxury! Thou curst by Heaven's decree. Oliver Goldsmith. BIrV *Fr.* Deserted Village, The.

O Lyric Love. Winfield Townley Scott. VGW

O Magi of the East, did you continue? Magi in Europe, The. Khalil Hawi. MAP, *tr. by* Diana Der Hovanessian and Lena Jayyusi

O Magnificent and Many. *Unknown.* SuSp, *tr. by* C. H. Wang

O, Magyar, think no German true. O, Magyar. *Unknown.* IQMS, *tr. by* Watson Kirkconnell

O maister deere and fader reverent! Thomas Hoccleve [*or* Occleve]. EBEV *Fr.* De Regimine Principum.

O Maistres Myn. *Unknown.* OxBS

O Maker of the starry world. Boethius. MLL *Fr.* Consolation of Philosophy, The ("De Consolacione Philosophie").

O Man, forgive thy mortal foe. Forgiving. Tennyson. SacPr

O Man! what Inspiration was thy Guide. Glass. Anne Finch, Countess of Winchilsea. OxBEV

O! Mankinde. See! Here, My Heart. *Unknown.* NoP-4

O, Mare Atlanticum. Sleep of My Lions, The. Douglas Livingstone. PeSAV

O Margie, Marge, Dear Margaret. Oswald von Wolkenstein. GePo, *tr. by* J. W. Thomas

O marvel, fruit of fruits, I pause. My Strawberry. Helen Hunt Jackson. SWaP

O Mary, go and call the cattle home. Forgotten Song. John Ashbery. HarvBoo

O Mary Hamilton to the kirk is gane. Mary Hamilton. *Unknown.* NOBE; OxBB

O Mary Mary lying on the wheel. Visitor's Parking. Anne Szumigalski. NOBC

O Master, Let Me Walk with Thee. Washington Gladden. AH; PWR

O Master Masons. Ernst Toller. TrJP, *tr. by* Ashley Dukes

O Master of the heart, whose magic skill. To the Author of Clarissa. Thomas Edwards. Son

O Master-Workman of the Race. Jay Thomas Stocking. AH

O May she comes, and May she goes. Bonny Hind, The. *Unknown.* ESPB

O me, oh my, oh you. Does the Spearmint Lose Its Flavor on the Bedpost Overnight? Billy Rose. OBAL

O-mei Mountain Moon. Li Po. CrYelRi, *tr. by* Sam Hamill

O 'Melia, my dear, this does everything crown! Ruined Maid, The. Thomas Hardy. BoLoP; FaBoVe; HeIP-4; NAEL-5v2; NAEL-6v2; NBLV; NIL-7; NOBL; OxBTC; PAI; PeLV; PeVV; SCV; TFi; TRP

O Meliwa, I come, a messenger of the Beautiful Ones. "Advice" to a Young Poet. Raymond Mazisi Kunene. PeSAV, *tr. by* the author

O melody, what children strange are these. Lines. Ina Coolbrith. SWaP

O memory! that which I gave thee. Flight. Charles Stuart Calverley. OBCoV

O Memory, Thou Fond Deceiver' Oliver Goldsmith. OxBSP *Fr.* Captivity, The.

O men, walk on the hills. Poem. Maxwell Bodenheim. TrJP

O merchants! oh turn to the Lord! Having Prayed for, and Made Much Mention of the Merchants, She Sings the Following Hymn to Them. Anna Trapnell. EMWP

O Merlin in your crystal cave. Merlin. Edwin Muir. FaBoTw; NePenScot; OxBS; RB

O! mestress, why. Distant as the Duchess of Savoy. *Unknown.* MiEL

O Michael, servant of the eternal King. Dedication to St. Michael. Alcuin. MLL, *tr. by* Helen Waddell

O mickle yeuks the keckle doup. Justice to Scotland. *Unknown.* NBLV

O might those sigh[e]s and tear[e]s return[e] again[e]. John Donne. SacPr *Fr.* Holy Sonnets.

O mighty Cæsar! dost thou lie so low? William Shakespeare. OxAEP-1 *Fr.* Julius Caesar.

O mighty-mouthed [*or* mouth'd] inventor of harmonies. Milton [Alcaics]. Tennyson. PeECV

O Mighty Nothing! unto thee. And He Answered Them Nothing. Richard Crashaw. ChIV-2; SacPr

O mightye Muse. George Puttenham. PBRV *Fr.* Partheniades.

O mine own sweet heart. Simon and Susan. *Unknown.* OxBoLi

O miraculous blown country. Mental Traveller's Landfall, The. Chris Wallace-Crabbe. BMAP

O Mistris mine where are you roming? William Shakespeare. *See* O[h] mistress mine, where are you roaming?

O months of blossoming, months of transfigurations. Lilacs and the Roses, The. Louis Aragon. OBWP, *tr. by* Louis MacNeice

O morning glory. Shohi. JDP, *tr. by* Yoel Hoffmann

O Mors! Quam Amara Est Memoria Tua Homini Pacem Habenti In Substantiis Suis. Ernest Christopher Dowson. OBMV

O mortal boy we cannot stop. To the Powers of Desolation. Genevieve Taggard. APT-2

O mortal folk you may behold and see. Stephen Hawes. EBEV; NoSic; OBEV *Fr.* Pastime of Pleasure, The.

O mortal man, that lives by bread. Sally Birkett's Ale. Julius Caesar Ibbetson. FaBoEE

O mortal virtue and immortal sin. Pride. Mary Elizabeth Coleridge. ViWPN

O Most High, you willed to create me a poet and now it is time for me to present a report. Report. Czeslaw Milosz. BodElec

O Mother-heart! when fast the arrows flew. Niobe. Henrietta Cordelia Ray. CBWP-3

O mother, open the window wide. At Last. Elizabeth Siddal. VWP

O Mother Race! to thee I bring. Ode to Ethiopia. Paul Laurence Dunbar. NAAAL

O mother / what have I left out. Allen Ginsberg. BB *Fr.* Kaddish.

O mountain Stream! the Shepherd and his Cot. William Wordsworth. CenSon *Fr.* River Duddon [A Series of Sonnets], The.

O move in me, my darling. Woman's Song. Judith Wright. PAI

O Muse! relate (for you can tell alone). Pope. OxBEV *Fr.* Dunciad, The.

O Muses! I beseech you, fire my heart with song. Ekaterina Urusova. ARWW, *tr. by* Catriona Kelly *Fr.* Heroides: Dedicated to the Muses.

O my agèd Uncle Arly! Edward Lear. *See* O [*or* Oh] my aged uncle Arly!

O my bright star. Star. Pavel Davydovich Kogan. TCRP, *tr. by* Albert C. Todd

O my chief good. Good Friday. George Herbert. GeHe

O my chief good! Passion, The. Henry Vaughan. ESCV

O my coy darling, still. Ode to a Dressmaker's Dummy. Donald Justice. NoAM

O my daughters. Behold This and Always Love It. Meridel Le Sueur. HW

O my dear father! Restoration, hang. William Shakespeare. OxAEP-1 *Fr.* King Lear.

O my deir hert, young Jesus sweit. Balulalow. John James. OBEV

O my eyes where are you, you found a face so wonderful? Old Age. Milán Füst. IQMS, *tr. by* Edwin Morgan

O my fair warrior! William Shakespeare. OxAEP-1 *Fr.* Othello.

O my friends. Mirabai [*or* Mira Bai]. EnlH

O My God Do Not Part Me from Thee. Esrefoğlu. WoPoe, *tr. by* Taner Baybars

O my God do not part me from thee. O My God Do Not Part Me from Thee. Esrefoğlu. WoPoe, *tr. by* Taner Baybars

O, My Heart Is Woe. *Unknown.* ChIV-2

O my Heart, my Mother, my Heart, my Mother. *Unknown.* AWP *Fr.* Book of the Dead.

O my heart's heart, and you who are to me. Christina Georgina Rossetti. OxBSo *Fr.* Monna Innominata.

O my hornbill husband, you have a bad smell. Lament for a Husband. *Unknown.* BoWoP, *tr. by* Don Laycock

O my Hornby and my Barlow long ago! (LL) At Lord's. Francis Thompson. EBVV; OPOU; OxBSP; PeLV

O my insatiable muse. Alfred de Musset. WoPoe, *tr. by* Claire Nicholas White *Fr.* Night in May, A.

O My Invisible Estate. Bruce Smith. Son

O my Joseph, Jacob's son. *Unknown.* ASW *Fr.* Christ 1.

O my lady, the Anunna, the great gods. Inanna and the Anunna. Enheduanna. BoWoP

O my land! O my love! Lament for Banba. Egan [*or* Aodhagán] O'Rahilly [*or* O'Reilly *or* Ó Rathaille]. AWP, *tr. by* James Clarence Mangan

O my Lord. Rabi'a al-Adawiyya. WPoS, *tr. by* Jane Hirshfield

O my Lord, if I worship you from fear of Hell. Rabi'a al-Adawiyya. BoWoP, *tr. by* Willis Barnstone

O my Lord, the stars glitter and eyes of men are closed. Rabi'a al-Adawiyya. BoWoP, *tr. by* Willis Barnstone

O my lost husband! let me ever mourn. Homer. OBVE, *tr. by* William Congreve *Fr.* Iliad, The.

O my love, my wife! William Shakespeare. OxAEP-1 *Fr.* Romeo and Juliet.

O my love's [*or* luve's *or* love is *or* luve is] like a red, red rose. Song. Robert Burns. AWP; BoLoP; GTBS-P; HAP; HeIP-4; ITBLP; NAEL-5v2;

NAEL-6v2; NePenScot; NUL-7; NIP-4; NOBE; NPeEn; OBEV; OxAEP-2; OxBEX; PAI; TF1

O my love / The pretty towns. Kenneth Patchen. VGW

O my love, what gift of mine. Gift. Rabindranath Tagore. AmFaPo, tr. by William Radice

O my lover, blind me. Tired Woman, The. Anna Wickham. MoBrPo

O my Lucasia, let us speak our love. To My Lucasia, in Defence of Declared Friendship. Katherine Philips. MeLP

O my merciful Lord God, you, who are one in three. Jane Vaughan. EMWP

O my mother Nut. Hymn to Nut. Unknown. HW

O my much praised but-not-altogether-satisfactory lady. (LL) Bathtub [or Bath Tub], The. Ezra Pound. NIP-4; TRP; WeW-3

O! my offense is rank, it smells to heaven. William Shakespeare. OxAEP-1 Fr. Hamlet.

O my people, O my people, how to love you delicately? (LL) Song of the African Middle Class. Molara Ogundipe-Leslie. HBAPE; PBMAP

O My Poor Darling. Wilfred Watson. EnLoPo

O my pretty pink frock. Pink Frock, The. Thomas Hardy. OxBSP

O my seven-stringed board. Drawer. Zbigniew Herbert. VCWP, tr. by Czeslaw Miosz and Peter Dale Scott

O my slender boy! (LL) Love Song. Unknown. BoWoP; WoPoe, tr. by Ulli Beier and H. Gaden

O my son, farewell! Song for a Fallen Warrior. Unknown. APN-2, tr. by John Mason Browne

O My songs. Coda. Ezra Pound. NOBA

O, my strong-minded sisters, aspiring to vote. Advice Gratis to Certain Women. Phoebe Cary. APN-2

O My Swallows! Ernst Toller. TrJP, tr. by Ashley Dukes

O Mzingeli son of the illustrious clans. Elegy. Raymond Mazisi Kunene. PBMAP

O Nature! I do not aspire. Nature. Henry David Thoreau. AiP

O Nature, thou to me was cruel. Address to Nature on its Cruelty, An. Ellen Johnston. VWP

O Nature! thou whom I have thought to love. Emily Jane Pfeiffer. ViWPN Fr. To Nature.

O Nectar! O Delicious Stream! Love. Thomas Traherne. GeHe

O New England, thou canst not boast. Word to New England, A. William Bradford. SCAP

O NICIAS, there is no other remedy for love. Theocritus. NoSic

O Night and Dark. Hymn for Morning. Prudentius. MLL, tr. by Helen Waddell

O night betrayed by darkness not its own. (LL) Night, Death, Mississippi. Robert Earl Hayden. LCAP-2; VCAP; VGW

O night cold without your nearness. Love. Elolongue Epanya Yondo. NegPo, tr. by Ellen Conroy Kennedy

O Night! dark Night! wrapped round with Stygian gloom! New Night Thoughts on Death; a Parody. William Whitehead. NOEC

O Night, O sleepless tossing, longing. Night Alone, The. Meleager. AWTN, tr. by Dudley Fitts

O Nightingale, That on Yon Bloomy Spray. John Milton. SCGP (To the Nightingale.) OWoS

O, No, John [or The One Answer]. Unknown. PeLV

O Noble and Most High in Beauty, Thou. Luis de Góngora y Argote. SpanPo, tr. by Ian Fletcher

O nocturnal garden, secret organ. Nocturnal Garden. Nikolai Alekseievich Zabolotsky [or Zabolotskii]. TCRusP, tr. by Kathy Lewis and Bob Perelman

O no[e], more pit[t]y he[e] had sure bestowed [or beestow'd]. (LL) Mary Sidney Wroth, Countess of Montgomery. BASC; BWW Fr. Pamphilia to Amphilanthus.

O none but gods have power their love to hide. Christopher Marlowe. OxAEP-1 Fr. Hero and Leander.

O! nothing earthly save the ray. Edgar Allan Poe. APN-1

O nothing in this corporal earth of man. Francis Thompson. MoBrPo; OBMV; Son Fr. Heart, The.

O Now the Drenched Land Wakes. Kenneth Patchen. CLPP

O now you come in rut. To Frighten a Storm. Gladys Cardiff. CDW

O nymph, compar'd with whose young bloom. To Lady Anne Fitzpatrick, When about Five Years Old, with a Present of Shells, 1772. Horace Walpole, 4th Earl of Orford. NOEC

O Nymphs, did Daphnis, passing by. Pan and the Nymphs. Glaukos. GrAn, tr. by Dudley Fitts

O nymphs that haunt the old Sicilian stream. Lament for Damon. John Milton. MLL, tr. by Helen Waddell

O, one I need to love me. Friends—With a Difference. Mary Elizabeth Coleridge. VWP

O, Open the Door to Me, O! Robert Burns. See Open the Door to Me, Oh!

O [or A or Oh] ye wha are sae guid yoursel. Address to the Unco Guid, or the Rigidly Righteous. Robert Burns. ChIV-1; NOBE; NOCV; OxBEV; OxBS

O! [or Oh] for a bowl of fat canary. John Lyly. NOBE; NoSic Fr. Alexander and Campaspe.

O [or Oh] listen, listen, ladies gay! Sir Walter Scott. GTBS-P Fr. Lay of the Last Minstrel, The.

O [or Oh] lovers' eyes are sharp to see. Maid of Neidpath, The. Sir Walter Scott. GTBS-P

O [or Oh] Mary, at the window be. Mary Morison. Robert Burns. GTBS-P; NePenScot; OBEV; OxBS

O [or Oh] Mary, go and call the cattle home. Charles Kingsley. EBVV; OxAEP-2; TreFP Fr. Alton Locke.

O [or Oh] my aged uncle Arly! Incidents in the Life of My Uncle Arly. Edward Lear. OBCoV; OxBoLi

O [or Oh] my dark Rosaleen. Dark Rosaleen. Owen Roe MacWard. AWP; BIrV; NOIV; OBEV; OxAEP-2, tr. by James Clarence Mangan

O [or Oh], never say that I was false of heart. William Shakespeare. NOBE; OBEV; OxAEP-1 Fr. Sonnets.

O [or Oh] Paddy, dear, and [or an'] did you hear the news that's going [or goin'] 'round? Wearing of [or Wearin' o'] the Green, The. Unknown. AWP; OxBoLi

O [or Oh] rare Harry Parry. Harry Parry. Unknown. OxNR

O [or Oh] silver-throated swan. Dying Swan, The. Thomas Sturge Moore. OBMV

O [or Oh] snatch'd away in beauty's bloom! Elegy. Byron. GTBS-P

O [or Oh] that 'twere possible. Tennyson. BoLoP; NAEL-5v2; NAEL-6v2; NOBE; NOBVV; OBEV; PoE Fr. Maud [A Monodrama].

O [or Oh] the French are on the sea. Shan Van Vocht, The. Unknown. OxBoLi

O [or Oh] there was a woman, and she was a widow. Flowers in the Valley. Unknown. OxBoLi

O [or Oh], to have a little house! Old Woman of the Roads, The. Padraic Colum. MoBrPo; NOIV; OBEV; PoRA

O [or Oh] turn away those cruel eyes. Relapse, The. Thomas Stanley. BeJo; NOSC; OBEV

O [or Oh] Wert Thou in the Cauld Blast. Robert Burns. EBEV; FaBoVe; HAP; NOBE; NPeEn; NePenScot; NoP-4; OxAEP-2; OxBS; PoPoPo; SCGP

O [or Oh] whare hae ye been a' day, my bonnie wee croodlin dow? Lord Randal. Unknown. ESPB

O [or Oh] when our clergy at the dreadful day. On Those That Deserve It. Francis Quarles. NOCV; NOSC

O [or Oh] when the saints go marchin' [or marching] in. When the Saints Go Marchin' [or Marching] In. Unknown. TCAPo

O [or Oh] where are you going? says [or said] Milder to Malder. Cutty Wren, The. Unknown. OxBoLi; UV

O Osbert father Osbert. To Osbert Sitwell. Cyril Connolly. OBCoV

O our Mother the Earth, O our Father the Sky. Song of the Sky Loom. Tewa Oral Tradition. WoPoe, tr. by Herbert J. Spinden

O owl! Issa. EH, tr. by Robert Hass

O Painter of the fruits and flowers. Garden. John Greenleaf Whittier. OBGa

O Paleys [or palace], whylom [or whilom] croune [or crown] of houses all[e]. Geoffrey Chaucer. NOBE; OBEV Fr. Troilus and Criseyde [or Criseide].

O Parcy Reed has Crozer ta'en. Parcy Reed. Unknown. OxBB

O, pardon me, thou bleeding piece of earth. William Shakespeare. OxAEP-1 Fr. Julius Caesar.

O Passenger, pray list and catch. Levelled Churchyard, The. Thomas Hardy. NOBL

O patient shore, that canst not go to meet. Tides. Helen Hunt Jackson. LW

O Peace, O Dove, O shape of the Holy Ghost. To Peace. Richard Watson Dixon. OxAEP-2

O peerless marble marvel! what of grace. Venus of Milo, The. Henrietta Cordelia Ray. CBWP-3

O people who live in the world. Andal. BoWoP

O perfite light, quhilk schaid away. Alexander Hume. NOCV; NePenScot; NPeEn; OxBS

O pine-tree standing. Var. authors. AWP; TAL Fr. Manyo Shu, Part 3 of 4.

O Pioneers! John Peale Bishop. VGW

O Pioneers! Jane Miller. GifTon

O Pity Our Small Size. Benjamin Rosenbaum. TrJP

O place us, dear Saviour! in some small retreat. Eliza Robertson. PoBW Fr. Poetical Epistle to an Absent Friend, A.

O pleasant exercise of hope and joy! William Wordsworth. HAP; NAEL-6v2 Fr. Prelude, The; Growth of a Poet's Mind [1850 vers.].

O Pleasing Thoughts. Thomas Lodge. Son Fr. Phyllis.

O, po' sinner, O, now is yo' time. What Yo' Gwine to [or t'] Do When Yo' [or de] Lamp Burn Down? Unknown. APN-2; BPo

O Poesy! for thee I hold my pen. John Keats. FHYEP Fr. Sleep and Poetry.

O poet gifted with the sight divine! Milton. Henrietta Cordelia Ray. BlSi; CBWP-3

O poet rare and old! Astræa. John Greenleaf Whittier. APN-1

O poet strutting from the sandbagged portal. As One Non-Combatant to Another. George Orwell. OxBTC

O Polly, you might have toy'd and kist. John Gay. EnLoPo *Fr.* Begger's Opera.

O poor me! / Who am going out to fight the enemy. Song of the Lenape Warriors Going against the Enemy, The. *Unknown.* APN-2, *tr. by* John Heckwelder

O poverty, by thee the soul is wrapp'd. Guido Cavalcanti. EaItPo, *tr. by* Dante Gabriel Rossetti

O Powers Celestial, with what sophistry. Barnabe Barnes. EnLoPo *Fr.* Parthenophil and Parthenophe.

O pr / gress verily thou art m. E. E. Cummings. UV

O pray! Example take too, and have care. (LL) After the Pleasure Party. Herman Melville. APN-2; NAAL-2v1; NAAL-3

O precious codex [*or* code], volume, tome. To a Thesaurus. Franklin Pierce Adams. NBLV

O Quadriga. Charles Olson. BodElec

O queen o sludge, maist royal mousse. To a Mousse. W. N. Herbert. NeBl

O quick quick quick, quick hear the song sparrow. T. S. Eliot. NAEL-5v2; NAEL-6v2; NoAM *Fr.* Landscapes.

O quondam pre-and-post-bellum. Bitch-Kitty, The. Jonathan Williams. PoM

O radiance, into which I go on dying . . . (LL) Monet: "Les Nymphéas." W. D. Snodgrass. CoAP; CoAmPo

O radiant luminary of light interminable. Prayer to the Father of [*or* in] Heaven, A. John Skelton. SacPr

O raging seas, and mighty Neptune's reign! Coming Homeward out of Spain. Barnabe Googe. NoSic

O rain, depart with blessings. Song of the Dew. *Unknown.* TrJP, *tr. by* Solomon Solis-Cohen

O! raise the woefull Pillalu. Irish Lamentation, An. Goethe. AWP, *tr. by* James Clarence Mangan

O rare Narcissus! sunny-haired! Echo's Complaint. Henrietta Cordelia Ray. CBWP-3

O're [*or* O'er] the smooth enamel'd [*or* enameled *or* enamelled] green. John Milton. OBEV; OxBSP *Fr.* Arcades.

O Realm Bejewelled. Forugh Farrokhzad. WPOW, *tr. by* Amin Banani and Jascha Kessler

O! Reason! vaunted Sovereign of the mind! Rejects the Influence of Reason. Mary Robinson. CenSon; RWP

O, red-hot pepper pod. Hymn to the Pepper. Novella Nikolaevna Matveyeva [*or* Matveieva]. TCRP, *tr. by* Deming Brown

O, remember me in your garden. Letter, A. Viktor Aleksandrovich Sosnora. ItGoST, *tr. by* Maia Tekses

O restless, caressing eyes. *Unknown.* PGA

O Restless Heart, Be Still! Henrietta Cordelia Ray. CBWP-3

O Ride On, Jesus. *Unknown.* AH

O Risen Lord upon the Throne. Louis FitzGerald Benson. AH

O road in dizzy moonlight bleak and blue. La Quinque Rue. Edmund Charles Blunden. PeFWW

O Robertson of Inverawe. Song of Sorrow, A. Mary Cameron (Mairi Chamaran, Nighean Fream Challaird). EMWP

O rocking boat, rocking boat poised on the wave. Boat Song. Henrietta Cordelia Ray. CBWP-3

O Roger, Mackerel, Riley, Ned, Nellie, Chester, Lady Ghost. (LL) Names of Horses. Donald Hall. AmFaPo; HAP; InPK-6; SoSe-8; TRP

O rosary that recalled my tear. Aithbhreac Inghean Corcadail. NePenScot, *tr. by* Derick Thomson

O Rose the Red and White Lil[l]y. Rose the Red and White Lil[l]y. *Unknown.* ESPB; OxBB

O Rose, thou art sick. William Blake. AWP; BoLoP; ClHu; EnLoPo; FHYEP; HAP; HeIP-4; InPK-6; NAEL-5v2; NAEL-6v2; NAWM-7v2; NIP-4; NOBE; NOBRP; NOEC; NPeEn; OPOU; OxAEP-2; OxBEV; OxBSP; PoE; RB; SCGP; SoSe-8; TFi; TRP; WeW-3 *Fr.* Songs of Experience.

O Ross, thou wale of hearty cocks. To Mr. Alexander Ross. James Beattie. OxBS

O rosy red, O torrent splendour. Come On, My Lucky Lads. Edmund Charles Blunden. PeFWW

O Rourk's noble fare. Description of an Irish Feast, The. Hugh MacGowran. NOIV; OBCoV, *tr. by* Jonathan Swift

O'Rourke's Feast. Hugh MacGowran. BIrV, *tr. by* Charles Wilson (Description of an Irish Feast, The.) OBVE, *tr. by* Jonathan Swift

O ruddier than the cherry! John Gay. NAEL-5v1; NAEL-6v1; NOEC *Fr.* Acis and Galatea.

O ruined father dead, long sweetly rotten. For the Word Is Flesh. Stanley Kunitz. VGW

O Sacred Head Now Wounded. Paul Gerhardt. SacPr, *tr. by* James Waddell Alexander

O sacred head, now wounded. Paul Gerhardt. GePo

O sacred Head, now wounded, With grief and shame weighed down. O Sacred Head Now Wounded. Paul Gerhardt. SacPr, *tr. by* James Waddell Alexander

O sacred Providence, who from end to end.Providence. George Herbert. BASC

O sacred Providence, who from end to end. George Herbert. AngWePo *Fr.* Providence.

O sacred spirit. Hokuso. JDP, *tr. by* Yoel Hoffmann

O sad Ulysses in decline, seer. Ulysses. Umberto Saba. WoPoe, *tr. by* Stephen Sartarelli

O sage of the stage, Shaw of Shaws! Limerick. Harold Ellis. PeLi

O sailing stars! Star Song. Henrietta Cordelia Ray. CBWP-3

O Saisons, O Châteaux. Arthur Rimbaud. WoPoe, *tr. by* Padraic Fallon

O salty sea, how much of your salt. Portuguese Sea, The. Fernando Pessoa. PeSAV

O save thy children blue Ontario! John Neal. APN-1 *Fr.* Battle of Niagara, The.

O Saviour of a World Undone. Leonard Withington. AH

O saw ye bonny Lesley. Bonnie Lesley. Robert Burns. CTC; GTBS-P; NOBE; OBEV

O saw ye my father? or saw ye my mother? Grey Cock, or, Saw You My Father?, The. *Unknown.* ESPB

O saw ye not fair Ines? Fair Ines. Thomas Hood. OBEV

O say can u see. On Watching a World Series Game. Sonia Sanchez. NBV

O! say can you see, by the dawn's early light. Francis Scott Key. *See* Oh [*or* O] say, [*or* O! say] can you see by the dawn's early light

O say, have you seen at the Willows so green. Ballad of the Emeu, The. Bret Harte. NBLV

O say not thou art left of God. Desolation. John Henry, Cardinal Newman. SacPr

O say what is that thing call'd Light. Blind Boy, The. Colley Cibber. GTBS-P; NOEC

O sea goddess Nuliajuk. Magic Words for Hunting Seal. *Unknown.* STP, *tr. by* Edward Field

O sea-gulls that are crying. *Unknown.* TAL

O Sea, take all, since thou hast taken him. Henry I to the Sea. Eugene Lee-Hamilton. PeVV

O seasons, O châteaux. O Saisons, O Châteaux. Arthur Rimbaud. WoPoe, *tr. by* Padraic Fallon

O seasons, o châteaux. Arthur Rimbaud. SxFrPo, *tr. by* Martin Sorrell

O see how narrow are our days. Prayer of the Maidens to Mary. Rainer Maria Rilke. AWP, *tr. by* Jethro Bithell

O, Seeger, the night you tied the cabbie. Quarry/Rock. Paul Mariah. GLP

O! seize again thy golden quill. To Della Crusca. The Pen. Hannah Cowley. NOBRP

O Shadow, in thy fleeting form I see. Shadow, The. John Banister Tabb. APN-2

O she looked out of the window. Two Magicians, The. *Unknown.* OxBoLi

O she took the babe still sick slick from the waterbag. Four Black Bogmen, The. Elder Olson. APT-2

O she was full of loving fuss. One of the Principal Causes of War. Hugh MacDiarmid. OxBSP

O shield me from his rage, celestial Powers! Esther Johnson. *See* Oh, shield me from his rage, celestial Powers!

O short shrift's the best shrift to give to this *Festschrift*! Unlikely Obbligato of Andersonstown. Kit Wright. OBCoV

O Silent God, Thou whose voice afar in mist and mystery hath left our ears anhungered in these fearful days. Litany of [*or* at] Atlanta, A. William Edward Burghardt DuBois. APT-1; TCAPo

O silent wood, I enter thee. Silent Wood, A. Elizabeth Siddal. NOBVV

O silver splendor, marvelous! Vision of Moonlight, A. Henrietta Cordelia Ray. CBWP-3

O, silver tree! Langston Hughes. *See* Oh, silver tree!

O Simplicitas. Madeleine L'Engle. OBCP *Fr.* Three Songs of Mary.

O Sing to Me of Heaven. Mary Stanley Bunce Dana. AH

O! sing ye a dirge for the loved and the lost. Tribute to a Lost Steamer. Mary Weston Fordham. CBWP-2

O singer of Persephone! Theocritus. Oscar Wilde. NOBE

O Sion, Haste, Thy Mission High Fulfilling. Mary A. Thomson. AH

O, Sire, is this the path? "H. D." NAAL-5 *Fr.* Walls Do Not Fall, The.

O Sister. Nelly Sachs. AF, *tr. by* Matthew Mead

O sister of wealth. Andal. WPoS *Fr.* Tiruppavai, The.

O sister, / where do you pitch your tent? O Sister. Nelly Sachs. AF, *tr. by* Matthew Mead

O sky & earth! How ye are linked together. Lago Maggiore. Thomas Cole. APN-1

O Sleep, O tranquil son of noiseless Night. To Sleep. Giovanni Della Casa. AWP, *tr. by* John Addington Symonds

O sleepy city of reeling wheelchairs. Wheelchair Butterfly, The. James Tate. LCAP-2; NoAM

O sluggish, hard, ingrate, what doest thou?   Guido Cavalcanti.   EaItPo, *tr. by* Dante Gabriel Rossetti

O small and squat.   Songs of the Fruits and Sweets of Childhood.   Lorna Goodison.   VCWP

O smooth flatterers, go over sea.   Reflection and Advice.   Ezra Pound.   OBSV

O snowflake clouds, O feath'ry clouds.   Cloud Song.   Henrietta Cordelia Ray.   CBWP-3

O so white, O so soft, O so sweet is she! (LL)   Ben Jonson.   BASC; CTC; EBEV; NAEL-6v1; NAEL-7v1; NOSC; NPeEn; NoP-4   *Fr.* Celebration of Charis in Ten Lyric[k] Pieces [*or* Peeces], A.

O soft embalmer of the still midnight!   To Sleep.   John Keats.   NIP-4; OBEV; OxBSo; Son

O soldier, O soldier, won't you marry me now.   Soldier, Won't You Marry Me?   *Unknown.*   OxBoLi; PeLV

O soldiers, soldiers, get ye back, I pray!   Saved.   Adah Isaacs Menken.   CBWP-1

O solitary wand'rer! whither stray.   Laura to Petrarch.   Mary Robinson.   CenSon

O Solitude, I said, sweet Solitude!   Solitude.   Helen Hunt Jackson.   SWaP

O Solitude! If I Must With Thee Dwell.   John Keats.   AmFaPo; CenSon

O Solitude! to thy sequester'd vale.   By the Same. To Solitude.   Charlotte Smith.   CenSon; RWP

O solo mio, hot diggety, nix 'I wather think I can.'   Poem.   Frank O'Hara.   TTTS

O! Solomon! let us try again. (LL)   Solomon and the Witch.   W. B. Yeats.   ChIV-1; NoAM; WoPoe

O sometimes in the street, or in the Paris Metro.   Remembrance.   Antoni Slonimski.   TrJP, *tr. by* Frances Notley

O Son of God, it would be sweet.   Saint Columcille [*or* Columba].   NOIV

O son of man, by lying tongues adored.   On the Russian Persecution of the Jews.   Algernon Charles Swinburne.   OxBSo; Son

O Son of Man, Thou Madest Known.   Milton S. Littlefield.   AH

O son of man, when thou findest wine.   Five Arabic Verses in Praise of Wine.   *Unknown.*   TrJP, *tr. by* Hartwig Hirschfeld

O son of mine, when dusk shall find thee bending.   From Generation to Generation.   Sir Henry John Newbolt.   FaBoTw

O Son of the living God.   Manchán's Prayer.   Saint Manchán.   NOIV

O song as yet unsung!   Song as Yet Unsung, A.   "Yehoash."   TrJP, *tr. by* Isidore Goldstick

O Son[ne] of God, who seeing two things.   John Donne.   NOCV   *Fr.* Litany, A.

O Sorrow!   John Keats.   OBEV   *Fr.* Endymion: A Poetic Romance.

O Sorrow, cruel fellowship.   Tennyson.   HAP; NAEL-6v2; NAWM-7v2   *Fr.* In Memoriam A. H. H.

O Sorrow, wilt thou live with me.   Tennyson.   NAEL-6v2   *Fr.* In Memoriam A. H. H.

O sorrowful and ancient days.   Metrum Parhemiacum Tragicum.   Eugenius Vulgarius.   FaBoWar, *tr. by* Helen Waddell

O soul, canst thou not understand.   Aridity.   "Michael Field."   OBMV

O soul, 'tis thine in season meet.   Ode on Theoxenos.   Pindar.   CAGL, *tr. by* John Addington Symonds

O soul, why shouldst thou downcast be?   Hope Thou in God.   Josephine D. Henderson Heard.   CBWP-4

O Soul, with Storms Beset.   Solomon ibn Gabirol.   TrJP, *tr. by* Alice Lucas

O spare a tear for poor Tom Hood.   Elegy on Thomas Hood.   Martin Fagg.   NOBL; UV

O splendour of God's glory bright.   Saint Ambrose.   SacPr, *tr. by* Robert Bridges

O Spring, thou youthful beauty of the year.   Spring.   Giovanni Battista Guarini.   AWP, *tr. by* Leigh Hunt

O St. James Road.   Swath.   Federico García Lorca.   PFTM-1

O stagnant east-wind, palsied mare.   Room on a Garden, A.   Wallace Stevens.   OBGa

O Star (the fairest one in sight).   Choose Something like a Star.   Robert Frost.   APT-1; MoAmPo

O starry Temple of unvalted space.   William Alabaster.   ESCV   *Fr.* Divine Meditations.

O! Start a Revolution.   D. H. Lawrence.   FaBoEE

O stay, sweet warbling woodlark stay.   Address to the Woodlark.   Robert Burns.   OWoS

O stay that covetous hand! First turn all eye.   Upon the Curtain[e] of Lucasta's Picture [It Was Thus Wrought].   Richard Lovelace.   CaPo

O stiffly shapen houses that change not.   Suburbs on a Hazy Day.   D. H. Lawrence.   OBMV

O still small voice of calm. (LL)   John Greenleaf Whittier.   AH; NOCV; SacPr   *Fr.* Brewing of Soma, The.

O still their Tongues till morning comes! (LL)   Resentments Composed because of the Clamor of Town Topers Outside My Apartment.   Sarah Kemble Knight.   AiP; SCAP

O stony grey soil of Monaghan.   Stony Grey Soil.   Patrick Kavanagh.   CIP-2; HarvBoo; ModIr

O stormy, stormy world.   Happiness Makes Up in Height for What It Lacks in Length.   Robert Frost.   MoAmPo; SoSe-8

Ô[h] strive not[t] still to heap[e] disdain[e] on me[e].   Mary Sidney Wroth, Countess of Montgomery.   NOSC   *Fr.* Pamphilia to Amphilanthus.

O study Nature! and with thought profound.   *Unknown.*   OBGa   *Fr.* Rise and Progress of the Present Taste in Planning Parks, Pleasure Grounds, Gardens, etc, The.

O subtile secret of the air.   Distance.   Helen Hunt Jackson.   SWaP

O subtle, musky, slumbrous clime!   To the South.   Maurice Thompson.   CBCWP

O Suen, the usurper Lugalanne means nothing to me!   Appeal to the Moongod Nanna-Suen to Throw Out Lugalanne.   Enheduanna.   BoWoP, *tr. by* Aliki and Willis Barnstone

O suitably-attired-in-leather-boots.   Fragment of a Greek Tragedy.   A. E. Housman.   NOBL; PeLV; WoPoe

O summer snail.   Issa.   SoOfWa, *tr. by* Sam Hamill

O sun, and moonlight shining in the woods.   Carmen Saeculare.   Charles Hubert Sisson.   OBVE, *tr. by* Christopher Smart

O sun, be his protection.   Branwen's Starling.   R. Williams Parry.   OBWVE, *tr. by* Gwyn Jones

O Sun! O age-old labor mutely mixed with ocean.   Edouard Glissant.   NegPo   *Fr.* Indies, The.

O suns [*or* sun] and skies and clouds of June.   October's Bright Blue Weather.   Helen Hunt Jackson.   ITBLP

O supercilious delicious Rhodope.   Irenaeus Referendarius.   GrAn

O Swallow, Swallow, flying, flying south.   O Swallow, Swallow.   Tennyson.   SCGP

O sway, and swing, and sway.   First Extra, The.   Amy Levy.   ViWPN

O, sweep of stars over Harlem streets.   Stars.   Langston Hughes.   GLP

O SWEET and bitter monuments of pain.   Upon the Ensigns of Christ's Crucifying.   William Alabaster.   NoSic

O sweet dead artist and seer, O tender prophetic priest.   Ernest Francisco Fenollosa.   APN-2   *Fr.* East and West.

O sweet everlasting Voices be still.   Everlasting Voices, The.   W. B. Yeats.   AWP

O sweet frustrations, I shall be back for more. (LL)   Voice from under the Table, A.   Richard Wilbur.   HAP; NOBA

O sweet incendiary! shew here thy art.   Richard Crashaw.   NPeEn   *Fr.* Flaming Heart, The.

O sweet, sad, singing river.   Song.   Henrietta Cordelia Ray.   CBWP-3

O Sweet Spontaneous.   E. E. Cummings.   NAAL-2v2; NAAL-5; NoAM; PAI; RaBo; TCAPo

O sweet woods, the delight of solitariness!   Sir Philip Sidney.   NoSic   *Fr.* Arcadia.

O sweete and bitter monuments of paine.   William Alabaster.   ESCV   *Fr.* Divine Meditations.

O Sweetie, O Hon, in this weather—split sea pea.   Crossed-Over, Fiend-Snitched, X-ed Out.   Mary Jo Bang.   BAP-01

O swiftly, re-light the flame.   "H. D."   NALW   *Fr.* Tribute to the Angels.

O sylvan priest of nature! rightly thou.   Thought at Walden, A.   Henrietta Cordelia Ray.   CBWP-3

O Sylvan prophet, whose eternal fame.   Hymn for St. John's Eve.   *Unknown.*   AWP, *tr. by* John Dryden

O Sylvia, Sylvia.   Sylvia's Death.   Anne Sexton.   LCAP-2; NAAL-2v2; NAAL-5; NALW

O! synge untoe mie roundelaie.   Thomas Chatterton.   *See* Oh! sing unto my roundelay [*or* O! Synge untoe mie roundelaie]

O-ta-pa! / I am creeping on your track.   *Unknown.*   APN-2   *Fr.* War Dance.

O-ta-pa! / Why run you from us when you.   *Unknown.*   APN-2   *Fr.* War Dance.

O talk not to me of a name great in story.   Byron.   *See* Oh, talk not to me of a name great in story

O Tan-Faced Prairie-Boy.   Walt Whitman.   CAGL

O Taste and See.   Denise Levertov.   ChIV-1; NoP-4; PoPoPo; TAP

O tears, no tears, but rain from beauty's skies.   Sir Philip Sidney.   Son   *Fr.* Astrophil and Stella.

O tell me, pretty river!   River, The.   *Unknown.*   PWR

O tell me where, in lands or seas.   Ballade of the Ladies of Time Past.   François Villon.   WoPoe, *tr. by* Richard Wilbur

O tender time that love thinks long to see.   Vision of Spring in Winter, A.   Algernon Charles Swinburne.   NPeEn

O Tender under Her Right Breast.   George Barker.   MoBrPo   *Fr.* Second Cycle of Love Poems.

O terrible is the highest thing.   Kenneth Patchen.   VGW

O Thalassa! Thalassa! Where, where.   Singers, The.   George Bruce.   OxBS

O that a town thus yields itself to view.   View from the Kobenzl.   Friedrich Torberg.   AuPH, *tr. by* Lowell A. Bangerter

O that I could a sin once see!   Sin.   George Herbert.   OxBSP

"O that mastering tune!" And up in the bed. Thomas Hardy. InPK-6 *Fr.* Satires of Circumstance in Fifteen Glimpses.

O that mine eyes might closed be. Prayer, A. Thomas Elwood. PWR

O that my prayers could raiment you in splendour. Fair Raiment. John Oxenham. SacPr

O, that the Holy Angels would indite. Quarto Centennial, The. Josephine D. Henderson Heard. CBWP-4

O that the lilies and roses were mine. J. Gordon Coogler. VerBaPo

O that the rain would come—the rain in big battalions. Precursors. Louis MacNeice. OxBSP

O, that the years had language! time would / tell. Judith. Eloise Bibb. CBWP-4

O, that there were, indeed, some hidden charm—. To Ancestry. John Thelwall. CenSon

O! that this too too solid flesh would melt. William Shakespeare. OxAEP-1; SCV *Fr.* Hamlet.

O! that we now had here. William Shakespeare. FaBoWar; OxAEP-1 *Fr.* King Henry V.

O the beautiful garment. "H. D." HarvBoo *Fr.* Flowering of the Rod, The.

O the Chimneys. Nelly Sachs. AF; HP; PoetW, tr. by Michael Roloff

O! / The constellation glitters. Stars abound. Passages 37. Robert Duncan. FTOS

O the cuckoo she's a pretty bird. Cuckoo, The. *Unknown.* RB

O the days gone by! O the days gone by! Days Gone By, The. James Whitcomb Riley. APN-2; OBCA

O the days of the Messiah are at hand, are at hand! Ballad of the Days of the Messiah. Abraham Moses Klein. TrJP

O the deep, deep love of Jesus! Samuel Trevor Francis. SacPr

O the engineer's joys! to go with a locomotive! Walt Whitman. HHAm *Fr.* Song of Joys, A.

O the goose and the gander walk'd over the green. Goose and the Gander, The. *Unknown.* RB

O the Harbour of Fowey. Harbour of Fowey, The. Sir Arthur Thomas Quiller-Couch. OBCoV

O the hurt, the hurt, and the hurt of love! Hurt of Love, The. George Macdonald. TrCP

O the little rusty dusty miller. *Unknown.* OxNR

O the month of May, the merry month of May. Thomas Dekker. NoSic *Fr.* Shoemaker's Holiday, The.

O the Night of the Weeping Children! Nelly Sachs. HP, tr. by Michael Hamburger

O the opal and the sapphire of that wandering western sea. Beeny Cliff. Thomas Hardy. CABP; OxAEP-2; RB

O the Ploughboy was a-ploughing. Simple Ploughboy, The. *Unknown.* FaBoCh

O The Raggedy Man! He works fer Pa. Raggedy Man, The. James Whitcomb Riley. ITBLP; OBCA

O, the rain, the weary, dreary rain. Twenty Golden Years Ago. James Clarence Mangan. NOBVV; OxBEV

O the sad day! Sad Day, The. Thomas Flatman. OBEV

O the Sad Moon. Sir Philip Sidney. *See* Astrophil and Stella

O the sweeping past of the ruined sky! (LL) Bracelet of Grass, The. William Vaughn Moody. APN-2; TCAPo

O, the Temeraire no more! (LL) *Temeraire,* The. Herman Melville. APN-2; FaBoWar

O the warm, sweet, mellow summer noon. Favorite Flower, The. Celia Laighton Thaxter. AiP

O, there be many things. Many Things. Oliver Wendell Holmes. PoToHe

O there is blessing in this gentle breeze. William Wordsworth. FHYEP; NAEL-6v2 *Fr.* Prelude, The; Growth of a Poet's Mind [1850 vers.].

O these wakeful[l] wounds of thine! On the Wounds of Our Crucified Lord. Richard Crashaw. NAEL-5v1; NAEL-6v1; NAEL-7v1

O, / these wild trees. Imamu Amiri Baraka. BB

O they took my blessed Lawd. He Never Said a Mumblin' Word. *Unknown.* APN-2

O this weather! this weather! Hot Day In Sydney, A. *Unknown.* NOBAu

O thou afflicted, drunken not with wine! Dirge for the Ninth of Ab. *Unknown.* TrJP, tr. by Nina Davis Salaman

O, thou art far away from me—dear boy! To My Brother. Mary Bryan. CenSon

O Thou, beloved of my twenty seven senses. Anna Blossom Has Wheels. Kurt Schwitters. PFTM-1

O thou bright jewel in my aim I strive. On Virtue. Phillis Wheatley. TAP

O thou, by Nature taught. Ode to Simplicity. William Collins. NOBE; OBEV; OxAEP-1

O Thou Eternal Victim Slain. Charles Wesley. NOCV

O thou Great Mantle which envelops us. Great Hymn. Ntsikana Gaba. PeSAV, tr. by Thomas Pringle

O thou great Wrong, that, through the slow-paced years. Death of Slavery, The. William Cullen Bryant. CBCWP

O Thou Hand of Fire. (LL) Hart Crane. NOBA; NoAM *Fr.* Bridge, The.

O thou! meek Orb! that stealing o'er the dale. Her Address to the Moon. Mary Robinson. CenSon; RWP

O thou Moor of Morería. Abenamar, Abenamar. *Unknown.* AWP, tr. by Robert Southey

O thou Most High, who rulest all. Upon My Dear and Loving Husband His Going into England. Anne Bradstreet. AH

O thou most terrible, most dreaded power. To Death. Mary Tighe. CenSon

O thou, my lovely boy, who in thy power. William Shakespeare. HeIP-4; NAEL-5v1; NAEL-6v1; NAEL-7v1 *Fr.* Sonnets.

O Thou my soule, Jehovah blesse. Bible, *O.T.* SCAP *Fr.* Bay Psalm Book, The.

O thou newcomer who seek'st Rome in Rome. Rome. Joachim Du Bellay. AWP; FaBoWar, tr. by Ezra Pound

O Thou of Little Faith! George Macdonald. SacPr

O thou sightd word, most like to *breath,* and made. Death. Mary Elizabeth Coleridge. ViWPN

O thou that after toil and storm. Tennyson. PeECV *Fr.* In Memoriam A. H. H.

O thou, that art my *Light,* my *Life,* my *Way.* (LL) Francis Quarles. BASC; MeLP; NOSC; OxAEP-1; SacPr *Fr.* Emblems.

O Thou, that dost cover the heavens. Song of the Wind and the Rain. Solomon ibn Gabirol. TrJP, tr. by Solomon Solis-Cohen

O thou that held'st the blessed Veda dry. Jayadeva. AWP, tr. by Sir Edwin Arnold *Fr.* Gita Govinda, The.

O Thou that in the heavens does dwell! Holy Willie's Prayer. Robert Burns. EBEV; NAEL-6v2; NOBRP; NOEC; OBCoV; OBSV; OxBS; PoE; TFi

O thou that lovest a pure, and whitend soul! Dressing. Henry Vaughan. ESCV

O thou that often hast within thine eyes. Sonnet: He Speaks of a Third Love of His. Guido Cavalcanti. AWP; EaItPo, tr. by Dante Gabriel Rossetti

O Thou, that sit'st upon a throne. Christopher Smart. NAEL-5v1; NAEL-6v1; NAEL-7v1; NOBE; OBWVE; PoE

O Thou That Sleep'st like Pig in Straw. Sir William Davenant [or D'Avenant]. NOSC

O Thou! the first fruits of the dead. Burial. Henry Vaughan. GeHe

O Thou, the first, the greatest friend. *First Six Verses* of the Ninetieth Psalm, The. Robert Burns. ChIV-1

O thou, the wonder of all day[e]s! Dirge of Jephthah's Daughter, The. Robert Herrick. ChIV-1

O Thou, to Whom in Ancient Time. John Pierpont. TCAPo

O thou undaunted daughter of desires! Richard Crashaw. HAP; NOBE; OBEV; WoPoe *Fr.* Flaming Heart, The.

O Thou unknown, Almighty Cause. Prayer, in the Prospect of Death, A. Robert Burns. TreFP

O thou unknown disturber of my rest. To———. Mary Bryan. CenSon

O Thou vast Ocean! ever-sounding Sea! Address to the Ocean. "Barry Cornwall." TreFP

O Thou, wha in the heavens dost dwell. Robert Burns. *See* O Thou that in the heavens does dwell!

O thou! whatever title suit thee. Address to the Deil. Robert Burns. NOEC; NePenScot; OxBS

O thou who didst furnish. Hymn to Moloch. Ralph Hodgson. OxBTC

O Thou, Who Didst Ordain the Word. Edwin Hubbell Chapin. AH

O thou! / Who from *"a wilderness of Suns"* Ode to Della Crusca. Hannah Cowley. NOBRP

O thou who never harbored fear. Sonnet. Eloise Bibb. CBWP-4

O Thou who speedest Time's advancing wing. *Unknown.* AWP *Fr.* Book of the Dead.

O thou who standest 'mid the bards of old. On Kean's Hamlet. Washington Allston. APN-1

O thou who sweetly bend'st my stubborn will. In Desolation. John Beaumont. SacPr

O thou whom Poetry [or Poesy] abhors. On Elphinston's Translation of Martial. Robert Burns. FaBoEE

O thou, whose eyes were closed in death's pale night. Epitaph on a Child Killed by Procured Abortion. *Unknown.* NOEC

O Thou Whose Face Hath Felt the Winter's Wind. John Keats. CenSon (What the Thrush Said.) EBEV

O Thou Whose Feet Have Climbed Life's Hill. Louis FitzGerald Benson. AH

O Thou Whose Gracious Presence Shone. Marion Franklin Ham. AH

O Thou! whose name too often is profaned. To Friendship. Charlotte Smith. RWP

O Thou Whose Own Vast Temple Stands. William Cullen Bryant. AH

O thou whose pow'r o'er moving worlds presides. Boethius. OBVE *Fr.* Consolation of Philosophy, The ("De Consolacione Philosophie").

O Thou! Whose Presence Went Before. John Greenleaf Whittier. AH

O Thou whose reason guides the universe. Boethius. MLL *Fr.* Consolation of Philosophy, The ("De Consolacione Philosophie").

O thou, with dewy locks, who lookest down.   To Spring.   William Blake.   NAEL-5v2; NAEL-6v2; NOEC; OBEV; SCGP

O Thought, now you'll have to think the same thing forever! (LL)   Fourth Floor, Dawn, Up All Night Writing Letters.   Allen Ginsberg.   HarvBoo; InvLad

O thow archbishop and metropolitan.   *Unknown.*   NOIV   *Fr.* Letter Sent by the Mayor and Inhabitants of the, A.

O thow Minstral that cannest so note and pipe.   John Lydgate.   OxBEV   *Fr.* Daunce of Death, The.

O three-toned green little place with trees.   Waxwings.   Milton Kessler.   InvLad

O! thy bright eyes must answer now.   Emily Jane Brontë.   *See* God of Visions

O Tim, my own Tim I must call 'ee—I will!   Thomas Hardy.   FaBoVe   *Fr.* Bride-Night Fire, The.

O Time the fatal wrack of mortal things.   Anne Bradstreet.   ColAP; WPOW   *Fr.* Contemplations.

O Time! who know'st a lenient hand to lay.   William Lisle Bowles.   *See* Time and Grief

O timeless guest!—so soon returned art thou.   To———.   Mary Bryan.   CenSon

O Times most bad.   Upon the Troublesome Times.   Robert Herrick.   CaPo; CavPo

O To Be A Dragon.   Marianne Craig Moore.   APT-1; CTC; ChIV-1; NAAL-5; NALW

O to be blind!   Blind Man at the Fair, The.   Joseph Campbell.   AWP

O to be in the news again—now as fashion runs.   Robert Adamson.   BMAP   *Fr.* Sonnets to be Written from Prison.

O to be Up and Doing.   Robert Louis Stevenson.   ITBLP

O to break loose, like the chinook.   Waking Early Sunday Morning.   Robert Lowell.   FaBoMo; HCAP; HarvBoo; NOBA; OxBC; VCAP

O to scuttle from the battle and to settle on an atoll far from brutal mortal neath a wattle portal!   O To Scuttle From the Battle.   Justin Richardson.   UV

O tongue / licking.   To an Old Jaundiced Woman.   William Carlos Williams.   APT-1

O tragic hours when lovers leave each other!   Partings.   Charles Guérin.   AWP, *tr.* by Jethro Bithell

O treacherous scent, O thorny sight.   Another for the Briar Rose.   William Morris.   NOBVV; OxBEV

O trees, to whom the darkness is a child.   Advice to a Forest.   Maxwell Bodenheim.   TrJP

O tremble, all ye earthly princes.   Revolutionaries, The.   Richard Percival Lister.   NOBL

O Troy Muir, my lily-flower.   Queen of Scotland, The.   *Unknown.*   ESPB

O Turn Ye, O Turn Ye.   Josiah Hopkins.   AH

O Tweed! a stranger, that with wandering feet.   Tweed Visited, The.   William Lisle Bowles.   Son

O two-horned moon, you love the parties that last all night.   Philodemus.   HePo   *Fr.* Epigrams.

O-U-G-H.   Charles Battell Loomis.   NBLV

O uncreated Lord of all creation.   Prayer to God the Father.   Marbod of Rennes.   MLL, *tr.* by Helen Waddell

O universal Mother, who dost keep.   *Unknown.*   AWP, *tr.* by Percy Bysshe Shelley   *Fr.* Homeric Hymns.

O vale and lake, within your mountain-urn.   Remembrance of Grasmere, A.   Felicia Dorothea Hemans.   CenSon

O Virtuous Light.   Elinor Wylie.   MoAmPo

O Vocables of Love.   Laura Riding Jackson.   APT-2

O Vorarlberg, 'tis you I greet.   My Vorarlberg.   Natalie Beer.   AuPH, *tr.* by Lowell A. Bangerter

O wad this braw hie-heapit toun.   Prows O' Reekie, The.   Lewis Spence.   NePenScot; OxBS

O wall-flower! or ever thy bright leaves fade.   Wall-Flower, The.   Henrik Arnold Thaulov Wergeland.   AWP, *tr.* by Sir Edmund William Gosse

O waly, waly, my gay goss-hawk.   Gay Goshawk [*or* Goss-Hawk], The.   Anna Gordon Brown.   ESPB; OxBB; WPE

O warm, enthusiastic maid.   Joseph Warton.   NOEC   *Fr.* Ode to Fancy.

O, Was my Heart but form'd for Woe.   One Thing Needful Generally Neglected, The.   Samuel Davies.   SacPr

O wastfull riot, never well content.   Lucan.   OBVE   *Fr.* Pharsalia.

O wat ye what my Minnie did.   Wat ye what my Minnie did.   Robert Burns.   EroLit

O waters running pure and crystal clear.   Baldomero Garcilaso de la Vega.   SpanPo, *tr.* by Edwin Morgan   *Fr.* Eclogue 1.

O Wave God   who broke through me today.   Burning Island.   Gary Snyder.   APSN; VCAP

O! we know not we know not, what future joys.   There's a Silvery Lining to Every Cloud.   Matilda Caroline Edwards.   PWR

O, we loved long and happily, God knows!   Custom of the World, The.   Louis Simpson.   BoLoP

O we were sisters seven, Maisry.   Fair Mary of Wallington.   *Unknown.*   ESPB

O we were sisters, sisters seven.   Earl Crawford.   *Unknown.*   ESPB

O wearisome condition of humanity!   Fulke Greville, 1st Baron Brooke.   *See* O[h] wearisome condition of humanity

O weary Champion of the Cross, lie still.   Cardinal Newman.   Christina Georgina Rossetti.   NAEL-5v2; NAEL-6v2

O weary pilgrims, chanting of your woe.   Robert Bridges.   MoBrPo   *Fr.* Growth of Love, The.

O weep no more; thou art all wan with sighs. (LL)   Sonnet: To the Same Ladies; With Their Answer.   Dante Alighieri.   AWP; EaItPo, *tr.* by Dante Gabriel Rossetti

O wen, wen, O little wennikins.   Charm, A.   *Unknown.*   RB, *tr.* by Richard Hammer

O Wendy, Arthur.   Maurice Kenny.   HATNAP

O Were My Love Yon Lilac[k] Fair.   Robert Burns.   OBEV

O, Wert Thou in the Cauld Blast.   Robert Burns.   *See* O [*or* Oh] Wert Thou in the Cauld Blast

O wha my babie-clouts will buy?   Rantin' Dog, the Daddie o't, The.   Robert Burns.   FaBoVe; OxBoLi; PeLV

O Wha's the Bride?   Hugh MacDiarmid.   GTBS-P; OxBEV; RaBo

O wha' the bride that cairries the bunch.   Hugh MacDiarmid.   NPeEn   *Fr.* Drunk Man Looks at the Thistle, A.

O wha will bake my bridal bread.   Fair Annie.   *Unknown.*   ESPB

O wha will shoe my bonny foot?   Fair Isabell of Rochroyall.   *Unknown.*   OxBB

O wha will shoe my fair foot?   Lass of Roch Royal, The.   *Unknown.*   ESPB

O wha would [*or* wou'd] wish the win to blaw.   Brown Adam.   *Unknown.*   ESPB; OxBB

O whare are ye gaun? [*or* O where are you going?].   False Knight upon [*or* on] the Road, The.   *Unknown.*   ESPB

O whare hae ye been a' day, Lord Donald, my son?   Lord Randal.   *Unknown.*   ESPB

O whare hae ye been, my dearest dear.   Carpenter's Wife, The.   *Unknown.*   OxBB

O whare hae ye been, Peggy?   Young Peggy.   *Unknown.*   ESPB

O what a loud and fearful shriek was there.   Samuel Taylor Coleridge.   OxBSo   *Fr.* Effusions.

O what a magic comfort are boys to men!   Fragment 652.   Euripides.   CAGL, *tr.* by John Addington Symonds

O what a strange parcel of creatures are we.   On an Unsociable Family.   Elizabeth Hands.   ECWP; NPeEn; WoRP

O what a tangled web we weave.   Word of Encouragement, A.   J. R. Pope.   NBLV; NOBL

O! what a thing is Love? who can define.   Edward Taylor.   SacPr

O what a weary while it is to stand.   Eternity.   James Whitcomb Riley.   GSo

O, what can ail thee, knight at arms.   Answer to a Kind Enquiry.   Mary Holtby.   UV

O what can you give me?   Idris Davies.   AngWePo   *Fr.* Gwalia Deserta.

O what could be more nice.   Light Listened.   Theodore Roethke.   MoAmPo

O what harper could worthily harp it.   Schoolmaster Abroad with His Son, The.   Charles Stuart Calverley.   NOBL; PeLV

O What Is That Sound [Which So Thrills the Ear].   W. H. Auden.   FaBoWar; PoE

(Ballad.)   MoBrPo

O what's the blood that's [*or* at's] on your sword.   Son David.   *Unknown.*   OxBB; OxBS

O what's the weather in a Beard?   Dinky.   Theodore Roethke.   OBAL; OBCA; OxIBACP

O what tears in eyes now.   Marina Ivanovna Tsvetayeva [*or* Tsvetaeva].   TCRP   *Fr.* March.

O what their joy and their glory must be.   Hymn for the Close of the Week.   Peter Abelard.   TrCP

O what will a' the lads do.   When Maggy Gangs Away.   James Hogg.   CABP

O when, through ev'ry province, shall be raised.   John Dyer.   NOEC   *Fr.* Fleece, The.

O when you come in summer time.   Blue Tail Fly or Jimmy Cracked Corn, The.   Daniel Decatur Emmett.   TCAPo

O when you were little, you were really big.   Duet.   Theodore Roethke.   OBCoV

O where are Mina Bell's cows who gave no milk.   Mina Bell's Cows.   Wesley McNair.   TRP

O where are they now, your harridan nuns.   Nuns of Childhood: Two Views, The.   Maxine W. Kumin.   FFC

O where ha' you been, Lord Randal, my son?   *Unknown.*   *See* O[h] where have [*or* ha *or* hae] you [*or* ye] been, Lord Randal [*or* Rendal *or* Randall] my son?

O where [*or* whare] have you [*or* hae ye] been, my dear, dear [*or* dearest dear *or* long, long] love.   Demon Lover, The.   *Unknown.*   HAP; SCGP; TFi; UnPo; WeW-3

O, Where Were We Before Time Was.   Max Dunn.   NOBAu

O, where, where are the winter grounds of angels. Angels, The. Marguerite Young. WPE

O while within a Jewish breast. Hatikvah—a Song of Hope. Naphtali Herz Imber. TrJP, tr. by Henry Snowman

O whirly-water. Lawn Sprinkler, The. Queen Lili'u-o-ka-lani. WoPoe, tr. by Alfons L. Korn and Mary Kawena Pukui

O whisper, O my soul! The afternoon. Tired Worker, The. Claude McKay. BPo

O whistle, and I'll come to you [or ye], my lad. Whistle, and I'll Come to You, My Lad. Robert Burns. OxAEP-2; OxBoLi

O white chrysanthemum. Otsuchi. JDP, tr. by Yoel Hoffmann

O whitewashed chapel. Greece. Gunnar Ekelof. BLT

O whither dost thou fly? Cannot my vow. To the Moment Last Past. William Habington. OxBSo

O Whither will you lead the Fair. Countess of Anglesey lead Captive by the Rebels, at the Disforresting of Pewsam, The. Sir William Davenant [or D'Avenant]. PBRV

O who rides by night thro' the woodland so wild? Erl-King, The. Goethe. AWP; OBVE; STV

O who will show me those delights on high? Heaven. George Herbert. ESCV; GeHe; TTTS; TrCP; WoPoe

O who would not sleep with the brave? (LL) Lancer. A. E. Housman. MoBrPo; OBWP

O why do you walk through the fields in gloves. To a Fat Lady Seen from the Train. Frances Darwin Cornford. FaBoWP; MoBrPo; OBMV; OxBEV; UV; WeW-3

O! why should heavenly God to men have such regard? (LL) Edmund Spenser. NOCV; NoSic Fr. Faerie Queene, The.

O, why should Nature niggardly restraine! Michael Drayton. PBRV Fr. Idea.

O wife, wife, wife! As if the sacred name. Last Giustiniani, The. Edith Wharton. APN-2

O wild-reäven west winds, as you do roar on. Jenny out from Hwome. William Barnes. SCGP

O wild West Wind, thou breath of Autumn's being. Ode to the West Wind. Shelley. AWP; CenSon; ClHu; EBEV; FHYEP; GTBS-P; HAP; HeIP-4; MakPoe; NAEL-5v2; NAEL-6v2; NAWM-7v2; NIL-7; NIP-4; NOBE; NOBRP; NPeEn; NoP-4; OBEV; OxAEP-2; OxBEV; OxBSo; PAI; PeECV; PoE; PoPoPo; PoRA; SCGP; TFi; TRP; WeW-3

O Willie brew'd a peck o' maut. Willie Brew'd [or Brewed] a Peck o' Maut. Robert Burns. AWP; OxBS

O Willie's large o' limb and lith. Birth of Robin Hood, The. Unknown. OxBB

O Willy was as brave a lord. Willie o Douglas Dale. Unknown. ESPB

O wind, rend open the heat. "H. D." HeIP-4; InPK-6; MoAmPo; OxBA; TAP; TCAPo; TRP; UnPo Fr. Garden, The.

O Wind, thou hast thy kingdom in the trees. "Michael Field." VWP

O Winter Aphrodite! O acute. To the Winter Aphrodite. "Michael Field." VWP

O winter wind, lat grievin be. Villanelle. Margaret Winefride Simpson. OxBS

O, winter, your gesture. Winter. Bella [or Izabella] Akhatovna Akhmadulina. BoWoP, tr. by Barbara Einzig

O wistful eyes that haunt the gloom of sleep. Unborn. John Le Gay Brereton. NOBAu

O withering seas. George Oppen. NNaP Fr. Some San Francisco Poems.

O woe, woe, / People are born and die. Mr. Housman's Message. Ezra Pound. FaBoEE

O Woman of Three Cows, agra [or agragh] [don't let your tongue thus rattle!]. Woman of Three Cows, The. Unknown. NOIV; OBCoV, tr. by James Clarence Mangan

O Woman, Shapely as the Swan. Unknown. BIrV; CTC, tr. by Padraic Colum

O wonderful nonsense of lotions of Lucky Tiger. Haircut. Karl Shapiro. TwCP

O, wondrous depth to which my soul is stirr'd. Music. Josephine D. Henderson Heard. CBWP-4

O wondrous thing it is. Excitation. Lorenzo Thomas. FTOS

O words are lightly spoken. Rose Tree, The. W. B. Yeats. OBMV

O world, I cannot hold thee close enough! God's World. Edna St. Vincent Millay. APT-1; ITBLP; MoAmPo; TrCP

O world invisible, we view thee. Kingdom of God, The. Francis Thompson. GTBS-P; NOCV; SacPr

O world! O life! O time! Lament, A: "O world! O life! O time!" Shelley. GTBS-P; NOBE; PoRA

O world, thou choosest not the better part! George Santayana. APN-2; TCAPo Fr. Sonnets.

O worship the King all glorious above. Sir Robert Grant. SacPr

O would I were where I would be! Suspiria. Unknown. OBEV

O Wretch, Beware. William Dunbar. SacPr

O wretch! hath madness cured thy dire despair? On Seeing an Officer's Widow Distracted. Mary Barber. ECWP; NOEC

O ye, all ye that walk in Willowwood. Dante Gabriel Rossetti. NAEL-5v2; NAEL-6v2; OxBSo Fr. House of Life, The.

O ye dead Poets, who are living still. Poets, The. Henry Wadsworth Longfellow. GSo

O ye gentle breeze which wafts to me. Ku'u Pua I Paoakalani. Queen Lili'u-o-ka-lani. SWaP

O Ye That Would Swallow the Needy. Bible, O.T. TrJP Fr. Amos.

O Ye Tongues. Anne Sexton.
Third Psalm. NALW

O ye who ride upon the wandering gale. To the Clouds. Susan Evance. CenSon

O ye wretched Scots. John Skelton. OBSV Fr. How the Doughty Duke of Albany like a Coward Knight Ran Away Shamefully.

O yee, whome lorde of lande and waters wyde. Seneca. OBVE, tr. by Jasper Heywood Fr. Thyestes.

O' Yes. Lamont B. Steptoe. ISC

O yes, I love you, book of my confessions. Water under the Earth. Robert Bly. NNaP

O yes. I've had to give up somewhat here. Dry Eleven Months. John Berryman. BodElec

O yes, the Chinese Garden! Do you remember. Chinese Garden, The. Horace Gregory. OBGa

O yes—you understand, I say. "H. D." NALW Fr. Tribute to the Angels.

O Yes? Do they come on horses. So Mexicans Are Taking Jobs from Americans. Jimmy Santiago Baca. LTA; UnSA

O yesterday the cutting edge drank thirstily and deep. To-morrow. John Masefield. MoBrPo

O Yonge fresshe folks, he or she. Love Unfeigned, The. Geoffrey Chaucer. OBEV

O You among Women. Frederick Robert Higgins. BIrV

O you chorus of indolent reviewers. Hendecasyllabics. Tennyson. EBEV; NOBL; PeLV

O You Jolly Augustine. Unknown. AuPH, tr. by Lowell A. Bangerter

O you lovers that are so gentle, step occasionally. Rainer Maria Rilke. RaBo Fr. Sonnets to Orpheus.

O, you're braw wi' your pearls and your diamonds. Lassie, What Mair Wad You Hae? Heinrich Heine. OxBS, tr. by Alexander Gray

O you so long dead. To My Brother: Killed: Hammont Wood: October, 1918. Louise Bogan. AiP

O you, / Who came upon me once. Carrefour. Amy Lowell. BoWoP; LW

O you who eat with someone else's teeth. Toothpuller Who Wanted to Turn a Mouth into a Grinding Machine, The. Francisco de Quevedo y Villegas. WoPoe, tr. by Willis Barnstone

O you who guard over. Andal. WPoS Fr. Tiruppavai, The.

O You Whom I Often and Silently Come. Walt Whitman. APN-1

O you would clothe me in silken frocks. Wild Goat, The. Claude McKay. RACG

O, Young Lochinvar is come out of the west. Sir Walter Scott. See Oh [or O], young Lochinvar is come out of the west

O young man who composes the poem. Brigid O'Donnell (Bríd Inían Iarla Chille Dara). EMWP

O young Mariner. Merlin and the Gleam. Tennyson. FHYEP

O younge [or yonge] fres[s]he folkes, he or she. Geoffrey Chaucer. NOBE; OBEV Fr. Troilus and Criseyde [or Criseide].

O zummer clote! when the brook's a-glidèn [or a-sliden]. Clote (Water-Lily), The. William Barnes. FaBoVe; NPeEn

Oaf. Song of a Young Girl. Flavien Ranaivo. PBMAP

Oak, The. Aleksandr Semionovich Kushner. TCRusP, tr. by Daniel Weissbort

Oak, The. George Pope Morris. See Woodman, Spare That Tree

Oak and the Ash, The. Unknown. FaBoCh

Oak and the Olive, The. George Barker. FaBoMo

Oak coffin covered with vines, An. Furtherness. Mary Ruefle. BAP-01

Oak inns creak in their joints as light declines, The. Derek Walcott. NoAM Fr. Midsummer.

Oak tree, The. Basho. EH, tr. by Robert Hass

Oakland. Robert Grenier.
"Open the door Oakland." FTOS

Oakland Blues. Ishmael Reed. NAAAL

Oaks and Squirrels. Anne Porter. ChIV-1

Oaks are stricken by a serious illness, The. More than Suspect. André Breton. AF, tr. by Mary Ann Caws

Oaks, how subtle and marine, The. Bearded Oaks. Robert Penn Warren. APT-2; ColAP; FuPo; MoAmPo; NAAL-2v2; NAAL-5; NOBA; NoAM; NoP-4; PAI; PoE; TAP; TwCP

Oars fell from our hands, The. Island, The. George Woodcock. MoCV

Oars, heavy with seaweed, at rest in humid mists, The. Oars Heavy with Seaweed, The. Karel Van de Woestijne. TuT, tr. by Michael Longley

Oasis, An. Agnes Mary Frances Robinson. VWP

Oasis, light incarnate. (LL) "World Without Objects Is a Sensible Emptiness, A." Richard Wilbur. CoAmPo; MoAmPo; NAAL-2v2; NOBA; NoAM

Oath, The. Allen Tate. FaBoMo; OxBA; VGW

Oath of Friendship. *Unknown*. TTTS, *tr. by* Arthur Waley

Oaths. Thomas [*or* "Tom"] Brown. FaBoEE; OBCoV

Oaths of Friendship. *Unknown*. ChiP, *tr. by* Arthur Waley

Oatmeal. Galway Kinnell. EmeKit

Oatmeal was in their blood and in their names. Edwin John Pratt. MoCV *Fr.* Towards the Last Spike.

Ob all de subjects I kin read. De Men Folks ob Today. Maggie Pogue Johnson. CBWP-4

Obbligato from a Public Gallery. Jared Angira. NAfrP

Obeah Mama Dot. Frederick D'Aguiar. Oth

Obedience. George Herbert. ESCV; GeHe

Obedience of the Corpse. C. D. Wright. LCAP-2

Obedient Girl, The. Marjorie Agosin. ExTi

Obelisk Inscriptions. Queen Hatshepsut.
"I have done this with a loving heart for my father Amun." HAWP
"Now my heart turns to and fro." WPOW

Ober de mountains, slick as an eel. Boatman's Dance. Daniel Decatur Emmett. APN-1

Oberon's Feast. Robert Herrick. BeJo; CaPo; NOSC

Oberon's Palace. Robert Herrick. CaPo

Obey Your Parents. William Bingham Tappan. VerBaPo

Obit. Robert Lowell. HCAP; PoetW; VCAP

Obit on Parnassus. F. Scott Fitzgerald. NBLV

Obiter Dicta. Joseph Hilaire Pierre Belloc. OBCoV

Obituary. Conrad Potter Aiken. OBAL

Obituary. Steve Chimombo. HBAPE

Obituary. Kenneth Fearing. IllVoic; VGW

Object among dreams, you sit here with your shoes off, An. Girl in a Library, A. Randall Jarrell. NAAL-2v2; NOBA; NoAM

Object of Burial Is Intent, The. Rebecca Reynolds. AmPoNex

Objection Overruled. Jackie Hardy. NeBl

Objection to Being Stepped On, The. Robert Frost. NBLV; OBCoV

Objectivists are metaphysical. Edward Hopper. Anthony Rudolf. PoSol

Objects. Yevgeny [*or* Evgenii] Mikhailovich Vinokurov. TCRusP, *tr. by* Daniel Weissbort *Fr.* History.

Objects clutter the shiny air and flash. In Communication with a UFO. Helen Chasin. YaYoPo

Objects in Mirror are Closer Than They Appear. Jeffrey Skinner. PBCAP

Obligations of Civil to Religious Liberty. William Wordsworth. SacPr *Fr.* Ecclesiastical Sonnets.

Obliged by frequent visits of this man. Flecknoe, an English Priest at Rome. Andrew Marvell. BASC

Oblique cloud of purple smoke, An. Woman Walking. William Carlos Williams. ColAP

Oblique light on the trite, on brick and tile. Courtyards in Delft. Derek Mahon. CIP-2; ModIr; NPeEn; PBCIP; PNI

Oblique Prayer. Denise Levertov. SacPr

Oblique Rain. Fernando Pessoa.
"Inside, the church lights up today's rain." PFTM-1

Oblivion. Fanny Carrión de Fierro. TANSG, *tr. by* Sally Cheney Bell

Oblivion. Jessie Redmond Fauset. NegPo

Oblivion. Ellis Ayitey Komey. PBA; PBMAP

Oblivion. Ibrahim Naji. MAP, *tr. by* Issa Boullata and John Heath-Stubbs

"Oblivion, that's all. I never dream" he said. Dreaming. Fleur Adcock. OxBSo

Oboe. Laurence McKinney. NBLV

Obscur et froncé. Arthur Rimbaud. EroLit, *tr. by* Kenneth McLeish

Obscure, The. Norman Dubie. NoAM

Obscure and little seen my way. Charlotte Brontë. VWP

Obscure Night of the Soul, The. Saint John of the Cross. AWP; OBMV, *tr. by* Arthur Symons

Obscurely yet most surely called to praise. Praise in Summer. Richard Wilbur. NoP-4

Obscurest night involved [*or* involv'd] the sky. Castaway, The. William Cowper. NAEL-5v1; NOBE; NOBRP; NOEC; NPeEn; OxBEV; PoE; TRP

Obscurity has its tale to tell. Focus. Adrienne Rich. FaBoWP

Obscurity of Woman's Worth. Caroline Elizabeth Norton. VWP

Obsequies of Stuart. John Randolph Thompson. CBCWP

Obsequy for Dylan Thomas. James Keir Baxter. PeLV

Observance. Barbara Unger. TWW

Observant of the way she told. Tact. Edwin Arlington Robinson. NoAM

Observation. Robert Herrick. ChIV-2

Observation. Dorothy Parker. APT-1 *Fr.* Some Beautiful Letters.

Observation, An. Kay Sage. SurWo

Observation Car. Alec Derwent Hope. NoAM

Observation Car and Cigar. William Stafford. LCAP-2

Observation Generall from Their Eating, Etc., The. Roger Williams. SCAP; SacPr
(Of Eating and Entertainment.) TCAPo

Observation of a Bee. Leah Goldberg. WPOW, *tr. by* Stephen Mitchell

Observations. Hilaire Kirkland. PeNZ

Observations. Luvuyo Mkangelwa. NAfrP

Observations in a Cornish Teashop. Kenneth Rexroth. OBAL

Observations in the Art of English Poesie. Thomas Campion.
"Follow, follow[e] / Though with mischiefe." EnLoPo
(Laura.) NOBE; OBEV
Rose-cheeked Laura, Come. CABP; EnLoPo; InPK-6; NAEL-5v1; NAEL-6v1; NAEL-7v1; NOBE; NOSC; NoP-4; OBEV; PoE; TFi; TRP
("Rose-cheekt *Lawra* come.") NPeEn; OxBEV; PBRV

Observe how he negotiates his way. Swimmer. Robert Francis. APT-2; WeW-3

Observe the weary birds ere night be done. Orinda to Lucasia. Katherine Philips. BASC; NOSC

Observe the young and tender frond. Arthur Rex Dugard Fairburn. PeNZ *Fr.* Album Leaves.

Observed Observer, The. Alan Gould. BMAP

Obsessed by betrayal. Palm Leaf of Mary Magdalene. Cheryl Clarke. GLP; WiU

Obsession. Léon Damas. NegPo, *tr. by* Ellen Conroy Kennedy

Obsession. Robert Desnos. SurPaPo, *tr. by* Mary Ann Caws

Obsession. Angelina Muñiz Huberman. MirDau, *tr. by* Aurora Camacho

Obsidian sculpted lips slip. Doll Museum, The. Carlyle Reedy. Oth

Obvious, The. Anna Couani. BMAP

Obvious, The. Jeffrey McDaniel. AmPoNex

Obvious is the rottenness through your head. (LL) Penis, The. Dafydd [*or* David] ap Gwilym. EroLit; WoPoe, *tr. by* Dafydd Johnston

Occasion and expediency determines the form, The. (LL) Past Is the Present, The. Marianne Craig Moore. APT-1; NAAL-2v2

Occasional Man, An. Hugh Martin. ReLy

Occasional mornings when an early fog. Housewife. Josephine Miles. APT-2

Occasional Poem. Han Yü. SuSp, *tr. by* Charles Hartman

Occasional Poem. A. E. Housman. NOBL; PeLV

Occasional Poem, A. Lu Yu. SuSp, *tr. by* Chiang Yee

Occasional Poem, An. Ssu-k'ung Shu. SuSp, *tr. by* Irving Y. Lo

Occasional Poem 7.1.72. Roy Fisher. HarvBoo

Occasional Verse. Wang Ts'an. SuSp, *tr. by* Ronald C. Miao

Occasional Verses. Marilyn Hacker. Son

Occasioned by Reading Mrs. M. Robinson's Poems. Martha Hanson. CenSon

Occasioned by Seeing a Walk of Bay Trees. Mildmay Fane, 2d Earl of Westmorland. BeJo; NOSC; OxBSP

Occasional Poem: Upon Seeing Lotuses Bloom in a Vase. Wang Shih-chieng. SuSp, *tr. by* Richard John Lynn

Occupant of the Hose. Larissa Szporluk. NeAmPo

Occupation: Housewife. Phyllis McGinley. WPE *Fr.* I Know a Village.

Occupations of Hell. John Milton. NOSC *Fr.* Paradise Lost.

Occupy the poem. They stake. Abandoing All Pretense, the Vandals. Alan Michael Parker. NAPBL

Occurrences, The. George Oppen. APT-2

Occurrences and all that failed to occur. Didactic Poem on the Nature of History, A.D. 1954. Helmut Heissenbüttel. PFTM-2, *tr. by* Jerome Rothenberg

Ocean, The. Byron. *See* Childe Harold's Pilgrimage

Ocean, The. Nathaniel Hawthorne. APN-1

Ocean, The. Moschus. AWP; OBVE

Ocean, The. Charles Olson. APT-2 *Fr.* Maximus Poems, The.

Ocean air is heavy in autumn, The. Climbing to the Top of the City Walls at Kan-yü. Wang T'ing-hsiang. CoBLCP, *tr. by* Jonathan Chaves

Ocean begat ground. February Ground. Edward Dahlberg. APT-2

Ocean has its silent caves, The. Ocean, The. Nathaniel Hawthorne. APN-1

Ocean has not been so quiet for a long while, The. Evening Ebb. Robinson Jeffers. NoAM

Ocean Liner. Ko Changsu (Chang-soo Koh). WoPoe, *tr. by* the author

Ocean Musing, An. Henrietta Cordelia Ray. CBWP-3; SWaP

Ocean of Light. Phineas Fletcher. NOSC
(Vast Ocean of light, whose rayes surround.) PBRV

Ocean of the Streams of Story. Primus St. John. GT

Ocean's Love to Cynthia, The. Sir Walter Ralegh.
"Butt stay my thoughts, make end, geve fortune way." NPeEn
Ocean to Cynthia, The. NoSic

(21th: and last booke of the Ocean to Scinthia, The.) PBRV

("Sufficeth it to yow my joyes interred.") PBRV

Ocean Spirit. Song for Smooth Waters. Haida. CA

Ocean strives with forth the boat to kiss, The. (LL) Sonnet: "Slide soft, fair forth, and make a crystal plain." William Drummond, of Hawthornden. NOSC; OxBSo

Ocean tides curl in anger, swift winds rage. Inscribed on a Painting of Dragons by Ch'en So-weng. Hsieh Chin. CoBLCP, *tr. by* Jonathan Chaves

Ocean to Cynthia, The. Sir Walter Ralegh. NoSic *Fr.* Ocean's Love to Cynthia, The.

Ocean too has winter-Views serene, The. George Crabbe. WoPoe *Fr.* Borough, The.

Ocean with its large mouth swallowed him, The. Kenji Takezo Becomes Water. Rick Noguchi. NeAmPo

Och hey! for the splendour of tartans! Return, The. Pittendrigh Macgillivray. OxBS

Och hon for somebody! Somebody. *Unknown.* OxBS

Och, Johnny, I hardly knew ye!' (LL) Johnny, I Hardly Knew Ye. *Unknown.* BIrV; FaBoWar; NPeEn; OxBoLi

Oche Iron. Peter Blue Cloud. HATNAP

Ocol rejects the old type. Okot P'Bitek. PoetW *Fr.* Song of Lawino.

Octaves. Edwin Arlington Robinson.

("We lack the courage to be where we are.") NCAP

Octet Before Winter. Claire Malroux. VCWP, *tr. by* Marilyn Hacker

October. William Cullen Bryant. APN-1

October. Mary Weston Fordham. CBWP-2

October. Robert Earl Hayden. ESEAA

October. Paul Hamilton Hayne. APN-2

October. Helen Hunt Jackson. APN-2

October. Patrick Kavanagh. CIP-2; GTBS-P

October. Denise Levertov. TRP

October. Vladimir Ivanovich Narbut. TCRP, *tr. by* Lubov Yakovleva

October. Henrietta Cordelia Ray. CBWP-3

October. Folgore da San Geminiano [*or* Gimignano]. EaItPo, *tr. by* Dante Gabriel Rossetti *Fr.* Sonnets of the Months.

October. Edmund Spenser. NAEL-5v1; NAEL-6v1; NAEL-7v1 *Fr.* Shepheardes [*or* Shepeards *or* Shepherd's] Calender, The.

October. Edward Thomas. CABP; HarvBoo; NoAM

October. Yvor Winters. APT-2

October 1. Karl Shapiro. MoAmPo

October 23, 1983. June Jordan. SeSe

October 27th. Vera Gherarducci. CItWP, *tr. by* Cinzia Sartini Blum and Lara Trubowitz

October 31st 1994 7:30 am, on a street in Syracuse New York I'm a black female. "C" ing in Colors: Blue. Safiya Henderson-Holmes. SpirFl

October, A Copper-Crawed Cock. Nikolai Alekseievich Klyuyev [*or* Kliuev *or* Klyuev]. TCRusP, *tr. by* John Glad

October & winter had begun. My Indian Grandmother Speaks to Animals. John E. Smelcer. PoCoUp

October at last has come! The thicket has shaken. Autumn. Alexander Sergeyevich Pushkin. AWP, *tr. by* Max Eastman

October, 1803. William Wordsworth. CenSon

October Falls in Black and White. Joe Lothamer. GeoH

October, flower of my peril—. Indian Summer. Cristina Campo. CItWP, *tr. by* Cinzia Sartini Blum and Lara Trubowitz

October has come—already now the wood. Autumn (A Fragment). Alexander Sergeyevich Pushkin. WoPoe, *tr. by* Edwin Morgan

October in my country. Fugue. Shauqi Abi Shaqra. MAP, *tr. by* Sargon Boulus and Peter Porter

October in the Country: [1983]. James Simmons. BiHa; CIP-2

October Is Here. Mrs. Henry Linden. CBWP-4

October, Isle of Skye. Carter Revard. NoP-4

October its brilliance. In October. Claire Malroux. VCWP, *tr. by* Marilyn Hacker

October Journey. Margaret Walker Alexander. GT

October Morning, An. Jayanta Mahapatra. OMIP

October night nesting on the stadium. Halftime. Adam Lefevre. MoASP

October Observed, Hudson Falls, New York in Bill's Back Yard. Richard Elman. PoCoUp

October Poem. Tamura Ryuichi. AF, *tr. by* Christopher Drake

October Redbreast, The. Alice Thompson Meynell. MoBrPo

October robin kept, An. October Robin, An. Ted Hughes. NOxBChV

October's Bright Blue Weather. Helen Hunt Jackson. ITBLP

October's gold is dim—the forests rot. Sonnet. David Gray. OxAEP-2

October Salmon, An. Ted Hughes. EmeKit

October. They decide it is time to move. Sestina for the House. Ronald Wallace. PBCAP

October Tune. Joseph Brodsky. VCWP, *tr. by* Joseph Brodsky

October, Yellowstone Park. Maxine W. Kumin. ExTi

Octopus. Ghazi Al-Gosaibi. MAP, *tr. by* Charles Doria and Sharif Elmusa

Octopus. Arthur Clement Hilton. UV

Octopus, The. James Merrill. CoAP

Octopus, The. Ogden Nash. RB

Octopus in hot sauce. Just the Two of Us. Kate Jennings. BMAP

Odakyu line is always crowded I go on standing, The. Near Kitami Station on the Odakyū Line. Itō Hiromi. PFTM-2, *tr. by* Leith Morton

Odd day, An. For the first time in years. View from a Cab, The. Henry Taylor. NBLV

Odd, friendless boy raised by four aunts, The. Thumb. Philip Dacey. KaS

Odd gift, certainly, An. One. Spirit Level. Anthony Conran. TCAWP

Odd music, / cutting through horn blasts and squawks of traffic, asserts. Organist's Black Carnation, The. Laurence Lieberman. BodElec

Odd rot it what a shame it is. To Miss B. John Clare. NOBVV

Odd silence / Falls as we enter, An. Dreams of Water. Donald Justice. LCAP-2

Odd to close my eyes during the day and open them at night. Robert Glück. WiU *Fr.* Visit, The.

Odd, *You* should fear the touch. Ne Me Tangito. Charlotte Mew. VWP

Oddities composed the sum of the news. For the Lost Generation. Galway Kinnell. PAI

Odds were a hundred to one against me, The. They All Laughed. George Gershwin. APT-2; ReLy

Ode. Elizabeth Alexander. GT; PoPoPo

Ode. William Collins. *See* How Sleep the Brave

Ode. Ralph Waldo Emerson. *See* Ode, Inscribed to W.H. Channing

Ode. Thomas Gray. *See* Ode on the Death of a Favourite [*or* Favorite] Cat, Drowned in a Tub [*or* Bowl] of Gold Fishes

Ode. John Hoskyns [*or* Hoskins]. *See* Absence

Ode. Richard Lovelace. *See* To Lucasta: The Rose

Ode. Hugh Maxton. PBCIP

Ode on Intimations of Immortality from Recollections of Early Childhood. William Wordsworth. *See* Ode: Intimations of Immortality [from Recollections of Early Childhood]

Ode 3: "Of late, what time the Bear turned round." Anacreon. NoSic, *tr. by* Anomos *Fr.* Odes.

Ode V: "Of thee the Northman by his beachèd galley." George Santayana. APN-2

Ode XV. Thomas Stanley. ChIV-1

Ode: Against War. John Scott of Amwell. *See* Ode: "I hate that drum's discordant sound."

Ode, An: "Almighty Power, who rul'st this world of storms." Anne Batten Cristall. RWP

Ode, An: "High-spirited friend, / I send not balms, nor corsives to your wound." Ben Jonson. BeJo

(Noble Balm, The.) OBEV

Ode, An: "Merchant, to secure his treasure, The." Matthew Prior. AWP; EnLoPo; GTBS-P; NOEC; NPeEn; PoRA

(Song.) OBEV

Ode: "At her fair hands how have I grace entreated." Walter Davison. BoLoP

Ode: Autumn. Thomas Hood. *See* Autumn

Ode: "Bards of passion and of mirth." John Keats. FHYEP; OBEV; OxAEP-2

(Ode on the Poets.) GTBS-P

Ode Composed in Sleep, An. Judith Madan. ECWP

Ode for a Social Meeting. Oliver Wendell Holmes. OBAL

Ode for Him [*or* Ben Jonson], An. Robert Herrick. AWP; BASC; BeJo; CaPo; NOSC; SCGP

Ode for Soft Voice. Michael McClure. NeAP

Ode for the American Dead in Korea. Thomas McGrath. VGW

(Ode for the American Dead in Asia.) AiP; RaBo

Ode for the Dancing Khlysty. Yury [*or* Iurii] Ivask. TCRP; TCRusP, *tr. by* Alla Burago and Burton Raffel

Ode for the New Year, An. John Gay. OxBoLi

Ode for Three Koras and Balaphong. Léopold Sédar Senghor.

"After this day's hope—see how the Somme, the Seine, and the wild Slav." NegPo

Ode for Walt Whitman. Federico García Lorca. PFTM-1

Ode: Hastening His Friend into the Country. Eldred Revett. NOSC

Ode: "Here I'm perched on a sheer cliff." Attila József. IQMS, *tr. by* Suzanne K. Walther

Ode: "I hate that drum's discordant sound." John Scott of Amwell. NIP-4; NOEC; OxAEP-1; PAI

(Drum, The.) FaBoWar; PeFWW

(Ode: Against War.) ECEV

Ode: "I sing a song of sixpence, and of rye." Anthony C. Deane. NOBL

Ode: "Idea of justice may be precious, An." Frank O'Hara. NeAP

Ode: In a Few Hours. Hans Lodeizen. TuT, *tr. by* Eamon Grennan

Ode in Honour. Francis Scarfe. SPE

Ode in May. Sir William Watson. OBEV

Ode in Time of Hesitation, An. William Vaughn Moody. APN-2; CBCWP; OxBA

Ode Inscribed to the Infant Son of S. T. Coleridge, Esq. Mary Robinson. RWP

Ode, Inscribed to W. H. Channing. Ralph Waldo Emerson. APN-1; HAP; NAAL-2v1; NAAL-3; NOBA; OxBA; TAP; TCAPo
  (Ode.) ColAP; NCAP; NoP-4

Ode: Intimations of Immortality [from Recollections of Early Childhood]. William Wordsworth. AWP; FHYEP; HAP; HeIP-4; NAEL-6v2; NAWM-7v2; NOBE; NOBRP; NPeEn; NoP-4; OBEV; OxBEV; PoE; PoPoPo
  "Our birth is but a sleep and a forgetting." ITBLP
  "There was a time when meadow, grove and stream." NAEL-5v2; SCGP; TFi; TOF; TRP
  "Thought of our past years in me doth breed, The." SacPr

Ode Long Kesh. Barry MacSweeney. Oth

Ode: "Now each creature joys the other." Samuel Daniel. NoSic

Ode Occasioned by the Death of Mr. Thomson. William Collins. NOEC; PoE
  (Ode on the Death of [Mr.] Thomson.) NAEL-5v1; NAEL-6v1; NAEL-7v1

Ode of Imr El-Qais, The. Imr el [or ul] Kais [or Qais]. WoPoe, tr. by Robert Bringhurst

Ode of Signs. Muhammad ʿAbd al-Hayy. NAfrP, tr. by Alistair Elliot and Matthew Sorenson

Ode: Of Wit. Abraham Cowley. BeJo; MeLP; NAEL-5v1; NAEL-6v1; NAEL-7v1; NOSC
  (Ode to Wit.) OxAEP-1

Ode on a Bicycle on Halsted Street in a Sudden Summer Thunderstorm. Paul Carroll. IllVoic

Ode on a Distant Prospect of Eton College. Thomas Gray. GTBS-P; NAEL-5v1; NAEL-6v1; NAEL-7v1; NOBE; NOEC; NoP-4; OxAEP-1; PoE; SCGP

Ode on a Grecian Urn. John Keats. AWP; BRP; ClHu; EBEV; HAP; HeIP-4; MakPoe; NAEL-5v2; NAEL-6v2; NAWM-7v2; NIL-7; NIP-4; NOBE; NOBRP; NPeEn; OBEV; OxBEV; PoE; SCGP; TFi; TOF; UnPo

Ode on a Grecian Urn Summarized. Desmond Skirrow. NIL-7; NIP-4; NOBL

Ode on Arrival. Carl Rakosi. BodElec

Ode on Celestial Music. Brian Patten. OxBTC

Ode on Gas, An. Unknown. OBAL

Ode on His Majesty's Proclamation. Sir Richard Fanshawe. NOBE Fr. Il Pastor Fido.

Ode on Indolence. John Keats. NAEL-5v2; NAEL-6v2

Ode on Lord Macartney's Embassy to China. William Shepherd. NOEC

Ode on Melancholy. John Keats. CABP; FHYEP; HAP; InPK-6; NAEL-5v2; NAEL-6v2; NAWM-7v2; NIL-7; NOBE; NPeEn; NoP-4; OBEV; OxAEP-2; OxBEV; PoE; PoRA; SCGP; TFi

Ode on Reincarnation. Ernest Francisco Fenollosa.
  "Here let me sit, in this empty, cool, terraced hall." APN-2
  "I remember an ancient Chinese picture kept over there in Daitokuji." APN-2

Ode on Slate, The. Osip Emilevich Mandelstam [or Mandelshtam]. WoPoe, tr. by Bernard Meares

Ode on Solitude. Pope. AWP; FHYEP; HeIP-4; NAEL-5v1; NAEL-6v1; NIL-7; NOSC; PAI; PoRA; SacPr; SCGP
  (Quiet Life, The.) GTBS-P; PoToHe

Ode on the Birth of Our Saviour, An. Robert Herrick. ChrPo

Ode on the Death of a Favourite [or Favorite] Cat, Drowned in a Tub [or Bowl] of Gold Fishes. Thomas Gray. ClHu; EBEV; ECEV; FHYEP; NAEL-5v1; NAEL-6v1; NAEL-7v1; NBLV; NOBE; NOBL; NOEC; NoP-4; OBCoV; OxBEV; PeLV; PoE; PoRA; TFi
  (On a Favorite Cat Drowned in a Tub of Gold Fishes.) EBNV; GTBS-P; OxAEP-1

Ode on the Death of Haig's Horse. Douglas Garman.
  "Bury the Great Horse." UV

Ode on the Death of [Mr.] Thomson. William Collins. See Ode Occasioned by the Death of Mr. Thomson

Ode on the Hills of Georgia. Alexander Sergeyevich Pushkin. WoPoe, tr. by Peter Viereck

Ode on the Mammoth Cheese. James McIntyre. VerBaPo

Ode on the Morning of Christ's Nativity. John Milton. See On the Morning of Christ's Nativity

Ode on the Passion. Thomas Warton, the Elder. ChIV-2

Ode on the Pleasure Arising from Vicissitude. Thomas Gray.

Ode on the Poetical Character. William Collins. NAEL-5v1; NOEC; PoE

Ode on the Poets. John Keats. See Ode: "Bards of passion and of mirth."

Ode on the Popular Superstitions of the Highlands of Scotland, An. William Collins. NOEC; OxAEP-1

Stormy Hebrides, The. NOBE

Ode on the Revolution. Vladimir Vladimirovich Mayakovsky [or Maiakovskii]. TCRP, tr. by Daniel Weissbort

Ode on the Spring. Thomas Gray. GTBS-P; NOEC

Ode on the Twentieth Century. Henrietta Cordelia Ray. CBWP-3

Ode on the Visit of the Shah of Persia. Joseph Gwyer.
  "Intoxicating draughts he never does drink." VerBaPo

Ode on Theoxenos. Pindar. CAGL, tr. by John Addington Symonds

Ode on Truth: Addressed to George Dyer. Anne Batten Cristall. RWP

Ode: "Raven croaks before me, A." Theophile De Viau. WoPoe, tr. by Phillip Holland

Ode Recited at the Harvard Commemoration (July 21, 1865). James Russell Lowell. APN-1; CBCWP; NOBA; OBWP
  "I praise him not." AiP

Ode: Rule, Brittania! James Thomson. See Alfred: A Masque

Ode: Salute to the French Negro Poets. Frank O'Hara. GLP; NNaP; NeAP; PFTM-2; PoM

Ode: "Sleep sweetly in your humble graves." Henry Timrod. CBCWP; MakPoe; NOBA; OxBA; TAP
  (Sleep Sweetly.) AH
  (Lines.) APN-2
  (Ode Sung at Magnolia Cemetery.) TCAPo

Ode: "Spacious firmament on high, The." Joseph Addison. ChIV-1; ECEV; NOCV; NOEC; NPeEn; OxBEV; TOF

Ode Sung at Magnolia Cemetery. Henry Timrod. See Ode: "Sleep sweetly in your humble graves."

Ode: "That I have often been in love, deep love." "Peter Pindar." NOEC

Ode: The Dying Christian to His Soul. Pope. ChIV-2; SacPr
  (Dying Christian to His Soul, The.) AWP; OBEV

Ode: "They journeyed, / When the darkness of night." Ibn al-Arabi. AWP, tr. by R. A. Nicholson

Ode to a Country Hoyden. "Peter Pindar." NOEC

Ode to a Ditch. Unknown. VerBaPo

Ode to a Dressmaker's Dummy. Donald Justice. NoAM

Ode to a Jacobin. Unknown. UV

Ode to a Long Sorrow. Ricardo Molinari. TCLAP, tr. by Inés Probert

Ode to a Lost Cargo in a Ship Called Save. José Craveirinha. PeSAV, tr. by Chris Searle

Ode to a Maintenance Man and His Family. Kay Boyle. GifTon

Ode to a Model. Vladimir Vladimirovich Nabokov. OBAL

Ode to a Nightingale. John Keats. AWP; AmFaPo; BRP; CABP; ClHu; EBEV; GTBS-P; HAP; HeIP-4; NAEL-5v2; NAEL-6v2; NAWM-7v2; NIL-7; NOBE; NOBRP; NPeEn; NoP-4; OBEV; OWoS; OxBEV; PoE; PoPoPo; PoRA; RB; SCGP; SoSe-8; TFi; TOF; UnPo

Ode to a Pig while His Nose Was Being Bored. Robert Southey. NOBL

Ode to a Skylark. Shelley. See To a Skylark

Ode to Africa. Bernard Dadié. NegPo, tr. by Ellen Conroy Kennedy

Ode to Anactoria. Sappho. AWP, tr. by William Ellery Leonard

Ode to Aphrodite. Sappho. AWP, tr. by William Ellery Leonard

Ode to Autumn. John Keats. See To Autumn

Ode to Borrowdale in Cumberland. Amelia Alderson Opie. RWP

Ode to Brother Joe. Anthony McNeill. WaCA

Ode to César Vallejo. Pablo Neruda. TCLAP, tr. by Stephen Tapscott

Ode to Chaplin. Zoltán Jékely. IQMS, tr. by Joseph Leftwich

Ode to Charles Fourier. André Breton.
  "Fourier what have they done with your keyboard." PFTM-2, tr. by Kenneth White

Ode to Coit Tower. Gregory Corso. CLPP

Ode to Death. Charlotte Smith. NoP-4

Ode to Della Crusca. Hannah Cowley. NOBRP

Ode to Duty. William Wordsworth. AWP; FHYEP; GTBS-P; NAEL-5v2; NAEL-6v2; NOBRP; OBEV

Ode to Election Day. Anselm Berrigan. HeMarv

Ode to Ethiopia. Paul Laurence Dunbar. NAAAL

Ode to Evening. William Collins. AWP; CABP; HAP; NAEL-5v1; NAEL-6v1; NAEL-7v1; NOBE; NOEC; OBEV; OxAEP-1; PoE; SCGP; TFi
  (If ought of oaten stop, or pastoral song.) EBEV; ECEV; NPeEn; OxBEV
  (To Evening.) GTBS-P

Ode to Evening. Joseph Warton. OxAEP-1

Ode to Fancy. Joseph Warton.
  "O warm, enthusiastic maid." NOEC

Ode to Fear. William Collins. NOEC; SCGP

Ode to Francisco Salinas. Luís De León. SpanPo, tr. by Edwin Morgan

Ode to Governor Capper, An. J. P. Dunn. VerBaPo

Ode to Himself, An. Ben Jonson. BASC; BeJo; CABP; HAP; NOBE; NOSC; NPeEn; NoP-4; OxAEP-1; PBRV; SCGP

Ode to Himself[e]. Ben Jonson. BeJo
  (On The New Inn: Ode. To Himself.) BASC

Ode to Jackson Pollock. Michael McClure. PmAP

Ode to Joy. Frank O'Hara. GLP; NeAP; PmAP

Ode to Language. Robert Kelly. PFTM-2; SeSe

Ode to Laziness. Pablo Neruda. TCLAP, *tr.* by William Carlos Williams

Ode to Lovers. Sir John Suckling. UV

Ode to Master Endymion Porter, upon His Brother's Death, An. Robert Herrick. CaPo

Ode to Master [*or* Mr.] Anthony Stafford to Hasten Him into the Country, An. Thomas Randolph. BASC; BeJo; NOBE; NOSC; OBEV

Ode to Meaning. Robert Pinsky. MakPoe

Ode to Michael Goldberg's Birth and Other Births. Frank O'Hara. NeAP

Ode: To Miss Margaret Pulteney. Ambrose Philips. OxAEP-1; UV

Ode to Moderation. Annabella Plumptre.
   "To thee, whose cautious step and specious air." ECWP; NOEC

Ode to Mozart. Maura Stanton. MiVo

Ode to Mr. F— [*or* Mr. Forbes]. Allan Ramsay. NOEC; OBVE

Ode to Mr. Hobbes. Abraham Cowley. *See* To Mr. Hobbes [*or* Hobs]

Ode to My Car. Gig Ryan. BMAP

Ode: To My Pupils. W. H. Auden. MoBrPo

Ode to My Socks. Pablo Neruda. AmFaPo, *tr.* by Stephen Mitchell

Ode to My Socks. Pablo Neruda. RaBo; TCLAP; TRP, *tr.* by Robert Bly

Ode to Peace. Mary Weston Fordham. CBWP-2

Ode to Psyche. John Keats. FHYEP; NAEL-5v2; NAEL-6v2; NOBE; NOBRP; NoP-4; OBEV; OxAEP-2; PoE; TFi; TOF

Ode to Rhys ap Maredudd of Tywyn. Dafydd [*or* David] Nanmor. OBWVE, *tr.* by H. Idris Bell

Ode to Salt. Pablo Neruda. TCLAP, *tr.* by Margaret Sayers Peden

Ode to Salted Mutton Birds. Jim Everett. IBA

Ode to Sappho. Elizabeth Oakes-Smith. ColAP

Ode to Señor Leal's Goat. Gary Soto. OxIBACP

Ode to Simplicity. William Collins. NOBE; OBEV; OxAEP-1

Ode to Singer. Paul Van Ostaijen. TuT, *tr.* by Peter Van de Kamp

Ode. To Sir William Sydney, on His Birthday. Ben Jonson. BeJo

Ode to Society, An. Hester Lynch Salusbury Thrale [*later* Mrs. Piozzi]. ECWP

Ode to Spring. Anna Laetitia Barbauld. OxAEP-1

Ode to St Crispin's Day. R. H. Ellis.
   "Walk up, walk up, my bonny boys." FaBoWar

Ode to Stephen Dowling Bots, Dec'd. "Mark Twain." *See* Adventures of Huckleberry Finn, The

Ode to Suburbia. Eavan Boland. PBCIP

Ode to Swansea. Vernon Watkins. OBWVE

Ode to Terminus. W. H. Auden. HAP

Ode to the Angels Who Move Perpetually toward the Dayspring of Their Youth. Paul Carroll. IllVoic

Ode to the Cat. Pablo Neruda. VCWP, *tr.* by John Hollander

Ode to the Confederate Dead. Allen Tate. APT-2; AiP; CBCWP; ColAP; FaBoMo; FuPo; HeIP-4; MoAmPo; NAAL-2v2; NOBA; NoAM; NoP-4; OBWP; OxBA; TAP; TFi; UnPo

Ode: To the Cuckoo. Michael Bruce. *See* To the Cuckoo

Ode to the Diencephalon. W. H. Auden. OxAEP-2

Ode to the End of Summer. Phyllis McGinley. NBLV

Ode to the German Drama. *Unknown.* NOEC

Ode to the Human Heart. Edward Laman Blanchard. NOBL

Ode to the Lemon. Pablo Neruda. PoetW, *tr.* by Margaret Sayers Peden

Ode to the Maguire. Eochadh [*or* Eochy] O'Hussey [*or* O'Heughusa]. *See* O'Hussey's Ode to the Maguire

Ode to the Northeast Wind. Charles Kingsley. OxAEP-2

Ode to the Pious Memory of the Accomplished Young Lady, Mrs. Anne Killigrew. Dryden. *See* To the Pious Memory of the Accomplished [*or* Accomplisht] Young Lady, Mrs. Anne Killigrew, [Excellent in the Two Sister-Arts of Poesie and Painting]

Ode to the Poppy. Henrietta O'Neill. ECWP; WPE

Ode to the Sea. Howard Baker. OxBA

Ode to the Setting Sun. Francis Thompson.
   "Who lit the furnace of the mammoth's heart?" MoBrPo

Ode to the Severn Bridge. Harri Webb. TCAWP

Ode to the Sun. Eloise Bibb. CBWP-4

Ode. To the Virginian Voyage. Michael Drayton. *See* To the Virginian Voyage

Ode to the Watermelon. Pablo Neruda. SPE, *tr.* by Robert Bly

Ode to the West Wind. Shelley. AWP; CenSon; ClHu; EBEV; FHYEP; GTBS-P; HAP; HeIP-4; MakPoe; NAEL-5v2; NAEL-6v2; NAWM-7v2; NIL-7; NIP-4; NOBE; NOBRP; NPeEn; NoP-4; OBEV; OxAEP-2; OxBEV; OxBSo; PAI; PeECV; PoE; PoPoPo; PoRA; SCGP; TFi; TRP; WeW-3

Ode to Truth. Mary Whateley. ECWP

Ode to Winter. Thomas Campbell. GTBS-P

Ode to Wisdom. Elizabeth Carter. ECWP

Ode to Wit. Abraham Cowley. *See* Ode: Of Wit

Ode to Your Back. Gloria Vando. TouFir

Ode to Zion. Judah Halevi. TrJP, *tr.* by Nina Davis Salaman

Ode: "Until thine hands clasp girdlewise the waist of the Belov'd." Sadi [*or* Saadi *or* Sa'di]. AWP, *tr.* by R. A. Nicholson

Ode, upon a Question Moved, Whether Love Should Continue Forever?, An. Edward Herbert, 1st Baron Herbert of Cherbury. BASC; MeLP; NOBE; OxAEP-1; OxBEV

Ode upon Doctor Harvey. Abraham Cowley.
   "Coy Nature (which remain'd, though aged grown)." NPeEn

Ode: "Urals post-master, this is your." Barry MacSweeney. Oth

Ode: "Vengeance will sit above our faults; but till." John Donne. SacPr

Ode: "We are the music-makers." Arthur William Edgar O'Shaughnessy. OBEV

(We Are the Music Makers.) CABP

Ode: "Weep, ah weep love's losing, love's with its dwelling place." *Var. authors.* AWP; TAL, *tr.* by Wilfrid Scawen Blunt and Lady Anne Blunt Fr. Mu'allaqat, The.

Ode: "Where have you gone blue middle of a decade? the gates creak. a sigh is so vastly different." D. A. Powell. NAPBL

Ode, which Was Prefixed to a Little Prayer-Book Givin to a Young Gentlewoman, An. Richard Crashaw. ESCV

Ode: "Who can support the anguish of love?" Ibn al-Arabi. AWP, *tr.* by R. A. Nicholson

Ode: Written After Reading Some Modern Love-Verses. John Scott of Amwell. ECEV

Ode Written in MDCCXLVI. William Collins. *See* How Sleep the Brave

Ode Written in the Beginning of the Year 1746. William Collins. *See* How Sleep the Brave

Ode Written in the Peak[e], An. Michael Drayton. NOSC

Odell. James Stephens. MoBrPo

Odes. Anacreon.
   Ode 3: "Of late, what time the Bear turned round." NoSic, *tr.* by Anomos

Odes. Hafiz [*or* Hafez].
   "Comrades, the morning breaks, the sun is up." AWP
   "Days of spring are here, The! the eglantine." AWP
   "Flower-tinted cheek, the flowery close, A." TAL
   "From Canaan Joseph shall return, whose face." TAL
   "Grievous folly shames my sixtieth year, A." AWP
   "I cease not from desire till my desire." AWP; TAL
   "I have borne the anguish of love, which ask me not to describe." AWP
   "I said to heaven that glowed above." AWP
   "Jewel of the secret treasury, The." AWP
   "Lady that hast my heart within thy hand." AWP
   "Mirth, Spring, to linger in a garden fair." TAL
   "Oft have I said, I say it once more." AWP
   "Rose has flushed red, the bud has burst, The." TAL
   "Rose is not the rose unless thou see, The." AWP
   "Saki, for God's love, come and fill my glass." AWP
   "What is wrought in the forge of the living and life." TAL
   "Where is my ruined life, and where the fame." AWP; TAL
   "Wind from the east, oh Lapwing of the day." AWP; TAL

Odes. Horace.
   1.2: To Leuconoë. WoPoe, *tr.* by David Ferry
   1.3: To the Ship on Which Virgil Sailed to Athens ("Sic te diva potens Cyri"). AWP, *tr.* by Dryden
   1.5: Quis Multa Gracilis. WoPoe, *tr.* by Stephen Sandy
   (Fifth Ode of Horace, The.) EBEV; EnLoPo; NPeEn; OxBEV; PBRV, *tr.* by Milton
   ("Pyrrha, what slender well-shap'd beau.") OBVE, *tr.* by Anthony Horneck
   ("To whom now, Pyrrha, art thou kind?") OBVE, *tr.* by Abraham Cowley
   ("What stripling now thee discomposes.") OBVE, *tr.* by Sir Richard Fanshawe
   1.8. OBVE, *tr.* by Sir Richard Fanshawe
   1.9. OBVE, *tr.* by Dryden
   (To Thaliarchus ("Thou seest the hills").) OBVE, *tr.* by Sir Richard Fanshawe
   ("You see how, white with snows to the north of us.") STV, *tr.* by John Frederick Nims
   1.11: Ad Leuconoen. AWP, *tr.* by F. P. Adams
   ("Don't ask—knowing's taboo—what's in the cards, darling, for you, for me.") STV, *tr.* by John Frederick Nims
   1.14: Ship of State, The ("O navis, referent"). AWP, *tr.* by William Ewart Gladstone
   1.21: To Apollo and Diana ("Dianam tenerae dicite virgines"). OBVE, *tr.* by Branwell Brontë
   (Invocation: "Maidens young and virgins tender.") AWP, *tr.* by Louis Untermeyer

1.22. OBVE *tr. by* the Earl of Roscommon

("Man in righteousness arrayed, The.") AWP, *tr. by* John Quincy Adams

1.23: To Chloë ("Vitas hinnuleo"). AWP; OBVE

1.25: Ribald Romeos Less and Less Berattle ("Parcius iunctas quatiunt fenestras"). STV, *tr. by* John Frederick Nims

("Bloods and bucks of this lewd town, The.") OBVE, *tr. by* the Young Gentleman of Mr. Rule's Academy at Islington

(To Lydia.) OBVE, *tr. by* Philip Francis

("Young bloods come round less often now, The.") BoLoP, *tr. by* James Michie

1.31. CTC, *tr. by* Ezra Pound

1.33: Albi, Ne Doleas. AWP, *tr. by* Austin Dobson

1.38: Persicos odi, puer, apparatus.

("Ah child, no Persian—perfect art.") OBVE, *tr. by* Gerard Manley Hopkins

("Boy, I detest the Persian pomp.") InPK-6; NBLV, *tr. by* Eugene Field

("Davus, I detest.") NBLV, *tr. by* Austin Dobson

("Dear Lucy, you know what my wish is.") NBLV, *tr. by* William Makepeace Thackeray

("I do not share the common craze.") NBLV, *tr. by* Keith Preston

("Nay, nay, my boy—'tis not for me.") InPK-6, *tr. by* Hartley Coleridge

("Persian flummery.") NBLV, *tr. by* George F. Whicher

(Persian Fopperies.) AWP, *tr. by* William Cowper

("Persian pomps, boy, ever I renounce them.") OBVE, *tr. by* Christopher Smart

2.4: Ad Xanthiam Phoceum ("Ne sit ancillae"). AWP, *tr. by* Franklin P. Adams

2.7. OBWP, *tr. by* James Michie

2.8. STV, *tr. by* John Frederick Nims

2.10: To Licinius. AWP, *tr. by* William Cowper

("Of thy lyfe [*or* life], Thomas, this compass well mark.") OBVE, *tr. by* Henry Howard, Earl of Surrey

("You better sure shall live, not evermore.") OBVE, *tr. by* Sir Philip Sidney

2.11: To an Ambitious Friend ("Quid bellicosus"). AWP, *tr. by* Matthew Arnold

2.18. OBVE, *tr. by* Christopher Smart

3.1. AWP; OBVE, *tr. by* Abraham Cowley

3.2: OBWP, *tr. by* James Michie

3.5: Carthaginian Peace, The. MLL, *tr. by* Helen Waddell

3.7. OBVE, *tr. by* George Stepney

3.9: Dialogue between Horace and Lydia, A ("Donec gratus eram"). OBVE, *tr. by* Robert Herrick

(Reconciliation: A Modern Version, The.) NBLV, *tr. by* Franklin P. Adams

3.10: Extremum Tanain. AWP, *tr. by* Austin Dobson

3.13: To the Fountain[s] of Bandusia ("O fons Bandusiae"). AWP, *tr. by* Eugene Field

3.22: Pine Tree for Diana, The ("Montium custos nemorumque"). AWP, *tr. by* Louis Untermeyer

3.23: To Phidyle ("Caelo supinas si tuleris"). AWP, *tr. by* Austin Dobson

3.28: Holiday ("Festo quid potius die"). AWP, *tr. by* Louis Untermeyer

3.29. AWP; NPeEn; OBVE, *tr. by* Dryden

3.30: This Monument Will Outlast (Exegi monumentum aere perennius). CTC; WoPoe, *tr. by* Ezra Pound

4.1: To Venus. AWP; OBVE, *tr. by* Ben Jonson

4.7. NAEL-5v1; NAEL-6v1; NAEL-7v1, *tr. by* Samuel Johnson

(Diffugere Nives.) OBVE, *tr. by* Alfred Edward Housman

("Snows are thaw'd, now grass new cloaths the earth.") NPeEn, *tr. by* Sir Richard Fanshawe

("Snows dissolving, grass returns to meadow.") WoPoe, *tr. by* Michael O'Brien

4.13: Revenge ("Audivere, Lyce"). AWP, *tr. by* Louis Untermeyer

Odes and Days. Bruce Beaver.

Day 20. BMAP

Odes of Solomon, The. *Unknown.*

"My heart was split, and a flower." EnlH

Odes Sung in Commemoration of the Marine Society. Anne Penny.

Sung at Table by the Same Choir. ECWP

Sung by a Choir of Boys Marching Round the Room. ECWP

Odi et Amo. Catullus. WoPoe, *tr. by* Frank Bidart

Odi et Amo. Catullus. CTC, *tr. by* Ezra Pound

Odor has remained among the sugarcane, An. Dictators, The. Pablo Neruda. AF, *tr. by* Robert Bly

Odor of a Metal Is Not Strong, The. Merrill Moore. OxBSo

Odor of algaroba, lure of release. Fructus. Genevieve Taggard. APT-2

Odorous shade lingers the fair day's ghost, An. Night. Henri De Regnier. AWP, *tr. by* "Seumas" O'Sullivan

Odour I bequeath, The. (LL) Unprofitablenes. Henry Vaughan. ESCV; GeHe; NAEL-7v1; NOSC

Odour of sanctity, The. Candles. Little Cloth, The. Hilary Llewellyn-Williams. TCAWP

Odour. 2. Cor. 2, The. George Herbert. ChIV-2; ESCV

Odours of spring, my sense ye charm. On Receiving a Branch of Mezereon Which Flowered at Woodstock, December 1809. Mary Tighe. RWP

Odysseus. Padraic Fallon. CIP-2

Odysseus. Haim [*or* Chaim *or* Khayim] Guri [*or* Gouri]. MHP, *tr. by* Ruth Finer Mintz

Odysseus. W. S. Merwin. NOBA; NoP-4

Odysseus heard the sirens; they were singing. Sirens, The. John Streeter Manifold. MoBrPo; Son

Odysseus rested on his oar, and saw. Second Voyage, The. Eiléan Ní Chuilleanáin. EmeKit; ModIr; NPeEn

Odysseus to Telemachus. Joseph Brodsky. BLT; PAI, *tr. by* George L. Kline

Odysseus under wet snapping sheets. Christian Karlson Stead. PeNZ *Fr.* Quesada.

Odyssey. Homer.

"And now the Queene of women had intent." OBVE, *tr. by* George Chapman

Argos. ModIr, *tr. by* Michael Longley

Butchers, The. ModIr; NPeEn, *tr. by* Michael Longley

"Cave we found, but vacant all within, The." OBVE, *tr. by* Pope

"Downe to the king's most bright-kept baths they went." CTC, *tr. by* George Chapman

End of the Suitors, The. OBVE, *tr. by* George Chapman

Execution of the faithless maids. OBVE, *tr. by* Pope

"For my part, I'le not meddle with the cause." CTC, *tr. by* George Chapman

"From her bed's high and odoriferous roome." CTC, *tr. by* George Chapman

Gardens of Alcinous, The. OBGa; OBVE, *tr. by* Pope

Gardens of Alcinous, The. OBVE, *tr. by* George Chapman

"God who mounts the winged winds, The." OBVE, *tr. by* Pope

"He ended, nor the Argicide refus'd." OBVE, *tr. by* Pope

"Just then, forgetful of the strict command." OBVE, *tr. by* William Cowper

Laertes. ModIr, *tr. by* Michael Longley

"Mighty wave rush'd o'er him as he spoke, A." OBVE, *tr. by* Pope

"Now gently winding up the fair ascent." OBVE, *tr. by* Pope

"Now toils the Heroe; trees on trees o'erthrown." OBVE, *tr. by* Pope

"Nymph turnd home, The. He fell to felling downe." OBVE, *tr. by* George Chapman

Phemios and Medon. ModIr, *tr. by* Michael Longley

"She thus; when I had great desire to prove." OBVE, *tr. by* George Chapman

Suitors watch Ulysses string the bow, The. OBVE, *tr. by* Pope

"There grew two olives, closest of the grove." OBVE, *tr. by* Pope

"This spoke, a huge wave tooke him by the head." OBVE, *tr. by* George Chapman

"Thus charg'd he; nor Argicides denied." OBVE, *tr. by* George Chapman

"Trembling the spectres glide, and plaintive vent." OBVE, *tr. by* Pope

"Twelve herds of oxen, no less flockes of sheepe." CTC, *tr. by* George Chapman

Ulysses Insults over the Cyclops. NOSC, *tr. by* George Chapman

Ulysses Invokes the Dead. NOSC, *tr. by* George Chapman

Ulysses Reunited with Penelope. NOSC; OBVE, *tr. by* George Chapman

"Where neither King nor shepheard want comes neare." CTC, *tr. by* George Chapman

"While thus he thought, a monst'rous wave up-bore." OBVE, *tr. by* Pope

"With many a weary step, and many a groan." UV

"Youth there was, Elpenor was he nam'd, A." OBVE, *tr. by* Pope

Odyssey. Homer. NAWM-5v1; NAWM-7v1, *tr. by* Robert Fitzgerald

"We bore down on the ship at sea's edge." WoPoe, *tr. by* Robert Fitzgerald

Odyssey, The. Rick Bass. Unle

Odyssey, The. Andrew Lang. OBEV; PoRA

Odyssey, The. Sipho Sepamla. AF

Odyssey of Big Boy. Sterling Allen Brown. NAAAL

Odyssey or "On Absence," The. Chimako Tada. VCWP, *tr. by* Naoshi Koriyama

Oeconomy of Love; a Poetical Essay, The. John Armstrong.

Advice to Lovers. NOEC

Oedipus. Thomas Blackburn. FaBoTw

Oedipus. Dryden.

"When Athens all the Graecian state did guide." NOSC

Oedipus. David Ignatow. PAI

Oedipus. Josephine Miles. SoSe-8; WPE

Oedipus and the Riddle. Jorge Luis Borges. WoPoe, *tr. by* John Hollander

Oedipus at Colonus. Sophocles.

Chorus: "What man is he that yearneth." AWP

Colonus' Praise. OBVE

"Endure what life God gives and ask no longer span." OBMV

Oedipus said to the Sphinx. Limerick: "Oedipus said to the Sphinx." Victor Gray. PeLi

Oedipus the King [or Oedipus Rex]. Sophocles. NAWM-5v1

Oenone and Paris. George Peele. See Arraignment of Paris, The

Oeuvre. Lucien Stryk. IllVoic

Of a child in Brooklyn. (LL) Locket, The. John Montague. BiHa; PBCIP

Of a cold day. (LL) Early in the Morning. Louis Simpson. CoAmPo; TRP

Of a Country Life. James Thomson.
  "How sweet and innocent are country sports." UV

Of a day I had rued. (LL) Dust of Snow. Robert Frost. APT-1; ChAP; OxBA; OxBSP; PAI; SAmP; SoSe-8; TAP; UnPo; WeW-3

Of a demon in my view—. (LL) "Alone." Edgar Allan Poe. APN-1; NAAL-2v1; NAAL-3

Of a Fair Shrew. Sir John Harington [or Harrington]. See Fair, Rich, and Young

Of a fallen sparrow, the prairie dog first softens. Gnawing the Breast. Sandra McPherson. LCAP-2

Of a full feast; and the out-courts of glory. (LL) Son-Days [dayes]. Henry Vaughan. AngWePo; GeHe; NOSC

Of a Good Prince and an Evil. Timothy Kendall. NoSic

Of a good universe next door≤t's go. (LL) E. E. Cummings. HarvBoo; NAAL-2v2; NOBA; OxBA; TAP

Of a horse shoe nail. (LL) Mother Goose. OxNR; ReMoGo

Of a hungry devil. (LL) Kasa no Iratsume. BoWoP; WPOW

Of a Husbandman. Joshua Sylvester. NOSC

Of a lady fair to see. Lines to Mrs. M. C. Turner. Eloise Bibb. CBWP-4

Of a little take a little. Unknown. OxNR

Of a love or a season? (LL) Reluctance. Robert Frost. ITBLP; MoAmPo; NOBA; OxBA

Of a mon Matheu thoghte. Unknown. MiEL

Of a newborn child. (LL) John Berryman. HCAP; PoPoPo; VCAP Fr. Dream Songs.

Of a rose, a lovely rose. Unknown.

Of a Rose, a Lovely Rose. Unknown. OBEV; OHMEL

Of a sudden, the great prima donna. Limerick. Unknown. PeLi

Of a tall stature and of sable hue. Charles II. Unknown. FaBoEE

Of A' the Airts [the Wind Can Blaw]. Robert Burns. AWP; NoP-4; OxBS
  (I Love My Jean.) OxBEV
  (Jean.) GTBS-P; OBEV

Of a' the maids o' fair Scotland. Young Benjie. Unknown. ESPB; OxBB

Of a vast expanding pearl. (LL) Kenneth Rexroth. APSN; APT-2 Fr. Love Poems of Marichiko, The.

Of a Zealous Lady. Sir John Harington [or Harrington]. FaBoEE

Of about one year and a half. (LL) Henry Reed. BoLoP; GTBS-P; NAEL-6v2; NIL-7; NIP-4; NOBE; NPeEn; NoP-4; OxBEV; PoWW Fr. Lessons of the War.

Of Adam's first wife, Lilith, it is told. Dante Gabriel Rossetti. Son Fr. House of Life, The.

Of age of ours. Age of the Rubber Seals. Buland Al-Haidari [or Al-Haydari]. MAP, tr. by Patricia Alanah Byrne and Salma Khadra Jayyusi

Of age's beauty 'tis a measure. Age. Ferdinand von Saar. AuPH, tr. by Lowell A. Bangerter

Of aid from them—She was the Universe. (LL) Darkness. Byron. CABP; NAEL-5v2; NAEL-6v2; PoE; TreFP

Of all are living, or have been. (LL) Queens. John Millington Synge. MoBrPo; OBMV; PeVV

Of all creatures women be best. What Women Are Not. Unknown. MiEL

Of all despondencies, death-despair must be the worst. Of All Despondencies. Enrique Lihn. VCWP, tr. by Alastair Reid

Of All Distances the Best Possible One. Patrizia Cavalli. CItWP, tr. by Cinzia Sartini Blum and Lara Trubowitz

Of All Garments. Dhu'l-Rumma. ArPe, tr. by Omar S. Pound

Of all God's jokes none is bluer. Limerick. A. Cinna. PeLi

Of all God's mercies, is my posy [or posie] still. (LL) Posy [or Posie], The. George Herbert. ChIV-1; NOSC

Of all great Nature's tones that sweep. Implicit Faith. Aubrey Thomas De Vere. SacPr

Of all I ever did. (LL) A. E. Housman. NOBVV; OxBEV

Of all implements, the pitchfork was the one. Pitchfork, The. Seamus Heaney. OxBEV

Of all sins of the flesh, that reprobate. Hangover Mass. X. J. Kennedy. DiPo

Of all that God has shown me. Mechthild von Magdeburg. EnlH; WPoS

Of all that Orient lands can vaunt. Haschish, The. John Greenleaf Whittier. APN-1; NCAP; OBAL

Of all that shines below. (LL) Sun-Flower, The. Dora Greenwell. EroLit; VWP; WPE

Of all the animals, my heart belongs to the camel. Camel. Boris Alekseievich Chichibabin. TCRP, tr. by Albert C. Todd

Of all the Bible stories that they tell. Revenge 1. Giuseppe Gioacchino Belli. WoPoe, tr. by Anthony Burgess

Of all the birds I know, few can. Toucan, The. Pyke, Jr. Johnson. NTCP

Of all the birds that rove and sing. Jenny Wren. Walter De la Mare. OWoS

Of all the brave captains that ever were seen. Sir Dilberry Diddle, Captain of Militia. Unknown. NOEC

Of all the causes which conspire to blind. Pope. MakPoe; NoP-4; OxAEP-1 Fr. Essay on Criticism, An.

Of all the cities far and wide. Sandblast Girl and the Acid Man, The. May Kendall. ViWPN

Of all the cities in Romanian lands. Dryden. EBNV; NOSC Fr. Theodore and Honoria, from [Fables Ancient and Modern from] Boccace.

Of all the creatures, in the world, that be. John Oldham. OBVE Fr. Satires.

Of all the flowers rising now. Maritae Suae. William Philpot. OBEV

Of all the girls that are so smart. Sally in Our Alley. Henry Carey. AWP; BoLoP; GTBS-P; NOBE; OBEV; OxAEP-1

Of all the huntresses. Patrizia Cavalli. NeIt

Of all the kings that ever here did reign. Sir Philip Sidney. NoSic Fr. Astrophil and Stella.

Of all the lives I cannot live. Dickinson. Anne Finch (b. 1908). FFC

Of all the mighty nations of the sun. (LL) Africa. Claude McKay. APT-1; NAAAL; NAAL-5; Son

Of all the people who went into the snowy mountains. Gu Cheng. PFTM-2; VCWP, tr. by Eva Hung Fr. Bulin File, The.

Of all the plants, bamboo is the most difficult to paint. Painting Bamboo, a Song. Po Chü-i. SuSp, tr. by Irving Lo

Of all the pleasant ways. Driving in the Park. Unknown. OxBoLi; PeLV

Of all the rides since the birth of time. Skipper Ireson's Ride. John Greenleaf Whittier. APN-1; NCAP; NOBA; OBAL; OBCA; OxBA

Of all the sayings in this world. Unknown. OxNR

Of all the seas that's coming. Unknown. EBEV

Of all the ships upon the blue. Captain Reece. Sir William Schwenck Gilbert. OBCoV

Of all the Souls that stand create—. Choice. Emily Dickinson. NAAL-2v1; NAAL-3

Of all the Sounds despatched abroad. Wind, The. Emily Dickinson. APN-2

Of all the thoughts of God that are. Sleep, The. Elizabeth Barrett Browning. ChIV-1; OxAEP-2

Of all the times when not to speak is best. Three Silences. Rachel Hadas. RA

Of all the torments, all the cares. Rivals. William Walsh. OBEV

Of all the wild deeds upon murder's black list. Verses on Daniel Good. Unknown. OxBB

Of all the world's enjoyments. Fisherman's Song, The. Thomas D'Urfey [or Durfey]. NOSC

Of All There Is. C. Mikal Oness. GeoHom

Of all thes kene conquerours to carpe it were kynde. Tournament of Tottenham, The. Unknown. OxBoLi

Of All Things for You to Go Away Mad. Joanne Kyger. PoM

Of all things living. Sweet Potato. Shinkichi Takahashi. ZenPo, tr. by Takashi Ikemoto and Lucien Stryk

Of all those streets that wander to the west. Limits. Jorge Luis Borges. PoetW, tr. by Alastair Reid

Of all those who reach earth by falling. (LL) Sudden Journey. Tess Gallagher. NIL-7; NIP-4

Of alle the enemies that I can fynde. Unknown. OHMEL

Of Althea and Flaxie. Cheryl Clarke. GLP

Of an Heroical Answer of a Great Roman Lady to Her Husband. Sir John Harington [or Harrington]. BoLoP

Of an old King in a story. Variations on an Air: after W. B. Yeats. Gilbert Keith Chesterton. NOBL

Of an Orchard. Katharine Tynan. SacPr

Of an unvisited garden in Mexico. (LL) Dream Record: June 8 1955. Allen Ginsberg. CoAmPo; NOBA

Of Angels and of Angel-men the King. (LL) Hymn for Christmas Day, A. John Byrom. ECEV; NOCV

Of animals' houses / Two sorts are found. Animals' Houses. James Reeves. OTCP

Of Another Fashion. Emilio Ballagas. CAGL, tr. by Fanny Arango-Ramos and William Keeth

Of asphodel, that greeny flower, the least. William Carlos Williams. HarvBoo Fr. Asphodel, That Greeny Flower.

Of attractions the Sabines ain't stinted. Limerick. D. W. Barker. PeLi

Of August strikes like a hawk the crouching hare. (LL) Emblems. Allen Tate. AWP; VGW

Of Autumn. Veronica Porumbacu. BoWoP

Of banks and stones and every blooming thing. (LL) Inniskeen Road: July Evening. Patrick Kavanagh. CIP-2; NPeEn; NoAM; OxBSo

Of beasts am I, of men was he most brave.   Lion over the Tomb of Leonidas, The.   *Unknown.*   AWP, *tr. by* Walter Leaf

Of Beauty.   Sir Richard Fanshawe.   BoLoP   *Fr.* Il Pastor Fido.

Of Being Numerous.   George Oppen.
   "It is difficult now to speak of poetry."   NNaP

Of Bison Men.   James Fenton.   PeLV   *Fr.* Wild Life Studies.

Of black flesh after flame. (LL)   Portrait in Georgia.   Jean Toomer.   APT-2; NoP-4

Of black silent waters weep. (LL)   Thrushes.   Ted Hughes.   FaBoMo; TRP

Of blackberry-eating in late September. (LL)   Blackberry Eating.   Galway Kinnell.   InPK-6; InvLad; NIL-7; NIP-4; SoSe-8

Of boats, of boats.   Passage.   Peter Rafferty.   NLP

Of Boston in New England.   William Bradford.   SCAP

Of Breakfast, then of walking to the pond.   Good Appetite.   Mark Van Doren.   OxBSP; Spl

Of bricks. . . Who built it? Like some crazy balloon.   Our Youth.   John Ashbery.   CoAmPo; VGW

Of bright cities / and citrus.   Florida.   Carl Rakosi.   TAP

Of British beasts the Buck is king.   Upon the Duke of Buckingham.   *Unknown.*   BASC

Of Bronze—and Blaze.   Aurora.   Emily Dickinson.   APN-2; NCAP

Of Byron and Shelley and Keats. (LL)   Dorothy Parker.   APT-1; NALW   *Fr.* Pig's-Eye View of Literature, A.

Of carrying a stick? (LL)   Critics and Connoisseurs.   Marianne Craig Moore.   APT-1; FaBoWP; NOBA; NoAM; OxBA

Of cat-gut lace. (LL)   Boogie: 1 A.M.   Langston Hughes.   APSN; APT-2

Of cat-gut lace. (LL)   Nightmare Boogie.   Langston Hughes.   APSN; APT-2

Of Caution.   Francesco da Barberini.   AWP; EaItPo, *tr. by* Dante Gabriel Rossetti

Of Change of Opinions.   Victor Gustave Plarr.   NOBVV

Of Choice.   William Meredith.   VCAP   *Fr.* Consequences.

Of Cold Winds.   Margaret Lucas Cavendish, Duchess of Newcastle.   EMWP

Of colour, wilting a little in the unseasonable heat. (LL)   Pink Rose Rings, The.   Tracey Herd.   MFPA; NeBl

Of Colours and Shadows.   Ahmed Tidjani-Cissé.   PBMAP

Of Common Devotion.   Francis Quarles.   FaBoEE; OxBSP

Of composts shall the Muse descend to sing.   James Grainger.   NOEC   *Fr.* Sugar Cane, The.

Of composts shall the Muse disdain to sing?   James Grainger.   VerBaPo   *Fr.* Sugar Cane, The.

Of Constance holy legends tell.   Nun, The.   Edward Moore.   ECEV

Of cord and cassia-wood is the lute compounded;.   Old Lute, The.   Po Chü-i.   ChiP, *tr. by* Arthur Waley

Of course, I don't know very much.   Aunt Chloe's Politics.   Frances Ellen Watkins Harper.   NAAAL; NALW

Of Course—I prayed.   Emily Dickinson.   APN-2; BoWoP; MoAmPo; TCAPo

Of course I tried to tell him.   Poets Hitchhiking on the Highway.   Gregory Corso.   BB; NeAP; PoM

Of course it had been madness even to bring it up.   E Pur Si Muove.   George Bradley.   YaYoPo

Of course it's all over the morning news.   Through These Halls.   Judy Jordan.   AmPoNex

Of course no one sets out to discover.   Discovery.   Brian Henry.   AmPoNex

Of course only days after I meet you I am imagining.   Only Days.   Melanie Hope.   WiU

Of course, something is missing.   Moving and St Rage.   Kathy Fagan.   ExTi

Of course, the entire effort is to put my [*or* one] self.   Thoughts during an Air Raid.   Stephen Spender.   MoBrPo

Of course, the familiar rustling of programs.   Peripeteia.   Anthony Hecht.   VCAP

Of course there's always a last everything.   Sonnet: The Last Things.   Gavin Ewart.   OxBSo

Of course they had servants, dressed for dinner.   Andrew Taylor.   BMAP   *Fr.* Travelling to Gleis-Binario.

Of course, wait. (LL)   Dinner Guest: Me.   Langston Hughes.   BPo; LTA; SSLK

Of course, we have Guide Dogs for The Blind.   Who Likes the Idea of Guide Cats?   Gavin Ewart.   NOxBChV

Of course, we must die.   Charles Reznikoff.   APT-2

Of course, we would wish them angelic lookouts.   Irving Feldman.   VCAP   *Fr.* All of Us Here.

Of course what called you was lovely. A girl gone.   Beauty, That Lying Bitch.   Paula McLain.   AmPoNex

Of course Zimmer was late for the gig.   Duke Ellington Dream, The.   Paul Zimmer.   PBCAP

Of Courtesy.   Arthur Guiterman.   Spl

Of Dancing.   Alan Brownjohn.   FaBoMo

Of Dandelions & Tourists.   Joe Rosenblatt.   NOBC

Of De Witt Williams on His Way to Lincoln Cemetery.   Gwendolyn Brooks.   ESEAA; NOBA; NoAM   *Fr.* Street in Bronzeville, A.

Of Difference Does It Make.   Tom Paulin.   BiHa

Of Distress Being Humiliated by the Classical Chinese Poets.   Hayden Carruth.   WoPoe

Of diverse monsters I have sometimes read.   Strange Monsters.   Rowland Watkyns.   FaBoEE

Of Dogs and Ostriches.   Eve Merriam.   TaR

Of Drunkenness.   George Turberville.   NBLV

Of dust the primal Adam came.   Kosmos.   Julia Ward Howe.   ColAP

Of dying. (LL)   I Give You Back.   Joy Harjo.   HATNAP; LoL

Of each bruised and heart- / Shaped petal. (LL)   Wild Dog Rose, The.   John Montague.   BIrV; CIP-2; PBCIP; PoE

Of eager and extravagant anger. (LL)   Lovers, The.   William Robert Rodgers.   BIrV; OxBSP; PNI

Of earthly civilization, what shall we say?   Tidings.   Czeslaw Milosz.   BodElec, *tr. by* Lillian Vallee

Of Earthly Love.   Susanna Valentine Mitchell.   LW

Of Eating and Entertainment.   Roger Williams.   *See* Observation General from Their Eating, Etc., The

Of Edenhall the youthful lord.   Luck of Edenhall, The.   Ludwig Uhland.   AWP, *tr. by* Henry Wadsworth Longfellow

Of elephop and telephong! (LL)   Eletelephony.   Laura Elizabeth Richards.   NBLV; NOxBChV; NTCP; OBCA; OxIBACP

Of Elizabeth, frigidly stretched. (LL)   This Houre Her Vigill.   Valentin Iremonger.   CIP-2; ModIr; NOIV; OxBTC

Of England, and of Its Marvels.   Fazio degli Uberti.   AWP; EaItPo, *tr. by* Dante Gabriel Rossetti

Of English Verse.   Edmund Waller.   BeJo; CABP; NAEL-5v1; NOSC; PoE

Of every kinne [*or* everykune] tree, of every kinne [*or* everykune] tree.   Hawthorn, The.   *Unknown.*   MiEL

Of every vice pursued by those.   Gambling.   Royall Tyler.   TAP

Of everything, a little stayed.   Residue.   Carlos Drummond de Andrade.   TCLAP, *tr. by* Virginia de Araújo

Of fading pleasures in successive flight. (LL)   Sonnet 6. To the Torrid Zone.   Helen Maria Williams.   CenSon; NOBRP

Of fantasye is all oure fare.   John Gower.   SacPr   *Fr.* This World fares as a Fantasy.

Of feathered fouls, that fan the buxom air.   Fashioned after the Manner of Master Geoffrey Chaucer in His Assembly of Fowls.   Thomas Warton, the Elder.   ChIV-1

Of February, 1918. (LL)   In the Waiting Room.   Elizabeth Bishop.   APT-2; FaBoWP; HeIP-4; LCAP-2; NAAL-2v2; NAAL-5; NALW; NOBA; NoAM; PoE; PoetW; VCAP

Of feeling no pain? (LL)   Painkillers.   Thom Gunn.   AllShUp; SwNoth

Of festive goodness in back of their hard, or veiled, or shining, / unknowable gaze. (LL)   Olga Poems.   Denise Levertov.   LCAP-2; NNaP

Of Fiammetta Singing.   Giovanni Boccaccio.   AWP; EaItPo, *tr. by* Dante Gabriel Rossetti   *Fr.* Sonnets.

Of finite hearts that yearn. (LL)   Two in the Campagna.   Robert Browning.   EBEV; EBVV; FHYEP; GTBS-P; NAEL-5v2; NAEL-6v2; NOBE; NOBVV; NPeEn; NoP-4; OxAEP-2; OxBEV; PoE; SCGP; TFi; TOF

Of fleissh and bon and full of lif. (LL)   John Gower.   NPeEn; OxBEV   *Fr.* Confessio Amantis.

Of flesh. O star of men! (LL)   Camp in the Prussian Forest, A.   Randall Jarrell.   FaBoWar; MoAmPo; OBWP; OxBC; PoWW

Of Forced Sightes and Trusty Ferefulness.   Jorie Graham.   PoPoPo

Of Gardens.   Rene Rapin.
  Of Gardens.   OBGa, *tr. by* John, the Younger Evelyn

Of gasoline and desert air. (LL)   At Barstow.   Charles Tomlinson.   NoAM; TwCP

Of George and Caroline! (LL)   Lilliputian Ode on Their Majesties' Accession, A.   Henry Carey.   FaBoVe; NOEC; NPeEn; OBCoV

Of Gods Omnipotencie.   Alexander Hume.   NOCV

Of gold or gowns my mother had not much.   She Would Have Roses.   Nicholas Lloyd Ingraham.   PWR

Of gold then but now locked in brass.   Epitaph: Chryseomallus the Mime.   Paulus [*or* Paulos] Silentiarius.   GrAn, *tr. by* Andrew Miller

Of grass, the myriad dewdrops twinkle round. (LL)   James Thomson.   NAEL-6v1; NAEL-7v1   *Fr.* Seasons, The.

Of Gravity and Angels.   Jane Hirshfield.   PasH

Of Green Steps and Laundry.   Ralph Gustafson.   NoP-4

Of guns punched dark holes in the sky. (LL)   Seals in Penobscot Bay, The.   Daniel Gerard Hoffman.   TwCP; YaYoPo

Of hacked, beheaded coconuts towards home. (LL)   Nights in the Gardens of Port of Spain.   Derek Walcott.   NAEL-5v2; NAEL-6v2; OxBC; PoetW

Of happiness, haply hysterics. Is. (LL)   Gwendolyn Brooks.   BPo; HAP; NAAAL; NoP-4; WPE; WeW-3   *Fr.* Womanhood, The.

Of Heaven, and hope to have it after all. (LL)   Argument of His Book, The.   Robert Herrick.   AWP; BASC; BeJo; CaPo; CavPo; EBEV; HAP; NAEL-

5v1; NAEL-6v1; NAEL-7v1; NOSC; NPeEn; NoP-4; OxAEP-1; PeECV; PoE; PoPoPo; PoRA; SacPr; TFi; TTTS; WoPoe

Of heaven, and, waking in the darkness, screams. (LL)   Nerves.   Arthur Symons.   CABP; FaBoTw

Of Heaven or Hell I have no power to sing.   William Morris.   AWP; EBVV; NAEL-5v2; NAEL-6v2   *Fr.* Earthly Paradise, The.

Of Helen's brothers, one was born to die.   George Santayana.   APN-2   *Fr.* Sonnets.

Of her, her only, of herself alone! (LL)   Petrarch.   NAWM-5v1; NAWM-7v1, *tr. by* Joseph Auslander   *Fr.* Sonnets to Laura.

Of her Jacks, Latin.   Jane.   Philip Hammial.   BMAP

Of her removed and soul-infused regard.   George Chapman.   OxBSo   *Fr.* Coronet for His Mistress Philosophy, A.

Of her soft armory. (LL)   Catch, The.   Richard Wilbur.   DiPo; WeW-3

Of him, even third or fourth hand. (LL)   Has Anyone Seen the Boy?   Jelaluddin [*or* Jalal al-Din] Rumi.   RaBo; WoPoe, *tr. by* Coleman Barks and John Moyne

Of Himself.   Meleager.   AWP, *tr. by* Richard Garnett

Of hireling wolves whose Gospel[l] is their maw. (LL)   To the Lord General Cromwell.   John Milton.   NAEL-5v1; NAEL-6v1; NOSC; SCGP; Son

Of His Conversion.   William Alabaster.   NPeEn
   (Away feare with thy projectes, noe false fyre.)   NPeEn

Of His Dear Son, Gervase.   Sir John Beaumont.   OBEV   *Fr.* Of My Dear Son, Gervase Beaumont.

Of His Death.   Meleager.   AWP, *tr. by* Andrew Lang

Of his glory. *So farewell.* (LL)   Upon Ben Jo[h]nson.   Robert Herrick.   BeJo; CaPo; FaBoEE

Of his hands and fingers, we know nothing. (LL)   Incident.   Imamu Amiri Baraka.   AF; NoAM

Of His Lady in Heaven.   Jacopo da Lentino.   AWP; EaItPo, *tr. by* Dante Gabriel Rossetti

Of His Lady's Face.   Jacopo da Lentino.   EaItPo, *tr. by* Dante Gabriel Rossetti (Sonnet.)   AWP

Of His Lady's Old Age.   Pierre de Ronsard.   AWP; CTC, *tr. by* Andrew Lang

Of His Last Sight of Fiammetta.   Giovanni Boccaccio.   AWP; EaItPo, *tr. by* Dante Gabriel Rossetti   *Fr.* Sonnets.

Of His Life.   Wayne Dodd.   BLT

Of his long marvellous letters but kept none. (LL)   Who's Who.   W. H. Auden.   MoBrPo; NoAM; Son

Of his Mistress, upon Occasion of her Walking in a Garden.   Henry Constable.   NIL-7; NIP-4; OBGa   *Fr.* Diana.

Of honest Theft. To my good friend Master Samuel Daniel.   Sir John Harington [*or* Harrington].   PBRV

Of hope, and smiles on you with cheer sublime. (LL)   Steamboats, Viaducts, and Railways.   William Wordsworth.   CenSon; NAEL-5v2; NAEL-6v2

Of horrors that happen so? (LL)   Apparition—A Retrospect, The.   Herman Melville.   APN-2; NCAP; TCAPo

Of human bliss to human woe. (LL)   Translation of Lines by Benserade.   Isaac de Benserade.   FaBoEE; WoPoe, *tr. by* Samuel Johnson

Of Human Knowledge.   Sir John Davies.
   "Why did my parents send me to the schools."   ChIV-1

Of idleness are still left to live. (LL)   Temple, The.   Po Chü-i.   ChiP; OBMV, *tr. by* Arthur Waley

Of imagery. I love you, I'd like to go. (LL)   Tom Clark.   PmAP; SPE   *Fr.* You.

Of it all. (LL)   Personal Letter No. 3.   Sonia Sanchez.   ESEAA; SSLK

Of Jacopo del Sellaio.   Ezra Pound.   APT-1

Of Jesu Christ I Sing.   *Unknown.*   PoE

Of John Bunyan's Life.   John James.   SCAP

Of John Cabanis' wrath and of the strife.   Edgar Lee Masters.   OBAL   *Fr.* Spoon River Anthology.

Of John Davidson.   Hugh MacDiarmid.   HarvBoo; NePenScot; OxBEV

Of joy. (LL)   Making Chicago.   Dennis Schmitz.   IllVoic; LCAP-2

Of Joy Illimited: Polyphonic Soundings: Shore to Ship.   Anna Rabinowitz.   KGB

Of joy that's left behind us. (LL)   Journey Onwards, The.   Thomas Moore.   GTBS-P; OxAEP-2

Of Kate's Baldness.   John Davies of Hereford.   FaBoEE

Of Late.   George Starbuck.   VGW

Of late it has dawned on me that it's futile.   Tune: "Rouged Lips."   Wang Kuo-wei.   ColAnChi, *tr. by* Jiaosheng Wang

Of late the nights.   Buson.   JDP, *tr. by* Yoel Hoffmann

Of late / thin little Vanya.   Smells.   Yelena [*or* Elena] Sergeievna, Countess de Carli Shchapova.   TCRP, *tr. by* Bradley Jordan

Of late, what time the Bear turned round.   Anacreon.   NoSic, *tr. by* Anomos   *Fr.* Odes.

Of lead and emerald.   Note to Olga (1966), A.   Denise Levertov.   NALW

Of Lentren in the first morning.   All Erdly Joy Returns in Pane.   William Dunbar.   SacPr

Of Liberty, Reforms and Rights I sing.   Instructions, Supposed to Be Written in Paris, for the Mob in England.   Mary Alcock.   ECWP

Of Life and Death.   Ben Jonson.   TreFP

Of life, of a cloud, of height. (LL)   Call of the Lake, The.   Andrey [*or* Andrei] Andreievich Voznesensky [*or* Voznesenskii].   TCRP; VCWP

Of little use the man you may suppose.   Pope.   EBEV   *Fr.* First Epistle of the Second Book of Horace Imitated, The.

Of longing, Termia, the sharp specifics know.   End of July.   John Peck.   HarvBoo

Of Lord Althorpe's—now Earl Spencer. (LL)   Thomas Hood.   OBCoV; OxBoLi; PeLV   *Fr.* Miss Kilmansegg and Her Precious Leg.

Of lost connections. (LL)   Memories of West Street and Lepke.   Robert Lowell.   AF; EmeKit; NAAL-2v2; NAAL-5; NOBA; NoAM; PoE; VCAP

Of Love.   William Meredith.   VCAP   *Fr.* Consequences.

Of love.   Sappho.   SaLy, *tr. by* Diane Rayor

Of love and death in the Garrison State I sing.   Karl Shapiro.   BodElec   *Fr.* Bourgeois Poet, The.

Of Love, Death and the Sea-Squirt.   Chris Greenhalgh.   NeBl

Of love he sang, full hearted one.   Forced Music, A.   Robert Graves.   MoBrPo

Of love's austere and lonely offices? (LL)   Those Winter Sundays.   Robert Earl Hayden.   APT-2; AmFaPo; ChAP; ColAP; ESEAA; HAP; HCAP; ISC; InPK-6; LCAP-2; MakPoe; NAAL-5; NIL-7; NIP-4; NoAM; NoP-4; PoPoPo; RaBo; SSLK; SoSe-8; TFi; UnPo; WeW-3

Of Loving at First Sight.   Edmund Waller.   NOSC

Of madness cured me. (LL)   For My Contemporaries.   James Vincent Cunningham.   APT-2; CoAP; VCAP

Of making many books there is no end.   Of Modern Books.   Carolyn Wells.   SWaP

Of Mal Bay. (LL)   Recessional.   Thomas MacGreevy [*or* McGreevy].   CIP-2; ModIr

Of man's delight and man's desire.   Ballad of Passive Paederasty, A.   Aleister Crowley.   CAGL

Of Man's First Disobedience, and the Fruit.   John Milton.   EBEV; FHYEP; NAEL-5v1; NAEL-6v1; NAWM-5v1; NAWM-7v1; NIL-7; NIP-4; NOSC; NPeEn; OxAEP-1; OxBEV; PeECV; SCV; TOF   *Fr.* Paradise Lost.

Of mankind. (LL)   Thread suns.   Paul Celan.   BBASP; OBVE; VCWP, *tr. by* Michael Hamburger

Of many things adulterate.   Epitaph.   Tristan Corbière.   AWP, *tr. by* Joseph T. Shipley

Of Many Worlds in This World.   Margaret Lucas Cavendish, Duchess of Newcastle.   NOSC; NPeEn

Of Mary.   Sister Mary Madeleva.
   Dumb Oxen.   CRP

Of May.   Alexander Scott.   OxBS

Of meat. To stay alive this way, it's hard. (LL)   Surviving.   James Welch.   CDW; HATNAP

Of memory there was also a song of.   Under My Breath.   Anne Waldman.   BodElec

Of men and girls. (LL)   Charles Olson.   APT-2; PmAP   *Fr.* Maximus Poems, The.

Of mercy by a gracious God. (LL)   To Retiredness.   Mildmay Fane, 2d Earl of Westmorland.   BeJo; NOSC

Of Mere Being.   Wallace Stevens.   APT-1; HCAP; NoP-4; WoPoe

Of Mere Plastic.   David Trinidad.   KGB

Of mighty love the wings for this me give. (LL)   In Spayn.   Sir Thomas Wyatt.   NoSic; OPOU; SCGP

Of Miles Davis.   William Ford.   SeSe

Of-millions-of sea. (LL)   Boat Poem.   Bernard Spencer.   EmeKit; FaBoTw; OxBTC

Of Modern Books.   Carolyn Wells.   SWaP

Of modern Manners let me sing.   Modern Manners.   Mary Alcock.   ECWP

Of Modern Poetry.   Wallace Stevens.   ColAP; NAAL-2v2; NAAL-5; NoAM; OxBA; TAP

Of Mohenjo Daro at Oxford.   Keki N. Daruwalla.   OMIP

Of Money.   Barnabe Googe.   NBLV; NoSic; SoSe-8

Of Mortmain.   Herman Melville.   APN-2   *Fr.* Clarel: A Poem and Pilgrimage in the Holy Land.

Of Moulds and Mushrooms.   Ruthven Todd.   NePenScot

Of Movement towards a Natural Place.   J. H. Prynne.   PFTM-2

Of my crust.   I Undressed Myself.   Thérèse 'Awwad.   PoArWo, *tr. by* Kamal Boullata

Of My Dear Son [*or* Deare Sonne], Gervase Beaumont.   Sir John Beaumont.   NOBE

Of My Dear Son, Gervase Beaumont.   Sir John Beaumont.   NOBE
   Of His Dear Son, Gervase.   OBEV

Of my drowsy mouth. (LL)   Breasts.   Charles Simic.   NNaP; RaBo

Of my husband I do not ask much.   Limerick.   *Unknown.*   PeLi

Of My Lady Isabella Playing on the Lute.   Edmund Waller.   HAP

Of my life / toward home. (LL)   I Am Singing the Cold Rain.   Lance Henson. HATNAP; STP

Of My Nipple Ring Halos.   Edwin Torres.   HeMarv

Of my shoulder and quickly, too quickly, I am gone? (LL)   Angel Surrounded by Paysans.   Wallace Stevens.   HCAP; LCAP-2

Of Myself.   Leah Goldberg.   BoWoP, *tr. by* Ramah Commanday

Of Myself [*or* My Self].   Abraham Cowley.   BASC

Of nearness to her sundered Things.   Emily Dickinson.   PoE

Of Necco Wafers, Nibs, and Juju Beads. (LL)   Ex-Basketball Player.   John Updike.   InPK-6; TRP

Of Nelson and the North.   Battle of the Baltic.   Thomas Campbell.   GTBS-P; OBEV

Of Neptune's empire [*or* Empyre] let us sing.   Hymn in Praise of Neptune, A.   Thomas Campion.   NOBE; OBEV

Of no removes. (LL)   John Dowland.   NPeEn; PBRV

Of no removes! (LL)   Fine Knacks for Ladies.   *Unknown*.   EBEV; HAP; NoP-4; NoSic

Of Nobility.   Fulke Greville, 1st Baron Brooke.   *Fr.* Treatise of Monarchy, A.

Of nomads entering a subcontinent through a narrow pass. (LL)   My Father Travels.   Dilip Chitre.   OMIP; WoPoe

Of nothing, nothing, nothing—nothing at all. (LL)   End of the World, The.   Archibald MacLeish.   GSo; InPK-6; MoAmPo; NOBA; NoAM; OBAL; OxBA; OxBSo; PAI; Son; TAP; TFi; VGW

Of now done darkness I wretch lay wrestling with (my God!) my God. (LL)   Carrion Comfort.   Gerard Manley Hopkins.   BBASP; GSo; HeIP-4; MakPoe; NAEL-5v2; NAEL-6v2; NoAM; PoE; Son; TFi; TOF

Of obedience, faith, adhesiveness.   Thought.   Walt Whitman.   HHAm

Of Objects Considered as Fortresses in a Baleful Place.   Hyam Plutzik.   VGW

Of of Titmouse.   Michael Portnoy.   HeMarv

Of old when folk lay sick and sorely tried.   On Hygiene.   Joseph Hilaire Pierre Belloc.   MoBrPo

Of old when Nature, in her verve defiant.   Giantess, The.   Charles Baudelaire. OBVE, *tr. by* Roy Campbell

Of old when Nature, in her verve defiant.   Giantess, The.   Charles Baudelaire. OBVE, *tr. by* Roy Campbell

Of old, when Scarron his companions invited.   Oliver Goldsmith.   NOIV; OxBoLi   *Fr.* Retaliation.

Of One That Had a Great Nose.   George Turberville.   FaBoEE

Of one who grew up at Gallipoli.   War Story.   Jon Stallworthy.   OxBC

Of one whose occupation was to die. (LL)   Souvenir.   Edwin Arlington Robinson.   APT-1; NoAM

Of our chosen place.   Map Burnt Through.   Joanna Rawson.   AmPoNex

Of our dear West. (LL)   David Jones.   HarvBoo; NoAM   *Fr.* Anathemata, The.

Of our desires the farther [*or* farder] down[e] to slide. (LL)   Mary Sidney Wroth, Countess of Montgomery.   BASC; NAEL-5v1; NAEL-6v1; NAEL-7v1; PEW   *Fr.* Pamphilia to Amphilanthus.

Of our jasmine-white Lord. (LL)   Mahadevi.   WPoS; WoPoe, *tr. by* Jane Hirshfield

Of our like minds. (LL)   Fan Letter, A.   Amy Gerstler.   BAP-97; BodElec

Of our losse by Adam, and our gayne by Christ.   Alice Sutcliffe.   *Fr.* Meditations of Man's Mortalitie; or, A Way to True Blessedness.

Of our white-on-white. (LL)   Snow Light, The.   May Sarton.   APT-2; NBLV

Of Oxfordshire and Gloucestershire. (LL)   Adlestrop.   Edward Thomas. HAP; HarvBoo; NAEL-5v2; NAEL-6v2; NOBE; NoP-4; OBEV; OxBTC; UV

Of pale cold light that was alive. (LL)   Signature of All Things, The.   Kenneth Rexroth.   APSN; APT-2; NNaP; TRP

Of past misadventure? (LL)   "H. D."   HarvBoo; NAAL-5   *Fr.* Walls Do Not Fall, The.

Of Paul and Silas it is said.   Emily Dickinson.   ChIV-2; SacPr

Of Peace.   Fulke Greville, 1st Baron Brooke.   *Fr.* Treatise of Monarchy, A.

Of people running down the street.   Picture, A.   Howard Nemerov.   OxBC

Of person rare, strong limbs, and manly shape.   Sonnet Written upon My Lord Admiral Seymour, A.   John Harington.   NoSic

Of pinyon / pine. (LL)   Gary Snyder.   APSN; PFTM-2   *Fr.* Mountains and Rivers without End: The Market.

Of pleasure. (LL)   Word *Plum*, The.   Helen Chasin.   NIL-7; NIP-4

Of Poor B.B.   Bertolt Brecht.   RB; WoPoe, *tr. by* Michael Hamburger

Of Potatoes.   Trish Reeves.   SpudSo

Of Power, Money, Cheese, Real Estate, Conboberation, Hoohah.   Mac Wellman.   FTOS   *Fr.* Terminal Hip.

Of Promises and Prophecy.   Steve Chimombo.   HBAPE

Of Rain and Air.   Wayne Dodd.   BLT

Of rapid floods and cruel winds.   Rapid Floods.   Kata Szidónia Petróczy [*or* Petróczi].   IQMS, *tr. by* Marie B. Jaffe

Of red berries. Will he wake? (LL)   Scenes from the Life of the Peppertrees. Denise Levertov.   NeAP; PoM

Of remembrance, whispers out of time. (LL)   Self-Portrait in a Convex Mirror. John Ashbery.   HCAP; NAAL-2v2

Of Robert Frost.   Gwendolyn Brooks.   NOBA; NoAM

Of Rome.   Herman Melville.   OxBA   *Fr.* Clarel: A Poem and Pilgrimage in the Holy Land.

Of room to lodge th' inhabitant. (LL)   Another [Epitaph on the Lady Mary Villiers].   Thomas Carew.   BeJo; CaPo

Of roses thrown on marble stairs. (LL)   Gift of God, The.   Edwin Arlington Robinson.   MoAmPo; OxBA

Of Saint Theresa in her wild lament. (LL)   Groundhog, The.   Richard Eberhart. APT-2; FaBoMo; MoAmPo; NoAM; PAI; RaBo; TAP; TFi; TRP; UnPo

Of Scolding Wives and the Third Day Ague.   Henricus Selyns.   AiP; SCAP

Of simple choice they are the villagers; their clothes come.   Adrienne Rich. HCAP   *Fr.* Shooting Script.

Of simple tastes and mind content! (LL)   Oliver Wendell Holmes.   APN-1; OxBA; PWR   *Fr.* Autocrat of the Breakfast Table, The.

Sir Frauncis Walsingham Sir Phillipp Sydney, and Sir Christopher Hatton, Lord Chancelor.   *Unknown*.   PBRV

Of Sleep.   Martha, Lady Giffard.   EMWP

Of solanum tuberosum, that vagrant vegetable.   William Matthews.   SpudSo

Of Solitude.   Abraham Cowley.   BASC

Of some Pharaoh's daughter. (LL)   Language Issue, The.   Nuala Ni Dhomhnaill.   ModIr; NPeEn, *tr. by* Paul Muldoon

Of someone greater than I can understand? (LL)   Empty Church, The.   Ronald Stuart Thomas.   AngWePo; EmeKit

Of Spring water—thirty or forty miles.   How I Sailed on the Lake till I Came to the Eastern Stream.   Lu Yu.   ChiP, *tr. by* Arthur Waley

Of St. Stephen.   Francis Quarles.   NOSC

Of Stars.   Margaret Lucas Cavendish, Duchess of Newcastle.   NOSC

Of such a time as this.   Shiei.   JDP, *tr. by* Yoel Hoffmann

Of such a wit the world should have no more. (LL)   Ode for Him [*or* Ben Jonson], An.   Robert Herrick.   AWP; BASC; BeJo; CaPo; NOSC; SCGP

Of such an intense azure.   Blue City, The.   Alfred Wellington Purdy.   NoP-4

Of Suicide.   John Berryman.   NoAM

Of Sweet Rest.   Joyce Mansour.   HAWP, *tr. by* Mary Beach

Of Taste; an Essay.   James Cawthorn.
Englishman at the Table, The.   ECEV; NOEC

Of th'eternal silence. (LL)   Noel; Christmas Eve, 1913.   Robert Bridges. ChrPo; NOCV; OBCP; SacPr

Of that late death took all my heart for speech. (LL)   In Memory of Major Robert Gregory.   W. B. Yeats.   EBEV; NAEL-6v2; SCGP

Of that medusa strange.   Statue of Medusa, The.   William Drummond.   GS

Of that mysterious race. (LL)   Poem: "At night Chinamen jump."   Frank O'Hara.   NOBA; NoAM; PmAP

Of that passion *that light within*.   To the Poets: To Make Much of the World. George Oppen.   BodElec

Of that table in the café.   Cafe.   Czeslaw Milosz.   PoSu, *tr. by* Jan Darowski

Of that wherein thou art a questioner.   To Dante Alighieri: He Interprets Dante Alighieri's Dream.   Dante da Maiano.   AWP; EaItPo, *tr. by* Dante Gabriel Rossetti

Of that which once was great, is [*or* has] passed [*or* pass'd] away. (LL)   On the Extinction of the Venetian Republic.   William Wordsworth.   GTBS-P; NOBE; OBEV

Of the Animal Spirits.   Margaret Lucas Cavendish, Duchess of Newcastle. PEW

Of the beauty of kindness I speak.   Kindness.   Thomas Sturge Moore. OBMV

Of the Birth and Bringing up of Desire.   Edward de Vere, 17th Earl of Oxford. FaBoEE; NoSic; SCGP

Of the Blessed Sacrament of the Altar [*or* Aulter].   Robert Southwell.   OBEV (Angells' eyes, whome veyles cannot deceive, The.)   SacPr

Of the brave! (LL)   Battle of the Baltic.   Thomas Campbell.   GTBS-P; OBEV

Of the breakers of stone. (LL)   Race Relations.   Carolyn Kizer.   CarOv; LTA

Of the broad road that stretches and the roadside fire. (LL)   Song of a Traveller, The.   Robert Louis Stevenson.   EBVV; MoBrPo; OBEV

Of the broken pieces of our lives. (LL)   Liberation.   Abena Busia.   HAWP; PoetW

Of the cave must tell you, "Yes, you can go back." (LL)   Return, The.   Molly Peacock.   PasH; RA

Of the Changes of Life.   William Dunbar.   WoPoe, *tr. by* Andrew Glaze

Of the Colossal substance / Of Immortality. (LL)   Emily Dickinson.   APN-2; EnlH

Of the Cosmic Light! (LL)   O Lord of Light! A Mystic Sage Returns to Realms of Eternity!   Askia Muhammad Touré.   SeSe; SpirFl

Of the country of my pleasure. (LL)   History of Sexual Preference, A.   Robin Becker.   BodElec; ExTi

Of the Courtier's Life.   Sir Thomas Wyatt.   NPeEn; NoSic; OBSV; OBVE; SCGP   *Fr.* Satires.

Of the Creator. And he waits for the world to begin. (LL)　Leviathan.　W. S. Merwin.　ChIV-1; NOBA; NoAM

Of the dark past.　Ecce Puer.　James Joyce.　AmFaPo; BIrV; ChIV-2; EBEV; NoAM; TrCP

Of the Day Estivall.　Alexander Hume.　NOCV; NePenScot; OxBS
"O perfite light, quhilk schaid away."　NPeEn

Of the dear little fish that I just now ate! (LL)　Considerate Crocodile, The.　Amos Russel Wells.　OBCA; OxIBACP

Of the Earth, Earthy.　Rosamund Marriott Watson.　ViWPN

Of the Epiphany.　John Beaumont.　SacPr

Of the Ever-Changing Agitation in the Air.　Jorie Graham.　ExTi

Of the eyes of my Annie. (LL)　For Annie.　Edgar Allan Poe.　APN-1; ColAP; NOBA; OBEV; OxBA; TCAPo

Of the far sea, / Tho' far off it be. (LL)　Christina Georgina Rossetti.　GTBS-P; PoE; WPE　Fr. Spring Fancies.

Of the far Waterfall like Doom. (LL)　Tarantella.　Joseph Hilaire Pierre Belloc.　FaBoCh; MoBrPo; OBMV; RB; UV

Of the Father's love begotten Ere the worlds began to be.　Prudentius.　SacPr, tr. by John Mason Neale

Of the fathoms of set eyes. (LL)　Fire at Alexandria, The.　Theodore Weiss.　NoAM; SAmP; TAP

Of the Finished World.　Lucie Brock-Broido.　MakPoe

Of the first league out from land? (LL)　Emily Dickinson.　APN-2; TCAPo

Of the first Paradice there's nothing found.　On St. James's Park, as Lately Improved by His Majesty.　Edmund Waller.　BASC; BeJo; NOSC; OBGa

Of the forest bees? (LL)　Carrefour.　Amy Lowell.　BoWoP; LW

Of the four fuschia plants that hung.　Robin's Nest, A.　Mary Jo Salter.　OWoS

Of the French Kings Nativity.　Benjamin Harris.　SCAP

Of the Gentle Heart.　Guido Guinicelli.　AWP; CTC; EaItPo; OBVE, tr. by Dante Gabriel Rossetti

Of the Great and Famous. . . Sir Francis Drake, and of My Little-Little Selfe.　Robert Hayman.　FaBoCh

Of the great moon. (LL)　Letter, The.　Amy Lowell.　NALW; PoBW

Of the Great Worm in the Sky? (LL)　Hornworm: Autumn Lamentation.　Stanley Kunitz.　AmFaPo; BodElec

Of the grieved lands of Africa. (LL)　Grieved Lands, The.　Agostinho Neto.　PBMAP; PoetW, tr. by Michael Wolfers

Of the ills we daily see.　Social Life, The.　Lizelia Augusta Jenkins Moorer.　CBWP-3

Of the Indigo Combo. (LL)　Melvin B. Tolson.　APT-2; PFTM-1　Fr. Harlem Gallery.

Of the Lady Pietra degli Scrovigni.　Dante Alighieri.　AWP; EaItPo; MakPoe; NPeEn; OBVE, tr. by Dante Gabriel Rossetti

Of the lapsing, unsoilable, Whispering sea. (LL)　Ringsend.　Oliver St. John Gogarty.　OBMV; OxBTC

Of the Last Verses in the Book.　Edmund Waller.　BASC; BeJo; EBEV; HAP; NOSC; NPeEn; NoP-4; OxBEV; PeECV; PoPoPo; SCGP; SacPr
"Seas are quiet when the winds give o'er, The."　NOBE; NOCV; OBEV

Of the long sepulcher that hid death and hides me? (LL)　How Much Longer Will I Be Able to Inhabit the Divine Sepulcher.　John Ashbery.　FTOS; HarvBoo; NeAP; PmAP; PoM

Of the look of a room on returning thence. (LL)　Walk, The.　Thomas Hardy.　NAEL-5v2; NAEL-6v2; NPeEn; OxBEV; PoE

Of the Loss of Time.　John Hoskyns [or Hoskins].　FaBoEE

Of the loud languorous nightingale. (LL)　Fantoches.　Paul Verlaine.　AWP; OBMV, tr. by Arthur Symons

Of the many known and proven.　Curing Homosexuality.　Jim Everhard.　CAGL; GLP

Of the many men whom I am, whom we are.　We Are Many.　Pablo Neruda.　VCWP, tr. by Alastair Reid

Of the Marriage of the Dwarfs.　Edmund Waller.　NPeEn

Of the million or two, more or less.　Instans Tyrannus.　Robert Browning.　EBEV

Of the moon. They can't see / Not yet. (LL)　Small Frogs Killed on the Highway.　James Wright (1927–80).　HCAP; NNaP; NoAM

Of the night. (LL)　Poem at Thirty.　Sonia Sanchez.　BPo; BlSi; NAAAL

Of the no need.　"H. D."　NALW　Fr. Tribute to the Angels.

Of the not born, yet buried, here's the tomb. (LL)　To Fine Lady Would-Be.　Ben Jonson.　FaBoEE; NOSC; NoP-4; OxBSP

Of the old Egyptian boys. (LL)　Travel.　Robert Louis Stevenson.　FaBoCh; OTCP

Of the old house, only a few crumbled.　House That Was, The.　Laurence Binyon.　MoBrPo

Of the petrel and the porpoise. In the end is my beginning. (LL)　T. S. Eliot.　HAP; VGW　Fr. Four Quartets.

Of the planet of which they were part. (LL)　Planet on the Table, The.　Wallace Stevens.　APT-1; HAP; HCAP; PoPoPo; SAmP

Of the primeval Priests assum'd power.　Book of Urizen [or First Book of Urizen], The.　William Blake.　NOBRP

Of the Progres[se] of the Soule; the Second Anniversarie.　John Donne.
Second Anniversary [or Anniversarie], The.　ESCV
"We now lament not, but congratulate."　NOSC

Of the Pythagorean Philosophy.　Ovid.　OBVE, tr. by John Dryden　Fr. Metamorphoses.

Of the Realme of Scotland.　Sir David Lindsay [or Lyndsay].　OxBS　Fr. Dreme, The.

Of the Reed That the Jews Set in Our Saviour's Hand.　William Alabaster.　NPeEn; NoSic

Of the Remembered.　David St. John.
"I will tell you. Maybe."　GeoHom
"Twin memory, we all seek it."　GeoHom

Of the Resurrection.　Miles Coverdale.　ChIV-2

Of the Resurrection of the Body.　Marbod of Rennes.　MLL, tr. by Helen Waddell

Of the right way.　As to How Much.　Louis Zukofsky.　APT-2

Of the salted bream. (LL)　Basho.　WoPoe; ZenPo, tr. by Takashi Ikemoto and Lucien Stryk

Of the same Love who holds me weeping now. (LL)　Dante Alighieri.　AWP; EaItPo, tr. by Dante Gabriel Rossetti　Fr. La Vita Nuova.

Of the Scythians.　Katha Pollitt.　DiPo

Of the shocked boy's twenty-year-old jacket. (LL)　Weakness, The.　Bernard O'Donoghue.　ModIr; NoP-4

Of the sixty-two.　Poetry of America, The.　Juan Felipe Herrera.　TouFir

Of the sky, and the wind thereof is my body. (LL)　De Aegypto.　Ezra Pound.　APT-1; VGW

Of the sound of jade tinkling on your bridle-straps. (LL)　To Li Chien.　Po Chü-i.　AWP; ChiP, tr. by Arthur Waley

Of the Terrible Doubt of Appearances.　Walt Whitman.　APN-1; CAGL

Of the Theam of Love.　Margaret Lucas Cavendish, Duchess of Newcastle.
See Of the Theme of Love

Of the Theme of Love.　Margaret Lucas Cavendish, Duchess of Newcastle.　OxBSP; PEW

Of the three, one blackheart man lives.　Black Heart.　Kwame Dawes.　WaCA

Of the toy's purchase with the length of life. (LL)　Blight.　Ralph Waldo Emerson.　APN-1; NCAP; NOBA; TCAPo

Of the unforgivable landscape. (LL)　Mouth of the Hudson, The.　Robert Lowell.　AiP; VCAP

Of the unnamed poor. (LL)　Minneapolis Poem, The.　James Wright (1927–80).　NoAM; UnPo

Of the very world he made. (LL)　Christopher Smart.　ChrPo; NOCV; NPeEn; OxBEV; SacPr　Fr. Hymns and Spiritual Songs for the Fasts and Festivals of the Church of England.

Of the war's obscenity. (LL)　Fabrication of Ancestors.　Alan Dugan.　CBCWP; NoAM

Of the Wars in Ireland.　John Harington.　NoSic

Of the Weather.　John Gay.　NPeEn　Fr. Trivia; or, The Art of Walking the Streets of London.

Of the world's business. (LL)　Mrs. Small.　Gwendolyn Brooks.　GT; ItWoWo

Of thee and thy house, which doth in eating heal. (LL)　John Donne.　BASC; ChIV-1; NAEL-5v1; NAEL-6v1; NAEL-7v1; NIP-4; NoP-4; OxBSo; PoE; Son　Fr. Holy Sonnets.

Of Thee I Sing.　George Gershwin.　ReLy

Of thee, kind boy, I ask no red and white.　Sonnet.　Sir John Suckling.　BASC; BeJo; CaPo; CavPo; MeLP; NOSC; NoP-4; OxBoLi

Of thee the Northman by his beachèd galley.　Ode V.　George Santayana.　APN-2

Of their iniquity. (LL)　Ballad Which Anne Askew Made and Sang When She Was in Newgate, The.　Anne Askew.　CABP; EMWP; NoSic; WPE

Of their passage. (LL)　On Third Avenue.　Mina Loy.　APT-1; HarvBoo

Of their unthinking Drums. (LL)　Emily Dickinson.　APN-2; HAP; MoAmPo; NAAL-2v1; NAAL-3; NAAL-5

Of them and rolled her head away. (LL)　Last Words of My English Grandmother, The.　William Carlos Williams.　APT-1; RB; RaBo; SAmP

Of these houses.　San Martino del Carso.　Giuseppe Ungaretti.　PeFWW, tr. by David McDuff

Of these men and their music. (LL)　Here Where Coltrane Is.　Michael S. Harper.　ESEAA; NAAAL

Of these the false Achitophel was first.　Dryden.　HAP; NOBE; OxBEV　Fr. Absalom and Achitophel.

Of these yarns now (except in nightmares, of course)? (LL)　Whatever Happened?　Philip Larkin.　OxBSo; Son

Of these your words the other's sense denies. (LL)　Sonnet: To Dante Alighieri on the Last Sonnet of the Vita Nuova.　Cecco Angiolieri, da Siena.　AWP; EaItPo, tr. by Dante Gabriel Rossetti

Of things beyond our reason or control. (LL)　Sound of the Sea, The.　Henry Wadsworth Longfellow.　ITBLP; TCAPo

Of things exactly as they are. (LL)　Wallace Stevens.　NoAM; RaBo　Fr. Man with the Blue Guitar, The.

Of things moving back to where they came from. (LL)   Procession at Candlemas, A.   Amy Clampitt.   FaBoWP; HCAP; PoPoPo

Of this bad world the loveliest and the best.   On a Dead Hostess.   Joseph Hilaire Pierre Belloc.   MoBrPo

Of this cloth doll which.   Michael Palmer.   NoP-4

Of this day's glorious feast and revel.   *Unknown*.   ChiP   *Fr.* Seventeen Old Poems.

Of this fair[e] volume which we World do[e] name.   Book, The.   William Drummond, of Hawthornden.   ChIV-1

Of this handful of cyclamen. (LL)   Cyclamens.   "Michael Field."   NOBVV; VWP; ViWPN

Of this house I know the backwindow.   Eyeglasses.   Tom Clark.   CoAmPo

Of this ruined house. (LL)   Lady Izumi.   WPoS; WoPoe, *tr. by* Mariko Aratani and Jane Hirshfield

Of this world's Theatre in which we stay.   Edmund Spenser.   NAEL-5v1; NoP-4   *Fr.* Amoretti.

Of those base things called men. (LL)   To Celinda.   Elizabeth Singer Rowe.   BASC; PEW

Of those by whom I was subdued? (LL)   Trumpet, The.   Ilya Grigoryevich Ehrenburg [*or* Erenburg].   TCRP; TrJP, *tr. by* Yakov Hornstein

Of those calm solitudes, is there. (LL)   Oh [*or* O] Fairest of the Rural Maids.   William Cullen Bryant.   APN-1; TAP

Of those dancers hand in hand. (LL)   Ballad of the Ten Casino Dancers.   Cecilia Meireles.   BoWoP; TCLAP, *tr. by* James Merrill

Of those rebellions that we start in jest.   Fear Test: Integrity of Heroes.   James Simmons.   CIP-2

Of those, thou woundest with thy Dart! (LL)   Wounded Cupid, The.   Robert Herrick.   AWP; OBVE

Of Those Who Go, Not to Return.   Benyamin [*or* Benjamin] Galai.   MHP, *tr. by* Ruth Finer Mintz

Of three eyes, I would still give two for one.   Third Eye, The.   Jay Macpherson.   MoCV

Of Three Friendly Warnings This Is the Second.   *Unknown*.   STP, *tr. by* Richard Johnny John and Jerome Rothenberg

Of Three Friendly Warnings This Is the Third.   *Unknown*.   STP, *tr. by* Richard Johnny John and Jerome Rothenberg

Of Three Girls and of Their Talk.   Giovanni Boccaccio.   AWP; EaItPo, *tr. by* Dante Gabriel Rossetti   *Fr.* Sonnets.

Of thy departure, when thou wentest forth, it went out / after thee. (LL)   Parting.   Judah Halevi.   AWP; TrJP, *tr. by* Nina Davis Salaman

Of thy life [*or* lyfe], Thomas, this compass[e] well mark.   Golden Mean, The.   Henry Howard, Earl of Surrey.   OBVE

Of Time and the Line.   Charles Bernstein.   NIL-7; PFTM-2; PmAP; ReTh

Of too much was our talk, of.   Zürich, the Stork Inn.   Paul Celan.   BBASP; HP, *tr. by* Michael Hamburger

Of touch they are, and poor I am their straw. (LL)   Sir Philip Sidney.   NAEL-5v1; NAEL-6v1; NAEL-7v1   *Fr.* Astrophil and Stella.

Of Treason.   Sir John Harington [*or* Harrington].   FaBoEE; InPK-6; NPeEn; NoSic; OBCoV; OxBEV; OxBoLi; SoSe-8

(Epigram IV.v: of Treason.)   NOSC

(Treason doth never prosper.)   PBRV

Of two fair virgins, modest, though admired.   On a Nun.   Jacopo Vittorelli.   AWP, *tr. by* Byron

Of Tyndarus, That Frumped a Gentlewoman.   *Unknown*.   BIrV, *tr. by* Richard Stanyhurst

Of unapplauding hands and broken song. (LL)   My Dark Fathers.   Brendan Kennelly.   BIrV; CIP-2; PBCIP

Of under me you so quite new. (LL)   E. E. Cummings.   BoLoP; PasH; Son; VGW

Of underground streams, what I see is a limestone landscape. (LL)   In Praise of Limestone.   W. H. Auden.   HAP; HarvBoo; NAEL-5v2; NAEL-6v2; NoAM; NoP-4

Of unremembered seas. (LL)   So I Said I Am Ezra.   A. R. Ammons.   ColAP; NAAL-2v2; NAAL-5; NOBA; NoAM; PAI

Of unsaciable purchasers.   Robert Crowley.   PBRV

Of Use.   John Heywood.   FaBoEE

Of vacant darkness and to cease. (LL)   Tennyson.   FHYEP; NAEL-6v2   *Fr.* In Memoriam A. H. H.

Of vast import to the nation. (LL)   Pastoral: "When I was younger."   William Carlos Williams.   APT-1; OxBA; SAmP

Of veins, purple as violets? (LL)   Hippolytus Temporizes.   "H. D."   APT-1; HarvBoo; RACG

Of violets, and my soul's forgotten gleam. (LL)   Sonnet: "I had no thought of violets of late."   Alice Moore Dunbar-Nelson.   BISi; Son

Of virtues I most warmly bless.   Gerard Manley Hopkins.   FaBoEE   *Fr.* Seven Epigrams.

Of Walter White's Father in the Rain.   Houston A. Baker, Jr.   SeSe

Of wars o western.   Disasters.   George Oppen.   BodElec

Of water, water, water. (LL)   Lifeguard, The.   James Dickey.   NoP-4; SoSe-8

Of what a quality is courage made.   Donagh MacDonagh.   CIP-2   *Fr.* Charles Donnelly.

Of what avail are palaces in hell.   Mátyás Nyéki Vörös.   IQMS, *tr. by* Watson Kirkconnell   *Fr.* Hell.

Of what good can Paradise be.   Paradise.   Immanuel di Roma.   TrJP, *tr. by* J. Chotzner

Of what has had an end. (LL)   To My Infant Daughter.   Yvor Winters.   VGW; WoPoe   *Fr.* To My Infant Daughter.

Of what is past, or passing, or to come. (LL)   Sailing To Byzantium.   W. B. Yeats.   AmFaPo; CABP; ClHu; GTBS-P; HAP; HarvBoo; HeIP-4; InPK-6; MoBrPo; NAEL-5v2; NAEL-6v2; NAWM-7v2; NIL-7; NIP-4; NOBE; NPeEn; NoAM; NoP-4; OBMV; OWoS; OxBEV; OxBTC; PoE; PoPoPo; PoRA; RaBo; SCGP; SoSe-8; TFi; TOF; UnPo; WeW-3; WoPoe

Of what mould did Nature frame me[?].   Tinder, The.   Thomas Carew.   CaPo

Of what the others never set eyes on. (LL)   Desert Flowers.   Keith Douglas.   FaBoTw; HarvBoo; NPeEn

Of what use to me are the nights full of wine.   Nina Grachova [*or* Grachiova].   TCRP

Of what we are, together, here. (LL)   Arthur Hugh Clough.   ChIV-2; SacPr

Of which we are too distantly a part. (LL)   Less and Less Human, O Savage Spirit.   Wallace Stevens.   BBASP; VGW

Of Why He Is Unhanged.   Cecco Angiolieri, da Siena.   EaItPo, *tr. by* Dante Gabriel Rossetti

(Sonnet.)   AWP

Of wild geese. (LL)   Kikaku.   BLT; ZenPo, *tr. by* Takashi Ikemoto and Lucien Stryk

Of wilding in his hand. (LL)   Two April Mornings, The.   William Wordsworth.   EBEV; GTBS-P; NAEL-5v2; NAEL-6v2

Of woman and wine, of woods and spring.   Inexhaustible.   Israel Zangwill.   TrJP

Of Woman Torn.   Suheir Hammad.   PoArWo

Of woods, of plains, of hills and dales.   Upon a Rich Country Gentleman.   *Unknown*.   FaBoEE

Of world without integument.   Red Clay.   Candice Favilla.   ExTi

Of writing many books there is no end!   Elizabeth Barrett Browning.   NOBVV; VWP   *Fr.* Aurora Leigh.

Of you.   Little Mother.   Guido Gezelle.   TuT, *tr. by* Mary E. O'Donnell

Of young men and boys. (LL)   Thousand Killed, A.   Bernard Spencer.   FaBoWar; OBWP

Of your beloved in sleep. (LL)   He Hears the Cry of the Sedge.   W. B. Yeats.   OxBTC; RB

Of your daughters: Zeus, Father.   Korinna [*or* Corinna].   SaLy, *tr. by* Diane Rayor

Of your making, tell them I am. (LL)   Hand, The.   Ronald Stuart Thomas.   NOCV; OxBC

Of your misprision and my impotence. (LL)   On the Threshold.   Amy Levy.   LW; NOBVV

Of your path. (LL)   "H. D."   APT-1; HeIP-4; InPK-6; MoAmPo; NoAM; OxBA; TAP; TCAPo; TRP; UnPo   *Fr.* Garden, The.

Of your trouble, Ben, to ease me.   Ben Jonson.   NAEL-6v1; NAEL-7v1   *Fr.* Celebration of Charis in Ten Lyric[k] Pieces [*or* Peeces], A.

Of your white hand, they are mine. (LL)   On Mr. G. Herberts Booke, The Temple.   Richard Crashaw.   ESCV; GeHe

Of Youth He Singeth.   Robert Wever.   *See* Lusty Juventus

Ofatedo / seek it out upon the skin of Africa.   Edouard J. Maunick.   NegPo   *Fr.* As Far as Yoruba Land.

Ofay-Watcher Looks Back.   Mongane Wally Serote.   NAfrP; PBMAP

Off again, / thrusting up at scald.   Caliban in Blue.   Walter McDonald.   CDa

Off all the lords in faire Scottland.   Heir of Linne, The.   *Unknown*.   ESPB

Off an ancient story Ile tell you anon.   King John and the Bishop.   *Unknown*.   ESPB

Off at dawn to service in the walled and storied palace.   Lu Chi.   CoBCP   *Fr.* Two Poems Presented to the Gentleman in the Office of Palace Writers Ku Yen-hsien.

Off Brighton Pier.   Alan Ross.   OBWP

Off-color eyes that shine through lobes.   Studs.   Michael S. Harper.   ESEAA

Off Februar the fyiftene nycht.   Dance of the Sevin Deidly Synnis, The.   William Dunbar.   MiEL; NePenScot; OxBS; PoE

Off Ferry Road, the toilet of a garage where.   Brigitte Bardot in Grangetown.   Tony Curtis.   TCAWP

Off from Swing Shift.   Garrett Kaoru Hongo.   GeoHom; ReTh

Off go the crows from the roof.   Crows in a Strong Wind.   Cornelius Eady.   ESEAA; InvLad

Off Highway 106.   Cherrylog Road.   James Dickey.   CoAP; ColAP; HAP; HCAP; NAAL-2v2; NIL-7; NIP-4; TwCP; WeW-3

Off in the forest.   Found.   Goethe.   STV, *tr. by* John Frederick Nims

Off in the twilight hung the low full moon.   Full Moon.   Sappho.   AWP, *tr. by* William Ellery Leonard

Off in the wilderness bare and level.   Temptations of Saint Anthony, The.   Phyllis McGinley.   OxBSP

Off our New England coast the sea to-night. House of Falling Leaves, The. William Stanley Braithwaite. NAAAL

Off'rings of the Eastern[e] kings of old, The. Royal[l] Presents. Nathaniel Wanley. SacPr

Off Scollay Square, back from the subway, stands. Epitaph for the Old Howard. Byron Vazakas. APT-2

Off-shore, by islands hidden in the blood. Charles Olson. NOBA; NoAM; PmAP; PoM *Fr.* Maximus Poems, The.

Off that landspit of stony mouth-plugs. Medusa. Sylvia Plath. NALW

Off the Back of a Lorry. Tom Paulin. ModIr; PBCIP

Off the Beaten Track. Peter Rafferty. NLP

Off the Dutchesse. Elizabeth Taylor. EMWP

Off to hunt ducks. Song of the Duck Hunters. Kao Ch'i. CoBLCP, *tr. by* Jonathan Chaves

Off to Pasárgada. Manuel Bandeira. TCLAP, *tr. by* Candace Slater

Off to Patagonia. Theodore Weiss. TAP

Off to Philadelphia in the Morning. Dennis Brutus. GT

Off with sleep, love, up from bed. Love in May. Jean Passerat. AWP, *tr. by* Andrew Lang

Off with you, boy! Pretended prude! Strato [*or* Straton]. GrAn

Off Womanheid Ane Flour Delice. *Unknown.* OxBS

Offended, The. Anne Hébert. BoWoP, *tr. by* Willis Barnstone

Offensive, The. Keith Douglas. PoWW

Offer, An. Arthur Guiterman. TrJP

Offer it up plank it down. Ooftish. Samuel Beckett. NoAM

Offer varied attractions to Whistler. (LL) Limerick: "There's a combative artist named Whistler." Dante Gabriel Rossetti. FaBoEE; PeLi

Offered to a Man Who Sells Pines. Yü Wu-ling. SuSp, *tr. by* Edward H. Schafer

Offering. Debra Allbery. PBCAP

Offering. Thomas McGrath. RaBo

Offering. Sharan Strange. GT

Offering, An. Eloise Bibb. CBWP-4

Offering Congratulations to the Enlightened Reign. Ou-yang Chiung. ColAnChi, *tr. by* Lois Fusek

Offering for the Cat, An. Mei Yao Ch'en. CoBCP; ColAnChi, *tr. by* Burton Watson

Offering: Part One, The. Mary Lee, Lady Chudleigh. WPE

Offering Wine. Yü Wu-ling. CoBCP, *tr. by* Burton Watson

Offers the boon of Death. (LL) Compensation. Paul Laurence Dunbar. APN-2; BPo

Offers thee gold. (LL) And She Washed His Feet with Her Tear[e]s, and Wiped Them with the Hairs of Her Head. Sir Edward Sherburne. MeLP; NOSC

Office Friendships. Gavin Ewart. PeLV

Office Geraniums. Laura Newburn. UrbNat

Office Hour. Carol Lem. GeoHom

Office Party. Phyllis McGinley. ChrPo; OBSV

Office Window. Llewelyn Wyn Griffith. AngWePo

Office work: a wearisome jumble. Poem without a Category. Liu Cheng. CoBCP; ColAnChi, *tr. by* Burton Watson

Officer at the Rapids, The. Han Yü. SuSp, *tr. by* Charles Hartman

"Officer, I broke your gun." (LL) Mother Speaks: The Algiers Motel Incident, Detroit, A. Michael S. Harper. BPo; NBV

Officers. Josephine Miles. FaBoWP

Officers and Gentlemen down Under. John Brookes. FaBoWar

Officers' Mess. Gavin Ewart. FaBoWar; OxBTC

Official document blows through a forest, An. Long Picnic, The. Russell Edson. LCAP-2

Official Love Story. Linda Gregg. BodElec

Official Piety. John Greenleaf Whittier. NCAP

Officials are quick to disembark. Singing Girls (Written in Jest). Tu Fu. CrYelRi, *tr. by* Sam Hamill

Officials checked to make certain we'd. John Cage. APSN *Fr.* Diary: How to Improve the World (You Will Only Make Matters Worse).

Offspring. Naomi Long Madgett. GT; SoSe-8

Offspring of modern poetry, attend. Morning. *Unknown.* NOEC

Oft am I by the women told. Age. Abraham Cowley. AWP

Oft haive I hard, bot ofter fund it treu. Christen Lyndesay to Ro. Hudsone. Christian Lindsay. EMWP

Oft have I brooded on defeat and pain. Success. Emma Lazarus. SWaP

Oft have I heard thee mourn the wretched lot. Charles Churchill. OBSV *Fr.* Prophecy of Famine, The.

Oft have I said, I say it once more. Hafiz [*or* Hafez]. AWP *Fr.* Odes.

Oft have I said, the praise of doing well. Matthew Prior. ChIV-1 *Fr.* Pleasure: The Second Book of Solomon on the Vanity of the World.

Oft have I seen at some cathedral door. Henry Wadsworth Longfellow. APN-1; OxBA; TAP; TCAPo

Oft have I seen, ere Time had ploughed my cheek. Decay of Piety. William Wordsworth. TrCP

Oft have I seen, when that renewing breath. Resurrection and Immortality. Henry Vaughan. ESCV

Oft have I strove t'asscend that lofty ground. To Dame—Augustin nun on her curious gum-work. Jane Barker. EMWP

Oft have you hinted to your brother peer. Pope. OBGa *Fr.* Epistle to Lord Burlington.

Oft I had heard of Lucy Gray. Lucy Gray; or, Solitude. William Wordsworth. NAEL-5v2; NAEL-6v2; NOBRP; OxAEP-2

Oft I must strive with wind and wave. Cynewulf. AnOE, *tr. by* Charles W. Kennedy *Fr.* Riddles (Exeter Book).

Oft I've implored the gods in vain. Fanny [*or* Frances] Macartney Greville. ECWP; NOEC; OxBEV

Oft in Danger yet alive. To Mrs Thrale [on Her Thirty-fifth Birthday]. Samuel Johnson. FaBoEE

Oft in my thought full busily have I sought. Oft in My Thought. Charles D'Orleans. NoP-4

Oft in the hall I have heard my people. *Unknown.* HeIP-4 *Fr.* Beowulf.

Oft in the lone church-yard at night I've seen. Robert Blair. OxAEP-1 *Fr.* Grave, The.

Oft, in the silence of the night. Our Little Ghost. Louisa May Alcott. OBCA

Oft in the Silent Night. Otto Julius Bierbaum. AWP, *tr. by* Ludwig Lewisohn

Oft In the Stilly Night. Thomas Moore. SCGP

(Light of Other Days, The.) GTBS-P; NOBE; OBEV

Oft it befalls by the grace of God. Fates of Men (Exeter Book). *Unknown.* AnOE, *tr. by* Charles W. Kennedy

Oft let me wander, at the break of day. Sun-Rise: A Sonnet. Ann Radcliffe. CenSon

Oft mighty elephants by little Moors are led. Powerful Servants. Friedrich von Logau. GePo, *tr. by* George C. Schoolfield

Oft o'er my brain does that strange fancy roll. Sonnet Composed on a Journey Homeward; the Author Having Received Intelligence of the Birth of a Son, 20 September 1796. Samuel Taylor Coleridge. OxBSo

Oft-Repeated Dream, The. Robert Frost. TCAPo *Fr.* Hill Wife, The.

Oft to the Wanderer, weary of exile. Wanderer, The. *Unknown.* AnOE; NAWM-5v1, *tr. by* Charles William Kennedy

Oft when I'm sitting without anything to read. Lines to a World-famous Poet Who Failed to Complete a World-famous Poem; or, Come Clean, Mr. Guest! Ogden Nash. OBAL

Oft when I've seen some lonely mansion stand. Richard Payne Knight. OBGa *Fr.* Landscape, The.

Oft, when my lips I open to rehearse. To Shakspeare. Frances Anne [*or* "Fanny"] Kemble. SWaP

Oft when my spirit doth spread her bolder wings. Edmund Spenser. Son *Fr.* Amoretti.

Oft with true sighs, oft with uncalled tears. Sir Philip Sidney. NAEL-5v1; NAEL-6v1; NAEL-7v1 *Fr.* Astrophil and Stella.

Often. Jane Kenyon. LoL *Fr.* Having It Out With Melancholy.

Often a friend will greet me thus. Hartmann von Aue. GePo

Often after we make love. Old Man, The. Penelope Shuttle. LW

Often beneath the wave, wide from this ledge. At Melville's Tomb. Hart Crane. APT-2; HAP; HarvBoo; MoAmPo; NAAL-2v2; NAAL-5; NoAM; NoP-4; TAP; UnPo; VGW

Often, for pastime, mariners will ensnare. Albatross, The. Charles Baudelaire. OWoS, *tr. by* Richard Wilbur

Often, half-way to sleep. In Procession. Robert Graves. TwCP

Often I Am Permitted to Return to a Meadow. Robert Duncan. ColAP; HarvBoo; NOBA; PFTM-2; PmAP

Often I go to bed as soon after dinner. Jane Kenyon. LoL *Fr.* Having It Out With Melancholy.

Often I inhabit my body. Stepping Aside. Andrée Chedid. HAWP, *tr. by* Harriet Zinnes

Often I return to that room—abject. Denied, The. Lisa Sewell. AmPoNex

Often I sit in the sun and brooding over the city, always. Dennis Lee. NOBC *Fr.* Civil Elegies.

Often I think of my Jewish friends. Pripet Marshes, The. Irving Feldman. TaR

Often I think of the beautiful town. My Lost Youth. Henry Wadsworth Longfellow. APN-1; AWP; ITBLP; NAAL-2v1; NAAL-3; NOBA; OBEV; OxBA; PoRA; TAP; TCAPo; TFi

Often I turn on people / in rather strange and / inexplicable ways. Maxfield Parrish. Eileen Myles. WiU

Often I've wished that I'd been born a woman. Wish, A. Laurence David Lerner. OxBTC

Often, I wonder, who is this stranger. Keys. Barbara J. Garshman. PasH

Often in summer, on a tarred bridge plank standing. Wild Bees. James Keir Baxter. NoP-4

Often in the morning the fog is thick over Jersey. View of Jersey, A. Edward Field. NeAP

Often, in these blue meadows.   Pursuit from Under.   James Dickey.   HAP

Often keening on her daughter's tomb, Kleina.   Anyte [*or* Anytes].   SaLy, *tr. by* Diane Rayor

Often of late.   Images of San Luis.   Luis Lopez.   GeoH

Often on this her daughter's tomb did Cleina grieve.   Anyte [*or* Anytes].   HePo   *Fr.* Epigrams.

Often rebuked, yet always back returning.   Stanzas.   Emily Jane Brontë.   NALW; NOBVV; OBEV; OxBEV; PEW; SCGP; VWP

Often the day had a most joyful morn.   Simbuono Giudice.   EaItPo, *tr. by* Dante Gabriel Rossetti

Often the start went wrong.   Start.   Martin Sorescu.   VCWP, *tr. by* Michael Hamburger

Often this thought wakens me unawares.   Night.   Hermann Hesse.   AWP, *tr. by* Ludwig Lewisohn

Often times / parents.   Wishbone.   Frank X. Walker.   SpirFl

Often waking / before the sun decreed.   Author of *Christine,* The.   Richard Howard.   CoAP

Often when alone I liken my lord / to the cosmos.   Gaspara Stampa.   BoWoP

Often, when bored, the sailors of the crew.   Albatross, The.   Charles Baudelaire.   SxFrPo, *tr. by* James McGowan

Often, when I leave home.   On Shutting the Door.   Lotte Kramer.   Prnts

Often, when o'er tree and turret.   Hic Vir, Hic Est.   Charles Stuart Calverley.   OxBoLi; PeLV

Often When Warring.   Thomas Hardy.   GSo

Oftentimes, I grew dejected and sobbed.   Ch'u Yüan.   SuSp   *Fr.* Li Sao.

Ofttimes have I heard you speak of one who commits a.   Kahlil Gibran.   PoToHe   *Fr.* Prophet, The.

Og [and Doeg].   Dryden.   AWP   *Fr.* Absalom and Achitophel, Part 2.

Oggy! Oggy! Oggy!   Land of Song.   Nigel Jenkins.   AngWePo

Ogot, you invertebrate charlatan!   Entelechy on the Libidinal Fringe.   E. San Juan, Jr.   ReBoTo

Ogre does what ogres can, The.   August 1968.   W. H. Auden.   OxBSP

Ogres and Pygmies.   Robert Graves.   FaBoMo; NoAM

Oh, a day in the city-square, there is no such pleasure in life! (LL)   Up at a Villa—down in the City.   Robert Browning.   FHYEP; GTBS-P; NOBE; PoRA

Oh, a hidden power is in my breast.   Song of the Moon.   Priscilla Jane Thompson.   CBWP-2

Oh! a private buffoon is a light-hearted loon.   Sir William Schwenck Gilbert.   NBLV   *Fr.* Yeoman of the Guard.

Oh, a soldier told me, before he died.   Soldier's Tale, The.   *Unknown.*   PeLV

Oh, about the joy of owning a crab hut at Sung-chiang!   Chang Chih-ho.   SuSp   *Fr.* Fisherman's Songs.

Oh Achilles of the moleskins.   Frank Horne.   BPo   *Fr.* Letters [*or* Notes] Found near a Suicide.

O[h] *all ye,* who pass[e] by, whose eyes and mind[e].   Sacrifice, The.   George Herbert.   GeHe

Oh, America / The sun sets in you.   Evening Land, The.   D. H. Lawrence.   FaBoA

Oh amiable rain.   Rain.   Charlotte Gardelle.   CuPo

Oh, and yet I see that I will return to you anyway, and throw myself at your feet and cry a lot over my sins, until my crime will be pardoned.   Marino Ceccoli.   CAGL, *tr. by* Jill Claretta Robbins

Oh angels! will ye never sweep the drifts from my door?   Drifts That Bar My Door.   Adah Isaacs Menken.   CBWP-1

Oh, answer me! (LL)   Answer Me.   Adah Isaacs Menken.   CBWP-1; PoBW; ViWPN

Oh, Astonishing Love.   Javier Sologuren.   BLPSL, *tr. by* Rene de Costa, Rigas Kappatos and Eleni Paidoussi

Oh, Athelstane, the faithful!   Athelstane.   Priscilla Jane Thompson.   CBWP-2

Oh author of my being!—far more dear.   To Charles Burney.   Frances [*or* Fanny], Mme D'Arblay Burney.   ECWP

Oh, baby, baby, baby dear.   Song.   Edith Nesbit.   NOBVV; PEW

Oh, be but still, you half-part of my breast!   Departure Aria.   Johann Christian Günther.   GePo, *tr. by* George C. Schoolfield

Oh be thou blest with all that Heav'n can send.   To Mrs. M. B. on Her Birth-Day.   Pope.   EnLoPo

Oh Beloved, Since the Origin We Have Been.   Bâkî.   WoPoe, *tr. by* Walter Andrews, Najaat Black and Mehmet Kalpakli

Oh, big sighs. Windy sighs. And ghostly laughter. (LL)   News Update.   John Balaban.   AF; CDa

Oh, Bill / Why can't you behave.   Cole Porter.   ReLy

Oh, black Persian cat!   Mujer.   William Carlos Williams.   SAmP

Oh! blame not the bard, if he fly to the bowers.   Thomas Moore.   NOIV; NPeEn

Oh, blessed ease! no more of heaven I ask.   Written in the Workhouse.   Thomas Hood.   CenSon

Oh! blest beyond all daughters of the earth!   Mary at the Feet of Christ.   Felicia Dorothea Hemans.   CenSon

Oh Boney's on the sea.   Shan Van Vocht, The.   *Unknown.*   OxBoLi

Oh Boney was a warrior.   Boney.   *Unknown.*   FaBoVe

Oh bright-glancing Silver, who marriage has made.   Stroll-Joy.   Johann Klaj.   GePo, *tr. by* George C. Schoolfield

Oh, brown skinny girl with eyes like chips of mica.   Tita's Poem.   Aurora Levins Morales.   PueRic

Oh, but it is dirty!   Filling Station.   Elizabeth Bishop.   FaBoMo; HAP; HCAP; InPK-6; NoP-4; PoetW; VCAP; WeW-3

Oh but It Was Good.   Harold Littlebird.   VoR

Oh, but to fade, and live we know not where.   Shakespearian Readings.   Phoebe Cary.   SWaP

Oh! can'st thou bear to see this faded frame.   Her Last Appeal to Phaon.   Mary Robinson.   CenSon; RWP

Oh, can we love and live? Pray, let us die.   Love's Sun.   William Cavendish, Duke of Newcastle.   NOSC

Oh child let yourself.   Prayer of Mothers Who Unintentionally Failed Their Children.   Vivian Lamarque.   CItWP, *tr. by* Cinzia Sartini Blum and Lara Trubowitz

Oh Cibernetic Fairy.   Down with the Money-Exchange.   Carlos German Belli.   TCLAP, *tr. by* Maureen Ahern and David Tipton

Oh, come let us welcome sweet Sabbath the Queen!   Welcome, Queen Sabbath.   Zalman Schneour.   TrJP, *tr. by* Harry H. Fein

Oh come, my beloved! from thy winter abode.   California Madrigal.   Bret Harte.   APN-2

Oh, come to me in dreams, my love!   Stanzas.   Mary Wollstonecraft Shelley.   LW

Oh come with me by moonlight, love.   Cherokee Love Song, A.   John Rollin Ridge.   APN-2

Oh, come with old Khayyám and leave the Wise.   Omar Khayyám.   UV, *tr. by* Edward Fitzgerald   *Fr.* Rubáiyát of Omar Khayyám [of Naishápúr], The.

Oh, could I but sing as the minstrels of old!   Lines to Emma.   Priscilla Jane Thompson.   CBWP-2

Oh Could I Raise the Darken'd Veil.   Nathaniel Hawthorne.   APN-1

Oh! could I see as thou hast seen.   On Hearing a Description of a Prairie.   Fanny Crosby.   SWaP

Oh country, marvel of the earth!   Not Yet.   William Cullen Bryant.   NCAP

Oh! craven, craven! while my brothers fall.   George Henry Boker.   APN-2

Oh Cruel Was the Press-Gang.   *Unknown.*   FaBoWar

Oh Damon, if thou ever werst.   To Damon. To Inquire of Him if He Cou'd Tell Me by the Style, Who Writ Me a Copy of Verses that Came to Me in an Unknown Hand.   Aphra Behn.   EMWP

Oh, Day of Days.   LeRoy V. Brant.   AH

Oh, de ole sheep, dey know de road.   Ole Sheep Dey Know de Road, De.   *Unknown.*   BPo

Oh dead punk lady with the knack.   Victim, The.   Thom Gunn.   SwNoth

Oh, Dear!   *Unknown.*   ReMoGo

Oh dear, my heart was ready to burst! (LL)   King Charles the First.   *Unknown.*   FaBoCh; OxNR

Oh, dear! Oh, me! Oh, my!   Song.   Gregory Corso.   BB

Oh, dear! / The Christian virtues will disappear!   Christian Virtues.   Charlotte Perkins Stetson Gilman.   SWaP

O[h], Dear! What Can the Matter Be?   *Unknown.*   OxNR

Oh dear what can the matter be?   Saturday Night.   Victoria Wood.   OBCoV

Oh, dear, what can the matter be? / Two old women got up in an apple-tree.   Bunch of Blue Ribbons, The.   *Unknown.*   ReMoGo

"Oh, dearest grandpa, come and see."   Dead Sister, The.   Caroline Gilman.   OBCA

Oh, dearest loss, sweet illusion.   Sonnet 32.   Fernando de Herrera.   BLPSL, *tr. by* Rene de Costa, Rigas Kappatos and Eleni Paidoussi

Oh! Death will find me, long before I tire.   Sonnet.   Rupert Brooke.   NoP-4; PoRA

Oh, Dem Golden Slippers!   James A. Bland.   APN-2

Oh Dick! You may talk of your writing and reading.   Thomas Moore.   OBCoV   *Fr.* Fudge Family in Paris, The.

Oh, ditch of all ditches.   Ode to a Ditch.   *Unknown.*   VerBaPo

Oh, do you remember sweet Betsey from Pike.   Sweet Betsey from Pike.   *Unknown.*   OBAL; OxBoLi

Oh, Domjum!   Archie Weller.   IBA

Oh, don't you remember Sweet Betsey from Pike.   *Unknown.*   *See* Oh, do you remember sweet Betsey from Pike

"Oh! don't you see the turtle-dove."   Turtle-Dove, The.   *Unknown.*   OxBoLi

Oh Dreams, Oh Destinations.   Cecil Day Lewis.
Symbols of Gross Experience.   Son

Oh, East is East, and West is West, and never the twain shall meet.   Ballad of East and West, The.   Rudyard Kipling.   EBNV; OBNV

Oh, Eleazar Wheelock was a very pious man.   Eleazar Wheelock.   Richard Hovey.   OBAL

Oh Eliza look at your Uncle Jim!   Soldiers' Chorus from Faust.   *Unknown.*   NOBAu

Oh, England is a pleasant place for them that's rich and high. Last Buccaneer, The. Charles Kingsley. EBVV

Oh, England. / Sick in head and sick in heart. England. *Unknown.* FaBoEE; OxBSP

Oh! Erin my country, my ancestor's home! Song to Erin. Mary Weston Fordham. CBWP-2

Oh, ever beats withn your melodies. Even the Beating Heart Is Already Indicated. Ernst Waldinger. AuPH, *tr.* by Lowell A. Bangerter

Oh, ever skilled [*or* skill'd] to wear the form we love! To Hope. Helen Maria Williams. CenSon; ECWP; OxBSo

Oh! ever thus from childhood's hour. Thomas Moore. UV *Fr.* Lalla Rookh.

Oh, everything is far. Lament. Rainer Maria Rilke. TrJP, *tr.* by C. F. MacIntyre

Oh, face to face with trouble. Margaret Elizabeth Munson Sangster. PoToHe

Oh fate, take pity on my suffering country. Zrínyi's Second Song. Ferenc Kölcsey. IQMS, *tr.* by Adam Makkai

Oh father, now that I have touched. Oh Father. Wendy Rose. CDW

Oh feet, oh legs, oh thighs / that formed the deathrow. Philodemus. GrAn

Oh flame falling, as shaken, as the stories. Fire, The. Robert Creeley. NOBA

Oh, For a Bowl of Fat Canary. John Lyly. *See* Alexander and Campaspe

Oh! for a closer walk with God. William Cowper. ECEV; NOCV; NOEC; PeECV; SCGP; TOF *Fr.* Olney Hymns.

Oh, for a drink, to-night. Charmion's Lament. Eloise Bibb. CBWP-4

Oh for a lodge in some vast wilderness. William Cowper. NOEC *Fr.* Task, The.

Oh for a poet—for a beacon bright. Sonnet. Edwin Arlington Robinson. APN-2; NCAP; OxBA

Oh for boyhood's painless play. John Greenleaf Whittier. AiP *Fr.* Barefoot Boy, The.

Oh for far-off monkeyland. Monkeyland. Sándor Weöres. IQMS; RB; WoPoe, *tr.* by Edwin Morgan

Oh! for imperial Polydamna's art. Nepenthe. Charlotte Smith. NoP-4

O[h]! for some honest lover's ghost. Sonnet. Sir John Suckling. BASC; BeJo; CavPo; MeLP; OxBEV

Oh for that rose of Bolshevism which holds. Anathema. Maranatha! John Wheelwright. APT-2

Oh, for the veils of my far away youth. Lost Illusions. Georgia Douglas Johnson. NAAAL

Oh for the wings of a dove. Song. Agnes Mary Frances Robinson. VWP

Oh for words with which. In the Potting Shed. Sir Osbert Sitwell. OBGa

Oh fortune, [how] thy wresting wavering state. Written on a Wall at Woodstock. Queen of England Elizabeth I. WPE

Oh, foully slighted Ethiope maid! Song, The. Priscilla Jane Thompson. CBWP-2

Oh friend, we arrived too late. Friedrich Hölderlin. RaBo *Fr.* Bread and Wine.

Oh! Fucking Halkirk. *Unknown.* FaBoWar

Oh, gallant was our galley from her carven steering-wheel. Galley-Slave, The. Rudyard Kipling. PeVV

Oh, gallant was the first love, and glittering and fine. Pictures in the Smoke. Dorothy Parker. NBLV

Oh, gallantly they fared forth in khaki and in blue. America's Welcome Home. Henry Van Dyke. AiP

Oh, Galuppi, Baldassaro, this is very sad to find! Toccata of Galuppi's, A. Robert Browning. EBVV; FaBoVe; GTBS-P; HAP; NAEL-5v2; NAEL-6v2; NOBE; NOBVV; UV

Oh, genius of Stratford, return! To Shakespeare. Nina Nikolaevna Berberova. TCRusP, *tr.* by John Glad

O[h,] gentle Love, do not forsake the guide. Upon Some Alterations in My Mistress, after My Departure into France. Thomas Carew. CaPo

Oh gentle Venus, ease a tarse. John Wilmot, 2d Earl of Rochester. EroLit *Fr.* Sodom; or The Quintessence of Debauchery.

"Oh, get you forth, my son Willy." Marm Grayson's Guests. Mary Eleanor Wilkins Freeman. OBCA

Oh give it Motion—deck it sweet. Emily Dickinson. NCAP

Oh give me a home where the buffalo roam. Home on the Range, A. *Unknown.* APN-2

Oh give me that you prize the most. Her Gift. Annie Hindle. PoBW

Oh, give my youth, my faith, my sword. Louise Imogen Guiney. TCAPo *Fr.* Knight Errant, The.

Oh! give to me of the bright green leaves. I Am Fashion's Toy. Mary E. Tucker. CBWP-1

Oh, Give Us Back the Days of Old! John Mason Neale. NOCV

Oh, give us of your oil, our lamps go out. For Richer, For Poorer. Emily Hickey. PoBW

Oh, give us pleasure in the flowers today. Prayer in Spring, A. Robert Frost. AH; TrCP

Oh, God, beneath thy guiding hand. Pilgrim Fathers, The. Leonard Bacon. AH

Oh, God, beyond the wit of the genius. Prayer. Dániel Berzsenyi. IQMS, *tr.* by Peter Zollman

Oh God Forbid. Freddie Greenfield. GLP

Oh, God, God!—Calm down. Which One Is the Grown-up? Haiku. Liz Rosenberg. InvLad

Oh God! It's great! Chocolate Milk. Ron Padgett. TTTS

Oh God! my heart is thine. In the Valley. Priscilla Jane Thompson. CBWP-2

Oh God of mercy, oh wild God. (LL) Dancing, The. Gerald Stern. LCAP-2; LoL; UnSA

(Oh God, she said). Song My. Susan Griffin. WPOW

Oh God, that I were dead! (LL) Mariana. Tennyson. AWP; FHYEP; NAEL-5v2; NAEL-6v2; NOBE; NOBRP; OBEV; OxAEP-2; PeVV; PoE; SCGP; TFi; UnPo

Oh God! what a lovely war. Cavalier's Farewell, The. Guillaume Apollinaire. WoPoe, *tr.* by Anne Greet

Oh, golden flower opened up. Poem to the Mother of the Gods, A. *Unknown.* STP, *tr.* by Edward Kissam

Oh golden life, waken! Fortunate night! Johann Klaj. GePo

Oh! Golden Rose! Oh. Glittering Lilly White. Edward Taylor. SCAP *Fr.* Preparatory Meditations before My Approach to the Lord's Supper.

Oh, good gigantic smile o' the brown old earth. Robert Browning. OxBSP *Fr.* James Lee's Wife.

Oh! Good, good, good, my Lord. What more love yet. Edward Taylor. NOBA *Fr.* Preparatory Meditations Before My Approach to the Lord's Supper.

Oh green green willow wonderfully red flower. Ikkyu Sojun. WoPoe, *tr.* by Stephen Berg

Oh, hadst thou, cruel! been content to seize. Pope. EroLit *Fr.* Rape of the Lock, The.

"Oh, halt!" cried Virginia, "Enough!" Limerick. Otto Watteau. PeLi

Oh hame cam his guid horse, but never cam he. (LL) Bonnie [*or* Bonny] George [*or* James] Campbell. *Unknown.* OxBB; OxBoLi; SCGP

Oh happy hero come, oh enter, worthy groom. To Be Read above the Castle-Gate, When His Princely Highness Rode in to His Marriage Bed. Simon Dach. GePo, *tr.* by George C. Schoolfield

Oh happy shades—to me unblest! Shrubbery, The. William Cowper. NOBE; OBGa

Oh, hark the dogs are barking, love. Banks of the Condamine, The. *Unknown.* NOBAu

Oh, have you heard de lates'. Ballit of de Boll Weevil, De. *Unknown.* NOBA

Oh, have you seen the *Tattlesnake*. Journal of Society, The. Godfrey Turner. NOBL; PeLV

Oh he is worn with toil! the big drops run. Robert Southey. CenSon

Oh, he was a handsome trotter, and he couldn't be completer. How We Drove the Trotter. W. T. Goodge. NOBAu

Oh! hear a pensive prisoner's prayer. Mouse's Petition, The. Anna Laetitia Barbauld. ECWP

"Oh, hear you a horn, mother, behind the hill?" Horn, The. James Reeves. OTCP

Oh heart rejoice! For I Have Done a Good and Kindly Deed. Franz Werfel. TrJP, *tr.* by Edith Abercrombie Snow

Oh, Heaven! it was a frightful and pitiful sight to see. William McGonagall. VerBaPo

Oh heavens how these crying people spoil the beautiful geological scene. (LL) New Age, The. Stevie Smith. NAEL-5v2; NAEL-6v2

Oh hell, what do mine eyes. Milton by Firelight. Gary Snyder. CoAP; NAAL-2v2

Oh, her beauty—the tender maid! Its brilliance gives light. Ibn al-Arabi. TOF

Oh hey, All-Destroyer. Najrul Islām. SinGod, *tr.* by Rachel Fell McDermott

Oh hold me, for I am afraid. (LL) Woman to Man. Judith Wright. BMAP; CBAP; NoP-4; WPE

Oh, how can I live in a torture so wild. Disappointment. Mary E. Tucker. CBWP-1

Oh, how fastidious you once were. Georgy [*or* Georgii] Vladimirovich Ivanov. TCRusP, *tr.* by Daniel Weissbort

Oh! How his pointed language, like a dart. Cant. 5.6 & c. Elizabeth Singer. ChIV-1

Oh! How I Hate to Get up in the Morning. Irving Berlin. ReLy; TCAPo

Oh, how I love Humanity. World State, The. Gilbert Keith Chesterton. SacPr

OH HOW I WANT THEE FAME! Mad Sonnet: Fame. Michael McClure. BB

Oh how I wanted to be a dancer. Soul Train. Allison Joseph. AmPoNex; ExTi

Oh how I wish that an embargo. Nurse's Dole in the Medea, The. Byron. OBVE

O[h], how much more doth beauty beauteous seem. William Shakespeare. AWP; OBEV; PoE; SCGP *Fr.* Sonnets.

Oh, how slowly he goes. Chalk and Soot. Wassily Kandinsky [or Kandinskii]. PFTM-1

Oh how the force the water lifts! Before a Fountain. Karl Kraus. AuPH, *tr.* by Lowell A. Bangerter

Oh, How the Hand the Lover Ought to Prize. Aphra Behn. LW

Oh, how the lilacs are this May! Bulging-large bunches fell. Sergey Gandlevsky. ItGoST, *tr.* by Philip Metres

Oh, how the world has altered since some fifty years ago! Song of the Modern Time. Eliza Cook. VWP

Oh humming all and. Detach, Invading. Ron Padgett. FTOS

Oh hush thee, my baby. Carol, A. Cecil Day Lewis. ChrPo

Oh! I admit I'm dull and poor. Claim, The. Edith Nesbit. NOBVV

Oh I am a cat that likes to. Galloping Cat, The. Stevie Smith. BrRo

Oh I am a Yankee sailor boy. Sailor Boy's Song. *Unknown.* CA

Oh / I am thinking. Frances Densmore. APT-1 *Fr.* Chippewa Music.

Oh, I am wild—wild! Sale of Souls. Adah Isaacs Menken. CBWP-1

Oh, I can cook, too, on top of the rest. I Can Cook, Too. Betty Comden. ReLy

Oh, I can smile for you, and tilt my head. Certain Lady, A. Dorothy Parker. NIL-7; NIP-4

Oh I can't decide between my two loves *ei!* Women's Songs. *Unknown.* PeNZ, *tr.* by Margaret Orbell

Oh! I could toil for thee o'er burning plains. To Phaon. Mary Robinson. CenSon; RWP

Oh, I don't care. Bufu. JDP, *tr.* by Yoel Hoffmann

Oh / I got a message from below. Pack up Your Sins and Go to the Devil. Irving Berlin. ReLy

Oh, I got plenty o' nuthin'. I Got Plenty o' Nuthin'. George Gershwin. ReLy

Oh I got up and went to work. On a Seven-Day Diary. Alan Dugan. OBAL

Oh I have grown so shrivelled and sere. Body of John. Ronald Allison Kells Mason. PeNZ

Oh, I have no illusions as to what. Penelope. James [or Jim] Harrison. NIP-4

Oh! I have slipped the surly bonds of Earth. High Flight. John Gillespie, Jr. Magee. ITBLP; PoWW

Oh, I have told thee every secret care. Charles Lloyd. CenSon

Oh, I laugh to hear what grown folk. Mrs. Kriss Kringle. Edith Matilda Thomas. OBCA

Oh I'll die I'll die I'll die. Stark Electric Jesus. Malay Roy Choudhury. PFTM-2

Oh, I'm a good old Rebel. Rebel, The. Innes Randolph. NBLV; OBAL; OxBoLi

Oh I'm Dirty Dan, the world's dirtiest man. Dirtiest Man in the World, The. Shel [or Shelley] Silverstein. OBCA

Oh, I'm 10 Months Pregnant. Ntozake Shange. GT

Oh, I should love to be like one of those. Youth Dreams, The. Rainer Maria Rilke. AWP; TrJP, *tr.* by Ludwig Lewisohn

Oh, I used to sing a song. Endless Song, The. Ruth McEnery Stuart. OBAL

Oh, I went down South for to see my Sal. Polly Wolly Doodle. *Unknown.* TCAPo

Oh, I would have these tongues oracular. At a Symphony. Louise Imogen Guiney. APN-2

Oh, if my power might equal my desire. Lady Charlotte Guest. Goronva Camlan. AngWePo

Oh if the gods would make me rich, you said. Oh If the Gods Would Make Me Rich. Martial. WoPoe, *tr.* by William Matthews

Oh, If Thou Knew'st How Thou Thyself Dost Harm. Sir William Alexander, Earl of Stirling. Son *Fr.* Aurora.

Oh! if thou lov'st me, love me not so well! Jane Cross Simpson. CenSon

Oh, ill-starred Ethiopia. Address to Ethiopia. Priscilla Jane Thompson. CBWP-2

Oh in eighteen hundred and forty-one. Poor Paddy Works on the Railway. *Unknown.* GM

Oh, in the fourteenth the faith landed. Land Is Gone, The. *Unknown.* PeNZ, *tr.* by Margaret Orbell

Oh, in the merry month of May. Bonny Barbara Allan. *Unknown.* AWP; BoLoP; ESPB; HeIP-4; OxBB

Oh in the Stonegut Sugar Works. Ballad of the Stonegut Sugar Works. James Keir Baxter. PeNZ

Oh Indian watching from the doorway. Who Knows? José Santos Chocano. TCLAP, *tr.* by Andrew Rosing

Oh, Is It Love? Amy Levy. ViWPN

Oh, is it, then, Utopian. De Profundis. Dorothy Parker. NAAL-2v2

Oh, it is done, my love, my death, my life, my prize. To the Superhuman Adelmund, When She Would Undo the Kiss Already Done. Philipp von Zesen. GePo, *tr.* by George C. Schoolfield

Oh, it's fiddle-de-dum and fiddle-de-dee. Dancing Bear, The. Albert Bigelow Paine. OBCA

Oh, it's hard to grow up at the way-station side! Boatman's Song, A. Wang Chien. SuSp, *tr.* by William H. Nienhauser

O[h] joy[e]s! Infinite sweetness! with what flowers [or flowres]. Morning-Watch, The. Henry Vaughan. AngWePo; BASC; ESCV; GeHe; NOSC; PeECV

Oh Kali. Janine Canan. HW

Oh Kali Full of Brahman! Rāmprasād Sen. SinGod, *tr.* by Rachel Fell McDermott

Oh! kangaroos, sequins, chocolate sodas! Today. Frank O'Hara. TTTS

O[h] King of grief! (a title strange, yet true). Thanksgiving, The. George Herbert. ESCV; GeHe

Oh King of Saints, how great's thy work, say we. Edward Johnson. SCAP

Oh king, whose head alone can rule Earth's company. Concerning the King of Sweden. Georg Rudolph Weckherlin. GePo, *tr.* by George C. Schoolfield

Oh, Lady, Be Good! George Gershwin. ReLy

Oh Lana Turner we love you get up. (LL). Poem. Frank O'Hara. CLPP; FTOS; PmAP; VGW

Oh Lawd have mussy now upon us. Blessing without Company. *Unknown.* BPo

Oh lay me by yon peaceful stream. Aged Bard's Wish (Translation of a Gaelic Poem Composed in the Isle of Skye), The. Anne Grant. RWP

Oh leaden heeld. Lord, give, forgive I pray. Edward Taylor. SCAP *Fr.* Preparatory Meditations before My Approach to the Lord's Supper.

Oh! leave the Past to bury its own dead. To One Who Would Make a Confession. Wilfrid Scawen Blunt. GSo

Oh, let me lay my head tonight upon your breast. I Am Your Wife. *Unknown.* PoToHe

Oh, let me not serve so, as those men serve. John Donne. BASC *Fr.* Elegies.

Oh, let me run and hide. Spring Ecstasy. Lizette Woodworth Reese. MoAmPo

Oh! let that day from time be blotted quite. On the Fatal Day January 30, 1648. Thomas Fairfax, Baron Fairfax of Cameron. NOSC

Oh, let us fly without delay. Bungalow in Quogue. P. G. Wodehouse. ReLy

Oh! Liberty! transcendent and sublime! To Liberty. Mary Robinson. OxBSo

Oh, life is a glorious cycle of song. Dorothy Parker. NBLV; NIP-4; OBAL; OBCoV *Fr.* Some Beautiful Letters.

Oh life, long as an epic. Tatiana Bek. ItGoST, *tr.* by Richard McKane

Oh limpid spring! that dost surpass. To Mother Luddwels Cave and Spring. Martha, Lady Giffard. EMWP

Oh List to My Song! Clara Ann Thompson. CBWP-2

Oh, listen, sister. Can't Help Lovin' Dat Man. Jerome Kern. ReLy

Oh Living Lord, I still will laud thy name. Other Song of the Faithful, for the Mercies of God, An. Michael Drayton. ChIV-1

Oh London I once more to thee do speak. Mary Adams. EMWP

Oh, long, long / The snow has possessed the mountains. Grass on the Mountain, The. *Unknown.* APT-1; AWP, *tr.* by Mary Austin

Oh Lord Cozens Hardy. Lord Cozens Hardy. Sir John Betjeman. OxBTC

Oh, Lord! I lift my heart. Prayer, A. Priscilla Jane Thompson. CBWP-2

Oh, Lord, we call to you from our apartment. Gay Psalm from Fort Valley, A. Louie Crew. GLP

Oh Lord, when all our bones are thrust. Supplication. Edgar Lee Masters. TrCP

Oh, lost and unforgotten friend. Desiderato. William Johnson Cory. CAGL

Oh! Love, that stronger art than wine. Aphra Behn. WPE; WPOW *Fr.* Lucky Chance, The.

Oh, love this house, and make of it a Home—. For a New Home. Rosa Zagnoni Marinoni. PoToHe

Oh Lovely Fishermaiden. Heinrich Heine. AWP, *tr.* by Louis Untermeyer

Oh lustrous! the king's army. Great War Dance, The. *Unknown.* WoPoe, *tr.* by Constance A. Cook

Oh, ma honey. Alexander's Ragtime Band. Irving Berlin. ReLy; TCAPo

Oh Ma Kali, for a long time now. Mahendranāth Bhattācārya. SinGod, *tr.* by Rachel Fell McDermott

Oh, Magyar, keep immovably. Appeal. Mihály Vörösmarty. IQMS, *tr.* by Watson Kirkconnell

Oh, Maika in a maika, there's the smell of summer. Viktor Arkad'evich Urin. TCRP

Oh man, be born of God: for at His Godhead's throne. "Angelus Silesius." GePo, *tr.* by George C. Schoolfield *Fr.* Cherubical Wanderer, The.

Oh, man's capacity / For spiritual sorrow. Crucifixion, The. Alice Thompson Meynell. SacPr

Oh, Mary, this London's a wonderful sight. Mountains of Mourne, The. William Percy French. OBCoV

Oh Mary, this Tatton's a wonderful sight. Tatton Parachute Training School. *Unknown.* FaBoWar

Oh May, bonnie May is to the Yowe buchts gane. Laird o' Ochiltree Wa's, The. *Unknown.* OxBB

Oh me / is that the ambulance chasing out of town? Alan Brunton. PeNZ

O[h] me[e], the time is [*or* has] come to part.   Mary Sidney Wroth, Countess of Montgomery.   NOSC   *Fr.* Pamphilia to Amphilanthus.

Oh men are beaten, beaten, beaten down.   Land Laws, The.   Merimeri Penfold.   PeNZ, *tr. by* Margaret Orbell

Oh Menelaus.   On Hearing the First Cuckoo.   Richard Church.   OBMV

Oh, might it die or rest at last! (LL)   Shelley.   HeIP-4; NAEL-5v2; NoP-4; PoE   *Fr.* Hellas.

Oh Mind, you don't know how to farm.   Rāmprasād Sen.   SinGod, *tr. by* Rachel Fell McDermott

O[h] mistress mine, where are you roaming?   William Shakespeare.   AEP; AWP; BoLoP; CTC; ClHu; HAP; NAEL-5v1; NAEL-6v1; NBLV; NOBE; NoP-4; NoSic; OxBSP; OxBoLi; PoRA; SCGP; TFi; WoPoe   *Fr.* Twelfth Night.

Oh moon, oh moon!   *Unknown.*   BoWoP

Oh, morning glory.   Hakusen.   JDP, *tr. by* Yoel Hoffmann

Oh mother, holiest mother, mother night!   To Night, the Mother of Sleep and Death.   John Addington Symonds.   Son

Oh, mother, I shall be married to Mr. Punchinello.   To Mr. Punchinello.   *Unknown.*   OxNR

Oh, Mother, Mother, oh what a cipher.   Carl Michael Bellman.   WoPoe, *tr. by* Rika Lesser   *Fr.* Fredman's Epistlar, 1790.

Oh mother my mouth is full of stars.   Song of the Dying Gunner A.A.1.   Charles Causley.   FaBoWar; PoWW

Oh Mother, so many times.   Mother with Child.   Lenore Keeshig-Tobias.   FFC

Oh! mourn not for Anacreon dead.   On Tom Moore's Translation of Anacreon.   Thomas Erskine, 1st Baron Erskine.   FaBoEE

Oh Muse! I crave a favor.   Muse's Favor, The.   Priscilla Jane Thompson.   CBWP-2

Oh! must that task, that mournful task, be thine? (LL)   Laments her Early Misfortunes.   Mary Robinson.   CenSon; RWP

Oh, my belovèd, have you thought of this.   Sonnet.   Edna St. Vincent Millay.   HeIP-4; LW

Oh my black[e] soul[e]! now thou art summoned.   John Donne.   EBEV; OxAEP-1; Son; TOF   *Fr.* Holy Sonnets.

Oh my boy: Jesus.   Confession Stone, The.   Owen Dodson.   TTY

Oh my bride, my bride. (LL)   I Remember.   Stevie Smith.   BoLoP; BoWoP; FaBoWP; InPK-6; NIL-7; OxBC

Oh, my fine, my honey-colored Duke of Marmalade!   Elegy for the Duke of Marmalade.   Luis Palés Matos.   TCLAP, *tr. by* Ellen G. Matilla and Diego de la Texera

Oh, my God is in the whirlwind.   Song of the Whirlwind.   Fenton Johnson.   NAAAL

Oh, my golden slippers am [*or* are] laid away.   Oh, Dem Golden Slippers!   James A. Bland.   APN-2

Oh my Good, my Beauty!   Morning of Drunkenness.   Arthur Rimbaud.   SxFrPo, *tr. by* Martin Sorrell

Oh, my hatred, my majestic hatred.   Sacred Hatred.   João da Cruz e Sousa.   TCLAP, *tr. by* Flavia Vidal

Oh, my heart is beating wildly.   When I'm Not near the Girl I Love.   Burton Lane.   ReLy

Oh, my Lord.   My Lord, What a Morning.   Waring Cuney.   TTY

Oh, My Love Is Like a Red, Red Rose.   Robert Burns.   *See* Song: "O my love's [*or* luve's *or* luve is] like a red, red rose."

Oh my mimics, my gangly girls.   Daffodils.   Karen Volkman.   NeAmPo

Oh my Mind, worship Kali.   Rāmprasād Sen.   SinGod, *tr. by* Rachel Fell McDermott

Oh my Mind! You're just spinning.   Rāmprasād Sen.   SinGod, *tr. by* Rachel Fell McDermott

Oh, my mother's moaning by the river.   Lonely Mother, The.   Fenton Johnson.   NAAAL

Oh, my mother was frightened by a shotgun they say.   You Can't Get a Man with a Gun.   Irving Berlin.   ReLy

Oh My Own Little Daughter, Four Years Old.   *Unknown.*   ECWP

Oh My People I Remember.   Wendy Rose.   CDW

Oh, my pretty cock, oh, my handsome cock.   Cock-A-Doodle-Do.   *Unknown.*   ReMoGo

Oh, my rash hand! what has thou idly done?   Written at Rossana. November 18, 1799.   Mary Tighe.   CenSon

Oh! my sleigh and my fast horse!   Sleigh, The.   Sergey [*or* Sergei] Aleksandrovich Yesenin [*or* Essenin].   RusPo, *tr. by* Robert Arthur Douglas Ford

Oh, my truelove, is part of it.   Old Love in Song, An.   Elizabeth Madox Roberts.   APT-1

Oh, neighbours! what had I a-do for to marry!   Hooly and Fairly.   Joanna Baillie.   RACG; WoRP

Oh never marry Ishmael!   Song for Unbound Hair.   Genevieve Taggard.   PoRA

Oh never on my youthful ear.   My Mother's Voice.   Mary E. Tucker.   CBWP-1

Oh never on that mountain.   Frances Ellen Watkins Harper.   TCAPo   *Fr.* Moses: A Story of the Nile.

Oh, never say that you have reached the very end.   We Survive!   Hirsch [*or* Glik, Hirsh] Glick.   TrJP, *tr. by* Ruth Rubin

Oh never weep for love that's dead.   Dead Love.   Elizabeth Siddal.   LW; NOBVV

Oh nimber, nimber Will-o!   Chuck Will's Widow Song.   *Unknown.*   BPo

Oh No.   Robert Creeley.   HeIP-4; InPK-6

Oh no.   Oh Yes.   Joseph Stroud.   GeoHom

Oh, no one can deny.   Self's the Man.   Philip Larkin.   NOBL; PeLV

Oh, Noa, Noa!   William Cole.   NBLV

Oh nobody's a long time.   Lonesome Boy Blues.   Kenneth Patchen.   APT-2

Oh, not more subtly silence strays.   To the Beloved.   Alice Thompson Meynell.   VWP

Oh, not to be in England.   Abroad Thoughts.   Edward Blishen.   NOBL

Oh, Nothing.   John Ashbery.   NAAL-2v2

Oh, now I feel as though another sense.   On the Group of the Three Angels before the Tent of Abraham, by Raffaelle, in the Vatican.   Washington Allston.   APN-1

Oh, now, now the white fury of the spring.   White Fury of the Spring, The.   Lizette Woodworth Reese.   APT-1

Oh oh—ah ah.   *Ti-ch'ü* Song Words.   *Unknown.*   CoBCP, *tr. by* Burton Watson

Oh, you will be sorry for that word!   Edna St. Vincent Millay.   BoWoP; HeIP-4; NALW

Oh, on an early morning I think I shall live forever!   Poem in Three Parts.   Robert Bly.   CoAmPo; NOBA; PAI

Oh, once I was a policeman young and merry (young and merry).   Policeman's Lot, A.   Wendy Cope.   FaBoWP

Oh, open the door, some pity to shew.   Open the Door to Me, Oh!   Robert Burns.   SCGP

Oh [*or* O] Fairest of the Rural Maids.   William Cullen Bryant.   APN-1; TAP

Oh [*or* O] how comely it is and how reviving.   John Milton.   NOBE; NOCV; OBEV; OxAEP-1   *Fr.* Samson Agonistes.

Oh [*or* O] many a day have I made good ale in the glen.   Outlaw of Loch Lene, The.   *Unknown.*   BIrV; OBEV, *tr. by* Jeremiah Joseph Callanan

Oh [*or* O], my name it is Sam [*or* Samuel] Hall, it is Sam [*or* Samuel] Hall.   Sam [*or* Samuel] Hall.   *Unknown.*   UnPo

Oh [*or* O], no more, no more, too late.   John Ford.   NOBE; NOSC   *Fr.* Broken Heart, The.

Oh [*or* O] say, [*or* O! say] can you see, by the dawn's early light.   Star-Spangled Banner, The.   Francis Scott Key.   AiP; HHAm; TAP; UV

Oh [*or* O], slow to smite and swift to spare.   Death of Lincoln, The.   William Cullen Bryant.   NAAL-2v1; TAP

Oh [*or* O] that those lips had language! Life has passed [*or* pass'd].   William Cowper.   NOEC; OxAEP-1

Oh [*or* O] thou great Power, in whom I move.   Hymn to My God in a Night of My Late Sickness[e], A.   Sir Henry Wotton.   MeLP; NOSC

Oh [*or* O!] what a plague is Love!   Phillida Flouts Me [*or* The Disdainful Shepherdess].   *Unknown.*   OBEV

"Oh [*or* O], World-God, give me Wealth!" the Egyptian cried.   Gifts.   Emma Lazarus.   TrJP

Oh [*or* O], young Lochinvar is come out of the west.   Sir Walter Scott.   EBNV; NAEL-6v2; NOBE; NePenScot; OxAEP-2; OxBS; PoRA; TFi   *Fr.* Marmion.

Oh, Paddy dear! and did ye hear the news that's goin' round?   Wearin' o' the Green, The.   *Unknown.*   NOIV

Oh pale, white forms, clear forms.   Antiphony.   João da Cruz e Sousa.   TCLAP, *tr. by* Nancy Vieira Couto

Oh Pangs of Love!   Robert Desnos.   SurPaPo, *tr. by* Mary Ann Caws

Oh, Passage town is of great renown.   Town of Passage, The.   *Unknown.*   OxBoLi

Oh, pedestals of ivory, breathing structure.   To a Pair of Legs.   Francisco de Terrazas.   BLPSL, *tr. by* Rene de Costa, Rigas Kappatos and Eleni Paidoussi

Oh pile of white shirts who is coming.   Night of the Shirts, The.   W. S. Merwin.   VCMP

Oh, Pillykin Willykin Winky Wee!   Punkydoodle and Jollapin.   Laura Elizabeth Richards.   OBCA

Oh! place me where the burning noon.   Petrarch.   RWP, *tr. by* Charlotte Smith   *Fr.* Sonnets to Laura.

Oh, Poet of our Race.   Poet of Our Race.   Maggie Pogue Johnson.   CBWP-4

Oh praise Him, praise Him, praise without an end or aim.   Zealous Admonition to Praise.   Catharina Regina von Greiffenberg.   GePo, *tr. by* George C. Schoolfield

Oh, Priest Pangeivi, you let go.   Funeral Eva.   Koroneu.   RaBo

Oh princess of your land, whom Holstein cousin names.   To the Great City of Moscow, as He Was Leaving June 25, 1636.   Paul Fleming.   GePo, *tr. by* George C. Schoolfield

Oh, pure and sportive little child.   To a Little Colored Boy.   Priscilla Jane Thompson.   CBWP-2

Oh, quietly mad I'd like to be.   Ballad.   Vladislav Felitsianovich Khodasevich.   TCRP, *tr. by* Michael Frayn

Oh River, gentle River! gliding on.   Night Journey of a River, The.   William Cullen Bryant.   APN-1

Oh, rock-a-by, baby mouse, rock-a-by, so!   Mouse's Lullaby, The.   Palmer Cox.   NOxBChV; OBCA; OxIBACP; TLR

Oh rose, thou art sick.   William Blake.   *See* O Rose, thou art sick

Oh roses for the flush of youth.   Song.   Christina Georgina Rossetti.   GTBS-P; NOBVV

Oh sacred Time! how soon thou'rt gone!   Midnight Thought, A [on the Death of Mrs. *E. H.* and Her Little Daughter].   Elizabeth Thomas.   NOSC

Oh say not that my heart is cold.   Song.   Charles Wolfe.   OxAEP-2

Oh, say you can hear / On the Watergate tapes.   Final Curtain.   Roger Woddis.   UV

Oh! scorn me not as a fameless thing.   Song of the Rushlight.   Eliza Cook.   VWP

Oh see how thick the goldcup flowers.   A. E. Housman.   MoBrPo

Oh, see my little boat.   Boat, The.   Caroline Gilman.   OBCA

Oh send to me an apple that hasn't any kernel.   *Unknown*.   FaBoCh; WoPoe, *tr. by* Gwyn Williams

Oh Sensibility! Thou busy nurse.   Addressed to Sensibility.   Ann Yearsley.   RWP

Oh sensibility, thou dangerous gift.   On Sensibility: A Fragment.   Isabella Lickbarrow.   RWP

Oh! she is very old. I lay.   Africa.   Joaquin Miller.   APN-2

Oh, she may be weary.   Try a Little Tenderness.   Jimmy Campbell.   ReLy

Oh, she said.   For Elaine de Kooning.   Hilda Morley.   PmAP

Oh, she / the well remembered.   Cytherea.   Carlos Montemayor.   BLPSL, *tr. by* Rene de Costa, Rigas Kappatos and Eleni Paidoussi

Oh she thinks in song.   She Thinks in Song.   Femi Osofisan.   NAfrP

O[h], she walked unaware of her own increasing beauty.   She Walked Unaware.   Patrick MacDonogh.   BoLoP; FaBoTw

Oh! she was a lovely girl.   Only One Eye.   Lillian E. Curtis.   VerBaPo

Oh, she was almost speechless! nor could hold.   Charles Lloyd.   CenSon

Oh! Shepherd John is good and kind.   Shepherd John.   Mary Mapes Dodge.   SWaP

Oh, shield me from his rage, celestial Powers!   Jealousy.   Esther Johnson.   OxBSP

Oh ship! new billows sweep thee out.   Horace.   AWP, *tr. by* William Ewart Gladstone   *Fr.* Odes.

Oh, show us the way to the next whisky-bar.   Alabama Song.   Bertolt Brecht.   PFTM-1

Oh, sick I am to see you, will you never let me be?   New Mistress, The.   A. E. Housman.   MoBrPo

Oh Sigh! thou steal'st, the herald of the breast.   To a Sigh.   Mary Robinson.   CenSon; RWP

Oh, silver tree!   Jazzonia.   Langston Hughes.   ColAP

Oh, Sing to God.   Jacob Steendam.   AH

Oh! sing unto my roundelay [*or* O! Synge untoe mie roundelaie].   Thomas Chatterton.   HAP; NOBE; SCGP   *Fr.* Aella: a Tragycal Enterlude.

Oh sister, he is so swift and tall.   Apprehension.   Hannah Flagg Gould.   SWaP

"Oh, sleep forever in the Latmian cave."   Edna St. Vincent Millay.   GSo; MoAmPo; NALW; NoAM

Oh, slow to smite and swift to spare.   William Cullen Bryant.   *See* Oh [*or* O], slow to smite and swift to spare

Oh smooth adder / who with fanged kisses changedst my natural blood.   Augusta Davies Webster.   BrRo   *Fr.* Medea in Athens.

Oh so fickle, oh so vain, oh so false, so false is she! (LL)   Song to a Lute, A.   Sir John Suckling.   BeJo; CaPo

Oh some are fond of red wine, and some are fond of white.   Captain Stratton's Fancy.   John Masefield.   MoBrPo; OBEV

Oh spare me, spare me.   Maya Bejerano.   DTA, *tr. by* Tsipi Keller   *Fr.* Hymns of Job.

Oh! Stalin is my darling, my darling, my darling.   Stalin Moy Golubchik.   "Sagittarius."   OBCoV

Oh stay at home, my lad, and plough.   A. E. Housman.   FaBoWar

"Oh, stop your dodging, Mrs. C.!" (LL)   Dorothy Parker.   APT-1; NALW   *Fr.* Pig's-Eye View of Literature, A.

Oh strong-ridged and deeply hollowed.   Smell.   William Carlos Williams.   MoAmPo; RaBo; TAP

Oh Sumptuous moment.   Emily Dickinson.   NAAL-2v1; NAAL-3

Oh! surely for thee were the gates ajar.   Rev. Samuel Weston.   Mary Weston Fordham.   CBWP-2

Oh! surely 'tis a theme sublime.   Dedicated to the Right Rev'd D. A. Payne.   Mary Weston Fordham.   CBWP-2

Oh! Susanna.   Stephen Collins Foster.   OBAL; TCAPo   (Susanna.)   APN-2

Oh, sweet gifts brought forth for my misfortune.   Sonnet 10.   Baldomero Garcilaso de la Vega.   BLPSL, *tr. by* Rene de Costa, Rigas Kappatos and Eleni Paidoussi

Oh swings: beyond complete immortal now. (LL)   Soledad.   Robert Earl Hayden.   APT-2; NAAAL

Oh, talk not to me of a name great in story.   Stanzas Written on the Road between Florence and Pisa.   Byron.   NAEL-5v2; NAEL-6v2

Oh, tell me why you make the school.   Retrospection.   Dunstan Shaw.   NOBAu

Oh thank you cowboy with four-wheel drive.   For Drum Hadley.   Harold Littlebird.   VoR

Oh thank you for giving me the chance.   Thank You.   Kenneth Koch.   NeAP; PoM

Oh that girl with the Binh Tien hairdo.   Girl with the Binh Tien Hairdo, The.   *Vietnamese Oral Tradition*.   CaDao, *tr. by* John Balaban

Oh that horse I see so high.   Gift of Great Value, A.   Robert Creeley.   LCAP-2

Oh, that I felt the touch of.   Asoka's Love Song.   Alexander Lernet-Holenia.   AuPH, *tr. by* Lowell A. Bangerter

Oh that I was the Bird of Paradise!   Edward Taylor.   NOCV   *Fr.* Preparatory Meditations before My Approach to the Lord's Supper.

Oh! That I were a poet now in grain!   Urian Oakes.   SCAP

Oh that I were all soul, that I might prove.   Upon Platonic Love: To Mistress Cicely Crofts, Maid of Honour.   Sir Robert Aytoun [*or* Ayton].   NOSC

Oh That I Were in the Wilderness.   Bible, *O.T.*   TrJP   *Fr.* Jeremiah.

Oh that I were / Where I would be.   *Unknown*.   OxNR

Oh That My Lungs.   *Unknown*.   NOBL   (Non-sense.)   NPeEn

Oh! that my young life were a lasting dream!   Edgar Allan Poe.   NCAP; OxBA; TAP   *Fr.* Dreams.

Oh, that they had pity, the men we serve so truly!   Cry of the Animals, The.   Mary Howitt.   VWP

Oh [*or* O] that those lips had language! Life has passed [*or* pass'd].   On the Receipt of My Mother's Picture out of Norfolk, the Gift of My Cousin Ann Bodham.   William Cowper.   NOEC; OxAEP-1

Oh the anguish of these secret meetings.   Kenneth Rexroth.   APSN; APT-2   *Fr.* Love Poems of Marichiko, The.

Oh the charming month of May!   Song.   Joseph Addison.   NOEC

Oh, the comfort—the inexpressible comfort of feeling safe with a person.   Friendship.   Dinah Maria Mulock Craik.   ITBLP; PoToHe

Oh the corrugated-iron town.   Douglas Stewart.   CBAP   *Fr.* Birdsville Track, The.

Oh, the days when I was young.   Richard Brinsley Sheridan.   OxAEP-1   *Fr.* Duenna, The.

Oh! the dream, the dream!   Orphan, The.   Muhammad Al-Maghut.   MAP

Oh! the eastern winds are blowing.   Cornish Emigrant's Song, The.   Robert Stephen Hawker.   EBVV

Oh, the Gingkos.   Edward Field.   BodElec

Oh, the girl that I loved she was handsome.   Man on the Flying Trapeze, The.   *Unknown*.   OxBoLi

Oh! the Golden Age.   William Browne.   NOSC   *Fr.* Britannia's Pastorals.

Oh, the gorgeous leaves of autumn!   Autumn Leaves.   Clara Ann Thompson.   CBWP-2

Oh, the hireling sun in a slipshod way.   Field of the Cloth of Gold, The.   Patrick Joseph Hartigan.   NOBAu

Oh! the king's gane gyte.   Cophetua.   Hugh MacDiarmid.   OxBS

Oh, the long and dreary Winter!   Henry Wadsworth Longfellow.   TreFP   *Fr.* Song of Hiawatha, The.

Oh the maggots marched down Pitt Street.   Maggot Song.   *Unknown*.   NOBAu

Oh the magnificence of hell!   Hell.   Edith Södergran.   PFTM-1

Oh the many joys of a harlot's wedding.   Hail Wedded Love!   Jay Macpherson.   MoCV

Oh the north countree is a hard countree.   Ballad of Yukon Jake, The.   Edward E., Jr. Paramore.   TCAPo

Oh! the old swimmin'-hole! whare the crick so still and deep.   Old Swimmin'-Hole, The.   James Whitcomb Riley.   APN-2; BRP

Oh, the Pilliwinks lived by the portals of Loo.   Cooky-Nut Trees, The.   Albert Bigelow Paine.   OBCA

Oh the rocks and the thimble.   Meditations of a Parrot.   John Ashbery.   TTTS

Oh the rose of keenest thorn!   Iniquity of the Fathers upon the Children, The.   Christina Georgina Rossetti.   FaBoVe

Oh, the slimy, squirmy, slithery eel!   Song of Hate for Eels.   Arthur Guiterman.   OBAL

Oh the sound of her silk sleeves.   Liu Ch'e.   EaWin, *tr. by* W. S. Merwin

Oh the streams of lovely Nancy are divided into three parts.   Streams of Lovely Nancy, The.   *Unknown*.   OxBoLi

Oh, the sweet contentment.   Coridon's Song.   John Chalkhill.   NOSC

Oh! the time that is past.   *Unknown*.   BoLoP

Oh, the wild joys of living! the leaping from rock up to rock. Robert Browning. ITBLP *Fr.* Saul.

Oh! the world gives little of love or light. Song of the Ugly Maiden. Eliza Cook. VWP

Oh there hasn't been much change. Grange, The. Stevie Smith. OBCoV

Oh, there once was a Puffin. There Once Was a Puffin. Florence Page Jaques. NTCP

Oh, there was a youth and a noble youth. Bailiff's Daughter of Islington, The. *Unknown.* ESPB; OxBB; OxBoLi

Oh they came, their eyes blank. Voice for the Sirens, A. Maura Stanton. YaYoPo

Oh! / They say some people long ago. Birth of the Blues, The. Ray Henderson. ReLy

Oh this is the animal that never was. Rainer Maria Rilke. TTTS *Fr.* Unicorn, The.

Oh this man. Magnificat. Michele Roberts. BrRo; PoBW

Oh! thou dead / And everlasting witness! whose unsinking. Byron. ChIV-1 *Fr.* Cain: A Mystery.

Oh, thou eternal Homer! I have now. Byron. FaBoWar *Fr.* Don Juan.

Oh thou great Power, in whom I move. Hymn to my God in a night of my late Sicknesse, A. Sir Henry Wotton. SacPr

Oh, thou immortal bard! Byron. J. Gordon Coogler. OBAL; VerBaPo

Oh, thou! in Hellas deemed of heavenly birth. Byron. NAEL-5v2; NAEL-6v2 *Fr.* Childe Harold's Pilgrimage.

Oh thou, that dear and happy isle. Andrew Marvell. OxBoLi *Fr.* Upon Appleton House [To My Lord Fairfax].

Oh thou that sit'st upon a throne. Christopher Smart. SacPr *Fr.* Song to David, A.

O[h] thou that swingest [*or* swing'st] upon the waving hair[e] [*or* ear *or* eare]. Grasshopper, The. Richard Lovelace. BASC; BeJo; CaPo; CavPo; EBEV; NAEL-5v1; NAEL-6v1; NAEL-7v1; NOBE; NOSC; NoP-4; OBEV; SCGP; TFi

Oh! thou who dry'st the mourner's tear. Comforter, The. Thomas Moore. SacPr

Oh, thou! whose tender smile most partially. Sonnet Addressed to My Mother. Mary Tighe. NoP-4

Oh, 'tis my delight on a shining night, in the season of the year. (LL) Lincolnshire Poacher, The. *Unknown.* PeLV

Oh to be a bride. Bride, The. Bella [*or* Izabella] Akhatovna Akhmadulina. BoWoP; MPUn

Oh, to be a child again. Childhood Revisited. Gerry Bostock. IBA

Oh to be at Crowdieknowe. Crowdieknowe. Hugh MacDiarmid. OxBS

Oh, to be in England. Home-Thoughts, from Abroad. Robert Browning. AWP; CABP; ClHu; EBVV; FHYEP; HeiP-4; NAEL-5v2; NAEL-6v2; NOBE; NOBVV; NoP-4; OBEV; PoRA; TFi; UV

Oh, to be more than you can be. Recruiting Poster. Hillel Schwartz. BAP-97

Oh, to be somebody's moon! Looking at the Moon. Vivian Lamarque. CltWP, *tr. by* Cinzia Sartini Blum and Lara Trubowitz

Oh! to have hidden in the undergrowth. King Lot's Envoys. Drummond Allison. OxBSP

Oh, to my sobs, Galatea, you are harder than a stone. Baldomero Garcilaso de la Vega. BLPSL, *tr. by* Rene de Costa, Rigas Kappatos and Eleni Paidoussi *Fr.* First Eclogue.

Oh, to vex me, contraries [*or* contraryes] meet in one. John Donne. BASC; ChIV-2; NAEL-7v1; NOSC; Son *Fr.* Holy Sonnets.

Oh town of the hundred doors. Jerusalem. Manuela Fingueret. MirDau, *tr. by* Roberta Gordenstein

Oh Trial. *Unknown.* FaBoVe

Oh! true was his heart while he breathed. King of Thule, The. Goethe. AWP, *tr. by* James Clarence Mangan

Oh virgin queen of mountain-side and woodland. Horace. AWP *Fr.* Odes.

O[h] waly, waly, up the [*or* yon] bank. Waly, Waly [Love Be Bonny]. *Unknown.* EnLoPo; HAP; NOSC; OBEV; OxBS; TFi

Oh! waves in the sunlight gleaming. Sonnet to My First Born. Mary Weston Fordham. CBWP-2

Oh we know. (LL) Song for Those Who Know. Hans Magnus Enzensberger. PoSu; VCWP, *tr. by* Hans Magnus Enzensberger and Michael Hamburger

O[h] wearisome condition of humanity. Fulke Greville, 1st Baron Brooke. HAP; NAEL-5v1; NAEL-6v1; NAEL-7v1; NOBE; OxBEV *Fr.* Mustapha.

Oh, weep for Mr. and Mrs. Bryan! Lion, The. Ogden Nash. TLR; WHSW

Oh! Weep for Those. Byron. ChIV-1

Oh! weep with me the changing scene. Letter to My Love—All Alone, Past 12, in the Dumps, A. "The Amorous Lady." ECWP

Oh well tonight or some other night. Te Kaha. Rachel McAlpine. PeNZ

Oh were I at the moss house, where the birds do increase. Streams of Bunclody, The. *Unknown.* BIrV

Oh, What a Beautiful Mornin'! Richard Rodgers. ReLy

Oh, what a bevy of beauties. They Couldn't Compare to You. Cole Porter. ReLy

Oh! what a cruel wicked thing. Poem for Children; or, On Cruelty to the Irrational Creation, A. Jane Cave. ECWP

O[h] what a cunning guest. Confession. George Herbert. ESCV

Oh what a gay, what a rambling life a Settler's leading. Polyglot Medley. Andrew Geddes Bain. PeSAV

Oh, what a kiss. Modern Mother, The. Alice Thompson Meynell. VWP

Oh! what a pain is here! All through the night. What Cannot Be. John Addington Symonds. CAGL

Oh what a pity, Oh! don't you agree. Innocent England. D. H. Lawrence. NPeEn; OBCoV

Oh! what a thing is man? Lord, who am I? Edward Taylor. NAAL-2v1; NAAL-3; NOBA; OxBA *Fr.* Preparatory Meditations before My Approach to the Lord's Supper.

Oh, what a waste of feeling and of thought. Gifts Misused. Letitia [*or* Laetitia] Elizabeth Landon. VWP

Oh, what am I but an engine, shod. Nothing New. Ella Wheeler Wilcox. APN-2

O[h] what can ail thee, knight-at-arms [*or* wretched wight]. La Belle Dame sans Merci [A Ballad]. John Keats. AWP; BRP; CABP; ClHu; FHYEP; FaBoCh; GTBS-P; HAP; HeiP-4; NAEL-5v2; NAEL-6v2; NAWM-7v2; NOBE; NOBRP; NPeEn; NoP-4; OBEV; OBSP; OxAEP-2; OxBEV; PAI; PoE; PoPoPo; PoRA; RB; SCGP; SCV; SoSe-8; TFi; TRP; UV; UnPo; WoPoe

Oh, what delight to be given the right. Cocktails for Two. Sam Coslow. ReLy

Oh, what do we geese wear for clothes? What Do We Geese Wear For Clothes? *Unknown.* OWoS, *tr. by* William DeWitt Snodgrass

Oh / What has happened to me? Head over Heels in Love. Mack Gordon. ReLy

Oh, what hath death with souls like thine to do? (LL) To Elizabeth Barrett Browning, in 1861. Dora Greenwell. PoBW; VWP

Oh, what have you got for dinner, Mrs. Bond? Dilly Dilly. *Unknown.* OxNR

Oh what is Man, great Maker of mankind. Acclamation, An. John Davies. SacPr

Oh! What is the matter? *Unknown.* PGA

Oh! What It Seemed to Be. Bennie Benjamin. ReLy

Oh, what's the matter wi' [*or* with] you, my lass. Jimmy's Enlisted; or, The Recruited Collier. *Unknown.* EBEV

Oh, what sound of gold going. Sunset. Juan Ramón Jiménez. SpanPo, *tr. by* Kate Flores

Oh, when I come to die. Give Me Jesus. *Unknown.* BPo; SacPr

Oh when I think of my long-suffering race. Enslaved. Claude McKay. BPo; NAAAL

Oh, when I was in love with you. Oh, When I Was In Love. A. E. Housman. BoLoP; MoBrPo; TFi

Oh, When Shall I See Jesus? Ecstasy. *Unknown.* AH

Oh when the early morning at the seaside. East Anglian Bathe. Sir John Betjeman. NoP-4

Oh, when the sky is choked with smoke. Getting Away: Verses and Choruses for Various Voices. Wendell Berry. PoCoUp

Oh, when this earthly tenement. "Ada" (Sarah Louisa Forten). BlSi

Oh, Whence Comes the Gladness? Priscilla Jane Thompson. CBWP-2

O[h] where have [*or* ha *or* hae] you [*or* ye] been, Lord Randal [*or* Rendal *or* Randall] my son? Lord Randal[l]. *Unknown.* AWP; EBEV; EBNV; ESPB; HAP; HeiP-4; OxBB; OxBEV; OxBS; PAI; SCGP; TFi; TRP; WeW-3

Oh where, oh where has my little dog gone? Where Is He? Mother Goose. OxNR

Oh! where's the slave so lowly. Thomas Moore. NOIV

Oh! wherefore come ye forth, in triumph from the North. Battle of Naseby, The. Thomas Babington Macaulay, 1st Baron Macaulay. FaBoWar; OxAEP-2

Oh, whiffaree an' a-whiffo-rye. Honey, Take a Whiff on Me. *Unknown.* OxBoLi

Oh, who crumbles up the heavens! Song of the Snow. Zalman Schneour. MHP, *tr. by* Ruth Finer Mintz

Oh, who has not heard of the Wooyeo Ball. Wooyeo Ball, The. *Unknown.* NOBAu

Oh who is that young sinner with the handcuffs on his wrists? A. E. Housman. CAGL; FaBoTw; NOBVV; NPeEn; SoSe-8

Oh! who is there of us that has not felt. November. Frederick Goddard Tuckerman. NOBA

O[h], who shall from this dungeon raise. Dialogue between the Soul and [the] Body, A. Andrew Marvell. BASC; ESCV; FSCP; GeHe; HAP; MeLP; NAEL-5v1; NAEL-6v1; NAEL-7v1; NoP-4; OxAEP-1; OxBEV; SoSe-8; TFi

Oh who that ever lived and loved. Egg, The. Clarence Day. NBLV

Oh why are not all those close ties which enfold. Fragment 3. Sydney Owenson, Lady Morgan. PoBW

Oh why did I awake? when shall I sleep again? (LL) A. E. Housman. MoBrPo; NOBVV; SCGP

Oh! why hath not the mind. William Wordsworth. NAEL-6v2 *Fr.* Prelude; Growth of a Poet's Mind, The [1850 vers.].

Oh, why left I my hame? Exile's Song, The. Robert Gilfillan. TreFP

Oh, why so late, when tired leaves are falling. József Kiss. IQMS, *tr. by* Peter Zollman

Oh wide and sad land, alone. Oh Wide and Sad Land. N. P. van Wyk Louw. PeSAV, *tr. by* Adam Small

Oh! Wilberforce, our star of hope. Golden Jubilee of Wilberforce. Mrs. Henry Linden. CBWP-4

Oh! will you never let me be? These Foolish Things (Remind Me of You). James Strachey. ReLy

Oh, will you wear red? I'll Wear Me a Cotton Dress. *Unknown.* BPo

Oh Woman, Blessed Woman! Mrs. Henry Linden. CBWP-4

Oh, woman, woman, in thy brightest hour. Appeal to Women, An. "Ada" (Sarah Louisa Forten). SWaP

Oh, women dear, and did ye hear the news that's going round. Purple, White and Green, The. L. E. Morgan-Browne. BrRo

Oh! wondrous force of sympathy. Triumvirate, The. Elizabeth Thomas. ECWP

Oh World, Why Do You Thus Pursue Me? Sister Juana Inés de la Cruz. SpanPo, *tr. by* Muriel Kittel

Oh would I could subdue the flesh. Senex. Sir John Betjeman. RB

Oh, would that I knew, the day my loss is lamented. Oh, Would That I Knew. Al-Samau'al ibn Adiya. TrJP

Oh would to God he would but pitty mee. Richard Barnfield [*or* Barnefield]. CAGL *Fr.* Affectionate Shepherd [*or* Shephearde], The.

Oh would you know why Henry sleeps. Inhuman Henry. A. E. Housman. NBLV

Oh! ye bright Stars! that on the ebon fields. Sappho's Address to the Stars. Mary Robinson. CenSon; RWP

Oh, Ye Censurers. Al-Samau'al ibn Adiya. TrJP, *tr. by* Hartwig Hirschfeld

Oh, ye lost ones, ye departed, who have passed that silent shore. Beyond. *Unknown.* PWR

Oh Yes. Joseph Stroud. GeoHom

Oh, yes! they love through all this world of ours! Elizabeth Barrett Browning. CenSon *Fr.* Sonnets from the Portuguese.

O, yet we trust that somehow good. Tennyson. CABP; EBVV; FHYEP; NAEL-6v2; PeECV *Fr.* In Memoriam A. H. H.

Oh! you great big brute. You Can't Stop Me from Lovin' You. Mann Holiner. ReLy

'Oh you kid!' / Shouted Id. Adventures of Id, The. Morris Gilbert Bishop. OBCoV

Oh you, once mighty Hungary, gone to seed. To the Hungarians. Dániel Berzsenyi. IQMS, *tr. by* Adam Makkai

Ohakune Fires. Lauris Edmond. PeNZ, *tr. by* Margaret Orbell

Ohé, long-haired beauty! Distress. Flavien Ranaivo. NegPo, *tr. by* Ellen Conroy Kennedy

Ohhh break love with white things. Sacred Chant for the Return of Black Spirit and Power. Imamu Amiri Baraka. NBV

Ohio Valley Swains. James Wright (1927–80). NNaP

Ohioan Pastoral. James Wright (1927–80). LCAP-2

Ohlone walk among us, setting fire to the stipa, The. California Coast. Jean V. Gier. ReBoTo

Ohnedaruth. Angela Jackson. SeSe

Oil. Hansjörg Mayer. WeW-3

Oil brown smog over Denver. Who Runs America? Allen Ginsberg. FaBoA

Oil of Her Hands, The. Mark Nepo. GotH

Oil on Troubled Waters. Amryl Johnson. Oth *Fr.* Rainbow Dragon Trilogy.

Oil Slick. Judith Thurman. SSCS

Oil-slick, slack shocks, ancient engine. Apples on Champlain. Richard Kenney. NoP-4

Oileus by his brother's side stood close and would not thence. Homer. OBVE, *tr. by* George Chapman *Fr.* Iliad, The.

Oily rag at her feet in the warehouse of scents, An. Studio, The (Homeage to Alice Neel). Alicia Ostriker. ExTi

Oink as Taunt. Roger Fanning. NAPBL

Oister, The. William Drummond, of Hawthornden. NePenScot

Ojibwa War Songs. *Unknown.* AWP, *tr. by* H. H. Schoolcraft

Ojichan was a fisherman / farmer. Fisherman, The. Janice Mirikitani. OpBo

Ojistoh. Emily Pauline Johnson. NOBC

OK Corral East Brothers in the Nam. Horace Coleman. CDa

OK, it's imperishable or a world as Will. Same Old Jazz, The. Philip Whalen. NeAP

OK. So she got back the baby. Onesided Dialog. June Jordan. NoAM

Okato-Otaia. Sándor Petőfi. IQMS, *tr. by* Anton N. Nyerges

Okay, Let's Be Honest. Robert Walker. IBA

Okay let's go swimming. Trout Quintet, The. Frank O'Hara. BodElec

Okay, my starsick beauty. Unknown Shores. Théophile Gautier. WoPoe, *tr. by* D. M. Thomas

Okay "Negroes." June Jordan. BPo

Okay, Toots. Walter Donaldson. ReLy

Okay. We're stuck with our lives and those. Heartbreak Hotel Piano-Bar. Richard Speakes. SwNoth

Okeydoekey Tribe, The. Chrystos. WiU

Okies wrapped their, The. First Spring in California, 1936. Wilma Elizabeth McDaniel. GeoHom

Oklahoma Ligno and Lithograph Co, The. Corporate Entity. Archibald MacLeish. OBAL

Okra to Greens /. Ntozake Shange. Different Love Poem / We Need a Change, A. UnSA

Ol' Bunk's Band. William Carlos Williams. NOBA

Ol' Clothes. *Unknown.* PoToHe

Ol' Hannah. Doc Reese. PFTM-1

Ol' Man River. Oscar Hammerstein, II. APT-2; ReLy

Ol' plantation wither. For Consciousness. Mervyn Morris. WaCA

Old, The. Franz Wright. LCAP-2

Old Abram Brown is dead and gone. Abram Brown. *Unknown.* OxNR

Old Adam, The. Denise Levertov. UnPo

Old Adam, the Carrion Crow. Thomas Lovell Beddoes. EBEV; NAEL-5v2; TFi *Fr.* Death's Jest Book.

Old Age. Maxwell Bodenheim. TaR

Old Age. Anne Bradstreet. TCAPo *Fr.* Four Ages of Man, The.

Old Age. Caroline Clive. VWP

Old Age. Milán Füst. IQMS, *tr. by* Edwin Morgan

Old Age. E. Keary. NOBVV

Old Age. John Morris-Jones. OBWVE, *tr. by* Anthony Conran

Old Age. Ou-yang Hsiu. OHPC, *tr. by* Kenneth Rexroth

Old Age. Po Chü-i. ChiP, *tr. by* Arthur Waley

Old Age. Frederick Tennyson. NOBVV

Old Age Compensation. James Wright (1927–80). NNaP

Old Age Gets Up. Ted Hughes. NoAM

Old age has come and I am glad. Tune: "Nien-nu Is Charming." Chu Tun-ju. ColAnChi, *tr. by* J. R. Hightower

Old age has little joy. Fresh Flowers. Wang An-shih. CoBCP, *tr. by* Burton Watson

Old Age in His Ailing. Herman Melville. TAP

Old age in the towns. War. Miguel Hernández. AF; RaBo

Old age is. To Waken an Old Lady. William Carlos Williams. HAP; InPK-6; PAI; SoSe-8; WeW-3

"Old age never comes alone"—it brings sighs. Old Age. John Morris-Jones. OBWVE, *tr. by* Anthony Conran

Old age, wise curber of the blood's ebullience. Plea to Old Age. Lajos Áprily. IQMS, *tr. by* Doreen Bell

Old album, The. Elizabeth Searle Lamb. HA

Old and abandoned by each venal friend. On Lord Holland's Seat near Margate, Kent. Thomas Gray. NOEC; NPeEn

Old and New. *Unknown.* AWP; ChiP, *tr. by* Arthur Waley

Old and New Year Ditties. Christina Georgina Rossetti.

Old and sick, many strange broodings. Meng Chiao. SuSp *Fr.* Autumn Meditations.

Old and the New, The. Clara Ann Thompson. CBWP-2

Old and Traveling. Yuan Mei. GifTon, *tr. by* Jerome P. Seaton

Old and young, everyone's asleep. Cold Lantern, The. Yang Wan-li. SuSp, *tr. by* Jonathan Chaves

Old Anguish, The. Chu Shu-chen. BoWoP, *tr. by* Kenneth Rexroth (Sheltered from the Spring wind by.) OHPC, *tr. by* Kenneth Rexroth

Old anorak green. Catherine Walsh. Oth *Fr.* Wait, A.

Old April wanes, and her last dewy morn. Last of April, The. John Clare. CenSon

Old archaeologist, Throstle, An. Limerick. *Unknown.* PeLi

Old Arm-Chair, The. Eliza Cook. BrRo; InPK-6; VWP

Old as I am, for ladies' love unfit. Dryden. OBNV

Old astronomer there was, An. Marvel, A. Carolyn Wells. OBCA

Old Atheist Pauses by the Sea, An. Thomas Kinsella. PAI

Old Aussee. Martha Hoffmann. AuPH, *tr. by* Lowell A. Bangerter

Old Australian Ways. Andrew Barton Paterson. NOBAu

Old Bachelor Brother. Brad Leithauser. NoP-4; RA

Old Barbarossa. Sleeping Heroes. Edward Richard Burton Shanks. OBMV

Old Barbed Wire, The. *Unknown.* FaBoWar

Old battle field, fresh with Spring flowers again. All That Is Left. Basho. AWP, *tr. by* Curtis Hidden Page

Old Beauty, The. Phyllis McGinley. FaBoEE

Old Belle, An. Lizette Woodworth Reese. SWaP

Old Black ladies. Weeksville Women. Elouise Loftin. ISC

Old blanket, The. The crumbs of rubbed wool turning up. Adrienne Rich. HCAP *Fr.* Shooting Script.

Old Boast, The. W. S. Merwin. NOBA

Old Boatman of Death's River, The. R. Williams Parry. OBWVE, *tr. by* Joseph P. Clancy

Old Bob-white and Chipbird, The. Few of the Bird-Family, A. James Whitcomb Riley. NOxBChV

Old Boniface he loved good cheer. *Unknown.* OxNR

Old Books, The. Vernon Scannell. OxBC

Old boy's seventy-three this year, The. Eulogy on My Own Portrait, A. Yang Shih-ch'i. CoBLCP, *tr. by* Jonathan Chaves

Old boys, the cracked boards spread before. Bread. James Dickey. LCAP-2

Old brown thorn-trees break in two high over Cummen Strand, The. Red Hanrahan's Song about Ireland. W. B. Yeats. FaBoCh; NOIV

Old Buildings, The. Pedro Juan Pietri. UnSA

Old calendar, The. Buson. EH, *tr. by* Robert Hass

Old canoe in, The. Sunrise. Jim Tollerud. VoR

Old Cat Care. Richard Hughes. OBMV

Old Cat's Confessions, An. Christopher Pearse Cranch. APN-1; OBCA

Old Cat's Dying Soliloquy, An. Anna Seward. ECWP; NOEC; OxBEV

Old cat whose calm, The. Her Seventeenth Winter. John Leax. CRP

Old Chairs to Mend. *Unknown.* *See* Chairs to Mend

Old Champagne Glass. Eddy Van Vliet. VCWP

Old Charcoal Seller, An. Po Chü-i. SuSp, *tr. by* Eugene Eoyang

Old Chaucer, like the morning Star. On Mr. Abraham Cowley, His Death and Burial amongst the Ancient Poets. Sir John Denham. BeJo

Old, childless, husbandless, bereaved, alone. Old, Childless, Husbandless. Ruth Pitter. PoBW

Old Christmas Morning. Roy Helton. MoAmPo

Old chronicler. Iroko. Onwuchekwa Jemie. PBMAP

Old *Chüeh-chü. Unknown.* CoBCP, *tr. by* Burton Watson

Old Churchyard of Bonchurch, The. Philip Bourke Marston. EBVV

Old Circles. Jennifer Rankin. BMAP

Old Clock on the Stairs, The. Henry Wadsworth Longfellow. PWR; TreFP

Old Co'es. Jim Everett. IBA

Old cob swan his cygnets thus addressed, An. Edmund Wilson. OBCoV *Fr.* Easy Exercises in the Use of Difficult Words.

Old Complex, The. John Ashbery. FTOS

Old cormorant keeper, The. Buson. EH, *tr. by* Robert Hass

Old Countries. Aurora Levins Morales. PueRic

Old Country, The. Carl Rakosi. BodElec

Old Countryside. Louise Bogan. HAP; WPE

Old Couple. Charles Simic. HCAP; PoPoPo

Old Couple, The. F. Pratt Green. OxBTC

Old cow lags, The. John Wills. HA

Old Cowboy, The. Kao Ch'i. OHMPC, *tr. by* Kenneth Rexroth

Old Coyote. . . "If he hadn't looked back." Telling about Coyote. Simon J. Ortiz. STP

Old Cracked Tune, An. Stanley Kunitz. LoL; TaR

Old Creek. Muso Soseki. EaWin, *tr. by* W. S. Merwin

Old Crib, The. Mary E. Tucker. CBWP-1

Old crow of Shang Mountain, you are cruel! Song of the Crow Pecking at My Scarred Donkey. Wang Yü-ch'eng. SuSp; WoPoe, *tr. by* Jonathan Chaves

Old Currawong. Jennifer Rankin. BMAP

Old Dan'l. Leonard Alfred George Strong. MoBrPo

Old Danish jester named Yorick, An. Limerick. Ogden Nash. PeLi

Old daughter, small traveler. Making the Jam without You. Maxine W. Kumin. NALW

Old Davis owned a solid mica mountain. Fountain, a Bottle, a Donkey's Ears and Some Books, A. Robert Frost. VGW

Old dears gardening in fur coats. House next Door, The. Douglas Dunn. OxBC

Old Dedication. Luciana Frezza. CItWP, *tr. by* Cinzia Sartini Blum and Lara Trubowitz

Old Derzhavin. "David Samuilovich Samoylov." [*or* Samoilov]. TCRP, *tr. by* Lubov Yakovleva

Old Devil Moon. Burton Lane. ReLy

Old Doctor Foster. *Unknown.* OxNR

Old Dog. Michael L. Johnson. UrbNat

Old dog, The. Issa. EH, *tr. by* Robert Hass

Old dog barks backward without getting up, The. Robert Frost. SoSe-8 *Fr.* Ten Mills.

Old Dog in the Ruins of the Graves at Arles, The. James Wright (1927–80). NNaP

Old dog listens, The. Issa. SoOfWa, *tr. by* Sam Hamill

Old dog used to herd me through the street, The. Turnabout. Linda Pastan. NIP-4

Old dream comes again to me, The. Mir träumte wieder der alte Traum. Heinrich Heine. AWP, *tr. by* James Thomson

Old Dreams. Ivor Gurney. HarvBoo

Old Dust. Li Po. CrYelRi, *tr. by* Sam Hamill

Old Dutch Woman, The. Gary Snyder. NAAL-2v2

Old Eagle. Fred Emerson Brooks. "From thine eyrie, the crag." VerBaPo

Old earth, how she sulks. Jacaranda. Roo Borson. NOBC

Old East End worker called Jock, An. Limerick. Victor Gray. NOBL

Old Eben Flood, climbing alone one night. Mr Flood's Party. Edwin Arlington Robinson. APT-1; AWP; AmFaPo; ClHu; ColAP; EBNV; HAP; HeIP-4; MoAmPo; NAAL-2v2; NAAL-5; NIL-7; NIP-4; NOBA; NoAM; NoP-4; OxBA; PoE; PoRA; SoSe-8; TAP; TCAPo; TFi; TRP; UnPo; WeW-3

Old Eddie's face, wrinkled with river lights. Glory Trumpeter, The. Derek Walcott. GT; NAEL-5v2; NAEL-6v2; NoP-4; SeSe

Old Egyptians hid their wit, The. On Mr. Nash's Picture at Full Length. Jane Brereton. WPE

Old elm that murmured in our chimney top. Fallen Elm, The. John Clare. FHYEP

Old England has not lost her prayer. Robert Lloyd. ECEV *Fr.* Poetry Professors, The.

Old England is eaten by Knaves. Alexander McLachlan. NOBC *Fr.* Emigrant, The.

Old English Riddle. Cynewulf. OPOU, *tr. by* Gerald Benson *Fr.* Riddles (Exeter Book).

Old Familiar Faces, The. Charles Lamb. AWP; GTBS-P; NOBE; NOBRP; OBEV; OxAEP-2; OxBEV; RB

(Where are they gone, the old familiar faces?) NOBRP

Old fang in the boot trick. Five chambered. Heart. Catherine Bowman. ExTi

Old Farmer Giles. *Unknown.* OxNR

Old farmer, nearing death, asked, The. Field Day. William Robert Rodgers. BIrV; PNI

Old-Fashioned Garden, An. Cole Porter. OBGa

Old-Fashioned Song, An. John Hollander. NoP-4

Old-fashioned uncouth measurer of the day. To an Hour-Glass. John Clare. CenSon

Old Father Greybeard. *Unknown.* OxNR

Old feeble Winter to gay Spring resigns. On an Early Spring. Mary Julia Young. CenSon

Old fellow, old one. Poem for My Father. Graham Allen. AngWePo

Old Fisherman, The. Emily Grosholz. RA

Old fisherman spends his night beneath the western cliffs. Old Fisherman. Ou-yang Hsiu. BLT

Old Fisherman with Guitar. George Mackay Brown. OxBC

Old Fitz, who from your suburb grange. To E. Fitzgerald. Tennyson. NOBVV; NPeEn

Old Flame, The. Robert Lowell. BoLoP; NOBA; NoAM; PAI

Old Florist. Theodore Roethke. APT-2; OxBSP

Old Folks at Home[, The]. Stephen Collins Foster. APN-2

Old Folks' Room, The. *Unknown.* TreFP

Old Folsom Prison. William Matthews. OPRER

Old Fools, The. Philip Larkin. EmeKit; HarvBoo

Old Fortunatus. Thomas Dekker.
Fortune and Virtue. NoSic
Priest's Song, A. NoSic

Old Forty-five Per Cent. *Unknown.* FaBoEE

Old Freedman, The. Priscilla Jane Thompson. CBWP-2

Old Friend. Dimitris Tsaloumas. BMAP

Old friend from schooldays, An. Letter from Brazil, A. Louis Simpson. BodElec

Old friend, kind friend! lightly down. To My Old Schoolmaster. John Greenleaf Whittier. ColAP; NOBA

Old friend, you. Back from the Word-Processing Course, I Say to My Old Typewriter. Michael C. Blumenthal. NoAM

Old friends know what I like. T'ao Ch'ien [*or* T'ao Yuan-ming]. SuSp *Fr.* Drinking Wine.

Old friends sigh at long separation. Saying Farewell to Magistrate Ch'en Ta-yu. Lin Hung. SuSp, *tr. by* Irving Y. Lo

Old Furniture. Thomas Hardy. OxBTC

Old gardens, a ruined terrace, willow trees new. At Su Terrace Viewing the Past. Li Po. CoBCP, *tr. by* Burton Watson

Old General Artichoke lay bloated on his bed. Old Land Dog, The. Sir John Betjeman. OBCoV

Old gilt vane and spire receive, The. Late, Last Rook, The. Ralph Hodgson. MoBrPo

Old Gory, The. Gerald William Barrax. NBV

Old gourmet who's grown somewhat stout, An. Limerick. "Yorick." PeLi

Old Grahame he is to Carlisle gone. Bewick and Graham. *Unknown.* ESPB

Old Green River knife had to be scraped, An. Canst Thou Draw Out Leviathan with an Hook. Allen Curnow. PeNZ

Old green witch, An. *Unknown.* WoPoe, *tr. by* Siv Cedering Fox *Fr.* Two Swedish Riddles.

Old grey hearse goes rolling by, The. Hearse Song, The. *Unknown.* OxBoLi; RB

Old Grimes. Albert Gorton Greene. ReMoGo

Old Guidebook to Prague, An. Frank Kuppner.
"Architecture is when the sun shines on a facade daily." NePenScot

Old Guitar, The. John Hollander. DiPo

Old guy put down his beer, The. Do the Dead Know What Time It Is? Kenneth Patchen. MoAmPo

Old Harem, The. Li Shang-yin. OHMPC, *tr. by* Kenneth Rexroth

Old harem is quiet and deserted, The. Old Harem, The. Li Shang-yin. OHMPC, *tr. by* Kenneth Rexroth

Old Haven. Jean Garrigue. WPE

Old Hokum Buncombe, The. Robert E. Sherwood. NBLV

Old Home, The. Amanda Ros. VerBaPo

Old Homestead, The. Mattie J. Peterson.
"I sometimes alligators heard." VerBaPo

Old horse, I've pushed you hard. Sick Horse. Tu Fu. CrYelRi, *tr. by* Sam Hamill

Old House, The. Franta Bass. INSAB

Old House, The. Amy Levy. PEW; VWP; ViWPN

Old House Blues. William Kulik. BodElec

Old house felt unfriendly, The. Empty House, The. Max Williams. CBAP

Old house leans upon a tree, The. Deserted. Madison Cawein. TCAPo

Old house with trees and twisting river, An. Visit to Bridge House, A. Richard Weber. BIrV

Old Houses. Homer D'Lettuso. PoToHe

Old Houses. Jennie Romano. PoToHe

Old Houses. Melvin B. Tolson. GT

Old Houses of Flanders, The. Ford Madox Ford. CTC

Old Houses on the Quays. Augusta Peaux. TuT, *tr. by* Tony Curtis

Old houses were scaffolding once. Image. Thomas Ernest Hulme. InPK-6; NPeEn; OxBTC

Old Hundredth. Bible, *O.T.* NOCV *Fr.* Psalms.

Old Husband Suspects Adultery, An. Gavin Ewart. NoAM

Old Hut. Muso Soseki. EaWin, *tr. by* W. S. Merwin

Old I Am. Thomas Stanley. AWP

Old Ila, to show his fine delicate taste. On Lord Ila's Improvements, near Hounslow Heath. Philip Dormer Stanhope, 4th Earl of Chesterfield. OBGa

Old in Overijssel. René Van Riessen. TuT, *tr. by* Robert Greacen

Old Indian chief, Running B'ar, An. Limerick. Mary Rita Hurley. PeLi

Old Indian Granny, The. Chrystos. ReEnLa

Old inventive Poets, had they seen, The. William Wordsworth. CenSon *Fr.* River Duddon [A Series of Sonnets], The.

Old Ironsides. Oliver Wendell Holmes. APN-1; AiP; BRP; NAAL-2v1; NAAL-3; NCAP; PWR; TAP; TCAPo; TFi

Old Jason, the Argonaut, The. Denis Glover. PeNZ

Old Jockey, The. Frederick Robert Higgins. OBMV; OxBTC

Old Joe. *Unknown.* OxBoLi

Old Joe Clark. *Unknown.* APN-2

Old Joe is gone, who saw hot Percy goad. James Russell Lowell. TCAPo *Fr.* Biglow Papers, The.

Old Joe Jones and his old dog Bones. Old Joe Jones. Laura Elizabeth Richards. TLR

Old joy returns in holy presence, An. (LL) Come into Animal Presence. Denise Levertov. AmFaPo; HeIP-4

Old King Cabbage. Richard Kendall Munkittrick. OBCA

Old King Cole ("Me clairvoyant.") Gilbert Keith Chesterton. NOBL; UV *Fr.* Variations on an Air Composed on Having to Appear in a Pageant as Old King Cole.

Old King Cole was a merry old soul. Mother Goose. LB; OTCP; OxNR; ReMoGo

Old Ladies. Will Allen Dromgoole. WeW-3

Old Ladies, The. Colin Ellis. OxBTC

Old ladies and tulips, model boats. Kensington Gardens. Muriel Spark. OBGa

Old lady, I now celebrate. John Montague. CIP-2 *Fr.* Leaping Fire, The.

Old Lady of Harrow, An. *Unknown.* PeLi

Old Lady's Lament for Her Youth, The. François Villon. BoLoP, *tr. by* Robert Lowell

Old lady Shih, braving acerbity, pokes in her three-foot beak. To Go with Shih K'o's Painting of an Old Man Tasting Vinegar. Huang T'ing-chien. CoBCP; ColAnChi, *tr. by* Burton Watson

Old lady writes me in a spidery style, An. Letter from Brooklyn, A. Derek Walcott. OxBTC

Old Land Dog, The. Sir John Betjeman. OBCoV

Old Leaves from the Chinese Earth. Sadanand Rege. OMIP; WoPoe, *tr. by* Dilip Chitre

Old Lem. Sterling Allen Brown. APT-2; BPo; TTY

Old light & owl-light. 2nd Light Poem: For Diane Wakoski. Jackson Mac Low. PoM

Old light smoulders in her eye, An. Pity. Trumbull Stickney. ColAP

Old Lobsterman, The. John Townsend Trowbridge. APN-2

Old Love Butchered (Colorado Springs and Huachuca). Lance Jeffers. NBV

Old Love in Song, An. Elizabeth Madox Roberts. APT-1

Old Loves. Henry Murger. AWP, *tr. by* Andrew Lang

Old Lute, The. Po Chü-i. ChiP, *tr. by* Arthur Waley

Old Lutheran Bells at Home, The. Wallace Stevens. NoAM

Old, mad, blind, despised, and dying king, An. England in 1819. Shelley. CenSon; NAEL-5v2; NAEL-6v2; NAWM-7v2; NOBE; OxAEP-2; OxBEV; OxBSo; Son; TFi; UnPo

Old maid, an old maid, An. *Unknown.* OxNR

Old maid early eer I knew, An. William Blake. OxBSP

Old Maid's Soliloquy. Maggie Pogue Johnson. CBWP-4

Old Malediction, An. Horace. NoAM; OBCoV; WoPoe, *tr. by* Anthony Hecht

Old Man. James Henry. NOBVV

Old Man. Geoffrey Holloway. NLP

Old Man. Edward Thomas. HarvBoo; NPeEn; OxBEV; SCV; TCAWP

Old man. Chinese Figures 2. *Unknown.* EaWin, *tr. by* W. S. Merwin

Old man, The. Birdfoot's Grampa. Joseph Bruchac. UnSA

Old man, The. Buson. EH, *tr. by* Robert Hass

Old Man, The. Penelope Shuttle. LW

Old Man, The. He Was Lucky. Anna Swirszczynska. HP; PoSu

Old man, a slight smile on his lips, rides a grey deer, The. Song of the Painting of the Long-Life Star. Wang Chiu-ssu. CoBLCP, *tr. by* Jonathan Chaves

Old Man Advancing. Muso Soseki. EaWin, *tr. by* W. S. Merwin

Old Man at Leisure. Muso Soseki. EaWin, *tr. by* W. S. Merwin

Old Man at the Crossing, The. Leonard Alfred George Strong. OBMV

Old man babbles on! Ye gods, I swear, The. Idler Listening to Socrates Discussing Philosophy with His Boy-Friends, An. Edward Cracroft Lefroy. CAGL

Old man bending I come among new faces, An. Wound-Dresser, The. Walt Whitman. APN-1; CBCWP; ColAP; NAAL-2v1; NAAL-3; NAAL-5; NOBA; OBWP; TAP; TCAPo

Old Man by the Brook, The. William Wordsworth. TreFP

Old Man Chang, sick three years, finally up and died. Rain Cleared and the Breeze and Sunshine Are Superb as I Stroll Outside the Gate, The. Lu Yu. SuSp, *tr. by* Burton Watson

Old Man Climbs a Tree, The. Wendell Berry. PoCoUp

Old Man from Darjeeling. *Unknown.* NTCP

Old man from Hsin-feng, eighty-eight years old, An. Old Man of Hsin-feng witih the Broken Arm, The. Po Chü-i. SuSp, *tr. by* Eugene Eoyang

Old Man from Peru, An. *Unknown. See* Limerick: "There was an old man of [*or* from] Peru / Who dreamt [*or* dreamed] he was eating his shoe."

Old man gets up turns, An. Zeimbekiko. Robin Magowan. SPE

Old man going a lone highway, An. Building the Bridge. Will Allen Dromgoole. WeW-3

Old Man Ho. To Kengai Osho of Engaku-ji. Muso Soseki. EaWin, *tr. by* W. S. Merwin

Old man in a lodge within a park, An. Chaucer. Henry Wadsworth Longfellow. APN-1; AWP; HeIP-4; NOBA; OBEV; OxBA; PoE; PoRA; Son; TAP; TCAPo; TFi; WoPoe

Old Man in a Moon Loft. T. Glynne Davies. OBWVE, *tr. by* the author

Old Man in Retirement. Muso Soseki. EaWin, *tr. by* W. S. Merwin

Old man in the rushes the poet's suspicion. Basho 1. Cees Nooteboom. TuT, *tr. by* Michael O'Loughlin

Old Man Inside Me, The. Dambudzo Marechera. NAfrP

Old Man Is Like Moses, The. Vicente Aleixandre. GifTon, *tr. by* Lewis Hyde

Old man kicking up dust. Dust Storm. Beryl Philp-Carmichael (Yungha-Dhu). IBA

Old Man Know-All. *Unknown.* BPo

Old Man Mose. Jack Kerouac. NeAP *Fr.* Mexico City Blues.

Old man mumbling in his dotage, or crying child, unborn? (LL) For Malcolm X. Margaret Abigail Walker. BPo; NAAAL; Son

Old Man Ocean, how do you pound. Old Man Ocean. Russell Hoban. TLR

Old Man of Few Words. Muso Soseki. EaWin, *tr. by* W. S. Merwin

Old Man of Hsin-feng with the Broken Arm, The. Po Chü-i. SuSp, *tr. by* Eugene Eoyang

Old Man of Nantucket, The. *Unknown.* PeLi

Old Man of Nine Dragon Mountain, The. Long Handscroll of Bamboo by Wang Meng-tuan, The. Li Tung-yang. CoBLCP, *tr. by* Jonathan Chaves

Old Man of Verona, The.   Claudian.   AWP; OBVE, tr. by Abraham Cowley

Old Man of Verona, The.   Claudian.   MLL, tr. by Helen Waddell

Old Man on the River Bank, An.   George Seferis.   AmFaPo

Old Man, or Lad's-Love,—in the name there's nothing.   Old Man.   Edward Thomas.   HarvBoo; NPeEn; OxBEV; SCV; TCAWP

Old Man Pondered.   John Crowe Ransom.   MoAmPo

Old Man Potchikoo.   Louise Erdrich.   HATNAP

Old man pushing seventy.   Written in a Carefree Mood.   Lu Yu.   CoBCP; ColAnChi, tr. by Burton Watson

Old man's almost gone, The.   Last Fullblood, The.   Frank Doolan.   IBA

Old Man's Comforts and How He Gained Them, The.   Robert Southey.   UV; UnPo

   (Old Man's Comforts, The.)   TreFP

Old Man's Complaint, The.   Unknown.   OxBSP

Old man's eagle mind, An. (LL)   Acre of Grass, An.   W. B. Yeats.   HarvBoo; NoAM

Old man's fair-haired consort, whole dewy axle-tree, The.   Ovid.   AWP, tr. by Kirby Flower Smith   Fr. Elegies.

Old Man's Lazy, The.   Peter Blue Cloud.   HATNAP; LTA

Old Man's Sigh, The. A Sonnet.   Samuel Taylor Coleridge.   CenSon

Old Man's Son, An.   Russell Edson.   LCAP-2

Old Man's Song, about His Wife, The.   Unknown.   STP, tr. by Armand Schwerner

Old Man's Tale, The.   Brian [or Bryan] Merriman [or Merryman].   BIrV, tr. by David Marcus   Fr. Midnight Court, The.

Old Man's Thought of School, an.   Walt Whitman.   AmFaPo

Old Man's Winter Night, An.   Robert Frost.   APT-1; AWP; HAP; MoAmPo; NAAL-2v2; NoAM; OxBA; VGW

Old Man's Wish, The.   Walter Pope.   NOSC

Old man sat by the chimney side, The.   Old Folks' Room, The.   Unknown.   TreFP

Old man, seated, his boiled turnip eyes, The.   Miracle, The.   George Young.   BloBone

Old man selling charms in a cranny of the town wall, An.   Pedlar of Spells, The.   Lu Yu.   ChiP, tr. by Arthur Waley

Old man shuffles to the fish market, The.   Georgy [or Georgii] Vladimirovich Ivanov.   TCRusP, tr. by Daniel Weissbort

Old man sitting on the roof, The.   Above Vitebsk.   Shirley Kaufman.   TaR

Old Man Stirs the Fire to a Blaze, An.   W. B. Yeats.   RB   Fr. Wanderings of Oisin, The.

Old Man Sunshine—listen, you!   But Not for Me.   George Gershwin.   ReLy

Old Man to-the-Point.   Muso Soseki.   EaWin, tr. by W. S. Merwin

Old Man Told Me.   Lance Henson.   VoR

Old Man Travelling [Animal Tranquillity and Decay, a Sketch].   William Wordsworth.   FaBoCh; NPeEn; OBWP

Old man, we do not speak of crosses. (LL)   Father and Daughter.   Sonia Sanchez.   FFC; GT

Old man who seined.   Lorine Niedecker.   VGW

Old Man with a Beard.   Edward Lear.   See There Was an Old Man with a Beard

Old Man with the Broken Arm, The.   Po Chü-i.   ChiP, tr. by Arthur Waley

Old Mansion.   John Crowe Ransom.   FuPo; HeIP-4; NOBA; OxBA

Old Maps and New.   Norman MacCaig.   OxBC

Old Mare, The.   Elizabeth Jane Coatsworth.   MoAmPo

Old Marse John.   Unknown.   TTY

Old master held up fluff, The.   Kaigen.   ZenPo, tr. by Takashi Ikemoto and Lucien Stryk

Old master yourself now, Auden, An.   As You Like It.   Theodore Weiss.   TAP

Old mayor climbed the belfry tower, The.   High Tide on the Coast of Lincolnshire, 1571, The.   Jean Ingelow.   UV; OxAEP-2

Old Meg she was a gipsy [or gypsy].   Meg Merrilies [or Merrilees].   John Keats.   FaBoCh; NOxBChV

Old Memories of Earth.   Ronald Allison Kells Mason.   PeNZ

Old Men.   Ogden Nash.   RB

Old Men, The.   Walter De la Mare.   MoBrPo

Old Men, The.   Irving Feldman.   TwCP

Old Men, The.   Alexander Javitz.   TrJP

Old Men, The.   Rudyard Kipling.   OBSV

Old Men Admiring Themselves in the Water, The.   W. B. Yeats.   FaBoCh; KaS

Old Men and Old Women Going Home on the Street Car.   Merrill Moore.   MoAmPo

Old men and women, The.   July.   Sonia Sanchez.   GT

Old men are like little boys.   Han Yü.   CoBCP   Fr. Pond in a Jardiniere, A.

Old men, as time goes on, grow softer, sweeter.   Silence of Women, The.   Liz Rosenberg.   NIL-7

Old Men at Pevensey.   Rudyard Kipling.   NoAM   Fr. Puck of Pook's Hill.

Old men in blue: and heavily encumbered.   Pihsien Road.   "Robin Hyde."   WPE

Old men in the hills, The.   Perlas.   Víctor Hernández Cruz.   TouFir

Old Men in the Leaf Smoke, The.   Archibald MacLeish.   IllVoic

Old Men of Athens, The.   Gail Holst-Warhaft.   GI

Old Men Playing Basketball.   B. H. Fairchild.   MoASP

Old men rake the yards for winter, The.   Old Men in the Leaf Smoke, The.   Archibald MacLeish.   IllVoic

Old men's wives, The.   Old Men of Athens, The.   Gail Holst-Warhaft.   GI

Old men teach me animal spirits.   Animal Spirits.   John E. Smelcer.   PoCoUp

Old men, white-haired, beside the ancestral graves.   Basho.   AWP

Old Menalcas on a day.   Robert Greene.   CTC; NoSic; SCGP   Fr. Never Too Late.

Old Merina Theme.   Flavien Ranaivo.   NegPo, tr. by Ellen Conroy Kennedy

Old Micon, once, and Canthus, Micon's foster-child.   Titus Calpurnius Siculus.   RomPo, tr. by Guy Lee   Fr. Eclogues.

Old moder Phoebe how happy you be.   Moder Phoebe.   Unknown.   FaBoVe

Old Moke.   Harold Littlebird.   VoR

Old Molly Means was a hag and a witch.   Molly Means.   Margaret Abigail Walker.   BlSi; NALW

Old monastery north of the city, The.   Leaving Ch'in-chou.   Tu Fu.   CrYelRi, tr. by Sam Hamill

Old moon fades, the flies tune their voices, The.   New Days for Old, Old Days for New.   Philip Levine.   TaR

Old moon my eyes are new moon with human footprint.   Poem Rocket.   Allen Ginsberg.   TaR

Old moon, old moon / what do I tell you?   Crater.   Lisa Williams.   AmPoNex

Old Mortality.   Sir Walter Scott.

   (Call, The.)   OBEV

Sound, Sound the Clarion.   FaBoEE; NOBE; OxAEP-2

Old Mother, The.   Unknown.   PoToHe

Old Mother Goose.   Mother Goose.   ReMoGo

Old Mother Hubbard.   Comic Adventures of Old Mother Hubbard and Her Dog, The.   Sarah Catherine Martin.   OxNR; ReMoGo

Old Mother Nidditty Nod.   Unknown.   OxNR

Old Mother Shuttle.   Unknown.   OxNR

Old Mother Twitchett had [or has] but one eye.   Mother Goose.   NTCP; OxNR; ReMoGo

Old Mothers.   Charles Sarsfield Ross.   PoToHe

Old Mountain.   Muso Soseki.   EaWin, tr. by W. S. Merwin

Old mountain man is learning to garden, The.   Vegetable Garden.   Lu Yu.   CoBCP, tr. by Burton Watson

Old Mrs. Lazibones.   Gerda Mayer.   OTCP

Old Mrs. Thing-um-e-bob.   Charles Causley.   OTCP

Old Mythologies.   John Montague.   NoP-4

Old Neighborhood, The.   Gerald Costanzo.   OPRER

Old Nelly's Birthday.   Ruth Pitter.   NALW

Old newspapers nobody's ever got to read again. (LL)   Twenty-Year Marriage.   Ai.   BoWoP; GT; NoAM

Old Nico brought wreaths to the tomb of Melite.   Philip of Thessalonica.   GrAn

Old Noah he had an ostrich farm and fowls on the largest scale.   Gilbert Keith Chesterton.   ChIV-1; MoBrPo   Fr. Flying Inn, The.

Old Nobility, The.   Friedrich von Logau.   GePo, tr. by George C. Schoolfield

Old now.   Benjamin Banneker Sends His Almanac to Thomas Jefferson.   Jay Wright.   VCAP

Old oak, old timber, sunk and rooted.   G. M. B.   Donald Davie.   OxBC

Old Oak Tree at Hatfield Broadoak, The.   Frederick Locker-Lampson.   OxAEP-2

Old Oaken Bucket, The.   Samuel Woodworth.   BRP; TCAPo

   (Bucket, The.)   APN-1

Old, old house by the side of the sea, An.   Katrina on the Porch.   Alice Cary.   APN-2

Old, old / To live on, wretched to behold.   Owen Gruffydd.   OBWVE   Fr. Men That Once Were, The.

Old ones to the side.   Psalm.   Charles Simic.   LCAP-2

Old [or Ould] Orange Flute, The.   Unknown.   OBCoV; OxBoLi

Old Ottakring.   Josef Weinheber.   AuPH, tr. by Lowell A. Bangerter

Old Ox, The.   George Rostrevor Hamilton.   FaBoEE

Old Parson Beanes hunts six days [or dayes] of the week.   Upon Parson Beanes.   Robert Herrick.   BeJo

Old Penobscot Indian, The.   Flux.   Richard Eberhart.   VGW

Old People.   Michael Davitt.   PBCIP, tr. by Michael Hartnett

Old people are like birds.   City Pigeons.   Helen Chasin.   WeW-3

Old person of Troy, An.   First Limick.   Ogden Nash.   PeLi

Old Peter Grimes made fishing his employ.   George Crabbe.   EBNV; ECEV; FHYEP; OBNV   Fr. Borough, The.

Old Pettigrew.   Melvin B. Tolson.   GT

Old Photograph Album. Linda Pastan. TaR

Old photographs would have her bookish, sitting. Ma. Paul Muldoon. PNI

Old Picture, An. Howard Nemerov. OxBSP

Old Pilot, The. Donald Hall. LCAP-2

Old Pine, An. Wang An-shih. SuSp, *tr. by* Jan W. Walls

Old pine trees, their shaggy manes. Pei-mang Cemetery. Yüan Hung-tao. CoBLCP, *tr. by* Jonathan Chaves

Old Pirate in These Waters, An. Ali Püsküllüoğlu. WoPoe, *tr. by* Murat Nemet-Nejat

Old Place, The. Blanche Edith Baughan. PeNZ

Old Platthis often thrust away her morning's sleep. Leonidas of Tarentum. HePo   *Fr.* Epigrams.

Old Poem. *Unknown.* AWP; BoWoP, *tr. by* Arthur Waley

Old Poem. *Unknown.* WoPoe, *tr. by* Burton Watson

Old Poems. David Shapiro. KGB

Old poet called Omar cried: "Now", An. Limerick. "J. E. C." PeLi

Old pond, The. Basho. NIL-7, *tr. by* R. H. Blyth

Old pond, The. Basho. EH, *tr. by* Robert Hass

Old pond—a frog jumps in, kerplunk, The. Basho. NIL-7, *tr. by* Allen Ginsberg

Old pond, / frog jumps in. Basho. EnlH; TAL   *Fr.* Seventy-six Hokku.

Old pond—frogs jumped in—sound of water. Basho. NIL-7, *tr. by* Lafcadio Hearn

Old pond full of flags and fenced around, The. John Clare. NPeEn

Old pond / Leap-splash. Basho. ZenPo, *tr. by* Takashi Ikemoto and Lucien Stryk

Old pond— / the sound, An. Basho. OHPJ

Old Postcards. Günter Eich. AF, *tr. by* Stuart Friebert

Old Priest, The. Vladimir Holan. PoSu, *tr. by* George Theiner

Old priest Peter Gilligan, The. Ballad of Father Gilligan, The. W. B. Yeats. EBVV; MoBrPo; PoRA

Old Prison, The. Judith Wright. BMAP

Old Pro's Lament, The. Paul Petrie. TAP

Old Professor, The. John Holmes (1904–62). APT-2

Old professor of zoology, The. Parrot, The. James Elroy Flecker. FaBoTw

Old Pump-house, Llanwrtyd Wells. Ruth Bidgood. TCAWP

Old question, The. Will not God do right? (LL) Leper, The. Algernon Charles Swinburne. NOBVV; OxBEV

Old recluse lives under the cliff, The. Taoist Song. Wang Yang-ming. CrYelRi, *tr. by* Sam Hamill

Old Relative. Gwendolyn Brooks. ColAP   *Fr.* Notes from the Childhood and the Girlhood.

Old Rhythm, old Metre. Judith Wright. HarvBoo   *Fr.* Notes at Edge.

Old Road, The. Aimée Grunberger. PoCoUp

Old road curves off the highway, The. Old Road, The. Aimée Grunberger. PoCoUp

Old Roads. Eiléan Ní Chuilleanáin. CIP-2

Old Robin of Portingale. *Unknown.* ESPB

Old Roger. *Unknown.* OxBoLi

Old rooster crows, The. O. Mabson Southard. HA

Old Roscoff. Tristan Corbière. WoPoe, *tr. by* Derek Mahon

Old Rugged Cross, The. George Bennard. AH; TCAPo

Old Ruralities: A Regret. Charles Tennyson Turner. EBVV; Son

Old Russia's slavery rights. Boiler room. Night. Olga Beshenkovskaya [*or* Beshenkovskaia]. TCRP

Old Russian spits up a plum, The. Man Then Suddenly Stops Moving, A. Alberto A. Ríos. NoAM

Old Rustic Mill, The. George Sands Johnson. PWR

Old sailor in old times, An. Flying down to Rio. Vincent Youmans. ReLy

Old Sailor Looking at a Container Ship. Robert Carson. AiP

Old Saint's Prayer, The. Priscilla Jane Thompson. CBWP-2

Old saltman, hair turned white, The. Wu Chia-chi. CoBLCP

Old Sam. Stanley Holloway. OBCoV

Old-Saxon Fragment. *Unknown.* OBCoV

Old Scent of the Plum Tree. Ietaka. AWP, *tr. by* E. Powys Mathers

Old School, The. Sean Dunne. ModIr   *Fr.* Sydney Place.

Old Scotia's jocund Highland reel. Sydney Owenson, Lady Morgan. RWP   *Fr.* Lay of an Irish Harp, or Metrical Fragments, The.

Old Section Boss, The. *Unknown.* BPo

Old Shepherd's Prayer. Charlotte Mew. MoBrPo; OxBTC; WPE

Old Ships, The. James Elroy Flecker. MoBrPo; OBMV; PoRA

Old ships are preserved. George Oppen. NNaP   *Fr.* Some San Francisco Poems.

Old shoe, an old pot, an old skin, An. Autumn Sequence. Adrienne Rich. VGW

Old shrines defiled by the weaver's excrement, The. (LL) Weaver Bird, The. Kofi Awoonor. HBAPE; PBMAP

Old singer, a young stag, I am Deor, An. Deor. *Unknown.* WoPoe, *tr. by* Peter Russell

Old Sir Simon the king. *Unknown.* OxNR

Old Sister Death bit you off. On the Death of Muriel Rukeyser. Billy Marshall-Stoneking. BMAP

Old Skinflint. Wilfrid Wilson Gibson. OBMV

Old snake, old hole in the corner man. Dead Weasel, A. David Helwig. NOBC

Old Snapshot. Ronald G. Everson. MoCV

Old soak from Stoke, An. C. J. Parker. PeLi

Old Soldier. Padraic Colum. OBMV

Old—some eighty, or thereabouts. 'Nkongane. W. C. Scully. PeSAV

Old Song. Edward Fitzgerald. OBEV; OxAEP-2

Old Song. *Unknown.* ChinPo, *tr. by* Yip Wai-lim

Old Song. *Unknown.* RaBo

Old Song. Andrey [*or* Andrei] Andreievich Voznesensky [*or* Voznesenskii]. VCWP, *tr. by* Vera Dunham and William Jay Smith

Old Song, An. "Yehoash." AWP, *tr. by* Marie Syrkin

Old Song, The. Gilbert Keith Chesterton. FaBoTw

Old Song Ended, An. J. D. McClatchy. ChrPo

Old Song Ended, An. Dante Gabriel Rossetti. BoLoP; EBVV

Old Song of Rejoicing, An. *Unknown.* PeNZ, *tr. by* Margaret Orbell

Old Song of the Musk Ox People. Brian Swann. PoCoUp

Old Song Resung, An. W. B. Yeats. *See* Down by the Salley Gardens

Old song with new words, An. Song. Yen Shu. CrYelRi, *tr. by* Sam Hamill

Old Song, Wrote by One of Our First New-England Planters, An. *Unknown.* SCAP

Old South Boston Aquarium stands, The. For the Union Dead. Robert Lowell. CBCWP; CoAP; ColAP; HAP; HCAP; HarvBoo; HeIP-4; LCAP-2; NAAL-2v2; NAAL-5; NOBA; NoAM; NoP-4; OBWP; PoE; PoetW; SCV; TFi; TRP; TwCP; UnPo; VCAP; WeW-3

Old spider web, An. J. W. Hackett. HA

Old spoon, An. Spoon, The. Charles Simic. NNaP

Old Squire, The. Wilfrid Scawen Blunt. OBEV; SCGP

Old / star / shuts her bleary eyes, The. In a Corner of the Sky. Federico García Lorca. PFTM-1

Old Stephen. Charles Tennyson Turner. EBVV

Old Stoic, The. Emily Jane Brontë. BWW; NALW; NOBE; OBEV; OxAEP-2 (Riches I hold in light esteem.) VWP

Old Stone Age. Frances Angela. Prnts

Old Story. Lance Henson. VoR

Old Story, An. Edwin Arlington Robinson. MoAmPo; OxBSP

Old Story, The. Argentarius. AWP, *tr. by* E. A. Robinson

Old Story, The. *Var. authors.* AWP   *Fr.* Variations of Greek Themes.

Old Style Poem. Li Po. CrYelRi, *tr. by* Sam Hamill

Old Summerhouse, The. Walter De la Mare. GTBS-P

Old Susan. Walter De la Mare. MoBrPo

Old Sussex Road, The. Ian Serraillier. NTCP

Old Sweetheart of Mine, An. James Whitcomb Riley. BRP   "As one who cons at evening o'er an album, all alone." ITBLP

Old sweetheart of mine!—Is this her presence here with me, An. James Whitcomb Riley. BRP

Old Swimmin'-Hole, The. James Whitcomb Riley. APN-2; BRP

Old Tai's Wine Shop. Li Po. WoPoe, *tr. by* Elling O. Eide

Old tales were told of Sigemund's daring. *Unknown.* AnOE, *tr. by* Charles W. Kennedy   *Fr.* Beowulf.

Old temple leans against the green hillside, An. Tune: "Stretch of Cloud over Mount Wu, A." Li Hsün. SuSp, *tr. by* Hellmut Wilhelm

Old Testament, The. Philip Levine. TaR

Old-Testament Gospel. William Cowper. ChIV-2; TrCP   *Fr.* Olney Hymns.

Old, the mad, the blind have fairest daughters, The. Beauty of Job's Daughters, The. Jay Macpherson. ChIV-1; MoCV; NOBC

Old / Old winds that blew, The. Night Winds. Adelaide Crapsey. APT-1; TCAPo

Old, their big shoulders humped, The. Stations. Philip Booth. GM

Old-Time Childhood in Kentucky. Robert Penn Warren. AiP

Old Time is lame and halt. Wie langsam kriechet sie dahin. Heinrich Heine. AWP, *tr. by* Richard Monckton Milnes

Old time, old shifting trade—time there is for the luffing sheets. Pindar. WoPoe, *tr. by* Robert Fagles   *Fr.* Olympian Odes, The.

Old-time pond, from off whose shadowed depth, An. Basho. NIL-7, *tr. by* Clara A. Walsh

Old-time Priapuses could take their pick. *Unknown.* PriapPo, *tr. by* Richard W. Hooper   *Fr.* Priapus Poems, The.

Old-Time Religion. *Unknown.* APN-2

Old Timers. Carl Sandburg. NoAM

Old Times. Daniel Mark Epstein. DiPo

Old Tips. Jean Earle. TCAWP

Old Tongue, The.   Herbert Williams.   AngWePo; TCAWP

Old towel folding it again autumn evening.   Marlene Mountain.   HA

Old town lies afar, An.   There Is an Old City.   Karl Bulcke.   AWP, *tr. by* Ludwig Lewisohn

Old Trail Town, Cody, Wyoming.   John Garmon.   AMV-80

Old Trees with Hands Sawing the Air.   Margit Szécsi.   IQMS, *tr. by* Agnes Arany-Makkai

Old Triton Time.   Vernon Watkins.   OxBSP

Old Trojan Chiefs See Helen, The.   Homer.   OBVE, *tr. by* Alexander Pope *Fr.* Iliad, The.

Old Tune, An.   Gérard de Nerval.   AWP, *tr. by* Andrew Lang

Old Veteran and Napoleon, The.   János Garay.   IQMS, *tr. by* Watson Kirkconnell

Old Vicarage, Grantchester, The.   Rupert Brooke.   MoBrPo; NoP-4; OxBTC; PoRA

Old virgin, your airs are proper.   To an Elderly Virgin.   Mael Isu O Brolchain.   NOIV, *tr. by* Thomas Kinsella

Old walls creak.   Restoring the Ancestral House.   Katerina Te Hei Koko Mataira.   PeNZ, *tr. by* Katerina Te Hei Koko Mataira

Old Walt.   Langston Hughes.   HarvBoo; HeIP-4

Old War-Dreams.   Walt Whitman.   OxBSP

Old warder of these buried bones.   Tennyson.   NAEL-6v2; PeECV   *Fr.* In Memoriam A. H. H.

Old watch: their, The.   Vapor Trail Reflected in the Frog Pond.   Galway Kinnell.   OBWP; VCAP; VGW

Old well.   Buson.   EH, *tr. by* Robert Hass

Old West, the old time, The.   Spanish Johnny.   Willa Sibert Cather.   AiP

Old Wharf Canto.   Jared Angira.   NAfrP

Old Whim Horse, The.   Edward Dyson.   CBAP

Old White Russian, An.   Ch'en Meng-chia.   WoPoe, *tr. by* Harold Acton and Ch'en Shih-hsiang

Old Wife and the Ghost, The.   James Reeves.   OTCP

Old Wife in High Spirits.   Hugh MacDiarmid.   OxBTC; PoE

Old wine gone.   Tune: "Four Pieces of Jade."   Kuan Han-ch'ing.   ChinPo, *tr. by* Yip Wai-lim

Old wines for those who will.   Chanson Delice.   Beatrice E. Harmon.   YaYoPo

Old Witherington.   Dudley Randall.   NBV; NoAM

(Old Witherington had drunk too much again.)   CoAmPo

Old Wives' [*or* Wife's] Tale, The.   George Peele.

("And every sheave a goulden tree.") (LL)   OxBEV

Song

(Song for the Head.)   RB

"Spread, table, spread."   NoSic

(Summer Song, A.)   NOBE; OBEV

"Three merry men, and three merry men."   NoSic

(Voice from the Well [of Life Speaks to the Maiden], The.)   NOBE; NoSic

Voice [Speaks] from the Well, A.   FaBoCh; NOBE; OxBoLi

(When As the Rye Reach to the Chin.)   NoP-4

"Whenas [*or* When as] the Rye [*or* Rie] reach to the chin."   EnLoPo; FaBoCh; FaBoVe; NPeEn; NoSic; OxBEV; OxBoLi; TFi

Old Wives' Tales.   Constance Urdang.   PBCAP

Old Woman.   Iain Crichton Smith.   FaBoTw; HarvBoo; NePenScot; OxBEV; OxBTC

Old Woman, An.   David Gwenallt Jones.   OBWVE, *tr. by* H. Idris Bell

Old Woman, The.   Joseph Campbell.   AWP; MoBrPo; OxBTC; PoToHe

Old Woman, The.   Beatrix Potter.   NTCP

Old Woman, The.   Iain Crichton Smith.   WoPoe

Old woman across the way, The.   Whipping, The.   Robert Earl Hayden.   PAI; PoE; SSLK; SoSe-8

Old Woman and the Pedlar, The.   Mother Goose.   OxNR; ReMoGo

Old Woman and the Sandwiches, The.   Libby Houston.   OBSP

Old Woman Awaiting the Greyhound Bus.   Duane Niatum.   CDW

Old woman, blue eyed and sun burned.   Leah Goldberg.   MHP   *Fr.* On Blossoming.

Old Woman from France, The.   *Unknown.*   ReMoGo

Old woman in me walks patiently to the hospital, An.   Revelation.   Carole C. Gregory Clemmons.   BlSi

Old woman likes to melt her husband. She puts him in a, An.   Feeding the Dog.   Russell Edson.   RaBo

Old woman must stand, The.   *Unknown.*   OxNR

Old Woman Nature.   Gary Snyder.   BB; NoAM; RaBo

Old Woman of Beare, The.   *Unknown.*   WoPoe, *tr. by* Brendan Kenneally

Old Woman of Beare Regrets Lost Youth, The.   *Unknown.*   OBMV, *tr. by* Frank O'Connor

Old Woman of Gloucester, The.   *Unknown.*   ReMoGo

Old Woman of Harrow.   *Unknown.*   ReMoGo

Old Woman of Leeds, The.   *Unknown.*   ReMoGo

Old Woman of Surrey.   Mother Goose.   ReMoGo

Old Woman of the Roads, The.   Padraic Colum.   MoBrPo; NOIV; OBEV; PoRA

Old Woman, Old Woman.   Mother Goose.   LB; OxNR; ReMoGo

Old woman, old woman, / Shall we go a-shearing?   Shall We Go A-Shearing?   Mother Goose.   OxNR; ReMoGo

Old Woman, Outside the Abbey Theater, An.   Leonard Alfred George Strong.   MoBrPo

Old Woman Remembers, An.   Sterling Allen Brown.   ISC

Old Woman's Lamentations, An.   François Villon.   MoBrPo; OBMV, *tr. by* J. M. Synge

Old Woman's Song, An.   Akjartoq.   WPOW, *tr. by* Tom Lowenstein and Knud Rasmussen

Old woman sits on a bench before the door and quarrels, The.   Fawn's Foster-Mother.   Robinson Jeffers.   NOBA; NoAM

Old Woman Speaks of the Moon, An.   Ruth Pitter.   WPE

Old woman standing, An.   Saviour.   Zindzi Mandela.   HAWP

Old woman, time and your own.   To Grandmother on Her Going.   Gail Tremblay.   HATNAP

Old woman was struck down by a chance shot, The.   27 July 1830.   Georgy [*or* Georgii] Arkadevich Shengeli.   TCRP, *tr. by* Daniel Weissbort

Old woman was sweeping her house, and she found, An.   *Unknown.*   LB

Old woman went to market and bought a pig, An.   *Unknown.*   OxNR

Old Woman who lived in the Shoe, The.   Limerick.   Joyce Johnson.   PeLi

Old Women.   Judith Ortiz Cofer.   PueRic

Old Women, The.   George Mackay Brown.   NoP-4; OxBS

Old Women of Toronto.   Miriam Waddington.   NOBC

Old woodcutter of the sea, The.   Song of the Woodcutter of the Sea.   Pien Kung.   CoBLCP, *tr. by* Jonathan Chaves

Old wooden steps to the front door, The.   Time Past, A.   Denise Levertov.   NoAM

Old words sing.   Song of Words.   Konstantin Konstantinovich Vaginov.   TCRP, *tr. by* Nina Kossman

Old World Monkeys.   Sam Truitt.   AmPoNex   *Fr.* Anamorphosis Eisenhower.

Old-World Thicket, An.   Christina Georgina Rossetti.   VWP

Old wound aches and shews its fellow scar, The. (LL)   Scar, The.   John Hewitt.   CIP-2; PNI

Old wound in my ass, The.   Fabrication of Ancestors.   Alan Dugan.   CBCWP; NoAM

Old Year, The.   John Clare.   NOBVV; OBCP

Old Year, The.   Priscilla Jane Thompson.   CBWP-2

Old Year, The.   Clarence Thomas Urmy.   PoToHe

Old Year's gone away, The.   Old Year, The.   John Clare.   NOBVV; OBCP

Old Yellow Shop, The.   Abbie Huston Evans.   APT-1

Old yellow stucco, The.   Winter Nightfall.   Sir John Collings Squire.   OxBTC

Old yew, which graspest at the stones.   Tennyson.   EBVV; GTBS-P; NAEL-6v2; NAWM-7v2; NOBE; NPeEn; PAI; UnPo   *Fr.* In Memoriam A. H. H.

Olden Days, The.   Joseph Hall.   OBSV   *Fr.* Virgidemiarum.

Olden Love-making.   Nicholas Breton.   NoSic

Older American, The.   Cheryl Clarke.   GLP

Older, but no wiser than the defect of love. (LL)   New World, The.   Imamu Amiri Baraka.   NoAM; NoP-4; PmAP

Older Men.   Alfred Corn.   GLP

Older, more generous.   Gift, The.   N. Scott Momaday.   NoP-4

Older now, I know just how hard the going can be. (LL)   Blue Rapids.   Lu Yu.   CoBCP; ColAnChi; SuSp, *tr. by* Burton Watson

Older women wise and tell Anna, The.   Birth Stone.   Lorna Goodison.   VCWP

Oldest human fossil, The.   Fire.   Mark O'Connor.   NOBAu

Oldest Living Thing in L.A., The.   Larry Levis.   UrbNat

Oldest man in the world wears shoes, The.   Passage.   Billy Marshall-Stoneking.   BMAP; NOBAu

Oldest of us burst into tears and cried, The.   Allen Curnow.   PeNZ   *Fr.* Tomb of an Ancestor.

Oldest Place, The.   Thomas Kinsella.   PBCIP

Oldies But Goodies.   Grace Bauer.   MiVo

Ole Abe (God bless 'is ole soul!)   Negro Soldier's Civil War Chant.   *Unknown.*   BPo

Ole Aunt Dinah, she's jes lak me.   Jack and Dinah Want Freedom.   *Unknown.*   BPo; NAAAL

Ole Sheep Dey Know de Road, De.   *Unknown.*   BPo

Oleander: coral.   Garden, The.   Rae Armantrout.   FTOS

Oleander on the wall, The.   By the Arno.   Oscar Wilde.   EBVV

Olfactory paradise.   Love Poem.   E. K. Caldwell.   PasH

Olga Orozco.   Olga Orozco.   TCLAP, *tr. by* Stephen Tapscott

Olga Poems.   Denise Levertov.   LCAP-2; NNaP

"Everything flows."   NAAL-2v2

Olive, The.   A. E. Housman.   NoAM

Olive Garden, The. Rainer Maria Rilke. GI

Olive garden for the nightingales, The. (LL) Painted Head. John Crowe Ransom. APT-1; FuPo; NOBA; NoAM; OxBA

Olive Tree, The. Felicia Dorothea Hemans. CenSon

Olive Trees. Bernard Spencer. NoAM

Olive trees grow silently in patches on the shoulders, The. Los Olivos. Michael Lieberman. BloBone

Oliver's climbed upon a hilly crest. Unknown. FaBoWar, tr. by Dorothy Leigh Sayers Fr. Song of Roland, The.

Olivia's lewd, but looks devout. Olivia. Elijah Fenton. ECEV

Olivier Metra's Waltz of Roses. La Mélinite: Moulin-Rouge. Arthur Symons. PeVV

Olmos. Dennis Nurkse. OPRER

Olney Hymns. William Cowper.

    Contentment. ChIV-2

    (Contrite Heart, The.) NPeEn

    Ephraim Repenting. ChIV-1

    Exhortation to Prayer. NOCV

    "Far from the world, O Lord, I flee." SacPr

    (Fountain, The.) ChIV-1

    (From Olney Hymns.) NoP-4

    Future Peace and Glory of the Church, The. InvLi

    "Hear what God the Lord hath spoken." InvLi

    House of Prayer, The. ChIV-2

    (Hymn 10.) ChIV-1

    Hymn. SacPr

    Jehovah Our Righteousness. NOCV

    Joy and Peace in Believing. NOCV

    Light Shining out of Darkness. CABP; EBEV; ECEV; FHYEP; FaBoCh; NOBE; NOCV; NOEC; NPeEn; OxBEV; PWR; SCGP; SacPr; TFi; TOF

    Lord Will Happiness Divine, The. NOCV

    Love Constraining to Obedience. NOCV

    Lovest Thou Me? ChIV-2

    My Soul Thirsteth for God. TrCP

    Old-Testament Gospel. ChIV-2; TrCP

    Praise for the Fountain Opened. InPK-6

    Retirement. SacPr

    Sardis. ChIV-2

    Self-Acquaintance. NOCV

    Sower, The. ChIV-2

    Walking with God. ECEV; NOCV; NOEC; PeECV; SCGP; TOF

    Wisdom. ChIV-1

Olokun. J. P. Clark Bekederemo. PBMAP Fr. Reed in the Tide, A.

Olsanski Cemetery, The. Yury Iofe. TCRusP, tr. by John Glad

Olympia 11—For Agesidamus of the Westwind Locrians: Winner in the Boys' Boxing Match. Pindar. WoPoe, tr. by Robert Fagles Fr. Olympian Odes, The.

Olympian Eleven. Pindar. Fr. Olympian Odes, The.

Olympian [Muses], round my mind. Alcman. SaLy, tr. by Diane Rayor

Olympian Odes, The. Pindar.

    Olympian Eleven.

       Olympia 11—For Agesidamus of the Westwind Locrians: Winner in the Boys' Boxing Match. WoPoe, tr. by Robert Fagles

Olympicus, the welter-weight. Lucilius. GrAn

Olympus, no medal like the light in each other's eye. (LL) To Hermes. Alfred Corn. CAGL; WiU

Omagh Post Office Rhyme. Unknown. FaBoVe

Ombre and basset laid aside. Song on the South Sea, A. Anne Finch, Countess of Winchilsea. ECWP; NOEC

Omen. Birago Diop. NegPo, tr. by Ellen Conroy Kennedy

Omens. Unknown. RB; WoPoe, tr. by Alexander Carmichael

Omens on the Road to Burgos. Unknown. WoPoe, tr. by Paul Blackburn Fr. Poem of the Cid, The.

Omera. Marjorie Oludhe Macgoye. HBAPE

Omeros. Derek Walcott.

    "He yawned and watched the lilac horns of his island." NoP-4

"Omit needless words!" Preface Shrink Lit: Elements of Style. Maurice Sagoff. NBLV

Omnes gentes plaudite. Last Drink, A. Unknown. MiEL

Omnes Gentes Plaudite! Unknown. OxBSP

Omnia Somnia. Joshua Sylvester. FaBoEE

Omnibus, The. Vera Bulich. ARWW, tr. by Catriona Kelly

Omnibus across the bridge, An. Symphony in Yellow. Oscar Wilde. EBVV; MoBrPo; NOBVV; NoAM; OPOU; OxBSP

Omnipotent and steadfast God. Stephen Vincent Benét. CBCWP Fr. John Brown's Body.

Omnipotent Olympus' king meanwhile. Virgil [or Vergil]. NAWM-5v1;

NAWM-7v1, tr. by Robert Fitzgerald Fr. Aeneid [or Eneados, Aeneis], The.

Omoro Sōshi, The. Unknown.

    "Before light became time." WoPoe, tr. by Christopher Drake

On a Bank [or Banck] as I Sat[e] [a-]Fishing; a Description of the Spring. Sir Henry Wotton. AmFaPo; BASC; NOSC

On a Bas-relief of Pelops and Hippodameia. Mary Elizabeth Coleridge. ViWPN

On a Bashful Shepherd. "Ephelia." PEW

On a Bath-House in which Both Men and Women Bathe. Paulus [or Paulos] Silentiarius. GrAn, tr. by Andrew Miller

On a Beautiful Woman. Mary Russell Mitford. CenSon

On a Bed of Guernsey Lilies. Christopher Smart. BBASP; NOEC

    (Ye beauties! O how great the sum.) CABP; PoPoPo

On a Bird Singing in its Sleep. Robert Frost. APT-1

On a Birthday. John Millington Synge. OBMV

On a Blind Girl. Baha Ad-din Zuhayr. AWP, tr. by E. H. Palmer

On a Bougainvillaea Vine at the Summer Palace [or in Haiti]. Barbara Howes. MoAmPo

On a Box Containing his Own Works. Po Chü-i. ChiP, tr. by Arthur Waley

On a branch covered with jade-green moss. Tune: "Sparse Shadows"—Plum Blossoms. Chiang K'uei. SuSp, tr. by An-yan Tang

On a broad plain in a universe of. Matters of Policy. Charles Bernstein. FTOS

On a brown isle of Lough Corrib. Celibacy. Austin Clarke. ModIr

On a Calm Summer's Night. John Nicholson. EnLoPo

On a Carrier Who Died of Drunkenness. Byron. NBLV

On a Cat Aging. Sir Alexander Gray. TriCat

On a cat's fur soft as pollen. Spring is a Cat, The. Yi Jang'hi (Jang-hi Lee). WoPoe, tr. by Ko Changsu (Chang-soo Koh)

On a Catholic Childhood. Janet Campbell Hale. VoR

On a Certain Alderman. John Cunningham. FaBoEE

    (On Alderman W———: The History of His Life.) OBCoV

On a Certain Effeminate Peer. John Winstanley. FaBoEE

On a Certain Field in Auvers. John Haines. OPRER

On a Certain Lady at Court. Pope. NOBE; NOEC; OBEV; OxBSP

On a Certain Lord Giving Some Thousand Pounds for a House. David Garrick. FaBoEE

On a Chaplain's Nose. Francisco de Quevedo y Villegas. WoPoe, tr. by Roy Campbell

On a chilly, clear night. Peepers. Howard Nelson. MiVo

On a Clear Day You Can See Forever. Burton Lane. ReLy

On a clear night in Live Oak you can see. Walking down the Road. Adrienne Rich. NIL-7; NIP-4

On a clear spring windless sky. Feathered Robe, The. Gary Snyder. BodElec

On a clear winter's evening. Winter Twilight. Anne Porter. APT-2

On a Clergyman's Horse Biting Him. Unknown. FaBoEE; NBLV; OxBoLi

    (Steed Bit His Master, The.) ChIV-1

On a cloud of universal love. (LL) My Chakabuku Mama: A Comic Tale. Jewelle Gomez. BAP-01; GLP

On a Cock at Rochester. Sir Charles Sedley. FaBoEE; NOSC; NPeEn; OBCoV

On a Cold Autumn Day. Bonnie Nims. TLR

On a Cold Day I Climbed Tiger Hill With Professor Ho. at the Time, the Local Prefect Had Prohibited Pleasure Excursions and Feasts, But the Mountain Was Quiet and Tranquil, So We Stayed All Day. Mo Shih-lung. CoBLCP, tr. by Jonathan Chaves

On a cold frosty morning in the month of September. Wreck of the Old 97. David Graves George. GM

On a cold night. Solitary. Lance Henson. HATNAP

On a cold night I came through the cold rain. James Vincent Cunningham. HAP; TRP; VCAP

On a Columnar Self. Emily Dickinson. APN-2; NoP-4

On a Contentious Companion. John Hoskyns [or Hoskins]. FaBoEE

On a Crab. P'i Jih-hsiu. SuSp, tr. by William H. Nienhauser

On a Curate's Complaint of Hard Duty. Jonathan Swift. OBCoV; SCGP

On a Dark Night. John F. Deane. BiHa

On a date with a charming young bird. Limerick. Unknown. PeLi

On a day—alack the day! William Shakespeare. OBEV Fr. Love's Labour's Lost.

On a day when I would have believed. At Jonestown. Lucille Clifton. NAAAL

On a day when smoke lies down in alleys. Looking Both Ways before Crossing. John Woods. CoAmPo

On a Dead Child. Robert Bridges. EBEV; NOBE; NOBVV; NoAM; OBMV; OxAEP-2; SCGP

On a Dead Hostess. Joseph Hilaire Pierre Belloc. MoBrPo

On a Death's Head. Elizabeth Tollet. ECWP

On a dirt road lies a dead beetle. Seen from Above. Wislawa Szymborska. BLT

On a Discovery Made Too Late. Samuel Taylor Coleridge. CenSon; GSo; Son *Fr.* Effusions.

On a Distinguished Politician. J. E. Thorold Rogers. FaBoEE

On a Doctor of Divinity. Richard Porson. FaBoEE

On a Dog of Lord Eglinton's. Robert Burns. OxBSP

On a Dolphin. Anyte [*or* Anytes]. GrAn, *tr. by* John Heath-Stubbs and Carol A. Whiteside

On a Drawing by Flavio. Philip Levine. BodElec

On a Drop of Dew. Andrew Marvell. BASC; ESCV; FSCP; GeHe; HAP; MeLP; NIL-7; NOSC; SCGP

On a Fair Beggar. Philip Ayres. EnLoPo

On a Fair Lady, Looking in the Glass. Richard Leigh. NOSC

On a Falling Group in the Last Judgement of Michael Angelo, in the Cappella Sistina. Washington Allston. APN-1

On a Favorite Cat Drowned in a Tub of Gold Fishes. Thomas Gray. *See* Ode on the Death of a Favourite [*or* Favorite] Cat, Drowned in a Tub [*or* Bowl] of Gold Fishes

On a Feast. Francis Quarles. ChIV-2

On a Female Rope-Dancer. *Unknown.* NOEC

On a Field Trip at Fredericksburg. Dave Jeddie Smith. HCAP; PoPoPo

On a Fifteenth-Century Flemish Angel. David Ray. CRP

On a Fine Crop of Peas Being Spoiled by a Storm. Henry Jones. OBGa

On a flat road runs the well-train'd runner. Runner, The. Walt Whitman. BLT; InPK-6; SAmP

On a flat road runs the well-trained runner. Walt Whitman. *See* On a flat road runs the well-train'd runner

On a Flimmering Floom You Shall Ride. Carl Sandburg. APT-1; OBAL

On a Fly Drinking out of [*or* from] His Cup. William Oldys. OBEV; OxAEP-1; OxBEV

  (Fly, The.) SCGP

On a Forsaken Lark's Nest. Mathilde Blind. VWP; ViWPN

On a Fortification at Boston Begun by Women. Benjamin Tompson. NOSC; SCAP

On a Fowler. Isidorus. AWP, *tr. by* William Cowper

On a Friend's Taking a Journey. Elizabeth Teft. PoBW

On a Frightful Dream. John Codrington Bampfylde. CenSon; 3NOEC

On a General Election. Joseph Hilaire Pierre Belloc. FaBoEE; NOBE; NOBL; NPeEn; OBSV; OxBEV; OxBoLi; OxBTC

On a Gentleman Marrying His Cook. Colin Ellis. FaBoEE

On a Gentleman's Complaining to a Lady That He Could Not Eat Meat. *Unknown.* ECWP

On a Gentlewoman that Sung and Played upon a Lute. William Strode. NOSC

On a Gentlewoman Walking in the Snow. William Strode. *See* On Chloris Walking in the Snow

On a Girdle. Edmund Waller. AWP; BASC; BeJo; GTBS-P; InPK-6; NAEL-5v1; NOSC; NoP-4; OBEV; PoE; PoRA; SCGP; TFi

On a Girl Who Took Action for Breach of Promise. Amanda Ros. VerBaPo

On a gnarled and naked tree. (LL) Song for a Dark Girl. Langston Hughes. NAAAL; NAAL-2v2; NAAL-5; NoP-4; SAmP

On a Good Leg and Foot. William Strode. NOSC

On a Government Surveyor. Albert Brodrick. PeSAV

On a Great Election. Joseph Hilaire Pierre Belloc. *See* On a General Election

On a green island in the Main Street traffic. Pro Patria. Constance Carrier. WPE

On a Grey-haired Old Lady Knitting at an Orchestral Concert. Suzanne Gardinier. CBAP

On a High House in Byzantium. Paulus [*or* Paulos] Silentiarius. GrAn, *tr. by* Andrew Miller

On a highway over the marshland. Flames and Dangling Wire. Robert Gray. BMAP; NOBAu

On a hill far away stood an old rugged cross. Old Rugged Cross, The. George Bennard. AH; TCAPo

On a hill near Petersburg. James Hugo Johnston. Maggie Pogue Johnson. CBWP-4

On a holy day when sails were blowing southward. Straying Student, The. Austin Clarke. BIrV; CIP-2; ModIr; NOIV; NPeEn

On a Honey Bee [*or* To a Honey Bee]. Philip Freneau. TAP

On a Hopeful Youth. Owen Felltham [*or* Feltham]. NOSC

On a Hound. Simonides. PGA, *tr. by* Kenneth Rexroth

On a journey, ill. Basho. JDP, *tr. by* Yoel Hoffmann

On a July night, the country's. Introduction to a Poem. Nikolai Ivanovich Glazkov. TCRP, *tr. by* Daniel Weissbort

On a Juniper Tree, Cut down to Make Busks. Aphra Behn. BASC

On a Lady Indifferent to Poetry. Sappho. STV, *tr. by* John Frederick Nims

On a Lady, Preached into the Colic, by One of Her Lovers. Aaron Hill. ECEV

On a Lady's Writing. Anna Laetitia Barbauld. PEW

On a Lady Who P-ssed [*or* P———st] at the Tragedy of Cato. Pope. OxBSP

On a Landscape by Myself. Yün Shou-p'ing. CoBLCP, *tr. by* Jonathan Chaves

On a leaf, a leaf. O. Mabson Southard. HA

On a Line from Valéry. Carolyn Kizer. FFC; GifTon

On a Lock of Miss Sarah Seward's Hair Who Died in her Twentieth Year. Anna Seward. CenSon

On a Lover of Books. Geoffrey Grigson. FaBoEE

On a Magazine Sonnet. Russell Hillard Loines. OBAL

On a Maid of Honour Seen by a Scholar in Somerset Garden. Thomas Randolph. OBGa

  (As once in black I disrespected walked.) OBGa

On a Man Run over by an Omnibus. Henry Luttrell. FaBoEE

On a Midsummer Eve. Thomas Hardy. FaBoVe

On a midsummer night, on a night that was eerie with stars. August Night. Sara Teasdale. MoAmPo

On a Monday morning early as my wandering steps did lead me. Boys of Mullabaun [*or* Mullaghbawn], The. *Unknown.* BIrV

On a Monument to Martí. Walter Adolphe Roberts. TTY

On a moonlight evening, in the month of May. Julia A. Moore. VerBaPo *Fr.* Croquet by Moonlight.

On a Moonlit Night, Sent to my Brothers and Sisters. Po Chü-i. SuSp, *tr. by* Irving Lo

On a morning ramble I visit a great mountain. Seeking out Master Chan on Incense Mountain. Meng Hao Jan. ColAnChi, *tr. by* Daniel Bryant

On a morning such as this. Veteran. Lola Ridge. WPE

On a mossy bank reclined. Stolen Kiss, The. Robert Dodsley. ECEV

On a needful day. Comfort-Maker. Jerry W., Jr. Ward. ISC

On a New Duke. *Unknown.* FaBoEE

On a Night of Snow. Elizabeth Jane Coatsworth. MoAmPo; OBCA

On a Night of the Full Moon. Audre Lorde. NALW

On a Noisy Polemic. Robert Burns. FaBoEE

On a Nomination to the Legion of Honour. *Unknown.* FaBoEE

On a Nook Called Fairyland. Henrietta Cordelia Ray. CBWP-3

On a Note of Triumph. Norman Corwin.

  Man unto His Fellow Man. TrJP

On a Nun. Jacopo Vittorelli. AWP, *tr. by* Byron

On a [p < suddenly . . . on a > was shot thro with a dyed. Scattering as Behavior toward Risk. Susan Howe. PFTM-2

On a Painted Woman. Shelley. NBLV

On a Painting "Ancient Trees and Flowing Stream." Yün Shou-p'ing. CoBLCP, *tr. by* Jonathan Chaves

On a Painting by Hsia Kuei Entitled "Returning in Wind and Snow to a Village Home." Kao Ch'i. SuSp, *tr. by* Irving Y. Lo

On a Painting by Patient B of the Independence State Hospital for the Insane. Donald Justice. CoAP; CoAmPo; NoAM

On a Painting by Wang the Clerk of Yen Ling. Su Tung-p'o (Su Shih). BLT, *tr. by* Kenneth Rexroth

On a Painting of a Knight-Errant. Cheng Hsieh. CoBLCP, *tr. by* Jonathan Chaves

On a Painting of a Woman Shown Half-Length. T'ang Yin. CoBLCP, *tr. by* Jonathan Chaves

On a Painting of Ants and Butterflies. Huang T'ing-chien. SuSp, *tr. by* Michael E. Workman

On a Painting of Fish Being Caught, A Song. Li Tung-yang. ColAnChi, *tr. by* John Timothy Wixted

On a Painting of Mushrooms. Yün Shou-p'ing. CoBLCP, *tr. by* Jonathan Chaves

On a Painting of the Radiant Emperor's Night Revels by Candlelight. Kao Ch'i. SuSp, *tr. by* Irving Y. Lo

On a Parisian Boulevard. James Kenneth Stephen. NOBL *Fr.* England and America.

On a Peacock. Thomas Heyrick. OWoS

On a Pet Grasshopper. Aristodicus of Rhodes. PGA, *tr. by* Kenneth Rexroth

On a Photo of Sgt. Ciardi a Year Later. John Ciardi. AiP

On a Phrase from Southern Ohio. James Wright (1927–80). LTA

On a Picture of Your House. Douglas G. Jones. NOBC

On a Picture Painted by Herself [*or* Her self], Representing Two Nymphs [*or* Nimphs] of Diana's, One in a Posture to Hunt, the other Bath[e]ing. Anne Killigrew. BASC; NOSC

On a Piece of Tapestry. George Santayana. APN-2

On a piece of toilet paper. Bladder Song. Leonard Nathan. BLT

On a Piece of Unwrought Pipeclay. John Frederick Bryant. NOEC

On a Pig's Head. Charles Tomlinson. NoAM

On a Poet. Henry Parrot. FaBoEE

On a poet's lips I slept. Shelley. GTBS-P; TOF *Fr.* Prometheus Unbound [A Lyrical Drama in Four Acts].

On a Political Prisoner. W. B. Yeats. OBMV

On a Portrait of a Falcon. Tu Fu. CrYelRi, *tr. by* Sam Hamill

On a Portrait of the Poet. Po Chü-i. CrYelRi, *tr. by* Sam Hamill

On a Portrait of Wordsworth by B. R. Haydon. Elizabeth Barrett Browning. HeIP-4

On a Procession with the Prince of Wales. Joseph Gwyer. "At evening too the dazzled light." VerBaPo

On a Puritan. Joseph Hilaire Pierre Belloc. FaBoEE

On a Puritanicall Lock-Smith. William Camden. FaBoEE

On a purple, sun-shot evening. On a Sunny Evening. *Unknown, fr. Terezin Concentration Camp*. INSAB

On a Raft. Lőrinc Szabó. IQMS, *tr. by* Watson Kirkconnell *Fr.* Cricket Music.

On a rainy night, the house is desolate. On Seeing a Firefly in My Room. Yang Chi. CoBLCP, *tr. by* Jonathan Chaves

On a Raised Beach. Hugh MacDiarmid. NePenScot "All is lithogenesis – or lochia." NPeEn

On a Recollected Road. Amir Gilbo'a. MHP, *tr. by* Ruth Finer Mintz

On a Replica of the Parthenon. Donald Davidson. FuPo

On a Return from Egypt. Keith Douglas. NoP-4

On a Rhine Steamer. James Kenneth Stephen. FaBoA; NOBL; NOBVV; OBCoV; PeLV *Fr.* England and America.

On a Ring. Asclepiades. GrAn, *tr. by* Alan Marshfield

On a rock, Bishop of Cloyne. Berkeley. Mairtin O Direain. BiHa

On A Romantic Lady. Mary Monck. ECWP; NOEC; RACG

On a Rose in December. Ebenezer Elliott. FaBoEE

On a Ruined House in a Romantic Country. Samuel Taylor Coleridge. CenSon

On a Sabbath eve, at dusk on a summer day. Song of Lies on Sabbath Eve, A. Yehuda Amichai [*or* Amikhai]. PoSu, *tr. by* Chana Bloch

On a Sabbath late. Mountains. Gaylord Brewer. AmPoNex

On a saddle without a horse. Journey through Hell. Nicanor Parra. WoPoe, *tr. by* Miller Williams

On a Santiago street. Hero, The. Pablo Neruda. GifTon, *tr. by* William O'Daly

On a Saturday afternoon in summer. Under House Arrest. Dennis Brutus. AF

On a Sea-Storm nigh the Coast. Richard Steere. SCAP

On a Seal. Plato. AWP; FaBoEE, *tr. by* Thomas Stanley

On a September night, a man looks down. Age of Cruelty, The. Gregory Orfalea. GraLe

On a Seven-Day Diary. Alan Dugan. OBAL

On a sheet of paper. Arithmetical Progression of the Verb "to Be." Walter Conrad Arensberg. APT-1

On a Shipmate, Pero Moniz, Dying at Sea. Luis de Camões [*or* Camoens]. OxBEV; PeSAV; WoPoe, *tr. by* Roy Campbell

On a shore washed by desolate waves, *he* stood. Alexander Sergeyevich Pushkin. WoPoe, *tr. by* D. M. Thomas *Fr.* Bronze Horseman, The.

On a sideboard where the sun falls. (LL) Man in Blue, A. James Schuyler. FTOS; PmAP

On a Similar Occasion for the Year 1790. William Cowper. NOCV

On a Similar Occasion for the Year 1792. William Cowper. NOCV (Subjoined to the Yearly Bill of Mortality of the Parish of All Saints, Northampton, 1792.) SacPr

On a Small Bath. *Unknown*. GrAn, *tr. by* Robin Skelton

On a small six-acre farm dwelt John Grist the miller. Under the Drooping Willow Tree. *Unknown*. OxBoLi

On a Snail. Su Tung-p'o (Su Shih). SuSp, *tr. by* Irving Y. Lo *Fr.* Two Poems on Insect Painting by Candidate Yin.

On a snug evening I shall watch her fingers. Piano after War. Gwendolyn Brooks. ESEAA

On a Soldier Fallen in the Philippines. William Vaughn Moody. NOBA

On a Soldier Killed in the Great War. R. Williams Parry. OBWVE, *tr. by* H. Idris Bell

On a Spaniel Called Beau Killing a Young Bird. William Cowper. FaBoCh

On a spring hillside. Ki no Tsurayuki. WoPoe, *tr. by* Steven D. Carter

On a spring morning of young wood, green wood. Burning the Dreams. Muriel Rukeyser. AF

On a squeaking cart, they push the usual stuff. Removal from Terry Street, A. Douglas Dunn. FaBoMo; FaBoVe; NPeEn; NoP-4; OxBC

On a Squirrel Crossing the Road in Autumn, in New England. Richard Eberhart. APT-2; HeIP-4

On a starless night and still. On Being Asked to Write a School Hymn. Charles Causley. OxAEP-2

On a starred [*or* starr'd] night Prince Lucifer uprose. Lucifer in Starlight. George Meredith. AWP; CABP; ChIV-1; EBVV; GSo; HAP; InPK-6; NAEL-5v2; NAEL-6v2; NOBE; NOBVV; NoP-4; OBEV; OxBEV; OxBSo; PoE; SCGP; Son; TFi; UnPo

On a starry, wintry night. Christ Child, The. Mary Weston Fordham. CBWP-2

On a Statue of Pan. *Unknown*. GrAn, *tr. by* W. G. Shepherd

On a Stingy Beau. John Winstanley. FaBoEE

On a Stone Thrown at a Very Great Man, But Which Missed Him. "Peter Pindar." NBLV

On a summer day in the month of May. Big Rock Candy Mountains, The. *Unknown*. FaBoA; NOBA

On a Summer Night. Elmaz Abinader. GraLe

On a summer night in Odessa. (LL) Dvonya. Louis Simpson. NNaP; NOBA

On a summer Sunday I saw the sun. Summer Sunday. *Unknown*. WoPoe, *tr. by* John Gardner

On a Sunbeam. Thomas Heyrick. NOSC

On a Sundial. Joseph Hilaire Pierre Belloc. FaBoEE

On a sunny brae alone I lay. Day Dream, A. Emily Jane Brontë. NALW

On a Sunny Evening. *Unknown, fr. Terezin Concentration Camp*. INSAB

On a Theme from Nicolas of Cusa. Clive Staples Lewis. SacPr

On a throne of new gold the Son of the Sky. Emperor, The. Tu Fu. AWP, *tr. by* E. Powys Mathers

On a Toad. Su Tung-p'o (Su Shih). SuSp, *tr. by* Irving Y. Lo *Fr.* Two Poems on Insect Painting by Candidate Yin.

On a train in Texas German prisoners eat. Defeat. Witter Bynner. APT-1

On a Tree Fallen across the Road. Robert Frost. RB

On a tributary of the Amazon. Lass of Aughrim, The. Paul Muldoon. NoAM; PBCIP

On a Vase of Gold-Fish. Charles Tennyson Turner. NOBVV; NPeEn

On a verdant summer islet. Burial of a Fairy Queen. Mary E. Tucker. CBWP-1

On a very hot Independence Day. Sonnet No. 21. Mark Ameen. GLP

On a View of Pasadena from the Hills. Yvor Winters. HarvBoo

On a Violet in Her Breast. Thomas Stanley. NOSC

On a Virtuous Young Gentlewoman That Died Suddenly. William Cartwright. HAP; OBEV

On a Visit to Ch'ung Chen Taoist Temple. Yü Hsüan-chi. ColAnChi, *tr. by* Chung Ling and Kenneth Rexroth

On a Vulgar Error. Clive Staples Lewis. OxBTC

On a wet night, laden with books for luggage. Poet on the Island, The. Richard Murphy. CIP-2

On a Wet Summer. John Codrington Bampfylde. NOEC; OxBSo

On a Whore. John Hoskyns [*or* Hoskins]. FaBoEE

On A Wife. Francis Burdett Money-Coutts. OxBSP

On a Winter Night. May Sarton. ItWoWo

On a winter's night long time ago. Noël. Joseph Hilaire Pierre Belloc. UV

On a withered branch. Basho. TAL

On a Woman. Robert Williams. OBWVE, *tr. by* H. Idris Bell

On a Worthless Politician. *Unknown*. GrAn, *tr. by* Peter Jay

On a Young Man and an Old Man. Edward May. OxBSP

On a Young Wife. Julianus of Egypt. GrAn, *tr. by* Willis Barnstone

On African Writing. Jack A. Mapanje. HBAPE

On afternoons of drowsy calm. Afternoon Service at Mellstock. Thomas Hardy. PeECV

On Alabama Ave., Paterson, NJ, 1954. Rachel De Vries. UnSA

On Alderman W————: The History of His Life. John Cunningham. *See* On a Certain Alderman

On Alexis. Plato. AWP, *tr. by* Thomas Stanley

On All Fours. Benjamin Péret. PFTM-1

On all that strand. Roundelay. Samuel Beckett. ModIr; OxBEV

On an accordion which had seen plenty. Blind Man, The. Konstantin Mikhailovich Simonov. TCRP, *tr. by* Lubov Yakovleva

On an Æolian Harp. George Cabot Lodge. APN-2

On an Amorous Old Man. David Mallet. NePenScot

On an Ancient Tomb East of the Village. Po Chü-i. TAL

On an Anniversary. John Millington Synge. FaBoEE; NOIV; OBMV

On an apple-ripe September morning. Tarry Flynn. Patrick Kavanagh. ModIr

On an average afternoon men lay down. Reminder to the Current President, A. Christopher Howell. CDa

On an Early Spring. Mary Julia Young. CenSon

On an East Wind from the Wars. Alan Dugan. AF

On an Engraving by Casserius. Alec Derwent Hope. CBAP; HarvBoo

On an Hour[e]-Glass[e]. John Hall. MeLP

On an Indian Tomineois, the Least of Birds. Thomas Heyrick. NOSC (I'me made in sport by Nature, when.) NPeEn

On an Infant Dying as Soon as Born. Charles Lamb. GTBS-P; OBEV

On an Infant Which Died before Baptism. Samuel Taylor Coleridge. SacPr

On an Invitation to the United States. Thomas Hardy. AWP; AiP; FaBoA

On an Inyanga Road. Noel H. Brettell. PeSAV

On an Island. "Ethna Carbery." WPE

On an Island. John Millington Synge. BIrV; FaBoVe; MoBrPo; NPeEn; OxBEV; OxBSP; PeVV

On an Old Woman. Lucilius. AWP, tr. by William Cowper

On an Old Woman Who Sold Pots. Unknown. PAI

On an outing with seventeen Czechs. Limerick: "On an outing with seventeen Czechs." Unknown. PeLi

On an Unfinished Statue. George Santayana. APN-2

On an Unsociable Family. Elizabeth Hands. ECWP; NPeEn; WoRP

On and on, always on and on. Unknown. ChiP Fr. Seventeen Old Poems.

On and On: An Ancient Song (Yueh-Fu). Li Ho. ChinPo, tr. by Yip Wai-lim

On and on, going on and on. Unknown. See Going on always on and on

On and on in the white clouds. Sent to the Taoist of Dragon Mountain, Hsü Faleng. Liu Ch'ang-ch'ing. SuSp, tr. by William H. Nienhauser

On and on we go over steppes. Refugees. Ilya Krichevsky [or Krichevskii]. TCRP, tr. by Albert C. Todd

On Angels. Czeslaw Milosz. BBASP

On Angels. Czeslaw Milosz. AF, tr. by Czeslaw Milosz

On Angels. W. W. Eustace Ross. MoCV

On Anna Laetitia Aikin. Mary Scott. RWP

On Another's Sorrow. William Blake. AWP; FHYEP; InvLi; OxAEP-2 Fr. Songs of Innocence.

On any sheet the least display of mind. (LL) Considerable Speck, A. Robert Frost. MoAmPo; OBAL; SAmP

On Apologies. Valerie Jean. SpirFl

On Archaeanassa. Plato. AWP, tr. by Thomas Stanley

On Arno's bosom, as he calmly flows. John Pierpont. APN-1 Fr. Airs of Palestine.

On Arrival. Richard Howard. TAP

On Arthur Hugh Clough. Algernon Charles Swinburne. FaBoEE

On Asuka River. Unknown. OHMPJ

On Authors and Booksellers [or Publishers]. Pope. FaBoEE

On Autumn Lake. John Ashbery. LCAP-2

On autumn nights. David Vogel. FIT, tr. by Robert Friend

On Balaam's Ass. Francis Quarles. ChIV-1

On Ballycastle Beach. Medbh McGuckian. PBCIP

On Barclay's Apology for the Quakers. Matthew Green. NOEC

On Basho's "Frog." Sengai Gibon. ZenPo, tr. by Takashi Ikemoto and Lucien Stryk

On Bathing. Thomas Warton, the Younger. OxBSo

On Beauty [or Beauety]. James Thomson.
"This happy place with all delights abounds." UV

On Becoming a Tiger. Lorna Goodison. GT

On Beer. Emperor Julian. PGA, tr. by Kenneth Rexroth

On Being a Householder. Alan Dugan. NoAM

On Being a Poet in Sierra Leone. Syl Cheney-Coker. HBAPE; PBMAP

On Being Asked for a Peace Poem. Howard Nemerov. OxBC

On Being Asked for a War Poem. W. B. Yeats. FaBoWar; NIP-4; OBWP; OxAEP-2; PoWW

On Being Asked to Write a Poem against the War in Vietnam. Hayden Carruth. CDa

On Being Asked to Write a Poem for 1979. Jack A. Mapanje. AF; NAfrP; PBMAP

On Being Asked to Write a School Hymn. Charles Causley. OxAEP-2

On Being Assigned as Military Adviser to the Garrison Army, Written when Passing Ch'ü-a. T'ao Ch'ien [or T'ao Yuan-ming]. CoBCP, tr. by Burton Watson

On Being Brought from Africa to America. Phillis Wheatley. NAAL-2v1; NAAL-3; NAAL-5; NALW; NOBA; NOEC; OxBEV; RWP; SacPr; TAP; TTY; WPE

On Being Cautioned against Walking on an Headland Overlooking the Sea, because It Was Frequented by a Lunatic. Charlotte Smith. CenSon; ECWP; NPeEn; WoRP

On Being Charged with Writing Incorrectly. "The Amorous Lady." ECWP

On Being Disabled by Light at Dawn in the Wilderness. G. E. Murray. IllVoic

On Being Forced to Part with his Library for the Benefit of his Creditors. William Stanley Roscoe. CenSon

On Being Head of the English Department. Pinkie Gordon Lane. BlSi; GT

On Being in the Midwest. Diana Chang. FSt

On Being Kicked Out of the Harold Washington Library Center for Napping on the Floor. Thom Ward. OPRER

On Being Kind to Horses. Vladimir Vladimirovich Mayakovsky [or Maiakovskii]. TCRP, tr. by Bernard Meares

On being Removed from Hsün-yang and Sent to Chung-chou. Po Chü-i. ChiP, tr. by Arthur Waley

On Being Sixty. Po Chü-i. AWP; ChiP, tr. by Arthur Waley

On Being Told I Don't Speak Like a Black Person. Allison Joseph. OPRER

On Bellosguardo, when the year was young. To Vernon Lee. Amy Levy. VWP

On Belmont, low riders. Hotel Fresno. Dixie Salazar. GeoHom

On Ben Dorain. Duncan Ban MacIntyre. Fr. Last Farewell to the Hills.

On Ben Jonson. Sidney Godolphin. BeJo

On Ben Jonson. Mildmay Fane, 2d Earl of Westmorland. See In Obitum Ben. Jons

On Bertrand Russell's "Portraits from Memory." Donald Davie. FaBoTw

On Bishop Burnet's Being Set on Fire in His Closet. Thomas Parnell. ECEV

On Bismillah Khan's Shehnai. Chennavira Kanavi. OMIP, tr. by A. K. Ramanujan

On black bare trees a stale cream moon. Eau-Forte. Francis Stewart [or "Frank"] Flint. OxBTC

On blood, smoke, rain and the dead. Who Knows Where. Detlev, Freiherr von Liliencron. AWP, tr. by Ludwig Lewisohn

On Blossoming. Leah Goldberg.
"How shall we bring our dying heart up." MHP
"Old woman, blue eyed and sun burned." MHP
"Scarlet, warm and heavy in black velvet leaves." MHP
"That death in his windows would rise." MHP

On blue summer evenings I'll go down the pathways. Sensation. Arthur Rimbaud. TTTS, tr. by Kenneth Koch

On Board a Boat at Chi-ning. Yüan Hung-tao. CoBLCP, tr. by Jonathan Chaves

On Board Ship: Reading Yüan Chên's Poems. Po Chü-i. ChiP, tr. by Arthur Waley

On Board Starship Enterprise. Unknown. PeLi

On board the Victory Line Bus. Assimilation. Eugene Gloria. ReBoTo

On Bond the Usurer. Unknown. NOSC

On Boston Common a red star. Winter's Tale, A. Sylvia Plath. FaBoA

On Botching. John Heywood. FaBoEE

On boys and girls the middle parts get mated. Unknown. PriapPo, tr. by Richard W. Hooper Fr. Priapus Poems, The.

On Brooklyn Bridge I saw a man drop dead. Charles Reznikoff. APT-2

On Buddha's birthday. Basho. SoOfWa, tr. by Sam Hamill

On Buddha's birthday. Kikaku. SoOfWa, tr. by Sam Hamill

On Buddha's deathday. Basho. SoOfWa, tr. by Sam Hamill

On Burroughs' Work. Allen Ginsberg. NAAL-2v2; NOBA

On Butler who can think without rage. John Oldham. OBSV Fr. Satire, A.

On Button the Grave-Maker. Unknown. FaBoEE

On Buying a Dog. Edgar Klauber. NTCP

On Buying a Horse. Unknown. NBLV; RB

On came the whirlwind—like the last. Charge at Waterloo. Sir Walter Scott. FaBoWar

On Catania and Syracuse Swallowed up by an Earthquake, from the Italian of Filicaja. Anna Seward. Son

On Catullus. Walter Savage Landor. OBEV

On certain days a sweat folds in over her, covering her as weather covers a little city. Bathroom. Fanny Howe. ExTi

On Certain Ladies. Pope. FaBoEE
(Epigram: "When other Ladies to the Shades go down") OxBSP

On certain nights as soon as I lie down. Execution, The. Vladimir Vladimirovich Nabokov. TCRP, tr. by Vladimir Nabokov

On certain nights I hear within the screeching of the horn. Léon Laleau. NegPo, tr. by Ellen Conroy Kennedy Fr. Black Music.

On Certain Wits. Howard Nemerov. HCAP; OxBC

On Change of Weathers. Francis Quarles. OxBSP

On Chao Ch'ang's Flower Paintings in Wang Po-yang's Collection. Su Tungp'o (Su Shih).
Hibiscus. SuSp, tr. by Irving Y. Lo
Plum Blossoms. SuSp, tr. by Irving Y. Lo
Sunflower. SuSp, tr. by Irving Y. Lo

On charts they fall like lace. Delos. Lawrence Durrell. OxAEP-2

On Children. Kahlil Gibran. PoToHe Fr. Prophet, The.

On Chloris Walking in the Snow. William Strode. NPeEn
(Chloris in the Snow.) NOBE; OBEV
(On a Gentlewoman Walking in the Snow.) NOSC; OxBSP

On Christians, Mercy Will Fall. Unknown. OBWVE, tr. by D. Myrddin Lloyd

On Christmas. John Codrington Bampfylde. CenSon

On Christmas Day I weep. Christmas Mourning. Vassar Miller. ChIV-2; MoAmPo

On Christmas Day in the morning. (LL) As I Sat on a Sunny Bank. Unknown. OxBoLi; OxNR

On Christmas Day to My Heart. Clement Paman. ChrPo; NOSC

On Christmas Eve I turned the spit. Unknown. OxNR

On Chung Mountain. Wang An-shih. CrYelRi, tr. by Sam Hamill

On city breezes borne. (LL) London Plane-Tree, A. Amy Levy. PEW; ViWPN

On City Streets. Margaret E. Bruner. PoToHe

On Clarastella walking in Her Garden. Robert Heath. NOSC

On Clergymen Preaching Politics. John Byrom. ECEV

On Climbing the Heights on the Ninth Day of the Ninth Moon. Tu Fu. TAL

On Climbing the Highest Peak of Stone Gate Mountain. Hsieh Ling-yün. ColAnChi, *tr. by* Richard W. Bodman

On Climbing the Mountain Where Buddha Trained. Mokusen. ZenPo, *tr. by* Takashi Ikemoto and Lucien Stryk

On Climbing the Pagoda of the Temple of Gracious Benevolence with Kao Shih and Hsüeh Chü. Ts'en Shen. SuSp, *tr. by* Daniel Bryant

On Climbing the Phoenix Tower at Chinling. Li Po. TAL

On Clouds. Douglas Livingstone. PeSAV

On cold winter mornings. Winter Morning. Frank Flynn. OTCP

On Commonwealth Avenue and Brattle Street. Diana Der Hovanessian. UrbNat

On Commonwealth, on Marlborough. Technologies. George Starbuck. YaYoPo

On Communists. Ebenezer Elliott. *See* Epigram: "What is a communist? One who hath yearnings."

On Consulting "Contemporary Poets of the English Language." Anthony Thwaite. OxBEV; PeLV

On Contact Opens Its Indigo Pit. Coral Bracho. PFTM-2, *tr. by* Forrest Gander

On Covering the Bones of Chang Chin, the Hired Man. Liu Tsung-yüan. SuSp; WoPoe, *tr. by* Jan W. Walls

On Cupid's bow how are my heart-strings bent. Sir Philip Sidney. NoSic *Fr.* Astrophil and Stella.

On Damons Loving of Clora. Damaris, Lady Masham. EMWP

On dark nights, when thoughts fly like nightbirds. It Is Important. Gail Tremblay. WeW-3

On Death. Aleksandr Aleksandrovich Blok. TCRP, *tr. by* Geoffrey Thurley

On Death. Anne Killigrew. BoWoP; ChIV-1

(Tell me thou safest end of all our woe.) PEW

On Death. Francis Quarles. PeECV *Fr.* Divine Fancies.

On Death. Sándor Weöres. IQMS, *tr. by* Alan Dixon

On death and beauty—till a bullet stopped his song. (LL) All Day It Has Rained. Alun Lewis. AngWePo; GTBS-P; NAEL-5v2; NAEL-6v2; NOBE; NoP-4; OBWP; OBWVE; OxBTC; TCAWP

On Death and Love. Janet Campbell Hale. VoR

On Death's domain intent I fix my eyes. To a Gentleman and Lady on the Death of the Lady's Brother and Sister, and a Child of the Name Avis, Aged One Year. Phillis Wheatley. BlSi

On deck. And love's the burning boy. (LL) Casabianca. Elizabeth Bishop. FaBoWP; NIL-7; OxBSP; WoPoe

On Dennis. Pope. FaBoEE

On Desire A Pindarick. Aphra Behn. EMWP

On Details. Sami Mahdi. MAP, *tr. by* Charles Doria and May Jayyusi

On Dewdrop. Wei Ying-wu. SuSp, *tr. by* Irving Y. Lo

On Digital Extremities. Frank Gelett Burgess. PeLi

On Dinah. Francis Quarles. ChIV-1

On Diogenes the Cynic. Antiphilus [*or* Antiphilos]. GrAn

On Display. Thomas Sayers Ellis. InTrad

On Diverse Deviations. Maya Angelou. BlSi

On Don Surly. Ben Jonson. FaBoEE; NAEL-5v1; NAEL-6v1; NAEL-7v1

On Donne's Poetry. Samuel Taylor Coleridge. NAEL-5v2; NAEL-6v2; PAI; UV

On Dorinda. Charles Sackville, 6th Earl of Dorset. *See* On the Countess of Dorchester

On Dorothea Lange's Photograph "Migrant Mother" (1936). Helen Pinkerton. FFC

On Dove's green brink the fair TREMELLA stood. Erasmus Darwin. NOBRP *Fr.* Botanic Garden, The.

On Dover Cliffs. July 20, 1787. William Lisle Bowles. CenSon

(Dover Cliffs.) OxAEP-2

On Dr. Evans Cutting Down a Row of Trees. *Unknown.* FaBoEE

On Dr. Keene, Bishop of Chester. Thomas Gray. FaBoEE

On Dr. Lettsom. *Unknown.* FaBoEE

On Dragon Hill. Li Po. CrYelRi, *tr. by* Sam Hamill

On Dreams. Jonathan Swift. BIrV

On Dreams, October 15, 1782. Sir Samuel Egerton Brydges. CenSon; Son

On dull mornings. Mrs. Busk. Sir Osbert Sitwell. OxBTC

On Dullness. Pope. OxBSP

On Dutch's Death. Robert Coles. BloBone

On Dwelling. Robert Graves. FaBoMo; OxBSP

On ear and ear two noises too old to end. Sea and the Skylark, The. Gerard Manley Hopkins. OBMV

On Early Trains. Boris Leonidovich Pasternak. TCRP, *tr. by* George Reavey

On Earth. Olga Broumas. BodElec

On Earth. Forugh Farrokhzad. BoWoP, *tr. by* Girdhard Tikku

On earth as it is in heaven. (LL) Talk Show, The. Albert Goldbarth. IllVoic; ReTh

On earth but love there is no other pleasure. (LL) Henry Constable. EnLoPo; SCGP; Son *Fr.* Diana.

On Earth There Is a Lamb So Small. Nikolaus [*or* Nicolaus] Ludwig, Graf von Zinzendorf. AH, *tr. by* Sheema Z. Buehne

On Education, December 1789. Elizabeth Bentley. WoRP

On either side of a rock-paved lane. St Kilda's Parliament: 1879–1979. Douglas Dunn. NePenScot

On either side the *Jervis Bay* the convoy was dipping. Michael Thwaites. FaBoWar *Fr.* Jervis Bay, The.

On either side the river lie. Lady of Shalott, The. Tennyson. FHYEP; NAEL-5v2; NAEL-6v2; NOBE; NOBRP; NoP-4; OBEV; OBNV; OBSP; OxAEP-2; PoE; TFi; TOF

On El Camino del Mar. Variations for the Piano. Siv Cedering. MiVo

On Eleanor Freeman, Who Died 1650, Aged 21. *Unknown.* OBEV

On Elijah's Chariot. Endre Ady. IQMS, *tr. by* Anton N. Nyerges

On Elizabeth Ireland. *Unknown.* FaBoEE

On Elizabeth Montagu. Mary Scott. RWP

On Elphinston's Translation of Martial. Robert Burns. FaBoEE

On Enclosures. *Unknown.* FaBoEE

(Epigram: On Inclosures.) OxBoLi

On English Monsieur. Ben Jonson. AEP; NBLV; NoP-4

On Entering His Coffin. Baiho. ZenPo, *tr. by* Takashi Ikemoto and Lucien Stryk

On Entries Emptiness. Dennis Phillips. FTOS

On Epicurus and Themistokles. Menander. GrAn, *tr. by* Alan Marshfield

On Epiktetos the Stoic. *Unknown.* GrAn, *tr. by* Peter Jay

On Esthwaite Water. Isabella Lickbarrow. RWP

On every slave a pigeon loft to kick in the light of his decline. 9000 Jackals Swimming to Boston. "Lucebert." PFTM-2, *tr. by* Peter Nijmeijer

On every thought I have the countless shadows fall. Light and Shadow. Hugh MacDiarmid. HarvBoo

On Evolution. John Ciardi. OBAL

On Exodus 3: 14: "I am that I am." Matthew Prior. ChIV-1; NOCV

On extending the olive branch to my own self. Harriet Jacobs. SpirFl

On Failing the Examination. Meng Chiao. CoBCP; ColAnChi, *tr. by* Burton Watson

On Fairford Windows. William Strode. NOSC

On Falling Asleep by Firelight. William Meredith. ChIV-1; NoAM

On Fame. John Keats. CenSon *Fr.* Two Sonnets on Fame.

On Fields oer Which the Reaper's Hand Has Passed. Henry David Thoreau. APN-1

On File. John Kendrick Bangs. PoToHe

On Finding a Swastika Carved on a Tree in the Hills above Heidelberg. Kevin Prufer. AmPoNex

On Finding an Old Photograph. Wendy Cope. HarvBoo

On Finding Out that the One You Slept with the Night before Was Murdered the Next Day. Chuck Ortleb. GLP

On Finding the Truth. Jones Very. TrCP

On Fire. David Morley. NLP

On First Looking in on Blodgett's Keats's "Chapman's Homer." George Starbuck. OBAL

On First Looking into Chapman's Hesiod. Peter Porter. NOBAu

On First Looking into Chapman's Homer. John Keats. BRP; CABP; CenSon; ClHu; FHYEP; FaBoCh; GSo; GTBS-P; HAP; HeIP-4; InPK-6; NAEL-5v2; NAEL-6v2; NAWM-7v2; NIL-7; NIP-4; NOBE; NOBRP; NPeEn; NoP-4; OBAL; OBEV; OPOU; OxAEP-2; OxBEV; OxBSo; PoE; PoPoPo; SCGP; SoSe-8; Son; TFi; TRP; UV; WoPoe

On First Looking into Krafft-Ebing's *Psychopathosexualis* [*or* Psychopathia Sexualis]. Oliver St. John Gogarty. UV

On First Looking into Loeb's Horace. Lawrence Durrell. FaBoMo

On First Returning from Taking the Examinations: Feelings at Cloud-Stop Pavilion. Wen Cheng-ming. CoBLCP, *tr. by* Jonathan Chaves

On Flower Wreath Hill. Kenneth Rexroth. APT-2; BodElec

On foot. On Foot I Had to Walk through the Solar Systems. Edith Södergran. WPoS, *tr. by* Stina Katchadourian

On foot I climb Pei-mang Slope. Written on Parting from Mr. Ying. Ts'ao Chih. CoBCP, *tr. by* Burton Watson

On Foot I Had to Walk through the Solar Systems. Edith Södergran. WPoS, *tr. by* Stina Katchadourian

On Fortune. Queen of England Elizabeth I. WPE

On four-horse coach, whose luggage pierced the sky. Past and Present. R. E. Egerton Warburton. NOBVV

On Fourteen Maple Street. Barbara Winder. MiVo

On Francis Drake. *Unknown.* NOSC; NPeEn; PBRV

On Freedom and Ambition. Oliver Goldsmith. NOIV *Fr.* Travel[l]er; or, A Prospect of Society, The.

On Fridays we would gather at Lucy's. Last at Lucy's, The. John Tripp. TCAWP

On Frosty Days. David Campbell. CBAP

On Fruition. Sir Charles Sedley. NOSC

On Fujiyama / Under the midsummer moon. Akahito. OHPJ

On Gallia's land I saw thy faded form. To Freedom. Joseph Hucks. CenSon

On Galveston Beach. Barbara Howes. MoAmPo

On Gask's deserted ancient hall. Ghost of Fadon, The. Joanna Baillie. NOBRP

On gay Anacreon's joy-inspiring line. On the Translation of Anacreon. Horace Walpole, 4th Earl of Orford. FaBoEE

On Gay Wallpaper. William Carlos Williams. APT-1; MoAmPo; TAP

On General Paoli and the Corsican Struggle for Liberty. Anna Laetitia Barbauld. ECWP   Fr. Corsica.

On Genessarett. Josephine D. Henderson Heard. CBWP-4

On Geoffrey Grigson. Cyril Connolly. OBCoV

On George Herbert's "The Temple" Sent to a Gentlewoman. Richard Crashaw. See On Mr. G. Herberts Booke, The Temple

On getting a card. Poem. William Carlos Williams. VGW

On Giles and Joan. Ben Jonson. NAEL-5v1; NAEL-6v1; NAEL-7v1; NOBL

On Giving up Smoking. Lawrence Spooner. NOEC   Fr. Looking-Glass for Smokers, A.

On Glaister's Hill. William Jeffrey.
   Carlyle on Burns. OxBS

On God's Favour. Francis Quarles. PeECV   Fr. Divine Fancies.

On God's Law. Francis Quarles. ChIV-1

On Groin. Ben Jonson. NOSC

On Growing Old. John Masefield. MoBrPo; PoRA

On Growing up the Darker Berry. Harriet Jacobs. ISC

On Gustavus Adolphus, King of Sweden. Sir Thomas Roe. FaBoEE

On Gut. Ben Jonson. NPeEn; NoP-4; PoPoPo

On Happiness. Pacifico Massimi. CAGL, tr. by James J. Wilhelm   Fr. Hecateleguim.

On Harting Down. Thomas Sturge Moore. OxBTC

On Hats and Things. Mcavoy Layne. CDa

On Having Been an Experimental Sacred Cow for Four Years, and a Token African on Faculty. Kofi Awoonor. HBAPE

On Having Piles. Sir Walter Scott. FaBoEE

On Hayley. William Blake. FaBoEE

On Hearing a Description of a Prairie. Fanny Crosby. SWaP

On Hearing a Lady Praise a Certain Rev. Doctor's Eyes. George Outram. EBVV

On Hearing a Symphony of Beethoven. Edna St. Vincent Millay. MoAmPo

On Hearing It Has Been Ordered in the Chapterhouse of Ireland That the Friars Make No More Songs or Verses. Pádraigín Haicéad. NOIV, tr. by Thomas Kinsella

On Hearing of the Intention of a Gentleman to Purchase the Poet's Freedom. George Moses Horton. APN-1; NAAAL

On Hearing Someone Sing a Poem by Yüan Chên. Po Chü-i. ChiP, tr. by Arthur Waley

On Hearing that a Potato Costs $70 in Sarajevo. Gloria Vando. SpudSo

On hearing that a small herd of buffalo. Buffalo Poem #1. Geary Hobson. UrbNat

On Hearing that Holders of the Chin-shih Degree Are Dealing in Tea. Mei Yao Ch'en. SuSp, tr. by Jonathan Chaves

On Hearing That San-p'ing's Newly Brewed Chrysanthemum Wine Is Ready to Drink—Investigating with a Poem. Pien Kung. CoBLCP, tr. by Jonathan Chaves

On Hearing That the Sea-Barbarians Are about To Attack Hu-chou—Expressing My Feelings to Tzu-yü. Tsung Ch'en. CoBLCP, tr. by Jonathan Chaves

On Hearing That the Students of Our New University Have Joined the Agitation against Immoral Literature. W. B. Yeats. NoAM

On Hearing That Torture Was Suppressed throughout the Austrian Dominions. John Codrington Bampfylde. Son

On Hearing the First Cuckoo. Richard Church. OBMV

On Hearing the Marsh Bird's Water Cry. Duane Niatum. CDW

On Hearing the News of the Japanese Surrender. Liu Ya-tzu. SuSp, tr. by Wu-Chi Liu

On Heaven. Ford Madox Ford. CTC

On Hellespont, guilty of true love's blood. Christopher Marlowe. NoSic; PoE   Fr. Hero and Leander.

On her beautiful face there are smiles of grace. Pretty Girl, A. J. Gordon Coogler. OBAL

On Her Blindness. Priscilla Pointon. ECWP   Fr. To the Critics.

On Her Brother. Al-Khansa. BoWoP, tr. by Willis Barnstone

On Her Brother Sakhr. Al-Khansa. BoWoP, tr. by Willis Barnstone

On her chest. (LL) Motherhood. May Swenson. CoAP; NoP-4

On Her Decision to Stop Wearing Clothes. Mahadevi. ErotSp; WPoS, tr. by Jane Hirshfield

On her evening off. For the Woman Who Dressed up to Listen to Gigli on the Radio. Jane Duran. MFPA

On her head. (LL) Eight Sandbars on the Takano River. Gary Snyder. NOBA; VGW

On Her Loving Two Equally. Aphra Behn. NALW; NIL-7; NIP-4 (Song.) EMWP; OxAEP-1

On Her Own Birthday. Judith Madan. ECWP

On Her Portrait. Sister Juana Inés de la Cruz. WoPoe, tr. by Robert Mezey

On Her Portrait. Sister Juana Inés de la Cruz. SpanPo, tr. by Kate Flores

On her side, reclining on her elbow. So-and-So Reclining on Her Couch. Wallace Stevens. NOBA

On her soft lap he sat, and caught the sounds. (LL) Joseph Warton. ECEV; NOEC   Fr. Enthusiast, The; or, The Lover of Nature.

On her 36th birthday, Thomas had shown her. Wingfoot Lake. Rita Dove. PoPoPo

On Her Vanity. Wilfrid Scawen Blunt. GSo

On Her Way. Gertrude Stein. PFTM-1

On her way to the beach. Young Girl. Carl Rakosi. APT-2

On high may dwell with thee. (LL) Church's One Foundation, The. Samuel John Stone. SacPr; UV

On High Street. Andrea Hollander Budy. UrbNat

On highway edges the sparrows. Winter Landscape. Luciana Notari. CItWP, tr. by Cinzia Sartini Blum and Lara Trubowitz

On him the unpetitioned heavens descend. Counsel of Moderation, A. Francis Thompson. MoBrPo

On him who is burned up, yea, visibly. (LL) Canzone: He Speaks of His Condition through Love. Folcachiero de' Folcachieri. AWP; EaItPo, tr. by Dante Gabriel Rossetti

On Himself. Callimachus. GrAn, tr. by Peter Jay

On Himself. Cyril Connolly. OBCoV

On Himself. Robert Herrick. See On Himselfe

On Himself. Walter Savage Landor. FaBoEE

On Himself. William Oldys. FaBoEE

On Himself. Matthew Prior. FaBoEE (Epitaph on Himself.) OBCoV

On Himself. Dante Gabriel Rossetti. FaBoEE (There is a poor sneak called Rossetti.) PeLi

On Himself. David Wright. OPOU

On Himself, upon Hearing What Was His Sentence. James Graham, Marquess of Montrose. NOSC; NPeEn; NePenScot (His Metrical Prayer.) ChIV-2; OxBS (Verses Composed on the Eve of His Execution.) FaBoEE

On Himselfe. Robert Herrick. BASC; BeJo; CaPo; FaBoEE; NOSC; NPeEn (On Himself.) CavPo

On hire is al my lyf ylong. Unknown. OHMEL

On his airy perch among the branches. Fox and the Crow, The. Jean de La Fontaine. OBVE, tr. by Marianne Moore

On his Baldness. Po Chü-i. ChiP, tr. by Arthur Waley

On His Birthday. Greg Williamson. NAPBL

On His Blindness. John Milton. AWP; CABP; ChIV-2; GSo; HAP; HeIP-4; ITBLP; InPK-6; NAEL-5v1; NAEL-6v1; NIL-7; NOBE; NOSC; NPeEn; NoP-4; OBEV; OxBSo; PoE; PoPoPo; PoRA; SCGP; SacPr; SoSe-8; TFi; TRP; WeW-3 (Sonnet 19.) BASC

On His Books. Joseph Hilaire Pierre Belloc. FaBoEE; MoBrPo; NBLV; OxBoLi; WeW-3

On his death-bed poor Lubin lies. Reasonable Affliction, A. Matthew Prior. NOEC

On his deathbed lies our Tsar, Christian Orthodox Tsar! Death of Ivan, The. "David Samuilovich Samoylov." [or Samoilov]. TCRP, tr. by Lubov Yakovleva

On His Deceased Wife. John Milton. NPeEn; OBEV; OxBSo; PoE; SCV; SacPr; TFi (On His Dead Wife.) HAP; NOBE; WeW-3 (Methought I Saw My Late Espousèd Saint.) BoLoP; CABP; EnLoPo; NAEL-5v1; NAEL-6v1; PBRV; PeECV; SCGP (Sonnet.) EBEV; NOSC (Methought I Saw.) NoP-4; Son (Sonnet 23.) MakPoe

On his first visit to Puerto Rico. Coca-Cola and Coco Frío. Martín Espada. ReTh; UnSA

On his free weekends he took. Military-Industrial Complex, The. Robley, Jr. Wilson. PBCAP

On His Friend Megistias, Who Died at Thermopylai. Simonides. GrAn, tr. by Peter Jay

On His Garden Book. Francis Daniel Pastorius. SCAP

On His Lady's Waking. Pierre de Ronsard. AWP, tr. by Andrew Lang

On His Late Majesty's Gracious Gift to the Universities.   Joseph Trapp.
   OxBEV
  (King, observing with judicious eyes, The.)   FaBoEE
  (King surveying, with judicious Eyes, The.)   OxBEV
On His Mistress Drown'd.   Thomas Spratt.   EnLoPo
On His Mistress Going from Home [Song].   Unknown.   NOSC
On His Mistress Looking in a Glass.   Thomas Carew.   CaPo
On His Mistress [or Mistris].   John Donne.   BoLoP; CABP; EBEV; ESCV;
   FSCP; MeLP; NAEL-5v1; NAEL-6v1; NAEL-7v1; NPeEn; NoSic;
   OxAEP-1; SCGP   Fr. Elegies.
On His Mistress [or Mistris], the Queen of Bohemia.   Sir Henry Wotton.
   BASC; EnLoPo; HAP; MeLP; NOSC; NPeEn; OxBEV; SCGP; TFi
  (Elizabeth of Bohemia.)   BoLoP; FaBoCh; GTBS-P; NOBE; OBEV
On His Own Poetry.   Charles Churchill.   NOEC   Fr. Prophecy of Famine,
   The.
On His Queerness.   Christopher Isherwood.   OxBTC
On His Royal Blindness Paramount Chief Kwangala.   Jack A. Mapanje.   AF
On His Royal Highness His Expedition against the Dutch.   Elizabeth Polwhele.
   EMWP
On His Seventy-Fifth Birthday.   Walter Savage Landor.   AWP; EBEV;
   OxAEP-2; SCGP   Fr. Last Fruit Off an Old Tree, The.
On His Thirty-Third Birthday.   Ch'ang Kuo Fan.   OHMPC, tr. by Kenneth
   Rexroth
On his way to the open hearth where white-hot steel.   My Father's Garden.
   David Wagoner.   DiPo; NIL-7; NIP-4
On his wedding night.   Sons of War.   Samih Al-Qasim.   FaBoWar, tr. by
   Abdullah Al-Udhari
On His Writing Verses.   John Hawthorn.   NOEC
On Honour.   Bernard Mandeville.   NOEC
On Hope.   Abraham Cowley.   See Mistress, The
On Hope.   Richard Crashaw.   NOBE
  (Answer for Hope.)   MeLP
  (M. [or Mr.] Crashaw's Answer for Hope.)   NOSC
On Hope.   Sándor Petőfi.   IQMS, tr. by Peter Zollman
On horseback, I am crossing the river.   Crossing the River.   Yang Shih-ch'i.
   CoBLCP, tr. by Jonathan Chaves
On hot nights now, in the smell of trees and water.   Lazarus' Sister.   Elaine
   Feinstein.   HarvBoo
On hot summer mornings my aunt set glasses.   Water.   Leslie Norris.
   AngWePo; OBWVE
On How the Cobler.   Unknown.   SCAP
On "How to Make Bee-keeping Pay." (LL)   Opportunity.   Harry Graham.
   OBCoV; PeLV
On humming rubber along this white concrete.   Driving in Oklahoma.   Carter
   Revard.   HATNAP; VoR
On Hurricane Jackson.   Alan Dugan.   CoAP; PAI; TRP
On Hygiene.   Joseph Hilaire Pierre Belloc.   MoBrPo
On Imagination.   Phillis Wheatley.   BlSi; NAAAL; OxWW; RWP
On Imitation.   Samuel Taylor Coleridge.   OxBSP
On Induction of the Hand.   Clark Coolidge.   PmAP
On Inhabiting an Orange.   Josephine Miles.   NoAM
On Inheriting Departure.   HeidiLynn Nilsson.   NeAmPo
On its highest leaves.   Ibycus.   SaLy, tr. by Diane Rayor
On Its Way.   May Swenson.   SoSe-8; WPE
On its way I see.   Kathleen Jessie Raine.   NALW
On its way west.   Choshi.   JDP, tr. by Yoel Hoffmann
On J. M. S. Gent.   Pope.   FaBoEE
On J. W. Ward.   Samuel Rogers.   FaBoEE
On Jacob's Purchase.   Francis Quarles.   ChIV-1
On Jacob Tonson, His Publisher.   Dryden.   FaBoEE; OBSV
On Jam.   Joseph Hilaire Pierre Belloc.   NBLV
On Jealousy.   Esther Johnson.   See Jealousy
On Jocky Bell.   Unknown.   FaBoEE
On John So.   Unknown.   FaBoEE
On Jordan's Bank.   Byron.   ChIV-1
On Joshu's Nothingness.   Saisho.   ZenPo, tr. by Takashi Ikemoto and Lucien
   Stryk
On Judas Iscariot.   Francis Quarles.   FaBoEE
On Judgement Day.   Sipho Sepamla.   PBMAP
On July 5 the Associated Press gave the news to the world.   Harangue on the
   Death of Hayyim Nahman Bialik.   César Tiempo.   TrJP, tr. by Donald
   Devenish Walsh
On Justifying Cuckoo La Goose.   Marianne Vitale.
  "Who trusteth in hilarity."   HeMarv
On Kean's Hamlet.   Washington Allston.   APN-1
On Keats.   Shelley.   FaBoEE
On Killing a Tax Collector.   Murragh O'Daly.   WoPoe, tr. by Richard
   O'Connell

On King Arthur's Round Table, at Winchester.   Thomas Warton, the Younger.
   Son
On King Richard the Third, Who Lies Buried under Leicester Bridge.   Sir John
   Suckling.   CaPo
On Knighthood.   Folgore da San Geminiano [or Gimignano].   AWP, tr. by
   John Addington Symonds
On Komochi Mountain.   Unknown.   OHMPJ
On Kriton the Miser.   Lucilius.   GrAn, tr. by Dudley Fitts
On Lady A———.   Nicolas Bentley.   OBCoV
On Lady Anne Hamilton.   Richard Brinsley Sheridan.   FaBoEE; NPeEn;
   OBCoV
On Lady Poltagrue, A Public Peril.   Joseph Hilaire Pierre Belloc.   MoBrPo;
   OBCoV
On land and sea I strove with anxious care.   Rudyard Kipling.   WoPoe   Fr.
   Epitaphs of the War [1914–1918].
On Late-acquired Wealth or Riches.   Unknown.   OBVE, tr. by William Cowper
  (Riches.)   AWP
On late-night television, two U.S. scientists talk about why the U.S.   Simon J.
   Ortiz.   OPRER
On Lazarus Raised from Death.   Henry Colman.   ChIV-2
On Leander's Swimming over the Hellespont to Hero.   Thomas Warton, the
   Younger.   FaBoEE
On Leaping over the Moon.   Thomas Traherne.   GeHe; NAEL-5v1
On Learning.   Elizabeth Teft.   ECWP
On Learning to Adjust to Things.   John Ciardi.   KaS; OBCA
On leave, I sat on marsh grass, watched.   Soldier on the Marsh, A.   Andrew
   Hudgins.   CBCWP
On Leaving Baltimore.   Duane Niatum.   CDW
On Leaving Cuba, Her Native Land.   Gertrudis Gomez de Avellaneda.
   WPOW, tr. by Catherine Rodriguez-Nieto
On Leaving Prison.   Luís de León.   SpanPo, tr. by Brenda M. Sackett
On Leaving Some Friends at an Early Hour.   John Keats.   CenSon
On Leaving the Artists' Colony.   Bruce Bawer.   RA
On leaving the city.   Seven Beginnings.   Olesya [or Olesia] Nikolayeva [or
   Nikolaeva].   ItGoST, tr. by Richard Graves and Carol Ueland
On Lending a Punch-Bowl.   Oliver Wendell Holmes.   TreFP
On Liberty and Slavery.   George Moses Horton.   APN-1
On Lien-ch'ang Palace.   Yüan Chên.   SuSp, tr. by Angela Jung Palandri
On Lieutenant Shift.   Ben Jonson.   OBSV
On life and extinction with sea wind changes.   Open-Eyed Angel.   David
   Rokeah [or Rokeakh].   MHP, tr. by Ruth Finer Mintz
On light's reflected word. (LL)   Heron, The.   Vernon Watkins.   AngWePo;
   GTBS-P; TCAWP; TwCP; UnPo
On Linden, when the sun was low.   Hohenlinden.   Thomas Campbell.   CABP;
   FaBoCh; GTBS-P; NOBE; NOBRP; OBWP; TFi
On Lisi's Golden Hair.   Francisco de Quevedo y Villegas.   WoPoe, tr. by Roy
   Campbell
  (When You Shake Loose Your Hair.)   SpanPo
On little rented chairs with gilded backs. (LL)   Evening Musicale.   Phyllis
   McGinley.   OBAL; OBCoV; Son
On Living.   Nazim Hikmet.   PoetW, tr. by Randy Blasing and Mutlu Konuk
On Living with a Fat Woman in Heaven.   Sidney Burris.   SwNoth
On Loch Leven.   Christian Carstairs.   ECWP
On Lolham Brigs in wild and lonely mood.   Flood, The.   John Clare.   RB
On London fell a clearer light.   Summer in England, 1914.   Alice Thompson
   Meynell.   BrRo; SoSe-8; WPE
On Long Island, they moved my clapboard house.   Whitman.   Larry Levis.
   ReTh
On longer evenings.   Coming.   Philip Larkin.   MoBrPo; OxBTC
On Looking into E. V. Rieu's Homer.   Patrick Kavanagh.   NOIV
On Lookout Mountain.   Robert Earl Hayden.   PoE
On Lord Cobham's Garden.   Nathaniel Cotton.   OBGa
On Lord Galloway.   Robert Burns.   FaBoEE   Fr. Epigrams on Lord Galloway.
On Lord Holland's Seat near Margate, Kent.   Thomas Gray.   NOEC; NPeEn;
   OBGa
  (And foxes stunk and littered in St Paul's.) (LL)   OBGa
  (Old, and abandoned by each venal friend.)   OBGa
On Lord Ila's Improvements, near Hounslow Heath.   Philip Dormer Stanhope,
   4th Earl of Chesterfield.   OBGa
On Lot's Wife Turned to Salt.   Agathias.   GrAn, tr. by Dudley Fitts
On Love.   Diophanes of Myrina.   WoPoe, tr. by Dudley Fitts
On Love.   Hsü Tsai-ssu.   CrYelRi; ErotSp, tr. by Sam Hamill
On Love of the Homeland.   Ernst Waldinger.   AuPH, tr. by George C.
   Schoolfield
On love's worst ugly day.   Theodore Roethke.   LCAP-2; NOBA   Fr.
   Meditations of an Old Woman.
On Loving Once and Loving Often.   Elizabeth Tollet.   LW

On Lucretia Borgia's Hair. Walter Savage Landor. *See* On Seeing a Hair of Lucretia Borgia

On Lucy, Countess[e] of Bedford. Ben Jonson. BASC; BeJo; NAEL-7v1; NOSC

On Lydia Distracted. Philip Ayres. EnLoPo; Son

On Maguire's Winter Campaign. Eochaidh Ó Heóghusa. PBRV

On Maids and Cats. Henricus Selyns. SCAP

On makeshift. On Makeshift Bedding. Vidya. WoPoe, *tr.* by Andrew Schelling

On Mammon. Herman Melville. OxBA *Fr.* Clarel: A Poem and Pilgrimage in the Holy Land.

On Man, on Nature, and on Human Life. William Wordsworth. FHYEP; PoE *Fr.* Excursion, The.

On Man, on Nature, and on Human Life. William Wordsworth. NAEL-6v2 *Fr.* Recluse; Home at Grasmere, The.

On Mankind. Attila József. IQMS, *tr.* by Adam Makkai

On Mankind. Mihály Vörösmarty. IQMS, *tr.* by Valerie Becker Makkai and Neville Masterman

On Marriage. Richard Crashaw. FaBoEE

On Marriage. Thomas Flatman. NOBL; PeLV (Bachelor's Song, The.) EnLoPo

On May Day, the girls of Penzance. Limerick. *Unknown.* PeLi

On May-day, when the lark began to rise. *Unknown.* NoSic *Fr.* Court of Love, The.

On Meeting a Gentlewoman in the Dark. *Unknown.* FaBoEE

On Meeting——, Esq., in St. James's Park. *Unknown.* ECWP

On Melancholy. *Unknown.* NOSC

On Mercenary and Unjust Bailiffs. Henricus Selyns. SCAP

On Michael Angelo. Washington Allston. APN-1

On Mike O'Day. *Unknown.* FaBoEE

On ministers, on actors. Public Beach No. 2. Andrey [*or* Andrei] Andreievich Voznesensky [*or* Voznesenskii]. RusPo, *tr.* by Robert Arthur Douglas Ford

On miserable Nearchos' bones lie lightly, earth. Last Lines. X. J. Kennedy. OBAL

On Miss Eleanor Ambrose, a Celebrated Beauty in Dublin. Philip Dormer Stanhope, 4th Earl of Chesterfield. FaBoEE

On Mr. G. Herberts Booke, The Temple. Richard Crashaw. ESCV; GeHe (Know you fair, on what you look?) CABP (Know you faire, on what you looke.) FSCP (On George Herbert's "The Temple" Sent to a Gentlewoman.) OxAEP-1 (On Mr. G. Herberts booke intituled the Temple of Sacred Poems, sent to a Gentlewoman.) FSCP (On Mr. George Herbert's Book, The Temple.) CABP

On Mr Milton's "Paradise Lost." Andrew Marvell. BASC; CABP; FSCP; NOSC

On Mr. Pitt's [*or* Pit's] Hair-Powder Tax. Robert Burns. FaBoEE

On misty waters, vast and vague. Hearing a Flute at Broken Bridge. Yün Shou-p'ing. CoBLCP, *tr.* by Jonathan Chaves

On Monday man gave God. Adam and God. Anne Wilkinson. MoCV

On Monsieur's Departure. Queen of England Elizabeth I. CABP; NAEL-5v1; NAEL-6v1; NAEL-7v1; NALW; WPE

On moon-washed apples of wonder. (LL) Moonlit Apples. John Drinkwater. OBMV; OxBTC; PoRA

On moonlit heath and lonesome bank. A. E. Housman. SCGP

On moors where people get lost and die of air. Water. Ted Hughes. OxBSP

On Mortality. Henry Colman. ChIV-1

On most nights now. Papa. Barbara Marsh. Prnts

On Motel Walls. David Wagoner. DiPo

On Mother's Day. Aileen Fisher. NTCP

On Mr. Abraham Cowley, His Death and Burial amongst the Ancient Poets. Sir John Denham. BeJo

On Mr. Dryden, Renegade. Aphra Behn. FaBoVe

On Mr. Edward Howard, upon His British Princes. Charles Sackville, 6th Earl of Dorset. OBSV

On Mr. G. Herberts booke intituled the Temple of Sacred Poems, sent to a Gentlewoman. Richard Crashaw. *See* On Mr. G. Herberts Booke, The Temple

On Mr. George Herbert's Book, The Temple. Richard Crashaw. *See* On Mr. G. Herberts Booke, The Temple

On Mr. Nash's Picture at Full Length. Jane Brereton. WPE

On Mr. Nash's Present of His Own Picture at Full Length. Philip Dormer Stanhope, 4th Earl of Chesterfield. NOEC

On Mr. Paine's Rights of Man. Philip Freneau. NAAL-2v1; NAAL-3; NAAL-5 (Thus briefly sketched the sacred RIGHTS OF MAN.) ColAP

On Mr. Pricke. *Unknown.* FaBoEE

On Mr. Rice the Manciple of Christ Church in Oxford. Richard Corbet [*or* Corbett]. NOSC

On Mr. Shirley's Poems. Thomas Stanley. BeJo

On Mrs. Montagu. Ann Yearsley. ECWP; RWP

On Mundane Acquaintances. Joseph Hilaire Pierre Belloc. FaBoEE; OBCoV; OxBTC

On Muranowska Street. Myra Sklarew. TaR

On My Bed I Sought Him. Bible, *O.T.* TrJP, *tr.* by Willis Barnstone *Fr.* Song of Solomon, The [*or* The Song of Songs].

On My Birthday. Yehuda Amichai [*or* Amikhai]. MHP, *tr.* by Ruth Finer Mintz

On My Birthday, July 21. Matthew Prior. OBEV

On My Birthday—Sick. Li K'ai-hsien. CoBLCP, *tr.* by Jonathan Chaves

On My Boy Henry. Elizabeth, Lady Brackley Egerton. EMWP

On My Child's Death. Joseph, Freiherr von Eichendorff. WoPoe, *tr.* by William DeWitt Snodgrass and W. D. Snodgrass

On My Dear Grandchild Simon Bradstreet, [Who Died on 16TH November, 1669, Being But A Month And One Day Old]. Anne Bradstreet. ColAP; NAAL-2v1; NAAL-3; SCAP (No sooner came, but gone, and fall'n asleep.) ColAP

On my desk, a set of labels. City Gent. Craig Raine. NoAM

On my desk is a small bottle. Jasmine. E. Ethelbert Miller. GT

On My First Daughter. Ben Jonson. BASC; BeJo; EBEV; FaBoEE; NAEL-5v1; NAEL-6v1; NAEL-7v1; NOBE; NOSC; NoP-4; PoE

On My First Son[ne]. Ben Jonson. AWP; AmFaPo; BASC; BeJo; CABP; ClHu; EBEV; FaBoEE; HAP; InPK-6; MakPoe; NAEL-5v1; NAEL-6v1; NAEL-7v1; NIL-7; NIP-4; NOSC; NPeEn; NoP-4; OxBEV; OxBSP; PBRV; PoE; PoPoPo; RB; RaBo; SCGP; TFi; TRP; WeW-3; WoPoe (On My Son.) NOBE

On My Fortieth Birthday. John Tripp. AngWePo

On my fourteenth birthday. Curtis Fuller. Rick Madigan. SeSe

On My Fourteenth Wedding Anniversary I Ride on Trains. Cornelia Veenendaal. GM

On my honorable Grandmother, Elizabeth Countess of Shrewbury. Lady Jane Cavendish. EMWP

On My Joyful Departure from the Same City. Samuel Taylor Coleridge. NBLV

On my knees to cry, *Who the hell are you, kid?* (LL) Roundhouse Voices, The. Dave Jeddie Smith. NoAM; VCAP

On my land grew a green tree. Arthur Rex Dugard Fairburn. PeNZ *Fr.* Album Leaves.

On My Late Dear Wife. Jonathan Richardson. NOEC

On my living room wall hangs a Navajo rug. Storm Pattern. Greg Pape. PBCAP

On My Lord Bacon. John Danforth. SCAP

On my Northwest coast in the midst of the night a fisherman's group stands watching. Torch, The. Walt Whitman. SAmP

On my old battledress tonight, my sweet. (LL) Goodbye. Alun Lewis. AngWePo; BoLoP; NAEL-5v2; NAEL-6v2; NoP-4; OBWP; OxBTC; PoWW; TCAWP

On My Pneumonia. Mihály Csokonai Vitéz. IQMS, *tr.* by Joseph Leftwich

On my return. L. A. Davidson. HA

On my right hand I'll seat one of my loves. Denis Gennad'evich Novikov. TCRP

On my school notebooks. Paul Éluard. TTTS *Fr.* Liberty.

On My Son. Ben Jonson. *See* On My First Son[ne]

On My Sorrowful Life. Moses Ibn Ezra. TrJP, *tr.* by Solomon Solis-Cohen

On my thigh, and mockery was still the unforgivable sin. (LL) Blasphemy, A. Rodney Jones. IllVoic; WeW-3

On My Thirty-third Birthday. Byron. FaBoEE

On My Visitt to WS Which I Dreamt of That Night. Lucy Hutchinson. EMWP

On my wall hangs a Japanese carving. Mask of Evil, The. Bertolt Brecht. PoSu; WoPoe, *tr.* by Hoffman Reynolds Hays

On my walls there are three. Photographs of My Father. Judith Ortiz Cofer. ExTi

On My Way from South Mountain to North Mountain, I Glance at the Scenery from the Lake. Hsieh Ling-yün. ColAnChi, *tr.* by Kang-i Sun Chang

On my way home from school. Testing-Tree, The. Stanley Kunitz. APT-2; UnPo

On my way to Mass. Lass from Bally-na-Lee, The. Anthony [*or* Antoine] Raftery [*or* Raifteiri]. BIrV, *tr.* by Desmond O'Grady

On My Wedding Day. Sarah Fyge Egerton. EMWP

On my window sill. Before Their Tanks. Tawfiq Zayyad. MAP, *tr.* by Charles Doria and Sharif Elmusa

On my winter walk. Hugo Majer. Spl

On Myself. Edith Bone. FaBoEE

On Myself. Anne Finch, Countess of Winchilsea. OxBSP (Good Heav'n, I thank thee, since it was designed.) NoP-4

On Naucratius, Brother of St. Basil. Gregory of Nazianzus, Saint. GrAn, *tr.* by Robin Skelton

On Neal's Ashes. Allen Ginsberg. PmAP; PoM

On New Waters. Endre Ady. IQMS, tr. by Anton N. Nyerges

On New Year's Day. Basho. SoOfWa, tr. by Sam Hamill

On New Year's Day. Nantembo. ZenPo, tr. by Takashi Ikemoto and Lucien Stryk

On New Year's Day in the morning. (LL) Mother Goose. LB; OxNR

On New Year's Day of the Year Kuei-ssu (1533), Releasing Live Creatures. Wang T'ing-hsiang. CoBLCP, tr. by Jonathan Chaves

On New Year's Eve of the Year Hsin-wei (1751), Drinking Alone and Sadly Chanting Poems, I Remembered My Aged Wife Who Is Living at Twisting River. Chin Nung.

"Traveler, I've been through a thousand changes, A." CoBLCP

On News. Thomas Traherne. See Third Century, The

On nights like this, when bayou and lagoon. Orgie. Madison Cawein. APN-2

On nights when hail / falls noisily. Lady Izumi. BoWoP; WoPoe, tr. by Willis Barnstone

On No Work of Words. Dylan Thomas. OxBSP

On Noman, a Guest. Joseph Hilaire Pierre Belloc. FaBoEE

On Non-dependence of Mind. Dogen. EnlH

On Not Being Milton. Tony Harrison. CABP; HarvBoo; NoP-4 Fr. School of Eloquence, The.

On Not Being Your Lover. Medbh McGuckian. PBCIP; PNI

On Observing a Large Red-Streak Apple. Philip Freneau. NAAL-2v1; NAAL-3

On ochre walls in ice-formed caves shaggy Neanderthals. To My Son Parker, Asleep in the Next Room. Bob Kaufman. TwCP; VGW

On Old River Mountain. Fall River Song. Li Po. CrYelRi, tr. by Sam Hamill

On Oliver Goldsmith. David Garrick. FaBoEE; OxBEV

On, on, on. Dirigible, The. Chris Wallace-Crabbe. CBAP

On, on the vessel steals. On the Rhine. Charles Stuart Calverley. PeLV

On, on to the darkest continent. Dedicated to Dr. W. H. Sheppard. Maggie Pogue Johnson. CBWP-4

On One Condition. Charles Madge. SPE

On one fix'd point all nature moves. On the Uniformity and Perfection of Nature. Philip Freneau. TCAPo

On one of those days with the Legion. Day with the Foreign Legion, A. Reed Whittemore. CoAP; CoAmPo

On one side the hedge, on the other the brook:. Common Path, The. Glyn Jones. AngWePo

On one summer's day, sun was shining fine. Bill Bailey, Won't You Please Come Home. Hughie Cannon. OBAL

On One That Lived Ingloriously. John Hoskyns [or Hoskins]. FaBoEE

On One Who Died Discovering Her Kindness. John Sheffield, Duke of Buckingham and Normandy. OBEV

On open downland we're as open as he—. Long-Man. Grace Nichols. Oth

On Opening. Mark Wunderlich. NAPBL

On Originality. Bill Manhire. HarvBoo; PeNZ

On other fields and other scenes the morn. Burnt Lands. G. D. Roberts. GSo

On Our Crucified Lord, Naked and Bloody. Richard Crashaw. See Upon the Body of Our Blessed Lord, Naked and Bloody

On our last evening on this land we chop our days. On Our Last Evening on This Land. Mahmoud Darwish. PoetW, tr. by Agha Shahid Ali, Mona Anis, Ahmad Dallal and Nigel Ryan Fr. Eleven Stars over Andalusia.

On our meat and on us all. (LL) Grace for a Child. Robert Herrick. AWP; NAEL-5v1; NAEL-6v1; PoE; TFi

On our Pharsalian Plaines, comprizing space. Seaconk Plain Engagement. Benjamin Thompson. SCAP

On Our Saviour's Passion. Francis Quarles. PeECV Fr. Divine Fancies.

On our way home, leaving absolutely nothing behind us. (LL) Sunday in Great Tew. Peter McDonald. ModIr; PNI

On our wedding day we climbed the top. Manhattan Pastures. Sandra Hochman. YaYoPo

On Oxford. John Keats. SCGP

(Lines Rhymed in a Letter from Oxford.) OBCoV

(Lines Rhymed in a Letter Received (by J. H. R[eynolds]) from Oxford.) PeLV

(On Oxford. A Parody.) OxAEP-2

On pale afternoons. Autumnal. "Rubén Dario." SpanPo, tr. by Anita Volland

On parent knees, a naked new-born child. Epigram. Sir William Jones. FaBoEE; OBEV

On parquet. Simon Cutts. PoSol Fr. Pianostool Footnotes.

On Parting. Edward Coote [or Coate] Pinkney. APN-1; TCAPo

On Parting with a Friend. Mary Weston Fordham. CBWP-4

On Parting with Moses ibn Ezra. Judah Halevi. TrJP, tr. by Solomon Solis-Cohen

On Parting with the Buddhist Pilgrim Ling-Ch'ê. Liu Ch'ang-ch'ing. WoPoe, tr. by Witter Bynner

On Passing over a Dreary Tract of Country, and Near the Ruins of a Deserted Chapel, during a Tempest. Charlotte Smith. BoWoP; WPE Fr. Montalbert.

On Passing the New Menin Gate. Siegfried Sassoon. NAEL-5v2; NAEL-6v2; NoAM; NoP-4; OBMV; PoWW; Son

On, Pegasus! Why, whither turn ye? Survey of the Amphitheatre, A. Moses Browne. NOEC

On Peter Robinson. Francis, Lord Jeffrey Jeffrey. FaBoEE; NBLV

(Epitaph on Peter Robinson.) OxBoLi

On Philiphaugh a fray began. Battle of Philiphaugh, The. Unknown. ESPB

On Pilgrimage. Czeslaw Milosz. AmFaPo, tr. by Robert Hass

On Plato's Grave. Unknown. GrAn, tr. by William J. Philbin

On Platonic Love. Samuel Boyse. ECEV

On Playwright. Ben Jonson. NoP-4

On Plaza Garibaldi. Nellie Wong. OpBo

On Poet-Ape. Ben Jonson. Son

On Poetry. Franco Buffoni. ItPo, tr. by Gayle Ridinger

On Poetry. Yüan Hao-wen.

"Croaking frog in a well sees the sky from end to end, A." SuSp

"Fade the kingfisher blue, trim the red, blend the colors." SuSp

"Poet's heart is wrenched and wrenched again until his head turns white, A." SuSp

On Poetry: a Rhapsody. Jonathan Swift. OBSV

Critics. HAP; SCV

On Poets. Pope. FaBoEE

On polar and on southern seas. Nikolai Stepanovich Gumilyov [or Gumiliov or Gumilev]. TCRP Fr. Captains.

On Ponkawtasset, Since, We Took Our Way. Henry David Thoreau. NCAP

On Portents. Robert Graves. FaBoMo; HarvBoo

On prancing steed with nodding plume, I join their hunting sports. (LL) Tennyson's Poems. Josephine D. Henderson Heard. CBWP-4; SWaP

On Prince Frederick. Unknown. FaBoEE; NOBL

(Epitaph on Prince Frederick.) OxBoLi

On Professor Coué. Charles Cuthbert Inge. OBCoV

On Professor Drennan's Verse. Roy Campbell. GTBS-P

On Pym. William Drummond, of Hawthornden. NOSC

On quarry walls the spleenwort spreads. Rockferns. Norman Nicholson. MoBrPo

On Queen Caroline. Unknown. FaBoEE

(Queen Caroline.) OBCoV

On Queen Caroline's Deathbed. Pope. NPeEn

On Rachmaninoff's Birthday. Frank O'Hara. PoM

On Ragged Mountain birches twists from rifts in granite. Granite and Grass. Donald Hall. DiPo

On rainy leaves / Glow. Ōshima Ryōta. ZenPo, tr. by Takashi Ikemoto and Lucien Stryk

On rainy Monday nights of an eternal November. (LL) Classic Ballroom Dances. Charles Simic. LCAP-2; WeW-3

On Re-recording Mozart. Susan Wicks. OxBSo

On Reading a Love Poem. Kedarnath Singh. OMIP, tr. by Vinay Dharwadker

On Reading a Recent Greek Poet. Bertolt Brecht. WoPoe, tr. by John Peck

On Reading Aloud My Early Poems. John Williams. WeW-3

On Reading an Archeological Article. Molara Ogundipe-Leslie. HBAPE

On Reading "God." Gilbert Keith Chesterton. OBCoV

On Reading Poems to a Senior Class at South High. David Chapman Berry. SoSe-2

On Reading Rumi. Mimi Khalvati. MFPA

On Reading The Book of Odes. Cao Bá Quát. AWTN, tr. by Hunh Sanh Thông

On Reading the Life of Haroun Er Reshid. Madison Cawein. APN-2

On reading the new physics—Creation and Cosmology. Cosi Fabian. HW

On Reading the Seas and Mountains Classic. J. R. Hightower. ColAnChi

On Receiving a Branch of Mezereon Which Flowered at Woodstock, December 1809. Mary Tighe. RWP

On Receiving a Crown of Ivy from the Same. Leigh Hunt. Son

On Receiving My Letter of Termination. Yüan Hung-tao. CoBLCP; ColAnChi, tr. by Jonathan Chaves

On Receiving News of the War. Isaac Rosenberg. HarvBoo; MoBrPo; OBWP; OxAEP-2; PeFWW; PeSAV; PoWW

On Reconnaissance. Mikhail Arkadyevich [orArkad'evich] Svetlov. TCRP, tr. by Daniel Weissbort

On Recrossing the Rocky Mountains after Many Years. John Charles Frémont. AiP

On Red Square, on the chopping block. Yury [or Iurii] Pavlovich Odarchenko. TCRP

On Refusal of Aid between Nations. Dante Gabriel Rossetti. EBEV; OxAEP-2; SCGP

On Rembrant; Occasioned by His Picture of Jacob's Dream. Washington Allston. APN-1

On Returning to My Garden and Field. T'ao Ch'ien [or T'ao Yuan-ming].
  "I plant beans at the foot of the southern hill." SuSp
  "When I was young, I did not fit into the common mold." SuSp
On Returning to Sung Mountain. Wang Wei. SuSp, tr. by Paul W. Kroll
On Revisiting Cintra after the Death of Catarina. Luis de Camões [or
  Camões]. AWP, tr. by Richard Garnett
On Richmond Park. Stephen Duck.
On Riding to See Dean Swift in the Mist of the Morning. Pope. FaBoEE
  (Visiting Dr Swift.) OBCoV
On roads beyond the camp the Khamsin struck me. Yitzhak Lamdan. MHP
  Fr. In the Khamsin.
On roadsides, / in fall fields, / in rumpy bunches. Goldenrod. Mary Oliver.
  NIL-7
On Robert Buchanan, Who Attacked Him under the Pseudonym of "Thomas
  Maitland." Dante Gabriel Rossetti. FaBoEE
On Rodin's "L'Illusion, Sœur d'Icare." Trumbull Stickney. APN-2
On Roman Feet my stumbling Muse declines. Elegiack Verse on Mr. Elijah
  Corlet, An. Nehemiah Walter. SCAP
On Roofs of Terry Street. Douglas Dunn. NPeEn; OxBTC
On Rosh Hashanah, I didn't bow. Remembering Our Fathers. Chava Pinchas-
  Cohen. DTA, tr. by Miriyam Glazer
On Rÿneveld, an Unpopular Dutch Judge. Unknown. FaBoEE
On S. John the Baptist. Thomas Stanley. ChIV-2
On Saint-Urbain Street. Milton Acorn. NOBC
On Sanazar's being honoured with six hundred Duckets by the Clarissimi of
  Venice, for composing an Elegiack Hexastick of The City. A Satyre.
  Richard Lovelace. PBRV
On Sandro's Flora. Trumbull Stickney. APN-2
On Saturday night shall be [all] my care. Saturday, Sunday. Mother Goose.
  OxNR; ReMoGo
On Saturday with joy Bill dubs his half. Linen Weaver, The. Unknown.
  NOEC
On Saturn the sexes are three. Limerick. Unknown. PeLi
On Saul and David. Francis Quarles. ChIV-1
On Saying Goodbye to the Lady in Green. 'Ali 'Abdallah Khalifa. MAP, tr.
  by Alistair Elliot and Lena Jayyusi
On Scott's Poem "The Field of Waterloo." Thomas Erskine, 1st Baron Erskine.
  NBLV
On sea and land alike. Poseidippus. GrAn
On Seein an Aik-Tree Sprent Wi Galls. Robert Garioch. OxBS
On Seeing a Bird-Catcher. Eliza Cook. VWP
On Seeing a Firefly in My Room. Yang Chi. CoBLCP, tr. by Jonathan Chaves
On Seeing a Hair of Lucretia Borgia. Walter Savage Landor. HAP; NPeEn;
  WeW-3
  (On Lucretia Borgia's Hair.) SCGP
On Seeing a Little Child Spin a Coin of Alexander the Great. Charles
  Tennyson Turner. NOBVV
On Seeing a Painting of Plants and Insects by·Chü-ning. Mei Yao Ch'en.
  SuSp, tr. by Jonathan Chaves
On Seeing a Piece of Our Artillery Brought into Action. Wilfred Owen. GSo
On Seeing a Tapestry Chair-Bottom Beautifully Worked by His Daughter for
  Mrs Holroyd. Richard Owen Cambridge. ECEV
On Seeing an Officer's Widow Distracted. Mary Barber. ECWP; NOEC
On Seeing an Old Poet in the Café Royal. Sir John Betjeman. OxBEV; UV
On Seeing Francis Jeffrey Riding on a Donkey. Sydney Smith. FaBoEE
On Seeing the Elgin Marbles. John Keats. CenSon; GSo; NAEL-5v2; NAEL-
  6v2; NIL-7; NIP-4
On Seeing the Field Being Singed. Lady Ise. BoWoP, tr. by Etsuko Terasaki
On Seeing the Picture of Æolus by Pelegrino Tibalbi, in the Institute at Bologna.
  Washington Allston. APN-1
On Seeing the Reformation Memorial in Geneva. Gyula Illyés. IQMS, tr. by
  John Wilkinson
On Seeing Two Brown Boys in a Catholic Church. Frank Horne. TTY
On Seeing Weather-Beaten Trees. Adelaide Crapsey. APT-1
On Sensibility: A Fragment. Isabella Lickbarrow. RWP
On Shakespear[e]. John Milton. CABP; MeLP; NAEL-5v1; NoP-4; NOSC;
  PoE; PoPoPo; PoRA; SCGP
  (Epitaph on the Admirable Dramatic Poet, W. Shakespeare, An.) FaBoEE
  (What needs my Shakespeare for his honor'd bones.) CABP
  (What needs my Shakespeare for his honored bones.) NAEL-6v1; NAEL-
  7v1; NoP-4; PoPoPo
On Shakespeare and Voltaire. Thomas Holcroft. NOEC
On Shakespeare Critics. Alec Derwent Hope. OxBC Fr. Dunciad Minor.
On shallow straw, in shadeless glass. Take One Home for the Kiddies. Philip
  Larkin. OxBTC
On Sharing a Husband. Hồ Xuân Hu'o'ng. WoPoe, tr. by John Balaban
On shining heights where Thought with stately tread. Emerson. Henrietta
  Cordelia Ray. CBWP-3

On Shooting a Swallow in Early Youth. Charles Tennyson Turner. NOBVV
On Shutting the Door. Lotte Kramer. Prnts
On Sidewalks, on Streetcorners, as Girls. Allison Joseph. IllVoic
On Sight of a Gentlewoman's Face in the Water. Thomas Carew. CaPo
On Sir G. B. his defeat. Alexander Brome. PBRV
On Sir Henry Ferrett, M.P. John Bingham Morton. OBCoV
On Sir J—— S—— Saying in a Sarcastic Manner, My Books Would Make Me
  Mad; an Ode. Elizabeth Thomas. CABP; ECWP
On Sir John Calf. Unknown. FaBoEE
On Sir John Hill, M. D., Playwright. David Garrick. FaBoEE; NBLV
On Sir John Vanbrugh [Architect]. Abel Evans. FaBoEE; NPeEn
On Sir Nathaniel Wraxall the Historian. George, the Younger Colman.
  FaBoEE
On Sir Robert Cotton the Antiquary. Thomas Randolph. NOSC
On Sir Walter Rawleigh at His Execution. Unknown. NOSC
On Sitting down to Read "King Lear" Once Again. John Keats. CABP;
  EBEV; GSo; NAEL-5v2; NAEL-6v2; NoP-4; PoPoPo
On Sitting down to Write, I Decide Instead to Go to Fred Herko's Concert.
  Diane Di Prima. PmAP
On Slieve Gullion 'men and mountain meet." On Slieve Gullion. Michael
  Longley. BiHa
On Snow. Li K'ai-hsien.
  "Jade trees from the rear courtyard of the empire of Ch'en." CoBLCP
On Snuff-Taking. Elizabeth Teft. ECWP
On Solitude. Abraham Cowley. See Of Solitude
On Solomon Pavy, a Child of Queen Elizabeth's Chapel. Ben Jonson. See
  Epitaph on S. P. [Salomon or Salathiel Pavy], a Child of Q[ueen]
  El[izabeth's] Chapel
On some bright morning filled with loving kindness. (LL) Cups. Gwen
  Harwood. EmeKit; HarvBoo
On some island I long to be. Saint Columcille [or Columba]. BIrV
On some rude fragment of the rocky shore. Written on the Sea Shore.—
  October, 1784. Charlotte Smith. CenSon; RWP
On Some Shells Found Inland. Trumbull Stickney. APN-2; Son
On Some South African Novelists. Roy Campbell. FaBoEE; GTBS-P; InPK-
  6; MoBrPo; NOBL; OBCoV; OxAEP-2; OxBEV; OxBTC; PeLV
On some Vermont road. Mating the Goats. Aliki Barnstone. BoWoP
On Some Violets Planted in My Garden by a Friend. Elizabeth Cobbold.
  CenSon
On Something, that Walk[e]s Somewhere. Ben Jonson. BASC; BeJo; NAEL-
  5v1; NAEL-6v1; NAEL-7v1; OxBSP; PAI; PoE; SCGP
On Sound. Wei Ying-wu. SuSp, tr. by Irving Y. Lo
On South Africa. Kim C. Lee. InTrad
On South Street, above a burning trashcan, a rasta. Reel around the Shadow.
  James Harms. NAPBL
On Spies. Ben Jonson. BeJo; FaBoVe; NPeEn; NoP-4; OxBSP; WoPoe
On Springfield Mountain there did dwell. Springfield Mountain. Unknown.
  TCAPo
On St. James's Park, as Lately Improved by His Majesty. Edmund Waller.
  BASC; BeJo; NOSC; OBGa
On St. Martin's evening green. Nuns at Eve. John Malcolm Brinnin. TwCP
On starry heights. Conflict of Convictions, The. Herman Melville. APN-2;
  CBCWP; NOBA
On Stella's Birthday, 1718/1719. Jonathan Swift. See Stella's Birthday;
  Written in the Year 1718[9]
On sticky summer Sunday afternoons. Elwood Collins: Summer of 1932.
  Dave Etter. IllVoic
On Stony Pierian Spurs. Osip Emilevich Mandelstam [or Mandelshtam].
  TCRusP, tr. by John Glad
On street corners east and west. Girl from Flower Mountain, The. Han Yü.
  SuSp, tr. by Charles Hartman
On Stripping Bark from Myself. Alice Walker. NAAAL
On Sturminster Foot-Bridge. Thomas Hardy. OxBSP
On Such A Day. Song-Jook Park. FSt
On such a day as this. Soundings. Paula Gunn Allen. HATNAP
On such a morning as this. In Memory of Basil, Marquess of Dufferin and
  Ava. Sir John Betjeman. OBWP
On Such a Night As This. Hugh Martin. ReLy
On such a night, or such a night. Emily Dickinson. TCAPo
On summer evenings blue, pricked by the wheat. Sensation. Arthur Rimbaud.
  AWP
On Sunday Afternoons. Sunday Afternoons. Anthony Thwaite. OxBTC
On Sunday morning, then he comes. Mr. Wells. Elizabeth Madox Roberts.
  KaS
On Sunday the hawk fell on Bigging. Hawk, The. George Mackay Brown.
  NoP-4; RB
On Sundays, from upstairs, a grown man's voice. Light's Reading, The. Alan
  Williamson. PoSol

On Sundays I watch the hermits coming out of their holes.   Studying the Language.   Eiléan Ní Chuilleanáin.   EmeKit; NPeEn

On Sundays the children would go to check.   Petrograd Side, The.   Lev Vladimir Loseff [or Losev].   TCRusP, tr. by Henry Pickford

On Sundays when the weather's good, traditionally.   Provincial Sundays.   Ramón López Velarde.   TCLAP, tr. by Julián Manríquez

On sunnier days a new coat of arms made the ocean high.   Boats.   Bernadette Mayer.   FTOS

On sunny summer Sunday afternoons in Harlem.   Passing.   Langston Hughes.   APSN; APT-2; SAmP

On Sweet Coffee.   Ábrahám Barcsay.   IQMS, tr. by Thomas Kabdebo

On Sweet Coffee.   Ábrahám Barcsay.   IQMS, tr. by Peter Zollman

On Sweet Killen Hill.   Tom MacIntyre.   CIP-2

(Sweet Killen Hill.)   PBCIP

On Sympathisers with the American Revolution.   Charles Wesley.   NOCV

On t'other side there stood destruction bare.   Geoffrey Chaucer.   FaBoWar, tr. by John Dryden   Fr. Canterbury Tales, The.

On tape and late at night.   Late Night Radio.   Geoff Page.   BMAP

On Teaching the Young.   Yvor Winters.   APT-2; MakPoe; NOBA; NoAM

On that big estate there is no rain.   Monangamba.   Antonio Jacinto.   TTY

On that day in autumn, when winter.   Engraving, An.   Aleksandr Petrovich Tkachenko.   ItGoST, tr. by Maia Tekses

On that day there was a holiday on earth.   Remembrance of Yalta.   Bella [or Izabella] Akhatovna Akhmadulina.   TCRP, tr. by Albert C. Todd

On that day when I brought wine to Red Bridge.   Occasional Poem: Upon Seeing Lotuses Bloom in a Vase.   Wang Shih-chieng.   SuSp, tr. by Richard John Lynn

On that great, that awful day,   Dies IrÆ.   Thomas Babington Macaulay, 1st Baron Macaulay.   ChIV-2

On that last night before we went.   Tennyson.   NAEL-6v2   Fr. In Memoriam A. H. H.

On That Mountain.   Rachel Hadas.   ExTi

On that unfashionable gyre again. (LL)   Gyres, The.   W. B. Yeats.   GTBS-P; HAP; NoAM

On the 3 of September, 1651.   Katherine Philips.   BASC; EMWP; PBRV

On the 5th of December 1791 Wolfgang Amadeus.   Mozart in Heaven.   Manuel Bandeira.   TCLAP, tr. by Dudley Poore

On the 21st March 1960.   I Remember Sharpeville.   Sipho Sepamla.   AF

On the Adequacy of Landscape.   Wallace Stevens.   SAmP

On the advice of Praxilla.   Aristophanes of Byzantium.   WoPoe, tr. by Sam Hamill

On the Amtrak from Boston to New York City.   Sherman Alexie.   PoPoPo

On the Anniversary of My Father's Death.   Michael Lieberman.   BloBone

On the Anniversary of Your Death.   Karen L. Mitchell.   GT

On the Antiquity of Microbes.   Strickland W. Gillilan.   NBLV

On the Aphorism "L'Amitié est l'Amour sans Ailes."   Charlotte Smith.   CABP; PEW

On the Appeal from the Race of Sheba: II.   Léopold Sédar Senghor.   TTY

On the apple.   Raymond Roseliep.   HA

On the Approach of Autumn.   Amelia Alderson Opie.   CenSon

On the Armada That Battled against England.   Luis de Góngora y Argote.   SpanPo, tr. by Ian Fletcher and Brian Soper

On the Army of Spartans, Who Died at Thermopylae.   Simonides.   FaBoEE

On the Assumption.   Richard Crashaw.   ESCV

On the Astrologer and Almanac Maker, John Partridge.   Jonathan Swift.   FaBoEE

On the Asylum Road.   Charlotte Mew.   MoBrPo; VWP

On the Atchison, Topeka and the Santa Fe.   Johnny Mercer.   ReLy

On the Athenians Who Died at the Hellespont, 440–39 B.C..   Unknown.   GrAn, tr. by Peter Jay

On the Author's Husband Desiring Her to Write Some Verses.   Mary Whateley.   ECWP

On the Babel-Builders.   Francis Quarles.   ChIV-1

On the Back of a Photograph.   János Pilinszky.   PoSu, tr. by Peter Jay

On the back trails, in sun glasses.   Kenyatta Listening to Mozart.   Imamu Amiri Baraka.   PmAP

On the balcony of the tower.   Exile in Japan.   Su Man-shu.   BLT, tr. by Kenneth Rexroth

On the bald street breaks the blank day. (LL)   Tennyson.   EBEV; EBVV; FHYEP; GTBS-P; HAP; HeIP-4; NAEL-6v2; NAWM-7v2; NOBE; NPeEn; OxBEV; SCGP; SCV; SoSe-8; UnPo   Fr. In Memoriam A. H. H.

On the bank of Lake Rouge a chestnut steed treads proudly.   Su Man-shu.   SuSp   Fr. Poems Written during My Sojourn in Japan.

On the banks of her butterfly pond.   Fishing among the Learned.   Nikky Finney.   SpirFl

On the Banks of the Duero.   Antonio Machado Ruiz.   STV, tr. by John Frederick Nims

On the banks of the Lachlan they caught us.   Kiacatoo.   Kevin Gilbert.   IBA

On the Baptized Ethiopian.   Richard Crashaw.   ChIV-2; FaBoEE, tr. by Richard Crashaw

(Acts 8; On the Baptized Æthiopian.)   SacPr, tr. by Richard Crashaw

(Let it no longer be a forlorn hope.)   NoP-4

On the bare slope, wind in my hair.   Invasion.   Anna Enquist.   TuT, tr. by Peter Van de Kamp

On the bare veld where nothing ever grows.   Veld Eclogue: The Pioneers, A.   Roy Campbell.   OBSV

On the Bath of Pallas.   Callimachus.   HePo, tr. by Barbara Hughes Fowler Fr. Hymns.

On the Bay.   Richard Watson Gilder.   APN-2

On the Beach.   Tom Clark.   BodElec

On The Beach.   John Corben.   Spl

On the Beach.   Jane Hirshfield.   ExTi

On the Beach at Fontana.   James Joyce.   MoBrPo; OBMV; RB; RaBo

On the Beach at Night.   Walt Whitman.   APN-1; AWP; MoAmPo; NOBA; NoP-4; OxBA; SAmP; TCAPo

On the Beach at Night Alone.   Walt Whitman.   APN-1; TAP

"On the beach," said John sadly, "there's such."   Limerick.   Isaac Asimov.   PeLi

On the Bearing of Waitresses.   Rodney Jones.   ReTh

On the Bell Frieze of a Roman Church.   René Char.   WoPoe, tr. by Mark Rudman

On the bench I wait.   Kenneth Yasuda.   HA

On the Benefactions in the Late Frost.   Pope.   NOEC; OxBSP

On the beryl-rimmed rebecs of Ruby.   Lily Adair.   Thomas Holley Chivers.   APN-1; OBAL

On the Bible.   Thomas Traherne.   ChIV-1

On the Bible.   Unknown.   NOSC

On the Bird Which Still Flew, though Its Head Was Severed.   Janus Pannonius.   IQMS, tr. by Anthony Barrett

On the Birth-Day of Queen Katherine.   Anne Killigrew.   EMWP

On the Birth of His Son.   Su Tung-p'o (Su Shih).   AWP; OBVE; WoPoe, tr. by Arthur Waley

On the Birth of Jesus.   Andreas Gryphius.   GePo, tr. by George C. Schoolfield

On the birthday of our most Pure Savior.   Conversational Melody, A Good Verse, A.   Nikolai Alekseievich Klyuyev [or Kliuev or Klyuev].   TCRusP, tr. by John Glad

On the blackened ridge of Psara.   Destruction of Psara, The.   Dionysios Solomos.   WoPoe, tr. by Edmund Keeley and Philip Sherrard

On the blank stones of the landing. (LL)   Colossus, The.   Sylvia Plath.   FaBoWP; HCAP; NALW; NOBA; NoAM; NoP-4; TAP; VCAP; WoPoe

On the Blessed Virgins Bashfulnesse.   Richard Crashaw.   HAP; OxBSP

On the blue waves.   Muso Soseki.   EaWin, tr. by W. S. Merwin

On the bog road the blackthorn flowers, the turf-stacks.   Anthony Cronin.   BIrV   Fr. R.M.S. Titanic.

On the bonnie banks o' Fordie. (LL)   Babylon; or, The Bonnie Banks o' Fordie.   Unknown.   ESPB; OxBB

On the Border, First Series.   Tu Fu.   CoBCP, tr. by Burton Watson

On the bottom of the sky.   Burning Shewolf.   Vasco [or Vasko] Popa.   PFTM-2; VCWP, tr. by Charles Simic

On the boundary of snow and melting.   Georgy [or Georgii] Vladimirovich Ivanov.   TCRusP, tr. by Daniel Weissbort

On the bridges / And along the banks.   Kenneth Rexroth.   APSN   Fr. Love Poems of Marichiko, The.

On the bright road to Rome, beyond Mantua.   Italian Eclogues.   Derek Walcott.   BAP-97

On the Bright Side.   Carter Revard.   VoR

On the Brink of Death.   Michelangelo Buonarroti.   AWP, tr. by John Addington Symonds

On the broad River Huai, dotted with islets, a village suddenly appears.   Little Village, A.   Mei Yao Ch'en.   SuSp, tr. by Jonathan Chaves

On the Building of a New Church.   Unknown.   See Building of a New Church, The

On the Burial of His Brother.   Catullus.   AWP, tr. by Aubrey Beardsley   Fr. Carmina.

On the Buses with Dostoyevsky.   Geoff Hattersley.   NeBl

On the Butterflies.   T'ang Yin.   CoBLCP, tr. by Jonathan Chaves

On the cabin-roof I lie.   Strenuous Life, The.   Henry Sidgwick.   OBCoV

On the Candidates for the Laurel.   Pope.   FaBoEE

On the Card[e]s, and Dice.   Sir Walter Ralegh.   ChIV-2; RB

On the Carpet, Staring at Myself.   Slavko Mihalic.   PoSu, tr. by Peter Kastmiler

On the Castle of Chillon.   Byron.   See Prisoner of Chillon, The

On the ceiling.   Gary Hotham.   HA

On the ceiling of the dim pavilion.   End of the Affair, The.   E. San Juan, Jr.   ReBoTo

On the Changes in France.   János Batsányi.   IQMS, tr. by Matthew Mead

On the chest of a barmaid in Sale.   Limerick.   Unknown.   PeLi

On the child crying for the bird of the snow. (LL) Snow. Edward Thomas. FaBoTw; OPOU

On the Christmaswhite plains of the floured and flowering kitchen table. Bread of this World; Praises III, The. Thomas McGrath. RaBo

On the Cicada: In Prison. Lo Pin-wang. ColAnChi, tr. by Stephen Owen

On the Circuit. W. H. Auden. NOBL; OxBTC

(Among pelagian travelers.) FaBoA

On the Circumsision: New Year's Day. Luke Wadding [or Waddinge]. NOIV

On the city limits where I live. City Limits, The. Attila József. IQMS, tr. by Anton N. Nyerges

On the civic amenity landfill site. Mr and Mrs Scotland Are Dead. Kathleen Jamie. EmeKit

On the Civilization of the Western Aboriginal Country. Philip Freneau. APN-1

On the Clerk of a Country Parish. William Shenstone. FaBoEE

On the Closing of Millom Ironworks. Norman Nicholson. FaBoTw

On the Coast of Coromandel. Courtship of the Yonghy-Bonghy-Bo, The. Edward Lear. EnLoPo

On the Coast of Coromandel. Sir Osbert Sitwell. MoBrPo

On the Cold Food Festival, Entertaining at the Southern Estate—the Guests Were Li Chiu-ho, Ma Nan-yeh, Wei Tung-kao, Li Hu-ch'uan, Huang K'ung-ts'un, Li Lung-t'ang, and Hu Hu-shan. Li K'ai-hsien. CoBLCP; ColAnChi, tr. by Jonathan Chaves

On the Collar of Mrs. Dingley's Lap-Dog. Jonathan Swift. FaBoEE

On the Completion of the Pacific Telegraph. Jones Very. TAP

On the Concert. Trumbull Stickney. APN-2

On the Concord River. Henrietta Cordelia Ray. CBWP-3

On the Conditions of Place. Michael Anania. IllVoic

On the Conflagrations at Washington. Philip Freneau. APN-1

On the Congo. Harry Edmund Martinson. RB, tr. by Robert Bly

On the Corner. Kit Robinson. FTOS

On the corner—116th and Lenox. Harlem Freeze Frame. Lebert Bethune. GT

On the Countess Dowager of Pembroke. William Browne (1591–1643). AWP; BASC; HAP; PoRA; TFi

(Epitaph on the Countess[e] Dowager of Pembroke.) FaBoEE; NOBE; OBEV; SCGP

(On the Death of Marie, Countess[e] of Pembroke.) NOSC

(Underneath this sable hearse.) NoP-4

(Underneth this Marble Hearse.) NPeEn

On the Countess of Dorchester. Charles Sackville, 6th Earl of Dorset. OBEV

(On Dorinda.) OxBSP

(Song: "Dorinda's sparkling wit, and eyes") NOSC

On the cow shed. Basho. EH, tr. by Robert Hass

On the crooked arm of Columbus, on his cloak. Pigeons. Alastair Reid. TwCP

On the Cross. Alcuin. MLL, tr. by Helen Waddell

On the Cross. Anna Kamienska. GI, tr. by David Curzon and Grażyna Drabik

On the crowded subway. Bicentennial Anti-Poem for Italian-American Women. Daniela Gioseffi. UnSA

On the Dakota prairie an Indian girl was given many gifts. Calling up the Spirit of the Lost Child. Maggie Penn. TWW

On the damp margin of the sea-beat shore. Anna Seward. CenSon

On the dark distant flurry. (LL) Angle of Geese. N. Scott Momaday. CDW; HATNAP

On the dark earth. (LL) Holy Longing, The. Goethe. RaBo; WoPoe, tr. by Robert Bly

On the Dark, Still, Dry, Warm Weather Occasionally Happening in the Winter Months. Gilbert White. NOEC

On the darkening Green. (LL) William Blake. AmFaPo; FHYEP; NAEL-5v2; NAEL-6v2; OxAEP; PoE; UnPo   Fr. Songs of Innocence.

On the day a fourteen year old disappeared in Ojai, California. Use of Poetry, The. Michael Ryan. BodElec

On the day I was born. My Stars. Abraham Ibn Ezra. WoPoe, tr. by Robert Mezey

On the day I was born, many visitors came to see me. On My Birthday—Sick. Li K'ai-hsien. CoBLCP, tr. by Jonathan Chaves

On the day of a funeral. Mirrors. Marta Kornblith. MirDau, tr. by Roberta Gordenstein

On the Day of Atonement. Yehuda Amichai [or Amikhai]. TOF

On the Day of Cold Food. Spring Sun. Chu Hsi. OHPC, tr. by Kenneth Rexroth

On the day of the explosion. Explosion, The. Philip Larkin. EBEV; EmeKit; FaBoMo; HAP; MakPoe; NAEL-5v2; NAEL-6v2; NPeEn; NoAM; NoP-4; OxAEP-2; OxBC; PeECV; RB; SCV; WeW-3

On the Day of the Mid-Autumn Festival of the Year Ping-yin (1686), Together with Chang Han-chan, Ching-fan, and Ching-t'ien, I Saw the Kuei Blossoms at the Northern Garden of Jade Peak. Yün Shou-p'ing.

"In a hidden spot on the northern mountain." CoBLCP

On the Day of Washing the Buddha in the Year Ting-wei (1607), I Dreamed That My Late Son Shih-ch'ü Was Holding a Book, and Appeared To Be Quite Happy. He Said That He Had Earned His Chin-shih Degree in the Underworld. after We Sighed and La. T'ang Hsien-tsu. CoBLCP; ColAnChi, tr. by Jonathan Chaves

On the day the sienna-skinned man. Russia, 1927. Ai. NoAM

On the day the world ends. Song on the End of the World, A. Czeslaw Milosz. WoPoe, tr. by Tony Milosz and the author

On The Day They Buried My Mother. Miguel Piñero. PueRic

On the day when the Savoy. Projection. Langston Hughes. PFTM-1

On the dead oak tree bough. (LL) Gallows, The. Edward Thomas. MoBrPo; NoAM; PAI; SCGP; UnPo

On the Dead-Sea-shore. (LL) Mammon Marriage. George Macdonald. BoLoP; EBVV; SacPr

On the Death of a German Philosopher. Stevie Smith. OBCoV

On the Death of a Lady's Owl. Moses Mendes. TrJP

On the Death of a New Born Child. Mei Yao Ch'en. OHPC; WoPoe, tr. by Kenneth Rexroth

On the Death of a Nightingale. Thomas Randolph. BASC; BeJo

On the Death of a Particular Friend. James Thomson. OBEV; SCGP   Fr. On the Death of Mr. William Aikman the Painter.

On the Death of a Pious Lady. Olof Wexionius. AWP, tr. by Sir Edmund William Gosse

On the Death of a Young and Favorite Slave. Martial. AWP, tr. by Goldwin Smith

On the Death of a Young Gentleman. Phillis Wheatley. SacPr

On the Death of an Infant of Five Days Old. Elizabeth Boyd. ECWP

(On the Death of an Infant of Five Days Old, being a Beautiful but Abortive Birth.) CABP

On The Death of an Oxford Proctor. Thomas Vaughan.

"When he did read how did we flock to hear." AngWePo

On the Death of Anne Brontë. Charlotte Brontë. VWP; WPE

On the Death of Catarina de Attayda. Luis de Camões [or Camões]. AWP, tr. by R. F. Burton

On the Death of Cleopatra-Selene. Crinagoras. GrAn, tr. by Alistair Elliot

On the Death of Dr [or Mr] Robert Levet [a Practiser in Physic]. Samuel Johnson. ChIV-2; EBEV; NAEL-5v1; NAEL-6v1; NAEL-7v1; NOBE; NOEC; NPeEn; NoP-4; OBEV; OxAEP-1; OxBEV; PeECV; PoE; SCGP; SCV; TFi

On the Death of Donne. Thomas Carew. NOBE   Fr. Elegy upon the Death of the Dean of [St.] Paul's, Dr. John Donne, An.

On the Death of Emily Jane Brontë. Charlotte Brontë. VWP

On the Death of Friends in Childhood. Donald Justice. CoAmPo; ColAP; InPK-6; LCAP-2

On the Death of Henry the Lion. Hildebert. MLL, tr. by Helen Waddell

On the Death of Her Body. James Keir Baxter. PeNZ

On the Death of His Baby Son. Su Tung-p'o (Su Shih). OHPC, tr. by Kenneth Rexroth

On the Death of his Father. Wei Wên-Ti. ChiP, tr. by Arthur Waley

On the Death of His Son. Lewis Glyn Cothi. WoPoe, tr. by Gwyn Williams

On the Death of His Son. Charles Wesley. NOCV

On the Death of His Son Vincent. Leigh Hunt. NOBVV

On the Death of His Wife. Mei Yao Ch'en. OHPC, tr. by Kenneth Rexroth

On the Death of His Wife. Muireadhach Albanach O'Dalaigh. BIrV; CIP-2, tr. by Frank O'Connor

On the Death of Joseph Rodman Drake. Fitz-Greene Halleck. APN-1

On the Death of Karl Barth. Jack R. Clemo. NOCV

On The Death of King Matthias. Unknown. IQMS, tr. by Joseph Leftwich

On the Death of Lisa Lyman. Della Burt. BlSi

On the Death of Ludwig Erhard. Hal Colebatch. NOBAu

On the Death of Marie, Countess[e] of Pembroke. William Browne (1591–1643). See On the Countess Dowager of Pembroke

On the Death of Mistress Mary Prideaux. William Strode. NOSC

On the Death of Mr. Crashaw. Abraham Cowley. BASC; BeJo; MeLP

On the Death of Mr. Persall's Little Daughter, in the Beginning of the Spring, at Amsterdam. Unknown. NOSC

On the Death of Mr. Pope. Unknown. NOEC; NPeEn

On the Death of Mr. Richard West. Thomas Gray. See Sonnet [on the Death of Mr. Richard West]

On the Death of Mr. William Aikman the Painter. James Thomson.

On the Death of a Particular Friend. OBEV; SCGP

On the Death of Mr. William Hervey [or Harvey]. Abraham Cowley. EBEV; OBEV

"It was a dismal and a fearful night." BeJo; NOBE; OxAEP-1

On the Death of Mrs. Bowes. Lady Mary Wortley Montagu. BoWoP; LW

On the Death of Mrs. Rowe. Elizabeth Carter. ECWP

On the Death of Muriel Rukeyser. Billy Marshall-Stoneking. BMAP

On the Death of My Dear Friend and Play-Fellow Mrs. E. D. Having Dream'd the Night before I Heard Thereof that I Had Lost a Pearl. Jane Barker. EMWP; PoBW

On the Death of My First and Dearest Child[e], Hector Philip[p]s. Katherine Philips. NAEL-6v1; NAEL-7v1

(Orinda upon little Hector Philips.) BASC; PBRV

On the Death of My Tomcat Murr. Vladislav Felitsianovich Khodasevich. TCRusP, tr. by Mary Jane White

On the Death of Nizar Qabbani. Mohja Kahf. PoArWo

On the Death of Old Bennet the News-Crier. Unknown. NOEC

On the Death of Ronald Ryan. Bruce Dawe. BMAP

On the Death of Sir Philip Sidney. Henry Constable. OBEV

(To Sir Philip Sidney's Soul.) NoSic

On the Death of Squire Christopher. John Wigson. OxBSP

On the Death of Sylvia Plath. Judith Herzberg. WPOW

On the Death of the Duke of Clarence. Joseph Gwyer.

"Albert Victor loved his mother." VerBaPo

On the Death of the Ferryman, Glaucus. Antiphilus [or Antiphilos]. GrAn; WoPoe, tr. by W. S. Merwin

On the Death of the Giraffe. Thomas Hood. FaBoEE

On the Death of the Great Chef Alexis Soyer. Unknown. FaBoEE

On the Death of the Late Earl of Rochester. Aphra Behn. BASC; EMWP; NoP-4

On the Death of the Lord Treasurer. Unknown. FaBoEE

On the Death of the Noble and Gentle Woman, Lady Joanna Kelley. Elizabeth Jane Leon. EMWP

On the Death of the Poet's Daughter Sato. Issa. WoPoe, tr. by Conrad Totman

On the Death of the Rev. Dr. Kippis. Helen Maria Williams. ECWP

On the Death of the Rev. Mr. George Whitefield, 1770. Phillis Wheatley. ColAP; NAAAL; NAAL-2v1; NAAL-3; NAAL-5; SacPr

(On the Death of the Rev. Mr. George Whitefield.)

On the Death of William Linley, esq. William Lisle Bowles. OxBSo

On the Debt My Mother Owed to Sears Roebuck. Edward Dorn. CoAmPo; TRP

On the Decease of the Religious and Honourable Jno Haynes Esqr. John James. SCAP

On the Deception of Appearances. Sadi [or Saadi or Sa'di]. AWP, tr. by L. Cranmer-Byng Fr. Gulistan, The.

On the deck of Patrick Lynch's boat I sat in woeful plight. County of Mayo, The. Thomas Flavell [or Lavell]. BIrV; OBEV, tr. by George Fox

On the Departure of Sir Walter Scott from Abbotsford, for Naples. William Wordsworth. EBEV

On the Departure of the Nightingale. Charlotte Smith. RWP; WoRP

On the Departure Platform. Thomas Hardy. NOBE; OxBTC

On the Deputy of Ireland's Child. Sir John Davies. FaBoEE

On the desert, between pale mountains, our cries—. Two Songs of Advent. Yvor Winters. APT-2

On the Detraction Which Followed upon My Writing Certain Treatises. John Milton. NoP-4; OxBSo; PoE; Son

(Sonnet 12.) BASC

On the Doctors' Telling Him that till He Left off Making Verses He Was Not Fit to be Discharged. James Carkesse. NOSC

On the Dress of the Hungarians. József Gvadányi. IQMS, tr. by Watson Kirkconnell Fr. Village Notary's Journey to Buda, A.

On the Duke of Buckingham. James Shirley. FaBoEE

(Epitaph on the Duke of Buckingham.) NPeEn

On the Duke of Buckingham, Slain by Felton, the 23rd August, 1628. Owen Felltham [or Feltham]. NOSC

On the Dunes. Sara Teasdale. TCAPo

On the Earl of Leicester. Unknown. FaBoEE

On the earth again. (LL) Samuel Beckett. BIrV; ModIr Fr. Words and Music.

On the Eastern horizon. Kakinomoto no Hitomaro. OHMPJ

On the eastern seacoast lives a sick man. Inscribed on a Painting by Myself. Ni Tsan. CoBLCP; ColAnChi, tr. by Jonathan Chaves

On the Eastern Way at the city of Lo-yang. Song. Sung Tzu-hou. WoPoe, tr. by Arthur Waley

On the Edge. Philip Levine. CoAP; TAP

On the edge of the road. (LL) Old Cracked Tune, An. Stanley Kunitz. LoL; TaR

On the Edition of Mr. Pope's Works with a Commentary and Notes. Thomas Edwards. OxBSo

On the eighth day, the rain stopped before dusk. Loon's Egg, The. Peter Dale Scott. MoCV

On the 85th night of 19__ there were 280 days left in the year. My Broken Heart. Fanny Howe. ExTi

On the electrified ocean. Evening Scene, An. Zhao Zhenkai. VCWP, tr. by Chen Maiping and Bonnie S. McDougall

On the Elk, Unwitnessed. Alan Dugan. YaYoPo

On the Elvis Mailing List. Neal Bowers. AllShUp; SwNoth

On the embankment he washes himself. Troop Train. Aleksandr Petrovich Mezhirov. TCRP, tr. by Deming Brown

On the Emigration to America [and Peopling the Western Country]. Philip Freneau. ColAP; NAAL-2v1; NAAL-3; NAAL-5; TAP

On The Empress's Mind. John Ashbery. RACG

On the empty mountain, seeing no one. Deer Enclosure. Wang Wei. ColAnChi, tr. by Richard W. Bodman and Victor H. Mair

On the Entrance of the Castle Bridge. Simon Dach. GePo, tr. by George C. Schoolfield

On the Erection of Shakespeare's Statue in Westminster Abbey. Pope. FaBoEE

On the Erie Canal, it was. Aged Pilot Man, The. "Mark Twain." OBAL

On the eve of death. Masaoka Shiki. OHMPJ

On the Eve of His Execution. Prince Otsu. WoPoe

On the Eve of His Execution. Chidiock Tichborne [or Tichbourne]. See Tichborne's Elegy

On the Eve of Our Mutually Assured Destruction. C. D. Wright. LCAP-2

On the eve of the Festival of the Potato Harvest. Dionysus. Genrik Veniaminovich Sapgir. ItGoST, tr. by J. Kates

On the Eve of the Plebiscite. Kenneth Rexroth. NNaP

On the Eve of the Warsaw Uprising. Robin Becker. TaR

On the Expected General Rising of the French Nation. Anna Laetitia Barbauld. ECWP

(On the Expected General Rising of the French Nation in 1792.) CABP

On the Extinction of the Venetian Republic. William Wordsworth. GTBS-P; NOBE; OBEV

On the face. George Swede. HA

On the Facets: The Flashing. Coral Bracho. PFTM-2, tr. by Thomas Hoeksema

On the fair green hills of Rio. Burglar of Babylon, The. Elizabeth Bishop. RB

On the Famous Voyage. Ben Jonson. BeJo

"By this time had they reached the Stygian pool." NOSC

On the Far Edge of Kilmer. Gerald Stern. LoL

On the Farm. Ronald Stuart Thomas. NPeEn; NoP-4; OxBEV; OxBTC; TCAWP

On the farm it never mattered. Assistance, The. Paul Blackburn. NeAP; PoM

On the Farther Wall, Marc Chagall. Phyllis McGinley. OBSV Fr. Spectator's Guide to Contemporary Art.

On the Fatal Day January 30, 1648. Thomas Fairfax, Baron Fairfax of Cameron. NOSC

On the Ferris Wheel rising to the full moon. No Way Back to the Past. Allen Ginsberg. BodElec

On the Ferry, toward Patras. Emily Grosholz. RA

On the fibula of Sir—— or Sir—— (LL) Wishbone, The. Paul Muldoon. CIP-2; PBCIP

On the Fifteenth Day of the Eighth Month: Watching a Rainstorm from a Tower in Seoul. Liu E. CoBLCP, tr. by Jonathan Chaves

On the Fifteenth Day of the Ninth Month of the Year Kuei-mao of the Chih-cheng Period (Oct. 22, 1363), I Painted This to Send to the Summoned Scholar, Sheng-po, and Inscribed This Poem on It. Ni Tsan. CoBLCP, tr. by Jonathan Chaves

On the Fifteenth Day of the Seventh Month I Came Home Late from the City. Shen Chou. CoBLCP, tr. by Jonathan Chaves

On the fifth day after the rise of Spring. Parting from the Winter Stove. Po Chü-i. ChiP, tr. by Arthur Waley

On the first cool day in half a year. Sky. Richard Katrovas. LTA

On the first day. Pledge of Allegiance. Carl Hancock Rux. SpirFl

On the first day, eighth moon. Journey North, The. Tu Fu. CrYelRi, tr. by Sam Hamill

On the first day, gazing idly about him. Adam. Yevgeny [or Evgenii] Mikhailovich Vinokurov. TCRusP, tr. by Daniel Weissbort

On the first day of Christmas. Unknown. See First day of Christmas, The

On the first day of school the teacher asked me. How a Girl Got Her Chinese Name. Nellie Wong. WPOW

On the first day of spring. Virginia Brady Young. HA

On the first good day of yard work. Alchemy. Alan Michael Parker. AmPoNex

On the first hour of my first day. Rudyard Kipling. FaBoTw Fr. Epitaphs of the War [1914–18].

On the first of January. Clare Pollard. NeBl Fr. Friday Night at the End of a Millennium, A.

On the first of March. Rooks, The. Unknown. OxNR

On the first of May. Mountain Greenery. Richard Rodgers. OBAL; ReLy

On the first of the Feast of Feasts. Epilogue. Robert Browning. ChIV-2

On the first page of my dreambook. Empire of Dreams. Charles Simic. BLT; LCAP-2; VCAP

On the fleet streams, the Sun, that late arose. Anna Seward. WoRP *Fr.* Sonnets.

On the Flooding of Prague, which Arose from Continuous Rain in the Year 1596. Elizabeth Jane Leon. EMWP

On The Fly. Diana Chang. FSt

On the Fly-Leaf of Pound's Cantos. Basil Bunting. FaBoTw; HarvBoo; NoAM; OxBTC

On the Following Work and Its Author. Jonathan Mitchell. SCAP

On the forest path. Asagumori. Kenneth Rexroth. GifTon

On the Founding of Liberia. Melvin B. Tolson. UnPo *Fr.* Libretto for the Republic of Liberia.

On the fourteenth day of April. Dust Storm Disaster. Woody Guthrie. APT-2

On the fourth day of his fasting. Henry Wadsworth Longfellow. TCAPo *Fr.* Song of Hiawatha, The.

On the fourth day the phone wires talked. I-5 Incident. Juan Delgado. AmPoNex; GeoHom

On the Fragile Labyrinth. José Emilio Pacheco. STV, *tr.* by John Frederick Nims

On the Frequent Review of the Troops. "M." NOEC

On the Fringe. Amina Said. HAWP, *tr.* by Eric Sellin

On the fringe of nothingness. On the Fringe. Amina Said. HAWP, *tr.* by Eric Sellin

On the front page of the Chronicle. New Mr Barnsley Something, The. Geoff Hattersley. NeBl

On the Frozen Lake. William Wordsworth. FaBoCh; WoPoe *Fr.* Prelude; Growth of a Poet's Mind, The [1805 vers.].

On the Fruit-Providing Autumn Season. Catharina Regina von Greiffenberg. WPoS, *tr.* by Michael Hamburger

On the Funeral of Dr. Livingston. Joseph Gwyer. "Heap on more grass was his request." VerBaPo

On the Game. Linda France. What I Know Now. MFPA

On the Gift of a Knife. Muireadhach Albanach O'Dalaigh. NOIV

On the Glittering Beaches. Tracey Herd. MFPA

On the Good Ship Lollipop. Sidney Clare. ReLy

On The Gospel. Francis Quarles. ChIV-2

On the Grass. Paul Verlaine. SxFrPo, *tr.* by Martin Sorrell

On the grass airfield, a wife. Private Airplane. Chase Twichell. ExTi

On the Grasshopper and [the] Cricket. John Keats. CenSon; FHYEP; NIL-7; NIP-4; OxAEP-2; Son; TTTS

On the Great Fog in London, December 1762. James Eyre Weeks. NOEC

On the Great Frost (1634). William Cartwright. NOSC

On the Great Wall. Rudyard Kipling. *Fr.* Puck of Pook's Hill.

On the Great Western Canal of the State of New York. Philip Freneau. APN-1

On the green / with lignum vitae balls and ivory markers. Bowls. Marianne Craig Moore. APT-1

On the ground. Rogan. JDP, *tr.* by Yoel Hoffmann

On the ground are my sketches of the contours. Painter in the Lion Cage, The. Betti Alver. BoWoP, *tr.* by Willis Barnstone and Felix Oinas

On the Group of the Three Angels before the Tent of Abraham, by Raffaelle, in the Vatican. Washington Allston. APN-1; GS

On the half-finished bridge. (LL) Basho. EH; NIL-7, *tr.* by Robert Hass

On the Hall at Stowey. Charles Tomlinson. PoE

On the Hall of Precious Virtue. Yang Shih-ch'i. CoBLCP; ColAnChi, *tr.* by Jonathan Chaves

On the hall stand hangs a fur coat. Yevgeny [*or* Evgenii] Mikhailovich Vinokurov. TCRP

On the Happy Corydon and Phyllis. Sir Charles Sedley. BoLoP (Young Coridon and Phillis.) BASC

On the harbor freeway. Dog Suicide. Wanda Coleman. GeoHom

On the hard road of life and death. Requiem. Master Wŏlmyŏng. WoPoe, *tr.* by Peter H. Lee

On the Head of a Pin. Thomas McGrath. GifTon

On the Headland. Bayard Taylor. CAGL

On the headland's grassed and sheltered side. Storm. Judith Wright. WPE

On the Heart's Beginning to Cloud the Mind. Robert Frost. GM

On the Heights. Walter Savage Landor. FaBoEE

On the highway. Está Muy Caliente. George Bowering. MoCV

On the hill he had climbed all winter. Hunger of the Lemur, The. Matthew Rohrer. NeAmPo

On the hill tops I visit the snares. Love Song. *Unknown.* PeNZ, *tr.* by Margaret Orbell

On the hillside. Bilberries. Gerda Mayer. Spl

On the Historians Freeman and Stubbs. J. E. Thorold Rogers. FaBoEE (Two Historians.) OBCoV

On the holy day of your going out to war. Mohodahi. BoWoP

On the Holy Scriptures. Francis Quarles. ChIV-2

On the Hon. George Nathaniel Curzon, Commoner of Balliol. *Var. authors.* FaBoEE; NOBL; OBCoV; PeLV *Fr.* Balliol Rhymes.

On the Hoping Life. Hans Leifhelm. AuPH, *tr.* by Lowell A. Bangerter

On the idle hill of summer. A. E. Housman. FaBoWar; MoBrPo; NOBE; OBWP

On the Ile de Gorée, M. Diop elegant. Double Take at Relais de L'Espadon. Thadious M. Davis. BlSi

On the Imprint of the First English Edition of "The Works of Max Beerbohm." Max Beerbohm. InPK-6; OBCoV

On the Inclusion of Miniature Dinosaurs in Breakfast Cereal Boxes. John Updike. OBCoV

On the Ineffable Inspiration of the Holy Spirit. Catharina Regina von Greiffenberg. WPoS; WoPoe, *tr.* by Michael Hamburger

On the Inscription over the Head of Christ on the Cross. Henry Colman. ChIV-2

On the iris / Kite's. Buson. ZenPo, *tr.* by Takashi Ikemoto and Lucien Stryk

On the Irish Club. Jonathan Swift. OBSV

On the Island. Dennis Brutus. AF

On the Island of the Spirits of the Dead. Two Sisters, The. *Aborigine Oral Tradition.* NOBAu, *tr.* by Manoowa

On the Islands. Aleksandr Aleksandrovich Blok. TCRP, *tr.* by Geoffrey Thurley

On the Islands of All Winds. Aimé Césaire. VCWP

On the jewelweed. Larry Gates. HA

On the Jubilee of Queen Victoria. Tennyson. UnPo

On the Killing at Lindisfarne. Alcuin. MLL, *tr.* by Helen Waddell

On the kitchen wall a flash. World Outside, The. Denise Levertov. CoAmPo; TRP

On the Lady Arabella. Richard Corbet [*or* Corbett]. NOSC

On the Lake. Victoria Mary Sackville-West. OBMV

On the Lake Poets. Charles Townsend. FaBoEE

On the lake, the autumn wind blows blue ripples. As I Looked at a Lake, My Thoughts Turned to a Certain Friend. Chu Yün-ming. CoBLCP, *tr.* by Jonathan Chaves

On the Lamented Death of Mrs. Throckmorton's Bullfinch. William Cowper. NOEC

On the landscape, to make of us what we could. (LL) Street Musicians. John Ashbery. HCAP; PoPoPo

On the large highway of the awful air that flows. Fish-Hawk, The. John Hall Wheelock. APT-1

On the Last Day of the World. Sherod Santos. GeoHom

On the last day of the year we have so much to be thankful for. Last Day of the Year; or, New Year's Eve, The. Mrs. Henry Linden. CBWP-4

On the last words of what you write to me. Dante da Maiano. EaItPo, *tr.* by Dante Gabriel Rossetti

On the last year's trip I enjoyed this place. On the Road through Chang-te. Sun Yün-feng. BoWoP; WPOW

On the Late Improvements at Nuneham, the Seat of the Earl of Harcourt. William Whitehead. OBGa

On the Late Massacre [*or* Massacher] in Piedmont [*or* Piemont]. John Milton. AWP; CABP; GSo; GTBS-P; HAP; HeIP-4; NAEL-5v1; NAEL-6v1; NIL-7; NOBE; NOCV; NPeEn; NoP-4; OBWP; OxBEV; OxBSo; PoPoPo; SCGP; Son; TFi; TRP; UnPo; WeW-3

(Sonnet 18 [On the Late Massacre in Piedmont].) BASC

On the late shift, front desk. Transient Hotel Sky at the Hour of Sleep. Martín Espada. ReTh

On the Lawn at the Villa. Louis Simpson. CoAP; OBAL; OxBC

On the length and breadth of the marvellous marshes of Glynn. (LL) Sidney Lanier. NOBA; OxBA *Fr.* Hymns of the Marshes.

On the length and the breadth of the marvellous marshes of Glynn. (LL) Marshes of Glynn, The. Sidney Lanier. NOBA; OxBA; TCAPo

On the Life of Man. Francis Quarles. ChIV-2; PeECV *Fr.* Divine Fancies.

On the Life of Man. Sir Walter Ralegh. *See* What Is Our Life?

On the Line. Emmy Bridgwater. SurWo

On the Line. Ruth Padel. MFPA

On the lips a taste of tolling we are blind. (Poem) (Chicago) (The Were-Age). Bill Knott. SPE

On the long shore, lit by the moon. Goose Fish, The. Howard Nemerov. HeIP-4; NIL-7; NIP-4; NoAM; NoP-4; PoE

On the look of Death. (LL) There's a Certain Slant of Light. Emily Dickinson. APN-2; BoWoP; HAP; HeIP-4; MoAmPo; NAAL-2v1; NAAL-3; NALW; NAWM-7v2; NCAP; NOBA; NoAM; NoP-4; OxBA; PoE; RB; SAmP; SoSe-8; TCAPo; TFi; TOF; WPE

On the Lord Gen[eral] Fairfax at the Siege of Colchester. John Milton. NOSC (Sonnet 15.) BASC

On the Loss of Friends. James Montgomery. SacPr

On the Loss of the *Royal George*. William Cowper. EBEV; NOBE (Loss of the Royal George.) GTBS-P; OxAEP-1

On the Love of Two Boys. Angelo [or Andrea] Poliziano. CAGL, tr. by James J. Wilhelm Fr. Greek Epigrams.

On the low margin of a murmuring stream. Visions Appear to her in a Dream. Mary Robinson. CenSon; RWP

On the Luxembourg Gallery. Washington Allston. APN-1

On the mantelpiece. Studio Poem. Cilla McQueen. PeNZ

On the many-leafed bedscreens, gold flickers and fades. Tune: Deva-like Barbarian. Wen T'ing-yün. CoBCP, tr. by Burton Watson

On the Marginal Way. Richard Wilbur. CoAP; NOBA

On the Marriage at Cana. Rainer Maria Rilke. GI

On the Marriage of a Virgin. Dylan Thomas. EnLoPo

On the Marriage of T. K. and C. C.: The Morning Stormy. Thomas Carew. BoLoP

On the Masquerades. Christopher Pitt. ECEV; NOEC

On the Mediterranean coast, between the estuary and Jubail. Amin Al-Rihani. GraLe, tr. by Sharif Elmusa Fr. Gibran.

On the Medusa of Leonardo da Vinci in the Florentine Gallery. Shelley. GS

On the Meetings of the Scotch Covenanters. Unknown. FaBoEE

On the Memorial building's. Under Cancer. John Hollander. CoAP

On the merry-go-round. Alan Pizzarelli. HA

On the Metamorphoses Brought about by Emotion: The Rebellion of the Eyes. Andrey [or Andrei] Andreievich Voznesensky [or Voznesenskii]. PFTM-2, tr. by Anselm Hollo

On the metro the man across. Here's Looking at You Francis Bacon. Joan Retallack. FTOS

On the mid stairs, between the light and dark. Algernon Charles Swinburne. EBNV Fr. Tristram of Lyonesse.

On the Miracle of Loaves. Richard Crashaw. OxBSP

On the Miracle of Multiplied [or Multiplyed] Loaves. Richard Crashaw. OxBSP

On the Mississippi. Hamlin Garland. APN-2

On the moor of Kasuga. Var. authors. AWP Fr. Manyo Shu, Part 3 of 4.

On the Morning of Christ's Nativity. John Milton. BASC; ChRo; MeLP; NAEL-5v1; NAEL-6v1; NAEL-7v1; NOCV; NoP-4; PBRV; SCGP

  Hymn on the Morning of Christ's Nativity. NOBE; OBEV

  "But peaceful was the night." FaBoCh

  "It was the winter wild[e]." NPeEn; OxBEV

On the morning of the crowning we chorused our. Geoffrey Hill. HAP Fr. Mercian Hymns.

On the morning of the funeral. Winston Churchill. David Scott. NLP

On the Morning of the Third Night above Nisqually. W. M. Ransom. CDW

On the Motor Bus. Alfred Denis Godley. See Motor Bus

On the Mountain. Neidhart von Reuental. AWP, tr. by Jethro Bithell

On the Mountain. Ruth Stone. BoWoP

On the mountain, Epicydes the hunter seeks. Callimachus. HePo Fr. Epigrams.

On the mountain, in the old oak's domain. Isolation. Alphonse Marie Louis de Lamartine. SxFrPo, tr. by E. H. Blackmore and A. M. Blackmore

On the Mountain of Boiled Rice I met Tu Fu. To Tu Fu. Li Po. TAL

On the mountain, old trees, still green in autumn. Inscribed on a Painting. T'ang Yin. CoBLCP, tr. by Jonathan Chaves

On the mountain peak, called "Going-to-the-Sun." Apple-Barrel of Johnny Appleseed, The. Nicholas Vachel Lindsay. OxBA

On the mountain slope. Gerard John Conforti. HA

On the Move. Thom Gunn. HAP; NoP-4; OxAEP-2; OxBTC; PoE; TRP; TwCP

On the Murder of an Ice Cream Man. Hayan Charara. AmPoNex

On the Name of Jesus. Richard Crashaw. ESCV

  (And break before thee.) (LL) FSCP

  (To the Name above Every Name, the Name of Iesvs a Hymn.) FSCP

On the Nature of Food. Alberta Turner. LCAP-2

On the New Forcers of Conscience under the Long Parliament. John Milton. BASC; NAEL-5v1; NAEL-6v1; NOSC; PBRV; Son

On The New Inn: Ode. to Himself. Ben Jonson. See Ode to Himself[e]

On the New Year. Christopher Okigbo. PoetW

On the Night. Ivor Gurney. OxBSP

On the night beach, quiet beside the blue. Morning. Glyn Jones. AngWePo

On the Night in Question. Patricia Goedicke. TAP

On the night of the Belgian surrender the moon rose. Moon and the Night and the Men, The. John Berryman. CoAP; VCAP; VGW

On the Night of the Fifteenth of the First Month I Go Out and Return. Mei Yao Ch'en. SuSp, tr. by Jonathan Chaves

On the Night of the Sixteenth of the Eighth Month: Watching the Moon from the Deck of the Ship, Aimo-maru in the Black Water Sea. Liu E. CoBLCP, tr. by Jonathan Chaves

On the night road from El Rama the cows. Second Poem from Nicaragua Libre: War Zone. June Jordan. NoAM

On the ninth of November by the dawning of the day. Farewell to Kingsbridge. Unknown. ECEV

On the ninth, we entered the country on iron horse rails. Spirit of '76, The. Friederike Mayröcker. PFTM-2, tr. by Anselm Hollo

On the North Shore a reptile lay asleep. Edwin John Pratt. MoCV; NOBC Fr. Towards the Last Spike.

On the Numerous Access of the English to Wait upon the King in Flanders. Katherine Philips. BASC; NOSC

On the Occasion of One Dr. Fell's Challenge to Translate an Epigram of Martial's. Thomas [or "Tom"] Brown. See Doctor Fell

On the Occurrence of a Spell of Arctic Weather in May, 1858. Paul Hamilton Hayne. APN-2

On the Ocean Floor. Hugh MacDiarmid. FaBoMo; HAP

On the offering mound, a dead roe. Unknown. ColAnChi, tr. by Jeffrey Riegel Fr. Classic of Odes.

On the old plum tree. Ransetsu. SoOfWa, tr. by Sam Hamill

On the old scarecrow. Lorraine Ellis Harr. HA

On the one-ton temple bell. Buson. InPK-6

On the Oregon Coast. Robert Bly. BodElec

On the Oregon Coast. Galway Kinnell. NoAM

On the Origin of Evil. John Byrom. NOEC; NPeEn

On the Origin of the Contrary. Miroslav Holub. VCWP, tr. by Stuart Friebert

On the Other Side. Czeslaw Milosz. PoSu, tr. by Jan Darowski

On the other side. Ohioan Pastoral. James Wright. LCAP-2

On the other side of the border. Kith. Marion Lomax. NeBl

On the other side of the moon. Land Where the Good Songs Go, The. P. G. Wodehouse. ReLy

On the other side of the world I heard. Elegy for a Schoolmate. Vincent O'Sullivan. PeNZ

On the Otis Redding Bridge. Judson Mitcham. SwNoth

On the outskirts, dumplings of mud. Wang Fan-chih. SuSp

On the Oxford Book of Victorian Verse. Hugh MacDiarmid. MoBrPo

On the padlock. Penny Harter. HA

On the Pains of Translating Miklós Radnóti. Frederick Turner. RA

On the Painter Val Prinsep. Dante Gabriel Rossetti. FaBoEE

  (There is a creator called God.) OBCoV

On the Painting "Joys of Village Life." Yün Shou-p'ing.

  "For a hundred miles the west wind carries the fragrance of millet." CoBLCP

On the Painting, Mist over Ten Thousand Mountains by Shih-ku. Yün Shou-p'ing. CoBLCP, tr. by Jonathan Chaves

On the Painting of the Sistine Chapel. Michelangelo Buonarroti. WoPoe, tr. by John Addington Symonds

On the path. Under the Maud Moon. Galway Kinnell. NNaP

On the path, / by this wet site. Galway Kinnell. NNaP

On the path winding. Path among the Stones, The. Galway Kinnell. NNaP; NOBA

On the pathway mica glints. Water and Worship: An Open-Air Service on the Gatineau River. Margaret Avison. HAP

On the pavement a blind man walks. Blind Man, The. Ksenya [or Kseniia] Nekrasova. TCRP, tr. by Vera Rich

On the pennants of blue are bold characters. Reviewing the Troops at Kuei-lin with Military Inspectors Chiang and Chang. Yang Chi. CoBLCP, tr. by Jonathan Chaves

On the Phoenix. Jean Adams. ECWP

On the phoenix terrace, phoenix at play. Ascend the Phoenix Terrace. Li Po. ChinPo, tr. by Yip Wai-lim

On the phonograph, the voice. Reunion. Carolyn Forché. NoAM

On the Picture of a Child. Henrietta Cordelia Ray. CBWP-3

On the Pilgrim's Way in Kent, as It Leads to the Coldrum Stones. "Asphodel." BrRo

On the Plain of Kulikovo. Aleksandr Aleksandrovich Blok. TCRusP, tr. by Denis Johnson and Kathy Lewis

On the Ploughman [or Plough-Man]. Francis Quarles. NOSC; SacPr

On the Poet, Arthur O'Shaughnessy—. Dante Gabriel Rossetti. OBCoV; PeLi

On the Poet Coming of Age. Lorna Dee Cervantes. TouFir

On the poop-deck my sad heart drips. Cheated Heart. Arthur Rimbaud. SxFrPo, tr. by Martin Sorrell

On the Portrait of a Girl. Erinna. GrAn, tr. by Lenore Mayhew

On the Prince's Death, to the King. Sir Robert Aytoun [or Ayton]. NOSC

On the Projected Kendal and Windermere Railway. William Wordsworth. CenSon

On the Prospect from Westminster Bridge. Elizabeth Tollet. ECWP

On the Prospect of Peace. Thomas Tickell.

  "Ah! curst Ambition, to thy lures we owe." ECEV

On the Prospect of Planting Arts and Learning in America. George Berkeley. AiP; NOEC; OxBEV

  (Verses on the Prospect of Planting Arts and Learning in America.) FaBoA

On the quays of Papeete, the dawlding white-ducked colonists.   Derek Walcott.   NoAM   *Fr.* Midsummer.

On the Queen's Return from the Low Countries.   William Cartwright.   OBEV

On the Railway.   Aleksandr Aleksandrovich Blok.   TCRP, *tr.* by Geoffrey Thurley

On the Railway Platform.   Randall Jarrell.   GM

On the rank harvest of betrayal they feed.   Rank Harvest of Betrayal, The.   Wilma Stockenström.   PeSAV, *tr.* by Rosa Keet

On the Rapid Extension of the Suburbs.   John Thelwall.   CenSon

On the rapids of the St. Lawrence.   Henrietta Cordelia Ray.   CBWP-3

On the Receipt of My Mother's Picture out of Norfolk [the Gift of My Cousin Ann Bodham].   William Cowper.   NOEC; OxAEP-1

On the Reedy Lake.   János Vajda.   IQMS, *tr.* by Jean Overton Fuller

On the reef of Norman's Woe! (LL)   Wreck of the *Hesperus*, The.   Henry Wadsworth Longfellow.   APN-1; BRP; EBNV; OBCA; OBNV; TCAPo; TreFP

On the Relative Merit of Friend and Foe, Being Dead.   Donald Thompson.   FaBoWar

On the Religion of Nature.   Philip Freneau.   NAAL-2v1; NAAL-3; NAAL-5

On the Relinquishment of a Title.   Geoffrey Grigson.   FaBoEE

On the Removal of the Fascist American Right from Power.   Etheridge Knight.   BodElec

On the restaurant terrace, we're face to face.   Ordinary Song, An.   Chairil Anwar.   PoetW, *tr.* by Burton Raffel

On the Resurrection of Christ.   William Dunbar.   ChIV-2; NOCV; OxBS

On the Returne of King Charles 2nd.   Ann Lee.   EMWP

On the Reverend Jonathan Doe.   *Unknown.*   FaBoEE

On the Rhine.   Charles Stuart Calverley.   PeLV

On the River.   Ku K'uang.   SuSp, *tr.* by Irving Y. Lo

On the River.   Li Po.   CoBCP, *tr.* by Burton Watson

On the River.   Tu Fu.   CoBCP, *tr.* by Burton Watson

On the River.   Yü Hsüan-chi.   SuSp, *tr.* by Jan W. Walls

On the river, every day these heavy rains.   On the River.   Li Po.   CoBCP, *tr.* by Burton Watson

On the river, the spring tides are calm.   Inscribed on an Album Leaf Painted by Dr. Lin.   Pien Kung.   CoBLCP, *tr.* by Jonathan Chaves

On the Road.   Prodigal Son, The.   Leah Goldberg.   GI, *tr.* by Robert Friend

On the Road.   Seamus Heaney.   TOF   *Fr.* Sweeney Redivivus.

On the Road at Night There Stands the Man.   Dahlia Ravikovitch [*or* Ravikovich].   WPOW, *tr.* by Chana Bloch

On the road between Spanish-Town / and Kingston.   West Indian Primer.   Elizabeth Alexander.   NIL-7

On the Road Home.   C. G. Hanzlicek.   GeoHom

On the road, the mountains.   My Fifty-Plus Years Celebrate Spring.   Luis Omar Salinas.   GeoHom

On the Road through Chang-te.   Sun Yün-feng.   BoWoP; WPOW

On the Road through the Wu-i Mountains—Making Fun of Chia-tse for Falling Off His Horse.   Hsü Wei.   CoBLCP, *tr.* by Jonathan Chaves

On the road to Ch'ang-an my horse goes slowly.   Tune: "Wanderings of a Youth."   Liu Yung.   SuSp, *tr.* by Jerome P. Seaton

On the Road to Damascus, Maryland.   Enid Dame.   UnSA

On the Road to Erewhon.   Allen Curnow.   HarvBoo

On the road to Hallucination.   On a Certain Field in Auvers.   John Haines.   OPRER

On the Road to Hsin-ch'eng.   Su Tung-p'o (Su Shih).   CoBCP, *tr.* by Burton Watson

On the Road to Pyongyang—An Improvisation.   Liu E.   CoBLCP, *tr.* by Jonathan Chaves

On the Road to San Romano.   André Breton.   PFTM-1

On the Road to T'ien-t'ai.   Yuan Mei.   GifTon, *tr.* by Jerome P. Seaton

On the road to the bay was a lake of rushes.   Bay, The.   James Keir Baxter.   HarvBoo; PeNZ

On the Road to the Sea.   Charlotte Mew.   BrRo; FaBoWP; PoBW

On the Road to Western Hill.   Ch'ien Ch'ien-i [*or* Ch'ien Ch'ien-yi].   SuSp, *tr.* by Irving Y. Lo

On the road we met a blackman.   Twenty-Six Ways of Looking at a Blackman.   Raymond R. Patterson.   ESEAA

On the roads at night I saw the glitter of eyes.   Eyes of Night-Time.   Muriel Rukeyser.   BoWoP

On the rock of a living faith! (LL)   Nearer Home.   Phoebe Cary.   PWR; SacPr

On the rock / Waves can't reach.   Tantan.   ZenPo, *tr.* by Takashi Ikemoto and Lucien Stryk

On the rocks of my mind's country. (LL)   Back?   T. Harri Jones.   AngWePo; TCAWP

On the rocky grassy slope of this hill, Topsy and I.   On the Slope of this Hill.   Shamsher Bahadur Singh.   OMIP, *tr.* by Vinay Dharwadker

On the rocky slope, blossoming.   Hoin.   ZenPo, *tr.* by Takashi Ikemoto and Lucien Stryk

On the Rouge.   Raymond Souster.   NOBC

On the ruins of Synagogue Cheva Bikur, built in 1887.   Monarchs of Parque Tranquilidad.   Robin Becker.   UrbNat

On the runway at the Roxy, the drag queen.   Take Good Care of Yourself.   Mark Wunderlich.   NeAmPo; ReTh; WiU

On the Russian Persecution of the Jews.   Algernon Charles Swinburne.   OxBSo; Son

On the salt plaza.   Skull of the Horse.   Thomas McGrath.   BodElec

On the salt water streets.   Venice Recalled.   Bruce Boyd.   NeAP

On the Same.   Roy Campbell.   OBCoV; OxBTC

On the Same [Death of My Dear Brother, Mr. H. S., Drowned]: The Boat.   William Hammond.   NOSC

On the Same Picture.   Walt Whitman.   GS

On the Sand Dune.   Kawamura Yoichi.   GifTon, *tr.* by Naoshi Koriyama and Edward Lueders

On the sands is seen the sun rising.   Composed at Sunset at the Dunes of Ho-yen.   Ts'en Shen.   SuSp, *tr.* by Ronald C. Miao

On the school platform, draping the folding seats.   Political Meeting.   Abraham Moses Klein.   MoCV

On the Sea.   Judah Halevi.
"Greetings ladies, kith and kin."   WoPoe, *tr.* by Gabriel Levin

On the Sea.   John Keats.   NoP-4

On the Sea.   Gabriella Sica.   CItWP, *tr.* by Cinzia Sartini Blum and Lara Trubowitz

On the Sea.   Bayard Taylor.   TreFP

On the sea-floor a stone bell, tolling.   August Sleepwalker, The.   Zhao Zhenkai.   VCWP

On the Second Day of the Fifth Month—Written after Drink.   Liu Ya-tzu.   SuSp, *tr.* by Wu-Chi Liu

On the second floor of the Worcester Center Mall, 7:15 P.M., March 3.   Lines Started outside Filene's Basement.   James R. Scrimgeour.   OPRER

On the second of October, a Monday at noon.   Walter Lesly.   *Unknown.*   ESPB

On the Second Tristia of Ovid.   Elizabeth Jane Leon.   EMWP

On the secret map the assassins.   Rivers and Mountains.   John Ashbery.   CoAP; NOBA; NoAM; TRP

On the Setting Up of Mr. Butler's Monument in Westminster Abbey.   Samuel Wesley.   NBLV; NOEC; OxBSP

On the Seven Bishops.   Anne Fychan.   EMWP

On the seventh day.   Love Affair 36.   Jennifer Rankin.   BMAP

On the sheep-cropped summit, under hot sun.   Cat and Mouse.   Ted Hughes.   OxBSP

On the shingle.   Kakinomoto no Hitomaro.   OHPJ

On the shore fish toss in the stretched nets of Simon, James, and John.   Abundant Catch (Luke 5:4–10).   Czeslaw Milosz.   GI

On the shore of Nawa.   Hioki no Ko-Okima.   AWP   *Fr.* Manyo Shu, Part 3 of 4.

On the shores of my animal there was a zoo.   Letter to Einstein Beginning Dear Albert.   Paul Hoover.   IllVoic

On the Shores of Szántód.   Ferenc Jankovich.   IQMS, *tr.* by Madeline Mason

On the Sicilian strand a hare well wrought.   Ausonius.   OBVE

On the side of the vaulted library of Augustus.   Santa Maria Antiqua.   István Vas.   IQMS, *tr.* by George Gömöri and Clive Wilmer

On the sightless seas of ether.   Mikhail Yuryevich Lermontov.   AWP   *Fr.* Daemon, The.

On the Situation of Highbury.   Katherine Austen.   EMWP

On the Siu Cheng Road.   Su Tung-p'o (Su Shih).   OHPC, *tr.* by Kenneth Rexroth

On the Sixteenth Day I Visit the Temple Again.   Pien Kung.   CoBLCP, *tr.* by Jonathan Chaves

On the sixth day we came. (LL)   Animals, The.   Edwin Muir.   CRP; ChIV-1; EBEV; HeIP-4; MoBrPo

On the sixty-fifth floor where you wrote.   Peregrine Falcon, New York City.   Robert Cording.   UrbNat

On the Slave-Trade.   Isabella Lickbarrow.   RWP

On the Slope of Hua Mountain.   *Unknown.*   WoPoe, *tr.* by Chung Ling and Kenneth Rexroth

On the Slope of the Desolate River.   Rabindranath Tagore.   OBMV   *Fr.* Gitanjali.

On the Slope of this Hill.   Shamsher Bahadur Singh.   OMIP, *tr.* by Vinay Dharwadker

On the slopes of the mountain.   Clear Bright.   Huang T'ing-chien.   OHMPC, *tr.* by Kenneth Rexroth

On the Snuff of a Candle.   Sir Walter Ralegh.   FaBoEE

On the Soft and Gentle Motions of Eudora.   Anne Killigrew.   PoBW

On the Solitary Fells around Hawkshead.   William Wordsworth.   OxAEP-2   *Fr.* Prelude; Growth of a Poet's Mind [1805 vers.], The.

On the Sonnet.   John Keats.   *See* If by Dull Rhymes Our English Must Be Chained

On the South Coast of Cornwall.   John Gray.   NOBVV

On the South Downs. Sara Teasdale. MoAmPo
On the southwest side of Capri. Nude Swim, The. Anne Sexton. WPE
On the Spartan Dead at Thermopylae. Simonides. WeW-3, tr. by Peter Jay
 (For the Spartan Dead at Thermopylai (480 B.C.).) GrAn, tr. by Peter Jay
 (Inform the Lakedaimonians, friend—we rest.) GrAn, tr. by Peter Jay
 (Take this news to the Lakedaimonians, friend.) GrAn, tr. by Peter Jay
On the Spirit Adulterated by the Flesh. Thomas Warton, the Elder. ChIV-1
On the Spirit of the Heart as Moon-Disk. Kojijū. WPoS; WoPoe, tr. by Edwin A. Cranston
On the spring river, you depart. Tsung Ch'en. CoBLCP Fr. Song of Chiang-nan.
On the Spur of the Moment. Tu Fu. CoBCP, tr. by Burton Watson
On the stage I stumbled. Indian Blood. Mary Tallmountain. UnSA
On the stage, mirrored many times. Stripper, The. Anita Endrezze. CDW; ReTh
On the stairway fragrance assails the bosom. Spring Song of Tzu-yeh, A. Hsiao Yen. SuSp, tr. by Jan W. Walls
On the Statue of a Player at Svaika. Alexander Sergeyevich Pushkin. CAGL, tr. by Michael Green
On the Statue of an Angel, by Bienaimé, in the Possession of J. S. Copley Greene, Esq. Washington Allston. APN-1
On the Statue of Epaminondas in Thebes. Unknown. GrAn, tr. by Peter Levi
On the steps of the Pentagon I tucked my skull. Revised Notes for a Sonnet. "Edward Pygge." OBCoV
On the stiff twig up there. Black Rook in Rainy Weather. Sylvia Plath. NAAL-2v2; NIL-7; NoP-4
On the stillest day. Windmill. Gillian Clarke. TCAWP
On the Strange Apparitions at Christ's Death. Henry Colman. ChIV-2
On the Street. Constantine P. Cavafy. BoLoP, tr. by Rae Dalven
On the street of Lo-yang. Meng Hao Jan. SuSp, tr. by Paul W. Kroll
On the street / Slung on his shoulder is a handle half way across. Shovel Man, The. Carl Sandburg. HAP
On the Street Where You Live. Frederick Loewe. ReLy
On the Subject of Poetry. W. S. Merwin. PAI
On the Subject of Waves. Eldon Grier. MoCV
On the Subway. Sharon Olds. LTA
On the Suicide of a Friend. Reed Whittemore. CoAmPo
On the Suicide of Young Writers. Wilma Stockenström. PeSAV, tr. by Stephen Gray
On the summer road that ran by our front porch. Lizards and Snakes. Anthony Hecht. FaBoMo; TwCP
On the Sun Coming Out in the Afternoon. Henry David Thoreau. OxBSP
On the Sunny Side of the Street. Dorothy Fields. ReLy
On the surface, foam and roar. Under the Surface. Frances Ridley Havergal. SacPr
On the Swag. Ronald Allison Kells Mason. PeNZ; SacPr
On the Sweet Comfort Brought by Grace. Catharina Regina von Greiffenberg. "I look." WPoS
On the Symbolic Consideration of Hands and the Significance of Death. Miller Williams. InPK-6
On the table. Few Things, A. Gerhard Rühm. PFTM-2, tr. by Rosmarie Waldrop
On the table, a book of glass. Book of Glass, A. David Shapiro. PmAP
On the table, these last mouthfuls. (LL) Glass, The. Sharon Olds. NIL-7; NIP-4
On the Tack. Thomas Hearne. ECEV
On the Tattered Edges. Amina Said. HAWP; NAfrP, tr. by Eric Sellin
On the tattered edges of my unravelling memory. On the Tattered Edges. Amina Said. HAWP; NAfrP, tr. by Eric Sellin
On the Telescopic Moon. John Swanwick [or Swanick] Drennan. BIrV
On the temple bell. Spring Scene. Buson. TTTS, tr. by Harold Henderson and Kenneth Koch
On the temple porch of Syrian Astarte. To Astarte. Unknown. GrAn, tr. by Guy Davenport
On the Tennis Court at Night. Galway Kinnell. MoASP
On the tenth day of December. Musselburgh Field. Unknown. ESPB
On the Tercentenary of Milton's Death. Gavin Ewart. OxBC
On the Thessalians Who Fought at Marathon. Aeschylus. GrAn, tr. by Edwin Morgan
On the Third Day. János Pilinszky. IQMS, tr. by Adam Makkai
On the third day of the third month, in fresh weather. Elegant Women, The. Tu Fu. SuSp, tr. by Mark Perlberg
On the third day rose Arp. Resurrection of Arp. Arthur James Marshall Smith. MoCV; NOBC
On the third finger of my left hand. Ceremony. William Stafford. LCAP-2
On the third planet too, life is found. Excerpt from a Report to the Galactic Council. Robert Conquest. OxBC
On the Thirteenth Day of Christmas. Charles Causley. OBCP

On the Thirteenth Day of the Eleventh Month I Went to the Granary for the First Time since My Illness. Mei Yao Ch'en. SuSp, tr. by Jonathan Chaves
On the 30th of June to God. Lady Jane Cavendish. EMWP
On the thousand mile road through Yang Pass. Bidding Farewell to Secretary Chou. Yu Hsin. CrYelRi, tr. by Sam Hamill
On the Three Children in the Fiery Furnace. Henry Colman. ChIV-1
On the Threshold. Karl Kraus. TrJP, tr. by Albert Bloch
On the Threshold. Amy Levy. LW; NOBVV
On the Threshold. Pierre Reverdy. CuPo
On the threshold no one. Road. Pierre Reverdy. CuPo
On the threshold of heaven, the figures in the street. To an Old Philosopher in Rome. Wallace Stevens. APT-1; ColAP; EnlH; NOBA; NoAM
On the throne of many hues, Immortal Aphrodite. Sappho. SaLy, tr. by Diane Rayor
On the tidal mud, just before sunset. Daybreak. Galway Kinnell. BLT; ChAP
On the Tisza. Endre Ady. IQMS, tr. by Anton N. Nyerges
On the Tomb of Orpheus. Damagetus. GrAn, tr. by John Heath-Stubbs and Carol A. Whiteside
On the Tomb of the Unknown Soldier. László Mécs. IQMS, tr. by Watson Kirkconnell
On the Tombs in Westminster Abbey. Francis Beaumont.
 Lines on the Tombs in Westminster. NOBE; OBEV; SCGP
 (Memento for Mortality, A.) FaBoCh; HAP
 (On the Tombs in Westminster Abbey.) GTBS-P; OxAEP-1
On the top fence-rail. O. Mabson Southard. HA
On the top of the Crumpetty Tree. Quangle Wangle's Hat, The. Edward Lear. EBEV; PeVV
On the Tower. Annette von Droste-Hülshoff. WPOW, tr. by James Edward Tobin
On the Tower of Gathering Remoteness. Su Tung-p'o (Su Shih). TAL
On the Town's Honest Man. Ben Jonson. NOSC
On the train / old ladies playing football. Going Uptown to Visit Miriam. Víctor Hernández Cruz. PueRic
On the Transitory. Hugo von Hofmannsthal. WoPoe, tr. by Naomi Replansky
On the Translation of Anacreon. Horace Walpole, 4th Earl of Orford. FaBoEE
On the Treasury of the True Dharma Eye. Dogen. EnlH
On the tree or billow? (LL) World's Wanderers, The. Shelley. TTTS; TreFP
On the Triumph of Judith. Félix Lope de Vega Carpio. See Judith
On the trunk of a haunted tree. (LL) Haunted Oak, The. Paul Laurence Dunbar. ColAP; NAAAL; UnPo
On the twelfth floor. Martin Burke. HA
On the twentieth, at a certain moment. Christmas 1956. György Petri. VCWP, tr. by George Gömöri and Clive Wilmer
On the Twentieth Day. Ni Tsan. CoBLCP, tr. by Jonathan Chaves
On the 25th Anniversary of the Liberation of Auschwitz. Eli W. Mandel. NOBC
On the Twenty-First Day of the Fifth Month, I Reached Home. Yüan Mei. CoBLCP, tr. by Jonathan Chaves
On the Twenty-fourth: Improvisations. Liu E. CoBLCP, tr. by Jonathan Chaves
On the Twenty-fourth of the Third Month, in the Year Ting-wei Sailed across Lake T'ai from behind the Mountain. Wu Wei-yeh. SuSp, tr. by Chang Yin-nan
On the Two Great Floods. Francis Quarles. ChIV-1
On the Uniformity and Perfection of Nature. Philip Freneau. TCAPo
On the University Carrier Who Sick'n'd [or Sickened] in the Time of His Vacancy[, Being Forbid to go to London, by Reason of the Plague]. John Milton. EBEV; FaBoCh; FaBoEE; NOSC; OxAEP-1
On the Unusual Cold and Rainy [or Rainie] Weather in the Summer, 1648. Robert Heath. NOSC
On the up-platform at Morpeth station. Complaint of the Morpethshire Farmer, The. Basil Bunting. CTC
On the uptown lexington avenue express: Martin Luther King Day 1995. Duriel Harris. SpirFl
On the Use of Jayshus. Oliver St. John Gogarty. FaBoEE
On the Use of New and Old Words in Poetry. Anna Seward. Son
On the Vanity of Earthly Greatness. Arthur Guiterman. APT-1; HeIP-4; OBCA; PAI; TrJP
On the Venom Farm. Ruth Padel. EmeKit
On the Viking Raids. Unknown. WoPoe
On the Village Green. William Somervile [or Somerville]. ECEV Fr. Hobbinol.
On the Voyage to Jerusalem. Judah Halevi.
 "Watery waste the sinful world has grown, A." SWaP, tr. by Emma Lazarus
On the Wall. Immanuel di Roma. TrJP, tr. by Solomon Solis-Cohen
On the Wall of a KZ-Lager. János Pilinszky. AF; HP; PoSu
On the Wall of Cloud-Friend Hut. Muso Soseki. EaWin, tr. by W. S. Merwin

On the Wall of My Age. Lajos Áprily. IQMS, *tr.* by Paul Tabori

On the wan sea-strand. Heinrich Heine. AWP, *tr.* by John Todhunter *Fr.* North Sea, The.

On the warm July river. Inner Tube. Michael Ondaatje. NoAM

On the Water of Our Lord's Baptism[e]. Richard Crashaw. GeHe

On the Waterfront. Michael Foley. PNI

On the Watergate Women. Robin Morgan. GLP

On the Way Back. Bogomil Gjuzel. CarOv, *tr.* by Carolyn Kizer

On the way down. Way Down, The. Philip Levine. NOBA

On the way home from school, a child is struck. Acorn, The. Gail Mazur. ExTi

On the Way Out. Tu Fu. CarOv, *tr.* by Carolyn Kizer *Fr.* Adviser to the Court.

On the way to bed a) Take the staircase. In Case of Monsters. Stephen Knight. NeBl

On the way to God the difficulties. Lal Ded [*or* Lalla]. WPoS; WoPoe, *tr.* by Coleman Barks

On the Way to Hangchow: Anchored on the River at Night. Po Chü-i. ChiP, *tr.* by Arthur Waley

On the Way to Huang-ch'ang River. Wang Shih-chieng. SuSp, *tr.* by Richard John Lynn

On the Way to Kew. William Ernest Henley. MoBrPo *Fr.* Echoes.

On the Way to Mind. Milo de Angelis. NeIt, *tr.* by Lawrence Venuti

On the Way to Pa-ling. Yüan Mei. CoBLCP; ColAnChi, *tr.* by Jonathan Chaves

On the way to the grove you'll pass the Fates. Edgar Lee Masters. TCAPo *Fr.* Spoon River Anthology.

On the Way to the Mission. Duncan Campbell Scott. NOBC

On the way to the outhouse. Basho. EH, *tr.* by Robert Hass

On the way up from Sheet I met some children. To Edward Thomas. Alun Lewis. PoWW

On the Welch. *Unknown.* AngWePo

On the Welch Language. Katherine Philips. *See* On the Welsh Language

On the Welsh Language. Katherine Philips. EMWP; NOSC

  (If honor to an ancient name be due.) NoP-4

  (On the Welch Language.) NoP-4

On the wet sand the queen emerged from forest. Theseus: A Trilogy. Yvor Winters. NOBA

On the whole, we conclude the Romans won't do it, and I shan't. (LL) Arthur Hugh Clough. EBVV; FaBoWar; OxAEP-2 *Fr.* Amours de Voyage.

On the Wide Heath. Edna St. Vincent Millay. WPE

On the wide level of a mountain's head. Time, Real and Imaginary. Samuel Taylor Coleridge. NOBE; OBEV; OxBSP

On the Willow Bank. Yen Chen. WoPoe, *tr.* by Arthur Sze

On the wind, a drifting echo. Christmas Night. Lawrence Sail. OBCP

On the windows, the dirty film. Finder, The. Robin Blaser. FTOS

On the Wing. Christina Georgina Rossetti. VWP

On the wings of the buck and wing. (LL) Buckdancer's Choice. James Dickey. HeIP-4; NOBA; NoAM; NoP-4

On the World. Francis Quarles. HAP

On the Wounds of Our Crucified Lord. Richard Crashaw. NAEL-5v1; NAEL-6v1; NAEL-7v1

On the Yangtze. Wang An-shih. SuSp, *tr.* by Jan W. Walls

On the Yard. Etheridge Knight. RaBo

On the Yellow Footprints. Mcavoy Layne. CDa

On Theodoros. Simonides. GrAn, *tr.* by Peter Jay

On these southern roads. Buson. SoOfWa, *tr.* by Sam Hamill

On Things Seen. Tsung Ch'en.

  "Rebels' cavalry are everywhere, The." CoBLCP

On Thinking of Photographing My Fantasies. Nellie Wong. OpBo

On Third Avenue. Mina Loy. APT-1; HarvBoo

On this bald hill the new year hones its edge. Parliament Hill Fields. Sylvia Plath. HCAP; NALW

On this blest [*or* blessed] day may no dark cloud, or shower. To the Countess of A— Written on the Anniversary of Her Marriage. Charlotte Smith. RWP

On this bus to oblivion i bleed in the seat. Today I Am a Homicide in the North of the City. Wanda Coleman. NAAAL

On this cold. Marlene Mountain. HA

On This Day. M. B. Goffstein. NTCP

On This Day. Leah Goldberg. MHP, *tr.* by Ruth Finer Mintz

On This Day I Complete My Fortieth Year. Peter Porter. BMAP

On This Day I Complete My Thirty-sixth Year. Byron. CAGL; FHYEP; NAEL-6v2; NPeEn; NoP-4; OBWP; PoE

  (Messalonghi. January 22, 1824. On This Day I Complete My Thirty-sixth Year.) NOBRP

On this day of my birth, I see no visitors. Evening of My Birthday, The. Yang Shih-ch'i. CoBLCP, *tr.* by Jonathan Chaves

On this day, the sun. Hiroshima. "Agyeya." OMIP; WoPoe, *tr.* by Agyeya and Leonard Nathan

On this day they break bread. On This Day. Leah Goldberg. MHP, *tr.* by Ruth Finer Mintz

On this day tradition allots. New Year Greeting, A. W. H. Auden. HarvBoo

On this day when you have needed to sleep forever. Healing Animal. Joy Harjo. SeSe

On this earth, in this life, as I read your story, you're lonely. Adrienne Rich. NAAL-5 *Fr.* Atlas of the Difficult World, An.

On this feast day, oh, cursèd day and hour! Christopher Marlowe. NOBE *Fr.* Hero and Leander.

On this ground I may look for rest. My Detacted Villa. Li Shan-fu. SuSp, *tr.* by Edward H. Schafer

On this her daughter's tomb. Anyte [*or* Anytes]. GrAn

On this high hill in a year's turning. (LL) Poem in October. Dylan Thomas. AngWePo; NAEL-5v2; NAEL-6v2; NPeEn; NoAM; OxAEP-2; PoRA; RB; SoSe-8; TCAWP; UV

On this hotel, their rumpled royalties. West Forties: Morning, Noon, and Night, The. Louis Edward Sissman. CoAP

On This Island. W. H. Auden. HarvBoo; NAEL-5v2; NAEL-6v2; OxBEV; PoE

  (Seascape.) GTBS-P

On this island where I was born. I Never Saw Great Lakes. Nancy Morejón. TANSG, *tr.* by Joy Renjilian-Burgy

On this lone Isle, whose rugged rocks affright. Sonnet: Suppos'd to Be Written at Lemnos. Thomas Russell. NOBRP; NOEC

On this map white. A state thick as a fist. Map of Montana in Italy, A. Richard Hugo. LCAP-2

On this night. Seder Night with My Ancestors. Joanne Limburg. NeBl

On this resemblance, where we find. On a Death's Head. Elizabeth Tollet. ECWP

On this road / no one will follow me. Basho. OHPJ

On this side, and on that, men see their friends. Robert Blair. OxAEP-1 *Fr.* Grave, The.

On This Side of the River. Stephen Berg. GifTon

On this summer night. Chikako. WPoS; WoPoe, *tr.* by Edwin A. Cranston

On this tiny planet. Tune: "Full River Red"—A Reply to Kuo Mo-jo. Mao Tse-tung [*or* Mao Zedong]. SuSp, *tr.* by Eugene Eoyang

On this winter night. Lady Izumi. BoWoP

On Those That Deserve It. Francis Quarles. NOCV; NOSC

On Those That Hated "The Playboy of the Western World" 1907. W. B. Yeats. NOIV

On Those Two Unparalleld Friends, Sr: G: Lisle and Sr: C: Lucas, Who Were Shott to Death at Colechester. Hester Lee Pulter. EMWP

On three crosses of a tree. Charm Rhyme, A. *Unknown.* FaBoVe

On three sides / the sea's. On a High House in Byzantium. Paulus [*or* Paulos] Silentiarius. GrAn, *tr.* by Andrew Miller

On through it into the future, into the night. (LL) Six Years Later. Joseph Brodsky. TCRP; VCWP, *tr.* by Richard Wilbur

On thy grey bark, in witness of my flame. Pietro Metastasio. RWP, *tr.* by Charlotte Smith

On thy stars below in Frederick town! (LL) Barbara Frietchie. John Greenleaf Whittier. APN-1; AiP; CBCWP; CTC; ColAP; EBNV; HHAm; ITBLP; NCAP; NOBA; OBAL; OBCA; OxIBACP; TFi

On thy stupendous summit, rock sublime! Charlotte Smith. RWP

On thy wild banks, by frequent torrents worn. To the River Arun. Charlotte Smith. CenSon; RWP

On Time. Richard Hughes. MoBrPo

On Time. John Milton. OBEV; SCGP; SacPr

On Time, Death, and Eternity. Robert Peter. VerBaPo

On Tobacco. Charles Cotton. OBSV

On Tom Holland and Nell Cotton. *Unknown.* FaBoEE

On Tom Moore's Translation of Anacreon. Thomas Erskine, 1st Baron Erskine. FaBoEE

On Tom-o-Combe. *Unknown.* FaBoEE

On Tom Onslow, Earl of Onslow. *Unknown.* FaBoEE

On Tomato Ketchup. *Unknown.* NBLV; Spl

  (Tomato Ketchup.) Spl

On Top of It All. Keith Gilyard. SpirFl

On top of the Crumpetty Tree. Quangle Wangle's Hat, The. Edward Lear. OTCP

On top of two buildings. Gum. Jean Toomer. APT-2

On Track. Kathleene West. FFC

On Transitoriness. Hugo von Hofmannsthal. AuPH, *tr.* by Lowell A. Bangerter

On Translating "Eugene Onegin." Vladimir Vladimirovich Nabokov. APT-2

  (Eugene Onegin Stanza, The.) WoPoe

On Transportation. Benjamin Paloff. UrbNat

On Trash.   Vladimir Vladimirovich Mayakovsky [*or* Maiakovskii].   TCRP, *tr. by* Daniel Weissbort

On tree-topped hill, on tufted green.   Tree-topped Hill.   *Unknown.*   NOEC

On Trees.   Alan Dugan.   NoAM

On Trying to Imagine the Kiwi Pregnant.   Clarence Major.   GT

On TV.   Lyle Glazier.   OPRER

On Twisting River Is the Old Home of My Father. Now that My Illness Has Eased Up, I Have Written These Six Poems about the Place.   Chin Nung. "I remember when he took me on a trip to this place."   CoBLCP

On Two Brothers.   Simonides.   AWP, *tr. by* W. H. D. Rouse

On Two Monopolists.   John Byrom.   FaBoEE

On Two Souldiers Killing One Another for a Groat.   Samuel Wesley. "Full doelful Tales have oft been told."   VerBaPo

On vague hills the prophet bird.   Carol.   W. S. Merwin.   YaYoPo

On Vermeer's "Young Woman with a Water Jug" (1658) in the Metropolitan Museum.   Helen Pinkerton.   FFC

On Viewing Her Sleeping Infant.   Maria Frances Cecelia Cowper.   ECWP

On Viewing Herself in a Glass.   Elizabeth Teft.   ECWP

On village green, whose smooth and well-worn sod.   Disappointment, A. Joanna Baillie.   NOEC; WoRP

On vinegar and sour fish sauce Rome's legions stemmed avalanches.   Drugs of War, The.   Les A. Murray.   BMAP

On Virtue.   Phillis Wheatley.   TAP

On Visiting My Son, Port Angeles, Washington.   Duane Niatum.   CDW

On Visiting Shorin Temple, Where Bodhidharma Once Lived.   Soen.   ZenPo, *tr. by* Takashi Ikemoto and Lucien Stryk

On Visiting Sokei, Where the Sixth Patriarch Lived.   Tesshu.   ZenPo, *tr. by* Takashi Ikemoto and Lucien Stryk

On Visiting Taoist Recluse of Tai-Tien-Shan and Not Finding Him.   Li Po.   ChinPo, *tr. by* Yip Wai-lim

On Visiting the Graves of Hawthorne and Thoreau.   Jones Very.   TAP

On Visiting the M.D. Anderson.   Salma Khadra Jayyusi.   MAP, *tr. by* Charles Doria and the author

On Visiting Westminster Abbey.   Amanda Ros.   VerBaPo

On Vulture Peak.   Peak of the Held-Up Flower, The.   Muso Soseki.   EaWin, *tr. by* W. S. Merwin

On W. R———, Esq.   Robert Burns.   FaBoEE

On washday in the good old bad old days.   Washday Battles.   Geoffrey Summerfield.   NOxBChV

On Washington's Birthday Yancey the haberdasher.   Americana 3.   Carl Rakosi.   APT-2

On Watching a Caterpillar Become a Butterfly.   Clarence Major.   NAAAL

On Watching a World Series Game.   Sonia Sanchez.   NBV

On Watching Politicians Perform at Martin Luther King's Funeral.   Etheridge Knight.   NNaP

On water the Man-Fisher walks. (LL)   Drunken Fisherman, The.   Robert Lowell.   ChIV-2; NOBA; OxBA; VGW

On Waterloo's ensanguined plain.   On Scott's Poem "The Field of Waterloo." Thomas Erskine, 1st Baron Erskine.   NBLV

On Wednesday last, in the vicinity.   Lost and Found.   Jane Griffiths.   NeBl

On Wednesday night.   Wednesday Night Prayer Meeting.   Jay Wright.   ISC

On weekends we climbed the bus out of Paris.   To Valenton: Impressions circa 1947.   Liliane Richman.   TWW

On Wellington.   Byron.   FaBoWar; OBSV; OxAEP-2; OxBoLi   *Fr.* Don Juan.

On Wenlock Edge.   A. E. Housman.   GTBS-P; HarvBoo; MoBrPo; NAEL-5v2; NAEL-6v2; NOBE; NoP-4; OxAEP-2; OxBTC; PoRA; RB; SCGP; TFi

On Wenlock Edge the wood's in trouble.   On Wenlock Edge.   A. E. Housman.   GTBS-P; HarvBoo; MoBrPo; NAEL-5v2; NAEL-6v2; NOBE; NoP-4; OxAEP-2; OxBTC; PoRA; RB; SCGP; TFi

On went She, and due north her journey took. (LL)   With Ships the Sea Was Sprinkled Far and Nigh.   William Wordsworth.   CenSon; SCGP; WoPoe

On western hills the sun dies, eastern hills are dusking.   Song of the Sacred Strings.   Li Ho.   CoBCP, *tr. by* Burton Watson

On Westwall Downes [*or* On Westwell Downs].   William Strode.   NOSC; NPeEn

On wet sidewalks at the close of fall.   Witch-Hazel Wood, The.   Emily Hiestand.   UrbNat

On what a brave and curious whim.   Clocks.   Louis Ginsberg.   TrJP

On what foundation stands the warrior's pride.   Samuel Johnson.   FaBoWar; OBWP; OxBEV   *Fr.* Vanity of Human Wishes; The Tenth Satire of Juvenal Imitated, The.

On What the Army Does with Heads.   Michael Casey.   YaYoPo

On what they hunger to become. (LL)   Boat People.   Yusef Komunyakaa.   CDa; PoPoPo

On Whitsunday morning.   Dunt Dunt Dunt Pittie Pattie.   *Unknown.*   FaBoVe

On ["Who Wrote Icon Basilike" by Dr.] Christopher Wordsworth, Master of Trinity.   Benjamin Hall Kennedy.   FaBoEE; OBCoV

On William Prynne.   Samuel Butler.   FaBoEE

On William Wilson, Tailor.   *Unknown.*   FaBoEE

On Wilshire I lunched with a woman dead.   Brilliant Windows.   Larry Kramer.   GeoHom

On windy days.   Clothes on the Washing Line.   Frank Flynn.   OTCP

On windy days the mill.   Unfortunate Miller, The.   Alfred Edgar Coppard.   FaBoTw

On windy, woodchopping afternoons. (LL)   All I Want.   Luci Tapahonso.   ItWoWo; UnSA

On Winter.   Mary Leapor.   PEW

On winter afternoons.   Portrait of My Father, Militant Communist.   Jorge Teillier.   TCLAP, *tr. by* Carolyne Wright

On winter mornings.   Richard Wright.   APT-2

On winter nights.   Car Cemetery, The.   Ciaran Carson.   CIP-2

On Winter Nights.   Nijole Miliauskaite.   VCWP, *tr. by* Jonas Zdanys

On winter nights, when my grandmother.   On Winter Nights.   Nijole Miliauskaite.   VCWP, *tr. by* Jonas Zdanys

On Wishes.   Mahmoud Darwish.   VCWP, *tr. by* Denys Johnson-Davies

On Witch Mountain the fireflies flit in the autumn night.   Upon Seeing the Fireflies.   Tu Fu.   SuSp, *tr. by* Wu-Chi Liu

On with my coat and out into the night. (LL)   World's a Stage, The.   Joseph Hilaire Pierre Belloc.   OBCoV; OxBTC

On with the jalapeño Christmas lights! It's only the end.   Sabotage.   Anselm Berrigan.   HeMarv

On Wodin's day, sixth of December, thirty-nine.   *In re* Solomon Warshawer. Abraham Moses Klein.   MoCV

On Woman.   W. B. Yeats.   ChIV-1

On Women ("Britannia's daughters.").   Edward Young.   ECEV   *Fr.* Satires.

On Women ("Lavinia is polite.").   Edward Young.   ECEV   *Fr.* Satires.

On Words and Concepts and Things.   Paul Ramsey.   CRP

On Work.   Kahlil Gibran.   PoToHe   *Fr.* Prophet, The.

On Worldly Prelates.   Charles Wesley.   ChIV-2

On yeir begines ane other endis.   Godlie Instructione for Old and Young, Ane.   *Unknown.*   EMWP

On yon hill's top which this sweet plain commands.   Invites His Nymph to His Cottage.   Philip Ayres.   EnLoPo

On yonder hill there stands a creature.   O, No, John [*or* The One Answer]. *Unknown.*   PeLV

On yonder oak, upon its lordliest height.   Mistletoe.   Mary E. Tucker.   CBWP-1

On your bare rocks, O barren moors.   Barren Moors, The.   William Ellery Channing.   APN-1

On your dazzling throne, Aphrodite.   Sappho.   BoWoP

On your own premises. (LL)   I Am in Danger—Sir.   Adrienne Rich.   HCAP; HarvBoo; NAAL-5; NALW; NOBA

On your piano a plaster Beethoven stands.   Picture Postcard from Our Youth. Dan Pagis.   VCWP, *tr. by* Stephen Mitchell

On your slender body.   For the Courtesan Ch'ing Lin.   Wu Tsao.   BoWoP; WPOW; WoPoe, *tr. by* Chung Ling and Kenneth Rexroth

On your throne, a marvel of art, immortal.   Sappho.   STV

On Your Twenty-First Birthday.   Joan Austin Geier.   FFC

On Zacchaeus [*or* Zacheus].   Francis Quarles.   NOSC; OxBSP

On Zacheus [*or* Zacchaeus].   Francis Quarles.   HAP

On Zion and on Lebanon.   Henry Ustic Onderdonk.   AH

Once.   Alice Walker.   BlSi

Once.   Siv Widerberg.   NTCP, *tr. by* Verne Moberg

Once a boy beheld a bright.   Rose, The.   Goethe.   AWP, *tr. by* James Clarence Mangan

Once a day the rocks, with little warning.   Naskeag.   Alfred Corn.   VCAP

Once a dream did weave a shade.   William Blake.   FHYEP; NOBRP   *Fr.* Songs of Innocence.

Once a flock of stately peacocks.   Patrician Peacocks and the Overweening Jay, The.   Guy Wetmore Carryl.   TCAPo

Once a girl, all April-fresh.   Fazil Abdulovich Iskander.   ItGoST, *tr. by* Avril Pyman

Once a jolly swagman camped by a billabong.   Waltzing Matilda.   Andrew Barton Paterson.   CBAP

Once, a lady of the O Moores.   Parthenogenesis.   Nuala Ni Dhomhnaill.   CIP-2, *tr. by* Michael Hartnett

Once a little boy, Jack, was, oh! ever so good.   Sad Story of a Little boy That Cried, The.   *Unknown.*   OBSP

Once a little boy was dreaming.   Parables, I.   Antonio Machado Ruiz.   STV, *tr. by* John Frederick Nims

Once a little girl received a present.   Bear, The.   Vladimir Aleksandrovich Lugovskoy [*or* Lugovskoi].   TCRP, *tr. by* Gordon McVay

Once a man is born he has to die.   All Intents.   Larry Eigner.   VGW

Once a man jumped out of a streetcar, but so clumsily that he fell under an automobile.   Event on the Street, An.   Daniil Kharms.   AF

Once a pallid vestal.   Vestal, The.   Nathalia Crane.   TrJP

Once a poor widow, aging year by year. Geoffrey Chaucer. NAWM-5v1, tr. by Theodore Morrison Fr. Canterbury Tales, The.

Once, a pre-med white boy laced his fingers into mine. Warning to Young Bright Sisters / White AM. Culture 101A. Michelle T. Clinton. InTrad

Once a raven from Pluto's dark shore. True Facts of the Case, The. Anthony Euwer. OBAL; PeLi

Once a Shoot of Heaven. Beckian Fritz Goldberg. PuP-23

Once a snowflake fell. Winter Poem. Nikki Giovanni. PAI

Once a time is how the baby asks for a story. Height of the Season, The. Maxine W. Kumin. FFC

Once a two day holiday, the most sacred stretches. At the New Moon: Rosh Hodesh. Marge Piercy. TaR

Once a woman fell from the sky. This woman who fell from the sky was. Woman Who Fell from the Sky, The. Joy Harjo. BodElec

Once a woman who had nine sons. Dead Brother, The. Hungarian Oral Tradition. IQMS, tr. by Adam Makkai

Once a year up the long road from Jericho. Hot summer. Mothballs. Visiting the West Bank. S. V. Atalla. PoArWo

Once Again. Liz Sohappy Bahe. CDW

Once again. Isabel Meyrelles. SurWo, tr. by Jean R. Longland

Once Again, Anne Frank. Elina Wechsler. MirDau, tr. by Darrell Lockhart

Once again Love [Eros], the loosener of limbs, shakes me. Sappho. EroLit, tr. by Josephine Balmer

Once again love has hold. That Which Is Enough for Love. Luis Cernuda. CAGL, tr. by Rick Lipinski

Once again, my luggage packed, I'm returning to Wu. Mooring in the Rain at Sung-ling. Chin Nung. CoBLCP, tr. by Jonathan Chaves

Once again, once again. Velemir [or Viktor Vladimirovich] Khlebnikov. TCRP

Once again, someone took me. Line Up. Forrest Hamer. OPRER

Once again that loosener of limbs, Love. Sappho. SaLy, tr. by Diane Rayor

Once again the Mind. Faiz Ahmad Faiz. AF, tr. by Naomi Lazard

Once again the pine-tree sung. Ralph Waldo Emerson. APN-1 Fr. Woodnotes II ("As sunbeams stream through liberal space.").

Once again the scurry of feet those myriads. Face of the Waters, The. Robert David Fitzgerald. CBAP

Once Alien Here. John Hewitt. CABP; CIP-2; PNI

Once Allen Ginsberg stopped to pee at a bookstore in New Jersey. Allen Ginsberg. Toi Derricotte. PBCAP

Once, among the transports, was one with children—two freight. Children. Charles Reznikoff. FTOS

Once an ex-con told me. Rape Poem, The. Tommi Avicolli. GLP

Once, and but once found in thy company. John Donne. ESCV; FSCP; NoSic Fr. Elegies.

Once and for all. (LL) Dark Room, The. Enrique Lihn. TCLAP; VCWP, tr. by David Unger

Once and for all I will lie down here like a dead man. Faces I Love, The. Gerald Stern. LoL

Once and Upon. Madeline Gleason. NeAP

Once, as a child, I ate raspberries. And forgot. Raspberries. Laurence David Lerner. EBEV

Once as abroad I stray'd. Transfiguration. Ralph Chubb. CAGL

Once as I in my study sat and saw. Hourglass, The. Joseph Beaumont. NOSC

Once, as in the darkness I lay asleep by night. Nightmare, The. Wang Yen-Shou. ChiP, tr. by Arthur Waley

Once as it was morning and I was in the field. Poppies. Zalman Schneour. MHP, tr. by Ruth Finer Mintz

Once, as old Lord Gorbals motored. Lord Gorbals. Harry Graham. PeLV

Once as we were sitting by. Spring 1942. Roy Fuller. OxBTC

Once at a merry wedding feast. St. George Tucker. NBLV Fr. Cynic, The.

Once before I loved this quiet place. Returning to Lotus Village. Kao Ch'i. CoBLCP, tr. by Jonathan Chaves

Once between us the Atlantic. Sundered. Israel Zangwill. TrJP

Once, but is the eternity that awaits you. (LL) Bright Field, The. Ronald Stuart Thomas. AngWePo; TCAWP

Once by the Pacific. Robert Frost. APT-1; GSo; HAP; HeIP-4; MoAmPo; NAAL-2v2; NIL-7; NOBA; Son; TRP; VGW; WeW-3

Once careless of her children. Sioux Woman Defends Her Children, The. Chippewa Oral Tradition. NAAL-5

Once Cypris sent to Europa a sweet dream. Europa. Moschus. HePo, tr. by Barbara Hughes Fowler

Once Death has spoken, the words are final. To My Daughter. Margit Mikes. IQMS, tr. by Suzanne K. Walther

Once Delpho read—sage Delpho, learned and wise. Mary Leapor. ECWP Fr. Epistle to Artemisia.

Once der was a meetin' in de wilderness. Brer Rabbit, You's de Cutes' of 'Em All. James Weldon Johnson. APT-1

Once Did My Thoughts. Unknown. EBEV

Once did She hold the gorgeous east in fee. On the Extinction of the Venetian Republic. William Wordsworth. GTBS-P; NOBE; OBEV

Once down on my knees to growing plants. Mood Apart, A. Robert Frost. OxBSP

Once drunk, my delight knows no limits. Written When Drunk. Chang Yüeh. CoBCP, tr. by Burton Watson

Once, far over the breakers. Akiko Yosano. OHMPJ

Once Father raised. Transits. Sharan Strange. InTrad

Once, for a dare. After the Deluge. Wole Soyinka. HBAPE

Once, grave Laodicean profiteer. Lourenço Marques. Charles Eglington. PeSAV

Once, happier people lived here. Theresienstadt's Hospital. Unknown, fr. Terezin Concentration Camp. INSAB

Once haunted. Love Letter. Katayoon Zandvakili. AmPoNex

Once he asked me. Tales about My Father. 'Abd al-Karim Kassid. MAP, tr. by Lena Jayyusi and Anthony Thwaite

Once he puts out the light. Hermit Has a Visitor, The. Maxine W. Kumin. BoWoP

Once he will miss, twice he will miss. Unknown. AWP Fr. Thousand and One Nights, The.

Once home, you'll throw yourself on an unmade bed. Like Thousands of Others. Aleksandr Petrovich Tkachenko. ItGoST, tr. by Maia Tekses

Once I am sure there's nothing going on. Church Going. Philip Larkin. CABP; GTBS-P; HarvBoo; HeIP-4; MoBrPo; NAEL-5v2; NAEL-6v2; NIL-7; NIP-4; NoAM; NoP-4; PAI; SCV; SoSe-8; TFi; TwCP; UnPo

Once I belonged to Achaimenides. Field, A. Unknown. GrAn, tr. by Peter Jay

Once I came across / some beardless doctors. Strato [or Straton]. GrAn

Once I entered. Like Ana. Nina Cassian. PoSu, tr. by Nina Cassian

Once I followed horses. Denis Glover. PeNZ Fr. Sings Harry.

Once I found a cowboy who thought he could. Mae West Chats It Up with Bessie Smith. Colleen J. McElroy. BAP-01

Once I goosestepped across the square. Résumé. Bei Dao. AF, tr. by Bonnie S. McDougall

Once I gorged myself in a peach grove. To an Ancient Tune. Unknown. CrYelRi, tr. by Sam Hamill

Once, I grew long hair. Very True Confessions. Sidney Burris. SwNoth

Once I had a taste. Remembrance of Strange Hospitality. Yelena [or Elena] Shwarts [or Shvarts]. ItGoST; VCWP, tr. by Michael Molnar

Once I had dreamed of return to a sunlit land. Old Dreams. Ivor Gurney. HarvBoo

Once, I knew a fine song. Stephen Crane. APN-2 Fr. Black Riders [and Other Lines], The.

Once I learnt in wilful hour. On a Wife. Francis Burdett Money-Coutts. OxBSP

Once I liked pablum. Once. Siv Widerberg. NTCP, tr. by Verne Moberg

Once I lived in capitals. Italic. Roger McGough. OBCoV

Once I lived with my brothers, images. Centaur Overheard, The. Edgar Bowers. CoAmPo

Once I loved a man. Baby, Baby All the Time. Bobby Troup. ReLy

Once I loved a spider. Spider and the Ghost of the Fly, The. Nicholas Vachel Lindsay. VGW

Once I Pass'd through a Populous City. Walt Whitman. NAAL-2v1; NAAL-3; NAAL-5; OxBA; RaBo; SAmP

Once I read a story. Story, The. Dan Pagis. PoSu, tr. by Stephen Mitchell

Once I saw a Devil in a flame of fire. William Blake. NAEL-6v2 Fr. Marriage of Heaven and Hell, The.

Once I saw a little bird. Little Bird, The. Mother Goose. OxNR; ReMoGo

Once I seen a human ruin. Ambrose Bierce. APN-2; OBAL Fr. Devil's Dictionary, The.

Once I shone afar like a. Kenneth Rexroth. APSN Fr. Love Poems of Marichiko, The.

Once I used to brag about my handy man. My Handy Man Ain't Handy No More. Andy Razaf. ReLy

Once I was a cow, a horse. Wang An-shih. CoBCP Fr. Twenty Poems in Imitation of Han-shan and Shih-te.

Once I was a lizard. Look in the Past, A. Jared Angira. PBMAP

Once I was a sentimental thing. Spring Can Really Hang You Up the Most. Tommy Wolf. ReLy

Once I was in love. Who's been exempted? Philodemus. GrAn

Once I was in love with a woman. Temporary Situation, A. David St. John. BodElec

Once I was reading Hesiod. Argentarius. GrAn

Once I was wood from a worthless old fig tree. Horace. PriapPo, tr. by Richard W. Hooper Fr. Satires.

Once I was young / Yesterday, perhaps. I Didn't Know What Time It Was. Richard Rodgers. ReLy

Once I wished I might rehearse. Freedom. Ralph Waldo Emerson. APN-1

Once in a dream (for once I dreamed of you). On the Wing. Christina Georgina Rossetti. VWP

Once in a dream I saw a snake. Snake. Paresh Chandra Raut. OMIP, *tr. by* Jayanta Mahapatra

Once, in [a] finesse of fiddles found I ecstasy. Embankment (The fantasia of a fallen gentleman on a cold, bitter night), The. Thomas Ernest Hulme. EBEV; FaBoMo; GTBS-P; OPOU; OxBSP; OxBTC

Once, in a foreign country, I was suddenly ill. Widening Spell of the Leaves, The. Larry Levis. PBCAP

Once, in a house I will inherit in a land I can't explain. Comings and Goings. Ann Townsend. NAPBL

Once in a Lifetime, Snow. Les A. Murray. CBAP; NoP-4

Once in a Saintly Passion. James Thomson. NOBVV

Once in a seaside town with time to kill. John Hewitt. ModIr *Fr.* Freehold.

Once in a thousand years. Fragrance of the Udumbara, The. Muso Soseki. EaWin, *tr. by* W. S. Merwin

Once in a While a Protest Poem. David B. Axelrod. InPK-6

Once in a while somebody fights for breath. Vanishing Lung Syndrome. Miroslav Holub. VCWP

Once in a while / we'd find a patch. Children, The. William Carlos Williams. SAmP

Once in Berlin I rode. Germany, 1981. Phyllis Kahaney. GotH

Once in Canandaigua, hitchhiking from Ann Arbor. Faces. John Ciardi. WeW-3

Once in Love with Amy. Frank Loesser. ReLy

Once in Mexico an old man was. Visions. William Stafford. NoAM

Once, in my early thirties, I saw. Jane Kenyon. LoL *Fr.* Having It Out With Melancholy.

Once in our customed walk a wounded bird. To My Brother. Mary Bryan. CenSon

Once in our lives, / Let us drink to our wives. *Unknown.* FaBoEE

Once-in-Passing, The. Louis MacNeice. ModIr *Fr.* Hand of Snapshots, A.

Once, in summer, / in the blueberries. Picking Blueberries, Austerlitz, New York, 1957. Mary Oliver. NAAL-5

Once, in the Colosseum—that. Lizard, The. Alphonse Marie Louis de Lamartine. SxFrPo, *tr. by* E. H. Blackmore and A. M. Blackmore

Once in the dark of night. Dark Night, The. Saint John of the Cross. BBASP; STV; WeW-3, *tr. by* Kieran Kavanaugh and Otilio Rodriquez

Once, in the Giant's Ring, I closed my eyes. Home. Frank Ormsby. ModIr; PBCIP; PNI

Once in the Phoenix tower the phoenix made her nest. On Climbing the Phoenix Tower at Chinling. Li Po. TAL

Once in the winter. Forsaken, The. Duncan Campbell Scott. NOBC

Once it had gorged itself. On a Pig's Head. Charles Tomlinson. NoAM

Once it smiled a silent dell. Valley of Unrest, The. Edgar Allan Poe. APN-1; NAAL-2v1; NAAL-3

Once it was cards on the table. In Memory of Elizabeth Kearney, Blasket-Islander. Michael Davitt. BiHa, *tr. by* the author

Once it was enough simply. Reaching the Horizon. Robert Mezey. GeoHom

Once late at night staying in Menton. Laughing All the Way. Liz Cashdan. Prnts

Once, long ago, a friend gave me a book. Gift, The. Margaret E. Bruner. PoToHe

Once long ago a wolf strolled down. Wolf and the Sow, The. Marie de France. NAEL-7v1, *tr. by* Harriet Spiegel

Once long ago when at the desert's edge. Three Holy Kings, The. Rainer Maria Rilke. ChrPo, *tr. by* Edward Snow

Once looked Gudrun. *Unknown.* OBVE *Fr.* Elder Edda, The.

Once loving is a gen'ral Fashion. On Loving Once and Loving Often. Elizabeth Tollet. LW

Once More. Forugh Farrokhzad. BoWoP, *tr. by* Amin Banani and Jascha Kessler

Once more a winter sky surrounds my sight. Winter Sky. John Cope. GeoH

Once more around should do it, the man confided. Flight of the Roller Coaster. Raymond Souster. NOBC

Once more beneath my thumb the globe turns. Childhood. Donald Justice. LCAP-2

Once more by the brook the alder leaves. Hayden Carruth. NNaP

Once more by the roadside fallen, Lord. Until New Spring or Death. Árpád Tóth. IQMS, *tr. by* Madeline Mason

Once more, Cesario. William Shakespeare. SCV *Fr.* Twelfth Night.

Once more drifting clouds gather in the western sky. Dusk. Shuntaro Tanikawa. PoetW, *tr. by* Harold Wright

Once More Fields and Gardens. T'ao Ch'ien [*or* T'ao Yuan-ming]. AWP, *tr. by* Florence Ayscough and Amy Lowell

Once More Following the Rhymes of Pin-lao's Poem "Getting Up after Illness and Strolling in the Eastern Garden." Huang T'ing-chien. CoBCP, *tr. by* Burton Watson

(Once More Following the Rhymes of Pin-lao's Poem "Getting Up After Illness and Strolling in the Eastern Garden") CoBCP, *tr. by* Burton Watson

Once more he sees his companions' faces. Survivor, The. Primo Levi. HP, *tr. by* Ruth Feldman

Once more I come to the white page of art. Cost of Seriousness, The. Peter Porter. NoAM

Once more I visited the place. Female's Lamentations; or, The Village in Mourning, The. Hannah Wallis. ECWP

Once more, listening to the wind and rain. Return, The. Arna Bontemps. GT

Once more, O Lord. George Washington Doane. AH

Once More, Once More. Velemir [*or* Viktor Vladimirovich] Khlebnikov. TCRusP, *tr. by* Kathy Lewis and Bob Perelman

Once More, Our God, Vouchsafe to Shine! Samuel Sewall. AH; SacPr (Wednesday, January 1, 1701.) SCAP

Once more the changed year's turning wheel returns. Dante Gabriel Rossetti. EBVV; NoP-4 *Fr.* House of Life, The.

Once more the leaves. Seattle, Autumn, 1933. Alfred Encarnacion. OpBo

Once more the perfect pattern falls asleep. Replica, The. Vernon Watkins. AngWePo

Once more the poem woke me up. Little Furnace. Brenda Hillman. BodElec

Once more the storm is howling, and half hid. Prayer for My Daughter, A. W. B. Yeats. HAP; NAEL-5v2; NAEL-6v2; NoAM; NoP-4; OxBTC; PoRA; RaBo; TFi

Once more unto the breach, dear friends, once more. William Shakespeare. OxAEP-1 *Fr.* King Henry V.

Once more upon the waters! yet once more! Byron. FHYEP *Fr.* Childe Harold's Pilgrimage.

Once more you pass her house, deep in thought. Song Inscribed on an Earthenware Vessel. *Unknown.* WoPoe, *tr. by* John L. Foster

Once mother said: My little pet. Animal Crackers in My Soup. Ted Koehler. ReLy

Once, my braids swung heavy as ropes. Butcher's Wife, The. Louise Erdrich. HATNAP; NoP-4

Once my clothes were shabby. All I Need Is the Girl. Stephen Sondheim. ReLy

Once my parents were older. Chiyojo [*or* Chiyo *or* Chiyo-Ni *or* Kaga no Chiyo *or* Fukuda Chiyo-Ni]. BoWoP

Once naked, once even intangible. (LL) Pleasure. A. K. Ramanujan. PoetW; VCWP

Once near San Ysidro. Earth and Rain, the Plants & Sun. Simon J. Ortiz. NAAL-5

Once noble custom was: by blood on battleground. Old Nobility, The. Friedrich von Logau. GePo, *tr. by* George C. Schoolfield

Once on a charger there was laid. Salome. Charles Lamb. ChIV-2

Once, on a lone sorry night, your ruins, Fort Huszt, did I enter. Huszt. Ferenc Kölcsey. IQMS, *tr. by* Watson Kirkconnell

Once on a morning of sweet recreation. Blackbird, The. *Unknown.* NOIV

Once on a Night in the Delta: A Report from Hell. Etheridge Knight. BodElec

Once on a time, a monarch, tired with whooping. Apple Dumplings and a King, The. "Peter Pindar." OBSV

Once on a time a thousand different men. James Henry. NOBVV

Once on a time did Eucritus and I. Theocritus. AWP *Fr.* Idylls.

Once on a time I used to be. Harlot's Catch. Robert Malise Bowyer Nichols. FaBoTw

Once on a time, some centuries ago. Henry Wadsworth Longfellow. OxBA *Fr.* Tales of a Wayside Inn.

Once on a time there was a pool. James Russell Lowell. OBAL *Fr.* Biglow Papers, The.

Once on a train from Baden-Baden. Rizal's Ghost. Eugene Gloria. ReBoTo

Once, on that highway where a traveler works hard. Pornography, Nebraska. Sandra McPherson. ReTh

Once on the mountain's balmy lap reclined. James Montgomery. NOBRP *Fr.* Brahmin, The.

Once, once, in Washington. Patriotic Tour and Postulate of Joy. Robert Penn Warren. AiP

Once once only in the deluge. Fear. George Oppen. BodElec

Once . . . once upon a time. Martha. Walter De la Mare. MoBrPo

Once one year, and I don't know when. Wanderer's Bouquet. So Chong-Ju. WoPoe, *tr. by* David R. McCann

Once [*or* Ons], as methought, Fortune me kissed [*or* kist *or* kyst]. Promise, A. Sir Thomas Wyatt. BoLoP

Once or twice he eyed me oddly. Once. Temptations of St. Antony by His Housekeeper. Elizabeth Smither. PeNZ

Once our healing nurse, now you're. Venus de Milo. Gottfried Keller. WoPoe, *tr. by* John Peck

Once-over, The. Paul Blackburn. NeAP; PoM

Once past the icefalls and the teeth of. On the Road to Erewhon. Allen Curnow. HarvBoo

Once, playing cricket, beneath a toast-dry hill.   Curriculum Vitae.   Robert Gray.   NOBAu

Once public treasurer, a farmer now.   *Unknown.*   PriapPo, *tr. by* Richard W. Hooper   *Fr.* Priapus Poems, The.

Once riding in Old Baltimore.   Incident.   Countee Cullen.   APT-2; BPo; ChAP; KaS; NAAAL; NAAL-2v2; NAAL-5; NOxBChV; NTCP; NoAM; NoP-4; OBCA; OxIBACP; PoPoPo; SSLK; VGW

Once she dressed in silks and lace.   She's Funny That Way (I Got a Woman, Crazy for Me).   Neil Moret.   ReLy

Once, so long ago.   For Paddy Mac.   Padraic Fallon.   CIP-2

Once some people were visiting Chekhov.   Chocolates.   Louis Simpson.   OBCoV; OxBC

Once someone loved this piece of junk.   Garage Sale as a Spiritual Exercise, The.   Thomas M. [*or* "Tom"] Disch.   GI

Once, taking a train into Chicago.   Freight Cars.   Stephen Dobyns.   GM

Once the Days.   Denis Glover.   PeNZ   *Fr.* Sings Harry.

Once the goal's reached.   Kishu.   ZenPo, *tr. by* Takashi Ikemoto and Lucien Stryk

Once, the mighty waves of ocean.   Precious Pearl, The.   Priscilla Jane Thompson.   CBWP-2

Once the nation's chief was honored by the company of one.   Notable Dinner, A.   Lizelia Augusta Jenkins Moorer.   CBWP-3

Once there occurred a miracle.   Sheep School.   Sándor Weöres.   IQMS, *tr. by* Adam Makkai and Donald E. Morse

Once there was.   From an ass to an analyst and back.   Joyce Mansour.   MFP, *tr. by* Martin Sorrell

Once there was a chain; strong as a destiny.   Break, The.   Delmira Agustini.   TANSG, *tr. by* Mark McCaffrey

Once there was a father.   Sons Changed Into Stags, The.   József Erdélyi.   IQMS, *tr. by* Watson Kirkconnell

Once there was a fence here.   Former Barn Lot.   Mark Van Doren.   MoAmPo

Once there was a little boy.   Switch on the Night.   Ray Bradbury.   OBSP

Once there was a little girl.   Little Girl of the Black Forest.   Lise Deharme.   SurWo, *tr. by* Franklin Rosemont

Once there was a man.   Story of the Man Whose Tastes Were Too Refined.   Charles Rafferty.   AmPoNex

Once there was a man named Mr. Artesian and his activity was tremendous.   Mr. Artesian's Conscientiousness.   Ogden Nash.   NBLV

Once there was a shock.   After a Death.   Tomas Tranströmer.   VCWP, *tr. by* Robert Bly

Once there was a snowman.   Snowman, The.   *Unknown.*   OTCP

Once there was a soldier boy.   Bulat Shalvovich Okudzhava.   TCRusP, *tr. by* Daniel Weissbort

Once there was a thing called Spring.   Spring Is Here.   Richard Rodgers.   ReLy

Once there was a woman went out to pick beans.   Hairy Toe, The.   *Unknown.*   OBSP

Once there was an elephant.   Eletelephony.   Laura Elizabeth Richards.   NBLV; NOxBChV; NTCP; OBCA; OxIBACP

Once There Was Light.   Jane Kenyon.   LoL   *Fr.* Having It Out with Melancholy.

Once there were 50 Marías.   Other Marías.   Diana García.   TouFir

Once there were none and the dark air was dumb.   Nightingales, The.   Harri Webb.   AngWePo; TCAWP

Once there were peasant pots and a dry brown hare.   Joan Miró.   Ruthven Todd.   SPE

Once there were 3 little Indian girls.   Charité Espérance et Foi.   Earle Birney.   OxBC

Once they stood tiptoe, dewy, poised.   Dream Lover.   Mark DeFoe.   SwNoth

Once they were sticks and stones.   Names.   Robert Earl Hayden.   GT

Once three gypsies I chanced to find.   Three Gypsies, The.   Nikolaus Lenau.   AuPH, *tr. by* Winthrop H. Root

Once to life I said, yes!   To Life I Said Yes.   Chaim Grade.   TrJP, *tr. by* Joseph Leftwich

Once, twice, thrice / I give thee warning.   *Unknown.*   OxNR

Once upon.   Fairy Tale, A.   Bogdan Boychuk.   WoPoe, *tr. by* David Ignatow

Once upon a colony.   Can. Hist.   Earle Birney.   OxBC

Once upon a midnight dreary, while I pondered [*or* ponder'd], weak and weary.   Raven, The.   Edgar Allan Poe.   APN-1; BRP; ChAP; ColAP; EBNV; FaBoCh; HeIP-4; ITBLP; NAAL-2v1; NAAL-3; NAAL-5; NCAP; NIL-7; NIP-4; NOBA; NoP-4; OBCA; OBNV; OWoS; OxBA; PWR; PoRA; TAP; TCAPo; TFi; TreFP; UV

Once upon a Seesaw with Charlie Chan.   Cyn Zarco.   ReBoTo

Once upon a Time.   Lee Adams.   ReLy

Once upon a Time.   Gabriel Okara.   PBA

Once upon a time.   Chernobyl.   Mary Jo Salter.   FFC

Once upon a time a girl with moonlight in her eyes.   Once upon a Time.   Lee Adams.   ReLy

Once upon a time an ancient man had fine.   Splendid Stags, The.   József Erdélyi.   IQMS, *tr. by* Thomas Land

Once upon a time / Before I took up smiling.   Blue Moon.   Richard Rodgers.   ReLy

Once upon a time, children.   Storytime.   Judith Nicholls.   OBSP

Once upon a time / I caught a little rhyme.   Catch a Little Rhyme.   Eve Merriam.   OBCA; OxIBACP

Once upon a time / I composed a witty rhyme.   Minstrel's Last Lay, The.   John Barth.   OBAL

Once upon a time, I practiced moves in a mirror.   Resurrection of Elvis Presley, The.   Ai.   AllShUp

Once upon a time I was.   To the Tune "The Fall of a Little Wild Goose."   Huang O [*or* Huang Ho].   WPOW

Once upon a time in California.   Friend of the Family, A.   Louis Simpson.   NNaP

Once upon a time, the goddesses settled down.   First Merseburg Spell.   *Unknown.*   GePo, *tr. by* Carroll Hightower

Once upon a time there was a girl called Annabell.   Annabell and the Witches.   Mick Gowar.   OBSP

Once upon a time / there was a lonely wolf.   Fable.   János Pilinszky.   OBVE; PoSu; RB

Once upon a time there was a roof covered with tin.   Owl and the Mouse, The.   Viktor Aleksandrovich Sosnora.   TCRusP, *tr. by* Denis Johnson and Kathy Lewis

Once upon a time there was a triangle.   Vasco [*or* Vasko] Popa.   PoSu   *Fr.* Yawn of Yawns, The.

Once upon a time there was a yawn.   Vasco [*or* Vasko] Popa.   PoSu   *Fr.* Yawn of Yawns, The.

Once upon a time there was an infinity of echoes.   Vasco [*or* Vasko] Popa.   PoSu, *tr. by* Anne Pennington   *Fr.* Yawn of Yawns, The.

Once upon a time there were three.   Variations.   Maurice Scully.   Oth

Once upon the Iceland's solitary strand.   Broken Oar, The.   Henry Wadsworth Longfellow.   OxBSo

Once, walking home, I passed beneath a tree.   Music of a Tree, The.   Walter James Turner.   MoBrPo

Once was a boy, age fifteen year.   Hiram Helsel.   Julia A. Moore.   VerBaPo

Once we dreamed of eagles.   Reading Indian Poetry.   Ramona Wilson.   VoR

Once we had a knocker.   Lazy.   Lu Yu.   OHMPC, *tr. by* Kenneth Rexroth

Once we knew the world well.   Wislawa Szymborska.   AF, *tr. by* Grazyna Drabik

Once We Played.   Mathilde Blind.   LW

Once we played at love together.   Once We Played.   Mathilde Blind.   LW

Once we presumed to found ourselves for good.   Disappearing Island, The.   Seamus Heaney.   BodElec

Once we saw the nest.   Nest, The.   Carol Moldaw.   UrbNat

Once We Were Farmers.   Elsa Rediva E'der.   ReBoTo

Once we were wayfarers, then seafarers, then airfarers.   Post Early for Space.   Peter J. Henniker-Heaton.   HHAm

Once when by Trent's pellucid streams.   John Gilbert Cooper.   ECEV   *Fr.* Call of Aristippus, The.

Once, when Heracles was ten months old, Alcmena.   Theocritus.   HePo, *tr. by* Barbara Hughes Fowler   *Fr.* Idylls.

Once when I read the funnies.   Looking.   Robert Kelly.   FTOS

Once, when I ventured on your deeps, Piranha. (LL)   Old Malediction, An.   Horace.   NoAM; OBCoV; WoPoe, *tr. by* Anthony Hecht

Once when I walked into a room.   Between Ourselves.   Audre Lorde.   ISC; WPOW

Once when I was coming from art class they surprised me.   Daryl Hine.   GLP   *Fr.* March.

Once When I Was in the Eighth Grade.   Maurice Kilwein Guevara.   AmPoNex

Once when I was little I knelt before an onion.   Poem.   Bob Holman.   SpudSo

Once when I was tree.   Root Song.   Henry Dumas.   ISC

Once when I was very scared.   Riddle, A.   Charlotte Zolotow.   NTCP

Once, when I wasn't very big.   Cat and the Pig, The.   Gerard Benson.   NOxBChV

Once, when midnight smote the air.   On Those That Hated "The Playboy of the Western World" 1907.   W. B. Yeats.   NOIV

Once when our eyes were clean as noon, our rooms.   Cana.   Thomas Merton.   ChIV-2; TrCP

Once when the moon was out about three quarters.   White Clover.   Marvin Bell.   InvLad; VCAP

Once when the snow of the year was beginning to fall.   Runaway, The.   Robert Frost.   AWP; FaBoCh; MoAmPo; SAmP; TwCP; VGW

Once, when their hearts were wild with joy.   On Harting Down.   Thomas Sturge Moore.   OxBTC

Once, when walking down the wet grey streets.   Archie Weller.   IBA

Once when young I lay and listened.   To the Tune "The Fair Maid of Yu."   Chiang Chieh.   OHMPC, *tr. by* Kenneth Rexroth

Once, while a famous town lay torn and burning.   Braveries.   Robert Pinsky.   HarvBoo

Once while hunting in the shady lurking wood he [Dionysus] was delighted by the rosy form of a young comrade. Nonnus. CAGL, *tr. by* W. H. D. Rouse *Fr.* Dionysiaca.

Once, with a certain pride, we kept attempts. Spot the Ball. Frank Ormsby. CIP-2; PBCIP; PNI

Once within a little grove a shepherdess I spied. Encounter, An. Guido Cavalcanti. NAWM-7v1, *tr. by* James J. Wilhelm

Once, years after your death, I dreamt. Dream, The. Irving Feldman. TaR; VCAP

Once you said. What She Said to Her Girl-Friend. Maturaikkataiayattar Makan Vennakan. WoPoe, *tr. by* A. K. Ramanujan

Once you told me my father never wept. Ancestral Burden. Alfonsina Storni. TCLAP, *tr. by* Andrew Rosing

Once You've Been to War. Walter McDonald. CDa

Once your name was Bimbircokak. Dear Husband. Yambo Ouloguem. NegPo, *tr. by* Ellen Conroy Kennedy

Ondt and the Gracehoper, The. James Joyce. BIrV *Fr.* Finnegans Wake.

One. James Berry. NOxBChV

One. Federico García Lorca. PFTM-1

One. Marvin Hamlisch. ReLy

One. John Heath-Stubbs. OBCoV

1. Hsüeh T'ao. WoPoe, *tr. by* Jeanne Larsen *Fr.* Trying on New-Made Clothes: Three Poems.

One. Thomas Kinsella.

38 Phoenix Street. ModIr

One. Carolyn Kizer. VCAP *Fr.* Pro Femina.

1. Robert Malise Bowyer Nichols. CLPP *Fr.* Get-Away.

I. Charles Reznikoff. FTOS *Fr.* Jews in Babylonia.

One. Carolyn M. Rodgers. BPo

One. Constance Fenimore Woolson. SWaP *Fr.* Two Women.

One, The. James Dickey. BodElec

One, The. Patrick Kavanagh. MoBrPo

(1) A man and woman looking for lilies. Lily Events. *Unknown.* PFTM-1

One a part of his famous society. (LL) Abraham. Delmore Schwartz. ChIV-1; TaR

One admires the American form of these sightings. Apparition, The. Carol J. Pierman. ReTh

One after the other. Granada (1000 A.D.). Abu Ishaq al-Ilbin. ArPe, *tr. by* Omar S. Pound

One afternoon in her loft. Need for Shoes, The. Molly Bendall. InvLad

One afternoon in my room. True Story, A. Marvin Bell. BodElec

One afternoon the last week in April. Axe Handles. Gary Snyder. ColAP; LoL; NoAM; PmAP; PoPoPo; VCAP

One AM. Leroy Gorman. HA

One among the Roses. Edmund Charles Blunden. OBGa

One arch of the sky. Love in Labrador. Carl Sandburg. VGW

One arm circles my neck. Octopus. Ghazi Al-Gosaibi. MAP, *tr. by* Charles Doria and Sharif Elmusa

One arm hooked around the frayed strap. Yellow Light. Garrett Kaoru Hongo. GeoHom; OpBo

One-armed explorer, The. Gardens of Zuñi, The. W. S. Merwin. GifTon

One-Armed Man in the Undergrowth, The. Bertolt Brecht. PoSu, *tr. by* Derek Bowman

One Art. Elizabeth Bishop. APT-2; AmFaPo; DiPo; HAP; HarvBoo; MakPoe; NAAL-2v2; NAAL-5; NALW; NoAM; NoP-4; PoE; PoPoPo; PoetW; SoSe-8; VCAP

One at one table. Automat. David Ray. PoSol

One Autumn night, in Sudbury town. Henry Wadsworth Longfellow. APN-1 *Fr.* Tales of a Wayside Inn.

One bath / After another. Issa. ZenPo, *tr. by* Takashi Ikemoto and Lucien Stryk

One be the nail another the pincers. Vasco [*or* Vasko] Popa. PoSu *Fr.* Games.

One beautiful morning in the month of May all was serene and / quiet. May. Mrs. Henry Linden. CBWP-4

One being led, The? I don't know. Scaffold in Winter. János Pilinszky. PoSu, *tr. by* Peter Jay

One biting winter morning. Spider, The. Hannah Flagg Gould. OBCA

One Blessing had I than the rest. Emily Dickinson. SWaP

One bliss for which / There is no match. Taboo to Boot. Ogden Nash. RB

One Book, The. Velemir [*or* Viktor Vladimirovich] Khlebnikov. TCRusP, *tr. by* Kathy Lewis and Bob Perelman

One bough in the land of eternal banishment. Poem No. VII. Sang Yi. PFTM-1

One boy, Saint Dwyn, my bauble. Lament for Siôn y Glyn. Lewis Glyn Cothi. OBWVE, *tr. by* Joseph P. Clancy

One breaker crashes. O. Mabson Southard. HA

One Budding-Talent Wang. *Unknown.* ColAnChi, *tr. by* Red Pine

One button undone. George Swede. HA

One by one, as harvesters, all heavy laden. Sacheverell Sitwell. MoBrPo *Fr.* Agamemnon's Tomb.

One by one, I crushed the letters. Fire and Embers. Leonor Scliar-Cabral. MirDau, *tr. by* Regina Igel

One by one many leaves. It. Muso Soseki. EaWin, *tr. by* W. S. Merwin

One by one, the ancient. Next Year, in Jerusalem. Shirley Kaufman. UnSA

One by one they appear in. My Sad Captains. Thom Gunn. FaBoMo; NAEL-5v2; NAEL-6v2; NPeEn; NoAM; NoP-4; PoPoPo

One by one to the floor all of her shadows. George Swede. HA

One cadaver said to the other. Basic Science. Fanny Howe. ExTi

One can glimpse Apollo in the door of each thing. Deeds Done and Suffered by Light. Clayton Eshleman. APSN

One can't / have it. Coming Right Up. A. R. Ammons. OBCoV

One cannot begin it too soon. (LL) Brown Penny. W. B. Yeats. BoLoP; FaBoCh

One cannot possess. Heritage. Augustus Young. CIP-2

One Christmas Night in Pontgibaud. After Hilaire Belloc. Max Beerbohm. UV

One Christmas-time, / The day before the holidays began. William Wordsworth. RB *Fr.* Prelude; Growth of a Poet's Mind [1805 vers.], The.

One-coach Penn Central is bound, The. On My Fourteenth Wedding Anniversary I Ride on Trains. Cornelia Veenendaal. GM

One cold damp night, winds pierced the cliffs. January 1939. Ilya Grigoryevich Ehrenburg [*or* Erenburg]. TCRP, *tr. by* Cathy Porter

One combat and one victory. (LL) Dead, The. René Arcos. FaBoWar; PeFWW, *tr. by* Christopher Middleton

One comes to language from afar, the ear. Vulnerary, A. Jonathan Williams. PoM

One constant in a world of variables. Homo Suburbiensis. Bruce Dawe. BMAP

One could do worse than be a swinger of birches. (LL) Birches. Robert Frost. APT-1; AmFaPo; FaBoVe; HarvBoo; HeIP-4; ITBLP; MoAmPo; NAAL-2v2; NAAL-5; NoAM; NoP-4; OxBA; PAI; PoPoPo; PoRA; RB; SAmP; SoSe-8; TAP; TCAPo; TFi; TRP

One crown that no one seeks. Emily Dickinson. ChIV-2

One Crucifixion is recorded—only. Emily Dickinson. APN-2

One cunning bosom-sin blows quite away. (LL) Sin (1). George Herbert. GeHe; OxAEP-1

One dark and dusty day. Stackolee. *Unknown.* NAAAL

One day. Room of One's Own, A. Hoda Hussein. PoArWo, *tr. by* Cornelia Al-Khaled

One day. Imogene Elizabeth Kennedy. PFTM-2, *tr. by* Edward Kamau Brathwaite

One day. One day. Imogene Elizabeth Kennedy. PFTM-2, *tr. by* Edward Kamau Brathwaite

One Day. Ray Mathew. NOBAu

One Day. Bobbi Sykes. BMAP; IBA

One Day! J. Wilbur Chapman. SacPr

One day across the lake where echoes come now. Animal That Drank Up Sound, The. William Stafford. VGW

One day as he did raunge the fields abroad. Edmund Spenser. NoSic *Fr.* Faerie Queene, The.

One day at noon I crossed. Sandy Yard, The. Edith Jay Scovell. HarvBoo

One day He. Anne Sexton. BodElec *Fr.* Furies, The.

One day he perched on a tree with dew. Migratory Bird. Chenjerai Hove. HBAPE

One day he realized. Orpheus. Stephen Perry. MiVo

One day I complained about the periphery. Periphery. A. R. Ammons. NOBA

One day, I decided to postpone believing the tale until the school bell rings. Voices. Sumaiya El-Sousy. PoArWo, *tr. by* Atef Abu-Seif and Nathalie Handal

One day I dreamt myself. To the Child That Never Was. Emma Sepúlveda-Pulvirenti. TANSG, *tr. by* Shaun Griffin

One day I forgot Jerusalem and my right arm is withered. Warning, A. Grace Paley. TaR

One day I found a lost dog in the street. Dead Dog. Vernon Scannell. OxBC

One Day I Know the Page. Amina Said. PoArWo, *tr. by* Lucy McNair

One day I'll lift the telephone. Elegy for My Father, Who Is Not Dead. Andrew Hudgins. RA

One day I met you. Song of Meeting. Tsung Ch'en. CoBLCP, *tr. by* Jonathan Chaves

One day I observed a grey hair in my head. Grey Hair, The. Judah Halevi. TrJP, *tr. by* J. Chotzner

One day I saw a ship pass close by. Pelican, The. Adelia Prado. TCLAP, *tr. by* Marcia Kirinus

One day I saw Chicago river move. Chicago. Margaret Walker Alexander. GT

One day I went and bought a fake fur coat. How I Had to Act. Molly Peacock. FFC

One day I went walking and. Man in a Shell, The. Angela Ball. ExTi

One Day I Wrote Her Name upon the Strand. Edmund Spenser. *See* Amoretti

One day in a popular quarter of Kharkov. Images. Valery Larbaud. BLT, *tr. by* William Jay Smith

One day in March, I ranged a verdant plain. On Meeting——, Esq., in St. James's Park. *Unknown.* ECWP

One day in the bluest of summer weather. Bird Language. Christopher Pearse Cranch. APN-1

One day in the fall sun. Forty Three Years after Hitler My Parents Visit Eugene. Joan Dobbie. GotH

One day in the Library. Further Advantages of Learning. Kenneth Rexroth. TAP

One day my husband came home with a jar of generic peanut butter. Marriage. Stephanie Brown. BodElec

One day, not here, you will find a hand. Again. Charlotte Mew. MoBrPo

One-day-old baby in Wallabout, A. Limerick. Morris Gilbert Bishop. PeLi

One day one young Creole candio. Criole Candjo. George Washington Cable. APN-2

One day over the course of a week or so. Dream of the Artfairy. Carl Morse. GLP

One day some young poet. Jean-Joseph Rabéarivelo [*or* Rebéarivelo]. NegPo

One day soon he'll tell her it's time to start packing. Drifters. Bruce Dawe. BMAP; CBAP; NoAM

One day Sun found a new canyon. People of the South Wind. William Stafford. NNaP

One day the amorous Lysander. Disappointment, The. Aphra Behn. BASC; EMWP; EroLit; NAEL-7v1; NALW; NOSC; PEW

One day, / the apolitical. Apolitical Intellectuals. Otto René Castillo. AF, *tr. by* Margaret Randall

One day the Chinese Bird of Royalty, Fum. Fum and Hum, the Two Birds of Royalty. Thomas Moore. OBSV

One day the god of fond desire. To the God of Fond Desire. James Thomson. EnLoPo

One day the letters went to school. Letters at School, The. Mary Mapes Dodge. OBCA

One day the Nouns were clustered in the street. Permanently. Kenneth Koch. CoAP; NoP-4; PmAP; PoM

One day the time had come. Visit, The. Toon Tellegen. TuT, *tr. by* Peter Van de Kamp

One day they said. Purdah, 1. Imtiaz Dharker. NeBl; OMIP

One day—'twas on a gentle, autumn noon. Leigh Hunt. NOBRP *Fr.* Story of Rimini, The.

One day we notice that the sun. Feeding the Sun. Bill Knott. PBCAP

One day we took our lunches. Circus Parade, The. Katharine Pyle. OBCA

One day when Coyote. One for Coyote. *Unknown.* STP, *tr. by* Carl Cary

One day when heaven was filled with his praises. One Day! J. Wilbur Chapman. SacPr

One day when me 'n' Dunbar wuz a-hoein' in de co'n. Me 'n' Dunbar. James David Corrothers. NAAAL

One day when the great *Titanic* was sinking away. Shine and the *Titanic*. *Unknown.* NAAAL

One day when the sun shone on the water and Golden. Introduction to a Prayer. Fritzi Harmsen van Beek. WoPoe, *tr. by* Claire Nicholas White

One day you look at the mirror and it's open. Glass. W. S. Merwin. SPE

One day you will slip into an airport. Regret. Michael Lieberman. BloBone

One deaf man went to law with. Nicarchus of Alexandria. PGA

One December Night. Denise Levertov. BodElec

One Desiring Me to Read, But Slept It Out, Wakening. George Daniel. OxBSP

One died, and the soul was wrenched out. Street Musicians. John Ashbery. HCAP; PoPoPo

One Dismal Night. Saint John of the Cross. SpanPo, *tr. by* Kate Flores

One document at dawn, submitted to the nine-tiered palace. Written on My Way into Exile. Han Yü. CoBCP, *tr. by* Burton Watson

1. Don't see him. Don't phone or write a letter. Two Cures for Love. Wendy Cope. OBCoV

One door alone is shut, one chamber still. (LL) Gone. Mary Elizabeth Coleridge. OBEV; PoBW; VWP

One dot / Grainily shifting we at roadside and. Bee, The. James Dickey. AmFaPo

One doth not stroke me, nor the other strike. (LL) To Fool or Knave. Ben Jonson. FaBoEE; NoP-4

One dread knocked out another. Elegy 11: Ford. Eric Mottram. Oth

One dream of passion and of beauty more! Properzia Rossi. Felicia Dorothea Hemans. RWP; VWP; ViWPN

One drop of dharma water. Ancient Origin. Muso Soseki. EaWin, *tr. by* W. S. Merwin

One drop of wine wherewith wild rain has mixed. (LL) And in the Hanging Gardens. Conrad Potter Aiken. APT-1; MoAmPo

One duck stood on my toes. Feeding Ducks. Norman MacCaig. HarvBoo; OxBS

One Duke and twenty [*or* twentie] places. (LL) Epitaph on the Duke of Buckingham. *Unknown.* BASC; NPeEn; PBRV

I. EAST TEXAS. Travels in the South. Simon J. Ortiz. UnSA

01 84. Michael Haslam. Oth *Fr.* Continual Song.

One either believes in God. In California. Kathy Fagan. GeoHom

One end is moo, the other, milk. (LL) Cow, The. Ogden Nash. NBLV; NoP-4; RB

One-erum, two-erum. *Unknown.* OxNR

One-ery, two-ery, [*or* ore-ery], ickery, Ann. *Unknown.* OxNR

One-ery, two-ery, tickery, seven. *Unknown.* OxNR

One evening an exceptionally abstract communication came over the airwaves. Henri Michaux. PFTM-2, *tr. by* Pierre Joris *Fr.* Saisir.

One evening as the sun went down [*or* when the sun was low]. Big Rock Candy Mountains, The. *Unknown.* OBAL; TTTS

One evening, breaking a jeep journey at Capuzzo. Ninth Elegy: Fort Capuzzo. Hamish Henderson. FaBoWar

One evening in August, the light already failing. Elegy for the Unknown Soldier. Michael O'Loughlin. PBCIP

One evening in February I came near to dying here. Alone. Tomas Tranströmer. WoPoe, *tr. by* Robin Fulton

One evening (surely I was led by her). William Wordsworth. RB *Fr.* Prelude; Growth of a Poet's Mind [1805 vers.], The.

One evening, we entered our room with. Flight from the Marriage Bed. Lisa M. Carbone. PasH

One evening when a genial air. Nightfall. Gwen Harwood. BMAP

One evening, when gorse was burning. Early Days. John Stuart Williams. TCAWP

One evening, when the sun was just gone down. On the Death of Old Bennet the News-Crier. *Unknown.* NOEC

One evening when we were lounging in his apartment in a relaxed mood. Rain. Anselm Hollo. PoM

One ever hangs where shelled roads part. At a Calvary near the Ancre. Wilfred Owen. ChIV-2; GI

One ewe. Shepherd's Night Count. Jane Yolen. TLR

One Explanation of Beauty. Mark Wunderlich. AmPoNex

One eye crystal, one eye flame, it arrives. Mimi Khalvati. NewEx

One eye without a head to wear it. Phyllis McGinley. OBSV *Fr.* Spectator's Guide to Contemporary Art.

One-eyed prison-warder, A. Ayásma. Gunnar Ekelof. WoPoe, *tr. by* Wystan Hugh Auden and Leif Sjöberg

One-Eyed Seller of Arrows: Creature came shuffling where there sat, A. Cynewulf. ASW *Fr.* Riddles (Exeter Book).

One face looks out from all his canvas[s]es. In An Artist's Studio. Christina Georgina Rossetti. NAEL-5v2; NAEL-6v2; NALW; PAI; ViWPN

One failure on. Their Sex Life. A. R. Ammons. OBCoV

One Faith and No Faith. Friedrich von Logau. GePo, *tr. by* George C. Schoolfield

One fall after another. The snow. Mother Ruin. Linda Gregerson. ExTi

One fantee wave. Dame Edith Sitwell. OBMV *Fr.* Gold Coast Customs.

One fat poppy dawdles. Garden of Eden, The. Ágnes Nemes Nagy. IQMS, *tr. by* Hugh Maxton

One fatal mistake that is made today is gossip. Gossip. Mrs. Henry Linden. CBWP-4

One feather is a bird. Voice, The. Theodore Roethke. VGW

One feels like an animal. Sinking Feeling, A. Amy Gerstler. BodElec

One Final Fling. Kemal Khojandi. ArPe, *tr. by* Omar S. Pound

One finds in every boarding school. "Tropicals." René Maran. NegPo, *tr. by* Ellen Conroy Kennedy

One Fine Day. János Pilinszky. PoSu, *tr. by* Peter Jay

One fine day. Traumerei. David Shapiro. BodElec

One Flesh. Julia Casterton. Prnts

One Flesh. Elizabeth Jennings. FaBoWP; LW; NoP-4; OxAEP-2; OxBTC; Prnts

One flower at a time, please. Bouquets. Robert Francis. ChAP

One fly everywhere the heat. Marlene Mountain. HA

One Fond Embrace. Thomas Kinsella. "Enough." ModIr

One Foot in Eden. Edwin Muir. GTBS-P; NOBE; NoAM

One Foot in the Door. Anne Elder. CBAP

One foot on the floor, one knee in bed. Evening Wind. Robert Mezey. PoSol

One for a Keepsake Album. Ferenc Kölcsey. IQMS, *tr. by* Adam Makkai

One for Balassi. Ferenc Kölcsey. IQMS, *tr. by* George Sutherland Fraser

One for Charlie Mingus. Quincy Troupe. SpirFl

One for Coyote. *Unknown.* STP, *tr. by* Carl Cary

One for Miss Pardo's Travel Diary. Mihály Vörösmarty. IQMS, *tr. by* Adam Makkai

One for money. *Unknown.* OxNR

One for My Baby (And One More for the Road). Johnny Mercer. ReLy

One for Pope Paul. Janus Pannonius. IQMS, *tr. by* George Burrough and Adam Makkai

One for sorrow, two for joy. *Unknown.* OxNR

One for the "Ancient Gypsy." Gyula Juhász. IQMS, *tr. by* Adam Makkai

One for the Anthologies. Gavin Ewart. OBCoV

One forfeit more from life the current claimed. At the Discharge of Cannon Rise the Drowned. Hubert Witheford. PeNZ

One Friday morn when we set sail. Mermaid, The. *Unknown.* ESPB

One from One Leaves Two. Ogden Nash.

  "I pray the Lord my soul to take." NBLV

One Furrow, The. Ronald Stuart Thomas. OxBC

One garland. Divorcing. Denise Levertov. NALW

One Generation Passeth Away. Jones Very. ChIV-1

One Girl. Sappho. AWP, *tr. by* Dante Gabriel Rossetti

One Girl at the Boys Party, The. Sharon Olds. InPK-6

One girl in a red dress leaves the shopping center. Suburban Dusk. Bert Meyers. SPE

One Girl's Dance. Leah Aini. DTA, *tr. by* Miriyam Glazer

One girl's dance. One Girl's Dance. Leah Aini. DTA, *tr. by* Miriyam Glazer

1 go to Zoo. Bill Griffiths. Oth *Fr.* Building: The New London Hospital.

One good crucifixion and he rose from the dead. Easter. Charles Hubert Sisson. OxBSP

One good mistress deserves another. Paul Eluard. SurPaPo, *tr. by* Julien Levy *Fr.* 152 Proverbs Mis au Goût du Jour.

One goodness ruleth by its single will. Alcuin. MLL

One got peace of heart at last, the dark march over. After War. Ivor Gurney. HarvBoo; OxBSP

One grandchild runs with a net. Butterfly Net, The. John Bensko. YaYoPo

One grandma. Two Grandmas. Stanley H. Barkan. UnSA

One granite ridge. Piute Creek. Gary Snyder. CoAP; CoAmPo; NAAL-2v2; NOBA

One great truth in life I've found. Those We Love the Best. Ella Wheeler Wilcox. PoToHe

One grey and foaming day. R. P. Blackmur. APT-2

One gulp. Kimpu. JDP, *tr. by* Yoel Hoffmann

One had a lovely face. Memory. W. B. Yeats. BIrV; PoE

One half of me was up and dressed. Gentle Check, The. Joseph Beaumont. NOSC

One hand is smaller than the other. It. Man with One Small Hand. Patricia K. Page. MoCV

One hand on her hip, one hand. Song of the Andoumboulou. Nathaniel Mackey. NAAAL

One hand's arthritic and chained to the pendulum. Hands of the Old Métis, The. Maurice Kilwein Guevara. NAPBL

One hand, two hands. Nothing more. Sphinxes Inclined to Be. Olga Orozco. WPOW, *tr. by* Leslie Keffer

One hard cold after another came. Winter 1967. Lenard D. Moore. ISC

One Hard Look. Robert Graves. MoBrPo

One has a feeling it is all coming to an end. Feeling, The. William Bronk. VGW

One, he loves; two, he loves. *Unknown.* ReMoGo

One Heart's Enough for Me. Auguste Mignon. TreFP

One heaven and earth. Cave of the Thousand Pines. Muso Soseki. EaWin, *tr. by* W. S. Merwin

One heifer and one fleecy sheep. Aristeides. Antipater of Sidon. AWP, *tr. by* Charles Whibley

One Home. William Stafford. CoAP; VGW

One Hope, The. Dante Gabriel Rossetti. GSo; NAEL-5v2; NAEL-6v2 *Fr.* House of Life, The.

One Horse Chay, The. *Unknown.* OxBoLi

One horse you gave me, The. Appaloosa, The. Michael S. Weaver. GT

One hugs me. Vasco [*or* Vasko] Popa. PoSu, *tr. by* Anne Pennington *Fr.* Raw Flesh.

One human being. Issa. EH, *tr. by* Robert Hass

One Hundred and Eighty-Third Chorus. Jack Kerouac. NeAP *Fr.* Mexico City Blues.

One Hundred and Fifty Years. Jack Davis. BMAP

One Hundred and Forty-Ninth Chorus. Jack Kerouac. PmAP *Fr.* Mexico City Blues.

100 Differences Between Poetry and Prose. Tom Leonard. Oth

108 Tales of a Po 'Buckra. Will Inman.

  "Dark brother touches me, The." GLP

One Hundred Eighty. Giusi Busceti. ItPo, *tr. by* Gayle Ridinger

182nd Chorus. Jack Kerouac. NeAP *Fr.* Mexico City Blues.

One hundred feet from off the ground. Christopher Smart. NOCV *Fr.* Hymns for the Amusement of Children.

152 Into 5, *El Centro Palabra de Fe.* M. L. Williams. GeoHom

152 Proverbs Mis au Goût du Jour. Paul Eluard.

  "One good mistress deserves another." SurPaPo, *tr. by* Julien Levy

146th Chorus. Jack Kerouac. NeAP *Fr.* Mexico City Blues.

One Hundred Lines for the Coast. Kojo Laing. HBAPE

179th Chorus. Jack Kerouac. NeAP Fr. Mexico City Blues.

113th Chorus. Jack Kerouac. NeAP; PmAP *Fr.* Mexico City Blues.

125th Street. Langston Hughes. APT-2

127th Chorus. Jack Kerouac. NeAP; PmAP *Fr.* Mexico City Blues.

One Hut. Muso Soseki. EaWin, *tr. by* W. S. Merwin

One I loathed, my one malignant foe, The. Posthumous Revenge. Francis Saltus Saltus. VerBaPo

One I Love (Belongs to Someone Else), The. Walter Donaldson. ReLy

One I love, two I love. *Unknown.* LB; OxNR

One in All, The. Margaret Fuller. SWaP

One in the boat cried out. Door, The. Leonard Alfred George Strong. MoBrPo

One Inch Tall. Shel [*or* Shelley] Silverstein. OBCA

One instant I was asleep in bed; the next. You Missed the Earthquake, Bill. Charles Harper Webb. GeoHom

One instant is eternity. Wu-Men. EnlH

One is always nearer by not keeping still. (LL) On the Move. Thom Gunn. HAP; NoP-4; OxAEP-2; OxBTC; PoE; TRP; TwCP

One is enough, she cried. Technicalities for Jack Spicer. Philip Whalen. PoM

One is Genius Itself—the other Beauty. Fig Tree. Stephanie Strickland. ExTi

One is One. Marie Ponsot. ExTi

One is reminded of a certain person. Kite Poem. James Merrill. TwCP

One is so seldom struck by lightning. For the Poet Who Said Poets Are Struck by Lightning Only Two or Three Times. Peter Klappert. NBLV

One Kind of Freedom Speaks. Erich Fried. AF, *tr. by* Georg Rapp

One kind of logic is a road cut into the side of a steep, wooded hill. Glimpse of Terrain. Thomas Bolt. YaYoPo

One king's daughter said to anither. Sheath and Knife. *Unknown.* ESPB

One kisses Ramén goodnight on Bank Street in the Village. Kissing Ramén. Michael Lassell. WiU

One Knows Not What One Is. "Angelus Silesius." GePo, *tr. by* George C. Schoolfield *Fr.* Cherubical Wanderer, The.

One-l lama, The / He's a priest. Lama, The. Ogden Nash. FaBoCh

One lady poet was a nymphomaniac and wrote for Vanity Fair. Lady Poets with Foot Notes, The. Ernest Hemingway. IllVoic

One Last Word. John Glassco. NOBC

One leaf lets go, and. Ransetsu. JDP, *tr. by* Yoel Hoffmann

One less. Lost Body. Terry Ehret. GifTon

One Life. Andrew Motion. HarvBoo

One Life to Live. Kurt Weill. ReLy

One lifetime in office. Chinese Figures 1. *Unknown.* EaWin, *tr. by* W. S. Merwin

One lily scented all the dark. It grew. One Night. Lizette Woodworth Reese. APN-2

One Little Boy. *Unknown.* NOxBChV

One little kiss. Remember. Irving Berlin. ReLy

One little mess of whelks, so he may 'scape! (LL) Caliban upon Setebos; or, Natural Theology in the Island. Robert Browning. AWP; EBEV; FHYEP; NAEL-5v2; NAEL-6v2; NOBVV; OxAEP-2; PeVV

One long and humid afternoon. Love Song. Rofel G. Brion. ReBoTo

One Long Jump. Lenrie Peters. PBMAP

One looks around and sees. Perspectives. Chiqui Vicioso. TANSG, *tr. by* Emma Jane Robinett

One looks from the train. Orient Express, The. Randall Jarrell. CoAP; NOBA; PoE

One Lost, The. Isaac Rosenberg. MoBrPo

One lost track of the story. Among Strangers. Silvia Curbelo. OPRER

One lovely summer afternoon when balmy breezes blew. To Clements' Ferry. Josephine D. Henderson Heard. CBWP-4; SWaP

One Man. William Scammell. NLP

One man except, the only son of light. John Milton. NOSC *Fr.* Paradise Lost.

One man follows a straight path. Anna Andreyevna Akhmatova. TCRP

One man made a ladder. Return: Buffalo. Linda Hogan. BodElec

One man's dick had the quaint. Wayne Koestenbaum. WiU *Fr.* Erotic Collectibles.

One Man's Potato Chip. Dina von Zweck. SpudSo

One Man's Wife. Philip Booth. VGW

One man shall smile one day and say goodbye. Cambodia. James Fenton. AF

One man we claim of wrought renown. Stonewall Jackson. Herman Melville. NCAP

One man won't say anything. Star-Spangled. Michele Glazer. OPRER

One Meat Ball. Thomas Lux. ReTh

One midnight, deep in starlight still. Bankrupt. Cortlandt W. Sayres. PoToHe

One midnight, old D. G. Rossetti. Limerick. Victor Gray. PeLi

One minute of sitting, one inch of Buddha. Manzan. ZenPo, tr. by Takashi Ikemoto and Lucien Stryk

One misty, moisty morning. Mother Goose. LB; OxNR; ReMoGo

One Modern Poet. Carl Sandburg. OBAL

One Moment My Hope Rises Up on Wings. Baldomero Garcilaso de la Vega. SpanPo, tr. by Edwin Morgan

One moment past our bodies cast. Rudyard Kipling. NoAM Fr. Second Jungle Book, The.

One monk, you have dissolved phenomena. At the Mountain of the Mysterious Tomb Visiting Master P'ou. Wu Wei-yeh. CoBLCP, tr. by Jonathan Chaves

One moon. Shofu. JDP, tr. by Yoel Hoffmann

One moon of joy I knew. Neglected Wife, The. Yi Talch'ung. WoPoe, tr. by Jean S. Grigsby

One More Brevity. Robert Frost. APT-1

One More Bruised Heart! Louisa Sarah Bevington. VWP

One more bruised heart laid bare! one victim more! One More Bruised Heart! Louisa Sarah Bevington. VWP

One more day gone, / done, found in / the form of days. Again. Robert Creeley. VCAP

One More Day's Work for Jesus. Anna Bartlett Warner. AH

One More New Botched Beginning. Stephen Spender. NoAM

One more night my blood. O Wendy, Arthur. Maurice Kenny. HATNAP

One more of those perfections. You Get What You Pay For. Allen Curnow. HarvBoo

One More River. Unknown. APN-2

One More Sign. Roberta Hill Whiteman. HATNAP

One more unfortunate. Bridge of Sighs, The. Thomas Hood. BRP; EBEV; GTBS-P; OBEV; OxAEP-2; TreFP

One morn before me were three figures seen. Ode on Indolence. John Keats. NAEL-5v2; NAEL-6v2

One Morn I Left Him in His Bed. Elizabeth Stoddard. SWaP

One morn I rose and looked upon the world. Dawn, The. Unknown. PoToHe

One Morning. Timothy Steele. CRP

One morning, as we travelled in the fields. Riders Held Back, The. Louis Simpson. CoAmPo

One Morning beside a Pond. Rofel G. Brion. ReBoTo

One morning ere [or before] Titan had thought to stir [or thought of stirring] his feet. Vision, The. Egan [or Aodhagán] O'Rahilly [or O'Reilly or Ó Rathaille]. NOIV

One morning I got up. Little Bird, The. Unknown. PBA, tr. by Rolf Italiander

One morning I shall find. Maisie. James Merrill. HeIP-4

One morning in April, a short time ago. Julia A. Moore. VerBaPo Fr. Little Libbie.

One morning in June above Yosemite Valley, John Muir learned. Sierra Bear. David Bottoms. GifTon

One morning in spring. Fife Tune. John Streeter Manifold. CBAP; FaBoWar; NBLV; NOBAu

One morning of August. Lament for MacGregor of Glenstrae. MacGregor, Mrs., of Glenstrae. NePenScot, tr. by Iain Crichton Smith

One morning old Wilfrid Scawen Blunt. Limerick. Victor Gray. NOBL

One morning the Monarch said: "When." Limerick. D. W. Barker. PeLi

One morning with a 12-gauge my brother shot what he said was a linnet. Linnets. Larry Levis. LCAP-2

One mouse adds up to many mice. Singular Indeed. David McCord. OBCA

One Mr. B, / A joker he. Repartée. Charles Follen Adams. OBAL

One mummy walks on snow. Mummies. Nicanor Parra. TCLAP, tr. by Thomas Merton

One musician is sure. Harp, The. Ralph Waldo Emerson. APN-1

One musn't confuse the day and the night. Nobility. Oumar Ba. PBMAP

One must completely destroy all logic in Variety Theater performances. Filippo Tommaso Marinetti. PFTM-1 Fr. Variety Theater Manifesto, The.

One must have a mind of winter. Snow Man, The. Wallace Stevens. APT-1; AmFaPo; ColAP; EnlH; HAP; HCAP; HarvBoo; HeIP-4; NAAL-2v2; NAAL-5; NoAM; NoP-4; PAI; PoE; PoPoPo; SoSe-8; TCAPo; TRP; WeW-3

One must have breakfasted often on automobile primer. Note to Tony Towle (After WS), A. Charles North. FTOS; PmAP

One must, to find your tomb. Mariner's Ideal Epitaph. Juan Ramón Jiménez. SpanPo, tr. by Kate Flores

One need not be a Chamber—to be Haunted. Emily Dickinson. APN-2; NALW

One needs sand from the sea, we have known. Rossana Ombres. NeIt Fr. Excursion to Ravenna of a Young Girl with Her Parents.

One Night. Constantine P. Cavafy. CAGL; EroLit, tr. by Edmund Keeley and Philip Sherrard

One Night. Lizette Woodworth Reese. APN-2

"One night," a doctor said, "last fall." Ambrose Bierce. APN-2 Fr. Devil's Dictionary, The.

One night a score of Erris men. Danny. John Millington Synge. PeVV

One night, after a storm, the sort of storm. Peace of Lodi, The. Norman Dubie. BodElec

One night all tired with the weary day. Gnat, The. Joseph Beaumont. NOSC

One Night America: A Boy and His Blowtorch. M. Loncar. NAPBL

One night as I lay on my bed. Death. Unknown. OBWVE; RB, tr. by Aneirin Talfan Davies

One night as I lay on the green hill. My Father's Whistle. Len Roberts. MiVo

One night, as I was pondering of late. John Oldham. NOSC Fr. Satyr, A.

One Night at Victoria Beach. Gabriel Okara. PBMAP; PoetW

One Night away from Day. John Digby. SPE

One-Night Expensive Hotel. Ronald G. Everson. NOBC

One night he heard heart-breaking sound. Austin Clarke. CIP-2 Fr. Mnemosyne Lay in Dust.

One night I dreamt that in a gleaming hall. Digby Mackworth Dolben. OxBSo

One night i' th' yeare [or in the year], my dearest Beauties, come. To His Lovely Mistresses. Robert Herrick. CTC; CaPo

One night I was home alone. Eileen's Vision. Eileen Myles. BodElec

One night in late October. Judged by the Company One Keeps. Unknown. NBLV

One night / my father saw a saint in his dream. My Father's Dream. Sargon Boulus. MAP, tr. by Sargon Boulus and Alistair Elliot

One night of tempest I arose and went. Night and Morning. Unknown. OBWVE, tr. by R. S. Thomas

One night on Monterey Bay the death-freeze of the century. Adrienne Rich. GeoHom Fr. Atlas of the Difficult World, An.

One night / One night full of perfumes, music of wings and murmurs. Nocturne. José Asunción Silva. BLPSL, tr. by Rene de Costa, Rigas Kappatos and Eleni Paidoussi

One night our block leader set a competition. Soup. Tony Curtis. TCAWP

One night's east wind made a thousand trees burst into flower. Tune: "Green Jade Cup"—Lantern Festival. Hsin Ch'i-chi. SuSp, tr. by Irving Y. Lo

One Night Stand. Imamu Amiri Baraka. NeAP

One Night Stand. Kenward Elmslie. FTOS

One night the Brownies reached a mound. Brownies' Celebration, The. Palmer Cox. OBCA

One night, when I couldn't sleep. Trick, The. John Mole. NOxBChV

One Night When We Paused Half-way. Kate Clanchy. MFPA

One Night with a Stranger at 30. Lisa Glatt. AmPoNex

One night, your mother is listening to the walls. How You Get Born. Erica Jong. UnPo

One noonday, at my window in the town. Ball's Bluff. Herman Melville. CBCWP; FaBoWar; OBWP

One nostril means latin. Queer Things. Emanuel Carnevali. SPE

One, not quite ten. Sisters. Saleem Peeradina. OMIP

One. now another. one. W. D. Snodgrass. InvLad Fr. Snow Songs.

One o'Clock. Philippe Soupault. AF, tr. by Eden Paul

One o'clock in the letter-box. Meeting, The. Muriel Rukeyser. MoAmPo; TrJP

One / O-N-E. Sophie, Climbing the Stairs. Dolores Kendrick. ESEAA

One observes them, one expects them. Turkeys Observed. Seamus Heaney. OWoS

One of a much larger crowd. To a Cloud. Ida Schwarz. AuPH, tr. by Lowell A. Bangerter

One of King Henries Favorites beganne. Groome of the Chambers religion in King Henry the eights time, A. Sir John Harington [or Harrington]. PBRV

One of King Henry's favourites began. Groom of the Chamber's Religion in King Henry the Eighth's Time, A. John Harington. NoSic

One of Many. Stevie Smith. OxBC

One of midnight's charms is a muted terror—. Conversation at Midnight. "Adelina Efimovna Adalis." TCRP, tr. by Bernard Meares

One of our race's great lights has gone out to the world. Paul Laurence Dunbar. Mrs. Henry Linden. CBWP-4

One of our race's greatest needs in this country today. Y. M. C. A, The. Mrs. Henry Linden. CBWP-4

One of the Awl Songs. *Unknown.* APN-2, tr. by Washington Matthews *Fr.* Mountain Chant, The.

One of the Boys. James Simmons. ModIr; PNI

One of the criminals who were hanged railed at him. Jorge Luis Borges. GI *Fr.* St. Luke.

One of the difficulties is in being. Russian Asylum. Marilyn Bowering. NOBC

One of the Jews. Constantine P. Cavafy. TrJP

One of the Lords of Life. David J. Rothman. GeoH

One of the more intelligent members. For the Fly-Leaf of a School-Book. Norman Cameron. OxBS

One of the neat ones in your awkward squad. (LL) Forgive Me, Sire. Norman Cameron. FaBoEE; GTBS-P; OxBEV; OxBS; OxBSP

One of the ones that Midas touched. Emily Dickinson. APN-2

One of the oxen said. Christmas Poem, A. Dick Davis. ChrPo

One of the Principal Causes of War. Hugh MacDiarmid. OxBSP

One of the Strangest. May Swenson. APT-2; OWoS

One of the Years. William Stafford. KaS

One of them said: "One life is much too little." Georgy [or Georgii Viktorovich] Adamovich. TCRP

One of them takes himself to be an ox. Tune: "Song of Divination" Using Quotations from *Chuang-tzu.* Hsin Ch'i-chi. SuSp, tr. by Irving Y. Lo

One of them, taking advantage of the crew's momentary carelessness. Edouard Glissant. NegPo *Fr.* Indies, The.

One of these days she will lie there and be dead. Grimalkin. Thomas Lynch. EmeKit

One of these nights about twelve o'clock. Heavenly Aeroplane, The. *Unknown.* NOCV

One of those days. I Remember Dexedrine. 1970. Pamela Brown. BMAP

One of those great, garishly emerald flies that always look freshly generated from fresh excrement. My Fly. C. K. Williams. AmFaPo

One of those times I knew even then. Pleasure. Dean Young. IllVoic

One of us said, how odd. "H. D." NALW *Fr.* Tribute to the Angels.

One of Us Two. Ella Wheeler Wilcox. PoToHe

One of us / will / be. Devils. Norman Mailer. OBAL

One of you is a major made of cord and catskin. Lent in a Year of War. Thomas Merton. SPE

One of you is lying. (LL) Unfortunate Coincidence. Dorothy Parker. LW; NoP-4

One. One. Laurie Duggan. BMAP *Fr.* Ash Range, The.

One or More Together. John Godfrey. FTOS

One or two lines to thee I'll here commend. To the Reader, in Vindication of This Book. Elizabeth Bradford. EMWP

One ought not to have to care. Robert Frost. HAP; NoP-4; RACG; VGW *Fr.* Hill Wife, The.

One ought to learn. The Winter Trees. Winter Trees. Ágnes Nemes Nagy. IQMS, tr. by Ila Egon

One-Page Novel. David Gewanter. NAPBL

One pair ridiculous gorilla slippers; 3 pairs of cheap shit sunglasses. Kenneth Goldsmith. HeMarv *Fr.* Punk.

One peak, stripped sheer. Trip to Hua-yang Mountain, A. Tao-chi. CoBLCP, tr. by Jonathan Chaves

One Perfect Rose. Dorothy Parker. APT-1; NALW; NBLV; NIL-7; NIP-4; NoP-4; OBAL; OBCoV

One person. Issa. TTTS

One Person. Elinor Wylie.
 "In our content, before the autumn came." NAAL-2v2; NALW
 Little Beauty That I Was Allowed, The. Son
 (Sonnet from "One Person.") MoAmPo
 Sonnet: "I hereby swear that to uphold your house." NAAL-2v2; OxBA; Son
 Sonnet: "Let us leave talking of angelic hosts." OxBA

One plum blossom blooms. Ransetsu. OHMPJ

One Polar Bear, The. Peter Sears. OPRER

One Potato. Pat Mora. SpudSo

One Presenting a Rare Book to Madame Hull. John Saffin. SCAP

One quick scratch. Lighting a Fire. X. J. Kennedy. NOxBChV

One Reality, The. Frances Ridley Havergal. SacPr

One reason. Why Your Grandfather Stopped Playing the Viola. Alice Wirth Gray. MiVo

One Reason I Went to Prison. James Moore. CDa

One remains, the many change and pass, The. Shelley. NPeEn; SCV *Fr.* Adonais; An Elegy on the Death of John Keats.

One remembers hysterical laughter. Land of Cotton. Gilbert Sorrentino. FTOS

One ring of clear chimes through the evening mist. Inscribed on My Little Painting of Plum Blossom and Bamboo. Tao-chi. CoBLCP, tr. by Jonathan Chaves

One road leads to London. Roadways. John Masefield. OTCP

One Roman / Finis. (LL) Tenuous and Precarious. Stevie Smith. HarvBoo; OxBTC

One rooster does not weave a morning. Weaving the Morning. João Cabral de Melo Neto. TCLAP, tr. by Galway Kinnell

One's at God's finding; t'other at his owne, T'. (LL) On the Ploughman [or Plough-Man]. Francis Quarles. NOSC; SacPr

One's Correspondence. Connie Bensley. OBCoV

One's Country. Jonathan Griffin. Oth

One's grand flights, one's Sunday baths. Sense of the Sleight-of-Hand Man, The. Wallace Stevens. HAP; MoAmPo; NOBA; NoAM; TwCP; WeW-3

One's none. Little Hundred. *Unknown.* OxNR

One's own body from its instant and heat. (LL) Six Young Men. Ted Hughes. OBWP; PoWW

One's-Self I Sing. Walt Whitman. ColAP; NOBA; OxBA; TCAPo

One Saturday morning he went to the river to play. From the Childhood of Jesus. Robert Pinsky. EmeKit; HarvBoo

One scene as I bow to pour her coffee. Vacation. William Stafford. BLT

One scull in the spring wind, one leaf of a boat. Li Yü. CoBCP

One Seated on the Stones of Cheops, The. Marcelle Ferry. SurWo, tr. by Myrna Bell Rochester

One Second. Innokenty Fiodorovich Annensky. WoPoe, tr. by Stephen Berg

One Secret That Has Carried, The. Jason Shinder. OPRER

One seem'd all dark and red—a tract of sand. Tennyson. UnPo *Fr.* Palace of Art, The.

One Self. Laura Riding Jackson. HarvBoo

One Sentence on Tyranny. Gyula Illyés. IQMS, tr. by Adam Makkai, Károly Nagy and Vernon Watkins

One set on the highway to sing. Li Po. OxBA

One ship drives east and another drives west. Winds of Fate, The. Ella Wheeler Wilcox. BRP

One ship, one only. Few Days in the South in February, A. Eleanor Ross Taylor. CBCWP

One showing the eggs unbroken. (LL) Explosion, The. Philip Larkin. EBEV; EmeKit; FaBoMo; HAP; MakPoe; NAEL-5v2; NAEL-6v2; NPeEn; NoAM; NoP-4; OxAEP-2; OxBC; PeECV; RB; SCV; WeW-3

One side black sheen three side purple. Cold in the North (After Yueh-Fu). Li Ho. ChinPo, tr. by Yip Wai-lim

One side of his world is always missing. Riding a One-eyed Horse. Henry Taylor. HeIP-4; InPK-6

One side of the potato-pits was white frost. Patrick Kavanagh. ModIr

One Sided Shoot-out. Haki R. Madhubuti. BPo; NBV

One silent night of late. Cheat of Cupid; or, The Ungentle Guest, The. Robert Herrick. AWP; OBVE

One single word of heartfelt kindness. Kindness. Mary E. Tucker. CBWP-1

One singular sensation. One. Marvin Hamlisch. ReLy

One slit's enough to let adultery [or adultry] in. (LL) Upon Scobble [Epigram]. Robert Herrick. BeJo; CaPo; FaBoEE

One Snapshot I Couldn't Take in France, The. Al Young. SpirFl

One sneeze / Skylark's. Yayu. ZenPo, tr. by Takashi Ikemoto and Lucien Stryk

One son of God, The. *Unknown.* WoPoe, tr. by Keith Bosley *Fr.* Turo, Rescuer of the Sun and Moon.

One son was a jewel to me. On the Death of His Son. Lewis Glyn Cothi. WoPoe, tr. by Gwyn Williams

One Song. Geoffrey Philp. WaCA

One, sorrow. Magpies. *Unknown.* OWoS

One sound. Then the hiss and whir. Garden, The. Louise Glück. HCAP; NAAL-2v2; VCAP

One spot, alone. Gaki. JDP, tr. by Yoel Hoffmann

One star. Apostacy, The. Thomas Traherne. OxBEV; SacPr

One star fell and another as we walked. Conrad Potter Aiken. MoAmPo *Fr.* Preludes for Memnon; or, Preludes to Attitude.

One step. Climbing the Ridge. Rosemerry Wahtola Trommer. GeoH

One Step at a Time. Joseph Morris. ITBLP

One step at a time to return. Wisconsin Horse, The. Simon J. Ortiz. PFTM-2

One step twix't me and death, (twas Davids speech). Roger Williams. SCAP

One stone. Inventory. Jacques Prévert. STV, tr. by John Frederick Nims

One stone sufficeth (lo what death can do). On a Whore. John Hoskyns [or Hoskins]. FaBoEE

One stood still, looking stupid. The other. Willets, The. May Swenson. WPE

One stormy morn I chanced to meet. Kiss in the Rain, A. Samuel Minturn Peck. OBAL

One Strategy for Loving the World. Mona Van Duyn. ExTi

One! strikes the clock in the belfry tower. Frederick B. Needham. VerBaPo *Fr.* Round of the Clock, The.

One Struggle More, and I Am Free. Byron. CAGL

One student (white). Images. Naomi Long Madgett. LTA

One summer day. Old-Fashioned Garden, An. Cole Porter. OBGa

One summer, high in Wyoming. Before the Storm. Kenneth O. Hanson. CoAP

One summer I saw the old wing. Rebirth. Beckian Fritz Goldberg. ExTi

One Sunday morning as I went walking, by Brisbane waters I chanced to stray. Moreton Bay. *Unknown.* CBAP

One Sunday morning soft and fine. Brigadier. Arthur James Marshall Smith. MoCV

One surely tires eventually of the frequent references—the gossip. Reading the Unpublished Manuscripts of Louis MacNeice at Kinsale Harbour. Desmond O'Grady. PBCIP

One sweetly solemn thought. Nearer Home. Phoebe Cary. PWR; SacPr

One syllable from Pedasos, Erato. *Unknown.* PriapPo, *tr. by* Richard W. Hooper *Fr.* Priapus Poems, The.

One Talent, The. William Cutler. PWR

One That Died, The. William Daniel Ehrhart. CDa

One that is ever kind said yesterday. Folly of Being Comforted, The. W. B. Yeats. HeIP-4; NAEL-5v2; NAEL-6v2

One that works Hollyhock Alley, The. Saxophone Julie. Susan Firer. MiVo

One the Morening the King was Taken Ill my Dreame of Him. Frances Feilding. EMWP

One theory is that acid wastes in the blood. Nobody Sleeps. Stanley Plumly. BodElec

One, they're spooking, two, they're opening letters. Un-American Women, The. John Tranter. BMAP

One Thing at a Time. M. A. Stodart. PoToHe

One thing at a time. *Unknown.* OxNR

One thing does not exist: Oblivion. Everness. Jorge Luis Borges. TCLAP, *tr. by* Richard Wilbur

One thing has a shelving bank. Drumlin Woodchuck, A. Robert Frost. APT-1; NOBA; NoAM

One thing in all things have I seen. Secret, The. "Æ" MoBrPo

One thing is sure. Pulse, The. Mark Van Doren. MoAmPo

One Thing Needful Generally Neglected, the. Samuel Davies. SacPr

One Thing That Can Save America, The. John Ashbery. AiP; FaBoA; NOBA; NoAM; PmAP

One thing that literature would be greatly the better for. Very like a Whale. Ogden Nash. APT-2; HAP; InPK-6

One thing you left with us, Jack Johnson. Strange Legacies. Sterling Allen Brown. TTY

One thinks of *one* as a pronoun employed principally. One. John Heath-Stubbs. OBCoV

1.33: Albi, Ne Doleas. Horace. AWP, *tr. by* Austin Dobson *Fr.* Odes.

One: This is the way it must be. Erotic Suite. Olga Nolla. TANSG, *tr. by* Paula Vega

One Thousand Fearful Words for Fidel Castro. Lawrence Ferlinghetti. VGW

One thousand saxophones infiltrate the city. Battle Report. Bob Kaufman. ISC; TTY

1.3: To the Ship on Which Virgil Sailed to Athens ("Sic te diva potens Cyri"). Horace. AWP, *tr. by* John Dryden *Fr.* Odes.

One Time. Douglas Livingstone. NoP-4

One time at Springfield. (LL) Edgar Lee Masters. ColAP; IllVoic; NOBA; NoAM; OxBA; TAP *Fr.* Spoon River Anthology.

One time / Columbus said this island and the seas. Time of Turtles. Grace Perry. NOBAu

One Time Henry Dreamed the Number. Doughtry Long. BPo

One time I wanted two moons. Jacob Nibenegenesabe. STP *Fr.* Wishing Bone Cycle, The.

One time in Alexandria, in wicked Alexandria. Thaïs. Newman Levy. PeLV

One time in the middle of "Goin' Down Slow." Stereo Time with Booker Little. Rick Madigan. SeSe

One time of the year. It is as if infancy were the whole of incarnation. Luci Shaw. SacPr

One time, to a coast of light. (LL) Flames and Dangling Wire. Robert Gray. BMAP; NOBAu

One time when the wind blows it is years. Glimpses. William Stafford. BodElec

One to destroy, is murder by the law. Edward Young. FaBoWar

One to make ready. Start, The. *Unknown.* LB; OxNR

One to Nothing. Carolyn Kizer. OBAL

One to Ten. Mother Goose. ReMoGo

One to Ten. Janet S. Wong. OxIBACP

One Too Many Mornings. David Rivard. PBCAP

One Tourist's Cologne. Hal Colebatch. NOBAu

One truth is clear, WHATEVER IS, IS RIGHT. (LL) Pope. NAEL-5v1; NAEL-6v1; NAWM-7v2 *Fr.* Essay on Man, An.

One Tuesday in Summer. James McAuley. BMAP

1.25: Ribald Romeos Less and Less Berattle ("Parcius iunctas quatiunt fenestras"). Horace. STV *Fr.* Odes.

1.21: To Apollo and Diana ("Dianam tenerae dicite virgines"). Horace. OBVE, *tr. by* Branwell Brontë *Fr.* Odes.

One two. Ballad: Of Motion. Billy Mills. Oth

One, two, and three. Leaves. Countee Cullen. GT

One, two, / Buckle my shoe. Mother Goose. LB; OxNR; ReMoGo

One-two! One-two! Footsteps of an Owl and His Lament, The. Viktor Aleksandrovich Sosnora. TCRusP, *tr. by* Kathy Lewis

One Two or Three. Philippe Soupault. SurPaPo, *tr. by* Mary Ann Caws and Patricia Terry

One, two, three. Toward the Corner. Laura Riding Jackson. NOxBChV

One, Two, Three. Michael Rosen. OTCP

One—Two—Three. Hannah Senesh. WPOW, *tr. by* Peter Hay

One, two, three. Washington Square Park and a Game of Chess. Christopher Stanard. SpirFl

One, Two, Three, Four, Five! *Unknown.* LB; OxNR

1, 2, 3, 4, 5! / I caught a hare alive. One to Ten. Mother Goose. ReMoGo

One, two, three, four, five / Once I caught a fish alive. One, Two, Three, Four, Five! *Unknown.* LB; OxNR

One two three four five six seven eight nine and ten. Kneeling. Gertrude Stein. PFTM-1

One, two, three, four, / Mary at the cottage door. Mother Goose. LB; OxNR

One, Two, Three—Gough! Eve Merriam. NTCP

One, two, three, / I love coffee. *Unknown.* OxNR

1-2-3 was the number he played but today the number came 3-2-1. Dirge. Kenneth Fearing. APT-2; NIL-7; NIP-4; PoRA; RB; TrJP

1.2: To Leuconoë. Horace. WoPoe, *tr. by* David Ferry *Fr.* Odes.

One, two, whatever you do. *Unknown.* OxNR

One unkind word in the early morn. Boomerang, The. Carrie May Nichols. PoToHe

One-Upmanship. Miriam Chaikin. NTCP

One wading a Fall meadow finds on all sides. Beautiful Changes, The. Richard Wilbur. CoAP; HCAP; NAAL-5; NIL-7; PoE

One wants a Teller in a time like this. Gwendolyn Brooks. WPE *Fr.* Womanhood, The.

One was a stammerer, the other dumb. (LL) Tony Harrison. HarvBoo; NAEL-6v2 *Fr.* School of Eloquence, The.

One was kicked in the stomach. Gangrene. Philip Levine. VGW

One Was More Wise Than The Other. (LL) Stephen Crane. APN-2; NAAL-2v2; NoP-4 *Fr.* Black Riders [and Other Lines], The.

One watch had passed, and still sweet slumber shed. Firdowsi. TAL *Fr.* Shahnamah, The.

One Way of Looking at It. Arthur Joseph Munby. NOBVV

One-Way Song. Percy Wyndham Lewis. "I would set all things whatsoever front to back." CTC

One We Knew. Thomas Hardy. NAEL-5v2; NAEL-6v2

One went off to be. Headlands. Jack Hirschman. CLPP

One went spinning down the plughole. Yesterday the House Was Full of Flies. Geoffrey Summerfield. OTCP

One wept whose only child was dead. Maternity. Alice Thompson Meynell. OxBSP; PEW; VWP

One West Coast. Al Young. GeoHom

1. What? summer now? divisions ring. Morgan Llwyd. PBRV *Fr.* Summer, The.

One whistle, a short husky breath. Not There. Tess Gallagher. NIP-4

One White Face in the Place, The. Sydney Lea. SwNoth

One white foot, try him. On Buying a Horse. *Unknown.* NBLV; RB

One who could repeat the Summer day, The. Emily Dickinson. NCAP

One who first gave birth to our people, The. *Unknown.* ColAnChi, *tr. by* Jeffrey Riegel *Fr.* Classic of Odes.

One who gave the warning with his wings, The. Karl Shapiro. CRP *Fr.* Adam and Eve.

One who has pulled his oar in a start of storm, The. Simile. Ágnes Nemes Nagy. PoSu, *tr. by* Frederic Will

One Who Is at Home, The. Franciso Albanez. RaBo, *tr. by* Robert Bly

One who is not, we see: but one, whom we see not, is. Algernon Charles Swinburne. CABP; PeVV *Fr.* Heptalogia, The.

One Who Laughs and Laughs and Laughs, The. Unsi Al-Haj [*or* Hajj]. MAP, *tr. by* Sargon Boulus and Alistair Elliot

One who lifted his arms with joy, first time across the. Inventory. Joan Larkin. WiU

One who played tunes, nights under the limetrees. Musician, The. Martinus Nijhoff. TuT, *tr. by* Desmond Egan

One who rows a storm at the inception. Comparison, A. Ágnes Nemes Nagy. IQMS, *tr. by* Alan Dixon

One who says: I was almost alive or nearly dead, The. Angel Atrapado 7. John Yau. BodElec

One who speaks does not know; one who knows does not speak. After Reading Lao Tzu. Po Chü-i. CrYelRi, *tr. by* Sam Hamill

One Who Struggles, The. Ernst Toller. TrJP, *tr. by* E. Ellis Roberts

One Who Watches. Siegfried Sassoon. TrJP

One who works. One Who Works and Buys Himself Books. Samuel Ha-Nagid. WoPoe, *tr. by* Peter Cole

One Who Works and Buys Himself Books. Samuel Ha-Nagid. WoPoe, *tr. by* Peter Cole

One who writes us is now doing four plays a year, The. Paavo Haavikko. VCWP *Fr.* Short Year, The.

One whom I knew, a student and a poet. Epitaph. Alex Comfort. MoBrPo

One whose love will never end. Accompanying a Gift. Lizelia Augusta Jenkins Moorer. CBWP-3

One whose majestic presence ever here. In Memoriam Frederick Douglass. Henrietta Cordelia Ray. CBWP-3

One Whose Reproach I Cannot Evade, The. George Hitchcock. SPE

One Wife for One Man. Frank Aig-Imoukhuede. PBA
(I done try go church, I done go for court.) PBMAP

One windy days. Spring. Judith Ortiz Cofer. PueRic

One winter he was the best. In Memory of My Friend the Bassoonist John Lenox. Donald Justice. BodElec

One Winter Night in August. X. J. Kennedy. OBCA; OBSP; OxIBACP

One Wintry Day. Pyong-hwa Cho. PoetW, *tr. by* Peter H. Lee

One with eyes the fairest. Euripides. AWP *Fr.* Cyclops, The.

One with the Essence of the boundless world. (LL) Pantheist's Song of Immortality, The. Constance Naden. VWP; ViWPN

One with this world. *Unknown.* FaBoA, *tr. by* A. L. Kroeber

One without looks in to-night [*or* tonight]. Fallow Deer at the Lonely House, The. Thomas Hardy. AWP; OxBSP; RB; TTTS

One Woman. Sandra Maria Esteves. PueRic

One woman has nothing out of place. Criminal. Stephen Dunn. MoASP

One woman seeks more. One Woman. Sandra Maria Esteves. PueRic

One Word. Gabriela Mistral. TCLAP, *tr. by* Doris Dana

One word is too often profaned. To——. Shelley. BoLoP; GTBS-P; NOBE; OBEV; OxAEP-2; TFi

One word, no more, to say. (LL) Merops. Ralph Waldo Emerson. APN-1; OxBA

One word two vowels one active situation at a time. Never Too Late. John Taggart. FTOS

One world at a time, remarked Thoreau. Point of View, A. Constance Carrier. APT-2

One would be in less danger. Family Court. Ogden Nash. PeLV

One would continue to contend with one's ideas. (LL) Glass of Water, The. Wallace Stevens. MoAmPo; OxBA; TAP

One would never suspect there were so many vices. Destruction of Sodom, The. Daryl Hine. ChIV-1

One writes, that "Other friends remain." Tennyson. NAEL-6v2 *Fr.* In Memoriam A. H. H.

One Writing against His Prick. *Unknown.* NOSC

One X. E. E. Cummings. FaBoMo

1 x 2. Hedva Harechavi. DTA, *tr. by* Miriyam Glazer

One xxxvii. Laurie Duggan. BMAP *Fr.* Epigrams of Martial, The.

One Year. N. M. Bodecker. TLR

One Year Ago. Adah Isaacs Menken. CBWP-1

One year ago—a ringing voice. Only a Year. Harriet Beecher Stowe. TreFP

One year I lived in high romance. Deteriora. William Johnson Cory. CAGL

One year the town Republicans. Alderman. Marilyn Nelson Waniek. LTA

One year there were too many / frogs. Calendar. Cecil Bodker. BoWoP, *tr. by* Nadia Christensen and Alexander Taylor

One Year to Live. Mary Davis Reed. PoToHe

One You Wanted to Be Is the One You Are, The. Jean Valentine. BodElec; ExTi

Onely in thy wig, Sister, does the sky clear. Americana. Sam Witt. NeAmPo

Onely the Reverend Grave and Godly Mr. Buckly Remaines. Edward Johnson. SCAP

On[e]ly true in shreds and stuff[e]. (LL) Upon Some Women. Robert Herrick. BeJo; CaPo

Ones you fear most of all: ask where you were, The. (LL) For the Record. Adrienne Rich. NIL-7; NIP-4; VCAP

Oneself a living armoury? (LL) Dead Crab, The. Andrew Young. FaBoTw; RB

Oneself Miss Grant. Miss Grant. Freda Downie. FaBoWP

Onesided Dialog. June Jordan. NoAM

Onesided, stripped of its ghosts. Eccles Street, Bloomsday, 1982. Harry Clifton. PBCIP

OnGoing. Naomi Shihab Nye. PoArWo

Ongoing Story, The. John Ashbery. HCAP

Onion. Cynewulf. WoPoe, *tr. by* Lewis Turco *Fr.* Riddles (Exeter Book).

Onion. Katha Pollitt. RaBo

Onion. Wislawa Szymborska. PoSu, *tr. by* Grazyna Drabik

Onion, The. John Thompson. NOBC

Onion Bucket. Lorenzo Thomas. GT

Onion Days. Carl Sandburg. IllVoic

Onion Fields. Robert Francis. APT-2

Onion is frost, An. Lullaby of the Onion. Miguel Hernández. AF, *tr. by* Robert Bly

Onion, Memory, The. Craig Raine. NAEL-5v2; NAEL-6v2; NoAM; NoP-4

Onions. William Matthews. EmeKit

Onlookers. Luci Shaw. SacPr

Only a bell, a bird, the stillness break. Immense Hour. Juan Ramón Jiménez. SpanPo, *tr. by* Edward F. Gahan

Only a Blush. Mary E. Tucker. CBWP-1

Only a brief sleep everywhere. O God. Else Lasker-Schüler. BBASP, *tr. by* Robert P. Newton

Only a cottage border. Changes. May Probyn. VWP

Only a Curl. Elizabeth Barrett Browning. TreFP

Only a few hours ago the water with its hooves. Mud-Flat. Willem Jan Otten. TuT, *tr. by* Peter Van de Kamp

Only a few will really understand. One Sided Shoot-out. Haki R. Madhubuti. BPo; NBV

Only a fool would eat his heart out so. Ballad of the Bushman. Eileen Duggan. PeNZ

Only a Little Thing. M. P. Handy. PoToHe

Only a little shall we speak of thee. Mary Elizabeth Coleridge. PoBW; VWP

Only a man harrowing clods. In Time of "The Breaking of Nations." Thomas Hardy. BoLoP; ChIV-1; EBEV; HAP; HarvBoo; MoBrPo; NAEL-5v2; NAEL-6v2; NOBE; NoAM; NoP-4; OBEV; OBWP; OPOU; OxAEP-2; PoWW; RB; TFi; WeW-3

Only a part of me shall triumph in this. Boult to Marina. "Ern Malley." BMAP

Only a Pin. Isaac Hinton Brown. PWR

Only a single ray, but suddenly. Hayyim Nahman [*or* Khayim Nakhman *or* Chaim Nachman] Bialik. FIT, *tr. by* Robert Friend

Only a Year. Harriet Beecher Stowe. TreFP

Only Alice. Josephine Jacobsen. FFC

Only an avenue, dark, nameless, without end. (LL) Old Man. Edward Thomas. HarvBoo; NPeEn; OxBEV; SCV; TCAWP

Only Applebaum Can Make a Tree. Joanne Hart. MiVo

Only awake to Universal Mind. Jack Kerouac. NeAP *Fr.* Mexico City Blues.

Only brooms / Know the devil. Brooms. Charles Simic. NNaP

Only calm here is the trees, waiting, The. Girl Named Spring, A. Betsy Sholl. PBCAP

Only calmness will reassure. Honey. Robert Morgan. BLT

Only casually invited, and that several months ago. (LL) Poem: "Eager note on my door said 'Call me,' The." Frank O'Hara. NOBA; NoAM; PmAP; SPE

Only consonants and vowels. (LL) Survey of Literature. John Crowe Ransom. FaBoCh; NBLV; OBAL; TAP; TwCP; VGW

Only content and we are here, / My baby dear. (LL) Song: "Oh, baby, baby, baby dear." Edith Nesbit. NOBVV; PEW

Only cry for you a little. (LL) Offering for the Cat, An. Mei Yao Ch'en. CoBCP; ColAnChi, *tr. by* Burton Watson

Only Daughter, The. Laura Riding Jackson. FuPo

Only Days. Melanie Hope. WiU

Only Death. Pablo Neruda. *See* Nothing but Death

Only deposed kings can know. (LL) Deposition from Love, A. Thomas Carew. BASC; BeJo; CaPo; CavPo; MeLP

Only depression if I stay at home. On the Night of the Fifteenth Day of the First Month I Go Out and Return. Mei Yao Ch'en. SuSp, *tr. by* Jonathan Chaves

Only emperor is the emperor of ice-cream, The. (LL) Emperor of Ice-Cream, The. Wallace Stevens. APT-1; FaBoMo; HAP; HCAP; HeIP-4; InPK-6; NAAL-2v2; NAAL-5; NAWM-7v2; NIL-7; NIP-4; NOBA; NoAM; NoP-4; OxBA; PoE; PoPoPo; TAP; TCAPo; TFi; TRP; WeW-3

Only evidence remaining from his existence was his coat, The. Underneath Oblivion. Yannis Ritsos. AF, *tr. by* Minas Savas

Only for Morning Glories. Basho. PAI, *tr. by* Nobuyuki Yuasa

Only for You. Else Lasker-Schüler. BBASP, *tr. by* Robert P. Newton

Only for you my tea roses. Yury [*or* Iurii] Pavlovich Odarchenko. TCRusP, *tr. by* Theodore Weiss

Only Fortunate Thing, The. Joe Wenderoth. BodElec

Only genuine awakening results in that. Nensho. ZenPo, *tr. by* Takashi Ikemoto and Lucien Stryk

Only he's on a par with our times. About a Hat. Alexander Ilyich Bezymensky [*or* Bezymenskii]. TCRP, *tr. by* Daniel Weissbort

Only head in the sky, The. Giraffe. Stanley Plumly. ChAP

Only heaven. (LL)   Luck.   Langston Hughes.   APT-2; SAmP

Only here that I roll my dope.   Nursing the Sunburn.   Judith Vollmer.   SwNoth

Only His Son Is with God.   "Angelus Silesius."   GePo, *tr. by* George C. Schoolfield   *Fr.* Cherubical Wanderer, The.

Only I laugh.   Alexis Rotella.   HA

Only, I would like to be that unnoticed / and that necessary. (LL)   Variation on the Word *Sleep*.   Margaret Atwood.   AmFaPo; NOBC

Only in Creve Coeur.   In Creve Coeur, Missouri.   Rosanna Warren.   PoPoPo

Only in Poetry.   Ajip Rosidi.   WoPoe, *tr. by* Harry Aveling

Only in This Way.   Margaret Goss Burroughs.   BlSi

Only Indirectly.   Giulia Niccolai.   CItWP, *tr. by* Cinzia Sartini Blum and Lara Trubowitz

Only Jealousy of Emer, The.   *Unknown.*   BIrV, *tr. by* John Montague

Only job I didn't like, quit, The.   What I Wouldn't Do.   Dorianne Laux.   ExTi

Only joy, now here you are.   Sir Philip Sidney.   HAP; NAEL-5v1; NAEL-6v1; NAEL-7v1; NoP-4; NoSic   *Fr.* Astrophil and Stella.

Only kid, An! an only kid.   Had Gadyaa Kid, a Kid.   *Unknown.*   TrJP

Only last week, walking the hushed fields.   Father and Son.   Frederick Robert Higgins.   BIrV; OBMV

Only legend I have ever loved is, The.   Pomegranate, The.   Eavan Boland.   CABP; NoP-4

Only letting in the cat.   Penny Harter.   HA

Only miracle I ever wanted as a kid, The.   Blonde Ambition.   Maureen Seaton.   ReTh

Only monarch all obey, The. (LL)   Written for My Son, and Spoken by Him at His First Putting on Breeches.   Mary Barber.   CABP; ECEV; ECWP; NOEC

Only News I know, The.   Emily Dickinson.   APN-2; NOCV

Only night heals again. (LL)   "H. D."   APT-1; MoAmPo   *Fr.* Songs from Cyprus.

Only Now I Realize.   Luis Lopez.   GeoH

Only, of course, they can't sustain the part. (LL)   Fireflies in the Garden.   Robert Frost.   OxBSP; SAmP

Only of Myself I Knew How to Tell.   "Rachel" [*or* "Rahel"].   MHP, *tr. by* Ruth Finer Mintz

Only on the rarest occasions, when the blue air.   Mountain, The.   W. S. Merwin.   VGW

Only once more and not again—the larches.   In Ampezzo.   Trumbull Stickney.   APN-2

Only One Eye.   Lillian E. Curtis.   VerBaPo

Only one final trick remains—.   Sergey [*or* Sergei] Aleksandrovich Yesenin [*or* Essenin].   TCRP

Only one fleeting.   Ato Tobira.   ArkPo, *tr. by* Edwin A. Cranston

Only one guy and.   Issa.   InPK-6

Only One Life.   *Unknown.*   TreFP

Only one of me.   One.   James Berry.   NOxBChV

Only one old woman.   Fugue.   Stephen Perry.   MiVo

Only one thing is certain. We are too many. (LL)   On Consulting "Contemporary Poets of the English Language."   Anthony Thwaite.   OxBEV; PeLV

Only One Way.   Ella Wheeler Wilcox.   *See* Inspiration, An

Only [*or* Onely] a little more.   His Poetry His Pillar.   Robert Herrick.   BeJo; CaPo; NOSC

Only parts of the pain of living.   Detroit 1958.   Al Young.   ESEAA

Only passages of a poetry, no more. No matter how many times the cards are handled.   Structure of Rime XXIII.   Robert Duncan.   FTOS

Only people who should really sin, The.   Inter-Office Memorandum.   Ogden Nash.   APT-2

Only Poem, The.   Robert Penn Warren.   BodElec

Only poem to write I now have in mind, The.   Only Poem, The.   Robert Penn Warren.   BodElec

Only possible utilisation of electricity "in the arts," The.   Electricity Breadthwise.   Marcel Duchamp.   PFTM-1

Only record of our great affection, The.   Gravestone at Corinth, A.   *Unknown.*   GrAn, *tr. by* Peter Jay

Only relics left are those long, The.   Monuments for a Friendly Girl at a Tenth Grade Party.   William Stafford.   NoAM

Only response, The.Poem.   Bill Knott.   InPK-6

Only ribbon round it. (LL)   Mother Goose.   LB; OxBoLi; OxNR; ReMoGo

Only rule is enjoy yourself, The.   *Unknown.*   GrAn

Only serpents change their outward skin.   Memory.   Nikolai Stepanovich Gumilyov [*or* Gumiliov *or* Gumilev].   TCRP, *tr. by* Yakov Hornstein

Only Silly Faggots Know.   Perry Brass.   CAGL

Only teaching on Tuesdays, book-worming.   Memories of West Street and Lepke.   Robert Lowell.   AF; EmeKit; NAAL-2v2; NAAL-5; NOBA; NoAM; PoE; VCAP

Only temple He delights to fill, The. (LL)   Enoch.   Jones Very.   ChIV-1; HAP; TCAPo

Only the chemist can tell, and not always the chemist.   Trainor, the Druggist.   Edgar Lee Masters.   APT-1; IllVoic   *Fr.* Spoon River Anthology.

Only the clouds were new.   Beast with Two Backs, The.   Andrew Taylor.   NOBAu

Only the compass, keeping hope alive.   Logbook of a Lost Caravan.   Gyula Illyés.   PFTM-1

Only / the gray wind.   Something for Supper.   Carroll Arnett.   VoR

Only the Hand That Stirs Knows What's in the Pot.   Luz Maria Umpierre.   PueRic

Only the illegitimate are beautiful.   Thesis.   Edward Dorn.   NOBA

Only the light industry of snow.   Man in the White Suit, The.   Nick Drake.   NeBl

Only the lion and the cock.   After Galen.   Oliver St. John Gogarty.   FaBoEE; OBMV; PoRA

Only the moon.   Tagami Kikusha-Ni.   SoOfWa, *tr. by* Sam Hamill

Only the most obvious questions.   Hearing Loss.   Christian Wiman.   AmPoNex

Only the New Branches Bloom.   Samuel Hazo.   GraLe

Only the new dust falling through the air. (LL)   My Grandmother.   Elizabeth Jennings.   HarvBoo; NoP-4

Only the old man was there to see me off. (LL)   Recruiting Officer of Shih-hao.   Tu Fu.   ColAnChi; SuSp, *tr. by* Irving Y. Lo

Only the plants remain sinless and pure.   Carbon Dioxide.   Ágnes Nemes Nagy.   IQMS, *tr. by* Adam Makkai

Only the Polished Skeleton.   Countee Cullen.   VGW

Only the shoots.   Buson.   SoOfWa, *tr. by* Sam Hamill

Only the short, broad, splayed feet.   Young Shepherd Bathing His Feet.   Peter Clarke.   PBA

Only the Sun.   István Sinka.   IQMS, *tr. by* William Price Turner

Only the truly bourgeois.   Qantas Bags.   Laurie Duggan.   BMAP

Only the very worst despair is as cold.   December Offensive.   Anna Enquist.   TuT, *tr. by* Peter Van de Kamp

Only the wanderer.   Song.   Ivor Gurney.   HarvBoo

Only the wholesomest foods you eat.   Samuel Hoffenstein.   TrJP   *Fr.* Poems in Praise of Practically Nothing.

Only the wind sings.   Mary Celeste.   Judith Nicholls.   OBSP

Only the Zen-man knows tranquillity.   Fugai.   ZenPo, *tr. by* Takashi Ikemoto and Lucien Stryk

Only then and not before.   S.O.S.   Léon Damas.   PFTM-1

Only these black translucent wings.   Murmur.   Esther Iverem.   GT

Only they are left me, they are faithful still.   My Dead.   "Rachel" [*or* "Rahel"].   FIT, *tr. by* Robert Friend

Only thing I have of Jane MacNaughton, The.   Leap, The.   James Dickey.   NIL-7; NIP-4

Only thing that can be relied on, The.   Snow on Saddle Mountain, The.   Miyazawa Kenji.   ColAP; NOBA; NoAM; PAI, *tr. by* Gary Snyder

Only think, dearest Louisa, what fearful scenes we have witnessed!   Arthur Hugh Clough.   EBVV; NPeEn   *Fr.* Amours de Voyage.

Only this. (LL)   Missing You.   "Shu Ting."   CarOv; VCWP, *tr. by* Carolyn Kizer and Y. H. Zhao

Only this evening I saw again low in the sky.   Martial Cadenza.   Wallace Stevens.   OxBA; VGW

Only this table by the draughty window.   Autumn Supper.   Dimitris Tsaloumas.   BMAP

"Only through Me!" The clear, high call comes pealing.   Dies Ire-Dies Pacis.   John Oxenham.   SacPr

Only time I ever watched *Dallas*, The.   Soap.   Jane Coleman.   ReTh

Only to fail again! (LL)   Emily Dickinson.   NCAP; NOBA; SAmP

Only to feed her pride. (LL)   Love's Siege.   Sir John Suckling.   CaPo; NPeEn

Only to have a grief.   Peeling Onions.   Adrienne Rich.   BoWoP; HCAP; TAP

Only to say, Here I am in person. (LL)   Stumpfoot on 42nd Street.   Louis Simpson.   NNaP; UnPo; VGW

Only Tourist in Havana Turns His Thoughts Homeward, The.   Leonard Cohen.   MoCV

Only true likeness of myself, The. (LL)   My Shoes.   Charles Simic.   CoAP; EmeKit; HCAP; VCAP

Only truth you know now is your hunger, The.   Disorder, The.   Marilyn Chin.   LoL

Only two patient eyes to stare.   Faded Pictures.   William Vaughn Moody.   TCAPo

Only until this cigarette is ended.   Edna St. Vincent Millay.   HeIP-4

Only voice they will obey, The. (LL)   Gray Folk, The.   Edith Nesbit.   NOBVV; PEW

Only war that matters is the war against the imagination, The.   Diane Di Prima.   PFTM-2   *Fr.* Rant.

Only Way, The.   W. N. Ewer.   FaBoWar

Only way to be quiet, The.   Poetry.   Frank O'Hara.   HCAP

Only Way to Have a Friend, The.   *Unknown.*   PoToHe

Only we, blasting your three years of war.   Manifesto of the Presidents of the

Terrestrial Globe.   Velemir [or Viktor Vladimirovich] Khlebnikov.   TCRP, *tr. by* Gary Kern

Only, we die in earnest—that's no jest. (LL)   What Is Our Life?   Sir Walter Ralegh.   EBEV; FaBoEE; NAEL-7v1; NoSic; OxBSP; PAI; SCGP; SoSe-8

Only what is heroic and courageious moves our blood.   Flowers of Politics, II, The.   Michael McClure.   NeAP

Only When My Heart Freezes.   Alden Nowlan.   RaBo

Only winds and rivers, / Life and death. (LL)   Robert Louis Stevenson.   FaBoCh; OBEV; OxBS; SCGP

Only with Radiance.   Margit Szécsi.   IQMS, *tr. by* Kenneth McRobbie

Only Years.   Kenneth Rexroth.   TAP

Only You.   Fanny Carrión de Fierro.   TANSG, *tr. by* Sally Cheney Bell

Onoto-face.   Hammock.   Blaise Cendrars.   CuPo

1.23: To Chloë ("Vitas hinnuleo").   Horace.   AWP; OBVE   *Fr.* Odes.

Onset, The.   Robert Frost.   APT-1; MoAmPo; OxBA

Onto the hallowit steid bryng in, thai cry.   Virgil [or Vergil].   OBVE, *tr. by* Gawin [or Gavin] Douglas   *Fr.* Aeneid [or Eneados, Aeneis], The.

Onto the twin and contrasting altars I pour my libations.   Libations.   Ferenc Kölcsey.   IQMS, *tr. by* Adam Makkai

Ontogeny.   Jarold Ramsey.   NIP-4

Ontology.   Rutger Kopland.   TuT, *tr. by* Seamus Deane

Onward, Christian Soldiers.   Sabine Baring-Gould.   SacPr

Onward led the road again.   Hell Gate.   A. E. Housman.   NoAM; SCGP; UnPo

Onward, Onward, Men of Heaven.   Lydia Huntley Sigourney.   AH

Onward! though ever in our march.   William Bingham Tappan.   VerBaPo   *Fr.* Song of the Three Hundred Thousand Drunkards in the United States.

Onycha.   "Michael Field."   ViWPN

Onyons.   Jonathan Swift.   BIrV   *Fr.* Verses Made for the Women Who Cry Apples, etc.

Ooftish.   Samuel Beckett.   NoAM

Oom Gert's Story.   C. Louis Leipoldt.   PeSAV, *tr. by* C. J. D. Harvey

Oonu see mi dyin trail!   Jesus Is Condemned to Death.   Pamela Mordecai.   WaCA

Ooooh, oooooh, oooh, says the voice of a girl.   Nights.   Lyn Hejinian.   BAP-01

Oor best-lo'ed makar has but late grown cauld.   William Jeffrey.   OxBS   *Fr.* On Glaister's Hill.

Oor Location.   Janet Hamilton.   NePenScot

Opal.   Amy Lowell.   NALW

Opal heart of afternoon, The.   Bracelet of Grass, The.   William Vaughn Moody.   APN-2; TCAPo

Opal Sea, The.   Ella Higginson.   SWaP

Open.   Larry Eigner.   NeAP

Open Air Where.   Larry Eigner.   PmAP

Open and Closed Space.   Tomas Tranströmer.   SPE, *tr. by* Robert Bly

Open area outdoors, preferably the courtyard of a church or other religious structure, an.   Realtheater Piece Two.   Jerome Rothenberg.   FTOS

Open as experience, this day, this.   Tomarata.   Kendrick Smithyman.   PeNZ

Open Country.   Richard Hugo.   LCAP-2

Open Door, The.   Elizabeth Jane Coatsworth.   TLR

Open door: image, song of the Little Miss by the Green Rill.   Unknown.   ChinPo, *tr. by* Yip Wai-lim

Open eye, An. (LL)   Margaret Atwood.   InPK-6; NALW; NoAM

Open-Eyed Angel.   David Rokeah [or Rokeakh].   MHP, *tr. by* Ruth Finer Mintz

Open Heart.   Sekou Sundiata.   SpirFl

Open House.   Theodore Roethke.   NOBA; NoAM

Open it.   First Book, The.   Rita Dove.   LoL

Open Letter to All Black Poets, An.   Samuel F. Reynolds.   SpirFl

Open mouth open through.   Ted Greenwald.   FTOS   *Fr.* Word of Mouth.

Open-mouthed quail, The.   Something or Other.   Ron Padgett.   FTOS

Open one's hand.   Curriculum vitae.   Marie-Claire Bancquart.   MFP, *tr. by* Martin Sorrell

Open Poem.   Melinda Goodman.   WiU

Open Prospect.   William Wordsworth.   CenSon   *Fr.* River Duddon [A Series of Sonnets], The.

Open Sea, The.   William Meredith.   CoAP; TAP; UnPo

Open Secrets.   Gwendolyn MacEwen.   LW

Open sesame.   Venus.   Federico García Lorca.   PFTM-1

Open the book of tales you knew by heart.   Living Memory.   Adrienne Rich.   TRP

Open the cupboard, cherries rounded up in the darkness.   Swallower.   Beckian Fritz Goldberg.   ExTi

Open the door Oakland.   Robert Grenier.   FTOS   *Fr.* Oakland.

Open the Door to Me, Oh!   Robert Burns.   SCGP

  (O, Open the Door to Me, O!)   FaBoCh

Open the door where I knock weeping.   Traveller, The.   Guillaume Apollinaire.   WoPoe, *tr. by* Rachel Blau

Open the final book: November spills.   Of the Finished World.   Lucie Brock-Broido.   MakPoe

Open the Gates.   Unknown.   TrJP, *tr. by* Israel Zangwill

Open the gates.   Bonny Earl of Murray, The.   Unknown.   ESPB

Open the shutters.   Teikitsu.   JDP, *tr. by* Yoel Hoffmann

Open the windows.   Spring Forward.   Martin Steingesser.   PoCoUp

Open Thy Doors, O Lebanon.   Bible, *O.T.*   AWP   *Fr.* Zechariah.

Open thy gates.   To Heaven.   Robert Herrick.   ChIV-2

Open, Time.   Louise Imogen Guiney.   APN-2

Open to Me!   Unknown.   AWP   *Fr.* Book of the Dead.

Open up this door where I knock weeping.   Voyager, The.   Guillaume Apollinaire.   CuPo

Open Windows.   Victor Hugo.   SxFrPo, *tr. by* E. H. Blackmore and A. M. Blackmore

Open Windows.   Sara Teasdale.   ColAP

Open Your Eyes.   Emma Bridge Whisenand.   PoToHe

Open your eyes and stare.   Haka: Hinemotu.   Te Aomuhurangi te Maaka.   PeNZ

Open your eyes that you may see.   Open Your Eyes.   Emma Bridge Whisenand.   PoToHe

Open your palms.   Request.   Jared Angira.   PBMAP

Open? Open. Shut? Shut. (LL)   Cardinal Ideograms.   May Swenson.   NoP-4; OBCA; OxIBACP

Opened, clear as a child's geography.   Summer Countries, The.   Henry Rago.   VGW

Opener.   Chris Wallace-Crabbe.   BMAP   *Fr.* Bits and Pieces, The.

Opening a vein he called my radial.   40 Days and 40 Nights.   Henri Cole.   PoPoPo

Opening his.   Alexis Rotella.   HA

Opening Le Ba Khon's Dictionary.   John Balaban.   CDa

Opening of a Door, The.   Suspense.   Emily Dickinson.   AWP; MoAmPo; OxBA; TCAPo; WPE

Opening of an Offensive.   Hamish Henderson.   FaBoWar

Opening scene, The. The yellow, coal-fed fog.   Poem with Refrains.   Robert Pinsky.   TaR

Opening Service, An.   Clara Ann Thompson.   CBWP-2

Opening the Cage.   Edwin Morgan.   NIL-7

Opening the mailbox.   Alan Pizzarelli.   HA

Openly send word to Algol and Procyon. (LL)   For Heather, Entering Kindergarten.   Roberta Hill Whiteman.   HATNAP; NoAM

Openly, yes / with the naturalness.   Black Earth.   Marianne Craig Moore.   APT-1; FaBoMo

Opens blue and cool on a hot morning. (LL)   Pleasures.   Denise Levertov.   NOBA; NeAP; NoAM; PoE

Opera Teacher Neemed Enna, An.   Moss Rich.   PeLi

Operation, The.   W. D. Snodgrass.   InPK-6; TAP

Operators Are Standing By.   John Ashbery.   BodElec

Ophelia.   Christopher Pilling.   NLP

Ophelia.   Vernon Watkins.   TCAWP

Ophelia's Death.   William Shakespeare.   OxAEP-1; RB   *Fr.* Hamlet.

Ophelia's Song.   William Shakespeare.   EBEV; EnLoPo; NoSic; PoRA; SCGP   *Fr.* Hamlet.

Ophra.   Judah Halevi.   TrJP, *tr. by* Nina Davis Salaman

Opinion is a flitting thing.   Emily Dickinson.   SAmP

Opinion of Hagar, The.   Alicia Ostriker.   TaR

Opinions of the New Student.   Regino Pedroso.   TTY, *tr. by* Langston Hughes

Opium-Eater, The.   Mary E. Tucker.   CBWP-1

Opium Fantasy, An.   Maria White Lowell.   APN-2; InPK-6

Oppenheim's Cup and Saucer.   Carol Ann Duffy.   LW

Opportunity.   Harry Graham.   OBCoV; PeLV

Opportunity.   Helen Hunt Jackson.   SWaP

Opportunity.   Niccolò Machiavelli.   AWP, *tr. by* James Elroy Flecker

Opportunity.   Walter Malone.   PWR

Opportunity.   Edward Rowland Sill.   APN-2

  (Broken Sword, The.)   PoToHe

Opposite of Green, The.   Alvin Aubert.   ISC

Opposite of Ornate and Rhetorical Poetry, The.   José Martí.   TCLAP

Opposite to Melancholy.   William Strode.   NOSC

Oppositions.   Judith Wright.   HarvBoo   *Fr.* Shadow of Fire: Ghazals, The.

Oppression.   Jimmy Santiago Baca.   AF

Opprobrium.   Rosario Ferré.   TANSG

Optical Prodigal, The.   Russell Edson.   PmAP

Optician Has a Glass Heart, An.   H. C. Artmann.   PFTM-2, *tr. by* Harriett Watts

Optician has a glass heart with plexiglass hinges, An.   Optician Has a Glass Heart, An.   H. C. Artmann.   PFTM-2, *tr. by* Harriett Watts

Optimism. Ella Wheeler Wilcox. PWR

Optimism, / trust, / fearless. Scum & Slime. John Giorno. PmAP

Opting for Early Retirement. Tom Leonard. Oth

Opulence. Jorie Graham. NoP-4

Opulent oracle—it's a terrible thing! It's a Terrible Thing! Everett Hoagland. BPo

Opulent park: serene, we chose the heights, An. Lo Yu Park. Tu Fu. CarOv, *tr. by* Carolyn Kizer

Opus 2. Witter Bynner. APT-1, *tr. by* Emanuel Morgan

Opus 17. Witter Bynner. APT-1, *tr. by* Emanuel Morgan

Opus 118. Arthur Davison Ficke. APT-1, *tr. by* Anne Knish

Opus 131. Arthur Davison Ficke. APT-1, *tr. by* Anne Knish

Opus from Space. Pattiann Rogers. PoCoUp

Opusculum paedagogum. Study of Two Pears. Wallace Stevens. APT-1; BLT; NAAL-2v2; NoAM; OxBA

Or a kick on the arse. (LL) Description of an Irish Feast, The. Hugh MacGowran. NOIV; OBCoV, *tr. by* Jonathan Swift

Or a Play. Leslie Scalapino. FTOS

Or an old man upon a winter's night. (LL) On Being Asked for a War Poem. W. B. Yeats. FaBoWar; NIP-4; OBWP; OxAEP-2; PoWW

Or any other reason why. (LL) Catch, A. Henry Aldrich. FaBoEE; NOSC; OxBSP

Or anything resembling it. Michael Palmer. BodElec

Or anywhere. "H. D." NAAL-5 *Fr.* Walls Do Not Fall, The.

Or as in jewelry shops, do gems. (LL) Edward Taylor. NAAL-2v1; NAAL-3; NAAL-5; TCAPo *Fr.* Preparatory Meditations before My Approach to the Lord's Supper.

Or better, be with me— / Yours, Fly. (LL) Letter to Bee. Emily Dickinson. SAmP; TLR; TTTS

Or buried lie in purple beds of thyme. (LL) Frances Anne [*or* "Fanny"] Kemble. CenSon; SWaP

Or certain ones. There are Bed and Breakfast flags. Primer about the Flag, A. Marvin Bell. GifTon

Or come again. My Ben. Robert Herrick. BASC

Or, conversely, hungers. Beethoven, Opus 111. Amy Clampitt. NIP-4

Or curtained close such scene from ev'ry future view. (LL) Ode on the Poetical Character. William Collins. NAEL-5v1; NOEC; PoE

Or did I really fall out of love with my country?—. "Naum Korzhavin." TCRP

Or die and so forget what love ere meant. (LL) On Monsieur's Departure. Queen of England Elizabeth I. CABP; NAEL-5v1; NAEL-6v1; NAEL-7v1; NALW; WPE

Or does it explode? (LL) Langston Hughes. APSN; APT-2; AiP; GLP; GT; HCAP; HeIP-4; NAAAL; NoP-4; RaBo; SAmP; SSLK *Fr.* Lenox Avenue Mural.

Or else in exile like a fugitive. (LL) Sonnet 17: "I flee the city, temples, and each place." Louise Labé. BoWoP; WoPoe, *tr. by* Willis Barnstone

Or else quite extinguish mine. (LL) Prayer to the Wind, A. Thomas Carew. BeJo; CavPo

Or else this very moment dies— (LL) Strephon to Celia. Mary Leapor. ECWP; RACG

Or every man be blind. (LL) Emily Dickinson. APN-2; ColAP; HeIP-4; NAAL-2v1; NAAL-3; NALW; NAWM-7v2; NOBA; NoAM; NoP-4; TAP; TCAPo; UnPo; WeW-3

Or gathers seaward, ebbing out of mind. (LL) Slow Pacific Swell, The. Yvor Winters. APT-2; ColAP; HarvBoo; NOBA

Or give the mittee will, or give the gode man power. (LL) Excelente Balade of Charitie, An. Thomas Chatterton. EBEV; NOEC; OxAEP-1

Or glittering starlight without thee is sweet. (LL) John Milton. UV; WoPoe *Fr.* Paradise Lost.

Or hawk[e] of the tower [*or* towre]. (LL) John Skelton. EBEV; EnLoPo; NAEL-5v1; NAEL-6v1; NBLV; NOBE; NoP-4; NoSic; OBEV; OxBEV; PeLV; PoE; PoRA; SCGP; SCV; TFi *Fr.* Garland [*or* Garlande *or* Garlands] of Laurel[l], The.

Or hear old Triton blow his wreathèd horn. (LL) World Is Too Much with Us, The. William Wordsworth. AWP; BRP; CABP; CenSon; ClHu; FHYEP; GSo; GTBS-P; HAP; HeIP-4; InPK-6; NAEL-5v2; NAWM-7v2; NOBE; NOBRP; NoP-4; OBEV; PWR; PoE; PoPoPo; PoRA; RaBo; SCGP; SacPr; SoSe-8; Son; TFi; TRP; WeW-3

Or help to half-a-crown. (LL) Man He Killed, The. Thomas Hardy. ChAP; FaBoWar; HAP; HarvBoo; HeIP-4; MoBrPo; NIP-4; OBWP; PAI; RB; TFi; WeW-3

Or her kisses where a serpent hides. (LL) Returning, We Hear the Larks. Isaac Rosenberg. FaBoMo; HarvBoo; NAEL-5v2; NAEL-6v2; NoAM; OBWP; PeFWW; PoWW

Or hope relief. (LL) Elegy over a Tomb. Edward Herbert, 1st Baron Herbert of Cherbury. MeLP; NOBE; OBEV; OBWVE

Or how belovèd above all else that dies. (LL) Edna St. Vincent Millay. PoRA; TAP

Or I of her a sinner. (LL) Pious Selinda [*or* Celinda]. William Congreve. NOBE; NPeEn

Or I shall live your epitaph to make. William Shakespeare. OxAEP-1 *Fr.* Sonnets.

Or I suppose I can. (LL) Self's the Man. Philip Larkin. NOBL; PeLV

Or if I die. (LL) William Blake. NAEL-5v2; NAEL-6v2; NBLV *Fr.* Songs of Experience.

Or if I would delight my privat hours. John Milton. PeECV *Fr.* Paradise Regained [*or* Regain'd].

Or if thou dar'st to climb the highest trees. Richard Barnfield [*or* Barnefield]. *See* If thou wilt come and dwell with me at home

Or, in eternal slumbers bid them rest. (LL) Sappho's Conjectures. Mary Robinson. CenSon; RWP

Or is it a great tide that covers the rock-pool. "H. D." WPoS *Fr.* Sagesse.

Or is it a shadow? (LL) Tenebris. Angelina Weld Grimké. APT-1; NAAAL

Or it goes to the backyard and stands like an old horse cold in the pasture. (LL) Original Sin. Robert Penn Warren. NOCV; TAP

Or its advantage—Blue. (LL) Emily Dickinson. APN-2; NCAP

Or just some human sleep. (LL) After Apple-Picking. Robert Frost. APT-1; MoAmPo; NAAL-2v2; NAAL-5; NOBA; NoAM; OxBA; PAI; PoE; SAmP; SoSe-8; TAP; TCAPo; TFi; TRP; UnPo

Or known what death could do. (LL) Carentan O Carentan. Louis Simpson. CoAP; NOBA; OBWP; PoE; RB; WoPoe

Or lamps in ancient [*or* antient] urns. (LL) To Her Lover's Complaint. Jane Barker. NPeEn; OxBSP

Or lapse for ever into a classic fatigue. (LL) Consider. W. H. Auden. FaBoMo; OxAEP-2

Or looked [*or* lookt] I back unto the times hence flown. To M. Denham, on His Prospective Poem. Robert Herrick. BeJo

Or love, either. (LL) Spinster. Sylvia Plath. FaBoWP; LW; SoSe-8

Or love me [*or* mee] less [*or* lesse], or love me [*or* mee] more. Song. Sidney Godolphin. BeJo; NOSC

Or many things adulterate. Epitaph. Tristan Corbière. AWP, *tr. by* Joseph T. Shipley

Or Mists—the Apennine. (LL) Emily Dickinson. OxBA; TCAPo

Or More. (LL) Emily Dickinson. APN-2; NALW

Or music [*or* musique] be[e] but[t] in sweet [*or* deere] thoughts of love? (LL) Mary Sidney Wroth, Countess of Montgomery. BASC; PBRV; WPE *Fr.* Pamphilia to Amphilanthus.

Or music when the sound is spent. (LL) Thine Own. Josephine D. Henderson Heard. CBWP-4; SWaP

Or not untrue or not unkind. (LL) Talking in Bed. Philip Larkin. BoLoP; NAEL-5v2; NAEL-6v2; PoetW

Or nothing. (LL) Ourselves or Nothing. Carolyn Forché. BodElec; GifTon

Or of his hope / that heat would be arrested on its shore. (LL) Heat. Kenneth Mackenzie. BMAP; CBAP

Or other names. (LL) Leaving the Motel. W. D. Snodgrass. NIL-7; NIP-4

Or out of time will correct this. (LL) Country Clergy, The. Ronald Stuart Thomas. GTBS-P; OxBTC; PeECV

Or pleasures, seldom reached, again pursued. (LL) Nocturnal Reverie, A. Anne Finch, Countess of Winchilsea. BWW; EBEV; ECEV; ECWP; NAEL-5v1; NAEL-6v1; NAEL-7v1; NALW; NOEC; NoP-4; OxAEP-1; OxBEV; PoE; WPE

Or rather the sacred fish with the golden faces. Callimachus. HePo *Fr.* Galataea.

Or scorn[e], or pity [*or* pittie] on me take. Dream[e], The. Ben Jonson. BeJo; NOBE; NOSC

Or see the raincoats pass. (LL) Lobsters in the Window. W. D. Snodgrass. TAP; TRP

Or so men think who like a different tree. (LL) Aspens. Edward Thomas. FaBoVe; NPeEn; OxBEV

Or so very little longer! (LL) Lost Mistress, The. Robert Browning. BoLoP; NOBE; OBEV

Or something very like Him. (LL) Arthur Hugh Clough. CABP; NAEL-5v2; NOBE; NOBVV; NPeEn; NoP-4; OxBEV; SacPr *Fr.* Dipsychus [and the Spirit].

Or stain a point with blood. (LL) Ghostly Tree. Léonie Adams. APT-2; MoAmPo

Or stand all night watering roses, his feet blue in rubber boots. (LL) Old Florist. Theodore Roethke. APT-2; OxBSP

Or take a day or two, my days are numbered. (LL) Unborn Child, An. Derek Mahon. CABP; PNI; WoPoe

Or teach himself to pray. (LL) Lives. Derek Mahon. EmeKit; ModIr; PBCIP

Or, tell you what, let's save it for The End. (LL) Man Who Loved Islands, The. Derek Walcott. BodElec; NoAM

Or that of my Alexis, I am lost. (LL) On Her Loving Two Equally. Aphra Behn. NALW; NIL-7; NIP-4

Or the *Chaplain,* (for 'tis his *Trade*) as in Duty bound, shall ever *Pray.* (LL) To Their Excellencies the Lords Justices of Ireland, the Humble Petition of

Frances Harris, Who Must Starve, and Die a Maid if It Miscarries. Jonathan Swift.   NOEC; OxBEV

Or the Chinese chest of drawers taken.   Orchestrion.   Edward Kleinschmidt.   MiVo

Or the day's vanity, the night's remorse. (LL)   Choice, The.   W. B. Yeats.   NoAM; OxBSP; OxBTC

Or the dazzling crystal. (LL)   What I Expected.   Stephen Spender.   MoBrPo; NOBE; NoAM; OxAEP-2

Or the Earl—an Earl? (LL)   Emily Dickinson.   FaBoVe; NCAP

Or the first murther. (LL)   Doomsday.   Elinor Wylie.   NoP-4; SacPr

Or the image-kingdom's idol of the past generation.   Saul [or Shaul] Tchernichowsky [or Tchernichovsky].   MHP   Fr. To the Sun.

Or the old grasshopper molasses-mouthed. (LL)   Frederick Goddard Tuckerman.   APN-2; TAP   Fr. Sonnets.

Or the price of grass-seed? (LL)   Other Side, The.   Seamus Heaney.   CIP-2; PNI

Or the prophetic sibillance of song. (LL)   Mad Potter, The.   John Hollander.   ColAP; VCAP

Or the radiant sisters the Pleiades. (LL)   On the Beach at Night.   Walt Whitman.   APN-1; AWP; MoAmPo; NOBA; NoP-4; OxBA; SAmP; TCAPo

Or the rest will be wanting one too! (LL)   Limerick: "Epicure, Dining at Crewe, An."   Unknown.   NTCP; PeLi

Or the "sculpture" of rhyme. (LL)   Ezra Pound.   HAP; HarvBoo; MoAmPo; NPeEn; VGW   Fr. Hugh Selwyn Mauberley (Life and Contacts).

Or the songs of the butterflies be. (LL)   Eutopia.   Francis Turner Palgrave.   EBVV; OBGa

Or the spike.   Like a Bulrush.   Marianne Craig Moore.   APT-1

Or the tears of a girl remembering her dread. (LL)   Vaunting Oak.   John Crowe Ransom.   OxBA; VGW

Or the unimaginable touch of Time. (LL)   William Wordsworth.   CenSon; EBEV; HeIP-4; InPK-6; NAEL-6v2; NOBE; NoP-4; OBEV   Fr. Ecclesiastical Sonnets.

Or they had now been there. (LL)   Fair Margaret and Sweet William.   Unknown.   ESPB; OxBB

Or Think We've Met subhuman rights Before. (LL)   Salesman, A.   E. E. Cummings.   NoAM; OxBA

Or till blossomed stalks cannot weave a spell. (LL)   Spraying the Potatoes.   Patrick Kavanagh.   BIrV; CABP

Or to seal up the sun. (LL)   To Daisies, Not to Shut So Soon[e].   Robert Herrick.   BeJo; CaPo; OBEV; OxBSP

Or to the play goes but some purse to nip. (LL)   Sir Revel.   Samuel Rowlands.   NoSic; OBCoV

Or too much weight to fly. (LL)   Emily Dickinson.   APN-2; NOBA

Or turn within to look at my own heart. (LL)   To the Tune "Moon over West River."   Yang Shen.   CoBLCP; ColAnChi, tr. by Jonathan Chaves

Or Venus with her ecstasy. (LL)   Father Mat.   Patrick Kavanagh.   CIP-2; ModIr; PoE

Or view the Lord of the unerring bow.   Byron.   GS   Fr. Childe Harold's Pilgrimage.

Or was myself—too small? (LL)   Emily Dickinson.   ChIV-1; SAmP

Or we be lost among the stars. (LL)   Calverly's.   Edwin Arlington Robinson.   APT-1; NoAM

Or what death I should dee. (LL)   Mary Hamilton.   Unknown.   NOBE; OxBB

Or what is closer to the truth.   When I Buy Pictures.   Marianne Craig Moore.   APT-1; ColAP; OxBA

Or where is man so[e] uncontrolled [or uncontroul'd] a lord? (LL)   Verses Written by Mrs. Hutchinson.   Lucy Hutchinson.   BASC; NOSC

Or whether doth my mind, being crowned with you.   William Shakespeare.   SCGP   Fr. Sonnets.

Or whether we shall be victorious, or utterly quell'd and defeated. (LL)   As I Lay with My Head in Your Lap Camerado.   Walt Whitman.   CAGL; CBCWP; NAAL-2v1; NAAL-3; OxBA

Or whistling, I am not a little boy. (LL)   Ball Poem, The.   John Berryman.   ChAP; CoAP; MoAmPo; NOBA; NoAM

Or withoute quiete to have huge labour. (LL)   Inordinate Love.   Unknown.   EBEV; MiEL; OxBSP

Or yield or die's the word, what could he mean.   Ignotum per Ignotius, or a Furious Hodge-Podge of Nonsense; a Pindaric.   Unknown.   NOEC

Or you may guess. (LL)   Winter: My Secret.   Christina Georgina Rossetti.   BrRo; NAEL-5v2; NAEL-6v2; NOBVV; NPeEn; VWP

Oracle.   Fanny Carrión de Fierro.   TANSG, tr. by Sally Cheney Bell

Oracle Night.   Michael Brownstein.
   "Oracle night / the porch is frozen."   FTOS

Oracle of the Drowned, The.   Douglas Oliver.   Oth

Oracle of the market! thence you drew.   Camelus Saltat: Continued.   George Meredith.   OxBSo

Oracles, The.   A. E. Housman.   HAP

Oracles for Youth.   Caroline Gilman.
   What Will Be Your Destiny?   SWaP

Oracular Degeneration.   Karl Kirchwey.   KGB

Oral Messages.   Lawrence Ferlinghetti.
   "I am waiting for my case to come up."   AiP; PmAP

Oral Tradition, The.   Eavan Boland.   PBCIP

Orange, The.   Matthew Prior.   PeLV

Orange Birch Bolete (Leccinum versipelle).   Harry Gilonis.   Oth   Fr. Forty Fungi.

Orange Buds by Mail from Florida.   Walt Whitman.   NAAL-2v1; NAAL-3

Orange Chiffon.   Jayne Cortez.   BlSi

Orange in the middle of a table.   Against Still Life.   Margaret Atwood.   MoCV

Orange Jews.   Ted Berrigan.   SPE

Orange leaf on every finger bowl: a dozen tongues, An.   Imperfect Is Our Paradise, The.   Joy Katz.   NeAmPo

Orange leaves are gone.   Lady Izumi.   BoWoP

Orange Lily, The.   Unknown.   NOIV

Orange line splits the sky, An.   Flint Hills, The.   Lew Blockcolski.   VoR

Orange March.   Richard Murphy.   NOIV   Fr. Battle of Aughrim, The.

Orange on its way.   On Its Way.   May Swenson.   SoSe-8; WPE

Orange on the table, An.   Alicante.   Jacques Prévert.   BoLoP, tr. by Lawrence Ferlinghetti

Orange Poem, The.   George MacBeth [or Macbeth].   OBCoV

Orange Tree, The.   Ben Belitt.   APT-2

Orange Tree, The.   John Shaw Neilson.   CBAP

Oranges.   Fruit.   Kenward Elmslie.   FTOS

Oranges.   Gary Soto.   NoAM; WeW-3

Oranges, The.   Abu Dharr.   TTY, tr. by A. J. Arberry

Oranges and lemons, say the bells of St. Clement's.   Unknown.   OxBEV

Oranges Returned, The.   Gilbert Sorrentino.   FTOS

Orara.   Henry Clarence Kendall.   CBAP

Oration on Death, An.   Manoah Bodman.
   "What rich profusion here."   APN-1

Orator.   Ralph Waldo Emerson.   OxBA   Fr. Quatrains.

Orator Flaccus can commit solecisms.   Lucilius.   GrAn

Orator Prigg.   William Blake.   OBSV

Orator's Epitaph, The.   Henry Peter Brougham, 1st Baron Brougham and Vaux.   NBLV

Oratorio for a Concentration Camp.   János Pilinszky.   IQMS, tr. by Adam Makkai

Orbit.   Gig Ryan.   BMAP

Orbit I describe in my environment, The.   Orbits.   Nina Cassian.   PoSu, tr. by Naomi Lazard

Orbits.   'Aisha Arnaout.   PoArWo, tr. by Mona Fayad

Orbits.   Nina Cassian.   PoSu, tr. by Naomi Lazard

Orchard.   "H. D."   APT-1; MoAmPo; OxBA; TCAPo

Orchard at Avignon, An.   Agnes Mary Frances Robinson.   NOBVV

Orchard dying, The.   Mary Kinzie.   FFC

Orchard in the Spring.   Jane Rohrer.   BodElec

Orchard of Figs in the Fall, An.   Diana García.   TouFir

Orchard Pavilion.   Wang Pin-chih.   ChinPo, tr. by Yip Wai-lim

Orchard-Pit, The.   Dante Gabriel Rossetti.   EnLoPo; NAEL-5v2; NAEL-6v2; PeVV; SCV

Orchards in July.   Zbigniew Machej.   BLT

Orchestra, The.   William Carlos Williams.   HAP

Orchestra; or, A Poem[e] of Da[u]ncing.   Sir John Davies.   NoSic
   (Dancing Justified.)   NAEL-6v1
   Praise of Dancing, The.   NOBE
   "Sole heir of virtue, and of beauty both."   NAEL-5v1
   Speach of Love persuading men to learn Dancing, The.   NPeEn
   "What eye doth see the heaven but doth admire."   PeECV
   "Where lives the man that never yet did heare."   OxBEV

Orchestration.   Jane Mayes.   PasH

Orchestrion.   Edward Kleinschmidt.   MiVo

Orchid Door, The.   Unknown.   WoPoe, tr. by Jean S. Grigsby

Orchid House, The.   Medbh McGuckian.   CABP

Orchid-lipped, loose-jointed, purplish, indolent flowers.   Himalayan Balsam.   Anne Stevenson.   FaBoWP; OxAEP-2

Orchid Pavilion.   Sun Ch'o.   ChinPo, tr. by Yip Wai-lim

Orchid Pavilion.   Wang Hsi-chih.   ChinPo, tr. by Yip Wai-lim

Orchids.   Theodore Roethke.   ColAP; HarvBoo; TRP

Orchids grow through spring and summer.   Ch'en Tzu-ang.   SuSp   Fr. Impressions of Things Encountered.

Ordained I was a beggar.   File-Hewer's Lamentation, The.   Joseph Mather.   NOEC

Ordeal, The.   Olga Fiodorovna Berggolts [or Bergholts].   TCRP, tr. by Daniel Weissbort

Order and the Days, The.   Alicia Galaz Vivar.   TANSG, tr. by Oliver Welden

Order is a lovely thing. Monk in the Kitchen, The. Anna Hempstead Branch. APT-1; MoAmPo

Order of the Dead, The. John Pepper Clark Bekedermo. HBAPE

Ordered verbal syntactic space, An. Syntactic and Verbal. Giulia Niccolai. CItWP, *tr.* by Cinzia Sartini Blum and Lara Trubowitz

Ordering my tombstone. Raymond Roseliep. HA

Orderly traffic, a normal day. From Los Angeles Looking South. Eloise Klein Healy. WiU

Ordinance, The. Luis Cabalquinto. ReBoTo

Ordinance on Arrival. Naomi Lazard. BLT

Ordinarily / when the Messenger, otherwise known. Vocational Guidance, with Special Reference to the Annunciation of Simone Martini. Richard Howard. BodElec

Ordinary, as Love. Susan Griffin. GifTon

Ordinary God. Donald Davie. InvLi

Ordinary People in the Last Days. Jay Macpherson. PAI

Ordinary Song, An. Chairil Anwar. PoetW, *tr.* by Burton Raffel

Ordinary Women, The. Wallace Stevens. OxBA

Ordnance Survey in the Northern Counties. Mick North. NLP

Ordonnance. Thomas McGrath. GifTon

Ordovician Fossil Algae. Lindley Williams Hubbell. APT-2

Oread. "H. D." APT-1; AWP; ColAP; HeIP-4; MoAmPo; NAAL-2v2; NAAL-5; NALW; NOBA; NPeEn; NoAM; OxBA; PoPoPo; TAP; TCAPo

Oregon. Bob Kaufman. GT

Oregon Landscape with Lost Lover. Olga Broumas. GifTon

Oregon Message, An. William Stafford. CoAP

Orf. Ted Hughes. NoAM

Orfeo. Jack Spicer. APSN

Organist's Black Carnation, The. Laurence Lieberman. BodElec

Orgasm completely, The. Sonnet. Tom Clark. CoAP

Orgie. Madison Cawein. APN-2

Orgy. Norman MacCaig. OxBC

Orgy (That Is, Vegetable Market, at Sarno). Gina Labriola. WPOW, *tr.* by Edgar Pauk

Orgy was held on the lawn, The. Limerick. *Unknown.* PeLi

Orient Express, The. Randall Jarrell. CoAP; NOBA; PoE

Oriental Ballerina, The. Rita Dove. NAAL

Oriental histories relate, The. John 1:14 (1964). Jorge Luis Borges. GI

Oriental ink drawing, An. Counting. Judith Ortiz Cofer. PueRic

Oriental, you give and give. No Christian ever gave like you. Karl Shapiro. BodElec *Fr.* Bourgeois Poet, The.

Orientation from Afar. Silvana Colonna. ItPo, *tr.* by Gayle Ridinger

Oriflamme. Jessie Redmond Fauset. BlSi

Origami. Greg Williamson. NAPBL

Origin. "Eduard Georgievich Bagritzky" [*or* "Bagritsky"]. TCRP, *tr.* by Vera Dunham

Origin. Rosario Castellanos. TANSG, *tr.* by Magda Bogin

Origin Charm against Uncertain Injuries. Talvikki Ansel. NeAmPo

Origin-Legend of the Chou Tribe. *Unknown.* ChiP, *tr.* by Arthur Waley

Origin of Baseball, The. Kenneth Patchen. APT-2; CLPP

Origin of Landscape or the End of Mercy, The. Odysseus Elytis. VCWP

Origin of Man, I, The. Jones Very. APN-1

Origin of Music, The. Dannie Abse. BloBone

Origin of the Skagit Indians, The. Lucy Williams. STP, *tr.* by Carl Cary

Origin of the Snake, The. *Unknown.* NOxBChV; OxIBACP

Original. Gwendolyn Brooks. *See* Original. / Ragged-round.

Original Epitaph on a Drunkard. Royall Tyler. OBAL

Original. / Ragged-round. Malcolm X. Gwendolyn Brooks. IllVoic; TTY

Original Sequence. Philip Booth. ChIV-1

Original Sin. Robinson Jeffers. MoAmPo

Original Sin. Robert Penn Warren. NOCV; TAP

Original Strawberry. Nancy Willard. LCAP-2

Original Summer Girl, The. Carolyn Wells. SWaP

Originally it does not need. Laughing Mountain. Muso Soseki. EaWin, *tr.* by W. S. Merwin

Origins. Vincent Buckley. BMAP

Origins. Forrest Hamer. GeoHom

Origins. Joan Larkin. WiU

Origins. Leonard Nolens. TuT, *tr.* by Michael O'Loughlin

Origins. Eric Ormsby. NoP-4

Origins. Carl Rakosi. FTOS

Origins and History of Consciousness. Adrienne Rich. NIP-4

Origins, Divergences. Cynthia Ozick. TaR

Origins of Naval Artillery. Thomas Dibdin. FaBoWar

Oriki Erinle. *Unknown.* PBA; TTY, *tr.* by Ulli Beier

Orinda and Rosania. (LL) To Mrs M. A. at Parting. Katherine Philips. NAEL-6v1; NAEL-7v1

Orinda, and the Fair Astrea gone. To the Author of Agnes de Castro. Delariviere Manley. EMWP

Orinda to Lucasia. Katherine Philips. BASC; NOSC

Orinda to Lucasia Parting, October, 1661, at London. Katherine Philips. BASC

Orinda upon little Hector Philips. Katherine Philips. *See* On the Death of My First and Dearest Child[e], Hector Philip[p]s

Oriole. Yuan Chen. CrYelRi, *tr.* by Sam Hamill

Oriole at Dawn, An. Li Meng-yang. CoBLCP, *tr.* by Jonathan Chaves

Oriole eats yellow berries, The. Husband and Wife. *Vietnamese Oral Tradition.* CaDao, *tr.* by John Balaban

Oriole sings in the greening grove, The. Summer in the South. Paul Laurence Dunbar. GT

Oriole Song. Hsueh Chao-yun. CrYelRi, *tr.* by Sam Hamill

Oriole songs hold me to look at the mountains even longer, The. Describing My Feelings While Living in Retirement by the Riverside: Seven Poems to the Tune "Ch'ing-p'ing-yüeh." Yang Chi. CoBLCP, *tr.* by Jonathan Chaves

Orioles and orioles. Love Song. Ch'iao Chi. CrYelRi, *tr.* by Sam Hamill

Orioles warble / And flowers dance. Tune: "Telling of Innermost Feelings." Wen T'ing-yün. SuSp, *tr.* by William R. Schultz

Orion. Adrienne Rich. NAAL-2v2; NIP-4; NoAM; NoP-4; WPE

Orion. Charles Tennyson Turner. GSo

Orisha. Jayne Cortez. BlSi

Orlando Commercial, The. George MacBeth [*or* Macbeth]. NOBL; PeLV

Orlando Furioso. Ludovico Ariosto.
  "Alcyna met them at the outer gate." OBVE
  Astolfo flies by Chariot to the Moon, where he collects Orlando's lost wits. NPeEn
  "Blessed angell not a word replies, The." OBVE
  "Go soule, go sweetest soule for ever blest." OBVE
  "I say although the fire were wondrous hot." NPeEn
  "Masters go abrod to vew the towne, The." OxBEV, *tr.* by John Harington
  Medoro's Inscription Book XXIII. NOBRP, *tr.* by William Parsons
  "Soon after, he a crystal stream espying." NoSic
  "Thus much he prayed, and thence away he went." NoSic

Orlando's Rhymes. William Shakespeare. CTC *Fr.* As You Like It.

Ormerod was deeply troubled. Distractions and the Human Crowd. Stevie Smith. OxBC

Ormsby Slatter. Mr. Slatter. N. M. Bodecker. TLR

Ornamental bung, An. Gargoyle. Robert B. Shaw. CRP

Ornaments. Frank Ormsby. CIP-2

Ornithology. Lynda Hull. SeSe

Ornithology. Laini Mataka. ISC

Ornithomorphous monsters. Usurers, The. Nicolás Guillén. PFTM-1

Orotava Road, The. Basil Bunting. NoAM

Orphan, An. Thurayya Malhas. PoArWo, *tr.* by Nasser Farghaly

Orphan, The. Muhammad Al-Maghut. MAP

Orphan, The. Glover Davis. GeoHom

Orphan, The. *Unknown.* ChiP, *tr.* by Arthur Waley

Orphan beat of my heart, The. "Ping Hsin." BoWoP

Orphan Born. Robert Jones Burdette. OBAL

Orphan Child, The. Charlotte Brontë. VWP

Orphan Girl, An. Mrs. Henry Linden. CBWP-4

Orphan Miranda walks over my writing book. Tiger Lady. Miguel Algarin. PueRic

Orphanage in the rain. Promises of Leniency and Forgiveness. Charles Simic. LCAP-2

Orphanhood. Hayyim Nahman [*or* Khayim Nakhman *or* Chaim Nachman] Bialik. FIT, *tr.* by Robert Friend

Orpheus. John Fletcher. *See* King Henry VIII

Orpheus. Robert Herrick. CaPo

Orpheus. John Kinsella. BMAP

Orpheus. Linda Pastan. MiVo

Orpheus. Stephen Perry. MiVo

Orpheus. Elizabeth Madox Roberts. MoAmPo

Orpheus. Yvor Winters. NOBA; VGW

Orpheus and Eurydice. Robert Browning. CTC

Orpheus and Eurydice. Jorie Graham. VCAP

Orpheus and Eurydice. Robert Henryson.
  "Syne nethir-mare he went quhare Pluto was." NePenScot

Orpheus and Eurydice. Geoffrey Hill. TRP

Orpheus and Eurydice. Jean Valentine. FaBoWP; LCAP-2

Orpheus, dying, not all Music died. Leontius Scholasticus [*or* Leontius Referendarius]. GrAn

Orpheus, Eurydice, Hermes. Rainer Maria Rilke. WoPoe, *tr.* by Franz Wright

Orpheus he went (as poets tell). Orpheus. Robert Herrick. CaPo

Orpheus in the Underworld. David Gascoyne. FaBoTw
Orpheus liked the glad personal quality. Syringa. John Ashbery. APSN; HCAP; NoAM; VCAP
Orpheus to Beasts. Richard Lovelace. CaPo
Orpheus to Woods. Richard Lovelace. CaPo
Orpheus with his lute made trees. John Fletcher. FaBoCh; NOSC *Fr.* King Henry VIII.
Orpingalik's My Breath: Eskimo Song. Stephen Berg. GifTon
Ortho's Epitaph. Theocritus. FaBoEE, *tr. by* Charles Stuart Calverley
Orthodox, Orthodox, wha [*or* who] believe in John Knox. Kirk's Alarm, The. Robert Burns. OxBoLi
Orthography. Ambrose Bierce. APN-2; OBAL; PeLi *Fr.* Devil's Dictionary, The.
Orthone. Philip Pendleton Cooke. APN-1
Orts. Ted Hughes.
  Buzz in the Window. NoAM
Osawatomie. Carl Sandburg. OxBA
Oscar Hummel. Edgar Lee Masters. APT-1 *Fr.* Spoon River Anthology.
Oscar Wilde. Dorothy Parker. APT-1; NALW *Fr.* Pig's-Eye View of Literature, A.
Oscar Wilde. Algernon Charles Swinburne. PeVV
Osceola. Walt Whitman. NAAL-2v1; NAAL-3
Oshi. James L. White. ReTh
Oshi has a very large Buddha in him, one that can change. Oshi. James L. White. ReTh
Oshun, the River Goddess. *Unknown.* WoPoe, *tr. by* Ulli Beier
Osip Mandelstam. Seamus Deane. BiHa; PBCIP
Osiris. Jane Hirshfield. BodElec
Ostella forth of Town: To My Heart. John Tatham. NOSC
Ostia Will Receive You. Friederike Mayröcker. PFTM-2, *tr. by* Beth Bjorklund
Ostracized as we are with God. Apology of Genius. Mina Loy. APT-1
Ostrich fern on shore. Robert Spiess. HA
Ostrich Is a Silly Bird, The. Mary Eleanor Wilkins Freeman. KaS; OBCA; OxIBACP
Ostriches and Grandmothers! Imamu Amiri Baraka. NeAP
Oswald Dead. Ferreira Gullar. TCLAP, *tr. by* Renato Rezende
Otagamiad. Jane Johnston Schoolcraft. SWaP
Oteli Asia Palas, Inc. Denis Devlin. ModIr; NOIV *Fr.* Memoirs of a Turcoman Diplomat.
Othello. William Shakespeare.
  Death of Othello. OxAEP-1
  "Her father lov'd me; oft invited me." EBEV; FaBoWar; OxAEP-1; SCV
  "I will in Cassio's lodging lose this napkin." OxAEP-1
  "It is the cause, it is the cause, my soul [*or* (my soule)]." EBEV; OxBEV
  "O my fair warrior!" OxAEP-1
Othello loved Desdemona. Limerick. A. Cinna. PeLi
Other. Lance Henson. VoR
Other. Dorothy Livesay. NIL-7
Other. Ronald Stuart Thomas. AngWePo
Other, The. Rosario Castellanos. TCLAP, *tr. by* Maureen Ahern
Other, The. Ruth Fainlight. BrRo
Other, The. Ted Hughes. EmeKit
Other, The. Constance Fenimore Woolson. SWaP *Fr.* Two Women.
Other bright days of action have seemed great. John Masefield. OxBTC *Fr.* Biography.
Other country, is it anticipated or half-remembered? The. In Your Mind. Carol Ann Duffy. EmeKit
Other day, The. Old Country, The. Carl Rakosi. BodElec
Other day I chanced to meet a soldier friend of mine, The. Oh! How I Hate to Get Up in the Morning. Irving Berlin. ReLy; TCAPo
Other day i looked out of the window and saw a, The. Endangered Nouns. David Antin. PFTM-2
Other day I was loving a sweet little fruitpie-and-cream, The. Lines. Gavin Ewart. SPE
Other day, when I looked at a tree, The. Roots. Louis Ginsberg. TrJP
Other Forms of Slaughter. Catherine Obianuju Acholonu. HAWP; HBAPE
Other Half of Me, The. Stan Freeman. ReLy
Other Heritage, The. Aurora Levins Morales. PueRic
Other Life, The. Nina Cassian. PoSu, *tr. by* Cristian Andrei and Daniel Weissbort
Other Little Tune, T' Mother Goose. OxNR; ReMoGo
Other Lives of the Romantics. Jane Flanders. PBCAP
Other loves I have known. Proof. Bessie Calhoun Bird. BlSi
Other Marías. Diana García. TouFir
Other men are thorn. Mahadevi. BoWoP

Other mind, and stood still. (LL) Black Silk. Tess Gallagher. EmeKit; FaBoWP
Other new dresses, of bloodred velvet. (LL) Sunday Afternoon. Denise Levertov. CoAmPo; PAI
Other night from Court returning late, The. Upon Mr Thomas Murrays Fall. Sir Robert Aytoun [*or* Ayton]. NePenScot
Other night I had a dreadful cough, The. Forese Donati. EaItPo, *tr. by* Dante Gabriel Rossetti
Other oxen have long curly horns. Old Cowboy, The. Kao Ch'i. OHMPC, *tr. by* Kenneth Rexroth
Other patients are ill otherwise, and do. Robert Pinsky. NoAM *Fr.* Essay on Psychiatrists.
Other People's Glasshouses. Ruth Pitter. OBGa
Other Places, The. Charles E. Butler. YaYoPo
Other props are gone, The. Je T'Adore. Thomas Kinsella. NoAM
Other remains, The / passive today. (LL) Classic Scene. William Carlos Williams. NAAL-2v2; OxBA
Other Side, The. Roy Fuller. OxBC
Other Side, The. Seamus Heaney. CIP-2; PNI
Other Side, The. Minnie Bruce Pratt. WiU
Other Side of a Mirror, The. Mary Elizabeth Coleridge. BoWoP; NALW; VWP; ViWPN
Other Side of the River, The. Charles Wright. VCAP
Other Side of the Valley, The. *Unknown.* CoBCP, *tr. by* Burton Watson
Other Side of the Valley, The. *Unknown.* ChiP, *tr. by* Arthur Waley
Other Simulation, The. Patrizia Valduga. CItWP, *tr. by* Cinzia Sartini Blum and Lara Trubowitz
Other Song of the Faithful, for the Mercies of God, An. Michael Drayton. ChIV-1
Other Syllabus, The. Chenjerai Hove. HBAPE
Other than Your two red feet, Syama. Kamalākānta Bhattācārya. SinGod, *tr. by* Rachel Fell McDermott
Other Tiger, The. Jorge Luis Borges. PoetW, *tr. by* Alastair Reid
Other Tiger, The. Jorge Luis Borges. TCLAP, *tr. by* Norman Thomas Di Giovanni
Other to the Altars God, The. (LL) Two Went Up into the Temple to Pray. Richard Crashaw. ChIV-2; HAP
Other Tradition, The. John Ashbery. FTOS; PmAP
Other Voice, The. Tom Paulin. PNI
Other way Satan went down, Th' John Milton. NAEL-5v1; NAEL-6v1 *Fr.* Paradise Lost.
Other wings flew into the stone. (LL) Red Lilies. Barbara Guest. FTOS; PmAP; PoM
Other Woman, The. Marion Lomax. LW
Other World, The. Dmitry [*or* Dmitrii] Vasil'evich Bobyshev. ItGoST, *tr. by* Michael van Walleghen
Other World, The. *Unknown.* AWP, *tr. by* Robert Silliman Hillyer *Fr.* Book of the Dead.
Others. James Reeves. Spl
Others abide our question. Thou art free. Shakespeare. Matthew Arnold. FHYEP; HeIP-4; OBEV; OxAEP-2; OxBSo; SCGP; Son
Others are all from here, The. Address. Leonard Nolens. TuT, *tr. by* Michael O'Loughlin
Others argue, and not a few. Michael Wigglesworth. NAAL-3 *Fr.* Day of Doom, The.
Others because you did not keep. Deep-sworn Vow, A. W. B. Yeats. PoE; UnPo
Others have pleasantness and praise. Love's Votary. George Augustus Simcox. NOBVV
Others Hunters in the North the Cree, The. Jerome Rothenberg. PoM
Others, I am not the first. A. E. Housman. MoBrPo; NOBVV; OxBTC; PoE
Others made the decisions, others spoke on their behalf. They. Missing, The. Yannis Ritsos. AF, *tr. by* Edmund Keeley
Others may forget you, but not I. Empress Yamato-himé. OHPJ
Others may never feel tyrannic sway? (LL) Phillis Wheatley. BPo; TTY *Fr.* To the Right Honourable William, Earl of Dartmouth.
Others may pity me but you shall not be ashamed. To My Children. Karen Gershon. ItWoWo
Others plant for profit, The. Clear Skies, Still Sea. *Vietnamese Oral Tradition.* CaDao, *tr. by* John Balaban
Others see a rush, a carnival, a million. Some People. A. K. Ramanujan. VCWP
Others taunt me with having knelt at well-curbs. For Once, Then, Something. Robert Frost. APT-1; NOBA; NoAM
Others will gain what I lose. Memory's Usefulness. Maria Luisa Spaziani. CItWP, *tr. by* Cinzia Sartini Blum and Lara Trubowitz
Otherwise. Jane Kenyon. AmFaPo; LoL
Otherwise kill me. (LL) Prayer before Birth. Louis MacNeice. FaBoVe; GTBS-P; HarvBoo; PNI; TwCP

Otranto. Barbara Guest. FTOS

Ottava Rima would, I know, be proper. W. H. Auden. NOBL *Fr.* Letter to Lord Byron.

Ottave. Osip Emilevich Mandelstam [*or* Mandelshtam].
"Both Schubert on the waters and Mozart in the din of birds." TCRP
"Tell me, draftsman of the desert." TCRP

Otter, An. Ted Hughes. NoAM

Otter, The. Seamus Heaney. NoAM; PNI

Otto. Theodore Roethke. HarvBoo

Où sont les neiges des neiges? Ted Berrigan. BodElec

Ought to be told to come and take him in. (LL) Runaway, The. Robert Frost. AWP; FaBoCh; MoAmPo; SAmP; TwCP; VGW

Our age bereft of nobility. Poem for Painters, A. John Wieners. BB; NeAP; PoM

Our arms have grown. At the Black Edge. Ger Killeen. AmPoNex

Our Ashes. Horst Bienek. AF

Our Asian war is over; others have begun. In Celebration of Spring. John Balaban. CDa

Our Assholes Are Different. Arthur Rimbaud. CAGL, *tr. by* Paul Schmidt

Our assholes are different from theirs. I used to watch. Our Assholes Are Different. Arthur Rimbaud. CAGL, *tr. by* Paul Schmidt

Our author by experience finds it true. Dryden. OxBoLi *Fr.* Aureng-Zebe.

Our Backs Are to the Cypress. Leah Goldberg. BoWoP, *tr. by* Ramah Commanday

Our beauty is to us that which to men. Sir Richard Fanshawe. OBVE *Fr.* Il Pastor Fido.

Our best singers. Blues (in Two Parts), The. Val Ferdinand. NBV

Our Birth-Cord. Kofi Anyidoho. NAfrP

Our birth is but a sleep and a forgetting. William Wordsworth. ITBLP *Fr.* Ode: Intimations of Immortality [from Recollections of Early Childhood].

Our blue boat drifts. Birdwatching at Fan Lake. Anita Endrezze. HATNAP

Our boat going upstream barely moves by the inch. Sailing Through the Gorges. Yang Wan-li. WoPoe, *tr. by* Kuangchi C. Chang

Our boat touches the bank. Thomas A. Clark. Oth *Fr.* Sixteen Sonnets.

Our Bodies. Denise Levertov. ErotSp

Our Bog Is Dood. Stevie Smith. NAEL-5v2; NAEL-6v2; NBLV; NIL-7; PoE; WeW-3

Our Bondage It Shall End. Peter Cartwright. AH

Our brains ache, in the merciless iced east winds that knive us. Exposure. Wilfred Owen. FaBoMo; NoAM; OBWP; PeFWW; PoWW; RB; TCAWP

Our brigade's / On the Diyovka-Sukhachovka. Judge Gorba. "Mikhail Semionovich Golodny" [*or* "Golodnyi"]. TCRP, *tr. by* Simon Franklin

Our brown canal was endless to my thought. "George Eliot." NOBVV *Fr.* Brother and Sister.

Our bugles sang truce, for the night-cloud had lowered [*or* lower'd]. Soldier's Dream, The. Thomas Campbell. GTBS-P; OxAEP-2

Our Burden Bearer. Phillips Brooks. SacPr

Our candles, lit, re-lit, have gone down now. Twelfth Night. Peter Scupham. OBCP

Our canoe idles in the idling current. Floating. Kenneth Rexroth. BodElec

Our Canterburye's great Cathedrall Bell. Upon Arch-bishop Laud, Prisoner in the Tower. 1641. *Unknown.* PBRV

Our cars were always used and named after singers. Lips. Lance Larsen. AmPoNex

Our caves do not go Boom! and make one nervy. Sterkfontein. Ruth Miller. PeSAV

Our children have eaten supper. Brian Coffey. CIP-2 *Fr.* Missouri Sequence.

Our Christian savages expect. He Shook off the Beast. Charles Wesley. ChIV-2

Our Christmas Tree. Wendell Berry. ChrPo

Our Christmas tree is. Our Christmas Tree. Wendell Berry. ChrPo

Our city declines, the world is still bleak. Beginnings. Peter Sirr. PBCIP

Our Club Work. Mrs. Henry Linden. CBWP-4

Our couch shall be roses all spangled with dew. Sensible Girl's Reply to Moore's, A. Walter Savage Landor. FaBoEE

Our country, in fenced areas, in cool shady streets. (LL) One Thing That Can Save America, The. John Ashbery. AiP; FaBoA; NOBA; NoAM; PmAP

Our Country of Origin. Rafael Campo. WiU *Fr.* Song for My Lover.

Our cup of joy was overfilled. Dialogue, A. Lizelia Augusta Jenkins Moorer. CBWP-3

Our Daily Bread. César Vallejo. TCLAP, *tr. by* James Wright
(Breakfast is drunk down. . . Damp earth.) GI, *tr. by* James Wright

Our dancing and mortal wine. (LL) Horses in Flowers. Sappho. OBVE; WoPoe, *tr. by* Guy Davenport

Our darling's now completely frappé! (LL) L'Enfant Glacé. Harry Graham. NBLV; OBCoV; PeLV

Our day was composed of resemblances, take. Sail Away. Robert Adamson. CBAP

Our days, alas! our mortal days. Shortness and Misery of Life, The. Isaac Watts. NOCV

Our days were a joy, and our paths through flowers. (LL) After a Journey. Thomas Hardy. EBEV; EnLoPo; GTBS-P; HarvBoo; NPeEn; OxAEP-2; OxBEV; OxBTC; PoE

Our Dean of Something thought it would be good. Classroom at the Mall, The. R. S. Gwynn. RA

Our Dear Friend Charles. Collaboration: Letter to Charlie Chaplin. Peter Orlovsky. CLPP

Our Dog Chasing Swifts. U. A. Fanthorpe. Spl

Our dog Fred. Diners in the Kitchen, The. James Whitcomb Riley. OBAL

Our drift-wood fire burns drowsily. Florida Beach, The. Constance Fenimore Woolson. APN-2

Our dropping Autumn morning clears apace. Robert Browning. OBGa *Fr.* Sordello.

Our ears were stunned with noisy drum. To Laura, on the French Fleet Parading before Plymouth. Ann Thomas. ECWP

Our earth in 1969. Doggerel by a Senior Citizen. W. H. Auden. NBLV; NOBL

Our Earth Will Not Die. Niyi Osundare. HBAPE

Our eldest son is like Ishmael, Jacob is like you. Isreal I. Charles Reznikoff. ChIV-1

Our end is Life. Put out to sea. (LL) Thalassa. Louis MacNeice. BIrV; FaBoMo; NOBE; WoPoe

Our England is a garden that is full of stately views. Rudyard Kipling. OBGa

Our England's victor dead: who can express. Acrostick Eligie on the Death of the No less Prudent than Victorious Prince Oliver Lord Protector, An. Elianour Havey. EMWP

Our English gamesters scorne to stake. Roger Williams. SCAP

Our Ernest. "Elmo." PWR

Our existence would be that much grimmer ex-. Limerick. Robert Conquest. PeLi

Our eyes have viewed the burnished vineyards where. Letter to a Friend. Robert Penn Warren. MoAmPo

Our faces are the. Poem No. 1. Carolyn M. Rodgers. ISC

Our Fadder, Which are in Heaben! He Paid Me Seven. *Unknown.* BPo

Our famous Harvey hath made good. Circulation, The. Thomas Washbourne. NOCV

Our fancies are but joys all unexprest. Fragment, A. Henrietta Cordelia Ray. CBWP-3

Our Father. Eliza Cook. VWP

Our Father. Barbara Goldberg. GotH

Our Father. James Schuyler. ChIV-2

Our Father, by Whose Name. F. Bland Tucker. AH

Our Father, God. Adoniram Judson. AH

Our Father, grant us to lie down in peace. Evening Prayer. *Unknown.* TrJP, *tr. by* Solomon Solis-Cohen

Our Father in Heaven. Sarah Josepha Buell Hale. AH

Our Father, Our King. *Unknown.* TrJP

Our Father which art in heaven. Lord's Prayer. Nicanor Parra. GI, *tr. by* Miller Williams

Our Father! While Our Hearts Unlearn. Oliver Wendell Holmes. AH

Our Father who art in heaven, I am drunk. Praying Drunk. Andrew Hudgins. RA

Our Father, who art speechless. N. N. Tries to Remember the Words of a Prayer. Stanislaw Baranczak. GI, *tr. by* Kevin Windle

Our father works in us. Father of Women, A [Ad Sororem E. B.]. Alice Thompson Meynell. BrRo; NALW; WPE

Our Fathers. Bible, Apocrypha. OBVE; TrJP *Fr.* Ecclesiasticus.

Our fathers all were poor. Fathers, The. Edwin Muir. OxBS

Our Fathers' God. Benjamin Copeland. AH

Our fathers took oaths as of old they took wives. Oaths. Thomas [*or* "Tom"] Brown. FaBoEE; OBCoV

Our fathers were saved from the deaths. Babylon: 539 B.C.E. Charles Reznikoff. ChIV-1

Our fathers wrung their bread from stocks and stones. Children of Light. Robert Lowell. NAAL-2v2; OxBA

Our Fear. Zbigniew Herbert. VCWP

Our feet meet the earth in this place. Marble Floor. Karol Wojtyla. CRP

Our first ancestor (Abram) alone received his religion from Heaven. Therefore We Preserve Life. Shen Ch'üan. TrJP, *tr. by* William C. White

Our Flag. *Unknown.* CA

Our fleet divides, and straight the Dutch appear. Dryden. BASC; FaBoWar *Fr.* Annus Mirabilis.

Our flesh that was a battle-ground. Litany of the Dark People, The. Countee Cullen. ChIV-2

Our fontanelle, the trout's dimpled feet. (LL) Flower Master, The. Medbh McGuckian. ModIr; PNI

Our foot's in the door. (LL)   Mushrooms.   Sylvia Plath.   FaBoWP; RB; WPOW

Our footprints. (LL)   Day We Die, The.   *Southern Bushmen Oral Tradition.*   BLT; WoPoe, *tr. by* Arthur Markowitz

Our friend there—he's a little queer.   Herman Melville.   APN-2   *Fr.* Clarel: A Poem and Pilgrimage in the Holy Land.

Our friends go with us as we go.   Non Dolet.   Oliver St. John Gogarty.   OBMV

Our friendship, Robert, firm through twenty years.   Letter to Robert Frost, A.   Robert Silliman Hillyer.   MoAmPo

Our future plunges with the whale.   Whales.   Morton Marcus.   GeoHom

Our future will be marvelously exciting.   Make a Miracle.   Frank Loesser.   ReLy

Our gang dug down two feet. With two feet left.   Signalmen, The.   Philip Stephens.   AmPoNex

Our Gardener here, James Phillips see.   Philip Yorke.   OBGa

Our geodesic dome-shaped lodge.   Personification of a Name, The.   Ray A. Young Bear.   HATNAP

Our God and God of our fathers.   Prayer for Dew.   Eleazar ben Kalir.   TrJP, *tr. by* Israel Zangwill

Our God and soldiers we alike adore.   Of Common Devotion.   Francis Quarles.   FaBoEE; OxBSP

Our God, Our Help.   Isaac Watts.   *See* Man Frail, and God Eternal

Our God's forgotten, and our soldiers slighted. (LL)   Of Common Devotion.   Francis Quarles.   FaBoEE; OxBSP

Our golden age was then, when lamp and rug.   Family Prime.   Mark Van Doren.   VGW

Our Goodman.   *Unknown.*   ESPB

Our Grandsons Will Be Astonished.   Ilya Grigoryevich Ehrenburg [*or* Erenburg]   TCRusP, *tr. by* Denis Johnson

Our guest's wound went unnoticed.   Callimachus.   GrAn

Our guttural muse.   Traditions.   Seamus Heaney.   FaBoMo

Our Hamster's Life.   Kit Wright.   OTCP

Our hands crushed.   Elaine Randell.   Oth   *Fr.* Snoad Hill Poems, The.

Our hands grope in vain.   Going Home.   Catherine Obianuju Acholonu.   HAWP

Our Hands in the Garden.   Anne Hébert.   BoWoP, *tr. by* A. Poulin, Jr.

Our heads on fire. (LL)   Paper Matches.   Paulette Jiles.   NIL-7; NIP-4; NOBC

Our headteacher has a golden.   Goldfish.   Barrie Wade.   OTCP

Our hearths are gone out, and our fires are broken.   Raven Days, The.   Sidney Lanier.   APN-2; OxBA; TCAPo

Our hearts are filled with pride to-day.   Welcome to Hon. Frederick Douglass.   Josephine D. Henderson Heard.   CBWP-4

Our héarts' charity's héarth's fíre, our thóughts' chivalry's thróng's Lórd. (LL)   Gerard Manley Hopkins.   FaBoMo; NOBE; NoAM; OxAEP-2; OxBEV; PeECV

Our hearts still listen for the landward bells. (LL)   Irishman in Coventry, An.   John Hewitt.   BIrV; CIP-2; ModIr; PNI

Our heritage the sea. (LL)   Sea-Song, A.   Allan Cunningham.   GTBS-P; OxAEP-2

Our Hindi.   Raghuvir Sahay.   OMIP, *tr. by* Vinay Dharwadker

Our Hindi is a widower's new wife.   Our Hindi.   Raghuvir Sahay.   OMIP, *tr. by* Vinay Dharwadker

Our hips.   About our hips.   Harriet Jacobs.   SpirFl

Our hired man is the kindest man.   Hired Man's Way, The.   John Kendrick Bangs.   OBCA

Our home is all too fragile, rather like.   Creative Poverty.   László Szabédi.   IQMS, *tr. by* John Gordon Nichols

"Our hope is for knowledge," said Reb Mendel. But not all his disciples were of this opinion.   Edmond Jabès.   PFTM-2, *tr. by* Rosmarie Waldrop   *Fr.* Book of Questions, The.

Our house had filled with moths.   Moths, The.   Michael Jackson.   PeNZ

Our Hunting Fathers.   W. H. Auden.   FaBoMo; HarvBoo; NoAM

Our hut puffs streaks of hope.   Country Life.   Chenjerai Hove.   HBAPE

Our Island Home.   Charles Timothy Brooks.   APN-1

Our Jatti, palace wrestler of Mysore.   At Forty.   A. K. Ramanujan.   VCWP

Our jeep crawls to your village.   Election, The.   Sitakant Mahapatra.   OMIP, *tr. by* Sitakant Mahapatra

Our journey had advanced.   Emily Dickinson.   APN-2; NOCV; SoSe-8

Our joy, a rampart to the mind. (LL)   Passing Strange, The.   John Masefield.   MoBrPo; OBEV

Our karma led.   Reply to a Friend's Poem.   Muso Soseki.   EaWin, *tr. by* W. S. Merwin

Our Kind Creator.   Solomon Howe.   AH

Our king has wrote a lang letter.   Lord Derwentwater.   *Unknown.*   ESPB

Our king he has a secret to tell.   Bonny Lass of Anglesey, The.   *Unknown.*   ESPB

Our king he kept a false steward.   Sir Aldingar.   *Unknown.*   ESPB; OxBB

Our king lay at Westminster.   Hugh Spencer's Feats in France.   *Unknown.*   ESPB

Our kisses are mountain mallow.   Khobayza.   Zulaykha Abu-Risha.   PoArWo, *tr. by* Clarissa C. Burt and Nathalie Handal

Our kisses / Rhodope / let us steal.   Paulus [*or* Paulos] Silentiarius.   GrAn

Our Kitty.   Carol Muske.   BAP-01

Our knowledge is historical, flowing, and flown. (LL)   At the Fishhouses.   Elizabeth Bishop.   APT-2; AmFaPo; CoAP; FaBoWP; HAP; HCAP; LCAP-2; NAAL-2v2; NAAL-5; NALW; PoPoPo; PoRA; PoetW; VCAP

Our Lady.   Mary Elizabeth Coleridge.   OBEV; OBMV; ViWPN; WPE

Our Lady.   John Godfrey.   PmAP

Our Lady Moon still hidden.   Memory.   Federico García Lorca.   PFTM-1

Our Lady of Ardboe.   Paul Muldoon.   BiHa; PBCIP

Our Lady of the Caves.   Our Lady of the Three-Pronged Devil.   Clayton Eshleman.   PFTM-2

Our Lady of the Laundromat.   Belle Waring.   PBCAP

Our Lady of the Three-Pronged Devil.   Clayton Eshleman.   PFTM-2

Our Lady's Lullaby.   Richard Verstegan [*or* Verstegen].   *See* Lullaby: "Upon my lap my sovereign sits."

Our Lady's Song.   *Unknown.*   OBEV

Our Land.   Yannis Ritsos.   AmFaPo, *tr. by* Edmund Keeley

Our last free summer we mooned about at odd hours.   Chrysalides.   Thomas Kinsella.   BIrV; ModIr

Our last resort. Lovers wading back to shore.   Wellfleet.   Timothy Liu.   AmPoNex

Our Life.   Mbella Sonne Dipoko.   PBMAP

Our Life in California.   Gary Young.   GeoHom

Our life in the world is only a great dream.   Awakening from Drunkenness on a Spring Day.   Li Po.   TAL

Our Life in This World.   Sami Mansei.   WoPoe, *tr. by* Steven D. Carter

Our life is changed; their coming our beginning. (LL)   Horses, The.   Edwin Muir.   CABP; EmeKit; HAP; HeIP-4; MoBrPo; NOBE; NPeEn; NePenScot; NoAM; OxBTC; PoE; RB; TRP; WeW-3

Our life is like a forest, where the sun.   Charles Sangster.   NOBC   *Fr.* Sonnets Written in the Orillia Woods.

Our life's the model of a winter's day.   Francis Quarles.   PeECV   *Fr.* Divine Fancies.

Our life-sick hearts and turn them into dust. (LL)   Last Word, A.   Ernest Christopher Dowson.   GSo; MoBrPo

Our life—impossible to ignore. (LL)   Indian Singing in 20th Century America.   Gail Tremblay.   HATNAP; LTA; ReEnLa

Our Limitations.   Oliver Wendell Holmes.   NCAP

Our little Death from which we daily.   Sleep Is a Deep and Many Voiced Flood.   Robert Duncan.   CLPP

Our Little Ghost.   Louisa May Alcott.   OBCA

Our Little Sister Is Worried.   *Unknown.*   OHMPC; WoPoe, *tr. by* Kenneth Rexroth

Our little tantrum, flushed and misery-hollow.   Rebeca in a Mirror.   Judith Rodriguez.   CBAP

Our lives are Swiss.   Emily Dickinson.   APN-2; NOBA; TAP

Our lives avoided tragedy.   Pantoum of the Great Depression.   Donald Justice.   MakPoe

Our lives no longer feel ground under them.   Stalin Epigram, The.   Osip Emilevich Mandelstam [*or* Mandelshtam].   AF; WoPoe, *tr. by* Clarence Brown and W. S. Merwin

Our Lord.   Nezahualcoyotl.   WoPoe, *tr. by* Thelma D. Sullivan

Our Lord, Immanuel [*or* Our Lord Emmanuel!]. (LL)   O Little Town of Bethlehem.   Phillips Brooks.   AH; APN-2; ChrPo; SacPr; TCAPo

Our lords are to the mountains gane.   Hughie Graham.   Robert Burns.   OxBB

Our lost virginities will never be regained.   Labane.   Annette M'Baye d'Erneville.   HAWP, *tr. by* Brian Baer

Our Love.   Jo Nelson.   PasH

Our Love.   Xavier Villaurrutia.   TCLAP, *tr. by* Michael Surman

Our love is infinite.   *Unknown.*   OHMPJ

Our Love Is like Byzantium.   Henrik Nordbrandt.   VCWP, *tr. by* Henrik Norbrandt and Alexander Taylor

Our love is not found in our respective.   Poem.   Carlos German Belli.   BLPSL, *tr. by* Rene de Costa, Rigas Kappatos and Eleni Paidoussi

Our love is the autumn languish.   Our Love.   Jo Nelson.   PasH

Our love shall live, and later life renew. (LL)   Edmund Spenser.   AWP; BoLoP; EBEV; HAP; HeIP-4; NAEL-5v1; NAEL-6v1; NAEL-7v1; NoP-4; NoSic; OxBSo; PAI; PoE; PoPoPo; Son; TFi; WeW-3   *Fr.* Amoretti.

Our love was conceived in silence and must live silently.   At the Dark Hour.   Paul Dehn.   BoLoP

Our love was pure.   Song of Snow-white Heads.   Chuo Wen-chün.   BoWoP; ChiP, *tr. by* Arthur Waley

Our love which had a thousand leaves. (LL)   Winter.   Sheila Wingfield.   EnLoPo; LW

Our love will not come back on fortune's wheel.   Obit.   Robert Lowell.   HCAP; PoetW; VCAP

Our March.   Vladimir Vladimirovich Mayakovsky [or Maiakovskii].   AWP, tr. by Babette Deutsch and Avrahm Yarmolinsky

Our masks are gauze and screen our faces for those unlike us only.   Come Over and Help Us; a Rhapsody.   John Wheelwright.   APT-2

Our mind is full of sorrow, who will know of our grief? (LL)   Song of the Bowmen of Shu.   Ezra Pound.   FaBoWar; OBVE

Our morning hymn this is, and song at evening. (LL)   Sir Philip Sidney.   HAP; NAEL-5v1; NAEL-6v1; NOBE; NoSic   Fr. Arcadia.

Our mother.   Incidence.   Rae Armantrout.   FTOS

Our Mother.   Susan Griffin.   HW

Our Mother *Eve*, who tasted of the Tree.   Aemilia Bassano Lanyer.   PBRV   Fr. Salve Deus Rex Judaeorum.

Our mother is gone? (LL)   Harriet.   Audre Lorde.   BlSi; NAAL-5

Our mother was the pussy-cat, our father was the owl.   Children of the Owl and the Pussy-Cat, The.   Edward Lear.   OBCoV

Our mother who are of the universe.   Mother of the Universe.   Yoko Ono.   HW

Our Mother who art in Earth and Heaven.   New Our Father, The.   Priscilla Baird Hinckley.   HW

Our mothers wrung hell and hardtack from row.   American Sonnet (10).   Wanda Coleman.   NAAAL

Our moulting days are in the twilight stage.   Margaret Danner.   BPo   Fr. Far from Africa: Four Poems.

Our names do not appear. (LL)   Diving into the Wreck.   Adrienne Rich.   ColAP; EmeKit; HCAP; HarvBoo; HeIP-4; InPK-6; MakPoe; NAAL-2v2; NAAL-5; NALW; NIL-7; NIP-4; NOBA; NoAM; NoP-4; OxWW; PoPoPo

Our nation's future is coming into view.   Live at Club Mozambique.   Charles Simic.   BodElec

Our Natures Rise.   Kalamu ya Salaam.   SpirFl   Fr. New Orleans Haiku.

Our Naughty Time.   Friedrich von Logau.   GePo, tr. by George C. Schoolfield

Our Noble Booker T. Washington.   Mrs. Henry Linden.   CBWP-4

Our novels get longa and longa.   Limerick.   H. G. Wells.   PeLi

Our old cat has kittens three.   Choosing Their Names.   Thomas Hood.   NOxBChV

Our old neighbor.   Lost Wood, The.   Renée Weiss.   PoCoUp

Our oneness is the wrestlers', fierce and close.   Wrestling.   Louisa Sarah Bevington.   LW; PEW

Our orchestra / is the cat's nuts.   Shoot It Jimmy!   William Carlos Williams.   APT-1

Our Own.   Margaret Elizabeth Munson Sangster.   PoToHe

Our own calm journey on for human sake. (LL)   Nile, The.   Leigh Hunt.   CenSon; EBEV; GSo; NOBE

Our Own—Progression F.   James Russell Lowell.   "This hand-to-mouth, pert, rapid, nineteenth century."   TCAPo

Our Padre.   Sir John Betjeman.   PeLV

Our Paris part of Belfast has.   Intimate Letter 1973.   Padraic Fiacc.   PNI

Our park empty.   Three o'Clock Love Song.   Michael S. Harper.   GT

Our Parodies Are Ended.   Horace Twiss.   UV

Our parodies are ended. These our authors.   Our Parodies Are Ended.   Horace Twiss.   UV

Our party scattered at yellow dusk and I came home to bed.   After Getting Drunk, Becoming Sober in the Night.   Po Chü-i.   BLT; ChiP, tr. by Arthur Waley

Our passions are most like to floods and stream[e]s.   Sir Walter Ralegh to the Queen.   Sir Walter Ralegh.   NoSic

Our people spread the news each day.   Spartan Mother, The.   Benedek Virág.   IQMS, tr. by Joseph Leftwich

Our perverse old *pisatel'* Vladimir.   Something for My Russian Friends.   Edmund Wilson.   OBAL

Our Photograph[s].   Frederick Locker-Lampson.   NBLV; NOBL; PeLV

Our portion of fire.   Manichaeans, The.   Gary Snyder.   VGW

Our private green honey. (LL)   Gentle Communion.   Pat Mora.   NIL-7; NIP-4

Our prize fish is done!   Hedylos.   GrAn

Our provincial city's narrow streets send me a.   Lost behind the Back of God.   Gyula Juhász.   IQMS, tr. by Adam Makkai

Our quin's seek, an very seek.   Queen Eleanor's Confession.   Unknown.   ESPB

Our regimental stallion.   Stallion, The.   "Mikhail Semionovich Golodny" [or "Golodnyi"].   TCRP, tr. by Simon Franklin

Our revels now are ended. These our actors.   William Shakespeare.   RB; UV   Fr. Tempest, The.

Our Richard Allen in his early youth.   Rt. Rev. Richard Allen.   Josephine D. Henderson Heard.   CBWP-4

Our Rock with loving care.   Grace after Meals.   Unknown.   TrJP, tr. by Alice Lucas

Our romance won't end on a sorrowful note.   They Can't Take That Away from Me.   George Gershwin.   ReLy

Our roofs are adjacent.   Love Song.   Unknown.   BoWoP, tr. by Reza Baraheni and Zahra-Soltan Shokoohtaezeh

Our ruins run back to memory.   Cavafy in Redondo.   Mark Jarman.   GeoHom

Our sacred earth in our day is our curse. (LL)   Dead in Europe, The.   Robert Lowell.   OxBA; OxBC; WoPoe

Our sacred Muse, of Israel's Singer sings.   Michael Drayton.   ChIV-1   Fr. David and Goliath.

Our sad farewell at the red tower.   To the Tune: Beautiful Barbarian.   Wei Chuang.   CrYelRi, tr. by Sam Hamill

Our saints are poets, Milton and Blake.   Encounter.   Denis Devlin.   BIrV

Our sardine fishermen work at night in the dark of the moon; daylight or moonlight.   Purse-Seine, The.   Robinson Jeffers.   AmFaPo; HAP; NOBA; NoAM; OxBA; WeW-3

Our Savior Christ tracing the bordering hills,   Thomas Deloney.   ChIV-2   Fr. Destruction of Jerusalem, The.

Our Saviour's Passion.   Mary Sidney Herbert, Countess of Pembroke.   "He placed all rest, and had no resting place."   SacPr

Our Scholar travels yet the loved hill-side. (LL)   Matthew Arnold.   FHYEP; NAEL-5v2; NAEL-6v2; NOBE; OBEV

Our School Now Closes Out.   Edmund Dumas.   AH

Our senses, without reason, are naught worth.   Robert Hayman.   NOSC   Fr. Owen's Epigrams.

Our 17th Street Years.   Bruce Weigl.   BodElec

Our Sharpeville.   Ingrid De Kok.   HAWP

Our shells clacked on the plates.   Oysters.   Seamus Heaney.   UV

Our ship, the Sea Smithy, swerved out of the tradewinds.   On the Congo.   Harry Edmund Martinson.   RB, tr. by Robert Bly

Our single purpose was to walk through snow.   Polar Exploration.   Stephen Spender.   NoAM

Our sister dear, what joy for us!   Conversation between Me and the Women.   Anna Petrovna Bunina.   ARWW, tr. by Sibelan Forrester

Our Skin Is Paper.   Hilary Booth.   SurWo

Our skin loosely lies.   Long Division; a Tribal History.   Wendy Rose.   OPRER

Our skin, strenuously tutored to appreciate the vernacular.   Skin.   Marjorie Welish.   PmAP

Our skins ache of emergence / dark o' the moon. (LL)   Loba Addresses the Goddess, The / or The Poet as Priestess Addresses the Loba-Goddess.   Diane Di Prima.   HW; PmAP

Our Smoke Has Gone Four Ways.   Lance Henson.   CDW

Our Son's Profession.   Ha Thi Thao.   WoPoe, tr. by Nguyen Ngoc Bich

Our speech slurs now.   Nook.   George Barlow.   GT

Our Spring Needs Shoveling.   Haniel Long.   APT-1

Our States, O Lord.   John Mycall.   AH

Our storm[e] is past, and that storm[e]'s tyrannous rage.   Calm[e], The.   John Donne.   NoSic

Our story didn't make the six o'clock news. The other story did. The one.   Sand.   Dominique Parker.   SpirFl

Our story isn't a file of photographs.   For an Album.   Adrienne Rich.   VCAP

Our suffering would be unbearable if we couldn't regard it as a.   Letter to Youki.   Robert Desnos.   AF, tr. by Carolyn Forché

Our Sun.   George Seferis.   AF

Our Sunday Rest.   "Don Aminado."   TCRusP, tr. by John Glad

Our talk was of Too Much, of.   Zurich, at the Stork.   Paul Celan.   PoetW, tr. by John Felstiner

Our Task.   Henrietta Cordelia Ray.   CBWP-3

Our teachers prepared us years ahead.   Dancing the Tarantella at the County Farm.   Sandra Alcosser.   ExTi

Our Tense and Wintry Minds.   Hayden Carruth.   AH

Our Tongue.   Ferenc Kazinczy.   IQMS, tr. by Watson Kirkconnell

Our trees are aspens, but people.   Another Version.   Lisel Mueller.   IllVoic

Our two soules therefore, which are one.   John Donne.   UV   Fr. Valediction: Forbidding Mourning, A.

Our Two Worthies.   John Crowe Ransom.   OBAL

Our view of sky, jungle, and fields constricts.   Insert, The.   R. L. Barth.   CDa; InPK-6

Our Village—by a Villager.   Thomas Hood.   FaBoVe; OBSV

Our village pond named Mother Ganga.   Pond Named Ganga, A.   Chandrashekhar Kambar.   OMIP, tr. by A. K. Ramanujan

Our Village, that's to say not Miss Mitford's.   Our Village—by a Villager.   Thomas Hood.   FaBoVe; OBSV

Our vision is our voice.   Anthem, An.   Sonia Sanchez.   UnSA

Our Voice.   Noémia da Sousa.   HAWP, tr. by Jacques-Noël Gouat

Our voice has risen, conscious and barbarous.   Our Voice.   Noémia da Sousa.   HAWP, tr. by Jacques-Noël Gouat

Our voices waved upwards into a tide / that wrapped itself around the island.   Island within Island.   Henry Dumas.   GT

Our waking hours write bitter things.   Reconciliation.   Dora Greenwell.   PoBW

Our wandering eyes are sated with the dancer's skill.   Cock-fight, The.   Ts'ao Chih.   ChiP, *tr. by* Arthur Waley

Our way of life.   It's a Woman's World.   Eavan Boland.   CIP-2; ItWoWo

Our whole body frantic for the leap and the sweet light that follows. (LL)   Tagging.   Maureen Seaton.   ExTi; IllVoic

Our windows. Who is the maniac, and why everywhere at the same time. (LL)   Das Kapital.   Imamu Amiri Baraka.   PFTM-2; PoM

Our words are dead.   Silence.   Ghazi Al-Gosaibi.   MAP, *tr. by* Charles Doria and Sharif Elmusa

Our words do not lie apart.   Holy Order.   Gemino H. Abad.   ReBoTo

Our World Is Less Full Now That Mr. Fuller Is Gone.   Kalamu ya Salaam.   ISC

Our world is very little in the sky.   Measurements.   Louisa Sarah Bevington.   VWP

Our years are driven wild.   Yeti.   John Haines.   PoCoUp

Our Youth.   John Ashbery.   CoAmPo; VGW

Our youth was gay but rough.   One of the Boys.   James Simmons.   ModIr; PNI

Our youth was happy: why repine.   Walter Savage Landor.   FaBoEE; NPeEn

Oure Ho[o]ste gan to swere as he were wood.   Geoffrey Chaucer.   NAEL-6v1; NAEL-7v1   *Fr.* Canterbury Tales, The.

Ours are the streets where Bess first met her / cancer.   Bess.   William Stafford.   NNaP

Ours is group solitude.   Eugenio Montale.   ItPo, *tr. by* Gayle Ridinger

Ours is the ancient story.   For Daughters of Magdalen.   Countee Cullen.   ChIV-2

Ourselves become our own best sacrifice! (LL)   Richard Crashaw.   GeHe; NAEL-6v1; NAEL-7v1

Ourselves or Nothing.   Carolyn Forché.   BodElec; GifTon

Ourselves to end ourselves. (LL)   William Shakespeare.   EBEV; OxAEP-1   *Fr.* Antony and Cleopatra.

Ourselves we do inter with sweet derision.   Emily Dickinson.   APN-2; FaBoEE

Ousel cock, so black of hue, The.   William Shakespeare.   NoSic   *Fr.* Midsummer Night's Dream, A.

Out.   Eleanor Brown.   MFPA

Out.   Anderson Ferrell.   Unlie

Out.   Ted Hughes.   FaBoWar

Out and Back on the Fifteenth Night of the First Month.   Mei Yao Ch'en.   CoBCP, *tr. by* Burton Watson

Out back, Lotte's feeding pillow cases.   Typing the Letters.   John A. Scott.   BMAP

Out beyond ideas of wrongdoing and rightdoing.   Jelaluddin [*or* Jalal al-Din] Rumi.   BLT; EnlH

Out Early One Morning, I Met an Old Acquaintance.   Shen Yüeh.   CoBCP, *tr. by* Burton Watson

Out Early One Morning, I Met an Old Acquaintance.   Wang Seng-ta.   CoBCP, *tr. by* Burton Watson

Out Fishing.   Barbara Howes.   WPE

Out for a walk, after a week in bed.   Urban Convalescence, An.   James Merrill.   CoAP; ColAP; NAAL-2v2; NAAL-5; NOBA

Out from the tight railway seams along Highway 101.   Elkhorn Slough.   Abigail Albrecht.   GeoHom

Out Here.   Roger Mitchell.   PoCoUp

Out here in Ringoes.   Rural Recreation.   Lillian Morrison.   KaS

Out here in the exact middle of the day.   Edward Hopper and the House by the Railroad.   Edward Hirsch.   PoSol

Out here on Cottage Grove it matters. The galloping.   Pyrography.   John Ashbery.   HarvBoo; PoM; VCAP

Out here there are no hearthstones.   Sleep in the Mojave Desert.   Sylvia Plath.   AiP

Out here, where any rambling bed—of sea-.   Reach, The.   Carl Phillips.   GT

Out here where the crows turn around.   Country Wisdoms.   Maggie Anderson.   PBCAP

Out in a world of death, far to the northward lying.   Winter Lakes, The.   Wilfred Campbell.   NOBC

Out in Arizona where the bad men are.   Rag Time Cowboy Joe.   Grant Clarke.   ReLy

Out in the bushlands a creeper grows.   Songs of Courtship.   *Unknown.*   ChiP, *tr. by* Arthur Waley

Out in the Dark.   Edward Thomas.   GTBS-P; MoBrPo; NOBE; OBWVE; OxBEV; RB

Out in the dark over the snow.   Out in the Dark.   Edward Thomas.   GTBS-P; MoBrPo; NOBE; OBWVE; OxBEV; RB

Out in the Desert.   Josephine D. Henderson Heard.   CBWP-4

Out in the elegy country, summer evenings.   Blue Suburban.   Howard Nemerov.   ColAP

Out in the Fields [with God].   Elizabeth Barrett Browning.   ITBLP

Out in the high waves.   Saigyo.   WoPoe, *tr. by* Steven D. Carter

Out in the late amber afternoon.   In Shadow.   Hart Crane.   NOBA

Out in the marsh reeds.   Ki no Tsurayuki.   OHPJ; WoPoe, *tr. by* Kenneth Rexroth

Out in the rain a world is growing green.   Easter Monday.   Christina Georgina Rossetti.   NOCV

Out in the silent Rockies.   Outcast, The.   P. G. Wodehouse.   UV

Out in the sky the great dark clouds are massing.   Ships That Pass in the Night.   Paul Laurence Dunbar.   ColAP

Out in the Snow, Spending the Night at the New Stockade, Extremely Depressed.   Huang T'ing-chien.   SuSp, *tr. by* Michael E. Workman

Out in the street.   (What Did I Do to Be So) Black and Blue?   Andy Razaf.   NAAAL

Out in the sun the goldfinch flits.   Hollow Wood, The.   Edward Thomas.   OWoS

Out in this desert we are testing bombs.   Trying to Talk with a Man.   Adrienne Rich.   HCAP

Out-island once, on a south slope.   Deer Isle.   Philip Booth.   VGW

Out it spake Lizee Linzee.   Lizie Lindsay.   *Unknown.*   ESPB

Out, John.   Thomas Haynes Bayly.   OBCoV

Out my window, the loop canal.   Loop Canal, The.   Nikolai Alekseievich Zabolotsky [*or* Zabolotskii].   TCRusP, *tr. by* Denis Johnson and Kathy Lewis

Out of a clear blue sky.   All I Do Is Dream of You.   Arthur Freed.   ReLy

Out of a fired ship, which, by no way.   Burnt Ship, A.   John Donne.   EBEV; FaBoWar; InPK-6; OBWP

Out of a gothic North, the pallid children.   Good-Bye to the Mezzogiorno.   W. H. Auden.   OxBTC

Out of a hat.   Out of Our Hands.   Cathy Song.   UnSA

Out of a Sudden.   Tom Raworth.   Oth

Out of adult hearing.   Picture of Okinawa, A.   Dennis Schmitz.   LCAP-2

Out of Africa arises a silence.   Art of Hurricanes, The.   Víctor Hernández Cruz.   TouFir

Out of an Epigram of Martial.   Martial.   OBVE, *tr. by* Sir John Denham

Out of Bounds.   Priscilla Borthwick.   Prnts

Out of burlap sacks, out of bearing butter.   They Feed They Lion.   Philip Levine.   LCAP-2; NNaP; NOBA; NoAM; NoP-4; VCAP

Out of chaos.   Yün-k'an Tzu.   ColAnChi, *tr. by* Jerome P. Seaton

Out of Chaos Out of Order Out.   Michele Roberts.   BrRo

Out of Control; the Quarry.   Christopher Dewdney.   NOBC

Out of East Gate.   East Gate, The.   *Unknown.*   ChinPo, *tr. by* Yip Wai-lim

Out of French.   Sir Charles Sedley.   FaBoEE

Out of friendship and a slow retreat of the blood.   Ascending Red Cedar Moon.   Duane Niatum.   CDW

Out of gas south.   Autumn.   Philip Levine.   NNaP

Out of heaven on your bugles blown! (LL)   England, My England.   William Ernest Henley.   MoBrPo; OBEV

Out of Hellas if you please, Aristarchean pedants.   Herodicus.   GrAn

Out of his cottage to the sun.   Old Dan'l.   Leonard Alfred George Strong.   MoBrPo

Out of Horace.   James Wright.   NOSC

Out of Ireland.   Thomas Kinsella.
   Harmonies.   ModIr

Out of it all but this remains.   Dead Cities.   Madison Cawein.   APN-2

Out of it steps our future, through this door.   W. H. Auden.   Son   *Fr.* Quest, The.

Out of love for You.   Dīnrām.   SinGod, *tr. by* Rachel Fell McDermott

Out of Luck.   Abraham Ibn Ezra.   TrJP, *tr. by* Solomon Solis-Cohen

Out of me unworthy and unknown.   Edgar Lee Masters.   CBCWP; HAP; MoAmPo; NOBA; NoAM; OxBA; PAI; TFi   *Fr.* Spoon River Anthology.

Out of midsummer's blazing most not night.   E. E. Cummings.   NoAM

Out of my flesh that hungers.   On a Night of the Full Moon.   Audre Lorde.   NALW

Out of my heart, one day, I wrote a song.   Misapprehension.   Paul Laurence Dunbar.   BPo

Out of my mother's womb.   Job. I.   John Hall.   ChIV-1

Out of my own great woe.   Proem.   Heinrich Heine.   AWP, *tr. by* Elizabeth Barrett Browning

Out of My Own Pocket.   Martha Collins.   ExTi

Out of my window I could see.   Blossoms.   Frank Dempster Sherman.   OBCA

Out of one golden breath.   Love-Song.   Else Lasker-Schüler.   TrJP, *tr. by* Jethro Bithell

Out of our daylight into death you burn.   Paper Anarchist Addresses the Shade of Nancy Ling Perry.   George Woodcock.   NOBC

Out of Our Hands.   Cathy Song.   UnSA

Out of Our Shame.   Norman Rosten.   TrJP

Out of sight, out of mind.   Sand in My Shoes.   Victor Schertzinger.   ReLy

Out of that pain.   Rasta Reggae.   Mervyn Morris.   WaCA

Out of the American provinces. Cheerleaders. Lisa Coffman. AmPoNex

Out of the blackthorn hedges. Love Song. Ivor Gurney. EnLoPo

Out-of-the-Body Travel. Stanley Plumly. LCAP-2

Out of the bosom of the Air. Snow-Flakes. Henry Wadsworth Longfellow. APN-1; ITBLP; NCAP; NOBA; NoP-4; TAP; TCAPo; UnPo

Out of the church she followed [or follow'd] them. Maude Clare. Christina Georgina Rossetti. EBVV; ViWPN

Out of the clover and blue-eyed grass. Driving Home the Cows. Kate Putnam Osgood. CBCWP

Out of the complicated house, come I. Hills, The. Frances Darwin Cornford. MoBrPo

Out of the corpse-warm vestibule of heaven steps the sun. Ingeborg Bachmann. BoWoP

Out of the Cradle Endlessly Rocking. Walt Whitman. APN-1; AWP; HAP; HeIP-4; MoAmPo; NAAL-2v1; NAAL-3; NAAL-5; NAWM-7v2; NOBA; OWoS; OxBA; PoE; SAmP; TAP; TRP

Out of the crowd, I have seen you travelling south of Pardoo. Witch Doctor's Magic Flight, The. Smiler Narautjarri. NOBAu, tr. by George von Brandenstein

Out of the dark. Open Door, The. Elizabeth Jane Coatsworth. TLR

Out of the dark cup. From the Telephone. Florence Ripley Mastin. LW

Out of the dark theatre into sunlight. Recording History. Gail Newman. GotH

Out of the Darkness. Frankie Armstrong. BrRo

Out of the Darkness. Voltairine de Cleyre. SWaP

Out of the Darkness. Gertrud Kolmar. WPOW, tr. by Michael Hamburger

Out of the darks and deeps of space. Tryst, The. Harriet Prescott Spofford. SWaP

Out of the Deep. Clara Ann Thompson. CBWP-2

Out of the deep [or depths] have I called [or cried unto] thee, O Lord. Bible, O.T. TrJP Fr. Psalms.

Out of the Depths I Cry unto You, O Death! Tawfiq [or Taufiq] Sayigh. MAP, tr. by Samuel Hazo and Anne Royal

Out of the depths of a heart of love. Valentine, A. Priscilla Jane Thompson. CBWP-2

Out of the dusk a shadow. Evolution. John Banister Tabb. APN-2

Out of the earth. I Sing for the Animals. Teton Sioux Oral Tradition. TCAPo; TTTS

Out of the earth, out of the air, out of the water. Richard Murphy. BIrV; NOIV; PBCIP Fr. Battle of Aughrim, The.

Out of the earth to rest or range. Passing Strange, The. John Masefield. MoBrPo; OBEV

Out of the East in purple robes. Ancient "Kayán," The. Endre Ady. IQMS, tr. by Watson Kirkconnell

Out of the east window a storm. Wednesday of Holy Week, 1940. Kenneth Rexroth. ChIV-1

Out of the factory chimney tall. Smoke Animals. Rowena Bastin Bennett. CA

Out of the farmhouse. Revelation on a Summer Walk. John O'Brien. PoCoUp

Out of the focal and foremost fire. Little Giffen. Francis Orrery [or Orray] Ticknor. CBCWP

Out of the Frying Pan into the Fire. James Henry. NOBVV

Out of the garden comes the tree. Because Thou Did'st Give. Harry Morris. CRP

Out of the ghetto streets where a Jewboy. Autobiographical. Abraham Moses Klein. MoCV; NoAM

Out of the green of spring. Old Mountain. Muso Soseki. EaWin, tr. by W. S. Merwin

Out of the grey air grew snow and more snow. Snow. William Robert Rodgers. ModIr

Out of the hills of Habersham. Song of the Chattahoochee. Sidney Lanier. APN-2; ColAP; TCAPo

Out of the hills the trees bulge. Charles Reznikoff. APT-2

Out of the house or be the wife I want. Martial. RomPo, tr. by Peter Whigham

Out of the Hurly-Burly. "Max Adeler." OBAL

Out of the Identical. Gustaf Sobin. PmAP

Out of the Italain. Giambattista [or Giovanni Battista] Marino. OBVE, tr. by Richard Crashaw

Out of the lamplight. Mice in the Hay. Leslie Norris. NOxBChV; OBCP

Out of the Land of Heaven. Leonard Cohen. MoCV

Out of the least shift in the wind, out of. Shirt Collar, The. Ann Townsend. NAPBL

Out of the life lived, out of the love spent. (LL) Urban Convalescence, An. James Merrill. CoAP; ColAP; NAAL-2v2; NAAL-5; NOBA

Out of the marvellous as he had known it. (LL) Seamus Heaney. EmeKit; ModIr; NPeEn Fr. Lightenings.

Out of the maternal watery blue lines. Curlews Lift. Ted Hughes. OWoS

Out of the midnight sky a great dawn broke. Shepherd Speaks, The. John Erskine. TrCP

Out of the mud two strangers came. Two Tramps in Mud Time. Robert Frost. APT-1; MoAmPo; NAAL-2v2; NoAM; SAmP

Out of the Night. Emily Jane Pfeiffer.

"So the river—yes, the river; I have come to that at last." VWP

Out of the Past there has come a Face. Face from the Past, A. Menella Bute Smedley. VWP

Out of the shadow, I am come in to you whole a black holy man. Study Peace. Imamu Amiri Baraka. APSN

Out of the soil and rock. Gary Snyder. BodElec

Out of the table endlessly rocking. Just Friends. Robert Creeley. NeAP

Out of the tomb, we bring Badroulbadour. Worms at Heaven's Gate, The. Wallace Stevens. NoAM

Out of the tree of life. Best Is Yet to Come, The. Cy Coleman. ReLy

Out of the Wailing. Stephen Caldwell Wright. ISC

Out of the waste you can spin. Gavin Selerie. Oth Fr. Roxy.

Out of the Whirlwind. Bible, O.T. AWP Fr. Job.

Out of the wind's and the rain's way. (LL) Old Woman of the Roads, The. Padraic Colum. MoBrPo; NOIV; OBEV; PoRA

Out of the window a sea of green trees. Open Windows. Sara Teasdale. ColAP

Out of the wine-pot cry'd the fly. Fly, The. Philip Ayres. OBVE

Out of the wood of thoughts that grows by night. Cock-Crow. Edward Thomas. GTBS-P; MoBrPo; NPeEn; OxBSP; RB

Out of their slumber Europeans spun. Snow in Europe. David Gascoyne. NPeEn

Out of these depths. De Profundis. David Gascoyne. PoWW

Out of this ugliness may come. Glasgow Street. William Montgomerie. OxBS

Out of This World. Johnny Mercer. ReLy

Out of those wild, in-. Irises. Gustaf Sobin. APSN

Out of Time. Kenneth Slessor.

"Leaning against the golden undertow." CBAP

Out of tube and tune. South Bound: Facing North. Geraldine Monk. Oth

Out of Tune. William Ernest Henley. MoBrPo

Out of tune with the crowd since young. Home to Farm. Unknown. ChinPo, tr. by Yip Wai-lim

Out of waters warm. Man. Oscar Hahn. TCLAP, tr. by Sandy McKinney

Out of Work, Out of Touch, Out of Sorts. Catherine Davis. FFC

Out of your head the sky is taken. Monotones. B. P. Nichol. FTOS

Out of your whole life give but a moment! Now. Robert Browning. OxBSo

Out on a limb and frantically sawing. Martyrdom of Two Pagans. Philip Whalen. NeAP

Out on the bare grey roads, I pass. Touch It. Robert Mezey. GeoHom

Out on the lawn I lie in bed. Summer Night, A. W. H. Auden. NPeEn

Out on the wastes of the Never Never. Where the Dead Men Lie. Barcroft Henry Boake. CBAP

Out on the windy hill. Shepherd's Dog, The. Leslie Norris. OBCP

Out, Out. Robert Frost. APT-1; AmFaPo; ColAP; HAP; HarvBoo; HeIP-4; NAAL-2v2; NAAL-5; OxBA; PAI; RB; SoSe-8; TCAPo; TRP; UnPo; VGW

Out past the window two trees in splendor. Sentiments at Autumn. Han Yü. SuSp, tr. by Charles Hartman

Out scouting for sound counsels? How to prosper? Ausiàs March. STV

Out strolling on a spring day. Tune: "Thinking of the Imperial Capital." Wei Chuang. ColAnChi, tr. by John Timothy Wixted

Out the southern gate at sundown. Unknown. CoBCP Fr. Tzu Yeh Songs.

Out the window, a kid-robin on a branch. Volunteers. Hilda Raz. ExTi

Out the window, Colombia, out the window. Sharon Doubiago. PBCAP Fr. South America Mi Hija.

Out There. Breyten Breytenbach. VCWP

Out there, beyond the boundary fence, beyond. Singing Bones, The. Randolph Stow. BMAP; CBAP

Out there in the sun—in the rain. (LL) Rooms. Charlotte Mew. HarvBoo; PoBW

Out there, we've walked quite friendly up to Death. Next War, The. Wilfred Owen. Son

Out, thou silly moon-struck elf. Idiot-Born, The. Eliza Cook. VWP

Out through the fields and the woods. Reluctance. Robert Frost. ITBLP; MoAmPo; NOBA; OxBA

Out upon it! I have loved [or lov'd]. Sir John Suckling. BASC; BeJo; CavPo; NAEL-6v1; NAEL-7v1; NBLV; NOSC; NPeEn; NoP-4; OxAEP-1; OxBEV; PBRV; PeLV; PoE Fr. Poem with the Answer, A.

Out, upon the deep old ocean. On Genessaret. Josephine D. Henderson Heard. CBWP-4

Out upon you California. Pennsylvania Places. Thomas Augustin Daly. OBAL

Out walking in July. Released on Parole. James McAuley. BMAP

Out walking in the frozen swamp one gray [*or* grey] day.   Wood-Pile, The.   Robert Frost.   APT-1; InPK-6; NAAL-2v2; NAAL-5; NoAM; SAmP; VGW

Out West.   Bill Manhire.   EmeKit

Out West.   Gary Snyder.   NNaP

Out Where the West Begins.   Arthur Chapman.   AiP; BRP

Out with my dog at dawn—we couldn't sleep—.   Two Ember Days in Alabama.   Andrew Hudgins.   RA

Outbound, your bark awaits you. Were I one.   Godspeed.   John Greenleaf Whittier.   GSo; Son

Outbreak.   Bill Anderson.   VGW

Outcast.   Claude McKay.   APT-1

(For the dim regions whence my father came.)   NAAAL

Outcast.   Alice Walker.   NAAAL

Outcast[, The].   "Æ"   OxBSP

Outcast, The.   Josephine D. Henderson Heard.   CBWP-4

Outcast, The.   James Stephens.   MoBrPo

Outcast, The.   P. G. Wodehouse.   UV

Outcries.   Hélène d'Oettingen.   CuPo

Outcry upon Opportunity, An.   William Shakespeare.   NOBE   *Fr.* Rape of Lucrece, The.

Outdoor Chums in the Forest.   Ann Townsend.   ExTi

Outer.   (LL) Self-Hatred of Don L. Lee, The.   Haki R. Madhubuti.   BPo; ESEAA

Outer Banks, The.   Emily Grosholz.   RA

Outer Banks, The.   Muriel Rukeyser.   APT-2

Outer—from the Inner, The.   Emily Dickinson.   APN-2

Outer Layers of Nervousness, The.   Alan Davies.   FTOS

Outer provinces are never secure, The.   Peace with Honor.   Philip Appleman.   CDa

Outgoing Sabbath.   *Unknown.*   TrJP, *tr. by* Joseph Leftwich

Outing, The.   Marina Kudimova.   TCRP, *tr. by* Albert C. Todd

Outlanders, The.   William Morris.   EBVV   *Fr.* Earthly Paradise, The.

Outlaw, The.   Seamus Heaney.   NIL-7; OxBC

Outlaw Murray, The.   *Unknown.*   ESPB; OxBB

Outlaw of Loch Lene, The.   *Unknown.*   BIrV; OBEV, *tr. by* Jeremiah Joseph Callanan

Outlaw's Song, The.   Joanna Baillie.   OBEV

Outlines.   Audre Lorde.   GLP

Outliving / Them all, all.   Issa.   ZenPo, *tr. by* Takashi Ikemoto and Lucien Stryk

Outlook.   Crystal Bacon.   UrbNat

Outlook wasn't brilliant for the Mudville nine that day, The.   Casey at the Bat.   Ernest Lawrence Thayer.   APN-2; AiP; AmFaPo; BRP; FaBoA; OBAL; OBCA; OBCoV; OxIBACP; PoRA; TCAPo

Outpacing bargain, vocable and prayer. (LL) Hart Crane.   APT-2; NOBA; NoAM

Outpost Soldier, The.   *Vietnamese Oral Tradition.*   CaDao, *tr. by* John Balaban

Outposts.   F. W. D. Bendall.   FaBoWar

Outrigger.   Charles Bernstein.   PFTM-2

Outroars a dead lion. (LL) Koheleth.   Louis Untermeyer.   ChIV-1; TrJP

Outside.   Susan M. Whitmore.   SpudSo

Outside, a delicate arch.   Curse, The.   John Hollander.   UnPo

Outside / a moon starting up.   Sharing.   Alan Yount.   PasH

Outside a rain steady and hard as nails.   Dwelling.   Emily Warn.   GifTon

Outside, affectionate eyes.   Ursula.   David Ray.   VGW

Outside Bristol Rovers Football Ground.   Ballad of Billy Rose, The.   Leslie Norris.   AngWePo

Outside everything visible and invisible a blazing maple.   Testimony of Light, The.   Carolyn Forché.   ExTi

Outside Fargo, North Dakota.   James Wright.   LCAP-2; NNaP

(Along the sprawled body of the derailed Great Northern freight car.)   GM

Outside. Field. Food.   Katie's Words.   Lawrence Raab.   Unle

Outside, in fact, there wasn't any change.   Patrizia Cavalli.   NeIt

Outside in the Open.   Adriann Roland Holst.   TuT, *tr. by* Desmond Egan

Outside memory worship never dies.   Sappho's Gymnasium.   Olga Broumas.   GifTon

Outside my door.   To the Tune "The Drunken Young Lord."   *Unknown.*   WoPoe, *tr. by* C. H. Kwock and Vincent McHugh

Outside my window a cow is giving birth.   Calf.   Katrina Porteous.   NeBl

Outside my window a lorry misses gear.   Weekend at Home.   John Pook.   AngWePo

Outside nothing's really changed.   Patrizia Cavalli.   ItPo, *tr. by* Gayle Ridinger

Outside of Havana.   Jewish Cemetery in Guanabacoa, The.   Ruth Behar.   MirDau

Outside our bedroom window.   Descant.   Jane Mayes.   PasH

Outside / outside myself / there is a world.   William Carlos Williams.   NAAL-2v2; NoAM   *Fr.* Paterson.

Outside Pisa.   Chitra Divakaruni.   OpBo

Outside Room Six.   Lynn Emanuel.   ReTh

Outside somewhere, beneath an atmosphere.   Allegory.   Rafael Campo.   RA

Outside the Bureau all the trams and trains.   Laid Off.   Francis Webb.   BMAP

Outside the children play like flames.   Fever, The.   Rosemary Dobson.   FaBoWP

Outside the city, desolate, an ancient terrace.   Flower-Rain Terrace, The.   Tao-chi.   CoBLCP, *tr. by* Jonathan Chaves

Outside the curtain rain trickles on.   Tune: "Sand Washed by Waves."   Li Yü.   ColAnChi, *tr. by* Jiaosheng Wang

Outside the Depot.   Betsy Sholl.   LTA

Outside, the freezing desert night.   Jelaluddin [*or* Jalal al-Din] Rumi.   EnlH

Outside the Furnace.   Aziz Qaisi.   OMIP, *tr. by* Baidar Bakht

Outside the great clanging cathedrals of rust and smoke.   Poem Written under an Archway in a Discontinued Railroad Station, Fargo, North Dakota, A.   James Wright.   GM

Outside the Holy City.   James G. Gilkey.   AH

Outside the Hospital.   Joe Wenderoth.   BodElec

Outside the hospital the sun lighted the leaves.   Triptych.   Christopher Pilling.   NLP

Outside the hotel window, unenlightened pigeons.   Jain Bird Hospital in Delhi, The.   William Meredith.   VCAP

Outside the house an ash-tree hung its terrible whips.   Discord in Childhood.   D. H. Lawrence.   HarvBoo

Outside, the last kids holler.   Leaving the Motel.   W. D. Snodgrass.   NIL-7; NIP-4

Outside, the music is steeped.   In the Evening.   Anna Andreyevna Akhmatova.   TCRP, *tr. by* Daniel Weissbort

Outside the office of the principal. (LL) Zimmer in Grade School.   Paul Zimmer.   KaS; PBCAP

Outside the Party.   Julia Ward Howe.   SWaP   *Fr.* Lyrics of the Street.

Outside the pub.   Chuck Brickley.   HA

Outside the rain is falling down.   Season's Finished, The.   Hyllus Maris.   IBA

Outside, the rain, pinafore of gray water, dresses the town.   Child Beater.   Ai.   BoWoP

Outside the screen rain drips and splashes.   Tune: "Ripples Sifting Sand: A Song."   Li Yü.   SuSp, *tr. by* Daniel Bryant

Outside the second grade room.   Girl Who Loved the Sky, The.   Anita Endrezze.   HATNAP

Outside the Supermarket.   Roy Fuller.   OxBC

Outside the Terrace of Yellow Cranes.   Mooring at Hsia-k'ou at Night.   Li Meng-yang.   CoBLCP, *tr. by* Jonathan Chaves

Outside the tower, the east wind's early to arrive.   To the Tune "Chao-chūn's Sorrow."   Yang Shen.   CoBLCP, *tr. by* Jonathan Chaves

Outside the town I've built this little place.   Garden Living.   Wu Wei-yeh.   CoBLCP, *tr. by* Jonathan Chaves

Outside the world was full, plural.   Christmas Tree, The.   Patricia Beer.   OBCP

Outside their door, a tiny narcissus.   April, New Hampshire.   Sharon Olds.   BodElec

Outside where the storm goes cracked.   Caption for a Miniature.   Joanne Kyger.   BB

Outside your temple wall.   To the Unnamed Buddhist Nun Who Burned Herself to Death on the Night of June 3, 1966.   Diane Di Prima.   BB

Outsider, The.   Syl Cheney-Coker.   HBAPE

Outsider: Minnie Evans.   Sandra McPherson.   ExTi

Outskirts.   Tomas Tranströmer.   BLT, *tr. by* Robert Bly

Outspoken buttocks in pink beads.   Hart Crane.   NAAL-2v2; OxBA   *Fr.* Bridge, The.

Outward.   Louis Simpson.   EmeKit

Outward Bound.   James Simmons.   CIP-2

Outwit me, Lord, if ever hence.   Security.   Charles Leo O'Donnell.   SacPr

Outwitted.   Edwin Markham.   MoAmPo; PoToHe

Outworn year has altered his apparel, The.   Elegy.   Miklós Zrínyi.   IQMS, *tr. by* Watson Kirkconnell

Ovals of opal on dislustred seas.   Memoriter.   Charles Spear.   PeNZ

Oven.   Laura Kasischke.   NAPBL

Oven Bird, The.   Robert Frost.   APT-1; AWP; GSo; HeIP-4; NAAL-2v2; NAAL-5; NOBA; NoAM; NoP-4; OWoS; OxBA; PoE; Son; TAP; TCAPo

Oven of Lublin, The.   Theodor Kramer.   AuPH, *tr. by* Lowell A. Bangerter

Ovens. Women in line waiting for showers.   Anna's Dream.   Nancy Shiffrin.   GotH

Over a dark and quiet empire.   Two Poems.   Andrey [*or* Andrei] Andreievich Voznesensky [*or* Voznesenskii].   VCWP, *tr. by* Patricia Blake and William Jay Smith

Over a sea with death acquainted, yet forever chaste. (LL) Ragged Island.   Edna St. Vincent Millay.   ColAP; NAAL-2v2; NoP-4

Over a slow-dying fire.   Lachesis.   Victor James Daley.   CBAP

Over-all picture is winter, The. William Carlos Williams. LCAP-2 *Fr.* Pictures from Brueghel.

Over all the hills now. Song of the Traveler at Evening. Goethe. STV, *tr. by* John Frederick Nims

Over all their property. (LL) White Clover. Marvin Bell. InvLad; VCAP

Over an ash-fawn beach fronting a sea which keeps. Fiascherino. Charles Tomlinson. NoAM

Over an oil drum the workmen warm. Break. Ben Howard. UrbNat

Over and back. At Ithaca. "H. D." ColAP; VGW

Over and over. Anita Virgil. HA

Over and over again. (LL) Love Poem. Audre Lorde. GLP; NoAM; PoBW

Over and over again the papers print. Once in a While a Protest Poem. David B. Axelrod. InPK-6

Over and over again to people. Limits of Submission, The. Faarah Nuur. TTY, *tr. by* B. W. Andrejewski and I. M. Lewis

Over & over, bamming it in while I cry out your name I do love you please Master. (LL) Please Master. Allen Ginsberg. CAGL; GLP

Over and over, like a Tune. Emily Dickinson. TCAPo

Over and Over Stitch. Jorie Graham. HCAP; VCAP

Over and over, when the wayside dust had grayed us. To Be Said at the Seder. Karl Wolfskehl. TrJP, *tr. by* Ernst Morowitz and Carol North Valhope

Over back where they speak of life as staying. Investment, The. Robert Frost. APT-1; OxBA

Over bare hills pale and still. Landscape in Late Autumn. Ferdinand von Saar. AuPH, *tr. by* Lowell A. Bangerter

Over by the horses. Belle Isle Men, The. Anthony Butts. AmPoNex

Over Coffee. Bob Hicok. AmPoNex

Over deep cushions, drenched with drowsy scents. Damned Women. Charles Baudelaire. BoLoP, *tr. by* Roy Campbell

Over dried grass. David Lloyd. HA

Over every elm, the. You Too Lie Down. Dennis Lee. TLR

Over Fayetteville, Arkansas. Arkansas Testament, The. Derek Walcott. CBCWP

Over fishes, over stars. Smugglers. "Eduard Georgievich Bagritzky" [*or* "Bagritsky"]. TCRP, *tr. by* Vera Dunham

Over-Heart, The. John Greenleaf Whittier. ChIV-2; NOCV

Over here in England I'm helpin' wi' the hay. Corrymeela. "Moira O'Neill." AWP

Over his keys the musing organist. James Russell Lowell. APN-1 *Fr.* Vision of Sir Launfal, The.

Over in the fields the wind provokes. Malines. Paul Verlaine. SxFrPo, *tr. by* Martin Sorrell

Over Manhattan Bridge. Brooklyn. Michael S. Weaver. SpirFl

Over meadows of Brittany, the lark. Death of Time. Robert Penn Warren. BodElec

Over Mount Kemenes howls Boreas in rage. Horace. Dániel Berzsenyi. IQMS, *tr. by* Peter Zollman

Over Mtskheta falls a star. In Memory of Titian Tabidze. Yunna Petrovna [*or* Iunna Pinkhusovna] Moritz [*or* Morits]. TCRP, *tr. by* J. R. Rowland

Over my district north to south, when will my days in office end? Out in the Snow, Spending the Night at the New Stockade, Extremely Depressed. Huang T'ing-chien. SuSp, *tr. by* Michael E. Workman

Over my head. Roots in the Air. Shirley Kaufman. TaR

Over my head. Freedom in the Air. *Unknown.* NAAAL

Over my head, I see the bronze butterfly. Lying in a Hammock at William Duffy's Farm in Pine Island, Minnesota. James Wright. CoAmPo; ColAP; HAP; HCAP; MakPoe; NOBA; TRP; VCAP

Over My Shoulder. Harry Woods. ReLy

Over my shoulder in Danbury, Connecticut, as I drove. Wonder, The. Thylias Moss. ChAP

Over my wrong. (LL) In Prison. William Morris. FaBoWar; PeVV

Over northeast mountains. Voyeur's Dream. Barney Bush. HATNAP

Over now / The dream is over now. Never Again. Noël Coward. ReLy

Over, o over / the thorn. (LL) Psalm: "No one moulds us again out of earth and clay." Paul Celan. BBASP; HP; OBVE, *tr. by* Michael Hamburger

Over obscured by their long hair they seem / to be mourning. (LL) George Oppen. APSN; NNaP *Fr.* Some San Francisco Poems.

Over, oh over / the thorn. (LL) Psalm: "No one kneads us again out of earth and clay." Paul Celan. PoSu; PoetW, *tr. by* John Felstiner

Over our heads the missiles ran. Loss of an Oil Tanker. Charles Causley. OxBC

Over our naked guilt. (LL) Net, The. William Robert Rodgers. BoLoP; CIP-2; ModIr; PNI

Over, Over. Thomas Love Peacock. OxAEP-2 *Fr.* Maid Marian.

Over paddies / At its foot. Issa. ZenPo, *tr. by* Takashi Ikemoto and Lucien Stryk

Over rips and tears and / thin places. (LL) Nameless One, A. Margaret Avison. HeIP-4; NOBC

Over rock and wrinkled ground. Beagles. William Robert Rodgers. FaBoTw

Over sheer banks a menacing wind moves. Night. Tu Fu. SuSp, *tr. by* Jan W. Walls

Over Sir John's Hill. Dylan Thomas. AngWePo; NPeEn; TCAWP; TOF

Over that morn hung heaviness, until. Seascape. Francis Brett Young. OxBTC

Over the Arafura sea, the China sea. For John Chappell. Gary Snyder. NNaP

Over the ball of it. Pisgah-Sights. I. Robert Browning. ChIV-1

Over the bed's cliff my legs dangle. Miser. Elizabeth Garrett. NeBl

Over the clay-laden estuary a. Bye Bye Blackbird. John James. Oth

Over the clean sea-beach. (LL) Akahito. AWP; TAL *Fr.* Manyo Shu, Part 2 of 4.

Over the Coast Range, silver horns of cloud. House of Breath. Ken Gerner. GifTon

Over the cobbles, in a lost Spring. (LL) Kenneth Rexroth. APSN; VGW

Over the crying comes the sugar, the cooing. Part One: The Orders Begin. Carmen Naranjo. TANSG, *tr. by* Shaun Griffin and Emma Sepúlveda-Pulvirenti

Over the downs there were birds flying. On the South Downs. Sara Teasdale. MoAmPo

Over the dragon rock the moon appears. Lament for Prince Chagoo. *Unknown.* WoPoe, *tr. by* Jean S. Grigsby

Over the earth I come. Soldier's Song. *Unknown.* APN-2, *tr. by* Stephen Return Riggs

Over the Edge. Fleur Adcock. PeNZ

Over the empty fields a black kite hovers. Kite, The. Aleksandr Aleksandrovich Blok. FaBoWar, *tr. by* Frances Cornford and Esther Polinowsky Salaman

Over the fence. Emily Dickinson. FaBoVe

Over the fields of. Okano Kin'emon Kanehide. JDP, *tr. by* Yoel Hoffmann

Over the flat slope of St Eloi. Trenches: St Eloi. Thomas Ernest Hulme. PeFWW

Over the Garden Wall. Eleanor Farjeon. ChAP

Over the half-finished houses. Roofwalker, The. Adrienne Rich. CoAP; NAAL-2v2

Over the heather the wet wind blows. W. H. Auden. FaBoWar *Fr.* Twelve Songs.

Over the hill and over the dale. Dawlish Fair. John Keats. PeLV

Over the hill came horsemen, horsemen whistling. Stared Story, A. William Stafford. Son

Over the hill I have watched the dawning. Dawning. Richard Watson Dixon. NOBVV

Over the hills. Witches' Ride, The. Karla Kuskin. NOxBChV; OxIBACP; TLR

Over the Hills and far away. (LL) John Gay. EnLoPo; NAEL-5v1; NAEL-6v1; NPeEn; OxBEV; OxBoLi; PeLV *Fr.* Begger's Opera.

Over the Hills and Far Away. John Gay. *See* Begger's Opera

Over the hills and far away. (LL) Gypsy, The. Edward Thomas. NoAM; NoP-4

Over the hills the loose clouds rambled. Subjection of Women, The. Austin Clarke. CIP-2

Over the housetops. Captured Goddess, The. Amy Lowell. NAAL-5

Over the land freckled with snow half-thawed. Thaw. Edward Thomas. EBEV; FaBoTw; GTBS-P; MoBrPo; OxAEP-2; OxBEV; OxBSP; OxBTC; Spl

Over the last century. Song of Lin Liang's Painting "Two Horned Falcons." Li Meng-yang. CoBLCP, *tr. by* Jonathan Chaves

Over the lids of thine eye. Images. Richard von Schaukal. AWP, *tr. by* Ludwig Lewisohn

Over the long road. Kikaku. SoOfWa, *tr. by* Sam Hamill

Over the low, barnacled, elephant-colored rocks. Meditation at Oyster River. Theodore Roethke. MoAmPo *Fr.* North American Sequence.

Over the monstrous shambling sea. Sidney Lanier. NOBA; TCAPo *Fr.* Hymns of the Marshes.

Over the month of June the rain Is falling. Rain is Falling, The. Homero [*or* Umberto] Aridjis. STV; TCLAP, *tr. by* John Frederick Nims

Over the mountains a plane bumbles in. Night-Time: Starting to Write. Bernard Spencer. AWTN

Over the mountains / And over the waves. Love Will Find Out the Way. *Unknown.* FaBoCh; OBEV

Over the Neva. Wilgelm Aleksandrovich Zorgenfrey [*or* Zorgenfrei]. TCRP, *tr. by* Sophie Lund

Over the old honeymoon cottage. Akiko Yosano. OHMPJ

Over the one-strand river. (LL) Gray [*or* Grey] Goose and Gander. *Unknown.* OxBoLi; OxNR

Over the peak spreading clouds. Hakuyo. ZenPo, *tr. by* Takashi Ikemoto and Lucien Stryk

Over the quarry the children went rambling. Fossil Raindrops, The. Harriet Prescott Spofford. OBCA

Over the Rainbow. Harold Arlen. ReLy

Over the rainy day mountain. Wishes. Patty L. Harjo. VoR

Over the reeds the. *Unknown.* OHMPJ

Over the right / triangle formed. Slogan, The. Paul Blackburn. PoM

Over the rim of the glass. Ghost in the Martini, The. Anthony Hecht. DiPo; NoP-4; OxBC

Over the river and through the wood. Thanksgiving Day. Lydia Maria Child. NTCP; WHSW

Over the Roofs. Sara Teasdale. ColAP

Over the roofs go his eyes and outcry. (LL) Esther's Tomcat. Ted Hughes. OxBC; OxBEV

Over the salt and table at a friendly meal. (LL) Archilochus. OBVE; WoPoe, *tr.* by Guy Davenport

Over the sea our galleys went. Robert Browning. OBEV *Fr.* Paracelsus.

Over the Sea to Skye. Robert Louis Stevenson. NOBE

    (Sing Me a Song.) CABP

Over the soughing of the sombre wind. Summer Poem, A. Jayanta Mahapatra. VCWP

Over the stones still rattling, up Pall Mall. Byron. NOBL *Fr.* Don Juan.

Over the tender, bow'd locks of the corn. (LL) Summer Dawn. William Morris. GSo; NOBE; NOBVV; OBEV; OxAEP-2; OxBEV

Over the top! The wire's thin here, unbarbed. Night Patrol, The. Arthur Graeme West. FaBoWar

Over the Top with Pershing. Zelda Sayre Fitzgerald. AiP

Over the up-turned boat, at night. Boat on the Shore. Andrey [*or* Andrei] Andreievich Voznesensky [*or* Voznesenskii]. RusPo, *tr.* by Robert Arthur Douglas Ford

Over the utmost hill at length I sped. Shelley. OBWP *Fr.* Revolt of Islam, The.

Over the vast field of mustard flowers. Buson. OHPJ

Over the vast summer hills. Echoes, The. Raymond Mazisi Kunene. PBMAP

Over the Wall: Berlin, May 1975. Charles Hubert Sisson. OxBC

Over the water and over the lea [*or* sea]. *Unknown.* OxNR; ReMoGo

Over the water / and under the water. Ship's Nail, A. *Unknown.* ReMoGo

Over the wharves at Provincetown. At Provincetown. Daniel Gerard Hoffman. YaYoPo

Over the white steppes. Sad Voices, The. Ricardo Jaimes Freyre. TCLAP, *tr.* by Iver Lofving

Over the wide cold leaves of time you arrive, stained. Little Ode to Melancholy. Ricardo Molinari. TCLAP, *tr.* by Inés Probert

Over the years, a tip would take on time's finish. Old Tips. Jean Earle. TCAWP

Over the years, horses have changed to Land-Rovers. Judith Wright. BMAP *Fr.* For a Pastoral Family.

Over their edge of earth. Little Clan, The. Frederick Robert Higgins. OBMV

Over There. George M. Cohan. FaBoA; ReLy

Over there are faith, life, virtue in the sun. (LL) Report on Experience. Edmund Charles Blunden. FaBoTw; GTBS-P; NOBE; NPeEn; OBMV; OBWP; OxBEV; PeFWW

Over there, people. Veronique Tadjo. NAfrP, *tr.* by Faustine Boateng Gyima

Over there? / *Where?* (LL) Café: 3 A.M. Langston Hughes. GLP; HCAP

Over these blunted, these tormented hills. Kanheri Caves. Dom Moraes. NoP-4

Over this battered track. Express Train. Karl Kraus. TrJP, *tr.* by Albert Bloch

Over this the foresayd lay. John Skelton. PBRV *Fr.* Collyn Clout.

Over thresholds of welcome dream with wet and moonlit skin. (LL) Elegy for Drowned Children. Bruce Dawe. BMAP; NOBAu

Over 2000 Illustrations and a Complete Concordance. Elizabeth Bishop. APT-2; HCAP; HarvBoo; LCAP-2; NAAL-2v2; NoAM; PoetW; VCAP

Over us stands the broad electric face. Terminal. Karl Shapiro. GM

Over *Voice of America.* Dennis Finnell. SwNoth

Over water / Sharp sickles. Buson. ZenPo, *tr.* by Takashi Ikemoto and Lucien Stryk

Over you, Hermes fights. Korinna [*or* Corinna]. SaLy, *tr.* by Diane Rayor

Over your body the clouds go. Gulliver. Sylvia Plath. NOBA

Over your head to sleep I bow. (LL) Robert Browning. BoLoP; OBEV *Fr.* In a Gondola.

Overburdened with sorrow now. Another Song. William [*or* Villeam] Ross [*or* Ros]. NePenScot, *tr.* by Derick Thomson

Overcoat, The. Alda Merini. CltWP, *tr.* by Cinzia Sartini Blum and Lara Trubowitz

Overcome by fatigue, there Boaz lay. Boaz Asleep. Victor Hugo. SxFrPo

Overdue Balance Sheet. Thérèse Plantier. BoWoP, *tr.* by Maxine W. Kumin and Judith Kumin

Overflow. Nada El-Hage. PoArWo, *tr.* by Nathalie El-Hani

Overflow advances across strawberry. Natural Disaster. David Swanger. GeoHom

Overgrown roads around here refract water-and-mirror mirages, The. Island Celebration. Kenward Elmslie. FTOS

Overhead, as the day breaks, a child is crying. (LL) Juan Ramón Jiménez. SpanPo; WoPoe, *tr.* by James Wright *Fr.* Ten Short Poems.

Overhead at night, above the planet. Alice Notley. PFTM-2 *Fr.* Désamère.

Overhead, the match burns out. Disregard. Ai. NoAM

Overheard. Denise Levertov. PoM

Overheard / a brother saying. July 27. Norman Jordan. NBV

Overheard in County Sligo. Gillian Clarke. HarvBoo; TCAWP

Overheard in the Love Hotel. Robert Polito. KGB

Overheard over S. E. Asia. Denise Levertov. BoWoP

Overjoyed at Soviet Russia's Entry into the War. Liu Ya-tzu. SuSp, *tr.* by Wu-Chi Liu

Overland to the Islands. Denise Levertov. PmAP; UnPo

Overlander, The. *Unknown.* NOBAu

Overlooking the Desert. Tu Fu. OHPC, *tr.* by Kenneth Rexroth

Overlooking the water, a desolate city. Sha-ch'eng, "Sand City." Yang Shih-ch'i. CoBLCP, *tr.* by Jonathan Chaves

Overmastering of the mud, The. 4 Variations On. Gerrit Kouwenaar. PFTM-2, *tr.* by Peter Nijmeijer

Overnight / a playful pony. Pony in Kukutis's Ear, A. Marcelijus Martinaitis. TWW, *tr.* by Laima Sruoginis

Overnight clouds begin to scatter. Inscribed on the Painting "Spring Dawn at Peach Blossom Spring" by Scholar Shang Te-fu. Chao Meng-fu. CoBLCP, *tr.* by Jonathan Chaves

Overnight Guest. Ramona Wilson. VoR

Overnight, very. Mushrooms. Sylvia Plath. FaBoWP; RB; WPOW

Overripe Fruit. Kasmuneh. TrJP

Overruled. John Greenleaf Whittier. NCAP

Overshot. Wythop Mill. Annie Foster. NLP

Overspread with Salty Soil. Tayankannanar. WoPoe, *tr.* by George L. Hart III

Overtaken. Michael McClintock. HA

Overtired branches are fragile. Fazil Abdulovich Iskander. TCRP

Overture. A. V. Christie. NAPBL

Overture. Zuhur Dixon. MAP, *tr.* by Patricia Alanah Byrne and Salma Khadra Jayyusi

Overture. Christopher Okigbo. PBMAP *Fr.* Heavensgate (1961).

Overture. Linda Pastan. MiVo

Overture for Bubble-Gum and Flute. Alistair Paterson. PeNZ

Overture to a Dance of Locomotives. William Carlos Williams. GM

Overture: Watermelon City. Elizabeth Alexander. NAPBL

Overturned Lake, The. Charles Henri Ford. SPE

Overwhelmed by mist. By mist. O. Mabson Southard. HA

Overwhelmed with passion. (LL) To the Tune "A Floating Cloud Crosses Enchanted Mountain." Huang O [*or* Huang Ho]. BoWoP; WoPoe, *tr.* by Chung Ling and Kenneth Rexroth

Ovid in Love. Ovid. *Fr.* Amores.

Ovid in Love: 2. Ovid. WoPoe, *tr.* by Derek Mahon *Fr.* Amores.

Ovid in the Third Reich. Geoffrey Hill. CABP; FaBoMo; HP; HarvBoo; NPeEn; NoAM; OxBEV

Ovid is the surest guide. Written in an Ovid. Matthew Prior. FaBoEE; OBCoV

Ovid, Meet a Metamorphodite. Jonathan Williams. PoM

Ovid's Banquet of Sense. George Chapman.

    Corinna Bathes. OxAEP-1

    Ear's Delight, The. NoSic

Ovid's Metamorphoses Book 6. Arthur Golding.

    "This Damsell was not famous for the place." PBRV

Ovid Twice Exiled. Jerzy Ficowski. PoSu, *tr.* by Frank J. Corliss, Jr. and Grazyna Sandel

Ovid would never have guessed how far. Brueghel in Naples. Dannie Abse. NIP-4

Ovids Elegies Book 1. Christopher Marlowe.

    "Now ore the sea from her old Love comes she." PBRV

Owdham Footbo' Ammon Wrigley. FaBoVe

Owed to New York. Byron Rufus Newton. NBLV

Owen's Bracelet. Robert Hayman. NOSC *Fr.* Owen's Epigrams.

Owen's Epigrams. Robert Hayman.

    Owen's Bracelet. NOSC

    Saturn's Three Sons. NOSC

Owen Tudor. Hugh Holland. AngWePo

Owen Tudor to Queen Katherine. Michael Drayton. NoSic *Fr.* England's Heroical Epistles.

Owens. Biographia Literaria. Joan Retallack. FTOS

Ower t'ills o Bingley. Blake Morrison. FaBoVe *Fr.* Ballad of the Yorkshire Ripper, The.

Owl. John Hollander. OWoS

Owl. George MacBeth [*or* Macbeth]. EmeKit

Owl. Robert Mezey. AWTN

Owl. Sylvia Plath. OWoS

Owl. Night Song of the Los Angeles Basin. Gary Snyder. UrbNat

Owl. So Chong-Ju. WoPoe, *tr. by* Kevin O'Rourke

Owl. Ted Walker. NOxBChV

Owl, The. Chia Yi. ColAnChi, *tr. by* J. R. Hightower

Owl, The. Walter De la Mare. OWoS; OxBSP

Owl, The. Tennyson. FaBoCh

Owl, The. Edward Thomas. AF; ChAP; EBEV; FaBoTw; GTBS-P; NAEL-5v2; NAEL-6v2; NIP-4; NOBE; NoAM; NoP-4; OBWVE; OWoS; OxAEP-2; PeFWW; PoE; RB; SCGP; TCAWP; TFi; TRP; UnPo

Owl, The. Robert Penn Warren. MoAmPo

Owl and the Eel and the Warming-Pan, The. Laura Elizabeth Richards. OBCA

Owl and the Lightning, The. Martín Espada. TouFir; UrbNat

Owl and the Mouse, The. Viktor Aleksandrovich Sosnora. TCRusP, *tr. by* Denis Johnson and Kathy Lewis

Owl and the Pussy-Cat, The. Edward Lear. BRP; CABP; FaBoCh; GTBS-P; NBLV; NOBE; NOxBChV; NPeEn; NTCP; NoP-4; OBCoV; OBSP; OTCP; OWoS; OxBoLi; PeLV; PoRA; TFi; TLR; TTTS; TriCat; WoPoe

(Owl and the Pussycat, The.) ChAP

Owl, The / Au / The owl. Song of the Owl. *Unknown.* APN-2, *tr. by* Henry Wadsworth Longfellow

Owl-Critic, The. James Thomas Fields. OBAL

Owl drifts slowly through the canyon where three flickers worry a pitted oak for grubs, An. Gary Young. GeoHom *Fr.* If He Had.

Owl expires, The! Death gave the dreadful word. On the Death of a Lady's Owl. Moses Mendes. TrJP

Owl hid his eyes, The. Candle. Penelope Rosemont. SurWo

Owl In Daytime, The. Thylias Moss. GT

Owl in the Sarcophagus, The. Wallace Stevens. FaBoMo

Owl Is an Only Bird of Poetry, An. Robert Duncan. NeAP; PoM

Owl-light in a tree house [1", 2", 3", or 4" of silence]. 3rd Light Poem: For Spencer, Beate, & Sebastian Holst—12 June 1962. Jackson Mac Low. PFTM-2

Owl of Minerva Takes Flight in the Evening, The. E. San Juan, Jr. ReBoTo

Owl of the Greenwood. Patricia Hubbell. OTCP

Owl of the wildwood I. Owl, The. Walter De la Mare. OWoS

Owl's Landscape, An. Jon Veinberg. GeoHom

Owl's Song. Ted Hughes. PAI

Owl shriek'd at thy birth, an evil sign, The. William Shakespeare. OxAEP-1 *Fr.* King Henry VI, Pt. III.

Owl / Who? Owl of the Greenwood. Patricia Hubbell. OTCP

Owl, The / whose home was in the hemlock. *Unknown.* STP

Owl winks in the shadows, An. Mother Earth: Her Whales. Gary Snyder. LCAP-2

Owl Wives. Nigel Wells. AngWePo

Owl Woman's Death Song. *Unknown.* BoWoP, *tr. by* Ruth Underhill

Owl Writes a Detective Story, The. Gavin Ewart. OBCoV

Owls. Charles Baudelaire. OWoS, *tr. by* Richard Howard

Owls. Louise Erdrich. TRP

Owls are calling / "Come, come." Issa. ZenPo, *tr. by* Takashi Ikemoto and Lucien Stryk

Owls mimic human speech. Meng Chiao. SuSp *Fr.* Laments of the Gorges.

Own. (LL) Offspring. Naomi Long Madgett. GT; SoSe-8

Owned by a heat:—*There is something in my heart like a burning Fire—shut up in my bones*—hear me, hear me. Of Joy Illimited: Polyphonic Soundings: Shore to Ship. Anna Rabinowitz. KGB

Owner of My Face, The. Rodney Hall. CBAP

Owner of the cherry blossoms, The. Utsu. JDP, *tr. by* Yoel Hoffmann

Owner of the drink of life. Water Woman. Catherine Obianuju Acholonu. HAWP

Owner of the field, The. Buson. EH, *tr. by* Robert Hass

Ownership. Ina Coolbrith. SWaP

Ownership. Lizette Woodworth Reese. MoAmPo

Ox, The. Russell Edson. RaBo

Ox-Bow. Donald Davie. DiPo

Ox bridle tossed, vows taken. Reito. ZenPo, *tr. by* Takashi Ikemoto and Lucien Stryk

Ox Cart Man. Donald Hall. LCAP-2; LoL

Ox Looks at Man, An. Carlos Drummond de Andrade. PoetW; TCLAP, *tr. by* Mark Strand

Ox of my childhood, steaming. Far Away and Long Ago. "Rubén Dario." PFTM-1; SpanPo, *tr. by* Denise Levertov

Ox-sized cauldron, Kleubotos gave, An. Anyte [*or* Anytes]. SaLy, *tr. by* Diane Rayor

Ox-Soldier, The. Oumar Ba. PBMAP

Ox-Tamer, The. Walt Whitman. RB

Ox-team and the automobile, The. Meeting, The. Harriet Monroe. IllVoic

Ox Turned Loose. Muso Soseki. EaWin, *tr. by* W. S. Merwin

Oxaitoq's Song. *Inuit Oral Tradition.* ErotSp, *tr. by* Sam Hamill

Oxaitoq's Song. *Unknown.* APN-2, *tr. by* Franz Boas

Oxcarts Are Now on Their Way, The. Juan Ramón Jiménez. SpanPo, *tr. by* Alice Sternberg

Oxen, The. Thomas Hardy. CABP; ChAP; ChrPo; EBEV; HAP; HarvBoo; InPK-6; MoBrPo; NOBE; NoAM; OBCP; OxAEP-2; OxBTC; PeECV; RB; SoSe-8; TFi; TOF; TRP; WeW-3

Oxen: Ploughing at Fiesole. Charles Tomlinson. OxBTC

Oxen's muzzles drip with bloody slaver, The. Razglednica (3). Miklós Radnóti. IQMS, *tr. by* Peter Zollman

Oxford. W. H. Auden. OxAEP-2

Oxford. Edward Dorn.

    "Blocks, The/ which are the buildings and walls." NOBA

    Comforted by Limestone. NOBA

Oxford-Act, The. Alicia D'Anvers.

    "Half Choakt ith' Dust of our lewd Town." EMWP

    True Relation of their Practice at Oxford Town when there an Act is, A. EMWP

Oxford Booklicker. Gwyneth Lewis. NeBl *Fr.* Parables & Faxes.

Oxford Canal. James Elroy Flecker. OxBTC

Oxford Cheese Ode. James McIntyre.

    "Ancient poets ne'er did dream, The." VerBaPo

Oxford Gardens. Charles McDonald. NLP

Oxford Hysteria of English Poetry, The. Adrian Mitchell. PeLV

Oxford, since late I left thy peaceful shore. To Oxford. Thomas Russell. CenSon; Son

Oxhead Temple. Ssu-k'ung Shu. ColAnChi; SuSp, *tr. by* Hellmut Wilhelm

Oxota. Lyn Hejinian.

    Book 2. PFTM-2

    "Truth is not precision but evidence." PFTM-2

Oxota: A Short Russian Novel. Lyn Hejinian.

    "No form at all—it's impossible to imagine its being." FTOS

Oya Now. Ifi Amadiume. NAfrP

Oye Mundo/Sometimes. Jesús Papoleto Meléndez. UnSA

Oyster, The. Francis Ponge. PFTM-1

Oyster, The. Sir Walter Scott. FaBoCh *Fr.* Antiquary, The.

Oyster: Deep sea suckled me, the waves sounded over me. Cynewulf. ASW *Fr.* Riddles (Exeter Book).

Oyster-Eaters, The. John Blight. NOBAu

Oyster that went to bed x-million years ago, An. Goodnight. John Ciardi. OBAL

Oyster, the size of an average pebble, is of more rugged appearance, The. Oyster, The. Francis Ponge. PFTM-1

Oystercatchers. Christopher Middleton. FaBoTw

Oystering. Richard Howard. NoAM

Oysters. Seamus Heaney. UV

Oysters. Jonathan Swift. ErotSp

Ozymandias. Shelley. AWP; BRP; CABP; CenSon; ChAP; ClHu; FaBoCh; GSo; GTBS-P; HAP; HeIP-4; InPK-6; MakPoe; NAEL-5v2; NAEL-6v2; NIL-7; NIP-4; NOBE; NPeEn; NoP-4; OPOU; OxBEV; OxBSo; PAI; PoE; PoPoPo; PoRA; RB; SCGP; SCV; SoSe-8; Son; TFi; UV

Ozymandias. Horace [*or* Horatio] Smith. CenSon

Ozymandias II. Howard Nemerov. Son

Ozymandias Revisited. Morris Gilbert Bishop. NBLV; UV

P

P.C. Plod versus the Dale St. Dog Strangler. Roger McGough. OBSP

P'eng-li commands three rivers. Sailing into the South Lake. Chan Fang-sheng. ChinPo, *tr. by* Yip Wai-lim

P'eng-ya Road. Tu Fu. CrYelRi, *tr. by* Sam Hamill

P'i-p'a begins the dance, midst changing new sounds, The. Wang Ch'ang-ling. SuSp *Fr.* Following the Army on Campaign.

P. M. T. Dorothy Porter. BMAP

P.O.E. Lincoln Kirstein. APT-2; PoWW

P.S. I Love You. Johnny Mercer. ReLy

P Word Poem, The. Leticia R. Benson. InTrad

Pablo. Dieter Weslowski. InvLad

Pablo Neruda. Jose Angel Figueroa. PueRic

Pachycephalosaurus. Richard Armour. ChAP

Pacific Crossing. Vince Gotera. ReBoTo

Pacific is nothing like its name, The. Elegy as Evening, as Exodus. James Harms. GeoHom

Pacific 1945–1995. Allen Curnow. HarvBoo

Pacifist, The. Joseph Hilaire Pierre Belloc. FaBoWar; OBCoV

Pacifists. George Woodcock. NOBC

Pacing. Raymond Roseliep. HA

Pacing toward what I know. (LL) Farm on the Great Plains, The. William Stafford. HAP; VGW

Pacing with bag-pipe in a bosky square. Caledonia. Anthony Powell. NOBL

Pack, The. Frank Prewett. HATNAP

Pack, clouds, away; and welcome, day[!]. Thomas Heywood. GTBS-P *Fr.* Rape of Lucrece, The.

Pack of wild colts went smoking by, The. In Fields of Sleepdreaming. Delmira Agustini. TANSG, *tr. by* Mark McCaffrey

Pack train, stage coach, pony express, climb over the mountain passes. James Henry Daugherty. HHAm *Fr.* Trail Breakers.

Pack Up Your Sins and Go to the Devil. Irving Berlin. ReLy

Package for Another World. Jemal Sharah. NOBAu

Pact, A. Robert Hass. BodElec

Pact, A. Ezra Pound. APT-1; ColAP; NAAL-2v2; NAAL-5; NOBA; NoAM; OxBA; PAI; TAP

Pact, The. P. S. Rege. OMIP, *tr. by* Vinay Dharwadker

Pact that we made was the ordinary pact, The. From a Survivor. Adrienne Rich. LoL; NALW; PAI

Pad, Pad. Stevie Smith. NPeEn; OxBEV

Padding down the street, the. No Shoes No Shirt No Service. Gary Snyder. BB

Paddlin' Madelin' Home. Harry Woods. ReLy

Paddling Song. *Unknown.* PBA, *tr. by* Max Exner

Paddock's a lonely space to stay inside, The. Gate's Open, The. John Blight. CBAP

Paddy Biran's Song. Paddy Biran. CBAP, *tr. by* R. M. W. Dixon

Paddy, I have but stol'n your living. Ebenezer Elliott. FaBoEE

Padmapani. Breyten Breytenbach. PoetW, *tr. by* André Brink

Padraic O'Conaire—Gaelic Storyteller. Frederick Robert Higgins. OBMV

Padre, The. Frank Ormsby. BiHa

Padre ministers to stumps of men, The. Remembrance. M. R. Peacocke. NLP

Paean to Eve's Apple. James Liddy. CIP-2

Paean to Place. Lorine Niedecker. APSN; APT-2

(Fish / fowl.) FTOS

Paean to the Dawn, A. Bayard Taylor. CAGL

Pagan Fires. Tawfiq Zayyad. MAP, *tr. by* Charles Doria and Sharif Elmusa

Pagan Isms, The. Claude McKay. BPo

Pagan's myths through marble lips are spoken, The. Worship. John Greenleaf Whittier. ChIV-2; NOCV

Paganly. Trinidad Tarrosa Subido. InvLi

Pagans wild confesse the bonds, The. Roger Williams. SCAP

Page dramatically estranged, nor lacking, A. Casting Sequences. Marjorie Welish. FTOS

Page from a Diary. Desmond O'Grady. NoAM

Page from the New Diary, A. Nida Fazli. OMIP, *tr. by* Baidar Bakht

Page is being beaten, A. Let's Say. Bob Perelman. PmAP

Page is printed, The. (LL) Thought-Fox, The. Ted Hughes. FaBoMo; HeIP-4; MakPoe; NPeEn; NoAM; SCV

Page of Shelley, A. Rod Willmot. HA

Page of Short Poems, A. Eugene McCarthy.

"Ending." HHAm

Page 1, line 8, for incorrigible read unredeemable. Errata. Jane Griffiths. NeBl

Page opens to snow on a field: boot-holed month, black hour, The. Elegy. Carolyn Forché. ExTi; LoL

Page to Commemorate Colonel Suárez, Victor at Junín, A. Jorge Luis Borges. PoetW, *tr. by* Alastair Reid

Pageant of the Seasons and the Months, The. Edmund Spenser. OxAEP-1 *Fr.* Faerie Queene, The.

Pages of the album, The. Sonatina in Yellow. Donald Justice. ColAP; LCAP-2

Pagget, a schoolboy, got a sword, and then. Upon Pagget. Robert Herrick. CaPo; FaBoCh

Pagliacci Pizza wants me. Sweet Red Peppers, Sun-Drieds, the Hearts of Artichokes. Martha Silano. AmPoNex

Pāhkahkos. Louise Bernice Halfe. ReEnLa

"Paid by my lord, one portrait, Lady Anne." Child with a Cockatoo. Rosemary Dobson. CBAP

Paid homage to them of unevent. (LL) Love Story, A. Robert Graves. FaBoTw; NAEL-5v2; NAEL-6v2

Pain. "Æ" MoBrPo

Pain. Thomas Edward Brown. SacPr

Pain. Mbella Sonne Dipoko. PBMAP

Pain. Enrique Gonzáles Martínez. TCLAP, *tr. by* Samuel Beckett

Pain. James Henry. NOBVV

Pain. Dionisio D. Martinez. OPRER

Pain. Lupenga Mphande. NAfrP

Pain. Elsie Robinson. PoToHe

Pain. Edith Södergran. WPOW, *tr. by* Samuel Charters

Pain. Edith Södergran. WPOW, *tr. by* Jaakko A. Ahokas

Pain. Charles Simic. BodElec

Pain. Alfonsina Storni. WPOW, *tr. by* Merrilee Antrim

Pain, The. Jeni Couzyn. HAWP

Pain, The. John Graham-Pole. BloBone

Pain and labor of oppression gave the Western world its birth. Pharaohs of Today, The. Lizelia Augusta Jenkins Moorer. CBWP-3

Pain—expands the Time. Emily Dickinson. APN-2

Pain Has an Element of Blank. Emily Dickinson. APN-2; ColAP; HeIP-4; MoAmPo; NAAL-2v1; NAAL-3; SWaP; TCAPo

Pain—I'm pro it. First Chance Twice. Fanny Howe. FTOS

Pain is a blacksmith. Blacksmith Pain. Otto Julius Bierbaum. AWP, *tr. by* Jethro Bithell

Pain of loving you, The. Young Wife, A. D. H. Lawrence. MoBrPo

Pain or Joy. Christina Georgina Rossetti. OWoS

Pain Strikes Sparks on Me, the Pain of Terezin. *Unknown, fr. Terezin Concentration Camp.* INSAB

Pain was pulled down over his eyes like a fool's hat. God, A. Ted Hughes. GI

Pain we have to suffer seems so broad, The. Belief. Ella Wheeler Wilcox. PWR

"Pain, who made thee?" thus I said once. Pain. James Henry. NOBVV

Painful husbandman with sweaty brows, The. George Wither. NOSC *Fr.* Collection of Emblemes, Ancient and Moderne, A.

Painful to look up. Underneath (1). Jorie Graham. BodElec

Painkillers. Thom Gunn. AllShUp; SwNoth

Pains and Gains. Edward de Vere, 17th Earl of Oxford. NoSic

Pains flip me around, The. Conception. Joseph Ceravolo. FTOS

Pains of insecurity surround me. Back Again, Home. Haki R. Madhubuti. BPo; NAAAL

Pains of Sleep, The. Samuel Taylor Coleridge. AWTN; FHYEP; NAEL-5v2; NAEL-6v2

Paint Castlemaine in colours that will hold. Andrew Marvell. OBSV *Fr.* Last Instructions to a Painter, The.

Paint last the King, and a dead shade of night. Andrew Marvell. OBSV *Fr.* Last Instructions to a Painter, The.

Paint me a cavernous waste shore. Sweeney Erect. T. S. Eliot. OxBTC; VGW

Paintbrush and lute-string or new modeling clay. Izhab-O-Rasai. N. M. Rashid. CarOv, *tr. by* Carolyn Kizer

Painted Ceiling, The. Amy Lowell. OBAL

Painted Cup, The. William Cullen Bryant. APN-1

Painted Cup, The. Michael Palmer. FTOS

Painted Head. John Crowe Ransom. APT-1; FuPo; NOBA; NoAM; OxBA

(Painting: A Head.) MoAmPo

Painted Lady, The. Margaret Danner. BPo

Painted, perfect, patient, I couch myself. Pornography. Angela Shaw. PuP-23

Painted with fancies of malignant power! (LL) Philip Freneau. NAAL-2v1; NAAL-3; TCAPo *Fr.* House of Night, The.

Painter. Zbigniew Herbert. AF, *tr. by* John Carpenter

Painter, A. Thomas Cole. APN-1

Painter, The. John Ashbery. EmeKit; HCAP; NOBA; NoP-4; PoE; PoPoPo; YaYoPo

Painter and poet, runner and disk-thrower. One of the Jews. Constantine P. Cavafy. TrJP

Painter Asks, The. John Yau. BodElec

Painter, by unmatch'd desert. Picture, The. Anacreon. AWP, *tr. by* Thomas Stanley

Painter descends into the world, The. In the Labyrinth of Elements. Duane Niatum. PoCoUp

Painter, encumbered with cash, A. Limerick. Thomas Thorneley. PeLi

Painter in the Lion Cage, The. Betti Alver. BoWoP, *tr. by* Willis Barnstone and Felix Oinas

Painter of Destinies, A. Molly Bendall. NAPBL

Painter's Son, The. Frank O'Hara. BodElec

Painters. Muriel Rukeyser. NAAL-5

Painting. Chang Yü. CoBLCP, *tr. by* Jonathan Chaves

Painting. Jane Hirshfield. ExTi

Painting. André Salmon. CuPo

Painting, The. Jack Hirschman. BodElec

Painting, The. *Vietnamese Oral Tradition.* CaDao, *tr. by* John Balaban

Painting: A Head. John Crowe Ransom. *See* Painted Head

Painting a Picture, The Tranquil Boat—Sent to Ko Ju-ching. Wen Cheng-ming. CoBLCP, tr. by Jonathan Chaves
Painting Bamboo, a Song. Po Chü-i. SuSp, tr. by Irving Lo
Painting Drunken Twilight. George Barlow. GT
Painting / (Frida Kahlo). Elizabeth Alexander. GT
Painting Her Nails. Yang Wei-chen. CoBLCP, tr. by Jonathan Chaves
Painting in the Style of Secretary Kao, A. Yün Shou-p'ing. CoBLCP, tr. by Jonathan Chaves
Painting, "Mist and Rain on the Spring River," by Hsiao Chao, The. Tai Piao-yüan. CoBLCP, tr. by Jonathan Chaves
Painting Mount Taranaki. David Eggleton. PeNZ
Painting my age with beauty of thy days. (LL) William Shakespeare. EBEV; OxAEP-1 Fr. Sonnets.
Painting not to be surpassed even by the brush of Master Wu!, A. (LL) To Go with Shih K'o's Painting of an Old Man Tasting Vinegar. Huang T'ing-chien. CoBCP; ColAnChi, tr. by Burton Watson
Painting of an endless field where grass waits, A. Picture on the Purple Wall, the. Steve Wilson. AmPoNex
Painting of Bamboo by Ni Yün-lin, A. Yang Chi. CoBLCP, tr. by Jonathan Chaves
Painting of Chrysanthemums in the Boneless Style of Hsü Ch'ung-ssu, A. Yün Shou-p'ing. CoBLCP, tr. by Jonathan Chaves
Painting of My Father. Padraic Fallon. NOIV
Painting of One Hundred Wild Geese, A. Tai Piao-yüan. CoBLCP, tr. by Jonathan Chaves
Painting of Peach Blossom Spring, A. Shen Chou. CoBLCP, tr. by Jonathan Chaves
Painting of People Strolling through a Pine Forest, A. Hsü Wei. CoBLCP, tr. by Jonathan Chaves
Painting of the Butterfly Dream by the Master Artist Li Tsai, A. Chu Yün-ming. CoBLCP, tr. by Jonathan Chaves
Painting of Water Buffaloes, A. Yang Shih-ch'i.
   "Herdboy returns, none too early, The." CoBLCP
Painting of Yams, A. Yün Shou-p'ing. CoBLCP, tr. by Jonathan Chaves
Painting "Solitary Fisherman by a Spring River" The. Ni Tsan. CoBLCP, tr. by Jonathan Chaves
Painting the Eaves. Tony Towle. PmAP
Painting the Gate. May Swenson. TLR; WeW-3
Painting the Nude. Eric Dyer. BloBone
Painting with Words. Nizar Qabbani.
   "Twenty years on the road of love." MAP
Painting would have been the best way to get things over, A. In Memoriam. Martin Johnston. BMAP; NOBAu
Paintings. Chang Yü. CoBLCP, tr. by Jonathan Chaves
Paintings. Pien Kung. CoBLCP, tr. by Jonathan Chaves
Paintings of Fishermen. Wu Chen. CoBLCP, tr. by Jonathan Chaves
Paintings of Ladies Engaged in Four Springtime Occupations. Yang Chi. Springtime Embroidery. CoBLCP, tr. by Jonathan Chaves
Paintings of Various Subjects by Fang Jih-sheng: Baby Chicks Following Their Mother. Pien Kung. CoBLCP, tr. by Jonathan Chaves
Paintings on My Wall Have Been Damaged by the Weather, The. T'ang Hsien-tsu. CoBLCP, tr. by Jonathan Chaves
Paintings with stiff. Primitives. Dudley Randall. BPo; NBV
Paints one himself in oil. (LL) Two Artists, The. Constance Naden. VWP; ViWPN
Pair of blackbirds, A. In Modern Dress. Craig Raine. NoAM
Pair of brothers love me, A. Strato [or Straton]. GrAn
Pair of clouded yellows, A. Exits. Patricia Pogson. NLP
Pair of feet, born so nimble, A. Street Angel, The. K'o Chia Tsang. WoPoe, tr. by Kai-yu Hsu
Pair of Glasses, A. Savithri Rajeevan. OMIP, tr. by K. Ayyappa Paniker
Pair of golden orioles, A. Far Up the River. Tu Fu. OHPC, tr. by Kenneth Rexroth
Pair of green-painted eyebrows, A. Wang Chien. SuSp Fr. Palace Poems.
Pair of Shoes, A. Theodore Weiss. NoAM
Pair of soft, black eyes, A. Home Greeting, A. Priscilla Jane Thompson. CBWP-2
Pair of strange new birds in the maple tree, A. "Never Apologize; Never Explain." Philip Whalen. BB
Paired Lives. William Robert Rodgers. CIP-2
Paisleys squirm with spermatozoa. Neckties. Liz Lochhead. NePenScot; OBCoV
Paiute Ponies. Jim Barnes. CDW
Pajaro the men thigh deep in mud. Song of Pajaro. Jeff Tagami. OpBo
Palabrarmás. Cecilia Vicuña.
   "I saw a word in the air." TANSG, tr. by Suzanne Jill Levine
Palabras Grandiosas. Bayard Taylor. OBAL

Palace, The. Charles Stuart Calverley. EBVV
Palace at dusk, the pearl blind is lowered. Jade Steps Plaint. Hsieh T'iao. SuSp, tr. by Ronald C. Miao
Palace-Burner, The. Sarah Morgan Bryan Piatt. NCAP; SWaP
Palace Cook's Tale. Joan Aiken. NOxBChV
Palace girls up early. Wang Chien. SuSp Fr. Palace Poems.
Palace great is builded rich and round. Torquato Tasso. NoSic Fr. Godfrey of Bulloigne; or, The Recoverie of Jerusalem [Gerusalemme Liberata].
Palace in smoky light. Ezra Pound. APT-1 Fr. Cantos.
Palace of Art, The. Tennyson. NOBRP
   "One seem'd all dark and red—a tract of sand." UnPo
Palace of Fine Arts in San Francisco, The. Fidelito Cortes. ReBoTo
Palace of Pleasant Regard, The. The Lady of the Assembly. WPE Fr. Assembly of Ladies, The.
Palace of Rocks, THe. Yüan Chieh. SuSp, tr. by William H. Nienhauser
Palace of the Gnomes. Maria Gowen Brooks. APN-1 Fr. Zophiël [or, the Bride of Seven].
Palace Poem. Chu Ch'ing-yü. SuSp, tr. by Irving Y. Lo
Palace Poem. Ts'ao Ching-chao. WoPoe, tr. by Nancy Hodes and Tung Yuan-fang
Palace Poem. Wang Ya. SuSp, tr. by Irving Y. Lo
Palace Poems. Wang Chien.
   "At home I loved to wear old clothes." SuSp
   "Early autumn, white rabbits." SuSp
   "Her silken gown rustles." SuSp
   "Long the flimsy skirts." SuSp
   "Pair of green-painted eyebrows, A." SuSp
   "Palace girls up early." SuSp
   "Red lantern calls the spring clouds from my sleep, A." SuSp
   "Spring breeze blows the rain, A." SuSp
   "Wanting to welcome the emperor." SuSp
Palace Song. Wang Chien. CoBCP, tr. by Burton Watson
Palace with revolving doors was mine, The. Atameros. John Beevers. SPE
Palaces and hovels, the leaden eye of the authorities. Trotsky in Mexico. Dmitry [or Dmitrii] Vasil'evich Bobyshev. ItGoST, tr. by Michael Van Walleghen
Palaestral Study, A. Edward Cracroft Lefroy. CAGL
Palais des Arts. Louise Glück. VCAP
Palaver is finished, The. (LL) T. S. Eliot. NAEL-5v2; NAEL-6v2; NoAM Fr. Landscapes.
Palaver is silly. (LL) Air: Sentir avec Ardeur. Marie-Françoise-Catherine de, Marquise de Boufflers Beauveau. CTC; WPOW, tr. by Ezra Pound
Pale amber sunlight falls across. Autumnal. Ernest Christopher Dowson. EBVV
Pale Ant. Ellease Southerland. GT
Pale as the morning star. White Stallion, The. Abu-I-Salt Umayyah. WoPoe, tr. by Cola Franzen
Pale beech and pine-tree blue. In a Wood. Thomas Hardy. PAI
Pale blossoms, each balanced on a single jointed stem. Carnations. Theodore Roethke. BLT
Pale Blue Casket, The. Oliver Pitcher. TTY
Pale Blue Line in a Forced Episode, I Cut a Hole in the Flag of the Republic. Simone Yoyotte. SurWo, tr. by Myrna Bell Rochester
Pale brows, still hands and dim hair. Lover Mourns for the Loss of Love, The. W. B. Yeats. WeW-3
Pale Cynthia! lovely goddess of the night. Thoughts in Midnight Hours. Fanny Crosby. SWaP
Pale dawn moon, A. Lorraine Ellis Harr. HA
Pale, drooping girl and the swaggering soldier, The. Just an Old Sweet Song. Donagh MacDonagh. CIP-2
Pale Ebenezer thought it wrong to fight. Pacifist, The. Joseph Hilaire Pierre Belloc. FaBoWar; OBCoV
Pale grey, her guns hooded, decks clear of all impediment. H. M. S. Hero. Michael Roberts. OxBTC
Pale Heinrich he came sauntering by. Window-Glance, The. Heinrich Heine. AWP, tr. by John Todhunter
Pale moon disappears, The. In the Shadows of the Wu-t'ung Tree. Unknown. CrYelRi, tr. by Sam Hamill
Pale mornings, and. Magpie's Shadow, The. Yvor Winters. APT-2
Pale nuns of St. Joseph are here, The. Island of the Three Marias. Alberto A. Ríos. NoAM
Pale ocean rock! that, like a phantom shape. Rockall. Epes Sargent. APN-1
Pale ravener of horrible meat. (LL) Maldive Shark, The. Herman Melville. APN-2; ColAP; NAAL-2v1; NAAL-3; NCAP; NOBA; NoP-4; OxBA; PAI; PoE; RB; TAP; TCAPo
Pale, struggling blossoms of mankind. Our Father. Eliza Cook. VWP
Pale water flowers. Coralie. Frederick Goddard Tuckerman. NCAP
Paleness of hunger, The. Mutineer's Ballad, The. Peter Kocan. NOBAu

Palette of Grief.   Leonid Gubanov.   TCRP, *tr.* by Bradley Jordan
Palimpsest, A.   "Michael Field."   VWP; ViWPN
Palindrome.   Lisel Mueller.   WeW-3
Palinode.   "Ern Malley."   BMAP
Palinode.   Oliver St. John Gogarty.   OBMV
Palinode, A.   Edmund Bolton.   NoSic
Pall.   Laura Kasischke.   AmPoNex
Pall Hanging over Manila.   Mila D. Aguilar.   ReBoTo
Palladium.   Matthew Arnold.   GTBS-P
Pallas and / golden-shoed Hera.   Rufinus.   GrAn
Pallid and moonlike in the smog.   Man Can Complain, Can't He?, A.   Ogden Nash.   NBLV
Pallid Cuckoo.   David Campbell.   CBAP
Pallid cuckoo, The.   Late Winter.   James McAuley.   BMAP
Pallid Harrier.   Colin Simms.   Oth
Pallid young man with an ardent expression.   To a Young Poet.   Valery [*or* Valerii] Yakovlevich [*or* Iakovlevich] Bryusov [*or* Briusov].   TCRP, *tr.* by April FitzLyon
Pallor.   Agnes Mary Frances Robinson.   NOBVV; VWP
Palm.   Roy Campbell.   MoBrPo
Palm at the end of the mind, The.   Of Mere Being.   Wallace Stevens.   APT-1; HCAP; NoP-4; WoPoe
Palm leaf of Mary Magdalene.   Cheryl Clarke.   GLP; WiU
Palm leaf of Mary Magdalene. (LL)   Palm Leaf of Mary Magdalene.   Cheryl Clarke.   GLP; WiU
Palm of the hand, The. / Is not aware of dying as.   Fumi Saito.   BoWoP; WoPoe, *tr.* by Edith Marcombe Shiffert and Yuki Sawa
Palm Reader, The.   Nicholas Christopher.   NoP-4
Palm-Sunday Hymn, A.   William Herebert.   MiEL
Palm Sunday: Naples.   Arthur Symons.   PeVV
Palm—the Vine—the Cedar—each hath power.   Olive Tree, The.   Felicia Dorothea Hemans.   CenSon
Palm Tree, A.   Rosario Castellanos.   TCLAP, *tr.* by Myralyn F. Allgood
Palm Tree, The.   Abd-ar-Rahman I.   AWP, *tr.* by J. B. Trend
Palm-tree, The.   Felicia Dorothea Hemans.   ViWPN
Palm-tree, The.   Henry Vaughan.   ESCV
Palm-tree, The.   John Greenleaf Whittier.   NCAP
Palm Tree King.   John Agard.   EmeKit; Oth
Palm-trees do have.   Cloud Rains.   Oumarou Watta.   NAfrP
Palmer, The.   Robert Greene.   NoSic
Palmer's Ode, The.   Robert Greene.   CTC; NoSic; SCGP   *Fr.* Never Too Late.
Palms.   June Sylvester.   PasH
Palms, The.   David Knight.   MoCV
Palms and Myrtles.   Eleazar ben Kalir.   TrJP, *tr.* by Alice Lucas
Palo Alto: the Marshes.   Robert Hass.   GeoHom
Palsy shakes my pen, while I intend, A.   To His Honored Friend Thomas Stanley Esquire, Upon His Elegant Poems.   James Shirley.   BeJo
Paltry Nude Starts on a Spring Voyage, The.   Wallace Stevens.   HCAP
Pampas grass, all dry.   Hakukin.   JDP, *tr.* by Yoel Hoffmann
Pampas grass, now dry.   Shoro.   JDP, *tr.* by Yoel Hoffmann
Pampered Philainion stabbed me, The.   Asclepiades.   GrAn
Pamphilia's Sonnet.   Mary Sidney Wroth, Countess of Montgomery.   WPE   *Fr.* Urania.
Pamphilia to Amphilanthus.   Mary Sidney Wroth, Countess of Montgomery.
  "All night I weep[e], all day I cry, Ay me[e]."   NOSC
  "Am I thus conquered [*or* conquer'd]? have I lost the powers."   CABP; NAEL-5v1; NAEL-6v1; NAEL-7v1; NOSC
  "Be[e] you all pleased [*or* pleas'd]? your pleasures grieve not[t] me[e]."   BWW; NOSC
  ("Cloyed with the torments of a tedious night.")   BASC
  "Come darkest night, be[e]coming sorrow best."   BASC; EMWP; NOSC
  Crown[e] of Sonnets [*or* Sonetts] Dedicated to Love, A.
    ("And be in his brave court a glorious light.")   BASC
    "And burn[e], yet[t] burning you will love the smart."   BASC
    ("Be from the Court of Love, and Reason torn.")   BASC
    ("Be given to him who triumphs in his right.")   BASC
    ("But where they may return with honour's grace.")   BASC
    "Except my hart which you beestow'd before."   EMWP
    ("Except my heart which you bestowed before.")   BASC
    "Free from all fogs but[t] shining fair[e], and clear [*or* cleere]."   BASC; EMWP
    ("He may our prophet, and our tutor prove.")   BASC; NoP-4
    ("He that shuns love doth love himself the less.")   BASC
    "His flames ar[e] joy[e]s, his bands true lovers' might."   BASC
    "How blest be[e] they then, who his favo[u]rs prove."   BASC
    "Is to leave all, and take the thread of love."   BASC; EMWP
    Sonnet 1: "In this strang[e] labyrinth [*or* labourinth] how shall I turn[e]?"

      BASC; CABP; EMWP; NAEL-5v1; NAEL-6v1; NAEL-7v1; NPeEn; NoP-4; PBRV
    Sonnet 2: "Is to leave all, and take the thread of love."   BASC; EMWP
    Sonnet 3: "His flames ar[e] joy[e]s, his bands true lovers' might."   BASC
    Sonnet 5: "And burn[e], yet[t] burning you will love the smart."   BASC
    Sonnet 7: "How blest be[e] they then, who his favo[u]rs prove."   BASC
    Sonnet 11: "Unprofitably pleasing, and unsound."   BASC
    Sonnet 13: "Free from all fogs but[t] shining fair[e], and clear [*or* cleere.]"   BASC; EMWP
    Sonnet 14: "Except my hart which you beestow'd before.".   EMWP
    "Unprofitably pleasing, and unsound."   BASC
  (Cupid Lost.)   LW
  ("Dear famish not what you yourself gave food.")   BASC
  "Deare cherish this, and with it[t] my soules will."   BWW
  "Dearest [*or* Deerest] if I by my deserving."   EMWP
  "False [*or* Faulce] hope which feeds but[t] to destroy, and spill."   BASC; NAEL-5v1; NAEL-6v1; NAEL-7v1; PEW
  "Fie [*or* Fy] tedious Hope, why do[e] you still rebel[l]?"   NOSC
  "How fast thou fliest, O Time, on loves swift wings."   NOSC
  "How like a fire doth love increase in me[e]."   NOSC
  ("I but chameleon-like would live, and love.") (LL)   BASC
  "If ever love had force in huma[i]ne bre[a]st?"   BASC; BWW
  "Juno still jealous[e] of her husband Jove."   OxBSo
  "Late in the Forest I did Cupid See."   NPeEn; OxBSo; PBRV
  "Led by the pow'r [*or* powre] of grief[e], to wailings [*or* waylings] brought."   PEW
  "Like to the Indians, scorched with the sun[ne]."   BASC; EMWP; NOSC
  "Love a child is ever crying [*or* criing]."   BASC; LW; NAEL-6v1; NAEL-7v1; NOSC; NoP-4; OxBEV
  "Love leave to urge, thou know'st thou hast the hand."   BASC; Son
  "Love like a jugler, comes to play his prize [*or* prise]."   EMWP
  ("My heart is lost. What can I now expect?")   OxBSo
  "My muse now hap[p]ly, lay thy self to rest."   BASC; NAEL-7v1
  "My pain[e], still smothered [*or* smother'd] in my grieved bre[a]st."   NAEL-6v1; NAEL-7v1; NOSC; PEW
  "Night, welcome art thou to my mind destrest."   NoP-4
  ("No time, no room, no thought, or writing can.")   PEW
  "Ô[h] strive not[t] still to heap[e] disdain[e] on me[e]."   NOSC
  "O[h] me[e], the time is [*or* has] come to part."   NOSC
  Song 2: "All night I weep[e], all day I cry, Ay me[e]."   NOSC
  Song 4: "Sweetest love return[e] again[e]."   NAEL-6v1; NAEL-7v1
  Song: "Dearest [*or* Deerest] if I by my deserving."   EMWP
  Song: "Love a child is ever crying [*or* criing]."   BASC; LW; NAEL-6v1; NAEL-7v1; NOSC; NoP-4; OxBEV
  Song: "O[h] me[e], the time is [*or* has] come to part."   NOSC
  Sonnet 1: "When night's black mantle could most darknes[s] prove."   BASC; CABP; MakPoe; NAEL-5v1; NAEL-6v1; NAEL-7v1; Son
  Sonnet 2: "Late in the Forest I did Cupid See."   NPeEn; OxBSo; PBRV
  Sonnet 2: "Love like a jugler, comes to play his prize [*or* prise]."   EMWP
  Sonnet 3: "Juno still jealous[e] of her husband Jove."   OxBSo
  Sonnet 6: "My pain[e], still smothered [*or* smother'd] in my grieved bre[a]st."   NAEL-6v1; NAEL-7v1; NOSC; PEW
  Sonnet 6: "Ô[h] strive not[t] still to heap[e] disdain[e] on me[e]."   NOSC
  Sonnet 7: "Love leave to urge, thou know'st thou hast the hand."   BASC; Son
  Sonnet 8: "Led by the pow'r [*or* powre] of grief[e], to wailings [*or* waylings] brought."   PEW
  Sonnet 9: "Be[e] you all pleased [*or* pleas'd]? your pleasures grieve not[t] me[e]."   BWW; NOSC
  Sonnet 9: "My muse now hap[p]ly, lay thy self to rest."   BASC; NAEL-7v1
  Sonnet 14: "Am I thus conquered [*or* conquer'd]? have I lost the powers."   BASC; CABP; NAEL-5v1; NAEL-6v1; NAEL-7v1; NOSC
  Sonnet 19: "Come darkest night, be[e]coming sorrow best."   BASC; EMWP; NOSC
  Sonnet 21: "When last I saw thee, I did not[t] thee see."   PEW
  Sonnet 22: "Like to the Indians, scorched with the sun[ne]."   BASC; EMWP; NOSC
  Sonnet 23: "When every one to pleasing pastime hies."   BASC; PBRV; WPE
  Sonnet 26: "Deare cherish this, and with it[t] my soules will."   BWW
  Sonnet 27: "Fie [*or* Fy] tedious Hope, why do[e] you still rebel[l]?"   NOSC
  Sonnet 32: "How fast thou fliest, O Time, on loves swift wings."   NOSC
  Sonnet 34: "Take heed mine eyes, how you your look[e]s do[e] cast."   BASC; NAEL-7v1; PEW
  Sonnet 35: "False [*or* Faulce] hope which feeds but[t] to destroy, and spill."   BASC; NAEL-5v1; NAEL-6v1; NAEL-7v1; PEW
  Sonnet 37: "Night, welcome art thou to my mind destrest."   NoP-4
  Sonnet 38: "What pleasure can a bannish'd creature have."   EMWP
  Sonnet 42: "If ever love had force in huma[i]ne bre[a]st?"   BASC; BWW

Sonnet 48: "How like a fire doth love increase in me[e]." NOSC

"Sweetest love return[e] again[e]." NAEL-6v1; NAEL-7v1

"Take heed mine eyes, how you your look[e]s do[e] cast." BASC; NAEL-7v1; PEW

"What pleasure can a bannish'd creature have." EMWP

"When every one to pleasing pastime hies." BASC; PBRV; WPE

"When last I saw thee, I did not[t] thee see." PEW

"When night's black mantle could most darknes[s] prove." BASC; CABP; MakPoe; NAEL-5v1; NAEL-6v1; NAEL-7v1; Son

Pan and the Cherries. Paul Fort. AWP, *tr. by* Jethro Bithell

Pan and the Nymphs. Glaukos. GrAn, *tr. by* Dudley Fitts

Pan as the Son of Penelope. Joanne Kyger. BB

Pan Asks about Daphnis. Diodorus Zonas. GrAn, *tr. by* Alistair Elliot

Pan came out of the woods one day. Pan with Us. Robert Frost. OxBA

Pan Cogito on Virtue. Zbigniew Herbert. PoSu, *tr. by* Adam Czerniawski

Pan, Echo, and the Satyr. Moschus. OBVE, *tr. by* Percy Bysshe Shelley

Pan in Battle. *Unknown.* PeNZ

Pan loved his neighbour Echo—but that child. Pan, Echo, and the Satyr. Moschus. OBVE, *tr. by* Percy Bysshe Shelley

Pan Piping. Plato. FaBoEE, *tr. by* Thomas Stanley

Pan's Song. John Lyly. *See* Midas

Pan's/ spring rain. Jonathan Williams. VGW *Fr.* Mahler.

Pan's Syrinx. John Lyly. NPeEn; NoSic; SCGP *Fr.* Midas.

Pan's Syrinx was a girl[e] indeed. John Lyly. NPeEn; NoSic; SCGP *Fr.* Midas.

Pan with Us. Robert Frost. OxBA

Panama. Patrick Sylvain. InTrad

Pancake Collector, The. Jack Prelutsky. OBCA; OxIBACP

Pancake Day. Mother Goose. LB; OxNR; ReMoGo

Pancake with its burnt side down, A. Cakes Continue to Rise. Rick Agran. AmPoNex

Pancakes for the Queen of Babylon. Peter Levi.

"City built in darkness and cold air, A." CRP

Panchatantra, The. *Unknown.* AWP, *tr. by* Arthur Ryder

Pandora and the Moon. Merrill Moore. MoAmPo

Pandora's Box. Sarah Kirsch. PFTM-2, *tr. by* Wayne Kvam

Pandora's Songs. Trumbull Stickney. APN-2 *Fr.* Prometheus Pyrphoros.

Pane of glass and fifty yards away, A. (LL) West Strand Visions. James Simmons. ModIr; PBCIP

Panegyric to Sir Lewis Pemberton, A. Robert Herrick. CaPo

Panes of light cracking. Wet Night, A. Richard Ryan. CIP-2

Pang of the long century of rains, The. Lament of Edward Blastock, The. Dame Edith Sitwell. OBMV

Pangloss's Song: A Comic-Opera Lyric. Richard Wilbur. NBLV; NoAM

Pangolin, The. Marianne Craig Moore. APT-1; HAP; NOBA; NoAM

Pangur Ban. *Unknown.* TriCat, *tr. by* Robin Ernest William Flower

Pangur Bán. *Unknown.* FaBoCh; RB

Pangur Bán. *Unknown.* NOIV

Panic. Archibald MacLeish. MoAmPo

Panic Grass. Charles Upton.

"When I was very young." CLPP

Panic of Birds, The. Olena Kalytiak Davis. AmPoNex

Panmongolism. Vladimir Sergeievich Solovyov [*or* Solov'iov]. TCRP, *tr. by* April FitzLyon

Pannyra of the Golden Heel. Albert Samain. AWP, *tr. by* James Elroy Flecker

Panope. Dame Edith Sitwell. MoBrPo

Panopticon. Steve McCaffery.

"Homines qouque si taceant, vocem invenient libri." FTOS

Panorama. Romelia Alarcón de Folgar. TANSG, *tr. by* Alison Ridley

Panorama 2. Romelia Alarcón de Folgar. TANSG, *tr. by* Alison Ridley

Pansie, Thistle, all with prickles set, The. William Browne (1591–1643). NPeEn *Fr.* Britannia's Pastorals.

Pansy who lived in Khartoum, A. Limerick. *Unknown.* PeLi

Pantheist's Song of Immortality, The. Constance Naden. VWP; ViWPN

Panther, The. Ogden Nash. OBAL; OBCA; OxIBACP

Panther, The. Rainer Maria Rilke. WoPoe, *tr. by* William DeWitt Snodgrass

Panther, The. Rainer Maria Rilke. AuPH, *tr. by* Lowell A. Bangerter

Panther, The. Rainer Maria Rilke. NAWM-7v2, *tr. by* Stephen Mitchell

Panther, The. *Unknown.* ASW, *tr. by* Kevin Crossley-Holland

Panther and Peacock. Gwen Harwood. CBAP

Panther Man. James A. Emanuel. BPo; NBV

Panties on the clothesline lingering mist. George Swede. HA

Pantisocracy. Samuel Taylor Coleridge. CenSon

Pantomime. Paul Verlaine. AWP, *tr. by* Arthur Symons

Pantoum. John Ashbery. MakPoe

Pantoum of the Great Depression. Donald Justice. MakPoe

Pantoumstone for a Dying Breed. Beth Lisick. AmPoNex

Pantoun for Chinese Women. Shirley Lim. FSt

Pants. Lisa Vice. GLP

Pants blown off his seat, The. (LL) Jubilation T. Cornpone. Johnny Mercer. OBAL; OBCoV

Papa. Barbara Marsh. Prnts

Papa drank and ate. Ironing. Nellie Wong. FFC

Papa John. Jorge de Lima. TTY, *tr. by* John Nist

Papa Love Baby. Stevie Smith. NALW

Papa's Letter. *Unknown.* WeW-3

Papá smelled of the fine *tabaco* and the dried blood. Malibú, El. Richard Blanco. AmPoNex

Paparazzi, The. Ai. ExTi

Paper Anarchist Addresses the Shade of Nancy Ling Perry. George Woodcock. NOBC

Paper Anniversary. Muriel Rukeyser. NoAM

Paper arks drift on a concrete lake. Park, A. Theo Sontrop. TuT, *tr. by* Ruth Hooley

Paper come out—done strewed de news. Scottsboro. *Unknown.* InPK-6

Paper Doll. Johnny S. Black. ReLy

Paper gardens are perhaps richer in memories than, The. Accessories shop, The. Pierre McOrlan. MFP, *tr. by* Martin Sorrell

Paper Kite, The. Samuel Bowden.

"Kite, completed thus, is borne along, The." NOEC

Paper Matches. Paulette Jiles. NIL-7; NIP-4; NOBC

Paper Memorial Stone. Sang Yi. PFTM-1

Paper Nautilus, The. Marianne Craig Moore. FaBoWP; HarvBoo; MakPoe; NAAL-5; NALW; VGW

Paper on Humor. Andrei Codrescu. PmAP

Paper Soldier. Bulat Shalvovich Okudzhava. TCRP, *tr. by* Albert C. Todd

Paper tigers roar at noon, The. Tiger. Alec Derwent Hope. OxBC; RB

Paper was pale, The. Etching. Samuel Greenberg. APT-1

Papermill. Joseph Kalar. APT-2

Papers have been sold. In them it's all made clear, The. German Borisovich Plisetsky [*or* Plisetskii]. TCRP

Papers on my desk out of hand, The. Example, The. Paul Zimmer. OPRER

Papers say the heat is here to stay, The. Nocturne. David Barber. AmPoNex

Paperweight, The. Gjertrud Schnackenberg. VCAP

Paphnutius. Hroswitha von Gandersheim (or, Hroswitha).

"I bring you a goat." WPOW

Papi worked the factory. Workers. David Hernandez. IllVoic

Papistry Storm'd. William Tennant.

"I sing the steir, strabush, and strife." NePenScot

Sang First. NePenScot

Papyrus. Ezra Pound. APT-1; PFTM-1

Par avion. Aerogrammes. Russell Leong. OpBo

Parable. Bob Orr. PeNZ

Parable. Richard Wilbur. HarvBoo; OxBSP

Parable, A. Ch'en Tzu-lung. SuSp, *tr. by* Irving Y. Lo

Parable, A. Li K'ai-hsien. CoBLCP; ColAnChi, *tr. by* Jonathan Chaves

Parable of the Blind, The. William Carlos Williams. LCAP-2; SAmP *Fr.* Pictures from Brueghel.

Parable of the Boy and the Polar Bear. Roger Fanning. NAPBL

Parable of the Four-Poster. Erica Jong. LW

Parable of the Good Seed, The. Bible, *N.T.* InPK-6 *Fr.* St. Matthew.

Parable of the Old Men and the Young, The. Wilfred Owen. ChIV-1; HarvBoo; PAI

Parable of the Sower, The. Stephen Mitchell. GI

Parable of the Unfaithful Wife. Rosario Castellanos. TANSG, *tr. by* Magda Bogin

Parables, I. Antonio Machado Ruiz. STV, *tr. by* John Frederick Nims

Parables & Faxes. Gwyneth Lewis.

"And this, too, is love." NeBl

Chernobyl Icon. NeBl

"I saw a vision." NeBl

Oxford Booklicker. NeBl

"So the Lord said: Eat this scroll." NeBl

Parabola. Alec Derwent Hope. NOBAu

Parabola of the Heart, The. Jolanda Insana.

"I am unable to recapture the allbody poured." CItWP, *tr. by* Cinzia Sartini Blum and Lara Trubowitz

Parabolas of grief, the hills are never. In Africa. Roy Fuller. PoWW

Paracelsus. Robert Browning.

"Heap cassia, sandal-buds and stripes." OBEV

"Over the sea our galleys went." OBEV

Song: "Heap cassia, sandal-buds and stripes." OBEV

Thus the Mayne Glideth. OBEV

Wanderers, The. OBEV

Parachute Men. Lenrie Peters. PBMAP

Parachutes, My Love, Could Carry Us Higher. Barbara Guest. NeAP

Parachutist. Dylan Thomas.
"I shall never forget his blue eye." UV

Parade. Robert Creeley. BodElec

Parade. Rachel Lyman Field. OBCA *Fr.* Circus Garland, A.

Parade's End. Barbara Guest. PoM

Paradice on earth is found, A. Michael Prayton. PBRV *Fr.* Muses Elizium, The.

Paradigm. Babette Deutsch. TrJP

Paradigm, The. Allen Tate. NOBA

Parading with the Veterans of Foreign Wars. Carter Revard. OPRER

Paradise. Chora. JDP, *tr.* by Yoel Hoffmann

Paradise. Peter Damian. MLL, *tr.* by Helen Waddell

Paradise. Jill Alexander Essbaum. NAPBL

Paradise. George Herbert. AngWePo; BASC; GeHe; NOSC

Paradise. George Herbert. SacPr

Paradise. Immanuel di Roma. TrJP, *tr.* by J. Chotzner

Paradise. John Milton. NOSC *Fr.* Paradise Lost.

Paradise. Ron Silliman.
"Sentence in the evening. Today the boxscores are green. Tonight, A." PmAP

Paradise. Yaitsu. JDP, *tr.* by Yoel Hoffmann

Paradise Illustrated. Dennis Joseph Enright.
"Days of Adam were 930 years, The." OBCoV
"Rich soil," remarked the Landlord." OBCoV
"Why didn't we think of clothes before?" OBCoV

Paradise Lost. John Milton.
Book I. FHYEP; NAEL-5v1; NAEL-6v1; OxAEP-1
"Anon out of the earth a fabric huge." MakPoe
"Ascending pile, The." NOSC
"If thou beest he; but O how fall'n! how chang'd." SCV
Immortal Hate. NOBE
(Induction, The.) PoE
Mulciber. NOSC
"Next came one / Who mourn'd in earnest, when the Captive Ark." EBEV
"Of Man's First Disobedience, and the Fruit." EBEV; NAWM-5v1; NAWM-7v1; NIL-7; NIP-4; NOSC; NPeEn; OxBEV; PeECV; SCV; TOF
(Satan's Summons.) NOSC
(Satan with his Angels now fallen into Hell.) NPeEn
"There the companions of his fall, o'erwhelmed." NOBE
Book II. FHYEP; NAEL-5v1; NAEL-6v1; OxAEP-1
"High on a throne of royal state, which far." NIL-7; NIP-4
"Into this wild abyss." NOSC
"Meanwhile [*or* Mean while] the Adversary of God and Man." EBEV; OBNV
Occupations of Hell. NOSC
Satan's Journey. NOSC
Sin and Death. EBEV; OBNV
"Thus saying, from her side the fatal Key." EBEV
"Thus saying rose / The monarch, and prevented all reply." NOSC
Book III.
"For Man will hearken to his glozing lies." InvLi
Hail, Holy Light[!]. NAEL-5v1; NAEL-6v1; PeECV; SCV; TOF
"Hail holy Light, offspring [*or* offspring] of Heav'n [*or* Heaven] first-born." NAEL-5v1; NAEL-6v1; PeECV; SCV; TOF
(Holy Light.) NOBE
(Invocation to Light.) NOSC
(Light.) OBEV
"Now had th' Almighty Father from above." NIL-7; NIP-4
"Thus they in Heav'n, above the starry Sphear." EBEV
Book IV.
Adam and Eve. PeECV
Eden. PeECV
Eve to Adam. UV; WoPoe
"In narrow room nature's whole wealth, yea more." NOSC
"Into thir inmost bower." TOF
("Led on the eternal spring.") (LL) OBGa
"Me miserable! which way shall I fly." PoE
"O for that warning voice which he who saw." NAEL-5v1; NAWM-7v1; OxAEP-1
Paradise. NOSC
(Paradise Lost.) OBGa
Prospect of Eden, The. NAEL-5v1; NAWM-7v1; OxAEP-1
"So passed they naked on, nor shunned the sight." PeECV

"Thus talking hand in hand alone they pass'd." EBEV
"Thus was this place, / A happy rural seat of various view." PeECV
"Two of far nobler shape erect and tall." PeECV
(Unfallen Love.) NOSC
"While thus he spake, th' Angelic Squadron bright." SCV
"With thee conversing I forget all time." UV; WoPoe
Book V.
Adam Unfallen. NOCV
Ascent of Species. NOSC
"At once on th' Eastern cliff of Paradise." PeECV
"Nor delayed the wingèd saint." NOSC
"Now Morn her rosie steps in th' Eastern Clime." NAEL-5v1
("Now morn her rosy steps in th' eastern clime.") NAEL-6v1
"O favorable spirit, propitious guest." NOCV
Raphael's Descent. NOSC
"So to the sylvan lodge." NAEL-5v1; NAEL-6v1
"To whom the wingèd hierarch replied." NOSC
Book VI.
"He sat; and in the assembly next upstood." FaBoWar
"They ended parle, and both addressed for fight." OBWP
Book VII.
"And God said, Let the waters generate." NOSC
Creation. NOSC
"Descend from Heaven [*or* Heav'n], Urania, by that name." EBEV; NAEL-5v1; NAEL-6v1; NOSC; TOF
"Forthwith the sounds and seas, each creek and bay." ChIV-1
"Heaven opened wide / Her ever during gates, harmonious sound." ChIV-1; TreFP
Invocation to Urania. EBEV; NAEL-5v1; NAEL-6v1; NOSC; TOF
"Thus God the Heav'n created, thus the Earth." PeECV
Book VIII.
Adam Describes His Own Creation and That of Eve; Having Repeated His Warning, the Angel Departs. NAWM-7v1
"For man to tell how human life began." ChIV-1
"Love thou saist." TOF
"So spake the godlike power, and thus our sire." NAEL-5v1; NAEL-6v1
"Solicit not thy thoughts with matters hid." NAWM-7v1
Book IX. FHYEP; NAEL-5v1; NAEL-6v1; NAWM-5v1; NAWM-7v1
"As when of old some orator renowed." NPeEn
"For now, and since first break of dawne the Fiend." NPeEn
"Her long with ardent look his Eye pursu'd." UnPo
(Higher Argument.) NOSC
"How shall I behold the face." TOF
"No more of talk where God or Angel Guest." OxBEV; TOF
"Pleasing was his shape." EBNV
Serpent Finds Eve Alone, The. NPeEn
"Since first break of dawn the fiend." NOSC
Temptation of Eve, The. EBNV
Tempter Disarmed, The. NOSC
"To whom with healing words Adam replied." NOSC
Uncloistered Virtue. NOSC
What Words Have Passed. TrCP
Book X. FHYEP
"Be it so, for I submit; his doom is fair." NAWM-5v1
"Other way Satan went down, Th'" NAEL-5v1; NAEL-6v1
"Such was thir song." PeECV
"Thus began / Outrage from lifeless things; but Discord first." NAEL-5v1; NAEL-6v1; NAWM-7v1
Book XI.
Flood, The. NOSC
(Michael sets before Adam in vision what shall happ'n till the Flood.) NPeEn
"One man except, the only son of light." NOSC
"This most afflicts me, that departing hence." PeECV
"To whom the Father, without Cloud, serene." PeECV
Book XII.
Adam and Eve led out of Paradise. NPeEn
Adam Fallen. NAWM-5v1; NAWM-7v1
Adam Fallen. NOCV
"But now lead on." NPeEn
"Descended, Adam to the bower where Eve." NOCV
(Banishment, The.) NOBE
(Exile.) NOSC
Expulsion from Eden, The. OPOU
"He ended, and they both descend the hill." NAWM-5v1; NAWM-7v1
"He ended; and thus *Adam* last reply'd." HeIP-4

"In either hand the hast'ning angel caught."   OPOU
Paradise Lost.   OxAEP-1; PeECV
Retreat from Paradise, The.   HeIP-4
"So spake the [or th'] Archangel Michael; then paused."   NAEL-5v1;
    NAEL-6v1
"This having learnt, thou hast attained the summe."   SCV
("Thus saying, from her husband's hand her hand.")   OBGa
"To whom thus also th' Angel last repli'd."   OxAEP-1; PeECV
"All in a moment, through the gloom were seen."   TreFP
Evening in Paradise.   NOBE
"Hail holy Light, ofspring of Heav'n first-born."   OxBEV
"High on a Throne of Royal State, which far."   FHYEP; NAEL-5v1; NAEL-
    6v1; OxAEP-1
March of the Rebel Angels.   TreFP
"Meanwhile the heinous [or hainous] and despiteful [or despightfull] act."
    FHYEP
(Moon and the Nightingale, The.)   PeECV
("No more of talk where God or angel guest.")   NoP-4
"No more [of] talk where God or Angel Guest."   FHYEP; NAEL-5v1;
    NAEL-6v1; NAWM-5v1; NAWM-7v1
"Now came still evening [or Ev'ning] on, and twilight gray [or grey]."
    NOBE
"Of Man's [or Mans] First Disobedience, and the Fruit."   FHYEP; NAEL-
    5v1; NAEL-6v1; OxAEP-1
Paradise Lost as a Haiku.   Stanley J. Sharpless.   OBCoV
Paradise Lost, Book V: An Epitome.   Anthony Hecht.   NBLV
Paradise Lost, Book IV, lines 639—654.   Leslie Johnson.   UV
Paradise on earth— that's the city of Suchou!   Scene at Heaven Gate, The.
    T'ang Yin.   CoBLCP, *tr. by* Jonathan Chaves
Paradise Re-entered.   D. H. Lawrence.   ChIV-2
Paradise Regained.   Hendrik Marsman.   TuT, *tr. by* Michael Longley
Paradise Regained [or Regain'd].   John Milton.
    Book I.
       "I who erewhile the happy Garden sung."   PeECV
       Messiah, The.   PeECV
       "So spake our morning star then in his rise."   PeECV
       "So they in Heav'n their odes and vigils tun'd."   PeECV
    Book II.
       Banquet, The.   NOSC
       "But now I feel hunger, which declares."   InvLi
       "He spake no dream, for as his words had end."   NOSC
       "It was the hour of night, when thus the Son."   EBEV; PeECV
       "Set women in his eye and in his walk."   PeECV
       "Sometimes they thought he might be only shewn."   PeECV
       Table Richly Spread, A.   FaBoCh
    Book III.
       (Parthian Powers.)   NOSC
       "They err who think it glorious to subdue."   FaBoWar
    Book IV.
       Athens.   NOSC; PeECV
       "He brought our saviour to the western side."   NOSC
       "Look once more ere we leave this specular Mount."   NOSC; PeECV
       "Or if I would delight my privat hours."   PeECV
       Rome.   NOSC
       "To whom the fiend with fear abasht repli'd."   PeECV
       "To whom the Tempter impudent replied."   ChIV-2
Paradise reserved for me, A. (LL)   Meditations on the Sepulchre in the Garden.
    Philip Doddridge.   NOCV; NOEC; OBGa
Paradise Saved.   Alec Derwent Hope.   OxBC; OxBSo
Paradiso.   Dante Alighieri.   *Fr.* Divina Commedia.
Paradiso.   Dante Alighieri.   *Fr.* Divine Comedy, The (Mandelbaum
    Translation).
Paradox.   Anna Wickham.   LW
Paradox, The.   John Donne.   NOSC
Paradox, The.   Paul Laurence Dunbar.   TCAPo
Paradox, The.   Francesca Yetunde Pereira.   PBA
Paradox of Time, The.   Pierre de Ronsard.   AWP, *tr. by* Austin Dobson
Paradoxes and Oxymorons.   John Ashbery.   FTOS; HeIP-4; NoAM; PmAP;
    PoPoPo
Paragon, The.   Coventry Patmore.   NAEL-6v2   *Fr.* Angel in the House, The.
Paragon of Animals, The.   Pope.   ECEV; FHYEP; NAEL-5v1; NAEL-6v1;
    NAEL-7v1; NOEC; PAI; SacPr; TFi   *Fr.* Essay on Man, An.
Paragraph 36.   Hayden Carruth.   BodElec
Paragraphs.   Hayden Carruth.
    "In filthy Puerto Rico lives a bird with no."   BodElec
Paraguay.   Carl Rakosi.   FTOS
Parallax.   Arthur Sze.   GifTon

Parallel tracks of silver.   Cascades of Death.   Angelina Muñiz Huberman.
    MirDau, *tr. by* Aurora Camacho
Paralytic.   Sylvia Plath.   FaBoWP
Paranoia.   Salwa Al-Neimi.   PoArWo, *tr. by* Subhi Hadidi and Nathalie Handal
Paranoia.   Leonard Nolens.   TuT, *tr. by* Michael O'Loughlin
Paranoia in Crete.   Gregory Corso.   NeAP
Paraphrase.   Samuel Johnson.   ChIV-1
Paraphrase from the French, A.   Matthew Prior.   OxBoLi; PeLV
Paraphrase of Part of the Book of Ecclesiates, A.   Henry Howard, Earl of
    Surrey.
    "I, Solomon, David's son, King of Jerusalem."   ChIV-1
    "When I bethought me well, under the restless sun."   ChIV-1
    "When that repentant tears hath cleansed clear from ill."   ChIV-1
Paraphrase of the Latter part of the Sixth Chapter of St. Matthew, A.   James
    Thomson.   ChIV-2
Paraphrase on Oenone to Paris, A.   Aphra Behn.   EMWP
Paraphrase on the Canticles, A.   Elizabeth Singer Rowe.
    "At thy approach, my cheek with blushes glows."   PEW
    Chapter II.   PEW
Paraphrase on the Psalms of David.   George Sandys.
    ("O Thou, who all things hast of nothing made.")   SacPr
Paraphrase Upon Job, A.   George Sandys.
    "Again when all the radiant sons of light."   NOSC
    "O Father, I acknowledge, Job replied."   ChIV-1
Paraphrase Upon Part of the CXXXIX Psalm, A.   Thomas Stanley.   ChIV-1
Paraphrases.   Roy Fisher.   PeLV
Parapoetics.   Eugene B. Redmond.   NBV
Parcæ, The; or, Three Dainty Destinies: The Armilet.   Robert Herrick.   CaPo
Parchment and paper left clean.   Making of Color, The.   Hugh Seidman.
    YaYoPo
Parcy Reed.   *Unknown.*   OxBB
Pardon.   Jane Kenyon.   LoL   *Fr.* Having It Out With Melancholy.
Pardon, The.   Richard Wilbur.   NIL-7; NOBA; NoAM; PAI
Pardon, goddess of the night.   William Shakespeare.   NoSic   *Fr.* Much Ado
    about Nothing.
Pardon, Lord, the lips that dare.   John Greenleaf Whittier.   SacPr   *Fr.* Andrew
    Rykman's Prayer.
Pardon me, boy.   Chattanooga Choo-Choo.   Harry Warren.   ReLy
Pardon me buddy, I didn't mean to bug you.   Homeless Compleynt.   Allen
    Ginsberg.   BodElec
Pardon me, if when I want.   Pablo Neruda.   GifTon, *tr. by* William O'Daly
Pardon me, Miss.   Real Live Girl.   Cy Coleman.   ReLy
Pardon my boldness, madam; here's the clout. (LL)   To a Lady with Child that
    Asked [or Ask'd] an Old Shirt.   Richard Lovelace.   BASC; NOSC
Pardon, oh, pardon, that my soul should make.   Elizabeth Barrett Browning.
    CenSon   *Fr.* Sonnets from the Portuguese.
Pardon sweete flower of matchless Poetrie.   Choise of valentines, The.
    Thomas Nashe [or Nash].   PBRV
Pardon us for utteirng a handful.   New Netherland, 1654.   Grace Schulman.
    OPRER
Pardon, ye glowing ears; need will it out.   Joseph Hall.   NoSic   *Fr.*
    Virgidemiarum.
Pardoned in heaven, the first by the throne! (LL)   Lost Leader, The.   Robert
    Browning.   FHYEP; NAEL-5v2; NAEL-6v2; PWR; SCGP
Pardoner's Prologue, The.   Geoffrey Chaucer.   FHYEP; NAEL-6v1; NAWM-
    5v1; PoE   *Fr.* Canterbury Tales, The.
Pardoner's Tale, The.   Geoffrey Chaucer.   NAWM-5v1; NAWM-7v1, *tr. by*
    Theodore Morrison   *Fr.* Canterbury Tales, The.
Pardoner's Tale, The.   Geoffrey Chaucer.   FHYEP; NAEL-6v1; NAEL-7v1;
    NAWM-5v1; PoE   *Fr.* Canterbury Tales, The.
Paredón.   Ricardo Pau-Llosa.   OPRER
Paregoric Babies.   Jim Carroll.   PmAP
Parent.   Josephine Miles.   NALW
Parent, The.   Ogden Nash.   Spl
Parent to Children.   Robert Graves.   OxAEP-2
Parentage.   Alice Thompson Meynell.   NALW; NPeEn; PeVV; VWP
Parental Critic, The.   Keith Preston.   NBLV
Parental Ode to My Son, Aged Three Years and Five Months, A.   Thomas
    Hood.   OBCoV
Parental Recollections.   Mary Lamb.   OxBEV; OxBSP
    (Child, A.)   OBEV
Parents.   Vincent Buckley.   CBAP
Parents.   Marta Kornblith.   MirDau, *tr. by* Roberta Gordenstein
Parents.   Hilda Morley.   PmAP
Parents are sinful now, for they must whisper.   Marriage.   Austin Clarke.
    BIrV; GTBS-P
Parents far asleep in the next room.   First Snow.   Joseph Awad.   GraLe
Parents' Pantoum.   Carolyn Kizer.   MakPoe

Parents: People Like Our Marriage Maxie and Andrew, The.   Gwendolyn Brooks.   ColAP   *Fr.* Notes from the Childhood and the Girlhood.

Parents take their children into the deepest Oregon forests.   Robert Bly.   LoL   *Fr.* Anger Against Children.

Parfum Exotique.   Charles Baudelaire.   AWP, *tr. by* Arthur Symons

Parihaka.   W. H. Oliver.   PeNZ

Paring the Apple.   Charles Tomlinson.   OxBTC; PoE; TRP

Paris.   Ingeborg Bachmann.   VCWP, *tr. by* Mark Anderson

Paris.   Gregory Corso.   VGW

Paris.   Miklós Radnóti.   IQMS, *tr. by* Zsuzsanna Ozsváth and Frederick Turner

Paris.   Arthur Symons.   NOBVV

Paris and Menelaus.   Homer.   OBVE, *tr. by* Alexander Pope   *Fr.* Iliad, The.

Paris—Christmas 1938.   Edwin Rolfe.   APT-2

Paris Cinquième.   Antonio Cisneros.   TCLAP, *tr. by* Maureen Ahern and David Tipton   *Fr.* Loneliness.

Paris Honeymoon, A.   Frank Ormsby.
    L'Orangerie.   ModIr

Paris in the Snow.   Léopold Sédar Senghor.   PBA, *tr. by* Ulli Beier

Paris Is Not the Same.   James Strachey.   ReLy

Paris Is Paris Again.   Frederick Loewe.   ReLy

Paris is six feet higher than Mexico.   Rousseau Le Douanier.   "Lucebert."   PFTM-2, *tr. by* Peter Nijmeijer

Paris Latin Quarter.   Femi Osofisan.   NAfrP

Paris Visitation.   Michael Brownstein.   FTOS

Parish Poor-Officers, The.   Edward Ward.   NOEC   *Fr.* Journey to Hell, A; or, A Visit Paid to the Devil.

Parish priest, The.   Preacher's Mistake, The.   William Croswell Doane.   PoToHe

Parish-priest was of the pilgrim train, A.   Character of a Good Parson, The.   Dryden.   NOCV

Parish Register, The.   George Crabbe.
    Burials.
    Lady of the Manor, The.   NOBE

Parish Register, The.   George Crabbe.
    "Lo! now with red rent cloak and bonnet black."   EBEV

Park, A.   Theo Sontrop.   TuT, *tr. by* Ruth Hooley

Park Elms.   Charles Ghigna.   UrbNat

Park in Milan, The.   William Jay Smith.   CoAP

Park is filled with night and fog, The.   Spring Night.   Sara Teasdale.   MoAmPo

Park of the Dead.   Gerrit Komrij.   TuT, *tr. by* Peter Van de Kamp

Park Poem.   Paul Blackburn.   PmAP

Park, the heart, you see at town's center is soft, The.   Last Look at La Plata, Missouri.   Jim Barnes.   CDW

Parked in the fields.   Forms of Love, The.   George Oppen.   NNaP

Parked in the office john, going.   Value Added in Smashing a German Roach on the Bathroom Door, The.   Luis Cabalquinto.   ReBoTo

Parker's Mood.   Clarence Beeks.   NAAAL

Parlement of Foules, The.   Geoffrey Chaucer.
    "And whan this werk al brought was to an ende."   OWoS
    Catalogue of the Birds.   NPeEn
    Now Welcom[e], Somer [*or* Summer].   HAP
    (Qui Bien Aime A Tard Oublie.)   EnLoPo
    Rondel: "And whan this werk al brought was to an ende."   OWoS
    (Roundel.)   CTC; NPeEn; OPOU; OxBSP
    "Whan I was come aeyyn into the place."   NPeEn
    "With that mine hand in his he took anon."   OBGa

Parley of Beasts.   Hugh MacDiarmid.   ChIV-1; MoBrPo; NoAM; OBMV

Parliament Hill Fields.   Sir John Betjeman.   FaBoTw; NOBE

Parliament Hill Fields.   Sylvia Plath.   HCAP; NALW

Parmenides Machine, A.   Charles Stein.   PFTM-2

Parodies of Cole Porter's "Night and Day."   Ring Lardner.   OBAL

Parody.   Martha Paley Francescato.   BoWoP, *tr. by* Willis Barnstone

Parody, A.   Frederick Douglass.   NAAL-2v1; NAAL-3; NAWM-7v2   *Fr.* Narrative of the Life of Frederick Douglass, an American Slave.

Parody of Bishop Percy.   Samuel Johnson.   OBCoV
    (Another dish of tea.) (LL)   OxAEP-1

Parody [*or* Parodie], A.   George Herbert.   ESCV

Paros.   Robin Magowan.   SPE

Parrot.   Po Chü-i.   SuSp, *tr. by* Irving Y. Lo

Parrot, The.   Oleg Grigorevich Chukhonstev.   TCRP, *tr. by* Simon Franklin

Parrot, The.   James Elroy Flecker.   FaBoTw

Parrot, The.   Wilfrid Wilson Gibson.   OBMV

Parrot at Sea, A.   Yelena [*or* Elena] Shwarts [*or* Shvarts].   ItGoST, *tr. by* Catriona Kelly

Parrot Cry, The.   Hugh MacDiarmid.   OxBS

Parrot Fish, The.   James Merrill.   NOBA

Parrot's Complaint.   John Skelton.   NPeEn   *Fr.* Speak [*or* Speke], Parrot.

Parrot's Soliloquy.   John Skelton.   NoSic; OxBoLi   *Fr.* Speak [*or* Speke], Parrot.

Parrot's voice snaps out, The.   "Psittachus Eois Imitatrix Ales ab Indis."   Sacheverell Sitwell.   MoBrPo

Parrots dwell in the west country.   Han-shan.   SuSp

Parry, of all my friends the best.   Invitation, The.   Goronwy Owen.   OBWVE, *tr. by* George Borrow

Parsifal.   Paul Verlaine.   SxFrPo, *tr. by* Martin Sorrell

Parsifal has conquered the Maidens, their sweet.   Parsifal.   Paul Verlaine.   SxFrPo, *tr. by* Martin Sorrell

Parsley.   Rita Dove.   ESEAA; HCAP; LoL; NAAAL; NAAL-5; NIL-7; NoAM; NoP-4; PoPoPo; VCAP

Parsnip, The.   Ogden Nash.   ChAP

Parsnips, those rabbis, The.   In the Root Cellar.   Maxine W. Kumin.   FaBoWP

Parson and the Plowman Described, The.   Geoffrey Chaucer.   SacPr   *Fr.* Canterbury Tales, The.

Parson's Case, The.   Jonathan Swift.
    "Thy curate's place, thy fruitful wife."   UV

Parson's Introduction, The.   Geoffrey Chaucer.   NAEL-7v1   *Fr.* Canterbury Tales, The.

Parson's Looks, The.   Robert Burns.   OxBoLi

Parson, these things in thy possessing.   Happy Life of a Country Parson, The.   Pope.   UV

Parśvanatha.   Robert Bringhurst.   GifTon

Part 2.   Anne Grant.   *Fr.* Highlanders, The.

Part eye, part tear, unwilling to recognize us. (LL)   Stone Canyon Nocturne.   Charles Wright.   ColAP; GeoHom; HCAP; LCAP-2; VCAP

Part I.   Elizabeth Barrett Browning.   PEW   *Fr.* Casa Guidi Windows.

Part II.   Elizabeth Barrett Browning.   PEW

Part of a Bird.   Nina Cassian.   PoSu, *tr. by* Andrea Deletant and Brenda Walker

Part of a Letter to the Codignola Boy.   Pier Paolo Pasolini.   VCWP, *tr. by* David Stivender

Part of a Novel, Part of a Poem, Part of a Play.   Marianne Craig Moore.
    "Dürer would have seen a reason for living."   APT-1; BoWoP; ColAP; FaBoMo; FaBoWP; HAP; HarvBoo; NOBA; NoAM; NoP-4; OxBA; PoPoPo; WPE
    Hero, The.   NOBA; OxBA
    Steeple-Jack, The.   APT-1; BoWoP; ColAP; FaBoMo; FaBoWP; HAP; HarvBoo; NOBA; NoAM; NoP-4; OxBA; PoPoPo; WPE
    "Where there is personal liking we go."   NOBA; OxBA

Part of an Irregular Fragment, Found in a Dark Passage of the Tower.   Helen Maria Williams.   RWP

Part of an Ode, A.   Ben Jonson.   OBEV   *Fr.* To the Immortal[l] Memory [*or* Memorie] and Friendship of That Noble Pair[e], Sir Lucius Cary and Sir H. [*or* Henry] Morison.

Part of me is missing.   Missing: A Dog's Doggerel.   Mary Morris.   Unle

Part of my charm.   Look for You Yesterday, Here You Come Today.   LeRoi Jones.   SSLK

Part of our nation of our fanatic sun. (LL)   Soul and Body of John Brown, The.   Muriel Rukeyser.   CBCWP; MoAmPo

Part of the difference between floating and going down. (LL)   Yellow Glove.   Naomi Shihab Nye.   LoL; PoArWo

Part of the Effect of the Public Scene Is to Importune the Passing Viewer.   Erin Belieu.   AmPoNex

Part of the field, A. Trumpets sound and two men enter.   Joseph Brodsky.   TCRusP, *tr. by* Bernard Meares   *Fr.* Sonnets on the Statue of Mary, Queen of Scots, in the Luxembourg Gardens, Paris.

Part of the Lay of Sigrdrifa.   Unknown.   See Elder Edda, The

Part of the soul that doubts, again and again, The.   Cures.   David Rivard.   AllShUp; SwNoth

Part of the work[e] remains [*or* remaines]; one part is past.   End of His Work, The.   Robert Herrick.   CaPo

Part of What I Mean.   Frank Gaspar.   UrbNat

Part One.   Thomas McGrath.   *Fr.* Letter to an Imaginary Friend.

[Part One].   Tristan Tzara.   PFTM-1   *Fr.* Approximate Man, The.

Part One: The Orders Begin.   Carmen Naranjo.   TANSG, *tr. by* Shaun Griffin and Emma Sepúlveda-Pulvirenti

Part otter, part snake, part bird the bird Anhinga.   Waterbird.   May Swenson.   NoP-4

Part, Provence, he loved so well. (LL)   To Ford Madox Ford in Heaven.   William Carlos Williams.   ColAP; NOBA

Part-Sequence for Change, A.   Robert Duncan.   VGW

Part Three.   Thomas McGrath.   *Fr.* Letter to an Imaginary Friend.

Part Two.   Thomas McGrath.   *Fr.* Letter to an Imaginary Friend.

Parta Quies.   A. E. Housman.   NOBE

Partake as doth the Bee.   Emily Dickinson.   TCAPo

Parted.   Alice Thompson Meynell.   PeVV

Parted. Clara Ann Thompson. CBWP-2

Parted by death, we'd strangle on our tears. Dreaming of Li Po. Tu Fu. CrYelRi, *tr. by* Sam Hamill

Parted by death, we swallow remorse. Tu Fu. SuSp *Fr.* Dreaming of Li Po.

Parted me leaf and leaf, divided me, eyelid and eyelid of slumber. (LL) Moonrise. Gerard Manley Hopkins. MoBrPo; NOBVV; RB

Parterre, The. E. Harriet Palmer. NOBL; PeLV

Parthenea, an Elegy. Elizabeth Singer Rowe. PoBW

Partheniades. George Puttenham.

"O mightye Muse." PBRV

Parthenogenesis. Nuala Ni Dhomhnaill. CIP-2, *tr. by* Michael Hartnett

Parthenon, The. Herman Melville. NCAP

Parthenon at Nashville, The. Joe Bolton. AmPoNex

Parthenophil and Parthenophe. Barnabe Barnes.

"Eccho, what shall I do to my Nymphe, when I goe to behold her?" MakPoe

"Jove, for Europa[e]s love took[e] shape of bull." OxBSo

"Lovely Maya, Hermes' mother." NoSic

Mistress, Behold, in This True-Speaking Glass. Son

"O Powers Celestial, with what sophistry." EnLoPo

Sestina: "Then first with locks dishevelled and bare." NPeEn; NoSic

Sestine 4. MakPoe

"Soft, lovely, rose-like lips, conjoined with mine." EnLoPo

"Then first with locks dishevelled and bare." NPeEn; NoSic

"Why do I draw this coole releeving ayer." PBRV

Write! Write! Help! Help! Son

Parthian Powers. John Milton. NOSC *Fr.* Paradise Regained [*or* Regain'd].

Partholan went out one day. First Lawcase, The. *Unknown.* BIrV, *tr. by* John Montague

Partial Accounts. William Meredith. GLP

Partial Comfort. Dorothy Parker. OBAL

Partial Luetic History of an Individual at Risk. J. M. Regan. GLP

Partial muse has, from my earliest hours, The. Charlotte Smith. RWP

Partial Muse, has from my earliest hours, The. Charlotte Smith. BWW; CenSon

Partial Resemblance. Denise Levertov. CoAP

Parting. A. R. Ammons. NoAM

Parting. William Johnson Cory. CAGL

Parting. Judah Halevi. AWP; TrJP, *tr. by* Nina Davis Salaman

Parting. Frances Anne [*or* "Fanny"] Kemble. PoBW

Parting. Li Po. CrYelRi, *tr. by* Sam Hamill

Parting. Coventry Patmore. PoToHe

Parting. W. B. Yeats. FaBoTw

Parting, The. Sara Berkeley. PBCIP

Parting, The. Michael Drayton. OBEV; SCV *Fr.* Idea.

Parting, The. Josephine D. Henderson Heard. CBWP-4

Parting, a thousand cups won't wash away the sorrow. To Tzu-an. Yü Hsüan-chi. BoWoP, *tr. by* Geoffrey Waters

Parting as Descent. John Berryman. MoAmPo

Parting at Morning. Dietmar, von Aist [*or* Eist]. AWP, *tr. by* Frank C. Nicholson

Parting at Morning. Robert Browning. AWP; CABP; FHYEP; HeIP-4; NAEL-5v2; NAEL-6v2; NOBE; OBEV; OxBSP; PAI; SCGP; SoSe-8; TFi; UnPo

Parting from Liu Nan-chou. Hsieh Chin.

"Wait until I too hang up my carriage." CoBLCP

Parting from Su Wu. Li Ling. ChiP, *tr. by* Arthur Waley

Parting from the Courtier Sung. Yin Shih. CoBCP, *tr. by* Burton Watson

Parting from the dead, I've stifled my sobs. Dreaming of Li Po. Tu Fu. CoBCP, *tr. by* Burton Watson

Parting from the Winter Stove. Po Chü-i. ChiP, *tr. by* Arthur Waley

Parting from Wang Wei. Meng Hao Jan. SuSp, *tr. by* Daniel Bryant

Parting Gift. Elinor Wylie. APT-1; OxBA

Parting gift to my body. Ensei. JDP, *tr. by* Yoel Hoffmann

Parting Hymn, A. Charlotte Forten. BlSi

Parting Hymn, A. Charlotte L. Forten Grimke. NAAAL

Parting Hymn We Sing, A. Aaron R. Wolfe. AH

Parting in Wartime. Frances Darwin Cornford. FaBoWP; NIP-4

Parting Is Hard. *Unknown.* BoWoP, *tr. by* Geoffrey Waters

Parting Kiss, The. Josephine D. Henderson Heard. CBWP-4

Parting Lovers, The. Mrs. Henry Linden. CBWP-4

Parting of the Red Sea, The. *Unknown.* AnOE, *tr. by* Charles W. Kennedy *Fr.* Exodus.

Parting Roundel. Jemal Sharah. NOBAu

Parting Song, A. Felicia Dorothea Hemans. VWP

Parting sorrow shattered / Beyond the gauze window. Tune: "Full River Red." Hsin Ch'i-chi. SuSp, *tr. by* Irving Y. Lo

Parting the curtains on the other world. Yunna Petrovna [*or* Iunna Pinkhusovna] Moritz [*or* Morits]. ItGoST, *tr. by* Daniel Weissbort

Parting, without a Sequel. John Crowe Ransom. MoAmPo; NoP-4; OxBA; SoSe-8

Parting word?, A. Bokusui. JDP, *tr. by* Yoel Hoffmann

Partings. Charles Guérin. AWP, *tr. by* Jethro Bithell

Partition's people stitched. Sea Breeze, Bombay. Adil Jussawalla. OMIP

Partitions. Franco Buffoni. ItPo, *tr. by* Gayle Ridinger

Partner in thy destiny! (LL) To an Infant Expiring the Second Day of Its Birth. Mehetabel Wright. ECWP; NOEC

Partridge. Agathias. GrAn, *tr. by* Guy Davenport

Partridge in a pear tree, A. (LL) Twelve Days of Christmas, The. *Unknown.* ChPo; OxBoLi; OxNR

Partridges. John Masefield. OxBTC

Party. Eddy Van Vliet. VCWP, *tr. by* John Van Tiel

Party, The. Donald Finkel. OPRER

Party, The. Antigone Kefala. BMAP

Party, The. William Robert Rodgers. BIrV; PNI

Party, The. Ben Scammell. NLP

Party, The. Reed Whittemore. CoAP

Party at Hydra. Irving Layton. HeIP-4

Party balloons rub against each other. Balloons. Dan Pagis. FIT, *tr. by* Robert Friend

Party Favour. Daniel David Moses. HATNAP

Party for your Right to Fight. Public Enemy. ISC

Party holds you down and you lie still, The. Nguyễn Chí Thiện. VCWP *Fr.* Sundry Notes.

Party on Women's Day, A. Olesya [*or* Olesia] Nikolayeva [*or* Nikolaeva]. ItGoST, *tr. by* Paul Graves and Carol Ueland

Party Piece. Brian Patten. BoLoP

Party's Over, The. Jule Styne. ReLy

Party She Outdid Herself, The. Craig Arnold. NAPBL

Party Shrine. Thomas McCarthy. BiHa

Party suddenly condensed, The. Thirteen Ways of Looking at a Hoover. Anthony Conran. TCAWP

Party was no good again, The. Europa. Rolfe Humphries. APT-2

Partying by a river near Ellwood City, Pennsylvania. Coming Home in March. Harold Littlebird. VoR

Parvenant. Arthur Hugh Clough. OBCoV *Fr.* Spectator ab Extra.

Pas de Deux for Lovers. Michael Dransfield. CBAP

Paso Robles, San Luis Obispo, San Luis Obispo. David Oliveira. GeoHom

Pasolini. Robert Glück. WiU

Pass. Edmund Vance Cooke. PWR

Pass and let pass,—this counsel I would give,—. Pucciarello di Fiorenza. EaItPo, *tr. by* Dante Gabriel Rossetti

Pass, Crow. (LL) Examination at the Womb-Door. Ted Hughes. NAEL-5v2; NAEL-6v2; NoP-4; OxBC

Pass It On. Henry Burton. PWR

Pass it on. (LL) Listen Children. Lucille Clifton. ISC; NOxBChV; OxIBACP

Pass me the sweet earthenware jug. Zonas. PGA

Pass not, but wonder, and amazed stand. Upon the Much Lamented Death of the Right Honourable, the Lady Elizabeth Langham. Bathsua Pell Makin. EMWP

Pass of Death, The. George Darley. NOBRP

Pass Office Song. *Unknown.* PBA; TTY, *tr. by* Peggy Rutherford

Pass to thy Rendezvous of Light. Emily Dickinson. NAWM-7v2

Pass us the ills, which each man feels or dreads. Matthew Prior. NOEC *Fr.* Solomon on the Vanity of the World.

Passacaglia. Don Hymans. BAP-97

Passacaglia. Lequita Vance-Watkins. SpudSo

Passage. Elizabeth Alexander. ISC

Passage. Hart Crane. NOBA; PoE

Passage. Billy Marshall-Stoneking. BMAP; NOBAu

Passage. Peter Rafferty. NLP

Passage. Penelope Rosemont. SurWo

Passage. *Unknown.*

"See there, that tree is a digging stick." WoPoe, *tr. by* Billy Marshall-Stoneking

Passage, The. "Adonis" [*or* "Adunis"]. VCWP, *tr. by* Samuel Hazo

Passage, The. Rita Dove. ESEAA

Passage of the Mountain of St. Gothard, The. Georgiana Cavendish, Duchess of Devonshire. ECWP; RWP

Passage Over Water. Robert Duncan. NOBA; NoAM

Passage to India. Walt Whitman. APN-1; NAAL-2v1; NCAP

Passages. Robert Duncan.

"And to Her-Without-Bounds I send." APSN; NOBA

"Angel Syphilis in the circle of Signators, The." PFTM-2

At the Loom.   VGW
"Butcher had prepared the leg of the lamb, The."   APSN
"Cat's purr, A."   VGW
Envoy: "Good Night, at last."   VGW
Feast, The.   APSN
Fire, The.   APSN; VGW
In Blood's Domaine.   PFTM-2
"In the War they made a celestial cave."   APSN
"Jump stone hand leaf shadow sun."   APSN; VGW
Moon, The.   APSN
"Now Johnson would go up to join the [great] simulacra of men."   APSN; NNaP
"So pleasing a light."   APSN
Transgressing the Real.   APSN
Tribal Memories.   APSN; NOBA
Up Rising.   APSN; NNaP
Passages.   Larry Eigner.   NeAP
Passages 37.   Robert Duncan.   FTOS
Pass[e] rascal deer [or Rascall Deare], strike me the largest doe. (LL)   La Bella Bona-Roba.   Richard Lovelace.   BeJo; CaPo; EBEV; NOSC; OxBEV
Passed On.   Bernard Spencer.   FaBoWar
Passed Ruin'd Ilion.   Walter Savage Landor.   See Ianthe
Passenger feels the sparks penetrate his halo, The.   Real Moment, The.   Eduardo Anguita.   BLPSL, tr. by Rene de Costa, Rigas Kappatos and Eleni Paidoussi
Passenger Opposite, The.   Elma Mitchell.   NePenScot
Passenger Shanty.   W. H. Auden.   OBCoV
Passengers afloat on many thousand feet.   Night Flight.   Marion Alexopoulos.   NOBAu
Passengers, armed, we travel from room to room. (LL)   Palladas [or Pallades].   GrAn; WoPoe, tr. by Frank Kuenstler
Passer-by, A.   Robert Bridges.   MoBrPo; OBEV; OxBTC; SCGP
Passer-by, don't blame this memorial.   Carphyllides.   GrAn
Passer Mortuus Est.   Edna St. Vincent Millay.   FaBoWP; MoAmPo; OxBA
Passes are blocked by snow, The.   Persia.   Victoria Mary Sackville-West.   WPE
Passes wind through where white lilacs flower.   Blossoms.   Ernst Goll.   AuPH, tr. by Lowell A. Bangerter
Passing.   Cheryl Clarke.   WiU
Passing.   Toi Derricotte.   OPRER
Passing.   Langston Hughes.   APSN; APT-2; SAmP
Passing.   Carl Phillips.   PoPoPo
Passing a Ruined Palace.   Wen T'ing-yün.   OHMPC, tr. by Kenneth Rexroth
Passing Away.   Augusta Davies Webster.   ViWPN
Passing away from you, love.   Passing Away.   Augusta Davies Webster.   ViWPN
Passing By.   Thomas Ford.   See There Is a Lady Sweet and Kind
Passing by a Mountain Village: Evening.   Chia Tao.   SuSp, tr. by Stephen Owen
Passing by Huai-yin I Have Feelings.   Wu Wei-yeh.   CoBLCP, tr. by Jonathan Chaves
Passing by Kamata.   Su Man-shu.   SuSp, tr. by Wu-Chi Liu
Passing By the Battlefield at Feng-k'ou.   Kao Ch'i.   CoBLCP, tr. by Jonathan Chaves
Passing by the Hot Springs at Hua-ch'ing Palace.   Yüan Hung-tao.
   "Eastern mountains/ and western mountains."   CoBLCP
Passing By Waterwheel Bay.   Yang Wan-li.   SuSp, tr. by Jonathan Chaves
Passing Ch'ien-hsi as Military Adviser in the Third Month of the Year Yi-ssu.   T'ao Ch'ien [or T'ao Yuan-ming].   SuSp, tr. by Eugene Eoyang
Passing Chao-ling Again.   Tu Fu.   CoBCP, tr. by Burton Watson
Passing clouds only a stand of aspens is in light.   Matsuo Allard.   HA
Passing clouds roll grimly on, The.   Shower.   Jacob Winkler Prins.   TuT, tr. by Tony Curtis
Passing Hung-fu Monastery with Yüan-ming: Inscribed in Jest.   Huang T'ing-chien.   SuSp, tr. by Michael E. Workman
Passing into Storm.   Patrick Lane.   NOBC
Passing like a Strauss waltz.   Hoofer, The.   A. K. Redwing.   VoR
Passing Mr. Sung's Old House.   Tu Fu.   CrYelRi, tr. by Sam Hamill
Passing of a dream, The.   Stanzas.   John Clare.   NOBVV
Passing of Arthur, The.   Layamon.   PoE   Fr. Brut, The.
Passing of Arthur, The.   Tennyson.   FHYEP; NAEL-5v2; NAEL-6v2   Fr. Idylls of the King.
Passing of the bars has made his glance, The.   Panther, The.   Rainer Maria Rilke.   AuPH, tr. by Lowell A. Bangerter
Passing of the Forest, The.   William Pember Reeves.   PeNZ
Passing of the Old Year.   Mary Weston Fordham.   CBWP-2
Passing of the Poets, The.   Fearflatha O'Gnive [or O'Gnimh].   NOIV
Passing of the Shee, The.   John Millington Synge.   BIrV; FaBoEE

Passing Piedras Blancas.   Abigail Albrecht.   GeoHom
Passing Remark.   Tawfiq Zayyad.   MAP, tr. by Charles Doria and Sharif Elmusa
Passing Seven-League Rapids.   Meng Hao Jan.   ColAnChi, tr. by Daniel Bryant
Passing Show, The.   Ambrose Bierce.   APN-2
Passing Strange, The.   John Masefield.   MoBrPo; OBEV
Passing stranger! you do not know how longingly I look upon you.   To a Stranger.   Walt Whitman.   APN-1; NOBA; SAmP
Passing T'ien-mên Street in Ch'ang-an and Seeing a Distant View of Chung-nan Mountains.   Po Chü-i.   ChiP, tr. by Arthur Waley
Passing the bread shop with hungry eyes.   Making It.   Magdalena Gomez.   PueRic
Passing the Crematorium.   Frank Ormsby.   ModIr
Passing the great plane tree in the square.   Beginning of the End, The.   Jon Stallworthy.   OxBC
Passing the Night.   Tu Fu.   CrYelRi, tr. by Sam Hamill
Passing the Night on a River in Chien-te.   Meng Hao Jan.   SuSp, tr. by Paul W. Kroll
Passing the Temple of Teeming Fragrance.   Wang Wei.   ChinPo, tr. by Yip Wai-lim
Passing this tomb with no smile on his face.   Thermopylai.   Hegemon.   GrAn, tr. by Peter Jay
Passing Through.   Constantine P. Cavafy.   CAGL, tr. by Edmund Keeley and Philip Sherrard
Passing Through.   Stanley Kunitz.   BodElec; LoL
Passing Through.   Patrick Williams.   PNI
Passing Through Ch'ien-hsi, Third Month, 405.   T'ao Ch'ien [or T'ao Yuan-ming].   CrYelRi, tr. by Sam Hamill
Passing Through Experiences.   Robert Adamson.   BMAP
Passing through huddled and ugly walls.   Harbor, The.   Carl Sandburg.   APT-1; ColAP; TAP
Passing through My Shih-ning Estate.   Hsieh Ling-yün.   SuSp, tr. by Francis Westbrook
Passing through Rajasthan.   Umashankar Joshi.   OMIP, tr. by Niranjan Bhagat
Passing White Banks Pavilion.   Hsieh Ling-yün.   SuSp, tr. by Francis Westbrook
Passion.   Michael Ryan.   BodElec
Passion.   Penelope Shuttle.
   "He draws memory out of me with hands of fire."   LW
Passion.   LW
Passion.   Penelope Shuttle.   LW   Fr. Passion.
Passion, The.   Henry Vaughan.   ESCV
Passion and Exaltation of Christ, The.   Isaac Watts.   NOCV
Passion and Love.   Paul Laurence Dunbar.   ErotSp
Passion circles round our body, A.   Gregorio Scalise.   ItPo, tr. by Gayle Ridinger
Passion Drinker, The.   Anita Endrezze.   VoR
Passion Flower.   Christopher Okigbo.   PBMAP   Fr. Heavensgate (1961).
Passion of her white December?, The. (LL)   Ice.   Stephen Spender.   FaBoMo; GTBS-P
Passion of Jesus Considered as an Uphill Race, The.   Alfred Jarry.   PFTM-1
Passion of M'Phail, The.   Horace Gregory.
   This Is the Place to Wait.   MoAmPo
Passion of Our Lord painted by an anonymous hand from the Circle of Rhenish Masters, The.   Zbigniew Herbert.   GI, tr. by Adam Czerniawski
Passion of Ravensbrück.   János Pilinszky.   AF; GI; HP; IQMS; PoSu, tr. by Ted Hughes
Passion of the Queen, The.   Virgil [or Vergil].   NAWM-5v1; NAWM-7v1, tr. by Robert Fitzgerald   Fr. Aeneid [or Eneados, Aeneis], The.
Passion Week.   William Everson.   SacPr
Passionate angels serenaded today in Jerusalem.   Passover in Jerusalem.   Avigdor Hame'iri.   MHP, tr. by Ruth Finer Mintz
Passionate beyond the will. (LL)   Alchemist, The.   Louise Bogan.   APT-2; AWP; MoAmPo
Passionate love is temporary.   Landscape with Leaves and Figure.   Olga Broumas.   BoWoP
Passionate Man['])s Pilgrimage, The.   Sir Walter Ralegh.   ChIV-2; NOBE; NoP-4; NPeEn; NoSic; OxBEV; PeECV; PoE; PoRA; RB; SCGP; TFi
   (Give me my scallop-shell of quiet.)   NoP-4
   (Give mee my Escallope shell of Quiett.)   OxAEP-1
   (His Pilgrimage.)   OBEV
   (Verses made by Sir Walter Raleigh the Night before he was Beheaded.)   OxAEP-1
Passionate Pilgrim, The.   Var. authors.
   "As it fell upon a day."   NOBE; OBEV
   (Madrigal, A.)   GTBS-P
   (Nightingale, The.)   AWP; GTBS-P

Philomel. NOBE; OBEV

(Crabbed Age and Youth.) NoSic; OBEV

Passionate Professor, The. Bert Leston Taylor. NBLV

Passionate Profiteer to His Love, The. "Sagittarius." OBCoV

Passionate Sheepheard to his Love, The. Christopher Marlowe. *See* Passionate Shepherd To His Love, The

Passionate Shepherd, The. Nicholas Breton.

Merry Country Lad, The. NoSic

Passionate Shepherd To His Love, The. Christopher Marlowe. AWP; BoLoP; CTC; CIHu; GTBS-P; HAP; HeIP-4; ITBLP; InPK-6; MakPoe; NAEL-5v1; NAEL-6v1; NAEL-7v1; NBLV; NIL-7; NIP-4; NOBE; NoSic; OBEV; OxAEP-1; OxBEV; PAI; PoE; PoRA; RB; SCV; TFi; TRP; TTTS; WeW-3; WoPoe

(Come live with me and be my Love.) AEP; CABP; NoP-4; PoPoPo

(Come Live With Me and Be My Love.) UV

(Passionate Sheepheard to his Love, The.) NPeEn; PBRV

Passionate Shepherd to His Love, The. Delmore Schwartz. SCGP

Passionate Summer's dead! the sky's a-glow, The. October. Paul Hamilton Hayne. APN-2

Passionate Sword, The. Jean Starr Untermeyer. TrJP

Passions; an Ode for [*or* to] Music, The. William Collins. GTBS-P

Passive Participle's Petition, The. John Byrom. ECEV

Passive sea of white foam, A. Poetic Reflections Enroute to, and During, the Funeral and Burial of Henry Dumas, Poet. Eugene B. Redmond. ISC

Passover. Linda Pastan. TaR

Passover in Jerusalem. Avigdor Hame'iri. MHP, *tr.* by Ruth Finer Mintz

Passover: the Injections. William Heyen. HP

Passport check. George Swede. HA

Passport photo booth flashes, The. Sean Dunne. ModIr *Fr.* Sydney Place.

Password of the twentieth century: Communications (as if we had to invent them), The. Funeral of Poetry, The. Karl Shapiro. APT-2

Past. Pablo Neruda. VCWP, *tr.* by Alastair Reid

Past, The. Kwesi Brew. *See* Past / Is but the cinders, The

Past, The. Ralph Waldo Emerson. FaBoCh; TAP; WoPoe

Past, The. Mary Weston Fordham. CBWP-2

Past, The. Ha Jin. NIL-7

Past, The. Oodgeroo of the tribe Noonuccal (Kath Walker). IBA

Past, The. Betsy Sholl. ExTi

Past, The. Fyodor [*or* Feodor] Ivanovich Tyutchev. WoPoe, *tr.* by Charles Tomlinson

Past, The. Sarah Helen Whitman. TCAPo

Past, a glacier, gripped the mountain wall, The. Full Moon at Tierz; before the Storming of Huesca. John Cornford. OBWP

Past all accident. (LL) Ivy Crown, The. William Carlos Williams. NAAL-2v2; NoAM

Past All Understanding. Heather McHugh. ExTi

Past and Present. Thomas Hood. *See* I Remember, I Remember

Past and Present. R. E. Egerton Warburton. NOBVV

Past and present wilt—I have filled them, emptied them, The. Walt Whitman. CAGL; ColAP; NAWM-7v2 *Fr.* Song of Myself.

Past bush paths tarred by tireless treading. Excursion. Niyi Osundare. HBAPE

Past can be no more, The. Now. Thomas Ken. SacPr

Past castle, brewery, over a sandstone bridge. Cockermouth. David Wright. NLP

Past eddies dangerous and rock-reefs wild. Boat, The. Ferenc Kazinczy. IQMS, *tr.* by Watson Kirkconnell

Past empty rooms full of men, the. Robert Sheppard. Oth *Fr.* Empty Diaries/ Twentieth Century Blues 24.

Past exchanges have left orbits of rain around my face. Apology, An. Diane Wakoski. TAP

Past fifty and cloyed at last. Philetas. GrAn; PGA

Past hovering as it revisits the light, The. (LL) It Rains. Edward Thomas. OxBEV; OxBTC; PoE

Past hurts, George, but sing and be merry, The. Old Song. Andrey [*or* Andrei] Andreievich Voznesensky [*or* Voznesenskii]. VCWP, *tr.* by Vera Dunham and William Jay Smith

Past / Is but the cinders, The. Search, The. Kwesi Brew. PBA

Past Is Dark with Sin and Shame, The. Thomas Wentworth Higginson. AH

Past is past, and if one. Salute. James Schuyler. NeAP

Past Is the Present, The. Marianne Craig Moore. APT-1; NAAL-2v2

Past Midnight, My Daughter Awakened by Miles Davis'*Kind of Blue.* Kevin Stein. IllVoic

Past. No matter how poised the shape. Poet Dives, The. Willem Jan Otten. TuT, *tr.* by Micheal O'Siadhail

Past One O'Clock. Vladimir Vladimirovich Mayakovsky [*or* Maiakovskii]. AF, *tr.* by George Reavey

Past Perfect. Linda Gregg. BodElec

Past, present, future: unattainable. Hakuin. ZenPo, *tr.* by Takashi Ikemoto and Lucien Stryk

Past Ruin'd Ilion. John Lyle Donaghy. AWP

(To Ianthe.) NOBE

(Verse: "Past ruin'd [*or* ruined] Ilion Helen lives.") OBEV

Past Ruined Ilion. Walter Savage Landor. *See* Ianthe

Past ruined [*or* ruin'd] Ilion Helen lives. Walter Savage Landor. CTC; EnLoPo; HAP; NOBRP; NPeEn; OxBEV; PoRA; TFi; WeW-3 *Fr.* Ianthe.

Past second cock-crow yacht masts in the harbor go slowly white. Masts at Dawn. Robert Penn Warren. NAAL-2v2; NoP-4; VCAP

Past seven o'clock: time to be gone. Moonset. Sir Henry John Newbolt. EBVV

Past the angular maguey fields, a ride on the optic nerve. Into Mexico. Mona Van Duyn. VCAP

Past the fierce Guardians. Poem in November. Shirley Kaufman. GifTon

Past the fourth cloverleaf, by dwindling roads. Buckroe, After the Season, 1942. Virginia Hamilton Adair. APT-2

Past the house where he was got. Austin Clarke. PoE *Fr.* Mnemosyne Lay in Dust.

Past the salt flats, the grave of the sea, the sky. Erosion. Christopher Merrill. OPRER

Past the school and down. Directions to the Nomad. James Welch. CDW

Past Thinking of Solomon. Francis Thompson. ChIV-1

Past three again! Honest to God, what are you doing? Coffee Imp, The. Bella [*or* Izabella] Akhatovna Akhmadulina. ItGoST, *tr.* by F. D. Reeve

Past Time. Edith Jay Scovell. HarvBoo

Past Yü-ku Tower glides the river Ch'ing. Tune: "The Bodhisattva's Golden Headdress." Hsin Ch'i-chi. ColAnChi, *tr.* by Jiaosheng Wang

Pastel: Masks and Faces. Arthur Symons. NOBVV

Pastiche. Elinor Wylie. NALW

Pastime. Henry VIII, King of England. CTC; EBEV; NoSic

Pastime Café. W. M. Ransom. GifTon

Pastime of Pleasure, The. Stephen Hawes. OBGa

Epitaph of Graunde [*or* La Graunde] Amoure, The. EBEV; NoSic; OBEV

(Epitaphy of la Graunde Amoure.) FaBoEE

"For knighthood is not in the feats of war." OBEV

"O mortal folk you may behold and see." EBEV; NoSic; OBEV

True Knight [*or* True Knighthood], The. OBEV

Pastime of the Queen of Fairies, The. Margaret Lucas Cavendish, Duchess of Newcastle. BASC; NAEL-6v1

Pastime with good company. Pastime. Henry VIII, King of England. CTC; EBEV; NoSic

Pastora. Mario Florián. BLPSL, *tr.* by Rene de Costa, Rigas Kappatos and Eleni Paidoussi

Pastora. Pastora. Mario Florián. BLPSL, *tr.* by Rene de Costa, Rigas Kappatos and Eleni Paidoussi

Pastoral, A: "Mobile, immaculate and austere." Geoffrey Hill. NPeEn

Pastoral, A: "There went out in the dawning light." *Unknown.* AWP, *tr.* by John Addington Symonds

Pastoral: "Annette came through the meadows." Henrietta Cordelia Ray. CBWP-3

Pastoral Ballad by John Bull, A. Thomas Moore. BIrV; OBSV

Pastoral Courtship, A. Thomas Randolph. BASC

Phyllis. BoLoP

"Poor credulous and simple maid!" BoLoP

Pastoral: "Death. / The death of a million." Ron Loewinsohn. NeAP

Pastoral Dialogue. Anne Killigrew. LW

Pastoral Dialogue between Two Shepherdesses, A. Anne Finch, Countess of Winchilsea. ECWP

Pastoral: "Dominic Francis Xavier Brotherton-Chancery." Gavin Ewart. OxBC

Pastoral: "Dove walks with sticky feet, The." Kenneth Patchen. CLPP

Pastoral Eclogue upon the Death of Sir Philip Sidney Knight, A. Lodowick [*or* Lewis] Bryskett. NoSic

Pastoral Elegy, A. Tibullus. AWP, *tr.* by Sir Charles Abraham Elton

Pastoral: "I came to a field." Charles Simic. NNaP

Pastoral in Posters, A. Carolyn Wells. SWaP

Pastoral; in the Modern Style, A. "Worcester." NOEC

Pastoral: "Like an otter, but warm." Rita Dove. NAAAL

Pastoral: "Little sparrows, The." William Carlos Williams. SAmP; TwCP

Pastoral: "Lumpish trollop, The!" Dominic Bevan Wyndham Lewis. UV

Pastoral Muses once were scattered, The. Artemidorus. GrAn

Pastoral on the King's Death, The; [Written in 1648]. Alexander Brome. NOSC

Pastoral Poetry. John Clare. FHYEP

Pastoral: "Slopes of the sun and vine, and thou dark stream." George Cabot Lodge. APN-2

Pastoral: "So soft in the hemlock wood." Robert Silliman Hillyer. MoAmPo

Pastoral Song, A.   Anne Hunter.   ECWP

Pastoral: "When I was younger."   William Carlos Williams.   APT-1; OxBA; SAmP

Pastoral: "You see that forest on the height?"   John Stuart Williams.   TCAWP

Pastorale.   Michael Hofmann.   HarvBoo

Pastoral[l] Dialogue, A.   Thomas Carew.   CaPo

Pastoral[l] Hymn[e], A.   John Hall.   MeLP

Pastorals.   Pope.
  Summer, The Second Pastoral, or Alexis.
  "See what delights in sylvan scenes appear!"   NOBE
  Sylvan Delights.   NOBE

Pasture, The.   Robert Frost.   APT-1; MoAmPo; NAAL-2v2; NAAL-5; NOBA; OxBA; PoE; SAmP; TLR; TRP; TTTS; WHSW

Pasture is best, freshly, A.   How to Play Night Baseball.   Jonathan Holden.   MoASP

Pastures spewing infinite tiny bells. You pimp. (LL)   Labor Day.   Louise Glück.   NIL-7; NoAM

Pat-a-cake, pat-a-cake, baker's man.   Mother Goose.   LB; OxNR; ReMoGo

Pat Cloherty's Version of The Maisie.   Richard Murphy.   RB

Pat on the head, A.   To an Angel in the House.   John Sparrow.   OBCoV

Pat Taffe and Arkle.   Tracey Herd.   MFPA

Pat your foot.   Leadbelly Gives an Autograph.   Imamu Amiri Baraka.   PmAP

Patch of Old Snow, A.   Robert Frost.   OxBSP; WeW-3

Patch-Shaneen.   John Millington Synge.   FaBoVe

Patches.   Thomas Russell Shelton.   PWR

Patches of it.   Luminous, The.   Barbara Guest.   PoM

Patches of snow.   Robert Spiess.   HA

Pater and Ave for my peace. (LL)   Posthumous Coquetry.   Théophile Gautier.   AWP; PeVV, tr. by Arthur Symons

Pater Filio.   Robert Bridges.   OBEV

Paterson.   William Carlos Williams.
  "Beat hell out of it."   APT-1; OxBA
  Delineaments of the Giants, The.   NoAM; TAP
  "Edward/ Paterson has grown older."   NoAM
  Episode 17.   APT-1; OxBA
  "It is dangerous to leave written that which is badly written."   PFTM-2
  "Outside/ outside myself/ there is a world."   NAAL-2v2; NoAM
  "Paterson lies in the valley under the Passaic Falls."   NoAM; TAP
  Preface: "Rigor of beauty is the quest. But how will you find beauty when it is locked."   NoAM
  Preface: "To make a start."   NOBA; NoAM
  "Rigor of beauty is the quest. But how will you find beauty when it is locked."   NoAM
  Sunday in the Park.   NAAL-2v2; NoAM
  "There is a woman in our town."   PoE
  "To make a start."   NOBA; NoAM

Paterson, Book 5: The River of Heaven.   William Carlos Williams.   HarvBoo   Fr. Asphodel, That Greeny Flower.

Paterson lies in the valley under the Passaic Falls.   William Carlos Williams.   NoAM; TAP   Fr. Paterson.

Paterson: The Falls.   William Carlos Williams.   APT-1; ColAP

Paterson—the Strike.   William Carlos Williams.   TCAPo   Fr. Wanderer, The: A Rococo Study.

Path, The.   "Valery Frantsevich Pereleshin."   TCRP, tr. by Albert C. Todd

Path, The.   Konstantin Iakovlevich Vanshenkin.   TCRusP, tr. by Daniel Weissbort

Path among the Stones, The.   Galway Kinnell.   NNaP; NOBA

Path by which we twain did go, The.   Tennyson.   CAGL; EBVV; NAEL-6v2; NAWM-7v2; PeECV; SCV   Fr. In Memoriam A. H. H.

Path goes on and on, The.   Brussels: Simple Frescos 2.   Paul Verlaine.   SxFrPo, tr. by Martin Sorrell

Path I'm following, The.   Yury [or Iurii] Pavlovich Odarchenko.   TCRusP, tr. by Theodore Weiss

Path Is Long, The.   Nikolai Ivanovich Glazkov.   TCRP, tr. by Daniel Weissbort

Path leads up to your house, and stops, The.   Makpelah.   Anna Hajnal.   IQMS, tr. by Kenneth McRobbie

Path-let. . . leaving home, leading out.   Footpath.   Stella Ngatho.   WPOW

Path Marked with Breadcrumbs, A.   Tony Lopez.   Oth

Path of Affection, The.   Laila 'Allush.   PoArWo, tr. by Abdelwahab M. Elmessiri

Path of glory leads but to the grave, The.   Nicarchus of Alexandria.   GrAn

Path of Independence, The.   Unknown.   TreFP

Path of the Just, The.   John Henry, Cardinal Newman.   SacPr

Path of Wisdom, The.   Bible, Apocrypha.   TrJP   Fr. Baruch.

Path strewn with a sprinkling of red, A.   Tune: "Treading on Fragrant Grass."   Yen Shu.   ColAnChi, tr. by Jiaosheng Wang

Path that Leads to Nowhere, The.   Corinne Roosevelt Robinson.   ITBLP

Path the stream scribbles, The.   Sensualist Speaks on Faith, A.   Dina Ben-Lev.   AmPoNex

Path to paradise, The.   Masumi Kato (d. 1796).   JDP, tr. by Yoel Hoffmann

Path up the mountain is hard, The.   Amongst the Cliffs.   Han Yü.   OHMPC, tr. by Kenneth Rexroth

Path winds through secret peaks and valleys, The.   At the Hermitage of Master Fu.   Wang Wei.   CrYelRi, tr. by Sam Hamill

Pathetic Lament, A.   Eliza Cook.   VerBaPo

Pathetic were their words, and well they aimed.   Philip Freneau.   NAAL-3   Fr. House of Night, The.

Pathologist.   Ellen Dudley.   OPRER

Pathology literally speaking is a flower garden.   William Carlos Williams.   TCAPo   Fr. Kora in Hell.

Pathology of Colours.   Dannie Abse.   BloBone; NIP-4; NoAM; TCAWP

Pathology of Proximity, The.   Mark Bibbins.   AmPoNex

Pathos of the result. (LL)   Eagle Valor, Chicken Mind.   Robinson Jeffers.   OxBA; OxBSP

Paths of the Mirror.   Alejandra Pizarnik.   PFTM-2, tr. by Jason Weiss

Pathway of light! o'er thy empurpled zone.   Sonnet 6. To the Torrid Zone.   Helen Maria Williams.   CenSon; NOBRP

Pathway of the sinking moon, The.   On the Sea.   Bayard Taylor.   TreFP

Patience.   Elaine Feinstein.   BrRo; FaBoWP

Patience.   Sir William Schwenck Gilbert.
  (Aesthete, The.)   EBVV
  "Am I alone."   NAEL-5v2; NAEL-6v2; NBLV
  Bunthorne's Song.   CABP
  If You're Anxious for to Shine in the High Aesthetic Line.   NAEL-5v2; NAEL-6v2; NBLV
  "If you're anxious for to shine in the high aesthetic line as a man of culture rare."   CABP

Patience.   Frank Horne.   BPo

Patience.   Unknown.
  Jonah and the Whale.   NPeEn
  "Now is Jonas the Jwe jugged to drowne."   NPeEn

Patience! coy singers of the Delphic wood.   To Poets.   Walter Savage Landor.   FaBoEE

Patience, Hard Thing!   Gerard Manley Hopkins.   See Sonnet: "Patience, hard thing! the hard thing but to pray."

Patience, hard thing! the hard thing but to pray.   Sonnet: "Patience, hard thing! the hard thing but to pray."   Gerard Manley Hopkins.   NOBVV

Patience is a virtue.   Unknown.   OxNR

Patience of the lambs was exhausted, The.   Sacred Wrath.   Vahan Tekeyan.   GI

Patience, Though I Have Not.   Sir Thomas Wyatt.   NoP-4

Patience with the Living.   Margaret Elizabeth Munson Sangster.   PoToHe

Patience. . . patience.   Patience.   Frank Horne.   BPo

Patient, The.   Nicholas Moore.   SPE

Patient Griselda.   Geoffrey Chaucer.   PoRA   Fr. Canterbury Tales, The.

Patient is a twelve-year-old white female, The.   Rafael Campo.   WiU   Fr. Ten Patients, and Another.

Patient Joe; or, The Newcastle Collier.   Hannah More.   ECWP; WoRP

Patient Pan, The.   Ralph Waldo Emerson.   APN-1

Patient: Spode.   Full Neurological Work-up.   Padgett Powell.   Unle

Patio.   Jorge Luis Borges.   TCLAP, tr. by Robert Fitzgerald

Patio.   Manuel A. Viray.   ReBoTo

Patmos.   Friedrich Hölderlin.   OBVE; WoPoe, tr. by David Gascoyne

Patois.   Marianne Vitale.   HeMarv

Patriarch, The.   Robert Burns.   ChIV-1

Patriarch Peaks.   Muso Soseki.   EaWin, tr. by W. S. Merwin

Patriarch wrestled with the angel long, The.   Jacob Wrestling with the Angel.   Jones Very.   ChIV-1

Patrician Peacocks and the Overweening Jay, The.   Guy Wetmore Carryl.   TCAPo

Patricians, The.   Douglas Dunn.   OxBC

Patriot, The.   Nissim Ezekiel.   EmeKit; FaBoVe

Patriot living at Ewell, A.   Limerick.   Langford Reed.   PeLi

Patriot's Day.   Steve Hassett.   CDa

Patriot's Progress, The.   Horace Twiss.   UV

Patriot, The [An Old Story].   Robert Browning.   FHYEP

Patriotic Poem.   Diane Wakoski.   VGW

Patriotic Songs.   Yehuda Amichai [or Amikhai].
  "Even my loves are measured by wars."   PoSu
  "I have nothing to say about the war."   PoSu
  "Let the memorial hill remember, instead of me."   PoSu
  "Town I was born in was destroyed by shells, The."   PoSu
  "War broke out in autumn at the empty border, The."   PoSu

Patriotic Tour and Postulate of Joy.   Robert Penn Warren.   AiP

Patriotic turns to face, The.   Question of Covenants, A.   Gerald Dawe.   PNI

Patriotism.   Sir Walter Scott.   NOBE; OxAEP-2   *Fr.* Lay of the Last Minstrel, The.

Patroclus Fights and Dies.   Homer.   NAWM-7v1, *tr.* by Robert Fagles   *Fr.* Iliad, The.

Patroclus Spears Thestor.   Homer.   OBVE, *tr.* by William Cowper   *Fr.* Iliad, The.

Patrolling Barnegat.   Walt Whitman.   APN-1

Patrols.   D. F. Brown.   CDa

Patron of all those who do good by stealth.   December: Prayer to St. Nicholas.   John Heath-Stubbs.   OBCP

Patron of Flawless Serpent Beauty.   Friederike Mayröcker.   WPOW, *tr.* by Michael Hamburger

Patrons of My Early Song, The.   Mary Leapor.   ECWP   *Fr.* Epistle to Artemisia.

Patsy Cline.   Richard Speakes.   SwNoth

Patter of rain, A.   O. Mabson Southard.   HA

Patterdale.   Isabella Lickbarrow.   RWP

Pattern, The.   Paula Meehan.   ModIr

Pattern and mirror of the acts of earth, The. (LL)   To Christ Our Lord.   Galway Kinnell.   HeIP-4; TwCP

Pattern is only ever of animal success, The.   Museum.   Joe Wenderoth.   BodElec

Pattern[e] of your love, A. (LL)   Canonization, The.   John Donne.   BASC; CABP; ESCV; EnLoPo; FHYEP; FSCP; FaBoVe; HAP; NAEL-5v1; NAEL-6v1; NAEL-7v1; NAWM-5v1; NIL-7; NIP-4; NOBE; NOSC; NPeEn; NoP-4; PBRV; PoE; PoPoPo; SCGP; SoSe-8; TFi; TRP; UnPo; WoPoe

Patterns.   Amy Lowell.   APT-1; AWP; AmFaPo; BoWoP; MoAmPo; NoP-4; OxBA; WHSW

Patterns.   Roberta Hill Whiteman.   HATNAP

Patterns.   Judith Wright.   HarvBoo   *Fr.* Shadow of Fire: Ghazals, The.

Patty-cake, patty-cake / Marcus Antonius.   Tact.   Paul Pascal.   WeW-3

Patty:"Hi, Mom! I'm home!" / *Cathy:* From the beginning, I.   Double Trouble.   David Trinidad.   PmAP

Patty-Poem.   Nick Kenny.   PoToHe

Paudeen.   W. B. Yeats.   HAP; OxBSP

Paul Butterfield, Dead at 44.   Robert Gibb.   SwNoth

Paul Celan: A Grave and Mysterious Sentence.   Edward Hirsch.   TaR

Paul comes from Toronto on Sunday.   I Am Not a Conspiracy Everything Is Not Paranoid The Drug Enforcement Administration Is Not Everywhere.   Susan Musgrave.   NIL-7; NoAM

Paul Faber, Surgeon.   George Macdonald.
   That Holy Thing.   OBEV
   That Holy Thing.   SacPr
   "They all were looking for a king."   OBEV
   "They all were looking for a king."   SacPr

Paul Klee.   Ruthven Todd.   SPE

Paul Laurence Dunbar.   Robert Earl Hayden.   ESEAA; GT; NoP-4

Paul Laurence Dunbar.   Mrs. Henry Linden.   CBWP-4

Paul Laurence Dunbar in The Tenderloin.   Ishmael Reed.   ESEAA

Paul Revere's Ride [The Landlord's Tale].   Henry Wadsworth Longfellow.   AiP; BRP; EBNV; FaBoTw; HHAm; ITBLP; OBAL; OBCA; OBNV; PWR; TCAPo; TFi   *Fr.* Tales of a Wayside Inn.

Paul Revere Speaks.   Myra Cohn Livingston.   HHAm

Paul Revere's Ride.   Henry Wadsworth Longfellow.   *See* Tales of a Wayside Inn

Paul's clock struck twelve, 'twas time to go to bed.   Midnight Ramble, The.   Charles Woodward.   NOEC

Paul's Wife.   Robert Frost.   EBNV

Paul set the bags down, told how they had split.   Venison.   Karen Chase.   NIL-7

Paul the First.   Pavel Grigoryevich Antokolsky.   TCRP, *tr.* by Bernard Meares

Paul Verlaine at the Grave of Lucien Létinois.   Bin Ramke.   OPRER

Paul / when the leaves.   Lorine Niedecker.   APT-2

Paula Becker to Clara Westhoff.   Adrienne Rich.   NAAL-2v2; VCAP

Paula of the trembling brown cheeks and silent tears.   For Paula Cooper.   Jackie Warren-Moore.   SpirFl

Pauline.   Felicia Dorothea Hemans.   RWP

Pauline [*or* Pauline; A Fragment of a Confession].   Robert Browning.
   "O God, where do they tend—these struggling aims?"   SacPr

Pauper Woodland.   Ronald G. Everson.   NOBC

Pause.   Mary Ursula Bethell.   PeNZ

Pause.   Eamon Grennan.   NIL-7

Pause.   Octavio Paz.   STV, *tr.* by John Frederick Nims

Pause, A.   Christina Georgina Rossetti.   VWP

Pause of Joe, The.   Imamu Amiri Baraka.   FTOS

Pause of sorrow hangs upon the world, A.   Reflections on the Death of Louis XVI.   Ann Yearsley.   RWP

Pause of Thought, A.   Christina Georgina Rossetti.   NOBE   *Fr.* Three Stages.

Pauses to sing. (LL)   Buson.   WoPoe; ZenPo, *tr.* by Takashi Ikemoto and Lucien Stryk

Pausing.   Elizabeth Searle Lamb.   HA

Pausing at the edge of the wood.   Cassandra and Friend.   Norman Henry Pritchard, II.   GT

Pavane.   Ronald Stuart Thomas.   HarvBoo

Pavane for the Nursery, A.   William Jay Smith.   MoAmPo

Pavane on Mr Wray's Locations, A.   Tony Baker.   Oth

Pavement slippery, people sneezing.   January, 1795.   Mary Robinson.   ECWP; OxBEV; WoRP

Pavements lined.   Death of a Chief.   Khadambi Asalache.   PBMAP

Pavilion for Listening to Fragrance, The.   Chang Yü.   CoBLCP; WoPoe, *tr.* by Jonathan Chaves

Pavilion on the Pier, The.   Byron Vazakas.   APT-2

Pavilions of dance, terraces of song.   Ch'ien Ch'ien-i [*or* Ch'ien-yi].   CoBLCP   *Fr.* In Spring of the Year *Ping-shen.*

Pavillion-Where-the-Crane-Came, The.   Chao Meng-fu.   CoBLCP, *tr.* by Jonathan Chaves

Pavlov.   Naomi Long Madgett.   BPo

Pavlovsk.   Anna Andreyevna Akhmatova.   RusPo, *tr.* by Robert Arthur Douglas Ford

Pawiak 1943.   Jerzy Ficowski.   PoSu, *tr.* by Frank J. Corliss, Jr. and Grazyna Sandel

Pawing us who dealt them war and madness. (LL)   Mental Cases.   Wilfred Owen.   FaBoMo; NoAM; PeFWW

Pawky auld carle cam[e] ower [*or* owre *or* o'er] the lea [*or* lee], The.   Gaberlunzie Man, The.   *Unknown.*   OxBB; OxBS

Pawnee War-Song.   *Unknown.*   APN-2, *tr.* by Daniel Garrison Brinton

Pawnshop, The.   Chu Hsiang.   WoPoe, *tr.* by Kai-yu Hsu

Pax.   D. H. Lawrence.   EnlH; PeECV; TrCP

"Pax vobis," quod the fox.   Fox and the Goose, The.   *Unknown.*   MiEL

Pay Cash Only.   James Sherry.   FTOS

Pay close attention: the world that appears now.   Lesson in Observation, A.   Dan Pagis.   AF, *tr.* by Stephen Mitchell

Pay Up or Else.   Luci Tapahonso.   ReTh

Pay Your Debts.   Mrs. Henry Linden.   CBWP-4

Paying a price, at his right hand? (LL)   Johannes Agricola in Meditation.   Robert Browning.   SacPr; TOF

Paying a Sick-call to Yao Ts'un-tao in the Rain.   Shen Chou.   CoBLCP, *tr.* by Jonathan Chaves

Paying a Visit to Monk Yung's Cloister.   Meng Hao Jan.   SuSp, *tr.* by Joseph J. Lee

Payre: a metrical tag.   Throwing Out at / of (Com)pare (Dis)pair, A.   Tina Darragh.   FTOS

Paysage Choisi.   Francis Sparshott.   MoCV

Paysage Moralisé.   W. H. Auden.   HarvBoo; MoBrPo; UnPo

Paysagesque.   Norman Henry Pritchard, II.   GT

P.C., X, 36.   Max Beerbohm.   *See* Police Station Ditties

Pea-Fields, The.   Sir Charles G. D. Roberts.   NOBC   *Fr.* Songs of the Common Day.

Peace.   Jonetta Barras.   ISC

Peace.   Bhartrihari.   AWP, *tr.* by Paul Elmer More

Peace.   Rupert Brooke.   NPeEn; OBWP   *Fr.* 1914.

Peace.   Charles Stuart Calverley.   EBVV
   (Peace: A Study.)   NOBVV

Peace.   Walter De la Mare.   MoBrPo

Peace.   Irwin Edman.   TrJP

Peace.   John Gower.   SacPr   *Fr.* Address to the King, An.

Peace.   George Herbert.   AWP; ESCV; GeHe; NOCV; NOSC; TreFP

Peace.   Gerard Manley Hopkins.   GTBS-P; OxBSP; TrCP

Peace.   Langston Hughes.   BPo

Peace.   Michael Longley.   BiHa; CIP-2; PBCIP; PNI

Peace.   Samuel Speed.   SacPr

Peace.   *Unknown.*   MiEL

Peace.   Henry Vaughan.   AWP; EBEV; ESCV; FSCP; FaBoCh; GeHe; HAP; NOBE; NOCV; OBEV; OxAEP-1; OxBEV; PoE; SCGP; TFi; TOF; TrCP; WeW-3

Peace: A Study.   Charles Stuart Calverley.   *See* Peace

Peace and Love.   Ella Wheeler Wilcox.   PWR

Peace and Mercy and Jonathan.   First Thanksgiving of All.   Nancy Byrd Turner.   ChAP

Peace and the Desert.   Kevin Gilbert.   IBA

Peace, and this Cot, and Thee, heart-honored [*or* heart-honor'd] Maid! (LL)   Samuel Taylor Coleridge.   FHYEP; NAEL-5v2; NAEL-6v2; NOBRP; NPeEn   *Fr.* Effusions.

Peace and War. Rowland Watkyns. AngWePo

Peace at the Goal. Ella Wheeler Wilcox. PWR

Peace, Be at Peace, O Thou My Heaviness. Charles Baudelaire. InPK-6, *tr.* by Lord Alfred Bruce Douglas (Sois sage o ma douleur.) AWP

Peace Be Still. *Unknown.* NAAAL

Peace be unto you, / Ye ministering angels. Shalom Aleichem. *Unknown.* TrJP

Peace be with you, gentle scrivener. Sholom Aleichem. Elias Lieberman. TrJP

Peace be with you! Savage mountain roads don't seem to retard you. Eighth Eclogue. Miklós Radnóti. IQMS, *tr.* by Peter Zollman

Peace; come away: the song of woe. Tennyson. EBVV; FHYEP; NAEL-6v2 *Fr.* In Memoriam A. H. H.

Peace Discovers the Poet. George Chapman. NOSC *Fr.* Euthymiae Raptus; or, The Teares of Peace.

Peace, Horror. Miklós Radnóti. AF, *tr.* by Emery E. George

Peace Hymn of the Republic. Henry Van Dyke. AH

Peace in the Welsh Hills. Vernon Watkins. GTBS-P; OxBTC

Peace in thy hands / Peace in thine eyes. Ghost, The. Walter De la Mare. EnLoPo; MoBrPo; NOBE; OxBTC

Peace is declared, an' I return. Return, The. Rudyard Kipling. MoBrPo

Peace is like salt which seasons all our meat. Peace and War. Rowland Watkyns. AngWePo

Peace is made with a warlike man. *Unknown.* BIrV

Peace Is the Mind's Old Wilderness. John Holmes (1904–62). AH

Peace is the next in order, first in end. Fulke Greville, 1st Baron Brooke. NOSC *Fr.* Treatise of Monarchy, A.

Peace Maketh Plenty. *Unknown.* OxBSP

Peace, my heart's blab! Be ever dumb. Silence: A Sonnet. Henry King, Bishop of Chichester. NOSC

Peace #3. Alma Villanueva. FFC

Peace of Death, The. George Chapman. NOSC *Fr.* Euthymiae Raptus; or, The Teares of Peace.

Peace of great doors be for you, The. For You. Carl Sandburg. MoAmPo

Peace of Lodi, The. Norman Dubie. BodElec

Peace of Wild Things, The. Wendell Berry. VGW

Peace-Offering, The. Thomas Hardy. OxBSP

Peace on Earth. Bacchylides. AWP, *tr.* by John Addington Symonds

Peace! Peace! God of our fathers grant us Peace! Prayer for Peace, A. Severn Teackle Wallis. CBCWP

Peace, peace, my hony [*or* honey], do not cry. Edward Taylor. NAAL-2v1; NAAL-2 *Fr.* God's Determinations [touching his Elect].

Peace Plan: Meditation on the 9 Stages of "Peacemaking" as Tribute to Senator Claiborne Pell: 1997. Michael S. Harper. PuP-23

Peace prat[t]ler, do not lour [*or* lowre]. Conscience. George Herbert. ESCV

Peace, Shepherd, peace! What boots it singing on? Genius Loci. Margaret Louisa Woods. OBEV

Peace Studies. Lynne McMahon. ExTi

Peace that hallows rudest ways. (LL) Forerunners. Ralph Waldo Emerson. APN-1; OBEV; OxBA

Peace the End of the Good Man. Robert Blair. OxAEP-1 *Fr.* Grave, The.

Peace, the wild valley streaked with torrents. Straw, The. Robert Graves. OxBTC

Peace to all living things. One of the Lords of Life. David J. Rothman. GeoH

Peace to all such! but were there one whose fires. Pope. AWP; InPK-6; NOBE; OxBEV; TRP *Fr.* Epistle to Dr. Arbuthnot.

Peace to all such! but were there one whose fires. Pope. NPeEn *Fr.* Epistle to Dr. Arbuthnot.

Peace to each swain, who rural rapture owns. George, the Younger Colman. OBGa *Fr.* London Rurality.

Peace to Lord Hamlet, I have never heard. Grave Doubts. Patricia Beer. NoP-4

Peace to the odalisque, the facile slave. Emily Jane Pfeiffer. VWP "Peace to the odalisque, whose morning glory." ViWPN

Peace to the odalisque, whose morning glory. Emily Jane Pfeiffer. ViWPN *Fr.* Peace to the odalisque, the facile slave.

Peace to these little broken leaves. Leaves. William Henry Davies. MoBrPo

Peace to this awful dome!—when straight I heard. Philip Freneau. NAAL-3 *Fr.* House of Night, The.

"Peace upon earth!" was said. We sing it. Christmas: 1924. Thomas Hardy. FaBoEE; OBCP

Peace, war, religion. This Tokyo. Gary Snyder. NeAP

Peace! where art thou to be found? Enquiry after Peace. A Fragment. Anne Finch, Countess of Winchilsea. ECWP; PoE

Peace with Honor. Philip Appleman. CDa

Peace, you ungracious clamours! peace, rude sounds! William Shakespeare. OxAEP-1 *Fr.* Troilus and Cressida.

Peace? and to all the world? sure, one. Nativity, The. Henry Vaughan. ChrPo

Peaceable Kingdom. Barbara Leslie Jordan. ExTi

Peaceable Kingdom, The. Marge Piercy. TwCP

Peaceful and young, Herculean silence bore. George Chapman. NOSC *Fr.* Euthymiae Raptus; or, The Teares of Peace.

Peaceful eyes my only wealth. Paul Verlaine. SxFrPo, *tr.* by Martin Sorrell

Peaceful Our Valley, Fair and Green. Dorothy Wordsworth. NALW (Grasmere—a Fragment.) PEW

Peaceful Shepherd, The. Robert Frost. MoAmPo

Peaceful Sunday. Charlotte Gardelle. CuPo

Peacefully upon its plantlike stem. (LL) Flowers by the Sea. William Carlos Williams. APT-1; MoAmPo; NoAM; RB; TAP

Peacetime. Peter McDonald. ModIr

Peacetime. Tom Paulin. FaBoWar

Peach. Lance Larsen. AmPoNex

Peach. Rose Rauter. KaS

Peach, The. Shinkichi Takahashi. ZenPo, *tr.* by Takashi Ikemoto and Lucien Stryk

Peach and plum blossoms, speechless, keep swaying in the wind. Huang T'ing-chien. SuSp *Fr.* In My Study in Monastery, Rising after a Nap.

Peach and plum I planted were my own, The. Tu Fu. CrYelRi, *tr.* by Sam Hamill *Fr.* Random Pleasures.

Peach Blossom and Pigeon (painting by Kiso). Shinkichi Takahashi. ZenPo, *tr.* by Takashi Ikemoto and Lucien Stryk

Peach Blossom Stream. Chou Pang-yen. CrYelRi, *tr.* by Sam Hamill

Peach Blossoms. Yuan Chen. CrYelRi, *tr.* by Sam Hamill

Peach blossoms are red, willow catkins white. Spring Day. Yu Chien-wu. ColAnChi, *tr.* by Victor H. Mair and Tsu-Lin Mei

Peach Tree Young and Fresh. *Unknown.* CoBCP, *tr.* by Burton Watson

Peachblossom is redded because rain fell overnight, The. Morning. Wang Wei. TAL

Peaches. Siv Cedering Fox. PBCAP

Peaches. Donald Hall. NoP-4

Peaches and Cream. Mudrooroo Narogin. BMAP

Peachstone. Dannie Abse. AngWePo; OxBC; WeW-3

Peachtree, The. Denise Levertov. TaR *Fr.* During the Eichmann Trial.

Peacock. D. H. Lawrence. TTTS

Peacock, The. James Merrill. OWoS

"Peacock colored tears and rotten oranges." Midnight on Front Street. Roberta Hill Whiteman. CDW

Peacock Display. David Wagoner. OWoS

Peacock drags its tail with its long golden threads, The. Tune: "Eight-beat Barbarian Tune." Sun Kuang-hsien. SuSp, *tr.* by Hellmut Wilhelm

Peacock Flew, A. Lu Yün. ChiP, *tr.* by Arthur Waley

Peacock flew, far off to the south-east, A. Peacock Flew, A. Lu Yün. ChiP, *tr.* by Arthur Waley

Peacock Poems: 1, The. Sherley Anne Williams. NAAAL

Peacock's Eye, The. Gerard Manley Hopkins. OWoS

Peacock's Feather, A. Seamus Heaney. DiPo

Peacock Southeast Flew, A. *Unknown.* ColAnChi, *tr.* by Anne Birrell

Peacock southeast flew, A. Peacock Southeast Flew, A. *Unknown.* ColAnChi, *tr.* by Anne Birrell

Peacock takes its perch upon the county hall, A. Endre Ady. IQMS, *tr.* by Sir Maurice Bowra

Peak of the Held-Up Flower, The. Muso Soseki. EaWin, *tr.* by W. S. Merwin

Peaks gather. Tune: "Sheep on the Mountain Slope." Chang Yang-hao. ChinPo, *tr.* by Yip Wai-lim

Pealing, The. Olga Broumas. BodElec

Pealing again, prolonged the roar. (LL) In Romney Marsh. John Davidson. EBVV; OxBTC

Peanut Sat on a Railroad Track, A. *Unknown.* TLR

Pear blossoms are pure, The. Spring. Su Tung-p'o (Su Shih). OHPC, *tr.* by Kenneth Rexroth

Pear Leaves Redden, Cicada's Song is Done, The. Ou-yang Hsiu. GifTon, *tr.* by Jerome P. Seaton

Pear Tree. "H. D." BoWoP; ColAP; MoAmPo; NOBA; PoE; TCAPo; UnPo

Pear-Tree, The. Iwan [*or* Yvan] Goll. TrJP, *tr.* by Babette Deutsch and Avrahm Yarmolinsky

Pear Tree, The. Edna St. Vincent Millay. MoAmPo

Pear-Tree, The. *Unknown.* AWP, *tr.* by Allen Upward *Fr.* Shi King.

Pear tree that last year, The. Shimmer. James Schuyler. VCAP

Pearl. Irène Hamoir. SurWo, *tr.* by Myrna Bell Rochester

Pearl. Barry MacSweeney.

  Pearl Alone. Oth

  Pearl Says. Oth

  Shells Her Auburn Hair Did Show, The. Oth

Pearl. *Unknown.*

"Perle, plesaunte to prynces paye." EBEV

("Perle plesaunte to prynces paye Pearl, the precious prize of a king.") NoP-4

Pearl Alone. Barry MacSweeney. Oth *Fr.* Pearl.

Pearl Avenue runs past the high-school lot. Ex-Basketball Player. John Updike. InPK-6; TRP

Pearl of the sea! Star of the West! On Leaving Cuba, Her Native Land. Gertrudis Gomez de Avellaneda. WPOW, *tr. by* Catherine Rodriguez-Nieto

Pearl pellets, resplendent young dandies. On the Street of Lo-yang. Meng Hao Jan. SuSp, *tr. by* Paul W. Kroll

Pearl Perch. John Blight. CBAP

Pearl Says. Barry MacSweeney. Oth *Fr.* Pearl.

Pearl-teardrops roll and gather. Huang E. CoBLCP; ColAnChi, *tr. by* Jonathan Chaves

Pearl, The. Matth. 13:45. George Herbert. BASC; ChIV-2; EBEV; ESCV; FHYEP; FSCP; GeHe; HAP; NOCV; NOSC; OxBEV

Pearle's Poem. Primus St. John. GT

Pearlmother dawn. It is fairly true. Abhorring a Vacuum. Chris Wallace-Crabbe. BMAP

Pearls. Janet Fisher. MFPA

Pearls. Alan Gould. NOBAu

Pearls. Lee Ann Roripaugh. AmPoNex

Pearls. Léopold Sédar Senghor. VCWP, *tr. by* Melvin Dixon

Pears are green as new jade, The. Servant Boy Delivers, The. Tu Fu. CrYelRi, *tr. by* Sam Hamill

Peas. *Unknown.* NTCP

Peasant, A. Ronald Stuart Thomas. AngWePo; OBWVE; OxBEV

Peasant, The. Vladimir Uflyand [*or* Ufliand]. TCRusP, *tr. by* Daniel Weissbort

Peasant and the Sheep, The. Ivan Andreevich Kriloff. AWP, *tr. by* C. Fillingham Coxwell

Peasant Declares His Love, The. Emile Roumer. NegPo; TTY, *tr. by* John Peale Bishop

Peasant Girl of the Rhone, The. Felicia Dorothea Hemans. RWP

Peasant haled a sheep to court, A. Peasant and the Sheep, The. Ivan Andreevich Kriloff. AWP, *tr. by* C. Fillingham Coxwell

Peasant once unthinkingly, A. Monk and the Peasant, The. Margaret E. Bruner. PoToHe

Peasant oppressed by sorrow and misery, A. Song of a Farmer. P'i Jih-hsiu. SuSp, *tr. by* William H. Nienhauser

Peasant Poet, The. John Clare. FHYEP

Peasant's child, The. Basho. EH, *tr. by* Robert Hass

Peasant's shack beside the, A. Country Cottage. Tu Fu. OHPC, *tr. by* Kenneth Rexroth

Peasants. Syl Cheney-Coker. NAfrP

Peasants, The. Alun Lewis. OxBEV; PoWW; TCAWP

Peasants at Work. James Hurdis. ECEV *Fr.* Favourite Village, The.

Peasants watch them die, The. (LL) Peasants, The. Alun Lewis. OxBEV; PoWW; TCAWP

Pease porridge [*or* pudding] hot. Mother Goose. OxNR

Peau de Chagrin of State Street, The. Oliver Wendell Holmes. TCAPo

Pebble, The. Zbigniew Herbert. AmFaPo; PoetW, *tr. by* Czeslaw Milosz and Peter Dale Scott

Pebble, The. Elinor Wylie. ChIV-1; MoAmPo

Pebble falls, A. John Wills. HA

Pebble ripples the lake, A. By Water Divined. Kathleene West. GifTon

Pebble swells to a boulder at low speed, A. Electronic Sound. May Swenson. APT-2

Pebbles. Herman Melville. NCAP

Pecan, the Toucan, The. Robert Williams Wood. NBLV

Pedagogy. Lin Max. MiVo

Pedalling between lectures, spokes throwing off. Cricket at Oxford. Alan Ross. PeLV

Pedalling Man, The. Russell Hoban. NOxBChV

Pediatrics. Carol Muske. PBCAP

Pedigree of Honey, The. Emily Dickinson. NOBA; SAmP

Pedlar. Confucius. CTC; OBVE, *tr. by* Ezra Pound *Fr.* Wei Wind.

Pedlar, The. Charlotte Mew. NOxBChV

Pedlar I am, that take great care, A. Pedlar of Small-Wares, A. Sir John Suckling. CaPo

Pedlar of Small-Wares, A. Sir John Suckling. CaPo

Pedlar of Spells, The. Lu Yu. ChiP, *tr. by* Arthur Waley

Pedlar's Song, The. William Shakespeare. *See* Winter's Tale, The

Pedro's mother greets us on the street. Monday Night at Pedro's. Sandra M. Castillo. TouFir

Peekaboo, I Almost See You. Ogden Nash. PeLV

Peeking in through. Praxilla. ErotSp, *tr. by* Sam Hamill

Peel Me a Grape. Dave Frishberg. ReLy

Peel me a grape, crush me some ice. Peel Me a Grape. Dave Frishberg. ReLy

Peeling Onions. Adrienne Rich. BoWoP; HCAP; TAP

Peeling Pippins. Mary Tallmountain. HATNAP

Peeling Potatoes. Philip L. Miller. SpudSo

Peels an apple, while B kneels to God, A. Howard Nemerov. *See* A peels an apple, while B kneels to God

Peepers. Howard Nelson. MiVo

Peeping Tom Tom Girl. Marisela Norte. GeoHom

Peer now spreads the glittering forfex wide, The. Pope. EroLit *Fr.* Rape of the Lock, The.

Peer of the gods is that man, who. Sappho. OBVE, *tr. by* William Carlos Williams

Peer of the golden gods is he to Sappho. Ode to Anactoria. Sappho. AWP, *tr. by* William Ellery Leonard

Peering, in depth. Backgrounds Observed. Jean Earle. TCAWP

Peering into the depths of the stream. T'ao Ch'ien [*or* T'ao Yuan-ming]. SuSp *Fr.* Seasons Come and Go, The.

Peering out. Michael McClintock. HA

Peering stung. Poem: Tears, Spray and Steam. John Logan. BodElec

Pees maketh plente. Peace. *Unknown.* MiEL

Peeter a Whitfeild he hath slaine. Jock o' the Side. *Unknown.* ESPB

Pegasus. Varlam Tikhonovich Shalamov. TCRP, *tr. by* Bradley Jordan

Pegasus Lost. Elinor Wylie. MoAmPo

Peggy. Allan Ramsay. *See* Gentle Shepherd, The

Peggy Browne. Turlough Carolan [*or* O'Carolan]. BIrV; OxBEV, *tr. by* Austin Clarke

Pei-mang Cemetery. Yüan Hung-tao. CoBLCP, *tr. by* Jonathan Chaves

Pelican, The. Adelia Prado. TCLAP, *tr. by* Marcia Kirinus

Pelican Chorus, The. Edward Lear. OBSP

Pelicans. Robinson Jeffers. MoAmPo

Pelicans. Judith Wright. BMAP; OWoS

Pelicans in the Wilderness (A Grave near Halfa). Rudyard Kipling. PeFWW *Fr.* Epitaphs of the War [1914–1918].

Pelleas and Ettarre. Tennyson. NAEL-5v2; NAEL-6v2 *Fr.* Idylls of the King.

Peloria the dog's upper lip kept curling. Charles Olson. PFTM-2

Pembrokeshire Buzzards. Tony Curtis. TCAWP

Pemulwy—A Visitation. Beryl Philp-Carmichael (Yungha-Dhu). IBA

Pen, The. Muhammad Al-Ghuzzi. MAP; NAfrP, *tr. by* John Heath-Stubbs and May Jayyusi

Pen, The. Mary Weston Fordham. CBWP-2

Pen, The. Galway Kinnell. BodElec

Pen, The. Solomon ibn Gabirol. WoPoe, *tr. by* Peter Cole

Pen, The. Jean Valentine. BodElec

Pen and four fingers: I watched four fair creatures. Cynewulf. ASW *Fr.* Riddles (Exeter Book).

Pen filled with ink dark. Blood. Lucien Stryk. BodElec

Pen-guin. The Sword-fish, The. Robert Williams Wood. NBLV

Pen is an index finger, The. Castration of the Pen. Erica Jong. NALW

Pen slides, The. Valerio Magrelli. NeIt

Pen Vine and Scroll. John Taggart. FTOS

Penal Law. Austin Clarke. BoLoP; GTBS-P; ModIr; NOIV; OxBEV; PAI

Penal Servitude for Mrs. Maybrick. *Unknown.* OxBoLi

Penalty for Bigamy Is Two Wives, The. William Matthews. SwNoth

Penance. Sherman Alexie. MoASP

Penance, A. Francis Daniel Pastorius. NOSC

Pencil's Sleep, The. Tymoteusz Karpowicz. PoSu, *tr. by* Rzej Busza and Bogdan Czaykowski

Pencilled by the Rain. Peter Hooper. PeNZ

Pendulum, The. Árpád Tóth. IQMS, *tr. by* Watson Kirkconnell

Pendydd. Kingsley Amis. NOBL *Fr.* Evans Country, The.

Penelope. James [*or* Jim] Harrison. NIP-4

Penelope. Monique Laederach. BoWoP, *tr. by* Charles Guenther

Penelope. Dorothy Parker. FaBoWar

Penelope as a *garçon manqué.* Mythology. Marilyn Hacker. NoAM; ReTh

Penelope for her *Ulisses* sake. Edmund Spenser. NoP-4; PBRV

Penelope pulls home. Kiltartan Legend. Padraic Fallon. ModIr; NOIV

Penelope, who really cried. (LL) Ancient Gesture, An. Edna St. Vincent Millay. NALW; NIL-7

Penetration. "Michael Field." VWP

Penguin hailed me at the door, A. Penguins in the Home. Helen Smith Bevington. OBAL

Penguin Jane Austen, The. Debora Greger. OWoS

Penguins. Artur Miedzyrzecki. PoSu, *tr. by* John Batki and Artur Miedzyrzecki

Penguins in the Home. Helen Smith Bevington. OBAL

Peninsula, The.   Seamus Heaney.   HarvBoo

Peninsula church, A. October's last Sunday.   Within.   Philip Booth.   PoCoUp

Penis, The.   Dafydd [or David] ap Gwilym.   EroLit; WoPoe, tr. by Dafydd Johnston

Penitent, The.   Anne Brontë.   SacPr

Penitent Considers Another Coming of Mary, A.   Gwendolyn Brooks.   NoAM

Penitential Cries of Jupiter Hammond, The.   Gary Smith.   GT

Penitential Psalms.   Sir Thomas Wyatt.
     Prologue: "Love, to give law unto his subject hearts."   ChIV-1

Penn Central Station at Beacon, N.Y., The.   Ed Ochester.   GM

Pennies from Heaven.   Johnny Burke.   ReLy

Pennies in a stream.   Moonlight in Vermont.   John Blackburn.   ReLy

Penniless Indian fakirs and their camels, The.   Avarice.   Anthony Hecht.   OxBSP

Penniless Lovers.   Eugenio de Andrade.   VCWP, tr. by Alexis Levitin

Pennsylvania Deutsch.   Christopher Darlington Morley.   NBLV

Pennsylvania Places.   Thomas Augustin Daly.   OBAL

Pennsylvania spiders.   Morning Harvest.   Gerald Stern.   LCAP-2

Pennsylvania to the coast of Ecuador, my mother calling her aunt.   Long Distance.   Maurice Kilwein Guevara.   TouFir

Pennsylvania Winter Indian 1974.   Harold Littlebird.   VoR

Penny.   Unknown.   FaBoVe; MiEL

Penny and penny.   Unknown.   OxNR

Penny for You, A.   Uri Zvi Greenberg.   MHP, tr. by Ruth Finer Mintz

Penny for you, philosophers of eternity, A.   Penny for You, A.   Uri Zvi Greenberg.   MHP, tr. by Ruth Finer Mintz

Penny lost in the lak, The.   Unknown.   OxBS   Fr. Colkelbie Sow.

Penny Men.   Rigoberto González.   GeoHom

Penny Toys.   John Mole.
     Musical Monkey, The.   OBCoV
     Song of the Hat-Raising Doll.   OBCoV

Penny Whistle, The.   Edward Thomas.   MoBrPo

Pennycandystore beyond the El, The.   Lawrence Ferlinghetti.   HeIP-4; PoM; TAP

Penobscot.   George Oppen.   HarvBoo

Penological Study: Southern Exposure.   Robert Penn Warren.
     Wet Hair: If Now His Mother Should Come.   NoAM

Pension Day.   Charmaine Papertalk-Green.   IBA

Pensive at eve on the hard world I mus'd [or mused].   Samuel Taylor Coleridge.   CenSon   Fr. Sonnets Attempted in the Manner of Contemporary Writers.

Pensive gnu, the staid aardvark, The.   For an Amorous Lady.   Theodore Roethke.   NBLV

Pensive on Her Dead Gazing.   Walt Whitman.   RB

Pentecost.   Gerrit Achterberg.   TuT, tr. by Dennis O'Driscoll

Pentecost.   Gwyneth Lewis.   MFPA

Pentecost Castle, The.   Félix Lope de Vega Carpio.   HAP; HarvBoo, tr. by Geoffrey Hill
     "And you my spent heart's treasure."   HAP; OxBEV; WoPoe, tr. by Geoffrey Hill
     "Down in the orchard."   HAP; WoPoe, tr. by Geoffrey Hill
     "I shall go down."   HAP, tr. by Geoffrey Hill
     "Splendidly-shining darkness."   HAP; WoPoe, tr. by Geoffrey Hill
     "They slew by night."   HAP; WoPoe, tr. by Geoffrey Hill

Pentelogia.   Francis Quarles.
     "Can he be fair that withers at a blast."   PeECV

Pentelogia.   Francis Quarles.
     "What is the World? A great Exchange of ware."   PBRV

Poem Written under an Archway in a Discontinued Railroad Station, Fargo, North Dakota, A.   James Wright (1927–80).   GM

Peona! ever have I long'd to slake.   John Keats.   NAEL-5v2; NAEL-6v2   Fr. Endymion: A Poetic Romance.

Peonage System, The.   Lizelia Augusta Jenkins Moorer.   CBWP-3

Peonies.   Harry Edmund Martinson.   WoPoe, tr. by Leif Sjöberg and William Jay Smith

Peonies are heavy with dew, The.   To the Tune: Beautiful Barbarian.   Unknown.   CrYelRi, tr. by Sam Hamill

Peonies at Dusk.   Jane Kenyon.   LoL

Peonies scattering.   Buson.   EH, tr. by Robert Hass

Peony Afternoon.   So Chong-Ju.   VCWP, tr. by David R. McCann

Peony Lover.   Lee Ann Roripaugh.   AmPoNex

People.   Hans [or Jean] Arp.   PFTM-1

People.   Georgy [or Georgii] Vladimirovich Ivanov.   TCRP, tr. by Daniel Weissbort

People.   Bob Merrill.   ReLy

People.   Jean Toomer.   GT

People, The.   Tomasso Campanella.   AWP, tr. by John Addington Symonds

People, The.   Robert Creeley.   VGW

People, The.   Elizabeth Madox Roberts.   NOxBChV

People all say the southland's better.   Tune: Deva-like Barbarian.   Wei Chuang.   CoBCP, tr. by Burton Watson

People all say the southland's better.   Wen T'ing-yün.   CoBCP

People all talk about serving the King of Emptiness.   Sent to the Ch'an Master Wu-hsiang.   Lo Yin.   SuSp, tr. by Geoffrey R. Waters

People along the sand, The.   Neither Out Far Nor In Deep.   Robert Frost.   APT-1; HAP; NAAL-2v2; NOBA; NoAM; NoP-4; TAP; TRP; WeW-3; WoPoe

People always say to me.   Question, The.   Karla Kuskin.   NTCP

People and things crowd in.   Nature Morte.   Joseph Brodsky.   TCRP, tr. by George L. Kline

People Are Dropping Out of Our Lives.   Albert Goldbarth.   SwNoth

People are eating dinner in that country north of Legge's Lake, The.   Les A. Murray.   BMAP   Fr. Bulahdelah—Taree Holiday Song Cycle, The.

People are making a camp of branches in that country at Arnhem Bay, The.   Song Cycle of the Moon-Bone.   Unknown.   NOBAu, tr. by Ronald M. Berndt

People are of two kinds, and he.   Tribute on the Passing of a Very Real Person.   Unknown.   PoToHe

People are on the one side understandable.   Dmitry [or Dmitrii] Aleksandrovich Prigov.   TCRP

People are putting up storm windows now.   Storm Windows.   Howard Nemerov.   CoAmPo; InPK-6; VCAP

People are queer / They're always crowing.   Life Is Just a Bowl of Cherries.   Ray Henderson.   ReLy

People are saying that I am your enemy, The.   To Julia de Burgos.   Julia de Burgos.   TCLAP, tr. by Grace Schulman

People are saying that I am your enemy, The.   To Julia de Burgos.   Julia de Burgos.   BoWoP, tr. by Grace Schulman

People ask about Cold Mountain Way.   Han-shan.   WoPoe, tr. by E. Bruce Brooks

People ask the way to Cold Mountain.   Unknown.   ColAnChi, tr. by Red Pine

People at Night.   Denise Levertov.   CLPP

People at the Pay Telephone, The.   Victoria McCabe.   OPRER

People brag / People boast.   Is It True What They Say About Dixie?   Irving Caesar.   ReLy

People came to listen, The.   Chartist Meeting.   Mike Jenkins.   AngWePo

People chained to aurora, A.   Civilization and Its Discontents.   John Ashbery.   LCAP-2; TwCP

People come from all over to consult me, bringing their limbs.   Margaret Atwood.   NALW   Fr. Circe / Mud Poems.

People die from loneliness.   One.   Carolyn M. Rodgers.   BPo

People don't swallow bullshit wholesale like they used to.   What Becomes Us.   Sharon Mesmer.   HeMarv

People expect old men to die.   Old Men.   Ogden Nash.   RB

People Getting Divorced.   Lawrence Ferlinghetti.   NoAM

People go naked men and women, The.   Admirals (Columbus).   Suzanne Gardinier.   NeAmPo

People going straight up to heaven.   Amazing Grace.   Anselm Hollo.   PoM

People have the oddest kinks.   Martial.   EroLit, tr. by James Michie

People Hide Their Love.   Emperor Wu of Han [or Wu Ti or Ou-ty or Liu Ch'e or Liu Ch'u].   ChiP, tr. by Arthur Waley

People I love the best, The.   To Be of Use.   Marge Piercy.   WWork

People in his homeland thought him mad.   In Memory of Ho Chi-chen.   Li Po.   CrYelRi, tr. by Sam Hamill

People in My Family.   Grace Paley.   TaR

People in the houses behind Searsport are dancing, The.   Dancing in Vacationland.   Stephen Dobyns.   EmeKit

People is a beast of muddy brain, The.   People, The.   Tomasso Campanella.   AWP, tr. by John Addington Symonds

People know what the land knows, The.   Carl Sandburg.   APT-1   Fr. People, Yes, The.

People laugh at me for having no old lady.   Fêng Mêng-lung.   ColAnChi, tr. by Richard W. Bodman   Fr. Mountain Songs.

People live forever in Jacksonville and St. Petersburg and Tampa.   Come On In, the Senility Is Fine.   Ogden Nash.   AiP

People love each other and the light.   William Meredith.   VCAP   Fr. Consequences.

People, / male and female.   Mahadevi.   BoWoP

People, more people.   Tayo-jo.   SoOfWa, tr. by Sam Hamill

People need poetry, The.   Osip Mandelstam.   Seamus Deane.   BiHa; PBCIP

People, No, The.   Vicki Raymond.   NOBAu

People of Figs.   Nidaa Khoury.   DTA, tr. by Karen Alkalay-Gut

People of Fire.   Nidaa Khoury.   DTA, tr. by Karen Alkalay-Gut

People of Fire.   Nidaa Khoury.   PoArWo, tr. by Linda Zisquit

People of Grapes.   Nidaa Khoury.   PoArWo, tr. by Linda Zisquit

People of My Country, The. Salah Abd al-Sabur. MAP, *tr. by* John Heath-Stubbs and Lena Jayyusi

People of Olives. Nidaa Khoury. DTA, *tr. by* Karen Alkalay-Gut

People of Pomegranates. Nidaa Khoury. DTA, *tr. by* Karen Alkalay-Gut

People of the Future. Ted Berrigan. PFTM-2

People of the islands want a different poem, The. Different Poem, A. Onésima Silveira. PBMAP

People of the South Wind. William Stafford. NNaP

People of Unrest. Margaret Walker Alexander. GT

People one, and one supplies the King, The. (LL) Homer. OBGa; OBVE, *tr. by* Alexander Pope *Fr.* Odyssey.

People open up like doors. Gossip. Angela Sorby. AmPoNex

People—people of my kind, my own, The. To the Lacedemonians. Allen Tate. NAAL-2v2; NoAM

People / People who need people. People. Bob Merrill. ReLy

People Possess Four Things. Antonio Machado Ruiz. WoPoe, *tr. by* Robert Bly

People possess four things. People Possess Four Things. Antonio Machado Ruiz. WoPoe, *tr. by* Robert Bly

People's abuse. Muso Soseki. EaWin, *tr. by* W. S. Merwin

People's Literary, De. Maggie Pogue Johnson. CBWP-4

People said, "Indian children are hard to teach". Indian Children Speak. Juanita Bell. PAI

People sat up from skin-baking or shade-seeking. Diver-Bird. Mike Jenkins. TCAWP

People say they have a hard time. For de Lawd. Lucille Clifton. TAP; TwCP

People see gardens and houses. Mikhail Alekseievich Kuzmin. CAGL, *tr. by* Michael Green

People that build their houses inland. Inland. Edna St. Vincent Millay. HarvBoo

People that I sing to. (I'm So) Weary of It All. Noël Coward. ReLy

People the Churches love best, The. Limerick: "People the Churches love best, The." Patrick Braybrook. PeLi

People, then, knew what they wanted and how to get it, The. (LL) Hotel Lautréamont. John Ashbery. FTOS; HarvBoo

People visiting all day. Buson. EH, *tr. by* Robert Hass

People vs. the People, The. Kenneth Fearing. MoAmPo

People, when you see the smoke. Baika. JDP, *tr. by* Yoel Hoffmann

People who buy flowers in Ch'ang-an. Song of Selling Flowers. Tsung Ch'en. CoBLCP; ColAnChi, *tr. by* Jonathan Chaves

People who come out of nowhere to try to put into words any part of what. All Writing Is Garbage. Antonin Artaud. PFTM-1

People who have no children can be hard. Gwendolyn Brooks. NAAAL; WPE *Fr.* Womanhood, The.

People who have what they want are very fond of telling people. Terrible People, The. Ogden Nash. APT-2

People who live here, The. How the Heart Aches. N.V.M. Gonzalez. ReBoTo

People who want to live beside the ocean are fundamentalists. Lakes. David Donnell. NoAM

People who watch me hang my coat, The. Leaving the Old Gods. Janet McAdams. OPRER

People will live on, The. Carl Sandburg. MoAmPo; NOBA; NoAM; OxBA *Fr.* People, Yes, The.

People Will Say We're in Love. Richard Rodgers. ReLy

People working fields. Issa. SoOfWa, *tr. by* Sam Hamill

People, Yes, The. Carl Sandburg.
  "Little girl saw her first troop parade and asked, What are those?, The." HHAm
  "People know what the land knows, The." APT-1
  "People will live on, The." MoAmPo; NOBA; NoAM; OxBA
  "People, yes, the people, The." APT-1
  "They have yarns / Of a skyscraper so tall they had to put hinges." MoAmPo
  "What the people learn out of lifting and hauling and waiting and losing." OBAL
  "Who shall speak for the people?" OxBA
  "Why did the children." OBAL
  "Why repeat? I heard you the first time." OBAL
  "You can go now yes go now. Go east or west, go north or." HHAm

People, yes, the people, The. Carl Sandburg. APT-1 *Fr.* People, Yes, The.

Peoples House. Nikolai Alekseievich Zabolotsky [*or* Zabolotskii]. TCRP, *tr. by* Daniel Weissbort

Peoples of the Americas. Let Them Call It Jazz. Stewart Brown. WaCA

Peoria. M. Loncar. NAPBL

Pepper. Joe Osterhaus. NAPBL

Pepper in ashes, cassia branches broken, the good man grows old, The.

Sending Off O. E. Who Brought an Orchid Home to Japan. "Lu Hsün." SuSp, *tr. by* William R. Schultz

Peppergrass. Stanley Plumly. LCAP-2

Peppertrees, the peppertrees!, The. Scenes from the Life of the Peppertrees. Denise Levertov. NeAP; PoM

Per Iter Tenebricosum. Oliver St. John Gogarty. OBMV

Peradventure of old, some bard in Ionian Islands. Henry Wadsworth Longfellow. APN-1 *Fr.* Elegiac Verse.

Perambulator Poems, I-VII. David McCord.
  When I Was Christened. KaS; OBCA; OBCoV

Perceived she stirred, but did not see. (LL) Seeing Her Dancing. Robert Heath. NOSC; OxBSP

Perception of an object costs. Emily Dickinson. APN-2; NOBA

Perchance in days to come. Strange Love. Moses Ibn Ezra. TrJP, *tr. by* Solomon Solis-Cohen

Perchance that I might learn what pity is. Prayer for Purification, A. Michelangelo Buonarroti. AWP, *tr. by* John Addington Symonds

Perchance, the friend who cheered thy early years. Judge Not. Josephine D. Henderson Heard. CBWP-4

Perchance to Dream. Mary Low. SurWo

Perched in a tower of this ancestral Wall. At the Great Wall of China. Edmund Charles Blunden. GTBS-P

Perched on his balcony of pleasure. Dialogue, The. Funso Aiyejina. NAfrP

Perching bolt upright. O. Mabson Southard. HA

Percussion, Salt and Honey. Sappho. WoPoe, *tr. by* Guy Davenport

Perdam Sapientiam Sapientum. William Habington. ChIV-2

Père Lalement. Marjorie Lowry Christie Pickthall. NOBC

Peregrin, Wandering Hunter of Faces. José María Eguren. TCLAP, *tr. by* Iver Lofving

Peregrine. Barton Sutter. UrbNat

Peregrine Falcon, New York City. Robert Cording. UrbNat

Peregrine White and Virginia Dare. Rosemary Benét. OBCA

Peregrinus A. Two Strangers, The. Manuel A. Viray. ReBoTo

Perennial. Susan Hahn. IllVoic

Perennial tears descend in gems. (LL) Valley of Unrest, The. Edgar Allan Poe. APN-1; NAAL-2v1; NAAL-3

Perfect. Hugh MacDiarmid. NePenScot; NoP-4; OxBEV; RB; WoPoe

Perfect breakfast, all must own, The. Breakfast. Harry Graham. EBNV

Perfect Child, The. Adrian Porter. NBLV

Perfect Couple, The. Good Marriage, A. Giovanna Pollarolo. TANSG, *tr. by* Marjorie Agosin

Perfect Disc of the Moon, The. Richard Kenney. Son

Perfect Heart, The. Shara McCallum. AmPoNex

Perfect is the silence of this golden day. Elis. Georg Trakl. WoPoe, *tr. by* Robert Firmage

Perfect is the word I can never hear. Rhymes. Charles Tomlinson. DiPo

Perfect Life, The. Jorge Carrera Andrade. TCLAP, *tr. by* Dudley Fitts

Perfect little body, without fault or stain on thee. On a Dead Child. Robert Bridges. EBEV; NOBE; NOBVV; NoAM; OBMV; OxAEP-2; SCGP

Perfect Orchestra, The. Henrietta Cordelia Ray. CBWP-3

Perfect Peace. Frances Ridley Havergal. SacPr

Perfect Reactionary, The. Hughes Mearns. NTCP

Perfect Timing. Sarah Maguire. LW

Perfect Woman. William Wordsworth. GTBS-P; HeIP-4; OBEV; PWR; SCGP; TFi

(She Was a Phantom of Delight.) NoP-4

Perfection, if't hath ever been attayned. In the Due Honor of the Author Master Robert Norton. John Smith. SCAP

Perfection, of a kind, was what he was after. Epitaph on a Tyrant. W. H. Auden. AF; HeIP-4; NoAM; OxBEV; OxBSP; RB

Perfection of Dentistry, The. Marvin Bell. CoAP

Perfectly beautiful, perfectly ignorant of it. (LL) Piazza di Spagna, Early Morning. Richard Wilbur. OxBSP; VGW

Perfecto Flores. Jimmy Santiago Baca. TRP

Performance. Paul McRay. SwNoth

Performance, The. James Dickey. CoAP; CoAmPo; FaBoWar; PoE

Performance at Hog Theater, A. Russell Edson. PmAP

Performance Poem. Bob Holman. KGB

Performance Test. Prageeta Sharma. HeMarv

Performances, assortments, résumés. Hart Crane. MoAmPo; NAAL-5; OxBA *Fr.* Bridge, The.

Performing Seal, The. Rachel Lyman Field. OBCA *Fr.* Circus Garland, A.

Perfume, The. John Donne. ESCV; FSCP; NoSic *Fr.* Elegies.

Perfume, The. Robert Herrick. CaPo

Perfume blows from the kingfisher. Song of Liang Chou. Ou-yang Hsiu. OHPC, *tr. by* Kenneth Rexroth

Perfume / of flowers! A haw, The. Charles Olson. RaBo

Perfume of the ginger-flowers, The.   Ginger-flowers.   Kenneth Mackenzie. BMAP

Perfume of the red water lilies, The.   To the Tune, "Plum Blossoms Fall and Scatter."   Li Ch'ing-chao.   OHPC, tr. by Kenneth Rexroth

Perfume sweet I send you.   Not of Itself, But Thee.   Unknown.   GrAn, tr. by Dudley Fitts

Perhaps.   Sydney Thompson Dobell.   NOBVV

Perhaps.   Perhaps One Day There Will Be Ways.   Armanda Guiducci.   CItWP

Perhaps.   "Shu Ting."   BLT; CarOv, tr. by Carolyn Kizer and Y. H. Zhao

Perhaps he is of medium height.   Hungarian Medical Student: 1928, The. Evelyn Posamentier.   GotH

Perhaps he left the newspaper stand that morning.   Jack Johnson Does the Eagle Rock.   Cornelius Eady.   ESEAA; MoASP

Perhaps he will fall. (LL)   Wilderness Gothic.   Alfred Wellington Purdy. HeIP-4; MoCV; NOBC; NoP-4

Perhaps he will press his warm lips.   Lebanon.   Frank O'Hara.   CAGL

Perhaps I asked too large.   Emily Dickinson.   TCAPo

Perhaps I may allow, the Dean.   Jonathan Swift.   NOBE; OxBEV; PeLV   Fr. Verses on the Death of Dr. Swift, D.S.P.D.

Perhaps I've got to write better longer thinking of it.   On Induction of the Hand.   Clark Coolidge.   PmAP

Perhaps if she stood for an hour like that.   Woman at Lit Window.   Eamon Grennan.   BLT

Perhaps if we are lucky.   Zuni Oral Tradition.   NAWM-7v2, tr. by Ruth L. Bunzel   Fr. Prayer at the Winter Solstice, A.

Perhaps in hell time has.   Lover Digresses, The.   Luis Cernuda.   CAGL, tr. by Rick Lipinski

Perhaps it is to avoid some great sadness.   Sleeping on the Wing.   Frank O'Hara.   NAAL-2v2

Perhaps it's a question of what.   Black Poppy (At the Temple).   David St. John.   BodElec

Perhaps it's as You Say.   Peter Everwine.   GeoHom; NNaP

Perhaps it was the fishing boat.   My Father's Words.   Lucy Hamilton.   Prnts

Perhaps, like everything, it has its flow and ebb.   My Cousin Abe, Paul Antschel and Paul Celan.   Jacqueline Osherow.   TaR

Perhaps my mother murdered me. (LL)   Inquest, The.   William Henry Davies. AngWePo; GTBS-P; NOBE; OxBTC; RB

Perhaps No Poem at All But All I Can Say and I Cannot Be Silent.   Denise Levertov.   SacPr

Perhaps on a sunday.   Day Song.   Lance Henson.   HATNAP

Perhaps One Day There Will Be Ways.   Armanda Guiducci.   CItWP

Perhaps one morning the sky will be.   Imani in Sunburst Summer: A Chant. Askia M. Toure.   SpirFl

Perhaps she said, lively at first but once.   Farmer Goes Beserk.   Anne Elder. CBAP

Perhaps the ankle of a horse is holy.   There Are Two Worlds.   Larry Levis. BodElec

Perhaps the smile and tender tone.   Tennyson.   NAEL-6v2   Fr. Maud [A Monodrama].

Perhaps the Time of Blood.   Franco Fortini.   ItPo, tr. by Gayle Ridinger

Perhaps the time of blood is on the return.   Perhaps the Time of Blood. Franco Fortini.   ItPo, tr. by Gayle Ridinger

Perhaps the World Ends Here.   Joy Harjo.   MakPoe; ReEnLa

Perhaps the world will end at the kitchen table, while we are laughing and crying, eating of the last sweet bite. (LL)   Perhaps the World Ends Here. Joy Harjo.   MakPoe; ReEnLa

Perhaps there has never before been such an open sea.   Invisible Hand.   L. S. Asekoff.   BodElec

Perhaps these thoughts of ours.   Perhaps.   "Shu Ting."   BLT; CarOv, tr. by Carolyn Kizer and Y. H. Zhao

Perhaps they heard we don't understand them.   What the Japanese Perhaps Heard.   Rachel Rose.   BAP-01

Perhaps they'll have some more a year hence. (LL)   Byron.   CABP; FHYEP Fr. Don Juan.

Perhaps this valley too leads into the head of long-ago days.   Grand Abacus. John Ashbery.   SPE

Perhaps you expected a face that was free from tears.   Narcissus.   Paul Valéry. AWP, tr. by Joseph T. Shipley

Perhaps you have seen The Dinner Party, tables set with linens and.   Dinner, The.   Rosario Morales.   PueRic

Perhaps you have sworn.   Jane Duran.   Prnts   Fr. Silences from the Spanish Civil War.

Perhaps you may of Priam's Fate enquire.   Virgil [or Vergil].   NPeEn, tr. by John Dryden   Fr. Aeneid [or Eneados, Aeneis], The.

Pericles.   William Shakespeare.
   "Terrible child-bed hast thou had, my dear, A."   EBEV; OxAEP-1

Pericles and Aspasia.   Walter Savage Landor.
   "Beauty! thou art a wanderer on the earth."   SCGP
   Behold, O Aspasia! I Send You Verses.   SCGP

Corinna, from Athens, to Tanagra.   OBEV

(Corinna, to Tanagra, from Athens.)   NOBE

Dirce.   AWP; CTC; EBEV; FaBoEE; HAP; NAEL-6v2; NOBE; NPeEn; NoP-4; OBEV; OxAEP-2; OxBEV; OxBSP; PoRA; SCGP; TFi; WeW-3; WoPoe

"Stand close around, ye Stygian set."   AWP; CTC; EBEV; FaBoEE; HAP; NAEL-6v2; NOBE; NPeEn; NoP-4; OBEV; OxAEP-2; OxBEV; OxBSP; PoRA; SCGP; TFi; WeW-3; WoPoe

"Tanagra! think not I forget."   OBEV

Pericoloso Sporgersi.   Joyce Mansour.
   "Naked / I float among the wreckage with steel mustaches."   SurPaPo, tr. by Mary Ann Caws

Peridot.   Rebecca Reynolds.   AmPoNex

Period.   Ronald Stuart Thomas.   HarvBoo

Peripatetic Letter to Isabella Fey, A.   David Wright.
   "This was as far as I had got."   PeSAV

Peripeteia.   Anthony Hecht.   VCAP

Periphery.   A. R. Ammons.   NOBA

Periphery.   Ruth Stone.   NALW

Perirrhanterium.   George Herbert.   ESCV

Perish th' illiberal thought which would debase.   Hannah More.   ECWP   Fr. Slavery, a Poem.

Perishing Bird, The.   Douglas G. Jones.   MoCV

Periwig, A.   Rowland Watkyns.   NOSC

Perla at the Mexican Border Assembly Line of Dolls.   Rigoberto González. AmPoNex

Perlas.   Víctor Hernández Cruz.   TouFir

Perle, pleasunte to prynces paye.   Unknown.   EBEV   Fr. Pearl.

Perle pleasunte to prynces paye Pearl, the precious prize of a king.   Unknown. See Perle, pleasunte to prynces paye

Permanence in Change.   Goethe.   STV, tr. by John Frederick Nims

Permanence of the Young Men, The.   William Soutar.   OxBS

Permanent Delegate, The.   Yuri Suhl.   PAI, tr. by Walter Lowenfels and Max Rosenfeld

Permanent Tourists, The.   Patricia K. Page.   NOBC

Permanently.   Kenneth Koch.   CoAP; NoP-4; PmAP; PoM

Permit Marissa in an artless Lay.   To Almystrea.   Mary Lee, Lady Chudleigh. EMWP

Permit Me Voyage.   James Agee.   MoAmPo; YaYoPo

Permit me voyage, love, into your hands. (LL)   Hart Crane.   AmFaPo; ColAP; OxBA   Fr. Voyages.

Permit Us, Lord, to Consecrate.   Joseph Green.   AH

Peroration, Concerning Genius.   Robert Pinsky.   NoAM   Fr. Essay on Psychiatrists.

Perpetua.   Olga Broumas.   ErotSp

Perpetual Infirmity of Hope.   Sister Juana Inés de la Cruz.   SpanPo, tr. by Muriel Kittel

Perpetuum Immobile.   Bruce Dawe.   CBAP

Perpetuum Mobile: The City.   William Carlos Williams.   APT-1

Perplexity.   Ibrahim Tuqan.   MAP, tr. by John Heath-Stubbs and Christopher Tingley

Perplexity: A Poem.   Elizabeth Hands.   WoRP

Perse owt of[f] Northombarlande, The.   Chevy Chase.   Unknown.   OxBB

Persecutions Purifie.   Robert Herrick.   SacPr

Persephone.   Robert Duncan.   NOBA

Persephone.   Ziporah Hildebrandt.   HW

Persephone.   Michael Longley.   NPeEn; PBCIP

Persephone.   Kathleen Norris.   HW

Persephone Abducted.   Rita Dove.   NAAAL   Fr. Mother Love.

Persephone ate seven pomegranate seeds. So What? I'll tell you what.   Ovid. ModIr, tr. by Ciaran Carson   Fr. Metamorphoses.

Persephone, 1978.   Thomas McCarthy.   ModIr

Persephone's Journey.   Patricia Monaghan.   HW

Persephone That Is to Say Double Issue.   René Daumal.   PFTM-1

Persephone, to Demeter.   Marilyn Krysl.   HW

Persephone Underground.   Rita Dove.   FFC

Perseus.   Robert Earl Hayden.   NoAM

Perseverance.   Martin Sorescu.   VCWP, tr. by D. J Enright and Joana Russell-Gebbett

Persia.   Victoria Mary Sackville-West.   WPE

Persian, The.   Stevie Smith.   FaBoWP

Persian Fopperies.   Horace.   AWP, tr. by William Cowper   Fr. Odes.

Persian Miniature.   William Jay Smith.   CoAP

Persian Parables.   Aleksander Wat.
   "By a great, swift water."   AF; WoPoe, tr. by Czeslaw Milosz

Persian Song of Hafiz, A.   Hafiz [or Hafez].   AWP, tr. by Sir William Jones

Persian Version, The.   Robert Graves.   NOBL; NoAM; NoP-4; OBWP; WeW-3

Persicos Odi: Pocket Version. Horace. NBLV, *tr.* by Austin Dobson *Fr.*
    Odes.
Persimmons. Li-Young Lee. NAAL-5; NIL-7; NIP-4; NoP-4; OPRER
Persimmons. Virginia Brady Young. HA
Persistence of Nature in Our Lives, The. Andrew Hudgins. DiPo; WeW-3
Persistence of Song, The. Howard Moss. NoP-4
Persistent Explorer. John Crowe Ransom. OxBA
Person, The. Lyn Hejinian.
    "Solitude flared out, The." FTOS
Person, The. Charles Hubert Sisson. HarvBoo
Person as Dreamer: We Talk about the Future, The. Michael Hartnett. PBCIP
    Fr. Notes on My Contemporaries.
Person, for you, is a book, A. Writer. Joe Wenderoth. BodElec
Person from Porlock, A. Ronald Stuart Thomas. TOF
Person is very self-conscious about his head, A. Thoughts on One's Head.
    William Meredith. HAP; VCAP
Person place thing tree. Diana Helen Melhem. PoArWo *Fr.* Country.
Person's Tale, The. U. A. Fanthorpe. NoP-4
Person sleeping under the chair, The. Chair. Hagiwara Sakutaro. PFTM-1
Personae Separatae. Eugenio Montale. AF, *tr.* by William Arrowsmith
Personal. Langston Hughes. NOBA
Personal. Peter Rafferty. NLP
Personal Ad. Joanna Fuhrman. AmPoNex
Personal Atlas. Rosalie Moore. YaYoPo
Personal Column. Tom Paulin. PNI
Personal Footnote, A. Gavin Ewart. FaBoWar
Personal Helicon. Seamus Heaney. NPeEn
Personal Histories, The. Michael Burkard. BodElec
Personal History of Hands, A. Lori Jakiela. ReTh
Personal Letter No. 3. Sonia Sanchez. ESEAA; SSLK
Personal Poem. Frank O'Hara. CLPP; PmAP
Personal Poem #9. Ted Berrigan. PmAP *Fr.* Sonnets, The.
Personal Reflections. Ahmad al-Mushari Al-'Udwani.
    "I asked the grave-digger, Do you have." MAP
Personal Talk. William Wordsworth. NOBE
Personality. Agnes Mary Frances Robinson. VWP
Personality. Jimmy Van Heusen. ReLy
Personality syndrome, The. Alan Davies. FTOS *Fr.* Name.
Personals. Star Black. KGB
Personification of a Name, The. Ray A. Young Bear. HATNAP
Persons, people, and the years. Velemir [*or* Viktor Vladimirovich] Khlebnikov.
    TCRP
Persons Unknown. Aidan Carl Mathews. BiHa
Perspective. Coventry Patmore. FaBoEE *Fr.* Angel in the House, The.
"Perspective," he would mutter, going to bed. Perspective He Would Mutter
    Going to Bed. Jack Gilbert. YaYoPo
Perspective Lovesong. "Ern Malley." BMAP
Perspective of lines or, The. Arroyo, The. Brenda Hillman. ExTi
Perspectives. Chiqui Vicioso. TANSG, *tr.* by Emma Jane Robinett
Perspectives on the Second World War. Irena Klepfisz. TaR
Persuade our Feathers Home. (LL) Emily Dickinson. APN-2; BoWoP
Persuasion. Patty Seyburn. AmPoNex
Persuasion. William Wordsworth. OWoS *Fr.* Ecclesiastical Sonnets.
Persuasions to Enjoy. Thomas Carew. BeJo; NOBE
    (Persuasions to Joy; a Song.) OBEV
    (Song: Persuasions to Enjoy.) CaPo; NAEL-5v1; NOSC
Persuasions to Joy; a Song. Thomas Carew. *See* Persuasions to Enjoy
Peru Eye, the Heart of the Lamp. Clark Coolidge. APSN
Perugia. Art Lange. PmAP
Peruvian restaurant served, The. California Potatoes. Denise Low. SpudSo
Pervasive and. Theoretical People. Paul Hoover. IllVoic
Perverse habit of cat goddesses, A. Cat Goddesses. Robert Graves. OxBSP
Perversion, A. Christopher Reid. OBCoV
Pesach Has Come to the Ghetto Again. Binem Heller. TrJP, *tr.* by Max
    Rosenfeld
Pesci Misti. Leonard [*or* Lazarus] Aaronson. FaBoTw
Pessimist, The. Ben King. NBLV; OBAL
    (Sum of Life, The.) CTC
Pessimist, The. *Unknown.* PoToHe
Pessimist's a cheerless man, The. Pessimist, The. *Unknown.* PoToHe
Pessimist's Vision, The. Constance Naden. VWP; ViWPN
Pestel, the Poet, and Anna. "David Samuilovich Samoylov" [*or* Samoilov].
    TCRP, *tr.* by Lubov Yakovleva
Pet Deer, The. James Tate. SPE
Pet-name, a common name, A. Best-selling brand, curt. Geoffrey Hill.
    NoAM; WoPoe *Fr.* Mercian Hymns.

Pet Names. Bernard Cooper. Unle
Petal by petal, the Spring dissolves. Tu Fu. CarOv, *tr.* by Carolyn Kizer *Fr.*
    Meandering River Poems, The.
Petal shower, A. Basho. EH, *tr.* by Robert Hass
Petals fall, The. Buson. EH, *tr.* by Robert Hass
Petals fall from Heliodora's image, The. Meleager. GrAn
Petals fall in the fountain, The. Ts'ai Chi'h. Ezra Pound. NoP-4
Petals on a wet, black bough. (LL) In a Station of the Metro. Ezra Pound.
    APT-1; ChAP; ColAP; HAP; HeIP-4; InPK-6; MoAmPo; NAAL-2v2;
    NAAL-5; NIL-7; NIP-4; NOBA; NPeEn; NoAM; NoP-4; OxBA; PAI; PoE;
    PoPoPo; TAP; TCAPo; TFi; UnPo; VGW; WeW-3
Petals red and purple turn to mud, and mud to dust. Fallen Blossoms. Yang
    Wan-li. SuSp, *tr.* by Sherwin S. S. Fu
Pete at the Zoo. Gwendolyn Brooks. TLR
Petelia Tablet, The. *Unknown.* WoPoe, *tr.* by Robert Bringhurst
Peter. Marianne Craig Moore. APT-1; NAAL-2v2; NoP-4; OxBA
Peter and Aleksey. Yaroslav [*or* Iaroslav] Vasilevich Smelyakov [*or*
    Smeliakov]. TCRP, *tr.* by Simon Franklin and Albert C. Todd
Peter and John. Elinor Wylie. MakPoe; MoAmPo
Peter Bell the Third. Shelley.
    "Devil now knew his proper cue, The." OBSV
    "Hell is a city much like London." OBSV
Peter broke the ragged branch to push his nostrils closer. West Paddocks.
    Arthur Davies. NOBAu
Peter died in a paper tiara cut. Tiara. Mark Doty. MakPoe
Peter Grimes. George Crabbe. EBNV; ECEV; FHYEP; OBNV *Fr.* Borough,
    The.
Peter had experienced the tight, nauseous desire. Wickedness of Peter
    Shannon, The. Alden Nowlan. MoCV
Peter Pan in North America. Robin Becker. ReTh
Peter-penny, The. Robert Herrick. CaPo
Peter, Peter, pumpkin eater. Pumpkin-Eater, The. Mother Goose. OxNR;
    ReMoGo
Peter Piper picked a peck of pickled pepper[s]. Mother Goose. LB; OTCP;
    OxNR; ReMoGo
Peter Quince at the Clavier. Wallace Stevens. APT-1; HeIP-4; InPK-6;
    MoAmPo; NAAL-5; NAWM-7v2; NOBA; NoAM; NoP-4; OxBA; PAI;
    PoE; SAmP; TAP; TCAPo; TFi; TwCP
Peter Rabbit. Sandra McPherson. LCAP-2
Peter's not friendly. He gives me sideways looks. John Berryman. ChIV-2
    Fr. Dream Songs.
Peter the Great, first Bolshevik. Maksimilian Aleksandrovich Voloshin. TCRP
    Fr. Russia.
Peter, Tom, David, Jim and Howard are gone. Condemned Site. Mona Van
    Duyn. MakPoe
Peter White will ne'er go right. Mother Goose. OxBoLi; OxNR
Peterhead in May. Burns Singer. OxBS
Petersburg. Innokenty Fiodorovich Annensky. TCRP, *tr.* by Daniel Weissbort
    and Lubov Yakovleva
Petersburg Strophes. Osip Emilevich Mandelstam [*or* Mandelshtam]. TCRP,
    tr. by Bernard Meares
Petit Guignol. Philip Hammial. BMAP
Petit Testament. "Ern Malley." BMAP
Petit, the Poet. Edgar Lee Masters. ColAP; MoAmPo; NOBA; NoAM;
    OxBA; TAP; TCAPo *Fr.* Spoon River Anthology.
Petition. W. H. Auden. NAEL-5v2; NAEL-6v2; Son
Petition. Brigit Pegeen Kelly. ExTi
Petition. Ronald Stuart Thomas. FaBoMo
Petition, A. Frances Anne [*or* "Fanny"] Kemble. LW
Petition, The. Thomas Beedome. NOSC
Petition for an Absolute Retreat, The. Anne Finch, Countess of Winchilsea.
    WPE
    "Give me, O indulgent fate!" ECWP; NOSC
Petition for Reconciliation. Cynddelw Brydydd Mawr. OBWVE, *tr.* by Joseph
    P. Clancy
Petition from the Chain Gang at Newcastle to Captain Furlong the
    Superintendent, A. Francis MacNamara. NOBAu
Petition of the Gray Horse, Auld Dunbar, The. William Dunbar. OxBS
Petition of the Orangemen of Ireland, The. Thomas Moore. NOIV
Petition to Father and Son and Holy Ghost, A. *Unknown.* SacPr
Petitioners are full of prayers. Lament of Swordy Well, The. John Clare.
    FaBoVe
Petra. John William Burgon.
    "Match me such marvel save in Eastern clime." UV
Petrarch. Giosuè Carducci. AWP, *tr.* by William Dudley Foulke
Petrarch. Nicholas Kilmer.
    "In my first gentle days." PeECV
Petrarch watched a plague: it took. Prognosis. George Starbuck. YaYoPo

Petrified Echoes. Vasco [*or* Vasko] Popa. PoSu, *tr. by* Anne Pennington *Fr.* Yawn of Yawns, The.

Petrograd Side, The. Lev Vladimir Loseff [*or* Losev]. TCRusP, *tr. by* Henry Pickford

Petropolis. Osip Emilevich Mandelstam [*or* Mandelshtam]. PeFWW

Petrushka's valentine pivots on its pin. (LL) Wine Menagerie, The. Hart Crane. APT-2; NOBA; NoAM; OxBA; VGW

Petticoat, A. Gertrude Stein. TTTS *Fr.* Tender Buttons.

Pettitoes are little feet, The. *Unknown.* OxNR

Petty Bourgeoisie, The. Roque Dalton. TCLAP, *tr. by* Richard Schaaf

Petty sneaking Knave I knew, A. Mr. Cromek [*or* On Cromek]. William Blake. FaBoEE

Petulance is purple. Spectrum. Mari E. Evans. BPo

Peveril of the Peak. Sir Walter Scott.
"Speak not of niceness, when there's chance of wreck." FaBoEE

Pewits Nest. John Clare. FaBoVe

Pewter. Jack Gilbert. BodElec

Pewter loons, ceramic bunnies, and faux bamboo. Mail Order Catalogs. William Matthews. ReTh

Peyote Poem. Michael McClure. PoM
"Clear—the senses bright—sitting in the black chair—Rocker." BB; NeAP

Peyote Vision. Lew Blockcolski. VoR

Pfarr-Schmerz (Village-Anguish). Veronica Forrest-Thomson. HarvBoo

Phaedra. Osip Emilevich Mandelstam [*or* Mandelshtam]. OBVE, *tr. by* James Greene

Phaedria's Island: The Faerie Queene II.vi. 12–17. Edmund Spenser. *See* Faerie Queene, The

Phaenomena. Aratus.
"Beneath both the feet of Boötes you may see." HePo
Proem: "From Zeus let us begin, him we mortals never." HePo, *tr. by* Barbara Hughes Fowler
"Take as a sign of the rising wind the swelling sea." HePo, *tr. by* Barbara Hughes Fowler
Weather Signs. HePo, *tr. by* Barbara Hughes Fowler

Phallic Root. Kazuko Shiraishi. WPOW

Phallus. Kazuko Shiraishi. BoWoP, *tr. by* Ikuko Atsumi

Phantasia for Elvira Shatayev. Adrienne Rich. NALW; WWork

Phantasies. Emma Lazarus.
Evening. APN-2
"Rest, beauty, stillness: not a waif of cloud." APN-2

Phantasus. Arno Holz. AWP, *tr. by* Ludwig Lewisohn

Phantom. Samuel Taylor Coleridge. NAEL-5v2; NAEL-6v2; OxBSP

Phantom. Tawfiq [*or* Taufiq] Sayigh. MAP, *tr. by* Thomas G. Ezzy and Anne Royal

Phantom Anthems. Robert Grenier.
Easter Roses. FTOS
"So I experienced." FTOS

Phantom Haiku/Silent Film. Jacqueline Osherow. ExTi

Phantom Horsewoman, The. Thomas Hardy. NOBE

Phantom Light of All Our Day, The. Nathaniel Mackey. GT

Phantom of Clouds, A. Guillaume Apollinaire.
As it was the eve of the 14th of July. PFTM-1

Phantom streams were in the distance—mocking lights of lake and pool. Christmas Creek. Henry Clarence Kendall. CBAP

Phantom-Wooer, The. Thomas Lovell Beddoes. NAEL-5v2; NAEL-6v2

Phantoms approached, we were told, The. Bomb That Fell on Abdu's Farm, The. Gregory Orfalea. GraLe

Phaon Awakes. Mary Robinson. CenSon; RWP

Phaon Forsakes Her. Mary Robinson. CenSon; RWP

Pharao's Daughter. Michael Moran. BIrV; ChIV-1

Pharaoh. Jane Kenyon. LoL

Pharaoh's Palace. David Wojahn. AllShUp

Pharaohs of Today, The. Lizelia Augusta Jenkins Moorer. CBWP-3

Pharisee murmurs when the woman weeps, conscious of guilt, The. Sequaire. Godeschalk. CTC, *tr. by* Ezra Pound

Pharmacy. Aaron Anstett. AmPoNex

Pharoah's Army Got Drowned. Lynn Domina. OPRER

Pharonnida. William Chamberlayne.
Bad Landlord, The. NOSC

Pharsalia. Lucan.
"All great things crush themselves; such end the gods." NoSic
"Just and fit actions, Ptolemy (he saith)." OBVE, *tr. by* Ben Jonson
"O wastfull riot, never well content." OBVE
Speech out of Lucan, A. OBVE, *tr. by* Ben Jonson
"Thee Pompey thy past deeds by turns infest." OBVE
"When Caesar saw his army prone to war." NoSic

Phase Four. John Berryman. BodElec

Phases. Wallace Stevens.
"This was the salty taste of glory." FaBoWar
"What shall we say to the lovers of freedom." FaBoWar

Phases of Darkness, The. Paul Petrie. TAP

Pheasant. Sylvia Plath. RB

Pheasant cries, The. Issa. EH, *tr. by* Robert Hass

Pheasant of the mountain, The. Kakinomoto no Hitomaro. OHPJ

Pheasant on His Morning Flight, A. Hsiao Kang. ColAnChi, *tr. by* Victor H. Mair and Tsu-Lin Mei

Pheasant Plucker's Son, The. Mick North. NLP

Phebus fonde first the craft of medecine. *Unknown.* MiEL

Phemios and Medon. Homer. ModIr *Fr.* Odyssey.

Phenomena. Robinson Jeffers. NOBA; OxBA

Phenomenology of Anger, The. Adrienne Rich. PFTM-2; PoE

Phenomenology of Stones, The. Thomas McCarthy. PBCIP

Phenomenon, A. Job Degenaar. TuT, *tr. by* Aidan Sharkey

Pheobus, arise! / And paint the sable skies. Invocation. William Drummond, of Hawthornden. OBEV

Phido the miser's crying. Nicarchus of Alexandria. GrAn

Philadelphia / a disguised southern city. Elegy (for MOVE and Philadelphia). Sonia Sanchez. ESEAA

Philadelphia is burning and water. Overture: Watermelon City. Elizabeth Alexander. NAPBL

Philadelphia: Spring, 1985. Sonia Sanchez. ESEAA

Philaenion is small and swart, but her hair curls more. Philodemus. HePo *Fr.* Epigrams.

Philainion is short and. Philodemus. PGA

Philanthropist and the Jelly-fish, The. May Kendall. VWP; ViWPN

Philemon and Baucis. Ovid. CTC, *tr. by* Arthur Golding *Fr.* Metamorphoses.

Philip V of Macedon. Alcaeus [*or* Alkaios]. GrAn, *tr. by* Alistair Elliot

Philip and Mildred. Adelaide Anne Procter. VWP

Philip at Kynoskephalai. Alcaeus [*or* Alkaios]. GrAn, *tr. by* Alistair Elliot

Philip has stolen a tie. Philip the Store Policeman. Lesley Dauer. AmPoNex

Philip of Macedon. Alcaeus [*or* Alkaios]. GrAn, *tr. by* Alistair Elliot

Philip Sparrow. John Skelton. *See* Phyllyp Sparowe

Philip the Store Policeman. Lesley Dauer. AmPoNex

Philip van Artevelde. Sir Henry Taylor.
Elena's Song. OBEV; RACG
"Quoth tongue of neither maid nor wife." OBEV; RACG

Philip Whalen's Hat. Joanne Kyger. BB

Philip, your poems tell. It was your lot. Lament for Philip Larkin, A. Joseph Awad. GraLe

Philippians 1.23. Francis Quarles. ChIV-2

Philippine Figures. *Unknown.* EaWin, *tr. by* W. S. Merwin

Philistion of Nikaia lies here, whose laughter. Epitaph of a Nicene Actor. *Unknown.* GrAn, *tr. by* Dudley Fitts

Philistion's a hard bitch:/ in her book "penniless lover." Maccius. GrAn

Phillida and Coridon. *Var. authors.* NoSic; OBEV; TTTS *Fr.* Honourable Entertainment Given to the Queen's Majesty in Progress at Elvetham, 1591, The.

Phillida Flouts Me [*or* The Disdainful Shepherdess]. *Unknown.* OBEV

Phillip Sparow. John Skelton.
"Pla ce bo." NoP-4

Phillip Sparow. John Skelton. NoP-4 *Fr.* Phillip Sparow.

Phillips, whose touch harmonious could remove. Epitaph upon the Celebrated Claudy Phillips, Musician, Who Died Very Poor, An. Samuel Johnson. NOEC

Phillis 2. Thomas Lodge. *See* Phyllis

Phillis and Coridon. Robert Greene. NoSic

Phillis is my only joy. Song. Sir Charles Sedley. EnLoPo

Phillis, let's shun the common fate. Song. Sir Charles Sedley. NPeEn

Phillis's Age. Matthew Prior. EnLoPo
(Phyllis's Age.) FaBoEE

Phillis's Resolution. William Walsh. OxBSP

Philo the gentleman, the fortune teller. Sir John Davies. NoSic *Fr.* Epigrams.

Philocles. Leonidas of Tarentum. AWP, *tr. by* F. A. Wright

Philoctetes. John Byrne Leicester Warren, 3d Baron De Tabley. NOBVV

Philoctetes. Henry Reed. HarvBoo

Philodes, if Desire, sweet Blandishment. To Diodorus, Dorotheus, Callicrates et al. Meleager. CAGL, *tr. by* Daryl Hine

Philokles offers his bouncing. Leonidas. GrAn; PGA

Philomel. *Var. authors.* NOBE; OBEV *Fr.* Passionate Pilgrim, The.

Philomela. Matthew Arnold. FHYEP; OBEV; OWoS; UnPo

Philomela. John Crowe Ransom. APT-1; FuPo; NAAL-2v2; NOBA; NoAM; OBAL; OBSV; OxBA

Philomela. Sir Philip Sidney. *See* Nightingale, The

Philomena Andronico. William Carlos Williams. FaBoMo

Philon the Shepherd. *Unknown. See* Unfaithful Shepherdess, The

Philosopher, A. Sam Walter Foss. OBAL

Philosopher, The. Emily Jane Brontë. BWW

Philosopher, The. Syl Cheney-Coker. PBMAP *Fr.* Blood in the Desert's Eyes, The.

Philosopher, The. Sara Teasdale. PoToHe

Philosopher and the Birds, The. Richard Murphy. CIP-2

Philosopher and the Lover; To a Mistress Dying, The. Sir William Davenant [*or* D'Avenant]. *See* Lover and Philosopher

Philosopher Berkeley once said, The. Limerick. P. W. R. Foot. PeLi

Philosopher's Stone, The. Konrad Bayer.
  Electrical Hierarchy, The. PFTM-2, *tr.* by Walter Billeter

Philosophers have measured [*or* measur'd] mountains. Agony [*or* Agonie], The. George Herbert. ESCV; GeHe

Philosophers: Lao-Tzu, The. Po Chü-i. BLT, *tr.* by Arthur Waley

Philosophic Flight, The. Giordano Bruno. AWP, *tr.* by John Addington Symonds

Philosophic Taed, The. William Soutar. NePenScot

Philosophical Songs. Charles North. KGB

Philosophy. John Kendrick Bangs. PoToHe

Philosophy. Ray Catina. CDa

Philosophy. "Rubén Dario." SpanPo, *tr.* by Muna Lee

Philosophy. Paul Laurence Dunbar. BPo; NAAAL

Philosophy. Elsa Gidlow. PoBW

Philosophy. Amy Levy. ViWPN

Philosophy of Life. Dániel Berzsenyi. IQMS, *tr.* by Watson Kirkconnell

Philosophy of white blood cells, The. Immanuel Kant. Miroslav Holub. VCWP

Philosophy, the great and only heir. Abraham Cowley. BASC; BeJo

Philothea (Lydia Child). James Russell Lowell. TCAPo *Fr.* Fable for Critics, A.

Phineas dwelled midst lives of many pieces. Phineas Within and Without. Paul Zimmer. VGW

Phineas Within and Without. Paul Zimmer. VGW

Phlebas the Phoenician, a fortnight dead. T. S. Eliot. NPeEn; OBVE; OxBEV *Fr.* Waste Land, The.

Phlegmatic winter on a bed of snow. Born in Winter. Francis Quarles. NOSC

Phoebe in a Rosebush. Clyde Watson. NTCP

Phoebe's cry, A. Anita Virgil. HA

Phoebus. James Russell Lowell. TCAPo *Fr.* Fable for Critics, A.

Phoebus, accept this dinner that I bring you. Automedon. GrAn

Phoebus and Boreas. Jean de La Fontaine. WoPoe, *tr.* by Marianne Craig Moore

Phœbus Apollo, from Olympus driven. Christopher Pearse Cranch. APN-1 *Fr.* Seven Wonders of the World.

Phoebus, make haste, the day's too long, be gone. Another. Anne Bradstreet. BASC

Phoebus, sitting one day in a laurel tree's shade. James Russell Lowell. TCAPo *Fr.* Fable for Critics, A.

Phoebus was a herdsman. Antipater of Thessalonica. GrAn

Phoebus with Admetus. George Meredith. NOBE; OBEV

Phoenix. Elizabeth Kay. Prnts

Phoenix, The. Ilya Abu Madi. MAP, *tr.* by Issa Boullata and Naomi Shihab Nye

Phoenix, The. Arthur Christopher Benson. OBEV

Phoenix, The. Cynewulf.
  "When stars are hid in the western wave, dimmed at dawn." WoPoe, *tr.* by Frank Kuenstler

Phoenix, The. George Darley. NOBE *Fr.* Nepenthe.

Phoenix, The. *Unknown.*
  "I have heard that far from here." ASW
  "Lo! I have learned of the loveliest of lands." AnOE
  "When the wind is asleep and the weather set fair." ASW

Phoenix and the Turtle, The. William Shakespeare. NOBE; NoSic; OBEV; OxAEP-1; OxBEV; PeECV; SCGP
  (Let the bird of loudest lay.) CABP; NoP-4
  (Let the bird of lowdest lay.) PBRV
  (Phoenix and Turtle, The.) CABP; NPeEn; PBRV

Phoenix and Turtle, The. William Shakespeare. *See* Phoenix and the Turtle, The

Phoenix, bird of terrible pride. Sir Herbert Read. FaBoTw *Fr.* Mutations of the Phoenix.

Phoenix birds once frolicked on Phoenix Terrace, The. Climbing Phoenix Terrace at Chin-ling. Li Po. SuSp, *tr.* by Joseph J. Lee

Phoenix Hairpins. Lu Yu. OHPC, *tr.* by Kenneth Rexroth

Phoenix is rising, The. Transformation. Adria Klinger. PasH

Phoenix tail on scented silk, flimsy layer on layer. Li Shang-yin. WoPoe, *tr.* by A. C. Graham

Phoenixes and Sparrows. *Vietnamese Oral Tradition.* CaDao, *tr.* by John Balaban

Phoenixes compete, so do sparrows. Phoenixes and Sparrows. *Vietnamese Oral Tradition.* CaDao, *tr.* by John Balaban

Phol and Wotan rode through the forest. Second Merseburg Spell. *Unknown.* GePo, *tr.* by Carroll Hightower

Phone Booth at the Corner, The. Juan Delgado. TouFir

Phone call. Alexis Rotella. HA

Phone Call to Rutherford. Paul Blackburn. PFTM-2; PoM

Phone for the fish-knives, Norman. How to Get On in Society. Sir John Betjeman. NOBL; OBSV; OxBTC; UV

Phone Sex. Richard Tayson. WiU

Phonemics. Jack Spicer. PmAP

'Phoning. Peter Sirr. BiHa

Phooie! Robert Garioch. FaBoWar

Phosphor Reading by His Own Light. Wallace Stevens. APT-1

Photo Genic. Olga Broumas. ExTi

Photo—narrow, leonine, Hebraic, old. United Way, The. Jack Marshall. GraLe

Photo of My Father in a Snowbound Train. David Wojahn. GM

Photo of someone else's childhood, A. Old Adam, The. Denise Levertov. UnPo

Photo: on a hill a yellow house, white portico, A. From an Album. Genrik Veniaminovich Sapgir. ItGoST, *tr.* by J. Kates

Photo Safari. Bruce Berger. PoCoUp

Photo shows me, The. Others Hunters in the North the Cree, The. Jerome Rothenberg. PoM

Photo Taken in Winter, 1944. Barbara Unger. TWW

Photograph, The. Christopher Pearse Cranch. APN-1 *Fr.* Seven Wonders of the World.

Photograph, The. Myra Schneider. Prnts

Photograph and White Tulips. Dannie Abse. TCAWP

Photograph in a Stockholm Newspaper for March 13, 1910. Don Coles. NOBC

Photograph: Migrant Worker, Parlier, California, 1967. Larry Levis. GeoHom

Photograph of a Bawd Drinking Raleigh Rye. Natasha Trethewey. NeAmPo

Photograph of a Child, Japanese-American Evacuation, Bainbridge Island, Washington, March 30, 1942. James Masao Mitsui. OpBo

Photograph of Haymaker, 1890. Molly Holden. OxBTC

Photograph of My Parents. Silvia Curbelo. TouFir

Photograph of Survivors. Gail Newman. GotH

Photographs. Alec Wilder. ReLy

Photographs, fading already, recall my discomfort. Getting It Wrong, Again. Steve Griffiths. AngWePo

Photographs from a Book: Six Poems. David Ferry.
  "Poem again, of several parts, each having to do, A." FaBoA

Photographs of My Father. Judith Ortiz Cofer. ExTi

Photographs of Pioneer Women. Ruth Dallas. PeNZ

Photographs were yellow where death is a bidden slow form splitting cells through the day. Masters, The. Gillian Conoley. BodElec

Photoheliograph (For Lady A.). Harry Crosby. APT-2

Photos. Hugh Seidman. BodElec

Photos, The. Diane Wakoski. NIP-4

Photos and clippings fade. Archives. Michael S. Harper. MoASP

Photos of a Salt Mine. Patricia K. Page. NIP-4; NOBC; NoAM

Phrase-Book. Veronica Forrest-Thomson. HarvBoo

Phraseology. Jayne Cortez. BlSi

Phryne. John Donne. FaBoEE

Phyllidula. Ezra Pound. FaBoTw

Phyllis. Thomas Lodge.
  I Hope and Fear. Son
  Love Guards [*or* Guides] the Roses of Thy Lips. NoSic; Son
  ("Love guards the roses of thy lips.") AEP
  No Stars Her Eyes. Son
  O Pleasing Thoughts. Son
  (Phillis 2.) OBEV
  (Phillis 1.) OBEV

Phyllis. Thomas Randolph. BoLoP *Fr.* Pastoral Courtship, A.

Phillis 1. Thomas Lodge. OBEV *Fr.* Phyllis.

Phyllis Corydon clutched him. Catullus. BoLoP *Fr.* Carmina.

Phyllis, loving Demophoon. Cometas. ErotSp, *tr.* by Sam Hamill

Phyllis [*or* Phillis] [*or* Progress of Love, The]. Jonathan Swift. EBNV; OBCoV; OBSV; PoE

Phyllis's Age. Matthew Prior. *See* Phillis's Age

Phyllis! why should we delay. To Phyllis. Edmund Waller. BeJo

Phyllyp Sparowe. John Skelton. OxBoLi

  (Philip Sparrow.) NOBE; OBCoV; PeLV

Phyllyp Sparowe [*or* Philip Sparrow]. John Skelton.

  (Cat of Carlyshe Kynde, A.) TriCat

  "*Pla ce bo!* Who is there, who?" NOBE; NoSic; OxBoLi

  Sparrow's Dirge, The. FaBoCh

  ("Whan I remembre agayn.") NPeEn

  "When I remember again." FaBoCh

Physical Comparison with Professors and Others. Robert Pinsky. NoP-4

Physical-education slides. Hullo, Inside. Max Fatchen. NOxBChV

Physician of eminence, some years ago, A. Lady and the Doctor, The. Helen Leigh. WoRP

Physicians' Fortune, The. Friedrich von Logau. GePo, *tr. by* George C. Schoolfield

Physics of Ochun, The. Víctor Hernández Cruz. PueRic

Physiologus. *Unknown.*

  "Now I will fashion the tale of a fish." AnOE

  ("Now I will sing about a kind of fish.") ASW, *tr. by* Kevin Crossley-Holland

  Whale, The. AnOE

    "To explain the nature of fishes in craft of verse." EBEV, *tr. by* Gavin Bone

  Whale, The. EBEV, *tr. by* Gavin Bone

π. Wislawa Szymborska. PoSu, *tr. by* Adam Czerniawski

π deserves our full admiration. π. Wislawa Szymborska. PoSu, *tr. by* Adam Czerniawski

Pianist Joe Sullivan, The. Thing About Joe Sullivan, The. Roy Fisher. HarvBoo

Pianist's funeral passes, The. Sean Dunne. ModIr *Fr.* Sydney Place.

Piano. D. H. Lawrence. CABP; GTBS-P; HAP; HarvBoo; HeIP-4; InPK-6; MoBrPo; NAEL-5v2; NAEL-6v2; NIL-7; NOBE; NoAM; NoP-4; OPOU; OxBSP; PAI; PoE; RB; SCGP; TFi; TRP; UnPo; WeW-3

Piano, The. Frank Daley. NOBC

Piano, The. D. H. Lawrence. WeW-3

Piano after War. Gwendolyn Brooks. ESEAA

Piano and Drums. Gabriel Okara. NIP-4; PBA; TTY

Piano has crawled into the quarry, The. Hauled. War Ballad. Andrey [*or* Andrei] Andreievich Voznesensky [*or* Voznesenskii]. WoPoe, *tr. by* Stanley Moss

Piano is correctly tuned slightly out of tune, The. Equal Temperament. Lin Max. MiVo

Piano keys sit stiff and stark, sterile, The. Echoes. Naomi Long Madgett. SeSe

Piano kissed by a slender hand, The. Paul Verlaine. SxFrPo, *tr. by* Martin Sorrell

Piano Pieces. Thomas William Shapcott. CBAP

Piano practice. Raymond Roseliep. HA

Piano Solo. Nicanor Parra. PoetW; TCLAP, *tr. by* William Carlos Williams

Piano, trembling, makes the lips grow dry, The. Boris Leonidovich Pasternak. TCRP

Piano Tuner's Wife, The. Karl Shapiro. NoAM

Pianostool Footnotes. Simon Cutts.

  "On parquet." PoSol

Piazza di Spagna, Early Morning. Richard Wilbur. OxBSP; VGW

  (I can't forget.) NoP-4

Piazza Piece. John Crowe Ransom. APT-1; BoLoP; ColAP; FuPo; HarvBoo; HeIP-4; MoAmPo; NAAL-2v2; NOBA; NoAM; NoP-4; OxBA; PAI; Son; TAP; TFi

Piazza Tragedy, A. Eugene Field. NBLV

Piazzas. Barbara Guest. NeAP

Pibroch. Ted Hughes. FaBoMo

Pibroch of Donald Dhu. Sir Walter Scott. *See* Pibroch of Donuil Dhu

Pibroch of Donuil Dhu. Sir Walter Scott. FaBoCh; OxBS

  (Gathering Song of Donald the Black.) GTBS-P

  (Pibroch of Donald Dhu.) FaBoWar

Picadilly or Paradise. John Yau. BodElec

Picasso and Anarchism. Leslie Scalapino. FTOS

Picasso flies into a rage at Braque. Picasso Visits Braque. Harold Norse. CLPP

Picasso Shag. M. Loncar. AmPoNex

Picasso Visits Braque. Harold Norse. CLPP

Picasso / you give us Things. E. E. Cummings. TCAPo

Piccolomini, The. Johann Christoph Friedrich von Schiller.

  "Cloud doth gather, the green wood roar, The." AWP

  Thekla's Song. AWP

Pick a card, any card. Tyranny of Choice. Elizabeth Garrett. NeBl

Pick a fern, pick a fern, ferns are high. Ezra Pound. OBVE

Pick ferns, pick ferns. *Unknown.* ChinPo, *tr. by* Yip Wai-lim

Pick-up truck. Marlene Mountain. HA

Pick Yourself Up. Dorothy Fields. ReLy

Picked offhand by the angels to demonstrate. Saint Ursula of Llangwyryfon. Gwyn Williams. AngWePo

Picket before Bull Run, The. John Day. TreFP

Picketing Supermarkets. Tom Wayman. NIP-4

Pickety fence, The. David McCord. NTCP

Pickin Em Up and Layin Em Down. Maya Angelou. NBLV

Picking at a bone. (LL) *Unknown.* LB; OxNR

Picking Blueberries, Austerlitz, New York, 1957. Mary Oliver. NAAL-5

Picking Grapes in an Abandoned Vineyard. Larry Levis. GeoHom

Picking Rushes. *Unknown.* CoBCP, *tr. by* Burton Watson

Picking Tea: A Ballad. Kao Ch'i. SuSp, *tr. by* Irving Y. Lo

Picking violets. Ryokan. WoPoe, *tr. by* Burton Watson

Pickle dogs come down. Emmett Williams. PFTM-2

Pickpocket leaves. Autumn. Robert Peterson. GeoHom

Pickpockets. John Gay. ECEV *Fr.* Trivia; or, The Art of Walking the Streets of London.

Picks up a water snake. Cobweb. Haniel Long. APT-1

Pickup. Paul Allen. ReTh

Picnic. Kenward Elmslie. FTOS

Picnic. Hugh Lofting. OTCP

  (Ella, fell a.) NOxBChV

Picnic. Nellie Wong. OpBo

Picnic, The. John Logan. CoAmPo; TRP

Picnic, an Homage to Civil Rights, The. Michael S. Weaver. ISC; LTA; PoPoPo

Picnic-goers beautified themselves, The. Embarkation for Cythera, The. David Ferry. GS

Picnic on the Bay Bridge. Morton Marcus. GeoHom

Picnic Remembered. Robert Penn Warren. NAAL-2v2

Picnic to the Earth. Shuntaro Tanikawa. PoetW, *tr. by* Harold Wright

Pict Song, A. Rudyard Kipling. NoAM *Fr.* Puck of Pook's Hill.

Pictor Ignotus. Robert Browning. CTC

Picture, A. "Michael Field." VWP

Picture, A. Dora Greenwell. EBVV

Picture, A. Aleksandr Semionovich Kushner. TCRusP, *tr. by* Daniel Weissbort

Picture, A. Howard Nemerov. OxBC

Picture, A. Henrietta Cordelia Ray. CBWP-3

Picture, A. B. P. Shillaber. TreFP

Picture, The. Anacreon. AWP, *tr. by* Thomas Stanley

Picture and book remain. Acre of Grass, An. W. B. Yeats. HarvBoo; NoAM

Picture Bride. Cathy Song. AiP

Picture has no grammar, A. It has neither evil nor good. Shall Gaelic Die? Iain Crichton Smith. NPeEn

Picture me. Postcard from Cuernavaca. Michael Hofmann. HarvBoo

Picture of a Fine Gentleman, The. Lady Sophia Burrell. ECWP

Picture of a Japanese Farmer, Woodland, California, May 20, 1942. James Masao Mitsui. OpBo

Picture of a Man. Calvin Forbes. ISC

Picture of a Nativity. Geoffrey Hill. NoAM; OxBC

Picture of Dorian Gray, The. Oscar Wilde.

  Preface: "Artist is the creator of beautiful things, The." NAEL-5v2

Picture of Eakins and a couple of other people, A. David Ferry. FaBoA

Picture of Elvis late at night at the piano, The. Elvis Sings Gospel. Fleda Brown Jackson. AllShUp

Picture of J. T. in a Prospect of Stone, The. Charles Tomlinson. NPeEn

  (What should one.) NoP-4

Picture of Little J. A. in a Prospect of Flowers, The. John Ashbery. CoAmPo; PmAP

Picture of Little T. C. in a Prospect of Flowers, The. Andrew Marvell. BASC; ESCV; FSCP; GeHe; MeLP; NAEL-5v1; NAEL-6v1; NAEL-7v1; NOBE; NoP-4; OBEV; OxAEP-1; PoE; SCGP; TFi

Picture of Loot. Alan Sillitoe. OxBTC

Picture of my Mother's Family, A. Wing Tek Lum. OpBo

Picture of Okinawa, A. Dennis Schmitz. LCAP-2

Picture of Sappho, The. Caroline Elizabeth Norton. VWP

Picture of the Body, The. Ben Jonson. NOSC *Fr.* Eupheme.

Picture on the front, The. Picture Postcard. Billy Marshall-Stoneking. BMAP

Picture on the Purple Wall, the. Steve Wilson. AmPoNex

Picture-Palaces. Philip Heseltine. *See* Limerick: "Young things who frequent picture-palaces, The."

Picture Postcard. Billy Marshall-Stoneking. BMAP

Picture Postcard from Our Youth. Dan Pagis. VCWP, *tr. by* Stephen Mitchell

Picture Postcard of a Zoo. Oscar Williams. Son

Picture Postcards. Miklós Radnóti. AF

Picture the lost world in. Critique. Anthony Barnett. Oth

Picture-Writing. Henry Wadsworth Longfellow. APN-1 *Fr.* Song of Hiawatha, The.

Pictures. Sarah Kirsch. AF, *tr. by* Wayne Kvam

Pictures and Stories. Amos Neufeld. GotH

Pictures come striding into the room, The. Evening. Mark McMorris. AmPoNex

Pictures from Brueghel. William Carlos Williams.
  ("According to Breughel.") PoPoPo
  "According to Breughel." LCAP-2; NAAL-2v2; NAAL-5; NoAM
  Haymaking. NoAM
  Hunters in the Snow, The. LCAP-2
  "In a red winter hat blue." LCAP-2
  ("In a red winter hat blue.") GI
  Landscape with the Fall of Icarus. LCAP-2; NAAL-2v2; NAAL-5; NoAM
  "Living quality of, The." NoAM
  "Over-all picture is winter, The." LCAP-2
  ("Over-all picture, The.") GS
  Parable of the Blind, The. LCAP-2; SAmP
  Self-Portrait. LCAP-2
  "This horrible but superb painting." LCAP-2; SAmP

Pictures in the Smoke. Dorothy Parker. NBLV

Pictures of a Gone World. Lawrence Ferlinghetti.
  "Away above a harborful." BoLoP; PoM
  "Dada would have liked a day like this." NeAP
  "Sarolla's women in their picture hats." NeAP; PoM

Pictures of the Floating World. Miyazawa Kenji. PFTM-1

Pictures of the Jews. Haim [*or* Chaim *or* Khayim] Guri [*or* Gouri]. MHP, *tr. by* Ruth Finer Mintz

Picturesque; a Fragment. John Aikin. NOEC

"Picturesque / common lot" the unwarranted light, The. George Oppen. APSN; NNaP *Fr.* Some San Francisco Poems.

Piddle-paddling race of critics, rhizome-fanciers. Antiphanes. GrAn, *tr. by* Edwin Morgan

Piece by piece I SEEM. Necessities of Life. Adrienne Rich. HCAP; NOBA

Piece of Advice, A. Gyula Illyés. IQMS, *tr. by* Adam Makkai

Piece of art, a scene, a poem, A. Silence, an Eloquent Applause. Leona Gregory. TrCP

Piece of Black Bread, A. "Eduard Georgievich Bagritzky" [*or* Bagritsky]. TrJP, *tr. by* C. M. Bowra

Piece of Bone, The. Katerina Pinosová. SurWo

Piece of burned meat, A. Jane Kenyon. LoL *Fr.* Having It Out With Melancholy.

Piece of buttered popcorn, A. Alan Pizzarelli. HA

Piece of Earth, A. Douglas Livingstone. PeSAV

Piece of forest, A. Still Life. Raymond Garlick. AngWePo

Piece of green pepper, A. Haiku Ambulance. Richard Brautigan. InPK-6

Piece of meat lost in cabbage stew, A. Our Birth-Cord. Kofi Anyidoho. NAfrP

Pieced together, never broken, never end. (LL) In Hayden's Collage. Michael S. Harper. ESEAA; NAAAL

Piecemeal the summer dies. Exeunt. Richard Wilbur. HeIP-4

Pieces. Duane Niatum. HATNAP

Pieces from a Mortal Duet. Mario Luzi.
  "As for Granata, the Siberian gulag, Ostia." ItPo, *tr. by* Gayle Ridinger
  Postscriptum. ItPo, *tr. by* Gayle Ridinger

Pieces of a green / bottle. (LL) Between Walls. William Carlos Williams. APT-1; TAP; VGW

Pieces of Coal. Huw Menai. AngWePo *Fr.* Back in the Return.

Pieces of coal, hewn from the deeps of earth. Huw Menai. AngWePo *Fr.* Back in the Return.

Pieces of Snot. *Unknown.* STP, *tr. by* Franz Boas

Pieces of the One and a Half Legged Man. Peter Klappert.
  Court of Divine Justice, The. YaYoPo

Pieces O'six—XVIII. Jackson Mac Low. FTOS

Pieces O'six—XXIV. Jackson Mac Low. FTOS

Pied Beauty. Gerard Manley Hopkins. AWP; AmFaPo; CABP; ChAP; ClHu; EBVV; EnlH; FaBoMo; GTBS-P; HAP; HeIP-4; ITBLP; InPK-6; InvLi; MoBrPo; NAEL-5v2; NAEL-6v2; NIL-7; NOBE; NOBVV; NPeEn; NoAM; NoP-4; OBEV; OBMV; OxAEP-2; OxBEV; OxBSP; PoE; PoPoPo; PoRA; RB; RaBo; SCGP; SCV; SacPr; SoSe-8; TFi; TTTS; UV; WeW-3

Pied Beauty. Stanley J. Sharpless. UV

Pied Piper, The. John Ashbery. YaYoPo

Pied Piper of Hamelin, The. Robert Browning. EBNV; FaBoCh; NOxBChV; OBNV; OBSP; PeLV
  "Into the street the Piper stept." OxAEP-2

Pier, The. Garrett Kaoru Hongo. OpBo

Pier, a great concrete semicircle, The. Pacific Crossing. Vince Gotera. ReBoTo

Pier-Glass, The. Robert Graves. NoAM

Pier: Under Pisces, The. James Merrill. LCAP-2; NoAM

Piercing brightness of the living ray, The. Dante Alighieri. TOF *Fr.* Divina Commedia.

Piercing Chill I Feel, The. Buson. InPK-6, *tr. by* Harold G. Henderson

Piercing winter frost, and winds, and darkened air, The. (LL) November. William Cullen Bryant. APN-1; GSo; Son; TreFP

Pierre Falcon. Le Tombeau de Pierre Falcon. James Reaney. MoCV

Pierrot, no sentimental swain. Pantomime. Paul Verlaine. AWP, *tr. by* Arthur Symons

Piers are pummelled by the waves, The. Fall of Rome, The. W. H. Auden. NPeEn; OxBEV; OxBTC; UnPo

Piers Gaveston. Michael Drayton.
  "And thus like slaves we sell our soules to sinne." CAGL
  "O breake my hart quoth he, O breake and dye." CAGL
  "This Edward in the Aprill of his age." CAGL
  "Why doe I quake my down-fall to reporte?" CAGL

Piers Plowman Shows the Way to Saint Truth. William Langland. NAEL-6v1; NAEL-7v1 *Fr.* Vision of Piers Plowman, The.

Pietà. Allen Afterman. NOBAu

Pietà. James McAuley. BMAP; CBAP

Pietà. Rainer Maria Rilke. GI

Pietà. Wislawa Szymborska. VCWP

Pietà. Ronald Stuart Thomas. NPeEn

Pietà's Over, The. Paul Durcan. PBCIP

Pietà's Over—and, now, my dear, droll, husband, The. Pietà's Over, The. Paul Durcan. PBCIP

"Pietrofesso," I'd repeat to Mr. Wright, the science teacher in / Junior High. Having the Wrong Name for Mr. Wright. Helen Barolini. UnSA

Pig. Anthony Hecht. OxBC
  (In the manger of course were crows and the Child Himself / Was like unto a lamb.) GI

Pig. Paul Éluard. TTTS, *tr. by* Kenneth Koch

Pig, The. Ogden Nash. RB

Pig, The. *Unknown.* FaBoEE; OBCoV

Pig and i spring rain. Marlene Mountain. HA

Pig, Goat, Sheep. Jean de La Fontaine. WoPoe, *tr. by* Bruce Boone and Robert Glück

Pig, if I am not mistaken, The. Pig, The. Ogden Nash. RB

Pig Island Letters. James Keir Baxter.
  "From an old house shaded with macrocarpas." PeNZ
  "When I was only semen in a gland." PeNZ

Pig lay on a barrow dead, The. View of a Pig. Ted Hughes. OxAEP-2; OxBEV; OxBTC; TwCP

Pig Melons. John Kinsella. NeBl

Pig's-Eye View of Literature, A. Dorothy Parker.
  Alexandre Dumas and His Son. APT-1
  Alfred, Lord Tennyson. APT-1; NALW
  "Although I work, and seldom cease." APT-1
  "Byron and Shelley and Keats." APT-1; NALW
  "Carlyle combined the lit'ry life." APT-1; NALW
  Charles Dickens. APT-1
  D. G. Rossetti. APT-1; NALW
  "Dante Gabriel Rossetti." APT-1; NALW
  George Gissing. APT-1
  George Sand. APT-1; NALW
  Harriet Beecher Stowe. APT-1; NALW
  "If with the literate, I am." APT-1; NALW
  Lives and Times of John Keats, Percy Bysshe Shelley, and George Gordon Noel, Lord Byron, The. APT-1; NALW
  Oscar Wilde. APT-1; NALW
  "Pure and worthy Mrs. Stowe, The." APT-1; NALW
  "Should Heaven send me any son." APT-1; NALW
  Thomas Carlyle. APT-1; NALW
  "Upon the work of Walter Landor." APT-1; NALW
  Walter Savage Landor. APT-1; NALW
  "What time the gifted lady took." APT-1; NALW
  "When I admit neglect of Gissing." APT-1
  "Who call him spurious and shoddy." APT-1

Pig's leg fills the plate, wine overflowing the cups, A. Fan Ch'eng-ta. SuSp, *tr. by* Wu-Chi Liu *Fr.* Four Songs in Imitation of Wang Chien.

Pig stands squarely, The. Transubstantiation. Gary Geddes. NOBC

Pigeon of My Childhood. Sergey Aleksandrovich Vasilyev [*or* Vasil'ev]. TCRP, *tr. by* Max Hayward and Lubov Yakovleva

Pigeon purrs in the wood; the wood has gone, The. Geoffrey Hill. NoAM; PoE *Fr.* Apology for the Revival of Christian Architecture in England, An.

Pigeon Rock: Lebanon. Elmaz Abinader. GraLe

Pigeons. David Hernandez. UnSA

Pigeons. Bert Meyers. SPE

Pigeons. Lilian Moore. SSCS

Pigeons. Alastair Reid. TwCP

Pigeons. Vikram Seth. OWoS

Pigeons. Daniel Tobin. UrbNat

Pigeons. Baron Wormser. UrbNat

Pigeons are cityfolk. Pigeons. Lilian Moore. SSCS

Pigeons are the spiks of Birdland. Pigeons. David Hernandez. UnSA

Pigeons do when they're knitting. (LL) Wild Oats. Norman MacCaig. NPeEn; NePenScot; OxBTC

Pigeons flutter'd fieldward, one and all, The. Gout and Wings. Charles Tennyson Turner. NOBVV

Pigeons have survived, The. Closure Opening Its Trap. Suzanne Wise. AmPoNex

Pigeons on the grass alas. Gertrude Stein. OWoS; TAP *Fr.* Four Saints in Three Acts.

Pigeons shake their wings on the copper church roof. Fourth Floor, Dawn, Up All Night Writing Letters. Allen Ginsberg. HarvBoo; InvLad

Pigeons swing across the square, The. Pigeons. Vikram Seth. OWoS

Pigeons that peck at the grass in Trinity Churchyard, The. Trinity Place. Phyllis McGinley. MoAmPo; OxBSP; SoSe-8

Piggish young person from Leeds, A. *Unknown.* KaS

Piggy-back. Langston Hughes. TLR

Pigmalion, whose hie love-hating minde. John Marston. PBRV *Fr.* Metamorphosis of Pigmalions Image, The.

Pigmies and Cranes. Walter Savage Landor. NOBVV

Pigs, The. Geoffrey Lehmann. CBAP

Pigs for Circe in May, The. Joanne Kyger. PoM

Pigsty did not reek, The. Barn-yard, The. Sheila Cussons. PeSAV, *tr.* by Johann de Lange

Pigtail. Tadeusz Różewicz. HP; PoSu

Pihsien Road. "Robin Hyde." WPE

Pike. Ted Hughes. FaBoMo; HAP; HeIP-4; NAEL-5v2; NAEL-6v2; NPeEn; OxBEV; OxBTC; PoE

Pike, The. Amy Lowell. APT-1

Pike, The. Theodore Roethke. MoASP

Pike Street Bus. Colleen J. McElroy. NAAAL

Pike, three inches long, perfect. Pike. Ted Hughes. FaBoMo; HAP; HeIP-4; NAEL-5v2; NAEL-6v2; NPeEn; OxBEV; OxBTC; PoE

Pilate Remembers. William E. Brooks. ChIV-2

Pilate's Wife. Nina Kossman. GI

Pilate's Wife's Dream. Charlotte Brontë. VWP

Pilchard-Curing Song, The. Alice Oswald. MFPA

Pile high the hickory and the light. Winter Night. Edna St. Vincent Millay. APT-1

Pile of discards on the sidewalk, A. Sunday Morning. David Ray. AllShUp

Pile of Feathers. Gerald Stern. LoL

Pile the bodies high at Austerlitz and Waterloo. Grass. Carl Sandburg. AWP; ColAP; FaBoWar; MoAmPo; NAAL-2v2; NOBA; NoAM; OBWP; OxBA; PeFWW; TCAPo; TFi

Piled deep below the screening apple-branch. Orchard-Pit, The. Dante Gabriel Rossetti. EnLoPo; NAEL-5v2; NAEL-6v2; PeVV; SCV

Piled for burning/ Brushwood. Boncho. ZenPo, *tr.* by Takashi Ikemoto and Lucien Stryk

Piled on a loading dock where I walked. Desks. Dave Jeddie Smith. HCAP

Piled snow hugs the bramble gates. Traveling Early through a Snowy Valley. Yü Chi. CoBLCP, *tr.* by Jonathan Chaves

Pilgrim, The. Emma Catherine Embury. OBCA

Pilgrim, The. Nicanor Parra. VCWP

Pilgrim, The. W. B. Yeats. RB

Pilgrim Cranes, The. John Byrne Leicester Warren, 3d Baron De Tabley. EBVV

Pilgrim Fathers, The. Leonard Bacon. AH

Pilgrim Fathers, The. William Wordsworth. AiP *Fr.* Ecclesiastical Sonnets.

Pilgrim from the East, The. Gustave Kahn. TrJP, *tr.* by Jethro Bithell

Pilgrim's Problem. Clive Staples Lewis. TrCP

Pilgrim's Progress, The. John Bunyan.
  Christian Loses His Burden. SacPr
  "He that is down, needs fear no fall." EBEV; NOBE; OBEV; SacPr
  Pilgrim Song, The. EBEV; NOCV; OxBEV
  Shepherd Boy Sings [in the Valley of Humiliation], The. EBEV; NOBE; OBEV; SacPr
  (Song of the Shepherd Boy.) OxBSP
  "Thus far I did come laden with my sin." SacPr

(Valiant-for-Truth's Song.) NPeEn

(Valiant's Song.) NOSC

"What danger is the pilgrim in." EBEV

"Who would true Valour see." EBEV; NOCV; OxBEV

Pilgrim's Viaticum; or, The Destitute, But Not Forlorn. Elizabeth Tipper.
  "More than a King's my Word dos rule to day." EMWP; NOSC
  To a Young Lady That Desired a Verse of My Being Servant One Day and Mistress Another. EMWP; NOSC

Pilgrim Song, The. John Bunyan. EBEV; NOCV; OxBEV *Fr.* Pilgrim's Progress, The.

Pilgrimage. Austin Clarke. CIP-2

Pilgrimage. Yoshioka Minoru. PFTM-2, *tr.* by Eric Selland

Pilgrimage, The. George Herbert. BASC; ESCV; GeHe; NAEL-5v1; NAEL-6v1; NAEL-7v1; NOSC; PAI; PoE

Pilgrimage, The. Henry Vaughan. ChIV-2; ESCV

Pilgrimage along the migratory roads, a voyage to ancestral / sources. Song of the Initiate. Léopold Sédar Senghor. VCWP, *tr.* by Melvin Dixon

Pilgrimage Song. *Unknown.* WPE, *tr.* by Mary Austin

Pilgrimage to Loango Strand. Jean-Baptiste Tati-Loutard. PBMAP

Pilgrims. Jean Valentine. LCAP-2; TAP

Pilgrims, The. Adelaide Anne Procter. SacPr

Pilgrims in Mexico. *Unknown.* OBCP

Pillar of Fame, The. Robert Herrick. BeJo; CaPo; NIP-4

Pillar of the Cloud, The. John Henry, Cardinal Newman. ChIV-1; InvLi; NPeEn; SacPr

Pillar [*or* Piller] perished [*or* pearisht] is whe[a]rto I le[a]nt, The. Sir Thomas Wyatt. NoSic; OBVE; OxBEV; PBRV

Pillow, The. Herman Melville. APN-2 *Fr.* Clarel: A Poem and Pilgrimage in the Holy Land.

Pillowed on your thighs in a dream garden. Song of the Dream Garden. Ikkyu Sojun. ErotSp, *tr.* by Sam Hamill

Pillows know, they say. Lady Ise. ArkPo, *tr.* by Helen Craig McCullough

Pilot, The. Russell Edson. LCAP-2

Pilot from the Carrier, A. Randall Jarrell. PoWW

Pilot's Psalm, The. *Unknown.* PoWW

Pilotless in youth was my life's ship. Ship of Life, The. Ahmad al-Safi Al-Najafi. MAP, *tr.* by John Heath-Stubbs and Salma Khadra Jayyusi

Pilots, Man Your Planes. Randall Jarrell. MoAmPo

Pin has a head, but has no hair, A. Christina Georgina Rossetti. VWP

Pin's Fee, or Painting with Star, A. David Shapiro. BodElec

Pin-swin or spine-swine, The. His Shield. Marianne Craig Moore. NALW

Pin your little tail on glittering star, come. Sarah Kirsch. PFTM-2, *tr.* by Wayne Kvam *Fr.* Kite-Flying.

Pinch him, pinch him black and blue. John Lyly. NoSic *Fr.* Endimion.

Pinch of Salt, A. Robert Graves. MoBrPo

Pindar. Antipater of Sidon. AWP, *tr.* by John Addington Symonds

Pindar. Plato. GrAn, *tr.* by Peter Jay

Pindar's Revenge. Edward Sanders. PoM

Pindaric on the Death of our Late Sovereign: With an Ancient Prophecy on His Present Majority, A. Aphra Behn. BASC

Pindaric on the Grunting of a Hog, A. Samuel Wesley. NOBL

Pindaric Poem, A. Anne Finch, Countess of Winchilsea.
  Hymn, The: "To the Almighty on his radiant throne." ChIV-1

Pindaric, to the Athenian Society, A. Elizabeth Singer Rowe. BASC

Pindarick to Mrs. Behn on her Poem on the Coronation, A. *Unknown.* EMWP

Pindaricque on the Grunting of a Hog, A. Samuel Wesley.
  "Freeborn Pindaric never does refuse." VerBaPo

Pinder. Mick North. NLP

Pine, The. Saunders Lewis. OBWVE, *tr.* by Gwyn Morgan

Pine boat a-shift. Ezra Pound. APSN; APT-1; OBVE

"Pine flower's blooming," says. Untitled. So Chong-Ju. VCWP, *tr.* by David R. McCann

Pine Is Standing Lonely, A. Heinrich Heine. NAWM-7v2, *tr.* by Hal Draper

Pine mushroom. Basho. EH, *tr.* by Robert Hass

Pine needles. Penny Harter. HA

Pine pierces the hills' whiteness, The. Epiphany. Andrea Zanzotto. VCWP, *tr.* by Ruth Feldman

Pine Planters, The. Thomas Hardy. FaBoVe

Pine seedling somewhere springs, A. Remember It, My Soul. Eduard Friedrich Mörike [*or* Möricke]. WoPoe, *tr.* by William DeWitt Snodgrass

Pine Shade. Muso Soseki. EaWin, *tr.* by W. S. Merwin

Pine Sounds. Po Chü-i. CoBCP, *tr.* by Burton Watson

Pine tree, A. Turtle Head Stupa. Muso Soseki. EaWin, *tr.* by W. S. Merwin

Pine-tree standeth lonely, A. Ein Fichtenbaum steht einsam. Heinrich Heine. AWP, *tr.* by James Thomson

Pine tree sways in the smoke, The. Wood in Sound, A. Shinkichi Takahashi. ZenPo, *tr.* by Takashi Ikemoto and Lucien Stryk

Pine Tree Tops. Gary Snyder. NOBA

Pine-trees in the Courtyard, The. Po Chü-i. ChiP, *tr.* by Arthur Waley

Pineneedles cast a quivering shadow on. Journey of a Doe. Chava Pinchas-Cohen. DTA, *tr.* by Miriyam Glazer

Pines and the Sea, The. Christopher Pearse Cranch. ColAP

Pines are capped with snow, The. Inscribed on a Painting. Yü Chi. CoBLCP, *tr.* by Jonathan Chaves

Pines moan when the wind passes, The. Beach. Sophia De Mello Breyner. VCWP, *tr.* by Ruth Fainlight

Pines were dark on Ramoth hill, The. My Playmate. John Greenleaf Whittier. APN-1; NOBA

Pines without Peer, The. Kelly Cherry. FFC

Pinetree. Ágnes Nemes Nagy. PoSu, *tr.* by Bruce Berlind

Pinionjay shits pebbles. *Unknown.* STP

Pinjarra warrior, where were you that day. Archie Weller. IBA

Pink and a bit soft-bodied, with a somewhat jazzy. Physical Comparison With Professors And Others. Robert Pinsky. NoP-4

Pink and white hands like roses and rice cake! Phoenix Hairpins. Lu Yu. OHPC, *tr.* by Kenneth Rexroth

Pink confused with white. Pot of Flowers, The. William Carlos Williams. APT-1

Pink creamy hands. Tune: "Phoenix Hairpin." Lu Yu. SuSp, *tr.* by James J. Y. Liu

Pink Dog. Elizabeth Bishop. NALW

Pink Frock, The. Thomas Hardy. OxBSP

Pink Locust, The. William Carlos Williams. SAmP

Pink Maniac, A. Ray DiPalma. PmAP

Pink neon lit window full of plaster of parts and resin, The. Real Indian Leans Against, The. Chrystos. UnSA

Pink petals of peach blossom. Peach Blossom and Pigeon (painting by Kiso). Shinkichi Takahashi. ZenPo, *tr.* by Takashi Ikemoto and Lucien Stryk

Pink Poem. Jackie Warren-Moore. SpirFl

Pink Rose Rings, The. Tracey Herd. MFPA; NeBl

Pink Slip at Tool & Dye. Dave Jeddie Smith. NoAM

Pink tender hand. Tune: Phoenix Hairpin. Lu Yu. CoBCP, *tr.* by Burton Watson

Pinned on our picnic blankets. Listening to Mozart at Meadow Brook. Patricia Hooper. MiVo

Piñon Nuts. Dixie Salazar. UnSA

Pinup of Rita Hayworth was taped, A. Post-Modernism. James Galvin. GifTon

Pioneer Lane. Michael Dransfield. NOBAu

Pioneer Village. Ruth Silcock. PeLi

Pioneer Woman. Vesta Pierce Crawford. AiP

Pioneers. Aileen Fisher. CA

Pioneers. Lillian M. Fisher. HHam

Pious magistrate! sound his praise throughout, A. Official Piety. John Greenleaf Whittier. NCAP

Pious One, The. Gabriela Mistral. BBASP, *tr.* by Doris Dana

Pious Selinda goes to prayers [or pray'rs]. Pious Selinda [or Celinda]. William Congreve. NOBE; NPeEn

Pious sire of Arla reared her youth. Enthusiast, The. Arla. Anne Batten Cristall. RWP

Pious wish to whiteness gone over, A / Or nothing. (LL) Queen-Anne's-Lace. William Carlos Williams. APT-1; MoAmPo; NAAL-2v2; NOBA; NoAM; TAP

Pip's sister, Mrs Joe Gargery. Hit Men, The. Philippa Lawrence. Prnts

Pipe, The. German Borisovich Plisetsky [or Plisetskii]. TCRP, *tr.* by Keith Boseley

Pipe, The. Shinkichi Takahashi. ZenPo, *tr.* by Takashi Ikemoto and Lucien Stryk

Pipe and Can, I. Robert Wisdome. *See* Religious Use of [Taking] Tobacco, A

Pipe and Can II. Thomas Bonham.
  (When as the chill charocco blows.) OBEV
  (When that the chill charocco blows.) FaBoCh

Pipe of Tobacco, A. Isaac Hawkins Browne.
  "Blest leaf! whose aromatic gales dispense." UV

Piper, The. William Blake. *See* Songs of Innocence

Piper, The. W. S. Merwin. NAAL-2v2

Piper and His Cow, THe. Mother Goose. OxNR; ReMoGo

Piper coming from far away is you, The. Keeping Going. Seamus Heaney. ModIr

Piper o' Dundee, The. *Unknown.* OxBS

Pipes at Lucknow, The. John Greenleaf Whittier. FaBoWar

Pipes in the streets were playing bravely, The. Cha Till Maccruimein (Departure of the 4th Camerons). Ewart Alan Mackintosh. FaBoWar

Pipes of the misty moorlands. Pipes at Lucknow, The. John Greenleaf Whittier. FaBoWar

Piping down the Valleys. William Blake. *See* Songs of Innocence

Piping Down the Valleys Wild. William Blake. ClHu; FaBoCh; HeIP-4; NAEL-5v2; NOBE; NOEC; NOxBChV; PoE; SoSe-8; TFi *Fr.* Songs of Innocence.

Piping hot, smoking hot. Hot Pease Man, The. Mother Goose. OxNR; ReMoGo

Piping of our slender, peaceful reeds, The. Prologue. Oliver Wendell Holmes. NCAP

Piping of plenty. (LL) To Waken an Old Lady. William Carlos Williams. HAP; InPK-6; PAI; SoSe-8; WeW-3

Piping Peace. James Shirley. NOBE *Fr.* Imposture, The.

Pipits sit up, sprinkle, dont give it motion, stay. Pallid Harrier. Colin Simms. Oth

Pipling. Theodore Roethke. OBCoV *Fr.* Three Epigrams.

Pippa Passes. Robert Browning.
  Pippa's Song. BRP; ITBLP; NTCP; OBEV; PAI; PoToHe; TrCP; UnPo (Song.) FHYEP; TFi
  "Year's at the spring, The." BRP; ITBLP; NTCP; OBEV; PAI; PoToHe; TrCP; UnPo

Pippa Passes, But I Can't Get Around This Truck. Margaret Blaker. NBLV

Pippa's Song. Robert Browning. BRP; ITBLP; NTCP; OBEV; PAI; PoToHe; TrCP; UnPo *Fr.* Pippa Passes.

Pique at Parting, A. Sarah Morgan Bryan Piatt. NCAP

Pirate Ditty. Robert Louis Stevenson. NOBVV; NPeEn *Fr.* Treasure Island.

Pirate Don Durk of Dowdee, The. Mildred Plew Meigs. ChAP

Pirate Story. Robert Louis Stevenson. NOxBChV

Pirates of Penzance, The. Sir William Schwenck Gilbert.
  I Am the Very Model [or Pattern] of a Modern Major-General. NOBL
  "I am the very pattern of a modern major-gineral." UV
  (Modern Major-General, The.) NBLV
  Policeman's Lot, A [or The]. NOBL; PeLV
  "When a felon's not engaged in his employment." NOBL; PeLV

Pirithous being over hault or mynde and such a one. Ovid. CTC, *tr.* by Arthur Golding *Fr.* Metamorphoses.

Pisan Canto 124. Ezra Pound.
  "Enormous tragedy of the dream in the peasant's bent / shoulders, The." AF

Pisces. Ronald Stuart Thomas. CABP; OxBC

Pisgah-Sights. I. Robert Browning. ChIV-1

Pisgah-Sights. II. Robert Browning. ChIV-1

Pismo, 1959. Robert Vasquez. GeoHom

Pissing in the snow. Issa. EH, *tr.* by Robert Hass

Pistachio Ice Cream. Annemarie Jacir. PoArWo

Pistyll Rhaeadr and Wrexham steeple. Seven Wonders of North Wales, The. *Unknown.* OBWVE

Pit, The. Su'ad al-Mubarak Al-Sabah. MAP, *tr.* by John Heath-Stubbs and May Jayyusi

Pit, The. David Ignatow. BodElec

Pit—but Heaven over it, A. Emily Dickinson. APN-2; NCAP

Pit indeed of Sin: No water's here, A. Edward Taylor. TCAPo *Fr.* Preparatory Meditations Before My Approach to the Lord's Supper.

Pit of Cologne, The. Boris Abramovich Slutsky [or Slutskii]. TCRP, *tr.* by J. R. Rowland

Pit of some fruit might be what I'm about, The. Riffing. Rick Barot. NeAmPo

Pit, pat, well-a-day. Mother Goose. OxNR

Pit Ponies, The. Leslie Norris. ChAP

Pit Viper. N. Scott Momaday. CDW; HATNAP

Pitch. Catherine Walsh.
  "Matter / of fact." Oth

Pitch-Ball. Yang Chi. CoBLCP, *tr.* by Jonathan Chaves *Fr.* Ten Poems on the Tuan-yang Festival.

Pitch black night gave me two deep black eyes, The. Generation, A. Gu Cheng. PFTM-2, VCWP, *tr.* by Sam Hamill

Pitch pines fade, The. Quiet Fog, The. Marge Piercy. UnPo

Pitcher, The. Robert Francis. MoASP; OxBSP; RaBo; WeW-3

Pitcher, The. Yüan Chên. AWP; ChiP, *tr.* by Arthur Waley

Pitcher shot her husband, The. Softball at Julia Tutwiler Prison. R. T. Smith. MoASP

Pitchfork, The. Seamus Heaney. OxBEV

Pitching Coups. Ron Wellburn. MoASP

Pitching the Potatoes. Martín Espada. SpudSo

Pite, that I have sought so yore agoo. Complaint unto Pity, The. Geoffrey Chaucer. MiEL

Pithecanthropus erectus. On Evolution. John Ciardi. OBAL

Pitiful dupes of old illusion, lost. Sparrows in a Hillside Drift. James Wright (1927–80). ColAP

Pitiless heat from heaven pours. Seasons, The. Kalidasa. AWP, *tr.* by Arthur W. Ryder

Pitiless war of love I fought, A. Sandro Penna. CAGL, *tr. by* John McRae
Pitman's Common Sense Arithmetic, 1917. Alan Brownjohn.
    "Agricultural labourer, who has, An." NOxBChV
    Common Sense. NOxBChV
Pitman's Lovesong, A. *Unknown.* FaBoVe
Pitt. Samuel Taylor Coleridge. CenSon *Fr.* Effusions.
Pitt-Rivers Museum, Oxford, The. James Fenton. FaBoMo *Fr.* Exempla.
Pittsburgh in Passing. Samuel Hazo. GraLe
Pity. Trumbull Stickney. ColAP
Pity, A. We Were Such a Good Invention. Yehuda Amichai [*or* Amikhai].
    FIT, *tr. by* Robert Friend
Pity beyond all telling, A. Pity of Love, The. W. B. Yeats. NOBVV
Pity, Lord, pity on my poor town. Pueblo. Luis Palés Matos. TCLAP, *tr. by*
    Barry Luby
Pity Me! Fu Hsüan. ColAnChi, *tr. by* Burton Watson
Pity me! my body is female. Pity Me! Fu Hsüan. ColAnChi, *tr. by* Burton
    Watson
Pity me not because the light of day. Edna St. Vincent Millay. FaBoWP;
    MoAmPo; OxBA
Pity not! The Army gave. Rudyard Kipling. HarvBoo *Fr.* Epitaphs of the
    War [1914–1918].
Pity of Love, The. W. B. Yeats. NOBVV
Pity of the Leaves, The. Edwin Arlington Robinson. APN-2; MoAmPo
Pity poor lovers who may not do what they please. Envy of Poor Lovers, The.
    Austin Clarke. CIP-2
Pity the heart, my lovely doe. Poem in Parts. Judah Halevi. WoPoe, *tr. by*
    Ammiel Alcalay
Pity the Man Who English Lacks. Michael Hartnett. CIP-2; PBCIP
Pity the nameless, and the unknown, where. Nameless Ones, The. Conrad
    Potter Aiken. OxBA
Pity the poor weightlifter. Baldanders. Christopher Reid. NPeEn
Pity the sorrows of a poor old man! Beggar, The. Thomas Moss. NOEC
Pity the tune bereft of singers. Song for the Music in the Warsaw Ghetto.
    Jacqueline Osherow. TaR
Pity this busy monster,manunkind. E. E. Cummings. HarvBoo; NAAL-2v2;
    NOBA; OxBA; TAP
Pity; We Were Such a Good Invention, A. Yehuda Amichai [*or* Amikhai].
    BoLoP, *tr. by* Assia Gutmann
Pity would be no more. William Blake. FHYEP; NAEL-5v2; NAEL-6v2;
    NOBRP; NOEC; OxAEP-2; PoE *Fr.* Songs of Experience.
Pitying the Farmer. Li Shen. CoBCP; ColAnChi, *tr. by* Burton Watson
Piute Creek. Gary Snyder. CoAP; CoAmPo; NAAL-2v2; NOBA
Piyyut for Rosh Hashana. Haim [*or* Chaim *or* Khayim] Guri [*or* Gouri].
    MHP, *tr. by* Ruth Finer Mintz
Pizza and Pretense. Nerissa S. Balce. ReBoTo
Pla ce bo. John Skelton. NoP-4 *Fr.* Phillip Sparow.
Pla ce bo / Who is there, who? Phyllyp Sparowe. John Skelton. OxBoLi
Pla ce bo! Who is there, who? John Skelton. NOBE; NoSic; OxBoLi *Fr.*
    Phyllyp Sparowe [*or* Philip Sparrow].
Place. Robert Creeley. LCAP-2
Place, The. Robert Creeley. BodElec
Place, The. Janet Frame. PeNZ
Place and Date. Leonard Nolens. TuT, *tr. by* Michael O'Loughlin
Place devoted to death, A. At noon, when I came out, the sun. Dossers at the
    Imperial War Museum. Joyce Herbert. TCAWP
Place for No Story, The. Robinson Jeffers. APT-1; AiP
Place has its undertone. Not all. Past, The. Fyodor [*or* Feodor] Ivanovich
    Tyutchev. WoPoe, *tr. by* Charles Tomlinson
Place is called the Golden Cock, The. Lunch at the Coq d'Or. Peter Davison.
    TwCP
Place is calm, dusty worries clear, The. On the Twentieth Day. Ni Tsan.
    CoBLCP, *tr. by* Jonathan Chaves
Place is growing difficult, The. Flails of bramble. Secret Garden, The.
    Thomas Kinsella. TwCP
Place is the corner of Empty and Bleak, The. Nighthawks. Samuel Yellen.
    PoSol
Place is the focus. What is the language. In Defence of Metaphysics. Charles
    Tomlinson. MoBrPo
Place Me in the Breach. Yehuda Karni. TrJP, *tr. by* Sholom J. Kahn
Place Names. Thomas Merton. ChIV-1 *Fr.* Geography of Lograire, The.
Place-Names of China. Alan Bennett. NOBL; UV
Place of Fire. Johannes Bobrowski. PoSu
Place of O, The. Ray A. Young Bear. VoR
Place of suffering, a golgotha, A. Black Flower. Walter Pavlich. TWW
Place of the Damned [*or* Damn'd], The. Jonathan Swift. ChIV-2; FaBoEE;
    OBSV
Place of the Fian is bare tonight, The. *Unknown.* NOIV
Place of V, The. Ray A. Young Bear. VoR

Place park. By the Light of the Silvery Moon. Edward Madden. ReLy
Place perpetually on heat, A. (LL) Antipater of Sidon. GrAn; WoPoe, *tr. by*
    Robin Skelton
Place Pigalle. Richard Wilbur. HeIP-4
Place, Places. Melvin Dixon. ISC
Place Setting. Johari M. Rashad. PasH
Place there is, where proudly raised there stands, A. Samuel Daniel. NoSic
    Fr. Civil Wars, The.
Place was famed for, The. Kris Hemensley. BMAP *Fr.* Mile from Poetry, A.
Place we could never enter hides away still, The. Last Visit. Robert Finch.
    NOBC
Place Where He Arose, The. George Barlow. GT
Place where I spend my days, The. *Unknown.* CoBCP
Place where I was born, The. Idea of Islands, The. Judith Ortiz Cofer.
    PueRic
Place Where the Rainbow Ends, The. Paul Laurence Dunbar. PWR; SacPr
Place you never thought to, A. Mad Wolf in Lunar Web, Mad Crow on the
    Beach. Mac Wellman. FTOS
Placed in the west, Manukau spreads out. Tamaki of a Hundred Lovers.
    Merimeri Penfold. PeNZ, *tr. by* Margaret Orbell
Placed midst the tempest, whose conflicting waves. On the Death of the Rev.
    Dr. Kippis. Helen Maria Williams. ECWP
Placed on this isthmus of a middle state. Pope. WeW-3 *Fr.* Essay on Man,
    An.
Placed these worlds in us. (LL) Lost Pilot, The. James Tate. CoAP; EmeKit;
    NoAM; OBWP; TwCP; UnPo
Placements I. Clayton Eshleman. PFTM-1
Places. Luciana Frezza. CItWP, *tr. by* Cinzia Sartini Blum and Lara
    Trubowitz
Places. Thomas Hardy. HarvBoo
Places and Ways to Live. Richard Hugo. NIP-4
Places I go, leaning on my bramble cane, The. Inscribed on a Painting. T'ang
    Yin. CoBLCP, *tr. by* Jonathan Chaves
Placid Man's Epitaph, A. Thomas Hardy. MoBrPo
Placing a $2 Bet for a Man Who Will Never Go to the Horse Races Any More.
    Diane Wakoski. UnPo
Plagiarism. Ben Marcus. HeMarv
Plagiarist, The. Bruce Berger. GeoH
Plague, The. Nikolai Stepanovich Gumilyov [*or* Gumiliov *or* Gumilev].
    TCRP, *tr. by* Simon Franklin
Plague and sores beyond relief. Les Congés du Lépreux. Jean Bodel.
    WoPoe, *tr. by* Frank Templeton Prince
Plague is Love, a plague, A! but yet. Little Love-God, The. Meleager. AWP,
    tr. by Walter Headlam
Plague of Dead Sharks. Alan Dugan. NoAM
Plague of God, the Rod of God, The. Sister Ann Zita Shows Us the
    Foolishness of the Forbidden Books. Len Roberts. BodElec
Plague of Starlings, A. Robert Earl Hayden. ESEAA; NoAM
Plague take all your pedants, say I! Robert Browning. CTC; EBVV *Fr.*
    Garden Fancies.
Plague take all your pedants, say I! Robert Browning. *See* Plague take all
    your pedants, say I!
Plague take them, every female! Girls of Llanbadarn, The. Dafydd [*or* David]
    ap Gwilym. DiPo, *tr. by* Leslie Norris
Plague to thy husband, scandal to thy sex. To Marina. Sarah Fyge Egerton.
    ECWP
Plague Victims Catapulted over Walls into Besieged City. Thomas Lux. KGB
Plaid is formed of yellow block and black, A. It Says, I Did So. Mary Jo
    Bang. KGB
Plain, The. Sándor Weöres. BLT
Plain and purl across the ribs of the world. (LL) Poem Ended by a Death.
    Fleur Adcock. NAEL-6v2; NoP-4; PeNZ
Plain be the phrase, yet apt the verse. Utilitarian View of the Monitor's Fight,
    A. Herman Melville. APN-2; ColAP; NAAL-2v1; NAAL-3; NCAP;
    UnPo
Plain Dealing. Alexander Brome. NOSC
Plain Dealing's Downfall. *Unknown.* OBSV
    (Long time plain dealing in the Hauty Town.) OxBEV
Plain Fare. Daryl Hine. CoAP
Plain Fools. Pope. OBSV *Fr.* Essay on Criticism, An.
Plain heart seeing into plain heart. (LL) Sun Bu-er. WPoS; WoPoe, *tr. by* Jane
    Hirshfield
Plain Language from Truthful James. Bret Harte. APN-2; CTC; EBNV;
    NOBL; OBAL; OBCoV; PeLV; UV
Plain of Adoration, The. *Unknown.* BIrV, *tr. by* John Montague
Plain of Donnerdale, The. William Wordsworth. CenSon *Fr.* River Duddon
    [A Series of Sonnets], The.
Plain Sense of Things, The. Wallace Stevens. APT-1; EmeKit; HCAP;
    NAAL-5; NoAM; PAI

Plain Song. Craig Raine. TOF

Plain Tales from the Hills. Rudyard Kipling.
　Kidnapped.
　　There Is a Tide. OxBSP
　Lispeth.
　　Look, You Have Cast Out Love! OxBSP

Plain Talk. William Jay Smith. MoAmPo

Plain truth would never serve. Take It from Me. Kenneth O. Hanson. CoAP

Plain verse to start, no tricky stuff. Poet's Progress, The. Chris Mann. PeSAV

Plain was grassy, wild and bare, The. Dying Swan, The. Tennyson. OWoS

Plain wood table, the obligatory, A. Art of Interpretation, The. Julia Copus. NeBl

Plainer Dubliners amaze us, The. On the Use of Jayshus. Oliver St. John Gogarty. FaBoEE

Plainest Narrative, The. William Bronk. APSN

Plainsong. Vladislav Felitsianovich Khodasevich. TCRP, tr. by Michael Frayn

Plaint. Chu Shu-chen. OHPC, tr. by Kenneth Rexroth

Plaint. Ebenezer Elliott. OBEV; SacPr

Plaint. Charles Henri Ford. SPE

Plaint of Flowers, A. Ernest Sandeen. CRP

Plaint of the Wife, The. *Unknown.* AWP, tr. by W. R. S. Ralston

Plainview: 3. N. Scott Momaday. CDW

Plaisir d'Amour. Patrick Galvin. BiHa

Plait of Hair, The. Alice V. Stuart. PoBW

Plaiting a dark red love-knot into her long black hair. (LL) Highwayman, The. Alfred Noyes. BRP; ChAP; EBNV; ITBLP; NOxBChV; OBNV; OBSP

Plaiting the generations. (LL) Combing. Gladys Cardiff. CDW; GifTon

Plan, The. Rae Armantrout. BAP-01

Plan, The. Jack Turner. BAP-97

Plan for a Curriculum of the Soul, A. Charles Olson. PFTM-2

Plan of the City of O. The great square. Michael Palmer. HarvBoo *Fr.* Series.

Plan of the Klan. Michelle T. Clinton. InTrad

Plane Debris. Stephen Rodefer.
　"My mind to me mangles iron. An error is mirror to the truth." PmAP

Plane Four. Velemir [or Viktor Vladimirovich] Khlebnikov. PFTM-1 *Fr.* Zangezi.

Plane tilts in to Nashville, The. Homecoming Singer, The. Jay Wright. VCAP

Planes flew low over the house, The. These Are Not Brushstrokes. Cyrus Cassells. GT

Planes Landing. Jamie Grant. NOBAu

"Planet doesn't explode of itself, A," said drily. Earth. John Hall Wheelock. SoSe-8

Planet Earth Speaks, The. Alma Villanueva. HW

Planet Jupiter, The. Epes Sargent. APN-1

Planet of Descendance, A. William Frederick Stevenson. NOBVV

Planet on the Table, The. Wallace Stevens. APT-1; HAP; HCAP; PoPoPo; SAmP

Planetarium. Adrienne Rich. FaBoWP; HCAP; NAAL-2v2; NALW; NIL-7; NIP-4; NOBA; NoAM; VCAP

Planh for the Young English King. Ezra Pound. APT-1

Planisféria, Map of the World, Lisbon, 1554. Ellen Hinsey. AmPoNex

Planning the Perfect Evening. Rita Dove. GT *Fr.* Suite for Augustus, A.

Plans. Brendan Kennelly. BiHa

Plans. Maxine W. Kumin. TLR

Plans Gone Up In Smoke. Sándor Petőfi. IQMS, tr. by Leslie A. Kery

Plant trees. Exactly against this tree. Paavo Haavikko. WoPoe, tr. by Anselm Hollo *Fr.* Fifteen Epigrams in Praise of the Tyrant.

Planted Heel, The. Sir Arthur Thomas Quiller-Couch. EBVV

Planter. Richard Murphy. BIrV *Fr.* Battle of Aughrim, The.

Planter's Daughter, The. Austin Clarke. CIP-2; ModIr; NPeEn; OxBEV; OxBTC

Planticru, The. Robert Rendall. OxBS

Planting. George Wither. NOSC *Fr.* Collection of Emblemes, Ancient and Moderne, A.

Planting. Okogbule Wonodi. PBMAP

Planting a Sequoia. Dana Gioia. GeoHom

Planting Flowers on the Eastern Embankment. Po Chü-i. OBGa, tr. by Arthur Waley
　(I TOOK money and brought flowering trees.) ChiP, tr. by Arthur Waley

Planting Initiation Song. *Unknown.* WPoS; WoPoe, tr. by Francis La Flesche

Planting Roses. Phillis Levin. FFC

Plants don't talk, people say. Rosalía de Castro. WPOW

Plants fruits of life and beauty there. (LL) William Blake. EBEV; FaBoEE; OxBEV *Fr.* Gnomic Verses.

Plants grow. Old Merina Theme. Flavien Ranaivo. NegPo, tr. by Ellen Conroy Kennedy

Plants succulent, distinct, each in its own atmosphere, The. At the Stanley Spencer Exhibition. John Riley. Oth

Plashes the Fountain. Paul Celan. OBVE, tr. by Michael Hamburger

Plasnewydd Square. Christopher Meredith. TCAWP

Plastic Cup, The. Kim Roberts. AmPoNex

Plastic freezer bag filled with cocaine, worn, A. Dancing to the Track Singers at the Nightclub. Judith Berke. SwNoth

Plastic transistor from Japan, A. First Radio. Michael McFee. SwNoth

Plate 134. By Eakins. "A cowboy in the West." David Ferry. FaBoA

Plateaus / The trunks of enormous. Savage, Our Fathers, The. B. H. Boston. GeoHom

Plates and bowls. Basho. EH, tr. by Robert Hass

Platinum blonde, Goldilocks, A. Limerick. Fiona Pitt-Kethley. PeLi

Platinum fur and brass revolver shine. Song. Michael McClure. BB

Platinum pens and Yellow Cake. Uranium. Gerry Bostock. IBA

Plato, despair! Meditation on Statistical Method. James Vincent Cunningham. CoAP; VGW

Plato excludes the poet from the city. My Dance. Blaise Cendrars. CuPo

Plato of the clear, dreaming eye and brave. Maidenhair. "Michael Field." OxBSo

Plato's Dog. John A. Scott. BMAP

Plato's Tomb. *Unknown. See* Spirit of Plato

Plato Told. E. E. Cummings. CTC
　(Plato Told Him.) NOBA; NoAM; OxBA; PoE

Plato Told Him. E. E. Cummings. CTC; NOBA; NoAM; OxBA; PoE

Plato told / him:he couldn't. Plato Told. E. E. Cummings. CTC

Plato was a fascist. Until He Comes. Trasi Johnson. InTrad

Platonic. Dudley North, 3d Baron North. NOSC

Platonic Blow, The. W. H. Auden.
　"Mad to be had, to be felt and smelled. My lips." EroLit

Platonic is a pretty name. Platonic. Dudley North, 3d Baron North. NOSC

Platonic Lady, The. John Wilmot, 2d Earl of Rochester. NOSC

Platonic Love. Abraham Cowley. *See* Mistress, The

Platonic Love. Edward Herbert, 1st Baron Herbert of Cherbury. NOSC

Platonic Love. Elizabeth Singer Rowe. BASC

Platonic love!—a pretty name. On Platonic Love. Samuel Boyse. ECEV

Platonic Subject. Ann Lauterbach. PmAP

Platonic[k] Love. Abraham Cowley. BeJo *Fr.* Mistress, The.

Platted quite neat to catch applause, with a sliding noose at the end. (LL) Character, A. William Blake. FaBoEE; InPK-6

Platypus, The. *Aborigine Oral Tradition.* NOBAu

Platypus, The. Oliver Herford. PeLV

Plaudite, or End of Life, The. Robert Herrick. CaPo

Play. Frank Asch. NTCP

Play 1. Identity A Poem. Gertrude Stein. PFTM-1

Play I could once; but, gentle friend, you see. To His Friend, on the Untunable Times. Robert Herrick. CaPo

Play is one paragraph, The. Realistic Bar and Grill, A. David Shapiro. PmAP

Play it across the table. Cahoots. Carl Sandburg. APT-1

Play It Again, Salmonella. Jeffrey McDaniel. AmPoNex

Play it once. Saturday Night. Langston Hughes. MoAmPo

Play No Ball. Gerard Benson. NOxBChV

Play, Phoebus, on thy lute. Canticle to Apollo, A. Robert Herrick. CaPo

Play Song. Peter Clarke. PBA

Play that thing. Jazz Band in a Parisian Cabaret. Langston Hughes. MoAmPo

Play that thing, you jazz mad fools! Jazz Band. Frank Marshall Davis. SeSe

Play the devil with one's emotions. (LL) Seven-Sided Poem. Carlos Drummond de Andrade. PoetW; TCLAP; VCWP, tr. by Elizabeth Bishop

"Play up! play up! and play the game!" (LL) Vitaï Lampada. Sir Henry John Newbolt. FaBoWar; OBWP; UV

Playboy. Richard Wilbur. NOBA; NoAM

Playboy of the Demi-World[: 1938], The. William Plomer. OxBTC; UV

Played backwards on his grandson's eyes. (LL) Grandfather. Michael S. Harper. ESEAA; LCAP-2; NAAAL; TAP; VCAP

Player Piano. John Updike. WeW-3

Player Piano, The. Randall Jarrell. NAAL-2v2

Players. E. Ethelbert Miller. SpirFl

Playful Poem on a Chicken Egg, A. Hsieh Chin. CoBLCP, tr. by Jonathan Chaves

Playground, The. Gregory Harrison. NOxBChV

Playhouse, The. Joseph Addison. ECEV

Playhouse Musings. James Smith. OxAEP-2

Playing at Cards. Belle Randall. CRP

Playing ball—so it's like paradise, not because it's in the past, we're on a. Leslie Scalapino. BodElec *Fr.* That they were at the beach—aeolotropic series.

Playing Basketball with the Viet Cong. Kevin Bowen. MoASP

Playing for England. David Scott. NLP

Playing for Time. Christopher Buckley. SeSe

Playing Monopoly's. It's a Bit Rich. Max Fatchen. OTCP

Playing once with facile. Asclepiades. PGA

Playing Pocahontas. Lew Blockcolski. VoR

Playing Solitaire. Thulani Davis. GT

Playing the Flute for the TMR Class. Jane Epton Seale. MiVo

Playing the Game. *Unknown.* PWR

Playing the Goldberg Variations on Sunday Morning. Bill Holm. MiVo

Playing the Machine. Howard Nemerov. BodElec

Playing the 7th. 48 Words for a Woman's Dance Song. Jerome Rothenberg. PoM

Playing with Fire. James Simmons. CIP-2

Playing your trumpets. Mosquitoes. Franz Wright. LCAP-2

Playland. Richard Foerster. SwNoth

Plays. Walter Savage Landor. NBLV; OxBSP; OxBoLi; PeLV

Playwright convict of public wrongs to men. On Playwright. Ben Jonson. NoP-4

Plaza and the Flaming Orange Trees, The. Antonio Machado Ruiz. SpanPo, *tr.* by Kate Flores

Plaza Has a Tower, The. Antonio Machado Ruiz. SpanPo, *tr.* by Angel Flores

Plea. John Ciardi. OxBSP

Plea for a Captive. W. S. Merwin. NoAM

Plea for Mercy, A. Kwesi Brew. PBA; PBMAP; WoPoe

Plea for My Heart's Sake. Naomi Long Madgett. SeSe

Plea for Peace. Frank Prewett. HATNAP

Plea for Tolerance. Margaret E. Bruner. PoToHe

Plea for Trigamy, A. Sir Owen Seaman. NOBL; PeLV

Plea to Boys and Girls, A. Robert Graves. GTBS-P; NAEL-5v2; NAEL-6v2

Plea to Old Age. Lajos Áprily. IQMS, *tr.* by Doreen Bell

Pleading eyebrows, intoxicating eyes! Song. Ch'in Kuan. CrYelRi, *tr.* by Sam Hamill

Pleasant Comedy of Patient Grissell [*or* Grissel *or* Grissill], The. Thomas Dekker.

　"Art thou poor, yet hast thou golden slumbers?" GTBS-P; HAP; NoSic; RB; SCGP; UnPo

　(Cradle Song, A: "Golden slumbers kiss your eyes.") SCGP

　Golden Slumbers. NoSic; OxAEP-1; OxBEV

　"Golden slumbers kiss[e] your eyes." NoSic; OxAEP-1; OxBEV

　Happy Heart, The. GTBS-P; HAP; NoSic; RB; SCGP; UnPo

　(Sweet Content.) OBEV

Pleasant Delusion of a Sumpteous Citty. Sarah Kemble Knight. SCAP

Pleasant it looked. This Newly Created World. *Unknown.* AiP

Pleasant Joys of Brotherhood, The. James Simmons. OBCoV; PBCIP

Pleasant land of counterpane, The. (LL) Land of Counterpane, The. Robert Louis Stevenson. ChAP; EBEV; NBLV; NTCP; PWR; TLR; WHSW

Pleasant Life in Newfoundland, The. Robert Hayman. NOBC

Pleasant place I was at today, A. Woodland Mass, The. Dafydd [*or* David] ap Gwilym. OBWVE, *tr.* by Gwyn Williams

Pleasant smell of frying sausages, A. Mixed Feelings. John Ashbery. HAP; WeW-3

Pleasant Songs of the Sweetheart Who Meets You in the Fields. *Unknown.* WoPoe, *tr.* by Ezra Pound and Noel Stock *Fr.* Conversations in Courtship.

Pleasant the House. *Unknown.* BIrV, *tr.* by John Montague

Pleasant to wander. Friedrich Hölderlin. WoPoe, *tr.* by David Gascoyne *Fr.* Tinian.

Pleasant winds brushing the forest grove. Su Tung-p'o (Su Shih). SuSp, *tr.* by Irving Y. Lo *Fr.* On Chao Ch'ang's Flower Paintings in Wang Po-yang's Collection.

Pleasantly, of the green wood and the dry. (LL) Rick of Green Wood, The. Edward Dorn. NeAP; PmAP; PoM

Pleasd with thy Place. Epictetus. NPeEn, *tr.* by George Chapman

Please. To One Afflicted with Adolescence. Anna Cascella. CItWP, *tr.* by Cinzia Sartini Blum and Lara Trubowitz

Please. Laura Kasischke. NAPBL

Please be silent, now my country, while I fill the speaker's place. Negro Schools, The. Lizelia Augusta Jenkins Moorer. CBWP-3

Please, Chung Tzu. *Unknown.* CoBCP, *tr.* by Burton Watson

Please come forth. Midwife's Invocation, A. *Unknown.* WPoS, *tr.* by Michael Coe and Whittaker Gordon

Please don't be offended if I preach to you a while. Look for the Silver Lining. B. G. DeSylva. ReLy; TCAPo

Please forgive this platitude. Fine and Dandy. Paul James. ReLy

Please Forward. James Welch. CDW

Please God, forsake your water and dry bread. To a Nun. John Ormond. EBEV; FaBoTw; NoP-4

Please hang a moon up and tune up the cellos. Here Come the Dreamers. Hugh Martin. ReLy

Please keep an eye on my house for a few moments. Vidya. BoWoP

Please Master. Allen Ginsberg. CAGL; GLP

Please master can I touch your cheek. Please Master. Allen Ginsberg. CAGL; GLP

Please mista do'n take me chilen, please mista do'n. Errol West. IBA

"Please, Please, Please" on the charts permits. David Wojahn. PBCAP *Fr.* Mystery Train: A Sequence.

Please refrain from frankly ogling your neighbor's. Locker Room Etiquette. Craig Arnold. MoASP

Please Say Something. Taeko Tomioka. WPOW

Please send me money enough for at least three weeks. (LL) Baudelaire. Delmore Schwartz. TwCP; VGW

Please, Sir Second-born. *Unknown.* ColAnChi, *tr.* by Jeffrey Riegel *Fr.* Classic of Odes.

Please teacher / Teach me something. Pick Yourself Up. Dorothy Fields. ReLy

Please, to finish my rhyme. (LL) Ballad of the Despairing Husband. Robert Creeley. NeAP; OBAL; RaBo

Please to remember / The fifth of November. Gunpowder Plot Day. *Unknown.* LB; OxNR

Please, when you ask me in this dream. Threnody for Sunrise. Richard Cecil. BodElec

Please you, draw near.—Louder the music there! William Shakespeare. EBEV *Fr.* King Lear.

Please your Grace, from out your store. Beggar to Mab, the Fairy [*or* Fairie] Queen, The. Robert Herrick. CaPo

Pleased am I, and more than willing. Lay of the Honeysuckle, The. Marie de France. WPE, *tr.* by Robin Johnson

Pleased in his loneliness, he often lies. Shepherd Boy, The. John Clare. CABP

Pleased to the last, she likes the luscious food. John Wilkes. EroLit *Fr.* Essay on Woman.

Pleasing was his shape. John Milton. EBNV *Fr.* Paradise Lost.

Pleasure. Allison Joseph. PasH

Pleasure. A. K. Ramanujan. PoetW; VCWP

Pleasure. Dean Young. IllVoic

Pleasure a writer knows is the pleasure all sages enjoy, The. Lu Chi. WoPoe, *tr.* by Sam Hamill *Fr.* Art of Writing, The.

Pleasure and pride are not, as duty knows. Vulgar Error, A. J. E. Thorold Rogers. FaBoEE

Pleasure Boat, The [*or* Pleasure-Boat, The]. Richard Henry Dana. APN-1

Pleasure Dome, The. Shrikant Verma. OMIP, *tr.* by Vinay Dahrwadker

PLEASURE FEARS ME, FOOT ROSE, FOOT BREATH. Michael McClure. BB *Fr.* Ghost Tantras.

Pleasure It Is. William Cornish. NPeEn

　(Gratitude.) CTC

Pleasure must slip. Condom Tree, The. Chase Twichell. EmeKit

Pleasure of Feeling Inside Your Body, The. Rochelle Lynn Holt. PasH

Pleasure of Imagination, The. Mark Akenside.

　Love of Nature. NOEC

Pleasure Reconciled to Virtue. Ben Jonson. NAEL-5v1; NAEL-6v1

　(Comus's Song.) OBCoV

　(Hymn to Comus.) NOSC; SCGP

Pleasure, sadness hold each other caught. Beethoven Sonata. Ernst Waldinger. AuPH, *tr.* by Lowell A. Bangerter

Pleasure: The Second Book of Solomon on the Vanity of the World. Matthew Prior.

　"Oft have I said, the praise of doing well." ChIV-1

Pleasures. Denise Levertov. NOBA; NeAP; NoAM; PoE

Pleasures among the Fields during the Four Seasons. Li K'ai-hsien. CoBLCP, *tr.* by Jonathan Chaves

Pleasures I took from life, The. Ghost of a Ghost, The. Brad Leithauser. RA

Pleasures of Darkness, The. Ahmad al-Safi Al-Najafi. MAP, *tr.* by John Heath-Stubbs and Salma Khadra Jayyusi

Pleasures of Heaven, The. Ben Jonson. TreFP

Pleasures of Hope, The. Thomas Campbell.

　At summer eve, when Heaven's ethereal bow.

　"'Tis summer eve, when heaven's ethereal bow." TreFP

Pleasures of Imagination, The. Mark Akenside.

　Creative Process, The. NOEC

　"Different task remains; the secret paths, A." NOEC

　(Love of Nature.) NOEC

　Poetic Genius. NOEC

　"Such is the secret union, when we feel." NOEC

Pleasures of Melancholy, The.   Thomas Warton, the Younger.
   "Beneath yon ruin'd abbey's moss-grown piles."   NOEC; OxAEP-1
   "Tapered choir, at the late hour of prayer, the."   ECEV
Pleasures of Merely Circulating, The.   Wallace Stevens.   OBAL
Pleasures of Retirement, The.   Edward Benlowes.   NOSC   *Fr.* Theophia.
Pleasures of Shinbashi.   Liu E.   CoBLCP, *tr. by* Jonathan Chaves
Pleasures of the Door, The.   Francis Ponge.   WoPoe, *tr. by* Raymond Federman
Pleasures of the Imagination.   Peter McDonald.   PNI
Pleasures of Thinking, The.   Thomas Vaux, 2d Baron Vaux of Harrowden.   NoSic
Pleaure Given by Suspicion with the Rhetoric of Crying, The.   Sister Juana Inés de la Cruz.   BLPSL, *tr. by* Rene de Costa, Rigas Kappatos and Eleni Paidoussi
Pledge at Spunky Point, The.   John Milton Hay.   OBAL
Pledge of Allegiance.   Carl Hancock Rux.   SpirFl
Pledge of Allegiance to the Family of Earth, A.   Mim Kelber.   HW
Pledged to the flood-tide of the sea. (LL)   Female.   Muhammad Al-Ghuzzi.   MAP; NAfrP, *tr. by* John Heath-Stubbs and May Jayyusi
Pleiades, The.   Mary Barnard.   APT-2
Pleiades, The.   S. E. K. Mqhayi.   PeSAV, *tr. by* Jeff Opland
Pleiades are sinking calm as paint, The.   Lesbos.   Lawrence Durrell.   EBEV
Pleiades disappear, The.   Sappho.   WoPoe, *tr. by* Sam Hamill
Plenteous place is Ireland for hospitable cheer, A.   Fair Hills of Ireland, The.   *Unknown.*   OBEV, *tr. by* Sir Samuel Ferguson
Plentiful light.   Electricity of Blossoms.   Lorenzo Thomas.   FTOS
Plenty of Flowers.   Two Songs about Flowers & Where I Was Walking.   *Unknown.*   STP, *tr. by* Johnny John and Jerome Rothenberg
Plenty Time Pass Fast, Fas Dey So.   Cheryl Boyce Taylor.   WiU
Plied for thee thy household tasks. (LL)   Saadi.   Ralph Waldo Emerson.   APN-1; OxBA
Plight, The.   James W. Thompson.   BPo
Plot, The.   William Dickey.   YaYoPo
Plot against the Giant, The.   Wallace Stevens.   OxBA; SAmP
Plot with Bitterness.   Vadim Gabrielevich Shershenevich.   TCRP, *tr. by* Daniel Weissbort
Plough, The.   Richard Henry [*or* Hengist] Horne.   OBEV
Plough and a Spade, A.   Nguyễn Trãi.   WoPoe, *tr. by* Nguyen Ngoc Bich
Plough and a spade, that's all, A.   Plough and a Spade, A.   Nguyễn Trãi.   WoPoe, *tr. by* Nguyen Ngoc Bich
Plough: I keep my snout to the ground; I burrow.   Cynewulf.   ASW   *Fr.* Riddles (Exeter Book).
Plough, sow and reap.   Charles Reznikoff.   FTOS   *Fr.* Jews in Babylonia.
Ploughing on Sunday.   Wallace Stevens.   RB; TTTS
Ploughing the land.   Basho.   EH, *tr. by* Robert Hass
Ploughing the seas like the pirate child.   On the Sea.   Gabriella Sica.   CItWP, *tr. by* Cinzia Sartini Blum and Lara Trubowitz
Ploughland has gone to bent, The.   Gin the Goodwife Stint.   Basil Bunting.   CTC
Ploughman.   John Tripp.   TCAWP
Ploughman, The.   Oliver Wendell Holmes.   CA
Ploughman, in Imitation of Milton, The.   Samuel Jones.   NOEC
Ploughman: In Welsh Uplands, The.   A. G. Prys-Jones.   AngWePo
Ploughman ploughing a level field.   To a Schoolboy.   *Unknown.*   RB, *tr. by* Anne Pennington
Ploughman's Horse, The.   Robert Bloomfield.   ECEV   *Fr.* Winter.
Ploughman's Song, The.   *Var. authors.*   *See* Honourable Entertainment Given to the Queen's Majesty in Progress at Elvetham, 1591, The
Ploughman, whose gnarly hand yet kindly wheeled.   Waving of the Corn, The.   Sidney Lanier.   APN-2
Plover rises, A.   Ryou.   JDP, *tr. by* Yoel Hoffmann
Plover wades through, A.   Teisa.   JDP, *tr. by* Yoel Hoffmann
Plovers cry, The.   Kakinomoto no Hitomaro.   OHMPJ
Plow: "My beak is bent downward, I burrow below."   Cynewulf.   AnOE   *Fr.* Riddles (Exeter Book).
Plowdens, Finns.   Robert Earl Hayden.   NAAL-5
Plower, The.   Padraic Colum.   MoBrPo
Plowing: A Memory.   Hamlin Garland.   ChAP
Plowing of Piers's Half-acre, The.   William Langland.   NAEL-6v1; NAEL-7v1   *Fr.* Vision of Piers Plowman, The.
Plowman.   Sidney Keyes.   PoRA
Plowman of Rákos Under the Turks.   Károly Kisfaludy.   IQMS, *tr. by* Watson Kirkconnell
Plows keep striking, large stones, their.   Harrowing.   Douglas Messerli.   FTOS
Pluck the Fruit and Taste the Pleasure.   Thomas Lodge.   OxAEP-1   *Fr.* Robert, Second Duke of Normandy.
Pluck Wins.   *Unknown.*   PWR

Plucke the fruite and tast the pleasure.   Thomas Lodge.   OxAEP-1   *Fr.* Robert, Second Duke of Normandy.
Plucking the Rushes.   *Unknown.*   BoLoP; ChiP; OBVE, *tr. by* Arthur Waley
Plug.   Edmund Vance Cooke.   PWR
Plum-blossom, The.   *Var. authors.*   AWP; TAL   *Fr.* Manyo Shu, Part 3 of 4.
Plum Blossoms.   Li Ch'ing-chao.   ErotSp, *tr. by* Sam Hamill   (To the Tune: Plum Blossoms.)   CrYelRi
Plum Blossoms.   Su Tung-p'o (Su Shih).   SuSp, *tr. by* Irving Y. Lo   *Fr.* On Chao Ch'ang's Flower Paintings in Wang Po-yang's Collection.
Plum blossoms float by on the spring water.   Song of the Yodo River.   Buson.   EH, *tr. by* Robert Hass
Plum blossoms here and there.   Buson.   EH, *tr. by* Robert Hass
Plum blossoms in bloom.   Buson.   SoOfWa, *tr. by* Sam Hamill
Plum Blossoms on Solitary Hill.   Wang An-shih.   SuSp, *tr. by* Jan W. Walls
Plum blossoms / One's nose.   Onitsura.   ZenPo, *tr. by* Takashi Ikemoto and Lucien Stryk
Plum blossoms scent.   Buson.   WoPoe, *tr. by* Tony Barnstone
Plum flowers all fallen and gone.   *Unknown.*   SuSp   *Fr.* Tzu-yeh Songs of the Four Seasons.
Plum in bloom.   Lucien Stryk.   IllVoic   *Fr.* Issa: A Suite of Haiku.
Plum petals falling.   Baiko.   JDP, *tr. by* Yoel Hoffmann
Plum Pudding, A.   Mother Goose.   OxNR; ReMoGo
Plum scent / Haloing.   Buson.   ZenPo, *tr. by* Takashi Ikemoto and Lucien Stryk
Plum tree breaks out in bees, The.   April.   Charles Wright.   GeoHom
Plum Tree by the House, The.   Oliver St. John Gogarty.   OBEV; PoRA
Plum Tree Drops Its Fruit, The.   *Unknown.*   CoBCP, *tr. by* Burton Watson
Plum-viewing.   Buson.   ZenPo, *tr. by* Takashi Ikemoto and Lucien Stryk
Plum Window.   Muso Soseki.   EaWin, *tr. by* W. S. Merwin
Plumber from Lowater Creek, A.   Limerick.   *Unknown.*   PeLi
Plumber may be a poet, but a poet is not likely, A.   Difference, The.   Stoddard King.   OBAL
Plumbers.   Susan Miles.   NOxBChV
Plumburst.   John Kinsella.   NeBl
Plume.   Richard Kenney.   NoP-4
Plumes of love are black, The!   Mad Sonnet 1.   Michael McClure.   PoM
Plumes of pampas grass.   Issa.   EH, *tr. by* Robert Hass
Plumpuppets, The.   Christopher Darlington Morley.   ChAP
Plums in blossom.   Buson.   EH, *tr. by* Robert Hass
Plums leave their tartness, weakening my teeth.   Early Summer Waking from a Nap.   Yang Wan-li.   SuSp, *tr. by* Sherwin S. S. Fu
Plunder.   Debra Bruce.   IllVoic
Plunge the green wave, and bid thy griefs subside. (LL)   Visions Appear to her in a Dream.   Mary Robinson.   CenSon; RWP
Plunging downward through the slimy water.   Death by Drowning.   Elizabeth Brewster.   NOBC
Plunging limbers over the shattered track, The.   Isaac Rosenberg.   FaBoMo; GTBS-P; NAEL-5v2; NAEL-6v2; NoAM; OBWP; PeFWW; PoWW; TrJP
Pluralist and Old Soldier, The.   John Collier.   NOEC
Plutarch.   Agathias.   AWP, *tr. by* John Dryden
Pluvius, this whole city on his nerves.   Spleen LXXV.   Charles Baudelaire.   SxFrPo, *tr. by* James McGowan
Pneumoconiosis.   Duncan Bush.   AngWePo; TCAWP
Po' los' boy, bebby, / Evahmo'. (LL)   Southern Road.   Sterling Allen Brown.   APT-2; BPo
Po, po, po, po.   *Unknown.*   MiEL
Po, the unrivalled poet.   To Li Po on a Spring Day.   Tu Fu.   TAL
Pobble Who Has No Toes, The.   Edward Lear.   FaBoCh; OTCP
Pocahontas.   William Makepeace Thackeray.
   "Wearied arm, and broken sword."   AiP
Pock-marked player of the accordion, The.   Wedding Party.   Donald Hall.   LCAP-2
Pocket, it is Poems by Pierre Reverdy. (LL)   Step Away from Them, A.   Frank O'Hara.   CoAmPo; HCAP; NAAL-2v2; VCAP; VGW; WoPoe
Pockets of our greatcoats full of barley, The.   Requiem for the Croppies.   Seamus Heaney.   BIrV; CIP-2; FaBoMo; OBWP
Pockets puffed with bottles.   Here.   Lawrence Joseph.   UrbNat
Poe.   James Russell Lowell.   *See* Fable for Critics, A
Poe.   Mina Loy.   APT-1
Poe and Longfellow.   James Russell Lowell.   APN-1; OxBA; TCAPo   *Fr.* Fable for Critics, A.
Poe Story, A.   Anthony Butts.   AmPoNex
Poem.   Tom Clark.   CoAmPo
   (Like Musical Instruments.)   PmAP
Poem.   "Paul Dermée."   CuPo
Poem.   Calvin C. Hernton.   GT
Poem.   Jack Kerouac.   CLPP
Poem.   Paul Klee.   PFTM-1

Poem. Pablo Neruda. CLPP, *tr.* by Kenneth Rexroth

Poem. Sterling Plumpp. GT

Poem, A. Boris Leonidovich Pasternak.
"I too have been in love, and my sleepless." TCRP

Poem, The. Homero [*or* Umberto] Aridjis. TCLAP, *tr.* by Eliot Weinberger

Poem 2 (for Duckie Simpson of Black Uhuru). Audrey Ingram-Roberts. WaCA

[Poem 2]: "Inside, the church lights up today's rain." Fernando Pessoa. PFTM-1 *Fr.* Oblique Rain.

Poem 12. Mary Oliver. PoCoUp *Fr.* West Wind.

Poem 15. Pablo Neruda. BLPSL, *tr.* by Rene de Costa, Rigas Kappatos and Eleni Paidoussi

Poem 20. Pablo Neruda. BLPSL, *tr.* by Rene de Costa, Rigas Kappatos and Eleni Paidoussi

Poem 143. Charles Olson. APSN; ColAP *Fr.* Maximus Poems, The.

Poem, A: "Gasp sounded, The." Mongane Wally Serote. PeSAV

Poem, A: "What is there that we can do or say." Ezekiel Mphahlele. AF

Poem about a Wolf Maybe Two Wolves, A. *Unknown.* STP, *tr.* by Richard Johnny John and Jerome Rothenberg

Poem about Breasts, A. James Wright (1927–80). TAP

Poem about Breath. David Wagoner. NoAM

Poem about Fan the Fourth, A. Li K'ai-hsien. CoBLCP, *tr.* by Jonathan Chaves

Poem about Intelligence for My Brothers and Sisters, A. June Jordan. PAI
(Few years back and they told me Black, A.) LTA; UnSA

Poem about My Rights. June Jordan. GLP; ISC; NAAAL; NoAM

Poem about People. Robert Pinsky. VCAP

Poem about Poems about Vietnam, A. Jon Stallworthy. NoAM

Poem about Rain. Nikolai Alekseievich Zabolotsky [*or* Zabolotskii]. TCRusP, *tr.* by Daniel Weissbort

Poem about the Blue Horse. Sergey Morozov. TCRusP, *tr.* by Daniel Weissbort

Poem about the Future. Hans Magnus Enzensberger. PoSu

Poem: "About the size of an old-style dollar bill." Elizabeth Bishop. HCAP; NoAM; PoPoPo; PoetW; VCAP

Poem about Youth and Romanticism, A. "Naum Korzhavin." TCRP, *tr.* by Vladimir Lunis and Albert C. Todd

Poem, after A. E. Housman. Hugh Kingsmill. NOBL; UV
(What, Still Alive.) NBLV
(What, Still Alive at Twenty–Two.) InPK-6

Poem: "After your death." Bill Knott. SPE

Poem again, of several parts, each having to do, A. David Ferry. FaBoA *Fr.* Photographs from a Book: Six Poems.

Poem against Catholics. John Fuller. OBSV; PeLV

Poem against the British. Robert Bly. CoAmPo

Poem against the Rich. Robert Bly. NOBA

Poem against the State (Of Things): 1975. June Jordan. ISC

Poem: "And if it snowed and snow covered the drive." Simon Armitage. HarvBoo

Poem: "And when I pay death's duty." Robin Blaser. NeAP

Poem Arrested at Daybreak. Julia de Burgos. TANSG, *tr.* by Heather Rosario Sievert

Poem: "As I traveled from the city." Salah Fa'iq. MAP, *tr.* by Patricia Alanah Byrne and Salma Khadra Jayyusi

Poem as Mask, The. Muriel Rukeyser. APT-2; NAAAL-5; NALW
(When I wrote of the women in their dances and wildness, it.) OxWW

Poem: "As the cat." William Carlos Williams. ChAP; HarvBoo; KaS; NoP-4; PAI; PoPoPo; SoSe-8; TTTS

Poem: "As the full moon rises." Kenneth Rexroth. GifTon

Poem ascends, The. (LL) Jacob's Ladder, The. Denise Levertov. APSN; ChIV-1; NAAL-5; PFTM-2; PoM

Poem: "At night Chinamen jump." Frank O'Hara. NOBA; NoAM; PmAP

Poem at Thirty. Sonia Sanchez. BPo; BiSi; NAAAL

Poem: "At your light side trees shy." Bill Knott. SPE

Poem before Departure. Jean Burden. WPE

Poem Beginning "The." Louis Zukofsky. APT-2
Fifth Movement: Autobiography. PFTM-1; TaR
"Speaking about epics, mother." PFTM-1; TaR

Poem Beginning with a Line by Cavafy. Derek Mahon. PNI

Poem Beginning with a Line by Pindar, A. Robert Duncan. NNaP; NeAP; PmAP; PoM; VCAP
(*Light foot hears you and the brightness begins, The.*) CoAmPo

Poem: "Between rebellion as a private study and the public." Charles Donnelly. *See* Last Poem

Poem: "Blue snow is turning black, The." Aleksandr Trifonovich Tvardovsky [*or* Tvardovskii]. RusPo, *tr.* by Robert Arthur Douglas Ford

Poem by a Perfectly Furious Academician. Shirley Brooks. NOBVV; PeLV

Poem by John Thorpe, A. Kris Hemensley. BMAP *Fr.* Mile from Poetry, A.

Poem by the Bridge at Ten-shin. Li Po. OBVE, *tr.* by Ezra Pound

Poem by the Charles River. Robin Blaser. NeAP

Poem: "By the road to the contagious hospital." William Carlos Williams.
See Spring and All

Poem: "Character of a landscape stands always in a mysterious relation, The." Charles Madge. SPE
(Landscape I.) SPE

(Poem) (Chicago) (The Were-Age). Bill Knott. SPE

Poem Circling Hamtramck, Michigan, All Night in Search of You, The. Philip Levine. NNaP

Poem: "Come, brother, and tell me your life." Jorge Rebelo. PBMAP, *tr.* by Margaret Dickinson

Poem Composed at the Command of the Emperor. Li Po. ChinPo, *tr.* by Yip Wai-lim

Poem Composed During a Brownout. Fidelito Cortes. ReBoTo

Poem: "Disturbing to have a person." Barbara Guest. FaBoWP

Poem: "Eager note on my door said 'Call me,' The." Frank O'Hara. NOBA; NoAM; PmAP; SPE

Poem Ended by a Death. Fleur Adcock. NAEL-6v2; NoP-4; PeNZ

Poem Entitled the Day and the War, A. James Madison Bell.
Though Tennyson the Poet King. CBCWP

Poem: "Every morning I forget how it is." Charles Simic. NNaP

Poem Expressing My Wife's Response to One I Sent Her, A. Li K'ai-hsien. CoBLCP, *tr.* by Jonathan Chaves

Poem Fifty. Nancy Morejón. TANSG, *tr.* by Joy Renjilian-Burgy

Poem: "Figures in the fields against the sky!" Antonio Machado Ruiz. AWP; WoPoe, *tr.* by John Dos Passos

Poem Films Itself, The. J. S. Harry. BMAP

Poem for a "Divorced" Daughter. Horace Coleman. ISC

Poem for a Guerrilla Leader. Syl Cheney-Coker. PBMAP

Poem for a Lost Lover. Syl Cheney-Coker. PBMAP

Poem for a Militant. Jorge Rebelo. PBMAP

Poem for a New Year. Rachel Wetzsteon. NeAmPo

Poem for a Younger Son. William Scammell. NLP

Poem for an Anniversary. Cecil Day Lewis. CABP

Poem for Aretha. Nikki Giovanni. BPo; WWork

Poem for Ben Barney. Leslie Marmon Silko. CDW; VoR

Poem for Black Boys. Nikki Giovanni. BPo

Poem for Black Hearts, A. Imamu Amiri Baraka. NAAAL; PoM

Poem for Black Hearts, A. LeRoi Jones. SSLK

Poem for Black Relocation Centers, A. Etheridge Knight. ESEAA *Fr.* Two Poems for Black Relocation Centers.

Poem for Carroll, Descendant of Chiefs. Lance Henson. VoR

Poem for Central America. Hilary Booth. SurWo

Poem for Children; or, On Cruelty to the Irrational Creation, A. Jane Cave. ECWP

Poem for Christmas, A. C. A. Snodgrass. PoToHe

Poem for Claude. Ray DiPalma. FTOS

Poem for Cocksuckers, A. John Wieners. CAGL

Poem for Deep Thinkers, A. Imamu Amiri Baraka. APSN

Poem for Diane Wakoski, A. Ray A. Young Bear. CDW

Poem for Easter. Robert Kelly. ErotSp; VGW

Poem for Ed "Whitey" Ford, A. Jonathan Holden. MoASP

Poem for Elliot Carter on His 90th Birthday. Alan Dugan. BodElec

Poem for Emily, A. Miller Williams. WeW-3

Poem for Etheridge. Sonia Sanchez. BPo

Poem for Flora. Nikki Giovanni. BPo

Poem for Garcia Lorca. George Woodcock. NOBC

Poem for George Helm: Aloha Week 1980. Eric Chock. OpBo

Poem for George Miles. Dennis Cooper. WiU

Poem for Gonzales, California, The. Morton Marcus. GeoHom

Poem for Guatemala. June Jordan. NAAAL

Poem for Half White College Students. Imamu Amiri Baraka. BPo; TAP; UnPo

Poem for Jacqueline Hill. *Unknown.* BrRo

Poem for Jan. Joseph Bruchac. CDW

Poem for July 4, 1994. Sonia Sanchez. SpirFl

Poem (for Langston Hughes), A. Nikki Giovanni. SSLK

Poem for "Magic," A. Quincy Troupe. ISC; LoL

Poem for Mankind and Its Hope. Clementina Suárez. TANSG, *tr.* by Janet N. Gold

Poem for Maurice O'Shea, A. Geoffrey Lehmann. NOBAu

Poem for Max Nordau, A. Edwin Arlington Robinson. APN-2

Poem for Melissa. Nuala Ni Dhomhnaill. BiHa

Poem for Mr. Li in Early Spring. Tu Fu. CrYelRi, *tr.* by Sam Hamill

Poem for museum goers, A. John Weiners. BB

Poem for Museum Goers, A. John Wieners. NeAP

Poem for My Brother Returning to My Farm. Tu Fu. CrYelRi, *tr. by* Sam Hamill

Poem for My Family: Hazel Griffin and Victor Hernandez Cruz. June Jordan. BPo

Poem for My Father. Graham Allen. AngWePo

Poem for My Father. Alejandra Piznarnick. TANSG, *tr. by* Susan Bassnett

Poem for My Father. Quincy Troupe. *See* Poem for My Father; for Quincy Trouppe, Sr

Poem for My Father, A. Sonia Sanchez. BPo

Poem for My Father; for Quincy Trouppe, Sr. Quincy Troupe. MoASP (Father, it was honor to be there, in the dugout.) AF (Poem for My Father.) AF; LTA

Poem for My Little Boy. Li Shang-yin. CoBCP, *tr. by* Burton Watson

Poem for My Nephew. Nikki Giovanni. NOxBChV

Poem for My Sister. Liz Lochhead. ItWoWo

Poem for My Sons. Minnie Bruce Pratt. WiU

Poem for My Wet Nurse, A. Cheng Hsieh. CoBLCP, *tr. by* Jonathan Chaves

Poem for Myself, A. Etheridge Knight. *See* Poem for Myself (Or Blues for a Mississippi Black Boy), A

Poem for Myself and Mei: Abortion. Leslie Marmon Silko. VoR

Poem for Myself (Or Blues for a Mississippi Black Boy), A. Etheridge Knight. PoPoPo (Poem for Myself, A.) AF

Poem for Nana. June Jordan. BlSi

Poem for Natalia Ginzburg. Anita Helle. OPRER

Poem for Painters, A. John Weiners. BB

Poem for Painters, A. John Wieners. NeAP; PoM

Poem for Players, A. Al Young. LTA

Poem for R. Kim Ly Bui-Burton. PasH

Poem for Shane on Her Brother's Birthday. Donald T. Sanders. TTTS

Poem for Sigmund. Lorna Crozier. LW

Poem for Some Black Women. Carolyn M. Rodgers. BlSi

Poem for Sophie. David Lampert. GotH

Poem for Speculative Hipsters, A. Imamu Amiri Baraka. NOBA; NoAM

Poem for Teacup Mantlepiece Poets Palpitating Poot Booty Plagiarists Imprisoned in Ivy League White Supremacist Mental Biological Warfare Labs. Tony Medina. InTrad

Poem for the Birthday of Huey P. Newton. Sotère Torregian. NBV

Poem for the Children. Carolyn Beard Whitlow. FFC

Poem for the End. Honor Moore. WiU

Poem for the Father. Alejandra Pizarnik. TCLAP, *tr. by* Frank Graziano and María Rosa Fort

Poem for the insane, A. John Weiners. *See* Poem for the Insane, A

Poem for the Insane, A. John Weiners. NeAP; PmAP; PoM (Poem for the insance, A.) BB

Poem for the Man Who Said Shit. David Clewell. OPRER

Poem for the Old Man, A. John Wieners. NeAP

Poem for the Sefirot as a Wheel of Light, A. Naftali Bacharach. PFTM-1

Poem for the Shechina. Cassia Berman. HW

Poem for the Womb. Jennifer O'Grady. AmPoNex

Poem for the Young White Man Who Asked Me How I, an Intelligent, Well-Read Person Could Believe in the War between Races. Lorna Dee Cervantes. PBCAP; PoPoPo; WPOW

Poem for Trapped Things, A. John Weiners. BB

Poem for Trapped Things, A. John Wieners. GLP; NeAP; PmAP; PoM

Poem for Trish, A. Gavin Moses. InTrad

Poem for Unwed Mothers. Nikki Giovanni. OBAL

Poem for vipers, A. John Weiners. BB

Poem for Willie Best, A. Imamu Amiri Baraka. NAAL-5

Poem for Writers, A. Lee Harwood. Oth

Poem: "For years I've heard." Robin Blaser. NeAP

Poem: "Form is the woods: the beast." James [*or* Jim] Harrison. VGW

Poem: "Frail sound of a tunic trailing, A." Antonio Machado Ruiz. AWP; WoPoe, *tr. by* John Dos Passos

Poem from Llanybri. Lynnette Roberts. AngWePo; TCAWP

Poem from Sierra Madre. Mila D. Aguilar. ReBoTo

Poem from the Empire State. June Jordan. BPo

Poem: "From us, like appendicitis." Andrey [*or* Andrei] Andreievich Voznesensky [*or* Voznesenskii]. RusPo, *tr. by* Robert Arthur Douglas Ford

Poem: "Geranium, houseleek, laid in oblong beds." John Gray. NOBVV

Poem: "Greater cities are, The." Víctor Hernández Cruz. PueRic

Poem: "Hasten on your childhood to the hour when white." Pablo Picasso. SPE, *tr. by* David Gascoyne (Poems.) SPE, *tr. by* David Gascoyne

Poem: "Hate is only one of many responses." Frank O'Hara. NeAP

Poem: "Here. Forget." Charles Bernstein. FTOS

Poem: "Horizon line." Raymond Radiguet. CuPo

Poem: "I do not want only." Colleen Thibaudeau. NOBC

Poem: "I don't know as I get what D. H. Lawrence is driving at." Frank O'Hara. LCAP-2

Poem: "I keep feeling all space as my image." Sanders Russell. SPE

Poem: "I know / how fascinated we are with clarity." Salah Fa'iq. MAP, *tr. by* Patricia Alanah Byrne and Salma Khadra Jayyusi

Poem: "I lived in the first century of world wars." Muriel Rukeyser. UnPo

Poem: "I loved my friend." Langston Hughes. NTCP

Poem: "I'm like all lovers, wanting love to be." Lesbia Harford. NOBAu

Poem: "I play tennis with the shells." "Paul Dermée." CuPo

Poem: "I sing th' adventures of mine worthy wights." Thomas Morton. SCAP

Poem: "I think I came close to being insane a few months ago." C. K. Williams. BodElec

Poem: "I walk at dawn across the hollow hills." Ruthven Todd. SPE

Poem: "I want to know today." Sargon Boulus. MAP, *tr. by* Sargon Boulus and Alistair Elliot

Poem: "If I held back each word, perhaps." Timothy Liu. AmPoNex

Poem: "If I speak always of the dead." Salah Fa'iq. MAP, *tr. by* Patricia Alanah Byrne and Salma Khadra Jayyusi

Poem: "In danger of which." Ray DiPalma. FTOS

Poem in Defense of Children. Joel Oppenheimer. CDa

Poem: "In its going down, the moon." Robert Hoggra. MoCV

Poem in November. Shirley Kaufman. GifTon

Poem in October. Dylan Thomas. AngWePo; NAEL-5v2; NAEL-6v2; NPeEn; NoAM; OxAEP-2; PoRA; RB; SoSe-8; TCAWP; UV

Poem in Parts. Judah Halevi. WoPoe, *tr. by* Ammiel Alcalay

Poem in Praise of Colum Cille, A. Dallán Forgaill. NOIV

Poem in Praise of My Husband (Taos). Diane Di Prima. BB

Poem in Rhyme-Prose Form. Pan Chieh-yû. CoBCP, *tr. by* Burton Watson

Poem: "In sand." Chimalum Nwankwo. NAfrP

Poem: "In the early evening, as now, a man is bending." Louise Glück. HCAP

Poem: "In the earnest path of duty." Charlotte Forten. BlSi

Poem in the Form of a Coffin-Puller's Song. Miu Hsi. CoBCP, *tr. by* Burton Watson

Poem in the Form of a Coffin-Puller's Song, No. 1. T'ao Ch'ien [*or* T'ao Yuan-ming]. CoBCP, *tr. by* Burton Watson

Poem in the Form of a Coffin-Puller's Song, No. 2. T'ao Ch'ien [*or* T'ao Yuan-ming]. CoBCP, *tr. by* Burton Watson

Poem in the Form of a Coffin-Puller's Song, No. 3. T'ao Ch'ien [*or* T'ao Yuan-ming]. CoBCP, *tr. by* Burton Watson

Poem in the Shape of a Saxophone. T. R. Hummer. SeSe

Poem: "In the stump of the old tree, where the heart has rotted out." Hugh Sykes Davies. SPE

Poem in Three Parts. Robert Bly. CoAmPo; NOBA; PAI

Poem in Three Parts. S. J. Marks. BodElec

Poem in Time of War. Ray Mathew. NOBAu; OBCoV

Poem in Which I Refuse Contemplation. Rita Dove. NAAL-5

Poem in Yellow after Tristan Tzara, A. Jerome Rothenberg. PoM

Poem Inscribed on a Landscape Painting. Chu Yün-ming. "Clouds are swept into the sunset—a sky beyond the sky." CoBLCP

Poem is the cry of its occasion, The. Another Duffer. Sam Hamill. BodElec

Poem is ugly and they make it uglier, The. Nokh Aushvits (After Auschwitz). Jerome Rothenberg. TaR

Poem: "It doesn't look like a finger it looks like a feather of broken glass." Hugh Sykes Davies. SPE

Poem: "Khrushchev is coming on the right day!" Frank O'Hara. NeAP; PoM

Poem: "Lana Turner has collapsed!" Frank O'Hara. CLPP; FTOS; PmAP; VGW

Poem: "Late butterflies gliding through the air—" Timothy Liu. NeAmPo

Poem Like a Grenade, A. John Haines. SPE

Poem: "Little bones of." Michael O'Brien. KGB

Poem Looking for a Reader, A. Haki R. Madhubuti. ISC

Poem looks at the paper, The. Creative Process, The. Amrita Pritam. OMIP, *tr. by* Amrita Pritam and Arlene Zide

Poem makes truth a little more disturbing, The. Hands. Donald Finkel. CoAP

Poem Making Fun of Chi-ti for His Eye Illness, A. Yang Chi. CoBLCP, *tr. by* Jonathan Chaves

Poem: "Mule kicked out in the trees, A. An Early." Norman Dubie. BodElec

Poem must complete the cycle of full release, A. Talking. Miguel Algarin. PueRic

Poem: "My little son, laughing, singing." Thomas McGrath. GifTon

Poem: "Naked is the earth." Antonio Machado Ruiz. AWP; WoPoe, *tr. by* John Dos Passos

Poem No. 1. Carolyn M. Rodgers. ISC

Poem No. II. Sang Yi. PFTM-1 *Fr.* Crow's-Eye View.

Poem No. III. Sang Yi. PFTM-1

Poem No. V. Sang Yi. PFTM-1

Poem No. VII. Sang Yi. PFTM-1

Poem No. X. Sang Yi. PFTM-1

Poem No. XV. Sang Yi. PFTM-1

Poem not flowery but bare, A. "David Samuilovich Samoylov" [or Samoilov]. TCRP

Poem: "Nothing is more cruel than to see." Salah Fa'iq. MAP, tr. by Patricia Alanah Byrne and Salma Khadra Jayyusi

Poem: "Nothing move thee." Saint Theresa [or Teresa] of Avila. CRP; WoPoe, tr. by Yvor Winters

Poem No. 286 (On Stalin). Osip Emilevich Mandelstam [or Mandelshtam]. TCRP

(We live, not feeling the ground under our feet.) PFTM-1

Poem No. 19 in the Old Manner. Li Po. CoBCP, tr. by Burton Watson

Poem: "O men, walk on the hills." Maxwell Bodenheim. TrJP

Poem: "O solo mio, hot diggety, nix 'I wather think I can'." Frank O'Hara. TTTS

Poem-Object. André Breton. PFTM-1

Poem of a Distant Childhood. Noémia da Sousa. HAWP, tr. by Allan Francovich and Kathleen Weaver

Poem of Alienation. Antonio Jacinto. PBMAP; PeSAV, tr. by Michael Wolfers

Poem of any Virgin. Jorge de Lima. PFTM-1

Poem of Attrition, A. Etheridge Knight. GT

Poem of Death, A. George MacBeth [or Macbeth]. HP Fr. Rumanian of Maria Banus, The.

Poem of Explanations. Dahlia Ravikovitch [or Ravikovich]. BoWoP, tr. by Chana Bloch

Poem of Holy Madness. Ray Bremser.
  "Let me lay it to you gently, Mr. Gone!" NeAP

Poem of Jacobus Sadoletus on the Statue of Laocoon, The. Jacopo Sadoleto. GS, tr. by H. S. Wilkinson

Poem of João, The. Noémia da Sousa. PeSAV, tr. by Margaret Dickinson

Poem of Medicine Puns. Unknown. ColAnChi; WoPoe, tr. by Victor H. Mair

Poem of My Sleeping Sorrow. Julia de Burgos. TANSG, tr. by Heather Rosario Sievert

Poem: "Of old, when Scarron his companions invited." Oliver Goldsmith. NOIV; OxBoLi Fr. Retaliation.

Poem of Prefectural Judge Yang T'ien-jui Righting a Wrong. Chao Meng-fu. CoBLCP, tr. by Jonathan Chaves

Poem of remembrance, a gift, a souvenir for you, A. (LL) Ballad of Remembrance, A. Robert Earl Hayden. BPo; ESEAA

Poem of Return. Jofre Rocha. NAfrP; PBMAP, tr. by Don Burness

Poem of the Cid, The. Unknown.
  Cid Calls His Vassals Together, The. They'll Go into Exile with Him. WoPoe, tr. by Paul Blackburn
  Cid Enters Burgos, The. WoPoe, tr. by Paul Blackburn
  "Cid Ruy Díaz came into Burgos, The." WoPoe, tr. by Paul Blackburn
  "Franks come down the hill with a random course, The." FaBoWar, tr. by John Hookham Frere
  "Gentlemen, for this day's work our chance has not been ill." FaBoWar, tr. by John Hookham Frere
  "He." WoPoe, tr. by Paul Blackburn
  No One Will Put the Cid up. Only a Small Girl Addresses Him and That to Tell Him to Go Away. The Cid Finds He Has to Make Camp Outside of Town, on the Sand of the Riverbank. WoPoe, tr. by Paul Blackburn
  Omens on the Road to Burgos. WoPoe, tr. by Paul Blackburn
  "Then they set spur to horse." WoPoe, tr. by Paul Blackburn
  "They would have invited him gladly." WoPoe, tr. by Paul Blackburn

Poem of the Conscripted Warrior. "Rui Nogar." TTY, tr. by Dorothy Guedes and Philippa Rumsey

Poem of the Dawn and the Night. Rodolfo Di Biasio. NeIt, tr. by Stephen Sartarelli

Poem of the End. Marina Ivanovna Tsvetayeva [or Tsvetaeva].
  ("And tomorrow / when / I am awake'?") (LL) PFTM-1
  Closely, like one creature, we.
  "Not quite remembering, not quite." TCRP
  ("End / as it ends.") (LL) BrRo
  I didn't want this, not. OBVE
  ("In silence— / something sinks like a ship.") (LL) PFTM-1
  ("In this most Christian of worlds / all poets are Jews.") (LL) PFTM-1
  "Last bridge I won't." EroLit, tr. by Elaine Feinstein
  "Like a thick horse's mane." WoPoe, tr. by David McDuff
  "Single post, a point of rusting, A." BrRo
  ("This is delirium, / please say this bridge cannot / end / as it ends.") (LL) PFTM-1

Poem of the Forty-eight States, A. Kenneth Koch. NNap; OBAL

Poem of the Frost and Snow. Lewis Morris. OBWVE, tr. by Anthony Conran

Poem of the Future Citizen. José Craveirinha. TTY, tr. by Dorothy Guedes and Philippa Rumsey

Poem of the Gifts. Jorge Luis Borges. TCLAP, tr. by Ben Belitt

Poem of the Girl from Velázquez. Ricardo Molinari. TCLAP, tr. by Inés Probert

Poem of the mind in the act of finding, The. Of Modern Poetry. Wallace Stevens. ColAP; NAAL-2v2; NAAL-5; NoAM; OxBA; TAP

Poem of the Sea and of Her. Carlos Oquendo de Amat. BLPSL, tr. by Rene de Costa, Rigas Kappatos and Eleni Paidoussi

Poem of the Universe, The. Charles Weldon. PWR

Poem of the Western Fields. Wu Wei-yeh. CoBLCP, tr. by Jonathan Chaves

Poem of Villeneuve St Georges, A. Mbella Sonne Dipoko. PBMAP

Poem on a Little Pine, A. Hsieh Chin. CoBLCP, tr. by Jonathan Chaves

Poem on Azure. Anna de Noailles. WPOW, tr. by Betty L. Schwimmer

Poem on Bread. Vernon Scannell. NOxBChV

Poem on Buddha's Begging Bowl—For Hui-ku, His Holiness Ming, A. Hsü Pen. CoBLCP, tr. by Jonathan Chaves

Poem on Canada. Patrick Anderson.
  Cold Colloquy. NOBC
  Coming of the White Man, The. MoCV

Poem on Coal, A. Yü Ch'ien. SuSp, tr. by Wu-Chi Liu

Poem on Divine Providence. Orientius.
  "Bulk of these years is already gone out of mind, The." WoPoe, tr. by John Peck

Poem on Drinking Wine with the Degree-Holder Ku. Ch'ien Ch'ien-i [or Ch'ien Ch'ien-yi]. CoBLCP, tr. by Jonathan Chaves

Poem on Dry Mountain (A Zen Garden). Muso Soseki. EaWin, tr. by W. S. Merwin

Poem on Elijahs Translation, A. Benjamin Colman. SCAP

Poem on Falling Leaves. Liu E. CoBLCP, tr. by Jonathan Chaves

Poem: "On getting a card." William Carlos Williams. VGW

Poem on His Death-Bed. Cynddelw Brydydd Mawr. OBWVE, tr. by Joseph P. Clancy

Poem on His Death-Bed. Meilyr Brydydd. OBWVE, tr. by Joseph P. Clancy

Poem on Losing One's Teeth. Han Yü. GifTon; SuSp, tr. by Kenneth O. Hanson

Poem on Passing by Hsin-k'ai Lake at Kao-yu in Light Rain, A. Yang Chi. CoBLCP, tr. by Jonathan Chaves

Poem on Returning to Dwell in the Country. T'ao Ch'ien [or T'ao Yuan-ming]. WoPoe, tr. by William Acker

Poem on the attitude adopted. Erol Güney's Cat. Orban Veli Kanik. WoPoe, tr. by Talat Sait Halman

Poem on the Bill Lately Passed for Regulating the Slave-Trade, A. Helen Maria Williams. RWP

Poem on the Fugitive Slave Law, A. Elymas Payson Rogers.
  In 'Fifty Congress Passed a Bill. CBCWP

Poem on the Supposition of an Advertisement; Appearing in a Morning Paper, of the Publication of a Volume of Poems, by a Servant-Maid, A. Elizabeth Hands. ECWP
  (Poem, on the Supposition of an Advertisement Appearing in a Morning Paper, of the Publication of a Volume of Poems, by a Serving-Maid, A.) WoRP

Poem on the Supposition of the Book Having Been Published and Read, A. Elizabeth Hands. ECWP; WoRP

Poem on the Wall, The. Po Chü-i. ChiP, tr. by Arthur Waley

Poem on the Wandering Immortal. Kuo P'o. CoBCP; ColAnChi, tr. by Burton Watson

Poem: "Once when I was little I knelt before an onion." Bob Holman. SpudSo

Poem: "Only response, The." Bill Knott. InPK-6

Poem, or Beauty Hurts Mr. Vinal. E. E. Cummings. FaBoA; HarvBoo; MoAmPo; NAAL-2v2; NAAL-5; OBAL; OxBA; PFTM-1; PeLV; TRP

Poem: "Our love is not found in our respective." Carlos German Belli. BLPSL, tr. by Rene de Costa, Rigas Kappatos and Eleni Paidoussi

Poem: "Puriri moth's wing, A." Jan Kemp. PeNZ

Poem: "Red eiderdown at the window, A." Raymond Radiguet. CuPo

Poem Rocket. Allen Ginsberg. VGW

Poem: "Rose fades, The." William Carlos Williams. NIL-7

Poem Seen in a Motel Fan. Alberto Blanco. CLPP, tr. by John Oliver Simon

Poem should be, as our best ever are, A. Whole Duty of a Poem, The. Arthur Guiterman. PoToHe

Poem should be palpable and mute, A. Ars Poetica. Archibald MacLeish. APT-1; AWP; ColAP; HAP; HeIP-4; IllVoic; InPK-6; MoAmPo; NAAL-2v2; NIP-4; NOBA; OxBA; PoRA; TAP; TFi; WeW-3

Poem: "So many pigeons at Columbus." Arthur Gregor. VGW

Poem: "So they begin. With two years gone." Boris Leonidovich Pasternak. TrJP, tr. by C. M. Bowra

Poem Some People Will Have to Understand, A. Imamu Amiri Baraka. BPo; GT; NOBA; RaBo

Poem: "Sometimes I wish that I were Helen-fair." Lesbia Harford. NOBAu

Poem spins over the head of a man, The. Poem, The. Homero [*or* Umberto] Aridjis. TCLAP, *tr. by* Eliot Weinberger

Poem Stalin, The. Adriano Spatola. PFTM-2, *tr. by* Paul Vangelisti

Poem: Tears, Spray and Steam. John Logan. BodElec

Poem That Took the Place of a Mountain, The. Wallace Stevens. LCAP-2

Poem That Was Once Called "Desperate" But Is Now Striving to Become the Perfect Love Poem. Richard Jackson. BAP-97

Poem, The: "If you start to write a poem." Clementina Suárez. TANSG, *tr. by* Janet N. Gold

Poem, The: "Rise Oedipus, and if thou canst unfold." Thomas Morton. NAAL-3; SCAP

Poem, The: "What ailes Pigmalion? Is it lunacy." Thomas Morton. SCAP

Poem Then, for Love. Michael Harlow.
   Anima Has a Predilection, The. PeNZ

Poem: "There I could never be a boy." Frank O'Hara. NNaP

Poem: "There is a wailing baby under every stone and you walk." Norman McCaig. SPE

Poem: "Think with your body." Víctor Hernández Cruz. PueRic

Poem: "Tiny new emotions, The." Tom Clark. CoAmPo

Poem to a Nigger Cop. Bobb Hamilton. TTY

Poem to a Redskin. Wendy Rose. CDW

Poem to al-Raihani. Ma'ruf Al-Rasafi. MAP, *tr. by* Issa Boullata and Christopher Middleton

Poem to Answer the Question: How Old Are Fleas? *Unknown.* Spl

Poem to Be Read and Sung. César Vallejo. TCLAP, *tr. by* Clayton Eshleman

Poem to Be Read and Sung. César Vallejo. SPE

Poem to Be Recited Every 8 Years While Eating Unleavened Tamales. *Unknown.* STP, *tr. by* Anselm Hollo

Poem to Be Said on Hearing the Birds Sing, A. Biddy Crummy. AWP, *tr. by* Douglas Hyde

Poem to Complement Other Poems, A. Haki R. Madhubuti. BPo; NBV

Poem to Complement Other Poems, A. Haki R. Madhubuti. NAAAL

Poem to Ease Birth. *Unknown.* BoWoP; STP, *tr. by* Anselm Hollo

Poem to Galway Kinnell, A. Etheridge Knight. BodElec; NNaP

Poem to Gentiles. Maxwell Bodenheim. TaR

Poem to Her Daughter. Mwana Kupona Msham.
   "Daughter, take this amulet." HAWP; WPOW

Poem to His Grace the Duke of Marlborough, A. Joseph Addison. OBWP
   Fr. Campaign, The.

Poem to Mary, A. Bláthmac Mac Con Brettan.
   "I call you with honest words." NOIV

Poem to My Death. Julia de Burgos. BoWoP; TCLAP, *tr. by* Grace Schulman

Poem to My Sister, Ethel Ennis, Who Sang "The Star-spangled Banner" at the Second Inauguration of Richard Milhous Nixon. June Jordan. TAP

Poem to Send to Friends in the Capital, A. Liu Tsung-yüan. CoBCP, *tr. by* Burton Watson

Poem to Shout in the Ruins. Louis Aragon. PFTM-1

Poem to Show the Trouble That Befell Him When He Was at Sea, A. Thomas Prys. OBWVE, *tr. by* Gwyn Williams

Poem to Some of my Recent Poems. James Tate. NoAM

Poem to the Mother of the Gods, A. *Unknown.* STP, *tr. by* Edward Kissam

Poem to the Sun. *Ancient Egyptian Oral Tradition.* TTTS, *tr. by* Christopher Wertz

Poem to the Tune of "Tsui hua yin." Li Ch'ing-chao. WPOW, *tr. by* Marsha Wagner

Poem to the Tune of "Yi chian mei." Li Ch'ing-chao. WPOW, *tr. by* Marsha Wagner

Poem to the Tune "Riverbank Willows." Yü Hsüan-chi. BoWoP, *tr. by* Geoffrey Waters

Poem: "Twenty-first, The. Night. Monday." Anna Andreyevna Akhmatova. RusPo, *tr. by* Robert Arthur Douglas Ford

Poem upon the Caelestial Embassy, A. Richard Steere. SCAP

Poem upon the Lisbon Disaster; or, An Inquiry into the Adage, "All Is for the Best." Voltaire.
   "Woeful mankind, born to a woeful earth!" WoPoe, *tr. by* Anthony Hecht

Poem upon the page is as massive as, The. Ted Berrigan. PFTM-2 *Fr.* Sonnets, The.

Poem upon the Triumphant Translation of. . . Mrs. Anne Eliot, A. John Danforth. SCAP

Poem: "Walls of the maelstrom are painted with trees, The." Charles Madge. SPE

Poem: "War and greed stop food." Hugh Seidman. BodElec

Poem, we're going this way. Pike Street Bus. Colleen J. McElroy. NAAAL

Poem: "We think to create festivals." Antonio Machado Ruiz. AWP; WoPoe, *tr. by* John Dos Passos

Poem: "Were I a king, I could command content." Edward de Vere, 17th Earl of Oxford. NoSic
   (Epigram: "Were I a king, I could command content.") FaBoEE; OxBSP
   (Weare I a Kinge I coulde commande content.) PBRV

Poem: "When I carry my little son in the cold." Thomas McGrath. GifTon

Poem: "When I look at the falling leaves." Marina Ivanovna Tsvetayeva [*or* Tsvetaeva]. RusPo, *tr. by* Robert Arthur Douglas Ford

Poem: "When I was still a child." Lesbia Harford. NOBAu

Poem: "When the dream departs leaving." Salah Fa'iq. MAP, *tr. by* Patricia Alanah Byrne and Salma Khadra Jayyusi

Poem: "When the rich pass proudly by." Wang Fan-chih. CrYelRi, *tr. by* Sam Hamill

Poem: "While we were walking under the top." John Ashbery. SPE

Poem with a Limp. Roger McGough. OBCoV

Poem with Capital Letters, A. Jane Cooper. FaBoWP

Poem with Light on Its Shoulder. Mary Ann Samyn. AmPoNex

Poem with Refrains. Robert Pinsky. TaR

Poem with Skin. Octavio Armand. TCLAP, *tr. by* Carol Maier

Poem with the Answer, A. Sir John Suckling.
   Constant Lover, A [*or* The]. BASC; BeJo; CavPo; NAEL-6v1; NAEL-7v1; NBLV; NOSC; NPeEn; NoP-4; OxAEP-1; OxBEV; PBRV; PeLV; PoE
   "Out upon it! I have loved [*or* lov'd]." BASC; BeJo; CavPo; NAEL-6v1; NAEL-7v1; NBLV; NOSC; NPeEn; NoP-4; OxAEP-1; OxBEV; PBRV; PeLV; PoE

Poem with Two Seasons Right Now. S. J. Marks. BodElec

Poem without a Category. Gensei. EnlH, *tr. by* Burton Watson

Poem without a Category. Liu Cheng. CoBCP; ColAnChi, *tr. by* Burton Watson

Poem without a Category, No. 4. T'ao Ch'ien [*or* T'ao Yuan-ming]. CoBCP, *tr. by* Burton Watson

Poem without a Category, No. 7. T'ao Ch'ien [*or* T'ao Yuan-ming]. CoBCP, *tr. by* Burton Watson

Poem without a Hero. Anna Andreyevna Akhmatova.
   Epilogue. PFTM-2, *tr. by* Lenore Mayhew and William McNaughton
   "Under the roof of the Fountain House." PFTM-2, *tr. by* Lenore Mayhew and William McNaughton

Poem Without a Single Bird in It, A. Jack Spicer. BodElec

Poem without a Title. Charles Simic. NNaP

Poem: "Word is fast asleep, The." Labhshankar Thacker. OMIP, *tr. by* Sitanshu Yashashchandra

Poem Written by Sir Henry Wotton, in His Youth, A. Sir Henry Wotton. NoSic

Poem Written During a Dream on the Twenty-Third Day of the Intercalary [Month After The] Fourth [Month]. Ch'ien Ch'ien-i [*or* Ch'ien Ch'ien-yi]. CoBLCP, *tr. by* Jonathan Chaves

Poem Written for the Celebration of the Fourth Anniversary of President Lincoln's Emancipation Proclamation, A. James M. Whitfield.
   From Year to Year the Contest Grew. CBCWP

Poem Written in a Copy of Beowulf. Jorge Luis Borges. PoetW, *tr. by* Alastair Reid

Poem Written in Answer to His Majesty's Question: "What Is There in the Mountains?" T'ao Hung Ching. ColAnChi, *tr. by* Stephen Owen

Poem Written in Time of Trouble by an Irish Priest Who Had Taken Orders in France, A. *Unknown.* OBMV, *tr. by* Augusta, Lady Gregory and Lady Gregory

Poem: "You are ill and so I lead you away." Alfred Wellington Purdy. NOBC

Poem You Asked For, The. Larry Levis. PBCAP

Poem: "You hear that heroic big land music?" Alice Notley. PmAP

Poem: "Your head it waves outside." Víctor Hernández Cruz. PueRic

Poema para los Californios Muertos. Lorna Dee Cervantes. PoPoPo

Poemectomy. John Dickson. IllVoic

Poèmes de la Mer (1968). Jean-Baptiste Tati-Loutard.
   "I am now very high upon the tree of the seasons." PBMAP
   News of My Mother. PBMAP

Poemes Negres. Tristan Tzara.
   Dance of the Greased Women, The. PFTM-1
   "(Steingeröll) new signs putting." PFTM-1

Poems. Philip O'Connor. *See* Poems (I-XI)

Poems. Pablo Picasso. *See* Poem: "Hasten on your childhood to the hour when white."

Poems. Helen Maria Williams.
   "Meek twilight! soften the declining day." CenSon
   Sonnet to Twilight. CenSon

Poems (I-XI). Philip O'Connor. SPE

Poems About Prison. Dennis Brutus. PBMAP

Poems after Beirut. Mahmoud Darwish. MAP, *tr. by* Lena Jayyusi and Christopher Middleton

"We travel like other people, but we return to nowhere. As if travelling." AF, *tr. by* Abdullah Al-Udhari

Poems After Drinking Wine. Ch'ien T'ao. ColAnChi, *tr. by* J. R. Hightower

Poems are bullshit unless they are. Black Art. Imamu Amiri Baraka. BPo; ESEAA; NAAAL

Poems are not places. Poem. Sterling Plumpp. GT

Poems at the Porthole. Lorine Niedecker. FTOS

Poems Come to Me in the Night. Alice Sadongei. HATNAP

Poems Composed or Suggested During a Tour, in the Summer of 1833. William Wordsworth.
  (Inner Vision, The.) GTBS-P
  Most Sweet It Is with Unuplifted Eyes. CenSon
  "Motions and Means, on land and sea at war." NAEL-5v2
  Steamboats, Viaducts and Railways. NAEL-5v2

Poems Expressing My Feelings. Juan Chi.
  "Autumn's onset means cooling breezes." SuSp
  "Deep in the night and unable to sleep." SuSp
  "Long ago there was an immortal man." SuSp

Poems for a Little Boy. Gabriella Sica.
  "I wish I were spring water." CItWP, *tr. by* Cinzia Sartini Blum and Lara Trubowitz

Poems for Lou. Guillaume Apollinaire.
  "My darling little Lou how I love you." PFTM-1

Poems for My Cousin. Josephine Jacobsen. APT-2

Poems for My Daughter. Horace Gregory. MoAmPo

Poems for the Game of Silence. *Unknown.* STP, *tr. by* Frances Densmore

Poems for Yukiko of Tamba. Liu E. CoBLCP, *tr. by* Jonathan Chaves

Poems from a Diary. Abraham Sutskever [*or* Sutzkever].
  "And when I go up as a pilgrim in winter, to recover." HP, *tr. by* Cynthia Ozick
  1980. HP, *tr. by* Cynthia Ozick
  1974. BBASP, *tr. by* Cynthia Ozick
  "Who will last? And what? The wind will stay." BBASP, *tr. by* Cynthia Ozick

Poems from Saint Pelagia Prison. Philippe Soupault. AF, *tr. by* Eden Paul

Poems from Subway to Work. Peter Orlovsky. CLPP

Poems from the Erotic Left. Ana María Rodas. TANSG, *tr. by* Zoë Anglesey

Poems from the Margins of Thom Gunn's Moly. Robert Duncan.
  "Childhood, boyhood, young manhood." FTOS

Poems from the Veterans Hospital. Simon J. Ortiz.
  8:50 AM Ft. Lyons VAH. NAAL-5
  "Man has been in the VAH Library all day long, A." NAAL-5
  Travelling. NAAL-5
  "Wisconsin Horse hears the geese, The." NAAL-5

Poems: "I think that I shall never read." Thomas M. [*or* "Tom"] Disch. UV

Poems in an Old Style. Li Po.
  "Ages have passed since the stately Odes flourished." ColAnChi, *tr. by* Victor H. Mair
  "My sword at my waist, I climb a high tower." ColAnChi, *tr. by* Victor H. Mair
  "There was a sojourner in Ying who intoned 'White Snows'" ColAnChi, *tr. by* Victor H. Mair

Poems in Depression, at Wei Village. Po Chü-i. ChiP, *tr. by* Arthur Waley

Poems in Praise of Practically Nothing. Samuel Hoffenstein.
  "Only the wholesomest foods you eat." TrJP
  "You buy some flowers for your table." OBCoV; TrJP
  "You buy yourself a new suit of clothes." OBCoV
  "You hire a cook, but she can't cook yet." OBCoV

Poems in the Greek Anthology Mode. Nissim Ezekiel.
  "When the female railway clerk." OBCoV

Poems Inscribed on Paintings. T'ang Yin. CoBLCP, *tr. by* Jonathan Chaves

Poems Inscribed on Paintings of Bamboo. Wu Chen. CoBLCP, *tr. by* Jonathan Chaves

Poems / let's / pretend. (LL) Love U.S.A. Kathleen Spivack. BoWoP; LW

Poems of Memory. Anne Cluysenaar.
  "Knife reduces a polished oval, The." Prnts

Poems of Our Climate, The. Wallace Stevens. APT-1; NoP-4; OxBA; SoSe-8; TwCP

Poems of Reflection on the Vicissitudes of Life. Ch'en Tzu-ang.
  "I close my door and trace the transformations of nature." ColAnChi, *tr. by* Victor H. Mair
  "I dwell in seclusion and observe the creative process." ColAnChi, *tr. by* Victor H. Mair
  "I dwell in the forest nursing a long illness." ColAnChi, *tr. by* Victor H. Mair
  "Men in the market pride themselves on their knowledge and craft, The." ColAnChi, *tr. by* Victor H. Mair

Poems of the Atomic Bomb. Tōge Sankichi.
  Dying. PFTM-2, *tr. by* Richard H. Minear
  "Loud in my ear: screams." PFTM-2, *tr. by* Richard H. Minear

Poems of the Pope, The. Nicanor Parra. VCWP, *tr. by* Edith Grossman

Poems on Man in His Various Aspects under the American Republic. Cornelius Mathews.
  "As shakes the canvass of a thousand ships." APN-1
  Journalist, The. APN-1
  "Leap into the light, ye living Forms!" APN-1
  Masses, The. APN-1
  Sculptor, The. APN-1
  "When, wild and high, the uproar swells." APN-1

Poems to Blok. Marina Ivanovna Tsvetayeva [*or* Tsvetaeva].
  "Cupolas flame, in Moscow where I live." TCRusP, *tr. by* Bob Perelman, Aleksandar Petrov and Shirley Rihner
  "Den—for the beast, A." TCRusP, *tr. by* Bob Perelman, Aleksandar Petrov and Shirley Rihner
  "Gentle ghost." TCRusP, *tr. by* Bob Perelman, Aleksandar Petrov and Shirley Rihner
  "They thought: Human!" TCRusP, *tr. by* Bob Perelman, Aleksandar Petrov and Shirley Rihner
  "You're going by, west of the sun." TCRusP, *tr. by* Bob Perelman, Aleksandar Petrov and Shirley Rihner
  "Your name—a bird on my hand." TCRusP, *tr. by* Bob Perelman, Aleksandar Petrov and Shirley Rihner

Poems to My Father. Mick North. NLP

Poems We Can Understand. Paul Hoover. PmAP

Poems Written during My Sojourn in Japan. Su Man-shu.
  "On the bank of Lake Rouge a chestnut steed treads proudly." SuSp
  "She puts on a silken blouse and comes down from the western chamber." SuSp
  "Shouldn't I pilfer wantonly this famed fragrance of a foreign land?" SuSp

Poems Written in Prison. Ch'ien Ch'ien-i [*or* Ch'ien Ch'ien-yi].
  "Fishing cove and long lines of fishermen's huts, A." SuSp
  "Nightly the watchman's rattle startles my sleep." SuSp
  "Spluttering burnt-out lamp blazes in the dusk." SuSp

Poesy. Oliver Wendell Holmes. TreFP

Poet. 'Ali Ja'far Al-Allaq. MAP, *tr. by* Sharif Elmusa and Thomas G. Ezzy

Poet. Ralph Waldo Emerson. OxBA; OxBSP; Spl; TCAPo   *Fr.* Quatrains.

Poet. Karl Shapiro. MoAmPo; NoAM

Poet. Peter Viereck. MoAmPo

Poet, A. Thomas Hardy. NoAM

Poet, The. Matthew Arnold. NPeEn   *Fr.* Resignation.

Poet, The. William Cullen Bryant. NAAL-2v1; NAAL-3; NCAP; TAP

Poet, The. Dale R. Carver. FaBoWar

Poet, The. Paul Laurence Dunbar. BPo; NAAAL; TCAPo

Poet, The. Padraic Fiacc. CIP-2

Poet, The. Gerrit Komrij. TuT

Poet, The. Alfred de Musset. WoPoe, *tr. by* Claire Nicholas White   *Fr.* Night in May, A.

Poet, The. Thomas Randolph. OxBSP

Poet, The. Sir Walter Scott. TreFP   *Fr.* Lay of the Last Minstrel, The.

Poet, The. Achsa W. Sprague.
  Scene 3.
    "'Tis near the time. I'm glad 'tis getting late." SWaP

Poet, The. Arseny [*or* Arsenii] Aleksandrovich Tarkovsky [*or* Tarkovskii]. TCRP, *tr. by* Peter Norman

Poet, The. Walt Whitman. MoAmPo   *Fr.* By Blue Ontario's Shore.

Poet: A Lying Word. Laura Riding Jackson. HarvBoo

Poet alone in my country, A. On Being a Poet in Sierra Leone. Syl Cheney-Coker. HBAPE; PBMAP

Poet Among Those Who Are Also Poets. Syl Cheney-Coker. NAfrP

Poet and Botanist. Constance Naden. VWP; ViWPN

Poet and Critic. Samuel Daniel. NoSiC; PBRV   *Fr.* Musophilus; or, Defence of All Learning.

Poet and His Book, The. Edna St. Vincent Millay. MoAmPo

Poet and His Patron, The. Edward Moore. ECEV
  "Why, Celia, is your spreading waist." ECEV

Poet and Person. Denise Levertov. GifTon

Poet and Saint! to thee alone are given. On the Death of Mr. Crashaw. Abraham Cowley. BASC; BeJo; MeLP

Poet and the Rose, The. John Gay. PeLV   *Fr.* Fables.

Poet and Tsar. Grigory [*or* Grigorii] Mikhailovich Pozhenyan [*or* Pozhenian]. TCRP, *tr. by* John Glad

Poet and War, The. Albert Ehrenstein. PeFWW, *tr. by* Christopher Middleton

Poet appointed dare not decline. Basil Bunting. *Fr.* Briggflatts [An Autobiography].

Poet as a penguin, The. Birds. Frieda Hughes. NeBl

Poet Asks His Love About the Enchanted City of Cuenca, The. Federico García Lorca. CAGL, *tr. by* David William Foster *Fr.* Sonetos del Amor Oscuro [Sonnets of Dark Love].

Poet Asks His Love to Write to Him, The. Federico García Lorca. CAGL, *tr. by* David William Foster *Fr.* Sonetos del Amor Oscuro [Sonnets of Dark Love].

Poet at Seven, The. Donald Justice. WeW-3

Poet at Seventeen, The. Larry Levis. GeoHom

Poet at Twenty, A. Donald Hall. SPE

(Images leap with him from branch to branch. His eyes.) SPE

Poet at Work. Richard Tipping. BMAP

Poet, be seated at the piano. Mozart, 1935. Wallace Stevens. MiVo

Poet by the fireside cries, A. Sean Dunne. ModIr *Fr.* Sydney Place.

Poet, conserver of the infinite faces of the living, The. René Char. PFTM-1 *Fr.* Leaves of Hypnos.

Poet Defended, A. Paul Ramsey. InPK-6

Poet Dives, The. Willem Jan Otten. TuT, *tr. by* Micheal O'Siadhail

Poet Dreamt of Heaven, The. *Unknown.* TreFP

Poet felt the rain, The. Rain. Margiad Evans. OBWVE

Poet from Cheltenham Spa, A. Limerick. Betty Morris. PeLi

Poet Grows Old, The. Oliver Wendell Holmes. TCAPo

Poet has by now travelled a distance, spanning mental universe, The. Iovis XIX: Why That's a Blade Can Float. Anne Waldman. PFTM-2

Poet Haunted, The. Wendy Rose. ReEnLa

Poet Hipponax lies here, The. Epitaph: Justice. Theocritus. WoPoe, *tr. by* Fred Chappell

Poet hung himself today, A. Mirrors in the Room. Rodney M. McNeil. InTrad

Poet! I like not mealy fruit; give me. Walter Savage Landor. FaBoEE

Poet in his lone yet genial hour, The. Apologia pro Vita Sua. Samuel Taylor Coleridge. OxBSP

Poet in Old Age Fishing at Evening, The. Desmond O'Grady. CIP-2

Poet in the Desert, The. Charles Erskine Scott Wood.

"I have entered into the Desert, the place of desolation." APT-1

Poet in the Kitchen. Margit Mikes. IQMS, *tr. by* Suzanne K. Walther

Poet, in the sunset? (LL) Poem: "Naked is the earth." Antonio Machado Ruiz. AWP; WoPoe, *tr. by* John Dos Passos

Poet in theory worships the moon, The. Moonlight and Gas. Constance Naden. VWP; ViWPN

Poet in Winter. Edward Lucie-Smith. TwCP

Poet is a fake, The. Autopsychography. Fernando Pessoa. WoPoe, *tr. by* Keith Bosley

Poet is a little God, The. (LL) Ars Poetica. Vincente Huidobro. PFTM-1; TCLAP, *tr. by* David Guss

Poet is a long animal, The. Another Genealogy. Luiza Neto Jorge. SurWo, *tr. by* Jean R. Longland

Poet is a pumping-station turning the landscape into words, The. Basho 4. Cees Nooteboom. TuT, *tr. by* Michael O'Loughlin

Poet is about to write a poem, The. Poem on Bread. Vernon Scannell. NOxBChV

Poet Is Dead, The. William Everson. NoAM

Poet Is Not a Jukebox, A. Dudley Randall. NoAM

Poet is one who writes verses, A. Who Is a Poet. Tadeusz Rózewicz. VCWP

Poet is priest. Death to Van Gogh's Ear! Allen Ginsberg. VGW

Poet Is Served Her Papers, The. Lorna Dee Cervantes. TouFir

Poet is working upstairs, The. Sean Dunne. ModIr *Fr.* Sydney Place.

Poet Laments the Coming of Old Age, The. Dame Edith Sitwell. NAEL-5v2; NAEL-6v2; NoAM

Poet, let passion sleep. Art, II. Alfred Noyes. OBEV

Poet Lied, The. Odia Ofeimun. HBAPE

Poet Loves a Mistress, but Not to Marry, The. Robert Herrick. CaPo

Poet man walks between dreams. Prologomena to a Poetics. Jerome Rothenberg. PFTM-2

Poet must work with brush and paper, The. Written on a Cold Evening. Yang Wan-li. ColAnChi, *tr. by* Jonathan Chaves

Poet nailed on, The. I am a Camera. Bob Kaufman. PFTM-2

Poet of Bray, The. John Heath-Stubbs. NOBL

Poet of Nature, thou hast wept to know. To Wordsworth. Shelley. CenSon; FHYEP; NAEL-5v2; NAEL-6v2; NPeEn; NoP-4; Son

Poet of Our Race. Maggie Pogue Johnson. CBWP-4

Poet of the dead leaves driven like ghosts. Shelley. Charles Simic. TRP

Poet of the Hortobágy, The. Endre Ady. IQMS, *tr. by* Anton N. Nyerges

Poet of the Mountains, The. Thomas McCarthy. CIP-2

Poet of the serene and thoughtful lay! Wordsworth. Charlotte L. Forten Grimke. TCAPo

Poet on the Island, The. Richard Murphy. CIP-2

Poet Pedro Pietri. Jose Angel Figueroa. PueRic

Poet put Old Prussian, A. Who Would Have Thought It. Marie Luise Kaschnitz. PFTM-2, *tr. by* Lisel Mueller

Poet Recognizing the Echo of the Voice, A. Diane Wakoski. NIP-4

Poet Reflects On Her Solitary Fate, The. Sandra Cisneros. FFC

Poet's Arbour in the Birchwood, The. Edward Williams. OBWVE, *tr. by* Kenneth Hurlstone Jackson

Poet's Biography. Belkis Cuza Malé. TANSG, *tr. by* Pamela Carmell

Poet's Calendar, The. Henry Wadsworth Longfellow. APN-1

Poet's Corner, The. Laura Riding Jackson. FuPo

Poet's daily chore, The. Lens. Anne Wilkinson. MoCV; NOBC

Poet's Day, The. Richard Weber. CIP-2

Poet's Death, A. Cheryl Clarke. WiU

Poet's death and sex thoughts rode me, A. Poet's Death, A. Cheryl Clarke. WiU

Poet's Delay, The. Henry David Thoreau. TCAPo

Poet's Destiny, The. Lady Jane Francesca Wilde. VWP

Poet's Dream, The. Shelley. GTBS-P; TOF *Fr.* Prometheus Unbound [A Lyrical Drama in Four Acts].

Poet's Fate, The. Thomas Hood. FaBoEE

Poet's Final Instructions, The. John Berryman. Son; VGW

Poet's Garret, The. Mary Robinson. RWP

Poet's Heart, The. Richard Jones. GifTon

Poet's heart is wrenched and wrenched again until his head turns white, A. Yüan Hao-wen. SuSp *Fr.* On Poetry.

Poet's Home, The. Mariella Bettarini.

"My home (did you know?)—my home." CItWP, *tr. by* Cinzia Sartini Blum and Lara Trubowitz

Poet's Ideal, The. Henrietta Cordelia Ray. CBWP-3

Poet's lovely faith creates, The. Poet's Lot, The. Letitia [*or* Laetitia] Elizabeth Landon. RWP

Poet's Loves, The. Hywel ab Owain Gwynedd. OBWVE, *tr. by* Gwyn Williams

Poet's Ministrants, The. Henrietta Cordelia Ray. CBWP-3

Poet's Obligation. Pablo Neruda. PoetW; VCWP, *tr. by* Alastair Reid

Poet's Prayer, The. *Unknown.* OBSV

Poet's Progress, The. Chris Mann. PeSAV

Poet's Request, The. *Unknown.* BIrV, *tr. by* John Montague

Poet's Resurrection, The. Jenő Dsida. IQMS, *tr. by* Peter Zollman

Poet's Shuffle, The. Calvin Forbes. GT; LTA

Poet's Song, The. Tennyson. EBVV

Poet's Terror at the Bailiffs of Exeter, The. Andrew Brice. NOEC *Fr.* Freedom; a Poem, Written in Time of Recess from the Rapacious Claws of Bailiffs.

Poet's Welcome to His Love-Begotten Daughter [the First Instance that Entitled Him to the Venerable Appellation of Father], A. Robert Burns. NOEC; OxBoLi

Poet's Wish; an Ode, The. Allan Ramsay. OBVE

Poet's Work. Lorine Niedecker. APT-2; HarvBoo

Poet should learn with his eyes, A. Kshemendra. EaWin; WoPoe, *tr. by* J. Moussaieff Masson and W. S. Merwin *Fr.* Kavikanthabharana.

Poet Sings His Painting, The. Lloyd Richardson. WaCA

Poet Speaks the Truth, The. Federico García Lorca. CAGL, *tr. by* David William Foster *Fr.* Sonetos del Amor Oscuro [Sonnets of Dark Love].

Poet Speaks with Love by Telephone, The. Federico García Lorca. CAGL, *tr. by* David William Foster *Fr.* Sonetos del Amor Oscuro [Sonnets of Dark Love].

Poet spilled my gin, The. Tropisms on John Berryman. Gerald Vizenor. VoR

Poet suffers making poems, A. Seeing Off Master Tan. Meng Chiao. SuSp, *tr. by* Stephen Owen

Poet the Dreamer, The. Norman Jordan. NBV

Poet Thinks, A. Lui Chi. AWP, *tr. by* E. Powys Mathers

Poet to a Painter, A. Aubrey Thomas De Vere. Son

Poet to Tiger. May Swenson. GLP; PoBW

Poet-Tree. Earle Birney. OxBC

Poet, Trying to Surprise God, The. Peter Meinke. PBCAP

Poet Turned Lawyer, The. John Donne. OBSV *Fr.* Satires.

Poet Upstairs, The. Sean Dunne. ModIr *Fr.* Sydney Place.

Poet Visits Egypt and Israel, The. Maxine W. Kumin. TaR

Poet vs. Parson. Ebenezer Elliott. Son

Poet walked with feet upon the ground, The. Rublyov XVth Century. Ksenya [*or* Kseniia] Nekrasova. TCRP, *tr. by* Vera Rich

Poet wears a hat, The. Siesta. Adelia Prado. TCLAP, *tr. by* Marcia Kirinus

Poet went to the Isthmian games, A. Cerealius. GrAn

Poet: What Ever Happened to Luther? Haki R. Madhubuti. SpirFl; UnSA

Poet, whoe'er thou art, God damn thee. John Wilmot, 2d Earl of Rochester. FaBoEE

Poet Wondering What He Is Up To. Dennis Joseph Enright. OxBC

Poet, write! / Not of a purpose dark and dire. Crime of the Ages, The. Augusta Cooper Bristol. APN-2

Poeta Fit, Non Nascitur. Lewis Carroll. OBSV

Poeta Fui. Julia Budenz. FFC

Poetaster, The. Ben Jonson.
  "If I freely may discover." BeJo
  "Swell me a bowl with lusty wine." BeJo

Poète Manqué. Ernest Sandeen. CRP

Poetess's Bouts-Rimés, The. *Unknown.* NOEC

Poetic Genius. Mark Akenside. NOEC *Fr.* Pleasures of Imagination, The.

Poetic License. Leonard Nolens. TuT, *tr. by* Michael O'Loughlin

Poetic Reflections Enroute To, and During, The Funeral and Burial of Henry Dumas, Poet. Eugene B. Redmond. ISC

Poetical Commandments. Byron. OxBoLi; PeLV *Fr.* Don Juan.

Poetical Epistle tae Cullybackey Auld Nummer. Thomas Given. FaBoVe

Poetical Epistle to an Absent Friend, A. Eliza Robertson.
  "O place us, dear Saviour! in some small retreat." PoBW

Poetical Happiness. Frederick Tennyson. CenSon

Poetical Question concerning the Jacobites, sent to the Athenians, A. Elizabeth Singer Rowe. BASC

Poetics. Manuel Bandeira. TCLAP, *tr. by* Candace Slater

Poetics. August Kleinzahler. PmAP

Poetics against the Angel of Death. Phyllis Webb. MoCV; NOBC

Poetograd. Nikolai Ivanovich Glazkov. TCRP, *tr. by* Daniel Weissbort

Poet[r]ess's Hasty Resolution, The. Margaret Lucas Cavendish, Duchess of Newcastle. BASC; NAEL-7v1

Poetress's Petition, The. Margaret Lucas Cavendish, Duchess of Newcastle. CABP
  (And for her glory, garlands of fresh bays.) (LL) CABP
  (Like to a fever's pulse my heart doth beat.) CABP
  (Poetress's Petition, The.) CABP

Poetry. Madison Cawein. APN-2

Poetry. Mary Elizabeth Fullerton. GI; NOBAu

Poetry. Jane Miller. GifTon

Poetry. Pablo Neruda. PoetW; VCWP, *tr. by* Alastair Reid

Poetry. Frank O'Hara. HCAP

Poetry. Lydia Huntley Sigourney. SWaP

Poetry. Xavier Villaurrutia. TCLAP, *tr. by* Dana Stangel

Poetry, a Natural Thing. Robert Duncan. NOBA; NoAM; PmAP; TRP

Poetry, almost blind like a camera. Jack Spicer. NeAP; PmAP *Fr.* Imaginary Elegies.

Poetry and Science. Hugh MacDiarmid. HarvBoo

Poetry and the Poet. Henry Cuyler Bunner. OBAL

Poetry Calendar, A. Chimako Tada. VCWP, *tr. by* Naoshi Koriyama

Poetry Concert. Michael S. Harper. TAP

Poetry Detective. Edwin Torres. HeMarv

Poetry Editor. Yevgeny [*or* Evgenii] Mikhailovich Vinokurov. TCRP, *tr. by* Daniel Weissbort

Poetry ends like a rope. (LL) Book of Music, A. Jack Spicer. APSN; PoM

Poetry for Supper. Ronald Stuart Thomas. OxBC

Poetry for the Goddess. William T. Crawley III. InTrad

Poetry: "I, too, dislike it: there are things that are important beyond all this fiddle." Marianne Craig Moore. APT-1; AmFaPo; BoWoP; ColAP; FaBoWP; HAP; HeIP-4; MoAmPo; NAAL-2v2; NAAL-5; NALW; NIP-4; NOBA; NoAM; NoP-4; OxBA; PAI; PoE; PoPoPo; TAP; TCAPo; TFi; UnPo
  (I, too, dislike it. / Reading it, however, with a perfect contempt for it, one discovers in.) HarvBoo; NIL-7

Poetry in England. Samuel Daniel. NoSic *Fr.* Musophilus; or, Defence of All Learning.

Poetry Is a Destructive Force. Wallace Stevens. APT-1; OxBA; RaBo

Poetry Is a Heavenly Crime. Vincente Huidobro. TCLAP, *tr. by* W. S. Merwin

Poetry is always seeking something special. To men with. From Hear to Air. Douglas Messerli. FTOS

Poetry is an applied science. Parapoetics. Eugene B. Redmond. NBV

Poetry is like a swoon, with this difference. Klupzy Girl, The. Charles Bernstein. PmAP

Poetry is made in bed like love. On the Road to San Romano. André Breton. PFTM-1

Poetry Is Not You. Rosario Castellanos. TANSG, *tr. by* Magda Bogin

Poetry / Is something refined. Sugar Poem. Aurora Levins Morales. PueRic

Poetry is the supreme fiction, madame. High-Toned Old Christian Woman, A. Wallace Stevens. NAAL-2v2; NAAL-5; NOBA; NoAM; TAP

Poetry Jump-Up. John Agard. NOxBChV

Poetry of America, The. Juan Felipe Herrera. TouFir

Poetry of Departures. Philip Larkin. HeIP-4; OxBC; PoE; TwCP

Poetry of Dress, The. Robert Herrick. *See* Delight in Disorder

Poetry of earth can never die, The. Grasshopper and the Cricket, The. Olga Sedakova. ItGoST, *tr. by* Catriona Kelly

Poetry of earth is never dead, The. On the Grasshopper and [the] Cricket. John Keats. CenSon; FHYEP; NIL-7; NIP-4; OxAEP-2; Son; TTTS

Poetry of Motion, The. Raymond Garlick. AngWePo

Poetry of Roses, The. Franco Fortini. ItPo, *tr. by* Gayle Ridinger

Poetry Paper. Andrei Codrescu. SPE

Poetry Perpetuates the Poet. Robert Herrick. BeJo; FaBoEE

Poetry Professors, The. Robert Lloyd.
  "Old England has not lost her prayer." ECEV
  "Yet matter must be gravely planned." ECEV

Poetry Reading. Vernon Scannell. NOBL

Poetry Reading. Anna Swirszczynska. BLT

Poetry's a gift wherein but few excell. Nathaniel Ward. SCAP

Poetry stops before the end of the margin. 100 Differences Between Poetry and Prose. Tom Leonard. Oth

Poetry sudden as rain flood, A. American Poetry. James Bertolino. SpudSo

Poetry wud go out of bizness. (LL) To P. J. (2 Yrs Old Who Sed Write a Poem for Me in Portland, Oregon). Sonia Sanchez. CA; OxIBACP

Poetry? It's a hobby. What the Chairman Told Tom. Basil Bunting. EmeKit; NoP-4; OxBTC

Poets. Gavin Ewart. PeLV

Poets. X. J. Kennedy. OPRER

Poets, The. Aleksandr Aleksandrovich Blok. TCRP, *tr. by* Geoffrey Thurley

Poets, The. Henry Wadsworth Longfellow. GSo

Poets Agree to Be Quiet by the Swamp, The. David Wagoner. CoAP; VGW

Poets and parents say he cannot die. Yet Another Poem about a Dying Child. Janet Frame. PeNZ

Poets and storytellers. American Literature. Lisel Mueller. PoSol

Poets are dying because they are told to die, The. Occasional Poem 7.1.72. Roy Fisher. HarvBoo

Poets are going home now, The. Ingathering. Carolyn Kizer. ExTi

Poets are usually pure, rugged. Lament for Lu Yin. Meng Chiao. SuSp, *tr. by* Stephen Owen

Poets arrive and shake hands, The. World Poetry Circuit. Alfred A. Yuson. ReBoTo

Poets' Corner. Robert Graves. FaBoEE

Poets for deciduous language., The. (LL) Postscript. Ronald Stuart Thomas. FaBoMo; OxBC

Poets have muddled all the little fountains, The. *Var. authors.* AWP, *tr. by* E. Powys Mathers *Fr.* Mu'allaqat, The.

Poets have often noticed. Bakhyt Kenzheyev [*or* Kenzheiev]. TCRP

Poets Have Their Ear to the Ground. Peter De Vries. UV

Poets Hitchhiking on the Highway. Gregory Corso. BB; NeAP; PoM

Poets, I want to follow them all. On Originality. Bill Manhire. HarvBoo; PeNZ

Poets / in a company. Dancing Concerning a Form of Women, A. Robert Duncan. FTOS

Poets in Late Winter. Mona Van Duyn. ExTi

Poets light but Lamps, The. Emily Dickinson. APN-2; HeIP-4; TCAPo

Poets loiter all their leisure. Hour Glass, The. Edward Quillinan. NOBRP

Poets make pets of pretty, docile words. Pretty Words. Elinor Wylie. NAAL-2v2

Poets may boast, as safely vain. Of English Verse. Edmund Waller. BeJo; CABP; NAEL-5v1; NOSC; PoE

Poets of Missouri stare at astonishing winter, The. Poets in Late Winter. Mona Van Duyn. ExTi

Poets often use many words to say a simple thing. Fly Me to the Moon (In Other Words). Bart Howard. ReLy

Poets on Poets. Nin Andrews. KGB

Poets on[e]ly that can tell, The. (LL) On a Picture Painted by Herself [*or* Her self], Representing Two Nymphs [*or* Nimphs] of Diana's, One in a Posture to Hunt, the other Bath[e]ing. Anne Killigrew. BASC; NOSC

Poets say that all who love are blind, The. I Got It Bad and That Ain't Good. Duke Ellington. ReLy

Poets, the sages, the seers of the land!, The. (LL) Woman's Future. May Kendall. VWP; ViWPN

Poggio. Lawrence Durrell. OxBTC

Pogrom. Ed. Hoornik. TuT, *tr. by* Mary E. O'Donnell

Pogrom. Phyllis Kahaney. GotH

Poh! did ever one see such a troublesome bear? Delia Very Angry. *Unknown.* NOEC

Point, The. David Bromige. FTOS

Point, The. Robert Earl Hayden. ESEAA

Point, The. Evan Jones. NOBAu

Point, The. John Montague. PNI

Point and Counter-Point in All Things. Jane Mead. NAPBL

Point at Issue, The. William Wordsworth. SacPr *Fr.* Ecclesiastical Sonnets.

Point, greatly enlarged, The. Thomas Kinsella. BiHa *Fr.* Technical Supplement, A.

Point Grey. Daryl Hine. NOBC

Point, I imagine, is, The. Point, The. Evan Jones. NOBAu

Point is not that Troy, The. On Living with a Fat Woman in Heaven. Sidney Burris. SwNoth

Point is not the point—, The. Point, The. David Bromige. FTOS

Point no scornful finger at Yoruba Land. Edouard J. Maunick. NegPo *Fr.* As Far as Yoruba Land.

Point of hill. Stairway to Heaven. Robert Creeley. FTOS

Point of moonlight, A. Inside: George Gaines at Graterford Prison, 1981. David Keplinger. AmPoNex

Point of No Return. Robert Graves. BIrV

Point of View, A. Constance Carrier. APT-2

Point Shirley. Sylvia Plath. NIL-7; NIP-4

Point your nose to the sun. Trajan. GrAn

Pointed houses lean so you would swear, The. Amsterdam. Francis Jammes. AWP, *tr. by* Jethro Bithell

Pointed out like the stars. Pointed Out Like the Stars. Alice Rahon. SurWo, *tr. by* Myrna Bell Rochester

Pointless homesickness. Pointless shudderings. Willow in Spring Wind: A Showing. Jorie Graham. ExTi

Pointless Journey. Yolanda Bedregal. TANSG, *tr. by* Carolyne Wright

Pointless Pride of Man, The. *Unknown.* FaBoVe

Poise of my hands reminded me of yours. (LL) Villanelle: "It is the pain, it is the pain, endures." William Empson. EnLoPo; HarvBoo; NoAM; PoE; TRP; UV

Poised between going on and back, pulled. Base Stealer, The. Robert Francis. NTCP

Poised smiling on your charger. Heavens Cherubim High Horsed or The Meeting of the Two Sevens (May 1977). Velma Pollard. WaCA

Poison, The. Hans Magnus Enzensberger. VCWP, *tr. by* Hans Magnus Enzensberger and Michael Hamburger

Poison Flower, The. Mary Elizabeth Coleridge. PEW

Poison flower that in my garden grew, The. Poison Flower, The. Mary Elizabeth Coleridge. PEW

Poison Tree, A. William Blake. AWP; FHYEP; HAP; NAEL-5v2; NAEL-6v2; NPeEn; OxAEP-2; OxBEV; RB; SCV; SoSe-8; TFi; WeW-3 *Fr.* Songs of Experience.

Poisoned Man, The. James Dickey. PAI

Poisoned wheat let. Garvey's Head as Value. Norman Weinstein. WaCA

Poisonfield. Glyn Maxwell. HarvBoo

Poland / 1931 "The Wedding." Jerome Rothenberg. PoM (Poland/1931.) FTOS

Poland works nicely. Story So Far, The. John Clarke. UV

Polar. Jacqueline Senard. SurWo, *tr. by* Myrna Bell Rochester

Polar Bear. William Jay Smith. TLR

Polar Bear never makes his bed, The. Polar Bear. William Jay Smith. TLR

Polar Cub. Judith Nicholls. NOxBChV

Polar DEW has just warned that, The. Your Attention Please. Peter Porter. OBWP; OxBTC

Polar Exploration. Stephen Spender. NoAM (North, The.) FaBoMo

Polarities. Kenneth Slessor. CBAP

Polderland. Hendrik Marsman. TuT, *tr. by* Seamus Deane

Pole at the Village Pagoda, The. *Vietnamese Oral Tradition.* CaDao, *tr. by* John Balaban

Pole Star, The. Coslett Coslett. OBWVE, *tr. by* Kenneth Hurlstone Jackson

Pole star and northern capital: equal as scepter and orb. Visit in Winter to the Temple of His Mystical Majesty, A. Tu Fu. CarOv, *tr. by* Carolyn Kizer

Pole Star for This Year. Archibald MacLeish. OxBA

Pole Vaulter. David Allan Evans. MoASP

Pole your three winged galleons. *Unknown.* ColAnChi, *tr. by* Red Pine

Poles, The. Paul Celan. PoetW, *tr. by* John Felstiner

Poles rode out from Warsaw against the German, The. Abnormal Is Not Courage, The. Jack Gilbert. CoAP; YaYoPo

Police are dragging for the bodies, The. Miners. James Wright (1927–80). CoAmPo

Police / being poisoned, The. List of the Delusions of the Insane / What They Are Afraid Of, A. David Antin. APSN

Police killed her brother. Rant, Rave and Ricochet. Luis J. Rodriguez. IllVoic

Police Station Ditties. Max Beerbohm. NOBL (P.C., X, 36.) UV (Police Station Ditty, A.) PeLV

Police Station Ditty, A. Max Beerbohm. *See* Police Station Ditties

Policeman buys shoes slow and careful, The. Psalm of Those Who Go Forth before Daylight. Carl Sandburg. OxBA

Policeman does not blow his whistle, The. A. Velichansky. TCRusP, *tr. by* Daniel Weissbort

Policeman from Nottingham Junction, A. Limerick. *Unknown.* PeLi

Policeman's Lot, A. Wendy Cope. FaBoWP

Policeman's Lot, A [*or* The]. Sir William Schwenck Gilbert. NOBL; PeLV *Fr.* Pirates of Penzance, The.

Pólis, place defended. Nanni Cagnone. ItPo, *tr. by* Gayle Ridinger *Fr.* Vaticinio.

Polis poutre catalane. Luis d'Antin Van Rooten. OBCoV *Fr.* Mots d'Heures: Gousses, Rames.

Polish Eagle, The. Kornel Ujejski. MLL, *tr. by* Helen Waddell

Polish Girl Standing on a Chair, A. J. B. Charles. TuT, *tr. by* Gregory O'Donoghue

Polish Knot, The. Tomasz Jastrun. AF, *tr. by* Michael March

Polish Rider, The. Derek Walcott. WoPoe

Polished and polished. Basho. SoOfWa, *tr. by* Sam Hamill

Polished now. Need for Armor, A. Eileen Stratidakis. PasH

Politer and politer and politer. (LL) City Christmas. Phyllis McGinley. ChrPo; OBCoV

Political. Rita Dove. FFC

Political Activist Living Alone. Pat Arrowsmith. BrRo

Political art, let it be, A. Short Speech to My Friends. Imamu Amiri Baraka. ESEAA

Political House that Jack Built, The. William Hone. NOBRP "This is THE MAN—all shaven and shorn." OBCoV

Political Intelligence. Arthur James Marshall Smith. SPE

Political Meeting. Abraham Moses Klein. MoCV

Political Orlando, The. George MacBeth [*or* Macbeth]. NOBL

Political Poem. Imamu Amiri Baraka. AF; CoAP; NAAL-2v2; NoAM; PmAP

Political Relations. Audre Lorde. GLP

"Political women," thought Yeats. Limerick. R. K. R. Thornton. PeLi

Politician is an arse upon, A. E. E. Cummings. FaBoEE; InPK-6; NBLV; OBAL

Politician's elephantine conk's, The. Maurus. Palladas [*or* Pallades]. GrAn, *tr. by* Tony Harrison

Politicians, heart and soul. Poll Star. Felicia Lamport. NBLV

Politicisation of the North Wind, The. David Morley. NLP

Politics. Tom Marshall. NOBC

Politics. W. B. Yeats. AmFaPo; HeIP-4; OxBTC; PoE; SCV

Politics of Envy. Duncan Forbes. PeLV

Politics of Rich Painters, The. Imamu Amiri Baraka. VGW

Polka. John Fuller. PeLV *Fr.* Fox-Trot.

Polka. Diane Jarvenpa. MiVo

Polka Dots and Moonbeams. Johnny Burke. ReLy

Poll Star. Felicia Lamport. NBLV

Pollen. Wyn Cooper. UrbNat

Polly; an Opera. John Gay. Air: "Sportsmen keep hawks, and their quarry they gain, The." NOEC "Honour plays a bubble's part." PeLV "Woman's like the flatt'ring ocean." PeLV

Polly and Sukey. Mother Goose. LB; OxNR; ReMoGo

Polly Be-en Upzides wi' Tom. William Barnes. NOBVV

Polly Perkins. *Unknown.* OBCoV; OxBoLi; PeLV

Polly put the kettle on. Polly and Sukey. Mother Goose. LB; OxNR; ReMoGo

Polly's Tree. Sylvia Plath. AmFaPo

Polly Wolly Doodle. *Unknown.* TCAPo

Polonius. Miroslav Holub. WoPoe, *tr. by* Ian Milner

Polonius is still alive. To be or not to be. Brian G. Gilmore. SpirFl

Polwart on the Green. Allan Ramsay. NOEC; NPeEn; OxBEV

Poly-Olbion Song 6. Michael Drayton. "What spirit can lift you up, to that immortall praise." PBRV

Polyaenus' daughter, Scyllis, came to the wide gates. Diotimus. HePo *Fr.* Epigrams.

Polychromatic beauty. Nectar of Ápan, The. Enrique Gonzáles Martínez. TCLAP, *tr. by* Elizabeth Gordon

Polychromatic springtime's gay cadenza. Vernal Equinox. Martin Johnston. CBAP

Polydamas, your depth in augry. Homer. NOSC, *tr. by* George Chapman *Fr.* Iliad, The.

Polydeukes. Alcman. SaLy, *tr. by* Diane Rayor

Polyglot Medley. Andrew Geddes Bain. PeSAV

Polyhedral kernels of wisdom. Mikhail Yeryomin. ItGoST, *tr. by* J. Kates

Polyhymnia. George Peele. (Farewell to Arms, A.) NOBE; OBEV; OBWP; OxAEP-1; PoRA (Farewell to the Court.) NoSic

His Golden Lock[e]s [Time Hath to Silver Turned].   NIP-4; NPeEn; NoP-4; OxBEV; SCGP; TFi

Polynesia.   Allen Curnow.   PeNZ

Polyolbion.   Michael Drayton.

"By thine own named town made famous in thy fall."   NOSC

"March strongly forth, my Muse, whilst yet the temperate air."   NOSC

"Then Frome (a nobler flood) the Muses doth implore."   NOSC

"Where she, of all the plains of Britain that doth bear."   NOSC

"With solitude what sorts, that here's not wondrous rife?"   NOSC

Polyphemus.   Virgil [or Vergil].   NoSic, tr. by Richard Stanyhurst   Fr. Aeneid [or Eneados, Aeneis], The.

"Polyphemus, Galatea with apples pelts your flocks."   Theocritus.   HePo, tr. by Barbara Hughes Fowler Fr. Idylls.

Polyphemus' Love Song.   Luis de Góngora y Argote.   SpanPo, tr. by Frances Fletcher   Fr. Fable of Polyphemus and Galatea.

Polystylistics.   Nina Iskrenko.   PFTM-2, tr. by John High

Polystylistics.   Nina Iskrenko.   TCRP, tr. by John High

Polystylistics is when a knight from the Middle Ages.   Polystylistics.   Nina Iskrenko.   PFTM-2, tr. by John High

Pomade.   Aleksei Eliseievich Kruchyonykh [or Kruchionykh or Kruchenykh].   "3 poems."   PFTM-1

Pomegranate.   Jean Janzen.   GeoHom

Pomegranate, The.   Eavan Boland.   CABP; NoP-4

Pomegranate grows in the garden front, The.   Forsaken Wife, The.   Ts'ao Chih.   CoBCP, tr. by Burton Watson

Pomegranate just splitting, a peach just furry, A.   Diodorus Zonas.   GrAn

Pomegranate speaks, The.   Unknown.   BoWoP

Pomelo, The.   Unknown.   WoPoe, tr. by Anne Birrell

Pomme arac.   Derek Walcott.   FaBoVe   Fr. Sainte Lucie.

Pomona.   William Morris.   NOBVV; NPeEn; OxBEV; WoPoe

Pompeii: Plaster Casts.   Peter Scupham.   HarvBoo

Pomposo (insolent and loud).   Charles Churchill.   OBSV   Fr. Ghost, The.

Pond, The.   Louise Glück.   ColAP

Pond in a Basin.   Tu Mu.   SuSp, tr. by Eddie Tsang

Pond in a Bowl, The.   Han Yü.   SuSp, tr. by Kenneth O. Hanson

Pond in a Jardiniere, A.   Han Yü.   CoBCP, tr. by Burton Watson

"My ceramic lake in dawn, water settled clear."   CoBCP

"Old men are like little boys."   CoBCP

"Pond shine and sky glow, blue matching blue."   CoBCP

Pond Named Ganga, A.   Chandrashekhar Kambar.   OMIP, tr. by A. K. Ramanujan

Pond shine and sky glow, blue matching blue.   Han Yü.   CoBCP   Fr. Pond in a Jardiniere, A.

Ponder, darling, these busted statues.   E. E. Cummings.   NIL-7; NIP-4; PoE

Ponder my words, if so that any be.   Request to the Graces, An.   Robert Herrick.   NOSC

Pondy Woods.   Robert Penn Warren.   MoAmPo

Ponies, Twynyrodyn.   Meic Stephens.   AngWePo

Ponnage Pool, The.   Helen B. Cruickshank.   NePenScot

Pont y Caniedydd.   Alun Llywelyn-Williams.   OBWVE, tr. by Joseph R. Clancy

Pontiac, The.   Meditation in Loudoun County.   Thomas Bolt.   YaYoPo

Pontiac, dressed in his French officer's uniform.   Starved Rock.   James Ballowe.   IllVoic

Pontius Pilate, remembered as a Roman.   And Pilate Said.   Joy Davidman.   YaYoPo

Pontoon.   Kit Robinson.   FTOS

Pontoosuce.   Herman Melville.   APN-2; NCAP; NOBA; TCAPo

Pontypool.   Richard Hall.   AngWePo

Pontypool! thou dirtiest of dirty places.   Pontypool.   Richard Hall.   AngWePo

Pony boy though it's spring we're still apart.   Thinking of My Little Boy.   Tu Fu.   ColAnChi; WoPoe, tr. by David Lattimore

Pony Farm.   Laura Jensen.   LCAP-2

Pony in Kukutis's Ear, A.   Marcelijus Martinaitis.   TWW, tr. by Laima Sruoginis

Pooh!   Walter De la Mare.   HAP; OBCoV; PeLV

Pool, The.   Hayyim Nahman [or Khayim Nakhman or Chaim Nachman] Bialik.   MHP, tr. by Ruth Finer Mintz

Pool, The.   Robert Creeley.   CoAP

Pool, The.   "H. D."   APT-1; HarvBoo

Pool is a Godless Sport.   James Haug.   MoASP

Pool is Full of Autumn Sky, Rippled by Gentle Breezes, The.   Ou-yang Hsiu.   ErotSp, tr. by Jerome P. Seaton

Pool light shimmers, The.   Weekend in Palm Springs.   Stewart Florsheim.   GotH

Pool of moonlight on my bed this late hour, A.   Quiet Night Thoughts.   Li Po.   CrYelRi, tr. by Sam Hamill

Poor.   Myra Cohn Livingston.   KaS

Poor, The.   Letitia [or Laetitia] Elizabeth Landon.   VWP

Poor, The.   John Langhorne.   NOEC   Fr. Country Justice, The.

Poor, The.   Emile Verhaeren.   AWP, tr. by Ludwig Lewisohn

Poor, The.   Jones Very.   SacPr

Poor, The.   William Carlos Williams.   MoAmPo

Poor Adam and Eve were from Eden turned out.   Unknown.   Spl

Poor beggars!—they'll never see 'ome! (LL)   Widow at Windsor, The.   Rudyard Kipling.   NAEL-5v2; NAEL-6v2; NoAM

Poor Bess Turpin, I pytty thy case as farr as I can.   Isobel Beaumont.   EMWP

Poor box, A.   Issa.   EH, tr. by Robert K. Haas

Poor boy. Poor boy.   I'm Glad I'm Not Young Any More.   Frederick Loewe.   ReLy

Poor Boy: Portrait of a Painting.   John Ash.   HarvBoo

Poor But Honest.   Unknown.   See She Was Poor but She Was Honest

Poor Calpurnius, the most Schweikian soldier in the land.   Lucilius.   GrAn

Poor child of sorrow! who did'st boldly spring.   To a Rejected Sonnet.   William Ewart Gladstone.   CenSon

Poor Children, The.   Victor Hugo.   AWP, tr. by Algernon Charles Swinburne

Poor Christian Looks at the Ghetto, A.   Czeslaw Milosz.   HP; PoSu; VCWP

Poor chum, dear chum, so here you lie at rest.   Monologue in a Rand Hospital.   William Elijah Hunter.   PeSAV

Poor crawlin' bodies, sair neglectit.   John Learmont.   NOEC   Fr. Address to the Plebeians, An.

Poor credulous and simple maid!   Thomas Randolph.   BoLoP   Fr. Pastoral Courtship, A.

Poor Crow!   Mary Mapes Dodge.   OBCA; SWaP

Poor Cupid sits and blows his nails for cold. (LL)   Blame Not My Cheekes.   Thomas Campion.   SCGP; UnPo

Poor dear dead have been laid out in vain, The.   Thomas Hood.   FaBoEE

Poor degenerate from the ape, A.   First Philosopher's Song.   Aldous Leonard Huxley.   AWP

Poor devil that I am, being so attacked.   Palladas [or Pallades].   OBVE

Poor Doctor Blow went out of church.   Queen Anne's Musicians.   Thomas Hennell.   FaBoTw

Poor Erin's daughter cross'd the main.   Erin's Daughter.   Lydia Huntley Sigourney.   SWaP

Poor fellow, what is it to you.   Verses.   Sir Charles Hanbury Williams.   OBWVE

Poor, fond deluded heart! wilt thou again.   Mary Tighe.   CenSon

Poor French Sailor's Scottish Sweetheart, A.   William Johnson Cory.   EBVV

Poor Girl's Meditation, The.   Unknown.   BIrV; OBMV, tr. by Padraic Colum

Poor Hal caught his death standing under a spout.   Fatal Love.   Matthew Prior.   NBLV

Poor have hands, and feet, and eyes, The.   Poor Man and His Parish Church, The.   Robert Stephen Hawker.   EBVV

Poor heart, unsatisfied!   Shadow and Sunrise.   Henrietta Cordelia Ray.   CBWP-3

Poor hill farmer astray in the grass.   Lonely Farmer, The.   Ronald Stuart Thomas.   NoP-4

Poor-House, The.   George Crabbe.   ECEV   Fr. Village, The.

Poor Houses, The.   Ed Roberson.   GT

Poor, impious Soul! that fixes its high hopes.   Aspiration.   Adah Isaacs Menken.   CBWP-1; ViWPN

Poor in my youth, and in life's later scenes.   On Late-acquired Wealth or Riches.   Unknown.   OBVE, tr. by William Cowper

Poor in spirit on their rosary rounds, The.   Lough Derg.   Denis Devlin.   BIrV; CIP-2

Poor John, who joined in make of wrong.   Welcome the Wrath.   Stanley Kunitz.   VGW

Poor Julia's heart was in an awkward state.   Byron.   NOBRP   Fr. Don Juan.

Poor Kid.   William Cole.   OBAL

Poor Kosai.   Kosai.   JDP, tr. by Yoel Hoffmann

Poor lad once and a lad so trim, A.   Jean Richepin's Song.   Herbert Trench.   OBMV

Poor Lazarus.   Unknown.   NAAAL

Poor Linley! I shall miss thee sadly, now.   On the Death of William Linley, esq.   William Lisle Bowles.   OxBSo

Poor little Ada Queetie has departed this life.   Nancy Luce.   VerBaPo   Fr. Poor Little Hearts.

Poor little diary, with its simple thoughts.   Augusta Davies Webster.   NPeEn; ViWPN   Fr. Castaway, A.

Poor little donkey! It's no joke.   Palladas [or Pallades].   GrAn

Poor little Foal of an oppressed Race!   Samuel Taylor Coleridge.   OxAEP-2   Fr. Effusions.

Poor Little Hearts.   Nancy Luce.

"Poor little Ada Queetie has departed this life."   VerBaPo

Poor little, pretty, fluttering [or flutt'ring] thing.   Adriani Morientis ad Animam Suam.   Emperor Hadrian.   OBVE; OxBSP, tr. by Matthew Prior

Poor Little Rich Girl.   Noël Coward.   ReLy

Poor Man and His Parish Church, The.   Robert Stephen Hawker.   EBVV

Poor man has misplaced the silk, The.   Stray Dogs, Foaming.   Thom Ward.   AmPoNex

Poor man's clothes are ragged, quick to soil, A.   Lice, The.   Mei Yao Ch'en.   CrYelRi, *tr. by* Sam Hamill

Poor man's clothes—ragged and easy to get dirty, A.   Shih-hou Pointed Out to Me That from Ancient Times There Had Never Been a Poem on the Subject of Lice.   Mei Yao Ch'en.   CoBCP; ColAnChi, *tr. by* Burton Watson

Poor Man's Pig, The.   Edmund Charles Blunden.   MoBrPo

Poor Man's Province, The.   John Wright.   NOEC

Poor man's sins are glaring, The.   Rich and Poor; or, Saint and Sinner.   Thomas Love Peacock.   NOBE; NOBL; OBSV; OxBEV; PeLV

Poor Man's Sunday Walk, The.   Charles MacKay.   EBVV

Poor melancholy bird—that all night long.   To a Nightingale.   Charlotte Smith.   CenSon; OxBSo; RWP

Poor Merry-Andrew, in the neuk.   Robert Burns.   OBCoV   *Fr.* Jolly Beggars, The.

Poor moth, I can't help you.   I Can't Help You.   Ryszard Krynicki.   BLT, *tr. by* Stanislaw Baranczak

Poor Mrs. Prior.   Gerda Mayer.   OTCP

Poor Naomi.   *Unknown.*   APN-2

Poor Negro Sadi, The.   Charlotte Dacre.   RWP

Poor of London, The.   William Forster.   CBAP

Poor old bait got sick & died, The.   Jackson Mac Low.   APSN   *Fr.* Presidents of the United States of America, The.

Poor Old Lady.   *Unknown.*   NOxBChV

   (Poor old lady, she swallowed a fly.)   NOxBChV

Poor Old Lady.   *Unknown.*   OBCA

Poor old lady, set her aside.   Old Mother, The.   *Unknown.*   PoToHe

Poor old man, The. (LL)   Note Left in Jimmy Leonard's Shack, A.   James Wright (1927–80).   HCAP; NoP-4

Poor old Mr. Bidery.   Mr. Bidery's Spidery Garden.   David McCord.   OTCP

Poor old Robinson Crusoe!   Mother Goose.   OxNR; ReMoGo

Poor Ophelia sighed: "I deplore."   Limerick.   Frank Richards.   PeLi

Poor [*or* Poore] bird! I do not envy thee.   Robin, The.   George Daniel.   NPeEn

Poor Paddy Maguire, a fourteen-hour day.   Patrick Kavanagh.   ModIr; NPeEn   *Fr.* Great Hunger, The.

Poor Paddy Works on the Railway.   *Unknown.*   GM

Poor Pemulwy.   Pemulwy—A Visitation.   Beryl Philp-Carmichael (Yungha-Dhu).   IBA

Poor people fish mostly with snare nets.   On a Painting of Fish Being Caught, A Song.   Li Tung-yang.   ColAnChi, *tr. by* John Timothy Wixted

Poor people use snare-nets, The.   Song of the Painting "Catching Fish."   Li Tung-yang.   CoBLCP, *tr. by* Jonathan Chaves

Poor Pierrot.   Otto Harbach.   ReLy

Poor Ploughman to a Gentleman for Whom He Had Taken a Little Pains, A.   George Turberville.   NoSic

Poor Poet-Ape, that would be thought our chief.   On Poet-Ape.   Ben Jonson.   Son

Poor Poll.   Robert Bridges.   EBEV; OxBTC; OxBoLi

Poor Professor Higgins!   Rain in Spain, The.   Frederick Loewe.   ReLy

Poor quarter, A.   Issa.   ZenPo, *tr. by* Takashi Ikemoto and Lucien Stryk

Poor Relation, The.   Edwin Arlington Robinson.   APT-1

Poor restless Dove, I pity thee.   Captive Dove, The.   Anne Brontë.   EBVV; VWP

Poor savage, doubting that a river flows.   Watching the Dance.   James Merrill.   NIL-7; NIP-4

Poor Scholar, The.   Abraham Ibn-Chasdai.   TrJP, *tr. by* J. Chotzner

Poor Scholar of the 'Forties, A.   Padraic Colum.   NOIV

Poor sheepish plaything.   For Sale.   Robert Lowell.   CoAmPo

Poor song.   Tape, The.   Myra Cohn Livingston.   NTCP

Poor soul, the center of my sinful earth.   William Shakespeare.   *See* Poor[e] soul[e], the centre of my sinful[l] earth

Poor thing stands their vainly, The.   Birdsong 2.   *Unknown, fr. Terezin Concentration Camp.*   INSAB

Poor tired Tim! It's sad for him.   Tired Tim.   Walter De la Mare.   NTCP

Poor Tom.   Charles Dibdin.   NOEC; OxBoLi

   (Tom Bowling.)   OxAEP-1

Poor vaunting earth, gloss'd with uncertain pride.   George Alsop.   SCAP

"Poor wanderer," said the leaden sky.   Subalterns, The.   Thomas Hardy.   MoBrPo; NOBVV; NoAM; PAI

Poor wayfaring man of grief, A.   Stranger and His Friend, The.   James Montgomery.   SacPr

Poor Wayfaring Stranger.   *Unknown.*   SacPr

   (I'm just a poor wayfaring stranger.)   TCAPo

Poor wearied pilgrim—in this toiling scene! (LL)   To the Moon.   Charlotte Smith.   BWW; CenSon; RWP; Son

Poor weaver, with the hopeless brow.   How Different!   Ebenezer Elliott.   EBEV

Poor who begs with bated breath, The.   Price of Begging, The.   Emmanuel [*or* Immanuel] ben David Frances.   TrJP, *tr. by* A. B. Rhine

Poore desolate Gardin, smile no more on me.   To the Gardin att O: [Owthorpe] 7:th.   Lucy Hutchinson.   EMWP

Poor[e] girl[e]s, neglected. (LL)   To Violets.   Robert Herrick.   CaPo; OBEV

Poor[e] soul[e] sat[e] sighing by a sycamore [*or* sicamore] tree, The.   Green Willow, The.   *Unknown.*   SCGP

Poor[e] soul[e], the centre of my sinful[l] earth.   William Shakespeare.   AWP; HAP; HeIP-4; NAEL-5v1; NAEL-6v1; NAEL-7v1; NOBE; NOCV; OBEV; OxAEP-1; PoE; SCGP; SacPr; Son; TFi   *Fr.* Sonnets.

Poore widwe [*or* widow], somdeel [*or* somedeal] stape in age, A.   Geoffrey Chaucer.   *See* Povre widwe [*or* wyde], somde[e]l stape in age, A

Poorer than X.   Vladimir Nikolaevich Kornilov.   TCRP

Poorly matched the world and she.   Poorly Matched.   Prageeta Sharma.   HeMarv

Pop bottles pop-bottles.   Song of the Pop-Bottlers.   Morris Gilbert Bishop.   KaS

Pop Goes the Weasel!   W. R. Mardale.   OxNR

Pop-out eyes belong to Baldwin, The.   Of Miles Davis.   William Ford.   SeSe

Pop's tops!   Limerick.   Bill Greenwell.   PeLi

Popcorn is greasy, and I forgot to bring a Kleenex, The.   James Bond Movie, The.   May Swenson.   FaBoWP

Pope.   Manuel González Prada.   SpanPo, *tr. by* William M. Davis

Pope, The.   A. E. Housman.   NPeEn; OBCoV

Pope Alexander VI.   Geoffrey Lehmann.   NOBAu

Pope from penance purgatorial, The.   James Vincent Cunningham.   OBVE

Pope John XXIII.   Ernst Waldinger.   AuPH, *tr. by* Lowell A. Bangerter

Pope's Carnations Knew Him.   Thom Gunn.   OBGa

Poplar.   Silver Poplar at Sunrise.   Constance Egemo.   PoCoUp

Poplar Field, The.   William Cowper.   FHYEP; HAP; NOBE; NOEC; OxBEV

Poplar Leaf, The.   George Seferis.   PFTM-1

Poplars.   Music.   Eugenio de Andrade.   VCWP, *tr. by* Alexis Levitin

Poplars are felled [*or* fell'd], farewell to the shade, The.   Poplar Field, The.   William Cowper.   FHYEP; HAP; NOBE; NOEC; OxBEV

Poplars are standing there still as death.   Southern Mansion.   Arna Bontemps.   APT-2; AiP; GT; NAAAL; TTY

Popol Vuh, The.   *Unknown.*   STP, *tr. by* Munro Edmonson

Poppa was a sugah daddy.   Poppa Chicken.   Margaret Abigail Walker.   NAAAL

Poppies.   Yolanda Bedregal.   TANSG, *tr. by* Carolyne Wright

Poppies.   Zalman Schneour.   MHP, *tr. by* Ruth Finer Mintz

Poppies in July.   Sylvia Plath.   FaBoWP; LCAP-2; RB

Poppies in October.   Sylvia Plath.   FaBoWP; HCAP; LCAP-2; NoAM

Poppies of This Year.   Gennady Aygi.   TCRusP, *tr. by* Peter France

Poppies on the Wheat.   Helen Hunt Jackson.   APN-2; ColAP

Poppies, that scattered o'er this arid plain.   Thomas Doubleday.   CenSon

Poppy, A.   Michael McClintock.   HA

Poppy, The.   Sarah Hamilton.   CenSon

Poppy, The.   Francis Thompson.   MoBrPo

Poppy Heads.   Neil Curry.   NLP

Poppy thane. Pendle dust. Boldo sachet gaudles.   Lesson from the Cockerel.   Maggie O'Sullivan.   Oth

Poppy there, companion to repose, The.   Philip Freneau.   NAAL-3   *Fr.* House of Night, The.

Poppy under a young.   Necromance.   Rae Armantrout.   FTOS; PmAP

Popryshchin.   Nikolai Alekseievich Zabolotsky [*or* Zabolotskii].   TCRusP, *tr. by* Daniel Weissbort

Popul Vuh, The.   *Unknown.*

   "Truly now."   WoPoe, *tr. by* Dennis Tedlock

   "Wait!"   WoPoe, *tr. by* Dennis Tedlock

Popular.   Tennyson.   NOBL

Popular Functionary, A.   Charles Dibdin.   NOEC

Popular Heart is a Cannon first, The.   Emily Dickinson.   TCAPo

Popular leader, national hero.   Finn's Wishes.   Desmond O'Grady.   CIP-2, *tr. by the author*

Popular Mechanics.   Charles Simic.   EmeKit

Popular Mythologies.   Vernon Scannell.   OBCoV

Popular, popular, unpopular!   Popular.   Tennyson.   NOBL

Popular Romance, A.   Kevin Ireland.   PeNZ

Popular Songs of Tuscany.   *Unknown.*   AWP, *tr. by* John Addington Symonds

Populated by dolls and clowns.   Waltz for Debby.   Gene Lees.   ReLy

Population Drifts.   Carl Sandburg.   OxBA

Porcelain Bells.   Medbh McGuckian.

   Speaking Into the Candles.   ModIr

Porcelain Couple, The.   Donald Hall.   BAP-97

"Porcelain is personal," he smiles. For His Ring and Watch on the Night Stand. Gladys Cardiff. HATNAP

Porcelain Pavilion, The. Nikolai Stepanovich Gumilyov [or Gumiliov or Gumilev]. TCRusP, tr. by Mary Jane White

Porch, The. Philip Pain. SCAP

Porch, The. Ronald Stuart Thomas. NOCV

Porch beats its yellow wings, The. Pavel Nikolaevich Vasilyev [or Vasil'ev]. TCRP, tr. by David Macduff Fr. Salt Riot, The.

Porch sitting hairbraiding. Initiation. Monifa Atungaye Love. ISC

Porchlight coming on again, The. 1926. Weldon Kees. CoAP

Porcupine, The. Galway Kinnell. NAAL-5; NOBA

Poring on Caesar's death with earnest eye. Julius Caesar and the Honey-Bee. Charles Tennyson Turner. OxBSo

Porirua Friday Night. Sam Hunt. PeNZ

Porno-Bach. Shuntaro Tanikawa. PoetW, tr. by Harold Wright

Pornographer, The. Robert Hass. YaYoPo

Pornographic Poem. John Giorno. CAGL

Pornography. Angela Shaw. PuP-23

Pornography, Nebraska. Sandra McPherson. ReTh

Porphyria's Lover. Robert Browning. AWP; FHYEP; HAP; NAEL-5v2; NAEL-6v2; OBEV; PAI

Porphyry of Elements, A. Garrett Kaoru Hongo. GeoHom Fr. Cruising 99.

Porpoises spout amid the waves. Tune: "Song of Shou-yang." Kuan Yün-shih. SuSp, tr. by Richard John Lynn

Porson on German Scholarship. Richard Porson. FaBoEE

Porson's Visit to the Continent. Richard Porson. FaBoEE

(Epigram on an Academic Visit to the Continent.) OxBoLi; PeLV

Port, The. Bernadette Mayer. FTOS

Port Bou. Stephen Spender. TwCP

Port of Holy Peter. John Masefield. OBMV

Port of Many Ships. John Masefield. OBMV

Port of Spain. Derek Walcott. NoAM

Port Phillip Night. Francis Webb. BMAP

Port Talbot. John Davies. AngWePo

Port, walls. Djinns, The. Victor Hugo. SxFrPo, tr. by E. H. and A. M. Blackmore

Porte Dorée. Léopold Sédar Senghor. PoetW, tr. by Melvin Dixon

Portent, The. Herman Melville. APN-2; CBCWP; ColAP; InPK-6; NAAL-2v1; NAAL-3; NCAP; NOBA; NoP-4; OBWP; OxBA; PoE; TAP; TCAPo

Porter. Marilyn Nelson Waniek. ESEAA

Porter and keepers, when they're civil. His Rule of Behaviour: If You Are Civil, I Am Sober. James Carkesse. NOSC

Porter's Love Song to a Chambermaid, A. James P. Johnson. ReLy

Porter to th' infernal[l] gate is Sin, The. Phineas Fletcher. NOSC Fr. Locusts, or Appolyonists, The.

Porth Cwyfan. Roland Mathias. AngWePo; TCAWP

Portinaio. Julie Agoos. YaYoPo

Portion of this yew. Transformations. Thomas Hardy. RB; TRP

Portishead Suite. Rick Barot. NeAmPo

Portly he was, in carriage somewhat grand. Bunch of Larks, The. Robert Leighton. EBVV

Portly prince, and goodly to the sight, A. Dryden. OBSV Fr. Hind and the Panther, The.

Portly pusher of waves, wind-slave. (LL) Winter Ocean. John Updike. InPK-6; PAI

Portrait. Manuel Bandeira. TCLAP, tr. by Candace Slater

Portrait. Antoine-Roger Bolamba. PBMAP

Portrait. E. E. Cummings. HeIP-4; InPK-6; NAAL-2v2; NIP-4; NOBA; OxBSP; PoE; RB; TAP; VGW

(Buffalo Bill's.) NAAL-5; NIL-7; TCAPo

Portrait. John Lyle Donaghy. BIrV

Portrait. Kenneth Fearing. APT-2; MoAmPo

Portrait. Gail Fox. NOBC

Portrait. Mary Leader. NAPBL

Portrait. Antonio Machado Ruiz. SpanPo, tr. by Doreen Bell

Portrait. Antonio Machado Ruiz. RaBo; STV; WoPoe, tr. by Robert Bly

Portrait. Cecília Meireles. TCLAP, tr. by Luiz Fernández García

Portrait. Hyam Plutzik. TaR

Portrait. Miklós Radnóti. IQMS, tr. by Thomas Land

Portrait. Yaroslav [or Iaroslav] Vasilevich Smelyakov [or Smeliakov]. TCRP, tr. by Simon Franklin

Portrait. Leopold Staff. PoSu, tr. by Adam Czerniawski

Portrait. Constance Urdang. OPRER

Portrait. Judith Wright. OxBSP; SoSe-8

Portrait, A. Walter De la Mare. NoAM

Portrait, A. Thomas Dekker. OxAEP-1

Portrait, A. "Michael Field." VWP

Portrait, The. Stanley Kunitz. InvLad; RaBo

Portrait by a Neighbour. Edna St. Vincent Millay. ItWoWo; OBCA

Portrait d'une Femme. Ezra Pound. APT-1; MoAmPo; NAAL-2v2; NAAL-5; NOBA; NoAM; NoP-4; PAI; TAP; TCAPo; TwCP

Portrait from the Infantry. Alan Dugan. AF

Portrait in a Brass Gong. Mick North. NLP

Portrait in Black Paint, with a Very Sparing Use of Whitewash. Elinor Wylie. NALW

Portrait in Georgia. Jean Toomer. APT-2; NAAL-2v2; NoP-4

Portrait in the Guards, A. Laurence Whistler. GTBS-P

Portrait of a Bishop. Evan Lloyd. AngWePo

Portrait of a Family. Carlos Drummond de Andrade. TCLAP, tr. by Virginia de Araújo

Portrait of a Girl. Conrad Potter Aiken. See Priapus and the Pool

Portrait of a Girl with Comic Book. Phyllis McGinley. APT-2

Portrait of a House Detective. Hans Magnus Enzensberger. HP; PoSu, tr. by Michael Hamburger

Portrait of a Jew Old Country Style. Jerome Rothenberg. NNaP

Portrait of a Lady. T. S. Eliot. APT-1; TwCP

Portrait of a Lady. Elizabeth Nannestad. PeNZ

Portrait of a Lady. William Carlos Williams. HarvBoo; NAAL-2v2; NAAL-5; NOBA; NoAM; OxBA

Portrait of a Lady in the Exhibition of the Royal Academy. Winthrop Mackworth Praed. NOBL; PeLV Fr. Every-Day Characters.

Portrait of a Lady Walking. Djuna Barnes. APT-1

Portrait of a Machine. Louis Untermeyer. MoAmPo

Portrait of a Married Couple. Margaret Scott. NOBAu

Portrait of a Motorcar. Carl Sandburg. APT-1

Portrait of a Nun. Bobi Jones. OBWVE, tr. by Joseph P. Clancy

Portrait of a Pregnant Woman. Bobi Jones. OBWVE, tr. by Joseph P. Clancy

Portrait of a Stupid Teacher of Rhetoric. Unknown. GrAn, tr. by Peter Jay

Portrait of a Young Girl Raped at a Suburban Party. Brian Patten. OxBTC

Portrait of an Engine Driver. Bobi Jones. OBWVE, tr. by Joseph P. Clancy

Portrait of Assimilation. Chrystos. UnSA

Portrait of Auntie Blodwen. Elwyn Davies. AngWePo

Portrait of Jonah with woman. Marie-Claire Bancquart. MFP, tr. by Martin Sorrell

Portrait of José Cemí. José Lezama Lima. TCLAP, tr. by Gregory Rabassa

Portrait of My Father and His Grandson. Richard Jones. IllVoic

Portrait of My Father, Militant Communist. Jorge Teillier. TCLAP, tr. by Carolyne Wright

Portrait of My Mother. Ilya [or Karl] L'vovich Selvinsky [or Sel'vinskii]. TCRP, tr. by Daniel Weissbort

Portrait of Myself with Arshile Gorky and Gertrude Stein. Jerome Rothenberg. FTOS

Portrait of Plisetskaya. Andrey [or Andrei] Andreievich Voznesensky [or Voznesenskii]. RusPo, tr. by Robert Arthur Douglas Ford

Portrait of Silverio Franconetti. Federico García Lorca. SpanPo, tr. by Rachel Benson and Robert O'Brien

Portrait of the Artist, A. Thomas Kinsella. HarvBoo

Portrait of the Artist, A. Mary Leapor. ECWP Fr. Mira's Picture, a Pastoral.

Portrait of the Artist as a Prematurely Old Man. Ogden Nash. APT-2

Portrait of the Artist as an Old Man. Michael Dransfield. BMAP; CBAP

Portrait of the Autist as a New World Driver. Les A. Murray. CBAP

Portrait of the Beautiful Unknown Woman. Juan Sánchez Peláez. BLPSL, tr. by Rene de Costa, Rigas Kappatos and Eleni Paidoussi

Portrait of the Boy as Artist. Barbara Howes. MoAmPo

Portrait of the Painter Hans Theo Richter and His Wife Gisela in Dresden, 1933. Tony Curtis. TCAWP

Portrait of the Poet as Landscape. Abraham Moses Klein. NOBC; NoAM

Portrait of Woman in Long Black Dress / Aurelia. Juan Felipe Herrera. TouFir

Portrait: The Freedom Fighter. George Jonas. NOBC

Portrait with Background. Oliver St. John Gogarty. OBMV

Portraits, The. Anna Maria Lenngren. WPOW, tr. by C. W. Stork

Portraits and Repetition. Gertrude Stein.

"How do you like what you have." AiP

Portraits of a Moment. Keith Gilyard. SpirFl

Portraits of Tudor Statesmen. U. A. Fanthorpe. EmeKit; OxBEV

Portrush. Walking dead streets in the dark. Archæologist, The. James Simmons. PBCIP

Ports of death are sins; of life, good deeds, The. Of Life and Death. Ben Jonson. TreFP

Portugal Laurel, The. John Wright. BloBone

Portuguese Mistake. Oswald de Andrade. TCLAP, tr. by Flavia Vidal

Portuguese Sea, The. Fernando Pessoa. PeSAV

Posies. Agnes Mary Frances Robinson. VWP

Posited. James McMichael. GeoHom

Position. Léon Damas. NegPo, *tr. by* Ellen Conroy Kennedy

Position is so well-known, The. Inside Diameter. Clarence Major. PmAP

Position is where you. Window, The. Robert Creeley. FTOS; NOBA; NoAM; PmAP; TAP; VGW

Position of Praise, The. Brendan Kennelly. BiHa

Position of the Sparrow. Shinkichi Takahashi. ZenPo, *tr. by* Takashi Ikemoto and Lucien Stryk

Positively on my own again, heart broken so long ago I hardly notice. Where the Weather Suits My Clothes. John Godfrey. PmAP

Positivists, The. Mortimer Collins. EBVV

Positivists ever talk in s- / Uch an epic style as Dawkins. *Var. authors.* FaBoEE   *Fr.* Balliol Rhymes.

Possessed. Charles Baudelaire. ErotSp, *tr. by* Richard Howard

Possessing what the owners can but own. (LL) Summer Morning, A. Richard Wilbur. FaBoMo; NBLV

Possession. Richard Aldington. MoBrPo

Possession. Marie Ponsot. VGW

Possession of Yesterday. Jorge Luis Borges. WoPoe, *tr. by* Nicomedes Suarez Arauz

Possessions. Ivor Gurney. NPeEn

Possessions. Ken Smith. SPE

Possessor. Things. W. S. Merwin. HAP

Possessor, The. Arthur Rex Dugard Fairburn. PeNZ   *Fr.* Album Leaves.

Possibilities: Remembering Malcolm X. Haki R. Madhubuti. SpirFl

Possibility. Charles Coe. UrbNat

Possibility. Tiziano Rossi. ItPo, *tr. by* Gayle Ridinger

Possibility, The. James Fenton. HarvBoo

Possibility of New Poetry, The. Robert Bly. CoAmPo

Possibility That Has Been Overlooked Is the Future, The. Michael Hartnett. NOIV

Possible. Ruth L. Schwartz. WiU

Possible Man, The. A. V. Christie. NAPBL

Possibly a child is not damaged immediately. Lackawanna. Galway Kinnell. GM

Possum with four crazed paws, The. Nest for Everyone, A. Roberta Spear. GeoHom

Post. Pierre Reverdy. CuPo

Post-boy drove with fierce career, The. Alice Fell; or, Poverty. William Wordsworth. OBNV

Post Card. Guillaume Apollinaire. AF; FaBoWar, *tr. by* Oliver Bernard

Post-Communion Striptease. Jill Alexander Essbaum. NAPBL

Post Early for Space. Peter J. Henniker-Heaton. HHAm

Post Heads. Johanna Kruit. TuT, *tr. by* Eamon Grennan

Post-historic herbivore, A. On the Inclusion of Miniature Dinosaurs in Breakfast Cereal Boxes. John Updike. OBCoV

Post-Modernism. James Galvin. GifTon

Post Mortem. Robinson Jeffers. MoAmPo

Post Mortem. Arthur Joseph Munby. NOBVV

Post Mortem. William Shakespeare. GTBS-P   *Fr.* Sonnets.

Post Mortem. Wole Soyinka. PoetW

Post-obits rarely reach a poet. (LL) Post-Obits and the Poets. Martial. AWP; FaBoEE; OBVE; RomPo, *tr. by* George Gordon Noel Byron, 6th Baron Byron

Post Operative. Thomas William Shapcott. BMAP

Post-Recessional. Gilbert Keith Chesterton. UV

Post-Script: for Gweno. Alun Lewis. AngWePo; BoLoP; GTBS-P

Post Scriptum. Mark Todd. GeoH

Post Ulixem Scriptum. James Joyce. OBCoV

Postcard. Margaret Atwood. NoAM

Postcard (Found on His body after He Was Killed by the Nazis). Miklós Radnóti. RaBo, *tr. by* Stephen Berg, S. J. Marks and Steven Polgar

(Nine miles from here.) HP, *tr. by* Stephen Berg, S. J. Marks and Steven Polgar

(Postcards.) HP, *tr. by* Stephen Berg, S. J. Marks and Steven Polgar

Postcard from a Travel Snob. Sophie Hannah. MFPA

Postcard from Berlin, A. Derek Mahon. BiHa

Postcard from Cuernavaca. Michael Hofmann. HarvBoo

Postcard from Kashmir. Agha Shahid Ali. NIL-7

Postcard from North Antrim, A. Seamus Heaney. PBCIP; PNI

Postcard from the Coast. Katrina Roberts. NAPBL

Postcard from the Garden. Marge Piercy. NoAM

Postcard from the Volcano, A. Wallace Stevens. APT-1; HAP; HCAP; NoAM; SAmP; WeW-3

Postcard from Trakl. John Yau. OpBo

Postcard to Send to Sumer, A. William Bronk. VGW

Postcards. Miklós Radnóti. *See* Postcard (Found on His body after He Was Killed by the Nazis)

Postcards from god (1). Imtiaz Dharker. NeBl

Postcolonial Tale, A. Joy Harjo. BodElec

Posted. John Masefield. Son

Poster. Ferreira Gullar. TCLAP, *tr. by* Renato Rezende

Poster Girl's Defence, The. Carolyn Wells. SWaP

Poster of Our Dazzling Victory at Saarbrucken, A. Arthur Rimbaud. OBWP, *tr. by* Robert Lowell   *Fr.* Eighteen-Seventy.

Poster with my picture on it, The. Unwanted. Edward Field. GLP

Posterity. Dennis Joseph Enright. OBCoV

Posterity. Philip Larkin. OxBC

Posterity hath many fates bemoaned. On Sir Robert Cotton the Antiquary. Thomas Randolph. NOSC

Posterity, thy name is Samuel Johnson. Dream of Judgement, A. Douglas Dunn. OxBC

Posterity was always a great reader. Posterity. Dennis Joseph Enright. OBCoV

Postfeminism. Brenda Shaughnessy. AmPoNex

Posthuman. Maura Stanton. BodElec

Posthumous. Michael O'Loughlin. PBCIP

Posthumous Coquetry. Théophile Gautier. AWP; PeVV, *tr. by* Arthur Symons

Posthumous Rehabilitation. Tadeusz Rózewicz. HP, *tr. by* Adam Czerniawski

Posthumous Revenge. Francis Saltus Saltus. VerBaPo

Postilion Has Been Struck by Lightning, The. Patricia Beer. OxBC

Postillion, The. Nikolaus Lenau. AuPH, *tr. by* Winthrop H. Root

Postman Cheval. André Breton. SPE, *tr. by* David Gascoyne

Postman comes when I am still in bed, The. Sick Child, A. Randall Jarrell. InPK-6; NoP-4; OxBC; VGW

Postman's Bell Is Answered Everywhere, The. Horace Gregory. MoAmPo

Postmaster-General cried: 'Arsehole!', The. Limerick. Victor Gray. PeLi

Postmen like doctors go from house to house. (LL) Aubade. Philip Larkin. AWTN; BodElec; CABP; NAEL-6v2; NoP-4; PoetW; SoSe-8; TRP

Postmodern: A Definition. Joseph Like. ReTh

Postmodern Maturity. Tony Towle. KGB

Postmortem. Maurice Kilwein Guevara. AmPoNex

Postponed Nightmare. Sandor Csoori. VCWP, *tr. by* Len Roberts and László Vértes

Postscript. R. L. Barth. CDa

Postscript. Henri Coulette. DiPo

Postscript. Ronald Stuart Thomas. FaBoMo; OxBC

Postscript, 1984. John Hewitt. BiHa

Postscript to a Pettiness. Arthur Seymour John Tessimond. OxBSP

Postscript to Orwell's *Animal Farm*, A. Miadesnia. PeLi

Postscript to Verses on the History of France, A. *Unknown.* NOIV

Postscripts 2. Dennis Brutus. HBAPE

Postscriptum. Mario Luzi. ItPo, *tr. by* Gayle Ridinger   *Fr.* Pieces from a Mortal Duet.

Posture of the tree, The. Lovers in Winter. Robert Graves. FaBoEE

Posy, A: "Dear love, I am resolved with thee to live." Sir Robert Aytoun [*or* Ayton]. NOSC

Posy [*or* Posie], The. George Herbert. ChIV-1; NOSC

Posy Ring, The. Clément Marot. AWP, *tr. by* Ford Madox Ford

Pot. Tiziano Rossi. ItPo, *tr. by* Gayle Ridinger

Pot Burial. Tom Paulin. ModIr

Pot of Flowers, The. William Carlos Williams. APT-1

Pot of Tea, A. Robert W. Service. PoWW

Pot of wine among flowers, A. Drinking Alone in the Moonlight. Li Po. AWP

Pot of wine among the flowers, A. Li Po. SuSp   *Fr.* Drinking Alone beneath the Moon.

Pot Roast. Mark Strand. AmFaPo

Pot Shot. Padraic Fallon. CIP-2

Potato. Michelle Boisseau. SpudSo

Potato. Jane Kenyon. SpudSo

Potato. Richard Wilbur. SpudSo

Potato, A. Robert Bly. SpudSo

Potato, The. Lillian E. Curtis. VerBaPo

Potato, The. Rochelle Ratner. SpudSo

Potato, The. Roderick Townley. SpudSo

Potato Blight. David Lindley. NLP

Potato Bug. Charles Webb. UrbNat

Potato Bug Exterminators. James McIntyre.
"When we do trace out nature's laws." VerBaPo

Potato Cellar. Meg Huber. SpudSo

Potato clock, a potato clock, A. Potato Clock. Roger McGough. OTCP

Potato Conflicts. Walter Bargen. SpudSo

Potato crops are flowering. Summer of Lost Rachel, The. Seamus Heaney. NIL-7

Potato Escape, A. Robley, Jr. Wilson. SpudSo

Potato: for want of it the Irish invaded Boston. On Hearing that a Potato Costs $70 in Sarajevo. Gloria Vando. SpudSo

Potato Garden. Jeanette Redenius. SpudSo

Potato Harvest, The. Sir Charles G. D. Roberts. NIL-7; NOBC

Potato is on the dishrack, The. Potato, The. Rochelle Ratner. SpudSo

Potato Pie. Abba Kovner. AF, *tr. by* Shirley Kaufman

Potato reminds one of an alert desert stone, The. And it belongs. Potato, A. Robert Bly. SpudSo

Potato, sojourner north, first sprung. In Praise of the Potato. David Williams. SpudSo

Potato Thief. Pentti Saarikoski. VCWP, *tr. by* Herbert Lomas

Potato was deep in the dark under ground. Tryst, The. John Banister Tabb. OBAL

Potato, you thunder along. Passacaglia. Lequita Vance-Watkins. SpudSo

Potatoes. David Donnell. NIP-4; NOBC; SpudSo

Potatoes. Eamon Grennan. SpudSo

Potatoes. Robert Peters. SpudSo

Potatoes. Daisy Rhau. SpudSo

Potatoes Coriander. Elise Paschen. SpudSo

Potatoes of the corner store sing, The. At Kino Viejo, Mexico. Alberto A. Ríos. NoAM

Potatoes of the Field, The. Thomas Michael McDade. SpudSo

Potatoes sit quietly on top of each other growing eyes, The. (LL) Potatoes. David Donnell. NIP-4; NOBC; SpudSo

Potatoes were a delicacy. Choice. Donna Trussell. SpudSo

Potflower on the windowsill says to me, The. Power of Suicide, The. Muriel Rukeyser. NALW

Potholes. Linda Hogan. UrbNat

Potlicker Blues. Calvin Forbes. GT

Potpourri from a Surrey Garden. Sir John Betjeman. NOBL; NPeEn

Potted Swan. Paul Dehn.

"Devil damn thee black, thou cream-faced loon—, The." OBCoV

Potter. Michael O'Reilly. BloBone

Potter, The. *Unknown.* TTY, *tr. by* Halim El-Dahb

Potter of Jaen, The. Ilya Grigoryevich Ehrenburg [*or* Erenburg]. TCRP, *tr. by* Cathy Porter

Potter's Field. Prageeta Sharma. HeMarv

Potter's Wheel, The. Calvin Forbes. GT

Potters I rose up with in a hurry. Contemporary. Alejandrino Hufana. ReBoTo

Pound at Spoleto. Lawrence Ferlinghetti. PoM

Pound bran all you please. Burmese Figures. *Unknown.* EaWin, *tr. by* W. S. Merwin

Pound-note was the best kind of passport, A. Emigration Trains, The. Thomas McCarthy. PBCIP

Pound stood at center stage of Caio Melisso. Two Worlds. Julia Older. TWW

Pounding Rain. Jackie Kay. MFPA; PoBW

Pour and say again and again and yet again. Meleager. HePo *Fr.* Epigrams.

Pour Commencer. Jon Stallworthy. NoAM

Pour for Heliodora Persuasion and pour for Cypris. Meleager. HePo *Fr.* Epigrams.

Pour l'Election de Son Sepulchre, I-V. Ezra Pound. *See* Hugh Selwyn Mauberley (Life and Contacts)

Pour O pour that parting soul in song. Song of the Son. Jean Toomer. ISC; MakPoe; NIL-7; NIP-4

Pour out the dark wine, Miriamne. Romancero. Lex Banning. NOBAu

Pour out, ye heav'ns, your veangence on his head. (LL) Philip Freneau. NAAL-2v1; NAAL-3 *Fr.* House of Night, The.

Pour out your light, O stars.Requiem. Ivor Gurney. FaBoEE; FaBoTw

Pour secrecy upon the dying page. (LL) I Held a Shelley Manuscript. Gregory Corso. BB; PmAP; VGW

Pour this wine. Meleager. GrAn

Pour Us Wine. *Var. authors.* AWP, *tr. by* E. Powys Mathers *Fr.* Mu'allaqat, The.

Pouring orange into GRAPE and grape into ORANGE forever. (LL) Ballad of Orange and Grape. Muriel Rukeyser. ChAP; NoAM; NoP-4

Pouring Out My Feelings after Parting from Yüan Chen. Po Chü-i. CoBCP, *tr. by* Burton Watson

Pousse y gâte, pousse y gâte. Luis d'Antin Van Rooten. OBCoV *Fr.* Mots d'Heures: Gousses, Rames.

Poussie, poussie, baudrons. *Unknown.* OxNR

Poverty. Theognis. AWP, *tr. by* John Hookham Frere

Poverty. Thomas Traherne. TrCP

Poverty. Yang Hsiung. ChiP, *tr. by* Arthur Waley

Poverty, in Imitation of Milton. Samuel Jones. NOEC

Poverty in London. Samuel Johnson. NOEC; NPeEn; OBSV; OxAEP-1 *Fr.* London: A Poem in Imitation of the Third Satire of Juvenal.

Poverty Knock. *Unknown.* FaBoVe

Poverty moved into my homestead. Abuse Poems: For Kodzo and Others. Komi Ekpe. PFTM-2, *tr. by* Kofi Awoonor

Poverty much maligned but beautiful. Mysteries of Small Houses. Alice Notley. ExTi

Poverty on the Bank. Mei Yao Ch'en. SuSp, *tr. by* Jonathan Chaves

Poverty, remorseless spectre. Christmas Eve, South, 1865. Mary E. Tucker. CBWP-1

Poverty? wealth? seek neither. Epigram. Kassia. WPOW, *tr. by* Patrick Diehl

Povre Ame Amoureuse. Louise Labé. AWP, *tr. by* Robert Bridges

Povre widwe [*or* wyde], somde[e]l stape in age, A. Geoffrey Chaucer. FHYEP; NAEL-6v1; NAWM-5v1 *Fr.* Canterbury Tales, The.

Powder-light let dust lie / On Musa, who had blue eyes. Epitaph in the Borghese Gardens. *Unknown.* GrAn, *tr. by* Peter Whigham

Powdered milk, chocolate bars, canned fruit, tea. Food Packages: 1947. Adrienne Rich. TaR

Powell (officer charged with the beating of rodney king). Lucille Clifton. RACG

(Powell march 1991.) ESEAA

Power. Hart Crane. MoAmPo *Fr.* Bridge, The.

Power. Audre Lorde. GLP; NoAM

Power. Adrienne Rich. ColAP; NALW; NIL-7; TAP

Power. Alma Villanueva. ItWoWo

Power above powers, O heavenly Eloquence. Samuel Daniel. NoSic *Fr.* Musophilus; or, Defence of All Learning.

Power and Light. James Dickey. NAAL-2v2

Power and Peace. Robert Herrick. CaPo

Power and the Glory, The. Siegfried Sassoon. OBMV

Power Cut. Seamus Deane. PBCIP

Power Equality. Party for your Right to Fight. Public Enemy. ISC

Power from God claimed [*or* claim'd *or* claym'd], than God himself[e] to trust. (LL) John Donne. BASC; EBEV; ESCV; FHYEP; FSCP; MeLP; NAEL-5v1; NAEL-6v1; NAEL-7v1; NoP-4; OxAEP-1; SacPr *Fr.* Satires.

Power-house, A. Classic Scene. William Carlos Williams. NAAL-2v2; OxBA

Power in the People, The. Robert Herrick. BASC; CaPo

Power is on the earth and in the air, A. Midsummer. William Cullen Bryant. GSo

Power of Destiny, The. Mary Whateley. ECWP

Power of Innocence, The. "C. G. H." NOEC

Power of Interval, The. John Byrne Leicester Warren, 3d Baron De Tabley. NOBVV; OxBSP

Power of Love, The. Charlotte Dacre. NOBRP

Power of Music, The. Thomas Lisle. NOBL

Power of One. Walta Borawski. CAGL

Power of Prayer, The. Samuel Johnson. NOBE *Fr.* Vanity of Human Wishes, The; The Tenth Satire of Juvenal Imitated.

Power of Prayer, The. Richard Chenevix Trench. PoToHe

Power of raven be thine. Good Wish. *Unknown.* FaBoCh

Power of Ridicule, The. Robert Bridges. NOBE

Power of Ridicule, The. Pope. *See* Epilogue to the Satires, in Two Dialogues

Power of Spleen, The. Anne Finch, Countess of Winchilsea. ECWP; NPeEn *Fr.* Spleen, a Pindaric Poem, The.

Power of Suicide, The. Muriel Rukeyser. NALW

Power of Taste, The. Zbigniew Herbert. PoSu; PoetW, *tr. by* John Carpenter and Bogdana Carpenter

Power of the awful wind, whose hollow blast. To Winter. Amelia Alderson Opie. CenSon

Power of the Soul. Sheilah Glover. HW

Power of Thought, The. Süsskind von Trimberg. TrJP

Power of Time, The. Jonathan Swift. FaBoEE

(Shall I Repine.) OxBSP

Power of Women, The. Matilda Barbara Betham-Edwards. ECWP

Power of Words, The. Letitia [*or* Laetitia] Elizabeth Landon. VWP

Power [*or* pow'r] must it maintain, A. (LL) Andrew Marvell. BASC; CABP; EBEV; ESCV; FSCP; GTBS-P; GeHe; HAP; NAEL-6v1; NAEL-7v1; NOBE; NOSC; NPeEn; NoP-4; OBEV; OBWP; OxAEP-1; OxBEV; PBRV; PoPoPo; SCGP; TFi

Power Quest, Sooke Park. Jarold Ramsey. PoCoUp

Power speaks only out of sleep and blackness, The. Below Loughrigg. Fleur Adcock. PeNZ

Power Station, The. James Merrill. CoAmPo

Power that dwelleth in sweet sounds to waken, The. Spirit's Mysteries, The. Felicia Dorothea Hemans. RWP

Power, that gives with liberal hand, The. On the Religion of Nature. Philip Freneau. NAAL-2v1; NAAL-3; NAAL-5

Power, the Enchanted World. George Oppen.

("Streets, in a poor district.") FTOS

Power Transformer. Ian Wedde. PeNZ *Fr.* Earthly: Sonnets for Carlos.

Powerful Servants. Friedrich von Logau. GePo, *tr. by* George C. Schoolfield

Powerless. Rawia Morra. PoArWo, *tr. by* Magdi Abdelhadi *Fr.* Ghurba.

Powerless emperor, The. Hard Listener, The. William Carlos Williams. OxBSP

Powerline Incarnation, The. Les A. Murray. CBAP

Powers of Darkness. Abraham Cowley. NOSC

Powers of the Pen, The. Evan Lloyd.
  Helen like the Rose. AngWePo; OBWVE

Powers of the Sonnet. Ebenezer Elliott. CenSon

Powers of Thirteen. John Hollander.
  "After the midwinter marriages—the bride of snow." VCAP
  "Like some ill-fated butterfly, the literalists." VCAP
  "So we came at last to meet, after the lights were out." VCAP
  "These two tales I tell of myself and the life I led." VCAP
  "What she and I had between us once, America." VCAP
  "Yes, go on! This is plain talk of plainer feelings now," VCAP

Powers that be in solemn conclave sat, The. A Bas la Gloire! Edward Wyndham Tennant. FaBoWar

Powhatan's Daughter. Hart Crane. *Fr.* Bridge, The.

P.O.W.s. R. L. Barth. CDa

Powwow. Carroll Arnett. LTA

Powwow. W. D. Snodgrass. SoSe-8

Powwow Polaroid. Sherman Alexie. UnSA

Powwow remnants. Lew Blockcolski. VoR

Pox fa that pultron Povertie. Francis Sempill. NePenScot *Fr.* Banishment of Poverty by His Royal Highness James Duke of Albany, The.

Pox of the statesman that's witty, A. Cabal at Nickey Nackey's, The. Aphra Behn. NOSC

Pox on't, says Time to Thomas Hearne. *Unknown.* FaBoEE

Pozo Basket, The. Glenna Luschei. GeoHom

Practice. Thomas Sayers Ellis. NAPBL; NeAmPo

Practice of Magical Evocation, The. Diane Di Prima. PmAP; PoM

"Practice your scream" I said. Jerome Rothenberg. FTOS; PFTM-2 *Fr.* Khurbn.

Practicing calligraphy, not noticing night had come. Calligraphy Practice. Ou-yang Hsiu. CoBCP, *tr. by* Burton Watson

Præfatory Poem to the Little Book, Entituled, Christianus per Ignem, A. Nicholas Noyes. SCAP

Prague in the Midday Sun. Vitězslau Nezval. AF, *tr. by* Ewald Osers

Prairie, The. Francis Ponge. AF, *tr. by* Beth Archer

Prairie Fires. Hamlin Garland. OBCA

Prairie-Grass Dividing, The. Walt Whitman. APN-1

Prairie Graveyard. Anne Marriott. NOBC

Prairie Houses. Barbara Guest. PmAP

Prairie Sunset, A. Walt Whitman. TCAPo

Prairie Waters by Night. Carl Sandburg. NAAL-2v2

Prairies, The. William Cullen Bryant. APN-1; ColAP; NAAL-2v1; NAAL-3; NAAL-5; NCAP; NOBA; OxBA; TAP; TCAPo
  "These are the gardens of the Desert, these." ITBLP

Prairies are broad, and the woodlands are wide, The. Stolen White Girl, The. John Rollin Ridge. APN-2

Praise. Jane Cooper. TAP

Praise. R. H. Grenville. PoToHe

Praise. Anne K. Smith. PasH

Praise. Henry Vaughan. ESCV

Praise (2). George Herbert. ChIV-1; ESCV

Praise and Prayer. Sir William Davenant [*or* D'Avenant]. OBEV *Fr.* Gondibert.

Praise Father, Son, and Holy Ghost. (LL) Morning Hymn. Thomas Ken. NOSC; SacPr

Praise for an Urn. Hart Crane. AWP; HAP; MoAmPo; NOBA; NoAM; OxBA; WeW-3

Praise for Mercies Spiritual and Temporal. Isaac Watts. NOEC

Praise for Sick Women. Gary Snyder. NeAP

Praise for the Fountain Opened. William Cowper. InPK-6 *Fr.* Olney Hymns.

"Praise God" said Spenser, "You live where you choose". Position of Praise, The. Brendan Kennelly. BiHa

Praise Hearst, from whom all blessings flow! Doxology. Bert Leston Taylor. OBAL

Praise him. (LL) Pied Beauty. Gerard Manley Hopkins. AWP; AmFaPo; CABP; ChAP; ClHu; EBVV; EnlH; FaBoMo; GTBS-P; HAP; HeIP-4; ITBLP; InPK-6; InvLi; MoBrPo; NAEL-5v2; NAEL-6v2; NIL-7; NOBE; NOBVV; NPeEn; NoAM; NoP-4; OBEV; OBMV; OxAEP-2; OxBEV; OxBSP; PoE; PoPoPo; PoRA; RB; RaBo; SCGP; SCV; SacPr; SoSe-8; TFi; TTTS; UV; WeW-3

Praise him that ay[e]. Bible, *O.T.* ChIV-1; OxBEV, *tr. by* Mary Sidney Herbert, Countess of Pembroke *Fr.* Psalms.

Praise Him Who Makes Us Happy. Mark Van Doren. AH

Praise in Summer. Richard Wilbur. NoP-4

Praise is a quiet and a gracious thing. Praise. R. H. Grenville. PoToHe

Praise is devotion fit for mighty minds. Sir William Davenant [*or* D'Avenant]. OBEV *Fr.* Gondibert.

Praise memory and forgetfulness! Macedonius. GrAn

Praise Now Your God. H. P. Brucker. AH

Praise of a Collie. Norman MacCaig. NePenScot; RB

Praise of a Yellow Skin, The, or An Elizabeth in Gold. John Collop. NOSC

Praise, of course, is best: plain speech breeds hate. Meditation. Palladas [*or* Pallades]. GrAn, *tr. by* Dudley Fitts

Praise of Dancing, The. Sir John Davies. NOBE *Fr.* Orchestra; or, A Poem[e] of Da[u]ncing.

Praise of Diseases. Jacopone da Todi. WoPoe, *tr. by* L. R. Lind

Praise of Dust, The. Gilbert Keith Chesterton. MoBrPo

Praise of Faith, The. John Hall. ChIV-2

Praise of God. *Unknown.* NOIV

Praise of Godly Love Out of 1 John. 4, The. John Hall. ChIV-2

Praise of His Lady, A. John Heywood. OBEV

Praise of Italian Chip-Shops. W. N. Herbert. NeBl

Praise of Little Women. Juan Ruiz, Archpriest of Hita. AWP, *tr. by* Henry Wadsworth Longfellow

Praise of Neptune's empery, The. (LL) Hymn in Praise of Neptune, A. Thomas Campion. NOBE; OBEV

Praise of Spenser. William Browne (1591–1643). OxAEP-1

Praise of Transitoriness. Hans Leifhelm. AuPH, *tr. by* Lowell A. Bangerter

Praise of Waterford, The. *Unknown.*
  "God of his goodnes, praysed that he be." NOIV

Praise of Women. Robert Mannyng [*or* Manning]. OBEV

Praise, Oh You Heavens, the Highest on High. Laurentius von Schnüffis. AuPH, *tr. by* Lowell A. Bangerter and George C. Schoolfield

Praise Poem to Christ, A. Catrin Ferch Gruffydd ab Ieuan ap Llywelyn Fychan. EMWP

Praise Psalm of the City-Dweller. April Bernard. NIL-7

Praise Song for My Mother. Grace Nichols. Prnts

Praise Song for the Oba of Benin. *Unknown.* WoPoe, *tr. by* John Bradbury

Praise the Lord. John Milton. FaBoCh

Praise the Tortilla, Praise the Menudo, Praise the Chorizo. Ray Gonzales. UnSA

Praise to God, immortal praise. Anna Laetitia Barbauld. SacPr

Praise to my older brother, the seventeen-year-old boy. Attic, The. Marie Howe. ExTi

Praise to skies. Hoyu. JDP, *tr. by* Yoel Hoffmann

Praise to the emptiness that blanks out existence. Existence. Jelaluddin [*or* Jalal al-Din] Rumi. EnlH

Praise to the End! Theodore Roethke.
  "Mips and ma the mooly moo." NBLV; RB

Praise to the Holiest in the height. John Henry, Cardinal Newman. NOCV *Fr.* Dream of Gerontius, The.

Praise to the Holy Creator, who has placed his throne upon. Invocation to the Conference of the Birds. Farid-uddin Attar. BBASP, *tr. by* C.S. Nott

Praise to the Lord, the Almighty, the King of creation. Praise to the Lord the Almighty. Joachim Neander. SacPr, *tr. by* Catherine Winkworth

Praise to the Rich. Marina Ivanovna Tsvetayeva [*or* Tsvetaeva]. TCRP, *tr. by* Elaine Feinstein and Angela Livingstone

Praise to the Tattoo Mistress. Mririda n'Ait Attik. WoPoe, *tr. by* Daniel Halpern and Paula Paley

Praise we the Lord / of Heaven's kingdom. Caedmon's Hymn. Caedmon. EBEV

Praise ye the Lord for the avenging of Israel. Bible, *O.T.* AWP; BoWoP *Fr.* Judges.

Praise Ye the Lord, O Celebrate His Fame. Peleg Folger. AH; ChIV-1

Praise you, "All these were lovely"; say, "He loved." (LL) Great Lover, The. Rupert Brooke. MoBrPo; PoRA

Praise youth's hot blood if you will, I think that happiness. Age in Prospect. Robinson Jeffers. MoAmPo

Prais[e]d be Diana[']s fair[e] and harmles[s] light. Homage to Diana. Sir Walter Ralegh. NPeEn; NoSic

Praised be God, and Lord Jesus, Lord Jesus. Three Kings of Bethlehem, The. Attila József. IQMS, *tr. by* Istvan Fekete

Praised be man, he is existing in milk. Jack Kerouac. NeAP; PmAP *Fr.* Mexico City Blues.

Praised be the moon of books! that doth above. In the Reading-Room of the Brtish Museum. Louise Imogen Guiney. APN-2

Praised be the name of the Lord, who created the wine. Five Arabic Verses in Praise of Wine. *Unknown.* TrJP, *tr. by* Hartwig Hirschfeld

Praised be the poet, who the sonnet's claim. To Mr. Henry Cary, On the Publication of his Sonnets. Anna Seward. CenSon

Praised beyond all Enids be. In Morfudd's Arms. Dafydd [*or* David] ap Gwilym. OBWVE, *tr. by* Rolfe Humphries

Praisers of women in their proud and beautiful poems, The. Not Marble nor the Gilded Monuments. Archibald MacLeish. BoLoP; PoRA; TwCP

Praises, The. Charles Olson. VGW

Praises of a Country Life, The. Horace. BASC, *tr. by* Ben Jonson *Fr.* Epodes.

Praises of Field-marshal J. C. Smuts, The. Nongejeni Zuma. PeSAV, *tr. by* Harry C. Lugg

Praises of the Bantu Kings (1–10). Jerome Rothenberg. FTOS

Praises of the Canna, The. *Unknown.* PeSAV, *tr. by* John Croumbie Brown

Praises, Tamalpais. Song of the Turkey Buzzard. Lew Welch. PoM

Praises to Him for aye! (LL) For Deliverance from a Fever. Anne Bradstreet. NAAL-2v1; NAAL-3; NALW

Praises to those who can wait. Zealots of Yearning. David Rokeah [*or* Rokeakh]. TrJP, *tr. by* I. M. Lask

Praising Thy worth, despite his cruel hand. (LL) William Shakespeare. CABP; EBEV; NAEL-7v1; NIP-4; NOBE; NoSic; OxAEP-1; OxBSo; PoRA; SCGP; Son; TFi; TreFP; UnPo *Fr.* Sonnets.

Prater's Tree-Lined Boulevard. Friedrich Torberg. AuPH, *tr. by* Lowell A. Bangerter

Praxinoa at home? Theocritus. HePo, *tr. by* Barbara Hughes Fowler *Fr.* Idylls.

Pray Billy Pitt explain thy rigs. On Mr. Pitt's [*or* Pit's] Hair-Powder Tax. Robert Burns. FaBoEE

Pray but one prayer for me 'twixt thy closed lips. Summer Dawn. William Morris. GSo; NOBE; NOBVV; OBEV; OxAEP-2; OxBEV

Pray for my soul. More things are wrought by prayer. Tennyson. SacPr *Fr.* Idylls of the King.

Pray for the Lovers. Jayne Cortez. ISC

Pray how did she look? Was she pale, was she wan? On Lady Anne Hamilton. Richard Brinsley Sheridan. FaBoEE; NPeEn; OBCoV

Pray keep them safe at home. (LL) Three Children. Mother Goose. LB; NOBL; OxNR; ReMoGo

Pray Remember the Poor. Christopher Smart. NOEC *Fr.* Hymns for the Amusement of Children.

Pray steal me not, I'm Mrs. Dingley's. On the Collar of Mrs. Dingley's Lap-Dog. Jonathan Swift. FaBoEE

Pray tell me, sir, whose dog are you? (LL) Epigram Engraved on the Collar of a Dog Given [*or* Which I Gave] to His Royal Highness. Pope. FaBoEE; InPK-6; KaS; NOEC; NTCP; OxBEV; OxBSP; PAI

Pray thee, take care, that tak'st my book[e] in hand. To the Reader. Ben Jonson. BASC; BeJo; NoP-4; PoE

Pray to What Earth Does This Sweet Cold Belong. Henry David Thoreau. NCAP; UnPo

Pray where would lamb and lion be. Nature Be Damned. Anne Wilkinson. NOBC

Pray who lies here? why don't you know. Original Epitaph on a Drunkard. Royall Tyler. OBAL

Pray why are you so bare, so bare. Haunted Oak, The. Paul Laurence Dunbar. ColAP; NAAAL; UnPo

Pray why should any man complain. On Sir G. B. his defeat. Alexander Brome. PBRV

Pray you fetch him hither. William Shakespeare. NPeEn *Fr.* Cymbeline.

Prayer. Daniel Berrigan. AF

Prayer. Lucille Clifton. NAAAL

Prayer. Hartley Coleridge. GSo

Prayer. Hartley Coleridge. GSo

Prayer. Hartley Coleridge. GSo

Prayer. Elaine Feinstein. HarvBoo

Prayer. Dana Gioia. NoP-4

Prayer. Dorianne Laux. OPRER

Prayer. Gabriela Mistral.

    "Like those jars that women put out to catch the dew of night." WPoS

Prayer. James Montgomery. SacPr

Prayer. Kathleen Jessie Raine. BBASP

Prayer. Rudaki. WoPoe, *tr. by* Geoffrey Squires

Prayer. Grace Schulman. PuP-23

Prayer. Jean Toomer. NAAAL

Prayer. Hugo Williams. EmeKit; NPeEn

Prayer, A. Max Ehrmann. PoToHe

Prayer, A. Sir Thomas More. InvLi

Prayer, A. Katharine Tynan. SacPr

Prayer, The. John Galsworthy. UV

Prayer, The. Jones Very. APN-1; OxBA; TrCP

Prayer (1): "Prayer the Church's banquet, Angels' age." George Herbert. AngWePo; BASC; EBEV; ESCV; GSo; GeHe; NAEL-5v1; NAEL-6v1;

NAEL-7v1; NOBE; NOSC; NoP-4; OBWVE; OxAEP-1; OxBSo; PeECV; PoE; PoPoPo; TFi; TOF

(Prayer the Churches banquet, Angels age.) FSCP; NPeEn; OxBEV; PBRV; SacPr

Prayer 20. Catherine of Siena (A. K. A. Saint Catherine).

    "We were enclosed." WPoS

Prayer, A: "Eternal God, our life is but." "Yehoash." TrJP, *tr. by* Isidore Goldstick

Prayer, A: "I pray Thee O Lord." Julian [*or* Juljan] Tuwim. TrJP, *tr. by* Wanda Dynowska

Prayer, A: "If I popped in at Downing Street." Max Beerbohm. UV

Prayer, A: "My soul doth pant towards thee." Jeremy Taylor. SacPr

Prayer, A: "O beauteous God! uncircumscribed treasure." Jeremy Taylor. SacPr

Prayer, A: "O Lord, the hard-won miles." Paul Laurence Dunbar. SacPr

Prayer, A: "O that mine eyes might closed be." Thomas Elwood. PWR

Prayer, A: "Oh, Lord! I lift my heart." Priscilla Jane Thompson. CBWP-2

Prayer, A: "Searcher of souls, you who in heaven abide." Samuel Butler (1835–1902). FaBoEE

Prayer, A: "When I look back upon my life nigh spent." George Macdonald. SacPr

Prayer After War. Endre Ady. IQMS, *tr. by* Anton N. Nyerges

Prayer after World War. Carl Sandburg. VGW

Prayer at Night. Alcuin. MLL, *tr. by* Helen Waddell

Prayer at the Winter Solstice, A. *Zuni Oral Tradition.*

    "Perhaps if we are lucky." NAWM-7v2, *tr. by* Ruth L. Bunzel

Prayer Before Birth. Louis MacNeice. FaBoVe; GTBS-P; HarvBoo; PNI; TwCP

Prayer before Sleep. Alice Lucas. TrJP

Prayer: "Fear of death disturbs me constantly, The." Gabrielle de Coignard. WPOW, *tr. by* Raymond Oliver

Prayer for a Day's Walk. Grace Noll Crowell. PoToHe

Prayer for a Second Flood. Hugh MacDiarmid. EBEV

Prayer for a Thief. Phil DuPlessis. PeSAV, *tr. by* the author

Prayer for Broken Little Families, A. Violet Alleyn Storey. PoToHe

Prayer for Charity, A. Jeremy Taylor. SacPr

Prayer for Dew. Eleazar ben Kalir. TrJP, *tr. by* Israel Zangwill

Prayer for Every Day. *Unknown.* PBA, *tr. by* Kweku Martin

Prayer for Every Day, A. Mary Carolyn Davies. PoToHe

Prayer for Faith, A. Margaret Elizabeth Sangster. PoToHe

Prayer for His Wife and Children, Written in Newgate. George Wither. SacPr

Prayer for Indifference, A. Fanny [*or* Frances] Macartney Greville. ECWP; NOEC; OxBEV

    ("I ask no kind return in love.") LW

    "I ask no kind return in love." OBEV

Prayer for Marilyn Monroe. Ernesto Cardenal. TCLAP, *tr. by* Robert Pring-Mill

Prayer for My Daughter, A. W. B. Yeats. HAP; NAEL-5v2; NAEL-6v2; NoAM; NoP-4; OxBTC; PoRA; RaBo; TFi

Prayer for My Son. James Applewhite. BLT

Prayer for My Son, A. W. B. Yeats. EBEV; OxAEP-2; RaBo

Prayer for Peace. Léopold Sédar Senghor.

    "Lord God, forgive white Europe!" TTY

    "Lord Jesus, at the end of this book which I offer you." NegPo

Prayer for Peace, A. Severn Teackle Wallis. CBCWP

Prayer for Purification, A. Michelangelo Buonarroti. AWP, *tr. by* John Addington Symonds

Prayer for Redemption. *Unknown.* TrJP

Prayer for Shut-Ins. Ruth Winant Wheeler. PoToHe

Prayer for Strength. Margaret E. Bruner. PoToHe

Prayer for the End of the Century, A. Heberto Padilla. VCWP

Prayer for the Great Family. Gary Snyder. HAP; WeW-3

Prayer for the Great Lunatic. László Mécs. IQMS, *tr. by* Paul Tabori

Prayer for the Journey. *Unknown.* SacPr

Prayer for the Little Daughter between Death and Burial. Diana Scott. BrRo

Prayer for the Living, A. Asha Bandele. InTrad

Prayer for the Speedy End of Three Great Misfortunes. *Unknown.* OBMV, *tr. by* Frank O'Connor

Prayer for This House. Louis Untermeyer. PoToHe

Prayer: "Forgive me, you whom they cast in a name." Avraham Shlonsky. MHP

Prayer Found in Chester Cathedral, A. Thomas Henry Basil Webb. PoToHe

Prayer: "God, I need a job because I need money." Alan Dugan. NoAM

Prayer: "God, though [*or* although] this life is but a wraith." Louis Untermeyer. MoAmPo; TrJP

Prayer: "Grant that no Hobgoblins fright me." John Day. Spl

Prayer: "If I must of my Senses lose." Theodore Roethke. TwCP

Prayer in Darkness, A. Gilbert Keith Chesterton. MoBrPo

Prayer in Four Verses. Pak Mokwŏl. WoPoe, *tr.* by Kim Chong-gil

Prayer in Spring, A. Robert Frost. AH; TrCP

Prayer: "In the bright bay of your morning, O God." Claire Goll. TrJP, *tr.* by Babette Deutsch and Avrahm Yarmolinsky

Prayer, in the Prospect of Death, A. Robert Burns. TreFP

Prayer is the little implement. Emily Dickinson. APN-2

Prayer: "Let my words." Joseph Bruchac. UnSA

Prayer, Living and Dying, A. Augustus Montague Toplady. *See* Rock of Ages

Prayer: "Lord I am not entirely selfish." Gavin Ewart. OxBC

Prayer: "Lord, stand up for the Soviets." Nikolai Ivanovich Glazkov. TCRP, *tr.* by Daniel Weissbort

Prayer: "Master, they say that when I seem." Clive Staples Lewis. SacPr; TrCP

Prayer: "Matthew, Mark, Luke, and John." *Unknown. See* Before Sleeping

Prayer: "Nobody understands so let the Rabbi." Stephen Berg. TaR

Prayer: "O Christ, who in Gethsemane." Henrietta Cordelia Ray. CBWP-3

Prayer: "O let me soar on steadfast wing." Dennis Brutus. AF

Prayer of a Woman in Charge of Berry Picking in Knights Inlet. *Unknown.* WPoS

Prayer of an Unbeliever. Lizette Woodworth Reese. SacPr

Prayer of an Unemployed Man. W. C. Ackerly. PoToHe

Prayer of Any Husband. Mazie V. Caruthers. PoToHe

Prayer of Columbus. Walt Whitman.

Prayer of Dedication. Cosi Fabian. HW

Prayer of Hezekiah, The. George Wither. ChIV-1

Prayer of Jabez, too, should be our prayer, The. Prayer of Jabez, The. Jones Very. ChIV-1

Prayer of Mothers Who Unintentionally Failed Their Children. Vivian Lamarque. CItWP, *tr.* by Cinzia Sartini Blum and Lara Trubowitz

Prayer of Nature, The. Byron. TreFP

Prayer of Nehemiah, The. George Wither. ChIV-1

Prayer of Richard De Castre. Richard of Caistre. SacPr

Prayer of St. Francis of Assisi for Peace. Saint Francis of Assisi. PoToHe

Prayer of the Maidens to Mary. Rainer Maria Rilke. AWP, *tr.* by Jethro Bithell

Prayer of the Old Woman. François Villon. MoBrPo; PeECV, *tr.* by J. M. Synge

Prayer of the Venerable Bede. The Venerable Bede. MLL, *tr.* by Helen Waddell

Prayer: "Oh, God, beyond the wit of the genius." Dániel Berzsenyi. IQMS, *tr.* by Peter Zollman

Prayer on the Threshold of Tomorrow. Vahan Tekeyan. AF, *tr.* by Diana Der Hovanessian and Marzbed Margossian

Prayer: "Pray for my soul. More things are wrought by prayer." Tennyson. SacPr *Fr.* Idylls of the King.

Prayer: "Some days, although we cannot pray, a prayer." Carol Ann Duffy. HarvBoo; NePenScot; NoP-4; OxBSo

Prayer That Will Be Answered, A. Anna Kamienska. BLT, *tr.* by Stanislaw Baranczak

Prayer the Church's banquet, Angels' age. Prayer (1): "Prayer the Church's banquet, Angels' age." George Herbert. AngWePo; BASC; EBEV; ESCV; GSo; GeHe; NAEL-5v1; NAEL-6v1; NAEL-7v1; NOBE; NOSC; NoP-4; OBWVE; OxAEP-1; OxBSo; PeECV; PoE; PoPoPo; TFi; TOF

Prayer the Churches banquet, Angels age. George Herbert. *See* Prayer the Church's banquet, Angels' age

Prayer: "Thy blessing on the boys—for time has come." Haim [*or* Chaim *or* Khayim] Guri [*or* Gouri]. TrJP, *tr.* by Ruth H. Lask

Prayer to Aphrodite. Sappho. WoPoe, *tr.* by Alfred Corn

Prayer to Be with Mercurial Women. Roddy Lumsden. NeBl

Prayer to Eve, A. Kathleen Norris. HW

Prayer to Go to Paradise with the Asses. Francis Jammes. AWP, *tr.* by Jethro Bithell

Prayer to Go to Paradise with the Donkeys, A. Francis Jammes. RB; WoPoe, *tr.* by Richard Wilbur

Prayer to God. Esther Kello. EMWP

Prayer to God. "Placido." TTY, *tr.* by Raoul Abdul

Prayer to God the Father. Hildebert. MLL, *tr.* by Helen Waddell

Prayer to God the Father. Marbod of Rennes. MLL, *tr.* by Helen Waddell

Prayer to Hermes. Robert Creeley. PoM

Prayer to Hymen. *Unknown.* NOSC

Prayer to Isis. Christina Walsh. BrRo

Prayer to Jesus 1. Richard Rolle of Hampole. SacPr

Prayer to my lady of Paphos. Sappho. HW, *tr.* by Mary Barnard

Prayer to My Mother. Pier Paolo Pasolini. VCWP

Prayer to Saint Grobianus. Roger McGough. NOxBChV

Prayer to the Divine Mother, A. Andrew Harvey. HW

Prayer to the Father of [*or* in] Heaven, A. John Skelton. SacPr

Prayer to the God Thot. *Unknown.* TTY, *tr.* by Ulli Beier

Prayer to the Gods of the Night. *Unknown.* WoPoe, *tr.* by David Ferry

Prayer to the Lord Ramakrishna, A. James Wright (1927–80). NNaP

Prayer to the Masks. Léopold Sédar Senghor. NegPo, *tr.* by Ellen Conroy Kennedy

Prayer to the Muse of Ordinary Life. Kate Daniels. ExTi

Prayer to the New Year, A. Fadwa Tuqan [*or* Tuquan]. PoArWo, *tr.* by Samira Kawar

Prayer to the Pacific. Leslie Marmon Silko. CDW; NoP-4; PoPoPo; VoR; WeW-3

Prayer to the Sockeye Salmon. *Unknown.* WPoS; WoPoe, *tr.* by Jane Hirshfield

Prayer to the Spirit of the New Year. Bobbi Sykes. IBA

Prayer to the Virgin of Chartres. Henry Adams. APT-1

Prayer to the Wind, A. Thomas Carew. BeJo; CavPo

Prayer unsaid, and mass unsung. George Darley. BIrV *Fr.* Syren Songs.

Prayer unto Christ the Judge of the World, A. Michael Wigglesworth. SCAP

Prayer upon Cutting down the Sacred Tree. *Unknown.* APN-2, *tr.* by John G. Bourke

Prayer: "What do you take." Bill Manhire. PeNZ

Prayer: "You dark eye, o rest upon me." Nikolaus Lenau. AuPH, *tr.* by Winthrop H. Root

Prayer: "You may be right, divinity." Francis Sullivan. CRP

Prayers. Henry Charles Beeching. OBEV; SacPr

Prayers, The. Brian Coffey. Oth

Prayers and Games of the Water People, The. Veno Taufer.
"Mother loves me loves me not." WoPoe, *tr.* by Milne Holton

Prayers, Dorcas, Fellowship, and Children's Groups! Gwladys Rhys. W. J. Gruffydd. OBWVE, *tr.* by Myrddin Lloyd

Prayers: I. Kadya Molodovsky [*or* Molodowsky]. WPoS, *tr.* by Kathryn Hellerstein

Prayers of Steel. Carl Sandburg. MoAmPo; SSCS; TrCP

Prayerwheel: 2. David Meltzer. NeAP

Praying. P. J. Kavanagh. OxBSP

Praying and to be married? It was rare. Isaac's Marriage. Henry Vaughan. ChIV-1

Praying Drunk. Andrew Hudgins. RA

Praying mantis doesn't pray, The. Mantis. David McCord. OBAL

Praysing that Greeke who did these mysteries find. Argument of the Third Booke, The. Lucy Hutchinson. EMWP

Pre-eminent among scholars. Martial. RomPo, *tr.* by Peter Whigham

Pre-Memory. Nikolai Stepanovich Gumilyov [*or* Gumiliov *or* Gumilev]. TCRusP, *tr.* by Denis Johnson and Kathy Lewis

Pre-Raphaelite Notebook, A. Geoffrey Hill. NoAM

Preacher, The. Al-Mahdi. TTY, *tr.* by A. J. Arberry

Preacher and the Slave, The. Joe Hill. APT-1

Preacher quoted, and the cranks, The. Bad Break!, A. W. T. Goodge. NOBAu

Preacher's Mistake, The. William Croswell Doane. PoToHe

Preacher, The: Ruminates behind the Sermon. Gwendolyn Brooks. InvLi; NAAAL *Fr.* Street in Bronzeville, A.

Preacher took from *Solomon's Song*, The. Rose Window. Herman Melville. APN-2

Preamble = sardanapalus. Tristan Tzara. PFTM-1 *Fr.* Dada Manifesto on Feeble and Bitter Love.

Precambrian [*or* Pre-Cambrian] Shield, The. Edwin John Pratt. MoCV; NOBC *Fr.* Towards the Last Spike.

Precautions. Martin Sorescu. VCWP, *tr.* by Paul Muldoon and Joana Russell-Gebbett

Precede me into this elusive country. Caravan, The. Gwendolyn MacEwen. MoCV

Precede us, O Lord, with Thy Grace. Limerick. Frank R. McManus. PeLi

Precedence. Horatius Bonar. SacPr

Precept of Silence, The. Lionel Pigot Johnson. MoBrPo; SacPr

Precepts for City Living. Vladimir Burich. TCRusP, *tr.* by Daniel Weissbort

Precepts He Gave His Folk. Elijah ben Menahem Hazaken, of LeMans. TrJP, *tr.* by Israel Zangwill

Precincts at day, quiet leisure of spring, The. Written in the Office Precincts. Wang T'ing-hsiang. CoBLCP, *tr.* by Jonathan Chaves

Preciosa and the Wind. Federico García Lorca. STV, *tr.* by John Frederick Nims

Precious Child, So Sweetly Sleeping. Anna Hoppe. AH

Precious Five. W. H. Auden. PeECV

Precious in the light of the early sun the Housatonic. From a Train Window. Edna St. Vincent Millay. GM

Precious Lord, take my hand. Take My Hand, Precious Lord. Thomas A. Dorsey. APT-2; ISC

Precious Lord, take my hand. Take My Hand, Precious Lord. *Unknown.* NAAAL

Precious—moldering pleasure—'tis, A. Emily Dickinson. APN-2

Precious Moments. Carl Sandburg. MoAmPo

Precious night-blooming cereus. Remembering Fannie Lou Hamer. Thadious M. Davis. BlSi

Precious Pearl, The. Priscilla Jane Thompson. CBWP-2

Precious Stones. Christina Georgina Rossetti. ChAP *Fr.* Sing-Song.

Precious stones that my mother. Yocheved Bat-Miriam. FIT, *tr. by* Robert Friend

Precious Things. *Unknown. See* Hold my Rooster

Precipice. Sang Yi. PFTM-1 *Fr.* Critical Condition.

Precipice, The. Judith Wright. BMAP

Precipitous point—river and lake. Climbing P'iao-miao Peak. Wu Wei-yeh. CoBLCP, *tr. by* Jonathan Chaves

Precise counterpart, The. Orchestra, The. William Carlos Williams. HAP

Precise German documentary reveals the horrors of Auschwitz, The. Shame. Matilde Salganicoff. MirDau, *tr. by* Celeste Kostopulos-Cooperman

Precisely because I do not have. Precisely. Daisy Zamora. LoL, *tr. by* Margaret Randall

Precisely because you are alive. Word before the Last about Loss, A. Linda Zisquit. DTA

Precisely the way you divide your small change between two. Paavo Haavikko. WoPoe, *tr. by* Anselm Hollo *Fr.* Fifteen Epigrams in Praise of the Tyrant.

Precisely their necessity. (LL) Emily Dickinson. PoToHe; Spl

Precision, A. Winter Voyage. Anne-Marie Albiach. PFTM-2, *tr. by* Joseph Simas

Precision, The. Yvor Winters. SPE

Precision German Craftsmanship. Matthew Rohrer. NAPBL; NeAmPo

Precursors. Louis MacNeice. OxBSP

Predator's excuse is always good, The. Lamb and the Wolves, The. Ignacy Krasicki. WoPoe, *tr. by* Jerzy Peterkiewicz and Burns Singer

Predestination. Robert Herrick. SacPr

Predicament: a corner of / a room. Tenant at Number 9. John Blight. CBAP

Predicter of Famine, The. William Carlos Williams. APT-1; VGW

Prediction. Michael Lieberman. BloBone

Prediction, The. Mark Strand. LCAP-2; NoP-4; SPE; VCAP

Preface: "Artist is the creator of beautiful things, The." Oscar Wilde. NAEL-5v2 *Fr.* Picture of Dorian Gray, The.

Preface or The Drama of Absence in an Eternal Heart. Roger Gilbert-Lecomte. PFTM-1

Preface: "Rigor of beauty is the quest. But how will you find beauty when it is locked." William Carlos Williams. NoAM *Fr.* Paterson.

Preface Shrink Lit: Elements of Style. Maurice Sagoff. NBLV

Preface: "Sonja Henie, the young girl." Theodore Weiss. VGW

Preface, The: "Infinity, when all things it beheld." Edward Taylor. HAP; NAAL-2v1; NAAL-3; NOBA; NOSC; OxBA; OxBEV; SCAP; TCAPo *Fr.* God's Determinations [touching his Elect].

Preface to a Twenty Volume Suicide Note. Imamu Amiri Baraka. AmFaPo; BB; ESEAA; NAAAL; PoM; TTY

Preface to I Am Rain. Hilary Booth. SurWo

Preface: "To make a start." William Carlos Williams. NOBA; NoAM *Fr.* Paterson.

Preface to the Memoirs, A. James Merrill. NOBA

Preface to *The Progress of Learning.* Sir John Denham. NOSC; OxBSP

Preface to the Suite: "Childhood, boyhood, young manhood." Robert Duncan. FTOS *Fr.* Poems from the Margins of Thom Gunn's Moly.

Prefatory Epistle, A. Maria Falconar. ECWP

Prefatory Poem, on. . . *Magnalia Christi Americana.* Nicholas Noyes. SCAP

Preference. Langston Hughes. APSN; HCAP; NOBA

Preference. Elinor Wylie. APT-1

Preference Declared, The. Horace. InPK-6; NBLV, *tr. by* Eugene Field *Fr.* Odes.

Pregnancy. Sandra McPherson. BoWoP; LoL

Pregnant again. Janice Bostok. HA

Pregnant girl, under sorrow's sign, A. Under Sorrow's Sign. Gofraidh Fionn O'Dalaigh. BIrV, *tr. by* John Montague

Pregnant lady playing tennis, The. Pregnant Lady Playing Tennis, The. Karen Volkman. AmPoNex

Pregnant Poets Swim Lake Tarleton, New Hampshire. Barbara Ras. NAPBL

Pregnant Woman. Ingrid Jonker. HAWP, *tr. by* Jack Cope and William Plomer

Prehistoric Burials. Siegfried Sassoon. MoBrPo

Preiching of the Swallow, The. Robert Henryson. OxBS

Prejudice. Lizelia Augusta Jenkins Moorer. CBWP-3

Prejudice against Colour. Langham Dale. PeSAV

Preliminary Poem. John Heath-Stubbs. OxBC

Preliminary Studies for the Frankfurt Readings 1984. Ernst Jandl. PFTM-2, *tr. by* Jerome Rothenberg

Preliminary to Classroom Lecture. Josephine Miles. NoAM

Prelude. Marilyn Chin. LoL

Prelude. René Depestre. NegPo, *tr. by* Ellen Conroy Kennedy *Fr.* Epiphanies of the Voodoo Gods.

Prelude. Federico García Lorca. PFTM-1

Prelude I: "Winter for a moment takes the mind; the snow." Conrad Potter Aiken. APT-1; OxBA *Fr.* Preludes for Memnon; or, Preludes to Attitude.

Prelude II: "Two coffees in the Español, the last." Conrad Potter Aiken. APT-1; NoAM *Fr.* Preludes for Memnon; or, Preludes to Attitude.

Prelude VI: "This is not you? These phrases are not you?" Conrad Potter Aiken. MoAmPo *Fr.* Preludes for Memnon; or, Preludes to Attitude.

Prelude VII: "Beloved, let us once more praise the rain." Conrad Potter Aiken. UnPo *Fr.* Preludes for Memnon; or, Preludes to Attitude.

Prelude XIV: "You went to the verge, you say, and came back safely." Conrad Potter Aiken. FaBoMo; TwCP *Fr.* Preludes for Memnon; or, Preludes to Attitude.

Prelude XIX: "Watch long enough, and you will see the leaf." Conrad Potter Aiken. OxBA *Fr.* Preludes for Memnon; or, Preludes to Attitude.

Prelude XXVIII: "Time has come, the clock says time has come, The." Conrad Potter Aiken. OxBA *Fr.* Preludes for Memnon; or, Preludes to Attitude.

Prelude XXIX: "What shall we do--what shall we think--what shall we say?" Conrad Potter Aiken. FaBoMo *Fr.* Preludes for Memnon; or, Preludes to Attitude.

Prelude XXXIII: "Then came I to the shoreless shore of silence." Conrad Potter Aiken. OxBA *Fr.* Preludes for Memnon; or, Preludes to Attitude.

Prelude XLII: "Keep in the heart the journal nature keeps." Conrad Potter Aiken. OxBA *Fr.* Preludes for Memnon; or, Preludes to Attitude.

Prelude LVI: "Rimbaud and Verlaine, precious pair of poets." Conrad Potter Aiken. FaBoMo; NoAM; TwCP *Fr.* Preludes for Memnon; or, Preludes to Attitude.

Prelude LVII: "One star fell and another as we walked." Conrad Potter Aiken. MoAmPo *Fr.* Preludes for Memnon; or, Preludes to Attitude.

Prelude: "Along the roadside, like the flowers of gold." John Greenleaf Whittier. APN-1; NAAL-2v1; OxBA *Fr.* Among the Hills.

Prelude: "As one, at midnight, wakened by the call." Wilfrid Wilson Gibson. MoBrPo

Prelude: "England! awake! awake! awake!" William Blake. FHYEP *Fr.* Jerusalem; The Emanation of the Giant Albion.

Prelude, Spoken to My Work Tools. Aleksey [*or* Aleksei] Ivanovich Parshchikov. TCRP, *tr. by* John High

Prelude: "Still south I went and west and south again." John Millington Synge. AWP; MoBrPo; OBMV

Prelude, The; Growth of a Poet's Mind [1850 vers.]. William Wordsworth. Books.

(Boy of Winander, The.) PoE

"He, who in his youth." TOF

"Here must we pause; this only let me add." NAEL-6v2

"Oh! why hath not the mind." NAEL-6v2

Cambridge and the Alps.

"That very day." NAEL-6v2

"When from the Vallais we had turned, and clomb." TOF

"When the third summer freed us from restraint." NAEL-6v2

France (Concluded).

"I summoned my best skill, and toiled, intent." NAEL-6v2

"O pleasant exercise of hope and joy!" HAP; NAEL-6v2

Imagination and Taste, How Impaired and Restored. NAEL-6v2

Spots of Time. TOF

"In one of those excursions (may they ne'er)." NAEL-6v2

Introduction—Childhood and School-Time. FHYEP; NAEL-6v2

("By day, and were a trouble to my dreams.") (LL) PoE

"Dust as we are, the immortal spirit grows." SCV

"Ere I had told / Ten birthdays when among the mountain-slopes." TOF

"Wisdom and Spirit of the universe!" AWP; OxBEV

("Work like a sea?") (LL) HAP

"Long time have human ignorance and guilt." NAEL-6v2

"O there is blessing in this gentle breeze." FHYEP; NAEL-6v2

Residence at Cambridge.

"Evangelist St John my patron was, The." HAP

"It was a dreary morning when the wheels." NAEL-6v2

Residence in France.

"Even as a river,—partly (it might seem)." NAEL-6v2

Residence in France and French Revolution.

"Cheared with this hope, to Paris I returned." NAEL-6v2

"Domestic carnage now filled the whole year." NAEL-6v2

Residence in London.

"As the black storm upon the mountain top." NAEL-6v2

"Rise up, thou monstrous ant-hill on the plain."   HAP

Retrospect Love of Nature Leading to Love of Mankind.
  "Rambling school-boy, thus, A."   NAEL-6v2

Same subject (Continued) [Imagination and Taste, How Impaired and Restored].
  "Here, calling up to mind what then I saw."   NAEL-6v2

School-Time.   FHYEP; NAEL-6v2
  "Blest the infant Babe."   TOF
  "But who shall parcel out."   TOF

Summer Vacation.
  "Among the favorites whom it pleased me well."   NAEL-6v2
  "As one who hangs down-bending from the side."   NAEL-6v2
  "Wildly he wandered on."   TOF

"Thus far, O Friend! have we, though leaving much."   FHYEP; NAEL-6v2

Prelude, The; Growth of a Poet's Mind [1805 vers.].   William Wordsworth.

Books.
  There Was a Boy.   RB
  "Thirteen years / Or haply less, I might have seen, when first."   OxAEP-2

Cambridge and the Alps.
  "I, too, have been a Wanderer; but, alas!"   OxAEP-2
  Simplon Pass, The.   CABP

Conclusion: "In one of these excursions, travelling then."
  "It was a Summer's night, a close warm night."   MakPoe
  Snowdon Sunrise, The.   OxAEP-2

Imagination, How Impaired and Restored.
  "One Christmas-time, / The day before the holidays began."   RB

Introduction—Childhood and School-Time.
  "And in the frosty season, when the sun."   FaBoCh; WoPoe
  "Fair seed-time had my soul, and I grew up."   OxAEP-2
  "One evening (surely I was led by her)."   RB
  "Was it for this."   RB
  "Wisdom and Spirit of the universe!"   NOBE

Residence in France.
  "I quitted and betook myself to France."   OxAEP-2

Residence in London.
  "Those days are now."   OxAEP-2

School-Time.
  "Nor should this, perchance."   OxAEP-2

Summer Vacation.
  "In a throng, / A festal company of Maids and Youths."   EBEV
  "While thus I wander'd, step by step led on."   OxAEP-1
  "Was it for this."   NPeEn
  "When from our better selves we have too long."   AmFaPo

Prelude: The Troops.   Siegfried Sassoon.   PeFWW

Prelude: The Wayside Inn.   Henry Wadsworth Longfellow.   APN-1   *Fr.* Tales of a Wayside Inn.

Prelude: "This fugitive between the Earth and Sky."   Tu Fu.   TAL

Prelude: "This short straight sword."   Ronald Allison Kells Mason.   PeNZ

Prelude to a Kiss.   Irving Gordon.   ReLy

Prelude to a Volume Printed in Raised Letters for the Blind.   Oliver Wendell Holmes.   APN-1

Prelude to Akwasidae.   *Unknown.*   TTY, *tr.* by Halim El-Dabh

Prelude to Among the Hills.   John Greenleaf Whittier.   *See* Among the Hills

Prelude to *An American Anthology.*   Edmund Clarence Stedman.   APN-2

Prelude to an Evening.   John Crowe Ransom.   MoAmPo; OxBA; SPE   *Fr.* Sixteen Poems in Eight Pairings.

Prelude to Memorial Song: 100 Years Later.   Phillip [or "Phil"] William George.   VoR

Prelude to Nothing.   Sonia Sanchez.   GT

Prelude to Part the First.   James Russell Lowell.   APN-1   *Fr.* Vision of Sir Launfal, The.

Prelude to Winter.   William Carlos Williams.   SAmP

Prelude: "Track is my companion, The."   Laury Wells.   IBA

Preludes (I–IV).   T. S. Eliot.   APT-1; HeIP-4; OBMV; TwCP; UnPo; VGW; WeW-3
  "His soul stretched tight across the skies."   TCAPo
  "Morning comes to consciousness, The."   TCAPo
  "Winter evening settles down, The."   OPOU; TCAPo
  "You tossed a blanket from the bed."   TCAPo

Preludes for Memnon; or, Preludes to Attitude.   Conrad Potter Aiken.
  Prelude I: "Winter for a moment takes the mind; the snow.".   APT-1; OxBA
  Prelude II: "Two coffees in the Español, the last.".   APT-1; NoAM
  Prelude VI: "This is not you? These phrases are not you?".   MoAmPo
  Prelude VII: "Beloved, let us once more praise the rain.".   UnPo
  Prelude XIV: "You went to the verge, you say, and came back safely.".   FaBoMo; TwCP

Prelude XIX: "Watch long enough, and you will see the leaf.".   OxBA

Prelude XXVIII: "Time has come, the clock says time has come, The.".   OxBA

Prelude XXIX: "What shall we do--what shall we think--what shall we say?".   FaBoMo

Prelude XXXIII: "Then came I to the shoreless shore of silence.".   OxBA

Prelude XLII: "Keep in the heart the journal nature keeps.".   OxBA

Prelude LVI: "Rimbaud and Verlaine, precious pair of poets.".   FaBoMo; NoAM; TwCP

Prelude LVII: "One star fell and another as we walked.".   MoAmPo

Prelusive.   Herman Melville.   *Fr.* Clarel: A Poem and Pilgrimage in the Holy Land.

Premeditations.   Geoff Page.   NOBAu

Premonition, The.   Theodore Roethke.   HarvBoo

Preparation.   Thomas Edward Brown.   OBEV

Preparation.   William Johnson Cory.   OxBSo

Preparation.   Czeslaw Milosz.   WoPoe

Preparations.   Tony Curtis.   TCAWP

Preparations.   Leslie Marmon Silko.   VoR

Preparations.   *Unknown.   See* Guest, The

Preparations for Seder.   Michael S. Glaser.   UnSA

Preparations for Victory.   Edmund Charles Blunden.   PeFWW

Preparative, The.   Thomas Traherne.   BASC; ESCV; GeHe

Preparatory Meditations Before My Approach to the Lord's Supper.   Edward Taylor.
  "All Dull, my Lord, my Spirits flat, and dead."   NOSC; TCAPo
  "Am I thy gold? Or purse, Lord, for thy wealth."   NOSC; OxBA; TAP; TCAPo
  "Apples of gold, in silver pictures shrined."   NAAL-2v1; NAAL-3; NAAL-5
  "Bran, a chaff, a very barley [y]awn, A."   ChIV-2; NOSC; TCAPo
  "But Woe is mee! who have so quick a Sent."   TCAPo
  "Deity of Love Incorporate, A."   TAP
  "Dull. Dull indeed! What shall it e'er be thus?"   ChIV-1
  "Guilty, my Lord, what can I more declare?"   ChIV-1; TCAPo
  "I kenning [*or* kening] through astronomy divine."   ChIV-2; ColAP; NAAL-2v1; NAAL-3; NAAL-5; NOBA; NoP-4; OxBA; SCAP; TAP
  "Leaf[e] gold, Lord of thy golden wedge o'erlaid."   NAAL-2v1; NAAL-3; NAAL-5
  "Like to the marigold, I blushing close."   ChIV-2; SCAP
  "Lord, art thou at the table head above."   ChIV-1; OxBA; TCAPo
  "Lord, can a crumb of dust the earth outweigh."   NAAL-2v1; NAAL-3; NAAL-5; TCAPo
  Meditation 8 (First Series).   ChIV-2; ColAP; NAAL-2v1; NAAL-3; NAAL-5; NOBA; NoP-4; OxBA; SCAP; TAP
  Meditation 16 (First Series).   NAAL-2v1; NAAL-3; NAAL-5
  Meditation 22 (First Series).   NAAL-2v1; NAAL-3; NAAL-5; TCAPo
  Meditation 26.   NAAL-2v1; NAAL-3
  Meditation 38.   NAAL-2v1; NAAL-3; NOBA; OxBA
  Meditation 42 (First Series).   NAAL-2v1; NAAL-3; NAAL-5
  Meditation 150 (Second Series).   ColAP; SCAP
  Meditation. Can. 1.3. Thy Good Ointment.   TCAPo
  Meditation. Col. 1.18. He is the Head of the Body.
    "My Metaphors are but dull Tacklings tag'd."   TCAPo
  Meditation. Heb. 13. 10. Wee have an Altar.   ChIV-2; NOSC; TCAPo
  Meditation. Joh. 15.5. Without me yee can do nothing.   TCAPo
  Meditation. Mal. 4.2. With Healing in His Wings.
    "Fiery Darts of Satan stob my heart, The."   TCAPo
  Meditation. Numb. 28.4.9. One Lamb shalt thou offer in the Morning, and the other at Even. And on the Sabbath day two Lambs etc.   ChIV-1; TCAPo
  Meditation on Gal. 3.16. And to thy Seed Which is Christ.
    "Lord with thine Altars Fire, mine Inward man."   TCAPo
  Meditation. Phil. 3 Ult. Our Vile Bodie.
    "Here is a Mudwall tent, whose Matters are."   TCAPo
  Meditation. Rom. 9.5. God blessed forever.   TCAPo
  Meditation. Zech. 9.11. The Pit wherein is no water.
    "Pit indeed of Sin: No water's here, A."   TCAPo
  "Methinks I spy Almighty holding in."   HAP
  "My Blessed Lord, how doth thy Beautious Spouse."   ColAP; SCAP
  "My Blessed Lord, that Golden Linck that joyns."   TCAPo
  "My gracious Lord, I would thee glory doe."   SCAP
  "My shattred phancy stole away from mee."   NOSC; SCAP
  "My sin! my sin, my God, these cursed dregs."   SCAP; TCAPo
  "Oh! Golden Rose! Oh. Glittering Lilly White."   SCAP
  "Oh! Good, good, good, my Lord. What more love yet."   NOBA
  "Oh leaden heeld. Lord, give, forgive I pray."   SCAP
  "Oh that I was the Bird of Paradise!"   NOCV; OxBEV

"Oh! what a thing is man? Lord, who am I?"   NAAL-2v1; NAAL-3; NOBA; OxBA

Prologue: "Lord, can a crumb of dust the earth outweigh."   NAAL-2v1; NAAL-3; NAAL-5; TCAPo

Should I with Silver Tooles Delve through the Hill.   ChIV-2; OxBA; SCAP

"State, a state, oh! dungeon state indeed, A."   ChIV-1

"Still I complain; I am complaining still."   OxBA; SacPr

"Stupendious love! all saints astonishment."   OxBA; SacPr

"Thy grace, dear Lord's my golden wrack I find."   SCAP

"Thy human frame, my glorious Lord, I spy."   ChIV-1

"Unclean, unclean: my Lord, undone, all vile."   NAAL-2v1; NAAL-3

"View, all ye eyes above, this sight which flings."   NOSC

"What love is this of thine, that cannot be."   NOCV; SCAP

"What shall I say, my Lord? With what begin?"   ChIV-2; HAP

"When, Lord, I seeke to shew thy praises, then."   TCAPo

"When thy bright beams, my Lord, do strike mine eye."   NAAL-2v1; NAAL-3; NAAL-5; TCAPo

"Why should my bells, which chime thy praise, when thou."   ChIV-2

"Ye angells bright, pluck from your wings a quill."   ChIV-2

Prepare for death. But how can you prepare.   Speculation.   Howard Nemerov.   TAP

"Prepare to meet the King of Terrors," cried.   Epigram.   Ebenezer Elliott.   NOBVV

Prepare your wreaths, Aonian maids divine.   To the Muses.   Mary Robinson.   CenSon; RWP

Prepare yourself to hear the worst!   That Was Before I Met You.   P. G. Wodehouse.   ReLy

Preparedness.   Edwin Markham.   MoAmPo

Preparing schmaltz for matzoh balls.   Preparations for Seder.   Michael S. Glaser.   UnSA

Preparing the Dead.   Paulette Roeske.   IllVoic

Preposterous is that Government, (and rude).   Ill Government.   Robert Herrick.   CavPo

Prerogative of Lieder, The.   Ray DiPalma.   FTOS

Presage and caveat not only seem.   Window Sill, The.   Robert Graves.   EnLoPo

Presage of mirth and hospitality. (LL)   Philip Freneau.   NAAL-2v1; NAAL-3; TCAPo   Fr. House of Night, The.

Presaging.   Rainer Maria Rilke.   AWP; TrJP, tr. by Jessie Lemont

Presbyterian Study.   Tom Paulin.   PBCIP

Presbyterians, The.   Dryden.   NOSC   Fr. Hind and the Panther, The.

Prescient.   Lucie Brock-Broido.   ExTi

Prescott, press my Ascot waistcoat.   Ascot Waistcoat.   David McCord.   NBLV

Prescription.   Donald Woods.   CAGL

Prescription of Painful Ends.   Robinson Jeffers.   APT-1; MoAmPo; OxBA

Presence, The.   Maxine W. Kumin.   WPE

Presence, The.   Medbh McGuckian.   PNI

Presence, The.   Dana Naone.   CDW

Presence, The.   Elder Olson.   IllVoic

Presence, The.   Pier Paolo Pasolini.   ItPo, tr. by Gayle Ridinger

Presence, The.   Jones Very.   HAP

Presence of the Dance / The Resolution of the Music, The.   Robert Duncan.   FTOS

Presence. Opposites. Absence. Forces exercising pressure against.   Alicia Kozameh.   MirDau, tr. by David Davis   Fr. Saltos Sobre El Exilio.

Presence was spectrum-blue, The.   "H. D."   APT-1   Fr. Walls Do Not Fall, The.

Presences Perfected.   Siegfried Sassoon.   MoBrPo

Present.   Sonia Sanchez.   WPOW

(This woman vomiting her.)   NAAAL; UnSA

Present, The.   Marie Laurencin.   CuPo

Present, The.   Adelaide Anne Procter.   TreFP

Present, The.   Maria Luisa Spaziani.   CItWP, tr. by Cinzia Sartini Blum and Lara Trubowitz

Present Age, The.   Frances Ellen Watkins Harper.   PWR

Present Crisis, The.   James Russell Lowell.   TreFP

Present Evening, The.   Eugenio Florit.   TCLAP, tr. by Hoffman Reynolds Hays

Present from the Emperor's New Concubine, A.   Pan Chieh-yû.   BoWoP; OHMPC; WoPoe, tr. by Kenneth Rexroth

Present in Abscence.   John Hoskyns [or Hoskins].   See Absence

Present is a Dangerous Place to Live, The.   Keorapetse Kgositsile.

"And at the door of the eye."   PBMAP

"Do not tell me, my brother, to reach."   PBMAP

Present of Butter, A.   Tadhg Dall O'Huiginn.   BIrV, tr. by The Earl of Longford

Present pain never come to an end. (LL)   Ejected Wife, The.   Yüan-ti.   OBVE; OxBEV, tr. by Arthur Waley

Present reigned supreme, The.   Home Coming.   Lenrie Peters.   HBAPE

Present Time Best Pleaseth, The.   Robert Herrick.   CavPo

Present to a Lady, A.   Unknown.   PeLV

Presentation of Two Birds to My Son, A.   James Wright (1927–80).   YaYoPo

Presente.   Inés Hernández-Ávila.   ReEnLa

Presented as a Farewell to Secretary Fu.   Pao Chao.   SuSp, tr. by Daniel Bryant

Presented to a Lady within the Palace.   Chang Yü.   SuSp, tr. by Ronald C. Miao

Presented to Liu Ching-wen.   Su Tung-p'o (Su Shih).   CoBCP, tr. by Burton Watson

Presented to Piao, the Prince of Pai-ma.   Ts'ao Chih.   CoBCP, tr. by Burton Watson

Presented to the Taoist Paragon Mao.   Cheng Huan.   ColAnChi, tr. by Edward H. Schafer

Presented to Wang Lun.   Li Po.   CoBCP, tr. by Burton Watson

Presented to Wang Wen-hsi.   Ho Ching-ming.   CoBLCP, tr. by Jonathan Chaves

Presented to Wei Pa, Gentleman in Retirement.   Tu Fu.   CoBCP, tr. by Burton Watson

Presentiment.   Emily Dickinson.   APN-2; HeIP-4; OxBA

Presentiment of life is alive until death, The.   Beast Flower.   Yelena [or Elena] Shwarts [or Shvarts].   TCRP, tr. by Nina Kossman

Presently.   Seven Stimuli.   Mei Ch'eng.   ColAnChi, tr. by Victor H. Mair

Presently at our touch the teacup stirred.   Voices from the Other World.   James Merrill.   TwCP; VCAP

Presents from My Aunts in Pakistan.   Moniza Alvi.   MFPA

Preserve for us rebellion, lightning, the illusory agreement, a laugh for.   Unbending Prayer.   René Char.   AF

Preserve my speech forever for its taste of sadness and smoke.   To A. A. A.   (Akhmatova).   Osip Emilevich Mandelstam [or Mandelshtam].   TCRP, tr. by Bernard Meares

Preserve thy sighs, unthrifty girl[e].   Soldier Going to the Field, The.   Sir William Davenant [or D'Avenant].   FaBoWar; NOBE; OBWP

Preserves its blue heat down my throat. (LL)   Song: "Yellow coverlet, A."   Rosanna Warren.   ExTi; MakPoe

Preserves us, not for specialists. (LL)   April Inventory.   W. D. Snodgrass.   CoAP; ColAP; HAP; NoAM; NoP-4; PAI; TAP; TRP; TwCP; VCAP

Preserving, The.   Kevin Young.   GT

President has thus disclosed, The.   Door of Hope, The.   Lizelia Augusta Jenkins Moorer.   CBWP-3

President Slumming, The.   James Tate.   OBAL

Presidents.   Michael Heffernan.   EmeKit

Presidents, The.   Lizelia Augusta Jenkins Moorer.   CBWP-3

Presidents of the United States of America, The.   Jackson Mac Low.

"Andrew Jackson & Martin Van Buren."   APSN

"Andrew Jackson's last name's the same as my first."   APSN

"George Washington never owned a camel."   APSN

"If Martin Van Buren ever swam in water."   APSN

"James Madison's hand cd lead an ox to water."   APSN

"James Monroe / laid a hand."   APSN

"John Adams knew the hand."   APSN

"John Quincy Adam's right hand."   APSN

"Marked by no fence."   APSN

"Poor old bait got sick & died, The."   APSN

"Tyler was no Whig at all & after his term's end."   APSN

Presocratic, Surfing, Breathing Cosmology Blues, The.   Christopher Buckley.   BodElec

Press, The.   Thomas Phipson.   PeSAV

Press ahead, beloved children.   Uncle Rube to the Young People.   Clara Ann Thompson.   CBWP-2

Press me to your bread-fruit chest.   Cultural Trip, A.   Opal Palmer Adisa.   GT

Press of the Spoon River Clarion was wrecked, The.   Edgar Lee Masters.   OBSV; PAI   Fr. Spoon River Anthology.

Press often for, (nor, than at this time, more).   Vox Oppressi, to the Lady Phipps.   Richard Henchman.   SCAP

Press on! surmount the rocky steeps.   Press On.   Park Benjamin.   TreFP

Pressed by the Moon, Mute Arbitress of Tides.   Charlotte Smith.   CenSon; NALW

(Sonnet. Written in the Church-Yard at Middleton in Sussex.)   CABP; ECWP; NOEC; NoP-4; NPeEn; PEW; WPE; WoRP

Pressed to the wall, dying, but—fighting back! (LL)   If We Must Die.   Claude McKay.   APT-1; BPo; ColAP; ISC; NAAAL; NAAL-5; NoAM; SSLK; Son; TFi; TTY; UnPo

Pressing for Tax Payment.   Fan Ch'eng-ta.   SuSp, tr. by Wu-Chi Liu   Fr. Four Songs in Imitation of Wang Chien.

Pressing my forehead.   Nicholas Virgilio.   HA

Pressing my lips. (LL)   Kenneth Rexroth.   APSN; APT-2   Fr. Love Poems of Marichiko, The.

Pressure.   Anne Waldman.   PoM

Pressure lamp hisses into the silence, The. African Student. Noel H. Brettell. PeSAV

Pressure of sun on the rockslide. Water. Gary Snyder. LCAP-2

Pressures, The. Imamu Amiri Baraka. BPo

Prestidigitator 1, The. Al Young. NBV

Prestidigitator 2, The. Al Young. NBV

Prestidigitator makes things disappear, A. Prestidigitator 1, The. Al Young. NBV

Presto, pronto! Two boys, two horses. Boy Riding Forward Backward. Robert Francis. LCAP-2

Preston. *Unknown.* FaBoVe

Pretences. Ibn Rashiq. TTY, *tr. by* A. J. Arberry

Pretext. Stephen Rodefer. PmAP

Prettiest shadows were impalpable, so I stored them, The. Izzy. Ira Sadoff. BodElec

Pretty. Stevie Smith. NAEL-5v2; NAEL-6v2; NoAM; NoP-4

Pretty Ambition, A. Mary Eleanor Wilkins Freeman. OBCA

Pretty Baby. Egbert Van Alstyne. ReLy

Pretty Bonnie, you are quick as a rabbit. Giving Rabbit to My Cat Bonnie. Anne Stevenson. FaBoWP

Pretty game, my girl, A. Flirt, The. William Henry Davies. EnLoPo

Pretty Girl, A. J. Gordon Coogler. OBAL

Pretty Girl Is Like a Melody, A. Irving Berlin. ReLy

Pretty John Watts. Mother Goose. OxNR; ReMoGo

Pretty Lady Carenza. Tenson. Carenza. WPOW, *tr. by* Bridget Connelly and Doris Earnshaw

Pretty maid, pretty maid, / Where have you been? Gift for the Queen. *Unknown.* OxNR

Pretty maid she died, she died, in love-bed as she lay, The. Ballade. Paul Fort. AWP, *tr. by* Frederick York Powell

Pretty matron, The. Clement Hoyt. HA

Pretty Miss Apathy. Pooh! Walter De la Mare. HAP

Pretty party for people, A. And. Robert Creeley. LCAP-2

Pretty song, this coming spring, A. Miss Betty's Singing-Bird. John Winstanley. NOEC

Pretty Soon. Edith Bruck. AF, *tr. by* Ruth Feldman

Pretty soon, the age of the talk show. Hush Yo Mouf. Thomas Sayers Ellis. InTrad

Pretty soon / when people hear a quiz show expert. Pretty Soon. Edith Bruck. AF, *tr. by* Ruth Feldman

Pretty Sport. William Habington. NOBE

Pretty Woman, A. Simon J. Ortiz. CDW

Pretty Words. Elinor Wylie. NAAL-2v2

Prevailing winds lied in intent, The. Statuary. John Ashbery. NoAM

Prevalent Poetry. Charles Follen Adams. PeLi

Prevention of Stacy Miller, The. Peter Miller. MoCV

Previous to her Interview with Phaon. Mary Robinson. CenSon; RWP

Previsioning death in advance, our doom is delayed. Foresight. Lincoln Kirstein. OBWP; PoWW

Prewar stadium and a prewar game, A. Dynamo Stadium, 1980. Aleksandr Petrovich Tkachenko. ItGoST, *tr. by* Maia Tekses

Prey. Michael Dorris. PoCoUp

Prey. Ken Gerner. GifTon

Prey. Peter Makuck. UrbNat

Prey swooped up, the iron love seat shudders. Up and Down. James Merrill. GLP

Prey to Prey. David Rowbotham. CBAP

Priam and Achilles. Homer. NOSC, *tr. by* George Chapman *Fr.* Iliad, The.

Priapean Corpus, The. *Unknown.*
"Bailiff, why your useless plaints about." RomPo, *tr. by* Eugene O'Connor
"Having left behind its cutting." RomPo, *tr. by* Eugene O'Connor
"I ask you to witness, Priapus." RomPo, *tr. by* Eugene O'Connor
"Romans, I appeal to you." RomPo, *tr. by* Eugene O'Connor
"To your question: why are my private parts." RomPo, *tr. by* Eugene O'Connor
"What business, this? What reason should we give." RomPo, *tr. by* Eugene O'Connor

Priapos of the Harbor. Antipater of Sidon. GrAn; WoPoe, *tr. by* Dudley Fitts

Priapus and the Pool. Conrad Potter Aiken.
This Is the Shape of the Leaf. NOBA; OxBA
(Portrait of a Girl.) MoAmPo
"When trout swim down Great Ormond Street." NOBA; NoAM

Priapus, may this shady roof forever. Tibullus. PriapPo, *tr. by* Richard W. Hooper

Priapus Poems, The. *Unknown.* PriapPo, *tr. by* Richard W. Hooper
"Bailiff of a fertile garden plot, The." PriapPo, *tr. by* Richard W. Hooper
"Beauty renders Hermes pleasing." PriapPo, *tr. by* Richard W. Hooper
"Beg your pardon, Lord Priapus." PriapPo, *tr. by* Richard W. Hooper

"Bunch of grapes leaves Bacchus satisfied, A." PriapPo, *tr. by* Richard W. Hooper

"But ain't it long, and ain't it good and thick." PriapPo, *tr. by* Richard W. Hooper

"Dear reader, though my uncombed verse be queer." PriapPo, *tr. by* Richard W. Hooper

"Don't assume each threat is uttered." PriapPo, *tr. by* Richard W. Hooper

"Don't pretend I didn't warn you." PriapPo, *tr. by* Richard W. Hooper

"Don't you believe it's enough that I'm stuck in this spot." PriapPo, *tr. by* Richard W. Hooper

"Drier than the sun-dried raisins." PriapPo, *tr. by* Richard W. Hooper

"Each of us has some bodily trait that's well known." PriapPo, *tr. by* Richard W. Hooper

"Famed Telethusa, of the downtown mob." PriapPo, *tr. by* Richard W. Hooper

"Farmer, what's the point complaining." PriapPo, *tr. by* Richard W. Hooper

"Forgive a hick unable to compete." PriapPo, *tr. by* Richard W. Hooper

"Friends, there has to be a limit." PriapPo, *tr. by* Richard W. Hooper

"Girl no whiter than the Moors are." PriapPo, *tr. by* Richard W. Hooper

"Girl, watch your cunt; boy, keep your ass from grief." PriapPo, *tr. by* Richard W. Hooper

"He whose not too honest fingers." PriapPo, *tr. by* Richard W. Hooper

"Here comes someone soft as goose down." PriapPo, *tr. by* Richard W. Hooper

"Honest matrons, pray retire." PriapPo, *tr. by* Richard W. Hooper

"I can't say words like *kiss, cuss, miss,* or *bless.*" PriapPo, *tr. by* Richard W. Hooper

"I could have said obscurely: Cast about." PriapPo, *tr. by* Richard W. Hooper

"I could simply die, Priapus." PriapPo, *tr. by* Richard W. Hooper

"I watch, O youths, this farmhouse and this place." PriapPo, *tr. by* Richard W. Hooper

"If boy, or man, or woman steals I hump." PriapPo, *tr. by* Richard W. Hooper

"If you could turn graffiti into gold." PriapPo, *tr. by* Richard W. Hooper

"If you should see unchaste obscenities." PriapPo, *tr. by* Richard W. Hooper

"If your mouth's all set for fig fruit." PriapPo, *tr. by* Richard W. Hooper

"Impose the letters *CD* on a staff." PriapPo, *tr. by* Richard W. Hooper

"In your honor, Lord Priapus." PriapPo, *tr. by* Richard W. Hooper

"It's me, O passerby, the poplar tree." PriapPo, *tr. by* Richard W. Hooper

"Jove wields the lightning, Neptune's trident-lord." PriapPo, *tr. by* Richard W. Hooper

"Jove, you hold Dodona sacred." PriapPo, *tr. by* Richard W. Hooper

"Just don't get caught. I won't exact a tithe." PriapPo, *tr. by* Richard W. Hooper

"Keep watch over the orchard, attentive Priapus!" PriapPo, *tr. by* Richard W. Hooper

"Law which (as they say) Priapus coined, The." PriapPo, *tr. by* Richard W. Hooper

"Let any thief whom we carelessly suffer to pass." PriapPo, *tr. by* Richard W. Hooper

"Look at how upset you've got me." PriapPo, *tr. by* Richard W. Hooper

"May all comers wax poetic." PriapPo, *tr. by* Richard W. Hooper

"May all the deities keep me from chewing like you." PriapPo, *tr. by* Richard W. Hooper

"My cock's great size results in one delight." PriapPo, *tr. by* Richard W. Hooper

"Old-time Priapuses could take their pick." PriapPo, *tr. by* Richard W. Hooper

"On boys and girls the middle parts get mated." PriapPo, *tr. by* Richard W. Hooper

"Once public treasurer, a farmer now." PriapPo, *tr. by* Richard W. Hooper

"One syllable from Pedasos, Erato." PriapPo, *tr. by* Richard W. Hooper

"Proud Aristagoras, whose vineyard lacks." PriapPo, *tr. by* Richard W. Hooper

"Public's darling Quintia, first-class, The." PriapPo, *tr. by* Richard W. Hooper

"Rot, old crow, a mausoleum." PriapPo, *tr. by* Richard W. Hooper

"Scythed god whose part is greater than the whole." PriapPo, *tr. by* Richard W. Hooper

"Should the bare-ass pavement-pounder." PriapPo, *tr. by* Richard W. Hooper

"Since you fail to ponder, scarcely." PriapPo, *tr. by* Richard W. Hooper

"Sleep soundly, dogs: the Dog Star and the Maid." PriapPo, *tr. by* Richard W. Hooper

"Some old lady scarcely younger." PriapPo, *tr. by* Richard W. Hooper

"Spring roses, autumn fruits, and summer grain." PriapPo, *tr. by* Richard W. Hooper

"Step right up, come one, come all, don't." PriapPo, *tr. by* Richard W. Hooper

"Such apples as once brought Atlanta down." PriapPo, *tr.* by Richard W. Hooper

"That hick farmer's got my number." PriapPo, *tr.* by Richard W. Hooper

"That that part of me is dripping." PriapPo, *tr.* by Richard W. Hooper

"Thief, you dare to laugh and even." PriapPo, *tr.* by Richard W. Hooper

"This heap betrays me: please, Priapus, say." PriapPo, *tr.* by Richard W. Hooper

"This proud scepter which now severed." PriapPo, *tr.* by Richard W. Hooper

"This victim from a lukewarm pigs' redoubt." PriapPo, *tr.* by Richard W. Hooper

"Though I'm just a wood Priapus." PriapPo, *tr.* by Richard W. Hooper

"Though, Priapus, you're stuck with a well-stiffened cock." PriapPo, *tr.* by Richard W. Hooper

"What's going on in my garden? Who can explain." PriapPo, *tr.* by Richard W. Hooper

"What's the difference if I'm aged." PriapPo, *tr.* by Richard W. Hooper

"What's the plaint against me, watchman?" PriapPo, *tr.* by Richard W. Hooper

"What's this? What does the anger of the gods ordain?" PriapPo, *tr.* by Richard W. Hooper

"Whatever it is, I shouldn't hesitate." PriapPo, *tr.* by Richard W. Hooper

"When the horny god saw someone." PriapPo, *tr.* by Richard W. Hooper

"When the horny god was feted." PriapPo, *tr.* by Richard W. Hooper

"Whichever one of you throwing a party at home." PriapPo, *tr.* by Richard W. Hooper

"While you acknowledge no wrongheaded wish to lay waste." PriapPo, *tr.* by Richard W. Hooper

"While you're alive I'm hopeful, rustic guard." PriapPo, *tr.* by Richard W. Hooper

"Who could believe it? O, the fates are fickle." PriapPo, *tr.* by Richard W. Hooper

"Whosoever steals a rosebud." PriapPo, *tr.* by Richard W. Hooper

"Why all these sidelong looks, you shameless tarts?" PriapPo, *tr.* by Richard W. Hooper

"Why the laughter, witless female?" PriapPo, *tr.* by Richard W. Hooper

"Why, you ask, do painted gonads." PriapPo, *tr.* by Richard W. Hooper

"With this gift of dirty pictures." PriapPo, *tr.* by Richard W. Hooper

"You ask why I don't hide my filthy charms?" PriapPo, *tr.* by Richard W. Hooper

"You'll get fucked, thief, for the first time." PriapPo, *tr.* by Richard W. Hooper

"You'll learn, should you steal apples in my care." PriapPo, *tr.* by Richard W. Hooper

"You there with the sticky fingers." PriapPo, *tr.* by Richard W. Hooper

"You, who to avoid my manhood." PriapPo, *tr.* by Richard W. Hooper

"You wonder, since I'm wooden front to rear." PriapPo, *tr.* by Richard W. Hooper

Priapus, seeing Cimon's rigid rod. Antipater of Thessalonica. CAGL, *tr.* by Daryl Hine

Priapus seeing Kimon with a stand. Antipater of Thessalonica. GrAn

Priapus the Scarecrow. Antistius Vetus. GrAn, *tr.* by Alistair Elliot

Price, The. John Davidson. EBVV

Price, The. Anne Stevenson. DiPo

Price of Begging, The. Emmanuel [*or* Immanuel] ben David Frances. TrJP, *tr.* by A. B. Rhine

Price of Disrespect, The. Lizelia Augusta Jenkins Moorer. CBWP-3

Price of Stone, The. Richard Murphy.

　Convenience. ModIr

　Kylemore Castle. ModIr

　Natural Son. ModIr

　Roof-Tree. BiHa; ModIr

Price seemed reasonable, location, The. Telephone Conversation. Wole Soyinka. NoP-4; PBMAP; PoetW; TTY

Priceless is one's incantation. Hakuin. ZenPo, *tr.* by Takashi Ikemoto and Lucien Stryk

Prices. Louis Ginsberg. TrJP

Prickle a lamb. Conjuring Roethke. James Tate. OBAL

Pride. Mary Elizabeth Coleridge. ViWPN

Pride. Violet Jacob. OxBS

Pride. Jackie Kay. NeBl

Pride, The. John Newlove. MoCV; NOBC

Pride cannot see itself by mid-day light. Barten Holyday. FaBoEE

Pride is his pity, artifice his praise. *Unknown.* FaBoEE

Pride, like a goldfish, flashed a sudden fin. (LL) Lesson, The. Edward Lucie-Smith. OxBTC; TwCP

Pride of a Jew, The. Judah Halevi. TrJP, *tr.* by Israel Cohen

Pride of all the village, The. Married to a Soldier. John Clare. SCGP

Pride of Ancestry. Robert Frost. OBAL

Pride of the Fourth and Liquid Element. Luis de Góngora y Argote. SpanPo, *tr.* by J. M. Cohen

Pride of the Peacock, The. William Blake. RaBo *Fr.* Marriage of Heaven and Hell, The.

Pride of Youth, The. Sir Walter Scott. *See* Heart of Midlothian, The

Priest. "H. D."

　"You come late." GifTon

Priest, The. Bob Boldman. HA

Priest and the Mulberry-Tree, The. Thomas Love Peacock. OxAEP-2 *Fr.* Crotchet Castle.

Priest attending, found he spoke at times, The. George Crabbe. PoE *Fr.* Borough, The.

Priest in the Sabbath Dawn Addresses His Somnolent Mistress, A. Peter Didsbury. EmeKit

Priest of Beauty, the Anointed One, The. Poet's Destiny, The. Lady Jane Francesca Wilde. VWP

Priest of Christ, The. Thomas Ken. SacPr

Priest of Felton. *Unknown.* OxNR

Priest of the spruce of the north, send all your people to work for us. Rain Song of the Shu'-wi Chai'än (Snake Society), A. *Unknown.* APN-2, *tr.* by Matilda Coxe Stevenson

Priest's Song, A. Thomas Dekker. NoSic *Fr.* Old Fortunatus.

Priest, the Levite, the Samaritan, and the man who fell among thieves meet in heaven to talk over old times, The. Good Samaritan et Al, The. Stephen Mitchell. GI

Priesthood, The. George Herbert. ESCV

Priestly poverty—. Buson. SoOfWa, *tr.* by Sam Hamill

Priests have a problem, The. Hakeldama. Zbigniew Herbert. GI, *tr.* by John Carpenter

Priests of Apollo, sacred be the room[e]. Sacrifice to Apollo, The. Michael Drayton. NOSC

Priests, prophets, helpless. She's beside herself. Virgil [*or* Vergil]. EroLit, *tr.* by Kenneth McLeish *Fr.* Aeneid [*or* Eneados, *Aeneis*], The.

Priests, the elders, and the scribes, The. Death and Resurrection. Priscilla Jane Thompson. CBWP-2

Prig offered Pig the first chance at dessert. Manners. Howard Nemerov. NBLV

Prikaz. André Salmon. CuPo

Primaleon of Greece. Anthony Munday.

　"Beauty sat bathing by a spring." NOBE; OBEV

　(Colin.) GTBS-P

Primaries, conventions, elections. Dream of Instant Total Representation, The. Anselm Hollo. PmAP

Primary Ground, A. Adrienne Rich. NNaP

Primavera. Antonio Machado Ruiz. WoPoe, *tr.* by Samuel Menashe

Prime. W. H. Auden. PoE *Fr.* Horae Canonicae.

Primer, The. Josephine Jacobsen. NoP-4

Primer about the Flag, A. Marvin Bell. GifTon

Primer for Blacks. Gwendolyn Brooks. ISC

Primer for Schoolchildren, A. Richard Weber. CIP-2

Primer Lesson. Carl Sandburg. MoAmPo

Primer of Plato. Jean Garrigue. NOBA

Primer of the Daily Round, A. Howard Nemerov. WeW-3

　(Peels an apple, while B kneels to God, A.) NoP-4

Primitive, The. Haki R. Madhubuti. BPo

Primitive like an Orb, A. Wallace Stevens. NOBA

Primitive Pithecanthropus erectus, The. Heredity. Arthur Guiterman. OBAL; PeLi

Primitive Place. Mildred Weston. FFC

Primitives. Dudley Randall. BPo; NBV

Primo Vere. Giosuè Carducci. AWP, *tr.* by John Bailey

Primos. Sandra M. Castillo. TouFir

Primrose, The. John Clare. CenSon

Primrose, The. Robert Herrick. OBEV

Primrose of the Rock, The. William Wordsworth. TreFP

Primrose there, the violet darkly blue, The. Philip Freneau. NAAL-3 *Fr.* House of Night, The.

Primroses; salutations; the miry skull. Pre-Raphaelite Notebook, A. Geoffrey Hill. NoAM

Primula veris. Randolph Healy. Oth

Prince. Ann Sansom. NeBl

Prince, The. Edgar Bowers. CoAmPo

Prince Alfred's Itinerary. *Unknown.*

　"I found in Munster, unfettered of any." BIrV

Prince-Archbishop, Father Adelhard. To Adelhard, Archbishop of Canterbury. Alcuin. MLL, *tr.* by Helen Waddell

Prince Charles in his Welsh principality. Limerick. Bernard Levin. PeLi

Prince Enters the Forest, The. Henri Cole. DiPo

Prince Eugenius, the knight so noble. Prince Eugene. *Unknown*. AuPH, *tr. by* Lowell A. Bangerter

Prince Foma. Pavel Nikolaevich Vasilyev [*or* Vasil'ev]. TCRP, *tr. by* David Macduff

Prince Hamlet thought Uncle a traitor. Hamlet. Stanley J. Sharpless. NBLV; PeLi

Prince Heathen. *Unknown*. ESPB

Prince New Year, welcome to thy throne. To the New Year. Priscilla Jane Thompson. CBWP-2

Prince of Love, The. William Blake. *See* How Sweet I Roamed [*or* Roam'd] from Field to Field

Prince of Peace His Banner Spreads, The. Harry Emerson Fosdick. AH

Prince Robert. *Unknown*. ESPB; OxBB

Prince Rupert's Drop, The. Jane Draycott. OxBSo

Prince's Progress, The. Christina Georgina Rossetti.
  "Too late for love, too late for joy." OBEV; WPE

Prince Tan of Yen knew how to treat a man—. In Praise of Ching K'o. Ch'ien T'ao. ColAnChi, *tr. by* J. R. Hightower

Prince Wen Hui's cook. Cutting up an Ox. Chuang Tzu. EnlH, *tr. by* Thomas Merton

Prince who said an English Senate can, The. Anne Merryweather. EMWP

Prince, with Wonder, sees the stately Tow'rs, The. Virgil [*or* Vergil]. OBVE, *tr. by* John Dryden [*or* Eneados, *Aeneis*], The.

Princely eagle, and the soaring hawke, The. William Wood. SCAP

Princes of Mercia were badger and raven, The. Thrall to their freedom, I dug and hoarded. Geoffrey Hill. HAP; NAEL-5v2; NAEL-6v2; NPeEn; NoAM; NoP-4; PoE; WoPoe *Fr.* Mercian Hymns.

Princess, The. Muhammad Al-As'ad. MAP, *tr. by* Charles Doria and Lena Jayyusi

Princess, The. Dame Edith Sitwell. BWW *Fr.* Sleeping Beauty, The.

Princess, The. Tennyson.
  "As through the land at eve we went." SCGP
  "Ask me no more: the moon may draw the sea." NAEL-5v2; NAEL-6v2
  Blow, Bugle, Blow. NOBE; OBEV; UnPo
  "Deep in the night I woke: she, near me, held." EroLit
  "Home they brought her warrior dead." OxAEP-2
  "So sang the gallant glorious chronicle." OBGa
  So was their sanctuary violated.
  "Blame not thyself too much, I said, nor blame." NAEL-5v2; NAEL-6v2
  "Come down, O maid, from yonder mountain height." EBVV; GTBS-P; NAEL-5v2; NAEL-6v2; NOBVV; NPeEn; OBEV; OxBEV; SCGP
  "Now sleeps the crimson petal, now the white." BoLoP; EBEV; EBVV; FHYEP; GTBS-P; NAEL-5v2; NAEL-6v2; NIL-7; NOBE; NPeEn; NoP-4; OxAEP-2; SCGP; SCV; TFi; WoPoe
  (Song.) OPOU
  (Summer Night.) OBEV
  "So she low-toned; while with shut eyes I lay." EBVV
  "Splendor falls on castle walls, The." AWP; ChAP; ClHu; EBVV; FHYEP; FaBoCh; GTBS-P; HeIP-4; InPK-6; NAEL-5v2; NAEL-6v2; NoP-4; PeVV; TFi
  "Sweet and low, sweet and low." ChAP; FHYEP; NAEL-5v2; NAEL-6v2; SCGP
  There sinks the nebulous star we call the Sun.
  "Tears, idle tears, I know not what they mean." AWP; CABP; EBVV; GTBS-P; HAP; NAEL-5v2; NAEL-6v2; NIL-7; NIP-4; NOBE; NoP-4; OxAEP-2; OxBEV; PoE; PoPoPo; SCGP; TFi; TreFP; UnPo
  (We Kiss'd Again with Tears.) PoToHe

Princess is sad, and in anguish reposes, The. Sonatina. "Rubén Dario." SpanPo, *tr. by* John Crow

Princess is sad, The. What ails the Princess? Sonatina. "Rubén Dario." TCLAP, *tr. by* Lysander Kemp

Princess of Scotland, The. Rachel Annand Taylor. NePenScot

Princess of the nights, be welcome. Night's Delights. Kaspar Stieler. GePo, *tr. by* Ingrid Waløe-Engel

Princess Parade. Sarah Gorham. FFC

Princess Sabbath. Heinrich Heine. TrJP, *tr. by* Charles Godfrey Leland

"Princess," said the Frog, "Do not wince." Limerick: "'Princess,' said the Frog, 'Do not wince.'" Gina Berkeley. PeLi

Princess that your love was not responded. Elegy for Joan the Mad One. Federico García Lorca. BLPSL, *tr. by* Rene de Costa, Rigas Kappatos and Eleni Paidoussi

Princess Victoria, The. Letitia [*or* Laetitia] Elizabeth Landon. RWP

Principles, When I Felt Them. Prageeta Sharma. HeMarv

Printed Words. Liz Sohappy Bahe. CDW

Printer's Error. P. G. Wodehouse. OBCoV

Printers. Denis Glover. PeNZ

Printing Bibles is Jenny's daily chore. Printing Jenny. Matthew Mitchell. OxBTC

Printing Jenny. Matthew Mitchell. OxBTC

Printing-Press, The. Christopher Pearse Cranch. APN-1 *Fr.* Seven Wonders of the World.

Printing the stones. (LL) Otter, The. Seamus Heaney. NoAM; PNI

Priorities at Friday Ranch. William Stafford. BodElec

Priory of St Saviour, Glendalough, The. Donald Davie. OxBC

Pripet Marshes, The. Irving Feldman. TaR

Prism crystal sets towards the axis, The. Chromatin. J. H. Prynne. PFTM-2

Prisms. Laura Riding Jackson. APT-2; ColAP

Prison. Mahmoud Darwish. AF, *tr. by* Denys Johnson-Davies

Prison, The. Samuel Ha-Nagid. WoPoe, *tr. by* T. Carmi

Prison, The. Maria Luisa Spaziani. CItWP, *tr. by* Cinzia Sartini Blum and Lara Trubowitz

Prison Daybreak, A. Faiz Ahmad Faiz. AF, *tr. by* Agha Shahid Ali

Prison Evening, A. Faiz Ahmad Faiz. VCWP, *tr. by* Agha Shahid Ali

Prison gets to be a friend, A. Emily Dickinson. APN-2; NCAP

Prison-house in which I live, The. Renewal of Strength. Frances Ellen Watkins Harper. PWR

Prison in Windsor Castle. Henry Howard, Earl of Surrey. NoSic; SCGP
  (In Windsor Castle.) NOBE
  (So Cruel Prison.) CABP; HAP; NoP-4

Prison Song. Alan Dugan. YaYoPo

Prisoned in Windsor, He Recounteth His Pleasure There Passed. Henry Howard, Earl of Surrey. NAEL-5v1; NAEL-6v1; NAEL-7v1 *Fr.* Windsor Castle.

Prisoner. Wole Soyinka. PBMAP *Fr.* Idanre and Other Poems (1967).

Prisoner, The. Emily Jane Brontë. NAEL-6v2; NALW; NOBVV
  "Still let my tyrants know, I am not doomed to wear." NOBE; NoP-4; OBEV

Prisoner, The. Keith Douglas. HarvBoo

Prisoner, The. Po Chü-i. ChiP, *tr. by* Arthur Waley

Prisoner of Chillon, The. Byron.
  "Kind of change came in my fate, A." NOBE
  Sonnet on Chillon. CenSon; GSo
  (On the Castle of Chillon.) GTBS-P

Prisoner of Los Angeles (2). Wanda Coleman. GeoHom

Prisoner of Love. Clarence Gaskill. ReLy

Prisoner of Zenda, The. Richard Wilbur. NBLV; OBCoV

Prisoner ran forward, The. First his head. Essay on Death. Hayden Carruth. BodElec

Prisoner's Dream, The. Eugenio Montale. PoetW, *tr. by* Jonathan Galassi

Prisoner's Lay, A. George Wither.
  "First think, my soul, if I have foes." SacPr

Prisoners. Randall Jarrell. OxBA

Prisoners. Denise Levertov. NoAM; VCAP

Prisoners, The. Alexander Brome.
  "Come a *brimmer* (my bullies) drink whole ones or nothing." PBRV

Prisoners, The. Stephen Spender. FaBoMo; MoBrPo

Prisoners, committed to death, The. Hunger. Jerome Rothenberg. APSN

Prisoners of Saint Lawrence, The. Martín Espada. TouFir

Prisoners of War. John Jarmain. FaBoWar

Prisons. Lőrinc Szabó. IQMS, *tr. by* Edwin Morgan

Prisons Are Full of Convicts, The. Yang Yi. SuSp, *tr. by* Jonathan Chaves

Prithee die and set me free. Out of an Epigram of Martial. Martial. OBVE, *tr. by* Sir John Denham

Prithee, fine lady, come under my bush. (LL) *Unknown*. FaBoVe; LB; OxNR

Privacy. Olga Broumas. PasH

Private, A. Edward Thomas. GTBS-P; PeFWW; TCAWP

Private, The. Robert Adamson. BMAP

Private Airplane. Chase Twichell. ExTi

Private Bottling, A. Don Paterson. EmeKit; NePenScot

Private But Sulphurous. Tom Matthews. PNI

Private Conference of Harry Fat, The. James Keir Baxter. PeLV

Private Dining Room, The. Ogden Nash. OBCoV

Private faces in public places. W. H. Auden. FaBoEE; PeLV *Fr.* Shorts [1927–1932].

Private First Class Brooks Morgenstein, U. S. M. C. Bryan Alec Floyd. CDa

Private Ian Godwin, U. S. M. C. Bryan Alec Floyd. CDa

Private Jack Smith, U. S. M. C. Bryan Alec Floyd. CDa

Private John Ball Wounded in the Wood. David Jones. TCAWP *Fr.* In Parenthesis.

Private Letter to Brazil, A. Gloria C. Oden. ESEAA; GT

Private madness has prevailed, A. O Virtuous Light. Elinor Wylie. MoAmPo

Private Means Is Dead. Stevie Smith. OxBC

Private Occasion in a Public Place, A. David Antin. PmAP

Private of the Buffs; or, The British Soldier in China. Sir Francis Hastings Doyle. FaBoWar; OBEV

Private Poem.   Strato [*or* Straton].   GrAn, *tr.* by Teddy Hogge

Private Sadness.   Bob Kaufman.   ISC

Private School for Girls, May 14, 1948, New York City, A.   Florence W. Freed.   GotH

Private Theatricals.   Louise Imogen Guiney.   PoBW

Private Transport.   Adrian Mitchell.   FaBoEE

Private Truce.   Lőrinc Szabó.   IQMS, *tr.* by Peter Zollman

Privets Come into Season at High Tide.   Ted Greenwald.   FTOS

Privilege of Being.   Robert Hass.   NIP-4

Privilege to die, The. (LL)   Heart asks Pleasure—first, The.   Emily Dickinson.   APN-2; MoAmPo; NAAL-2v1; NAAL-3; NOBA; NoP-4; OxBA; PoPoPo; TCAPo; WPE

Privileged fill the imperial ranks, The.   At Li's Mountain Hermitage.   Wang Wei.   CrYelRi, *tr.* by Sam Hamill

Privy Counsellors do not sleep in barns. (LL)   Lodging with the Old Man of the Stream.   Po Chü-i.   AWP; BLT; ChiP, *tr.* by Arthur Waley

Privy-Love for My Landlady.   George Farewell.   NOEC; OBCoV

Prize for Good Conduct.   Kenneth Allott.   OBWP

Prize-giving.   Gwen Harwood.   CBAP

Prize Riddle on Herself When 24, A.   Elizabeth Frances Amherst.   ECWP

Pro Eto.   Vladimir Vladimirovich Mayakovsky [*or* Maiakovskii].   "No matter how much more waiting I'll have to do."   TCRP

Pro Femina.   Carolyn Kizer.   "From Sappho to myself, consider the fate of women."   VCAP   "I take as my theme."The Independent Woman"   FFC; VCAP   "I will speak about women of letters, for I'm in the racket."   NALW

Pro Patria.   Constance Carrier.   WPE

Pro Patria.   Adah Isaacs Menken.   CBWP-1

Pro Patria Mori.   Thomas Moore.   GTBS-P; OxAEP-2

Pro patria mori. (LL)   Dulce et Decorum Est.   Wilfred Owen.   AmFaPo; CABP; FaBoTw; FaBoWar; HarvBoo; HeIP-4; InPK-6; MoBrPo; NAEL-5v2; NAEL-6v2; NIL-7; NIP-4; NoAM; NoP-4; OBWP; OxBEV; PeFWW; PoE; PoPoPo; PoWW; RaBo; TCAWP; TFi; TRP; UnPo

Pro Sua Vita.   Robert Penn Warren.   MoAmPo

Probable Cause.   Thomas McGrath.   GifTon

Probably.   Keith Preston.   NBLV

Probably the most human thing I do.   Eleanor Brown.   NeBl

Probably the song of a temple prostitute, priestess of the second caste.   Armand Schwerner.   PFTM-2   *Fr.* Tablets, The.

Probably to relate to the notes on 4-dim'l perspective.   Cast Shadows.   Marcel Duchamp.   PFTM-1

Probatioun Officeres Tale, The.   Gerard Benson.   NBLV

Problem, A.   Carolyn Wells.   SWaP

Problem, The.   Paul Blackburn.   NeAP

Problem, The.   Ralph Waldo Emerson.   APN-1; AWP; NAAL-2v1; NAAL-3; NOBA; OxBA; TAP

Problem here is that, The.   Sherbet.   Cornelius Eady.   GT; LTA

Problem in History, A.   Robert Wallace.   CRP

Problem is not the letter X, The.   Malcolm Is 'Bout More Than Wearing a Cap.   Michael Warr.   UnSA

Problem of Anxiety, The.   John Ashbery.   BAP-97

Problems With Hurricanes.   Víctor Hernández Cruz.   PmAP

Procedure.   Ann Lauterbach.   BodElec

Procedures for Underground.   Margaret Atwood.   NALW

Process.   John Montague.   CIP-2

Process.   Charles Leo O'Donnell.   SacPr

Process calls for twenty heads to stare, The.   David Wojahn.   PBCAP   *Fr.* Mystery Train: A Sequence.

Process of Conception, The.   Claude Quillet.   ECEV   *Fr.* Callipaedia; or, The Art of Getting Beautiful Children.

Processes activities break drop and disappear, The.   Allen Fisher.   Oth   *Fr.* Emergent Manner.

Processes of generation; deeds of settlement.   Geoffrey Hill.   NoP-4   *Fr.* Mercian Hymns.

Procession, The.   Sarah Rosenblatt.   AmPoNex

Procession, A. Southern wails. A yellow.   Southern Birth.   Kevin Powell.   AmPoNex; InTrad

Procession at Candlemas, A.   Amy Clampitt.   FaBoWP; HCAP; PoPoPo

Procession of ghosts shuffles by, The.   Carnival at the River.   Robert Greacen.   PNI

Procession of honest men, A.   Selah.   Ronald Stuart Thomas.   FaBoMo

Processions, The.   Mário de Andrade.   TCLAP, *tr.* by Jack E. Tomlins

Processions that lack high stilts have nothing that catches the eye.   High Talk.   W. B. Yeats.   FaBoVe; RaBo

Proclaim liberty throughout.   Inscription on the Liberty Bell.   Bible, *O.T.*   CA

Proclaim the Lofty Praise.   Sarah Judson.   AH

Proclamation, or Paper Bomb, The.   F. W. Reitz.   PeSAV, *tr.* by F. W. Reitz

Proclamation without Pretention.   Tristan Tzara.   NAWM-7v2, *tr.* by Mary Ann Caws

Procne.   Peter Quennell.   MoBrPo

Procne, Philomela, and Itylus.   Philomela.   John Crowe Ransom.   APT-1; FuPo; NAAL-2v2; NOBA; NoAM; OBAL; OBSV; OxBA

Proconsul of Bithynia.   To Petronius Arbiter.   Oliver St. John Gogarty.   OBMV

Procrastination.   George Crabbe.   NOBRP

Procrastination.   Martial.   AWP; FaBoEE; OBVE, *tr.* by Abraham Cowley

Procurers.   Novella Nikolaevna Matveyeva [*or* Matveieva].   TCRP, *tr.* by Deming Brown

Procuress, The.   Herodas.   HePo, *tr.* by Barbara Hughes Fowler

Prodigal, The.   Elizabeth Bishop.   APT-2; ChIV-2; CoAP; GI; LCAP-2; TwCP

Prodigal Daughter.   Angelina Muñiz Huberman.   MirDau, *tr.* by Aurora Camacho

Prodigal Son, The.   Robert Bly.   ChIV-2

Prodigal Son, The.   Leah Goldberg.   GI, *tr.* by Robert Friend

Prodigal Son, The.   Rudyard Kipling.   NoAM   *Fr.* Kim.

Prodigal Son, The.   W. S. Merwin.   "And the silence off on the hills might be an echo."   GI

Prodigal Son, The.   Edwin Arlington Robinson.   GI; MoAmPo

Prodigal Son is kneeling in the husks, The.   Prodigal Son, The.   Robert Bly.   ChIV-2

Prodigals.   Phoebe Cary.   SacPr

Prodigy.   Charles Simic.   AF; VCAP

Prodigy, The.   Lola Haskins.   MiVo

Prodike.   Rufinus.   GrAn, *tr.* by Alan Marshfield

Produce.   Debra Allbery.   PBCAP

Produce from the colonies.   Pierre McOrlan.   MFP, *tr.* by Martin Sorrell

Produce, Produce.   Susan Wheeler.   KGB

Produce the urn that Hannibal contains.   Juvenal.   OBVE, *tr.* by William Gifford   *Fr.* Satires.

Product.   George Oppen.   HarvBoo

Product of Evolution, I Invest in a Mutual Fund, A.   Amanda Pecor.   BodElec

Product of peoples on two sides of a narrow sea, The.   Lyle Donaghy, Poet, 1902–1949.   George Buchanan.   PNI

Proem: "From Zeus let us begin, him we mortals never."   Aratus.   HePo, *tr.* by Barbara Hughes Fowler   *Fr.* Phaenomena.

Proem: "I love the old melodious lays."   John Greenleaf Whittier.   APN-1; OxBA; TAP

Proem: "Lo, thus, as prostrate, 'In the dust I write'."   James Thomson.   OxBS   *Fr.* City of Dreadful Night, The.

Proem: "Out of my own great woe."   Heinrich Heine.   AWP, *tr.* by Elizabeth Barrett Browning

Proem: To Brooklyn Bridge.   Hart Crane.   *See* Bridge, The

Profane, The.   Horace.   AWP, *tr.* by Abraham Cowley   *Fr.* Odes.

Profaning the Dead.   Carole Bernstein.   AmPoNex

Professional, The.   David Ignatow.   NNaP

Professional Poet.   Bogomil Gjuzel.   CarOv, *tr.* by Carolyn Kizer

Professor and Ginger are standing in the space in front, The.   Gilligan's Island.   Tim Dlugos.   ReTh

Professor at the Breakfast Table, The.   Oliver Wendell Holmes.   Lord of All Being, Throned Afar.   AH   O Love Divine, That Stooped to Share.   AH

Professor Burke's symphony, "Colorado Vistas."   Cultural Notes.   Kenneth Fearing.   PoE

Professor Eisenbart, asked to attend.   Prize-giving.   Gwen Harwood.   CBAP

Professor Eisenbart, with grim distaste.   Panther and Peacock.   Gwen Harwood.   CBAP

Professor Gratt.   Donald Hall.   OBAL

Professor invites me to his "Black Lit" class; they're, A.   Passing.   Toi Derricotte.   OPRER

Professor Kelleher and the Charles River.   Desmond O'Grady.   CIP-2; PBCIP

Professor Noctutus.   George Macdonald.   NOBVV

Professor of Ethical Culture, A.   Limerick.   *Unknown.*   PeLi

Professor Palamedes darts down Westow Street.   News from Norwood.   Christopher Middleton.   FaBoMo

Professor Robinson each summer beats.   Don's Holiday.   George Rostrevor Hamilton.   OBCoV

Professor's Song, A.   John Berryman.   HeIP-4; NAAL-2v2; NOBA; NoAM; OxBC

Profile of Rose.   Glyn Jones.   OBWVE

Profile on the Pillow, The.   Dudley Randall.   BPo; TAP

Profiles of My Father.   Rhyll McMaster.   CBAP

Profit and Loss.   John Oxenham.   SacPr

Profit and Loss: An Elegy upon the Decease of Mrs. Mary Gerrish.   John Danforth.   SCAP

Profit may and will the pains requite, The. (LL)   Rachel Speght.   BASC; WPE

Profit?—Loss? Profit and Loss. John Oxenham. SacPr

Profiteers. Pope. ECEV; OBSV *Fr.* First Epistle of the First Book of Horace Imitated, The.

Profound the radiance issuing. Eve. David Gascoyne. GTBS-P

Profuse announcement. Paul Celan. PoetW, *tr. by* John Felstiner

Progeny of Cain, The. Nikolai Stepanovich Gumilyov [*or* Gumiliov *or* Gumilev]. TCRP, *tr. by* Simon Franklin

Prognosis. Debra Bruce. IllVoic

Prognosis. Louis MacNeice. NOBE

Prognosis. George Starbuck. YaYoPo

Prognostication on Will Laud, Late Archbishop of Canterbury, A. *Unknown.* OxBoLi

Program Notes. Ruth Roston. MiVo

Progress. Matthew Arnold. ChIV-2

Progress. Robert Conquest. OBCoV

Progress. Samuel Hoffenstein. OBCoV

Progress. Pope. ECEV *Fr.* Windsor-Forest [*or* Windsor Forest].

Progress. Barrett Watten.
"Relax, / stand at attention, and." PmAP
"Isolate *and*." FTOS

Progress of a Divine, The. Richard Savage.
"Now in the patron's mansion see the wight." OBSV

Progress of Liberty, The. Mary Robinson.
Book 1.
"Superstition, more destructive still." RWP

Progress of Love, The. Robert Dodsley. ECEV

Progress of Man, The. George Canning. NOBRP

Progress of Poesy, The. Matthew Arnold. NOBVV

Progress of Poesy, The. Thomas Gray. AWP; GTBS-P; NOEC; OBEV

Progress of Poesy, The. Thomas Gray. AWP; GTBS-P; NOEC; OBEV
"In climes beyond the solar road." OxAEP-1

Progress of Poetry, The. "Christopher Caudwell." OxBTC

Progress of Poetry, The. Jonathan Swift. NOIV

Progressions of Spacetime: I. Allen Fisher. Oth *Fr.* Stepping Out.

Progressive Man's Indignation, A. Dimitris Tsaloumas. BMAP

Prohibiting all hope. Dello da Signa. EaItPo, *tr. by* Dante Gabriel Rossetti

Prohibition, The. John Donne. MeLP; NOSC

Project. Piera Oppezzo. CItWP, *tr. by* Cinzia Sartini Blum and Lara Trubowitz

Project: Flag. Tadeusz Borowski. AF, *tr. by* Larry Rafferty

Project for Freight Trains, A. David Young. GM

Project of Linear Inquiry, The. Michael Palmer. PmAP

Projected Scenario of a Performance to Be Given Before the UN. Lawson Fusao Inada. FaBoA

Projection. Langston Hughes. PFTM-1

Projection, A. Reed Whittemore. AiP

Projector O film still! Capitalist Projections. Brenda Coultas. HeMarv

Prokosch in Tehran, 1978. Dominador I. Ilio. ReBoTo

Prolegomenon to a Theodicy, A. Kenneth Rexroth.
"Bell, The." PFTM-1

Proletarian Portrait. William Carlos Williams. BLT; OBAL; SAmP; TAP

"Prolific and the Devourer," The. W. H. Auden.
"Conversion of stones into bread would be a supernatural miracle, The." GI

Prologomena to a Poetics. Jerome Rothenberg. PFTM-2

Prologue. Oliver Wendell Holmes. NCAP

Prologue. Audre Lorde. ESEAA

Prologue. Archibald MacLeish. MoAmPo

Prologue. Milestone: The Birth of an Ancestor. Eugene B. Redmond. SpirFl

Prologue, The. Anne Bradstreet. BASC; BoWoP; EMWP; NAAL-2v1; NAAL-3; NAAL-5; NALW; NOBA; NoP-4; OxBA; PEW; PoE; SCAP; TAP; TCAPo; WPE
"I am obnoxious to each carping tongue." WoPoe

Prologue: "And the way goes on in the worn earth." Archibald MacLeish. NoAM *Fr.* Conquistador.

Prologue: "As needy gallants in the scriv'ners' hands." Dryden. OBSV *Fr.* Amboyna; or, The Cruelties of the Dutch to the English Merchants.

Prologue: "Exult each patriot heart!—this night is shewn." Royall Tyler. NAAL-3 *Fr.* Contrast, The.

Prologue from "Legacy." Patricia Parker. GLP

Prologue: "He who writ [*or* wrote] this, not without pains and thought." Dryden. PeLV *Fr.* Secret Love; or, The Maiden Queen.

Prologue: "I have come down." Odia Ofeimun. HBAPE; NAfrP

Prologue: "I'll mock those thoughts of yours." Vladimir Vladimirovich Mayakovsky [*or* Maiakovskii]. TCRP, *tr. by* Bernard Meares *Fr.* Cloud in Trousers, The.

Prologue: "I wrote this when the sky was still serene." Mihály Vörösmarty. IQMS, *tr. by* Peter Zollman

Prologue in Heaven. Goethe. *Fr.* Faust.

Prologue: "Lord, can a crumb of dust the earth outweigh." Edward Taylor. NAAL-2v1; NAAL-3; NAAL-5; TCAPo *Fr.* Preparatory Meditations Before My Approach to the Lord's Supper.

Prologue: "Love, to give law unto his subject hearts." Sir Thomas Wyatt. ChIV-1 *Fr.* Penitential Psalms.

Prologue: "Mirra Lokhvitskaia's ashes are now entombed." "Igor Severyanin [*or* Severianin]." TCRP, *tr. by* Bernard Meares

Prologue: "O love, the interest itself in thoughtless heaven." W. H. Auden. EBEV; FaBoMo

Prologue on the Old Winchester Playhouse over the Old Butchers' Shambles. Thomas Warton, the Younger. ECEV

Prologue: "Our author by experience finds it true." Dryden. OxBoLi *Fr.* Aureng-Zebe.

Prologue Spoken by Mr[.] Garrick at the Opening of the Theatre in Drury Lane, 1747. Samuel Johnson. EBEV; NAEL-5v1; NAEL-6v1; NAEL-7v1; NOEC; OxAEP-1

Prologue [Spoken by Mr. Horden]: "First Adventurer for her fame I stand, The." Delariviere Manley. EMWP *Fr.* Lost Lover, The.

Prologue: The Birth of Architecture. W. H. Auden. *Fr.* Thanksgiving for a Habitat.

Prologue: The rain fell hard on the Jacqueline Kennedy Onassis auction. Weather Report. Brenda Coultas. HeMarv

Prologue: The Wanderers. William Morris. EBVV *Fr.* Earthly Paradise, The.

Prologue to a Time That Is Not Itself. Eunice Odio. TCLAP, *tr. by* Martha Collins

Prologue to Hugh Kelly's *A Word to the Wise.* Samuel Johnson. EBEV; NPeEn; OxAEP-1

Prologue to "Love Triumphant." Dryden. OxBoLi *Fr.* Love Triumphant.

Prologue to Sir Thopas. Geoffrey Chaucer. NAEL-5v1 *Fr.* Canterbury Tales, The.

Prologue to the Aetia. Callimachus. WoPoe, *tr. by* Stanley Lombardo and Diane Rayor

Prologue to the Avowis of Alexander. John Barbour. OxBS *Fr.* Buik of Alexander, The.

Prologue to the Book "Anatol." Hugo von Hofmannsthal. AuPH, *tr. by* Lowell A. Bangerter

Prologue to The Collected Poems. Dylan Thomas. *See* Author's Prologue

Prologue to the First Satire. Persius. AWP, *tr. by* John Dryden *Fr.* Satires.

Prologue to "The Lakers; a Comic Opera." James Plumptre.
"Where Cumbria's mountains in the north arise." NOEC

Prologue to the Miller's Tale. Geoffrey Chaucer. NAWM-5v1; NAWM-7v1, *tr. by* Theodore Morrison *Fr.* Canterbury Tales, The.

Prologue to the Pardoner's Tale. Geoffrey Chaucer. NAWM-5v1; NAWM-7v1, *tr. by* Theodore Morrison *Fr.* Canterbury Tales, The.

Prologue: "Under the shadow of the gloomy night." Samuel Rowlands. NOSC

Prologue: "We Who with Songs Beguile Your Pilgrimage." James Elroy Flecker. OBMV; OxBTC; UV *Fr.* Golden Journey to Samarkand, The.

Prologues are over. It is a question, now, The. Asides on the Oboe. Wallace Stevens. FaBoMo; MoAmPo

Prolonged horizontal pleasures. Q.E.D. Mary Low. SurWo

Prolonged Sonnet: In the Last Days of the Emperor Henry VII. Simone dall' Antela. AWP; EaItPo, *tr. by* Dante Gabriel Rossetti

Prolonged Sonnet: When the Troops Were Returning from Milan. Niccolò degli Albizzi. AWP; EaItPo; FaBoWar; OBVE, *tr. by* Dante Gabriel Rossetti

Promachus hangs here. Mnasalcas. GrAn

Promenade. David Ignatow. TrJP

Promenade, The. U Tam'si Tchicaya. NegPo, *tr. by* Ellen Conroy Kennedy

Prometheus. Byron. NOBE; OxAEP-2

Prometheus. Goethe. AWP, *tr. by* John S. Dwight

Prometheus. Robert Horan. YaYoPo

Prometheus. Jenny Mastoraki. BoWoP, *tr. by* Nikos Germanakos

Prometheus. Charles Tomlinson. HarvBoo

Prometheus fashioned man. "Michael Field." ViWPN

Prometheus Pyrphoros. Trumbull Stickney.
Pandora's Songs. APN-2

Prometheus Unbound. Alec Derwent Hope. OxBC

Prometheus Unbound [A Lyrical Drama in Four Acts]. Shelley. NAEL-5v2; NAEL-6v2; NOBRP
"As I have said, I floated to the earth." FHYEP
"Crawling glaciers pierce me with the spears." FHYEP
Life of Life. NOBE; PoE
(Hymn to the Spirit of Nature.) GTBS-P
"My soul is enchanted boat." FHYEP
"On a poet's lips I slept." GTBS-P; TOF
"There the voluptuous nightingales." OWoS
"This is the day, which down the void abysm." FHYEP

"Thou, Earth, calm empire of a happy soul." PeECV

"Thou knowest that toads and snakes and loathly worms." PoE

PROMETHEUS, when first from heaven high. Sir Edward Dyer. NoSic

Promiscuity. Lisa Fishman. AmPoNex

Promise. Joe Wenderoth. BodElec

Promise, A. Sir Thomas Wyatt. BoLoP

Promise, The. Toi Derricotte. GT

Promise, The. Jewel C. Latimore. BlSi

Promise, The. Sharon Olds. ExTi

Promise, The. Heberto Padilla. TCLAP, *tr. by* Alexander Coleman and Alastair Reid

Promise, The. Jones Very. NCAP

Promise! Mafika Pascal Gwala. NAfrP

Promise me no promises. Promises like Pie-Crust. Christina Georgina Rossetti. NAEL-6v2; NOBVV; NPeEn

Promise of Peace. Robinson Jeffers. MoAmPo

Promise This, When You be Dying. Emily Dickinson. SWaP

Promise to California, A. Walt Whitman. APN-1

Promised Land, The. Jessie E. Sampter. TrJP

Promises. Richard Shelton. GifTon

Promises like Pie-Crust. Christina Georgina Rossetti. NAEL-6v2; NOBVV; NPeEn

Promises of Freedom. *Unknown.* BPo; NAAAL

Promises of Leniency and Forgiveness. Charles Simic. LCAP-2

Promising Author. Carolyn Kizer. GeoHom

Promontory. Arthur Rimbaud. SxFrPo, *tr. by* Martin Sorrell

Prompt sadness of Schumann and Tchaikovsky. From Bowling Green. Al Young. ESEAA

Prompting of my shadow, The. Roberto Juarroz. VCWP *Fr.* Seventh Vertical Poetry.

Prone couple still sleeps, A. First Light. Thomas Kinsella. BIrV; PoE

Prone, I stretch myself upon a mountain where it's grassy. Elegy on a Broom Bush. Árpád Tóth. IQMS, *tr. by* Neville Masterman

Pronouns, The—A Collection of 40 Dances—For the Dancers. Jackson Mac Low.

   1st Dance—Making Things New—6 February 1964. FTOS; PFTM-2; PmAP

   2nd Dance—Seeing Lines—6 February 1964. PFTM-2

   6th Dance—Doing Things With Pencils—17–18 February 1964. PmAP

   12th Dance—Getting Leather by Language—21 February 1964. PmAP

   27th Dance—Walking—22 March 1964. FTOS

Proof. Bessie Calhoun Bird. BlSi

Proof. Brendan Kennelly. CIP-2; PBCIP

Proof. Czeslaw Milosz. TOF, *tr. by* the author

Proof, The. Richard Wilbur. CRP; InvLi; OxBSP

Proofs. Tadeusz Rózewicz. PoSu, *tr. by* Adam Czerniawski

Proper Clay. Mark Van Doren. PoRA

Proper New Ballad Entitled [*or* Intituled] The Fairies' [*or* Faeryes] Farewell, or God-a-Mercy Will, A. Richard Corbet [*or* Corbett]. BASC; BeJo; NOSC; OxBEV; PBRV; PeLV

Proper Pride. D. H. Lawrence. FaBoEE

Proper scale would pat you on the head, The. Scales, The. William Empson. FaBoMo

Proper Song, Entitled: Fain Would I Have a Pretty Thing to Give unto My Lady, A. *Unknown.* NoSic

Proper way to eat a fig, in society, The. Figs. D. H. Lawrence. EroLit

Properties of a Good Greyhound, The. Dame Juliana Berners. RB; WoPoe, *tr. by* Seamus Heaney

Property. Robert Garioch. FaBoWar

Properzia Rossi. Felicia Dorothea Hemans. RWP; VWP; ViWPN

Prophecies or Memories or Display-Board Newspapers. Andrea Zanzotto.

   "Eva, forma futuri." ItPo, *tr. by* Gayle Ridinger

Prophecy. Eileen Duggan. PeNZ

Prophecy. Elinor Wylie. BoWoP; FaBoWP; ItWoWo; VGW

Prophecy, A. Allen Ginsberg. TAP

Prophecy, The. József Bajza. IQMS, *tr. by* Judith Kroll

Prophecy, The. Robert Wrigley. SwNoth

Prophecy of a Ten Ton Cheese. James McIntyre. VerBaPo

Prophecy of Famine, The. Charles Churchill.

   "For bards, like these, who neither sing nor say." NOEC

   "Oft have I heard thee mourn the wretched lot." OBSV

   "Two boys, whose birth beyond all question springs." OBSV

Prophet, The. Rose Drachler. TaR

Prophet, The. Kahlil Gibran.

   Crime and Punishment. PoToHe

   On Children. PoToHe

   On Work. PoToHe

Prophet, The. Alexander Sergeyevich Pushkin. AWP, *tr. by* Babette Deutsch and Avrahm Yarmolinsky

Prophet, The. Yevgeny [*or* Evgenii] Mikhailovich Vinokurov. TCRP, *tr. by* Daniel Weissbort

Prophet, The. "Yehoash." TrJP, *tr. by* Isidore Goldstick

Prophet digs with iron hands, The. Transfiguration. Djuna Barnes. SPE

Prophet, Go, Flee! Hayyim Nahman [*or* Khayim Nakhman *or* Chaim Nachman] Bialik. MHP, *tr. by* Ruth Finer Mintz

Prophet Jeremiah and the Personification of Israel, The. Eleazar ben Kalir. TrJP, *tr. by* Nina Davis Salaman

Prophet Lost in the Hills at Evening, The. Joseph Hilaire Pierre Belloc. SacPr

Prophet of the body's roving. Walt Whitman. Edwin Honig. TAP

Prophet's Lantern, The. David Lehman. KGB

Prophet speaks, The. Saint Malcolm. Jewel C. Latimore. BPo

Prophet stood, The. Psalm of Silk. Malachi. WaCA

Prophet tribe with burning eyes set forth, The. Gypsies on the Move. Charles Baudelaire. GS, *tr. by Unknown*

Prophet works hard at dreaming, The. Prophet, The. Rose Drachler. TaR

Prophetess, The. Dorothy Livesay. MoCV

Prophetic Powers. *Unknown.* APN-2, *tr. by* Henry Rowe Schoolcraft

Prophetic Soul. Dorothy Parker. LW

Prophetissa. Diane Di Prima. PFTM-2

Prophets at street corners, in neat grey suits. Saturday Night. Antigone Kefala. CBAP

Prophets for a New Day. Margaret Abigail Walker. BPo; NAAAL

Prophets say to Know Thyself: I say it can't be done, The. Karl Shapiro. BodElec *Fr.* Bourgeois Poet, The.

Proportion. Amy Lowell. BoWoP

Proportioned to the groove. (LL) Emily Dickinson. NOBA; TCAPo

Proposal. Maggie Nelson. HeMarv

Proposal. Bayard Taylor. TreFP

Proposition. Nicolás Guillén. TTY, *tr. by* Langston Hughes

Proposition. Robert Pinsky. HCAP; NoAM *Fr.* Essay on Psychiatrists.

Proposition II. Keith Waldrop. InPK-6

Proposition and Invocation. Homer. NOSC, *tr. by* George Chapman *Fr.* Iliad, The.

Propositions. Phyllis Webb. MoCV

Propped against the crowded bar. Naima. Edward Kamau Brathwaite. WoPoe

Propped boughs are heavy with apples. In the Huon Valley. James Philip McAuley. CBAP

Propped on pillows, not attending to business. Sick Leave. Po Chü-i. ChiP, *tr. by* Arthur Waley

Props assist the House, The. Emily Dickinson. APN-2; WPoS

Proputty, proputty, proputty—canter an' canter awaäy. (LL) Northern Farmer: New Style. Tennyson. NAEL-5v2; NAEL-6v2; OBCoV; OxAEP-2; PeVV

Pros-pectin' round about one day. Joe's Luck. Albert Brodrick. PeSAV

Prosaic miles of streets stretch all round. Seder-Night. Israel Zangwill. TrJP

Prosaics. Boris Abramovich Slutsky [*or* Slutskii]. TCRP, *tr. by* J. R. Rowland

Prose 22. Michael Palmer. HarvBoo *Fr.* Series.

Prose 31. Michael Palmer. HarvBoo *Fr.* Series.

Prose for Des Esseintes. Donald Davie. OBVE

Prose of the Trans-Siberian and Little Jean of France. Blaise Cendrars. CuPo

Prose of the Trans-Siberian and of Little Jeanne of France, The. Blaise Cendrars.

   "Back then I was still young." PFTM-1

Prose Poem. Humphrey Jennings. SPE

Prose Poems. Liz Rosenberg.

   "Edith B——and her mother on a Sunday afternoon." UnSA

Proserpine and Dis. Ovid. NPeEn, *tr. by* Arthur Golding *Fr.* Metamorphoses.

Proserpine's Ragout. Mary Leapor. ECWP

Prospect. Ambrose Bierce. APN-2; OBAL *Fr.* Devil's Dictionary, The.

Prospect Beach. Lou Lipsitz. VGW

Prospect of a Landscape, Beginning with a Grove, The. Jane Barker. BASC

Prospect of Eden, The. John Milton. NAEL-5v1; NAWM-7v1; OxAEP-1 *Fr.* Paradise Lost.

Prospect of Heaven Makes Death Easy, A. Isaac Watts. *See* Heaven

Prospect of the Future, The. Mrs. Henry Linden. CBWP-4

Prospect Park. David Schubert. APT-2

Prospect seen as false: the listening, The. Provisional. Reginald Shepherd. UrbNat

Prospecting. A. R. Ammons. CoAmPo

Prospective Immigrants Please Note. Adrienne Rich. AiP; AmFaPo; PoPoPo; VGW

Prospectors' Little Waltz, The. Aleksandr Arkadevich Galich. TCRP, *tr. by* Gene Sosin

Prospectus. William Wordsworth. FHYEP; PoE *Fr.* Excursion, The.

Prospectus and Specimen of an Intended National Work by William and Robert Whistlecraft . . . Relating to King Arthur and His Round Table. John Hookham Frere.

"I've often wish'd that I could write a book." NOBRP

Prospectus to *The Recluse.* William Wordsworth. NAEL-6v2 *Fr.* Recluse; Home at Grasmere, The.

Prosper / O / cell. Ronald Johnson. APSN *Fr.* Ark.

Prosperity and decline have no fixed dwelling. T'ao Ch'ien [*or* T'ao Yuanming]. CoBCP *Fr.* Drinking Wine.

Prospero Listens to the Night. Jack Gilbert. BodElec

Prosperous Villager, The. Li K'ai-hsien. CoBLCP, *tr. by* Jonathan Chaves

Prospice. Robert Browning. FHYEP; ITBLP; NAEL-5v2; NAEL-6v2; PoRA; TrCP

Prostitute living in London, A. Limerick. Douglas Catley. PeLi

Prostitute's shack, The. Issa. EH, *tr. by* Robert Hass

Prostitutes at Smiller's Bar beside the dusty road, The. Cheerful Girls at Smiller's Bar, 1971, The. Jack A. Mapanje. HBAPE; NAfrP; PBMAP; PeSAV

Prostitution. Bogomil Gjuzel. CarOv, *tr. by* Carolyn Kizer

Protect Me, My Talisman. Milo De Angelis. NeIt, *tr. by* Lawrence Venuti

Protect the gleaming, battered soul of her. Faith #1. Esther Iverem. InTrad

Protect us, the poets. Protect us. Reflections Near the House Where Titian Tabidze Lived. Bulat Shalvovich Okudzhava. TCRP, *tr. by* Deming Brown

Protected Species. Susan Wicks. MFPA

Protected Venezuela, the rare, The. Lost Plaza Is Everywhere, The. Rafael Campo. AmPoNex

Protection of a cheap coat suffices, The. Parmenion of Macedon. GrAn

Protective instinct among the Emperor penguins, The. Penguins. Artur Miedzyrzecki. PoSu, *tr. by* John Batki and Artur Miedzyrzecki

Protects the lingering dew-drop from the sun. (LL) To a Child [Written in Her Album]. William Wordsworth. OxBSP; Spl

Protest. Amal Al-Juburi. PoArWo, *tr. by* Salih J. Altoma

Protest. Romelia Alarcón de Folgar. TANSG, *tr. by* Alison Ridley

Protest in the Sixth Year of Ch'ien Fu, A. Ts'ao Sung. ChiP, *tr. by* Arthur Waley

Protest Poem. Vernon Scannell. OBCoV

Protestant graveyard was a forbidden place, The. Weeping Headstones of the Isaac Becketts, The. Paul Durcan. PBCIP

Protestation. Bertrans [*or* Bertran *or* Bertrand] de Born. WoPoe, *tr. by* John Peale Bishop

Protesting at the Nuclear Test Site. Denise Levertov. PoCoUp

Prothalamion. Robert Silliman Hillyer.

"Hills turn hugely in their sleep, The." MoAmPo

Prothalamion. Delmore Schwartz. OxBA

Prothalamion. Edmund Spenser. AWP; EBEV; GTBS-P; HAP; NPeEn; NoSic; OBEV; OxAEP-1; OxBEV; SCGP; TFi; WoPoe

"With that I saw two swans of goodly hue [*or* hew]." OWoS

Prothalamium. Donagh MacDonagh. BIrV

Protocols. Randall Jarrell. LCAP-2; OxBC; VGW

Proton Decay. Robert Pack. ColAP

Proud and beautiful city of Moscow, The. History Lessons. Seamus Deane. BiHa; PBCIP; PNI

Proud Aristagoras, whose vineyard lacks. *Unknown.* PriapPo, *tr. by* Richard W. Hooper *Fr.* Priapus Poems, The.

Proud as Apollo on his forked hill. Pope. OBSV *Fr.* Epistle to Dr. Arbuthnot.

Proud associate told me, A. Fresno Truth, The. Lawson Fusao Inada. GeoHom

Proud Egyptian [*or* Aegyptian] queen, her Roman guest, The. And She Washed His Feet with Her Tear[e]s, and Wiped Them with the Hairs of Her Head. Sir Edward Sherburne. MeLP; NOSC

Proud fountains, wave your plumes. Fountains. Sir Osbert Sitwell. MoBrPo

Proud Hogen Mogen's, we will make you bow. On His Royal Highness His Expedition Against the Dutch. Elizabeth Polwhele. EMWP

Proud in Thy Love. *Unknown.* Son *Fr.* Zepheria.

Proud is my Magyar descent, far to eastward my lineage sprouted. Kölcsey. Ferenc Kölcsey. IQMS, *tr. by* Watson Kirkconnell

Proud Lady Margaret. *Unknown. See* Proud Margret

Proud Maisie. Sir Walter Scott. CABP; FaBoCh; NAEL-5v2; NAEL-6v2; NOBRP; NePenScot; OBEV; OxBEV; OxBS; RACG; SCGP; TFi; UnPo *Fr.* Heart of Midlothian, The.

Proud, majestic Southern sun, The. Husband's Return, The. Priscilla Jane Thompson. CBWP-2

Proud Margret. *Unknown.* OxBB

(Proud Lady Margaret.) ESPB

Proud Music of the Storm. Walt Whitman. APN-1

Proud *Paulus* late my secrecies revealing. Of honest Theft. To my good friend Master Samuel Daniel. Sir John Harington [*or* Harrington]. PBRV

Proud Preston poor people. Preston. *Unknown.* FaBoVe

Proud Queen of the Earth Gods, Supreme Among the Heaven Gods. *Unknown.* HW, *tr. by* Samuel Noah Kramer and Diane Wolkstein *Fr.* Loud Thundering Storm.

Proud Riders. Harold Lenoir Davis. APT-2

Proud Upon an Alien Shore. Rose Furuya Hawkins.

Issei Men: The First Generation. FSt

Nisei Daughter: The Second Generation. FSt

Sansei: The Third Generation. FSt

Proud with success, richly pleased. Alexander Jannai. Constantine P. Cavafy. TrJP, *tr. by* Simon Chasen

Proud word you never spoke, but you will speak. Walter Savage Landor. EnLoPo; OBEV *Fr.* Ianthe.

Proudly swept the rain by the cliffs. Aloha'oe. Queen Lili'u-o-ka-lani. SWaP

Proust's Madeleine. Kenneth Rexroth. NoAM; TRP

Prove It on Me Blues. Gertrude "Ma" Rainey. NAAAL

Proverb. *Unknown.* ReMoGo

Proverb, XXX. John Hall. ChIV-1

Proverbial Advice on Marriage. *Unknown.* NBLV

Proverbios Morales. Santob [*or* Shem-Tob] De Carrion.

"What treasure greater than a friend." TrJP

Proverbs. Bible, *O.T.*

Drunkard, The. TrJP

Fear of the Lord, The. TrJP

Go to the Ant [Thou Sluggard]. TrJP

Happy he who has found wisdom. HW

Happy Is the Man. TrJP

Legacy, The. TrJP

Neither Poverty nor Riches. TrJP

She of the Impudent Face. TrJP

Virtuous Woman, The. TrJP

Words of Agur, The.

"There are three things which are too wonderful for me." TrJP

Proverbs. Teresa de Jesús. AF, *tr. by* Maria Proser

Proverbs. Samuel Ha-Nagid. TrJP, *tr. by* Israel Abrahams

Proverbs 6:6. David Curzon. ChIV-1

(Midrashim: Proverbs 6:6.) WoPoe

Proverbs of Alfred, The. Alfred, King of England. PoE

Proverbs of Hell. William Blake. *Fr.* Marriage of Heaven and Hell, The.

Provide, Provide. Robert Frost. APT-1; ChIV-1; HAP; HarvBoo; NAAL-2v2; NOBA; NoAM; NoP-4; PoE; TAP; TFi; TwCP; UnPo; WeW-3; WoPoe

Providence. George Herbert. BASC

"O sacred Providence, who from end to end." AngWePo

Providence heavenly passeth living thought. Edmund Spenser. NAEL-6v1; NAEL-7v1 *Fr.* Faerie Queene, The.

Providence Journal V: Israel of Puerto Rico. Michael S. Weaver. SpirFl

Province has set up shrines, The. Parihaka. W. H. Oliver. PeNZ

Province I govern is humble and remote, The. To Li Chien. Po Chü-i. AWP; ChiP, *tr. by* Arthur Waley

Province of the Saved, The. Emily Dickinson. TRP

Provinces. C. D. Wright. LCAP-2

Provincetown. Louis Dudek. MoCV

Provincia Deserta. Ezra Pound. OxBA

Provincial Adolescence, A. Michael Foley. PNI

Provincial Sundays. Ramón López Velarde. TCLAP, *tr. by* Julián Manríquez

Proving again that posture is everything. Helicopter Wrecked on a Hill. Christine Hume. BAP-97

Provision a ship for me like a great idea. Miraculous Ship, The. Delmira Agustini. TCLAP, *tr. by* Karl Kirchwey

Provisional. Reginald Shepherd. UrbNat

Provisionally. Ken Edwards. Oth

Provocatively, our epoch swings her breasts. Prostitution. Bogomil Gjuzel. CarOv, *tr. by* Carolyn Kizer

Prowling wolf, whose shaggy skin, A. Wolf and the Dog, The. Jean de La Fontaine. OBVE, *tr. by* Elizur Wright

Prows O' Reekie, The. Lewis Spence. NePenScot; OxBS

Prudence. Ralph Waldo Emerson. OBAL

Prudent Simplicity. Goronwy Owen. FaBoEE, *tr. by* William Cowper

Prudish old lady called Muir, A. Limerick. *Unknown.* PeLi

Prue, my dearest maid, is sick. Upon Prudence Baldwin Her Sickness[e]. Robert Herrick. BASC

Pruned Tree, The. Howard Moss. VCAP

Pruner, The. John Oxenham. SacPr

Pruning, The. Adam David Miller. NBV

Pruning Trees. Po Chü-i. ChiP, *tr. by* Arthur Waley

Pruzzian Elegy. Johannes Bobrowski. AF

Prytherch is dead. We have no right. Dai, Live. Jon Dressel. AngWePo

Psalm. Tudor Arghezi. AF, *tr. by* Andrei Bantas

Psalm. Lucian Blaga. PFTM-1

Psalm. Paul Celan. WoPoe, *tr. by* Margaret Guillemin and Katherine Washburn

Psalm. Peter Huchel. AF, *tr. by* Daniel Simko

Psalm 1. Genrik Veniaminovich Sapgir. ItGoST, *tr. by* J. Kates

Psalm 2. Mahmoud Darwish. AF, *tr. by* Denys Johnson-Davies

Psalm 3: "To God: to illuminate all men. Beginning with Skid Road." Allen Ginsberg. ChIV-1

Psalm 5. Ernesto Cardenal. TCLAP, *tr. by* Robert Marquez

Psalm 23 to the Singer's Nectar. 'Ali Al-Sharqawi.
  "I shall knock three times at the door." MAP

Psalm and Lament. Donald Justice. DiPo

Psalm Concerning the Castle. Denise Levertov. TwCP; WPE

Psalm for Christmas Day. Thomas Pestel [*or* Pestell]. SacPr

Psalm: "Happy is the man whom Thou hast set apart." "Yehoash." TrJP, *tr. by* Isidore Goldstick

Psalm: "In the small beauty of the forest." George Oppen. APT-2; HarvBoo; NNaP; PFTM-2; WoPoe

Psalm: "No one kneads us again out of earth and clay." Paul Celan. PoSu; PoetW, *tr. by* John Felstiner

Psalm: "No one moulds us again out of earth and clay." Paul Celan. BBASP; HP; OBVE, *tr. by* Michael Hamburger

Psalm of Battle. *Unknown.* AWP *Fr.* Thousand and One Nights, The.

Psalm of Christ, The. Chad Walsh. TrCP

Psalm of Life, A. Henry Wadsworth Longfellow. APN-1; AmFaPo; BRP; ITBLP; NAAL-2v1; NAAL-3; NAAL-5; OBCA; PWR; TAP; TCAPo
  "Tell me not in mournful numbers." AH

"Psalm of Life" for thee is o'er, The. Longfellow. Henrietta Cordelia Ray. CBWP-3

Psalm of Marriage. Phoebe Cary. PWR

Psalm of Praise, A. Richard Baxter.
  "Ye holy Angels bright." NOCV

Psalm of Silk. Malachi. WaCA

Psalm of Those Who Go Forth before Daylight. Carl Sandburg. OxBA

Psalm: "Old ones to the side." Charles Simic. LCAP-2

Psalm on the day, A. Psalm. Yehuda Amichai [*or* Amikhai]. BBASP, *tr. by* Chana Bloch

Psalm: The New Day. Mark Jarman. AWTN

Psalm to the Creatures. Gwilym R. Jones. OBWVE, *tr. by* Joseph P. Clancy

Psalm: "While Northward the hot sun was sinking o'er the trees." Robert Bridges. FaBoTw

Psalms. Bible, *O.T.*
  Psalm 1.
  ("Blessed are the man and the woman.") EnlH, *tr. by* Stephen Mitchell
  ("Blessed is the man that walketh not in the counsel of the ungodly [*or* wicked].") AWP
  (Happy Is the Man.) TrJP
  ("O blessed man, that in th' advice.") SCAP
  Psalm 2.
  ("Why do the Gentiles tumult, and the Nations.") OBVE
  ("Why do the heathen rage.") NAAL-2v1
  Psalm 3.
  ("Lord how many are my foes.") OBVE
  Psalm 6.
  ("O lord, I dred, and that I did not dred.") OBVE
  Psalm 8.
  (How Glorious Is Thy Name.) TrJP
  ("O Lord our Lord, how excellent is thy name in all the earth!") AWP; NAWM-5v1
  ("O Lord, that rul'st the human heart.") OBVE
  ("O Lorde oure gouvernoure, howe excellent is thy name.") OBVE
  Psalm 11.
  ("Since I do trust Jehova still.") OBVE
  Psalm 13.
  ("How long, O lord, shall I forgotten be?") NoSic; OBVE
  Psalm 14.
  ("Fool hath said in his heart, There is no God, The.") TrJP
  Psalm 17.
  ("My suite is just, just lord to my suite hark.") OBVE
  Psalm 19.
  (Glory of God, The.) TrJP
  ("Heavens declare God's glory, The.") EnlH
  ("Heavens declare the glory of God, The.") AWP; NAWM-5v1

("Heavens doe declare / The majesty of God, The.") SCAP

("Heavnly Frame sets forth the Fame, The.") OBVE

("Spacious firmament on high, The.") ChIV-1; TOF

Psalm 23.

("Happy me! o happy sheepe!") ChIV-1

("Lord is my herd, nae want sal fa' me, The.") ChIV-1

("Lord is my shepherd; I shall not want, The.") AWP; NAWM-5v1; NIL-7; NIP-4; TFi; TrJP

("Lord's my shepherd, I'll not want, The.") AH; TRP

("Lord to me a shepherd is, The.") OBCA; TCAPo

("Lorde is my shepherde, The; therefore can I lack nothing.") OBVE

Psalm 24.

("Earth is the Lord's and the fulness thereof, The.") AWP; TrJP

Psalm 29.

("Give unto the Lord, O ye mighty.") AWP

Psalm 39.

(Lord, Make Me to Know Mine End.) TrJP

Psalm 42.

("As the hart panteth after the water brooks.") AWP; TrJP

Psalm 46.

("God is our refuge and strength, a very present help in trouble.") AWP

Psalm 50.

("Mighty God, even the Lord, hath spoken, The.") BrRo

Psalm 52.

("Tyrant, why swel'st [*or* swell'st] thou thus.") NAEL-7v1; NoSic; OBVE

Psalm 55: Exaudi, Deus.

("Give ear to my prayer, O God.") AWP

("My God most glad to look, most prone to hear [*or* heere].") OBVE

Psalm 58: Si Vere Utique.

("And call ye this to utter what is just.") BoWoP; NAEL-5v1; NOCV; NoSic; WPE

("Do ye, o congregation.") NoP-4

("Judges, who rule the world by laws.") NoP-4

("Ye congregation of the tribes.") NoP-4

Psalm 59.

("Save me from such as me assail.") NoSic

Psalm 72.

("Looke how the woods, where enterlaced trees.") OBVE

Psalm 73.

("It is most true that God to Israel.") NoSic

Psalm 77.

("I cried unto God with my voice, even unto God with my voice.") AWP

Psalm 78.

("There where the deepe did show his sandy flore.") OBVE

Psalm 79.

(Heathen Are Come into Thine Inheritance, The.) TrJP

Psalm 83.

("O God, keep not Thou silence.") TrJP

Psalm 84.

("How lovely are thy tabernacles.") TrJP

Psalm 90.

("Lord, thou hast been our dwelling place in all generations.") AWP

Psalm 91.

("He that dwelleth in the secret place of the most High.") AWP

("Make the greate God thy Fort, and dwell.") NPeEn

Psalm 95.

("O come, let us sing unto the Lord.") AWP

Psalm 100.

("All people that on earth do dwell.") NOCV; SacPr

("O be joyful in the Lord, all ye lands.") PeECV

Psalm 102.

("Lord hear [*or* here] my prayer [*or* prayre] and let my cry[e] pass[e].") OBVE

Psalm 103.

("Bless the Lord, O my soul: and all that is within me.") AWP

("O Thou my soule, Jehovah blesse.") SCAP

("Praise, my soul, the King of heaven.") NOCV; SacPr

Psalm 104.

("Bless the Lord, O my soul. O Lord my God.") NAWM-5v1; TrJP

("Unnamable God, you are fathomless.") EnlH

Psalm 107.

("O Give yee thanks unto the Lord.") SCAP

Psalm 114.

(When Israel Came Forth out of Egypt.) TrJP

("When Israel came from Egypt's coast.") OBVE

("When Israel came out of Egypt.") CRP

Psalm 115.

("Not us, I say, not us.") NOCV

Psalm 118.

("O give thanks unto the Lord; for he is good: because his mercy endureth for ever.") TrJP

Psalm 119.

("How like to threads of flax.") ChIV-1

Psalm 121.

("I to the hills lift up mine eyes.") OBCA

("I will lift up mine eyes unto the hills.") AWP

("Now the twin-light of my eyes.") GePo

Psalm 124.

("Now Israel.") NPeEn

Psalm 126.

("When the Lord brought back those that returned to Zion.") TrJP

Psalm 127.

("They shall not be put to shame, / When they speak with their enemies in the gate.") TrJP

Psalm 130.

("From depth of sinn and from a diepe dispaire.") NoSic; OBVE; OxBEV

("Out of the deep [or depths] have I called [or cried unto] thee, O Lord.") TrJP

Psalm 131.

("Lord, my mind is not noisy with desires.") EnlH

Psalm 133.

("Behold, how good and how pleasant it is.") AWP

("Beholde, how good and joyfull a thinge it is, brethren to dwell to gether in unitye.") OBVE

(To Dwell Together in Unity.) TrJP

Psalm 134.

("You that Jehovah's servants are.") NoSic

Psalm 136.

("O give thanks unto the Lord; for he is good [or gracious]: for his mercy endureth for ever.") AWP

Psalm 137.

("By the rivers of Babylon, there we sat down, yea, we wept, when [or then] we remembered Zion.") AWP; NAWM-5v1; TrJP

("By the waters of Babylon we sat down and wept.") NPeEn; OBVE; WoPoe

("Sitting by the streams that glide.") ChIV-1

Psalm 139.

("O Lord, in me there lieth nought.") NAEL-7v1; NOCV; NoSic; OBVE

Psalm 147.

("Hosanna—musick is divine.") NOCV

("Sing to the Lord, for what can better be.") NOCV

Psalm 148.

("Hallelujah! kneel and sing / Praises to the heav'nly king.") OBVE,

("Hallelujah. Praise ye the Lord from the heavens.") TrJP

Psalms. Bible, O.T., tr. by Mary Sidney Herbert, Countess of Pembroke

Psalm 52. Quid Gloriaris? BASC; PBRV, tr. by Mary Sidney Herbert, Countess of Pembroke

Psalm 57. Miserere Mei Deus. EMWP; PEW, tr. by Mary Sidney Herbert, Countess of Pembroke

Psalm 58. Si Vere Utique. BASC; NPeEn; NoP-4; PEW, tr. by Mary Sidney Herbert, Countess of Pembroke

Psalm 72. Deus Judicium. EMWP, tr. by Mary Sidney Herbert, Countess of Pembroke

Psalm 74. Ut Quid, Deus. BASC; NOCV, tr. by Mary Sidney Herbert, Countess of Pembroke

Psalm 84. CABP, tr. by Mary Sidney Herbert, Countess of Pembroke

Psalm 89. Misericordias.

"Gods boundles bownties gods promise ever abyding." PBRV, tr. by Mary Sidney Herbert, Countess of Pembroke

Psalm 92. Bonum Est Confiteri. PEW, tr. by Mary Sidney Herbert, Countess of Pembroke

Psalm 100. CABP, tr. by Mary Sidney Herbert, Countess of Pembroke

Psalm 117. Laudate Dominum. ChIV-1; OxBEV, tr. by Mary Sidney Herbert, Countess of Pembroke

Psalm 120. Ad Dominum. BASC; OxBEV, tr. by Mary Sidney Herbert, Countess of Pembroke

Psalm 130. De Profundis. EMWP, tr. by Mary Sidney Herbert, Countess of Pembroke

Psalm 139. Domine, Probasti. PEW; WPE, tr. by Mary Sidney Herbert, Countess of Pembroke

"Each inmost peece in me is thine." NPeEn, tr. by Mary Sidney Herbert, Countess of Pembroke

Psalm 142. Voce mea ad Dominum. PBRV, tr. by Mary Sidney Herbert, Countess of Pembroke

Psalms. Bible, O.T., tr. by New Revised Standard Version

Psalm 8. InvLi, tr. by New Revised Standard Version

Psalm 23. InvLi, tr. by New Revised Standard Version

Psalm 50.

"Hear, O my people, and I will speak." InvLi, tr. by New Revised Standard Version

Psalms (Chapter 137, Verse 5–6). Manuela Fingueret. MirDau, tr. by Roberta Gordenstein

Psalms of Love. Peter Baum. AWP, tr. by Jethro Bithell

Psittachus Eois Imitatrix Ales ab Indis. Sacheverell Sitwell. MoBrPo

Psyche. Mary Tighe. RWP

"Illumined bright now shines the splendid dome." NOBRP

"Let not the rugged brow the rhymes accuse." NoP-4

"'Mid the thick covert of that woodland shade." NOBRP

Psyche, Before the Tribunal of Venus. Nathaniel Parker Willis. APN-1

Psychiatrist. Peter De Vries. OBAL

Psychiatrist fellow from Rye, A. Limerick. Stephen Cass. PeLi

Psychic researcher's elation, A. Limerick. Cyril Mountjoy. PeLi

Psycho. Peter Olds. PeNZ

Psychologia Christiana. Mihály Babits. IQMS, tr. by Peter Zollman

Psychopathology of Everyday Life, The. William Matthews. NIP-4

Psychozoia, or, the Life of the Soul. Henry More.

Contrition. NOSC

Psyllus lies here. Procuring was his trade. Argentarius. GrAn

Pub empties out, the moon sets. The stars, The. Time Now Please. Adriann Roland Holst. TuT, tr. by Paula Meehan

Pub empties, the moon is down, The. Time, Please. Adriann Roland Holst. TuT, tr. by Sean Dunne

Puberty Rite Dance Song (Traditional). Unknown. BoWoP, tr. by Willis Barnstone

Puberty Tree, The. D. M. Thomas. TOF

Pubescence at 39. Vickie Sears. GLP

Public Aid for Niagara Falls. Morris Gilbert Bishop. NBLV

Public Beach (Long Island Sound). Christopher Darlington Morley. NBLV

Public Beach No. 2. Andrey [or Andrei] Andreievich Voznesensky [or Voznesenskii]. RusPo, tr. by Robert Arthur Douglas Ford

Public Dinner, A. Thomas Hood. OBCoV

Public Garden, The. Arthur Hugh Clough. PeLV Fr. Dipsychus [and the Spirit].

Public Garden, The. Robert Lowell. OBGa; PoRA; TAP

Public has no belief, The. Obbligato from a Public Gallery. Jared Angira. NAfrP

Public house screaming. Drunk Man, The. Unknown. NOBAu

Public Journal. Phyllis McGinley. NBLV

Public Library. Dannie Abse. OxBC

Public Outcry. Karen Alkalay-Gut. DTA

Public Place (After Olga Broumas), The. Achy Obejas. WiU

Public Prayer. Delmira Agustini. TANSG, tr. by Mark McCaffrey

Public's darling Quintia, first-class, The. Unknown. PriapPo, tr. by Richard W. Hooper Fr. Priapus Poems, The.

Public School No. 18: Paterson, New Jersey. Maria Gillan. UnSA

Public Schools. Robert Lloyd. NOEC Fr. Familiar Epistle to J. B. Esq, A.

Public servant of men's private parts, The. Richard Murphy. ModIr Fr. Price of Stone, The.

Publication—is the Auction. Emily Dickinson. APN-2; NAAL-2v1; NAAL-3; NALW; NCAP; NoP-4; TCAPo

Publicity. (LL) Mouth, The. Ciaran Carson. ModIr; PNI

Publick Fast on Account of the Afflicted: March 31, 1692. Nicole Cooley. NeAmPo

Publisher's Party. Phyllis McGinley. OBAL

Publisher went off to France, A. Limerick. Unknown. PeLi

Puck of Pook's Hill. Rudyard Kipling.

Centurion of the Thirtieth, A.

Cities and Thrones and Powers. NOBE; NOxBChV; OxBTC

Knights of the Joyous Venture, The.

Harp Song of the Dane Women. HAP; HarvBoo; PoRA; RACG

Old Men at Pevensey. NoAM

Runes on Weland's Sword, The. NoAM

On the Great Wall.

Song to Mithras, A. NoAM

Puck's Song. FaBoCh

Winged Hats, The.

Pict Song, A. NoAM

Puck's Song. Rudyard Kipling. FaBoCh Fr. Puck of Pook's Hill.

Puckered breasts like Leiberman's. Grandma in the Shower. Dale M. Kushner. UnSA

Pueblo. Luis Palés Matos. TCLAP, tr. by Barry Luby

Puella Parvula. Wallace Stevens. HCAP; LCAP-2

Puerta Rica. Víctor Hernández Cruz. LoL

Puerto Rican Girls of French Hill, The. Sean Thomas Dougherty. AmPoNex

Puerto Rico Made in Japan. Jose Angel Figueroa. PueRic

Puerto Rico 1974. This Is Not the Place Where I was Born. Miguel Piñero. PueRic

Puerto Rico / You lovely island. America. Stephen Sondheim. ReLy

Puertoricanness. Aurora Levins Morales. PueRic

Puffy Jacket. Amy Fusselman. HeMarv

Pula. Matsemela Manaka.
   Chorus: "Babylon, I did not come to you for the sake of coming." PeSAV
   Chorus: "In the name of the people." PeSAV

Pulkovo Meridian, The. Vera Inber.
   "Teeth are bared, the mouth drawn tight, the face, The." FaBoWar, tr. by Alexander Kaun and Dorothea Prall Radin

Pull me down, ladybug. Ladybug. Raymond Souster. MoCV

Pull My Daisy. Allen Ginsberg. PoM

Pull over. Your car with its slow. Quivira City Limits. Kevin Young. NeAmPo

Pull the car off here. Loving Along Western Rivers. Stephen J. Lyons. PasH

Pull up the stems, grass doesn't die. Expressing My Feelings. Meng Chiao. SuSp, tr. by Stephen Owen

Pulley, The. George Herbert. AWP; BASC; BBASP; ChIV-1; FHYEP; FSCP; GeHe; HAP; HeIP-4; InPK-6; InvLi; NAEL-5v1; NAEL-6v1; NAEL-7v1; NOBE; NOCV; NOSC; NoP-4; OBEV; OxAEP-1; PAI; SCGP; TFi
   (Gifts of God, The.) GTBS-P; TreFP

Pullin me in off the corner to wash my face an. Black Jam for Dr. Negro. Mari E. Evans. BPo

Pulling in the Nets. C. Mikal Oness. GeoHom

Pulling in the Reins. Yoshimasu Gōzō. PFTM-2, tr. by Richard Arno

Pulling the Chain. Simon Rae. UV

Pulling the Ivy. Julia Copus. MFPA

Pulling up flax after the blue flowers have fallen. Linen Industry, The. Michael Longley. CIP-2; ModIr; NoP-4; PBCIP; PNI

Pulling up in my car, I went into the cottage. After Five Years. Augustus Young. BIrV

Pulls rabbits out of hats. Great Mutando, The. Deryn Rees-Jones. TCAWP

Pulmonary tuberculosis. Limerick. L. G. Udall. PeLi

Pulse. Jane Holland. MFPA

Pulse, The. Martha Kapos. Prnts

Pulse, The. Mark Van Doren. MoAmPo

Pulse of your revolt stilled, The. My Friendly People. Frank Mkalawile Chipasula. HBAPE

Puma called asking me to remind you. Rosa. Miguel Algarin. PueRic

Pumping Iron. Diane Ackerman. MoASP

Pumpkin-Eater, The. Mother Goose. OxNR; ReMoGo

Pumpkins' crooked grins. Harvest Moon. Jan Barry. CDa

Pumpkins rove the ground, The. In Hecate's Garden. Ziporah Hildebrandt. HW

Punch and Judy. Rose Fyleman. NOxBChV

'Punch,' said Judy. Punch and Judy. Rose Fyleman. NOxBChV

Punch, the Immortal Liar. Conrad Potter Aiken.
   Puppet Dreams, The. MoAmPo

Punctilio. Mary Elizabeth Coleridge. OBEV; PoBW

Punctual as bad luck. Family Goldschmitt, The. Henri Coulette. CoAP

Punctually at Christmas the soft plush. White Christmas. William Robert Rodgers. MoBrPo

Punica, The. Catius As Conius Silius Italicus.
   "At the city's heart stood the shrine to Dido's ghost." RomPo, tr. by Marcus Wilson
   "Death comes in strange forms and contrasting images." RomPo, tr. by Marcus Wilson
   "Furiously along the banks stormed Hannibal." RomPo, tr. by Marcus Wilson
   "Give me Maeonian Homer's resonant tongue." RomPo, tr. by Marcus Wilson
   "Horses which Titan when discharged for the night, The." RomPo, tr. by Marcus Wilson
   "Memories of past struggles were expelled by fear." RomPo, tr. by Marcus Wilson

Punished by crimes of which I would be quit. (LL) Allen Tate. ChrPo; Son Fr. Sonnets at Christmas.

Punishing God has taken all content. To His Wife. Fyodor [or Feodor] Ivanovich Tyutchev. OxBEV, tr. by Henry Gifford and Charles Tomlinson

Punishment. Seamus Heaney. EmeKit; NAEL-5v2; NAEL-6v2; NoAM; NoP-4; OxAEP-2; PBCIP; PoPoPo

Punishments. Rafael Alberti. AF, tr. by Geoffrey Connell

Punk. Kenneth Goldsmith.

"One pair ridiculous gorilla slippers; 3 pairs of cheap shit sunglasses." HeMarv

Punk Pantoum. Pamela Stewart. ReTh

Punkydoodle and Jollapin. Laura Elizabeth Richards. OBCA

Punt gliding under a chain of smiles, A. Tilla Brading. NewEx

Punting pole stuck in the reeds. Inscribed on a Painting of a Fisherman. T'ang Yin. CoBLCP, tr. by Jonathan Chaves

Punziplaze karmasokist DecoYen Pompieraeian. Purplexicon of Dissynthegrations, A. Abraham Lincoln Gillespie. APT-2

Pupa of pain, I sat and lay one July, A. Mockingbird Month. Mona Van Duyn. OWoS

Pupil of fever chills and bewilderment, A. Aleksey [or Aleksei] Petrovich Tsvetkov. TCRP

Puppet, The. Chuck Brickley. HA

Puppet Dreams, The. Conrad Potter Aiken. MoAmPo Fr. Punch, the Immortal Liar.

Puppet of the Wolf, The. Margaret Atwood. NoAM

Puppets. Patricia K. Page. MoCV

Puppets on stage let people do what they will. Tune: "Partridge Sky"—Puppet Theater. Ku T'ai-ch'ing. SuSp, tr. by Irving Y. Lo

Purcell in many victories of his. Bounty. Josephine Miles. NoAM

Purdah, 1. Imtiaz Dharker. NeBl; OMIP

Pure air trembles, O pitiless God, The. Noon. Robinson Jeffers. MoAmPo

Pure amnesia of her face, The. August, Los Angeles, Lullaby. Carol Muske. PBCAP

Pure and worthy Mrs. Stowe, The. Dorothy Parker. APT-1; NALW Fr. Pig's-Eye View of Literature, A.

Pure as a pane of ice. It's a gift. (LL) Love Letter. Sylvia Plath. LW; NOBA

Pure brush-clover / Basket of flowers. Ōshima Ryōta. ZenPo, tr. by Takashi Ikemoto and Lucien Stryk

Pure contralto sings in the organloft, The. Walt Whitman. FaBoA; TTTS Fr. Song of Myself.

Pure Death. Robert Graves. AWP; GTBS-P

Pure Dust. Maria Luisa Spaziani. NeIt, tr. by Beverly Allen

Pure Hypothesis, A. May Kendall. VWP

Pure in Heart Shall See God, The. Frances Ellen Watkins Harper. PWR

Pure is the body on the Earth. Unknown. AWP Fr. Book of the Dead.

Pure Loneliness, The. Michael Ryan. BodElec

Pure nothing, in the middle of the day. (LL) Daystar. Rita Dove. AmFaPo; LCAP-2; NAAAL; NIL-7; NIP-4; OxWW

Pure Pop. Allison Joseph. NeAmPo

Pure products of America, The. To Elsie. William Carlos Williams. APT-1; AmFaPo; NAAL-2v2; NAAL-5; NOBA; OxBA; PoE; PoPoPo

Pure Sound Pavilion. Wang Shih-chieng. ColAnChi, tr. by Richard John Lynn

Pure Sound Pavilion of the Riverside Temple, The. Muso Soseki. EaWin, tr. by W. S. Merwin

Pure stream, in whose transparent wave. To Leven Water. Tobias Smollett. OBEV

Pure sun dazzled, The. Glazier, The. Stéphane Mallarmé. OBVE, tr. by Keith Bosley

Pure sunlight is strewn all over the lawn. Saturday Afternoon, October. Jonathan Holden. OPRER

Pure white plum blossoms. Buson. SoOfWa, tr. by Sam Hamill

Pure woman is to man a crown. Virtuous Wife, The. Süsskind von Trimberg. TrJP

Pure? What does it mean? Fever 103°. Sylvia Plath. FaBoWP; NOBA; NoAM; VCAP; VGW

Purer than purest pure. E. E. Cummings. AH

Purest Rage, The. Charles Baxter. SwNoth

Purest soul that e'er was sent, The. Another [Epitaph on the Lady Mary Villiers]. Thomas Carew. BeJo; CaPo

Purgatorio. Dante Alighieri. Fr. Divina Commedia.

Purgatorio. Dante Alighieri. Fr. Divine Comedy, The (Mandelbaum Translation).

Purge, The. Michael Hartnett.
   "Hartnett, the poet, might as well be dead." BiHa

Puriri moth's wing, A. Poem. Jan Kemp. PeNZ

Purist, The. Ogden Nash. KaS; MoAmPo; NBLV; OBCA

Puritan, The. Karl Shapiro. MoAmPo

Puritan Lady, A. Lizette Woodworth Reese. MoAmPo

Puritan Sonnet, IV. Elinor Wylie. BoWoP; MoAmPo Fr. Wild Peaches.

Puritans. Elaine Equi. PmAP

Purity. Avigdor Hame'iri. MHP, tr. by Ruth Finer Mintz

Purity of the moonlight, The. Unknown. OHPJ

PURITY! PURITY! PURITY! Fanny Beznos. SurWo, tr. by Myrna Bell Rochester

Purple. Lullaby "Purple." Eve Merriam. NOxBChV

Purple Clover. Emily Dickinson. MoAmPo

Purple Cow, The. Frank Gelett Burgess. BRP; NBLV; NTCP; OBAL; OBCA; OBCoV; OxIBACP; TCAPo; TFi; TLR

Purple Cow, The: Suite. Frank Gelett Burgess. *See* Cinq Ans Après

Purple headland over yonder. Afternoon. Louisa Sarah Bevington. NOBVV; PEW

Purple Indians pas de bourrée. Lord Fluting Dreams of America on the Eve of His Departure from Liverpool. Paul Zimmer. VGW

Purple is the Color of Longing. David Steinberg. PasH

Purple Island, The. Phineas Fletcher.
　(Triumph of the Church, The.) SacPr
　"With her, her sister went, a warlike maid." NOSC

Purple Loosestrife. Ann Townsend. ExTi; NeAmPo

Purple Peach Tree, The. Su Tung-p'o (Su Shih). OHPC, *tr. by* Kenneth Rexroth

Purple pill rattles, The. Antidepressant. Adrienne Su. AmPoNex

Purple Precincts touch Longevity Mountain, The. I Was Received in an Early Audience at Heaven-Gate and Then at Noon I Was Summoned to the Yu-shun Gate. In the Evening I Withdrew, and Improvised This Poem. Yang Shih-ch'i. CoBLCP, *tr. by* Jonathan Chaves

Purple sleep of the golden wheatfield. Poppies. Yolanda Bedregal. TANSG, *tr. by* Carolyne Wright

Purple Spot, The. Ramón López Velarde. BLPSL, *tr. by* Rene de Costa, Rigas Kappatos and Eleni Paidoussi

Purple Thought, The. Houda Al-Na'mani. PoArWo, *tr. by* Richard McKane

Purple Valleys, The. Madison Cawein. APN-2

Purple, White and Green, The. L. E. Morgan-Browne. BrRo

Purple William or The Liar's Doom. A. E. Housman. NOxBChV

Purple, yellow, red and green. *Unknown.* OxNR

Purplexicon of Dissynthegrations, A. Abraham Lincoln Gillespie. APT-2

Purpose. Desmond O'Grady. PBCIP

Purpose of Fable-writing, The. Phaedrus. AWP, *tr. by* Christopher Smart

Purpose of Nuns, The. Judith Ortiz Cofer. TouFir

Purposes, to himself, in a broken sleep. (LL) House on a Cliff. Louis MacNeice. HarvBoo; ModIr; NOIV; NPeEn

Purr, The. Molly Peacock. ExTi; PasH

"Purr," says the cat. (LL) Mother Goose. OxNR; ReMoGo

Purse, A. Gertrude Stein. TCAPo *Fr.* Tender Buttons.

Purse be full again, or else I must die. This is the wish. That Been to Me My Lives Light and Saviour. Susan Wheeler. ExTi

Purse-Seine, The. Robinson Jeffers. AmFaPo; HAP; NOBA; NoAM; NoP-4; OxBA; WeW-3

Purse was not green, it was not straw color, it was hardly seen and, A. Gertrude Stein. TCAPo *Fr.* Tender Buttons.

Pursued by one nun or another. Class Bully. Thomas Reiter. SwNoth

Pursuing beauty, men descry. Song. Thomas Southerne. NOSC

Pursuit. "H. D." WPE

Pursuit. Julian [*or* Juljan] Tuwim. TrJP, *tr. by* Watson Kirkconnell

Pursuit. Robert Penn Warren. FuPo; HAP; MoAmPo; TwCP

Pursuit from Under. James Dickey. HAP

Pursuit[e], The. Henry Vaughan. AngWePo; GeHe; NOSC; SacPr; TrCP

Pusey Hughes, a low-grade voter. Unfortunate Occurrence at Cwm-Cadno. A. G. Prys-Jones. AngWePo

Push, push the heavy door. Skeleton House. Laurence Smith. OTCP

Pushan, God of golden day. *Unknown.* AWP *Fr.* Vedic Hymns.

Pushan, God of Pasture. *Unknown.* AWP *Fr.* Vedic Hymns.

Pushing. Christopher Gilbert. LTA; SoSe-8

Pushing. Michael McClintock. HA

Pushing the seed into the ground. Listening to a White Man Play the Blues. Silvia Curbelo. TouFir

Pushing up through smoke. Flames. Tōge Sankichi. FaBoWar, *tr. by* Richard H. Minear

Pushing young man in Patchogue, A. Limerick. Morris Gilbert Bishop. PeLi

Pushkin. Anna Andreyevna Akhmatova. TCRP, *tr. by* Daniel Weissbort

Puss came dancing out of a barn. *Unknown.* OxNR

Pussicat, wussicat, with a white foot. *Unknown.* OxNR

Pussies are not gods. They are created beings. Notes for a Sermon on the Mount. Nin Andrews. BAP-01

Pussy cat ate the dumplings. Pussycat. Mother Goose. OxNR; ReMoGo

Pussy-Cat Mew. *Unknown.* ReMoGo

Pussy Cat Mole. *Unknown.* OxNR

Pussy-Cat, Pussy-Cat / where have you been? Mother Goose. LB; OxNR; ReMoGo

Pussy said Meow, and Robin flew [*or* jumped] away. (LL) Catch. Mother Goose. LB; OxNR

Pussy sits beside the fire. By the Fire. Mother Goose. OxNR

Pussycat. Mother Goose. OxNR; ReMoGo

Puszta in Winter, The. Sándor Petőfi. IQMS, *tr. by* Watson Kirkconnell

Put a sun in Sunday, Sunday. Gertrude Stein. TCAPo *Fr.* Yet Dish.

Put dogs on the list. Before You Cut Loose. Simon Armitage. EmeKit

Put Down. Léon Damas. TTY, *tr. by* Seth L. Wolitz

Put down your weapons. Haka: The Blossoming. Pita Sharples. PeNZ, *tr. by* Pita Sharples

Put 'Em in a Box, Tie 'Em with a Ribbon (And Throw 'Em in the Deep Blue Sea). Sammy Cahn. ReLy

Put Forth, O God, Thy Spirit's Might. Howard Chandler Robbins. AH

Put forth thy leaf, thou lofty plane. In Stratis Viarum IV. Arthur Hugh Clough. EBEV

Put Hannibal i' th' scale. Juvenal. OBVE, *tr. by* Henry Vaughan *Fr.* Satires.

Put in something else like page bonded to a neutrality my brother. Remembered Sequel. Hannah Weiner. FTOS

Put it on record. Identity Card. Mahmoud Darwish. VCWP, *tr. by* Denys Johnson-Davies

Put me into the breach with every rolling stone. Put Me into the Breach. Yehuda Karni. MHP, *tr. by* Ruth Finer Mintz

Put off an important decision. 7th Light Poem: For John Cage—17 June 1962. Jackson Mac Low. FTOS

Put Off Constricting Day. Mary Stanley. PeNZ

Put off Thy robe of purple, then go on. Good Friday: Rex Tragicus, or, Christ Going to His Cross[e]. Robert Herrick. NOSC

Put on a Happy Face. Lee Adams. ReLy

Put on all the bracelets beads rings. Tuglik's Song. Tuglik. WoPoe, *tr. by* Stephen Berg

Put on that languor which the world frowns on. Sonnet 120. Marc André Raffalovich. CAGL

Put on yo' red silk stockings. Red Silk Stockings. Langston Hughes. NAAAL

Put on your silks, and piece by piece. To His Mistresses. Robert Herrick. CaPo

Put on your slumming clothes and get your car. Slumming on Park Avenue. Irving Berlin. APT-1

Put out my hand and touched the face of God. (LL) High Flight. John Gillespie, Jr. Magee. ITBLP; PoWW

Put out the lights and stop the clocks. Madrid—1937. Langston Hughes. AF

Put out the lights now! Christmas Tree, The. Cecil Day Lewis. ChrPo

Put out to sea, if wine thou wouldest make. Sent from Egypt with a Fair Robe of Tissue to a Sicilian Vinedresser. Thomas Sturge Moore. OBEV

Put the Blame on Mame. Doris Fisher. ReLy

Put the broidery-frame away. Bertha in the Lane. Elizabeth Barrett Browning. ViWPN

Put the sun a thought below his prime. Afternoon in the Garden. Ethel Louisa Mason Anderson. NOBAu

Put things in their place. Sky Is Blue, The. David Ignatow. NNaP

Put to sleep my mother's curse? (LL) Welsh Marches, The. A. E. Housman. FaBoTw; SCGP

Put to the door—the school's begun. Country School, The. *Unknown.* TCAPo

Put u red-eye in. Ron Welburn. NBV

Put up a windmill on. Midwest, Midcentury. Sharyn Jeanne Skeeter. ISC

Put up thy gold: go on,—here's gold,—go on. William Shakespeare. OxAEP-1 *Fr.* Timon of Athens.

Put up with them while they last—calm waters lie ahead. (LL) Song of Surfing on the Bore. Cheng Hsieh. CoBLCP; ColAnChi, *tr. by* Jonathan Chaves

Put Your Arms Around Me, Honey. Junie McCree. ReLy

Put your finger in Foxy's hole. *Unknown.* LB; OxNR

Put your head, darling, darling, darling. Dear Black Head. *Unknown.* BIrV, *tr. by* Sir Samuel Ferguson

Put　your / self　out. Chasm. A. R. Ammons. OBAL

Puttin' on the Ritz (Original Version). Irving Berlin. ReLy

Puttin' on the Ritz (Revised Version). Irving Berlin. ReLy

Putting an End to the War Stories. Larry Moffi. CDa

Putting in the Seed. Robert Frost. APT-1; NoAM; OxBA

Putting on Nightgown. *Unknown.* OxNR

Putting red reins on you, goat, with a noseband. Anyte [*or* Anytes]. SaLy, *tr. by* Diane Rayor

Putting soup in his mouth with a spoon. (LL) Soup. Carl Sandburg. HHAm; NOBA; NOBE; OBCA

Putting the World to Bed. Esther W. Buxton. NOxBChV

Puva, puva, puva. Lullaby. *Unknown.* TTTS, *tr. by* Natalie Curtis

Puzzle faces in the dying elms. 'Mystery Boy' Looks for Kin in Nashville. Robert Earl Hayden. LCAP-2; NoAM; NoP-4; PoE

Puzzle Pieces. Chana Bloch. ExTi

Puzzled. Carolyn Wells. OBCA

Pygmaleon. John Gower. NPeEn; OxBEV *Fr.* Confessio Amantis.

Pygmalion had seen the shameless lives. Ovid. NAWM-7v1, *tr. by* Allen Mandelbaum *Fr.* Metamorphoses.

Pygmalion's Image. Eiléan Ní Chuilleanáin. MakPoe

Pygmies Are Pygmies Still, Though Percht on Alps.   Gwendolyn Brooks.
   ColAP   *Fr.* Notes from the Childhood and the Girlhood.
Pylons, The.   Stephen Spender.   AWP; NoAM
Pyramids, The.   Nick Piombino.   FTOS
Pyrenees, The.   Jane Duran.   Prnts   *Fr.* Silences from the Spanish Civil War.
Pyres, The.   Virgil [*or* Vergil].   WoPoe, *tr. by* Robert Fitzgerald   *Fr.* Aeneid
   [*or* Eneados, *Aeneis*], The.
Pyrography.   John Ashbery.   HarvBoo; PoM; VCAP
Pythagoras planned it. Why did the people stare?   Statues, The.   W. B. Yeats.
   NoAM; WeW-3
Pythagorean Silence.   Susan Howe.
   "Age of earth and us all chattering."   PFTM-2
Pythagoric letter, two ways spread, The.   Pythagoric Letter, The.   Thomas
   Stanley.   NOSC
Pythian Odes.   Pindar.
   Pythian Ten.
   "Among them too are the Muses."   WoPoe, *tr. by* Padraic Fallon
   Pythian Twelve.
   "I ask you."   WoPoe, *tr. by* Thomas Meyer
Python-coils of leg and trunk.   Oliver Reynolds.   TCAWP   *Fr.* Tone Poem.
Pythoness, The.   Kathleen Jessie Raine.   MoBrPo

Q

Qadesha (Sacred Whore).   Cosi Fabian.   HW
Qantas Bags.   Laurie Duggan.   BMAP
Q:dwo / we know of anything which can.   E. E. Cummings.   OBAL
Q.E.D.   Mary Low.   SurWo
Qua Cursum Ventus.   Arthur Hugh Clough.   OBEV
Quack, quack, quack!   Dumpy Ducky.   Lucy Larcom.   OBCA
Quaco Sam.   *Unknown.*   FaBoVe
Quadratic function, ambitious, A.   Limerick.   Leo Moser.   PeLi
Quadroon mermaids, Afro angels, black saints.   Ballad of Remembrance, A.
   Robert Earl Hayden.   BPo; ESEAA
Quaerè.   George Farewell.   NOEC; NPeEn; OBCoV
Quail in Autumn.   William Jay Smith.   OWoS
Quail Sky.   Li Ch'ing-chao.   OHPC, *tr. by* Kenneth Rexroth
Quails.   Shinkichi Takahashi.   ZenPo, *tr. by* Takashi Ikemoto and Lucien Stryk
Quaint Mazes.   Geoffrey Hill.   NoAM   *Fr.* Apology for the Revival of
   Christian Architecture in England, An.
Quake Theory.   Sharon Olds.   PBCAP
Quaker Graveyard in Nantucket, The.   Robert Lowell.   ColAP; HAP; MakPoe;
   NAAL-2v2; NAAL-5; NOBA; NoAM; NoP-4; OxBA; PeECV; TAP; UnPo;
   VCAP
Quaker's stiffness, with a tradesman's grin, A.   Character, A.   Clara Reeve.
   ECWP
Quaker's wife got up to bake, The.   *Unknown.*   OxNR
QUALITY OF NIGHT THAT YOU HATE MOST IS ITS BLACK, THE.
   Three Movements and a Coda.   Imamu Amiri Baraka.   NAAAL
Quality of Sprawl, The.   Les A. Murray.   EmeKit; HarvBoo; NoP-4
Quality of the dirt, the fealty changing under my foot, The. (LL)   Derek
   Walcott.   NAEL-5v2; NAEL-6v2; NoP-4   *Fr.* Midsummer.
Quality of Wine.   Hayden Carruth.   BodElec
Quand on n'a pas ce que l'on aime, il faut aimer ce que l'on a—.   Stevie Smith.
   FaBoEE
Quangle Wangle's Hat, The.   Edward Lear.   EBEV; OTCP; PeVV
Quant Souvenir Me Ramentoit.   Charles, Duc d' Orléans.   WoPoe, *tr. by* Fred
   Chappell
Quantifiable griefs. The daily kill.   Pacific 1945–1995.   Allen Curnow.
   HarvBoo
Quantum.   Martin Johnston.   CBAP
Quantum Est Quod Desit.   Thomas Moore.   *See* Did Not
Quarrel, The.   Conrad Potter Aiken.   MoAmPo
Quarrel, The.   Federico García Lorca.   AF, *tr. by* Robert Bly
Quarrel, The.   Josephine D. Henderson Heard.   CBWP-4
Quarrel, The.   Stanley Kunitz.   APT-2; TaR
Quarrel of the sparrows in the eaves, The.   Sorrow of Love, The.   W. B. Yeats.
   MoBrPo; NOBVV; NPeEn; NoAM; OxBEV
Quarrel with Fortune, A.   Benjamin Colman.   SCAP
Quarreling person is none other than a person who had not been quarreling, A.
   Poem No. III.   Sang Yi.   PFTM-1
Quarrels have long been in vogue among sages.   Song from the Coptic, A.
   Goethe.   NOIV; WoPoe, *tr. by* James Clarence Mangan
Quarrelsome Bishop, A.   Walter Savage Landor.   FaBoEE
Quarries in Syracuse.   Louis Golding.   TrJP
Quarrle, The.   Mother Goose.   OxNR; ReMoGo
Quarry, The.   Vassar Miller.   WPE

Quarry Pool, The.   Denise Levertov.   VGW
Quarry/Rock.   Paul Mariah.   GLP
Quarter century ago, A.   Wilberforce.   Josephine D. Henderson Heard.
   CBWP-4
Quarter century of exile has passed, A.   Georgy [*or* Georgii] Vladimirovich
   Ivanov.   TCRusP, *tr. by* Daniel Weissbort
Quarter-Hour Between God and the Office.   Lőrinc Szabó.   IQMS, *tr. by* Egon
   F. Kunz
Quarter-million, the last great flock of passenger pigeons, A.   Derailment.
   William Heyen.   PoCoUp
Quarter Moon Rise.   Kalamu ya Salaam.   SpirFl   *Fr.* New Orleans Haiku.
Quarter of an hour to wait, A.   Underground.   May Kendall.   VWP; ViWPN
Quarterly, is it, money reproaches me.   Money.   Philip Larkin.   NPeEn
Quartermaster of the spring, The.   First Rondeau: After a French Poet of the
   Fourteenth Century.   Johann Nikolaus Götz.   GePo, *tr. by* George C.
   Schoolfield
Quartier Libre.   Jacques Prévert.   CLPP, *tr. by* Lawrence Ferlinghetti
Quarto Centennial, The.   Josephine D. Henderson Heard.   CBWP-4
Quartz Pebble, The.   Vasco [*or* Vasko] Popa.
   Adventure of the Quartz Pebble, The.   PoSu, *tr. by* Anne Pennington
   Dream of the Quartz Pebble, The.   PoSu, *tr. by* Anne Pennington
   Heart of the Quartz Pebble, The.   PoSu, *tr. by* Anne Pennington
   Love of the Quartz Pebble, The.   PoSu, *tr. by* Anne Pennington
   Quartz Pebble, The.   PoSu, *tr. by* Anne Pennington
   Secret of the Quartz Pebble, The.   PoSu, *tr. by* Anne Pennington
   Two Quartz Pebbles.   PoSu, *tr. by* Anne Pennington
Quasi-crazy tenement fleet, A.   Time Bum.   Jordan Davis.   HeMarv
Quaternary.   Gottfried Benn.   WoPoe, *tr. by* Teresa Iverson
Quatrain.   Sarah Norcliffe Cleghorn.   *See* Golf Links, The
Quatrain.   Ayn Al-Qozat Hamadani.   BBASP, *tr. by* Nasrollah Pourjavady and
   Peter Lamborn Wilson
Quatrain: "Above the creek dallies a bright moon."   Yüan Hao-wen.   SuSp, *tr.
   by* Irving Y. Lo
Quatrain at Chen-chou.   Wang Shih-chieng.   CoBLCP, *tr. by* Jonathan Chaves
Quatrain: "At this remote village, I have no neighbors."   Chang Yü.   CoBLCP,
   tr. by Jonathan Chaves
Quatrain: "Before you praise Spring's advent note."   Tu Fu.   TAL
Quatrain: "Beyond the gate the cormorant had gone and not returned."   Tu Fu.
   SuSp, *tr. by* Jerome P. Seaton
Quatrain: "Birds the more white, against green stream."   Tu Fu.   SuSp, *tr. by*
   Jerome P. Seaton
Quatrain: "France's I am; my lookout's glum."   François Villon.   WoPoe, *tr. by*
   Richard Wilbur
Quatrain: "I cry / but you want comforting."   Jelaluddin [*or* Jalal al-Din] Rumi.
   ArPe, *tr. by* Omar S. Pound
Quatrain: "I lounge on the jetty in the fragrance of catalpa."   Tu Fu.   SuSp, *tr.
   by* Jerome Seaton
Quatrain: "I saw that thieves had burgled as they do."   Ilyas Farhat.   MAP, *tr.
   by* John Heath-Stubbs and Salma Khadra Jayyusi
Quatrain: "I've learnt to laugh now at adversity."   Ilyas Farhat.   MAP, *tr. by*
   John Heath-Stubbs and Salma Khadra Jayyusi
Quatrain: "Just life and death make up our worldly state."   Ilyas Farhat.   MAP,
   tr. by John Heath-Stubbs and Salma Khadra Jayyusi
Quatrain: "Late sun, the stream and the hills; the beauty."   Tu Fu.   SuSp, *tr. by*
   Jerome Seaton
Quatrain: "My foolish heart keeps beckoning to me."   Ilyas Farhat.   MAP, *tr.
   by* John Heath-Stubbs and Salma Khadra Jayyusi
Quatrain: "O gold, a deep contempt for you I own."   Ilyas Farhat.   MAP, *tr. by*
   John Heath-Stubbs and Salma Khadra Jayyusi
Quatrain: "Sarmèd, whom they intoxicated from the cup of love."   Sarmèd the
   Yahud.   TrJP, *tr. by* David Shea
Quatrain: "Seekers of peace, enough hypocrisy!"   Ilyas Farhat.   MAP, *tr. by*
   John Heath-Stubbs and Salma Khadra Jayyusi
Quatrain: "This existence has, without the azure sphere, no reality."   Sarmèd the
   Yahud.   TrJP, *tr. by* David Shea
Quatrain: "Time promises, should I in that confide?"   Ilyas Farhat.   MAP, *tr. by*
   John Heath-Stubbs and Salma Khadra Jayyusi
Quatrain: "We're snug as a bug in a heated house."   Adriann Roland Holst.
   TuT, *tr. by* Sean Dunne
Quatrain: "With you away—despair!"   Rudaki.   ArPe, *tr. by* Omar S. Pound
Quatrain without Sparrows, Helpful Bells or Hope.   Thomas McCarthy.
   PBCIP
Quatrains.   Ralph Waldo Emerson.
   Climacteric.   TCAPo
   Fate.   APN-1; NoP-4
   Gardener.   OxBA
   Memory.   APN-1; TCAPo
   Orator.   OxBA
   Poet.   OxBA; OxBSP; Spl; TCAPo

Self-Reliance. APN-1

Shakspeare. TCAPo

Suum Cuique. APN-1

Quatrains. Salah Jahin. TTY, *tr. by* Samir M. Zoghby

Quatrains for Joy. Muhammad Al-Ghuzzi. MAP; NAfrP, *tr. by* John Heath-Stubbs and May Jayyusi

Quavering cry. Screech-owl? A. Night, Death, Mississippi. Robert Earl Hayden. LCAP-2; VCAP; VGW

Quay recedes, The. Hurrah! Ahead we go! Colonel's Soliloquy, The. Thomas Hardy. FaBoWar; OBWP

Quebec. Henrietta Cordelia Ray. CBWP-3

Quebec Farmhouse. John Glassco. NOBC

Queen, A. Bella [*or* Izabella] Akhatovna Akhmadulina. TCRusP, *tr. by* Daniel Weissbort

Queen and Huntress. Ben Jonson. NAEL-5v1; NAEL-6v1; NAEL-7v1; NoP-4 *Fr.* Cynthia's Revels.

Queen Anne's Lace. June Jordan. TAP

Queen-Anne's-Lace. William Carlos Williams. APT-1; MoAmPo; NAAL-2v2; NOBA; NoAM; TAP

(Queen-Ann's-Lace.) NoP-4

Queen Anne's Musicians. Thomas Hennell. FaBoTw

Queen asks, The. Kamalākānta Bhattācārya. SinGod, *tr. by* Rachel Fell McDermott

Queen Bess was Harry's daughter. Stand forward partners all! Looking Glass, The. Rudyard Kipling. FaBoTw; OBMV

Queen Caroline. *Unknown. See* On Queen Caroline

Queen Eleanor's Confession. *Unknown.* ESPB

Queen Esther Award, The. Richard Michelson. GotH

Queen, for her part, all that evening ached, The. Virgil [*or* Vergil]. NAWM-5v1; NAWM-7v1, *tr. by* Robert Fitzgerald *Fr.* Aeneid [*or* Eneados, *Aeneis*], The.

Queen Hera. Burleigh Mutén. HW

Queen Hera, may your [graceful form]. Sappho. SaLy, *tr. by* Diane Rayor

Queen Katherine to Owen Tudor. Michael Drayton. NoSic *Fr.* England's Heroical Epistles.

Queen-Like Closet, The. Hannah Wolley.

"Ladies, I do here present you." EMWP

Queen Mab's Chariot. Michael Drayton. NPeEn

Queen Medusa. Burleigh Mutén. HW

Queen Mother of the West peach tree is planted in my yard, A. Late Bloomer at the Front of My Garden. Li Po. ColAnChi, *tr. by* Elling O. Eide

Queen Mother to New Queen. Robert Graves. OBSV

Queen Nefertiti. *Unknown.* OTCP; TLR

Queen next morning fried, The. (LL) King Arthur. Mother Goose. LB; OxNR

Queen of black-earth Egypt, divine Isis. Philip of Thessalonica. GrAn

Queen of Carthage, The. Louise Glück. AmFaPo

Queen of Corinth, The. John Fletcher.

Weep No More. OBEV; OxAEP-1

Queen of Elfan's [*or* Elfland's] Nourice [*or* Nourrice], The. *Unknown.* ESPB

"I heard a cow low, a bonnie cow low." FaBoCh

Queen of fragrance, lovely rose. Rose-Bud, The. William Broome. OBEV

Queen of Hearts, The. Tarts, The. Mother Goose. LB; OxNR; ReMoGo

Queen of Hearts, The. Christina Georgina Rossetti. NPeEn; PeVV

Queen of Heaven Mausoleum. Dennis Schmitz. LCAP-2

Queen of herself, the world and me. (LL) Regina. Mary Elizabeth Coleridge. NALW; PoBW

Queen of Lydia, The. Charles Hubert Sisson. OxBC

Queen of martials, The. Homer. NOSC, *tr. by* George Chapman *Fr.* Iliad, The.

Queen of Prussia's Tomb, The. Felicia Dorothea Hemans. RWP

Queen of Scotland, The. *Unknown.* ESPB

Queen of Sheba, The. Kathleen Jamie. NePenScot

Queen of Swords, The. Joanne Limburg. NeBl

Queen of the Blues. Gwendolyn Brooks. NALW; SeSe

Queen of the differentiated sites, administratrix of the. David Jones. AngWePo; TCAWP *Fr.* Tutelar of the Place, The.

Queen of the River. Elizabeth Nannestad. PeNZ

Queen of the silver bow!—by thy pale beam. To the Moon. Charlotte Smith. BWW; CenSon; RWP; Son

Queen, Queen Caroline. *Unknown.* TLR

Queen's After-Dinner Speech, The. William Percy French. OBCoV

Queen's Answer, The. Queen of England Elizabeth I. EMWP

Queen's Dream, The. *Unknown.* PeVV

Queen's English, The. Tony Harrison. DiPo

Queen's Marie, The. *Unknown.* OBEV

Queen's Tears. Tony Curtis. TCAWP

Queen's Wake, The. James Hogg.

Kilmeny. OBEV; OxAEP-2

Thirteenth Bard's Song, The. NePenScot

Queen Sabbath. Hayyim Nahman [*or* Khayim Nakhman *or* Chaim Nachman] Bialik. TrJP, *tr. by* Jessie Sampter

Queen she kept high festival in Windsor's lordly hall, The. Royal Banquet, The. William Edmonstoune [*or* Edmondstoune] Aytoun. OBCoV

Queen she sent to look for me, The. Grenadier. A. E. Housman. OBMV; OBWP

Queen Virtue's court, which some call Stella's face. Sir Philip Sidney. NAEL-5v1; NAEL-6v1; NAEL-7v1 *Fr.* Astrophil and Stella.

Queen was beloved by a jester, A. Cap and Bells, The. W. B. Yeats. MoBrPo; NoAM

Queen wept but thought: It is not appropriate to show such grief, The. *Unknown.* WoPoe, *tr. by* Armand Schwerner *Fr.* Drimeh Kundan.

Queen Yang-Se-Fu / Has seventy great castles. Yang-Se-Fu. "Yehoash." TrJP, *tr. by* Isidore Goldstick

Queene *Vertues* court, which some call *Stellas* face. Sir Philip Sidney. *See* Queen Virtue's court, which some call Stella's face

Queenie. Mary Weston Fordham. CBWP-2

Queenie was a blonde, and her age stood still. Joseph Moncure March. OBCoV *Fr.* Wild Party, The.

Queens. John Millington Synge. MoBrPo; OBMV; PeVV

Queens of Hell had lissome necks to crane, The. Tall Girl, The. John Crowe Ransom. OxBSo; Son

Queer are the ways of a man I know. Phantom Horsewoman, The. Thomas Hardy. NOBE

Queer the way. Making Conversation. Maggie Hannan. MFPA

Queer Thing, A. Nancy Keesing. NOBAu

Queer thing about those waters: there are no, A. Across the Bay. Donald Davie. CABP; NoAM

Queer Things. Emanuel Carnevali. SPE

Queer, what a dim dark smudge you have disappeared into! (LL) Mosquito, The. D. H. Lawrence. NPeEn; RB

Quentin Durward. Sir Walter Scott.

Serenade, A: "Ah! County Guy, the hour is nigh." GTBS-P

La Querida. Bino A. Realuyo. ReBoTo

Querido Flaco, / The ride was cool, wasn't it? Us five. Letter to El Flaco on His Birthday. Richard Blanco. NAPBL

Quesada. Christian Karlson Stead.

"All over the plain of the world lovers are being hurt." PeNZ

"Odysseus under wet snapping sheets." PeNZ

"That the balls of the lover are not larger than the balls of the priest." PeNZ

Quest. Naomi Long Madgett. BPo

Quest, The. W. H. Auden.

Door, The. Son

Quest, The. Denise Levertov. LW

Quest of Silence, The. Christopher John Brennan.

"Fire in the heavens, and fire along the hills." CBAP; NOBAu

Quest of the Ideal, The. Henrietta Cordelia Ray. CBWP-3; SWaP

Quest of the Sancgreall, The. Thomas Westwood.

"Motionless sat the shadow at the helm." PeVV

Quest of the Sangraal, The. Robert Stephen Hawker.

"Land is lonely now, The: Anathema." EBVV

Questing-for-Spring Arbor. Huang Ching-jen. SuSp, *tr. by* Chang Yin-nan

Question. Langston Hughes. APSN

Question. Edith Södergran. WPoS

Question. May Swenson. APT-2; VGW

Question, A. John Millington Synge. MoBrPo; NOIV; OBMV; OxBTC; PAI

Question, A. *Unknown.* NOSC

Question, The. W. H. Auden. OxAEP-2

Question, The. Robert Duncan. NeAP

Question, The. Josephine D. Henderson Heard. CBWP-4

Question, The. Karla Kuskin. NTCP

Question, The. Frank Templeton Prince. BoLoP; GTBS-P

Question, The. Muriel Rukeyser. WPOW

Question, The. Shelley. OBEV; OxBEV

(Dream of the Unknown, The.) GTBS-P

Question, The. Shelley. OBEV

(Dream of the Unknown, The.) GTBS-P

Question, The. Frederick Goddard Tuckerman. APN-2; ColAP

Question Addressed to Liu Shih-chiu, A. Po Chü-i. CoBCP, *tr. by* Burton Watson

Question and Answer. Langston Hughes. BPo

Question and Answer. Kathleen Jessie Raine. MoBrPo

Question and Answer. William Carlos Williams. HarvBoo

Question and Answer, The. Thomas Beedome. NOSC

Question and the Answer, The.   Muhammad Al-Faituri [*or* Al-Fituri *or* Al-Fayturi].   MAP, *tr.* by Sargon Boulus and Peter Porter

Question Answered, The [*or* A].   William Blake.   ErotSp; FaBoEE; NoP-4; OxBEV; WoPoe   *Fr.* Several Questions Answered.

Question at Night.   Mihály Babits.   IQMS, *tr.* by Peter Zollman

Question clear, the answer deep, The.   Sodo.   ZenPo, *tr.* by Takashi Ikemoto and Lucien Stryk

Question for the Frankfurt School, A.   Heberto Padilla.   TCLAP, *tr.* by Andrew Hurley and Alastair Reid

Question is: how does one hold an apple, The.   George Oppen.   NNaP   *Fr.* Five Poems about Poetry.

Question me again. (LL)   Casualty.   Seamus Heaney.   ModIr; NAEL-5v2; NAEL-6v2; PBCIP; PoE

Question Not.   Adam Lindsay Gordon.   PoToHe

Question not, but live and labor.   Question Not.   Adam Lindsay Gordon.   PoToHe

Question of Climate, A.   Audre Lorde.   NoAM

Question of Covenants, A.   Gerald Dawe.   PNI

Question of Form and Content, A.   Jon Stallworthy.   OxBC

Question of Time, The.   William Peskett.   PNI

Question of Vitamins, A.   Ron Charach.   BloBone

Question then, to state it first, The.   Samuel Butler (1612–80).   NOBL   *Fr.* Hudibras.

Question Time.   Jack Lindsay.   NOBAu

Question Time.   Thomas McCarthy.   CIP-2

Question to Life.   Patrick Kavanagh.   MoBrPo

Question to Lisetta, The.   Matthew Prior.   OBEV

Question was an academic one, The.   Tomorrows.   James Merrill.   OBAL

Questioner Who Sits So Sly, The.   W. H. Auden.   OxAEP-2

Questioning.   Henrietta Cordelia Ray.   CBWP-3

Questioning Faces.   Robert Frost.   APT-1

Questioning Spirit, The.   Arthur Hugh Clough.   SacPr

Questionnaire.   Susan Saxe.   GLP

Questions, The.   Robert Pinsky.   ColAP; NoAM

Questions about Poetry since Auschwitz.   Tadeusz Rózewicz.   AF, *tr.* by Robert A. Maguire

Questions Answered.   Li Po.   CrYelRi, *tr.* by Sam Hamill

Questions My Son Asked Me, Answers I Never Gave Him.   Nancy Willard.   LCAP-2

Questions of Swimming, 1935.   Peter Davison.   DiPo

Questions of Travel.   Elizabeth Bishop.   ColAP; HarvBoo; NAAL-2v2; NOBA

Quetzalcoatl Looks Down on Mexico.   D. H. Lawrence.   PeECV

Queue.   Rashidah Ismaili.   HAWP

Queynt.   Anne Rouse.   NeBl

Quha Is Perfyte.   Alexander Scott.   OxBS

Quhen Flora Had O'erfret the Firth.   *Unknown.*   OBEV
   (Four May Poems.)   OxBS

Quhen he wes yung, and cled in grene.   Quhy Sowld Nocht Allane Honorit Be?   *Unknown.*   OxBS

Quhen [*or* Qwhen *or* When] Alexander [*or* Alysandyr] our kynge [*or* King] was dede.   Death of Alexander, The.   *Unknown.*   OxBS

Quhen [*or* When] Noy[e] had maid his Sacrifyce [*or* sacrifice].   Sir David Lindsay [*or* Lyndsay].   ChIV-1; OxBS   *Fr.* Monarche, The.

Quhen Tayis bank wes blumyt brycht.   Tayis Bank.   *Unknown.*   FaBoVe

Quhen that I had oversene this regioun.   Sir David Lindsay [*or* Lyndsay].   OxBS   *Fr.* Dreme, The.

Quhen thou art careit to that cuntree.   Virgil [*or* Vergil].   OBVE, *tr.* by Gawin [*or* Gavin] Douglas   *Fr.* Aeneid [*or* Eneados, *Aeneis*], The.

Quhilk send this summer day. (LL)   Alexander Hume.   NOCV; NePenScot; OxBS

Quhy Sowld Nocht Allane Honorit Be?   *Unknown.*   OxBS

Quhy will ye, merchantis of renoun.   To the Merchantis of Edinburgh.   William Dunbar.   OxBS

Qui Bien Aime a Tard Oublie.   Geoffrey Chaucer.   *See* Parlement of Foules, The

Quia Amore Langueo.   *Unknown.*   NOBE; NOCV; OBEV, *tr.* by Helen Gardner

Quia Pauper Amavi.   Ezra Pound.
   Three Cantos.
   "Another one, half-cracked: John Heydon."   TCAPo

Quick! a last poem before I go.   On Rachmaninoff's Birthday.   Frank O'Hara.   PoM

Quick and Bitter.   Yehuda Amichai [*or* Amikhai].   BoLoP; VCWP

Quick and the Dead, The.   Galway Kinnell.   BAP-01

Quick, at the feeder, pausing.   Nuthatch.   David Wagoner.   OWoS

Quick climb to the Incense Terrace, A.   In the Mountains, Parting from Master Ning As I Return to West Bank.   Kao Ch'i.   CoBLCP, *tr.* by Jonathan Chaves

Quick embrace.   Staircase.   Marina Ivanovna Tsvetayeva [*or* Tsvetaeva].   ARWW, *tr.* by Catriona Kelly

Quick-falling dew.   Basho.   AWP

Quick hands on spinning ropes.   Dead Horse Bay.   Robert Adamson.   NOBAu

Quick in spite I said unkind.   Brazen Tongue.   William Rose Benét.   MoAmPo

Quick in the April hedge.   House.   Robert Hass.   LoL

Quick Night / easy warmth.   World Is Full of Remarkable Things, The.   LeRoi Jones.   SSLK

Quick on my feet in those Novembers of my loneliness.   Mad Fight Song for William S. Carpenter, 1966, A.   James Wright (1927–80).   NoAM

Quick Sell the Pig.   Matthew Rohrer.   AmPoNex

Quick sounds.   Hogyoku.   JDP, *tr.* by Yoel Hoffmann

Quick sparks on the gorse bushes are leaping, The.   Wild Common, The.   D. H. Lawrence.   NoAM

Quick-Step.   Robert Creeley.   VGW

Quick, woman, in your net.   Net, The.   William Robert Rodgers.   BoLoP; CIP-2; ModIr; PNI

Quickened with touches of transporting fear. (LL)   Leigh Hunt.   HAP; NOBL; OBEV; OxBSo

Quickly, love, be lyrical & let.   La, La, La!   Thomas M. [*or* "Tom"] Disch.   NBLV

Quickly take a pen.   Of Sweet Rest.   Joyce Mansour.   HAWP, *tr.* by Mary Beach

Quickness.   Thomas Stanley.   GeHe; MeLP; NOBE; NOCV; NOSC

Quickness.   Henry Vaughan.   BBASP

Quickness which my God hath kissed, A. (LL)   Quickness.   Thomas Stanley.   GeHe; MeLP; NOBE; NOCV; NOSC

Quicksilver song, The.   Insomnia at the Solstice.   Jane Kenyon.   AWTN

Quid, omit, my simple friend.   Horace.   AWP, *tr.* by Matthew Arnold   *Fr.* Odes.

Quid Sit Futurum Cras Fuge Quaerere.   Matthew Prior.   FaBoEE

Quid the Cynic's Song.   William Blake.   RB   *Fr.* Island in the Moon, An.

Quidditie [*or* Quiddity], The.   George Herbert.   GeHe; NOSC

Quiddity i cannot penetrate or name. (LL)   [American Journal].   Robert Earl Hayden.   ESEAA; ISC

Quiescent, a Person Sits Heart and Soul.   Ring Lardner.   OBAL

Quiet.   Marjorie Lowry Christie Pickthall.   NOBC; SacPr

Quiet after the Rain of Morning.   Trumbull Stickney.   ColAP

Quiet afternoon.   Anita Virgil.   HA

Quiet among the leaves, a wren.   Wren, A.   Denise Levertov.   PoCoUp

Quiet beyond recall, / Into irrelevance. (LL)   To the Holy Spirit.   Yvor Winters.   MoAmPo; VGW

Quiet courtyard fills with greenery, The.   Wen Cheng-ming.   CoBLCP   *Fr.* What It's Like Living in My Studio Late in Spring.

Quiet day, A.   Marlene Mountain.   HA

Quiet Days.   Mildred T. Mey.   PoToHe

Quiet deepens, The. You will not persuade.   Farewell to Van Gogh.   Charles Tomlinson.   GTBS-P; NoP-4; PoE

Quiet Earth, The.   Heid E. Erdrich.   AmPoNex

Quiet Evening, Home Away.   Joann Balingit.   ReBoTo

Quiet Fog, The.   Marge Piercy.   UnPo

Quiet Glades of Eden, The.   Robert Graves.   BoLoP

Quiet Has a Hidden Sound.   William Stanley Braithwaite.   NAAAL

Quiet House, The.   Charlotte Mew.   BrRo; EBEV; HarvBoo; NALW; NPeEn

Quiet House in Ch'ang-lo Ward, A.   Po Chü-i.   CoBCP, *tr.* by Burton Watson

Quiet Kingdom, The.   Carl Busse.   AWP, *tr.* by Ludwig Lewisohn

Quiet left by a departing soul, The. (LL)   Rafael Campo.   AmPoNex; WiU   *Fr.* Ten Patients, and Another.

Quiet Life, The.   William Byrd.   NoSic
   (Herdmen, The.)   NOBE

Quiet Life, The.   Pope.   *See* Ode on Solitude

Quiet Mind, The.   *Unknown.*   NoSic

Quiet moon, immaculate of face, The.   "William Baylebridge."   CBAP   *Fr.* Love Redeemed.

Quiet Neighbour, A.   John Heywood.   NoSic

Quiet night is solemn and still, The.   Sent to the Hsiu-ts'ai on His Entry into the Army.   Hsi K'ang.   CoBCP, *tr.* by Burton Watson

Quiet Night Thoughts.   Li Po.   EaWin, *tr.* by W. S. Merwin

Quiet Night Thoughts.   Li Po.   CrYelRi, *tr.* by Sam Hamill

Quiet Nights.   Raymond Carver.   EmeKit

Quiet Nights of Quiet Stars (Corcovado).   Antonio Carlos Jobim.   ReLy, *tr.* by Gene Lees

Quiet Normal Life, A.   Wallace Stevens.   NAAL-2v2; NAAL-5; NoAM

Quiet now, feel the kindly pressure of darkness.   Winter Solstice Poem.   Diana Scott.   BrRo

Quiet, quiet / spring clouds float.   Flower Shadows.   Mo Shih-lung.   CoBLCP, *tr.* by Jonathan Chaves

Quiet room, the flowers, the perfumed calm, The. Schumann's Sonata in A Minor. Celia Laighton Thaxter. AiP

Quiet rustle, A. Rod Willmot. HA

Quiet season of flowering, the courtyard gate is shut. Palace Poem. Chu Ch'ing-yü. SuSp, tr. by Irving Y. Lo

Quiet Sitting. Wang Chiu-ssu. CoBLCP, tr. by Jonathan Chaves

Quiet Soul, A. John Oldham. OBEV

Quiet Spaces. Vincente Huidobro. TCLAP, tr. by Stephen Fredman

Quiet (Thames' or Don's or Salween's) *waters by, The.* (LL) Whit Monday. Louis MacNeice. ChIV-1; PeECV

Quiet Thing, A. Fred Ebb. ReLy

Quiet Until the Thaw. Jacob Nibenegenesabe. AmFaPo, tr. by Howard Norman

Quiet upon the terraces. Chairs in Snow. Elwyn Brooks White. ChAP

Quietly. Gary Hotham. HA

Quietly. Kenneth Rexroth. ErotSp

Quietly and while at rest on the trim grass I have gazed. Air of June Sings, The. Edward Dorn. NeAP; PoM

Quietly dozing. Eric Amann. HA

Quietly I enter the closet. Communion. P. M. Snider. PoToHe

Quietly shaping. David Lloyd. HA

Quietly shining to the quiet Moon. (LL) Samuel Taylor Coleridge. CABP; EBEV; FHYEP; HAP; NAEL-5v2; NAEL-6v2; NOBE; NPeEn; NoP-4; PoE; TFi; TOF

Quietly step onto a land. Kayenta Times Yet Dreaming On. Nia Francisco. HATNAP

Quietly the world lay sleeping. Birth of Jesus, The. Josephine D. Henderson Heard. CBWP-4

Quietly, they take on the color and shape. Danger, Men in Trees. Doris Safie. GraLe; PoArWo

Quilt of Rights. Sandra McPherson. LoL

Quilts. Kathleen Peirce. PBCAP

Quince Preserved through the Winter, Given to a Lady, A. Antiphilus [or Antiphilos]. GrAn

Quinn the Eskimo. "Bob Dylan." RaBo

Quinnapoxet. Stanley Kunitz. LoL

Quinquireme of Nineveh from distant Ophir. Cargoes. John Masefield. BRP; CABP; InPK-6; MoBrPo; NOBE; OBEV; OBMV; PAI; PoRA; TFi

Quintana Lay in the Shallow Grave of Coral. Karl Shapiro. VGW

Quintana lay in the shallow grave of coral. Karl Shapiro. BodElec Fr. Bourgeois Poet, The.

Quintina of Crosses, A. Chad Walsh. TrCP

Quip, The. George Herbert. BASC; GeHe; NOSC; OxAEP-1; OxBEV

Quirky old gent, name of Freud, A. Limerick. Martin Fagg. PeLi

Quis Optimus Reipublicae Status. Sir Thomas More. PBRV

Quite a posh old house was this. Recollections of an Old Spook. Richard Edwards [or Edwardes]. NOxBChV

Quite Apart from the Holy Ghost. Adrian Mitchell. OBSV

Quite for no reason. I've Been to a Marvelous Party. Noël Coward. NBLV; ReLy

Quite Forsaken. D. H. Lawrence. SCGP

Quite horfen, fer a lark, coves on a ship. Helbatrawss, The. Kingsley Amis. NOBL

Quite is high. Styro. Clark Coolidge. PmAP

Quite, quite. / Oh I agree. Restricted. Eve Merriam. TrJP

Quite spent with thoughts I left my cell, and lay. Vanity of Spirit. Henry Vaughan. ESCV; GeHe; NOSC; TOF

Quite unexpectedly as Vasserot. End of the World, The. Archibald MacLeish. GSo; InPK-6; MoAmPo; NOBA; NoAM; OBAL; OxBA; OxBSo; PAI; Son; TAP; TFi; VGW

Quits. Matthew Prior. *See* Epigram: "To John I ow'd great obligation."

Quivering together /Ears of barley. Kana-jo, Lady. ZenPo, tr. by Takashi Ikemoto and Lucien Stryk

Quivira City Limits. Kevin Young. NeAmPo

Quo life, the warld is mine. Flyting o' Life and Daith, The. Hamish Henderson. OxBS

Quod Dunbar to Kennedy. William Dunbar. OxBoLi

Quondam was I in my lady's grace. Sir Thomas Wyatt. NoSic

Quoof. Paul Muldoon. FaBoVe; NPeEn; PBCIP; PNI

Quotations. George Oppen. NNaP

Quote Me Wrong Again and I'll Slit the Throat of Your Pet Iguana. David St. John. RACG

Quoth a cow in the marshes of Glynne. Limerick. Conrad Potter Aiken. PeLi

Quoth Cibber to Pope, tho' in verse you foreclose. Pope. FaBoEE

Quoth Elizabeth prisoner. (LL) Written with a Diamond On Her Window at Woodstock. Queen of England Elizabeth I. PEW; WPE

Quoth he, My faith as adamantine. Samuel Butler (1612–80). OBSV Fr. Hudibras.

Quoth he, to bid me not to love. Samuel Butler (1612–80). NOBL Fr. Hudibras.

Quoth the Duchess of Cleveland to counselor Knight. Song. John Wilmot, 2d Earl of Rochester. BASC

Quoth tongue of neither maid nor wife. Sir Henry Taylor. OBEV; RACG Fr. Philip van Artevelde.

Quotidian, The. Claudia Rankine. AmPoNex

Qwhen Alexander our kynge was dede. *Unknown.* NePenScot

R

R.A.F. (Aged Eighteen). Rudyard Kipling. PoWW Fr. Epitaphs of the War [1914–1918].

R. Alcona to J. Brenzaida. Emily Jane Brontë. *See* Remembrance

R-and-R Centre: An Incident from the Vietnam War. Dennis Joseph Enright. OxBC

R-E-M-O-R-S-E. George Ade. NBLV; OBAL; OBCoV; PeLV

R', n.1. lo. Lattice at/of (Com)pare (Dis)pair. Tina Darragh. FTOS

R-p-o-p-h-e-s-s-a-g-r. E. E. Cummings. PoE

R the reviewer, reviewing my book. Joseph Hilaire Pierre Belloc. NoAM Fr. Moral Alphabet, A.

Rabbi Abe Rosen returned. Genuine Jewish Flesh. Richard Michelson. GotH

Rabbi Ben Ezra. Robert Browning. NAEL-5v2; NAEL-6v2 "Grow old along with me!" ITBLP; PoToHe

Rabbi Ben Levi, on the Sabbath, read. Henry Wadsworth Longfellow. NCAP; TCAPo Fr. Tales of a Wayside Inn.

Rabbi Eleazer opened the palm of his hand. Circle of the Golem, The. Angelina Muñiz Huberman. MirDau, tr. by Aurora Camacho

Rabbi's Song, The. Rudyard Kipling. ChIV-1

Rabbi tells us music on the Sabbath, The. No Music. Richard Chess. TaR

Rabbi Yom-Tob of Mayence Petitions His God. Abraham Moses Klein. TrJP

Rabbi Yussel Luksh of Chelm. Jacob Glatstein [or Glatsteyn]. TrJP, tr. by Nathan Halper

Rabbit, The. Nina Cassian. PoSu, tr. by Christopher Hewitt

Rabbit, The. Elizabeth Madox Roberts. OBCA; OxIBACP

Rabbit Is King of the Ghosts, A. Wallace Stevens. NoAM; TTTS

Rabbit Shoeshine. S. K. Kelen. BMAP

Rabbit: timid brother! My teacher and philosopher! Perfect Life, The. Jorge Carrera Andrade. TCLAP, tr. by Dudley Fitts

Rabbiters: A Pastoral, The. John Kinsella. NeBl

Rabble of six arrived at my house, A. Satire on the O'Haras, A. Tadhg Dall O'Huiginn. NOIV

(.rabid or dog-dull.) Let me tell you how. Professor's Song, A. John Berryman. HeIP-4; NAAL-2v2; NOBA; NoAM; OxBC

Rabinal-Achí. *Unknown.* "Cala-Achí! Ha! Aha! Yeha! Ahau! Wow! Achí!" STP

Raccoon. Kenneth Rexroth. KaS; NNaP Fr. Bestiary, A.

Raccoon wears a black mask, The. Kenneth Rexroth. KaS; NNaP Fr. Bestiary, A.

Raccoons have invaded the crawl space. In the Old Neighborhood. Rita Dove. SpirFl

Race. Karen Gershon. HP

Race. Orkhan Muyassar. MAP, tr. by Samuel Hazo and Lena Jayyusi

Race, The. Nuala Ni Dhomhnaill. CIP-2; PBCIP, tr. by Michael Hartnett

Race, The. Sharon Olds. InvLad; RaBo

Race and Battle. D. H. Lawrence. ChIV-1

Race is not to the swift, The. Race and Battle. D. H. Lawrence. ChIV-1

Race of the Kingfishers. Ray A. Young Bear. HATNAP

Race on Gathering Bites. Kojo Laing. HBAPE

Race Question, The. Naomi Long Madgett. BPo; LTA

Race Relations. Carolyn Kizer. CarOv; LTA

Race round the track of the stadium pupil. (LL) Stenographers, The. Patricia K. Page. HeIP-4; NALW; NoAM

Race to freedom and herself to fame, A. (LL) Harriet Beecher Stowe. Paul Laurence Dunbar. BPo; PoPoPo

Racehorses assemble at the starting barrier, The. Flemington Racecourse. Kevin Hart. NOBAu

Racer's Widow, The. Louise Glück. MoASP

Races will disappear. Nikolai Ivanovich Glazkov. TCRP

Rachel. Lizette Woodworth Reese. TCAPo

Rachel. Bobbi Sykes. IBA

Rachel. Joy Williams. IBA

Rachel (rā'chal), a Ewe. Linda Pastan. TaR

Rachmaninoff played, Chaliapin sang. Return. Dmitry [or Dmitrii] Vasil'evich Bobyshev. ItGoST, tr. by Michael Van Walleghen

Racing, reckoning fingers flick. Palladas [or Pallades]. GrAn; OBVE

Racist Psychotherapy. Isaac J. Black. NBV

Racists. C. K. Williams. LTA

Raderus. John Donne. PeLV

Radial wheels of the season spiked with knives, The. Charles Tomlinson. NewEx

Radiance of that star that leans on me, The. Delay. Elizabeth Jennings. NIL-7; NIP-4; OPOU; OxBTC

Radiant. James Sherry. FTOS

Radiant Dog. John Godfrey. FTOS

Radiant Ranks of Seraphim. Valery [or Valerii] Yakovlevich [or Iakovlevich] Bryusov [or Briusov]. AWP, tr. by Babette Deutsch and Avrahm Yarmolinsky

Radiant silence in Fiesole. Art of the Fugue: A Prayer, The. James Wright (1927–80). BBASP

Radiant Silhouette I. John Yau. OpBo

Radiant Silhouette II. John Yau. OpBo

Radiant Silhouette III. John Yau. OpBo

Radiant Silhouette IV. John Yau. OpBo

Radiant Silhouette V. John Yau. OpBo

Radiant soda of the seashore fashions, The. Far Rockaway. Delmore Schwartz. APT-2

Radiant with vernal grace and summer flowers. Mothers. Francis Saltus Saltus. VerBaPo

Radiating Naïveté. Lucie Brock-Broido. OPRER

Radiation bubbles beneath the skin. Nostradamus Predicts the Destruction of Chicago. Maureen Seaton. IllVoic

Radiation Victim. Colin Thiele. NOBAu

Radiator. Kimiko Hahn. ExTi

Radiator's hissing hot, The. Studio Up Over In Your Ear. Al Young. GT

Radical War Song, A. Thomas Babington Macaulay, 1st Baron Macaulay. OBSV

Radio. Cornelius Eady. ESEAA

Radio. Harriet Monroe. APT-1

Radio. Barrett Watten. PmAP

Radio Cradle-song. Eugène Marais. PeSAV, tr. by Stephen Gray

Radio Gibberish. Genrikh Sabgir. TCRusP, tr. by Daniel Weissbort

Radio grovels from over the fence, A. Sydney. Robert Harris. NOBAu

Radio is playing downstairs in the kitchen, The. Distances. Eavan Boland. HarvBoo

Radio is teaching my goldfish Jujitsu, The. Heavy Water Blues. Bob Kaufman. NBV

Radio Nebraska. Erin Belieu. NAPBL

Radio's reality when. Monday, Monday. David Trinidad. SwNoth

Radioactive. Janine Canan. HW

Radish. N. M. Bodecker. Spl

Radish is / the only dish, The. Radish. N. M. Bodecker. Spl

Radius of the bomb was twelve inches. Yehuda Amichai [or Amikhai]. FaBoWar, tr. by Benjamin Harshav and Barbara Harshav Fr. Time.

Raft drifted, The. John Heath-Stubbs. PeECV Fr. Artorius.

Raftsmen on their floats. Buson. TAL

Rag of black plastic, shred of a kite. Goodbye, Goldeneye. May Swenson. NoP-4

Rag Time Cowboy Joe. Grant Clarke. ReLy

Raga of the drum, the drum the drum the drum the drum, the heartbeat. Unanimity Has Been Achieved, Not a Dot Less for Its Accidentalness. Bob Kaufman. NAAAL

Ragas. David Meltzer. NeAP

Rage—goddess, sing the rage of Peleus' son Achilles. Homer. NAWM-7v1, tr. by Robert Fagles Fr. Iliad, The.

Rage of Achilles, The. Homer. NAWM-7v1, tr. by Robert Fagles Fr. Iliad, The.

Rage of yellow asters, A. Still-Life. Maurice Kenny. UrbNat

Rage, rage against the dying of the light. (LL) Do Not Go Gentle into That Good Night. Dylan Thomas. AmFaPo; CABP; ChAP; ClHu; HAP; HarvBoo; HeIP-4; ITBLP; InPK-6; MakPoe; MoBrPo; NAEL-5v2; NAEL-6v2; NIL-7; NIP-4; NOBE; NPeEn; NoAM; NoP-4; OxAEP-2; OxBTC; PAI; PeECV; PoE; PoPoPo; RB; SCV; SoSe-8; TCAWP; TFi; TOF; TRP; TwCP; UV; UnPo; WeW-3

Ragged Island. Edna St. Vincent Millay. ColAP; NAAL-2v2; NoP-4

Raggedy Ann. Anne Caldwell. ReLy

Raggedy Man, The. James Whitcomb Riley. ITBLP; OBCA

Raggedy! Raggedy! Raggedy Man! (LL) Raggedy Man, The. James Whitcomb Riley. ITBLP; OBCA

Raging cannon-thunder rolls from Bulgaria, A. Razglednica (1). Miklós Radnóti. IQMS, tr. by Peter Zollman

Raging sea, A. Choha. JDP, tr. by Yoel Hoffmann

Ragwort. Anne Stevenson. OPOU

Rahab. Diane Glancy. CRP

Raid, The. William Everson. NoAM

Raid of the Reidswire, The. Unknown. IBB

Raider, The. William Robert Rodgers. MoBrPo

Raiders' Dawn. Alun Lewis. AngWePo; NPeEn

Railing Rimes Returned upon the Author by Mistress Mary Wrothe. Mary Sidney Wroth, Countess of Montgomery. EMWP

Railings. Sean Dunne. ModIr Fr. Sydney Place.

Railings of iron. Anna Andreyevna Akhmatova. TCRP

Railroad and a river and a road, A. Low-Level Cross-Country. Howard Nemerov. GM

Railroad Avenue. Langston Hughes. APT-2

Railroad Bill, A Conjure Man. Ishmael Reed. GM; NAAAL

Railroad Bill was free. (LL) Railroad Bill, A Conjure Man. Ishmael Reed. GM; NAAAL

Railroad Blues, The. Unknown. GM

Railroad bridge's, De. Homesick Blues. Langston Hughes. MoAmPo

Railroad Cars Are Coming, The. Unknown. HHAm

Railroad Man for Me, A. Unknown. CA

Railroad Section Leader's Song. Unknown. GM

Railroad Station. Shinkichi Takahashi. ZenPo, tr. by Takashi Ikemoto and Lucien Stryk

Railroad station, a few, A. Railroad Station. Shinkichi Takahashi. ZenPo, tr. by Takashi Ikemoto and Lucien Stryk

Railroad track is miles away, The. Travel. Edna St. Vincent Millay. OBCA

Railroad yard in San Jose. In Back of the Real. Allen Ginsberg. HeIP-4

Railroads and Freight Handler to the Nation. (LL) Chicago. Carl Sandburg. APT-1; AiP; AmFaPo; BRP; ColAP; IllVoic; MoAmPo; NAAL-2v2; NOBA; NoAM; OxBA; TAP; TFi; TRP; UnPo; VGW

Railway Allotments. M. R. Peacocke. OBGa

Railway Bridge of the Silvery Tay. William McGonagall. NePenScot "Beautiful Railway Bridge of the Silvery Tay!" VerBaPo

Railway Children, The. Seamus Heaney. OPOU

Railway Junction, The. Walter De la Mare. OxBTC

Railway Signals. Sheenagh Pugh. TCAWP

Railway Station, The. Jejuri Arun Kolatkar. EmeKit

Raiment We Put On, The. Kelly Cherry. FFC

Rain. John Ashbery. FTOS

Rain. Nicaragua Water Fire. Gioconda Belli. TANSG, tr. by Steven F. White

Rain. Roo Borson. NoP-4

Rain. Emanuel DiPasquale. InPK-6; KaS

Rain. Margiad Evans. OBWVE

Rain. Charlotte Gardelle. CuPo

Rain. Jeff Gundy. IllVoic

Rain. Amy Hempel. Unle

Rain. Lance Henson. VoR

Rain. Anselm Hollo. PoM

Rain. Nicholas Vachel Lindsay. RaBo

Rain. Dunya Mikhail. PoArWo, tr. by Nathalie Handal and Samira Kawar

Rain. Marlene Mountain. HA

Rain. Paul Murray. BIrV

Rain. Po Chü-i. BLT, tr. by Arthur Waley

Rain. Po Chü-i. ChiP, tr. by Arthur Waley

Rain. Danton R. Remoto. ReBoTo

Rain. Raymond Roseliep. HA

Rain. Gary Soto. NoAM Fr. Elements of San Joaquin, The.

Rain. Robert Louis Stevenson. NTCP

Rain. Shinkichi Takahashi. ZenPo, tr. by Takashi Ikemoto and Lucien Stryk

Rain. Edward Thomas. FaBoWar; HarvBoo; MakPoe; NAEL-5v2; NAEL-6v2; NPeEn; NoP-4; OBWP; OxBEV; OxBTC; PeFWW; PoWW

Rain. Leslie Ullman. YaYoPo

Rain. Konstantin Iakovlevich Vanshenkin. TCRusP, tr. by Daniel Weissbort

Rain. Sándor Weöres. BLT

Rain, the. Muhammad al-Mahdi Al-Majdhoub. MAP, tr. by Matthew Sorenson

Rain, The. Robert Creeley. AmFaPo; CoAP; CoAmPo; ColAP; ErotSp; InvLad; PmAP; PoE; RaBo; TRP; VGW

Rain, The. William Henry Davies. OxBTC

Rain, The. Zbigniew Herbert. PoetW, tr. by John Carpenter and Bogdana Carpenter

Rain, The. Valerie Patterson Napanangka. IBA

Rain, The. Unknown. OxNR

Rain after a Vaudeville Show. Stephen Vincent Benét. MoAmPo

Rain, and a flurry of wind shaking the pear's white blossom. Christian Karlson Stead. PeNZ Fr. Twenty-one Sonnets.

Rain: and over the thorned, cliff-eaten. Rainy Easter. William Everson. APT-2

Rain and the Tyrants. Jules Supervielle. WoPoe, tr. by David Gascoyne

Rain and thunder beat down and flooded the streets. Cartagena. Gary Snyder. BB

Rain at Cold-Food Festival. Su Tung-p'o (Su Shih). "Since coming to Huang-chou." SuSp

"Spring flood is coming up to my door." SuSp

Rain at Night. Jakov [or Jacob] Steinberg. FIT, tr. by Robert Friend

Rain at Noon-time. Molara Ogundipe-Leslie. HAWP

Rain beats on trees south of the river. Tune: "Mountain Hawthorns." Wang An-shih. SuSp, tr. by James J. Y. Liu

Rain before [or Raan afoor] seven. Unknown. FaBoVe; OxNR

Rain brings flowers to this road each spring. From a Dream. Ch'in Kuan. CrYelRi, tr. by Sam Hamill

Rain brings me back, The. Patrizia Cavalli. NeIt

Rain by my throw in a. Subtracted Words. P. Inman. FTOS

Rain came. Fog out of the slough and horses. Day after Chasing Porcupines. James Welch.

Rain Cleared and the Breeze and Sunshine Are Superb as I Stroll Outside the Gate, The. Lu Yu. SuSp, tr. by Burton Watson

Rain clouds clear away. Seishu. JDP, tr. by Yoel Hoffmann

Rain, Clouds, Eight Thousand Miles of Roads. Wang Ping. "No cloud or rain all night long." KGB

Rain comes and goes. Green Refrain, The. Avraham Huss. MHP, tr. by Ruth Finer Mintz

Rain comes down, it comes without our call, The. Winter Rain, The. Jones Very. NCAP

Rain comes flapping through the yard, The. Gathering Mushrooms. Paul Muldoon. BiHa; CIP-2; HarvBoo; ModIr; NoP-4; PBCIP; PNI

Rain comes over the hills, The. Archie Weller. IBA

Rain dampens Sung-ling, spring fills with mist. Hsiu-chou. T'ang Hsien-tsu. CoBLCP, tr. by Jonathan Chaves

Rain Dance. Susan Wicks. MFPA

Rain Ditch. Pinkie Gordon Lane. ISC

Rain Down. Mary Ellen Solt. BoWoP

Rain Downriver. Philip Levine. VCAP

Rain drifts forever in this place. Falls of Glomach, The. Andrew Young. OxBS

Rain drips through. Laurie Duggan. BMAP Fr. Dogs.

Rain During the Cold Food Festival. Su Tung-p'o (Su Shih). CrYelRi, tr. by Sam Hamill

Rain falls on fallen flowers. To the Tune: The Wine Spring. Li Hsun. CrYelRi; ErotSp, tr. by Sam Hamill

Rain falls on the grass. Buson. SoOfWa, tr. by Sam Hamill

Rain Forest. Eric Rolls. NOBAu

Rain Forest. Dave Jeddie Smith. HCAP

Rain, Four Poems. Tu Fu. "Light rain doesn't slick the road." SuSp

"This southern rain nourishes the mossy stones." SuSp

Rain had fallen, the Poet arose, The. Poet's Song, The. Tennyson. EBVV

Rain has beaded the panes. At the Office Early. Ted Kooser. PBCAP

Rain has come, and the earth must be very glad, The. Soaking, The. Ivor Gurney. OxBEV

Rain has passed, The. Birth. Amir Gilbo'a. MHP

Rain hisses off the bus and car and taxi tires. Matins. Molly Peacock. ExTi

Rain hushes the surfaces of tin porches, The. (LL) Rain. Emanuel DiPasquale. InPK-6; KaS

Rain in gusts. John Wills. HA

Rain in May. Jane Hirshfield. GeoHom

Rain in my ears: impatiently there raps. Robert David Fitzgerald. CBAP Fr. Essay on Memory.

Rain in Ohio. Mary Oliver. InPK-6

Rain in Spain, The. Frederick Loewe. ReLy

Rain in Summer. Henry Wadsworth Longfellow. TreFP

Rain in the Aspens. Su Tung-p'o (Su Shih). OHPC, tr. by Kenneth Rexroth

Rain in torrents has washed out the road. Midsummer. Patricia Cumming. WWork

Rain is due to fall, The. Poet Thinks, A. Lui Chi. AWP, tr. by E. Powys Mathers

Rain is Falling, The. Homero [or Umberto] Aridjis. STV; TCLAP, tr. by John Frederick Nims

Rain is not the shape of water most like love. Shape of Water Most Like Love, The. David J. Rothman. GeoH

Rain is over and gone, The. (LL) Written in March [While Resting on the Bridge at the Foot of Brother's Water]. William Wordsworth. ChAP; NAEL-5v2; NAEL-6v2; NTCP; SCGP; UnPo

Rain is pissing down, The. Night Song of the Personal Shadow. György Petri. VCWP, tr. by George Gömöri and Clive Wilmer

Rain is raining all around, The. Rain. Robert Louis Stevenson. NTCP

RAIN is speaking it pelts, THE / THE POEM is moving by itself. Then and Now. James Laughlin. PmAP

Rain It Raineth, The. Charles Synge Christopher Bowen, Baron Bowen. NBLV; NTCP

Rain it raineth all around, The. Rain It Raineth, The. Charles Synge Christopher Bowen, Baron Bowen. NBLV; NTCP

Rain it raineth every day, The. Pennsylvania Deutsch. Christopher Darlington Morley. NBLV

Rain keeps falling, The. Rain. Shinkichi Takahashi. ZenPo, tr. by Takashi Ikemoto and Lucien Stryk

Rain Man. Drahomira Vandas. SurWo, tr. by Guy Ducornet

Rain, midnight rain, nothing but the wild rain. Rain. Edward Thomas. FaBoWar; HarvBoo; MakPoe; NAEL-5v2; NAEL-6v2; NPeEn; NoP-4; OBWP; OxBEV; OxBTC; PeFWW; PoWW

Rain mixed with sleet. Rosamond Haas. HA

Rain Moving In. John Ashbery. NoP-4

Rain Near Heart Lake. Reg Saner. PoCoUp

Rain now stopped on the plain to the west. Composed at the West Wall of Tsou-p'ing Three Days After the Festival of Pure Brightness. Wang Shih-chieng. ColAnChi, tr. by Richard John Lynn

Rain of hollow malice, A. Cesare Greppi. ItPo, tr. by Gayle Ridinger

Rain of London pimples, The. London Rain. Louis MacNeice. NoP-4

Rain on a Grave. Thomas Hardy. OxAEP-2

Rain on lilac leaves. In the dusk. Taid's Grave. Gillian Clarke. OPOU

Rain on the far tip of the grove. Scattered Leaves. Lance Henson. VoR

Rain on the green grass. Rain, The. Unknown. OxNR

Rain on the high prairies. Big Swimming. Edwin Ford Piper. APT-1

Rain on the River. Lu Yu. OHMPC; OHPC tr. by Kenneth Rexroth

Rain on the West Side Highway. Adrienne Rich. NAAL-2v2 Fr. Twenty-one Love Poems.

Rain or shine each day. Kalamu ya Salaam. SpirFl Fr. New Orleans Haiku.

Rain patters on a sea that tilts and sighs. Absences. Philip Larkin. OxBEV

Rain, people, rain! Mocking-Bird's Song, The. Unknown. APN-2, tr. by Alice C. Fletcher

Rain Please Fall. Shuntaro Tanikawa. PoetW, tr. by Harold Wright

Rain Poem. Gabriel Preil. FIT, tr. by Robert Friend

Rain Psalm. Leopoldo Lugones. TCLAP, tr. by Julie Schumacher

Rain, rain, go away. Unknown. OxNR; ReMoGo

Rain, rain, go to Spain. Mother Goose. FaBoVe; ReMoGo

Rain rains sair on Duriesdyke, The. Duriesdyke. Algernon Charles Swinburne. OxBB

Rain rins doun through Mirry-land toune, The. Sir Hugh; or, The Jew's Daughter. Unknown. ESPB

Rain roared through, now. Moon, Rain, Riverbank. Tu Fu. CrYelRi, tr. by Sam Hamill

Rain runs down the glass, The. Wish you were here. (LL) Belvedere Marittimo. Greg Williamson. AmPoNex; NeAmPo

Rain's all right. The boys who physic. Biography of Southern Rain. Kenneth Patchen. VGW

Rain's cold grains are silver-gray, The. Crowded Trolley Car, A. Elinor Wylie. SacPr

Rain's feet, The. Sublimated Mercury. Alice Rahon. SurWo, tr. by Myrna Bell Rochester

Rain's pounding away, The. Rain. Sándor Weöres. BLT

Rain, said the first, as it falls in Venice. Song Tournament: New Style. Louis Untermeyer. OBAL

Rain set early in tonight, The. Porphyria's Lover. Robert Browning. AWP; FHYEP; HAP; NAEL-5v2; NAEL-6v2; OBEV; PAI

Rain sets more flowers blooming. Tune: "Happiness Approaches." Ch'in Kuan. ColAnChi, tr. by Jiaosheng Wang

Rain smell comes with the wind. Love Poem. Leslie Marmon Silko. UnPo; VoR

Rain Song. Badr Shakir Al-Sayyab. MAP, tr. by Lena Jayyusi and Christopher Middleton

Rain Song. Robert Loveman. See April Rain

Rain Song of the Quer'ränna Chai'än, A. Unknown. APN-2, tr. by Matilda Coxe Stevenson

Rain Song of the Shu'-wi Chai'än (Snake Society), A. Unknown. APN-2, tr. by Matilda Coxe Stevenson

Rain sounded just like that, he said, on the roofs there, The. (LL) Nineteen. Elizabeth Alexander. GT; InTrad

Rain stopped for one afternoon, The. Easter: Wahiawa, 1959. Cathy Song. OpBo

Rain stops falling in this river village, The. In a Village by the River. Li Po. CrYelRi, tr. by Sam Hamill

Rain-sunken roof, grown green and thin. Barn, The. Edmund Charles Blunden. MoBrPo

Rain sweeps in as the gale begins to blow. Wet Day. James McAuley. BMAP

Rain the rain the rain, The.   Massacre Sandhill.   Grandfather Koori.   IBA

Rain There.   Tu Fu.   CarOv, *tr. by* Carolyn Kizer   *Fr.* Meandering River Poems, The.

Rain thunders on the roof, The.   Different Morning Altogether, A.   Dima Hilal.   PoArWo

Rain thunderstorms over the Potomac, in Georgetown.   Rainscapes, Hydrangeas, Roses, and Singing Birds.   Richard Eberhart.   MoAmPo

Rain to the Tribe. ·Al-Khansa.   BoWoP, *tr. by* Willis Barnstone and Tony Nawfal

Rain Travel.   W. S. Merwin.   ColAP

Rain tries the one small foot and at length the other.   Towards the Land of the Composer.   Francis Webb.   BMAP

Rain washed his paw, The.   Rain.   Amy Hempel.   Unle

Rain, wind and fire! The secret, bestial peace! (LL)   Card-Players, The.   Philip Larkin.   BLT; OxBC

Rain with its hair gilded by the sun, The.   Transfiguration of the Rain.   Jorge Carrera Andrade.   TCLAP, *tr. by* Michael Surman

Rain with the old sound, with the country sough.   Under Cover.   Abbie Huston Evans.   APT-1

Rainbow, A.   Alexis Rotella.   HA

Rainbow, The.   Opal Palmer Adisa.   GT

Rainbow, The.   Gerard Manley Hopkins.   OxBSP

Rainbow, The.   John Keble.   TreFP

Rainbow, The.   Coventry Patmore.   GTBS-P   *Fr.* Angel in the House, The.

Rainbow, The.   Henry Vaughan.   GeHe

Rainbow, The.   William Wordsworth.   OBEV
 (My Heart Leaps Up When I Behold.)   ChAP

Rainbow at Night.   Antonio Machado.   AF; BLT, *tr. by* Robert Bly

Rainbow-Colored Whale, The.   Ferenc Juhász.   WoPoe, *tr. by* David Wevill

Rainbow Dragon Trilogy.   Amryl Johnson.
 Oil on Troubled Waters.   Oth

Rainbow faded, the animals dispersed, The.   Return to Ararat.   Martyn Halsall.   TrCP

Rainbow for the Christian West, A.   René Depestre.
 Baron-Samedi.   PFTM-2, *tr. by* Joan Dayan
 Cap'tain Zombi.   PFTM-2, *tr. by* Joan Dayan
 Chango.   PFTM-2, *tr. by* Joan Dayan

Rainbow i'th'morning.   *Unknown.*   FaBoVe

Rainbow; or Curious Covenant, The.   Robert Herrick.   ChIV-1

Rainbow Over the Seine, A.   Mary Jo Salter.   ExTi

Rainbows hang in the eddies.   City Out of the Boy, The.   Jeffrey Skinner.   UrbNat

Raindrops.   György Sárközi.   IQMS, *tr. by* Roy Fuller

Raindrops fall.   To a Man Who is Rob Southland.   Nia Francisco.   HATNAP

Raindrops on roses and whiskers on kittens.   My Favorite Things.   Richard Rodgers.   ReLy

Rainer, / the man who was about to celebrate his 52nd birthday.   Death of Europe, The.   Charles Olson.   NeAP

Rainforest.   Judith Wright.   OPOU

Rainier.   Jim Tollerud.   VoR

Raining at every window.   Cor Van den Heuvel.   HA

Rainmakers, The.   Robert Kelly.   PmAP

Rainpoem.   Michael Dransfield.   CBAP

Rains are driven by stiff winds, The.   Traveler's Life, A.   Sung Fang-hu.   CrYelRi, *tr. by* Sam Hamill

Rains have come, The.   Poem from Sierra Madre.   Mila D. Aguilar.   ReBoTo

Rains have come, the frogs are bursting with joy, The.   Frogs.   Buddhadeva Bose.   OMIP, *tr. by* Buddhadeva Bose

Rains have come, the winds are shrill, The.   Rainy Season in California, The.   John Rollin Ridge.   APN-2

Rains Pass.   Yüan Mei.   CoBLCP, *tr. by* Jonathan Chaves

Rainscapes, Hydrangeas, Roses, and Singing Birds.   Richard Eberhart.   MoAmPo

Rainstorm Has Dragged On for Ten Days Now, and There Is No Fire in the Kitchen. Moistening My Inkstone and Chewing on My Brush, I've Lived in Isolation Like a Monk—and Completed Eight Quatrains to Express My Feelings, A.   T'ang Yin.
 "Ten days of wind and rain, depressing darkness!"   CoBLCP

Rainy day, A.   Anita Virgil.   HA

Rainy Day, The.   Henry Wadsworth Longfellow.   AWP

Rainy Easter.   William Everson.   APT-2

Rainy Mountain Cemetery.   N. Scott Momaday.   CDW; HATNAP

Rainy Night.   Ho Ching-ming.   CoBLCP, *tr. by* Jonathan Chaves

Rainy Night.   Juana de Ibarbourou.   TCLAP, *tr. by* Sophie Cabot Black

Rainy Night at the Writers' Colony.   Josephine Jacobsen.   TAP

Rainy Pleiads Wester, The.   A. E. Housman.   BoLoP

Rainy Season.   Charles Reznikoff.   APT-2

Rainy Season, The.   Linda Hogan.   HATNAP; TRP

Rainy Season in California, The.   John Rollin Ridge.   APN-2

Rainy skies, misty mountains.   Fifty.   Kenneth Rexroth.   TAP

Rainy Summer, The.   Alice Thompson Meynell.   OxBSP; OxBTC

Rainy summer night.   Gustave Keyser.   HA

Rainy winter evening.   Martin Burke.   HA

Raise a "Rucus" To-Night.   *Unknown.*   BPo; TAP

Raise girls but not too many.   *Unknown.*   ColAnChi, *tr. by* Red Pine

Raise high the roof.   Sappho.   SaLy, *tr. by* Diane Rayor

Raise him a tombstone of snow. (LL)   Last Rites.   Christina Georgina Rossetti.   FaBoVe; NPeEn

Raise the Cromlech high!   Lament of Maev Leith-Dherg, The.   *Unknown.*   OBWP, *tr. by* Thomas W. H. Rolleston

Raise the oars, be carried.   Mortal Practice.   Gabriel Zaid.   TCLAP, *tr. by* Mónica Hernández-Cancio

Raise the shade.   E. E. Cummings.   VGW

Raise up your valorous right arm, O Spain.   On the Armada That Battled Against England.   Luis de Góngora y Argote.   SpanPo, *tr. by* Ian Fletcher and Brian Soper

Raises up both hands and shouts three times! (LL)   Meeting the Mountains.   Gary Snyder.   NoAM; TAP

Raisin, The.   Donald Hall.   TAP

Raising a Humid Flag.   Thylias Moss.   GT

Raising its radiance to the moon. (LL)   Bread.   W. S. Merwin.   SPE; VCAP

Raising my drooping Head, o'er charg'd with Thought.   My Fate.   Anne Wharton.   EMWP

Raising that truncheon of an arm.   When I Think About America Sometimes (I Think of Ralph Kramden).   Dorothy Barresi.   ExTi; ReTh

Raising the Dead.   Fatima Lim-Wilson.   ReBoTo

Raising the Flag.   Gerald Vizenor.   VoR

Raising the Mediating Center and the Field of Evil with the Twenty-Five Thousand Accounts and the Chant of the Ancients.   Eduardo Calderón.   PFTM-2, *tr. by* F. Kaye Sharon

Raizan has died.   Konishi Raizan.   JDP, *tr. by* Yoel Hoffmann

Raja, I wish I knew.   To Raja Rao.   Czeslaw Milosz.   TOF

Rajah doesn't like Nirvana but he seems.   Rajah in Babylon.   David Wojahn.   IllVoic

Rajah in Babylon.   David Wojahn.   IllVoic

Raka.   N. P. van Wyk Louw.
 Coming of Raka, The.   PeSAV, *tr. by* Guy Butler

Rake, The.   Abu Nuwas.   ArPe, *tr. by* Omar S. Pound

Rakes of Mallow, The.   *Unknown.*   OBCoV

Raking leaves / brown as his robe.   My Favorite Monk Is.   Connie Deanovich.   AmPoNex

Ralegh's Prizes.   Robert Pinsky.   DiPo; VCAP

Raleigh Was Right.   William Carlos Williams.   NIL-7; NIP-4; NoAM; RB; WoPoe

Rally Song.   Mary Weston Fordham.   CBWP-2

Ralph Ellison didn't.   Forgive and Live.   Yusef Komunyakaa.   BodElec

Ralph Leech Believes.   Ebenezer Elliott.   Son   *Fr.* Year of Seeds, The.

Ralph Rhodes.   Edgar Lee Masters.   APT-1   *Fr.* Spoon River Anthology.

Ram.   Gillian Clarke.   AngWePo

Ram came last of all. And Abraham, The.   Heritage.   Haim Gouri.   HP

Ram's Horn, The.   John Hewitt.   BIrV; ModIr; PNI

Rama Kam.   David Diop.   NegPo, *tr. by* Ellen Conroy Kennedy

Rama says.   Two Women Knitting.   Mrinal Pande.   OMIP, *tr. by* Mrinal Pande

Ramat Gan houseware shop, The.   Liquidation.   Leah Aini.   DTA, *tr. by* Miriyam Glazer

Ramble in St. James's Park, A.   John Wilmot, 2d Earl of Rochester.   BASC; PeLV

Ramble of the Gods through Birmingham.   James Bisset.
 Next day they rambled round the town, and swore.   NOEC

Rambling Sailor, The.   Charlotte Mew.   PoRA

Rambling school-boy, thus, A.   William Wordsworth.   NAEL-6v2   *Fr.* Prelude, The; Growth of a Poet's Mind [1850 vers.].

Rampaging spectral images.   Just Another Gig.   Baron James Ashanti.   SeSe

Ramshackles, archipelagoes, loose constellations.   Unifying Principle, The.   A. R. Ammons.   NOBA

Rana, I know you gave me poison.   Mirabai [*or* Mira Bai].   BoWoP, *tr. by* Willis Barnstone and Usha Nilsson

Rana, why do you treat me as your enemy?   Mirabai [*or* Mira Bai].   BoWoP

Randall, My Son.   Donald Davidson.   FuPo

Randall, my son, before you came just now.   Randall, My Son.   Donald Davidson.   FuPo

Random Generation of English Sentences; or, The Revenge of the Poets.   William Jay Smith.   OBAL

Random Pleasures.   Tu Fu.   SuSp, *tr. by* Irving Y. Lo

Random Pleasures.   Tu Fu.

"All day, all night, I worry." CrYelRi, *tr. by* Sam Hamill

"Blown by winds, the thistledown." CrYelRi, *tr. by* Sam Hamill

"Dragon sleeps three winter months, A." CrYelRi, *tr. by* Sam Hamill

"Grieved, I idle and doze." CrYelRi, *tr. by* Sam Hamill

"Peach and plum I planted were my own, The." CrYelRi, *tr. by* Sam Hamill

"River swallows know my shack is humble." CrYelRi, *tr. by* Sam Hamill

"T'ao Ch'ien withdrew from all the world." CrYelRi, *tr. by* Sam Hamill

"Unemployed and lazy, I wander around the village." CrYelRi, *tr. by* Sam Hamill

"West of my hut, I grow mulberry." CrYelRi, *tr. by* Sam Hamill

Random (Re-arrangeable) Study for *Views*. Tony Towle. PmAP

Random talk has blown in. Raisa Blokh. TCRP

Random Thoughts Written in Spring. Wang Yü-ch'eng. SuSp, *tr. by* Irving Y. Lo

Random Verses on Mountain Life. Yüan Hao-wen.

"Clustered trees filled with the sounds of autumn." SuSp

"Winding creek and scattered maple groves, A." SuSp

Randy young girl called Miranda, A. Limerick. Peter Alexander. PeLi

Range-finding. Robert Frost. NIL-7; NIP-4; NoAM; OBWP; RB

Range in the Desert, The. Randall Jarrell. NOBA; PoWW

Range is French and has a mind of its own, The. Collector's Marginalia, The. Peter Sirr. PBCIP

Range of It, The. Michael Klein. WiU

Range Rovers carry. Three xlvii. Laurie Duggan. BMAP

Ranges / of clinker heaps. John Maydew or The Allotment. Charles Tomlinson. OBGa

Rank. Lincoln Kirstein. FaBoA; OBWP

Rank Harvest of Betrayal, The. Wilma Stockenström. PeSAV, *tr. by* Rosa Keet

Rank stench of those bodies haunts me still, The. Siegfried Sassoon. PeFWW

Rankles in a livid spot. (LL) Fifth-Floor Window, The. Lola Ridge. APT-1; WPE

Ranks of electroplated cubes, dwindling to glitters. Fixed Ideas. Kenneth Slessor. BMAP

Rannoch, by Glencoe. T. S. Eliot. NAEL-5v2; NAEL-6v2 *Fr.* Landscapes.

Ransomed soul, A. (LL) My Faith Looks Up to Thee. Ray Palmer. AH; SacPr

Ransomed Spirit to Her Home, The. William Bingham Tappan. AH

Rant. Diane Di Prima.

"Only war that matters is the war against the imagination, The." PFTM-2

Rant Block. Michael McClure. SPE

Rant, Rave and Ricochet. Luis J. Rodriguez. IllVoic

Rantin' Dog, the Daddie o't, The. Robert Burns. FaBoVe; OxBoLi; PeLV

Rantin Laddie, The. Robert Burns. ESPB

Rantin, Rovin Robin. Robert Burns. OxBS

Rap Is. Christopher Stanard. SpirFl

Rap is no mystery. Rap Is. Christopher Stanard. SpirFl

Rape. Jayne Cortez. GT; PmAP

Rape. Joan Larkin. GLP

Rape. Tom Pickard. FaBoTw

Rape of Lucrece, The. John Gower. NPeEn, *tr. by* John Gower *Fr.* Confessio Amantis.

Rape of Lucrece, The. Thomas Heywood.

Good Morrow. GTBS-P

(Matin Song.) OBEV

Rape of Lucrece, The. William Shakespeare.

("At last shee cals to mind where hangs a peece.") PBRV

[Before the Rape] NoSic

Lucrece's Death. · NoSic

(Outcry upon Opportunity, An.) NOBE

Rape of the Lock, The. Pope.

"Adventurous baron the bright locks admired, The." EroLit

"For ever cursed be this detested day." EroLit

"Oh, hadst thou, cruel! been content to seize." EroLit

"Peer now spreads the glittering forfex wide, The." EroLit

"Then flashed the living lightning from her eyes." EroLit

Rape of the Lock; an Heroi-Comical Poem, The. Pope. CABP; FHYEP; HAP; NAEL-6v1; NAEL-7v1; NAWM-7v2; NoP-4; OBNV; PeLV

"And now, unveiled, the toilet stands displayed." ECEV; NOBE; OxAEP-1; OxBEV

"But anxious cares the pensive nymph oppressed." EBNV; OxAEP-1

"But when to mischief mortals bend their will." OxAEP-1

"Close by those meads, for ever crowned with flow'rs." EBNV; OBSV; OxBoLi

"For lo! the board with cups and spoons is crown'd." UV

Hampton Court. EBNV; OBSV; OxBoLi

"Hither the heroes and the nymphs resort." ECEV

"Not with more glories, in th'ethereal plain." EBEV; EBNV; ECEV; NOBE; NOEC; OxAEP-1

"Restore the lock!" she cries; and all around." OxAEP-1

"Say why are beauties praised and honoured most" ECEV

"She said: the pitying audience melt in tears." EBNV

"Sol through white curtains shot a tim'rous ray." ECEV; NPeEn

"Then grave Clarissa graceful wav'd her fan." NPeEn; OxBEV

Toilet, The. ECEV; NOBE; OxAEP-1; OxBEV

Voyage on the Thames, The. EBEV; EBNV; ECEV; NOBE; NOEC; OxAEP-1

"What dire offence from am'rous causes springs." EBNV; NOEC

Rape Poem, The. Tommi Avicolli. GLP

Raphael. Henrietta Cordelia Ray. CBWP-3

Raphael. Priscilla Jane Thompson. CBWP-2

Raphael's Descent. John Milton. NOSC *Fr.* Paradise Lost.

Rapid day is gone; her banner swings the night, The. Evening. Andreas Gryphius. GePo, *tr. by* George C. Schoolfield

Rapid Floods. Kata Szidónia Petröczy [*or* Petröczi]. IQMS, *tr. by* Marie B. Jaffe

Rapid Transit. James Agee. MoAmPo

Rapid Transit. William Carlos Williams. APT-1

Rapier of Treason, A. *Unknown.* BoWoP, *tr. by* Willis Barnstone

Rapist's Villanelle, The. Thomas M. [*or* "Tom"] Disch. RA

Rapist, who reeked of cheap booze, A. Limerick. *Unknown.* PeLi

Rapparees. Richard Murphy. BIrV; NOIV; PBCIP *Fr.* Battle of Aughrim, The.

Rapt. Irene McKinney. PBCAP

Rapt with the rage of mine own ravisht thought. Edmund Spenser. PeECV *Fr.* Fowre Hymnes.

Raptor. Ronald Stuart Thomas. EmeKit

Rapture. Stefan George. AWP, *tr. by* Ludwig Lewisohn

Rapture, A. Thomas Carew. BASC; BeJo; CABP; CaPo; NAEL-5v1; NAEL-6v1; NAEL-7v1; OxAEP-1

"Come, then, and mounted on the wings of Love." EroLit

"I will enjoy thee now my Celia, come." PBRV

"Now in more subtle wreaths I will entwine." EroLit

Rapture, The. Henry Baker. NOEC

Rapture, The. Adam Cornford.

"And it came to pass just as they had foretold." CLPP

Rapture, The. Thomas Traherne. GeHe; NOSC

Rapunzel. Olga Broumas. ReTh

Rapunzel Rapunzel let down your hair. After-Thought, The. Stevie Smith. OxBC

Rare are thy cheeks, Susanna, which do show. Upon Mistresse Susanna Southwell, Her Cheeks. Robert Herrick. BeJo

Rare composition of a poet-knight. Sonnet to a Sonnet. Thomas Hood. CenSon

Rare flower, leaf-fringed, or tender yellow gold. Yellow Sunflower of Szechwan. Chang Yü. SuSp, *tr. by* Irving Y. Lo

Rare Is the Wheat-Field in Which There's No Blemish. *Hungarian Oral Tradition.* IQMS, *tr. by* Adam Makkai

Rare medieval Spirit! brooding seer! Dante. Henrietta Cordelia Ray. CBWP-3

Rare sight, a woman lost in the trance. *Unknown.* GifTon, *tr. by* David Ray

Rare smile, The. Portrait. Manuel Bandeira. TCLAP, *tr. by* Candace Slater

Rare temples thou hast seen, I know. Fairy Temple; or, Oberon's Chapel, The. Robert Herrick. CaPo

Rare, twice-in-a-lifetime form of sport, A. Retort Perfect, The. Justin Richardson. OBCoV

Rare type of gentrie, and true Vertues Starr. Joshua Sylvester. OxBSo *Fr.* Du Bartas: His Divine Weeks and Works.

Rare Willie Drowned in Yarrow; or, The Water o Gamrie. *Unknown.* ESPB (Rare Willy.) OxBB

Rare Willy. *Unknown. See* Rare Willie Drowned in Yarrow; or, The Water o Gamrie

Rarely, rarely, comest thou. Song. Shelley. FHYEP

Rarest of the esculents, its distribution. Roger Garfitt. NewEx

Rarity and value of scientific knowledge, The. Poetry and Science. Hugh MacDiarmid. HarvBoo

Rascal far gone in treachery, A. Limerick. *Unknown.* PeLi

Raspberries. Laurence David Lerner. EBEV

Raspberry in the Pudding, The. Philip O'Connor. SPE

Rasta Reggae. Mervyn Morris. WaCA

Rat, The. William Henry Davies. OBWVE; OxBTC

Rat, The. Karen Kipp. BodElec

Rat, The. *Unknown.* WoPoe, *tr. by* John S. Major

Rat and the Elephant, The. Jean de La Fontaine. OBVE, *tr. by* Marianne Moore

Rat-fink Baby. Brothers at the Bar. Naomi Long Madgett. NBV

Rat Jelly. Michael Ondaatje. EmeKit

Rat Minaret: Miniaturist-Divan, The. Mac Wellman.

"All the way clear to Aliquippa." HeMarv

"Blue sky in a human face." HeMarv

"Endowed fiction of a mouse ear." HeMarv

"Evil Raven, have paper pity upon those." HeMarv

"Lost from an airy." HeMarv

"Most simple things repel." HeMarv

"Moth house is taking over, Sir Footfall." HeMarv

"Needle growing in ancient basalt." HeMarv

"No point mortgages wilt in daynights." HeMarv

"No tongue but bumbles, has." HeMarv

"Silvery tells no sphere to go and." HeMarv

"So perfectly done and yet." HeMarv

"United bolt and screw." HeMarv

"Who lowers the unseen hat from on high." HeMarv

Rat, O Rat. Christopher Logue. EmeKit

Rat Song. Margaret Atwood. NIP-4 *Fr.* Songs of the Transformed.

Rat too has a skin (to tan), A. Confucius. WoPoe, *tr. by* Ezra Pound *Fr.* Yung Wind.

Rat Trap. Mick Gowar. NOxBChV

Rat will have carried her into his hole, The. (LL) What Invisible Rat. Jean-Joseph Rabéarivelo [*or* Rebéarivelo]. NegPo; PBMAP; TTY

Rata blooms explode, the bow-legged tomcat, The. James Keir Baxter. PeNZ *Fr.* Autumn Testament.

Ratatouille. Gina Berkeley. PeLi

Ratcatcher's Daughter, The. *Unknown.* OxBoLi

Rath in front of the oak wood, The. *Unknown.* NOIV

Rather, cars will honk as if to say it's easier. Strictly Speaking. Debra Gregerman. AmPoNex

Rather extreme vegetarian, A. Limerick. "Sagittarius." PeLi

Rather notice, mon cher. To a Solitary Disciple. William Carlos Williams. VGW

Rather obese Master Shuang, A. Tune: "Po Pu-tuan" Fat Couple. Wang Ho-ch'ing. ColAnChi, *tr. by* James I. Crump

Rather remote, all of it. Vanished Work. Hans Magnus Enzensberger. VCWP, *tr. by* Hans Magnus Enzensberger and Michael Hamburger

Rather skinny beauty, you'll find, / is Diocleia, A. Argentarius. GrAn

Rather than attribute, towards the brush with open sea. (LL) Note to Tony Towle (After WS), A. Charles North. FTOS; PmAP

Rather than leave behind me. Jikko. JDP, *tr. by* Yoel Hoffmann

Rather than our bodies the sand. Army Beach with Trumpets. Jack Spicer. APSN

Rather than your fine hotels. Sightseers in a Courtyard. Nicolás Guillén. TTY, *tr. by* Langston Hughes

Rather the Bird Flying By and Leaving No Trace. Fernando Pessoa. WoPoe, *tr. by* Edwin Honig

Rathlin. Derek Mahon. ModIr

Ration books voided, there was little to eat. Tía Olivia Serves Wallace Stevens a Cuban Egg. Richard Blanco. NAPBL

Ration Card, The. Liz Sohappy Bahe. CDW

Rational. Helen Chalakee Burgess. ReEnLa

Rational Man. Muriel Rukeyser. AF

Rats by night such mischief did, The. Fable XXI: The Rat-catcher and Cats. John Gay. OxAEP-1

Rattan bed, paper netting. I wake from morning sleep. Li Ch'ing-chao. BoWoP, *tr. by* Willis Barnstone and Sun Chu-chin

Rattle. Peter Blue Cloud. HATNAP

Rattle Bag, The. Dafydd [*or* David] ap Gwilym. NBLV; RB; WoPoe, *tr. by* Joseph P. Clancy

Rattler, Alert. Brewster Ghiselin. HAP; WeW-3

Rattlesnake Country. Robert Penn Warren. NAAL-2v2; VCAP

Rattling little cart and patches of yellow dust at dusk. Ballad of the Little Cart, A. Ch'en Tzu-lung. SuSp, *tr. by* Wu-Chi Liu

Rauf Coilyear. *Unknown.*

"Coilyear, gudlie in feir, tuke him be the hand, The." OxBS

Rav / of Northern White Russia declined, The. Illustrious Ancestors. Denise Levertov. NAAL-2v2; NOBA; PmAP; TaR; VGW

Ravaged Villa, The. Herman Melville. APN-2; CTC; NOBA; TCAPo

(In Shards the Sylvan Vases Lie.) NCAP

Ravel: Bolero. Al Young. SpirFl

Raven, The. Samuel Taylor Coleridge. NOxBChV

Raven, The. Nikolai Ivanovich Glazkov. TCRP, *tr. by* Daniel Weissbort

Raven, The. Edgar Allan Poe. APN-1; BRP; ChAP; ColAP; EBNV; FaBoCh; HeIP-4; ITBLP; NAAL-2v1; NAAL-3; NAAL-5; NCAP; NIL-7; NIP-4; NOBA; NoP-4; OBCA; OBNV; OWoS; OxBA; PWR; PoRA; TAP; TCAPo; TFi; TreFP; UV

Raven, The. Edwin Arlington Robinson. AWP; FaBoEE; OBAL

Raven, The. *Var. authors.* AWP; FaBoEE; OBAL *Fr.* Variations of Greek Themes.

Raven croaks before me, A. Ode. Theophile De Viau. WoPoe, *tr. by* Phillip Holland

Raven Days, The. Sidney Lanier. APN-2; OxBA; TCAPo

Raven dies, The. (LL) Raven, The. Edwin Arlington Robinson. AWP; FaBoEE; OBAL

Raven eyes blink. Raven Is Two-Faced. Robert H. Davis. HATNAP

Raven, gather us to that dark breast. Raven Tells Stories. Robert H. Davis. HATNAP

Raven Is Two-Faced. Robert H. Davis. HATNAP

Raven/Moon. Anita Endrezze. VoR

Raven sat upon a tree, A. Sycophantic Fox and the Gullible Raven, The. Guy Wetmore Carryl. NBLV; OBCA

Raven Tells Stories. Robert H. Davis. HATNAP

Ravening Coyote comes. Three Songs of Mad Coyote. *Unknown.* STP, *tr. by* Herbert J. Spinden

Ravenna Bridge. Leslie Norris. AngWePo

Ravine on a Cold Evening. Li Ho. ColAnChi; SuSp, *tr. by* Maureen Robertson

Raw cabbage marinated in vinegar with chilies. Kimchee in Worchester (Mass.). Alfred Corn. WiU

Raw Fish and Vegetables. Shinkichi Takahashi. ZenPo, *tr. by* Takashi Ikemoto and Lucien Stryk

Raw Flesh. Vasco [*or* Vasko] Popa.

"After the third evening roud." PoSu, *tr. by* Anne Pennington

("After the third evening round.") HP, *tr. by* Anne Pennington

Be Seeing You. PoSu, *tr. by* Anne Pennington

In the Village of My Forefathers. PoSu, *tr. by* Anne Pennington

"One hugs me." PoSu, *tr. by* Anne Pennington

"Sweeper collects dry leaves with his broom, The." PoSu, *tr. by* Anne Pennington

Time Swept Up. PoSu, *tr. by* Anne Pennington

Rawk o' the autumn, The. John Clare. SCGP

Rawk o' the autumn hangs over the woodlands, The. Rawk o' the autumn, The. John Clare. SCGP

Ray Charles at Mississippi State. Tom Dent. NBV

Ray Charles! His voice. Hannoi Hanna. Yusef Komunyakaa. SwNoth

Ray of light slants through the windows, A. Wedding. Nikolai Alekseievich Zabolotsky [*or* Zabolotskii]. TCRP, *tr. by* Daniel Weissbort

Ray's third new car in half as many years. Family Reunion. Louise Erdrich. HATNAP; NoAM

Rayboy Blk & Bluz. Shirley Bradley LeFlore. SpirFl

Rayflower / About the head. Sándor Weöres. IQMS, *tr. by* Edwin Morgan

Raymond Chandler: The Big Sleep. Basil Ransome-Davies. OBCoV

Raymond of the Rooftops. Paul Durcan. EmeKit

Raynsford, a knight, fit to have served King Arthur. Sir John Raynsford's Confession. John Harington. NoSic

Razglednica (1). Miklós Radnóti. IQMS, *tr. by* Peter Zollman

Razglednica (2). Miklós Radnóti. IQMS, *tr. by* Peter Zollman

Razglednica (3). Miklós Radnóti. IQMS, *tr. by* Peter Zollman

Razglednica (4). Miklós Radnóti. IQMS, *tr. by* Peter Zollman

Razglednica (4). Miklós Radnóti. IQMS, *tr. by* Zsuzsanna Ozsváth and Frederick Turner

Razglednica (4). Miklós Radnóti. IQMS, *tr. by* George Gömöri and Clive Wilmer

Razglednica (4). Miklós Radnóti. IQMS, *tr. by* Iain MacLeod

Razors pain you. Dorothy Parker. APT-1; HeIP-4; InPK-6; NAAL-2v2; NALW; NBLV; NoP-4; OBAL; TrJP; UV *Fr.* Some Beautiful Letters.

Razzle Dazzle! Whiskers Meets Polly. Michael Stillman. TLR

Razzle dazzle maggots are summary, The. Easter. Frank O'Hara. SPE

Razzmatazz. Gilbert Sorrentino. FTOS

Re-act for Action. Haki R. Madhubuti. BPo

Re-born Sun, The. (LL) "H. D." APT-1; NAAL-5 *Fr.* Walls Do Not Fall, The.

Re-Conversion. Novella Nikolaevna Matveyeva [*or* Matveieva]. TCRusP, *tr. by* Nigel Stott

Re-Emergence of the Trombone, The. Fred Muratori. MiVo

Re-encounter. Joaquim Paço D'Arcos. PeSAV, *tr. by* Roy Campbell

Re-forming the Crystal. Adrienne Rich. TAP

Re-member Us. Judith Anderson. HW

Re-member us, / you who are living. Re-member Us. Judith Anderson. HW

Re-reading Jane. Anne Stevenson. NALW

Re:searches (Fragments, after Anakreon, for Emily Dickinson). Kathleen Fraser. PmAP

Re that winter cloak. Slow Giving. Ibn al-Rumi. ArPe, *tr. by* Omar S. Pound

Re: the question of poems. Memo from the Desk of X. Donald Justice. TwCP

Re-Verse. Diane Ward. FTOS

Reach, The. Carl Phillips. GT

Reach and you set this whole harp. Harp/Desire. Katherine Soniat. MiVo

Reach back and bring me the firmness of her hand. (LL) Request to a Year. Judith Wright. CBAP; FaBoWP; ItWoWo; NALW; NoAM; NoP-4

Reach for arrows of falling light. A man once sang. Falling Moon. Roberta Hill Whiteman. CDW

Reach, with your whiter hands, to me. To the Water Nymphs, Drinking at the Fountain. Robert Herrick. BeJo; CaPo; NAEL-5v1; NAEL-6v1

Reaches down like a hood. Although the Sky. Elmaz Abinader. PoArWo

Reaches Sicily. Mary Robinson. CenSon; RWP

Reaching Forty. 'Abd al-Razzaq 'Abd al-Wahid. MAP, tr. by Diana Der Hovanessian and Lena Jayyusi

Reaching out into the sea, passing the waves its exhaust smoking. Mission Work-Boat. Unknown. NOBAu, tr. by Mungayana Nundhirribala

Reaching the Horizon. Robert Mezey. GeoHom

Reaching Yellow River. Roberta Hill Whiteman. HATNAP

Reactionary Poet, The. Ishmael Reed. ESEAA; GT

Read about the Buddhist monk. Dilemma. Patricia Beer. OxBC

Read and committed to the flames, I call. Tony Harrison. CABP; HarvBoo; NoP-4 Fr. School of Eloquence, The.

Read here: / This is the story of Evarra-man. Evarra and His Gods. Rudyard Kipling. MoBrPo

Read it not, noble lords. William Shakespeare. OxAEP-1 Fr. Coriolanus.

Read me Euripides. Follies of Adam, The. Theodore Roethke. ChIV-1

Read my riddle, I pray. Equal, An. Unknown. ReMoGo

Read of Thyestes, Oedipus, dark suns. Martial. RomPo, tr. by Peter Whigham

Read some lines a poet wrote in the exile of his town. Town. Marie-Claire Bancquart. MFP, tr. by Martin Sorrell

Read—Sweet—how others—strove. Emily Dickinson. AH; NOCV

Read the Bible, it will tell. Bible, The. Lizelia Augusta Jenkins Moorer. CBWP-3

Read this Song of Hiawatha! (LL) Henry Wadsworth Longfellow. ColAP; NOBA; PoE Fr. Song of Hiawatha, The.

Reader. Epitaph on Sir Philip Sidney Lying in St Paul's without a Monument, to Be Fastned upon the Church Door. Edward Herbert, 1st Baron Herbert of Cherbury. NPeEn

Reader, The. Janet Lewis. APT-2

Reader, The. Thomas Merton. CRP

Reader, The. Wallace Stevens. SAmP

Reader, behold! this monster wild. Infant Innocence. A. E. Housman. NOBL

Reader, beneath this turf I lie. Thomas [or "Tom"] Brown. FaBoEE

Reader! I am no poet: but I grieve! To the Reader. Urian Oakes. SCAP

Reader, I was born and cried. Epitaph on the Fart in the Parliament House. John Hoskyns [or Hoskins]. FaBoEE

Reader, I would not have thee mistake. His Own Epitaph, When He Was Sick. John Hoskyns [or Hoskins]. FaBoEE

Reader / If thou be a Christian and a Freeman. Epitaph for Jonathan Robbins. Philip Freneau. TCAPo

Reader of Poetry, The. Ilya [or Karl] L'vovich Selvinsky [or Sel'vinskii]. TCRP, tr. by Daniel Weissbort

Reader of This Page. Maurice Kilwein Guevara. NAPBL

Reader over My Shoulder, The. Robert Graves. NAEL-5v2; NAEL-6v2

Reader, pass on, nor idly waste [or don't waste] your time. In Peterborough Churchyard. Paulus [or Paulos] Silentiarius. FaBoEE; NOBL

Reader, stay, / And if I had no more to say. Epitaph on Master Philip Gray, An. Ben Jonson. FaBoEE

Reader unmov'd and Reader unshaken, Reader unsedc'd. Sweet Reader, Flanneled and Tulled. Olena Kalytiak Davis. BAP-01; NAPBL

Reader, when these dumb stones have told. Another [On the Duke of Buckingham]. Thomas Carew. NOSC

Readers and the hearers like my books, The. Critics. Martial. AWP, tr. by Sir John Harington \VP/[or Harrington]

Readers, forgive me. Ten ii. Laurie Duggan. BMAP

Readers of Newspapers. Marina Ivanovna Tsvetayeva [or Tsvetaeva]. TCRP, tr. by Elaine Feinstein and Angela Livingstone

Readers of the Boston Evening Transcript, The. Boston Evening Transcript, The. T. S. Eliot. inPK-6; TCAPo

READIE-SOUNDPIECE (after a suggestion of Hilaire Hiler) (synchro-with Orchestrauto maton). Abraham Lincoln Gillespie. PFTM-2 Fr. Readie-Soundpiece (For Bob Brown's Reading Machine).

Readie-Soundpiece (For Bob Brown's Reading Machine). Abraham Lincoln Gillespie.

"READIE-SOUNDPIECE (after a suggestion of Hilaire Hiler) (synchro-with Orchestrauto maton)." PFTM-2

Reading. Joanne Burns. BMAP

Reading. P'i Jih-hsiu. SuSp, tr. by William H. Nienhauser

Reading. Jean-Joseph Rabéarivelo [or Rebéarivelo]. NegPo, tr. by Ellen Conroy Kennedy

Reading. Ruth Stone. ExTi

Reading, A. Virginia Hooper. KGB

Reading, The. Gabriel Gbadamosi. HBAPE

Reading a Medal. Terence Tiller. FaBoTw; GTBS-P

Reading, and reading—little is the gain. Suspiria Noctis. Henry Howard Brownell. APN-2

Reading Aquinas. Michael Heffernan. WeW-3

Reading Before We Read, Horoscope and Weather. Wyatt Prunty. RA

Reading Bonjour, Tristesse at the Florence Crittenden Home for Unwed Mothers. Diane Wakoski. GeoHom

Reading by Mechanic Light. Thomas McGrath. BodElec; GifTon

Reading clouds beyond the road. Getting Your Rocks Off. Melvin Dixon. CAGL

Reading, Dreaming, Hiding. Kelly Cherry. FFC

Reading Emerson. Cottonmouths are moving mildly. Lake Drummond Dream. Dave Jeddie Smith. VCAP

Reading Frank O'Hara in a Mexican Rainstorm. Michael McClure. BB

Reading Hamlet. Anna Andreyevna Akhmatova. PoetW, tr. by Max Hayward and Stanley Kunitz

Reading how even the Swiss had thrown the sponge. Beyond the Alps. Robert Lowell. LCAP-2; NOBA

Reading I spilled the wine. Untoward. Ann Lauterbach. BodElec

Reading in Li Po. After the Last Dynasty. Stanley Kunitz. InvLad; TAP

Reading in my palanquin, I fall asleep and dream. Passing By Waterwheel Bay. Yang Wan-li. SuSp, tr. by Jonathan Chaves

Reading in the heat of noon. Summer Day. Yüan Mei. OHMPC, tr. by Kenneth Rexroth

Reading in the Night. Roy Fuller. OxBC

Reading Indian Poetry. Ramona Wilson. VoR

Reading Lesson, The. Richard Murphy. PBCIP

Reading Milosz. Lev Vladimir Loseff [/or Losev]. TCRP, tr. by G. S. Smith

Reading my verses, I liked [or like't] them so well. Poet[r]ess's Hasty Resolution, The. Margaret Lucas Cavendish, Duchess of Newcastle. BASC; NAEL-7v1

Reading Myself. Robert Lowell. HCAP; NAAL-2v5; TAP; VCAP

Reading Paradise Lost in Protestant Ulster 1984. Seamus Deane. BiHa; PBCIP

Reading Pornography in Old Age. Howard Nemerov. NoAM

Reading Room. Allison Joseph. NAPBL

Reading Scheme. Wendy Cope. MakPoe

Reading Seferis. Sam Hamill. GifTon

Reading some Russian novel. White Gloves. William Plomer. PeSAV

Reading the Annals of Emperor Wu of the Han Dynasty. Wu Wei-yeh. CoBLCP, tr. by Jonathan Chaves

Reading the Bible Backwards. Eleanor Wilner. NoP-4

Reading the Book of Hills and Seas. Ch'ien T'ao. ChiP, tr. by Arthur Waley

Reading the Books Our Children Have Written. Dave Jeddie Smith. HCAP

Reading The Classic of Hills and Seas. T'ao Ch'ien [or T'ao Yuan-ming]. CoBCP, tr. by Burton Watson

Reading the Collected Works of Li Po and Tu Fu: A Colophon. Po Chü-i. SuSp, tr. by Irving Y. Lo

Reading the Elephant. Andrew Motion. HarvBoo

Reading the I Ching. Raquel Chalfi. DTA, tr. by Karen Alkalay-Gut

Reading the Japanese Poet Issa: (1762–1826). Czeslaw Milosz. WoPoe, tr. by Robert K. Haas

Reading the Names of the Vietnam War Dead. Thomas McGrath. CDa

Reading the Newspaper. William Cowper. ECEV Fr. Task, The.

Reading the Poems of an Absent Friend. Ou-yang Hsiu. OHPC, tr. by Kenneth Rexroth

Reading the Poetry Collection of Lü Fang-ch'ing. Chang Yü. CoBLCP, tr. by Jonathan Chaves

Reading the Poetry of Meng Chiao: Two Poems. Su Tung-p'o (Su Shih). ColAnChi; WoPoe, tr. by Burton Watson

Reading the Unpublished Manuscripts of Louis MacNeice at Kinsale Harbour. Desmond O'Grady. PBCIP

Reading Time : 1 Minute 26 Seconds. Muriel Rukeyser. NIL-7

Reading Walt Whitman. Calvin Forbes. ESEAA; NBV

Reading Whitman in a Toilet Stall. Timothy Liu. WiU

Reading won't save us from death. Unknown. ColAnChi, tr. by Red Pine

Reading your poems I am aware. Letter to Peter Levi, A. Elizabeth Jennings. OxAEP-3

Reading Yuan Chen on a Boat. Po Chü-i. CrYelRi, tr. by Sam Hamill

Readings. Armanda Guiducci. CltWP, tr. by Cinzia Sartini Blum and Lara Trubowitz

Readings. Czeslaw Milosz. GI

Readings, Forecasts, Personal Guidance. Kenneth Fearing. MoAmPo

Readings of History. Adrienne Rich. CoAmPo

Ready. Dan Pagis. FIT, *tr. by* Robert Friend

Ready. Margaret Junkin Preston. PWR

Ready for Flight. Eavan Boland. OxBSo

Ready-Made World. Piera Oppezzo. CItWP, *tr. by* Cinzia Sartini Blum and Lara Trubowitz

Readymade. John Perreault. SPE

Real Chocolate. Stewart Florsheim. GotH

Real collision, The. (LL) What are We Playing at? Andrée Chedid. BoWoP; HAWP, *tr. by* Mirène Ghossein and Samuel Hazo

Real Comfort. Mary Stanley Bunce Dana. SWaP

Real danger. gambles. and the edge of death. (LL) What You Should Know to Be a Poet. Gary Snyder. APSN; NNaP; PFTM-2; PoM

Real duel of Apollo, The. Apollo and Marsyas. Zbigniew Herbert. PoSu; WoPoe, *tr. by* Czeslaw Milosz and Peter Dale Scott

Real Estate. David Antin. FTOS

Real Estate. Michael Hannon. GeoHom

Real horse is good, A. Wooden Horse, The. Mary Mapes Dodge. SWaP

Real Indian Leans Against, The. Chrystos. UnSA

Real Live. Ted Berrigan. FTOS *Fr.* Sonnets, The.

Real Live Girl. Cy Coleman. ReLy

Real Love Isn't What It Seems. Dahlia Ravikovitch [*or* Ravikovich]. DTA, *tr. by* Chana Bloch

Real Moment, The. Eduardo Anguita. BLPSL, *tr. by* Rene de Costa, Rigas Kappatos and Eleni Paidoussi

Real poems are being written in outports, The. Without Benefit of Tape. Dorothy Livesay. NOBC

Real Romance, A. Henry Cuyler Bunner. VerBaPo *Fr.* In School House.

Real teeth. (LL) Big Momma. Haki R. Madhubuti. AmFaPo; BPo

Real Thing, The. Eiléan Ní Chuilleanáin. ModIr

Real unabstract snow, The. (LL) Malcolm Mooney's Land. William Sydney Graham. NPeEn; NePenScot

Realism. Carla Harryman. PmAP

Realism. Tom Mandel. PmAP

Realist, The. Carl H. Greene. NBV

Realist of 1939–40, A. Wilma Elizabeth McDaniel. GeoHom

Realistic Bar and Grill, A. David Shapiro. PmAP

Realistic dreams with a whiff of terror. 29-77-02. Artur Miedzyrzecki. PoSu, *tr. by* Stanislaw Baranczak

Reality. Léon Damas. NegPo, *tr. by* Ellen Conroy Kennedy

Reality. Sir Aubrey De Vere. SacPr

Reality and Desire. Olga Orozco. TCLAP, *tr. by* Stephen Tapscott

Reality Demands. Wislawa Szymborska. VCWP, *tr. by* Stanislaw Baranczak

Reality is a question. Terms in Which I Think of Reality, The. Allen Ginsberg. AmFaPo

Reality Is an Activity of the Most August Imagination. Wallace Stevens. APT-1; NoAM

Reality is flowerlike. Shagai. JDP, *tr. by* Yoel Hoffmann

Reality of Autumn, The. Duane Niatum. HATNAP

Reality, yes, reality. Reality and Desire. Olga Orozco. TCLAP, *tr. by* Stephen Tapscott

Realization, The. Yvor Winters. APT-2; HarvBoo

Realizing the Futility of Life. Po Chü-i. ChiP, *tr. by* Arthur Waley

Really Long Ride, The. Rick Noguchi. NeAmPo

Realm is here of masquing light, A. Light at Equinox. Léonie Adams. ColAP

Realm of Fancy, The. John Keats. *See* Fancy

Realm of Jabberwocks and Angels' Wings, Widows' Kisses, Corpse Revivers, The. (LL) Cocktails. Ciaran Carson. BiHa; ModIr; PBCIP

Realtheater Piece Two. Jerome Rothenberg. FTOS

Reaper, The. William Wordsworth. *See* Solitary Reaper, The

Reapers. Mathilde Blind. WPE

Reapers. Jean Toomer. APT-2; BPo; ColAP; GT; HAP; NIL-7; NoAM; NoP-4; SoSe-8; TRP; WeW-3

Reappearing like bindweed. Candid Camera. Angelo Lumelli. ItPo, *tr. by* Gayle Ridinger

Rear-Guard, The. Siegfried Sassoon. MoBrPo; NAEL-5v2; NAEL-6v2; NoAM; OBWP; PoWW

Rear Porches of an Apartment Building. Maxwell Bodenheim. APT-1

Rear ruth as the seat, rear her ureaus, cart cheer there. Archeus Terrae. John Peck. HarvBoo

Rear Window. Angela Shaw. NeAmPo

Reared within the Mountains! *Unknown.* APN-2; TCAPo, *tr. by* Washington Matthews *Fr.* Mountain Chant, The.

Rearmament. Robinson Jeffers. OxBA

Rearrange a "Wife's" affection! Emily Dickinson. NALW

Reason. Charlotte Brontë. VWP

Reason. Abraham Cowley. SacPr

Reason. Ralph Hodgson. *See* Reason Has Moons

Reason. Philippe Jaccottet. MFP, *tr. by* Martin Sorrell

Reason. Clive Staples Lewis. SacPr

Reason. Josephine Miles. InPK-6; NALW; NoAM; TAP

Reason, The. Eric Pankey. GI

Reason, The. Chris Van Wyk. PeSAV

Reason and Faith. Cecil Frances Alexander. SacPr

Reason for Poetry, The. Nancy Morejón. WPOW, *tr. by* Anita Whitney

Reason for Refusal. Martin Bell. FaBoWar

Reason for Silence, A. Louise Imogen Guiney. SWaP

Reason Has Moons. Ralph Hodgson. FaBoCh; OxBSP (Reason.) MoBrPo

Reason, in faith thou art well served, that still. Sir Philip Sidney. NAEL-5v1; NAEL-6v1; NAEL-7v1 *Fr.* Astrophil and Stella.

Reason of the saint that he is saintly, The. Reasons of Each, The. Laura Riding Jackson. HarvBoo

Reason, Reason is my middle name. (LL) Reason. Josephine Miles. InPK-6; NALW; NoAM; TAP

Reason we do not learn from history is, The. Ultima Ratio Reagan. Howard Nemerov. AF

Reason we're asked to endure, The. Limerick. Bill Greenwell. PeLi

Reason why, The. Reason, The. Chris Van Wyk. PeSAV

Reason why the Park is closed, The. Deceit in the Park. Patrick Hare. OBGa

Reasonable Affliction, A. Matthew Prior. NOEC (Cause and Effect.) NBLV

Reasons drawn from Divinity. Sir John Davies. SacPr *Fr.* Nosce Teipsum.

Reasons for and against Marrying Widows. Henricus Selyns. SCAP

Reasons for Attendance. Philip Larkin. PoPoPo

Reasons for Loving the Harmonica. Julie Kane. MiVo

Reasons for the Beginning. Milo De Angelis. ItPo, *tr. by* Gayle Ridinger

Reasons of Each, The. Laura Riding Jackson. HarvBoo

Reasons That Induced Dr. Swift to Write a Poem Called "The Lady's Dressing-Room," The. Lady Mary Wortley Montagu. NAEL-7v1

Reassurance, The. Thom Gunn. NPeEn

Reassured when the moon's pale flesh. Famine's End. Judy Longley. SpudSo

Rebeca in a Mirror. Judith Rodriguez. CBAP

Rebecca. Vadim Leonidovich Andreyev [*or* Andreiev]. TCRP, *tr. by* Olga Carlisle

Rebecca. E. Ethelbert Miller. ISC

Rebecca Cutlet. Bill Berkson. PmAP

Rebecca's maid: a girl come from afar. Jacob and Esau. Else Lasker-Schüler. BoWoP, *tr. by* Rosmarie Waldrop

Rebecca, Who Slammed Doors for Fun and Perished Miserably. Joseph Hilaire Pierre Belloc. NOBL

Rebel, A. John Gould Fletcher. MoAmPo

Rebel, The. Mari E. Evans. CRP

Rebel, The. Innes Randolph. NBLV; OBAL; OxBoLi

Rebel General, The. Chris Wallace-Crabbe. CBAP

Rebel's Progress. Tom Earley. OBWVE

Rebel Scot, The. John Cleveland. BASC

"He that saw hell in his melancholy dream." NOSC

"How? 'Providence', and yet a Scottish crew?" NOSC

"Lord! what a goodly thing is want of shirts." OBSV

"Nature herself doth Scotchmen beasts confess." OBSV

Rebel Soldier, The. *Unknown.* OxBoLi

Rebellion against the North Side. Naomi Shihab Nye. WeW-3

Rebellion of the Waters, The. George Darley. NOBRP

Rebellion shook an ancient dust. April Mortality. Léonie Adams. APT-2; MoAmPo

Rebellious fools that scorn to bow. Bracelet, The. Thomas Stanley. BeJo

Rebels' cavalry are everywhere, The. Tsung Ch'en. CoBLCP *Fr.* On Things Seen.

Rebirth. Margaret E. Bruner. PoToHe

Rebirth. Beckian Fritz Goldberg. ExTi

Rebirth. Man Giac. EaWin; WoPoe, *tr. by* W. S. Merwin and Nguyen Ngoc Bich

Rebirth. Catriona Stamp. BrRo

Rebirth of Venus, The. Mary Jo Salter. FFC

Rebis. Mitch Highfill. HeMarv

Reborn. Kingsley Amis. OxBC

Reborn. Edison Mpina. NAfrP

Rebuke by the Bishop of London, A. Limerick. Victor Gray. PeLi

Rebuke Me Not. John Addington Symonds. Son

Rebuke to Robert Southey, A. *Unknown.* ECWP

Rebus Tact. Ray DiPalma. PmAP

Rebuttal of Tung-p'o's Poem on "Bathing the Infant," A. Ch'ien Ch'ien-i [or Ch'ien Ch'ien-yi]. SuSp, tr. by Irving Y. Lo

Recalcitrant, the empire sleeves of her dress hold back. Diagnosis: My Mother's Breast. Lisa Fishman. AmPoNex

Recall how she lolly-gagged beneath. Forgetting the Sixties. Mark DeFoe. SwNoth

Recalling a Visit from His Majesty. Princess Uchiko. WoPoe

Recalling now the pleasures of the South. Tune: "The Bodhisattva Foreigner." Wei Chuang. ColAnChi, tr. by John Timothy Wixted

Recalling our agony, and the way we danced. / The music! (LL) Tree Telling of Orpheus, A. Denise Levertov. APSN; MiVo

Recalling the dead. (LL) Picture of a Nativity. Geoffrey Hill. NoAM; OxBC

Recalling the past years, my heart is often bewildered. Tune: "Decorous and Pretty." Kung Tzu-chen. SuSp, tr. by An-yan Tang

Recalling War. Robert Graves. AF; HarvBoo; NoAM; OBWP; PeFWW; PoWW

Recalling When I Was Drunk. Yüan Chên. SuSp, tr. by Dell R. Hales

Recantation. Minuchihri. ArPe, tr. by Omar S. Pound

Recapitulations. Karl Shapiro. TaR

Receipt for the Vapours. Lady Mary Wortley Montagu. See Receipt to Cure [or for] the Vapours, A

Receipt for Writing a Novel, A. Mary Alcock. ECWP

Receipt to Cure a Love Fit, A. Unknown. NOEC

Receipt to Cure [or for] the Vapours, A. Lady Mary Wortley Montagu. ECWP; NOEC; NoP-4; NPeEn; OxBEV; PeLV; PEW

Receives its annual reply! (LL) Emily Dickinson. OxBA; SoSe-8

Recent earthquake, A. Lucilius. GrAn

Recent Past, The. C. S. Giscombe. GT

Recently displayed at the Times Square station, a new Vandyke on the face-cream girl. Art Review. Kenneth Fearing. APT-2

Recently in Sokol. Igor Kholin. TCRP

Reception, The. June Jordan. FaBoWP

Reception Good. Kenneth Fearing. APT-2

Receptive, soft, and absolute. (LL) Sundays of Satin-Legs Smith, The. Gwendolyn Brooks. NAAAL; SeSe

Recessional. Robert Kelly. FTOS

Recessional. Rudyard Kipling. AWP; BRP; CABP; InvLi; MoBrPo; NAEL-6v2; NOBE; NOBVV; NPeEn; NoAM; NoP-4; OBEV; OxAEP-2; OxBEV; PWR; SCGP; TFi; UV; UnPo

Recessional. Thomas MacGreevy [or McGreevy]. CIP-2; ModIr

Recife. Evocation of Recife. Manuel Bandeira. TCLAP, tr. by Candace Slater

Recipe for a Salad. Sydney Goodsir Smith. See Salad, A

Recipe for a Warsaw Novel. Cyprian Norwid. WoPoe, tr. by Jerzy Peterkiewicz, Burns Singer and Jon Stallworthy

Recipe for an Ocean in the Absence of the Sea. Richard Howard. TAP

Recipe for Living. Alfred Grant Walton. PoToHe

Reciprocal love, the only love that should concern us here, is the love that. Paul Eluard. PFTM-1 Fr. Immaculate Conception, The.

Reciprocity. Walter Kent. ReLy

Recital. Muhammad 'Afifi Matar. MAP, tr. by Ferial Ghazoul and Desmond O'Grady

Recital. John Updike. OBAL

Recitation. Ellease Southerland. GT

Recitative. Hart Crane. FaBoMo

Recitative. Iwan [or Yvan] Goll. PeFWW, tr. by Patrick Bridgwater Fr. Requiem for the Dead of Europe.

Recitative: "Farmer's son is good and mad," The. Ronald McCuaig. NOBAu

Recite the dangers chiselled on this face. Lines for a Tomb. Donald Davidson. FuPo

Reckoning. Fay Zwicky. NOBAu

"Reclining Figure." Donald Hall. LCAP-2

Recluse, The. Herman Melville. APN-2 Fr. Clarel: A Poem and Pilgrimage in the Holy Land.

Recluse; Home at Grasmere, The. William Wordsworth. Prospectus to The Recluse. NAEL-6v2

Recluses, The. Stuart Z. Perkoff. NeAP

Reclusive. Wang Fan-chih. CrYelRi, tr. by Sam Hamill

Recogitabo Tibi Omnes Annos Meos. William Habington. ChIV-1

Recognition. Kate Clanchy. MFPA

Recognition. Alejandra Piznarnick. TANSG, tr. by Susan Bassnett

Recognition. Eve Wood. BAP-97

Recognition, The. John Berryman. BodElec

Recognition, The. Denise Levertov. VGW

Recognition of Eve, The. Karl Shapiro. ChIV-1 Fr. Adam and Eve.

Recognized Futures. Lisa Suhair Majaj. UnSA

Recollect thou, in thunder. Tallulah. James Matthew Legaré. APN-2

Recollection, A. John Peale Bishop. Son

Recollection, A. Frances Darwin Cornford. FaBoWP

Recollection, The. Shelley. GTBS-P

Recollection of Gabriela Mistral. Claudia Lars. TCLAP, tr. by Nancy Christoph

Recollections of an Old Spook. Richard Edwards [or Edwardes]. NOxBChV

Recollections of "Lalla Rookh." John Townsend Trowbridge. APN-2; OBAL

Recollections of Love. Samuel Taylor Coleridge. NAEL-5v2; NAEL-6v2

Recollections of Siberia. Bella [or Izabella] Akhatovna Akhmadulina. RusPo, tr. by Robert Arthur Douglas Ford

Recollections of The Arabian Nights. Tennyson. OBGa

Recollections of the Cross. Vladimir Nikolaevich Sokolov. TCRP, tr. by Albert C. Todd

Recommendation. Andrey [or Andrei] Andreievich Voznesensky [or Voznesenskii]. RusPo, tr. by Robert Arthur Douglas Ford

Recommitted. Juan Delgado. TouFir

Recompensed? Henrietta Cordelia Ray. CBWP-3

Reconciled Flame. Alessandro Ceni. ItPo, tr. by Gayle Ridinger

Reconcilement, The. John Sheffield, Duke of Buckingham and Normandy. OBEV

Reconciliation. "Æ." OBMV; TrCP

Reconciliation. Cecil Day Lewis. PoWW; TwCP

Reconciliation. Dora Greenwell. PoBW

Reconciliation. Walt Whitman. APN-1; FaBoWar; HAP; MoAmPo; NAAL-2v1; NAAL-3; NAAL-5; NoP-4; OBWP; OxBA; OxBSP; PAI; WeW-3; WoPoe

Reconciliation, The. Archibald MacLeish. MoAmPo

Reconciliation: A Modern Version, The. Horace. See Odes

Recondite familiar to your candour, The. (LL) Divestment of Beauty. Laura Riding Jackson. APT-2; HarvBoo

Reconnaissance. Arna Bontemps. APT-2; BPo

"Reconnaissance in force"—just three brief words. Ilya Grigoryevich Ehrenburg [or Erenburg]. TCRP

Reconsideration of the Blackbird, A. Thylias Moss. ESEAA

Record is nothing, and the hero great. Sonnet. John Byrne Leicester Warren, 3d Baron De Tabley. EBVV; OxBSo

Record of a Past Affair, A. Li K'ai-hsien. CoBLCP, tr. by Jonathan Chaves

Record of My Trip to Mount She, A. Yüan Hung-tao. CoBLCP, tr. by Jonathan Chaves

Recorders Ages Hence. Walt Whitman. HeIP-4; MoAmPo; SAmP

Recording a Dream. Yang Shih-ch'i. CoBLCP, tr. by Jonathan Chaves

Recording a Weird Happening. Li K'ai-hsien. CoBLCP, tr. by Jonathan Chaves

Recording History. Gail Newman. GotH

Recording My Happiness. Wang Chiu-ssu. CoBLCP, tr. by Jonathan Chaves

Recording My Happiness upon Returning Home. Wen Cheng-ming. CoBLCP, tr. by Jonathan Chaves

Records all agree, The. Alistair Campbell. PeNZ Fr. Sanctuary of Spirits.

Recovering Henry levelled and confronted. 4th Weekend. John Berryman. BodElec

Recovery. M. Wyrebek. AmPoNex

Recovery, The. Edmund Charles Blunden. MoBrPo

Recovery, The. Thomas Traherne. ESCV Fr. Third Century, The.

REcreation. Askhari. InTrad

Recreation. Audre Lorde. NIL-7

Recreation. Jane Taylor. OBCoV; OxBoLi; PEW; WoRP

Recreational Mathematics. Steve Wilson. AmPoNex

Recruiting Drive. Charles Causley. OxBTC

Recruiting Officer of Shih-hao. Tu Fu. ColAnChi; SuSp, tr. by Irving Y. Lo

Recruiting Poster. Hillel Schwartz. BAP-97

Recruiting Serjeant, The. Isaac Bickerstaffe. "What a charming thing's a battle!" NOEC; OBCoV

Recruiting Song. Michael Foster. UV

Rectitude, and the terrible upstanding member. Washington in Love. John Berryman. LCAP-2

Recuerdo. Edna St. Vincent Millay. APT-1; ChAP; NAAL-2v2; NAAL-5; NoAM; OxBA; TAP

Reculver Bay. Vicki Raymond. NOBAu

Recumbent. Carl Phillips. NAPBL

Recumbent against any mirror, any stardom. Mimetic. Ann Lauterbach. PmAP

Recuperating in Chang Villa. Huang Tsun-hsien. SuSp, tr. by Irving Y. Lo

Recurrence. Michael White. GifTon

Recurrences. / Coppery light hesitates. Measure. Robert Hass. YaYoPo

Recursus. Michael Palmer. APSN

Red. Eugene Field. CA

Red. Lance Larsen. AmPoNex

Red. W. Les Russell. IBA

Red. Jean Yamasaki Toyama. FSt

Red Admiral, The. Charles Hubert Sisson. HarvBoo

Red and green neon lights, the jazz hysteria. Nuit Blanche: North End. Conrad Potter Aiken. OxBA

Red and the Green, The. Anne Wilkinson. MoCV

Red Ant Way. *Unknown.*
Song: "Red young men under the ground, The." STP, *tr. by* Jerome Rothenberg

Red as his guide-book grows, moves on, and offers up a prayer for France. (LL) Three Musicians, The. Aubrey Beardsley. NOBVV; PeVV

Red as the guardroom lamp. Heartbreak Camp. Roy Campbell. OxBTC

Red berries wiping rain at the window. Old Circles. Jennifer Rankin. BMAP

Red Bird. Gerald Stern. UrbNat

Red, black and yellow are the. Rest Our Spiritual Dead. Jim Everett. IBA

Red blossoms of mountain peach crowd the uplands. Bamboo Branch Song. Liu Yu Hsi. CoBCP, *tr. by* Burton Watson

Red Book of Hergest, The. *Unknown.*
Lament for Urien, The. OBMV, *tr. by* Ernest Rhys

Red Boots On. Kit Wright. PeLV

Red Brick and Brown Stone. James Schuyler. BodElec

Red brick monastery in, The. Semblables, The. William Carlos Williams. FaBoMo; NOBA

Red brick [*or* bricks] in the suburbs, white horse on the wall. Ballad to a Traditional Refrain. Maurice James Craig. BIrV

Red-bud, the Kentucky tree, The. Christmas at Freelands. James Stephens. TrCP

Red canna blooms, A. Canna. Shinkichi Takahashi. ZenPo, *tr. by* Takashi Ikemoto and Lucien Stryk

Red cassia flowers. If Hot Flowers Come to the Street. R. Meenakshi. OMIP; WoPoe, *tr. by* Martha Ann Selby

Red Chair (for three voices), The. Emmett Williams.
"He said it two days ago." PFTM-2

Red Clay. Candice Favilla. ExTi

Red Cliff, The. Su Tung-p'o (Su Shih). OHPC, *tr. by* Kenneth Rexroth

Red cliffs arise. And up them service lifts. NW5 and N6. Sir John Betjeman. SCV

Red Clock. A., Jr. Poulin. OPRER

Red Cloth, The. *Vietnamese Oral Tradition.* CaDao, *tr. by* John Balaban

Red Cloud's Song. *Unknown.* APN-2, *tr. by* Stephen Powers *Fr.* Sacred Songs of the Konkau.

Red Cockatoo, The. Po Chü-i. *See* Red Cuckatoo, The

Red cockatoo crests caught on coral-trees. Early Arrival: Sydney. Vivian Smith. NOBAu

Red comb on its head needs no adorning, The. Inscribed on a Painting of a Cock. T'ang Yin. SuSp, *tr. by* Chiang Yee

Red Cow Is Dead, The. Elwyn Brooks White. NBLV

Red Cross Telegram, The. Lotte Kramer. HP

Red Cuckatoo, The. Po Chü-i. WoPoe, *tr. by* Arthur Waley
(Red Cockatoo, The.) ChiP, *tr. by* Arthur Waley

Red dawn clouds coming up! the heavens proclaim you. Morning Light Song. Philip Lamantia. NeAP

Red Desiré. Mick North. NLP

Red dew on floral chamber, white honeycomb. Boudoir Feelings. Li Shang-yin. SuSp, *tr. by* Eugene Eoyang

Red Dog, The. Laura Jensen. LCAP-2

Red Dress, The. Dorothy Parker. APT-1

Red-Dress Girl. Ann Turner. SSCS

Red Dust. Philip Levine. NNaP; NoAM

Red Dye. Barbara Guest. BodElec

Red eiderdown at the window, A. Poem. Raymond Radiguet. CuPo

Red Embankment. Tu Mu. ColAnChi; SuSp, *tr. by* John M. Ortinau

Red Embroidered Carpet. Po Chü-i. SuSp, *tr. by* Wu-Chi Liu

Red eye, red foot: the pigeons are finding. Warmer. Martha Collins. UrbNat

Red eyes of rabbits, The. Springtime, The. Denise Levertov. CoAP; CoAmPo

Red Flag, The. Michael Jackson. PeNZ

Red flag is up, The. We Meet in the Lives of Animals. Peter Everwine. NNaP

Red-flashing lights. Martin Shea. HA

Red flipped out. Anita Virgil. HA

Red Flower. Ann Turner. SSCS

Red fool, my laughing comrade. To a Comrade in Arms. Alun Lewis. FaBoTw; MoBrPo

Red fox, the vixen, The. Abnegation. Adrienne Rich. WPE

Red Geranium and Godly Mignonette. D. H. Lawrence. GTBS-P; NoAM

Red gladioli of bleeding feathers. Gladioli by the Sea. Oscar Hahn. TCLAP, *tr. by* Isabel Bize

Red globes of light, the liquor-green, The. William Street. Kenneth Slessor. BMAP; CBAP

Red Glow in the Sky, A. Aleksandr Aleksandrovich Blok. OBVE

Red-Gold Rain, The. Sacheverell Sitwell. MoBrPo

Red granite and black diorite, with the blue. Skeleton of the Future, The. Hugh MacDiarmid. MoBrPo; OBMV

Red Guard. Maksimilian Aleksandrovich Voloshin. TCRP, *tr. by* Albert C. Todd

Red-haired hard-of-hearing woman. (LL) Romance. Ann Sansom. MFPA; NeBl

Red-haired Man's Wife, The. James Stephens. MoBrPo

Red Hanrahan's Song about Ireland. W. B. Yeats. FaBoCh; NOIV

Red Harlaw. Sir Walter Scott. OxBB *Fr.* Antiquary, The.

Red Hat, The. Rachel Hadas. RA

Red-head swallows swoop and clip the waves in pairs, so light! Crossing the Yangtze in a Strong Wind. Wang Shih-chieng. CoBLCP, *tr. by* Jonathan Chaves

Red-headed G.I.'s favourite, The. Bombshell. Tracey Herd. NeBl

Red-Headed Intern, Taking Notes. Ramon Guthrie. APT-2

Red Heart Station. Yang Shih-ch'i. CoBLCP, *tr. by* Jonathan Chaves

Red Hills of Home. Chenjerai Hove. HBAPE; NAfrP

Red horse, A. Louis Zukofsky. PFTM-2 *Fr.* A.

Red Hot. Laurie Anderson. OxWW

Red, Hot and Blue. Cole Porter. ReLy

Red Indian Corpse. Peter Redgrove. OxBC

Red is the colour. Red. W. Les Russell. IBA

Red is the down which is covering me. Ankotarinya. *Unknown.* CBAP, *tr. by* T. G. H. Strehlow

Red Jacket. Fitz-Greene Halleck. APN-1

Red Judge, The. D. M. Black. EmeKit

Red lantern calls the spring clouds from my sleep, A. Wang Chien. SuSp *Fr.* Palace Poems.

Red leaped. Moon, The. Witter Bynner. APT-1

Red Light District Nurse, The. John Fuller. OBCoV

Red light is stuck, A. Why We Are Late. Josephine Miles. NALW

Red Lilies. Barbara Guest. FTOS; PmAP; PoM

Red lips are not so red. Greater Love. Wilfred Owen. EnLoPo; FaBoMo; GTBS-P; MoBrPo; NoAM; TFi

Red Lipstick on a Straw. Michael Melo. ReBoTo

Red lotus incense fades on / the jewelled curtain. Li Ch'ing-chao. BoWoP; OHMPC

Red-Man, The. Frank Prewett. HATNAP

Red men embraced my body's whiteness. Birch Canoe. Carter Revard. NoP-4

Red morning sky. Issa. EH, *tr. by* Robert Hass

Red mouths of lads for love God made. De Puerorum osculis. Giles de Gillies. CAGL

Red mullet, rosy in its sleep. Beaulieu. Clarence Major. FTOS

Red o'er the forest glows the setting sun. John Keble. OBEV *Fr.* Forest Leaves in Autumn.

Red oak leaves rustle in the wind. Leaves of a Dream Are the Leaves of an Onion, The. Arthur Sze. OpBo

Red of the dawn! Dawn, The. Tennyson. NAEL-5v2; NAEL-6v2

Red on sun sky sail. Six Eagles. Thomas Love Peacock. VoR

Red, orange, yellow, green, turquoise, blue, violet. Tune: "Deva-like Barbarian"—Ta-po-ti. Mao Tse-tung [*or* Mao Zedong]. SuSp, *tr. by* Eugene Eoyang

Red Peonies. Wang Wei. SuSp, *tr. by* Irving Y. Lo

Red pepper hangs from a nail, The. Mal'Occhio. Jennifer Martelli. OPRER

Red poppy. Ghazal 21. Mirza Asadullah Khan Ghalib. EaWin, *tr. by* Aijaz Ahmad and W. S. Merwin

Red, Red Rose, A. Robert Burns. *See* Song: "O my love's [*or* luve's *or* love is *or* luve is] like a red, red rose."

Red Ridinghood. Nathan [*or* Natan] Alterman. MHP, *tr. by* Ruth Finer Mintz

Red River. Molly Fisk. PasH

Red river, red river. T. S. Eliot. FaBoA; InPK-6 *Fr.* Landscapes.

Red Rock Ceremonies. Anita Endrezze. CDW; VoR

Red rock wilderness, The. Sidney Keyes. OBWP; PoWW *Fr.* Wilderness, The.

Red Rose and a Beggar. "H. D." APSN; PFTM-2 *Fr.* Hermetic Definition.

Red Rose, proud Rose, sad Rose of all my days! To the Rose upon the Rood of Time. W. B. Yeats. NoAM

Red rose whispers of passion, The. White Rose, A. John Boyle O'Reilly. OBEV

Red Roses. Anne Sexton. EmeKit

Red Roses. Gertrude Stein. TTTS *Fr.* Tender Buttons.

Red roses, in the slender vases burning. Forlorn. William Dean Howells. APN-2

Red round sun, The. Louise Herlin. MFP, *tr. by* Martin Sorrell

Red Salamander—Video Store Parking Lot. Mark DeFoe. UrbNat

Red Shirt, The. Philip Levine. BodElec

Red silk lines the chamber curtains, their tassels fringed with gold. Ravine on a Cold Evening. Li Ho. SuSp, *tr. by* Maureen Robertson

Red Silk Stockings. Langston Hughes. NAAAL

Red sky at night. *Unknown.* OxNR

Red sky at night, A. *Unknown.* OBCoV

Red sky at night is the shepherd's delight, A. *Unknown. See* Red sky at night

Red spattered on an orchard path. Thats all. Seed. Charles Buckmaster. BMAP

Red Squirrel. Bruce Weigl. BodElec

Red stockings, blue stockings. *Unknown.* OxNR

Red String. Minnie Bruce Pratt. WiU

Red sun fills the sky and the earth, The. Suffering from Heat. Wang Wei. SuSp, *tr. by* Hugh M. Stimson

Red Sunsets, 1883, The. Mathilde Blind. ViWPN

Red that iron becomes when held, The. San Joaquin. David Oliveira. GeoHom

Red Trousseau. Carol Muske. BodElec

Red varnish / Warm flitch. Louis Zukofsky. APT-2 *Fr.* 29 Poems.

Red Velvet Jacket. Lynda Hull. ExTi

Red walls of the old temple emerge from the blur of the blue-green mountain. Lieh Mountain. Wang Shih-chieng. SuSp, *tr. by* Richard John Lynn

Red Water. Dana Levin. AmPoNex

Red Wheelbarrow, The. William Carlos Williams. APT-1; BLT; ChAP; ColAP; HarvBoo; HeIP-4; InPK-6; MoAmPo; NAAL-2v2; NAAL-5; NIL-7; NIP-4; NOBA; NoAM; NoP-4; PAI; PoE; SAmP; SoSe-8; TAP; TFi; TRP; TTTS; UnPo; WeW-3

Red young men under the ground, The. *Unknown.* STP, *tr. by* Jerome Rothenberg *Fr.* Red Ant Way.

Redbreast, The. Anthony Rye. Spl

Redbreast smoulders in the waste of snow, The. Redbreast, The. Anthony Rye. Spl

Redeem Time Past. William Drummond, of Hawthornden. OxAEP-1

Redeemer, The. Cynewulf. *Fr.* Ascension, The.

Redefining "Orthodoxy." Pier Paolo Pasolini. ItPo, *tr. by* Gayle Ridinger

Redemption. George Herbert. BASC; CABP; ESCV; FSCP; GSo; GeHe; HAP; InPK-6; MeLP; NAEL-5v1; NAEL-6v1; NOBE; NOCV; NOSC; NPeEn; NoP-4; OxBEV; OxBSo; PBRV; PeECV; PoE; PoPoPo; SCGP; SCV; SoSe-8; TFi; TrCP; WeW-3

Redemption. Pauli Murray. GT

Redemption hangs upon the nails. (LL) He. Stanley Kunitz. NoP-4; VGW

Redemption's problem unto thee well solved. (LL) Milton. Henrietta Cordelia Ray. BlSi; CBWP-3

Redeployment. Howard Nemerov. OBWP; PoWW; TrJP

Redesdale and Wise William. *Unknown.* ESPB

Redfern at Night. Stephen Clayton. IBA

Redingote and the Vamoose, The. Richard Kendall Munkittrick. OBCA

Rediscovery. Kofi Awoonor. TTY

Redivivus. Donald Davidson. FuPo

Redness: Thinking it Through. Garrett Kaoru Hongo. LTA

Redress: to receive something, get in exchange. Redness: Thinking it Through. Garrett Kaoru Hongo. LTA

Reds in the Bed. Peter Finch. Oth

Redshanks, The. Julian Bell. OBMV

Redwing. R. P. Blackmur. APT-2

Redwing Sonnets. Julia Alvarez. BodElec

Redwings. James Wright (1927–80). NNaP

Redwoods, The. Louis Simpson. CoAP

Reed, The. Mikhail Yuryevich Lermontov. AWP, *tr. by* J. J. Robbins

Reed: I sank roots first of all, stood. Cynewulf. ASW *Fr.* Riddles (Exeter Book).

Reed in the Tide, A. J. P. Clark Bekederemo.
  Olokun. PBMAP
  Night Rain. PBMAP
  For Granny (from Hospital). PBMAP
  Cry of Birth. PBMAP
  Abiku. PBMAP
  Child Asleep, A. PBMAP

Reeds give, The. Small Song. A. R. Ammons. NoAM

Reeds of Innocence. William Blake. *See* Songs of Innocence

Reeking of unsolved crimes, the cop. Two Hookers. A. K. Redwing. VoR

Reel Around the Shadow. James Harms. NAPBL

Reel unrolling towards the river, The. (LL) Three Fates, The. Rosemary Dobson. BMAP; BoWoP

Reeling Silk. Fan Ch'eng-ta. SuSp, *tr. by* Wu-Chi Liu *Fr.* Four Songs in Imitation of Wang Chien.

Reencounrter with the Goddess. Olga Nolla. TANSG, *tr. by* Paula Vega

Reever ryves at the gullie, The. Wemen's Wather. T. S. Law. OxBS

Refined by bile as yellow as a lump of gold. (LL) For George Santayana. Robert Lowell. NAAL-2v2; VGW

Refined Man, The. Rudyard Kipling. FaBoEE; FaBoTw; NPeEn; PeFWW *Fr.* Epitaphs of the War [1914–1918].

Refiner's Gold, The. Frances Ellen Watkins Harper. PWR

Refining Fire. Lizelia Augusta Jenkins Moorer. CBWP-3

Reflected / In the dragonfly's eye. Issa. ZenPo, *tr. by* Takashi Ikemoto and Lucien Stryk

Reflected in the plate glass, the pies. Night Waitress. Lynda Hull. SwNoth

Reflection. Elisabeth Eybers. PeSAV, *tr. by the* author

Reflection. Christina Georgina Rossetti. VWP

Reflection. Walter James Turner. OBMV

Reflection, A. Thomas Hood. FaBoEE; PAI

Reflection, The. Elizabeth Singer Rowe. EMWP

Reflection and Advice. Ezra Pound. OBSV

Reflection by a Mailbox. Stanley Kunitz. TrJP

Reflection from Sea and Sky. Walter Savage Landor. FaBoEE

Reflection in a Green Arena. Gregory Corso. VGW

Reflection Kiss, one given, The. Some Kisses from *The Kama Sutra.* Hugo Williams. BoLoP

Reflection on Babies. Ogden Nash. NBLV

Reflection on El Train Glass. Luis J. Rodriguez. IllVoic

Reflection on Ingenuity. Ogden Nash. RB

Reflections. George Crabbe.
  Late Wisdom. OBEV

Reflections. Vivian Smith. CBAP

Reflections After the June 12th March for Disarmament. Sonia Sanchez. ESEAA

Reflections at Dawn. Phyllis McGinley. NBLV; NOBL

Reflections at Lake Louise. Allen Ginsberg. BBASP

Reflections in a Slum. Hugh MacDiarmid. FaBoTw

Reflections Near the House Where Titian Tabidze Lived. Bulat Shalvovich Okudzhava. TCRP, *tr. by* Deming Brown

Reflections on a Dove. Hamutal Bar Yosef. DTA, *tr. by* Shirley Kaufman

Reflections on a Visit to the Burke Museum, University of Washington, Seattle. Gail Tremblay. HATNAP

Reflections on Growing Older. Quincy Troupe. GT

Reflections on Hillsborough in Memoriam. T. H. Naisby. NOBAu

Reflections on Ice-breaking. Ogden Nash. APT-2; AiP; NBLV; OBAL; PeLV (Candy.) NIL-7; NoP-4

Reflections on Mirrors. Elder Olson. CRP

Reflections on the Death of Louis XVI. Ann Yearsley. RWP

Reflections, Written on Visiting the Grave of a Venerated Friend. Ann Plato. BlSi

Reflective. A. R. Ammons. HCAP; VCAP

Reflective life separates us from the sources of reflection. Mario Luzi. ItPo, *tr. by* Gayle Ridinger *Fr.* In the Dark Body of Metamorphosis.

Reflexion, The. Edward Taylor. ChIV-1; OxBA; TCAPo *Fr.* Preparatory Meditations Before My Approach to the Lord's Supper.

Reflexions on suicide, & on my father, possess me. Of Suicide. John Berryman. NoAM

Reflexions on the Seizure of the Suez, and on a Proposal to Line the Banks of That Canal with Billboard Advertisements. Howard Nemerov. NBLV

Reforma Agraria. Ian Duhig. ModIr

Reformation. Anne Finch, Countess of Winchilsea. ECWP

Reformation of Manners. Daniel Defoe.
  London. NOEC
  "Search all the Christian climes from pole to pole." OBSV
  "Yet Ostia boasts of her regeneration." OBSV

Reformer to His Father, A. James Simmons. BIrV

Refracted through years, this neon light comes back. Poem in the Shape of a Saxophone. T. R. Hummer. SeSe

Refresh my thoughts of Penelope again. Pan as the Son of Penelope. Joanne Kyger. BB

Refreshing, the wind against the waterfall. Jakushitsu. ZenPo, *tr. by* Takashi Ikemoto and Lucien Stryk

Refrigerium. Frederick Goddard Tuckerman. TCAPo

Refuge. Gyula Illyés. IQMS, *tr. by* Peter Zollman

Refuge at the One Step Down. Belle Waring. PBCAP; SeSe

Refugee. Laila Halaby. PoArWo

Refugee, A. Lee Ranaldo. HeMarv

Refugee Blues. W. H. Auden. AmFaPo; HP; OxAEP-2 *Fr.* Ten Songs.

Refugee Ship. Lorna Dee Cervantes. PoPoPo

Refugees. Donald Davidson. FuPo

Refugees. Chaim Grade. HP, *tr. by* Marc Kaminsky

Refugees. Ilya Krichevsky [or Krichevskii]. TCRP, tr. by Albert C. Todd
Refugees, The. Randall Jarrell. MoAmPo
Refugees, The. Edwin Muir. NoAM
Refugees at Cobh. Sean Dunne. BiHa
Refusal to Inter. Mohammed Khaïr-Eddine. PFTM-2, tr. by Pierre Joris
Refusal to Mourn, A. Derek Mahon. ModIr; PNI
Refusal to Mourn the Death, by Fire, of a Child in London, A. Dylan Thomas.
    AF; EBEV; FaBoMo; FaBoWar; GTBS-P; HarvBoo; HeIP-4; MoBrPo;
    NOBE; NoAM; NoP-4; OBWVE; OxAEP-2; OxBTC; PAI; PoE; PoWW;
    TFi; TwCP; UnPo
Refusing the Call. Enid Shomer. TaR
Refusing worldly worries. Lu-lung Village, Autumn. Hsu Hsuan. CrYelRi,
    tr. by Sam Hamill
Refuting the "Invitation to Hiding." Wang K'ang-chü. CoBCP, tr. by Burton
    Watson
Reg wished me to go with him to the field. My Mother. Claude McKay. GT
Regal is the pleasure, afoot, threading the trees. Spring. Ferenc Faludi.
    IQMS, tr. by Donald Davie
Regalia Figure. Carl Phillips. NAPBL
Regalia in Immediate Demand! Philip Whalen. BB
Regard, O reader, how it is with me. Look, in the Labyrinth of Memory.
    Delmore Schwartz. TrJP
Regard the capture here, O Janus-faced. Recitative. Hart Crane. FaBoMo
Regarding Music. Siv Cedering. MiVo
Regarding yours, dear Mrs Nightingale. Mrs Nightingale. Martin Fagg. UV
Regarding yours, dear Mrs Worthington. Noël Coward. ReLy; UV Fr. Mrs
    Worthingtion.
Regeneration. Henry Vaughan. BASC; ChIV-1; ESCV; FSCP; GeHe; MeLP;
    NAEL-5v1; NAEL-6v1; NAEL-7v1; NoP-4; PoE
Regeneration. Leo Vroman. TuT, tr. by James Liddy
Reggae. Vejay Steede. WaCA
Reggae Cat (for Boston Jack). Kendel Hippolyte. WaCA
Reggae Prophecy. Marion Bethel. WaCA
Reggae Sounds. Linton Kwesi Johnson. WaCA
Régime. Karel Soudijn. TuT, tr. by Ruth Hooley
Regina. Mary Elizabeth Coleridge. NALW; PoBW
Reginald Pugh, the Man Who Came from the Army. Emma Lee Warrior.
    HATNAP
Region of life and light! Life of the Blessed, The. Luís De León. AWP, tr.
    by William Cullen Bryant
Region of Unlikeness, The. Jorie Graham. HarvBoo
Regions of Tyre are noted, The. Meleager. GrAn
Regret. Michael Lieberman. BloBone
Regret. Yuan Chi. ChiP, tr. by Arthur Waley
Regret for the Mourning Doves Who Failed to Mate. Bruce Weigl. UrbNat
Regretful Thoughts. Yü Hsüan-chi. BoWoP, tr. by Geoffrey Waters
Regrets. Joachim Du Bellay.
    "Given all my worries over each day's trivia." WoPoe, tr. by David Curzon
    "To walk with sober step, to raise the eyebrow." WoPoe, tr. by Denis Devlin
Regrets untold! Tune: "Memories of the South." Li Yü. ColAnChi, tr. by
    Jiaosheng Wang
Regretting the Past. Narihira (Ariwara no Narihira). WoPoe, tr. by F. Vos Fr.
    Ise Monogatari, The.
Regular Bobbsey Twins. / That story. (LL) Cinderella. Anne Sexton. HeIP-
    4; NAAL-2v2
Regulation equipment. Joyce Mansour. MFP, tr. by Martin Sorrell
Rehabilitative Report: We Can Still Laugh. Daniel Berrigan. AF
Rehearsal, The. Horace Gregory. VGW
Reid in the Loch Sayis, The. Unknown. OxBS
Reification won't get you out of the parking lot. Things. Bob Perelman.
    PmAP
Reign of Chaos, The. Pope. EBEV; NoP-4; SCV Fr. Dunciad, The.
Rein up. Ode of Imr El-Qais, The. Imr el [or ul] Kais [or Qais]. WoPoe, tr.
    by Robert Bringhurst
Reincarnation. Mudrooroo Narogin. IBA
Reindeer and Engine. Josephine Jacobsen. WPE
Reindeer Report. U. A. Fanthorpe. OBCP
Reinvent it on earth / as song. (LL) Last Songs. Galway Kinnell. PAI;
    VCAP
Reisebilder. Edoardo Sanguineti.
    "I defended Genet on the subject of terror in London." ItPo, tr. by Gayle
        Ridinger
    "I tell you it was a hard punch to my brain." ItPo, tr. by Gayle Ridinger
    "So it takes very little indeed: a brasserie." ItPo, tr. by Gayle Ridinger
    "To the mini-skirted customs official who with sibyl-dove eyes." ItPo, tr. by
        Gayle Ridinger
Reizan Osho Visits Me. Muso Soseki. EaWin, tr. by W. S. Merwin
Reject Jell-o. Lucille Day. MPUn

Rejected. Lord Alfred Bruce Douglas. PeVV
Rejected Gift, The. Ida G. M. Gerhardt. TuT, tr. by Ruth Hooley
Rejected Gift, The. Ida G. M. Gerhardt. TuT, tr. by Peter Van de Kamp
Rejected "National Hymns," The. "Orpheus C. Kerr." OBAL
Rejection, The. Sir Robert Aytoun [or Ayton]. NOSC
Rejects the Influence of Reason. Mary Robinson. CenSon; RWP
"Rejoice holy bundles, sacred bundles." They Went to the Moon Mother.
    Unknown. STP, tr. by Barbara Tedlock
Rejoice in God that I am gon. Isabella Whitney. BWW Fr. Manner of Her
    Will and What She Left to London and to All Those in It, at Her Departing,
    The.
Rejoice in the Abyss. Stephen Spender. AF
Rejoice, join. Bill Griffiths. Oth Fr. Building: The New London Hospital.
Rejoice, Let Alleluias Ring. Sister M. Cherubim Schaefer. AH
Rejoice, O Bridegroom! Unknown. TrJP, tr. by Israel Abrahams
Rejoice, O youth, in the lovely hind. Moses Ibn Ezra. TrJP Fr. Wedding
    Song in honor of R. Solomon ben Matir.
Rejoice! The Lord is King. Charles Wesley. SacPr
Rejoicing at the Arrival of Ch'ên Hsiung. Po Chü-i. See Rejoicing at the
    Arrival of Chi'en Hsiung
Rejoicing at the Arrival of Chi'en Hsiung. Po Chü-i. AWP, tr. by Arthur
    Waley
    (Rejoicing at the Arrival of Ch'ên Hsiung.) ChiP, tr. by Arthur Waley
Rejoicing / because we had met again. Good Dream, The. Denise Levertov.
    NNaP
Rejoicing That Attend the Murder of Famous Men, The. Robley, Jr. Wilson.
    PBCAP
Rejoicing that the Zen Master Pao Has Arrived from Dragon Mountain. Liu
    Ch'ang-ch'ing. CoBCP, ColAnChi, tr. by Burton Watson
Rejoicing the Spirits. Fan Ch'eng-ta. SuSp, tr. by Wu-Chi Liu Fr. Four
    Songs in Imitation of Wang Chien.
Rejoinder to a Critic. Donald Davie. CABP; NoP-4
Relapse, The. Thomas Stanley. BeJo; NOSC; OBEV
Relapse, The. Henry Vaughan. ESCV; TrCP
Relationship. János Pilinszky. IQMS, tr. by Peter Jay
Relative Thing, A. William Daniel Ehrhart. CDa
Relatives are leaning over, staring expectantly, The. "Dreadful Has Already
    Happened, The." Mark Strand. HCAP; NoAM; VCAP
Relax for one moment, my Jerry. Cole Porter. ReLy
Relax, / stand at attention, and. Barrett Watten. PmAP Fr. Progress.
Relaxed Abalone, The. Rosmarie Waldrop. InPK-6
Relaxed, nothing to do. Letting My Feelings Out. Yü Hsüan-chi. BoWoP, tr.
    by Geoffrey Waters
Relaxing all day in this tropical atmosphere. Foreign Aid. Lionel Kearns.
    NOBC
Relaxing in the Evening in My Study, the Wo-chih-chai. Yang Wan-li.
    CoBCP, tr. by Burton Watson
Relearning the Alphabet. Denise Levertov. NOBA
Release. Adelaide Crapsey. APT-1
Release. R. S. Gwynn. RA
Release. Femi Osofisan. NAfrP
Release. Lisa Sewell. AmPoNex
Release, The. Adah Isaacs Menken. CBWP-1
Released from your cell. For Lolita Lebron. Sandra Maria Esteves. PueRic
Released on Parole. James McAuley. BMAP
Released [or Releas'd] from the noise of the butcher and baker. Jinny the Just.
    Matthew Prior. NOBE; NOEC; OBEV
Releasing a Migrant 'Yen' (Wild Goose). Po Chü-i. ChiP, tr. by Arthur Waley
Relent at last, you, lightnings wrought of steel. To Pál Ányos. Ábrahám
    Barcsay. IQMS, tr. by Adam Makkai
Relent, my dear yet unkind Coelia. William Percy. Son Fr. Coelia.
Relentless, black on white, the cable runs. T-Bar. Patricia K. Page. NOBC;
    NoAM
Relentlessly Lovelorn, the Non-Sleeper Whispers and Re-Whispers a Magic
    Charm Against His Wound's Roar. Stephen Margulies. AWTN
Reliance. Henry Van Dyke. ITBLP
Relic. Ted Hughes. NAEL-5v2; NAEL-6v2; NoP-4
Relic, The. John Donne. BASC; FHYEP; FSCP; HAP; HeIP-4; NAEL-6v1;
    NAEL-7v1; NOBE; NOSC; NoP-4; TFi
    (Relique, The.) ESCV; MeLP; SCGP
Relief. Charles Vildrac. PeFWW, tr. by Christopher Middleton
Relief of Myopia, The. U. A. Fanthorpe. Spl
Relieved, I let the book fall behind a stone. Depressed by a Book of Bad
    Poetry, I Walk toward an Unused Pasture and Invite the Insects to Join Me.
    James Wright (1927–80). EmeKit
Religio Laici. Dryden.
    "But if there be a power too just and strong." NOCV
Conclusion, The. BASC

"Dim, as the borrow'd beams of moon and stars."   BASC; NOSC

"Thus man by his own strength to Heaven would soar."   NOCV

"What then remains, but, waiving each extreme."   BASC

Religio Medici.   Sir Thomas Browne.

  Colloquy with God, A.   SacPr

Religion.   Gwendolyn Brooks.   OxWW   *Fr.* Ulysses.

Religion.   Henry Vaughan.   ESCV; NOCV; OxAEP-1; PeECV; TOF

Religion and the Lower Classes.   Evan Lloyd.   NOEC   *Fr.* Methodist, The.

Religion Back Home.   William Stafford.   OBAL

Religion Is That I Love You.   Kenneth Patchen.   APT-2

Religion stands on tip-toe in our land.   George Herbert.   PBRV   *Fr.* Church Militant, The.

Religion stands, the church blocking the sun. (LL)   Landscape near an Aerodrome, The.   Stephen Spender.   MoBrPo; NoAM; OxBTC

Religious man practises reversals, The.   B. P. Nichol.   PFTM-2   *Fr.* Martyrology 7, The.

Religious Use of [Taking] Tobacco, A.   Robert Wisdome.   OBCoV; SCGP (Pipe and Can, I.)   OBEV

Religious wars of Europe have been numbered with the past, The.   Peonage System, The.   Lizelia Augusta Jenkins Moorer.   CBWP-3

Relinquishment.   Elsa Gidlow.   PoBW

Reliquaries, The.   Valerie Martínez.   TouFir

Relique, The.   John Donne.   *See* Relic, The

Relish honey. If you please.   To a Swallow.   Euenos.   GrAn; OBVE, *tr. by* John Peale Bishop

Reluctance.   Robert Frost.   ITBLP; MoAmPo; NOBA; OxBA

Reluctant, I must take leave from war.   Farewell Rhyme.   Tu Fu.   CrYelRi, *tr. by* Sam Hamill

Reluctant prophet.   Luci Shaw.   SacPr

Remain, Ah Not in Youth Alone.   Walter Savage Landor.   HAP   *Fr.* Ianthe.

Remain, Rata.   Te Puea Herangi.   PeNZ, *tr. by* Margaret Orbell

Remain within its sanctuary! (LL)   Sleeping Beauty, The.   Samuel Rogers.   GTBS-P; OxAEP-2

Remains.   Tony Harrison.   FaBoVe

Remains of an Indian Village.   Alfred Wellington Purdy.   NOBC

Remark.   Charles Spear.   PeNZ

Remarkable race are the Persians, A.   Limerick.   *Unknown.*   PeLi

Remarkable that the skin has such resiliency.   Monster's Dream, The.   William Reichard.   AmPoNex

Remarked [*or* remark'd] how ill we all dissembled. (LL)   Ode, An: "Merchant, to secure his treasure, The."   Matthew Prior.   AWP; EnLoPo; GTBS-P; NOEC; NPeEn; PoRA

Rembrandt—Self Portrait.   Gregory Corso.   BB

Remedia Amoris.   Elizabeth Thomas.   LW

Remedy Worse than the Disease, The.   Matthew Prior.   FaBoEE

Remeidis of Luve.   *Unknown.*   OxBS

Remember.   Irving Berlin.   ReLy

Remember.   Ion Caraion.   AF, *tr. by* Marguerite Dorian

Remember.   Joy Harjo.   LoL; OxWW

  (Remember the sky you were born under.)   NOxBChV

Remember.   Christina Georgina Rossetti.   *See* Remember [Me]

Remember a while ago we happened to meet.   My Neighbor to the South, the Office Clerk Hsiao, Came in the Evening to Say Good-bye.   Harry Mathews.   CoBCP, *tr. by* Burton Watson

Remember a while ago we happened to meet.   My Neighbor to the South, the Office Clerk Hsiao, Came in the Evening to Say Good-bye.   Mei Yao Ch'en.   CoBCP, *tr. by* Burton Watson

Remember, Alyosha, the roads of Smolensk.   Konstantin Mikhailovich Simonov.   TCRP

Remember Barbara.   Barbara.   Jacques Prévert.   AF

Remember Dear Mary.   John Clare.   WeW-3

Remember, do you remember those solemn words.   Thymocles.   GrAn

Remember Euboulos [*or* Eubolus], who lived and died sober?   Leonidas of Tarentum.   GrAn

Remember he was poor and country-bred;.   Abraham Lincoln.   Mildred Plew Meigs.   CA

Remember how unimportant.   Milkweed.   Philip Levine.   LCAP-2

Remember how we spread our hair on the sea.   Lines in Dejection.   Jean Valentine.   YaYoPo

Remember how you always bore me! (LL)   Villeggiature.   Edith Nesbit.   LW; NOBVV; PEW

Remember I am a garnet woman.   If I Am Too Brown or Too White for You.   Wendy Rose.   HATNAP

Remember, imbeciles and wits.   Basil Bunting.   NPeEn; OxBEV   *Fr.* Villon.

Remember, Imbeciles and Wits.   François Villon.   WoPoe, *tr. by* Basil Bunting

Remember It, My Soul.   Eduard Friedrich Mörike [*or* Möricke].   WoPoe, *tr. by* William DeWitt Snodgrass

Remember last summer when God turned on the heat.   Honeymoon, The.   James Simmons.   PNI

Remember, Man, Death's grief and sorrow.   Remembrance of Death.   András Batizi.   IQMS, *tr. by* Adam Makkai

Remember [Me].   Christina Georgina Rossetti.   AWP; BoLoP; EnLoPo; NOBE; OBEV; OxAEP-2; PoRA; TFi

  (Remember.)   ChAP; GSo; LW; NoP-4; PEW; VWP

"Remember me" implored the Thief!   Emily Dickinson.   ChIV-2; SacPr

Remember me this summer.   New England Wind.   Eileen Myles.   PmAP

Remember me when I am dead.   Simplify Me When I'm Dead.   Keith Douglas.   FaBoWar; NoAM; OxBTC

Remember me when I am gone away.   Remember [Me].   Christina Georgina Rossetti.   AWP; BoLoP; EnLoPo; NOBE; OBEV; OxAEP-2; PoRA; TFi

Remember me when thou comest into thy Kingdom.   Discourse of the Good Thief, The.   Nicanor Parra.   GI, *tr. by* Miller Williams

Remember me?   Remember?   Alice Walker.   InvLad

Remember Me?   Harry Warren.   ReLy

Remember my little granite pail?   Lorine Niedecker.   APT-2

Remember, my love, the item you saw.   Carcass, A.   Charles Baudelaire.   NAWM-7v2, *tr. by* James McGowan

Remember, my love, the object we saw.   Carcass, A.   Charles Baudelaire.   SxFrPo, *tr. by* James McGowan

Remember now, my Love, what piteous thing.   Carrion, A.   Charles Baudelaire.   AWP, *tr. by* Allen Tate

Remember Now Thy Creator.   Bible, *O.T.*   AWP; OBVE   *Fr.* Ecclesiastes.

Remember now thy Creator in the days of thy youth.   Bible, *O.T.*   AWP; OBVE   *Fr.* Ecclesiastes.

Remember now? Do you.   Thymocles.   PGA

Remember, Sinful Youth.   *Unknown.*   AH

Remember Something Like This.   Lionel Fogarty.   BMAP

Remember Suez?   Adrian Mitchell.   OxBTC

Remember Tam o' Shanter's mare! (LL)   Tam o' Shanter; A Tale.   Robert Burns.   CABP; EBNV; NAEL-5v2; NAEL-6v2; NPeEn; NePenScot; NoP-4; OBNV; OxBS; PeLV

Remember That Country.   Jean Garrigue.   VGW

Remember that June before our wedding we spent.   First Mango.   Vince Gotera.   ReBoTo

Remember that night.   *Unknown.*   NOIV

Remember the blackness of that flesh.   Memento.   Stephen Spender.   HP

Remember the boy who played with a rope.   Emperor of China, The.   Shirley Kaufman.   BAP-01

Remember the Christmas morning long ago.   Happy Time, The.   John Kander.   ReLy

Remember the covenant of our youth.   Dying Wife to Her Husband, A.   Moses Ibn Ezra.   TrJP

Remember the Giver fading off the lip. (LL)   Drink of Water, A.   Seamus Heaney.   OxBC; TRP

Remember the goose that.   Dario Villa.   ItPo, *tr. by* Gayle Ridinger

Remember the hate.   Same Old Problem.   Kevin Gilbert.   IBA

Remember the Island Where They Build the Fire.   Yves Bonnefoy.   WoPoe, *tr. by* Galway Kinnell and Richard Pevear

Remember—the noise of moonlight.   In the Lebanese Mountains.   Nadia Tuéni.   PoArWo, *tr. by* Samuel Hazo

Remember the old hawker.   Ballad of the Cadger.   May Kendall.   ViWPN

Remember the Poor.   Matilda Caroline Edwards.   PWR

Remember the sky that you were born under.   Remember.   Joy Harjo.   LoL; OxWW

Remember the sky you were born under.   Joy Harjo.   *See* Remember the sky that you were born under

Remember the sun in the autumn, its rays.   Secret Town, The.   Abraham Sutskever [*or* Sutzkever].   TrJP, *tr. by* Jacob Sonntag

Remember Thee! Remember Thee!   Byron.   BoLoP; NPeEn; OxBSP

Remember then this lullaby! (LL)   Lullaby [*or* Lullabie] of a Lover, The.   George Gascoigne.   EBEV; HAP; NAEL-5v1; NAEL-6v1; SCGP

Remember this.   Fury.   Lucille Clifton.   LoL

Remember Thy Creator Now.   Peter Long.   AH

Remember us, remember our names! (LL)   Barbershop Ritual.   Sharan Strange.   ISC; InTrad

Remember when.   Sisters.   Kimberly Ann Collins.   InTrad

Remember when.   Among Strangers.   William Stafford.   NNaP

Remember when you are bemusing.   Limerick.   Cyril Hughes.   PeLi

Remember when you hear them beginning to say Freedom.   Alex Comfort.   MoBrPo   *Fr.* Song of Lazarus, The.

Remember when you love, from that same hour.   Pastoral Dialogue.   Anne Killigrew.   LW

Remember when you were the first one awake, the first.   Little Girl Wakes Early.   Robert Penn Warren.   PoE

Remember, while you are sleeping here, offshore.   Evolution.   John Blight.   CBAP

Remember your grandfather tall and straight. Grandfather: Frailty Is Not the Story. Diana Helen Melhem. GraLe

Remember? Eva Johnson. IBA

Remember? Stephen Sondheim. ReLy

Remember? Alice Walker. InvLad

Remember? Remember? Remember? Stephen Sondheim. ReLy

Remembered. Sterling Plumpp. GT

Remembered Morning. Janet Lewis. MakPoe; SoSe-8; WPE

Remembered Music. James Russell Lowell. APN-1

Remembered on waking. (LL) I Love All Beauteous Things. Robert Bridges. EBEV; OxAEP-2; TrCP

Remembered Sequel. Hannah Weiner. FTOS

Remembering. László Kálnoky. IQMS, tr. by Kenneth McRobbie and Zita McRobbie

Remembering. Stephen J. Lyons. PasH

Remembering. Yuan Chen. CrYelRi; ErotSp, tr. by Sam Hamill

Remembering Ancient Days in Yueh. Li Po. CrYelRi, tr. by Sam Hamill

Remembering Carrigskeewaun. Michael Longley. PBCIP

Remembering dark trees of home that keep. Pan in Battle. *Unknown*. PeNZ

Remembering Dennis's Eyes. Geoff Hattersley. NeBl

Remembering Dresden. Van K. Brock. HP

Remembering East Mountain. Li Po. CrYelRi, tr. by Sam Hamill

Remembering Fannie Lou Hamer. Thadious M. Davis. BlSi

Remembering Golden Bells. Po Chü-i. AWP; ChiP, tr. by Arthur Waley

Remembering how. Buson. EH, tr. by Robert Hass

Remembering Leopardi's Moon. Giacomo Leopardi. WoPoe, tr. by Stephen Berg

Remembering Love. Aleksandr Semionovich Kushner. TCRP, tr. by Paul Graves and Carol Uel

Remembering Lunch. Douglas Dunn. OxBC

Remembering Min Ch'e. Su Tung-p'o (Su Shih). OHMPC, tr. by Kenneth Rexroth

Remembering My Father. Zbigniew Herbert. VCWP, tr. by John Carpenter

Remembering My Late Wife. Chu Yün-ming. CoBLCP, tr. by Jonathan Chaves

Remembering My Wife. Su Tung-p'o (Su Shih). ErotSp, tr. by Sam Hamill

Remembering Our Excursion in the Past. Li Po. ChinPo, tr. by Yip Wai-lim

Remembering Our Fathers. Chava Pinchas-Cohen. DTA, tr. by Miriyam Glazer

Remembering Priest Quang Tri. Doan Van Kham. WoPoe, tr. by Nguyen Ngoc Bich

Remembering that war, I'd near believe. Night Operations, Coastal Command RAF. Howard Nemerov. AF

Remembering the Ardèche. Emily Grosholz. RA

Remembering the Night Fountains. I. K. Bonset. TuT, tr. by Desmond Egan

Remembering the Pacific. Diane Wakoski. GeoHom

Remembering the Past. Al Robles. ReBoTo

Remembering the shot that seemed to burst with no. Slaughter. Susan Stewart. BodElec

Remembering the Strait of Belle Isle or. Large Bad Picture. Elizabeth Bishop. OxBC

Remembering the 'Thirties. Donald Davie. HarvBoo; NoP-4; OxBTC

Remembering this—how Love. Jacopo da Lentino. EaItPo, tr. by Dante Gabriel Rossetti

Remembering what passed. Old Scent of the Plum Tree. Ietaka. AWP, tr. by E. Powys Mathers

Remembering Yeats. Francis Stuart. BiHa

Remembering your face, I see it here. On Dorothea Lange's Photograph "Migrant Mother" (1936). Helen Pinkerton. FFC

Remembers thou in Æsope of a taill. Alexander Montgomerie. PBRV

Remembrance. Emily Jane Brontë. BoLoP; BoWoP; CABP; EBEV; EnLoPo; HAP; MakPoe; NAEL-5v2; NAEL-6v2; NOBE; NOBVV; NPeEn; NoP-4; OxAEP-2; OxBEV; PEW; PoE; PoPoPo; TFi; VWP; WPE; WeW-3

(R. Alcona to J. Brenzaida.) BrRo; EBVV; NALW

Remembrance. Margaret E. Bruner. PoToHe

Remembrance. M. R. Peacocke. NLP

Remembrance. William Shakespeare. *See* Sonnets

Remembrance. Antoni Słonimski. TrJP, tr. by Frances Notley

Remembrance. Robert Southey. TreFP

Remembrance. Sir Thomas Wyatt. *See* Lover Showeth How He Is Forsaken of Such as He Sometime Enjoyed, The

Remembrance Day. Ida G. M. Gerhardt. TuT, tr. by Michael Longley

Remembrance Day. Ida G. M. Gerhardt. TuT, tr. by Robert Greacen

Remembrance of a Color inside a Forest, A. Ray A. Young Bear. CDW

Remembrance of Beginnings of Things. Leah Goldberg. MHP, tr. by Ruth Finer Mintz

Remembrance of Death. András Batizi. IQMS, tr. by Adam Makkai

Remembrance of Five Loaves. Mikhail Pozdnyayev [or Pozdniaev]. TCRP, tr. by Vladimir Lunis and Albert C. Todd

Remembrance of Grasmere, A. Felicia Dorothea Hemans. CenSon

Remembrance of My Friend Mr. Thomas Morley, A. John Davies of Hereford. OxBSP

Remembrance of Strange Hospitality. Yelena [or Elena] Shwarts [or Shvarts]. ItGoST; VCWP, tr. by Michael Molnar

Remembrance of the Founts of Night. Theo Van Doesburg. PFTM-1

Remembrance of Things Past. Horace Coleman. CDa

Remembrance of Yalta. Bella [or Izabella] Akhatovna Akhmadulina. TCRP, tr. by Albert C. Todd

Remembrance Sunday. Dennis Joseph Enright. NPeEn

Remembrancer of joys long passed away. To a Golden Heart, Worn round His Neck. Goethe. AWP, tr. by Margaret Fuller Ossoli

Remind Me. Dorothy Fields. ReLy

Remind me who I am. (LL) Touch Me. Stanley Kunitz. APT-2; NoP-4

Remind you, that there was darkness in my heart. Canticle of Darkness. Wilfred Watson. MoCV

Reminder, The. Thomas Hardy. ChAP; OBCP

Reminder, The. Denise Levertov. PoCoUp

Reminder to the Current President, A. Christopher Howell. CDa

Reminiscence. Vladimir Holan. PoSu, tr. by George Theiner

Reminiscence. Wallace Irwin. NOBL

Reminiscence, A. Anne Brontë. WPE

Reminiscence, A. Amy Levy. VWP

Remission. Katherine Frost. Prnts

Remittance Man. Judith Wright. NoAM

Remnant Ghosts at Dawn. Oliver La Grone. NBV

Remnants and relics of a thousand years—here in a pit full of dust. Book-burning Pit, The. Lo Yin. SuSp, tr. by Edward H. Schafer

Remnants of a rainbow fall to the western bank at dawn, The. Poem on Passing by Hsin-k'ai Lake at Kao-yu in Light Rain, A. Yang Chi. CoBLCP, tr. by Jonathan Chaves

Remnants of counterclockwise. If I Blindfold You. Marjorie Welish. FTOS

Remonstrance, A. John Gerrard. NOEC

Remonstrance, A. James Kenneth Stephen. NOBVV

Remonstrance in the Platonic Shade. Flourishing on an Height. Ann Yearsley. "These feeble sounds." ECWP

Remonstrance to the King. William Dunbar. OxBS

Remorse. Sir John Betjeman. MoBrPo; OxBSP

Remorse. Samuel Taylor Coleridge.
Invocation, An: "Hear, sweet spirit, hear the spell." PeECV

Remorse. Shelley. *See* Stanzas—April, 1814

Remorse for Time, The. Howard Nemerov. Son

Remorse—is Memory—awake. Emily Dickinson. NAAL-2v1; NAAL-3; NOBA; NOCV; NoP-4; SAmP

Remote and ineffectual Don. Lines to a Don. Joseph Hilaire Pierre Belloc. MoBrPo; OBSV

Remote, unfriended, melancholy, slow. Oliver Goldsmith. BIrV *Fr.* Travel[l]er; or, A Prospect of Society, The.

Removal, The. *Unknown*. STP, tr. by Frances Densmore

Removal from Terry Street, A. Douglas Dunn. FaBoMo; FaBoVe; NPeEn; NoP-4; OxBC

Removal: Last Part. Carroll Arnett. VoR

Removal of Our Village, KwaBhanya, The. Mbuyiseni Oswald Mtshali. PeSAV, tr. by the author

Removed from Europe's feuds, a hateful scene. Warning to America, A. Philip Freneau. TAP

Removing the Plate of the Pump on the Hydraulic System of the Backhoe. Gary Snyder. LoL

Renaissance Drunk, A. George Evans. PmAP

Renaissance of wonder, A. (LL) Lawrence Ferlinghetti. AiP; PmAP *Fr.* Oral Messages.

Renaming, The. Valerie Sinason. BrRo

Renascence. Edna St. Vincent Millay. BRP; ColAP; MoAmPo
"All I could see from where I stood." MoAmPo; TCAPo

Renato O. Jones, you maintain my beliefs. Ode to a Maintenance Man and His Family. Kay Boyle. GifTon

Rendez-vous Manqué dans la Rue Racine. John Millington Synge. BIrV

Rendezvous. Mary Scott Fitzgerald. PoToHe

Rendezvous. Edna St. Vincent Millay. APT-1; NALW

Rendezvous. Alan Seeger. *See* I Have a Rendezvous with Death

Rendezvous, The. Bernard Spencer. GTBS-P

Rendezvous in the Cave. Ahmad 'Abd al-Mu'ti Hijazi. MAP, tr. by Sargon Boulus and Peter Porter

Rendezvous of river. Appellants, The. Alice Rahon. SurWo, tr. by Myrna Bell Rochester

How did you come to develop the concept of Negritude? Aime Cesaire. PFTM-1 *Fr.* Discourse on Colonialism.
René's Songs. T. Carmi.
 "Bright-haired am I, my face and body white." MHP, *tr. by* Ruth Finer Mintz
 First Song. MHP, *tr. by* Ruth Finer Mintz
 "Lo-Imi, Lo-Imi!" MHP, *tr. by* Ruth Finer Mintz
 "My brothers are big, so much bigger than I." MHP, *tr. by* Ruth Finer Mintz
 Second Song. MHP, *tr. by* Ruth Finer Mintz
 Third Song. MHP, *tr. by* Ruth Finer Mintz
Renegade. Andrée Chedid. PoArWo, *tr. by* Lucy McNair
Renegade, The. David Diop. PBMAP
Renegade Wants Words, The. James Welch. CDW
Renewal. "Michael Field." ViWPN
Renewal, A. James Merrill. OxBSP; VCAP
Renewal, The. Theodore Roethke. VGW
Renewal by Her Element. Denis Devlin. CIP-2; ModIr
Renewal Notice. Bruce Dawe. BMAP
Renewal of Strength. Frances Ellen Watkins Harper. PWR
Renoir. Rosanna Warren. GS
Renoir's Bathers. Julie Moulds. AmPoNex
Renouncement. Alice Thompson Meynell. BoLoP; GSo; LW; MoBrPo; NOBE; OBEV; OBMV; OxBSo; PEW; Son; VWP; WPE
Renouncing of Love, A. Sir Thomas Wyatt. Son
 (Sonnet: "Farewell, Love.") AEP
Renowned as Black Geordie. Sporting the Plaid. Chris Wallace-Crabbe. NOBAu
Renowned Empress, and Great Britain's Queen. Aemilia Bassano Lanyer. NAEL-7v1 *Fr.* Salve Deus Rex Judaeorum.
Renowned Generations, The. W. B. Yeats. OxBoLi
Renowned interpreter of, A. If You're Lost. S. B. Sowbel. SpudSo
Renowned musician, freeman of the world. To Ferencz Liszt. Mihály Vörösmarty. IQMS, *tr. by* Alan Dixon
Rent. Jane Cooper. TAP
Rent man knocked, The. Madam and the Rent Man. Langston Hughes. SAmP
Rent overdue. Not a Care in the World. Vernon Duke. ReLy
Renting a Room. Sarah Kirsch. PFTM-2, *tr. by* Wayne Kvam *Fr.* Kite-Flying.
Renunciation. Emily Dickinson. APN-2; MoAmPo; NAAL-2v1; NAAL-3; NOBA
Renunciation. Padraic Pearse. NOIV, *tr. by* the author
Renunciation. Lizette Woodworth Reese. TCAPo
Renunciation, A. Edward de Vere, 17th Earl of Oxford. *See* If Women Could Be Fair
Renunciation, A. Henry King, Bishop of Chichester. OBEV
Renunciation—is a piercing Virtue. Emily Dickinson. APN-2; NoP-4
Renunciation's agonies. Dīnrām. SinGod, *tr. by* Rachel Fell McDermott
Repartée. Charles Follen Adams. OBAL
Repeat that, repeat. Cuckoo, The. Gerard Manley Hopkins. MoBrPo; OxBSP; RB; TTTS
Repeating fly, blueback, thumbthick—so gross, A. Harriet. Robert Lowell. NoP-4
Repeats one note. (LL) Xenophanes. Ralph Waldo Emerson. APN-1; NOBA
Repentance. George Alexander Stevens. NOEC
Repentance. Louis Untermeyer. NBLV
Repetition of Words and Weather. Ruth Stone. BoWoP
Repetitive Heart, The. Delmore Schwartz.
 All Clowns Are Masked. OxBA
 (For Rhoda.) MoAmPo; OxBA
 Heavy Bear Who Goes with Me, The. APT-2; ColAP; NOBA; NoAM; TAP; TrJP; TwCP; UnPo
Replacing rings on her hands. Cat's Cradle. Lynne Wycherley. Prnts
Replica, the. Vernon Watkins. AngWePo
Replies. *Vietnamese Oral Tradition.* CaDao, *tr. by* John Balaban
Reply. Reiner Kunze. PoSu, *tr. by* Ewald Osers
Reply, A. *Unknown.* NBLV; NOBL; OxBEV; PeLi
Reply From His Coy Mistress, A. Anne Finch (b. 1908). FFC
Reply to a Friend's Advice. Tu Fu. CarOv, *tr. by* Carolyn Kizer *Fr.* Adviser to the Court.
Reply to a Friend's Poem. Muso Soseki. EaWin, *tr. by* W. S. Merwin
Reply to a Magistrate. Wang Wei. CrYelRi, *tr. by* Sam Hamill
Reply to Bukko Zenji's Poem at Seiken-ji. Muso Soseki. EaWin, *tr. by* W. S. Merwin
Reply to Gen'no Osho's Poem. Muso Soseki. EaWin, *tr. by* W. S. Merwin
Reply to Mr.———, The. Elizabeth Singer Rowe. BASC
Reply to Petőfi. János Arany. IQMS, *tr. by* Madeline Mason

Reply to Prefect Liu. T'ao Ch'ien [*or* T'ao Yuan-ming]. CrYelRi, *tr. by* Sam Hamill
Reply to Reizan Osho. Muso Soseki. EaWin, *tr. by* W. S. Merwin
Reply to Suzan Osho's Snow Poem. Muso Soseki. EaWin, *tr. by* W. S. Merwin
Reply to the Committed Intellectual. Francis Sparshott. NOBC
Replycacion, A. John Skelton.
 "Than, if this noble kyng." PBRV
Replying to a Poem by a New Graduate Lamenting the Loss of His Wife. Yü Hsüan-chi. SuSp, *tr. by* Geoffrey R. Waters
Replying to a Poem by Li T'ien-lin. Yang Wan-li. SuSp, *tr. by* Sherwin S. S. Fu
Replying to a Poem by the Monk Ling-yi at the New Spring. Liu Ch'ang-ch'ing. SuSp, *tr. by* William H. Nienhauser
Replying to a Poem from My Cousin Hui-lien. Hsieh Ling-yün. CoBCP, *tr. by* Burton Watson
Replying to Hsi-mei's "Thoughts in Early Autumn." Lu Kuei Meng. SuSp, *tr. by* Robin D. S. Yates
Replying to "On the Occasion of Morning Audience after Snow" Poem by Assistant Secretary Wang of the Board of Sacrifices. Ts'en Shen. SuSp, *tr. by* Daniel Bryant
Report. Czeslaw Milosz. BodElec
Report from an Unappointed Committee. William Stafford. CDa
Report from Germany, 1944. Ernst Waldinger. AuPH, *tr. by* Lowell A. Bangerter
Report from the Besieged City. Zbigniew Herbert. AF, *tr. by* John Carpenter
Report from the Skull's Diorama. Yusef Komunyakaa. LTA
Report on Experience. Edmund Charles Blunden. FaBoTw; GTBS-P; NOBE; NPeEn; OBMV; OBWP; OxBEV; PeFWW
Report on Her Remains. Daniel David Moses. HATNAP
Report on the Protest in Front of the United States Embassy by the Pino Grande Movement, A. Daisy Zamora. CLPP, *tr. by* Barbara Paschke
Report Song [in a Dream], A. Nicholas Breton. NoSic
 (Wooing in a Dream.) NOBE
Report to Crazy Horse. William Stafford. NoAM
Report to the Stockholders. Reg Saner. PoCoUp
Reported Missing. John Clifford Bayliss. PoWW
Reporter of the courage of heroes. Antipater of Sidon. GrAn
Reporting to a future difficult. 'From Escomb, County Durham:' July 1990. John Seed. Oth
Reportless Subjects, to the Quick. Emily Dickinson. NOBA
Repose. Henrietta Cordelia Ray. CBWP-3
Repose of Rivers. Hart Crane. APT-2; AWP; ColAP; MoAmPo; NOBA; OxBA; PoE
Repression. C. K. Williams. NoP-4
Repression of War Experience. Siegfried Sassoon. AF; NoAM; PeFWW; PoE
Repressive desublimation. Lines. David Bromige. FTOS
Reprieve, The. Hans Magnus Enzensberger. PoSu *Fr.* Sinking of the Titanic, The.
Reprieve, The. Elizabeth Garrett. NeBl
Reprieve on the Stoop. Belle Waring. PBCAP
Reprisal[1], The. George Herbert. ESCV; GeHe
Reprisals. W. B. Yeats. OBWP; PoWW
Reproach. Elizabeth Cobbold. CenSon *Fr.* Sonnets of Laura.
Reproach to Dead Poets. Archibald MacLeish. NAAL-2v2
Reproach to Julia. Robert Graves. FaBoEE
Reproaches Phaon. Mary Robinson. CenSon
Reproachful eyes' / beauty but the. Wrath to Sadness. Robert Grenier. PmAP
Reproduction of Profiles, The. Rosmarie Waldrop.
 Feverish Propositions. FTOS; PFTM-2
Reproof Deserved; or After the Lecture. Sir John Betjeman. OBCoV
Reptilian green the wrinkled throat. Sir Gawaine and the Green Knight. Yvor Winters. NoAM; PoRA; VGW
Republic of the West. James Kenneth Stephen. FaBoA; NOBL; NOBVV; OBCoV; PeLV *Fr.* England and America.
Republicans? We've got a few. In fact. Hayden Carruth. GifTon *Fr.* Vermont.
Repudiate the Forge. (LL) Emily Dickinson. APN-2; NALW; TCAPo; WPoS
Repulse, The. Thomas Stanley. BeJo; MeLP
Repulse Bay. Marilyn Chin. OpBo
Repulse to Alcander, The. Sarah Fyge Egerton. ECWP
 (What is't you mean, that I am thus approach'd.) CABP
Request. Jared Angira. PBMAP
Request. Langston Hughes. APT-2
 (Gimme $25.00 / and the change.) PFTM-1
Request. Shuntaro Tanikawa. VCWP, *tr. by* Harold Wright
Request, The. Sharon Olds. BodElec

Request for Meat and Drink. Sedulius Scottus. NOIV

Request of a Dying Child. Lydia Huntley Sigourney. OBCA

Request of Alexis, The. Sarah Dixon. LW

Request to a Year. Judith Wright. CBAP; FaBoWP; ItWoWo; NALW; NoAM; NoP-4

Request to the Graces, An. Robert Herrick. NOSC

Requiem. Anna Andreyevna Akhmatova. NAWM-7v2, tr. by Judith Hemschemeyer

Requiem. Anna Andreyevna Akhmatova. TCRusP, tr. by Daniel Weissbort

Requiem. Annette M'Baye d'Erneville. HAWP, tr. by Brian Baer

Requiem. Bobbi Sykes. IBA

Requiem. Master Wŏlmyŏng. WoPoe, tr. by Peter H. Lee

Requiem aeternam dona eis, Domine!. (LL) John Skelton. NOBE; NoSic; OxBoLi Fr. Phyllyp Sparowe [or Philip Sparrow].

Requiem for "Bird" Parker, Musician. Gregory Corso. BB

Requiem for Eduard Streltsov. Aleksandr Petrovich Tkachenko. TCRP, tr. by Bradley Jordan

Requiem[:] for Soldiers Lost in Ocean Transports, A. Herman Melville. APN-2

Requiem for the Croppies. Seamus Heaney. BIrV; CIP-2; FaBoMo; OBWP

Requiem for the Dead of Europe. Iwan [or Yvan] Goll.
   "Let me lament the exodus of so many men from their." PeFWW, tr. by Patrick Bridgwater
   "Like a grey wall around Europe." PeFWW, tr. by Patrick Bridgwater
   Recitative. PeFWW, tr. by Patrick Bridgwater
   Recitative. PeFWW, tr. by Patrick Bridgwater

Requiem for the Left Hand. Nancy Morejón. TANSG, tr. by Joy Renjilian-Burgy

Requiem for the Plantagenet Kings. Geoffrey Hill. CABP; NAEL-5v2; NAEL-6v2; NoAM

Requiem: "Houses in country and city." Wang Fan-chih. CrYelRi, tr. by Sam Hamill

Requiem in C. Biagio Cepollaro. ItPo, tr. by Gayle Ridinger

Requiem 1935–1940. Anna Andreyevna Akhmatova. BoWoP, tr. by Richard McKane
   ("Choir of angels glorified the hour, A.") GI, tr. by Max Hayward and Stanley Jasspon Kunitz
   ("Into her secret eyes. Nobody dared.") (LL) GI, tr. by Max Hayward and Stanley Jasspon Kunitz
   ("No, it was not under a strange sky.") PFTM-1

Requiem: "No foreign sky protected me." Anna Andreyevna Akhmatova. AF; PoetW; TCRP; WoPoe, tr. by Max Hayward and Stanley Kunitz

Requiem: "O, insatiable monster! Could'st thou not." Mary Weston Fordham. CBWP-2

Requiem on Poros. Yannis Ritsos. VCWP, tr. by Edmund Keeley

Requiem: "Pour out your light, O stars." Ivor Gurney. FaBoEE; FaBoTw

Requiem: "There was a young belle of old Natchez." Ogden Nash. KaS; NoP-4

Requiem: "They say 'the lighthouse keeper's world is round'." Sam Hunt. PeNZ

Requiem: "Under the wide and starry sky." Robert Louis Stevenson. BRP; EBVV; MoBrPo; NBLV; NOBE; NOBVV; NePenScot; OBEV; OxBEV; PoRA; SCGP; TFi

Requiem: "Your names ring clearly." Annette Bialik Harchik. GotH

Requiescam. Trumbull Stickney. ColAP

Requiescat. Matthew Arnold. AWP; FHYEP; NOBE; OBEV; PoRA

Requiescat. Haim [or Chaim or Khayim] Guri [or Gouri]. MHP, tr. by Ruth Finer Mintz

Requiescat. Leo Ross. TuT, tr. by Sean Dunne

Requiescat. Leo Ross. TuT, tr. by Eamon Grennan

Requiescat. Oscar Wilde. EBVV; MoBrPo; PeVV

Required, as a necessity requires. (LL) Plain Sense of Things, The. Wallace Stevens. APT-1; EmeKit; HCAP; NAAL-5; NoAM; PAI

Required of You This Night. Peter Redgrove. PoE

Requirements for Suggesting Fats Waller. Connie Deanovich. AmPoNex

Requiring no shoes, O my children! (LL) Gazelle Calf, The. D. H. Lawrence. OxBTC; RB

Requiring something lovely on his arm. Labor Day. Louise Glück. NIL-7; NoAM

Rereading Old Writing. David Ferry. DiPo

Rescue. James Tate. YaYoPo

Rescue, The. Robert Creeley. CRP; VCAP

Rescue, The. John Logan. CoAP

Rescue the Dead. David Ignatow. VGW; WoPoe

Rescued Year, The. William Stafford. ColAP; LCAP-2

Rescues them at last, as a star absorbs the night. (LL) Other Tradition, The. John Ashbery. FTOS; PmAP

Rescuing gate is wide, The. Like a Mourningless Child. Kenneth Patchen. MoAmPo

Research has shown that ballads were produced by all of society. Hotel Lautréamont. John Ashbery. FTOS; HarvBoo

Resentment. Richard Aldington. PeFWW

Resentment Near the Jade Steps. Li Po. ErotSp, tr. by Sam Hamill (Complaint near the Jade Steps.) CrYelRi

Resentments Composed because of the Clamor of Town Topers Outside My Apartment. Sarah Kemble Knight. AiP; SCAP

Reservation, The. Susan Clements. UnSA

Reservation Love Song. Sherman Alexie. PoPoPo

Reservation Special. Lew Blockcolski. VoR

Reserve. Lizette Woodworth Reese. SWaP

Reserved. Walter De la Mare. GTBS-P

Reserved Sacrament. James Schuyler. BodElec

Reservoirs. Ronald Stuart Thomas. AngWePo

Residence at Cambridge. William Wordsworth. Fr. Prelude, The; Growth of a Poet's Mind [1850 vers.].

Residence in France. William Wordsworth. Fr. Prelude, The; Growth of a Poet's Mind [1850 vers.].

Residence in France and French Revolution. William Wordsworth. Fr. Prelude, The; Growth of a Poet's Mind [1850 vers.].

Residence in London. William Wordsworth. Fr. Prelude, The; Growth of a Poet's Mind [1850 vers.].

Residence of the Emperors of Ch'en, The. Yang Wei-chen. CoBLCP, tr. by Jonathan Chaves

Resident doctor said, The. Notice. Robert Lowell. NoAM

Residue. Carlos Drummond de Andrade. TCLAP, tr. by Virginia de Araújo

Residue. Carlos Drummond de Andrade. PoetW; VCWP, tr. by Mark Strand

Residue. Paula McLain. AmPoNex

Residues: Thronging the Heart. Gael Turnbull. Oth

Resign the rhapsody, the dream. To the Muse. Robert Louis Stevenson. EBEV

Resignation. Matthew Arnold. FHYEP
   Poet, The. NPeEn

Resignation. Thomas Chatterton. TrCP

Resignation. Santob [or Shem-Tob] De Carrion. TrJP, tr. by George Ticknor

Resignation. Paul Laurence Dunbar. SacPr

Resignation. Po Chü-i. ChiP, tr. by Arthur Waley

Resignation; an Ode to the Journeyman Shoemakers. "Peter Pindar."
   "Sons of Saint Crispin, 'tis in vain!" NOEC

Resigning from a Job in a Defense Industry. Sandra McPherson. LCAP-2

Resin. Patricia Pogson. NLP

Resist Confinement. Joette Harland-Watts. InTrad

Resistance. Horst Bienek. AF

Resistance. Susan Dambroff. GotH

Resisting, by embracing, nothingness. (LL) In Santa Maria del Popolo. Thom Gunn. FaBoMo; GTBS-P; HarvBoo; NPeEn; OxBC; PoE

Resolute Desire That Enters, The. Arnaut Daniel. STV, tr. by John Frederick Nims

Resolution. Charles Leo O'Donnell. SacPr

Resolution, The. Richard Baxter. SacPr

Resolution and Independence. William Wordsworth. EBEV; FHYEP; HAP; NAEL-6v2; NOBE; NOBRP; NOCV; NoP-4; OxAEP-2; TFi
   "Now, whether it were by peculiar grace." UV
   "There was a roaring in the wind all night." ITBLP; WoPoe

Resolution in Four Sonnets, of a Poetical Question Put to Me by a Friend, Concerning Four Rural Sisters. Charles Cotton. OxBSo; Son
   "Alice is tall and upright as a pine." BoLoP; EnLoPo
   "Marg'ret of humbler stature by the head." BoLoP; EnLoPo

Resolution of Dependence. George Barker. FaBoTw

Resolve. Charlotte Perkins Stetson Gilman. PoToHe

Resolve. Leslie Ullman. ExTi

Resolve, The. Alexander Brome. NOSC; OBEV

Resolve, The. Mary Lee, Lady Chudleigh. ECWP; WPE

Resolve, The. Lady Mary Wortley Montagu. See Lady's Resolve, The

Resolve, The. Henry Vaughan. ESCV

Resolve to make the best of life. Beyond the Beaten Way. George Sands Johnson. PWR

Resolved to love, unworthy to obtain. Henry Constable. Son Fr. Diana.

Resolves to Take the Leap of Leucata. Mary Robinson. CenSon; RWP

Resonance. Christopher Gilbert. ESEAA

Resonance. Ruth Stone. BodElec

Resort. George Oppen. FTOS

Respect for Law and Order, A. John Hughes. PNI

Respect the dreams of old men, said the cricket. Song for September. Robert Fitzgerald. VGW

Respect yourself, my brother. Brothers Loving Brothers. Vega. ISC

Respectability. Robert Browning. EnLoPo

Respectable Burgher, The. Thomas Hardy. ChIV-2; NoAM

Respectable House. Anne Stevenson. NALW

Respected, Feared, and Somehow Loved. Marjorie Welish. PmAP

Respice Finem. Thomas Proctor. NoSic

Respite, The. Ingeborg Bachmann. WPOW, tr. by Michael Hamburger

Resplendent chariot of the sun goes down inside, The. Evening. Mihály Csokonai Vitéz. IQMS, tr. by Madeline Mason

Resplendent studs of heaven's frame. *Unknown.* SCAP

Respondez! Walt Whitman. NoAM
 (Chants Democratic and Native American: 5.) APN-1

Response. Mary Ursula Bethell. FaBoWP; PeNZ

Response to Rimbaud's Later Manner. Thomas Sturge Moore. CABP; OBMV

Response to Wang Ssu-yüan's Poem on the Moon, A. Shen Yüeh. SuSp, tr. by Richard B. Mather

Responses to Montale. Brian Turner. PeNZ

Responsibilities. Anthony Cronin. PBCIP

Responsibility. Lisa Lewis. BodElec

Responsive to the tune of lawns and trees. Dogs in the Morning Light. Bruce Dawe. NoAM

Responsory, 1948, A. Thomas Merton. VGW

Ressaif My Saul. R. Crombie Saunders. OxBS

Rest. George Macdonald. SacPr

Rest. Christina Georgina Rossetti. GSo; NOBE; OBEV

Rest. *Unknown.* PoToHe

Rest, The. Ezra Pound. MoAmPo; NOBA; NoAM; OxBA *Fr.* Lustra.

Rest, and be thankful! On the verge. Adam Lindsay Gordon. CBAP *Fr.* Hippodramania; or, Whiffs from the Pipe.

Rest, beauty, stillness: not a waif of cloud. Emma Lazarus. APN-2 *Fr.* Phantasies.

Rest, Christ! from tireless war. See, it's midsummer. Derek Walcott. TOF *Fr.* Midsummer.

Rest from Loving and Be Living. Cecil Day Lewis. MoBrPo; OBMV

Rest in Love. Diana Helen Melhem.
 "It was warm in Grandma's kitchen. Throughout this, her second." GraLe
 "Say french." PoArWo

Rest in peace, warriors of Soweto. Elegy for the Dead of Soweto. Thembinkosi Ndlovu. PeSAV, tr. by Chris Mann

Rest Is Grace, The. János Pilinszky. IQMS, tr. by Adam Makkai

Rest is vanity of vanities, The. (LL) Ecclesiastes. Gilbert Keith Chesterton. ChIV-1; MoBrPo; OxBSP

Rest lightly O Earth upon this wretched Nearchos. Epitaph of Nearchos. Ammianus. WeW-3, tr. by Dudley Fitts

Rest, little guest. After Annunciation. Anna Wickham. MoBrPo

Rest me with Chinese colours. Song of the Degrees, A. Ezra Pound. APT-1

Rest / Of our life must be a palimpsest, The. Palimpsest, A. "Michael Field." VWP; ViWPN

Rest of the way will be only going down, The. (LL) Long Hill, The. Sara Teasdale. MoAmPo; TCAPo

Rest Only in the Grave. James Clarence Mangan. BIrV

Rest Our Spiritual Dead. Jim Everett. IBA

Rest, rest, and rest again. (LL) Nod. Walter De la Mare. MoBrPo; OxBTC

Rest thee aged pilgrim, now thy toils are o'er. Death of a Grandparent. Mrs. Jennette Bonneau. Mary Weston Fordham. CBWP-2

Rest! This little Fountain runs. For a Fountain. "Barry Cornwall." OBEV

Restaurant. Maxine Hong Kingston. OpBo

Resting. Josephine D. Henderson Heard. CBWP-4

Resting-Place, The. William Wordsworth. CenSon *Fr.* River Duddon [A Series of Sonnets], The.

Restless and discontent. Agathias. GrAn; PGA

Restless as a Wolf. Moyshe-Leyb [*or* Moishe-Leib *or* Leyb] Halpern. TrJP, tr. by Jacob Sloan

Restless before the canary, wave of traffic on an inhale, I can just barely see on a dark blue ground black arabesques. Killarney Clary. GeoHom

Restless he rolls about from whore to whore. John Wilmot, 2d Earl of Rochester. OBSV *Fr.* Satire on Charles II, A.

Restless Night. Tu Fu. CoBCP, tr. by Burton Watson

Restless Night in Camp, A. Tu Fu. OHPC, tr. by Kenneth Rexroth

Restless she stirs as she reclines. Sun and the Woman, The. Salah Abd al-Sabur. MAP, tr. by John Heath-Stubbs and Lena Jayyusi

Restoration. Jeffrey Skinner. PBCAP

Restoration of Enheduanna to Her Former Station, The. Enheduanna. BoWoP

"Restore the lock!" she cries; and all around. Pope. OxAEP-1 *Fr.* Rape of the Lock, The; an Heroi-Comical Poem.

Restored Terrace is new and fresh, The. *Unknown.* ColAnChi, tr. by Jeffrey Riegel *Fr.* Classic of Odes.

Restores the else-betrayed, too-human heart. (LL) At a Bach Concert. Adrienne Rich. NIL-7; NIP-4; YaYoPo

Restoring the Ancestral House. Katerina Te Hei Koko Mataira. PeNZ, tr. by Katerina Te Hei Koko Mataira

Restricted. Eve Merriam. TrJP

Restroom. Chitra Divakaruni. UnSA

Résumé. Bei Dao. AF, tr. by Bonnie S. McDougall

Résumé. Dorothy Parker. APT-1; HeIP-4; InPK-6; NAAL-2v2; NALW; NBLV; NoP-4; OBAL; TrJP; UV *Fr.* Some Beautiful Letters.

Resurgam. Adah Isaacs Menken. CBWP-1

Resurgam. Marjorie Lowry Christie Pickthall. SacPr; TrCP

Resurrection. George Crabbe. SacPr

Resurrection. Margiad Evans. OBWVE

Resurrection. Kenneth Fearing. PoE

Resurrection. Joy Harjo. HATNAP

Resurrection. Vladimir Holan. PoSu
 (After this life here, we're to be awakened one day.) AF, tr. by C. G. Hanzlicek

Resurrection. Marie Luise Kaschnitz. WPOW, tr. by Michael Hamburger

Resurrection. Karl Kraus. AuPH, tr. by Lowell A. Bangerter

Resurrection. Alfred Noyes. SacPr

Resurrection, The. Abraham Cowley. ChIV-2

Resurrection, The. Elizabeth Jennings. HarvBoo

Resurrection, The. Nathaniel Wanley. NPeEn

Resurrection, The. W. B. Yeats.
 "I saw a staring virgin stand." FaBoTw; HAP; NOBE; PoE
 Two Songs from a Play. FaBoTw; HAP; NOBE; PoE

Resurrection: An Easter Sequence. William Robert Rodgers.
 "It was a lovely night." PNI

Resurrection and Immortality. Henry Vaughan. ESCV

Resurrection, Imperfect. John Donne. ChIV-2

Resurrection of a Mouse. David J. Rothman. GeoH

Resurrection of Arp. Arthur James Marshall Smith. MoCV; NOBC

Resurrection of Elvis Presley, The. Ai. AllShUp

Resurrection of the Flesh, The. Juan Felipe Herrera. TouFir

Resurrection of the Right Side. Muriel Rukeyser. LCAP-2

Resurrection Song. Thomas Lovell Beddoes. FaBoEE

Resuscitation Team. U. A. Fanthorpe. FaBoWP

Retaliation. Margaret E. Bruner. PoToHe

Retaliation. Oliver Goldsmith. OxBoLi
 David Garrick. NOEC; NPeEn; OxBEV
 Edmund Burke. FaBoEE; NOEC; NPeEn; OxBEV
 (Joshua Reynolds.) NPeEn
 Poem: "Of old, when Scarron his companions invited." NOIV; OxBoLi
 Sir Joshua Reynolds. FaBoEE; NoEC; OBCoV; OxBEV

Rethink in the hair department. Time maybe to move on from the fags. (LL) Time Out. Maurice Riordan. EmeKit; ModIr

Reticence. May Muzaffar. PoArWo, tr. by Tahia Abdel Nasser

Reticulations creep upon the slack stream's face. On Sturminster Foot-Bridge. Thomas Hardy. OxBSP

Retina fills with skies and expanses of grass, The. Martyrdom. Yolanda Bedregal. TANSG, tr. by Carolyne Wright

Retinal burn of warm November light. Dan Guillory. IllVoic *Fr.* Snowpoems.

Retire, my daughter. Fragment of an English Opera. A. E. Housman. OBCoV

Retired, a lonely figure, to lay eggs at Bordighera. (LL) I Had a Duck-billed Platypus. Patrick Barrington. OBCoV; PeLV

Retired Ballerinas, Central Park West. Lawrence Ferlinghetti. NoAM

Retired Civil Servant from Gateley, A. Limerick. Ida Thurtle. PeLi

Retired Friendship, to Ardelia, A. Katherine Philips. BASC

Retired general is talking about restraint, The. Nightline: An Interview with the General. Ronald Wallace. PBCAP

Retired Greyhound, I. Natalie Kusz. Unle

Retired Greyhound, II. Natalie Kusz. Unle

Retired man showed the town, The. His Waves. Rick Noguchi. AmPoNex

Retired [*or* Retyrèd] thought[e]s enjoy their own[e] delight[e]s. Look[e] Home. Robert Southwell. ESCV; NOCV; NoSic

Retired Pilot to Himself, The. Walter McDonald. CDa

Retirement. William Cowper. SacPr *Fr.* Olney Hymns.

Retirement. Henry Timrod. APN-2

Retirement. Henry Vaughan. GeHe
 (Retirement (I).) NOSC

Retirement. Henry Vaughan. ChIV-1

Retirement. Yuan Chen. CrYelRi, tr. by Sam Hamill

Retirement (I). Henry Vaughan. *See* Retirement

Retort Perfect, The. Justin Richardson. OBCoV

Retort to Jesus. D. H. Lawrence. PeECV

Retreat. Árpád Tóth. IQMS, *tr. by* Watson Kirkconnell

Retreat from Paradise, The. John Milton. HeIP-4 *Fr.* Paradise Lost.

Retreat of Ita Cagney, The. Michael Hartnett. CIP-2; PBCIP

Retreat of Liu Kuo-pao, The. Chang Yü. CoBLCP, *tr. by* Jonathan Chaves

Retreat of Sun Ching-hsiang, The. Chang Yü. CoBLCP, *tr. by* Jonathan Chaves

Retreat[e], The. Henry Vaughan. AWP; BASC; CABP; ClHu; ESCV; FSCP; GTBS-P; GeHe; HAP; InPK-6; MeLP; NAEL-5v1; NAEL-6v1; NAEL-7v1; NIP-4; NOBE; NOCV; NOSC; NPeEn; NoP-4; OBEV; OBWVE; OxBEV; PBRV; PeECV; PoE; PoRA; SCGP; TFi; TOF

Retribution. Aleksandr Aleksandrovich Blok.
"In those far years of inertia." TCRP

Retribution. Ilya Grigoryevich Ehrenburg [*or* Erenburg]. TCRP, *tr. by* Gordon McVay

Retribution. Friedrich von Logau. PoToHe, *tr. by* Henry Wadsworth Longfellow

Retribution. Lizelia Augusta Jenkins Moorer. CBWP-3

Retrieval System, The. Maxine W. Kumin. FaBoWP; InvLad; WeW-3

Retrieving is uncertain work. Lab Lines. Robert Hugh Benson. Unle

"Retro Me, Sathana." Dante Gabriel Rossetti. ChIV-2

Retrospect. Josephine D. Henderson Heard. CBWP-4

Retrospect Love of Nature Leading to Love of Mankind. William Wordsworth. *Fr.* Prelude, The; Growth of a Poet's Mind [1850 vers.].

Retrospection. Charlotte Brontë.
"Dream that stole o'er us in the time." PEW

Retrospection. Henrietta Cordelia Ray. CBWP-3

Retrospection. Dunstan Shaw. NOBAu

Retrospective. Ogata Kenzon. WoPoe, *tr. by* Richard L. Wilson

Retrospective. William Scammell. NLP

Return. Dmitry [*or* Dmitrii] Vasil'evich Bobyshev. ItGoST, *tr. by* Michael Van Walleghen

Return. Constantine P. Cavafy. PasH, *tr. by* Rae Dalven

Return. Seamus Deane. BIrV; PBCIP; PNI

Return. Carolyn Forché. BodElec

Return. Robinson Jeffers. HarvBoo

Return. Jewel C. Latimore. BlSi

Return. Archibald MacLeish. APT-1

Return. John Wilmot, 2d Earl of Rochester. *See* Song: "Absent from thee, I languish still."

Return. William Wordsworth. CenSon; HAP *Fr.* River Duddon [A Series of Sonnets], The.

Return, The. John Peale Bishop. APT-1; OxBA

Return, The. Arna Bontemps. GT

Return, The. Alistair Campbell. PeNZ

Return, The. Rosario Castellanos. TANSG; TCLAP, *tr. by* Magda Bogin

Return, The. Emily Dickinson. MoAmPo

Return, The. Felicia Dorothea Hemans. RWP

Return, The. Julio Herrera y Reissig. TCLAP, *tr. by* Andrew Rosing

Return, The. Dalia Hertz. FIT, *tr. by* Robert Friend

Return, The. Rudyard Kipling. MoBrPo

Return, The. Joanne Limburg. NeBl

Return, The. Pittendrigh Macgillivray. OxBS

Return, The. Thomas McGrath. GifTon

Return, The. Edna St. Vincent Millay. MoAmPo; NoAM; OxBA

Return, The. Molly Peacock. PasH; RA

Return, The. Ezra Pound. APT-1; HAP; MoAmPo; NOBA; NPeEn; NoAM; OxBA; PoE; RB; TRP; VGW; WeW-3

Return, The. Tadeusz Różewicz. HP, *tr. by* Adam Czerniawski

Return, The. Yevgeny [*or* Evgenii] Borisovich Rein. ItGoST, *tr. by* Judith Hemschemeyer

Return, The. T'ao Ch'ien [*or* T'ao Yuan-ming]. ColAnChi, *tr. by* J. R. Hightower

Return, The. Evan J. Thomas. AngWePo

Return, The. Thomas Traherne. GeHe

Return, The. Tu Fu. TAL

Return 2. Tamara Kamenszain. MirDau, *tr. by* Roberta Gordenstein

Return Alpheus, the dread voice is past. John Milton. PeECV *Fr.* Lycidas.

Return: An Elegy, The. Robert Penn Warren. APT-2

Return and dwell with me. (LL) Shall Earth no more inspire thee. Emily Jane Brontë. BWW; VWP

Return, blessed years, when not the jocund spring. Anna Seward. RWP *Fr.* Llangollen Vale.

Return: Buffalo. Linda Hogan. BodElec

Return, Content! for fondly I pursued. William Wordsworth. CenSon *Fr.* River Duddon [A Series of Sonnets], The.

Return from Battle. *Unknown.* ChiP, *tr. by* Arthur Waley

Return from Luluabourg. Michael Jackson. PeNZ

Return Home 1918, The. Franz Theodor Csokor. AuPH, *tr. by* Lowell A. Bangerter

Return is not a way of going forward. Roman Poem Number Nine. June Jordan. GT

Return, my joys, and hither bring. Opposite to Melancholy. William Strode. NOSC

Return of a Popular Statesman. Vincent Buckley. CBAP

Return of an Ikon. Dimitris Tsaloumas. BMAP

Return of Astraea, The. Ben Jonson. NOBE

Return of Persephone, The. Alec Derwent Hope. BMAP

Return of Robinson Jeffers, The. Robert Hass. GeoHom

Return of the Banished. Li Po. CrYelRi, *tr. by* Sam Hamill

Return of the Greeks, The. Edwin Muir. NoP-4; PoE

Return of the Native. Imamu Amiri Baraka. APSN; BPo (Harlem is vicious.) ColAP

Return of the Proconsul, The. Zbigniew Herbert. PoSu

Return of the Prodigal Son. Léopold Sédar Senghor.
"Elephant of Moissel, hear my pious prayer." NegPo

Return of the Sire de Nesle A.D. 16, The. Herman Melville. NOBA

Return of the Wolves. Anita Endrezze. HATNAP

Return of Youth, The. William Cullen Bryant. TreFP

Return often and take me. Return. Constantine P. Cavafy. PasH, *tr. by* Rae Dalven

Return, Return, O Shulammite. Bible, *O.T.* TrJP *Fr.* Song of Solomon, The [*or* The Song of Songs].

Return, Sweet Horse, rise. Cortez's Horse. Pat Mora. UnSA

Return thee, heart. Alexander Scott. NePenScot

Return thee, heart, hamewart again. Return thee, heart. Alexander Scott. NePenScot

Return to Ararat. Martyn Halsall. TrCP

Return to Cardiff. Dannie Abse. AngWePo; TCAWP

Return to DeKalb. Lucien Stryk. IllVoic

Return to Frankfurt. Marie Luise Kaschnitz.
"Girl thinks if I can only manage, The." ItWoWo, *tr. by* Beatrice Cameron

Return to Harmony 3. Agha Shahid Ali. BAP-97

Return to La Plata, Missouri. Jim Barnes. HATNAP

Return to My Native Land. Aimé Césaire. NegPo, *tr. by* Emile Snyders
"I shall not regard my swelled head as a sign of real glory." TTY

Return to Paris. Jules Supervielle. MFP, *tr. by* Martin Sorrell

Return to Scalpay. Norman MacCaig. NePenScot

Return to Shaoshan. Mao Tse-tung [*or* Mao Zedong]. WoPoe, *tr. by* Willis Barnstone and Ko Ching-po

Return to Temptation. Mary Weems. SpirFl

Return to the Homeland. Adelina da Silva. NAfrP, *tr. by* Don Burness

Return to the Native Land, A. Aimé Césaire.
"This flat city shortly after dawn." NegPo

Return to the Tree of Time, A. Vesna Parun. WPOW, *tr. by* Vasa D. Mihailovich and Ronald Morgan

Return to Wang River. Wang Wei. CrYelRi, *tr. by* Sam Hamill

Returned from California. Simon J. Ortiz. HATNAP

Returned from college R——gets a wife. Discontented Student, The. St. George Tucker. OBAL

Returned Heart, The. Sarah Dixon. ECWP

Returned Soldier, The. John Clare. FaBoWar

Returned to Say. William Stafford. CoAmPo

Returning. Linda Pastan. WeW-3

Returning. Victor Vroomkoning. TuT, *tr. by* Ruth Hooley

Returning a Lawn to the Field It Was. Brendan Galvin. PoCoUp

Returning as it came. Shidoken. JDP, *tr. by* Yoel Hoffmann

Returning at Night. James [*or* Jim] Harrison. VGW

Returning / By an unused path—violets. Bakusui. ZenPo, *tr. by* Takashi Ikemoto and Lucien Stryk

Returning by Night to Lu-Men. Meng Hao Jan. OHMPC, *tr. by* Kenneth Rexroth

Returning coiling on the misty steps, just like a snail! (LL) Red Embankment. Tu Mu. ColAnChi; SuSp, *tr. by* John M. Ortinau

Returning Fire. D. F. Brown. CDa

Returning from a funeral. Mukai Kyorai. SoOfWa, *tr. by* Sam Hamill

Returning from court day after day, I pawn my spring clothes. Tu Fu. SuSp *Fr.* Meandering River.

Returning from its daily quest, my Spirit. To Dante [*or* Sonnet: Guido Cavalcanti to Dante Alighieri]. Guido Cavalcanti. AWP; OBVE, *tr. by* Percy Bysshe Shelley

Returning from Kuang-ling. Ch'in Kuan. SuSp, *tr. by* Stephen West

Returning from the Seventy-Two Mountains. Hsü Wei. CoBLCP, *tr. by* Jonathan Chaves

Returning Home. "Shu Ting." CarOv, *tr.* by Carolyn Kizer and Y. H. Zhao

Returning Home. Tu Mu. SuSp, *tr.* by John M. Ortinau

Returning Home. Yüan Mei. CoBLCP, *tr.* by Jonathan Chaves

Returning Home at Dusk from Town, on the Fifteenth of the Seventh Month. Shen Chou. SuSp, *tr.* by Irving Y. Lo

Returning in Wind and Drizzle to My Home. S. J. Marks. BodElec

Returning Late to Lu-men Shan. Meng Hao Jan. CrYelRi, *tr.* by Sam Hamill

Returning Spring. Pauli Murray. GT

Returning thanks. Goshi. JDP, *tr.* by Yoel Hoffmann

Returning to Goleufryn. Vernon Watkins. AngWePo; OBWVE

Returning to Lotus Village. Kao Ch'i. CoBLCP, *tr.* by Jonathan Chaves

Returning to My Fields and Gardens. T'ao Ch'ien [*or* T'ao Yuan-ming]. CrYelRi, *tr.* by Sam Hamill

Returning to My Garden Home: In Respectful Response to the Master of Hua-yang. Shen Yüeh. ColAnChi, *tr.* by Richard Mather

Returning to my grandfather's house, after this exile. Returning to Goleufryn. Vernon Watkins. AngWePo; OBWVE

Returning to My Home in the Country, No. 1. T'ao Ch'ien [*or* T'ao Yuan-ming]. CoBCP, *tr.* by Burton Watson

Returning to My Home in the Country, No. 2. T'ao Ch'ien [*or* T'ao Yuan-ming]. CoBCP, *tr.* by Burton Watson

Returning to My Home in the Country, No. 3. T'ao Ch'ien [*or* T'ao Yuan-ming]. CoBCP, *tr.* by Burton Watson

Returning to My Home in the Country, No. 4. T'ao Ch'ien [*or* T'ao Yuan-ming]. CoBCP, *tr.* by Burton Watson

Returning to the Alluvial Fields. Wu Chia-chi.

"In the morning they build embankments against floods." CoBLCP

Returning to the Fields. Ch'ien T'ao. ChiP, *tr.* by Arthur Waley

Returning to the Port of Authority: A Picaresque. Constance Urdang. PBCAP

Returning to the Town Where We Used to Live. Susan Musgrave. NOBC

Returning to Yin-ch'eng Early in the Year *Ting-ch'ou* (1277). Tai Piao-yüan. CoBLCP, *tr.* by Jonathan Chaves

Returning, We Hear the Larks. Isaac Rosenberg. FaBoMo; HarvBoo; NAEL-5v2; NAEL-6v2; NoAM; OBWP; PeFWW; PoWW

Reuben Bright. Edwin Arlington Robinson. APN-2; MoAmPo; NOBA; Son; TAP

Reuben Pantier. Edgar Lee Masters. APT-1 *Fr.* Spoon River Anthology.

Reuben, Reuben. Michael S. Harper. LoL; PoE

Reuben, Reuben, I've been thinking. How 'Ya Gonna Keep 'Em Down on the Farm? (After They've Seen Paree). Sam M. Lewis. ReLy

Reunion. T. Crunk. YaYoPo

Reunion. Carolyn Forché. NoAM

Reunion. Judith Herzberg. BoWoP, *tr.* by Shirley Kaufman

Reunion. Carolyn Kizer. ExTi

Reunion. Edwin Arlington Robinson. NOBA

Reunion. Tu Fu. CarOv, *tr.* by Carolyn Kizer *Fr.* Banishment.

Reunited. Sir Gilbert Parker. OBEV

Reunited. Henrietta Cordelia Ray. CBWP-3

Rev. Andrew Brown, over the Hill to Rest. Josephine D. Henderson Heard. CBWP-4

Rev. Homer Wilbur's "Festina Lente." James Russell Lowell. OBAL *Fr.* Biglow Papers, The.

Rev. Nicholas Noyes to the Rev. Cotton Mather, The. Nicholas Noyes. SCAP

Rev Owl. Abraham Moses Klein. TrJP

Rev'rend Father stood inculcating, The. Luis de Camões [*or* Camõens]. PeSAV *Fr.* Lusiads, The.

Rev. Samuel Weston. Mary Weston Fordham. CBWP-2

Reveal Code: Indra's Net 8. John Cayley.

"Code key." PFTM-2

Four Screen Shots. PFTM-2

Revealing Oneself to a Woman. Bin Ramke. YaYoPo

Reveille. A. E. Housman. CABP; HarvBoo; MoBrPo; NoP-4

Reveille. Primo Levi. HP, *tr.* by Ruth Feldman

Réveille. Lola Ridge. WPE

Reveille Matin, or Good Morrow to a Friend. Mildmay Fane, 2d Earl of Westmorland. NOSC

Revel pauses and the room is still, The. Pannyra of the Golden Heel. Albert Samain. AWP, *tr.* by James Elroy Flecker

Revelation. Carole C. Gregory Clemmons. BlSi

Revelation. Robert Frost. ChIV-2

Revelation. Sir Edmund William Gosse. OBEV

Revelation. Sir Edmund William Gosse. OBEV

Revelation. Robert Penn Warren. NoAM

Revelation, The. Stanley Crouch. SeSe

Revelation, The. Coventry Patmore. EnLoPo; GTBS-P; HAP; OxBSP *Fr.* Angel in the House, The.

Revelation, The. William Carlos Williams. SAmP

Revelation, The. James Wright (1927–80). PAI

Revelation 5, October 8. Anne Wentworth. EMWP

Revelation 8, March 31. Anne Wentworth. EMWP

Revelation and Decline. Georg Trakl. PFTM-1

Revelation in the Mother Lode. George Evans. AF; PmAP

Revelation of St. John the Divine, The. Bible, *N.T.*

"Spirit saith, come, The." EMWP, *tr.* by Bathsheba Bowers

Revelation on a Summer Walk. John O'Brien. PoCoUp

Revelation: The Movie. Elton Glaser. PBCAP

Revelations. David Meltzer. NeAP

Revelations—we've come to the lewd. Limerick. *Unknown.* PeLi

Revellers, The. Felicia Dorothea Hemans. TreFP

Revelry in Black-and-White. Ann Lauterbach. BodElec

Revelry was had, A. The chair came to pieces. Fall of Because, The. David Baratier. AmPoNex

Revenge. Letitia [*or* Laetitia] Elizabeth Landon. NOBRP; NPeEn

Revenge. Amado Nervo. TCLAP, *tr.* by Sue Standing

Revenge. Mary E. Tucker. CBWP-1

Revenge, The. Pierre de Ronsard. AWP, *tr.* by Thomas Stanley

Revenge, The. Tennyson. EBVV; FaBoCh; PoRA

"At Flores in the Azores Sir Richard Grenville lay." EBNV; OBWP

Revenge 1. Giuseppe Gioacchino Belli. WoPoe, *tr.* by Anthony Burgess

Revenge—? Heinrich Heine. WoPoe, *tr.* by Mark Rudman

Revenge—?—as if it were a cure. Revenge—? Heinrich Heine. WoPoe, *tr.* by Mark Rudman

Revenge of America, The. Joseph Warton. ECEV

Revenge of Hamish, The. Sidney Lanier. APN-2; EBNV; NCAP

Revenge of the Hunted. Robert Arthur Douglas Ford. MoCV

Revenge to Come. Propertius. AWP, *tr.* by Kirby Flower Smith *Fr.* Elegies.

Revenger's Tragedy, The. Cyril Tourneur.

"Art thou beguild now? tut, a Lady can." OxBEV

"Duke: royall letcher; goe, gray hayrde adultery." OxBEV

Reverberation. Maurice Kenny. HATNAP

Reverend Butler came by. Madam and the Minister. Langston Hughes. NOBA

Reverend Henry Ward Beecher, The. Limerick. Oliver Wendell Holmes. PeLi

Reverend mothers, The. Foretold Futures. Giovanna Pollarolo. TANSG, *tr.* by Marjorie Agosin

Reverend Mr, The Higginson. Edward Johnson. SCAP

Reverend Mr. Uprightly, The. Limerick. *Unknown.* PeLi

Reverie. Henrietta Cordelia Ray. CBWP-3

Reverie, A. Joanna Baillie. ECWP; WoRP

Reverie, A. Mary Weston Fordham. CBWP-2

Reverie of a Mum. Nancy Keesing. CBAP; NOBAu

Reverie of Poor Susan, The. William Wordsworth. GTBS-P; OxBoLi

Reverse Order. Steve Benson.

"As sincerely as possible." FTOS

Reverse the flight of Lucifer. Task, The. Ruth Pitter. MoBrPo

Reversible Stitches: my mother and I leaned over a single piece of English. Mary Warren's Sampler. Nicole Cooley. NeAmPo

Reversionary. Stevie Smith. FaBoEE

Review from Staten Island. Gloria C. Oden. GT

Reviewing me without undue elation. Choice of Weapons, A. Stanley Kunitz. VGW

Reviewing Past Lives while Leaf-Burning. Anita Endrezze. HATNAP

Reviewing the Situation. Lionel Bart. ReLy

Reviewing the Troops at Kuei-lin with Military Inspectors Chiang And Chang. Yang Chi. CoBLCP, *tr.* by Jonathan Chaves

Reviews are gaudy shows—allowed. On the Frequent Review of the Troops. "M." NOEC

Revised Notes for a Sonnet. "Edward Pygge." OBCoV

Revisionary Instruments 1. Kathy Fagan. ExTi

Revisionism. Joanne Burns. BMAP

Revival. Arthur Hugh Clough. SacPr

Revival. Steve Crow. HATNAP

Revival, The. Henry Vaughan. InvLi; NOCV

Revo Lyric. Kendel Hippolyte. WaCA

Revocation, A. Sir Thomas Wyatt. *See* Farewell: "What should I say."

Revolt of immense estates, The. (LL) In the Miscroscope. Miroslav Holub. PoSu; WoPoe, *tr.* by Ian Milner and Jarmila Milner

Revolt of Islam, The. Shelley.

"Over the utmost hill at length I sped." OBWP

Revolting against the lips. Dracula. Salwa Al-Neimi. PoArWo, *tr.* by Subhi Hadidi

Revolution. Brian G. Gilmore. SpirFl

Revolution. Enrique Lihn. TCLAP, *tr.* by Jonathan Cohen

Revolution, The. Jack Gilbert. BodElec

Revolution is conceived, The. Cycle. Bobbi Sykes. BMAP; IBA
Revolution of the Aged, The. Njabulo S. Ndebele. PeSAV
"Revolution," said Mr. Adams, The. Canto 32. Ezra Pound. PFTM-1
Revolution Will Not Be Televised!, The. Gil Scott-Heron. NAAAL
Revolutionaries, The. Richard Percival Lister. NOBL
Revolutionaries, The. Unknown. NOBL
Revolutionary. Willie Perdomo. InTrad
Revolutionary, The. Dezső Kosztolányi. IQMS, tr. by Peter Zollman
Revolutionary Letter #1. Diane Di Prima. CLPP
Revolutionary Petunias. Alice Walker. BlSi; NIL-7
Revolutionary Vision, The. Ira B. Jones. InTrad
Revolutions. William Shakespeare. See Sonnets
Revolving auger. (LL) Leonidas. GrAn; PGA
Revolving door. Ron Silliman. PFTM-2 Fr. Ketjak.
Reward. Shimon Halkin. MHP, tr. by Ruth Finer Mintz
Reward. Kevin Young. SpirFl
Rewarded porters opening their smiles, The. On the Railway Platform. Randall Jarrell. GM
Rewards and Fairies. Roger Woddis. UV
Rewind. Ger Killeen. AmPoNex
Rex Mundi. David Gascoyne. NoP-4
Rex regum, for whom praise flows freely. Poem on His Death-Bed. Meilyr Brydydd. OBWVE, tr. by Joseph P. Clancy
Rex Whistler—or is it Joe Isuzu?—stretches. Society. Tom Clark. PmAP
Reynard the Fox. John Masefield.
  "Ducks flew up from the Morton Pond, The." EBNV
  "Fox knew well, that before they tore him, The." OBNV
  "Meet was at 'The Cock and Pye,' The." OxBTC
  Run to Mourne End Wood, The. EBNV
Rhapsody. William Stanley Braithwaite. TCAPo
Rhapsody. Frank O'Hara. NoAM
Rhapsody, A. Henry Vaughan. BeJo; NAEL-5v1; NAEL-6v1
  "Should we go now a wandering [or a-wand'ring], we should meet." BASC
Rhapsody for the Mule. José Lezama Lima. TCLAP, tr. by Dudley Fitts, José Rodríguez Feo and Donald D. Walsh
Rhapsody: Keeping Faith. István Vas. IQMS, tr. by George Szirtes
Rhapsody of Old Men, A. Dimitris Tsaloumas.
  "They brought him one morning." CBAP
Rhapsody on a Windy Night. T. S. Eliot. HeIP-4; PoE
Rhapsody on Main Street. Patrick Williams. PNI
Rhapsody on Whistling. Ch'eng-kung Sui. ColAnChi, tr. by Douglass A. White
Rhapsody, Written at the Lakes in Westmorland, A. John Brown. NOEC
Rheia, submissive in love to Kronos, Hesiod. RaBo, tr. by Richmond Lattimore Fr. Theogony.
Rhetoric. Francis Ponge. WoPoe, tr. by Serge Gavronsky
Rhetoric of Langston Hughes, The. Margaret Danner. BlSi
Rhiannon. Christine Furnival. TCAWP
Rhiannon. T. Harri Jones. AngWePo
Rhinoceros, The. Ogden Nash. MoAmPo; OBAL
Rhodanthe. Agathias. AWP, tr. by Andrew Lang
Rhode Island. William Meredith. NoP-4
Rhode Island Is Famous for You. Howard Dietz. ReLy
Rhodoclea, I send you this wreath which I wove with my own hands. Rufinus. HePo, tr. by Barbara Hughes Fowler
Rhododaphne. Thomas Love Peacock.
  "Magic and mystery, spells Circæan." NOBRP
Rhododendron is happy. Its aloof yet sexual, The. It's a Party (1959). Baron Wormser. SeSe
Rhododendrons. Larry Levis. GeoHom
Rhodope is so stuck up / because of her beauty. Rufinus. GrAn
Rhodope, Melite and Rhodoklea / contested. Rufinus. GrAn
Rhodora, The [On Being Asked Whence Is the Flower]. Ralph Waldo Emerson. APN-1; AWP; AmFaPo; ITBLP; NAAL-2v1; NAAL-3; NAAL-5; NOBA; NoP-4; OxBA; PWR; PoE; TAP; TCAPo; TFi
Rhodri. Ronald Stuart Thomas. OxAEP-2
Rhodri Theophilus Owen. Rhodri. Ronald Stuart Thomas. OxAEP-2
Rhonda, Age 15, Emergency Room. Letta Neely. WiU
Rhotruda. Frederick Goddard Tuckerman. NCAP
Rhudine Rhudine. Tony Medina. InTrad
Rhydcymerau. David Gwenallt Jones. OBWVE, tr. by Anthony Conran
Rhyfel y Sais Bach. John Stuart Williams. TCAWP
Rhyme. James Laughlin. WeW-3
Rhyme. Sylvia Plath. BodElec
Rhyme for a Child Viewing a Naked Venus in a Painting [of "The Judgement of Paris"]. Robert Browning. NPeEn; OBCoV
Rhyme for Halloween, A. Maurice Kilwein Guevara. TouFir

Rhyme for Night. Joan Aiken. TLR
Rhyme for the Child as a Wet Dog. Judith Johnson Sherwin. TAP
Rhyme from Lincolnshire, A. Unknown. NPeEn
Rhyme is after, The. For W.C.W. Robert Creeley. FTOS; LCAP-2
Rhyme Is Running Out, The. József Kiss. IQMS, tr. by Anthony Edkins
Rhyme nor mars, nor makes, His Defence Against the Idle Critic. Michael Drayton. NOSC
Rhyme of My Inheritance. Joan Larkin. GLP
Rhyme of Sir Christopher, The. Henry Wadsworth Longfellow. NCAP
Rhyme of the Antique Forest. Henrietta Cordelia Ray. CBWP-3
Rhyme of the Flying Bomb, The. Mervyn Laurence Peake.
  "Babe was born in the reign of George, A." FaBoWar
Rhyme of the Sun-Dial, A. William Bell Scott. NOBVV
Rhyme [or Rime], the rack of finest wits. Fit of Rhyme [or Rime] against Rhyme [or Rime], A. Ben Jonson. BeJo
Rhyme-Prose on the Desolate City. Pao Chao. CoBCP, tr. by Burton Watson
Rhyme-Prose on the Idle Life. P'an Yüeh. CoBCP, tr. by Burton Watson
Rhyme-Prose on the Owl. Chia Yi. CoBCP, tr. by Burton Watson
Rhyme-Prose on the Snow. Hsieh Hui-lien. CoBCP, tr. by Burton Watson
Rhyme, the rack of finest wits. Ben Jonson. See Rhyme [or Rime], the rack of finest wits
Rhymed Words Sent to My Eldest Son. Yang Shih-ch'i. CoBLCP, tr. by Jonathan Chaves
Rhymeprose on an Owl. Chia Yi.
  "Year was tan-wo, it was the fourth month, summer's first, The." WoPoe, tr. by J. R. Hightower
Rhymeprose on the Sword Gallery. Li Po. ColAnChi, tr. by Elling O. Eide
Rhymes. Charles Tomlinson. DiPo
Rhymes (?). Henry Sambrooke Leigh. NOBL
Rhymes for a Modern Nursery. Paul Dehn.
  In a cavern, in a canyon. KaS
  "Jack and Jill went up the hill/ To fetch some heavy water." ReMoGo
Rhymes on the Road. Thomas Moore.
  "And is there then no earthly place." OBSV
Rhyming a Friend's Poem. Yü Hsüan-chi. BoWoP, tr. by Geoffrey Waters
Rhyming with a Friend. Yü Hsüan-chi. BoWoP, tr. by Geoffrey Waters
Rhyming with Tzu-yu's "Treading the Green." Su Tung-p'o (Su Shih). CoBCP, tr. by Burton Watson
  (Spring wind raises fine dust from the road, The.) OHPC, tr. by Kenneth Rexroth
  (Walk in the Country, A.) OHPC, tr. by Kenneth Rexroth
Rhythm. Yevgeny [or Evgenii] Mikhailovich Vinokurov. TCRP, tr. by Daniel Weissbort
Rhythm Is Only a Servant. János Batsányi. IQMS, tr. by Joseph Leftwich
Rhythm of the Pestle. Richard Ntiru.
  "Listen—listen." EroLit
Rib Sandwich. William J. Harris. UnSA
Ribald Romeos less and less berattle. Horace. STV Fr. Odes.
Ribbe ne rele ne spinne ich ne may. Servant-Girl's Holiday, A. Unknown. MiEL
Ribbon-Fish, The. Robert Adamson. CBAP
Ribbons of iodine. Kelp. Nora Dauenhauer. HATNAP
Ribes rubrum. Elizabeth Garrett. NeBl
Ribh Considers Christian Love Insufficient. W. B. Yeats. BBASP; RaBo
Ribs and terrors in the whale, The. Herman Melville. APN-2; ChIV-1 Fr. Moby Dick.
Ribs of leaves lie in the dust, The. Coming of the Cold, The. Theodore Roethke. OBCP
Rice. Chemmanam Chacko. OMIP, tr. by K. Ayyappa Paniker
Rice. Mary Oliver. PoCoUp
Rice around the lingam stone will be distributed in the dying sun, The. Karl Shapiro. BodElec Fr. Bourgeois Poet, The.
Rice Comes to El Volcán. Virgil Suárez. AmPoNex
Rice is cut and clouds glisten in the fields, The. After the Harvest. Tu Fu. CrYelRi, tr. by Sam Hamill
Rice this year ripens so late! Lament of the Farm Wife of Wu. Su Tung-p'o (Su Shih). CoBCP; ColAnChi, tr. by Burton Watson
Rice Will Grow Again. Frank A. Cross. CDa
Rich and Poor; or, Saint and Sinner. Thomas Love Peacock. NOBE; NOBL; OBSV; OxBEV; PeLV
Rich, black humus, airborne, glimmers gold, The. Descano, California. Chryss Yost. GeoHom
Rich blood disturbed my thought. Arrival. John Wain. EBEV
Rich earth has not pressed down. Epitaph for Mael Mhuru. Unknown. NOIV
Rich families ordered everything in crystal, The. Waterford. Medbh McGuckian. BiHa
Rich, flashy, puffy-faced. Cabaret. Sterling Allen Brown. APT-2; NAAAL

Rich Harvest. Max Fleischer. AuPH, *tr. by* Lowell A. Bangerter

Rich Is the Year with Much Millet and Rice. *Unknown.* CoBCP, *tr. by* Burton Watson

Rich jigsaw'd gone, A. Bill Griffiths. Oth *Fr.* Building: The New London Hospital.

Rich *Lazarus!* richer in those gems, thy teares. Upon Lazarus His Teares. Richard Crashaw. GeHe

Rich little circle south. Bruce Andrews. FTOS

Rich Man, The. Franklin Pierce Adams. NBLV; OBAL

Rich man bought a swan and goose, A. Swan and the Goose, The. Aesop. AWP, *tr. by* William Ellery Leonard

Rich man has his motorcar, The. Rich Man, The. Franklin Pierce Adams. NBLV; OBAL

Rich night. Will They Always Remember. Tracy Clarke. InTrad

Rich nights in another climate. Emblems. Douglas Dunn. FaBoMo

"Rich soil," remarked the Landlord. Dennis Joseph Enright. OBCoV *Fr.* Paradise Illustrated.

Rich Statue, double-faced. To the New Yeere [*or* Year]. Michael Drayton. NOSC

Rich surplus of consciousness rots at the wharves, The. Clouds. Francis Webb. BMAP

Rich tuft of ivy, A. Suibne Geilt. NOIV

Rich, voluptuous languor of dim pain, A. Vanitas Vanitatum. Israel Zangwill. TrJP

Rich Words! HEAV'N, HEAV'N WILL MAKE AMENDS FOR ALL. (LL) Cotton Mather. AiP; SCAP

Richard II. Veronica Forrest-Thomson. Oth

Richard 2. William Shakespeare. OBGa *Fr.* King Richard II.

Richard Brought His Flute. Nancy Morejón. TCLAP, *tr. by* Kathleen Weaver

Richard Cory. Edwin Arlington Robinson. APN-2; ChAP; ColAP; HAP; InPK-6; MoAmPo; NAAL-2v2; NAAL-5; NCAP; NOBA; NoP-4; OxBA; PAI; PoPoPo; PoRA; TAP; TCAPo; TFi

Richard Cory. Paul Simon. InPK-6

Richard Dick upon a stick. *Unknown.* OxNR

Richard II Forty. Louis Aragon. WoPoe, *tr. by* Peter Dale

Richard's Blues. Richard Cecil. SeSe

Riches. *Unknown. See* On Late-acquired Wealth *or* Riches

Riches and honours Buckley layes aside. Onely the Reverend Grave and Godly Mr. Buckly Remaines. Edward Johnson. SCAP

Riches I hold in light esteem. Emily Jane Brontë. VWP
(Old Stoic, The.) BWW; NALW; NOBE; OBEV; OxAEP-2

Richie Story. *Unknown.* ESPB

Richly Painted Zither, The. Li Shang-yin. SuSp, *tr. by* James J. Y. Liu

Richly painted zither, for no reason, has fifty strings, The. Richly Painted Zither, The. Li Shang-yin. SuSp, *tr. by* James J. Y. Liu

Richmond. John Updike. CBCWP

Richmond Gardens: A Poem. *Unknown.*
"Hail! Richmond, hail! thy matchless beauties." OBGa

Richmond Hill. Thomas Maurice.
Chiswick. OBGa

Rick of Green Wood, The. Edward Dorn. NeAP; PmAP; PoM

Rickety chimney suggests, A. Caravan. Michael Longley. CIP-2; ModIr; PNI

Riddim an' Hardtimes. Lillian Allen. WaCA

Riddle. Gharib Nawaz. BBASP, *tr. by* Nasrollah Pourjavady and Peter Lamborn Wilson

Riddle, The. "H. E. H." PoToHe

Riddle, A: "Once when I was very scared." Charlotte Zolotow. NTCP

Riddle, a riddle / As I suppose, A. Sieve, A. Mother Goose. OxNR; ReMoGo

Riddle a riddle as I suppose, A. Riddle. *Unknown.* FaBoVe

Riddle, A: "'Twas in heaven pronounced, and 'twas muttered in hell." Catherine Maria Fanshawe. NOBRP; OxBEV

Riddle, A: "Upon a bed of humble clay." Thomas Parnell. ECEV

Riddle, A: "Yon laddie wi' the gowdan pow." William Soutar. OxBS

Riddle: "As I went down that yella bank." *Unknown.* FaBoVe

Riddle: "As I went through a guttery gap / I met a wee man with a red cap." *Unknown.* FaBoVe

Riddle: "As I went through yon guttery gap / I met my Uncle Davy." *Unknown.* FaBoVe

Riddle: "Black'm saut'm rough'm glower'm saw." *Unknown.* FaBoVe

Riddle: "Chip chip cherry." *Unknown.* FaBoVe

Riddle: Cuckoo. Cynewulf. ASW; AnOE *Fr.* Riddles (Exeter Book).

Riddle: "Cuckoo and the gowk, the." *Unknown.* FaBoVe

Riddle cum diddle cum dido. Kindness to Animals. Laura Elizabeth Richards. NTCP

Riddle: "From Belsen a crate of gold teeth." William Heyen. HP; SoSe-8

Riddle: "He went to the wood and caught it." *Unknown.* OxNR

Riddle: "Hickamore hackamore." *Unknown.* FaBoVe

Riddle: "High as the sky it flies." *Unknown.* FaBoVe

Riddle: "Highty, tighty, paradighty, clothed [all] in green." *Unknown.* OxNR

Riddle: "Hopper o'ditches, A." *Unknown.* FaBoVe

Riddle: "House full, [a] yard full, [A]." *Unknown.* LB; NTCP

Riddle: "I'm a strange creature, for I satisfy women." Cynewulf. ASW, *tr. by* Kevin Crossley-Holland *Fr.* Riddles (Exeter Book).

Riddle in the Garden. Robert Penn Warren. NoAM

Riddle: "Invisible, chimerical." Daryl Hine. NoP-4

Riddle: "It has a head like a cat, feet like a cat." *Unknown.* NTCP

Riddle: "Land was white, The." *Unknown.* FaBoVe; OxNR

Riddle: "Little trotty hetty coat." *Unknown.* FaBoVe

Riddle: "Lives in winter." *Unknown.* NTCP
(Icicles, An.) ReMoGo

Riddle: "Long slick black feller." *Unknown.* FaBoVe

Riddle-Me-Ree. Liz Lochhead. OPOU

Riddle me, riddle me ree. Mother Goose. OxNR

Riddle: "No more, no more, / We are already pined [pin'd]." Alexander Brome. NOSC

Riddle of Noah, The. Maxine W. Kumin. OPRER

Riddle: On a Kiss, A. William Strode. NOSC

Riddle: "Riddle a riddle as I suppose, A." *Unknown.* FaBoVe

Riddle: "Riddlum riddlum ranty pole." *Unknown.* FaBoVe

Riddle: "Round the round and round the house / and there lies a black glove in the window." *Unknown.* FaBoVe

Riddle: "Round the house and round the house / and there lies a white glove in the window." *Unknown.* FaBoVe

Riddle: "Shoemaker makes shoes without leather, A." *Unknown.* OxNR

Riddle silently sees its image. It spins evening, The. Dusk in the Country. Harry Edmund Martinson. RB, *tr. by* Robert Bly

Riddle: "Their tongues are knives, their forks are hands and feet." Adrian Mitchell. FaBoEE; OxBSP

Riddle: "Two legs sat upon three legs." Mother Goose. LB; NTCP; OxNR

Riddle we can guess, The. Emily Dickinson. SAmP

Riddle: "White bird featherless." *Unknown.* FaBoVe; OxBEV; OxNR

Riddle: "White sheep, white sheep, on a blue hill." *Unknown.* FaBoVe

Riddle: "Wooden belly iron back." *Unknown.* FaBoVe

Riddles. Ilya Abu Madi. GraLe, *tr. by* Andrew Ghareeb

Riddles. *Unknown.* NoP-4

Riddles (Exeter Book). Cynewulf.
"Anchor: I must fight with the waves whipped up by the wind." ASW

Anchor: "Oft I must strive with wind and wave" AnOE, *tr. by* Charles W. Kennedy

"At times I resort, beyond man's discerning." AnOE

"Bellows: O wise man, weigh your words." ASW

"Book: Enemey ended my life, deprived me, An." ASW

Book Moth: "Moth ate a word. To me it seemed, A." AnOE

("Bookmoth: A moth devoured words. When I heard.") ASW, *tr. by* Kevin Crossley-Holland

Bookworm. WoPoe, *tr. by* Edwin Morgan

"Bread: I'm told a certain object grows." ASW

"Chalice: I heard a radiant ring, with no tongue." ASW

("Churning (or lovemaking): Young man made for the corner, A.") ASW, *tr. by* Kevin Crossley-Holland

"Clothes make no sound when I tread ground." RB; WoPoe, *tr. by* Geoffrey Grigson

"Coat-of-Mail: Dank earth, wondrously cold, The." ASW

"Cock and Hen: I watched a couple of curious creatures." ASW

"Creation: Enduring the Creator, He who now guides." ASW

"Cuckoo: In former days my father and mother [*or* mother and father]." ASW; AnOE

"Fire: On earth there's a warrior of curious origin." ASW

Fish in River: "My house is not quiet, I am not loud." AnOE, *tr. by* Charles W. Kennedy

Honey-Mead: "I am valued by men, fetched from afar." AnOE, *tr. by* Charles W. Kennedy

"Horn: I'm loved by my lord, and his shoulder." ASW

Horn: "Time was when I was weapon and warrior." AnOE, *tr. by* Charles W. Kennedy

"House Martins: This wind wafts little creatures." ASW

"I am valued by men, fetched from afar." AnOE, *tr. by* Charles W. Kennedy

"I'm a strange creature, for I satisfy women." ASW, *tr. by* Kevin Crossley-Holland

"I puff my breast out, my neck swells." RB

"I saw a strange creature." ASW; WoPoe, *tr. by* Kevin Crossley-Holland

"Ice: On the way a miracle: water become bone." ASW

"Iceberg: Curious, fair creature came floating on the waves, A." ASW

"Jay: I've one mouth but many voices." ASW

"Leather: I travel by foot, trample the ground." ASW

"Lonely wanderer, wounded with iron, A." AnOE, *tr. by* Charles W. Kennedy

"Lot and his two daughters and their sons: Man sat sozzled with his two wives, A." ASW

"Meal of words made by a moth, A." WoPoe, *tr. by* Edwin Morgan

"Moth ate a word. To me it seemed, A." AnOE

"Moth, I thought, munching a word, A." OPOU, *tr. by* Gerard Benson

"My attire is noiseless when I tread the earth." AnOE, *tr. by* Charles W. Kennedy

"My beak is bent downward, I burrow below." AnOE

"My house is not quiet, I am not loud." AnOE, *tr. by* Charles W. Kennedy

"Oft I must strive with wind and wave." AnOE, *tr. by* Charles W. Kennedy

Old English Riddle. OPOU, *tr. by* Gerard Benson

"One-Eyed Seller of Arrows: Creature came shuffling where there sat, A." ASW

Onion. WoPoe, *tr. by* Lewis Turco

"Oyster: Deep sea suckled me, the waves sounded over me." ASW

"Pen and four fingers: I watched four fair creatures." ASW

"Plough: I keep my snout to the ground; I burrow." ASW

Plow: "My beak is bent downward, I burrow below" AnOE

"Reed: I sank roots first of all, stood." ASW

Riddle: Cuckoo. ASW; AnOE

Riddle: "I'm a strange creature, for I satisfy women." ASW, *tr. by* Kevin Crossley-Holland

"Shield: I'm by nature solitary, scarred by spear." ASW

Shield: "Lonely wanderer, wounded with iron, A." AnOE, *tr. by* Charles W. Kennedy

"Soul and Body: I've heard tell of a noble guest." ASW

"Storm at Sea: Sometimes I plunge through the press of waves." ASW

"Strange thing hangs by man's hip, A." PeLV, *tr. by* Kevin Crossley-Holland

Sun and Moon. ASW; WoPoe, *tr. by* Kevin Crossley-Holland

"Swan: Silent is my dress when I step across the earth." ASW, *tr. by* Kevin Crossley-Holland

Swan, The. RB; WoPoe, *tr. by* Geoffrey Grigson

Swan, The: "Silent is my dress when I step across the earth." ASW, *tr. by* Kevin Crossley-Holland

"This knave came in where he knew she'd be." EroLit, *tr. by* Michael Alexander

Three Riddles from *The Exeter Book.* PeLV, *tr. by* Kevin Crossley-Holland

"Time was when I was weapon and warrior." AnOE, *tr. by* Charles W. Kennedy

("Weathercock: My breast is puffed up and my neck is swollen.") ASW, *tr. by* Kevin Crossley-Holland

Weathercock, The: "I puff my breast out, my neck swells." RB

Wild Swan: "My attire is noiseless when I tread the earth." AnOE, *tr. by* Charles W. Kennedy

Wind: "At times I resort, beyond man's discerning." AnOE

"World's wonder, I liven wenches, The." WoPoe, *tr. by* Lewis Turco

"Young man made for the corner, A." PeLV, *tr. by* Kevin Crossley-Holland

Riddles Wisely Expounded. *Unknown.* ESPB

(Jennifer Gentle and Rosemary.) OxBoLi

Riddling Knight, The. *Unknown.* FaBoCh

"Riddling world, A!" one cried. Two Questions, The. Alice Thompson Meynell. WPE

Riddlum riddlum ranty pole. Riddle. *Unknown.* FaBoVe

Riddym Ravings (The Mad Woman's Poem). Jean Binta Breeze. WaCA

Ride. Josephine Miles. FaBoWP

Ride, The. Lucinda Roy. GT

Ride a cock-horse [*or* a-cock horse] to Banbury Cross, / To see a fine lady upon a white horse. Mother Goose. OxBoLi; OxNR

Ride a cock-horse to Banbury Cross. *Unknown.* OxBEV

Ride a cock-horse to Banbury Cross / To buy little Johnny a galloping horse. *Unknown.* OxNR

Ride a cock-horse to Banbury Cross / To see what Tommy can buy. *Unknown.* OxNR

Ride away, ride away / Johnny shall ride. Mother Goose. OxNR; ReMoGo

Ride-by-Nights, The. Walter De la Mare. ChAP

Ride Fortune's chariot with care and doubt. Fickle Fortune. Ferenc Faludi. IQMS, *tr. by* Watson Kirkconnell and John Gordon Nichols

Ride out against the horizon and the orange sun! (LL) Feminine Intuition. Stephanie Brown. AmPoNex; NoPo

Ride, ride together, for ever ride? (LL) Last Ride Together, The. Robert Browning. BoLoP; EroLit; FHYEP; ITBLP; NAEL-5v2; NAEL-6v2; OBEV; UnPo

Ride round the Parapet, The. Friedrich Rückert. AWP, *tr. by* James Clarence Mangan

Ride the Turtle's Back. Beth Brant. ItWoWo

Ride upon the Death Chariot. Mbuyiseni Oswald Mtshali. PBMAP

Rider. Mark Rudman.

   "What about that girl in first grade? The one who hopped up on her desk." TaR

Rider, The. Sarah Manguso. BAP-01

Rider and horse,—friend, foe,—in one red burial blent! (LL) Byron. NAEL-5v2; NAEL-6v2 *Fr.* Childe Harold's Pilgrimage.

Rider in stone, A. To the Gods the Shades Flavinus of the Cavalry Regiment. David Wright. NLP

Riders, The. Ann Stanford. WPE

Riders Held Back, The. Louis Simpson. CoAmPo

Ridge, The. John Cowper Powys.

   "Aye! What a thing is the passing of Cronos, the angular-minded." OBWVE

Ridiculous dreamer. Events Like Palaces. Paz Molina. TANSG, *tr. by* Steven F. White

Ridiculous / How the space between three violins. Cantata. Jack Spicer. APSN

Ridiculous shack of frost is slush, faded, The. March Elegy. Arkadii Dragomoschenko. ItGoST, *tr. by* Elena Balashova and Lyn Hejinian

Ridin' High. Cole Porter. ReLy

Riding. Buson. EH, *tr. by* Robert Hass

Riding a Boat on Wu-ling Stream. Tao-chi. CoBLCP, *tr. by* Jonathan Chaves

Riding a One-eyed Horse. Henry Taylor. HeIP-4; InPK-6

Riding Across John Lee's Finger. Stanley Crouch. GT

Riding across the town in a dirty carriage. Riding Over Belmore Park. Robert Harris. BMAP

Riding at dawn, riding alone. Gillespie. Sir Henry John Newbolt. PeVV

Riding backwards this wooden horse. Kukoku. ZenPo, *tr. by* Takashi Ikemoto and Lucien Stryk

Riding high into the night. Gas. Gerry Gordon. MiVo

Riding into California. Shirley Lim. GeoHom

Riding Lesson. Henry Taylor. NBLV

Riding on a Streetcar with My Father. Mary Ann Larkin. AiP

Riding on the Coast Starlight. Ursula K. Le Guin. PoCoUp

Riding Out at Evening. Linda McCarriston. BBASP

Riding Over Belmore Park. Robert Harris. BMAP

Riding silk, adrift at noon. Basil Bunting. WoPoe *Fr.* Briggflatts [An Autobiography].

Riding the "A." May Swenson. APT-2; GM

Riding the black express from heaven to hell. Lucifer in the Train. Adrienne Rich. GM

Riding the blue sapphire mountains. Mahadevi. BoWoP

Riding the Empire Builder, 1948. David Wojahn. GM

Riding the Lion, Riding the Lamb. Karen Chamberlain. GeoH

Riding the North Point Ferry. Wing Tek Lum. OpBo

Riding the Rock Island Through Kansas. Dave Etter. GM

Riding the wide leaf. Kikaku. SoOfWa, *tr. by* Sam Hamill

Riding through life. (LL) Poem of Alienation. Antonio Jacinto. PBMAP; PeSAV, *tr. by* Michael Wolfers

Riding Together. William Morris. NOBE

Riding Westward. John Balaban. GifTon

Rifacimento. Paul Violi. PmAP

Riffing. Rick Barot. NeAmPo

Rifle, The. Tymoteusz Karpowicz. PoSu, *tr. by* Jan Darowski

Rifled honeycomb, The. John Montague. CIP-2; ModIr *Fr.* Cave of Night, The.

Rig Veda. *Unknown. Fr.* Vedic Hymns.

Rigadoon, rigadoon, now let him fly. *Unknown.* OxNR

Rigamarole. William Carlos Williams. APT-1

Rigby. Mark Todd. GeoH

Right after her birth, they crowded in. Anaesthesia. Jean Valentine. TAP

Right among the people coming and going. Lodging House in Town, A. Muso Soseki. EaWin, *tr. by* W. S. Merwin

Right Arm, The. Paul Muldoon. NoAM

"Right as a Ribstone Pippin!" But it lied. (LL) False Heart, The. Joseph Hilaire Pierre Belloc. FaBoCh; FaBoEE; OxBSP

Right at the end of night. Philippe Jaccottet. VCWP, *tr. by* Derek Mahon

Right back on in. (LL) My Mama Moved among the Days. Lucille Clifton. BlSi; ItWoWo

Right best beloved and most in assurance. *Unknown.* EMWP

Right Cross, The. Philip Levine. MoASP

Right down the shocked street with a siren-blast. Fire-Truck, A. Richard Wilbur. AiP

Right from the ambiguous start. D-Zug. Julian Croft. NOBAu

Right from the start I have stood on my own feet. I Have Done My Reckoning. Attila József. IQMS, *tr. by* Michael Hatwell

Right from the start I knew I'd follow you like a grenadier his banner. To a

Dead Lady. Antonio Cisneros. TCLAP, *tr.* by Maureen Ahern and David Tipton

Right Hand, The. Robert Herrick. CavPo

Right here I was nearly killed one night in February. Solitude. Tomas Tranströmer. RB, *tr.* by Robert Bly

Right here the other night something. E. E. Cummings. NoAM

Right here with the others. (LL) Language of the Brag, The. Sharon Olds. MakPoe; PBCAP

Right in the middle. Arizona Zipper. HA

Right in the Trail. Gary Snyder. PmAP

Right Kind of People, The. Edwin Markham. PoToHe

Right Meaning, The. César Vallejo. RaBo, *tr.* by Robert Bly

Right Must Win, The. Frederick William Faber. PWR

Right now I am the flower girl. Flowers. Margaret Atwood. NoP-4

Right now my love for you is a baby elephant. Baby Elephant, A. Nikolai Stepanovich Gumilyov [*or* Gumiliov *or* Gumilev]. TCRusP, *tr.* by Carl R. Proffer

Right now two black people sit in a jury room. Affirmative Action Blues (1993). Elizabeth Alexander. ExTi

Right of Way. Barry Sternlieb. GM

Right of Way, The. William Carlos Williams. APT-1

Right-of-Way: 1865, A. William Plomer. PeLV

Right On: White America. Sonia Sanchez. ISC

Right or ruth. Susan Howe. PmAP *Fr.* Speeches at the Barriers.

Rt. Rev. Richard Allen. Josephine D. Henderson Heard. CBWP-4

Right Thing, The. Theodore Roethke. PeECV

Right to Be. Eva Johnson. IBA

Right to Grief, The. Carl Sandburg. IllVoic

Right to Love, The. Gene Lees. ReLy

Right to the end you never got it straight. Mother's Room. Nicky Rice. Prnts

Right under their noses, the green. Dusk of Horses, The. James Dickey. ColAP

Right Use of Prayer, The. Sir Aubrey De Vere. SacPr

Right waves gather, The. (LL) From the Wave. Thom Gunn. NAEL-5v2; NAEL-6v2; NoP-4

Right well I know thou'rt Alighieri's son. Forese Donati. EaItPo, *tr.* by Dante Gabriel Rossetti

Right well I w[r]ote most mighty Soueraine [*or* soveraine]. Edmund Spenser. NoSic *Fr.* Faerie Queene, The.

Right words elude me, The. Love. Joan Gordon. Prnts

Righteous Anger. James Stephens. *See* Glass of Beer, A

Righteous Man, The. Samuel Butler (1835–1902). OBSV

Rightful One, The. David Ignatow. TaR

Rights of Way. Thomas Reiter. GM

Rights of Woman, The. Anna Laetitia Barbauld. CABP; ECWP; NAEL-6v2; NOEC; NoP-4; PEW; WoRP

Rigid Body Sings. James Clerk Maxwell. UV

Rigoletto. Newman Levy. OBAL

Rigor of beauty is the quest. But how will you find beauty when it is locked. William Carlos Williams. NoAM *Fr.* Paterson.

Rilke's Letter from Rome. Star Black. KGB

Rill of the House of the Luans. Wang Wei. ChinPo, *tr.* by Yip Wai-lim

Rillons, Rillettes. Richard Wilbur. OBCoV

Rillons, Rillettes, they taste the same. Rillons, Rillettes. Richard Wilbur. OBCoV

Rilly, / im a brown man. Not no socialism/communism classical, but some power to the people jazz. Daniel Gray-Kontar. SpirFl

Rimbaud and Verlaine, precious pair of poets. Conrad Potter Aiken. FaBoMo; NoAM; TwCP *Fr.* Preludes for Memnon; *or*, Preludes to Attitude.

Rimbaud Having a Bath. Robert Adamson. BMAP

Rime of the Ancient Feminist, The. Stephanie Markman. BrRo
  "They lived out in a women's house."

Rime of the Ancient Mariner, The. Samuel Taylor Coleridge. CABP; EBEV; EBNV; FHYEP; FaBoCh; HAP; HeIP-4; NAEL-6v2; NOBE; NoP-4; OBEV; OBNV; OxAEP-2; OxBEV; PeECV; PoE; PoPoPo; SCGP; TFi; TOF
  "And now the Storm-blast came, and he." OWoS
  "I fear thee, ancient Mariner!" NPeEn
  "It is an ancient Mariner." AmFaPo
  ("It is an ancyent Marinere.") NPeEn

Rime of the Ancyent Marinere, In Seven Parts, The. Samuel Taylor Coleridge. *See* Rime of the Ancient Mariner, The

Rime of the Auncient Waggonere, The. William Maginn. ClHu

Rime, the rack of finest wits. Ben Jonson.
  See Rhyme [*or* Rime], the rack of finest wits

Rimer. Ambrose Bierce. APN-2 *Fr.* Devil's Dictionary, The.

Rimer quenches his unheeded fires, The. Ambrose Bierce. APN-2 *Fr.* Devil's Dictionary, The.

Rimrock, Where It Is. Hayden Carruth. NNaP

Rims of Distinction: I. Allen Fisher. Oth *Fr.* Stepping Out.

Rin and rout, rin and rout. Deevil's Waltz, The. Sydney Goodsir Smith. FaBoTw

Rincón. Sandra M. Castillo. TouFir

Ring-a-ring o' roses. Mother Goose. LB; OxNR; ReMoGo

Ring and the Book, The. Robert Browning.
  "Do you see this square old yellow Book, I toss." FaBoVe

Ring in the Christ that is to be. (LL) Tennyson. ChrPo; EBVV; FHYEP; NAEL-6v2; NAWM-7v2; OxAEP-2; PeECV; TreFP *Fr.* In Memoriam A. H. H.

Ring into golden bowls. (LL) Opium Fantasy, An. Maria White Lowell. APN-2; InPK-6

Ring, joyous chords!—ring out again! Revellers, The. Felicia Dorothea Hemans. TreFP

Ring of, The. Charles Olson. NOBA; VGW

Ring of Irony, The. Diane Wakoski. NIL-7

Ring of the moon, starshine, swept away as I watch. Traveler's Thoughts. Tu Hsün-ho. CoBCP, *tr.* by Burton Watson

Ring on the Finger. Harold Rome. ReLy

Ring out the silence I am nourished by. (LL) Allen Tate. ChrPo; NAAL-2v2; Son *Fr.* Sonnets at Christmas.

Ring Out, Wild Bells. Tennyson. ChrPo; EBVV; FHYEP; NAEL-6v2; NAWM-7v2; OxAEP-2; PeECV; TreFP *Fr.* In Memoriam A. H. H.

Ring out, wild bells, to the wild sky. Tennyson. ChrPo; EBVV; FHYEP; NAEL-6v2; NAWM-7v2; OxAEP-2; PeECV; TreFP *Fr.* In Memoriam A. H. H.

Ring Out Your Bells. Sir Philip Sidney. *See* Dirge

Ring out your bells [*or* belles], let mourning shows [*or* shewes] be spread. Dirge: "Ring out your bells [*or* belles], let mourning shows [*or* shewes] be spread." Sir Philip Sidney. NoSic

Ring Presented to Julia, A. Robert Herrick. PeLV

Ring ring ring ring ring!/ Catholic bells—! (LL) Catholic Bells, The. William Carlos Williams. NOBA; OxBA; SAmP

Ring so worn as you behold, The. Marriage Ring, The. George Crabbe. BoLoP; EnLoPo; OBEV; OxBEV

Ring Sonnet. Betty Scott Stam. SacPr

Ring That Controlled Erections, The. *Unknown.* NAWM-7v1, *tr.* by Ned Dubin

Ring the bells, ring! Dunce, The. *Unknown.* OxNR

Ringed Plover by a Water's Edge. Norman MacCaig. NoP-4; OxBC

Ringing out from our blue heavens. Journey. Breyten Breytenbach. AF, *tr.* by Denis Hirson

Ringing phone and a hushed voice, A. Prayer for the Living, A. Asha Bandele. InTrad

Ringing the Bells. Anne Sexton. HCAP; PoE; TAP; VGW

Ringing tire iron, A. Some Good Things to Be Said for the Iron Age. Gary Snyder. TTTS

Ringing Words. Mary Kinzie. FFC

Ringless. Diane Wakoski. NALW

Ringlety-jing! Nonsense Rhyme, A. James Whitcomb Riley. NOxBChV

Ringmaster's Wife. Fatima Lim-Wilson. ReBoTo

Rings. Joan Michelson. Prnts *Fr.* Departures.

Rings on a stump, The. Wood. Novella Nikolaevna Matveyeva [*or* Matveieva]. TCRP, *tr.* by Deming Brown

Ringsend. Oliver St. John Gogarty. OBMV; OxBTC

Rinsing the choked mud, keeping the colours new. (LL) In Carrowdore Churchyard. Derek Mahon. CIP-2; NoP-4; PBCIP; PNI

Riot. Gwendolyn Brooks. BPo; NAAAL; NALW; NBV; SSLK; TAP

Riot, A. Mrs. Henry Linden. CBWP-4

Riot Act, April 29, 1992. Ai. ESEAA; NIL-7

Riot at Winchell's. Bruce Jackson. AmPoNex

Riot in the lute song's propinquity. Propose to be guided by the. Pieces O'six—XXIV. Jackson Mac Low. FTOS

Riot of forsythia, a six-pack, A. Vandals in the Garden. Alan Michael Parker. NAPBL

Riot; or, Half a Loaf Is Better than No Bread, The. Hannah More. NOEC
  (Riot; or Half a Loaf is Better than No Bread In a Dialogue between Jack Anvil and Tom Hod, The.) PEW

Riot; or Half a Loaf is Better than No Bread In a Dialogue between Jack Anvil and Tom Hod, The. Hannah More. *See* Riot; or, Half a Loaf Is Better than No Bread, The

Rioupéroux. James Elroy Flecker. OBEV

Ripe, Being Plunged into Fire. Friedrich Hölderlin. OBVE, *tr.* by James Blair Leishman

Ripe cherries and ripe maidens. Cherries. Zalman Schneour. TrJP, *tr.* by Joseph Leftwich

Ripe Plums. *Unknown.* TAL

Ripe plums are dropping. Ripe Plums. *Unknown.* TAL

Ripeness is all; her in her cooling planet. To an Old Lady. William Empson. FaBoTw; GTBS-P; NOBE; NoAM; OxAEP-2; OxBEV

Ripeness Is Rapid. Rosalie Moore. YaYoPo

Ripeness is rapid as plum-drop, as invader. Ripeness Is Rapid. Rosalie Moore. YaYoPo

Ripening. Wendell Berry. RaBo

Ripperty! Kye! Ahoo! Henry Lawson. CBAP

Ripple-topped stream in its best suit, in the ground. (LL) Mi Abuelo. Alberto A. Ríos. NIL-7; PoPoPo

Rippled nut, The. Empty Walnut, The. Gabriela Mistral. TANSG, *tr. by* Maria Jacketti

Ripples lap the sand on the beach of Parrot Isle. Tune: "Ripples Sifting Sand." Liu Yu Hsi. SuSp, *tr. by* Daniel Bryant

Rippling hospital sheets. Grandmother: Crossing Jordan. Melvin Dixon. ESEAA

Rippling in the ocean of that darkening room. Woman at the Piano. Marya Alexandrovna Zaturenska. MoAmPo

Riprap. Gary Snyder. HCAP; NAAL-2v2; NAAL-5; NOBA; NeAP; NoAM; PmAP; PoM; PoPoPo; VCAP

Rise. Brenda Shaughnessy. AmPoNex

Rise and deride this sepulchre of crime. (LL) On Passing the New Menin Gate. Siegfried Sassoon. NAEL-5v2; NAEL-6v2; NoAM; NoP-4; OBMV; PoWW; Son

Rise and fall like waves. I regret nothing. (LL) Portrait of the Artist as an Old Man. Michael Dransfield. BMAP; CBAP

Rise and hold up the curved glass. *Var. authors.* AWP, *tr. by* E. Powys Mathers *Fr.* Mu'allaqat, The.

Rise and Progress of the Present Taste in Planning Parks, Pleasure Grounds, Gardens, etc, The. *Unknown.*

"O study Nature! and with thought profound." OBGa

Rise, blossom of the spring. To a Lady on the Rise of Morn. Anne Batten Cristall. RWP

Rise, crowned with light, imperial Salem, rise! Pope. SacPr *Fr.* Messiah [a Sacred Eclogue, in Imitation of Virgil's Pollio].

Rise from the wrist, o kestrel. Sonnets for the Novachord. "Ern Malley." BMAP

Rise from Your Bed of Languor. Stevie Smith. BWW

Rise from your virgin sheets, that be. Epithalamium: To Mistress M. A. Martin Lluellyn [*or* Lluelyn]. NOSC

Rise heart; thy Lord is risen. Sing his praise. Easter. George Herbert. ESCV; GeHe; NAEL-5v1; NAEL-6v1; NOSC; PeECV; TrCP

Rise, let us go. Fujo. JDP, *tr. by* Yoel Hoffmann

Rise, mighty nation, in thy strength. On the Expected General Rising of the French Nation. Anna Laetitia Barbauld. ECWP

Rise odors of ploughed field or flowery mead. (LL) Chaucer. Henry Wadsworth Longfellow. APN-1; AWP; HeIP-4; NOBA; OBEV; OxBA; PoE; PoRA; Son; TAP; TCAPo; TFi; WoPoe

Rise Oedipus, and if thou canst unfold. Poem, The. Thomas Morton. NAAL-3; SCAP

Rise of capitalism parallels the advance of romanticism, The. Definition of Blue. John Ashbery. NAAL-2v2

Rise of the Afternoon is a Wide Glory, The. Jeannette Miller. TANSG, *tr. by* Paula Vega

Rise, shining martyrs. With Meaning. John Weiners. BB

Rise up, brother, be born with me. Pablo Neruda. TCLAP, *tr. by* David Young *Fr.* Heights of Macchu Picchu, The.

Rise up, Magyar, the country calls! National Song. Sándor Petőfi. IQMS, *tr. by* Adam Makkai

Rise Up, O Men of God. William Pierson Merrill. AH

Rise up, Oh, Tihany's clamorous daughter. To the Echo of Tihany. Mihály Csokonai Vitéz. IQMS, *tr. by* Adam Makkai

Rise up, rise up, / And, as the trumpet blowing. Trumpet, The. Edward Thomas. MoBrPo

Rise up, thou monstrous ant-hill on the plain. William Wordsworth. HAP *Fr.* Prelude, The; Growth of a Poet's Mind [1850 vers.].

Rise winds of night! Relentless tempests rise! Part of an Irregular Fragment, Found in a Dark Passage of the Tower. Helen Maria Williams. RWP

Rise, Ye Children. Justus Falckner. AH, *tr. by* Emma Frances Bevan

Risen from rented rooms, old ghosts. Winter Ode to the Old Men of Lummus Park, Miami, Florida, A. Donald Justice. WeW-3

Risen from the artificial lake. Porcelain Pavilion, The. Nikolai Stepanovich Gumilyov [*or* Gumiliov *or* Gumilev]. TCRusP, *tr. by* Mary Jane White

Risen in a / welter of waters. Birth of Venus, The. Muriel Rukeyser. NALW

Rises at five, just when a late moon. Insomniac Sleeps Well for Once and, The. Hayden Carruth. NNaP

Rises toward her day after day, like a terrible fish. (LL) Mirror. Sylvia Plath. FaBoWP; HAP; NIL-7; NIP-4; PAI

Risest thou thus, dim dawn, again. Tennyson. NAEL-6v2; PeECV *Fr.* In Memoriam A. H. H.

Risest thou thus, dim dawn, again. Tennyson. EBVV; NAEL-6v2 *Fr.* In Memoriam A. H. H.

Rising, The. Jayne Cortez. NBV

Rising Asleep. Penelope Rosemont. SurWo

Rising deluge he descried, The. Vision of Noah, The. May Kendall. VWP

Rising Drunk on a Spring Day. Li Po. CrYelRi, *tr. by* Sam Hamill

Rising Early in the Morning. Chao Yi. SuSp, *tr. by* Chang Yin-nan

Rising from Sleep. Wang Chiu-ssu. CoBLCP, *tr. by* Jonathan Chaves

Rising Glory of America, The. Hugh Henry Brackenridge. AiP

Rising hills, the slopes, The. For the Children. Gary Snyder. PAI

Rising in the North, The. *Unknown.* ESPB

Rising in Winter. Hsiao Kang. OHMPC, *tr. by* Kenneth Rexroth

Rising Late, and Playing with A-ts'ui, Aged Two. Po Chü-i. ChiP, *tr. by* Arthur Waley

Rising moon revenges herself, The. Lunatics. Bella [*or* Izabella] Akhatovna Akhmadulina. TCRusP, *tr. by* Daniel Weissbort

Rising of the Session, The. Robert Fergusson. OxBS

Rising Spring Waters. Tu Fu. CrYelRi, *tr. by* Sam Hamill

Rising toward New England along the throughway. Summers of Vietnam. Mary Kinzie. IllVoic

Rising up in time, michael jordan hangs like an icon, suspended in space. Forty-one Seconds on a Sunday in June, in Salt Lake City, Utah. Quincy Troupe. MoASP

Rising Village, The. Oliver, the Younger Goldsmith.

Lonely Settler, The. NOBC

Risk, The. Anne Sexton. BoWoP

Risk is moral death each time we act, The. Some Girls. Susanne Doyle. FFC

Risk of Abstraction, The. Adriano Spatola. PFTM-2, *tr. by* Paul Vangelisti

Risk of Birth, The. Madeleine L'Engle. SacPr

Risks. Malcolm Glass. SpudSo

Rispond Miser, The. Robert MacKay (Macaoidh, Rob Donn). NePenScot, *tr. by* Derick Thomson

Rite of Spring. Seamus Heaney. OxBC

Rites. Edward Kamau Brathwaite.

"Look wha' happen las' week at de Oval!" FaBoVe

Rites for Cousin Vit, The. Gwendolyn Brooks. BPo; HAP; NAAAL; NoP-4; WPE; WeW-3 *Fr.* Womanhood, The.

Rites of Manhood, The. Alden Nowlan. RaBo

Rites of Participation. Robert Duncan.

"Drama of our time is the coming of all men into one fate, The." PFTM-1

Ritual. Rosita Kalina. MirDau, *tr. by* Roberta Gordenstein

Ritual done, sterile as Pilate. Contact. Alison Chisholm. Prnts

Ritual Girl. Frank Mkalawile Chipasula. HBAPE

Ritual Murder. Aig Higo. PBMAP

Ritual of Departure. Thomas Kinsella. CIP-2

Ritual Three. David Ignatow. CoAmPo

Ritual to Read to Each Other, A. William Stafford. RaBo

Rituals, Yours—and Mine. Kimberly M. Blaeser. ReEnLa

Rival, A. Rachel Wetzsteon. NeAmPo

Rival, The. Sylvia Plath. PAI

Rival, The. Sylvia Townsend Warner. MoBrPo

Rival Curates, The. Sir William Schwenck Gilbert. PeLV

Rival Queens; or, Alexander the Great, The. Nathaniel Lee.

"Nay, *Clytus*, you that cou'd advise—" FaBoWar

Rivals. William Walsh. OBEV

Rivals, The. James Stephens. OBEV; OBMV

Riven Quarry, The. Gloria C. Oden. GT

River. Ted Hughes. NAEL-5v2; NAEL-6v2; NoP-4

River. Shuntaro Tanikawa. VCWP, *tr. by* Harold Wright

River, The. Hart Crane. GM; MoAmPo; NAAL-5; NOBA; OxBA *Fr.* Bridge, The.

River, The. Jacques Prévert. MFP, *tr. by* Martin Sorrell

River, The. Patti Tana. PasH

River, The. *Unknown.* PWR

River, The. John Wills. HA

River Afram. Andrew Amankwa Opoku. PBA

River and Death, The. Badr Shakir Al-Sayyab. PFTM-2, *tr. by* Pierre Joris

River and Fountain. Michael Longley. ModIr

River bank is white like silver, The. On the Willow Bank. Yen Chen. WoPoe, *tr. by* Arthur Sze

River bank—the evening tides have started to ebb. On the Fifteenth Day of the Ninth Month of the Year Kuei-mao of the Chih-cheng Period (Oct. 22, 1363), I Painted This to Send to the Summoned Scholar, Sheng-po, and Inscribed This Poem on It. Ni Tsan. CoBLCP, *tr. by* Jonathan Chaves

River Bend. Judith Wright. BMAP

River Bidgee. Iris Clayton. IBA

River brought down, The. How We Heard the Name. Alan Dugan. CoAP; NoAM; YaYoPo

River called the Snake, A. Blueprint for Disaster. Christian Morgenstern. WoPoe, *tr. by* David R. Slavitt

River Crossing, The. Denis Glover. PeNZ *Fr.* Arawata Bill.

River Darkens on an Autumn Night, The. Yi Jung. WoPoe, *tr. by* Virginia Olsen Baron and Chung Seuk Park

River Dove: a Lyric Pastoral, The. Samuel Bently. VerBaPo

River drops from Dragon Gate, The. Descending Through Dragon Gate. Tu Fu. CrYelRi, *tr. by* Sam Hamill

River Duddon [A Series of Sonnets], The. William Wordsworth.

After-Thought. CenSon

American Tradition. CenSon

"But here no cannon thunders to the gale." CenSon

Change Me, Some God, Into That Breathing Rose! CenSon; Son

"Child of the clouds! remote from every taint." CenSon

Conclusion: "But here no cannon thunders to the gale." CenSon

"Dark plume fetch me from yon blasted yew, A." CenSon; HAP

"Ere yet our course was graced with social trees." CenSon

Faery Chasm, The. CenSon; OxBSo

Flowers. CenSon

"From this deep chasm, where quivering sunbeams play." CenSon

"Hail to the fields—with Dwellings sprinkled o'er." CenSon

"How shall I paint thee?—Be this naked stone." CenSon

"I rose while yet the cattle, heat-opprest [*or* oppressed]." CenSon

"I thought of Thee, my partner and my guide." CenSon

Journey Renewed. CenSon

"KIRK OF ULPHA to the pilgrim's eye, The." CenSon

("Leave them—and, if thou canst, without regret!") (LL) CenSon

"Love-lorn Maid, at some far distant time, A." CenSon

"Methinks 'twere no unprecedented feat." CenSon

"Mid-noon is past;—upon the sultry mead." CenSon

"My frame hath often trembled with delight." CenSon

"No fiction was it of the antique age." CenSon; OxBSo

"No record tells of lance opposed to lance." CenSon

("Not envying shades which haply yet may throw.") CenSon

"Not hurled precipitous from steep to steep." CenSon

"Not so that Pair whose youthful spirits dance." CenSon

"O mountain Stream! the Shepherd and his Cot." CenSon

"Old inventive Poets, had they seen, The." CenSon

Open Prospect. CenSon

Plain of Donnerdale, The. CenSon

Resting-Place, The. CenSon

Return. CenSon; HAP

"Return, Content! for fondly I pursued." CenSon

"Sacred Religion! 'mother of form and fear.'" CenSon

("Sad thoughts, avaunt!—the fervor of the year.") CenSon

Same Subject, The. CenSon

Seathwaite Chapel. CenSon

"Sole listener, Duddon! to the breeze that played." CenSon

Stepping-Stones, The. CenSon

"Struggling Rill insensibly is grown, The." CenSon

"Such fruitless questions may not long beguile." CenSon

"Take, cradled Nursling of the mountains, take." CenSon

Tradition. CenSon

Tributary Stream. CenSon

(Valediction to the River Duddon.) NOBE

(Valedictory Sonnet to the River Duddon.) OBEV

"What aspect bore the Man who roved or fled." CenSon

"Whence that low voice?—A whisper from the heart." CenSon

"Who swerves from innocence, who makes divorce." CenSon

River flows to the East, The. Red Cliff, The. Su Tung-p'o (Su Shih). OHPC, *tr. by* Kenneth Rexroth

River Flute. Po Chü-i. CrYelRi, *tr. by* Sam Hamill

River-Fog. Kiyowara Fukuyabu. AWP, *tr. by* Arthur Waley

River-Fog. *Var. authors.* AWP *Fr.* Shui Shu.

River God, The. Sacheverell Sitwell. MoBrPo

River God, The. Stevie Smith. BrRo; FaBoTw; FaBoWP

River[-]God's Song, The. John Fletcher. NOSC *Fr.* Faithful Shepherdess, The.

River Guadalquivir, The. Little Ballad of the Three Rivers. Federico García Lorca. BLPSL, *tr. by* Rene de Costa, Rigas Kappatos and Eleni Paidoussi

River gulls bob and toss in reed-flower autumn. Song of the Clear River. Huang T'ing-chien. CoBCP, *tr. by* Burton Watson

River, I am passing. River Afram. Andrew Amankwa Opoku. PBA

River in its abundance, The. Eros at Temple Stream. Denise Levertov. NALW

River in March, The. Ted Hughes. OxBC

River in the Meadows, The. Léonie Adams. MoAmPo

River in the street!, A. Streets 2. Paul Verlaine. SxFrPo, *tr. by* Martin Sorrell

River inn spring hangover—half a day's delay. At Ta-an I Got Sick from Wine and Had to Lay Over for Half a Day. Governor Wang Invited Me to His Place Again. Lu Yu. ColAnChi, *tr. by* Burton Watson

River is calm, the moon reflected in its waters, The. Noble Scholar Playing the Lute, A. Yang Chi. CoBLCP, *tr. by* Jonathan Chaves

River is famous to the fish, The. Famous. Naomi Shihab Nye. LoL

River is largely implicit here, but part, The. Waterborne. Linda Gregerson. BAP-01

River is lined with the, The. At Ch'en Ch'u. Wang Shih-chieng. OHMPC, *tr. by* Kenneth Rexroth

River is rising, *Ngoho,* the river, The. In a Storm. Antoine-Roger Bolamba. NegPo, *tr. by* Ellen Conroy Kennedy

River is smooth and calm this evening, The. Spring River Flowers Moon Night. Emperor Yang of Sui. OHMPC, *tr. by* Kenneth Rexroth

River is so much mica, The. River; North of Guelph, The. Douglas G. Jones. NOBC

River Izumi, The. Fujiwara no Go-Kanesuke. OHPJ

River jordan run red. Emmett Till. Wanda Coleman. NAAAL

River Mang has always been clear—not a trace of mud, The. Recording a Weird Happening. Li K'ai-hsien. CoBLCP, *tr. by* Jonathan Chaves

River-Mates. Padraic Colum. AWP

River-Merchant's Wife: A Letter, The. Ezra Pound. ColAP

River-Merchant's Wife: A Letter, The. Ezra Pound. AmFaPo; HarvBoo; NAAL-5; NIL-7; NoP-4; PoPoPo; RACG; TCAPo

River-Merchant's Wife: A Letter, The. Rihaku. APT-1; NPeEn, *tr. by* Ezra Pound

River Merchant's Wife, The; a Letter. Li Po. AWP; BoLoP; ClHu; HAP; HeIP-4; InPK-6; MoAmPo; NAAL-2v2; NIP-4; NOBA; NOBE; NoAM; OBMV; OBVE; OxBA; RB; RaBo; TAP; TFi; TRP; TTTS; TwCP; UnPo; WeW-3, *tr. by* Ezra Pound

River-mirror mirrors the cold sky, The. Mists Over the River. William Carlos Williams. ColAP

River; North of Guelph, The. Douglas G. Jones. NOBC

River Now, The. Richard Hugo. VCAP

River of Bees, The. W. S. Merwin. HeIP-4; LCAP-2; VCAP

River of Bones and Flesh and Blood. Eugene B. Redmond. IllVoic

River of diaphanous waters, The. Blue River. Muhammad ibn Ghalib al-Rusafi. WoPoe, *tr. by* Cola Franzen

River of Heaven, The. *Var. authors.* AWP, *tr. by* Lafcadio Hearn *Fr.* Manyo Shu, Part 3 of 4.

River of Life, The. Thomas Campbell. GTBS-P

River of Rivers in Connecticut, The. Wallace Stevens. APT-1; FaBoA; HAP; HCAP; NOBA; VCAP

River of Seville. Seguidillas of the Guadalquivir River. Félix Lope de Vega Carpio. SpanPo, *tr. by* Denise Levertov

River of sudden, The. Waterfall. Gareth Owen. Spl

River of Time. River of Bones and Flesh and Blood. Eugene B. Redmond. IllVoic

River Path, The. John Greenleaf Whittier. TreFP

River Pavilion. Tu Fu. CrYelRi, *tr. by* Sam Hamill

River Road. Stanley Kunitz. NoAM

River Road Studio. Barbara Guest. PmAP; PoM

River Roads. Carl Sandburg. VGW

River's Answer, The. Ben Howard. PoCoUp

River's glint and mountain mist were floating in green. Composed on Horseback, Returning from Lakeview Pavilion at Hangchow, Presented to Yü-ju and Lo-tao. Wang An-shih. SuSp, *tr. by* Jan W. Walls

River's just beyond that hill, The. Tugela River. William Plomer. PeSAV

River's tent is broken: the last fingers of leaf, The. T. S. Eliot. HarvBoo *Fr.* Waste Land, The.

River's up two feet overnight, The. Rising Spring Waters. Tu Fu. CrYelRi, *tr. by* Sam Hamill

River Scamander Attacks Achilles. Homer. OBVE, *tr. by* Alexander Pope *Fr.* Iliad, The.

River seemed a broad stream, fenced with folk, The. János Arany. IQMS, *tr. by* Watson Kirkconnell *Fr.* Toldi.

River shaking in the sun, A. (LL) Windigo. Louise Erdrich. NoAM; PoPoPo

River Silence, The. Leonid Nikolaevich Martynov. TCRP, *tr. by* J. R. Rowland

River slopes, already into the midmonth of spring. On the Spur of the Moment. Tu Fu. CoBCP, *tr. by* Burton Watson

River Snow. Liu Tsung-yüan. ChinPo, *tr. by* Yip Wai-lim

River Snow. Liu Tsung-yüan. CoBCP, *tr. by* Burton Watson

River Snow. Gary Snyder. ColAnChi

River Song. Ben Howard. PoCoUp

River Song. Li Po. ChinPo, tr. by Yip Wai-lim

River Song. Roberta Spear. GeoHom

River Song, The. Wang Yung. ChinPo, tr. by Yip Wai-lim

River, Stay 'Way from My Door. Mort Dixon. ReLy

River Steamer, The. Edith Jay Scovell. HarvBoo

River Still to Be Found, A. Lawrence Ferlinghetti. BB

River stretches wide, The. It flows on tiredly. On the Plain of Kulikovo.
     Aleksandr Aleksandrovich Blok. TCRusP, tr. by Denis Johnson and Kathy
     Lewis

River swallows know my shack is humble. Tu Fu. CrYelRi, tr. by Sam
     Hamill Fr. Random Pleasures.

River Swelleth More and More, The. Henry David Thoreau. NOBA

River swells onto the flooded banks, The. Cortes Swamp, The. Clovis L.
     Nazareno. ReBoTo

River takes the land, and leaves nothing, The. Slip, The. Wendell Berry.
     NOCV

River that flows nowhere, like a sea, The. (LL) River of Rivers in Connecticut,
     The. Wallace Stevens. APT-1; FaBoA; HAP; HCAP; NOBA; VGW

River That Flows through Our Land, The. Jeremy Cronin. PeSAV

River Town Packin House Blues. Quincy Troupe. LoL

River turns, The. Pike, The. Theodore Roethke. MoASP

River Walk. John Stuart Williams. AngWePo

River Wandering Down. Robert Creeley. FTOS

River was announcing, The. Denis Glover. PeNZ Fr. Arawata Bill.

River waters ruffled in the west wind. By the River. Wang An-shih. CoBCP,
     tr. by Burton Watson

River waters shiver in the west wind. On the Yangtze. Wang An-shih. SuSp,
     tr. by Jan W. Walls

River, why in ceaseless flow. Maiden and River. Mary Weston Fordham.
     CBWP-2

Riverbank Blues. Sterling Allen Brown. MakPoe

Riverbank, the long rigs. Broagh. Seamus Heaney. FaBoVe; ModIr; NPeEn

Riverbed, The. Vona Groarke. MFPA

Rivercraft: Carey neon. Dove-webbing fatigues. 2nd Lesson from the Cockerel.
     Maggie O'Sullivan. Oth

Riverrun where can you guess? Limerick. Unknown. PeLi

Rivers. Homero [or Umberto] Aridjis. PoCoUp, tr. by George McWhirter

Rivers. Thomas Storer. FaBoCh

Rivers. Giuseppe Ungaretti. PeFWW, tr. by Jon Silkin

Rivers, The. Giuseppe Ungaretti. PFTM-1

Rivers and Mountains. John Ashbery. CoAP; NOBA; NoAM; TRP

Rivers and winds among the twisted hills. Robert Louis Stevenson.
     "As with heaped bees at hiving time." NOBVV

Rivers level granite mountains. Sulpicius Lupercus Servasius. PGA; WoPoe,
     tr. by Kenneth Rexroth

Rivers of wings surround us and vast tribulation. (LL) Glazunoviana. John
     Ashbery. LCAP-2; VCAP

Riverside willows sway their green mist, The. To the Retired Scholar Chang.
     Ni Tsan. CoBLCP, tr. by Jonathan Chaves

Riversongs of Arion, The. Michael Anania. NoAM

Riviera, The. Joseph McCarthy, Jr. ReLy

Riviera, The / On every street a gay casino. Riviera, The. Joseph McCarthy,
     Jr. ReLy

Rivulet, The. William Cullen Bryant. APN-1

Rivulet-loving wanderer Abraham, The. Abraham. Edwin Muir. ChIV-1

Rizal's Ghost. Eugene Gloria. ReBoTo

Rizpah. Tennyson. NPeEn; PeVV
     (Wailing, wailing, wailing, the wind over the land and sea.) RACG

R.M.S. Titanic. Anthony Cronin.
     "On the bog road the blackthorn flowers, the turf-stacks." BIrV
     "Trembling with engines, gulping oil, the river." PBCIP

Roach, The. John Raven. BPo

Roach / came struttin, A. Roach, The. John Raven. BPo

Road. Pierre Reverdy. CuPo

Road, The. Conrad Potter Aiken. MoAmPo; PAI

Road, The. Robert Creeley. BodElec

Road, The. Helene Johnson. BlSi

Road, The. Herbert Morris. DiPo

Road, The. Nikolay Platonovich Ogarev. AWP, tr. by P. E. Matheson

Road, The. Zalman Schneour. TrJP, tr. by Joseph Leftwich

Road ahead, The. Seamus Heaney. TOF Fr. Sweeney Redivivus.

Road at My Door, The. W. B. Yeats. BIrV; NOBE; NPeEn; PoE Fr.
     Meditations in Time of Civil War.

Road at the top of the rise, The. Middleness of the Road, The. Robert Frost.
     NOBA

Road beneath the giant original trees, The. Sanctuary. Judith Wright. WPE

Road can't be as sad as a shoe is sad, A. Shoe. John Perreault. SPE

Road climbs, villages, The. Going. Peter Everwine. NNaP

Road crowds houses almost into the lake, The. Along Overgrown Paths.
     James Schuyler. BAP-01

Road he took was virgin territory, The. Theaitetos. Callimachus. GrAn, tr.
     by Peter Jay

Road I take, The. Sokin. JDP, tr. by Yoel Hoffmann

Road in Kentucky, A. Robert Earl Hayden. ColAP

Road Is Wider than Long, The. Roland Penrose.
     Road is Wider Than Long: An Image Diary from the Balkans, July–August
     1938, The. SPE

Road is Wider Than Long: An Image Diary from the Balkans, July–August
     1938, The. Roland Penrose. SPE Fr. Road Is Wider than Long, The.

Road Not Taken, The. Robert Frost. APT-1; AiP; ChAP; FaBoCh; HAP;
     HarvBoo; HeIP-4; ITBLP; MoAmPo; NAAL-2v2; NAAL-5; NIP-4; NoAM;
     NoP-4; OxBA; PoPoPo; SAmP; SoSe-8; TAP; TCAPo; TFi; TRP;
     TwCP

Road of terror! Ice of Ladoga, The. Aleksandr Petrovich Mezhirov. TCRP,
     tr. by Deming Brown

Road of the Dread, The. Lorna Goodison. VCWP

Road reaches beyond mountains, The. Stayover at Pei-Ku-Shan. Wang Wan.
     ChinPo, tr. by Yip Wai-lim

Road Show. Geoff Page. BMAP

Road that I came by mounts eight thousand feet, The. Waters of Lung-t'ou,
     The. HSü Ling. ChiP, tr. by Arthur Waley

Road to Exile Thinking of Vallejo, The. Syl Cheney-Coker. PBMAP

Road to Hogan's Gap, The. Andrew Barton Paterson. CBAP

Road to Morocco, The. Jimmy Van Heusen. ReLy

Road to Patmos, The. John Ennis. PBCIP

Road to Shu Is Hard, The. Li Po. WoPoe, tr. by Elling O. Eide

Road to Shu Is Hard, The. Li Po. SuSp, tr. by Irving Y. Lo

Road to Terezin, The. Ilse Weber. AuPH, tr. by Lowell A. Bangerter

Road turned out to be a cul-de-sac, The. Brother and Sisters. Judith Wright.
     BMAP; FaBoWP

Road turns back, the desolate mountain parts, The. Passing By the Battlefield
     at Feng-k'ou. Kao Ch'i. CoBLCP, tr. by Jonathan Chaves

Road unravels as I go, The. Minstrel. Michael Dransfield. BMAP

Road where Ts'ao Chih watched the fighting cocks, The. Spending the Night in
     the Eastern Park. Shen Yüeh. SuSp, tr. by Richard B. Mather

Roadkill Coyote. Art Goodtimes. GeoH

Roadmap. Harryette Mullen. ISC

Roads. Peter Huchel. AF, tr. by Daniel S. Simko

Roads. Peter Huchel. HP; PoSu, tr. by Michael Hamburger

Roads. (LL) I Am Alone. Léopold Sédar Senghor. PoetW; VCWP, tr. by
     Melvin Dixon

Roads. Edward Thomas. HarvBoo; PeFWW

Roads Also, The. Wilfred Owen. EBEV

Roadside flowers are blooming, butterflies on the wing. Su Tung-p'o (Su Shih).
     WoPoe, tr. by Burton Watson Fr. Roadside Flowers, Three Poems with
     Introduction.

Roadside Flowers, Three Poems with Introduction. Su Tung-p'o (Su Shih).
     "Roadside flowers are blooming, butterflies on the wing." WoPoe, tr. by
     Burton Watson
     "Wealth and honor in life were dew on the grass leaf." WoPoe, tr. by Burton
     Watson
     "Wild roadside flowers, blooming in boundless numbers." WoPoe, tr. by
     Burton Watson

Roadside thistle, eager, The. Basho. AWP

Roadside Weeds. John Haines. PoCoUp

Roadways. John Masefield. OTCP

Roaming Immortal. Ts'ao Chih. SuSp, tr. by Ronald C. Miao

Roaming life's ocean, if your damaged vessel. Haven of Rest. Mihály Tompa.
     IQMS, tr. by Doreen Bell

Roaming the East Field. Hsieh T'iao. ChinPo, tr. by Yip Wai-lim

Roaming the Via degli Alfani. Late Apostasy, A. V. Penelope Pelizzon.
     AmPoNex

Roaming through a fenceless world. (LL) Stephen Crane. APN-2; NAAL-2v2
     Fr. War Is Kind.

Roar of the Sea and the Darkness, The. Malcolm Lowry.
     "Lighthouse invites the storm and lights it, The." NOBC

Roar of welkome though the welkin, A. Elk, the Whelk, The. Robert
     Williams Wood. NBLV

Roar, raging torrent! and thou, mighty river. Niagara. Joseph Rodman Drake.
     APN-1

Roaring alongside he takes for granted, The. Sandpiper. Elizabeth Bishop.
     APT-2; AiP; HeIP-4; OWoS; RB; TOF

Roaring Frost, The. Alice Thompson Meynell. EBVV; WPE

Roaring of the wheels has filled my ears, The.   Cry from the Ghetto, A.
    Morris Jacob Rosenfeld.   TrJP, *tr. by* Charles Weber Linn
Roaring waterfall, the.   Su Tung-p'o (Su Shih).   EnlH
Roars on the coast at Ise. (LL)   Kasa no Iratsume.   OHPJ; WoPoe, *tr. by*
    Kenneth Rexroth
"Roast chestnuts, a shilling."   Walking against the Wind.   Jon Stallworthy.
    OxBC
Roasting alive of rabbis, The.   In the Absence of Bliss.   Maxine W. Kumin.
    NoAM; TaR
Roasting chestnuts.   Ishii Rogetsu.   OHMPJ
Roasting Potatoes.   Denise Levertov.   SpudSo
Rob me and maim me! Why, man, take such pains.   To One Who Quotes and
    Detracts.   Walter Savage Landor.   FaBoEE
Rob Roy.   *Unknown.*   ESPB
Robben Island Sequence.   Dennis Brutus.   HBAPE
Robber, The.   Hugh MacDiarmid.   OBVE
Robber, The.   Walter James Turner.   MoBrPo
Robber Bridegroom, The.   Margaret Atwood.   LCAP-2
Robber of Kuan-shan, The.   Wang Chiu-ssu.
    "Today I am a farmer in the fields."   CoBLCP
Robber, with a pike in his hand. (LL)   Petrarch.   BIrV; OBMV; OxBEV;
    WoPoe, *tr. by* John Millington Synge and J. M. Synge   *Fr.* Sonnets to
    Laura.
Robby, git down wi'tha, wilt tha?   Tennyson.   FaBoVe   *Fr.* Spinster's Sweet-
    Arts, The.
Robe, The.   Martha Rhodes.   ExTi
Robe, The.   Jones Very.   NCAP
Robe of Golden Thread, The.   Autumn Maid Tu (Tu Ch'iu-niang).   ColAnChi,
    tr. by Victor H. Mair
Robed Heart, The.   Elizabeth Spires.   ExTi
Robene and Makyne.   Robert Henryson.   *See* Robin [*or* Robene] and Makyne
Robene sat on gud grene [*or* green] hill.   Robert Henryson.   *See* Robin [*or*
    Robene] sat on gude green [*or* gud grene] hill
Robert.   Wendy Rose.   HATNAP
Robert Barnes, or [my] fellow fine.   Mother Goose.   OxNR; ReMoGo
Robert Bruce's Address to His Army.   Robert Burns.   FaBoWar
    (Before Bannockburn.)   FaBoCh
    (Robert Bruce's March to Bannockburn.)   NePenScot
Robert Bruce's March to Bannockburn.   Robert Burns.   NePenScot
    (Before Bannockburn.)   FaBoCh
    (Robert Bruce's Address to His Army.)   FaBoWar
Robert E. Lee.   Julia Ward Howe.   CBCWP
Robert Frost.   Robert Lowell.   NAAL-2v2; NoAM; PAI; Son   *Fr.* Writers.
Robert Frost.   Novella Nikolaevna Matveyeva [*or* Matveieva].   TCRP, *tr. by*
    Deming Brown
Robert G. Shaw.   Henrietta Cordelia Ray.   BlSi; CBWP-3; Son
Robert Gould Shaw.   Paul Laurence Dunbar.   CBCWP; PoPoPo; Son
Robert Graves.   Gavin Ewart.   NoAM
Robert Graves saw—not the male-womb made scary in Euripides.   Image-
    Nation 22.   Robin Blaser.   PFTM-2
Robert Lowell's Notebook.   "Edward Pygge."   OBCoV
Robert of Lincoln.   William Cullen Bryant.   OBCA
Robert Penn Warren's Book.   Anthony Lawrence.   BMAP
Robert Rowley rolled a round roll round.   Mother Goose.   OxNR
Robert Sat.   Tom Matthews.   PNI
Robert, Second Duke of Normandy.   Thomas Lodge.
    Pluck the Fruit and Taste the Pleasure.   OxAEP-1
Robert the Bruce.   Edwin Muir.   OxBS
Robert Whitmore.   Frank Marshall Davis.   BPo
Robert Wilson.   Michael Collier.   OPRER
Robes loosely flowing and aspect as free.   Seeing Her Dancing.   Robert Heath.
    NOSC; OxBSP
Robespierre and Mozart as Stage.   Robert Lowell.   FaBoMo
Robespierre could live with himself: "The Republic."   Robespierre and Mozart
    as Stage.   Robert Lowell.   FaBoMo
Robin, The.   George Daniel.   NPeEn
Robin, The.   Jones Very.   Son
Robin, The.   John Greenleaf Whittier.   OWoS
Robin-a-Bobbin.   *Unknown.*   OxNR; ReMoGo
Robin-a-bobin.   Mother Goose.   OxNR
Robin; a Pastoral Elegy.   John Dobson.   NOEC
Robin and a robin's son, A.   *Unknown.*   OxNR
Robin and Richard.   Mother Goose.   OxBoLi; OxNR; ReMoGo
Robin and Richard / Were two pretty men.   Robin and Richard.   Mother
    Goose.   OxBoLi; OxNR; ReMoGo
Robin and the red-breast, The.   Warning, A.   *Unknown.*   OxNR
Robin and the wren, The.   Greed.   *Unknown.*   OxNR

Robin cries: *rain!*, The.   Rain in Ohio.   Mary Oliver.   InPK-6
Robin Goodfellow.   *Unknown.*   FaBoCh
Robin he's gane to the wast.   Wife Wrapt [*or* Wrapped] in Wether's Skin, The.
    Unknown.   ESPB
Robin Hode and the Munkee.   *Unknown.*   *See* Robin Hood and the Monk
Robin Hood.   John Keats.   AWP; SCGP
Robin Hood.   Phyllis McGinley.   OBSV   *Fr.* Speaking of Television.
Robin Hood.   *Unknown.*   OxNR
Robin Hood and Allen [*or* Allin] -a-Dale.   *Unknown.*   ESPB; OxAEP-1
Robin Hood and Guy of Gisborne.   *Unknown.*   ESPB
Robin Hood and Little John.   *Unknown.*   ESPB
Robin Hood and Little John.   *Unknown.*   ReMoGo
Robin Hood and Maid Marian.   *Unknown.*   ESPB
Robin Hood and Queen Katherine.   *Unknown.*   ESPB
Robin Hood and the Beggar, I.   *Unknown.*   ESPB
Robin Hood and the Beggar, II.   *Unknown.*   ESPB
Robin Hood and the Bishop.   *Unknown.*   ESPB
Robin Hood and the Bishop of Hereford.   *Unknown.*   ESPB
Robin Hood and the Butcher.   *Unknown.*   ESPB
Robin Hood and the Curtal Friar.   *Unknown.*   ESPB
Robin Hood and the Golden Arrow.   *Unknown.*   ESPB
Robin Hood and the Grey Friars.   Thomas Love Peacock.   OxAEP-2   *Fr.*
    Maid Marian.
Robin Hood and the Monk.   *Unknown.*   ESPB; OBNV
    (Robin Hode and the Munkee.)   EBNV
Robin Hood and the Pedlars.   *Unknown.*   ESPB
Robin Hood and the Potter.   *Unknown.*   ESPB
Robin Hood and the Prince of Aragon.   *Unknown.*   ESPB
Robin Hood and the Ranger.   *Unknown.*   ESPB
Robin Hood and the Scotchman.   *Unknown.*   ESPB
Robin Hood and the Shepherd.   *Unknown.*   ESPB
Robin Hood and the Tanner.   *Unknown.*   ESPB
Robin Hood and the Three Squires.   *Unknown.*   *See* Robin Hood Rescuing
    Three Squires
Robin Hood and the Tinker.   *Unknown.*   ESPB
Robin Hood and the Valiant Knight.   *Unknown.*   ESPB
Robin Hood Book, A.   Alan Halsey.
    "His acre. His arbour."   Oth
    "Saracen SAS or Assasseen called Nasir claims on HTV, A."   Oth
    "32s. 6d. for the chattels of Robert Hod, fugitive, Michaelmas 1230 at York."
    Oth
    "Weakened by loss of blood Robin's last act was to slash his sword."   Oth
Robin Hood / Has gone to the wood.   Robin Hood.   *Unknown.*   OxNR
Robin Hood he was [*or* hee was] and a tall young man.   Robin Hood's Progress
    to Nottingham.   *Unknown.*   ESPB
Robin Hood Newly Revived.   *Unknown.*   ESPB
Robin Hood Rescuing Three Squires.   *Unknown.*   ESPB
    (Robin Hood and the Three Squires.)   NAEL-5v1
Robin Hood Rescuing Will Stutly.   *Unknown.*   ESPB
Robin Hood, Robin Hood, / Is in the mickle wood.   Mother Goose.   OxNR
Robin Hood, Robin Hood, / Is in the mickle wood!   Robin Hood and Little
    John.   *Unknown.*   ReMoGo
Robin Hood's Birth, Breeding, Valor, and Marriage.   *Unknown.*   ESPB
Robin Hood's Chase.   *Unknown.*   ESPB
Robin Hood's Death.   *Unknown.*   ESPB
Robin Hood's Delight.   *Unknown.*   ESPB
Robin Hood's Golden Prize.   *Unknown.*   ESPB
Robin Hood's Progress to Nottingham.   *Unknown.*   ESPB
Robin is a lovely lad.   Thomas Campion.   FaBoCh   *Fr.* Ayres that Were Sung
    and Played, at *Brougham Castle* in *Westmerland*, in the Kings
    Entertainment, The.
Robin listens, A.   William J. Higginson.   HA
Robin [*or* Robene] and Makyne.   Robert Henryson.   OBEV; PeLV
    (Robene and Makyne.)   BoLoP; MiEL; PoE
    (Robene sat on gud grene [*or* green] hill.)   BoLoP
Robin pipeth now, The. (LL)   Song: "Feathers of the willow, The."   Richard
    Watson Dixon.   FaBoCh; GTBS-P; NOBE
Robin Redbreast in a cage, A.   William Blake.   OWoS; OxBoLi   *Fr.* Auguries
    of Innocence.
Robin! Robin! call the Springtime.   March.   Henrietta Cordelia Ray.   CBWP-3
Robin's Nest, A.   Mary Jo Salter.   OWoS
Robin the Bobbin.   Robin-a-Bobbin.   *Unknown.*   OxNR; ReMoGo
Robinets and Jenny Wrens.   *Unknown.*   OxNR
Robins' green-blue eggs, The.   Morning.   Louise Bogan.   APT-2
Robinson at cards at the Algonquin; a thin.   Aspects of Robinson.   Weldon
    Kees.   CoAP
Robinson at Home.   Weldon Kees.   CoAP

Robinson Crusoe. Soubhagya Kumar Mishra. OMIP, *tr.* by Jayanta Mahapatra

Robinson Crusoe breaks a plate on his way out. Revolution, The. Jack Gilbert. BodElec

Robinson Crusoe Daniel Defoe. Maurice Sagoff. NBLV

Robinson Crusoe's Story. Charles Edward Carryl. PoRA *Fr.* Davy and the Goblin.

Robinson's Resignation. Simon Armitage. HarvBoo

Robo. Nick Carbó. NAPBL

Robot Camera. Robert Johnstone. PNI

Robyn and Gandeleyn. *Unknown.* ESPB; OxBB

Robyn lyæth in grene wode bowndyn. (LL) Robyn and Gandeleyn. *Unknown.* ESPB; OxBB

Roc, The. Mohja Kahf. PoArWo

Roça. Maria Manuela Margarido. HAWP, *tr.* by Julia Kirst

Rochester Extempore. John Wilmot, 2d Earl of Rochester. ChIV-1

Rock, The. T. S. Eliot.

   "It is hard for those who have never known persecution." SacPr

   "O Light Invisible, we praise Thee!" SacPr

Rock, The. Elizabeth Spires. ExTi

Rock, The. Wallace Stevens. APT-1

Rock, The. Jones Very. InvLi

"Rock-a-by, baby, up in the tree-top!" In the Tree-Top. Lucy Larcom. OBCA

Rock-a-bye, baby, thy cradle is green. Mother Goose. OxNR; ReMoGo

   (Rock-a-bye, baby.) LB

Rock-a-Bye Your Baby with a Dixie Melody. Jean Schwartz. ReLy

Rock and Hawk. Robinson Jeffers. APT-1; ColAP; NOBA; NoAM; OxBA

Rock and precipice. Landscape. Octavio Paz. OBVE, *tr.* by Charles Tomlinson

Rock, Ball, Fiddle. *Unknown.* OxBoLi; OxNR

Rock Bottom. Michael Ondaatje.

   "For you I have slept." NoP-4

Rock Climbers, The. Robert Francis. MoASP

Rock Crumbles, The. Else Lasker-Schüler. TrJP

   (My People.) WPOW, *tr.* by Michael Hamburger

Rock grows brittle, The. My People. Else Lasker-Schüler. WPOW, *tr.* by Michael Hamburger

Rock-like the souls of men. Men Fade Like Rocks. Walter James Turner. OBMV

Rock Me to Sleep[, Mother]. Elizabeth Akers Allen. APN-2; BRP; ITBLP; OBCA; SWaP

Rock 'n Roll. Peter Balakian. SwNoth

Rock 'n' Roll. Lesley Frost. AiP

Rock O' My Soul. *Unknown.* TCAPo

Rock o' my soul in de bosom of Abraham. Rock O' My Soul. *Unknown.* TCAPo

Rock of Ages. Augustus Montague Toplady. NOCV; SCGP; SacPr

   (Living and Dying Prayer for the Holiest Believer in the World, A.) NOEC

   (Prayer, Living and Dying, A.) ECEV

Rock of ages, cleft for me. Rock of Ages. Augustus Montague Toplady. NOCV; SCGP; SacPr

Rock of Cader Idris, The. Felicia Dorothea Hemans. RWP

Rock of My Salvation. Mordecai ben Isaac. TrJP, *tr.* by Solomon Solis-Cohen

Rock Painting. Carroll Arnett. VoR

Rock Pilgrim. Herbert Edward Palmer. OxBTC

Rock, Rock, Sleep, My Baby. Clyde Watson. NTCP

Rock's gray place is precise, The. Translation. Nicholas Samaras. YaYoPo

Rock-shores of the world and the secret waters. (LL) Birds. Robinson Jeffers. APT-1; VGW

Rock the child, rock the small one. *Unknown.* WoPoe, *tr.* by Keith Bosley *Fr.* Kanteletar, The.

Rock there is whose homely front, A. Primrose of the Rock, The. William Wordsworth. TreFP

Rock Thrown into the Water Does Not Fear the Cold, A. Audre Lorde. NAAL-2v2

Rockall. Epes Sargent. APN-1

Rockall. Malin. Dogger. Finisterre. (LL) Prayer: "Some days, although we cannot pray, a prayer." Carol Ann Duffy. HarvBoo; NePenScot; NoP-4; OxBSo

Rock[e] them, rock[e] them, lullaby [*or* lullabie]. (LL) Thomas Dekker. NoSic; OxAEP-1; OxBEV *Fr.* Pleasant Comedy of Patient Grissell [*or* Grissel *or* Grissill], The.

Rocked in the Cradle of the Deep. Emma Hart Willard. PWR

Rocked on this dreamy and indifferent tide. (LL) Absinthe-Drinker, The. Arthur Symons. FaBoTw; NOBVV

Rockefeller the Center. Marie Ponsot. CLPP

Rockes turn to Rivers, Rivers turn to Men. (LL) To Dean-bourn, a Rude River

in Devon, by Which Sometimes He Lived. Robert Herrick. BeJo; CaPo; PBRV

Rocket and the car, The. (LL) Window Ledge in the Atom Age. Elwyn Brooks White. NBLV; OBAL

Rocket Attack. Walter McDonald. CDa

Rocket to Russia. Alison Stone. SwNoth

Rockferns. Norman Nicholson. MoBrPo

Rockin' A Man, Stone Blind. Carolyn Beard Whitlow. FFC

Rockin' Chair. Hoagy Carmichael. ReLy

Rocking. Gabriela Mistral. TANSG, *tr.* by Maria Jacketti

Rocking. Gabriela Mistral. BBASP, *tr.* by Doris Dana

Rocking. Gabriela Mistral. SpanPo, *tr.* by Muriel Kittel

Rocking Chair, The. Abraham Moses Klein. HeIP-4

   (It seconds the crickets of the province. Heard.) NoP-4

Rockland. Julia Randall. WPE

Rockpool. Judith Wright. HarvBoo *Fr.* Shadow of Fire: Ghazals, The.

Rocks. Florence Parry Heide. NTCP

Rocks. Shinkichi Takahashi. ZenPo, *tr.* by Takashi Ikemoto and Lucien Stryk

Rocks, The. (LL) Sort of a Song, A. William Carlos Williams. APT-1; NAAL-2v2; OxBSP; TAP; WoPoe

Rocks Along the Coast, The. Jerry Martien. GeoHom

Rocks fallout on us. Rocket Attack. Walter McDonald. CDa

Rocks jagged in the morning mist. Point, The. John Montague. PNI

Rocks spear upward: sky's face split. Trip on Mount T'ai-P'ing. K'ung Chih-kuei. ChinPo, *tr.* by Yip Wai-lim

Rocky Acres. Robert Graves. NoAM; UnPo

Rod, The. Georgy [*or* Georgii] Nikolaevich Obolduyev [*or* Obolduev]. TCRP, *tr.* by Vera Dunham

Rod full of wind and moon, A. Tune: "Immortal at the Magpie Bridge." Lu Yu. SuSp, *tr.* by James J. Y. Liu

Rod of Jesse, The. Bible, *O.T.* AWP; OBVE; TrJP *Fr.* Isaiah.

Rodeo Tangent. Kendra Borgmann. MoASP

Rodez. Donald Davie. HarvBoo

Rodin's "Gates of Hell." Jane Greer. FFC

Rodomontade on His Cruel Mistress, A. John Wilmot, 2d Earl of Rochester. OxBSP

Rods and Kisses. Coventry Patmore. SacPr

Roe (and my joy to name) th'art now, to go. To William Roe. Ben Jonson. BeJo

Roe-Deer. Ted Hughes. NOxBChV; NoAM; OxAEP-2

Roethke Plain. John Malcolm Brinnin. TAP

Rogation Day: Portrush. James Simmons. PBCIP

Roger a doleful widower. Widower's Courtship, The. Elizabeth Hands. WoRP

Roger and Dolly. Henry Carey. NOEC; OxNR

   (Young Roger and Dolly.) ReMoGo

Roger the Dog. Ted Hughes. ChAP

Rogero's Song. George Canning. NOEC; OBCoV *Fr.* Rovers, The.

Rogers in Italy. Frank O'Hara. FTOS

Roget, Papier, Schism! Michael Portnoy. HeMarv

Rogue and Jar: 4/27/77. Thulani Davis. SeSe

Róisín, have no sorrow for all that has happened you. Little Black Rose. *Unknown.* NOIV, *tr.* by Thomas Kinsella

Roistering I'll Chaff. Luis de Góngora y Argote. SpanPo, *tr.* by William M. Davis

Rokeby Venus, The. Robert Conquest. GS

Roland is dead and the ivory broken. Rockefeller the Center. Marie Ponsot. CLPP

Role Reversal. Maria Luisa Spaziani. CItWP, *tr.* by Cinzia Sartini Blum and Lara Trubowitz

Rolfe and the Palm. Herman Melville. NCAP

Roll back, you fabulous animal. Carnal Knowledge. Gwen Harwood. CBAP

Roll Call, The. Dan Pagis. HP, *tr.* by Stephen Mitchell

Roll-Call in the Concentration Camp. Dan Pagis. FIT; PoSu, *tr.* by Robert Friend

Roll forth, my song, like the rushing river. Nameless One, The. James Clarence Mangan. BIrV; NOIV; OBEV

Roll on, sad world! Not Mercury or Mars. Frederick Goddard Tuckerman. APN-2 *Fr.* Sonnets.

Roll on, thou ball, roll on! To the Terrestrial Globe. Sir William Schwenck Gilbert. NBLV

Roll on, thou deep and dark blue ocean—roll! Byron. NOBRP; UV *Fr.* Childe Harold's Pilgrimage.

Roll On, Time, Roll On. Julia A. Moore.

   "Some people are getting so they think a poor girl." VerBaPo

Roll the stone from its grave away! (LL) John Greenleaf Whittier. APN-1; BRP; TAP; TreFP

Roll them overboard and sleep. (LL) W. H. Auden. BoLoP; FaBoTw *Fr.* Sea and the Mirror, The.

Roll within themselves. People of Pomegranates. Nidaa Khoury. DTA, *tr. by* Karen Alkalay-Gut

Rollcall of Bones, The. César Vallejo. AF, *tr. by* Robert Bly

Rolled in your fragrances, beautiful turning Earth. Sphere. Jules Supervielle. MFP, *tr. by* Martin Sorrell

Roller Coaster. Nicanor Parra. TCLAP, *tr. by* Miller Williams

Roller, pitch, and stumps, and all, The. (LL) Brahma. Andrew Lang. NOBL; PeLV; UV

Rollercoaster. Cris Cheek. Oth

Rolling Chinese Wall, The. Roger Woddis. UV

Rolling English Road, The. Gilbert Keith Chesterton. FaBoCh; NOBE; NOBL; OBEV; OBMV; OxAEP-2; OxBTC; UV

Rolling from St. Patrick's, The. Burial of an Irish President. Austin Clarke. BIrV

Rolling mountains push toward the city. Lang Mountain Monastery. Yang Yi. SuSp, *tr. by* Jonathan Chaves

Rolling the Lawn. William Empson. HarvBoo; MoBrPo; OBGa

Rolls and harrows lie at rest beside, The. Sky Lark, The. John Clare. NPeEn

And do they so? Henry Vaughan. BASC; ESCV; GeHe; MeLP; SacPr

Roma. Rutilius. CTC, *tr. by* Ezra Pound

Roma Higgins. Dave Etter. IllVoic

Roman Arbor, The. Ellen Hinsey. YaYoPo

Roman Baths at Nîmes, The. Henri Cole. MakPoe

Roman Earl, The. *Unknown.* OBVE, *tr. by* Douglas Hyde

Roman Elegies. Joseph Brodsky. VCWP, *tr. by* Joseph Brodsky

Roman Elegies, The. Goethe.

  "Here my garden is growing, the flowers of Eros I tend here." EroLit, *tr. by* David Luke

  "When you tell me that you were unpopular as a child." WoPoe, *tr. by* David Ferry

Roman Evening. Pier Paolo Pasolini. CLPP

Roman Fountain. Louise Bogan. APT-2; NoP-4; WPOW

Roman Fountain. Rainer Maria Rilke. GS, *tr. by* Edward Snow

Roman had an, A/ artist, a freedman. Marianne Craig Moore. NALW

Roman miniature urchin, A. Seeking an Explanation. Richard Emil Braun. NoAM

Roman Numerals. *Unknown.* OxNR

Roman Officer Writes, A. Charles Montague Doughty. FaBoTw *Fr.* Dawn in Britain, The.

Roman Poem Number Nine. June Jordan. GT

Roman Presents. Martial. OBCP, *tr. by* James Michie

Roman Road, The. Thomas Hardy. MoBrPo; NOBE

Roman Stage, The. Lionel Pigot Johnson. NOBVV

Roman Study. Louise Glück. BodElec

Roman Temple, A. 'Umar Abu Risha. MAP, *tr. by* Issa Boullata and Thomas G. Ezzy

Roman Thank-You Letter, A. Martial. OBCP, *tr. by* James Michie

Roman threw us a road, a road, The. Gilbert Keith Chesterton. OBSV *Fr.* Songs of Education.

Roman Virgil [*or* Vergil], thou that singest. To Virgil [*or* Vergil]. Tennyson. AWP; GTBS-P; NAEL-6v2

Roman Wall Blues. W. H. Auden. FaBoWar *Fr.* Twelve Songs.

Roman was the victor of the world, The. Petronius Arbiter. MLL *Fr.* Satyricon.

Roman Women. Thomas Edward Brown.

  "O Englishwoman on the Pincian." NOBVV

Romance. Andrew Lang. NePenScot

Romance. Edgar Allan Poe. APN-1; NCAP; OxBA

  (Introduction.) NAAL-2v1; NAAL-3; NOBA

  (Preface.) NAAL-3

Romance. Arthur Rimbaud. AmFaPo, *tr. by* Paul Schmidt

Romance. Ann Sansom. MFPA; NeBl

Romance. Walter James Turner. MoBrPo; NOBAu; NOBE; NOxBChV; OBMV; PoRA

Romance. Paul Zimmer. ReTh

Romance is a world, tiny and curved, reflected in a spoon. Perilous as a. Marriage. Amy Gerstler. PmAP

Romance Moderne. William Carlos Williams. APT-1

Romance of Love. *Unknown.* BLPSL, *tr. by* Rene de Costa, Rigas Kappatos and Eleni Paidoussi

Romance of the Swan's Nest, The. Elizabeth Barrett Browning. VWP

Romance [*or* Romaunt] of the Rose, The. Guillaume de Lorris.

  ("Garden *or* gardin was, by measuring, The.") OBGa, *tr. by* Geoffrey Chaucer

  ("That casten up full good savour.") (LL) OBGa, *tr. by* Geoffrey Chaucer

Romance to Night, A. Georg Trakl. AF, *tr. by* Daniel Simko

Romance, who loves to nod and sing. Romance. Edgar Allan Poe. APN-1; NCAP; OxBA

Romancero. Lex Banning. NOBAu

Romania, Romania. Gerald Stern. LCAP-2; MiVo

Romans Angry about the Inner World. Robert Bly. NOBA

Romans, I appeal to you. *Unknown.* RomPo, *tr. by* Eugene O'Connor *Fr.* Priapean Corpus, The.

Romans once indeavoured all they could, The. Upon a Joynted Ring. Francellina Stapleton. EMWP

Romantic Movement, The. Philip Lamantia. CLPP

Romanus Sum. István Vas. IQMS, *tr. by* George Gömöri and Clive Wilmer

Romanus sum—and I held my hand in fire. Romanus Sum. István Vas. IQMS, *tr. by* George Gömöri and Clive Wilmer

Rome. Madison Cawein. APN-2

Rome. Arthur Hugh Clough. EBVV; OxAEP-2 *Fr.* Amours de Voyage.

Rome. James Vincent Cunningham. OBVE

Rome. Joachim Du Bellay. WoPoe, *tr. by* Yvor Winters

Rome. Joachim Du Bellay. AWP; FaBoWar, *tr. by* Ezra Pound

Rome. Hildebert. MLL, *tr. by* Helen Waddell

Rome. John Milton. NOSC *Fr.* Paradise Regained [*or* Regain'd].

Rome: Building a New Street in the Ancient Quarter. Thomas Hardy. Son

Rome, Conqueror, Conquered. Joshua Sylvester. FaBoEE

Rome disappoints me still; but I shrink and adapt myself to it. Arthur Hugh Clough. EBVV; OxAEP-2 *Fr.* Amours de Voyage.

Rome, do not ask for the Pontiff Paul to be testicle-tested! One For Pope Paul. Janus Pannonius. IQMS, *tr. by* George Burrough and Adam Makkai

Rome has a thousand fountains, and in May they sing. Maria Luisa Spaziani. NeIt

Rome, I am Scorpus, foremost in the race. Martial. RomPo, *tr. by* Brian Hill

Rome never looks where she treads. Rudyard Kipling. NoAM *Fr.* Puck of Pook's Hill.

Rome, queen of all, your fame will never die. Constantinople (New Rome). *Unknown.* GrAn, *tr. by* Peter Jay

Rome's guns are spiked; and they'll stay so. Herman Melville. OxBA *Fr.* Clarel: A Poem and Pilgrimage in the Holy Land.

Rome still lies gleaming in a yellowish-golden hue. Marcus Aurelius. Dezső Kosztolányi. IQMS, *tr. by* Earl M. Herrick

Romeo and Juliet. William Shakespeare.

  "Even or odd, of all days in the year." SCV

  "He jests at scars [that never felt a wound]." PAI

  ("I dreampt a dreame to night.") OxBEV

  "If I profane with my unworthiest hand." OxAEP-1; SoSe-8; Son

  Living Juliet, The. PAI

  Mercutio's Queen Mab Speech.

    Mercutio Describes Queen Mab. RB

  "O my love, my wife!" OxAEP-1

Romeo, Grown Old. James Wright (1927–80). BodElec

Romira, stay. Call, The. John Hall. MeLP; NOSC

Romney! expert infallibly to trace. To George Romney, Esq. William Cowper. OxBSo

Romp. Dave Etter. WeW-3

Ron. Beatrix Gates. WiU *Fr.* Triptych.

Ron Mason. Hone Tuwhare. PeNZ

Ronald Reagan screamed out in dismay. Limerick. Frank Richards. PeLi

Ronald Wyn. Robert Bagg. TwCP

Roncevalles. *Unknown.* WoPoe, *tr. by* Charles Hubert Sisson *Fr.* Song of Roland, The.

Rondeau, A. Leigh Hunt. *See* Rondeau: "Jenny kissed [*or* kiss'd] me when we met."

Rondeau after a Transatlantic Telephone Call. Marilyn Hacker. ColAP; NoAM

Rondeau at the Train Stop. Erin Belieu. GifTon; NeAmPo

Rondeau: "Fleas, stink, pigs, mold." Eustache Deschamps. WoPoe, *tr. by* David Curzon and Jeffrey Fiskin

Rondeau for You. Mário de Andrade. TTY, *tr. by* John Nist

Rondeau: "Jenny kissed [*or* kiss'd] me when we met." Leigh Hunt. CABP; NBLV; NIL-7; NTCP; OBEV; OxAEP-2; OxBEV; PeLV; PoRA

  (Jenny Kiss'd Me.) BRP

  (Jenny Kissed Me.) ITBLP; TFi; UV

  (Rondeau, A.) InPK-6; NOBE; NOBVV; SCGP

Rondeau: "Lord, I'm done for: now Margot." Vincent Voiture. WoPoe, *tr. by* William Jay Smith

Rondeau of the Little Horses. Manuel Bandeira. TCLAP, *tr. by* Candace Slater

Rondeau Redoublé. Wendy Cope. HarvBoo

Rondeau Tempo. Rossana Ombres. CItWP, *tr. by* Cinzia Sartini Blum and Lara Trubowitz

Rondeau: "They are bodies left unburied." Cheryl Clarke. FFC

Rondel: "And whan this werk al brought was to an ende."   Geoffrey Chaucer. OWoS   *Fr.* Parlement of Foules, The.

Rondel: "Good-by, the tears are in my eyes."   François Villon.   AWP, *tr. by* Andrew Lang

Rondel: "Love, love, what wilt thou with this heart of mine?"   Jean Froissart. AWP, *tr. by* Henry Wadsworth Longfellow

Rondel: "Now that I am fifty-six."   Muriel Rukeyser.   NoP-4

Rondel of Luve [*or* Love], A.   Alexander Scott.   BoLoP; OBEV; OxBEV; OxBS

Rondel: "Strengthen, my Love, this castle of my heart."   Charles, Duc d' Orléans.   AWP, *tr. by* Andrew Lang

Rondelet: "Say what you please."   May Probyn.   VWP

Rondelet: "Which way he went?"   May Probyn.   VWP

Rondels.   Aleister Crowley.   CAGL

Rondo for the Poet's Children.   Jean-Joseph Rabéarivelo [*or* Rebéarivelo]. NegPo, *tr. by* Ellen Conroy Kennedy

Roof and spire and darkened vane.   Autumn Rain, The.   Christopher Pearse Cranch.   TCAPo

Roof caves in, A.   English Sampler, An.   Frederick D'Aguiar.   Oth

Roof Garden.   James Schuyler.   OBGa

Roof it down. Batten down. Dig in.   Seamus Heaney.   PoetW   *Fr.* Squarings.

Roof-poles in those days, The.   Tel Aviv 1935.   Leah Goldberg.   FIT, *tr. by* Robert Friend

Roof-Tops.   Charles Hanson Towne.   PoToHe

Roof-tops, roof-tops, what do you cover?   Roof-Tops.   Charles Hanson Towne. PoToHe

Roof-Tree.   Richard Murphy.   BiHa; ModIr   *Fr.* Price of Stone, The.

Roofs of cars were crusted thick with frost, The.   Citizen.   Chris Wallace-Crabbe.   CBAP

Roofs over the shops, The.   Christmas Eve.   Patricia Beer.   OBCP

Rooftop.   James Kimbrell.   AmPoNex

Rooftop Piper.   David Hernandez.   IllVoic

Roofwalker, The.   Adrienne Rich.   CoAP; NAAL-2v2

Rook's nest do rock on the tree-top, The.   Lullaby.   William Barnes.   SCGP

Rook[e] he sells feathers, yet he still doth cry.   Upon Rook: Epigram.   Robert Herrick.   CaPo

Rookhope Ryde.   *Unknown.*   ESPB; IBB

Rookhope stands in a pleasant place.   Rookhope Ryde.   *Unknown.*   ESPB; IBB

Rooks.   Charles Hamilton Sorley.   MoBrPo

Rooks, The.   Arthur Rimbaud.   FaBoWar, *tr. by* Norman Cameron

Rooks, The.   *Unknown.*   OxNR

Rooks are cawing up and down the trees!, The.   Nests in Elms.   "Michael Field."   VWP

Rooks are raging where great elms were felled.   World of Simon Raven, The. Peter Porter.   PeLV

Rooks: December.   Huw Menai.   AngWePo

Rooks love excitement.   Ted Hughes.   NOxBChV

Rooks love excitement. When I walked in under the rookery.   Rooks love excitement.   Ted Hughes.   NOxBChV

Room.   Robert Finch.   MoCV

Room.   Ruth Stone.   BoWoP

Room, The.   Conrad Potter Aiken.   APT-1; MoAmPo; NOBA

Room, The.   W. S. Merwin.   NOBA

Room, The.   William Soutar.   EBEV; NePenScot

Room 5600.   Ernesto Cardenal.   CLPP, *tr. by* Jonathan Cohen

Room above the Square, The.   Stephen Spender.   NOBE

Room after room.   Love in a Life.   Robert Browning.   FHYEP; NOBE; NOBVV; NPeEn; OxBEV

Room beneath the Rafters, The.   Ella Wheeler Wilcox.   PWR

Room contains no sound, The.   At 3 A.M.   Wendy Cope.   LW

Room fell silent, and all eyes were on him, The.   Virgil [*or* Vergil].   NAWM-5v1; NAWM-7v1, *tr. by* Robert Fitzgerald   *Fr.* Aeneid [*or* Eneados, Aeneis], The.

Room for a Jovial Tinker: Old Brass to Mend.   *Unknown.*   OxBB

Room for All.   Timothy Holmes.   PeSAV

Room grew dark and at my work desk stood two spirits, The.   Visitation. Adriann Roland Holst.   TuT, *tr. by* Paula Meehan

Room in Bloomsbury, A.   Sandy Wilson.   ReLy

Room is already white, The. Trim it in blue.   Life in the City: In Memoriam Edward Gibbon.   Philip Whalen.   PoM

Room is full of gold, The.   Jason.   Anthony Hecht.   ColAP

Room is prepared, the incense burned, The.   Southern Room Over the River, The.   Su Tung-p'o (Su Shih).   OHPC, *tr. by* Kenneth Rexroth

Room is sparsely furnished, The.   Thrall.   Carolyn Kizer.   GifTon

Room itself, The. The women. The absence of women, The.   Dionisio D. Martinez. NoP-4   *Fr.* What the Men Talk About When the Women Leave the Room.

Room of Leaves.   Amanda Dalton.

Almost Bird.   NeBl

In Love.   NeBl

Nest.   NeBl

Room of My Life, The.   Anne Sexton.   VCAP

Room of One's Own, A.   Hoda Hussein.   PoArWo, *tr. by* Cornelia Al-Khaled

Room on a Garden, A.   Wallace Stevens.   OBGa

Room sometimes vacant, sometimes engaged, A. A red-light district, just. Poem for the Womb.   Jennifer O'Grady.   AmPoNex

Room was cheap and sordid, The.   One Night.   Constantine P. Cavafy. CAGL; EroLit, *tr. by* Edmund Keeley and Philip Sherrard

Room was divided by a curtain, The.   Tailor's Wedding, The.   Louis Simpson. NNaP

Room was suddenly rich and the great bay-window was, The.   Snow.   Louis MacNeice.   CIP-2; FaBoMo; HarvBoo; ModIr; NOBE; NPeEn; NoAM; OPOU; OxAEP-2; OxBEV; OxBSP; OxBTC; PNI

Room with a View, A.   Noël Coward.   PeLV

Rooms.   Charlotte Mew.   HarvBoo; PoBW

Rooms.   Gertrude Stein.

"Light in the moon the only light is on Sunday, A."   TCAPo

Rooster.   James Tate.   LCAP-2

Rooster, The.   Abu'l Qasim As'ad Ibn Billita.   WoPoe, *tr. by* Leticia Garza-Falcón and Christopher Middleton

Rooster, The.   Aleksandr Semionovich Kushner.   ItGoST, *tr. by* Paul Graves and Carol Ueland

Rooster and the Pearl, The.   Max Jacob.   CuPo

Rooster crows like someone being sick, The.   City Girl in the Country. Elizabeth Smither.   PeNZ

Rooster had hardly crowed when Timofey jumped out of the win-, The. Beginning of a Beautiful Day (A Symphony), The.   Daniil Kharms.   AF, *tr. by* George Gibian

Rooster nights with crests of screams; sleep that's gotten old.   Clothes without the Monk, The.   Silvio Giussani.   ItPo, *tr. by* Gayle Ridinger

Rooster, you monster with a blood-red crest, a jagged.   Rooster, The. Aleksandr Semionovich Kushner.   ItGoST, *tr. by* Paul Graves and Carol Ueland

Roosters.   Elizabeth Bishop.   APT-2; ChIV-2; NALW

Root.   Miklós Radnóti.   IQMS, *tr. by* Peter Zollman

Root Cellar.   Theodore Roethke.   ColAP; HarvBoo; HeIP-4; InPK-6; NoP-4; PAI; VCAP

Root of Our Evil, The.   D. H. Lawrence.   ChIV-2

Root of our present evil is that we buy and sell, The.   Root of Our Evil, The. D. H. Lawrence.   ChIV-2

Root Song.   Henry Dumas.   ISC

Root stirs with rushing power, The.   Root.   Miklós Radnóti.   IQMS, *tr. by* Peter Zollman

Rooting, The.   Jolanda Insana.

"She doesn't feel the need to erect pergolas."   CItWP, *tr. by* Cinzia Sartini Blum and Lara Trubowitz

Rootless tree, A.   Sozan-Kyonin.   ZenPo, *tr. by* Takashi Ikemoto and Lucien Stryk

Roots.   Seamus Deane.   PNI

Roots.   Louis Ginsberg.   TrJP

Roots.   Seymour Mayne.   NOBC

Roots.   Charlotte Watson Sherman.   ISC

Roots and Branches.   Robert Duncan.   FTOS; VGW

Roots and Leaves Themselves Alone.   Walt Whitman.   APN-1

Roots around your soul and eyes, The.   Sweating It Out on Winding Stair Mountain.   Jim Barnes.   CDW

Roots in the Air.   Shirley Kaufman.   TaR

Roots of Blue Bells.   Nia Francisco.   HATNAP

Roots of mankind are tangled in my hair, The.   Epitaph.   Wendy Rose.   CDW

Roots of your hair / what, The.   Nappy Edges.   Ntozake Shange.   NAAAL

Roots: To My Daughter.   Virginia R. Terris.   SpudSo

Rope and candle gout.   Tselkov: An Interpretation.   Lev Vladimir Loseff [*or* Losev].   TCRP, *tr. by* Walter Arndt

Rope is braided in colors of love, The.   Wind Turns, The.   Nicole Espagnol. SurWo, *tr. by* Myrna Bell Rochester

Rope swings in, The.   Red-Dress Girl.   Ann Turner.   SSCS

Ropero, so sad and so forlorn.   El Ropero.   Antonio Di Montorio.   TrJP

Ropes, pull them tight!, The.   Fishermen's Song.   *Unknown.*   PeNZ, *tr. by* Margaret Orbell

Ropewalk, The.   Henry Wadsworth Longfellow.   NCAP

Ropey, lippy, loopy, scribbly.   Nasturtium Scanned.   Judith Rodriguez. BMAP

Rosa.   Miguel Algarin.   PueRic

Rosa.   Rita Dove.   ExTi

Rosa dances her feet out.   Nudo de Claridad.   Miguel Algarin.   PmAP

Rosa/Filí.   Maria Arrillaga.   TANSG

Rosa Luxembourg. Eileen Duggan. PeNZ

Rosa Rosarum. Agnes Mary Frances Robinson. PoBW

Rosa's body stopped growing. Water, White Cotton, and the Rich Man. Martín Espada. PueRic

Rosabel. Angelina Weld Grimké. PoBW

Rosabelle. Sir Walter Scott. GTBS-P *Fr.* Lay of the Last Minstrel, The.

Rosalind, in a négligée. Early Unfinished Sketch. Austin Clarke. ModIr

Rosalind's Madrigal. Thomas Lodge. *See* Rosalynde; or Euphues' Golden Legacy

Rosalind's [*or* Rosalynd's] Madrigal[l]. Thomas Lodge. NOBE; NoSic; OBEV *Fr.* Rosalynde; or Euphues' Golden Legacy.

Rosalind's [*or* Rosalynde's] Description. Thomas Lodge. *See* Rosalynde; or Euphues' Golden Legacy

Rosaline. Thomas Lodge. GTBS-P; OBEV *Fr.* Rosalynde; or Euphues' Golden Legacy.

Rosalynde; or Euphues' Golden Legacy. Thomas Lodge.

  (Love in My Bosom.) SCGP

  (Rosalind's Madrigal.) NoP-4; RACG

  Rosalind's [*or* Rosalynd's] Madrigal[l]. NOBE; NoSic; OBEV

  (Rosalind's [*or* Rosalynde's] Description.) OxAEP-1

  Rosaline. GTBS-P; OBEV

Rosary Beads. Herman Melville. NCAP

Rosciad, The.   Charles Churchill.

  Character of a Critic. NOEC

Roscoe's strictly a meat-and-potatoes man. Arsh Potatoes. Robert Phillips. SpudSo

Rose. Kathleen Jessie Raine. WPE

Rose, A. William Browne (1591–1643). OBEV *Fr.* Visions.

Rose, A. Sir Richard Fanshawe. OBEV *Fr.* Il Pastor Fido.

Rose, The. "Angelus Silesius." GePo, *tr.* by George C. Schoolfield *Fr.* Cherubical Wanderer, The.

Rose, The. Goethe. AWP, *tr.* by James Clarence Mangan

Rose, The. Gabriela Mistral. SpanPo, *tr.* by Kate Flores

Rose, The. Gabriela Mistral. WPoS, *tr.* by Langston Hughes

Rose, The. Theodore Roethke. APT-2; NOBA; TRP

Rose, The. Theodore Roethke. NOBA; TRP *Fr.* North American Sequence.

Rose, The. Pierre de Ronsard. AWP, *tr.* by Andrew Lang

Rose, The. Elizabeth Tollet. ECWP

Rose, The. William Carlos Williams. NOBA

Rose, The. William Carlos Williams. APT-1

Rose among thorns, The. Life Is Life. Robert Walker. IBA

Rose and gold and violet, The. Afterglow, The. Henrietta Cordelia Ray. CBWP-3

Rose and grape, pear and bean. *Unknown.* BoWoP

Rose and the lily, the moon and the dove, The. Rose, die Lilie, die Taube, die Sonne, Die. Heinrich Heine. AWP

Rose and went a-roving, mother. Lass A-Laundering. *Unknown.* STV, *tr.* by John Frederick Nims

Rose Aylmer. Walter Savage Landor. AWP; BoLoP; EnLoPo; HAP; NAEL-5v2; NAEL-6v2; NOBE; NOBRP; OBEV; OxAEP-2; SCGP; TFi; UnPo; WeW-3

  (Ah what avails the sceptered race.) NoP-4

  (Ah what avails the sceptred race!) CABP

Rose both white and Rede, The. John Skelton. PBRV *Fr.* Lawde and Prayse Made for Our Sovereigne Lord the Kyng, A.

Rose-Bud, The. William Broome. OBEV

Rose by the Wayside, The. D.A. Drown. TreFP

Rose-Cheek'd Laura, Come. Thomas Campion. *See* Observations in the Art of English Poesie

Rose-cheeked Laura, Come. Thomas Campion. EnLoPo; InPK-6; NAEL-5v1; NAEL-6v1; NAEL-7v1; NOSC; NoP-4; PoE; TFi; TRP *Fr.* Observations in the Art of English Poesie.

Rose, die Lilie, die Taube, die Sonne, Die. Heinrich Heine. AWP

  (Love's Resume.) TrJP, *tr.* by "J. F. C."

Rose fades, The. Poem. William Carlos Williams. NIL-7

Rose Family, The. Robert Frost. NIL-7; OBAL; OBCA

Rose Farmer, The. Herman Melville. APN-2

Rose for a young head, A. Watcher, The. James Stephens. MoBrPo; OBEV

Rose from al-Mutanabbi's Blood, A. 'Abd-Allah Al-Baraduni.

  "His fame stole his real name." MAP

Rose-Geranium, The. Eiléan Ní Chuilleanáin. CIP-2

Rose gives a tremulous glance, The. Limerick. Anne Norris. PeLi

Rose Growing into the House, The. Gibbons Ruark. InPK-6

Rose, harsh rose. Sea Rose. "H. D." APT-1; FaBoMo; HeIP-4; NIL-7; NoAM; NoP-4; OxWW; TRP

Rose has flushed red, the bud has burst, The. Hafiz [*or* Hafez]. TAL *Fr.* Odes.

Rose in her hand, a rose in her breast, A. Kyrielle. May Probyn. VWP

Rose in October, A. James Whitcomb Riley. OBAL

Rose in the Afternoon. Jenny Joseph. BrRo

Rose is a rose, The. Rose Family, The. Robert Frost. NIL-7; OBAL; OBCA

Rose is a Rose is a Rose is a Rose is a Rose. Emmett Williams. PFTM-2 *Fr.* Ultimate Poem, The.

Rose is a Violin is a Codpiece. Emmett Williams. PFTM-2 *Fr.* Ultimate Poem, The.

Rose is not the rose unless thou see, The. Hafiz [*or* Hafez]. AWP *Fr.* Odes.

Rose is red, the grass is green, The. *Unknown.* OxNR

Rose is red, the rose is white, The. *Unknown.* OxNR

Rose is red, the violet's blue, The. *Unknown.* OxNR

Rose-Leaves. Austin Dobson.

  Urceus Exit. OBEV

Rose Leaves When the Rose Is Dead. Marc André Raffalovich. CAGL

Rose might of the winds. Ronald Johnson. FTOS *Fr.* Ark.

Rose of all the world is not for me, The. Little White Rose, The. Hugh MacDiarmid. NePenScot

Rose of Brooklyn, The. Gregory Orfalea. GraLe

Rose of England, The. *Unknown.* ESPB

Rose of Fire. Antonio Machado Ruiz. SpanPo, *tr.* by Kate Flores

Rose of Life, The. Sir Richard Fanshawe. *See* Il Pastor Fido

Rose of Sharon, A. Myung Mi Kim. FSt

Rose of Sharon / I lost in the tortured night, The. For the New Union Dead in Alabama. Edward Dorn. PoM

Rose of Silence. Gennady Aygi. ItGoST, *tr.* by Peter France

Rose of that Garland! fairest and sweetest. To the Most Beautiful Lady, the Lady Bridget Manners. Barnabe Barnes. EnLoPo

Rose of the World, The. John Masefield. PoRA

Rose of the World, The. W. B. Yeats. MoBrPo; NAEL-5v2; NAEL-6v2

Rose, Oh Pure Contradiction. Rainer Maria Rilke. TTTS, *tr.* by Stephen Mitchell

Rose, oh pure contradiction, joy. Rainer Maria Rilke. EnlH

Rose on My Cake, The. Karla Kuskin. TLR

Rose Quartz. Leslie Ullman. ExTi

Rose, regarded here by your external eyes, The. "Angelus Silesius." GePo, *tr.* by George C. Schoolfield *Fr.* Cherubical Wanderer, The.

Rose That Bore Jesu, The. *Unknown.* NPeEn

Rose the Red and White Lil[l]y. *Unknown.* ESPB; OxBB

Rose to the living is more than, A. Nixon Waterman. PoToHe

Rose Tree, The. W. B. Yeats. OBMV

Rose was sick and smiling died [*or* di'd], The. Funeral[l] Rites of the Rose, The. Robert Herrick. CaPo; NOSC; OBEV

Rose, were you not extremely sick? (LL) True Maid, A. Matthew Prior. FaBoEE; NAEL-5v1; NAEL-6v1; NAEL-7v1; NIP-4; NOEC; NPeEn; PeLV

Rose Window. Herman Melville. APN-2

Rose Wreaths, The. Friedrich Gottlieb Klopstock. GePo, *tr.* by J. W. Thomas

Rosebud in the Heather. Goethe. STV, *tr.* by John Frederick Nims

Rosebush, Less Presumption. Francisco de Quevedo y Villegas. SpanPo, *tr.* by William M. Davis

Rosemary. John A. Stone. BloBone

Rosemary, Rosemary. Stephen Vincent Benét. *See* Rosemary, Rosemary, let down your hair!

Rosemary, Rosemary, let down your hair! Nonsense Song, A. Stephen Vincent Benét. OBAL

Rosemary Spray, The. Luis de Góngora y Argote. AWP, *tr.* by E. Churton

Roses. Anacreon. AWP, *tr.* by Thomas Stanley

Roses. Barbara Guest. NoP-4

Roses. Geoffrey Lehmann.

  "At night, circling weightless, we dreamed of roses." BMAP

Roses. Pierre de Ronsard. WoPoe, *tr.* by Vernon Watkins

Roses. Pierre de Ronsard. AWP, *tr.* by Andrew Lang

Roses, The. Jennifer Snyder. BodElec

Roses and Revolutions. Dudley Randall. BPo; CoAmPo; TAP

Roses are already here. Philodemus. PGA

Roses are red. *Unknown.* OxNR

Roses at first were white. How Roses Came Red. Robert Herrick. BeJo; CaPo; NAEL-7v1

Roses caged in windows, heighten. Julia Ward Howe. SWaP *Fr.* Lyrics of the Street.

Roses every one were red, The. Spleen. John Gray. NOBVV

Roses first came red, The. (LL) How Roses Came Red. Robert Herrick. BeJo; CaPo; NAEL-7v1

Roses hence, or Lil[l]ies rather. (LL) Upon the Infant Martyrs. Richard Crashaw. GeHe; NPeEn; PAI

Roses in breathing forth their scent. Celia Singing. Thomas Stanley. BeJo; NOSC

Roses, Late Summer. Mary Oliver. NIL-7

Roses (Love's delight) let's join. Roses. Anacreon. AWP, *tr. by* Thomas Stanley

Roses of Sa'adi, The. Marceline Desbordes-Valmore. BoWoP, *tr. by* Barbara Howes

Roses of Saadi, The. Marceline Desbordes-Valmore. WPOW, *tr. by* Deirdre Lashgari

Roses Red. Arno Holz. AWP, *tr. by* Jethro Bithell

Roses red upon my neighbor's vine, The. My Neighbor's Roses. Abraham L. Gruber. PoToHe

Roses, rose-red and white, and green. Alleluya. "Rubén Dario." TTY, *tr. by* Lysander Kemp

Roses, roses of dust, how much hardness. Poetry of Roses, The. Franco Fortini. ItPo, *tr. by* Gayle Ridinger

Roses, roses, roses. June. Henrietta Cordelia Ray. CBWP-3

Roses, their sharp spines being gone. John Fletcher. NOBE; NOSC; NoSic *Fr.* Two Noble Kinsmen, The.

Roses used to bloom in spring. Crinagoras. GrAn

Roses were bright red, The. Spleen. Paul Verlaine. SxFrPo, *tr. by* Martin Sorrell

Rosh Chodesh Tisheri. Vicki Hollander. HW

Rosie. Andrew Hudgins. Unle

Rosina Alcona to Julius Brenzaida. Judith Wright. NALW

Roslyn Malamud the Coup. Anna Deavere Smith. OxWW *Fr.* Fires in the Mirror.

Ross's Poems. Geoffrey Lehmann. CBAP

  "What's that bird, Mr Long?" BMAP

Rostov. George Sutherland Fraser. PoWW

Rosy Bosom'd Hours, The. Coventry Patmore. EnLoPo; NOBVV

Rosy from wine, she rises. Drinking All Night, Sleeping All Day. Li Ho. CrYelRi, *tr. by* Sam Hamill

Rosy shield upon its back, A. Dead Crab, The. Andrew Young. FaBoTw; RB

Rot, old crow, a mausoleum. *Unknown.* PriapPo, *tr. by* Richard W. Hooper *Fr.* Priapus Poems, The.

Rot on the vine: in that land were we born. (LL) Mediterranean, The. Allen Tate. APT-2; FaBoMo; FuPo; HAP; MoAmPo; VGW; WoPoe

Rotating Tombs. Mikhail Naimy. GraLe, *tr. by* Sharif Elmusa and Gregory Orfalea

Rothko's Yellow. Dean Young. IllVoic

Rotten wood is unfit for carving, so I slept at noon. For Guests after Their Visit. SuSp, *tr. by* Wu-Chi Liu

Rotting Ginsberg, I stared in the mirror naked today. Mescaline. Allen Ginsberg. PFTM-2

Rotting Symbols. Eileen Myles. BodElec

Rottnest Island. Nicholas Hasluck.

  "All day the bicycles come and go." NOBAu

  "Christmas Day. 1696." NOBAu

Rotund, stubby fingered. Tale. Jennifer Rankin. BMAP

Rou-cou spoke the dove. Song of Fixed Accord. Wallace Stevens. SAmP

Rouen. May Wedderburn Cannan. NAEL-5v2; NAEL-6v2; OBWP; OxBTC

Rouen, Place de la Pucelle. Maria White Lowell. APN-2

Rouge. Ann Townsend. ExTi

Rouged hands. Tune: "Hairpin Phoenix." Lu Yu. ChinPo, *tr. by* Yip Wai-lim

Rough Are the Roads. Baldomero Garcilaso de la Vega. SpanPo, *tr. by* Edwin Morgan

Rough are the roads that led me to this place. Rough Are the Roads. Baldomero Garcilaso de la Vega. SpanPo, *tr. by* Edwin Morgan

Rough articles likesiding at others plug making plug. Accessories are. Hints at Distance. Michael Portnoy. HeMarv

Rough Boys. Sam Adams. TCAWP

Rough fir, hauled from the hills. Making of the Cross, The. William Everson. VGW

Rough hail rattles thro the trees, The. Eild. Robert Tannahill. NePenScot

Rough man entered the lover's garden, The. Ilahi. Pir Sultan Abdal. WoPoe, *tr. by* Murat Nemet-Nejat

Rough Music. Deborah Digges. ExTi

Rough Ridge. Yüan Mei. CoBLCP, *tr. by* Jonathan Chaves

Rough wind, that moanest loud. Dirge, A. Shelley. NAEL-5v2; NOBE; PoRA; SCGP

Roughly estimated ones, who do not sort well, The. Monuments of Hiroshima, The. Dennis Joseph Enright. OxBSP

Roughly figured, this man of moderate habits. Life Cycle of Common Man. Howard Nemerov. NBLV

Roughly-silvered leaves that are the snow. Song from Armenia, A. Geoffrey Hill. FaBoMo

Round, A. *Unknown. See* Hey Nonny No!

Round, The. Stanley Kunitz. BodElec

Round a cleft in the cliffs to come upon. Venus of the Salty Shell. Denis Devlin. BIrV; NOIV

Round a flame. Kaikai. JDP, *tr. by* Yoel Hoffmann

Round About. Ogden Nash. ReLy

Round about Me. Sappho. AWP, *tr. by* William Ellery Leonard

Round about, round about, / Catch a wee mouse. *Unknown.* OxNR

Round about, round about, here sits the hare. *Unknown.* OxNR

Round about, round about, / maggotty pie. *Unknown.* OxNR

Round about the rosebush. *Unknown.* OxNR

Round about there / Sat a little hare. *Unknown.* OxNR

Round and round. Private Transport. Adrian Mitchell. FaBoEE

Round and round the cornfield. *Unknown.* LB

Round and round the garden. *Unknown.* OxNR

Round and round the rugged rock. *Unknown.* OxNR

Round-bottomed babe from Mobile, A. Limerick. *Unknown.* PeLi

Round dance of day has gone. Sitting Alone in Tulsa Three A.M. Lance Henson. VoR

Round her red garland and her golden hair. Giovanni Boccaccio. AWP; EaItPo, *tr. by* Dante Gabriel Rossetti *Fr.* Sonnets.

Round his left shoulder, as he got up slowly. Lazarus. Ágnes Nemes Nagy. IQMS, *tr. by* Hugh Maxton

Round Irving High School. Cheryl Boyce Taylor. WiU

'Round Killar. Eric Dyer. BloBone

Round like a circle in a spiral. Windmills of Your Mind, The. Alan Bergman. ReLy

Round living bulge, more certain today, The. Delivery. Alicia Galaz Vivar. TANSG, *tr. by* Dave Oliphant

Round Midnight. Clarence Major. NAAAL

'Round Midnight. Thelonius Monk. ReLy

Round Midnight, Place de Congo. Kalamu ya Salaam. SpirFl *Fr.* New Orleans Haiku.

Round my neck a rosary of fine beads. Anna Andreyevna Akhmatova. TCRP

Round Nights black Axle-tree, bright Stars, farewel. (LL) Theocritus. CTC; OBVE *Fr.* Idylls.

Round—oblong—like jam. Contours. Noël Coward. UV

Round of the Clock, The. Frederick B. Needham.

  "One! strikes the clock in the belfry tower." VerBaPo

Round Song, A. Rhyll McMaster. CBAP

Round the cape of a sudden came the sea. Parting at Morning. Robert Browning. AWP; CABP; FHYEP; HeIP-4; NAEL-5v2; NAEL-6v2; NOBE; OBEV; OxBSP; PAI; SCGP; SoSe-8; TFi; UnPo

Round the house and round the house / and there lies a black glove in the window. Riddle. *Unknown.* FaBoVe

Round the house and round the house / and there lies a white glove in the window. Riddle. *Unknown.* FaBoVe

Round the island of Zipangu. Mimshi Maiden, The. Hugh Raymond McCrae. NOBAu

Round the streets of this city I rode you. Farewell to My Scooter. Mbuyiseni Oswald Mtshali. PeSAV

Round the World with the Rumpus God. Meret Oppenheim. SurPaPo; SurWo, *tr. by* Catherine Schelbert

Round this particular date I have drawn a circle. Sulpicia. Michael Longley. OxBSo; RACG

Round universe, where only spheres can range. Emblem 51. Zbigniew Morsztyn. WoPoe, *tr. by* Jerzy Peterkiewicz and Burns Singer

Round: "'Wondrous life!' cried Marvell at Appleton House." Weldon Kees. CoAP

Roundabout winds wearily down, The. Poem about the Blue Horse. Sergey Morozov. TCRusP, *tr. by* Daniel Weissbort

Rounded Catalogue Divine Complete, The. Walt Whitman. NAAL-2v1; NAAL-3

Rounded world is fair to see, The. Nature [1844]. Ralph Waldo Emerson. APN-1

Roundel. Geoffrey Chaucer. *See* Parlement of Foules, The

Roundel: "Take, take this cosse, atonys, atonys, my hert!" Charles, Duc d' Orléans. NPeEn

Roundelay, A: "It fell upon a holy eve." Edmund Spenser. NPeEn *Fr.* Shepheardes [*or* Shepeards *or* Shepherd's] Calender, The.

Roundelay Between Two Shepherds, A. Michael Drayton. NoP-4

Roundelay: "On all that strand." Samuel Beckett. ModIr; OxBEV

Roundhouse Voices, The. Dave Jeddie Smith. NoAM; VCAP

  (In full glare of sunlight I came here, man-tall but thin.) ColAP; GM

Rounding a slip of the marsh, the boat skids. Looking for the Melungeon. Dave Jeddie Smith. HCAP

Rounding steeps and jostles were one thing, The. Ferris Wheel, The. Wyatt Prunty. RA

Rounding the Horn. L. S. Asekoff. BAP-97

Rounding the Horn. John Masefield. MoBrPo *Fr.* Dauber.

Roundness. Pierre Drieu la Rochelle. CuPo

Rounds, The. G. E. Murray. IllVoic

Rounds and Garlands Done, The. Léonie Adams. APT-2

Rouse for Stevens, A. Theodore Roethke. OBAL

Rouse thee, old Time, thy folded pinions shake. To Time. Mary Julia Young. CenSon

Roused by November seas, wrecked on Italian rocks. Theodoridas. GrAn

Rousseau in His Day. Donald Davie. DiPo

Rousseau Le Douanier. "Lucebert." PFTM-2, tr. by Peter Nijmeijer

Rousseau, Voltaire, our Gibbon, and De Staël. Sonnet to Lake Leman. Byron. CenSon; Son

Route. George Oppen. AF; APSN; APT-2

Route. Philippe Soupault. PFTM-1

Route of Evanescence, A. Hummingbird, A. Emily Dickinson. APN-2; HeIP-4; NAAL-2v1; NAAL-3; NoP-4; SoSe-3; TCAPo

Route of the Táin, The. Thomas Kinsella. PBCIP

Route Six. Stanley Kunitz. APT-2

Routes. Peter Everwine. NNaP

Routine Day Sonnet. A. K. Ramanujan. EmeKit

Rover, The. Sir Walter Scott. GTBS-P

Rover killed the goat. Brave Rover. Max Beerbohm. NBLV

Rover or The Banished Cavaliers, The. Aphra Behn. BWW

Rovers, The. George Canning.
  Rogero's Song. NOEC; OBCoV
  (Song of One Eleven Years in Prison.) PeLV

Roving breezes come and go, the reed-beds sweep and sway, The. Travelling Post Office, The. Andrew Barton Paterson. CBAP; NOBAu

Row after row. Mule, The. Boynton, Jr. Merrill. CRP

Row after row with strict impunity. Ode to the Confederate Dead. Allen Tate. APT-2; AiP; CBCWP; ColAP; FaBoMo; FuPo; HeIP-4; MoAmPo; NAAL-2v2; NOBA; NoAM; NoP-4; OBWP; OxBA; TAP; TFi; UnPo

Row gently here, my gondolier; so softly wake the tide. Venetian Air. Thomas Moore. OxBSP

Row of Stalls, A. Raymond Knister.
  Nell. NOBC
  "Nellie Rakerfield." NOBC

Row of willow trees, almost green for the spring, A. Two Fish by a Willow Embankment. Hsü Wei. CoBLCP, tr. by Jonathan Chaves

Row, Row, Row. William Jerome. ReLy

Row us out from Desenzano, to your Sirmione row! Frater Ave Atque Vale. Tennyson. EBVV; GTBS-P; HAP; NAEL-5v2; NAEL-6v2; NoP-4; OxBSP

Rowan like a lip-sticked girl, A. Song. Seamus Heaney. TRP

Rowan Tree Fire, The. Sergey [or Sergei] Aleksandrovich Yesenin [or Essenin]. TCRP, tr. by Geoffrey Thurley

Rowing. Larry Gates. HA

Rowing. Anne Sexton. BoWoP; LCAP-2

Rowing between Pond and Western Islands. Loon Call, A. Richard Eberhart. ColAP

Rowing downstream. Michael McClintock. HA

Rowing in Familiar January. Milo De Angelis. NeIt, tr. by Lawrence Venuti

Rows of carriages, grooms at rest. Occasional Verse. Wang Ts'an. SuSp, tr. by Ronald C. Miao

Rows of cells are unroofed, The. Old Prison, The. Judith Wright. BMAP

Rows of Cold Trees, The. Yvor Winters. NOBA

Roxy. Gavin Selerie.
  "Angel of moment is dust, The." Oth
  "Hungry bower of drolleries" Oth
  "Out of the waste you can spin." Oth

Roy Bean. Unknown. OBAL

Roy Kloof. Sydney Clouts. PeSAV

Royal Angler, The. Unknown.
  "Me thinks I see our mighty monarch stand." OBSV

Royal Banquet, The. William Edmonstoune [or Edmondstoune] Aytoun. OBCoV

Royal Charlie's now awa. Will He No Come Back Again? Unknown. OBEV

Royal Crown, The. Solomon ibn Gabirol. AWP, tr. by Israel Zangwill
  My God. TrJP, tr. by Alice Lucas
  "My God, I know that those who plead." TrJP, tr. by Alice Lucas

Royal Dwellings. Juntoku, Emperor. WoPoe, tr. by Howard S. Levy

Royal Education. Winthrop Mackworth Praed. OBSV

Royal feast was done; the King, The. Edward Rowland Sill. APN-2; ITBLP

Royal health to the Rising Sun, The. Unknown. BASC

Royal in splendour went down the day. Indian City, The. Felicia Dorothea Hemans. RWP

Royal Manor Road. Gerald Stern. InvLad

Royal Palm. Hart Crane. MoAmPo; NoAM

Royal Portraits, The. William Dean Howells. APN-2

Royal Princess, A. Christina Georgina Rossetti. BrRo

Royal Procession. Ernst Goll. AuPH, tr. by Lowell A. Bangerter

Royal Review, The. William McGonagall.
  "All hail to the Empress of India, Great Britain's Queen." VerBaPo

Royal roads were cow paths, The. Seamus Heaney. PoetW Fr. Sweeney Redivivus.

Royal Stag, The. Hugh MacDiarmid. FaBoMo

Royal Tour, The. "Peter Pindar." OxBoLi; PeLV

Royal Tour, and Weymouth Amusements, The. "Peter Pindar." OxBoLi
  George III and the Sailor. NOEC

Royall Palace of the Heichest Hewin, The. Alexander Montgomerie. NePenScot

Royal[l] Presents. Nathaniel Wanley. SacPr

Royals. James Schuyler. FTOS

Royalties. Dennis Joseph Enright. NOBL; PeLV

Roye Robert the Bruss the rayke he avowit, The. Sir Richard Holland. OxBS
  Fr. Buke of the Howlat, The.

Roys, The. Arvind Krishna Mehrotra. OMIP

Roysters give Roome, for here comes a Lass. Elizabeth Banckes. EMWP

Rrrrrrrraaarghr / We have paid you back. Fury against the Moslems at Uhud. Hind bint Utba. WPOW, tr. by Bridget Connelly and Deirdre Lashgari

Rub, A. John Banister Tabb. OBAL

Rub a dub dub. Mother Goose. NOBL; OxNR

Rub a Dub Style inna Regent Park. Lillian Allen. WaCA

Rubai. Nazim Hikmet. WoPoe, tr. by Taner Baybars

Rubaiyat. Mimi Khalvati. MFPA

Rubáiyát of Omar Khayyám [of Naishápúr], The. Omar Khayyám. AWP; EBVV; HAP; NAEL-5v2; NAEL-6v2; NoP-4; TRP, tr. by Edward Fitzgerald
  "Ah, with the grape my fading life provide." EBEV; GTBS-P, tr. by Edward Fitzgerald
  "And when like her, oh Sákí, you shall pass." TRP, tr. by Edward Fitzgerald
  "Awake! for morning in the bowl of night." NOBVV; NPeEn; OxAEP-2; OxBEV; PeVV; TAL; UV, tr. by Edward Fitzgerald
  "Book of verses underneath the bough, A." CABP; NOBE; OBEV; TRP; WoPoe, tr. by Edward Fitzgerald
  "But leave the Wise to wrangle, and with me." OxBEV
  "Come, fill the cup, and in the fire of spring." TRP; UV, tr. by Edward Fitzgerald
  "For some we loved, the loveliest and the best." TRP, tr. by Edward Fitzgerald
  "Here with a Loaf of Bread beneath the Bough." UV, tr. by Edward Fitzgerald
  "'How sweet is mortal Sovranty!'— think some." UV, tr. by Edward Fitzgerald
  "I sometimes think that never blows so red." TRP, tr. by Edward Fitzgerald
  "Iram indeed is gone with all his rose." OBVE, tr. by Edward Fitzgerald
  "Moving Finger writes; and, having writ, The." TRP, tr. by Edward Fitzgerald
  "Myself when young did eagerly frequent." TRP, tr. by Edward Fitzgerald
  "Oh, come with old Khayyam and leave the Wise." UV, tr. by Edward Fitzgerald
  "Some for the Glories of This World; and some." TRP, tr. by Edward Fitzgerald
  "They say the lion and the lizard keep." EBEV, tr. by Edward Fitzgerald
  "Wake! for the sun, who scattered [or scatter'd] into flight." TRP, tr. by Edward Fitzgerald
  "Yon rising Moon that looks for us again." TRP, tr. by Edward Fitzgerald

Rubber. Rolf Jacobsen. BLT, tr. by Roger Greenwald
  (One pale morning in June at four o'clock.) BLT, tr. by Roger Greenwald

Rubber penis, the wig, false breasts, The. Poggio. Lawrence Durrell. OxBTC

Rubbing its hands. (LL) Void, The. G. M. Muktibodh. OMIP; WoPoe, tr. by Vinay Dharwadker

Rubbish Bags. Victor Vroomkoning. TuT, tr. by Dennis O'Driscoll

Rubens. Washington Allston. APN-1

Rubens. Harriet Monroe. IllVoic

Rublyov XVth Century. Ksenya [or Kseniia] Nekrasova. TCRP, tr. by Vera Rich

Rubric, The. Virgil [or Vergil]. OBVE, tr. by Gawin [or Gavin] Douglas Fr. Aeneid [or Eneados, Aeneis], The.

Ruby and amethyst eyes of anemones, The. Charles Brasch. PeNZ Fr. Night Cries, Wakari Hospital.

Ruby Red's Migrant Camp. Wilma Elizabeth McDaniel. GeoHom

Ruddigore. Sir William Schwenck Gilbert.
  Darned Mounseer, The. NOBL
  Thought from Ruddigore, A. OBCoV

Ruddy drop of manly blood, A. Friendship. Ralph Waldo Emerson. CAGL

Ruddy fire-glow, like her sister's eyes, The. Lot and His Daughters I. Alec Derwent Hope. ChIV-1

Ruddy-skinned pears. (LL) Late Aubade, A. Richard Wilbur. PAI; SoSe-8

Rude, from the wide extended Chesapeke. Philip Freneau. TCAPo *Fr.* House of Night, The.

Rude Mars had th' ordering of their spirits; of Greeks, the learned Maid. Homer. FaBoWar, *tr. by* George Chapman *Fr.* Iliad, The.

Rude mass of earth, from which moilèd hands. On a Piece of Unwrought Pipeclay. John Frederick Bryant. NOEC

Rudolph Reed was oaken. Ballad of Rudolph Reed, The. Gwendolyn Brooks. RB

Rue de Rosiers: To My Brother Fred. Liliane Richman. TWW

Ruffed blue-green garden, red blossoms. Tune: "Butterflies Lingering over Flowers." Ou-yang Hsiu. SuSp, *tr. by* Jerome P. Seaton

"Rufinianus" was once just Rufus. *Unknown.* GrAn

Rufous Hummingbird. Duane Niatum. PoCoUp

Rufus Prays. Leonard Alfred George Strong. MoBrPo

Rug, The. Michael McClure. NeAP

Rug of dead butterflies at my feet, A. Ghost. Nina Cassian. PoSu, *tr. by* Christopher Hewitt

Rugby Chapel. Matthew Arnold. PeECV

Rugged billion Miles, A. (LL) Emily Dickinson. ChrPo; SacPr

Ruin, The. Dafydd [*or* David] ap Gwilym. OBWVE, *tr. by* Rolfe Humphries

Ruin, The. Richard Hughes. OBMV

Ruin, The. *Unknown.* NAWM-7v1, *tr. by* Lee Patterson

Ruin, The. *Unknown.* WoPoe, *tr. by* Michael O'Brien

Ruin, The. *Unknown.* EBEV, *tr. by* Gavin Bone

Ruin, The. *Unknown.* AnOE, *tr. by* Charles W. Kennedy

Ruin seize thee, ruthless King! Thomas Gray. GTBS-P; NOBE; NOEC; OxAEP-1

Ruine of this Island, The. Margaret Lucas Cavendish, Duchess of Newcastle. EMWP

Ruined Altar, A. Rosamund Marriott Watson. ViWPN

Ruined and ill—a man of two score. Remembering Golden Bells. Po Chü-i. AWP; ChiP, *tr. by* Arthur Waley

Ruined City, The. Pao Chao. WoPoe, *tr. by* Michael Bullock and C. J. Chen

Ruined Cottage, The. William Wordsworth. NAEL-6v2; NoP-4

Ruined Maid, The. Thomas Hardy. BoLoP; FaBoVe; HeIP-4; NAEL-5v2; NAEL-6v2; NBLV; NIL-7; NOBL; OxBTC; PAI; PeLV; PeVV; SCV; TFi; TRP

(O'Melia, my dear, this does everything crown!) NoP-4; PoPoPo

Ruined Motel, The. Reginald Gibbons. BodElec

Ruined stone temple by the side of a lake, A. Ian Hamilton Finlay. PFTM-2 *Fr.* Images from the Arcadian Dream Garden.

Ruined, time ruined, all these once good things. Rimrock, Where It Is. Hayden Carruth. NNaP

Ruines of Rome: by Bellay. Edmund Spenser.

    "Who lists to see, what ever nature, arte." PBRV

Ruines of Time, The. Edmund Spenser. OxAEP-1

Ruinous Rains. Fu Hsien. CoBCP, *tr. by* Burton Watson

Ruins of a Great House. Derek Walcott. TwCP

    (Stones only, the disjecta membra of this.) PoPoPo

Ruins of Corinth, The. Antipater of Sidon. GrAn, *tr. by* Peter Jay

Ruins of Drégel have sunk in the clouds, The. Two Pages of Szondi, The. János Arany. IQMS, *tr. by* Adam Makkai

Ruins of Lo-yang, The. Ts'ao Chih. ChiP, *tr. by* Arthur Waley

Ruins of Rome. Joachim Du Bellay.

    Antiquitez de Rome. OBVE, *tr. by* Edmund Spenser

    "Hope ye, my verses, that posterity." PoE

    "Who list the Romane greatnes forth to figure." OBVE

Ruins of the City of Hay. Randolph Stow. CBAP

Ruins of Time, The. Luis de Góngora y Argote. WoPoe, *tr. by* Robert Lowell

Ruins of Walsingham, The. *Unknown.* NoSic

    (In the wrackes of walsingam.) PBRV

    (In the wracks of Walsingham.) NoP-4

    (Lament for Our Lady's Shrine at Walsingham, A.) NPeEn; NoP-4; PBRV

    (Walsingam oh farewell.) (LL) PBRV

Ruins under the Stars. Galway Kinnell. LCAP-2

Ruispiri—A Comic Ballad. Bulat Shalvovich Okudzhava. RusPo, *tr. by* Robert Arthur Douglas Ford

Rule, Britannia! James Thomson. GTBS-P; NOEC; OBWP; TreFP *Fr.* Alfred: A Masque.

RULE: It is important not to wear out the freshness and original taste of a person's. Art of the Nickname, The. Dominique Parker. SpirFl

Rule of Thirds, The. Jack Coulehan. BloBone

Rule over myself He has taken away from me. (LL) James Keir Baxter. HarvBoo; PeNZ *Fr.* Jerusalem Sonnets.

Rule well v, and come to hevyn. (LL) Ten Commandments, Seven Deadly Sins, and Five Wits. *Unknown.* FaBoEE; MiEL

Rule which by obeying grows. Intellect. Ralph Waldo Emerson. APN-1; NoP-4

Ruler, The. Robin Blaser. FTOS

Rules and Lessons. Henry Vaughan. ESCV

Rules and Ranges for Ian Tyson. Roy Fisher. Oth

Rules and Regulations. Lewis Carroll. NOBVV; PeVV

Rules of Sleep. Howard Moss. VCAP

Rules of the Road, The. Cy Coleman. ReLy

Rum Tum Tugger, The. T. S. Eliot. TriCat

Rumanian of Maria Banus, The. George MacBeth [*or* Macbeth]. Poem of Death, A. HP

Rumba. José Zacarías Tallet. TTY, *tr. by* Sangodare Akanji

Rumble, A. Virginia Schonborg. SSCS

Rumble on, machines of the gold mines. In the Gold Mines. B. W. Vilakazi. TTY

Rumbling in the chimneys. Windy Nights. Rodney Bennett. KaS

Rumbling sound of man. Buzz. Jim Tollerud. VoR

Rumbling under blackened girders, Midland, bound for Cricklewood. Parliament Hill Fields. Sir John Betjeman. FaBoTw; NOBE

Ruminant pillows! Gregarious soft boulders! Black Faced Sheep, The. Donald Hall. LCAP-2

Rummaging a drawer I found the bee glue. Resin. Patricia Pogson. NLP

Rummle an' dunt o' watter. Sumburgh Heid. George Bruce. OxBS

Rumor had it there had been. Storm Surf. Greg Pape. MoASP

Rumor's Rooster. Ray DiPalma. PmAP

Rumors fly and you can't tell where they start. They Say It's Wonderful. Irving Berlin. ReLy

Rumors from an Aeolian Harp. Henry David Thoreau. APN-1

Rumors of it kept my doors sealed. Potato Bug. Charles Webb. UrbNat

Rumoured thief. Sam Smith. NewEx

Rumpelstiltskin Convention. Charles Webb. ReTh

Rumpelstiltskin. Glyn Maxwell. OBCoV

Rumpty-iddity, row, row, row. *Unknown.* OxNR

RUN AWAY from this sub- / scriber for the second time. Reward. Kevin Young. SpirFl

Run before Dawn. William Stafford. MoASP

Run down by fate's spite. Lament for Five Sons Lost in a Plague. Abu Dhu'ayb al-Hudhali. ArPe; WoPoe, *tr. by* Omar Pound and Omar S. Pound

Run like rats from the plague in you. Saint Coleman's Song for Flight/ An Ite Missa Est. Padraic Fiacc. PNI

Run, my verse, my hound—fetch it! Prelude, Spoken to My Work Tools. Aleksey [*or* Aleksei] Ivanovich Parshchikov. TCRP, *tr. by* John High

Run, Nigger, Run! *Unknown.* BPo

Run out the boat, my broken comrades. Thalassa. Louis MacNeice. BIrV; FaBoMo; NOBE; WoPoe

Run, tailors, run / or she'll kill you all e'en now. (LL) Snail, The. Mother Goose. LB; OxNR; ReMoGo

Run to Death. Amy Levy. ViWPN

Run to Mourne End Wood, The. John Masefield. EBNV *Fr.* Reynard the Fox.

Run toward the Nightland. *Unknown.*

    "Now! The Red Tobacco has come to strike your soul." STP

Runagate Runagate. Robert Earl Hayden. APT-2; BPo; ESEAA; GM; LCAP-2; NAAAL; SSLK

    (I runs falls rises stumbles on from darkness into darkness.) ISC

Runaway. Honor Moore. Unle

Runaway, The. Robert Frost. AWP; FaBoCh; MoAmPo; SAmP; TwCP; VGW

Runaway Cow, A. Cathal Ó Searcaigh. ModIr, *tr. by* Patrick Crotty

Runaway Slave at Pilgrim's Point, The. Elizabeth Barrett Browning. BrRo; NALW; VWP; ViWPN

Runaway slave came to my house and stopt outside, The. Walt Whitman. HHAm *Fr.* Song of Myself.

Runaway son, A. Wandering. Muso Soseki. EaWin, *tr. by* W. S. Merwin

Runaways, The. Mark Van Doren. PoRA

Runaways Café II. Marilyn Hacker. NoAM

Rundown Church (Ballad of the First World War). Federico García Lorca. RaBo, *tr. by* Robert Bly

    (Rundown Church.) AF, *tr. by* Robert Bly

Rune-Maker, The. Frederick Feirstein. RA

Rune of the Finland Woman. Marilyn Hacker. RA

Rune Poem, The. *Unknown.*

    "We love the daylight." WoPoe, *tr. by* James Paul

Runes on Weland's Sword, The. Rudyard Kipling. NoAM *Fr.* Puck of Pook's Hill.

Rung from their Marble Caves, repent, repent. (LL)   For the Baptiste.   William Drummond, of Hawthornden.   NPeEn; OxBEV; PBRV

Rung from their marble [or flinty] caves "Repent! Repent!" (LL)   Saint John Baptist.   William Drummond, of Hawthornden.   GTBS-P; NOBE; OBEV; OxAEP-1; TrCP

Runnable Stag, A.   John Davidson.   EBNV; HAP; OBEV; OxBTC

Runner, The.   Gary Gildner.   TAP

Runner, The.   Louis Simpson.   AF

Runner, The.   Walt Whitman.   BLT; InPK-6; SAmP
    (On a flat road runs the well-trained runner.)   KaS

Runner in the Skies, The.   James Oppenheim.   TrJP

Runners creak, The. Dead snow broke like day.   Winter Sonnets, The.   Vyacheslav Ivanovich Ivanov.   TCRusP, tr. by Mary Jane White

Runnin' scared—runnin' scared.   Running Scared.   Miguel Piñero.   PueRic

Running.   Brendan Galvin.   MoASP

Running.   Leslie Ullman.   PBCAP

Running.   Richard Wilbur.   CoAP; MoASP

Running Battle, A.   Brendan Kennelly.   BiHa

Running down the fell, I round a rock.   Yew.   Elizabeth Delmore.   NLP

Running downhill, spilling over, searching and spilling.   Flood Water.   Unknown.   NOBAu, tr. by Mungayana Nundhirribala

Running from death.   Death and the Dancer.   Muriel Rukeyser.   AF

Running from his eye to his ear. (LL)   Middleaged Man, The.   Louis Simpson.   BodElec; NNaP

Running from Trouble.   Tu Fu.   CrYelRi, tr. by Sam Hamill

Running Hares.   Tessa Rose Chester.   MFPA

Running Lightly over Spongy Ground.   Theodore Roethke.   RB

Running on Empty.   Robert Phillips.   InPK-6

Running over the fields. (LL)   Days.   Philip Larkin.   EBEV; FaBoMo; NPeEn; OxAEP-2; OxBC; OxBEV; OxBSP; PeECV; PoetW; RB; TOF; WoPoe

Running Scared.   Miguel Piñero.   PueRic

Running shallow.   Arimaru.   JDP, tr. by Yoel Hoffmann

Running stream, The.   Chiboku.   JDP, tr. by Yoel Hoffmann

Running through the thick wiry grasses to the pond.   Shore.   Jean Garrigue.   TAP

Running to Paradise.   W. B. Yeats.   OxBoLi

Running waters, crystal clear and pure.   Nemoroso.   Baldomero Garcilaso de la Vega.   BLPSL, tr. by Rene de Costa, Rigas Kappatos and Eleni Paidoussi

Runoff.   William Everson.   NoAM

Runs falls rises stumbles on from darkness into darkness.   Runagate Runagate.   Robert Earl Hayden.   APT-2; BPo; ESEAA; GM; LCAP-2; NAAAL; SSLK

Runs on the standing windows and away. (LL)   Storm Windows.   Howard Nemerov.   CoAmPo; InPK-6; VCAP

Runt of a Dream, A.   Arthur Rimbaud.   WoPoe, tr. by Denis Goacher

Rupert Murdoch, with glee, shouted: "What."   Limerick.   Frank Richards.   PeLi

Rural Colloquy with a Painter.   Timothy Steele.   CRP

Rural Dance about the Maypole, The.   Unknown.   OxBoLi

Rural Lass, The.   Catherine Jemmat.   ECWP; NOEC

Rural letter box said Toffile Lajway, The. (LL)   Robert Frost.   APT-1; NOBA; NoAM; PoE   Fr. Two Witches.

Rural Life.   George Crabbe.   NOBE   Fr. Village, The.

Rural Lyre, The.   Ann Yearsley.   RWP

Rural Mail, The.   John Glassco.   MoCV

Rural Recreation.   Lillian Morrison.   KaS

Rural Scenes.   John Clare.   CenSon

Rural Simplicity.   Henry James Byron.   NOBL

Rush hour. I board the train.   Notes from the Defense of Colin Ferguson.   Sekou Sundiata.   ESEAA

Rushes daily grow taller, The.   Farm Routine.   Ch'u Kuang-hsi.   SuSp, tr. by Joseph J. Lee

Rushing.   Ray A. Young Bear.   CDW

Rushing at times.   Rushing at Times Like Flames.   Nelly Sachs.   WPoS, tr. by Matthew Mead and Ruth Mead

Rushing at Times Like Flames.   Nelly Sachs.   WPoS, tr. by Matthew Mead and Ruth Mead

Ruskie's Boy.   Víctor Hernández Cruz.   PueRic

Russ Joy Little League.   Douglas Carlson.   MoASP

Russia.   Aleksandr Aleksandrovich Blok.   AWP, tr. by Babette Deutsch and Avrahm Yarmolinsky

Russia.   Maksimilian Aleksandrovich Voloshin.
    "Peter the Great, first Bolshevik."   TCRP

Russia.   William Carlos Williams.   VGW

Russia can't be grasped by the mind.   Mariya [or Mariia] Avakkumova.   TCRP

Russia 1812.   Victor Hugo.   FaBoWar; OBWP, tr. by Robert Lowell

Russia has lost Russia in Russia.   Loss.   Yevgeny Aleksandrovich Yevtushenko [or Evtushenko].   TCRP, tr. by James Reagan and Yevgeny Yevtushenko

Russia, 1927.   Ai.   NoAM

Russia's Resentment.   Lizelia Augusta Jenkins Moorer.   CBWP-3

Russia set thousands and thousands free.   Me and Russia.   Velemir [or Viktor Vladimirovich] Khlebnikov.   TCRusP, tr. by Kathy Lewis and Bob Perelman

Russian Asylum.   Marilyn Bowering.   NOBC

Russian cemetery is too shabby for dawdlers, The.   Olsanski Cemetery, The.   Yury Iofe.   TCRusP, tr. by John Glad

Russian Cradle Song, A.   David Nomberg.   TrJP, tr. by Alter Brody

Russian God, The.   Prince P. A. Vyazemsky.   WoPoe, tr. by Alan Meyers and Alan Myers

Russian Gods, The.   Daniil Leonidovich Andreyev [or Andreiev].
    "Night winds! Dark mountainous skies."   TCRP

Russian Mind, The.   Vyacheslav Ivanovich Ivanov.   TCRP, tr. by Albert C. Todd

Russian New Year.   Bill Berkson.   PmAP

Russian sailed over the blue Black Sea, A.   "Soldier, Rest!"   Robert Jones Burdette.   OBAL

Russian Soul II, The.   John Hollander.   NBLV

Russian Student's Tale, The.   Mathilde Blind.   VWP

Russian Woman.   "Igor Severyanin [or Severianin]."   TCRP, tr. by Bernard Meares

Russians.   Keith Douglas.   OxBTC

Russians Breathing.   Philip Hammial.   NOBAu

Rust and silence fill the thatch.   Wole Soyinka.   HBAPE

Rust is ripeness, rust.   Wole Soyinka.   PBMAP   Fr. Idanre and Other Poems (1967).

Rustic Courtship.   Robert Dodsley.   ECEV   Fr. Agriculture.

Rustic inn, our evening resting place, A. (LL)   Ruined Cottage, The.   William Wordsworth.   NAEL-6v2; NoP-4

Rustic mango-stone, The.   Family Pride.   T. S. Venugopalan.   OMIP, tr. by Rajagopal Parthasarathy

Rustic person like me seldom spends a night in a mountain home, A.   Viewing Mr. Yü's Landscape Painting on the Wall.   Wang Chi.   SuSp, tr. by Joseph J. Lee

Rustic Temple Is Hidden, The.   Chu Chen Po.   OHMPC, tr. by Kenneth Rexroth

Rustily creak the crickets: Jack Frost came down last night.   Jack Frost.   Celia Laighton Thaxter.   OBCA

Rustle of Birches.   Gennady Aygi.   TCRusP, tr. by Peter France

Rustle of each falling leaf, The.   Love.   Samuele Romanelli.   TrJP, tr. by A. B. Rhine

Rustle of whispering wind over leaves, A.   Kingfisher Flat.   William Everson.   PoM

Rustler.   William Stroud.   Spl

Rustling across the wild barley's withered blade. (LL)   Letters from the Ming Dynasty.   Joseph Brodsky.   PoetW; TCRP, tr. by Derek Walcott

Rustling dry paper.   Richard Wright.   APT-2

Rustling of the silk is discontinued, The.   Liu Ch'e.   Ezra Pound.   APT-1; OBVE; VGW

Rusty.   Gordon Lish.   Unle

Rusty Man, The.   Herman Melville.   NCAP

Ruth.   Bible, O.T.
    "And Naomi said/ Unto her two daughters-in-law."   TrJP
    Naomi and Ruth.   TrJP

Ruth.   Mary Crockett Hill.   AmPoNex

Ruth.   Thomas Hood.   BoLoP; ChIV-1; EnLoPo; NOBE; OBEV

Ruth.   Elizaveta Kuzmina-Karavayeva.   ARWW, tr. by Catriona Kelly

Ruth.   Norman J. Loftis.   SpirFl

Ruth.   Colleen J. McElroy.   BlSi

Ruth [or, The Influences of Nature].   William Wordsworth.   GTBS-P

Rutherford McDowell.   Edgar Lee Masters.   OxBA   Fr. Spoon River Anthology.

Rwose in the Dark, The.   William Barnes.   NOBVV

Rye Bread.   William Stanley Braithwaite.   GT

Rye, flax, horses, platinum, timber, and fur. (LL)   Monkeys, The.   Marianne Craig Moore.   APT-1; NOBA; OxBA

Rye Whiskey.   Unknown.   OxBoLi

Rye Whisky.   Unknown.   OxBoLi

(Ryokan's scroll).   Louis Zukofsky.   APT-2

S

S.F. homebound kearny street.   Manong with a Thousand Tribal Visions, The.   Al Robles.   ReBoTo

S.F. Southward. Allen Ginsberg. NAAL-2v2 *Fr.* Continuation of a Long Poem of These States.

S.L.A.M. Giovanna Pollarolo. TANSG, *tr. by* Marjorie Agosin

S'posin'. Paul Denniker. ReLy

S sz sz SZ sz SZ sz ZS zs Zs zs zs z. Siesta of a Hungarian Snake. Edwin Morgan. HarvBoo; InPK-6

S. W. Rafael Campo. BloBone

'S Wonderful. George Gershwin. ReLy

Saadi. Ralph Waldo Emerson. APN-1; OxBA

Sabbath. John Berryman. LCAP-2 *Fr.* Dream Songs.

Sabbath and sweet spices. Susan Howe. PmAP *Fr.* Speeches at the Barriers.

Sabbath Bells. John Clare. FHYEP

Sabbath Bells. Josephine D. Henderson Heard. CBWP-4

Sabbath Day Was By, The. Howard Chandler Robbins. AH

Sabbath Morning. Marcia Falk. TaR

Sabbath, My Love. Judah Halevi. TrJP, *tr. by* Solomon Solis-Cohen

Sabbath of Rest, A. Isaac Luria. TrJP, *tr. by* Nina Davis Salaman

Sabbath Sonnet. Felicia Dorothea Hemans. Son

Sabbath, the pious carry no money. Voice out of the Sabbaths, A. Derek Walcott. WeW-3

Sabbaths. Robert Herrick. SacPr

Sabbaths are threefold (as S. Austine sayes). Sabbaths. Robert Herrick. SacPr

Sable arrested a fine comb. Jack Spicer. FTOS *Fr.* Love Poems.

Sabotage. Anselm Berrigan. HeMarv

Saboteur autumn has riddled the pampered folds. Wild Honey. Francis Webb. NOBAu

Sabrina. John Milton. *See* Comus; a Masque Presented at Ludlow Castle

Sabrina Fair. John Milton. EBEV; FaBoCh; OxBEV; WoPoe *Fr.* Comus; a Masque Presented at Ludlow Castle.

Sabrina's Song. John Milton. *See* Comus; a Masque Presented at Ludlow Castle

Sack of kittens, The. Nicholas Virgilio. HA

Sacrament of Poverty, The. Marilyn Nelson. ExTi; GT

Sacrament of the Altar, The. *Unknown.* NoP-4

Sacré Dieu, I said for the very first time. Hinglish. Gerald Stern. BodElec

Sacred. Gertrude Stein. OBAL

Sacred and Profane Love, or, There's Nothing New under the Moon Either. Peter De Vries. NBLV; OBCoV

Sacred and secular. Inauguration of Fukusan Dormitory. Muso Soseki. EaWin, *tr. by* W. S. Merwin

Sacred Book, The. Zoroaster [*or* Zarathustra]. AWP, *tr. by* A. V. Williams Jackson

Sacred Chant for the Return of Black Spirit and Power. Imamu Amiri Baraka. NBV

Sacred Children, The. Hoffman Reynolds Hays. SPE

Sacred Cow of Hardship, The. Agi Mishol. DTA, *tr. by* Tsipi Keller

Sacred Dramas. Hannah More. RWP

Sacred Formula to Destroy Life. *Unknown.* PAI, *tr. by* James Mooney

Sacred Grove, A. Edward Cracroft Lefroy. AWP *Fr.* Echoes from Theocritus.

Sacred Grove, A. Fran Winant. BrRo

Sacred Hatred. João da Cruz e Sousa. TCLAP, *tr. by* Flavia Vidal

Sacred Hearth, The. David Gascoyne. FaBoTw

Sacred Heliconian spring, The. Clara Reeve. ECWP *Fr.* To My Friend Mrs.———, on Her Holding an Argument in Favour of the Natural Equality of Both the Sexes.

Sacred marble, clothed in spirit and strength. Venus de Milo. Charles Marie René Leconte de Lisle. GS, *tr. by Unknown*

Sacred mouthpiece of the Muses Pindar. Nine Lyric Poets, The. *Unknown.* GrAn, *tr. by* Peter Jay

Sacred Mt. Hua, terrace of clouds. Seeing Off Han Ju-ch'ing as He Returns to the Land Within the Passes. Ho Ching-ming. CoBLCP, *tr. by* Jonathan Chaves

Sacred muse that first[e] made love divine [*or* devine], The. Sir John Davies. NoSic; OxBSo; PBRV *Fr.* Gulling[e] Sonnets, The.

Sacred night / Through masks. Kikaku. ZenPo, *tr. by* Takashi Ikemoto and Lucien Stryk

Sacred or secular. Old Man at Leisure. Muso Soseki. EaWin, *tr. by* W. S. Merwin

Sacred Religion, mother of form and fear. Samuel Daniel. NoSic *Fr.* Musophilus; or, Defence of All Learning.

Sacred Religion! "mother of form and fear." William Wordsworth. CenSon *Fr.* River Duddon [A Series of Sonnets], The.

Sacred Songs of the Konkau. *Unknown.*

 Acorn Song, The. APN-2, *tr. by* Stephen Powers

 Ki-u-nad'-dis-si's Song. APN-2, *tr. by* Stephen Powers

 Red Cloud's Song. APN-2, *tr. by* Stephen Powers

Sacred tree midst the fair orchard grew, The. Tree of Knowledge, The. Abraham Cowley. ChIV-1

Sacred Trees. Jayne Cortez. SurWo

Sacred words?, The. (LL) Ka 'Ba. Imamu Amiri Baraka. BPo; ISC; NBV; PmAP; TAP

Sacred Wrath. Vahan Tekeyan. GI

Sacrifice. Albania and the Death of Enver Hoxha. Will Alexander. PFTM-2

Sacrifice. Melanie Hope. WiU

Sacrifice. Gyula Illyés. IQMS, *tr. by* Marie B. Jaffe

Sacrifice. Nana Issaia. BoWoP, *tr. by* Helle Tzalopoulou Barnstone

Sacrifice. Léon Laleau. NegPo, *tr. by* Ellen Conroy Kennedy *Fr.* Black Music.

Sacrifice. Christopher Okigbo. PBMAP

Sacrifice, A. Robert Davenport. NOSC

Sacrifice, The. Frank Bidart. GLP; VCAP

Sacrifice, The. George Herbert. GeHe

Sacrifice, The. Gertrud Kolmar. AF, *tr. by* David Kipp

Sacrifice: An Epistle to Celia, The. Mary Leapor. PEW

Sacrifice of Er-Heb, The. Rudyard Kipling. PeVV

Sacrifice of Isaac, The. Rabbi Ephraim ben Jacob. NAWM-7v1, *tr. by* Judah Goldin

Sacrifice to Apollo, The. Michael Drayton. NOSC

Sacrifice to Apollo, The. Homer. OBVE, *tr. by* John Dryden *Fr.* Iliad, The.

Sacrificed Author, A. Howard Nemerov. GI *Fr.* Gnomes.

Sacrificial Wolf. Anne Rouse. MFPA; NeBl

Sad and great evil is the expectation of death, A. Palladas [*or* Pallades]. GrAn

Sad and lonely, I sew a bag that holds heaven. From So Mountain. *Vietnamese Oral Tradition.* CaDao, *tr. by* John Balaban

Sad and solemn night, The. Hymn to the North Star. William Cullen Bryant. NCAP

Sad and solemn verse doth please the mind, A. Discourse of Melancholy, A. Margaret Lucas Cavendish, Duchess of Newcastle. NOSC

Sad beauty? Basho. EH, *tr. by* Robert Hass

Sad Birds, The. Harry Mathews. PmAP

Sad Boy, The. Laura Riding Jackson. RB

Sad Children's Song, The. Grace Paley. SoSe-8; TaR

Sad Day, The. Thomas Flatman. OBEV

Sad for those without sweet Anglo-Saxon. Change, The. David [*or* Daibhi][*or* Daithi] O'Bruadair [*or* Ó Bruadair]. BIrV, *tr. by* Austin Clarke

Sad Green. Sylvia Townsend Warner. MoBrPo

Sad guard / Haven't you slept? Dialogue. Buland Al-Haidari [*or* Al-Haydari]. MAP, *tr. by* Patricia Alanah Byrne and Salma Khadra Jayyusi

Sad-hearted, be at peace: the snowdrop lies. O Thou of Little Faith! George Macdonald. SacPr

Sad Hesper o'er the buried sun. Tennyson. EBVV; NAEL-6v2 *Fr.* In Memoriam A. H. H.

Sad, I blame Mister Sky. Tao. *Vietnamese Oral Tradition.* CaDao, *tr. by* John Balaban

Sad, idle, I think of my dead mother. Red Cloth, The. *Vietnamese Oral Tradition.* CaDao, *tr. by* John Balaban

Sad is our home. Mumbling. Enrique Banchs. BLPSL, *tr. by* Rene de Costa, Rigas Kappatos and Eleni Paidoussi

Sad is the burying in the sunshine. Rhyme from Lincolnshire, A. *Unknown.* NPeEn

Sad is the man who is asked for a story. Story, A. Li-Young Lee. LoL; RaBo

Sad Joke on a Marae. Apirana Taylor. PeNZ

Sad, lost in thought, and mute I go. *Unknown.* AWP

Sad music from vermilion strings. Telling My Feelings. Yü Hsüan-chi. BoWoP, *tr. by* Geoffrey Waters

Sad nodes. Basho. EH, *tr. by* Robert Hass

Sad Ode. Alma Johanna Koenig. AuPH, *tr. by* Lowell A. Bangerter

Sad, on Broadway next afternoon. Francis Saltus Saltus. VerBaPo *Fr.* In a Book-store.

Sad, purple well! whose bubbling eye. Abel's Blood. Henry Vaughan. OBWVE

Sad refrain I heard, from poet sad, A. Forevermore. Jones Very. NCAP

Sad Remembrance. Mei Yao Ch'en. CoBCP; ColAnChi, *tr. by* Burton Watson

Sad, sad—lean with long illness. Illness. Po Chü-i. ChiP, *tr. by* Arthur Waley

Sad, sad they leave their old village. Tu Fu. SuSp *Fr.* Frontier Songs, First Series.

Sad seamstress, The. House Guest. Elizabeth Bishop. TAP

Sad Sestina. Robin Becker. BodElec

Sad Shepherd, The. Ben Jonson.

 Death and Love. NOBE

 Here She Was Wont to Go. BeJo; OxBSP

"Though I am young, and cannot tell." NOBE

Sad Song. Laura Kasischke. PuP-23

Sad Song. *Unknown.* ChinPo, *tr. by* Yip Wai-lim

Sad Song. *Unknown.* CoBCP, *tr. by* Burton Watson

Sad Song, A. Stephen Vincent Benét. *See* Nonsense Song, A

Sad song for weeping. Sad Song. *Unknown.* ChinPo, *tr. by* Yip Wai-lim

Sad songs of Autumn mirth. (LL) Digging. Edward Thomas. MoBrPo; OxBTC

Sad Spring-Song. Sarah Morgan Bryan Piatt. NCAP

Sad Steps. Philip Larkin. NAEL-6v2; NoAM; NoP-4

Sad Story of a Little boy That Cried, The. *Unknown.* OBSP

Sad Strains of a Gay Waltz. Wallace Stevens. OxBA

Sad Thyrsis weeps till his blue eyes are dim. Edward Cracroft Lefroy. AWP *Fr.* Echoes from Theocritus.

Sad, to shut / to shut other. Nearly Circle. Heather Ramsdell. AmPoNex

Sad Voices, The. Ricardo Jaimes Freyre. TCLAP, *tr. by* Iver Lofving

Sad was his countenance, if we can call. Philip Freneau. NAAL-2v1; NAAL-3 *Fr.* House of Night, The.

Sad was the morn', the sadder week began. Pindaric on the Death of our Late Sovereign: With an Ancient Prophecy on His Present Majority, A. Aphra Behn. BASC

Sad? / (admit it). Picasso Shag. M. Loncar. AmPoNex

Saddest day will have an eve, The. Hope. Clara Ann Thompson. CBWP-2

Saddest noise, the sweetest noise, The. Emily Dickinson. OWoS

Saddhu of Couva, The. Derek Walcott. BodElec

Saddle and Cell. The Three Marias. BoWoP, *tr. by* Helen R. Lane

Saddled and briddled. Bonnie James Campbell. *Unknown.* ESPB

Saddled Ass, The. Jean de La Fontaine. NBLV, *tr. by* Deems Taylor

Sadie. Philip Hammial. BMAP

Sadie and Maud. Gwendolyn Brooks. ESEAA; InPK-6; NAAAL; NOBA; NoAM; TAP *Fr.* Street in Bronzeville, A

Sadie Snuffs a Candle. Dolores Kendrick. ESEAA

Sadie, who was only twelve, wrote each letter down. Ellis Island, September 1907. Andrea Hollander Budy. OPRER

Sadistic Love. Julio Herrera y Reissig. BLPSL, *tr. by* Rene de Costa, Rigas Kappatos and Eleni Paidoussi

Sadly I see. Chine. JDP, *tr. by* Yoel Hoffmann

Sadly, sadly the season draws to an end. Hsü Kan. SuSp *Fr.* Boudoir Thoughts.

Sadly the dead leaves rustle in the whistling wind. Church of a Dream, The. Lionel Pigot Johnson. CABP; OBMV

Sadly unroll sleepingbag. 25:I:68. Philip Whalen. PoM

Sadness. Mary Elizabeth Coleridge. ViWPN

Sadness. Shuntaro Tanikawa. VCWP, *tr. by* Harold Wright

Sadness. Tennyson. FaBoEE

Sadness and grace are closely linked, with feeling. Mozart, Piano Concerto No. 20 in D Minor, K.466. Ernst Waldinger. AuPH, *tr. by* Lowell A. Bangerter

Sadness in Spring. *Unknown.* OBVVE, *tr. by* Gwyn Jones

Sadness in the Autumn Chambers. Yün Shou-p'ing. CoBLCP, *tr. by* Jonathan Chaves

Sadness in the human visage stares, The. At an Exhibition of Historical Paintings, Hobart. Vivian Smith. CBAP; NOBAu

Sadness of afternoons was unmistakable, The. After the War; When Coltrane Only Wanted to Play Dance Tunes. Matthew Graham. SeSe

Sadness of Couples, The. Barbara Ras. NAPBL

Sadness of Leaving, The. Eileen Myles. PmAP

Sadness of Memory, The. Barbara Ras. NAPBL

Sadness of the Sea, The. William Carlos Williams. ColAP

Sadness, stillness in the room. Illness. Franta Bass. INSAB

Sadness, the languor of the human body, The. Paul Verlaine. SxFrPo, *tr. by* Martin Sorrell

Sae let the Lord be thankit. (LL) Grace at Kirkudbright. Robert Burns. OxBEV; OxBSP

Safaddan. Ruth Bidgood. TCAWP

Safe. James Walker. OBCP

Safe-Conduct. Ingeborg Bachmann. PoSu, *tr. by* Daniel Huws

Safe from the wolf's [*or* wolves] black jaw, and the dull ass's [*or* Asses] hoof[e]. (LL) Ode To Himself, An. Ben Jonson. BASC; BeJo; CABP; HAP; NOBE; NOSC; NPeEn; NoP-4; OxAEP-1; PBRV; SCGP

Safe is the man with blunderbuss. Ernest. Malcolm Cowley. APT-2

Safe-T-Man. Kate Light. AmPoNex *Fr.* Five Urban Love Songs.

Safe upon the solid rock the ugly houses stand. Second Fig. Edna St. Vincent Millay. APT-1; NALW; NoP-4

Safety. Rupert Brooke. EnLoPo *Fr.* 1914.

Safety-Clutch. Ambrose Bierce. APN-2; OBAL *Fr.* Devil's Dictionary, The.

Saffron-colored leaves are cresting into their moment, The. It's. Autumnal. Mark Irwin. PuP-23

Sag' Mir Wer Einst die Uhren Erfund. Heinrich Heine. *See* Who Was It, Tell Me

Sag', wo ist dein schönes Liebchen. Heinrich Heine. AWP, *tr. by* James Thomson

Saga. Andrey [*or* Andrei] Andreievich Voznesensky [*or* Voznesenskii]. TCRP, *tr. by* Vera Dunham and William Jay Smith

Saga of Gisli, The. *Unknown.* OBVE, *tr. by* George Johnston

Saga of Jenny, The. Kurt Weill. ReLy

Sagacity. William Rose Benét. MoAmPo

Sagamore, The. B. P. Shillaber. TreFP

Sage and the ordinary man both have bodies, The. Poem on Buddha's Begging Bowl—For Hui-ku, His Holiness Ming, A. Hsü Pen. CoBLCP, *tr. by* Jonathan Chaves

Sage Counsel. Sir Arthur Thomas Quiller-Couch. NBLV

Sage in Unison, The. Harold Stewart. NOBAu

Sage nor saint nor soldier—these were not. At the Monument to Pierre Louÿs. Richard Howard. VCAP

Sage Philosophy. Richard Jago. ECEV *Fr.* Edge-Hill; or, The Rural Prospect Delineated and Moralised.

Sagebrush (*Artemisia*) is of the sunflower family, or Compositae. It is. Gary Snyder. APSN *Fr.* Mountains and Rivers without End: The Market.

Sagesse. "H. D."

"You look at me, a hut or cage contains." NOCV

"Or is it a great tide that covers the rock-pool." WPoS

Sagesse. Paul Verlaine.

"Sky is up above the roof, The." AWP

"Slumber dark and deep." AWP

Sagest of women, even of widows, she. Byron. NOBL; PeLV *Fr.* Don Juan.

Sagimusume: The White Heron Maiden. Jonny Kyoko Sullivan. WPOW

Saginaw Song, The. Theodore Roethke. NBLV; RB

Sahara. Coventry Patmore. EBVV *Fr.* Angel in the House, The.

Sahara to America, The. Aleksei Eliseievich Kruchyonykh [*or* Kruchionykh *or* Kruchenykh].

"Who wants to think of us as five? Five keen-nosed grey-maned black-." PFTM-1

Said. George Starbuck. OBAL

Said a boastful young student from Hayes. Limerick. Frank Richards. PeLi

Said a diffident lady named Drood. Limerick. *Unknown.* PeLi

Said a dreadfully literate cat. Limerick. Conrad Potter Aiken. PeLi

Said a fair-headed maiden of Klondike. Limerick. Langford Reed. PeLi

Said a famous old writer called Fender. Limerick. Victor Gray. PeLi

Said a fervent young lady of Hammels. Limerick. Morris Gilbert Bishop. PeLi

Said a foolish young lady of Wales. Limerick. Langford Reed. PeLi

Said a girl in green Mansfield Park. Limerick. E. O. Parrott. PeLi

Said a gloomy young fellow called Fart. Limerick. Victor Gray. PeLi

Said a God-fearing lady called Whitehouse. Limerick. Roger Woddis. PeLi

Said a herring one day to a sole. Limerick. Stanley J. Sharpless. PeLi

Said a luscious young lady called Wade. Limerick. *Unknown.* PeLi

Said a maid: "I will marry for lucre." Limerick. *Unknown.* PeLi

Said a Marxist who stood on the pier. Limerick. W. H. G. Price. PeLi

Said a medical student, unmanned. Limerick. Allan M. Laing. PeLi

Said a parson, addressing his flock. Limerick. W. J. Strachan. PeLi

Said a practical thinker: "One should." Limerick. Frank Watson. PeLi

Said a pupil of Einstein: "It's rotten." Limerick. C. F. Best. PeLi

Said a scarecrow swingin' on a pole. If I Only Had a Brain (If I Only Had a Heart) (If I Only Had the Nerve). Harold Arlen. ReLy

Said a Tripper: "O joy, to have found." Limerick. Thomas Thorneley. PeLi

Said a wife to her husband near Scole. Limerick. Ida Thurtle. PeLi

Said / Agatha Christie to. George Starbuck. OBCoV

Said an ape as he swung by his tail. Limerick. *Unknown.* PeLi

Said an elderly Bishop called Greville. Limerick. "Little Billee." PeLi

Said an eminent, erudite ermine. Limerick. *Unknown.* PeLi

Said an erudite sinologue: "How." Limerick. R. J. P. Hewison. OBCoV; PeLi

Said Arnold to Arthur Hugh Clough. Limerick. Victor Gray. PeLi

Said Dorothy Hughes to Helen Hocking. William Jay Smith. KaS

Said Fading-leaf to Fallen-leaf. Fading-Leaf and Fallen-Leaf. Richard Garnett. EBVV

Said Freud: "I've discovered the Id." Limerick. Frank Richards. PeLi

Said God, "You sisters, ere ye go." Hope and Despair. Lascelles Abercrombie. OBMV

Said Harry to Holyoake. Private Conference of Harry Fat, The. James Keir Baxter. PeLV

Said I many times. I'm Glad There Is You (In This World of Ordinary People). Paul Madeira. ReLy

Said, I, Oh, give me simplicity. Rural Simplicity. Henry James Byron. NOBL

Said Isolde to Tristan: "How curious!" Limerick. Conrad Potter Aiken. PeLi

Said Jerome K. Jerome to Ford Madox Ford. Mutual Problem. William Cole. OBAL; OBCoV

Said King Pompey. Dame Edith Sitwell. BWW; UV

Said lady once to lover. Three Bushes, The. W. B. Yeats. EBNV

Said Little Boy Blue. W. S. Brownlee. PeLi

Said Mario Praz to Mario Pei. Miniature Dialogue. Edmund Wilson. OBCoV

Said Marlowe: "Bay City's a drag." Limerick. Peter Alexander. PeLi

Said Mars when entangled with Venus. Limerick. Mary Holtby. PeLi

Said Miss Farrow, on one of her larks. Limerick. *Unknown.* PeLi

Said Nelson at his most la-di-da-di. Limerick. A. Cinna. PeLi

Said Old Father William: "I'm humble." Limerick. Conrad Potter Aiken. PeLi

Said Old Nick: "Mister Lewis and me." Limerick. M. Cassell. PeLi

Said Orville to Wilbur "Hold tight!" Limerick. Stanley J. Sharpless. PeLi

Said Paisley: "I've given up hope." Limerick. Frank Richards. PeLi

Said Philip Sidney, buttoning his jerkin. Edmund Wilson. OBCoV *Fr.* Easy Exercises in the Use of Difficult Words.

Said philosopher-physicist Jeans. Limerick. R. C. Owen. PeLi

Said Plato: "The things that we feel." Limerick. Basil Ransome-Davies. PeLi

Said Powell: "Don't call me insane." Limerick. Roger Woddis. PeLi

Said, Pull her up a bit will you, Mac, I want to unload there. Reason. Josephine Miles. InPK-6; NALW; NoAM; TAP

Said Queen Isabella of Spain. Limerick. *Unknown.* PeLi

Said Tebbitt: "I don't understand 'em." Limerick. Gerry Hamill. PeLi

Said Tennyson: "Yes, *Locksley Hall*'s." Limerick. Victor Gray. PeLi

Said the boy driving home towards Clere. Limerick. Ida Thurtle. PeLi

Said the Canoe. Isabella Valancy Crawford. NOBC

Said the chief of the marriage feast to the groom, Wedding Feast, The. Edgar Lee Masters. ChIV-2

Said the Chinese philosopher, Lin. Limerick. Len. PeLi

Said the Duchess of Alba to Goya. Limerick. *Unknown.* PeLi

Said the Englishman: "W'at's all this bloomin' wow?" Foreigners at the Fair. Fred Emerson Brooks. OBAL

Said the famous philosopher, Russell. Limerick. Victor Gray. PeLi

Said the lady, Can you do. Langston Hughes. APSN

Said the Lion: "On music I dote." Musical Lion, The. Oliver Herford. OBCA

Said the Lion to the Lioness—"When you are amber dust." Heart and Mind. Dame Edith Sitwell. LW; OxBTC; TwCP

Said the mythical King of Algiers. Limerick. *Unknown.* PeLi

Said the newly-weds staying near Kitely. Limerick. *Unknown.* PeLi

Said the Queen to her favourite ghillie. Limerick. A. Cinna. PeLi

Said the Stoic, tormented by gout. Limerick. Thomas Thorneley. PeLi

Said the table to the chair. Table and the Chair, The. Edward Lear. ITBLP

Said the Undertaker to the Overtaker. Tweedledee and Tweedledoom. Ogden Nash. OBCoV

Said the vet as he looked at my pet. Limerick. Frank Richards. PeLi

Said the Wind to the Moon, 'I will blow you out' Wind and the Moon, The. George Macdonald. NOxBChV

Said to the children, and they fell asleep. (LL) My Father in the Night Commanding No. Louis Simpson. CoAP; CoAmPo; HeIP-4; NOBA; NoAM; PAI; TAP; TwCP; VGW

Said Uncle Sam to Harry Fat. Harry Fat and Uncle Sam. James Keir Baxter. PeLV

Said Wellington: "What's the location." Limerick. Frank Richards. PeLi

Said Wilbur Wright, "Oh, this is grand." Limerick. Frank Richards. PeLi

Said Wittgenstein: "Don't be misled!" Limerick. Peter Alexander. PeLi

Said Zwingli to Muntzer. How to Start a War. Phyllis McGinley. OBSV

Saies, "Come here, cuzen Gawaine so gay." King Arthur and King Cornwall. *Unknown.* ESPB

Saigon River, The. *Vietnamese Oral Tradition.* CaDao, *tr.* by John Balaban

Saigon River slides past the Old Market, The. Saigon River, The. *Vietnamese Oral Tradition.* CaDao, *tr.* by John Balaban

Sail, A. Mikhail Yuryevich Lermontov. AWP, *tr.* by Max Eastman

Sail Away. Robert Adamson. CBAP

Sail Away. Noël Coward. ReLy

Sail before the morning breeze. Archipelago, The. Herman Melville. APN-2

Sail is up, Fortune ruleth our helm, The. John Skelton. NoSic *Fr.* Bouge of Court, The.

Sail, Monarchs, rising and falling. Roots and Branches. Robert Duncan. FTOS; VGW

Sail Peacefully Home. Simeon Grigoryevich Frug. TrJP

Sailboats in line. Hokushi. ZenPo, *tr.* by Takashi Ikemoto and Lucien Stryk

Sailed. Aaron Shurin. FTOS

Sailing. Richard Kenney. YaYoPo

Sailing. Henrik Nordbrandt. VCWP, *tr.* by Henrik Norbrandt and Alexander Taylor

Sailing along the Tai Stream from Stone Bridge to the Foot of Mo-ho Peak. Wang Shih-chieng. SuSp, *tr.* by Chang Yin-nan

Sailing at Dusk from T'u-sung. Wu Wei-yeh. SuSp, *tr.* by Chang Yin-nan

Sailing at Night on Flowing-sand River. Lin Hung. SuSp, *tr.* by Irving Y. Lo

Sailing Back to the Capital. Chan Fang-sheng. ChinPo, *tr.* by Yip Wai-lim

Sailing Down the Han. Wang Wei. CrYelRi, *tr.* by Sam Hamill

Sailing from the United States. Stanley Moss. VGW

Sailing Home from Rapallo. Robert Lowell. HCAP; PoPoPo; PoetW; TAP

Sailing Homeward. Chan Fang-sheng. AWP; ChiP; FaBoCh, *tr.* by Arthur Waley

Sailing into the South Lake. Chan Fang-sheng. ChinPo, *tr.* by Yip Wai-lim

Sailing on Men River, I heard. Soan. ZenPo, *tr.* by Takashi Ikemoto and Lucien Stryk

Sailing on the Lake to the Ching River. Lu Yu. OHPC, *tr.* by Kenneth Rexroth

Sailing through the Gorges. Yang Wan-li. WoPoe, *tr.* by Kuangchi C. Chang

Sailing to an Island. Richard Murphy. ModIr; PBCIP

Sailing to Bien Hoa. Bruce Weigl. CDa

Sailing to Byzantium. W. B. Yeats. AmFaPo; CABP; ClHu; GTBS-P; HAP; HarvBoo; HeIP-4; InPK-6; MoBrPo; NAEL-5v2; NAEL-6v2; NAWM-7v2; NIL-7; NIP-4; NOBE; NPeEn; NoAM; NoP-4; OBMV; OWoS; OxBEV; OxBTC; PoE; PoPoPo; PoRA; RaBo; SCGP; SoSe-8; TFi; TOF; UnPo; WeW-3; WoPoe

Sailing to Italy—fitting out / commissioning—to see the friends. Crinagoras. GrAn

Sailor. Vincente Huidobro. TCLAP, *tr.* by David Guss

Sailor. Gerry Gomez Pearlberg. WiU

Sailor, The. Safaa Fathy. PoArWo, *tr.* by S. V. Atalla

Sailor, The. Raymond Roseliep. HA

Sailor, The. Sylvia Townsend Warner. OBMV

Sailor and the Shark, The. Paul Fort. OBMV, *tr.* by Frederick York Powell

Sailor, ask not whose this tomb. *Unknown.* GrAn

Sailor Boy, The. Tennyson. SCGP

Sailor Boy's Song. *Unknown.* CA

Sailor fishes for herring, The. Aria. Irène Hamoir. SurWo, *tr.* by Myrna Bell Rochester

Sailor leaning on the rail thinks of home, The. One Day. Ray Mathew. NOBAu

Sailor pops upon the Royal Pair, A. "Peter Pindar." NOEC *Fr.* Royal Tour, and Weymouth Amusements, The.

Sailor rescued from his buffeting, The. Alcuin. MLL

Sailor's Carol. Charles Causley. OBCP; PeECV

Sailor's Harbor. Henry Reed. MoBrPo

Sailor's Return, The. *Unknown.* OxBoLi

Sailor's Song. Slavko Janevski. WoPoe

Sailor's Wife, The. William Julius Mickle. GTBS-P
(There's Nae Luck about the House.) NOEC; OxAEP-1

Sailor, we all stare at you. Wynyard Sailor. Ray Mathew. CBAP

"Sailorman, I'll give to you." Silver Penny, The. Walter De la Mare. NOxBChV; OBMV

Sailors come / To the drum. Dame Edith Sitwell. FaBoMo; GTBS-P *Fr.* Façade.

Sailors, I wish you safety on sea and land. *Unknown.* GrAn

Sailors' Song. Thomas Lovell Beddoes. OxAEP-2 *Fr.* Death's Jest Book.

Sailors there are of gentlest breed. Commemorative of a Naval Victory. Herman Melville. HAP; UnPo

Sails falshing to the wind like weapons. Robert Earl Hayden. *See* Jesús, Estrella, Esperanza, Mercy

Sails out of sleep / Steering for dream. (LL) E. E. Cummings. EmeKit; Spl

Sails shred, the steering goes, and waves roar doom. Storm, The. Adam Mickiewicz. WoPoe, *tr.* by Vyt Bakaitis

Saint. Stéphane Mallarmé. NAWM-7v2, *tr.* by Henry Weinfield

Saint. Stéphane Mallarmé. SxFrPo, *tr.* by E. H. Blackmore and A. M. Blackmore

St Agnes' Eve—Ah, bitter chill it was! Eve of St Agnes, The. John Keats. CABP; EBNV; FHYEP; HAP; NAEL-5v2; NAEL-6v2; NOBRP; NPeEn; NoP-4; OBNV; OxAEP-2; PoE; TFi; TRP

Saint Augustine, thy praise was sung by one. Richard Henry Wilde. APN-1 *Fr.* Hesperia.

St. Bartholomew's Night. Bella [*or* Izabala] Akhatovna Akhmadulina. TCRP, *tr.* by Albert C. Todd

Saint Bernards carry the food bowl, not him. Pasting relics, The. Abel and Abel. Silvio Giussani. ItPo, *tr.* by Gayle Ridinger

Saint Bridget was / A problem child. Giveaway, The. Phyllis McGinley. PoRA

Saint Called "Truth," A. William Langland. NOCV *Fr.* Vision of Piers Plowman, The.

Saint Coleman's Song for Flight/ An Ite Missa Est.   Padraic Fiacc.   PNI

St. Dunstan, as the story goes.   *Unknown*.   OxNR

St. Eustace.   Derek Mahon.   BiHa

St Francias came to me alive last night and tole me.   I Dream of St. Francis.   Peter Orlovsky.   BB

Saint Francis and the Sow.   Galway Kinnell.   AmFaPo; ChAP; InPK-6; NAAL-5; RB

St. Govan.   A. G. Prys-Jones.   OBWVE

Saint Harmony my patroness.   Paul Goodman.   VGW

St. Helena Lullaby, A.   Rudyard Kipling.   EBEV; FaBoCh; FaBoWar; OBMV

St. Isaac's Church, Petrograd.   Claude McKay.   NAAAL

Saint Jerome lived with a community.   Elegy for Wright & Hugo.   Norman Dubie.   NoAM

Saint John Baptist.   William Drummond, of Hawthornden.   GTBS-P; NOBE; OBEV; OxAEP-1; TrCP

  (For the Baptist.)   ChIV-2; SCGP

Saint John divinely counsels us.   Praise of Godly Love Out of 1 John. 4, The.   John Hall.   ChIV-2

Saint Judas.   James Wright (1927–80).   CoAmPo; GI; LCAP-2; NOBA; PAI

Saint-Just 1767–93.   Robert Lowell.   FaBoMo

Saint-Lô.   Samuel Beckett.   NOIV; NPeEn

St. Louis / such a colored town / a whiskey.   Nappy Edges (A Cross Country Sojourn).   Ntozake Shange.   BlSi

Saint Luke the Painter.   Dante Gabriel Rossetti.   SacPr

St. Malachy.   Thomas Merton.   VGW

Saint Malcolm.   Jewel C. Latimore.   BPo

Saint Margaret of Cortona.   Eiléan Ní Chuilleanáin.   ModIr

Saint Margaret's Legend.   Endre Ady.   IQMS, *tr. by* Anton N. Nyerges

Saint Martha.   Anna Kamienska.   GI, *tr. by* David Curzon and Grażyna Drabik

Saint Mary Magdalene or The Weeper.   Richard Crashaw.   BASC; ChIV-2; GeHe; MeLP

  (Weeper, The.)   ESCV; OBEV

St. Michael and all Angels.   Christina Georgina Rossetti.   SacPr

Saint Nicholas.   Marianne Craig Moore.   WPE

Saint Patrick's Breastplate.   *Unknown*.   NOIV

Saint Patrick's Day, 1973.   Wendy Rose.   CDW

St Patrick's Breastplate.   Saint Patrick.   FaBoCh; SacPr, *tr. by* Frances Alexander

St. Patrick's Dean, your country's pride.   To Dr. Swift on His Birthday, 30th November 1721.   Esther Johnson.   EnLoPo

St. Paul.   Thomas Merton.   ChIV-2

St. Peter.   Christina Georgina Rossetti.   ChIV-2; NOCV

St. Peter Claver.   Toi Derricotte.   LTA; PBCAP

St. Peter once: "Lord, dost Thou wash my feet?"   St. Peter.   Christina Georgina Rossetti.   ChIV-2; NOCV

Saint Peter sat by the celestial gate.   Byron.   NAEL-6v2

St. Peter's Day was celebrated by St. Brendan at sea.   Fish at Mass, The.   *Unknown*.   BIrV, *tr. by* J. F. Webb

St. Philip and St. James.   Christopher Smart.   NOCV; NOEC   *Fr.* Hymns and Spiritual Songs for the Fasts and Festivals of the Church of England.

Saint Pumpkin.   Nancy Willard.   LCAP-2

Saint Ras.   Anthony McNeill.   WaCA

St. Roach.   Muriel Rukeyser.   GLP

Saint Rose of Lima.   Judith Ortiz Cofer.   PueRic; TouFir

Saint's Bridge.   Lola Ridge.   WPE

Saint's Logic.   Linda Gregerson.   ExTi

St. Simeon Stylites.   Tennyson.   NOBVV

St. Stephen and King Herod.   *Unknown*.   ESPB; OxBoLi

  (Seynt Stevyn and Herowdes.)   OxBB

Saint Stephen's.   Martina Wied.   AuPH, *tr. by* Lowell A. Bangerter

St. Stephen's Day.   John Hewitt.   CIP-2

St. Thomas.   Christopher Smart.   ChIV-2   *Fr.* Hymns and Spiritual Songs for the Fasts and Festivals of the Church of England.

St. Thomas Aquinas thought.   Kenneth Rexroth.   NNaP   *Fr.* Bestiary, A.

St. Thomas's Day is past and gone.   *Unknown*.   OxNR

Saint Ursula of Llangwyryfon.   Gwyn Williams.   AngWePo

Saint Vitus's Dance in October 10.   Leonard Nolens.   TuT, *tr. by* Michael O'Loughlin

Saint, who overlaps.   John Logan.   CRP   *Fr.* Cycle for Mother Cabrini, A.

Sainte-Chapelle.   John Taggart.   FTOS

Sainte Lucie.   Derek Walcott.

  "Pomme arac."   FaBoVe

Saints.   Amy Gerstler.   ExTi

Saints and Strangers.   Andrew Hudgins.   RA

Saints are gathering at the real, The.   Confirmers, The.   A. R. Ammons.   TAP

Saints are in such wise from God's own godhead drunk, The.   "Angelus

Silesius."   GePo, *tr. by* George C. Schoolfield   *Fr.* Cherubical Wanderer, The.

Saints' Encouragement, The.   Alexander Brome.   BASC

Saints have adored the lofty soul of you.   Charles Hamilton Sorley.   PeFWW   *Fr.* Two Sonnets.

Saints, I give myself up to thee.   Jack Kerouac.   NeAP   *Fr.* Mexico City Blues.

Saints in Glory, We Together.   Nehemiah Adams.   AH

Saints of Jazz.   Yevgeny Aleksandrovich Yevtushenko [*or* Evtushenko].   SeSe

Saints of Jazz are playing, The.   Saints of Jazz.   Yevgeny Aleksandrovich Yevtushenko [*or* Evtushenko].   SeSe

Saisir.   Henri Michaux.

  "One evening an exceptionally abstract communication came over the airwaves."   PFTM-2, *tr. by* Pierre Joris

Sakhara.   Robert Arthur Douglas Ford.   NOBC

Saki, for God's love, come and fill my glass.   Hafiz [*or* Hafez].   AWP   *Fr.* Odes.

Salaam.   Mangesh Padgaonkar.   OMIP, *tr. by* Vinay Dharwadker

Salaam, / to everyone, salaam.   Salaam.   Mangesh Padgaonkar.   OMIP, *tr. by* Vinay Dharwadker

Salad, A.   Sydney Goodsir Smith.   NBLV

  (Recipe for a Salad.)   OBCoV

Salad Days.   Bruce Berger.   SwNoth

Salad Days.   Susan Musgrave.   NoAM

Salad La Raza.   Janet Campbell Hale.   VoR

Salad of greens! Salad of greens!   Universal Favorite, The.   Carolyn Wells.   NBLV

Salamanders.   A. K. Ramanujan.   PoetW

Salami.   Philip Levine.   NNaP; NOBA; TAP; TRP

Salaziennes, Les.   Auguste Lacaussade.

  "My lips from this day forgot how to smile."   TTY

Sale.   Josephine Miles.   APT-2; WPE

Sale began—young girls were there, The.   Slave Auction, The.   Frances Ellen Watkins Harper.   APN-2; BPo; ColAP; ISC; TTY

Sale of a Historian's Library.   Yelena [*or* Elena] Shwarts [*or* Shvarts].   ARWW, *tr. by* Catriona Kelly

Sale of Souls.   Adah Isaacs Menken.   CBWP-1

Salem.   Robert Lowell.   AiP; Son

Sales.   Arthur Rimbaud.   SxFrPo, *tr. by* Martin Sorrell

Sales Talk for Annie.   Morris Gilbert Bishop.   NBLV

Salesman, A.   E. E. Cummings.   NoAM; OxBA

Salesman is an it that stinks excuse, A.   Salesman, A.   E. E. Cummings.   NoAM; OxBA

Salina sauntering in a shade.   Slattern, The.   Sarah Dixon.   ECWP

Salisbury Plain.   Elizabeth Robinson.   AmPoNex

Salisbury; the Cathedral Close.   Coventry Patmore.   EBVV   *Fr.* Angel in the House, The.

Sallie sits beside me as we wait for you and studies the painting of the hot-air ballon.   Revisionary Instruments 1.   Kathy Fagan.   ExTi

Sally.   Cynthia Heimel.   Unle

Sally Birkett's Ale.   Julius Caesar Ibbetson.   FaBoEE

Sally go round the sun.   *Unknown*.   OxNR

Sally, having swallowed cheese.   Cruel, Clever Cat.   Geoffrey Taylor.   FaBoEE

Sally in Our Alley.   Henry Carey.   AWP; BoLoP; GTBS-P; NOBE; OBEV; OxAEP-1

  (Ballad of Sally in Our Alley, The.)   NOEC

Sally is gone that was so kindly.   Ha'nacker Mill.   Joseph Hilaire Pierre Belloc.   MoBrPo; OxBTC; RB

Sally, Sally Waters.   *Unknown*.   OxNR

Sally Simpkin's Lament.   Thomas Hood.   CABP

Sally, tell my Mother I shall never come back. (LL)   Gypsies in the Wood.   *Unknown*.   OxBSP; OxBoLi; OxNR

Sally: Twelfth Street.   Naomi Long Madgett.   NBV

Salma.   Ilyas Farhat.   MAP, *tr. by* John Heath-Stubbs and Salma Khadra Jayyusi

Salma in Wonderland.   Mona Fayad.   PoArWo

Salman.   Tawfiq Zayyad.   MAP, *tr. by* Charles Doria and Sharif Elmusa

Salmon, The.   Duane Niatum.   PoCoUp

Salmon Brook.   Henry David Thoreau.   TCAPo

Salmon Drowns Eagle.   Malcolm Lowry.   MoCV

Salmon Fishing.   Robinson Jeffers.   APT-1

Salmon lying in the depths of Llyn Llifon, The.   Ancients of the World, The.   Ronald Stuart Thomas.   OPOU; RB

Salmon's leap, The.   Shannon Estuary Welcomes the Fish, The.   Nuala Ni Dhomhnaill.   ModIr, *tr. by* Patrick Crotty

Salome.   Ai.   NoAM

Salomé.   Silvia Grénier.   SurWo, *tr. by* Natalie Kenvin

Salome. Charles Lamb. ChIV-2

Salon de Vers. Orrick Johns. APT-1

Saloon is gone up the creek, The. William Carlos Williams. APT-1; PoRA
   Fr. Folded Skyscraper, A.

Saloon is sometimes called a Bar, The. Bar, The. *Unknown.* PoToHe

Saloon with Birds. Christopher Middleton. HarvBoo

Salopian student of Greek, A. Limerick. Martin Fagg. PeLi

Salsabíl. Jamíl. ArPe, *tr. by* Omar S. Pound

Salt. George Barlow. GT

Salt. Viktor Fiodorovich Bokov. TCRP, *tr. by* Bernard Meares

Salt. Anne Hartigan. CIP-2

Salt. Yusef Komunyakaa. OPRER; UnSA

Salt creek mouths unflushed by the sea. South Coast, The. William Everson. NeAP

Salt Garden, The. Howard Nemerov. OBGa

Salt Lake, The. Iwan [*or* Yvan] Goll. WoPoe, *tr. by* George Hitchcock

Salt Longing. Austin Hummell. AmPoNex

Salt Pork, The. Robert Clayton Casto. HeIP-4

Salt Riot, The. Pavel Nikolaevich Vasilyev [*or* Vasil'ev].
   Wedding, The. TCRP, *tr. by* David Macduff

Salt shining behind its glass cylinder. Morning. Mary Oliver. NIL-7

Salt sprays deluge it, wild waves buffet it, hurricanes rave. Sir Lewis Morris.
   AngWePo *Fr.* St. David's Head.

Salt Water Story. Richard Hugo. NAAL-2v2; NoAM

Saltmarsh on the horizon, The. Estuarial Republic, The. Douglas Dunn.
   FaBoMo

Saltos Sobre El Exilio. Alicia Kozameh.
   "It's absorbed, perceived, partially picked up. The brightness envelops."
   MirDau, *tr. by* David Davis
   "Presence. Opposites. Absence. Forces exercising pressure against." MirDau,
   tr. by David Davis
   "We will mention it. We will remember and mention." MirDau, *tr. by* David
   Davis

Salty like my seashores. Maysoun Saqr Al-Qasimi. PoArWo, *tr. by* Subhi
   Hadidi *Fr.* Morning of Every Sin, The.

Salty spray glistens on the fence, The. Sleep, My Beloved. Yevgeny
   Aleksandrovich Yevtushenko [*or* Evtushenko]. TCRP, *tr. by* Geoffrey
   Dutton and Tina Tupkina-Glaessner

Saluste du Bartas' Devine Weekes. Joshua Sylvester.
   "Cunning Painter, that with curious care, The." PBRV

Salutation. Robert Herrick. CavPo; ChIV-2

Salutation. Ezra Pound. HeIP-4; MoAmPo; NOBA; OxBA; TAP; VGW

Salutation, A. Louise Imogen Guiney. APN-2

Salutation, The. Thomas Traherne. *See* Salutation [*or* Salutations], The

Salutation [*or* Salutations], The. Thomas Traherne. ESCV; EnlH; GeHe;
   NOCV; SacPr
   (Salutation, The.) NoP-4
   (These little limbs.) NoP-4

Salutation the Second. Ezra Pound. NOBA; OxBA

Salutation to the Dawn. Kalidasa. PoToHe

Salutations. Shanmuga Subbiah. OMIP, *tr. by* T. K. Doraiswamy

Salutations to the goddess who dwells in all things as. Tantric Praise of the
   Goddess. *Unknown.* HW, *tr. by* Jalaja Bonheim

Salute. James Schuyler. NeAP

Salute, Friends! Vladimir Salimon. TCRP, *tr. by* Albert C. Todd

Salute to Icheke. Okogbule Wonodi. PBMAP

Salute we must, nor strangers, kin, or friends. (LL) Salutation. Robert
   Herrick. CavPo; ChIV-2

Salvador Dali. David Gascoyne. OxBTC; SPE
   (In Defence of Humanism.) FaBoMo

Salvation, and bliss. (LL) Ode for the Dancing Khlysty. Yury [*or* Iurii] Ivask.
   TCRP; TCRusP, *tr. by* Alla Burago and Burton Raffel

Salvation Army lass, The. Lola Ridge. WPE *Fr.* Ward X.

Salvation bought, sin sold. Hermit with Landscape. Daniel Hall. YaYoPo

Salvation is of Christ the Lord. (LL) St Patrick's Breastplate. Saint Patrick.
   FaBoCh; SacPr, *tr. by* Frances Alexander

Salvation lassie named Claire, A. Limerick. *Unknown.* PeLi

Salvation to all that will is nigh. John Donne. TrCP *Fr.* Holy Sonnets.

Salve! Thomas Edward Brown. OBEV

Salve Deus Rex Judaeorum. Emilia [*or* Aemelia] Lanier [*or* Lanyer].
   (Eve's Apology in Defense of Women.) NAEL-7v1
   Eves Apologie. BoWoP
   "Now Pontius Pilate is to judge the cause." EMWP; NAEL-6v1; NALW;
   NOSC

Salve Deus Rex Judaeorum. Aemilia Bassano Lanyer.
   "Our Mother *Eve,* who tasted of the Tree." PBRV
   "Sith Cynthia is ascended to that rest." BASC; NoP-4

To the Queen's Most Excellent Majesty. NAEL-7v1

Salve Regina. *Unknown.* MiEL

Sam. Lucille Clifton. UnSA

Sam. Walter De la Mare. MoBrPo

Sam and Bob. William Barnes. PeVV, *tr. by* Hualing Nieh *Fr.* Best Man in
   the Vield, The.

Sam'el Down vrom Lon'on. William Barnes. PeVV

Sam Jackson. Frank Marshall Davis. APT-2

Sam [*or* Samuel] Hall. *Unknown.* UnPo

Sam's Ghazals. Elise Paschen. Unle

Sam, Sam, the butcher man. *Unknown.* TLR

Sam Smiley. Sterling Allen Brown. NAAAL

Samantha. Edward Albee. Unle

Samantha is my. Samantha Is My Negro Cat. William J. Harris. GT

Samantha Is My Negro Cat. William J. Harris. GT

Same, The. Dante Gabriel Rossetti. CenSon

Same as ever to the sight, The. (LL) Mill, The. Edwin Arlington Robinson.
   APT-1; HAP; NAAL-2v2; NoAM; NoP-4; PAI; WeW-3

Same Corpse, The. Kojo Laing. HBAPE

Same Cottage—But Another Song, of Another Season. Max Beerbohm. UV

Same Gesture, The. John Montague. BIrV; ModIr; PNI

Same in Blues. Langston Hughes. APSN; APT-2; SSLK *Fr.* Lenox Avenue
   Mural.

Same Inside, The. Anna Swirszczynska. BLT

Same leaves over and over again, The! In Hardwood Groves. Robert Frost.
   HAP

Same look which she turn'd [*or* turned] when he rose, The. (LL) Believe Me,
   If All Those Endearing Young Charms. Thomas Moore. NAEL-5v2;
   NAEL-6v2

Same low sky, The. Every Metaphor. Milo De Angelis. ItPo, *tr. by* Gayle
   Ridinger

Same Month They Bombed Cambodia, The. Amy Uyematsu. OpBo

Same Old Jazz, The. Philip Whalen. NeAP

Same Old Problem. Kevin Gilbert. IBA

Same Old Way, The. "Igor Severyanin [*or* Severianin]." TCRP, *tr. by* Bernard
   Meares

Same Side of the Canoe, The. Alda do Espirito Santo. HAWP, *tr. by* Allan
   Francovich and Kathleen Weaver

Same Subject, The. William Wordsworth. CenSon *Fr.* River Duddon [A
   Series of Sonnets], The.

Same subject (Continued) [Imagination and Taste, How Impaired and Restored].
   William Wordsworth. *Fr.* Prelude, The; Growth of a Poet's Mind [1850
   vers.].

Same, The [London, MDCCII]. William Wordsworth. *See* London 1802

Samela. Robert Greene. NOBE; OBEV *Fr.* Menaphon.

Sammy Lou of Rue. Revolutionary Petunias. Alice Walker. BlSi; NIL-7

Samos. James Merrill. HCAP *Fr.* Scripts for the Pageant.

Sampler from Haworth. Frances Minturn Howard. WPE

Sampson Imitated. Benjamin Franklin. FaBoEE
   (Impromptu.) NOBL

Samson Agonistes. John Milton. BASC; FHYEP; NAEL-6v1
   "All is best, though we oft doubt." NOBE; NOSC; OBEV; OxBEV
   ("But chief of all.") NPeEn
   "But see here comes thy reverend Sire." EBEV
   "But what is strength without a double share." ChIV-1
   "Chief of all." NOSC
   Deliverer, The. NOBE; NOCV; OBEV; OxAEP-1
   "Feast and noon grew high, and Sacrifice, The." EBEV
   "Just are the ways of God." InvLi
   "Let me obtain forgiveness of thee, Samson." EBEV
   "Little onward lend thy guiding hand, A." OxAEP-1; WoPoe
   "Oh [*or* O] how comely it is and how reviving." NOBE; NOCV; OBEV;
   OxAEP-1
   Samson before the Prison in Gaza. OxAEP-1; WoPoe
   Samson Fallen. UnPo
   Samson's Complaint. NOSC
   "This, this is he; softly a while." UnPo
   "Wilt thou then serve the Philistines with that gift." EBEV

Samson Agonistes. Ogden Nash. APT-2; OBCoV

Samson before the Prison in Gaza. John Milton. OxAEP-1; WoPoe *Fr.*
   Samson Agonistes.

Samson Fallen. John Milton. UnPo *Fr.* Samson Agonistes.

Samson's Complaint. John Milton. NOSC *Fr.* Samson Agonistes.

Samson to His De [*or* a] lilah. Richard Crashaw. ChIV-1

Samuel. Judith Baumel. TaR

Samuel. Anté Popovski.
   "There was nothing left for man." CarOv, *tr. by* Carolyn Kizer

Samuel Brown. Phoebe Cary. APN-2; OBAL

Samuel Hearne in Wintertime. John Newlove. NOBC

Samuel's Prayer. John Keble. ChIV-1

Samuel Sewall. Anthony Hecht. NBLV; PeLV; PoRA; TwCP
(Samuel Sewall, in a world of wigs.) CoAmPo

San Buenaventura. Maurina Sherman. GeoHom

San Diego (On a rainy day). Lamea Abbas Amara. PoArWo, tr. by Nathalie Handal and Mike Maggio

San Diego Poem, A. Simon J. Ortiz. CDW

San Francisco Poem. John Logan. NNaP

San Francisco remains in grave personal. Jeane Dixon's America. Gerald Costanzo. ReTh

San Francisco Sunrise. Diane Ackerman. UrbNat

San Fransisco. Miguel Algarin. PmAP

San Jacinto Plaza. Ray Gonzalez. UrbNat

San Joaquín. David Oliveira. GeoHom

San Juan. Myrna Peña Reyes. FSt

San Martino del Carso. Giuseppe Ungaretti. PeFWW, tr. by David McDuff

San Pedro Road. Robert Hass. GeoHom

San Quentin 1968. Robert Peterson. GeoHom

San Sepolcro. Jorie Graham. HCAP; VCAP

Sanct Christopher II. Robert Garioch. OBVE

Sancta Maria, ora pro nobis. James Ryman. OHMEL

Sanctification. Joseph Ibn Abithur. TOF, tr. by David Goldstein

Sanctity. Patrick Kavanagh. BIrV; NOIV; NoP-4

Sanctity, The. C. K. Williams. BodElec

Sanctuary. Bruce Boyd. NeAP

Sanctuary. Donald Davidson. APT-1; FuPo

Sanctuary. Norman Dubie. BodElec

Sanctuary. Dorothy Hewett. CBAP

Sanctuary. Angelina Muñiz Huberman. MirDau, tr. by Aurora Camacho

Sanctuary. Dorothy Parker. NBLV

Sanctuary. Judith Wright. WPE

Sanctuary. Elinor Wylie. BoWoP; MoAmPo

Sanctuary, The. Sara Teasdale. APT-1

Sanctuary of Spirits. Alistair Campbell.
    Against Te Rauparaha. PeNZ
    "Records all agree, The." PeNZ

Sand. Nina Cassian. PoSu, tr. by Nina Cassian and Naomi Lazard

Sand. John Jarmain. FaBoWar

Sand. Dominique Parker. SpirFl

Sand. Hannah Weiner. PFTM-2

Sand birds fly east, they flee the spread net. Following the Rhymes of Bamboo Branch Songs in Response to Yüan Po-chang. Yü Chi. CoBLCP, tr. by Jonathan Chaves

Sand, caravans, and teetering sea-edge graves. Earthen Lot, The. Tony Harrison. NPeEn

Sand Creek. Charles G. Ballard. UnPo; VoR

Sand Dunes. Robert Frost. MoAmPo

Sand has the ants, clay ferny weeds for play. Possessions. Ivor Gurney. NPeEn

Sand in Flames. Nujoum Al-Ghanim. PoArWo, tr. by Clarissa C. Burt

Sand in My Shoes. Victor Schertzinger. ReLy

Sand is a fine grit, The. Dry Root in a Wash. Simon J. Ortiz. HATNAP

Sand is swift, overflowing, The. Snake. Dan Pagis. WoPoe, tr. by Stephen Mitchell

Sand Martin, The. John Clare. NPeEn

Sand modeller always began by heaping the sand, The. Entertainer, The. Bruce Beaver. NOBAu

Sand Nigger. Lawrence Joseph. GraLe; OPRER

Sand of the Desert in an Hour-Glass. Henry Wadsworth Longfellow. NCAP

Sand pyramid, size of a child, each September. Ant Hill, The. Cynthia Zarin. NoP-4

Sand-Quarry with Moving Figures. Muriel Rukeyser. NoP-4

Sand Roads. Marge Piercy.
    "Bulldozers come, they rip, The." NBLV
    Development, The. NBLV

Sand, sand. In the university the halls. Poet Visits Egypt and Israel, The. Maxine W. Kumin. TaR

Sand Seer, The. Niyi Osundare. PBMAP

Sand Shark. Nancy Willard. PoCoUp

Sand-slums are hunble townships, the. Saturday in the Sand-Slums. Agostinho Neto. PoetW, tr. by Michael Wolfers

Sand Wet and Cool, The. Dennis Brutus. GT

Sandal and garment of yellow and lotus garlands upon his body of blue. Jayadeva. TAL Fr. Gita Govinda, The.

Sandal Mountain. Hsieh Chin. CoBLCP, tr. by Jonathan Chaves

Sandalphon. Henry Wadsworth Longfellow. TCAPo

Sandalphon. Ezra Pound. TCAPo

Sandals on my feet. (LL) Basho. EH; NIL-7, tr. by Robert Hass

Sandalwood Comes to My Mind. Carl Rakosi. ChIV-1 Fr. Exercises in Scriptural Writing.

Sandalwood the hawser-ties, silk the puller ropes. Song to the Tune "Perching Crows." Wu Wei-yeh. CoBLCP, tr. by Jonathan Chaves

Sandbags of sugar cannot conceal the gloomy fact. And the World was Calm. Chris Wallace-Crabbe. BMAP

Sandbar at Moore's Creek. Judy Jordan. AmPoNex

Sandblast Girl and the Acid Man, The. May Kendall. ViWPN

Sanderlings. Roland Mathias. TCAWP

Sandlewood comes to my mind. Carl Rakosi. ChIV-1 Fr. Exercises in Scriptural Writing.

Sandpiper. Elizabeth Bishop. APT-2; AiP; HeIP-4; OWoS; RB; TOF

Sandpiper, The. Celia Laighton Thaxter. OBCA; PWR

Sandra. Demetrice A. Worley. SpirFl

Sandra: At the Beaver Trap. Michael S. Harper. NoAM

Sands at my feet, The. (LL) Venus Transiens. Amy Lowell. APT-1; NAAL-5; NALW

Sands of Dee, The. Charles Kingsley. EBVV; OxAEP-2; TreFP Fr. Alton Locke.

Sands of time are sinking, The. In Emmanuel's Land. Anne R. Cousin. SacPr

Sands stretch away like snow, The. Listening to a Flute at Night near the City Wall. Li Yi. CrYelRi, tr. by Sam Hamill

Sandwich Man, The. Ron Padgett. CoAmPo

Sandwiches. David Donnell. NoAM

Sandy and Jockie. Robert Burns. OxBSP

Sandy cat by the Farmer's chair, The. Summer Evening. Walter De la Mare. MoBrPo

Sandy he belongs to the mill. Unknown. OxNR

Sandy Kildandy. Unknown. OxNR

Sandy road, the bright green two-inch lizard, The. Pen, The. Jean Valentine. BodElec

Sandy Yard, The. Edith Jay Scovell. HarvBoo

Sang. Robert MacLellan. OxBS

Sang. Allan Ramsay. See Gentle Shepherd, The

Sang a maiden in a meadow. Reunited. Henrietta Cordelia Ray. CBWP-3

Sang First. William Tennant. NePenScot Fr. Papistry Storm'd.

Sang of the Outlaw Murray, The. Unknown. IBB

Sang unmeanig down the stream. (LL) Orpheus. Yvor Winters. NOBA; VGW

Sango. Gabriel Gbadamosi.
    "Sango's son came down to the river." HBAPE

Sango's son came down to the river. Gabriel Gbadamosi. HBAPE Fr. Sango.

Sanitized Sonnets, The. Peter Porter.
    "It's there, somewhere in the Platonic cold store." OxBSo
    "Now it's in all the novels, what's pornography to do?" OBCoV

Sank through easeful. Diver, The. Robert Earl Hayden. BPo; MoASP

Sanoe. Queen Lili'u-o-ka-lani. SWaP

Sanquhar, whom this earth could scarce contain. William Drummond, of Hawthornden. FaBoEE

Sans Culotte. Pavel Grigoryevich Antokolsky. TCRP, tr. by Bernard Meares

Sans Equity and sans Poise. Confucius. WoPoe, tr. by Ezra Pound Fr. Yung Wind.

Sans teeth, sans eyes, sans taste, sans everything. (LL) William Shakespeare. ITBLP; RB; UV Fr. As You Like It.

Sansei: The Third Generation. Rose Furuya Hawkins. FSt Fr. Proud Upon an Alien Shore.

Sanskrit. Jayanta Mahapatra. VCWP

Santa Claus. Christopher Vernon Hassall. OxBTC

Santa Claus. Dom Moraes. NoAM

Santa Claus. Howard Nemerov. HAP

Santa Claus Is Comin' to Town. J. Fred Coots. ReLy

Santa Decca. Oscar Wilde. OxBSo

Santa Fe, still the one, The. American Trains. Reginald Gibbons. GM

Santa Fe Trail. Barbara Guest. FTOS; NeAP; PoM

Santa Filomena. Henry Wadsworth Longfellow. FaBoWar

Santa Maria Antiqua. István Vas. IQMS, tr. by George Gömöri and Clive Wilmer

Santa Monica. Charlie Smith. KGB

Santhal Poems, 1. Bishnu De. OMIP, tr. by Samir Dasgupta

Santo Domingo Corn Dance. Lynn Riggs. APT-2

Santo Domingo, DemRep, March 1965. War Poem. Simon J. Ortiz. CDa

Santorin. James Elroy Flecker. FaBoTw; OBMV

Santorini Daughter. Julie Fay. NAPBL

São Paulo! tumult of my life. Inspiration. Mário de Andrade. TCLAP, *tr. by* Jack E. Tomlins

Saon of Acanthus. Callimachus. AWP, *tr. by* John Addington Symonds

Sap. Robert Minhinnick. AngWePo

Sap, The. Henry Vaughan. ESCV

Sap is going out of my fingers, The. In Autumn. Charles Hubert Sisson. PeECV

Sap rises from the sodden ditch. For Jane Myers. Louise Glück. FaBoWP

Sap weeps, The. Why the Wind Comes. Hirini Melbourne. PeNZ

Saphire (Metamorpho's Chick). Joe Rosenblatt. MoCV

Sapho and Phao. John Lyly.
   "My shag-hair Cyclops, come, lets ply." EBEV
   "O cruel Love! on thee I lay." NoSic
   Sapho's Song. NoSic
   (Song in Making of the Arrows, The.) NoSic
   Vulcan's Song. EBEV

Sapho's Kiss. Efrén Rebolledo. BLPSL, *tr. by* Rene de Costa, Rigas Kappatos and Eleni Paidoussi

Sapho's Song. John Lyly. NoSic *Fr.* Sapho and Phao.

Sapho to Philaenis. John Donne. RACG *Fr.* Elegies.

Saplings of the green-tipped birch, The. Never Tell. *Unknown.* OBWVE, *tr. by* Anthony Conran

Sapphic Fragment. Thomas Hardy. OBVE
   (Achtung.) CTC

Sapphics. George Canning. *See* Friend of Humanity and the Knife Grinder, The

Sapphics. Dominic Bevan Wyndham Lewis. NOBL; PeLV

Sapphics. Algernon Charles Swinburne. NPeEn

Sapphics: At the Mohawk-Castle, Canada. Thomas Morris. NOEC

Sapphics for Patience. Anne Finch (b. 1908). FFC

Sapphire, nor diamond, nor emerald. Jacopo da Lentino. EaItPo, *tr. by* Dante Gabriel Rossetti

Sappho. Catullus. AWP, *tr. by* William Ellery Leonard *Fr.* Carmina.

Sappho. Plato. GrAn, *tr. by* Peter Jay

Sappho. Christina Georgina Rossetti. VWP

Sappho. James Wright (1927–80). NoAM

Sappho Burns Her Books and Cultivates the Culinary Arts. Elizabeth Moody. ECWP

Sappho Discovers her Passion. Mary Robinson. CenSon; RWP

"Sappho, if you do not come out." Sappho. BoWoP

Sappho; or, The Resolve. Charlotte Dacre. NOBRP

Sappho Rejects Hope. Mary Robinson. CenSon; RWP

Sappho's Address to the Stars. Mary Robinson. CenSon; RWP

Sappho's Conjectures. Mary Robinson. CenSon; RWP

Sappho's Gymnasium. Olga Broumas. GifTon

Sappho's Leap. Howard Baker. APT-2

Sappho's Prayer to Venus. Mary Robinson. CenSon

Sappho's Prayer to Venus. Mary Robinson. RWP

Sappho's Reply. Rita Mae Brown. OxWW

Sappho's Song. Letitia [*or* Laetitia] Elizabeth Landon. RWP; VWP *Fr.* Improvisatrice, The.

Sappho was neither woman or man. Greek Metamorphosis. Belkis Cuza Malé. TANSG, *tr. by* Pamela Carmell

Sara in Her Father's Arms. George Oppen. NNaP

Saraband. Austin Hummell. AmPoNex

Sarabande on Attaining the Age of Seventy-Seven. Anthony Hecht. BAP-01

Saracen SAS or Assasseen called Nasir claims on HTV, A. Alan Halsey. Oth *Fr.* Robin Hood Book, A.

Sarah. Delmore Schwartz. ChIV-1; TaR

Sarah Byng. Joseph Hilaire Pierre Belloc. NoAM

Sarah Cynthia Sylvia Stout Would Not Take the Garbage Out. Shel [*or* Shelley] Silverstein. OBCA; OxIBACP

Sarah Hazard's Love Letter. John Ellis. NOEC

Sarah, my rose, where are you off? Please stop a minute. Lover Under Suspicion. Ádám Pálóczi Horváth. IQMS, *tr. by* John Gordon Nichols

Sarah's Choice. Eleanor Wilner. TaR

Sarajevo. Lawrence Durrell. GTBS-P

Sarcophagus. Pauline Stainer. NeBl

Sardanapalus. Henry Howard, Earl of Surrey. NAEL-6v1; NAEL-7v1; NoSic

Sardines seem to get out of hand. Limerick. Leslie Johnson. PeLi

Sardis. William Cowper. ChIV-2 *Fr.* Olney Hymns.

Sardis. Sappho. SaLy, *tr. by* Diane Rayor

Sardis, the old city of Gyges and Alyattes. Bianor. GrAn

Saris go by me from the embassies, The. Woman at the Washington Zoo, The. Randall Jarrell. CoAP; HAP; HCAP; OxBC; TAP; TwCP; UnPo; VCAP

Sarmèd, whom they intoxicated from the cup of love. Quatrain. Sarmèd the Yahud. TrJP, *tr. by* David Shea

Sarolla's women in their picture hats. Lawrence Ferlinghetti. NeAP; PoM *Fr.* Pictures of a Gone World.

Sarpedon's Speech to Glaucus. Homer. NPeEn; OBVE, *tr. by* Sir John Denham *Fr.* Iliad, The.

Sartor Resartus. Art Goodtimes. GeoH

Sasha and the Poet. Jean Valentine. VGW

Sassafras. Barbara Guest. FTOS

Sat a damsel on the hillside. Messengers, The. Henrietta Cordelia Ray. CBWP-3

Sat down. Michael McClintock. HA

Sat for three days in a white room. Heroin. Jim Carroll. OBCoV

Sat in the pub. Diet, The. Maureen Burge. BrRo

Sat up all night and lugged at the moon. Critter. W. M. Ransom. CDW

Sat Will & Kate. Those Troublesome Disguises. Jonathan Williams. NeAP

Satan. Jamil. B. Holway. GraLe, *tr. by* George Dimitri Selim

Satan came to me in my dream. Satan. Jamil. B. Holway. GraLe, *tr. by* George Dimitri Selim

Satan has enough in hell. (LL) For a Mouthy Woman. Countee Cullen. ChIV-1; OBAL

Satan Is on Your Tongue. George Barker. MoBrPo *Fr.* Secular Elegies.

Satan's Journey. John Milton. NOSC *Fr.* Paradise Lost.

Satan's Summons. John Milton. NOSC *Fr.* Paradise Lost.

Satan Says. Sharon Olds. PBCAP

Satan with his Angels now fallen into Hell. John Milton. NPeEn *Fr.* Paradise Lost.

Satasai, The. Bihari.
   "What she said to her companion." WoPoe, *tr. by* Krishna P. Bahadur

Satchmo. Melvin B. Tolson. BPo; NAAAL

Sated with home, of wife, of children tired. Cui Bono? Horace Smith. NOBRP

Sather Gate Illumination. Allen Ginsberg. NeAP

Satia Te Sanguine. Algernon Charles Swinburne. PeVV

Satie, at the End of Term. Simon Curtis. NOBL; PeLV

Satin-Clad. Stevie Smith. OxBC

Satin Doll. Johnny Mercer. ReLy

Satin Doll. David Wojahn. PBCAP

Satire. Ibn Sharaf. WoPoe, *tr. by* Leticia Garza-Falcón and Christopher Middleton

Satire. *Unknown.* WoPoe, *tr. by* Sir Arthur Grimble

Satire, A. John Oldham.
   "On Butler who can think without rage." OBSV

Satire 1 [A London Street]. John Donne. NoSic *Fr.* Satires.

Satire 1. Juvenal. RompPo, *tr. by* Peter Green *Fr.* Satires.

Satire 1. Persius. RompPo, *tr. by* Richard Emil Braun

Satire 2. John Donne. *Fr.* Satires.

Satire 2. Juvenal. *Fr.* Satires.

Satire 3 [Religion]. John Donne. BASC; EBEV; ESCV; FHYEP; FSCP; MeLP; NAEL-5v1; NAEL-6v1; NAEL-7v1; NoP-4; OxAEP-1; SacPr *Fr.* Satires.

Satire 4. John Donne. OBSV *Fr.* Satires.
   "Then, as if he would have sold." PBRV

Satire 5. John Donne. OBSV *Fr.* Satires.

Satire 5. Persius. RompPo, *tr. by* Richard Emil Braun

Satire 6. Juvenal. RompPo, *tr. by* Peter Green *Fr.* Satires.

Satire 6. Persius. RompPo, *tr. by* Richard Emil Braun

Satire VIII. Joseph Hall. ChIV-2

Satire 10. Juvenal. RompPo, *tr. by* Peter Green *Fr.* Satires.

Satire against Reason and Mankind, A. Grace Buchanan Sherwood. NoP-4

Satire on Charles II, A. John Wilmot, 2d Earl of Rochester.
   "Restless he rolls about from whore to whore." OBSV

Satire on Charles II, A. John Wilmot, 2d Earl of Rochester. NOSC; PeLV

Satire on Paying Calls in August. Ch'ĕng Hsiao. ChiP, *tr. by* Arthur Waley

Satire on the O'Haras, A. Tadhg Dall O'Huiginn. NOIV

Satire on the Rebellion, A. Alexander Brome. BASC

Satire [*or* Satyre *or* Satyr] against [Reason and] Mankind, A. John Wilmot, 2d Earl of Rochester. BASC; NOSC; OBSV; SCV
   "Were I (who to my cost already am)." CABP; NPeEn; OxBEV; SCV
   "You see how far Mans wisedom here extends." OxBEV

Satire: "This way of writing I observed by some." *Unknown.* BASC

Satire upon the Licentious Age of Charles II. Samuel Butler (1612–80).
   "How silly were those sages heretofore." NOBL

Satires. John Donne.
   "Away thou fondling motley humourist." NoSic
   "Kind pity [*or* Kinde pitty] chokes my spleen[e]; brave scorn forbids." BASC; EBEV; ESCV; FHYEP; FSCP; MeLP; NAEL-5v1; NAEL-6v1; NAEL-7v1; NoP-4; OxAEP-1; SacPr
   Satire 1 [A London Street]. NoSic

Satire 2.
  Poet Turned Lawyer, The.   OBSV
Satire 3 [Religion].   BASC; EBEV; ESCV; FHYEP; FSCP; MeLP; NAEL-5v1; NAEL-6v1; NAEL-7v1; NoP-4; OxAEP-1; SacPr
  Hill of Truth, The.   OBSV
  Seek True Religion!   NOBE
Satire 4.   OBSV
Satire 5.   OBSV
(Satyre 3 [On Religion].)   PBRV
(Satyre: Of Religion.)   PoE
"Thou shalt not laugh in this leaf, Muse, nor they."   OBSV
(Search for True Religion, The.)   NoSic
"Well, I may now receive, and die: my sin."   OBSV
Satires. Horace.
  "Once I was wood from a worthless old fig tree."   PriapPo, tr. by Richard W. Hooper
  1.8.   PriapPo, tr. by Richard W. Hooper
Satires. Juvenal.
  "But of all the plagues, the greatest is untold."   OBSV
  Celestial Wisdom.   AWP, tr. by Samuel Johnson
  "During Saturn's reign I believe that Chastity still."   RomPo, tr. by Peter Green
  "Give store of days, good Jove, give length of years."   OBSV
  Hannibal ("Produce the urn that Hannibal contains").   OBVE, tr. by William Gifford
  Hannibal ("Put Hannibal i' th' scale").   OBVE, tr. by Henry Vaughan
  Hannibal ("Throw Hannibal on the scales, how many pounds").   OBVE, tr. by Robert Lowell
  "How many men are killed by power, by power."   OBVE, tr. by Robert Lowell
  "Life! length of life!" for this, with earnest cries."   OBVE
  "Must hapless man, in ignorance sedate."   AWP, tr. by Samuel Johnson
  "Must I always be stuck in the audience at these poetry-readings, never."   RomPo, tr. by Peter Green
  "Produce the urn that Hannibal contains."   OBVE, tr. by William Gifford
  "Put Hannibal i' th' scale."   OBVE, tr. by Henry Vaughan
  Satire 1.   RomPo, tr. by Peter Green
  Satire 2.
    "Northward beyond the Lapps to the world's end, the frozen."   CAGL, tr. by Peter Green
  Satire 6.   RomPo, tr. by Peter Green
  Satire 10.   RomPo, tr. by Peter Green
  "Search every land, from Cadiz to the dawn-streaked shores."   RomPo, tr. by Peter Green
  Sejanus ("How many men are killed by power, by power").   OBVE, tr. by Robert Lowell
  Sejanus ("Some ask for envy'd pow'r; which publick hate").   OBVE, tr. by John Dryden
  Sejanus ("What crowds by envied power, the wish of all").   OBVE, tr. by William Gifford
  Sixth Satire.
    "But of all plagues, the greatest is untold."   BASC, tr. by John Dryden
    Empress Messalina, The.   BASC, tr. by John Dryden
    Gaudy Gossip, The.   BASC, tr. by John Dryden
    "Gaudy gossip, when she's set agog, The."   BASC, tr. by John Dryden
    "In Saturn's reign, at Nature's early birth."   NPeEn; OBSV; OBVE; OxBEV, tr. by John Dryden
    Learned Wife, The.   BASC, tr. by John Dryden
    "This was a private crime; but you shall hear."   BASC, tr. by John Dryden
    "What care our Drunken Dames to whom they spread?"   OxBEV, tr. by John Dryden
  "Some ask for envy'd pow'r; which publick hate."   OBVE, tr. by John Dryden
  Tenth Satire.
    "In his own age, Democritus could find."   BASC, tr. by John Dryden
  Sejanus.   BASC, tr. by John Dryden
  "Throw Hannibal on the scales, how many pounds."   OBVE, tr. by Robert Lowell
  "What crowds by envied power, the wish of all."   OBVE, tr. by William Gifford
  "When the last Flavius, drunk with fury, tore."   OBVE
Satires. John Marston.
  Cynic Satire, A.   NoSic
  Humours.   NoSic
  "Man, a man, a kingdom for a man!, A."   NoSic
  "Sleep, grim Reproof; my jocund muse doth sing."   NoSic
Satires. John Oldham.
  "Of all the creatures, in the world, that be."   OBVE

Satires. Persius.
  "I never did on cleft Parnassus dream."   AWP, tr. by John Dryden
  Prologue to the First Satire.   AWP, tr. by John Dryden
Satires. Sir Thomas Wyatt.
  "Mine [or Myne] own[e] John Poyntz, since [or sins] ye delight to know."   NPeEn; NoSic; OBSV; OBVE; SCGP
  (Mine Own John Poins.)   NAEL-7v1; NoP-4
  (Mine Own John Poins.)   NAEL-6v1
  ("Mine own John Poins, since ye delight to know.")   NoP-4
  "My mother's maids [or maydes] when they did sew [or sowe] and spin [or spynne]."   NoSic
  (Myn owne John poyntz sins ye delight to know.)   PBRV
  Of the Courtier's Life.   NPeEn; NoSic; OBSV; OBVE; SCGP
  "Spending hand that alway poureth [or powreth] out [or owte], A."   NoSic
  To Sir Francis Brian.   NoSic
Satires. Edward Young.   ECEV
  On Women ("Britannia's daughters").   ECEV
  On Women ("Lavinia is polite").   ECEV
Satires of Circumstance in Fifteen Glimpses.   Thomas Hardy.
  "And now to God the Father, he ends."   InPK-6; MoBrPo; SCV
  At the Altar-Rail.   MoBrPo
  At the Draper's.   MoBrPo
  "But hear. If you stay, and the child be born."   MoBrPo
  By Her Aunt's Grave.   MoBrPo
  "I stood at the back of the shop, my dear."   MoBrPo
  In Church.   InPK-6; MoBrPo; SCV
  In the Cemetery.   InPK-6; Son
  In the Moonlight.   NoAM
  In the Nuptial Chamber.   InPK-6
  In the Restaurant.   MoBrPo
  In the Room of the Bride-Elect.   InPK-6
  "My bride is not coming, alas! says the groom."   MoBrPo
  "O lonely workman, standing there."   NoAM
  "O that mastering tune! And up in the bed."   InPK-6
  "Sixpence a week, says the girl to her lover."   MoBrPo
  "Would it had been the man of our wish!"   InPK-6
  "You see those mothers squabbling there?"   InPK-6; Son
Satiric and Censorious Epistle.   Francisco de Quevedo y Villegas.
  "I'll not be silent, though you put your finger."   SpanPo, tr. by Denise Levertov
Satirical Elegy on the Death of a Late Famous General, A.   Jonathan Swift.   NBLV; NPeEn; OBSV; PoE
Satis Passio.   Les A. Murray.   HarvBoo
Satisfaction Coal Company, The.   Rita Dove.   LCAP-2
Satisfaction—is the Agent.   Emily Dickinson.   NOBA; TCAPo
Satisfied, unsatisfied.   "H. D."   APT-1   Fr. Flowering of the Rod, The.
Satori.   Gayl Jones.   BlSi
Saturated.   Aaron Shurin.   FTOS
Saturday.   New Comers.   Melinda Goodman.   WiU
Saturday Afternoon at the Movies.   John Logan.   NNaP
Saturday Afternoon, October.   Jonathan Holden.   OPRER
Saturday Afternoon, When Chores Are Done.   Harryette Mullen.   ISC
Saturday, April 26, 1973.   Poem to Galway Kinnell, A.   Etheridge Knight.   BodElec; NNaP
Saturday at the Border.   Hayden Carruth.   MakPoe
Saturday grieves.   To the New World.   Claudia Keelan.   BodElec
Saturday in the Sand-Slums.   Agostinho Neto.   PoetW, tr. by Michael Wolfers
Saturday in the '20s.   Jean Earle.   AngWePo
Saturday, March the first, she rings.   Chords.   Eamer O'Keefe.   Prnts
Saturday Market.   Charlotte Mew.   WPE
Saturday Morning, A.   Manuel A. Viray.   ReBoTo
Saturday morning, Motown.   Collection Day.   Natasha Trethewey.   SpirFl
Saturday morning, Wolverhampton market.   Red Desiré.   Mick North.   NLP
Saturday mornings, before.   Bait, The.   Eric Chock.   OpBo
Saturday Night.   I Can't Get Started.   Ai.   GT
Saturday Night.   Clark Coolidge.   FTOS
Saturday Night.   Sir Alan Patrick Herbert.   NBLV
Saturday Night.   Langston Hughes.   MoAmPo
Saturday Night.   Antigone Kefala.   CBAP
Saturday Night.   Victoria Wood.   OBCoV
Saturday Night Decades.   Sterling Plumpp.   IllVoic
Saturday night in August when, A.   Last Meeting.   Robert Penn Warren.   DiPo
Saturday Night in the Parthenon.   Kenneth Patchen.   SPE
Saturday Night in the Village.   Giacomo Leopardi.   OBVE; WoPoe, tr. by Robert Lowell

Saturday night November 1980. Lullabye for a Butch. Melinda Goodman. WiU

Saturday night she comes in her little boat. Music on the Water. George Johnston. MoCV

Saturday on Seventh Street. Fields, The. W. S. Merwin. HCAP

Saturday Review, The. Dora Greenwell. EBVV

Saturday's Child. Countee Cullen. NAAAL; PAI

Saturday 6 A.M. Charles Wright. GeoHom

Saturday, Sunday. Mother Goose. OxNR; ReMoGo

Saturday: The Small-Pox. Lady Mary Wortley Montagu. BWW; ECWP; NOEC; WPE Fr. Six Town Eclogues.

Saturday Tub, The. Mary Gilmore. NOBAu

Saturday with Dad. Liz Houghton. Prnts

Saturn. Geoffrey Chaucer. NPeEn Fr. Canterbury Tales, The.

Saturn. Günter Grass. AF

Saturn. John Keats. FHYEP; NOBRP; OxAEP-2; OxBEV Fr. Hyperion.

Saturn. Sharon Olds. RaBo

Saturn Declining. Sándor Weöres. IQMS, tr. by Alan Dixon

Saturn's Three Sons. Robert Hayman. NOSC Fr. Owen's Epigrams.

Satyr, A. John Oldham.
    London. NOSC
    "One night, as I was pondering of late." NOSC
    "Sir, to be short, in this expensive town." NOSC

Satyr Address'd to a Friend That Is About to Leave the University, and Come Abroad in the World, A. John Oldham.
    If you for orders, and a gown design.
    "If you're so out of love with happiness." OBSV

Satyr by Diodorus, A. Plato the Younger. GrAn, tr. by G. R. H. Wright

Satyr, Cunnilinguent: To Herman Melville. Charles Martin. RA

Satyr O never ask how I came to this place. Michael Drayton. AEP Fr. Muses' Elysium X, The.

Satyr's Song, The ("Softly Gliding as I Go"). John Fletcher. NOSC Fr. Faithful Shepherdess, The.

Satyre 3 [On Religion]. John Donne. See Satires

Satyre: Of Religion. John Donne. See Satires

Satyricon. Petronius Arbiter.
    "Fate brought three men to birth." MLL
    "From the high Alpine pass." MLL
    "However, Eumolpus, our champion in time of trouble and the author of the present harmony." EroLit, tr. by J. P. Sullivan
    "Roman was the victor of the world, The." MLL
    "Such flowers as Earth our Mother." MLL

Satyrs used to fall for nymphs. Love-Songs, at Once Tender and Informative. Samuel Hoffenstein. OBAL

Satyrus Peregrinans. William Rankins.
    "By this time long-gowned Lumen walked abroad." OBSV

Sauchs in the Reuch Heuch Hauch, The. Hugh MacDiarmid. NoAM

Saucy [or Saucie] Subjects still will bear[e] the sway, The. (LL) Power in the People, The. Robert Herrick. BASC; CaPo

Saul. Nathan [or Natan] Alterman. TrJP, tr. by Dov Vardi

Saul. Robert Browning.
    "Oh, the wild joys of living! the leaping from rock up to rock." ITBLP

Saul did much care and diligence express. Rowland Watkyns. FaBoEE

Sauna 2. Karina Africa-Bolasco. ReBoTo

Sauntering home from church we lingered. Mary Ursula Bethell. PeNZ Fr. By the River Ashley.

Sausage. Edgar Albert Guest. OBAL

Sausalito, / Little Willow. Sausalito Trash Prayer. Lew Welch. BB

Sausalito Trash Prayer. Lew Welch. BB

Sautéed, baked or fried. Kalamu ya Salaam. SpirFl Fr. New Orleans Haiku.

Savage cold of Russian winters, The. Natalya [or Natal'ia] Gorbanevskaya [or Gorbanyevskaya orGorbanevskaia]. TCRusP, tr. by Daniel Weissbort

Savage Memories. Yehuda Amichai [or Amikhai]. FIT, tr. by Robert Friend

Savage of Aveyron, The. Mary Robinson. RWP

Savage, Our Fathers, The. B. H. Boston. GeoHom

Savage's romance, The. New York. Marianne Craig Moore. NAAL-2v2

Savage the sea leaped high; on the rocks plunged ponderous breakers. Tempest. Theodore H. Banks, Jr. YaYoPo

Save As: Salvation. Bill Knott. BodElec

Save breed to brave him when he takes thee hence. (LL) William Shakespeare. AWP; HeIP-4; NAEL-5v1; NAEL-6v1; NAEL-7v1; NoSic; SCGP; Son; WoPoe Fr. Sonnets.

Save by the Old Road none attain the new. Coventry Patmore. FaBoEE

Save her? What for? To act this wedded life! (LL) George Meredith. NAEL-5v2; NAEL-6v2 Fr. Modern Love.

Save it all; you do not know. 1915: A Pre-Raphaelite Ending, London. Richard Howard. RACG

Save of him who, desiring, honors her. (LL) Ballata: He Will Gaze upon Beatrice. Dante Alighieri. AWP; EaItPo, tr. by Dante Gabriel Rossetti

Save only that of death. (LL) Ambrose Bierce. APN-2; OBAL Fr. Devil's Dictionary, The.

Save that I know Roger Parry and he does not? (LL) Porth Cwyfan. Roland Mathias. AngWePo; TCAWP

Save that the curtains, drawn. New York Minute. Joe Osterhaus. AmPoNex

Save that to die, I leave my love alone. (LL) William Shakespeare. AWP; CTC; EBEV; HAP; NOBE; NoSic; OxAEP-1; TFi; WeW-3 Fr. Sonnets.

Save the Boys. Frances Ellen Watkins Harper. PWR

Save there. / There / No flower. (LL) In the Grave No Flower. Edna St. Vincent Millay. NAAL-2v2; NAAL-5

Save thou, my rose; in it thou art my all. (LL) William Shakespeare. NOBE; OBEV; OxAEP-1 Fr. Sonnets.

Save to one man, and unto God. (LL) Precept of Silence, The. Lionel Pigot Johnson. MoBrPo; SacPr

Save Us From. Roo Borson. NIL-7

Save us from night. Save Us From. Roo Borson. NIL-7

Save us, the poets, save us, we have but. Bulat Shalvovich Okudzhava. TCRusP, tr. by Denis Johnson, Aleksandar Petrov and Shirley Rihner

Save yourself. Run and leave me. I must go back. Clive Staples Lewis. EBEV Fr. Epigrams and Epitaphs.

Saved. Adah Isaacs Menken. CBWP-1

Saving the Appearances. Charles Tomlinson. OxBEV

Saving the Harvest. Geoffrey Lehmann. CBAP

Savior. Ray Gonzalez. TouFir

Savior! I've no one else to tell. Emily Dickinson. TrCP

Savior Is Abducted in Puerto Rico, The. Martín Espada. TRP

Savior looked on Peter, The. Ay, no word. Look, The. Elizabeth Barrett Browning. TrCP

Savior must have been, The. Emily Dickinson. ChrPo; SacPr

Saviour. Zindzi Mandela. HAWP

Saviour of mankind, Man, Emmanuel! Hymn Written at the Holy Sepulchre in Jerusalem. George Sandys. SacPr

Saviour, Sprinkle Many Nations. Arthur Cleveland Coxe. AH

Saviour, Thy Dying Love. Sylvanus D. Phelps. AH

Saviour, Who Thy Flock Art Feeding. William Augustus Mühlenberg. AH

Sâvitrî; or, Love and Death. Unknown. TAL Fr. Mahabharata, The.

Savoir Faire. Claribel Alegría. VCWP

Savonarola. Edmund Clerihew Bentley. OxBoLi

Savouring the shade of our teacher's willow. Dog Day Lesson. John Hughes. PNI

Savoy / The home of sweet romance. Stompin' at the Savoy. Edgar Sampson. ReLy

Saw a home movie this afternoon. Uncle Charles. Uncle Charles: A Home Movie. J. Bernlef. TuT, tr. by Peter Van de Kamp

Saw a lamb being born. Lamb. Michael Dennis Browne. RaBo

Saw my shadow on the wall. Shadow Returns, The. Phillis Levin. RA

Saw someone yesterday looked like you did. In the Post Office. Thom Gunn. CAGL

Saw the Cloud Lynx. Samuel Makidemewabe. STP, tr. by Howard Norman

Saw them glittering in the trees. Blake. Lucille Clifton. ExTi

Saw whites clap during a sacred dance. Today Was a Bad Day Like TB. Chrystos. UnSA

Saw ye aught of my love a-coming from the market? My Love. Unknown. ReMoGo

Saw Ye Bonny Lesley. Robert Burns. See Bonnie Lesley

Saw ye Jenny Nettles. Jenny Nettles. Unknown. NePenScot

Sawmill. Richard Kenney. NoP-4

Sawyers lie outside the shed, The. Boathouse, The. Robert Minhinnick. AngWePo

Saxon Legend of Language, The. Mary Weston Fordham. CBWP-2

Saxons of Flint, The. Unknown. OBWVE, tr. by Mary C. Llewelyn

Saxophone Julie. Susan Firer. MiVo

Say "Cheese!" Tommy Wolf. ReLy

Say, crimson rose and dainty daffodil. Nosegay, A. John Reynolds. OBEV

Say, dear Maria! is the modish life. Familiar Epistle, A. Ann Murry. WPE

Say, dear Sophia! gentle friend. To Miss Sophia Headle. Dorothea Primrose Campbell. PoBW

Say, Dwarf, for it seems to me. Unknown. OBVE, tr. by Wystan Hugh Auden and Paul B. Taylor Fr. Elder Edda, The.

Say, earth, why hast thou got thee new attire. Giles Fletcher, the Younger. NOCV Fr. Christ's Victory and Triumph.

Say french. Diana Helen Melhem. PoArWo Fr. Rest in Love.

Say Girls in Shoe Ads: "I Go for a Man Who's Tall!" Robley, Jr. Wilson. PBCAP

Say good-by er howdy-do. Good-by er Howdy-do. James Whitcomb Riley. CTC

Say Good-bye to Big Daddy. Randall Jarrell. MoASP

Say happiness is possible, or more than possible. On Track. Kathleene West. FFC

Say, hast thou track'd a traveller's round. Taormini. John Henry, Cardinal Newman. SacPr

Say! Have you ever met the girl who's the toast of the town. Lady in Red, The. Allie Wruber. ReLy

Say Hello to John. Sherley Anne Williams. BlSi

Say, how shall thoughtless, easy-natured youth. Stanzas Imitated From Psalm CXIX. Thomas Warton, the Elder. ChIV-1

Say, I come tomorrow [or to-morrow]. (LL) Westphalian Song. Unknown. AWP; OBVE, tr. by Samuel Taylor Coleridge

Say I were not sixty. Make Believe. Gerda Mayer. Prnts

Say It. Jayne Cortez. SurWo

Say it and cry aloud. I Am a Negro. Muhammad Al-Faituri [or Al-Fituri or Al-Fayturi]. TTY, tr. by Halim El-Dabh

Say it is Tuesday. Tuesday Shaman. Maurice Kilwein Guevara. TouFir

Say it isn't real. Bedtime Stories. Silvia Curbelo. TouFir

Say It Isn't So. Irving Berlin. ReLy

Say It Loud—I'm Black and I'm Proud. James Brown. ISC

Say it's an important event like this. Off to Patagonia. Theodore Weiss. TAP

Say Ja. Tom Mandel. PmAP

Say life is the one-way trip, the one-way flight. Watchmaker God. Robert Lowell. HCAP; InvLi; SoSe-8

Say, little honey / I haven't any money. Great Big Bunch of You, A. Harry Warren. ReLy

Say, lovely Tory, why the jest. To Miss Eleanor Ambrose on the Occasion of Her Wearing an Orange Lily at a Ball in Dublin Castle on July the 12th. Philip Dormer Stanhope, 4th Earl of Chesterfield. EnLoPo

Say me, wight in the brom [or broom]. Tell Me, Wight in the Broom. Unknown. MiEL; NAEL-5v1; NAEL-6v1

Say, mighty Love, and teach my song. Few Happy Matches. Isaac Watts. NOEC

Say, Montagu, can this unartful verse. On Elizabeth Montagu. Mary Scott. RWP

Say Muses, say; who now in those rich fields. Phineas Fletcher. ChIV-1 Fr. Locusts, or Appolyonists, The.

Say nay, say nay! (LL) Lover's Appeal, The. Sir Thomas Wyatt. EnLoPo; GTBS-P; NAEL-5v1; NoSic; SCGP

Say not, because no more you see. On the Death of Mr. Persall's Little Daughter, in the Beginning of the Spring, at Amsterdam. Unknown. NOSC

Say not of beauty she is good. Beauty. Elinor Wylie. APT-1; NAAL-2v2; OxBA

Say not of me that weakly I declined. Robert Louis Stevenson. PeVV

Say not the age is hard and cold. Present Age, The. Frances Ellen Watkins Harper. PWR

Say not the mermaid is a myth. Mermaid, The. Ogden Nash. Spl

Say Not the Struggle Nought Availeth. Arthur Hugh Clough. AWP; EBVV; GTBS-P; ITBLP; NAEL-5v2; NAEL-6v2; NOBE; NOBVV; NoP-4; OBEV; OxBEV; SCGP; SacPr; TFi

Say not the struggle nought [or naught] availeth. Say Not the Struggle Nought Availeth. Arthur Hugh Clough. AWP; EBVV; GTBS-P; ITBLP; NAEL-5v2; NAEL-6v2; NOBE; NOBVV; NoP-4; OBEV; OxBEV; SCGP; SacPr; TFi

Say over again, and yet once over again. Elizabeth Barrett Browning. CenSon; NAEL-5v2; NAEL-6v2; OxBSo Fr. Sonnets from the Portuguese.

Say proudly yet—''Twas hers who loved me well!' (LL) Properzia Rossi. Felicia Dorothea Hemans. RWP; VWP; ViWPN

Say, reverend man, why midst this stormy night. Blind Man, The. Anne Batten Cristall. ECWP

Say—So I'll Say. Giancarlo Majorino. ItPo, tr. by Gayle Ridinger

Say, spotless plume, if Damon bade thee go. To My Pen. Mary Julia Young. CenSon

Say, stranger, that this is the tomb of the mare Aethyia. Mnasalcas. HePo Fr. Epigrams.

Say, sweet, my grief and I, we may not brook. Je ne veux de personne aupres de ma tristesse. Henri De Regnier. AWP, tr. by "Seumas" O'Sullivan

Say (sweetest) whether thou didst use me well. To Cynthia on Her Being an Incendiary. Sir Francis Kynaston. HAP

Say that a ballad. Susan Howe. PmAP Fr. Speeches at the Barriers.

Say that I should say I love ye. Assurance, An. Nicholas Breton. SCGP

Say that thou didst forsake me for some fault. William Shakespeare. OxAEP-1 Fr. Sonnets.

Say that you're lying comfortably under. Journey Out. Rachel Hadas. RA

Say the need's born within the tree. Gum-trees Stripping. Judith Wright. BMAP

Say the words I am. Examining the I. Jean V. Gier. ReBoTo

Say, there's a lamb in the daisies. (LL) For a Lamb. Richard Eberhart. ColAP; OxBSP; RB; SoSe-8

Say this city has ten million souls. W. H. Auden. AmFaPo; HP; OxAEP-2 Fr. Ten Songs.

Say this to the king: men wrought this shrine. Last Oracle from Delphi. Unknown. WoPoe, tr. by Katherine Washburn

Say to me: out there are only streets, and cars. Lullaby. Constance Merritt. AmPoNex

Say tyrant Custom, why must we obey. Emulation, The. Sarah Fyge Egerton. CABP; ECWP; NOEC; PEW

Say well and do well. Unknown. OxNR

Say! what is life? 'Tis to be born. Story of Life, The. John Godfrey Saxe. PoToHe

Say what remains when Hope is fled? Boy of Egremond, The. Samuel Rogers. NOBRP

Say what you please. Rondelet. May Probyn. VWP

Say what you want about doctors or priests. Lightning Rod Salesman, The. M. L. Hester. CRP

Say what you will in two. Air: Sentir avec Ardeur. Marie-Françoise-Catherine de, Marquise de Boufflers Beauveau. CTC; WPOW, tr. by Ezra Pound

"Say, where is the maiden sweet." Sag', wo ist dein schönes Liebchen. Heinrich Heine. AWP, tr. by James Thomson

Say wherefore is't that Damon flys. On Damons Loveing of Clora. Damaris, Lady Masham. EMWP

"Say why are beauties praised and honoured most." Pope. ECEV Fr. Rape of the Lock, The; an Heroi-Comical Poem.

Say witty fair one, from what sphere. To the Most Excellently Accomplished Mrs. Katherine Philips. Henry Vaughan. CABP

Say, wouldst thou guard thy son. Of Caution. Francesco da Barberini. AWP; EaItPo, tr. by Dante Gabriel Rossetti

Say "Yes," if you please. (LL) Sukey [or Suky], you shall be my wife. Unknown. OxNR; TLR

Say Yes Quickly. Jelaluddin [or Jalal al-Din] Rumi. EnlH; RaBo

Say you needed some ideas. Journals, The. Gaylord Brewer. AmPoNex

Say you want to sing right now. Worry. Aaron Anstett. AmPoNex

Sayatasha's Night Chant. Zuni Oral Tradition. Fr. Shalako.

Sayes "Christ thee saue, good Child of Ell!" Earl Brand. Unknown. ESPB

Saying blackberry, blackberry, blackberry. (LL) Meditation at Lagunitas. Robert Hass. AmFaPo; ColAP; GeoHom; MakPoe; NoP-4; VCAP

Saying Dante Aloud. James Wright (1927–80). InPK-6

Saying Dear child, and all time has disproved. (LL) Faith Healing. Philip Larkin. ChIV-2; GI; NoAM; OxBEV

Saying Farewell to a Friend. Li Po. TAL

Saying Farewell to Magistrate Ch'en Ta-yu. Lin Hung. SuSp, tr. by Irving Y. Lo

Saying for ever to the spirit, "Sigh!" (LL) Dante Alighieri. AWP; EaItPo, tr. by Dante Gabriel Rossetti Fr. La Vita Nuova.

Saying Good-bye in a Ch'in-ling Wineshop. Li Po. CrYelRi, tr. by Sam Hamill

Saying Good-bye to a Singing Girl Who Has Decided to Become a Nun. Mo Shih-lung. CoBLCP; ColAnChi; WoPoe, tr. by Jonathan Chaves

Saying Good-Bye to Feng the Hermit. Mo Shih-lung. CoBLCP, tr. by Jonathan Chaves

Saying Good-bye to Meng Hao-jan at Yellow Crane Pavilion. Li Po. CrYelRi, tr. by Sam Hamill

Saying Goodby to the Monk Ling-ch'e. Liu Ch'ang-ch'ing. SuSp, tr. by Dell R. Hales

Saying Goodbye to a Monk from Japan. Hsü Pen. CoBLCP, tr. by Jonathan Chaves

Saying to her too, Ease and peace thou art. (LL) Sonnet: Death Is Not without but within Him. Cino da Pistoia. AWP; EaItPo, tr. by Dante Gabriel Rossetti

Sayings in Verse. Arthur Schnitzler. AuPH, tr. by Lowell A. Bangerter

Says a Reverend Priest to a less Rev'rend friend. Epigram. Unknown. NOBRP

Says Body to Mind, "'Tis amazing to see." Dialogue, A. Elizabeth Carter. ECWP

Says Come here, says. Whistle. Janet Holmes. ExTi

Says it. His is. Zeimbekiko. Robin Magowan. SPE

Says Jone to his woife on a whot summer's day. Jone o' Grinfilt. Joseph Lees. NOBRP

Says my Uncle, I pray you discover. Molly Mog [or The Fair Maid of the Inn]. John Gay. OBCoV

Says Tom to Jack, ''Tis very odd.' Methodist, The. Thomas Chatterton. ECEV

Says Tweed tae Till. Unknown. See Tweed and Till

Says Tweed to [tae] Till. Tweed and Till. Unknown. FaBoCh; NPeEn; OxBSP

Says yes. Lao Figures. Unknown. EaWin, tr. by W. S. Merwin

Scaffold, The. Amal Dunqul. MAP; NAfrP, *tr.* by Sharif Elmusa and Thomas G. Ezzy

Scaffold in Winter. János Pilinszky. PoSu, *tr.* by Peter Jay

Scaffolding. Seamus Heaney. ChAP

Scald it and scour it like a doorstep. (LL) View of a Pig. Ted Hughes. OxAEP-2; OxBEV; OxBTC; TwCP

Scale Force, Cumberland. Letitia [*or* Laetitia] Elizabeth Landon. RWP

Scale of Being, The. Pope. WoPoe *Fr.* Essay on Man, An.

Scale of dragon, tooth of wolf. William Shakespeare. UV *Fr.* Macbeth.

Scales, The. William Empson. FaBoMo

Scales of pearly cloud inlay. Holiday at Hampton Court. John Davidson. EBVV

Scallion stands, gruel shops—half are run by ex-scholars! Inscribed on the Wall of a Rice Cake Shop. Chin Nung. CoBLCP, *tr.* by Jonathan Chaves

Scalloped synecdoches of satin cloud. Shells. Rachel Hadas. ExTi

Scalp Dance, The. *Zuni Oral Tradition.*
"Indeed, the enemy." NAWM-7v2, *tr.* by Ruth L. Bunzel

Scalpel finds the heart, The. The heart is still. Rafael Campo. WiU *Fr.* Song for My Lover.

Scalpel in Hand. Marjorie Welish. FTOS

Scampering the pasture, that's how now. Calf and the Ox, The. Avianus. WoPoe, *tr.* by David R. Slavitt

Scan. Gillian Ferguson. NeBl

Scandal of this universe, The. Door of the Cities. Munia Samara. PoArWo, *tr.* by Amal Amireh

Scandal or two, A. Tattle. Godfrey Turner. NOBL

Scandalous man, A. Mr. Tom Narrow. James Reeves. OBSP

Scant and straggling her yellow hair, from her lip. Old Woman, An. David Gwenallt Jones. OBWVE, *tr.* by H. Idris Bell

Scape-Goat, The. Agnes Mary Frances Robinson. VWP

Scaped. Stephen Crane. APN-2 *Fr.* Black Riders [and Other Lines], The.

Scapegoat. William Robert Rodgers. CIP-2

Scapular of birds hung fast, A. Eclipses. Nancy Sullivan. TAP

Scar, The. John Hewitt. CIP-2; PNI

Scarabæus Sisyphus. Mathilde Blind. ViWPN

Scaramouche and Pulcinella. Weird as Puppets. Paul Verlaine. SxFrPo, *tr.* by Martin Sorrell

Scaramouche waves a threatening hand. Fantoches. Paul Verlaine. AWP; OBMV, *tr.* by Arthur Symons

Scarborough Fair. *Unknown.* OxBoLi; PeLV

Scarce a breeze on the lake, with four oars to our boat. On Loch Leven. Christian Carstairs. ECWP

Scarce do I pass a day, but that I hear. Meditation 8. Philip Pain. NOBA; NOSC; OxBSP

Scarce had I slept my wonted round. Dream, A. Sir John Suckling. ChIV-2

SCARCE had the morning star hid from the light. Affectionate Shepherd, The. Richard Barnfield [*or* Barnefield]. NoSic

Scarce had the morning starre hid from the light. Richard Barnfield [*or* Barnefield]. CAGL *Fr.* Affectionate Shepherd [*or* Shephearde], The.

Scarce warms the surface of the deepest pool? (LL) August. Elinor Wylie. APT-1; MoAmPo

Scarcely. Alfonso Reyes. TCLAP, *tr.* by Samuel Beckett

Scarcely a street, too few houses. Village, The. Ronald Stuart Thomas. HarvBoo

Scarcely, I think; yet it indeed *may* be. For "An Allegorical Dance of Women" by Andrea Mantegna. Dante Gabriel Rossetti. CenSon

Scar[e]-Fire, The. Robert Herrick. HAP

Scarecrow. Alan Pizzarelli. HA

Scarecrow, The. Walter De la Mare. MoBrPo; OxBTC

Scarecrow, The. Andrew Young. FaBoTw

Scarecrows. James Kirkup. NOxBChV

Scared Cows. Douglas Messerli. FTOS

Scared? / are responsible negros running. Concerning One Responsible Negro with Too Much Power. Nikki Giovanni. BPo

Scaring Crows. *Unknown.* OxNR

Scaring Hens. Peter Finch. Oth

Scarlet. Arrow Song. *Unknown.* TCAPo

Scarlet Crown. Marc J. Straus. BloBone

Scarlet Skirt. Víctor Hernández Cruz. TouFir

Scarlet, warm and heavy in black velvet leaves. Leah Goldberg. MHP *Fr.* On Blossoming.

Scarred by flame, hollowed out by waves. To the Wooden Hermit. Han Yü. SuSp, *tr.* by Kenneth O. Hanson

Scarred hemlock roots. Down Stream. Louise Imogen Guiney. SWaP

Scars. William Stafford. AmFaPo

Scars take us back to places we have been, The. Memoranda. William Dickey. YaYoPo

Scartabello. Edoardo Sanguineti.

"And now a few questions to end with." ItPo, *tr.* by Gayle Ridinger

"At the offset it was calculated." ItPo, *tr.* by Gayle Ridinger

"Like a disk, a trembling coin spinning on its own diameter." ItPo, *tr.* by Gayle Ridinger

"What you're reading (if you're reading me) are the effects." ItPo, *tr.* by Gayle Ridinger

"Wind shoves my New Year's Day sun in my face, The." ItPo, *tr.* by Gayle Ridinger

Scattered, aslant. Fathers. Robert Creeley. FTOS

Scattered brainscape while the fan. Summertime Late Show. Edwin Torres. HeMarv

Scattered Congregation, The. Tomas Tranströmer. RaBo, *tr.* by Robert Bly

Scattered Leaves. Lance Henson. VoR

Scattered Light. Fanny Howe. FTOS

Scattered milkweed, valentine. To My Soul. Jean Valentine. YaYoPo

Scattered Moluccas. Ezra Pound. TCAPo *Fr.* Hugh Selwyn Mauberley (Life and Contacts).

Scattering as Behavior Toward Risk. Susan Howe. PFTM-2

Scattering Ashes. David Scott. NLP

Scattering bloom, The. Buson. TAL

Scattering Flowers. George Hitchcock. CDa

Scattering of mottled seeds, spots, A. My Shining Archipelago. Talvikki Ansel. NeAmPo

Scazons. Clive Staples Lewis. EBEV

Scel Lem Duib. *Unknown. See* Season Song

Scenario is: I'm six, and an invincible Venusian army of robots, The. Meop. Albert Goldbarth. IllVoic

Scene, The. Ágnes Nemes Nagy. PoSu, *tr.* by Bruce Berlind

Scene 3. Achsa W. Sprague. *Fr.* Poet, The.

Scene: A Bedside in the Witches' Kitchen. Ramon Guthrie. APT-2

Scene after Hunting at Swallowfield in Berkshire, A. Sneyd Davies. NOEC

Scene at Heaven Gate, The. T'ang Yin. CoBLCP, *tr.* by Jonathan Chaves

Scène de Boudoir. Edmund Wilson. OBCoV *Fr.* Easy Exercises in the Use of Difficult Words.

Scene for the Mornings Preceding the Fire, A. Ghada El-Shafa'i. PoArWo, *tr.* by Atef Abu-Seif and Nathalie Handal

Scene from a Play, Acted at Oxford, Called "Matriculation." Thomas Moore. OBSV

Scene from South Hill to North Hill Passing the Lake. Hsieh Ling-yün. ChinPo, *tr.* by Yip Wai-lim

Scene from the Movie *Giant.* Tino Villanueva. ReTh

Scene is different, and the place, The. Arthur Hugh Clough. PeVV *Fr.* Dipsychus [and the Spirit].

Scene is set for dreaming, The. My Foolish Heart. Ned Washington. ReLy

Scene of Return is Sketched, A. Mercedes Roffé. MirDau

Scene of superfluous grace, and wasted bloom. Anna Seward. PEW *Fr.* Colebrook Dale.

Scene on the Northern Shore of Sicily. Ann Radcliffe. RWP

Scene-Script. Giancarlo Majorino. ItPo, *tr.* by Gayle Ridinger

Scene with Figure. Babette Deutsch. TrJP

Scene within the paperweight is calm, The. Paperweight, The. Gjertrud Schnackenberg. VCAP

Scenes. Yang Chi.
"Eastern neighbor, western neighbor." CoBLCP

Scènes de la Vie de Bohème. Arthur Symons.
Episode of a Night of May. PeVV

Scenes for an Elegy. Michael Klein. WiU

Scenes from the Door. Gertrude Stein. AF

Scenes from the Life of the Peppertrees. Denise Levertov. NeAP; PoM (Peppertrees, the peppertrees!, The.) NoP-4

Scenes from the Mesozoic. Clarence Day.
"Yesterday explorers found." OBCoV

Scenes in London: Piccadilly. Letitia [*or* Laetitia] Elizabeth Landon. RWP

Scenes of Childhood. James Merrill. CoAP

Scenes of Childhood. Carl Morse. GLP

Scenes of my childhood, how oft I recall!, The. My Infundibuliform Hat. Charles Follen Adams. OBAL

Scent of hyacinths, like a pale mist, lies between me and my book, The. Vernal Equinox. Amy Lowell. APT-1

Scent of pencil, a house full, The. How Garnett Mims and the Enchanters Came into Your Life. Bruce Smith. SwNoth

Scent of ripeness from over a wall, A. Unharvested. Robert Frost. APT-1; SAmP

Scent of unseen jasmine on the warm night beach, The. Málaga. Pearse Hutchinson. BIrV; ModIr; PBCIP

Scented Herbage of My Breast. Walt Whitman. APN-1; NAAL-2v1; NAAL-3

Scented with days to come. (LL) Girl Help. Janet Lewis. APT-2; HeIP-4; InPK-6

Scentless laurel a broad leaf displays, The. Walter Savage Landor. FaBoEE

Schadenfreude. Stephanie Brown. BodElec

Sche broghte him to his chambre tho. John Gower. NPeEn, *tr.* by John Gower *Fr.* Confessio Amantis.

Schemhammphorasch. Rose Terry Cooke. SWaP

Schemmelfennig. Bret Harte. OBAL

Scherzo. Pamela Alexander. YaYoPo

Scherzo, A. Dora Greenwell. NOBVV; NPeEn
    (Scherzo A Shy Person's Wishes, A.) PEW

Scherzo A Shy Person's Wishes, A. Dora Greenwell. *See* Scherzo, A

Schicksalslied. Friedrich Hölderlin. WoPoe, *tr.* by M. L. Rosenthal *Fr.* Hyperion.

Schir William Wallace. Henry the Minstrel. OxBS

Schir, ye have mony servitouris. Remonstrance to the King. William Dunbar. OxBS

Schizophrenic. Patricia K. Page. HeIP-4

Schizophrenic, wrenched by two styles. Codicil. Derek Walcott. NoAM

Schluf mine faygele. Lullaby. Breyten Breytenbach. · VCWP, *tr.* by Breyten Breytenbach

Scholar, The. Austin Clarke. RB

Scholar, The. Frances Darwin Cornford. BrRo

Scholar, The. Vijay Seshadri. KGB

Scholar, The. Robert Southey. GTBS-P
    (Among His Books.) OxAEP-2
    (His Books.) OBEV

Scholar I. Seamus Deane. NOIV

Scholar II. Seamus Deane. CIP-2; NOIV

Scholar and the Cat, The. *Unknown.* WoPoe, *tr.* by Frank O'Connor

Scholar, compose me a Magyar song. Matthias' Demented Scholar. Endre Ady. IQMS, *tr.* by Anton N. Nyerges

Scholar first my Love implor'd, A. Song. Dorothea Du Bois. LW

Scholar first my love implored, A. Song. Lady Dorothea Dubois. ECWP

Scholar Gypsy, The. Matthew Arnold. EBEV; EBVV; FHYEP; HAP; NAEL-5v2; NAEL-6v2; NOBE; NOBVV; NoP-4; OBEV; OxAEP-1; PoE; SCGP; TFi
    "O born in days when wits were fresh and clear." OxBEV

Scholar in the Narrow Street, The. Tso Ssu. AWP; ChiP, *tr.* by Arthur Waley

Scholar of Oxford, while tipsy, A. Tribute to Matthew Arnold in a Moment of Self-Abuse, A. Richard Shepherd. PeLi

Scholar Recruit. Pao Chao. FaBoWar, *tr.* by Arthur Waley

Scholar's Cat, The. János Arany. IQMS, *tr.* by Neville Masterman

Scholar's Life, The. Samuel Johnson. NOBE; NPeEn; OBSV *Fr.* Vanity of Human Wishes; The Tenth Satire of Juvenal Imitated, The.

Scholar's Life, The. *Unknown.* NOIV, *tr.* by Thomas Kinsella

Scholars. Walter De la Mare. NoAM

Scholars, The. W. B. Yeats. NoP-4

Scholars at the Orchid Pavilion. John Berryman. HarvBoo; PoE

School and Nature. Jean Follain. BLT, *tr.* by W. S. Merwin

School and Schoolfellows. Winthrop Mackworth Praed. OxAEP-2

School-Boy, The. William Blake. FHYEP; FaBoCh; OxAEP-2 *Fr.* Songs of Experience.

School Cadets. Anne Elder. CBAP

School Children, The. Louise Glück. ColAP; HCAP; PoPoPo; WeW-3

School Days. Maltbie Davenport Babcock. PWR

School Days. William Stafford. LCAP-2

School for Satire, The. Lady Sophia Burrell. ECWP

School for Scandal, The. Richard Brinsley Sheridan.
    Drinking Song. NOIV; NPeEn; OxBEV
    (Song: "Here's to the maiden [*or* maid] of bashful fifteen.") NOEC; OxAEP-1; OxBoLi; PeLV; PoRA

School Globe, The. James Reaney. NOBC

School is gone from Belgrave Place, The. Sean Dunne. ModIr *Fr.* Sydney Place.

School is long closed down, The. A Nos Glorieux Morts. Jan Eijkelboom. TuT, *tr.* by Michael O'Loughlin

School is over. It is too hot. Lonely Street, The. William Carlos Williams. APT-1; TwCP

School-Master and the Truants, The. "John Brownjohn." OBCA

School-Mistress, The. William Shenstone. NOEC

School of Beauty's a tavern now, The. Gwendolyn Brooks. VGW *Fr.* Street in Bronzeville, A.

School of clouds and a bunch, A. Fish. Mariana Romo-Carmona. WiU

School of Denial. Mary Ruefle. ExTi

School of Eloquence, The. Tony Harrison.
    Book Ends. DiPo; NAEL-5v2; NAEL-6v2
    "Bottomless pits. There's one in Castleton." HarvBoo; NAEL-5v2; NAEL-6v2

    Classics Society. NoP-4
    "Gold survives the fire that's hot enough." EmeKit; HarvBoo
    Heredity. HarvBoo; NAEL-6v2
    "I thought it made me look more "working class." NAEL-6v2
    Long Distance. NAEL-5v2; NAEL-6v2
    Marked with D. NAEL-5v2; NAEL-6v2
    National Trust. HarvBoo; NAEL-5v2; NAEL-6v2
    On Not Being Milton. CABP; HarvBoo; NoP-4
    Timer. EmeKit; HarvBoo
    Turns. NAEL-6v2

School of Fish. Eileen Myles. WiU

School Parted Us. "George Eliot." Son *Fr.* Brother and Sister.

School's Out. William Henry Davies. OBMV

School-Time. William Wordsworth. FHYEP; NAEL-6v2 *Fr.* Prelude, The; Growth of a Poet's Mind [1850 vers.].

School-Time. William Wordsworth. *Fr.* Prelude, The; Growth of a Poet's Mind [1805 vers.].

Schoolbag, The. Seamus Heaney. BiHa

Schoolboy's Lot, A. *Unknown.* MiEL

Schoolgirls Hastening. John Shaw Neilson. NOBAu

Schooling, A. Seamus Deane. CIP-2; PNI

Schoolmaster. George Rostrevor Hamilton. FaBoEE

Schoolmaster, The. Herodas. HePo, *tr.* by Barbara Hughes Fowler

Schoolmaster Abroad with His Son, The. Charles Stuart Calverley. NOBL; PeLV

Schools. George Crabbe. CTC *Fr.* Borough, The.

Schools break up tonight, The. Lament for Fearghal Ruadh. Tadhg Og O'Huiginn. NOIV

Schooner Flight, The. Derek Walcott. ESEAA; HarvBoo; NoP-4
    Adios, Carenage. PoetW

Schooners with their pale green lights, The. Dream within a Song, A. Henrietta Cordelia Ray. CBWP-3

Schsssssssss. Martin Steingesser. MoASP

Schubert. Michael Klieba. AuPH, *tr.* by Lowell A. Bangerter

Schule Laddie's Lament on the Lateness o' the Season, A. James Logie Robertson. NOBVV

Schumann's Sonata in A Minor. Celia Laighton Thaxter. AiP

Schute, Bell, Badgery, Lumby. Country Song, A. Douglas Stewart. NOBAu

Schwerner, Chaney, Goodman. Raymond R. Patterson. NBV

Schwinn rests in back seat. American Odalisque. Jane Miller. GifTon

Science. Samuel Davies. SacPr

Science. Robinson Jeffers. OxBA

Science and Human Behavior. John Hollander. YaYoPo

Science and Poetry. James Russell Lowell. NCAP

Science! bright Beam of Light Divine! Science. Samuel Davies. SacPr

Science Fiction. Kingsley Amis. NoAM

Science finds out ingenious ways to kill. Modern World, The. Colin Ellis. FaBoEE

Science! meet daughter of old time thou art. Sonnet—To Science. Edgar Allan Poe. NAAL-2v1; NAAL-3; NAAL-5

Science of Geology, The. James Milligan.
    "In ages past [animals] lived and died." VerBaPo

Science of the Night, The. Stanley Kunitz. APT-2; ColAP; MoAmPo; TwCP

Science, science, science! Venus Hottentot, The. Elizabeth Alexander. ESEAA; InTrad

Science, the agile ape, may well. Coventry Patmore. FaBoEE

Science! thou fair effusive ray. Hymn to Science. Mark Akenside. ECEV

Science! true daughter of Old Time thou art! Sonnet—To Science. Edgar Allan Poe. OxBA; OxBSo; Son; TAP; TCAPo

Scientific inquiry, seen in a very broad perspective may. Not a Cage. Joan Retallack. FTOS

Scientific Wooing. Constance Naden. VWP *Fr.* Evolutional Erotics.

Scientist has a test tube full of sheep, A. Counting Sheep. Russell Edson. LCAP-2

Scientist living at Staines, A. Genius. R. J. P. Hewison. PeLi

Scientists and technicians! Arab Traveler in a Space Ship, An. Muhammad Al-Maghut. MAP

Scillaes Metamorphosis. Thomas Lodge.
    "Minde through thee divines on endlesse things, The." PBRV

Scion of Boston society, A. Limerick. Conrad Potter Aiken. PeLi

Scissor-Man. George MacBeth [*or* Macbeth]. FaBoMo

Scissors and string, scissors and string. *Unknown.* OxNR

Scissors Ceremony, The. Michael Longley. EmeKit

Scissors cut the long-grown hair, The. Upon Shaving Off One's Beard. John Updike. OxBSP

Scissors cut you? What tender ears! On Words and Concepts and Things. Paul Ramsey. CRP

Scissors Strokes by the Clock. Laurence Iché. SurWo, *tr. by* Myrna Bell Rochester

Scissortails. Teresa Whitman. TWW

Scobble for whoredom[e] whips his wife, and cries [*or* cryes]. Upon Scobble [Epigram]. Robert Herrick. BeJo; CaPo; FaBoEE

Scoffers, The. William Blake. *See* Mock On, Mock On, Voltaire, Rousseau

Scolded like an impolite child. Saint Martha. Anna Kamienska. GI, *tr. by* David Curzon and Grażyna Drabik

Scones. *Unknown.* OBCoV

Scorched with love, the cicada. Kenneth Rexroth. APSN *Fr.* Love Poems of Marichiko, The.

Scorn Not the Sonnet. William Wordsworth. GSo; NoP-4

  (Scorne: "Scorn not the sonnet; critic, you have frowned.") OBEV

Scorn not the Sonnet; Critic, you have frowned. Sonnet. William Wordsworth. CenSon; EBEV; HeIP-4; OxBSo; Son

"Scorn not the sonnet," though its strength be sapped. On a Magazine Sonnet. Russell Hillard Loines. OBAL

Scorner, The. U Tam'si Tchicaya. PBMAP *Fr.* Epitomé (1962).

Scorner, The. Felix Tchicaya [*or* TchiKaya] U'Tamsi. TTY

  (I drink to your glory, God.) NegPo, *tr. by* Ellen Conroy Kennedy

Scorning religion all thy lifetime past. On Mr. Dryden, Renegade. Aphra Behn. FaBoVe

Scorpion. Stevie Smith. EBEV; FaBoWP; NPeEn; OxAEP-2; PeECV; PoE

Scorpion, The. William Plomer. OBMV; PeSAV

Scorpion's tails, silver hooks. Yün Shou-p'ing. CoBLCP *Fr.* In the Tenth Month of the Year Jen-tzu (1672) the Imperial Censor Tan Chiang-shang, Mountain Man Wang Shih-ku and I Traveled by Boat to Pi-ling and Moored There. We Lingered among the Frosty Trees and Red Leaves. Wang Was Entrusted with the Task of P.

Scorpion so wishes to be gone. (LL) Scorpion. Stevie Smith. EBEV; FaBoWP; NPeEn; OxAEP-2; PeECV; PoE

Scorpions, the. Alfonso X. NAWM-7v1, *tr. by* Peter Dronke

Scotch. Ruth Padel. MFPA

Scotch Drink. Robert Burns. ChIV-1

Scotch God / Kent His / Faither. Alexander Scott. OBCoV; WoPoe *Fr.* Scotched.

Scotch Rhapsody. Dame Edith Sitwell. TwCP

Scotch Song, A. Joanna Baillie. *See* Trysting Bush, The

Scotch Te Deum. William Kethe. SacPr

  (Psalm C.) NOCV

  (Psalm 100. 'O Be Joyful in the Lord, All Ye Lands') PeECV

Scotched. Alexander Scott.

  "*Scotch God* / Kent His / Faither." OBCoV; WoPoe

Scotland. Sir Alexander Gray. OxBS

Scotland. Alastair Reid. NePenScot

Scotland. Frederick Seidel. BodElec

Scotland. William Soutar. OxBS

Scotland 1941. Edwin Muir. CABP; NePenScot; OxBS

Scotland's Winter. Edwin Muir. NePenScot; OxBS; OxBTC

Scotland Small? Hugh MacDiarmid. NePenScot; RB

Scotland, when it is given to me. With a Lifting of the Head. Hugh MacDiarmid. MoBrPo

Scotland, you have invoked her name. Queen of Sheba, The. Kathleen Jamie. NePenScot

Scots steel tempered wi' Irish fire. Weapon, The. Hugh MacDiarmid. RB

Scots, wha hae wi' Wallace bled. Robert Bruce's March to Bannockburn. Robert Burns. NAEL-5v2; NAEL-6v2; OxBS

Scott and I bent. Heaven. Gary Soto. SwNoth

Scott Joplin. Bill Holm. MiVo

Scot[t]ish Field[e]. *Unknown.*

  Battle of Flodden, The. NoSic

Scottsboro. *Unknown.* InPK-6

Scotty Has His Say. Sterling Allen Brown. APT-2

Scoundrel carries his baseness around like an ID card, The. Answer. Bei Dao. PoetW; VCWP, *tr. by* Donald Finkel

Scourge deep, and quick be done. Martyr. Mary Elizabeth Fullerton. CBAP

Scourge of Folly, The. John Davies of Hereford.

  Author Loving These Homely Meats, The. NPeEn; OBCoV; Son

  (Homely Meats.) FaBoCh

Scourge of Villainy [*or* Villanie], The. John Marston.

  To Detraction I Present My Poesie. NoSic

  To Everlasting Oblivion. NoSic; SCGP

  "Fy Satyre fie, shall each mechanick slave." PBRV

Scouring pans. Larry Wiggin. HA

Scrabble. David Starkey. ReTh

Scrambled Eggs and Garlic Pork. Michael Melo. ReBoTo

Scrap. Tomasz Jastrun. AF, *tr. by* Daniel Bourne

Scrape the bottom of the hole: gather up the stuff! Digger's Song, The. Barcroft Henry Boake. NOBAu

Scrapping Limits. Salma Khadra Jayyusi. MAP, *tr. by* Charles Doria and the author

Scraps of Time. Mrs. Henry Linden. CBWP-4

Scraptures: 7th Sequence. B. P. Nichol. FTOS

Scraptures: 17th Sequence. B. P. Nichol. PFTM-2 *Fr.* Martyrology 7, The.

Scratch a Jew and you'll find a Wailing Wall. Wall, The. Eve Merriam. TaR; TrJP

Scrawled in a rage by Dublin's poor. (LL) Inscription for a Headstone. Austin Clarke. BIrV; CIP-2

Scrawled in Pencil in a Sealed Car. Dan Pagis. PoSu, *tr. by* Robert Friend

Scream, A. Muhammad Al-Faituri [*or* Al-Fituri *or* Al-Fayturi]. MAP, *tr. by* Sargon Boulus and Peter Porter

Scream, The. Donald Hall. GS

Scream is a Kind of Coffin, The. Paz Molina. TANSG, *tr. by* Steven F. White

Scream of Abû Nuwâs, The. Jolanda Insana.

  "From wonder to wonder." CItWP, *tr. by* Cinzia Sartini Blum and Lara Trubowitz

Scream that climbs a candle, A. Screams in the Dark. Slavko Mihalic. PoSu, *tr. by* Charles Simic

Screamer Discusses Methods of Screaming, A. James Schevill. TAP

Screaming and laughing; soaked right through. (LL) Pounding Rain. Jackie Kay. MFPA; PoBW

Screaming My Head Off. Vladimir Vladimirovich Mayakovsky [*or* Maiakovskii]. PFTM-1

Screams in the Dark. Slavko Mihalic. PoSu, *tr. by* Charles Simic

Screams round the Arch-druid's brow the sea-mew—white. William Wordsworth. Son *Fr.* Ecclesiastical Sonnets.

Screech owls moan in the yellowing. Travelling Northward. Tu Fu. BLT; OHPC, *tr. by* Kenneth Rexroth

Screen of supreme good fortune curved, The. Young Son, The. John Ashbery. YaYoPo

Screen Porch. Frederick Marchant. UrbNat

Screening its face amongst lotus stalks. Mahendranâth Bhattâcârya. SinGod, *tr. by* Rachel Fell McDermott

Screens. Barry Silesky. IllVoic

Screes, The. William Scammell. NLP

Screes are speeding down at perfect pitch, The. Screes, The. William Scammell. NLP

Screw-Guns. Rudyard Kipling. FaBoWar

Screw the fate that makes you share a man. On Sharing a Husband. Hồ Xuân Hu'o'ng. WoPoe, *tr. by* John Balaban

Scribbled at a Cabinet Meeting. Sir Edward Carlson. FaBoVe

Scribblers, The. Walter Savage Landor. OBSV

  (Why should scribblers discompose.) FaBoEE

Scribe, The. Walter De la Mare. FaBoCh; OBMV; TrCP

Scribe, to the vulgar inclined, A. Limerick. Douglas Catley. PeLi

Scribes, The. Suzanne Noguere. FFC

Scribes have cast the blame, The. Bible, *O.T.* WoPoe, *tr. by* Susan Stewart *Fr.* Lamentations.

Scrimmage of appetite everywhere, The. (LL) Delmore Schwartz. APT-2; ColAP; NOBA; NoAM; TAP; TrJP; TwCP; UnPo *Fr.* Repetitive Heart, The.

Script Conference. John Hartley Williams. EmeKit

Scripts for the Pageant. James Merrill.

  Samos. HCAP

Scripts I used to write for the young actor, The. Written, Directed by and Starring. James Simmons. PBCIP

Scripture of the Golden Eternity, The. Jack Kerouac.

  "Did I create that sky? Yes, for, if it was." CLPP

Scroll is open, The. "Ada" (Sarah Louisa Forten). SWaP

Scroll is open—many a name is written, The. Scroll is open, The. "Ada" (Sarah Louisa Forten). SWaP

Scroll of blue, an exquisite thought, A. Ball. Birago Diop. PBMAP

Scrotal burning, night, all day, night two, A. Recognition, The. John Berryman. BodElec

Scrub. Edna St. Vincent Millay. APT-1

Scrub woman for the old bank and jailhouse, The. Lamentations. Norman Dubie. NoAM

Scrutiny [*or* Scrutinie], The. Richard Lovelace. BeJo; BoLoP; CaPo; EnLoPo; MeLP

  (Song: The Scrutiny.) NOSC

  (Why should you swear I am forsworn.) CavPo

Scuba Diver Recovers the Body of a Drowned Child, The. Gerald William Barrax. GT; NBV

Scudamor in the Temple of Venus. Edmund Spenser. PoE *Fr.* Faerie Queene, The.

Sculler, The. John Taylor.

"As Gold is better that's in fire tride." PBRV

Sculptor, The. Cornelius Mathews. APN-1 *Fr.* Poems on Man in His Various Aspects under the American Republic.

Sculptor, The. *Unknown.* PoToHe

Sculptor musing sat one eve, A. Sculptor's Vision, The. Henrietta Cordelia Ray. CBWP-3

Sculptor remarked: "I'm afraid," A. Limerick. *Unknown.* PeLi

Sculptor's Vision, The. Henrietta Cordelia Ray. CBWP-3

Sculpture Garden. Austin Hummell. AmPoNex

Sculpture, heroic as it is, over the ages. Variations on a Theme. Joseph Awad. GraLe

Sculpture in a bare white gallery, A. Field, The. Jean Valentine. LCAP-2

Scum & Slime. John Giorno. PmAP

Scunner. Hugh MacDiarmid. FaBoTw; NePenScot

Scyld was still a strong man when his time came. Ship of Death, A. Seamus Heaney. NAEL-6v2; NoP-4

Scylla and Charybdis. Thomas Kinsella. OxBTC

Scythed god whose part is greater than the whole. *Unknown.* PriapPo, *tr. by* Richard W. Hooper *Fr.* Priapus Poems, The.

Scythians, The. Aleksandr Aleksandrovich Blok. AWP

(You are millions, we are multitude.) TCRP, *tr. by* Babette Deutsch

Se Aprovechan. Irving Feldman. GS

Sè Stesso, A. Giacomo Leopardi. AWP

Sea. Marie-Claire Bancquart. MFP, *tr. by* Martin Sorrell

Sea. Valerie Wohlfeld. YaYoPo

Sea, The. Jorge Luis Borges. TCLAP, *tr. by* John Updike

Sea, The. William Henry Davies. FaBoTw

Sea, The. E. A. Markham. EmeKit

Sea, The. James Reeves. NOxBChV

Sea, The. Francis Webb. CBAP

Sea and a crescent strip of beach, The. George Oppen. APSN; NNaP *Fr.* Some San Francisco Poems.

Sea and Other Stories, The. Jennifer Rankin. NOBAu

Sea and Ourselves at Cape Ann, The. Lawrence Ferlinghetti. PoM

Sea and set it blooming, The. (LL) Lady Ise. BoWoP; WoPoe, *tr. by* Irma Brandeis and Etsuko Terasaki

Sea and the Canefield, The. João Cabral de Melo Neto. TCLAP, *tr. by* Louis Simpson

Sea and the Hills, The. Rudyard Kipling. SCGP

Sea and the Man, The. Anna Swirszczynska. BLT

Sea and the Mirror, The. W. H. Auden.
  Supporting Cast, Sotto Voce, The.
  ("And the high green hill sits always by the sea.") (LL) RACG
  "At Dirty Dick's and Sloppy Joe's." BoLoP; FaBoTw
  Miranda. NPeEn; NoAM
  "My Dear One is mine as mirrors are lonely." NPeEn; NoAM
  Song of the Master and Boatswain. BoLoP; FaBoTw

Sea and the Skylark, The. Gerard Manley Hopkins. OBMV

Sea and You, The. Julia de Burgos. TANSG, *tr. by* Heather Rosario Sievert

Sea Anemones, The. Gwen Harwood. BMAP

Sea at evening moves across the sand, The. Soldiers Bathing. Frank Templeton Prince. GTBS-P; MoBrPo; NOCV; OBWP; OxBTC

Sea at this town's neat threshold spills its gloss. At the Sea's Edge. Gwen Harwood. CBAP

Sea awoke at midnight from its sleep, The. Sound of the Sea, The. Henry Wadsworth Longfellow. ITBLP; TCAPo

Sea bird knows the coming of storm, A. To Secretary Lu Ch'ien of Jen City. Li Po. SuSp, *tr. by* Joseph J. Lee

Sea Breeze. Mitch Highfill. HeMarv

Sea Breeze. Stéphane Mallarmé. WoPoe, *tr. by* Louis Simpson

Sea Breeze. Stéphane Mallarmé. SxFrPo, *tr. by* E. H. Blackmore and A. M. Blackmore

Sea-Breeze at Matanzas, The. Epes Sargent. APN-1

Sea Breeze, Bombay. Adil Jussawalla. OMIP

Sea-bundle. Jennifer Rankin. BMAP

Sea Cadences. Henrietta Cordelia Ray. CBWP-3

Sea Calm. Langston Hughes. APT-2

Sea Canes. Derek Walcott. HeIP-4

Sea Change. John Masefield. FaBoTw; OBMV; RB

Sea-Chantey, A. Derek Walcott. RB
  "In the middle of the harbour." TTY

Sea Chanty. Gregory Corso. BB

Sea-Chaplain's Petition to the Lieutenants in the Ward-Room, for the Use of the Quarter-Gallery, A. "J. T." NOEC

Sea-Chill. Arthur Guiterman. UV

Sea crawls from the shore, The. Old Woman of Beare, The. *Unknown.* WoPoe, *tr. by* Brendan Kenneally and Brendan Kennelly

Sea cries with its meaningless voice, The. Pibroch. Ted Hughes. FaBoMo

Sea-Cucumber, The. Martin Johnston. BMAP

Sea darkening, The. Basho. EH, *tr. by* Robert Hass

Sea Desires. Laila Al-Saih. MAP, *tr. by* Patricia Alanah Byrne and Salma Khadra Jayyusi

Sea Dialogue, A. Oliver Wendell Holmes. OBAL

Sea Dirge. Archias of Byzantium. AWP, *tr. by* Andrew Lang

Sea Dirge, A. William Shakespeare. *See* Tempest, The

Sea does not, The. Those Others. Ian Wedde. PeNZ

Sea Dreams. Rosita Copioli. CItWP, *tr. by* Cinzia Sartini Blum and Lara Trubowitz

Sea drew back uninjured with the blood of giant squids, The. Beat It Night Dog. Aimé Césaire. NegPo, *tr. by* Clayton Eshleman and Denis Kelly

Sea Eats the Land at Home, The. Kofi Awoonor. EmeKit; PBMAP

Sea-Elephant, The. William Carlos Williams. SAmP

Sea, False Philosophy. Laura Riding Jackson. APT-2

Sea Fever. John Masefield. BRP; CABP; ChAP; ITBLP; MoBrPo; OxAEP-2; OxBTC; UV

Sea flat out / the light far out, The. Mazatlan: Sea. Robert Creeley. APSN

Sea Flower. Mary Dorcey. BrRo

Sea gleamed deep blue in the sunlight, The. Homage to Marcel Proust. Thomas MacGreevy [*or* McGreevy]. CIP-2

Sea go dark, dark with wind. Wild Iron. Allen Curnow. RB

Sea-god, when he walked the beach, shared out, The. Foam. Roland Jones. WoPoe, *tr. by* Anthony Conran

Sea goes flick-flack or the light does, The. Sheep Dipping. Norman MacCaig. OxBC

Sea Grapes. Derek Walcott. PoetW; TRP
  (Sour Grapes.) BodElec

Sea, great mercury mirror, The. Symphony in Gray Major. "Rubén Dario." SpanPo, *tr. by* Denise Levertov

Sea guards warily its treasures, The. Heart, The. Jakov [*or* Jacob] Steinberg. TrJP, *tr. by* Harry H. Fein

Sea-Gull, The. Ogden Nash. OWoS

Sea-Gull and the Ea-Gull, The. Ogden Nash. ReLy

Sea-gull *is* so sorry!, The. Sorrowful Sea-Gull, The. Menella Bute Smedley. VWP

Sea-gull met an ea-gull, A. Sea-Gull and the Ea-Gull, The. Ogden Nash. ReLy

Sea gull / who flaps his wings. Magic Words to Feel Better. Nakasuk. STP, *tr. by* Jerome Rothenberg

Sea Gypsy, The. Richard Hovey. BRP; TCAPo
  (I am fever'd with the sunset.) ChAP

Sea has it this way: if you see, The. Cormorants. John Blight. CBAP

Sea has made a wall for its defence, The. Shoreline. Mary Barnard. APT-2

Sea Hath Its Pearls, The. Heinrich Heine. AWP, *tr. by* Henry Wadsworth Longfellow

Sea hath tempered it; the mighty sun, The. Fountain, The. Don Allen Johnson. AWP, *tr. by* Dulcie L. Smith

Sea-Hawk. Richard Eberhart. RB

Sea Holly. Conrad Potter Aiken. APT-1

Sea Horse, The. Robert Graves. FaBoMo

Sea howling and moaning by itself, The. Guillaume Apollinaire. PFTM-1 *Fr.* Victoire.

Sea Inside the Sea. Tess Gallagher. PasH

Sea Iris. "H. D." APT-1

Sea is a blue garden of crystal flowers, The. Sea Surrounded. Dulce Maria Loynaz. TANSG, *tr. by* Alan West

Sea is a circuit of holes, The. Coral Reef, The. Laurence Lieberman. CoAP

Sea is a hungry dog, The. Sea, The. James Reeves. NOxBChV

Sea is an acre of dull glass, the land is a table, The. Lusty Juventus. Charles Madge. FaBoMo

'Sea is Awash with Roses, The.' Kenneth Patchen. CLPP
  (Upon the land.) (LL) CLPP

Sea is calm tonight [*or* to-night], The. Dover Beach. Matthew Arnold. AWP; AmFaPo; BRP; CABP; CIHu; EBVV; GTBS-P; HAP; HeIP-4; ITBLP; InPK-6; MakPoe; NAEL-5v2; NAEL-6v2; NIL-7; NIP-4; NOBE; NOBVV; NPeEn; NoP-4; OxBEV; PAI; PeVV; PoE; PoPoPo; PoRA; SCGP; SCV; TFi; TOF; WoPoe

Sea Is Enormous, The. Juan Ramón Jiménez. SpanPo, *tr. by* James Wright

Sea is flecked with bars of grey, The. Oscar Wilde. EBVV *Fr.* Impressions.

Sea is made of ponds—a cairn of rain, The. Sea Sonnet. Alice Oswald. OxBSo

Sea is the Aegean Sea which goes beyond Alicante. In Honor of the Sardana and the Tenora. Max Jacob. CuPo

Sea-lashed coast outside the gate reaches to the hedge. Bamboo Branch Song of the Seacoast. Yang Wei-chen. CoBLCP, *tr. by* Jonathan Chaves

Sea-Limits, The. Dante Gabriel Rossetti. NAEL-5v2; NAEL-6v2 *Fr.* House of Life, The.

Sea Love. Charlotte Mew. LW; MoBrPo; OxAEP-2; OxBEV; OxBTC

Sea love song, The. Lilies for the Prophet. Nazik Al-Mala'ika. MAP

Sea Marke. John Smith. SCAP; TCAPo

Sea Monkeys, The. Barbara J. Orton. NeAmPo

Sea Nocturne. U Tam'si Tchicaya. NegPo, *tr.* by Ellen Conroy Kennedy

Sea of living silver. Visions. Elsa Cross. TANSG, *tr.* by Patricia Dubrava

Sea of Oblivion. Shinkichi Takahashi. ZenPo, *tr.* by Takashi Ikemoto and Lucien Stryk

Sea or Sky? Medbh McGuckian. PBCIP

Sea Owl. Dave Jeddie Smith. HCAP

Sea-perch over paddocks. Dunes. Salt light everywhere low down. Greenhouse Vanity, The. Les A. Murray. FaBoVe

Sea-Polyp, The. Julia Copus. NeBl

Sea Poppies. "H. D." APT-1; NALW

Sea-preserved, heaped with sea-spoils. Picture of a Nativity. Geoffrey Hill. NoAM; OxBC

Sea Replies to Byron, The. Gilbert Keith Chesterton. UV

Sea retreats as I advance, The. Sea Nocturne. U Tam'si Tchicaya. NegPo, *tr.* by Ellen Conroy Kennedy

Sea-Ritual, The. George Darley. BIrV   *Fr.* Syren Songs.

Sea rocks her thousand of waves, The. Rocking. Gabriela Mistral. BBASP, *tr.* by Doris Dana

Sea Rose. "H. D." APT-1; FaBoMo; HeIP-4; NIL-7; NoAM; NoP-4; OxWW; TRP

Sea's Abundant Progeny, The. William Wood. NOSC; SCAP

Sea serpent is, The. CXXXIV. Pita Amor. TANSG, *tr.* by Shaun Griffin and Emma Sepúlveda-Pulvirenti

Sea shone, The. During War, the Timeless Air. John Seed. Oth

Sea-Shore. Ralph Waldo Emerson. APN-1; ColAP; OxBA

Sea Shroud, The. Jack Kerouac. PoM

Sea-Sickness. Heinrich Heine. WoPoe, *tr.* by Vernon Watkins

Sea-Side Cave, The. Alice Cary. APN-2; ColAP

Sea sighs, thieves fly, The. Sigh, The. Nathalie Handal. PoArWo

Sea Similized to Meadows and Pastures: the Mariners, to Shepherds: the Mast, to a May-Pole: the Fish, to Beasts, The. Margaret Lucas Cavendish, Duchess of Newcastle. NoP-4

Sea slaps the sleeping beach's ear, The. Beyond the breakers. Joyce Mansour. MFP, *tr.* by Martin Sorrell

Sea Song. Luis Omar Salinas. GeoHom

Sea-Song, A. Allan Cunningham. GTBS-P; OxAEP-2

Sea Song, A. Digby Mackworth Dolben. EBVV

Sea Song, A. William Shakespeare. *See* Tempest, The

Sea Sonnet. Alice Oswald. OxBSo

Sea Spray. Marion Margaret Boyd. YaYoPo

Sea Sprite, Hermosa Beach, The. Maurya Simon. GeoHom

Sea stares at my dream, The. Gulf. Dhabya Khamees. PoArWo, *tr.* by Clarissa C. Burt

Sea sucks at its own, The. Landcrab II. Margaret Atwood. NIP-4

Sea Surface Full of Clouds. Wallace Stevens. APT-1; MoAmPo; VGW

Sea Surrounded. Dulce Maria Loynaz. TANSG, *tr.* by Alan West

Sea, The—quick pugilist. Training. Herrera S. Demetrio. TTY, *tr.* by Dudley Fitts

Sea Things. Gwendolyn MacEwen. FaBoWP

Sea took a sailor to its deep.—, The. Supplication. Constantine P. Cavafy. BLT, *tr.* by Rae Dalven

Sea—turn yr Back on, The. Charles Olson. PFTM-2   *Fr.* Maximus Poems, The.

Sea Unicorns and Land Unicorns. Marianne Craig Moore. NALW; PFTM-1

Sea-View, A. Ann Radcliffe. RWP

Sea View, The. Charlotte Smith. CenSon; ECWP

Sea View, Water's Edge, Atlantis. Double Writing. Stephen Knight. NeBl

Sea Violet. "H. D." APT-1; NoP-4

Sea-Voyage from Tenby to Bristol, A. Katherine Philips. WPE

Sea voyagers talk about fairy islands. T'ien-mu Mountain Ascended in a Dream: A Farewell Song. Li Po. SuSP, *tr.* by Wu-Chi Liu

Sea-Wash. Carl Sandburg. OBCA

Sea-wash never ends, The. Sea-Wash. Carl Sandburg. OBCA

Sea waves are green and wet. Sand Dunes. Robert Frost. MoAmPo

Sea We Read About, The. Philip Levine. GeoHom

Sea-Weed. D. H. Lawrence. RB

Sea whisper'd [*or* whispered] me, The. (LL) Out of the Cradle Endlessly Rocking. Walt Whitman. APN-1; AWP; HAP; HeIP-4; MoAmPo; NAAL-2v1; NAAL-3; NAAL-5; NAWM-7v2; NOBA; OWoS; OxBA; PoE; SAmP; TAP; TRP

Sea-Wind. Stéphane Mallarmé. AWP, *tr.* by Arthur Symons

Sea-wind and fog hover over the river's waves. Returning in Wind and Drizzle to My Home. S. J. Marks. BodElec

Sea without Poets. Branko Miljkovic. WoPoe, *tr.* by Charles Simic

Sea World. Eric Berlin. OPRER

Sea yes learns from the canefield, The. Sea and the Canefield, The. João Cabral de Melo Neto. TCLAP, *tr.* by Louis Simpson

Sea yes teaches the canefield, The. Canefield and the Sea, The. Joao Cabral de Melo Neto. TCLAP, *tr.* by Louis Simpson

Seacoast wears you out with damp and heat. White Crane Hill. Su Tung-p'o (Su Shih). CoBCP; ColAnChi; GifTon, *tr.* by Burton Watson

Seaconk or Rehoboths Fate. Benjamin Tompson. SCAP

Seaconk Plain Engagement. Benjamin Thompson. SCAP

Seafarer. *Unknown.* PoE, *tr.* by Kemp Malone

Seafarer, The. Ezra Pound. APT-1; CTC; FaBoTw; HeIP-4; NoP-4; OxBA; TCAPo; WoPoe

Seafarer, The. Henry Howard, Earl of Surrey. NPeEn; NoSic; SCGP

(Complaint of the Absence of Her Lover Being upon the Sea.) EBEV; NOBE; OBEV

(O Happy Dames, That May Embrace.) NAEL-6v1; NAEL-7v1

Seafarer, The. *Unknown.* EBEV, *tr.* by John Wain

Seafarer, The. *Unknown.* SacPr, *tr.* by Margaret Williams

Seafarer, The. *Unknown.* AnOE, *tr.* by Charles W. Kennedy

Seafarer, The. *Unknown.* OBVE, *tr.* by Michael Alexander

Seafarer, The. *Unknown.* NoP-4

Seafarer, The. *Unknown.*

"I can sing a true song about myself." ASW

"I can sing of myself a true song." PoRA

"My purpose is to tell my own true tale." EBEV

"Song I sing of my sea adventure, A." AnOE

"Tale I frame shall be found to tally." OBVE

Seafarer (c. 10th century), The. *Unknown.*

"Mæg ic be me sylfum so???ogied wrecan." CABP

Seafarers. Georg Heym. WoPoe, *tr.* by Christopher Benfey

Seagull, The. Dafydd [*or* David] ap Gwilym. OBWVE; TCAWP, *tr.* by Glyn Jones

Seagull, The. Siôn Phylip. OBWVE, *tr.* by Joseph P. Clancy

(Fair seagull on the water's edge, bright-feathered breast, rich your state.) PBRV

Seagulls. Judith Herzberg. TuT, *tr.* by Greg Delanty

Seagulls. Daria Menicanti. CItWP, *tr.* by Cinzia Sartini Blum and Lara Trubowitz

Seagulls. John Updike. OWoS

Seal at Stinson Beach. Roberta Hill Whiteman. VoR

Seal Cave. Brenda Chamberlain. TCAWP

Seal Island. Tom Sexton. PoCoUp

Seal's cry has lain against my leg, A. Sheila Nickerson. GifTon

Seal's wide spindrift gaze toward paradise, The. (LL) Hart Crane. ColAP; HAP; MoAmPo; OxBA; PoE; RaBo; TRP; UnPo; VGW; WoPoe   *Fr.* Voyages.

Seal swims like a poodle through the sheet, A. Flaw, The. Robert Lowell. HarvBoo

Seal up the book, all vision's at an end. On the Death of Mr. Pope. *Unknown.* NOEC; NPeEn

Seal up your soul with tears, and never blame me. (LL) I Am the Great Sun. Charles Causley. OxBSo; PeECV; TOF

Sealed epistle submitted / at dawn to Nine-fold Heaven, A. Demoted I Arrive at Lan-t'ien Pass and Show This Poem to My Brother's Grandson Han Hsiang. Han Yü. SuSP, *tr.* by Charles Hartman

Sealed in rainlight one. Magic Apple Tree, The. Elaine Feinstein. BrRo; HarvBoo

Sealed in your pewter coat. Sand Shark. Nancy Willard. PoCoUp

Sealink. Brendan Cleary. NeBl

Seals, The. Pauline Stainer. NeBl

Seals at High Island. Richard Murphy. BiHa; CIP-2; ModIr; PBCIP

Seals at play off Western Isle, The. Seals, Terns, Time. Richard Eberhart. MoAmPo

Seals in Penobscot Bay, The. Daniel Gerard Hoffman. TwCP; YaYoPo

Seals of love, but seal'd in vain, seal'd in vain! (LL) William Shakespeare. AWP; EBEV; EnLoPo; NoSic; OBEV; SCGP; TFi   *Fr.* Measure for Measure.

Seals, Terns, Time. Richard Eberhart. MoAmPo

Seaman, 1941. Molly Holden. FaBoWP

Seamen's Mission. Gerald Dawe. PNI

Seamless. Gojusan. ZenPo, *tr.* by Takashi Ikemoto and Lucien Stryk

Seams. Hazel Hall. APT-1

Seamstress, The. Harry Clifton. BiHa

Seamstress. Zinaida Nikolayevna [*or* Nikolaevna] Gippius. ARWW, *tr.* by Catriona Kelly

Seamstress stitches on a sewing machine, The. Mikhail Yeryomin. ItGoST, *tr.* by J. Kates

Seamus, Light-hearted and Loving Friend of My Brea. Owen Roe O'Sullivan.

"Seamus, light-hearted and loving friend of my breast." NOIV

Seamus, light-hearted and loving friend of my breast. Owen Roe O'Sullivan. NOIV *Fr.* Seamus, Light-hearted and Loving Friend of My Brea.

Seamus of the Smart Suit, box player, made. Thomas Kinsella. ModIr *Fr.* Out of Ireland.

Seance. Edouard Roditi. SPE

Seance. Raymond Roseliep. HA

Search. Claribel Alegría. BoWoP, *tr. by* Aliki Barnstone and Willis Barnstone

Search. Eleanor Slater. YaYoPo

Search, The. Kwesi Brew. PBA

(Past, The.) PBMAP

Search, The. George Herbert. ESCV

Search, The. John Hewitt. PNI

Search, The. Inge Hoogerhuis. HW

Search, The. Charles Shaw. NOBAu

Search, The. Maurya Simon. ExTi

Search, The. Henry Vaughan. ChIV-2; ESCV; GeHe

"Leave, leave, thy gadding thoughts." SacPr

Search after Happiness, The. Hannah More.

Epilogue: "Child! we must quit these visionary scenes." ECWP

Search all the Christian climes from pole to pole. Daniel Defoe. OBSV *Fr.* Reformation of Manners.

Search and Destroy. Dale Ritterbusch. CDa

Search every land, from Cadiz to the dawn-streaked shores. Juvenal. RomPo, *tr. by* Peter Green *Fr.* Satires.

Search for Apollo, A. Agnes Mary Frances Robinson. VWP

Search for My Tongue. Sujata Bhatt.

"You ask me what I mean." PFTM-2

Search. Search. Seek. Seek. Weary Song to a Slow Sad Tune, A. Li Ch'ing-chao. BoWoP; OHMPC, *tr. by* Kenneth Rexroth

Searcher of souls, you who in heaven abide. Prayer, A. Samuel Butler (1835–1902). FaBoEE

Searching. Cathy Grindrod. Prnts

Searching, The. Alice S. Cobb. BlSi

Searching for Gathered Fragrance Temple. Way to the Temple, The. Wang Wei. CrYelRi, *tr. by* Sam Hamill

Searching for Herb Brazier and Cinnabar Well, I Also Saw the Waterfall of Singing Strings. Alongside Was the Cliff of the Lord of the Mountain. Tao-chi. CoBLCP, *tr. by* Jonathan Chaves

Searching for *Melinda's Magic Moment*. Allison Joseph. NAPBL

Searching for the Ruins of the Pavilion of the Drunken Old Man. Yang Shih-ch'i. CoBLCP, *tr. by* Jonathan Chaves

Searching Him took. Keppo. ZenPo, *tr. by* Takashi Ikemoto and Lucien Stryk

Searching my heart for its true sorrow. Exiled. Edna St. Vincent Millay. PoRA

Searching on the wind. J. W. Hackett. HA

Searching, seeking. Long Melancholy Tune, A. Li Ch'ing-chao. ColAnChi, *tr. by* Jiaosheng Wang

Searching storehouse eaves. Basho. SoOfWa, *tr. by* Sam Hamill

Searching was easy and memory ripens, The. Blood Donor. Robert Morgan. AngWePo; TCAWP

Searchlights. Kenneth Mackenzie. BMAP

Seas are quiet when the winds give o'er, The. Edmund Waller. NOBE; NOCV; OBEV *Fr.* Of the Last Verses in the Book.

Seas Incarnadine. R. P. Blackmur. APT-2

Seas of Sorrow boil with a rage, Magyar, The. To the Hungarians. Dániel Berzsenyi. IQMS, *tr. by* Adam Makkai

Seas slowly darken. Basho. SoOfWa, *tr. by* Sam Hamill

Sea's Wash in the Hollow of the Heart, The. Denise Levertov. LW

Seascape. W. H. Auden. *See* On This Island

Seascape. Elizabeth Bishop. ColAP; FaBoWP; OxBC

Seascape. Arthur Rimbaud. SxFrPo, *tr. by* Martin Sorrell

Seascape. Francis Brett Young. OxBTC

Seashell. "Rubén Dario." SpanPo, *tr. by* Anita Volland

Seashell, The. "Rubén Dario." TCLAP, *tr. by* Lysander Kemp

Seashore, The. Leonid Nikolaevich Martynov. TCRP, *tr. by* J. R. Rowland

Seaside, and the fragment of one running. Reliquaries, The. Valerie Martínez. TouFir

Seaside: In and Out of the Season, The. Charles Tennyson Turner. Son

Season. Wole Soyinka. PBMAP *Fr.* Idanre and Other Poems (1967).

Season in Hell, A. Arthur Rimbaud.

Dawn. TTTS

Season is fall and the moon's full too, The. Accidental Meeting with an Old Friend While Traveling at Night, An. Tai Shu-lun. SuSp, *tr. by* William H. Nienhauser

Season late, day late, sun just down, and the sky. Birth of Love. Robert Penn Warren. APT-2; UnPo; VCAP

Season of Anger. René Depestre. PFTM-2, *tr. by* Pierre Joris

Season of Beginning and End. Zuhur Dixon. MAP, *tr. by* Patricia Alanah Byrne and Salma Khadra Jayyusi

Season of Locking-In, The. Christiane Jacox Kyle. YaYoPo

Season of Loss, A. Jim Barnes. HATNAP

Season of mists and mellow fruitfulness. To Autumn. John Keats. AWP; ClHu; EBEV; FHYEP; HAP; HeIP-4; ITBLP; InPK-6; MakPoe; NAEL-5v2; NAEL-6v2; NAWM-7v2; NIL-7; NIP-4; NOBE; NOBRP; NPeEn; OBEV; OxAEP-2; OxBEV; PAI; PoE; RB; RaBo; SCGP; SCV; SoSe-8; TFi; TRP; UnPo; WeW-3

Season of Omens. J. P. Clark Bekedermo. PBMAP *Fr.* Casualties (1970).

Season of Phantasmal Peace, The. Derek Walcott. EmeKit; PoPoPo; PoetW; VCWP

Season of rains: the horizon like an illness. Autumn 1942. Roy Fuller. PoWW

Season of ships is here, The. Spring on the Coast. Leonidas of Tarentum. GrAn, *tr. by* Clive Sansom

Season of the Rains, The. Simon Mpondo. PBMAP

Season's anguish, crashing whirlwind, ice, The. Winter Garden. David Gascoyne. GTBS-P

Season's Finished, The. Hyllus Maris. IBA

Season's Lovers, The. Miriam Waddington. MoCV

Season Song. Judith Nicholls. Spl

Season Song. *Unknown.* RB; WoPoe, *tr. by* Flann O'Brien and Flann O'Brien (Scel Lem Duib.) BIrV

Season 'tis, my lovely lambs, The. E. E. Cummings. UnPo

Seasonal. Karen Volkman. AmPoNex

Seasonal Poems on Fields and Gardens. Fan Ch'eng-ta.

Autumn. SuSp, *tr. by* Irving Y. Lo

"Behind a vermilion gate, on the eve of the Skills Festival." SuSp, *tr. by* Irving Y. Lo

"Crow after crow darts into the woods; the passers-by are few." SuSp, *tr. by* Irving Y. Lo

Late Spring. SuSp, *tr. by* Irving Y. Lo

"Myriad cicadas seethe and buzz in the setting sun." SuSp, *tr. by* Irving Y. Lo

Summer. SuSp, *tr. by* Irving Y. Lo

"Under the eaves, their back burned by the sun as hot as fire." SuSp, *tr. by* Irving Y. Lo

Winter. SuSp, *tr. by* Irving Y. Lo

Seasoned with sage and onions, and port wine. (LL) To a Goose [*or* Gosse]. Robert Southey. CenSon; NOBL; PeLV; Son

Seasons. Christine Busta. AuPH, *tr. by* Lowell A. Bangerter

Seasons. Safaa Fathy. PoArWo, *tr. by* S. V. Atalla

Seasons. Giampiero Neri. ItPo, *tr. by* Gayle Ridinger

Seasons, The. Friedrich Hölderlin.

Autumn. WoPoe, *tr. by* David Rattray

"Myths of separation from the Earth, The." WoPoe, *tr. by* David Rattray

Spring. WoPoe, *tr. by* David Rattray

Summer. WoPoe, *tr. by* David Rattray

"When Light returns to face the Earth anew." WoPoe, *tr. by* David Rattray

"When seasons' images pass out of sight and mind." WoPoe, *tr. by* David Rattray

"Wherever Summer is a country still." WoPoe, *tr. by* David Rattray

Winter. WoPoe, *tr. by* David Rattray

Seasons, The. Thomas Holcroft. NOEC

Seasons, The. Kalidasa. AWP, *tr. by* Arthur W. Ryder

Seasons, The. James Thomson.

Autumn.

Evening and Night. NAEL-6v1; NAEL-7v1

Hymn on the Seasons, A. CABP

"These, as they change, Almighty Father! these." InvLi; TreFP

Spring.

"Behold yon breathing prospect bids the Muse." PoE

"Flushed by the spirit of the genial year." OxAEP-1

Spring Flowers. NOBE

Summer.

"And what, my thoughtless sons, should fire you more." ECEV

Forenoon. Summer Insects Described. NPeEn

Night. Summer Meteors. A Comet. NPeEn

"'Tis raging noon; and vertical, the sun." EBEV

"These, as they change, Almighty Father! these." CABP

Winter.

"For, see! where Winter comes, himself, confest." NePenScot

"Keener tempests come, The: and fuming dun." EBEV

"Now, when the cheerless empire of the sky." OxBA

"'Tis done! Dread Winter spreads his latest glooms." OxAEP-1

"What art thou, frost? and whence are thy keen stores." OxBS

"When from the pallid sky the sun descends." OxBS

Winter Night, A. NOBE

Winter Tragedy, A. ECEV

Seasons and Times. William Barnes. NOBVV

Seasons are spirits, you said, each. Grandmother. Regina DeCormier-Shekejian. TWW

Seasons burn, The. The wind is dry. Earthquake. Robert Arthur Douglas Ford. NOBC

Seasons Come and Go, The. T'ao Ch'ien [or T'ao Yuan-ming].

"Bank to bank, the stream is wide." SuSp

"By and by, the seasons come and go." SuSp

"In the morning and at night." SuSp

"Peering into the depths of the stream." SuSp

Seasons in Santa Fe. Gerald Vizenor. HATNAP

Seasons of Fire, The. Billy Marshall-Stoneking. NOBAu

Seasons of the Soul. Allen Tate. FuPo; OxBA

Seated on her bed legs spread open. Joyce Mansour. BoWoP; HAWP; WoPoe, tr. by Willis Barnstone

Seated one day at the organ. Lost Chord, The. Dominic Bevan Wyndham Lewis. UV

Seated one day at the Organ. Lost Chord, A. Adelaide Anne Procter. ITBLP; SacPr; UV; VWP

Seated statue of himself he seems, A. Farm Boy after Summer. Robert Francis. APT-2

Seathwaite Chapel. William Wordsworth. CenSon Fr. River Duddon [A Series of Sonnets], The.

Seattle, Autumn, 1933. Alfred Encarnacion. OpBo

Seaweed. Henry Wadsworth Longfellow. APN-1; ColAP; OxBA; TAP

Seaweed / Between rocks—. Takai Kito. ZenPo, tr. by Takashi Ikemoto and Lucien Stryk

Sebastopol. Ilya [or Karl] L'vovich Selvinsky [or Sel'vinskii]. TCRP, tr. by Daniel Weissbort

Secluded from domestic strife. Double Transformation, The. Oliver Goldsmith. OBCoV; OBNV

Secluded gentleman, The. Rhapsody on Whistling. Ch'eng-kung Sui. ColAnChi, tr. by Douglass A. White

Secluded in my chamber. To the Tune: Lips Painted Red. Li Ch'ing-chao. CrYelRi, tr. by Sam Hamill

Secluded myself. I found one word. Thérèse 'Awwad. PoArWo, tr. by Kamal Boullata

Secluded within the women's quarters—that was sad enough. Tomb of the Singing Girl Ch'iung-i, The. Hsü Pen. CoBLCP, tr. by Jonathan Chaves

Second Advent, The. Thomas Kelly. SacPr

Second after, / the first boat touched the shore, A. Settlers, The. Margaret Atwood. MoCV

2nd afternoon I come, The. Poem for the Insane, A. John Weiners. NeAP; PmAP; PoM

Second Air Force. Randall Jarrell. NAAL-2v2; NAAL-5

Second and third month of sunny spring, The. Song of the Thoroughfare. Hsieh Shang. CoBCP, tr. by Burton Watson

Second Anniversary. Federico García Lorca. SpanPo, tr. by Rachel Benson and Robert O'Brien

Second Anniversary [or Anniversarie], The. John Donne. ESCV Fr. Of the Progres[se] of the Soule; the Second Anniversarie.

Second Ascension of Christ, The. John Wheelwright. NOCV Fr. Forty Days.

Second Best. Rupert Brooke. MoBrPo

Second Book of Theognis, The. Theognis.

"Boy and horse, a similar brain: the horse doesn't cry when its rider lies in the dust." CAGL, tr. by Peter Bing and Rip Cohen

"It's a thrill to love a boy: even Kronos' son, king of immortals, once longed for Ganymede." CAGL, tr. by Peter Bing and Rip Cohen

"Man who doesn't love boys and single-foot horses and dogs, his heart will never know pleasure, The." CAGL, tr. by Peter Bing and Rip Cohen

Second bounding snow, The. (LL) Mill, A. William Allingham. FaBoEE; OxBSP

Second Brother, The. Thomas Lovell Beddoes.

Song: "Strew not earth with empty stars." OxBSP

Second Carolina Said-Song. A. R. Ammons. OBAL

Second Class Citizen. Jennifer Lagier. UnSA

Second-Class Citizen. Slavko Mihalic. PoSu, tr. by Charles Simic

Second Coming. Adam Small. PeSAV, tr. by Carrol Lasker

Second Coming, The. Mohammad Bennis. MAP, tr. by Charles Doria and Sharif Elmusa

Second Coming, The. Suzanne Benton. HW

Second Coming, The. W. B. Yeats. BlrV; CABP; ChIV-2; ClHu; FaBoMo; GI; GTBS-P; HAP; HarvBoo; HeIP-4; InPK-6; MoBrPo; NAAL-3; NAEL-5v2; NAEL-6v2; NIL-7; NIP-4; NOBE; NoAM; NoP-4; OxAEP-2;

OxBEV; OxBTC; PoE; PoPoPo; RaBo; SCV; SoSe-8; TFi; TRP; UnPo; WoPoe

Second Cycle of Love Poems. George Barker.

O Tender under Her Right Breast. MoBrPo

2nd Dance—Seeing Lines—6 February 1964. Jackson Mac Low. PFTM-2 Fr. Pronouns, The—A Collection of 40 Dances—For the Dancers.

Second Dream, The. Jean Valentine. LCAP-2

Second Elegy. Aida Cartagena de Portalatin. TANSG, tr. by Emma Jane Robinett

Second Epistle of the Second Book of Horace Imitated, The. Pope. TOF

Second Epistle to Davie. Robert Burns. NePenScot

Second Epitaph, A. Unknown. MiEL

Second Epode of Horace Translated, The. Thomas Randolph. BASC

Second Evening. Mary F. Johnson. CenSon

Second Fig. Edna St. Vincent Millay. APT-1; NALW; NoP-4

Second Glance at a Jaguar. Ted Hughes. NoAM

Second Half of Our Lives, The. Sarah Rosenblatt. AmPoNex

Second-Hand Elegy, A. Michael Anania. CDa

Second-hand platitudes like antique watches. Catching One Clear Thought Alive. Paula Gunn Allen. WPOW

Second Hand Rose. Grant Clarke. ReLy

Second Honeymoon. Unknown. BIrV, tr. by Augustus Young

Second Image Sequence. Umberto Piersanti. NeIt, tr. by Stephen Sartarelli

Second Jungle Book, The. Rudyard Kipling.

Letting in the Jungle.

Morning Song in the Jungle. NoAM

Mowgli's Song Against People. NOxBChV

2nd Lesson from the Cockerel. Maggie O'Sullivan. Oth

Second Life, The. Edwin Morgan. OxBS

Second Life of Lazarus, The. Gwen Harwood. CBAP

Second Life of My Mother. Jorge Carrera Andrade. TCLAP, tr. by Muna Lee

2nd Light Poem: For Diane Wakoski. Jackson Mac Low. PoM

Second Love, she is so like to me, The. (LL) Dante Alighieri. AWP; EaItPo, tr. by Dante Gabriel Rossetti Fr. La Vita Nuova.

Second Madrigal, The. Anna Swirszczynska. BLT

Second Marriage. Mei Yao Ch'en. SuSp, tr. by Jonathan Chaves

Second Merseburg Spell. Unknown. GePo, tr. by Carroll Hightower

Second month. Jowa. JDP, tr. by Yoel Hoffmann

Second month, The. Gohei. JDP, tr. by Yoel Hoffmann

Second Nature. Paul Eluard. SurPaPo, tr. by Samuel Beckett

Second of the second month, The. Unrei. JDP, tr. by Yoel Hoffmann

Second passerby (he reads):"The Tables of Destiny! I carve you in letters." Velemir [or Viktor Vladimirovich] Khlebnikov. PFTM-1 Fr. Zangezi.

Second Philosopher's Song. Aldous Leonard Huxley. OBCoV

Second Poem. Peter Orlovsky. NeAP

Second Poem, The. Paavo Haavikko. PFTM-2, tr. by Anselm Hollo Fr. Winter Palace, The.

Second Poem from Nicaragua Libre: War Zone. June Jordan. NoAM

Second Poem the Night-Walker Wrote, The. Goethe. AWP, tr. by Robert Bly Fr. Wanderer's Night-Songs.

Second Portrait. Manuela Fingueret. MirDau, tr. by Roberta Gordenstein

Second Psalm: The Signals. W. S. Merwin. GifTon

Second Rapture, The. Thomas Carew. BASC; CaPo

Second Review of the Grand Army, A. Bret Harte. CBCWP

Second Rondeau. Johann Nikolaus Götz. GePo, tr. by George C. Schoolfield

Second Samuel. Bible, O.T.

("Beauty of Israel is slain upon thy high places: how are the mighty fallen!, The.") FaBoWar

"Beauty of Israel is slain[e] upon thy high places, The." NPeEn; OBVE; OBWP; TrJP

David's Lament. NPeEn; OBVE; OBWP; TrJP

(David's Lament for Saul and Jonathan.) AWP

Second Satire of the Second Book of Horace Imitated, The. Pope.

"With all a woman's virtues but the pox." OBSV

Second Series. Yannis Ritsos. PFTM-2, tr. by Kostas Myrsiades Fr. 3 x 111 Tristychs.

Second Sermon on the Warpland, The. Gwendolyn Brooks. BPo; NOBA

Second Shaman Song. Gary Snyder. NOBA; NeAP; PoM Fr. Myths and Texts.

Second Shepherd's Play, The. Unknown. NAEL-5v1; NAEL-7v1

(Haylle, Comly and Clene.) OBEV; OxBoLi

Second Sight. Felicia Dorothea Hemans. RWP

Second Skins—a Peyote Song. Joseph Bruchac. CDW

Second Song. T. Carmi. MHP, tr. by Ruth Finer Mintz Fr. René's Songs.

Second Song for the Worship of the Goddess at Yu Mountain: "Bidding the Goddess Farewell." Wang Wei. ColAnChi, tr. by Stephen Owen

Second Stanza for Dr. Johnson, A. Donald Hall. KaS

Second Thoughts. "Michael Field." LW; ViWPN

Second Time Around, The. Jimmy Van Heusen. ReLy

Second time the comet swung by, The. Gwyneth Lewis. NeBl

Second Viennese Elegy. Ferdinand von Saar. AuPH, *tr. by* Lowell A. Bangerter

Second Voyage, The. Eiléan Ní Chuilleanáin. EmeKit; ModIr; NPeEn

Second Warning Sign: the Game Heats Up. Edoardo Cacciatore. ItPo, *tr. by* Gayle Ridinger *Fr.* Full Powers: Five Warning Signs.

Second World War, The. Elizabeth Jennings. ItWoWo

Second year of the emperor's reign, in autumn, The. Journey North. Tu Fu. ColAnChi; SuSp, *tr. by* Hugh M. Stimson

(Secondary experience, nouns). Zen Buddhism and Psychoanalysis / Psychoanalysis and Zen Buddhism. Jackson Mac Low. PoM

Secondhand Coat. Ruth Stone. NALW; NIL-7; NIP-4

Secondline Send Off. Kalamu ya Salaam. SpirFl *Fr.* New Orleans Haiku.

Secrecy. Samuel Greenberg. APT-1

Secrecy of Mirrors, The. Al-Zahra Al-Mansouri. PoArWo, *tr. by* Nathalie Handal, Richard McKane and Tahia Abdel Nasser

Secrecy [*or* Secresie] Protested. Thomas Carew. CaPo

Secret. Gwendolyn B. Bennett. BlSi

Secret. Pierre Reverdy. PFTM-1

Secret, The. "Æ" MoBrPo

Secret, The. Charles Bukowski. RaBo

Secret, The. Peter Cooley. PoCoUp

Secret, The. Fanny Carrión de Fierro. TANSG, *tr. by* Sally Cheney Bell

Secret, The. Suzanne Noguere. FFC

Secret, a secret, A. If This Isn't Love. Burton Lane. ReLy

Secret Agent, A. Yevgeny [*or* Evgenii] Borisovich Rein. ItGoST, *tr. by* Judith Hemschemeyer

Secret cistern, forcing its way at last, the. (LL) Fifth Stanzas. De Arte Poetica. Olga Sedakova. ARWW; ItGoST, *tr. by* Catriona Kelly

Secret Flowers. Katherine Mansfield. LW

Secret Garden, The. Rita Dove. NoAM

Secret Garden, The. Thomas Kinsella. TwCP

Secret Garden, The. Eleanor Wilner. GifTon

Secret Gratitude, A. James Wright (1927–80). NoAM

Secret History of the Dividing Line. Susan Howe.
  "In its first dumb form." FTOS

Secret History of the Mongols, The. *Unknown*.
  "As he rode back Yesugei came on a camp of the Tatar." WoPoe, *tr. by* Paul Kahn
  "Chingis Khan left his camp on Mount Chasutu." WoPoe, *tr. by* Paul Kahn
  Death of Yesugei, The. WoPoe, *tr. by* Paul Kahn
  Last Battle and Death of Chingis Khan, The. WoPoe, *tr. by* Paul Kahn
  Temujin Becomes Chingis Khan. WoPoe, *tr. by* Paul Kahn
  "Then they moved the whole camp." WoPoe, *tr. by* Paul Kahn

Secret in the Cat, The. May Swenson. PAI

Secret in the Roar, The. Luis H. Francia. ReBoTo

Secret kept from all the rest, / Between yourself and me, A. (LL) Lewis Carroll. GTBS-P; NOBVV; NPeEn; OxBoLi; PeLV *Fr.* Alice's Adventures in Wonderland.

Secret Life of Gilbert Bond, The. Joan Retallack. FTOS

Secret like a lodestar, a ball of pure lead, I thought, A. Dust Storm. Gray Jacobik. BAP-97

Secret Love. John Clare. FHYEP; PoE; SCGP
  (Song). NAEL-6v2; NOBVV; OxBEV; RB

Secret Love. Sammy Fain. ReLy

Secret Love. Milton Kessler. UnSA

Secret Love; or, The Maiden Queen. Dryden.
  (Hidden Flame.) OBEV
  Prologue: "He who writ [*or* wrote] this, not without pains and thought." PeLV
  Song: "I feed a flame within, which so torments me." AWP

Secret many years unseen, A. Chess Play, The. Nicholas Breton. NoSic

Secret Melodies. Debra Taub. SurWo

SECRET murder hath been done of late. *Unknown*. NoSic

Secret Notebook. "Eduard Veniaminovich Limonov."
  "And it's the summer civil war." TCRusP, *tr. by* William Tjalsma
  "Fantastic!" TCRusP, *tr. by* William Tjalsma
  For whisper and orchestra. TCRusP, *tr. by* William Tjalsma
  "I kiss my Russian Revolution." TCRusP, *tr. by* William Tjalsma
  "It is good in May, in marvelous wet May, to be the chairman of the All-Russian Extraordinary Committee in the city of Odessa." TCRusP, *tr. by* William Tjalsma
  "Japanese restaurant is good in autumn—in dank weather—the hot napkins, the warm sake, The." TCRusP, *tr. by* William Tjalsma

Secret of the Quartz Pebble, The. Vasco [*or* Vasko] Popa. PoSu, *tr. by* Anne Pennington *Fr.* Quartz Pebble, The.

Secret of these hills was stone, and cottages, The. Pylons, The. Stephen Spender. AWP; NoAM

Secret People, The. Gilbert Keith Chesterton. OxBTC

Secret Rose, The. W. B. Yeats. NAEL-5v2; NAEL-6v2

Secret Sits, The. Robert Frost. InPK-6

Secret Song, The. Margaret Wise Brown. OBCA

Secret Song of the Heretics. Kitahara Hakushū. WoPoe, *tr. by* Donald Keene

Secret they are, sealed, annealed, and brainless. Oystering. Richard Howard. NoAM

Secret Thoughts. Ella Wheeler Wilcox. PWR

Secret Town, The. Abraham Sutskever [*or* Sutzkever]. TrJP, *tr. by* Jacob Sonntag

Secret Virginity, The. "Angelus Silesius." GePo, *tr. by* George C. Schoolfield *Fr.* Cherubical Wanderer, The.

Secretary, The. Peter Redgrove. OxBTC

Secreted by long minds, antenna shell. Night Sky Hiss. Jonathan Griffin. Oth

Secrets. Ahmad 'Abd al-Mu'ti Hijazi. MAP, *tr. by* Sargon Boulus and Peter Porter

Secrets. Letitia [*or* Laetitia] Elizabeth Landon. VWP *Fr.* Fragments.

Secrets of the Earth, The. William Blake. NOBE *Fr.* Book of Thel, The.

Secrets of the Landscape, The. Jacob [*or*Jakov] Fichman. FIT, *tr. by* Robert Friend

Section: America (2): Seen as a Bird. Nathaniel Tarn. APSN *Fr.* Lyrics for the Bride of God.

Section II. "Mang Ke." PFTM-2, *tr. by* Nicholas Jose and Wu Baohe *Fr.* Apeherd.

Section VI. George Barker. SPE *Fr.* Calamiterror.

Section V. Jacques Roubaud. PFTM-2, *tr. by* Rosmarie Waldrop *Fr.* Some Thing Black.

Secular. Natasha Trethewey. SpirFl

Secular, The. Chris Wallace-Crabbe. NOBAu

Secular Elegies. George Barker.
  O Golden Fleece. MoBrPo
  Satan Is on Your Tongue. MoBrPo

Secular Masque, The. Dryden. BASC; NAEL-5v1; NAEL-6v1; NPeEn; OxAEP-1; OxBEV; PoE; SCGP
  All, All of a Piece Throughout. HAP
  (Chorus to the Gods.) OxBSP
  Diana's Hunting-Song. NOBE
  Momus' Song to Mars. OxBSP
  (Song: "All, all of a piece throughout") WeW-3

Secure in death he keeps the hearts he had. Death's Guerdon. Lizette Woodworth Reese. APN-2

Security. Shirley Kaufman. DTA

Security. Charles Leo O'Donnell. SacPr

Security-man who stood, arms crossed, outside, The. Reading Whitman in a Toilet Stall. Timothy Liu. WiU

Sed Non Frustra. Anton Korteweg. TuT, *tr. by* Seamus Deane

Sed non satiata. Charles Baudelaire. SxFrPo, *tr. by* James McGowan

Sedans cruised past our bench. Wayne Koestenbaum. WiU *Fr.* Erotic Collectibles.

Seder, The. Enid Dame. UnSA

Seder-Night. Israel Zangwill. TrJP

Seder Night with My Ancestors. Joanne Limburg. NeBl

Sediment of Lukewarm and Radiant Rain. Coral Bracho. TANSG, *tr. by* Celeste Kostopulos-Cooperman

Seduced by Analogy. Bob Perelman. FTOS

Seduced Girl. Hedylos. BoLoP, *tr. by* Louis Untermeyer

Seducin me. Asante. Leticia R. Benson. InTrad

Seduction. Jo Ann Hall-Evans. BlSi

Seduction, The. Archilochus.
  "I said, Be mine." EroLit, *tr. by* Kenneth McLeish

See. LZ Gator Body Collector, The. Michael Casey. YaYoPo

See. Ginko. JDP, *tr. by* Yoel Hoffmann

See a man who so loves you as your fond S. T. COLERIDGE. (LL) Metrical Feet. Samuel Taylor Coleridge. FHYEP; NIL-7; NIP-4

See a pin and pick it up. *Unknown*. ITBLP; LB; ReMoGo

See a traveler in sorrow: deeper is his grief. Random Pleasures. Tu Fu. SuSp, *tr. by* Irving Y. Lo

See an old unhappy bull. Bull, The. Ralph Hodgson. MoBrPo; OBMV; OxBTC

See, and not see; and if thou chance t' espy [*or* espie]. To the Generous Reader. Robert Herrick. CaPo

See, Ben, the water. To Ben, at the Lake. Cilla McQueen. PeNZ

See, Chloris, how the clouds.   To Chloris.   William Drummond, of Hawthornden.   OxBSP

See columns rang'd in proud Palladian style!   *Unknown.*   FaBoEE

See dear Pater with the bills.   Christmas Bills.   Joseph Hatton.   OBCP

See Florio in his *vis-à-vis.*   Picture of a Fine Gentleman, The.   Lady Sophia Burrell.   ECWP

See for yourself? (LL)   Telephone Conversation.   Wole Soyinka.   NoP-4; PBMAP; PoetW; TTY

See! from the brake the whirring Pheasant springs.   Pope.   ECEV; FHYEP   *Fr.* Windsor-Forest [or Windsor Forest].

See, hear, and am silent. (LL)   I Sit and Look Out.   Walt Whitman.   NAAL-2v1; NAAL-3; OxBA; PAI; SAmP; TAP

See her caught in the throb of a drum.   Agbor Dancer.   J. P. Clark Bekederemo.   PBA

See her come bearing down, a tidy craft!   Note on Wyatt, A.   Kingsley Amis.   WeW-3

See her eager face.   Not Mine.   Adolph Green.   ReLy

See her there, Francie-the-Mad.   Francie-the-Possessed.   Oswald Durand.   NegPo, *tr.* by Ellen Conroy Kennedy

See here an easy [*or* easie] Feast that know[e]s no wound.   On the Miracle of Multiplied [*or* Multiplyed] Loaves.   Richard Crashaw.   OxBSP

See, here is eternity's shore.   Arrival in Hades.   Edith Södergran.   WoPoe, *tr.* by David McDuff

See! Here, My Heart.   *Unknown.*   NoP-4

See here, nice Death, to please his palate.   Epitaph.   Pope.   FaBoEE

See, here's the grand approach.   Verses on Blenheim.   Martial.   AWP, *tr.* by Jonathan Swift

See, here's the workbox, little wife.   Workbox, The.   Thomas Hardy.   InPK-6; NAEL-5v2; NAEL-6v2; UnPo

See: here, the bougainvillea.   Floating Petals.   Jan Barry.   CDa

See him recall the day by moral trace, a squint.   Of Movement towards a Natural Place.   J. H. Prynne.   PFTM-2

See His face, and sing His praise! (LL)   Cradle Hymn, A.   Isaac Watts.   OBEV; SCGP

See how Flora smiles to see.   On Clarastella walking in Her Garden.   Robert Heath.   NOSC

See how he loves me.   Generations.   Joseph Awad.   GraLe

See how our works endure! (LL)   Rudyard Kipling.   NOBE; NOxBChV; OxBTC   *Fr.* Puck of Pook's Hill.

See how she strips her lily for the sun.   Double Looking Glass, The.   Alec Derwent Hope.   CBAP

See how that pair of billing doves.   Verses Written in a Garden.   Lady Mary Wortley Montagu.   ECWP

See how that royal fights.   Christopher Logue.   FaBoWar   *Fr.* War Music.

See how the archèd earth does here.   Upon the Hill and Grove at Bilbrough.   Andrew Marvell.   BASC

See how the cottonwood bends at the waist.   At the Rio Grande Near the End of the Century.   Ray Gonzalez.   HCAP

See how the flowers, as at parade.   Andrew Marvell.   OBEV   *Fr.* Upon Appleton House [To My Lord Fairfax].

See, how the human animal is fed.   Sir Richard Blackmore.   ECEV   *Fr.* Creation.

See! How the Nations Rage Together.   Richard Allen.   TCAPo

See how the orient dew.   On a Drop of Dew.   Andrew Marvell.   BASC; ESCV; FSCP; GeHe; HAP; MeLP; NIL-7; NOSC; SCGP

See how the rainbow in the sky.   Justification.   William Strode.   NOSC

See How the Rising Sun.   Elizabeth Scott.   AH

See,—how the shining share.   God Save the Plough.   Lydia Huntley Sigourney.   OBAL

See how the willing earth gave way.   Fall, The.   Edmund Waller.   NOSC

See how they hurry.   At Luca Signorelli's Resurrection of the Body.   Jorie Graham.   HCAP

See / how they trace.   Birds in Snow.   "H. D."   APT-1

See how this ivy strives to twine.   Love's Innocence.   Thomas Stanley.   BeJo

See how this violet which before.   On a Violet in Her Breast.   Thomas Stanley.   NOSC

See! Hymen comes; how his torch blazes!   Sir Charles Sedley.   NOSC

See, I was raised on the wild side, border country.   How the Wild South East Was Lost.   Kit Wright.   OBCoV

See It Does Rise.   April Bernard.   KGB

See it does rise, and will not be stalled.   See It Does Rise.   April Bernard.   KGB

See lightning is flashing.   Storm, The.   Sara Coleridge.   NOxBChV

See Lucifer Like Lightning Fall.   John Keble.   ChIV-2

See me, the lord of deep-bosomed earth, who turned Acmonides upside down.   Wings.   *Unknown.*   HePo, *tr.* by Barbara Hughes Fowler

See me with all the terrors on my roads.   Face, The.   Edwin Muir.   GTBS-P

See, Mignonne, hath not the Rose.   Rose, The.   Pierre de Ronsard.   AWP, *tr.* by Andrew Lang

See No Indian, Hear No Indian.   Victoria Lena Manyarrows.   TWW

"See, nothing has happened to her," said my guide.   Seeing Oloalok.   Marilyn Bowering.   NOBC

See now, tender anemones are lifting up.   To Spring.   Mihály Fazekas.   IQMS, *tr.* by Watson Kirkconnell

See, o'er its withering leaves, the musk-rose bend.   Written in a Shrubbery Towards the Decline of Autumn.   Mrs. B. Finch.   CenSon

See on one hand.   Rainbow, The.   Gerard Manley Hopkins.   OxBSP

See on yon verdant lawn, the gathering crowd.   William Somervile [*or* Somerville].   ECEV   *Fr.* Hobbinol.

See, one physician, like a sculler, plies.   Joseph Jekyll.   FaBoEE

See, our languishing park's finery fades and falls.   Approaching Winter, The.   Dániel Berzsenyi.   IQMS, *tr.* by Peter Zollman

See-saw, down in my lap.   *Unknown.*   OxNR

See-saw, Margery Daw.   *Unknown.*   LB; OxBEV

See-saw, Margery Daw, / Jack[y] shall have a new master.   Mother Goose.   OxNR; ReMoGo

See-saw, Margery Daw, / Sold her bed and lay upon straw.   *Unknown.*   OxNR

See-saw, Margery Daw, / The old hen flew over the malt house.   Mother Goose.   OxNR

See-saw, sacradown [*or* Sacaradown].   Mother Goose.   OxNR

See, See Rider.   Gertrude "Ma" Rainey.   NAAAL

See, see, she wakes, Sabina wakes!   William Congreve.   NOEC; OxBSP

See, see, what shall I see?   Mother Goose.   OxNR; ReMoGo

See'st thou o'er my shoulders falling.   Love Song.   Judah Halevi.   TrJP, *tr.* by Emma Lazarus

See'st thou that Cloud as silver cleare.   Her Bed.   Robert Herrick.   PBRV

See that day, Lord, did you hear what happened then.   Twelve Bar Bessie.   Jackie Kay.   NeBl

See that lady / Dressed so fine?   Lady's Boogie.   Langston Hughes.   APT-2

See that sun in the morning.   Side by Side.   Harry Woods.   ReLy

See the chariot at hand here of Love.   Ben Jonson.   BASC; CTC; EBEV; NAEL-6v1; NAEL-7v1; NOSC; NPeEn; NoP-4   *Fr.* Celebration of Charis in Ten Lyric[k] Pieces [*or* Peeces], A.

See the Condemned alone within his cell.   William Wordsworth.   SacPr   *Fr.* Sonnets upon the Punishment of Death.

See the Conqueror mounts in triumph.   Christopher Wordsworth.   SacPr

See, the Day Begins to Break.   John Fletcher.   SCGP   *Fr.* Faithful Shepherdess, The.

See the dazzled stripling stand.   Goliath and David.   Louis Untermeyer.   TrJP

See the great vultures.   *Unknown.*   WoPoe, *tr.* by Anselm Hollo   *Fr.* Three Gypsy Songs.

See the handsome hippopotamus.   Hippopotamus.   Joanna Cole.   NTCP

See the kitten on the wall.   William Wordsworth.   ChAP   *Fr.* Kitten and [the] Falling Leaves, The.

See the man sit in the center there naked.   Sale of a Historian's Library.   Yelena [*or* Elena] Shwarts [*or* Shvarts].   ARWW, *tr.* by Catriona Kelly

See! the moon is smiling.   Eliza in Uncle Tom's Cabin.   Eloise Bibb.   CBWP-4

See the Rat—at Least It's Got a Hide.   *Unknown.*   CoBCP, *tr.* by Burton Watson

See the rat in the jelly.   Rat Jelly.   Michael Ondaatje.   EmeKit

See, the smelle of my sone is as the smell of a feld.   Bible, *O.T.*   OBVE   *Fr.* Genesis.

See[!] the smoking bowl before us.   Robert Burns.   NPeEn; NePenScot; PoE   *Fr.* Jolly Beggars, The.

See the Spring herself discloses.   Spring.   Anacreon.   AWP, *tr.* by Thomas Stanley

See the whole panoply of love. (LL)   Philetas.   GrAn; PGA

See the world! the tussles.   Annunciation, The.   Douglas Messerli.   FTOS

See the young man I've laid out.   Funeral Lament (Kommos) from Epiros.   *Unknown.*   BoWoP, *tr.* by Elene Margot Kolb

See them joined by strings to history.   Puppets.   Patricia K. Page.   MoCV

See them sprawl with earth for bed.   Angry Dusk.   Jack Lindsay.   NOBAu

See! There he stands; not brave, but with an air.   Brothers.   James Weldon Johnson.   NAAAL

See! there she goes.   William Somervile [*or* Somerville].   ECEV   *Fr.* Chase, The.

See there, that tree is a digging stick.   *Unknown.*   WoPoe, *tr.* by Billy Marshall-Stoneking   *Fr.* Passage.

See these happy youths, now made.   Anne Penny.   ECWP   *Fr.* Odes Sung in Commemoration of the Marine Society.

See, they are clearing the sawdust course.   Rachel Lyman Field.   OBCA   *Fr.* Circus Garland, A.

See, they return; ah, see the tentative.   Return, The.   Ezra Pound.   APT-1; HAP; MoAmPo; NOBA; NPeEn; NoAM; OxBA; PoE; RB; TRP; VGW; WeW-3

See this air, how empty it is of angels.   Five for the Grace of Man.   Winfield Townley Scott.   VGW

See those cherries, how they cover. Cherries; a Parable, The. Thomas Moore. OBSV

See those resplendent creatures, as they glide. Fashion. Ada Cambridge. NOBAu

See, through this air, this ocean, and this earth. Pope. InvLi *Fr.* Essay on Man, An.

See what a clouded Majesty, and eyes. To My Worthy Friend Mr. Peter Lely [*or* Lilly]. Richard Lovelace. BASC; CaPo; CavPo; GS; NOSC

See what a mass of gems the city wears. Impression de Nuit; London. Lord Alfred Bruce Douglas. OBEV

See what delights in sylvan scenes appear! Pope. NOBE *Fr.* Pastorals.

See what the boys in the backroom will have. Boys in the Backroom, The. Frederick Hollander. ReLy

See, when a fireship in mid ocean blazes. Surrender to Christ. Frederic William Henry Myers. SacPr

See when my English cousin comes. English Cousin Comes to Scotland. Jackie Kay. NOxBChV

See where Capella with her golden kids. Edna St. Vincent Millay. MoAmPo *Fr.* Epitaph for the Race of Man.

See where she sits upon the grassie [*or* grassy] green[e]. Edmund Spenser. OBEV *Fr.* Shepheardes [*or* Shepeards *or* Shepherd's] Calender, The.

See where the falling day. Tomorrow. Anna Laetitia Barbauld. ECWP; PEW

See where the windows are boarded up. Where Are the Waters of Childhood? Mark Strand. EmeKit; HCAP; LCAP-2; VCAP; WeW-3

See where they blur, and die, and are outsoared. (LL) Camping Out. William Empson. FaBoMo; OxBTC

See Willow. James Bertolino. PoCoUp

See with what constant Motion. Gratiana Dancing [*or* Dauncing] and [*or* &] Singing. Richard Lovelace. BeJo; CaPo; MeLP; OBEV

See with what simplicity. Picture of Little T. C. in a Prospect of Flowers, The. Andrew Marvell. BASC; ESCV; FSCP; GeHe; MeLP; NAEL-5v1; NAEL-6v1; NAEL-7v1; NOBE; NoP-4; OBEV; OxAEP-1; PoE; SCGP; TFi

See yonder hallow'd fane, the pious work. Robert Blair. OxAEP-1 *Fr.* Grave, The.

See yonder, where a gem of night. Es fällt ein Stern herunter. Heinrich Heine. AWP, *tr. by* Richard Garnett

See you not Heng Mountain towering over Hunan hills. Song of the Vermeil Phoenix. Tu Fu. TAL

See you the ferny ride that steals. Rudyard Kipling. FaBoCh *Fr.* Puck of Pook's Hill.

Seed. Charles Buckmaster. BMAP

Seed, The. Tomasz Jastrun. AF, *tr. by* Michael March

Seed, The. Vasco [*or* Vasko] Popa. PoSu *Fr.* Games.

Seed catalog in the mailbox cold drizzle. Marlene Mountain. HA

Seed Cutters, The. Seamus Heaney. PNI *Fr.* Mossbawn.

Seed dazzled over the footbattered blaze of the earth. (LL) Vapor Trail Reflected in the Frog Pond. Galway Kinnell. OBWP; VCAP; VGW

Seed Growing Secretly, The. Henry Vaughan. ChIV-2; ESCV; GeHe

Seed is dug under, A. Shekhinah. Karl Wolfskehl. TrJP

Seed is in Me, The. José Craveirinha. PBMAP

Seed Journey. Gregory Corso. VGW

Seed, Lord, falls on stony ground, The. Process. Charles Leo O'Donnell. SacPr

Seed-Picture, The. Medbh McGuckian. ModIr; PNI

Seed pods of frost falling in autumn. Trail among the Pines, A. Lin Pu. SuSp, *tr. by* Irving Y. Lo

Seeded in the mud on turtle's back. Sweetgrass. Maurice Kenny. HATNAP

Seeds clutched in my hand. Hunting. "Yehoash." TrJP, *tr. by* Isidore Goldstick

Seeds in a dry pod, tick, tick, tick. Edgar Lee Masters. ColAP; MoAmPo; NOBA; NoAM; OxBA; TAP; TCAPo *Fr.* Spoon River Anthology.

Seeds of certain grasses that once grew, The. Metaphor of Grass in California. Charles Martin. RA

Seeds of Kindness. *Unknown.* PoToHe
  (Speak Out.) PWR

Seeds of Love, The. Mrs. Fleetwood Habergham. FaBoCh; OxBoLi
  (Unfortunate Damsel, The.) LW

Seedsman of old Saturn's land. Herman Melville. APN-2 *Fr.* Clarel: A Poem and Pilgrimage in the Holy Land.

Seedsmen of old Saturn's land. Herman Melville. *See* Seedsman of old Saturn's land

Seedy Henry rose up shy in de world. John Berryman. HCAP; VCAP *Fr.* Dream Songs.

Seeing. At the Castle. Jerome Rothenberg. FTOS

Seeing a Basket of Lobelia the Color of a Bathrobe. Molly Peacock. SpudSo

Seeing a Friend Off. Li Po. CoBCP, *tr. by* Burton Watson

Seeing as I was willing to give up my seat for the person who said. Instead of an Animal. Leslie Scalapino. PFTM-2

Seeing as the father saw the rosy morn. Ovid. OBVE *Fr.* Metamorphoses.

Seeing Flowers I Remember My Late Daughter, Shu. Kao Ch'i. CoBLCP, *tr. by* Jonathan Chaves

Seeing for a Moment. Denise Levertov. VCAP

Seeing good places / for my hands. Time We Climbed Snake Mountain, The. Leslie Marmon Silko. VoR

Seeing Her Dancing. Robert Heath. NOSC; OxBSP

Seeing Hsia Chan off by River. Po Chü-i. TAL

Seeing is believing. On Sir Henry Ferrett, M.P. John Bingham Morton. OBCoV

Seeing Meng Hao-jan Off to Kuang-ling. Li Po. SuSp, *tr. by* Paul W. Kroll

Seeing Off a Friend. Stephen Dobyns. EmeKit

Seeing Off a Friend. Li Po. CrYelRi, *tr. by* Sam Hamill

Seeing Off Commander In Chief Li to Yün-chung. Li Meng-yang. CoBLCP, *tr. by* Jonathan Chaves

Seeing Off Editor Wang Chou-tz'u and Secretary Lin Shih-lai on Their Mission as Envoys to the Ryūkyū Islands. Wang Shih-chieng. CoBLCP, *tr. by* Jonathan Chaves

Seeing Off Han Ju-ch'ing as He Returns to the Land Within the Passes. Ho Ching-ming. CoBLCP, *tr. by* Jonathan Chaves

Seeing Off Master Tan. Meng Chiao. SuSp, *tr. by* Stephen Owen

Seeing Off Mr. Yang on His Journey to Wu-wei Prefecture. Yün Shou-p'ing. "War ships, cold tides." CoBLCP

Seeing Off Sun Ling-hsiu on His Journey to Chen-ting. Wu Wei-yeh. CoBLCP, *tr. by* Jonathan Chaves

Seeing Off Wang Yüan-chao—Reprise. Wu Wei-yeh. CoBLCP, *tr. by* Jonathan Chaves

Seeing Oloalok. Marilyn Bowering. NOBC

Seeing people off. Basho. EH, *tr. by* R. H. Blyth

Seeing Someone Off. Wang Wei. CoBCP, *tr. by* Burton Watson

Seeing Someone Off. Wang Wei. SuSp, *tr. by* Irving Y. Lo

Seeing St. James's. Ray Mathew. NOBAu

Seeing that there's no other way. After a Death. Roo Borson. NIL-7

Seeing the Beloved in a Dream. Shen Yüeh. ColAnChi, *tr. by* Richard Mather

Seeing the block of flats, I remember. Where All Were Good to Me, God Knows. Glyn Jones. TCAWP

Seeing the Bones. Maxine W. Kumin. NoAM

Seeing the Documentary by the British Liberating Bergen-Belsen. Lyn Lifshin. GotH

Seeing the Eclipse in Maine. Robert Bly. InvLad

Seeing the Plum Blossoms by the River. Lady Ise. BoWoP, *tr. by* Etsuko Terasaki

SEEING the plum-tree I thought of the Western Island. Ballad of the Western Island in the North Country. *Unknown.* ChiP, *tr. by* Arthur Waley

Seeing the Returning Geese. Lady Ise. BoWoP; WoPoe, *tr. by* Irma Brandeis and Etsuko Terasaki

Seeing the snowman standing all alone. Boy at the Window. Richard Wilbur. RaBo

Seeing the year end at my brother's home. New Year's Eve at the Home of Tu Wei. Tu Fu. CrYelRi, *tr. by* Sam Hamill

Seeing them like this. Toys. Carl Phillips. ReTh

Seeing Things. Seamus Heaney.
  "*Claritas.* The dry-eyed Latin word." HarvBoo
  "Inishbofin on a Sunday morning." HarvBoo

Seeing thou art fair, I bar not thy false playing. Ovid. OBVE, *tr. by* Christopher Marlowe *Fr.* Elegies.

Seeing thou art faire, I barre not thy false playing. Ovid. *See* Seeing thou art fair, I bar not thy false playing

Seeing through the Sun. Linda Hogan. HATNAP

Seeing You Stand Once More before My Eyes. Amy Lowell. Son *Fr.* Eleanora Duse.

Seek not, my Lesbia, the sequestered dale. Anna Seward. CenSon

Seek not the spirit, if it hide. Sursum Corda. Ralph Waldo Emerson. APN-1

Seek Out Another Heart. Mikha'il Nu'aima [*or* Nuaymah]. MAP, *tr. by* Sargon Boulus and Thomas G. Ezzy

Seek the Lord. Thomas Campion. SacPr; TrCP

Seek True Religion! John Donne. NOBE *Fr.* Satires.

Seek true religion. O where? Mirreus. John Donne. OBSV *Fr.* Satires.

Seek[e] Flowers of Heaven. Robert Southwell. TrCP

Seeker, The. Matthew Green. ECEV

Seekers of peace, enough hypocrisy! Quatrain. Ilyas Farhat. MAP, *tr. by* John Heath-Stubbs and Salma Khadra Jayyusi

Seeking a Mooring. Wang Wei. BoWoP; WPOW

Seeking an Explanation. Richard Emil Braun. NoAM

Seeking heat men become cold, and look for meaning. David Foster. NOBAu *Fr.* Fleeing Atalanta, The.

Seeking Hsin E in the Western Hills. Meng Hao Jan. SuSp, *tr. by* Daniel Bryant

Seeking marsh. Wind. Hsüeh T'ao. ColAnChi, *tr. by* Jeanne Larsen

Seeking out Hermit Hu.   Kao Ch'i.   CoBLCP, *tr.* by Jonathan Chaves

Seeking Out His face in a Cup.   Fanny Howe.   FTOS

Seeking out Master Chan on Incense Mountain.   Meng Hao Jan.   ColAnChi, *tr.* by Daniel Bryant

Seeking Spring Beyond the city.   Su Tung-p'o (Su Shih).   TAL

Seeking Te Iwi-ika's death.   Lament for Te Iwi—ika.   *Unknown.*   PeNZ, *tr.* by Margaret Orbell

Seeking the words.   Poem for Jan.   Joseph Bruchac.   CDW

Seekonk Woods, The.   Galway Kinnell.   NoAM

Seele im Raum.   Randall Jarrell.   LCAP-2

Seem with their quiet to have stilled in life's dream / All sorrowing now. (LL) Ghost, The.   Walter De la Mare.   EnLoPo; MoBrPo; NOBE; OxBTC

Seemèd that Man had them devoured all.   Giles Fletcher, the Younger.   PeECV *Fr.* Christ's Victory and Triumph.

Seems I'm always making resolutions.   Call Me Irresponsible.   Jimmy Van Heusen.   ReLy

Seems lak to me de stars don't shine so bright.   Sence You Went Away.   James Weldon Johnson.   ISC; NAAAL

Seems like I heard.   Sunnyland.   Elmore James.   NAAAL

Seems that I read, or somebody said.   I Thought about You.   Johnny Mercer.   ReLy

Seen.   Issa.   EH, *tr.* by Robert Hass

Seen from Above.   Wislawa Szymborska.   PoSu, *tr.* by Grazyna Drabik

Seen from Above.   Wislawa Szymborska.   BLT

Seen from close up, my heart is a lake. (LL)   Here I am Once More.   Rachida Madani.   HAWP; NAfrP, *tr.* by Eric Sellin

Seen from the air. (LL)   Lamentations.   Louise Glück.   BoWoP; HCAP; VCAP

Seen from within a heated room.   Tough Guy of London, The.   Kojo Gyinaye Kyei.   EmeKit

Seen in plain daylight.   Basho.   SoOfWa, *tr.* by Sam Hamill

Seen my lady home las' night.   Negro Love Song, A.   Paul Laurence Dunbar.   APN-2; ColAP; NAAAL; SSLK

Seen on the sea, no sign; no sign, no sign.   Dead Wingman, The.   Randall Jarrell.   PoWW

Seen Words.   Hannah Weiner.   FTOS   *Fr.* Spoke Aug 19.

Seep yourself, clear as water.   Exits.   Jean Earle.   TCAWP

Seer, The.   János Batsányi.   IQMS, *tr.* by John Fuller

Sees not my love how time resumes.   To a Lady in a Garden.   Edmund Waller.   BeJo; NPeEn

Seest thou those diamonds which she wears.   Robert Herrick.   NOSC

Seest thou yonder craggy rock.   Complaint of a Lover, The.   Anne Killigrew.   BASC

Seething over inwardly.   His Confession.   *Unknown.*   NAWM-7v1, *tr.* by Helen Waddell

Sefarad.   Olga Klein Weisz.   MirDau, *tr.* by Leslie MacIntosh

Sefarad, it is I who abandons.   Sefarad.   Olga Klein Weisz.   MirDau, *tr.* by Leslie MacIntosh

Seferis.   Lawrence Durrell.   EBEV

Segmented line, The.   Line of a Poem.   Zali Gurevitch.   FIT, *tr.* by Robert Friend

Segregated Railway Diner—1946.   Robert Winner.   LTA

Segregation #1.   Carlos German Belli.   TCLAP, *tr.* by Isabel Bize

Segue O Teu Destino.   Fernando Pessoa.   WoPoe, *tr.* by David Wright

Seguidillas of the Guadalquivir River.   Félix Lope de Vega Carpio.   SpanPo, *tr.* by Denise Levertov

Sehnsucht.   Anna Wickham.   MoBrPo

Seil o'yer face! the send has come.   Fleggit Bride, The.   Hugh MacDiarmid.   OxBS

16 heures / l'Etoile.   Two X.   E. E. Cummings.   FaBoMo

Seize the moment!   *Unknown.*   ColAnChi, *tr.* by Jeanne Larsen   *Fr.* Midnight Songs.

Seized with a sudden fancy for fresh meat.   *Unknown.*   OBVE, *tr.* by Percy Bysshe Shelley   *Fr.* Homeric Hymns.

Seizing the Day.   Judith Ortiz Cofer.   PueRic; SwNoth

Sejanus.   Juvenal.   BASC, *tr.* by John Dryden   *Fr.* Satires.

Sejanus ("How many men are killed by power, by power").   Juvenal.   OBVE, *tr.* by Robert Lowell   *Fr.* Satires.

Sejanus ("Some ask for envy'd pow'r; which publick hate").   Juvenal.   OBVE, *tr.* by John Dryden   *Fr.* Satires.

Sejanus ("What crowds by envied power, the wish of all").   Juvenal.   OBVE, *tr.* by William Gifford   *Fr.* Satires.

Selah.   Ronald Stuart Thomas.   FaBoMo

"Seldom we find," says Solomon Don Dunce.   Enigma, An.   Edgar Allan Poe.   Son

Select fine arrows and call for falcons.   Lu Lun.   SuSp   *Fr.* Frontier Songs.

Selecting a loose vibration from the taut air.   Soundwaves.   Andrew Sant.   NOBAu

Selecting a Reader.   Ted Kooser.   PBCAP

Selection of Heaven, The.   Paul Blackburn.   "Mind returns to it always, The."   APSN

Selenologist, The.   Bill Manhire.   PeNZ

Self-abandonment.   Li Po.   ChiP, *tr.* by Arthur Waley

Self-Acquaintance.   William Cowper.   NOCV   *Fr.* Olney Hymns.

Self-analysis.   Michael Dransfield.   BMAP

Self-Analysis.   Anna Wickham.   MoBrPo

Self and the Mulberry, The.   Marvin Bell.   BodElec

Self-brewing of the amaryllis rising before me, The.   Opulence.   Jorie Graham.   NoP-4

Self-Consciousness Makes All Changes Happy; Ode.   Jonathan Richardson.   NOEC

Self crowned the day displays its plumage.   Hymn Among the Ruins.   Octavio Paz.   PFTM-1; TCLAP, *tr.* by William Carlos Williams

Self-Deceaver, The.   Thomas Stanley.   OBVE

Self Defense.   Ai.   ESEAA

Self-Defense.   Santob [*or* Shem-Tob] De Carrion.   TrJP, *tr.* by George Ticknor

Self-Devoted, The.   Agnes Strickland.   CenSon

Self Dirge.   Wendy Rose.   CDW

Self-Discipline.   "Æ"   MoBrPo

Self-employed.   David Ignatow.   NNaP

Self-Evident.   James Robinson Planché.   OBCoV

Self-Examination.   Elaine Terranova.   GifTon

Self-Examination, The.   *Unknown.*   ECWP

Self-Hatred of Don L. Lee, The.   Haki R. Madhubuti.   BPo; ESEAA

Self-Heal.   Michael Longley.   ModIr   *Fr.* Mayo Monologues.

Self, I want you now to be.   Thing Is Violent, The.   Gwendolyn MacEwen.   MoCV; NOBC

Self in 1958.   Anne Sexton.   HCAP

Self-Mastery.   Henrietta Cordelia Ray.   CBWP-3; SWaP

Self-mockery.   "Lu Hsün."   SuSp, *tr.* by William R. Schultz

Self must hide from wind and dust, The.   On Reading *The Book of Odes.*   Cao Bá Quát.   AWTN, *tr.* by Hunh Sanh Thông

Self-Pity.   Philip Hodgins.   NOBAu

Self-Pity.   D. H. Lawrence.   OxBTC; RB

Self-Pity Is a Kind of Lying, Too.   James Schuyler.   BodElec; PoM

Self-Portrait.   Frank Bidart.   HCAP

Self-Portrait.   Cecil Bodker.   BoWoP, *tr.* by Nadia Christensen

Self-Portrait.   Michelangelo Coviello.   ItPo, *tr.* by Gayle Ridinger   *Fr.* Caravaggio.

Self-Portrait.   Robert Creeley.   NoAM; PmAP

Self-Portrait.   Milán Füst.   IQMS, *tr.* by Paul Tabori

Self-Portrait.   Moses Mendelssohn.   TrJP

Self-Portrait.   Linda Pastan.   ExTi

Self-Portrait.   A. K. Ramanujan.   NoP-4; PoetW

Self-Portrait.   So Chong-Ju.   WoPoe, *tr.* by Peter H. Lee

Self-Portrait.   Gerald Stern.   TaR

Self-Portrait.   William Carlos Williams.   LCAP-2   *Fr.* Pictures from Brueghel.

Self-Portrait.   Charles Wright.   PoPoPo

Self-Portrait.   Elinor Wylie.   APT-1

Self Portrait 4.   Tove Ditlevsen.   WPOW, *tr.* by Ann Freeman

Self-Portrait Approaching Promontory, Utah.   Michael Pettit.   GM

Self Portrait as Nancy Drew, Girl Sleuth.   Kristy Nielsen.   ReTh

Self-Portrait as Somebody Else.   Laura Mullen.   ExTi

Self-Portrait at Thirty-Nine.   Ted Kooser.   PBCAP

Self-Portrait in a Convex Mirror.   John Ashbery.   HCAP; NAAL-2v2

Self-Portrait in the Third Person.   Biancamaria Frabotta.   CItWP, *tr.* by Cinzia Sartini Blum and Lara Trubowitz

Self-Portrait, Jackson.   James Kimbrell.   NAPBL

Self-Portrait of the Laureate of Nonsense.   Edward Lear.   *See* How Pleasant to Know Mr. Lear

Self-Portrait of the Other.   Heberto Padilla.   TCLAP; VCWP, *tr.* by Andrew Hurley and Alastair Reid

Self-Portrait on a Summer Evening.   Eavan Boland.   NPeEn

Self-Portraits.   Takahashi Mutsuo.   Myself in the Disguise of an Ancient Queen.   PFTM-2, *tr.* by Hiroaki Sato   Myself with a Glory Hole.   PFTM-2, *tr.* by Hiroaki Sato

Self-portraits by Frida Kahlo.   Joanna Rawson.   BodElec

Self-Protection.   D. H. Lawrence.   NoP-4

Self-Reliance.   Ralph Waldo Emerson.   APN-1   *Fr.* Quatrains.

Self-Reliance.   James M. Whitfield.   NAAAL

Self-renewing vegetable bliss?, A. (LL)   Sonnet Made upon the Groves near Merlou [*or* Merlow] Castle.   Edward Herbert, 1st Baron Herbert of Cherbury.   NOSC; NPeEn

Self's the Man.   Philip Larkin.   NOBL; PeLV

Self-same Power that brought me there brought you, The. (LL)   Rhodora, The [On Being Asked Whence Is the Flower].   Ralph Waldo Emerson.   APN-

1; AWP; AmFaPo; ITBLP; NAAL-2v1; NAAL-3; NAAL-5; NOBA; NoP-4; OxBA; PWR; PoE; TAP; TCAPo; TFi

Self-same thing will be, The [*or* It's the self same thing to me]. (LL) As I Walked [*or* Walk'd] by Myself. *Unknown*. FaBoEE; OxBSP; OxNR; ReMoGo

Self-slaved, The. Patrick Kavanagh. MoBrPo

Self-styled reluctant womaniser; less. Tragic Hero. Eleanor Brown. MFPA

Self-Transformation. Willem Kloos. TuT, *tr. by* Desmond Egan

Self-Unseeing, The. Thomas Hardy. EBEV; HAP; MoBrPo; NOBE; NOBVV; OxAEP-2; OxBEV; RB; WeW-3

Self World. Clarence Major. NBV

Self[e] Accuser, A. John Donne. FaBoEE; PeLV

Selfishness. Margaret E. Bruner. PoToHe

Selfsame surface that billowed once with, The. Skin Flick. Fred Chappell. InPK-6

Selfsame toothless voice for death or bridal, The. Bell Speech. Richard Wilbur. MoAmPo

Sell it, though it sleeps still at its mother's breast! Meleager. HePo *Fr.* Epigrams.

Sell Out. Léon Damas. NegPo, *tr. by* Ellen Conroy Kennedy

Selling My Official Robe. Yang Chi. CoBLCP, *tr. by* Jonathan Chaves

Selling Ruined Peonies. Yü Hsüan-chi. BoWoP, *tr. by* Geoffrey Waters

Selva Oscura. Louis MacNeice. HarvBoo

Semantic Limerick According to Dr. Johnson's Dictionary (Edition of 1765), The. Gavin Ewart. OBCoV

Semantic Limerick According to the Shorter Oxford English Dictionary (1933), The. Gavin Ewart. OBCoV

Semblables, The. William Carlos Williams. FaBoMo; NOBA

Semblance of my elusive love, hold still. Which Contains a Fantasy Satisfied with a Love Befitting It. Sister Juana Inés de la Cruz. ErotSp, *tr. by* Alan S. Trueblood

Semele Recycled. Carolyn Kizer. NALW

Semele to Jupiter. William Congreve. OBCoV

Semen. Martha Paley Francescato. BoWoP, *tr. by* Willis Barnstone

Semi-Skilled Lover. Maureen Duffy. LW

Seminar for Backward Pupils. Günter Eich. AF, *tr. by* David Young

Semiotics not of sex but of concealment, the lessons, The. My Father's Pornography. David Wojahn. ReTh

Semphill, his hat stuck full of hooks. Trout Fisher. George Mackay Brown. OxBC

Sempronius,/ Sends greeting, warden of this Roman shore. Charles Montague Doughty. FaBoTw *Fr.* Dawn in Britain, The.

Sen Habbie's dead. (LL) Life and Death of [Habbie Simson] the Piper of Kilbarchan, The. Robert Sempill. NPeEn; OxBS

Senate Hearings. Michael McClure. BB

Senator Smoot (Republican, Ut.). Invocation. Ogden Nash. OBAL

Sence You Went Away. James Weldon Johnson. ISC; NAAAL

Send for Lord Timothy. John Heath-Stubbs. OxBC

Send Forth, O God, Thy Light and Truth. John Quincy Adams. AH

Send forth your songs like the doe and the fawn. Memento of Roads. Nathan [*or* Natan] Alterman. MHP, *tr. by* Ruth Finer Mintz

Send Him Back Hard By Your Lady's Small Window. *Unknown*. WoPoe, *tr. by* John L. Foster

Send home my long strayed [*or* long-strayed *or* long-strayd] eyes to me[e]. Message, The. John Donne. MeLP

Send in the Clowns. Stephen Sondheim. ReLy

Send me a shirt and neck-tie. (LL) Home News. Ahmed Tidjani-Cissé. NAfrP; PBMAP

Send me jewels from starboard. What It Takes. John Godfrey. FTOS

Send My Spinach. Douglas Florian. NOxBChV

Send New Beasts. Joe Wenderoth. BodElec

Send-Off, The. Wilfred Owen. HarvBoo; MoBrPo; NPeEn; OBWP; OBWVE; OxBEV; OxBTC; PeFWW; PoWW; RB; TCAWP

Sending Off O. E. Who Brought an Orchid Home to Japan. "Lu Hsün." SuSp, *tr. by* William R. Schultz

Sending Tzu-lung Off to a Post in Chi-chou. Lu Yu. CoBCP, *tr. by* Burton Watson

Seneca Journal 1: "A Poem of Beavers." Jerome Rothenberg. APSN

Seneca's Troas. Act 2. Chorus. Seneca. *See* Troades

Senex. Sir John Betjeman. RB

Senful man, bethink and see. *Unknown*. MiEL

Senilio Passes, Singing. Martin Bell. OBCoV

Senilio's Weather Saw. Martin Bell. PeLV

Senior Lady Sells Garden Eggs. Kojo Laing. HBAPE

Senior Members. Sean Lucy. CIP-2

Senlin; a Biography. Conrad Potter Aiken.

"It is morning, Senlin says, and in the morning." NoAM

Morning Song. NoAM

(Morning Song of Senlin.) APT-1; MoAmPo; OxBA

Señorita Nina. Nina. Noël Coward. ReLy

Señorita who strolled on the Corso, A. Limerick. *Unknown*. PeLi

Sens Plastique. Malcolm de Chazal.

"Bicycle rolls on the road, A." SurPaPo, *tr. by* Patricia Terry

Sensation. Arthur Rimbaud. TTTS, *tr. by* Kenneth Koch

Sensation. Arthur Rimbaud. AWP

Sensation Type and His Friends, The. Michael Davidson. FTOS

Sense. Rae Armantrout. FTOS

Sense of Coolness, A. Quincy Troupe. GT

Sense of danger must not disappear, The. Leap Before You Look. W. H. Auden. NoAM

Sense of obligation, A. (LL) Stephen Crane. APN-2; BRP; FaBoEE; NAAL-2v2; OBAL; OBSV; TAP; TCAPo; WeW-3 *Fr.* War Is Kind.

Sense of the Sleight-of-Hand Man, The. Wallace Stevens. HAP; MoAmPo; NOBA; NoAM; TwCP; WeW-3

Sense of the world is short, The. Eros. Ralph Waldo Emerson. APN-1

Sense with keenest edge unused. Pater Filio. Robert Bridges. OBEV

Sensemayá. Nicolás Guillén. PFTM-1

Sensibility; a Poetical Epistle. Hannah More.

Sensibility: A Poetical Epistle to the Hon. Mrs Boscawen. ECWP

Sensibility: A Poetical Epistle to the Hon. Mrs Boscawen. Hannah More. ECWP *Fr.* Sensibility; a Poetical Epistle.

Sensible Girl's Reply to Moore's, A. Walter Savage Landor. FaBoEE

Sensible Is the Label. Eldon Grier. MoCV

Sensing the next. Re-Verse. Diane Ward. FTOS

Sensitive girl called O'Neill, A. Limerick. *Unknown*. PeLi

Sensitive male minus labour pains equals poem. Baby Poem Industry Poem, The. W. N. Herbert. NeBl

Sensitive Plant, The. Shelley. FHYEP

Conclusion. NPeEn

"Whether the sensitive plant, or that." NPeEn

Sensitive, Seldom and Sad. Mervyn Laurence Peake. OTCP

Sensitiveness. John Henry, Cardinal Newman. TrCP

Sensual world, remote, extinct, is found, A. (LL) Under the Hill. Daryl Hine. MakPoe; MoCV

Sensualist Speaks on Faith, A. Dina Ben-Lev. AmPoNex

Sensuous and hilarious wit. Marathon. Cyrus Cassells. WiU

Sensuous / sloe eyed. Seduction. Jo Ann Hall-Evans. BlSi

Sent as a present from Annam. Red Cuckatoo, The. Po Chü-i. WoPoe, *tr. by* Arthur Waley

Sent by another world, I wonder. Another World. Sándor Weöres. IQMS, *tr. by* Adam Makkai and Donald E. Morse

Sent for You Yesterday. Jimmy Rushing. NAAAL

Sent forth the beams and made so fair my race. (LL) Sir Philip Sidney. HAP; NAEL-5v1; NAEL-6v1; NAEL-7v1; PoE; Son *Fr.* Astrophil and Stella.

Sent from Egypt with a Fair Robe of Tissue to a Sicilian Vinedresser. Thomas Sturge Moore. OBEV

Sent from the Capital to Her Elder Daughter. Lady Otomo no Sakanoé. BoWoP; WPOW, *tr. by* Geoffrey Bownas

Sent from the Power. Nag Hammadi Library. WPoS *Fr.* Thunder: Perfect Mind, The.

Sent in Lieu of a Letter to Shih-wu, Lan-ku, and Other Friends. Huang Tsun-hsien. SuSp, *tr. by* An-yan Tang

Sent in Parting. Tu Mu. CoBCP, *tr. by* Burton Watson

Sent in Parting to Yen Kung-su. Shen Chou. CoBLCP, *tr. by* Jonathan Chaves

Sent myself the length. Eleven Rock Poems. Gustaf Sobin. PmAP

Sent out of sight, somewhere becoming rain. (LL) Whitsun Weddings, The. Philip Larkin. FaBoMo; HeIP-4; NoAM; NoP-4; OxAEP-2; OxBTC

Sent to a Ch'an Master. Han Wo. SuSp, *tr. by* Irving Y. Lo

Sent to All My Nephews and Nieces at Tung-ch'eng. Yang Shih-ch'i.

"I've drawn a salary in the capital for forty years now." CoBLCP

Sent to Be Inscribed on the Temple of P'u-jun (Universal Fructification) at Lou-fu Mountain. Yü Chi. CoBLCP, *tr. by* Jonathan Chaves

Sent to Chief Abbot of Tung-lin Monastery. Su Tung-p'o (Su Shih). SuSp, *tr. by* Chiang Yee

Sent to Lo-t'ien for Thinking of Me after the Rainfall. Yüan Chên. SuSp, *tr. by* Angela Jung Palandri

Sent to My Fourth Son, Shao-Wu (to the Tune "Southern Countryside"). Liang Te-sheng. WoPoe, *tr. by* Nancy Hodes and Tung Yuan-fang

Sent to My Two Little Children in the East of Lu. Li Po. CoBCP, *tr. by* Burton Watson

Sent to Recluse Ch'eng. Wang Chi. SuSp, *tr. by* Hellmut Wilhelm

Sent to the Ch'an Master Wu-hsiang. Lo Yin. SuSp, *tr. by* Geoffrey R. Waters

Sent to the Hsiu-ts'ai on His Entry into the Army. Hsi K'ang. CoBCP, *tr. by* Burton Watson

Sent to the Magistrate of P'eng-chou. Tu Fu. CrYelRi, *tr. by* Sam Hamill

Sent to the Master Physician, "Almond Orchard" Shih. Li K'ai-hsien. CoBLCP; ColAnChi, *tr. by* Jonathan Chaves

Sent to the Painter, Lu Hsiao-feng. Li K'ai-hsien. CoBLCP, *tr. by* Jonathan Chaves

Sent to the Taoist Holy Man of Ch'üan-chiao. Wei Ying-wu. CoBCP, *tr. by* Burton Watson

Sent to the Taoist of Dragon Mountain, Hsü Fa-leng. Liu Ch'ang-ch'ing. SuSp, *tr. by* William H. Nienhauser

Sent to the Taoist of Dragon Mountain, Hsu Fa-leng. William H. Nienhauser. ColAnChi

Sent to Wen T'ing-yün on a Winter Night. Yü Hsüan-chi. BoWoP, *tr. by* Geoffrey Waters

Sent to Yü Te-fu upon His Receipt of an Official Commission to the Two Che's. Tsung Ch'en.
"When you enter Chin-hua Mountain." CoBLCP

Sentence, The. Anna Andreyevna Akhmatova. AmFaPo, *tr. by* Judith Hemschemeyer

Sentence, The. Yuly [*or* Iulii] Markovich Daniel. TCRP, *tr. by* Arthur Boyars and David Burg

Sentence in the evening, A. Today the boxscores are green. Tonight. Ron Silliman. PmAP *Fr.* Paradise.

Sentence—Life without a prison—struck, The. Divorcee. C. Webster Wheelock. SoSe-8

Sentence, unapproved, and overruled by Heaven, A. (LL) Emily Jane Brontë. NAEL-6v2; NALW; NOBVV

Sentences. Nicanor Parra. AF, *tr. by* Miller Williams

Sentences After *Defence of Poetry*. Paul Goodman. BodElec

Sentences for Matthew Ready, Series 2. Paul Goodman.
"Now only praise makes me cry." BodElec

Sentences we studied are rungs upon the ladder Jacob saw, The. Luzzato. Charles Reznikoff. BBASP

Sentences While Remembering Hiraethog. T. Glynne Davies. OBWVE, *tr. by* R. Gerallt Jones

Sentiment. Thomas Chatterton. NOEC

Sentiment. Sa'di Yusuf. MAP, *tr. by* Lena Jayyusi and Naomi Shihab Nye

Sentimental Education. Rachel Hadas. RA

Sentimental Elegy, A. Arkadii Dragomoschenko. PFTM-2, *tr. by* Elena Balashova and Lyn Hejinian

Sentimental Journey. Les Brown. ReLy

Sentimental Poem. Po Chü-i. CoBCP, *tr. by* Burton Watson

Sentimental Suffering of the Oyster of Smoke. Rossana Ombres. CItWP, *tr. by* Cinzia Sartini Blum and Lara Trubowitz

Sentiments at Autumn. Han Yü. SuSp, *tr. by* Charles Hartman

Sentiments for a Dedication. Archibald MacLeish. APT-1

Sentiments on New Year's Eve in the Year Kuei-ssu. Huang Ching-jen. SuSp, *tr. by* Chang Yin-nan

Sentimientos pour from your teeth. Tato—Reading at the Nuyorican Poets' Cafe. Miguel Algarin. PmAP

Sentinel of the grave who counts us all! (LL) Ode to the Confederate Dead. Allen Tate. APT-2; AiP; CBCWP; ColAP; FaBoMo; FuPo; HeIP-4; MoAmPo; NAAL-2v2; NOBA; NoAM; NoP-4; OBWP; OxBA; TAP; TFi; UnPo

Sentinels, The. Robert Duncan. HarvBoo

Sentry. Dennis Saleh. GeoHom

Sentry, The. Alun Lewis. AngWePo; PoWW; TCAWP

Sentry, The. Wilfred Owen. EBNV; PeFWW; PoWW
"We'd found an old Boche dug-out, and he knew." FaBoWar

Sentry, sentry, what did you see. Outposts. F. W. D. Bendall. FaBoWar

Separated East, The. Ernest Francisco Fenollosa. APN-2 *Fr.* East and West.

Separated West, The. Ernest Francisco Fenollosa. *Fr.* East and West.

Separating one by one. Island Waters. Tony Beyer. PeNZ

Separation. Walter Savage Landor. NPeEn

Separation. W. S. Merwin. HAP; NoP-4

Separation. Po Chü-i. ChiP, *tr. by* Arthur Waley

Separation by Death. Ibn Hazm al-Andalusi. RaBo, *tr. by* A. R. Nykl

Separation from Clorila, The. José Manuel Martínez de Navarrete. BLPSL, *tr. by* Rene de Costa, Rigas Kappatos and Eleni Paidoussi

Separation from the Torah. Solomon ibn Gabirol. TOF, *tr. by* David Goldstein

Separation on the River Kiang. Li Po. UnPo, *tr. by* Ezra Pound

Separations begin with placement. River Road Studio. Barbara Guest. PmAP; PoM

Sephestia's Lullaby. Robert Greene. *See* Menaphon

Sephestia's Song to Her Child[e]. Robert Greene. NoSic; OxAEP-1 *Fr.* Menaphon.

Sephirot. Leonor Scliar-Cabral. MirDau, *tr. by* Regina Igel

Sepia Fashion Show. Maya Angelou. BlSi

Sepr. ye 6th 1666 Thursday A Thanks Geving for the Stoping of the Fire in London. Elizabeth, Viscountess Mordaunt. EMWP

September. Mary Elizabeth Coleridge. ViWPN

September. Ted Hughes. BoLoP

September. Aldous Leonard Huxley. EBEV

September. Linda Pastan. InvLad

September. Henrietta Cordelia Ray. CBWP-3

September. Folgore da San Geminiano [*or* Gimignano]. EaItPo, *tr. by* Dante Gabriel Rossetti *Fr.* Sonnets of the Months.

September. Herta Felicia Staub. AuPH

September. John Updike. KaS

September 5. Robert Peterson. GeoHom

September 11, 1973. Emma Sepúlveda-Pulvirenti. TANSG, *tr. by* Shaun Griffin

September 18, 1958 I took the day off to be born. Human Museum, The. Brenda Coultas. HeMarv

September 22nd. Vera Gherarducci. CItWP, *tr. by* Cinzia Sartini Blum and Lara Trubowitz

September, 1918. Amy Lowell. NAAL-5

September Afternoon at Four O'Clock. Marge Piercy. NIP-4

September came on Tuesday. Joseph Brodsky. WoPoe, *tr. by* George L. Kline *Fr.* New Stanzas to Augusta.

September City. Gerald Hausman. UrbNat

September [Days Are Here]. Helen Hunt Jackson. APN-2

September evenings they are here after work. Surfers. Robert Minhinnick. TCAWP

September has come and I wake. Louis MacNeice. NoP-4 *Fr.* Autumn Journal.

September in the Rain. Harry Warren. ReLy

September Night, A. George Marion McClellan. TCAPo

September 1913. W. B. Yeats. GTBS-P; HAP; HarvBoo; NAEL-5v2; NAEL-6v2; NoAM; PoRA

September 1, 1939. W. H. Auden. AF; HarvBoo; MoBrPo; OxAEP-2; OxBA; PoE

September 1, 1802. William Wordsworth. OxBSo

September rain falls on the house. Sestina. Elizabeth Bishop. APT-2; InPK-6; LCAP-2; NAAL-5; NIL-7; NoP-4; PoE; PoPoPo; PoetW

September Song. Geoffrey Hill. FaBoWar; HP; HarvBoo; NAEL-5v2; NAEL-6v2; NPeEn; NoAM; NoP-4; OBWP; OxBEV

September Song. Kurt Weill. ReLy

September, the First Day of School. Howard Nemerov. OxBC

September. The gypsy and the nightingale. Autumn. Itsik [*or* Itzik *or* Itzig] Manger. TrJP, *tr. by* Ruth Whitman

SEPTEMBER *twenty-second*, Sir: today. After the Surprising Conversions. Robert Lowell. CoAmPo; HAP; NAAL-2v2; NoAM; PAI; TRP

September was when it began. Coming of the Plague, The. Weldon Kees. ChIV-1; VGW

September, you who red and gold. September. Herta Felicia Staub. AuPH

Sepulchre. George Herbert. ESCV; MiEL

Sepulchres, how thick they stand, The. Meditations on the Sepulchre in the Garden. Philip Doddridge. NOCV; NOEC; OBGa

Sepulchrum Domus Mea Est. William Austin. NOSC

Seq. Maggie Hannan. NLP

Sequaire. Godeschalk. CTC, *tr. by* Ezra Pound

Sequel of Appomattox. Donald Davidson. CBCWP; FuPo

Sequel to "A Reminiscence," The. Amy Levy. VWP

Sequence. Kenneth Irby. FTOS

Sere of the sun exploded in the sea. (LL) O Carib Isle! Hart Crane. APT-2; NoAM; PFTM-1; VGW

Serenade. Emanuel Carnevali. APT-2

Serenade. Angie Estes. GeoHom

Serenade. Adelia Prado. TANSG, *tr. by* Ellen Watson

Serenade, A. Thomas Hood. NBLV *Fr.* Domestic Poems.

Serenade, A: "Ah! County Guy, the hour is nigh." Sir Walter Scott. GTBS-P *Fr.* Quentin Durward.

Serenade: Any Man to Any Woman. Dame Edith Sitwell. NALW

Serenade at Dawn. Árpád Tóth. IQMS, *tr. by* Jess Perlman

Serenade: "Come now, and let us wake them: time." *Unknown*. AWP, *tr. by* Jethro Bithell

Serenade for Ilonka. Jenő Dsida. IQMS, *tr. by* Joseph Leftwich

Serenade for Two Poplars, A. Esther Raab. FIT, *tr. by* Robert Friend and Shimon Sandbank

Serenade in Blue. Harry Warren. ReLy

Serenade: "Look out upon the stars, my love." Edward Coote [*or* Coate] Pinkney. APN-1

Serenade of a Loyal Martyr. George Darley. *See* Song: "Sweet in her green dell the flower of beauty slumbers."

Serenade: "Sleep, love sleep." Mary Weston Fordham. CBWP-2; SWaP

Serenade: "Softly, O midnight Hours!" Aubrey Thomas De Vere. OBEV

Serenade: "Who is it sings the gypsies' song to-night." Rosamund Marriott Watson. ViWPN

Serenader, The. *Unknown.* GrAn, *tr. by* Dudley Fitts

Serenades in Virginia. Andrew Hudgins. CBCWP

Serene and outraged in a trenchcoat. Severances. Aidan Carl Mathews. CIP-2

Serene Words. Gabriela Mistral. SpanPo, *tr. by* Muriel Kittel

Serenity. Philippe Jaccottet. MFP, *tr. by* Martin Sorrell

Serenity in Stones, The. Simon J. Ortiz. CDW; ColAP

Serepta Mason. Edgar Lee Masters. APT-1 *Fr.* Spoon River Anthology.

Serf, The. Roy Campbell. GTBS-P; MoBrPo; OBMV

Serfs are glad through Lara's wide domain, The. Byron. *Fr.* Lara.

Sergeant Brandon Just, U. S. M. C. Bryan Alec Floyd. CDa

Sergeant Brown's Parrot. Kit Wright. OPOU

Sergeant laughs with strong teeth, The. At Rest from the Grim Place. Arthur Nortje. PBMAP

Sergeant-Major Money. Robert Graves. FaBoWar; OBWP

Sergeant of the Lawe, war and wys, A. Geoffrey Chaucer. CTC *Fr.* Canterbury Tales, The.

Sergeant's been on a gas course. Gas Drill. Tom Rawling. FaBoWar

Sergeant's Weddin', The. Rudyard Kipling. OBCoV; OxBTC

Sgt. stands so fluently in leather, The. On a Photo of Sgt. Ciardi a Year Later. John Ciardi. AiP

Sergeant to Enyalios. Archilochus. GrAn

Seriema Song. Albert Goldbarth. UrbNat

Series. Michael Palmer.

  "Logical principle is said to be an empty, A." HarvBoo

  "Plan of the City of O. The great square." HarvBoo

  Prose 22. HarvBoo

  Prose 31. HarvBoo

Series—3, The. Leslie Scalapino. PmAP *Fr.* Crowd and Not Evening Or Light.

Serious Concerns. Wendy Cope. OBCoV

Serious Merriment of Women, The. Patricia Goedicke. TAP

Serious of Photographs, A. Iain Sinclair. Oth *Fr.* Ebbing of Kraft, The.

Serious over my cereals I broke one breakfast my fast. Breakfast with Gerard Manley Hopkins. Anthony Brode. NOBL

Serious Readers. Peter Redgrove. OxBC

Serious young lady from Welwyn, A. Limerick. C. Armstrong Gibbs. PeLi

Seriously, these sorts. Gradation. Charles Bernstein. FTOS

Sermon. Emanuel Carnevali. APT-2

Sermon, The. Richard Hughes. OBMV

Sermon at Clevedon, a. Thomas Edward Brown. NOBVV

Sermon on Swift, A. Austin Clarke. BIrV

Sermon on the Warpland, The. Gwendolyn Brooks. BPo; NOBA

Sermon our Pastor, Rt. Rev., The. Limerick. *Unknown.* PeLi

Serpent, The. Theodore Roethke. NOxBChV

Serpent, The. Jones Very. NCAP

Serpent Finds Eve Alone, The. John Milton. NPeEn *Fr.* Paradise Lost.

Serpent Knowledge. Robert Pinsky. ColAP *Fr.* Explanation of America, An.

Serpent Knowledge. Robert Pinsky. NAAL-2v2 *Fr.* Explanation of America, An.

Serpent with a voyce, so slie and fine, The. Samuel Gorton. SCAP

Serpent with the eagle in the boughs, The. (LL) Hart Crane. MoAmPo; NAAL-5; OxBA *Fr.* Bridge, The.

Serpentine Voices. Diana García. TouFir

Serried hosts stood man to man, The. Oranges, The. Abu Dharr. TTY, *tr. by* A. J. Arberry

"Serva tibi minas!" Judge with the Sore Rump, The. St. George Tucker. OBAL

Servant, A. Rudyard Kipling. HarvBoo; NPeEn; PeFWW *Fr.* Epitaphs of the War [1914–1918].

Servant Boy Delivers, The. Tu Fu. CrYelRi, *tr. by* Sam Hamill

Servant-Girl's Holiday, A. *Unknown.* MiEL

Servant of the House. "Sagittarius." UV

Servant of the world's welfare once were you—god bless. Humiliating the Laser-Beam. Ödön Palasovszky. IQMS, *tr. by* Kenneth McRobbie

Servant to Servants, A. Robert Frost. NAAL-2v2

Servant When He Reigneth, A. Rudyard Kipling. ChIV-1

Service. Peter Scupham. HarvBoo

Service and strength, God's Angels and Archangels. St. Michael and all Angels. Christina Georgina Rossetti. SacPr

Service Is No Heritage. Nicholas Breton. NoSic

Service Wash. Deryn Rees-Jones. MFPA

Services. Carl Rakosi. ChIV-1

Servile Blood. Vasily [*or* Vasilii Dmitrievich] Fyodorov [*or* Fiodorov]. TCRP, *tr. by* Lubov Yakovleva

Servile Herd, The. Pope. OBSV *Fr.* Essay on Criticism, An.

Serving Maid, The. Arthur Joseph Munby. NOBVV

Serving man. Curled my hair, A. Thom Gunn. OxBC *Fr.* Misanthropos.

Serving-man to be a queen, A. (LL) Famous Flower of Serving-Men; or, The Lady Turn'd Serving-Man, The. *Unknown.* ESPB; OxBB

Serving Men's Song, A. John Lyly. NOBE; NoSic *Fr.* Alexander and Campaspe.

Serving the Shogun in the capital. Kodo. ZenPo, *tr. by* Takashi Ikemoto and Lucien Stryk

Serving with Gideon. William Stafford. LCAP-2

Session[s] was held the other day, A. Sir John Suckling. BASC; BeJo; CABP; CaPo

Sestina: Altaforte. Ezra Pound. APT-1; ColAP; FaBoTw; MakPoe; MoAmPo; NOBA; TCAPo

Sestina: "Body of my love is a familiar country, The." Mary Stanley. PeNZ

Sestina d'Inverno. Anthony Hecht. NoAM

Sestina for the House. Ronald Wallace. PBCAP

Sestina for the Ladies of Tehuántepec. Earle Birney. PeLV

Sestina: "I have reached, alas, the long shadow." Dante Alighieri. WoPoe, *tr. by* James Schuyler

Sestina: "I saw my soul at rest upon a day." Algernon Charles Swinburne. MakPoe

Sestina in a Cantina. Malcolm Lowry. MoCV

Sestina: "In fair Provence, the land of lute and rose." Sir Edmund William Gosse. MakPoe

Sestina of the Tramp-Royal. Rudyard Kipling. MakPoe; MoBrPo

Sestina: "September sunlight on the house." Elizabeth Bishop. APT-2; InPK-6; LCAP-2; NAAL-5; NIL-7; NoP-4; PoE; PoPoPo; PoetW

Sestina: "Then first with locks dishevelled and bare." Barnabe Barnes. NPeEn; NoSic *Fr.* Parthenophil and Parthenophe.

Sestina with Refrain. Thomas William Shapcott. CBAP

Sestine 4. Barnabe Barnes. MakPoe *Fr.* Parthenophil and Parthenophe.

Set foot once beyond Nilotic Meroë. Paulus [*or* Paulos] Silentiarius. GrAn

Set golden butter out in a dish. Fanny Howe. FTOS *Fr.* "O'clock."

Set Him Apart! Victor Hugo. SxFrPo, *tr. by* E. H. Blackmore and A. M. Blackmore

Set in their studious corners, the players. Chess. Jorge Luis Borges. PoetW, *tr. by* Alastair Reid

Set in this stormy northern sea. Ave Imperatrix! Oscar Wilde. PeVV

Set Love in order, thou that lovest Me. Cantica: Our Lord Christ: Of Order. Saint Francis of Assisi. AWP; EaItPo; OBVE, *tr. by* Dante Gabriel Rossetti

Set me as a seal on your heart. Bible, *O.T.* BoWoP; TrJP, *tr. by* Willis Barnstone *Fr.* Song of Solomon, The [*or* The Song of Songs].

Set me free, flagpole, why must you deny me the free wind? Conversation. Ágnes Nemes Nagy. IQMS, *tr. by* Adam Makkai

Set me to sound for you. Jay Macpherson. NOBC *Fr.* Ark, The.

Set me whereas the sun[ne] doth[e] parch [*or* perche] the green [*or* grene]. Petrarch. AWP; HAP; NoSic; OxBSo, *tr. by* Henry Howard, Earl of Surrey *Fr.* Sonnets to Laura.

Set on rising ground above the village. Caleb Barnes. David Wright. NLP

Set on the soul's acropolis the reason stands. Reason. Clive Staples Lewis. SacPr

Set on this bubble of dead stone and sand. On an Engraving by Casserius. Alec Derwent Hope. CBAP; HarvBoo

Set silver cone to tulip flame! Inscription for a Mirror in a Deserted Dwelling. William Rose Benét. MoAmPo

Set up the drum. December. Maurice Kenny. HATNAP

Set where the upper streams of Simois flow. Palladium. Matthew Arnold. GTBS-P

Set women in his eye and in his walk. John Milton. PeECV *Fr.* Paradise Regained [*or* Regain'd].

Set your fir-tree / In a pot. Advice to a Child. Eleanor Farjeon. OTCP

Seth Bingham. William W. Cook. SpirFl

Setting a trotline after sundown. In the Deep Channel. William Stafford. RB

Setting in the house with everything on my mind. In the House Blues. Bessie Smith. NAAAL

Setting Out at Dawn. Wu Wei-yeh. CoBLCP, *tr. by* Jonathan Chaves

Setting out over the sea to the south. At Kan's Embarkation for Yuan China. Muso Soseki. EaWin, *tr. by* W. S. Merwin

Setting sun—a pool of molten gold, The. Tune: "Joy of Eternal Union." Li Ch'ing-chao. ColAnChi, *tr. by* Jiaosheng Wang

Setting sun about to vanish west of the Hsien Hill, The. Song of Hsiang-yang. Li Po. SuSp, *tr. by* Joseph J. Lee

Setting sun illuminates half the river, The. Walk to the Eastern River Bank, A. Kao Ch'i. CoBLCP, *tr. by* Jonathan Chaves

Setting their country free. Mnasalcas. GrAn

Settled In. Michael David Madonick. IllVoic

Settlement. Ingeborg Bachmann. PoSu, *tr. by* Daniel Huws

Settler, The. Jones Very. SacPr

Settlers. Tom Paulin. PNI

Settlers, The. Margaret Atwood. MoCV

Settlers abandoned our country long ago. Pauper Woodland. Ronald G. Everson. NOBC

Settling, white dew. Nishiyama Soin. SoOfWa, *tr. by* Sam Hamill

Seumas Beg. James Stephens. OxBTC

Seven. Natan Zach. FIT, *tr. by* Robert Friend

Seven, The. *Unknown.* RB; WoPoe, *tr. by* Jerome Rothenberg and Jerome K. Rothenberg

Seven Activities for a Young Child. Alan Brownjohn. OTCP

Seven against Thebes, The. Aeschylus.
  Lament for the Two Brothers Slain by Each Other's Hand. AWP

Seven ages, first puking and mewling. "All the World's a Stage." Victor Gray. NBLV; PeLi

Seven Ages of Man, The. William Shakespeare. ITBLP; RB; UV *Fr.* As You Like It.

Seven Beginnings. Olesya [*or* Olesia] Nikolayeva [*or* Nikolaeva]. ItGoST, *tr. by* Richard Graves and Carol Ueland

Seven Beginnings. Olesya [*or* Olesia] Nikolayeva [*or* Nikolaeva]. TCRP, *tr. by* Vera Dunham

Seven candles in silver sticks. Richard Murphy. BIrV *Fr.* Battle of Aughrim, The.

Seven Cuban / army officers. Pornographic Poem. John Giorno. CAGL

Seven Days. J. R. Rowland. PAI

Seven Days of Creation, The. James McAuley.
  Seventh Day, The. BMAP

Seven Days of the Sun, The. Walter James Turner. OBMV

Seven Deadly Sins. Yusef Komunyakaa. BAP-01

Seven dog-days we let pass. Queens. John Millington Synge. MoBrPo; OBMV; PeVV

Seven Dreams. John Clifford Bayliss. SPE

Seven Epigrams. Gerard Manley Hopkins.
  "Of virtues I most warmly bless." FaBoEE

Seven Fiddlers, The. Sebastian Evans. EBVV

7:v:60 (an interesting *lapsus calami*). For Kai Snyder. Philip Whalen. PoM

Seven Forbidden Words. Michael Palmer. HarvBoo

747 (London–Chicago). Robert Conquest. OxBC

Seven full-paunched eunuchs came to me. King, The. Skipwith Cannell. APT-1

Seven Gifts of the Holy Ghost, The. John Audelay [*or* Awdelay]. SacPr

Seven Hells of Jigoku Zoshi, The. Jerome Rothenberg. NNaP

Seven hills shudder in silence, The. Agony . . . A Resurrection, An. Assumpta Acam-Oturu. HAWP; NAfrP

700 years ago. Slim Man Canyon. Leslie Marmon Silko. VoR

Seven Laments for the War-Dead. Yehuda Amichai [*or* Amikhai]. PoetW, *tr. by* Chana Bloch

Seven lang years I hae served the King. Whummil Bore, The. *Unknown.* ESPB

Seven Metal Mountains. Bible, Pseudepigrapha. TrJP *Fr.* Enoch.

Seven o'clock. The seventh day of the seventh month of the. Birth, The. Paul Muldoon. EmeKit

Seven Old Men, The. Charles Baudelaire. OBVE, *tr. by* Roy Campbell

Seven Old Men, The. Charles Baudelaire. SxFrPo, *tr. by* James McGowan

Seven pairs of leopard-skin underpants. Leopard Skin. Douglas Stewart. NOBAu

Seven Pilgrims: A Monk. Geoffrey Chaucer. OBCoV *Fr.* Canterbury Tales, The.

Seven Pilgrims: A Prioress[e]. Geoffrey Chaucer. CTC; NPeEn *Fr.* Canterbury Tales, The.

Seven Pilgrims: A Wyf of Bathe. Geoffrey Chaucer. EBEV *Fr.* Canterbury Tales, The.

Seven plus thirty years are gone. Philodemus. GrAn

Seven pm in Redfern, apprehension showing. Redfern at Night. Stephen Clayton. IBA

Seven Poems of Lament. Ts'ao Chih. SuSp, *tr. by* Ronald C. Miao

Seven Poems of Lament. Wang Ts'an.
  "Land of the Ching tribes is not my home, The." SuSp
  "This frontier post brings me sorrow." SuSp
  "Western Capital is in turmoil, The." SuSp

Seven Poems on Living in the Mountains: Seeing Off. Chang Yü. CoBLCP, *tr. by* Jonathan Chaves

Seven Rainy Months. William Plomer. OxBTC

Seven Sages, The. W. B. Yeats. NOIV

Seven scythes leaned at the wall. Taxman. George Mackay Brown. NePenScot

Seven Seages, The. John Rolland.
  "In haist ga hy thee to sum hoill." OxBS

Seven seas sucked up together, The. Gesshu Soko. ZenPo, *tr. by* Takashi Ikemoto and Lucien Stryk

Seven-Sided Poem. Carlos Drummond de Andrade. PoetW; TCLAP; VCWP, *tr. by* Elizabeth Bishop

Seven Sides and Seven Syllables. Edouard J. Maunick. CarOv; NegPo; VCWP, *tr. by* Carolyn Kizer

Seven Sins, The. *Unknown.* SacPr
  (Wyth a gerlond of thornes kene.) OHMEL

Seven Songs. Cheng Hsieh. CoBLCP, *tr. by* Jonathan Chaves

Seven Songs and Song Pictures. *Unknown.* PFTM-1

Seven Songs Written During the Ch'ien-yüan Era. Tu Fu. CoBCP, *tr. by* Burton Watson
  "I have a sister, little sister, living in Chung-li." CoBCP
  "I have brothers, younger brothers in a place far away." CoBCP
  "Long hoe, long hoe, handle of white wood." CoBCP
  "To the south there is a dragon living in a mountain pool." CoBCP
  "Traveler, a traveler, Tzu-mei his name, A." CoBCP

Seven Songs Written while Living at T'ung-ku in 759. Tu Fu. ColAnChi; SuSp, *tr. by* Geoffrey Waters and Goeffrey Waters

Seven Sorrows. Wang Ts'an. ColAnChi

Seven Sorrows. Wang Ts'an. CoBCP, *tr. by* Burton Watson
  "Tribes of Ching—that's not my home." CoBCP

Seven Sorrows, The. Ted Hughes. NAEL-5v2; NAEL-6v2

Seven Spiritual Ages of Mrs. Marmaduke Moore, The. Ogden Nash. MoAmPo

Seven Stages, The. Kahlil Gibran. BBASP, *tr. by* Michael Beard and Adnan Haydar

Seven Stanzas at Easter. John Updike. TrCP

Seven stars in the still water. Dole of the King's Daughter, The. *Unknown.* AWP, *tr. by* Oscar Wilde

Seven Stimuli. Mei Ch'eng. ColAnChi, *tr. by* Victor H. Mair

Seven Stones. Marjorie Agosin. TANSG, *tr. by* Cola Franzen

Seven Strangely Exciting Lies. Denise Riley.
  Disintegrate Me. Oth
  Flip, Flop. Oth
  I Take Two of These Tablets Tonight and in the Morning Go on Living. Oth
  "So get up speed. So you're sick with fear again so what so what." Oth
  "There was such brilliance lifting off the sea, its aquamarine strip." Oth
  "What clicks and rattles coloured strings of plastic curtains all the afternoon." Oth

Seven threads make the shroud. Shroud. George Mackay Brown. NoP-4; RB

Seven Times Three—Love. Jean Ingelow. TreFP *Fr.* Songs of Seven.

Seven Virgins, The. *Unknown.* OBEV

Seven wealthy towns contend for Homer dead. Cure for Poetry, A. *Unknown, after the Latin of* George Buchanan. FaBoEE

Seven weeks of sea, and twice seven days of storm. Gibraltar. Wilfrid Scawen Blunt. OBEV

Seven white peacocks against the castle wall, The. What the Orderly Dog Saw. Ford Madox Ford. CTC

Seven wise men, seven fit in their wisdom—seven heroes. On the Seven Bishops. Anne Fychan. EMWP

Seven Wonders of North Wales, The. *Unknown.* OBWVE

Seven Wonders of the World. Christopher Pearse Cranch.
  Locomotive, The. APN-1; GM
  Photograph, The. APN-1
  Printing-Press, The. APN-1

Seven Woodland Crows. Gerald Vizenor. VoR

Seven Words, The. Jerzy Ficowski. PoSu, *tr. by* Keith Bosley and Krystyna Wandycz

Seven years ago / at forty five. Now or Never. "Astra." BrRo

Seven years ago I went into. Water's Chant, The. Philip Levine. GeoHom

Seven years I have kept him, dead. Corpse-Keeper, The. *Unknown.* BoWoP

Seven years lived in Italy leave me convinced. Oak and the Olive, The. George Barker. FaBoMo

"Seven years ye shall be a stone." Maid and the Palmer, The. *Unknown.* ESPB

1780 A.D. in the street they flung foam about and a young. Poems (I–XI). Philip O'Connor. SPE

1789. Jackson Mac Low. APSN *Fr.* Presidents of the United States of America, The.

1711. Fugitive Slaves. Gale Jackson. SpirFl

Seventeen feet of canvas. Shoeing the Currach. Mary O'Malley. MakPoe

17:II:82. David Meltzer. SeSe

17. IV. 71. Paul Blackburn. PoM

Seventeen hundred and sixty yards. Enigma No. 6. Augusta Davies Webster. VWP

Seventeen hundred and thirty-nine. Ballad of 'Beau Brocade,' The. Austin Dobson. OxAEP-2

1797. Jackson Mac Low. APSN   *Fr.* Presidents of the United States of America, The.

Seventeen Old Poems. *Unknown.*
   "Bright moon, oh how white it shines, The."   ChiP
   "Crossing the river I pluck the lotus flowers.;"   ChiP
   "Dead are gone and with them we cannot converse, The."   ChiP
   "Eastern Wall stands high and long, The."   ChiP
   "Green, green."   ChiP
   "In the north-west there is a high house."   ChiP
   "Of this day's glorious feast and revel."   ChiP
   "On and on, always on and on."   ChiP
   "Turning my chariot I yoke my horses and go."   ChiP
   "Years of a lifetime do not reach a hundred, The."   ChiP

Seventeen years ago come March. (LL)   Crusoe in England.   Elizabeth Bishop. APT-2; EmeKit; FaBoVe; HCAP; PoPoPo; RACG

Seventeen years ago you said. À Quoi Bon Dire.   Charlotte Mew.   MakPoe; NPeEn; OxBEV; OxBTC; VWP

Seventeenth stanza, The. My heart aches, my tears fall.   Ts'ai Yen.   WPOW   *Fr.* Eighteen Verses Sung to a Tatar Reed Whistle.

Seventh, The. Attila József.   AF; RB, *tr.* by John Batki

Seventh Avenue. Muriel Rukeyser.   NoAM

Seventh Birthday of the First Child.   Sharon Olds.   PBCAP

Seventh Day, The. James McAuley.   BMAP   *Fr.* Seven Days of Creation, The.

Seventh Day Seventh Month.   Kuan Yun She.   OHMPC, *tr.* by Kenneth Rexroth

Seventh Eclogue. Miklós Radnóti. IQMS, *tr.* by Peter Zollman

Seventh Eclogue. Miklós Radnóti. PFTM-1

7th Light Poem: For John Cage—17 June 1962.   Jackson Mac Low.   FTOS

Seventh month. Chinese Figures 3.   *Unknown.*   EaWin, *tr.* by W. S. Merwin

Seventh of July, the suith to say, The.   Raid of the Reidswire, The.   *Unknown.* IBB

Seventh Street. Jean Toomer.   APT-2; NAAL-2v2

Seventh Symphony, The.   Sándor Weöres.   IQMS, *tr.* by Bruce Berlind and Mária Kőrösy

7th Untitled Poem. Pedro Juan Pietri.   PueRic

Seventh Vertical Poetry.   Roberto Juarroz.
   "Prompting of my shadow, The."   VCWP

Seventies, The. Louis Johnson.   PeNZ

Seventy-eight awkward years.   Ichigen.   ZenPo, *tr.* by Takashi Ikemoto and Lucien Stryk

Seventy Feet Down.   Philip Larkin.   NPeEn; RB   *Fr.* Livings.

Seventy-five Are My Abyssed Forests.   Shimon Halkin.   MHP, *tr.* by Ruth Finer Mintz

74th Street. Myra Cohn Livingston.   SSCS

Seventy-one! Kigen.   JDP, *tr.* by Yoel Hoffmann

Seventy-six: done. Fuyo-Dokai.   ZenPo, *tr.* by Takashi Ikemoto and Lucien Stryk

Seventy-six Hokku. Basho.
   "Old pond, / frog jumps in."   EnlH

Seventy Six Trombones.   Meredith Willson.   ReLy

Seventy-two years I've hung.   Ikuo-Myotan.   ZenPo, *tr.* by Takashi Ikemoto and Lucien Stryk

Seventy years and more.   Tosui Unkei.   JDP, *tr.* by Yoel Hoffmann

Seventy Years Are Few.   Lu Chih.   WoPoe, *tr.* by Bruce Carpenter

Several months after we lost our way.   Natives, The.   David Mura.   CDa; WeW-3

Several of us are quiet in a ring.   Manuscript with Illumination.   Robert Fitzgerald.   APT-2

Several Questions Answered.   William Blake.
   Eternity.   AWP; AmFaPo; EBEV; EnlH; FaBoEE; NOBE; NoP-4; OxBSP; RB; SCGP; SoSe-8; Spl
   "Look of love alarms, The."   WoPoe
   Question Answered, The [*or* A].   ErotSp; FaBoEE; NoP-4; OxBEV; WoPoe
   "What is it men in women do require?"   ErotSp; FaBoEE; NoP-4; OxBEV; WoPoe

Several sentences appear.   Konrad Bayer.   PFTM-2, *tr.* by Walter Billeter   *Fr.* Philosopher's Stone, The.

Several Voices Out of a Cloud.   Louise Bogan.   APT-2; NALW

Severance. Kit Robinson.   FTOS

Severance of Connections, 1946.   Louis Edward Sissman.   TwCP

Severances. Aidan Carl Mathews.   CIP-2

Severed Selves. Dante Gabriel Rossetti.   BoLoP   *Fr.* House of Life, The.

Severer Service of Myself.   Emily Dickinson.   TRP

Severity of Heaven calls out the angry winds, The.   On the Flooding of Prague, which Arose from Continuous Rain in the Year 1596.   Elizabeth Jane Leon.   EMWP

Severn and Vaga, each old Cambria's pride.   Thoughts on Happiness.   Francis Homfray.   AngWePo

Severn Bore. Catherine Fisher.   AngWePo; TCAWP

Sevint Buik, Lines 1029–92, The.   Blind Harry.   NePenScot   *Fr.* Actis and Deidis of the Illustere and Vailyeand Campioun Schir William Wallace, Knicht of Ellerslie, The.

Sew a Pocket. Jessie Welborn Smith.   PWR

Sewing a Dress. Lorine Niedecker.   APT-2

Sewing Lesson, The.   Kate Lilley.   BMAP

Sewing the long white seam. (LL)   Long White Seam, The.   Jean Ingelow. NOBVV; OxBEV

Sewing without Mother: A Zuihitsu.   Kimiko Hahn.   PuP-23

Sewing Woman. Alison Kim.   FSt

Sex. Stefan Brecht.
   "Here then is the life-giving activity given to every man: the sexual / act, vivificator."   CLPP

Sex. Jean Valentine.   FaBoWP

Sex—A Five-Minute Briefing.   Nina Iskrenko.   ItGoST, *tr.* by Patrick Henry, John High and Katya Olmsted

Sex and the Over Forties.   Peter Porter.   BMAP

Sex and the Single Spud.   Ann Slegman.   SpudSo

Sex, as they harshly call it.   Adrienne Rich.   EmeKit; NIL-7

Sex, as they harshly call it.   Adrienne Rich.   NIP-4; NOBA; TAP   *Fr.* Two Songs.

Sex, Consolation for Misery.   Pier Paolo Pasolini.   CLPP

Sex fingers toes. Dear John, Dear Coltrane.   Michael S. Harper.   ISC; NAAL-5; NIL-7; NIP-4; VCAP

Sex floated like a moon.   Circle, a Square, a Triangle and a Ripple of Water, A.   Jane Cooper.   TAP

Sex Has a Way. Wendy Lee.   PasH

Sex has a way of softening limbs.   Sex Has a Way.   Wendy Lee.   PasH

Sex is the curse of life! (LL)   Margaret Fuller Slack.   Edgar Lee Masters. APT-1; IllVoic; RACG   *Fr.* Spoon River Anthology.

Sex-life of Fish, The.   William Diaper.   ECEV; OBVE   *Fr.* Halieutica.

Sex violent as an object (whitened quarry of marble).   Amelia Rosselli.   ItPo, *tr.* by Gayle Ridinger

Sex with a Famous Poet.   Denise Duhamel.   KGB; NeAmPo

Sex without Love. Sharon Olds.   HeIP-4; NIL-7; NIP-4; TRP

Sexes waking, now separate and sore, The.   Martyrs, The.   Jay Macpherson. MoCV

Sexsmith the Dentist.   Edgar Lee Masters.   GeoHom   *Fr.* Spoon River Anthology.

Sextain: "Sith gone is my delight and only pleasure."   William Drummond, of Hawthornden.   NOSC

Sextain: "With elegies, sad songs, and mourning lays."   William Drummond, of Hawthornden.   NOSC

Sextet. Joseph Brodsky.   TCRP, *tr.* by Joseph Brodsky

Sexton is opening up the grave, The.   Third Light, The.   Michael Longley. PNI

Sexton tolled the bell, The. (LL)   Faithless Sally Brown.   Thomas Hood. NOBL; OBNV

Sextus the Usurer. Martial.   AWP, *tr.* by Kirby Flower Smith

Sexual intercourse began.   Annus Mirabilis.   Philip Larkin.   NBLV; NIP-4; NOBL; OBAL

Sexual Privacy of Women on Welfare.   Pinkie Gordon Lane.   BlSi

Sexual Water. Pablo Neruda.   PFTM-1

Sexy talk show host nods and nods, The.   Beside her.   Broken Helix.   Dina Ben-Lev.   AmPoNex

Sexy young student once toyed, A.   Limerick.   Richard Taylor.   PeLi

Sey me, wight in the broom.   *Unknown. See* Say me, wight in the brom [*or* broom]

Seynt Stevene was a clerk.   St. Stephen and King Herod.   *Unknown.*   ESPB; OxBoLi

Seynt Stevyn and Herowdes.   *Unknown. See* St. Stephen and King Herod

Seyton!—I am sick at heart.   William Shakespeare.   OxAEP-1   *Fr.* Macbeth.

Sgt. Christopher and I are.   OK Corral East Brothers in the Nam.   Horace Coleman.   CDa

Sha-ch'eng, "Sand City."   Yang Shih-ch'i.   CoBLCP, *tr.* by Jonathan Chaves

Shabby Old Dad. Anne Campbell.   PoToHe

Shabine sang to you from the depths of the sea. (LL)   Derek Walcott.   ESEAA; HarvBoo; NoP-4

Shack and a few trees, The.   After Work.   Gary Snyder.   NNaP

Shade and Noon Sun.   Muhammad Al-Maghut.   MAP, *tr.* by John Heath-Stubbs and May Jayyusi

Shade of His hand shall cover us, The.   His Hand Shall Cover Us.   Isaac ben Samuel of Dampière.   TrJP, *tr.* by Nina Davis Salaman

Shade-Seller, The.   Josephine Jacobsen.   TAP

Shade springs open, the.   Alan Pizzarelli.   HA

Shade upon the mind there passes, A.   Emily Dickinson.   APN-2

Shaded lamp and a waving blind, A. August Midnight, An. Thomas Hardy. NOBVV

Shades. Minnie Bruce Pratt. ExTi

Shades of Callimachus, Coan ghosts of Philetas. Ezra Pound. APT-1; HAP; NOBA; OBVE; OxBA; WoPoe *Fr.* Homage to Sextus Propertius.

Shades of eve are quickly closing in, The. Night. Josephine D. Henderson Heard. CBWP-4

Shades of Night, The. A. E. Housman. NBLV; OBCoV; UV

Shades of night were falling fast, The. Shades of Night, The. A. E. Housman. NBLV; OBCoV; UV

Shades of night were falling fast, The. Excelsior. Henry Wadsworth Longfellow. BRP; NAAL-2v1; NAAL-3; OBCA; OBSP; TCAPo; UV

Shades of old Lucretia Borgia! Witchcraft. Cy Coleman. ReLy

Shades of Pharoah Sanders Blues for My Baby. John O'Neal. NBV

Shades of the Newly Buried Complain to the Gods, The. *Unknown.* WoPoe, *tr. by* John S. Major

Shading his eyes. Cor Van den Heuvel. HA

Shadow. Guillaume Apollinaire. PeFWW, *tr. by* Christopher Middleton

Shadow. Mary Elizabeth Coleridge. VWP

Shadow. Josip Novakovich. BAP-97

Shadow, The. Nathan [*or* Natan] Alterman. FIT, *tr. by* Robert Friend

Shadow, The. Luis Cernuda. CAGL, *tr. by* Rick Lipinski

Shadow, The. Ben Jonson. *See* Song. That Women Are But Men's Shadows

Shadow, The. John Banister Tabb. APN-2

Shadow 1. Miyoshi Toyoichiro. GifTon, *tr. by* Naoshi Koriyama and Edward Lueders

Shadow and caress- / ing a disguise!, A. (LL) Image of Leda, An. Frank O'Hara. HCAP; LCAP-2

Shadow and Shade. Allen Tate. VGW

Shadow and Sunrise. Henrietta Cordelia Ray. CBWP-3

Shadow Beds. Delmira Agustini. TANSG, *tr. by* Mark McCaffrey

Shadow boxer, fighting. Father of Famine. Richard Ryan. PBCIP

Shadow-Casting. James Galvin. MoASP

Shadow does not leave my feet, The. David. Charles Reznikoff. ChIV-1

Shadow extends the tree. Thomas A. Clark. Oth

Shadow faces / In the shadow night. Chord. Langston Hughes. APSN

Shadow fruit is falling from the walls. Songs from an Island. Ingeborg Bachmann. VCWP, *tr. by* Mark Anderson

Shadow Grammar. Terence Winch. BAP-97

Shadow his father makes with joined hands, A. Alphabets. Seamus Heaney. NoAM

Shadow in Stone. Janice Mirikitani. OpBo

Shadow in the folded napkin, The. Cor Van den Heuvel. HA

Shadow is floating through the moonlight, A. Bird of Night, The. Randall Jarrell. KaS

Shadow of a Branch, The. Edith Marcombe Shiffert. WPE

Shadow of a fat man in the moonlight, The. Things to Come. James Reeves. OxBSP

Shadow of Cain, The. Dame Edith Sitwell. OxBTC

Shadow of Darkness. Gladys May Casely Hayford. HAWP; PBA

Shadow of Days to Come. Alejandra Piznarnick. TANSG, *tr. by* Susan Bassnett

Shadow of Fire: Ghazals, The. Judith Wright.

    Dust. HarvBoo

    Oppositions. HarvBoo

    Patterns. HarvBoo

    Rockpool. HarvBoo

    Summer. HarvBoo

    Winter. HarvBoo

Shadow of Flowers, The. Su Tung-p'o (Su Shih). OHPC, *tr. by* Kenneth Rexroth

Shadow of Himself, The. William Renton. NOBVV

Shadow of Life, The. Vicki Davey. IBA

Shadow of the little fishing launch, The. Parrot Fish, The. James Merrill. NOBA

Shadow of the night comes on, The. (LL) You, Andrew Marvell. Archibald MacLeish. APT-1; AWP; ColAP; HAP; HeIP-4; MoAmPo; NAAL-2v2; NOBA; NoAM; NoP-4; OxBA; PoRA; SoSe-8; TFi; TRP; TwCP

Shadow of the Rock, The. Frederick William Faber. SacPr

Shadow of the trees, The. Kenneth Yasuda. HA

Shadow of the Venetian blind on the painted wall, The. Forties Flick. John Ashbery. FTOS; NoAM

Shadow of War, 1941. Thomas William Shapcott. BMAP

Shadow of wings grew, The. Fight With An Angel. Tadeusz Różewicz. PoSu, *tr. by* Victor Contoski

Shadow on shadow his mind. Remembering Yeats. Francis Stuart. BiHa

Shadow Returns, The. Phillis Levin. RA

Shadow sits and waits for me, The. (LL) Tennyson. CAGL; EBVV; NAEL-6v2; NAWM-7v2; PeECV; SCV *Fr.* In Memoriam A. H. H.

Shadow, stone, linen, lime, the. Seventh Symphony, The. Sándor Weöres. IQMS, *tr. by* Bruce Berlind and Mária Kőrösy

Shadow streamed into the wall, The. Shadow and Shade. Allen Tate. VGW

Shadow Train. John Ashbery. LCAP-2

Shadow Valley. Robert Morgan. AngWePo

Shadow within the light, The. Serenity. Philippe Jaccottet. MFP, *tr. by* Martin Sorrell

Shadowboxing. James Tate. MoASP

Shadowless sun on male bodies. Sandro Penna. CAGL, *tr. by* John McRae

Shadows. John Clare. CenSon

Shadows. Samuel Daniel. *See* Tethy's Festival

Shadows. Patricia Hubbell. Spl

Shadows. Richard Jackson. SeSe

Shadows. D. H. Lawrence. OxBTC

Shadows. Victor Gustave Plarr. NOBVV

Shadows. Joy Williams. IBA

Shadows. "Yehoash." TrJP, *tr. by* Elias Lieberman

Shadows are descending, The. Outgoing Sabbath. *Unknown.* TrJP, *tr. by* Joseph Leftwich

Shadows become familiar. My Neighborhood. Stuart Dybek. PBCAP

Shadows from a lingering sun. Soko. JDP, *tr. by* Yoel Hoffmann

Shadows in his eye sockets like shades, The. Richmond. John Updike. CBCWP

Shadows in the grass. Rod Willmot. HA

Shadows in the Water. Thomas Traherne. GeHe; HAP; NoP-4; SCGP; WoPoe (In unexperienc'd infancy.) CABP; NPeEn

Shadows, like Navahoes, wear velvet. Tourist Country. William Stafford. NoAM

Shadows of Chrysanthemums. Edith Jay Scovell. HarvBoo

Shadows of His Lady. Jacques Tahureau. AWP, *tr. by* Andrew Lang

Shadows of ringdoves chanting, but easing nothing, The. (LL) Winter Trees. Sylvia Plath. HCAP; LCAP-2

Shadows of the cypresses, The. Wind Tossed Dragons. Hsieh Ngao. OHMPC, *tr. by* Kenneth Rexroth

Shadows of the sails pass across his windows. Visiting the Garden at Monk Wen Ko's Home. Wu Wei-yeh. SuSp, *tr. by* Chang Yin-nan

Shadows of the t'ung tree, glistening and clear. In a Dream. Lu Yu. SuSp, *tr. by* Irving Y. Lo

Shadows on the wall. Life Doesn't Frighten Me. Maya Angelou. ChAP

Shadowy as a blueprint is. Building the Dam. Reuel Denney. YaYoPo

Shadrach O'Leary. Edwin Arlington Robinson. APT-1

Shadwell Stair. Wilfred Owen. FaBoTw

Shady Grove. *Unknown.* APN-2

Shady grove, my true love. Shady Grove. *Unknown.* APN-2

Shady, Shady. T'ao Ch'ien [*or* T'ao Yuan-ming]. AWP, *tr. by* Arthur Waley

Shady, shady the wood in front of the Hall. Ch'ien T'ao. ChiP

Shaemus. Conrad Potter Aiken. OxBA

Shaft, The. Charles Tomlinson. DiPo

Shaft extracted does not cure the wound!, The. (LL) Petrarch. CenSon; RWP, *tr. by* Charlotte Smith *Fr.* Sonnets to Laura.

Shaft of narrative peers down, The. Soul, The. Ira Sadoff. BodElec

Shaft we raise to them and thee, The. (LL) Concord Hymn. Ralph Waldo Emerson. AWP; AiP; BRP; ClHu; ColAP; FaBoA; HAP; HeIP-4; NOBA; NoP-4; OBWP; OxBA; PeECV; PoPoPo; TAP; TCAPo; TFi

Shaft[e]sbury. Dryden. NOSC *Fr.* Absalom and Achitophel.

Shaftesbury. Dryden. NPeEn *Fr.* Absalom and Achitophel.

Shag, The. Eileen Duggan. PeNZ

Shag Rock. "Paul Henderson." PeNZ

Shagbark. Faye George. PoCoUp

Shahnamah, The. Firdowsi.

    Birth of Sohráb, The. TAL

    Death of Sohráb, The. TAL

Shaka, King of the Zulus. *Unknown.* PBA; TTY, *tr. by* A. C. Jordan

Shake Down the Stars. Eddie DeLange. ReLy

Shake hands, we shall never be friends, all's over. A. E. Housman. CAGL

Shake hole. Marks the English Left on the Map. Peter Finch. Oth

Shake'nbake Ballad. Peter Van Toorn. NOBC

Shake off this sadness, and recover your spirit. Throw Yourself Like Seed. Miguel de Unamuno. RaBo, *tr. by* Robert Bly

Shake the bed, the blackened child whimpers. Cotton Flannelette. Les A. Murray. PoetW

Shaken already, I know. Goodbye, Sally. James Simmons. BIrV

Shakeout. Diane Ward. FTOS

Shakespeare. Matthew Arnold. FHYEP; HeIP-4; OBEV; OxAEP-2; OxBSo; SCGP; Son

Shakespeare. Henry Wadsworth Longfellow. AWP

Shakespeare. Henrietta Cordelia Ray. CBWP-3

Shakespeare; an Epistle to David Garrick, Esq. Robert Lloyd. "Shall ancient worth, or ancient fame." NOEC True Genius. NOEC

Shakespeare stand-ins, same string hair, gay, dirty. Ulysses. Robert Lowell. NAAL-2v2

Shakespeare!—to such name's sounding, what succeeds. Names, The. Robert Browning. OxBSo

Shakespeare, whose heartfelt scenes shall ever give. To Shakespeare. Thomas Edwards. Son

Shakespearean fish swam the sea, far away from land. Three Movements. W. B. Yeats. FaBoEE

Shakespearian Readings. Phoebe Cary. SWaP

Shakin All Over. John James. Oth

Shaking Hands with Mongo. Martín Espada. SeSe

Shaking in my hands, The. Letter. Sam Hamod. GraLe

Shaking my head, I let the world of red dust. Tune: "Happy Events Approaching." Chu Tun-ju. SuSp, tr. by James J. Y. Liu

Shaking the snow from your hair, bowl cut. Huy Nguyen: Brothers, Drowning Cries. David Mura. CDa

(Shaking with light—) is born. (LL) Thinking. Jorie Graham. BAP-97; ExTi

Shako, The. Robert Lowell. Son

Shakspeare. Ralph Waldo Emerson. TCAPo Fr. Quatrains.

Shakti. Rae Desmond Jones. BMAP

Shalako. Zuni Oral Tradition. Sayatasha's Night Chant. Dismissal of the Koyemshi. NAWM-7v2, tr. by Ruth L. Bunzel House Blessing. NAWM-7v2, tr. by Ruth L. Bunzel "Then my father's rain-filled room." NAWM-7v2, tr. by Ruth L. Bunzel "This many are the days." NAWM-7v2, tr. by Ruth L. Bunzel

Shale. Vona Groarke. MFPA

Shall ancient worth, or ancient fame. Robert Lloyd. NOEC Fr. Shakespeare; an Epistle to David Garrick, Esq.

Shall be a soldier's sepulchre. (LL) Hohenlinden. Thomas Campbell. CABP; FaBoCh; GTBS-P; NOBE; NOBRP; OBWP; TFi

Shall be lifted—nevermore! (LL) Raven, The. Edgar Allan Poe. APN-1; BRP; ChAP; ColAP; EBNV; FaBoCh; HeIP-4; ITBLP; NAAL-2v1; NAAL-3; NAAL-5; NCAP; NIL-7; NIP-4; NOBA; NoP-4; OBCA; OBNV; OWoS; OxBA; PWR; PoRA; TAP; TCAPo; TFi; TreFP; UV

Shall be the Psalms sung forth in gracious layes. (LL) Edward Taylor. ChIV-2; SCAP Fr. Preparatory Meditations Before My Approach to the Lord's Supper.

Shall both rise with me. (LL) Cherry-Tree Carol, The. Unknown. ChrPo; EBEV; ESPB; HeIP-4; MakPoe; OxBB; OxBoLi; PeECV; SCGP; TFi

Shall bring my boats ashore. (LL) Where Go the Boats? Robert Louis Stevenson. FaBoCh; NOxBChV; NTCP; TLR; WHSW

Shall brothers [or brithers] be for a' that. (LL) For A' That and A' That ["Is there, for honest poverty"]. Robert Burns. NAEL-5v2; NAEL-6v2; OxAEP-2; TFi; TreFP; UV

Shall buffet the vexed forests in his rage. (LL) Winter Piece, A. William Cullen Bryant. APN-1; ColAP; OxBA

Shall do it reverence. (LL) City in the Sea, The. Edgar Allan Poe. APN-1; NAAL-2v1; NAAL-3; NCAP; NOBA; NoP-4; OxBA; PoE; SCV; TAP; TCAPo; TFi; TRP

Shall draw the Thing as he sees It for the God of Things as They are! (LL) L'Envoi. Rudyard Kipling. BRP; PWR

Shall Earth no more inspire me. Emily Jane Brontë. BWW; VWP

Shall fear to seem untrue. Rejection, The. Sir Robert Aytoun [or Ayton]. NOSC

Shall find wings waiting there. (LL) Going Down Hill on a Bicycle. Henry Charles Beeching. NOxBChV; OBEV

Shall flock about thee, and keep time with kisses. (LL) On the Death of a Nightingale. Thomas Randolph. BASC; BeJo

Shall fly, the feathered arrow of the foam. (LL) Choosing a Mast. Roy Campbell. FaBoTw; NoP-4

Shall Gaelic Die? Iain Crichton Smith. NPeEn

Shall have a [or the] gold fiddle. (LL) Rock, Ball, Fiddle. Unknown. OxBoLi; OxNR

Shall hearts that beat no base retreat. Enthusiast, The. Herman Melville. ChIV-1; NAAL-2v1; NAAL-3

Shall henceforth wash the river Rhine? (LL) Cologne. Samuel Taylor Coleridge. FaBoEE; NBLV

Shall I ask the willow trees on the dike. Longing in My Heart. Wei Ying-wu. SuSp, tr. by Irving Y. Lo

Shall I be child of the full moon. Bloody Masculinity. Ifi Amadiume. HAWP

Shall I be one of those obsequious Fools. Liberty, The. Sarah Fyge Egerton. EMWP

Shall I charge like a bull. Auvaiyar. WPOW

Shall I come, if I swim? wide are the waves, you see. Thomas Campion. EnLoPo

Shall I Come, Sweet Love. Thomas Campion. EBEV; HAP; OxAEP-1; OxBoLi (Lover's Plea, A.) NOBE

Shall I come there, or you here? Hafsa bint al-Hajj. WPOW

Shall I compare her to a summer play? Sonnet on Famous and Familiar Sonnets and Experiences. Delmore Schwartz. Son; TRP

Shall I Compare Thee to a Summer's Day? Howard Moss. InPK-6

Shall I Complain. Louise Chandler Moulton. PoToHe

Shall I complain because the feast is o'er. Shall I Complain. Louise Chandler Moulton. PoToHe

Shall I connect for this world's eyes. Dumb World, The. William Henry Davies. OxBTC

Shall I Do This. Swami Purohit. OBMV

Shall I embrace my disease. Monologue of a Dying Beast. Mark Ameen. GLP

Shall I get drunk or cut myself a piece of cake. Cairo Jag. Keith Douglas. HarvBoo; PoWW

"Shall I go with you [or thee]? Ay, by-and-by" (LL) Old Woman, Old Woman. Mother Goose. LB; OxNR

Shall I have jealous thoughts to nurse. No Man's Wood. William Henry Davies. OBGa

Shall I, I wonder, ever find. Peace. Irwin Edman. TrJP

Shall I love God for causing me to be? Proof, The. Richard Wilbur. CRP; InvLi; OxBSP

Shall I place a tin wreath upon! (LL) Ezra Pound. ColAP; HarvBoo; MoAmPo; NOBE Fr. Hugh Selwyn Mauberley (Life and Contacts).

Shall I rebuke thee, Ocean, my old love. To the Ocean. Thomas Hood. CenSon

Shall I Repine. Jonathan Swift. See Power of Time, The

Shall I say how it is in your clothes? How It Is. Maxine W. Kumin. NALW; NoAM

Shall I see it again. Shunzei. WoPoe, tr. by Valerie Durham

Shall I sonnet-sing you about myself? House. Robert Browning. NAEL-5v2; NAEL-6v2

Shall I strew on thee rose or rue or laurel. Ave atque Vale. Algernon Charles Swinburne. NAEL-5v2; NAEL-6v2; NOBE; OBEV

Shall I tell you the signs of a New Age coming? New Age, The. Stevie Smith. NAEL-5v2; NAEL-6v2

Shall I tell you whom I love? William Browne (1591–1643). NOSC Fr. Britannia's Pastorals.

Shall I then praise the heavens, the trees, the earth. Anne Bradstreet. NOSC Fr. Contemplations.

Shall I, Wasting in Despair. George Wither. OxAEP-1; SCGP Fr. Fair Virtue, the Mistress of Philarete.

Shall keep the blessed spirit that I praise. (LL) Canzone: He Beseeches Death for the Life of Beatrice. Dante Alighieri. AWP; EaItPo, tr. by Dante Gabriel Rossetti

Shall last and shine when all of these are gone. (LL) Anne Bradstreet. ColAP; WPOW Fr. Contemplations.

Shall, like a hallowed [or hallow'd] Lamp, for ever burn. (LL) Eternity of Love Protested. Thomas Carew. BeJo; MeLP

Shall live my Highland Mary. (LL) Highland Mary. Robert Burns. AWP; GTBS-P; OBEV

Shall make sweet music blossomed Thy praise. (LL) Edward Taylor. NAAL-2v1; NAAL-3 Fr. Preparatory Meditations Before My Approach to the Lord's Supper.

Shall make thy actions with their ends to meet. (LL) Matins [or Mattens], or Morning Prayer. Robert Herrick. BASC; CaPo

Shall Man, O God of Light. Timothy Dwight. AH

Shall multi . . . pl . . . p. (LL) Spring's Last Drop, The. Catherine Obianuju Acholonu. HAWP; NAfrP

Shall never be beloved by men. (LL) William Blake. OWoS; OxBoLi Fr. Auguries of Innocence.

Shall no more blackened and obscured be. (LL) October. Edward Thomas. CABP; HarvBoo; NoAM

Shall not be seen upon thy hand again. (LL) Thy Brother's Blood. Jones Very. APN-1; NOBA; TAP

Shall paint this happiest scene with pencil soft. (LL) Written at the Eagle's Nest, Killarney. July 26, 1800. Mary Tighe. CenSon; OxBSo

Shall pause at the song of their captive and weep! (LL) Thomas Moore. NOIV; NPeEn

Shall pour such splendour as your heart to me. (LL) Most Lovely Shade. Dame Edith Sitwell. FaBoTw; GTBS-P

Shall pride a heap of sculptur'd marble raise. Epitaph on Laurence Sterne. David Garrick. FaBoEE

Shall royal praise be rhym'd by such a ribald. On the Candidates for the Laurel. Pope. FaBoEE

Shall silence shroud such sin.   Declaration of the Death of John Lewes, A.   Thomas Gilbart.   NoSic

Shall speak to me in their fattening echo, and purr: penetralia.   Waterfowl Descending.   Sam Witt.   NeAmPo

Shall the Dead Praise Thee?   George Macdonald.   TrCP

Shall Then Another.   Kenneth Mackenzie.   NOBAu

Shall then another do what I have done.   Shall Then Another.   Kenneth Mackenzie.   NOBAu

Shall turn and welcome me at the door. (LL)   Wizard's Funeral, The.   Richard Watson Dixon.   NOBVV; PeVV

Shall we behold "no classes" on God's earth. (LL)   No Classes!   Ella Wheeler Wilcox.   APN-2; SWaP

Shall We Dance.   Joe Osterhaus.   NAPBL

Shall We Dance?   Richard Rodgers.   ReLy

Shall we forget the shiver.   Yury [or Iurii] Ivask.   TCRP; TCRusP, tr. by John Glad

Shall we gather at the river.   Beautiful River.   Robert Lowry.   APN-2

Shall We Go a-Shearing?   Mother Goose.   OxNR; ReMoGo

Shall we go dance the hay? The hay?   Report Song [in a Dream], A.   Nicholas Breton.   NoSic

Shall we have a family born.   For Walter Lowenfels.   Wendy Rose.   CDW

Shall we hear you again soon, soon? (LL)   Nightingales, The.   Harri Webb.   AngWePo; TCAWP

Shall We Join the Ladies?   David Ross.   ReLy

Shall we leave it unabated in its place? (LL)   Mesopotamia.   Rudyard Kipling.   HarvBoo; PoWW

Shall we make love.   Var. authors.   AWP   Fr. Manyo Shu, Part 3 of 4.

Shall we stay in the.   Unknown.   OHMPJ

Shall we win at love or shall we lose.   Hôtel Transylvanie.   Frank O'Hara.   NeAP; PoM

Shall whet their knives, and think of you. (LL)   Poem, after A. E. Housman.   Hugh Kingsmill.   NOBL; UV

Shall you be overcome. (LL)   Conscientious Objector.   Edna St. Vincent Millay.   FaBoWar; WPOW

Shall yourselves find blessing. (LL)   Good King Wenceslas.   Unknown.   ChrPo; SacPr, tr. by John Mason Neale

Shallow-Water Warning.   Helen Adam.   APT-2

Shallows, brighter, The.   Pier: Under Pisces, The.   James Merrill.   LCAP-2; NoAM

Shalom Aleichem.   Unknown.   TrJP

Shaman.   María Sabina.   WPOW, tr. by Henry Munn

Shaman and the Red God, The.   Nakkiranar.   WoPoe

Shaman Breaks.   Gerald Vizenor.   HATNAP

Shaman's Song.   Hungarian Oral Tradition.   IQMS, tr. by Adam Makkai

Shaman Song.   Luswat.   STP, tr. by James Koller

Shaman Song.   Uvavnuk.   WoPoe, tr. by Jane Hirshfield

Shamash of the glade, The.   Venerable Bee, The.   Abraham Moses Klein.   TrJP

Shame.   Vern Rutsala.   OPRER

Shame.   Matilde Salganicoff.   MirDau, tr. by Celeste Kostopulos-Cooperman

Shame.   Lőrinc Szabó.   IQMS, tr. by John Gordon Nichols   Fr. Cricket Music.

Shame.   Richard Wilbur.   CoAmPo; EmeKit; FaBoMo; OBCoV; OxBC

Shame Kept My Tears Away.   Mutanabbi.   ArPe, tr. by Omar S. Pound

Shame, No Statist.   Robert Herrick.   BASC

Shame on You.   Langston Hughes.   APT-2

Shamed by the Creature.   Mildmay Fane, 2d Earl of Westmorland.   NOSC

Shameful / Dead grass.   Shoha.   ZenPo, tr. by Takashi Ikemoto and Lucien Stryk

Shameful Death.   William Morris.   GTBS-P; PeVV

Shameful mask hid his teeth, The.   Squares.   Pierre Reverdy.   PFTM-1

Shameful / These clothes.   Sono-Jo, Lady.   ZenPo, tr. by Takashi Ikemoto and Lucien Stryk

Shampoo, The.   Elizabeth Bishop.   APT-2; FaBoWP; HarvBoo; OxBC; VCAP

Shan Van Vocht, The.   Unknown.   OxBoLi

Shancoduff.   Patrick Kavanagh.   BIrV; CIP-2; FaBoTw; HarvBoo; WoPoe

Shandon Bells, The.   Francis Sylvester Mahony.   See Bells of Shandon, The

Shane O'Neill's Cairn.   Robinson Jeffers.   NOBA; NoAM

Shaneen and Maurya Prendergast.   Patch-Shaneen.   John Millington Synge.   FaBoVe

Shang Cup.   Louis Zukofsky.   APT-2

Shang ya!   Oath of Friendship.   Unknown.   TTTS, tr. by Arthur Waley

Shango.   Unknown.   PBA; TTY, tr. by Ulli Beier and Bakare Gbadamosi

Shannon Estuary Welcomes the Fish, The.   Nuala Ni Dhomhnaill.   ModIr, tr. by Patrick Crotty

Shannon Estuary Welcoming the Fish, The.   Nuala Ni Dhomhnaill.   CIP-2, tr. by the author

Shantih shantih shantih. (LL)   T. S. Eliot.   APT-1; CABP; FaBoMo; HAP; MoAmPo; NAAL-2v2; NAAL-5; NAEL-5v2; NAEL-6v2; NAWM-7v2;

NOBA; NOBE; NoAM; NoP-4; OxAEP-2; OxBA; OxBTC; PoE; TAP; TCAPo; TFi; UnPo

Shanty shade figured among the makers, A.   Revelry in Black-and-White.   Ann Lauterbach.   BodElec

Shao and the South.   Confucius.   CTC, tr. by Ezra Pound

Shap.   Mick North.   NLP

Shapcot, to the thee Fairy [or faery] State.   Oberon's Feast.   Robert Herrick.   BeJo; CaPo; NOSC

Shape-Changer, The.   Chris Wallace-Crabbe.   NOBAu

Shape of Death, The.   May Swenson.   APT-2; TAP

Shape of talk would sag, The.   Ongoing.   Naomi Shihab Nye.   PoArWo

Shape of the Fire, The.   Theodore Roethke.   LCAP-2; VCAP

Shape of Things, The.   Lavinia Greenlaw.   MFPA

Shape of Water Most Like Love, The.   David J. Rothman.   GeoH

Shape ships to seek some shining shore.   Vladislav Felitsianovich Khodasevich.   TCRP

Shape the lips to an o, say a.   Ö.   Rita Dove.   HCAP; WeW-3

Shaped and vacated.   Event, The.   Thomas Sturge Moore.   OBMV

Shaped new to your measure.   Jay Macpherson.   NOBC   Fr. Ark, The.

Shapeless mass of wreck and rubbish lies, A. (LL)   Warning, The.   Henry Wadsworth Longfellow.   APN-1; ChIV-1; NCAP; TCAPo

Shapeless, the waves rise toward their elements, where the foam of.   Orbits.   'Aisha Arnaout.   PoArWo, tr. by Mona Fayad

Shapelessness, the endlessness, The.   Ágnes Nemes Nagy.   IQMS, tr. by Alan Dixon

Shapes of Death, The.   Stephen Spender.   OBMV

Shapeshifter Poems.   Lucille Clifton.   BodElec; LoL

Shapeshifting.   Isabel Gowdie.   EMWP

Shards.   Enid Shomer.   TaR

Shards, The.   Michael O'Loughlin.   Bunkers, The.   PBCIP

Shards of sunlight touch me here.   Massacre, October '66.   Wole Soyinka.   AF; PBMAP

Share-Croppers.   Langston Hughes.   SAmP

Share fear. Repeat with one lip what.   Poem with Skin.   Octavio Armand.   TCLAP, tr. by Carol Maier

Share in perdition. (LL)   Lost Soul, A.   Jay Macpherson.   NOBC; NoP-4

Share my harvest and my home. (LL)   Ruth.   Thomas Hood.   BoLoP; ChIV-1; EnLoPo; NOBE; OBEV

Shari Wag El Burka.   Unknown.   FaBoWar

Sharing.   Alan Yount.   PasH

Sharing, The.   Bruce Weigl.   CDa

Sharing bread.   Truth.   Jean Valentine.   BodElec

Sharing Eve's Apple.   John Keats.   ChIV-1; ErotSp; NBLV; PeLV

Sharing Lodging with Hsieh Shih-hou.   Mei Yao Ch'en.   CoBCP; ColAnChi, tr. by Burton Watson

Shark, The.   Edwin John Pratt.   NOBC

Shark, with your mouth tucked under.   Thom Gunn.   NOxBChV   Fr. Three for Children.

Sharks, The.   Denise Levertov.   NeAP

Sharks tooth is perfect for biting, The.   Canticle.   Michael McClure.   NeAP; PoM

Sharp as an arrow Orpheus.   Orfeo.   Jack Spicer.   APSN

Sharp facets.   Jewel Cliff.   Muso Soseki.   EaWin, tr. by W. S. Merwin

Sharp howling winds scattering grit.   Desert Crossing.   Dambudzo Marechera.   NAfrP

Sharp Ridge, The.   Robert Graves.   FaBoEE

Sharpen the sword in the Sobbing Waters.   Tu Fu.   SuSp   Fr. Frontier Songs, First Series.

Shatter.   Elizabeth Robinson.   AmPoNex

Shattered membranes of the fly, The. (LL)   Range in the Desert, The.   Randall Jarrell.   NOBA; PoWW

Shattered water made a misty din, The.   Once by the Pacific.   Robert Frost.   APT-1; GSo; HAP; HeIP-4; MoAmPo; NAAL-2v2; NIL-7; NOBA; Son; TRP; VGW; WeW-3

Shatterfall. Scutter.   Mark, The.   Robert Dana.   OPRER

Shaving.   Richard Blanco.   AmPoNex; NAPBL

Shavings, fall from the carved stick.   Working Song.   Buluguru.   CBAP, tr. by E. A. Worms

She.   Lynn Emanuel.   BodElec

She.   Zinaida Nikolayevna [or Nikolaevna] Gippius.   WPOW, tr. by Dianne Levitin

She.   Jean-Joseph Rabéarivelo [or Rebéarivelo].   See Here is

She.   Theodore Roethke.   BoLoP; NIL-7

She.   Yevgeny [or Evgenii] Mikhailovich Vinokurov.   TCRP, tr. by Daniel Weissbort

She.   Richard Wilbur.   CoAmPo; NIL-7

She adjusts my hip, spine, shoulder.   Chest X-Ray.   Paula Tatarunis.   BloBone

She aims her spears at the cardinal points. Spark of Green. Maria Luisa Spaziani. CItWP, tr. by Cinzia Sartini Blum and Lara Trubowitz

She alone still cracks about why where whys are crimes. (LL) Making Our Clowns Martyrs. Jack A. Mapanje. HBAPE; NAfrP

She always said "tu." in such a way. Dark Portrait, A. Lawrence Ferlinghetti. PmAP

"She always seems so tied" is what friends say. Just to Be Needed. Mary Eversley. PoToHe

She, and comparisons are odious. (LL) John Donne. BASC; PeLV Fr. Elegies.

She and I. Norman Cameron. OxBSP; RB

She answers the bothersome telephone, takes the message, forgets the message, forgets who called. Alzheimer's: The Wife. C. K. Williams. VCAP

She asked brown eyes, "Burn me loose." Seal at Stinson Beach. Roberta Hill Whiteman. VoR

She asked for bread. Mother. Isobel Thrilling. Prnts

She asked me to luncheon in fur. Far from. Oppenheim's Cup and Saucer. Carol Ann Duffy. LW

She asked me why I did such things. Dialogue. Jared Angira. NAfrP

She Attempts to Refute the Praises That Truth, Which She Calls Passion, Inscribed on a Portrait of the Poet. Sister Juana Inés de la Cruz. BoWoP

She Attempts to Tell The Truth About True Romance. Kathy Fagan. ExTi

She begins, and my grandmother joins her. I Ask My Mother to Sing. Li-Young Lee. IllVoic; InvLad; LoL; OpBo; UnSA

She begins to board the flight. White Bear. Joy Harjo. NAAL-5

She being Brand. E. E. Cummings. EroLit; NOBA; OxBA; PeLV

She believed she was cursed. She believed her guardian angel had. Three Observations on Belief. Tarin Towers. AmPoNex

She Bewitched Me. Thomas Burbidge. EnLoPo

She bites into the red skin. My Love Eats an Apple. Ralph Gustafson. MoCV

She blossomed in the country. Country Lassie, The. Unknown. TreFP

She Boasts of Her Constancy. Johann Rist. GePo, tr. by George C. Schoolfield

She boned three chickens—all except the wings. Bacchanal. Barbara J. Orton. NeAmPo

She bounded o'er the graves. Anna Playing in a Graveyard. Caroline Gilman. OBCA

She bows her head. Annunciation, The. Samuel Menashe. GI

She brings that breath, and music too. Visitor, The. William Henry Davies. OBWVE

She brought a drinking-cup to him. Two. Hugo von Hofmannsthal. TrJP, tr. by Jethro Bithell

She brought her to her ioyous Paradize. Edmund Spenser. See Shee brought her to her ioyous paradize

She brought us a month noisy with rain. Full Moon in Malta. "Asphodel." BrRo

She burnt like ho[ll]y gren. (LL) Young Hunting. Unknown. ESPB; OxBB

She buys a potato. One Potato. Pat Mora. SpudSo

She called me the man of sands. Gist of the Story, The. Salah Abd al-Sabur. MAP, tr. by John Heath-Stubbs and Lena Jayyusi

She calls herself the plain girl, but I. Handbook of Sex of the Plain Girl, The. Marian Yee. FSt

She Calms the Savage Beast with Her Aubade. Grace Bauer. MiVo

She came among us from the South. Enrica, 1865. Christina Georgina Rossetti. NALW

She came and spoke low. Velemir [or Viktor Vladimirovich] Khlebnikov. TCRP Fr. Night Before the Soviets, The.

She came as a falling star to the lakes. She lithesome virgin not to be turned into. My Mother, Life. John Godfrey. FTOS

She came every morning to draw water. Drink of Water, A. Seamus Heaney. OxBC; TRP

She came, fair Friendship came, with aspect bland. Friendship. Mary Julia Young. CenSon

"She came home, my Lord, and smashed-in the television." Wife Who Smashed Television Gets Jail. Paul Durcan. CABP; CIP-2

She came in from the snowing air. Ice. Stephen Spender. FaBoMo; GTBS-P

She came in glowing. Visitor. Aleksandr Aleksandrovich Blok. TCRusP, tr. by Geoffrey Thurley

She came on Earth soon after the creation. Fairy Maimounè, The. John Moultrie. NOBRP

She came through the room like an answer in long division. Victorian Idyll, A. David Wagoner. NoAM

She came to him in dreams—her ears. Cowper's Tame Hare. Norman Nicholson. RB

She came to the village church. Tennyson. EBVV; NAEL-5v2; NAEL-6v2 Fr. Maud [A Monodrama].

She came to this local bar. Performance. Paul McRay. SwNoth

She came to us walking, at night. Shoemaker's Wife, The. Lotte Kramer. HP

She came up the hill carrying water. Achill Woman, The. Eavan Boland. BiHa; HarvBoo

She came walking. Parable. Bob Orr. PeNZ

She cannot leave it alone. New Toy, The. Thomas Hardy. ChAP

She cannot read or write. Um Hakeem. Salah Niyazi [or Niazi]. MAP, tr. by Charles Doria and Lena Jayyusi

She carried a book, either to imply. "H. D." NALW Fr. Tribute to the Angels.

She carries it unsteadily, warily. Young Girl with a Pitcher Full of Water, A. David Wagoner. NoAM

She cat, The. Basho. EH, tr. by Robert Hass

She channelled love under my skin. Finding. Celia Barry. Prnts

She chooses her clothes in subdued colours. Other Woman, The. Marion Lomax. LW

She clasps the cup with both her hands. In a Café. Rosemary Dobson. CBAP

She cleaned house, and then lay down long. Secret Gratitude, A. James Wright (1927–80). NoAM

She climbs the stairs to the fifth floor. Portrait of My Mother. Ilya [or Karl] L'vovich Selvinsky [or Sel'vinskii]. TCRP, tr. by Daniel Weissbort

She closes the bathroom door to secure her privacy, slips off her robe. Shower Scene in Psycho, The. David Trinidad. ReTh

She closes the gate. Times Like This. Richard Jones. GifTon

She coaxes her fat in front of her. New Day. Naomi Long Madgett. BlSi

She comes in late, then settles like a sigh. Introduction to Poetry. Paul Lake. RA

She comes level with him at. Donahue's Sister. Thom Gunn. NoAM

She Comes Not When Noon Is on the Roses. Herbert Trench. OBEV

She comes! she comes! the sable throne behold. Pope. ECEV Fr. Dunciad, The.

She comes with fairy footsteps. Little Rose. Unknown. TreFP

She concerned him. Melon Grower, The. Alice Oswald. MFPA

She could be seen undressing. Gesture and Flight. Ann Lauterbach. BodElec

She could bind the world's winds in a single strand. Rune of the Finland Woman. Marilyn Hacker. RA

She could die laughing. Minnie and Mrs. Hoyne. Kenneth Fearing. PoRA

She cried out for Mama, who did not. Rita Dove. NAAAL Fr. Mother Love.

She Cries. John Montague. BiHa

She cursed the circumstance. (LL) Ballad of Sue Ellen Westerfield, The. Robert Earl Hayden. ESEAA; NoAM

She'd always been there. Interface. Gloria Anzaldúa. GLP

She'd always peeled them. Mushrooms. Moira Clark. Prnts

She'd looks, she'd style. Ovid. EroLit, tr. by Kenneth McLeish Fr. Amores.

She'd Say. Frank Davey. NOBC

She'd thrust the canyon out of her mind; she never thought of the whispering fall, the ferns, the hawk-haunted. Home. Robinson Jeffers. BodElec

She'd want, if we were given what we want. (LL) What Do Women Want? Mary Jo Salter. FFC; RA

She dealt her pretty words like Blades. Emily Dickinson. HAP; NIL-7

She delighted to hold a slip of myrtle. Archilochus. SaLy, tr. by Diane Rayor

She dens in a garret. Fruit and Flower Painter. Herman Melville. NCAP

She detaches herself from her shadow. She is an old woman and still beautiful. Gloria Gervitz. MirDau, tr. by Stephen Tapscott Fr. Yiskor.

She dialed a number and said. How to Live Through This Night (A Dream). Nina Iskrenko. ItGoST, tr. by Patrick Henry, John High and Katya Olmsted

"She did not climb the April hill." April Hill, The. Janet Lewis. CRP

She did not love to love, but hated him. End of It, The. Francis Thompson. NOBVV; OxBSP

She Didn't Say "Yes." Otto Harbach. ReLy

She died after the beautiful snow had melted. In Memorial. J. Gordon Coogler. OBAL

"She died as she lived, sniffing cocaine" (LL) Cocaine Lil [and Morphine Sue]. Unknown. OxBoLi; RB

She died full long agone! (LL) Meg Merrilies [or Merrilees]. John Keats. FaBoCh; NOxBChV

She died in the upstairs bedroom. Death in Leamington. Sir John Betjeman. MakPoe; NoP-4; OxAEP-2; RB

She does not know. No Images. Waring Cuney. APT-2; NIP-4; SSLK; TTY

She does not move. Jean Daive. MFP, tr. by Martin Sorrell

She does not move. Takes the man's. She does not move. Jean Daive. MFP, tr. by Martin Sorrell

She Does Not Remember. Anna Swirszczynska. BLT

She does not speak. Jacqueline Goldberg. MirDau, tr. by Joanne Friedman Fr. Luba.

She doesn't feel the need to erect pergolas. Jolanda Insana. CItWP, tr. by Cinzia Sartini Blum and Lara Trubowitz Fr. Rooting, The.

She doesn't say a word, concentrating on one thing only.   Balgu Song.   *Unknown*.   CBAP, *tr.* by Clancy McKenna

She doesn't want.   Pumping Iron.   Diane Ackerman.   MoASP

She doesn't wear.   Gwendolyn Brooks.   Haki R. Madhubuti.   ESEAA; OPRER

She don't have no sense. (LL)   Admonitions.   Lucille Clifton.   BPo; NALW

She don't look Indian all the time.   Rational.   Helen Chalakee Burgess.   ReEnLa

She done put huh little hands.   Conjured.   Sterling Allen Brown.   NoP-4

She drawled, When Ah itchez, Ah scratchez! (LL)   Requiem: "There was a young belle of old Natchez."   Ogden Nash.   KaS; NoP-4

She dreamed along the beaches of this coast.   Palo Alto: the Marshes.   Robert Hass.   GeoHom

She dreams the baby's so small she keeps.   Motherhood.   Rita Dove.   NAAAL

She drew an angel down[!]. (LL)   Alexander's Feast; or, The Power of Music [*or* Musique].   Dryden.   GTBS-P; NAEL-5v1; NAEL-6v1; NAEL-7v1; NOBE; PeECV; TFi

She drew back; he was calm.   Subverted Flower, The.   Robert Frost.   APT-1; ColAP; HAP; NOBA; NoAM; OxBA; PoE

She dried her tears, and they did smile.   Emily Jane Brontë.   NOBVV

She Drove a 'Seventies Plymouth.   Robert Minhinnick.   TCAWP

She dwelt among the untrodden ways.   William Wordsworth.   AWP; BoLoP; EnLoPo; GTBS-P; HAP; HeIP-4; NAEL-6v2; NIL-7; NIP-4; NPeEn; OxAEP-2; OxBSP; PAI; PWR; UV; UnPo; WeW-3   *Fr.* Lucy.

She Endeavors to Fascinate Him.   Mary Robinson.   CenSon; RWP

She even meditates on rites of passage.   Gooseflesh.   Janet Fisher.   MFPA

She even thinks that up in heaven.   Countee Cullen.   APT-2; HeIP-4; InPK-6; NIL-7; NIP-4; OBAL; SSLK; TAP; TRP   *Fr.* Four Epitaphs.

She extends the empty cup of her body.   Diminutive.   Nancy Steele.   GifTon

She eyes herself in the mirror.   Salma in Wonderland.   Mona Fayad.   PoArWo

She falls for him, conventional longing well.   Robert Sheppard.   Oth   *Fr.* Empty Diaries/Twentieth Century Blues 24.

She Fans the Word.   Sharif Elmusa.   GraLe

She fears him, and will always ask.   Eros Turannos.   Edwin Arlington Robinson.   APT-1; AmFaPo; HAP; HeIP-4; MoAmPo; NAAL-2v2; NOBA; NoAM; NoP-4; OxBA; PoE; PoPoPo; TAP; TCAPo; TFi; TRP; WoPoe

She feels her hands, scabrous as fish.   Washerwoman, The.   Veronica Volkow.   VCWP, *tr.* by Forrest Gander

She fell asleep on Christmas Eve.   My Sister's Sleep.   Dante Gabriel Rossetti.   NAEL-5v2; NAEL-6v2

She fell away in her first ages spring.   Edmund Spenser.   OBEV   *Fr.* Daphnaïda.

She flees, she flees through flat white lands, as patiently I take my aim.   Song of the Initiate.   Léopold Sédar Senghor.   NegPo, *tr.* by Ellen Conroy Kennedy

She flies she flies through the white flat lands, and patiently I take my aim.   Nocturne (She Flies She Flies).   Léopold Sédar Senghor.   WoPoe, *tr.* by John Reed and Olive Wake

She flitted by me on the stair.   Meeting, The.   Isabel Ecclestone MacKay.   PoBW

She flourished in the 'Twenties, "hectic" days of peace.   Mews Flat Mona.   William Plomer.   FaBoTw

She folds her wings about her sleeping child. (LL)   Bats.   Randall Jarrell.   ChAP; NTCP; OBCA; PAI

She gave it out as if it were.   Aphrodisiac, The.   Medbh McGuckian.   PBCIP

She gave me childhood's flowers.   Heirloom.   Kathleen Jessie Raine.   NALW

"She gives herself;" there's a poetic thought.   Portrait in Black Paint, with a Very Sparing Use of Whitewash.   Elinor Wylie.   NALW

She gives him paper and a fine-nibbed pen.   Trois Petits Tours et Puis . . .   Marie Ponsot.   ExTi

She glided into.   Youth.   Vernon Rowe.   BloBone

She goes but softly, but she goeth sure.   Upon the [*or* a] Snail.   John Bunyan.   OxBSP

She goes on with her story.   Mother and Son.   Alden Nowlan.   RaBo

She goes to different bars.   There Is a Woman in This Town.   Patricia Parker.   BlSi

She goes upstairs early.   Double Bed.   Carol Rumens.   LW

She got pulled down and learned to like it.   Falling.   Joy Katz.   NeAmPo

She grew ninety years through sombre winter.   Epitaph on a Fir-Tree.   Richard Murphy.   FaBoTw

She grew up in bedeviled southern wilderness.   Ballad of Sue Ellen Westerfield, The.   Robert Earl Hayden.   ESEAA; NoAM

She Had a Name.   Edward Thomas.   OxBSP

She had already kissed Antony's dead lips.   Cleopatra.   Anna Andreyevna Akhmatova.   PoetW, *tr.* by Max Hayward and Stanley Kunitz

She had become, the preacher hollows his voice.   Saint Margaret of Cortona.   Eiléan Ní Chuilleanáin.   ModIr

She had blue eyes and light flaxen hair.   Julia A. Moore.   VerBaPo   *Fr.* Hattie House.

She had from Monsieur d'Elbœuf. (LL)   Alas! Poor Queen.   Marion Angus.   NPeEn; NePenScot

She had in her favor.   Magical Devices.   Clara Silva.   TANSG, *tr.* by Celeste Kostopulos-Cooperman

She Had Known Brothers.   Sherley Anne Williams.   GT

She had life in the blood of her eyes, history in her body. With a.   Felipa, La Filosofa de Rincon que Nació a los 98 Años.   Jose Angel Figueroa.   PueRic

She had never desired him in that way.   Maura.   Thomas Lynch.   EmeKit

She had no saying dark enough.   Robert Frost.   TCAPo   *Fr.* Hill Wife, The.

She had nothing.   Girl of Six from the Ghetto Begging in Smolna Street in 1942, A.   Jerzy Ficowski.   HP, *tr.* by Keith Bosley

She had raised the window.   Destination: Tule Lake Relocation Center, May 20, 1942.   James Masao Mitsui.   OpBo

She Had Some Horses.   Joy Harjo.   HATNAP; LoL

Drowning Horses.   NAAL-5

She had the fewer for what she did. (LL)   Cynewulf.   ASW; AnOE   *Fr.* Riddles (Exeter Book).

She had the stance of a snowdrop.   Elaine Randell.   Oth   *Fr.* Snoad Hill Poems, The.

She had thought the studio would keep itself.   Living in Sin.   Adrienne Rich.   NIL-7; NIP-4; NoP-4; SoSe-8; TAP; UnPo

She had to be Milked by a Man and his Wife. (LL)   Cow, The.   Theodore Roethke.   OBAL; OBCA

She had too much so with a smile you took some.   Other, The.   Ted Hughes.   EmeKit

She had travelled through nights and days.   End of the Journey, The.   May Probyn.   VWP

She hadn't found a speck of death. (LL)   How I Learned to Sweep.   Julia Alvarez.   FFC; RA

She hangs out his shirts.   Shirts.   Nigel Jenkins.   TCAWP

She has a full beard when I first meet her.   Hand.   Robert E. Penn.   WiU

She has already kissed Antony's dead lips.   Cleopatra.   Anna Andreyevna Akhmatova.   FaBoWar, *tr.* by Max Hayward and Stanley Kunitz

She has always been clever and poor.   Clever and Poor.   V. Penelope Pelizzon.   AmPoNex

She has been burning palaces. "To see."   Palace-Burner, The.   Sarah Morgan Bryan Piatt.   NCAP; SWaP

She has been condemned to death by hanging.   Marrying the Hangman.   Margaret Atwood.   NOBC

She has been packing all night.   Leaving Yuba City.   Chitra Divakaruni.   GeoHom

She has begun to see men invite themselves.   Professional, The.   David Ignatow.   NNaP

She has calld to her her bower-maidens.   Young Hunting.   *Unknown*.   ESPB

She has decided that she no longer loves me.   Wind in the Tree, The.   Frank Templeton Prince.   OxBSP

She has finished and sealed the letter.   Parting, without a Sequel.   John Crowe Ransom.   MoAmPo; NoP-4; OxBA; SoSe-8

She has gone.   Richard Crist.   HA

She has had to bear. (LL)   Whipping, The.   Robert Earl Hayden.   PAI; PoE; SSLK; SoSe-8

She has left me, my pretty.   Song.   Sylvia Townsend Warner.   MoBrPo

She has no bosom and no behind. (LL)   This Englishwoman.   Stevie Smith.   FaBoEE; NALW

She has not come.   Paulus [*or* Paulos] Silentiarius.   GrAn

She has one good bumblebee.   Head of a White Woman Winking.   James Tate.   BodElec

She has returned, and she has returned.   Morning.   Gabriela Mistral.   TANSG, *tr.* by Maria Jacketti

She has taken a woman lover.   Judy Grahn.   WPOW   *Fr.* Common Woman, The.

She has to pity him after what happened.   Job's Wife.   Shirley Kaufman.   DTA

She has wounded me.   Wound of Love, The.   Heinrich von Morungen.   NAWM-7v1, *tr.* by Peter Dronke

She hated a *mown lawn*.   Mown Lawn, A.   Lydia Davis.   BAP-01

She hath an art[e] to break[e] them with her eyes. (LL)   Thrice Toss[e] These Oaken Ashes in the Air [*or* Ayre].   Thomas Campion.   EBEV; EnLoPo; FaBoCh; HAP; OxBSP; OxBSo; PoRA; SCGP; TFi; WeW-3

She hath forsaken courtly halls and bowers.   Self-Devoted, The.   Agnes Strickland.   CenSon

She hath her reward. (LL)   Man Who Married Magdalene, The.   Anthony Hecht.   ChIV-2; PeLV

She having gainèd both the Wind and Sun. (LL)   Fair Singer, The.   Andrew Marvell.   EnLoPo; FSCP; MeLP; NOBE; NoP-4; SCGP

She heard the mourners wailing one night.   Silent Tear, The.   Ilya Abu Madi.   GraLe, *tr.* by George Dimitri Selim

She hears the infantry of eyes advance. (LL)   Retreat of Ita Cagney, The. Michael Hartnett.   CIP-2; PBCIP

She Hears The Storm.   Thomas Hardy.   NAEL-5v2; NAEL-6v2

She hers, he his, pursuing. (LL)   Dalliance of the Eagles, The.   Walt Whitman. HAP; HeIP-4; NAAL-2v1; NAAL-3; NoP-4; SAmP; TAP; TCAPo; TRP

She holds a candle, advances.   Brides of Elvis, The.   David Ray.   AllShUp

She / holds th mirror to her eye.   My Lai / Remuera / Ponsonby.   David Mitchell.   PeNZ

She holds things together, collects bail,   Judy Grahn.   NALW   *Fr.* Common Woman, The.

She holds to the idea.   Visit.   Gerald William Barrax.   GT

She hopes to hear a word from her.   Adoration of the Anchor.   Laura Jensen. LCAP-2

She hovered hooded, blue-eyed.   Catechism, 1958.   W. M. Ransom.   CDW

She Hugged Me and Kissed Me.   *Unknown.*   BPo

She hung away her years, her eyes grew young.   Waiting for the Bus.   Dennis Joseph Enright.   OxBTC

She I love leaves me, and I leave my friends.   False Bay.   Frank Templeton Prince.   HarvBoo

She in whose lipservice.   Goddess, The.   Denise Levertov.   NALW; NOBA; NeAP; PoM

She is a black crow being driven out of sight.   Drinking the Wind.   "Tan Ying."   WPOW

She is a file.   Necromancy.   Rikki Ducornet.   SurWo

She is a mermaid caught in a net.   Scherzo.   Pamela Alexander.   YaYoPo

She is a reed swaying in blue.   Love Song.   Earle Thompson.   HATNAP

She is about to come. This time.   Lovers, The.   Dorianne Laux.   BodElec; ErotSp

She is all so slight.   After Two Years.   Richard Aldington.   MoBrPo

She is all there.   For My Lover, Returning to His Wife.   Anne Sexton. HCAP; UnPo; WPE

She Is Always Unwilling to Understand.   Paul Éluard.   NAWM-7v2, tr. by Lloyd Alexander

She is always unwilling to understand, to listen.   She Is Always Unwilling to Understand.   Paul Éluard.   NAWM-7v2, *tr. by* Lloyd Alexander

She is as in a field a silken tent.   Silken Tent, The.   Robert Frost.   APT-1; ColAP; InPK-6; NOBA; NoP-4; OxBSo; Son; TAP; TRP; TwCP; WeW-3

She is carried in with half her buttocks gone.   Kim-San.   Steve Denning. CDa

She is crying.   Gloria Gervitz.   MirDau, *tr. by* Stephen Tapscott   *Fr.* Yiskor.

She is dead.   Birthdays.   Hilde Domin.   BoWoP, *tr. by* Tudor Morris

She is facetious, of a gentle nature.   Epigram VII: Winifred.   Hugh Crompton. NOSC

She Is Far from the Land.   Thomas Moore.   NOIV; OxAEP-2

She is Flat on Her Back.   E. Ethelbert Miller.   GT

She is gathering lotos-seed in the river of Yueh.   Girl of Yueh, The.   Li Po. TAL

She is gesture.   Isn't She Not a Bird.   Nina Iskrenko.   PFTM-2, *tr. by* Forrest Gander and Mala Kotamraju

She is gone! The occasion for ever is past!   Lines Written Immediately after Parting from a Lady.   Sir Samuel Egerton Brydges.   NOEC

She is invigilator; her name is knife.   Mother, Dear Mother.   Elma Mitchell. Prnts

She is large and matronly.   Lui et Elle.   D. H. Lawrence.   NoAM

She is like this.   My Mother.   Virginia Cerenio.   ReBoTo

She is liquid darkness occult with desire.   Christopher Dewdney.   FTOS   *Fr.* Concordat Proviso Ascendant.

She is lovely. Her eyes are big almonds.   Sub Shop Girl.   Michael S. Weaver. SpirFl

She is madonna in an art.   Nicholas Vachel Lindsay.   APT-1   *Fr.* Mae Marsh, Motion Picture Actress.

She is my right hand woman, my best friend. I know.   My Muse, the Whore. Linda France.   NeBl

She is neither pink nor pale.   Witch-Wife.   Edna St. Vincent Millay.   APT-1

She Is No Liar.   Robert Graves.   OxBSP

She is no woman, but a sencelesse stone. (LL)   Edmund Spenser.   NAEL-5v1; NoP-4   *Fr.* Amoretti.

She is not dead, but sleepeth.   Mrs. Rebecca Weston.   Mary Weston Fordham. CBWP-2

She is not fair to outward view.   Song.   Hartley Coleridge.   GTBS-P; OBEV

She is not happy as the Poets say.   On Sandro's Flora.   Trumbull Stickney. APN-2

She is old, and bent, and wrinkled.   Marching Still.   Minna Irving.   CBCWP

She is older than the rocks among which she sits.   Mona Lisa.   Walter Pater. OBMV

She is one with your joy. (LL)   How to Get a Baby.   Judith Ortiz Cofer.   NIL-7; PueRic

She is pale, her eyes baggy.   At Breakfast.   Giovanna Pollarolo.   TANSG, *tr. by* Marjorie Agosin

She is rising. Yes.   From the Healing Dark.   Alma Villanueva.   HW

She is shameless, despicable, vile. She.   Zinaida Nikolayevna [*or* Nikolaevna] Gippius.   WPOW, *tr. by* Dianne Levitin

She is Singing to Thee, *Domine!.*   "Michael Field."   VWP

She is sixty. She lives.   Greatest Love, The.   Anna Swirszczynska.   PoSu

She is sleeping, so it's quiet. Then it snows in the rooms.   Tributary.   Leonard Nolens.   TuT, *tr. by* Michael O'Loughlin

She is slim again.   Baby in the House, A.   Patrick Williams.   PNI

She is standing on my eyelids.   Woman in Love.   Paul Éluard.   NAWM-7v2, *tr. by* Lloyd Alexander

She is standing on my lids.   Lady Love.   Paul Éluard.   OBVE; SurPaPo; WoPoe, *tr. by* Samuel Beckett

She is still unborn.   Silentium.   Osip Emilevich Mandelstam [*or* Mandelshtam].   TCRP, *tr. by* Albert C. Todd

She is swinging in a contraption above the heads.   Our Kitty.   Carol Muske. BAP-01

She is talking aesthetics, the dear clever creature.   "Owen Meredith."   VerBaPo   *Fr.* Midges.

She is the fairies' midwife, and she comes.   William Shakespeare.   RB   *Fr.* Romeo and Juliet.

She Is the Greatest Wealth.   Georg Rudolph Weckherlin.   GePo, *tr. by* George C. Schoolfield

She is the one you call sister.   Mirror in Which Two Are Seen as One, The. Adrienne Rich.   NAAL-2v2; NNaP

She is the thing that she despises. (LL)   Hue and Cry after Fair Amoret, A. William Congreve.   NOEC; NPeEn; OBEV; OxBEV

She is the woman hanging from the 13th floor.   Woman Hanging from the Thirteenth Floor Window, The.   Joy Harjo.   GLP; HATNAP

She is tougher than me, harder.   For My Mother.   Iain Crichton Smith.   OxBS

She is weeping for her lost right arm.   Weeping Woman.   Denise Levertov. AF

She issues radiant from her dressing-room.   George Meredith.   NOBVV   *Fr.* Modern Love.

She juliets him from a window in Soho.   Short Time.   Gavin Ewart.   NoAM

She just got here yesterday.   Sweet Georgia Brown.   Kenneth Casey.   ReLy

She keeps the memory-game.   Net, The.   Fleur Adcock.   PeNZ

She kept an antique shop—or it kept her.   My Grandmother.   Elizabeth Jennings.   HarvBoo; NoP-4

She kept her secret well, oh, yes.   My Angeline.   Harry Bache Smith.   NBLV

She kept her songs, they took so little space.   Love Songs in Age.   Philip Larkin.   OxBEV

She: King. Father. Mother. Husband. Wife.   Testing the Confucian Ideal. *Vietnamese Oral Tradition.*   CaDao, *tr. by* John Balaban

She kissed me for good-night. So you'll not tell. (LL)   Match with the Moon, A.   Dante Gabriel Rossetti.   NOBVV; NPeEn; OxBEV

She knelt in prayer. A stream of sunset fell.   Costanza.   Felicia Dorothea Hemans.   RWP

She knew more about me *than* let us say.   Isolate.   Clarence Major.   PmAP

She knows them all. Urchins. Beggars.   Left Eye of Odin, The.   Regina DeCormier-Shekejian.   TWW

She knows where to get cracked eggs, does Nelly.   Old Nelly's Birthday.   Ruth Pitter.   NALW

She languorously swings her tongue.   Domesticity of Giraffes, The.   Judith Beveridge.   BMAP

She Lay All Naked.   *Unknown.*   BoLoP

She Lay All Naked in Her Bed.   She Lay All Naked.   *Unknown.*   BoLoP

She lay all night beside me.   Paulus [*or* Paulos] Silentiarius.   GrAn

She lay, and serving-men her lithe arms took.   Abishag.   Rainer Maria Rilke. AWP, *tr. by* Jethro Bithell

She lay beside me in the dawn. (LL)   Alba.   Ezra Pound.   HAP; TCAPo; WeW-3

She lay beside the bridge. The German troops had reckoned.   Retribution.   Ilya Grigoryevich Ehrenburg [*or* Erenburg].   TCRP, *tr. by* Gordon McVay

She lay in her girlish sleep at ninety-six.   Castoff Skin.   Ruth Whitman. InPK-6

She Lay Wrapped.   Gail Fox.   NOBC

She leaned her back unto a thorn.   Cruel Mother, The.   *Unknown.*   ESPB

She leaned her head upon her hand.   Vashti.   Frances Ellen Watkins Harper. BlSi; NALW

She leaned in a small fist on the cushions, buds in her pajamas. "Make me a story."   Blue Shade.   Aaron Shurin.   FTOS

She leaves.   Michael McClintock.   HA

She left me at the silent time.   Lines Written in the Bay of Lerici.   Shelley. NAEL-6v2

She left then, spitting the reek of soil.   Shipping the Pictures from Belfast. Catherine Byron.   Prnts

She licked my salty nose.   Old People.   Michael Davitt.   PBCIP, *tr. by* Michael Hartnett

She lied as much as she could, while she lived.   Epitaph: On the Near-Death Experience.   Ellis Owen.   WoPoe, *tr.* by Anthony Conran

She Lies Silent.   Christopher Pilling.   NLP

She lies silent, her head in The Plague.   She Lies Silent.   Christopher Pilling. NLP

She lies tonight.   Melancholic.   Li Ho.   CrYelRi; ErotSp, *tr.* by Sam Hamill

She liked mornings the best—Thomas gone.   Weathering Out.   Rita Dove. ESEAA; LCAP-2; NoAM

She liked the blue drapes. They made a star.   Couple in the Next Room, The. John Ashbery.   BodElec

She likes it, the conjugal act.   *Unknown.*   GifTon, *tr.* by David Ray

She Lived.   Lucille Clifton.   LoL

She lived in the hovel alone, the beautiful child.   Scape-Goat, The.   Agnes Mary Frances Robinson.   VWP

She lives a prisoner within.   Shut-In, The.   Nellie De Hearn.   PoToHe

She lives alone now.   Poet Reflects On Her Solitary Fate, The.   Sandra Cisneros.   FFC

She lives in the porter's room; the plush is nicotined.   Bitter Sanctuary.   Harold Monro.   FaBoMo; OBMV

She Looked at the Sun.   Tadeusz Rózewicz.   PoSu, *tr.* by Magnus F. Krynski

She looked over his shoulder.   Shield of Achilles, The.   W. H. Auden.   EBEV; FaBoMo; GTBS-P; HAP; NAEL-5v2; NAEL-6v2; NOBE; NOCV; NPeEn; NoAM; NoP-4; OxBEV; PeECV; PoE; WeW-3

She love me, loves me not.   Vladimir Vladimirovich Mayakovsky [*or* Maiakovskii].   *See* She loves me? She loves me not?

She Loves.   Olga Broumas.   GLP

She loves, and she confesses too.   Honour.   Abraham Cowley.   BoLoP

She loves him. . . and what small child could deny.   Americanized.   Bruce Dawe.   CBAP

She Loves Me.   Sheldon Harnick.   ReLy

She Loves Me, She Loves Me Not.   Dmitry [*or* Dmitrii] Sergeievich Merezhkovsky [*or* Merezhkovskii].   TCRP, *tr.* by Albert C. Todd

She loves me? She loves me not?   Mayakovsky's Suicide Note.   Vladimir Vladimirovich Mayakovsky [*or* Maiakovskii].   TCRP

She lowers her fragrant curtain.   Song.   Liu Yung.   ErotSp, *tr.* by Sam Hamill

She made him an amulet.   Wanderer in the Night of the World, A.   N. V. M. Gonzalez.   ReBoTo

She made the trip daily, though.   Drapery Factory, Gulfport, Mississippi, 1956. Natasha Trethewey.   SpirFl

She makes her way through the dark trees.   Country Wife, The.   Dana Gioia. RA

She may count three little daisies very well.   Gertrude Stein.   NoP-4   *Fr.* Stanzas in Meditation.

She may not accuse me.   Friedrich von Hausen.   GePo

She means two things.   Stereograph: 1903.   Julie Fay.   NAPBL

She Mends an Ancient Wireless.   Paul Durcan.   PBCIP

She might, so noble from head.   Thought from Propertius, A.   W. B. Yeats. OxBSP

She minds the lilacs.   Hopper's Women.   Sue Standing.   PoSol

She most, and in her look sums all delight. (LL)   John Milton.   OxAEP-1; PeECV   *Fr.* Paradise Lost.

She mourned the long-ears.   Jugged Hare.   Jean Earle.   TCAWP

She Moved through the Fair.   Padraic Colum.   BIrV; NOIV

She never puts her toys away.   Patty-Poem.   Nick Kenny.   PoToHe

She never will say no. (LL)   I Care Not for These Ladies.   Thomas Campion. HAP; NAEL-5v1; NAEL-7v1; NoP-4; NoSic; PoE; SCGP

She / not to be confused with she, a dog.   Lady Tactics.   Anne Waldman. PoM

She of the Impudent Face.   Bible, *O.T.*   TrJP   *Fr.* Proverbs.

She, only she, can please the taste! (LL)   To an Author.   Philip Freneau. ColAP; NOBA; OxBA

She passed away like morning dew.   Early Death.   Hartley Coleridge.   OBEV

She passed with her mother. What rare beauty!   Cowardice.   Amado Nervo. BLPSL, *tr.* by Rene de Costa, Rigas Kappatos and Eleni Paidoussi

She peeked out from under.   Missing Patriarch, The.   Michael S. Weaver. PBCAP

She picks me.   Women.   Zakiyya Malallah.   PoArWo, *tr.* by Wen Chin Ouyang

She played me false, but that's not why.   Our Photograph[s].   Frederick Locker-Lampson.   NBLV; NOBL; PeLV

She plays Miles, rolls another joint.   Shunning an Imperative.   Carl Hancock Rux.   HeMarv

She plucked one thread.   Paulus [*or* Paulos] Silentiarius.   GrAn

She points to a star.   Fortune Teller, The.   Fu'ad [*or* Fuad] Rifqa [*or* Rifka]. BBASP; MAP, *tr.* by Sargon Boulus and Samuel Hazo

She practices a fugue, though it can matter.   Suburban Sonnet.   Gwen Harwood.   CBAP

She presses her dark lips.   Girl/Spit.   Lisa Coffman.   AmPoNex

She Proves the Inconsistency of the Desires and Criticism of Men Who Accuse Women of What They Themselves Cause.   Sister Juana Inés de la Cruz. BoWoP, *tr.* by Aliki and Willis Barnstone

She put away her hats.   Mistress, The.   Pamela Gillilan.   Prnts

She puts her face against the wall.   She Cries.   John Montague.   BiHa

She puts on a silken blouse and comes down from the western chamber.   Su Man-shu.   SuSp   *Fr.* Poems Written during My Sojourn in Japan.

She raised her head. With hot and glittering eye.   Mother's Charge, The.   Charlotte Perkins Stetson Gilman.   SWaP

She re-enters her life.   Returning.   Linda Pastan.   WeW-3

She reads, of course, what he's doing, shaking Nixon's hand.   Women Who Love Elvis All Their Lives, The.   Fleda Brown Jackson.   AllShUp

She remarks how the style of a whole age.   Moment of Waking, The.   John Tranter.   BMAP

She remembered seeing the underpass up ahead.   Pink Rose Rings, The. Tracey Herd.   MFPA; NeBl

She remembered to the very end.   Annunciations.   Nuala Ni Dhomhnaill. ModIr, *tr.* by Michael Hartnett

She retires from life's uncertainties, he plunges.   Kundiman.   Bataan Faigao. ReBoTo

She rises among boulders. Naked, alone.   Bath of Aphrodite.   Brewster Ghiselin.   APT-2

She rises mostly every day.   On a Girl Who Took Action for Breach of Promise.   Amanda Ros.   VerBaPo

She roamed the meadows long in hope.   Recompensed?   Henrietta Cordelia Ray.   CBWP-3

She rose from the water like a mermaid.   Mermaid's Song.   James C. McCullagh.   PoCoUp

She Rose to His Requirement—Dropt.   Emily Dickinson.   NALW

She rose upon her feet.   Minor Elegy, A.   "Igor Severyanin" [*or* Severianin]. TCRP, *tr.* by Bernard Meares

She's a big teaser. She took him half the way there.   Big Tease.   Ania Walwicz.   BMAP

She's a copperheaded waitress.   Judy Grahn.   NALW   *Fr.* Common Woman, The.

She's a Latin from Manhattan.   Harry Warren.   ReLy

She's always expecting disaster.   Why She Hurries Out, Then Home.   Martha Rhodes.   OPRER

She's combed his neckties out of her hair.   Widow, A.   Ted Kooser.   PBCAP

She's daft to refuse the laird o' Cockpen. (LL)   Laird o' Cockpen, The. Carolina Oliphant, Baroness Nairne.   NOBRP; NPeEn; OxBEV; WPE

She's empty: hark, she sounds: there's nothing there.   Nahum 2.10.   Francis Quarles.   ChIV-1

She's Free!   Frances Ellen Watkins Harper.   BlSi; Son

She's Funny That Way (I Got a Woman, Crazy for Me).   Neil Moret.   ReLy

She's gone! Call Rape! Call Robbers! Violence!.   Meleager.   GrAn

She's gone. She was my love, my moon or more.   Complaint.   James Wright (1927–80).   NOBA; TAP; VGW

She's heating you some soup. (LL)   Old Woman Nature.   Gary Snyder.   BB; NoAM; RaBo

She's looking out of the picture. The bars across her face hold her in the picture and.   Motive for Mayhem, A.   Abigail Child.   FTOS

She's my lover.   One or More Together.   John Godfrey.   FTOS

She's no more wit to ask than to deny. (LL)   Charles Cotton.   OxBSo; Son

She's not a faultless woman; no!   James Kenneth Stephen.   EBVV; NOBVV   *Fr.* After the Golden Wedding.

She's not and never can be mine. (LL)   Coventry Patmore.   OBEV; OxAEP-2; SacPr   *Fr.* Angel in the House, The.

She's now yo' own. Salute yo' bride! (LL)   Slave Marriage Ceremony Supplement.   *Unknown.*   BPo; TAP

She's out there again with her five-cent.   Another Spring on Olmstead Street. Len Roberts.   UrbNat

She's put the child to sleep.   Issa.   EH, *tr.* by Robert Hass

She's resting in the bosom of Jesus. (LL)   Go Down Death.   James Weldon Johnson.   ISC; SacPr

She's slim and seems distracted, the social worker.   Midlife.   Joseph Millar. OPRER

She's somewhere in the sunlight strong.   Song.   Richard Le Gallienne.   OBEV

She's the camera.   Judy-One.   Haki R. Madhubuti.   TAP

She's there in the way you mark a cross.   There.   Caroline Natzler.   Prnts

She said, I am wrong to want something more, it's true.   Words in the Shadow. Victor Hugo.   WoPoe, *tr.* by Louis Simpson

She said: "I'm god and all."   Against a Sickness: To the Female Double Principle God.   Alan Dugan.   NoAM

She said, "I was not born to mope at home in loneliness."   Ride round the Parapet, The.   Friedrich Rückert.   AWP, *tr.* by James Clarence Mangan

She said, If tomorrow my world were torn in two.   Phyllis McGinley.   APT-2; WPE   *Fr.* I Know a Village.

She said it was a better way to die. Her Final Show. Rafael Campo.
   BloBone
She said she'd do. Love Before Dinner. Alfred A. Yuson. ReBoTo
She said she don't love me anymore because I drink whiskey. *Unknown*. STP
   Fr. Kiowa "49" Songs.
She said she forgave me. Parted. Clara Ann Thompson. CBWP-2
She said she would come. Sosei. OHPJ
She said she would marry him. Listen. Marylin Butler. CDa
She said that underneath the surface. American Variation on How Rilke Loved
   a Princess and Got to Stay in Her Castle. Alan Dugan. BodElec
She said the Jehovah Witness man. Gayl Jones. BlSi *Fr.* Journal.
She said: the pitying audience melt in tears. Pope. EBNV *Fr.* Rape of the
   Lock; an Heroi-Comical Poem, The.
She said, "They gave me of their best." After Aughrim. Emily Lawless.
   OBEV
She said to one: "How glows." Subalterns. Elizabeth Daryush. OBWP
She said, Wear my leather jacket, a looser. How to Dress Like a Scary Dyke.
   Jane Barnes. GLP
She sang beyond the genius of the sea. Idea of Order at Key West, The.
   Wallace Stevens. APT-1; AmFaPo; ColAP; HAP; HCAP; HarvBoo; HeIP-
   4; MakPoe; MoAmPo; NAAL-2v2; NAAL-5; NAWM-7v2; NIL-7; NIP-4;
   NOBA; NoAM; NoP-4; OxBA; PoE; PoPoPo; SAmP; TAP; TFi
She sang this "Song of the Shirt!" (LL) Song of the Shirt, The. Thomas
   Hood. BRP; EBVV
She sat and looked at a picture. Her Son. Ebba M. Leaf. PWR
She sat and sang alway. Song. Christina Georgina Rossetti. NAEL-5v2;
   NAEL-6v2
She sat and wept beside His feet; the weight. "Multum Dilexit." Hartley
   Coleridge. SacPr
She sat at tea just like the others. First. Going Blind. Rainer Maria Rilke.
   BLT, *tr. by* Walter Arndt
She sat by the fire and told many a fine tale. (LL) Clever Hen, The.
   Unknown. LB; ReMoGo
She sat down below a thorn. Cruel Mother, The. *Unknown*. ESPB; InPK-6;
   OxBB
She sat on a shelf. Motherhood. May Swenson. CoAP; NoP-4
She sat on a willow-trunk. Fly, The. Miroslav Holub. NPeEn; PoSu; PoetW;
   RB, *tr. by* Ian Milner and George Theiner
She sat on the willow bark. Miroslav Holub. *See* She sat on a willow-trunk
She sat up on her pillows, receiving guests. Douglas Dunn. NoP-4 *Fr.*
   Elegies.
She saw Africa as a continent. White Poetess. Musaemura Bonus Zimunya.
   PeSAV
She saw on her home street. Survivor, The. Thomas Dorsett. BloBone
She saying, You don't have to do anything. One You Wanted to Be Is the One
   You Are, The. Jean Valentine. BodElec; ExTi
She says. So Now You're Chicana. Carol Lem. GeoHom
She Says, Cocks Are Crowing! *Unknown*. CoBCP, *tr. by* Burton Watson
She says "How was you?" Kissing. "Come on in." Unrecorded Speech. Anna
   Adams. BrRo
She says she is going to kill. Joy Harjo. NAAL-5 *Fr.* She Had Some
   Horses.
She Schools the Flighty Pupils of Her Eyes. Gerard Manley Hopkins. OxBSP
She seemed to be a witch. (LL) John Skelton. EBEV; PoE *Fr.* Tunnyng [*or*
   Tunning] of Elynour [*or* Elinor] Rummyng [*or* Rumming], The.
She seems to come by wing. Jackson Mac Low. PFTM-2 *Fr.* Pronouns,
   The—A Collection of 40 Dances—For the Dancers.
She sells sea-shells on the sea shore. She Sells Sea-shells. *Unknown*. OTCP
She Sent Him Away. Clara Ann Thompson. CBWP-2
She sent him off to war for nothing but a title. (LL) Silent at Her Window.
   Wang Ch'ang-ling. ColAnChi; CrYelRi, *tr. by* Sam Hamill
She shakes feathers toward him. Pay Cash Only. James Sherry. FTOS
She shakes in the take-off lounge. Frightened Flier Goes North, The. Judith
   Kazantzis. BrRo
She shall live in the proud memorial of your arms! (LL) Appeal. Noémia da
   Sousa. PBMAP; TTY; WPOW
She sharpened her knife both sharp and keen. Young Hunting. *Unknown*.
   OxBoLi
She, she and she and she. Divestment of Beauty. Laura Riding Jackson.
   APT-2; HarvBoo
She should have died hereafter. William Shakespeare. SoSe-8 *Fr.* Macbeth.
She shuffles to the door on faded scuffs. Curandera, La. Diana García.
   TouFir
She shuts out the city now. Lonely Woman's Room, The. Ahmad 'Abd al-
   Mu'ti Hijazi. MAP, *tr. by* Sargon Boulus and Peter Porter
She sights a Bird—she chuckles—. Cat. Emily Dickinson. SAmP
She sits beside: through four low panes of glass. Nightfall. "Michael Field."
   VWP

She sits in her glass garden. One Whose Reproach I Cannot Evade, The.
   George Hitchcock. SPE
She sits in the marketplace. Pearle's Poem. Primus St. John. GT
She sits in the park. Her clothes are out of date. In The Park. Gwen
   Harwood. BMAP; CBAP; NIL-7
She sits in the tawny vapour. Wife in London, A. Thomas Hardy. NOBVV;
   OBWP
She sits naked on a rock. Last Gods. Galway Kinnell. PasH; RaBo
She sits on a smoldering couch. Woman on the Dump, The. Elizabeth Spires.
   EmeKit
She sits on the mountain that is her home. Night Music. Linda Gregg. BLT
She sits on tumulus Savoor, and stares. Flax. Ivan Alekseievich Bunin.
   AWP, *tr. by* Babette Deutsch and Avrahm Yarmolinsky
She sits there. Girl at the Window. Pinkie Gordon Lane. GT
She sits with. Young Woman at a Window. William Carlos Williams.
   HHAm
She sits with one hand poised against her head, the. Dialogue. Adrienne Rich.
   NIL-7; TAP
She skimmed the yellow water like a moth. My Grandmother's Ghost. James
   Wright (1927–80). Son
She skips on to the day's next blue radius. Maggie. Duane Niatum.
   HATNAP
She Sleeps. T. Carmi. MHP, *tr. by* Ruth Finer Mintz
She sleeps and rests on the candor of the sand. Negro Mask. Léopold Sédar
   Senghor. NegPo, *tr. by* Ellen Conroy Kennedy
She sleeps so lightly, that in trembling fear. Hush. Mary Elizabeth Coleridge.
   PoBW
She sleeps: yet is her hand awake. She Sleeps. T. Carmi. MHP, *tr. by* Ruth
   Finer Mintz
She slings her rugs faithfully. Beatings. Will Wells. GotH
She slipped. Heels over head she landed. Portrait. Gail Fox. NOBC
She smelled like bananas just as sure. Nature of Braille, The. Anthony Butts.
   AmPoNex
She smiled behind a lawny cloud. Fancy Dress. Dorothea MacKellar.
   NOBAu
She Smiled like a Holiday. *Unknown*. OxBoLi
She sought him east, she sought him west. Rare Willie Drowned in Yarrow; or,
   The Water o Gamrie. *Unknown*. ESPB
She Speaks the Morning's Filigree. Philip Lamantia. VGW
She Speaks to Her Husband, Asleep. Robert Schultz. AWTN
She speaks with the accent of her wild seas. Stranger, The. Gabriela Mistral.
   SpanPo, *tr. by* Kate Flores
She spent her money with such perfect style. Rapist's Villanelle, The.
   Thomas M. [*or* "Tom"] Disch. RA
She spent three hundred and sixty four days a year. Grandmother Jackson.
   David Jackson. OBCP
She spreads her pale legs. In the Purple Bar. Gig Ryan. BMAP
She springs from the ground-clinging thicket, her face. Veneris Venefica
   Agrestis. Lucio Piccolo. OBVE, *tr. by* Charles Tomlinson
She stamps and shivers. Entering the Mare. Katie Donovan. NeBl
She stands as pale as Parian statues stand. Soul, A. Christina Georgina
   Rossetti. NALW; WPOW
She stands as pale as Parian statues stand. Study (A Soul), A. Christina
   Georgina Rossetti. VWP
She stands by the table, poised. Vermeer. Stephen Mitchell. GI
She started up from where the lizard lies. On Rodin's "L'Illusion, Sœur
   d'Icare." Trumbull Stickney. APN-2
She stitched her story on black. Constellation Quilt, The. Mei-Mei
   Berssenbrugge. OpBo
She stole my pencil-case, red leather. Thief, The. Josephine Jacobsen. WPE
She stood breast-high amid the corn. Ruth. Thomas Hood. BoLoP; ChIV-1;
   EnLoPo; NOBE; OBEV
She stood close to a tree and wrinkled. Tree Old Woman. Samuel
   Makidemewabe. STP, *tr. by* Howard Norman
She stood in her scarlet gown. *Unknown*. MLL *Fr.* Carmina Burana.
She stood nakedly. After Her Man Had Left Her for the Sixth Time That Year
   (An Uncommon Occurrence). Haki R. Madhubuti. GT
She Stoops to Conquer. Oliver Goldsmith.
   Song: "Let school-masters puzzle their brain." BIrV; NOIV
   (Three Jolly Pigeons, The.) PoRA
She stopped traffic. Tribal Marks. Saundra Sharp. SpirFl
She stops combing her hair. Tune: Dreaming of the South. Wen T'ing-yün.
   CoBCP, *tr. by* Burton Watson
She strolls in the valley, alone. Madwoman at Rodmell. Michele Roberts.
   BrRo
She swam smiling in the river. Waiting to Be Fed. Ray A. Young Bear.
   CDW
She talks not, plays not, visits not, in bed. *Unknown*. FaBoEE
She Teaches Him to Reach Out. Martha Elizabeth. PasH

She Tells Her Love While Half Asleep. Robert Graves. BoLoP; EBEV; FaBoTw; NOBE; OxBTC

She tells me she will find a letter. Woman of Three Minds, The. Thomas Centolella. GifTon

She tells me with claret she cannot agree. Drinking Song. *Unknown*. NOBL

She tells us she felt. Clinic, The. Grace Herman. BloBone

She tests the curb with a chubby boot. For Heather, Entering Kindergarten. Roberta Hill Whiteman. HATNAP; NoAM

She that but little patience knew. On a Political Prisoner. W. B. Yeats. OBMV

She, / the eskimo's woman. Eskimo's Woman, The. Anabel Torres. TANSG, *tr. by* Celeste Kostopulos-Cooperman

She, the river. Woman. Hira Bansode. ItWoWo; OMIP; WoPoe, *tr. by* Vinay Dharwadker

She, the sensual creature, the green singer. Slow Dancer That No One Hears but You. Duane Niatum. CDW

She Thinks in Song. Femi Osofisan. NAfrP

She Thinks of Her Beloved. Lu Chi. OHMPC, *tr. by* Kenneth Rexroth

She thus; when I had great desire to prove. Homer. OBVE *Fr.* Odyssey.

She Tied Up Her Few Things. John Clare. HAP

She Ties Her Bandanna. Beth Cuthand. ReEnLa

She, to Him. Thomas Hardy.
   "This love puts all humanity from me." TOF
   "When you shall see me in the toils of Time." OxBTC

She told how they used to form for the country dances. One We Knew. Thomas Hardy. NAEL-5v2; NAEL-6v2

She told me she had always fantasized. Black Slip. Terry Wolverton. WiU

She told the story, and the whole world wept. Harriet Beecher Stowe. Paul Laurence Dunbar. BPo; PoPoPo

She, too, the voyaging in doors and Keys. This Alice. Herbert Morris. PoRA

She too went dark as dusk began, though rising. On the Death of Cleopatra-Selene. Crinagoras. GrAn, *tr. by* Alistair Elliot

She took such good care of him. Widower. David Ray. SpudSo

She took the dappled partridge flecked [*or* fleckt] with blood. Sonnet. Tennyson. NAEL-5v2; NAEL-6v2

She tosses and rumples alone on the double bed. Flying Fox. Thomas William Shapcott. CBAP

She touches me. Her fingers nibble gently. In Love. David Wevill. MoCV

She transplanted each spruce, blue as the. Spruce. Phillip [*or* "Phil"] William George. VoR

She tried to warn us. Justice of the Peace, The. Alison Luterman. MPUn

She trips across the meadows. April. Henrietta Cordelia Ray. CBWP-3

She turned in the high pew, until her sight. Church Romance, A. Thomas Hardy. FaBoTw; NOBE; OxAEP-2; OxBSo; OxBTC; PeECV

She turns and calls him by name. His Wife. "Rachel" [*or* "Rahel"]. WPOW, *tr. by* Sholom J. Kahn

She turns onions into zeroes on the cutting board. Household Rules. Farwell Avenue, Chicago, 1946. Lisa Ress. GotH

She turns the child. Anita Virgil. HA

She turns them over in her slow hands. Mongoloid Child Handling Shells on the Beach, A. Richard Snyder. InPK-6; NIL-7

She twirled the string of golden beads. Illustration of a Picture. Oliver Wendell Holmes. TreFP

She used to. Emily Dickinson's Defunct. Marilyn Nelson Waniek. ESEAA

She used to flash her fingers through the flame. Heroine. Paul Groves. AngWePo

She used to let her golden hair fly free. Petrarch. NAWM-5v1; NAWM-7v1, *tr. by* Morris Gilbert Bishop *Fr.* Sonnets to Laura.

She wadna bake, she wadna brew. Wife Wrapt in Wether's Skin, The. *Unknown*. ESPB

She waited on the 7th floor. Frank Albert and Viola Benzena Owens. Ntozake Shange. BlSi

She / wakes up each day with the dawn. Crazed Woman, The. Jeannette Miller. TANSG, *tr. by* Paula Vega

She walked in the garden. Che Sara Sara. Rose Terry Cooke. SWaP

She walked nude beside them. Springtime. Norman Henry Pritchard, II. GT

She Walked Unaware. Patrick MacDonogh. BoLoP; FaBoTw

She walks down the road. Girl with the Green Skirt. Dana Naone. CDW

She Walks in Beauty. Byron. AWP; AmFaPo; BRP; BoLoP; CABP; FHYEP; GTBS-P; HeIP-4; ITBLP; NAEL-5v2; NAEL-6v2; NOBE; NOBRP; NePenScot; NoP-4; OBEV; OxAEP-2; OxBEV; PoE; PoPoPo; SCGP; TFi

She walks in beauty like the night. She Walks In Beauty. Byron. AWP; AmFaPo; BRP; BoLoP; CABP; FHYEP; GTBS-P; HeIP-4; ITBLP; NAEL-5v2; NAEL-6v2; NOBE; NOBRP; NePenScot; NoP-4; OBEV; OxAEP-2; OxBEV; PoE; PoPoPo; SCGP; TFi

She walks—the lady of my delight. Shepherdess, The. Alice Thompson Meynell. AWP; MoBrPo; NOBVV

She wanted a little room for thinking. Daystar. Rita Dove. AmFaPo; LCAP-2; NAAAL; NIL-7; NIP-4; OxWW

She wanted her ashes scattered. Marty's Mother. Stephen Kessler. GeoHom

She wanted pretty fine. Aunt Jessie. Wanda Coleman. GT

She wanted rain. Dust. Kathleen Spivack. BoWoP

She wanted to tread the surge of the sea. Beams. Paul Verlaine. SxFrPo, *tr. by* Martin Sorrell

She Wants. David Baratier. AmPoNex

She wants a man she can just. Roadmap. Harryette Mullen. ISC

She wants me to hear the whole story. Coincidentally. Frederic W. Platt. BloBone

She wants to hear. Sunday Greens. Rita Dove. GT; LCAP-2

She Warns Him. Frances Darwin Cornford. EnLoPo

She was a beautiful animal. Nijinksy's Dog. Susan Hahn. IllVoic

She was a brazen package of smoulder. Party, The. Ben Scammell. NLP

She was a child's purse, full of useless things. (LL) Death of an Irishwoman. Michael Hartnett. CIP-2; EmeKit; PBCIP

She was a dear little dicky bird. She Was One of the Early Birds. T. W. Connor. OBCoV

She was a maid of high degree. He Took Her. Tom Masson. OBAL

She Was a Phantom of Delight. William Wordsworth. *See* Perfect Woman

She Was a Queen. Hartley Coleridge. OxAEP-2

She was a queen of noble Nature's crowning. She Was a Queen. Hartley Coleridge. OxAEP-2

She was a small dog, neat and fluid. Praise of a Collie. Norman MacCaig. NePenScot; RB

She was a woman obsessed by an old book. Beyond Phigalia. Alec Derwent Hope. BMAP

She was a year younger. Picture Bride. Cathy Song. AiP

She was able to kill herself. Way Down, The. Ernest Sandeen. CRP

She was all woman, all women to me. One Flesh. Julia Casterton. Prnts

She was alone that evening—and alone. Lonely Lady, The. Charlotte Brontë. VWP

She was already lean when. Parting. A. R. Ammons. NoAM

She was an evil stepmother. She Does Not Remember. Anna Swirszczynska. BLT

She was at work on a poem about breath. Poem about Breath. David Wagoner. NoAM

She was blushing in the misty green of August. Good Night! Gilbert Sorrentino. FTOS

She was born with sand in her mouth. Urban Aboriginal. Jack Davis. IBA

She was buying an elixir. Buying. Jean Follain. BLT, *tr. by* Heather McHugh

She was caught, a young girl of Uttoxeter. Limerick. Tim Hopkins. PeLi

She was cleaning—there is always. Black Silk. Tess Gallagher. EmeKit; FaBoWP

She was four, he was one, it was raining, we had colds. Clasp, The. Sharon Olds. BodElec

She was given to fits. Crazy Girl, The. Sharan Strange. InTrad

She was going on the bus he could see. Woman Looking Through a Viewmaster. C. D. Wright. LCAP-2

She was in terrible pain the whole day. Wedding, A. James Tate. NoAM

She was just risen from her bended knee. Girl at Her Devotions, A. Letitia [*or* Laetitia] Elizabeth Landon. VWP

She was little. To My Little Girl. Shakuntala Hawoldar. HAWP

She was made from scratch in Wisconsin. American Cheese. G. E. Murray. IllVoic

She was most like a rose, when it flushes rarest. Gone Before. Christina Georgina Rossetti. PoBW

She was my staff and I am blind. Jana Bai. BoWoP

She was old. She lived alone in a small house. Knife. Gloria Vando. TouFir

She Was One of the Early Birds. T. W. Connor. OBCoV

She Was Poor but She Was Honest. *Unknown*. NOBL
(Poor But Honest.) NBLV; RB

She was pure and white, resembling the sun as it rises. Separation by Death. Ibn Hazm al-Andalusi. RaBo, *tr. by* A. R. Nykl

She was skilled in music and the dance. Alas! Poor Queen. Marion Angus. NPeEn; NePenScot

She was so aesthetic and culchud. Cultured Girl Again, The. Ben King. OBAL

She was so small, that sometimes I would walk into. Her First Week. Sharon Olds. ExTi

She was still upset. Bubba Esther, 1888. Ruth Whitman. TaR

She Was Telling It This Way. Laura Tohe. ReEnLa

She was the daughter of a fishmonger, she stood. Theatrical Venus. George Buchanan. PNI

She was the joke of the angels—a girl. Saint Rose of Lima. Judith Ortiz Cofer. PueRic; TouFir

She was the one who lived up country. After Reading "The Country of the Pointed Firs." Jean Garrigue. VCAP

She was the woman who drank us up. Woman Who Drank Us Up, The. Lesley Quayle. Prnts

She was there on the mountain. Flower No More Than Itself, A. Linda Gregg. BBASP

She was thinner, with a mannered gauntness. Bistro Styx, The. Rita Dove. NoP-4

She was too kind, wooed too persistently. Samuel Butler (1835–1902). OxBSo

She was urgent to speak of the moon: she offered delight. Old Woman Speaks of the Moon, An. Ruth Pitter. WPE

She was young! She was pure! She was new! She was nice! Have Some Madeira, M'dear? Michael Flanders. OBCoV

She washed and washed the pity from her hands. (LL) Intruder, The. Carolyn Kizer. BoWoP; InPK-6

She watched all day that she might see him pass. "George Eliot." LW Fr. How Lisa Loved the King.

She watches him reaching for oranges. Art History (Sandro Botticelli). Alena N´dvorníková. SurWo

She wears her middle age like a cowled. From a Correct Address in a Suburb of a Major City. Helen Sorrells. PAI; WPE

She weaves away at the bower. To-and-Fro of Saint Theresa. Alfonso Reyes. WoPoe, tr. by Samuel Beckett

She weighed / three hundred pounds. Walking the Dog. John Wright. BloBone

She went along the road. Hagar. Francis Lauderdale Adams. OxBS

She went back to her hometown. Mom and Dad Getting Older. Sarah Rosenblatt. AmPoNex

She went out making hats when she was young. Hats. Jean Pedrick. WWork

She Went to Stay. Robert Creeley. OBAL

She went up the hill to pick angelica. Old Poem. Unknown. WoPoe, tr. by Burton Watson

She went up the mountain to pluck wild herbs. Old and New. Unknown. AWP; ChiP, tr. by Arthur Waley

She Wept, She Railed. Stanley Kunitz. VGW

She whispers to me she says to me she says to me to me she she. Her, Me, and Yochanan. Chava Pinchas-Cohen. DTA, tr. by Miriyam Glazer

She, who could neither rest nor sleep. Sadi [or Saadi or Sa'di]. AWP, tr. by L. Cranmer-Byng Fr. Gulistan, The.

She Who First Bore Our People. Unknown. CoBCP, tr. by Burton Watson

She who has forgotten. Yr Iaith. Nigel Jenkins. AngWePo

She who has no love for women. Calliope in the Labour Ward. Elaine Feinstein. BrRo

She who hath felt a real pain. John Gay. EnLoPo

She who in the beginning gave birth to the people. Origin-Legend of the Chou Tribe. Unknown. ChiP, tr. by Arthur Waley

She Who Is Always in My Thoughts. Bhartrihari. BoLoP, tr. by John Brough

She who is always in my thoughts prefers. She Who Is Always In My Thoughts. Bhartrihari. BoLoP, tr. by John Brough

She Who Listens. Elana Klugman. HW

She who shook and swayed among the chorus. Macedonius. GrAn

She who to Heaven more Heaven doth annex. On a Virtuous Young Gentlewoman That Died Suddenly. William Cartwright. HAP; OBEV

She who was burned more than half her body skipped out of death. Praises, The. Charles Olson. VGW

She-Who-Watches . . . The Names are Prayer. Elizabeth Woody. OPRER

She who worked patiently. Charles Reznikoff. APT-2

She Will Gather Roses. Unknown. OxIBACP

She will know. (LL) Scuba Diver Recovers the Body of a Drowned Child, The. Gerald William Barrax. GT; NBV

She will not have it that my day wanes low. Augusta Davies Webster. OxBSo; ViWPN Fr. Mother and Daughter.

She will run to you for love whoever. Children. Sandra McPherson. FaBoWP

She wonders how people get babies. Facts of Life, The. Ronald Wallace. PBCAP

She wore a new 'terra-cotta' dress. Thunderstorm in Town, A. Thomas Hardy. BoLoP; EnLoPo; OxBSP

She worked in the newsagent, redhaired. Graffiti. Julian Croft. NOBAu

She works with the Moors. Showing some skin she lures a. Sadie. Philip Hammial. BMAP

She Would Have Roses. Nicholas Lloyd Ingraham. PWR

She would not see. (LL) Leave-taking, A. Algernon Charles Swinburne. NOBE; NOBVV; OxBEV

She wreaks such havoc in my library. Minding Ruth. Aidan Carl Mathews. BiHa; CIP-2; PBCIP

She writes to me as if we still shared. Letter from Home in Spanish. Judith Ortiz Cofer. ExTi

Sheaf Mark. Ray DiPalma. FTOS

Sheafe of snakes used heretofore to be, A. To Mr. George Herbert. John Donne. OBVE

Shealtiel, governor of Judah. Haggai. John Chagy. ChIV-1

Shearer man like toast and butter. Indian Bagman's Toast. Unknown. FaBoVe

Shearer's Wife, The. Louis Esson. NOBAu

Shearing, The. Unknown. OBWVE, tr. by Glyn Jones

Sheath and Knife. Unknown. ESPB

Sheaves, The. Edwin Arlington Robinson. APT-1; AWP; HAP; MoAmPo; NOBA; NoAM; OxBA; SoSe-8; TAP

Sheaves are ripe now for the tying, The. Rich Harvest. Max Fleischer. AuPH, tr. by Lowell A. Bangerter

Sheaves of drooping dandelions to the courts of Kentish town. (LL) Parliament Hill Fields. Sir John Betjeman. FaBoTw; NOBE

Shed, The. Frank Flynn. OTCP

Shed a tear for the WREN named McGinnis. Limerick. Unknown. PeLi

Shed the Fear. Anselm Hollo. PmAP

Shed, the wall, and the anonymous cross. (LL) Daryl Hine. GS; NoAM

Shee brought her to her joyous paradize. Edmund Spenser. NOBE Fr. Faerie Queene, The.

Sheen of the willows spreads ten thousand feet, The. "Song of Farewell" in the Tartar Mode. Chang Yü. SuSp, tr. by Irving Y. Lo

Sheep. William Henry Davies. MoBrPo; NPeEn; RB

Sheep. Robert Francis. LCAP-2

Sheep. Samuel Hoffenstein. TrJP

Sheep. Shinkichi Takahashi. ZenPo, tr. by Takashi Ikemoto and Lucien Stryk

Sheep and Lambs. Katharine Tynan. OBEV; SacPr

Sheep and the Goat, The. George Macdonald. EBVV; SacPr

Sheep Child, The. James Dickey. EmeKit; HCAP; NOBA; NoAM; TAP; VCAP

Sheep Dipping. Norman MacCaig. OxBC

Sheep-folds, holy spring of the Nymphs. Leonidas of Tarentum. GrAn

Sheep in Fog. Sylvia Plath. FaBoWP; HCAP; LCAP-2; NPeEn

Sheep is blind; a passing Owl, The. Blind Sheep, The. Randall Jarrell. OBAL

Sheep School. Sándor Weöres. IQMS, tr. by Adam Makkai and Donald E. Morse

Sheep was. And a purse dangled from his arm. A sporran jogged between his lies, A. Tune. Robert Kelly. FTOS

Sheepdog Trials in Hyde Park. Cecil Day Lewis. NoAM; OxBTC

Sheepheard, what's Love, I pray thee tell? Sheepheards Description of Love, The. Unknown. NPeEn

Sheepheards Description of Love, The. Unknown. NPeEn

Sheepheards Sorrow, Being Disdained in Love, The. Thomas Lodge. See Shepherd's Sorrow, Being Disdained in Love, The

Sheer, bright-shining spring, spring as it used to be. After Liberation. J. C. Bloem. TuT, tr. by Seamus Heaney

Sheer cliff, far mountains. Inscribed on My Large Landscape Hanging Scroll "Listening to a Waterfall." Tao-chi. CoBLCP, tr. by Jonathan Chaves

Sheer naked rock. From the high cliff-cut. Stone Face Falls. William Everson. APT-2

Sheet lightning. Chuck Brickley. HA

Sheet of paper, placed, A. Lakshmi. Padraic Fallon. NOIV

Sheet of rain, A. Issa. SoOfWa, tr. by Sam Hamill

Sheet of writing paper, The. Alchemist, The. Richard Church. OxBTC

Sheets, The. Timothy Steele. DiPo

Sheets on the floor, a stick. Distance between Bodies, The. Bill Manhire. HarvBoo

Sheets were frozen hard, and they cut the naked hand, The. Christmas at Sea. Robert Louis Stevenson. ChrPo; EBVV; NePenScot; PeVV

Sheila and I spent the night talking about French. Scrambled Eggs and Garlic Pork. Michael Melo. ReBoTo

Sheila-na-gig, I will make myself a hat. Sheila the Hat. Pat Parnell. HW

Sheila the Hat. Pat Parnell. HW

Shekhinah. Karl Wolfskehl. TrJP

Shekinah is She Who Dwells Within. Meditation on the Feminine Nature of Shekinah, A. Ann Gottlieb. HW

Shell. Shinkichi Takahashi. ZenPo, tr. by Takashi Ikemoto and Lucien Stryk

Shell, The. Thomas Holley Chivers. TCAPo

Shell, The. H. M. Sarson. PoWW

Shell, The. James Stephens. MoBrPo

Shell-bursting births, comas, and the mute. Eclogue 4. Andrea Zanzotto. ItPo, tr. by Gayle Ridinger

Shell of objects inwardly consumed, The. My Last Dance. Julia Ward Howe. APN-1

Shell / sitting still. Wingaersheek Beach. Marsden Hartley. APT-1

Shellbrook. William Barnes. OxBEV

Shelley. Charles Simic. TRP

Shelley and jazz and lieder and love and hymn-tunes. Louis MacNeice. NOBL; NPeEn *Fr.* Autumn Journal.

Shelley's death—was it really his wish. Limerick. Bill Greenwell. PeLi

Shelley's Skylark. Thomas Hardy. CABP

Shelley's Vision. Herman Melville. APN-2

Shells. Rachel Hadas. ExTi

Shells Her Auburn Hair Did Show, The. Barry MacSweeney. Oth *Fr.* Pearl.

Shelly Beach. Christopher Koch. NOBAu

Shelter. R. S. Jones. Unle

Sheltered beneath white hawthorn boughs. En un Vergier Soiz Folha D'Albespi. *Unknown.* WoPoe, *tr.* by Stanley Burnshaw

Sheltered from the spring wind by / A silver screen. Old Anguish, The. Chu Shu-chen. BoWoP, *tr.* by Kenneth Rexroth

Sheltered garden sleeps among the tall, The. Battledore. John Gray. NOBVV

Sheltering Ground, The. Sherod Santos. Son

Sheltering Places. Gerald Dawe. PNI

Shemà. Primo Levi. AF; FaBoWar; HP, *tr.* by Ruth Feldman and Ruth Feldman

Shema Yisrael. *Unknown.* TrJP

Shen is very sick these days, he's fading away. On the Road Through the Wu-i Mountains—Making Fun of Chia-tse for Falling Off His Horse. Hsü Wei. CoBLCP, *tr.* by Jonathan Chaves

Shenandoah. Delmore Schwartz.
  Let Us Consider Where the Great Men Are. MoAmPo

Shep'erd Bwoy, The. William Barnes. EBVV

Shep lies long-bodied upon the auburn grass. February's Forgotten Mitts. Raymond Knister. NOBC

Shephard loveth thow me vell? Song. Jean Passerat. NPeEn; OBVE, *tr.* by William, of Hawthornden Drummond

Shephe[a]rd's Hunting, The. George Wither.
  Sonnet: "I that erstwhile the world's sweet air did draw." NOSC

Shepheardes [*or* Shepeards *or* Shepherd's] Calender, The. Edmund Spenser.
  Aprill. NAEL-5v1; NAEL-6v1; OBEV
    Ditty, A: In Praise of Eliza, Queen of the Shepherds. OBEV
    (Ditty, A: "See where she sits upon the grassy green") FaBoCh
    (Lay to Eliza, The.) NOBE
    "See where she sits upon the grassie [*or* grassy] green[e]." OBEV
  August.
    (Roundelay, A: "It fell upon a holy eve") NPeEn
    "Ye wastefull woodes bear witness of my woe." MakPoe
  "Cuddie [*or* Cuddy], for shame hold up thy heavy[e] head." NAEL-5v1; NAEL-6v1; NAEL-7v1
  "Goe little booke: thy selfe present." NAEL-6v1; NAEL-7v1
  "Is not thilke the mery moneth of May." PBRV
  June. AEP
  "Lo, Collin, here the place whose pleasant syte." AEP
  May. PBRV
  October. NAEL-5v1; NAEL-6v1; NAEL-7v1
  ("Shepheardes boye (no better do him call), A.") CAGL
  "Tell me, good Hobbinoll, what garres thee greete?" NAEL-5v1; NAEL-6v1; OBEV
  To His Booke. NAEL-6v1; NAEL-7v1

Shepherd. Sheila Kohler. Unle

Shepherd. Avraham Shlonsky. MHP, *tr.* by Ruth Finer Mintz

Shepherd, The. William Blake. ChAP; FHYEP *Fr.* Songs of Innocence.

Shepherd and Shepherdess. Thomas Hennell. FaBoTw

Shepherd Boy, The. John Clare. CABP; NOBVV

Shepherd-Boy and the Wolf, The. Aesop. AWP, *tr.* by William Ellery Leonard

Shepherd Boy Sings [in the Valley of Humiliation], The. John Bunyan. EBEV; NOBE; OBEV; SacPr *Fr.* Pilgrim's Progress, The.

Shepherd cheerfully, The. Hildebert. MLL

Shepherd Corydon burned with fire for fair Alexis, The. Virgil [*or* Vergil]. CAGL, *tr.* by Byrne Fone *Fr.* Eclogues.

Shepherd is blind, the sheep are made of stone, The. To Ovid. Elena Ignatova. ItGoST, *tr.* by Sibelan Forrester

Shepherd John. Mary Mapes Dodge. SWaP

Shepherd Left Behind, The. Mildred Plew Meigs. TrCP

Shepherd, Ned Vaughan, A. Ned Vaughan. Walter De la Mare. FaBoEE

Shepherd Paris bore the Spartan bride, The. Theocritus. OBVE *Fr.* Idylls.

Shepherd plays his flute, The. Hollow Echo. Fazil Hüsnü Daglarca. CRP

Shepherd Rides on Donkey-Back, The. Sándor Petőfi. IQMS, *tr.* by Peter Zollman

Shepherd's Calendar. Bill Griffiths. Oth *Fr.* Building: The New London Hospital.

Shepherd's Calendar cont'd. Bill Griffiths. Oth *Fr.* Building: The New London Hospital.

Shepherd's Calendar, 'June,' The. Edmund Spenser.
  "Lo, Colin, here the place whose pleasant site." AEP

Shepherd's Dale, The. Herman Melville. *See* Clarel: A Poem and Pilgrimage in the Holy Land

Shepherd's daughter watching sheep, A. Knight and the Shepherd's Daughter, The. *Unknown.* ESPB

Shepherd's Dog, The. Leslie Norris. OBCP

Shepherd's Garland, The. Michael Drayton.
  (Daffodil Song, The.) AEP
  "Shepherd, why creep we in this lowly vein." NoSic

Shepherd's Gift, A. Anyte [*or* Anytes]. AWP, *tr.* by John William Burgon

Shepherd's Gratitude, The. Virgil [*or* Vergil]. AWP, *tr.* by Charles Stuart Calverley *Fr.* Eclogues.

Shepherd's Hut, The. Andrew Young. OxBTC

Shepherd's Lament, The. Goethe. AWP, *tr.* by Bayard Taylor

Shepherd's Night Count. Jane Yolen. TLR

Shepherd's [*or* Shepheards] Calendar, The. John Clare.
  February. NOBE
  "Snow has left the cottage top, The." NOBE

Shepherd's Song at Christmas. Langston Hughes. ChrPo

Shepherd's Sorrow, Being Disdained in Love, The. Thomas Lodge. NoSic (Sheepheards Sorrow, Being Disdained in Love, The.) NPeEn

Shepherd's star with trembling glint, The. En Bateau. Paul Verlaine. AWP, *tr.* by Arthur Symons

Shepherd's Tale, The. James Kirkup. OBCP

Shepherd's Tree, The. John Clare. CenSon

Shepherd's Week, The. John Gay.
  Tuesday; or, the Ditty. NOEC

Shepherd's Wife's Farewell to the Old Pasture, The. István Sinka. IQMS, *tr.* by Gavin Ewart

Shepherd's Wife's Song, The. Robert Greene. HAP; NoSic; RACG *Fr.* Greene's Mourning Garment.

Shepherd, Shepherd, Hark. Saint Theresa [*or* Teresa] of Avila. AWP, *tr.* by Arthur Symons

Shepherd, Show Me How to Go. Mary Baker Eddy. AH

Shepherd-Song. Sigmund von Birken. GePo, *tr.* by George C. Schoolfield

Shepherd Speaks, The. John Erskine. TrCP

Shepherd stands at one end of the arena, A. Sheepdog Trials in Hyde Park. Cecil Day Lewis. NoAM; OxBTC

Shepherd Thirsis longed to die, The. Giovanni Battista Guarini. EroLit, *tr.* by Sir Robert Aytoun \VP/[*or* Ayton]

Shepherd who lived up in Gwent, A. Limerick. E. O. Parrott. PeLi

Shepherd Who with Your Tender Calls. Félix Lope de Vega Carpio. SpanPo, *tr.* by Kate Flores

Shepherd, why creep we in this lowly vein. Michael Drayton. NoSic *Fr.* Shepherd's Garland, The.

Shepherd, Young and Mournful, Grieves Alone, A. Saint John of the Cross. SpanPo, *tr.* by James Edward Tobin

Shepherdess. Norman Cameron. OxBS *Fr.* Three Love Poems.

Shepherdess, The. Alice Thompson Meynell. *See* Shepherdress, The

Shepherdess—/ A fair one are you. William Shakespeare. PoE *Fr.* Winter's Tale, The.

Shepherdess of sheep, A. (LL) Shepherdress, The. Alice Thompson Meynell. AWP; MoBrPo; NOBVV

Shepherdress, The. Alice Thompson Meynell. AWP; CABP; MoBrPo; NOBVV; RACG
  (Lady of the Lambs, The.) OBEV

Shepherds and angels sing in unison. Harmony. *Unknown.* GrAn, *tr.* by William J. Philbin

Shepherds and Flocks. Victor Hugo. SxFrPo, *tr.* by E. H. Blackmore and A. M. Blackmore

Shepherds armed with staff and sling. Carol of Patience. Robert Graves. OBCP

Shepherds' Carol. Norman Nicholson. OBCP

Shepherd's Dochter, The. *Unknown. See* Knight and the Shepherd's Daughter, The

Shepherds' Hymn, The. Richard Crashaw. NOBE *Fr.* In the Holy Nativity of Our Lord God.

Shepherds, I sing you, this winter's night. For the Nativity. John Heath-Stubbs. ChrPo

Shepherds on old hills, with robber. Gallery Shepherds. Patricia Beer. OxBC

Shepherds [*or* Shepheards], The. Henry Vaughan. ChIV-2; ESCV

Shepherds that on this mountain ridge abide. Cleitagoras. Leonidas of Tarentum. AWP, *tr.* by William M. Hardinge

Shepherds went their hasty way, The. Christmas Carol, A. Samuel Taylor Coleridge. ChrPo

Sherbet. Cornelius Eady. GT; LTA

Sheridan at Cedar Creek.   Herman Melville.   CBCWP

Sheridan's Ride.   Thomas Buchanan Read.   APN-2; CBCWP

Sherri told me they had been.   Drooling Madness at St. Liz.   Charles Bukowski.   BodElec

Sherwood.   Alfred Noyes.   MoBrPo

Shew, weakenes speaks in prose, but powre in verse. (LL)   Samuel Daniel.   NoSic; PBRV   Fr. Musophilus; or, Defence of All Learning.

Shi King.   Unknown.
  Chou and the South.   CTC, tr. by Ezra Pound
  How Goes the Night?   AWP, tr. by Helen Waddell
  I Wait My Lord.   AWP, tr. by Helen Waddell
  Maytime.   AWP, tr. by L. Cranmer-Byng
  Morning Glory, The.   AWP, tr. by Helen Waddell
  Pear-Tree, The.   AWP, tr. by Allen Upward
  Under the Pondweed.   AWP, tr. by Helen Waddell
  Woman.   AWP, tr. by H. A. Giles
  You Will Die.   AWP, tr. by H. A. Giles

Shibboleth.   Paul Celan.   PoetW, tr. by Michael Hamburger

Shickered As He Could Be.   Unknown.   NOBAu

Shield: I'm by nature solitary, scarred by spear.   Cynewulf.   ASW   Fr. Riddles (Exeter Book).

Shield: "Lonely wanderer, wounded with iron, A."   Cynewulf.   AnOE, tr. by Charles W. Kennedy   Fr. Riddles (Exeter Book).

Shield of Achilles, The.   W. H. Auden.   EBEV; FaBoMo; GTBS-P; HAP; NAEL-5v2; NAEL-6v2; NOBE; NOCV; NPeEn; NoAM; NoP-4; OxAEP-2; OxBEV; PeECV; PoE; WeW-3

Shield of Achilles, The.   Homer.   NOSC, tr. by George Chapman   Fr. Iliad, The.

Shield of Achilles, The.   Homer.   NAWM-7v1, tr. by Robert Fagles   Fr. Iliad, The.

Shield of Aeneas, The.   Virgil [or Vergil].   NAWM-5v1; NAWM-7v1, tr. by Robert Fitzgerald   Fr. Aeneid [or Eneados, Aeneis], The.

Shields Bruttians threw from their doomed shoulders.   Nossis.   SaLy, tr. by Diane Rayor

Shields Strong, Nulla Nullas Alive.   Lionel Fogarty.   IBA

Shift.   Aaron Anstett.   AmPoNex

Shift[,] here, in town, not meanest among squires.   On Lieutenant Shift.   Ben Jonson.   OBSV

Shifting Colors.   Robert Lowell.   BodElec; HCAP

Shifting riddle glitters, The.   Highest Sickness, The.   Boris Leonidovich Pasternak.   TCRP

Shiftless young fellow of Kent, A.   Limerick.   Unknown.   PeLi

Shih Ching.   Unknown.
  "Cloth-plant grew till it covered the thorn bush, The."   BoWoP; ChiP, tr. by Arthur Waley
  "Very handsome gentleman, A."   BoWoP
  Widow's Lament.   BoWoP, tr. by Arthur Waley

Shih-hou Pointed Out to Me That from Ancient Times There Had Never Been a Poem on the Subject of Lice.   Mei Yao Ch'en.   CoBCP; ColAnChi, tr. by Burton Watson

Shillin' a Day.   Rudyard Kipling.   NoAM

Shilling life will give you all the facts, A.   Who's Who.   W. H. Auden.   MoBrPo; NoAM; Son

Shillong.   Bernard Gutteridge.   PoWW

Shiloh [A Requiem].   Herman Melville.   APN-2; CBCWP; ColAP; NOBA; NoP-4; OBWP; OxBA; SCV; TCAPo

Shilpit dog fucks grimly by the close, a.   Edwin Morgan.   OxBSo

Shimá Shil hoolne'   She Was Telling It This Way.   Laura Tohe.   ReEnLa

Shimmer.   James Schuyler.   VCAP

Shimmering beneath the glaze.   Elizabeth Searle Lamb.   HA

Shimmering in the scrub-brush, A.   Little Overture.   David Barber.   AmPoNex

Shimmering sea is still, The.   Dolphins.   Bryn Griffiths.   TCAWP

Shimmering water at its full—sunny day is best.   Drinking at the Lake, First It's Sunny, Then It Rains.   Su Tung-p'o (Su Shih).   SuSp, tr. by Irving Y. Lo

Shinano.   Issa.   EH, tr. by Robert Hass

Shine.   Léon Damas.   NegPo, tr. by Ellen Conroy Kennedy

Shine and the Titanic.   Unknown.   NAAAL

Shine, "O world!" don't weary the gulping Pole.   Frank O'Hara.   UnPo   Fr. Life on Earth.

Shine out, resplendent God of day.   Laplander's Song to His Mistress, A.   Elizabeth Singer Rowe.   ECWP

Shine, Perishing Republic.   Robinson Jeffers.   APT-1; HarvBoo; NAAL-2v2; NAAL-5; NOBA; NoAM; NoP-4; OxBA; PAI; PoPoPo; TAP; TFi; UnPo; VGW

Shine was up in Harlem damn near drunk. (LL)   Dark Prophecy: I Sing of Shine.   Etheridge Knight.   BPo; ESEAA; LTA; PBCAP

Shiner.   Maggie Nelson.   AmPoNex

Shines / in the mind of heaven God.   Canto 51.   Ezra Pound.   PFTM-1

Shinier than transparent marble.   Sapho's Kiss.   Efrén Rebolledo.   BLPSL, tr. by Rene de Costa, Rigas Kappatos and Eleni Paidoussi

Shining cup of earthly joy, The.   Earthly Joy.   Sydney E. Jerrold.   SacPr

Shining Eye of Horus cometh, The.   Unknown.   AWP   Fr. Book of the Dead.

Shining fauna of that fire, The. (LL)   Burning the Christmas Greens.   William Carlos Williams.   APT-1; ChrPo; NAAL-2v2; NAAL-5; NOBA; NoAM

Shining in his stickiness and glistening with honey.   Friendly Cinnamon Bun, The.   Russell Hoban.   OTCP

Shining like a star.   Hunting Song.   Unknown.   STP, tr. by Jerome Rothenberg

Shining to the perfect day. (LL)   Morning Hymn.   Charles Wesley.   NPeEn; TOF

Shiny record albums scattered over.   As You Leave Me.   Etheridge Knight.   NNaP

Ship, The.   Bill Griffiths.   Oth   Fr. Building: The New London Hospital.

Ship, The.   Robert Southey.   TreFP

Ship at rock, wakes, terns, A.   Going to Sea.   Douglas Messerli.   FTOS

Ship-broken Men Whom Stormy Seas Sore Toss.   William Fowler.   NPeEn

Ship I have got in the North Country, A.   Golden Vanity, The.   Unknown.   FaBoCh

Ship Is Lost, The.   William Falconer.   OxAEP-1   Fr. Shipwreck, The.

Ship, leaving or arriving, of my lover.   After a Passage in Baudelaire.   Robert Duncan.   PoE

Ship of Death, A.   Seamus Heaney.   NAEL-6v2; NoP-4

Ship of Death, The.   D. H. Lawrence.   FaBoTw; GTBS-P; MoBrPo; NAEL-5v2; NAEL-6v2; NoAM; NoP-4; OxAEP-2; OxBEV

Ship of Life, The.   Ahmad al-Safi Al-Najafi.   MAP, tr. by John Heath-Stubbs and Salma Khadra Jayyusi

Ship of Love, The.   Salma Khadra Jayyusi.   MAP, tr. by Charles Doria and the author

Ship of Redemption.   Vietnamese Oral Tradition.   CaDao, tr. by John Balaban

Ship of State, The.   Henry Wadsworth Longfellow.   PWR   Fr. Building of the Ship, The.

Ship of the body, ship of the soul, voyaging, voyaging, voyaging. (LL)   Aboard at a Ship's Helm.   Walt Whitman.   APN-1; NOBA; OxBA

Ship's Cook, a Captive Sings, The.   Hugo von Hofmannsthal.   TrJP, tr. by Charles Wharton Stork

Ship's master:/ before him, in the waist and before it.   David Jones.   FaBoTw; WoPoe   Fr. Anathemata, The.

Ship's Nail, A.   Unknown.   ReMoGo

Ship Sets out, the.   William Falconer.   OxAEP-1   Fr. Shipwreck, The.

Ship sets sail, the ship is journeying, The.   Stoker, The.   Shin Shalom.   MHP, tr. by Ruth Finer Mintz

Ship Starting, The.   Walt Whitman.   TCAPo

Ship That Sails, The.   Unknown.   PoToHe

Ship That Went Down, The.   Adah Isaacs Menken.   CBWP-1

Ship Waits in the Harbor, The.   Gabriella Leto.   CItWP, tr. by Cinzia Sartini Blum and Lara Trubowitz

Ship was large, The.   Ode to a Lost Cargo in a Ship Called Save.   José Craveirinha.   PeSAV, tr. by Chris Searle

Ship weighed twenty thousand ton, The.   Passenger Shanty.   W. H. Auden.   OBCoV

Ship Without a Sail, A.   Richard Rodgers.   ReLy

Ship you've boarded, The.   Ark.   Gu Cheng.   VCWP

Shipboard Song.   Yüan Chüeh.   ColAnChi, tr. by John Timothy Wixted

Shiperd-boy, what is yer trade?   Beggar-Laddie, The.   Unknown.   ESPB

Shipment to Maidanek.   Ephim G. Fogel.   HP; OBWP; TrJP

Shipping the Pictures from Belfast.   Catherine Byron.   Prnts

Ships of state, The.   Australorp.   Edith Speers.   NOBAu

Ships That Pass in the Night.   Paul Laurence Dunbar.   ColAP

Ships that pass in the night, and speak each other in passing.   Henry Wadsworth Longfellow.   PoToHe   Fr. Tales of a Wayside Inn.

Ships that sail forth.   Yury [or Iurii] Konstantinovich Terapiano.   TCRP

Shipwreck.   Mary Weston Fordham.   CBWP-2

Shipwreck.   Biancamaria Frabotta.   CItWP, tr. by Cinzia Sartini Blum and Lara Trubowitz

Shipwreck.   Rosalie Moore.   YaYoPo

Shipwreck, The.   Byron.   NPeEn   Fr. Don Juan.

Shipwreck, The.   William Falconer.
  "Amid this fearful trance, a thundering sound."   ECEV
  "And now, lash'd on by destiny severe."   OxAEP-1
  Ship Is Lost, The.   OxAEP-1
  Ship Sets out, the.   OxAEP-1
  "Sun's bright orb, declining all serene, The."   OxAEP-1

Shipwreck in Haven, A.   Keith Waldrop.
  "Balancing. Austere. Life."   PmAP

Shipwreck Poem.   Karen Volkman.   NeAmPo

Shipyard cranes have come down again.   Landscape with One Figure.   Douglas Dunn.   NePenScot

Shirt. Robert Pinsky. ColAP; HarvBoo; NAAL-5

Shirt. Carl Sandburg. CA

Shirt. Charles Simic. HCAP

Shirt blows across the field, A. Storm. Ágnes Nemes Nagy. IQMS, tr. by Hugh Maxton

Shirt Collar, The. Ann Townsend. NAPBL

Shirt I sleep in, The. Dux Bellorum. Max Winter. NeAmPo

Shirt of a Lad, The. Unknown. OBWVE, tr. by Anthony Conran

Shirts. Nigel Jenkins. TCAWP

Shitting in the winter turnip field. Masaoka Shiki. OHMPJ

Shitty. Kingsley Amis. OxBC

Shiva. Robinson Jeffers. NOBA; NoAM; Son

Shiva's Prowess. Maurya Simon. ErotSp

Shivering. Emperor, The. Jonathan Griffin. Oth

Shivering and hoping no one. Grandma's Bureau. Robert Morgan. WeW-3

Shlup, shlup, the dog. Denise Levertov. HeIP-4; InPK-6 Fr. Six Variations.

Shma—listen, receive. She Who Listens. Elana Klugman. HW

Shoal of Silver Angelfish, A. Edward B. Koster. TuT, tr. by Tony Curtis

Shock. C. K. Williams. UrbNat

Shock-black bubble-doun-beat bouncing. Reggae Sounds. Linton Kwesi Johnson. WaCA

Shocks of dizziness. Incantations of the Sea: Moando Coast. Mukula Kadima-Nzuji. NAfrP, tr. by Gerald Moore

Shoe. John Perreault. SPE

Shoe a little horse. Unknown. OxNR

Shoe Shop. Barton Sutter. SoSe-8

Shoe the colt, shoe the colt. Shoeing. Mother Goose. OxNR; ReMoGo

Shoe the little horse. Unknown. LB

Shoe the steed with silver. Sheridan at Cedar Creek. Herman Melville. CBCWP

Shoe with legs, A. Lobster. Anne Sexton. ChAP

Shoeing. Mother Goose. OxNR; ReMoGo

Shoeing the Currach. Mary O'Malley. MakPoe

Shoemaker makes shoes without leather, A. Riddle. Unknown. OxNR

Shoemaker's Holiday, The. Thomas Dekker.
     O, the Month of May. NoSic

Shoemaker's Wife, The. Lotte Kramer. HP

Shoemakker, The. Unknown. FaBoVe

Shoes, secret face of my inner life. My Shoes. Charles Simic. CoAP; EmeKit; HCAP; VCAP

Shoeshine Boy. Maria Eugénia Lima. HAWP, tr. by Julia Kirst

Shoeshine, master?, A. Shoeshine Boy. Maria Eugénia Lima. HAWP, tr. by Julia Kirst

Shoichi brushed the black. Awakening. Lucien Stryk. BodElec

Sholom Aleichem. Elias Lieberman. TrJP

Sholto Peach Harrison you are no son of mine. Correspondence between Mr. Harrison in Newcastle and Mr. Sholto Peach Harrison in Hull. Stevie Smith. NBLV; OxBC

Shon a Morgan. Unknown. OxNR

Shona married a Ndebele, A. Maze of Blood, A. N. C. G. Mathema. PeSAV

Shone through her body visibly. (LL) Phantom. Samuel Taylor Coleridge. NAEL-5v2; NAEL-6v2; OxBSP

Shoni Onions. Sheenagh Pugh. AngWePo

Shoo the orioles, drive them away. Spring Grievance. Chin Ch'ang-hsü. CoBCP, tr. by Burton Watson

Sho[o]e Tying, The. Robert Herrick. CaPo

Shoot It Jimmy! William Carlos Williams. APT-1

Shooting a Farmhouse. Ted Kooser. PBCAP

Shooting Back. Thomas Sayers Ellis. GT

Shooting Crows. Peter Markus. AmPoNex

Shooting, Killing, Drug Busts, Cover-Ups. Bruce Jackson. AmPoNex

Shooting of Dan McGrew, The. Robert W. Service. BRP; EBNV; PoRA; RB; UV

Shooting of His Dear. Unknown. OxBoLi

Shooting of John Dillinger outside the Biograph Theater July 22, 1934, The. David Wagoner. CoAP; RB

Shooting Script. Adrienne Rich.
     "Mare's skeleton in the clearing: another sign of life, The." FaBoWP
     Newsreel. FaBoWP; HCAP
     "Of simple choice they are the villagers; their clothes come." HCAP
     "Old blanket, The. The crumbs of rubbed wool turning up." HCAP
     "They come to you with their descriptions of your soul." HCAP
     "This would not be the war we fought in. See, the foliage." FaBoWP; HCAP
     "We are driven to odd attempts; once it would not have occurred to." HCAP
     "Whatever it was: the grains of the glacier caked in the boot-cleats." FaBoWP; HCAP

Shooting Script, A. Seamus Heaney. BodElec

Shooting Star, A. Edith Matilda Thomas. ChAP

Shooting the Dogs. Philip Hodgins. BMAP

Shooting the rapids! Robert Spiess. HA

Shooting Whales. Mark Strand. ColAP

Shootingway Ceremony Prayer. Unknown. WPoS; WoPe, tr. by Gladys A. Reichard

Shop o' Meat-Weare. William Barnes. NOBVV

Shop Talk. Roy Fuller. OxBC

Shopgirls leave their work, The. Charles Reznikoff. APT-2

Shopkeepers at the Party Meeting. Thomas McCarthy. BiHa

Shoplifters. Maura Stanton. ReTh

Shoplifting. Baron Wormser. ReTh

Shopping. Agi Mishol. DTA, tr. by Tsipi Keller

Shopping for Midnight. G. E. Murray. ReTh

Shops, the streets are full of old men, The. Talk. Roo Borson. NIP-4; NOBC

Shore. Jean Garrigue. TAP

Shore Bird. Brewster Ghiselin. APT-2

Shore Grass. Amy Lowell. APT-1

Shore looked wild, without a trace of man, The. Byron. HAP Fr. Don Juan.

Shore of Life, The. Robert Fitzgerald. VGW

Shore people worshipped, we are told, the Mother. Peter Davison. YaYoPo Fr. Breaking of the Day, The.

Shore Tullye. Robert Rendall. OxBS

Shoreless breeze from heaven over an endless road. In a Dream I Traveled among Ten Thousand Acres of Lotuses. Lu Yu. SuSp, tr. by Irving Y. Lo

Shoreline. Mary Barnard. APT-2

Shoreline After Storm. Eamon Grennan. PoCoUp

Shores of my native land. Farewell. Isaac Toussaint L'Ouverture. TTY, tr. by Edna Worthley Underwood

Shores of Styx are lone for evermore, The. Idle Charon. Eugene Lee-Hamilton. NOBVV

Shoriken. Charles Brasch. PeNZ

Shoring up the ocean. A railroad track. Blood-Sister. Adrienne Rich. NAAL-2v2

Shorn of landmarks, glued to a sere promontory. "No!" He Said. Wole Soyinka. HBAPE

Short afternoon ends, and the year is over, The. New Year. Philip Larkin. ChRPo

Short and Sweet Sonnet Made by One of the Maids of Honour, upon the Death of Queen Elizabeth, which She Sewed upon a Sampler, in Red Silke, A. Unknown. EMWP

Short, big-nosed men with nasty conical caps. Hittites, The. Roy Fuller. OxBSP

Short Circuit. Daniel Hall. OWoS

Short cut home lay through the cemetery, The. Mistress, The. Joan Barton. OxBTC

Short day has grown, A. Place of V, The. Ray A. Young Bear. VoR

Short direction / To avoid dejection, A. Rules and Regulations. Lewis Carroll. NOBVV; PeVV

Short History of Autumn, A. Anselm Berrigan. HeMarv

Short History of British India, A. Geoffrey Hill. OxBC

Short History of Illumination, A. Matthew Rohrer. AmPoNex

Short History of the Bourgeoisie. Hans Magnus Enzensberger. VCWP, tr. by Hans Magnus Enzensberger and Michael Hamburger

Short in measure, narrow in theme. Erinna's Distaff. Antipater of Sidon. GrAn, tr. by Peter Jay

Short Lexicon of Torture in the Eighties, A. Edward Hirsch. VCAP

Short Life of the Hermit, A. John Logan.
     "He told the crowd The devils" CRP

Short nap / Waking. Buson. ZenPo, tr. by Takashi Ikemoto and Lucien Stryk

Short Narrative of Breasts and Wombs in Service of Plot Entitled, A. Claudia Rankine. BAP-01

Short Narrative of Hand and Face in Service of PLOT, Entitled, A. Claudia Rankine. NAPBL

Short night, A. Yayu. JDP, tr. by Yoel Hoffmann

Short night, The. Buson. EH, tr. by Robert Hass

Short night / Scarlet flower. Issa. ZenPo, tr. by Takashi Ikemoto and Lucien Stryk

Short Note on the Sparseness of the Language. Diane Di Prima. BB

Short Oblation of This Smal Work by the Writer Gatherer Thereof to Our Most Sweet and Merciful God, A. Dame Gertrude More. EMWP

Short on brains, long on stupidity, the mantis seizes the cicada. Huang T'ing-chien. SuSp Fr. In My Study in Monastery, Rising after a Nap.

Short-Order Cook. Jim Daniels. ReTh

Short Poem. Kenneth Carroll. SpirFl

Short Poem. William Carlos Williams. SAmP

Short Poem for Armistice Day, A. Sir Herbert Read. PeFWW

Short Prayer for a Loyalist Hero. César Vallejo. TCLAP, *tr.* by Clayton Eshleman *Fr.* Spain, Take This Cup from Me.
Short Revelation Concerning Death and Chaos. René Daumal. PFTM-1
Short service, to be sure, A. Lament for a Leg. John Ormond. AngWePo; NoP-4; OBWVE
Short Song. T. Carmi. WoPoe, *tr.* by Grace Schulman
Short Song of Congratulation [*or* To a Young Heir], A. Samuel Johnson. EBEV; HAP; InPK-6; NAEL-6v1; NOBE; NOEC; NPeEn; OBCoV; OBSV; OxAEP-1; OxBEV; PeLV; PoE; TFi; UnPo; WoPoe
  (To a Young Heir.)   SCGP
Short Speech to My Friends. Imamu Amiri Baraka. ESEAA
Short Story. Maura Stanton. BodElec
Short Story, A. David Escobar Galindo. ChAP, *tr.* by Jorge Piche
Short Summary. Louise Bogan. APT-2
Short Testimony for Anne Whitehead, A. Jane Sowle. EMWP
Short Time. Gavin Ewart. NoAM
Short Wave. Hilary Llewellyn-Williams. TCAWP
Short Year, The. Paavo Haavikko.
  "One who writes us is now doing four plays a year, The."   VCWP
Shortcut, A. Buson. EH, *tr.* by Robert Hass
Shortened History in Pictures, A. Jamie McKendrick. OxBSo
Shortening the Road. Michael Davitt. PBCIP, *tr.* by Philip Casey
Shorter and shorter now the twilight clips. Autumn. Alice Cary. APN-2
Shorter she grows, The. (LL) Candle, A. Mother Goose. LB; OxNR; ReMoGo
Shortest and Sweetest of Songs, The. George Macdonald. NOBVV
Shorthand. Theodore Weiss. BodElec
Shortly after midnight, certain creatures become what they really. Nocturne. Angie Estes. GeoHom
Shortness and Misery of Life, The. Isaac Watts. NOCV
Shortness of Life. Thomas Fairfax, Baron Fairfax of Cameron. NOSC
Shorts I. W. H. Auden.
  Lost. FaBoEE
  "Lost on a fog-bound spit of sand." FaBoEE
Shorts / Excerpts. Bill Knott. PBCAP
Shorts [1948–1957]. W. H. Auden.
  (Aesthetic Point of View, The.) NBLV; OBAL; OBCoV
  "Behold the manly mesomorph." OxBSP
  Give Me A Doctor. OBCoV
  Limerick: "As the poets have mournfully sung." PeLi
Shorts [1939–1947]. W. H. Auden.
  Statesmen. OBCoV
  "When Statesmen gravely say, We must be realistic" OBCoV
  Words. OxBSP; PeLV
Shorts [1927–32]. W. H. Auden.
  Dedication: "Let us honour if we can." PeLV
  Dedication: "Private faces in public places." FaBoEE; PeLV
Shot at Random, A. Dominic Bevan Wyndham Lewis. UV
Shot down from its enskied formation. Angel in Blythburgh Church, An. Peter Porter. NoP-4
Shot Forth. Paul Celan. WoPoe, *tr.* by Margaret Guillemin and Katherine Washburn
Shot gold, maroon and violet, dazzling silver, emerald, fawn. Prairie Sunset, A. Walt Whitman. TCAPo
Shot of War, A. J. S. Harry. BMAP
Shot through with silver gray light. One Snapshot I Couldn't Take in France, The. Al Young. SpirFl
Shot Who? Jim Lane! Merrill Moore. MoAmPo
Shot? so quick, so clean an ending? A. E. Housman. CAGL
Shotgun. Patti See. MPUn
Shotgun / blossoming / outward. Maxine Chernoff. PmAP *Fr.* Japan.
Shots at Otters. Colin Simms.
  "Lochside silverschistsand disturbed-to-black-below distributed." Oth
Should any ask me on this hour to dwell. Sadi [*or* Saadi *or* Sa'di]. AWP, *tr.* by L. Cranmer-Byng *Fr.* Gulistan, The.
Should any to himself for safety fly? To Whom Else Can We Fly? Giles Fletcher, the Younger. SacPr
Should auld acquaintance be forgot. Auld Lang Syne. Robert Burns. AWP; NAEL-5v2; NAEL-6v2; NOBE; NOSC; NePenScot; OBEV; OxAEP-2; OxBEV; OxBS; SCGP
Should be congealed with sorrow like this? (LL) Tune: "Eight Beats of a Kan-chou Song." Liu Yung. ColAnChi; SuSp, *tr.* by James J. Y. Liu
Should be very quiet this morning. Sunday Morning. Robert Grenier. PmAP
Should Dennis print how once you robb'd your brother. On Dennis. Pope. FaBoEE
Should ever be forgot. (LL) Gunpowder Plot Day. *Unknown.* LB; OxNR
Should find brief solace there, as I have found. (LL) Sonnet: "Nuns fret not at

their convent's narrow room." William Wordsworth. EBEV; NIP-4; OBEV; Son
Should Heaven send me any son. Dorothy Parker. APT-1; NALW *Fr.* Pig's-Eye View of Literature, A.
Should I Be a Rabbi? Hayyim Nahman [*or* Khayim Nakhman *or* Chaim Nachman] Bialik. TrJP, *tr.* by Grace Goldin
Should I believe you, e'en my oaths are witty. *Unknown.* FaBoEE
Should I ever fall ill. Yaroslav [*or* Iaroslav] Vasilevich Smelyakov [*or* Smeliakov]. TCRP
Should I forget your scales. Walking Buddha. Barbara Guest. FTOS
Should I get married? Should I be good? Marriage. Gregory Corso. CoAP; NeAP; NoP-4; OBAL; PeLV; PmAP; TAP; TRP
Should I give in to sleep? This fire's warm. Reading *Paradise Lost* in Protestant Ulster 1984. Seamus Deane. BiHa; PBCIP
Should I know this room. Locale. Penelope Shuttle. BrRo
Should I return to consciousness or stay. Conciousness. Ágnes Nemes Nagy. IQMS, *tr.* by Doreen Bell
Should I say the eyes were laced and that the laces were snakes. How Should I Say This? Robert Dow. BAP-97
Should I see a cloud high up in the sky. Yury [*or* Iurii] Kuznetsov. TCRP
Should I simplify my life for you? Adrienne Rich. NIL-7 *Fr.* Inscriptions.
Should I Stay or Should I Go? Sarah Rosenblatt. AmPoNex
Should I tell of all the absolute fools. Georgy [*or* Georgii] Vladimirovich Ivanov. TCRusP, *tr.* by Daniel Weissbort
Should I tell what a miracle she was. (LL) Relic, The. John Donne. BASC; FHYEP; FSCP; HAP; HeIP-4; NAEL-6v1; NAEL-7v1; NOBE; NOSC; NoP-4; TFi
Should I wear a shadowed eye. Acceptance. John Wieners. FTOS
Should I with Silver Tooles Delve through the Hill. Edward Taylor. ChIV-2; OxBA; SCAP *Fr.* Preparatory Meditations Before My Approach to the Lord's Supper.
Should Lanterns Shine. Dylan Thomas. OxBEV
Should make men atheists, and not women whores. (LL) Thomas Carew. BASC; BeJo; CABP; CaPo; NAEL-5v1; NAEL-6v1; NAEL-7v1; OxAEP-1
Should never be light. That kind of thing feels. Your One Good Dress. Brenda Shaughnessy. AmPoNex
Should smile like you, and perish as they smile! (LL) Sonnet 5: "Evening, as slow thy placid shades descend." William Lisle Bowles. NOBRP; NOEC
Should some ill Painter in a wild design. Horace. OBVE *Fr.* Art of Poetry, The.
Should the bare-ass pavement-pounder. *Unknown.* PriapPo, *tr.* by Richard W. Hooper *Fr.* Priapus Poems, The.
Should the building totter, run for an archway! Fallen Tower of Siloam, The. Robert Graves. ChIV-2
Should the lone Wanderer, fainting on his way. Charlotte Smith. RWP
Should the pillar sing, should salt. Lot. David Helwig. NIP-4
Should the wide world roll away. Stephen Crane. APN-2 *Fr.* Black Riders [and Other Lines], The.
Should they not have the best of both worlds? Mules. Paul Muldoon. HarvBoo
Should toss with tangle and with shells. (LL) Tennyson. EBVV; NAEL-6v2; NAWM-7v2 *Fr.* In Memoriam A. H. H.
Should we go now a wandering [*or* a-wand'ring], we should meet. Henry Vaughan. BASC *Fr.* Rhapsody, A.
Should wear all Time's destruction for a dress. (LL) Poet Laments the Coming of Old Age, The. Dame Edith Sitwell. NAEL-5v2; NAEL-6v2; NoAM
Should weep? (LL) Night Winds. Adelaide Crapsey. APT-1; TCAPo
Should you ask me, whence these stories? Henry Wadsworth Longfellow. ColAP; NOBA; PoE *Fr.* Song of Hiawatha, The.
Should you come to me. Years from Now. Kim Sowŏl. WoPoe, *tr.* by Kevin O'Rourke
Should you ever forsake me. Soul and Love, The. Albert Verwey. TuT, *tr.* by Tony Curtis
Should You Go First. Albert K. Rowswell. PoToHe
Should You, My Lord. Phillis Wheatley. BPo; TTY *Fr.* To the Right Honourable William, Earl of Dartmouth.
Should you, my lord, while you pursue my song. Phillis Wheatley. BPo; TTY *Fr.* To the Right Honourable William, Earl of Dartmouth.
Should you revisit us. New Approach Needed. Kingsley Amis. NoAM; OxBTC
Shoulder-bag, cloak, unleavened barley-cake, stick. On Diogenes the Cynic. Antiphilus [*or* Antiphilos]. GrAn
Shoulder of rock, A. High Island. Richard Murphy. CIP-2; NOIV
Shouldering a lance, wandering aimlessly, alone. (LL) Hesitation. "Lu Hsün." SuSp; WoPoe, *tr.* by William R. Schultz
Shouldering its way and shedding the earth crumbs. (LL) Putting in the Seed. Robert Frost. APT-1; NoAM; OxBA
Shouldering shapes of the skies of Broceliande. Taliessin's Song of the Unicorn. Charles Williams. FaBoTw

Shouldn't I pilfer wantonly this famed fragrance of a foreign land? Su Man-shu. SuSp *Fr.* Poems Written during My Sojourn in Japan.

Shout came from the loquacious ones, A. Welsh Ballad, A. Edmwnd Prys. OBWVE, *tr. by* Gwyn Williams

Shout, shout, up with your song! March of the Women, The. Cicely Hamilton. BrRo

Shovel Man, The. Carl Sandburg. HAP

Shoving another quarter home to make. Honky-Tonk Blues. Walter McDonald. SwNoth

Show, The. Wilfred Owen. MoBrPo; OBWVE; OxBEV; OxBTC; PeFWW

Show a prosperous year ahead. (LL) Silkworm Song of Torchlit Fields. Kao Ch'i. CoBLCP; ColAnChi, *tr. by* Jonathan Chaves

Show an affirming flame. (LL) September 1, 1939. W. H. Auden. AF; HarvBoo; MoBrPo; OxAEP-2; OxBA; PoE

Show and Tell. Roddy Lumsden. NeBl

Show Biz Parties. Elizabeth Claman. OPRER

Show Me a Rose. John Godfrey. FTOS

Show me again the time. Lines to a Movement in Mozart's E-Flat Symphony. Thomas Hardy. NoAM

Show me dear[e] Christ, thy spouse, so bright and clear[e]. John Donne. BASC; FSCP; MeLP; NAEL-5v1; NAEL-6v1; NAEL-7v1; NOSC; OxBSo; PeECV; PoE; Son *Fr.* Holy Sonnets.

Show me himself, himself (bright Sir) O show. Come See the Place Where the Lord Lay. Richard Crashaw. ChIV-2

Show me the flames you brag of, you that be. On the Great Frost (1634). William Cartwright. NOSC

Show me the woman. Black. Grace Nichols. Oth

Show me thy feet, show me thy legs, thy thighs. Robert Herrick. *See* Show [*or* Shew] me thy feet; show [*or* shew] me thy legs, thy thighs

"Show me your God!" the doubter cries. Blind. John Kendrick Bangs. PoToHe

Show of arrogant spirit fills the road, A. Light Furs, Fat Horses. Po Chü-i. CoBCP, *tr. by* Burton Watson

Show [*or* Shew] me thy feet; show [*or* shew] me thy legs, thy thighs. To Dianeme. Robert Herrick. CaPo; NOSC

Show the runner coming through the shadows. Runner, The. Gary Gildner. TAP

Show them this day you were on Calvary. (LL) Petrarch. NAWM-5v1; NAWM-7v1, *tr. by* Bernard Bergonzi *Fr.* Sonnets to Laura.

Show us there's chance at least of winning through. (LL) To Whistler, American. Ezra Pound. AiP; FaBoA; NAAL-2v2

Shower. Leah Aini. DTA, *tr. by* Linda Zisquit

Shower. Jacob Winkler Prins. TuT, *tr. by* Tony Curtis

Shower, A. Amy Lowell. PoBW

Shower, The. Linda Smukler. GLP

Shower of Secret Things, The. Nathaniel Mackey. PmAP

Shower [*or* Showre], The. Henry Vaughan. ESCV; GeHe

Shower Scene in *Psycho*, The. David Trinidad. ReTh

Showering, I see more than the single showerhead. Learnng the Ropes. Custer Street. Evanston, 1949. Lisa Ress. GotH

Showing. Liam Rector. TRP

Showing a torn sleeve, with stiff and shaking fingers the old man. Charles Reznikoff. WoPoe

Shown to My Son Yü. Lu Yu. SuSp, *tr. by* Irving Y. Lo

Shows. Yevgeny [*or* Evgenii] Mikhailovich Vinokurov. TCRP, *tr. by* Daniel Weissbort

Shows blank Orion where to dip his hand. (LL) Bride's Hours, A. Jean Valentine. FaBoWP; MPUn

Shoyn Fergéssin: "I've Forgotten" in Yiddish. Albert Goldbarth. TaR

Shrapnel lives in Morton's neck, so his head stays. Refuge at the One Step Down. Belle Waring. PBCAP; SeSe

Shred in his little fist. (LL) Balloons. Sylvia Plath. FaBoWP; PoE

Shrew, The. Rowland Watkyns. AngWePo

Shrewd star, who crudes our naming: you should be flame. Untitled. Karen Volkman. NAPBL; NeAmPo

Shrewish, barren, bony, nosy servant, A. David [*or* Daibhi][*or* Daithi] O'Bruadair [*or* Ó Bruadair]. NOIV

Shriek said the saw smile said the mice. To the Age's Insanities. Marie Ponsot. VGW

Shrieking its message the flying death. Shell, The. H. M. Sarson. PoWW

Shrieking man stood in the square, A. Ballad of the Shrieking Man, The. James Fenton. EmeKit

Shrieking plovers / Calling darkness. Basho. ZenPo, *tr. by* Takashi Ikemoto and Lucien Stryk

Shrill sentence: God is love, The. (LL) On the Farm. Ronald Stuart Thomas. NPeEn; NoP-4; OxBEV; OxBTC; TCAWP

Shrill winds, high sky, monkeys' heart-rending cry. Climbing on the Double Ninth Day. Tu Fu. ChinPo, *tr. by* Yip Wai-lim

Shrilling cicada, drunk on drops of dew, you sing. Meleager. HePo *Fr.* Epigrams.

Shrimp, The. Moses Browne.
  "Shrimp, A! Black thing as widow's crape." NOEC

Shrimp, A! Black thing as widow's crape. Moses Browne. NOEC *Fr.* Shrimp, The.

Shrimp and Her Daughter, The. Jean de La Fontaine. WoPoe, *tr. by* Bruce Boone and Robert Glück

Shrimp Boats, Biloxi. Campbell McGrath. AmPoNex

Shrimps. Nguyễn Văn Lạc. WoPoe, *tr. by* Hunh Sanh Thông

Shrine. Octavio Paz. EroLit

Shrine, The. "H. D." ColAP

Shrine, The. Sara Teasdale. APT-1

Shrine gate / Through morning mist. Kikaku. ZenPo, *tr. by* Takashi Ikemoto and Lucien Stryk

Shrine of General Pien, The. Chu Yün-ming. CoBLCP, *tr. by* Jonathan Chaves

"Shrink" is a misnomer. The religious. Robert Pinsky. HCAP *Fr.* Essay on Psychiatrists.

Shrinking brain, sick of an inner war, The. (LL) Sidney Keyes. NoP-4; OBWP *Fr.* Foreign Gate, The.

Shrinking Lonesome Sestina, The. Miller Williams. MakPoe

Shropshire Lad, A. Sir John Betjeman. HarvBoo

Shroud. George Mackay Brown. NoP-4; RB

Shroud, The. Galway Kinnell. LCAP-2

Shroud of Color, The. Countee Cullen. NAAAL

Shrouded Stranger, The. Allen Ginsberg. NeAP

Shrouding of the Duchess of Malfi, The. John Webster. *See* Duchess of Malfi, The

Shrubbery, The. William Cowper. NOBE; OBGa

Shrunken world, A. Epistle. To Enrique Caracciolo Trejo. Donald Davie. HarvBoo

Shu Has Gone Hunting. *Unknown.* CoBCP, *tr. by* Arthur Waley

Shu in the hunting-fields. Shu Has Gone Hunting. *Unknown.* CoBCP, *tr. by* Arthur Waley

Shu is away in the hunting-fields. *Unknown.* WoPoe, *tr. by* Arthur Waley

Shu' Shu' of Delgo. Albert Brodrick. PeSAV

Shu Swamp, Spring. May Swenson. APT-2

Shubble, The. Walter De la Mare. OBCoV

Shuffle Off to Buffalo. Harry Warren. ReLy

Shuffling papers. Certificate of Live Birth. Kimberly M. Blaeser. UnSA

Shui Shu. *Var. authors.* AWP, *tr. by* Arthur Waley
  River-Fog. AWP

Shulamit in Her Dreams. Marcia Falk. TaR

Shumeekuli, The. Andrew Peynetsa. PFTM-2, *tr. by* Dennis Tedlock

Shun[ne] delay[e]s, they breed[e] remorse. Loss[e] in Delay[e]. Robert Southwell. NoSic

Shunning an Imperative. Carl Hancock Rux. HeMarv

Shush, cicada / Old Whiskers. Issa. ZenPo, *tr. by* Takashi Ikemoto and Lucien Stryk

Shut In. Robert B. Shaw. SoSe-8

Shut-In, The. Nellie De Hearn. PoToHe

Shut in from all the world without. John Greenleaf Whittier. OBCP *Fr.* Snow-Bound [*or* Snow-Bound; a Winter Idyl].

Shut not me alive away. Commuted Sentence, The. Stevie Smith. OxAEP-2

Shut not so soon; the dull-eyed night. To Daisies, Not to Shut So Soon[e]. Robert Herrick. BeJo; CaPo; OBEV; OxBSP

Shut Not Your Doors. Walt Whitman. NOBA; OxBA

Shut Out. Christina Georgina Rossetti. NALW

Shut Out That Moon. Thomas Hardy. NOBE; NoAM

Shut, shut the door, good John! (fatigu'd [*or* fatigued] I said). Pope. FHYEP; NAEL-6v1; NAEL-7v1; OxAEP-1; PoE; TFi

Shut the Seven Seas against Us. George Barker. MoBrPo *Fr.* Third Cycle of Love Poems.

Shut up. Shut up. There's nobody here. Beast in the Space, The. William Sydney Graham. EmeKit; FaBoTw; OxAEP-2

Shut-winged fish, brown as mushroom. Swifts. Glyn Jones. AngWePo

Shut your eyes then. Nursery Rhyme. May Sarton. NOxBChV

Shuts up the story of our days. (LL) Nature, That Washed [*or* Washt] Her Hands in Milk[e]. Sir Walter Ralegh. NAEL-6v1; NAEL-7v1

Shutting my gate, I walk away. All Souls' Ruth Bidgood. AngWePo

Shuttle in the Crypt, The. Wole Soyinka.
  Bearings III: Amber Wall. PBMAP
  Ujamaa. PBMAP

Shuttles of trains going north, going south, drawing threads of blue. Morning Sun. Louis MacNeice. MoBrPo; TwCP

Shy and timid, Gloom to me. Outcast, The. James Stephens. MoBrPo

Shy dawn tenderly. Kalamu ya Salaam. SpirFl *Fr.* New Orleans Haiku.

Shy Geordie. Helen B. Cruickshank. OxBS

Shy one, shy one. To an Isle in the Water. W. B. Yeats. AWP; TTTS

Shy Request. Mihály Csokonai Vitéz. IQMS, *tr. by* Adam Makkai and Ena Roberts

Shy speechless sound, The. Osip Emilevich Mandelstam [*or* Mandelshtam]. Spl

Shyly she knits her brows. Tune: "Drunk in Fairyland." Ou-yang Hsiu. ColAnChi, *tr. by* J. R. Hightower

Shyly the silver-hatted mushrooms make. May. John Shaw Neilson. NOBAu

Shyness and modesty, they said. Disillusionment. Virginia Graham. NBLV

Si, señor, is halligators here, your guidebook say it. Sinalóa. Earle Birney. MoCV; OxBC; PeLV

Siamese Twins in Love. Susan Swartwout. ReTh

Siamese twins: one, maddened by. Twins. Robert Graves. FaBoEE; OBCoV

Siberia. James Clarence Mangan. BIrV; NOBVV; NOIV; NPeEn

Siberian Wooing. Yevgeny Aleksandrovich Yevtushenko [*or* Evtushenko]. VCWP, *tr. by* Albert C. Todd

Sibilla's Dirge. Thomas Lovell Beddoes. NOBE *Fr.* Death's Jest Book.

Sibrandus Schafnaburgensis. Robert Browning. CTC; EBVV *Fr.* Garden Fancies.

Sibyl. Robert Adamson. BMAP

Sibyl, The. Agnes Mary Frances Robinson. VWP

Sibyl's Song, The. Michele Roberts. BrRo

Sibylla Palmifera. Dante Gabriel Rossetti. *See* House of Life, The

Sibylline, yet benign. (LL) Formerly a Slave. Herman Melville. APN-2; TAP

Sic et Non. Sir Herbert Read. FaBoTw

Sic Itur. Arthur Hugh Clough. EBVV

Sic Vita. William Stanley Braithwaite. NAAAL

Sic Vita. Henry King, Bishop of Chichester. BASC; NOBE; NOSC; OxBSP; PAI; SCGP

Sic Vita. Henry David Thoreau. *See* I Am a Parcel of Vain Strivings Tied

Siccine separat amara mors? Knowledge after Death. Henry Charles Beeching. SacPr

Sich a Nice Man Too! Albert Chevalier.
    "There's parties ad yer meets about." UV

Sicilian Cyclamens. D. H. Lawrence. NoAM

Sicilian Muse, begin a loftier strain. Virgil [*or* Vergil]. AWP *Fr.* Eclogues.

Sicilian Muses, sing we greater things. Virgil [*or* Vergil]. *See* Sicilian Muse, begin a loftier strain

Sick. Shel [*or* Shelley] Silverstein. ChAP

Sick Child, A. Randall Jarrell. InPK-6; NoP-4; OxBC; VGW

Sick cicada, unable now to fly, A. Sick Cicada. Chia Tao. SuSp, *tr. by* Stephen Owen

Sick Horse. Tu Fu. CrYelRi, *tr. by* Sam Hamill

Sick Image of My Father Fades, The. John Horder. RaBo

Sick Leave. Po Chü-i. ChiP, *tr. by* Arthur Waley

Sick, lost traveler, wandering in the mists of night, A. Sonnet 103. Luis de Góngora y Argote. BLPSL, *tr. by* Rene de Costa, Rigas Kappatos and Eleni Paidoussi

Sick Love. Robert Graves. BoLoP; EBEV; GTBS-P; HAP; HarvBoo; NOBE; NPeEn; OxAEP-2
    (O Love in Me.) FaBoMo

Sick Man, The. E. du Perron. TuT, *tr. by* Pat Boran

Sick man passing. Buson. EH, *tr. by* Robert Hass

Sick Men Sleeping. Kenneth Mackenzie. BMAP

Sick Nought, The. Randall Jarrell. OxBA

Sick of all his women. Gambit. Tony Curtis. AngWePo

Sick of the piercing company of women. Country Walk, A. Thomas Kinsella. CIP-2

Sick on a journey. Basho. EH, *tr. by* Robert Hass

Sick on a journey / Over parched fields. Basho. ZenPo, *tr. by* Takashi Ikemoto and Lucien Stryk

Sick on my journey. Basho. SoOfWa, *tr. by* Sam Hamill

Sick Rose, The. William Blake. AWP; BoLoP; ClHu; EnLoPo; FHYEP; HAP; HeIP-4; InPK-6; NAEL-5v2; NAEL-6v2; NAWM-7v2; NIP-4; NOBE; NOBRP; NOEC; NPeEn; OPOU; OxAEP-2; OxBEV; OxBSP; PoE; RB; SCGP; SoSe-8; TFi; TRP; WeW-3 *Fr.* Songs of Experience.

Sick Stockrider, The. Adam Lindsay Gordon. CBAP

Sick Woman. John Kinsella. BMAP

Sick, you said goodbye to me. Lamenting for My Wife. Wang Shih-chieng. CoBLCP, *tr. by* Jonathan Chaves

Sickens my gut, Yellow Bittern. Yellow Bittern, The. Tom MacIntyre. PBCIP

Sickens my gut, Yellow Bittern. Yellow Bittern, The. *Unknown.* CIP-2, *tr. by* Tom MacIntyre

Sickles sound. Harvest Song. Ludwig Heinrich Christoph Hölty. AWP, *tr. by* Charles T. Brooks

Sickly. Basho. EH, *tr. by* Robert Hass

Sickly taper / By glimmering through thy low-browed misty vaults, The. Robert Blair. ECEV *Fr.* Grave, The.

Sickly wolfberry shrub, A. Eve's Monologue. Bella Abramovna Dizhur. ItGoST, *tr. by* Sarah Bliumis

Sickness. William Thompson.
    "Next, in a low-browed cave, a little hell." ECEV

Sickness is upon me, it will not leave! Beauty. "Badawi al-Jabal." MAP, *tr. by* John Heath-Stubbs and Matthew Sorenson

Sickness of Adam, The. Karl Shapiro. CRP *Fr.* Adam and Eve.

Sick. . . Sick. . . I will lie down and die. How. Isaac Rosenberg. PeFWW *Fr.* Unicorn, The.

Sidanen. Ludovic Lloyd.
    "Flee, stately Juno, Samos fro." AngWePo

Side 4. Víctor Hernández Cruz. PueRic

Side 12. Víctor Hernández Cruz. PueRic

Side 18. Víctor Hernández Cruz. PueRic

Side 20. Víctor Hernández Cruz. PueRic

Side 21. Víctor Hernández Cruz. PueRic

Side 22. Víctor Hernández Cruz. PueRic

Side 26. Víctor Hernández Cruz. PueRic

Side 32. Víctor Hernández Cruz. PueRic

Side by side. September City. Gerald Hausman. UrbNat

Side by Side. Harry Woods. ReLy

Side by side after the meal. Valerio Magrelli. NeIt

Side by side on the narrow bed. That Room. John Montague. CIP-2

Side by side, their faces blurred. Arundel Tomb, An. Philip Larkin. NoP-4; OxAEP-2

Side by side, we ride out of the city. Tsung Ch'en. CoBLCP *Fr.* Excursion to the Suburbs, An.

Side-canyon, A. Michael McClintock. HA

Side-room has sweated years and patience, rolls its one eye, The. Hospital Night. Francis Webb. BMAP

Sidera Cadentia. Ford Madox Ford. OxBSP

Sidewalk joins the concrete wall around the vacant lot, The. Where or When. Philip Whalen. PoM

Sidewalk Racer Or, On the Skateboard, The. Lillian Morrison. NTCP
    (Skimming.) KaS

Sidewalks of New York, The. James W. Blake. TCAPo

Sidney, Looking for Her Mother. Dolores Kendrick. ISC

Sidrophel, the Rosicrucian Conjurer. Samuel Butler (1612–80). OxBoLi *Fr.* Hudibras.

Siege. Sargon Boulus. MAP, *tr. by* Sargon Boulus and Alistair Elliot

Siege. Edna St. Vincent Millay. APT-1

Siege of Valencia, The. Felicia Dorothea Hemans.
    Dirge: "Calm on the bosom of thy God." OBEV; WoRP
    Meeting of the Bards, The. Written for an Eisteddford, or Meeting of Welsh Bards, Held in London, 22 May 1822. RWP

Siena. Lily Thicknesse. LW

Siena Mi Fe'; Disfecemi Maremma. Ezra Pound. MoAmPo *Fr.* Hugh Selwyn Mauberley (Life and Contacts).

Sierra Bear. David Bottoms. GifTon

Sierra Cup. Reg Saner. PoCoUp

Sierra Kid. Philip Levine. GeoHom

Sierra Noon. C. G. Hanzlicek. GeoHom

Sierras. Joaquin Miller. APN-2

Siesta. Antonio Machado Ruiz. SpanPo, *tr. by* Kate Flores

Siesta. Leslie Anne McIlroy. AmPoNex

Siesta. Adelia Prado. TCLAP, *tr. by* Marcia Kirinus

Siesta, The. *Unknown.* AWP, *tr. by* William Cullen Bryant

Siesta in Xbalba. Allen Ginsberg.
    "So I dream nightly of an embarkation." CLPP

Siesta of a Hungarian Snake. Edwin Morgan. HarvBoo; InPK-6

Sieve, A. Mother Goose. OxNR; ReMoGo

Sifting fronds of your hair, she talks "style." Hairdressing. Patricia Pogson. NLP

Sigh. Stéphane Mallarmé. AWP, *tr. by* Arthur Symons

Sigh, A. Witter Bynner. APT-1

Sigh, A. Anne Finch, Countess of Winchilsea. ECWP; OxBEV

Sigh, The. Nathalie Handal. PoArWo

Sigh, heart, and break not; rest, lark, and wake not! Nuptial Song. John Byrne Leicester Warren, 3d Baron De Tabley. GTBS-P; PeVV

Sigh, in the wind fall flowers, their petals dance. Selling Ruined Peonies. Yü Hsüan-chi. BoWoP, *tr. by* Geoffrey Waters

Sigh no more, dealers, sigh no more.   Much Ado about Nothing in the City. *Unknown.* UV

Sigh no more, ladies [sigh no more].   William Shakespeare.   AWP; CTC; NoSic; PAI; UV   *Fr.* Much Ado about Nothing.

Sigh not, Parthenia, that I'me doom'd to dye.   To My Most Honord Cosen, Mrs Somerset on the Unjust Censure Past Upon My Poore Marcelia.   Frances Boothby.   EMWP

Sigh sounds and a sough replies, A.   Ballad of Mulan, The.   *Unknown.* SuSp, *tr. by* William H. Nienhauser

Sigh then beyond my song: whirl & rejoice! (LL)   Canto Amor.   John Berryman.   CoAP; MoAmPo; VGW

Sigh, wind in the pine.   Douglas Stewart.   CBAP   *Fr.* Glencoe.

Sigh with her bosom over me. (LL)   Kingfisher, The.   William Henry Davies.   AngWePo; NOBE; OBEV; OBWVE

Sighed a dear little shipboard divinity.   Limerick.   Conrad Potter Aiken.   OBAL; PeLi

Sighing.   József Bajza.   IQMS, *tr. by* Watson Kirkconnell

Sighing, and sadly sitting by my Love.   Richard Barnfield [*or* Barnefield].   CAGL; PBRV   *Fr.* Cynthia, with Certain[e] Sonnets.

Sighing high and / again a sigh!   Weaving at the Window.   Wang Chien.   SuSp, *tr. by* William H. Nienhauser

Sighing I murmur, 'O mihi pratterritos!' (LL)   Eheu Fugaces.   "Thomas Ingoldsby."   FaBoEE; OxBoLi

Sighing I see yon little troop at play.   Charlotte Smith.   RWP

Sighing, O greet you and mourn you, O meadow of burial, Mohács.   Károly Kisfaludy.   IQMS, *tr. by* Watson Kirkconnell   *Fr.* Mohács.

Sighing over Flowers.   Tu Mu.   SuSp, *tr. by* Eddie Tsang

Sighs Are Air, and Go to the Air.   Gustavo Adolfo Bécquer.   SpanPo, *tr. by* Kate Flores

Sighs are my food, drink are my tears.   Sir Thomas Wyatt.   NoSic; OxBSP

Sighs of the Gunner from Dakar, The.   Guillaume Apollinaire.   PeFWW, *tr. by* Anne Hyde Greet

Sight.   Wilfrid Wilson Gibson.   MoBrPo

Sight and hearing finely tuned.   When I Was Young, I Stopped by a Wine Shop in Chi-men and Wrote This Poem, Inscribed It and Signed It, "Written by Lien the Eighteenth." The People of That District Have Since Taken It to Be a Poem of [the God] Lü Tung-pin! I Have Re.   Yü Chi.   CoBLCP, *tr. by* Jonathan Chaves

Sight grows dim—my power.   Arseny [*or* Arsenii] Aleksandrovich Tarkovsky [*or* Tarkovskii].   TCRP

Sight in Camp [in the Daybreak Gray and Dim], A.   Walt Whitman.   BLT; CBCWP; NAAL-2v1; NAAL-3; NAAL-5; NoAM; OxBA; PAI; PoE; SAmP; TAP

Sight of a lark's, The.   Virginia Brady Young.   HA

Sight of the coffee was good for sore eyes, The.   Upon Receipt of a Pound of Coffee in 1863.   Mary E. Tucker.   CBWP-1

Sight of the English is getting me down, The.   Hiraeth in N.W.3.   Wynford Vaughan-Thomas.   NOBL

Sight seems colored by the hour.   On Being Disabled by Light at Dawn in the Wilderness.   G. E. Murray.   IllVoic

Sight Unseen.   Kingsley Amis.   NoAM

Sighting down the long black barrel.   Hunting.   William Daniel Ehrhart.   CDa

Sighting the Slave Ship.   Pauline Stainer.   NeBl

Sightseeing.   Rita Dove.   GT

Sightseers, The.   Paul Muldoon.   BiHa; CIP-2

Sightseers in a Courtyard.   Nicolás Guillén.   TTY, *tr. by* Langston Hughes

Sigil.   "H. D."
    "Are these ashes in my hand."   APT-1
    "If you take the moon in your hands."   APT-1; BoWoP; FaBoWP
    Moon in Your Hands, The.   APT-1; BoWoP; FaBoWP
    "Now let the cycle sweep us here and there."   APT-1; VGW

Sigmund Freud says that one who reflects.   Limerick.   Peter Alexander.   PeLi

Sign.   Linda Smukler.   WiU

Sign Illuminated, A.   Roy Fisher.   EmeKit

Sign of the Times.   Remco Campert.   TuT, *tr. by* Desmond Egan

Sign your name in the book. It's just ink.   Limerick.   Sydney Bernard Smith.   PeLi

Signal, The.   David Ignatow.   NNaP

Signal Fire, The.   Aeschylus.   CTC, *tr. by* Dallam Simpson   *Fr.* Agamemnon.

Signal Gun, The.   Mary E. Tucker.   CBWP-1

Signal; or, A Satire against Modesty, The.   Francis Hawling.
    Author Consults a Critic and Sells His Manuscript, The.   NOEC

Signalmen, The.   Philip Stephens.   AmPoNex

Signature for Tempo.   Archibald MacLeish.   CRP; VGW

Signature of All Things, The.   Kenneth Rexroth.   APSN; APT-2; NNaP; TRP

Signatures.   Daniel Gerard Hoffman.   VGW

Signboard, The.   Robert Creeley.   CoAmPo

Signed by Franz Paul Stangl, Commandant.   Trains, The.   William Heyen.   GotH

Signet ring of Heaven, The. (LL)   Death of an Infant.   Lydia Huntley Sigourney.   SWaP; TCAPo

Significance of a Water Animal, The.   Ray A. Young Bear.   HATNAP

Significant Fevers.   Alison Fell.   BrRo

Signify the strength of the waves' lash. (LL)   Lear.   William Carlos Williams.   NAAL-2v2; NAAL-5; NOBA

Signifying Monkey, The.   *Unknown.* NAAAL

Signior Dildo.   John Wilmot, 2d Earl of Rochester.   BASC

Signs.   Ahmad al-Mushari Al-'Udwani.
    "Mysterious things within you, The."   BBASP; MAP, *tr. by* Charles Doria and Hilary Kilpatrick
    "You I give no name to / The mysterious things within you / are an untrodden bower."   BBASP; MAP, *tr. by* Charles Doria and Hilary Kilpatrick
    "You I give no name to / The mysterious things within you / are fragrance, light and melody."   BBASP; MAP, *tr. by* Charles Doria and Hilary Kilpatrick

Signs.   Silvia Grénier.   SurWo, *tr. by* Myrna Bell Rochester

Signs.   Wendy Mnookin.   UrbNat

Signs.   Mariana Romo-Carmona.   WiU

Signs.   Gjertrud Schnackenberg.   InPK-6; VCAP

Signs, The.   Norman Henry Pritchard, II.   NBV

Signs of Love.   Petrarch.   AWP   *Fr.* Sonnets to Laura.

Signs of Spring.   Sir Thomas Browne.   NOSC

Signs of the Times.   Paul Laurence Dunbar.   APN-2

Signs of the Zodiac are fading, The.   Nikolai Alekseievich Zabolotsky [*or* Zabolotskii].   TCRP; WoPoe, *tr. by* Daniel Weissbort

Signs of wear.   Monogram 29.   Martina Werner.   BoWoP, *tr. by* Rosmarie Waldrop

Signs on 42nd Street.   Flash.   Lee Bennett Hopkins.   SSCS

Signs on the Table, The.   Amanda Berenguer.   TANSG, *tr. by* Louise B. Popkin

Sigurd of yore.   *Unknown.* AWP, *tr. by* Eirikr Magnusson and William Morris   *Fr.* Elder Edda, The.

Sila.   Robert Penn Warren.   NoP-4

Sile Na gCioch.   Pat Parnell.   HW

Silence.   Bella [*or* Izabella] Akhatovna Akhmadulina.   BoWoP, *tr. by* Daniel Halpern

Silence.   Ghazi Al-Gosaibi.   MAP, *tr. by* Charles Doria and Sharif Elmusa

Silence.   Claribel Alegría.   TANSG, *tr. by* Darwin Flakoll

Silence.   Eugenio de Andrade.   VCWP, *tr. by* Alexis Levitin

Silence.   Stefan Brecht.   CLPP

Silence.   Bella Abramovna Dizhur.   ItGoST, *tr. by* Sarah Bliumis

Silence.   Miroslav Holub.   PoSu, *tr. by* Ian Milner and Jarmila Milner

Silence.   Thomas Hood.   EBEV; GSo; NOBE; OBEV; OxBSo; Son

Silence.   Slavko Janevski.   WoPoe, *tr. by* Charles Simic

Silence.   Tymoteusz Karpowicz.   PoSu, *tr. by* Jan Darowski

Silence.   Asymmetry 205.   Jackson Mac Low.   PFTM-2

Silence.   René Maran.   NegPo, *tr. by* Ellen Conroy Kennedy

Silence.   Edgar Lee Masters.   MoAmPo; PoToHe

Silence.   Marianne Craig Moore.   APT-1; FaBoMo; FaBoWP; HarvBoo; NALW; NOBA; PAI; TRP; WoPoe

Silence.   Edgar Allan Poe.   *See* Sonnet—Silence

Silence.   James Whitcomb Riley.   GSo

Silence.   Walter James Turner.   MoBrPo

Silence.   William Carlos Williams.   SAmP

Silence, The.   Robert Mezey.   TaR

Silence, The.   Vern Rutsala.   CDa

Silence, The.   Myra Scovel.   HA

Silence, The.   Virginia Brady Young.   HA

Silence, 2.   Stefan Brecht.   CLPP

Silence, 2.   Sipho Sepamla.   AF

Silence a droplet of water trickles down a stone, The.   Matsuo Allard.   HA

Silence: A Sonnet.   Henry King, Bishop of Chichester.   NOSC

Silence aimlessly.   Silent Time.   Hannie Rouweler.   TuT, *tr. by* Aidan Sharkey

Silence all flesh, your selves prepare.   Judicious Observation of That Dreadful Comet, A.   Ichabod Wiswall.   SCAP

Silence, an Eloquent Applause.   Leona Gregory.   TrCP

Silence and aura. An ancient Yemenite woman gathers dry.   Gleaning.   David Shimoni.   MHP, *tr. by* Ruth Finer Mintz

Silence and sleep like fields / Of amaranth lie. (LL)   All That's Past.   Walter De la Mare.   NOBE; OBMV; OxBTC

Silence and Solitude may hint.   Uninscribed Monument on One of the Battlefields of the Wilderness, An.   Herman Melville.   CBCWP

Silence and solitude were vacancy? (LL)   Mont Blanc.   Shelley.   NAEL-5v2; NAEL-6v2; NIP-4; NOBRP; NoP-4

Silence, and stealth of day[e]s! 'tis now.   Silence and Stealth of Day[e]s!   Henry Vaughan.   ESCV; NAEL-5v1; NAEL-6v1; NAEL-7v1; NPeEn

Silence, and whirling worlds afar.   Night.   Paul Laurence Dunbar.   InvLi

Silence Around an Ancient Stone.   Rosario Castellanos.   TANSG, *tr. by* Magda Bogin

Silence augmenteth grief, writing increaseth rage.   Epitaph on Sir Philip Sidney.   Fulke Greville, 1st Baron Brooke.   SCGP

Silence between drops of rain, The. (LL)   Why Must You Know?   John Wheelwright.   APT-2; VGW

Silence / between the floorboards.   Neighbor.   Bahiyyih Maroon.   SpirFl

Silence braided her fingers in my hair.   Dumb.   Hildegarde Flanner.   APT-2

Silence brought by the dark night: Eryri's.   Nightfall.   Walter Davies.   OBWVE; WoPoe, *tr. by* Anthony Conran

Silence, cooked like gold, in.   Alchemical.   Paul Celan.   VCWP, *tr. by* Michael Hamburger

Silence I identify with silence.   Silences.   Alejandra Pizarnik.   BLPSL, *tr. by* Rene de Costa, Rigas Kappatos and Eleni Paidoussi

Silence I speak of, The.   Silence: 2.   Sipho Sepamla.   AF

Silence / .is / a / looking.   E. E. Cummings.   PoE

Silence is a task that will last all her life. It continues.   Gloria Gervitz.   MirDau, *tr. by* Stephen Tapscott   *Fr.* Yiskor.

Silence is harder, Una said.   Cup, The.   Judith Wright.   FaBoWP

Silence is sucking the earth dry.   Silence.   Tymoteusz Karpowicz.   PoSu, *tr. by* Jan Darowski

Silence. Noon. The tower of sun, its rapt, circled crowd.   Indian Rope Trick.   Geoffrey Holloway.   NLP

Silence, now the bells are still.   Sunday.   J. C. Bloem.   TuT, *tr. by* Desmond Egan

Silence of love that cannot sing again. (LL)   Christina Georgina Rossetti.   GSo; OxBSo; Son   *Fr.* Monna Innominata.

Silence of the night, a sad, nocturnal.   Nocturne.   "Rubén Dario."   TCLAP, *tr. by* Lysander Kemp

Silence of the suburb, The.   Suburbia.   David Ignatow.   PoCoUp

Silence of Women, The.   Liz Rosenberg.   NIL-7

Silence on silence treads at each low morn.   Philoctetes.   John Byrne Leicester Warren, 3d Baron De Tabley.   NOBVV

Silence slipping around like death, A.   Winter Twilight, A.   Angelina Weld Grimké.   NAAAL

Silence Spoken Here.   Samuel Hazo.   GraLe

Silence the Eyes! Becalm the Senses!   Michael McClure.   PFTM-2   *Fr.* Ghost Tantras.

Silence Wager Stories.   Susan Howe.   BodElec; FTOS

Silence wells up at the mouth, A.   Whapmagoostui.   Charles Fishman.   PoCoUp

Silence where hope was. (LL)   Autumn.   Walter De la Mare.   NPeEn; OxBTC

Silence whistles in the open spaces.   Summer Night.   Nathan [*or* Natan] Alterman.   FIT, *tr. by* Robert Friend

Silences.   David Mitchell.   PeNZ

Silences.   Alejandra Pizarnik.   BLPSL, *tr. by* Rene de Costa, Rigas Kappatos and Eleni Paidoussi

Silences.   Edwin John Pratt.   NOBC

Silences; a Dream of Governments.   Jean Valentine.   LCAP-2

Silences from the Spanish Civil War.   Jane Duran.
Pyrenees, The.   Prnts
Spanish Peasant Boy.   Prnts

Silent, The.   Jones Very.   NCAP

Silent and alone, I ascend the west tower.   To the Tune "Meeting Happiness."   Li Yü.   WoPoe, *tr. by* Arthur Sze

Silent and small in your wet sleep.   Winter's Tale, A.   Wyatt Prunty.   RA

Silent Angel, The.   James Wright (1927–80).   BodElec

Silent as a nun Aleng Maria prays.   Aleng Maria.   Eugene Gloria.   ReBoTo

Silent as Roses.   Gillian Ferguson.   NeBl

Silent at Her Window.   Wang Ch'ang-ling.   ColAnChi; CrYelRi, *tr. by* Sam Hamill

Silent Buddha, The.   Larry Gates.   HA

Silent companions of the lonely hour.   To My Books.   Caroline Elizabeth Norton.   CenSon

Silent conquering army, A.   Kirkyard.   George Mackay Brown.   NPeEn; NePenScot

Silent crowd, The.   L. A. Davidson.   HA

Silent deer the sound of a waterfall.   Lenard D. Moore.   HA

Silent, draped in the garments of sacrifice.   Adelaida Gertsyk.   ARWW, *tr. by* Catriona Kelly

Silent friend of many distances, feel.   Rainer Maria Rilke.   EnlH   *Fr.* Sonnets to Orpheus.

Silent Globe.   Debra Gregerman.   AmPoNex

Silent hammers of decay. (LL)   Hammers, The.   Ralph Hodgson.   MoBrPo; NOBE; OxBTC

Silent Hour.   Rainer Maria Rilke.   AWP, *tr. by* Jessie Lemont

Silent hush, the rusted hinges, The.   Who Will Live in Our Houses When We Die?   Michael C. Blumenthal.   NoAM

Silent I gaze at the cataract.   By the Waterfall.   Friedrich Adler.   TrJP, *tr. by* Jethro Bithell

Silent, I go up alone to the Western Pavilion.   Tune: "Joy at Meeting."   Li Yü.   SuSp, *tr. by* Eugene Eoyang

Silent in the moonlight, no beginning or end.   Two Ramages for Old Masters.   Robert Bly.   BodElec

Silent is the house: all are laid asleep.   Visionary, The.   Emily Jane Brontë.   BrRo; NOBE; NOBVV; NPeEn; OxBEV; SCGP; SCV

Silent Lover, The.   Sir Walter Ralegh.   OBEV

Silent Night.   Joseph Mohr.   ChrPo, *tr. by* John Freeman Young

Silent Night, The.   Mrs. Henry Linden.   CBWP-4

Silent night, hallowed night!   Christmas Song.   Joseph Mohr.   AuPH, *tr. by* Lowell A. Bangerter

Silent night, holy night.   Silent Night.   Joseph Mohr.   ChrPo, *tr. by* John Freeman Young

Silent Night! Holy Night!   Joseph Mohr.   SacPr, *tr. by* Jane Campbell

Silent Noon.   Dante Gabriel Rossetti.   GSo; HAP; NAEL-5v2; NAEL-6v2; NoP-4   *Fr.* House of Life, The.

Silent Nymph, with curious eye!   John Dyer.   CABP; NOEC; NoP-4; OxAEP-1

Silent, O Moyle, be the roar of thy water.   Song of Fionnuala, The.   Thomas Moore.   BIrV

Silent old man, The.   Old Man of Few Words.   Muso Soseki.   EaWin, *tr. by* W. S. Merwin

Silent One, The.   Ivor Gurney.
"Who died on the wires, and hung there, one of two."   HarvBoo; NAEL-5v2; NAEL-6v2; NPeEn; NoP-4; OBWP; PeFWW; PoWW

Silent Piano, The.   Louis Simpson.   EmeKit

Silent Poem.   Robert Francis.   CRP; LCAP-2

Silent Prophet, The.   Norman Jordan.   NBV

Silent Room, The.   Kingsley Amis.   OxBC

Silent room—gray with a dusty blight, A.   Among His Books.   Edith Nesbit.   NOBVV

Silent room—grey with a dusty blight, A.   Edith Nesbit.   *See* Silent room— gray with a dusty blight, A

Silent Slain, The.   Archibald MacLeish.   *See* Too-Late Born, The

Silent Tear, The.   Ilya Abu Madi.   GraLe, *tr. by* George Dimitri Selim

Silent, thatched hut deep among the trees, A.   Little Landscape, A.   Chu Yün-ming.   CoBLCP, *tr. by* Jonathan Chaves

Silent, the autumn river, fishermen's fires sparse.   Spending the Night on the River.   T'ang Hsien-tsu.   CoBLCP, *tr. by* Jonathan Chaves

Silent the girl at the spindle.   Spinner, The.   Nathan [*or* Natan] Alterman.   FIT, *tr. by* Robert Friend

Silent the maid with the spindle spun.   Maid, The.   Nathan [*or* Natan] Alterman.   MHP, *tr. by* Ruth Finer Mintz

Silent Time.   Hannie Rouweler.   TuT, *tr. by* Aidan Sharkey

Silent Town, The.   Richard Dehmel.   AWP, *tr. by* Jethro Bithell

Silent, upon a peak in Darien. (LL)   On First Looking into Chapman's Homer.   John Keats.   BRP; CABP; CenSon; CIHu; FHYEP; FaBoCh; GSo; GTBS-P; HAP; HeIP-4; InPK-6; NAEL-5v2; NAEL-6v2; NAWM-7v2; NIL-7; NIP-4; NOBE; NOBRP; NPeEn; NoP-4; OBAL; OBEV; OPOU; OxAEP-2; OxBEV; OxBSo; PoE; PoPoPo; SCGP; SoSe-8; Son; TFi; TRP; UV; WoPoe

Silent Woman to the University of Oxford, The.   Dryden.
"What Greece, when learning flourished, only knew."   NOSC

Silent Wood, A.   Elizabeth Siddal.   NOBVV

Silent Words, The.   Haim [*or* Chaim *or* Khayim] Guri [*or* Gouri].   MHP, *tr. by* Ruth Finer Mintz

Silent World Is Our Only Homeland, The.   Francis Ponge.   AF, *tr. by* Beth Archer

Silentium.   Osip Emilevich Mandelstam [*or* Mandelshtam].   TCRP, *tr. by* Albert C. Todd

Silentium.   Fyodor [*or* Feodor] Ivanovich Tyutchev.   WoPoe, *tr. by* Charles Tomlinson

Silently and very fast. (LL)   Fall of Rome, The.   W. H. Auden.   NPeEn; OxBEV; OxBTC; UnPo

Silently my wife walks on the still wet furze.   Berry Picking.   Irving Layton.   HeIP-4; MoCV; NIP-4; NoP-4

Silently / or LOUD. (LL)   Black Art.   Imamu Amiri Baraka.   BPo; ESEAA; NAAAL

Silently / she was quieter than breathing now.   Juliet's Garden.   Charles Tomlinson.   OBGa

Silently, slowly falls the snow from an ashen sky.   Snowfall.   Giosuè Carducci.   AWP, *tr. by* Romilda Rendel

Silently the sleepy dray cart crawls.   In the Moldavian Steppe.   Aleksandr [*or* Viktor Fyodorovich] Vertinsky [*or* Vertinskii].   TCRP, *tr. by* Daniel Weissbort

Silently you stand before me.   David Vogel.   FIT, *tr. by* Robert Friend

Silesian Weavers, The.   Heinrich Heine.   NAWM-7v2, *tr. by* Hal Draper

Silet.   Ezra Pound.   MoAmPo; Son

Silhouette. Langston Hughes. NAAL-5

Silhouettes, they lean against a ringed moon. Paiute Ponies. Jim Barnes. CDW

Silk Robe. Jeffrey Skinner. PBCAP

Silk, / Satin. *Unknown.* OxNR

Silken Snake, The. Robert Herrick. OxBSP; PBRV

Silken Tent, The. Robert Frost. APT-1; ColAP; InPK-6; NOBA; NoP-4; OxBSo; Son; TAP; TRP; TwCP; WeW-3

Silken threads by viewless spinner spun, The. Crossed Threads. Helen Hunt Jackson. APN-2

Silkworm Song of Torchlit Fields. Kao Ch'i. CoBLCP; ColAnChi, *tr. by* Jonathan Chaves

Silkworms, The. Douglas Stewart. CBAP

Silkworms enter cocoons: harvest time. At the Temple of Kuan Yin in the Rain. Su Tung-p'o (Su Shih). CrYelRi, *tr. by* Sam Hamill

Siller Croun, The. Susanna Blamire. ECWP; LW

Silly Boy. *Unknown.* NOSC

Silly boy, 'tis ful[l] moon[e] yet, thy night as day shines clearly [*or* clearly]. First Love. Thomas Campion. OxBoLi

Silly boy, wert you but wise. Silly Boy. *Unknown.* NOSC

Silly country maiden went, A. Leda in Stratford, Ont. Anne Wilkinson. MoCV

Silly Fool, The. W. H. Auden. OBMV

Silly girl! Yet morning lies. To a Pretty Girl. Israel Zangwill. TrJP

Silly Song. Federico García Lorca. TTTS, *tr. by* M. D. Herter Norton

Silly Spring. Marcelijus Martinaitis. TWW, *tr. by* Laima Sruogins

Silo Treading. Bruce Beaver. BMAP

Silouette of a woman appears in my mind as if from a sixteen millimeter film, The. Thoughts about Sari's Jump. Devorah Amir. DTA, *tr. by* Miriyam Glazer

Silver. A. R. Ammons. NoP-4

Silver. Walter De la Mare. MoBrPo; PoRA; TTTS

Silver answer rang,—"Not Death, but Love," The. (LL) Elizabeth Barrett Browning. BWW; CenSon; EBVV; NOBE; NoP-4; OBEV; OxAEP-2; PoPoPo; WPE *Fr.* Sonnets from the Portuguese.

Silver as / The needle's eye. George Oppen. NNaP *Fr.* Some San Francisco Poems.

Silver as / The needle's eye. George Oppen. *See* Old ships are preserved

Silver bark of beech, and sallow. Counting-out Rhyme. Edna St. Vincent Millay. InPK-6; NOxBChV; OxIBACP; SoSe-8; TTTS

Silver birch is a dainty lady, The. Child's Song in Spring. Edith Nesbit. NOxBChV

Silver Bowl, The. Joseph Ezobi.
  "And like thy father sing in tunefulness." TrJP, *tr. by* D. I. Friedmann
  Barren Soul, A. TrJP, *tr. by* D. I. Friedmann

Silver chariots, and copper. Seascape. Arthur Rimbaud. SxFrPo, *tr. by* Martin Sorrell

Silver chatter in parks. Silver Talk. Remco Campert. TuT, *tr. by* Theo Dorgan

Silver Clasps. "Paul Dermée." CuPo

Silver dust. Pear Tree. "H. D." BoWoP; ColAP; MoAmPo; NOBA; PoE; TCAPo; UnPo

Silver Eros the ankle bracelet, The. Leonidas of Tarentum. GrAn

Silver flash from the sinking sun, A. Sunset in the Tropics. James Weldon Johnson. APT-1

Silver Flask, The. John Montague. CIP-2; PNI

Silver-footed girl was bathing, letting the water, The. Rufinus. HePo, *tr. by* Barbara Hughes Fowler

Silver herring throbbed thick in my seine, The. Kenneth Leslie. NOBC; OxBSo *Fr.* By Stubborn Stars.

Silver, into which I force. Paavo Haavikko. PFTM-2, *tr. by* Anselm Hollo *Fr.* Winter Palace, The.

Silver Jubilee. Llewelyn Wyn Griffith. OBWVE

Silver Love, an anklet, A. Leonidas of Tarentum. PGA

Silver Lucifer. A. Lunar Baedeker. Mina Loy. APT-1; VGW

Silver Mist, The. John Clare. FHYEP

Silver mist more lowly swims, The. Silver Mist, The. John Clare. FHYEP

Silver-Paced. Bruce Berger. UrbNat

Silver Penny, The. Walter De la Mare. NOxBChV; OBMV

Silver Poplar at Sunrise. Constance Egemo. PoCoUp

Silver rubs rocks and furs the twig. Bounding Line. Genevieve Taggard. APT-2

Silver Sands, The. Richard Blanco. AmPoNex; NAPBL

Silver-scaled Dragon with jaws flaming red, A. Toaster, The. William Jay Smith. NOxBChV; OTCP

Silver Spoon, The. Po Chü-i. ChiP, *tr. by* Arthur Waley

Silver Swan, The. Orlando Gibbons. FaBoCh; HAP; HeIP-4; NAEL-5v1; NAEL-6v1; OPOU; OWoS; OxBSP; PAI

(Silver Swan[ne], Who Living Had No Note, The.) InPK-6; RB; WoPoe

Silver Swan, The. *Unknown.* NoP-4

Silver swan, who living had no note, The. Silver Swan, The. Orlando Gibbons. FaBoCh; HAP; HeIP-4; NAEL-5v1; NAEL-6v1; OPOU; OWoS; OxBSP; PAI

Silver swan, who living had no note, The. Silver Swan, The. *Unknown.* NoP-4

Silver Swan[ne], Who Living Had No Note, The. Orlando Gibbons. *See* Silver Swan, The

Silver Talk. Remco Campert. TuT, *tr. by* Theo Dorgan

Silver Tassie, The. Robert Burns. NOBE; OBEV; WoPoe
  (Soldier's Farewell, A.) FaBoWar

Silver trumpets rang across the Dome, The. Easter Day. Oscar Wilde. OxAEP-2

Silver-vested monkey trips, A. Cortège. Paul Verlaine. AWP; OBVE, *tr. by* Arthur Symons

Silver Wedding. Ralph Hodgson. OxBTC

Silverhaired guard at the museum of fine arts, The. "Moscow" Pool. Pyotr Vegin. TCRusP, *tr. by* Daniel Weissbort

Silverthorn Bush. Robert Finch. NOBC

Silvertoed virgin, A. Rufinus. GrAn

Silvery Fountain. Mary E. Tucker. CBWP-1

Silvery tells no sphere to go and. Mac Wellman. HeMarv *Fr.* Rat Minaret: Miniaturist-Divan, The.

Silvia. William Shakespeare. *See* Two Gentlemen of Verona, The

Silvia pretty nymph! within this shade. Pastoral Dialogue between Two Shepherdesses, A. Anne Finch, Countess of Winchilsea. ECWP

Silvio's Complaint: A Song, To a Fine Scotch Tune. Aphra Behn. EMWP
  (In the Blooming Time o'th'year.) RACG

Simchas Torah. Morris Jacob Rosenfeld. TrJP

Simcox. John Heath-Stubbs. OBCoV

Simcox was one of several rather uninteresting. Simcox. John Heath-Stubbs. OBCoV

Simhat Torah. Judah Leib Gordon. TrJP, *tr. by* Helena Frank and Alice Lucas

Simile. N. Scott Momaday. CDW

Simile. Ágnes Nemes Nagy. PoSu, *tr. by* Frederic Will

Simile, A. Matthew Prior. NOEC

Simile for Her Smile, A. Richard Wilbur. InPK-6

Similes. Charles Reznikoff. APT-2

Similes for Two Political Characters of 1819. Shelley. RB
  (As from their ancestral oak.) NAEL-5v2; NAEL-6v2
  (To Sidmouth and Castlereagh.) NAEL-5v2; NAEL-6v2

Similie. Charlotte Dacre. NOBRP

Simon and Susan. *Unknown.* OxBoLi

Simon and the Tarantula. James Wright (1927–80). NNaP

Simon Gerty. Elinor Wylie. OBAL

Simon Lee [the Old Huntsman]. William Wordsworth. GTBS-P; NAEL-5v2; NAEL-6v2

Simon Legree—A Negro Sermon. Nicholas Vachel Lindsay. TAP *Fr.* Booker Washington Trilogy, The.

Simon my son, son of my Nuptiall knot. Lamentation on My Dear Son Simon, A. John Saffin. SCAP

Simon the Cyrenian Speaks. Countee Cullen. BPo; ChIV-2; HAP; MoAmPo; TTY; TrCP

Simone, laying her life in Perrin's hands, has yet. Intact. Stephanie Strickland. ExTi

Simone Weil: In Assisi. Edward Hirsch. BBASP

Simple. Naomi Long Madgett. GT

Simple ain't it? Genius Child. Kevin Powell. AmPoNex

Simple Autumnal. Louise Bogan. MoAmPo; Son

Simple child, A. Solstice for John. John Cope. GeoH

Simple child, A. William Wordsworth. NAEL-5v2; NAEL-6v2; NOBRP

Simple contact with a wooden spoon and the word, The. Words. Barbara Guest. FTOS

Simple Faith. William Cowper. FHYEP

Simple food, coarse clothing are all you need. Bamboo Villa, The. Shen Chou. CoBLCP, *tr. by* Jonathan Chaves

Simple Gifts. *Unknown.* APN-2

Simple Like That. Wil'um Lee. InTrad

Simple living was clearly the nub. Limerick. Joyce Johnson. PeLi

Simple lust is all my woe, A. Dennis Brutus. HBAPE

Simple Man, A. Nikolai Ivanovich Glazkov. TCRP, *tr. by* Daniel Weissbort

Simple Matter, A. Gloria Rawlinson. PeNZ

Simple nosegay! was that much to ask?, A. Troll's Nosegay, The. Robert Graves. OxBSo; Son

Simple Outlines, Human Shapes. Irving Feldman. VCAP *Fr.* All of Us Here.

Simple outlines, human shapes, daily acts, plain poses. Irving Feldman. VCAP *Fr.* All of Us Here.

Simple Pastoral, A. George Alexander Stevens. NOEC

Simple Ploughboy, The. *Unknown.* FaBoCh

Simple Poem. Anthony Thwaite. DiPo

Simple Purification, The. Kabir. EnlH; WoPoe, *tr. by* Robert Bly

Simple Rustic You Seemed, A. *Unknown.* SuSp, *tr. by* Wu-Chi Liu

Simple Simon. Mother Goose. LB; OTCP; OxNR; ReMoGo

Simple Story, A. Gwen Harwood. FaBoWP; NOBAu

Simple Thing, A. Leatha Kendrick. SpudSo

Simple Truth, The. Philip Levine. NoP-4

Simple Verses. José Martí. TTY, *tr. by* Seymour Resnick
  "I am an honest man." TCLAP, *tr. by* Elinore Randall
  "I know: from flesh." TCLAP, *tr. by* Elinore Randall
  "In the shadow of a wing." TCLAP, *tr. by* Elinore Randall
  "Lonely trembling soul can ache, The." TCLAP, *tr. by* Elinore Randall

Simplest, The. Occurrences, The. George Oppen. APT-2

Simplest and the Hardest, The. Margaret Lloyd. OPRER

Simplex Munditiis. Ben Jonson. AWP; NOBE; OBEV *Fr.* Epicoene; or, The Silent Woman.

Simplicity Aims Circularly. Anna Walters. VoR

Simplicity and Sweet Neglect. Ben Jonson. OxAEP-1 *Fr.* Epicoene; or, The Silent Woman.

Simplicity's Song. Robert Wilson. CTC *Fr.* Three Ladies of London, The.

Simplicity sings it and 'sperience doth prove. Robert Wilson. CTC *Fr.* Three Ladies of London, The.

Simplicity so graven hurts the sense. So Graven. Josephine Miles. NoAM

Simplify Me When I'm Dead. Keith Douglas. FaBoWar; NoAM; OxBTC

Simplify Your Combination Therapy. Mark Wunderlich. NAPBL

Simplon Pass, The. William Wordsworth. NPeEn

Simplon Pass, The. William Wordsworth. CABP *Fr.* Prelude, The; Growth of a Poet's Mind [1805 vers.].

Simply by sailing in a new direction. Landfall in Unknown Seas. Allen Curnow. NoP-4

Simply I would sing for the time being. Interlude. Keidrych Rhys. AngWePo

Simply to leave him out of the scene forever. (LL) Anonymous Drawing. Donald Justice. CoAP; HeIP-4

Simultaneously. David Ignatow. TwCP

Simultaneously, as soundlessly. W. H. Auden. PoE *Fr.* Horae Canonicae.

Sin. "Angelus Silesius." GePo, *tr. by* George C. Schoolfield *Fr.* Cherubical Wanderer, The.

Sin. Ben Scammell. NLP

Sin (1). George Herbert. GeHe; OxAEP-1
  (Sin (I).) NoP-4

Sin and Death. John Milton. EBEV; OBNV *Fr.* Paradise Lost.

Sin and Despair Have So Possess'd My Heart. Anne Vaughan Locke. CABP

Sin, Despair, and Lucifer. Phineas Fletcher. NOSC *Fr.* Locusts, or Appolyonists, The.

Sin (I). George Herbert. *See* Sin (1)

Sin I am free, I counte him not a bene. (LL) Geoffrey Chaucer. BoLoP; NAEL-5v1; NAEL-6v1; SCGP *Fr.* Merciles[s] Beaute [*or* Beautée *or* Beauty].

Sin!/ O only fatal Woe. Thomas Traherne. ESCV *Fr.* Third Century, The.

Sin: "O that I could a sin once see!" George Herbert. OxBSP

Sin of Omission, The. Margaret Elizabeth Munson Sangster. *See* At Sunset

Sin's Round. George Herbert. NOSC

Sin' they nailed him to the tree. (LL) Ballad of the Goodly Fere. Ezra Pound. ChIV-2; MoAmPo; PoRA; TrCP

Sin! wilt thou vanquish me! Thomas Traherne. ESCV *Fr.* Third Century, The.

Sinalóa. Earle Birney. MoCV; OxBC; PeLV

Since Akkad, Since Elam, Since Sumer. Aimé Césaire. WoPoe, *tr. by* Gregson Davis

Since all our keys are lost or broken. Art of Poetry, An. James Philip McAuley. NOCV

Since all shall be nothing a hundred years hence. (LL) Careless Gallant, The. Thomas Jordan. HAP; OxBoLi

Since all that beat about in Nature's range. Constancy to an Ideal Object. Samuel Taylor Coleridge. NAEL-5v2; NAEL-6v2; NOBRP

Since all that I can ever do for thee. Last Wish, The. "Owen Meredith." OxBSP

Since apes are still able to learn. Shih Te. SuSp

Since as in night's deck-watch ye show. Herman Melville. APN-2 *Fr.* John Marr.

Since autumn attached itself to the humid streets of this city. Return 2. Tamara Kamenszain. MirDau, *tr. by* Roberta Gordenstein

Since before anyone remembers. Old Creek. Muso Soseki. EaWin, *tr. by* W. S. Merwin

Since Bonny-Boots Was Dead. *Unknown.* NPeEn
  (Madrigal: "Since Bonny-boots was dead, that so divinely") OxBoLi

Since brass, nor stone, nor earth, nor boundless sea. William Shakespeare. AWP; HAP; NAEL-5v1; NAEL-6v1; NAEL-7v1; NOBE; NoSic; OxAEP-1; OxBSo; PoRA; RaBo; SCGP; Son; TFi; TreFP; UnPo *Fr.* Sonnets.

Since Cassius first did whet me against Cæsar. William Shakespeare. OxAEP-1 *Fr.* Julius Caesar.

Since certainly it is mine. (LL) Lilacs. Amy Lowell. APT-1; MoAmPo; OxBA; PoRA

Since Christmas they have lived with us. Balloons. Sylvia Plath. FaBoWP; PoE

Since clarity suggests simplicity. Counterpart, The. Elizabeth Jennings. TOF

Since coming to Huang-chou. Su Tung-p'o (Su Shih). SuSp *Fr.* Rain at Cold-Food Festival.

Since, Coridon, you have a hart can pay. To a Gentleman that Courted Several Ladys. *Poets of the Tixall Circle.* EMWP

Since drums and parchment were invented. (LL) John Gay. NOEC; NPeEn *Fr.* Fables.

Since earnestly studying the Buddhist doctrine of emptiness. Idle Droning. Po Chü-i. CoBCP, *tr. by* Burton Watson

Since earth has put you away, O sons of Barmak. *Unknown.* AWP *Fr.* Thousand and One Nights, The.

Since every quill is silent to relate. Monumental Memorial of Marine Mercy, A. Richard Steere. SCAP; TCAPo

Since feeling is first. E. E. Cummings. MoAmPo; NoP-4

Since first break of dawn the fiend. John Milton. NOSC *Fr.* Paradise Lost.

Since First I Saw Your Face. *Unknown.* OBEV; OxBSP

Since first my little one lay on my breast. Augusta Davies Webster. VWP; ViWPN *Fr.* Mother and Daughter.

Since first we met. Encounter. Mary Low. SurWo

Since first you knew my am'rous smart. Epigram. Robert Nugent. NOEC

Since God through Jordan leadest me. (LL) He Leadeth Me. Joseph Henry Gilmore. AH; SacPr

Since he came back. Private Jack Smith, U. S. M. C. Bryan Alec Floyd. CDa

Since he kissed them and put them there. (LL) Little Boy Blue. Eugene Field. BRP; ChAP; ITBLP; OBAL; OBCA; SoSe-8

Since I abandoned and tied my soul to your sweet appearance and manners oh Sir, guide and light of my life, will I ever see you before I die? Cecco Nuccoli. CAGL, *tr. by* Jill Claretta Robbins

Since I am coming [*or* comming] to that holy room[e]. Hymn[e] to God My God, in My Sickness[e], A. John Donne. BASC; EBEV; ESCV; HeIP-4; MeLP; NAEL-5v1; NAEL-6v1; NAEL-7v1; NOSC; NoP-4; OxAEP-1; PBRV; PoE; SoSe-8; TFi; TOF

Since I am convinced. Saigyo. AWP

Since I am the bookish, just like you, abuelita. Memoranda for Rosario. Maria Elena Caballero-Robb. ReBoTo

Since I believe in God the Father Almighty. Johannes Milton, Senex. Robert Bridges. PeECV

Since I do not hope to return ever. Ballata II: Last Song: from Exile. Guido Cavalcanti. WoPoe, *tr. by* George Sutherland Fraser and G. S. Fraser

Since I don't wake with her. Thin, Black Band, A. Sandor Csoori. VCWP

Since I emerged that day from the labyrinth. Labyrinth, The. Edwin Muir. MoBrPo

Since I entered the inner rooms. Written on a Leaf. *Unknown.* BoWoP, *tr. by* Geoffrey Waters

Since I got my cat Five White. Offering for the Cat, An. Mei Yao Ch'en. CoBCP; ColAnChi, *tr. by* Burton Watson

Since I have seen a bird one day. Truth, The. William Henry Davies. FaBoTw

Since I have set my lips to your full cup, my sweet. More Strong Than Time. Victor Hugo. AWP, *tr. by* Andrew Lang

Since I heard. *Var. authors.* AWP *Fr.* Kokin Shu.

Since I Lay Ill. Po Chü-i. ChiP, *tr. by* Arthur Waley

Since I lay ill, how long has passed? Since I Lay Ill. Po Chü-i. ChiP, *tr. by* Arthur Waley

Since I left her. Mibu no Tadami. OHPJ

Since I left you, mine eye is in my mind. William Shakespeare. SCGP *Fr.* Sonnets.

Since I lived a stranger in the City of Hsün-yang. Rain. Po Chü-i. BLT, *tr. by* Arthur Waley

Since I lived a stranger in the City of Hsün-yang. Rain. Po Chü-i. ChiP, *tr. by* Arthur Waley

Since I'm a girl. *Unknown.* BoWoP

Since I must love your north. To My Mountain. Kathleen Jessie Raine. OxBS

Since I must needs into thy school[e] return[e]. Lady's Prayer to Cupid, A. Thomas Carew. CaPo

Since I noo mwore do zee your feäce. Wife A-Lost, The. William Barnes. BoLoP; EBVV; EnLoPo; HAP; OBEV; SCGP

Since I parted from you, immortal bird. For Several Days I Have Not Visited the Garden Pavilion—A Poem Sent to My Pet Crane. Wang Chiu-ssu. CoBLCP, *tr. by* Jonathan Chaves

Since I reached the charming age of puberty. Where Is the Life That Late I Led? Cole Porter. ReLy

Since I've been in this colony I've written many a song. Flash Colonial Barman, The. William W. Coxon. NOBAu

Since I've felt this pain. Ono no Komachi. WPOW, *tr. by* Rob Swigart

Since I was born. Kisei. JDP, *tr. by* Yoel Hoffmann

Since I was in Syracuse is a month ago. Quarries in Syracuse. Louis Golding. TrJP

Since I Was Thrown Inside. Nazim Hikmet. AF

Since in a land not barren still. Love and Discipline. Henry Vaughan. GeHe; SacPr

Since in religion all men disagree. To Caelia. *Unknown*. FaBoEE

Since, in the loop of time this will return. Love's Parallel. Elizabeth Garrett. MFPA

Since it must be so. New-Courtier, The. Alexander Brome. BASC

Since last September I've been trying to describe. Edward Lear in February. Christopher Middleton. TwCP

Since last the tutelary hearth. Christmas Family Reunion. Peter De Vries. NBLV; NOBL

Since last we met, thou and thy horse, my dear. Henry Vaughan. AngWePo *Fr.* Invitation to Brecknock, An.

Since laws were made for ev'ry degree. John Gay. NAEL-6v1; NOEC *Fr.* Begger's Opera.

Since life is nothing in your philosophy. Nothing. Julia de Burgos. BoWoP, *tr. by* Aliki and Willis Barnstone

Since, Lord, to thee / A narrow way and little gate. Holy Baptism (2). George Herbert. ChIV-2

Since Love is shivering. Sister Juana Inés de la Cruz. WPoS *Fr.* First Villancico, Written for the Nativity of Our Lord, Puebla, 1689, The.

Since man has been articulate. Every Thing. Harold Monro. MoBrPo

Since Man's a little world, to make it great. Epigram on Woman, An. Philip Ayres. FaBoEE

Since man's life is nothing but a bit of action at a distance. Piano Solo. Nicanor Parra. PoetW; TCLAP, *tr. by* William Carlos Williams

Since man went out from the fields of paradise. On the Killing at Lindisfarne. Alcuin. MLL, *tr. by* Helen Waddell

Since man with that inconstancy was born. To Alexis in Answer to His Poem against Fruition. Aphra Behn. LW

Since *metaphor* derives from *transferring*. Welcome to Ithaca. Rebecca Seiferle. ExTi

Since morning glories. Chiyojo [*or* Chiyo *or* Chiyo-Ni *or* Kaga no Chiyo *or* Fukuda Chiyo-Ni]. SoOfWa, *tr. by* Sam Hamill

"Since mountains sink to vales, and valleys die." Bathos, The. Richard Porson. FaBoEE

Since my hair was plaited and we became man and wife. To His Wife. Su Wu. ChiP, *tr. by* Arthur Waley

Since my overdraft threatens to be. Limerick. S. Tonkin. PeLi

Since my Vivian left me. Daniel Mark Epstein. DiPo *Fr.* Homage to Mallarmé.

Since my wife was born. Notes for the Legend of Salad Woman. Michael Ondaatje. NoAM

Since Naturally Black is Naturally Beautiful. Naturally. Audre Lorde. BlSi; ISC

Since nought avails, let me arise and leave. Sadi [*or* Saadi *or* Sa'di]. AWP, *tr. by* L. Cranmer-Byng *Fr.* Gulistan, The.

Since now I dare not ask. Sharp Ridge, The. Robert Graves. FaBoEE

Since now I have a mind to sing. William of Aquitaine. MLL

Since now in every public place. Sea Horse, The. Robert Graves. FaBoMo

Since now, once more beside this mound. Sing Again Together. William Barnes. SCGP

Since observed by Yours faithfully, God. (LL) Reply, A. *Unknown*. NBLV; NOBL; OxBEV; PeLi

Since of no creature living the last breath. Edna St. Vincent Millay. HeIP-4; VGW

Since one anthologist put in his book. Anthologistics. Arthur Guiterman. NBLV

Since our Country, our God—Oh, my Sire! Jephtha's Daughter. Byron. ChIV-1

Since Potiphar made you his overseer. Israel II. Charles Reznikoff. ChIV-1

Since Reverend Doctors now declare. Respectable Burgher, The. Thomas Hardy. ChIV-2; NoAM

Since Rose is a classic taste possessed. Beau Ideal, The. Jessie Pope. FaBoWar

Since She Gives So Little Pay. Steinmar. GePo, *tr. by* J. W. Thomas

Since she must go, and I must mourn, come night. John Donne. EBEV *Fr.* Elegies.

Since she was lovelier than any of you. (LL) Blue Girls. John Crowe Ransom. APT-1; ColAP; MoAmPo; NoAM; NoP-4; RB; TAP; VGW; WeW-3

Since whom[e] I loved [*or* lov'd *or* lovd] hath paid [*or* payd] her last debt. John Donne. BASC; FSCP; NAEL-5v1; NAEL-6v1; NAEL-7v1; NOSC; PBRV; Son *Fr.* Holy Sonnets.

Since Shylock's book has walk'd the circles here. To a Noisy Politician. Philip Freneau. TAP

Since 1619. Margaret Abigail Walker. NoP-4

Since that day. Abortion. Iman Mirsal. NAfrP, *tr. by* Clarissa C. Burt

Since that first morning when I crawled. Hornworm: Autumn Lamentation. Stanley Kunitz. AmFaPo; BodElec

Since that night / I cannot know myself. Lady Izumi. BoWoP

Since that this thing we call the world. Epicurean Ode, An. John Hall. MeLP; NOSC; NPeEn

Since the Conquest none of us. Conquest, The. Oliver St. John Gogarty. OBMV

Since the first toss of gale that blew. Valentine Ackland. PoBW

Since the good Bishop left his name. To Mr. Wren, My Valentine Six Year Old. Jane Holt. ECWP

Since the night is dark. *Unknown*. BoWoP

Since the sky started crying. Flood at the International Writer's Workshop. Bogomil Gjuzel. CarOv, *tr. by* Carolyn Kizer

Since the / Spirit's omnipresent, there's a difference. John Cage. APSN *Fr.* Diary: How to Improve the World (You Will Only Make Matters Worse).

Since the storm two nights ago. Recognition, The. Denise Levertov. VGW

Since the world, the base world has no pleasure for me. (LL) Stanzas: "In this vain, busy world, where the good and the gay." Mary Robinson. ECWP; WoRP

Since their dream has / come true. (LL) Passing. Langston Hughes. APSN; APT-2; SAmP

Since Then. Dennis Joseph Enright. OBSV

Since then I was. Significance of a Water Animal, The. Ray A. Young Bear. HATNAP

Since there are depths. Though. Composition. Hugh Seidman. BodElec

Since There's No Help. Michael Drayton. CABP; PoPoPo *Fr.* Idea.

Since There's No Help. R. P. Blackmur. APT-2

Since there your elements assemble. (LL) In Me, Past, Present, Future Meet. Siegfried Sassoon. OBEV; OxBSP

Since Those We Love and Those We Hate. William Ernest Henley. OBMV

Since thou art gone, my friend, I seek in vain for peace. On Parting with Moses ibn Ezra. Judah Halevi. TrJP, *tr. by* Solomon Solis-Cohen

Since thou fayre soule, art warblinge to a spheare. Elegie Written by the Lady A. S. to the Countesse of London Derrye Supposyenge Hir to be Dead by Hir Long Silence, An. Lady Anne Harris Southwell. EMWP

Since thou hast viewed [*or* view'd] some Gorgon, and art grown. Double Rock, The. Henry King, Bishop of Chichester. NOSC

Since thou wou'dst [*or* wouldst] needs, bewitcht [*or* bewitched] with some ill charms. To One Married to an Old Man. Edmund Waller. FaBoEE; OxBSP

Since Thursday last the bare living-room. Bicycle. David Malouf. BMAP

Since thy third curing of the French infection. Against an Old Lecher. Sir John Harington [*or* Harrington]. FaBoEE

Since time began. Nandai. JDP, *tr. by* Yoel Hoffmann

Since Tyndareos. Stesichoros. SaLy, *tr. by* Diane Rayor

Since wailing is a bud of causeful sorrow. Sir Philip Sidney. MakPoe *Fr.* Arcadia.

Since we agreed to let the road between us. No Road. Philip Larkin. EBEV; MoBrPo; OxAEP-2

Since we can die but once, what matters it. Sentiment. Thomas Chatterton. NOEC

Since we'd always sky about. Can. Lit. Earle Birney. NOBC

Since we had changed. Message. Allen Ginsberg. CoAmPo; NeAP; VGW

Since we halved the hairpin. Tune: "Slow Song of Chu Ying-t'ai"—Late Spring. Hsin Ch'i-chi. SuSp, *tr. by* Irving Y. Lo

Since we must soon be fed. Philosophy. Elsa Gidlow. PoBW

Since we parted, spring half over. Tune: Pure Serene Music. Li Yü. CoBCP, *tr. by* Burton Watson

Since we through war awhile must part. At Parting. Anne Ridler. FaBoWar; LW

Since we were first married. On the Death of His Wife. Mei Yao Ch'en. OHPC, *tr. by* Kenneth Rexroth

Since worms and dust must be your fate. Ausonius. MLL

Since yes you [were] once a child. Sappho. SaLy, *tr. by* Diane Rayor

Since you are dead, Timon, tell me which. Callimachus. GrAn

Since you are this way and they are that. Dreams of the One, The. Lőrinc Szabó. IQMS, *tr. by* Edwin Morgan

Since you ask, most days I cannot remember. Wanting to Die. Anne Sexton. CoAmPo; ColAP; NoAM; TAP; TRP; VCAP

Since you, Charmenion, come from Corinth. Martial. RomPo, *tr. by* Dorothea Wender

Since you dare Brave me, with a Rivals Name. To My Rival. "Ephelia." LW

Since you fail to ponder, scarcely. *Unknown.* PriapPo, *tr. by* Richard W. Hooper *Fr.* Priapus Poems, The.

Since you have turned unkind. To a Lady Friend. William Henry Davies. MoBrPo

Since You Left. Chang Chiu-ling. OHMPC, *tr. by* Kenneth Rexroth

Since you left, my lover. Since You Left. Chang Chiu-ling. OHMPC, *tr. by* Kenneth Rexroth

Since you're asking so many questions I'll be off to Tuia and seek ship. Song by a Woman Accused of Adultery. Kie Tapu. PeNZ, *tr. by* Margaret Orbell

Since you walked out on me. Lady of Miracles. Nina Cassian. WPOW, *tr. by* Laura Schiff

Since you went away. In Imitation of Hsü Kan. Liu Chün. SuSp, *tr. by* Jan W. Walls

Since you went away, oh. Added to a Letter Sent to a Traveler. Pao Ling-hui. ColAnChi, *tr. by* Anne Birrell and Jeanne Larsen

Since you will needs my hart possesse. Confession, A. *Poets of the Tixall Circle.* EMWP

Since you wrote a poem. What Color Is Lonely. Carolyn M. Rodgers. BPo

Since your marriage you have lost the look. Martial. PGA

Sincere and most Peruvian mechanics. Telluric and Magnetic. César Vallejo. PFTM-1

Sincere Flattery of R. B. James Kenneth Stephen. NOBL

Sincere Flattery of W. W. (Americanus). James Kenneth Stephen. NOBL

Sincere Man, The. Alfred Grant Walton. PoToHe

Sincerity. Ágnes Nemes Nagy. VCWP, *tr. by* Hugh Maxton

Sindhi Woman. Jon Stallworthy. OxBC

Sine qua non of bed wetting. Air and Angels. Charles North. FTOS

Sinfonia Domestica. Jean Starr Untermeyer. MoAmPo

Sinfonia Eroica. Amy Levy. ViWPN

Sing a last song. Locket, The. John Montague. BiHa; PBCIP

Sing a song o' [*or of*] sixpence. Song of Sixpence. *Unknown.* OxBoLi

Sing a song of critics. Valentine. Ernest Hemingway. IllVoic; OBAL

Sing a Song of People. Lois Lenski. NOxBCh; OTCP

Sing a song of rugby. Vive Le Sport. Harri Webb. TCAWP

Sing a song of sad young men. Ballad of the Sad Young Men, The. Tommy Wolf. ReLy

Sing a song of sixpence. Mother Goose. OxBEV; OxNR

Sing a Song of Sixpence. *Unknown. See* Song of Sixpence

Sing a Song of Subways. Eve Merriam. KaS

Sing Again Together. William Barnes. SCGP

Sing agreeably, agreeably, agreeably of love. (LL) W. H. Auden. FaBoTw; RB *Fr.* Ten Songs.

Sing, Brothers, Sing! William Robert Rodgers. MoBrPo

Sing, cuccu, nu. Sing cuccu. Cuckoo Song, The. *Unknown.* OWoS

Sing cuccu [*or* cuckoo]! Sing cuccu [*or* cuckoo] nu [*or* now]! (LL) Sumer Is Icumen In. *Unknown.* AWP; HAP; HeIP-4; MiEL; OPOU; OxBEV

Sing goddamm, sing goddamm, DAMM. (LL) Ancient Music. Ezra Pound. HeIP-4; NBLV; OBAL; OBCoV; OxBA; PeLV; TCAPo; UV

Sing!/ Great dark oak. Lines to the Black Oak. Oliver La Grone. NBV

Sing his praises that doth keep. John Fletcher. NOBE; OBEV *Fr.* Faithful Shepherdess, The.

Sing in me, Muse, and through me tell the story. Homer. NAWM-5v1; NAWM-7v1, *tr. by* Robert Fitzgerald

Sing Ivy. *Unknown.* OxNR

Sing lullaby, as women do. George Gascoigne. *See* Sing lullaby [*or* lullabie] as women do[e]

Sing lullaby, mine only joy! (LL) Lullaby: "Upon my lap my sovereign sits." Richard Verstegan [*or* Verstegen]. OBEV; SCGP

Sing lullaby [*or* lullabie] as women do[e]. Lullaby [*or* Lullabie] of a Lover, The. George Gascoigne. EBEV; HAP; NAEL-5v1; NAEL-6v1; SCGP

Sing, magnarello, merrily. Leaf-picking, The. Frédéric Mistral. AWP, *tr. by* Harriet Waters Preston

Sing Me a Song. Robert Louis Stevenson. *See* Over the Sea to Skye

Sing me a song of a lad that is gone. Over the Sea to Skye. Robert Louis Stevenson. NOBE

Sing me a song of the dead. Dead Man Asks for a Song, The. *Unknown.* WoPoe, *tr. by* Willard Trask

Sing me a thrush, bone. Anne Sexton. BodElec *Fr.* Furies, The.

Sing me the men ere this. He Would Have His Lady Sing. Digby Mackworth Dolben. EBEV

Sing me "Woe," you glades and Dorian water. Moschus. *See* Ye mountain valleys, pitifully groan!

"Sing, my golden cock, I'll give thee grain!" Neidhart von Reuental. GePo

Sing, My Heart. Ted Koehler. ReLy

Sing, My Soul. *Unknown.* AH

Sing Not for Others, But for Me. Lady Caroline Lamb. RWP

Sing of lusty foods. Kalamu ya Salaam. SpirFl *Fr.* New Orleans Haiku.

Sing on a brittle sea of glass! Morgan Llwyd. AngWePo *Fr.* 1648.

Sing out, my soul, thy songs of joy. Songs of Joy. William Henry Davies. MoBrPo

Sing out pent soul[e]s, sing cheerfully! Vintage to the Dungeon, The. Richard Lovelace. BeJo; CaPo

Sing, Poet, 'tis a merry world. Alexander Smith. NePenScot *Fr.* Glasgow.

Sing, Sing, Sing, Numen, Lumen, Numen. To Her Modest Mirth-Making Friend, Mr Robert Dover. Sibella Cole Dover. EMWP

Sing, sing, / What shall I sing? Mother Goose. LB; ReMoGo

Sing so dogs bark, oxen bolt. Singer with a Bad Voice, The. *Vietnamese Oral Tradition.* CaDao, *tr. by* John Balaban

Sing-Song. Christina Georgina Rossetti.
   "Brown and furry." FaBoVe
   Caterpillar, The. FaBoVe
   City Mouse and the Garden Mouse, The. NTCP
   Ferry Me across the Water. TLR
   "Horses of the sea, The." NTCP
   Hurt No Living Thing. OTCP
   Let's Be Merry. TLR
   Mix a Pancake. NTCP
   "Mother shake the cherry-tree." TLR
   (Precious Stones.) ChAP

Sing the Alpha forest gods. Walt Whitman. Edward Dahlberg. APT-2

Sing to Apollo, God of Day. John Lyly. NoSic *Fr.* Midas.

Sing to Ashtaroth and Bel. To Ashtaroth and Bel. Saul [*or* Shaul] Tchernichowsky [*or* Tchernichovsky]. TrJP, *tr. by* L. V. Snowman

Sing to the Lord Most High. Timothy Dwight. AH

'Sing to us Sappho!' cried the crowd. "Michael Field." ViWPN

Sing We and Chant It. Thomas Morley. EBEV; NoSic

Sing we for love and idleness. Immorality, An. Ezra Pound. MoAmPo; NOBA; OBAL; TCAPo

Sing we now merily. Thomas Ravenscroft. PBRV

Sing what God doth, and do[o] what men may sing. (LL) To the Thrice-Sacred Queen Elizabeth. Mary Sidney Herbert, Countess of Pembroke. NALW; NoP-4

Sing with Your Body. Janice Mirikitani. WPOW

Sing, women o' the Earth. Mune Rune. Helen Adam. APT-2

Singapore. Mary Oliver. NIL-7

Singapore, July 4th. Sascha Feinstein. AmPoNex

Singe we alle and say we thus. My Purse. *Unknown.* EBEV

Singer, The. Gerald William Barrax. ESEAA

Singer, The. Edward Dowden. OxBSo *Fr.* In the Garden.

Singer, The. Diane Wakoski. HeIP-4

Singer, The. Anna Wickham. MoBrPo

Singer of sweet Colonus, and its child. (LL) To a Friend. Matthew Arnold. NAEL-5v2; NAEL-6v2; Son

Singer's House, The. Seamus Heaney. EBEV

Singer, the song, and the sung. (LL) Blessed Lord, What It Is to Be Young. David McCord. KaS; NTCP

Singer with a Bad Voice, The. *Vietnamese Oral Tradition.* CaDao, *tr. by* John Balaban

Singers, The. George Bruce. OxBS

Singers are gone from the Cornmarket-place, The. Thomas Hardy. HAP *Fr.* At Casterbridge Fair.

Singers Change, the Music Goes On, The. Linda Gregg. BAP-01

Singers have hushed their notes of shrill song, The. Five-string, The. Po Chü-i. ChiP, *tr. by* Arthur Waley

Singers of serenades, The. Mandoline. Paul Verlaine. AWP; OBMV, *tr. by* Arthur Symons

Singers to Come. Alice Thompson Meynell. WPE

Singin' in the Rain. Arthur Freed. ReLy

Singing. Geoff Hattersley. NeBl

Singing about her head, as she rode by. (LL) Love without Hope. Robert Graves. BoLoP; FaBoEE; GTBS-P; NAEL-5v2; NAEL-6v2; NOxBChV; NPeEn; NoP-4; OPOU; OxBEV; Spl

Singing Alone. Nancy Cox. MiVo

Singing & Doubling Together. A. R. Ammons. NAAL-2v2; NoAM

Singing Bones, The. Randolph Stow. BMAP; CBAP

Singing Cat, The. Stevie Smith. OxBTC

Singing, dancing—handsome actors entertain. On the Cold Food Festival, Entertaining at the Southern Estate—the Guests Were Li Chiu-ho, Ma Nan-yeh, Wei Tung-kao, Li Hu-ch'uan, Huang K'ung-ts'un, Li Lung-t'ang, and Hu Hu-shan. Li K'ai-hsien. CoBLCP; ColAnChi, *tr. by* Jonathan Chaves

Singing down the Breadfruit. Pauline Stewart. NOxBChV

Singing Drum, The. Frank Mkalawile Chipasula. NAfrP

Singing Flower, The. "Shu Ting." CarOv, *tr. by* Carolyn Kizer and Y. H. Zhao

Singing, flying, singing. Basho. EH, *tr. by* Robert Hass

Singing Girls (Written in Jest). Tu Fu. CrYelRi, *tr. by* Sam Hamill

Singing Hallelujia. Fenton Johnson. NAAAL

Singing his name. Sweet Bread. Frank X. Walker. SpirFl

Singing I saw, with others who sat round. (LL) Giovanni Boccaccio. AWP; EaItPo, *tr. by* Dante Gabriel Rossetti *Fr.* Sonnets.

Singing Image of Fire. Kukai. EnlH, *tr. by* Stephen Mitchell

Singing in the Streets. Leonard Clark. NOxBChV

Singing in the Toyota. Dave Etter. IllVoic

Singing is sweet; but be sure of this. James Thomson. NOBVV *Fr.* Art.

Singing Lesson, The. David Wagoner. NoAM

Singing Lute, The. Ibn Arfa' Ra'suh. NAWM-7v1, *tr. by* James T. Monroe

Singing my days. Walt Whitman. APN-1; NAAL-2v1; NCAP

Singing nature when I need sing my nature nevermore. (LL) Singing & Doubling Together. A. R. Ammons. NAAL-2v2; NoAM

Singing of Niagara, and the Huron squaws. Possibility of New Poetry, The. Robert Bly. CoAmPo

Singing of the Source of Holy Church. Wu Li. ColAnChi, *tr. by* Jonathan Chaves

Singing of Thoughts. Juan Chi. CoBCP, *tr. by* Burton Watson

"Beautiful trees make paths beneath themselves." CoBCP, *tr. by* Burton Watson

"In North Ward they do many strange dances." CoBCP

"Long ago, at fourteen or fifteen." CoBCP

"This summer's burning heat." CoBCP

"Tung-ling melons—men say that long ago." CoBCP

"Years ago, when I was young." CoBCP

Singing, planting rice. Basho. SoOfWa, *tr. by* Sam Hamill

Singing School. Seamus Heaney.

Constable Calls, A. EmeKit; NOIV

Singing to Tony Bennett's Cock. Victoria Redel. KGB

Singing, today I married my white girl. Epithalamion. Dannie Abse. OBWVE

Singing under ice. (LL) Uninvited, The. Dorothy Livesay. NOBC; NoP-4

Singing we ride over the field. Vasco [*or* Vasko] Popa. PoSu; WoPoe, *tr. by* Anne Pennington *Fr.* Blackbird's Field, The.

Singing with open mouths their strong melodious songs. (LL) I Hear America Singing. Walt Whitman. AWP; AiP; HAP; HHAm; ITBLP; MoAmPo; NIL-7; SAmP; TFi; WeW-3

Single and last carriage is ready for the journey, A. David Vogel. FIT, *tr. by* Robert Friend

Single bird sang, A. Bird. Yona Volach. DTA, *tr. by* Miriyam Glazer

Single clenched fist lifted and ready, The. Choose. Carl Sandburg. Spl

Single Eye All Light, no Darkness, A. Laurence Clarkson.

"Behold, the King of glory now is come." PBRV

Single-eyed to child and sunbeam. Blue-eyed Mary. Mary Eleanor Wilkins Freeman. OBCA

Single fact is matter, The. Chronic Meanings. Bob Perelman. PmAP

Single flow'r he sent me, since we met, A. One Perfect Rose. Dorothy Parker. APT-1; NALW; NBLV; NIL-7; NIP-4; NoP-4; OBAL; OBCoV

Single illness has lasted three months, A. Written While Sick. Wen Cheng-ming. CoBLCP, *tr. by* Jonathan Chaves

Single leaf falls, A. Ransetsu. SoOfWa, *tr. by* Sam Hamill

Single man stands like a bird-watcher, A. Mouth of the Hudson, The. Robert Lowell. AiP; VCAP

Single pavilion looms dark against clouds and forest, A. Deepening-Green Pavilion. Chu Yi-tsun. SuSp, *tr. by* Chang Yin-nan

Single pearl of dew suspended clear and chill, A. Tune: "Lotus-leaf Cup." Wen T'ing-yün. SuSp, *tr. by* William R. Schultz

Single petal swirling diminishes the spring, A. Tu Fu. SuSp *Fr.* Meandering River.

Single post, a point of rusting, A. Marina Ivanovna Tsvetayeva [*or* Tsvetaeva]. BrRo *Fr.* Poem of the End.

Single ripple starts from where he stood, A. (LL) Heron, The. Theodore Roethke. APT-2; OWoS

Single rock from Cinnabar Hill, A. On a Painting of Mushrooms. Yün Shou-p'ing. CoBLCP, *tr. by* Jonathan Chaves

Single rose-red tile, A. Visiting Light. Jean Earle. TCAWP

Single Screw of Flesh, A. Emily Dickinson. APN-2

Single sleeper lying here, The. Epitaph for the Poet. George Barker. OxBSP

Single slender crescent brow before her dressing mirror, A. Tune: "Echoing Heaven's Everlastingness." Li Ching. SuSp, *tr. by* Daniel Bryant

Single Sonnet. Louise Bogan. Son

Single soul that lacks a sweet crystalline cry, A. (LL) Paudeen. W. B. Yeats. HAP; OxBSP

Single spot slides the trumpet's flare then stops, A. Lost Fugue for Chet. Lynda Hull. SeSe

Single thought which benefits and harms me, A. Verses in Italian and French, Written by the Queen of Scots to the Queen of England. Mary Stuart, Queen of Scots. EMWP

Single true man, A. For Myo's Departure for Shofuku-ji. Muso Soseki. EaWin, *tr. by* W. S. Merwin

Single tulip!, A. Michael McClintock. HA

Single, unpropped, and nodding to my fall. (LL) Sonnet on a Family Picture. Thomas Edwards. CenSon; NOEC

Single wild goose climbs into the void, A. (LL) Clear After Rain. Tu Fu. BLT; OHPC, *tr. by* Kenneth Rexroth

Single yam leaf, A. Kikaku. SoOfWa, *tr. by* Sam Hamill

Sings Harry. Denis Glover.

"Once I followed horses." PeNZ

Once the Days. PeNZ

Song: "If everywhere in the street" PeNZ

"These songs will not stand." PeNZ

Thistledown. PeNZ

"When I am old." PeNZ

Singular goddess, brown as night, and wild. Sed non satiata. Charles Baudelaire. SxFrPo, *tr. by* James McGowan

Singular Indeed. David McCord. OBCA

Singular Metamorphosis, A. Howard Nemerov. CoAmPo

Sinhala New Year 1975. Anne Ranasinghe. GotH

Sink into its havoc. (LL) Saint-Lô. Samuel Beckett. NOIV; NPeEn

Sink is choked with dirty plates, The. Daedalus. Stephen Knight. TCAWP

Sinking, below the star-several harps. Old Poems. David Shapiro. KGB

Sinking Feeling, A. Amy Gerstler. BodElec

Sinking into sound grief. Rebus Tact. Ray DiPalma. PmAP

Sinking of Clay City, The. Robert Wrigley. GifTon

Sinking of the *Titanic*. *Unknown.* NAAAL

Sinking of the Titanic, The. Hans Magnus Enzensberger.

Reprieve, The. PoSu

Sixteenth Canto. PoSu

Thirty-third Canto. PoSu

Twenty-ninth Canto. PoSu

Sinking of the *Titanic proceeds according to plan, The.* Hans Magnus Enzensberger. PoSu *Fr.* Sinking of the Titanic, The.

Sinless Child, The. Elizabeth Oakes-Smith.

"'Tis the summer prime, when the noiseless air." SWaP

Sin[ne] of self[e]-love possesseth all mine eye [*or* eie]. William Shakespeare. EBEV; OxAEP-1 *Fr.* Sonnets.

Sinner, The. Margaret E. Bruner. PoToHe

Sinner, Is Thy Heart at Rest? Jared Bell Waterbury. AH

Sinner Kissed an Angel, A. Ray Joseph. ReLy

Sinner's Rue. A. E. Housman. PeVV

Sinners, abhor the Fiend. Charles Wesley. NOCV *Fr.* Horrible Decree, The.

Sinners, Will You Scorn the Message? Jonathan Allen. AH

Sinnes Heavie Loade. Robert Southwell. ESCV

Sins of Kalamazoo, The. Carl Sandburg. VGW

Sins of Kalamazoo are neither scarlet nor crimson, The. Sins of Kalamazoo, The. Carl Sandburg. VGW

Sion. George Herbert. ChIV-1; ESCV

Sion lies [*or* Syon lyes] waste, and thy Jerusalem. Fulke Greville, 1st Baron Brooke. ChIV-1; NoSic; PeECV *Fr.* Caelica.

Sion Lies Waste. Fulke Greville, 1st Baron Brooke. ChIV-1; NoSic; PeECV *Fr.* Caelica.

Sioux Metamorphoses. *Unknown.* STP, *tr. by* James Koller

Sioux Woman Defends Her Children, The. *Chippewa Oral Tradition.* NAAL-5

Sioux women, The. Sioux Women Gather Up Their Wounded, The. *Chippewa Oral Tradition.* NAAL-5

Sioux Women Gather Up Their Wounded, The. *Chippewa Oral Tradition.* NAAL-5

Sip a little. Baby's Drinking Song. James Kirkup. NTCP; OTCP

Sipping whiskey and gin. Analysands. Dudley Randall. BPo

Sir, after all that sweet cod. Dafydd's Seagull and the West Wind. Glyn Jones. TCAWP

Sir, after you have wip'd the eyes. Consolatory Poem Dedicated unto Mr. Cotton Mather, A. Nicholas Noyes. SCAP

Sir Aldingar. *Unknown.* ESPB; OxBB

Sir Andrew Bart[t]on. *Unknown.* ESPB; OxBB

Sir Anthony Habberton, Justice and Knight. Obiter Dicta. Joseph Hilaire Pierre Belloc. OBCoV

Sir Balaam. Pope. NPeEn *Fr.* Epistle III, to Allen Lord Bathurst.

Sir Beelzebub. Dame Edith Sitwell. BoWoP; FaBoMo; FaBoWP; MoBrPo; NALW; OBCoV; OxBTC *Fr.* Façade.

Sir Brian had a battleaxe with great big knobs on. Bad Sir Brian Botany. Alan Alexander Milne. NOxBChV

Sir Bumper was a baron bold. Lover's Leap; a Tale, The. Andrew Macdonald. NOEC

Sir Cawline. *Unknown.* ESPB

Sir Charles into my chamber coming in. Courting the Faerie Queen. Margaret Lucas Cavendish, Duchess of Newcastle. NOSC

Sir Christopher Wren. Edmund Clerihew Bentley. NBLV; PeLV *Fr.* Clerihews.

Sir Colin. *Unknown.* OxBB

Sir Dilberry Diddle, Captain of Militia. *Unknown.* NOEC

Sir Eglamour. Samuel Rowlands. FaBoCh *Fr.* Melancholy Knight, The.

Sir Egrabell had sonnes three. Sir Lionel. *Unknown.* ESPB

Sir, / Ere you pass this threshold, stay. To the King, at His Entrance into Saxham: By Master John Crofts. Thomas Carew. CaPo

Sir Eustace Grey. George Crabbe.

    Frenzy. NOBE

Sir Fantasy. Ssu-ma Hsiang-ju. ColAnChi, *tr.* by Burton Watson

Sir Francis, Sir Francis, Sir Francis is come. Upon Sir Francis Drake's Return from His Voyage about the World, and the Queen's Meeting Him. *Unknown.* FaBoCh

Sir *Frauncis* and *Sir Phillip* have noe Tombe. Of Sir Frauncis Walsingham Sir Phillipp Sydney, and Sir Christopher Hatton, Lord Chancelor. *Unknown.* PBRV

Sir Gawain and the Green Knight. *Unknown.* NAEL-6v1; NAEL-7v1; NAWM-7v1, *tr.* by Brian Stone

    "But the lady's longing would not allow her to sleep." EroLit

    "For that noble princess pressed him so hard." EroLit

    Gawain and the Lady of the Castle. EBEV

    Gawain Journeys North. NPeEn

    "He dwelt there all that day, and at dawn on the morrow." FaBoWar

    "Mony klyf he overclambe in contrayes straunge." FaBoVe

    "Noble sighed ceaselessly in restless slumber, The." EroLit

    "Then the drawbridge came down, and the thick gates." WoPoe, *tr.* by Burton Raffel

    "This kyng lay at Camylot upon Krystmasse." PoE

    "Those words, said the lady, are the worst there could be." EroLit

Sir Gawaine and the Green Knight. Yvor Winters. NoAM; PoRA; VGW

Sir Gelli Meurig. Ronald Stuart Thomas. AngWePo

Sir Gelli to R. S. Roland Mathias. AngWePo

Sir Geoffrey Chaucer. Robert Greene. *See* Greene's Vision

Sir Gregory Nonsense's News from No Place. John Taylor.

    "It was in June the eight and thirtieth day." NOSC

Sir Halewyn. Sir Alexander Gray. OxBB

Sir, How much do you need. Follow Me. Nada El-Hage. PoArWo, *tr.* by Nathalie El-Hani

Sir Hudibras his passing worth. Samuel Butler (1612–80). BASC; EBEV; NAEL-5v1; NAEL-6v1; NAEL-7v1 *Fr.* Hudibras.

Sir Hudson Lowe, Sir Hudson *Low.* To Sir Hudson Lowe. Thomas Moore. OBSV

Sir Hugh; or, The Jew's Daughter. *Unknown.* ESPB

    (Hugh of Lincoln.) OxBB

Sir Humphry Davy. Edmund Clerihew Bentley. OxBEV *Fr.* Clerihews.

Sir, I admit your general [*or* gen'ral] Rule. Epigram from the French. Pope. FaBoEE

Sir, I am not a bird of prey. Reply from His Coy Mistress, A. Anne Finch (b. 1908). FFC

Sir, I Ham a very Bad Hand at Righting. (LL) Tony Harrison. CABP; HarvBoo; NoP-4 *Fr.* School of Eloquence, The.

Sir, I have remained so overcome, that I can no longer suffer your attacks. Marino Ceccoli. CAGL, *tr.* by Jill Claretta Robbins

Sir Isaac Newton. *Unknown.* WeW-3

Sir James Murray. Edwin Morgan. HarvBoo

Sir James the Rose. *Unknown.* ESPB

Sir John addressed the Snake-god in his temple. Robert Graves. PeLV *Fr.* Grotesques.

Sir John Butler. *Unknown.* ESPB

Sir John Raynsford's Confession. John Harington. NoSic

Sir John Shagbag (Conservative, Nore). Limerick. Victor Gray. PeLi

Sir John, The Hero. Sándor Petőfi.

    "Upon the shepherd-boy the summer sun." IQMS, *tr.* by Watson Kirkconnell

Sir Joshua Reynolds. William Blake. FaBoEE; OxBoLi; PeLV

Sir Joshua Reynolds. Oliver Goldsmith. FaBoEE; NOEC; OBCoV; OxBEV *Fr.* Retaliation.

Sir knights, take heed hither in hie. York Play of the Crucifixion, The. *Unknown.* NAEL-5v1

Sir, laugh no more at Pliny and the rest. Animal Weather-Forecasting. Thomas Lodge. NoSic

Sir Lionel. *Unknown.* ESPB

Sir, more than kisses, letters mingle souls. To Sir Henry Wotton. John Donne. NoSic

Sir, no man's enemy, forgiving all. Petition. W. H. Auden. NAEL-5v2; NAEL-6v2; Son

Sir Nose D'VoidofFunk. Thomas Sayers Ellis. NeAmPo

Sir, / not that we did not hear the noise. What Her Girl Friend Said to Him. Kannan. WoPoe, *tr.* by A. K. Ramanujan

Sir, now unravelled [*or* unravell'd] is the Golden Fleece. To Dr. F. B. on His Book of Chess[e]. Richard Lovelace. CaPo

Sir Olaf. Johann Gottfried von Herder. AWP, *tr.* by Elizabeth Craigmyle

Sir Oluf he rideth over the plain. Elected Knight, The. *Unknown.* AWP, *tr.* by Henry Wadsworth Longfellow

Sir Patient Fancy. Aphra Behn.

    "What has poor Woman done, that she must be." WPOW

Sir Patrick Spens [*or* Spence]. *Unknown.* AWP; ClHu; EBEV; ESPB; FaBoCh; HAP; InPK-6; MakPoe; NAEL-5v1; NAEL-6v1; NAEL-7v1; NIP-4; NOBE; NPeEn; NePenScot; OBEV; OBSP; OxBB; OxBEV; OxBS; PoE; RB; SCGP; TFi; UnPo; WeW-3

    (King sits in Dumferling town, The.) NoP-4; PoPoPo

Sir Revel. Samuel Rowlands. NoSic; OBCoV

Sir Robert Bolton had three sons. Sir Lionel. *Unknown.* ESPB

Sir Roland; a Fragment. Robert Merry. NOEC

Sir, say no more. Dramatic Fragment. Trumbull Stickney. InPK-6; OxBA; OxBSP

Sir, say no more. Trumbull Stickney. APN-2; InPK-6; OxBA; OxBSP *Fr.* Dramatic Fragments.

Sir, so suspicious. *Unknown.* NOIV

Sir Thomas Maitland's Satyr upon Sir Niel Laing. Sir Thomas Maitland. NePenScot

Sir, though (I thank God for it) I do hate. John Donne. OBSV *Fr.* Satires.

Sir, to be short, in this expensive town. John Oldham. NOSC *Fr.* Satyr, A.

Sir Tristrem. Thomas of Erceldoune.

    Tristrem and the Hunters. OxBS

Sir Walter, oh, oh, my own Sir Walter. Lady Ralegh's Lament. Robert Lowell. OxBSP

Sir Walter Ralegh to the Queen. Sir Walter Ralegh. NoSic

Sir Walter Raleigh Sailing in the Lowlands. *Unknown.* OxBoLi

Sir Walter Ra[u]le[i]gh to His Son[ne]. Sir Walter Ralegh. GSo; NAEL-5v1; NAEL-6v1; NAEL-7v1; NPeEn; NoSic; OxBSo; RB; Son; WoPoe

    (To His Son.) OxBSP; SCGP

Sir Walter Scott at the Tomb of the Stuarts in St. Peter's. Richard Monckton, 1st Baron Houghton Milnes. EBVV

Sir! when I flew to seize the bird. Beau's Reply. William Cowper. FaBoCh

Sir, / Whether these lines do find you out. Summons to Town, A. Sir John Suckling. NOSC

Sir William Dyer, Knight. Lady Catherine [*or* Katherine] Dyer.

    (Epitaph on Sir William Dyer.) NPeEn

    Epitaph on the Monument of Sir William Dyer at Colmworth, 1641. BoLoP; EnLoPo

Sir, you are sealèd of the tribe of Ben. (LL) Ben Jonson. BASC; BeJo

Sir, / You need no Parian or Egyptian stone. To Sir Henry Newton, upon His Re-edifying the Church of Charleton in Kent. Thomas Philipott. NOSC

Sir, you should notice me: I am the Man. Epitaph. Lascelles Abercrombie. MoBrPo

Sir, you were a credit to whatever. To a Teacher of French. Donald Davie. OxBC

Sire. W. S. Merwin. CoAP; VGW

Siren. Amy Gerstler. ExTi

Siren. Anna Semionovna Prismanova. TCRP, *tr.* by Bradley Jordan

Siren, The. "Violet Fane." VWP

Siren, The. Alfonsina Storni. TANSG, *tr.* by Mark McCaffrey

Siren Bird, The. Henrietta Cordelia Ray. CBWP-3

Siren Chorus. George Darley. *See* Syren Songs

Siren sang, and Europe turned away, A. To the Western World. Louis Simpson. CoAP; CoAmPo; NOBA; TAP; TRP

Siren Song. Margaret Atwood. HAP; NIL-7; NIP-4; WeW-3 *Fr.* Songs of the Transformed.

Sirena. Michael Drayton. OBEV

Sirens, The. Gordon Challis. PeNZ

Sirens, The. John Streeter Manifold. MoBrPo; Son

Sirens are those journeys, The. Wound-dresser's Dream, The. Pauline Stainer. NeBl

Sirens' Song. William Browne (1591–1643). NOBE; OBEV *Fr.* Inner Temple Masque, The.

Sirhan Drinks His Coffee in the Cafeteria.   Mahmoud Darwish.   VCWP, *tr. by* Rana Kabbani

Sirius.   "H. D."   NAAL-5   *Fr.* Walls Do Not Fall, The.

Sirmio.   Catullus.   *See* Carmina

Sirmione.   James Wright (1927–80).   BodElec

Sirs—though we fail you—let us live.   To Men.   Anna Wickham.   MoBrPo

Sirventes.   Bertrans [*or* Bertran *or* Bertrand] de Born.   WoPoe, *tr. by* Paul Blackburn

Sirventes.   Paul Blackburn.   NeAP; PoM

Sis Boom Ba.   Tina Darragh.   FTOS

Sis co wet.   Sis Boom Ba.   Tina Darragh.   FTOS

Sister.   Magali Alabaú.   TANSG, *tr. by* Mary Jane Treacy

Sister.   Langston Hughes.   APSN

Sister.   Gabriela Mistral.   BoWoP, *tr. by* Langston Hughes

Sister, a sister calling.   Gerard Manley Hopkins.   FaBoVe   *Fr.* Wreck of the Deutschland, The.

Sister Agnes Writes to Her Beloved Mother.   Paul Durcan.   OBCoV

Sister and mother and diviner love.   To the One of Fictive Music.   Wallace Stevens.   APT-1; MoAmPo; NoP-4; TCAPo

Sister Ann Zita Shows Us the Foolishness of the Forbidden Books.   Len Roberts.   BodElec

Sister, Awake!   *Unknown.*   NOBE; OBEV

Sister, come to the chestnut toll.   Last Night, The.   Alfred Austin.   PeVV

Sister darling, ope the window, let the balmy air once more.   Dying Girl, The.   Mary Weston Fordham.   CBWP-2

Sister Death.   Penny Harter.   TWW

Sister Emma, O you must come down to the mire.   Down to the Mire.   *Unknown.*   WPoS

Sister Gone.   William Barnes.   OxBEV

Sister has been raped, they said, The.   Fallin'   Bobbi Sykes.   IBA

Sister, I have come to take your place.   Anna Andreyevna Akhmatova.   ARWW, *tr. by* Catriona Kelly

Sister Johnson's Speech.   Maggie Pogue Johnson.   CBWP-4

Sister Lakin and Lally.   Dorothy Perry Thompson.   SpirFl

Sister Lou.   Sterling Allen Brown.   APT-2
   (Honey.)   GM; ISC

Sister Margaret Clare.   In the middle of Priest Lake.   Madeline DeFrees.   ExTi

Sister Midnight.   John James.   Oth

Sister Muse, lament for my pain.   Elegy on Reichenau.   Walafrid Strabo.   NAWM-7v1, *tr. by* Peter Godman

Sister of Mercy, The.   Constance Naden.   VWP; ViWPN

Sister on the Tracks, A.   Donald Hall.   GM

Sister once of weeds and a dark water that held still.   Family Romance.   Larry Levis.   BodElec

Sister saying—"Soon you'll be back in the ward."   In the Theatre.   Dannie Abse.   BloBone; NoAM; TCAWP

Sister, sister.   What Danger We Court.   Luci Tapahonso.   ReEnLa

Sister sister go to bed!   Brother and Sister.   Lewis Carroll.   NOxBChV

Sister Songs.   Francis Thompson.
   "But lo! at length the day is lingered out."   OBMV

Sister Swallow to Swinburne.   Mary Holtby.   UV

Sister, the stars have no children.   Mother of Nothing.   Naomi Shihab Nye.   GraLe

Sister was wedged beside the wicker basket.   Burned Bridge, The.   Ruth Stone.   WPE

Sister, You Cannot Think a Baby Out!   Irène Assiba d'Almeida.   HAWP

Sisters.   Kimberly Ann Collins.   InTrad

Sisters.   Wendy Cope.   ItWoWo

Sisters.   Saleem Peeradina.   OMIP

Sisters.   Haunani-Kay Trask.   ReEnLa

Sisters, The.   Roy Campbell.   BoLoP; FaBoTw; NoP-4; OBMV

Sisters, The.   Melissa Cannon.   FFC

Sisters, The.   Alexis De Veaux.   GLP

Sisters, The.   Nicki Jackowska.   BrRo

Sisters, The.   Amy Lowell.   NALW

Sisters, The.   John Banister Tabb.   APN-2

Sisters, The.   Tennyson.   PAI

Sisters, The.   John Greenleaf Whittier.   AWP

Sisters, The.   Judith Wright.   NALW

Sisters are always drying their hair.   Triolet Against Sisters.   Phyllis McGinley.   KaS; OBCA; OxIBACP

Sisters Newyearsgift from Elizabeth to Mary a Happie Mother of Good Children, The.   Elizabeth Cromwell.   EMWP

Sisters of Sexual Treasure, The.   Sharon Olds.   PBCAP

Sisters! sisters! who sent you here?   Fire, Famine, and Slaughter.   Samuel Taylor Coleridge.   FaBoWar

Sisters / Where there is cold silence.   To Black Women.   Gwendolyn Brooks.   IllVoic

Sistine Chapel.   Raymond Roseliep.   HA

Sistrum.   Margaret Fuller.   APN-1

Sit as close to the stage as possible.   Michael Lassell.   GLP   *Fr.* Times Square Poems.

Sit down in the shade of this fine spreading laurel.   Anyte [*or* Anytes].   GrAn

Sit down under the high crown.   Plato.   PGA

Sit down with me awhile beside the heath-corner.   Erica.   Mary Ursula Bethell.   PeNZ

Sit Down, You're Rockin' the Boat.   Frank Loesser.   ReLy

Sit, everyone, under the luxuriant laurel.   Anyte [*or* Anytes].   SaLy, *tr. by* Diane Rayor

Sit for a while on a stone.   Thomas A. Clark.   Oth

Sit here and guard the household.   To My Dog, Swan.   Dezső Kosztolányi.   IQMS, *tr. by* Lydia Pasternak-Slater

Sit on the bed. I'm blind, and three parts shell.   A Terre.   Wilfred Owen.   FaBoWar; OxBTC; PAI; PeFWW; PoWW

Sit, she said. The wolf sat. Shake, she said.   Manners.   Pamela Alexander.   ExTi

Sit there and count your fingers.   Lorenz Hart.   *See* When I was very young

Sit too close.   My Mother Spinning.   Peter Olds.   PeNZ

Site of Ambush.   Eiléan Ní Chuilleanáin.
   "At alarming bell daybreak, before."   CIP-2

Site of My Grandfather's House, The.   Dominador I. Ilio.   ReBoTo

Sith al that in this world hath ben in rerum natura.   *Unknown.*   OHMEL

Sith Cynthia is ascended to that rest.   Aemilia Bassano Lanyer.   BASC; NoP-4   *Fr.* Salve Deus Rex Judaeorum.

Sith gone is my delight and only pleasure.   Sextain.   William Drummond, of Hawthornden.   NOSC

Sith, in dark speech, Carvilios hymn unfolds.   Charles Montague Doughty.   FaBoTw   *Fr.* Dawn in Britain, The.

Sith my life from life is parted.   Marie [*or* Mary] Magdalens Complaint at Christs Death.   Robert Southwell.   ChIV-2; ESCV

Sith sickles and the shearing scythe.   Hawking for the Partridge.   Thomas Ravenscroft.   OxBoLi

Sith Venus had her mole, Helen her stain.   Against Proud Poor Phryna.   John Davies of Hereford.   FaBoEE

Sits at the window, waits the threatened steel.   Medusa.   Vincent O'Sullivan.   PAI

Sitter Bitter.   Miss Bitter.   N. M. Bodecker.   NTCP

Sitters on the mead-bench, quaffing among questions.   Exeter Riddle, An.   Gavin Ewart.   OxBC

Sitteth alle stille and herkneth to me.   Song of Lewes, The.   *Unknown.*   OxBoLi

Sittin' on the Porch.   Edgar Albert Guest.   ITBLP

Sittin' on the porch at night when all the tasks are done.   Sittin' on the Porch.   Edgar Albert Guest.   ITBLP

Sitting.   Bob Boldman.   HA

Sitting, The.   Medbh McGuckian.   CABP; ModIr; PNI

Sitting alone (as one forsook).   Vision, The.   Robert Herrick.   CaPo; CavPo; SCGP

Sitting Alone in Ching-t'ing Mountain.   Li Po.   SuSp, *tr. by* Irving Y. Lo

Sitting Alone in the Courtyard.   Yü Chi.   CoBLCP, *tr. by* Jonathan Chaves

Sitting alone in the empty hall.   Sitting Alone on an Autumn Night.   Wang Wei.   CrYelRi, *tr. by* Sam Hamill

Sitting Alone in Tulsa Three A.M.   Lance Henson.   VoR

Sitting Alone on an Autumn Night.   Wang Wei.   CrYelRi, *tr. by* Sam Hamill

SITTING alone upon my thought, in melancholy mood.   Edward de Vere, 17th Earl of Oxford.   NoSic

Sitting, and ready to be drawn.   Ben Jonson.   NOSC   *Fr.* Eupheme.

Sitting at crossings and waiting for freights to pass, we have all noticed.   Project for Freight Trains, A.   David Young.   GM

Sitting at her table, she serves.   Nani.   Alberto A. Ríos.   MakPoe; SoSe-8; UnSA

Sitting at Night.   Po Chü-i.   TAL

Sitting at Night on the Front Porch.   Charles Wright.   ColAP; GeoHom; LCAP-2

Sitting at Night on the Moon-viewing Terrace.   Yang Wan-li.   SuSp, *tr. by* Jonathan Chaves

Sitting at Night on the Moonlit Terrace.   Yang Wan-li.   CoBCP, *tr. by* Burton Watson

Sitting at Night with My Nephew Who Has Just Come from Afar.   Su Tung-p'o (Su Shih).   TAL

Sitting Bard, The.   Sir Owen Seaman.   NOBL

Sitting between the sea and the buildings.   Painter, The.   John Ashbery.   EmeKit; HCAP; NOBA; NoP-4; PoE; PoPoPo; YaYoPo

Sitting Bull's Will versus the Sioux Treaty of 1868 and Monty Hall.   A. K. Redwing.   VoR

Sitting by a Bush in Broad Daylight. Robert Frost. ChIV-1

Sitting by Myself. K'ang Hai. CoBLCP, tr. by Jonathan Chaves

Sitting by the barbecue. Dinner Together. Diana Rivera. InvLad

Sitting by the streams that glide. Bible, O.T. See By the rivers of Babylon, there we sat down, yea, we wept, when [or then] we remembered Zion

Sitting dead in 'Death Valley.' Death Valley. Sorley MacLean (Somhairle MacGill-Eain). FaBoWar; NePenScot

Sitting here alone, in peace. Private Sadness. Bob Kaufman. ISC

Sitting in cold fear, boys, waiting for the end? (LL) Just a Smack at Auden. William Empson. MoBrPo; PeLV; UV; UnPo

Sitting in sunlight, the child. Eleven A.M. on My Day Off, My Sister Phones Desperate for a Babysitter. Sharon Hashimoto. FSt; OpBo

Sitting, legs crossed, copper-toned old man. My Song. King D. Kuka. VoR

Sitting on a Rock by Mountain Stream. Ch'en Yü-yi. SuSp, tr. by Irving Y. Lo

Sitting on a windowsill, swinging. Blue Moon. Mimi Khalvati. MFPA

Sitting on the Brooklyn Bridge at night. Side 4. Víctor Hernández Cruz. PueRic

Sitting on the grass. In the Park. Judith Beveridge. BMAP

Sitting Outdoors. Lu Yu. CoBCP, tr. by Burton Watson

Sitting over words. Utterance. W. S. Merwin. BLT

Sitting shoulder to shoulder. Kim Roberts. AmPoNex Fr. Constellation Frigidaire, The.

Sitting straightbacked, a modest Irish miss. Lesson in Love, A. Philip Hobsbaum. OxBTC

Sitting up. (LL) First Trimester, The. Campbell McGrath. NeAmPo; UrbNat

Sitting Up at Night. Lu Yu. CoBCP, tr. by Burton Watson

Sitting Up with My Wife on New Year's Eve. Hsü Chün-ch'ien. CoBCP, tr. by Burton Watson

Sitting with Lester Young. Paul Zimmer. SeSe

Sitting, wondering, do I have a place here? Errol West. IBA

Situation. Langston Hughes. APSN; OBAL

Situation. Kaa Naa Subramanyam. OMIP, tr. by Kaa Naa Subramanyam

6. Jack Spicer. FTOS Fr. Love Poems.

6. Raúl Zurita. TCLAP, tr. by Jack Schmitt

6 A.M. All over the world. Rosemary. John A. Stone. BloBone

Six and sixty. Usei. JDP, tr. by Yoel Hoffmann

Six black ibis. Snapshots. Mary Oliver. PoCoUp

Six Choruses. Tu Fu. CrYelRi, tr. by Sam Hamill

Six Commissioned Texts. W. H. Auden.
    Ballad of Barnaby, The. OBNV

Six Cranes at Dusk. Henri Faust. YaYoPo

Six crock bowls the bride smashed. Angry Bride, The. Unknown. WoPoe, tr. by Kevin O'Rourke

Six-cylinder car and two Fords in the middle of / the fields, A. Harvest. Blaise Cendrars. BLT, tr. by Monique Chefdor

Six days ago the water fell. Peacock's Feather, A. Seamus Heaney. DiPo

Six decades gone and one to come. Juxtapositions. David Wright. NLP

Six discs / with Decca. (LL) Be-Bop Boys. Langston Hughes. APSN; APT-2; OBAL

Six Eagles. Thomas Love Peacock. VoR

Six Feet Under. Janet Campbell Hale. VoR

Six-foot nest of the sea-hawk, The. Sea-Hawk. Richard Eberhart. RB

Six green plums bottoms. Wickson Plums. William Corbett. PmAP

Six hundred dark feet from the cliffs. "But Still in Israel's Paths They Shine." Carter Revard. VoR

Six in the morning, a weekday in May. Highland, 1955. Kevin Fitzpatrick. MiVo

"Six Lectures in Verse." Czeslaw Milosz.
    "Christ has risen. Whoever believes that / Should not behave as we do." GI

Six little mice sat down to spin. Six Little Mice. Mother Goose. OxNR

Six Local Poems. David Avidan. FIT, tr. by Robert Friend

Six Movements on a Theme. David Ignatow. NNaP

Six Nations Museum Onchiota, New York—January. Wendy Rose. HATNAP

Six Nuns Die in Convent Inferno. Paul Durcan.
    "We resided in a Loreto convent in the centre of Dublin city." ModIr

Six o'Clock. Trumbull Stickney. APN-2; OxBA

6 : o'clock our passageway. Travois of the Nameless. Sotère Torregian. NBV

Six o'clock: the kitchen bulbs which blister. Ode to Suburbia. Eavan Boland. PBCIP

Six of them, The. These Six. Sean Lucy. CIP-2

Six or seven rows of waves struggle landward. On the Oregon Coast. Galway Kinnell. NoAM

Six Poems of Loneliness. Enrique Lihn. VCWP, tr. by David Unger

Six Poems on Nothing. Gwyneth Lewis. HarvBoo

Six Poems on Remembering. Shen Yüeh. CoBCP, tr. by Burton Watson
    "I think of when she comes." CoBCP

Six-Quart Basket, The. Raymond Souster. MoCV

Six Reasons for Drinking. Vernon Scannell. OxBC

Six, seven years ago. He Makes a House Call. John A. Stone. BloBone

Six Small Fires. Paul Jenkins. OPRER

Six stone in weight and so disconsolate. Society Woman, The. Dezső Kosztolányi. IQMS, tr. by Peter Zollman

Six street ends come together here. Blue Island Intersection. Carl Sandburg. MoAmPo

Six Strings, The. Federico García Lorca. RB, tr. by Donald Hall

Six Ten Sixty-Nine. Conyus. GT

Six to Six. Unknown. PBA, tr. by A. C. Jordan

Six Town Eclogues. Lady Mary Wortley Montagu.
    Saturday: The Small-Pox. BWW; ECWP; NOEC; WPE

6/20/97. Harvey Shapiro. KGB

Six Variations. Denise Levertov. CoAmPo; LCAP-2
    "Shlup, shlup, the dog." HeIP-4; InPK-6

Six Ways. Issa. EH, tr. by Robert Hass

Six Winter Privacy Poems. Robert Bly. LCAP-2

Six Years Later. Joseph Brodsky. TCRP; VCWP, tr. by Richard Wilbur

Six years the moon shone at mid-autumn. Mid-Autumn Moon. Su Tung-p'o (Su Shih). CoBCP; GifTon, tr. by Burton Watson

Six Young Men. Ted Hughes. OBWP; PoWW

"Sixpence a week," says the girl to her lover. Thomas Hardy. MoBrPo Fr. Satires of Circumstance in Fifteen Glimpses.

Sixteen Dead Men. W. B. Yeats. OBWP

1686–1802 / Toll taker at Dunk's Ferry, Pennsylvania. Alice. Gale Jackson. SpirFl

1648. Morgan Llwyd.
    Excuse, The. AngWePo
    Harvest, The. AngWePo
    Spring, The. AngWePo
    Summer, The. AngWePo
    Winter, The. AngWePo

Sixteen Poems in Eight Pairings. John Crowe Ransom.
    Agitato Ma Non Troppo. OxBA
    (Conrad in Twilight.) FuPo; OxBA
    "Do not enforce the tired wolf." MoAmPo; OxBA
    ("Grim in my tight black coat as the sleazy beetle.") FuPo
    Here Lies a Lady. APT-1; AWP; HAP; MoAmPo; NAAL-2v2; NoAM; PoRA; RB; TAP; VGW
    ("Hush, O hush, he is come!") (LL) FuPo
    Prelude to an Evening. MoAmPo; OxBA; SPE
    (Vanity of the Bright Young Men, The.) FuPo

1668. Dom Moraes. EmeKit

Sixteen Sonnets. Thomas A. Clark.
    "As I walked out early." Oth
    "Our boat touches the bank." Oth

16 years old. My Old Man. Charles Bukowski. PmAP

Sixteen years old and crooked. Meeting Mescalito at Oak Hill Cemetery. Lorna Dee Cervantes. PBCAP

Sixteenth Canto. Hans Magnus Enzensberger. PoSu Fr. Sinking of the Titanic, The.

6th Dance—Doing Things With Pencils—17–18 February 1964. Jackson Mac Low. PmAP Fr. Pronouns, The—A Collection of 40 Dances—For the Dancers.

Sixth Grade. Melanie Hope. WiU

Sixth Grade. Marie Howe. KGB

6th Grade—Our Lady of Pompeii. Vittoria Repetto. UnSA

6th grade—our lady of pompeii. 6th Grade—Our Lady of Pompeii. Vittoria Repetto. UnSA

Sixth-Month Song in the Foothills. Gary Snyder. HCAP

Sixth Psalm. Anne Sexton. LCAP-2

Sixth Satire. Juvenal. Fr. Satires.

Sixth Sense, The. Nikolai Stepanovich Gumilyov [or Gumiliov or Gumilev]. TCRP, tr. by Yakov Hornstein

Sixth Song of the Holy Young Men. Unknown. APN-2, tr. by Washington Matthews Fr. Mountain Chant, The.

Sixth Vertical Poetry. Roberto Juarroz.
    "Bell is full of wind, The." VCWP

Sixties brought a clash of arms, The. Emancipation Day. Lizelia Augusta Jenkins Moorer. CBWP-3

Sixties, I think, were not a total loss, The. January 15 as a National Holiday. Carter Revard. VoR

Sixty-Eighth Birthday. James Russell Lowell. OxBSP

Sixty-five years. Unpo Bun-Etsu. ZenPo, tr. by Takashi Ikemoto and Lucien Stryk

Sixty-four Tanka. Saigyo.

("Why should I be bitter.") OHMPJ, *tr.* by Kenneth Rexroth

Sixty-one? I thought you were that back. Swallows of Salangan. Gloria Vando. TouFir

Sixty percent of the universe's energy is missing. Beneath Cold Mountain. Michael Hannon. GeoHom

Sixty second / August. Maxine Chernoff. PmAP *Fr.* Japan.

67. Edmund Spenser. *See* Amoretti

Sixty-Six. Philip Booth. BodElec

66°7' N/22°17' W. Peter Rafferty. NLP

Sixty-Six Poems for a Blackfoot Bundle. *Unknown.* STP, *tr.* by Jerome Rothenberg

Sixty-six years. Tendo-Nyojo. ZenPo, *tr.* by Takashi Ikemoto and Lucien Stryk

Sixty sun-decked years Charito has gotten to. Philodemus. GrAn

63rd and Broadway. Reuben Jackson. ESEAA

Size, The. George Herbert. GeHe

Size of It, The. Timothy Liu. WiU

Size of This Universe, The. Randolph Healy. Oth

Sizeline. Felix Mnthali. PeSAV

Sizing. Heather McHugh. ExTi

Sizing up an adversary is a matter of estimating his familiarity with pain. Battle at Horizon. Ben Marcus. HeMarv

Sizing up our present situation. Woman's Intuition, A. Victor Young. ReLy

Skaian Gate, The. Geoffrey Scott.
"Hector, the captain bronzed, from simple fight." OBMV

Skara Brae. Michael Longley. PBCIP

Skateboard. Thom Gunn. MoASP

Skater, The. Hester Knibbe. TuT, *tr.* by Micheal O'Siadhail

Skater, The. Sir Charles G. D. Roberts. NOBC

Skaters, The. John Ashbery.
"These decibels / Are a kind of flagellation, an entity of sound." PmAP
"Wind thrashes the maple seed-pods, The." APSN

Skaters, The. John Gould Fletcher. KaS; MoAmPo

Skein, The. Carolyn Kizer. VGW

Skeleton, The. Gilbert Keith Chesterton. FaBoTw

Skeleton House. Laurence Smith. OTCP

Skeleton in Armor [*or* Armour], The. Henry Wadsworth Longfellow. APN-1; AWP; TreFP

Skeleton in the Cupboard, The. Dora Sigerson Shorter. VWP

Skeleton is hiding in the closet as it should, The. Everything in Its Place. Arthur Guiterman. NBLV; OBAL; OBCoV

Skeleton of the Future, The. Hugh MacDiarmid. MoBrPo; OBMV

Skeleton of the Great Moa in the Canterbury Museum, Christchurch, The. Allen Curnow. PeNZ

Skeleton of Winter. Joy Harjo. LoL

Skeleton Parade. Jack Prelutsky. NTCP

Skeletons are out tonight, The. Skeleton Parade. Jack Prelutsky. NTCP

Skengeh, A. Eena Mi Corner. Jean Binta Breeze. WaCA

Skeptic, The. Clara Ann Thompson. CBWP-2

Sketch. Cecília Meireles. TCLAP, *tr.* by Luiz Fernández García

Sketch, A. Christina Georgina Rossetti. GTBS-P; VWP

Sketch for an Aesthetic Project. Jay Wright. GT

Sketch in October. Tomas Tranströmer. VCWP, *tr.* by Robin Fulton

Sketch of Lord Byron's Life. Julia A. Moore. OBAL

Sketch of Mount Chung, A. Wang An-shih. SuSp, *tr.* by Jan W. Walls

Sketch of the Frontier Woman. Claudia Lars. TCLAP, *tr.* by Donald D. Walsh

Sketches. Federico García Lorca. PFTM-1

Sketches from History. Sergey [*or* Sergei] Drofenko. TCRP, *tr.* by Lubov Yakovleva

Skialetheia Satire 5. Everard Guilpin.
"What more variety of pleasures can." PBRV

Skibbereen the Famine Pit. John Knoepfle. SpudSo

Skiddaw House. David Scott. NLP

Skies ain't gonna cloud no mo' Happiness Is Just a Thing Called Joe. Harold Arlen. ReLy

Skies and god's mystery look on, The. Another Alexandra. Mongane Wally Serote. PeSAV

Skies are cold and hard; the dead lights trail, The. Departure, The. Trumbull Stickney. ColAP

Skies at dawn. Shiba Sonome. JDP, *tr.* by Yoel Hoffmann

Skies gan scowl, o'ercast with misty clouds, The. George Gascoigne. ChIV-1 *Fr.* De Profundis.

Skies o'ercast and fierce winds blow, The. December. Josephine D. Henderson Heard. CBWP-4

Skies remind one of one of those mounds of custard, The. Lollipops of the Pomeranian Baroque. James Fenton. PeLV

Skies they were ashen and sober, The. Ulalume [*or* Ulalume—a Ballad].

Edgar Allan Poe. APN-1; AWP; NAAL-2v1; NAAL-5; NCAP; NOBA; OxBA; TAP; TCAPo

Skiing on Russian Christmas. Nora Dauenhauer. HATNAP

Skill is leaching from his hands, moment, The. Allegiance. Sheenagh Pugh. TCAWP

Skill originated in the West, The. Lines in Praise of a Self-Chiming Clock. Hsüan-yeh. ColAnChi, *tr.* by Jonathan Spence and Jonathan D. Spence

Skilled to pull wires, he baffles Nature's hope. Boss, The. James Russell Lowell. NCAP; OBAL

Skillful mistress of guilty glances. Osip Emilevich Mandelstam [*or* Mandelshtam]. TCRP

Skim from curb to curb like regatta. Island Women of Paris, The. Rita Dove. LoL

Skimbleshanks: The Railway Cat. T. S. Eliot. NOBL

Skimming. Lillian Morrison. *See* Skimming / an asphalt sea

Skimming / an asphalt sea. Sidewalk Racer Or, On the Skateboard, The. Lillian Morrison. NTCP

Skimming lightly, wheeling still. Shiloh [A Requiem]. Herman Melville. APN-2; CBCWP; ColAP; NOBA; NoP-4; OBWP; OxBA; SCV; TCAPo

Skimming the Ice. Tom Sexton. PoCoUp

Skimming the waves, deep in the night. Sandal Mountain. Hsieh Chin. CoBLCP, *tr.* by Jonathan Chaves

Skin. Anthony Butts. AmPoNex

Skin. Sari Friedman. GotH

Skin. Brian Henry. AmPoNex

Skin. Linda Hogan. ReEnLa

Skin. Mary Leader. NAPBL

Skin. Lucia Maria Perillo. IllVoic

Skin. Marjorie Welish. PmAP

Skin Canoes. Carolyn Forché. YaYoPo

Skin Color from the Sun. Daryl Ngee Chinn. LTA

Skin Diving in the Virgins. John Malcolm Brinnin. TAP

Skin Flick. Fred Chappell. InPK-6

Skin / Meat / BONES. Anne Waldman. PmAP

Skin meeting skin, we want to think. Touching Each Other's Surfaces. Carol Jane Bangs. NIP-4

Skin of ice. Lyrics to the Tune "Fairy Grotto." Su Tung-p'o (Su Shih). WoPoe, *tr.* by Greg Whincup

Skin of the night bristling with stars. Night, I Know All About You. Yolanda Bedregal. TANSG, *tr.* by Carolyne Wright

Skin ripples over my body like moon-wooed water, The. Prison Song. Alan Dugan. YaYoPo

Skin the Goat's Curse on Carey. *Unknown.* BlrV

Skinful of bowls, he bowls them. Second Glance at a Jaguar. Ted Hughes. NoAM

Skinning. Dan Quisenberry. SpudSo

Skinny Girl, The. Anne Hébert. BoWoP, *tr.* by Willis Barnstone

Skinny rocks—verdigris green. Crossing Ts'en River. Yang Wan-li. SuSp, *tr.* by Jonathan Chaves

Skinny waterfalls, footpaths, The. Lastness. Galway Kinnell. NNaP

Skins. Charles Wright. HCAP

Skins. Judith Wright. BMAP

Skins of flayed authors, husks of dead reviews. After-Dinner Poem (Terpsichore), An. Oliver Wendell Holmes. TCAPo

Skip, The. James Fenton. HarvBoo

Skipper Ireson's Ride. John Greenleaf Whittier. APN-1; NCAP; NOBA; OBAL; OBCA; OxBA

Skipping along the footpath. Wind Debates Asian Immigration, The. Peter Rose. BMAP

Skirting the river road, (my forenoon walk, my rest,). Dalliance of the Eagles, The. Walt Whitman. HAP; HeIP-4; NAAL-2v1; NAAL-3; NoP-4; SAmP; TAP; TCAPo; TRP

Skreak and skritter of evening gone, The. Autumn Refrain. Wallace Stevens. APT-1

Skull. Edward Weismiller. YaYoPo

Skull of the Horse. Thomas McGrath. BodElec

Skunk, The. Seamus Heaney. NAEL-5v2; NAEL-6v2; NoP-4; OxBC; PoE

Skunk cabbage with its smug and opulent smell, The. Skunk Cabbage. Eric Ormsby. NoP-4

Skunk Hour. Robert Lowell. CoAP; CoAmPo; ColAP; EmeKit; FaBoMo; HAP; HCAP; HarvBoo; HeIP-4; InPK-6; LCAP-2; MoAmPo; NAAL-2v2; NAAL-5; NIL-7; NIP-4; NOBA; NoAM; NoP-4; OxBC; PAI; PoE; PoPoPo; PoetW; SCV; TAP; TFi; TRP; VCAP

Skunks fight under the house and keep us. Bureau 2. Josephine Miles. NALW

Sky. James Harms. NAPBL

Sky. Richard Katrovas. LTA

Sky. Raymond Roseliep. KaS

Sky. Shinkichi Takahashi. ZenPo, *tr.* by Takashi Ikemoto and Lucien Stryk

Sky, The. April 5th. Vera Gherarducci. CItWP, *tr.* by Cinzia Sartini Blum and Lara Trubowitz

Sky, The. Vladimir Nikolaevich Kornilov. TCRP, *tr.* by Daniel Weissbort

Sky, The. Elizabeth Madox Roberts. MoAmPo

Sky, The. *Unknown.* TTY, *tr.* by Ulli Beier

Sky a black sphere, The. Lighthouse in the Night. Alfonsina Storni. BoWoP, *tr.* by Aliki and Willis Barnstone

Sky above the roof's, The. Paul Verlaine. SxFrPo, *tr.* by Martin Sorrell

Sky above us was silent and empty, The. Yiddish Poets in America. Richard Chess. TaR

Sky at night is like a big city, The. Sky, The. *Unknown.* TTY, *tr.* by Ulli Beier

Sky becomes one with its clouds, The. Fisherman's Honor, The. Li Ch'ing-chao. WPoS, *tr.* by Jane Hirshfield

Sky-black gull. Interstices. William J. Higginson. HA

Sky ceases. There is only. Michael Dransfield. CBAP *Fr.* Geography.

Sky Clears, The. *Unknown.* OBVE, *tr.* by Frances Densmore

Sky drank in sparrows making lucid the oaks, The. Sky Drank In, The. Gillian Conoley. BAP-97

Sky extends upwards for ninety thousand miles, The. Buddhist Monk Cut and Burned His Own Flesh to Make the Rains Stop—A Man from His Native Place Asked Me to Write a Poem to Send to Him, A. Hsü Wei. CoBLCP; ColAnChi, *tr.* by Jonathan Chaves

Sky full of autumn. Autumn. Ngo Chi Lan. EaWin, *tr.* by Nguyen Ngoh Bich, W. S. Merwin, M. S. Merwin and Nguyen Ngoc Bich

Sky full of cymbals, of fiddles and lutes. Spring Joy Praising God. Catharina Regina von Greiffenberg. AuPH; GePo, *tr.* by George C. Schoolfield

Sky grew darker with each minute, The. Before the Storm. Richard Dehmel. AWP, *tr.* by Ludwig Lewisohn

Sky has been dark, The. Youngest Daughter, The. Cathy Song. NoAM

Sky has recovered, The. Louise Herlin. MFP, *tr.* by Martin Sorrell

Sky is a dark bowl, the stars die and fall, The. *Unknown.* WoPoe, *tr.* by Willis Barnstone and Tony Barnstone *Fr.* Cannibal Hymn, The.

Sky Is Blue, The. David Ignatow. NNaP

Sky is changed!—and such a change! Oh night, The. Byron. NOBRP *Fr.* Childe Harold's Pilgrimage.

Sky is cloudy, yellowed by the smoke, The. In a London Drawingroom. "George Eliot." NPeEn

Sky is covered with stars, like a body with sores, The. Svetlana Kekova. ItGoST, *tr.* by Judith Hemschemeyer

Sky is dotted like th' unleavened bread, The. Haggadah. Abraham Moses Klein. TrJP

Sky is gray with rain that will not fall, The. At the Zoo. Israel Zangwill. TrJP

Sky is green, ands there is no book to tell us what it means. It has. Engines of Gloom and Affection. John Yau. PmAP

Sky is heavy, it is raining stars, The. Cannibal Hymn, The. *Unknown.* TTY, *tr.* by Samuel A. B. Mercer

Sky is hot and yellow, filled, The. Brides Come to Yuba City, The. Chitra Divakaruni. OpBo; UnSA

Sky is letting its blue eyes close, The. Lullaby. Attila József. IQMS, *tr.* by Vernon Watkins

Sky is low—the Clouds are mean, The. Emily Dickinson. MoAmPo; OxBA

Sky is overcast and behind it an infinite regress, The. Within This Book, Called Marguerite. Marjorie Welish. FTOS; PmAP

Sky is strewn with stars, The. *Unknown.* WoPoe, *tr.* by Charles Simic

Sky is up above the roof, The. Paul Verlaine. AWP *Fr.* Sagesse.

Sky Lark, The. John Clare. NPeEn

Sky, lazily disdaining to pursue, The. Georgia Dusk. Jean Toomer. APT-2; BPo; NAAL-2v2; NAAL-5; NoAM; NoP-4

Sky Lies Blue—Like a Sea, The. Nikolai Alekseievich Klyuyev [*or* Kliuev *or* Klyuev]. TCRusP, *tr.* by John Glad

Sky links cloud waves, links dawn fog. Li Ch'ing-chao. BoWoP

Sky low down in distant West, The. To Mary. Mary E. Tucker. CBWP-1

Sky of churning cogs and work without weekends, A. First Circle, The. S. K. Kelen. BMAP

Sky on this mountain. Water Lilies. Ralph J. Mills, Jr. IllVoic

Sky or an edge or a beach or a wall or a room or a, A. Nursery Rhyme. Kit Robinson. FTOS

Sky overpowering, grey; beneath it. Holland. Hendrik Marsman. TuT, *tr.* by Michael Longley

Sky Picture. Henrietta Cordelia Ray. CBWP-3

Sky-piercing sword, gleaming cold. Zuian. ZenPo, *tr.* by Takashi Ikemoto and Lucien Stryk

Sky possesses the moon, The. You're Mine, You! Edward Heyman. ReLy

Sky rumbles. Gathers. Rain. Virgil [*or* Vergil]. EroLit, *tr.* by Kenneth McLeish *Fr.* Aeneid [*or* Eneados, *Aeneis*], The.

Sky's are a pitiful lot, The. Limerick. Bob Scott. PeLi

Sky's as blue and black as ink, The. Calligram, 15 May 1915. Guillaume Apollinaire. OBWP, *tr.* by O. Bernard

Sky's not high, earth not solid. Seiho. ZenPo, *tr.* by Takashi Ikemoto and Lucien Stryk

Sky's unresting cloudland, that with varying play, The. Robert Bridges. EBEV *Fr.* Testament of Beauty, The.

Sky Scrape / City Scape. Jane Yolen. SSCS

Sky so pale, and the trees, such frail things, The. Á la Promenade. Paul Verlaine. AWP; OBVE, *tr.* by Arthur Symons

Sky that has never known sun, moon, or stars, A. Rear Porches of an Apartment Building. Maxwell Bodenheim. APT-1

Sky that is the limit is the one, The. Incomplete Scenario Involving What the Voice Said. Jane Mead. NAPBL

Sky the color of a wren's [*or* wrens] breath, A. At Chadwicks Bar and Grill. Lance Henson. HATNAP

Sky very blue. Raul Bopp. TCLAP, *tr.* by Renato Rezende *Fr.* Black Snake.

Sky was a somber cave of water, The. Rain Psalm. Leopoldo Lugones. TCLAP, *tr.* by Julie Schumacher

Sky was a street map with stars for, The. Ode. Elizabeth Alexander. GT; PoPoPo

Sky was battened down, The. On Galveston Beach. Barbara Howes. MoAmPo

Sky was blue, so blue, that day, The. For the Candle Light. Angelina Weld Grimké. BlSi; NAAAL

Sky was carpeted with Italian flak. Crump!, The. Malta. John Forbes. NOBAu

Sky was gold in those days, The. In the Beginning. Valerie Sinason. BrRo

Sky was low, the sounding rain was falling dense and dark, The. Late Passenger, The. Clive Staples Lewis. TrCP

Sky was red and the earth got hot, The. When One Is Feeling One's Way. Lawrence Joseph. KGB

Sky wears in a belt of clouds, The. Only for You. Else Lasker-Schüler. BBASP, *tr.* by Robert P. Newton

Sky will extinguish its stars, and the sun, The. Philip of Thessalonica. GrAn

Sky Will Resound, The. Frances Densmore. APT-1 *Fr.* Chippewa Music.

Skylark. Basho. WoPoe; ZenPo, *tr.* by Takashi Ikemoto and Lucien Stryk

Skylark. Johnny Mercer. ReLy

Skylark / Have you anything to say to me? Skylark. Johnny Mercer. ReLy

Skylark's melody is sealed in ice, The. Coronach. Tracey Herd. NeBl

Skylark school, The. Prince Shiki. SoOfWa, *tr.* by Sam Hamill

Skylark / Soaring—her young. Sora. ZenPo, *tr.* by Takashi Ikemoto and Lucien Stryk

Skylark, what prompts your silver song. Nature Poem. Adrian Mitchell. Spl

Skylarks. Ted Hughes.

"All the dreary Sunday morning." HAP

"Crueller than owl or eagle." HAP

"I suppose you just gape and let your gaspings." HAP

"Lark begins to go up, The." HAP

"Like those flailing flames." HAP

"My idleness curdles." HAP

Skylarks and Fuji. Kusano Shimpei. PFTM-1

Skylarks singing / The farmer. Issa. ZenPo, *tr.* by Takashi Ikemoto and Lucien Stryk

Skylight, The. Seamus Heaney. OxBSo *Fr.* Glanmore Revisited.

Skylike limpid eyes, The. Ezra Pound. MoAmPo *Fr.* Hugh Selwyn Mauberley (Life and Contacts).

Skyline of New York does not excite me, The. Review from Staten Island. Gloria C. Oden. GT

Skyline of New York is a splendid sight, The. It's So Peaceful in the Country. Alec Wilder. ReLy

Skymen coming down out the clouds land. Poem for Deep Thinkers, A. Imamu Amiri Baraka. APSN

Skyscraper. Carl Sandburg. HHAm

Skyscrapers. Rachel Lyman Field. ChAP; NOxBChV; SSCS

Skywriting. Jamie Grant. EmeKit

Slain. T. W. H. Crosland. OBWP

Slain Lamb of God. Nikolaus [*or* Nicolaus] Ludwig, Graf von Zinzendorf. AH, *tr.* by Sheema Z. Buehne

Slam, Dunk, and Hook. Yusef Komunyakaa. ISC; MoASP

Slander. Anna Andreyevna Akhmatova. TCRP, *tr.* by Daniel Weissbort

Slant of Sun [on Dull Brown Walls], A. Stephen Crane. NAAL-2v2 *Fr.* War Is Kind.

Slanting ray of evening light, A. Squire's Pew, The. Jane Taylor. PEW

Slanting rays shine on the hamlet. Farms at Wei River, The. Wang Wei. SuSp, *tr.* by Paul W. Kroll

Slanting wind, misty rain. Tune: "The Charm of a Maiden Singer;" Spring Thoughts. Jiaosheng Wang. ColAnChi

Slap in the Face of Public Taste, A. D. Burliuk.

"To the readers of our New First Unexpected." PFTM-1

Slashed and dumped. (LL)   Grauballe Man, The.   Seamus Heaney.   OxBEV; PoetW

Slate.   Richard Murphy.   PBCIP   *Fr.* Battle of Aughrim, The.

Slate-gray waves of day.   Sunset.   John Cope.   GeoH

Slate I picked from a nettlebed.   Richard Murphy.   PBCIP   *Fr.* Battle of Aughrim, The.

Slate Quay: Felinheli.   Peter Gruffydd.   AngWePo

Slate Street School.   Ciaran Carson.   CABP

Slated for demolition.   Cathedral Is, The.   John Ashbery.   InPK-6

Slattern, The.   Sarah Dixon.   ECWP

Slaughter.   Susan Stewart.   BodElec

Slaughter of the Laird of Mellerstain, The.   *Unknown.*   ESPB

Slave, The.   James Oppenheim.   TrJP

Slave, The.   Jones Very.   TAP

Slave and the Iron Lace, The.   Margaret Danner.   BPo

Slave Auction, The.   Frances Ellen Watkins Harper.   APN-2; BPo; ColAP; ISC; TTY

Slave Cabin, Sotterly Plantation, Maryland, 1989.   Lucille Clifton.   LoL

Slave Girl, The.   Rufinus.   GrAn, *tr. by* Alan Marshfield

Slave Girl's Song.   *Unknown.*   PeNZ, *tr. by* Margaret Orbell

Slave in the Dismal Swamp, The.   Henry Wadsworth Longfellow.   TCAPo

Slave Marriage Ceremony Supplement.   *Unknown.*   BPo; TAP

Slave Mother, The.   Frances Ellen Watkins Harper.   ColAP

Slave Ritual.   Carolyn M. Rodgers.   ISC

Slave's Dream, The.   Henry Wadsworth Longfellow.   NAAL-2v1; NAAL-3; NAAL-5

Slave's Lament, The.   Massillon Coicou.   NegPo, *tr. by* Ellen Conroy Kennedy

Slave-Ships, The.   John Greenleaf Whittier.   TCAPo

Slave systems of Rome and Greece, and no one agreed, The. (LL)   Sleet Storm on the Merritt Parkway.   Robert Bly.   CoAmPo; NOBA

Slave Trade, The.   Hannah More.
    "Strange power of song! the strain that warms the heart."   NoP-4

Slavery.   Hannah More.   RWP; WoRP

Slavery.   Jones Very.   NCAP

Slavery, a Poem.   Hannah More.
    "Perish th' illiberal thought which would debase."   ECWP

Slaves.   James Grainger.   NOEC   *Fr.* Sugar Cane, The.

Slaves are dragging the last, The.   Rain.   Leslie Ullman.   YaYoPo

Slaves to London, I'll deceive you.   Song, A.   Peter Anthony Motteux.   NOSC

Slaveship.   Lucille Clifton.   ESEAA
    (Slaveships.)   OPRER

Sld bar 1.99 + drnk.   'Merican Fst Fd.   Thom Tammaro.   ReTh

Sled Burial, Dream Ceremony.   James Dickey.   NoP-4

Sleek, dark-suited.   Elegist, The.   Geoff Page.   BMAP

Sleek mechanical dart: the syringe noses into the blue vein marking the target of me.   D. A. Powell.   NeAmPo

Sleep.   Theophile De Viau.   AWP, *tr. by* Sir Edmund William Gosse

Sleep.   Mary Crockett Hill.   AmPoNex

Sleep.   Jane Holland.   NeBl

Sleep.   Bravig Imbs.   SPE

Sleep.   Bill Knott.   SPE

Sleep.   Dana Naone.   CDW

Sleep.   James Schuyler.   GLP

Sleep.   Sir Philip Sidney.   *See* Astrophil and Stella

Sleep.   Charles Simic.   CoAP

Sleep.   Kenneth Slessor.   BMAP

Sleep.   Publius Papinius Statius.   AWP, *tr. by* W. H. Fyfe

Sleep, The.   Elizabeth Barrett Browning.   ChIV-1; OxAEP-2

Sleep, America.   Bedtime Story.   Gustav Hasford.   CDa

Sleep and death, the dusky eagles.   Lament.   Georg Trakl.   PeFWW, *tr. by* Michael Hamburger

Sleep and oblivion / Reign over all. (LL)   Curfew.   Henry Wadsworth Longfellow.   APN-1; OxBA

Sleep and Poetry.   John Keats.
    "And can I ever bid these joys farewell?"   TOF
    "O for ten years, that I may overwhelm."   NAEL-5v2; NAEL-6v2
    "O Poesy! for thee I hold my pen."   FHYEP

Sleep and rain, two gangsters.   Lullaby.   Alan Michael Parker.   AmPoNex

Sleep, angry beauty, sleep, and fear[e] not me.   Sleep, Angry Beauty.   Thomas Campion.   OxBSP

Sleep, baby mine, Desire; nurse Beauty singeth.   Sleep, Baby Mine, Desire.   Sir Philip Sidney.   OxBSP

Sleep, baby, sleep.   Lullaby.   *Unknown.*   NOBE, *tr. by* Geoffrey Bownas

Sleep, baby, sleep.   *Unknown.*   LB

Sleep, baby, sleep, / Our cottage vale is deep.   *Unknown.*   ReMoGo

Sleep, Big Baby, sleep your fill. (LL)   Lullaby: "Din of work is subdued, The."   W. H. Auden.   FaBoMo; GLP; NoAM

Sleep Brought Me Vision.   John Peale Bishop.   Son

Sleep, Christian warrior, sleep.   To Rev. Thaddeus Saltus.   Mary Weston Fordham.   CBWP-2

Sleep cold at someone's.   Callimachus.   GrAn

Sleep Drops Its Nets.   Jean Valentine.   YaYoPo

Sleep drops its nets for monsters old as the flood.   Sleep Drops Its Nets.   Jean Valentine.   YaYoPo

Sleep, grim Reproof; my jocund muse doth sing.   John Marston.   NoSic   *Fr.* Satires.

Sleep in the Mojave Desert.   Sylvia Plath.   AiP

Sleep is a country of water.   Country of Water.   Bernice Ames.   WPE

Sleep Is a Deep and Many Voiced Flood.   Robert Duncan.   CLPP

Sleep is 20.   20.   Barbara Guest.   PoM

Sleep, King Jesus.   Mary's Song.   Charles Causley.   OBCP

Sleep, kinsman thou to death and trance.   Tennyson.   NAEL-6v2   *Fr.* In Memoriam A. H. H.

Sleep, little architect. It is your mother's wish.   Lullaby.   Joan Murray.   YaYoPo

Sleep. little Baby, kip in peace through the night.   Radio Cradle-song.   Eugène Marais.   PeSAV, *tr. by* Stephen Gray

Sleep, love sleep.   Serenade.   Mary Weston Fordham.   CBWP-2; SWaP

Sleep, McKade.   Evening Song.   Kenneth Fearing.   SPE

Sleep, My Beloved.   Yevgeny Aleksandrovich Yevtushenko [*or* Evtushenko].   TCRP, *tr. by* Geoffrey Dutton and Tina Tupkina-Glaessner

Sleep, My Child.   "Sholom Aleichem."   TrJP, *tr. by* Alter Brody

Sleep, my child; because of you.   Night.   Gabriela Mistral.   WoPoe, *tr. by* Alice Jane McVan

Sleep, my child, it's late, go to rest.   Lullaby for Mirjam.   Richard Beer-Hofmann.   AuPH, *tr. by* Naemah Beer-Hofmann

Sleep, my child, my little daughter.   Cradle Song.   *Unknown.*   TrJP, *tr. by* Joseph Leftwich

Sleep, my child, sleep.   Lullaby.   Elolongue Epanya Yondo.   NegPo, *tr. by* Ellen Conroy Kennedy

Sleep, my little baby, sleep.   Lullaby.   Samuel Hoffenstein.   TrJP

Sleep My Little Love.   Breyten Breytenbach.   PeSAV, *tr. by* Stephen Gray

Sleep, my little one, sleep, my pretty / one, sleep. (LL)   Tennyson.   FHYEP; NAEL-5v2; NAEL-6v2; SCGP   *Fr.* Princess, The.

Sleep, my love, and peace attend thee.   All Through the Night.   *Unknown.*   ITBLP

Sleep, my sweet girl! and all the sleep.   La Promessa Sposa.   Walter Savage Landor.   NOBVV

Sleep of Adam, The.   John Hejduk.   ChIV-1

Sleep of Beasts, The.   Peter Cooley.   UrbNat

Sleep of My Lions, The.   Douglas Livingstone.   PeSAV

Sleep of Palinurus, The.   Virgil [*or* Vergil].   WoPoe, *tr. by* Cecil Day Lewis   *Fr.* Aeneid [*or* Eneados, *Aeneis*], The.

Sleep of the Brave, The.   Odysseus Elytis.   AF

Sleep of the Insomniac, The.   William Virgil Davis.   YaYoPo

Sleep of the Painted Ladies, The.   Nancy Willard.   LCAP-2

Sleep of this night deepens, The.   Under Stars.   Tess Gallagher.   InPK-6

Sleep on, and dream of Heaven awhile.   Sleeping Beauty, The.   Samuel Rogers.   GTBS-P; OxAEP-2

Sleep on, I lie at heaven's high oriels.   Nirvana.   John Hall Wheelock.   MoAmPo

Sleep, our lord, and for thy peace.   Night Song for a Child.   Charles Williams.   OBEV

Sleep'ry Sim of the Lamb-kill.   Fray of Suport, The.   *Unknown.*   IBB

Sleep's dream / the nerve-flash in the blood.   Subliminal.   Lorine Niedecker.   PFTM-1

Sleep's Underside.   Melissa Kirsch.   AWTN

Sleep's very dear to me, but being stone's.   "Night" in the Medici Chapel.   Michelangelo Buonarroti.   WoPoe, *tr. by* William Jay Smith

Sleep, Silence' Child.   William Drummond, of Hawthornden.   NePenScot; Son (Sonet to Sleepe.)   OxBS
    (Sonnet: "Sleep, silence' child, sweet father of soft rest")   NOSC

Sleep, sleep, beauty bright.   Cradle Song, A.   William Blake.   OBEV

Sleep sleep old sun, thou canst not have repast [*or* repassed].   Resurrection, Imperfect.   John Donne.   ChIV-2

Sleep Softly.   John Macrae (Mhurchaidh, Ian Mac).   NePenScot, *tr. by* Derick Thomson

Sleep softly . . . eagle forgotten . . . under the stone.   Eagle That Is Forgotten, The.   Nicholas Vachel Lindsay.   APT-1; AWP; MoAmPo; NOBA; OxBA

Sleep Song.   John Fletcher.   *See* Tragedy of Valentinian, The

Sleep soundly, dogs: the Dog Star and the Maid.   *Unknown.*   PriapPo, *tr. by* Richard W. Hooper   *Fr.* Priapus Poems, The.

Sleep Spaces.   Robert Desnos.   SurPaPo, *tr. by* Mary Ann Caws

Sleep sweetly in your humble graves. Ode. Henry Timrod. CBCWP; MakPoe; NOBA; OxBA; TAP

Sleep tried to split us apart. Meeting with Vilakazi, the Great Zulu Poet, A. Raymond Mazisi Kunene. PeSAV, *tr.* by the author

Sleep-walking vapor, like a visitant ghost. Still Life. Anthony Hecht. NoP-4

Sleep Watch. Lance Henson. VoR

Sleep well, my love, sleep well. Nightsong: City. Dennis Brutus. HBAPE; PBMAP; PoetW; WoPoe

Sleep will He give His beloved? Nirvana. Rosamund Marriott Watson. VWP

Sleep-Worker, The. Thomas Hardy. OxBSo

Sleep, You hungry people, sleep! Lullaby for the Hungry. Muhammad Mahdi Al-Jawahiri. MAP, *tr.* by Issa Boullata and John Heath-Stubbs

Sleep you shipwrecked sailor! (LL) Brief Lessons in Eroticism 1. Gioconda Belli. ErotSp; TANSG, *tr.* by Steven F. White

Sleep your sleep softly, my darling, my love. Sleep Softly. John Macrae (Mhurchaidh, Ian Mac). NePenScot, *tr.* by Derick Thomson

Sleepe after our short light / One everlasting night. (LL) Catullus. FaBoEE; NoSic; OBVE, *tr.* by Sir Walter Alexander Raleigh *Fr.* Carmina.

Sleeper. Amy Fusselman. HeMarv

Sleeper. Patricia Pogson. NLP

Sleeper, The. Walter De la Mare. MoBrPo

Sleeper, The. Edgar Allan Poe. NAAL-2v1; NAAL-3; NCAP; NOBA; OxBA; TAP

Sleeper, The. *Unknown.* AWP *Fr.* Thousand and One Nights, The.

Sleeper in the Valley, The. Arthur Rimbaud. OBWP; WoPoe, *tr.* by William Jay Smith

Sleeper in the Valley, The. Arthur Rimbaud. OBWP *Fr.* Eighteen-Seventy.

Sleeper of the Valley, The. Arthur Rimbaud. AWP, *tr.* by Ludwig Lewisohn

Sleeper sinks down in soft pillows and fine, The. Summer Night. Ludwig Goldscheider. AuPH, *tr.* by Lowell A. Bangerter

Sleeper, the palm-trees drink the breathless noon. *Unknown.* AWP *Fr.* Thousand and One Nights, The.

Sleepers. Branko Miljkovic. WoPoe, *tr.* by Charles Simic

Sleepers, The. Peter Kocan. CBAP

Sleepers, The. Walt Whitman. NAAL-2v1; NAAL-3
 "I wander all night in my vision." AWTN
 "Now what my mother told me one day as we sat at dinner / together." BLT

Sleepers humped down on the benches, The. Night Raid. Desmond Hawkins. PoWW

Sleeping. (LL) Weep [*or* Weepe] You No More [Sad Fountains]. *Unknown.* EBEV; EnLoPo; HAP; NOSC; NoSic; PoE; TFi

Sleeping, The. Lynn Emanuel. AiP

Sleeping armies of the living God, The. Death of Saul, The. Philip Levine. ChIV-1

Sleeping at last, the trouble and tumult over. Sleeping at Last. Christina Georgina Rossetti. NAEL-5v2; NAEL-6v2

Sleeping Beauty, The. Hayden Carruth.
 "Called him "Big Joe" yes and Joe Turner it was his name." GifTon
 "Your dream: / The letters HIV appear." GifTon

Sleeping Beauty, The. Samuel Rogers. GTBS-P; OxAEP-2

Sleeping Beauty, The. Dame Edith Sitwell.
 Governante, The. BWW
 Innocent Spring, The. NOBE; OxBTC
 Princess, The. BWW
 "When we come to that dark house." OBMV

Sleeping Compartment. Norman MacCaig. EmeKit

Sleeping Father. David Chin. InvLad

Sleeping Fury, The. Louise Bogan. NALW

Sleeping Giant, The. Donald Hall. PAI; TwCP

Sleeping Heroes. Edward Richard Burton Shanks. OBMV

Sleeping in their sheen. (LL) Willie Macintosh. *Unknown.* ESPB; OxBoLi

Sleeping late. Buson. EH, *tr.* by Robert Hass

Sleeping Lord, The. David Jones.
 "Does he cock his weather-ear, enquiringly." TCAWP
 "Tawny-black sky-scurries." OBWVE

Sleeping Man Must Be Awakened to Be Killed, A. Erin Belieu. NeAmPo

Sleeping on Horseback. Po Chü-i. BLT; ChiP, *tr.* by Arthur Waley

Sleeping on the Ceiling. Elizabeth Bishop. APT-2; OBGa; TTTS

Sleeping on the Wing. Frank O'Hara. NAAL-2v2

Sleeping They Bear Me. Alfred Mombert. AWP, *tr.* by Jethro Bithell

Sleeping, turning in turn like planets. Adrienne Rich. TRP *Fr.* Twenty-one Love Poems.

Sleeping with Foxes. Roberta Hill Whiteman. CDW

Sleeping with Women. Kenneth Koch. PoM

Sleeping woman dreams she wakes, A. Nightmare. Isabella Gardner. CoAP

Sleepless. Al-Khansa. BoWoP, *tr.* by Willis Barnstone

Sleepless. Ch'in Kuan. CrYelRi, *tr.* by Sam Hamill

Sleepless. Eileen Myles. WiU

Sleepless as Prospero back in his bedroom. Darwin in 1881. Gjertrud Schnackenberg. NoAM; NoP-4

Sleepless at Crown Point. Richard Wilbur. InPK-6; WeW-3

Sleepless, I stare. Broken Dark, The. Robert Earl Hayden. AWTN; GT

Sleepless Night. Léon Damas. NegPo, *tr.* by Ellen Conroy Kennedy

Sleepless Night, A. Philip Levine. BLT

Sleepless Nights. Tu Fu. CrYelRi, *tr.* by Sam Hamill

Sleepless Nights. Marilyn Nelson Waniek. ISC

Sleepless nights, The. I Wish I Were in Love Again. Lorenz Hart. OBCoV

Sleepless with cold commemorative eyes. (LL) Dante Gabriel Rossetti. EBVV; GSo; GTBS-P; NAEL-5v2; NAEL-6v2; NoP-4 *Fr.* House of Life, The.

Sleepless, with pleasure and expiring fears. Walter Savage Landor. NOBRP *Fr.* Gebir.

Sleepless, you hear the neighboring temple bell. Poem Making Fun of Chi-ti for His Eye Illness, A. Yang Chi. CoBLCP, *tr.* by Jonathan Chaves

Sleeplessness. Michelle Boisseau. ExTi

Sleeplessness. Gerardo Diego. BLPSL, *tr.* by Rene de Costa, Rigas Kappatos and Eleni Paidoussi

Sleeplessness. Luigi Fontanella. NeIt, *tr.* by W. S. Di Piero

Sleepwalkers. Bella [*or* Izabella] Akhatovna Akhmadulina. BoWoP, *tr.* by Barbara Einzig

Sleepwalkers' Ballad. Federico García Lorca. STV; WeW-3, *tr.* by John Frederick Nims

Sleepwalking Ballad, The. Federico García Lorca. WoPoe, *tr.* by Michael Hartnett

Sleepwalking Soho. Stuart Dybek. IllVoic

Sleepy Giant, The. Charles Edward Carryl. NOxBChV; OTCP

Sleepy lagoon, A. Sleepy Lagoon. Eric Coates. ReLy

Sleepy Time Gal. Raymond B. Egan. ReLy

Sleet. Norman MacCaig. OBCP

Sleet and rain, as if the pot were boiling. Bad Government. Kuan Hsiu. WoPoe, *tr.* by Jerome P. Seaton

Sleet Storm on the Merritt Parkway. Robert Bly. CoAmPo; NOBA

Sleigh, The. Sergey [*or* Sergei] Aleksandrovich Yesenin [*or* Essenin]. RusPo, *tr.* by Robert Arthur Douglas Ford

Sleigh Ride in July. Jimmy Van Heusen. ReLy

Slender as a needle. Awotunde Aworinde. PFTM-1 *Fr.* If a Suite in Praise of the Yoruba Oracle.

Slender bamboo is like a hermit, The. On a Painting by Wang the Clerk of Yen Ling. Su Tung-p'o (Su Shih). BLT, *tr.* by Kenneth Rexroth

Slender Fingers. Chao Luan-luan. BoWoP

Slender grasses. Traveling at Night. Tu Fu. WoPoe, *tr.* by Greg Whincup

Slender Lad, The. *Unknown.* OBWVE, *tr.* by Kenneth Hurlstone Jackson

Slender plank above a waterhole, A. Founding of New Hampshire, The. Carl Rakosi. FTOS

Slender rays: a chord barely seen. New Moon. Tu Fu. ChinPo, *tr.* by Yip Wai-lim

Slept, and there was no pursuit. (LL) Hell Gate. A. E. Housman. NoAM; SCGP; UnPo

Slice of Wedding Cake, A. Robert Graves. BoLoP; NAEL-5v2; NAEL-6v2; NOBE; OxBTC

Slices of Knowledge. Henri Michaux.
 "He who knows how to shave the razor, will know how to erase the." PFTM-1

Slicing my head off shaving I think of Charles I. Notes for a Revised Sonnet. "Edward Pygge." OBCoV

Slick. Víctor Hernández Cruz. PueRic

Slide soft, fair forth, and make a crystal plain. Sonnet. William Drummond, of Hawthornden. NOSC; OxBSo

Slides. Jennifer Maiden. CBAP

Slides by on grease. (LL) For the Union Dead. Robert Lowell. CBCWP; CoAP; ColAP; HAP; HCAP; HarvBoo; HeIP-4; LCAP-2; NAAL-2v2; NAAL-5; NOBA; NoAM; NoP-4; OBWP; PoE; PoetW; SCV; TFi; TRP; TwCP; UnPo; VCAP; WeW-3

Sliding. Sam Adams. AngWePo

Sliding from half-up the eucalyptus trees, the wild desert pigs practice flight. Border, The. Joanna Rawson. BodElec

Sliding Trombone. Georges Ribemont-Dessaignes. SPE, *tr.* by David Gascoyne

Slight as thou art, thou art enough to hide. To a Daisy. Alice Thompson Meynell. MoBrPo; SacPr; Son; VWP

Slight unpremeditated Words are borne. Love's Witness. Aphra Behn. BoWoP; LW

Slighted Lady, The. Anna Wickham. LW

Slighted Wife, The. Aaron Hodza. PeSAV, *tr.* by George Fortune

Slightest vacuum when the concrete-mixer stops, The. Michael Haslam. Oth *Fr.* Continual Song.

Slightly before the middle of Congressman Pudd. E. E. Cummings. FaBoEE; OBAL

Slim and singing copper girl, A. Early Copper. Carl Sandburg. HeIP-4

Slim Cunning Hands. Walter De la Mare. FaBoEE; NIL-7; NIP-4; WeW-3

Slim cunning hands at rest, and cozening eyes. Slim Cunning Hands. Walter De la Mare. FaBoEE; NIL-7; NIP-4; WeW-3

Slim Greer. Sterling Allen Brown. NAAAL

Slim Greer went to heaven. Slim in Hell. Sterling Allen Brown. BPo

Slim in Atlanta. Sterling Allen Brown. APT-2; NoP-4

Slim in Hell. Sterling Allen Brown. BPo

Slim Man Canyon. Leslie Marmon Silko. VoR

Slim sentinels. Trees at Night. Helene Johnson. BlSi

Slim / young fascist, A. On the Yard. Etheridge Knight. RaBo

Slime clung, The. Isaac Rosenberg. PeFWW Fr. Amulet, The.

Slimy obscene creatures, insane. Nigga Section, The. Welton Smith. BPo

Sling me under the sea. Bones. Carl Sandburg. TCAPo

Slip, The. Wendell Berry. NOCV

Slip of loveliness, slim, seemly. In Praise of a Girl. Huw Morus. OBWVE, tr. by Gwyn Williams

Slip of the tong. (LL) Lapsus Linguae. Keith Preston. NBLV; OBAL; OBCoV

Slip off that gown. Paulus [or Paulos] Silentiarius. GrAn

Slippery twitch near my loafer, toy so. Red Salamander—Video Store Parking Lot. Mark DeFoe. UrbNat

Slipping in blood, by his own hand, through pride. To an Artist, to Take Heart. Louise Bogan. PAI; TRP

Slipping in the snow. Chuck Brickley. HA

Slipping—is Crash's law. (LL) Emily Dickinson. NOBA; TCAPo

Slipshod writing, premature publication. Martial. RomPo, tr. by Peter Whigham

Slithergadee has crawled out of the sea, The. Not Me. Shel [or Shelley] Silverstein. NBLV; OBCoV

Sliver of Sermon. Langston Hughes. APT-2

Sloe Gin. Seamus Heaney. PNI

Slog brute streets with rebel tramping! Our March. Vladimir Vladimirovich Mayakovsky [or Maiakovskii]. AWP, tr. by Babette Deutsch and Avrahm Yarmolinsky

Slogan, The. Paul Blackburn. PoM

Slop Barrel, The. Philip Whalen. PmAP

Slope of it. Body. Robert Creeley. FTOS

Slope woods' snows melt. Easter Sunday. Allen Ginsberg. FTOS

Slopes of the sun and vine, and thou dark stream. Pastoral. George Cabot Lodge. APN-2

Sloth, The. Theodore Roethke. ChAP; OBAL; OBCA; OxIBACP; TRP

Slouch. Brendan Cleary. NeBl

Slouches towards Bethlehem to be born? (LL) Second Coming, The. W. B. Yeats. BIrV; CABP; ChIV-2; ClHu; FaBoMo; GI; GTBS-P; HAP; HarvBoo; HeIP-4; InPK-6; MoBrPo; NAAL-3; NAEL-5v2; NAEL-6v2; NIL-7; NIP-4; NOBE; NoAM; NoP-4; OxAEP-2; OxBEV; OxBTC; PoE; PoPoPo; RaBo; SCV; SoSe-8; TFi; TRP; UnPo; WoPoe

Slough. Sir John Betjeman. HarvBoo; MoBrPo; NoAM; OxAEP-2

Slow. Marvin Bell. MoASP

Slow. Robert Francis. APT-2

Slow, blue shadows of the olive groves, The. Good Men. Roberta Spear. GeoHom

Slow by slow people come. Christmas Eve: Nuyorican Café. Miguel Algarin. PueRic

Slow clear. That More Simple Natural Time Tone Distortion. Tom Raworth. Oth

Slow, cold breathing, The. Marsh, New Year's Day, The. Peter Everwine. NNaP

Slow Curtain. John Wheelwright. APT-2

Slow Dance. David St. John. LCAP-2

Slow Dancer That No One Hears But You. Duane Niatum. CDW

Slow Delight. Leopoldo Lugones. BLPSL, tr. by Rene de Costa, Rigas Kappatos and Eleni Paidoussi

Slow-footed stockman called Beales, A. Limerick. Cyril Mountjoy. PeLi

Slow for the sake of flowers as they turn. Release. R. S. Gwynn. RA

Slow Giving. Ibn al-Rumi. ArPe, tr. by Omar S. Pound

Slow in the Wintry Morn, the struggling light. Charlotte Smith. RWP

Slow moves the pageant of a climbing race. Slow Through the Dark. Paul Laurence Dunbar. GSo; SacPr

Slow Night on Texas Street, A. James Kimbrell. NAPBL

Slow on the leash / Pallid the leash-men! (LL) Return, The. Ezra Pound. APT-1; HAP; MoAmPo; NOBA; NPeEn; NoAM; OxBA; PoE; RB; TRP; VGW; WeW-3

Slow overture of rain, The. Mind. Jorie Graham. HCAP

Slow Pacific Swell, The. Yvor Winters. APT-2; ColAP; HarvBoo; NOBA

Slow pass the hours—ah, passing slow! Ballade Tragique à Double Refrain. Max Beerbohm. OBSV

Slow-rolling beauty. Mountains of California: Part 2, The. Al Young. GeoHom

Slow, Slow, Fresh Fount. Ben Jonson. See Cynthia's Revels

Slow, slow, fresh fount, keep time with my salt tears. Ben Jonson. NOSC Fr. Cynthia's Revels.

Slow—slow—slow—slow. (LL) Swing Song, A. William Allingham. OTCP; TLR

Slow Song for Mark Rothko. John Taggart. PFTM-2

Slow splashing splashing. Malay Figures. Unknown. EaWin, tr. by W. S. Merwin

Slow the limpid currents twining. Canzonet. Mary Robinson. NOBRP

Slow Through the Dark. Paul Laurence Dunbar. GSo; SacPr

Slow to Come, Quick a-Gone. William Barnes. NOBVV

Slow toiling upward from the misty vale. Nearing the Snow-Line. Oliver Wendell Holmes. APN-1

Slow train, A. Few travellers. If. Eleanor Maxted. NewEx

Slow vengeance, like a blood-hound at his heels. (LL) To the Earl of Oxford, Late Lord Treasurer. Jonathan Swift. FaBoWar; OBVE

Slow wand'ring came the sightless sire and she. Antigone and Oedipus. Henrietta Cordelia Ray. BlSi; CBWP-3

Slowly. James Reeves. NOxBChV

Slowly, and flake by flake. . . At the drifted fond. Winter Night: Mount Royal. Abraham Moses Klein. NoAM

Slowly, by God's Hand Unfurled. William Henry Furness. AH

Slowly, carefully. I live. (LL) Clouded Sky. Miklós Radnóti. GifTon; HP, tr. by Stephen Berg, S. J. Marks, F. J. Marks and Steven Polgar

Slowly flutters the snow from ash-coloured heavens in silence. Snowfall. Giosuè Carducci. AWP, tr. by Romilda Rendel

Slowly he moves. Boy on a Swing. Mbuyiseni Oswald Mtshali. NIL-7

Slowly he sways that head that cannot hear. Rattler, Alert. Brewster Ghiselin. HAP; WeW-3

Slowly he turns himself round and round. Dancing Bear, The. Rachel Lyman Field. KaS; NTCP

Slowly in three to four weeks. My Girlfriends. Erich Fried. AF, tr. by Georg Rapp

Slowly / like a crippled cow. Jean-Joseph Rabéarivelo [or Rebéarivelo]. NegPo

Slowly, like a hot tear tracing the skin's folds. Doomsday. Maurya Simon. ExTi

Slowly out of the sun-blackened landscape. (LL) Rivers and Mountains. John Ashbery. CoAP; NOBA; NoAM; TRP

Slowly / Over cedars. Gyodai. ZenPo, tr. by Takashi Ikemoto and Lucien Stryk

Slowly, silently, now the moon. Silver. Walter De la Mare. MoBrPo; PoRA; TTTS

Slowly, slowly. David Steinberg. PasH

Slowly, Slowly Poem, The. Yüan Hung-tao. CoBLCP; ColAnChi, tr. by Jonathan Chaves

Slowly the Moon her banderoles of light. Battle, A. Isabella Valancy Crawford. NOBC

Slowly the moon is rising out of the ruddy haze. Aware. D. H. Lawrence. MoBrPo; NoAM

Slowly the ocean-liner. Ocean Liner. Ko Changsu (Chang-soo Koh). WoPoe, tr. by the author

Slowly the old stone building walls downtown dissolve. Kenneth Irby. PFTM-2

Slowly the poison the whole blood stream fills. Missing Dates. William Empson. HAP; HarvBoo; MakPoe; MoBrPo; NOBE; NPeEn; NoAM; OxBEV; PoE; UnPo

Slowly the ponderous doors of lead imponderous. Sleep. Bravig Imbs. SPE

Slowly the tide creeps up the sand. Slowly. James Reeves. NOxBChV

Slowly the vision grows. Lakeside Incident. Robin Skelton. NOBC

Slowly the women file to where he stands. Faith Healing. Philip Larkin. ChIV-2; GI; NoAM; OxBEV

Slowly the world contracts about my ears. Flagpole Sitter, The. Donald Finkel. CoAP

Slowly the world freezes into me. Ice. Ágnes Nemes Nagy. IQMS, tr. by Ila Egon

Slowness of Belief in a Spiritual World, The. Jones Very. NCAP

Slug in Woods. Earle Birney. NOBC; NoP-4

Slugabed. Sydney Goodsir Smith. OxBS Fr. Under the Eildon Tree.

Sluggard, The. William Henry Davies. OBMV

Sluggard, The. Isaac Watts. ECEV; HAP; NOEC; OxBEV; OxBoLi; UV

Sluggish morne as yet undrest, The. Upon Phillis Walking in a Morning before Sun-Rising. John Cleveland. MeLP

Sluggy and slowe, in spetinge muiche. Unknown. MiEL

Slugs. Gillian Ferguson. MFPA

Slum Dwelling. Jack Davis. IBA

Slum man they killed, the mountain man lives on, The. (LL) Early Lynching. Carl Sandburg. ChIV-2; MoAmPo

Slumber dark and deep. Paul Verlaine. AWP *Fr.* Sagesse.

Slumber pours down. (LL) About the Cool Water. Sappho. OBVE; PGA, *tr. by* Kenneth Rexroth

Slumber Song of the Gardens, A. John Runcie. PeSAV

Slumbering Passion. Josephine D. Henderson Heard. CBWP-4

Slumming on Park Avenue. Irving Berlin. APT-1

Slump. Vassar Miller. BoWoP

Slumped on a chair, his body is an S. Lavatory Attendant, The. Wendy Cope. UV

Slumped on a pallet of winter-withered grass. Cross Cut. Peter Davison. ColAP

Slumped under the impressive genitals. Boston Common. John Berryman. CBCWP

Slung over a screen. Buson. SoOfWa, *tr. by* Sam Hamill

Sma' was I, amang brether o' mine. David and Goliath. P. Hately Waddell. ChIV-1

Small Acts. Thomas Centolella. GifTon

Small Aircraft. Bella [*or* Izabella] Akhatovna Akhmadulina. BoWoP, *tr. by* Daniel Halpern

Small and emptied woman you lie here a thousand years dead. In the Museum. Isabella Gardner. SoSe-8

Small and little thing!, A. (LL) Thomas Traherne. NOBE; OBEV *Fr.* Third Century, The.

Small / & with intensely. Parents. Hilda Morley. PmAP

Small arena almost filled, The. Event. Kim Addonizio. MoASP

Small as he is he can nimbly dance. Tune: "Hung Hsiu-hsieh." To a Flea. Yang Na. ColAnChi, *tr. by* James I. Crump

Small bird, The. North-East. *Unknown.* WoPoe, *tr. by* Seamus Heaney

Small bird, forgive me. *Unknown.* KaS

Small Bird's Nest Made of White Reed Fiber, A. Robert Bly. NNaP

Small bird / tracks. Rain. Lance Henson. VoR

Small boat lurches, drifting, The. Gwbert: Mackerel Fishing. Sam Adams. TCAWP

Small boy drove the shaggy ass, The. Turf-Carrier [*or* Turf Carrier] on Aranmore. John Hewitt. PoRA

Small bundle of bones, small bundle of fingers, of plumpness, of heart. Song for the Spirit of Natalie Going. Susan Wheeler. ExTi

Small, busy flames play through the fresh-laid coals. To My Brothers. John Keats. Son

Small but splendid is. Smell. 'Enayat Jaber. PoArWo, *tr. by* Wen Chin Ouyang

Small Celandine, The. William Wordsworth. *See* Lesson, A

Small change and hums back to it its slow vowels. (LL) Mongoloid Child Handling Shells on the Beach, A. Richard Snyder. InPK-6; NIL-7

Small change, when we'are [*or* we are *or* we're] to bodies gone. (LL) Ecstasy, The. John Donne. BASC; BoLoP; CABP; FHYEP; FSCP; HAP; NAEL-5v1; NAEL-6v1; NAEL-7v1; NOBE; NoP-4; OBEV; OxBEV; PoE; TFi; TOF

Small Country. Claribel Alegría. BoWoP, *tr. by* Aliki and Willis Barnstone

Small doses, effleurage will do. Sea or Sky? Medbh McGuckian. PBCIP

Small Dream. Fujii Sadakazu. PFTM-2, *tr. by* Christopher Drake *Fr.* Where is Japanese Poetry?

Small eyes water on the branch. Another Face. Ray A. Young Bear. CDW

Small fact and fingers and farthest one from me. Poem for Emily, A. Miller Williams. WeW-3

Small Faculty Stag for the Visiting Poet, A. Earle Birney. OxBC; PeLV

Small Farm, A. Michael Hartnett. CIP-2; PBCIP

Small Fat Boy Walking Backwards, A. Gerry Murphy. BiHa

Small Female Skull. Carol Ann Duffy. EmeKit; HarvBoo

Small Fig Tree, A. Donald Hall. ChIV-2; GI

Small fish-boats / After what. Kagami Shiko. ZenPo, *tr. by* Takashi Ikemoto and Lucien Stryk

Small fists waving. Baby Hilary, Sir Edmund, The. Kathleen Leland Baker. NBLV

Small Frogs Killed on the Highway. James Wright (1927–80). HCAP; NNaP; NoAM

   (Still.) PoPoPo

Small Garden, The. Cheng Hsieh. SuSp, *tr. by* Wu-Chi Liu

Small girl, A. Michael McClintock. HA

Small Girl Brings an Injured Bird into the Surgery, A. Michael O'Reilly. BloBone

Small girls on trikes. Christmas Day. Roy Fuller. OBCP

Small gleams on the bank. (LL) Bog Queen. Seamus Heaney. NoAM; PAI; RACG

Small gnats that fly. One Hard Look. Robert Graves. MoBrPo

Small gray cloudy louse that nests in my beard, The. James Keir Baxter. *See* Small grey cloudy louse that nests in my beard, The

Small grey cloudy louse that nests in my beard, The. James Keir Baxter. PeNZ *Fr.* Jerusalem Sonnets.

Small hills upon small hills: sungold sheen comes and goes. Tune: "Beautiful Barbarians." Wen T'ing-yün. ChinPo, *tr. by* Yip Wai-lim

Small Hours. David Barber. AmPoNex

Small householder now comes out warily, The. Spring Voices. Louis MacNeice. Son

Small Joys. May Sarton. FFC

Small Kulak Landowner. Innokenty Fiodorovich Annensky. TCRP, *tr. by* Daniel Weissbort and Lubov Yakovleva

Small Light, A. Cathy Song. TRP

Small lights pirouette. Peterhead in May. Burns Singer. OxBS

Small Lochs. Norman MacCaig. NePenScot

Small man suffers the indignities of childhood, The. Paul Klee. Ruthven Todd. SPE

Small. Miniaturized, yet you insist. Country of Dust, The. Vahan Tekeyan. AF, *tr. by* Diana Der Hovanessian and Marzbed Margossian

Small Miracle, A. Anabel Torres. TANSG, *tr. by* Celeste Kostopulos-Cooperman

Small Miseries. Letitia [*or* Laetitia] Elizabeth Landon. VWP

Small Moon on the Shoulder of New York. George Keithley. UrbNat

Small-mouth bass breaks water, gorged with spawn, The. (LL) After the Surprising Conversions. Robert Lowell. CoAmPo; HAP; NAAL-2v2; NoAM; PAI; TRP

Small noise, A. Rod Willmot. HA

Small Number, A. Olena Kalytiak Davis. NAPBL

Small Ode to a Black Cuban Boxer. Nicolás Guillén. TCLAP, *tr. by* Robert Marquez and David Arthur McMurray

Small part of it will die if I'm not around / feeding it anymore, A. (LL) Chicago Poem. Lew Welch. NeAP; PoM

Small Passing. Ingrid De Kok. HAWP

Small Patch of Ice, A. Betsy Sholl. PBCAP

Small Paths. Henriëtte Roland-Holst. WPOW, *tr. by* Jonathan Crewe

Small Pleasures. Angela Shaw. NeAmPo

Small Prayer. Weldon Kees. VGW

Small Rains. N. M. Bodecker. Spl

Small Room with Large Windows, A. Allen Curnow. PeNZ

Small room with one table and one chair, A. Poet in Winter. Edward Lucie-Smith. TwCP

Small sad man with a hat, A. At Last. John Montague. PBCIP

Small-scale Reflections on a Great House. A. K. Ramanujan. OxBC

Small script take thy swift way across the sea. For His Friends. Alcuin. MLL, *tr. by* Helen Waddell

Small Secret Book, A. Michael McClure. PFTM-2

Small Secrets. John Montague. ModIr

Small service is true service while it lasts. To a Child [Written in Her Album]. William Wordsworth. OxBSP; Spl

Small Sins. Maram Masri. PoArWo, *tr. by* Amal Amireh

Small Song. A. R. Ammons. NoAM

Small space. Two Tile Beaks. Maria Amalia Fonte Boa. BoWoP, *tr. by* Willis Barnstone and Nelson Cerqueira

Small Square, The. Sophia de Mello Breyner Andresen. WPOW, *tr. by* Alexis Levitin

Small Square, The. Sophia De Mello Breyner. VCWP, *tr. by* Ruth Fainlight

Small Talk in a Garden. O. B. Hardison, Jr. CRP

Small thing and moreover black is she, A. Philodemus. GrAn

Small things, like the turning of a key. Chimes. Michael Smith. PBCIP

Small Town. Rita Dove. GT

Small-town Gladys. David Campbell. BMAP

Small Town with One Road. Gary Soto. SoSe-8

Small type of great ones, that do hum. Fly Caught in a Cobweb, A. Richard Lovelace. BeJo; CaPo

Small vampire, gorger at your mother's teat. Last Child. X. J. Kennedy. OxBSP

Small Variation. Octavio Paz. VCWP, *tr. by* Mark Strand

Small Vases from Hebron, The. Naomi Shihab Nye. PoArWo

Small, viewless Æronaut, that by the line. To the Insect of the Gossamer. Charlotte Smith. OxBSo

Small wind lightly, A. Count Carrots. Gerda Mayer. OBSP

Small wind whispers through the leafless hedge, The. Winter. John Clare. CenSon

Small Wire. Anne Sexton. InvLi

Small Woman on Swallow Street. W. S. Merwin. CoAmPo; CoAP

Small Wonder. Brock. Paul Muldoon. NoAM; NoP-4

Smaller and clearer as the years go by. (LL) Lines on a Young Lady's Photograph Album. Philip Larkin. EnLoPo; HAP

Smaller, older *Girl at a Sewing Machine*, The. Two Hoppers. John Updike. PoSol

Smaller than the small. Canticle of the Void, The. Paul Murray. InvLi

Smaller—that Covered Vision—Here. (LL) Emily Dickinson. APN-2; NoP-4

Smallest bark on life's tumultuous ocean, The. Influence. Sarah Knowles Bolton. PWR

Smallest sting can wound the breast of Love, The. (LL) To the Eolian Harp. Mary Robinson. CenSon; RWP

Smallpox, insurrection. Was her kingdom not ravaged enough already? Empress Shōtoku Invents Printing in 1770. Teresa D. Cader. ExTi

Smalltown Memorials. Geoff Page. BMAP

Smart. Fêng Mêng-lung. ColAnChi; WoPoe, tr. by Richard W. Bodman *Fr.* Mountain Songs.

Smart and cannot fish there. (LL) Limbo. Seamus Heaney. CIP-2; NoAM; OxBC

Smart armadillo stays, The. Dead Armadillos. Gail White. UrbNat

Smart man was Bishop Colenso, A. Colenso Rhymes for Orthodox Children. Bret Harte. OBAL

Smash Your Fist. Anabel Torres. TANSG, tr. by Celeste Kostopulos-Cooperman

Smear of blue peat smoke, The. Shepherd's Hut, The. Andrew Young. OxBTC

Smeared with the gold of the opulent sun. (LL) Postcard from the Volcano, A. Wallace Stevens. APT-1; HAP; HCAP; NoAM; SAmP; WeW-3

Smell. 'Enayat Jaber. PoArWo, tr. by Wen Chin Ouyang

Smell. William Carlos Williams. MoAmPo; RaBo; SAmP; TAP

Smell of autumn / Heart longs. Basho. ZenPo, tr. by Takashi Ikemoto and Lucien Stryk

Smell of Coal Smoke, The. Les A. Murray. NOBAu

Smell of death was in the air, The. Farewell. John Press. PoRA

Smell of gasoline. (LL) Moose, The. Elizabeth Bishop. DiPo; FaBoWP; NAAL-2v2; NAAL-5; NALW

Smell of piss guides us down the halls. Hospital State, The. Betsy Sholl. PBCAP

Smell of potatoes just taken out of the earth, The. Chilean Elegies: 5, The. The Interior. Tom Wayman. NOBC

Smell of snow, stinging in nostrils as the wind lifts it from a beach, The. Crystal Lithium, The. James Schuyler. PmAP; PoM; VCAP

Smell of the heat is boxwood, The. To Daphne and Virginia. William Carlos Williams. APT-1

Smell sweet and blossom in their dust. (LL) James Shirley. BASC; BeJo; FaBoWar; GTBS-P; HAP; NOBE; NPeEn; OBEV; OxBEV; PBRV; PeECV; PoRA; SCGP; UnPo; WoPoe *Fr.* Contention of Ajax and Ulysses, The.

Smells. Yelena [*or* Elena] Sergeievna, Countess de Carli Shchapova. TCRP, tr. by Bradley Jordan

Smells distinctly of the cold. (LL) Eggplants Have Pins and Needles, The. Novella Nikolaevna Matveyeva [*or* Matveieva]. TCRusP; WPOW, tr. by Daniel Weissbort

Smilax in our homes entwine, The. Christmas Eve. Lizelia Augusta Jenkins Moorer. CBWP-3

Smile, A. Tzu Yeh. CrYelRi; ErotSp, tr. by Sam Hamill

Smile, A. *Unknown.* PoToHe

Smile, The. William Blake. RB

Smile, The. Luciana Frezza. CItWP, tr. by Cinzia Sartini Blum and Lara Trubowitz

Smile at us, pay us, pass us; but do not quite forget. Secret People, The. Gilbert Keith Chesterton. OxBTC

Smile costs nothing but gives much—, A. Smile, A. *Unknown.* PoToHe

Smile, Death. Charlotte Mew. WPE; WPOW

Smile fell in the grass, A. Night Dances, The. Sylvia Plath. AmFaPo; LCAP-2

Smile for Daddy. Elizabeth Bartlett. Prnts

Smile his lips, A. Richard Wagner (1813–83). EroLit, tr. by Alfred Forman *Fr.* Tristan and Isolde.

Smile of the Goat has a meaning that few, The. Smile of the Goat, The. Oliver Herford. OBCoV; PeLV

Smile of the Walrus is wild and distraught, The. Smile of the Walrus, The. Oliver Herford. OBCoV

Smile on the famed Mona Lisa, The. Limerick. Stanley J. Sharpless. PeLi

Smile, smile / Blest isle! Lilliputian Ode on Their Majesties' Accession, A. Henry Carey. FaBoVe; NOEC; NPeEn; OBCoV

Smile, Smile, Smile. Wilfred Owen. PeFWW

Smile / to see the lake. Lorine Niedecker. VGW

Smiled at me and said, Yeah honey I guess I sure am. (LL) Waiting on Elvis, 1956. Joyce Carol Oates. AllShUp; SwNoth

Smiling and haunted, to a dark morning. (LL) To the Snake. Denise Levertov. NAAL-5; PAI

Smiling becomes. Smile, The. Luciana Frezza. CItWP, tr. by Cinzia Sartini Blum and Lara Trubowitz

Smiling Dawn, with diadem of dew, The. Poet's Ministrants, The. Henrietta Cordelia Ray. CBWP-3

Smiling girls, rosy boys. Mother Goose. OxNR

Smiling mouth and laughing eyen gray, The. Smiling Mouth, The. Charles D'Orleans. HAP; MiEL; NoP-4

Smiling mouth and laughing eyn grey, The. Smiling Mouth and Laughing Eyen Grey, The. Charles, Duc d' Orléans. HAP; MiEL

Smiling, sweet girl, this proffered toy approve. To a Lady, with a Present of a Fan. Charles Brandling. NOEC

Smiling Through. Reed Whittemore. BodElec

Smiling, we set the testing tray before the hall. Wen Cheng-ming. CoBLCP *Fr.* My Son's One-Year Test: Improvised.

Smith makes me, A. Rudyard Kipling. NoAM *Fr.* Puck of Pook's Hill.

Smith of Maudlin. George Walter Thornbury. PeVV

Smithereens. Dante Gabriel Rossetti. NOBVV

Smithfield Ham. Dave Jeddie Smith. HCAP

Smiths, The. E. G. Murphy. NOBAu

Smitten Purist, The. James Whitcomb Riley. VerBaPo

Smitten with sorrow, overcast with gloom. Roaming the East Field. Hsieh T'iao. ChinPo, tr. by Yip Wai-lim

Smoke. Rubén Bonitaz Nuño. STV, tr. by John Frederick Nims

Smoke. Philip Levine. MakPoe

Smoke. Susan Mitchell. EmeKit

Smoke. Henry David Thoreau. *See* Walden

Smoke. Smoke Rose. Itamar Ya'oz-kest. HP, tr. by Glenda Abramson

Smoke and nothing the breath of being. Living and Dying. Manuel González Prada. SpanPo, tr. by Kate Flores

Smoke and Steel. Carl Sandburg.
    "Bar of steel—it is only, A." AiP
    "Smoke of the fields in spring is one." MoAmPo

Smoke Animals. Rowena Bastin Bennett. CA

Smoke-Blackened Smiths. *Unknown.* OBCoV
    (Blacksmiths, The.) CABP

Smoke contending with smoke which will be maddest. Portrait of an Engine Driver. Bobi Jones. OBWVE, tr. by Joseph P. Clancy

Smoke from a neighbor's chimney loneliness. Marlene Mountain. HA

Smoke from the train-gulf hid by hoardings blunders upward. Birmingham. Louis MacNeice. MoBrPo; OxAEP-2

Smoke Gets in Your Eyes. Otto Harbach. ReLy

Smoke of the fields in spring is one. Carl Sandburg. MoAmPo *Fr.* Smoke and Steel.

Smoke on, salt swamps. Do Not Have Pity. Aimé Césaire. NAWM-7v2, tr. by Gregson Davis

Smoke rises. Never before, The. Achaian Invasion of Sparta, The. *Unknown.* GrAn, tr. by Peter Jay

Smoke Rose. Itamar Ya'oz-kest. HP, tr. by Glenda Abramson

Smoke should dry me well before I slept, The. (LL) John Davies of Hereford. NPeEn; OBCoV; Son *Fr.* Scourge of Folly, The.

Smoke shrouds cold water, moonlight shrouds sand. Mooring at River Ch'in-Huai. Tu Mu. ChinPo, tr. by Yip Wai-lim

Smoke twisting over the scorched ground. This Curious Involvement, a Dominant Species. John Seed. Oth

Smoke when the sun fell and when it rose. Peter Levi. FaBoTw *Fr.* Life Is a Platform.

Smokehouse, The. Yusef Komunyakaa. NoP-4

Smokey's Getting Old. Jessica Tarahata Hagedorn. OpBo

Smokin' my pipe on the mountings, sniffin' the mornin'-cool. Screw-Guns. Rudyard Kipling. FaBoWar

Smoking. Elton Glaser. BAP-97

Smoking. Ronald Wallace. SwNoth

Smoking and shaving and drinking the dry beer. (LL) Way of Life, A. Howard Nemerov. NIL-7; NIP-4

Smoking in an Open Grave. David Bottoms. InPK-6

Smoking swamp before a cottage door, A. Irish Picture, An. J. Stanyan Bigg. NOBVV

Smoky as peat your lank hair on my pillow. Nest in a Wall, A. Richard Murphy. BiHa; CIP-2

Smoky mist weaves through cold mountain forests. To the Tune: Beautiful Barbarian. Li Po. CrYelRi, tr. by Sam Hamill

Smoky rain riddles the ocean plains, A. My Father Paints the Summer. Richard Wilbur. NOBA

Smoky summer evening, The. Window, The. Dino Campana. STV, tr. by John Frederick Nims

Smoky sunset. I dab my eyes, A. Required of You This Night. Peter Redgrove. PoE

Smoldering dry fern. And What of Me? Liz Sohappy Bahe. CDW

Smooth Divine, The. Timothy Dwight. SacPr *Fr.* Triumph of Infidelity, The.

Smooth Gnarled Crape Myrtle. Marianne Craig Moore. APT-1

Smooth simple path! whose undulating line.   To a Gravel Walk.   William Mason.   OBGa

Smooth smell of Manhattan taxis, The.   Dance of the Infidels.   Al Young.   ESEAA; NBV; SeSe

Smoothing the heads of the hungry children. (LL)   John Crowe Ransom.   MoAmPo; OxBA   Fr. Sixteen Poems in Eight Pairings.

Smoothness of onions infuriates him, The.   Onion.   Katha Pollitt.   RaBo

Smothered Fires.   Georgia Douglas Johnson.   BlSi

Smuggled human hair from Mexico.   David Wojahn.   PBCAP   Fr. Mystery Train: A Sequence.

Smugglers.   "Eduard Georgievich Bagritzky" [or Bagritsky].   TCRP, tr. by Vera Dunham

Smuggling you in. (LL)   White Porch, The.   Cathy Song.   NAAL-5; YaYoPo

Sn wfl k s.   Marlene Mountain.   HA

Snail.   Elisabeth Eybers.   PeSAV, tr. by Elisabeth Eybers

Snail, The.   Vincent Bourne.   NPeEn; OBVE, tr. by William Cowper

Snail, The.   Mother Goose.   LB; OxNR; ReMoGo

Snail—baring / Shoulders.   Lucien Stryk.   IllVoic   Fr. Issa: A Suite of Haiku.

Snail gets up.   Issa.   EH; NIL-7, tr. by Robert Hass

Snail moves like a, The.   Hedgehog.   Paul Muldoon.   BIrV; NoAM; PBCIP

Snail [or Snayl], The.   Richard Lovelace.   BeJo; CaPo; NPeEn   (Wise Emblem of our Politick World.)   PBRV

Snail Poem.   Peter Orlovsky.   BB

Snail pushes through a green, The.   Considering the Snail.   Thom Gunn.   NAEL-5v2; NAEL-6v2; OxBEV; TwCP

Snail River.   James Bertolino.   PoCoUp

Snail's Lesson, The.   Priscilla Jane Thompson.   CBWP-2

Snail, snail, put out your horns.   Unknown.   OxNR

Snails.   E. D. Blodgett.   NOBC

Snails.   Liagarang.   CBAP, tr. by Ronald M. Berndt

Snails have made a garden of green lace, The.   After Rain.   Patricia K. Page.   NOBC; PoE

Snaith Marsh; a Yorkshire Pastoral.   "Ophelia."   ECWP

Snake.   Dannie Abse.   NoAM

Snake.   D. H. Lawrence.   AmFaPo; CABP; ChAP; EBNV; FaBoMo; HarvBoo; HeIP-4; NAEL-6v2; NOBE; NoAM; NoP-4; OxBEV; PoRA; TFi; UV

Snake.   Dan Pagis.   WoPoe, tr. by Stephen Mitchell

Snake.   Paresh Chandra Raut.   OMIP, tr. by Jayanta Mahapatra

Snake.   Theodore Roethke.   NOBA

Snake, The.   Emily Dickinson.   BoWoP; ClHu; HAP; HeIP-4; NAAL-2v1; NAAL-3; NALW; NIP-4; NOBA; NoAM; NoP-4; OBCA; OxBA; PAI; PoE; RB; SAmP; SoSe-8; TAP; TFi; TRP; WeW-3; WoPoe   (Narrow Fellow in the Grass, A.)   BLT; ChAP; ColAP; PoPoPo

Snake, The.   Vance Palmer.   NOBAu

Snake, The.   Andrew Suknaski.   NOBC

Snake came to my water-trough, A.   D. H. Lawrence.   AmFaPo; CABP; ChAP; EBNV; FaBoMo; HarvBoo; HeIP-4; NAEL-6v2; NOBE; NoAM; NoP-4; OxBEV; PoRA; TFi; UV

Snake Eyes.   Imamu Amiri Baraka.   VGW

Snake on D. H. Lawrence, The.   N. J. Warburton.   UV

Snake snatched, The.   Horned Snake, The.   Louis Oliver.   HATNAP

Snake swam across the blue stream.   Four Divine Animals.   Shinkichi Takahashi.   ZenPo, tr. by Takashi Ikemoto and Lucien Stryk

Snake that Dances, The.   Charles Baudelaire.   EroLit

Snake Trying, The.   W. W. Eustace Ross.   MoCV; NOBC

Snakeroot.   J. L. Jacobs.   AmPoNex

Snakes.   A. K. Ramanujan.   NoP-4

Snakes.   Nikolai Alekseievich Zabolotsky [or Zabolotskii].   TCRusP, tr. by Denis Johnson and Kathy Lewis

Snakes of September, The.   Stanley Kunitz.   ColAP

Snap tempered tooth chips.   Sawmill.   Richard Kenney.   NoP-4

Snapping of the Bow, The.   James David Corrothers.   NAAAL

Snaps for Dinner, Snaps for Breakfast, and Snaps for Supper.   George Moses Horton.   OBAL

Snaps its twig-tethermounts.   Dove, A.   Ted Hughes.   OxBC

Snaps of Immigration.   Víctor Hernández Cruz.   TouFir

Snapshot.   Lajos Kassák.   IQMS, tr. by Edwin Morgan

Snapshot of a Crab-Picker among Barrels Spilling Over, Apparently at the End of Her Shift.   Dave Jeddie Smith.   NoAM

Snapshots.   Sharif Elmusa.   GraLe

Snapshots.   Mary Oliver.   PoCoUp

Snapshots.   John Updike.   NoP-4

Snapshots of a Daughter-in-Law.   Adrienne Rich.   FaBoWP; HCAP; NAAL-2v2; NALW; NIP-4; NoAM; NoP-4; VCAP

Snapshots of the Chameleon Woman.   Perla Schwartz.   TANSG, tr. by Celeste Kostopulos-Cooperman

Snare, The.   James Stephens.   SCGP

Snatch out of time the passionate transitory. (LL)   Hospital, The.   Patrick Kavanagh.   BIrV; CABP; CIP-2; EmeKit; ModIr; NPeEn

Sneaked about here.   By the Road.   Geoffrey Grigson.   OxBTC

Sneeze, A.   So Chong-Ju.   VCWP, tr. by David R. McCann

Sneeze on [a] Monday, [You] sneeze for danger.   Sneezing.   Unknown.   LB; NBLV; OTCP

Sneeze on [a] Saturday, see your true love tomorrow. (LL)   Sneezing.   Unknown.   LB; NBLV; OTCP

Sneezing.   Unknown.   LB; NBLV; OTCP

Sneezing.   Unknown.   ReMoGo

Sniff.   Lily Tuck.   Unle

Sniff for madness—you'll find ripped-up quartets.   Stout Brahms.   Bruce Berger.   GeoH

Sniff of the real, that's, The.   Autobiography.   Thom Gunn.   NoAM

Sniffed, dilating my nostrils.   Elvin's Blues.   Michael S. Harper.   BPo; LoL

Snoad Hill Poems, The.   Elaine Randell.
   "And if my light should."   Oth
   "Hedge breaks out in bud, The."   Oth
   "Its this familiar black line from the tops."   Oth
   "Jetty, The."   Oth
   "O house, o sloping field, o poplar trees whose tall arms salute."   Oth
   "Our hands crushed."   Oth
   "She had the stance of a snowdrop."   Oth
   "Temperament is related to physique."   Oth
   "Waiting."   Oth
   "Walking towards the village."   Oth

Snore in the foam: the night is vast and blind.   Tristan da Cunha.   Roy Campbell.   MoBrPo

Snoring Bedmate, The.   Unknown.   BIrV, tr. by John V. Kelleher

Snoring of the storm in Melleray last night, The.   Mount Melleray.   Sean O Riordain.   ModIr, tr. by Patrick Crotty

Snot goes down.   Pieces of Snot.   Unknown.   STP, tr. by Franz Boas

Snow.   Innokenty Fiodorovich Annensky.   TCRP, tr. by Daniel Weissbort and Lubov Yakovleva

Snow.   Margaret Avison.   NOBC

Snow.   Adelaide Crapsey.   APT-1

Snow.   John Davidson.   NPeEn; NePenScot

Snow.   William Virgil Davis.   YaYoPo

Snow.   Walter De la Mare.   OxAEP-2

Snow.   Regina DeCormier-Shekejian.   TWW

Snow.   George Dillon.   IllVoic

Snow.   Vladimir Nikolaevich Kornilov.   TCRP, tr. by Daniel Weissbort

Snow.   Philip Levine.   ColAP; UrbNat

Snow.   Dulce Maria Loynaz.   TANSG, tr. by Alan West

Snow.   Louis MacNeice.   CIP-2; FaBoMo; HarvBoo; ModIr; NOBE; NPeEn; NoAM; OPOU; OxAEP-2; OxBEV; OxBSP; OxBTC; PNI

Snow.   David Malouf.   CBAP

Snow.   Muso Soseki.   EaWin, tr. by W. S. Merwin

Snow.   William Robert Rodgers.   ModIr

Snow.   Edward Thomas.   FaBoTw; OPOU

Snow.   David Wevill.   MoCV

Snow.   Charles Wright.   ColAP; LCAP-2

Snow, The.   Emily Dickinson.   SoSe-8; WHSW

Snow, The.   June Jordan.   GLP

Snow and then rain. The roads are wet. A car.   Edgar Bowers.   VCAP   Fr. Autumn Shade.

Snow astonishing their hammered faces.   Prisoners of Saint Lawrence, The.   Martín Espada.   TouFir

Snow at dusk.   Betty Drevniok.   HA

Snow at Rohatsu Sesshin.   Muso Soseki.   EaWin, tr. by W. S. Merwin

Snow-Ball, The.   Soame Jenyns.   OBVE

Snow-Ball, The.   Thomas Stanley.   NPeEn

Snow bared the black lines of hedges in thorn.   Wishes.   Ger Killeen.   AmPoNex

Snow-Bound [or Snow-Bound; a Winter Idyl].   John Greenleaf Whittier.   APN-1; NAAL-3; NAAL-5; NOBA; OxBA; TAP; TFi
   Firelight.   OBCP
   "Sun that brief December day, The."   AiP; TCAPo

Snow by the window paper flowers gathering dust.   Matsuo Allard.   HA

Snow came down last night like moths, The.   First Snow in Alsace.   Richard Wilbur.   NoP-4; OBWP

Snow came early here, and hard.   Blizzard of Sixty-Six, The.   William Daniel Ehrhart.   CDa

Snow Climbers.   Steve Wiesinger.   PasH

Snow, clothing sky & mountain.   Apollonides.   GrAn

Snow Country Weavers.   James Welch.   CDW; HATNAP

Snow-covered and bleeding, he came home. Feeding Ground. Thomas McCarthy. CIP-2

Snow-covered dead, The. Dead, The. José María Eguren. TCLAP, *tr. by* Iver Lofving

Snow crept up overnight as we slept. Vanishing Point, The. Peter Davison. DiPo

Snow-Day. Judith Baumel. KGB

Snow Day. Billy Collins. BAP-01

Snow dissolv'd no more is seen, The. Horace. NAEL-5v1; NAEL-6v1; NAEL-7v1, *tr. by* Samuel Johnson *Fr.* Odes.

Snow falling. Eric Amann. HA

Snow falling. Snowfall. Artis Bernard. NTCP

Snow falling and night falling fast oh fast. Desert Places. Robert Frost. APT-1; HarvBoo; InPK-6; MoAmPo; NAAL-2v2; NAAL-5; NOBA; NoAM; OxBA; PoE; RB; SoSe-8; TAP; TRP; UnPo

Snow falling around the man in the naked woods, The. White Heart of God, The. Jack Gilbert. BodElec

Snow falling in the pine forest. Chŏng Ch'ŏl. WoPoe, *tr. by* Kevin O'Rourke *Fr.* Snow Falling in the Pine Forest: Two Poems.

Snow Falling in the Pine Forest: Two Poems. Chŏng Ch'ŏl.
   "Snow falling in the pine forest." WoPoe, *tr. by* Kevin O'Rourke
   "Why does that pine tree stand." WoPoe, *tr. by* Kevin O'Rourke

Snow falls and falls, The. Ōkura Ichijitsu. OHMPJ

Snow falls from trees. Alan Pizzarelli. HA

Snow falls on the cars in Doctors' Row and hoods the headlights. Doctors' Row. Conrad Potter Aiken. HAP

Snow falls so hard the neighbors' windows seem. Hangman. Philip Stephens. AmPoNex

Snow falls with, The. If You Listen. Rosemerry Wahtola Trommer. GeoH

Snow fell, and its power was multiplied, The. Russia 1812. Victor Hugo. FaBoWar; OBWP, *tr. by* Robert Lowell

Snow-Fiend, The. Anne Batten Cristall. RWP

Snow-filled Nest, The. Rose Terry Cooke. OBCA

Snow fills heaven and earth. On a Painting of a Knight-Errant. Cheng Hsieh. CoBLCP, *tr. by* Jonathan Chaves

Snow fills the fields like milk. Mother: Dorcas Good, The. Nicole Cooley. NeAmPo

Snow fills the leaves that haven't blown. Quiet Earth, The. Heid E. Erdrich. AmPoNex

Snow-Flakes. Henry Wadsworth Longfellow. APN-1; ITBLP; NCAP; NOBA; NoP-4; TAP; TCAPo; UnPo

Snow-Flakes, The. Priscilla Jane Thompson. CBWP-2

Snow Garden. Muso Soseki. EaWin, *tr. by* W. S. Merwin

Snow had begun in the gloaming, The. First Snowfall [*or* Snow-Fall], The. James Russell Lowell. AmFaPo; TAP

Snow had buried Stuyvesant, The. Inauguration Day: January 1953. Robert Lowell. OxBSo

Snow had fallen many nights and days, The. End of the World, The. Gordon Bottomley. MoBrPo

Snow, hail and smut the sky. Asclepiades. GrAn

Snow! Hail! Lower! Lightning! Thunder! Asclepiades. PGA

Snow has covered the next line of tracks. Looking at New-Fallen Snow from a Train. Robert Bly. GM

Snow has drifted. Quietness descends, The. Twilight. Vladislav Felitsianovich Khodasevich. TCRP, *tr. by* Michael Frayn

Snow has gone from Chung-nan; spring is almost come, The. Passing T'ien-mên Street in Ch'ang-an and Seeing a Distant View of Chung-nan Mountains. Po Chü-i. ChiP, *tr. by* Arthur Waley

Snow has left the cottage top, The. John Clare. NOBE *Fr.* Shepherd's [*or* Shepheards] Calendar, The.

Snow has melted now, The. January. Douglas Gibson. OBCP

Snow hurries. Love in the Weather's Bells. Jay Wright. ESEAA

Snow in Europe. David Gascoyne. NPeEn

Snow in October. Alice Moore Dunbar-Nelson. BlSi

Snow in the Suburbs. Thomas Hardy. MoBrPo; OBMV; OxBTC

Snow is a mind. Revival. Steve Crow. HATNAP

Snow is a strange white word. On Receiving News of the War. Isaac Rosenberg. HarvBoo; MoBrPo; OBWP; OxAEP-2; PeFWW; PeSAV; PoWW

Snow is falling, snow is falling. Snow Is Falling. Boris Leonidovich Pasternak. ChAP

Snow is knee-deep in the courtyard, The. Cucumber, The. Nazim Hikmet. VCWP

Snow is melting, The. Issa. EH, *tr. by* Robert Hass

Snow is sick, The. The pure. March Snow. Don McKay. NOBC

Snow is snowing, The. I've Got My Love to Keep Me Warm. Irving Berlin. ReLy

Snow is water. Snow. Dulce Maria Loynaz. TANSG, *tr. by* Alan West

Snow is weaving a soft, white, shroud, The. Dying Year, The. Clara Ann Thompson. CBWP-2

Snow is white on wood and wold, The. Kiss, The. Edith Nesbit. LW

Snow is witherin' off'n the' gress, T' Drained Cup, The. D. H. Lawrence. FaBoVe

Snow-laden bushes. O. Mabson Southard. HA

Snow-Leopard, The. Randall Jarrell. TwCP

Snow lies deep: nor sun nor melting shower, The. Winter at Tomi. Ovid. AWP, *tr. by* F. A. Wright

Snow Lies Sprinkled on the Beach, The. Robert Bridges. NoAM

Snow lies there—ro'rāni'!, The. *Unknown.* APN-2 *Fr.* Ghost-Dance Songs.

Snow Light, The. May Sarton. APT-2; NBLV

Snow Lip. Iain Sinclair. Oth *Fr.* Ebbing of Kraft, The.

Snow Maiden, The. Bella [*or* Izabella] Akhatovna Akhmadulina. TCRusP, *tr. by* Daniel Weissbort

Snow-Man, The. "Marian Douglas." OBCA

Snow Man, The. Wallace Stevens. APT-1; AmFaPo; ColAP; EnlH; HAP; HCAP; HarvBoo; HeIP-4; NAAL-2v2; NAAL-5; NoAM; NoP-4; PAI; PoE; PoPoPo; SoSe-8; TCAPo; TRP; WeW-3

Snow, not the rare snow of Jerusalem. Little Research in Snow, A. Gabriel Preil. FIT, *tr. by* Robert Friend

Snow of yesterday, The. Gozan. JDP, *tr. by* Yoel Hoffmann

Snow on a Mountain. Dom Moraes. NoP-4

Snow on Lotus Mountain. Liu Ch'ang-ch'ing. OHMPC, *tr. by* Kenneth Rexroth

Snow on my ladder's rungs, The. Winter Regrets. Bill Knott. BodElec

Snow on Saddle Mountain, The. Miyazawa Kenji. ColAP; NOBA; NoAM; PAI, *tr. by* Gary Snyder

Snow on Stone Gate. Crossing the Lang-yeh Mountain with a Friend. Wei Ying-wu. SuSp, *tr. by* Wu-Chi Liu

Snow on the pines. Shiyo. JDP, *tr. by* Yoel Hoffmann

Snow panels, ice pipes, house the afternoon. January of a Gnat, The. Carl Rakosi. APT-2; FTOS

Snow Party, The. Derek Mahon. CIP-2; HarvBoo; ModIr; NPeEn; OxBC; PBCIP; PNI

Snow Poem. Rodolfo Di Biasio. NeIt, *tr. by* Stephen Sartarelli

Snow Poem. Roger McGough. Spl

Snow powder, flowery. Kuan Han-ch'ing. SuSp *Fr.* Tune: "Song of Great Virtue"—Winter.

Snow, rocks darker than any shadow in the world. Undiscovered Country. James Longenbach. NAPBL

Snow's white pencil outlining the buildings. Vladimir Nikolaevich Sokolov. TCRP

Snow Signs. Charles Tomlinson. NoAM

Snow, snow faster. *Unknown.* OxNR

Snow Song. Henrietta Cordelia Ray. CBWP-3

Snow Songs. W. D. Snodgrass.
   "One. now another. one." InvLad

Snow Storm. Tu Fu. BLT; OHPC, *tr. by* Kenneth Rexroth

Snow Storm, The. Mary Weston Fordham. CBWP-2

Snow Storm, The. Edna St. Vincent Millay. NAAL-2v2

Snow-Storm [*or* Snowstorm], The. Ralph Waldo Emerson. APN-1; ITBLP; NAAL-2v1; NAAL-3; NCAP; NOBA; NoP-4; OxBA; PoE; PoPoPo; TAP; TCAPo; TFi; TreFP; UnPo

Snow sweeps through February. Poem in Three Parts. S. J. Marks. BodElec

Snow Valley. Muso Soseki. EaWin, *tr. by* W. S. Merwin

Snow whispers about me, The. Falling Snow. Amy Lowell. ColAP

Snow White and the Seven Deadly Sins. R. S. Gwynn. SoSe-8

Snow White and the Seven Dwarfs. Anne Sexton. HCAP; PoPoPo

Snow-white terrier brushes the ground as it walks. Palace Poem. Wang Ya. SuSp, *tr. by* Irving Y. Lo

Snow White was nude at her wedding, she's so white. Lessons from a Mirror. Thylias Moss. ESEAA; LTA

Snow wind-whipt to ice. Winter. Richard Hughes. OBMV; OBWVE

Snowbanks North of the House. Robert Bly. AiP; BodElec; LCAP-2; RaBo

Snowbound City, The. John Haines. SPE

Snowdon Sunrise, The. William Wordsworth. OxAEP-2 *Fr.* Prelude; Growth of a Poet's Mind, The [1805 vers.].

Snowdrop. Ted Hughes. FaBoMo; HarvBoo

Snowdrop, The. Mary Weston Fordham. CBWP-2

Snowdrop of dogs, with ear of brownest dye. Sonnet: To Tartar, a Terrier Beauty. Thomas Lovell Beddoes. NOBVV; OxBSo

Snowdrops. Margiad Evans. OBWVE

Snowdrops. George MacBeth [*or* Macbeth]. OBCP

Snowed. Some of Betty's Story Round 1850. Gale Jackson. SpirFl

Snowed-in cross within the woods, A. Woodland Cross, The. Endre Ady. IQMS, *tr. by* Anton N. Nyerges

Snowfall. Bella [*or* Izabella] Akhatovna Akhmadulina. TCRP, *tr. by* Albert C. Todd

Snowfall. Artis Bernard. NTCP

Snowfall. Giosuè Carducci. AWP, *tr. by* Romilda Rendel

Snowfall. W. S. Merwin. NNaP

Snowfall, The. Donald Justice. CRP; VGW

Snowfall, The. Gwerfyl Mechain. OBWVE, *tr. by* Kenneth Hurlstone Jackson

Snowfall; a Poem about Spring. James Wright (1927–80). NoAM

Snowfall in the Afternoon. Robert Bly. NOBA; SPE

Snowfall on a College Garden. Cecil Day Lewis. OBGa

Snowflake. First Snowflake. N. M. Bodecker. TLR

Snowflake Which Is Now and Hence Forever, The. Archibald MacLeish. NoP-4

Snowflakes. Penny Harter. HA

Snowflakes. Howard Nemerov. HCAP

Snowflakes. Clive Sansom. OBCP

Snowflakes were teeming down. Jerzy Ficowski. HP, *tr. by* Keith Bosley *Fr.* Assumption of Miriam from the Street in the Winter of 1942, The.

Snowman, The. Roger McGough. OTCP

Snowman, The. Patricia K. Page. NOBC

Snowman, The. *Unknown.* OTCP

Snowman in a field. Roger McGough. Spl

Snowman in the yard is frozen hard, The. Let It Snow! Let It Snow! Let It Snow! Jule Styne. ReLy

Snowman's eyes, The. Mabutsu (d. 1696). JDP, *tr. by* Yoel Hoffmann

Snowman Sniffles. N. M. Bodecker. TLR

Snowmelt pond warm granite. Bedrock. Gary Snyder. PoE

Snowpoems. Dan Guillory.
      "Retinal burn of warm November light." IllVoic

Snows are fled away, leaves on the shaws, The. Diffugere Nives. A. E. Housman. AmFaPo

Snows are thaw'd, now grass new cloaths the earth. Horace. NPeEn, *tr. by* Sir Richard Fanshawe *Fr.* Odes.

Snows dissolving, grass returns to meadow. Horace. WoPoe, *tr. by* Michael O'Brien *Fr.* Odes.

Snows of February had buried Christmas, The. Christmas Robin, The. Robert Graves. ChrPo

Snows that glittered on the disk of Mars, The. Oliver Wendell Holmes. APN-1 *Fr.* Wind-Clouds and Star-Drifts.

Snowstorm: At a Gathering at Chang Chu-fu's House, with Tzu-yeh Attending, We All Wrote Poems on This Subject—I Got the Rhyme-Word, "Hu." Tsung Ch'en. CoBLCP, *tr. by* Jonathan Chaves

Snowstorm made the earth tremble, A. Winter Night. Boris Leonidovich Pasternak. WoPoe, *tr. by* Edwin Morgan

Snowstorm shook its cloak—, The. Ballad about the Circus. Aleksandr Petrovich Mezhirov. TCRP, *tr. by* Deming Brown

Snowy Benches. Aileen Fisher. KaS

Snowy coats and snowy crests and beaks of blue jade. Egrets. Tu Mu. WoPoe, *tr. by* A. C. Graham

Snowy curtain / slides up the sky, A. Noon Office. James Schuyler. BodElec

Snowy Day, A. *Unknown.* OBWVE, *tr. by* H. Idris Bell

Snowy Egret. Bruce Weigl. UrbNat

Snowy morning, A. Basho. EH, *tr. by* Robert Hass

Snowy Mountains. Tsung Ch'en. CoBLCP, *tr. by* Jonathan Chaves

Snowy Owl. Matthew J. Spireng. PoCoUp

Snowy Owl near Ocean Shores. Duane Niatum. HATNAP

Snowy River. Liu Tsung-yüan. CrYelRi, *tr. by* Sam Hamill

Snowy Sky. Shinkichi Takahashi. ZenPo, *tr. by* Takashi Ikemoto and Lucien Stryk

Snub-nosed, bone-fingered, deft with engraving tools. Death the Painter. Anthony Hecht. NoP-4

Snug—the robe sewn from coarse cotton. Lu Yu. CoBCP *Fr.* Farm Families.

So. Citadel. Edward Kamau Brathwaite. VCWP

So Abram rose, and clave the wood, and went. Parable of the Old Men and the Young, The. Wilfred Owen. ChIV-1; HarvBoo; PAI

So all day long the noise of battle rolled. Tennyson. EBNV; NIP-4; NOBVV; OBNV; OxAEP-2 *Fr.* Morte d'Arthur.

So all through Troy the men who had fled like panicked fawns. Homer. NAWM-7v1, *tr. by* Robert Fagles *Fr.* Iliad, The.

So all waited for manna. Manna. Jared Angira. PBMAP

So all within be livelier than before. (LL) Forerunners, The. George Herbert. AngWePo; ESCV; GeHe; NAEL-5v1; NAEL-6v1; NAEL-7v1; NoP-4; TOF

So am I as the rich, whose blessed key. William Shakespeare. OxAEP-1 *Fr.* Sonnets.

So an age ended, and its last deliverer died. W. H. Auden. PoE *Fr.* Sonnets from China.

So-and-So Reclining on Her Couch. Wallace Stevens. NOBA

So angels love and all the rest is dross. Platonic Love. Elizabeth Singer Rowe. BASC

So apparent, wanting so much that it bothers me. (LL) Rondeau at the Train Stop. Erin Belieu. GifTon; NeAmPo

So bandit-eyed, so undovelike a bird. Blue Jay [*or* Bluejay]. Robert Francis. LCAP-2

So Bartas-like thy fine spun poems been. Anagram, An. *Unknown.* TCAPo

So Be It. Ruth Stone. ExTi

So be it. I am. Hayden Carruth. VGW

So be merry, so be dead. (LL) All the Hills and Vales Along. Charles Hamilton Sorley. EBEV; FaBoCh; MoBrPo; OBWP; OxAEP-2; PeFWW; PoWW

So Beautiful. Indran Amirthanayagam. OpBo

So beautiful—God himself quailed. Woman, The. Ronald Stuart Thomas. OxBC

So Beautiful Is the Tree of Night. Pauline Hanson. TAP

So beautiful that couple. So Beautiful. Indran Amirthanayagam. OpBo

So beautiful the lungs. From "Songs of a Wanderer." Aleksander Wat. BLT

So, because you chose to follow me into the subtle sadness of night. Giving Back the Flower. Sarah Morgan Bryan Piatt. APN-2

So, behind the heavy backyard orchard. We Wondered about the Mellow Peaches. Jack A. Mapanje. HBAPE

So big in life, head like a chopping block. Kookaburra. Frieda Hughes. NeBl

So blest are they who round a family board. Family, The. Donna R. Lydston. PoToHe

So, bored with dragons, he lay down to sleep. Beowulf. Kingsley Amis. OxBC

So Bring the Order for My Execution. Faiz Ahmad Faiz. VCWP, *tr. by* Agha Shahid Ali

"So careful of the type?" but no. Tennyson. EBVV; FHYEP; HAP; NAEL-6v2; NAWM-7v2; NPeEn; TOF *Fr.* In Memoriam A. H. H.

So, circling about my head, a fly. For Mao Tse-tung; a Meditation on Flies and Kings. Irving Layton. NOBC

So cold and lost for ever evermore. (LL) Dead before Death. Christina Georgina Rossetti. NAEL-5v2; NAEL-6v2; NALW

So cold? (LL) Warning, The. Adelaide Crapsey. APT-1; Spl; TCAPo; WPE

So confortand his levis unto me bene. (LL) To a Lady[e]. William Dunbar. EBEV; OBEV; OxBS; PeLV

So covetous Ballaam with fond intent. Abraham Cowley. ChIV-1 *Fr.* Davideis.

So coy, pretending shyness. (LL) Li Po. CrYelRi; ErotSp, *tr. by* Sam Hamill *Fr.* Women of Yueh.

So cruel [*or* cruell *or* crewell] prison how could betide [*or* howe coulde betyde], alas. Prison in Windsor Castle. Henry Howard, Earl of Surrey. NoSic; SCGP

So Cruel Prison. Henry Howard, Earl of Surrey. *See* Prison in Windsor Castle

So cruel prison how could betide, alas. Henry Howard, Earl of Surrey. NAEL-5v1; NAEL-6v1; NAEL-7v1 *Fr.* Windsor Castle.

So Da-da-da-daddy might spank. (LL) My Heart Belongs to Daddy. Cole Porter. OBAL; ReLy

So, Dear, your mother says you got a divorce. Family Reunion—Aunt Vern's Two Cents. Beth Gylys. AmPoNex

So died John So. On John So. *Unknown.* FaBoEE

So does the sun withdraw his beam[e]s. On His Mistress Going from Home [Song]. *Unknown.* NOSC

So, driven to new shoes incessantly. Lake, The. Alphonse Marie Louis de Lamartine. SxFrPo, *tr. by* E. H. Blackmore and A. M. Blackmore

So drunk, I enfold the seas of forgetfulness. So Drunk Am I with the Night, the Air, and the Trees. Mona Saudi. PoArWo, *tr. by* Kamal Boullata

So earth's inclined toward the one invisible. Winter Scene. Marguerite Young. WPE

So elegant, so simple, yet thought. Insulin Receptor. H. J. Van Peenen. BloBone

So ended Saturn; and the God of the Sea. John Keats. FHYEP *Fr.* Hyperion.

So even *he* was not so lazy as I. (LL) Lazy Man's Song. Po Chü-i. ChiP; OBVE, *tr. by* Arthur Waley

So fair thy vision that the night. Milton. John Banister Tabb. APN-2

So faire, so fressh, so goodly on-to see. *Unknown.* OHMEL

So fairely mounted in fertile Soile. On the Situation of Highbury. Katherine Austen. EMWP

So fallen! so lost! the light withdrawn. Ichabod[!]. John Greenleaf Whittier. APN-1; NAAL-2v1; NAAL-3; NAAL-5; NOBA; OxBA; TAP; TCAPo

So far doth my heart utter, and then sighs. (LL) Dante Alighieri. AWP; EaItPo, *tr. by* Dante Gabriel Rossetti *Fr.* La Vita Nuova.

So far, have managed, Not. Small Number, A. Olena Kalytiak Davis. NAPBL

So. Farewell Krishna. In Memoriam Krishna Menon. E. J. Thribb. OBCoV

So. Farewell / Then / Larry Parnes. In Memoriam Larry Parnes ("Mr Parnes Shillings and Pence"). E. J. Thribb. OBCoV

So fine, the boards of magnolia. Wrecked Boat on the River Shore. Chiang Lu. CoBCP, *tr.* by Burton Watson

So first there's the chemo: three sticks, once a week. Needles. Lucia Maria Perillo. IllVoic

So, forgetful Mahadeva. Kamalākānta Bhattācārya. SinGod, *tr.* by Rachel Fell McDermott

So forlorn am I. Lady Izumi. WoPoe, *tr.* by Steven D. Carter

So forth she comes, and to her coche does clyme. Edmund Spenser. NAEL-5v1 *Fr.* Faerie Queene, The.

So Foul Is Sin and Loathsome in Thy Sight. Anne Vaughan Locke. CABP

So friendly, and so rich. (LL) On the Circuit. W. H. Auden. NOBL; OxBTC

So frisky and fit. Simchas Torah. Morris Jacob Rosenfeld. TrJP

So from the bosom of darkness our days come roaring and gleaming. Fragment: August 4, 1856. Henry Wadsworth Longfellow. TCAPo

So from the ground we felt that virtue branch. Transfiguration, The. Edwin Muir. ChIV-2; OxBS

So full of courtly reverence. Air. Dudley North, 3d Baron North. OxBSP

So furze tell me what you mean and don't make such a rhubarb. (LL) Poem of Medicine Puns. *Unknown.* ColAnChi; WoPoe, *tr.* by Victor H. Mair

So gentle and so beautiful, should perish with the flowers. (LL) Death of the Flowers, The. William Cullen Bryant. OBCA; TreFP

So Get Over It, Honey. Belle Waring. ExTi

So get up speed. So you're sick with fear again so what so what. Denise Riley. Oth *Fr.* Seven Strangely Exciting Lies.

So glad that your especial sperm. Birthday, A. Anne Rouse. MFPA

So God spoke to her. Ann Griffith. Ronald Stuart Thomas. PeECV

So good luck came, and on my roof[e] did light. Coming of Good Luck, The. Robert Herrick. FaBoEE; NPeEn; OxBEV; OxBSP; Spl

So, good night, with lullaby. (LL) William Shakespeare. NOBE; NoSic; PoRA; SCGP *Fr.* Midsummer Night's Dream, A.

So goodbye, Mrs. Brown. To-Day I Leave Mrs. Brown's Lodgings. Sir Walter Scott. FaBoEE

So goodly wonne with her owne will beguyld. (LL) Edmund Spenser. HeIP-4; NAEL-5v1; PoE; Son *Fr.* Amoretti.

So Graven. Josephine Miles. NoAM

So greatly thy great pleasaunce pleasured me. Dante da Maiano. EaItPo, *tr.* by Dante Gabriel Rossetti

So Han-shan writes you these words. *Unknown.* CoBCP

So hand in glove. (LL) Line Drive Caught by the Grace of God. Linda Gregerson. ExTi; MoASP

So hard for women to believe each other. Apron Strings. Marge Piercy. TAP

So hard to say I love you madly. Love Song for Difficult Times. Maria Elena Cruz Varela. VCWP, *tr.* by Mairym Cruz-Bernal

So hath been dawning another blue day. Today. Thomas Carlyle. PWR

So have I heard and do in part believe it. (LL) William Shakespeare. PeECV; TOF *Fr.* Hamlet.

So have I seen a little silly fly. Quarrel with Fortune, A. Benjamin Colman. SCAP

So having ended, silence long ensewed. Edmund Spenser. MakPoe; NOBE *Fr.* Faerie Queene, The.

So he came to write again. Burning Hills. Michael Ondaatje. NOBC; NoAM

So he'd be sure to see me, we came in late. Versification of a Passage from Penthouse. Andrew Hudgins. AllShUp

So he that saileth in this world of pleasure. Anne Bradstreet. WPOW *Fr.* Contemplations.

So he was exiled from rome. Ovid Twice Exiled. Jerzy Ficowski. PoSu, *tr.* by Frank J. Corliss, Jr. and Grazyna Sandel

So Hector Protector was sent back again. (LL) Mother Goose. OxNR; ReMoGo

So. / Hello then / Dali. In Memoriam Salvador Dali. E. J. Thribb. OBCoV

So her close beauties further blaze her fame. George Chapman. OxBSo; Son *Fr.* Coronet for His Mistress Philosophy, A.

So here comes this mf (excuse me). Whole Truth So Help Me God—Also Known as the Gettin' Rid of Nigguz Business. Lorena M. Craighead. InTrad

So here I am again thinking of you—. Mother Tongue. Rebecca Seiferle. ExTi

So, here, tied in that crooked line. Chart Showing Rain, Winds, Isothermal Lines and Ocean Currents. Louise Owen. YaYoPo

So him at first *De Nance* commanded was to kill. Anne Dowriche. PBRV *Fr.* French Historie, The.

So how is life with your new bloke? Attempt at Jealousy, An. Craig Raine. NoAM

So, how was I to know, when he invited. Helen. James [*or* Jim] Harrison. NBLV

So Hrothgar's men lived happy in his hall. *Unknown.* PoE *Fr.* Beowulf.

So humble things thou hast borne for us, O God. Veni Creator. Alice Thompson Meynell. WPE

So I came. (LL) Mary's Dream. Van K. Brock. AllShUp; SwNoth

So I came down the steps to Lenin. Dorothy Wellesley, Duchess of Wellington. OBMV *Fr.* Lenin.

So I can join you to bob on the waves? (LL) Poem without a Category. Liu Cheng. CoBCP; ColAnChi, *tr.* by Burton Watson

So I did sit and eat. (LL) Love (3). George Herbert. AWP; BASC; BBASP; CABP; ChIV-2; ClHu; EBEV; ESCV; EnlH; FHYEP; FSCP; FaBoVe; GeHe; HeIP-4; InPK-6; InvLi; MeLP; NAEL-5v1; NAEL-6v1; NAEL-7v1; NOBE; NOCV; NOSC; NPeEn; NoP-4; OBEV; OBWVE; OxAEP-1; OxBEV; PBRV; PoPoPo; SCV; TFi; TOF; TrCP; WeW-3

"So I don't have to think / any / more" (LL) How to Meditate. Jack Kerouac. BB; PoM

So I dream nightly of an embarkation. Allen Ginsberg. CLPP *Fr.* Siesta in Xbalba.

So I experienced. Robert Grenier. FTOS *Fr.* Phantom Anthems.

So I fled into the thing for him. Walter Lowenfels. APT-2 *Fr.* Elegy in the Manner of a Requiem in Memory of D.H. Lawrence.

So, I have seen a man killed! Arthur Hugh Clough. EBVV; NPeEn; PeVV *Fr.* Amours de Voyage.

So I'le not feare the Judge, or thee. (LL) To His Conscience. Robert Herrick. BeJo; ChIV-1; NAEL-5v1

So I'll keep repeating in my mind. (LL) Look for the Silver Lining. B. G. DeSylva. ReLy; TCAPo

So I Lost My Temper. Rose Romano. UnSA

So I'm an alcoholic Catholic mother-lover. Jack Would Speak Through the Imperfect Medium of Alice. Alice Notley. PmAP

So I may say. Epitaph. "H. D." APT-1

So, I Remained Alone. Anna Andreyevna Akhmatova. TCRusP, *tr.* by Daniel Weissbort

So I Said I Am Ezra. A. R. Ammons. ColAP; NAAL-2v2; NAAL-5; NOBA; NoAM; PAI

So I shall never hear from his own lips. Donald Evans. Witter Bynner. APT-1

So I took her to the riverside. Unfaithful Wife, The. Federico García Lorca. EroLit, *tr.* by Alan Bold

So I wait—bereft of 2,000 years and the bath of life. (LL) Marriage. Gregory Corso. CoAP; NeAP; NoP-4; OBAL; PeLV; PmAP; TAP; TRP

So I walk a little too fast. End of a Love Affair, The. Edward C. Redding. ReLy

So I walked her down to the river. Unfaithful Wife, The. Federico García Lorca. STV, *tr.* by John Frederick Nims

So I was past caring so many, too many men. Paragraph 36. Hayden Carruth. BodElec

So I went wrong. Revival. Arthur Hugh Clough. SacPr

So I wish you a gude morning. (LL) Johnnie Cope. Adam Skirving. NePenScot; OxBS

So I would hear out those lungs. Buckdancer's Choice. James Dickey. HeIP-4; NOBA; NoAM; NoP-4

So I would rather drown, remembering. "H. D." APT-1 *Fr.* Flowering of the Rod, The.

So if all do their duty, they need not fear harm. (LL) William Blake. FHYEP; HeIP-4; InPK-6; NAEL-5v2; NAEL-6v2; NAWM-7v2; NOEC; OxAEP-2; PAI; PoE; SCGP; SoSe-8; TFi *Fr.* Songs of Innocence.

So in hers am I buried this night. (LL) Barnabe Barnes. NPeEn; NoSic *Fr.* Parthenophil and Parthenophe.

So in Love. Cole Porter. ReLy

So, in the nocturnal stream. Daedalus. Leonid Nikolaevich Martynov. TCRP, *tr.* by J. R. Rowland

So inferred. From the Novissimi. Giulia Niccolai. PFTM-2, *tr.* by Paul Vangelisti

So Inferred. Giulia Niccolai. CItWP, *tr.* by Cinzia Sartini Blum and Lara Trubowitz

So is coal, but alight it shines like roses. (LL) Asclepiades. GrAn; PGA, *tr.* by Kenneth Rexroth

So is it not with me as with that Muse. William Shakespeare. HeIP-4 *Fr.* Sonnets.

So it always was, so shall ever be! (LL) Robert Browning. FHYEP; SCGP

So it begins. Adam is in his earth. James Agee. APT-2 *Fr.* Sonnets.

So it came in a dream I was bound. Being. Adriann Roland Holst. TuT, *tr.* by Paula Meehan

So it came time. Mansion. A. R. Ammons. AmFaPo

So it had to be—. Akhmatova. Deborah Digges. ExTi

So it is. Coleman Barks. CRP *Fr.* New Words.

So it is because. *Unknown.* ArkPo, *tr.* by Edwin A. Cranston

So it is, my dear. Even So. Dante Gabriel Rossetti. NOBE; NOBVV

So it is whispered here and there. Lesson in a Picture, A. Sarah Morgan Bryan Piatt. NCAP

So it's hullo now. Rufinus. GrAn

So, it's like this. Reading the I Ching. Raquel Chalfi. DTA, *tr.* by Karen Alkalay-Gut

So it's one of those bars, see. Plastic Cup, The. Kim Roberts. AmPoNex

So it takes very little indeed: a brasserie. Edoardo Sanguineti. ItPo, *tr. by* Gayle Ridinger *Fr.* Reisebilder.

So it tries to reach her inside her mind. Silvana Colonna. ItPo, *tr. by* Gayle Ridinger

So Jah Sey. Kendel Hippolyte. WaCA

So jealous of your beauty. "Michael Field." VWP

So late in my life, some things I have remembered. Childhood. Syl Cheney-Coker. NAfrP

So late, so late, so haunting. On the Threshold. Karl Kraus. TrJP, *tr. by* Albert Bloch

So learned men in controversies spend. George Chapman. NOSC *Fr.* Euthymiae Raptus; or, The Teares of Peace.

So let all thine enemies perish, O Lord: but let them that love him be as the sun when he goeth forth in his might. And the land had rest forty years. (LL) Bible, *O.T.* AWP; BoWoP *Fr.* Judges.

So let's live—really live!—for love and loving. Catullus. *See* Lesbia / live with me

So Let's Look at It Another Way. John Godfrey. PmAP

So light no one noticed. Song, The. Edward Dorn. VGW

So like a harrow pin. Iron Spike. Seamus Heaney. BodElec; TRP

So Little and So Much. John Oxenham. SacPr

So little Master Wagtail I'll bid you a 'Good-bye.' (LL) Little Trotty Wagtail. John Clare. NOxBChV; RB; SCGP; UnPo

So little there is of Life: of Letters, page on page! Rhapsody: Keeping Faith. István Vas. IQMS, *tr. by* George Szirtes

So live, so love, so use that fragile hour. Robert Louis Stevenson. NOBVV

So live, that when thy summons comes to join. William Cullen Bryant. PoToHe; TreFP *Fr.* Thanatopsis.

So lonely am I. Ono no Komachi. BoWoP

So Long. Jayne Cortez. BoWoP; LW

So long. James Dickey. AiP *Fr.* For the First Manned Moon Orbit.

So Long. Langston Hughes. APSN; APT-2

So Long Ago. Morris Jacob Rosenfeld. TrJP, *tr. by* Elbert Aidline

So long as days shall be. (LL) Bible, *O.T.* OBCA; TCAPo *Fr.* Bay Psalm Book, The.

So long as I loved shadows, the shadows of vain gods. Christian Rome. Hildebert. MLL, *tr. by* Helen Waddell

So long as this breath fills your nostrils. Mahadevi. WPoS

So long as you live and move. Teach Us to Mark This, God. Franz Werfel. TrJP, *tr. by* Jacob Sloan

So long gone from life itself, so many things have changed. (LL) Immigrants in Our Own Land. Jimmy Santiago Baca. AF; UnSA

So long had life together been that now. Six Years Later. Joseph Brodsky. TCRP; VCWP, *tr. by* Richard Wilbur

So long lives this, and this gives life to thee. (LL) William Shakespeare. AEP; AmFaPo; BoLoP; CABP; CTC; ClHu; EnLoPo; HAP; HeIP-4; ITBLP; InPK-6; MakPoe; NAEL-6v1; NAEL-7v1; NIL-7; NOBE; NPeEn; NoSic; OBEV; OxBEV; OxBSo; PoE; PoPoPo; PoRA; SCGP; SCV; Son; TFi; WeW-3 *Fr.* Sonnets.

So Long, Mary. George M. Cohan. ReLy

So long, sad times! Happy Days Are Here Again. Jack Yellen. ReLy

So long to love / so long. (LL) So Long. Jayne Cortez. BoWoP; LW

So long you wandered on the dusky plain. To His Friend in Elysium. Joachim Du Bellay. AWP, *tr. by* Andrew Lang

So Long? Stevens. John Berryman. HAP; HCAP; NOBA *Fr.* Dream Songs.

So looks Anthea, when in bed she lyes. To Anthea Lying in Bed. Robert Herrick. BeJo

So lost a thing as thou hadst been. (LL) Upon My Lady Carlisle's Walking in Hampton Court Garden. Sir John Suckling. BeJo; CaPo

So Love and Folly were in hell. (LL) Barley-Break, A. Sir John Suckling. BASC; CaPo; CavPo

So luminous around them lay the air. Oystercatchers. Christopher Middleton. FaBoTw

So. Magnus / Magnusson. Lines on the Award "Pipe Man of the Year" to Magnus Magnusson. E. J. Thribb. OBCoV

So many boulders have been cast at me. Solitude. Anna Andreyevna Akhmatova. ARWW, *tr. by* Catriona Kelly

So many cloisters closed. John Skelton. PeECV *Fr.* Manner of the World Nowadays, The.

So many convolutions and not enough simplicity! To Marina. Kenneth Koch. NoAM

So many days spent tracking the desert. Argument, The. Christiane Jacox Kyle. YaYoPo

So many delights the excitement has no end. Sitting Up with My Wife on New Year's Eve. Hsü Chün-ch'ien. CoBCP, *tr. by* Burton Watson

So Many Feathers. Jayne Cortez. BlSi; ISC

So many flea bites. Issa. SoOfWa, *tr. by* Sam Hamill

So many kinds of sadness. Sotto Voce. M. Vasalis. TuT, *tr. by* Peter Van de Kamp

So many kisses. Kisses that have pulled me. Kisses. Giancarlo Majorino. ItPo, *tr. by* Gayle Ridinger

So many new crimes since then! Since Then. Dennis Joseph Enright. OBSV

So many nights the solitary lamp had burned. Rousseau in His Day. Donald Davie. DiPo

So many people lie in this alley. Neighborhood House, The. Jay Wright. NBV

So many people, not to speak of the dog. (LL) Taxis, The. Louis MacNeice. EmeKit; NPeEn; OxBTC; PNI

So many pigeons at Columbus. Poem. Arthur Gregor. VGW

So Many Summers. Norman MacCaig. HarvBoo

So many thousands for a house! On a Certain Lord Giving Some Thousand Pounds for a House. David Garrick. FaBoEE

So many times I've seen hand-to-hand combat. Yuliya [*or* Iuliia] Vladimirovna Drunina. TCRP

So many times / I walked and walked. By Forty-Sixth. Fernando D'Almeida. NAfrP, *tr. by* Faustine Boateng Gyima

So many times since antiquity. Lamenting the Civil War. Muso Soseki. EaWin, *tr. by* W. S. Merwin

So many traces, fragile monuments. So many traces. Louise Herlin. MFP, *tr. by* Martin Sorrell

So many want to be lifted by song and dancing. Dark Thing Inside the Day, A. Linda Gregg. BLT

So many women are murdered because some man. Body Count. Leonard Nathan. PBCAP

So many years have passed. Charlotte Smith. ECWP *Fr.* Emigrants, The.

So many years I've seen the sun. Mystery of Life, The. John Gambold. NOEC

So Mary died last night! To-day. Twilight. Amy Levy. VWP

So may the auspicious Queen of Love. Horace. AWP, *tr. by* John Dryden *Fr.* Odes.

So may the relation of each man be clipped. (LL) Comedian as the Letter C, The. Wallace Stevens. OxBA; TCAPo

So mean I. (LL) Waiting Both. Thomas Hardy. MoBrPo; OxBoLi; TTTS

So merrily march the merchant men. (LL) Merchants of London, The. Mother Goose. OxNR; ReMoGo

So Mexicans Are Taking Jobs from Americans. Jimmy Santiago Baca. LTA; UnSA

So, midst the wither'd waste of life, those tears would flow to me. (LL) Stanzas for Music. Byron. HAP; NOBRP; NPeEn

So Might is Right, you say; I fight in vain. "Might Is Right." Israel Zangwill. TrJP

So, Mind / You've decided to go on pilgrimage? Rāmprasād Sen. SinGod, *tr. by* Rachel Fell McDermott

So mine be your eyes!. (LL) To Morfydd. Lionel Pigot Johnson. MoBrPo; OBMV

So Miss Myrtle is going to marry? Charming Woman, The. Helen Selina Blackwood, Countess of Dufferin. VWP

So Miss Myrtle is going to marry? Charming Woman, The. Helen Selina Sheridan. WPE

So, Mister Moneybags, you're loaded? So? Palladas [*or* Pallades]. GrAn

So Motown taught me all about men. Men worshipped. Patricia Smith. UnSA *Fr.* Sweet Daddy.

So mourn'd Pelides his late loss, so weighty were his moans. Homer. FaBoWar, *tr. by* George Chapman *Fr.* Iliad, The.

So much depends. Red Wheelbarrow, The. William Carlos Williams. APT-1; BLT; ChAP; ColAP; HarvBoo; HeIP-4; InPK-6; MoAmPo; NAAL-2v2; NAAL-5; NIL-7; NIP-4; NOBA; NoAM; NoP-4; PAI; PoE; SAmP; SoSe-8; TAP; TFi; TRP; TTTS; UnPo; WeW-3

So much for Julia. Now we'll turn to Juan. Byron. NPeEn *Fr.* Don Juan.

So much for the elves' wergild, the true governance. Geoffrey Hill. NoAM; WoPoe *Fr.* Mercian Hymns.

So much Summer. Emily Dickinson. SWaP

So much sweeter here than in other lands? (LL) Columbus Day. Jimmie Durham. HATNAP; LTA

So much time has gone by! Napoleon's house. Day We Visited New Orleans, The. Robert Bly. KGB

So much to tell you. 2 Variations: All About Love. Philip Whalen. NeAP

So—Murray to Byron in Italy. Kaleidoscope. G. K. Page. NoAM

So my mother begins. Nice Thing about Counting Stars, The. Dwight Okita. UnSA

So my pictures are in prison, instead of in the Zoo. (LL) Innocent England. D. H. Lawrence. NPeEn; OBCoV

So my soul can sing. (LL) Feeling Fucked/Up Up. Etheridge Knight. GT; NNaP; PBCAP; RaBo

So name her Vivian. I, scarecrow Merlin. Elegy for Mélusine from the Intensive Care Ward. Ramon Guthrie. APT-2

So not doing anything, how much. Mountain Forest. "Aleksandr Borisovich Kusikov." TCRP, *tr.* by Albert C. Todd

So nothing is left of your agony. Talking to Jim. Walta Borawski. CAGL

So, now I have confess'd that he is thine. William Shakespeare. HeIP-4; OxAEP-1 *Fr.* Sonnets.

So now I have to pack my forests. Leaving. Pamela Brown. BMAP

So now I'm brooding moodily upon. Simple Matter, A. Gloria Rawlinson. PeNZ

So now it's your turn. Instructions to the Double. Tess Gallagher. FaBoWP

So now just suppose that someone wanted to know. Surgery. Kenneth Pitchford. CAGL; GLP

So now the sun moves to die at mid-morning. Harvest of Hate. Wole Soyinka. AF

So now the very bones of you are gone. Doricha. Poseidippus. AWP; FaBoEE; OBVE; WoPoe, *tr.* by Edwin Arlington Robinson *Fr.* Variations of Greek Themes.

So now, this poet, who forsakes the stage. Dryden. OxBoLi *Fr.* Love Triumphant.

So now, you quiet house, adieu! Farewell. Ferdinand Raimund. AuPH, *tr.* by Lowell A. Bangerter

So Now You're Chicana. Carol Lem. GeoHom

So now you want to move still deeper into the clouds. (LL) To a Hermit in the Mountains. Hsü Pen. CoBLCP; ColAnChi, *tr.* by Jonathan Chaves

So obese is my cousin from Hendon. Limerick. A. H. Baynes. PeLi

So oft as I her beauty do behold. Edmund Spenser. Son *Fr.* Amoretti.

So Often. Léon Damas. NegPo, *tr.* by Ellen Conroy Kennedy

So often,it appears like an escape. Works of Art. Elizabeth Jennings. PeECV

So often it has been displayed to us, the hourglass. Testament. Hayden Carruth. GifTon

So often my feeling of race. So Often. Léon Damas. NegPo, *tr.* by Ellen Conroy Kennedy

So often true back then. One White Face in the Place, The. Sydney Lea. SwNoth

So often we hear of the vacant chair. Chair That Is Filled, The. Carrie Biggs. PWR

So on his Nightmare through the evening fog. Erasmus Darwin. NOEC *Fr.* Botanic Garden, The.

So on she goes, and in her idle flight. Christopher Marlowe. PoE *Fr.* Hero and Leander.

So, on the bloody sand, Sohrab lay dead. Matthew Arnold. GTBS-P; NOBE; PeVV *Fr.* Sohrab and Rustum.

So open was his mind, so wide. Independent, The. Phyllis McGinley. FaBoEE

So Paradise was brightened, so 'twas blest. To Philomela. Benjamin Colman. SCAP

So passed they naked on, nor shunned the sight. John Milton. PeECV *Fr.* Paradise Lost.

So perfectly done and yet. Mac Wellman. HeMarv *Fr.* Rat Minaret: Miniaturist-Divan, The.

So pleasing a light. Robert Duncan. APSN *Fr.* Passages.

So plentiful, the babes-in-a-pot. *Unknown.* ColAnChi, *tr.* by Jeffrey Riegel *Fr.* Classic of Odes.

So prayis me as ye think caus quhy. Remeidis of Luve. *Unknown.* OxBS

So proper and polite. Night Is Young and You're So Beautiful, The. Dana Suesse. ReLy

So proud she was to die. Emily Dickinson. NOBA

So prudent and so young a wife! To Geron. Hildebrand Jacob. NOEC

So quiet it was in that high, sun-steeped room. Nuremberg. Kenneth Slessor. BMAP

So's Liberty. (LL) Emily Dickinson. NALW; TCAPo

So sang he: and as meeting rose and rose. Dante Gabriel Rossetti. NAEL-5v2; NAEL-6v2; OxBSo *Fr.* House of Life, The.

So sang the gallant glorious chronicle. Tennyson. OBGa *Fr.* Princess, The.

So say, This earth untouched is ruptured enough to grieve. (LL) Testimonial. Claudia Rankine. ExTi; NeAmPo

So saying, light-foot Iris passed away. Homer. OBVE, *tr.* by Alfred Tennyson, 1st Baron Tennyson *Fr.* Iliad, The.

So several factions from this first ferment. Dryden. NOBE *Fr.* Absalom and Achitophel.

So shaken as we are, so wan with care. William Shakespeare. OxAEP-1 *Fr.* King Henry IV, Pt. I.

So shall ye waste to dust. (LL) Aged Lover Renounceth Love, The. Thomas Vaux, 2d Baron Vaux of Harrowden. NoSic; SCGP

So she became a bird and bird-like danced. Procne. Peter Quennell. MoBrPo

So she came back into his house again. Edna St. Vincent Millay. ColAP *Fr.* Sonnets from an Ungrafted Tree.

So she'll lift me up, turn me loose to head for the blue clouds! (LL) *Unknown.* CoBCP; ColAnChi, *tr.* by Burton Watson *Fr.* Four *Tz'u* from Tun-huang.

So she low-toned; while with shut eyes I lay. Tennyson. EBVV *Fr.* Princess, The.

So she must have been pleased with us, "H. D." NALW *Fr.* Tribute to the Angels.

So she sat down. For P—Celtic: found text from Machen. Bill Griffiths. Oth

So she sd, if u lose me, u lose a good thing. Next Door. Laini Mataka. ISC

So she went into the garden. Great Panjandrum [Himself], The. Samuel Foote. FaBoCh

So shoots a star as doth my mistress glide. John Davies of Hereford. OxBSo *Fr.* Wit's Pilgrimage.

So-shu dreamed. Ancient Wisdom, Rather Cosmic. Ezra Pound. NOBA

So shuts the marigold her leaves. William Browne (1591–1643). OBEV *Fr.* Britannia's Pastorals.

So Simple. Mark Van Doren. APT-2

So, since your heart is set on those sweet fields. To Colman Returning. *Unknown.* BIrV, *tr.* by Helen Waddell

So sits enthroned in vegetable pride. Erasmus Darwin. OBGa *Fr.* Botanic Garden, The.

So slight a ritual can still remind. Apprehension. Jeremy Ingalls. YaYoPo

"So small and young" the silver moon with its spoons hung. Donagh MacDonagh. James Liddy. BiHa

So small are the flowers of Seamu. *Unknown.* BoWoP

So smell those odours that do rise. To the Most Fair and Lovely Mistress Anne Soame, Now Lady Abdie. Robert Herrick. CaPo; NOBE; NOSC

So smelling their sweetness would be no theft. (LL) Unharvested. Robert Frost. APT-1; SAmP

So smooth, so sweet, so silv'ry is thy voice. Upon Julia's Voice. Robert Herrick. InPK-6; NOBE; NPeEn; SoSe-8

So, so, break[e] off this last lamenting kiss[e]. Expiration, The. John Donne. MeLP; OxBSP

So soft in the hemlock wood. Pastoral. Robert Silliman Hillyer. MoAmPo

So soft streams meet, so springs with gladder smiles. Welcome to Sack, The. Robert Herrick. BeJo; CaPo

So Soon. Mieke Tillema. TuT, *tr.* by Medbh McGuckian

So Soon. Mieke Tillema. TuT, *tr.* by Joan McBreen

So soon, so tired. So Soon. Mieke Tillema. TuT, *tr.* by Joan McBreen

So soon—so without tomorrow. So Soon. Mieke Tillema. TuT, *tr.* by Medbh McGuckian

So soon. Today, love, we. Tzu Yeh. WoPoe, *tr.* by Jeanne Larsen

So soon. Today, love, we. *Unknown.* ColAnChi, *tr.* by Jeanne Larsen *Fr.* Midnight Songs.

So spake our morning star then in his rise. John Milton. PeECV *Fr.* Paradise Regained [*or* Regain'd].

So spake the godlike power, and thus our sire. John Milton. NAEL-5v1; NAEL-6v1 *Fr.* Paradise Lost.

So spake the [*or* th'] Archangel Michael; then paused. John Milton. NAEL-5v1; NAEL-6v1 *Fr.* Paradise Lost.

So spends a summer's jasper century. (LL) Slug in Woods. Earle Birney. NOBC; NoP-4

So strange to hear that song again tonight. Cruising with the Beach Boys. Dana Gioia. GeoHom; SwNoth

So strong you thump O terrible drums—so loud you bugles blow. (LL) Beat! Beat! Drums! Walt Whitman. CBCWP; FaBoWar; HeIP-4; InPK-6; NAAL-2v1; NAAL-3; NAAL-5; NCAP; OBWP

So suddenly. Martha Anthony. InTrad

So summer comes in the end to these few stains. Beginning, The. Wallace Stevens. VGW

So sung the BARD—and Nansie's waws. Robert Burns. PoE *Fr.* Jolly Beggars, The.

So sweet, all sweet—the body as the shyer. Sweet-Briar in Rose. "Michael Field." VWP

So sweet, so golden. Christian Hofmann von Hofmannswaldau. GePo, *tr.* by Alexander Gode

So swete a kis yistrene fra thee I reft. To His Maistres [*or* Mistress]. Alexander Montgomerie. OxBS

So talks as it's most used to do. (LL) Samuel Taylor Coleridge. FHYEP; NAEL-5v2; NAEL-6v2; NOBRP

So tell me about fever dreams. Poet Is Served Her Papers, The. Lorna Dee Cervantes. TouFir

So terrible a scold above the squat adobe. Magpie. Alan Michael Parker. AmPoNex

So Terrifyingly Melancholy. Hagiwara Sakutaro. PFTM-1

So that each person may quickly find that. Johann Joachim Quantz's Five Lessons. William Sydney Graham. EmeKit; FaBoMo; HarvBoo

So, that girl with the gazelle eyes. Tanka. Nikolai Stepanovich Gumilyov [*or* Gumiliov *or* Gumilev]. TCRP, *tr.* by Simon Franklin

So that good and evil may die in equal hope. (LL) May, 1945. Peter Porter. HP; OxBC

So that I make you a microcosm or symbolic center of the public. Duration of Water. Mei-Mei Berssenbrugge. FSt

So that I might see you. Gift, The. Edgar Silex. NAPBL

So that I understand it, ladies mine. (LL) Dante Alighieri. AWP; CTC; EaItPo, *tr.* by Dante Gabriel Rossetti *Fr.* La Vita Nuova.

So that is his mother. Born of Woman. Wislawa Szymborska. GI

So that the cheek blanches and then blushes. (LL) At First Sight. Robert Graves. FaBoEE; OxBSP

So that the vines burst from my fingers. Ezra Pound. APT-1; NAAL-2v2; OBMV *Fr.* Cantos.

So the blues are again requiem. Paul Butterfield, Dead at 44. Robert Gibb. SwNoth

So / the body. 4/30/92 for rodney king. Lucille Clifton. ESEAA

So. The curtain has come. In Memoriam the Master—Noel Coward (1900–1973). E. J. Thribb. PeLV

So the cyclo driver. Dead for Two Years, Erhart Arranges to Meet Me in a Dream. John Balaban. CDa

So the distances are Galatea. Distances, The. Charles Olson. NAAL-2v2; NeAP

So the fight went on, like an inextinguishable fire. Homer. CAGL, *tr.* by Emile Victor Rieu *Fr.* Iliad, The.

So the last day's come at last, the close of my fifteen year. Old Place, The. Blanche Edith Baughan. PeNZ

So the Lord said: 'Eat this scroll.' Gwyneth Lewis. NeBl *Fr.* Parables & Faxes.

So the man spread his blanket on the field. Tall Man Executes a Jig, A. Irving Layton. MoCV; NOBC; NoAM

So the men fought on like a mass of whirling fire. Homer. NAWM-7v1, *tr.* by Robert Fagles *Fr.* Iliad, The.

So the milk carton which used to wobble. They Are Planning to Cancel the School Milk Program to Fund a Tax Cut for the Middle Class. Liz Rosenberg. InvLad

So the old man might sail his own boat to Hades. (LL) On the Death of the Ferryman, Glaucus. Antiphilus [*or* Antiphilos]. GrAn; WoPoe, *tr.* by W. S. Merwin

So the rain falls. Cornkind. Frank O'Hara. CLPP

So the river—yes, the river; I have come to that at last. Emily Jane Pfeiffer. VWP *Fr.* Out of the Night.

So the sky wounded you, jagged at the heart. Daylights. Rosanna Warren. NoAM

So the soldier replied to the poet. Volunteer's Reply to the Poet, The. Roy Campbell. FaBoWar

So the Trojans held their watch that night but not the Achaeans. Homer. NAWM-7v1, *tr.* by Robert Fagles *Fr.* Iliad, The.

So the villa, having learned its many skills. Madrid. Jay Wright. ESEAA

So the World Changes. Kofi Awoonor. VCWP

So the world offers itself in love. Sunday Park. Gwyneth Lewis. TCAWP

So, the year's done with! Robert Browning. EnLoPo *Fr.* Earth's Immortalities.

So the years go by. Song for a Seed. Violeta Parra. TANSG, *tr.* by Bonnie Shepard

So then the sunken heart was hauled up, nearly breaking. Poem That Was Once Called "Desperate" But Is Now Striving to Become the Perfect Love Poem. Richard Jackson. BAP-97

"So then you won't fight?" Dooley Is a Traitor. James Michie. OxBTC

So there it is. Painting, The. Jack Hirschman. BodElec

So there stood Matthew Arnold and this girl. Dover Bitch, The. Anthony Hecht. NBLV; NIL-7; NIP-4; NOBA; NOBL; OBAL; PeLV; UnPo; VGW

So there was no one left but me. (LL) Good Play, A. Robert Louis Stevenson. OTCP; PWR

So there will be no more people who must sell their daughters and sons? (LL) Ballad of Selling a Child. Wang Chiu-ssu. CoBLCP; ColAnChi, *tr.* by Jonathan Chaves

So there you are, in wispy veil and hat. Tea Party. Nancy Vieira Couto. PBCAP

So these are the Himalayas. Notes from a Nonexistent Himalayan Expedition. Wislawa Szymborska. AmFaPo, *tr.* by Stanislaw Baranczak and Clare Cavanagh

So these are the ropes. Rules of the Road, The. Cy Coleman. ReLy

So these two faced each other there. Portrait in the Guards, A. Laurence Whistler. GTBS-P

So they appeared before their lord the king. Dynastic Hymn. *Unknown.* ChiP, *tr.* by Arthur Waley

So they begin. With two years gone. Poem. Boris Leonidovich Pasternak. TrJP, *tr.* by C. M. Bowra

So they canonized him by the name of Jem Crow! (LL) "Thomas Ingoldsby." EBNV; OBCoV; OBNV; OBSP *Fr.* Ingoldsby Legends, The.

So they get this and we're coming off some it's like and. Et in Leucadia Ego. Michael Davidson. PmAP

So they have got you down at last, omera. Omera. Marjorie Oludhe Macgoye. HBAPE

So they in Heav'n their odes and vigils tun'd. John Milton. PeECV *Fr.* Paradise Regained [*or* Regain'd].

So they passed. Group Shot. Basil T. Paquet. CDa

So they smashed that old man of Whitehaven. (LL) Limerick: "There was an old man of Whitehaven." Edward Lear. EBEV; NPeEn; OxAEP-2

So they went, leaving a picnic-litter of talk. Party, The. William Robert Rodgers. BIrV; PNI

So this is all of life! Whirling, singing. Pre-Memory. Nikolai Stepanovich Gumilyov [*or* Gumiliov *or* Gumilev]. TCRusP, *tr.* by Denis Johnson and Kathy Lewis

So this is death. Jules Pascin. Mina Loy. HarvBoo

So this is, Jimmy, where we live. Urgent Letter, An. Hugh Maxton. PBCIP

So This Is Love. Lorna Crozier. LW

So this is the dust that passes through porcelain. Iron Lung, The. Stanley Plumly. LCAP-2

So this is the fruit that made us all human. Bruce Guernsey. IllVoic

So this is the man you dreamt I had betrayed. Gwyneth Lewis. TCAWP *Fr.* Welsh Espionage.

So this is the way it happens. Dreaded Road. 'Abd al-Razzaq 'Abd al-Wahid. MAP, *tr.* by Diana Der Hovanessian and Lena Jayyusi

So this is utopia, is it? Well. In a Copy of More's (or Shaw's or Wells's or Plato's or Anybody's) Utopia. Max Beerbohm. OBCoV

So this is what it's like being a wife. Being a Wife. Selima Hill. EmeKit

So this is what the afterlife is like! Man's Country. Daryl Hine. IllVoic

So this is women's work: folding. St Bride's. Kathleen Jamie. NePenScot

So thou art come again, old black-winged night. To Night. Thomas Lovell Beddoes. CenSon; Son

So through that unripe day you bore your head. Philip Larkin. NoAM

So through the night rode Paul Revere. Henry Wadsworth Longfellow. *See* Listen my children, and you shall hear

So thus he sorrowed till it was day. David Jones. NoAM *Fr.* In Parenthesis.

So tired! so weary. Catharine of Arragon. Eloise Bibb. CBWP-4

So tired, your footsteps drag. You Rise among Truths. 'Abd al-Razzaq 'Abd al-Wahid. MAP, *tr.* by Diana Der Hovanessian and Lena Jayyusi

So, 'tis enough. (LL) Kissing. Edward Herbert, 1st Baron Herbert of Cherbury. EnLoPo; NOSC

So to Tell the Truth. Janet Dubé. BrRo

So to the sylvan lodge. John Milton. NAEL-5v1; NAEL-6v1 *Fr.* Paradise Lost.

So Touch Our Hearts with Loveliness. Gail Brook Burket. AH

So turbid though I am. Edith Jay Scovell. HarvBoo *Fr.* Water Images.

So unwarely was never no man caught [*or* cawght]. Sir Thomas Wyatt. OxBEV

So, up the steep side of the rugged hill. Jack and Jill. A. E. Housman. UV

So vast, our Goddess Night, she rises. *Unknown.* WoPoe, *tr.* by Peter Dent and Edwin Gerow *Fr.* Vedic Hymns.

So very sad. (LL) First Circle, The. Kofi Awoonor. HBAPE; PBMAP; VCWP

So very still, even. Fuhaku. SoOfWa, *tr.* by Sam Hamill

So vile was poor Wat, such a miscreant slave. On W. R————, Esq. Robert Burns. FaBoEE

So warm I may melt. Sunday Morning. Christina Jenkins. BrRo

So was it even then. So soundlessly. Trysting, A. Richard Dehmel. AWP, *tr.* by Jethro Bithell

So was their sanctuary violated. Tennyson. *Fr.* Princess, The.

So we are taking off our masks, are we, and keeping. Homosexuality. Frank O'Hara. CAGL; LCAP-2; PFTM-2; TAP

So we begin to plan. Karen Alkalay-Gut. DTA *Fr.* Between Bombardments: A Journal.

So we came at last to meet, after the lights were out. John Hollander. VCAP *Fr.* Powers of Thirteen.

So we'd shine like dimes. (LL) Momma Sayings. Harryette Mullen. ISC; ItWoWo

So, we got you in the heel. Goodnight, Achilles. Enrique Lihn. VCWP, *tr.* by Alastair Reid

So We'll Go No More a-Roving. Byron. AWP; BoLoP; CABP; ChAP; ClHu; FHYEP; HAP; HeIP-4; MakPoe; NAEL-5v2; NAEL-6v2; NOBE; NPeEn; NePenScot; NoP-4; OPOU; OxBS; OxBSP; PAI; PoE; PoRA; SCGP; TFi; TTTS; WoPoe

(We'll Go No More a-Roving.) OBEV

So we march into the present. Rosemary Benét. HHAm *Fr.* U. S. A.

So we move now. Sam Hamod. GraLe; UnSA *Fr.* Moving.

So we must part, my body, you and I. Any Soul to Any Body. Cosmo Monkhouse. NOBVV; OxBEV

So we must say Goodbye, my darling. Goodbye. Alun Lewis. AngWePo; BoLoP; NAEL-5v2; NAEL-6v2; NoP-4; OBWP; OxBTC; PoWW; TCAWP

So we pass our time together, calm and delighted. (LL) For My Son Noah, Ten Years Old. Robert Bly. LoL; RaBo

So, we're estranged again—how it goes on! Drought. David Holbrook. OxBTC

So we sat there all afternoon. (LL) On the Lawn at the Villa. Louis Simpson. CoAP; OBAL; OxBC

So we wait on the verge of. Sequence. Kenneth Irby. FTOS

So we were together. "H. D." FaBoWP Fr. Winter Love.

So well is me begone. Unknown. MiEL

So well that I can live without. Emily Dickinson. TCAPo

So/ Went this little pig from the mainland to the market. Louis Untermeyer. MoAmPo Fr. Mother Goose Up-to-Date.

So what if clowns and gnomes. Golden Age, The. Artur Miedzyrzecki. PoSu, tr. by Stanislaw Baranczak

So what if Lowry got spooked by sea-birds and volcanoes crossing. Imperfect Sestina. Phyllis Webb. NOBC

So what if next year the deep pink burst. Perennial. Susan Hahn. IllVoic

So, what more do you want from me? Return, The. Yevgeny [or Evgenii] Borisovich Rein. ItGoST, tr. by Judith Hemschemeyer

So what said the others and the sun went down. Mrs. Alfred Uruguay. Wallace Stevens. TwCP

So what would you do? (LL) What? Langston Hughes. NBLV; OBAL

So, when he lost his temper, the Owl lost its life. (LL) Lewis Carroll. NOBL; OBCoV; PeLV; UV Fr. Alice's Adventures in Wonderland.

So, when she saw Narcissus wandering through the lonely countryside, Echo fell in love with him, and followed secretly in his steps. Ovid. EroLit, tr. by Mary M. Innes Fr. Metamorphoses.

So when the Queen of Love rose from the Seas. To a Very Young Gentleman at a Dancing-School. Elizabeth Singer Rowe. EMWP

So when you see the desolating sacrilege spoken of by the prophet Daniel. W. B. Yeats. GI Fr. St. Matthew.

So where is that guy who left us piles. Mikhail Aizenberg. ItGoST, tr. by J. Kates

So while you bloom, adopt a more becoming demeanor. (LL) Marbod of Rennes. CAGL; EroLit, tr. by John Boswell Fr. Unyielding Youth, The.

So White, So Soft, So Sweet. Ben Jonson. FaBoCh Fr. Devil Is an Ass, The.

So who of us. Vsevolod Nekrasov. ItGoST, tr. by Gerald Janecek

So wide the wells of darkness sink. Fragmentary Stars. Léonie Adams. APT-2

So winter closed its fist. Rite of Spring. Seamus Heaney. OxBC

So with my moan I left the mountain-side. (LL) Sonnet: Of the Grave of Selvaggia, on the Monte della Sambuca. Cino da Pistoia. AWP; EaItPo, tr. by Dante Gabriel Rossetti

So would I to the hills again. Christopher Okigbo. PBMAP Fr. Heavensgate (1961).

So would this be how I'd remember my hands. Lament in Good Weather. Lucia Maria Perillo. ExTi

So write, before I die, "'E liked it all!" (LL) Sestina of the Tramp-Royal. Rudyard Kipling. MakPoe; MoBrPo

So you alone are blessed with thought, free-thinking man. Golden Sayings. Gérard de Nerval. WoPoe, tr. by Richard Sieburth

So, you and I are dethroned, divorced. Garland, The. Vladimir Nikolaevich Sokolov. TCRP, tr. by Albert C. Todd

So you are married, girl. It makes me sad. Epithalamium. Roy McFadden. PNI

So you aren't Tolstoy or Saint Francis. So? Leonard Nathan. PBCAP

So you come with these maps in your head. Man Who Makes Brooms, The. Naomi Shihab Nye. LoL

So you fought for the Jews. To an Anti-Semite. Carl Rakosi. APT-2

So, you have gone my erstwhile glad boy. Ballygrand Widow. Deborah Randall. NeBl

So you have swept me back. "H. D." NALW; VGW Fr. Eurydice.

So you're a windmill. Vincente Huidobro. TCLAP, tr. by Stephen Fredman Fr. Altazor.

So you've reached your thirty-eighth birthday. My Husband's Birthday. Josephine D. Henderson Heard. CBWP-4

So you wanna kill white people. Something easy for Ultra Black nationalists. Kenneth Carroll. SpirFl

So You Want to Hear the Blues. Grace Bauer. MiVo

So. You were. Lines on the Hundredth Anniversary of the Birth of W. Somerset Maugham. E. J. Thribb. PeLV

So you were David's father. In Memoriam[, Private D. Sutherland]. Ewart Alan Mackintosh. PoWW

So you will presently my loving hands abjure. To This Book. Martin Opitz. GePo, tr. by George C. Schoolfield

So You Would Listen to Me. Laura Riesco. TANSG, tr. by Shaun Griffin and Emma Sepúlveda-Pulvirenti

So your daughter had a white dress, and once you saw. Stopwatch. Mary Ruefle. ExTi

So? Leonard Nathan. PBCAP

Soaked into a paste fine breaker slant. Ken Edwards. Oth Fr. 3600 Weekends.

Soaked to the skin I peer through the drizzle, and I perceive. Hans Magnus Enzensberger. PoSu Fr. Sinking of the Titanic, The.

Soaking, The. Ivor Gurney. OxBEV

Soap. Jane Coleman. ReTh

Soap. M. R. Peacocke. NLP

Soap. Gerald Stern. TaR

Soap (II). Jerome Rothenberg. NNaP

Soap Bubbles. Chrystos. ReTh

Soap-Pig, The. Paul Muldoon. PBCIP

Soap Suds. Louis MacNeice. EmeKit; FaBoMo; ModIr; NAEL-5v2; NAEL-6v2; NOIV; NPeEn; SCV

Soar[e] up[p], my soul[e], unto thy rest[e]. Seek[e] Flowers of Heaven. Robert Southwell. TrCP

Soaring again from the Leukadian Rock. Anacreon. SaLy, tr. by Diane Rayor

Soaring hawk from fist that flies, The. Lover Compareth Himself to the Painful Falconer, The. Unknown. NoSic

Soaring into the distant sky, a lone bird disappears. Climbing Up to the Lo-yu Plain. Tu Mu. SuSp, tr. by Irving Y. Lo

Sober, he thinks of her; so he gets drunk. Man and Woman. Robert Conquest. OxBTC

Sobering Up. Yüan Chên. SuSp, tr. by Dell R. Hales

Soccer. Nikolai Alekseievich Zabolotsky [or Zabolotskii]. TCRP, tr. by Daniel Weissbort

Social Glass, The. Lizelia Augusta Jenkins Moorer. CBWP-3

Social Life, The. Lizelia Augusta Jenkins Moorer. CBWP-3

Social Note. Dorothy Parker. LW Fr. Some Beautiful Letters.

Social Virtue's liberal plan. Anne Penny. ECWP Fr. Odes Sung in Commemoration of the Marine Society.

Social Worship. Bishop Richard Mant. SacPr

Socialist Manifesto for East Balgillo, The. W. N. Herbert. NePenScot

Society. Tom Clark. PmAP

Society, gregarious dame! Ode to Society, An. Hester Lynch Salusbury Thrale [later Mrs. Piozzi]. ECWP

Society has quite forsaken all her wicked courses. Sir William Schwenck Gilbert. OBSV Fr. Utopia Limited.

Society Upon the Stanislaus, The. Bret Harte. OBAL

Society Woman, The. Dezső Kosztolányi. IQMS, tr. by Peter Zollman

Socope. Maria Manuela Margarido. HAWP, tr. by Julia Kirst

Socrates' Death. Michael Jackson. PeNZ

Soda Jerk. Cynthia Rylant.
  Living in Cheston. HHAm

Soda pop. (LL) You Too? Me Too—Why Not? Soda Pop. Robert Hollander. NIL-7; NIP-4

Sodeynly affrayed, half wakyng, half slepyng. Unknown. OHMEL

Sodger laddie's socht a hoose, A. Under the Greenwood Tree. Hugh MacDiarmid. FaBoWar; OBVE

Sodom. Chaim Grade. TrJP, tr. by Joseph Leftwich

Sodom; or The Quintessence of Debauchery. John Wilmot, 2d Earl of Rochester.
  Song: "Oh gentle Venus, ease a tarse." EroLit

Soeur Louise de la Miséricorde (1674). Christina Georgina Rossetti. VWP

Sofa, The. William Cowper. Fr. Task, The.

Sofa, The. Medbh McGuckian. PBCIP; PNI

Sofa in the Forties, A. Seamus Heaney. EmeKit

Sofia. John Seed. Oth

Soft are Sappho's kisses. Paulus [or Paulos] Silentiarius. GrAn

Soft as old silk. Loving You. Frances Horovitz. LW

Soft Black Eyes. Priscilla Jane Thompson. CBWP-2

Soft blushing flower! my bosom grieves. To a Llangollen Rose, the Day after It Had Been Given by Miss Ponsonby. Matilda Barbara Betham-Edwards. CenSon

Soft-boiled egg is emptied, The. History Goes to Work. Elizabeth Garrett. MFPA; NeBl

Soft breeze! / Whispering trees! Strange Music. Edvard Grieg. ReLy

Soft colored clouds obscured by the sun. Tune: "Song of the Southern Country"—Spring Thoughts at Pearl River. Chu Yi-tsun. SuSp, tr. by Irving Y. Lo

Soft drinks and hot music. Jukebox Saturday Night. Paul McGrane. ReLy

Soft falls the sweet evening. Song. John Clare. NOBVV

Soft grasses, a plain of sedge fresh with passing rain. Tune: Sand of Silk-washing Stream. Su Tung-p'o (Su Shih). CoBCP, tr. by Burton Watson

Soft grasses, a plain of sedge fresh with passing rain. Su Tung-p'o (Su Shih). CoBCP, tr. by Burton Watson Fr. Along the Road to Stone Lake.

Soft greens, deep reds, really fresh colors. On the Butterflies. T'ang Yin. CoBLCP, tr. by Jonathan Chaves

Soft hangs the opiate in the brain. Opium Fantasy, An. Maria White Lowell. APN-2; InPK-6

Soft haze upon the mountain and a haze upon the sea. Slumber Song of the Gardens, A. John Runcie. PeSAV

Soft kisses may be innocent. Caution, The. Catherine Cockburn. LW

Soft, lovely, rose-like lips, conjoined with mine. Barnabe Barnes. EnLoPo Fr. Parthenophil and Parthenophe.

Soft moon shimmers out. Kalamu ya Salaam. SpirFl Fr. New Orleans Haiku.

Soft moonlight shines upon the corner store. Night in Kolozsvár. Lajos Áprily. IQMS, tr. by Watson Kirkconnell

Soft murmur in the walnut leaf. Insect. Sándor Weöres. IQMS, tr. by Peter Zollman

Soft new grass is creeping o'er the graves, The. By the Potomac. Thomas Bailey Aldrich. Son

Soft on the wave the oars at distance sound. Netley Abbey; Midnight. William Sotheby. NOEC

Soft, our poem begins as vandals dreams. (LL) Vandals, Horses. Alan Michael Parker. NAPBL; PuP-23

Soft quem quam will be Scops the Owl, The. Acropolis. Lawrence Durrell. OxAEP-2

Soft ridge of cloud or mountain! which thou art. Malvern at a Distance. John Keble. OxBSo

Soft Sea washed around the House, A. Emily Dickinson. SAmP

Soft Snow. William Blake. SoSe-8

Soft sound of his steps on the pier, The. Photograph of a Child, Japanese-American Evacuation, Bainbridge Island, Washington, March 30, 1942. James Masao Mitsui. OpBo

Soft sounds and odours brim up through the night. Guided Missiles Experimental Range. Robert Conquest. OxBC

Soft Swimmer, Winter Swan. Robert Horan. YaYoPo

Soft Targets. Essex Hemphill. GT

Soft through the silent air descend the feathery snow-flakes. Fragment: December 18, 1847. Henry Wadsworth Longfellow. APN-1; TCAPo

Soft Time of the Year, The. Hayden Carruth. PoCoUp

Soft, to Your Places. Thomas Kinsella. HarvBoo

Soft, to your places, animals. Soft, To Your Places. Thomas Kinsella. HarvBoo

Soft-toned clock upon the stair chimed three, The. Dawn. Ella Higginson. SWaP

Soft toys that make to seem girls. Strip-tease. Lawrence Durrell. OxAEP-2

Soft White. Lee Harwood. SPE

Soft wind southwesterly, something like, A. Vermont Thaw. Robert Penn Warren. BodElec

Soft winds circle the mountain head. Whisky Lovers. Vietnamese Oral Tradition. CaDao, tr. by John Balaban

Soft you; a word or two before you go. William Shakespeare. OxAEP-1 Fr. Othello.

Softball at Julia Tutwiler Prison. R. T. Smith. MoASP

Softened by Time's consummate plush. Emily Dickinson. NOBA

Softly. Nighttime. René Crevel. CAGL, tr. by Michael Taylor

Softly along the road of evening. Nod. Walter De la Mare. MoBrPo; OxBTC

Softly and humbly to the Gulf of Arabs. Beach Burial. Kenneth Slessor. CBAP

Softly croons the radiogram, loudly hoot the owls. Invasion Exercise on the Poultry Farm. Sir John Betjeman. NOBL

Softly Fades the Twilight Ray. Samuel Francis Smith. AH

Softly gliding I go. John Fletcher. NOSC Fr. Faithful Shepherdess, The.

Softly, in the dusk, a woman is singing to me. Piano. D. H. Lawrence. CABP; GTBS-P; HAP; HarvBoo; HeIP-4; InPK-6; MoBrPo; NAEL-5v2; NAEL-6v2; NIL-7; NOBE; NoAM; NoP-4; OPOU; OxBSP; PAI; PoE; RB; SCGP; TFi; TRP; UnPo; WeW-3

Softly now the day is dawning. Signal Gun, The. Mary E. Tucker. CBWP-1

Softly now the light of day. Evening Contemplation. George Washington Doane. AH

Softly, O midnight Hours! Serenade. Aubrey Thomas De Vere. OBEV

Softly rustled the oaks, whispered low in my ear. Graveyard, The. Hayyim Nahman [or Khayim Nakhman or Chaim Nachman] Bialik. TrJP, tr. by Bertha Beinkinstadt

Softly sighs the April air. Bel m'es quan lo vens m'alena. Arnaut Daniel. AWP, tr. by Harriet Waters Preston

Softly, softly, the rhyme is running out. Rhyme Is Running Out, The. József Kiss. IQMS, tr. by Anthony Edkins

Softly the civilized. Raiders' Dawn. Alun Lewis. AngWePo; NPeEn

Softly the linden grows green in the opening summer. Early Noon. Ingeborg Bachmann. AF, tr. by Mark Anderson

Softly the waters ripple. Albert Ehrenstein. TrJP, tr. by Babette Deutsch and Avrahm Yarmolinsky

Soho Hospital for Women, The. Fleur Adcock. NAEL-6v2; NoP-4

Sohrab and Rustum. Matthew Arnold. EBNV; OBNV
"And night came down over the solemn waste." OxBEV

Sohrab Dead. GTBS-P; NOBE; PeVV
"Then Sohrab with his sword smote Rustum's helm." OBWP

Soil between balls of thumb and forefinger crumbled / falls. Skylarks and Fuji. Kusano Shimpei. PFTM-1

Soil is freshly dug, the half-faded wreaths of leaves, The. Heraclitus of Halicarnassus. GrAn; WoPoe, tr. by Edwin Morgan

Soil now gets a rumpling soft and damp, The. Strong Are Saying Nothing, The. Robert Frost. APT-1

Soil was deep and the field well-sited, The. Failure, A. Cecil Day Lewis. NOBE

Soirée. Ezra Pound. OBCoV

Sois sage, ô ma douleur. . . I don't. Michael Foley. PNI Fr. True Life Love Stories.

Sois sage o ma douleur. Charles Baudelaire. See Peace, Be at Peace, O Thou My Heaviness

Soissons. Keith Douglas. NoAM

Sojourn in the Whale. Marianne Craig Moore. NALW

Sojourners, The. Bino A. Realuyo. ReBoTo

Sokoya, I said, looking through. There Is No Word for Goodbye. Mary Tallmountain. HATNAP; LoL

Sokrates to Agathon. Plato. GrAn, tr. by Peter Jay

Sokrates to Xanthippé. Plato. GrAn, tr. by Peter Jay

Sol through white curtains shot a tim'rous ray. Pope. ECEV; NPeEn Fr. Rape of the Lock, The; an Heroi-Comical Poem.

Sol took his nightcap off and gazed. After the Storm. Henrietta Cordelia Ray. CBWP-3

Solace. Josephine D. Henderson Heard. CBWP-4

Solace hast thou for pain! (LL) Dying Words of Stonewall Jackson, The. Sidney Lanier. APN-2; CBCWP

Solace in Age. Sir Richard Maitland. OxBS

Solange. Rashidah Ismaili. HAWP

Solanum tuberosum. Alice Potato. Thomas Zvi Wilson. SpudSo

Solar Creation. Charles Madge. FaBoMo; OBMV; OxBTC

Solar Loneliness. "Strannik." TCRP, tr. by April FitzLyon

Solar Myth. Genevieve Taggard. MoAmPo

Solar Years. David Rokeah [or Rokeakh]. MHP, tr. by Ruth Finer Mintz

Soldier, A. Sir John Suckling. PoE

Soldier, The. Rupert Brooke. AmFaPo; CABP; FaBoWar; GSo; HeIP-4; MoBrPo; NAEL-5v2; NAEL-6v2; NOBE; NoP-4; OBEV; OBWP; OxBTC; PeFWW; PoRA; PoWW; Son; TFi; UV Fr. 1914.

Soldier, The. John Clare. FaBoWar

Soldier, The. Gerard Manley Hopkins. FaBoWar

Soldier Addresses His Body, The. Edgell Rickword. PeFWW; PoWW

Soldier Bathing. Frank Ormsby. PNI Fr. Northern Spring, A.

Soldier, beware of mrs smith. (LL) E. E. Cummings. NOBA; OBSV

Soldier Boy's Dream, The. Mary E. Tucker. CBWP-1

Soldier brave, sailor true. Unknown. OxNR

Soldier came back home one day, A. Ground Glass. Irina Odoyevtseva [or Odoevtseva]. TCRP, tr. by Bradley Jordan

Soldier from the Wars Returning. A. E. Housman. OBMV

Soldier, full of battles and renown, The. Returned Soldier, The. John Clare. FaBoWar

Soldier Going to the Field, The. Sir William Davenant [or D'Avenant]. FaBoWar; NOBE; OBWP

Soldier in the Park, The. Elizabeth Riddell. CBAP

Soldier Is Home, The. John Shaw Neilson. CBAP

Soldier maimed and in the beggars' list, A. Pluralist and Old Soldier, The. John Collier. NOEC

Soldier of the Legion lay dying in Algiers, A. Bingen on the Rhine. Caroline Elizabeth Norton. TreFP

Soldier of Urbina, A. Jorge Luis Borges. PoetW, tr. by Alastair Reid

Soldier on the Marsh, A. Andrew Hudgins. CBCWP

Soldier passed me in the freshly fallen snow, A. To a Conscript of 1940. Sir Herbert Read. OBWP; PoWW

Soldier, past full retreat, is marching out of the grave, The. Go Ask the Dead. Thomas McGrath. AF

"Soldier, Rest!" Robert Jones Burdette. OBAL

Soldier Rest! [Thy Warfare O'er]. Sir Walter Scott. AWP; NOBE; PoRA Fr. Lady of the Lake, The.

Soldier's Betrothed, The. Richard Billinger. AuPH, tr. by Lowell A. Bangerter

Soldier's Ditty, A. Bulat Shalvovich Okudzhava. TCRP, tr. by Deming Brown

Soldier's Dream, The. Thomas Campbell. GTBS-P; OxAEP-2

Soldier's Farewell, A. Robert Burns. See Silver Tassie, The

Soldier's Rest. Roque Dalton. TCLAP, tr. by Richard Schaaf

Soldier's Song. Bálint Balassi. IQMS, tr. by Joseph Leftwich

Soldier's Song. Goethe. AWP, tr. by Bayard Taylor Fr. Faust.

Soldier's Song. Helene Kafka. AuPH, *tr. by* Lowell A. Bangerter

Soldier's Song. *Unknown.* APN-2, *tr. by* Stephen Return Riggs

Soldier's Tale, The. *Unknown.* PeLV

Soldier's Wife, The. Robert Southey. FaBoWar; OxBSP

Soldier's Wound, The. Wallace Stevens. NOBA   *Fr.* Esthétique du Mal.

Soldier stalks before my door, A. (LL) Contrary Theses (I). Wallace Stevens. OxBA; SAmP

Soldier stood at the pearly gate. *Unknown.* FaBoWar

Soldier That Has Seen Service, The. *Unknown.* NOEC

Soldier, There Is a War between the Mind. Wallace Stevens. NoAM   *Fr.* Notes toward a Supreme Fiction.

Soldier, think before you marry. John Gay. PeLV   *Fr.* Achilles.

Soldier: Twentieth Century. Isaac Rosenberg. PoWW

Soldier waits until he's called—then, A. Alfonzo Prepares to Go Over the Top. Rita Dove. LoL

Soldier Walks under the Trees of the University, The. Randall Jarrell. OxBA

Soldier Who Crucified Jesus, The. Martinus Nijhoff. TuT, *tr. by* Desmond Egan

Soldier, Won't You Marry Me? *Unknown.* OxBoLi; PeLV

Soldiers. Sutardji Calzoum Bachri. WoPoe, *tr. by* Harry Aveling

Soldiers. Padraic Fiacc. PNI

Soldiers. Giuseppe Ungaretti. PFTM-1

Soldiers. *Unknown.* FaBoEE; FaBoWar

Soldiers and poor, unable to rejoice. (LL) Owl, The. Edward Thomas. AF; ChAP; EBEV; FaBoTw; GTBS-P; NAEL-5v2; NAEL-6v2; NIP-4; NOBE; NoAM; NoP-4; OBWVE; OWoS; OxAEP-2; PeFWW; PoE; RB; SCGP; TCAWP; TFi; TRP; UnPo

Soldiers are citizens of death's grey land. Dreamers. Siegfried Sassoon. MoBrPo; NoAM; Son

Soldiers Bathing. Frank Templeton Prince. GTBS-P; MoBrPo; NOCV; OBWP; OxBTC

Soldiers, behold, and captains, mark it well. George Gascoigne. FaBoWar   *Fr.* Fruits of War, The.

Soldiers came, brewed tea in Snoddy's field, The. After the War. Douglas Dunn. OxBC

Soldiers' Chorus from Faust. *Unknown.* NOBAu

Soldiers have to fight and swear. Unequal Distribution. Samuel Hoffenstein. TrJP

Soldiers never do die well. Champs d'Honneur. Ernest Hemingway. AiP; IllVoic

Soldiers of Christ, arise. Whole Armour of God, The. Charles Wesley. NOCV

Soldiers' Songs of the First World War. *Unknown.*

   "Bells of hell go ting-a-ling-a-ling, The." OBCoV

   I Don't Want to be a Soldier. PoWW

   "I have no pain, dear mother, now." OBCoV

   "Sure, a little bit of shrapnel fell from out the sky one day." OBCoV

   "Wash me in the water." OBCoV

   "We are Fred Karno's army." OBCoV

Soldiers, what finer worth. Soldier's Song. Bálint Balassi. IQMS, *tr. by* Joseph Leftwich

Soldiers who wish to be a hero. Soldiers. *Unknown.* FaBoEE; FaBoWar

Sole heir of virtue, and of beauty both. Sir John Davies. NAEL-5v1   *Fr.* Orchestra; or, A Poem[e] of Da[u]ncing.

Sole listener, Duddon! to the breeze that played. William Wordsworth. CenSon   *Fr.* River Duddon [A Series of Sonnets], The.

Sole necessity of Earth and Heaven!, The. (LL) John Greenleaf Whittier. APN-1; NAAL-2v1; OxBA   *Fr.* Among the Hills.

Sole science to remain standing, The. Story of Every Day, The. Eugenio Montale. ItPo, *tr. by* Gayle Ridinger

Sole watchman of the flying stars, guard me. John Berryman. UnPo   *Fr.* Eleven Addresses to the Lord.

Soledad. Robert Earl Hayden. APT-2; NAAAL

Soledad. = f.*Solitude, loneliness, homesickness; lonely retreat.* Adrienne Rich. GeoHom   *Fr.* Atlas of the Difficult World, An.

Solemn Douglas firs stride slowly. Confirmation, A. William Daniel Ehrhart. CDa

Solemn Hour. Rainer Maria Rilke. TrJP, *tr. by* C. F. MacIntyre

Solemn Meditation, A. William Shenstone. NOEC

Solemn moon-beams fall, soft dews distill, The. Invocation to the Spirit Said to Haunt Wroxall Down. Mary F. Johnson. CenSon

Solemn plain-faced child stands gazing there, A. Portrait, A. Walter De la Mare. NoAM

Solemn receptions given by death. Two of the Festivals of Death. João Cabral de Melo Neto. TCLAP, *tr. by* W. S. Merwin

Solemn, solemn the coachman gets ready to go. To His Wife. Ch'in Chia. ChiP, *tr. by* Arthur Waley

Solemn thing—it was—I said, A. Emily Dickinson. NALW

Solemn Vow, A. Mikhail Naimy. GraLe

Solemne Long Enduring Passion, A. Nicholas Breton.

   "I have neither Plummes nor Cherries." NPeEn

   "Let mee thinke no more on thee." NPeEn

   "Wearie thoughts doe waite upon me." NPeEn

Solemnly, mournfully, / Dealing its dole. Curfew. Henry Wadsworth Longfellow. APN-1; OxBA

Solicit not thy thoughts with matters hid. John Milton. NAWM-7v1   *Fr.* Paradise Lost.

Solicitudes canine, four-footed amities. (LL) Sonnet: To Tartar, a Terrier Beauty. Thomas Lovell Beddoes. NOBVV; OxBSo

Solid houses in the mist, The. Charles Reznikoff. TaR; VGW

Soliloquies on Temporal Indigence. Mary Latter.

   "Now calumnies arise, and black reproach." ECWP

   "Strangers to meek compassion's tender touch." ECWP

   "With tearful eye, how frequent have I seen." ECWP

Soliloquy. Eugenio Montale. ItPo, *tr. by* Gayle Ridinger

Soliloquy. Richard Rodgers. ReLy

Soliloquy. George Sewell. *See* Dying Man in His Garden, The

Soliloquy at Potsdam. Peter Porter. NOBAu

Soliloquy in the Suburbs, A. Charles Jenner. NOEC   *Fr.* Eclogue IV: The Poet.

Soliloquy of a Beauty in the Country. George Lyttelton. ECEV

Soliloquy of a Maiden Aunt. Dollie Radford. NOBVV; OxBEV

Soliloquy of a Turkey. Paul Laurence Dunbar. BPo

Soliloquy of One of the Spies Left in the Wilderness, A. Gerard Manley Hopkins. TrCP

Soliloquy of the Night, The. Mihály Vörösmarty. IQMS, *tr. by* Peter Zollman   *Fr.* Csongor and Tünde.

Soliloquy of the Solipsist. Sylvia Plath. HarvBoo

Soliloquy of the Spanish Cloister. Robert Browning. FHYEP; FaBoVe; InPK-6; NAEL-5v2; NAEL-6v2; NIL-7; NIP-4; NOBL; NOBVV; NoP-4; OxBEV; PAI; PeVV; TOF; UV

Soliloquy on an Empty Purse. Mary Jones. ECWP

   (Alas! my Purse! how lean and low!) PEW

Soliloquy on Death. F. K. Fiawoo. PBA

Soliloquy to Absent Friends. Douglas G. Jones. MoCV

Soliloquy: "What folly to complain." Ann Yearsley. NOBRP

Solipsist with triplets said: "Though," A. Limerick. Lupellus. PeLi

Solitaire. Conrad Potter Aiken. ColAP

Solitaire. George Hitchcock. GifTon

Solitaire. Amy Lowell. MoAmPo; TCAPo

Solitariness. Sir Philip Sidney. *See* Arcadia

Solitary. Lance Henson. HATNAP

Solitary. Samar Sen. WoPoe, *tr. by* Pritish Nandy

Solitary, A. Basho. SoOfWa, *tr. by* Sam Hamill

Solitary, The. Mary Barnard. APT-2

Solitary, The. Friedrich Wilhelm Nietzsche. AWP, *tr. by* Ludwig Lewisohn

Solitary, The. Rainer Maria Rilke. TrJP, *tr. by* C. F. MacIntyre

Solitary, The. Sara Teasdale. MoAmPo

Solitary bird of night, The. Ode to Wisdom. Elizabeth Carter. ECWP

Solitary Canto to Chloris the Disdainful, A. John Smith. NOEC

Solitary city. Lamentation After Jeremiah to Exorcise High Rental / High Rise Building Scheduled for Construction with Public Funds. Diana Helen Melhem. GraLe

Solitary Confinement. Robert Walker. IBA; NOBAu

Solitary crow. Norman MacCaig. NoP-4

Solitary Falcon above the Buddha Hall of the Monastery of Universal Purity, A. Mei Yao Ch'en. SuSp; WoPoe, *tr. by* Jonathan Chaves

Solitary fly, nice, and content, A. All Soul's Day. Willem Jan Otten. TuT, *tr. by* Micheal O'Siadhail

Solitary invalid in a fuchsia garden, A. Philosopher and the Birds, The. Richard Murphy. CIP-2

Solitary life beside Chi River, A. Chi River Gardens and Fields. Wang Wei. CrYelRi, *tr. by* Sam Hamill

Solitary molar of a whore, The. Cycle. Gottfried Benn. PFTM-1

Solitary Reaper, The. William Wordsworth. AWP; CABP; ClHu; FHYEP; FaBoCh; HAP; HeIP-4; NAEL-5v2; NAEL-6v2; NOBE; NOBRP; NoP-4; OBEV; OxAEP-2; OxBEV; PAI; PoPoPo; PoRA; SCGP; SCV; SoSe-8; TFi; UnPo; WeW-3

   (Reaper, The.) GTBS-P

Solitude. Anna Andreyevna Akhmatova. ARWW, *tr. by* Catriona Kelly

Solitude. Dániel Berzsenyi. IQMS, *tr. by* Watson Kirkconnell

Solitude. Byron. *See* Childe Harold's Pilgrimage

Solitude. John Clare. NOBVV; OxBSP

Solitude. Abraham Cowley. *See* Of Solitude

Solitude. Michael Cuddihy. GifTon

Solitude. Babette Deutsch. LW

Solitude. Duke Ellington. ReLy

Solitude. Andreas Gryphius. GePo, *tr.* by George C. Schoolfield

Solitude. 'Enayat Jaber. PoArWo, *tr.* by Wen Chin Ouyang

Solitude. Helen Hunt Jackson. SWaP

Solitude. Mary Mollineux. NOSC

Solitude. Harold Monro. MoBrPo

Solitude. Rainer Maria Rilke. TrJP, *tr.* by C. F. MacIntyre

Solitude. Tomas Transtromer. RB, *tr.* by Robert Bly

Solitude. Ella Wheeler Wilcox. BRP; PWR; SWaP; TCAPo

Solitude: An Ode. James Grainger. ECEV

Solitude Exercises. Iman Mersal. PoArWo, *tr.* by Khaled Mattawa

Solitude flared out, The. Lyn Hejinian. FTOS *Fr.* Person, The.

Solitude is like rain. Solitude. Rainer Maria Rilke. TrJP, *tr.* by C. F. MacIntyre

Solitude Late at Night in the Woods. Robert Bly. VGW

Solitude of Alexander Selkirk, The. William Cowper. *See* Verses Supposed to Be Written by Alexander Selkirk during His Solitary Abode on the Island of Juan Fernandez

Solitude of Glass, The. Yvor Winters. APT-2

Solitude, solitude so sought after . . . I love you. XXX. Dulce Maria Loynaz. TANSG, *tr.* by Alan West

Solitude supporting solitude on two pergolas. Poem for a Guerrilla Leader. Syl Cheney-Coker. PBMAP

Solitude that unmakes me one of men. Compensation. Robinson Jeffers. MoAmPo

Solitude: you must be very strong. Lines from the Testament. Pier Paolo Pasolini. VCWP, *tr.* by Norman MacAfee

Solitudes, The. Luis de Góngora y Argote.

   "It was the flowery season of the year." SpanPo, *tr.* by Edward E. Wilson

Wedding Hymn.

      "Come Hymen come, for here to thee we bring." SpanPo, *tr.* by Edward E. Wilson

Solo. Mary Elizabeth Coleridge. VWP; ViWPN

Solo for Ear-Trumpet. Dame Edith Sitwell. MoBrPo

Solo for Two Voices. Octavio Paz. STV, *tr.* by John Frederick Nims

Solo for Voice 17 Song with Electronics (Relevant). John Cage. PFTM-2 *Fr.* Song Books.

Solo Native. Thomas Lux. LCAP-2

Solo or in the ride out gliding and. Barney Bigard. Suzanne Noguere. FFC

Solo Palabras. Magdalena Gomez. PueRic

Solo: The Good Blues. Dolores Kendrick. FFC

Solo with Chorus. Rose Fyleman. NOxBChV

Soloing. Philip Levine. OPRER

Soloists, The. Mingus Speaks: Found Poems. George Barlow. ISC

Solomon. Heinrich Heine. TrJP, *tr.* by Emma Lazarus

Solomon and Balkis. Robert Browning. ChIV-1

Solomon and the Witch. W. B. Yeats. ChIV-1; NoAM; WoPoe

Solomon Grundy. Mother Goose. LB; NBLV; OTCP; OxBoLi; OxNR; PeLV; ReMoGo

Solomon Grundy / Bored on Tuesday. Senilio Passes, Singing. Martin Bell. OBCoV

Solomon King of the Jews and the Queen of Sheba, Balkis. Solomon and Balkis. Robert Browning. ChIV-1

Solomon on the Vanity of the World. Matthew Prior.

   "Pass we the ills, which each man feels or dreads." NOEC

Solomon Redivivus, 1886. Constance Naden. VWP *Fr.* Evolutional Erotics.

Solomon's Seal, False and True. Graveyard at Bald Eagle Ridge. John Balaban. CDa

Solsequium, The. Alexander Montgomerie. OxBS

Solstice. Gerald Dawe. PNI

Solstice for John. John Cope. GeoH

Soluble Noughts and Crosses; or, California, Here I Come. Roger Roughton. SPE

Solum Mihi Superest Sepulchrum. William Habington. ChIV-1; NOSC

Solution. Ralph Waldo Emerson. OBAL

Solution, The. Bertolt Brecht. PoSu, *tr.* by Dereck Bowman

Solution, The. Brian [*or* Bryan] Merriman [*or* Merryman]. BIrV, *tr.* by Arland Ussher *Fr.* Midnight Court, The.

Solvitur Acris Hiems. Horace. WoPoe, *tr.* by Louis MacNeice *Fr.* Three Odes of Horace.

Soma. Suzanne Noguere. FFC

Soma haoma avestan haoma. Hymn to the Sacred Mushroom. Bob Cobbing. Oth

Somber empress. To Death, from the Genie of My Poetry. Delmira Agustini. TANSG, *tr.* by Mark McCaffrey

Sombra? Shade-Seller, The. Josephine Jacobsen. TAP

Sombre as the heavens when morning clouds arise. Lychee-tree, The. Wang I. ChiP, *tr.* by Arthur Waley

Sombre [*or* Somber] and rich, the skies. By the Statue of King Charles [*or* I] at Charing Cross. Lionel Pigot Johnson. MoBrPo; NOBE; OBEV; OBMV; PeVV

Sombre the night is. Returning, We Hear the Larks. Isaac Rosenberg. FaBoMo; HarvBoo; NAEL-5v2; NAEL-6v2; NoAM; OBWP; PeFWW; PoWW

Some Account of Anne Whitehead's Early Experience, as Written by Her Near Thirty Years Ago. Anne Greenwell. EMWP

Some act of Love's bound to rehearse. Why I Write Not of Love. Ben Jonson. BeJo; OxBSP

Some Adventures of John Kennedy Jr. Dennis Cooper.

   In New York. ReTh

   In School. ReTh; WiU

Some affairs are hard to relate and painful to hear. On the Second Day of the Fifth Month—Written after Drink. Liu Ya-tzu. SuSp, *tr.* by Wu-Chi Liu

Some ages hence, for it must not decay. Under a Lady's Picture. Edmund Waller. EnLoPo

Some are & are going to my howinouse. 12th Horse Song of Frank Mitchell (Blue), The. Frank Mitchell. APSN; STP, *tr.* by Jerome Rothenberg

Some are and are going to my howinouse baheegwing hawuNnawu. 12th Horse-Song of Frank Mitchell (Blue), The. Jerome Rothenberg. FTOS

Some are bewildered in the maze of Schools. Pope. OBSV *Fr.* Essay on Criticism, An.

Some are plain lucky—we ourselves among them. Lost Soul, A. Jay Macpherson. NOBC; NoP-4

Some are pure business, land deals, receipts, a contract. You Sort Old Letters. Robert Penn Warren. BodElec

Some are teethed on a silver spoon. Saturday's Child. Countee Cullen. NAAAL; PAI

Some ask for envy'd pow'r; which publick hate. Juvenal. OBVE, *tr.* by John Dryden *Fr.* Satires.

Some autumn leaves a painter took. Sumach Leaves, The. Jones Very. ColAP; NOBA

Some banks cropped close, and lawns smooth mown and green. Hill-Side Park, The. William Henry Davies. OBGa

Some Beasts. Pablo Neruda. TCLAP, *tr.* by James Wright and James Wright

Some beauties yet no precepts can declare. Pope. HAP *Fr.* Essay on Criticism, An.

Some Beautiful Letters. Dorothy Parker.

   Comment. NBLV; NIP-4; OBAL; OBCoV

   News Item. APT-1; NALW; OBAL

   Observation. APT-1

   Résumé APT-1; HeIP-4; InPK-6; NAAL-2v2; NALW; NBLV; NoP-4; OBAL; TrJP; UV

   Social Note. LW

Some believe the end will come in the form of a mathematical equation. Rider, The. Sarah Manguso. BAP-01

Some Biographical Data. Cees Buddingh' TuT, *tr.* by Mary E. O'Donnell

Some bite off the others'/ Arm. Vasco [*or* Vasko] Popa. PoSu, *tr.* by Anne Pennington *Fr.* Games.

Some blaze the precious beauties of their loves. John Davies of Hereford. Son *Fr.* Wit's Pilgrimage.

Some books are lies frae end to end. Death and Doctor Hornbook [A True Story]. Robert Burns. OxBS

Some Boys. Chuck Ortleb. GLP

Some broken. State of Nature, A. John Hollander. AiP; NIL-7

Some by their friends, more by themselves thought wise. Dryden. ChIV-1; OBSV *Fr.* Absalom and Achitophel.

Some call Experience. (LL) Emily Dickinson. NOBA; NOCV; OxBSP; SAmP; TCAPo

Some call that deep-deep bell. "H. D." NALW *Fr.* Tribute to the Angels.

Some can gaze and not be sick. A. E. Housman. FaBoEE; NOBVV; OBSV; OxBEV

Some can leave the truth unspoken. Truth. Eileen Duggan. PeNZ

Some candle clear burns somewhere I come by. Candle Indoors, The. Gerard Manley Hopkins. ChIV-1; OxAEP-2

Some celebration. / One by one they all left me. On the Carpet, Staring at Myself. Slavko Mihalic. PoSu, *tr.* by Peter Kastmiler

Some Contemplations of the Poor, and Desolate State of the Church at Deerfield. John Williams. SCAP

Some Cool. Alice Fulton. AllShUp

Some creep came to my water trough. Snake on D. H. Lawrence, The. N. J. Warburton. UV

Some cry up Haydn, some Mozart. Free Thoughts on Several Eminent Composers. Charles Lamb. OxBoLi; PeLV

Some curse that traitor Judas life and limb. On Judas Iscariot. Francis Quarles. FaBoEE

Some Day. Darío Jaramillo Agudelo. BLPSL, *tr.* by Rene de Costa, Rigas Kappatos and Eleni Paidoussi

Some day.—Alas, alas! (LL) Near Lanivet, 1872. Thomas Hardy. AWP; NoAM

Some day, all unawares, alone in the deep forest.　My Death.　Carl Zuckmayer. TrJP, *tr. by* E. B. Ashton

Some day I'm going to have a store.　General Store.　Rachel Lyman Field. ChAP

Some day I will go to Aarhus.　Tollund Man, The.　Seamus Heaney.　BIrV; CABP; CIP-2; EBEV; FaBoMo; ModIr; NPeEn; PBCIP; PNI; WoPoe

Some day I will write a poem for you that will not mention the air or the night. Some Day.　Darío Jaramillo Agudelo.　BLPSL, *tr. by* Rene de Costa, Rigas Kappatos and Eleni Paidoussi

Some day in six inches of.　Kenneth Rexroth.　APSN; APT-2　*Fr.* Love Poems of Marichiko, The.

Some day shall I be the one who let.　Some day shall I be.　Jules Supervielle. MFP, *tr. by* Martin Sorrell

Some Day, Some Day.　Cristóbal de Castillejo.　AWP, *tr. by* Henry Wadsworth Longfellow

Some day when I'm awf'ly low.　Way You Look Tonight, The.　Dorothy Fields.　ReLy

Some days ago I remarried.　Marrying Again.　Mei Yao Ch'en.　CoBCP; ColAnChi, *tr. by* Burton Watson

Some days, although we cannot pray, a prayer.　Prayer.　Carol Ann Duffy. HarvBoo; NePenScot; NoP-4; OxBSo

Some days, anything is wonderful. In its.　Mishipasinghan, Lumchipamudana, Etc.　Albert Goldbarth.　SpudSo

Some days he would wander around his attic-room.　Wisdom of AE, The. Thomas McCarthy.　PBCIP

Some days I am lonesome   I want to talk to my mother.　Grace Paley.　TaR

Some days I do feel better. Then I know.　Worst Fear, The.　George MacBeth [*or* Macbeth].　OxBSo

Some days in May, little stars.　Long Branch Song, A.　Robert Pinsky.　NoP-4

Some days start already swung from rafters.　Here and There.　Ann Lauterbach.　BodElec

Some define the happening. (LL)　Native's Letter.　Arthur Nortje.　HBAPE; PeSAV

Some Die of Light.　Simeon Dumdum.　ReBoTo

Some die too late and some too soon.　Lost Occasion, The.　John Greenleaf Whittier.　NOBA

Some distance away.　Letter from An Hoc (4), by a Seedbed.　R. L. Barth. CDa

Some dreams are like glass.　Lake Has Swallowed the Whole Sky, The.　Silvia Curbelo.　TouFir

Some Dreams They Forgot.　Elizabeth Bishop.　NoAM

Some dreams we have are nothing else but dreams.　Thomas Hood.　EBEV

Some Early gardenists.　William Mason.　OBGa　*Fr.* English Garden, The.

Some Enchanted Evening.　Richard Rodgers.　ReLy

Some Experimental Passages of My Life, with Reflections upon Jacob's Words, Few and Evil Have the Days of the Years of My Life Been.　Elizabeth Tipper.　EMWP

Some eyes condemn the earth they gaze upon.　Some Eyes Condemn.　Edward Thomas.　NoAM; OxBSo

Some Feelings.　Michael Benedikt.　CoAmPo

Some fellers love to Tip-Toe Through the Tulips.　Bidin' My Time.　George Gershwin.　ReLy

Some folks in looks take so much pride.　*Unknown.*　PoToHe

Some folks transplant rice for wages.　Farmer's Pride, The.　*Unknown.* WoPoe, *tr. by* Nguyen Ngoc Bich

Some fools once were listening to a poet reading his poem.　William Carlos Williams.　TCAPo　*Fr.* Kora in Hell.

Some for the Glories of This World; and some.　Omar Khayyám.　TRP, *tr. by* Edward Fitzgerald　*Fr.* Rubáiyát of Omar Khayyám [of Naishápúr], The.

Some Foreign Letters.　Anne Sexton.　MoAmPo

Some formula for sacred council as not to weep.　Potter's Field.　Prageeta Sharma.　HeMarv

Some fowls there be that have so perfect sight.　Petrarch.　SCGP, *tr. by* Sir Thomas Wyatt　*Fr.* Sonnets to Laura.

Some Frenchmen.　John Updike.　NBLV

Some generous painter now assist my pen.　True Effigies of a Certain Squire: Inscribed to Clemena, The.　Elizabeth Thomas.　ECWP

Some Girls.　Susanne Doyle.　FFC

Some Glow on the Sill.　Clark Coolidge.　FTOS

Some glowing in the common blood. / Some specialness within. (LL)　Of Robert Frost.　Gwendolyn Brooks.　NOBA; NoAM

Some gold lies veiled behind each evening cloud.　Hidden Essence.　Henrietta Cordelia Ray.　CBWP-3

Some good people, daring and subtle voices.　John Berryman.　HCAP　*Fr.* Dream Songs.

Some Good Things to Be Said for the Iron Age.　Gary Snyder.　TTTS

Some Grand River Blues.　Daniel David Moses.　HATNAP

Some guy in the miserable convoy.　Last Lie, The.　Bruce Weigl.　AF

Some guys show up.　Lawrence Ferlinghetti.　*See* Sometime during eternity / some guys show up

Some hae meat that canna eat.　*Unknown.*　FaBoCh　*Fr.* Two Graces.

Some Harvard men, stalwart and hairy.　Limerick.　Edward Gorey.　OBAL; OBCoV

Some have no money.　John Skelton.　NAEL-7v1　*Fr.* Tunnyng [*or* Tunning] of Elynour [*or* Elinor] Rummyng [*or* Rumming], The.

Some have [*or* hae] meat and cannot [*or* canna] eat.　Grace at Kirkudbright. Robert Burns.　OxBEV; OxBSP

Some heaps of trash upon a vacant lot.　Ambrose Bierce.　APN-2　*Fr.* Devil's Dictionary, The.

Some hearts go hungering thro' the world.　Hungering Hearts.　*Unknown.* PoToHe

Some in a Child Would Live, Some in a Book.　Mary Elizabeth Coleridge. ViWPN

Some in the Godspeed, the Susan C.　Enough.　Marianne Craig Moore. NOBA

Some Indian Uses of History on a Rainy Day.　A. K. Ramanujan.　OxBC

Some interiors keep their shade.　Some Die of Light.　Simeon Dumdum. ReBoTo

Some keep the Sabbath going to Church.　Emily Dickinson.　HeIP-4; MoAmPo; PAI; TCAPo

Some kind, a prodigy, a maimed one. (LL)　Geoffrey Hill.　NoAM; WoPoe *Fr.* Mercian Hymns.

Some Kind of Crazy.　Major L. Jackson.　SpirFl

Some kinds of trees seem ever eager.　Mast Year, The.　Medbh McGuckian. CIP-2

Some Kisses from *The Kama Sutra.*　Hugo Williams.　BoLoP

Some ladies smoke too much and some ladies drink too much and some ladies pray too much.　Curl Up and Diet.　Ogden Nash.　OBCoV

Some Lapland Views.　Christian Dotremont.　PFTM-2, *tr. by* Pierre Joris

Some Last Questions.　W. S. Merwin.　HCAP; VCAP

Some leading thoroughfares of man.　Herman Melville.　APN-2; NCAP　*Fr.* Clarel: A Poem and Pilgrimage in the Holy Land.

Some like cats, and some like dogs.　Cats and Dogs.　N. M. Bodecker.　TLR

Some like drink.　Not I.　Robert Louis Stevenson.　NOBL

Some like them gentle and sweet.　I Like Them Fluffy.　Sir Alan Patrick Herbert.　NBLV

Some Lines on My Mother's Illness.　Yunna Petrovna [*or* Iunna Pinkhusovna] Moritz [*or* Morits].　TCRP, *tr. by* Bernard Meares

Some Litanies.　Michael Benedikt.　CoAP; TwCP

Some lives are so odd—you agree?　Limerick.　*Unknown.*　PeLi

Some love a laundress and others love a duchess.　My Love.　"Sasha Chorny" [*or* Chiornyi].　TCRP, *tr. by* Bernard Meares

Some lovers speak, when they their Muses entertain.　Sir Philip Sidney. NAEL-5v1; NAEL-6v1; NAEL-7v1; NoSic; Son　*Fr.* Astrophil and Stella.

Some lucky day each November great waves awake and are drawn.　November Surf.　Robinson Jeffers.　NAAL-2v2; OxBA

Some Magic.　James Koller.　PoM

Some man unworthy to be possessor.　Confined Love.　John Donne.　BASC

Some marring in the glass of the body.　Shatter.　Elizabeth Robinson. AmPoNex

Some may occasion snatch to carp.　Harp, The.　Ralph Knevet.　ChIV-2

Some may wish for city streets, jewels or silken gown.　Wishes.　A. C. Child. PoToHe

Some men break your heart in two.　Experience.　Dorothy Parker.　NAAL-2v2

Some men deem.　Ideals.　Robert Greene.　PoToHe

Some men marriage do commend.　De Se.　John Weever.　FaBoEE

Some men never think of it.　Flowers.　Wendy Cope.　NoP-4

Some men, some men.　Chant for Dark Hours.　Dorothy Parker.　ItWoWo

Some men to carriages aspire.　Ballade of an Omnibus.　Amy Levy.　ViWPN

Some men wash their hands five times a day.　Hygiene.　Reginald Shepherd. ReTh

Some Metaphysics of Junior Wells.　Sandra McPherson.　SeSe

Some, misbelieving and profane in love.　Michael Drayton.　AEP　*Fr.* Idea.

Some moments stolen by a slave.　Frozen Witness, The.　Nick Piombino. FTOS

Some moralist or mythological poet.　W. B. Yeats.　PoE　*Fr.* Nineteen Hundred and Nineteen.

Some More Scruples Clear'd.　Elizabeth Hincks.　EMWP

Some must employ the scythe.　Dedicated, The.　Philip Larkin.　OxBC

Some names are ominous, wherein wise fate.　Of St Stephen.　Francis Quarles. NOSC

Some names there are that win the best applause.　William Lloyd Garrison. Henrietta Cordelia Ray.　CBWP-3

Some ne'er advance a judgment of their own.　Pope.　OBSV　*Fr.* Essay on Criticism, An.

Some Nets.　B. P. Nichol.　FTOS

Some newness of the heart I would discern.　Mid Winter.　Hubert Witheford. PeNZ, *tr. by* Sam Karetu

Some night under a pale moon and geraniums. Serenade. Adelia Prado. TANSG, *tr. by* Ellen Watson

Some nights it's bound to be your best way out. Insomnia I. Howard Nemerov. DiPo

Some nights the quiet is all wrong. A tape. Over *Voice of America.* Dennis Finnell. SwNoth

Some nineteen German planes, they say. Reprisals. W. B. Yeats. OBWP; PoWW

Some of Betty's Story Round 1850. Gale Jackson. SpirFl

Some of his messages were personal. Passed On. Bernard Spencer. FaBoWar

Some of the girls are playing jacks. Narcissa. Gwendolyn Brooks. NTCP

Some of the time. Working with Mother. Myra Cohn Livingston. TLR

Some of their chiefs were princes of the land. Dryden. EBEV; OxBEV; SCV *Fr.* Absalom and Achitophel.

Some of them with staves. Basho. TAL

Some of These Days. Shelton Brooks. ReLy

Some of us are telling secrets. Late Night Radio. Aleda Shirley. ExTi

Some of us believe. Night Game, The. Robert Pinsky. TaR

Some of us know. Intelligence Quotients. Dorothy Perry Thompson. SpirFl

Some of us stayed forever, under the lough. Frank Ormsby. CIP-2 *Fr.* Northern Spring, A.

Some of Us Wear Pink Triangles. Walta Borawski. CAGL

Some Old How. Sándor Petőfi. IQMS, *tr. by* Peter Zollman

Some old lady scarcely younger. *Unknown.* PriapPo, *tr. by* Richard W. Hooper *Fr.* Priapus Poems, The.

Some One. Walter De la Mare. TLR

Some one calls out, and some one else. Sick Men Sleeping. Kenneth Mackenzie. BMAP

Some One Liked Me when I Was Twelve. Peter Orlovsky. GLP

Some one prepared this mighty show. Emily Dickinson. SAmP

Some Opposites. Richard Wilbur. OBCA; OxIBACP

Some Other Time. Leonard Bernstein. ReLy

Some pages have eyes, some mouths. They desire. Family Album, The. Lisa Ress. GotH

Some patios won't allow the shadow of a maid. Scattered Light. Fanny Howe. FTOS

Some People. Rachel Lyman Field. ChAP; NTCP

Some People. A. K. Ramanujan. VCWP

Some People. Stephen Sondheim. ReLy

Some People Are about Jam. Sandra Maria Esteves. PueRic

Some people are getting so they think a poor girl. Julia A. Moore. VerBaPo *Fr.* Roll On, Time, Roll On.

Some people are incurably gentle. Portrait of a Lady. Elizabeth Nannestad. PeNZ

Some people as they die grow fierce, afraid. Hereafter, The. Andrew Hudgins. RA

Some people can get a thrill. Some People. Stephen Sondheim. ReLy

Some people cannot endure. Going the Rounds; a Sort of Love Poem. Anthony Hecht. BoLoP

Some people go their whole lives. Dream On. James Tate. BodElec

Some people hang portraits up. Robert Browning. CTC

Some people in the sky. Song for a Scalp Dance. *Unknown.* STP, *tr. by* Jerome Rothenberg

Some people know how to love. Poem of Explanations. Dahlia Ravikovitch [*or* Ravikovich]. BoWoP, *tr. by* Chana Bloch

Some People Laugh, Some People Cry. Sri Sri.
  "Man walks on the bridge and gives away the change in his, A." OMIP

Some people may think I'm a bit la-di. Limerick. C. Vita-Finzi. PeLi

Some people need a lot of money. I'm Just a Lucky So-and-So. Duke Ellington. ReLy

Some people, / no matter what you give them. Adam's Complaint. Denise Levertov. BoWoP; NNaP

Some people see only you. Couple, The. Ana Blandiana. WPOW, *tr. by* William M. Murray and the author

Some people should take a break. Have you ever. Mercy Flight. Anselm Berrigan. HeMarv

Some people terrified for their lives cut. Karen Alkalay-Gut. DTA *Fr.* Between Bombardments: A Journal.

Some people weren't meant to eat a New York Strip. Angel Finally Admits What She Knows to Lou Binkler of Bethany, Missouri, An. Catie Rosemurgy. AmPoNex

Some pimps wear summer hats. What? Langston Hughes. NBLV; OBAL

Some pleasure for our punishment! (LL) Argument, An. Thomas Moore. BoLoP; EnLoPo; OxBSP

Some prefer a glory of horsemen; warships. Sappho. STV

Some primal termite knocked on wood. Termite, The. Ogden Nash. KaS; OBCA

Some prowl sea-beds, some hurtle to a star. X-Ray. Dannie Abse. AngWePo; BloBone

Some queen has left her mirror on the grass. Frozen Tarn. Catherine Fisher. TCAWP

Some Questions You Might Ask. Mary Oliver. ColAP

Some 're lovely N nawu nnnn but some 're & are at my hawuz nawu wnn. 13th Horse Song of Frank Mitchell (White), The. Frank Mitchell. STP

Some Reflections. Anne Finch, Countess of Winchilsea. ChIV-1

Some rose from the underground. Civil War. Maksimilian Aleksandrovich Voloshin. TCRP, *tr. by* Albert C. Todd

Some Ruthless Rhymes. Harry Graham.
  Calculating Clara. PeLV
  Compensation. PeLV
  Englishman's Home, The. PeLV
  Mr Jones. PeLV
  Necessity. PeLV
  Stern parent, The. PeLV
  Tender-Heartedness. NBLV; NOxBChV; PeLV

Some San Francisco Poems. George Oppen.
  And Their Winter and Night in Disguise. APSN; NNaP
  Anniversary Poem. APSN; NNaP
  But So As By Fire. APT-2; NNaP
  Impossible Poem, The. NNaP
  Morality Play: Preface, A. APSN; NNaP
  "Moving over the hills, crossing the irrigation." APSN; NNaP
  "O withering seas." NNaP
  ("Silver as / The needle's eye.") FTOS; NNaP
  Taste, The. NNaP
  Translucent Mechanics, The. NNaP

Some say an army of horsemen, others. Sappho. SaLy, *tr. by* Diane Rayor

Some say cavalry and others claim. Sappho. BoWoP

Some say, compar'd to Bononcini. Epigram on the Feuds between Handel and Bononcini. John Byrom. FaBoEE; NOBL; NOEC

Some say that Chattanooga is the. Chattanooga. Ishmael Reed. NAAAL

Some say that love is sweet as a rose. Candy. Alex Kramer. ReLy

Some say that my teaching is nonsense. Lao Tzu. EnlH *Fr.* Tao Te Ching.

Some say the deil's deid. *Unknown.* FaBoCh

Some say the radiance around the body. 11/10 Again. Lucille Clifton. GT

Some say the world's / A hopeless case. How I See It. Kit Wright. OTCP

Some say the world will end in fire. Fire and Ice. Robert Frost. APT-1; BRP; ColAP; FaBoEE; HeIP-4; InPK-6; MoAmPo; NAAL-2v2; NAAL-5; NOBA; NoAM; OxBA; PAI; RaBo; SoSe-8; TAP; TFi

Some say there are nine Muses: but they're wrong. Sappho. Plato. GrAn, *tr. by* Peter Jay

Some say you dye your hair, Nikylla. Lucilius. GrAn

Some seven score Bishops late at Lambeth sat. Lambeth Lyric. Lionel Pigot Johnson. NOBVV

Some Sights Sometimes Seen and Seldom Seen. William Cole. TLR

Some silent movie star. Flicker, The. Lew Blockcolski. VoR

Some silver-fingered fountain steals the world. (LL) Sonnet IV. E. E. Cummings. ChIV-1; MoAmPo

Some sit and stare. Common Grave, The. James Dickey. CoAP

Some Sixties. Ray Gonzalez. MiVo

Some slumbring thoughts possess'd my brain. Golden Island, The; or, the Darian Song. *Unknown.* EMWP

Some small grey fur is pulsing in its grip. (LL) End of the Weekend, The. Anthony Hecht. CoAmPo; FaBoMo; HAP; WeW-3

Some songs by women. Some Songs Women Sing. Peter Harris. ISC

Some Songs Women Sing. Peter Harris. ISC

Some Stories of the Beauty Wapiti. Ebbe Borregaard. NeAP

Some, striving knowledge to refine. Thought on Human Life, A. *Unknown.* OxBSP

Some Syrian rainmaker. Assumption. Padraic Fallon. BIrV; NOIV

Some talk of Alexander, and some of Hercules. British Grenadiers, The. *Unknown.* FaBoWar; OxBoLi

Some Tears. Kees Ouwens. TuT, *tr. by* Peter Van de Kamp

Some Tentative Definitions 1. Kwame Dawes. WaCA

Some Tentative Definitions 4. Kwame Dawes. WaCA

Some Tentative Definitions 7. Kwame Dawes. WaCA

Some Tentative Definitions 11. Kwame Dawes. WaCA

Some Terms. Robert Pinsky. HCAP *Fr.* Essay on Psychiatrists.

Some that have deeper digged love's mine [*or* myne] than [*or* then] I. Love's Alchemy [*or* Alchemie]. John Donne. BASC; ESCV; NAEL-5v1; NAEL-6v1; NAEL-7v1; NoP-4; PoE

Some—the ones with fish names—grow so north. Wildflower. Stanley Plumly. LCAP-2

Some there are who are present at such occasions. On the Suicide of a Friend. Reed Whittemore. CoAmPo

Some there are who say that the fairest thing seen. Sappho. NAWM-7v1; WPOW, *tr. by* Richmond Lattimore

Some they will talk of bold Robin Hood. Robin Hood and the Bishop of Hereford. *Unknown.* ESPB

Some Thing Black. Jacques Roubaud.
Section V. PFTM-2, *tr. by* Rosmarie Waldrop

Some thing is lost in me. Man Thinking about Woman. Haki R. Madhubuti. PAI

Some things a man must surely know. Recipe for Living. Alfred Grant Walton. PoToHe

Some things are truly lost. Think of a sun-hat. Richard Wilbur. LCAP-2; NAAL-2v2; NoAM

Some things are very dear to me. Sonnet—2. Gwendolyn B. Bennett. NAAAL

Some things I do not profess. Abduction, The. Stanley Kunitz. WeW-3

Some things I have to say aren't getting said. Bilingual Sestina. Julia Alvarez. ExTi; FFC

Some things persist by suffering change, others. Homage to the Philosopher. Babette Deutsch. TrJP

Some things that fly there be. Emily Dickinson. NCAP; OxBA

Some things you should forget. But Bird. Paul Zimmer. SeSe

Some think that in the Christian scheme. Christopher Smart. NOCV *Fr.* Hymns for the Amusement of Children.

Some thirty inches from my nose. W. H. Auden. FaBoEE *Fr.* Thanksgiving for a Habitat.

Some Thracian exults in an excellent shield. Archilochus. SaLy, *tr. by* Diane Rayor

Some three or four mile out of town. Robert Lloyd. *See* Wealthy Cit, grown old in trade, The

Some Time After. Anne Ridler. SacPr

Some time ago a soul, now erased, was mine. Sweet Reliquaries, The. Delmira Agustini. TANSG, *tr. by* Mark McCaffrey

Some time in the dark hours. Snowfall. W. S. Merwin. NNaP

Some time now past in the autumnal tide. Anne Bradstreet. ColAP; NAAL-3; NAAL-5; SCAP; TCAPo; WPE

Some time when the river is ice ask me. Ask Me. William Stafford. LoL

Some / times. "5 Minutes, Mr. Salaam." Kalamu ya Salaam. SpirFl

Some to Conceit alone their taste confine. Pope. OxAEP-1 *Fr.* Essay on Criticism, An.

Some Trees. John Ashbery. CoAmPo; HCAP; NAAL-2v2; YaYoPo

Some truths may pierce the spirit's deeper gloom. Frederick Goddard Tuckerman. APN-2 *Fr.* Sonnets.

Some unknown sound. Foster Jewell. HA

Some vex their souls with jealous pain. On One Who Died Discovering Her Kindness. John Sheffield, Duke of Buckingham and Normandy. OBEV

Some Walks with You. John Hollander. BodElec

Some walls enclosing furniture. (LL) Key, The. John Ormond. AngWePo; TCAWP

Some waves / a wave of now. Latin and Soul for Joe Bataan. Víctor Hernández Cruz. PueRic

Some were for setting up a king. Samuel Butler (1612–80). EBEV *Fr.* Hudibras.

Some with sharp swords, to tell O most accursed! Margaret Lucas Cavendish, Duchess of Newcastle. PEW *Fr.* Fort or Castle of Hope, The.

Some without remote interview. Shakeout. Diane Ward. FTOS

Some women marry houses. Housewife. Anne Sexton. NALW

Some women save their sanity with needles. Mr. McGregor's Garden. Medbh McGuckian. CIP-2; PNI

Some Words for President Wilson. Samuel Hazo. GraLe

Some write of angels, some of goddess. Gentleman's Study, in Answer to The Lady's Dressing-Room, The. "Miss W——." ECWP

Some years ago, ere time and taste. Winthrop Mackworth Praed. OBEV; OxAEP-2 *Fr.* Every-Day Characters.

Somebodies walked the woods. North, The. Barry McKinnon. NOBC

Somebody. Tennyson. FaBoEE; NOBL
(Somebody Being a Nobody.) OxBSP

Somebody. *Unknown.* OxBS

Somebody almost walked off wid alla my stuff. Ntozake Shange. NAAAL; WPOW

Somebody being a nobody. Somebody. Tennyson. FaBoEE; NOBL

Somebody Consoles Me with a Poem. Sandor Csoori. GifTon, *tr. by* Len Roberts and László Vértes

Somebody Died. Robert Creeley. LCAP-2

Somebody dies every four minutes. Rapid Transit. William Carlos Williams. APT-1

Somebody Else. Jackie Kay. NeBl

Somebody has given my. Proust's Madeleine. Kenneth Rexroth. NoAM; TRP

Somebody is shooting at something in our town. Swarm, The. Sylvia Plath. NALW

Somebody loses whenever somebody wins. Crapshooters. Carl Sandburg. VGW

Somebody Loves Me. Ballard MacDonald. ReLy

Somebody loves us all. (LL) Filling Station. Elizabeth Bishop. FaBoMo; HAP; HCAP; InPK-6; NoP-4; PoetW; VCAP; WeW-3

Somebody muffed it? Somebody wanted to joke. (LL) Sunset of the City, A. Gwendolyn Brooks. FaBoWP; LCAP-2

Somebody's Darling. Marie La Coste. UnPo

Somebody's done for. (LL) Death and Co. Sylvia Plath. CoAmPo; EmeKit; LCAP-2

Somebody's Gone. Charles Henri Ford. SPE

Somebody's in there. Saint Pumpkin. Nancy Willard. LCAP-2

Somebody's knockin' at th' door. Collier's Wife, The. D. H. Lawrence. FaBoVe; OxBTC

Somebody's Mother. *Unknown.* ChAP

Somebody said that it couldn't be done. It Couldn't Be Done. Edgar Albert Guest. BRP; ITBLP

Somebody said when snubbed, "Is Damon so." Diodes. CAGL, *tr. by* Daryl Hine

Somebody said wrecks. Drowned, The. Norman MacCaig. OxBC

Somebody, Somewhere. Frank Loesser. ReLy

Somebody, somewhere. Somebody, Somewhere. Frank Loesser. ReLy

Somebody threw away a piano. Street Music. Barbara Angell. AiP

Somebody told me you were dead. Callimachus. PGA

Somebody, when I was young, stole my toy horse. Toy Horse, The. Valentin Iremonger. NOIV

Somebody who should have been born. Abortion, The. Anne Sexton. LCAP-2; VGW

Someday he'll leave me: then what will I do? (LL) How Lies Grow. Maxine Chernoff. IllVoic; PmAP

Someday I will leave this town and not look back. Suture. Mark Wunderlich. AmPoNex

Someday the phoebe bird will sing. Occupant of the Hose. Larissa Szporluk. NeAmPo

Someday they'll find me out, and my lavish hands. Self-Portrait. Charles Wright. PoPoPo

Somehow I never stopped to notice. His Costume. Sharon Olds. BAP-01

Somehow I really want to go. Vsevolod Nekrasov. ItGoST, *tr. by* Gerald Janecek

Somehow it got into my room. My Life. Joe Wenderoth. BodElec; NAPBL

Somehow myself survived the Night. Emily Dickinson. APN-2

Somehow or other. Senkei. JDP, *tr. by* Yoel Hoffmann

Somehow the tutorial takes an unplanned direction. How Come the Truck-Loads? Judith Rodriguez. FaBoWP

Someone. Ruth Forman. AmPoNex

Someone. Someone Will Take The Ball. Nelly Sachs. BBASP; WPoS, *tr. by* Matthew Mead and Ruth Mead

Someone anonymous in the anonymous throng. Writing on a Tombstone. J. C. Bloem. TuT, *tr. by* Desmond Egan

Someone approaches to say his life is ruined. Dream, The. David Ignatow. CoAP; NNaP; PAI

Someone Asked the Publisher. John Bingham Morton. UV *Fr.* When We Were Very Silly.

Someone brought them to Palma. Toward the Jurassic Age. Claribel Alegría. TCLAP, *tr. by* Carolyn Forché

Someone came knocking. Someone [*or* Some One]. Walter De la Mare. MoBrPo

Someone dancing inside us. Advice. Bill Holm. RaBo

Someone Digging in the Ground. Jelaluddin [*or* Jalal al-Din] Rumi. RaBo, *tr. by* Coleman Barks

Someone drove a two-by-four. Child's Grave, Hale County, Alabama. Jim Simmerman. WeW-3

Someone else cut off my head. Bread. Brendan Kennelly. PBCIP

Someone else / looked at the sky. Lady Izumi. BoWoP

Someone had been walking in and out. Origin of Baseball, The. Kenneth Patchen. APT-2; CLPP

Someone hands you an English thriller. This Is Bad. Gottfried Benn. WoPoe, *tr. by* Harvey Shapiro

Someone is remembered to dry the dishes. Red Lilies. Barbara Guest. FTOS; PmAP; PoM

Someone has shut the shining eyes, straightened and folded. Beside the Bed. Charlotte Mew. BWW; MoBrPo; OxBSP; WPE

Someone, I tell you, / will remember us. Sappho. BoWoP

Someone, if you pay the price, can hypnotize. Interview with an Alchemist in the New Age. Stephanie Brown. BodElec

Someone in Quaker meeting talks about greed and aggression. Greed and Aggression. Sharon Olds. RaBo

Someone in the Garden. Mary Mapes Dodge. SWaP

Someone in the garden murmurs all the day. Someone in the Garden. Mary Mapes Dodge. SWaP

Someone in the next apartment. Room. Ruth Stone. BoWoP

Someone Is Beating a Woman. Andrey [or Andrei] Andreievich Voznesensky [or Voznesenskii]. VCWP, tr. by Jean Garrigue

Someone is breathing in the room. Waking. Hugh Maxton. BIrV; CIP-2

Someone is dead. Lament. Anne Sexton. CoAmPo; WPE

Someone is glad that I, Theodorus, am dead. On Theodoros. Simonides. GrAn, tr. by Peter Jay

Someone is leaving town as clean smoke. Passing the Crematorium. Frank Ormsby. ModIr

Someone is locking out the stars and the yellow flowers. Old Man in a Moon Loft. T. Glynne Davies. OBWVE, tr. by the author

Someone Is Probably Dead. Marvin Bell. BodElec

Someone is sitting in the red house. Small Town. Rita Dove. GT

Someone is walking through the snow. Hearing Steps. Charles Simic. HCAP

Someone Knocks. Peter Everwine. NNaP

Someone later may hear these playthings, thinking. Strato [or Straton]. GrAn

Someone like No One Else. Forugh Farrokhzad. WPOW, tr. by Deirdre Lashgari

Someone lives in a cave. Anne Sexton. BodElec Fr. Furies, The.

Someone lives in the old house. Visting Malacca. Shirley Lim. FSt

Someone might live. Dark Spaces: Thoughts on All Souls Day. John Knoepfle. IllVoic

Someone might think that because New Jersey is a relatively easy concept. Dinner in the Sun. Donald Berger. NAPBL

Someone [or Some One]. Walter De la Mare. MoBrPo

Someone passes. Murasaki Shikibu. BoWoP; OHPJ

Someone runs about. Bullfight. Miroslav Holub. RB, tr. by Ian Milner and Jarmila Milner

Someone's absence you. Sofia. John Seed. Oth

Someone's Been Sending Me Flowers. Sheldon Harnick. ReLy

Someone's licked a finger, touched it to the mirror. Ghazal on signs of Love and Occupation. Philip Salom. BMAP

Someone's lifeless body lies in the street. Corpse, The. Jagannath Prasad Das. OMIP, tr. by Jayanta Mahapatra

Someone's newspaper. Jack Cain. HA

Someone's old parents in the desert on folding chairs. Giants. Jane Miller. ExTi

Someone said dead men make islands in the sea. Fishermen, Drowned beyond the West Coast. Vivian Smith. CBAP

Someone said, "Our right hand is in the book. But the left has the / privilege of opening and closing." Book, The. Edmond Jabès. AF, tr. by Rosmarie Waldrop

Someone sits in a mountain gorge. Han-shan. GifTon, tr. by Red Pine

Someone, somewhere, is always starting trouble. Beware. Kenneth Fearing. APT-2

Someone sows someone. Vasco [or Vasko] Popa. PoSu Fr. Games.

Someone spoke of your death, Herakleitos. It brought me. Callimachus. GrAn

Someone stirs above me. Night Flute, The. Beryle Williams. MiVo

Someone Talking to Himself. Richard Wilbur. HarvBoo

Someone that I belong to. Prisoner of Love. Clarence Gaskill. ReLy

Someone throws stones at my roof, then. Revenge. Amado Nervo. TCLAP, tr. by Sue Standing

Someone to Watch over Me. George Gershwin. ReLy

Someone told me. Patrizia Cavalli. NeIt

Someone told me, Heracleitus. Callimachus. HePo Fr. Epigrams.

Someone was searching for a Form of Fire. Create Desire. Karen Volkman. KGB; NAPBL

Someone was writing this incredibly personal poem. Santa Monica. Charlie Smith. KGB

Someone who well knew how she'd toss her chin. Loose Woman. X. J. Kennedy. WeW-3

Someone, whose morals need mending. Time's Betrayal. Herman Melville. NCAP

Someone will consider something you do prolific. Estrella's Prophecies #47. David Baratier. AmPoNex

Someone will reap you like a field. To One Loved Wholly within Wisdom. Genevieve Taggard. APT-2

Someone Will Take the Ball. Nelly Sachs. BBASP, tr. by Matthew Mead and Ruth Mead

Someone would like to have you for her child. Lullaby. Unknown. TTTS; WoPoe, tr. by Kwabenia Nketia

Someone writes kike on. Being Jewish in a Small Town. Lyn Lifshin. UnSA

Someone yelled come home, but we were dancing in the night. (LL) Jungle Music. Warren Woessner. MiVo; SwNoth

Somer is comen and winter gon. Unknown. MiEL

Somer is comen with love to toune. Unknown. MiEL

Something. (LL) Jackson Mac Low. FTOS; PFTM-2; PmAP Fr. Pronouns, The—A Collection of 40 Dances—For the Dancers.

Something. Design. Mary Oliver. PoCoUp

Something, The. Charles Simic. BAP-97

Something about Being an Indian. Adrian C. Louis. UnSA

Something about Silence. Elizabeth Hincks. EMWP

Something about the idea. Abandonment of Autos. Bruce Dawe. CBAP

Something about You. Jessica Tarahata Hagedorn. PmAP

Something better forgotten. (LL) Ki no Tsurayuki. OHPJ; WoPoe, tr. by Kenneth Rexroth

Something / cold is in the air. Anne Sexton. BodElec Fr. Furies, The.

Something Cool. Billy Barnes. ReLy

Something cracks every moment because. Brief Thoughts on Cracks. Miroslav Holub. PoSu, tr. by Ian Milner and Jarmila Milner

Something drained our blood and it wasn't the leeches. Anorexia. Peter Hollenbeck. CDa

Something easy for Ultra Black nationalists. Kenneth Carroll. SpirFl

Something Else. Paul Muldoon. ModIr

Something familiar / Something peculiar. Comedy Tonight. Stephen Sondheim. ReLy

Something for Easter. Robert Creeley. InvLad

Something for her lips. Oh dare, oh share. Something. Bernice Got Next to Isis. Leslie Simon. FFC

Something for My Russian Friends. Edmund Wilson. OBAL

Something for Supper. Carroll Arnett. VoR

Something forgotten for twenty years: though my fathers. Map of the Western Part of the County of Essex in England, A. Denise Levertov. CoAP; NAAL-2v2

Something forgotten twenty years: though my fathers. Denise Levertov. See Something forgotten for twenty years: though my fathers

Something Goes By. May Swenson. BodElec

Something hangs in back of me. Wings, The. Denise Levertov. APSN; NALW

Something has ceased to come along with me. Death of a Son. Jon Silkin. GTBS-P; OxBTC

Something has happened to me. Kofi Awoonor. HBAPE

Something has happened to my name. Catalogue Army. Naomi Shihab Nye. ReTh

Something has reached out and taken in the beams of my eyes. All I Was Doing Was Breathing. Mirabai [or Mira Bai]. WoPoe, tr. by Robert Bly

Something I'm Not. Liz Lochhead. NePenScot

Something I saw or thought I saw. On the Heart's Beginning to Cloud the Mind. Robert Frost. GM

Something immense and lonely. Foreboding. John Haines. CoAmPo

Something in the letter found in the box, and something just out there. Meditation Brought About by George Bogin's Translation of Jules Supervielle's Poem "The Sea." Michael Burkard. BodElec

Something / in the way these alleys twist and. Reggae Cat (for Boston Jack). Kendel Hippolyte. WaCA

Something in their psyche insists on Elvis. Them and Us. Lucille Clifton. AllShUp

Something inspires the only cow of late. Cow in Apple Time, The. Robert Frost. MoAmPo; OxBSP

Something is bound to happen yet to my head. Thin Wire. Leo Vroman. TuT, tr. by Desmond Egan

Something is going to go, baby. Cyril Connolly. OBCoV Fr. Where Engels Fears to Tread.

Something is happening. Dear Jesse Helms. Lucille Clifton. GifTon

Something is in the line and air along edges. Mountains. Alice Oswald. MFPA

Something is pushing against my blood. Posthumous. Michael O'Loughlin. PBCIP

Something is taking its course. Harvest of War. Catherine Obianuju Acholonu. HAWP; NAfrP

Something Like a Sonnet for Phillis Miracle Wheatley. June Jordan. NIL-7

Something like volcanic ash wafted in air. Cabbage Butterfly, The. Henri Cole. UrbNat

Something must be done right away. Song for Those Who Know. Hans Magnus Enzensberger. PoSu; VCWP, tr. by Hans Magnus Enzensberger and Michael Hamburger

Something occurred after the operation. Surgical Ward: Men. Robert Graves. FaBoMo

Something of a Departure. Paul Muldoon. PBCIP

Something of glass about her, of dead water. Circe. Louis MacNeice. OBMV

Something old and tyrannical burning there. Coal Fire in Winter, A. Thomas McGrath. ErotSp; GifTon; RaBo

Something Old, Something New.   Carl H. Greene.   NBV

Something or Other.   Ron Padgett.   FTOS

Something out of it, I think. (LL)   Best, The.   Elizabeth Barrett Browning. OxBEV; OxBSP

Something removed roars in the ears of this house.   Missing the Sea.   Derek Walcott.   OxBEV

Something's Gotta Give.   Johnny Mercer.   ReLy

Something's there, by Pan there's something hidden—.   Callimachus.   GrAn

Something said: You have nothing to fear.   Heard by a Girl.   Louise Bogan. APT-2

Something stands here to peril our advance.   Thomas Hardy.   FaBoWar   *Fr.* Dynasts, Part 2, The.

Something Starting Over.   Thomas Hornsby Ferril.   APT-2

Something startles me where I thought I was safest.   This Compost.   Walt Whitman.   AWP; MoAmPo; NAAL-2v1; NAAL-3; PFTM-1

Something strange happened yesterday.   After-Word.   Ras Baraka.   InTrad

Something strange I do not comprehend.   Literature: The God, Its Ritual. Merrill Moore.   FuPo

Something There.   Samuel Beckett.   OxBEV

Something there is that doesn't love a wall.   Mending Wall.   Robert Frost. APT-1; BRP; ChAP; ClHu; HAP; HarvBoo; HeIP-4; ITBLP; MoAmPo; NAAL-2v2; NAAL-5; NOBA; NoAM; NoP-4; OxBA; PAI; PoE; PoPoPo; SAmP; SCV; SoSe-8; TAP; TCAPo; TFi; VGW; WeW-3

Something they said beside me.   At the Cafe Door.   Constantine P. Cavafy. CAGL, *tr. by* Edmund Keeley and Philip Sherrard

Something this foggy day, a something which.   Christina Georgina Rossetti. NAEL-5v2; NAEL-6v2   *Fr.* Later Life: A Double Sonnet of Sonnets.

Something to be tinkered with at their leisure. (LL)   Talk.   Roo Borson.   NIP-4; NOBC

Something to Live For.   Billy Strayhorn.   ReLy

Something to Remember You By.   Arthur Schwartz.   ReLy

Something to Say.   Betsy Sholl.   ExTi

Something to talk about. (LL)   Admonition to Myself, An.   Chao Meng-fu. CoBLCP; WoPoe, *tr. by* Jonathan Chaves

Something told the wild geese.   Rachel Lyman Field.   ChAP; NTCP; OBCA; OxIBACP

Something uncertain moves.   Again.   Lenard D. Moore.   GT

Something went crabwise.   Presence, The.   Maxine W. Kumin.   WPE

Something you said—I found it written down.   Postcard to Send to Sumer, A. William Bronk.   VGW

Something you won't ever bring pressure to bear on.   James Sutherland-Smith. NewEx

Sometime a while back it seemed real clear to me.   Just Word Wranglin'   John Nelson.   GeoH

Sometime during eternity / some guys show up.   Sometime During Eternity. Lawrence Ferlinghetti.   NoAM

   (Some guys show up.)   NoP-4

Sometime during the night there are three mushrooms which are the.   Moon Poem.   Max Jacob.   AF, *tr. by* Michael Brownstein

Sometime I fled the fire that me brent.   Sir Thomas Wyatt.   NoSic

Sometime in the night I stir, rain.   Loft.   Michael Dransfield.   CBAP

Sometime the world seems sad and lonely.   Lonely World.   Mrs. Henry Linden.   CBWP-4

Sometimes.   Jan Eijkelboom.   TuT, *tr. by* Peter Van de Kamp

Sometimes.   Maggie Pogue Johnson.   CBWP-4

Sometimes.   Woman, 2.   Jyotsna Milan.   OMIP, *tr. by* Mrinal Pande

Sometimes.   Lilian Moore.   TLR

Sometimes.   Sheenagh Pugh.   OPOU; TCAWP

Sometimes a button. Sometimes a rat. (LL)   Residue.   Carlos Drummond de Andrade.   PoetW; VCWP, *tr. by* Mark Strand

Sometimes a crumb falls.   Luck.   Langston Hughes.   APT-2; SAmP

Sometimes a lantern moves along the night.   Lantern Out of Doors, The. Gerard Manley Hopkins.   SacPr; TrCP

Sometimes a light surprizes.   William Cowper.   NOCV   *Fr.* Olney Hymns.

Sometimes a Man Stands Up During Supper.   Rainer Maria Rilke.   BBASP; RaBo, *tr. by* Robert Bly

Sometimes a mesh of ideas.   Dennis Brutus.   HBAPE

Sometimes / A night funeral.   Dead in There.   Langston Hughes.   APSN

Sometimes a word will start it, like.   Variant.   John Ashbery.   BodElec

Sometimes alone at night.   Vanderdecken.   Douglas Livingstone.   PeSAV

Sometimes an effluence rises.   Scarcely.   Alfonso Reyes.   TCLAP, *tr. by* Samuel Beckett

Sometimes and always, with mixed feelings? (LL)   At North Farm.   John Ashbery.   ColAP; HCAP; HarvBoo; PoE

Sometimes, as a Child.   Olga Broumas.   YaYoPo

Sometimes, as young things will, she vexes me.   Augusta Davies Webster. ViWPN   *Fr.* Mother and Daughter.

Sometimes at night, when I sit and write.   In the Night.   Ella Wheeler Wilcox. SWaP

Sometimes at night when the heart stumbles and stops.   Caesura.   Kenneth Mackenzie.   CBAP; NOBAu

Sometimes before great events a person will try.   Things That Happen. William Stafford.   NNaP

Sometimes by night I don't know why.   Anne Carson.   BodElec   *Fr.* Truth About God, The.

Sometimes, childishly watching a beetle, thrush or trout.   Clarence Mangan. Thomas Kinsella.   CIP-2

Sometimes colored tears play.   George Grosz.   Else Lasker-Schüler.   PFTM-1

Sometimes Damocles is less afraid that the sword may drop.   Comic Look at Damocles, A.   Bill Knott.   BodElec

Sometimes, Doctor, I awake.   Dario Villa.   ItPo, *tr. by* Gayle Ridinger

Sometimes Even Parents Win.   John Ciardi.   NOxBChV

Sometimes, everywhere I look.   Kabir.   ErotSp, *tr. by* Sam Hamill

Sometimes Feel.   Pearse Hutchinson.   ModIr

Sometimes God will drop a fit on you.   Anne Carson.   BodElec   *Fr.* Truth About God, The.

Sometimes grown-ups forget you're down there.   Battered Toddler, Page B6. Ellen Watson.   OPRER

Sometimes he steps out with the class.   Some Biographical Data.   Cees Buddingh'   TuT, *tr. by* Mary E. O'Donnell

Sometimes he walked to occupy / his feet.   Generations 2.   Sam Cornish.   GT

Sometimes he will break.   I, the Neighbor Mr. Uskovich, Watch Every Morning Kenji Takezo Hold His Breath.   Rick Noguchi.   NeAmPo

Sometimes I am so lonely the phone.   Phone Sex.   Richard Tayson.   WiU

Sometimes I call X nostalgia.   Little Ode for X.   Maura Stanton.   IllVoic

Sometimes I catch a glimpse of it.   Presence, The.   Dana Naone.   CDW

Sometimes I do despatch my heart.   "Michael Field."   VWP

Sometimes I dress, with women sit.   Matthew Green.   ECEV; NPeEn; OBCoV   *Fr.* Spleen, The.

Sometimes I feel discouraged, and think my work's in vain.   There Is a Balm in Gilead.   *Unknown.*   TCAPo

Sometimes I feel like a motherless child.   *Unknown.*   APN-2

Sometimes I feel like I will never stop.   To Satch.   Samuel Allen.   ISC; MoASP; PAI; TTY

Sometimes I feel like my money's gone to Heaven.   Product of Evolution, I Invest in a Mutual Fund, A.   Amanda Pecor.   BodElec

Sometimes I get up at daybreak, thirsty.   Murmur.   Adelia Prado.   TANSG, *tr. by* Ellen Watson

Sometimes / I go about pitying myself.   Song of the Thunders.   *Unknown.* OBVE, *tr. by* Frances Densmore

Sometimes I Go about Pitying Myself.   *Unknown.*   RaBo; WoPoe, *tr. by* Robert Bly and Frances Densmore

Sometimes I Go to Camarillo and Sit in the Lounge.   K. Curtis Lyle.   NBV

Sometimes I go to the pornos.   No God.   Dennis Cooper.   PmAP

Sometimes I have wanted.   Coat.   Vicki Feaver.   LW

Sometimes I hear haunted mouths.   Few Picnics in Illinois, A.   Maura Stanton. IllVoic

Sometimes I know the way.   Absence.   Charlotte Mew.   MoBrPo

Sometimes I lie in wait.   Full face.   Andrée Chedid.   PoArWo, *tr. by* Lucy McNair

Sometimes I look at the needle.   Joy Williams.   IBA

Sometimes I'm Happy.   Irving Caesar.   ReLy

Sometimes I'm happy: la la la la la la la.   Joy Sonnet in a Random Universe. Helen Chasin.   NIL-7

Sometimes I must smell that sulphur pit.   Sometimes.   Jan Eijkelboom.   TuT, *tr. by* Peter Van de Kamp

Sometimes I pause and sadly think.   It Might Have Been Worse.   G. J. Russell. PoToHe

Sometimes I plunge into the ocean.   Heberto Padilla.   AF, *tr. by* Alastair Reid

Sometimes I recall how, in the early eighteen-eighties.   Stars in Sand.   Francis Carey Slater.   PeSAV

Sometimes I remember you, little Ruth.   Little Ruth.   Yehuda Amichai [*or* Amikhai].   VCWP, *tr. by* Benjamin Harshav

Sometimes I sauntered from my lone abode.   *Unknown.*   CAGL   *Fr.* Don Leon.

Sometimes I see churches.   Winter Walking.   Alfred Wellington Purdy. NoAM

Sometimes I see my spirit, swiftly unsheathed.   Saddhu of Couva, The.   Derek Walcott.   BodElec

Sometimes I sit in the balcony.   Symphony from the Balcony.   Jared Angira. NAfrP

Sometimes I stare into an awning of spirit.   Sometimes I Go to Camarillo and Sit in the Lounge.   K. Curtis Lyle.   NBV

Sometimes I stop on the street afraid.   Materialism.   Lőrinc Szabó.   IQMS, *tr. by* Laurence James

Sometimes I think of its bright cramped spaces.   Dancing at Oakmead Road. Maura Dooley.   NeBl

Sometimes I think that nothing. Small-scale Reflections on a Great House. A. K. Ramanujan. OxBC

Sometimes I think you're. Everything You Own. Gerald Costanzo. GifTon

Sometimes I walk where the deep water dips. Frederick Goddard Tuckerman. APN-2; NOBA Fr. Sonnets.

Sometimes I watch the moon at night. Moon and a Cloud, The. William Henry Davies. RB

Sometimes I wish that I his pillow were. Richard Barnfield [or Barnefield]. PBRV Fr. Cynthia, with Certain[e] Sonnets.

Sometimes I wish that I were Helen-fair. Poem. Lesbia Harford. NOBAu

Sometimes in early June I am standing. It Arrives Suddenly and Carries Us Off As Usual. Marge Piercy. PasH

Sometimes in summer months, the gestate earth. Summer Idyll. George Barker. FaBoMo

Sometimes in the dark I fear trampling. Fear of Subways. Maureen Seaton. FFC

Sometimes in the evening when love. Sometimes Mysteriously. Luis Omar Salinas. GeoHom

Sometimes in the over-heated house, but not for long. Fame. Charlotte Mew. BrRo; HarvBoo; InPK-6; NPeEn; VWP

Sometimes it frightens me. Coincidence. Aida Gelbtrunk. MirDau, tr. by Roberta Gordenstein

Sometimes it's difficult, isn't it, not to grow grim and rancorous. Necessary Dirge, A. Ogden Nash. APT-2

Sometimes it's salt. Getting to Know Her. Jacqueline Berger. AmPoNex

Sometimes it's the flagrant accentuation. Jazz as Was. Al Young. ESEAA

Sometimes it seems almost beyond belief. Whirling Round the Sun. Suzanne Noguere. FFC

Sometimes love comes. Phenomenon, A. Job Degenaar. TuT, tr. by Aidan Sharkey

Sometimes memory fails: meanings get forgotten. Earlobe. Leonid Andreievich Zavalnyuk [or Zaval'niuk]. TCRP, tr. by Albert C. Todd

Sometimes Mysteriously. Luis Omar Salinas. GeoHom

Sometimes / on windless nights. After the Vietnam War. Steven Ford Brown. CDa

Sometimes pus / Sometimes a poem. Ibn Gabirol. Yehuda Amichai [or Amikhai]. AF, tr. by Assia Gutmann

Sometimes, riding in a car, in Wisconsin. Three Kinds of Pleasures. Robert Bly. AiP

Sometimes she climbed. Old Stone Age. Frances Angela. Prnts

Sometimes she is a child within mine arms. Dante Gabriel Rossetti. Son Fr. House of Life, The.

Sometimes she is like sherry, like the sun through a vessel of glass. Polarities. Kenneth Slessor. CBAP

Sometimes, she remembers, a chipped flint. Imago. Amy Clampitt. VCAP

Sometimes still in my deepest sleep. Vietnam Dream. Ron Carter. CDa

Sometimes the Mind. Jane Mead. NAPBL

Sometimes the moon. Homage to Robert Johnson. David St. John. SwNoth

Sometimes the mountain. Witness. Denise Levertov. BLT

Sometimes the night echoes to prideless wailing. John Berryman. NoAM Fr. Sonnets to Chris.

Sometimes the rapid-fire channel switching is like eye music. Grazing. Ira Sadoff. BodElec

Sometimes the weather goes on for days. Mystery of Emily Dickinson, The. Marvin Bell. InvLad

Sometimes the words are so close I am. Julia Alvarez. FFC Fr. ("33").

Sometimes there are airs grave and gentle. Limerick. Unknown. PeLi

Sometimes there has been enough writing. Pickup. Paul Allen. ReTh

Sometimes there is steam in the apartment. Celebration of Home Birth: November 15th, 1981, A. Sandra Maria Esteves. PueRic

Sometimes they cross an avenue at dusk. Survivors. Frank Ormsby. CIP-2

Sometimes, they open a new highway, and let it roll, open wide. Etel Adnan. GraLe Fr. Journey to Mount Tamalipais.

Sometimes, they save people from drowning in the river. Angels of Juárez, Mexico, The. Ray Gonzalez. TouFir

Sometimes they thought he might be only shewn. John Milton. PeECV Fr. Paradise Regained [or Regain'd].

Sometimes things don't go, after all. Sometimes. Sheenagh Pugh. OPOU; TCAWP

Sometimes to think about age. Age. Rae Desmond Jones. CBAP

Sometimes too personal, sun, you. Sun. John Blight. BMAP

Sometimes up out of this land. Bi-Focal. William Stafford. RB

Sometimes waking, sometimes sleeping. Nestus Gurley. Randall Jarrell. HeIP-4; TwCP

Sometimes walking late at night. Butcher Shop. Charles Simic. AF; InPK-6; LCAP; NNaP

Sometimes we collide, tectonic plates merging. Implications of One Plus One. Marge Piercy. PasH

Sometimes we get up. Resurrection. Marie Luise Kaschnitz. WPOW, tr. by Michael Hamburger

Sometimes we go our way carefree. Rebirth. Margaret E. Bruner. PoToHe

Sometimes we sit in Phil's. My Care. Peter Fallon. CIP-2

Sometimes when. Each Happiness Ringed by Lions. Jane Hirshfield. ExTi

Sometimes when alone. Outcast[, The]. "Æ" OxBSP

Sometimes when clouds float. At the Edge of Town. William Stafford. NNaP

Sometimes when I feel bad. If You Were the Only Girl in the World. Clifford Grey. ReLy

Sometimes when I feel hurried or dismayed. For One Who Is Serene. Margaret E. Bruner. PoToHe

Sometimes when I have dropped to sleep. Room beneath the Rafters, The. Ella Wheeler Wilcox. PWR

Sometimes when I hold. School Globe, The. James Reaney. NOBC

Sometimes when I'm lonely. Hope. Langston Hughes. OBAL; OBCA; OxIBACP; TRP

Sometimes When It Rains. Gcina Mhlophe. HAWP; NAfrP

Sometimes when my eyes are red. My Sad Self. Allen Ginsberg. UnPo; VCAP

Sometimes When Night. Victoria Mary Sackville-West. WPE

Sometimes (/ when the night air feels chevere). Oye Mundo/Sometimes. Jesús Papoleto Meléndez. UnSA

Sometimes, when winding slow by brook and bower. Sonnets: First Series. Frederick Goddard Tuckerman. NCAP

Sometimes, when you're away from home. Away from Home. Unknown. PWR

Sometimes, when you're called a bastard. When Something Happens. James A., Jr. Randall. BPo; SSLK

Sometimes while I sleep. Edwin Honig. NoAM Fr. To Restore a Dead Child.

Sometimes with One I Love. Walt Whitman. APN-1; OxBSP; SAmP

Sometimes you almost get a punch in. Shadowboxing. James Tate. MoASP

Sometimes you appear in the swampy twilight. Meeting. László Kálnoky. IQMS, tr. by Kenneth McRobbie and Zita McRobbie

Sometimes you can hear the naked will. Death on Columbus Day. James Tate. YaYoPo

Sometimes / you feel / like / a / bottle. No Deposit. Earle Thompson. HATNAP

Sometimes, you give way to sickness. Igor Vladimirovich Chinnov. TCRP

Sometimes you hear, fifth-hand. Philip Larkin. HeIP-4; OxBC; PoE; TwCP

Sometimes your writing is a lush web of fine thoughts. Lu Chi. WoPoe, tr. by Tony Barnstone and Chou Ping Fr. Art of Writing, The.

Somewhat back from the village street. Old Clock on the Stairs, The. Henry Wadsworth Longfellow. PWR; TreFP

Somewhat more splendid in dress, in a waistcoat work of a lady. Arthur Hugh Clough. FaBoVe Fr. Bothie of Tober-na-Vuolich, The [A Long-Vacation Pastoral].

Somewhere. Sir Edwin Arnold. PoToHe

Somewhere. Robert Creeley. NoAM

Somewhere. Sneeze, A. So Chong-Ju. VCWP, tr. by David R. McCann

Somewhere. Stephen Sondheim. ReLy

Somewhere, a cup tinkles in its saucer. English Earthquake, The. Eva Salzman. MFPA

Somewhere a forest, every. These Leaves. William Stafford. NNaP

Somewhere / a niche. Wish. Lance Henson. CDW

Somewhere afield here something lies. Shelley's Skylark. Thomas Hardy. CABP

Somewhere behind me. Foster Jewell. HA

Somewhere beneath that piano's superb sleek black. Piano, The. D. H. Lawrence. WeW-3

Somewhere between a bird's nest and a solar system whom did. Station (4). James Galvin. GifTon

Somewhere between Amazing Grace. Death of Chet Baker, The. Miller Williams. SeSe

Somewhere between faith and grace there is the footprint of logic lost. Before. Khaled Mattawa. NeAmPo

Somewhere deep in the San Joaquin Valley. Orchard of Figs in the Fall, An. Diana García. TouFir

Somewhere does the sky bend into itself. Show Me a Rose. John Godfrey. FTOS

Somewhere his number must have been betrayed. Common Man, The. Arthur James Marshall Smith. NOBC

Somewhere i have never travelled, gladly beyond. E. E. Cummings. BoLoP; MoAmPo; NAAL-2v2; NAAL-5; NoP-4; TwCP; VGW

Somewhere I read that high and loe notes. Comfort. Maura Stanton. SoSe-8

Somewhere, I think in Dakota. Sound from the Earth, A. William Stafford. NNaP

Somewhere in a field near Magadan. Nikolai Alekseievich Zabolotsky [*or* Zabolotskii*]. TCRP

Somewhere in Africa. Anne Sexton. NALW

Somewhere—in desolate wind-swept space. Identity. Thomas Bailey Aldrich. TCAPo

Somewhere in everyone's head something points toward home. Shrinking Lonesome Sestina, The. Miller Williams. MakPoe

Somewhere in his body a blood-clot is moving. Little Death. Gwyn Thomas. OBWVE, *tr. by* Joseph P. Clancy

Somewhere in Mauriac a girl. Frank Templeton Prince. PeSAV   *Fr.* Memoirs in Oxford.

Somewhere / in the light above the womb. My Grandfather Walks in the Woods. Marilyn Nelson Waniek. ESEAA

Somewhere in the Midwest. Crabapples. Michael Van Walleghen. IllVoic

Somewhere in the mountains. Puerto Rico Made in Japan. Jose Angel Figueroa. PueRic

Somewhere in the next block. Early Sunday Morning. John A. Stone. PoSol

Somewhere in the world my tree stands, for I know that every person. Mail. Sarah Kirsch. AF, *tr. by* Wayne Kvam

Somewhere inside me. Coming Back Home. Ray A. Young Bear. CDW

Somewhere is the software to ID all. Save As: Salvation. Bill Knott. BodElec

Somewhere it being yesterday. Song of Mary, A. Lucille Clifton. NALW

Somewhere Near Phu Bai. Yusef Komunyakaa. CDa

Somewhere now she takes off the dress I am putting. Palindrome. Lisel Mueller. WeW-3

Somewhere nowhere in Utah, a boy by the roadside. Utah. Anne Stevenson. FaBoVe

Somewhere on his travels the strange Child. Santa Claus. Howard Nemerov. HAP

Somewhere on the other side of this wide night. Words, Wide Night. Carol Ann Duffy. NePenScot

Somewhere or Other. Christina Georgina Rossetti. FaBoVe; NOBE; NOBVV; OxBEV

Somewhere out there the sea has shrugged its shoulders. Severn Bore. Catherine Fisher. AngWePo; TCAWP

Somewhere outside your window. Sense of Coolness, A. Quincy Troupe. GT

Somewhere someone is traveling furiously toward you. At North Farm. John Ashbery. ColAP; HCAP; HarvBoo; PoE

Somewhere, sometime, in an April twilight. Willa Sibert Cather. WPE

Somewhere, somewhere it is so. (LL) But for Lust. Ruth Pitter. FaBoTw; NPeEn; OxBTC

Somewhere the deer lies on the ground, I think; I walk about. Hunter's Song. *Unknown.* APN-2, *tr. by* Albert S. Gatschet

Somewhere there has to be. Other Half of Me, The. Stan Freeman. ReLy

Somewhere there is Grace, Lord. Latter Day Psalms. Cliff Ashby. NOCV

Somewhere There's a Man. Roberto Juarroz. TCLAP, *tr. by* W. S. Merwin

Somewhere there's music. How High the Moon. Nancy Hamilton. ReLy

Somewhere under sand. Primitive Place. Mildred Weston. FFC

Somewhere you are always going home. Sums, The. Lauris Edmond. FaBoWP

Somnambulist. Adele Ne Jame. PoArWo

Somnambulist Ballad. Federico García Lorca. SpanPo, *tr. by* Robert O'Brien

Somnolence of star-stones, ice-tears, The. Laurentia. Medbh McGuckian. BiHa

Somnolent through landscapes and by trees. Permanent Tourists, The. Patricia K. Page. NOBC

Somnus, the humble god, that dwells. Song, A. Sir John Denham. BeJo

Somonour was ther with us in that place, A. Geoffrey Chaucer. OBCoV   *Fr.* Canterbury Tales, The.

Somtyme the pryde of mye assured trothe. Argument, The. Sir Thomas Wyatt. SacPr

Somtyme this world was so stedfast and stable. Lak of Stedfastnesse. Geoffrey Chaucer. AWP; MiEL

Son. Pavel Grigoryevich Antokolsky.
    "We are not always dependent on memory." TCRusP, *tr. by* Bob Perelman and Shirley Rihner
    "You must dig in black ashes a long time." TCRusP, *tr. by* Bob Perelman and Shirley Rihner
    "You share your mourning with all Moscow. There." TCRusP, *tr. by* Bob Perelman and Shirley Rihner

Son, A. Rudyard Kipling. FaBoEE; NPeEn; PeFWW   *Fr.* Epitaphs of the War [1914–18].

Son, The. John Donne. NOCV   *Fr.* Litany, A.

Son, The. Denise Levertov. NALW

Son, The. Frederic Ridgely Torrence. TCAPo

Son, The. Jones Very. NCAP

Son'ahchi. Boy and the Deer, The. Andrew Peynetsa. STP, *tr. by* Dennis Tedlock

Son, come tell me 'bout the meetin. Old and the New, The. Clara Ann Thompson. CBWP-2

Son David. *Unknown.* OxBB; OxBS

Son-Days [dayes]. Henry Vaughan. AngWePo; GeHe; NOSC

Son et Lumière. Mark Todd. GeoH

Son, I am going: the morning. Mitayo, The. Manuel González Prada. SpanPo, *tr. by* Kate Flores

Son, my son! Lament of a Man for His Son. *Unknown.* AWP, *tr. by* Mary Austin

Son of a mystic race, he came. Heinrich Heine. Ludwig Lewisohn. TrJP

Son of Enops, Thestor next he smote, The. Homer. OBVE, *tr. by* William Cowper   *Fr.* Iliad, The.

Son, of great fortune have I none. Christine to Her Son. Christine de Pisan. BoWoP, *tr. by* Barbara Howes

Son of the Bone Speaks, The. Roger Gilbert-Lecomte. PFTM-1

Son of the ocean isle! England's Dead. Felicia Dorothea Hemans. NAEL-6v2; NoP-4

Son of the Romanovs, A. Louis Simpson. OxBC

Son replied, "For all your good advice," The. To His Father on Praising the Honest Life of the Peasant. Parvin E'tesami. WPOW, *tr. by* Deirdre Lashgari

Son's a poor, wretched, unfortunate creature, The. James Henry. NPeEn

Son singin. Imamu Amiri Baraka. FTOS   *Fr.* Why's/Wise.

Son who came forth on a winter's morning. Song for Te Hauapu. Noho-mai-te-Rangi. PeNZ, *tr. by* Margaret Orbell

Sonata. John Fuller. DiPo

Sonata. Alvaro Mutis. TCLAP, *tr. by* Sophie Cabot Black and Maria Negroni

Sonatina. "Rubén Dario." TCLAP, *tr. by* Lysander Kemp

Sonatina. "Rubén Dario." SpanPo, *tr. by* John Crow

Sonatina in Yellow. Donald Justice. ColAP; LCAP-2

Sonet. Mark Alexander Boyd. *See* Fra Bank to Bank, Fra Wood to Wood I Rin

Sonet: "Fra bank [*or* banc] to bank [*or* banc], fra wood [*or* wod] to wood [*or* wod] I rin." Mark Alexander Boyd. *See* Fra Bank to Bank, Fra Wood to Wood I Rin

Sonet. In Orknay. William Fowler. *See* In Orknay

Sonet: "Thocht Polibus, pisander, and with them." Alexander Montgomerie. NePenScot

Sonet to Sleepe. William Drummond, of Hawthornden. *See* Sleep, Silence' Child

Sonet written in prayse of the brown beautie, A. George Gascoigne. PBRV

Sonetos del Amor Oscuro [Sonnets of Dark Love]. Federico García Lorca.
    "Ah secret voice of dark love! Ah bleating without wool! Ah wound! Ah prick of gall, sunken camellia!" CAGL, *tr. by* David William Foster
    "Did you like the city the water wrought drop by drop in the center of the pines?" CAGL, *tr. by* David William Foster
    "I am afraid of losing the marvel of your eyes of a statue, and the accent the solitary rose of your breath lays on my cheek at night." CAGL, *tr. by* David William Foster
    "I want to cry my pain and I am telling you so you will love me and cry for me in a nightfall of nightingales with a dagger, with kisses and with you." CAGL, *tr. by* David William Foster
    "Love of my heart, living death, I await in vain your written word and I think with the dying flower, that if I live without myself I want to lose you." CAGL, *tr. by* David William Foster
    Night of Sleepless Love. CAGL, *tr. by* David William Foster
    Poet Asks His Love about the Enchanted City of Cuenca, The. CAGL, *tr. by* David William Foster
    Poet Asks His Love to Write to Him, The. CAGL, *tr. by* David William Foster
    Poet Speaks the Truth, The. CAGL, *tr. by* David William Foster
    Poet Speaks with Love by Telephone, The. CAGL, *tr. by* David William Foster
    Sonnet of Sweet Weeping. CAGL, *tr. by* David William Foster

Sonetto XXXV: To Guido Orlando. Guido Cavalcanti. CTC, *tr. by* Ezra Pound

Song. Thomas Lovell Beddoes. *See* Death's Jest Book

Song. Aphra Behn. *See* On Her Loving Two Equally

Song. William Blake. *See* How Sweet I Roamed [*or* Roam'd] from Field to Field

Song. Anne Brontë. PEW

Song. Emily Jane Brontë. FaBoCh; NPeEn; OxBSP

Song. Robert Browning. *See* Pippa Passes

Song. Robert Burns. *See* Ae Fond Kiss

Song. Robert Burns. BoLoP; NOBRP; PeLV

    (Corn Rigs Are Bonnie.) OxBS

Song. Byron. *See* Maid of Athens, Ere We Part

Song. Thomas Carew. *See* To My Inconstant Mistress [*or* Mistris]

Song. John Clare. *See* Secret Love

Song. Hartley Coleridge. OxAEP-2

Song. Anne Collins. PEW

Song. William Congreve. *See* False Though She Be

Song. William Congreve. *See* Pious Selinda [*or* Celinda]

Song. Robert Creeley. FTOS

Song. George Darley. *See* Song: "Sweet in her green dell the flower of beauty slumbers."

Song. Thomas Dekker. NOSC

Song. Dryden. *See* Song: "SYLVIA the fair, in the bloom of fifteen."

One Happy Moment. Dryden. OBEV

Song. Cornelius Eady. ESEAA; GT

Song. Ebenezer Elliott. *See* Song: "When working blackguards come to blows."

Song: "Do not fear to put thy feet." John Fletcher. *See* Faithful Shepherdess, The

Song. Kath Fraser. LW

Song. Oliver Goldsmith. AWP; BoLoP; FHYEP; NOBE; NOEC; OxAEP-1 *Fr.* Vicar of Wakefield, The.

Clerimont's Song. Ben Jonson. BASC; NOSC; PoE *Fr.* Epicoene; or, The Silent Woman.

Song. Ben Jonson. OxBSP *Fr.* Epicoene; or, The Silent Woman.

Song. Ben Jonson. *See* Gypsies Metamorphosed, The

To Celia. Ben Jonson. *See* Volpone

Song. Letitia [*or* Laetitia] Elizabeth Landon. VWP

Song. Alun Lewis. *See* Song (On Seeing Dead Bodies Floating Off the Cape)

Song: To Amarantha, That She Would Dishevel Her Hair. Richard Lovelace. *See* To Amarantha, That She Would Dishevel[l] Her Hair[e]

Song. Richard Lovelace. *See* To Amarantha, That She Would Dishevel[l] Her Hair[e]

Song: To Lucasta, Going beyond the Seas. Richard Lovelace. *See* To Lucasta, [on] Going beyond the Seas

Song. Richard Lovelace. *See* To Lucasta, [on] Going beyond the Seas

Song: The Scrutiny. Richard Lovelace. *See* Scrutiny [*or* Scrutinie], The

Song. Richard Lovelace. *See* Scrutiny [*or* Scrutinie], The

Song. George Macdonald. NePenScot

Song. Philip Massinger. OxAEP-1

Song. John Milton. PBRV

(And welcom thee, and wish thee long.) (LL) PBRV

(Now the bright morning Star, Dayes harbinger.) PBRV

Song. John Milton. *See* Comus; a Masque Presented at Ludlow Castle

Song. Gabriela Mistral. WPoS, *tr. by* Langston Hughes

Song. Matthew Prior. *See* Ode, An: "Merchant, to secure his treasure, The."

Song. Sir Walter Scott. *See* Marmion

Rover's Adieu [*or* Farewell], The. Sir Walter Scott. NOBE; OBEV

Song. Sir Walter Scott. EnLoPo

Song. William Shakespeare. *See* As You Like It

Song. William Shakespeare. *See* Cymbeline

Song. William Shakespeare. *See* Merchant of Venice, The

Song. James Shirley. BeJo

Song. Primus St. John. GT

Song. Tennyson. GTBS-P; HeIP-4; OBGa

Song. Tennyson. *See* Maud [A Monodrama]

Song. Tennyson. OPOU *Fr.* Princess, The.

Song. Anne Wharton. EMWP; LW

Song. William Wordsworth. *See* Lucy

Song, A. George Darley. *See* It Is Not Beauty I Demand

Song, A. Edward Dorn. CoAmPo

Song, A. Richard Duke. BoLoP; ECEV

Song, A. George Farquhar. NOSC

Song, A. Laetitia Pilkington. PEW

Song, A. Shelley. *See* Charles the First

Song, The. George Herbert. *See* Easter

Song, The. Balakrishna Sama. PoetW

Song 2: "All night I weep[e], all day I cry, Ay me[e]." Mary Sidney Wroth, Countess of Montgomery. NOSC *Fr.* Pamphilia to Amphilanthus.

Song 3: "Surrounded by the gentle sound." Baldomero Garcilaso de la Vega. SpanPo, *tr. by* Frances Fletcher

Song 4: "Sweetest love return[e] again[e]." Mary Sidney Wroth, Countess of Montgomery. NAEL-6v1; NAEL-7v1 *Fr.* Pamphilia to Amphilanthus.

Song 9. Harry Gilonis. Oth

Song XI: "Lay your sleeping head, my love." W. H. Auden. *See* Lullaby: "Lay your sleeping head, my love."

Song, [A]: "Ask[e] me no more where Jove bestow[e]s." Thomas Carew. AWP; BASC; BeJo; CaPo; CavPo; ClHu; EnLoPo; HAP; MeLP; NAEL-

5v1; NAEL-6v1; NAEL-7v1; NOBE; NOSC; NoP-4; OBEV; OxBEV; PAI; PoE; PoRA; SCGP; TFi

(Aske me no more whither doe stray.) NPeEn

Song, A: "Farewell my Betty, and farewell my Annie." Christian Carstairs. ECWP

Song, A: "For mercy, courage, kindness, mirth." Laurence Binyon. MoBrPo

Song, A: "In the north there is a lovely woman." Li Yen-nien. ColAnChi, *tr. by* Anne Birrell

Song, A: "Lying is an occupation." Laetitia Pilkington. PEW; WPE

Song, A: "Men of England." Shelley. *See* Song to the Men of England

Song, A: "Morpheus, the humble god, that dwells." Sir John Denham. NOSC

Song, A: "Music, thou queen of souls, get up and string." Thomas Randolph. OxBSP

Song, A: "My head on moss reclining." *Unknown.* NOEC

Song, A: "No riches from his scanty store." Helen Maria Williams. WoRP

Song, A: "Nymph in vain bestows her pains, The." Anne Finch, Countess of Winchilsea. OxBSP

Song, A: "O close of night, I would have you linger." "Adonis" [*or* "Adunis"]. MAP, *tr. by* John Heath-Stubbs and Lena Jayyusi

Song, A: On His Mistress. Sir Robert Aytoun [*or* Ayton]. NOSC

Song, a poem of itself—the word itself a dirge, A. Yonnondio. Walt Whitman. NAAL-2v1; NAAL-3

Song, A: "Slaves to London, I'll deceive you." Peter Anthony Motteux. NOSC

Song, A: "Somnus, the humble god, that dwells." Sir John Denham. BeJo

Song, A: "Song of grass, A, / A song of earth." "Yehoash." TrJP, *tr. by* Isidore Goldstick

Song, A: "Strephon, your breach of faith and trust." Laetitia Pilkington. LW

Song, A: "What torments must the virgin prove." Charlotte Lennox. ECWP

Song, A: "While a thousand fine projects are planned ev'ry day." *Unknown.* NOEC

Song, A: "World is young today, The." Digby Mackworth Dolben. NOBVV

Song about a Dead Person—or Was It a Mole?, A. *Unknown.* STP, *tr. by* Richard Johnny John and Jerome Rothenberg

Song About Benedek Virág. Dezső Kosztolányi. IQMS, *tr. by* Watson Kirkconnell

Song about Kőrösi Csoma. Gyula Juhász. IQMS, *tr. by* Watson Kirkconnell

Song about Major Eatherly, A. John Wain. OxBTC

Song about Myself, A. John Keats.

Song: "Absent from thee, I languish still." John Wilmot, 2d Earl of Rochester. BoLoP; EnLoPo; NPeEn; OxBEV

(Return.) NOBE; OBEV

Song: "After the eating, the drinking, the singing." Liu Yung. CrYelRi, *tr. by* Sam Hamill

Song: "Afternoon cooking in the fall sun." Robert Hass. LoL

Song against Grocers, The. Gilbert Keith Chesterton. OBCoV

Song: "Age is when to a man." Samuel Beckett. BIrV; ModIr *Fr.* Words and Music.

Song: "Ah, Dangerous Swain, tell me no more." Mary De La Rivíere Manley. LW

Song: "Ah false Amyntas, can that hour." Aphra Behn. WPE *Fr.* Dutch Lover, The.

Song: "Ah, vale of woe, of gloom and darkness moulded." Rachel [*or* Rahel] Morpurgo. TrJP, *tr. by* Nina Davis Salaman

Song: "All, all of a piece throughout." Dryden. *See* Secular Masque, The

Song: "All joy to mortals, joy and mirth." Aphra Behn. WPE *Fr.* Emperor of the Moon.

Song: "All roocoogirls." Hans Andreus. TuT, *tr. by* Peter Van de Kamp

Song: "Among the clamor the single shout." Blanca Wiethüchter. TANSG, *tr. by* Shaun Griffin and Emma Sepúlveda-Pulvirenti

Song and Musick, Set by Mr. Eccles, and Sung by Mrs. Leveridge. Delariviere Manley. EMWP

Song and Poetry. *Unknown.* OBWVE, *tr. by* Gwyn Jones

Song: "April, April, / Laugh thy girlish laughter." Sir William Watson. OBEV

Song: "As F———at her Toliet sat." Margaret, Lady Godolphin. EMWP

Song: "As I walked out one evening." W. H. Auden. *See* As I Walked Out One Evening

Song as Yet Unsung, A. "Yehoash." TrJP, *tr. by* Isidore Goldstick

Song at Graveside. Ewald von Kleist. GePo, *tr. by* George C. Schoolfield

Song at midnight. Lucille Clifton. ErotSp; UnSA

Song at Night. Norman Nicholson. FaBoTw

Song: "At night on my bed I longed for." Bible, *O.T.* WPoS *Fr.* Song of Solomon.

Song at the African Middle Class. Molara Ogundipe-Leslie. HBAPE; PBMAP

Song at the Beginning of Autumn. Elizabeth Jennings. OxBTC

Song: "At the center of the earth." *Unknown.* STP, *tr. by* Jerome Rothenberg

Song at the End of a Meal. John Hollander. TaR

Song: "Balkis was in her marble town." Lascelles Abercrombie. MoBrPo *Fr.* Judith.

Song: "Balmy comforts that are fled, The." Anne Batten Cristall. RWP

Song: "Because I know deep in my own heart." Pauli Murray. BlSi

Song: "Because spring brings miserable green and painful red." Liu Yung. CrYelRi, *tr. by* Sam Hamill

Song: "Before the barn-door crowing." John Gay. OxBSP *Fr.* Begger's Opera.

Song: "Beloved, it is morn!" Emily Hickey. SacPr

Song Bewailing the Time of Christmas, So Much Decayed in England, A. *Unknown.* NoP-4

Song: "Boat is chafing at our long delay, The." John Davidson. OBEV

Song Books. John Cage.
Solo for Voice 17 Song with Electronics (Relevant). PFTM-2

Song: "Both gloomy and dark was the shadowy night." Anne Batten Cristall. RWP

Song: Boundless Space. Sándor Weöres. WoPoe, *tr. by* William Jay Smith

Song by a Woman Accused of Adultery. Kie Tapu. PeNZ, *tr. by* Margaret Orbell

Song: "By all love's soft, yet mighty powers." John Wilmot, 2d Earl of Rochester. BASC

Song by Isbrand. Thomas Lovell Beddoes. NOBVV; OxBEV *Fr.* Death's Jest Book.

Song: "By the rushy-fringèd bank." John Milton. OxBEV *Fr.* Comus; a Masque Presented at Ludlow Castle.

Song by the Shore, A. Richard Hovey. APN-2

Song: "By vulgar Eros long misled." Sarah Ponsonby. PoBW

Song: "Can love be controlled by advice?" John Gay. OxBSP *Fr.* Begger's Opera.

Song. Celia singing. Thomas Carew. NPeEn
(Harke how my Celia, with the choyce.) NPeEn

Song: "Chestnuts shine through the cloven rind, The." Thomas Bailey Aldrich. TreFP

Song: "Chloris, forbear a while." Henry Bold. NOSC

Song: "Chloris, it is not thy disdaine." Sidney Godolphin. MeLP

Song Circle of Jacky. Mudrooroo Narogin. IBA

Song: "Clawed green-eyed." Lenrie Peters. PBMAP

Song: "Come, let us dance and sing." Anne Batten Cristall. RWP

Song: "Come, live with me and be my love." Cecil Day Lewis. BoLoP; NIP-4; OBMV *Fr.* Two Songs.

Song: "Come, my beloved." Bible, *O.T.* WPoS *Fr.* Song of Solomon, The.

Song Composed in Time of the Civill Warr, when the Wicked Did Much Insult over the Godly, A. Anne Collins. EMWP

Song: "Curse upon that faithless maid, A." Aphra Behn. WPE *Fr.* Emperor of the Moon.

Song Cycle of Jacky, The. Mudrooroo Narogin.
Song Thirty-Four. BMAP

Song Cycle of the Moon-Bone. *Unknown.* NOBAu, *tr. by* Ronald M. Berndt

Song: "Day will rise and the sun from eastward." George Campbell Hay. OxBS

Song: "Dearest [*or* Deerest] if I by my deserving." Mary Sidney Wroth, Countess of Montgomery. EMWP *Fr.* Pamphilia to Amphilanthus.

Song: "Deftly, admiral, cast your fly." W. H. Auden. GTBS-P *Fr.* Five Songs.

Song: "Did you see me walking by the Buick Repairs?" Frank O'Hara. TTTS

Song: "Distil not poison in mine ears." John Hall. OxBSP

Song: "Does the policeman sleep with his boots on." Gerda Mayer. PeLV

Song: "Donought would have everything." Ebenezer Elliott. NOBVV

Song: "Dorinda's sparkling wit, and eyes." Charles Sackville, 6th Earl of Dorset. *See* On the Countess of Dorchester

Song: "Drinke and be merry, merry, merry boyes." Thomas Morton. SCAP

Song: Endimion Porter and Olivia. Sir William Davenant [*or* D'Avenant]. *See* Endimion Porter and Olivia

Song: Eternity of Love Protested. Thomas Carew. *See* Eternity of Love Protested

Song: "Eve descends with radiant streaks, The." Anne Batten Cristall. RWP

Song: "Fair Chloris in a pigsty lay." John Wilmot, 2d Earl of Rochester. NOSC

Song: "Fair Iris I love, and hourly I die." Dryden. AWP *Fr.* Amphitryon.

Song: "Fairest things are those which live, The." Mary Russell Mitford. NOBRP

Song: "Feathers of the willow, The." Richard Watson Dixon. FaBoCh; GTBS-P; NOBE
(Willow.) OBEV

Song: "Flowers that in thy garden rise, The." Sir Henry John Newbolt. FaBoTw

Song: "Fool, take up thy shaft again." Thomas Stanley. EnLoPo

Song: "Foolish eyes, thy streams give over." Martha Sansom. ECWP

Song for a Birth or a Death. Elizabeth Jennings. EBEV; HarvBoo

Song for a Dance. Francis Beaumont. FaBoCh *Fr.* Masque of the Inner Temple and Gray's Inne, The.

Song for a Dancer. Kenneth Rexroth. TAP

Song for a Dark Girl. Langston Hughes. NAAAL; NAAL-2v2; NAAL-5; NoP-4; SAmP

Song for a Fallen Warrior. *Unknown.* APN-2, *tr. by* John Mason Browne

Song for a Forgotten Shrine to Pan. John Chipman Farrar. YaYoPo

Song for a Girl. Dryden. ErotSp

Song for a Girl on Her First Menstruation. *Unknown.* BoWoP, *tr. by* Joe Prentuo

Song for a Jewess. Iwan [*or* Yvan] Goll. TrJP, *tr. by* Joseph T. Shipley

Song for a Scalp Dance. *Unknown.* STP, *tr. by* Jerome Rothenberg

Song for a Seed. Violeta Parra. TANSG, *tr. by* Bonnie Shepard

Song: For A' That and A' That. Robert Burns. *See* For A' That and A' That ["Is there, for honest poverty"]

Song for a Thin Sister. Audre Lorde. OxWW

Song for a Young General. Tu Fu. CrYelRi, *tr. by* Sam Hamill

Song for a Young Girl's Puberty Ceremony. *Unknown.* ChAP; ItWoWo, *tr. by* Frances Densmore

Song for All Seas, All Ships. Walt Whitman. APN-1

Song for Annie. Harry Gilonis. Oth

Song for "Buvez les Vins du Postillion"—Advt. Jean Garrigue. TAP

Song for February, A. Thomas Given. FaBoVe

Song for Fine Weather. *Unknown.* AWP, *tr. by* Constance Lindsay Skinner *Fr.* Three Songs from the Haida.

Song for Gwydion. Ronald Stuart Thomas. HarvBoo

Song for Healing. Roberta Hill Whiteman. CDW

Song: "For her gait, if she be walking." William Browne (1591–1643). OBEV
(Sonnet.) NOSC

Song for Ilva Mackay and Mongane. Keorapetse Kgositsile. PBMAP

Song for Ishtar. Denise Levertov. NALW; NoAM; PoM

Song for Joseph. *Unknown.* PeNZ, *tr. by* Margaret Orbell

Song for My Lover. Rafael Campo.
Medical Student Learns Love and Death, A. WiU
Our Country of Origin. WiU

Song for My Shadow, A. Kim Pyŏngyŏn. WoPoe, *tr. by* Richard John Lynn

Song for Occupations, A. Walt Whitman.
"Will you seek afar off? you surely come back at last." ChIV-1

Song for Past Midnight. Geoffrey Lehmann. CBAP

Song for Ranelagh. William Whitehead. ECEV

Song for St Cecilia's Day, 1687, A. Dryden. AWP; BASC; FHYEP; FaBoTw; GTBS-P; HAP; NAEL-6v1; NAEL-7v1; NOSC; OBEV; OxAEP-1; SCGP; TFi; TreFP; WoPoe
"Trumpet's loud clangor, The." FaBoWar

Song/for Sanna. Olga Broumas. PoBW

Song for September. Robert Fitzgerald. VGW

Song for Simeon, A. T. S. Eliot. ChIV-2; NOCV
(Lord, the Roman hyacinths are blooming in bowls.) GI

Song for Smooth Waters. Haida. CA

Song for St. Cecilia's Day. W. H. Auden. FaBoTw; TwCP

Song for Straphangers. George Buchanan. PNI

Song for Te Hauapu. Noho-mai-te-Rangi. PeNZ, *tr. by* Margaret Orbell

Song for the Cattle. David Campbell. NOBAu

Song for the Clatter-Bones. Frederick Robert Higgins. ChIV-1; OBMV

Song for the Dead, III. *Unknown.* TTY, *tr. by* Frances S. Herskovits

Song for the Head. George Peele. RB *Fr.* Old Wives' [*or* Wife's] Tale, The.

Song for the Heroes. Alex Comfort. MoBrPo

Song for "The Jacquerie." Sidney Lanier. NCAP

Song for the Last Act. Louise Bogan. NoP-4; UnPo; WPE

Song for the Lost Private. Bruce Weigl. CDa

Song for the Middle of the Night, A. James Wright (1927–80). WeW-3

Song for the Moon. Nazik Al-Mala'ika. BBASP; MAP, *tr. by* Christopher Middleton and Matthew Sorenson

Song for the Music in the Warsaw Ghetto. Jacqueline Osherow. TaR

Song for the Newborn. *Unknown.* WPE, *tr. by* Mary Austin

Song for the Rainy Season. Elizabeth Bishop. APT-2

Song for the Richest Woman in Wrangell. Guxnawu. STP, *tr. by* James Koller

Song for the Single Table on New Year's Day, A. Elizabeth Frances Amherst. ECWP

Song for the Spirit of Natalie Going. Susan Wheeler. ExTi

Song for the Squeeze-Box. Theodore Roethke. NBLV

Song for the Sugar Cane. Virgil Suárez. AmPoNex

Song for the Sun That Disappeared behind the Rainclouds. *Hottentot Oral Tradition.* TTTS; TTY, *tr. by* Ulli Beier

Song for the Sun That Disappeared behind the Rainclouds. *Unknown.* ChAP

Song for the unsung heroes who rose in the country's need, A.   Unsung Heroes, The.   Paul Laurence Dunbar.   BPo; CBCWP

Song for the Workers, A.   Eliza Cook.   VWP

Song for the Year's End, A.   Louis Zukofsky.   TaR

Song for Those Who Know.   Hans Magnus Enzensberger.   PoSu; VCWP, tr. by Hans Magnus Enzensberger and Michael Hamburger

Song for Unbound Hair.   Genevieve Taggard.   PoRA

Song for Wei City, A.   Wang Wei.   TAL

Song Form.   Imamu Amiri Baraka.   ChAP; TTTS

Song: "Fresh from the dewy hill, the merry year."   William Blake.   PeECV

Song from Armenia, A.   Geoffrey Hill.   FaBoMo

Song from "Chartivel."   Marie de France.   AWP; EnLoPo; WPOW   Fr. Chartivel.

Song from Mardi.   Herman Melville.   APN-2

Song from Shakespeare's Cymbeline, A.   William Collins.   See Fidele, A

Song from the Bride of Smithfield.   Sylvia Townsend Warner.   MoBrPo

Song from the Coptic, A.   Goethe.   NOIV; WoPoe, tr. by James Clarence Mangan

Song from The Indian Emperor.   Dryden.   NoP-4

Song from the Occupation Time.   Ion Caraion.   AF, tr. by Marguerite Dorian

Song from the Waters.   Thomas Lovell Beddoes.   NOBE   Fr. Death's Jest Book.

Song from Troilus and Cressida.   Dryden.   NoP-4

Song: "Give Isaac the nymph who no beauty can boast."   Richard Brinsley Sheridan.   NOIV   Fr. Duenna, The.

Song: "Give me leave to rail at you."   John Wilmot, 2d Earl of Rochester.   NOSC

Song gives birth to. . . The woman with white hair.   Song of Ancient Ways, The.   William Oandasan.   HATNAP

Song: "Go and catch a falling star."   John Donne.   AWP; ClHu; EBEV; FHYEP; FSCP; HAP; HeIP-4; InPK-6; NAEL-5v1; NAEL-6v1; NAEL-7v1; NAWM-5v1; NIL-7; NIP-4; NOBE; NOSC; NoP-4; NoSic; OBEV; OxAEP-1; PoE; SoSe-8; TFi; WoPoe

(Goe and catche a falling starre.)   ESCV; MeLP; NBLV; OxBEV

Song: "Go[e], lovely rose."   Edmund Waller.   AWP; BASC; BeJo; BoLoP; CABP; CTC; ClHu; EnLoPo; GTBS-P; HAP; HeIP-4; InPK-6; NAEL-5v1; NAEL-6v1; NAEL-7v1; NIL-7; NOBE; NOSC; NPeEn; NoP-4; OBEV; OxAEP-1; OxBEV; PBRV; PoE; PoPoPo; PoRA; SoSe-8; TFi; UnPo; WeW-3; WoPoe

Song: "Goe turne away those Cruell Eyes."   Barbara Syms.   EMWP

Song: Good Counsel to a Young Maid.   Thomas Carew.   CaPo

(Gaze not on thy beauty's pride.)   CavPo

(Good Counsel to a Young Maid.)   CavPo

(Perpetual blush to thine, A.) (LL)   CavPo

Song: Green Grow the Rashes.   Robert Burns.   See Green Grow the Rashes [A Fragment]

Song: Green Water, Singing Girl.   Li Ho.   CrYelRi, tr. by Sam Hamill

Song: "Hang sorrow, cast away care."   Unknown.   NOSC

Song: "Hark! hark! the lark at heaven's gate sings."   William Shakespeare.   NOSC   Fr. Cymbeline.

Song: "Hast thou seen the down i' th' air."   Sir John Suckling.   See Song to a Lute, A

Song: "Heap cassia, sandal-buds and stripes."   Robert Browning.   OBEV   Fr. Paracelsus.

Song: "Hear me, ye smokeless skies and grass-green earth."   Charles Mair.   NOBC   Fr. Last Bison, The.

Song: "Hears not my Phillis how the birds."   Sir Charles Sedley.   EnLoPo

Song: "Here's to the maiden [or maid] of bashful fifteen."   Richard Brinsley Sheridan.   See School for Scandal, The

Song: "Hold back thy hours, dark night, till we have done."   Francis Beaumont.   OxBSP   Fr. Maid's Tragedy, The.

Song: "How many times do I love thee, dear?"   Thomas Lovell Beddoes.   NAEL-6v2   Fr. Torrismond.

Song: "I am dark, daughters of Jerusalem."   Bible, O.T.   WPoS   Fr. Song of Solomon, The.

Song: "I am weaving a song of waters."   Gwendolyn B. Bennett.   BlSi

Song: "I carouse all night."   Cho-yong.   WoPoe, tr. by Okhee Yoo and Michael Stephens

Song: "I chuck my Bible in the parlour fire."   Peter Redgrove.   EmeKit

Song: "I feed a flame within, which so torments me."   Dryden.   AWP   Fr. Secret Love; or, The Maiden Queen.

Song: "I have heard the silvery note."   Sándor Kisfaludy.   IQMS, tr. by Anthony Edkins

Song: "I have so little sorrow."   Patricia Jones.   ISC

Song: "I keep running around."   Unknown.   STP, tr. by Jerome Rothenberg

Song: "I know that any weed can tell."   Louis Ginsberg.   TrJP

Song: "I led my Silvia to a grove."   Aphra Behn.   BASC

Song: "I'm about to go shopping."   James Schuyler.   TTTS

Song: "I'm living in a cave."   Unknown.   STP, tr. by Jerome Rothenberg

Song: "I made another garden, yea."   Arthur William Edgar O'Shaughnessy.   OBEV

Song: "I make my shroud but no one knows."   Adelaide Crapsey.   APT-1

Song: "I peeled bits of straw and I got switches too."   John Clare.   NAEL-5v2; NAEL-6v2

Song: "I placed my dream in a boat."   Cecília Meireles.   WPOW, tr. by Eloah F. Giacomelli

Song: "I prithee let my heart alone."   Thomas Stanley.   BeJo

Song: "I prithee spare me, gentle boy."   Sir John Suckling.   BeJo; CavPo

Song I sing of my sea adventure, A.   Unknown.   AnOE tr. by Charles W. Kennedy   Fr. Seafarer, The.

Song I sing of sorrow unceasing, A.   Unknown.   See I make this song about me full sadly

Song I sing of sorrow unceasing, A.   Wife's Lament, The.   Unknown.   AnOE

Song: I Want a Witness.   Michael S. Harper.   LTA

Song: "I was asleep but my heart stayed awake."   Bible, O.T.   WPoS

Song: "I was so chill, and overworn, and sad."   Anna Wickham.   MoBrPo

Song: "I watered my horse at the Long Wall caves."   Susan Ch'en Lin.   CoBCP; ColAnChi, tr. by Burton Watson

Song: "I went my Sunday mornings round."   John Clare.   NOBVV

Song: "If any wench Venus's girdle wear."   John Gay.   PeLV   Fr. Begger's Opera.

Song: "If everywhere in the street."   Denis Glover.   PeNZ   Fr. Sings Harry.

Song: "If I freely may discover."   Ben Jonson.   BeJo   Fr. Poetaster, The.

Song: "If I were tortur'd with greensickness."   Elizabeth Polwhele.   EMWP

Song: "If she be not as kind as fair."   William Walsh.   NOSC

Song: "If the scorn of your bright eyne."   William Shakespeare.   CTC   Fr. As You Like It.

Song: "If thou art sleeping, maiden."   Gil Vicente.   AWP; CTC, tr. by Henry Wadsworth Longfellow

Song: "If to your ear it wonder bring."   Ben Jonson.   OxBEV   Fr. Key Keeper, The.

Song: "In a maiden-time professed."   Thomas Middleton.   OxBSP   Fr. Witch, The.

Song in August.   Badr Shakir Al-Sayyab.   MAP, tr. by Lena Jayyusi and Christopher Middleton

Song in Making of the Arrows, The.   John Lyly.   See Sapho and Phao

Song: "In mine one [or own] monument I lie [or lye]."   Richard Lovelace.   OxBSP

Song in Passing, A.   Yvor Winters.   CRP; VGW

Song in Praise of a Favourite Humming-Top, A.   Hone Tuwhare.   PeNZ

Song in Sligo.   Jean Garrigue.   APT-2

Song in Spite of Myself.   Countee Cullen.   ISC

Song in the Blood.   Jacques Prévert.   AF, tr. by Lawrence Ferlinghetti

Song in the Front Yard, A.   Gwendolyn Brooks.   ESEAA; NAAAL; NAAL-2v2; NOBA; NOxBChV; NoAM   Fr. Street in Bronzeville, A.

Song: "In the middle of the sea."   Unknown.   STP, tr. by Jerome Rothenberg

Song in the Symbol, The.   Grandfather Koori.   IBA

Song in the valley of Nemea, A.   Nemea.   Lawrence Durrell.   FaBoTw; GTBS-P

Song in the Wood.   John Fletcher.   NOSC   Fr. Little French Lawyer, The.

Song in Time of Plague.   Thomas Nashe [or Nash].   See Summer's Last Will and Testament

Song Inscribed on an Earthenware Vessel.   Unknown.   WoPoe, tr. by John L. Foster

Song Is Ended (But the Melody Lingers On), The.   Irving Berlin.   ReLy

Song is gone; the dance, The.   Bora Ring.   Judith Wright.   NoAM

Song is in the air.   You and the Night and the Music.   Arthur Schwartz.   ReLy

Song Is You, The.   Jerome Kern.   ReLy

Song: "Isle!/ Island of the syllables of flame!"   Jacques Rabémanganjara.   NegPo, tr. by Ellen Conroy Kennedy

Song: "It is not now I learn."   Louise Bogan.   APT-2

Song: "It's the wine, this ache, this longing."   Liu Yung.   CrYelRi, tr. by Sam Hamill

Song: "Jog on, jog on, the footpath way."   William Shakespeare.   See Winter's Tale, The

Song: "Keep the dream alive and growing always."   Edwin Rolfe.   TrJP

Song: "Kind lovers, love on."   John Crowne.   OxBSP   Fr. Calisto.

Song: "Know what I'll promise you?"   Unknown.   STP, tr. by Jerome Rothenberg

Song: "Ladies, though to your conquering eyes."   Sir George Etherege.   OxBSP   Fr. Comical Revenge, The.

Song: "Lark now leaves his wat'ry [or watery] nest, The."   Sir William Davenant [or D'Avenant].   See Lark Now Leaves His Watery [or Wat'ry] Nest

Song: "Leave this gaudy gilded stage."   John Wilmot, 2d Earl of Rochester.   OxBSP

Song: "Let it be forgotten, as a flower is forgotten."   Sara Teasdale.   MoAmPo; TCAPo

Song: "Let not the sluggish sleep." William Byrd. OxBSP; SacPr

Song: "Let school-masters puzzle their brain." Oliver Goldsmith. BIrV; NOIV *Fr.* She Stoops to Conquer.

Song: Lift-Boy. Robert Graves. OxAEP-2

Song: "Linnet in the rocky dells, The." Emily Jane Brontë. HAP; RACG (Linnet in the rocky dells, The.) VWP (My Lady's Grave.) OxAEP-2

Song: "Listen: there was a goat's head hanging by ropes in a tree." Brigit Pegeen Kelly. ExTi; IllVoic *Fr.* Southern Review, The.

Song: Little Black Rose, The. Aubrey Thomas De Vere. BIrV

Song: "Little onion lay by the fireplace, A." Nicholas Moore. SPE

Song: "Longing, I watch out the open window." Tzu Yeh. CrYelRi, *tr. by* Sam Hamill

Song: "Lord, when the sense of Thy sweet grace." Richard Crashaw. InvLi (Ecstacy, An.) OxAEP-1

Song: "Love a child is ever crying [*or* criing]." Mary Sidney Wroth, Countess of Montgomery. BASC; LW; NAEL-6v1; NAEL-7v1; NOSC; NoP-4; OxBEV *Fr.* Pamphilia to Amphilanthus.

Song: "Love a woman? You're [*or* Y'are] an ass." John Wilmot, 2d Earl of Rochester. NBLV; NOBL; NOSC; PeLV; WoPoe

Song: Love Armed [*or* Arm'd]. Aphra Behn. BASC; NALW; NOBE; NOSC; NPeEn; NoP-4; OBEV; OxAEP-1; OxBEV; PEW; WPE; WeW-3 *Fr.* Abdelazer.

Song: "Love is a green girl." Michael Stillman. TLR

Song: Love Lives Beyond the Tomb. John Clare. *See* Loves Lives Beyond the Tomb

Song: "Love, love today, my dear." Charlotte Mew. MoBrPo

Song: "Love still has something of the sea." Sir Charles Sedley. NOBE; OxAEP-1; OxBEV

Song: "Love that is hoarded, moulds at last." Harold C. Sandall. PoToHe

Song: "Love what art thou? A vain thought." Mary Sidney Wroth, Countess of Montgomery. NAEL-5v1; NAEL-6v1; NAEL-7v1; NoP-4 *Fr.* Urania.

Song: "Lovely hill-torrents are." Walter James Turner. MoBrPo

Song: "Lovers in ladies' magazines." Thomas McGrath. VGW

Song-Maker. Anita Endrezze. HATNAP

Song-Maker, The. Anna Wickham. MoBrPo

Song: "Man's a poor deluded bubble." Robert Dodsley. OxBSP

Song: Mary Morison. Robert Burns. *See* Mary Morison

Song: "Master, the swabber, the boatswain and I, The." William Shakespeare. NOBL; OxBSP *Fr.* Tempest, The.

Song: "Memory, hither come." William Blake. NAEL-5v2; NAEL-6v2

Song: "Might have known it." *Unknown.* STP, *tr. by* Jerome Rothenberg

Song: Miss Penelope Burgess, Balling the Jack. Thomas McGrath. MiVo

Song: "Mist rauk is hanging, The." John Clare. NOBVV

Song: Montrose. Charles Cotton. NOSC

Song: "Moth's kiss, first, The!" Robert Browning. BoLoP; OBEV *Fr.* In a Gondola.

Song: "Mother Mother shave me." *Unknown.* BoWoP, *tr. by* Ulli Beier

Song My. Susan Griffin. WPOW

Song: "My cabinets are oyster-shells." Margaret Lucas Cavendish, Duchess of Newcastle. WPE

Song: "My heart is like the failing hearth." Letitia [*or* Laetitia] Elizabeth Landon. NOBRP *Fr.* Golden Violet, The.

Song: "My heart, my dove, my snail, my sail, my." Cynthia Zarin. NIL-7; NoP-4

Song: "My silks and fine array." William Blake. RACG; SCGP

Song: "My straying thoughts, reduced stay." Anne Collins. WPE

Song: "Neath blue-bell or streamer." Edgar Allan Poe. OxBA *Fr.* Al Aaraaf.

Song: "Never take her away." Vinícius de Moraes. WoPoe, *tr. by* Richard Wilbur

Song No. 2: "I say. all you young girls waiting to live." Sonia Sanchez. FFC

Song No. 3: "Cain't nobody tell me any different." Sonia Sanchez. FFC; NOxBChV

Song: "No, no, fair heretic[k], it needs must be." Sir John Suckling. BeJo; CaPo *Fr.* Aglaura.

Song: "No use to aim that sextant now." Reuel Denney. YaYoPo

Song: "Noe more unto my thoughts appeare." Sidney Godolphin. MeLP

Song: "Nothing ades to Loves fond fire." Elizabeth Wilmot, Countess of Rochester. EMWP; LW

Song: "Now and then there will arise." *Unknown.* OBVE, *tr. by* Frances Densmore

Song: "Now that Fate is dead and gone." Dame Edith Sitwell. MoBrPo

Song: "Now the moon is rising." Antonio Machado Ruiz. SpanPo, *tr. by* Kate Flores

Song: "Now this bloody war is over." George Barker. PeLV

Song: "Nymphs and Shepherds dance no more." John Milton. OxBEV *Fr.* Arcades.

Song: "O lovely April, rich and bright." Gustave Kahn. TrJP, *tr. by* Ludwig Lewisohn

Song: "O my love's [*or* luve's *or* love is *or* luve is] like a red, red rose." Robert Burns. GTBS-P (My luve [*or* love] is like a red, red rose.) OxBEV; UV (Oh, My Love Is Like a Red, Red Rose.) InPK-6 (Red, Red Rose, A.) AWP; BoLoP; ChAP; HAP; HeIP-4; ITBLP; NAEL-5v2; NAEL-6v2; NIL-7; NIP-4; NOBE; NOBRP; NOEC; NPeEn; NePenScot; NoP-4; OBEV; OxAEP-2; OxBEV; OxBS; PAI; PoPoPo; SCGP; TFi; UV

Song: "O're [*or* O'er] the smooth enamel'd [*or* enameled *or* enamelled] green." John Milton. OBEV; OxBSP *Fr.* Arcades.

Song: "O ruddier than the cherry." John Gay. *See* Acis and Galatea

Song: "O sing into my roundelay." Thomas Chatterton. *See* Aella; a Tragycal Enterlude

Song: "O sweet, sad, singing river." Henrietta Cordelia Ray. CBWP-3

Song of a Common Lover. Flavien Ranaivo. TTY, *tr. by* Alan Ryder (Don't love me, my dear.) PBMAP

Song of a Dream Journey over the Vast Sea. Yang Wei-chen. CoBLCP, *tr. by* Jonathan Chaves

Song of a Dream Visit to T'ien-mu: Farewell to Those I Leave Behind. Li Po. CoBCP, *tr. by* Burton Watson

Song of a Farmer. P'i Jih-hsiu. SuSp, *tr. by* William H. Nienhauser

Song of a Hungarian Jacobin. Endre Ady. IQMS, *tr. by* Sir Maurice Bowra

Song of a Jewish Boy. "M. J." TrJP, *tr. by* A. Glanz-Leyeles

Song of a Man in the Dark. "Adonis" [*or* "Adunis"]. VCWP, *tr. by* Samuel Hazo

Song of a Man Who Has Come Through. D. H. Lawrence. FaBoMo; GTBS-P; HarvBoo; OxBTC; PeFWW; PoE; RaBo; TRP

Song of a Man Who Has Come Through. D. H. Lawrence. "Not I, not I, but the wind that blows through me!" FaBoMo; GTBS-P; OxBTC; PeFWW; PoE; RaBo; TRP

Song of a Marriageable Girl. *Unknown.* WoPoe, *tr. by* Willard Trask

Song of a Prisoner. Jack Spicer. APSN

Song of a Second April. Edna St. Vincent Millay. OxBA

Song of a Spirit. Ann Radcliffe. ECWP; RWP

Song of a Thousand Empty Hands. Adele Ne Jame. PoArWo

Song of a Traveller, The. Robert Louis Stevenson. EBVV; MoBrPo; OBEV

Song of a Woman Abandoned by the Tribe. *Unknown.* WPE, *tr. by* Mary Austin

Song of a Young Girl. Flavien Ranaivo. PBMAP

Song of a Young Lady to Her Ancient Lover, A. John Wilmot, 2d Earl of Rochester. BASC; BoLoP; EBEV; NOSC; NPeEn; NoP-4; OxAEP-1; OxBEV

Song of Absinthe Granny, The. Ruth Stone. NALW

Song of Ale, A. William Stevenson. *See* Gammer Gurton's Needle

Song of an Autumn Night. Chao Meng-fu. CoBLCP, *tr. by* Jonathan Chaves

Song of an Impossible Blue. "Porfirio Barba-Jacob." Song of the Fleeting Day. CAGL, *tr. by* Jeff Bingham and Juan Antonio Serna Servin

Song of an Old Gray Wolf. *Unknown.* APN-2, *tr. by* Alfred Kroeber

Song of Ancient Ways, The. William Oandasan. HATNAP

Song of Apollo. John Lyly. NoSic *Fr.* Midas.

Song of Apollo. Shelley. NAEL-5v2; NAEL-6v2

Song Of Arla, Written During Her Enthusiasm, A. Anne Batten Cristall. RWP

Song of Autumn I. Charles Baudelaire. NAWM-7v2, *tr. by* Carlyle Ferren MacIntyre and C. F. MacIntyre

Song of Autumn Night. Wang Ya. SuSp, *tr. by* Irving Y. Lo

Song of Battle. Bertrans [*or* Bertran *or* Bertrand] de Born. AWP, *tr. by* Ezra Pound (War Song, A.) FaBoWar

Song of Becoming. Fadwa Tuqan [*or* Tuquan]. AF, *tr. by* Naomi Shihab Nye

Song of Bekotsidi, The. *Unknown.* OBVE, *tr. by* Washington Matthews

Song of Bliss. Edmund Spenser. OBVE *Fr.* Faerie Queene, The.

Song of Blodeuwedd, The. *Unknown.* NoP-4; WoPoe, *tr. by* Robert Graves

Song of Blue and Red, A. Amir Gilbo'a. MHP, *tr. by* Ruth Finer Mintz

Song of Breath. Peire Vidal. AWP, *tr. by* Ezra Pound

Song of Bullets, The. Jessica Hagedorn. FSt

Song of Callicles, The. Matthew Arnold. GTBS-P; NOBE; OBEV *Fr.* Empedocles on Etna.

Song of canaries, The. Canary, The. Ogden Nash. PeLV

Song of Catching Tigers. Hsü Chung-hsing. "How brave the peasant who lives beside the lake." CoBLCP

Song of Cayetano's Circus, The. George Washington Cable. APN-2

Song Of Ch'ang-Kan (Yueh-Fu), The. Li Po. ChinPo, *tr. by* Yip Wai-lim

Song Of Chang Ching-Yüan Picking Lotus Flowers, A. Wen T'ing-yün. SuSp, *tr. by* William R. Schultz

Song of Chess, The. Abraham Ibn Ezra. TrJP, *tr. by* Nina Davis Salaman

Song of Chiang-nan. Tsung Ch'en.
  "On the spring river, you depart." CoBLCP
Song of Crede, The. *Unknown.* BIrV, *tr. by* Alfred Perceval Graves
Song of Cursive Calligraphy. Hsieh Chin. CoBLCP; ColAnChi, *tr. by*
  Jonathan Chaves
Song of Dachau. Jura Soyfer. AuPH, *tr. by* Lowell A. Bangerter
Song of Dalliance, A. William Cartwright. NOSC
Song of Deborah, The. Bible, *O.T.* AWP; BoWoP *Fr.* Judges.
Song of Degrees, A. Howard Nemerov. TaR
Song of Delight. Shao Yung. CoBCP, *tr. by* Burton Watson
Song of Derivations, A. Alice Thompson Meynell. CABP
Song of Devotion to the Forest. David Henderson. GT
Song of Diamond Eyes, The. Franco Buffoni. ItPo, *tr. by* Gayle Ridinger
Song of Distant Waters, A. Wen T'ing-yün. SuSp, *tr. by* William R. Schultz
Song of Dust, A. John Byrne Leicester Warren, 3d Baron De Tabley. EnLoPo
Song of Earth. Uri Zvi Greenberg. FIT, *tr. by* Robert Friend
Song of Ecstasy. Abu al-Qasim Al-Shabbi.
  "Cupbearer, take your wine away." MAP
Song of Emigration. Felicia Dorothea Hemans. VWP
Song of Emptiness to Fill up the Empty Pages Following, A. Michael
  Wigglesworth. SCAP
Song of Esechia, The. John Hall. ChIV-1
Song of Everlasting Sorrow. Po Chü-i. WoPoe, *tr. by* Dore J. Levy
Song of Exile. Antônio Gonçalves Dias.
  "There are palm trees in my homeland." TTY
Song of Expectancy. George Hitchcock. SPE
Song of Faith Forsworn, A. John Byrne Leicester Warren, 3d Baron De Tabley.
  PeVV
"Song of Farewell" in the Tartar Mode. Chang Yü. SuSp, *tr. by* Irving Y. Lo
Song of Finis, The. Walter De la Mare. MoBrPo
Song of Fionnuala, The. Thomas Moore. BIrV
Song of Fixed Accord. Wallace Stevens. SAmP
Song of grass, A, / A song of earth. Song, A. "Yehoash." TrJP, *tr. by* Isidore
  Goldstick
Song of "Hand-in-Hand", A. Ou-yang Hsiu. SuSp, *tr. by* Irving Y. Lo
Song of Hannah, The. Bible, *O.T. See* First Samuel
Song of Hate. Jacob ben David Frances. TrJP, *tr. by* A. B. Rhine
Song of Hate for Eels. Arthur Guiterman. OBAL
Song of Heavenly Ascent. Ts'ao Chih. SuSp, *tr. by* Ronald C. Miao
Song of Hiawatha, The. Henry Wadsworth Longfellow.
  Famine, The. TreFP
  Four Winds, The.
  Hiawatha's Departure.
    "Heavy with the heat and silence." APN-1
  Hiawatha's Fasting.
    "On the fourth day of his fasting." TCAPo
  Hiawatha's Wooing. EBNV
  Introduction: "Should you ask me, whence these stories?" ColAP; NOBA;
    PoE
  Picture-Writing. APN-1
  White Man's Foot, The.
    Hiawatha: The White Man's Foot. NCAP
Song of Home. Mida Huber. AuPH, *tr. by* Lowell A. Bangerter
Song of Honor [*or* Honour], The. Ralph Hodgson. MoBrPo
Song of Hsiang-yang. Li Po. SuSp, *tr. by* Joseph J. Lee
Song of Hungarrda, The. Ngunaitponi. NOBAu
Song of Igor's Campaign, The. *Unknown.*
  "And in the mountains of Kiev, Sviatoslav." WoPoe, *tr. by* Harry
    Strickhausen
Song of Instruction, A. Te Kooti Rikirangi. PeNZ, *tr. by* Margaret Orbell
Song of Job, A. Khalil Touma. MAP, *tr. by* Samuel Hazo and Lena Jayyusi
Song of Jonah in the Whale's Belly, The. Michael Drayton. ChIV-1
Song of Joys, A. Walt Whitman.
  "O the engineer's joys! to go with a locomotive!" HHAm
Song of Kai-hsia. Hsiang Chi. SuSp, *tr. by* Ronald C. Miao
Song of "Kornél Esti," The. Dezső Kosztolányi. IQMS, *tr. by* Adam Makkai
Song of Krishna: The Fourth Song, Sung with Raga "Ramakari." Jayadeva.
  WoPoe, *tr. by* Barbara Stoler Miller *Fr.* Gita Govinda, The.
Song of Kuk-ook, the Bad Boy, The. *Eskimo Oral Tradition.* TTTS
Song of Lament, A. Ts'ao Chih. SuSp, *tr. by* Hans H. Frankel
Song of Lasting Regret, The. Po Chü-i. ColAnChi, *tr. by* Paul W. Kroll
Song of Lawino. Okot P'Bitek.
  Woman with Whom I Share My Husband, The. PoetW
Song of Lazarus, The. Alex Comfort.
  Notes for My Son. MoBrPo
Song of Lewes, The. *Unknown.* OxBoLi

Song of Liang Chou. Ou-yang Hsiu. OHPC, *tr. by* Kenneth Rexroth
Song of Liberty, A. William Blake. NAEL-6v2 *Fr.* Marriage of Heaven and
  Hell, The.
Song of Lies on Sabbath Eve, A. Yehuda Amichai [*or* Amikhai]. PoSu, *tr. by*
  Chana Bloch
Song of Life, A. Franz Werfel. TrJP, *tr. by* Edith Abercrombie Snow
Song of Lin Liang's Painting "Two Horned Falcons." Li Meng-yang.
  CoBLCP, *tr. by* Jonathan Chaves
Song of Lo-fu, The. *Unknown.* AWP; ChiP, *tr. by* Arthur Waley
Song of Loneliness. Judah Halevi. TrJP, *tr. by* Nina Davis Salaman
Song of Love, The. Rainer Maria Rilke. AWP, *tr. by* Ludwig Lewisohn
Song of Lung-hsi. Ch'en Tao. CoBCP, *tr. by* Burton Watson
Song of Man Chipping an Arrowhead. W. S. Merwin. InPK-6
Song of Marke Anthony, A. John Cleveland. NPeEn
  (When as the Nightingall chanted her Vesper.) NPeEn
Song of Mary, A. Lucille Clifton. NALW
Song of Meeting. Tsung Ch'en. CoBLCP, *tr. by* Jonathan Chaves
Song of Mehitabel, The. Don Marquis. APT-1; OBCoV; TriCat *Fr.* Archy
  and Mehitabel.
Song of Milkanwatha, The. George A. Strong.
  "He [*or* When he] killed the noble Mudjokivis." OBCoV; PeLV; UV
  Modern Hiawatha, The. OBCoV; PeLV; UV
Song of Mount T'ai. Lu Chi. CrYelRi, *tr. by* Sam Hamill
Song of Mr Toad, The. Kenneth Grahame. NOBL; NOxBChV *Fr.* Wind in
  the Willows, The.
Song of My People-Forest, People-Sea. Uri Zvi Greenberg. FIT, *tr. by* Robert
  Friend
Song of My Song, in Three Parts, A. *Unknown.* STP, *tr. by* Richard Johnny
  John and Jerome Rothenberg
Song of My Soul. Ralph Chubb. CAGL
Song of Myself. Walt Whitman. MoAmPo; NAAL-3; NAAL-5; NOBA;
  OxBA
  "Alone far in the wilds and mountains I hunt." SAmP
  (Battle of the *Bonhomme Richard* and the *Serapis.*) RB; UnPo
  "Big doors of the country stand open and ready, The." ColAP; ITBLP
  "Blind loving wrestling touch! Sheathed hooded sharptoothed touch!"
    CAGL
  Child said *What is the grass?* fetching it to me with full hands, A. ColAP;
    ITBLP; NoP-4; SAmP
  From Pent-up Aching Rivers.
    "From pent-up aching rivers." EroLit
  "Has any one supposed it lucky to be born?" NAWM-7v2
  Heroes. SAmP
  "Houses and rooms are full of perfumes." CAGL; UnPo
  ("Houses and rooms are full of perfumes, the shelves are crowded with
    perfumes.") ColAP
  Hub of the Universe, The. EnlH
  "I am of old and young, of the foolish as much as the wise." NAWM-7v2
  "I am the poet of the Body and I am the poet of the Soul." CAGL; ColAP;
    NAWM-7v2; WeW-3
  "I am the teacher of athletes." CAGL; ColAP
  "I believe a leaf of grass is no less than the journey-work of the stars."
    SAmP
  I believe in you my soul. CAGL
    Swiftly Arose. TrCP
  "I believe in you my soul." CAGL
  ("I believe in you my soul, the other I am must not abase itself to you.")
    ColAP
  ("I celebrate myself.") CAGL
  "I celebrate myself, and sing myself." ColAP; FaBoVe; NAWM-7v2; NCAP;
    NIL-7; NoAM; PoE; PoPoPo; RaBo; SAmP; TCAPo
  "I have heard what the talkers were talking. . . . the talk of the beginning and
    the end." CAGL; ColAP
  "I have said that the soul is not more than the body." ColAP; EnlH
  ("I know I have the best of time and space—and that I was never measured,
    and never will be measured.") AmFaPo; CAGL
  "I know I have the best of time and space, and was never measured and will
    never be measured." ColAP; NAWM-7v2; NoAM
  "I think I could turn and live with animals, they are so placid and self-
    contained." HAP; NAWM-7v2; SAmP; WeW-3
  "I understand the large hearts of heroes." SAmP
  "Is this then a touch? . . . quivering me to a new identity." CAGL
  "Little one sleeps in its cradle, The." ColAP; SAmP
  "Now I will do nothing but listen." SAmP
  "Past and present wilt—I have filled them, emptied them, The." CAGL;
    ColAP; NAWM-7v2
  "Pure contralto sings in the organloft, The." FaBoA; TTTS
  "Runaway slave came to my house and stopt outside, The." HHAm

"Spotted hawk swoops by and accuses me, he complains of my gab and my loitering, The." AmFaPo; CAGL; ColAP; NAWM-7v2; SAmP

("Stretch'd and still lies the midnight.") ColAP

"There is that in me . . . .I do not know what it is . . . .but I know it is in me." CAGL; ColAP

"This is the meal pleasantly set . . . .this is the meat and drink for natural hunger." CAGL

"To be in any form, what is that?" CAGL

"Trippers and askers surround me." CAGL; ColAP; EnlH; NAWM-7v2; UnPo

"Twenty-eight young men bathe by the shore." CAGL; ColAP; HAP; NoP-4; SAmP

"Walt Whitman, a kosmos, of Manhattan the son." ColAP; NAWM-7v2; NoP-4; SAmP; SCV

"Walt Whitman, an American, one of the roughs, a kosmos." CAGL

"Who goes there! hankering, gross, mystical, nude?" CAGL; ColAP

Would You Hear of an Old-Time [or Old-Fashioned] Sea fight? SAmP

"You sea! I resign myself to you also—I guess what you mean." CAGL

"Wild gander leads his flock through the cool night, The." ColAP

"Dazzling and tremendous how quick the sun-rise would kill me." ColAP

"All truths wait in all things." ColAP

"And as to you Death, and you bitter hug of mortality, it is idle to try to alarm." ColAP

Song of Napalm. Bruce Weigl. CDa

Song of Nature. Ralph Waldo Emerson. APN-1

Song of "Night After Night," A. Ou-yang Hsiu. SuSp, *tr. by* Irving Y. Lo

Song of Obstacles. Louise Glück. LW   *Fr.* Marathon.

Song of One Eleven Years in Prison. George Canning. *See* Rovers, The

Song of One of the Girls. Dorothy Parker. NALW

Song of P'eng-ya. Tu Fu. CoBCP, *tr. by* Burton Watson

Song of Pajaro. Jeff Tagami. OpBo

Song of Parable, A. *Unknown.* SuSp, *tr. by* Jan W. Walls

Song of Parents Who Want to Wake Up Their Son. *Unknown.* TTTS

Song of Parting. Wang Po-ch'eng. CrYelRi, *tr. by* Sam Hamill

Song of Peach Blossom Retreat. T'ang Yin. CoBLCP, *tr. by* Jonathan Chaves

Song of Peach Tree Spring. Wang Wei. WoPoe, *tr. by* Willis Barnstone, Tony Barnstone and Xu Haixin

Song of Picking Mulberry. Ou-yang Hsiu. CoBCP, *tr. by* Burton Watson

Song of Ptahhotep, The. Robert Bringhurst. GifTon

Song of Pursuit. Gabriel Zaid. TCLAP, *tr. by* Mónica Hernández-Cancio

Song of Quavering, A. Jerome Rothenberg. FTOS

Song of Racquetball. David Allan Evans. MoASP

Song of Reasons. Robert Pinsky. HCAP

Song of Regret. Pan Chieh-yû. CoBCP, *tr. by* Burton Watson

Song of Reply. Alda Merini. CItWP, *tr. by* Cinzia Sartini Blum and Lara Trubowitz

Song of Reproach. Ferenc Apáti. IQMS, *tr. by* Adam Makkai

Song of Roland, The. *Unknown.*

"Charles the King, our Emperor, the great." NAWM-5v1; NAWM-7v1, *tr. by* Frederick Goldin

"In wrath and grief away the Paynims fly." OBWP

"Marsilion sees his people's martyrdom." NAWM-5v1; NAWM-7v1, *tr. by* Frederick Goldin

"Night passes on, and the bright day appears." NAWM-7v1, *tr. by* Frederick Goldin

"Now Roland feels that he is at death's door." FaBoWar, *tr. by* Dorothy Leigh Sayers

"Oliver's climbed upon a hilly crest." FaBoWar, *tr. by* Dorothy Leigh Sayers Roncevalles. WoPoe, *tr. by* Charles Hubert Sisson

"They arm themselves with Saracen hauberks." NAWM-5v1; NAWM-7v1, *tr. by* Frederick Goldin

Song of Samuel Sweet, The. Charles Causley. OBNV

Song of Saul before His Last Battle. Byron. ChIV-1

Song of Selling Flowers. Tsung Ch'en. CoBLCP; ColAnChi, *tr. by* Jonathan Chaves

Song of Sequence. *Unknown. See* Mountain Chant, The

Song of Seyd [or Seid] Nimetollah of Kuhistan. Seid [or Sayyid] Nimatullah [or Ni'matu'llah]. NOBA, *tr. by* Ralph Waldo Emerson

Song of shadows: never glory was, A. Shadows. Victor Gustave Plarr. NOBVV

Song of Shem. James Philip McAuley. ChIV-1   *Fr.* Family of Love, The.

Song of Sixpence. *Unknown.* OxBoLi

(Sing a Song of Sixpence.) ReMoGo

Song of skylark. Lucien Stryk. IllVoic   *Fr.* Issa: A Suite of Haiku.

Song of Slaves in the Desert. John Greenleaf Whittier. APN-1; OxBA

Song of Snow-white Heads. Chuo Wen-chün. BoWoP, *tr. by* Arthur Waley

Song of Solomon. Bible, *O.T.*

Song: "At night on my bed I longed for." WPoS

Song of Solomon, The. Bible, *O.T.*

"Garden inclosed is my sister, my spouse; a spring shut up, a fountain / sealed, A." OBGa

Song of Solomon, The. Bible, *O.T.*

Song: "I am dark, daughters of Jerusalem." WPoS

Song of Solomon, The. Bible, *O.T.*

Song: "Come, my beloved.". WPoS

Song of Solomon, The [or The Song of Songs]. Bible, *O.T.* AWP

As a Seal upon Thy Heart. BoWoP; TrJP, *tr. by* Willis Barnstone

"Behold, thou art fair." TrJP

"Give me all the kisses of your mouth." ErotSp, *tr. by* Sam Hamill

Hark! My Beloved! TrJP, *tr. by* Willis Barnstone

"How beautiful are thy feet with shoes." EroLit, *tr. by* King James Version

"I am come into my garden, my sister, my spouse." OBVE; TOF

"I am come into my garden, my sister, my spouse." EroLit, *tr. by* King James Version

I Am My Beloved's. BoWoP; TrJP, *tr. by* Willis Barnstone

I Am the Rose of Sharon. BoLoP; OBVE

I Sleep, but My Heart Waketh. BoWoP; TrJP, *tr. by* Willis Barnstone

"I was drowsy, but my heart was awake. Listen!" WoPoe, *tr. by* Peter Jay

("In my bed at night.") BoWoP, *tr. by* Willis Barnstone

"My beloved spake, and said unto me." OPOU

"My love has gone down to his garden." BoWoP

"My love is white and ruddy." BoWoP

On My Bed I Sought Him. TrJP, *tr. by* Willis Barnstone

Return, Return, O Shulammite. TrJP

"Song of songs, which is Solomon's, The." OBVE

"Sound of my lover, The." WoPoe, *tr. by* Marcia Falk

("Voice of my darling, The.") BoWoP, *tr. by* Willis Barnstone

Song of Songs. Yelena [or Elena] Kryukova [or Kriukova]. TCRP, *tr. by* Albert C. Todd

Song of Songs, The. Heinrich Heine. EroLit, *tr. by* Louis Untermeyer

Song of songs, which is Solomon's, The. Bible, *O.T.* OBVE   *Fr.* Song of Solomon, The [or The Song of Songs].

Song of Sorrow. *Unknown.* CoBCP, *tr. by* Burton Watson

Song of Sorrow, A. Mary Cameron (Mairi Chamaran, Nighean Fream Challaird). EMWP

Song of Spring. Wu Chün. CoBCP, *tr. by* Burton Watson

Song of Spring, A. Frances Densmore. APT-1   *Fr.* Chippewa Music.

Song of Spring at West Lake, Sent to Circuit Officer Hsieh, A. Ou-yang Hsiu. SuSp, *tr. by* Irving Y. Lo

Song of Spring Journeying. Wang Ya. SuSp, *tr. by* Irving Y. Lo

Song of Spring Replying to a Poem by Po Chü-yi, A. Liu Yu Hsi. SuSp, *tr. by* Daniel Bryant and Ronald C. Miao

Song of Starvation. *Unknown.* STP, *tr. by* Jerome Rothenberg

Song of Summer. Paul Laurence Dunbar. APN-2

Song of Summer. Alexander MacDonald.

"Month of plants and of honey." NePenScot, *tr. by* Derick Thomson

Song of Summer. *Unknown.* NAWM-7v1, *tr. by* Jan Ziolkowski

Song of Surfing on the Bore. Cheng Hsieh. CoBLCP; ColAnChi, *tr. by* Jonathan Chaves

Song of T'ung-ku. Tu Fu. CrYelRi, *tr. by* Sam Hamill

Song of Thanks. Martin Joseph Prandstetter. AuPH, *tr. by* Lowell A. Bangerter

Song of the Alpine Hunter. Paul Van Ostaijen. TuT, *tr. by* Theo Dorgan

Song of the Andoumboulou. Nathaniel Mackey. NAAAL

Song of the Andoumboulou: 6. Nathaniel Mackey. FTOS

Song of the Andoumboulou: 7. Nathaniel Mackey. FTOS

Song of the Andoumboulou: 12. Nathaniel Mackey. FTOS

Song of the Andoumboulou: 15. Nathaniel Mackey. PFTM-2

Song of the Angels. Lizelia Augusta Jenkins Moorer. CBWP-3

Song of the Autumn Wind. Emperor Wu of Han [or Wu Ti or Ou-ty or Liu Ch'e or Liu Ch'u]. CoBCP, *tr. by* Burton Watson

Song of the Bald Eagle. *Unknown.* APN-2   *Fr.* Minnetare Songs.

Song of the Banjo, The. Rudyard Kipling. FaBoCh

Song of the Barren Orange Tree. Federico García Lorca. AmFaPo, *tr. by* W. S. Merwin

Song of the Bay Steed of Governor Wei, A. Ts'en Shen. SuSp, *tr. by* Daniel Bryant

Song of the Bear. *Unknown.* APN-2   *Fr.* Minnetare Songs.

Song of the Beautiful Ladies. Tu Fu. CoBCP, *tr. by* Burton Watson

Song of the Beggars. W. H. Auden. PeLV   *Fr.* Twelve Songs.

Song of the Black Bear, The. *Unknown.* RaBo

Song of the Boat-Pullers. Pien Kung. CoBLCP, *tr. by* Jonathan Chaves

Song of the Boatswain of Yüeh. *Unknown.* SuSp, tr. by Irving Y. Lo

Song of the Borderguard, The. Robert Duncan. NeAP; PoM

Song of the Bounder, The. Edgar Wallace. PeSAV

Song of the Bowmen of Shu. Ezra Pound. FaBoWar; OBVE

Song of the Breaking of the Willow. *Unknown.* CoBCP; ColAnChi, tr. by Burton Watson

Song of the Brightness of Water. Karol Wojtyla. CRP

Song of the Broad-Axe [*or* Broad-Ax]. Walt Whitman.
   Broad-Ax, The. MoAmPo

Song of the Burning. David Wojahn. SwNoth

Song of the Butterfly, The. Frances Densmore. APT-1 *Fr.* Chippewa Music.

Song of the Camel, The. Charles Edward Carryl. OTCP *Fr.* Admiral's Caravan, The.

Song of the Cannibals, A. Anne Finch, Countess of Winchilsea. PoE

Song of the Captive Sioux Woman. *Chippewa Oral Tradition.* NAAL-5

Song of the Ch'in-Dynasty Mirror—Written for Yüan Sung-li. Wang Shih-chieng. CoBLCP, tr. by Jonathan Chaves

Song of the Chattahoochee. Sidney Lanier. APN-2; ColAP; TCAPo

Song of the Clear River. Huang T'ing-chien. CoBCP, tr. by Burton Watson

Song of the Clouds. Aristophanes. AWP *Fr.* Clouds, The.

Song of the Crab Medicine-Bag. *Unknown.* STP, tr. by Jerome Rothenberg

Song of the Crow Pecking at My Scarred Donkey. Wang Yü-ch'eng. SuSp; WoPoe, tr. by Jonathan Chaves

Song of the Crows. *Chippewa Oral Tradition.* NAAL-5

Song of the Cuban Blacks. Federico García Lorca. RaBo, tr. by Robert Bly
   (When the full moon comes.) RaBo, tr. by Robert Bly

Song of the Dead Soldier, The. Christopher Logue. FaBoWar

Song of the Degrees, A. Ezra Pound. APT-1

Song of the Dew. *Unknown.* TrJP, tr. by Solomon Solis-Cohen

Song of the Dogs, The. Sándor Petőfi. IQMS, tr. by George Sutherland Fraser

Song of the Dove, The. Alexander Robertson. APT-1

Song of the Dream Garden. Ikkyu Sojun. ErotSp, tr. by Sam Hamill

Song of the Duck Hunters. Kao Ch'i. CoBLCP, tr. by Jonathan Chaves

Song of the Dying Gunner A.A.1. Charles Causley. FaBoWar; PoWW

Song of the Eiffel Tower. David Shapiro. BodElec

Song of the Elk. *Unknown.* APN-2 *Fr.* Minnetare Songs.

Song of the Emigrants in Bermuda. Andrew Marvell. *See* Bermudas

Song of the English Bowmen. *Unknown.* FaBoWar

Song of the Eucharist, A. James Ryman. SacPr

Song of the Exposition. Walt Whitman.
   Muse in the New World, The. MoAmPo

Song of the Faithful, A. Michael Drayton. ChIV-1

Song of the Fallen Deer. *Unknown.* OBVE, tr. by Frank Russell

Song of the Fire-Charm. *Unknown.* STP, tr. by Frances Densmore and Jerome Rothenberg

Song of the Flea. Judah Al-Harizi. TrJP

Song of the Fleeting Day. "Porfirio Barba-Jacob." CAGL, tr. by Jeff Bingham and Juan Antonio Serna Servin *Fr.* Song of an Impossible Blue.

Song of the Flood. *Unknown.* TTTS

Song of the flute, O sister, is madness, The. Mirabai [*or* Mira Bai]. WPoS

Song of the Fucked Duck. Marge Piercy. BoWoP

Song of the Galley, The. *Unknown.* AWP, tr. by John Gibson Lockhart

Song of the Galley-Slaves. Rudyard Kipling. GTBS-P; HAP; SCGP

Song of the GPO, A. Gerry Hamill. NOBL

Song of the Graves, The. *Unknown.* OBMV, tr. by Ernest Rhys *Fr.* Black Book of Carmarthen, The.

Song of the Great Mind. Uri Zvi Greenberg. FIT, tr. by Robert Friend

Song of the Great Wind. Liu Pang. ColAnChi, tr. by Victor H. Mair

Song of the Great Wind. Liu Pang. SuSp, tr. by Ronald C. Miao

Song of the Gun. *Unknown.* APN-2 *Fr.* Minnetare Songs.

Song of the Happy Shepherd, The. W. B. Yeats. NoAM

Song of the Harlot. Bible, *O.T.* TrJP *Fr.* Isaiah.

Song of the Hat-Raising Doll. John Mole. OBCoV *Fr.* Penny Toys.

Song of the Highest Tower. Arthur Rimbaud. AWP, tr. by Edgell Rickword

Song of the Horse. *Unknown.* AWP, tr. by Natalie Curtis Burlin

Song of the Ill-Married. *Unknown.* BoWoP, tr. by Patricia Terry

Song of the Imprisoned Bird. Eliza Cook. VWP

Song of the Indian Maid. John Keats. OBEV *Fr.* Endymion: A Poetic Romance.

Song of the Indian Wars, The. John Gneisenau Neihardt.
   "Summer turned." GM

Song of the Initiate. Patrice Kayo. PBMAP

Song of the Initiate. Léopold Sédar Senghor. NegPo, tr. by Ellen Conroy Kennedy

Song of the Initiate. Léopold Sédar Senghor. VCWP, tr. by Melvin Dixon

Song of the Jellicles, The. T. S. Eliot. FaBoCh

Song of the Juggler. Heberto Padilla. AF, tr. by Alastair Reid

Song of the Lenape Warriors Going against the Enemy, The. *Unknown.* APN-2, tr. by John Heckwelder

Song of the Lioness for Her Cub. *Unknown.* BoWoP, tr. by Thomas Hahn

Song of the Little Miss by the Green Rill. *Unknown.* ChinPo, tr. by Yip Wai-lim

Song of the Lotus-Eaters. Tennyson. NOBE; OBEV *Fr.* Lotus-Eaters, The.

Song of the Low, The. Ernest Charles Jones. NOBVV

Song of the Lute. Po Chü-i. CoBCP, tr. by Burton Watson

Song of the Mad Prince, The. Walter De la Mare. EBEV; FaBoCh; MakPoe; NOBE; NoAM; OxAEP-2

Song of the Maidens. Yüan Hao-wen. SuSp, tr. by Stephen West

Song of the Man of Green Hill, The. Kao Ch'i. CoBLCP; ColAnChi, tr. by Jonathan Chaves

Song of the Man Who Succeeded. *Unknown.* STP, tr. by Jerome Rothenberg

Song of the Master and Boatswain. W. H. Auden. BoLoP; FaBoTw *Fr.* Sea and the Mirror, The.

Song of the Men of Chin-ling. Hsieh T'iao. ChiP, tr. by Arthur Waley

Song of the Merchant's Wife. Yang Sheh-ch'i. CoBLCP, tr. by Jonathan Chaves

Song of the Messiah, The. John Gneisenau Neihardt.
   "In vain against the formless wolves of air." APT-1

Song of the Militant Romance, The. Percy Wyndham Lewis. FaBoTw; OxBTC

Song of the Mischievous Dog, The. Dylan Thomas. OBCoV

Song of the Mock Turtle, The. Lewis Carroll. UV *Fr.* Alice's Adventures in Wonderland.

Song of the Modern Time. Eliza Cook. VWP

Song of the Moderns. John Gould Fletcher. AWP

Song of the Moon. Priscilla Jane Thompson. CBWP-2

Song of the Narcissus, The. *Unknown.* AWP *Fr.* Thousand and One Nights, The.

Song of the Oktahutchee. Alexander L. Posey. APN-2

Song of the Old Man. Richard Jones. IllVoic

Song of the Old Mother, The. W. B. Yeats. MoBrPo

Song of the Old Oak. Chang Yü. CoBLCP, tr. by Jonathan Chaves

Song of the Old Woman. *Unknown.* BoWoP, tr. by Armand Schwerner and Paul-Emile Victor

Song of the Open Road. Ogden Nash. APT-2; OBAL

Song of the Open Road. Walt Whitman. NOBA
   "Earth expanding right hand and left hand, The." AmFaPo
   "Efflux of the soul is happiness, here is happiness, The." AmFaPo

Song of the Open Road, A. *Unknown.* AWP, tr. by John Addington Symonds

Song of the Owl. *Unknown.* APN-2, tr. by Henry Wadsworth Longfellow

Song of the Owl, The. Richard Kendall Munkittrick. OBCA

Song of the P'i-P'a. Po Chü-i. ChinPo, tr. by Yip Wai-lim

Song of the Painting "Catching Fish." Li Tung-yang. CoBLCP, tr. by Jonathan Chaves

Song of the Painting of the Long-Life Star. Wang Chiu-ssu. CoBLCP, tr. by Jonathan Chaves

Song of the Painting "River and Mountains," by Wu Wei. Ho Ching-ming. CoBLCP, tr. by Jonathan Chaves

Song of the Palace of Ch'en. Kuan Hsiu. WoPoe, tr. by Jerome P. Seaton

Song of the Passion, A. Richard Rolle of Hampole. SacPr

Song of the Pen, The. Judah Al-Harizi. TrJP, tr. by J. Chotzner

Song of the Pheasant. *Unknown.* APN-2 *Fr.* Minnetare Songs.

Song of the pines. Po Chü-i. TAL

Song of the Pleiades. *Unknown.* TCAPo

Song of the Poor Man. *Unknown.* TTY, tr. by Anselm Hollo

Song of the Pop-Bottlers. Morris Gilbert Bishop. KaS

Song of the Promise of the Buffalo. *Unknown.* APN-2, tr. by Alice C. Fletcher *Fr.* Hako, The.

Song of the Prophet. *Unknown.* APN-2, tr. by Washington Matthews *Fr.* Mountain Chant, The.

Song of the Rabbits Outside the Tavern, The. Elizabeth Jane Coatsworth. OBCA; OxIBACP; SoSe-8

Song of the Radiant Lady. Wang An-shih. SuSp, tr. by Jan W. Walls

Song of the Radiant Lady, Replying to a Poem by Wang Chieh-fu. Ou-yang Hsiu. SuSp, tr. by Irving Y. Lo

Song of the Rain. Hugh Raymond McCrae. CBAP

Song of the Rain Chant. *Unknown.* AWP, tr. by Natalie Curtis Burlin

Song of the Rear Palace. Po Chü-i. SuSp, tr. by Ronald C. Miao

Song of the Red & Green Buffalo, A. *Unknown.* STP, tr. by William Whitman

Song of the Rejected Woman. Kibkarjuk. WPOW, tr. by Tom Lowenstein and Knud Rasmussen

Song of the Rider. Federico García Lorca. WoPoe, tr. by Edwin Honig

Song of the Riders. Stephen Vincent Benét. MoAmPo *Fr.* John Brown's Body.

Song of the Rising Sun Dance. *Unknown.* APN-2, *tr. by* Washington Matthews *Fr.* Mountain Chant, The.

Song of the Running Horse River: Presented on Saying Farewell to the Army Going on Campaign to the West, A. Ts'en Shen. ColAnChi, *tr. by* Daniel Bryant

Song of the Running Horse River: Presented on Seeing General Feng Off on a Campaign to the West, A. Ts'en Shen. SuSp, *tr. by* Daniel Bryant

Song of the Rushlight. Eliza Cook. VWP

Song of the Sabbath. Kadya Molodovsky [*or* Molodowsky]. WPOW, *tr. by* Jean Valentine

Song of the Sacred Strings. Li Ho. CoBCP, *tr. by* Burton Watson

Song of the Sea Weed. Eliza Cook.
 "Many a lip is gaping for drink." VerBaPo

Song of the Seeress. *Unknown.* NAWM-5v1

Song of the Self: The Grandmother. Alma Villanueva. HW

Song of the Shadows, The. Walter De la Mare. MoBrPo

Song of the Shepherd Boy. John Bunyan. *See* Pilgrim's Progress, The

Song of the Shirt, The. Thomas Hood. BRP; EBVV

Song of the Silent Land. Johann Gaudenz von Salis-Seewis. AWP, *tr. by* Henry Wadsworth Longfellow

Song of the Silent Night. Aurelio Arturo. BLPSL, *tr. by* Rene de Costa, Rigas Kappatos and Eleni Paidoussi

Song of the Sky Loom. *Tewa Oral Tradition.* WoPoe, *tr. by* Herbert J. Spinden

Song of the Smoke, The. William Edward Burghardt DuBois. ISC; SSLK; UnPo

Song of the snails on their way to a funeral. Jacques Prévert. MFP, *tr. by* Martin Sorrell

Song of the Snow. Zalman Schneour. MHP, *tr. by* Ruth Finer Mintz

Song of the Snow-white Heads. *Unknown.* ChiP, *tr. by* Arthur Waley

Song of the Son. Jean Toomer. ISC; MakPoe; NIL-7; NIP-4

Song of the Soul that Rejoices in Knowing God through Faith. Saint John of the Cross. TOF, *tr. by* K. Kavanaugh and O. Rodrigues

Song of the spheres in their revolutions, The. Jelaluddin [*or* Jalal al-Din] Rumi. TOF

Song of the Stars. William Cullen Bryant. TreFP

Song of the Stars, The. *Unknown.* APN-2, *tr. by* Charles Godfrey Leland

Song of the Stormy Petrel. "Maksim Gorky" [*or* Gorkii]. TCRP, *tr. by* Albert C. Todd

Song of the Strange Woman. Leah Goldberg. FIT, *tr. by* Robert Friend

Song of The Suffering Servant, The. Bible, *O.T.* NAWM-5v1 *Fr.* Isaiah.

Song of the Sword. William Ernest Henley.
 "I am the feast-maker." FaBoWar

Song of the Taste. Gary Snyder. LCAP-2

Song of the Third Generation. Julia Lisella. UnSA

Song of the Thoroughfare. Hsieh Shang. CoBCP, *tr. by* Burton Watson

Song of the Three Hundred Thousand Drunkards in the United States. William Bingham Tappan.
 "Onward! though ever in our march." VerBaPo

Song of the Thunders. *Unknown.* OBVE, *tr. by* Frances Densmore

Song of the Tölös. Hulü Chin. ColAnChi, *tr. by* Victor H. Mair

Song of the Tortured Girl, The. John Berryman. CoAP

Song of the Tower of Skulls. Vasco [*or* Vasko] Popa. WoPoe, *tr. by* Anne Pennington

Song of the Train. David McCord. NTCP

Song of the Transport Workers—Seeing Off Fang Wen-yü on His Way to His Post as Inspector of Transportation. Pien Kung. CoBLCP, *tr. by* Jonathan Chaves

Song of the Transportationist, The. *Unknown.* NOBAu

Song of the Traveler at Evening. Goethe. STV, *tr. by* John Frederick Nims

Song of the Trees. *Unknown.* OBVE, *tr. by* Frances Densmore

Song of the Turkey Buzzard. Lew Welch. PoM
 (Praises, Tamalpais, / Perfect in Wisdom and Beauty.) BB

Song of the Ugly Maiden. Eliza Cook. VWP

Song of the Ungirt Runners, The. Charles Hamilton Sorley. MoBrPo; OBEV

Song of the Vermeil Phoenix. Tu Fu. TAL

Song of the Viet Boatman. *Unknown.* ColAnChi, *tr. by* Anne Birrell

Song of the Virgin Mary, The. Miles Coverdale. ChIV-2

Song of the Virgin Mother, A. Félix Lope de Vega Carpio. AWP, *tr. by* Ezra Pound

Song of the Wagon-whip, A. Samuel Cron Cronwright. PeSAV

Song of the Wanderer. Wang T'ing-hsiang. CoBLCP, *tr. by* Jonathan Chaves

Song of the War-Chariots (Yueh-Fu). Tu Fu. ChinPo, *tr. by* Yip Wai-lim

Song of the War Wagons. Tu Fu. CrYelRi, *tr. by* Sam Hamill

Song of the Waterfall at Mount Lu. Yang Wei-chen. CoBLCP, *tr. by* Jonathan Chaves

Song of the Wave. Kahlil Gibran. GraLe, *tr. by* H. M. Nahmad

Song of the Weasel. *Unknown.* APN-2 *Fr.* Minnetare Songs.

Song of the Weaving Woman. Yüan Chên. SuSp, *tr. by* Wu-Chi Liu

Song of the Well. Bible, *O.T.* TrJP *Fr.* Numbers.

Song of the Whirlwind. Fenton Johnson. NAAAL

Song of the White Man. *Unknown.* APN-2 *Fr.* Minnetare Songs.

Song of the White Snow: Saying Farewell to Supervisor Wu Returning to the Capital. Ts'en Shen. SuSp, *tr. by* C. H. Wang

Song of the Wind and the Rain. Solomon ibn Gabirol. TrJP, *tr. by* Solomon Solis-Cohen

Song of the Wolves, The. Sándor Petőfi. IQMS, *tr. by* George Sutherland Fraser

Song of the Woman with Her Parts Coming Out, The. Susan Griffin. GLP

Song of the Woodcutter of the Sea. Pien Kung. CoBLCP, *tr. by* Jonathan Chaves

Song of the Yellow Cedar Face, A. George Clutesi. HATNAP

Song of the Yodo River. Buson. EH, *tr. by* Robert Hass

Song of Three Smiles. W. S. Merwin. CoAP; NOBA; VGW

Song of Troylus, The. Geoffrey Chaucer. AWP *Fr.* Troilus and Criseyde [*or* Criseide].

Song of Tzu-yeh. *Unknown.* SuSp, *tr. by* Ronald C. Miao

Song of Ullikummi, The. Charles Olson. PFTM-1

Song of Venus. Dryden. OxBoLi *Fr.* King Arthur.

Song Of Wandering Aengus, The. W. B. Yeats. ChAP; FaBoCh; MoBrPo; OTCP; PoRA; RaBo; TFi; TTTS

Song of War. Kofi Awoonor. *See* Songs of Sorrow

Song of War. Kofi Awoonor. PBMAP; PoetW

Song of War, A. Li Po. TAL

Song of Wildfire, A. Wen T'ing-yün. SuSp, *tr. by* William R. Schultz

Song of Winnie. Gwendolyn Brooks. ESEAA *Fr.* Winnie.

Song of Winter, A. Emily Jane Pfeiffer. OBWVE

Song of Woe. Shen Yüeh. SuSp, *tr. by* Richard B. Mather

Song of Words. Konstantin Konstantinovich Vaginov. TCRP, *tr. by* Nina Kossman

Song of Wu-ch'eng. Wang T'ing-hsiang.
 "Don't ask about the Six Dynasties of the Sui Palace." CoBLCP

Song of Yearning, A. Kohine Whakarua Ponika. PeNZ, *tr. by* the author

Song of Yen. Kao Shih. SuSp, *tr. by* Joseph J. Lee

Song of Yen. Ts'ao P'i. SuSp, *tr. by* Ronald C. Miao

Song: "Oh, baby, baby, baby dear." Edith Nesbit. NOBVV; PEW

Song: "Oh, dear! Oh, me! Oh, my!" Gregory Corso. BB

Song: "Oh for the wings of a dove." Agnes Mary Frances Robinson. VWP

Song: "Oh gentle Venus, ease a tarse." John Wilmot, 2d Earl of Rochester. EroLit *Fr.* Sodom; or The Quintessence of Debauchery.

Song: "Oh! Love, that stronger art than wine." Aphra Behn. WPE; WPOW *Fr.* Lucky Chance, The.

Song: "O[h] me[e], the time is [*or* has] come to part." Mary Sidney Wroth, Countess of Montgomery. NOSC *Fr.* Pamphilia to Amphilanthus.

Song: "Oh no more, no more, too late." John Ford. *See* Broken Heart, The

Song: "Oh roses for the flush of youth." Christina Georgina Rossetti. GTBS-P; NOBVV

Song: "Oh say not that my heart is cold." Charles Wolfe. OxAEP-2

Song: "Oh the charming month of May!" Joseph Addison. NOEC

Song: "Old England is eaten by Knaves." Alexander McLachlan. NOBC *Fr.* Emigrant, The.

Song: "Old song with new words, An." Yen Shu. CrYelRi, *tr. by* Sam Hamill

Song on Being Too Lazy to Get Up. Shao Yung. CoBCP, *tr. by* Burton Watson

Song on Climbing the Gate Tower at Yu-chou, A. Ch'en Tzu-ang. SuSp, *tr. by* Wu-Chi Liu

Song on Climbing Yu-chou Gate Tower. Ch'en Tzu-ang. CoBCP, *tr. by* Burton Watson

Song on Enduring the Cold. Ts'ao Ts'ao. CoBCP; ColAnChi, *tr. by* Burton Watson

Song on Leaving the Country Early in the Spring. Anne Batten Cristall. RWP

Song (On Seeing Dead Bodies Floating Off the Cape). Alun Lewis. NAEL-5v2; NAEL-6v2; NoP-4; OBWP

Song: "On the Eastern Way at the city of Lo-yang." Sung Tzu-hou. WoPoe, *tr. by* Arthur Waley

Song on the End of the World, A. Czeslaw Milosz. WoPoe, *tr. by* Tony Milosz and the author

Song on the South Sea, A. Anne Finch, Countess of Winchilsea. ECWP; NOEC

Song on the Water. Thomas Lovell Beddoes. FaBoCh; WoPoe *Fr.* Death's Jest Book.

Song on the Way to Jail. Kakayek. STP, *tr. by* James Koller

Song: "Only the wanderer." Ivor Gurney. HarvBoo

Song: "Or love me less, or love me more." Sidney Godolphin. BeJo; NOSC

Song Out of Season, A. May Probyn. VWP

Song: "Pardon, goddess of the night." William Shakespeare. CTC *Fr.* Much Ado about Nothing.

Song: Persuasions to Enjoy. Thomas Carew. *See* Persuasions to Enjoy

Song: "Phillis is my only joy." Sir Charles Sedley. EnLoPo

Song: "Phillis, let's shun the common fate." Sir Charles Sedley. NPeEn

Pious Selinda [*or* Celinda]. William Congreve. NOBE; NPeEn

(Song.) BoLoP; ECEV; NBLV; NOEC; OxBEV; OxBSP

Song: "Platinum fur and brass revolver shine." Michael McClure. BB

Song: "Pleading eyebrows, intoxicating eyes!" Ch'in Kuan. CrYelRi, *tr.* by Sam Hamill

Song Poem, The. Lenard D. Moore. SpirFl

Song (Poverty Parts Good Company, For an Old Scotch Air. Joanna Baillie. RWP

Song: "Pursuing beauty, men descry." Thomas Southerne. NOSC

Song: "Quoth the Duchess of Cleveland to counselor Knight." John Wilmot, 2d Earl of Rochester. BASC

Song: "Rarely, rarely, comest thou." Shelley. FHYEP

(Invocation.) GTBS-P

Song: "Red young men under the ground, The." *Unknown.* STP, *tr.* by Jerome Rothenberg *Fr.* Red Ant Way.

Song: "Rowan like a lip-sticked girl, A." Seamus Heaney. TRP

Song's Eternity. John Clare. FaBoCh

Song: "Scholar first my Love implor'd, A." Dorothea Du Bois. LW

Song: "Scholar first my love implored, A." Lady Dorothea Dubois. ECWP

Song Set by John Farmer. *Unknown.* CTC; NoSic

Song Set by Nicholas Yonge. *Unknown.* CTC

Song: "She has left me, my pretty." Sylvia Townsend Warner. MoBrPo

Song: "She lowers her fragrant curtain." Liu Yung. ErotSp, *tr.* by Sam Hamill

Song: "She's somewhere in the sunlight strong." Richard Le Gallienne. OBEV

Song: "She sat and sang alway." Christina Georgina Rossetti. NAEL-5v2; NAEL-6v2

Song: "Shephard loveth thow me vell?" Jean Passerat. NPeEn; OBVE, *tr.* by William, of Hawthornden Drummond

Song: "Slow, slow fresh fount, keep time with my salt tears." Ben Jonson. *See* Cynthia's Revels

Song: "Soft falls the sweet evening." John Clare. NOBVV

Song: "Soules joy, now I am gone." William Herbert, Earl of Pembroke. ESCV

Song: "Sound is fading out." *Unknown.* STP, *tr.* by Jerome Rothenberg

Song: "Stay Phoebus, stay." Edmund Waller. BeJo

Song: "Stop all the clocks, cut off the telephone." W. H. Auden. CAGL; MoBrPo; OPOU; RB *Fr.* Twelve Songs.

Song: "Stranger, you who hide my love." Stephen Spender. FaBoTw

Song: "Strew not earth with empty stars." Thomas Lovell Beddoes. OxBSP *Fr.* Second Brother, The.

Song: "Strive not, vain Lover, to be fine." Richard Lovelace. CavPo

Song: "Sun sets in night, and the stars shun the day, The." Royall Tyler. NAAL-3 *Fr.* Contrast, The.

Song Sung by Egistus and Clytemnestra. John Pickering [*or* Pikerying]. NoSic *Fr.* Horestes.

Song: "Sure thing / I'm a spirit!" *Unknown.* STP, *tr.* by Jerome Rothenberg

Song: "Sweet are the thoughts that savour of content." Robert Greene. PoToHe *Fr.* Greene's Farewell to Folly.

Song: "Sweet beast, I have gone prowling." W. D. Snodgrass. MoAmPo

Song: "Sweet in her green dell the flower of beauty slumbers." George Darley. OBEV; OxAEP-2

(Serenade of a Loyal Martyr.) NOBE

Song: "Sweetest love, I do not go[e]." John Donne. AWP; BoLoP; ESCV; FHYEP; HeIP-4; MeLP; NAEL-7v1; NOBE; NoP-4; NoSic; PAI; TFi

(Sweetest love, I do not go for weariness of thee.) FSCP

Song: "SYLVIA the fair, in the bloom of fifteen." Dryden. EBEV

(Song.) OxAEP-1

(Sylvia the Fair.) PoPoPo

Song Taught to Joseph, The. Ray A. Young Bear. AF

Song that I came to sing remains unsung to this day, The. Song That I Came to Sing, The. Rabindranath Tagore. WoPoe

Song that I'm going to sing, The. Crafty Farmer, The. *Unknown.* ESPB

Song that she sang was all written, The. Moon of Mobile, The. Thomas Holley Chivers. OBAL

Song. That Women Are But Men's Shadows. Ben Jonson. BeJo; OxBSP

(Shadow, The.) NOBE; OBEV

Song, The: "Beauty no more the subject be." Thomas Nabbes. NOSC

Song, The: "Beehive source." Anne Baring. HW

Song, The: "Drink and be merry, merry, merry boys." Thomas Morton. NAAL-3

Song, The: "Oh, foully slighted Ethiope maid!" Priscilla Jane Thompson. CBWP-2

Song: The Railway Train. *Unknown.* NOBAu, *tr.* by George Taplin

Song, The: "So light no one noticed." Edward Dorn. VGW

Song, The: "That day, in the slipping of torsos and straining flanks." Lola Ridge. WPE

Song, The: "When I would sing of crooked streams and fields." Jones Very. APN-1

Song: The Willing Mistriss. Aphra Behn. PEW *Fr.* Dutch Lover, The.

Song: The Willing Prisoner to His Mistress. Thomas Carew. CaPo

Song: "There never was." Carl Rakosi. BodElec

Song: "There's a barrel of porter at Tammany Hall." Fitz-Greene Halleck. OBAL

Song: "There's a beautiful woman in the north." Li Yen-nien. CrYelRi, *tr.* by Sam Hamill

Song: "There stands a lonely pine-tree." Heinrich Heine. TrJP, *tr.* by Emma Lazarus

Song: "These songs will not stand." Denis Glover. PeNZ *Fr.* Sings Harry.

Song: "Think of dress in every light." John Gay. OxBSP *Fr.* Achilles.

Song Thirty-Four. Mudrooroo Narogin. BMAP *Fr.* Song Cycle of Jacky, The.

Song: "This is a song for the speechless." Edward Hirsch. OPRER

Song: "Those rivers run from that land." Robert Creeley. VGW

Song: "Though regions farr divided." Aurelian Townshend [*or* Townsend]. NOSC

Song: "Three little maidens they have slain." Maurice Maeterlinck. AWP, *tr.* by Jethro Bithell

Song: "Through springtime walks, with flowers perfumed." Anne Batten Cristall. ECWP; RWP

Song: "'Tis affection but dissembled." Sidney Godolphin. BeJo

Song: "'Tis light to love thee living, girl, when hope is full and fair." Thomas Tod Stoddart. NOBRP *Fr.* Death-Wake, The; or, Lunacy.

Song, 'tis my will that thou do seek out Love. Dante Alighieri. AWP; EaItPo, *tr.* by Dante Gabriel Rossetti *Fr.* La Vita Nuova.

Song: "'Tis true our life is but a long dis-ease." Katherine Philips. OxBSP (To my Lord Biron's Tune of—Adieu Phillis.) NPeEn

Song to a Child. *Unknown.* WoPoe, *tr.* by Anthony Conran

Song to a Fair Young Lady, Going Out of the Town in the Spring. Dryden. OBEV

Song to a Lover. *Unknown.* BoWoP, *tr.* by Willis Barnstone

Song to a Lute, A. Sir John Suckling. BeJo; CaPo

(Song: "Hast thou seen the down i' th' air.") EnLoPo

Song to Alasdair Mac Colla, A. Dorothy Brown (Diorbhail nic a Bhriuthainn). EMWP

Song to Amoret, A. Henry Vaughan. NAEL-7v1

Song to be Shouted Out. Nissim Ezekiel. OBCoV *Fr.* Songs for Nandu Bhende.

Song to Be Sung by the Father of Infant Female Children. Ogden Nash. MoAmPo

Song to Be Written on a Wave. José Emilio Pacheco. STV, *tr.* by John Frederick Nims

Song to Bring Fair Weather. *Unknown.* WoPoe, *tr.* by Frances Densmore

Song: To Celia. Ben Jonson. AWP; AmFaPo; BeJo; ClHu; NAEL-5v1; NAEL-6v1; NAEL-7v1; NOSC; OxAEP-1; OxBEV; PoE; SoSe-8; UV

(Drink to Me Only with Thine Eyes.) TFi

(Drinke to me onley with thine eyes.) SCGP

(Song: To Celia (II).) NoP-4

(To Celia.) BoLoP; EnLoPo; GTBS-P; InPK-6; NOBE; OBEV; OBVE; SCGP

Song. To Celia. Ben Jonson. BeJo; NPeEn; NoP-4; OxBEV, *tr.* by Ben Jonson *Fr.* Volpone.

Song to Celia. Sir Charles Sedley. GTBS-P; OxBEV

(To Celia.) AWP; NOBE; OBEV

Song: To Celia (II). Ben Jonson. *See* Song: To Celia

Song to David, A. Christopher Smart. NAEL-5v1; NAEL-6v1; NAEL-7v1; NOBE; OBWVE; PoE

"Glorious the sun in mid career." FaBoCh

"O David, highest in the list." NOEC; NPeEn; OxBEV

"Oh thou that sit'st upon a throne." SacPr

Strength. UV

"Strong is the lion – like a coal." HAP

"Sublime – invention ever young." OBEV

Song to Erin. Mary Weston Fordham. CBWP-2

Song to Fidel. Ernesto "Che" Guevara. TCLAP, *tr.* by Gordon Brotherston and Edward Dorn

Song to Heaven. Uri Zvi Greenberg. FIT, *tr.* by Robert Friend

Song to Hymen: 1942. Anthony Richardson. PoWW

Song: To Mary. Charles Wolfe. *See* To Mary

Song to Mary, A. William of Shoreham. MiEL

Song to Mithras, A. Rudyard Kipling. NoAM *Fr.* Puck of Pook's Hill.

Song to Promote Growth. *Unknown.* OBVE, *tr.* by Washington Matthews

Song to Sleep. John Fletcher. *See* Tragedy of Valentinian, The

Song to the Alpaca. Denise Y. Arnold. PoCoUp

Song to the Banyan. Virgil Suárez. AmPoNex

Song to the Creator. Hildegard von Bingen. WPoS, *tr.* by Barbara Newman

Song to the Masquers. James Shirley. OxBSP *Fr.* Triumph of Peace, The.

Song to the Men of England. Shelley. CABP; NAEL-6v2; PAI (Song, A: "Men of England.") NAEL-5v2

Song to the Mother of the World. Suzanne Ironbiter. HW

Song to the Mountains. *Unknown.* AWP, *tr.* by Alice C. Fletcher

Song: "To the old, long life and treasure." Ben Jonson. OxBSP *Fr.* Gypsies Metamorphosed, The.

Song to the Runaway Slave. *Unknown.* BPo

Song to the Trees and Streams. *Unknown.* APN-2, *tr.* by Alice C. Fletcher *Fr.* Hako, The.

Song to the Tune "Perching Crows." Wu Wei-yeh. CoBLCP, *tr.* by Jonathan Chaves

Song to the Tune "Ting Feng Po." Liu Yung. WoPoe, *tr.* by Sam Hamill

Song to the Virgin Mary. András Vásárhelyi. IQMS, *tr.* by René Bonnerjea

Song to the Wife of His Youth, The. Nathan [*or* Natan] Alterman. MHP, *tr.* by Ruth Finer Mintz *Fr.* Joy of the Poor, The.

Song to the Wind, A. Taliesin. FaBoCh, *tr.* by A. P. Graves

Song: "Tomorrow is saint valentine's day." William Shakespeare. EnLoPo; NoSic *Fr.* Hamlet.

Song: "Tomorrow is Saint Valentine's Day." William Shakespeare. *See* Hamlet

Song: "Tossed midst life's terrific storms." Anne Batten Cristall. RWP

Song Tournament: New Style. Louis Untermeyer. OBAL

Song: "Turn, turn thy beauteous face away." Francis Beaumont. NOSC *Fr.* Love's Cure.

Song upon Miss Harriet Hanbury, Addressed to the Revd Mr Birt. Sir Charles Hanbury Williams. OBCoV

Song: "Wandering in the still of eve." Anne Batten Cristall. RWP

Song Wants to Be Light, The. Federico García Lorca. SpanPo, *tr.* by Rachel Benson and Robert O'Brien

Song: "Water's flowing." *Unknown.* STP, *tr.* by Jerome Rothenberg

Song: "We are the darkness in the heat of the day." Dame Edith Sitwell. BWW

Song: "We have bathed, where none have seen us." Thomas Lovell Beddoes. NOBVV *Fr.* Death's Jest Book.

Song: "We'll, placed in Love's triumphant chariot high." William Cavendish, Duke of Newcastle. OxBSP *Fr.* Humorous Lovers, The.

Song: "We raise de wheat." *Unknown.* BPo; NAAAL; PAI; TAP

Song went to the garden, The. Where the Song Went Where She Went & What Happened When They Met. *Unknown.* STP, *tr.* by Richard Johnny John and Jerome Rothenberg

Song: "Were I laid on Greenland's coast." John Gay. EnLoPo; NAEL-5v1; NAEL-6v1; NPeEn; OxBEV; OxBoLi; PeLV *Fr.* Begger's Opera.

Song: "What a dainty life the milkmaid leads!" Thomas Nabbes. NOSC

Song: "What mak's me so unnimbly ryse." Aurelian Townshend [*or* Townsend]. OxBEV *Fr.* Albion's Triumph.

Song: "What means this strangeness now of late." Sir Robert Aytoun [*or* Ayton]. NOSC

(What meanes this strangeness now of late.) NePenScot

Song: "What shall he have that kill'd the dear?" William Shakespeare. *See* As You Like It

Song: "What voice is this, thou evening gale!" Joanna Baillie. RWP; WoRP

Song: "Whaur yon broken brig hings owre." William Soutar. OxBS

Song: "When, dearest, I but think on [*or* of] thee." Sir John Suckling. OBEV (Ensuing Copy the Late Printer Hath Been Pleased to Honour, by Mistaking It Among Those of the Most Ingenious and Too Early Lost Sir John Suckling, The.) NOSC

Song: "When I am dead, my dearest." Christina Georgina Rossetti. AWP; BoLoP; CABP; EBEV; NAEL-5v2; NAEL-6v2; NOBE; NOBVV; NPeEn; NoP-4; OBEV; OxAEP-2; PoRA; SCV; VWP; ViWPN; WPE

(When I Am Dead [My Dearest].) TFi

Song: "When I am old." Denis Glover. PeNZ *Fr.* Sings Harry.

Song: "When I show up." *Unknown.* STP, *tr.* by Jerome Rothenberg

Song: "When I was a greenhorn and young." Charles Kingsley. NOBVV

Song: "When o'er the wold the heedless lamb." Thomas Holcroft. NOEC

Song: "When that I was and a little tiny boy." William Shakespeare. EBEV; FaBoCh; NOBE; NoSic; OxAEP-1; PoRA; SCGP; TFi *Fr.* Twelfth Night.

Song: "When the echo of the last footstep dies." Eli W. Mandel. MoCV

Song: "When the heart's feeling." Thomas Moore. OxBSP

Song: "When the Sex War ended with the slaughter of the Grandmothers." W. H. Auden. PeLV

Song: "When the water's calm." *Unknown.* STP, *tr.* by Jerome Rothenberg

Song: "When thy beauty appears." Thomas Parnell. OBEV; OxAEP-1

Song: "When working blackguards come to blows." Ebenezer Elliott. EBEV; OxAEP-2

Song: "Whenas [*or* When as] the Rye [*or* Rie] reach to the chin." George Peele. EnLoPo; FaBoCh; FaBoVe; NPeEn; NoSic; OxBEV; OxBoLi; TFi *Fr.* Old Wives' [*or* Wife's] Tale, The.

Song: "Whenever, Chloe, I begin." Philip Dormer Stanhope, 4th Earl of Chesterfield. NOEC

Song: "Where did you borrow that last sigh." Sir William Berkeley. OxBSP *Fr.* Lost Lady, The.

Song: "Where in blind files." Eavan Boland. CIP-2

Song: "Where is all the bright company gone." Dame Edith Sitwell. NALW

Song: "Where is the nymph, whose azure eye." Thomas Moore. EnLoPo

Song: "Where, O! where's the chain to fling." Letitia [*or* Laetitia] Elizabeth Landon. NOBRP *Fr.* Golden Violet, The.

Song: "Where shall Celia fly for shelter." Christopher Smart. EnLoPo

Song: "Whilst Alexis lay pressed." Dryden. BoLoP *Fr.* Marriage à la Mode.

Song: "Who can say." Tennyson. FaBoCh

Song: "Why Damon, why, why, why so pressing?" Mary Lee, Lady Chudleigh. LW

Song: "Why should a foolish marriage vow." Dryden. AWP *Fr.* Marriage à la Mode.

Song: "Why so pale and wan, fond lover?" Sir John Suckling. AWP; BASC; BeJo; BoLoP; CaPo; CavPo; ClHu; EnLoPo; GTBS-P; HAP; HeIP-4; ITBLP; NAEL-5v1; NAEL-6v1; NAEL-7v1; NBLV; NIL-7; NIP-4; NOBE; NPeEn; NoP-4; OBEV; OxAEP-1; OxBEV; PAI; PoE; PoRA; TFi; UnPo *Fr.* Aglaura.

Song will deceive you, the scent will incite you to sing, The. You Cannot Go Down to the Spring. John Shaw Neilson. CBAP

Song: "Winter skies are cold and low." Tzu Yeh. CrYelRi; ErotSp, *tr.* by Sam Hamill

Song with Words. James Agee. ChIV-1; MoAmPo

Song: "Woman sits on her porch." Earle Thompson. HATNAP

Song: Woo'd and married and a' Joanna Baillie. NAEL-6v2; NoP-4

Song Written at Sea in the First Dutch War (1665), the Night before an Engagement. Charles Sackville, 6th Earl of Dorset. EnLoPo; NOBE; OBEV; OBWP; OxAEP-1

(Written at Sea, in the First Dutch War.) NOSC

Song—Written at the North. Samuel Henry Dickson. APN-1

Song: "Yellow coverlet, A." Rosanna Warren. ExTi; MakPoe

Song: "Yellow dust drifts down the road to Ch'ang-an." *Unknown.* CrYelRi, *tr.* by Sam Hamill

Song Yet Song. Amir Gilbo'a. MHP, *tr.* by Ruth Finer Mintz

Song: "Yi surta." Tom Leonard. Oth

Song: "You are as gold." "H. D." APT-1; MoAmPo; TCAPo

Song: "You are the sandstorm beneath my skin." Odia Ofeimun. NAfrP

Song: "You bound strong sandals on my feet." Sara Teasdale. PoBW

Song: "You're wondering if I'm lonely." Adrienne Rich. InPK-6

Song: "You wear the morning like your dress." Joseph Hilaire Pierre Belloc. OBEV

Song: "You wrong me, Strephon, when you say." "Ephelia." EMWP

Song: "Young flowers were whispering in melody." Edgar Allan Poe. NOBA *Fr.* Al Aaraaf.

Songbirds in the public boughs, The. (LL) After the Last Bulletins. Richard Wilbur. CoAP; CoAmPo; MoAmPo

Songe 17: "Sun is set, and masked night, The." Robert Sidney. NoSic

(Sunn is set, and masked night, The.) PBRV

Songe bewailinge the tyme of Christmas, So much decayed in Englande, A. *Unknown.* PBRV

Songe d'Athalie. Stevie Smith. OxBEV

Songe Made by Her Majestie and Songe before Her at Her Cominge from White Hall to Powles through Fleete Streete in Anno Domini 1588, A. Queen of England Elizabeth I. EMWP

Songless Land, The. Francis Carey Slater. PeSAV

Songs. Steve Crow.

    "They say a man dies." HATNAP

Songs. Langston Hughes. APT-2

Songs about Life and Brighter Things Yet. Samuel Hoffenstein. NBLV

Songs and Chants. *Unknown.* APN-2, *tr.* by John Wesley Powell

Songs are thoughts, sung out with the breath when people are moved by great forces and ordinary speech no longer suffices. "Songs are Thoughts, Sung Out with the Breath." Orpingalik. PFTM-1

Songs, but the bloody revolution goes unnoticed. When People Rise from Cheese, Statement #1. Duo Duo (Li Shizheng). PFTM-2, *tr.* by John Rosenwald

Songs crying out their ironies, The. (LL) Achill Woman, The. Eavan Boland. BiHa; HarvBoo

Songs for a Colored Singer. Elizabeth Bishop. RB

Songs for a Three-String Guitar. Léopold Sédar Senghor. PBA, *tr.* by Miriam Koshl

Songs for Eve. Archibald MacLeish.
What the Serpent Said to Adam. ChIV-1
Songs for Nandu Bhende. Nissim Ezekiel.
Family. OBCoV
Song to be Shouted Out. OBCoV
Songs for Signare. Léopold Sédar Senghor.
"I walked you to the village where the granaries are at the threshold of
Night." NegPo
"Long, long between your hands you held the warrior's black face." NegPo
"We shall bathe, my love, in an African presence." NegPo
"Your face, the beauty of a time long past evokes the perfumed robes in faded
hues." NegPo
Songs for the Four Parts of the Night. Tohono O'odham (Owl Woman) (Juana
Manwell). WPoS, tr. by Frances Densmore
Songs for the People. Frances Ellen Watkins Harper. NAAAL; PWR
Songs for the Sleepless. Elaine Randell. Oth
Songs from an Island. Ingeborg Bachmann. VCWP, tr. by Mark Anderson
Songs from Cyprus. "H. D."
"Gather for festival." MoAmPo
"Where is the nightingale." APT-1; MoAmPo
Songs from the Great Feast to the Dead. Unknown. APN-2, tr. by Edward
William Nelson
Songs from the Society of the Mystic Animals. Richard Johnny John.
Two Songs About a Dead Person or a Mole—Whichever It Was. PFTM-1
Songs I wrote when I was young and ardent, The. Boethius. MLL Fr.
Consolation of Philosophy, The ("De Consolacione Philosophie").
Songs in Flight. Ingeborg Bachmann.
"Instructed in love." WPOW
Songs in the Desert! songs of husky breath. James Thomson. SacPr
Songs of an Other. Robert Duncan. PmAP
Songs of birds which leaps from leaf to leaf, The. Canto de li Augei di Frunda
in Frunda, Il. Matteo Maria Boiardo. WoPoe, tr. by Peter Russell
Songs of Ch'ang-kan. Ts'ui Hao. CoBCP, tr. by Burton Watson
Songs of Ch'en. Confucius. CTC, tr. by Ezra Pound
Songs of Ch'iu-p'u. Li Po.
"Ch'iu-p-u teems with white gibbons." SuSp
"Furnace fire lights up earth and sky, The." SuSp
"How like a bolt of white silk is this water." SuSp
"My white hair of thirty thousand feet." SuSp
Songs of Cheng. Confucius. CTC, tr. by Ezra Pound
Songs of Chiang-nan. Wang T'ing-hsiang. CoBLCP, tr. by Jonathan Chaves
Songs of Conn the Fool, The. Fannie Stearns Gifford.
Moon Folly. RACG
Songs of Courtship. Unknown. ChiP, tr. by Arthur Waley
Songs of Degrees. Louis Zukofsky.
"William / Carlos / Williams / alive!" PFTM-1
Songs of Depression. Yang Wan-li.
"I don't feel like reading another book." ColAnChi; SuSp, tr. by Jonathan
Chaves
"I finish chanting my new poems." SuSp
Songs of Divorce. Jane Green. WPOW, tr. by Frances Densmore
Songs of Education. Gilbert Keith Chesterton.
Geography. OBSV
History. OBSV
Songs of Experience. William Blake.
Ah, Sun-Flower [or Ah! Sun-Flower]. AWP; EBEV; FHYEP; HAP; NAEL-
6v2; NIP-4; NOBRP; NOEC; NPeEn; NoP-4; PoE; PoPoPo; RB; SCGP;
TFi; TOF; UnPo; WeW-3
"All the night in woe." FHYEP; NOBRP
Angel, The. FHYEP; RACG
"Children of the future age." FHYEP
Chimney Sweeper, The. FHYEP; NAEL-5v2; NAEL-6v2; NAWM-7v2;
NOEC; RB
Clod and the Pebble, The. EnLoPo; FHYEP; NAEL-5v2; NAEL-6v1;
NOBE; NPeEn; NoP-4; OxAEP-2; OxBEV; OxBSP; PoE; RB; SCGP; SCV;
TFi
"Cruelty has a Human heart." ChIV-1; NAEL-5v2; NAEL-6v2; NoP-4; RB
"Dear Mother, dear Mother, the Church is cold." FHYEP; NBLV; OBSV
Divine Image, A. ChIV-1; NAEL-5v2; NAEL-6v2; NoP-4; RB
"Earth rais'd up her head." ChIV-1; FHYEP; NAEL-5v2; NAEL-6v2;
NOBRP; NOEC; PoE
("Earth raised up her head.") NAWM-7v2
Earth's Answer. ChIV-1; FHYEP; NAEL-5v2; NAEL-6v2; NOBRP; NOEC;
PoE
"Flower was offered [or offerd] to me, A." BoLoP; FHYEP; NAEL-5v2;
NAEL-6v2; NOBRP
(Fly, The.) FHYEP; NOBRP; NOxBChV; OxAEP-2

Garden of Love, The. AWP; EnLoPo; FHYEP; HAP; NAEL-5v2; NAEL-
6v2; NPeEn; NoP-4; OBGa; OxAEP-2; OxBEV; PoE; PoPoPo; RB; SCGP;
TFi; TOF; TRP
(Hear the Voice.) OBEV
Holy Thursday [2]. FHYEP; NAEL-5v2; NAEL-6v2; NOBRP; NOEC;
NoP-4
(Holy Thursday (Experience).) NOxBChV
Human Abstract, The. FHYEP; NAEL-5v2; NAEL-6v2; NOBRP; NOEC;
OxAEP-2; PoE
"I Dreamt a Dream—What can it mean?" FHYEP; RACG
"I love to rise in a summer morn." FHYEP; FaBoCh; OxAEP-2
"I wander through [or thro'] each chartered [or charter'd] street." AWP;
CABP; ClHu; FHYEP; HAP; HeIP-4; InPK-6; NAEL-5v2; NAEL-6v2;
NAWM-7v2; NIL-7; NIP-4; NOBE; NOBRP; NOEC; NPeEn; NoP-4;
OxAEP-2; OxBEV; PoE; PoPoPo; RB; SCGP; SCV; TFi; TRP; UnPo;
WeW-3
"I was angry with my friend." AWP; FHYEP; HAP; NAEL-5v2; NAEL-
6v2; NPeEn; OxAEP-2; OxBEV; RB; SCV; SoSe-8; TFi; WeW-3
"I went to the Garden of Love." AWP; EnLoPo; FHYEP; HAP; NAEL-5v2;
NAEL-6v2; NPeEn; NoP-4; OBGa; OxAEP-2; OxBEV; PoE; PoPoPo; RB;
SCGP; TFi; TOF; TRP
"In futurity / I prophetic see." FHYEP; NOBRP
Infant Sorrow. FHYEP; NAEL-5v2; NAEL-6v2; OxAEP-2; OxBEV;
OxBSP; PoPoPo; RB
Introduction: "Hear the voice of the Bard!" ChIV-1; EBEV; FHYEP; HAP;
NAEL-5v2; NAEL-6v2; NAWM-7v2; NOBE; NOBRP; NOEC; NPeEn;
NoP-4; OxBEV; PoE; RB; TFi
"Is this a holy thing to see." FHYEP; NAEL-5v2; NAEL-6v2; NOBRP;
NOEC; NoP-4
Lily, The. FHYEP; NOBRP
"Little black thing among the snow, A." FHYEP; NAEL-5v2; NAEL-6v2;
NAWM-7v2; NOEC; RB
Little Boy Lost, A. FHYEP; PeECV
Little Fly. NAEL-5v2; NAEL-6v2; NBLV
Little Girl Found, The. FHYEP; NOBRP
Little Girl Lost, A. FHYEP
Little Girl Lost, The. FHYEP; NOBRP
Little Vagabond, The. FHYEP; NBLV; OBSV
London. AWP; CABP; ClHu; FHYEP; HAP; HeIP-4; InPK-6; NAEL-5v2;
NAEL-6v2; NAWM-7v2; NIL-7; NIP-4; NOBE; NOBRP; NOEC; NPeEn;
NoP-4; OxAEP-2; OxBEV; PoE; PoPoPo; RB; SCGP; SCV; TFi; TRP;
UnPo; WeW-3
"Love seeketh not Itself to please." EnLoPo; FHYEP; NAEL-5v2; NAEL-
6v1; NOBE; NPeEn; NoP-4; OxAEP-2; OxBEV; OxBSP; PoE; RB; SCGP;
SCV; TFi
"Modest rose puts forth a thorn, The." FHYEP; NOBRP
"My mother groaned! [or groan'd!, or groand!] my father wept." FHYEP;
NAEL-5v2; NAEL-6v2; OxAEP-2; OxBEV; OxBSP; PoPoPo; RB
My Pretty Rose-Tree. BoLoP; FHYEP; NAEL-5v2; NAEL-6v2; NOBRP
"Nought loves another as itself." FHYEP; PeECV
Nurse's Song. FHYEP
"Pity would be no more." FHYEP; NAEL-5v2; NAEL-6v2; NOBRP;
NOEC; OxAEP-2; PoE
Poison Tree, A. AWP; FHYEP; HAP; NAEL-5v2; NAEL-6v2; NPeEn;
OxAEP-2; OxBEV; RB; SCV; SoSe-8; TFi; WeW-3
School-Boy, The. FHYEP; FaBoCh; OxAEP-2
Sick Rose, The. AWP; BoLoP; CABP; ClHu; EnLoPo; FHYEP; HAP; HeIP-
4; InPK-6; NAEL-5v2; NAEL-6v2; NAWM-7v2; NIL-7; NIP-4; NOBE;
NOBRP; NOEC; NoP-4; NPeEn; OPOU; OxAEP-2; OxBEV; OxBSP; PoE;
PoPoPo; RB; SCGP; SoSe-8; TFi; TRP; WeW-3
To Tirzah. FHYEP; NAEL-5v2; NAEL-6v2; NOBE
"Tyger Tyger [or Tyger! Tyger! or Tiger! Tiger!] burning bright." AWP;
BBASP; BRP; ChAP; ClHu; FaBoCh; HAP; HeIP-4; ITBLP; InPK-6;
MakPoe; NAEL-6v2; NAWM-7v2; NIL-7; NIP-4; NOBE; NOBRP; NOEC;
NOxBChV; NPeEn; NoP-4; OBEV; OPOU; OxBEV; PeECV; PoE; PoPoPo;
PoRA; RB; SCGP; SCV; SoSe-8; TFi; TTTS; UnPo; WHSW
Voice of the Ancient Bard, The. FHYEP
"Whate'er is Born of Mortal Birth." FHYEP; NAEL-5v2; NAEL-6v2;
NOBE
"When the voices of children are heard on the green / And whisperings [or
whisprings] are in the dale." FHYEP
"Youth of delight, come hither." FHYEP
Songs of Fairly Utter Despair. Samuel Hoffenstein.
"Now, alas, it is too late." OBCoV
Songs of Innocence. William Blake.
"All the night in woe." FHYEP; NOBRP
Blossom, The. FHYEP
"Can I see another's woe." AWP; FHYEP; InvLi; OxAEP-2
Chimney Sweeper, The. FHYEP; HeIP-4; InPK-6; NAEL-5v2; NAEL-6v2;
NAWM-7v2; NOEC; OxAEP-2; PAI; PoE; SCGP; SoSe-8; TFi

Cradle Song, A: "Sweet dreams form a shade." FHYEP; OBCP

Divine Image, The. BBASP; ChAP; FHYEP; InvLi; NAEL-5v2; NAEL-6v2; NOBE; NOBRP; NOEC; NoP-4; OxBEV; PeECV; PoE

Dream, A. FHYEP; NOBRP

Echoing [or Ecchoing] Green, The. AmFaPo; FHYEP; NAEL-5v2; NAEL-6v2; OxAEP-2; PoE; UnPo

"Father, father, where are you going?" FHYEP

(From Songs of Innocence.) NoP-4

Holy Thursday [1]. FHYEP; NAEL-5v2; NAEL-6v2; NAWM-7v2; NOBE; NOBRP; NOEC; NPeEn; NoP-4; PeECV; PoE; SCV; TFi; TrCP

(Holy Thursday (Innocence).) NOxBChV

"How sweet is the Shepherd's sweet lot!" ChAP; FHYEP

"I have no name." FHYEP; NAEL-5v2; OxAEP-2; OxBSP; PoPoPo

"In futurity / I prophetic see." FHYEP; NOBRP

Infant Joy. FHYEP; NAEL-5v2; OxAEP-2; OxBSP

(Introduction.) NAEL-6v2; NAWM-7v2; NOBRP

Lamb, The. ChIV-2; FHYEP; FaBoCh; HeIP-4; ITBLP; NAEL-5v2; NAEL-6v2; NAWM-7v2; NIL-7; NIP-4; NOBRP; NOEC; NoP-4; OxAEP-2; PAI; PoE; PoPoPo; SoSe-8; TFi; TRP; TrCP; UnPo

(Laughing Song.) FHYEP; NAEL-5v2

Little Black Boy, The. AWP; AmFaPo; CABP; ChAP; FHYEP; HeIP-4; NAEL-5v2; NAEL-6v2; NAWM-7v2; NOBRP; NOEC; NoP-4; OBEV; PeECV; PoE; PoPoPo; SCGP; TFi

Little Boy Found, The. FHYEP; NoP-4

"Little boy lost in the lonely fen, The." FHYEP; NoP-4

Little Boy Lost, The. FHYEP

Little Girl Found, The. FHYEP; NOBRP

Little Girl Lost, The. FHYEP; NOBRP

"Merry Merry Sparrow!" FHYEP

"My mother bore me in the southern wild." AWP; AmFaPo; CABP; ChAP; FHYEP; HeIP-4; NAEL-5v2; NAEL-6v2; NAWM-7v2; NOBRP; NOEC; NoP-4; OBEV; PeECV; PoE; PoPoPo; SCGP; TFi

Night. FHYEP; ITBLP; OBEV

Nurse's Song. AWP; FHYEP; NAEL-5v2; NAEL-6v2; PeLV; RACG; SCGP

On Another's Sorrow. AWP; FHYEP; InvLi; OxAEP-2

"Once a dream did weave a shade." FHYEP; NOBRP

(Piper, The.) AWP

(Piping down the Valleys.) ChAP

Piping Down the Valleys Wild. ClHu; FaBoCh; HeIP-4; NAEL-5v2; NOBE; NOEC; NOxBChV; PoE; SoSe-8; TFi

(Reeds of Innocence.) OBEV

Shepherd, The. ChAP; FHYEP

"Sound the Flute!" FHYEP; FaBoCh; NOxBChV; TTTS

Spring. FHYEP; FaBoCh; NOxBChV; TTTS

"Sun descending in the west, The." FHYEP; ITBLP; OBEV

"Sun does [or doth] arise, The." AmFaPo; FHYEP; NAEL-5v2; NAEL-6v2; OxAEP-2; PoE; UnPo

"Sweet dreams form a shade." FHYEP; OBCP

"To Mercy, Pity, Peace and Love." BBASP; ChAP; FHYEP; InvLi; NAEL-5v2; NAEL-6v2; NOBE; NOBRP; NOEC; NoP-4; OxBEV; PeECV; PoE

"'Twas on a Holy Thursday, their innocent faces clean." FHYEP; NAEL-5v2; NAEL-6v2; NAWM-7v2; NOBE; NOBRP; NOEC; NPeEn; NoP-4; PeECV; PoE; SCV; TFi; TrCP

"When my mother died I was very young." FHYEP; HeIP-4; InPK-4; NAEL-5v2; NAEL-6v2; NAWM-7v2; NOEC; OxAEP-2; PAI; PoE; SCGP; SoSe-8; TFi

When the Green Woods Laugh. NBLV

"When the voices of children are heard on the green." AWP; FHYEP; NAEL-5v2; NAEL-6v2; PeLV; RACG; SCGP

Songs of Innocence. Attila József. IQMS, tr. by Thomas Kabdebo and Anton N. Nyerges

Songs of Joy. William Henry Davies. MoBrPo

Songs of Lake Tung-t'ing. Yang Wei-chen. CoBLCP, tr. by Jonathan Chaves

Songs of Maximus. Charles Olson. NeAP Fr. Maximus Poems, The.

Songs of My Soul. Juan Chi.

"Confucianist is versed in the Six Arts, The." ColAnChi

"Elder lives by the side of the river, An." ColAnChi

"Hibiscus grows lushly on the grave mounds, The." ColAnChi

"It is the middle of the night—I cannot sleep." ColAnChi

"Lucent dew congeals into frost, The." ColAnChi

"My steps lead me to a junction of three roads." ColAnChi

"Whether one is eminent or humble depends on Fate." ColAnChi

Songs of Rescue. Jacques Dupin.

"From a thread in space, endless and unbroken. Without unravelling." VCWP

Songs of Seven. Jean Ingelow.

Giving in Marriage. TreFP

Seven Times Three—Love. TreFP

Songs of shepherds and rustical roundelays. Hunting of the Gods, The. Unknown. OxBoLi

Songs of Sorrow. Kofi Awoonor. HBAPE; PBMAP

(I shall sleep in white calico.) PBMAP

(Song of War.) PBMAP

Songs of Spirits. Unknown. APN-2, tr. by Jeremiah Curtin

Songs of T'ang. Confucius.

Alba. CTC, tr. by Ezra Pound

Songs of the Arapaho. Unknown. APN-2, tr. by James Mooney Fr. Ghost-Dance Songs.

Songs of the Common Day. Sir Charles G. D. Roberts.

Herring Weir, The. NOBC

Pea-Fields, The. NOBC

Songs of the Frontier. Li K'ai-hsien. CoBLCP, tr. by Jonathan Chaves

Songs of the Fruits and Sweets of Childhood. Lorna Goodison. VCWP

Songs of the Kiowa. Unknown. APN-2, tr. by James Mooney Fr. Ghost-Dance Songs.

Songs of the Kwakiutl Indians. Unknown.

Girl's Song, A. APN-2, tr. by Franz Boas

Love Song: "Like pain of fire runs down my body my love to you, my dear!" APN-2, tr. by Franz Boas

Warsong of the Kwakiutl. APN-2, tr. by Franz Boas

Songs of the Paiute. Unknown. APN-2 Fr. Ghost-Dance Songs.

Songs of the People. Hayyim Nahman [or Khayim Nakhman or Chaim Nachman] Bialik. AWP, tr. by Maurice Samuel

Songs of the Psyche. Thomas Kinsella.

"Character, indistinct, entered, A." NoAM

Songs of the Sacred Mysteries. Unknown. APN-2, tr. by Alfred Longley Riggs

Songs of the Sioux. Unknown. APN-2 Fr. Ghost-Dance Songs.

Songs of the Squatters. Robert Lowe, Viscount Sherbrooke.

"Commissioner bet me a pony, I won, The." NOBAu

"Gum has no shade, The." NOBAu

Songs of the Stream. Leah Goldberg.

Blade of Grass Sings to the River, The. TrJP, tr. by Robert Friend

Blade of Grass Sings to the Stream, The. MHP, tr. by Ruth Finer Mintz

Girl Sings to the Stream, The. MHP, tr. by Ruth Finer Mintz

Moon Sings to the Stream, The. MHP, tr. by Ruth Finer Mintz

Stream Sings to the Stone, The. MHP, tr. by Ruth Finer Mintz

Tree Sings to the Stream, The. MHP, tr. by Ruth Finer Mintz

Songs of the Transformed. Margaret Atwood.

Rat Song. NIP-4

Siren Song. HAP; NIL-7; NIP-4; WeW-3

Songs of the Valley. John Koethe. BAP-01

Songs of Yen-ching. Hsü Wei. CoBLCP, tr. by Jonathan Chaves

Songs, so old and bitter, The. Coffin, the. Heinrich Heine. AWP, tr. by Louis Untermeyer

Songs to Joannes. Mina Loy. APT-1

Songs to Seraphine. Heinrich Heine. TrJP, tr. by Emma Lazarus

Songs to Welcome the Society of the Mystic Animals. Unknown. STP, tr. by Richard Johnny John and Jerome Rothenberg

Songs We Fought For, The. Walter McDonald. SwNoth

Songs without Words. John Ashbery. NAAL-2v2

Songs you sent me I have read, The. Hildebert. MLL

Sonia at 32. Morrie Warshawski. GotH

Sonja Henie, the young girl. Preface. Theodore Weiss. VGW

Son[ne], The. George Herbert. AngWePo; GeHe; PeECV

Sonnet. William Browne (1591–1643). See Song: "For her gait, if she be walking."

Sonnet. Thomas Gray. See Sonnet [on the Death of Mr. Richard West]

"No Worst, There Is None. Pitched Past Pitch of Grief." Gerard Manley Hopkins. See No Worst, There Is None. Pitched Past Pitch of Grief

Sonnet. Willem Kloos. TuT, tr. by Tony Curtis

Sonnet. James Russell Lowell. NCAP

Sonnet. John Milton. See When the Assault Was Intended to the City

Sonnet. John Milton. See To Mr. Cyriack Skinner upon His Blindness

Sonnet. John Milton. See To Cyriack Skinner

Sonnet. John Milton. See To Mr. Lawrence

Sonnet. John Milton. See On His Deceased Wife

Sonnet. John Milton. See Sonnet: On the Religious Memorie of Mrs. Catherine Thomason My Christian Freind Deceas'd Decem. 1646

Sonnet. Ed Roberson. GT

Sonnet, A [or "A Sonnet is a moment's monument"]. Dante Gabriel Rossetti. GSo; NIL-7; Son Fr. House of Life, The.

Sonnet. William Shakespeare. See also Sonnets

Sonnet. Henry Howard, Earl of Surrey. See Complaint by Night, A

Sonnet. Henry Howard, Earl of Surrey. See Soote Season, The

Sonnet. Frederick Goddard Tuckerman. *See* Sonnets: "Starry flower, the flower-like stars that fade, The."

Sonnet, A. James Kenneth Stephen. *See* Sonnet, A: "Two voices are there: one is of the deep."

Sonnet, The. Richard Watson Gilder. APN-2

Sonnet, The. Dante Gabriel Rossetti. *See* House of Life, The

Sonnet, The. Ella Wheeler Wilcox. APN-2

Sonnet 1. George Herbert. *See* Sonnet: "My God, where is that ancient heat towards Thee."

Sonnet 1. William Shakespeare. CTC; HeIP-4; NAEL-6v1; NAEL-7v1 *Fr.* Sonnets.

Sonnet 1: "Everything that happens to me these days." Julia Alvarez. FFC *Fr.* ("33").

Sonnet 1: "Happy ye leaves! whenas those lily hands." Edmund Spenser. EBVV; NAEL-5v1; PoE; Son *Fr.* Amoretti.

Sonnet I: "His piercing pince-nez. Some dim frieze." Ted Berrigan. FTOS *Fr.* Sonnets, The.

Sonnet 1: "I thought once how Theocritus had sung." Elizabeth Barrett Browning. BWW; CenSon; EBVV; NOBE; NoP-4; OBEV; OxAEP-2; PoPoPo; WPE *Fr.* Sonnets from the Portuguese.

Sonnet I: "If it must be; if it must be, O God!" David Gray. OxBS *Fr.* In the Shadows.

Sonnet 1: "In this strang[e] labyrinth [*or* labourinth] how shall I turn[e]?" Mary Sidney Wroth, Countess of Montgomery. BASC; CABP; EMWP; NAEL-5v1; NAEL-6v1; NAEL-7v1; NPeEn; NoP-4; PBRV *Fr.* Pamphilia to Amphilanthus.

Sonnet 1: "Loving in truth, and fain[e] in verse my love to show." Sir Philip Sidney. AWP; CABP; EBEV; HAP; NAEL-5v1; NAEL-6v1; NAEL-7v1; NPeEn; NoP-4; NoSic; OxAEP-1; OxBSo; PoE; SCGP; Son; TFi *Fr.* Astrophil and Stella.

Sonnet 1: "Not Ulysses, no, nor any other man." Louise Labé. BoWoP, *tr. by* Willis Barnstone

Sonnet 1: "When night's black mantle could most darknes[s] prove." Mary Sidney Wroth, Countess of Montgomery. BASC; CABP; MakPoe; NAEL-5v1; NAEL-6v1; NAEL-7v1; Son *Fr.* Pamphilia to Amphilanthus.

Sonnet 2. George Herbert. *See* Sonnet: "Sure Lord, there is enough in thee to dry."

Sonnet 2. William Shakespeare. HeIP-4; NoSic; SCGP; Son *Fr.* Sonnets.

Sonnet 2: "But only three in all God's universe." Elizabeth Barrett Browning. CenSon *Fr.* Sonnets from the Portuguese.

Sonnet 2: "Deep in her seventh month, my sister dozes." Debra Bruce. FFC *Fr.* ("The Light They Make").

Sonnet 2: "Is to leave all, and take the thread of love." Mary Sidney Wroth, Countess of Montgomery. BASC; EMWP *Fr.* Pamphilia to Amphilanthus.

Sonnet 2: "Late in the Forest I did Cupid See." Mary Sidney Wroth, Countess of Montgomery. NPeEn; OxBSo; PBRV *Fr.* Pamphilia to Amphilanthus.

Sonnet 2: "Love like a jugler, comes to play his prize [*or* prise]." Mary Sidney Wroth, Countess of Montgomery. EMWP *Fr.* Pamphilia to Amphilanthus.

Sonnet 2: "My own heart let me have. More pity on." Nell Altizer. FFC *Fr.* ("Love Letters to Her Who Lives [Alas!] Away").

Sonnet 2: "Not at [the] first sight, nor with a dribbed shot." Sir Philip Sidney. NAEL-5v1; NAEL-6v1; NAEL-7v1 *Fr.* Astrophil and Stella.

Sonnet 2: "O handsome chestnut eyes, evasive gaze." Louise Labé. BoWoP, *tr. by* Willis Barnstone

Sonnet—2: "Some things are very dear to me" Gwendolyn B. Bennett. NAAAL

Sonnet 3. William Shakespeare. NAEL-5v1; NAEL-6v1; NAEL-7v1; NoP-4; SCGP *Fr.* Sonnets.

Song 3: "As Phyllis the gay, at the break of the day." Edward Moore. ECEV

Sonnet 3: "His flames ar[e] joy[e]s, his bands true lovers' might." Mary Sidney Wroth, Countess of Montgomery. BASC *Fr.* Pamphilia to Amphilanthus.

Sonnet 3: "Juno still jealous[e] of her husband Jove." Mary Sidney Wroth, Countess of Montgomery. OxBSo *Fr.* Pamphilia to Amphilanthus.

Sonnet 3: "Let dainty wits cry on the sisters nine." Sir Philip Sidney. NoSic; Son *Fr.* Astrophil and Stella.

Sonnet 3: "O interminable desires, O futile hope." Louise Labé. BoWoP, *tr. by* Willis Barnstone

Sonnet III: "Stronger than alcohol, more great than song." Ted Berrigan. FTOS *Fr.* Sonnets, The.

Sonnet 3: "The sovereign beauty." Edmund Spenser. AEP *Fr.* Amoretti.

Sonnet 3: "Unlike are we, unlike, O princely Heart!" Elizabeth Barrett Browning. BWW; CABP; CenSon; OBEV; OxAEP-2 *Fr.* Sonnets from the Portuguese.

Sonnet IV. E. E. Cummings. ChIV-1; MoAmPo

Sonnet 4. Pablo Neruda. BLPSL, *tr. by* Rene de Costa, Rigas Kappatos and Eleni Paidoussi

Sonnet IV. Chris Wallace-Crabbe. BMAP *Fr.* Sonnets to the Left.

Sonnet 4: "From that first flash when awful Love took flame." Louise Labé. BoWoP, *tr. by* Willis Barnstone

Sonnet 4: "New year, forth looking out of Janus' gate." Edmund Spenser. NoSic *Fr.* Amoretti.

Sonnet 4: "Thou hast thy calling to some palace-floor." Elizabeth Barrett Browning. CenSon; OxAEP-2; Son; VWP *Fr.* Sonnets from the Portuguese.

Sonnet 4: "Wet streets, black trees, a gold leaf smacked." Debra Bruce. FFC *Fr.* ("The Light They Make").

Sonnet 5. Baldomero Garcilaso de la Vega. BLPSL, *tr. by* Rene de Costa, Rigas Kappatos and Eleni Paidoussi

Sonnet 5: "And burn[e], yet[t] burning you will love the smart." Mary Sidney Wroth, Countess of Montgomery. BASC *Fr.* Pamphilia to Amphilanthus.

Sonnet V: "Dreamt I today [*or* to-day] the dream of yesternight." George Santayana. APN-2 *Fr.* Sonnets.

Sonnet 5: "Evening, as slow thy placid shades descend." William Lisle Bowles. NOBRP; NOEC

Sonnet 5: "I lift my heavy heart up solemnly." Elizabeth Barrett Browning. CenSon; LW; NALW; PEW; VWP *Fr.* Sonnets from the Portuguese.

Sonnet 5: "It is most true that eyes are formed to serve." Sir Philip Sidney. NAEL-5v1; NAEL-6v1; NAEL-7v1; NoSic; Son *Fr.* Astrophil and Stella.

Sonnet 5: "No, I'll not, carrion, comfort you. Comfort." Nell Altizer. FFC

Sonnet 5: "Those hours that with gentle work." William Shakespeare. AEP *Fr.* Sonnets.

Sonnet 5: "Whilst Youth and Error." Samuel Daniel. AEP *Fr.* Delia.

Sonnet 5: "White Venus limpid wandering in the sky." Louise Labé. BoWoP, *tr. by* Aliki and Willis Barnstone

Sonnet 6: "Coming of that limpid star is twice, The." Louise Labé. BoWoP, *tr. by* Willis Barnstone

Sonnet 6: "Go from me. Yet I feel that I shall stand." Elizabeth Barrett Browning. BWW; CenSon; LW; OBEV; OxAEP-2 *Fr.* Sonnets from the Portuguese.

Sonnet 6: "How many paltry, foolish, painted things." Michael Drayton. *See* Idea

Sonnet 6: "My pain[e], still smothered [*or* smother'd] in my grieved bre[a]st." Mary Sidney Wroth, Countess of Montgomery. NAEL-6v1; NAEL-7v1; NOSC; PEW *Fr.* Pamphilia to Amphilanthus.

Sonnet 6: "Ô[h] strive not[t] still to heap[e] disdain[e] on me[e]." Mary Sidney Wroth, Countess of Montgomery. NOSC *Fr.* Pamphilia to Amphilanthus.

Sonnet 6: "Some lovers speak, when they their Muses entertain." Sir Philip Sidney. NAEL-5v1; NAEL-6v1; NAEL-7v1; NoSic; Son *Fr.* Astrophil and Stella.

Sonnet 6. To the Torrid Zone. Helen Maria Williams. CenSon; NOBRP; NoP-4

Sonnet 7. John Milton. BASC

(On His Being Arrived to the Age of Twenty-Three.) GSo

Sonnet 7: "By Derwent's rapid stream as oft I strayed." Anna Seward. CenSon *Fr.* Sonnets.

Sonnet 7: "Face of all the world is changed, I think, The." Elizabeth Barrett Browning. CTC; CenSon *Fr.* Sonnets from the Portuguese.

Sonnet 7: "How blest be[e] they then, who his favo[u]rs prove." Mary Sidney Wroth, Countess of Montgomery. BASC *Fr.* Pamphilia to Amphilanthus.

Sonnet 007: "Like an enfranchised bird, who wildly springs." Caroline Elizabeth Norton. CenSon; VWP

Sonnet 7: "Love leave to urge, thou know'st thou hast the hand." Mary Sidney Wroth, Countess of Montgomery. BASC; Son *Fr.* Pamphilia to Amphilanthus.

Sonnet 7: "We see each living thing finally die." Louise Labé. BoWoP, *tr. by* Willis Barnstone

Sonnet 7: "When Nature made her chief work, Stella's eyes." Sir Philip Sidney. NAEL-5v1; NAEL-6v1; NAEL-7v1; NIL-7; NIP-4; Son *Fr.* Astrophil and Stella.

Sonnet [*or* Sonetto] 7: "Who is she that comes, makyng turn every man's eye." Guido Cavalcanti. CTC; OBVE, *tr. by* Ezra Pound

Sonnet 8: "I live, I die, I burn myself and drown." Louise Labé. BoWoP, *tr. by* Willis Barnstone

Sonnet 8: "Led by the pow'r [*or* powre] of grief[e], to wailings [*or* waylings] brought." Mary Sidney Wroth, Countess of Montgomery. PEW *Fr.* Pamphilia to Amphilanthus.

Sonnet 8: "More than most fair [*or* fayre], full of the living fire [*or* fyre]." Edmund Spenser. OxBSo; PoE; Son *Fr.* Amoretti.

Sonnet 8: "What can I give thee back, O liberal." Elizabeth Barrett Browning. BWW; CenSon; OxAEP-2 *Fr.* Sonnets from the Portuguese.

Sonnet 9: "As soon as I lie down in my soft bed." Louise Labé. BoWoP, *tr. by* Willis Barnstone

Sonnet 9: "Be[e] you all pleased [*or* pleas'd]? your pleasures grieve not[t] me[e]." Mary Sidney Wroth, Countess of Montgomery. BWW; NOSC *Fr.* Pamphilia to Amphilanthus.

Sonnet 9: "Can it be right to give what I can give?" Elizabeth Barrett Browning. CTC; CenSon; Son *Fr.* Sonnets from the Portuguese.

Sonnet 9: "Ladie [*or* Lady], that in the prime of earliest youth." John Milton. OxBSo

(Lady That in the Prime.) Son

(Sonnet: Lady, That in the Prime.)   ChIV-2

Sonnet 9: "My muse now hap[p]y, lay thy self to rest."   Mary Sidney Wroth, Countess of Montgomery.   BASC; NAEL-7v1   Fr. Pamphilia to Amphilanthus.

Sonnet 9: "Queen Virtue's court, which some call Stella's face."   Sir Philip Sidney.   NAEL-5v1; NAEL-6v1; NAEL-7v1   Fr. Astrophil and Stella.

Sonnet 10.   Baldomero Garcilaso de la Vega.   BLPSL, tr. by Rene de Costa, Rigas Kappatos and Eleni Paidoussi

Sonnet 10: "Reason, in faith thou art well served, that still."   Sir Philip Sidney.   NAEL-5v1; NAEL-6v1; NAEL-7v1   Fr. Astrophil and Stella.

Sonnet 10: "Unrighteous Lord of Love."   Edmund Spenser.   AEP   Fr. Amoretti.

Sonnet 10: "When I perceive your blond and graceful head."   Louise Labé.   BoWoP

Sonnet 10: "Yet, love, mere love, is beautiful indeed."   Elizabeth Barrett Browning.   BWW; CTC; CenSon; OxAEP-2   Fr. Sonnets from the Portuguese.

Sonnet 11: "And therefore if to love can be desert."   Elizabeth Barrett Browning.   CenSon   Fr. Sonnets from the Portuguese.

Sonnet 11: "In truth, O Love, with what a boyish kind."   Sir Philip Sidney.   OxBSo; PoE   Fr. Astrophil and Stella.

Sonnet 11: "O eyes clear with beauty, O tender gaze."   Louise Labé.   BoWoP, tr. by Willis Barnstone

Sonnet 11: "Unprofitably pleasing, and unsound."   Mary Sidney Wroth, Countess of Montgomery.   BASC   Fr. Pamphilia to Amphilanthus.

Sonnet 12.   Francesco de Aldana.   BLPSL, tr. by Rene de Costa, Rigas Kappatos and Eleni Paidoussi

Sonnet 12.   William Shakespeare.   AWP; HeIP-4; NAEL-5v1; NAEL-6v1; NAEL-7v1; NoSic; SCGP; Son; WoPoe   Fr. Sonnets.

Sonnet 12: "I saw an ugly beast come from the sea."   Edmund Spenser.   ChIV-2

Sonnet 12: "Indeed this very love which is my boast."   Elizabeth Barrett Browning.   CenSon   Fr. Sonnets from the Portuguese.

Sonnet 12: "Lute, companion of my calamity."   Louise Labé.   BoWoP, tr. by Aliki and Willis Barnstone

Sonnet 12: On the Detraction Which Followed upon My Writing Certain Treatises.   John Milton.   See On the Detraction Which Followed upon My Writing Certain Treatises

Sonnet 13: "And wilt thou have me fashion into speech."   Elizabeth Barrett Browning.   BWW; BrRo; CABP; CenSon; VWP   Fr. Sonnets from the Portuguese.

Sonnet 13: "Free from all fogs but[t] shining fair[e], and clear [or cleere]."   Mary Sidney Wroth, Countess of Montgomery.   BASC; EMWP   Fr. Pamphilia to Amphilanthus.

Sonnet 13: "I saw a woman sitting on a beast."   Edmund Spenser.   ChIV-2

Sonnet 13: "If I could linger on his lovely chest."   Louise Labé.   BoWoP, tr. by Aliki and Willis Barnstone

Sonnet 13: "In That proud port, which her so goodly graceth."   Edmund Spenser.   Son   Fr. Amoretti.

Sonnet XIV.   Louise Labé.   BoWoP, tr. by Willis Barnstone

Sonnet 14.   William Shakespeare.   Son   Fr. Sonnets.

Sonnet 14: "Alas, have I not pain enough, my friend."   Sir Philip Sidney.   NoP-4; NoSic   Fr. Astrophil and Stella.

Sonnet 14: "Am I thus conquered [or conquer'd]? have I lost the powers."   Mary Sidney Wroth, Countess of Montgomery.   BASC; CABP; NAEL-5v1; NAEL-6v1; NAEL-7v1; NOSC   Fr. Pamphilia to Amphilanthus.

Sonnet 14: "Except my hart which you beestow'd before."   Mary Sidney Wroth, Countess of Montgomery.   EMWP   Fr. Pamphilia to Amphilanthus.

Sonnet 14: "If thou must love me, let it be for nought [or naught]."   Elizabeth Barrett Browning.   BWW; CTC; CenSon; GSo; HeIP-4; LW; OBEV; OxAEP-2; OxBSo; SoSe-8   Fr. Sonnets from the Portuguese.

Sonnet 14: "Not Wordsworth's genius, Pestalozzi's love."   Amos Bronson Alcott.   APN-1

Sonnet 14: "Then might I see upon a white horse set."   Edmund Spenser.   ChIV-2

Sonnet 15 [On the Lord General Fairfax at the Siege of Colchester].   John Milton.   See On the Lord Gen[eral] Fairfax at the Siege of Colchester

Sonnet 15.   William Shakespeare.   AWP; NAEL-5v1; NAEL-6v1; NAEL-7v1; NoSic; SCGP; Son   Fr. Sonnets.

Sonnet 15: "Accuse me not, beseech thee, that I wear."   Elizabeth Barrett Browning.   CenSon   Fr. Sonnets from the Portuguese.

Sonnet 15: "I saw new Earth, new Heaven, said Saint John."   Edmund Spenser.   ChIV-2

Sonnet 15: "To honor the return of sparkling sun."   Louise Labé.   BoWoP, tr. by Willis Barnstone

Sonnet 15: "Ye tradeful merchants that, with weary toil."   Edmund Spenser.   HeIP-4; NIP-4; Son   Fr. Amoretti.

Sonnet 15: "You that do search for every purling spring."   Sir Philip Sidney.   NAEL-5v1; NoSic; OxAEP-1; Son   Fr. Astrophil and Stella.

Sonnet XVI: "After an age when thunderbolts and hail."   Louise Labé.   BoWoP, tr. by Willis Barnstone

Sonnet 16: "And yet, because thou overcomest so."   Elizabeth Barrett Browning.   CenSon   Fr. Sonnets from the Portuguese.

Sonnet 16: "In nature apt to like when I did see."   Sir Philip Sidney.   NAEL-5v1; NAEL-6v1; NAEL-7v1   Fr. Astrophil and Stella.

Sonnet 17.   Edna St. Vincent Millay.   APT-1   Fr. Sonnets from an Ungrafted Tree.

Sonnet 17: "I flee the city, temples, and each place."   Louise Labé.   BoWoP; WoPoe, tr. by Willis Barnstone

Sonnet 17: "My poet, thou canst touch on all the notes."   Elizabeth Barrett Browning.   BrRo; CenSon   Fr. Sonnets from the Portuguese.

Sonnet 18.   William Shakespeare.   AEP; AmFaPo; BoLoP; CABP; CTC; ClHu; EnLoPo; HAP; HeIP-4; ITBLP; InPK-6; MakPoe; NAEL-6v1; NAEL-7v1; NIL-7; NOBE; NPeEn; NoSic; OxBEV; OxBSo; PoE; PoPoPo; PoRA; SCGP; SCV; Son; TFi; WeW-3   Fr. Sonnets.

Sonnet 18: "Adventurous mariner! in whose gray skiff."   Amos Bronson Alcott.   APN-1

Sonnet 18: "I never gave a lock of hair away."   Elizabeth Barrett Browning.   CenSon; EBVV; HAP; OxBSo   Fr. Sonnets from the Portuguese.

Sonnet 18: "Kiss me again, re-kiss and kiss me whole."   Louise Labé.   WPOW (Sonnet XVIII: "Kiss me again, rekiss, kiss me more")   BoWoP, tr. by Willis Barnstone

Sonnet 18 [On the Late Massacre in Piedmont].   John Milton.   See On the Late Massacre [or Massacher] in Piedmont [or Piemont]

Sonnet 18: "With what sharp checks I in myself am shent."   Sir Philip Sidney.   NAEL-5v1; NAEL-6v1; NAEL-7v1; NoSic   Fr. Astrophil and Stella.

Sonnet 19.   Amos Bronson Alcott.   APN-1

Sonnet 19.   John Milton.   See On His Blindness

Sonnet 019.   Anna Seward.   CenSon

Sonnet 19.   William Shakespeare.   AWP; EBEV; HeIP-4; NAEL-5v1; NAEL-6v1; NAEL-7v1; NoSic; OxAEP-1; PoE; SCGP   Fr. Sonnets.

Sonnet XIX: "After having slain very many beasts."   Louise Labé.   BoWoP, tr. by Willis Barnstone

Sonnet 19: "Come darkest night, be[e]coming sorrow best."   Mary Sidney Wroth, Countess of Montgomery.   BASC; EMWP; NOSC   Fr. Pamphilia to Amphilanthus.

Sonnet 19: "On Cupid's bow how are my heart-strings bent."   Sir Philip Sidney.   NoSic   Fr. Astrophil and Stella.

Sonnet 19: "Soul's Rialto hath its merchandise, The."   Elizabeth Barrett Browning.   CenSon   Fr. Sonnets from the Portuguese.

Sonnet XX.   Louise Labé.   BoWoP, tr. by Willis Barnstone

Sonnet 20.   William Shakespeare.   CAGL; HeIP-4; NAEL-5v1; NAEL-6v1; NAEL-7v1; NoP-4; NoSic; OxAEP-1   Fr. Sonnets.

Sonnet 20: "Beloved, my Beloved, when I think."   Elizabeth Barrett Browning.   CenSon; Son; WPE   Fr. Sonnets from the Portuguese.

Sonnet 20: "Fly, fly, my friends."   Sir Philip Sidney.   NAEL-7v1; NoSic   Fr. Astrophil and Stella.

Sonnet 20: Remembering, from a Nazi Prison, a Teacher Years Before.   William Pitt Root.   MiVo

Sonnet 21.   William Shakespeare.   HeIP-4   Fr. Sonnets.

Sonnet 21: "I start awake at night afraid of death."   Paul Goodman.   VGW

Sonnet 21: "Say over again, and yet once over again."   Elizabeth Barrett Browning.   CenSon; NAEL-5v2; NAEL-6v2; OxBSo   Fr. Sonnets from the Portuguese.

Sonnet 21: "What grandeur makes a man seem venerable?"   Louise Labé.   BoWoP, tr. by Willis Barnstone

Sonnet 21: "When last I saw thee, I did not[t] thee see."   Mary Sidney Wroth, Countess of Montgomery.   PEW   Fr. Pamphilia to Amphilanthus.

Sonnet 21: "Your words my friend (right healthful caustics) blame."   Sir Philip Sidney.   NAEL-5v1; NAEL-7v1; NoSic; PoE   Fr. Astrophil and Stella.

Sonnet 22.   William Shakespeare.   Son

Sonnet 22: "In highest way of heav'n the sun did ride."   Sir Philip Sidney.   Son   Fr. Astrophil and Stella.

Sonnet 22: "Like to the Indians, scorched with the sun[ne]."   Mary Sidney Wroth, Countess of Montgomery.   BASC; EMWP; NOSC   Fr. Pamphilia to Amphilanthus.

Sonnet 22: "O blazing Sun, how happy you are there."   Louise Labé.   BoWoP, tr. by Willis Barnstone

Sonnet 22: "This holy season, fit to fast and pray."   Edmund Spenser.   PoE   Fr. Amoretti.

Sonnet 22: "When our two souls stand up erect and strong."   Elizabeth Barrett Browning.   BWW; BoWoP; CenSon; LW; NAEL-5v2; NAEL-6v2; NALW; NOBE; OBEV; WPE   Fr. Sonnets from the Portuguese.

Sonnet 23.   John Milton.   See On His Deceased Wife

Sonnet 23.   William Shakespeare.   NoSic; Son   Fr. Sonnets.

Sonnet 23: "Is it indeed so? If I lay here dead."   Elizabeth Barrett Browning.   CenSon   Fr. Sonnets from the Portuguese.

Sonnet 23: "What good is it to me if long ago."   Louise Labé.   BoWoP, tr. by Willis Barnstone

Sonnet 23: "When every one to pleasing pastime hies." Mary Sidney Wroth, Countess of Montgomery. BASC; PBRV; WPE *Fr.* Pamphilia to Amphilanthus.

Sonnet 24: "Don't blame me, ladies, if I've loved. No sneers." Louise Labé. BoWoP

Sonnet 24: "Let the world's sharpness, like a clasping knife." Elizabeth Barrett Browning. CenSon; NOBVV; OxBEV *Fr.* Sonnets from the Portuguese.

Sonnet 25. William Shakespeare. FaBoWar; OxAEP-1; SCGP *Fr.* Sonnets.

Sonnet XXV: "As in the midst of battle there is room." George Santayana. APN-2; AWP *Fr.* Sonnets.

Sonnet 25: "Heavy heart, Beloved, have I borne, A." Elizabeth Barrett Browning. CenSon *Fr.* Sonnets from the Portuguese.

Sonnet 25: "Wisest scholar of the wight most wise, The." Sir Philip Sidney. NoP-4 *Fr.* Astrophil and Stella.

Sonnet 25: "Yow that take pleasure in yowr cruelty." Robert Sidney. PBRV

Sonnet 26. Christina Georgina Rossetti. *See* Later Life: A Double Sonnet of Sonnets

Sonnet 26. William Shakespeare. HeIP-4 *Fr.* Sonnets.

Sonnet 26: "Deare cherish this, and with it[t] my soules will." Mary Sidney Wroth, Countess of Montgomery. BWW *Fr.* Pamphilia to Amphilanthus.

Sonnet 26: "I lived with visions for my company." Elizabeth Barrett Browning. BWW; CenSon *Fr.* Sonnets from the Portuguese.

Sonnet 26: "Though dusty wits dare scorn astrology." Sir Philip Sidney. Son *Fr.* Astrophil and Stella.

Sonnet 27. William Shakespeare. AWTN; CAGL; HeIP-4; NoSic; SCGP *Fr.* Sonnets.

Sonnet 27: "Because I oft, in dark abstracted guise." Sir Philip Sidney. NoSic *Fr.* Astrophil and Stella.

Sonnet 27: "Fair proud, now tell me, why should fair be proud." Edmund Spenser. Son *Fr.* Amoretti.

Sonnet 27: "Fie [*or* Fy] tedious Hope, why do[e] you still rebel[l]?" Mary Sidney Wroth, Countess of Montgomery. NOSC *Fr.* Pamphilia to Amphilanthus.

Sonnet 27: "My own Beloved, who hast lifted me." Elizabeth Barrett Browning. CenSon *Fr.* Sonnets from the Portuguese.

Sonnet 28. William Shakespeare. AWTN *Fr.* Sonnets.

Sonnet 28: "My letters! all dead paper, mute and white." Elizabeth Barrett Browning. CenSon; HAP; OxAEP-2 *Fr.* Sonnets from the Portuguese.

Sonnet 28: "You that with allegory's curious frame." Sir Philip Sidney. NAEL-7v1; NoSic *Fr.* Astrophil and Stella.

Sonnet XXIX. Elizabeth Barrett Browning. *See* Sonnets from the Portuguese.

Sonnet 29. William Shakespeare. AWP; AmFaPo; CTC; EBEV; HAP; HeIP-4; ITBLP; InPK-6; NAEL-5v1; NAEL-6v1; NAEL-7v1; NOBE; NoP-4; NoSic; OBEV; OPOU; OxAEP-1; PoPoPo; SCGP; Son; TFi; WeW-3; WoPoe *Fr.* Sonnets.

Sonnet 29: "Am I failing? For no longer can I cast." George Meredith. SCGP *Fr.* Modern Love.

Sonnet 29: "I think of thee!—My thoughts do twine and bud." Elizabeth Barrett Browning. CenSon *Fr.* Sonnets from the Portuguese.

Sonnet 29: "When in disgrace with Fortune." William Shakespeare. *See* Sonnets

Sonnet 30. William Shakespeare. AWP; CTC; ClHu; EBEV; HAP; HeIP-4; NAEL-5v1; NAEL-6v1; NAEL-7v1; NOBE; NoSic; OBEV; OxAEP-1; PAI; PoE; PoRA; SCGP; TFi *Fr.* Sonnets.

Sonnet 30: "I see thine image through my tears tonight." Elizabeth Barrett Browning. CenSon *Fr.* Sonnets from the Portuguese.

Sonnet 30: "My love is like to ice, and I to fire." Edmund Spenser. PAI *Fr.* Amoretti.

Sonnet 30: "Whether the Turkish new moon minded be." Sir Philip Sidney. NoSic; PoE *Fr.* Astrophil and Stella.

Sonnet 31. Anna Seward. PoBW

Sonnet 31. William Shakespeare. NOBE; OBEV *Fr.* Sonnets.

Sonnet 31: "Thou comest! all is said without a word." Elizabeth Barrett Browning. BWW; CenSon *Fr.* Sonnets from the Portuguese.

Sonnet 31: "With how sad steps, O Moon[e], thou climb'st the skies." Sir Philip Sidney. AEP; AWP; BoLoP; CABP; EnLoPo; GSo; HAP; HeIP-4; NAEL-5v1; NAEL-6v1; NAEL-7v1; NPeEn; NoSic; OxAEP-1; OxBSo; PoE; PoRA; SCGP; Son; TFi; TRP *Fr.* Astrophil and Stella.

Sonnet 32. Fernando de Herrera. BLPSL, *tr. by* Rene de Costa, Rigas Kappatos and Eleni Paidoussi

Sonnet 32: "First time that the sun rose on thine oath, The." Elizabeth Barrett Browning. CenSon; NAEL-5v2; NAEL-6v2; WPE *Fr.* Sonnets from the Portuguese.

Sonnet 32: "How fast thou fliest, O Time, on loves swift wings." Mary Sidney Wroth, Countess of Montgomery. NOSC *Fr.* Pamphilia to Amphilanthus.

Sonnet 33. William Shakespeare. AWP; EBEV; HAP; NAEL-7v1; NIP-4; NoP-4; NoSic; OxAEP-1; PoRA; SCGP; Son; TFi; WeW-3 *Fr.* Sonnets.

Sonnet 33: "I might, unhappy word, O me, I might." Sir Philip Sidney. NPeEn *Fr.* Astrophil and Stella.

Sonnet 33: "When men shall find thy flower." Samuel Daniel. *See* To Delia

Sonnet 33: "Yes, call me by my pet-name! let me hear." Elizabeth Barrett Browning. CenSon *Fr.* Sonnets from the Portuguese.

Sonnet 34. William Shakespeare. HeIP-4; OxAEP-1 *Fr.* Sonnets.

Sonnet 34: "Like as a ship, that through the ocean wide." Edmund Spenser. NAEL-5v1; PoE *Fr.* Amoretti.

Sonnet 34: "Take heed mine eyes, how you your look[e]s do[e] cast." Mary Sidney Wroth, Countess of Montgomery. BASC; NAEL-7v1; PEW *Fr.* Pamphilia to Amphilanthus.

Sonnet XXXIV: "Time flies by like a great whale." Ted Berrigan. FTOS *Fr.* Sonnets, The.

Sonnet 34: "With the same heart, I said, I'll answer thee." Elizabeth Barrett Browning. CenSon *Fr.* Sonnets from the Portuguese.

Sonnet 35. William Shakespeare. HeIP-4; NAEL-5v1; NAEL-6v1; NAEL-7v1; NoSic; OxAEP-1; PoE; SCGP; UnPo *Fr.* Sonnets.

Sonnet 35: "False [*or* Faulce] hope which feeds but[t] to destroy, and spill." Mary Sidney Wroth, Countess of Montgomery. BASC; NAEL-5v1; NAEL-6v1; NAEL-7v1; PEW *Fr.* Pamphilia to Amphilanthus.

Sonnet 35: "If I leave all for thee, wilt thou exchange." Elizabeth Barrett Browning. CenSon; Son *Fr.* Sonnets from the Portuguese.

Sonnet 35: "Some, misbelieving and profane." Michael Drayton. AEP *Fr.* Idea.

Sonnet XXXV: "You can make this swooped transition on your lips." Ted Berrigan. FTOS *Fr.* Sonnets, The.

Sonnet 36. William Shakespeare. HeIP-4 *Fr.* Sonnets.

Sonnet 36: "When we first met and loved, I did not build." Elizabeth Barrett Browning. CenSon *Fr.* Sonnets from the Portuguese.

Sonnet 37: "I'd decided I initiate most." Phyllis Koestenbaum. FFC

Sonnet 37: "My mouth doth water, and my breast doth swell." Sir Philip Sidney. NAEL-5v1; NAEL-6v1; NAEL-7v1; Son *Fr.* Astrophil and Stella.

Sonnet 37: "Night, welcome art thou to my mind destrest." Mary Sidney Wroth, Countess of Montgomery. NoP-4 *Fr.* Pamphilia to Amphilanthus.

Sonnet 37: "Pardon, oh, pardon, that my soul should make." Elizabeth Barrett Browning. CenSon *Fr.* Sonnets from the Portuguese.

Sonnet 37: "What guile [*or* guyle] is this, that those her golden tresses." Edmund Spenser. NAEL-5v1; NAEL-6v1; PAI; Son *Fr.* Amoretti.

Sonnet 38: "First time he kissed me, he but only kissed." Elizabeth Barrett Browning. CTC; CenSon; ITBLP; LW *Fr.* Sonnets from the Portuguese.

Sonnet 38: "What pleasure can a bannish'd creature have." Mary Sidney Wroth, Countess of Montgomery. EMWP *Fr.* Pamphilia to Amphilanthus.

Sonnet 39: "Because thou hast the power and own'st the grace." Elizabeth Barrett Browning. CenSon *Fr.* Sonnets from the Portuguese.

Sonnet 39: "Come Sleep! O sleep the certain knot of peace." Sir Philip Sidney. GSo; NAEL-5v1; NAEL-6v1; NAEL-7v1; NoSic; OxAEP-1; OxBSo; PoE; PoRA; SCGP; SCV; Son; TFi *Fr.* Astrophil and Stella.

Sonnet 40. William Shakespeare. HeIP-4; OxAEP-1; SCGP *Fr.* Sonnets.

Sonnet 40: "As good to write as for to lie and groan." Sir Philip Sidney. NoSic *Fr.* Astrophil and Stella.

Sonnet 40: "Oh, yes! they love through all this world of ours!" Elizabeth Barrett Browning. CenSon *Fr.* Sonnets from the Portuguese.

Sonnet 41. Francisco de Medrano. BLPSL, *tr. by* Rene de Costa, Rigas Kappatos and Eleni Paidoussi

Sonnet 41. William Shakespeare. OxAEP-1 *Fr.* Sonnets.

Sonnet 41: "Having this day my horse, my hand, my lance." Sir Philip Sidney. HAP; NAEL-5v1; NAEL-6v1; NAEL-7v1; PoE; Son *Fr.* Astrophil and Stella.

Sonnet 41: "Having this day my horse, my lance." Sir Philip Sidney. *See* Astrophil and Stella

Sonnet 41: "I thank all who have loved me in their hearts." Elizabeth Barrett Browning. CenSon *Fr.* Sonnets from the Portuguese.

Sonnet 42. William Shakespeare. HeIP-4; OxAEP-1 *Fr.* Sonnets.

Sonnet 42: "How do I love thee? Let me count the ways." Elizabeth Barrett Browning. AmFaPo; BWW; BoLoP; CTC; CenSon; EBVV; GSo; HeIP-4; ITBLP; InPK-6; MakPoe; NAEL-5v2; NAEL-6v2; NALW; NIL-7; NIP-4; NoP-4; OPOU; OxAEP-2; OxBSo; PoE; PoPoPo; PoRA; PoToHe; Son; TFi; UV; UnPo; VWP; WPE *Fr.* Sonnets from the Portuguese.

Sonnet 42: "If ever love had force in huma[i]ne bre[a]st?" Mary Sidney Wroth, Countess of Montgomery. BASC; BWW *Fr.* Pamphilia to Amphilanthus.

Sonnet 42: "Sometimes the words are so close I am." Julia Alvarez. FFC *Fr.* ("33").

Sonnet 43. Eleanor Brown. MFPA

Sonnet 43. Elizabeth Barrett Browning. *See* Sonnets from the Portuguese

Sonnet XLIII: "Candour of the gods is in thy gaze, The." George Santayana. APN-2 *Fr.* Sonnets.

Sonnet 44. William Shakespeare. Son *Fr.* Sonnets.

Sonnet 44: "Beloved, thou hast brought me many flowers." Elizabeth Barrett Browning. CenSon; EBVV; LW; OxBSo; WPE *Fr.* Sonnets from the Portuguese.

Sonnet 44: "When those renowned noble peers of Greece." Edmund Spenser. PoE *Fr.* Amoretti.

45. Samuel Daniel. *See* To Delia

Sonnet 45: "Stella oft sees the very face of woe." Sir Philip Sidney. NAEL-5v1; NAEL-6v1; NAEL-7v1; NoSic; PoE *Fr.* Astrophil and Stella.

Sonnet 46. William Shakespeare. HeIP-4 *Fr.* Sonnets.

Sonnet 47: "What, have I thus betrayed my liberty?" Sir Philip Sidney. NAEL-5v1; NAEL-6v1; NAEL-7v1; NoP-4 *Fr.* Astrophil and Stella.

Sonnet 48: "How like a fire doth love increase in me[e]." Mary Sidney Wroth, Countess of Montgomery. NOSC *Fr.* Pamphilia to Amphilanthus.

Sonnet XLVIII: "Of Helen's brothers, one was born to die." George Santayana. APN-2 *Fr.* Sonnets.

Sonnet 48: "Soul's joy, bend not those morning stars from me." Sir Philip Sidney. NoP-4 *Fr.* Astrophil and Stella.

Sonnet 49. William Shakespeare. OxAEP-1 *Fr.* Sonnets.

Sonnet 49: "I on my horse, and Love on me doth try." Sir Philip Sidney. NAEL-5v1; NAEL-6v1; NAEL-7v1; NoP-4; PoE *Fr.* Astrophil and Stella.

Sonnet 50. William Shakespeare. OxAEP-1 *Fr.* Sonnets.

Sonnet 52. William Shakespeare. OxAEP-1 *Fr.* Sonnets.

Sonnet 52: "Strife is grown between Virtue and Love, A." Sir Philip Sidney. NAEL-5v1; NAEL-6v1; NAEL-7v1; NoP-4 *Fr.* Astrophil and Stella.

Sonnet 53. William Shakespeare. CTC; EBEV; NoSic; OBEV; OxAEP-1; OxBEV; SCGP *Fr.* Sonnets.

Sonnet 53: "In martial sports I had my cunning tried." Sir Philip Sidney. NAEL-5v1; NAEL-6v1; NAEL-7v1; NoSic *Fr.* Astrophil and Stella.

Sonnet 54. William Shakespeare. AWP; OBEV; PoE; SCGP *Fr.* Sonnets.

Sonnet 54: "Because I breathe not love to every one." Sir Philip Sidney. NoSic *Fr.* Astrophil and Stella.

Sonnet 54: "O how much more doth beauty." William Shakespeare. *See* Sonnets

Sonnet 54: "Of this world's Theatre in which we stay." Edmund Spenser. NAEL-5v1; NoP-4 *Fr.* Amoretti.

Sonnet 55. William Shakespeare. AEP; AWP; CABP; CTC; HeIP-4; NAEL-5v1; NAEL-6v1; NAEL-7v1; NIP-4; NOBE; NoP-4; NoSic; OxAEP-1; OxBSo; PAI; PoE; PoRA; SCGP; Son *Fr.* Sonnets.

Sonnet LV: "Grace to be born and live as variously as possible." Ted Berrigan. FTOS; PFTM-2 *Fr.* Sonnets, The.

Sonnet 55: "So oft as I her beauty do behold." Edmund Spenser. Son *Fr.* Amoretti.

Sonnet 56. William Shakespeare. SCGP *Fr.* Sonnets.

Sonnet 56: "Fair ye be sure, but cruel and unkind." Edmund Spenser. Son *Fr.* Amoretti.

Sonnet 56: "Fie, school of Patience, fie; your lesson is." Sir Philip Sidney. NAEL-5v1; NAEL-6v1; NAEL-7v1 *Fr.* Astrophil and Stella.

Sonnet 57. William Shakespeare. CAGL; HAP; NoSic; OBEV *Fr.* Sonnets.

Sonnet 57. Edmund Spenser. OxBSo *Fr.* Amoretti.

Sonnet 59. William Shakespeare. TreFP *Fr.* Sonnets.

Sonnet 60. William Shakespeare. CABP; EBEV; NAEL-7v1; NIP-4; NOBE; NoSic; OxAEP-1; OxBSo; PoRA; SCGP; Son; TFi; TreFP; UnPo *Fr.* Sonnets.

Sonnet 61. Félix Lope de Vega Carpio. BLPSL, *tr.* by Rene de Costa, Rigas Kappatos and Eleni Paidoussi

Sonnet 61. William Shakespeare. AWTN; CAGL *Fr.* Sonnets.

Sonnet 61: "Glorious image of the Maker's beauty, The." Edmund Spenser. SacPr; Son *Fr.* Amoretti.

Sonnet 61: "Oft with true sighs, oft with uncalled tears." Sir Philip Sidney. NAEL-5v1; NAEL-6v1; NAEL-7v1 *Fr.* Astrophil and Stella.

Sonnet 62. William Shakespeare. EBEV; OxAEP-1 *Fr.* Sonnets.

Sonnet 64. William Shakespeare. AWP; EnLoPo; HAP; HeIP-4; NOBE; NoSic; OxAEP-1; PoE; PoRA; SCGP; Son; TreFP *Fr.* Sonnets.

Sonnet 64: "Coming [*or* Comming] to kiss[e] her lips [*or* lyps], such grace I found." Edmund Spenser. EBEV; NAEL-5v1; NAEL-6v1; OxBSo; Son *Fr.* Amoretti.

Sonnet 64: "No more, my dear, no more these counsels try." Sir Philip Sidney. SCGP *Fr.* Astrophil and Stella.

Sonnet 65. William Shakespeare. AWP; HAP; NAEL-5v1; NAEL-6v1; NAEL-7v1; NOBE; NoSic; OxAEP-1; OxBSo; PoRA; RaBo; SCGP; Son; TFi; TreFP; UnPo *Fr.* Sonnets.

Sonnet 65: "Doubt which ye misdeeme, fayre love, is vaine, The." Edmund Spenser. NAEL-5v1; NAEL-6v1; NAEL-7v1 *Fr.* Amoretti.

Sonnet 65: "Love, by sure proof I may call thee unkind." Sir Philip Sidney. Son *Fr.* Astrophil and Stella.

Sonnet 65: "The doubt which ye misdeem." Edmund Spenser. *See* Amoretti

Sonnet 66. William Shakespeare. AWP; CTC; EBEV; HAP; NOBE; NoSic; OxAEP-1; TFi; WeW-3 *Fr.* Sonnets.

Sonnet 67. William Shakespeare. SCGP *Fr.* Sonnets.

Sonnet 67: "Like a huntsman after weary chase." Edmund Spenser. HeIP-4; NAEL-5v1; PoE; Son *Fr.* Amoretti.

Sonnet 68. William Shakespeare. SCGP *Fr.* Sonnets.

Sonnet 68: "Most glorious Lord of Life that on this day." Edmund Spenser. ChIV-2; HAP; NAEL-5v1; NOCV; NoSic; PoE; SacPr; Son *Fr.* Amoretti.

Sonnet 69: "O joy, too high for my low style to show." Sir Philip Sidney. NAEL-5v1; NAEL-6v1; NAEL-7v1; OxAEP-1 *Fr.* Astrophil and Stella.

Sonnet 70. William Shakespeare. OxAEP-1; SCGP *Fr.* Sonnets.

Sonnet 70: "Fresh Spring the herald of love's mighty king." Edmund Spenser. AWP; HAP; OBEV; PoE; Son *Fr.* Amoretti.

Sonnet LXX: "Sweeter than sour apples flesh to boys." Ted Berrigan. FTOS *Fr.* Sonnets, The.

Sonnet 71. William Shakespeare. AWP; EBEV; HAP; HeIP-4; NAEL-5v1; NAEL-6v1; NAEL-7v1; NoSic; OxAEP-1; PAI; PoRA; SCGP; Son; TFi *Fr.* Sonnets.

Sonnet 71: "I joy to see how in your drawen work." Edmund Spenser. NoP-4; PBRV; PoE *Fr.* Amoretti.

Sonnet 71: "Who will in fairest book of Nature know." Sir Philip Sidney. NAEL-5v1; NAEL-6v1; NAEL-7v1; NoP-4; NoSic; PoE *Fr.* Astrophil and Stella.

Sonnet 72. William Shakespeare. OxAEP-1 *Fr.* Sonnets.

Sonnet 72: "Desire, though thou my old companion art." Sir Philip Sidney. NAEL-5v1; NAEL-6v1; NAEL-7v1 *Fr.* Astrophil and Stella.

Sonnet 72: "Oft when my spirit doth spread her bolder wings." Edmund Spenser. Son *Fr.* Amoretti.

Sonnet 73. William Shakespeare. AEP; AWP; BoLoP; CABP; CTC; ClHu; EBEV; GTBS-P; HAP; HeIP-4; InPK-6; NAEL-5v1; NAEL-6v1; NAEL-7v1; NIP-4; NOBE; NoP-4; NoSic; OBEV; OxBSo; PoE; PoRA; SCGP; SoSe-8; Son; TFi; UnPo; WeW-3 *Fr.* Sonnets.

Sonnet 73: "Being my self captived here." Edmund Spenser. AEP

Sonnet 74. William Shakespeare. NAEL-5v1; NAEL-6v1; NAEL-7v1; OxAEP-1; Son *Fr.* Sonnets.

Sonnet 74: "I never drank of Aganippe well." Sir Philip Sidney. NAEL-5v1; NAEL-6v1; NAEL-7v1; NoSic; Son *Fr.* Astrophil and Stella.

Sonnet 74: "Love still a boy, and oft a wanton is." Sir Philip Sidney. Son *Fr.* Astrophil and Stella.

Sonnet 74: "Most happy letters framed by skilfull trade." Edmund Spenser. NAEL-5v1 *Fr.* Amoretti.

Sonnet 75: "Of all the kings that ever here did reign." Sir Philip Sidney. NoSic *Fr.* Astrophil and Stella.

Sonnet 75: "One day I wrote her name upon the strand." Edmund Spenser. AWP; BoLoP; EBEV; HAP; HeIP-4; NAEL-5v1; NAEL-6v1; NAEL-7v1; NoP-4; NoSic; OxBSo; PAI; PoE; PoPoPo; Son; TFi; WeW-3 *Fr.* Amoretti.

Sonnet 77: "Was it a dream, or did I see it plain." Edmund Spenser. NIP-4; OxBSo *Fr.* Amoretti.

Sonnet 76. William Shakespeare. EBEV; NoSic; OxAEP-1 *Fr.* Sonnets.

Sonnet 76: "Fair bosom! fraught with virtue's richest treasure." Edmund Spenser. NIP-4 *Fr.* Amoretti.

Sonnet 77. William Shakespeare. HeIP-4 *Fr.* Sonnets.

Sonnet 78: "Lacking my love, I go from place to place." Edmund Spenser. NoSic *Fr.* Amoretti.

Sonnet 78: "Little Hearts, where light-wing'd Passion raignes, The." Fulke Greville, 1st Baron Brooke. PBRV *Fr.* Cælica.

Sonnet 78: "So oft have I invok'd thee." William Shakespeare. AEP *Fr.* Sonnets.

Sonnet 79: "Men call you fair [*or* fayre], and you do[e] credit it." Edmund Spenser. AWP; NAEL-5v1; Son *Fr.* Amoretti.

Sonnet 80. William Shakespeare. CAGL; OxAEP-1 *Fr.* Sonnets.

Sonnet 80. Edmund Spenser. CABP *Fr.* Amoretti.

Sonnet 81. William Shakespeare. OxAEP-1 *Fr.* Sonnets.

Sonnet 81: "Fair [*or* Fayre] is my love, when her fair [*or* fayre] golden heares." Edmund Spenser. Son *Fr.* Amoretti.

Sonnet 81: "O kiss, which dost those ruddy gems impart." Sir Philip Sidney. NAEL-5v1; NAEL-6v1; NAEL-7v1; OxBSo; Son *Fr.* Astrophil and Stella.

Sonnet 82. Luis de Góngora y Argote. BLPSL, *tr.* by Rene de Costa, Rigas Kappatos and Eleni Paidoussi

Sonnet 82: "Joy of my life, full oft for loving you." Edmund Spenser. HeIP-4 *Fr.* Amoretti.

Sonnet 82: "Nymph of the garden where all beauties be." Sir Philip Sidney. PoE *Fr.* Astrophil and Stella.

Sonnet 84: "Highway, since you my chief Parnassus be." Sir Philip Sidney. SCGP *Fr.* Astrophil and Stella.

Sonnet 85. William Shakespeare. Son *Fr.* Sonnets.

Sonnet 86. William Shakespeare. CABP; NoSic; OxAEP-1; SCGP; Son *Fr.* Sonnets.

Sonnet 87. William Shakespeare. CAGL; EBEV; GTBS-P; NAEL-5v1; NAEL-6v1; NOBE; NoSic; OBEV; OxAEP-1; Son; TFi *Fr.* Sonnets.

Sonnet 87: "When I was forced from Stella ever dear." Sir Philip Sidney. NAEL-5v1; NAEL-6v1; NAEL-7v1 *Fr.* Astrophil and Stella.

Sonnet 88. William Shakespeare. OxAEP-1 *Fr.* Sonnets.

Sonnet 89. William Shakespeare. OxAEP-1 *Fr.* Sonnets.

Sonnet 89: "Like as the culver on the bared bough." Edmund Spenser. PoE *Fr.* Amoretti.

Sonnet 89: "Now that of absence the most irksome night." Sir Philip Sidney. NAEL-5v1; NAEL-6v1; NAEL-7v1 *Fr.* Astrophil and Stella.

Sonnet 90. William Shakespeare. AWP; EBEV; NOBE; NoSic; OBEV; OxAEP-1 *Fr.* Sonnets.

Sonnet 90: "Stella, think not that I by verse seek fame." Sir Philip Sidney. NoP-4; NoSic *Fr.* Astrophil and Stella.

Sonnet 91: "Stella, while now by honour's cruel might." Sir Philip Sidney. NAEL-5v1; NAEL-6v1; NAEL-7v1; PoE *Fr.* Astrophil and Stella.

Sonnet 92. William Shakespeare. HeIP-4 *Fr.* Sonnets.

Sonnet 92: "Be your words made (good sir) of Indian ware." Sir Philip Sidney. NoSic *Fr.* Astrophil and Stella.

Sonnet 94. William Shakespeare. NAEL-5v1; NAEL-6v1; NAEL-7v1; NIL-7; NOBE; NoSic; OBEV; OxAEP-1; OxBEV; OxBSo; PoE; SCGP; SCV; Son; TRP; WoPoe *Fr.* Sonnets.

Sonnet 95. William Shakespeare. HeIP-4; SCGP *Fr.* Sonnets.

Sonnet 97. William Shakespeare. AWP; EnLoPo; GTBS-P; HeIP-4; NAEL-5v1; NAEL-6v1; NAEL-7v1; NOBE; NoSic; OBEV; OxAEP-1; PoRA; SCGP; Son; TFi *Fr.* Sonnets.

Sonnet 97: "How like a winter." William Shakespeare. *See* Sonnets

Sonnet 98. William Shakespeare. AWP; EBEV; NAEL-5v1; NAEL-6v1; NAEL-7v1; NOBE; NoSic; OBEV; OxAEP-1 *Fr.* Sonnets.

Sonnet 98: "Ah bed, the field where joy's peace some do see." Sir Philip Sidney. EnLoPo *Fr.* Astrophil and Stella.

Sonnet 99. William Shakespeare. OxAEP-1 *Fr.* Sonnets.

Sonnet 99: "When far-spent night persuades each mortal eye." Sir Philip Sidney. NoSic; PoE; Son *Fr.* Astrophil and Stella.

Sonnet 100. William Shakespeare. TreFP *Fr.* Sonnets.

Sonnet 100: "O tears, no tears, but rain from beauty's skies." Sir Philip Sidney. Son *Fr.* Astrophil and Stella.

Sonnet 102. William Shakespeare. AWP; OBEV *Fr.* Sonnets.

Sonnet 103. Luis de Góngora y Argote. BLPSL, *tr.* by Rene de Costa, Rigas Kappatos and Eleni Paidoussi

Sonnet 103: "O happy Thames, that didst my Stella bear." Sir Philip Sidney. OxAEP-1 *Fr.* Astrophil and Stella.

Sonnet 104. William Shakespeare. GTBS-P; HeIP-4; NoSic; OBEV; OxAEP-1; SCGP *Fr.* Sonnets.

Sonnet 104: "Envious wits, what hath been mine offence." Sir Philip Sidney. PoE; Son *Fr.* Astrophil and Stella.

Sonnet 106. William Shakespeare. AWP; CTC; EnLoPo; FaBoCh; NAEL-5v1; NAEL-6v1; NAEL-7v1; NOBE; NoSic; OBEV; OxAEP-1; PoRA; SCGP; Son; WoPoe *Fr.* Sonnets.

Sonnet 107. William Shakespeare. AWP; CTC; EBEV; HAP; NAEL-5v1; NAEL-6v1; NAEL-7v1; NoSic; OxAEP-1; SCGP *Fr.* Sonnets.

Sonnet 107: "Stella, since thou so right a Princess art." Sir Philip Sidney. NoP-4; OxAEP-1 *Fr.* Astrophil and Stella.

Sonnet 108. William Shakespeare. TreFP *Fr.* Sonnets.

Sonnet 108: "When sorrow (using mine own fire's might)." Sir Philip Sidney. NAEL-6v1; NAEL-7v1 *Fr.* Astrophil and Stella.

Sonnet 109. William Shakespeare. NOBE; OBEV; OxAEP-1 *Fr.* Sonnets.

Sonnet 110. William Shakespeare. EBEV; NAEL-6v1; NAEL-7v1; NoSic; OxAEP-1 *Fr.* Sonnets.

Sonnet 110: "Alas, 'tis true." William Shakespeare. *See* Sonnets

Sonnet 111. William Shakespeare. OxAEP-1 *Fr.* Sonnets.

Sonnet 113. William Shakespeare. SCGP *Fr.* Sonnets.

Sonnet 114. William Shakespeare. SCGP *Fr.* Sonnets.

Sonnet 115: "All we were going strong last night this time." John Berryman. FaBoMo *Fr.* Sonnets to Chris.

Sonnet 116. William Shakespeare. AEP; AWP; CABP; ClHu; EnLoPo; GSo; HAP; HeIP-4; NAEL-5v1; NAEL-6v1; NAEL-7v1; NIP-4; NOBE; NPeEn; NoSic; OBEV; OxAEP-1; OxBEV; OxBSo; PoE; PoPoPo; PoRA; SCGP; SCV; SoSe-8; Son; TFi; TRP; UnPo; WeW-3 *Fr.* Sonnets.

Sonnet 118. William Shakespeare. SCGP *Fr.* Sonnets.

Sonnet 119. William Shakespeare. OxAEP-1 *Fr.* Sonnets.

Sonnet 120. Marc André Raffalovich. CAGL

Sonnet 120. William Shakespeare. OxAEP-1 *Fr.* Sonnets.

Sonnet 121. William Shakespeare. CAGL; NoSic; OxAEP-1; SCGP *Fr.* Sonnets.

Sonnet 123. William Shakespeare. OxAEP-1; Son *Fr.* Sonnets.

Sonnet 124. William Shakespeare. NoSic *Fr.* Sonnets.

Sonnet 125. William Shakespeare. NoSic *Fr.* Sonnets.

Sonnet 125: "Were't aught to me." William Shakespeare. *See* Sonnets

Sonnet 126. William Shakespeare. HeIP-4; NAEL-5v1; NAEL-6v1; NAEL-7v1 *Fr.* Sonnets.

Sonnet 127. William Shakespeare. NAEL-6v1; NAEL-7v1; OxAEP-1 *Fr.* Sonnets.

Sonnet 128. William Shakespeare. NAEL-5v1; NAEL-6v1; NAEL-7v1; OxAEP-1; PoE *Fr.* Sonnets.

Sonnet 129. William Shakespeare. AWP; EBEV; ErotSp; HAP; HeIP-4; NAEL-5v1; NAEL-6v1; NAEL-7v1; NIL-7; NIP-4; NOBE; NoSic; OBEV;

OxAEP-1; OxBEV; PAI; PoE; SCGP; SCV; Son; TFi; UnPo; WoPoe *Fr.* Sonnets.

Sonnet 130. William Shakespeare. AWP; BoLoP; CABP; EBEV; HAP; HeIP-4; InPK-6; NAEL-5v1; NAEL-6v1; NAEL-7v1; NIL-7; NIP-4; NoSic; OxAEP-1; OxBEV; PAI; PoE; PoPoPo; SoSe-8; Son; TFi; WeW-3 *Fr.* Sonnets.

Sonnet 130: My Mistress' Eyes Are Nothing Like the Sun. William Shakespeare. *See* Sonnets

Sonnet 132. William Shakespeare. OxAEP-1 *Fr.* Sonnets.

Sonnet 133. William Shakespeare. OxAEP-1 *Fr.* Sonnets.

Sonnet 134. William Shakespeare. HeIP-4; OxAEP-1 *Fr.* Sonnets.

Sonnet 135. William Shakespeare. NAEL-5v1; NAEL-6v1; NAEL-7v1 *Fr.* Sonnets.

Sonnet 138. William Shakespeare. AWP; AmFaPo; EBEV; HeIP-4; NAEL-5v1; NAEL-7v1; NPeEn; NoSic; OxAEP-1; OxBEV; PAI; SoSe-8 *Fr.* Sonnets.

Sonnet 140. William Shakespeare. NoSic *Fr.* Sonnets.

Sonnet 144. William Shakespeare. EBEV; HeIP-4; NAEL-5v1; NAEL-6v1; NAEL-7v1; NIL-7; NIP-4; OxBSo; Son *Fr.* Sonnets.

Sonnet 144: "Two loves I have." William Shakespeare. *See* Sonnets

Sonnet 145. William Shakespeare. Son *Fr.* Sonnets.

Sonnet 146. William Shakespeare. AWP; HAP; HeIP-4; NAEL-5v1; NAEL-6v1; NAEL-7v1; NOBE; NOCV; OBEV; OxAEP-1; PoE; SCGP; SacPr; Son; TFi *Fr.* Sonnets.

Sonnet 147. William Shakespeare. EBEV; NAEL-5v1; NAEL-6v1; NAEL-7v1; OxAEP-1 *Fr.* Sonnets.

Sonnet 147: "My love is as a fever." William Shakespeare. *See* Sonnets

Sonnet 148. William Shakespeare. SCGP *Fr.* Sonnets.

Sonnet 150. William Shakespeare. OxAEP-1; SCGP *Fr.* Sonnets.

Sonnet 151. William Shakespeare. EBEV; HeIP-4; NoSic; OxAEP-1; PoE *Fr.* Sonnets.

Sonnet 188. Félix Lope de Vega Carpio. BLPSL, *tr.* by Rene de Costa, Rigas Kappatos and Eleni Paidoussi

Sonnet, A: "O lovely O most charming pug." Marjory Fleming. NBLV

Sonnet: A Rapture Concerning His Lady. Guido Cavalcanti. AWP; EaItPo, *tr.* by Dante Gabriel Rossetti

Sonnet; A Still Place. "Barry Cornwall." NOBRP

Sonnet: A Trance of Love. Cino da Pistoia. AWP; EaItPo, *tr.* by Dante Gabriel Rossetti

Sonnet, A: "Two voices are there: one is of the deep." James Kenneth Stephen. CABP; NOBL; UV

(Sonnet, A.) PeLV

Sonnet, A: "Weeping, murmuring, complaining." Oliver Goldsmith. NOIV

Sonnet Addressed to Henry III on the Death of Thulène, the King's Fool. Jean Passerat. WoPoe, *tr.* by Richmond Lattimore

Sonnet Addressed to My Mother. Mary Tighe. NoP-4

Sonnet Against Nuclear Weapons. Jane Miller. ExTi

Sonnet: "Alexis, here she stayed; among these pines." William Drummond, of Hawthornden. NOSC

(Spring Bereaved.) OBEV

Sonnet ("All my senses, like beacon's flame"). Fulke Greville, 1st Baron Brooke. CABP; NOSC; NoSic *Fr.* Caelica.

Sonnet: "All my thoughts always speak to me of love." Dante Alighieri. AWP; EaItPo, *tr.* by Dante Gabriel Rossetti *Fr.* La Vita Nuova.

Sonnet All of a Sudden, A. Félix Lope de Vega Carpio. SpanPo, *tr.* by Doreen Bell

Sonnet: "Alone, in mourning, wearing an archaic black gown." J. V. Foix. WoPoe, *tr.* by M. L. Rosenthal

Sonnet: "And so, as this great sphere (now turning slow)." Frederick Goddard Tuckerman. ColAP

Sonnet: "And then I sat me down, and gave the rein." Gustav Rosenhane. AWP, *tr.* by Sir Edmund William Gosse

Sonnet Around Stephanie. Lee Ann Brown. BAP-01

Sonnet: "As in a duskie [*or* dusky] and tempestuous night." William Drummond, of Hawthornden. NOSC; OxAEP-1

Sonnet: At Ostend. William Lisle Bowles. NOEC

Sonnet: "Beauty of songs your absence I should not show." Bernadette Mayer. PmAP

Sonnet: "Beauty, sweet love, is like the morning dew." Samuel Daniel. NOBE; NoSic; OBEV *Fr.* To Delia.

Sonnet: "Because my grief seems quiet and apart." Robert Nathan. TrJP

Sonnet: "Beckie, my luve!—What is't, ye twa-faced tod?" George Campbell Hay. OxBS

Sonnet: "Bible says Sennacherib's campaign was spoiled, The." Clive Staples Lewis. TrCP

Sonnet: "Caelica, I overnight was finely used." Fulke Greville, 1st Baron Brooke. NAEL-6v1; Son *Fr.* Caelica.

Sonnet: "Caught—the bubble." Elizabeth Bishop. APT-2

Sonnet: "Cleare moving cristall, pure as the Sunne beames." Sir William Alexander, Earl of Stirling. OxBS *Fr.* Aurora.

Sonnet Composed on a Journey Homeward; the Author Having Received Intelligence of the Birth of a Son, 20 September 1796. Samuel Taylor Coleridge. OxBSo

(Composed on a Journey Homeward; the Author Having Received Intelligence of the Birth of a Son.) Son

[Sonnet] Conclusive. Mary Robinson. CenSon; RWP

Sonnet: "Cry, crow." Hayden Carruth. NNaP; Son

Sonnet: Death Is Not without but within Him. Cino da Pistoia. AWP; EaItPo, *tr.* by Dante Gabriel Rossetti

Sonnet: Death Warnings. Francisco de Quevedo y Villegas. AWP; OxBEV; WoPoe, *tr.* by John Masefield

Sonnet: Death Will Find Me. Rupert Brooke. *See* Sonnet: "Oh! Death will find me, long before I tire."

Sonnet: "Deep in a vale where rocks on every side." Gustav Rosenhane. AWP, *tr.* by Sir Edmund William Gosse

Sonnet: "Dost see how unregarded now." Sir John Suckling. BASC; BeJo; CaPo; CavPo; NOSC

Sonnet: "Down[e] in the depth of mine iniquity." Fulke Greville, 1st Baron Brooke. CABP; NOSC; NoSic *Fr.* Caelica.

Sonnet: "Earth with thunder torn, with fire blasted, The." Fulke Greville, 1st Baron Brooke. NoSic *Fr.* Caelica.

Sonnet: England in 1819. Shelley. *See* England in 1819

Sonnet: "England! the time is come when thou shouldst wean." William Wordsworth. Son

Sonnet: Equality of the Sexes. Gavin Ewart. Son

Sonnet: "Eternall Truth, almighty, infinite." Fulke Greville, 1st Baron Brooke. NoSic; SacPo *Fr.* Caelica.

Sonnet: "Farewell, Love." Sir Thomas Wyatt. AEP

(Renouncing of Love, A.) Son

Sonnet for a Picture. Algernon Charles Swinburne. OxBSo; UV *Fr.* Heptalogia, The.

Sonnet for Christmas. Judith Wright. LW

Sonnet for July. Rosemerry Wahtola Trommer. GeoH

Sonnet for Minimalists. Mona Van Duyn. FFC; WeW-3

Sonnet for the Season. Art Lange. PmAP

Sonnet: "From a rived tree, that stands beside the grave." Anna Seward. ECWP

Sonnet from Below the Age Gap. Keith Sinclair. PeNZ

Sonnet from "One Person." Elinor Wylie. *See* One Person

Sonnet: [From the Italian of Dante.] Dante Alighieri to Guido Cavalcanti. Dante Alighieri. *See* Sonnet: To Guido Cavalcanti

Sonnet: "Go, thou that vainly dost mine eyes invite." Henry King, Bishop of Chichester. OxBSP

Sonnet: "Guido, I wish that you and Lapo and I." Dante Alighieri. RB; TTTS, *tr.* by Kenneth Koch

Sonnet: He Argues His Case with Death. Cecco Angiolieri, da Siena. AWP; EaItPo, *tr.* by Dante Gabriel Rossetti

Sonnet: He Compares All Things with His Lady, and Finds Them Wanting. Guido Cavalcanti. AWP; EaItPo, *tr.* by Dante Gabriel Rossetti

Sonnet: He Craves Interpreting of a Dream of His. Dante da Maiano. AWP; EaItPo, *tr.* by Dante Gabriel Rossetti

Sonnet: He Is Past All Help. Cecco Angiolieri, da Siena. AWP; EaItPo, *tr.* by Dante Gabriel Rossetti

Sonnet: He Jests Concerning His Poverty. Bartolomeo di Sant' Angelo. AWP; EaItPo, *tr.* by Dante Gabriel Rossetti

Sonnet: He Rails against Dante, Who Had Censured His Homage to Becchina. Cecco Angiolieri, da Siena. AWP; EaItPo, *tr.* by Dante Gabriel Rossetti

Sonnet: He Speaks of a Third Love of His. Guido Cavalcanti. AWP; EaItPo, *tr.* by Dante Gabriel Rossetti

Sonnet: He Will Not Be Too Deeply in Love. Cecco Angiolieri, da Siena. AWP; *tr.* by Dante Gabriel Rossetti

Sonnet: He Will Praise His Lady. Guido Guinicelli. AWP; EaItPo, *tr.* by Dante Gabriel Rossetti

Sonnet: "Here in the self is all that men can know." John Masefield. AWP *Fr.* Lollingdon Downs.

Sonnet: "Here lies the noble flesh of Spartacus the knave." Daniel Casper von Lohenstein. GePo *Fr.* Arminius.

Sonnet: "How do I hate you? Let me count the ways." Stanley J. Sharpless. UV

Sonnet: "How many faults you might accuse me of." Elinor Wylie. NAAL-2v2

Sonnet: "How many times Nights silent Queene her Face." William Drummond, of Hawthornden. NPeEn

Sonnet: "I am an honest man." Octavio Armand. TCLAP, *tr.* by Jason Shinder

Sonnet: "I dreamed the nymph that o'er my fancy reigns." Sir William Alexander, Earl of Stirling. NOSC *Fr.* Aurora.

Sonnet: "I feel I am;—I only know I am." John Clare. *See* I Feel I Am

Sonnet: "I had no thought of violets of late." Alice Moore Dunbar-Nelson. BlSi; Son

Sonnet: "I hate the Spring in parti-coloured vest." Mary Locke. CenSon; ECWP

Sonnet: "I hereby swear that to uphold your house." Elinor Wylie. NAAL-2v2; OxBA; Son *Fr.* One Person.

Sonnet: "I know that all beneath the moon decays." William Drummond, of Hawthornden. Son

("I Know That All Beneath The Moon Decays") GSo

Sonnet: "I saw magic on a green country road." Michael Hartnett. BIrV; PBCIP *Fr.* Thirteen Sonnets.

Sonnet: "I still shall smile and go my careless way." Mamie A. Richardson. LW

Sonnet: "I that erstwhile the world's sweet air did draw." George Wither. NOSC *Fr.* Shephe[a]rd's Hunting, The.

Sonnet: "I wandered out a while agone." George Wither. NOSC *Fr.* Fair Virtue, the Mistress of Philarete.

Sonnet: "If it be night." Alec Brock Stevenson. FuPo

Sonnet: "If love is chaste, what bears adultery?" Sibylla Schwarz. GePo, *tr.* by George C. Schoolfield

Sonnet: "If there were any power in human love." Frances Anne [*or* "Fanny"] Kemble. VWP

Sonnet (III), The. John Addington Symonds. GSo

Sonnet: "Ile give thee leave my love, in beauties field." Sir William Alexander, Earl of Stirling. *Fr.* Aurora.

Sonnet: In Absence from Becchina. Cecco Angiolieri, da Siena. AWP; EaItPo, *tr.* by Dante Gabriel Rossetti

Sonnet: "In every dream thy lovely features rise." William Barnes. BoLoP

Sonnet: In Time of Revolt. Rupert Brooke. OBCoV

Sonnet: Ingratitude. Anna Seward. CenSon; ECWP; NOEC

Sonnet Introductory. Mary Robinson. CenSon; RWP

Sonnet is a moment's monument, A. Dante Gabriel Rossetti. GSo; NIL-7; Son *Fr.* House of Life, The.

Sonnet is a world, where feelings caught, The. Sonnet (III), The. John Addington Symonds. GSo

Sonnet: Kamikaze: "Dawn and night of fighting, lovers like actual wars." Bernadette Mayer. FTOS

Sonnet: Lady, That in the Prime. John Milton. *See* Sonnet 9: "Ladie [*or* Lady], that in the prime of earliest youth."

Sonnet: "Leave me, all sweet refrains my lip hath made." Luis de Camões [*or* Camõens]. AWP, *tr.* by Richard Garnett

Sonnet: "Let others sing of knights and paladin[e]s." Samuel Daniel. NAEL-7v1; NOBE; NoSic; OBEV; SCGP *Fr.* To Delia.

Sonnet: "Let us leave talking of angelic hosts." Elinor Wylie. OxBA *Fr.* One Person.

Sonnet: Lift Not the Painted Veil: "Lift not the painted veil which those who live." Shelley. CenSon; FHYEP; GSo; NOBRP; Son

Sonnet: "Light-spring, oh sun, in light our wedding joys immure." Daniel Casper von Lohenstein. GePo *Fr.* Arminius.

Sonnet: "Love and the gentle heart are one same thing." Dante Alighieri. AWP; EaItPo, *tr.* by Dante Gabriel Rossetti *Fr.* La Vita Nuova.

Sonnet: "Love and the gentle heart are one thing." Dante Alighieri. NAWM-7v1, *tr.* by Dino Cervigni and Edward Vasta *Fr.* La Vita Nuova.

Sonnet: "Love is the peace, whereto all thoughts do strive." Fulke Greville, 1st Baron Brooke. NPeEn; NoSic *Fr.* Caelica.

Sonnet Made upon the Groves near Merlou [*or* Merlow] Castle. Edward Herbert, 1st Baron Herbert of Cherbury. NOSC; NPeEn

Sonnet: "Man, dream[e] no more of curious mysteries." Fulke Greville, 1st Baron Brooke. NOSC; NoSic *Fr.* Caelica.

Sonnet: "Master and the slave go hand in hand, The." Edwin Arlington Robinson. APN2

Sonnet: "Morsels of my lifework: the story of a professional party hostess." D. A. Powell. NeAmPo

Sonnet: "My dream a drink with Lonnie Johnson we discuss the code." Ted Berrigan. NoAM *Fr.* Sonnets, The.

Sonnet: My Errors My Loves My Unlucky Star. Luis de Camões [*or* Camõens]. WoPoe, *tr.* by David Wevill

Sonnet: "My galley charged." Sir Thomas Wyatt. AEP

Sonnet: "My God, where is that ancient heat towards Thee." George Herbert. ESCV; GeHe; NOSC

(Sonnet 1.) FSCP

Sonnet: "My love, if I write a song for you." Veronica Forrest-Thomson. HarvBoo

Sonnet: "My meditation turns to thinking." Giorgio Baffo. EroLit, *tr.* by Wayland Young

Sonnet: "My soul surcharged with grief now loud complains." Rachel [*or* Rahel] Morpurgo. TrJP, *tr.* by Nina Davis Salaman

Sonnet No. 22. Mark Ameen. GLP

Sonnet: "Now I see them sitting me before a mirror." Michael Palmer. HarvBoo; MakPoe

Sonnet: "Now the bat circles on the breeze of eve." Ann Radcliffe. CenSon; WPE

Sonnet No. 21. Mark Ameen. GLP

Sonnet: "Nuns fret not at their convent's narrow room." William Wordsworth. EBEV; GSo; NIP-4; NoP-4; OBEV; Son

(Nuns Fret Not.) NIL-7

Sonnet: "O false and treacherous Probability." Fulke Greville, 1st Baron Brooke. SacPr Fr. Caelica.

Sonnet: "O thou who never harbored fear." Eloise Bibb. CBWP-4

Sonnet: "October's gold is dim—the forests rot." David Gray. OxAEP-2

Sonnet: Of All He Would Do. Cecco Angiolieri, da Siena. AWP; EaItPo, tr. by Dante Gabriel Rossetti

Sonnet: Of an Ill-Favored Lady. Guido Cavalcanti. AWP; EaItPo, tr. by Dante Gabriel Rossetti

Sonnet: Of Beatrice de' Portinari, on All Saints' Day. Dante Alighieri. AWP; EaItPo, tr. by Dante Gabriel Rossetti

Sonnet: Of Beauty and Duty. Dante Alighieri. AWP; EaItPo, tr. by Dante Gabriel Rossetti

Sonnet: Of Becchina in a Rage. Cecco Angiolieri, da Siena. AWP; EaItPo, tr. by Dante Gabriel Rossetti

Sonnet: Of Becchina, the Shoemaker's Daughter. Cecco Angiolieri, da Siena. AWP; EaItPo, tr. by Dante Gabriel Rossetti

Sonnet of Black Beauty. Edward Herbert, 1st Baron Herbert of Cherbury. NOSC

Sonnet of Brotherhood. Ronald Allison Kells Mason. PeNZ

Sonnet of Fishes. George Barker. FaBoMo; Son

Sonnet: Of His Lady's Face. Jacopo da Lentino. See Of His Lady's Face

Sonnet: Of His Pain from a New Love. Guido Cavalcanti. AWP; EaItPo, tr. by Dante Gabriel Rossetti

Sonnet: Of Love, in Honor of His Mistress Becchina. Cecco Angiolieri, da Siena. AWP; EaItPo, tr. by Dante Gabriel Rossetti

Sonnet: Of Love in Men and Devils. Cecco Angiolieri, da Siena. AWP; EaItPo, tr. by Dante Gabriel Rossetti

Sonnet: Of Moderation and Tolerance. Guido Guinicelli. AWP; EaItPo, tr. by Dante Gabriel Rossetti

Sonnet of Sweet Complaint. Federico García Lorca. BLPSL, tr. by Rene de Costa, Rigas Kappatos and Eleni Paidoussi

Sonnet of Sweet Weeping. Federico García Lorca. CAGL, tr. by David William Foster Fr. Sonetos del Amor Oscuro [Sonnets of Dark Love].

Sonnet: Of the Eyes of a Certain Mandetta. Guido Cavalcanti. AWP; EaItPo, tr. by Dante Gabriel Rossetti

Sonnet: Of the Grave of Selvaggia, on the Monte della Sambuca. Cino da Pistoia. AWP; EaItPo, tr. by Dante Gabriel Rossetti

Sonnet: Of the Making of Master Messerin. Rustico Di Filippo. AWP; EaItPo, tr. by Dante Gabriel Rossetti

Sonnet of the Mountain, The. Mellin de Saint-Gelais. AWP, tr. by Austin Dobson

Sonnet: Of the 20th of June 1291. Cecco Angiolieri, da Siena. AWP; EaItPo, tr. by Dante Gabriel Rossetti

Sonnet: "Of thee, kind boy, I ask no red and white." Sir John Suckling. BASC; BeJo; CaPo; CavPo; MeLP; NOSC; NoP-4; OxBoLi

Sonnet: Of Virtue. Folgore da San Geminiano [or Gimignano]. AWP; EaItPo, tr. by Dante Gabriel Rossetti

Sonnet: Of Why He Is Unchanged. Cecco Angiolieri, da Siena. See Of Why He Is Unhanged

Sonnet: Of Why He Would Be a Scullion. Cecco Angiolieri, da Siena. AWP; EaItPo, tr. by Dante Gabriel Rossetti

Sonnet: "Oh! Death will find me, long before I tire." Rupert Brooke. NoP-4; PoRA

(Sonnet: Death Will Find Me.) MoBrPo; Son

Sonnet: "Oh for a poet—for a beacon bright." Edwin Arlington Robinson. APN-2; NCAP; OxBA

Sonnet: "O[h]! for some honest lover's ghost." Sir John Suckling. BASC; BeJo; CavPo; MeLP; OxBEV

(Doubt of Martyrdom, A.) BoLoP; CaPo; NOBE; OBEV

Sonnet: "Oh, my belovèd, have you thought of this." Edna St. Vincent Millay. HeIP-4; LW

Sonnet on a Family Picture. Thomas Edwards. CenSon; NOEC

Sonnet on Catherine Wordsworth. William Wordsworth. CenSon; OxBSo; SCGP

(Desideria.) GTBS-P; OBEV

(Surprised by Joy.) BoLoP; CABP; GSo; HAP; NAEL-5v2; NAEL-6v2; NOBE; NoP-4; PoE; Son; TFi

Sonnet on Chillon. Byron. CenSon; GSo Fr. Prisoner of Chillon, The.

Sonnet on Famous and Familiar Sonnets and Experiences. Delmore Schwartz. Son; TRP

Sonnet: on Loss. Sir Robert Aytoun [or Ayton]. NOSC

Sonnet on Reading the Poem upon the Mountain Daisy, by Mr. Burns. Helen Maria Williams. ECWP

Sonnet on Sir William Alexander's Harsh Verses after the English Fashion, A. James I, King of England. Son

Sonnet: On the 9th of June 1290. Dante Alighieri. AWP; EaItPo, tr. by Dante Gabriel Rossetti

Sonnet on the Crimean War. William Forster. CBAP

Sonnet [on the Death of Mr. Richard West]. Thomas Gray. CenSon; NOEC; OxBSo; PoE

(In vain to me the smiling mornings shine.) GSo; NoP-4

(On the Death of Mr. Richard West.) GSo; NOBE; Son

(Sonnet.) NoP-4

Sonnet on the Death of the Man Who Invented Plastic Roses. Peter Meinke. PBCAP

Sonnet: On the Detection of a False Friend. Guido Cavalcanti. AWP; EaItPo, tr. by Dante Gabriel Rossetti

Sonnet: On the Religious Memorie of Mrs. Catherine Thomason My Christian Freind Deceas'd Decem. 1646. John Milton. ChIV-2

(Sonnet.) OxAEP-1

Sonnet: On the River Tweed. Sir Robert Aytoun [or Ayton]. NOSC

(Faire famous flood, which sometyme did devyde.) NePenScot

Sonnet: "Orgasm completely, The." Tom Clark. CoAP

Sonnet: "Patience, hard thing! the hard thing but to pray." Gerard Manley Hopkins. NOBVV

(Patience, Hard Thing!) Son

Sonnet: Political Greatness. Shelley. CenSon

Sonnet: "Record is nothing, and the hero great." John Byrne Leicester Warren, 3d Baron De Tabley. EBVV; OxBSo

Sonnet Reversed. Rupert Brooke. NOBL; OxBSo; PeLV

Sonnet Right off the Bat. Félix Lope de Vega Carpio. STV, tr. by John Frederick Nims

Sonnet's Voice, The. Theodore Watts-Dunton. GSo

Sonnet: "Scorn not the sonnet; critic, you have frowned." William Wordsworth. OBEV

(Scorn Not the Sonnet.) GSo; NoP-4

Sonnet sent to Blackness to Mr. John Welsch, by the Lady Culross, A. Elizabeth Melville, Lady Culross. EMWP

Sonnet: "She took the dappled partridge flecked [or fleckt] with blood." Tennyson. NAEL-5v2; NAEL-6v2

Sonnet—Silence. Edgar Allan Poe. ColAP; NOBA; TCAPo

(Silence.) APN-1; GSo; NCAP

Sonnet: "Sleep, silence' child, sweet father of soft rest." William Drummond, of Hawthornden. See Sleep, Silence' Child

Sonnet: "Slide soft, fair forth, and make a crystal plain." William Drummond, of Hawthornden. NOSC; OxBSo

Sonnet: "Stranger, when o'er yon slant, warm field no cloud." Anna Seward. NOBRP

Sonnet: Supernatural Beings. Gavin Ewart. Son

Sonnet: Suppos'd to Be Written at Lemnos. Thomas Russell. NOBRP; NOEC

Sonnet: "Sure Lord, there is enough in thee to dry." George Herbert. GeHe; NOSC

(Sonnet 2.) FSCP

Sonnet: "Tell me[e] no more how fair[e] she[e] is." Henry King, Bishop of Chichester. EnLoPo; MeLP; OxBEV

Sonnet: That Sad and Joyful Dawn. Luis de Camões [or Camõens]. WoPoe, tr. by David Wevill

Sonnet: The Beautiful American Word, Sure. Delmore Schwartz. See Beautiful American Word, Sure, The

Sonnet: The Ladies' Home Journal. Sandra M. Gilbert. See Ladies' Home Journal, The

Sonnet: The Last Things. Gavin Ewart. OxBSo

Sonnet: "The long love." Sir Thomas Wyatt. See Long love that in my thought doth harbo[u]r, The

Sonnet: "There are strange shadows fostered on the moon." Arthur Davison Ficke. TCAPo

Sonnet: "There, on the darkened deathbed, dies the brain." John Masefield. EBEV

Sonnet: "This infant world has taken long to make." George Macdonald. SacPr

Sonnet: "Thou poisonous laurel leaf, that in the soil." Frances Anne [or "Fanny"] Kemble. SWaP

Sonnet: "Thousand apples you might put in your theories." Bernadette Mayer. PmAP

Sonnet: "Three things there be in mans opinion dear[e]" Fulke Greville, 1st Baron Brooke. NOCV; NOSC; NoSic Fr. Caelica.

Sonnet: "Time and the mortal will stand never fast." Luis de Camões [or Camõens]. AWP, tr. by Richard Garnett

Sonnet: "'Tis dead of night; storms rend the troubled air." Mary Locke. ECWP

Sonnet, to a Child. Wilfred Owen. NOxBChV

Sonnet to a Friend Who Asked How I Felt When the Nurse First Presented My Infant to Me. Samuel Taylor Coleridge. CenSon

Sonnet: To a Friend Who Does Not Pity His Love. Guido Cavalcanti. AWP; EaItPo, *tr. by* Dante Gabriel Rossetti

Sonnet to a Negro in Harlem. Helene Johnson. APT-2; NAAAL; NIL-7; NIP-4; SSLK

Sonnet: To a Portrait of Hart Crane. Allen Tate. GS

Sonnet to a Sonnet. Thomas Hood. CenSon

Sonnet—To an American Painter Departing for Europe. William Cullen Bryant. *See* To Cole, the Painter, Departing for Europe

Sonnet to Be Written from Prison. Robert Adamson. CBAP

Sonnet to Britain. William Edmonstoune [*or* Edmondstoune] Aytoun. OxBSo

Sonnet: To Brunetto Latini. Dante Alighieri. AWP; EaItPo, *tr. by* Dante Gabriel Rossetti

Sonnet: To Certain Ladies; When Beatrice Was Lamenting Her Father's Death. Dante Alighieri. AWP; EaItPo, *tr. by* Dante Gabriel Rossetti

Sonnet: To Dante Alighieri (He Writes to Dante, Then in Exile at Verona, Defying Him as No Better Than Himself). Cecco Angiolieri, da Siena. AWP; EaItPo, *tr. by* Dante Gabriel Rossetti

Sonnet: To Dante Alighieri on the Last Sonnet of the Vita Nuova. Cecco Angiolieri, da Siena. AWP; EaItPo, *tr. by* Dante Gabriel Rossetti

Sonnet to France On Her Present Exertions. Anna Laetitia Barbauld. RWP

Sonnet to Gath. Edna St. Vincent Millay. BoWoP; MoAmPo

Sonnet: To Guido Cavalcanti. Dante Alighieri. AWP

(Sonnet: [From the Italian of Dante.] Dante Alighieri to Guido Cavalcanti.) OBVE; WoPoe

Sonnet to Heavenly Beauty, A. Joachim Du Bellay. AWP; CTC, *tr. by* Andrew Lang

Sonnet: To His Lady Joan, of Florence. Guido Cavalcanti. AWP; EaItPo, *tr. by* Dante Gabriel Rossetti

Sonnet to Lake Leman. Byron. CenSon; Son

Sonnet: To Love, In Great Bitterness. Cino da Pistoia. AWP, *tr. by* Dante Gabriel Rossetti

Sonnet: To Mr. H. Lawes, on His Air[e]s. John Milton. *See* To Mr. H. Lawes On His Airs

Sonnet to My First Born. Mary Weston Fordham. CBWP-2

Sonnet to My Mother. George Barker. OxBSo; RaBo

(To My Mother.) FaBoMo; MakPoe; OxAEP-2; OxBTC; PoWW; Son; TwCP

Sonnet to My Mother, A. Heinrich Heine. TrJP, *tr. by* Emma Lazarus

Sonnet to My Mother, A. Heinrich Heine. *See* To My Mother

Sonnet to Nothing. Thomas Beck. NOBRP

Sonnet to Opium; Celebrating Its Virtues, A. "Orestes." NOEC

Sonnet—To Science. Edgar Allan Poe. NAAL-2v1; NAAL-3; NAAL-5; OxBA; OxBSo; Son; TAP; TCAPo

(To Science.) APN-1; GSo

Sonnet: "To see a woman long oppressed by fear." Hayden Carruth. ErotSp *Fr.* Sonnets.

Sonnet to Sleep. John Keats. *See* To Sleep

Sonnet: To Tartar, a Terrier Beauty. Thomas Lovell Beddoes. NOBVV; OxBSo

Sonnet to the Asshole. Paul Verlaine. CAGL, *tr. by* Alan Stone

Sonnet to the Imagination. Robin Becker. BodElec

Sonnet: To the Lady Pietra degli Scrovigni. Dante Alighieri. AWP; EaItPo, *tr. by* Dante Gabriel Rossetti

Sonnet to the "Most Distinguished Chancellor" that Oxford Has Had. Max Beerbohm. UV

Sonnet to the Noble Lady, the Lady Mary Wroth, A. Ben Jonson. BeJo; NAEL-7v1; NoP-4

Sonnet: To the River Lodon. Thomas Warton, the Younger. CenSon; NOEC; OxBSo

Sonnet to the River Otter. Samuel Taylor Coleridge. CenSon; OxBSo

(To the River Otter.) Son

Sonnet, to the Same. Byron. OxBSo

Sonnet: To the Same Ladies; With Their Answer. Dante Alighieri. AWP; EaItPo, *tr. by* Dante Gabriel Rossetti

Sonnet to Twilight. Helen Maria Williams. CenSon *Fr.* Poems.

Sonnet to Valclusa. Thomas Russell. NOBRP

(What though, Valclusa, the fond Bard be fled.) CenSon

Sonnet to Vauxhall. Thomas Hood. NPeEn; OBCoV; OxBSo

Sonnet: "To work away in art's traditional measure." Goethe. STV, *tr. by* John Frederick Nims

Sonnet: "Triumphing chariots, statues, crowns of bay." William Drummond, of Hawthornden. NOSC *Fr.* Urania, or Spiritual Poems.

Sonnet upon Sonnets, A. Robert Burns. GSo; Son

Sonnet Variations. Peyton Houston. Son

Sonnet: "Way the world is not, The." Bill Knott. PBCAP

Sonnet: "We often pass a night warm and intimate." Feng Chih. WoPoe, *tr. by* Yip Wai-lim

Sonnet: "We will not whisper, we have found the place." Joseph Hilaire Pierre Belloc. MoBrPo

Sonnet: "Well, she told me I had an aura. 'What?' I said." Hayden Carruth. GifTon

Sonnet: "What is my lady like? thou fain would'st know." Frances Anne [*or* "Fanny"] Kemble. SWaP

Sonnet: "What lips my lips have kissed, and where, and why." Edna St. Vincent Millay. APT-1; BoLoP; HeIP-4; MakPoe; MoAmPo; NAAL-2v2; NIP-4; OPOU; Son

(What lips my lips have kissed.) GSo; NIL-7

Sonnet: "When I was marked for suffering, Love forswore." Miguel de Cervantes Saavedra. AWP, *tr. by* Sir Edmund William Gosse

Sonnet: "When men shall find thy flower, thy glory, pass." Samuel Daniel. NAEL-5v1; NOBE; NoSic; OBEV; SCGP; Son *Fr.* To Delia.

Sonnet: "When Phoebe formed a wanton smile." William Collins. EnLoPo; OxBSP

Sonnet: "When she walks by here." Petrarch. WoPoe, *tr. by* Nicholas Kilmer

Sonnet: "When you see millions of the mouthless dead." Charles Hamilton Sorley. FaBoWar; NPeEn; OBWP; OxBSo; PeFWW; PoWW

Sonnet: "Whenas [*or* When as] man's life, the light of human lust." Fulke Greville, 1st Baron Brooke. CABP; NOSC; NoSic *Fr.* Caelica.

Sonnet: Where Lies the Land. William Wordsworth. CenSon

Sonnet: "Winter deepening, the hay all in, The." Richard Wilbur. OxBSo; Son

Sonnet: "Wisest of all men lies buried on this spot, The." Daniel Casper von Lohenstein. GePo *Fr.* Arminius.

Sonnet with a Different Letter at the End of Every Line. George Starbuck. OBAL

Sonnet-writing. To F. W. F. Frederick William Faber. CenSon

Sonnet Written at the Close of Spring [*or* Elegiac Sonnet]. Charlotte Smith. CenSon; ECWP; RWP

(Written at the Close of Spring.) NAEL-6v2

Sonnet Written from an Eastern Apartment in the Bishop's Palace at Lichfield, Which Commands a View of Stowe Valley. Anna Seward. RWP

Sonnet. Written in the Church-Yard at Middleton in Sussex. Charlotte Smith. *See* Pressed by the Moon, Mute Arbitress of Tides

Sonnet Written in Tintern Abbey, Monmouthshire. Edmund Gardner. NOEC

Sonnet Written upon My Lord Admiral Seymour, A. John Harington. NoSic

Sonnet: "Ye praise the humble: of the meek ye say." Sir Aubrey De Vere. SacPr

Sonnet: "You are the faintest freckles on the hide." Elinor Wylie. APT-1

Sonnet: "You know all those sonnets the ones where I said, I love you, well." Tom Devaney. AmPoNex

Sonnet: "You rose from our embrace and the small light spread." Hayden Carruth. ErotSp *Fr.* Sonnets.

Sonnet: "You were born; must die; were loved; must love." Stephen Spender. MoBrPo; Son

Sonnets. James Agee. MoAmPo

"Now stands our love on that still verge of day." APT-2

"So it begins. Adam is in his earth." APT-2

Sonnets. John Berryman. Son

Sonnets. Giovanni Boccaccio.

Inscription for a Portrait of Dante. AWP; EaItPo, *tr. by* Dante Gabriel Rossetti

Of Fiammetta Singing. AWP; EaItPo, *tr. by* Dante Gabriel Rossetti

Of His Last Sight of Fiammetta. AWP; EaItPo, *tr. by* Dante Gabriel Rossetti

Of Three Girls and of Their Talk. AWP; EaItPo, *tr. by* Dante Gabriel Rossetti

To Dante in Paradise, after Fiammetta's Death. AWP; EaItPo, *tr. by* Dante Gabriel Rossetti

To One Who Had Censured His Public Exposition of Dante. AWP; EaItPo, *tr. by* Dante Gabriel Rossetti

Sonnets. Hayden Carruth.

Sonnet: "To see a woman long oppressed by fear.". ErotSp

Sonnet: "You rose from our embrace and the small light spread.". ErotSp

"To see a woman long oppressed by fear." ErotSp

"You rose from our embrace and the small light spread." ErotSp

Sonnets. John Masefield.

"Is there a great green commonwealth of Thought." MoBrPo

Sonnets. George Santayana.

"As in the midst of battle there is room." APN-2; AWP

"Candour of the gods is in thy gaze, The." APN-2

"Dreamt I today [*or* to-day] the dream of yesternight." APN-2

"O world, thou choosest not the better part!" APN-2; TCAPo

"Of Helen's brothers, one was born to die." APN-2

Sonnet V: "Dreamt I today [*or* to-day] the dream of yesternight." APN-2

Sonnet XXV: "As in the midst of battle there is room." APN-2; AWP

Sonnet XLIII: "Candour of the gods is in thy gaze, The" APN-2

Sonnet XLVIII: "Of Helen's brothers, one was born to die." APN-2

Sonnets. Anna Seward.

"Behold that tree, in Autumn's dim decay." WoRP

"On the fleet streams, the Sun, that late arose." WoRP

"While one sere leaf, that parting autumn yields." WoRP

Sonnets. Anna Seward.

Sonnet 7: "By Derwent's rapid stream as oft I strayed." CenSon

Sonnets. William Shakespeare.

(Absence.) GTBS-P

"Against that time, if ever that time come." OxAEP-1

"Ah! wherefore with infection should he live." SCGP

"Alas, 'tis true I have gone here and there." EBEV; NAEL-6v1; NAEL-7v1; NoSic; OxAEP-1

"As an unperfect actor on the stage." NoSic; Son

"Be wise as thou art cruel; do not press." NoSic

"Being your slave, what should I do[e] but tend." CAGL; HAP; NoSic; OBEV

"Beshrew that heart that makes my heart to groan." OxAEP-1

(Blind Love.) GTBS-P

("But be contended when that fell arest.") PBRV

"But be contented: when that fell arest." NAEL-5v1; NAEL-6v1; NAEL-7v1; OxAEP-1; Son

(Consolation, A.) GTBS-P

"Devouring Time, blunt thou the lion's paws." AWP; EBEV; HeIP-4; NAEL-5v1; NAEL-6v1; NAEL-7v1; NoSic; OxAEP-1; PoE; SCGP

("Devouring time blunt thou the Lyons pawes.") PBRV

("Expence of Spirit in a waste of shame, Th'") NPeEn; PBRV

"Expense of spirit in a waste of shame, The [or Th']." AWP; EBEV; ErotSp; HAP; HeIP-4; NAEL-5v1; NAEL-6v1; NAEL-7v1; NIL-7; NIP-4; NOBE; NoSic; OBEV; OxAEP-1; OxBEV; PAI; PoE; SCGP; SCV; Son; TFi; UnPo; WoPoe

("Farewell: thou art too dear for my possessing.") NAEL-7v1

"Farewell! Thou art too dear[e] for my possessing." CAGL; EBEV; GTBS-P; NAEL-5v1; NAEL-6v1; NOBE; NoSic; OBEV; OxAEP-1; Son; TFi

"Forward violet thus did I chide, The." OxAEP-1

"From fairest creatures we desire increase." CTC; HeIP-4; NAEL-6v1; NAEL-7v1

(From Sonnets.) NoP-4

"From you have I been absent in the spring." AWP; EBEV; NAEL-5v1; NAEL-6v1; NAEL-7v1; NOBE; NoSic; OBEV; OxAEP-1

(Full Many a Glorious Morning.) NIL-7

"Full many a glorious morning have I seen[e]." AWP; EBEV; HAP; NAEL-7v1; NIP-4; NoP-4; NoSic; OxAEP-1; PoRA; Son; TFi; WeW-3

"How can I then return in happy plight." AWTN

"How heavy do I journey on the way." OxAEP-1

"How like a winter hath my absence been[e]." AWP; EnLoPo; GTBS-P; HeIP-4; NAEL-6v1; NAEL-7v1; NOBE; NoSic; OBEV; OxAEP-1; PoRA; SCGP; Son; TFi

"How oft, when thou, my music, music play'st." NAEL-5v1; NAEL-6v1; NAEL-7v1; OxAEP-1; PoE

"How sweet and lovely dost thou make the shame." HeIP-4; SCGP

"If my dear love were but the child of state." NoSic

"If the dull substance of my flesh were thought." Son

"If there be nothing new, but that which is." TreFP

"In faith, I do[e] not love thee with mine eyes." HeIP-4; OxAEP-1

"In loving thee thou know'st I am forsworn." HeIP-4

"In the old age black was not counted fair." NAEL-6v1; NAEL-7v1; OxAEP-1

"Is it thy will thy image should keep open." AWTN; CAGL

"Let me confess that we two must be twain." HeIP-4

("Let me confesse that we two must be twaine.") PBRV

"Let those who are in favour with their stars." FaBoWar; OxAEP-1; SCGP

(Life without Passion, The.) GTBS-P

(Like as the Waves.) NIL-7

("Like as the waves make toward the pebbled shore.") PoPoPo

("Like as the waves make toward the pibled shore.") NAEL-6v1; NPeEn; OxBEV

"Like as the waves make towards the pebbled shore." CABP; EBEV; NAEL-7v1; NIP-4; NOBE; NoSic; OxAEP-1; OxBSo; PoRA; SCGP; Son; TFi; TreFP; UnPo

"Like as, to make our appetites more keen." SCGP

"Lo! as a careful housewife runs to catch." SCGP

"Look in thy glass and tell the face thou viewest." NAEL-5v1; NAEL-6v1; NAEL-7v1; NoP-4; SCGP

"Lord of my love, to whom in vassalage." HeIP-4

"Love is too young to know what conscience is." EBEV; HeIP-4; NoSic; OxAEP-1; PoE

(Love's Not Time's Fool.) ITBLP

"Mine eye and heart are at a mortal war." HeIP-4

"My glass shall not persuade me I am old." Son

("My love is as a fever, longing still.") AEP

"My love is as a fever [or feaver],k longing still." EBEV; NAEL-5v1; NAEL-6v1; NAEL-7v1; OxAEP-1

"My love is strengthen'd, though more weak in seeming." AWP; OBEV

"My mistress' eyes are nothing like the sun." AWP; BoLoP; CABP; EBEV; HAP; HeIP-4; InPK-6; NAEL-5v1; NAEL-6v1; NAEL-7v1; NIL-7; NIP-4; NoSic; OxAEP-1; OxBEV; PAI; PoE; PoPoPo; SoSe-8; Son; TFi; WeW-3

"My tongue-tied Muse in manners holds her still." Son

"No longer mourn for me when I am dead." AWP; EBEV; HAP; HeIP-4; NAEL-5v1; NAEL-6v1; NAEL-7v1; NoSic; OxAEP-1; PAI; PoRA; SCGP; Son; TFi

"No more be grieved at that which thou hast done." HeIP-4; NAEL-5v1; NAEL-6v1; NAEL-7v1; NoSic; OxAEP-1; PoE; SCGP; UnPo

("No more bee greev'd at that which thou hast done.") PBRV

"No, Time, thou shalt not boast that I do change." OxAEP-1; Son

"Not from the stars do I my judgement pluck." Son

(Not Marble, Nor The Gilded Monuments.) GSo; NIL-7

("Not marble, nor the guilded monuments.") NPeEn; PBRV

"Not mine own fears nor the prophetic soul." AWP; CTC; EBEV; HAP; NAEL-5v1; NAEL-6v1; NAEL-7v1; NoSic; OxAEP-1; SCGP

("Not mine owne feares, nor the prophetick soule.") NPeEn

"O, for my sake do you with Fortune chide." OxAEP-1

"O, from [or O! From] what power hast thou this powerful might." OxAEP-1; SCGP

"O, how I faint when I of you do write." CAGL; OxAEP-1

("O how much more cloth beauty beauteous seem.") AEP

"O! Lest the world should task you to recite." OxAEP-1

"O [or Oh], never say that I was false of heart." NOBE; OBEV; OxAEP-1

"O thou, my lovely boy, who in thy power." HeIP-4; NAEL-5v1; NAEL-6v1; NAEL-7v1

"O[h], how much more doth beauty beauteous seem." AWP; OBEV; PoE; SCGP

"Or I shall live your epitaph to make." OxAEP-1

"Or whether doth my mind, being crowned with you." SCGP

("Poor soul, the center of my sinful earth.") NoP-4

"Poor[e] soul[e], the centre of my sinful[l] earth." AWP; HAP; HeIP-4; NAEL-5v1; NAEL-6v1; NAEL-7v1; NOBE; NOCV; OBEV; OxAEP-1; PoE; SCGP; SacPr; Son; TFi

(Post Mortem.) GTBS-P

(Remembrance.) GTBS-P

(Revolutions.) GTBS-P

"Say that thou didst forsake me for some fault." OxAEP-1

"Since brass, nor stone, nor earth, nor boundless sea." AWP; HAP; NAEL-5v1; NAEL-6v1; NAEL-7v1; NOBE; NoSic; OxAEP-1; OxBSo; PoRA; RaBo; SCGP; Son; TFi; TreFP; UnPo

"Since I left you, mine eye is in my mind." SCGP

"Sin[ne] of self[e]-love possesseth all mine eye [or eie]." EBEV; OxAEP-1

"So am I as the rich, whose blessed key." OxAEP-1

"So is it not with me as with that Muse." HeIP-4

"So, now I have confess'd that he is thine." HeIP-4; OxAEP-1

("So oft have I invok'd thee for my muse.") AEP

Sonnet 1. CTC; HeIP-4; NAEL-6v1; NAEL-7v1

Sonnet 2. HeIP-4; NoSic; SCGP; Son

Sonnet 3. NAEL-5v1; NAEL-6v1; NAEL-7v1; NoP-4; SCGP

(Sonnet 5: 'Those hours that with gentle work') AEP

Sonnet 12. AWP; HeIP-4; NAEL-5v1; NAEL-6v1; NAEL-7v1; NoSic; SCGP; Son; WoPoe

Sonnet 14. Son

Sonnet 15. AWP; NAEL-5v1; NAEL-6v1; NAEL-7v1; NoSic; SCGP; Son

Sonnet 18. AEP; AmFaPo; BoLoP; CABP; CTC; ClHu; EnLoPo; HAP; HeIP-4; ITBLP; InPK-6; MakPoe; NAEL-6v1; NAEL-7v1; NIL-7; NOBE; NPeEn; NoSic; OBEV; OxBEV; OxBSo; PoE; PoPoPo; PoRA; SCGP; SCV; Son; TFi; WeW-3

Sonnet 19. AWP; EBEV; HeIP-4; NAEL-5v1; NAEL-6v1; NAEL-7v1; NoSic; OxAEP-1; PoE; SCGP

Sonnet 20. CAGL; HeIP-4; NAEL-5v1; NAEL-6v1; NAEL-7v1; NoP-4; NoSic; OxAEP-1

Sonnet 21. HeIP-4

Sonnet 22. Son

Sonnet 23. NoSic; Son

Sonnet 25. FaBoWar; OxAEP-1; SCGP

Sonnet 26. HeIP-4

Sonnet 27. AWTN; CAGL; HeIP-4; NoSic; SCGP

Sonnet 28. AWTN

Sonnet 29. AWP; AmFaPo; CTC; EBEV; HAP; HeIP-4; ITBLP; InPK-6;

NAEL-5v1; NAEL-6v1; NAEL-7v1; NOBE; NoP-4; NoSic; OBEV; OPOU; OxAEP-1; PoPoPo; SCGP; Son; TFi; WeW-3; WoPoe

(Sonnet 29: 'When in disgrace with Fortune')　AEP

Sonnet 30.　AWP; CTC; ClHu; EBEV; HAP; HeIP-4; NAEL-5v1; NAEL-6v1; NAEL-7v1; NOBE; NoSic; OBEV; OxAEP-1; PAI; PoE; PoRA; SCGP; TFi

Sonnet 31.　NOBE; OBEV

Sonnet 33.　AWP; EBEV; HAP; NAEL-7v1; NIP-4; NoP-4; NoSic; OxAEP-1; PoRA; SCGP; Son; TFi; WeW-3

Sonnet 34.　HeIP-4; OxAEP-1

Sonnet 35.　HeIP-4; NAEL-5v1; NAEL-6v1; NAEL-7v1; NoSic; OxAEP-1; PoE; SCGP; UnPo

Sonnet 36.　HeIP-4

Sonnet 40.　HeIP-4; OxAEP-1; SCGP

Sonnet 41.　OxAEP-1

Sonnet 42.　HeIP-4; OxAEP-1

Sonnet 44.　Son

Sonnet 46.　HeIP-4

Sonnet 49.　OxAEP-1

Sonnet 50.　OxAEP-1

Sonnet 52.　OxAEP-1

Sonnet 53.　CTC; EBEV; NoSic; OBEV; OxAEP-1; OxBEV; SCGP

Sonnet 54.　AWP; OBEV; PoE; SCGP

(Sonnet 54: 'O how much more doth beauty')　AEP

Sonnet 55.　AEP; AWP; CABP; CTC; HeIP-4; NAEL-5v1; NAEL-6v1; NAEL-7v1; NIP-4; NOBE; NoP-4; NoSic; OxAEP-1; OxBSo; PAI; PoE; PoRA; SCGP; Son

Sonnet 56.　SCGP

Sonnet 57.　CAGL; HAP; NoSic; OBEV

Sonnet 59.　TreFP

Sonnet 60.　CABP; EBEV; NAEL-7v1; NIP-4; NOBE; NoSic; OxAEP-1; OxBSo; PoRA; SCGP; Son; TFi; TreFP; UnPo

Sonnet 61.　AWTN; CAGL

Sonnet 62.　EBEV; OxAEP-1

Sonnet 64.　AWP; EnLoPo; HAP; HeIP-4; NOBE; OxAEP-1; PoE; PoRA; SCGP; Son; TreFP

Sonnet 65.　AWP; HAP; NAEL-5v1; NAEL-6v1; NAEL-7v1; NOBE; NoSic; OxAEP-1; OxBSo; PoRA; RaBo; SCGP; Son; TFi; TreFP; UnPo

Sonnet 66.　AWP; CTC; EBEV; HAP; NOBE; NoSic; OxAEP-1; TFi; WeW-3

Sonnet 67.　SCGP

Sonnet 68.　SCGP

Sonnet 70.　OxAEP-1; SCGP

Sonnet 71.　AWP; EBEV; HAP; HeIP-4; NAEL-5v1; NAEL-6v1; NAEL-7v1; NoSic; OxAEP-1; PAI; PoRA; SCGP; Son; TFi

Sonnet 72.　OxAEP-1

Sonnet 73.　AEP; AWP; BoLoP; CABP; CTC; ClHu; EBEV; GTBS-P; HAP; HeIP-4; InPK-6; NAEL-5v1; NAEL-6v1; NAEL-7v1; NIP-4; NOBE; NoP-4; NoSic; OBEV; OxBSo; PoE; PoRA; SCGP; SoSe-8; Son; TFi; UnPo; WeW-3

(That Time of Year Thou Mayst in Me Behold.)　NIL-7

Sonnet 74.　NAEL-5v1; NAEL-6v1; NAEL-7v1; OxAEP-1; Son

Sonnet 76.　EBEV; NoSic; OxAEP-1

Sonnet 77.　HeIP-4

(Sonnet 78: 'So oft have I invok'd thee')　AEP

Sonnet 80.　CAGL; OxAEP-1

Sonnet 81.　OxAEP-1

Sonnet 85.　Son

Sonnet 86.　CABP; NoSic; OxAEP-1; SCGP; Son

Sonnet 87.　CAGL; EBEV; GTBS-P; NAEL-5v1; NAEL-6v1; NOBE; NoSic; OBEV; OxAEP-1; Son; TFi

Sonnet 88.　OxAEP-1

Sonnet 89.　OxAEP-1

Sonnet 90.　AWP; EBEV; NOBE; NoSic; OBEV; OxAEP-1

Sonnet 92.　HeIP-4

Sonnet 94.　NAEL-5v1; NAEL-6v1; NAEL-7v1; NIL-7; NOBE; NoSic; OBEV; OxAEP-1; OxBEV; OxBSo; PoE; SCGP; SCV; Son; TRP; WoPoe

Sonnet 95.　HeIP-4; SCGP

Sonnet 97.　AWP; EnLoPo; GTBS-P; HeIP-4; NAEL-5v1; NAEL-6v1; NAEL-7v1; NOBE; NoSic; OBEV; OxAEP-1; PoRA; SCGP; Son; TFi

(Sonnet 97: 'How like a winter')　AEP

Sonnet 98.　AWP; EBEV; NAEL-5v1; NAEL-7v1; NOBE; NoSic; OBEV; OxAEP-1

Sonnet 99.　OxAEP-1

Sonnet 100.　TreFP

Sonnet 102.　AWP; OBEV

Sonnet 104.　GTBS-P; HeIP-4; NoSic; OBEV; OxAEP-1; SCGP

Sonnet 106.　AWP; CTC; EnLoPo; FaBoCh; NAEL-5v1; NAEL-6v1; NAEL-7v1; NOBE; NoSic; OBEV; OxAEP-1; PoRA; SCGP; Son; WoPoe

Sonnet 107.　AWP; CTC; EBEV; HAP; NAEL-5v1; NAEL-6v1; NAEL-7v1; NoSic; OxAEP-1; SCGP

Sonnet 108.　TreFP

Sonnet 109.　NOBE; OBEV; OxAEP-1

Sonnet 110.　EBEV; NAEL-6v1; NAEL-7v1; NoSic; OxAEP-1

(Sonnet 110: 'Alas, 'tis true')　AEP

Sonnet 111.　OxAEP-1

Sonnet 113.　SCGP

Sonnet 114.　SCGP

Sonnet 116.　AEP; AWP; CABP; ClHu; EnLoPo; GSo; HAP; HeIP-4; NAEL-5v1; NAEL-6v1; NAEL-7v1; NIP-4; NOBE; NPeEn; NoSic; OBEV; OxAEP-1; OxBEV; OxBSo; PoE; PoPoPo; PoRA; SCGP; SCV; SoSe-8; Son; TFi; TRP; UnPo; WeW-3

Sonnet 118.　SCGP

Sonnet 119.　OxAEP-1

Sonnet 120.　OxAEP-1

Sonnet 121.　CAGL; NoSic; OxAEP-1; SCGP

Sonnet 123.　OxAEP-1; Son

Sonnet 124.　NoSic

Sonnet 125.　NoSic

(Sonnet 125: 'Were't aught to me')　AEP

Sonnet 126.　HeIP-4; NAEL-5v1; NAEL-6v1; NAEL-7v1

Sonnet 127.　NAEL-6v1; NAEL-7v1; OxAEP-1

Sonnet 128.　NAEL-5v1; NAEL-6v1; NAEL-7v1; OxAEP-1; PoE

Sonnet 129.　AWP; EBEV; ErotSp; HAP; HeIP-4; NAEL-5v1; NAEL-6v1; NAEL-7v1; NIL-7; NIP-4; NOBE; NoSic; OBEV; OxAEP-1; OxBEV; PAI; PoE; SCGP; SCV; Son; TFi; UnPo; WoPoe

Sonnet 130.　AWP; BoLoP; CABP; EBEV; HAP; HeIP-4; InPK-6; NAEL-5v1; NAEL-6v1; NAEL-7v1; NIL-7; NIP-4; NoSic; OxAEP-1; OxBEV; PAI; PoE; PoPoPo; SoSe-8; Son; TFi; WeW-3

(Sonnet 130: My Mistress' Eyes Are Nothing Like the Sun.)　AEP

Sonnet 132.　OxAEP-1

Sonnet 133.　OxAEP-1

Sonnet 134.　HeIP-4; OxAEP-1

Sonnet 135.　NAEL-5v1; NAEL-6v1; NAEL-7v1

Sonnet 138.　AWP; AmFaPo; EBEV; HeIP-4; NAEL-5v1; NAEL-7v1; NPeEn; NoSic; OxAEP-1; OxBEV; PAI; SoSe-8

Sonnet 140.　NoSic

Sonnet 144.　EBEV; HeIP-4; NAEL-5v1; NAEL-6v1; NAEL-7v1; NIL-7; NIP-4; OxBSo; Son

(Sonnet 144: 'Two loves I have')　AEP

Sonnet 145.　Son

Sonnet 146.　AWP; HAP; HeIP-4; NAEL-5v1; NAEL-6v1; NAEL-7v1; NOBE; NOCV; OBEV; OxAEP-1; PoE; SCGP; SacPr; Son; TFi

Sonnet 147.　EBEV; NAEL-5v1; NAEL-6v1; NAEL-7v1; OxAEP-1

(Sonnet 147: 'My love is as a fever')　AEP

Sonnet 148.　SCGP

Sonnet 150.　OxAEP-1; SCGP

Sonnet 151.　EBEV; HeIP-4; NoSic; OxAEP-1; PoE

Sonnet 151.　HeIP-4; OxAEP-1

(Soul and Body.)　GTBS-P

"Sweet love renew thy force."　SCGP

"Take all my loves, my Love, yea, take them all."　HeIP-4; OxAEP-1; SCGP

("Th' expense of spirit in a waste of shame.")　PoPoPo

("Th'expense of spirit in a waste of shame.")　CABP

"That thou art blamed shall not be thy defect."　OxAEP-1; SCGP

"That thou hast her, it is not all my grief[e]."　HeIP-4; OxAEP-1

"That time of year thou may'st [or maist] in me behold."　AEP; AWP; BoLoP; CABP; CTC; ClHu; EBEV; GTBS-P; HAP; HeIP-4; InPK-6; NAEL-5v1; NAEL-6v1; NAEL-7v1; NIP-4; NOBE; NoP-4; NoSic; OBEV; OxBSo; PoE; PoRA; SCGP; SoSe-8; Son; TFi; UnPo; WeW-3

("That time of yeeare thou maist in me behold.")　NPeEn

"That you were once unkind befriends me now."　OxAEP-1

"Then hate me when thou wilt; if ever, now."　AWP; EBEV; NOBE; NoSic; OBEV; OxAEP-1

("They that have pow'r to hurt, and will do none.")　CABP

("They that have power to hurt and will do none.")　NoP-4

"They that have power to hurt[e], and will do[e] none."　NAEL-5v1; NAEL-6v1; NAEL-7v1; NIL-7; NOBE; NoSic; OBEV; OxAEP-1; OxBEV; OxBSo; PoE; SCGP; SCV; Son; TRP; WoPoe

("They that have powre to hurt, and will doe none.")　NPeEn; PBRV

"Thine eyes I love, and they, as pitying me."　OxAEP-1

"Those lips that Love's own hand did make."　Son

"Those petty [or pretty] wrongs that liberty commits."　OxAEP-1

"Thus is his cheek the map of days outworn."　SCGP

"Thy bosom is endeared with all hearts."　NOBE; OBEV

"Thy glass will show thee how thy beauties wear." HeIP-4
(Time and Love, I.) GTBS-P
(Time and Love, II.) GTBS-P
"Tired [or Tyr'd, or Tir'd] with all these, for restful death I cry." AWP; CTC; EBEV; HAP; NOBE; NoSic; OxAEP-1; TFi; WeW-3
("Tired with all these, for restful death I cry.") CABP; PoPoPo
"'Tis better to be vile than vile esteem'd." CAGL; NoSic; OxAEP-1; SCGP
("'Tis better to be vile then vile esteemed.") PBRV
(To His Love.) GTBS-P
"To me, fair[e] Friend, you never can be old." GTBS-P; HeIP-4; NoSic; OBEV; OxAEP-1; SCGP
(Triumph of Death, The.) GTBS-P
(True Love.) GTBS-P
(Let Me Not to the Marriage of True Minds.) GSo; NIL-7
"Two loves I have of comfort and despair." EBEV; HeIP-4; NAEL-5v1; NAEL-6v1; NAEL-7v1; NIL-7; NIP-4; OxBSo; Son
("Two loves I have of comfort and dispaire.") NPeEn; PBRV
("Tyr'd with all these for restfull death I cry.") NPeEn; PBRV
(Unchangeable, The.) GTBS-P
"Was it the proud full sail[e] of his great verse." CABP; NoSic; OxAEP-1; SCGP; Son
"Weary with toil, I haste me to my bed." AWTN; CAGL; HeIP-4; NoSic; SCGP
"Were't aught to me I bore the canopy." NoSic
"What is your substance, whereof are you made." CTC; EBEV; NoSic; OBEV; OxAEP-1; OxBEV; SCGP
"What potions have I drunk of Siren tears." OxAEP-1
"What's in the brain that ink may character." TreFP
("What's in the braine that Inck may character.") PBRV
"When forty winters shall besiege thy brow." HeIP-4; NoSic; SCGP; Son
"When I consider everything that grows." AWP; NAEL-5v1; NAEL-6v1; NAEL-7v1; NoSic; SCGP; Son
("When I do count the clock that tells the time") GSo
"When I have seen by Time's fell hand defac'd [or defaced]." AEP; AWP; EnLoPo; HAP; HeIP-4; NOBE; NoSic; OxAEP-1; PoE; PoRA; SCGP; Son; TreFP
("When in disgrace with Fortune and men's eyes") GSo
"When in the chronicle of wasted time." AWP; CTC; EnLoPo; FaBoCh; NAEL-5v1; NAEL-6v1; NAEL-7v1; NOBE; NoSic; OBEV; OxAEP-1; PoRA; SCGP; Son; WoPoe
"When my love swear[e]s that she is made of truth." AWP; AmFaPo; CABP; EBEV; HeIP-4; NAEL-5v1; NAEL-7v1; NPeEn; NoP-4; NoSic; OxAEP-1; OxBEV; PAI; PBRV; SoSe-3
"When thou shalt be dispos'd to set me light." OxAEP-1
("When to the sessions of sweet silent thought") GSo
"Where art thou, Muse, that thou forget'st so long." TreFP
("Who ever hath her wish, thou hast thy *Will,.*") PBRV
"Whoever hath her wish, thou hast thy Will." NAEL-5v1; NAEL-6v1; NAEL-7v1
"Why didst thou promise such a beauteous day." HeIP-4; OxAEP-1
"Why is my verse so barren of new pride." EBEV; NoSic; OxAEP-1
"Woman's face with Nature's own hand painted, A." CAGL; HeIP-4; NAEL-5v1; NAEL-6v1; NAEL-7v1; NoP-4; NoSic; OxAEP-1
("Womans face with natures owne hand painted, A.") PBRV
(World's Way, The.) GTBS-P
("Yf my deare love were but the childe of state.") NPeEn; PBRV
Sonnets. Frederick Goddard Tuckerman.
"And change[,] with hurried hand, has swept these scenes." APN-2; HAP; NOBA; TAP; TCAPo
"And two I knew, an old man and a boy." APN-2
"As when, down some broad River dropping,we." APN-2
"But war his overturning trumpet blew." APN-2
"But we are set to strive to make our mark." TrCP
"Dark fens of cedar; hemlock-branches gray." APN-2
"Gertrude and Gulielma, sister-twins." HAP
"Hast thou seen reversed the prophet's miracle." NOBA
"Here, where the red man swept the leaves away." NOBA; TAP
"His heart was in his garden; but his brain." APN-2; NoP-4; TCAPo
"How oft in schoolboy-days, from the school's sway." APN-2; NoP-4; Son
"How well do I recall that walk in state." APN-2
"Let me give something!—as the years unfold." APN-2
"Let me give something!—though my spring be done." APN-2
"Morning comes; not slow, with reddening gold, The." APN-2
"No! Cover not the fault. The wise revere." TCAPo
"Nor strange it is, to us who walk in bonds." APN-2; TCAPo
"Not sometimes, but to him that heeds the whole." TCAPo
"Roll on, sad world! Not Mercury or Mars." APN-2

"Some truths may pierce the spirit's deeper gloom." APN-2
"Sometimes I walk where the deep water dips." APN-2; NOBA
"Still pressing through these weeping solitudes." NOBA
"Thin little leaves of wood fern, ribbed and toothed." APN-2; TAP
"Under the mountain, as when first I knew." APN-2; HAP; TAP
"Yes: though the brine may from the desert deep." HAP
"Yet, even 'mid merry boyhood's tricks and scapes." APN-2
Sonnets, The. Ted Berrigan.
"Academy of the future is opening its doors, The." PFTM-2
"(Clarity! clarity!) a semblance of motion, omniscience." PFTM-2
"Dear Margie, hello. It is 5:15 A.M." PmAP
Final Sonnet, A. FTOS; PFTM-2; PmAP
"How strange to be gone in a minute? A man." FTOS; PFTM-2; PmAP
"It is a human universe: & I." PFTM-2
"It is night. You are asleep. And beautiful tears." PFTM-2
("It is 3:17 A.M. in New York city, yes, it is.") FTOS
"It's 8:54 A.M. in Brooklyn it's the 28th [or 26th] of July [and]." PmAP
Personal Poem #9. PmAP
"Poem upon the page is as massive as, The." PFTM-2
("Snake, The.") (LL) FTOS
Sonnet I: "His piercing pince-nez. Some dim frieze." FTOS
Sonnet III: "Stronger than alcohol, more great than song." FTOS
Sonnet LV: "Grace to be born and live as variously as possible." FTOS; PFTM-2
Sonnet LXX: "Sweeter than sour apples flesh to boys." FTOS
Sonnet: "My dream a drink with Lonnie Johnson we discuss the code." NoAM
Sonnets, The. Ted Berrigan.
"He eats of the fruits of the great Speckle." FTOS
Real Live. FTOS
Sonnets, The. Ted Berrigan.
Sonnet XXXIV: "Time flies by like a great whale." FTOS
Sonnets, The. Ted Berrigan.
Sonnet XXXV: "You can make this swooped transition on your lips." FTOS
Sonnets: A Sequence on Profane Love. George Henry Boker.
"Ah, lute, how well I know each tone of thee." APN-2
"As stands a statue on its pedestal." APN-2
"Farewell once more,—and yet again farewell!" APN-2
"If she should give me all I ask of her." APN-2
"Leaden eyelids of wan twilight close, The." APN-2
"My darling's features, painted by the light." APN-2
Sonnets at Christmas. Allen Tate. APT-2; HAP; NOBA; OxBA; VGW
"Ah, Christ, I love you rings to the wild sky." ChrPo; Son
"This is the day His hour of life draws near." ChrPo; NAAL-2v2; Son
Sonnets Attempted in the Manner of Contemporary Writers. Samuel Taylor Coleridge. Son
"Pensive at eve on the hard world I mus'd [or mused]." CenSon
To Simplicity. CenSon
Sonnets: First Series. Frederick Goddard Tuckerman. NCAP
Sonnets for Roberta (1954). John Hewitt.
"How have I served you? I have let you waste." PNI
"If I had given you that love and care." PNI
Sonnets for Stan Gage (1945–1992). Sascha Feinstein. SeSe
Sonnets for the Novachord. "Ern Malley." BMAP
Sonnets from a Lock Box. Anna Hempstead Branch.
"Around this rod my writhing self might twist." APT-1
"I say that words are men and when we spell." APT-1; NALW
"I used to think. . . number was fixed and still." APT-1
"Into the void behold my shuddering flight," NALW
"What witchlike spell weaves here its deep design." APT-1; NALW
Sonnets from an Ungrafted Tree. Edna St. Vincent Millay. NALW
"So she came back into his house again." ColAP
Sonnet 17. APT-1
Sonnets from China. W. H. Auden.
("And the age ended, and the last deliverer died.") Son
"Far from a cultural centre he was used." NoAM
"He turned his field into a meeting-place." SCV
"Here war is harmless like a monument." OBWP
("Here war is simple like a monument.") OxBSo
"So an age ended, and its last deliverer died." PoE
"They wondered why the fruit had been forbidden." ChIV-1; Son
Sonnets from Greece. Trumbull Stickney. APN-1
Mount Lykaion. OxBA; Son
Sonnets from Scotland. Edwin Morgan.
Coin, The. NePenScot
Sonnets from the Portuguese. Elizabeth Barrett Browning.

"Accuse me not, beseech thee, that I wear." CenSon

"And therefore if to love can be desert." CenSon

"And wilt thou have me fashion into speech." BWW; BrRo; CABP; CenSon; VWP

"And yet, because thou overcomest so." CenSon

"Because thou hast the power and own'st the grace." CenSon

"Beloved, my Beloved, when I think." CenSon; Son; WPE

"Beloved, thou hast brought me many flowers." CenSon; EBVV; LW; OxBSo; WPE

"But only three in all God's universe." CenSon

"Can it be right to give what I can give?" CTC; CenSon; Son

"Face of all the world is changed, I think, The." CTC; CenSon

"First time he kissed me, he but only kissed." CTC; CenSon; ITBLP; LW

"First time that the sun rose on thine oath, The." CenSon; NAEL-5v2; WPE

(For Love's Sake Only.) PoToHe

"Go from me. Yet I feel that I shall stand." BWW; CenSon; LW; OBEV; OxAEP-2

"Heavy heart, Beloved, have I borne, A." CenSon

"I lift my heavy heart up solemnly." CenSon; LW; NALW; PEW; VWP

"I lived with visions for my company." BWW; CenSon

"I never gave a lock of hair away." CenSon; EBVV; HAP; OxBSo

"I see thine image through my tears tonight." CenSon

"I thank all who have loved me in their hearts." CenSon

"I think of thee!—My thoughts do twine and bud." CenSon

"I thought once how Theocritus had sung." BWW; CenSon; EBVV; NOBE; NoP-4; OBEV; OxAEP-2; PoPoPo; WPE

"If I leave all for thee, wilt thou exchange." CenSon; Son

"If thou must love me, let it be for nought [or naught]." BWW; CTC; CenSon; GSo; HeIP-4; LW; OBEV; OxAEP-2; OxBSo; SoSe-8

"Indeed this very love which is my boast." CenSon

"Is it indeed so? If I lay here dead." CenSon

"Let the world's sharpness, like a clasping knife." CenSon; NOBVV; OxBEV

"My letters! all dead paper, mute and white." CenSon; HAP; OxAEP-2

"My own Beloved, who hast lifted me." CenSon

"My poet, thou canst touch on all the notes." BrRo; CenSon

"Oh, yes! they love through all this world of ours!" CenSon

"Pardon, oh, pardon, that my soul should make." CenSon

"Say over again, and yet once over again." CenSon; NAEL-5v2; NAEL-6v2; OxBSo

Sonnet 1: "I thought once how Theocritus had sung." BWW; CenSon; EBVV; NOBE; NoP-4; OBEV; OxAEP-2; PoPoPo; WPE

Sonnet 2: "But only three in all God's universe." CenSon

Sonnet 3: "Unlike are we, unlike, O princely Heart!" BWW; CABP; CenSon; OBEV; OxAEP-2

Sonnet 4: "Thou hast thy calling to some palace-floor." CenSon; OxAEP-2; Son; VWP

Sonnet 5: "I lift my heavy heart up solemnly." CenSon; LW; NALW; PEW; VWP

Sonnet 6: "Go from me. Yet I feel that I shall stand." BWW; CenSon; LW; OBEV; OxAEP-2

Sonnet 7: "Face of all the world is changed, I think, The." CTC; CenSon

Sonnet 8: "What can I give thee back, O liberal." BWW; CenSon; OxAEP-2

Sonnet 9: "Can it be right to give what I can give?" CTC; CenSon; Son

Sonnet 10: "Yet, love, mere love, is beautiful indeed." BWW; CTC; CenSon; OxAEP-2

Sonnet 11: "And therefore if to love can be desert." CenSon

Sonnet 12: "Indeed this very love which is my boast." CenSon

Sonnet 13: "And wilt thou have me fashion into speech." BWW; BrRo; CABP; CenSon; VWP

Sonnet 14: "If thou must love me, let it be for nought [or naught]." BWW; CTC; CenSon; GSo; HeIP-4; LW; OBEV; OxAEP-2; OxBSo; SoSe-8

Sonnet 15: "Accuse me not, beseech thee, that I wear." CenSon

Sonnet 16: "And yet, because thou overcomest so." CenSon

Sonnet 17: "My poet, thou canst touch on all the notes." BrRo; CenSon

Sonnet 18: "I never gave a lock of hair away." CenSon; EBVV; HAP; OxBSo

Sonnet 19: "Soul's Rialto hath its merchandise, The." CenSon

Sonnet 20: "Beloved, my Beloved, when I think." CenSon; Son; WPE

Sonnet 21: "Say over again, and yet once over again." CenSon; NAEL-5v2; NAEL-6v2; OxBSo

Sonnet 22: "When our two souls stand up erect and strong." BWW; BoWoP; CenSon; LW; NAEL-5v2; NAEL-6v2; NALW; NOBE; OBEV; WPE

Sonnet 23: "Is it indeed so? If I lay here dead." CenSon

Sonnet 24: "Let the world's sharpness, like a clasping knife." NOBVV; OxBEV

Sonnet 25: "Heavy heart, Beloved, have I borne, A." CenSon

Sonnet 26: "I lived with visions for my company." BWW; CenSon

Sonnet 27: "My own Beloved, who hast lifted me." CenSon

Sonnet 28: "My letters! all dead paper, mute and white." CenSon; HAP; OxAEP-2

(Sonnet XXIX.) PEW

Sonnet 29: "I think of thee!—My thoughts do twine and bud." CenSon

Sonnet 30: "I see thine image through my tears tonight." CenSon

Sonnet 31: "Thou comest! all is said without a word." BWW; CenSon

Sonnet 32: "First time that the sun rose on thine oath, The." CenSon; NAEL-5v2; NAEL-6v2; WPE

Sonnet 33: "Yes, call me by my pet-name! let me hear." CenSon

Sonnet 34: "With the same heart, I said, I'll answer thee." CenSon

Sonnet 35: "If I leave all for thee, wilt thou exchange." CenSon; Son

Sonnet 36: "When we first met and loved, I did not build." CenSon

Sonnet 37: "Pardon, oh, pardon, that my soul should make." CenSon

Sonnet 38: "First time he kissed me, he but only kissed." CTC; CenSon; ITBLP; LW

Sonnet 39: "Because thou hast the power and own'st the grace." CenSon

Sonnet 40: "Oh, yes! they love through all this world of ours!" CenSon

Sonnet 41: "I thank all who have loved me in their hearts." CenSon

Sonnet 42: "How do I love thee? Let me count the ways." AmFaPo; BWW; BoLoP; CTC; CenSon; EBVV; GSo; HeIP-4; ITBLP; InPK-6; MakPoe; NAEL-5v2; NAEL-6v2; NALW; NIL-7; NIP-4; NoP-4; OPOU; OxAEP-2; OxBSo; PoE; PoPoPo; PoRA; PoToHe; Son; TFi; UV; UnPo; VWP; WPE

(Sonnet 43.) CABP

Sonnet 44: "Beloved, thou hast brought me many flowers." CenSon; EBVV; LW; OxBSo; WPE

"Soul's Rialto hath its merchandise, The." CenSon

"Thou comest! all is said without a word." BWW; CenSon

"Thou hast thy calling to some palace-floor." CenSon; OxAEP-2; Son; VWP

"Unlike are we, unlike, O princely Heart!" BWW; CABP; CenSon; OBEV; OxAEP-2

"What can I give thee back, O liberal." BWW; CenSon; OxAEP-2

"When our two souls stand up erect and strong." BWW; BoWoP; CenSon; LW; NAEL-5v2; NAEL-6v2; NALW; NOBE; OBEV; WPE

"When we first met and loved, I did not build." CenSon

"When we met first and loved, I did not build." CenSon

"With the same heart, I said, I'll answer thee." CenSon

"Yes, call me by my pet-name! let me hear." CenSon

"Yet, love, mere love, is beautiful indeed." BWW; CTC; CenSon; OxAEP-2

Sonnets in Quaker Language. Hildegarde Flanner. WPE

Sonnets of English Dramatic Poets. Algernon Charles Swinburne. Son

Sonnets of Laura. Elizabeth Cobbold.

   Absence. CenSon

   Reproach. CenSon

   Veil, The. CenSon

Sonnets of Michelangelo, The. Elizabeth Jennings.

   "I wish, God, for some end I do not will." PeECV; TOF

Sonnets of the Months. Folgore da San Geminiano [or Gimignano]. AWP, tr. by Dante Gabriel Rossetti

   April. EaItPo, tr. by Dante Gabriel Rossetti

   August. CTC; EaItPo, tr. by Dante Gabriel Rossetti

   December. EaItPo, tr. by Dante Gabriel Rossetti

   Dedication: "Unto the blithe and lordly fellowship." EaItPo, tr. by Dante Gabriel Rossetti

   February. EaItPo, tr. by Dante Gabriel Rossetti

   "For July, in Siena, by the willow-tree." EaItPo, tr. by Dante Gabriel Rossetti

   January. EaItPo, tr. by Dante Gabriel Rossetti

   July. EaItPo, tr. by Dante Gabriel Rossetti

   June. EaItPo, tr. by Dante Gabriel Rossetti

   March. EaItPo, tr. by Dante Gabriel Rossetti

   May. EaItPo, tr. by Dante Gabriel Rossetti

   November. EaItPo, tr. by Dante Gabriel Rossetti

   October. EaItPo, tr. by Dante Gabriel Rossetti

   September. EaItPo, tr. by Dante Gabriel Rossetti

   "Unto the blithe and lordly fellowship." EaItPo, tr. by Dante Gabriel Rossetti

Sonnets of the Months: Conclusion. Folgore da San Geminiano [or Gimignano]. AWP; EaItPo, tr. by Dante Gabriel Rossetti

Sonnets of the Months: September. Folgore da San Geminiano [or Gimignano]. AWP, tr. by Dante Gabriel Rossetti

Sonnets on the Statue of Mary, Queen of Scots, in the Luxembourg Gardens, Paris. Joseph Brodsky.

   "In my declining years, in a land beyond the ocean." TCRusP, tr. by Bernard Meares

   "Mary, the Scots are sots in any case." TCRusP, tr. by Bernard Meares

"Part of the field, A. Trumpets sound and two men enter." TCRusP, *tr. by* Bernard Meares

"That which ripped an amazed scream." TCRusP, *tr. by* Bernard Meares

"Will a mouth that's muttered its goodbyes." TCRusP, *tr. by* Bernard Meares

"With a simple, truly unrebellious pen." TCRusP, *tr. by* Bernard Meares

Sonnets: "Starry flower, the flower-like stars that fade, The." Frederick Goddard Tuckerman. APN-2

(Sonnet.) ColAP

Sonnets to Aurelia. Robert Malise Bowyer Nichols. OBMV

Sonnets to be Written from Prison. Robert Adamson.

"O to be in the news again—now as fashion runs." BMAP

Sonnets to Bothwell. Mary Stuart, Queen of Scots.

"For him also I powrit out mony teiris." NePenScot, *tr. by* Unknown

Sonnets to Chris. John Berryman.

"Astronomies and slangs to find you, dear." AWTN

"I've found out why, that day, that suicide." PoE

"Nothing there? nothing up the sky alive." BoLoP

"Sometimes the night echoes to prideless wailing." NoAM

Sonnet 115: "All we were going strong last night this time." FaBoMo

Sonnets to Helen. Pierre de Ronsard.

"By looking too long on your perfect face." EroLit

"When you are old, at evening candle-lit." WoPoe, *tr. by* Humbert Wolfe

Sonnets to Laura. Petrarch.

"Apollo, if the sweet desire is still alive that inflamed you beside." NAWM-7v1, *tr. by* Robert M. Durling

"Being one day at my window all alone." AWP

"Blest be the day, and blest the month and year." NAWM-5v1; NAWM-7v1, *tr. by* Joseph Auslander

"Clear, fresh, sweet waters, where she who alone seems lady." NAWM-7v1, *tr. by* Robert M. Durling

Complaint of a Lover Rebuked. HeIP-4; NAEL-5v1; OBVE, *tr. by* Henry Howard, Earl of Surrey

Description of the Contrarious Passions in a Lover. OBVE; Son, *tr. by* Sir Thomas Wyatt

"Eyes that drew from me such fervent praise, The." NAWM-5v1

"Father in heaven, after each lost day." NAWM-5v1; NAWM-7v1, *tr. by* Bernard Bergonzi

"First day she passed up and down through the Heavens, The." OBMV

Galley, The. HAP; OBVE; OxBEV; SCGP; Son; WeW-3, *tr. by* Sir Thomas Wyatt

"Go, grieving rimes of mine, to that hard stone." NAWM-5v1; NAWM-7v1, *tr. by* Morris Gilbert Bishop

"Great is my envy of you, earth, in your greed." NAWM-5v1

He Understands the Great Cruelty of Death. BIrV; OBMV; OxBEV; WoPoe, *tr. by* John Millington Synge and J. M. Synge

Heart on the Hill, The. AWP

How the Lover Perisheth in His Delight, As the Fly in the Fire. SCGP, *tr. by* Sir Thomas Wyatt

"I find no peace and all my war[r] is done." OBVE; Son, *tr. by* Sir Thomas Wyatt

I saw a Phoenix in the Wood Alone. AWP, *tr. by* Edmund Spenser

"If amorous faith, a heart of guileless ways." AWP

If It Be Destined. AWP, *tr. by* Edward Fitzgerald

"In the years of her age the most beautiful." OBMV

"It was the day when the sun's rays turned pale with grief for his." NAWM-7v1, *tr. by* Robert M. Durling

"It was the morning of that blessed day." NAWM-5v1

"Long[e] love that in my thought do[e]th [*or* I] harbour [*or* harber *or* harbar], The." NPeEn, *tr. by* Sir Thomas Wyatt

"Loose to the wind her golden tresses streamed." CenSon; RWP, *tr. by* Charlotte Smith

Love's Fidelity. AWP; HAP; NoSic; OxBSo, *tr. by* Henry Howard, Earl of Surrey

"Love, That Doth Reign [*or* Raine] and Live Within My Thought." HeIP-4; NAEL-5v1; OBVE, *tr. by* Henry Howard, Earl of Surrey

("Love that liveth and reigneth in my thought.") AWP; Son

Lover for Shamefastness Hideth His Desire within His Faithful Heart. NPeEn, *tr. by* Sir Thomas Wyatt

"My flowery and green age was passing away." BIrV; OBMV; OxBEV; WoPoe, *tr. by* John Millington Synge and J. M. Synge

(My Galley.) NAEL-6v1; WoPoe

"My galley [*or* galy] charged with forgetfulness." HAP; OBVE; OxBEV; SCGP; Son; WeW-3, *tr. by* Sir Thomas Wyatt

"My ship laden with forgetfulness passes through a harsh sea, at." NAWM-7v1, *tr. by* Robert M. Durling

"Oh! place me where the burning noon." RWP, *tr. by* Charlotte Smith

"Set me whereas the sun[ne] doth[e] parch [*or* perche] the green [*or* grene]." AWP; HAP; NoSic; OxBSo, *tr. by* Henry Howard, Earl of Surrey

"She used to let her golden hair fly free." NAWM-5v1; NAWM-7v1, *tr. by* Morris Gilbert Bishop

Signs of Love. AWP

("Snatched from a world of woe, survives in bliss above!") (LL) RWP

"Some fowls there be that have so perfect sight." SCGP, *tr. by* Sir Thomas Wyatt

"Thou green and blooming, cool and shaded hill." AWP

Translation from Petrarch, A. MoBrPo, *tr. by* J. M. Synge

Visions, The. AWP

"What a grudge I am bearing the earth." MoBrPo, *tr. by* J. M. Synge

"When Simon received the high idea which, for my sake, put his." NAWM-7v1, *tr. by* Robert M. Durling

"Ye vales and woods! fair scenes of happier hours." RWP, *tr. by* Charlotte Smith

"You who hear in scattered rhymes the sound of those sighs with." NAWM-7v1, *tr. by* Robert M. Durling

Sonnets to Orpheus. Rainer Maria Rilke.

"As once the winged energy of delight." EnlH

"Be ahead of all parting, as though it already were." EnlH

"Call me to the one among your moments." EnlH

"Silent friend of many distances, feel." EnlH

Sonnets to Orpheus, The. RaBo

"This is the creature there has never been." OBVE

"Tree ascending there. O pure transcension, A." TOF

"We are the driving ones." EnlH

"Where in what ever-blissfully watered gardens, upon what trees." OBVE

"Where praise already is is the only place Grief." RaBo

Sonnets to the Left. Chris Wallace-Crabbe.

Sonnet IV. BMAP

Sonnets to the Seasons. Hartley Coleridge.

November. CenSon

Sonnets upon the Punishment of Death. William Wordsworth.

"See the Condemned alone within his cell." SacPr

Sonnets Written in the Orillia Woods. Charles Sangster.

"Our life is like a forest, where the sun." NOBC

Sonny. Ku K'uang. SuSp, *tr. by* Irving Y. Lo

Sonny grows up in Fukien. Sonny. Ku K'uang. SuSp, *tr. by* Irving Y. Lo

Sonny's Purple Heart. Adrian C. Louis. ReTh

Sonrisas. Pat Mora. NIL-7; NIP-4

Sons and Fathers. Larry Mitchell. GLP

Sons Changed Into Stags, The. József Erdélyi. IQMS, *tr. by* Watson Kirkconnell

Li Sons d'un Cornet. *Unknown.* WoPoe, *tr. by* Willard Trask

Sons of Martha, The. Rudyard Kipling. ChIV-2

(Sons of Mary seldom bother, The.) GI

Sons of Mary seldom bother, for they have inherited that good part, The. Sons of Martha, The. Rudyard Kipling. ChIV-2

Sons of Our Sons, The. Ilya Grigoryevich Ehrenburg [*or* Erenburg]. TrJP, *tr. by* Babette Deutsch

Sons of Promise. Thomas Curtis Clark. PoToHe

Sons of Saint Crispin, 'tis in vain! "Peter Pindar." NOEC *Fr.* Resignation; an Ode to the Journeyman Shoemakers.

Sons of War. Samih Al-Qasim. FaBoWar, *tr. by* Abdullah Al-Udhari

Sons of War sometimes are known, The. Evan Lloyd. OBSV *Fr.* Methodist, The.

Sonsy Milkmaid, The. Emily Jane Pfeiffer. ViWPN

Soon. Pamela Alexander. ExTi

Soon. James Harms. NeAmPo

(Soon after). Tune: "Drunk in the East Wind." Lu Chih. ChinPo, *tr. by* Yip Wai-lim

Soon after, he a crystal stream espying. Ludovico Ariosto. NoSic *Fr.* Orlando Furioso.

Soon and silently. Peter Reading. NewEx

Soon as the Azure-colored Gates. Richard Lynche. Son *Fr.* Diella.

Soon as the harvest hath laid bare the plains. Stephen Duck. NOEC *Fr.* Thresher's Labour, The.

Soon as the sun forsook the eastern main. Hymn to the Evening, An. Phillis Wheatley. WPE

Soon as / you stop. Cleavage. A. R. Ammons. OBAL

Soon at Last My Sighs and Moans. Louis Ginsberg. TrJP

Soon I shall hear. Takuro. JDP, *tr. by* Yoel Hoffmann

Soon I shall take more. Rotting Symbols. Eileen Myles. BodElec

Soon I Will Be Done. *Unknown.* NAAAL

Soon I will climb the hill to the sunlight. From the Rain Forest. Desiré Flynn. BrRo

Soon it will be thirteen years since the nightingale. Letters from the Ming Dynasty. Joseph Brodsky. PoetW; TCRP, *tr. by* Derek Walcott

Soon it will be twenty years. Barcelona Days. Jaime Manrique. WiU, *tr. by* Edith Grossman

Soon kindled and soon spent, we that were the pick of many. (LL) Old Woman's Lamentations, An. François Villon. MoBrPo; OBMV, *tr. by* J. M. Synge

Soon one more goes thither! (LL) Exeunt Omnes. Thomas Hardy. FaBoVe; UV

Soon the last trains will be backed. Last Trains, The. C. G. Hanzlicek. GM

Soon we entered in the woods. Alexander McLachlan. NOBC *Fr.* Emigrant, The.

Soon we shall be truly wedded. Some Old How. Sándor Petőfi. IQMS, *tr. by* Peter Zollman

Soon we shall plunge into the chilly fogs. Song of Autumn I. Charles Baudelaire. NAWM-7v2, *tr. by* Carlyle Ferren MacIntyre and C. F. MacIntyre

Sooner I may some fixed statue be. On the Duke of Buckingham, Slain by Felton, the 23rd August, 1628. Owen Felltham [*or* Feltham]. NOSC

Sooner or late—in earnest or in jest. Rudyard Kipling. OxBSo *Fr.* Land and Sea Tales.

Sooner or Later. John Digby. SPE

Sooner or later the sun cracks rebecca. Fragment. Ray DiPalma. FTOS

Sooner tears than sleep this midnight. Wind's Lament, The. John Morris-Jones. OBWVE, *tr. by* Anthony Conran

Soonest Mended. John Ashbery. HCAP; NAAL-2v2; NAAL-5; PoetW; VCAP

Soot season, that bud and bloom forth brings, The. Henry Howard, Earl of Surrey. *See* Soote season, that bud and bloom forth brings, The

Soote Season, The. Henry Howard, Earl of Surrey. NAEL-5v1; NAEL-6v1; NAEL-7v1; NoP-4; NoSic; Son

  (Description of Spring.) SCGP

  (Description of Spring, Wherein Each Thing Renews Save Only the Lover.) OBEV

  (Sonnet.) AEP

  (Soot season, that bud and bloom forth brings, The.) AEP

  (Soote season, that bud and blome furth bringes, The.) OxBEV; PBRV

Soote season, that bud and bloom forth brings, The. Soote Season, The. Henry Howard, Earl of Surrey. NAEL-5v1; NAEL-6v1; NAEL-7v1; NoP-4; NoSic; Son

Sooth-Sayer, The. Sadi [*or* Saadi *or* Sa'di]. AWP, *tr. by* Sir Edwin Arnold *Fr.* Gulistan, The.

Soothed by the murmurs on the sea-beat shore. To the Curlew. Helen Maria Williams. CenSon; WoRP

Sooty, swart smiths, smattered with smoke. Blacksmiths, The. *Unknown.* WoPoe, *tr. by* Wesli Court

Sophia. Joyce Rupp. HW

Sophia! Antiphon for Divine Wisdom. Hildegard von Bingen. WPoS, *tr. by* Barbara Newman

Sophia, / to you I come. Sophia. Joyce Rupp. HW

Sophie, Climbing the Stairs. Dolores Kendrick. ESEAA

Sophisticated Lady. Mitchell Parish. ReLy

Sophocles. *Unknown.* GrAn, *tr. by* Lee T. Pearcy

Sopolis. Callimachus. AWP, *tr. by* William M. Hardinge

Soraidh Slan Don Oidhche Areir. Niall Mor MacMuireadach. BIrV, *tr. by* Maire Cruise O'Brien

Sorcerer, The. Laury Wells. IBA

Sorcerer sang the spring to sleep, The. Aleksandr Aleksandrovich Blok. TCRP

Sordello. Robert Browning.
  "Our dropping Autumn morning clears apace." OBGa

Sordello. Robert Browning. OBGa *Fr.* Sordello.

Sordid, unfeeling, reprobate, degraded / Spiritless outcast! (LL) Friend of Humanity and the Knife Grinder, The. George Canning. OBCoV; UV

Sorrow. Chu Shu-chen. BoWoP; OHMPC, *tr. by* Kenneth Rexroth

Sorrow. Aubrey Thomas De Vere. SacPr

Sorrow. D. H. Lawrence. GTBS-P; NPeEn; OBMV

Sorrow. Mei Yao Ch'en. OHPC; WoPoe, *tr. by* Kenneth Rexroth

Sorrow. Edna St. Vincent Millay. APT-1

Sorrow. Laetitia Pilkington. ECWP

Sorrow. Alfonsina Storni. TCLAP, *tr. by* Andrew Rosing

Sorrow. *Unknown.* AWP, *tr. by* W. R. S. Ralston

Sorrow and Rapture. Maura Stanton. IllVoic

Sorrow Garden, The. Thomas McCarthy. BiHa

Sorrow heaped on sorrow, ruin on disaster. On My Sorrowful Life. Moses Ibn Ezra. TrJP, *tr. by* Solomon Solis-Cohen

Sorrow I'll [*or* I'le] wed: Despair [*or* Dispaire] thus governs me[e]. (LL) Mary Sidney Wroth, Countess of Montgomery. BWW; NOSC *Fr.* Pamphilia to Amphilanthus.

Sorrow in the Harem, A. Wang Ch'ang-ling. OHMPC, *tr. by* Kenneth Rexroth

Sorrow is my own yard. Widow's Lament in Springtime, The. William Carlos Williams. APT-1; HAP; NAAL-2v2; NAAL-5; NOBA; NoAM; PoE; SAmP; SoSe-8; TAP; TCAPo

Sorrow lay upon my breast more heavily than winter clay. "Desolation Is a Delicate Thing." Elinor Wylie. MoAmPo

Sorrow, mute, a guitar. Luzumiyya. Abdul Wahab [*or* 'Abd al-Wahhab] Al-Bayati [*or* Al-Bayyati]. MAP, *tr. by* Salma Khadra Jayyusi and Christopher Middleton

Sorrow of Kodio, The. *Unknown.* PBA, *tr. by* Miriam Koshl

Sorrow of Love, The. W. B. Yeats. MoBrPo; NAEL-5v2; NAEL-6v2; NOBVV; NPeEn; NoAM; OxBEV; PeVV

Sorrow of Mydath. John Masefield. MoBrPo

Sorrow Since Sitting Bull, A. Christopher Gilbert. ESEAA

Sorrow, since you cannot make me. Sorrow Vanquished. Amado Nervo. TCLAP, *tr. by* Sue Standing

Sorrow Song. Lucille Clifton. BodElec

Sorrow Vanquished. Amado Nervo. TCLAP, *tr. by* Sue Standing

Sorrow? A Great Ocean. Sándor Petőfi. IQMS, *tr. by* Wystan Hugh Auden *Fr.* Clouds, The.

Sorrowful Sea-Gull, The. Menella Bute Smedley. VWP

Sorrowful Shadow, The. Julio Herrera y Reissig. TCLAP, *tr. by* Andrew Rosing

Sorrowing for the Past at Western Pass Mountain. Liu Yu Hsi. SuSp, *tr. by* Daniel Bryant

Sorrows of an Abandoned Queen. Nguyễn Gia Thiều.
  "You were a fool, Old Man of the Moon." WoPoe, *tr. by* Nguyen Ngoc Bich

Sorrows of my heart enlarged are, The. Some Contemplations of the Poor, and Desolate State of the Church at Deerfield. John Williams. SCAP

Sorrows of Sunday; an Elegy, The. "Peter Pindar."
  "Susan, the constant slave to mop and broom." NOEC

Sorrows of Werther, The. William Makepeace Thackeray. NBLV; NOBL; NOBVV; OBCoV; PeLV

Sorry. Julie Watson Nungarrayi. IBA

Sorry, Hank. / Found out / The Hard / Way. Hank Mobley's. Cornelius Eady. SeSe

Sorry I am, my God, sorry I am. Sin's Round. George Herbert. NOSC

Sorry I'm late. I had to drive way out of my. Mrs. Eden in Town for the Day. Richard Howard. KGB

Sort of a Song, A. William Carlos Williams. APT-1; NAAL-2v2; OxBSP; TAP; WoPoe

Sort of attachment to the family tree, A. Lilith, Adam's First Companion. Elina Wechsler. MirDau, *tr. by* Darrell Lockhart

Sort of extra hunger, A. Poet Wondering What He Is Up To. Dennis Joseph Enright. OxBC

Sort of meaning that comes back, A. (LL) Sonatina in Yellow. Donald Justice. ColAP; LCAP-2

Sortie, The. Miklós Zrínyi. IQMS, *tr. by* Thomas Kabdebo

Sorting Laundry. Elisavietta Ritchie. SoSe-8

Sorting out letters and piles of my old. Mementos, 1. W. D. Snodgrass. MoAmPo; NoP-4; UnPo; VCAP

Sorting Things Out. Wanda Barford. Prnts

Sory beverech [*or* beuerech] it is and sore it is abought [*or* a-bouth], A. Christ's Prayer in Gethsemane. *Unknown.* MiEL; SacPr

SOS. Imamu Amiri Baraka. BPo; NAAAL

S.O.S. Léon Damas. PFTM-1

Sosicles the farmer dedicated these sheaves. Philip of Thessalonica. GrAn

Sōsos the cattleman slew the lion. Leonidas of Tarentum. GrAn

Sospetto d'Herode. Giambattista [*or* Giovanni Battista] Marino. *Fr.* Strage degli innocenti, La.

Sot-Weed Factor, The. Ebenezer Cook. TCAPo

Soto, a Character. Mary Leapor. ECWP

Sotto Voce. M. Vasalis. TuT, *tr. by* Peter Van de Kamp

Sotto voce / cynics pass the word. But God is Silent / Psalm 114. Daniel Berrigan. InvLi

Sottoportico San Zaccaria. Kenneth Rexroth. ErotSp

Sought by the world, and hath the world disdained. Love's Ending. *Unknown.* NoSic

Soul, A. Christina Georgina Rossetti. NALW; WPOW

Soul, The. Joseph Addison. TreFP *Fr.* Cato.

Soul, The. Ira Sadoff. BodElec

Soul a crystal is, the Godhead is its shine, The. "Angelus Silesius." GePo, *tr. by* George C. Schoolfield *Fr.* Cherubical Wanderer, The.

Soul against the state, The. Paavo Haavikko. WoPoe, *tr. by* Anselm Hollo

Soul and Body. Margaret Lucas Cavendish, Duchess of Newcastle. OxBSP
  (Soule, and Body.) PEW

Soul and Body. Friedrich von Logau. GePo, *tr. by* George C. Schoolfield

Soul and Body. William Shakespeare. *See* Sonnets

Soul and Body: I've heard tell of a noble guest. Cynewulf. ASW *Fr.* Riddles (Exeter Book).

Soul and Body of John Brown, The. Muriel Rukeyser. CBCWP; MoAmPo

Soul and fire of windsongs must not be neutral, The. Killing Memory. Haki R. Madhubuti. IllVoic

Soul and Love, The. Albert Verwey. TuT, *tr. by* Tony Curtis

Soul and race. Here Where Coltrane Is. Michael S. Harper. ESEAA; NAAAL

Soul and the Body, The. Sir John Davies. CTC; NOBE *Fr.* Nosce Teipsum.

Soul-animating strains—alas, too few! (LL) Sonnet: "Scorn not the sonnet; critic, you have frowned." William Wordsworth. CenSon; EBEV; HeIP-4; OxBSo; Son

Soul counsels flight. Meleager. GrAn

Soul Food. Janice Mirikitani. OpBo

Soul has Bandaged moments, The. Emily Dickinson. NALW; TRP

Soul-Hunter, The. Julia Ward Howe. SWaP *Fr.* Lyrics of the Street.

Soul Incense. Henrietta Cordelia Ray. CBWP-3

Soul is a beautiful thing, The. Three Days/out of Franklin. Víctor Hernández Cruz. PueRic

Soul is a prisoner, and body is its jail. Soul and Body. Friedrich von Logau. GePo, *tr. by* George C. Schoolfield

Soul is a region without definite boundaries, The. Terrain. A. R. Ammons. CoAmPo; VCAP

Soul is lonely, The. La Selva. Cid Corman. VGW

Soul lies buried in the ink that writes, The. (LL) Fragment: "Language has not the power to speak what love indites." John Clare. FaBoEE; OxBSP

Soul, like the moon, The. Lal Ded [*or* Lalla]. WPoS; WoPoe, *tr. by* Coleman Barks

Soul, little wandering friend. Emperor Hadrian on his Soul. Emperor Hadrian. WoPoe, *tr. by* Frederick Morgan

Soul Make a Path Through Shouting. Cyrus Cassells. GT; GifTon; OPRER; UnSA

Soul Music. Stephen Clayton. IBA

Soul Music. Baron Wormser. LTA; SwNoth

Soul Music: The Derry Air. Eamon Grennan. BiHa; PBCIP

Soul of a Man, The. Ferenc Kazinczy. IQMS, *tr. by* Adam Makkai

Soul of Jesus Is Restless, The. Cyprus R. Mitchell. TrCP

Soul of my inner face, face of my race. Ernest Francisco Fenollosa. APN-2 *Fr.* East and West.

Soul of the Black Land, The. Guy Tirolien. NegPo, *tr. by* Ellen Conroy Kennedy

Soul's Beauty. Dante Gabriel Rossetti. OBEV *Fr.* House of Life, The.

Soul's Courts, The. Henrietta Cordelia Ray. CBWP-3

Soul's Desire, The. *Unknown.* SacPr, *tr. by* Eleanor Hull

Soul's distinct connection, The. Emily Dickinson. SAmP

Soul's Garment, The. Margaret Lucas Cavendish, Duchess of Newcastle. WPE

Soul's Groan to Christ for Succo[u]r, The. Edward Taylor. NAAL-2v1; NAAL-3 *Fr.* God's Determinations [touching his Elect].

Soul's joy, bend not thou those morning stars from me. Sir Philip Sidney. NoP-4 *Fr.* Astrophil and Stella.

Soul's joy, when thou art gone. Parody [*or* Parodie], A. George Herbert. ESCV

Soul's Liberty. Anna Wickham. MoBrPo; OxBSP

Soul's Rialto hath its merchandise, The. Elizabeth Barrett Browning. CenSon *Fr.* Sonnets from the Portuguese.

Soul's Superior instants, The. Emily Dickinson. APN-2; EnlH

Soul Says. Jorie Graham. PoPoPo

Soul, secure in her existence, smiles, The. Joseph Addison. TreFP *Fr.* Cato.

Soul selects her own Society, The. Emily Dickinson. APN-2; AWP; BoWoP; HeIP-4; InPK-6; MoAmPo; NAAL-2v1; NAAL-3; NAAL-5; NALW; NAWM-7v2; NOBA; NoAM; NoP-4; OxBA; OxWW; PAI; PoE; PoPoPo; SAmP; TAP; TCAPo; TFi; UnPo; WPE

Soul-soothing drug! your virtues let me laud. Sonnet to Opium; Celebrating Its Virtues, A. "Orestes." NOEC

Soul Speaks, The. *Unknown.*
"Beguines who hear these words." WPoS

Soul that hath a Guest, The. Emily Dickinson. APN-2

Soul that must endure it, The. (LL) "All Is Vanity, Saith the Preacher." Byron. ChIV-1; TrCP

Soul that's fed on Nature is content, The. Nature's Uplifting. Henrietta Cordelia Ray. CBWP-3

Soul, thou must seek thyself in Me. Saint Theresa [*or* Teresa] of Avila. TOF

Soul Train. Allison Joseph. AmPoNex; ExTi

Soul tries a thousand remedies in vain, The. Michelangelo Buonarroti. CAGL, *tr. by* James M. Saslow

Soul-troubled at the febrile ways of breath. For Hazel Hall, American Poet. Countee Cullen. APT-2

Soul which doth with God unite, The. Cupio Dissolvi. William Habington. ChIV-2

Soul Woven of Shadows. Árpád Tóth. IQMS, *tr. by* Edmund Charles Blunden and John Gordon Nichols

Soule, and Body. Margaret Lucas Cavendish, Duchess of Newcastle. *See* Soul and Body

Soul[e] of my soul[e]! my Joy, my crown, my friend! L'Amitie: To Mrs. Mary [*or* M.] Awbrey. Katherine Philips. NIL-7; NOSC

Soule, which to Hell wast thrall. Faith Above Reason. William Drummond, of Hawthornden. SacPr

Soules joy, now I am gone. Song: "Soules joy, now I am gone." William Herbert, Earl of Pembroke. ESCV

Soulfolk, think a minute. To Soulfolk. Margaret Goss Burroughs. BlSi

Souls. Paul Wertheimer. TrJP, *tr. by* Jethro Bithell

Souls Lake. Robert Fitzgerald. APT-2; TwCP

Souls of Poets dead and gone. Lines on the Mermaid Tavern. John Keats. FHYEP; PoRA; SCGP

Sound. James [*or* Jim] Harrison. VGW

Sound, A. Gertrude Stein. TTTS *Fr.* Tender Buttons.

Sound, The. Robert Kelly. PoM

Sound Advice. *Unknown.* NBLV

Sound, and the imagination of the sound—a place, The. (LL) Triphammer Bridge. A. R. Ammons. ColAP; NAAL-2v2; NOBA

Sound Bite. Frederick D'Aguiar. Oth

Sound bubbled up, The. Jah Music. Lorna Goodison. WaCA

Sound from the Earth, A. William Stafford. NNaP

Sound I Listened For, The. Robert Francis. APT-2

Sound is fading away, The. Frances Densmore. APT-1 *Fr.* Chippewa Music.

Sound is fading out. Song. *Unknown.* STP, *tr. by* Jerome Rothenberg

Sound is forced [*or* forc'd], the notes are few, The. (LL) To the Muses. William Blake. HAP; HeIP-4; NAEL-5v2; NAEL-6v2; NOBE; NOEC; OBEV; SCGP

Sound is sea: pattern lapping pattern. If we erase the air and slow the. Ronald Johnson. APSN *Fr.* Ark.

Sound like a great big crowd. (LL) Morning After. Langston Hughes. NAAL-2v2; NBLV; NoAM; OBCoV

Sound like a rusty pump beneath our window, A. Blue Jay. Paul Lake. RA

Sound like hundreds of barbers, A. Night Dust-off. Basil T. Paquet. CDa

Sound like I can hear this morning. Death Bells. Lightnin' Hopkins. APT-2

Sound of a bell. Buson. EH, *tr. by* Robert Hass

Sound of a melody. Tomoemon. JDP, *tr. by* Yoel Hoffmann

Sound of a saw. Buson. EH, *tr. by* Robert Hass

Sound of autumn from a stretch of reed flowers, The. Tune: "Song of Plucking Cassia." Ch'iao Chi. SuSp, *tr. by* Sherwin S. S. Fu

Sound of Birds at Noon, The. Dahlia Ravikovitch [*or* Ravikovich]. VCWP

Sound of Breaking. Conrad Potter Aiken. AWP

Sound of gunfire—dilutes the bloody terror of revolution, The. Duo Duo (Li Shizheng). AF, *tr. by* Gregory Lee *Fr.* Thoughts and Recollections.

Sound of Guns, The. Gerald McCarthy. CDa

Sound of guns from beleaguered Donelson, The. Lines Written for Allen Tate on His Sixtieth Anniversary. Donald Davidson. FuPo

Sound of happy laughter leap with shadows on the walls. Taos Winter. Patty L. Harjo. VoR

sound of her silk skirt has stopped, The. Li Fu-Jên. Emperor Wu of Han [*or* Wu Ti *or* Ou-ty *or* Liu Ch'e *or* Liu Ch'u]. ChiP, *tr. by* Arthur Waley

Sound of Music, The. Richard Rodgers. ReLy

Sound of my lover, The. Bible, *O.T.* WoPoe, *tr. by* Marcia Falk *Fr.* Song of Solomon, The [*or* The Song of Songs].

Sound of My Sneezing Nose, The. Te Whetu. PeNZ, *tr. by* Margaret Orbell

Sound of Night, The. Maxine W. Kumin. SoSe-8; WPE

Sound of Rain, The. Bella [*or* Izabella] Akhatovna Akhmadulina. BoWoP, *tr. by* Daniel Halpern and Albert Todd

Sound of rain, The. (LL) On Gay Wallpaper. William Carlos Williams. APT-1; MoAmPo; TAP

Sound of shoes going down to the grave in the dark, The. Shadow 1. Miyoshi Toyoichiro. GifTon, *tr. by* Naoshi Koriyama and Edward Lueders

Sound of snails—crying. Snails. Liagarang. CBAP, *tr. by* Ronald M. Berndt

Sound of tears on the wind, The. Lament. Máire Mhac an tSaoi. ModIr, *tr. by* Patrick Crotty

Sound of tears the moment after, A. (LL) Dream, A [*or* The]. William Allingham. BIrV; NOBVV

Sound of the fifth watch! Dawn hastens to obey. Tu Fu. CarOv, *tr. by* Carolyn Kizer *Fr.* Adviser to the Court.

Sound of the Horn, The. Alfred de Vigny. AWP, *tr. by* Wilfred Thorley

Sound of the rain, The. Richard Wright. APT-2

Sound of the Sea, The. Henry Wadsworth Longfellow. ITBLP; TCAPo

Sound of the Trees, The. Robert Frost. *See* Sound of Trees, The

Sound of the waves in the silence, The. Yocheved Bat-Miriam. FIT, *tr. by* Robert Friend

Sound of the Wind That Is Blowing, The. J. Kitchener Davies.

"Today,/ there came a breeze thin as the needle of a syringe." OBWVE

Sound of Trees, The. Robert Frost. APT-1; NoAM; OxBA

Sound of Water. Mary O'Neill. NTCP

Sound of words as they fall away from our mouths, The. Duet for a Chair and a Table. Jack Spicer. APSN

Sound on, thou dark unslumbering sea! Last Song of Sappho, The. Felicia Dorothea Hemans. VWP

Sound, sound forever, trumpet-calls of thought! Victor Hugo. SxFrPo, tr. by E. H. Blackmore and A. M. Blackmore

Sound, Sound the Clarion. Thomas Osbert Mordaunt. EBEV; FaBoEE; NOBE Fr. Verses Written during the War, 1756–1763.

Sound, Sound the Clarion. Sir Walter Scott. FaBoEE; NOBE; OxAEP-2 Fr. Old Mortality.

Sound Systems. Ronald Wallace. SwNoth

Sound the Flute! William Blake. FHYEP; FaBoCh; NOxBChV; TTTS Fr. Songs of Innocence.

Sound the Loud timbrel o'er Egypt's dark sea! Sound the Loud Timbrel. Thomas Moore. ChIV-1

Sound trumpets, ho!—weigh anchor—loosen sail. Voyager's Song, The. Edward Coote [or Coate] Pinkney. APN-1

Sound Waves. Mary Kinzie. FFC

Soundings. Paula Gunn Allen. HATNAP

Soundless as dots—on a Disc of Snow. (LL) Emily Dickinson. APN-2; NAAL-2v1; NOBA; OxBA; RaBo; TCAPo; WPE; WoPoe

Soundlessly, a tide at the ear. Awakening. John Haines. SPE

Sounds. Lindley Williams Hubbell. APT-2

Sounds. Wassily Kandinsky [or Kandinskii]. PFTM-1

Sounds, The. Summer Night. Langston Hughes. APT-2

Sounds, The. Gerald Stern. BodElec

Sounds are heard too high for ears. Watching Television. Robert Bly. CoAP

Sounds Begin Again, The. Dennis Brutus. HBAPE

Sounds in the dim washed room. Learning to Count. Sara Berkeley. BiHa

Sounds like big. Waking from a Nap on the Beach. May Swenson. NTCP

Sounds of a Dreamer. James Berry. WaCA

Sounds of Autumn. Lu Yu. SuSp, tr. by Irving Y. Lo

Sounds of Ireland, The. Windharp. John Montague. CIP-2; PNI

Sounds of the Day. Norman MacCaig. RB

Sounds of the Resurrected Dead Man's Footsteps #15. Marvin Bell. SpudSo

Sounds of the stream, The. Incomparable-Verse Valley. Muso Soseki. EaWin, tr. by W. S. Merwin

Sounds our parents heard echoing over, The. Strangers Like Us: Pittsburgh, Raleigh, 1945–1985. Gerald William Barrax. ISC

Sounds That Arrived, The. Milo De Angelis. NeIt, tr. by Lawrence Venuti

Soundtracks. Timothy Geiger. AmPoNex

Soundwaves. Andrew Sant. NOBAu

Soup. Tony Curtis. TCAWP

Soup. Carl Sandburg. HHAm; NOBA; NOBE; OBCA

Soup, The. Gary Soto. NoP-4

Soup and Slavery. Myra Schneider. Prnts

Soup Kitchen. Betsy Sholl. PBCAP

Soup Kitchen Song. Unknown. NOBAu

Sour daylight cracks through my sleep-caked lids, The. Distant Winter, The. Philip Levine. VGW

Sour fiend, go home and tell the Pit. Ghoul Care. Ralph Hodgson. MoBrPo

Sour Grapes. Derek Walcott. See Sea Grapes

Sour grapes I saw in Aleppo, The. Camel's Bite. Ben Bennani. GraLe

Sour smell, The. Getting in the Wood. Gary Snyder. NoAM

Source, The. David Wagoner. VCAP

Sources of My Being, The. Moses Ibn Ezra. TOF, tr. by David Goldstein

Sources of the Delaware. Dean Young. BAP-01

Sourdough mountain called a fire in. Gary Snyder. NAAL-2v2 Fr. Myths and Texts.

Sourdough Mountain Lookout. Philip Whalen. BB; NeAP; PoM

Sous-Entendu. Anne Stevenson. LW; OxBSP

South. Blaise Cendrars. BLT, tr. by Monique Chefdor

South. Aurora Levins Morales. PueRic

South. M. L. Williams. GeoHom

South, The. Emma Lazarus. APN-2; ColAP

South, The. Wang Chien. AWP; BLT; ChiP, tr. by Arthur Waley

South African Exhibition, 1907. Kingsley Fairbridge. PeSAV

South America Mi Hija. Sharon Doubiago. PueRic

"Out the window, Colombia, out the window." PBCAP

South America, Take It Away! Harold Rome. ReLy

South American stories. Tangerine. Johnny Mercer. ReLy

South Bound: Facing North. Geraldine Monk. Oth

South Bronx appears on the TV screen, The. Getting Out Alive. Rosario Morales. PueRic

South Bronx Testimonial. Sandra Maria Esteves. UnSA

South China Sea drives in, The. Break from the Bush, A. Yusef Komunyakaa. CDa

South Coast, The. William Everson. NeAP

South Coast Haiku. Laurie Duggan. BMAP Fr. Dogs.

South Country. Kenneth Slessor. BMAP; CBAP

South Country, The. Joseph Hilaire Pierre Belloc. MoBrPo; OxAEP-2

South End. Conrad Potter Aiken. OxBA

South-Folk in Cold Country. Ezra Pound. OBVE

South Mount Soaring High. Unknown. SuSp, tr. by C. H. Wang

South Mountain! So full of sorrows! In Protest. Li Ho. SuSp, tr. by Maureen Robertson

South, North, East, West, inland and seaboard, we will surely awake. (LL) To the States, To Identify the 16th, 17th, or 18th Presidentiad. Walt Whitman. CTC; NAAL-2v1; NAAL-3; RaBo

South of Boston, south of Washington. Robert Lowell. HCAP Fr. Mexico.

South of house, north of house, all spring water. Guest, A. Tu Fu. ChinPo, tr. by Yip Wai-lim

South of Hsien-yang. Rhymeprose on the Sword Gallery. Li Po. ColAnChi, tr. by Elling O. Eide

South of My Days. Judith Wright. FaBoWP; WPE

South of the Bridge. Shen Chou. CoBLCP Fr. Stone Bridge, The.

South of the Great Sea. Unknown. ChiP, tr. by Arthur Waley

South of the house, north of the house. Tai Piao-yüan. CoBLCP Fr. Following His Rhymes and Answering the Poems of My Friend Next Door on Recent Events.

South of the Line, inland from far Durban. Christmas Ghost-Story, A. Thomas Hardy. ChrPo; OBWP

South of the river: to pluck lotus. South of the Yangtze. Unknown. ChinPo, tr. by Yip Wai-lim

South of the Yangtze. Unknown. ChinPo, tr. by Yip Wai-lim

South Sea Ballad, A. Edward Ward. OBCoV

South Side. Robert Fitzgerald. APT-2

South Song. Bill Griffiths. Oth Fr. Building: The New London Hospital.

South Texas Summer Rain. Rebecca Gonzales. AiP

South Wind. Tu Fu. BLT; OHPC, tr. by Kenneth Rexroth

South wind blows open the folds of my dress, The. Spring Longing. Amy Lowell. APT-1

South-wind brings, The. Ralph Waldo Emerson. APN-1; TCAPo

South wind does not shed so great a cast, The. Callimachus. HePo Fr. Hecale.

South-wind strengthens to a gale, The. Low Barometer. Robert Bridges. CABP; NOCV; NoAM; SCGP

Southbound on the Freeway. May Swenson. NTCP

Southeast, and storm, and every weathervane. Hatteras Calling. Conrad Potter Aiken. ColAP; NOBA; TAP

Southeast at low tide. Skiing on Russian Christmas. Nora Dauenhauer. HATNAP

Southeast Corner. Gwendolyn Brooks. VGW Fr. Street in Bronzeville, A.

Southeast the Peacock Flies. Unknown. CoBCP, tr. by Burton Watson

Southern Africa. Nguno Wakolele. PeSAV

Southern Birth. Kevin Powell. AmPoNex; InTrad

Southern Blues. Unknown. APT-1

Southern Blues, The. Big Bill Broonzy. GM

Southern Cop. Sterling Allen Brown. SoSe-8

Southern Crescent Was on time, The. Andrew Hudgins. GM

Southern Cross. Herman Melville. TCAPo Fr. Clarel: A Poem and Pilgrimage in the Holy Land.

Southern Dawn. Pier Paolo Pasolini. VCWP, tr. by Norman MacAfee

Southern gentle lady, / Do not swoon. Silhouette. Langston Hughes. NAAL-5

Southern hill-billy named Hollis, A. Limerick. Unknown. PeLi

Southern Mansion. Arna Bontemps. APT-2; AiP; GT; NAAAL; TTY

Southern Mountains. Han Yü. SuSp, tr. by Charles Hartman

Southern Pacific. Carl Sandburg. GM

Southern Paiute Poetry. Unknown. APN-2, tr. by John Wesley Powell

Southern Press, The. Lizelia Augusta Jenkins Moorer. CBWP-3

Southern Pulpit, The. Lizelia Augusta Jenkins Moorer. CBWP-3

Southern Review, The. Brigit Pegeen Kelly.

Song: "Listen: there was a goat's head hanging by ropes in a tree." ExTi; IllVoic

Southern Road. Sterling Allen Brown. APT-2; BPo

Southern Road. Mwatabu Okantah. SeSe

Southern Road, The. Dudley Randall. GM

Southern Room Over the River, The. Su Tung-p'o (Su Shih). OHPC, tr. by Kenneth Rexroth

Southern Scene, A. Priscilla Jane Thompson. CBWP-2

Southern trees bear a strange fruit. Strange Fruit. Lewis Allan. ReLy

Southern University, 1962. Kevin Young. SpirFl

Southern women have alabaster skin. Li Po. CrYelRi; ErotSp, tr. by Sam Hamill Fr. Women of Yueh.

Southern Work of Dr. and Mrs. L. M. Dunton. Lizelia Augusta Jenkins Moorer. CBWP-3

Southward bound over sixty days. Officer at the Rapids, The. Han Yü. SuSp, tr. by Charles Hartman

Southward from hence ten miles, where Derwent laves. Charles Cotton. OBGa Fr. Wonders of the Peak, The.

Southward I once traveled, crossing mountain passes. Su Tung-p'o (Su Shih). SuSp, tr. by Irving Y. Lo Fr. On Chao Ch'ang's Flower Paintings in Wang Po-yang's Collection.

Southwest. Viktor Krivulin. TCRusP, tr. by Anna Barker and Daniel Weissbort

Souvenir. Naomi Long Madgett. NBV

Souvenir. Alfred de Musset. AWP, tr. by George Santayana

Souvenir. Edwin Arlington Robinson. APT-1; NoAM

Souvenir. Paul Van Ostaijen. TuT, tr. by Tony Curtis

Souvenir de Monsieur Poop. Stevie Smith. NALW

Souvenirs. Jessica Tarahata Hagedorn. ReBoTo

Souvenirs. Dudley Randall. BPo

Souvenirs. Elizabeth Rosner. GotH

Sovereign and Transforming Grace. Frederic Henry Hedge. AH

Sovereign Queen. Padeshah Khatun. WPOW, tr. by Deirdre Lashgari

Sovereign soul, The/ Of him who lives self-governed and at peace. Unknown. TOF Fr. Bhagavad-Gita, The.

Sovereignty, His. Kalonymos ben Moses of Lucca. TrJP, tr. by Nina Davis Salaman

Sow came in with the saddle, The. Mother Goose. OxNR

Sow of Feeling, The. Robert Fergusson. NOEC

Sower, The. Mathilde Blind. WPE

Sower, The. William Cowper. ChIV-2 Fr. Olney Hymns.

Sower, The. Jones Very. SacPr

Sower's Song, The. Thomas Carlyle. SCGP

Sower went forth to sow, A. Parable of the Sower, The. Stephen Mitchell. GI

Sown in dishonor! Emily Dickinson. ChIV-2

Soy Inés Tohmahtohlahkikt. Presente. Inés Hernández-Ávila. ReEnLa

Soyer is gone! Then be it said. On the Death of the Great Chef Alexis Soyer. Unknown. FaBoEE

Soyŏng Problems. Sang Yi. PFTM-1

Sozzled, Mo-tsu, after a silence, vouchsafed. Scholars at the Orchid Pavilion. John Berryman. HarvBoo; PoE

Space. Maura Stanton. OPRER

Space. Urdeath. August Stramm. PFTM-1

Space and stars. Below. Federico García Lorca. PFTM-1

Space beats the ruddy freedom of their limbs. Daughters of War. Isaac Rosenberg. PeFWW

Space being(don't forget to remember)Curved. E. E. Cummings. NoAM

Space Between, The. Elena Georgiou. WiU

Space in the Air, A. Jon Silkin. TrJP

Space Instead. Jean Daive. MFP, tr. by Martin Sorrell

Space instead of furniture. Space Instead. Jean Daive. MFP, tr. by Martin Sorrell

Space Invaders Machine, The. Pita Sharples. PeNZ, tr. by the author

Space is ample, east and west. Unity. Ralph Waldo Emerson. TCAPo

Space is too full. Did nothing happen here? American Farm, 1934. Genevieve Taggard. VGW

Space Memorabilia Auction, Superior Stamp and Coin, Beverly Hills, California. Joel Brouwer. AmPoNex

Space Needle, The. Roger Fanning. NAPBL

Space Needle works like a pushpin, The. Space Needle, The. Roger Fanning. NAPBL

Space Parable. Max Winter. NeAmPo

Space Song. Alfonso Cortes. TCLAP, tr. by Thomas Merton

Space-vase . . . the past is lioness to swallow. Next Two Tablets, The. Armand Schwerner. BodElec

Space was easier then, and time slower. Planisféria, Map of the World, Lisbon, 1554. Ellen Hinsey. AmPoNex

Space with figure who holds the newspaper. Doing. Giancarlo Majorino. ItPo, tr. by Gayle Ridinger

Spacepod shrunk to microscopic, The. Undetectable. Justin Chin. WiU

Spaces We Leave Empty. Cathy Song. YaYoPo

Spaceship drifting up, The. Christmas. Peter McDonald. PNI

Spacious firmament on high, The. Ode. Joseph Addison. ChIV-1; ECEV; NOCV; NOEC; NPeEn; OxBEV; TOF

Spacious firmament on high, The. Bible, O.T. See Heavens declare the glory of God, The

Spade, The. George Wither. NOSC Fr. Collection of Emblemes, Ancient and Moderne, A.

Spade and the Wreath, The. George Wither. NOSC Fr. Collection of Emblemes, Ancient and Moderne, A.

Spade-bearded grandfather, squat Lenin. Summer Pogrom. Fay Zwicky. CBAP

Spade, for labour stands. The ball with wings, The. George Wither. NOSC Fr. Collection of Emblemes, Ancient and Moderne, A.

Spades take up leaves. Gathering Leaves. Robert Frost. RB; VGW

Spaewife, The. Robert Louis Stevenson. OxBS

Spain. Dorothy Livesay. NOBC

Spain, 1809. Frank Lawrence Lucas. EBNV

Spain frightened you. Spain. You Hated Spain. Ted Hughes. EmeKit

Spain! much more beautiful than Egypt! Madrid. Frank O'Hara. FTOS

Spain 1937. W. H. Auden. AF; NAEL-5v2; NAEL-6v2; NoP-4; OBWP

Spain, Take This Cup from Me. César Vallejo.
Mass. TCLAP, tr. by Clayton Eshleman
Short Prayer for a Loyalist Hero. TCLAP, tr. by Clayton Eshleman

Spain. The wild dust, the whipped corn, earth easy for. Teresa of Avila. Elizabeth Jennings. PeECV; TOF

Span of Life, The. Robert Frost. SoSe-8 Fr. Ten Mills.

Spaniard That Blighted My Life, The. Billy Merson. OBCoV

Spaniel, Beau, that fares like you, A. On a Spaniel Called Beau Killing a Young Bird. William Cowper. FaBoCh

Spanish Curate, The. John Fletcher.
"Let the bells ring, and let the boys sing." SCGP

Spanish Dancer. Oliver Reynolds. TCAWP

Spanish Dancer. Rainer Maria Rilke. NAWM-7v2, tr. by Stephen Mitchell

Spanish Descent, The. Daniel Defoe.
"Word's gone out, and now they spread the main, The." OBWP

Spanish Folk Songs. Antonio Machado Ruiz. AWP, tr. by Havelock Ellis

Spanish Friar [or Fryar], The. Dryden.
("Farewell, ungrateful traitor!") RACG
"Farewell ungrateful[l] traitor [or traytor], / Farewell my perjured swain." BoLoP; EnLoPo; HAP; NOBE
"Twere well your judgments but in plays did range." OBSV

Spanish Generosity. Max Jacob. CuPo

Spanish is the lovin' tongue. Border Affair, A. Charles Badger, Jr. Clark. APT-1

Spanish Jake. Irving Caesar. ReLy

Spanish Jew's Tale: Azrael, The. Henry Wadsworth Longfellow. APN-1; TCAPo Fr. Tales of a Wayside Inn.

Spanish Jew's Tale: The Legend of Rabbi Ben Levi, The. Henry Wadsworth Longfellow. NCAP; TCAPo Fr. Tales of a Wayside Inn.

Spanish Johnny. Willa Sibert Cather. AiP

Spanish Ladies. Unknown. FaBoCh

Spanish of Our Out-Loud Dreams, The. Martín Espada. PueRic

Spanish Peasant Boy. Jane Duran. Prnts Fr. Silences from the Spanish Civil War.

Spanish record turns, The. By the Campfire. Konstantin Mikhailovich Simonov. TCRP, tr. by Lubov Yakovleva

Spanish War, The. Hugh MacDiarmid. NOBC

Sparafucile fought his peasant war. Dead Fly. Eiléan Ní Chuilleanáin. CIP-2

Spare, gen'rous victor, spare the slave. To a Lady: She Refusing to Continue a Dispute with Me, and Leaving Me in the Argument. Matthew Prior. NoP-4

Spare Professor, grave and bald, The. At a Reading. Thomas Bailey Aldrich. OBAL

Spare the mother of acorns, man. Cut down some paliurus. Diodorus Zonas. GrAn

Spare then the person, and expose the vice. Pope. OBSV Fr. Epilògue to the Satires, in Two Dialogues.

Spare Us, O Lord, Aloud We Pray. Isaac Watts. AH

Sparhawk [or Sparrow-hawk] proud did hold in wicked jail, A. Sparrow-Hawk, A. Unknown. EBEV

Spark, A. Alan Pizzarelli. HA

Spark, The. Joseph Mary Plunkett. AWP

Spark of Green. Maria Luisa Spaziani. CItWP, tr. by Cinzia Sartini Blum and Lara Trubowitz

Spark's Farewell to Its Clay, The. Ronald Allison Kells Mason. PeNZ

Sparkler goes out, The. Lorraine Ellis Harr. HA

Sparkles from the Wheel. Walt Whitman. NAAL-2v1; NAAL-3; SAmP

Sparkling Beaches, The. Raúl Zurita. TCLAP, tr. by Jack Schmitt

Sparrow. Reginald Gibbons. IllVoic

Sparrow, The. William Carlos Williams. LCAP-2; VGW

Sparrow and Bird-Net Building. Shinkichi Takahashi. ZenPo, tr. by Takashi Ikemoto and Lucien Stryk

Sparrow dips in his wheel-rut bath, The. Five Students, The. Thomas Hardy. GTBS-P

Sparrow dives from roof to ground. Flight of the Sparrow. Shinkichi Takahashi. ZenPo, *tr. by* Takashi Ikemoto and Lucien Stryk

Sparrow has cut the day in half, The. Position of the Sparrow. Shinkichi Takahashi. ZenPo, *tr. by* Takashi Ikemoto and Lucien Stryk

Sparrow-Hawk, A. *Unknown.* EBEV

Sparrow hawk drops to the cornfield, The. Sound of Guns, The. Gerald McCarthy. CDa

Sparrow Hills. Robley, Jr. Wilson. PBCAP

Sparrow in the Dust, A. Ruth Domino. BoWoP, *tr. by* Daniel Hoffman and Jerre Mangione

Sparrow in Withered Field. Shinkichi Takahashi. ZenPo, *tr. by* Takashi Ikemoto and Lucien Stryk

Sparrow's always sleeping. Sparrow and Bird-Net Building. Shinkichi Takahashi. ZenPo, *tr. by* Takashi Ikemoto and Lucien Stryk

Sparrow's Dirge, The. John Skelton. FaBoCh *Fr.* Phyllyp Sparowe [*or* Philip Sparrow].

Sparrow's Fall, The. Frances Ellen Watkins Harper. PWR

Sparrow's Skull, The. Ruth Pitter. FaBoWP

Sparrow singing. Buson. EH, *tr. by* Robert Hass

Sparrow, you darling pet of my beloved. 2. Catullus. NAWM-7v1, *tr. by* Charles Martin

Sparrows in a Hillside Drift. James Wright (1927–80). ColAP

Sparrows sunning. Martin Shea. HA

Sparrows were feeding in a freezing drizzle. Because You Asked about the Line between Prose and Poetry. Howard Nemerov. VCAP; WeW-3

Sparse fence, winding path, a small farmhouse. Chou Pang-yen. SuSp *Fr.* Tune: "Beautiful Lady Yü, The."

Sparse season, the lean, The. Disconsolate Morning. Elizabeth Madox Roberts. APT-1

Spartan Mother, The. Benedek Virág. IQMS, *tr. by* Joseph Leftwich

Spasibo. Thanks. O.K. (LL) Adrienne Rich. EmeKit; NIL-7

Spate in Winter Midnight. Norman MacCaig. GTBS-P

Spatulate is the word *Glamour Magazine* uses. Personal History of Hands, A. Lori Jakiela. ReTh

Spawn of fantasies. Love Songs. Mina Loy. VGW; WPE

Spawn of Slums, The. James W. Thompson. BPo

Speach of Love persuading men to learn Dancing, The. Sir John Davies. NPeEn *Fr.* Orchestra; or, A Poem[e] of Da[u]ncing.

Speak. James Wright (1927–80). HAP; NoP-4; TAP

Speak. Benjamin Zephaniah. Oth

Speak! William Wordsworth. OBEV
(To a Distant Friend.) GTBS-P

Speak! And I'll say what you are. 'Tis enough! Altogether I know you. Merits of Writers. Ferenc Kazinczy. IQMS, *tr. by* Watson Kirkconnell

Speak, daughter, speak; art speaking now? Demeter and Cora. Dora Greenwell. VWP

Speak earth and bless me with what is richest. Love Poem. Audre Lorde. GLP; NoAM; PoBW

Speak! fairy Moon, interpret this! (LL) Dawn of Love, The. Henrietta Cordelia Ray. BlSi; CBWP-3

SPEAK, gentlemen, what shall we do today? Sir Revel. Samuel Rowlands. NoSic; OBCoV

Speak Gently. David Bates. PWR

Speak gently; it is better far. Speak Gently. G. W. Langford. PoToHe; UV

Speak Low. Ogden Nash. ReLy

Speak low to me, my Saviour, low and sweet. Comfort. Elizabeth Barrett Browning. SacPr

Speak low when you speak love. Speak Low. Ogden Nash. ReLy

Speak my name, call to me, call. (LL) To My Sister. Olga Fiodorovna Berggolts [*or* Bergholts]. BoWoP; TCRusP, *tr. by* Daniel Weissbort

Speak not ill of womankind. Against Blame of Woman. Gerald Fitzgerald, 4th Earl of Desmond. BIrV, *tr. by* The Earl of Longford

Speak not of niceness, when there's chance of wreck. Sir Walter Scott. FaBoEE *Fr.* Peveril of the Peak.

Speak not of passion, for my heart is tired. Sister of Mercy, The. Constance Naden. VWP; ViWPN

Speak [*or* Speke], Parrot. John Skelton.
"Now, Parrot, my sweet bird, speak our yet once again." NoSic
("Nowe, Parott, my swete byrde, speke owte yet ons agayn.") NPeEn
(Parrot's Complaint.) NPeEn
Parrot's Soliloquy. NoSic; OxBoLi

Speak Out. *Unknown.* PWR
(Seeds of Kindness.) PoToHe

Speak out, speak well. József Katona. IQMS, *tr. by* Gavin Ewart and Paul Tabori *Fr.* Bánk the Palatine.

Speak out your secret, bellowing waves. Lines: Composed at the Old Temples of Maralipoor. Charles Timothy Brooks. APN-1

Speak roughly to your little boy. Lewis Carroll. FaBoCh; NBLV; UV *Fr.* Alice's Adventures in Wonderland.

Speak! speak! thou fearful guest! Skeleton in Armor [*or* Armour], The. Henry Wadsworth Longfellow. APN-1; AWP; TreFP

Speak to Her Tenderly. Mary E. Tucker. CBWP-1

Speak to Me. Fanny Carrión de Fierro. TANSG, *tr. by* Sally Cheney Bell

Speak to me. Take my hand. What are you now? Effort at Speech between Two People. Muriel Rukeyser. MoAmPo; NAAL-5; PAI; TrJP; TwCP

Speak when I have nothing to say. (LL) Lady Love. Paul Éluard. OBVE; SurPaPo; WoPoe, *tr. by* Samuel Beckett

Speak when you're spoken to, *l* Come for one call. Mother Goose. OxNR

Speak You Too. Paul Celan. PoetW, *tr. by* John Felstiner

Speaker, The. Charles G. Ballard. VoR

Speaker in the Square, A. George Buchanan. PNI

Speakin' in general, I 'ave tried 'em all. Sestina of the Tramp-Royal. Rudyard Kipling. MakPoe; MoBrPo

Speaking. Simon J. Ortiz. NIL-7

Speaking. Michael Ryan. SoSe-8

Speaking about epics, mother. Louis Zukofsky. PFTM-1; TaR *Fr.* Poem Beginning "The."

Speaking and Kissing. Thomas Stanley. BeJo

Speaking as one Jew to another. Of Dogs and Ostriches. Eve Merriam. TaR

Speaking in a state of fidelity to the subject, living flesh though it may. My Story. Carla Harryman. PmAP

Speaking Into the Candles. Medbh McGuckian. ModIr *Fr.* Porcelain Bells.

Speaking like wind. Swimmer. Gladys Cardiff. CDW

Speaking My Mind. Chung-ch'ang T'ung. CoBCP, *tr. by* Burton Watson

Speaking of Gabriel. Rosario Castellanos. TANSG, *tr. by* Magda Bogin

Speaking of Gethsemane in Yoruba Land. Edouard J. Maunick. NegPo *Fr.* As Far as Yoruba Land.

Speaking of marvels, I am alive. Alive Together. Lisel Mueller. IllVoic

Speaking of peaceful trees / another village explodes. (LL) It Is Dangerous to Read Newspapers. Margaret Atwood. HeIP-4; OBWP

Speaking of Places. Rajagopal Parthasarathy. OMIP

Speaking of Poetry. John Peale Bishop. APT-1; OxBA

Speaking of sunsets. Never Again the Same. James Tate. BodElec

Speaking of Television. Phyllis McGinley.
Robin Hood. OBSV
"Zounds, gramercy, and rootity-toot!" OBSV

Speaking Through White: For My Mother. Kyoko Mori. UnSA

Speaking Tree, The. Muriel Rukeyser. VGW

Speaking with Hands. Luis J. Rodriguez. UnSA

Speaking Your Name. Alejandra Piznarnick. TANSG, *tr. by* Susan Bassnett

Speaks a new scene; the last act crowns the play. (LL) Epigram: "My soul, sit thou a patient looker-on." Francis Quarles. NOBE; PoToHe

Speaks Bito's tomb to whomsoever reads. Nicaenetus. GrAn

Speaks to spirits. Abu Salim, Healer. Rachel Tzvia Back. DTA

Speargrass crackles under the billy and overhead is the winter sun, The. While the Billy Boils. David McKee Wright. PeNZ, *tr. by* Margaret Orbell

Spearo's Blues (or: Ode to a Grecian Yearn). Eugene B. Redmond. NBV

Special Branch are after my neck, The. Everything to Declare. Frank Mkalawile Chipasula. NAfrP

Special Jurymen of England! who admire your country's laws. Damages, Two Hundred Pounds. William Makepeace Thackeray. OBSV

Special Theory came to me, The. Naming the Living God. Kathleen Norris. InvLi

Special Train, A. Daniel Gerard Hoffman. CDa

Specially for me, she had some breaded. Breaded Fish. A. K. Ramanujan. NoP-4

Species. Charles Boyle. EmeKit

Species Means Guilt. Bruce Andrews. PmAP

Specifically the rose window specifically the center. Sainte-Chapelle. John Taggart. FTOS

Specimen. Christopher Pilling. NLP

Specimens of Indian Songs. *Unknown.* APN-2, *tr. by* Lewis Cass

Speck of protoplasm in a finch's egg, The. Birdsong. Burns Singer. FaBoTw

Speck Speaks, A. Adrian Mitchell. OBSP

Speck that would have been beneath my sight, A. Considerable Speck, A. Robert Frost. MoAmPo; OBAL; SAmP

Speckled cat and a tame hare, A. Two Songs of a Fool. W. B. Yeats. RB

Speckled Hen's Morning Song to Biddy Early, The. Nancy Willard. FFC

Spectacular. Lilian Moore. KaS

Spectacular Blossom. Allen Curnow. PeNZ

Spectator, The. Evan J. Thomas. AngWePo

Spectator ab Extra. Arthur Hugh Clough. OBCoV; OxBoLi; PeLV; PeVV
As I Sat at the Café GTBS-P; NBLV; OBCoV; OxBoLi
(How Pleasant It Is to Have Money.) NOBE
Le Diner. OBCoV; OBSV

Parvenant. OBCoV

Spectator's Guide to Contemporary Art. Phyllis McGinley.
  On the Farther Wall, Marc Chagall. OBSV
  Squeeze Play. FaBoEE; OBCoV; OBSV
Spectators only on this bustling stage. Charles Churchill. OBSV *Fr.* Night; an Epistle to Robert Lloyd.
Specter, The. Anna Andreyevna Akhmatova. TCRP, *tr. by* Daniel Weissbort
Specter, The. Ernst Hardt. AWP, *tr. by* Jethro Bithell
Spectra. Witter Bynner.
  "If I were only dafter." TCAPo
Spectral Attitudes, The. André Breton. SPE, *tr. by* David Gascoyne
Spectral Dues. Pimone Triplett. AmPoNex
Spectral Lovers. John Crowe Ransom. APT-1; HeIP-4
Spectre is haunting America—the spectre of hoodooism, A. Black Power Poem. Ishmael Reed. BPo
Spectre of the Rose, The. Luis de Góngora y Argote.
  Allegory of the Brevity of Things Human. SpanPo; WoPoe, *tr. by* Roy Campbell
Spectrum. Mari E. Evans. BPo
Spectrum. Aidan Carl Mathews. PBCIP
Spectrum Trench. Autumn. Nineteen-Sixteen. Dead Soldiers, The. Max Plowman. PoWW
Specula. Gauze in a halo of disinfectant. Depth of Field. Linda Bierds. ExTi
Speculate on anxiety, courtesy of midnight. Dissonances. Giusi Busceti. ItPo, *tr. by* Gayle Ridinger
Speculation. Howard Nemerov. TAP
Speculations. Marcel Duchamp. PFTM-1
Speculations on the Present through the Prism of the Past. June Jordan. GT
Speculations on the Subject of Barabbas. Zbigniew Herbert. GI, *tr. by* John Carpenter
Speculators, The. William Makepeace Thackeray. OBCoV; OBSV
Speech. Chief Mothibi. PeSAV
Speech. Leopold Staff. PoSu, *tr. by* Adam Czerniawski
Speech. Henry Taylor. NBLV
Speech after long silence; it is right. After Long Silence. W. B. Yeats. BoLoP; EnLoPo; HeIP-4; NAEL-5v2; NAEL-6v2; OBMV; UnPo
Speech Against Stone. Charles Martin. RA
Speech and Image: An African Tradition of the Surreal. Léopold Sédar Senghor. PFTM-1
Speech Before Harfleur, The. William Shakespeare. *See* King Henry V
Speech for Psyche in the Golden Book of Apuleius. Ezra Pound. HarvBoo
Speech of the Nymph. Anna Seward. NOBRP
Speech out of Lucan, A. Lucan. OBVE, *tr. by* Ben Jonson *Fr.* Pharsalia.
Speech seems to us the main instrument of thought, emotion and action.
  Speech and Image: An African Tradition of the Surreal. Léopold Sédar Senghor. PFTM-1
Speech to a Crowd. Archibald MacLeish. MoAmPo
Speech to Those Who Say Comrade. Archibald MacLeish. OxBA
Speech Warts. Myra Sklarew. CRP
Speeches at the Barriers. Susan Howe.
  "Right or ruth." PmAP
  "Sabbath and sweet spices." PmAP
  "Say that a ballad." PmAP
  "Twenty lines of." PmAP
Speechless, considering, feet well apart. Still Life in Garden. Rachel Hadas. ExTi
Speechless moment thins my blood, A. At the Havana Hilton. Sandra M. Castillo. TouFir
Speechless, speechless, you testify against us. (LL) On the Wall of a KZ-Lager. János Pilinszky. AF; HP; PoSu
Speechless: Upon the Marriage of Two Deaf and Dumb Persons. Philip Bourke Marston. EBVV; OxBSo
Speechless[e] still, and never cry [or crie]. (LL) Epitaph on the Earl of Strafford. John Cleveland. BASC; FaBoEE; NOBE; NOSC; NPeEn; OxBEV; PeECV
Speed, a Pastoral. John Forbes. BMAP
Speed Ball. Yusef Komunyakaa. SeSe
Speed of Darkness, The. Muriel Rukeyser. APSN; APT-2; GLP; LCAP-2; PFTM-2
  "My night awake." AWTN
Speed of the punch. Homage to the Brown Bomber. Michael S. Harper. MoASP
Speeding carriage climbs through eastern gate, A. *Unknown.* SuSp
Speeding flowers along the shores mirror my boat red. Journeying to Hsiang-yi. Ch'en Yü-yi. SuSp, *tr. by* Irving Y. Lo
Speir [or Spier] ye for Maggie Lauder. (LL) Maggie Lauder. Francis Sempill. NePenScot; OxBS
Spell. Anuradha Mahapatra. OMIP, *tr. by* Jyotirmoy Dutta

Spell, A. *Unknown.* WoPoe, *tr. by* Siv Cedering Fox *Fr.* Three Swedish Spells.
Spell, The. Robert Herrick. CaPo
Spell, The. Molly Peacock. FFC
Spell against Predatory Animals. *Unknown.* WoPoe, *tr. by* Siv Cedering Fox *Fr.* Three Swedish Spells.
Spell against Twisting an Ankle. *Unknown.* WoPoe, *tr. by* Siv Cedering Fox *Fr.* Three Swedish Spells.
Spell for Birth. Jeni Couzyn. HAWP
Spell for Jealousy. Jeni Couzyn. HAWP
Spell for Making the First Man. *Unknown.* PeNZ, *tr. by* Margaret Orbell
Spell for Sleeping, A. Alastair Reid. NOxBChV
Spell of Blazing Trees, The. Sa'adyya Muffareh. PoArWo, *tr. by* Mona Fayad
Spell of Creation. Kathleen Jessie Raine. FaBoCh; OxBS
Spell of Weather, A. Eve Merriam. CA
Spell to Cure Barrenness. Jeni Couzyn. HAWP
Spell to Protect Our Love. Jeni Couzyn. HAWP
Spell, treasure-bearing spell, prop up the sky standing above. Lament. *Unknown.* PeNZ, *tr. by* Margaret Orbell
Spellbinding image, A. De Pisis--Piacenza Papers. Franco Buffoni. ItPo, *tr. by* Gayle Ridinger
Spellbound. Emily Jane Brontë. NOBE; NOBVV; NPeEn
  (Night is darkening round me, The.) VWP
Spelling. Margaret Atwood. NALW; NoAM
Spelling reformer indicted, A. Ambrose Bierce. APN-2; OBAL; PeLi *Fr.* Devil's Dictionary, The.
Spelt from Sibyl's Leaves. Gerard Manley Hopkins. FaBoMo; NOBVV; NPeEn; OxBEV; OxBSo; TOF
Spend the years of learning squandering. Gnome. Samuel Beckett. BIrV; OxBSP
Spende and god schall sende. Penny. *Unknown.* FaBoVe; MiEL
Spending beyond their income on gifts for Christmas. Christmas Shopping. Louis MacNeice. OBCP
Spending hand that alway poureth [or powreth] out [or owte], A. Sir Thomas Wyatt. NoSic *Fr.* Satires.
Spending the Night at a Mountain Temple. Chia Tao. SuSp, *tr. by* Stephen Owen
Spending the Night at the Hillside Lodge of Master Yeh and Waiting for My Friend Ting. Meng Hao Jan. SuSp, *tr. by* Daniel Bryant
Spending the Night in an Inn at Swatow and Writing about My Feelings, Sent to Liang Shih-wu. Huang Tsun-hsien. SuSp, *tr. by* An-yan Tang
Spending the Night in the Eastern Park. Shen Yüeh. SuSp, *tr. by* Richard B. Mather
Spending the Night on Stone Gate Mountain. Hsieh Ling-yün. SuSp, *tr. by* Francis Westbrook
Spending the Night on the River. T'ang Hsien-tsu. CoBLCP, *tr. by* Jonathan Chaves
Spending these lonesome evenings. Why Was I Born? Jerome Kern. ReLy
Spendthrift, disinherited and graceless, The. Remittance Man. Judith Wright. NoAM
Spenser's Ireland. Marianne Craig Moore. FaBoWP; NOBA; NoAM; OxBA; TAP
Spent a night in Pratt, Kansas. Dead Center. Alfred A. Yuson. ReBoTo
Spent purpose of a perfectly marvellous, The. In Favor of One's Time. Frank O'Hara. NeAP
Spermal Chimney. Francis Picabia. PFTM-1
Sperrins surround it, the Faughan flows by, The. Claudy. James Simmons. BiHa; CIP-2; PBCIP
Spes mea in Deo est. My Hope Is in God. *Unknown.* SacPr
Speshal Rikwes. Ahdri Zhina Mandiela. WaCA
Spesse Fiate Vegnonmi a la Mente. Dante Alighieri. WoPoe
Spew out thy filth, thy flesh abjure. Instruction, The. Thomas Traherne. BASC
Sphere. A. R. Ammons.
  "I don't know about you,/ but I'm sick of good poems." HCAP
  "I was pulling veronica out of the lawn when this hornet came." NoAM
  "There is a faculty or knack, smallish, in the mind that can turn." NoAM
Sphere. Jules Supervielle. MFP, *tr. by* Martin Sorrell
Spheroid. Eggplant. Ibn Sara. WoPoe, *tr. by* Leticia Garza-Falcón and Christopher Middleton
Sphinx. Van K. Brock. AllShUp; SwNoth
Sphinx. Robert Earl Hayden. GT; HCAP
Sphinx, The. W. H. Auden. OxBSo *Fr.* Voyage, A.
Sphinx, The. Ralph Waldo Emerson. APN-1; NOBA; OxBA; TCAPo
Sphinx, The. Oscar Wilde.
  Fin-de-Siècle Cat. TriCat
  "How subtle-secret is your smile! Did you love none then? Nay, I know." MoBrPo

Sphinx slinks above the blond commotion, The. Lust. Star Black. KGB

Sphinxes. Sandra Hochman. YaYoPo

Sphinxes Inclined to Be. Olga Orozco. WPOW, tr. by Leslie Keffer

Spice and pungent air of the earth, The. Confession of Cleopas, The. Eric Pankey. GI

Spice of Life, The. Kalamu ya Salaam. SpirFl Fr. New Orleans Haiku.

Spicewood. Lizette Woodworth Reese. MoAmPo

Spider. Basho. TTTS

Spider. William Virgil Davis. YaYoPo

Spider. Joan Swift. UrbNat

Spider, The. Richard Eberhart. NoAM

Spider, The. Hannah Flagg Gould. OBCA

Spider, The. Edward Littleton. NOEC

Spider, The. César Vallejo. RaBo, tr. by Robert Bly

Spider and the Fly, The. Mary Howitt. ITBLP; OTCP; PWR; UV

Spider and the Ghost of the Fly, The. Nicholas Vachel Lindsay. VGW

Spider, cork, pearl. In Portuguese. Adelia Prado. TCLAP, tr. by Marcia Kirinus

Spider crouching on the ledge above the sink, The. James Keir Baxter. PeNZ Fr. Autumn Testament.

Spider Crystal Ascension. Charles Wright. HCAP; LCAP-2; VCAP

Spider expects the cold of winter, The. Spider, The. Richard Eberhart. NoAM

Spider, from his flaming sleep. Little City. Robert Horan. YaYoPo

Spider Hangs Too Far from the Ground, The. Antonio Cisneros. TCLAP, tr. by William Rowe

Spider holds a Silver Ball, The. Emily Dickinson. WPOW

Spider in the bath, A. The image noted. Image, The. Roy Fuller. GTBS-P; OxBTC

Spider, juiced crystal and Milky Way, drifts on his web through the night sky, The. Spider Crystal Ascension. Charles Wright. HCAP; LCAP-2; VCAP

Spider of Doubt. Pimone Triplett. AmPoNex

Spider, salute the Sun! No rancor show. Philosophy. "Rubén Dario." SpanPo, tr. by Muna Lee

Spider sewed at Night, A. Emily Dickinson. NAAL-2v1; NAAL-3; NALW

Spiders. David Wevill. MoCV

Spiders started out to go with the wind on its pilgrimage, The. Broken, The. W. S. Merwin. LCAP-2

Spiderwebs on the casement. Old Times. Daniel Mark Epstein. DiPo

Spiel of [the] Three Mountebanks. John Crowe Ransom. MoAmPo

Spies' March, The. Rudyard Kipling. FaBoWar

Spies whisper through my air condition units. Light Reading. Vassar Miller. FFC

Spies, you are lights in state, but of base stuff. On Spies. Ben Jonson. BeJo; FaBoVe; NPeEn; NoP-4; OxBSP; WoPoe

Spiked thorns all over, and a thirty-foot wall. Ballad of the Government Granary Clerk. Ho Ching-ming. CoBLCP; ColAnChi, tr. by Jonathan Chaves

Spilled into the cup. Bubbling Wine. Abu Zakariya. TTY, tr. by A. J. Arberry

Spilling out / into the world. (LL) Where Mountain Lion Lay [or Laid] Down with Deer. Leslie Marmon Silko. TRP; VoR; WPOW

Spilt blood and tears like rivers flow. Archie Weller. IBA

Spilt Milk. Sarah Maguire. EmeKit; LW; MFPA

Spilt Milk. W. B. Yeats. OxBSP

Spin. Tracy Ryan. NeBl

Spin a coin, spin a coin. Queen Nefertiti. Unknown. OTCP; TLR

Spin-Cycle. Jane Holland. MFPA

Spin, Dame, spin. Unknown. OxNR

Spin the ball! I reel, I burn. Song of Seyd [or Seid] Nimetollah of Kuhistan. Seid [or Sayyid] Nimatullah [or Ni'matu'llah]. NOBA, tr. by Ralph Waldo Emerson

Spinal Cord. 'Aisha Arnaout. PoArWo, tr. by Mona Fayad

Spine doesn't give or arch to it, The. Not-loving. Sylvia Kantaris. LW

Spine has been tingled; the horn has been swoggled, The. Woolly Words. Robert N. Feinstein. NBLV

Spineless and eyeless we spend our days. Sea-Polyp, The. Julia Copus. NeBl

Spinner, The. Nathan [or Natan] Alterman. FIT, tr. by Robert Friend

Spinners' lights from house to house brighten the deep night. Sitting Up at Night. Lu Yu. CoBCP, tr. by Burton Watson

Spinning. May Muzaffar. PoArWo, tr. by Tahia Abdel Nasser

Spinning. Alfred Wellington Purdy. NOBC; NoAM

Spinning Dharma Wheel. Shinkichi Takahashi. ZenPo, tr. by Takashi Ikemoto and Lucien Stryk

Spinning Song. Dame Edith Sitwell. MoBrPo

Spinning top. (LL) Leonidas. GrAn; PGA

Spinning Woman, The. Leonidas of Tarentum. AWP, tr. by Andrew Lang Fr. Epigrams.

Spinoza. Jorge Luis Borges. TCLAP, tr. by Richard Howard and César Rennert

Spinoza / Collected curiosa. Clerihew. Unknown. NOBL

Spinster. Sylvia Plath. FaBoWP; LW; SoSe-8

Spinster near Gyöngyös displays, A. Unspeakable. Ferenc Faludi. IQMS, tr. by John Gordon Nichols

Spinster's Lullaby. Vassar Miller. BoWoP

Spinster's Sweet-Arts, The. Tennyson.
    "Robby, git down wi'tha, wilt tha?" FaBoVe

Spinster Song: African-American Woman Guild. Angela Jackson. IllVoic

Spinster with a mouth like a dam and a heart, A. Lizzie. Nancy Vieira Couto. PBCAP

Spiralwise it spins. Time. Ralph Hodgson. GTBS-P

Spire, The. Ellen Bryant Voigt. NoAM

Spirella lady sipped tea, The. Fitting. Pauline Prior-Pitt. Prnts

Spires, firm on their monster feet rose light and thin, The. Denis Devlin. CIP-2 Fr. Heavenly Foreigner, The.

Spires of Oxford, The. Winifred M. Letts. PoRA

Spirit, The. Jones Very. NCAP

Spirit appeared to me, and said, A. Spirit Appeared to Me, A. Herman Melville. ChIV-1

Spirit came upon me in the night, A. After-State. Frederick William Faber. CenSon

Spirit Craft, The. Charles G. Ballard. VoR

Spirit Epiloguizes, The. John Milton. See Comus; a Masque Presented at Ludlow Castle

Spirit Flowers. Della Burt. BlSi

Spirit from Perfecter Ages. Arthur Hugh Clough. EBEV; OxAEP-2 Fr. Amours de Voyage.

Spirit in Our Hearts, The. Henry Ustic Onderdonk. AH

Spirit in the sky. Spirit Song. Unknown. WoPoe, tr. by Stephen Berg

Spirit is lame and in the pale flesh, The. Landing Area. J. H. Prynne. PFTM-2

Spirit Is Too Blunt an Instrument, The. Anne Stevenson. ColAP

Spirit Land, The. Jones Very. HAP

Spirit lasts, but in what mode, The. Emily Dickinson. APN-2

Spirit Level. Anthony Conran. TCAWP

Spirit Level, The. David Barber. AmPoNex

Spirit of dreams, that when the dark hours steep. Invocation, To the Genius of Slumber Written Oct. 1787. Anna Seward. PEW

Spirit of evil, with which the earth is rife. Charles Johnston. CenSon

Spirit of Gama! round the stormy Cape. Cape of Storms, The. John Wheatley. PeSAV

Spirit of God, The. Antiphon for the Holy Spirit. Hildegard von Bingen. WPoS, tr. by Barbara Newman

Spirit of God! descend upon my heart. Supplication, A. George Croly. SacPr

Spirit of Life, in This New Dawn. Earl Bowman Marlatt. AH

Spirit of light, whose eye unfolds. Ode Inscribed to the Infant Son of S.T. Coleridge, Esq. Mary Robinson. RWP

Spirit of Love, with Love's intelligence, A. Noffo Bonaguida. EaItPo, tr. by Dante Gabriel Rossetti

Spirit of Plato. Unknown. AWP; OBVE
    (Plato's Tomb.) FaBoCh

Spirit of Poetry, The. Henry Wadsworth Longfellow. APN-1

Spirit of pure benevolence, descend. On the Slave-Trade. Isabella Lickbarrow. RWP

Spirit of '76, The. Friederike Mayröcker. PFTM-2, tr. by Anselm Hollo

Spirit of spirits, who, through ev'ry part. Hymn to Na'ra'yena, A. Sir William Jones. NOBRP

Spirit of the Age, The. Christopher Pearse Cranch. APN-1

Spirit of the Place, The. Tony Curtis. AngWePo

Spirit of the Wind. Gabriel Okara. PBMAP

Spirit Papers. Teresa D. Cader. ExTi

Spirit Pass'd Before Me, A. Byron. ChIV-1

Spirit's Epilogue, The. John Milton. See Comus; a Masque Presented at Ludlow Castle

Spirit's Epochs, The. Coventry Patmore. EBEV; OxBSP Fr. Angel in the House, The.

Spirit's Mysteries, The. Felicia Dorothea Hemans. RWP

Spirit's Odyssey, The. M. Krishnamurti. InPK-6

Spirit saith, come, The. Bible, N.T. EMWP, tr. by Bathsheba Bowers Fr. Revelation of St. John the Divine, The.

Spirit seems to pass, A. Lausanne: In Gibbon's Old Garden: 11–12 p.m. Thomas Hardy. FaBoTw

Spirit sets about its task, but slowly, The.   J. D. McClatchy.   WiU   *Fr.* First Steps.

Spirit, Silken Thread.   Margot Ruddock.   OBMV

Spirit Song.   *Unknown.*   WoPoe, *tr.* by Stephen Berg

Spirit sweats—the horizon's, The.   Moochkap.   Boris Leonidovich Pasternak.   TCRusP, *tr.* by Bogdan Boychuk and Mark Rudman

Spirit! What art thou erecting.   Poet's Ideal, The.   Henrietta Cordelia Ray.   CBWP-3

Spirit Whose Work Is Done.   Walt Whitman.   CBCWP; NAAL-2v1; NAAL-3

Spirited light! on the edge.   Antiphon for the Angels.   Hildegard von Bingen.   WPoS, *tr.* by Barbara Newman

Spirits.   Robert Bridges.   OBEV

Spirits.   Birago Diop.   NegPo, *tr.* by Ellen Conroy Kennedy

Spirits.   Víctor Hernández Cruz.   PueRic

Spirits, Dancing.   Arthur Gregor.   VGW

Spirits Everywhere.   Ludwig Uhland.   AWP, *tr.* by James Clarence Mangan

Spirits of old that bore me.   Louise Imogen Guiney.   RACG

Spirits of the dead lights.   Jerome Rothenberg.   PFTM-2   *Fr.* Khurbn.

Spirits of well-shot woodcock, partridge, snipe.   Death of King George V.   Sir John Betjeman.   NOBE; OxBEV; OxBoLi

Spiritual, A.   Paul Laurence Dunbar.   BPo; SacPr

Spiritual Alchemy, The.   "Angelus Silesius."   GePo, *tr.* by George C. Schoolfield   *Fr.* Cherubical Wanderer, The.

Spiritual Ark And The Manna-Vessel, The.   "Angelus Silesius."   GePo, *tr.* by George C. Schoolfield   *Fr.* Cherubical Wanderer, The.

Spiritual athlete often changes the color of his clothes, The.   Hopeful Spiritual Athlete, The.   Kabir.   RaBo, *tr.* by Robert Bly

Spiritual Canticle.   Saint John of the Cross.   SpanPo; STV, *tr.* by John Frederick Nims

Spiritual Geography.   Kalamu ya Salaam.   SpirFl   *Fr.* New Orleans Haiku.

Spiritual: "How did you feel when you come out the wilderness?"   William W. Cook.   SpirFl

Spiritual Impregnation, The.   "Angelus Silesius."   GePo, *tr.* by George C. Schoolfield   *Fr.* Cherubical Wanderer, The.

Spiritual Isolation.   Isaac Rosenberg.   TrJP

Spiritual Land.   Elizabeth Brown.   IBA

Spiritual Laws.   Ralph Waldo Emerson.   APN-1

Spiritual Meditation upon a Bee, A.   Amey Hayward.   EMWP

Spiritual Morning.   Robin Becker.   TaR

Spiritual Song of the Aborigine.   Hyllus Maris.   IBA

Spiritual, the carnal, are one, The.   Dorothy Wellesley, Duchess of Wellington.   OBMV   *Fr.* Matrix.

Spiritual Wedding.   Manuel Bandeira.   TCLAP, *tr.* by Candace Slater

Spirituality vs. the Temporality, The.   John Skelton.   NAEL-6v1   *Fr.* Colin Clout.

Spit.   A. R. Ammons.   BodElec

Spit.   C. K. Williams.   GotH; TaR

Spit in my face ye [*or* you] Jew[e]s, and pierce my side.   John Donne.   BASC; Son; TOF   *Fr.* Holy Sonnets.

Spit of sky, awash with Venetian gold, A.   Sunset at Wellfleet.   Jean Valentine.   YaYoPo

Spite made the architects put the front desk of the hotel.   Hard Put.   Catie Rosemurgy.   AmPoNex

Spitfire! from *BlackFleshMotors*.   Dance Bodies #1.   Eugene B. Redmond.   ISC

Spits of glitter in lowgrade ore.   Conserving the Magnitude of Uselessness.   A. R. Ammons.   NoAM

Spitting blood.   Sunao.   JDP, *tr.* by Yoel Hoffmann

Spitting—from lips once sanctified by Hers. (LL)   To Edward FitzGerald.   Robert Browning.   NAEL-5v2; NAEL-6v2; OxBSP

Spitting in the Leaves.   Maggie Anderson.   PBCAP

Spittle beads as ice along.   Wrong Way Will Haunt You, The.   Sydney Lea.   RA

Splash water on level ground.   Pao Chao.   ChinPo, *tr.* by Yip Wai-lim   *Fr.* Weary Road, The.

Splashing paint from a glass.   But Could You?   Vladimir Vladimirovich Mayakovsky [*or* Maiakovskii].   TCRP, *tr.* by Bernard Meares

Splashing—that is now some stone. (LL)   These.   William Carlos Williams.   APT-1; MoAmPo; NOBA; OxBA

Splat of bare feet on wet tile, The.   Women's Locker Room.   Marilyn Nelson Waniek.   LTA

Spleen.   Ernest Christopher Dowson.   MoBrPo; NOBVV

Spleen.   John Gray.   NOBVV

Spleen.   August Kleinzahler.   PmAP

Spleen.   Paul Verlaine.   AWP, *tr.* by Ernest Dowson

Spleen.   Paul Verlaine.   SxFrPo, *tr.* by Martin Sorrell

Spleen, The.   Matthew Green.

　"First know, my friend, I do not mean."   ECEV; NOEC

　"Forced by soft violence of prayer."   ECEV

　"Sometimes I dress, with women sit."   ECEV; NPeEn; OBCoV

　"To cure the mind's wrong bias, Spleen."   ECEV; NPeEn

　"When by its magic lantern Spleen."   OxAEP-1

Spleen, The.   Matthew Green.

　"I always choose the plainest food."   VerBaPo

　"This motley piece to you I send."   NoP-4

Spleen, The.   Anne Finch, Countess of Winchilsea.   NALW; NOSC

Spleen LXXV.   Charles Baudelaire.   SxFrPo, *tr.* by James McGowan

Spleen LXXVI.   Charles Baudelaire.   SxFrPo, *tr.* by James McGowan

Spleen LXXVII.   Charles Baudelaire.   SxFrPo, *tr.* by James McGowan

Spleen LXXVIII.   Charles Baudelaire.   SxFrPo, *tr.* by James McGowan

Spleen LXXVIII.   Charles Baudelaire.   NAWM-7v2

Spleen LXXIX.   Charles Baudelaire.   NAWM-7v2

Spleen LXXXI.   Charles Baudelaire.   NAWM-7v2

Spleen, a Pindaric Poem, The.   Anne Finch, Countess of Winchilsea.   Power of Spleen, The.   ECWP; NPeEn

Splendid Bankrupt, The.   Arthur A. Sykes.   UV

Splendid coat that wrapped the favored son, The.   Woman of Color.   Constance Merritt.   AmPoNex

Splendid Shilling, The.   John Phillips.

　"Happy the man, who, void of cares and strife."   NOEC

Splendid Stags, The.   József Erdélyi.   IQMS, *tr.* by Thomas Land

Splendid Village, The.   Ebenezer Elliott.

　"Village! thy butcher's son, the steward now."   OBSV

Splendidly-shining darkness.   Félix Lope de Vega Carpio.   HAP; WoPoe, *tr.* by Geoffrey Hill   *Fr.* Pentecost Castle, The.

Splendor and pride I celebrate.   Angelo Politziano.   WoPoe, *tr.* by Guy Davenport   *Fr.* Tournament, The.

Splendor Falls, The.   Tennyson.   *See* Princess, The

Splendor falls on castle walls, The.   Tennyson.   AWP; ClHu; EBVV; FHYEP; FaBoCh; GTBS-P; HeIP-4; InPK-6; NAEL-5v2; NoP-4; PeVV; TFi   *Fr.* Princess, The

Splendor in the Wind.   Raúl Zurita.   TCLAP, *tr.* by Jack Schmitt

Splendor of the moon shines down on quiet night.   Response to Wang Ssu-yüan's Poem on the Moon, A.   Shen Yüeh.   SuSp, *tr.* by Richard B. Mather

Splendor of Thine Eyes, The.   Moses Ibn Ezra.   TrJP, *tr.* by Solomon Solis-Cohen

Splendour Falls, The.   Tennyson.   AWP; ClHu; EBVV; FHYEP; FaBoCh; GTBS-P; HeIP-4; InPK-6; NAEL-5v2; NoP-4; PeVV; TFi   *Fr.* Princess, The.

Splendour falls on castle walls, The.   Tennyson.   *See* Splendor falls on castle walls, The

Splendour of life so splendidly contained.   Geoffrey Hill.   NoAM   *Fr.* Lachrimae; or Seven Tears Figured in Seven Passionate Pavans.

Splendour of my Spring I destroy here, The. Not knowing.   Abishag.   Jacob [*or*Jakov] Fichman.   TrJP, *tr.* by Sholom J. Kahn

Splendour recurrent.   Confucius.   CTC; OBVE   *Fr.* Deer Sing.

Splinter.   Carl Sandburg.   KaS; OBCA; SoSe-8; Spl

Splinter under nail.   Spell to Cure Barrenness.   Jeni Couzyn.   HAWP

Splintered the crystal of identity.   "H. D."   NAAL-5   *Fr.* Walls Do Not Fall, The.

Splinters of information, stones of information.   Minerals of Cornwall, Stones of Cornwall.   Peter Redgrove.   FaBoMo

Splish splosh, February-fill-the-dike.   February.   John Heath-Stubbs.   OBCP

Split open the massive chaos to obtain black gold.   Poem on Coal, A.   Yü Ch'ien.   SuSp, *tr.* by Wu-Chi Liu

Split the Lark—and you'll find the Music.   Emily Dickinson.   APN-2; ChIV-2; NoP-4; TCAPo

Splitting birches, spiky thicket, kinship.   Black Bread.   Tom Paulin.   CIP-2

Splitting the void in half.   Nanei.   ZenPo, *tr.* by Takashi Ikemoto and Lucien Stryk

Splitting Wood Near Morris, Oklahoma on Robbie and Lesa McMurtry's Farm.   Lance Henson.   HATNAP

Splittings.   Adrienne Rich.   HarvBoo

Spluttering burnt-out lamp blazes in the dusk.   Ch'ien Ch'ien-i [*or* Ch'ien Ch'ien-yi].   SuSp   *Fr.* Poems Written in Prison.

Spofford Hall.   Alison Stone.   SwNoth

Spoils.   Robert Graves.   HAP; Son; WeW-3

Spoils of Annwn, The.   *Unknown.*   WoPoe, *tr.* by Anthony Conran

Spokane Falls.   Phillip [*or* "Phil"] William George.   VoR

Spoke Aug 19.   Hannah Weiner.

　Seen Words.   FTOS

Spoken by Venus on Seeing Her Statue Done by Praxiteles.   *Unknown.*   FaBoEE

Spoken Extempore on the Death of Mr. Pope.   *Unknown.*   NOEC

Spoken to Pines and Bamboos.   Wei Chuang.   SuSp, *tr.* by Robin D. S. Yates

Spontaneous Me. Walt Whitman. NAAL-2v1; NAAL-3; NAAL-5; OxBA

Spontaneous momentum, A. Sheaf Mark. Ray DiPalma. FTOS

Spontaneous Requiem For the American Indian. Gregory Corso. PoM
(Wakonda! Talako! **deathonic** turkey gobbling in the soft-.) BB

Spoon, The. Charles Simic. NNaP

Spoon Maker's Daughter, The. Susan Utting. Prnts

Spoon of your head, The. Rain. John Ashbery. FTOS

Spoon River Anthology. Edgar Lee Masters.
  A. D. Blood. APT-1
  Amanda Barker. APT-1; NoAM
  Anne Rutledge. CBCWP; HAP; MoAmPo; NOBA; NoAM; OxBA; PAI; TFi
  Archibald Higbie. APT-1
  Benjamin Pantier. APT-1
  "Butch" Weldy. APT-1
  Carl Hamblin. OBSV; PAI
  Cassius Hueffer. OxBA
  Circuit Judge, The. FaBoEE
  Constance Hately. APT-1
  Daisy Fraser. HAP; PoE
  Doctor Meyers. APT-1; IllVoic
  Dora Williams. HAP
  Editor Whedon. APT-1; FaBoEE; NOBA; OBSV; OxBA; PoE
  Elliott Hawkins. OxBA
  Elsa Wertman. NoAM; OxBA; PAI
  Emily Sparks. APT-1
  English Thornton. OxBA
  Father Malloy. OxBA
  Fiddler Jones. IllVoic; NoAM; OxBA; TAP
  Flossie Cabanis. APT-1
  Hamilton Greene. NoAM; OxBA; PAI
  Harry Williams. APT-1
  Henry C. Calhoun.
    "On the way to the grove you'll pass the Fates." TCAPo
  Herman Altman. OxBA
  Hill, The. ColAP; IllVoic; NOBA; NoAM; OxBA; TAP
  "I looked like Abraham Lincoln." OxBA
  "I staggered on through darkness." APT-1
  "If you in the village think that my work was a good one." APT-1
  Indignation Jones. APT-1
  "It is true, fellow citizens." APT-1
  Jonathan Houghton. OxBA
  Jonathan Swift Somers. OBAL
  Judge Somers. FaBoEE; OBSV
  Justice Arnett. APT-1
  Knowlt Hoheimer. OxBA
  Lucinda Matlock. HAP; IllVoic; MoAmPo; NOBA; NoAM; OxBA
  Margaret Fuller Slack. APT-1; IllVoic; RACG
  Minerva Jones. APT-1; IllVoic
  Mrs. Benjamin Pantier. APT-1
  Mrs. Meyers. APT-1; IllVoic
  Oscar Hummel. APT-1
  Petit, the Poet. ColAP; MoAmPo; NOBA; NoAM; OxBA; TAP; TCAPo
  Ralph Rhodes. APT-1
  Reuben Pantier. APT-1
  Rutherford McDowell. OxBA
  Serepta Mason. APT-1
  Sexsmith the Dentist. GeoHom
  Spooniad, The. OBAL
  Starved Rock. GeoHom
  Trainor, the Druggist. APT-1; IllVoic
  Webster Ford. APT-1
  Willie Metcalf. APT-1

Spoon River Sadie Louise. Anne Lamott. Unle

Spooniad, The. Edgar Lee Masters. OBAL *Fr.* Spoon River Anthology.

Sporting Acquaintances. Siegfried Sassoon. OxBSo; OxBTC

Sporting as fancie, setting light by love. Richard Barnfield [*or* Barnefield].
  CAGL *Fr.* Cynthia, with Certain[e] Sonnets.

Sporting Beasley. Sterling Allen Brown. APT-2; NAAAL

Sporting Goods. Philippe Soupault. TTTS, *tr. by* Rosmarie Waldrop
  (Brave as a postage stamp, he went his way.) PFTM-1

Sporting people, The. Free Fantasia: Tiger Flowers. Robert Earl Hayden.
  ESEAA

Sporting the Plaid. Chris Wallace-Crabbe. NOBAu

Sports and gallantries, the stage, the arts, the antics of dancers. Boats in a Fog.
  Robinson Jeffers. NAAL-2v2; NoP-4; OxBA

Sportsmen. Keith Douglas. *See* Aristocrats

Sportsmen keep hawks, and their quarry they gain, The. John Gay. NOEC
  Fr. Polly; an Opera.

Sporus. Pope. AWP; NOBE; OBSV; OxBEV; SCV *Fr.* Epistle to Dr.
  Arbuthnot.

Spot her, but don't lock on her. How to Approach Your Lover's Wife. Amy
  Bottke. OPRER

Spot the Ball. Frank Ormsby. CIP-2; PBCIP; PNI

Spotlights had you covered, The. Poem about Poems about Vietnam, A. Jon
  Stallworthy. NoAM

Spots of Blood. Phyllis Webb. NOBC

Spots of Time. William Wordsworth. TOF *Fr.* Prelude, The; Growth of a
  Poet's Mind [1850 vers.].

Spots triumphed in the afternoon light, The. After the Rain. Kristina
  Rungano. HAWP

Spotted Flycatcher, The. Walter De la Mare. OxBSP

Spotted hawk swoops by and accuses me, he complains of my gab and my
  loitering, The. Walt Whitman. AmFaPo; CAGL; ColAP; NAWM-7v2;
  SAmP *Fr.* Song of Myself.

Spouse of Jesus Laments Her Heart's Flame, The. Friedrich Spee. GePo, *tr.*
  by George C. Schoolfield

Spouse to the Younglings, The. William Baldwin. *See* Christ, My Beloved

Spraggy cod'll grow ni fatter, A. Fisherman's Rhyme. *Unknown.* FaBoVe

Sprawl is the quality. Quality of Sprawl, The. Les A. Murray. EmeKit;
  HarvBoo; NoP-4

Sprawled belly-down on the damp planks. Bullhead. John Engels. MoASP

Sprawled in the pigsty. For a Young Artist. Robert Earl Hayden. NoAM

Sprawled, like park derelicts, about. Sleepers, The. Peter Kocan. CBAP

Sprawled / on our faces in the spring. Hen Flower, The. Galway Kinnell.
  NNaP

Sprawled on the crates and sacks in the rear of the truck. Green, Green Is El
  Aghir. Norman Cameron. NPeEn; NePenScot; OBWP; OxBTC

Sprawls across the centerline. Roadkill Coyote. Art Goodtimes. GeoH

Spray. Biddy Jenkinson. ModIr, *tr. by* Alex Osborne

Spray of pine-needles, A. Nullo. Jean Toomer. APT-2

Spray-painted across a garage door. Strange Fruit. Timothy Liu. WiU

Sprayed with strong poison. Paul Goodman. InPK-6

Spraying the Potatoes. Patrick Kavanagh. BIrV; CABP

Spread a Little Happiness. Clifford Grey. ReLy

Spread eagle sheep legs wide. Mantanza to Welcome Spring. Jimmy Santiago
  Baca. PmAP

Spread on the roadway. Cyclists, The. Amy Lowell. WPE

Spread over the earth! Autumn Leaves. Mikhail Naimy. GraLe, *tr. by* Sharif
  Elmusa and Gregory Orfalea

Spread Rhythm. C. D. Wright. LCAP-2

Spread, table, spread. George Peele. NoSic *Fr.* Old Wives' [*or* Wife's] Tale,
  The.

Spread the board with linen snow. Invitation to the Dance. Apollinaris
  Sidonius. AWP, *tr. by* Howard Mumford Jones

Spread their gay wings before the Throne, and smile. (LL) Epitaph on the
  Tombstone of a Child, the Last of Seven That Died Before. Aphra Behn.
  CABP; NOSC; OxBSo

Spreadeagled for sleep, godlike, on your back. Contrary Motion. Elizabeth
  Garrett. NeBl

Spreadeagled in the empty air / of existence. (LL) Constantly Risking
  Absurdity. Lawrence Ferlinghetti. NeAP; PmAP; PoM; TAP

Spreadin' Rhythm Around. Ted Koehler. ReLy

Spreading fragrant grass, random spring clouds. Tune: "Full Moon in the
  Human World"—Spring Evening: Replying to a Song. *Unknown.* SuSp,
  tr. by Sherwin S. S. Fu

Spreading here, spreading there, the grasses on the plain. Grass on Ancient
  Plain, a Song of Farewell. Po Chü-i. SuSp, *tr. by* Irving Y. Lo

Spreading o'er the hills' domain. Waldviertel. Lower Austria. Alma Johanna
  Koenig. AuPH, *tr. by* Lowell A. Bangerter

Spreading Wings on Wind. Simon J. Ortiz. HATNAP

Spree. Maxine W. Kumin. NoAM

Sprig of Karo, A. Murray Edmond. PeNZ

Sprig of Lime, The. Robert Malise Bowyer Nichols. GTBS-P

Sprig of Moss, The. William McGonagall.
  "By taking the impressions of watch-cases he discovered, one day."
  VerBaPo

Spring. Anacreon. AWP, *tr. by* Thomas Stanley

Spring. William Blake. FHYEP; FaBoCh; NOxBChV; TTTS *Fr.* Songs of
  Innocence.

Spring. Reed Bye. TTTS

Spring. Chu Shu-chen. OHPC, *tr. by* Kenneth Rexroth

Spring. Judith Ortiz Cofer. PueRic

Spring. "Rubén Darío. SpanPo, *tr. by* Anita Volland

Spring. Ebenezer Elliott. OxAEP-2

Spring. Ferenc Faludi. IQMS, *tr. by* Donald Davie

Spring. Adelaida Gertsyk. ARWW, *tr. by* Catriona Kelly
Spring. Giovanni Battista Guarini. AWP, *tr. by* Leigh Hunt
Spring. Margherita Guidacci. CItWP, *tr. by* Cinzia Sartini Blum and Lara Trubowitz
Spring. Friedrich Hölderlin. WoPoe, *tr. by* David Rattray *Fr.* Seasons, The.
Spring. Michael Hogan. InPK-6
Spring. Gerard Manley Hopkins. EBVV; GSo; HAP; MoBrPo; NAEL-5v2; NAEL-6v2; NOBE; NOBVV; NoAM; OBMV; RB; TFi; TrCP
Spring. Iio Sogi. WoPoe, *tr. by* Steven D. Carter
Spring. Pinkie Gordon Lane. GT
Spring. Philip Larkin. MoBrPo
Spring. Hugo Majer. Spl
Spring. Meleager. AWP, *tr. by* William M. Hardinge
Spring. Edna St. Vincent Millay. APT-1; BoWoP; MoAmPo; NoP-4
Spring. Thomas Nashe [*or* Nash]. *See* Summer's Last Will and Testament
Spring. Charles, Duc d' Orléans. AWP; CTC, *tr. by* Andrew Lang
Spring. Papyrus. Ezra Pound. APT-1; PFTM-1
Spring. Lola Ridge. WPE
Spring. Isaac Rosenberg. TrJP
Spring. Rudaki. WoPoe, *tr. by* Geoffrey Squires
Spring. William Shakespeare. HAP; InPK-6; NAEL-5v1; NAEL-6v1; NBLV; NIL-7; NIP-4; NOBE; NoSic; OBEV; PAI; PoRA; SCGP; TFi; UnPo *Fr.* Love's Labour's Lost.
Spring. André Spire. AWP, *tr. by* Jethro Bithell
Spring. Su Tung-p'o (Su Shih). OHPC, *tr. by* Kenneth Rexroth
Spring. Shinkichi Takahashi. ZenPo, *tr. by* Takashi Ikemoto and Lucien Stryk
Spring. James Thomson. *Fr.* Seasons, The.
Spring. Tu Fu. TAL
Spring. Mary E. Tucker. CBWP-1
Spring. *Unknown.* SuSp *Fr.* Tzu-yeh Songs of the Four Seasons.
Spring, The. Thomas Carew. BeJo; CaPo; CavPo; NoP-4; PBRV; PoE
Spring, The. Abraham Cowley. BeJo; HAP; MeLP; OxAEP-1 *Fr.* Mistress, The.
Spring, The. Morgan Llwyd. AngWePo *Fr.* 1648.
Spring! Basho. EH, *tr. by* Robert Hass
Spring 61. Lenore Kandel. BB
Spring after spring, I sat before my mirror. Boat of Stars. Li Ch'ing-chao. ErotSp, *tr. by* Sam Hamill
Spring, and a new pair of moccasins! Sunflower Moccasins. Phillip [*or* "Phil"] William George. VoR
Spring and All. William Carlos Williams. APT-1; ChAP; ColAP; HAP; InPK-6; MakPoe; NAAL-2v2; NAAL-5; NOBA; NoAM; OxBA; PoE; PoPoPo; TAP; TCAPo; TFi; TRP
   (Poem: "By the road to the contagious hospital.") MoAmPo; UnPo
Spring, and all over town. Signs. Wendy Mnookin. UrbNat
Spring and Autumn. William James Linton. EBVV
Spring and Fall. Gerard Manley Hopkins. CABP; EBEV; GTBS-P; HAP; HeIP-4; InPK-6; NAEL-5v2; NAEL-6v2; NIL-7; NOBE; NoAM; NoP-4; OPOU; PAI; PeVV; PoE; PoPoPo; RB; SCGP; SCV; TFi; TOF; TRP
   (Spring and Fall: To a Young Child.) ClHu; OxAEP-2
Spring / and for you, spring—isn't it spring? Kukutis's Swallow's Hymn. Marcelijus Martinaitis. TWW, *tr. by* Laima Sruoginis
Spring and the Ashura. Miyazawa Kenji. PFTM-1
Spring, and the Blind Children. Alfred Noyes. OxBTC
Spring and the girls are twirling batons. Twirling. Jane Flanders. ItWoWo; PBCAP
Spring appears, in which the earth, The. *Unknown.* AWP
Spring at Fort Okanogan. Ramona Wilson. VoR
Spring at Nant Dywelan. Bobi Jones. OBWVE, *tr. by* Joseph P. Clancy
Spring at Wu Ling. Li Ch'ing-chao. ErotSp, *tr. by* Sam Hamill
   (To the Tune: Spring at Wu Ling.) CrYelRi
Spring at Yesan Station. Sub-ok. WPoS, *tr. by* Julie Pickering
Spring being at her blessed carpentry, The. Garden Chidings. Louise Imogen Guiney. SWaP
Spring Bereaved. William Drummond, of Hawthornden. *See* Sonnet: "Alexis, here she stayed; among these pines."
Spring Bereaved. William Drummond, of Hawthornden. OBEV
Spring Bereaved 2. William Drummond, of Hawthornden. OBEV
   (Sweet Spring.) Son
Spring blooms, autumn moon, when will they end? Tune: "Beautiful Lady Yü, The." Li Yü. SuSp, *tr. by* Eugene Eoyang
Spring blossoms, autumn moon. To the Tune: Beautiful Lady Yu. Li Yu. CrYelRi, *tr. by* Sam Hamill
Spring blossoms, honey-bee, in the colours you parade. Nicias. GrAn
Spring Breeze. Ho Hsun. OHMPC, *tr. by* Kenneth Rexroth
Spring breeze. Anita Virgil. HA
Spring breeze blows the rain, A. Wang Chien. SuSp *Fr.* Palace Poems.

Spring breeze stirs a springtime heart. *Unknown.* SuSp *Fr.* Tzu-yeh Songs of the Four Seasons.
Spring breezes erase the flowers. Spring Evening on Pan Mountain. Wang An-shih. CrYelRi, *tr. by* Sam Hamill
Spring breezes waft along the avenue. Horseman at the Roadside, The. Yang Wei-chen. CoBLCP, *tr. by* Jonathan Chaves
Spring came. Spring. Rudaki. WoPoe, *tr. by* Geoffrey Squires
Spring came, with orioles singing. Farmer's Thoughts, A. Ch'u Kuang-hsi. CoBCP, *tr. by* Burton Watson
Spring Can Really Hang You Up the Most. Tommy Wolf. ReLy
Spring Cleaning. Phillip [*or* "Phil"] William George. VoR
Spring Cliff. Muso Soseki. EaWin, *tr. by* W. S. Merwin
Spring clouds look like beasts. Random Thoughts Written in Spring. Wang Yü-ch'eng. SuSp, *tr. by* Irving Y. Lo
Spring clouds rest on the walls of the Royal Park. Tu Fu. CarOv, *tr. by* Carolyn Kizer *Fr.* Meandering River Poems, The.
Spring, Coast Range. Kenneth Rexroth. APT-2
Spring comes early to the gardens. Green Jade Plum Trees in Spring. Ou-yang Hsiu. OHPC, *tr. by* Kenneth Rexroth
Spring comes: the flowers learn their coloured shapes. Vision, A. Maria Konopnicka. WPOW, *tr. by* Jerzy Peterkiewicz and Burns Singer
Spring Comes to Chicago. Campbell McGrath. NeAmPo
Spring Comes to Murray Hill. Ogden Nash. APT-2
Spring Comes to the Suburbs. Phyllis McGinley. APT-2
Spring Coming. A. R. Ammons. HeIP-4; InPK-6
Spring Dawn. Meng Hao Jan. ColAnChi, *tr. by* Elling O. Eide
Spring Day. John Ashbery. ColAP; NOBA
Spring Day. "Igor Severyanin [*or* Severianin]." TCRP, *tr. by* Bernard Meares
Spring Day. Su Tung-p'o (Su Shih). SuSp, *tr. by* Irving Y. Lo
Spring Day. Yu Chien-wu. ColAnChi, *tr. by* Victor H. Mair and Tsu-Lin Mei
Spring day, The. Issa. EH, *tr. by* Robert Hass
Spring Day in the Countryside, A. Wen T'ing-yün. SuSp, *tr. by* William R. Schultz
Spring Day on West Lake. Ou-yang Hsiu. OHPC, *tr. by* Kenneth Rexroth
Spring Day—Remembering Living on the River, A. Kao Ch'i. CoBLCP, *tr. by* Jonathan Chaves
Spring Day: Thinking of Li Po. Tu Fu. ChinPo, *tr. by* Yip Wai-lim
Spring Days in My Home Town. Yang Chi.
   "Thousands of flowers, thousands of petals." CoBLCP
Spring does not flow now, the stream is quite dry, The. Spring Does Not Flow Now, The. Rosalía de Castro. SpanPo, *tr. by* Muriel Kittel
Spring Dreams. Meng Hao Jan. CrYelRi, *tr. by* Sam Hamill
Spring Dreams. Yang Chi. CoBLCP, *tr. by* Jonathan Chaves
Spring dusk. (LL) Basho. EH; NIL-7, *tr. by* Robert Hass
Spring Ecstasy. Lizette Woodworth Reese. MoAmPo
Spring Equinox. Peter Blue Cloud. ChAP *Fr.* Within the Seasons.
Spring evening. Chuck Brickley. HA
Spring Evening. Frederick Turner. RA
Spring Evening on Pan Mountain. Wang An-shih. CrYelRi, *tr. by* Sam Hamill
Spring Fancies. Christina Georgina Rossetti.
   "Gone were but the Winter." GTBS-P; PoE; WPE
   Spring Quiet. GTBS-P; PoE; WPE
Spring Fever. Rosario Morales. PueRic
Spring Fiord. *Unknown.* STP, *tr. by* Armand Schwerner
Spring flood is coming up to my door. Su Tung-p'o (Su Shih). SuSp *Fr.* Rain at Cold-Food Festival.
Spring Flowers. James Thomson. NOBE *Fr.* Seasons, The.
Spring flowers and autumn moon enter poems. For Hidden Mist Pavilion. Yü Hsüan-chi. BoWoP, *tr. by* Geoffrey Waters
Spring flowers, autumn moon: when to end? Tune: "Beauty Yu." Li Yü. ChinPo, *tr. by* Yip Wai-lim
Spring flowers, Autumn moons. Plaint. Chu Shu-chen. OHPC, *tr. by* Kenneth Rexroth
Spring Flowers Own, The. Etel Adnan.
   "Butterfly came to die, A." PoArWo
Spring Forward. Martin Steingesser. PoCoUp
Spring Forward, Fall Back. Alpay Ulku. AmPoNex
Spring from the earth, food for our children. Give us good health. Let us grow up, and become ripe. *Unknown.* APN-2 *Fr.* Minnetare Songs.
Spring garden is *Irish* green, The. British Garden, A. Wes Magee. OBGa
Spring garlands the earth with leaves. *Unknown.* GrAn
Spring-gazing Song. Hsüeh T'ao. BoWoP, *tr. by* Carolyn Kizer
Spring Goes. Tu Fu. CarOv, *tr. by* Carolyn Kizer *Fr.* Meandering River Poems, The.
Spring goes, and the hundred flowers. Rebirth. Man Giac. EaWin; WoPoe, *tr. by* W. S. Merwin and Nguyen Ngoc Bich
Spring goes, spring comes, spring again will be spring. Tune: "Willow Branches." *Unknown.* SuSp, *tr. by* Hellmut Wilhelm

Spring going. Basho. EH, *tr.* by Robert Hass
Spring Grievance. Chin Ch'ang-hsü. CoBCP, *tr.* by Burton Watson
Spring groves: flowers, such charm. Spring Song from "Tzu-Yeh" Songs of the Four Seasons. *Unknown.* ChinPo, *tr.* by Yip Wai-lim
Spring hailstones would drive us. Because of My Father's Job. James Masao Mitsui. NIL-7; OpBo; UnSA
Spring Has Come. Antonio Machado Ruiz. SpanPo, *tr.* by Kate Flores
Spring has come and the snow has gone. Captive. Peretz Hirshbein. TrJP, *tr.* by Joseph Leftwich
Spring has come. I try to forget. Spring. Chu Shu-chen. OHPC, *tr.* by Kenneth Rexroth
Spring has come to the gate—spring's grasses green. Tune: "Manifold Little Hills." Li Ch'ing-chao. SuSp, *tr.* by Eugene Eoyang
Spring has come to the Pass. Two Springs. Li Ch'ing-chao. BoWoP; OHPC, *tr.* by Kenneth Rexroth
Spring has darkened with activity, The. Time and the Garden. Yvor Winters. APT-2; HarvBoo; MoAmPo; NoAM; VGW
Spring has returned. The earth is. Spring Has Returned. Rainer Maria Rilke. WoPoe, *tr.* by Charles Haseloff
Spring has swept the ice from all my frozen rivers, The. Blues. Léopold Sédar Senghor. PBMAP
Spring has vanished. End to Spring, An. Tzu Yeh. CrYelRi, *tr.* by Sam Hamill
Spring here in Tien-nan, The. To the Tune "Chiang ch'eng tzu." Yang Shen. CoBLCP, *tr.* by Jonathan Chaves
Spring Homecoming. Tu Fu. CrYelRi, *tr.* by Sam Hamill
Spring in a Mountain Village. Noin. WoPoe, *tr.* by Steven D. Carter
"Spring in Ch'in's Garden." Mao Tse-tung [*or* Mao Zedong]. SuSp, *tr.* by Eugene Eoyang
Spring in London. John Bingham Morton. OBCoV
Spring in New Hampshire. Claude McKay. BPo; ChAP
Spring in the Bronx. *Unknown.* OBCoV
Spring in the Students' Quarter. Henry Murger. AWP, *tr.* by Andrew Lang
Spring in Tien is fine! To the Tune "Spring in Tien Is Fine." Yang Shen. CoBLCP, *tr.* by Jonathan Chaves
Spring in Virginia. Ramona Wilson. VoR
Spring is a Cat, The. Yi Jang'hi (Jang-hi Lee). WoPoe, *tr.* by Ko Changsu (Chang-soo Koh)
Spring is a juice, a rejoicing, forcing. Sirventes. Bertrans [*or* Bertran *or* Bertrand] de Born. WoPoe, *tr.* by Paul Blackburn
Spring is a-rising. Young Miracle Stag, The. László Nagy. IQMS, *tr.* by Adam Makkai
Spring is cheap, but clean of sky. Long after she used to. In the Clear Long After. Olena Kalytiak Davis. NAPBL
Spring is come at last, my freens, cheer up, you sons of toil, The. Working Man, The. Ellen Johnston. VWP
Spring is early this year. Kenneth Rexroth. APSN *Fr.* Love Poems of Marichiko, The.
Spring is going, gone! Tune: "Memories of the South." Liu Yu Hsi. ColAnChi, *tr.* by Jiaosheng Wang
Spring is half gone since we parted. Tune: "Pure Serene Music." Li Yü. ColAnChi, *tr.* by Jiaosheng Wang
Spring Is Here. Richard Rodgers. ReLy
Spring is here / I'm a fool if I fall again. Fun to be Fooled. Harold Arlen. ReLy
Spring is like a perhaps hand. E. E. Cummings. NoP-4; TAP; VGW
Spring is not so beautiful there, The. Water-Front Streets. Langston Hughes. SAmP
Spring is past and over these many days. September. Aldous Leonard Huxley. EBEV
Spring is short. Akiko Yosano. BoWoP
Spring is sprung. Spring in the Bronx. *Unknown.* OBCoV
Spring is the Period. Emily Dickinson. TAP
Spring is when the grass turns green and glad. Lines Written for Gene Kelly to Dance To. Carl Sandburg. AiP
Spring isn't ev'rything, it's true. Spring Isn't Everything. Harry Warren. ReLy
Spring Joy Praising God. Catharina Regina von Greiffenberg. AuPH; GePo, *tr.* by George C. Schoolfield
Spring-Joy Praising God; Praise of the Sun. Catharina Regina von Greiffenberg. WPOW, *tr.* by George C. Schoolfield
Spring Landscape. Augusta Peaux. TuT, *tr.* by Tony Curtis
Spring lingers on, The. Richard Wright. APT-2
Spring Longing. Amy Lowell. APT-1
Spring moon, The. (LL) Springtime, The. Denise Levertov. CoAP; CoAmPo
Spring moon. Basho. Spl
Spring moonrise. Haiku. Lenard D. Moore. SpirFl
Spring Morning. Ch'en Yü-i. OHMPC, *tr.* by Kenneth Rexroth
Spring Morning. D. H. Lawrence. MoBrPo

Spring, my dear, The. Out of Tune. William Ernest Henley. MoBrPo
Spring Night. Hagiwara Sakutaro. PFTM-1
Spring night. Masaoka Shiki. OHMPJ
Spring Night. Su Tung-p'o (Su Shih). CoBCP, *tr.* by Burton Watson
Spring Night. Sara Teasdale. MoAmPo
Spring Night, A—Rejoicing in Rain. Tu Fu. SuSp, *tr.* by William H. Nienhauser
Spring Night at Bamboo Pavillion, Presenting a Poem to Subprefect Qian about His Staying for Good in Blue Field Mountains. Wang Wei. WoPoe, *tr.* by Willis Barnstone, Tony Barnstone and Xu Haixin
Spring Night in Lo-Yang—Hearing a Flute. Li Po. CoBCP; TTTS, *tr.* by Burton Watson
Spring Night in Shokoku-ji, A. Gary Snyder. VGW *Fr.* Four Poems for Robin.
Spring night's, The. Fujiwara no Teika. OHMPJ
Spring 1942. Roy Fuller. OxBTC
Spring Nocturne. Abraham Liessin. TrJP
Spring of the Thief. John Logan. NNaP
Spring of Work Storm. Joseph Ceravolo. FTOS
Spring Offensive. Wilfred Owen. GTBS-P; PeFWW
Spring Offensive of the Snail, The. Marge Piercy. TAP
Spring omnipotent goddess thou dost. E. E. Cummings. NBLV; OxBA
Spring on the Coast. Leonidas of Tarentum. GrAn, *tr.* by Clive Sansom
Spring one hundred years ago. Spring. Shinkichi Takahashi. ZenPo, *tr.* by Takashi Ikemoto and Lucien Stryk
Spring Pastoral. Elinor Wylie. TCAPo
Spring Peepers. Joseph Bruchac. PoCoUp
Spring plain / Gulped. Yamei. ZenPo, *tr.* by Takashi Ikemoto and Lucien Stryk
Spring Poem, The. Dave Jeddie Smith. PoPoPo
Spring Pools. Robert Frost. APT-1; ColAP; NAAL-2v2; NOBA; NoAM; OxBA
Spring Prospect. Tu Fu. CoBCP, *tr.* by Burton Watson
Spring quickly passes. Yosano Akiko. ErotSp, *tr.* by Sam Hamill
Spring Quiet. Christina Georgina Rossetti. GTBS-P; PoE; WPE *Fr.* Spring Fancies.
Spring rain. Basho. EH, *tr.* by Robert Hass
Spring Rain. Ch'in Kuan. SuSp, *tr.* by Stephen West
Spring Rain. Robert Hass. BodElec
Spring Rain. William Hawkins. MoCV
Spring rain. Issa. EH, *tr.* by Robert Hass
Spring Rain. Li Shang-yin. ChinPo, *tr.* by Yip Wai-lim
Spring Rain. Li Shang-yin. CoBCP, *tr.* by Burton Watson
Spring Rain. Tu Fu. OHMPC, *tr.* by Kenneth Rexroth
Spring rain! And as yet. Buson. TAL
Spring returns to Peach Blossom River. Heading South. Tu Fu. CrYelRi, *tr.* by Sam Hamill
Spring—River—Flower—Moon—Night. T'ang Yin.
"Fog of night envelops the flowering trees, The." CoBLCP
Spring River Flowers Moon Night. Emperor Yang of Sui. OHMPC, *tr.* by Kenneth Rexroth
Spring roses, autumn fruits, and summer grain. *Unknown.* PriapPo, *tr.* by Richard W. Hooper *Fr.* Priapus Poems, The.
Spring's dewy hand on this fair summit weaves. Written in Farm Wood, South Downs, in May 1784. Charlotte Smith. RWP
Spring's end: washing in clear water. Third Day of the Third Month at the Meandering River, The. Yu Ch'an. ChinPo, *tr.* by Yip Wai-lim
Spring's Last Drop, The. Catherine Obianuju Acholonu. HAWP; NAfrP
Spring's second month. Things Seen on Spring Days. Yüan Mei. CoBLCP, *tr.* by Jonathan Chaves
Spring's sun has just turned, the year's about to end. New Year's Eve. Yang Wen-li. WoPoe, *tr.* by Nancy Hodes and Tung Yuan-fang
Spring's sweet attendant! modest simple flower. To a Violet. Susan Evance. CenSon
Spring's Welcome. John Lyly. *See* Alexander and Campaspe
Spring said nothing to me—it couldn't. Georgy [*or* Georgii] Vladimirovich Ivanov. TCRP
Spring scarlet of the forest blossoms fades and falls, The. Tune: "Crows Crying at Night." Li Yü. SuSp, *tr.* by Daniel Bryant
Spring Scene. Buson. TTTS, *tr.* by Harold Henderson and Kenneth Koch
Spring Scene. Su Tung-p'o (Su Shih). TAL
Spring Scene. Tu Fu. ChinPo, *tr.* by Yip Wai-lim
Spring sea rising, The. Buson. EH, *tr.* by Robert Hass
Spring Sentiments. Chao Yi. SuSp, *tr.* by Chang Yin-nan
Spring Shade. Robert Fitzgerald. APT-2
Spring shakes the windows; doors whang to. Spring Wind, A. Bernard Spencer. GTBS-P
Spring / slips / silent / snowdrops. Spring. Hugo Majer. Spl

Spring Snow and Tui. Mary Ursula Bethell. PeNZ

Spring Song. Peter Fallon. CIP-2; PBCIP

Spring Song. Federico García Lorca. SpanPo, tr. by Rachel Benson and Robert O'Brien

Spring Song. Hermann Hesse. AWP, tr. by Ludwig Lewisohn

Spring Song. John Milton. MLL, tr. by Helen Waddell

Spring Song. Nahum. TrJP, tr. by Emma Lazarus

Spring Song. Unknown. OBVE, tr. by Frances Densmore

Spring Song. William of Aquitaine. NAWM-7v1, tr. by Peter Dronke

Spring Song from "Tzu-Yeh" Songs of the Four Seasons. Unknown. ChinPo, tr. by Yip Wai-lim

Spring Song of A Civil Servant. James Keir Baxter. PeLV

Spring Song of the Birds. James I, King of Scotland. OBEV

Spring Song of Tzu-yeh, A. Hsiao Yen. SuSp, tr. by Jan W. Walls

Spring Sorrow. Chin Ch'ang-hsü. OHMPC, tr. by Kenneth Rexroth

Spring stirs slowly, shuffles, hops;. Season Song. Judith Nicholls. Spl

Spring Storm. Johanna Rayl. PasH

Spring storm shakes the old peach tree, A. Garden Note I, Los Altos. Janet Lewis. APT-2

Spring Strains. William Carlos Williams. APT-1; TCAPo

Spring Street Bar. Mei-Mei Berssenbrugge. WPOW

Spring Sun. Chu Hsi. OHPC, tr. by Kenneth Rexroth

Spring that I was six I found in the woods, The. Paul Smyth. CRP Fr. Frame for the Angels, A.

Spring. The golfball head. Bash on Basho: Six of the Best. Geoffrey Holloway. NLP

Spring the purple Violet. (LL) Upon Prue [or Prew], His Maid. Robert Herrick. BeJo; CaPo; NAEL-5v1; NAEL-6v1; NAEL-7v1; NPeEn; PAI

Spring, the Sweet Spring. Thomas Nashe [or Nash]. NAEL-5v1; NAEL-6v1; NoP-4; NoSic; TFi Fr. Summer's Last Will and Testament.

Spring Thoughts. Li Po. WoPoe, tr. by Elling O. Eide

Spring Thoughts Sent to Tzu-an. Yü Hsüan-chi. BoWoP; WoPoe, tr. by Geoffrey Waters

Spring-Tide. Unknown. See Lenten Is [or Ys] Come [with Love to Toune]

Spring Time. John Milton. MLL, tr. by Helen Waddell

Spring Trances in the Control Emerald Night. Christopher Dewdney. "August a haze amniotic our dream aether and lens of distance. Tree sentinels in." FTOS

Spring twilight. Noin. OHMPJ

Spring under a Thorn, The. Unknown. MiEL

Spring up, O well--sing ye unto it. Bible, O.T. TrJP Fr. Numbers.

Spring Vacation, The. Derek Mahon. PNI

Spring View. Tran Nhan-tong. WoPoe, tr. by Nguyen Ngoc Bich

Spring View. Tu Fu. ColAnChi, tr. by Gary Snyder

Spring Vigil in the Imperial Chancellery. Tu Fu. ChinPo, tr. by Yip Wai-lim

Spring Vista from the Tower of Illuminated Distance. Li Meng-yang. CoBLCP, tr. by Jonathan Chaves

Spring Voices. Louis MacNeice. Son

Spring Walk to the Pavilion of Good Crops and Peace. Ou-yang Hsiu. OHPC, tr. by Kenneth Rexroth

Spring was coming, brimful. Yellow Spring. Juan Ramón Jiménez. SpanPo, tr. by Angel Flores

Spring Waters. "Ping Hsin." "In shaping the snow into blossoms." BoWoP; WPOW "O, Lord/ If in life eternal." WPOW

Spring waters run north and south from here. To a Guest. Tu Fu. CrYelRi, tr. by Sam Hamill

Spring we don't see, The. Basho. EH, tr. by Robert Hass

Spring we went into the heat of lilacs. For My Father. Philip Schultz. TaR

Spring—where has it come from. Song of Spring. Wu Chün. CoBCP, tr. by Burton Watson

Spring Whistles. Lucy Larcom. OBCA

Spring Will Be a Little Late This Year. Frank Loesser. ReLy

Spring will be reborn under our bright steps. (LL) Vultures, The. David Diop. PBA; TTY; WoPoe, tr. by Ulli Beier and Gerald Moore

Spring will meet this year. Gosen. JDP, tr. by Yoel Hoffmann

Spring Wind, A. Bernard Spencer. GTBS-P

Spring wind in North Park. Tune: "Courtyard Full of Fragrance, The." Huang T'ing-chien. ColAnChi, tr. by J. R. Hightower

Spring wind on the Bowery, A. Spring. Lola Ridge. WPE

Spring Wind on the Riverbank at Kema. Buson. EH, tr. by Robert Hass

Spring wind, proud rider! To the Tune "Shui hsien-tzu." Ma Chih-yüan. CoBLCP, tr. by Jonathan Chaves

Spring wind raises fine dust from the road, The. Su Tung-p'o (Su Shih). See East wind stirs fine dust on the roads

Spring wind will never reach, The. Answer to Ting Yuan Ch'en, An. Ou-yang Hsiu. OHPC, tr. by Kenneth Rexroth

Spring winds perfume the shop. Saying Good-bye in a Ch'in-ling Wineshop. Li Po. CrYelRi, tr. by Sam Hamill

Springfield Mountain. Unknown. TCAPo

Springtime. "Rubén Darío." TCLAP, tr. by Lysander Kemp

Springtime. Nikki Giovanni. TLR

Springtime. Norman Henry Pritchard, II. GT

Springtime, The. Denise Levertov. CoAP; CoAmPo

Springtime—and the green willow catkins. To the Tune "Bamboo at West Lake." Shen Chou. CoBLCP, tr. by Jonathan Chaves

Springtime at Twilight. Michael S. Smith. PasH

Springtime Cometh, The. Sammy Fain. ReLy

Springtime Embroidery. Yang Chi. CoBLCP, tr. by Jonathan Chaves Fr. Paintings of Ladies Engaged in Four Springtime Occupations.

Springtime It Brings On the Shearing, The. E. J. Overbury. NOBAu

Springtime of low walls and flowery darkness. In Harmony with Kao "The Second" Ch'i's Poem "On Hearing a P'i-p'a Played Next Door." Hsü Pen. CoBLCP, tr. by Jonathan Chaves

Springtime Sleep. Meng Hao Jan. ChinPo, tr. by Yip Wai-lim

Springtime sleep: too deep to know dawn. Springtime Sleep. Meng Hao Jan. ChinPo, tr. by Yip Wai-lim

Springtime South of the Yangtze. K'o Chun. CrYelRi, tr. by Sam Hamill

Springtime South of the Yangtze. Li Po. CrYelRi, tr. by Sam Hamill

Sprinkle water wide / For the sparrow. Kikaku. ZenPo, tr. by Takashi Ikemoto and Lucien Stryk

Sprinkler had come out on the road with a green hiss, The. Aridness of Air, The. Silvio Giussani. ItPo, tr. by Gayle Ridinger

Sprinkler twirls, The. John Updike. OBCA Fr. Child's Calendar, A.

Sprinter from Carmarthen disgorges, The. Intercity, Swansea-London. Jon Dressel. TCAWP

Spritely Dead, The. Oscar Williams. Son Fr. Variations on a Theme.

Spruce. Phillip [or "Phil"] William George. VoR

Spry, wry, and gray as these March sticks. Among the Narcissi. Sylvia Plath. FaBoMo; RB; SCV

Spuds. Brian Daldorph. SpudSo

Spunk Talking. Anne Rouse. MFPA; NeBl

Spur, The. W. B. Yeats. OxAEP-2; WeW-3

Spur of Love, The. Hugh MacDiarmid. OxBEV

Spurskricksspurskricksspurskricksspurskricksspurskni. My Knicks Are Going to Beat Your Spurs—NBA Souvenir Bracelet 1999 for My Long Distance Love. Catherine Bowman. MoASP

Spurt of Blood, The. Antonin Artaud. PFTM-1

Spy bears his bald intent like a maniac, The. John Tranter. CBAP Fr. Crying in Early Infancy.

Spyglass Conversations. Unknown. STP, tr. by Frances Densmore

Squabbling gods the fight forsake, The. Thomas Bridges. FaBoWar Fr. Homer Travestie.

Squadrons swoop down, shrieking. Invaders from South of the Border Imperil Native Population. Charles Harper Webb. GeoHom

Squalid, empty-headed hen, A. Hen under Bay-Tree. Ruth Pitter. OxBTC

Squalid street after squalid street. Great Industrial Centre, A. Edith Nesbit. VWP

Squall. Stanley Moss. CoAP

Squander for me no scent of myrrh. Epitaph on a Tomb near Rome. Unknown. GrAn, tr. by Frank Kuenstler

Square. Rob MacKenzie. Oth

Square along the couch, and stark. George Meredith. PeVV Fr. Nuptials of Attila, The.

Square as a seed-box, in their attic stands. Handloom, The. Judith Rodriguez. FaBoWP

Square of the Holy Passion, gaze on the demonstrators. Natalya [or Natal'ia] Gorbanevskaya [or Gorbanyevskaya or Gorbanevskaia]. TCRusP, tr. by Daniel Weissbort

Square, squat room (a cellar on promotion), A. William Ernest Henley. NAEL-5v2; NAEL-6v2; NOBVV; NPeEn Fr. In Hospital.

Squares. Pierre Reverdy. PFTM-1

Squares and Courtyards. Marilyn Hacker. WiU

Squaring the Names. Diana García. TouFir

Squarings. Seamus Heaney. "Be literal a moment. Recollect." PoetW "Deserted harbour stillness. Every stone." PoetW "Roof it down. Batten down. Dig in." PoetW "Visible sea at a distance from the shore, The." PoetW

Squat in swamp shadows. Gary Snyder. NOBA; NeAP; PoM Fr. Myths and Texts.

Squat man under the hoop, The. Winter Ball. August Kleinzahler. MoASP

Squats on a toad-stool under a tree. Thomas Lovell Beddoes. NOBVV; OxBEV Fr. Death's Jest Book.

Squatter in the Foreground. Kenward Elmslie. FTOS

Squatting a day in the sun.   Fire in the Hole.   Gary Snyder.   NAAL-2v2
Squeal.   Louis Simpson.   UnPo
Squealing under city stone.   Rapid Transit.   James Agee.   MoAmPo
Squeeze.   Abigail Child.   FTOS
Squeeze Play.   Phyllis McGinley.   FaBoEE; OBCoV; OBSV   *Fr.* Spectator's Guide to Contemporary Art.
Squeezes.   Brian Patten.   OTCP; Spl
Squid seller's call, The.   Basho.   EH, *tr. by* Robert Hass
Squinting against neon signs.   Eclipse.   Anita Endrezze.   CDW
Squinting though eye-slits in our balaclavas.   Crossing the Square.   Grace Schulman.   ExTi
Squire and Milkmaid; or, Blackberry Fold.   *Unknown.*   OxBB
Squire he had whose name was Ralph, A.   Samuel Butler (1612–80).   NOBE   *Fr.* Hudibras.
Squire is in his library, The. He is rather worried.   Send for Lord Timothy.   John Heath-Stubbs.   OxBC
Squire Meldrum at Carrickfergus.   Sir David Lindsay [*or* Lyndsay].   OxBS   *Fr.* Historie of Squyer William Meldrum, The.
Squire nagged and bullied till I went to fight.   Memorial Tablet.   Siegfried Sassoon.   PoWW
Squire's Pew, The.   Jane Taylor.   PEW
Squire sat alone beside the board, The.   Little Fay's Thanksgiving.   Henrietta Cordelia Ray.   CBWP-3
Squire Squint, shooting at a pheasant.   G. J. Blundell.   UV
Squirrel, The.   Saleem Barakat.   MAP, *tr. by* Lena Jayyusi and Naomi Shihab Nye
Squirrel, The.   *Unknown.*   OxNR
Squirrel crosses / my way while on a trip, A.   If.   Jared Angira.   PBMAP
Squirrel in his shirt, The.   Ground-Squirrel Song.   *Navajo Oral Tradition.*   TTTS
Squirrel near Library.   Genevieve Taggard.   WPE
Sri Nityananda Mandir (The Temple of Nityananda).   Elsa Cross.   TANSG, *tr. by* Patricia Dubrava
Sssnnnwhufffll?   Loch Ness Monster's Song, The.   Edwin Morgan.   NePenScot; OPOU
Sssssoundcheck.   Doggin the Rockman.   Paul Beatty.   InTrad
St. Agnes' Eve.   Tennyson.   OBEV; SacPr
St Andrew's Day, blind November fumbling.   St. Andrew's Day.   Robert Greacen.   PNI
St. Andrew's Voyage to Mermedonia.   *Unknown.*   AnOE, *tr. by* Charles W. Kennedy   *Fr.* Andreas.
St Andrews town may look right gawsy.   To the Principal and Professors of the University of St Andrews, on their Superb Treat to Dr Samuel Johnson.   Robert Fergusson.   NePenScot
St. Anthony and His Pig; a Cantata.   Frederick Forrest.   NOEC
St. Anzas VI.   B. P. Nichol.   FTOS
St. Anzas IX.   B. P. Nichol.   FTOS
St. Asaph's.   Kingsley Amis.   OxBTC
St. Aubin d'Aubigne.   Paul Dehn.   OBWP
St Bees in Winter.   William Scammell.   NLP
St Bride's.   Kathleen Jamie.   NePenScot
St. Bridget's Cross.   Anne Hartigan.   CIP-2
St Cecilia's Day Epigram.   Peter Porter.   PeLV
St Christopher.   Austin Clarke.   ModIr
St. Clare's Underwear.   Barbara Hamby.   ReTh
St. Columcille the Scribe.   Saint Columcille [*or* Columba].   BIrV
St. David's Head.   Sir Lewis Morris.
  "Salt sprays deluge it, wild waves buffet it, hurricanes rave."   AngWePo
St. Francis and the Nun.   Carl Dennis.   KGB
St. Francis Speaks to Me at a Young Age.   Vic Coccimiglio.   InvLad
St. Gervais.   Michael Roberts.   FaBoCh
St Jerome in his study kept a great big cat.   St Jerome and His Lion.   *Unknown.*   TriCat
St. John.   Bible, *N.T.*
  "I am the true vine, and my Father is the husbandman."   OBVE
  "In the beginnin o aa things the Wurd wis there ense."   FaBoVe
  John 3; But Men Loved Darknesse Rather than Light.   ChIV-2, *tr. by* Richard Crashaw
St. John.   Jorge Luis Borges.
  John 1:14; And the Word became flesh and dwelt among us.   GI
St. John.   Mary Elizabeth Fullerton.
  John 14:1–2.   GI
  "Let not your heart be troubled."   GI
St. John.   Gail Holst-Warhaft.
  "In the beginning was the Word."   GI
  John 1:1 and 14.   GI
St. John.   Nina Kossman.
  John 13:21–30; When Jesus had thus said, he was troubled.   GI

St. John.   Howard Nemerov.
  John 3:1–15; Now there was a man.   GI
St. John.   Pier Paolo Pasolini.
  John 12:24–25; Truly, truly, I say to you.   GI
St. John.   Rainer Maria Rilke.
  John 2:1–12; On the third day there was a marriage.   GI
  John 11:30–44; Now Jesus had not yet come to the village.   GI
  John 20:11–18; But Mary stood weeping outside the tomb.   GI
St John of the Cross: Song of the Soul That Is Glad to Know God by Faith.   Roy Campbell.   PeECV
St John of the Cross: Songs of the Soul in Rapture.   Roy Campbell.   PeECV
St Kilda.   Neil Curry.   NLP
St Kilda's Parliament: 1879–1979.   Douglas Dunn.   NePenScot
St. Lawrence and the Saguenay.   Charles Sangster.
  Thousand Islands, The.   NOBC
St. Louis.   Amy Lowell.   NAAL-5
St. Louis Cemetery Crypt.   Kalamu ya Salaam.   SpirFl   *Fr.* New Orleans Haiku.
St. Luke.   W. H. Auden.
  Luke 23:26–38; And as they led him away.   GI
St. Luke.   Bible, *N.T.*
  "And it came to pass in those days, that there went out a decree from Caesar Augustus."   NAWM-5v1
  ("And Marie said, My soule doth magnifie the Lord.")   OBVE
  Blessed be the Paps which Thou hast Sucked.   ChIV-2; NOSC, *tr. by* Richard Crashaw
  "Feare not, litle flocke, for it is your fathers good pleasure to give you the kingdome."   OBVE
  "Her eyes flood lickes his feets faire staine."   NOSC; SacPr, *tr. by* Richard Crashaw
  Luke 7; She Began To Wash His Feet with Teares and Wipe Them with the Haires of Her Head.   NOSC; SacPr, *tr. by* Richard Crashaw
  Magnificat, The.   BoWoP
  "Suppose he had been Tabled at thy Teates."   ChIV-2; NOSC, *tr. by* Richard Crashaw
  "Then drew near unto him all the publicans and sinners."   NAWM-5v1
St. Luke.   Jorge Luis Borges.
  Luke 23:39–43; One of the criminals.   GI
St. Luke.   Bertolt Brecht.
  Luke 2:8–20; And in that region there were shepherds.   GI
St. Luke.   Ernesto Cardenal.
  Luke 16:1–9; He also said to the disciples.   GI
St. Luke.   T. S. Eliot.
  Luke 2:21–40; And at the end of eight days, when he was circumcised.   GI
St. Luke.   Robert Frost.
  Luke 16:19–26; "There was a rich man."   GI
St. Luke.   Louise Glück.
  Luke 2:1–7; In those days a decree went out from Caesar Augustus.   GI
St. Luke.   Alec Derwent Hope.
  Luke 24:36–49; As they were saying this, Jesus.   GI
St. Luke.   Anna Kamienska.
  Luke 1:26–38; In the sixth month the angel Gabriel.   GI
  Luke 10:38–42; Now as they went on their way.   GI
St. Luke.   Czeslaw Milosz.
  Luke 5:1–11; While the people pressed upon him.   GI
St. Luke.   Stephen Mitchell.
  Luke 10:25–37; And behold, a lawyer.   GI
St. Luke.   Eric Pankey.
  Luke: 24:13–32; That very day two of them.   GI
St. Luke.   Rainer Maria Rilke.
  Luke 1:39–56; In those days Mary arose.   GI
  Luke 15:11–19; And he said, "There was a man."   GI
St. Luke.   Edwin Arlington Robinson.
  Luke 15:20–32; And he arose and came.   GI
St. Mark.   Bible, *N.T.*
  "Aa this while, Peter wis doun ablò i the yaird."   FaBoVe
  "And he said, So is the kingdome of God."   OBVE
  And he said, So soule doth magnifie the Lord.   OBVE
St. Mark.   Czeslaw Milosz.
  Mark 5:21–43; And when Jesus had crossed.   GI
St. Mark.   Boris Leonidovich Pasternak.
  Mark 14:26–42; And when they had sung.   GI
St. Matthew.   Philip Appleman.
  Matthew 1:18–25: Now the birth of Jesus Christ took place.   GI
St. Matthew.   Bible, *N.T.*
  "And seeing the multitudes, he went up."   NAWM-5v1

Beatitudes, The. OBVE

("Father our, he-who is at-the-height, name Thy let-it-be.") PeSAV

"In the end of the sabbath, as it began to dawn toward the first day of the week." NAWM-5v1

"No man can serve two masters." OBVE

Parable of the Good Seed, The. InPK-6

"Then one of the twelve, called Judas Iscariot." NAWM-5v1

"When morning has come, all the chief priests and elders of the people." NAWM-5v1

St. Matthew. Jorge Luis Borges.
Matthew 5:1–12; Seeing the crowds, he went up on the mountain. GI
Matthew 25:14–30; "For it will be as when a man." GI

St. Matthew. René Daumal.
Matthew 27:11–24; Now Jesus stood before. GI

St. Matthew. T. S. Eliot.
Matthew 2:1–12; Now when Jesus was born. GI

St. Matthew. Jacob Glatstein [or Glatsteyn].
Matthew 5:38–48; "You have heard that it was said, 'An eye.'" GI

St. Matthew. Donald Hall.
Matthew 21:18–22; In the morning. GI

St. Matthew. Julia Hartwig.
Matthew 2:16–18; Then Herod, when he saw. GI

St. Matthew. Zbigniew Herbert.
Matthew 27:3–10; When Judas, his betrayer, saw. GI

St. Matthew. Gail Holst-Warhaft.
Matthew 5:13; You are the salt of the earth. GI
Matthew 5:27–30; You have heard that it was said. GI

St. Matthew. Ted Hughes.
Matthew 27:45–56; Now from the sixth hour there was darkness. GI

St. Matthew. Anna Kamienska.
Matthew 19:16–24; And behold, one came up to him. GI

St. Matthew. Karl Kirchwey.
Matthew 8:20; And Jesus said to him. GI

St. Matthew. Philip Larkin.
Matthew 10:1. GI

St. Matthew. D. H. Lawrence.
Matthew 6:7–15; "And in praying do not heap up empty." GI

St. Matthew. Desanka Maksimovic.
Matthew 22:15–22; Then the Pharisees went and. GI

St. Matthew. Czeslaw Milosz.
Matthew 4:1–11; Then Jesus was led up by the spirit. GIt
Matthew 28:1–6; Now after the sabbath. GI

St. Matthew. Stephen Mitchell.
Matthew 13:1–9; That same day Jesus. GI

St. Matthew. Boris Leonidovich Pasternak.
Matthew 21:1–11. GI
Matthew 26:47–56; While he was still speaking, Judas came. GI

St. Matthew. Rainer Maria Rilke.
Matthew 26:17–29. GIh
Matthew 27:57–61; When it was evening, there came a rich man. GI

St. Matthew. Edwin Arlington Robinson.
Matthew 22:1–14; And again Jesus spoke to them. GI

St. Matthew. Theodore Roethke.
Matthew 7:1–2; "Judge not, that you be not" GI

St. Matthew. Richard Wilbur.
Matthew 8:28–34; And when he came to the other side. GI

St. Matthew. W. B. Yeats.
Matthew 24:15–31. GI
Matthew 28:16–20; Now the eleven disciples went to Galilee. GI

St. Matthew; He also told them a parable. William Carlos Williams.
Luke 6:39. GI

St Merri district, The. Robert Desnos. MFP, tr. by Martin Sorrell

St. Michael's Square in night so deep. Night Walk Through the Burg. Hans Just. AuPH, tr. by Lowell A. Bangerter

St. Patrick's Hymn Before Tara. James Clarence Mangan.
"Christ, as a light." SacPr

St. Paul's Steeple. Unknown. LB; OxNR

St. Peter and the Angel. Denise Levertov. SacPr

St Sava's Forge. Vasco [or Vasko] Popa. PoSu, tr. by Anne Pennington Fr. St Sava's Spring.

St Sava's Journey. Vasco [or Vasko] Popa. PoSu; WoPoe, tr. by Anne Pennington Fr. St Sava's Spring.

St Sava's Spring. Vasco [or Vasko] Popa.
"From the besieged hills." PoSu, tr. by Anne Pennington
"He journeys over the dark land." PoSu; WoPoe, tr. by Anne Pennington

"Hungry and thirsty for holiness." PoSu, tr. by Anne Pennington

Life of St Sava, The. PoSu, tr. by Anne Pennington

St Sava's Forge. PoSu, tr. by Anne Pennington

St Sava's Journey. PoSu; WoPoe, tr. by Anne Pennington

St. Saviour's, Aberdeen Park, Highbury, London, N. Sir John Betjeman. SacPr

St. Sophia. John Fuller. DiPo

St. Stephen's Day. Patric Dickinson. OBCP

St. Stephen's is a stage. Patriot's Progress, The. Horace Twiss. UV

St. Swithin's Day, if thou dost rain. Unknown. LB

St. Thomas's Day. Gillian Clarke. HarvBoo

St. Valentine's Day. Wilfrid Scawen Blunt. EnLoPo Fr. Love Sonnets of Proteus, The.

St. Vincent's. W. S. Merwin. VCAP

Stabbed, clubbed, and slashed, I stand. Wound Man, The. D. A. Feinfeld. BloBone

Stable-lamp is lighted, A. Christmas Hymn, A. Richard Wilbur. ChIV-2; ChrPo; OBCP; TrCP

Stack of summer suits makes a better emblem than a piano, A. Requirements for Suggesting Fats Waller. Connie Deanovich. AmPoNex

Stackalee. Unknown. APN-2

Stacking the Straw. Amy Clampitt. VCAP

Stackolee. Unknown. NAAAL

Stadium, The. William Heyen. MoASP

Staff and slippers hang here, Kypris, A. Leonidas. PGA

Staff slips from the hand, The. Outward. Louis Simpson. EmeKit

Staff[e] is now greased [or greas'd], The. Hag, The. Robert Herrick. CaPo

Stag does not lay his side to sleep. Grania's Song to Diarmuid. Unknown. WoPoe, tr. by Frank O'Connor

Stag lifts his nostrils to the morning, A. Scotland. Frederick Seidel. BodElec

Stag of Irisoda, The. Lajos Áprily. IQMS, tr. by Adam Makkai

Stag on the westward ride, melodious. Unknown. WoPoe, tr. by Austin Clarke Fr. Sweeney Astray.

Stag, the runnable stag, The. (LL) Runnable Stag, A. John Davidson. EBNV; HAP; OBEV; OxBTC

Stag was very proud of his swiftness, The. Ballade 1. Eustache Deschamps. WoPoe, tr. by David Curzon and Jeffrey Fiskin

Stage and Screen, 1989. Carol Muske. BodElec

Stage-Driver's Story, The. Bret Harte. EBNV

Stage Duo. Kenward Elmslie. FTOS

Stage is about to be swept of corpses, The. Horatian Epode to the Duchess of Malfi. Allen Tate. FaBoMo

Stage-lit streets. Allen Ginsberg. NAAL-2v2 Fr. Continuation of a Long Poem of These States.

Stage was set, the house was packed, The. Concert Party: Busseboom. Edmund Charles Blunden. FaBoWar

Stages on a Journey Westward. James Wright (1927–80). LCAP-2

Staggering down the road at midnite. Encounter, The. Paul Blackburn. NeAP

Stagnant pond, A. John Wills. HA

Stagolee. Unknown. OxBoLi; TTY

Stags from the foundry bugle from the front door. Trophy Homes. Bruce Berger. GeoH

Staid schizophrenic named Struther, A. Limerick. Unknown. NIP-4

Stained Glass Window. Adelia Prado. TCLAP, tr. by Marcia Kirinus

Staircase. Marina Ivanovna Tsvetayeva [or Tsvetaeva]. ARWW, tr. by Catriona Kelly

Staircase with a Hundred Steps, The. Benjamin Péret. SPE, tr. by David Gascoyne

Stairs are dark, the steps are high, The. Up in Mabel's Room. Kenneth Slessor. BMAP

Stairway is not, The. Jacob's Ladder, The. Denise Levertov. APSN; ChIV-1; NAAL-5; PFTM-2; PoM

Stairway to Heaven. Robert Creeley. FTOS

Stairway to Paradise. B. G. DeSylva. TCAPo

Stalagmites in spring caves rise to more stalactites. Red Embankment. Tu Mu. ColAnChi; SuSp, tr. by John M. Ortinau

Stalin. Robert Lowell. HCAP

Stalin Epigram, The. Osip Emilevich Mandelstam [or Mandelshtam]. AF; WoPoe, tr. by Clarence Brown and W. S. Merwin

Stalin Moy Golubchik. "Sagittarius." OBCoV

Stalin's falcons proudly soar. Year 1937, The. Timur Kibirov. TCRP, tr. by Vera Dunham

Stalin's Genius. Bruce Andrews. PmAP

Stalin stood committed to peasant hunger. Reply to the Committed Intellectual. Francis Sparshott. NOBC

Stalingrad Theater. Mikhail Kuz'mich Lukonin. TCRP, tr. by Albert C. Todd

Stalker. Jeanne Schinto. Unle

Stalking. Where Seed Falls. Essex Hemphill. GT

Stalking before the lords of life, one came. Circumstance. John Townsend Trowbridge. APN-2

Stall Me Out. Paul Beatty. AmPoNex

Stall so tight he can't raise heels or knees, The. Bronco Busting, Event #1. May Swenson. APT-2

Stalled before my metal shaving mirror. Notes for a Sonnet. "Edward Pygge." OBCoV

Stalled car. Gary Hotham. HA

Stallion, The. "Mikhail Semionovich Golodny [or Golodnyi]. TCRP, tr. by Simon Franklin

Stallion, The. Tudur Aled. OBWVE, tr. by Joseph P. Clancy

Stamp, roar like our Russian poets, like Derzhavin. Ode for the Dancing Khlysty. Yury [or Iurii] Ivask. TCRP; TCRusP, tr. by Alla Burago and Burton Raffel

Stand back, bright morning. Black Song. Amin Nakhla. MAP, tr. by Matthew Sorenson

'Stand back, Tom Devil, I'm gonna rule Hell by myself.' (LL) Stagolee. Unknown. OxBoLi; TTY

Stand back, ye sleeping jacks at home. John Pickering [or Pikerying]. NoSic Fr. Horestes.

Stand by Me. Charles A. Tindley. InvLi; NAAAL

Stand by me, Death, lest these dark days. Three Pleas. Henry Treece. PoWW

Stand by me, stand by me. (LL) Stand by Me. Charles A. Tindley. InvLi; NAAAL

Stand close around, ye Stygian set. Walter Savage Landor. AWP; CTC; EBEV; FaBoEE; HAP; NAEL-6v2; NOBE; NPeEn; NoP-4; OBEV; OxAEP-2; OxBEV; OxBSP; PoRA; SCGP; TFi; WeW-3; WoPoe Fr. Pericles and Aspasia.

Stand fast, my child, and after all. Christopher Smart. ChIV-2 Fr. Hymns for the Amusement of Children.

Stand here, says the professional TV person. Telyric. Andrei Codrescu. PmAP

Stand in a field long enough, and the sounds. Becoming a Redwood. Dana Gioia. GeoHom

Stand in a row and learn. (LL) Drunk in the Furnace, The. W. S. Merwin. NAAL-2v2; NoAM; NoP-4; PoE; TwCP

Stand like a beaten anvil, when thy dream. Anvil, The. Alfred Noyes. SacPr

Stand not uttering sedately. Epitaphium Citharistriae. Victor Gustave Plarr. EnLoPo; NBLV

Stand Not Uttering Sedately. Victor Gustave Plarr. See Epitaphium Citharistriae

Stand off, daughter of the dusk, Gwendolyn Brooks. NALW Fr. Womanhood, The.

Stand off, physician! Let me frolic. On Melancholy. Unknown. NOSC

Stand on the highest pavement of the stair. La Figlia Che Piange. T. S. Eliot. APT-1; FaBoTw; HarvBoo; HeIP-4; OxBEV; OxBTC; TCAPo; UnPo; VGW

Stand [or Stond] who so list upon the slipper top[pe]. Seneca. NPeEn; NoSic; OBVE; OxBEV, tr. by Sir Thomas Wyatt Fr. Thyestes.

Stand out, maids, and look on the land of Cynddylan. Unknown. OBWVE Fr. Elegy on Cynddylan.

Stand out the bright steamers / to kingdom come. (LL) Lawrence Ferlinghetti. BoLoP; PoM

Stand still. In the Fog. Lilian Moore. TLR

Stand Still. Jim Peterson. PoCoUp

Stand- / Still). (LL) E. E. Cummings. EroLit; NOBA; OxBA; PeLV

Stand still, and I will read to thee. Lecture upon the Shadow, A. John Donne. AWP; ESCV; NAEL-5v1; NAEL-6v1; NAEL-7v1; NoSic; SCGP; UnPo

Stand Still, and See. Betty Scott Stam. SacPr

Stand still, yet we will make him run. (LL) To His Coy Mistress. Andrew Marvell. AWP; AmFaPo; BASC; BoLoP; CABP; ClHu; EBEV; ESCV; EnLoPo; EroLit; ErotSp; FHYEP; FSCP; GeHe; HAP; HeIP-4; InPK-6; MeLP; NAEL-5v1; NAEL-6v1; NAEL-7v1; NIL-7; NIP-4; NOBE; NOSC; NPeEn; NoP-4; OBEV; OxAEP-1; OxBEV; PBRV; PoE; PoPoPo; PoRA; SCGP; SCV; TFi; TRP; UV; WoPoe

Stand still, you floods! do[e] not deface. On Sight of a Gentlewoman's Face in the Water. Thomas Carew. CaPo

Stand there just a moment. Moonlight Becomes You. Johnny Burke. ReLy

Stand there, manslaying spear; no longer drip. Anyte [or Anytes]. SaLy, tr. by Diane Rayor

Stand-To, The. Cecil Day Lewis. NoP-4; OBWP

Stand-to: Good Friday Morning. Siegfried Sassoon. FaBoTw

Stand to one side. No, over here with me. Venetian Interior, 1889. Richard Howard. VCAP

Stand Up! D. H. Lawrence. OxBTC

Stand up, be proud. Jim Carlson. IBA

Stand Up! Stand Up for Jesus. George, Jr. Duffield. AH; SacPr; TCAPo

Stand! Who goes there? John Lyly. NoSic; OBCoV Fr. Endimion.

Stand whoso list upon the slipper top. Stand Whoso List. Sir Thomas Wyatt. NAEL-7v1; NoP-4

Stand with thy nose against. Of One That Had a Great Nose. George Turberville. FaBoEE

Stand you here, murdering shaft, no longer. Dedication: A Spear. Anyte [or Anytes]. GrAn, tr. by John Heath-Stubbs and Carol A. Whiteside

Stand your ground, soul. Strong Beams. Mairtin O Direain. ModIr, tr. by Patrick Crotty

Standard Time. Ira Sadoff. BodElec

Standard Time: Novena for My Father. Dionisio D. Martinez. TouFir

Standards of the King go forth, The. Saint Venantius Fortunatus. MLL

Standing all day on Lake View Tower. Written on Lake View Tower. P'an Lang. SuSp, tr. by Jonathan Chaves

Standing alone on the highway. (Here Am I) Broken Hearted. Lew Brown. ReLy

Standing aloof in giant ignorance. To Homer. John Keats. EBEV; NAEL-5v2; NAEL-6v2; NoP-4; Son

Standing at dawn where Union and Burnside. Closer to Home. Floyd Skloot. UrbNat

Standing at my stove, potatoes to be mashed. Simple Thing, A. Leatha Kendrick. SpudSo

Standing at Pasternak's Table, Peredelkino. James Ragan. TWW

Standing beside you, fiddler. Unknown. GrAn

Standing Between Two Ideas. Maurya Simon. InvLad

Standing Coffin. Tamura Ryuichi. AF, tr. by Christopher Drake

Standing corn is green, the wild in flower, The. Nunc Viridant Segetes. Sedulius Scottus. BIrV; NAWM-5v1, tr. by Helen Waddell

Standing erect in the mire. Sketch of the Frontier Woman. Claudia Lars. TCLAP, tr. by Donald D. Walsh

Standing in a stillness that now is yours. (LL) Water Island. Howard Moss. CoAP; NoP-4

Standing in ribbons, over our heads, for an hour. (LL) End of the Picnic. Francis Webb. BMAP; NOBAu

Standing in the Doorway, I Watch the Young Child Sleep. Sharon Hashimoto. FSt; OpBo

Standing in the hall against the wall. Listening to Grownups Quarreling. Ruth Whitman. NTCP

Standing knee-deep in Oak Creek. Dog Days and Delta Nights. Franz Douskey. PasH

Standing on the Corner. Philip Levine. NNaP

Standing Stone. Ruth Bidgood. AngWePo

Standing there they began to grow skins. Pilgrims. Jean Valentine. LCAP-2; TAP

Standing Trains, The. Thomas McCarthy. ModIr

Standing under the greengrocer's awning. Hailstone, The. Peter Didsbury. NPeEn

Standing Up. Tomas Tranströmer. "It's been a hard winter, but summer is here and the fields." RaBo

Standing upon a hill of fancies high. Landscape, A. Margaret Lucas Cavendish, Duchess of Newcastle. NOSC

Standing While We Die. Qasim Haddad. "Book of the defeated man." MAP

Standing, with your back turned, taut at work. Vista. Elizabeth Garrett. NeBl

Standing Worship. Dhabya Khamees. PoArWo, tr. by Clarissa C. Burt

Stands be within me, let me be where it is. (LL) Psalm Concerning the Castle. Denise Levertov. TwCP; WPE

Stands for hope. (LL) Marianne Craig Moore. APT-1; BoWoP; ColAP; FaBoMo; FaBoWP; HAP; HarvBoo; NOBA; NoAM; NoP-4; OxBA; PoPoPo; WPE Fr. Part of a Novel, Part of a Poem, Part of a Play.

Stands the moon, brilliant, cloudless. (LL) Chikako. WPoS; WoPoe, tr. by Edwin A. Cranston

Stanley Matthews. Alan Ross. OxBTC

Stanley Meets Mutesa. James David Rubadiri. PBA

Stanza 10. Gertrude Stein. APT-1 Fr. Stanzas in Meditation.

Stanza: "What, my Lord, shall I do with." Unknown. WoPoe, tr. by Lewis Turco

Stanza Written in Jest. Yang Wan-li. SuSp, tr. by Sherwin S. S. Fu

Stanzas. Thomas Hood. NPeEn

Stanzas. John Keats. OBEV (Happy Insensibility.) GTBS-P

Stanzas. Osip Emilevich Mandelstam [or Mandelshtam]. "And then my country spoke to me." TCRP "And you, my sister Moscow, are at ease." TCRP

Stanzas. Charles Newton. "Fresh were the breathings of the nightborn gale." NOEC Wild Nature. NOEC

Stanzas. Edgar Allan Poe. NCAP

Stanzas Against Forgetting. Guillaume Apollinaire. AF, *tr. by* Carolyn Forché

Stanzas: "Ah! think'st thou, Laura, then, that wealth." Charlotte Smith. NoP-4

Stanzas—April, 1814. Shelley. SCGP

(Remorse.) OBEV

Stanzas: "Black absence hides upon the past." John Clare. EnLoPo; NOBVV

Stanzas Concerning an Ecstasy Experienced in High Contemplation. Saint John of the Cross. TOF, *tr. by* K. Kavanaugh and O. Rodrigues

Stanzas Concerning Love. Stefan George. AWP, *tr. by* Ludwig Lewisohn

Stanzas for an Imaginary Garden. Octavio Paz. OBGa

Stanzas for Music. Byron. HAP; NOBRP; NPeEn

(Youth and Age.) GTBS-P

Stanzas for Music. Byron. AWP; GTBS-P; HAP; NAEL-5v2; NAEL-6v2; OxBSP; PoRA

(They say that Hope is happiness.) NAEL-6v2

Stanzas from the Grande Chartreuse. Matthew Arnold. EBVV; NAEL-5v2; NAEL-6v2; PoE

"For rigorous teachers seized my youth." FHYEP

Stanzas: "How often we forget all time, when lone." Edgar Allan Poe. APN-1

Stanzas: "How smooth that lake expands its ample breast!" Ann Radcliffe. WPE

Stanzas: "I'll not weep that thou art going to leave me." Emily Jane Brontë. WPE

Stanzas Imitated From Psalm CXIX. Thomas Warton, the Elder. ChIV-1

Stanzas in Bloomsbury. Richard Howard. MakPoe

Stanzas in Meditation. Gertrude Stein.

Stanza 10. APT-1

Stanzas in Meditation. Gertrude Stein.

From Stanzas in Meditation. NoP-4

Stanzas: "In this vain, busy world, where the good and the gay." Mary Robinson. ECWP; WoRP

Stanzas Occasioned by the Ruins of a Country Inn *or* On the Ruins of a Country Inn. Philip Freneau. OxBA

Stanzas of the Graves, The. *Unknown.*

"Graves the rain makes wet and sleek, The." OBWVE

Stanzas of the Soul that Suffers with Longing to See God. Saint John of the Cross. TOF, *tr. by* K. Kavanaugh and O. Rodrigues

Stanzas: "Often rebuked, yet always back returning." Emily Jane Brontë. NALW; NOBVV; OBEV; OxBEV; PEW; SCGP; VWP

Stanzas: "Oh, come to me in dreams, my love!" Mary Wollstonecraft Shelley. LW

Stanzas on Charles Armitage Brown. John Keats. UV

Stanzas on Mutability. Hugo von Hofmannsthal. AWP; TrJP, *tr. by* Jethro Bithell

Stanzas on the Death of Mrs Hemans. Letitia [*or* Laetitia] Elizabeth Landon. VWP *Fr.* New Monthly Magazine, 44 286–8.

Stanzas on the Psalms. Thomas Warton, the Elder. ChIV-1

Stanzas: "Passing of a dream, The." John Clare. NOBVV

Stanzas Subjoined to the Yearly Bill of Mortality of the Parish of All Saints, Northampton; for the Year 1787. William Cowper. NOCV

Stanzas to———. Emily Jane Brontë. WPE

(Well, some may hate and some may scorn.) VWP

Stanzas to the Memory of the Late King. Felicia Dorothea Hemans. RWP

Stanzas to the Speaker Asleep. Winthrop Mackworth Praed. OBSV

Stanzas: "When a man hath no freedom to fight for at home." Byron. FaBoEE; NAEL-5v2; NAEL-6v2; NBLV; NoP-4; OxAEP-2; PAI; TRP

Stanzas: "With tears thy grief thou dost bemoan." Solomon ibn Gabirol. TrJP, *tr. by* Emma Lazarus

Stanzas: "With youthful loss of memory, in my voiceless land." Viktor Korkiya [*or* Korkiia]. TCRP, *tr. by* Vera Dunham

Stanzas Written between Dover and Calais, in July, 1792. Martha Robinson. ECWP

Stanzas Written in Dejection, near Naples [*or*—December 1818, near Naples]. Shelley. GTBS-P; NAEL-5v2; NAEL-6v2; NAWM-7v2; NoP-4; PoRA

Stanzas Written in London in 1773. Edward Williams.

"Why, Cambria did I quit thy shore." AngWePo

Stanzas Written on the Road between Florence and Pisa. Byron. NAEL-5v2; NAEL-6v2

(All for Love.) GTBS-P

(O talk not to me of a name great in story.) GTBS-P

Star. Pavel Davydovich Kogan. TCRP, *tr. by* Albert C. Todd

Star, A. Federico García Lorca. PFTM-1

Star, The. Jane Taylor. NOBRP; NOxBChV; NTCP; OTCP; OxBEV; OxNR; UV

(Twinkle Twinkle Little Star.) ChAP

Star & Garter Theater. Dennis Schmitz. LCAP-2

Star and Sea. William Peskett. PNI

Star Blanket. Ray A. Young Bear. CDW

Star burns out over the tree tops, The. Aleksandr Semionovich Kushner. TCRusP, *tr. by* Daniel Weissbort

Star Child. Thomas Sayers Ellis. NeAmPo

Star crashes in a small plaza and a bird loses its eyes, A. Things I Say Are True, The. Blanca Varela. BoWoP, *tr. by* Donald Yates

Star-crowned solitude of thine oblivious hours!, The. (LL) To One in Bedlam. Ernest Christopher Dowson. GSo; MoBrPo; OBMV; Son

Star Dust. Mitchell Parish. ReLy

Star exploding in the body, The. Cancer and Nova. Hyam Plutzik. AmFaPo

Star-filled seas are smooth to-night, The. Isle of Portland, The. A. E. Housman. MoBrPo

Star-Fix. Marilyn Nelson Waniek. ESEAA; LTA

Star frightens the steeple cross, A. Guard-Duty. August Stramm. PeFWW, *tr. by* Patrick Bridgwater

Star-Gazer. Louis MacNeice. ModIr; NAEL-5v2; NAEL-6v2; NoP-4

Star-Gazing. Ptolemy. GrAn, *tr. by* Dudley Fitts

Star, / If you are. Christmas Tree, A. William Burford. SoSe-8

Star in a Stoneboat, A. Robert Frost. APT-1

Star is gone, A! a star is gone! Fallen Star, The. George Darley. OBEV

Star Journey. Naomi Long Madgett. BPo

Star light, star bright. Wishing Poem. *Unknown.* NTCP; OxNR

Star looks down at me, A. Waiting Both. Thomas Hardy. MoBrPo; OxBoLi; TTTS

Star Morals. Friedrich Wilhelm Nietzsche. AWP, *tr. by* Ludwig Lewisohn

Star of Evening. Sappho. WoPoe, *tr. by* Paul Roche

Star of Free Will, The. Maria Luisa Spaziani.

"I shall find in paradise that emaciated rose shoot." NeIt

"Sunday in the provinces, a plaintive Norman bell-peal." NeIt

"Traveling with too much baggage is not a good idea." NeIt

Star of the Evening. James M. Sayles. UV

Star of the North! though naught winds drift. Fugitive Slave's Apostrophe to the North Star, The. John Pierpont. APN-1

Star of the sea, surest point of brightness. Stella Maris. O. B. Hardison, Jr. CRP

Star over all. Christmas Tree. Laurence Smith. OBCP

Star Quilt. Roberta Hill Whiteman. CDW; NoAM

Star's Whole Secret, The. Mary Jo Bang. NAPBL

Star Song. Henrietta Cordelia Ray. CBWP-3

Star-Spangled. Michele Glazer. OPRER

Star-Spangled Banner, The. Francis Scott Key. AiP; HHAm; TAP; UV

(Defense of Fort McHenry.) APN-1; NoP-4

(O! say can you see, by the dawn's early light.) NoP-4

Star-Struck Utopias of 2000. "Antler." PoCoUp

Star System, The. Richard Wilbur. NBLV *Fr.* Flippancies.

Star-Talk. Robert Graves. MoBrPo; OxBTC

Star That Bids the Shepherd Fold, The. John Milton. FaBoCh; NPeEn; OBEV *Fr.* Comus; a Masque Presented at Ludlow Castle.

Star that bringest home the bee. To the Evening Star. Thomas Campbell. GTBS-P; NePenScot

Star Trek III. Richard Harteis. GLP

Star-Tribes, The. *Aborigine Oral Tradition.* NOBAu, *tr. by* Fred Biggs

Star Watcher, The. Peter Davison. TwCP; YaYoPo

Star Wish. *Unknown. See* Wishing Poem

Stardust Sequence, The. Dermot Bolger.

"Last night in swirling colour we daced again." BiHa

Stare at the stars, the stars say. Look at me. Ego. Norman MacCaig. GTBS-P

Stare from your pillow into the sun. People of Unrest. Margaret Walker Alexander. GT

Stare's Nest by My Window, The. W. B. Yeats. BIrV; GTBS-P; NOBE *Fr.* Meditations in Time of Civil War.

Stared, astonied all. È, the Feasting Florentines. Daniel Gerard Hoffman. VGW

Stared Story, A. William Stafford. Son

Starfish. Lorna Dee Cervantes. TouFir

Starfish. Eric Ormsby. NoP-4

Starfish Waving to Me from the Sand. Matthew Rohrer. NAPBL

Staring Aristogoras in the face. To Aristogoras. Meleager. CAGL, *tr. by* Daryl Hine

Staring at the almost. Mother's Day. Steve Hassett. CDa

Staring at the Sea on the Day of the Death of Another. May Swenson. APT-2

Staring down the mountainous wall. Paredón. Ricardo Pau-Llosa. OPRER

Staring, you look for clues. Vanishing Point. Gary Metras. PasH

Stark Electric Jesus. Malay Roy Choudhury. PFTM-2

Stark Major. Hart Crane. FuPo

Starless and chill is the night. Heinrich Heine. AWP, *tr. by* Howard Mumford Jones *Fr.* North Sea, The.

Starless and fatherless, a dark water. (LL)   Sheep in Fog.   Sylvia Plath. FaBoWP; HCAP; LCAP-2; NPeEn

Starlet.   Fanny Howe.   ExTi

Starlight.   Freda Downie.   FaBoWP

Starlight Haven.   Shirley Lim.   UnSA

Starlight like Intuition Pierced the Twelve.   Delmore Schwartz.   ChIV-2

Starlight Night, The.   Gerard Manley Hopkins.   GTBS-P; MoBrPo; NAEL-5v2; NAEL-6v2; PoE

Starlight's intuitions pierced the twelve, The.   Starlight like Intuition Pierced the Twelve.   Delmore Schwartz.   ChIV-2

Starlight Scope Myopia.   Yusef Komunyakaa.   MakPoe

Starling, The.   John Heath-Stubbs.   OWoS

Starling and a willow-wren, A.   W. H. Auden.   FaBoMo   *Fr.* Five Songs.

Starling is my darling, although, The.   Starling, The.   John Heath-Stubbs. OWoS

Starling Lake, The.   "Seumas O'Sullivan."   AWP

Starling Migration, The.   Jeffrey Skinner.   PBCAP

Star[re], The.   George Herbert.   ESCV; PeECV

Starre, The.   Henry Vaughan.   ESCV

Starry flower, the flower-like stars that fade, The.   Sonnets.   Frederick Goddard Tuckerman.   APN-2

Starry frost descends, The.   Suibne Geilt.   NOIV

Starry hosts whose far-flung cohorts gleam, The.   Human Greatness.   Edwin Barclay.   PBA

Starry Night, The.   Anne Sexton.   ColAP; NAAL-5; NoAM; PoE; VCAP

StarrynightIenteryourmirror.   Alexis Rotella.   HA

Stars.   Emily Jane Brontë.   AWTN; BrRo; NAEL-5v2; NAEL-6v2; NALW (Ah! Why, Because the Dazzling Sun.)   VWP

Stars.   George Mackay Brown.   OxBS

Stars.   Nikki Giovanni.   KaS

Stars.   Robert Earl Hayden.   LCAP-2

Stars.   Langston Hughes.   GLP

Stars.   Lenard D. Moore.   HA

Stars.   Carl Sandburg.   NOxBChV

Stars, The.   Madison Cawein.   APN-2

Stars, The.   "Ping Hsin."   WPOW, *tr.* by Kai-yu Hsu

Stars, The.   Lydia Huntley Sigourney.   ColAP; TCAPo

Stars all fell out of the sky, The.   Guy Fawkes '58.   Fiona Kidman.   PeNZ

Stars, all the years of our lives. (LL)   National Cold Storage Company.   Harvey Shapiro.   VGW; WoPoe

Stars and grass.   Weeds.   James Dickey.   BodElec

Stars and Moon on the River.   Tu Fu.   OHPC, *tr.* by Kenneth Rexroth (Autumn night is clear, The.)   OHPC, *tr.* by Kenneth Rexroth (Frost glitters on the chrysanthemums.) (LL)   OHPC, *tr.* by Kenneth Rexroth

Stars and Planets.   Norman MacCaig.   OPOU; OxBSP

Stars and Stripes.   Mary Weston Fordham.   CBWP-2

Stars are a memory system, The.   Notes on the Art of Memory.   Diane Di Prima.   SeSe

Stars are dredging, The.   Richard Wright.   APT-2

Stars are forth, the moon above the tops, The.   Byron.   AmFaPo; TreFP   *Fr.* Manfred.

Stars are gone out spark by spark, The.   At Cockcrow.   Lizette Woodworth Reese.   SacPr

Stars Are Lit, The.   Hayyim Nahman [*or* Khayim Nakhman *or* Chaim Nachman] Bialik.   TrJP, *tr.* by Florence L. Friedman

Stars are old and wise, The. Tonight they look.   Very Young Man Speaks, A. "Paul Tanaquil."   YaYoPo

Stars are shining (the eyes of men are closed.   Rabi'a al-Adawiyya.   WPOW

Stars are still on high, The.   There's a Lull in My Life.   Mack Gordon.   ReLy

Stars are too many to count, The.   Stars.   Carl Sandburg.   NOxBChV

Stars around the fair moon, The.   Sappho.   SaLy, *tr.* by Diane Rayor

Stars around the luminous moon—how soon they.   Sappho.   STV

Stars at Tallapoosa.   Wallace Stevens.   WoPoe

Stars Begin to Fall.   *Unknown.*   SacPr

Stars crickets.   George Swede.   HA

Stars dead heroes in the sky, The.   Offensive, The.   Keith Douglas.   PoWW

Stars / Expanding with the starr'd nocturnal flowers. (LL)   From My Diary, July 1914.   Wilfred Owen.   FaBoMo; MoBrPo

Stars Fade.   Peretz Hirshbein.   TrJP, *tr.* by Joseph Leftwich

Stars Fell on Alabama.   Mitchell Parish.   ReLy

Stars Go Over the Lonely Ocean, The.   Robinson Jeffers.   HarvBoo

Stars, gold specks, are piercing the dark leaves, The.   At the Window in the Dark.   Victor Hugo.   SxFrPo, *tr.* by E. H. Blackmore and A. M. Blackmore

Stars had the look of dogs to him sometimes.   Star Watcher, The.   Peter Davison.   TwCP; YaYoPo

Stars have not dealt me the worst they could do, The.   Stars Have Not Dealt Me, The.   A. E. Housman.   EBEV; GTBS-P; OxBoLi

Stars have not yet retired, and the sky is still dark, The.   Women Transport Corps.   *Unknown.*   WPOW, *tr.* by Kai-yu Hsu

Stars Heng and Chi never halt their courses, The.   Fulling Cloth for Clothes.   Hsieh Hui-lien.   CoBCP, *tr.* by Burton Watson

Stars hidden by dark clouds.   Boethius.   MLL   *Fr.* Consolation of Philosophy, The ("De Consolacione Philosophie").

Stars. I have confidence in my grandfather's building. (LL)   Wild Night at Treweithan.   Gwyn Williams.   AngWePo; TCAWP

Stars, I Have Seen Them Fall.   A. E. Housman.   OxBSP

Stars in Apple Cores.   Luci Shaw.   TrCP

Stars in profusion.   World to Come, A.   Bernard Dadié.   NegPo, *tr.* by Ellen Conroy Kennedy

Stars in Sand.   Francis Carey Slater.   PeSAV

Stars in the sky are as big as coins.   Turkish Love Songs.   *Unknown.*   BoWoP, *tr.* by Reza Baraheni and Zahra-Soltan Shokoohtaezeh

Stars in their calm, The. (LL)   Matthew Arnold.   NOBE; OBEV   *Fr.* Empedocles on Etna.

Stars in your face, The.   In Missing.   Ray A. Young Bear.   CDW

Stars moving from their summertime.   Book, for Growing Old, The.   Yves Bonnefoy.   PoetW, *tr.* by Emily Grosholz

Stars of Night contain the glittering Day, The.   Dying Words of Stonewall Jackson, The.   Sidney Lanier.   APN-2; CBCWP

Stars over snow.   Night.   Sara Teasdale.   NOxBChV

Stars rest cold by shoals of cloud.   Li Ho.   CoBCP   *Fr.* For the Examination at Ho-nan-fu: Songs of the Twelve Months.

Stars shine and go out.   Hayyim Nahman [*or* Khayim Nakhman *or* Chaim Nachman] Bialik.   FIT, *tr.* by Robert Friend

Stars Stand Up in the Air, The.   *Unknown.*   BIrV, *tr.* by Thomas Macdonagh

Stars walk downhill.   Concert.   Robert Sward.   VGW

Stars were strange lightbulbs, the moon was half, The.   Alas, That Is the Name of Our Town; I Have Been Concealing It All This Time.   Joshua Clover.   NeAmPo

Stars wheel in purple, yours is not so rare.   "H. D."   APT-1; MoAmPo; NOBA; TAP   *Fr.* Let Zeus Record.

Start.   Martin Sorescu.   VCWP, *tr.* by Michael Hamburger

Start, The.   *Unknown.*   LB; OxNR

Start from death's slumbers to eternity. (LL)   New Birth, The.   Jones Very.   APN-1; NCAP; NOBA; SacPr

Start like pieces of string.   Advice to the Orchestra.   David Wagoner.   NoAM

Start my good song.   Song of "Kornél Esti", The.   Dezső Kosztolányi.   IQMS, *tr.* by Adam Makkai

Start not at her, who, in fantastic guise.   Idiot Girl, The.   Mary F. Johnson.   CenSon

Start of summer, grass and trees grown tall.   Reading *The Classic of Hills and Seas.*   T'ao Ch'ien [*or* T'ao Yuan-ming].   CoBCP, *tr.* by Burton Watson

Start over, all over again. (LL)   Who Remains Standing?   Andrée Chedid.   HAWP; WoPoe, *tr.* by Mirène Ghossein and Samuel Haze

Start slowly and simply—warming up is crucial.   Recreational Mathematics.   Steve Wilson.   AmPoNex

Start where you stand and never mind the past.   Start Where You Stand.   Berton Braley.   PoToHe

Started as arr.   Crow.   Robert Grenier.   PmAP

Starting again.   Dark Country, A.   Derek Mahon.   BIrV

Starting at the center.   Tables in Pictures.   Diane Ward.   FTOS

Starting-cry of a race, The. A name to conjure with. (LL)   Geoffrey Hill.   NoAM; WoPoe   *Fr.* Mercian Hymns.

Starting Early from the Ch'u-ch'êng Inn.   Po Chü-i.   ChiP; OBVE, *tr.* by Arthur Waley (Starting Early.)   BLT, *tr.* by Arthur Waley

Starting Early from Yü-p'u Deep.   Meng Hao Jan.   SuSp, *tr.* by Daniel Bryant

Starting from Central Station.   David Campbell. ("Moon hangs in the air, A.")   BMAP (I Starting from Central Station.)   BMAP

Starting from San Francisco.   Lawrence Ferlinghetti.   GM

Starting in a long swale between the Sierras.   Garrett Kaoru Hongo.   GeoHom   *Fr.* Cruising 99.

Starting 1973: What to Do Now that Peace Has Been Announced.   Joseph Cady.   CDa

Starting now the hours of the clock.   Against the Laws.   Friedrich Wilhelm Nietzsche.   WoPoe, *tr.* by W. S. Merwin

Starting School.   Annie Foster.   NLP

Starting to rise.   Cor Van den Heuvel.   HA

Starting. Words which begin, A.   Zoetropes.   Bill Manhire.   PeNZ

Startle, and stare out. (LL)   Psalm: "In the small beauty of the forest."   George Oppen.   APT-2; HarvBoo; NNaP; PFTM-2; WoPoe

Startled / By a single scream.   Saigyo.   AWP

Startled into Life Like Fire.   Charles Bukowski.   PmAP

Startled stag, the blue-grey night, A.   Dark Stag, The.   Isabella Valancy Crawford.   NOBC

Startling reality of things / Is my discovery every single day, The. "Startling Reality of Things," The. Fernando Pessoa. PFTM-1

Starts for a moment from its dust. (LL) Crows. Lizette Woodworth Reese. APT-1; TCAPo

Starvation Camp near Jaslo. Wislawa Szymborska. WPOW
(Hunger Camp at Jaso.) AF, tr. by Grazyna Drabik
(Write it. Write. In ordinary ink.) AF, tr. by Grazyna Drabik

Starved. Laura Riding Jackson. FuPo

Starved old gelding, blind and lamed, A. Brian [or Bryan] Merriman [or Merryman]. BIrV, tr. by Frank O'Connor Fr. Midnight Court, The.

Starved Rock. James Ballowe. IllVoic

Starved Rock. Edgar Lee Masters. GeoHom Fr. Spoon River Anthology.

"Starved to death." In Memoriam. Bernard Dadié. NegPo, tr. by Ellen Conroy Kennedy

Starving to Death on a Government Claim. Unknown. OBAL
(Frank Baker's my name, and a bachelor I am.) APN-2

Starwork. L. S. Asekoff. BodElec

Stasis in darkness. Ariel. Sylvia Plath. HCAP; HeIP-4; LCAP-2; NAAL-2v2; NALW; NOBA; NoAM; NoP-4; PoE; VCAP

State, a state, oh! dungeon state indeed, A. Edward Taylor. ChIV-1 Fr. Preparatory Meditations Before My Approach to the Lord's Supper.

State Funeral. Thomas McCarthy. CIP-2; ModIr

State of Arkansas, The. Unknown. APN-2

State of Butterfly. Ahmed Taha. NAfrP, tr. by Clarissa C. Burt

State of Fever, A. Sa'di Yusuf. MAP, tr. by Lena Jayyusi and Naomi Shihab Nye

State of Innocence, The. Dryden. NOCV

State of Nature, A. John Hollander. AiP; NIL-7

State of Preservation. Celeste Turner Wright. FFC

State of Seige. Teresa Calderón. TANSG, tr. by Celeste Kostopulos-Cooperman

State of the Nation, The. Kenneth Patchen. CLPP

State of the Union. Aimé Césaire. NegPo, tr. by Denis Kelly

State Poetry Day. Ronald Wallace. PBCAP

State Street's cold mingling. Chicago/3 Hours. Victor Hernández Cruz. PueRic

State Will Be Served Even By Poets, The. Julian Beck. PFTM-2

State with the prettiest name, The. Florida. Elizabeth Bishop. TwCP

Statecraft and Foresight have gone to their mountain council. Bowmen, The. Paavo Haavikko. WoPoe, tr. by Anselm Hollo

Stately as a Galleon. Joyce Grenfell. OBCoV

Stately home where doves, in dovecotes, coo, A. Owl Writes a Detective Story, The. Gavin Ewart. OBCoV

Stately Homes of England, The. Noël Coward. UV
(Lord Elderley, Lord Borrowmere, Lord Sickert and Lord Camp.) OBCoV

Stately Homes of England, The. Noël Coward. OBCoV

Stately Homes of England, The. Noël Coward. UV Fr. Stately Homes of England, The.

Stately homes of England, The. Homes of England, The. Felicia Dorothea Hemans. NOBRP; PEW; RWP; UV; ViWPN; WPE

Stately palace in which the queen dwells, The. Her Descending Down. Margaret Lucas Cavendish, Duchess of Newcastle. BASC; NOSC

Stately rainbow came and stood, A. Coventry Patmore. GTBS-P Fr. Angel in the House, The.

Stately Structure of This Earth, The. Martha Brewster. AH

Stately yon vessel sails adown the tide. Ship, The. Robert Southey. TreFP

State/meant. Imamu Amiri Baraka. BB

Statement on Our Higher Education. W. M. Ransom. CDW

States of War. Maya Bejerano. DTA, tr. by Miriyam Glazer

States when they black out and lie there rolling when they turn, The. Falling. James Dickey. LCAP-2; NoAM

Statesman, The. Joseph Hilaire Pierre Belloc. NOBE

Statesman's Holiday, The. W. B. Yeats. OxBTC

Statesmen. W. H. Auden. OBCoV Fr. Shorts [1939–1947].

Statesmen, The. Ambrose Bierce. APN-2

Statesmen, in your exalted station know. Unknown. CAGL Fr. Don Leon.

Static. Mary Barnard. APT-2

Static, The. Lewis Warsh. FTOS

Station. Sharon Olds. PBCAP

Station (1). James Galvin. GifTon

Station (2). James Galvin. GifTon

Station (4). James Galvin. GifTon

Station Island. Seamus Heaney.
"Black water. White waves. Furrows snowcapped." NoAM
"I had come to the edge of the water." NPeEn; PBCIP
"Like a convalescent, I took the hand." NAEL-5v2; NAEL-6v2; NoAM; TOF
"My brain dried like spread turf, my stomach." CIP-2

Stationmaster is garrulous in, The. Daphne Stillorgan. Denis Devlin. CIP-2

Stations. Philip Booth. GM

Stations. Ted Hughes.
"I can understand the haggard eyes." NoAM
"Suddenly his poor body." NoAM
"Whether you say it, think it, know it." NoAM
"You are a wild look—out of an egg." NoAM

Statistic. Michelle Parkerson. ISC

Statistic: The Witness. Rita Dove. NAAAL Fr. Mother Love.

Statistics. Stephen Spender. MoBrPo

Statistics. Barrett Watten. PmAP

Statuary. John Ashbery. NoAM

Statuary Christ bleeds sweating grief, A. Bookbuying in the Tenderloin. Robert Hass. YaYoPo

Statue, The. Kenneth Allott. SPE

Statue, The. Joseph Hilaire Pierre Belloc. OxAEP-2

Statue, The. Robert Creeley. LCAP-2

Statue, The. Ivano Fermini. ItPo, tr. by Gayle Ridinger

Statue, The. John Fuller. NOBE

Statue, The. Ella Higginson. SWaP

Statue, The. Orkhan Muyassar. MAP, tr. by Samuel Hazo and Lena Jayyusi

Statue, The. Luz Maria Umpierre. PueRic

Statue and Birds. Louise Bogan. MoAmPo

Statue of Bereniké, A. Callimachus. GrAn, tr. by Peter Jay

Statue Of Eros, A. Zenodotus. GrAn, tr. by Peter Jay

Statue of Medusa, The. William Drummond. GS

Statue of Nemesis at Rhamnus, The. Parmenion of Macedon. GrAn, tr. by Alistair Elliot

Statue of the Dying Gladiator, The. Felicia Dorothea Hemans. RWP

Statues. Lisel Mueller. ExTi

Statues, The. Laurence Binyon. OBEV

Statues, The. W. B. Yeats. NoAM; WeW-3

Statues in the Public Gardens, The. Howard Nemerov. CoAmPo

Statues with exposed hearts and barbed-wire crowns. Mud Vision, The. Seamus Heaney. PBCIP

Status Symbol. Mari E. Evans. NAAAL

Stay. Ben Sonnenberg. Unle

Stay, and behold; and see the greatest wonder. Essay upon Good-Friday, An. Anne King. EMWP

Stay Behind, The. Andrew Elliott. PNI

Stay! Beneath your feet is a wonder of women. On a Woman. Robert Williams. OBWVE, tr. by H. Idris Bell

Stay, Death. Not mine the Christus-wand. Herman Melville. APN-1; NCAP Fr. Clarel: A Poem and Pilgrimage in the Holy Land.

Stay, fairest Chari[e]ssa, stay and mark. Glowworm, The. Thomas Stanley. BeJo; NOSC

Stay, gentle Child of Taste! who'er thou art. Prefatory Epistle, A. Maria Falconar. ECWP

Stay here, fond youth, and ask no more. Against Fruition. Sir John Suckling. BeJo; CaPo; CavPo; NOSC

Stay in this world with me. Please. Laura Kasischke. NAPBL

Stay, my tendrils, where hung. Asclepiades. GrAn

Stay near me. Speak my name. Oh, do not wander. Midcentury Love Letter. Phyllis McGinley. LW

Stay now with me, and listen to my sighs. Dante Alighieri. AWP; EaItPo, tr. by Dante Gabriel Rossetti Fr. La Vita Nuova.

Stay of your secure firm dry embrace, The. (LL) Hug, The. Thom Gunn. HarvBoo; NPeEn

Stay off from me, wild sea. Tomb on the Shore, A. Asclepiades. GrAn, tr. by Alan Marshfield

Stay, passenger, and lend a tear. On a Hopeful Youth. Owen Felltham [or Feltham]. NOSC

Stay Phoebus, stay. Song. Edmund Waller. BeJo

'Stay!' said the child. The bird said, 'No.' Footprint on the Air, A. Naomi Lewis. NOxBChV

Stay, shade of my shy treasure! Oh, remain. Sister Juana Inés de la Cruz. WPOW

Stay, Spring. Andrew Young. FaBoTw

Stay weary traveler, stay! Fountain at the Tomb, The. Nicias. AWP, tr. by Charles Merivale

Stay with poetry, and with God above. (LL) Song for the Moon. Nazik Al-Mala'ika. BBASP; MAP, tr. by Christopher Middleton and Matthew Sorenson

Stay within yourself, Mind. Kamalākānta Bhattācārya. SinGod, tr. by Rachel Fell McDermott

Stay yet, pale flower, though coming storms will tear thee. On a Rose in December. Ebenezer Elliott. FaBoEE

Stayed by what was, and pulled by what would be. (LL)   She.   Theodore Roethke.   BoLoP; NIL-7

Stayed late in town, sped home in my boat.   On the Fifteenth Day of the Seventh Month I Came Home Late from the City.   Shen Chou.   CoBLCP, tr. by Jonathan Chaves

Staying Alive.   Denise Levertov.
   "Went with some of my students to work in the People's."   CDa

Staying Alive.   David Wagoner.   CoAP; InPK-6

Staying alive the boy on the screen is doing it.   Breakdancing.   Jorie Graham.   BodElec

Staying at an inn.   Basho.   EH, tr. by Robert Hass

Staying at Ed's Place.   May Swenson.   VCAP

Staying in the Mountains in Summer.   Yü Hsüan-chi.   BoWoP, tr. by Geoffrey Waters

Staying Overnight at Blue Cloud Temple.   Mo Shih-lung.   CoBLCP, tr. by Jonathan Chaves

Staying Overnight at Spirit-Source Temple.   Wen Cheng-ming.   CoBLCP, tr. by Jonathan Chaves

Staying Overnight at T'ien-ning Ch'an Temple.   Chang Yü.   CoBLCP, tr. by Jonathan Chaves

Staying Overnight at the Temple of the Holy Vulture.   Yang Wan-li.   SuSp, tr. by Sherwin S. S. Fu

Staying Overnight on the Banks of Embroidered River.   Li K'ai-hsien.   CoBLCP, tr. by Jonathan Chaves

Staying up to eat and play all night.   All the Stars Are Foxfire.   Van K. Brock.   AllShUp

Staying with a friend, you leave his mother's kitchen.   In the Outhouse.   Katherine Pierpoint.   MFPA

Staying Young.   Bob Merrill.   ReLy

Stayover at Chien-Teh River.   Meng Hao Jan.   ChinPo, tr. by Yip Wai-lim

Stayover at Pei-Ku-Shan.   Wang Wan.   ChinPo, tr. by Yip Wai-lim

Steadfast a lamp burns sheltered from the wind.   Unknown.   TOF   Fr. Bhagavad-Gita, the.

Steadfastness.   Sir Thomas Wyatt.   FaBoVe; HAP; NAEL-5v1; NOBE; NoSic; OBEV; SCGP
   (Forget Not Yet.)   AmFaPo; NAEL-6v1; NAEL-7v1; NoP-4; PoPoPo
   (Forget not yet the tryde entent.)   NPeEn
   (Supplication, A.)   GTBS-P

Steadily it snows.   O. Mabson Southard.   HA

Steady advance of the darkness.   Night.   Boris Leonidovich Pasternak.   TCRP, tr. by Edwin Morgan

Steady, the evening fades.   Buffalo Evening.   Robert Creeley.   BodElec

Steal Away to Jesus.   Unknown.   BPo; NAAAL; NoP-4
   (Steal Away.)   APN-2; ISC

Steal from the world, and not a stone / Tell where I lie. (LL)   Ode on Solitude.   Pope.   AWP; FHYEP; HeIP-4; NAEL-5v1; NAEL-6v1; NIL-7; NOSC; PAI; PoRA; SCGP

Stealing.   Carol Ann Duffy.   EmeKit

Stealing of Apollo's Cattle, The.   Unknown.   WoPoe, tr. by Padraic Fallon   Fr. Homeric Hymns.

Steam-cleaned, so groundless you'd believe.   Dirty English Potatoes.   X. J. Kennedy.   SpudSo

Steam Engine; or, The Power of the Flame, The.   Thomas Baker.
   "Lord Stanhope hit upon a novel plan."   VerBaPo

Steam in Sacrifice.   Robert Herrick.   CaPo

Steam Power.   Erasmus Darwin.   NOEC   Fr. Botanic Garden, The.

Steam rises over my nose.   Coffee.   Wanda Coleman.   ISC

Steam rising wherever the edge may be?, The. (LL)   Tractatus.   Derek Mahon.   ModIr; OxBSP

Steam Shovel.   Charles Malam.   NTCP

Steam was what she thought.   Birthday.   Christine Hume.   AmPoNex

Steam whistle cleaves to the wind, The.   Spring at Yesan Station.   Sub-ok.   WPoS, tr. by Julie Pickering

Steamboats, Viaducts and Railways.   William Wordsworth.   CenSon; NAEL-5v2; NAEL-6v2   Fr. Poems Composed or Suggested During a Tour, in the Summer of 1833.

Steamer left he black and oozy wharves, The.   Alexander Smith.   PeVV   Fr. Boy's Poem, A.

Steaming hunk of meat, A.   Hero's Portion.   John Montague.   NOIV

Steddefast cross, inmong aile other.   William Herebert.   SacPr

Stedefast [or Steddefast or Steadfast] cross[e], inmong [or among] alle [or all] other.   Holy Cross.   Venantius Fortunatus.   MiEL

Stedfast and enduring bone, The. (LL)   Immortal Part, The.   A. E. Housman.   MoBrPo; SCGP; SoSe-8; UnPo

Steed bit his master, The.   On a Clergyman's Horse Biting Him.   Unknown.   FaBoEE; NBLV; OxBoLi

Steed Bit His Master, The.   Unknown.   See On a Clergyman's Horse Biting Him

Steekit, consecrat, fou o fire but fuel.   Douglas Young.   OBVE   Fr. Kirkyaird by the Sea, The.

Steel.   Lee Ranaldo.   HeMarv

Steel fibrous slant & ribboned glint, The.   Turncoat, The.   Imamu Amiri Baraka.   NeAP; PoE

Steel Usurps the Forests; Silence Dethrones Dialogue.   Bible, Apocrypha.   HBAPE

Steele Glas, The.   George Gascoigne.
   "These knacks, my lord, I cannot call to mind."   SacPr

Steelhead in the Whitehorse Rearing Pond.   Joan Swift.   PoCoUp

Steely train in the stupid green, The.   Train: Abstraction.   Genevieve Taggard.   WPE

Steep Acquisitions Motionless Fears.   Gabriella Leto.   CItWP, tr. by Cinzia Sartini Blum and Lara Trubowitz

Steep cliffs pierce the sky.   Mount T'ai P'ing.   Ch'ien Ch'i.   OHMPC, tr. by Kenneth Rexroth

Steep from an ocean where no landfall can be. (LL)   Voyage West.   Archibald MacLeish.   APT-1; VGW

Steep frowning glories of dark Loch na Garr!, The. (LL)   Lachin y Gair.   Byron.   NePenScot; OxBS

Steep mountains.   Tiger Valley.   Muso Soseki.   EaWin, tr. by W. S. Merwin

Steep slope hangs above, The.   On Visiting Shorin Temple, Where Bodhidharma Once Lived.   Soen.   ZenPo, tr. by Takashi Ikemoto and Lucien Stryk

Steep, steep the lofty mountain peak.   Hsü Kan.   SuSp   Fr. Boudoir Thoughts.

Steep valley overhung by trees, A.   Plea for Peace.   Frank Prewett.   HATNAP

Steeped in ecstasies of perfume.   Spring Nocturne.   Abraham Liessin.   TrJP

Steepies for the bairnie.   Supper.   William Soutar.   OxBS

Steeple-Jack, The.   Marianne Craig Moore.   APT-1; BoWoP; ColAP; FaBoMo; FaBoWP; HAP; HarvBoo; NOBA; NoAM; NoP-4; OxBA; PoPoPo; WPE   Fr. Part of a Novel, Part of a Poem, Part of a Play.

Steeplejack.   Katherine Pierpoint.   MFPA

Steer hither, steer your wingéd pines.   William Browne (1591–1643).   NOBE; OBEV   Fr. Inner Temple Masque, The.

Steerage.   Albert Goldbarth.   TaR

Steered straight into this century I see narrowboats.   Homage to the Canal People.   Andrew Sant.   NOBAu

Stefansson: a walrus of a man.   Stefansson Island.   Philip Booth.   SoSe-8

Stefansson Island.   Philip Booth.   SoSe-8

(Steingeröll) new signs putting.   Tristan Tzara.   PFTM-1   Fr. Poemes Negres.

Stele and my Sirens and mournful pitcher that hold.   Erinna.   HePo   Fr. Epigrams.

Stele and my sirens and mournful urn.   Erinna.   SaLy, tr. by Diane Rayor

Stele (1–2 c. B.C.).   Denise Levertov.   BodElec

Stella and Flavia every hour.   Stella and Flavia.   Mary Barber.   ECWP

Stella at Wood-Park.   Jonathan Swift.   BIrV

Stella behold, and then begin t'indite. (LL)   Sir Philip Sidney.   NAEL-5v1; NoSic; OxAEP-1; Son   Fr. Astrophil and Stella.

Stella Maris.   O. B. Hardison, Jr.   CRP

Stella oft sees the very face of woe.   Sir Philip Sidney.   NAEL-5v1; NAEL-6v1; NAEL-7v1; NoSic; PoE   Fr. Astrophil and Stella.

Stella's Birthday ([March 13,] 1727).   Jonathan Swift.   NoP-4; PoE; SCGP

Stella's Birthday [1721].   Jonathan Swift.   NAEL-5v1; NAEL-6v1; OxAEP-1

Stella's Birthday; Written in the Year 1718[/9].   Jonathan Swift.   EnLoPo
   (On Stella's Birthday, 1718/1719.)   InPK-6; NIP-4; NOIV

Stella's Epitaph.   Mary Jones.   ECWP

Stella's Kiss.   Sir Philip Sidney.   NoSic   Fr. Astrophil and Stella.

Stella, since thou so right a Princess art.   Sir Philip Sidney.   NoP-4; OxAEP-1   Fr. Astrophil and Stella.

Stella, think not that I by verse seek fame.   Sir Philip Sidney.   NoP-4; NoSic   Fr. Astrophil and Stella.

Stella this day is thirty-four.   Stella's Birthday; Written in the Year 1718[/9].   Jonathan Swift.   EnLoPo

Stella, while now by honour's cruel might.   Sir Philip Sidney.   NAEL-5v1; NAEL-6v1; NAEL-7v1; PoE   Fr. Astrophil and Stella.

Stellar sea crawler, maw, The.   Starfish.   Eric Ormsby.   NoP-4

Stella's Birthday, 1725.   Jonathan Swift.   CABP; NOEC

Stem heaped up, heaped, heaped up.   Spell for Making the First Man.   Unknown.   PeNZ, tr. by Margaret Orbell

Stendhal.   Sergey [or Sergei] Nikolaevich Markov.   TCRP, tr. by Lubov Yakovleva

Stenographers, The.   Patricia K. Page.   HeIP-4; NALW; NoAM

Step aside, you ornery tenderfeet.   I'm an Old Cowhand.   Johnny Mercer.   OBAL

Step Away from Them, A.   Frank O'Hara.   CoAmPo; HCAP; NAAL-2v2; VCAP; VGW; WoPoe

Step on His Head.   James Laughlin.   VGW

"Step on it," said Aunt Alice, "for God's sake."   Ascension: 1925, The.   John Malcolm Brinnin.   InPK-6

Step or two inside the door, A. Murphy's Law. Alan Jenkins. OxBSo

Step right up, come one, come all, don't. *Unknown.* PriapPo, *tr. by* Richard W. Hooper *Fr.* Priapus Poems, The.

Stepback, stepforward; it was that kind of rhythm. Frederick D'Aguiar. WaCA *Fr.* GDR.

Stepfathers. David Donnell. NOBC

Stephano Remembers. James Simmons. PBCIP; PNI

Stephen Smith, University of Iowa sophomore, burned what he said was his draft card. Of Late. George Starbuck. VGW

Stephen to Lazarus. Clive Staples Lewis. ChIV-2; SacPr

Stepmother. Dinah Livingstone. Prnts

Stepmother, The. Tatiana Shcherbina. ItGoST, *tr. by* J. Kates

Stepping Aside. Andrée Chedid. HAWP, *tr. by* Harriet Zinnes

Stepping down from the swing. Tune: "Rouged Lips." Li Ch'ing-chao. ColAnChi, *tr. by* Jiaosheng Wang

Stepping gingerly. Cat in the Snow. Aileen Fisher. NTCP

Stepping in the Same River. Karen Chamberlain. GeoH

Stepping into the field, sadness fills my deep heart. Love Lament. *Vietnamese Oral Tradition.* CaDao, *tr. by* John Balaban

Stepping Out. Michael Brownstein. FTOS

Stepping Out. Allen Fisher.
  Progressions of Spacetime: I. Oth
  Rims of Distinction: I. Oth
  Stepping Out: 2. Oth
  Stepping Out: I. Oth

Stepping Out. Maureen Watson. IBA

Stepping Out: I. Allen Fisher. Oth *Fr.* Stepping Out.

Stepping Out: 2. Allen Fisher. Oth *Fr.* Stepping Out.

Stepping out of my apartment building. Ordinance, The. Luis Cabalquinto. ReBoTo

Stepping out through the west-wall gate. Leaving West Archery Hall at Dusk. Hsieh Ling-yün. SuSp, *tr. by* Francis Westbrook

Stepping Out With Edvard Munch. Elma Van Haren. TuT, *tr. by* Anne Kennedy

Stepping Out With Edvard Munch. Elma Van Haren. TuT, *tr. by* Medbh McGuckian

Stepping-Stones, The. William Wordsworth. CenSon *Fr.* River Duddon [A Series of Sonnets], The.

Stepping to da Muse/Sic. Afua Cooper. WaCA

Stepping Westward. Denise Levertov. NALW; VGW

Stepping Westward. William Wordsworth. SCGP

Steps. Kojo Laing. NAfrP

Steps. Naomi Shihab Nye. ExTi

Steps. Frank O'Hara. CoAmPo; PmAP

Steps. Roberta Hill Whiteman. VoR

Steps in the Night. Mahmoud Darwish. VCWP, *tr. by* Denys Johnson-Davies

Steps out / from a lily. Woman. Carl Rakosi. TAP

Steps to the Temple. Giambattista [*or* Giovanni Battista] Marino. SacPr *Fr.* Strage degli innocenti, La.

Stereo Time with Booker Little. Rick Madigan. SeSe

Stereograph: 1903. Julie Fay. NAPBL

Sterile and impotent and justified. (LL) Paradise Saved. Alec Derwent Hope. OxBC; OxBSo

Sterile Dish, The. Lenka Valachová. SurWo, *tr. by* Katerina Pinosová

Sterile line glows, The. Poem for Claude. Ray DiPalma. FTOS

Sterkfontein. Ruth Miller. PeSAV

Sterling Williams has a nosebleed. Sterling Williams' Nosebleed. David Chin. InvLad

Sterling Williams' Nosebleed. David Chin. InvLad

Stern Daughter of the Voice of God! Ode to Duty. William Wordsworth. AWP; FHYEP; GTBS-P; NAEL-5v2; NAEL-6v2; NOBRP; OBEV

Stern Master Munchem, rod in hand, stole out of school one day. School-Master and the Truants, The. "John Brownjohn." OBCA

Stern Miss Frugle always said. What Happened to Miss Frugle. Brian Patten. OBSP

Stern parent, The. Harry Graham. PeLV *Fr.* Some Ruthless Rhymes.

Stern Truth. Letitia [*or* Laetitia] Elizabeth Landon. VWP

Stethoscope, The. Dannie Abse. BloBone

Stethoscope tells what everyone fears, The. Academic. Theodore Roethke. FaBoEE; OBAL

Steve Biko is Dead. Jack A. Mapanje. PeSAV

Steve's Commando Paintball, San Adriano, California. Joel Brouwer. AmPoNex

Steveston. Daphne Marlatt.
  Imagine: A Town. NOBC

Sthenelais. *Unknown.* GrAn, *tr. by* Guy Davenport

Sticheron for Matins, Wednesday of Holy Week. Kassia. WPOW, *tr. by* Patrick Diehl

Stick and Hat. King Lê Thánh–tông. WoPoe, *tr. by* John S. Major

Stick goes over the falls at sunset, A. Cor Van den Heuvel. HA

Stick he used to tap out feet, The. Phanias. GrAn

Stick of Incense, A. W. B. Yeats. ChIV-2

Stick your patent name on a signboard. Hart Crane. GM; MoAmPo; NAAL-5; NOBA; OxBA *Fr.* Bridge, The.

Sticking morphine in the arm and eating meat. (LL) Last Night in Calcutta. Allen Ginsberg. FTOS; NoAM

Sticks. Thomas Sayers Ellis. NAPBL

Sticks and stones may break my bones. Truth. Barrie Wade. OTCP

Sticks-in-a-drowse droop over sugary loam. Cuttings. Theodore Roethke. APT-2; HCAP; LCAP-2; NAAL-2v2; NAAL-5; NOBA; NoAM; OBGa; TAP; UnPo

Sticky inside their winter suits. Thaw. Margaret Avison. FaBoWP; NOBC

Stiff lines of the twigs, The. April. Charles Reznikoff. APT-2

Stiff spokes of this wheel, The. July in Washington. Robert Lowell. LCAP-2; NAAL-2v2

Stiff, still features, The. (LL) Ezra Pound. NOBA; NoAM *Fr.* Cantos.

Stiff winds blow. *Unknown.* OHMPJ

Stiff with weapons, fighting back over the same ground. (LL) Thistles. Ted Hughes. FaBoVe; NPeEn; NoAM; OxBSP; OxBTC; SoSe-8

Stigmata. Patrick Lane. NOBC

Stike up, Gypsy, you have quaffed your wages. Ancient Gypsy, The. Mihály Vörösmarty. IQMS, *tr. by* Peter Zollman

Still. Jack Marshall. GraLe

Still. Wislawa Szymborska. AF, *tr. by* Robert A. Maguire

Still. Ronald Stuart Thomas. TCAWP

Still. James Wright (1927–80). *See* Still, / I would leap too

Still alive. Basho. EH, *tr. by* Robert Hass

Still and All. Burns Singer. HarvBoo; OxBS

Still are there wonders of the dark and day. To Keep the Memory of Charlotte Forten Grimké. Angelina Weld Grimké. BlSi

Still as. Moon-Shadows. Adelaide Crapsey. APT-1

Still as a moth face on the water. Memory of Quiet. Rosalie Moore. APT-2

Still asleep his body wakes from sleep. Day. Khairi Mansour. MAP, *tr. by* Charles Doria and Lena Jayyusi

Still blooming on, when Summer-flowers all fade. Autumn Flowers. Jones Very. APN-1

Still-born silence, thou that art. Invocation of Silence. Richard Flecknoe. OxBSP

Still burning. (LL) Portrait, The. Stanley Kunitz. InvLad; RaBo

Still Century. Tom Paulin. BiHa

Still, Citizen Sparrow. Richard Wilbur. ColAP; NoAM; TRP

Still clear, that morning his family moved. After a Friendship. Robert Minhinnick. AngWePo

Still clinging to your shirt. (LL) My Papa's Waltz. Theodore Roethke. APT-2; AmFaPo; ClHu; ColAP; HAP; HCAP; HeIP-4; InPK-6; LCAP-2; NAAL-2v2; NAAL-5; NBLV; NIL-7; NIP-4; NOBA; NOxBChV; NoAM; NoP-4; PAI; PoE; PoPoPo; RaBo; TAP; TFi; TRP; VGW

Still Do I Keep My Look, My Identity. Gwendolyn Brooks. IllVoic *Fr.* Gay Chaps at the Bar.

Still do I love, still shed my innocent light, my Blood, for thee. (LL) Still Falls the Rain. Dame Edith Sitwell. BoWoP; CABP; MoBrPo; NAEL-5v2; NAEL-6v2; NOBE; NoAM; OBWP; PFTM-1; PeECV; TFi; TwCP

Still do the stars impart their light. Falsehood. William Cartwright. OBEV

Still drone of the time, The. What She Said. Patumanār. AWTN, *tr. by* A. K. Ramanujan

Still exhausted at dawn, she plays. She Calms the Savage Beast with Her Aubade. Grace Bauer. MiVo

Still explosions on the rocks, The. Shampoo, The. Elizabeth Bishop. APT-2; FaBoWP; HarvBoo; OxBC; VCAP

Still Falls the Rain. Dame Edith Sitwell. BoWoP; CABP; MoBrPo; NAEL-5v2; NAEL-6v2; NOBE; NoAM; OBWP; PFTM-1; PeECV; TFi; TwCP

Still far from patriarch or sage. Osip Emilevich Mandelstam [*or* Mandelshtam]. TCRP

Still fettered, still unconquered, still in pain. Prometheus Unbound. Alec Derwent Hope. OxBC

Still for the world he lives, and lives in bliss. Written on the Anniversary of Our Father's Death. Hartley Coleridge. Son

Still green on the limbs o' the woak wer the leaves. Which Road? William Barnes. NOBVV

Still had hair! (LL) For Emily (Dickinson). Maureen Owen. PmAP; ReTh

Still-Heart. Frank Pearce Sturm. OBMV

Still Here. Langston Hughes. SAmP
  (I been scarred and battered.) BPo

Still holding and feeding the stem of the contained flower. (LL) Shape of the Fire, The. Theodore Roethke. LCAP-2; VCAP

Still hovering round the fair at sixty-four. On an Amorous Old Man. David Mallet. NePenScot

Still, I am here. Pablo Neruda. GifTon, *tr.* by William O'Daly

Still I complain; I am complaining still. Edward Taylor. OxBA; SacPr *Fr.* Preparatory Meditations Before My Approach to the Lord's Supper.

Still, I lay awake in the dark. Call, The. Robert Harris. BMAP

Still I Rise. Maya Angelou. BlSi; NAAAL

Still, / I would leap too. Small Frogs Killed on the Highway. James Wright (1927–80). HCAP; NNaP; NoAM

Still in her purity. (LL) Ballata: In Exile at Sarzana. Guido Cavalcanti. AWP; EaltPo, *tr.* by Dante Gabriel Rossetti

Still in his mother's lap the baby Love played. Meleager. HePo *Fr.* Epigrams.

Still in October, the woodcock. On the Mountain. Ruth Stone. BoWoP

Still in one body, locked and barred. Prisons. Lőrinc Szabó. IQMS, *tr.* by Edwin Morgan

Still in sleeping bags, the promised delivery. Bats. Dave Jeddie Smith. NoAM

Still, in some hidden towns of our Dispersion. Talmud Student, The. Hayyim Nahman [*or* Khayim Nakhman *or* Chaim Nachman] Bialik. TrJP, *tr.* by Helena Frank

Still in the cool[e], and silent shades of sleep. (LL) To Perilla. Robert Herrick. BeJo; CaPo; NOSC; SCGP

Still in the published city but not yet. John Ashbery. PmAP *Fr.* Flow Chart.

Still is my love telling what is told. (LL) William Shakespeare. EBEV; NoSic; OxAEP-1 *Fr.* Sonnets.

Still it is raining lightly. Love Medicine, A. Louise Erdrich. HATNAP

Still Later There Are War Stories. D. F. Brown. CDa

Still, leagues beyond those leagues, there is more sea. (LL) Dante Gabriel Rossetti. GTBS-P; OBEV *Fr.* House of Life, The.

Still let my tyrants know, I am not doomed to wear. Emily Jane Brontë. NOBE; NoP-4; OBEV *Fr.* Prisoner, The.

Still-Life. Elizabeth Daryush. FaBoWP; NPeEn; OxBEV; WPE

Still Life. Raymond Garlick. AngWePo

Still Life. Anthony Hecht. NoP-4

Still-Life. Maurice Kenny. UrbNat

Still-Life. "Shahryar." OMIP, *tr.* by Gopi Chand Narang

Still-Life. Tatiana Shcherbina. ItGoST, *tr.* by J. Kates

Still Life. Sharan Strange. GT

Still Life. Francis Sullivan. CRP

Still Life. Reed Whittemore. CoAP; CoAmPo

Still Life in Garden. Rachel Hadas. ExTi

Still Life: The Table. Theo Van Doesburg. PFTM-1

Still Life with Endings. Ray Gonzalez. TouFir

Still-Life with Woodstove. William W. Cook. SpirFl

Still looking for a scoot-hole, Phemios the poet. Homer. ModIr *Fr.* Odyssey.

Still must I tamely. Sigh, A. Witter Bynner. APT-1

Still night. The old clock Ticks. Last Night in Calcutta. Allen Ginsberg. FTOS; NoAM

Still Night Thoughts. Li Po. CoBCP; ColAnChi; TTTS, *tr.* by Burton Watson

Still, O Lord, for Thee I Tarry. Charles Wesley. SacPr

Still old pond, The. Basho. NIL-7, *tr.* by Earl Miner

Still on my cheeks I feel their fondling breath. Stanzas on Mutability. Hugo von Hofmannsthal. AWP; TrJP, *tr.* by Jethro Bithell

Still one more year of preparation. Preparation. Czeslaw Milosz. WoPoe

Still onward winds the dreary way. Tennyson. NAEL-6v2 *Fr.* In Memoriam A. H. H.

Still Poem 9. Philip Lamantia. NeAP

Still pressing through these weeping solitudes. Frederick Goddard Tuckerman. NOBA *Fr.* Sonnets.

Still round thy towers descend the fertile rain! Cordova. Ibn Zaydun. AWP, *tr.* by H. A. R. Gibb

Still seems to need. (LL) Memories of a Lost War. Louis Simpson. OBWP; VGW

Still Shines When You Think of It. Vincent O'Sullivan. PeNZ

Still singing. (LL) Issa. EH; NIL-7, *tr.* by Robert Hass

Stil sits the school-house by the road. In School-Days. John Greenleaf Whittier. OBCA

Still small voice unto, The. Successful Summer, A. David Schubert. APT-2; ChIV-1

Still south I went and west and south again. Prelude. John Millington Synge. AWP; MoBrPo; OBMV

Still, still my eye will gaze long-fixed on thee. Columbine, The. Jones Very. ColAP; GSo; NOBA

Still, Still, with Thee. Harriet Beecher Stowe. AH

Still sunlit, one tree. O. Mabson Southard. HA

Still the balance stays. City Park. Erika Mitterer. AuPH, *tr.* by Lowell A. Bangerter

Still the loud death drum, thundering from afar. Eighteen Hundred and Eleven. Anna Laetitia Barbauld. NOBRP; RWP

Still the Messerschmitts claw at the heart. Hospital, The. Boris Abramovich Slutsky [*or* Slutskii]. TCRusP, *tr.* by Daniel Weissbort

Still the mighty mountains stand. Epilogue to Alun Mabon. John Ceiriog Hughes. OBWVE, *tr.* by H. Idris Bell

Still the walls do not fall. "H. D." NAAL-5 *Fr.* Walls Do Not Fall, The.

Still There's No Trace. Zim Mnotoza. PeSAV

Still, there was quite a decent turn-out really. New Rock n Roll, The. Brendan Cleary. NeBl

Still tied to the world. Ozui. JDP, *tr.* by Yoel Hoffmann

Still to be neat, still to be dressed [*or* Drest]. Ben Jonson. BeJo; HAP; NAEL-5v1; NAEL-6v1; NAEL-7v1; NIL-7; NPeEn; NoP-4; PAI; PoPoPo; TFi; WeW-3 *Fr.* Epicoene; or, The Silent Woman.

Still to my sight thy love doth rise. To a Friend, Who Gave the Author a Reading Glass. Elizabeth Moody. PoBW

Still to survive in my immortal song. (LL) Michael Drayton. EnLoPo; HAP; HeIP-4; NAEL-5v1; NAEL-7v1; NIP-4; NOSC; SCGP *Fr.* Idea.

Still Waiting for My Winter Coat: A Sequence of Fragments. Hipponax. WoPoe, *tr.* by Anselm Hollo

Still waiting for the pool to fill. (LL) Audubon Drive, Memphis. James Seay. AllShUp; SwNoth

Still was the night, serene and bright. Michael Wigglesworth. ColAP; NAAL-3; TCAPo *Fr.* Day of Doom, The.

Still Without Life. Rosalie Moore. YaYoPo

Still young and fine! but what is still in view. Rainbow, The. Henry Vaughan. GeHe

Still your people and mine were tearing each other to pieces when we. Letter to the Actor Charles Laughton concerning the Work on the Play "The Life of Galileo." Bertolt Brecht. PoSu, *tr.* by Michael Hamburger

Stillborn. Jane Duran. MFPA

Stillborn Night. Beth Brant. ReEnLa

Stilled is the lute string after hours of song. Orchid Door, The. *Unknown.* WoPoe, *tr.* by Jean S. Grigsby

Stilled room to which I am called, A. Call, The. Dennis Haskell. NOBAu

Stillness. Basho. EH, *tr.* by Robert Hass

Stillness. James Elroy Flecker. MoBrPo

Stillness. Exclamation. Octavio Paz. ChAP, *tr.* by Eliot Weinberger

Stillness! Down the dripping ride. Tunstall Forest. Donald Davie. OxBEV

Stillness is highest act. James McAuley. BMAP *Fr.* Seven Days of Creation, The.

Stillness of dawn, The. J. W. Hackett. HA

Stillness of the jungle, The. Stillness of the Poem, The. Ron Loewinsohn. NeAP; PoM

Stillness of the Poem, The. Ron Loewinsohn. NeAP; PoM

Stillness of the rose, The. Rose, The. William Carlos Williams. NOBA

Stillness, / of the wood, The. Figures, The. Robert Creeley. UnPo

Still. . . some echo. Elizabeth Searle Lamb. HA

Stilt-walker. Susan Wicks. Prnts

Stimulus beyond the Grave, The. Emily Dickinson. OxBSP

Stincher, The. Jackie Kay. NOxBChV

Sting, The. Tom Paulin. EmeKit

Sting of Death, The. Frederick George Scott. SacPr

Stinging / gold swarms. Sunset. E. E. Cummings. MoAmPo

Stingo! to thy bar-room skip. Anacreontic to Flip. Royall Tyler. OBAL

Stings. Sylvia Plath. NALW

Stink and are thrown away. End fair enough. (LL) On Spies. Ben Jonson. BeJo; FaBoVe; NPeEn; NoP-4; OxBSP; WoPoe

Stinking of chlorine and sweit, the sweirt recruits. 1941. Robert Garioch. FaBoWar

Stinking Rose, The. Sujata Bhatt. HarvBoo

Stir not the sand too much, for there lies Stuyvesant. Epitaph for Peter Stuyvesant. Henricus Selyns. SCAP

Stir of the world, the music of the mountain, The. (LL) Fawn's Foster-Mother. Robinson Jeffers. NOBA; NoAM

Stirring, A. Octavio Paz. PFTM-2, *tr.* by Eliot Weinberger *Fr.* Blanco.

Stirring as among / cattle, A. Snow. David Malouf. CBAP

Stirring in safety, smiling at being a Jew. (LL) Wall, The. Eve Merriam. TaR; TrJP

Stirring of a feathering cloud, The. Nature's Minor Chords. Henrietta Cordelia Ray. CBWP-3

Stirring the red: a single boat. Tune: "Charm of Nien-nu." Chiang K'uei. SuSp, *tr.* by James J. Y. Liu

Stirs its ashes and embers, its burnt sticks. Old Age Gets Up. Ted Hughes. NoAM

Stirs the Culprit—Life! (LL) Emily Dickinson. SAmP; TAP; TCAPo

Stitch in the side. Want of %&$ Want of — +. Anne Szumigalski. FaBoWP

Stitches. Debra Kang Dean. NAPBL

Stitches. Shinkichi Takahashi. ZenPo, *tr.* by Takashi Ikemoto and Lucien Stryk

Stockdoves, The. Andrew Young. NePenScot

Stocking Up. Sylvia Kantaris. LW

Stocky woman at the door, The. Last Day and the First, The. Theodore Weiss. TwCP; VGW

Stockyard, The. Sir John Collings Squire. OxBTC

Stoic: for Laura von Courten, The. Edgar Bowers. CoAP

Stoker, The. Shin Shalom. MHP, tr. by Ruth Finer Mintz

Stoklewath; or, The Cumbrian Village. Susanna Blamire. "From where dark clouds of curling smoke arise." ECWP; NOEC

Stolen Away.˙ Joseph Ceravolo. FTOS

Stolen Child, The. W. B. Yeats. NAEL-5v2; NAEL-6v2; NoP-4

Stolen Kiss, The. Robert Dodsley. ECEV

Stolen Pleasure. William Drummond, of Hawthornden. EnLoPo

Stolen Visit, A. Rosa Mulholland. PoBW

Stolen White Girl, The. John Rollin Ridge. APN-2

Stomach. Kathleen Norris. OBAL

Stomach of goat, crushed. Salami. Philip Levine. NNaP; NOBA; TAP; TRP

Stomp of feet, A bevy of swift hands, A. (LL) Woman Me. Maya Angelou. BlSi; OxWW

Stompin' at the Savoy. Edgar Sampson. ReLy

Stomping to the house. To Kill Stray Dogs. Mark Todd. GeoH

Stond well, moder, under Rode. Unknown. MiEL

Stone. Edward Kamau Brathwaite. PFTM-2; WaCA

Stone. Donald Justice. CRP Fr. Things.

Stone. Charles Simic. ChAP

Stone, A. Yves Bonnefoy. VCWP, tr. by John Naughton

Stone, The. Walter De la Mare. WeW-3

Stone, The. Wilfrid Wilson Gibson. MoBrPo

Stone, The. Henry Vaughan. ChIV-1

Stone, The. Thomas Vaughan. OBWVE

Stone and Fern. Leslie Norris. AngWePo

Stone and Light. Shuntaro Tanikawa. VCWP, tr. by Harold Wright

Stone and Sky. Nikolay Novikov. "In our world it's unusual." TCRusP, tr. by Daniel Weissbort

Stone / and that hard. Lorine Niedecker. APT-2

Stone at dawn, A. Easter Morning. Amy Clampitt. ChIV-2

Stone at the Bottom, The. Manuel Ulacia. VCWP, tr. by Reginald Gibbons

Stone at the Tip of the Tongue, A. Oumarou Watta. NAfrP

Stone bell tolls on the seabed, The. August Sleepwalker, The. Bei Dao. PFTM-2, tr. by Bonnie S. McDougall

Stone Bridge, The. Shen Chou. "South of the Bridge." CoBLCP

Stone, bronze, stone, steel, stone, oakleaves, horses' heels. T. S. Eliot. OBWP Fr. Coriolan.

Stone Canyon Nocturne. Charles Wright. ColAP; GeoHom; HCAP; LCAP-2; VCAP

Stone Castle Music. Unknown. CoBCP, tr. by Burton Watson

Stone cliffs, no clouds. Early Summer in the Year Jen-tzu (1672)—Playfully Painted in the Manner of Ts'ao Yün-hsi. Yün Shou-p'ing. CoBLCP, tr. by Jonathan Chaves

Stone / cold / daylight. Poem for Etheridge. Sonia Sanchez. BPo

Stone cries from the wall, The. Epitaph. Unknown. TrJP

Stone cries to stone. Jerusalem. James Fenton. HarvBoo

Stone-cutters fighting time with marble, you foredefeated. To the Stone-Cutters. Robinson Jeffers. ColAP; MoAmPo; NAAL-2v2; NAAL-5; NOBA; OxBA; PAI; PoRA

Stone Diary, A. Pat Lowther. NOBC

Stone doesn't repel the light, The. Stone and Light. Shuntaro Tanikawa. VCWP, tr. by Harold Wright

Stone Dog, The. King Lê Thánh–tông. WoPoe, tr. by Nguyen Ngoc Bich

Stone Dolphin, The. Fay Zwicky. BMAP Fr. Three Songs of Love and Hate.

Stone Face, The. Harri Webb. AngWePo

Stone Face Falls. William Everson. APT-2

Stone Fish Lake. Yüan Chieh. ChiP, tr. by Arthur Waley

Stone for a Statue. Sarah Morgan Bryan Piatt. NCAP

Stone for the sake of the souls of the slain birds sailing. (LL) Over Sir John's Hill. Dylan Thomas. AngWePo; NPeEn; TCAWP; TOF

Stone Gentleman, The. James Reeves. OxBSP

Stone Giant. Joseph Bruchac. CDW

Stone gullets among. Stone Gullets. May Swenson. VCAP

Stone had skidded arc'd and bloomed into islands, The. Calypso. Edward Kamau Brathwaite. HarvBoo

Stone Hammer Poem. Robert Kroetsch. NOBC

Stone Idol, The. Ivan Alekseievich Bunin. TCRP, tr. by Simon Franklin

Stone in your face, The. Ode to César Vallejo. Pablo Neruda. TCLAP, tr. by Stephen Tapscott

Stone. Love this man. (LL) Distances, The. Charles Olson. NAAL-2v2; NeAP

Stone-masons give stones dreams to dream. Stone-masons, My Father, and Me. Namdeo Dhasal. OMIP, tr. by Vinay Dharwadker

Stone-masons, My Father, and Me. Namdeo Dhasal. OMIP, tr. by Vinay Dharwadker

Stone of Megakles who's dead, The. Simonides. GrAn

Stone of Patience. Mimi Khalvati. MFPA

Stone / On summer plain. Masaoka Shiki. ZenPo, tr. by Takashi Ikemoto and Lucien Stryk

Stone on the Hilltop, The. Lu Yu. CoBCP; ColAnChi, tr. by Burton Watson

Stone relief I never tire of, A. Spinning Dharma Wheel. Shinkichi Takahashi. ZenPo, tr. by Takashi Ikemoto and Lucien Stryk

Stone says that it covers here the white dog, The. Tymnes. HePo Fr. Epigrams.

Stone Speech. Charles Tomlinson. NPeEn

Stone stands among new firs, The. Standing Stone. Ruth Bidgood. AngWePo

Stone that God whets laws with, The. Trinity. Gerrit Achterberg. TuT, tr. by Dennis O'Driscoll

Stone upon stone, and man, where was he? Pablo Neruda. TCLAP, tr. by John Felstiner Fr. Heights of Macchu Picchu, The.

Stone Wall. Shinkichi Takahashi. ZenPo, tr. by Takashi Ikemoto and Lucien Stryk

Stone Wall and Celebration. János Pilinszky. PoSu, tr. by Peter Jay

Stone Wall and Fiesta. János Pilinszky. IQMS, tr. by Adam Makkai

Stone, who was his father that lies beneath you? Hektor of Troy. Archias of Macedon. GrAn, tr. by Dudley Fitts

Stone Will Talk, The. Houda Al-Na'mani. PoArWo

Stone within stone, and man, where was he? Pablo Neruda. VCWP Fr. Heights of Macchu Picchu, The.

Stone you let fall in me will not resile, The. Edith Jay Scovell. HarvBoo Fr. Water Images.

Stoned & / singing Indian scat. River Still To Be Found, A. Lawrence Ferlinghetti. BB

Stonehenge. Samuel Daniel. NPeEn Fr. Musophilus; or, Defence of All Learning.

Stonemason, The. Valery [or Valerii] Yakovlevich [or Iakovlevich] Bryusov [or Briusov]. TCRP, tr. by April FitzLyon

Stonemason wanted. . . he dared to want, A. Tomb of the Imagination. Miguel Hernández. AF, tr. by Tom Jones

Stones. William Jeffrey. OxBS

Stones. Shirley Kaufman. DTA

Stones (a miracle to mortal view), The. Ovid. OBVE Fr. Metamorphoses.

Stones and Bones. Christopher Reid. NPeEn

Stones and Snow. Homer. OBVE, tr. by Alexander Pope Fr. Iliad, The.

Stones are time, The. Village. Octavio Paz. TCLAP, tr. by Charles Tomlinson

Stones in Jordan's stream, The. Stones. William Jeffrey. OxBS

Stones in my Passway. Robert Johnson. APT-2

Stones must form a circle first not a wall. First Rule. Maurice Kenny. HATNAP

Stones no longer interest me, The. In the Roman Forum. István Vas. IQMS, tr. by Bruce Berlind

Stones of Time, The. Kenneth Koch. NoAM Fr. Days and Nights.

Stones only, the disjecta membra of this Great House. Ruins of a Great House. Derek Walcott. TwCP

Stones only, the disjecta membra of this. Derek Walcott. See Stones only, the disjecta membra of this Great House

Stones Speak of an Earthless Sky. Duane Niatum. PoCoUp

Stonewall Jackson. Herman Melville. NCAP

Stonewall Jackson's Way. John Williamson Palmer. CBCWP

Stoney Ridge Dance Hall. Alden Nowlan. MoCV

Stony Grey Soil. Patrick Kavanagh. CIP-2; HarvBoo; ModIr

Stony Lonesome. Langston Hughes. NOBA; SAmP

Stony lonesome reached out and grabbed me. Dannemora Contraband. Jackie Warren-Moore. SpirFl

Stood off shrouded in his loneliness. (LL) Watchmaker God. Robert Lowell. HCAP; InvLi; SoSe-8

Stood on the top of a spur once. Still Shines When You Think of It. Vincent O'Sullivan. PeNZ

Stood there then among. Robert Earl Hayden. LCAP-2

Stood watching the boat disappear on the black waters of Lethe? (LL) Supermarket in California, A. Allen Ginsberg. CAGL; CoAP; HAP; HCAP; HeIP-4; InPK-6; NAAL-2v2; NAAL-5; NIL-7; NOBA; NeAP; NoAM; PmAP; PoM; ReTh; TAP; TFi; TwCP; UnPo; WeW-3

Stoop, and begin the ancient croaking. (LL) Poets Agree to Be Quiet by the Swamp, The. David Wagoner. CoAP; VGW

Stoop on the log-house is brown with sweet rain-rot, The. Joan Finnigan. WPE *Fr.* May Day Rounds: Renfrew County.

Stooping to pull up a weed. Taproot. Debra Kang Dean. NAPBL

Stop. Richard Wilbur. LCAP-2

Stop all the clocks. W. H. Auden. *See* Twelve Songs

Stop all the clocks, cut off the telephone. W. H. Auden. CAGL; MoBrPo; OPOU; RB *Fr.* Twelve Songs.

Stop bleeding said the knife. Bleeding. May Swenson. NALW

Stop, Christian passer-by!—Stop, child of God. Epitaph. Samuel Taylor Coleridge. NAEL-5v2; NAEL-6v2; NOCV; SacPr

Stop! cried the knight. No more of this, good sir. Geoffrey Chaucer. NAWM-5v1, *tr. by* Theodore Morrison *Fr.* Canterbury Tales, The.

Stop, cried the wolf to the lamb seven. Failure. Natan Zach. FIT, *tr. by* Robert Friend

Stop! Don't touch me. *Unknown.* BoWoP

Stop Fooling. Velemir [*or* Viktor Vladimirovich] Khlebnikov. TCRP, *tr. by* Gary Kern

Stop!—for thy tread is on an Empire's dust! Byron. NAEL-5v2; NAEL-6v2 *Fr.* Childe Harold's Pilgrimage.

Stop!—Gaze thro' this hushed gallery! The air. Benjamin Paul Blood. APN-2 *Fr.* Bride of the Iconoclasts, The.

Stop, let me have the truth of that! Dîs Aliter Visum; or, Le Byron de Nos Jours. Robert Browning. NAEL-5v2; NAEL-6v2

Stop looking like a purse. How could a purse. Toad. Norman MacCaig. HarvBoo

Stop, my Augustine, stop: ere you will God explain. "Angelus Silesius." GePo, *tr. by* George C. Schoolfield *Fr.* Cherubical Wanderer, The.

Stop, passenger! a wondrous tale to list. Epitaph on Mr W———. Felicia Dorothea Hemans. ViWPN

Stop, shadow of my tricky fate. In Containing a Thought Satisfied with Chaste Love. Sister Juana Inés de la Cruz. BLPSL, *tr. by* Rene de Costa, Rigas Kappatos and Eleni Paidoussi

Stop, stop and listen for the bough top. Blackbird of Derrycairn, The. *Unknown.* BIrV, *tr. by* Austin Clarke

Stop this motherfucking Limo, says the King. Elvis Moving a Small Cloud: The Desert Near Las Vegas, 1976. David Wojahn. AllShUp

Stop you my mouth with still still kissing me. (LL) Sir Philip Sidney. NAEL-5v1; NAEL-6v1; NAEL-7v1; OxBSo; Son *Fr.* Astrophil and Stella.

Stop! You're Breakin' My Heart. Ted Koehler. ReLy

Stopless wind, here are the columbine seeds I have. Of Forced Sightes and Trusty Ferefulness. Jorie Graham. PoPoPo

Stoplights edged the licorice street with ribbon. Leap in the Dark. Roberta Hill Whiteman. WPOW

Stopping at a Friend's Farm. Meng Hao Jan. SuSp, *tr. by* Daniel Bryant

Stopping at the Mayflower. Joseph Awad. GraLe

Stopping by Woods on a Snowy Evening. Robert Frost. APT-1; BRP; ChAP; ClHu; ColAP; FaBoCh; HAP; HarvBoo; HeIP-4; ITBLP; InPK-6; MoAmPo; NAAL-2v2; NAAL-5; NIL-7; NIP-4; NOBA; NTCP; NoAM; NoP-4; OBCA; OxBA; PAI; PoE; PoPoPo; PoRA; RB; SAmP; SCV; SoSe-8; TAP; TFi; TOF; TRP; TTTS

Stopping the diary. Forget What Did. Philip Larkin. NoAM

Stopping the Night at Jung-yang. Po Chü-i. ChiP, *tr. by* Arthur Waley

Stopping to Take Notes. Michael Smith. PBCIP

Stopping Wine. T'ao Ch'ien [*or* T'ao Yuan-ming]. CoBCP, *tr. by* Burton Watson

Stopwatch. Mary Ruefle. ExTi

Store dick lays a hand on your shoulder, The. Shoplifting. Baron Wormser. ReTh

Stored in the attic, even in sleep. To Atlas in the Attic. Julie Agoos. YaYoPo

Stores and filling stations prefer a roof. Christmas Tree. Stanley Cook. OBCP

Stores lit up with their goods, The. (LL) Dream, The. David Ignatow. CoAP; NNaP; PAI

Stores were bright, and not too far from home, The. From the Porch. John Koethe. MakPoe

Storied cliffs were the fortune I cast. Han-shan. GifTon, *tr. by* Red Pine

Storied Sonnet. Ann Radcliffe. CenSon

Stories. J. Patrick Lewis. NOxBChV

Stories of Snow. Patricia K. Page. NOBC; NoP-4

Stories / would be braided in my hair, The. Story Keeper. Wendy Rose. UnSA

Storing Memories. Belinda Zubicueta Carmona. TANSG, *tr. by* Celeste Kostopulos-Cooperman

Stork questioned the swan whose moving song, The. Aria Senza da Capo. Robert Finch. MoCV

Storks are coming now, The. Spirit of the Wind. Gabriel Okara. PBMAP

Storks like elbows had a fit of falling, The. There's No Place to Sleep in This Bed, Tanguy. Charles Henri Ford. SPE

Storm. Emily Dickinson. NAAL-2v1; NAAL-3; OxBSP

Storm. "H. D." APT-1

Storm. Roger McGough. OTCP

Storm. Ágnes Nemes Nagy. IQMS, *tr. by* Hugh Maxton

Storm. Judith Wright. WPE

Storm, A. "Nikolai Nikolaevich Morshen." TCRusP, *tr. by* John Glad

Storm, The. Alcaeus [*or* Alkaios]. AWP, *tr. by* John Hermann Merivale

Storm, The. Elizabeth Jane Coatsworth. OBCA

Storm, The. Sara Coleridge. NOxBChV

Storm, The. Walter De la Mare. NOxBChV

Storm, The. Heinrich Heine. AWP, *tr. by* Louis Untermeyer

Storm, The. George Herbert. ESCV

Storm, The. Adam Mickiewicz. WoPoe, *tr. by* Vyt Bakaitis

Storm, The. Eugenio Montale. AF, *tr. by* William Arrowsmith

Storm, The. Coventry Patmore. EnLoPo

Storm, The. Jirka Polak. INSAB

Storm, The. Margaret Stanley-Wrench. LW

Storm, an Endless Instant. Boris Leonidovich Pasternak. TCRusP, *tr. by* Bogdan Boychuk and Mark Rudman

Storm and Calm: Sent from Embden to M. Edw. Ma. and M. Tho. Ly, The. Nicholas Murford. NOSC

Storm at Sea. Rumann, Son of Colman. WoPoe, *tr. by* Frank O'Connor

Storm at Sea, A. John Donne. NOBE *Fr.* Storm[e], The.

Storm at Sea: Sometimes I plunge through the press of waves. Cynewulf. ASW *Fr.* Riddles (Exeter Book).

Storm-Beaten. Clara Ann Thompson. CBWP-2

Storm-beaten old watch-tower, A. Symbols. W. B. Yeats. OBMV

Storm blew in last night and knocked out, A. Window, The. Raymond Carver. BLT

Storm blew up so suddenly, The. In Rough Weather. Paul Lake. RA

Storm—chestnuts / Race along. Masaoka Shiki. ZenPo, *tr. by* Takashi Ikemoto and Lucien Stryk

Storm-Cock's Song, The. Hugh MacDiarmid. OxBTC

Storm Cone, The. Rudyard Kipling. NoAM; OxBTC

Storm cries every night, The. Spring Song. Hermann Hesse. AWP, *tr. by* Ludwig Lewisohn

Storm-dances of gulls, the barking game of seals, The. Divinely Superfluous Beauty. Robinson Jeffers. HeIP-4; MoAmPo

Storm Ending. Jean Toomer. APT-2

Storm Fear. Robert Frost. APT-1; ColAP; OxBA; TCAPo

Storm from the Far Heights. Sándor Weöres. IQMS, *tr. by* Adam Makkai and Donald E. Morse

Storm has ended and death steps back, The. On the Beach. Tom Clark. BodElec

Storm hath ceased: yet still I have, The. Ghona Widow's Lullaby, The. Thomas Pringle. PeSAV

Storm high. Brown Rosellen. FFC

Storm House, The. Elizabeth Jennings. WPE

Storm in Summer, A. Wilfrid Scawen Blunt. FaBoTw

Storm in the Black Forest. D. H. Lawrence. FaBoVe

Storm is over, the land hushes to rest, The. Robert Bridges. GTBS-P; OBMV

Storm is sweeping o'er the land, The. Wild Night, A. Julia Ward Howe. ColAP

Storm not, brave Friend, that thou hast never yet. To Scilla. Sir Charles Sedley. FaBoEE

Storm, park, and restless. Christopher Street 1979. Walter Holland. CAGL

Storm Pattern. Greg Pape. PBCAP

Storm's still everywhere I step, The. Abbott's Lagoon. Dennis Schmitz. GeoHom

Storm splattering the tough magnolia, The. Storm, The. Eugenio Montale. AF, *tr. by* William Arrowsmith

Storm Surf. Greg Pape. MoASP

Storm Warnings. Adrienne Rich. AiP; NAAL-2v2; NAAL-5; NIL-7; NIP-4; YaYoPo

Storm was coming, that was why it was dark, A. Sudden Things. Donald Hall. SPE

Storm-wearied Argo slept upon the water. Bayard Taylor. CAGL *Fr.* Hylas.

Storm-Wind, The. William Barnes. NOBE

Storm Windows. Howard Nemerov. CoAmPo; InPK-6; VCAP

Storm winds carry snow. Deer Song. Leslie Marmon Silko. VoR

Stormalong! *Unknown.* FaBoVe

Storm[e], The. John Donne. NAEL-6v1; NAEL-7v1; NoSic Storm at Sea, A. NOBE

Stormeys' dead that good old man. Stormalong! *Unknown.* FaBoVe

Stormpetrel. Richard Murphy. ModIr

Storms lend you wings, destroyer of the lands. Inanna and Enlil. Enheduanna. BoWoP

Stormy are the waters of Waiapu. Waters of Waiapu, The. Pairare Henare Tomoana. PeNZ, *tr. by* Margaret Orbell

Stormy Hebrides, The. William Collins. NOBE *Fr.* Ode on the Popular Superstitions of the Highlands of Scotland, An.

Stormy Night. William Robert Rodgers. ModIr; PNI

Stormy Night in Autumn. Chu Shu-chen. BoWoP; OHPC, *tr.* by Kenneth Rexroth

Stormy Weather (Keeps Rainin' All the Time). Ted Koehler. ReLy

Stornelli and Strambotti. Agnes Mary Frances Robinson. VWP

Story. John Balaban. CDa

Story. Eavan Boland. HarvBoo

Story, A. Yusuf Al-Sa'igh. MAP, *tr.* by Diana Der Hovanessian and Salma Khadra Jayyusi

Story, A. Margaret Avison. MoCV

Story, A. Jane Hirshfield. BLT

Story, A. Jean Ingelow. VWP

Story, A. Li-Young Lee. LoL; RaBo

Story, A. William Stafford. NNaP

Story, The. Muhammad Al-Faituri [*or* Al-Fituri *or* Al-Fayturi]. MAP, *tr.* by Sargon Boulus and Peter Porter

Story, The. Kevin Hart. BMAP

Story, The. Dan Pagis. PoSu, *tr.* by Stephen Mitchell

Story, The. Charles Simic. NNaP

Story, a story, A! Rowing. Anne Sexton. BoWoP; LCAP-2

Story About Chicken Soup, A. Louis Simpson. NNaP; PoE; PoWW; TAP; UnSA

Story about Indians, A. Climate of Paradise, The. Louis Simpson. NOBA

Story about the Body, A. Robert Hass. RaBo

Story After the Story, The. Marie Ponsot. ExTi

Story Books on a Kitchen Table. Audre Lorde.

   ("For the vanished mother / of a Black girl.") (LL) GT

Story comes apart near Gala's eyebrows, The. Hallucinogenic Bullfighter. Juan Felipe Herrera. BodElec

Story goes, from evil, The. Alcaeus [*or* Alkaios]. SaLy, *tr.* by Diane Rayor

Story goes like this: the light, The. Juliana Spahr. NAPBL *Fr.* We.

Story I Like to Tell, The. Robin Becker. PBCAP

Story I shall tell today, The. Nightingale, The. Marie de France. BoWoP, *tr.* by Patricia Terry

Story is simple, The. Linda. Jack Lawrence. ReLy

Story is true, The. (LL) Bresson's Movies. Robert Creeley. NoP-4; PmAP

Story Keeper. Wendy Rose. UnSA

Story of a Hotel Room. Rosemary Tonks. LW; OxBTC

Story of a Well-made Shield, The. N. Scott Momaday. CDW; HATNAP

Story of Abraham, The. Alicia Ostriker. InvLi

Story of Augustus Who Would Not Have Any Soup, The. Heinrich Hoffmann. NBLV

Story of Canobie Dick, The. Libby Houston. OBSP

Story of Every Day, The. Eugenio Montale. ItPo, *tr.* by Gayle Ridinger

Story of Frankie. . . My Man, The. Archie Weller. BMAP

Story of How a Wall Stands, A. Simon J. Ortiz. HATNAP

Story of Inkle and Yarico, The. Frances Seymour, Countess of Hertford. ECWP

Story of Joshua. Alicia Ostriker. ChIV-1

Story of Keys, The. Richard Garcia. TouFir

Story of Life, The. John Godfrey Saxe. PoToHe

Story of Lovers Leap, The. Maggie Pogue Johnson. CBWP-4

Story of My Life, The. Carroll Arnett. VoR

Story of My Life, The. Liz Rosenberg. PBCAP

Story of my skin, The. Autobiographical Poem. Elaine Equi. KGB

Story of Our Lives, The. Mark Strand. VCAP

Story of Phoebus and Daphne Applied, [etc.], The. Edmund Waller. NAEL-5v1; NOSC

   (Story of Phœbus and Daphne appli'd, The.) PBRV

   (*Thirsis* a youth of the inspired train.) PBRV

Story of Rimini, The. Leigh Hunt.

   "Noble range it was, of many a rood, A." OBGa

   "One day—'twas on a gentle, autumn noon." NOBRP

   Story of Rimini, The. OBGa

Story of Stonewall goes like this: On the night of Judy Garland's, A. Story of Stonewall, A. Maureen Seaton. ReTh

Story of the Eaters, A. Santiago Mendes Zapata. STP

Story of the Man Whose Tastes Were Too Refined. Charles Rafferty. AmPoNex

Story of Uriah, The. Rudyard Kipling. NOBVV; OxBEV; PeVV; SCV

Story Often Told in Bars, A: The *Reader's Digest* Version. William Matthews. ReTh

Story So Far, The. John Clarke. UV

Story That Could Be True, A. William Stafford. KaS; NTCP; RaBo

Story: There was a cow in the road, struck by a semi, A. Difficult Body. Mark Wunderlich. NAPBL

Story We Know, The. Martha Collins. SoSe-8

Storys to rede ar delitabill. John Barbour. OxBS *Fr.* Bruce, The.

Storytime. Judith Nicholls. OBSP

Stout Brahms. Bruce Berger. GeoH

Stow, birde, stow, stow! John Skelton. NoSic *Fr.* Magnificence.

Stowe, the Gardens of the Rt. Hon. Richard Lord Viscount Cobham. Gilbert West. OBGa *Fr.* Stowe, the Gardens of the Rt. Hon. Richard Lord Viscount Cobham.

   "Hence thro' the windings of the mazy wood." OBGa

Stowed away in a Montreal lumber room. O God! O Montreal! Samuel Butler (1835–1902). OBSV; OxBoLi; PeLV

Strage degli innocenti, La. Giambattista [*or* Giovanni Battista] Marino. Sospetto d'Herode.

   Steps to the Temple. SacPr

Straggled soldier halted—stared at Him, The. Christ and the Soldier. Siegfried Sassoon. NoP-4

Strahan, Tonson, Lintot of the times. To Mr. Murray. Byron. UV

Straight from the east the wind blows sharp with rain. April in Town. Lizette Woodworth Reese. APN-2

Straight from the heart. Love Is a Random Thing. George, Jr. Marion. ReLy

Straight out of the blue. Pigeon of My Childhood. Sergey Aleksandrovich Vasilyev [*or* Vasil'ev]. TCRP, *tr.* by Max Hayward and Lubov Yakovleva

Straight remnant, of the spiry birchen bough. Elegiac Sonnet to a Mopstick. William Beckford. CenSon

Straight rye whiskey, 100 proof. Brooklyn Narcissus. Paul Blackburn. PmAP

Straight Talk from Plain Women. Sherley Anne Williams. GT

Straight through the air my mooring line to you. (LL) Kenneth Leslie. NOBC; OxBSo *Fr.* By Stubborn Stars.

Straining at the padlock. Jack Kerouac. HA

Strains of Sight. Robert Duncan. PoE

Strand at Lough Beg, The. Seamus Heaney. CIP-2; NPeEn; NoAM; OBWP

Strand Hotel, Rosslare, The. James Liddy. CIP-2

Strand-Thistle. Gustav Falke. AWP, *tr.* by Jethro Bithell

Stranded in My Ontario. Ronald G. Everson. NOBC

Stranded on the moon. Moon-Man. Dorothy Hewett. CBAP

Stranded Whales, The. Geoffrey Dutton. CBAP

Strange. Stanley Burnshaw. TrJP

Strange. Kirby Doyle. NeAP

Strange. To a Fair Lady Playing with a Snake. Edmund Waller. CABP; EBEV; NOSC; PoE

Strange Adventure. Rossana Ombres. NeIt, *tr.* by Ruth Feldman

Strange and slow work: they dug in turn. Well, The. Philip Salom. NOBAu

Strange and unnatural! lets stay and see. Destinie. Abraham Cowley. MeLP

Strange are the feelings arising within me. Love of Hell, The. Abraham Burstein. TrJP

Strange are the paths of mankind in the night. Revelation and Decline. Georg Trakl. PFTM-1

Strange arrangement to comfort the heart, A. Fragrant Hands. Faiz Ahmad Faiz. VCWP, *tr.* by Agha Shahid Ali

Strange, beautiful girl, A. By T'ing Yang Waterfall. Hsieh Ling-yün. OHMPC, *tr.* by Kenneth Rexroth

Strange beauty, eight-limbed and eight-handed. Octopus. Arthur Clement Hilton. UV

Strange Bird, A. Michael Dransfield. BMAP

Strange Business. Jelaluddin [*or* Jalal al-Din] Rumi. LoL, *tr.* by Coleman Barks

Strange calling; to play the minor effects, A. Foley Artist, The. Nick Drake. NeBl

Strange Case, The. Michael Ondaatje. EmeKit

Strange church smelled a bit 'high,' of censers, The. Geoffrey Hill. EmeKit; PoE *Fr.* Mercian Hymns.

Strange Country. Julie Parson-Nesbitt. MPUn

Strange, dear, but true, dear. So in Love. Cole Porter. ReLy

Strange Fits of Passion Have I Known. William Wordsworth. EBEV; NAEL-5v2; NAEL-6v2; NOBE; OBEV; PoE

Strange Fruit. Lewis Allan. ReLy

Strange Fruit. Joy Harjo. SeSe

Strange Fruit. Timothy Liu. WiU

Strange grows the river on the sunless evenings! Vesperal. Ernest Christopher Dowson. OBMV

Strange Hells. Ivor Gurney. FaBoWar; OxBTC; PeFWW

Strange Hurt. Langston Hughes. APT-2

Strange Legacies. Sterling Allen Brown. TTY

Strange—like messengers. Kaiga. JDP, *tr.* by Yoel Hoffmann

Strange Love. Moses Ibn Ezra. TrJP, *tr.* by Solomon Solis-Cohen

Strange Meeting. Wilfred Owen. FaBoMo; FaBoWar; GTBS-P; HarvBoo; HeIP-4; MakPoe; MoBrPo; NAEL-5v2; NAEL-6v2; NOBE; NoAM; NoP-4; OBWP; OxAEP-2; OxBEV; PeFWW; PoE; PoWW; RB; SCV; TCAWP; TFi

Strange Meetings. Harold Monro.
   Flower Is Looking, A. MoBrPo
   If Suddenly a Clod of Earth. MoBrPo

Strange Monsters. Rowland Watkyns. FaBoEE

Strange Music. Edvard Grieg. ReLy

Strange mysterious God visits the forest, A. Eternal Farewell. Ricardo Jaimes Freyre. TCLAP, tr. by Victor Tulli

Strange now to think of you, gone without corsets & eyes. Kaddish. Allen Ginsberg. HCAP; NAAL-2v2; NOBA; NeAP; PmAP; PoM

Strange old man, A. Kakinomoto no Hitomaro. OHPJ

Strange Old Woman, A. Mother Goose. FaBoCh; LB; ReMoGo

Strange paradise, complete with worms. Ware Collection of Glass Flowers and Fruit, Harvard Museum, The. Mark Doty. HarvBoo

Strange Peak. Muso Soseki. EaWin, tr. by W. S. Merwin

Strange People, The. Louise Erdrich. PoPoPo

Strange power, I know not what thou art. To Memory. Mary Elizabeth Coleridge. ViWPN

Strange Power! I trust thy might; trust thou my constancy. (LL) Visionary, The. Emily Jane Brontë. BrRo; NOBE; NOBVV; NPeEn; OxBEV; SCGP; SCV

Strange power of song! the strain that warms the heart. Hannah More. NoP-4 Fr. Slave Trade, The.

Strange race of critics, A. Antiphanes. WoPoe, tr. by Sam Hamill

Strange room, from this angle. Soho Hospital for Women, The. Fleur Adcock. NAEL-6v2; NoP-4

Strange Shepherd, Set My Bellwether Free. Félix Lope de Vega Carpio. SpanPo, tr. by W. S. Merwin

Strange spirit with inky hair. Lion, The. Walter James Turner. MoBrPo

Strange Tears. Liu Ya-tzu. SuSp, tr. by Wu-Chi Liu

Strange that I did not know him then. Old Story, An. Edwin Arlington Robinson. MoAmPo; OxBSP

Strange / That in this nigger place. Esthete in Harlem. Langston Hughes. BPo; ColAP

Strange that your image should occur to me. Grudge, The. Dimitris Tsaloumas. BMAP

Strange the formation of the eely race. William Diaper. ECEV; OBVE Fr. Halieutica.

Strange thing hangs by man's hip, A. Cynewulf. PeLV, tr. by Kevin Crossley-Holland Fr. Riddles (Exeter Book).

Strange things indeed Are seen in the sea-world. Nature of the Siren, The. Cynewulf. WoPoe, tr. by Richard Wilbur

Strange to be torn away from your embrace. Strange. Stanley Burnshaw. TrJP

Strange to behold, unmingled with surprize. On the Civilization of the Western Aboriginal Country. Philip Freneau. APN-1

Strange to step straight into the beautiful dawn. Miraculous Dawn. R. Williams Parry. OBWVE, tr. by Joseph P. Clancy

Strange tropic warmth and hints of summer seas. (LL) Ethnogenesis. Henry Timrod. APN-2; NOBA; OxBA; TCAPo

Strange Type. Malcolm Lowry. NPeEn

Strange Visitor, The. Unknown. FaBoCh

Strange walkers! See their processional. Mushroom Gatherers, The. Donald Davie. OxBEV

Strange was the way of my life—its paths were paths of wonder. Orphanhood. Hayyim Nahman [or Khayim Nakhman or Chaim Nachman] Bialik. FIT, tr. by Robert Friend

Strangely assorted, the shape of song and the bloody man. Military Harpist, The. Ruth Pitter. FaBoTw; NALW

Strangeness of Heart. Siegfried Sassoon. TrJP

Stranger. Elizabeth Madox Roberts. MoAmPo

Stranger, A. Lionel Pigot Johnson. NOBVV

Stranger, The. Aleksandr Aleksandrovich Blok. TCRP

Stranger, The. Walter De la Mare. OxBTC

Stranger, The. Jean Garrigue. NOBA; TwCP

Stranger, The. Gerald Locklin. OPRER

Stranger, The. Gabriela Mistral. SpanPo, tr. by Kate Flores

Stranger, The. Aldo Palazzeschi. PFTM-1

Stranger, The. Adrienne Rich. NNaP

Stranger. A curious hand touches the snow raising pigeons. Jungle Book. Tom Raworth. PFTM-2

Stranger and His Friend, The. James Montgomery. SacPr

Stranger! Approach this spot with gravity! Dentist, A. Unknown. FaBoEE

Stranger asked me what my country was, The. Answer, An. Ahmad al-Mushari Al-'Udwani. MAP, tr. by Charles Doria and Hilary Kilpatrick

Stranger, below the boulder rest your spent limbs. Anyte [or Anytes]. SaLy, tr. by Diane Rayor

Stranger, beware! This terrible tomb. Philip of Thessalonica. GrAn

Stranger by the roadside, do not smile. Epitaph of a Dog. Unknown. GrAn, tr. by Dudley Fitts

Stranger here, as all my fathers were, A. Motet. John Amner. OxBSP

Stranger, if thou hast learned [or learnt] a truth which needs. Inscription for the Entrance to a Wood. William Cullen Bryant. APN-1; OxBA; TAP

Stranger, if you sail to the land of lovely dances, Mitylene. Nossis. SaLy, tr. by Diane Rayor

Stranger in Louisiana, The. Felicia Dorothea Hemans. RWP

Stranger in Paradise. George Forrest. ReLy

Stranger in the Pumpkin, The. John Ciardi. NTCP

Stranger in the street, A. (LL) Sword of Surprise, The. Gilbert Keith Chesterton. MoBrPo; SacPr

Stranger in This Land, A. Cliff Ashby. NOCV

Stranger Not Ourselves, The. William Stafford. NNaP

Stranger passing, A. Alan Pizzarelli. HA

Stranger's heart! Oh! wound it not!, The. Stranger's Heart, The. Felicia Dorothea Hemans. VWP

Stranger, Stranger. Jorge de Lima. TCLAP, tr. by Luiz Fernández García

Stranger! Tell the people of Śpoon River two things. Edgar Lee Masters. NoAM; TAP Fr. New Spoon River, The.

Stranger than the Worst. Babette Deutsch. WPE

Stranger to a Small Child. Ben Scammell. NLP

Stranger to Europe, waiting release. Stranger to Europe. Guy Butler. PeSAV

Stranger to Love, Whoever Loves Not Thee. Félix Lope de Vega Carpio. SpanPo, tr. by Ian Fletcher

Stranger walks into the dark room, The. Seance. Edouard Roditi. SPE

Stranger was short: let my verse be such, The. Callimachus. GrAn

Stranger, when o'er yon slant, warm field no cloud. Sonnet. Anna Seward. NOBRP

Stranger, when you come to / Lakedaimon. Simonides. OBVE; PGA

Stranger, whoe'er thou art, whose ling'ring feet. Sonnet Written in Tintern Abbey, Monmouthshire. Edmund Gardner. NOEC

Stranger, wond'ring, stalks, and stares upon, The. Rome, Conqueror, Conquered. Joshua Sylvester. FaBoEE

Stranger, you who hide my love. Song. Stephen Spender. FaBoTw

Strangers. Huda Ablan. PoArWo, tr. by Nathalie Handal and Ibrahim Muhawi

Strangers. William Stafford. NNaP

Strangers, The. Jones Very. APN-1; OxBA

Strangers: An Essay. Jim Elledge. SwNoth

Strangers are people we haven't seen before. Conversations with Strangers. George Buchanan. PNI

Strangers Are We All upon the Earth. Franz Werfel. TrJP, tr. by Edith Abercrombie Snow

"Strangers are we and pilgrims here!" At a Friends' Meeting. Mary Elizabeth Coleridge. WPE

Strangers Like Us: Pittsburgh, Raleigh, 1945–1985. Gerald William Barrax. ISC

Strangers on a train. Travels with the Band-Aid Army. Lance Henson. VoR

Strangers to meek compassion's tender touch. Mary Latter. ECWP Fr. Soliloquies on Temporal Indigence.

Stranglehold of English Lit, The. Felix Mnthali. PBMAP

Strangling women in the suburban bush. Das Kapital. Imamu Amiri Baraka. PFTM-2; PoM

Strapped at the center of the blazing wheel. Pilot from the Carrier, A. Randall Jarrell. PoWW

Strapped helpless, monarchs and prelates, round they swung. Wheel of Fortune, The. Thom Gunn. OxBC

Strapped to my seat, I turn. Above It All. Philip Levine. NOBA

Strategy. Archilochus. WoPoe, tr. by Guy Davenport

Stratis the Sailor by the Dead Sea. George Seferis. WoPoe, tr. by Rex Warner

Stratton Water. Dante Gabriel Rossetti. OxBB

Stravinsky in L.A. Elizabeth Alexander. AmPoNex

Straw, The. Robert Graves. OxBTC

Straw Hat. Rita Dove. NAAL-5 Fr. Thomas and Beulah.

Straw Hat in the Rain. Harry Akst. ReLy

Straw in the Street. Amy Levy. VWP

Straw in the street where I pass to-day. Straw in the Street. Amy Levy. VWP

Straw reed climbs the car antenna, A. Götterdämmerung. Rita Dove. ExTi

Straw rustling everywhere. Clearing-Station. Wilhelm Klemm. PeFWW, tr. by Patrick Bridgwater

Straw sandal half sunk. Buson. EH, tr. by Yoel Hoffmann

Strawberries. W. S. Merwin. AmFaPo; NoP-4

Strawberries. Edwin Morgan. BoLoP; NoP-4

Strawberries in Mexico. Ron Padgett. SPE

Strawberries that in gardens grow. Wild Strawberries. Robert Graves. FaBoCh

Strawberry, The. Maggie Pogue Johnson. CBWP-4

Strawberry blooms upon its lowly bed, The. To the Strawberry. Helen Maria Williams. CenSon; OxBSo; RWP

Strawberry Picking. Alexander the Wild. NAWM-7v1, *tr.* by Peter Dronke

Strawberry Shrub, The. Edna St. Vincent Millay. FaBoWP

Strawberrying. Maurice Kenny. HATNAP

Strawberrying. May Swenson. VCAP

Straws like tame lightnings lie about the grass. Summer Farm. Norman MacCaig. NPeEn; NePenScot; OxBTC

Stray Animals. James Tate. NoAM

Stray bullet, A. Angel. Marisela Norte. GeoHom

Stray Dogs, Foaming. Thom Ward. AmPoNex

Strayed Reveller, The. Matthew Arnold.

    Strayed Reveller to Ulysses, The. OBEV

Straying Student, The. Austin Clarke. BIrV; CIP-2; ModIr; NOIV; NPeEn

Streak, The. Julia Kasdorf. AmPoNex

Streak of Sappho, it is said, A. Mould of Castile. Jack R. Clemo. NOCV

Streak of world blurred charcoal and scarlet, the El slows. Window, The. Lynda Hull. ExTi

Streaked and fretted with effort, the thick. Street, The. Robert Pinsky. NAAL-5; NoP-4

Stream, The. Edith Jay Scovell. HarvBoo *Fr.* Water Images.

Stream, The. Mona Van Duyn. VCAP

Stream flowing steadily over a stone does not wet its core, A. Elder's Reproof to his Wife, An. 'Abdillaahi Muuse. TTY, *tr.* by B. W. Andrejewski and I. M. Lewis

Stream of rain off metal awning. View Café, The. Jonathan Johnson. AmPoNex

Stream rills softly, the carp, The. Carp, The. *Vietnamese Oral Tradition.* CaDao, *tr.* by John Balaban

Stream ripples pure, The. By a Stream on Mount T'ien-t'ung. Wang An-shih. SuSp, *tr.* by Jan W. Walls

Stream runs clear to its stones, The. Painting, The. *Vietnamese Oral Tradition.* CaDao, *tr.* by John Balaban

Stream's Song, The. Lascelles Abercrombie. OBMV

Stream Sings to the Stone, The. Leah Goldberg. MHP, *tr.* by Ruth Finer Mintz *Fr.* Songs of the Stream.

Stream sorrow, eyes. Elegy for Her Brother Sakhr. Al-Khansa. BoWoP; WPOW

Stream was swift, and so cold, The. Captivity. Louise Erdrich. HATNAP; NoAM

Streamed from my eyes and fell on the collar of my dress. (LL) Pitcher, The. Yüan Chên. AWP; ChiP, *tr.* by Arthur Waley

Streamers. Sandra McPherson. VCAP

Streamers of crepe idling before doors. Epidemic. Charles Reznikoff. APT-2

Streamful of flowing water, A. Spring Day—Remembering Living on the River, a. Kao Ch'i. CoBLCP, *tr.* by Jonathan Chaves

Streaming into the heart. (LL) Exiles, The. Iain Crichton Smith. HarvBoo; NePenScot

Streamlet! methinks thy lot resembles mine. John F. M. Dovaston. CenSon

Streams are fettered, and with us as rare, The. Thomas Shipman. NOSC *Fr.* Frost, 1654, The: To Mr. W.L.

Streams fall down and through the darkness bear, The. Spate in Winter Midnight. Norman MacCaig. GTBS-P

Streams of Bunclody, The. *Unknown.* BIrV

Streams of Lovely Nancy, The. *Unknown.* OxBoLi

Street. Eiléan Ní Chuilleanáin. EmeKit

Street. Gary Soto. GeoHom

Street, The. James Russell Lowell. GSo; Son

Street, The. Ksenya [*or* Kseniia] Nekrasova. TCRP, *tr.* by Vera Rich

Street, The. Robert Pinsky. NAAL-5; NoP-4

Street Angel, The. K'o Chia Tsang. WoPoe, *tr.* by Kai-yu Hsu

Street Corner College. Kenneth Patchen. APT-2; CLPP; MoAmPo

Street Cries. Sidney Lanier.

    To Richard Wagner. APN-2; NCAP

Street Demonstration. Margaret Abigail Walker. BPo

Street Fair: The Quartet. Marvin Bell. BodElec

Street Fight. Harold Monro. FaBoTw

Street Funeral. Irving Layton. NIL-7

Street in Agrigento. Salvatore Quasimodo. WoPoe, *tr.* by Denis Devlin

Street in Bronzeville, A. Gwendolyn Brooks. BPo; BlSi; FaBoWP

    Hunchback Girl: She Thinks of Heaven. ChAP

    Kitchenette Building. BPo; FaBoWP; GT; NAAL; NAAL-2v2; NAAL-5; NoP-4; PoE; PoPoPo; UnPo

    "Mrs. Coley's three-flat brick." NAAL; NAAL-2v2; NOBA; NoAM

    Mother, The. ESEAA; ISC; IllVoic; NAAL; NAAL-5; NALW; PoPoPo

    Of De Witt Williams on His Way to Lincoln Cemetery. ESEAA; NOBA; NoAM

Preacher, The: Ruminates behind the Sermon. InvLi; NAAAL

Sadie and Maud. ESEAA; InPK-6; NAAAL; NOBA; NoAM; TAP

Song in the Front Yard, A. ESEAA; NAAAL; NAAL-2v2; NOBA; NOxBChV; NoAM

Southeast Corner. VGW

Vacant Lot, The. NAAAL; NAAL-2v2; NOBA; NoAM

Street Instructions at the Crotch. Edward Field. CAGL

Street is soon there, The. To Ride. Paul Éluard. TTTS, *tr.* by Kenneth Koch

Street Is Waiting for the Night, The. Juan Ramón Jiménez. SpanPo, *tr.* by Lysander Kemp

Street is waiting for the night, The. Street Is Waiting for the Night, The. Juan Ramón Jiménez. SpanPo, *tr.* by Lysander Kemp

Street lamp. Something missing. Drugstore. Mikhail Yeryomin. ItGoST, *tr.* by J. Kates

Street Lanterns. Mary Elizabeth Coleridge. PoRA

Street Music. Elizabeth Akers Allen. SWaP

Street Music. Barbara Angell. AiP

Street Music. Greg Pape. PBCAP

Street Musicians. John Ashbery. HCAP; PoPoPo

Street of Dreams. Victor Young. ReLy

Street of Nectar, Street of Contingency. Bruce Smith. Son *Fr.* In My Father's House.

Street Performers, 1851. Terence Tiller. GTBS-P

Street Scene, A. Lizette Woodworth Reese. OBCA

Street Song. Thom Gunn. HeIP-4; OxBC

Street Song. Langston Hughes. APT-2

Street Song. Sylvia Plath. MiVo

Street there is in Paris famous, A. William Makepeace Thackeray. OBEV; OxAEP-2

Street threatened, The. Aerial, The. Reiner Kunze. PoSu, *tr.* by Ewald Osers

Street-traders were roaring and steaming, The. Combustion Engine. Katherine Pierpoint. MFPA

Street was strange. Things made me wonder, The. Tram That Lost Its Way, The. Nikolai Stepanovich Gumilyov [*or* Gumiliov *or* Gumilev]. TCRP, *tr.* by Yakov Hornstein

Street Yarn. Julia Ward Howe. SWaP *Fr.* Lyrics of the Street.

Streetcar Named Poetry, A. Yevgeny Aleksandrovich Yevtushenko [*or* Evtushenko]. RusPo, *tr.* by Robert Arthur Douglas Ford

Streetcar That Lost Its Way, The. Nikolai Stepanovich Gumilyov [*or* Gumiliov *or* Gumilev]. TCRusP, *tr.* by Denis Johnson and Kathy Lewis

Streetcleaner's Lament, The. Patricia Hubbell. SSCS

Streetcorner Church. Sharan Strange. InTrad

Streets. Mudrooroo Narogin. IBA

Streets. Henrik Nordbrandt. VCWP, *tr.* by Henrik Norbrandt and Alexander Taylor

Streets 1. Paul Verlaine. SxFrPo, *tr.* by Martin Sorrell

Streets 2. Paul Verlaine. SxFrPo, *tr.* by Martin Sorrell

Streets are quiet as a fall of snow, The. (LL) Big Parade, The. Stephen Knight. NeBl; TCAWP

Streets are waiting for a snow, The. Dundee. John Burnside. NePenScot

Streets of Ch'ang-an. Ch'u Kuang-hsi. ColAnChi, *tr.* by Burton Watson

Streets of Ch'ang-an, The. Ch'u Kuang-hsi. CoBCP, *tr.* by Burton Watson

Streets of Forbes, The. Jack McGuire. CBAP; NOBAu

Streets of Laredo, The. Louis MacNeice. FaBoWar; OBWP

Streets of Laredo, The. *Unknown.* *See* Cowboy's Lament, The

Streets of the roaring town. On a Soldier Fallen in the Philippines. William Vaughn Moody. NOBA

Streets of your glances, The. Vasco [*or* Vasko] Popa. PoSu *Fr.* Far Within Us.

Streets outside have ice on them, The. My Grandfather Always Promised Us. Liam Rector. UrbNat

Streets we live by fall away, The. Potholes. Linda Hogan. UrbNat

Streets were clogged with garbage, The. New Brooms, The. Odia Ofeimun. NAfrP

Strength. Helen Chasin. YaYoPo

Strength. Christopher Smart. UV *Fr.* Song to David, A.

Strength for To-Day. *Unknown.* PWR

Strength I had to uproot hills. Song of Kai-hsia. Hsiang Chi. SuSp, *tr.* by Ronald C. Miao

Strength of Fate, The. Euripides. AWP, *tr.* by A. E. Housman *Fr.* Alcestis.

Strength of Fields, The. James Dickey. VCAP

Strength through Joy. Kenneth Rexroth. VGW

Strengthen, my Love, this castle of my heart. Rondel. Charles, Duc d' Orléans. AWP, *tr.* by Andrew Lang

Strengthened to live, strengthened to die for. In Distrust of Merits. Marianne Craig Moore. APT-1; ColAP; MoAmPo; NAAL-2v2; NAAL-5; OBWP; OxBA

Strenuous faithful buckled to their prayers, The. (LL)   Robert Louis Stevenson. NOBVV; NPeEn

Strenuous Life, The.   Henry Sidgwick.   OBCoV

Strephon kissed me in the spring.   Look, The.   Sara Teasdale.   APT-1; LW

Strephon to Celia.   Mary Leapor.   ECWP; RACG

Strephon, your breach of faith and trust.   Song, A.   Laetitia Pilkington.   PEW

Strephon, your breach of faith and trust.   Song, A.   Laetitia Pilkington.   LW

Stress of his anger set me back.   Revelation, The.   James Wright (1927–80).   PAI

Stretch cast out night's long,'d, The.   Lakefront, Cleveland.   Russell Atkins.   GT

Stretch of wall, The.   Volga Towns, The.   Johannes Bobrowski.   PoSu, tr. by Matthew Mead and Ruth Mead

Stretch out your hands to me.   Bei Dao.   AF, tr. by Bonnie S. McDougall

Stretched in the shadow of the broad beech.   Virgil [or Vergil].   AWP, tr. by Charles Stuart Calverley   Fr. Eclogues.

Stretched Out in Solitude.   Belinda Zubicueta Carmona.   TANSG, tr. by Celeste Kostopulos-Cooperman

Stretched out on a roof.   Potato Cellar.   Meg Huber.   SpudSo

Stretched out under the oak, in the wood's new leaves.   Forest Murmurs. Eduard Friedrich Mörike [or Möricke].   WoPoe, tr. by Randall Jarrell

Stretching.   Robert Morgan.   WeW-3

Stretching before and after. (LL)   T. S. Eliot.   APT-1; HarvBoo; MoAmPo; NAAL-2v2; NAAL-5; PoE   Fr. Four Quartets.

Stretching into the distance.   By the sea.   Muso Soseki.   EaWin, tr. by W. S. Merwin

Strew not earth with empty stars.   Thomas Lovell Beddoes.   OxBSP   Fr. Second Brother, The.

Strew on her roses, roses.   Requiescat.   Matthew Arnold.   AWP; FHYEP; NOBE; OBEV; PoRA

Stricken Deer, The.   William Cowper.   NAEL-5v1; NAEL-6v1; NAEL-7v1; PAI   Fr. Task, The.

Strict hairshirt of circumstance tears the flesh.   Veterans, The.   Donagh MacDonagh.   CIP-2

Strictly for Posterity.   Charles Simic.   NNaP

Strictly Germ-proof.   Arthur Guiterman.   TrJP

Strictly Speaking.   Debra Gregerman.   AmPoNex

Striding, shuddering.   Lina Tibi.   PoArWo, tr. by Subhi Hadidi and Nathalie Handal

Striding up to his bed, you.   Confabulation.   John A. Stone.   BloBone

Strife is grown between Virtue and Love, A.   Sir Philip Sidney.   NAEL-5v1; NAEL-6v1; NAEL-7v1; NoP-4   Fr. Astrophil and Stella.

Strike, churl; hurl, cheerless wind, then; heltering hail.   Hailstorm in May. Gerard Manley Hopkins.   Spl

Strike Up the Band.   George Gershwin.   ReLy

Strike up, you lusty gallants, with music [or musick] and sound of drum. Captain Ward and the *Rainbow*.   *Unknown*.   ESPB

Strikers in Hyde Park.   Louise Imogen Guiney.   APN-2

String.   Dennis Schmitz.   LCAP-2

Stringer's Field.   Roy McFadden.   PNI

Stringing red serrano peppers, crushing.   Desert Landscape.   Agha Shahid Ali. OMIP

Strings' Excitement, The.   W. H. Auden.   MoBrPo

Stringybark Cockatoo, The.   *Unknown*.   NOBAu

Strip.   A. R. Ammons.
   "Wdn't it be silly to be serious, now."   BAP-97

Strip her first of home and family.   Out.   Eleanor Brown.   MFPA

"Strip," Leofric said, "and you'll find."   Limerick.   Harry Thomas.   PeLi

Strip Me Naked, or Royal Gin for Ever; a Picture.   *Unknown*.   NOEC

Strip-tease.   Lawrence Durrell.   OxAEP-2

Striped blouse in a clearing by Bazille, A.   Ceremony.   Richard Wilbur. CoAP; NAAL-2v2; NAAL-5; NoAM

Striped suit.   New Suit, The.   Nidia Sanabria de Romero.   ChAP, tr. by Arnaldo D. Larrosa and Naomi Shihab Nye

Stripped of his crown.   Bombax Tree, The.   Fily-Dabo Sissoko.   NegPo, tr. by Ellen Conroy Kennedy

Stripper, The.   Anita Endrezze.   CDW; ReTh

Stripping and Putting on.   May Swenson.   WeW-3

Strips of adhesive tape criss-crossed the windowpane cutting.   After Fall, 1956. Devorah Amir.   DTA, tr. by Miriyam Glazer

Striptease.   Andrey [or Andrei] Andreievich Voznesensky [or Voznesenskii]. TCRusP, tr. by Daniel Weissbort

Strive in this, and love the strife. (LL)   Banquet, The.   George Herbert. ESCV; GeHe

Strive not, vain Lover, to be fine.   Song: "Strive not, vain Lover, to be fine." Richard Lovelace.   CavPo

Strive: yet I do not promise.   Strive, Wait, and Pray.   Adelaide Anne Procter. TreFP

Stroke.   Vincent Buckley.
   "In the faint blue light."   BMAP

Stroke.   Arthur Ginsberg.   BloBone

Stroke.   Hugh Seidman.   BodElec

Stroke the small silk with your whispering hands.   Geoffrey Hill.   NPeEn; OxBEV   Fr. Apology for the Revival of Christian Architecture in England, An.

Strokes.   William Stafford.   CoAmPo

Strokes are pulses: from my shapely cloud, The.   Minor Van Gogh (He Speaks), A.   Alicia Ostriker.   RACG

Strokes the fern's / voluptuous braille. (LL)   Fish in the Stone, The.   Rita Dove.   EmeKit; HCAP

Stroll-Joy.   Johann Klaj.   GePo, tr. by George C. Schoolfield

Stroll on, thou dark not deep "blue" dandy, stroll.   Sea Replies to Byron, The. Gilbert Keith Chesterton.   UV

Stroll to Parfondeval, A.   Remco Campert.   TuT, tr. by Theo Dorgan

Strolling along the Riverbank, Looking for Flowers.   Tu Fu.
   "Masses of flowers and plants envelop the riverbanks."   SuSp
   "'Tis not I pity the flowers are about to die."   SuSp

Strolling in the Countryside.   Chao Yi.   SuSp, tr. by Chang Yin-nan

Strolling Musicians.   Nikolai Alekseievich Zabolotsky [or Zabolotskii].   TCRP, tr. by Daniel Weissbort

Strolling one day, beyond the Kalends, on Mount Cyllene.   Austin Clarke. ModIr   Fr. Tiresias.

Strong and slippery / half for the midnight grass-party.   Peter.   Marianne Craig Moore.   APT-1; NAAL-2v2; NoP-4; OxBA

Strong ankled, sun burned, almost naked.   Vitamins and Roughage.   Kenneth Rexroth.   NoAM

Strong Are Saying Nothing, The.   Robert Frost.   APT-1

Strong Beams.   Mairtin O Direain.   ModIr, tr. by Patrick Crotty

Strong Bond, The.   Juana de Ibarbourou.   TCLAP, tr. by Sophie Cabot Black, Maria Negroni and Linda Scheer

Strong Draughts of Their Refreshing Minds.   Emily Dickinson.   SWaP

Strong drink, hundred-year-old, A.   Soul Music: The Derry Air.   Eamon Grennan.   BiHa; PBCIP

Strong enough to trust to. (LL)   Paper Nautilus, The.   Marianne Craig Moore. FaBoWP; HarvBoo; MakPoe; NAAL-5; NALW; VGW

Strong extreme speed, that the brain burries with.   Dante Gabriel Rossetti. PeVV   Fr. Trip to Paris and Belgium, A.

Strong God which made the topmost stars.   Prophet Lost in the Hills at Evening, The.   Joseph Hilaire Pierre Belloc.   SacPr

Strong is the horse upon his speed.   Christopher Smart.   UV   Fr. Song to David, A.

Strong is the lion – like a coal.   Christopher Smart.   HAP   Fr. Song to David, A.

Strong is your hold O Love. (LL)   Last Invocation, The.   Walt Whitman. MoAmPo; OxBA

Strong Men.   Sterling Allen Brown.   BPo; TTY
   (Stronger.) (LL)   ISC; NAAAL
   (They dragged you from homeland.)   ISC; NAAAL

Strong men keep coming on, The.   Upstream.   Carl Sandburg.   MoAmPo

Strong Men, Riding Horses / Lester after the Western.   Gwendolyn Brooks. GT
   (Pasted to stars already. . . .) (LL)   GT

Strong rods for sceptors to bear sway.   On the Decease of the Religious and Honourable Jno Haynes Esqr.   John James.   SCAP

Strong Room of the House, The.   William Bronk.   APSN

Strong saturation of sea! O widely flown.   George Cabot Lodge.   APN-2

Strong-shouldered mole.   Dead Mole, A.   Andrew Young.   GTBS-P; NePenScot; OxBSP

Strong sob of the chafing stream, The.   Orara.   Henry Clarence Kendall. CBAP

Strong Son of God, immortal Love.   Tennyson.   EBVV; HAP; NAEL-6v2; NAWM-7v2; SacPr; TrCP   Fr. In Memoriam A. H. H.

Strong Wind, A.   Austin Clarke.   RB

Strong Winds Below the Canyons.   Larry Kramer.   GeoHom

Strong without rage, without o'erflowing full. (LL)   Sir John Denham.   NAEL-5v1; NAEL-6v1; NOSC; NPeEn; OxAEP-1; OxBEV   Fr. Cooper's Hill.

Strong women told the faggots that there are two important, The.   Women Wisdom.   Larry Mitchell.   GLP

Stronger than alcohol, more great than song.   Ted Berrigan.   FTOS   Fr. Sonnets, The.

Strongest, The.   "Yehoash."   TrJP, tr. by Marie Syrkin

Strongest parts of language are lonely, desolate women, singing, The. Fragments to Overcome Silence.   Alejandra Piznarnick.   TANSG, tr. by Susan Bassnett

Strongest thing in the world, The.   Ring on the Finger.   Harold Rome.   ReLy

Strongly it bears us along in swelling and limitless billows.   Homeric Hexameter, The.   Samuel Taylor Coleridge.   OxAEP-2

Strongly worded to say on the subject. (LL) Seascape. Elizabeth Bishop. ColAP; FaBoWP; OxBC

Struck out of dim fluctuant forces and shock of electrical vapour. Mathilde Blind. VWP *Fr.* Ascent of Man, The.

Struck through such a dome. Baroque Sunburst, A. Amy Clampitt. ColAP

Struck to the heart by this sad pageantry. Shelley. OxBEV *Fr.* Triumph of Life, The.

Struck, was I, not yet by Lightning. Emily Dickinson. NCAP

Struck with huge Love, of what is to be possest. Prefatory Poem, on. . . *Magnalia Christi Americana*. Nicholas Noyes. SCAP

Structural Study of Myth, The. Jerome Rothenberg. FTOS; PoM

Structure of process, The. Process. John Montague. CIP-2

Structure of Rime XVIII. Robert Duncan. FTOS

Structure of Rime XXIII. Robert Duncan. FTOS

Structure of the soul, The. States of War. Maya Bejerano. DTA, *tr. by* Miriyam Glazer

Structure, yes. You'd hardly say a house, A. At the Flyfisher's Shack. Sydney Lea. RA

Struggle. Sidney Lanier. OxBA

Struggle, The. Toi Derricotte. LTA; PBCAP

Struggle, The. René François Armand Sully-Prudhomme. AWP, *tr. by* Arthur O'Shaughnessy

Struggle for Life. Frigyes Karinthy. IQMS, *tr. by* Peter Zollman

Struggle for the Taal, The. Breyten Breytenbach. AF, *tr. by* Denis Hirson

Struggle-Road Dance. Ahmos, II Zu-Bolton. ISC

Struggle to preserve once spoken words, The. Tony Harrison. HarvBoo

Struggling Rill insensibly is grown, The. William Wordsworth. CenSon *Fr.* River Duddon [A Series of Sonnets], The.

Strugnell's Bargain. Wendy Cope. UV

Strugnell's Rubáiyát. Wendy Cope. UV

Strumming and patter / the meaningful glances, The. Philodemus. GrAn

Strut for Roethke, A. John Berryman. NOBA

Stubble Burning, The. Sarah Ruden. AmPoNex

Stuck. Cheryl Clarke. WiU

Stuck in an unnamed place. Space Between, The. Elena Georgiou. WiU

Stud. Michael Lassell. GLP *Fr.* Times Square Poems.

Student, The. Shauqi Abi Shaqra. MAP, *tr. by* Sargon Boulus and Peter Porter

Student, The. Marianne Craig Moore. NAAL-2v2; TwCP

Student, The. *Unknown.* OBMV, *tr. by* Frank O'Connor

Student, do the simple purification. Simple Purification, The. Kabir. EnlH; WoPoe, *tr. by* Robert Bly

Student from Pembroke once said, A. Limerick. Andrew Stoker. PeLi

Student of nuclear fission, A. Limerick. W. Bernard Wake. PeLi

Student's life is pleasant, The. Student, The. *Unknown.* OBMV, *tr. by* Frank O'Connor

Student who sat facing me on the Osaka express, A. Lindley Williams Hubbell. APT-2

Students, like students, form and fly. "When the Students Resisted, a Minor Clash Ensued." David Knight. MoCV

Studied slouch of nouns, The. Dementia. John Cope. GeoH

Studies. Carlos Pellicer. TCLAP, *tr. by* Donald Justice

Studies at Delhi, 1876. Sir Alfred Comyn Lyall.

 Badminton. PeVV

 "Hardly a shot from the gate we stormed." PeVV

Studies from the Antique. Emily Jane Pfeiffer. ViWPN

Studies in Desire. Pimone Triplett. AmPoNex

Studies in Light. Diane Di Prima. PFTM-2

Studio for Listening to the Snow, The. Yang Chi. CoBLCP, *tr. by* Jonathan Chaves

Studio Poem. Cilla McQueen. PeNZ

Studio, The (Homeage to Alice Neel). Alicia Ostriker. ExTi

Studio Up Over In Your Ear. Al Young. GT

Studley Park. John Langhorne. OBGa

Studs. Michael S. Harper. ESEAA

Studs and Rings: Favors of the Piercing Party. D. A. Powell. WiU

Study. Tony Harrison. CABP

Study, A. Alice Thompson Meynell. VWP

Study (A Soul), A. Christina Georgina Rossetti. VWP

Study in Aesthetics, The. Ezra Pound. APT-1; NOBA

Study in Blue. Evan Jones. NOBAu

Study of a Spider, The. John Byrne Leicester Warren, 3d Baron De Tabley. NOBVV

Study of Reading Habits, A. Philip Larkin. InPK-6; NOBL; OBCoV

Study of Two Pears. Wallace Stevens. APT-1; BLT; NAAL-2v2; NoAM; OxBA

Study Peace. Imamu Amiri Baraka. APSN

Studying history. History. Juan Gelman. TCLAP, *tr. by* Robert Marquez

Studying Horses. Robert Kelly. APSN

Studying Physics with My Daughter. Jeanne Murray Walker. WeW-3

Studying the ancient manuscript crumbly with age. Following the Rhymes of Chang Hsün, in My Study in Late Spring. Huang T'ing-chien. SuSp, *tr. by* Michael E. Workman

Studying the Language. Eiléan Ní Chuilleanáin. EmeKit; NPeEn

Studying the Signs. Allen Ginsberg. FTOS

Stuff. Linda Gregg. ExTi

Stuff of the moon. Nocturne in a Deserted Brickyard. Carl Sandburg. APT-1; MoAmPo

Stuffed owls drum in my heart. Fear. Thomas Love Peacock. VoR

Stuffed pink stocking, the neck. One of the Strangest. May Swenson. APT-2; OWoS

Stuffed quail, A. October Tune. Joseph Brodsky. VCWP, *tr. by* Joseph Brodsky

Stuffy chill of clouded Summer, crowdsmell, booksmell. Supervising Examinations. Sean Lucy. CIP-2

Stuffy Turkey. Dave Etter. SeSe

Stumble. Getsurei. JDP, *tr. by* Yoel Hoffmann

Stumbling along a sidewalk clogged with snow. Falcon. Rachel Hadas. ExTi

Stumpfoot on 42nd Street. Louis Simpson. NNaP; UnPo; VGW

Stunned by Freedom. Eva Svankmajerová. SurWo, *tr. by* Katerina Pinosová

Stunned I Was Looking for Reasons. Patrizia Cavalli. CItWP, *tr. by* Cinzia Sartini Blum and Lara Trubowitz

Stunned in the stone light, laid among the lilies. Ophelia. Vernon Watkins. TCAWP

Stuntman. Lionel Kearns. MoCV

Stupendious love! all saints astonishment. Edward Taylor. OxBA; SacPr *Fr.* Preparatory Meditations Before My Approach to the Lord's Supper.

Stupid and abiding jelly, The. (LL) Bacchanal. Peter De Vries. NBLV; NOBL; OBAL

Stupid Leander. Colombine. Paul Verlaine. SxFrPo, *tr. by* Martin Sorrell

Stupid of me to think you were salmon. American Tourist. B. C. Ramachandra Sharma. OMIP, *tr. by* A. K. Ramanujan

Stupidity. Mary Elizabeth Fullerton. CBAP

Stupidity achieves the crime. Martyr. Mary Elizabeth Fullerton. CBAP

Stupidity Street. Ralph Hodgson. MoBrPo; OxBTC

Sturdy ploughman doth the soldier see, The. Joseph Hall. OBSV *Fr.* Virgidemiarum.

Sturm und Drang narcissus, loose petals. At the Freud Hilton. Campbell McGrath. AmPoNex

Sturts quick as fear, and seeks its hidden lair. (LL) Hares at Play. John Clare. RB; WoPoe

Stuttering Lover, The. Fred Emerson Brooks. VerBaPo

Stuttering rain at the window. Sister Midnight. John James. Oth

Stwonen Steps, The. William Barnes. NOBVV

Style. Howard Nemerov. NoAM

Style is the water out of Homer. Garden God, The. Richard Eberhart. OBGa

Style thee a most great fool, but no great man. (LL) On Don Surly. Ben Jonson. FaBoEE; NAEL-5v1; NAEL-6v1; NAEL-7v1

Styled [*or* Stil'd] but the shadows [*or* shaddowes] of us men? (LL) Song. That Women Are But Men's Shadows. Ben Jonson. BeJo; OxBSP

Stylized Donkey, A. "Sasha Chorny [*or* Chiornyi]. TCRP, *tr. by* Bernard Meares

Styro. Clark Coolidge. PmAP

Styx. Robert Duncan. VCAP

Suave and paltry man, my enemy, A. In the Tail of the Scorpion. Genevieve Taggard. VGW

Suave Mari Magno. Lucretius. AWP, *tr. by* W. H. Mallock *Fr.* De Rerum Natura (On the Nature of Things).

Sub Contra. Louise Bogan. APT-2

Sub Shop Girl. Michael S. Weaver. SpirFl

Subaltern's Love-Song, A. Sir John Betjeman. BoLoP; HAP; NOBL; NoAM; OxAEP-2; OxBTC; TwCP

Subalterns. Elizabeth Daryush. OBWP

Subalterns, The. Thomas Hardy. MoBrPo; NOBVV; NoAM; PAI

Subject. Marie Ponsot. VGW

Subject for a Story. Nikolai Ivanovich Glazkov. TCRP, *tr. by* Daniel Weissbort

Subject of people unverifiable, The. Patois. Marianne Vitale. HeMarv

Subjection of Women, The. Austin Clarke. CIP-2

Subjoined to the Yearly Bill of Mortality of the Parish of All Saints, Northampton, 1792. William Cowper. *See* On a Similar Occasion for the Year 1792

Sublimed Mercury. Alice Rahon. SurWo, *tr. by* Myrna Bell Rochester

Sublime – invention ever young. Christopher Smart. OBEV *Fr.* Song to David, A.

Sublime was he, stupendous in invention. Wangsun, The. Wang Yen-Shou. ChiP, *tr. by* Arthur Waley

Subliminal. Lorine Niedecker. PFTM-1

Submarine Tombs. Jean-Baptiste Tati-Loutard. PBMAP

Submission. Clara Ann Thompson. CBWP-2

Submission to Afflictive Providences. Isaac Watts. NOCV

Submitting a Memorial Requesting Permission to Return Home and Care for My Parents. Yang Chi. CoBLCP, *tr. by* Jonathan Chaves

Subnarcosis. Andrea Zanzotto. ItPo, *tr. by* Gayle Ridinger

Substance and Shadow. John Hewitt. ModIr; PNI

Substance, Shadow, and Spirit. Ch'ien T'ao. ChiP, *tr. by* Arthur Waley

Substance, Shadow, and Spirit. T'ao Ch'ien [*or* T'ao Yuan-ming]. ColAnChi, *tr. by* J. R. Hightower

Substance, Shadow, and Spirit. T'ao Ch'ien [*or* T'ao Yuan-ming]. CoBCP, *tr. by* Burton Watson

Substance that stirs in my palm, The. Ash. Jayanta Mahapatra. VCWP

Substituted Poem of Laureate Quynh, The. *Unknown*. EaWin, *tr. by* W. S. Merwin and Nguyen Ngoc Bich

Substitution. Elizabeth Barrett Browning. SacPr

Substitution. Anne Spencer. BlSi

Subterranean. Michael Hannon. GeoHom

Subterranean geography. Elena Clementelli. CItWP, *tr. by* Cinzia Sartini Blum and Lara Trubowitz *Fr.* Etruscan Notebook.

Subtle almost beyond thought are these dim colours. Dun-Colour [*or* Dun-Color]. Ruth Pitter. PoRA

Subtle capering on a simple thought. Fleadh Cheoil. Pearse Hutchinson. PBCIP

Subtle chain of countless rings, A. Nature [1836]. Ralph Waldo Emerson. APN-1; AWP

Subtle erratic vocation, A. Cesare Greppi. ItPo, *tr. by* Gayle Ridinger

Subtlest strain a great musician weaves, The. Limitations. Henrietta Cordelia Ray. CBWP-3

Subtracted Words. P. Inman. FTOS

Suburban. John Ciardi. NBLV

Suburban Childhood, A. Liz Rosenberg. PBCAP

Suburban Dreams. Edwin Muir. OxBTC

Suburban Dusk. Bert Meyers. SPE
    (One girl in a red dress leaves the shopping center with.) SPE

Suburban Lovers. Bruce Dawe. NOBAu

Suburban Song. Elizabeth Riddell. CBAP; NOBAu

Suburban Sonnet. Gwen Harwood. CBAP

Suburbia. David Ignatow. PoCoUp

Suburbs on a Hazy Day. D. H. Lawrence. OBMV

Subverted Flower, The. Robert Frost. APT-1; ColAP; HAP; NOBA; NoAM; OxBA; PoE

Subway, The. Edwin Denby. APT-2

Subway, The. Allen Tate. NOBA

Subway Face. Langston Hughes. APT-2

Subway flatters like the dope habit, The. Subway, The. Edwin Denby. APT-2

Subway Rush Hour. Langston Hughes. InPK-6
    (Mingled.) KaS

Subway train, the, / subway train, The. Subway Train, The. Leland B. Jacobs. SSCS

Subway Wind. Claude McKay. APT-1

Subway Witnesses, The. Lorenzo Thomas. GT

Subways Are People. Lee Bennett Hopkins. HHAm

Success. Berton Braley. PoToHe

Success. Rupert Brooke. OxBTC

Success. C. C. Cameron.
    Don't Give Up. PoToHe

Success. Cornelius Eady. ISC

Success. William Empson. OxBTC

Success. Emma Lazarus. SWaP

Success. *Unknown*. PoToHe

Success and failure are not our affairs. Seeing Off Sun Ling-hsiu on His Journey to Chen-ting. Wu Wei-yeh. CoBLCP, *tr. by* Jonathan Chaves

Success is like some horrible disaster. After Publication of Under the Volcano. Malcolm Lowry. FaBoTw

Success is speaking words of praise. Success. *Unknown*. PoToHe

Successful Summer, A. David Schubert. APT-2; ChIV-1

Successive Deaths. Adelia Prado. TANSG, *tr. by* Ellen Watson

Succubus, The. Harriet Rose. BrRo

Such a Boat of Land. Lamont B. Steptoe. UnSA

Such a flow of language! Rebecca Cutlet. Bill Berkson. PmAP

Such a fool as I am you had better ignore. Usk, The. Charles Hubert Sisson. HarvBoo; NOCV

Such a funny word. Chalazion. Allison Joseph. NAPBL

Such a gentleman, lowering black wool. In Kind. Linda France. NeBl

Such a gloomy day. Meditation by the Xerox Machine. Doris Safie. GraLe; PoArWo

'Such a little king's eye,' said my mother. Roy Kloof. Sydney Clouts. PeSAV

Such a moon. Buson. WoPoe; ZenPo, *tr. by* Takashi Ikemoto and Lucien Stryk

Such a Parcel of Rogues in a Nation. Robert Burns. NePenScot; OxBS

Such a peculiar lot. James Berry. EmeKit *Fr.* Fantasy of an African Boy.

Such a prelate, I trow. John Skelton. OBSV *Fr.* Why Come Ye Not to Court.

Such a result so soon—and from such a beginning! (LL) Hand-Mirror, A. Walt Whitman. NAAL-2v1; NAAL-3; OxBA; PoPoPo

Such a splendid place! The cedar and elm are whispering. More about God (But with Some Reservations). Victor Hugo. SxFrPo, *tr. by* E. H. Blackmore and A. M. Blackmore

Such a time of it they had. Stanley Meets Mutesa. James David Rubadiri. PBA

Such a Way to Go. Martha Silano. AmPoNex

Such a wizened creature. Old Age. E. Keary. NOBVV

Such accidents do happen. Blues 2. Barry Wallenstein. SeSe

Such an itch and tickle of slow. Stretching. Robert Morgan. WeW-3

Such apples as once brought Atlanta down. *Unknown*. PriapPo, *tr. by* Richard W. Hooper *Fr.* Priapus Poems, The.

Such are our habits. To My Friends. Nikolai Ivanovich Glazkov. TCRP, *tr. by* Daniel Weissbort

Such as in God the Lord Do Trust. William Kethe. AH

Such as mine has been! (LL) *Var. authors*. AWP; TAL *Fr.* Manyo Shu, Part 2 of 4.

Such as, retired from sight of men, like thee. To Saint Mary Magdalen. Henry Constable. Son

Such as she was, such as she would become. (LL) Gift Outright, The. Robert Frost. AiP; ColAP; FaBoA; HHAm; HarvBoo; MoAmPo; NAAL-2v2; NAAL-5; NOBA; NoAM; NoP-4; OxBA; PoPoPo; TFi; TRP

Such be the dog, I charge, thou mean'st to train. Thomas Tickell. ECEV *Fr.* Fragment of a Poem on Hunting, A.

Such beautiful, beautiful hands! My Mother's Hands. *Unknown*. ITBLP

Such brazen slatterns. Dandelions. Gerda Mayer. Spl

Such Cloe is, and common as the air. (LL) Cloe. George Granville [*or* Grenville], Baron Lansdowne. FaBoEE; NIP-4; OxBEV

Such closets to search, such alcoves to importune! (LL) Love in a Life. Robert Browning. FHYEP; NOBE; NOBVV; NPeEn; OxBEV

Such counsels ye gave to me, O! (LL) Edward [*or* Edward, Edward]. *Unknown*. ClHu; EBEV; ESPB; HAP; InPK-6; NAEL-5v1; NOBE; OBEV; OxBB; OxBEV; OxBS; PAI; PoRA; SCGP; SoSe-8; TFi; TRP

Such days as these there are before the spring. Such Days as These. Anna Andreyevna Akhmatova. RusPo, *tr. by* Robert Arthur Douglas Ford

Such eyes, such hair, such wit, and such a hand? (LL) Conquest [*or* His Lady's Might]. Philippe Desportes. AWP; NoSic

Such familiar space. This House. Robert Creeley. BodElec

Such flowers as Earth our Mother. Petronius Arbiter. MLL *Fr.* Satyricon.

Such fruitless questions may not long beguile. William Wordsworth. CenSon *Fr.* River Duddon [A Series of Sonnets], The.

Such grace, so self-contained, was the best escape to know. (LL) Ballet of the Fifth Year, The. Delmore Schwartz. APT-2; OxBA; TwCP

Such haukes, such hounds, and such a leman. (LL) Three Ravens, The. *Unknown*. ESPB; HeIP-4; InPK-6; NAEL-5v1; OBEV; OxBB; PAI; PoE; SCGP; TFi; UnPo

Such heate they cast as lifts the Spirit high. (LL) To Music Bent Is My Retired Mind. Thomas Campion. NOCV; PeECV

Such ills attend. John Armstrong. NOEC *Fr.* Oeconomy of Love; a Poetical Essay, The.

Such Is the Grief of the Grey-Haired Man. *Unknown*. WoPoe, *tr. by* Michael O'Brien *Fr.* Beowulf.

Such is the grief of the grey-haired man. *Unknown*. WoPoe, *tr. by* Michael O'Brien *Fr.* Beowulf.

Such is the secret union, when we feel. Mark Akenside. NOEC *Fr.* Pleasures of Imagination, The.

Such is the way of the world. "St.-John Perse." OBVE *Fr.* Anabasis.

Such is the world's way. Tanehiko. JDP, *tr. by* Yoel Hoffmann

Such let me seem till such I be. Mignon Aspiring to Heaven. Goethe. TreFP

Such light in sense, with such a darkened [*or* darken'd] mind. (LL) Sir Philip Sidney. NoSic; PoE; Son *Fr.* Astrophil and Stella.

Such light is in sea-caves. Musica No. 3. Richard Duerden. NeAP

Such maner time there was (what time I n'ot). Sir Philip Sidney. PBRV *Fr.* Countesse of Pembrokes Arcadia, The.

Such marvellous ways to kill a man! Bofors A. A. Gun, The. Gavin Ewart. PoWW

Such men as sideling ride the ambling Muse. Homer and the Brazen Head of Rumour. George Chapman. NOSC

Such moving sounds from such a careless touch.   Of My Lady Isabella Playing on the Lute.   Edmund Waller.   HAP

Such nice machines. (LL)   Spring Coming.   A. R. Ammons.   HeIP-4; InPK-6

Such passion for love coiled in my heart.   Archilochus.   SaLy, *tr. by* Diane Rayor.

Such pretious perils for mankind! (LL)   Boethius.   NOSC; OBVE; PAI, *tr. by* Henry Vaughan   *Fr.* Consolation of Philosophy, The ("De Consolacione Philosophie").

Such radiance of green.   Red Peonies.   Wang Wei.   SuSp, *tr. by* Irving Y. Lo

Such shameless bards we have; and yet 'tis true.   Pope.   OBSV   *Fr.* Essay on Criticism, An.

Such should this day be, so the sun should hide.   On the Marriage of T. K. and C. C.: The Morning Stormy.   Thomas Carew.   BoLoP

Such silence falls. (LL)   Anna Andreyevna Akhmatova.   FaBoWar; PoetW, *tr. by* Max Hayward   *Fr.* In 1940.

Such silence / Snow tracing smiles.   Masaoka Shiki.   ZenPo, *tr. by* Takashi Ikemoto and Lucien Stryk

Such skill, matcht with such courage as he had.   Edmund Spenser.   OBWP   *Fr.* Astrophel.

Such stillness.   Basho.   WoPoe, *tr. by* Donald Keene

Such subtile filigranity and nobless of construccion.   "Wellcome, to the Caves of Artá!"   Robert Graves.   NBLV; NOBL; PeLV

Such, such is Death: no triumph: no defeat.   Charles Hamilton Sorley.   PeFWW   *Fr.* Two Sonnets.

Such such is life (LL)   Cold Are the Crabs.   Edward Lear.   NAEL-5v2; NAEL-6v2

Such Sweet Sorrow.   Elizabeth Delmore.   NLP

Such Tophet was; so looked the grinning fiend.   Tophet.   Thomas Gray.   ChIV-1; FaBoEE; NOEC; OxBSP

Such violence. And such repose. (LL)   Tywater.   Richard Wilbur.   CoAmPo; TRP

Such was thir song.   John Milton.   PeECV   *Fr.* Paradise Lost.

Such wisdom as a little child displays.   Bonaggiunta Urbiciani.   EaItPo, *tr. by* Dante Gabriel Rossetti

Such wrong, as when a married man doth woo[e]. (LL)   Break[e] of Day.   John Donne.   NAEL-5v1; NAEL-6v1; NAEL-7v1; SoSe-8

Suck, The.   John Wieners.   FTOS

Suck, baby, suck, mother's love grows by giving.   Gipsy's Malison, The.   Charles Lamb.   OxBSo

Sudden a thought came like a full-blown rose.   John Keats.   EroLit   *Fr.* Eve of St. Agnes, The.

Sudden Appearance of a Monster at a Window.   Lawrence Raab.   BLT

Sudden blow, A! And she claims me for child.   Neither Innocence or Experience.   Dambudzo Marechera.   NAfrP

Sudden blow: a great bird lifts us, A.   Notion of Grace, A.   Brenda J. Moossy.   PoArWo

Sudden blow: the great wings beating still, A.   Leda and the Swan.   W. B. Yeats.   CABP; ClHu; EBEV; EroLit; GSo; GTBS-P; HAP; HarvBoo; HeIP-4; InPK-6; MoBrPo; NAEL-5v2; NAEL-6v2; NAWM-7v2; NIL-7; NIP-4; NOBE; NPeEn; NoAM; NoP-4; OWoS; OxAEP-2; OxBEV; OxBSo; PAI; PoE; PoPoPo; SCV; SoSe-8; Son; TFi; TRP; WeW-3

Sudden chill, A / In our room my dead wife's.   Buson.   ZenPo, *tr. by* Takashi Ikemoto and Lucien Stryk

Sudden Journey.   Tess Gallagher.   NIL-7; NIP-4

Sudden Light.   Dante Gabriel Rossetti.   BoLoP; CABP; CTC; NOBE; NOBVV; NPeEn; NoP-4; OxBEV

Sudden rain / Rows of horses.   Masaoka Shiki.   ZenPo, *tr. by* Takashi Ikemoto and Lucien Stryk

Sudden rain this afternoon.   Evening after Rain.   Tu Fu.   CrYelRi, *tr. by* Sam Hamill

Sudden sad mischance, A.   Looking-Glass for Men and Maids, A.   *Unknown.*   BASC

Sudden shower.   Buson.   EH, *tr. by* Robert Hass

Sudden Shower.   John Clare.   OxAEP-2

Sudden shower / Cooling lava.   Sodo.   ZenPo, *tr. by* Takashi Ikemoto and Lucien Stryk

Sudden snowfall comes in darkness, A.   Snowy Mountains.   Tsung Ch'en.   CoBLCP, *tr. by* Jonathan Chaves

Sudden strong squalls from the sou'-west.   Leonidas of Tarentum.   GrAn

Sudden the desert changes.   Bridge-Guard in the Karroo.   Rudyard Kipling.   OBWP

Sudden Things.   Donald Hall.   SPE

Sudden, unexpected movement; his hand, A.   Audible and Inaudible.   Yannis Ritsos.   AF, *tr. by* Minas Savas

Sudden wakin', a sudden weepin', A.   Man's Days.   Eden Phillpotts.   OBEV; OxBTC

Suddenly.   Yusuf Al-Sa'igh.   MAP, *tr. by* Diana Der Hovanessian and Salma Khadra Jayyusi

Suddenly.   Robin Blaser.   FTOS; PoM

Suddenly.   Semyon [*or* Semion] Isaakovich Kirsanov.   RusPo, *tr. by* Robert Arthur Douglas Ford

Suddenly after a few years of abject misery, depression and paralysis.   Obvious, The.   Anna Couani.   BMAP

Suddenly, after the quarrel, while we waited.   Quarrel, The.   Conrad Potter Aiken.   MoAmPo

Suddenly an old man on the threshold of the age.   Joseph Miezan Bognini.   PBMAP   *Fr.* Herbe Féconde (1973).

Suddenly as the riot squad moved in, it was raining exclamation marks.   Belfast Confetti.   Ciaran Carson.   BiHa; CIP-2; NPeEn; PNI

Suddenly aware that the good year is almost over.   Autumn Thoughts.   Ts'en Shen.   SuSp, *tr. by* C. H. Wang

Suddenly becoming talkative.   Christopher Okigbo.   PBMAP   *Fr.* Limits (1962).

Suddenly everything stops.   Slump.   Vassar Miller.   BoWoP

Suddenly half in jest.   Album Leaf.   Stéphane Mallarmé.   OBVE, *tr. by* Keith Bosley

Suddenly his mouth filled with sand.   Death of a Poet.   Charles Causley.   EmeKit; OxBSP

Suddenly his poor body.   Ted Hughes.   NoAM   *Fr.* Stations.

Suddenly horizons clouded.   Vision, The.   Muhammad Al-Faituri [*or* Al-Fituri *or* Al-Fayturi].   MAP, *tr. by* Sargon Boulus and Peter Porter

Suddenly / I am the same age.   Suddenly.   Semyon [*or* Semion] Isaakovich Kirsanov.   RusPo, *tr. by* Robert Arthur Douglas Ford

Suddenly I meet your face. (LL)   Deep-sworn Vow, A.   W. B. Yeats.   PoE; UnPo

Suddenly I remembered.   Lord of Nature.   Leonid Nikolaevich Martynov.   TCRP, *tr. by* J. R. Rowland

Suddenly I saw the cold and rook-delighting heaven.   Cold Heaven, The.   W. B. Yeats.   AWP; CTC; GTBS-P; HAP; NPeEn; NoAM; OxBSP; RB

Suddenly I was stabbed from behind.   Maya Bejerano.   DTA, *tr. by* Tsipi Keller   *Fr.* Hymns of Job.

Suddenly I would like prison. (LL)   Now that the time seems all mine.   Patrizia Cavalli.   NeIt; VCWP, *tr. by* Judith Baumel

Suddenly / in middle age.   Icons.   Miriam Waddington.   NOBC

Suddenly in the dark wood.   Her Voice Could Not Be Softer.   Austin Clarke.   NOIV

Suddenly in the midnight on mortal men.   *Unknown.*   AnOE, *tr. by* Charles W. Kennedy   *Fr.* Christ 3.

Suddenly in the midst of a game of lotto with his sisters.   Louis Armstrong.   Ernst Moerman.   SeSe

Suddenly, like an arrow from the East.   Woodpecker.   Gerald Bullett.   OWoS

Suddenly my father lifted up his nightie, I.   Lifting, The.   Sharon Olds.   NIL-7

Suddenly my father lifted up his nightie, I.   In the Hospital Near the End.   Sharon Olds.   NIP-4

Suddenly night crushed out the day and hurled.   Unreturning, The.   Wilfred Owen.   MoBrPo

Suddenly on a day in July.   Giusi Busceti.   ItPo, *tr. by* Gayle Ridinger

Suddenly out of its still and drowsy lair, the lair of slaves.   Europe, the 72d and 73d Year of These States.   Walt Whitman.   TCAPo

"Suddenly she slapped me, hard across the face."   Elizabeth in Italy.   Richard Weber.   BoLoP

Suddenly startled at the fresh sound, the stabbing dagger.   Suddenly Startled.   Léopold Sédar Senghor.   PoetW, *tr. by* Melvin Dixon

Suddenly the golden grove stopped.   Golden Grove, The.   Sergey [*or* Sergei] Aleksandrovich Yesenin [*or* Essenin].   RusPo, *tr. by* Robert Arthur Douglas Ford and R.A.D. Ford

Suddenly, the legs want a different sort of work.   April.   Cornelius Eady.   ESEAA

Suddenly the phoenix trees stop swaying.   Unexpected Meeting.   "Shu Ting."   CarOv, *tr. by* Carolyn Kizer and Y. H. Zhao

Suddenly the swallow's shadow reaped the glances of its nostalgia: / Noon.   Origin of Landscape or the End of Mercy, The.   Odysseus Elytis.   VCWP

Suddenly the window will open.   Return, The.   Tadeusz Różewicz.   HP, *tr. by* Adam Czerniawski

Suddenly there was a dress.   White Notes.   Donald Justice.   LCAP-2

Suddenly there were forms there.   Horses.   Gwyn Thomas.   OBWVE, *tr. by* Joseph P. Clancy

Suddenly they all stopped talking about it. Yet I.   John Ashbery.   PFTM-2   *Fr.* Flow Chart.

Suddenly they came flying, like a long scarf of smoke.   Thing, The.   Theodore Roethke.   APT-2

Suddenly to become John Benbow, walking down William Street.   Metempsychosis.   Kenneth Slessor.   NOBAu

Suddenly wait against the moon's face. (LL)   E. E. Cummings.   HarvBoo; MoAmPo

Suddenly we're sons of Noah.   From the Theater of Wine.   Cyrus Cassells.   GifTon

Suddenly we will wake from sleep at night.   Suddenly We Will Wake.   Shin Shalom.   MHP, *tr. by* Ruth Finer Mintz.

Suddenly / when I hear airplanes overhead.   Porter.   Marilyn Nelson Waniek.   ESEAA

Suddenly / (yet somehow expected).   Thief in the Night, A.   Jelaluddin [*or* Jalal al-Din] Rumi.   BBASP, *tr. by* Nasrollah Pourjavady and Peter Lamborn Wilson

Suddenly you felt it. And under the white.   Roman Arbor, The.   Ellen Hinsey.   YaYoPo

Sueden chance ded mak me mues, The.   Lady Margaret Howard.   EMWP

Suelick is the greatest Indian power.   Origin of the Skagit Indians, The.   Lucy Williams.   STP, *tr. by* Carl Cary

Suffer, Poor Negro!   David Diop.   PBA, *tr. by* Langston Hughes

Sufferance of her race is shown, The.   Formerly a Slave.   Herman Melville.   APN-2; TAP

Suffering.   Albert Ehrenstein.   TrJP, *tr. by* Babette Deutsch

Suffering.   Miroslav Holub.   PoSu, *tr. by* Ian Milner and George Theiner

Suffering.   Patricia K. Page.   NoAM

Suffering from Heat.   Wang Wei.   SuSp, *tr. by* Hugh M. Stimson

Suffering the Sea Change: All My Pretty Ones.   Lucinda Roy.   GT

Suffice they show I lived, and loved thee dear. (LL)   Samuel Daniel.   NAEL-7v1; NOBE; NoSic; OBEV; SCGP   *Fr.* To Delia.

Suffice, thou shalt be loved as well as she. (LL)   Samuel Daniel.   NoSic; Son   *Fr.* To Delia.

Suffolk Miracle, The.   *Unknown.*   ESPB

Suffused in April twilight.   Redemption.   Pauli Murray.   GT

Sufi, The.   Kahlil Gibran.   GraLe, *tr. by* Andrew Ghareeb

Sufi Quatrain.   Rabi'a bint Isma'il of Syria.   WPOW, *tr. by* Deirdre Lashgari

Sugar and cream. (LL)   Mother Goose.   LB; OxNR; ReMoGo

Sugar Cane, The.   James Grainger.
     Compost.   NOEC
     "Of composts shall the Muse disdain to sing?"   VerBaPo
     Slaves.   NOEC

Sugar in the Cane.   Tennessee Williams.   OBAL

Sugar-Plum Tree, The.   Eugene Field.   ITBLP; NBLV; OTCP

Sugar Poem.   Aurora Levins Morales.   PueRic

Suggested by a Picture of Peele Castle, in a Storm, Painted by Sir George Beaumont.   William Wordsworth.   *See* Elegiac Stanzas Suggested by a Picture of Peele Castle, in a Storm, Painted by Sir George Beaumont

Suggestion from a Friend.   Jane Kenyon.   LoL   *Fr.* Having It Out With Melancholy.

Suggestion Made by the Posters of the *Globe*, A.   J. E. Thorold Rogers.   FaBoEE

Suggestion of chill pervades the little bower, A.   Tune: "Sand of Silk-Washing Brook."   Ch'in Kuan.   ColAnChi, *tr. by* Jiaosheng Wang

Sui Veneris/The Poet of No Return.   Ricardo M. de Ungria.   ReBoTo

Suicide.   Robert Lowell.   PoE

Suicide.   Anne Stevenson.   FaBoWP

Suicide.   Lina Tibi.   PoArWo, *tr. by* Subhi Hadidi and Nathalie Handal

Suicide, The.   Louis MacNeice.   ModIr

Suicide applicant, A.   Ant Dodger.   Bill Knott.   PBCAP

Suicide in [the] Trenches.   Siegfried Sassoon.   FaBoWar; PoWW

Suicide is a duel with yourself.   Sergey [*or* Sergei] Chudakov.   TCRusP, *tr. by* Daniel Weissbort

Suicide Note.   Janice Mirikitani.   OxWW

Suicide on Pentwyn Bridge.   Gillian Clarke.   AngWePo

Suicide Rates, The.   Lewis Warsh.   FTOS

Suicide's Note.   Langston Hughes.   APT-2; PoPoPo; SAmP

Suicide with Squirtgun.   Tom Clark.   PmAP

Suicide Year, The.   Alice Anderson.   AmPoNex

Suilven.   Andrew Young.   OxBS

Suilven and the Eagle.   Gordon Bottomley.
     Eagle Song.   MoBrPo

Suit of Nettles, A.   James Reaney.
     Branwell's Sestina.   MoCV

Suitable for a gentleman with medals.   War Lord in the Early Evening.   Patricia K. Page.   NoAM

Suitcases, The.   'Abd al-Karim Kassid.   MAP, *tr. by* Lena Jayyusi and Anthony Thwaite

Suite for Augustus, A.   Rita Dove.
     Planning the Perfect Evening.   GT

Suite for Marriage, A.   David Ignatow.   NNaP

Suite in the Ch'ing-p'ing Mode, A.   Li Po.   ColAnChi, *tr. by* Elling O. Eide

Suite Repose.   Carl Hancock Rux.   SpirFl

Suitor, The.   Jane Kenyon.   InPK-6

Suitors watch Ulysses string the bow, The.   Homer.   OBVE, *tr. by* Alexander Pope   *Fr.* Odyssey.

Sukey [*or* Suky], you shall be my wife.   *Unknown.*   OxNR; TLR

Sukhanovo.   Natalya [*or* Natal'ia] Gorbanevskaya [*or* Gorbanyevskaya *or* Gorbanevskaia].   AF, *tr. by* Daniel Weissbort

Sulkily the sticks burn, and though they crackle.   Under the Pot.   Robert Graves.   FaBoEE

Sulking in the Seventies.   Kris Hemensley.   BMAP

Sulky old gray brute!, The.   Bristol Channel, The.   Thomas Edward Brown.   NOBVV

Sulky Sue.   Mother Goose.   OxNR; ReMoGo

Sullen, sullen, my brows are ever knit.   To his Brother Hsing-chien, Who was Serving in Tung-ch'uan.   Po Chü-i.   ChiP, *tr. by* Arthur Waley

Sullenness.   "Michael Field."   VWP

Sulpicia.   Michael Longley.   OxBSo; RACG

Sultan of the animals is the night, The.   Sultan of the Animals Is the Night, The.   Fazil Hüsnü Daglarca.   WoPoe, *tr. by* Ahmet Ö Evin

Sultry air, the smoke of shavings.   Night in a Village, A.   Ivan Savvich Nikitin.   AWP, *tr. by* P. E. Matheson

Sultry heat; dry, dead grass; endless steppes.   Stone Idol, The.   Ivan Alekseievich Bunin.   TCRP, *tr. by* Simon Franklin

Sultry Night, A.   Boris Leonidovich Pasternak.   TCRusP, *tr. by* Bogdan Boychuk and Mark Rudman

Sultry noon, not in the summer's prime, A.   Carlos Wilcox.   APN-1   *Fr.* Age of Benevolence, The.

Sum, A.   Lewis Carroll.   Spl

Sum of Life, The.   Ben King.   CTC

Sum speiks of lords, sum speiks of lairds.   Johnie Armstrang.   *Unknown.*   ESPB; IBB; OxBB

Sumac showing faint traces of red.   Autumn Thoughts.   Lu Yu.   SuSp, *tr. by* Burton Watson

Sumach Leaves, The.   Jones Very.   ColAP; NOBA

Sumburgh Heid.   George Bruce.   OxBS

Sumer is comen and winter gon.   Easter Song, An.   *Unknown.*   MiEL

Sumer Is Icumen [*or* Ycomen] In.   *Unknown.*   AWP; HAP; HeIP-4; MiEL; OPOU; OxBEV
     (Cuckoo Song, The.)   NAEL-7v1; NBLV; NOBE; NoP-4; OBEV; PeLV; TFi
     (Sing cuccu nu.)   EBEV; NoP-4; UV
     (Somer is i-comen in.)   OHMEL
     (Summer is acoming in.)   InPK-6
     (Summer [*or* Sumer] is y-comen [*or* y-cumen] in.)   NAEL-7v1; NBLV; NOBE; PeLV

Summa is i-cumen in.   Baccalaureate.   David McCord.   NBLV; OBAL

Summary.   Sonia Sanchez.   BPo

Summary.   Jaime Torres Bodet.   TCLAP, *tr. by* Sonja Karsen

Summary for Alastor.   Laura Riding Jackson.   FuPo; WoPoe

Summary of Lord Lyttleton's 'Advice to a Lady,' A.   Lady Mary Wortley Montagu.   FaBoEE; OxBEV

Summe men sayen that I am blac.   *Unknown.*   MiEL

Summer.   Conrad Potter Aiken.   NoAM

Summer.   Frank Asch.   NTCP

Summer.   John Ashbery.   NAAL-2v2

Summer.   Sir John Betjeman.   PeLi

Summer.   Fan Ch'eng-ta.   SuSp, *tr. by* Irving Y. Lo   *Fr.* Seasonal Poems on Fields and Gardens.

Summer.   Luciana Frezza.   CItWP, *tr. by* Cinzia Sartini Blum and Lara Trubowitz

Summer.   Friedrich Hölderlin.   WoPoe, *tr. by* David Rattray   *Fr.* Seasons, The.

Summer.   Judah Halevi.   NAWM-7v1, *tr. by* William M. Davis

Summer.   Kassan.   JDP, *tr. by* Yoel Hoffmann

Summer.   Tom Marshall.   NOBC

Summer.   Josephine Miles.   FaBoWP; WPE

Summer.   David Oliveira.   GeoHom

Summer.   Dennis Saleh.   GeoHom

Summer.   James Thomson.   *Fr.* Seasons, The.

Summer.   *Unknown.*   SuSp, *tr. by* Michael E. Workman   *Fr.* Tzu-yeh Songs of the Four Seasons.

Summer.   Diane Wakoski.   VGW

Summer.   Ramona Wilson.   VoR

Summer.   Judith Wright.   HarvBoo   *Fr.* Shadow of Fire: Ghazals, The.

Summer, The.   Morgan Llwyd.   AngWePo   *Fr.* 1648.
     "1. What? summer now? divisions ring."   PBRV

Summer, adieu.   Ode to the End of Summer.   Phyllis McGinley.   NBLV

Summer Again.   Yves Bonnefoy.   VCWP, *tr. by* Lisa Sapinkopf

Summer airing / On one pole.   Morikawa Kyoroku.   ZenPo, *tr. by* Takashi Ikemoto and Lucien Stryk

Summer airing / Trying on a quilt.   Kikaku.   ZenPo, *tr. by* Takashi Ikemoto and Lucien Stryk

Summer, and a woman lowers her jug to the river. She bathes and sings the word "why."   White Nile Elegy.   Khaled Mattawa.   NAPBL

Summer and dawn. It's Visitation Day. Sándor Sík. IQMS, *tr. by* Watson Kirkconnell

Summer and Winter. Shelley. OxAEP-2; SCGP

Summer Band Concert. Vivian Smith. CBAP

Summer Beach. Frances Darwin Cornford. BrRo

Summer blew its little drifts of sound, The. Army of Occupation. Sarah Morgan Bryan Piatt. NCAP

Summer breeze. Cor Van den Heuvel. HA

Summer brought fireflies in swarms. Childhood. Sharan Strange. GT

Summer came too fast, The. Chocolate Confessions. Magdalena Gomez. PueRic

Summer Christmas in Australia, A. Douglas Brook Wheelton Sladen. OBCP

Summer Cloud, A. Waldo Williams. OBWVE, *tr. by* Joseph P. Clancy

Summer come soon and turn the sickness from my house. Entreaty. Robert Fitzgerald. OxBSP

Summer comes. Magalu. Helene Johnson. APT-2; BlSi

Summer Countries, The. Henry Rago. VGW

Summer Dawn. William Morris. GSo; NOBE; NOBVV; OBEV; OxAEP-2; OxBEV

Summer Day. Yüan Mei. OHMPC, *tr. by* Kenneth Rexroth

Summer Day, A. Joanna Baillie.
    Evening. ECWP

Summer Day, A. Robert Greacen. PNI

Summer Day, The. Mary Oliver. AmFaPo

Summer Day in the Mountains. Li Po. CoBCP, *tr. by* Burton Watson

Summer day suffocates, smothers, pants, The. Poem on Azure. Anna de Noailles. WPOW, *tr. by* Betty L. Schwimmer

Summer Days. Wathen Mark Wilks Call. EBVV

Summer days are noticeably shortening, The. Margarita Iosifovna Aliger. TCRP

Summer Days in the Mountains. Li Po. CrYelRi, *tr. by* Sam Hamill

Summer delights the scholar. Scholar, The. Austin Clarke. RB

Summer dream beneath the shrubbery? The. (LL) Sonnet—To Science. Edgar Allan Poe. NAAL-2v1; NAAL-3; NAAL-5

Summer dream beneath the tamarind tree? The. (LL) Sonnet—To Science. Edgar Allan Poe. OxBA; OxBSo; Son; TAP; TCAPo

Summer drizzle. John Wills. HA

Summer ends now; now, barbarous in beauty, the stooks [a]rise. Hurrahing in Harvest. Gerard Manley Hopkins. MoBrPo; NAEL-5v2; NAEL-6v2; OxBSo; PeECV; PoE; SacPr; TOF

Summer Eve's Vision, A. Maria Jane Jewsbury. VWP

Summer evening. Chuck Brickley. HA

Summer Evening. Walter De la Mare. MoBrPo

Summer Evening, A. Geoffrey Nutter.
    "Toward the substation in the testing wind." BAP-97

Summer Farm. Norman MacCaig. NPeEn; NePenScot; OxBTC

Summer Fires of Mulanje Mountain. Edison Mpina. NAfrP

Summer Garden. Anna Andreyevna Akhmatova. BoWoP, *tr. by* Stephen Stepanchev

Summer Garden, The. Elena Ignatova. ItGoST, *tr. by* Sibelan Forrester

Summer grass. Basho. EH, *tr. by* Robert Hass

Summer grasses. Basho. SoOfWa, *tr. by* Sam Hamill

Summer grasses. Basho. Spl

Summer grasses / All that remains. Basho. ZenPo, *tr. by* Takashi Ikemoto and Lucien Stryk

Summer grasses grow, The. Basho. TAL

Summer grew, broadened out. Peonies. Harry Edmund Martinson. WoPoe, *tr. by* Leif Sjöberg and William Jay Smith

Summer grows old, cold-blooded mother. Frog Autumn. Sylvia Plath. OxBSP

Summer Harvest Spreads the Fields, The. Nathan Strong. AH

Summer Heat. Edward Carpenter. CAGL *Fr.* Towards Democracy.

Summer Holiday. Robinson Jeffers. MoAmPo; OxBA

Summer Home. Seamus Heaney. PBCIP

Summer I killed my pet chicken, The. Summer of the New Well. David Marlatt. AmPoNex

Summer I slept, The. My Cockroach Lover. Martín Espada. UrbNat

Summer I Taught English to the French, The. Abigail Mozley. PeLV

Summer Idyll. George Barker. FaBoMo

Summer in England, 1914. Alice Thompson Meynell. BrRo; SoSe-8; WPE

Summer in the South. Paul Laurence Dunbar. GT

Summer Is a-Comin' In. Vernon Duke. ReLy

Summer Is a Poem by Ovid. Douglas G. Jones. NIP-4

Summer Is By. William Soutar. FaBoVe

Summer is dying in the purple and gold and russet. Hayyim Nahman [*or* Khayim Nakhman *or* Chaim Nachman] Bialik. FIT, *tr. by* Robert Friend

Summer Is Ended. Christina Georgina Rossetti. NOBVV; NPeEn; OxBEV

Summer is fading. Afternoons. Philip Larkin. NPeEn; OxBEV; PoetW

Summer Is Gone. *Unknown.* FaBoCh, *tr. by* Kuno Meyer

Summer is happening above the heads of the dead. Blue Dome, The. Deborah Randall. NeBl

Summer is late, my heart. Touch Me. Stanley Kunitz. APT-2; NoP-4

Summer is over and. Bashō, A Departure. Robert Hass. LoL

Summer is over, the old cow said. Moo! Robert Silliman Hillyer. OBAL

Summer journeys to Niag'ra. Manhattan. Richard Rodgers. OBAL; ReLy

Summer Lost. Harriet Hamilton King. VWP

Summer Matures. Helene Johnson. BlSi

Summer Me, Winter Me. Michel Legrand. ReLy

Summer me, winter me. Summer Me, Winter Me. Michel Legrand. ReLy

Summer meant peeling: peaches. Preserving, The. Kevin Young. GT

Summer moon. William J. Higginson. HA

Summer Morning, A. Rachel Lyman Field. ChAP

Summer Morning, A. Richard Wilbur. FaBoMo; NBLV

Summer mornings we. Sherley Anne Williams. GeoHom *Fr.* Iconography of Childhood, The.

Summer, my dearest, turns again to the dark. Two of Us Together, Each of Us Alone, The. Yehuda Amichai [*or* Amikhai]. FIT, *tr. by* Robert Friend

Summer near the River. Carolyn Kizer. CoAP; VGW

Summer nests uncovered by autumn wind, The. Birds' Nests. Edward Thomas. OWoS

Summer Night. Nathan [*or* Natan] Alterman. FIT, *tr. by* Robert Friend

Summer Night. Hayyim Nahman [*or* Khayim Nakhman *or* Chaim Nachman] Bialik. FIT, *tr. by* Robert Friend

Summer Night. Ludwig Goldscheider. AuPH, *tr. by* Lowell A. Bangerter

Summer Night. Langston Hughes. APT-2

Summer night. Issa. EH, *tr. by* Robert Hass

Summer night. Peggy Lyles. HA

Summer Night. Antonio Machado. BLT, *tr. by* Willis Barnstone

Summer Night. Antonio Machado Ruiz. WoPoe, *tr. by* Willis Barnstone

Summer night. George Swede. HA

Summer Night. Tennyson. OBEV *Fr.* Princess, The.

Summer Night. Tu Fu. TAL

Summer Night, A. W. H. Auden. NPeEn

Summer Night, The. Friedrich Gottlieb Klopstock. GePo, *tr. by* George C. Schoolfield

Summer night—a night whose wide-spread wings, A. Infinite in the Skies, The. Alphonse Marie Louis de Lamartine. SxFrPo, *tr. by* E. H. Blackmore and A. M. Blackmore

Summer night clothes whirling in a dryer. Marlene Mountain. HA

Summer Night, Riverside. Sara Teasdale. APT-1

Summer nights I loved the cool pillow. Screen Porch. Frederick Marchant. UrbNat

Summer Niight. *Unknown.* SuSp, *tr. by* Edward H. Schafer

Summer 1984. Duncan Bush. TCAWP

Summer 1983. Mary Jo Salter. RA

Summer nineteen seventy. Lindiwe Mabuza. WPOW

Summer nineteen sixty nine. Seamus Heaney. CIP-2

Summer noon. Lenard D. Moore. HA

Summer Noon: 1941. Yvor Winters. ColAP

Summer Nostalgia. Virginia E. Escandor. ReBoTo

Summer, now we must live without your sweet weather. Neidhart von Reuental. GePo

Summer of Lost Rachel, The. Seamus Heaney. NIL-7

Summer of nineteen eighteen, The. Bad Old Days, The. Kenneth Rexroth. NNaP; NoAM; PAI

Summer of 'sixty-three, sir, and Conrad was gone away. Kentucky Belle. Constance Fenimore Woolson. CBCWP

Summer of strike and drought. Summer 1984. Duncan Bush. TCAWP

Summer of the New Well. David Marlatt. AmPoNex

Summer or Its Ending. Yehuda Amichai [*or* Amikhai]. PoSu, *tr. by* Dennis Silk

Summer Oracle. Audre Lorde. BlSi

Summer Palace burnt, the Winter Palace, wherever it was, The. 10:X:57, 45 Years Since the Fall of the Ch'ing Dynasty. Philip Whalen. PoM

Summer passed through the cool rooms, violent. Stone, A. Yves Bonnefoy. VCWP, *tr. by* John Naughton

Summer Poem, A. Jayanta Mahapatra. VCWP

Summer Pogrom. Fay Zwicky. CBAP

Summer pours its fullness out abroad, The. Summer Stanzas. Carl Dallago. AuPH, *tr. by* Lowell A. Bangerter

Summer rain isn't here yet, The. Language of Weather, The. Ray A. Young Bear. HATNAP

Summer Recital. Cynthia S. Pederson. MiVo

Summer's Day, A. Joanna Baillie. WoRP

Summer's Dream, A. Elizabeth Bishop. OxBC

Summer's Last Will and Testament. Thomas Nashe [*or* Nash].

("Adieu; fare-well earth's bliss.") SacPr

Adieu, Farewell, Earth's Bliss[e]. EBEV; HAP; HeIP-4; NPeEn; NoP-4; NoSic; OxBEV; TFi; TRP

Autumn. NoSic; SCGP

(Baning Summer.) OxBSP; SCGP

Fair Summer Droops. NoSic

("Fayre Summer droops, droope men and beasts therefore.") NPeEn

(In a Time of Pestilence.) OBEV

(In Plague Time.) FaBoCh

(In Time of Pestilence.) NOBE; PeECV; WoPoe

(Litany in Time of Plague, A.) ClHu; NAEL-5v1; NAEL-6v1; NAEL-7v1; NIL-7; NIP-4; PoPoPo; PoRA; SacPr

(Song in Time of Plague.) SCV

(Spring.) GTBS-P; NOBE; OBEV; SCGP

Spring, the Sweet Spring. NAEL-5v1; NAEL-6v1; NoP-4; NoSic; TFi

("Spring, the sweete spring, is the yeres pleasant King.") OxBEV

Summer's Night, A. Paul Laurence Dunbar. APN-2

Summer's night, A. Summer's Night, A. Antonio Machado Ruiz. SpanPo, tr. by James Duffy

Summer Sabbath. Jessie E. Sampter. TrJP

Summer Seeming. John Riley. Oth

Summer set lip to earth's bosom bare. Poppy, The. Francis Thompson. MoBrPo

Summer Shower. David McCord. TLR

Summer Shower, The. Thomas Buchanan Read. TreFP

Summer Sketches. Bessie Rayner Parkes. Lilian's Second Letter. VWP

Summer sky / Clear after rain. Masaoka Shiki. ZenPo, tr. by Takashi Ikemoto and Lucien Stryk

Summer slams the tropic sun, The. Country Club Romance, A. Derek Walcott. OxBC

Summer Solstice. George Bowering. "I am slowly dying, water evaporating." NOBC

Summer Solstice. Alan Garner. NOxBChV

Summer Solstice. Dorothy Hewett. "Sunset flames over the city, The." BMAP

Summer Song. Unknown. APN-2, tr. by Franz Boas

Summer Song. Emperor Wu of Han [or Wu Ti or Ou-ty or Liu Ch'e or Liu Ch'u]. ChiP, tr. by Arthur Waley

Summer Song, A. George Peele. See Old Wives' [or Wife's] Tale, The

Summer Song I. George Barker. HarvBoo

Summer, splendid summer, nourishing the poet on the milk of your light. Midnight Elegy. Léopold Sédar Senghor. NegPo, tr. by Ellen Conroy Kennedy

Summer Stanzas. Carl Dallago. AuPH, tr. by Lowell A. Bangerter

Summer stillness. Peggy Lyles. HA

Summer Storm. Dana Gioia. RA

Summer Storm. Louis Simpson. OxBC; OxBSo

Summer Sun. Robert Louis Stevenson. MoBrPo; PWR

Summer sun ray, The. Noon Walk on the Asylum Lawn. Anne Sexton. OBGa

Summer Sunday. Unknown. WoPoe, tr. by John Gardner

Summer swells like a fruit. Heat. Maura Dooley. NeBl

Summer that I was ten, The. Centaur, The. May Swenson. APT-2; FaBoWP; TwCP

Summer the Beatles Went Over Seven Minutes on a Single, The. Doyle Wesley Walls. SwNoth

Summer, The Second Pastoral, or Alexis. Pope. Fr. Pastorals.

Summer, this is our flesh. Seasons of the Soul. Allen Tate. FuPo; OxBA

Summer thunder darkens, and its climbing. Prometheus. Charles Tomlinson. HarvBoo

Summer Time on Bredon. Hugh Kingsmill. NOBL; UV

Summer turned. John Gneisenau Neihardt. GM Fr. Song of the Indian Wars, The.

Summer twilight, The. (LL) Sone Yoshitada. AmFaPo; OHMPJ, tr. by Kenneth Rexroth

Summer Vacation. William Wordsworth. Fr. Prelude, The; Growth of a Poet's Mind [1850 vers.].

Summer was dry, dry the garden. On the Debt My Mother Owed to Sears Roebuck. Edward Dorn. CoAmPo; TRP

Summer waves goodbye to the wayside. Storm, an Endless Instant. Boris Leonidovich Pasternak. TCRusP, tr. by Bogdan Boychuk and Mark Rudman

Summer when our life was fair, The. (LL) Musings. William Barnes. HAP; NOBE

Summer Wind. William Cullen Bryant. APN-1

Summer with Monika. Roger McGough. "Away from you." OBCoV

Summer Words of [or for] a Sistuh [or Sister] Addict. Sonia Sanchez. BPo; BlSi; UnPo

Summerfield. Jim Barnes. HATNAP Fr. Ex-Deputy Sheriff Remembers the Eastern Oklahoma Murderers, An.

Summerhouse Piano. Sascha Feinstein. AmPoNex

Summers and summers have come, and gone with the flight of the swallow. Tantramar Revisited, The. Sir Charles G. D. Roberts. NOBC

Summers of Vietnam. Mary Kinzie. IllVoic

Summertime. Su Shun-ch'in. SuSp, tr. by Michael E. Workman

Summertime and the livin' is easy. Summertime. DuBose Heyward. ReLy

Summertime and the Living. Robert Earl Hayden. TwCP

Summertime Late Show. Edwin Torres. HeMarv

Summing Up. Claribel Alegría. LoL

Summing-up, The. Stanley Kunitz. OBAL

Summit, A. Tu Fu. CrYelRi, tr. by Sam Hamill

Summit, The. Kathleen Jessie Raine. OxBS Fr. Beinn Naomh.

Summit Temple, The. Li Po. TAL

Summon now the kings of the forest. Mmenson. Edward Kamau Brathwaite. OPOU

Summon one's powers. (LL) George Oppen. APT-2; NNaP Fr. Some San Francisco Poems.

Summon the Earth (the fair Astrea's gone). Unknown. EMWP

Summoned by Bells. Sir John Betjeman. "My dear deaf father, how I loved him then." OxBTC

Summoned by conscious recollection, she. Misery and Splendor. Robert Hass. VCAP

Summons. Christian Morgenstern. WoPoe, tr. by David R. Slavitt

Summons. David Rivard. OPRER

Summons of the Soul, The. Ch'u Yüan. WoPoe, tr. by David Hawkes

Summons to Love. William Drummond, of Hawthornden. See Invocation: "Pheobus, arise! / And paint the sable skies."

Summons to Town, A. Sir John Suckling. NOSC

Sums, The. Lauris Edmond. FaBoWP

Sun. John Blight. BMAP

Sun. Omer Hillel. MHP, tr. by Ruth Finer Mintz

Sun. Morning. Vincente Huidobro. CuPo

Sun. Michael Palmer. APSN; PFTM-2 "Lines through these words, The." PFTM-2

Sun. Henry Rowe. OBEV

Sun. Gary Soto. TRP

Sun. Valerie Worth. NOxBChV

Sun, The. Judah Al-Harizi. BLT, tr. by T. Carmi

Sun, The. Hugo Ball. PFTM-1

Sun, The. John Drinkwater. NTCP

Sun, The. Czeslaw Milosz. ChAP

Sun, The. Sweet Brown Rice and Red Bones. Lamont B. Steptoe. SpirFl

Sun, The. Francis Thompson. MoBrPo Fr. Ode to the Setting Sun.

Sun, The. Walter James Turner. MoBrPo

Sun, The. Vidya. "I praise the disk of the rising sun." WPOW

Sun, The. Sun. Valerie Worth. NOxBChV

Sun, The. Benjamin Zephaniah. Oth

Sun-a-shine, Rain-a-fall. Valerie Bloom. NOxBChV

Sun above the hills raged in the height, The. Lot and His Daughters II. Alec Derwent Hope. ChIV-1

Sun and Fog contested, The. Sun and Fog Contested, The. Emily Dickinson. Spl

Sun and Moon. Cynewulf. ASW; WoPoe, tr. by Kevin Crossley-Holland Fr. Riddles (Exeter Book).

Sun and moon. Gary Hotham. HA

Sun and Moon. Mary Kinzie. FFC

Sun and Moon So High and Bright, The. Unknown. AH

Sun and moon, that ceaselessly obey, The. Immortal Israel. Judah Halevi. TrJP, tr. by Solomon Solis-Cohen

Sun and rain at work together. Red-Gold Rain, The. Sacheverell Sitwell. MoBrPo

Sun and the north wind observed a traveler, The. Phoebus and Boreas. Jean de La Fontaine. WoPoe, tr. by Marianne Craig Moore

Sun and the Ocean, The. Gravestone, August 8, 1968, A. Paul Goodman. BodElec

Sun and the sea have erupted, sheet-lightning, The. Paradise Regained. Hendrik Marsman. TuT, tr. by Michael Longley

Sun and the Woman, The. Salah Abd al-Sabur. MAP, tr. by John Heath-Stubbs and Lena Jayyusi

Sun appearing: a pendant, The. Plainview: 3. N. Scott Momaday. CDW

Sun as a Spinning Top (I), The. Francis Ponge. AF, tr. by Serge Gavronsky

Sun as zenith; the sun-cross is hoisted. Ants and the Sun. Khalil Khouri. MAP, tr. by Sharif Elmusa and Christopher Middleton

Sun at noon to higher air, The. March. A. E. Housman. FaBoCh

Sun-beams of thy face, The. (LL) Bible, *O.T.* EMWP; PEW, *tr.* by Mary Sidney Herbert, Countess of Pembroke *Fr.* Psalms.

Sun, beholding so as he does pass, The. On a Fair Lady, Looking in the Glass. Richard Leigh. NOSC

Sun blazed while the thunder yet, The. Mill-Pond, The. Edward Thomas. RB

Sun blazing slowly in its last hour, The. Evening, An. Robert Mezey. GeoHom

Sun blooms in our bodies. Summer. Tom Marshall. NOBC

Sun brightens. Alan Pizzarelli. HA

Sun burning down on back and loins, penetrating the skin, bathing their flanks in sweat. Edward Carpenter. CAGL *Fr.* Towards Democracy.

Sun bursts through the window, The. Poet in the Kitchen. Margit Mikes. IQMS, *tr.* by Suzanne K. Walther

Sun Children. Leslie Marmon Silko. VoR

Sun comes up. Sun: Day, The. Bert Schierbeek. PFTM-2, *tr.* by Charles McGeehan

Sun comes up, The. Losing My Mind. Stephen Sondheim. ReLy

Sun comes up, wind starts to ripple, The. Going to the Ministry with Chao Tzu-ch'i. Yü Chi. CoBLCP, *tr.* by Jonathan Chaves

Sun creeps under the caves. Reader, The. Janet Lewis. APT-2

Sun, dear Haemon, in its far domain, The. Antigone. Lajos Áprily. IQMS, *tr.* by Watson Kirkconnell

Sun descended on the top of the mountain, The. Who Can Understand This? László Mécs. IQMS, *tr.* by Kenneth Thomas

Sun descending in the west, The. William Blake. FHYEP; ITBLP; OBEV *Fr.* Songs of Innocence.

Sun-Dial, The. Adelaide Crapsey. APT-1

Sun does [*or* doth] arise, The. William Blake. AmFaPo; FHYEP; NAEL-5v2; NAEL-6v2; OxAEP-2; PoE; UnPo *Fr.* Songs of Innocence.

Sun drew off at last his piercing fires, The. Witchcraft: New Style. Lascelles Abercrombie. MoBrPo

Sun dries me as I dance, The. (LL) Gary Snyder. NOBA; NeAP; PoM *Fr.* Myths and Texts.

Sun drops below the elms. Routes. Peter Everwine. NNaP

Sun drops luridly into the west, The. Augusta Davies Webster. PeVV; VWP *Fr.* Circe.

Sun Exercises. Michael Dennis Browne.

"You, I accuse." SpudSo

Sun-flames of springtime, The. March in Transylvania. Lajos Áprily. IQMS, *tr.* by Adam Makkai

Sun-Flower, The. Dora Greenwell. EroLit; VWP; WPE

(Sunflower, The.) PEW

Sun frets, a fat wafer falling like a trap of failed mesh, The. Hole, Where Once in Passion We Swam. Dave Jeddie Smith. NoAM

Sun from the east tips the mountains with gold, The. Paul Whitehead. OxBoLi *Fr.* Apollo and Daphne.

Sun-god was reclining on a couch of rosy shells, The. Sunset Picture. Henrietta Cordelia Ray. CBWP-3

Sun goes. David Chapman Berry. CDa

Sun goes down, The. Evening in Terezin, An. Eva Schulzová. INSAB

Sun goes down, The. Cor Van den Heuvel. HA

Sun goes down, and over all, The. Low Tide on Grand Pré. Bliss Carman. NOBC

Sun goes down for hours, taking more of her along, The. Lady in the Pink Mustang, The. Louise Erdrich. HATNAP; OPRER; ReTh

Sun going down. Sundown Blues. Raymond R. Patterson. SeSe

Sun had begun in the gloaming, The. First Snow-fall, The. James Russell Lowell. ITBLP

Sun had stooped, his westward clouds to win. Nutting. John Clare. CenSon

Sun had thrown its noontide ray, The. Noon. Lysander. Anne Batten Cristall. RWP

Sun had wheeled from Grey's to Dammer's Crest, The. Burghers, The. Thomas Hardy. EBNV

Sun has come, I know, The. Sun, The. Walter James Turner. MoBrPo

Sun has risen on the eastern brim of the world, The. Song of Lo-fu, The. *Unknown.* AWP; ChiP, *tr.* by Arthur Waley

Sun has rung, The. Summer. Dennis Saleh. GeoHom

Sun has set, and the long grass now, The. Emily Jane Brontë. UnPo

Sun has set, the moon is in darkness, The. Swarming Mosquitoes. Mei Yao Ch'en. SuSp, *tr.* by Jonathan Chaves

Sun has sunk 'neath yonder distant hill, The. Belshazzer's Feast. Eloise Bibb. CBWP-4

Sun hath run his course through all the Signes, The. George Wither. PBRV *Fr.* Vox Pacifica.

Sun House. Haki R. Madhubuti. ESEAA

Sun, hung by a string, The. Diptych. Birago Diop. NegPo, *tr.* by Ellen Conroy Kennedy

Sun-Hunters, The. Mark O'Connor. NOBAu

Sun, in clownish yellow, but not a clown, The. Wallace Stevens. NOBA *Fr.* Esthétique du Mal.

Sun, / in her memory, The. Lost in the Desert. Clarence Major. FTOS

Sun in the mouth of the day. Envoi. Robley, Jr. Wilson. InvLad; PBCAP

Sun in the south ranges a winter heaven, The. South Side. Robert Fitzgerald. APT-2

Sun is a huntress young, The. Nicholas Vachel Lindsay. IllVoic

SUN IS A NEGRO, THE. Untitled. Bob Kaufman. ISC

Sun is about to set when I board the boat, The. Sailing at Night on Flowing-sand River. Lin Hung. SuSp, *tr.* by Irving Y. Lo

Sun is blazing and the sky is blue, The. Pink Dog. Elizabeth Bishop. NALW

Sun is blue and scarlet on my page, The. Falling Asleep over the Aeneid. Robert Lowell. MoAmPo; OxBA

Sun is bright,—the air is clear, The. It Is Not Always May. Henry Wadsworth Longfellow. PWR

Sun is falling as the peasant girl, The. Village Saturday, The. Giacomo Leopardi. NAWM-7v2, *tr.* by Ottavio M. Casale

Sun is folding, cars stall and rise, The. New World, The. Imamu Amiri Baraka. NoAM; NoP-4; PmAP

Sun is going down, The. Aranda Song. *Unknown.* CBAP, *tr.* by T. G. H. Strehlow

Sun is in Capricorn, The. Joyce Mansour. HAWP, *tr.* by Carol Cosman

Sun is in mourning, The. Be like the sun. Possessed. Charles Baudelaire. ErotSp, *tr.* by Richard Howard

Sun is in the west. Fishing boats, The. Drinking at Night with Yen Kung-mou. Shen Chou. CoBLCP, *tr.* by Jonathan Chaves

Sun is lord and god, sublime, serene, The. Lake of Gaube, The. Algernon Charles Swinburne. CABP; NAEL-5v2; NAEL-6v2

Sun is nigh the verge, The. Soon we must part. Walk, A. Hedwig Lachmann. TrJP, *tr.* by Jethro Bithell

Sun is not in love with us, The. Isles of Greece, The. Demetrios Capetanakis. GTBS-P

Sun is on the crowded street, The. Scenes in London: Piccadilly. Letitia [*or* Laetitia] Elizabeth Landon. RWP

Sun is rising, The. Healing Song. *Unknown.* OBVE, *tr.* by Frances Densmore

Sun is set, and masked night, The. Songe 17. Robert Sidney. NoSic

Sun is shining, the grass is green, The. White Christmas. Irving Berlin. ReLy

Sun is sinking low, The. Deep Purple. Mitchell Parish. ReLy

Sun is warm, the sky is clear, The. Stanzas Written in Dejection, near Naples [*or*—December 1818, near Naples]. Shelley. GTBS-P; NAEL-5v2; NAEL-6v2; NAWM-7v2; PoRA

Sun kept setting—setting—still, The. Emily Dickinson. APN-2

Sun-light recedes on the mountains, in long gold shafts. Interlude. Maxwell Bodenheim. APT-1

Sun lights my hand writing, The. Sun On My Hand, The. Bert Voeten. TuT, *tr.* by James Simmons

Sun lights up a distant ridge another, The. John Wills. HA

Sun like a sleepy giant, The. Narcolepsy. Maureen Owen. TTTS

Sun like an orange mousse through the trees. Dog Day Vespers. Charles Wright. LCAP-2

Sun May Set, The. Catullus. FaBoEE; NoSic; OBVE, *tr.* by Sir Walter Alexander Raleigh *Fr.* Carmina.

Sun moon stars rain. (LL) Anyone Lived in a Pretty How Town. E. E. Cummings. ChAP; ColAP; HAP; InPK-6; MoAmPo; NAAL-2v2; NAAL-5; NOBA; NoP-4; PoPoPo; RB; TAP; TFi; TwCP; VGW

Sun now darts his fervid rays, The. Lines Written in the Dog-Days. William Woty. NOEC

Sun Now Risen, The. Johann Conrad Beissel. AH

Sun of Auschwitz, The. Tadeusz Borowski. AF, *tr.* by Larry Rafferty

Sun of Auschwitz, The. Tadeusz Borowski. HP, *tr.* by Tadeuszt Pióro

Sun of my soul, thou Saviour dear. John Keble. SacPr

Sun of Our Existence, The. Mrs. Henry Linden. CBWP-4

Sun, of whose terrain we creatures are, The. Solar Creation. Charles Madge. FaBoMo; OBMV; OxBTC

Sun on hillsides, wind on seas. Desolation. *Unknown.* OBWVE, *tr.* by Aneirin Talfan Davies

Sun On My Hand, The. Bert Voeten. TuT, *tr.* by Tony Curtis

Sun On My Hand, The. Bert Voeten. TuT, *tr.* by James Simmons

Sun on the tree-tops no longer is seen, The. Queen Sabbath. Hayyim Nahman [*or* Khayim Nakhman *or* Chaim Nachman] Bialik. TrJP, *tr.* by Jessie Sampter

Sun plants a foot in the pasture, The. Goree. Niyi Osundare. HBAPE

Sun pours over me, The. Loneliness. Dhabya Khamees. PoArWo, *tr.* by Clarissa C. Burt

Sun-Rise: Sonnet, A. Ann Radcliffe. CenSon

Sun rises, The.   In Fields of Summer.   Galway Kinnell.   VGW

Sun rises at the southeastern corner, The.   Mulberry by the Path.   *Unknown.* SuSp; WoPoe, *tr. by* Hans H. Frankel

Sun rises going the rounds.   Tatar Songs.   *Unknown.*   EaWin, *tr. by* W. S. Merwin

Sun rises in the ancient east, The.   Ode to Governor Capper, An.   J. P. Dunn. VerBaPo

Sun rises in the southeast corner, The.   Ballad of the Mulberry Road. *Unknown.*   ChinPo, *tr. by* Yip Wai-lim

Sun rises over eastern seas, The.   Six Choruses.   Tu Fu.   CrYelRi, *tr. by* Sam Hamill

Sun Rising, The.   John Donne.   BASC; BoLoP; CABP; ClHu; ESCV; FHYEP; FSCP; HAP; HeIP-4; MeLP; NAEL-5v1; NAEL-6v1; NAEL-7v1; NIL-7; NIP-4; NOBE; NOSC; NoP-4; PAI; PBRV; PoE; PoPoPo; SCV; TFi; WeW-3

  (Busie old foole, unruly Sunne.)   PBRV

Sun rising over the mountains, The.   Right Cross, The.   Philip Levine. MoASP

Sun rushed up the sky, The; the taxi flew.   Parting as Descent.   John Berryman. MoAmPo

Sun's accomplice, the tree. / Maurice. (LL)   Dusting.   Rita Dove.   ESEAA; HCAP; HeIP-4; LCAP-2

Sun's bright orb, declining all serene, The.   William Falconer.   OxAEP-1   *Fr.* Shipwreck, The.

Sun's fair rays are shining, The.   Yun Sŏndo.   WoPoe, *tr. by* Peter H. Lee   *Fr.* Angler's Calendar, The.

Sun's high, I've slept enough, still too lazy to get up, The.   Writing Again on the Same Theme.   Po Chü-i.   CoBCP, *tr. by* Burton Watson

Sun's Perpendicular Rays, The.   William Lort Mansel.   FaBoEE

Sun's rays that shoot up, stretched out, The.   Old Song of Rejoicing, An. *Unknown.*   PeNZ, *tr. by* Margaret Orbell

Sun's return is magical, The.   Carnival.   Primus St. John.   GT

Sun sank in the thunderous sky of the town, The.   Marriage.   Walter James Turner.   NOBAu

Sun says she is there, The.   White Deer, The.   Jay Wright.   ESEAA

Sun serpent: eye beguiling my eye.   Sun Serpent.   Aimé Césaire.   NAWM-7v2, *tr. by* Gregson Davis

Sun set, but set not his hope, The.   Character.   Ralph Waldo Emerson. OxBSP

Sun set early on the forest, The.   After the Wedding Party.   Matthew Rohrer. ReTh

Sun sets brightly—but a ruddier glow, The.   Wife of Asdrubal, The.   Felicia Dorothea Hemans.   ViWPN

Sun sets in night, and the stars shun the day, The.   North American Death Song. Anne Hunter.   ECWP

Sun sets in night, and the stars shun the day, The.   Royall Tyler.   NAAL-3   *Fr.* Contrast, The.

Sun sets in the cold without friends, The.   Dusk in Winter.   W. S. Merwin. BLT

Sun sets on the dike where I walk.   Song of "Hand-in-Hand," A.   Ou-yang Hsiu.   SuSp, *tr. by* Irving Y. Lo

Sun sets, the pagoda is darkened, The.   Evening Bell from a Misty Temple. Wen Cheng-ming.   CoBLCP, *tr. by* Jonathan Chaves

Sun sets, The. The wind moans.   Ts'ai Yen.   BoWoP; WPOW   *Fr.* Eighteen Verses Sung to a Tatar Reed Whistle.

Sun shines, The.   Tommies in the Train.   D. H. Lawrence.   PoWW

Sun shines bright, but sadly, The.   Autumn.   Priscilla Jane Thompson. CBWP-2

Sun shines bright in the old Kentucky home, The.   My Old Kentucky Home[, Good Night!].   Stephen Collins Foster.   APN-2

Sun shines high on yonder hill, The.   False Lover Won Back, The.   *Unknown.* ESPB; OxBB

Sun shines in disarray, The.   Maybe There's a God Around.   Aleksandr Ivanovich Vvedensky [*or* Vvedenskii].   TCRP, *tr. by* Bradley Jordan

Sun shone in my hut, The.   He Who Has Lost All.   David Diop.   TTY, *tr. by* Anne Atik

Sun shows thin through hail, wallpaper-pale, and falls, The.   Soft Swimmer, Winter Swan.   Robert Horan.   YaYoPo

Sun sinks low, The. I.   *Unknown.*   ColAnChi, *tr. by* Jeanne Larsen   *Fr.* Midnight Songs.

Sun sinks towards the horizon, The.   Clear Evening after Rain.   Tu Fu. OHPC, *tr. by* Kenneth Rexroth

Sun smudge on the smoky water.   Autumn.   Archibald MacLeish.   IllVoic

Sun sought thy dim bed and brought forth light, The.   Africa.   Claude McKay. APT-1; NAAAL; NAAL-5; Son

Sun stares, The.   Tall Walking Woman.   Pat Mora.   OxIBACP

Sun still proud, the shadow still disdained, The. (LL)   Follow Thy Fair Sun[ne] [Unhappy Shadow].   Thomas Campion.   EnLoPo; NOBE; NOSC; NoSic; SCGP; UnPo

Sun stood still, The.   Day They Came for Our House, The.   Don Mattera. PeSAV

Sun-Struck Eagle, The.   Eleanor Percy Lee.   SWaP

Sun, sweet girl, hath run his year-long race.   First Birthday, The.   Hartley Coleridge.   CenSon

Sun-swept beaches with a light wind blowing.   Unchanging, The.   Sara Teasdale.   APT-1

Sun-tanned men and women, toiling there together.   Reapers.   Mathilde Blind. WPE

Sun, that brave man, The.   Brave Man, The.   Wallace Stevens.   SAmP

Sun that brief December day, The.   John Greenleaf Whittier.   APN-1; NAAL-3; NAAL-5; NOBA; OxBA; TAP; TFi

Sun that brief December day, The.   John Greenleaf Whittier.   AiP; TCAPo   *Fr.* Snow-Bound [*or* Snow-Bound; a Winter Idyl].

Sun, The: Day.   Bert Schierbeek.   PFTM-2, *tr. by* Charles McGeehan

Sun the executioner the press of the masses, The.   Day and Night.   Aimé Césaire.   NAWM-7v2, *tr. by* Gregson Davis

Sun the First.   Odysseus Elytis.   GifTon, *tr. by* Olga Broumas

Sun, the moon, the stars, the seas, the hills and the plains, The.   Higher Pantheism, The.   Tennyson.   CABP; InvLi

Sun, the rose, the lily, the dove, The.   Love's Résumé.   Heinrich Heine.   TrJP, *tr. by* J. F. C.

Sun This March, The.   Wallace Stevens.   APT-1; HarvBoo

Sun Underfoot Among the Sundews, The.   Amy Clampitt.   NoP-4

Sun upon the lake is low, The.   Datur Hora Quieti.   Sir Walter Scott.   GTBS-P

Sun upon the Weirdlaw Hill, The.   Dreary Change, The.   Sir Walter Scott. NAEL-5v2; NAEL-6v2

Sun used to shine while we two walked, The.   Sun Used to Shine, The. Edward Thomas.   FaBoTw

Sun was black with judgment, and the moon, The.   Femina Contra Mundum. Gilbert Keith Chesterton.   OxAEP-2

Sun was down, and twilight grey, The.   In the Room.   James Thomson. NOBVV; NePenScot; OxBEV; PeVV

Sun was now withdrawn, The.   Damon and Cupid.   John Gay.   EnLoPo

Sun was shining on the sea, The.   Lewis Carroll.   CABP; ChAP; ITBLP; NAEL-5v2; NAEL-6v2; NOBL; NOBVV; NoAM; OBSP; OTCP; OxAEP-2; PeLV; PoRA; TFi   *Fr.* Through the Looking-Glass.

Sun, when he enamels day, The.   Praise of a Yellow Skin, The, or An Elizabeth in Gold.   John Collop.   NOSC

Sun, which doth the greatest comfort bring, The.   Letter to Ben Jonson, A. Francis Beaumont.   BeJo

Sun whirls an axle on fire, The.   Leonidas of Tarentum.   GrAn

Sun will never see you, The.   On a Pet Grasshopper.   Aristodicus of Rhodes. PGA, *tr. by* Kenneth Rexroth

Sun woke me this morning loud, The.   True Account of Talking to the Sun at Fire Island, A.   Frank O'Hara.   AmFaPo; EmeKit; HCAP; NNaP; RB; TTTS

Sun—a shadow of a magnitude, A. (LL)   On Seeing the Elgin Marbles.   John Keats.   CenSon; GSo; NAEL-5v2; NAEL-6v2; NIL-7; NIP-4

Sunbathing.   Nancy Travis.   ISC

Sunbeams.   Avner Trainin.   MHP, *tr. by* Ruth Finer Mintz

Sunbeams streamed without, The.   In the Morgue.   Israel Zangwill.   TrJP

Sunburned eyes.   Man Is Dead, A.   Claire Gebeyli.   PoArWo, *tr. by* Mona Takyeddine Amyuni

Suncoming.   Oliver La Grone.   NBV

Sunday.   Mário de Andrade.   TCLAP, *tr. by* Jack E. Tomlins

Sunday.   J. C. Bloem.   TuT, *tr. by* Desmond Egan

Sunday.   Jorge Carrera Andrade.   TCLAP, *tr. by* Muna Lee

Sunday.   George Herbert.   GeHe; PeECV; TrCP

Sunday.   Timothy Liu.   NeAmPo

Sunday.   Achy Obejas.   WiU

Sunday.   Carl Phillips.   GT

Sunday.   James Schuyler.   TTTS

Sunday.   Philippe Soupault.   PFTM-1

Sunday.   Primus St. John.   ISC

Sunday: A Fragment Transcribed from a Ms. in Chatterton's Handwriting. Thomas Chatterton.   ECEV

Sunday A.M. Not in Manhattan.   John Hollander.   PoSol

Sunday A.M. so early even FM crackles church service.   In the Kingdom of Perpetual Repair.   Kevin Stein.   IllVoic

Sunday Afternoon.   Denise Levertov.   CoAmPo; PAI

Sunday afternoon and the water.   Fording the River.   Seamus Deane.   PBCIP; PNI

Sunday Afternoon Service in St. Enodoc Church, Cornwall.   Sir John Betjeman. NOCV

Sunday Afternoons.   Herbert Asquith.   NAAAL

Sunday Afternoons.   Anthony Thwaite.   OxBTC

Sunday, and the thin lull of evening.   San Buenaventura.   Maurina Sherman. GeoHom

Sunday at the State Hospital. David Ignatow. RaBo

Sunday Brunch. Reuben Jackson. ISC

Sunday by the Combination. Langston Hughes. APT-2

Sunday Chicken. Gwendolyn Brooks. ColAP *Fr.* Notes from the Childhood and the Girlhood.

Sunday Chimes in the City. Louise Imogen Guiney. APN-2

Sunday Dreamer's Guide to Yarrow, Missouri, A. Jim Barnes. HATNAP

Sunday Evening. Barbara Guest. NeAP

Sunday Evening. Sam Hunt. PeNZ

Sunday Evening in the Common. John Hall Wheelock. MoAmPo

Sunday Greens. Rita Dove. GT; LCAP-2

Sunday heavy potlid on the boiling blood. Tristan Tzara. PFTM-1 *Fr.* Approximate Man, The.

Sunday in Glastonbury. Robert Bly. CoAmPo

Sunday in Great Tew. Peter McDonald. ModIr; PNI

Sunday in the Park. William Carlos Williams. NAAL-2v2; NoAM *Fr.* Paterson.

Sunday in the provinces, a plaintive Norman bell-peal. Maria Luisa Spaziani. NeIt *Fr.* Star of Free Will, The.

Sunday in the snow. Fall, The. Michael Anania. IllVoic

Sunday is wringing its discoloured hands. Mild Citizen. Glyn Maxwell. HarvBoo

Sunday lamb cracks in its fat, The. Mary's Song. Sylvia Plath. ChIV-2; FaBoMo; FaBoWP

Sunday Matinee. Sybil Kollar. FFC

Sunday Morning. Robert Grenier. PmAP

Sunday Morning. Christina Jenkins. BrRo

Sunday Morning. Louis MacNeice. FaBoMo; MoBrPo; NAEL-5v2; NAEL-6v2; NIP-4; OxAEP-2; Son

Sunday Morning. Robert Minhinnick. TCAWP

Sunday Morning. David Ray. AllShUp

Sunday Morning. Anne Rouse. NeBl

Sunday Morning. Wallace Stevens. APT-1; BBASP; ColAP; HAP; HCAP; HarvBoo; HeIP-4; MoAmPo; NAAL-2v2; NAAL-5; NAWM-7v2; NIL-7; NIP-4; NOBA; NoAM; NoP-4; OxBA; PoE; PoPoPo; SAmP; SoSe-8; TAP; TCAPo; TFi; TRP

Sunday Morning Apples. Hart Crane. HarvBoo

Sunday Morning in Old San Juan. Julio Marzán. PueRic

Sunday Morning, King's Cambridge. Sir John Betjeman. PeECV

Sunday Morning, 1950. Irene McKinney. PBCAP

Sunday Morning Through Binoculars. Eamon Grennan. PBCIP

Sunday News, The. Dana Gioia. WeW-3

Sunday night, 2:00 A.M. Night Call. George Young. BloBone

Sunday Park. Gwyneth Lewis. TCAWP

Sunday Piece. Jules Laforgue. WoPoe, *tr.* by William Jay Smith

Sunday's bad. Why do you bother. Too Bad. Gig Ryan. NOBAu

Sunday Schools. Anna Sawyer. ECWP

Sunday shuts down on this twentieth-century evening. Boy with His Hair Cut Short. Muriel Rukeyser. NALW; NoAM; TwCP; VGW; WPE

Sunday Skaters. Mary Jo Salter. MoASP

Sunday swallows edged the sky, The. Omnibus, The. Vera Bulich. ARWW, *tr.* by Catriona Kelly

Sunday the only day we don't work. Walk, A. Gary Snyder. NOBA

Sunday the Power Went Off, The. Duncan Bush. TCAWP

Sunday up the River. James Thomson.

    Gifts. OBEV

    "Give a man a horse he can ride." OBEV

    "Wine of Love is music, The." OBEV

Sunday Visit. Antigone Kefala. BMAP

Sundays of Satin-Legs Smith, The. Gwendolyn Brooks. NAAAL; SeSe

Sundays too my father got up early. Those Winter Sundays. Robert Earl Hayden. APT-2; AmFaPo; ChAP; ColAP; ESEAA; HAP; HCAP; ISC; InPK-6; LCAP-2; MakPoe; NAAL-5; NIL-7; NIP-4; NoAM; NoP-4; PoPoPo; RaBo; SSLK; SoSe-8; TFi; UnPo; WeW-3

Sunder me from my bones, O sword of God. Sword of Surprise, The. Gilbert Keith Chesterton. MoBrPo; SacPr

Sundered. Israel Zangwill. TrJP

Sunderland Children, The. Alice Thompson Meynell. NALW

Sundew, The. Algernon Charles Swinburne. PeVV

Sundial. Gabriel Zaid. TCLAP, *tr.* by Adrian Hernandez

Sundial, The. Austin Dobson. OBGa

Sundial, The. Douglas Dunn. NPeEn

Sundown. Léonie Adams. MoAmPo

Sundown at Darlington 1878. Lance Henson. VoR

Sundown Blues. Raymond R. Patterson. SeSe

Sundown on the sand, and your shadow. Air Dagger. Jack Marshall. GeoHom

Sundown splendid and serene / Death, The. (LL) William Ernest Henley. MoBrPo; NOBE; OBEV *Fr.* Echoes.

Sundowner, The. John Shaw Neilson. CBAP

Sundry Christian Passions Contained in Two Hundred. Henry Lok. Son

Sundry Notes. Nguyễn Chí Thiện.

    "Party holds you down and you lie still, The." VCWP

Sunfish Races. James Preston. InPK-6

Sunflakes. Frank Asch. NTCP

Sunflower. Mack David. ReLy

Sunflower. Rolf Jacobsen. RaBo, *tr.* by Robert Bly

Sunflower. Kao Ch'i. SuSp, *tr.* by Irving Y. Lo

Sunflower. Leonid Nikolaevich Martynov. TCRP, *tr.* by J. R. Rowland

Sunflower. Tuvia Rivner. MHP, *tr.* by Ruth Finer Mintz

Sunflower. Su Tung-p'o (Su Shih). SuSp, *tr.* by Irving Y. Lo *Fr.* On Chao Ch'ang's Flower Paintings in Wang Po-yang's Collection.

Sunflower, The. Dora Greenwell. *See* Sun-Flower, The

Sunflower! gross of leaf and porous. Wild Sunflower. Yvor Winters. APT-2

Sunflower Moccasins. Phillip [*or* "Phil"] William George. VoR

Sunflower Sonnet Number One. June Jordan. Son

Sunflower Sutra. Allen Ginsberg. CoAP; HCAP; NAAL-2v2; NOBA; NeAP; VCAP

    (I walked on the banks of the tincan banana dock and sat down.) GM; PoPoPo

Sunflowers and Saturdays. Melba Joyce Boyd. BlSi

Sung at Table by the Same Choir. Anne Penny. ECWP *Fr.* Odes Sung in Commemoration of the Marine Society.

Sung by a Choir of Boys Marching Round the Room. Anne Penny. ECWP *Fr.* Odes Sung in Commemoration of the Marine Society.

Sung in a Graveyard. Anna Wickham. ItWoWo

Sung-ling road in setting sunlight. Feelings Come As I Pass through Wu-chiang. Wu Wei-yeh. CoBLCP, *tr.* by Jonathan Chaves

Sunheat was equivalent, The. Still There's No Trace. Zim Mnotoza. PeSAV

Sunk in slate-gray plastic panels. Ancestral Echoes/Rap Music. Charles Lynch. SwNoth

Sunk Lyonesse. Walter De la Mare. FaBoCh

Sunken Gold. Eugene Lee-Hamilton. GSo; NOBVV

Sunken Road, Antietam 1980, The. Gregory Orfalea. GraLe

Sunken Sailor. Francis Claiborne Mason. YaYoPo

Sunken Ship, The. Salma Khadra Jayyusi. PoArWo, *tr.* by Suneet Chopra

Sunlight still on me, you row'd in clood, The. At My Father's Grave. Hugh MacDiarmid. GTBS-P; HarvBoo; NePenScot

Sunlight. Seamus Heaney. *See* Mossbawn

Sunlight climbs the snowpeak. Late October Camping in the Sawtooths. Gary Snyder. BLT

Sunlight drawing from shadow, up and down the street. Passages. Larry Eigner. NeAP

Sunlight dried the last small patches of moisture. In Ferrara. John Jenkins. BMAP

Sunlight in a, The. At the Faucet of June. William Carlos Williams. APT-1

Sunlight in spring explodes in your eyes. Verses about a Nightingale and a Poet. "Eduard Georgievich Bagritzky" [*or* Bagritsky]. TCRP, *tr.* by Vera Dunham

Sunlight in the alleys. There is always a window. Puzzle Pieces. Chana Bloch. ExTi

Sunlight in the house. Maritimes. Penelope Shuttle. BrRo

Sunlight on the Garden, The. Louis MacNeice. EBEV; GTBS-P; HAP; HarvBoo; NAEL-5v2; NAEL-6v2; NOBE; NOIV; NPeEn; NoP-4; OxAEP-2; OxBTC; PNI; TRP; TwCP; WoPoe

Sunlight steams the river stones. Waterfall at Lu-shan. Li Po. CrYelRi, *tr.* by Sam Hamill

Sunlight streaming on Incense Stone kindles violet smoke. Viewing the Waterfall at Mount Lu. Li Po. CoBCP; ColAnChi; TTTS, *tr.* by Burton Watson

Sunlight strikes a glass of grapefruit juice. Morning in the Hospital Solarium. Sylvia Plath. BodElec

Sunlight that pulls itself over the rooftops looks vacant, The. Inertia. Kirti Chaudhari. WPOW, *tr.* by Leonard Nathan

Sunlight the tall women may never have seen. Children, the Sandbar, That Summer. Muriel Rukeyser. LCAP-2

Sunne begins uppon my heart to shine, The. William Alabaster. ESCV *Fr.* Divine Meditations.

Sunne may set and rise, The. Catullus. FaBoEE; NoSic; OBVE, *tr.* by Sir Walter Alexander Raleigh *Fr.* Carmina.

Sunne Rising, The. John Donne. *See* Sun Rising, The

Sunny afternoons. Sunny Afternoon Dream, The. Giovanna Pollarolo. TANSG, *tr.* by Marjorie Agosin

Sunny Disposish. Philip Charig. ReLy

Sunny Gale. Hugh MacDiarmid. FaBoVe

Sunny Prestatyn. John Davies. TCAWP

Sunny Prestatyn. Philip Larkin. NoAM; OBCoV

Sunny shaft did I behold, A. Samuel Taylor Coleridge. OBEV Fr. Zapolya.

Sunny Side Up. Ray Henderson. ReLy

Sunnyland. Elmore James. NAAAL

Sunrise. Sidney Lanier. Fr. Hymns of the Marshes.

Sunrise. Henrietta Cordelia Ray. BlSi Fr. Idyl.

Sunrise. Jim Tollerud. VoR

Sunrise at the southeast corner. Mulberry up the Lane. Unknown. ColAnChi, tr. by Anne Birrell

Sunrise brightens my autumn window. Traveler's Pavilion. Tu Fu. CrYelRi, tr. by Sam Hamill

Sunrise Comes to Second Avenue. Thylias Moss. TRP

Sunrise on the River. Kalamu ya Salaam. SpirFl Fr. New Orleans Haiku.

Sunrise path. Ruth Yarrow. HA

Sunrise runs for Both, The. Emily Dickinson. SWaP

Sunrise Sequence. Unknown. NOBAu, tr. by Ronald M. Berndt Fr. Dulngulg Song Cycle, The.

Sunrise, Sunset. Sheldon Harnick. ReLy

Sunrise Trumpets. Joseph Auslander. TrJP

Sunrise with Sea Monster. Charles North. FTOS

Sunrise. . . & toward the sunrise stands the village of the Bow People. Muu's Way; or Pictures from the Uterine World. Unknown. STP, tr. by Jerome Rothenberg

Sunrising and sunsetting evermore. (LL) James Henry. NOBVV; NPeEn; OxBEV

Suns eye gleams on the burnt black prairie, The. Confluence. John Knoepfle. IllVoic

Suns in a skein, the uncut stones of night. Roy Fuller. GTBS-P Fr. Mythological Sonnets.

Suns of the world may stain when heaven's sun staineth. (LL) William Shakespeare. AWP; EBEV; HAP; NAEL-7v1; NIP-4; NoP-4; NoSic; OxAEP-1; PoRA; SCGP; Son; TFi; WeW-3 Fr. Sonnets.

Sunset. Hayyim Nahman [or Khayim Nakhman or Chaim Nachman] Bialik. TrJP, tr. by Helena Frank

Sunset. Joseph Ceravolo. FTOS

Sunset. John Cope. GeoH

Sunset. E. E. Cummings. MoAmPo

Sunset. Mary Weston Fordham. CBWP-2

Sunset. Jim Handlin. HA

Sunset. Juan Ramón Jiménez. SpanPo, tr. by Kate Flores

Sunset. Henrietta Cordelia Ray. BlSi Fr. Idyl.

Sunset. Tu Fu. CrYelRi, tr. by Sam Hamill

Sunset. Tu Fu. BLT; OHPC, tr. by Kenneth Rexroth

Sunset, A. Samuel Taylor Coleridge. OxBSP

Sunset, A. Victor Hugo. AWP, tr. by Francis Thompson Fr. Feuilles d'Automne.

Sunset, a huge flower, wilts on the horizon, The. Flowers. Roo Borson. NOBC

Sunset and evening star. Crossing the Bar. Tennyson. BRP; ChIV-2; ClHu; EBVV; HeIP-4; ITBLP; NAEL-5v2; NAEL-6v2; NOBE; NOBVV; NoP-4; OBEV; PWR; PeECV; PoRA; SacPr; SoSe-8; TFi; TrCP

Sunset and silence! A man: around him earth savage, earth broken. Plower, The. Padraic Colum. MoBrPo

Sunset at Twin Lake. Anita Endrezze. HATNAP

Sunset at Wellfleet. Jean Valentine. YaYoPo

Sunset. Blue peaks vanish in dusk. Snow on Lotus Mountain. Liu Ch'ang-ch'ing. OHMPC, tr. by Kenneth Rexroth

Sunset by the lake. Lake Murry. Pinkie Gordon Lane. GT

Sunset dying. Gary Hotham. HA

Sunset fades, and from the little hill, The. Konstantin Iakovlevich Vanshenkin. TCRusP, tr. by Daniel Weissbort

Sunset eye flames over the city, The. Dorothy Hewett. BMAP Fr. Summer Solstice.

Sunset Frisco hilly tincan evening sitdown vision. (LL) Sunflower Sutra. Allen Ginsberg. CoAP; HCAP; NAAL-2v2; NOBA; NeAP; VCAP

Sunset from Omaha Hotel Window. Carl Sandburg. APT-1; AiP

Sunset glitters on the beads. Sunset. Tu Fu. BLT; OHPC, tr. by Kenneth Rexroth

Sunset—God's face from which grief radiates. Sodom. Chaim Grade. TrJP, tr. by Joseph Leftwich

Sunset in the Tropics. James Weldon Johnson. APT-1

Sunset knocks the edge from the. Green Eyed Monsters of the Valley Dusk, The. Shirley Anne Williams. GeoHom

Sunset like the grasshopper flying. (LL) Ezra Pound. APT-1; NAAL-2v2; OBMV Fr. Cantos.

Sunset nails the lip of a building. Harlem: Neo-Image. Kevin Powell. AmPoNex

Sunset of the City, A. Gwendolyn Brooks. FaBoWP; LCAP-2

(Sunset of the City / Kathleen Eileen, A.) GT

Sunset on Calvary. Unknown. See Now Goeth [or goth or goothe] Sun [or Sonne or Sunne] under Wood

Sunset Picture. Henrietta Cordelia Ray. CBWP-3

Sunset pours its gold through jade-colored clouds. To the Tune: Eternal Joy. Li Ch'ing-chao. CrYelRi, tr. by Sam Hamill

Sunset's mounded cloud, A. Evening, An. William Allingham. EnLoPo; NOBVV

Sunset Stripping: Visiting L.A. Michael Lassell. WiU

Sunset: the blaze of evening burns. Hospital Evening. Gwen Harwood. EmeKit; FaBoWP

Sunset, the cheapest of all picture-shows. Frederiksted, Dusk. Derek Walcott. NoAM

Sunset was thick with the feel of rain. Miscellaneous Poem on Rural Life. Liu Yin. ColAnChi, tr. by John Timothy Wixted

Sunsets. Carl Sandburg. MoAmPo

Sunshade, The. Thomas Hardy. OxBTC

Sunshine. Mother Goose. OxNR; ReMoGo

Sunshine after Cloud. Josephine D. Henderson Heard. CBWP-4

Sunshine and Music. Unknown. PoToHe

Sunshine and shadow play amid the trees. July. Henrietta Cordelia Ray. CBWP-3

Sunshine not yet through. (LL) Poem for Ben Barney. Leslie Marmon Silko. CDW; VoR

Sunshine Prisoner "470." Stephen Clayton. IBA

Sunshiny shower, A. Unknown. LB; OxNR; ReMoGo

Sunstone. Octavio Paz.
  "All is transformed and is sacred." BLPSL, tr. by Rene de Costa, Rigas Kappatos and Eleni Paidoussi
  "Crystal willow, a poplar of water, A." WoPoe, tr. by Eliot Weinberger
  "I travel your body as I would travel the world." BLPSL, tr. by Rene de Costa, Rigas Kappatos and Eleni Paidoussi
  "Madrid, 1937." BLPSL, tr. by Rene de Costa, Rigas Kappatos and Eleni Paidoussi
  Names, Places, Streets, Faces: The Universe in Flame.
  "And the banquet, the exile, the first crime." PoetW, tr. by Eliot Weinberger
  "Better the crime." PoetW, tr. by Eliot Weinberger
  "Was it I making plans." PoetW, tr. by Eliot Weinberger

Sunstruck spray sifts back breakwater waves, A. Pavilion on the Pier, The. Byron Vazakas. APT-2

Sunt Lacrimae Rerum et Mentem Mortalia Tangunt. R. P. Blackmur. APT-2

Sunt Leones. Stevie Smith. NoAM

Super-cool / ultrablack. But He Was Cool; or, He Even Stopped for Green Lights. Haki R. Madhubuti. BPo

Super-suburbia of the Southern Seas. Farewell to New Zealand. Wynford Vaughan-Thomas. NOBL

Superb and sole, upon a plumèd spray. Mocking Bird, The. Sidney Lanier. APN-2; TCAPo

Superballs. Tom Clark. SPE

Supererogatory divinations one is. Unknown, The. Denise Levertov. NAAL-2v2

Superhighway elegy in a pink convertible / It was 1956. Western CIV, 4 and 5. Joan Retallack. FTOS

Superior, as a singer from Lesbos to those of other lands. Sappho. SaLy, tr. by Diane Rayor

Superliminare. George Herbert. ESCV; NOSC

Superman Is Dead. Rafael Campo. ReTh

Supermarket. Felice Holman. OTCP

Supermarket. Peter Meinke. PBCAP

Supermarket in California, A. Allen Ginsberg. CAGL; CoAP; HAP; HCAP; HeIP-4; InPK-6; NAAL-2v2; NAAL-5; NIL-7; NOBA; NeAP; NoAM; PmAP; PoM; ReTh; TAP; TFi; TwCP; UnPo; WeW-3

Supernatural Love. Gjertrud Schnackenberg. DiPo; MakPoe; NoAM; NoP-4; VCAP

Superscription, A. Dante Gabriel Rossetti. EBVV; GSo; GTBS-P; NAEL-5v2; NAEL-6v2; NoP-4 Fr. House of Life, The.

Superstition. Minji Karibo. WPOW

Superstition, more destructive still. Mary Robinson. RWP Fr. Progress of Liberty, The.

Superstitions. Maggie Pogue Johnson. CBWP-4

Supervising Examinations. Sean Lucy. CIP-2

Supervisor, Han Chün-mei, Has Shown Me Five Poems He Has Written Called, The Trees Flourish in Early Summer. I Have Therefore Written Down My Own Ignoble Feelings and Sent Them Via Inspector Juan. At This Time, Chün-mei Is Lecturing to the. Tai Piao-yüan. CoBLCP, tr. by Jonathan Chaves

Supine the Wanderer lay. William Wordsworth. NOBRP Fr. Excursion, The.

Supper. William Soutar. OxBS

Supper after the Last, The. Galway Kinnell. NOBA

Supper at Apelles'/ was a garden-butcher's work. Ammianus. GrAn

Supper Time. Irving Berlin. ReLy

Supper time / I should set the table. Supper Time. Irving Berlin. ReLy

Supple / slender. Tyger, Tyger. Isabel Meyrelles. SurWo, tr. by Penelope Rosemont

Supplement, A. Benjamin Tompson. SCAP

Supplement of an Imperfect Copy of Verses of Mr. Will. Shakespeare's, by the Author, A. Sir John Suckling. CavPo

Supplementary to the account. Wrong Side of the Door, The. Ray DiPalma. FTOS

Supplication. Constantine P. Cavafy. BLT, tr. by Rae Dalven

Supplication. Edgar Lee Masters. TrCP

Supplication, A. Abraham Cowley. GTBS-P Fr. Davideis.

Supplication, A. George Croly. SacPr

Supplication, A. Sir Thomas Wyatt. See Steadfastness

Supplied [or Supply'd] the epithalamy [or Epithalamie]. (LL) Upon a Maid That Died [or Dyed] the Day She Was Married [or Marryed]. Meleager. AWP; OBVE, tr. by Robert Herrick

Support act, The. Nigger and Some Poofters, A. Nigel Roberts. BMAP

Support Your Local Police Dog. Carter Revard. VoR

Supporting Cast, Sotto Voce, The. W. H. Auden. Fr. Sea and the Mirror, The.

Suppose an Eyes. Gertrude Stein. PFTM-1

Suppose Gauguin had never seen Tahiti. Suppose the. Wheatfield Under Clouded Sky. Campbell McGrath. NeAmPo

Suppose he had been Tabled at thy Teates. Bible, N.T. ChIV-2; NAEL-7v1; NOSC, tr. by Richard Crashaw Fr. St. Luke.

Suppose I can convince myself this world. Summons. David Rivard. OPRER

Suppose I Make a Timepiece of Humanity. Velemir [or Viktor Vladimirovich] Khlebnikov. AF, tr. by Paul Schmidt

Suppose it, for the last time, in that moment. Patrick Anderson. MoCV Fr. Poem on Canada.

Suppose it is within a gate which open is open at the hour of closing summer that is to say so. Suppose an Eyes. Gertrude Stein. PFTM-1

Suppose me dead; and then suppose. Jonathan Swift. NOBE; NOEC; OxBoLi; PeLV Fr. Verses on the Death of Dr. Swift, D.S.P.D.

Suppose one thing. For Those Who Always Fear the Worst. Unknown. NBLV

Suppose the Ceiling went Outside. Ceiling, The. Theodore Roethke. KaS

Suppose the dead could crown their wit. Responsory, 1948, A. Thomas Merton. VGW

Suppose This Moment Some Stupendous Question. Alden Nowlan. NOBC

Suppose we are standing together a minute. April. Jean Valentine. TAP

Suppose we could telephone the dead. Hotel de Dream. Jane Cooper. ExTi

Suppose you're a solo native here. Solo Native. Thomas Lux. LCAP-2

Suppose you screeve? or go cheap-jack? Villon's Straight Tip to All Cross Coves. William Ernest Henley. AWP; OxAEP-2

Suppose you slosh gin deep into a glass. Cheers. Charles McDonald. NLP

Suppose you want to write. Adrienne Rich. LoL Fr. North American Time.

Supposed Dancer, The. Roy Fisher. HarvBoo

Supposed To Be Written by Werter. Charlotte Smith. CenSon; RWP

Supposing all the things on the playground. On a Cold Autumn Day. Bonnie Nims. TLR

Supposing that one walks out into the air. Kenneth Koch. OBCoV Fr. Fresh Air.

Supposing we could just go on and on as two. Sunflower Sonnet Number Two. June Jordan. Son

Suppression. Jayne Cortez. NBV

Supremacy. Edwin Arlington Robinson. APN-2; NoAM

Supreme Death. Douglas Dunn. FaBoMo

Supreme Fortune Falls Soonest. Robert Herrick. CaPo

Supreme Hour, The. Viktor Aleksandrovich Sosnora. ItGoST, tr. by F. D. Reeve

Supreme my holdings, greater yet my need. John Berryman. CRP Fr. Dream Songs.

Supreme Savior of Sinners. Rāmprasād Sen. SinGod, tr. by Rachel Fell McDermott

Supremer Sacrifice, The. Suzanne Gardinier. CBAP

Supremes, The. Mark Jarman. GeoHom; SwNoth

Supremes done gone, The. Memorial. Sonia Sanchez. BlSi

SURcenSURE. Marcel Duchamp. PFTM-1

Sure, a little bit of shrapnel fell from out the sky one day. Unknown. OBCoV Fr. Soldiers' Songs of the First World War.

Sure an' twas a / fine st. patrick's day. Saint Patrick's Day, 1973. Wendy Rose. CDW

Sure, if those Babel-builders had thought good. On the Babel-Builders. Francis Quarles. ChIV-1

Sure It was so. Man in those early days. Corruption. Henry Vaughan. ESCV; GeHe; NAEL-5v1; NAEL-6v1; NAEL-7v1; NOCV; NOSC

Sure Jo & I used to spend hours doin' it. Boys' Own. Brendan Cleary. NeBl

Sure John and I are more than quit. (LL) Epigram: "To John I ow'd great obligation." Matthew Prior. FaBoEE; OBVE; OxBEV

Sure Lord, there is enough in thee to dry. Sonnet. George Herbert. GeHe; NOSC

Sure, Saul as little looked to be a king. On Saul and David. Francis Quarles. ChIV-1

Sure some malignant star diffused its ray. Power of Destiny, The. Mary Whateley. ECWP

Sure Test, A. Unknown. OxNR; ReMoGo

Sure the last end. Robert Blair. OxAEP-1 Fr. Grave, The.

Sure there are Poets which did never dream. Sir John Denham. BeJo; CABP; PBRV

Sure there are some differences. I'm no virgin. Self Portrait as Nancy Drew, Girl Sleuth. Kristy Nielsen. ReTh

Sure, there are times when one cries with acidity. To An Undiscerning Critic. Sir Arthur Conan Doyle. OBCoV

Sure there is lots of trouble. Up and Doing. Douglas Malloch. ITBLP

Sure, there's a tie of bodies! and as they. Henry Vaughan. GeHe

Sure thing / I'm a spirit! Song. Unknown. STP, tr. by Jerome Rothenberg

Sure thing / I'm a spirit! / see me becoming visible? Seven Songs and Song Pictures. Unknown. PFTM-1

Sure thou didst flourish once! and many springs. Timber, The. Henry Vaughan. GeHe; OBEV

Sure, to the mansions of the blest. To a Bereaved Mother. John Quincy Adams. SacPr

Sure we have poets, that did never dream. Sir John Denham. See Sure there are Poets which did never dream

Surely! Sir Fantasy. Ssu-ma Hsiang-ju. ColAnChi, tr. by Burton Watson

Surely among a rich man's flowering lawns. W. B. Yeats. OBGa Fr. Meditations in Time of Civil War.

Surely he is more than reason. (LL) Inscribed on a Painting by Myself. Ni Tsan. CoBLCP; ColAnChi, tr. by Jonathan Chaves

Surely, I suffer on your account. Once More to Lilla. Mihály Csokonai Vitéz. IQMS, tr. by Adam Makkai

Surely it is death to come here. Tlanusi' Yi, the Leech Place. Gladys Cardiff. CDW

Surely My Soul. . . . Jacob Cohen. TrJP, tr. by I. M. Lask

Surely one of my finest days, I'd just. Extract from Memoirs. Howard Nemerov. OxBC

Surely the air must still have human warmth. Air. Jennifer Maiden. BMAP

Surely the opposite shall come to pass. (LL) To Dante Alighieri. Guido Cavalcanti. AWP; EaItPo, tr. by Dante Gabriel Rossetti

Surely there's a teahouse. Shiyo. JDP, tr. by Yoel Hoffmann

Surely They're Just So Large. Irving Feldman. VCAP Fr. All of Us Here.

Surely they're just so large as their burdens allow. Irving Feldman. VCAP Fr. All of Us Here.

Surely you paused at this roadside oasis. Garage in Co. Cork, A. Derek Mahon. DiPo; PBCIP

Surely You Remember. Dahlia Ravikovitch [or Ravikovich]. VCWP

Surely you would not ask me to have known. Question to Life. Patrick Kavanagh. MoBrPo

Surf. Lillian Morrison. NTCP

(Waves want.) KaS

Surf. Kiyoko Nagase. ItWoWo, tr. by Kijima Hajime

Surf-casting. W. S. Merwin. NOBA

Surf is a partial deafness islanders. Polynesia. Allen Curnow. PeNZ

Surf Motel, The. Stephen Knight. NeBl

Surf washed up its rows of green, The. Continent's Edge. Mark Wunderlich. WiU

Surface, The. Jorie Graham. HarvBoo

Surface, The. Masumi Kato (d. 1825). JDP, tr. by Yoel Hoffmann

Surfaces. Kay Ryan. ExTi

Surfaces serve. Surfaces. Kay Ryan. ExTi

Surfer, The. Judith Wright. WPE

Surfers. Robert Minhinnick. TCAWP

Surfing on the dance floor. Trickster 4 (for Sister Patra). Kwame Dawes. WaCA

Surge, The. Molly Peacock. PasH

Surge and thunder of the Odyssey, The. (LL) Odyssey, The. Andrew Lang. OBEV; PoRA

Surge of spirit that goes with using an axe, The. Felling a Tree. Ivor Gurney. FaBoVe

Surgeon's Knife, The. Eliza Cook. VWP

"There are hearts—stout hearts,—that own no fear." VerBaPo

Surgeons must be very careful. Emily Dickinson. SAmP; TAP; TCAPo

Surgery. Kenneth Pitchford. CAGL; GLP

Surgical Moves. Rachel Wetzsteon. AmPoNex; ExTi

Surgical Ward: Men. Robert Graves. FaBoMo

Surplice, The. David Scott. NLP

Surplus. Abigail Child. FTOS

Surplus. Rebecca Reynolds. AmPoNex

Surprise. Richard Brautigan. KaS

Surprise in the Peninsula, A. Fleur Adcock. EmeKit

Surprise, Surprise. *Unknown.* EroLit, *tr.* by Derek Parker

Surprised and ungrateful eye, The. (LL) Cutting Greens. Lucille Clifton. ESEAA; GT

Surprised by Evening. Robert Bly. VGW

Surprised by Joy. William Wordsworth. *See* Sonnet on Catherine Wordsworth

Surprising my dupe by his egg of Oedipus. Dirge for Three Trumpets. *Unknown.* SPE

Surprisingly easy to cook a meal now. Turning Fifty. Thomas William Shapcott. BMAP

Surrealism, *n.* Psychic automatism in its pure state. André Breton. PFTM-1 *Fr.* Manifesto of Surrealism (1924).

Surrender. "Rachel" [*or* "Rahel"]. FIT, *tr.* by Robert Friend

Surrender, The. Henry King, Bishop of Chichester. BoLoP; EBEV; NOSC

Surrender to Christ. Frederic William Henry Myers. SacPr

Surrendered Names. Gerald Vizenor. HATNAP

Surrendering the joys that they condemn. (LL) Geoffrey Hill. NAEL-5v2; NAEL-6v2; NoAM *Fr.* Lachrimae; or Seven Tears Figured in Seven Passionate Pavans.

Surrendering to a rain-washed stone. Alexis Rotella. HA

Surrexit Dominus de sepulchro. (LL) On the Resurrection of Christ. William Dunbar. NPeEn; NePenScot; OxBEV

Surrey with the Fringe on Top, The. Richard Rodgers. ReLy

Surrogate Mothers. Andrea M. Wren. InTrad

Surrounded by eunuchs and limp as a tissue. Martial. WoPoe, *tr.* by William Matthews *Fr.* Epigrams.

Surrounded by my shields, am. Song of the Self: The Grandmother. Alma Villanueva. HW

Surrounded by scientists in a faculty. Homage to the New World. Michael S. Harper. ESEAA; LCAP-2

Surrounded by the gentle sound. Song 3. Baldomero Garcilaso de la Vega. SpanPo, *tr.* by Frances Fletcher

Surrounding Blues on the Way Down. Bruce Weigl. CDa

Surrounding boxes alarm you, The. Sojourners, The. Bino A. Realuyo. ReBoTo

Surroundings. Joseph A. Soldati. CDa

Sursum Corda. Ralph Waldo Emerson. APN-1

Surveillances. Tom Paulin. CIP-2; PNI

Survey, A. William Stafford. RB

Survey of Literature. John Crowe Ransom. FaBoCh; NBLV; OBAL; TAP; TwCP; VGW

Survey of the Amphitheatre, A. Moses Browne. NOEC

Surveying Britain's battled coast. Servant of the House. "Sagittarius." UV

Survival, The. Edmund Charles Blunden. OBEV; OBMV

Survival 1. Chiqui Vicioso. TANSG, *tr.* by Emma Jane Robinett

Survival 2. Chiqui Vicioso. TANSG, *tr.* by Emma Jane Robinett

Survival, I know how this way. Survival This Way. Simon J. Ortiz. CDW

Survival: Infantry. George Oppen. FTOS

Survival Motion: Notice. Melvin E. Brown. ISC

Survival This Way. Simon J. Ortiz. CDW

Survivals. Ruth Behar. MirDau

Surviving. James Welch. CDW; HATNAP

Surviving is keeping your eyes open. Portraits of Tudor Statesmen. U. A. Fanthorpe. EmeKit; OxBEV

Survivor. Barbara Goldberg. GotH

Survivor. Mike Jenkins. TCAWP

Survivor. Roger McGough. OBCoV

Survivor. Barry Sternlieb. GotH

Survivor. Florence Weinberger. GotH

Survivor, The. Thomas Dorsett. BloBone

Survivor, The. Primo Levi. HP, *tr.* by Ruth Feldman

Survivor, The. Tadeusz Rózewicz. HP; PoSu, *tr.* by Adam Czerniawski

Survivor, The. Ronald Stuart Thomas. FaBoTw

Survivor of that time, that place. (LL) Requiem: "No foreign sky protected me." Anna Andreyevna Akhmatova. AF; PoetW; TCRP; WoPoe, *tr.* by Max Hayward and Stanley Kunitz

Survivor sole, and hardly such, of all. Yardley Oak. William Cowper. NOEC

Survivor speaks, A. Treblinka. Michael Hamburger. HP

Survivors. Frank Ormsby. CIP-2

Survivors. Sterling Plumpp. UrbNat

Survivors, The. Tracey Herd. NeBl

Survivors, The. Daryl Hine. TwCP

Survivors will be human. (LL) Deathwatch. Michael S. Harper. NAAAL; NAAL-5

"Susaddah!" exclaimed Ibsen. Edmund Clerihew Bentley. OBCoV *Fr.* Clerihews.

Susan. Robin Magowan. SPE

Susan and Charlotte and Letty and all. Welford Wedding, The. Elizabeth Frances Amherst. ECWP

Susan B.'s voice: We cannot retrace our steps, going forward may be the. Gertrude Stein. PFTM-2 *Fr.* Mother of Us All, The.

Susan, the constant slave to mop and broom. "Peter Pindar." NOEC *Fr.* Sorrows of Sunday; an Elegy, The.

Susanna. Stephen Collins Foster. *See* Oh! Susanna

Susanna and the Elders. Adelaide Crapsey. APT-1; TCAPo; WPE

Susanna: girl and bride. Man-Fate, The. William Everson. NoAM

Susannah. Thulani Davis. GT

Susannah and the Elders. *Unknown.* PeLV

Susannah Bathing. Ödön Palasovszky. IQMS, *tr.* by Kenneth McRobbie

Susannah Prout. Walter De la Mare. FaBoEE

Susannah the fair. Susannah and the Elders. *Unknown.* PeLV

Susans. Susan Clements. UnSA

Sushi. Paul Muldoon. CABP; CIP-2

Susie Asado. Gertrude Stein. APT-1; NoAM; TAP

Susie's galoshes. Galoshes. Rhoda Warner Bacmeister. NTCP

Susie's Lament for Johnny. Mihály Csokonai Vitéz. IQMS, *tr.* by Anthony Edkins

Susie Wong was at the Starlight Haven. Starlight Haven. Shirley Lim. UnSA

Suspects his Constancy. Mary Robinson. CenSon; RWP

Suspended from / your animal form. Marvelous Beast. Patti Tana. PasH

Suspended in a sea of blue-gray slate. American Dreams. "Sapphire." AfrBLW

Suspense. Emily Dickinson. AWP; MoAmPo; OxBA; TCAPo; WPE

Suspense. D. H. Lawrence. MoBrPo

Suspension: Junior Wells on a Small Stage in a Converted Barn. Sandra McPherson. SeSe

Suspicion. Alejandra Piznarnick. TANSG, *tr.* by Susan Bassnett

Suspiria. *Unknown.* OBEV

Suspiria Noctis. Henry Howard Brownell. APN-2

Sussex Street sleeps in mists of nickel moonlight. Night Flower. Geoffrey Lehmann. NOBAu

Sustain tomorrow's road. (LL) Survival, The. Edmund Charles Blunden. OBEV; OBMV

Sustenance. Jason Santalucia. SpudSo

Suture. Mark Wunderlich. AmPoNex

Suum Cuique. Ralph Waldo Emerson. APN-1 *Fr.* Quatrains.

Suzan Oshos's Visit to My West Mountain Hut. Muso Soseki. EaWin, *tr.* by W. S. Merwin

Suzie Wong Doesn't Live Here. Diane Mei Lin Mark. ReTh

Suzie, you picked a hell of a time. " . . the light that cannot fade. . . " William Daniel Ehrhart. CDa

Suzy Wong's Been Dead a Long Time. Kitty Tsui. ReTh

Svidrigailov's Last Night. László Kálnoky. IQMS, *tr.* by Kenneth McRobbie and Zita McRobbie

Swain, give o'er your fond pretension. Hildebrand Jacob. FaBoEE

Swallow. Cloud's Anchor, The. Ian Hamilton Finlay. NePenScot

Swallow, The. Abraham Cowley. EBEV; OBEV; OxAEP-1

Swallow, The. Thomas Stanley. AWP

Swallow flies away, The. *Unknown.* ColAnChi, *tr.* by Jeffrey Riegel *Fr.* Classic of Odes.

Swallow has set her six young on the rail, The. Robert Browning. SCGP *Fr.* James Lee's Wife.

Swallow, my sister, O sister swallow. Itylus. Algernon Charles Swinburne. NPeEn; UV

Swallow nothing but light. (LL) Envoi: "Sun in the mouth of the day." Robley, Jr. Wilson. InvLad; PBCAP

Swallow's Flight, The. Louis Levy. TrJP, *tr.* by Martin S. Alwood and Sanford Kaufman

Swallow sings "Dawn," The. *Unknown.* BoWoP

Swallow the Lake. Clarence Major. ESEAA; FTOS; GT; NAAAL; PmAP

Swallower. Beckian Fritz Goldberg. ExTi

Swallowing raindrops / clear from China. (LL) Prayer to the Pacific. Leslie Marmon Silko. CDW; NoP-4; PoPoPo; VoR; WeW-3

Swallowing the dark truths at my sides. I Have Lost A Verse. Julia de Burgos. TANSG, *tr.* by Heather Rosario Sievert

Swallowing words in water. Rebis. Mitch Highfill. HeMarv

Swallows, The. Elizabeth Jane Coatsworth. TLR

Swallows and Tortoises. Neil Curry. NLP

Swallows are passing, The. (LL) They've Come. Alfonsina Storni. BoWoP; WPOW

Swallows carve lake wind. Skin Canoes. Carolyn Forché. YaYoPo

Swallows / In eaves of mansions. Buson. ZenPo, *tr. by* Takashi Ikemoto and Lucien Stryk

Swallows of Salangan. Gloria Vando. TouFir

Swallows travel to and fro. Robert Louis Stevenson. EBVV

Swam too far out: the swell took him. Elegy for a School-Friend. Augustus Young. BIrV

Swamp. Roberta Hill Whiteman. VoR

Swamp Angel, The. Herman Melville. APN-2

Swampland Mulberries Are Lovely. *Unknown.* CoBCP, *tr. by* Burton Watson

Swamps, marshes, borrow-pits and other. Culture as Exhibit. "Ern Malley." BMAP

Swan. D. H. Lawrence. PoE

Swan. Edward Lowbury. GTBS-P

Swan, The. Delmira Agustini. TANSG, *tr. by* Mark McCaffrey

Swan, The. Charles Baudelaire. WoPoe, *tr. by* Louis Simpson

Swan, The. Charles Baudelaire. SxFrPo, *tr. by* James McGowan

Swan, The. Mei-Mei Berssenbrugge. OpBo

Swan, The. Cynewulf. RB; WoPoe, *tr. by* Geoffrey Grigson *Fr.* Riddles (Exeter Book).

Swan, The. "Rubén Dario." TCLAP, *tr. by* Lysander Kemp

Swan, The. Jay Macpherson. NoP-4

Swan, The. Rainer Maria Rilke. NAWM-7v2; OWoS, *tr. by* Stephen Mitchell

Swan, The. William Robert Rodgers. PNI

Swan, The. Theodore Roethke. VGW

Swan, The. *Unknown.* OxNR; ReMoGo

Swan among the shadows is like snow, The. Leda. "Rubén Dario." SpanPo, *tr. by* Doreen Bell

Swan and Shadow. John Hollander. InPK-6; VCAP
  (Dusk.) NoP-4

Swan and the Goose, The. Aesop. AWP, *tr. by* William Ellery Leonard

Swan Bathing, The. Ruth Pitter. MoBrPo

Swan existing, The. Voyage à l'Infini. Walter Conrad Arensberg. APT-1

Swan's Feet, The. Edith Jay Scovell. FaBoWP; OxBTC

Swan's head, The. Anita Virgil. HA

Swan sail with her young beneath her wings, The. (LL) George Meredith. EnLoPo; GTBS-P; NOBE; NOBVV; OxBEV *Fr.* Modern Love.

Swan Sequence, The. *Unknown.* WoPoe, *tr. by* Denis Goacher

Swan: Silent is my dress when I step across the earth. Cynewulf. ASW, *tr. by* Kevin Crossley-Holland *Fr.* Riddles (Exeter Book).

Swan swam [*or* swan] over the sea. Swan, The. *Unknown.* OxNR; ReMoGo

Swan, tell my your old story. Kabir. EnlH

Swan, The: "Silent is my dress when I step across the earth." Cynewulf. ASW, *tr. by* Kevin Crossley-Holland *Fr.* Riddles (Exeter Book).

Swans. Lawrence Durrell. MoBrPo

Swans, The. "Rubén Dario." SpanPo, *tr. by* Doreen Bell

Swans, The. Clifford Dyment. TCAWP

Swans, The. Dame Edith Sitwell. WPE

Swans' Book, The. Víctor Hernández Cruz. PueRic

Swans Mating. Michael Longley. PNI

Swans of Vadstena, The. Ralph Gustafson. MoCV

Swans on the River Ayr. Mary Oliver. UrbNat

Swans stir of his breath against my hair. Alexis Rotella. HA

Swansea Bay. Julia Ann Hatton. AngWePo

Swarm, The. Sylvia Plath. NALW

Swarm is copulating in the blood, A. Babel. Giuseppe Ungaretti. PFTM-1

Swarm of bees in May, A. Swarm of Bees, A. *Unknown.* LB; OxNR; ReMoGo

Swarming Bees, The. James Laughlin. VGW

Swarming Mosquitoes. Mei Yao Ch'en. SuSp, *tr. by* Jonathan Chaves

Swarms of flies crowd my sick horse. Ballad of Ching Mountain. Meng Chiao. SuSp, *tr. by* Stephen Owen

Swart Italian with his breast of fur, The. Public Beach (Long Island Sound). Christopher Darlington Morley. NBLV

Swart swarthy smiths besmattered with smoke. Blacksmiths, The. *Unknown.* RB

Swarte-smeked smethes, smatered with smoke. Smoke-Blackened Smiths. *Unknown.* OBCoV

Swarthy bee is a buccaneer, The. More Ancient Mariner, A. Bliss Carman. OBAL

Swath. Federico García Lorca. PFTM-1

Sway. Louis Simpson. NoAM

Sway song. Eye of God. Jim Tollerud. VoR

Swaying, the trembling, The. In the Dark World. Haniel Long. APT-1

Swear. Virtual Reality. Charles Bernstein. FTOS

Swear by what the sages spoke. W. B. Yeats. HAP; NAEL-5v2; NAEL-6v2; NoAM; NoP-4; OxBTC

Swear to me, pine. Koseki. JDP, *tr. by* Yoel Hoffmann

Sweat-House Ritual No. 1. *Unknown.* STP, *tr. by* Alia Fletcher, Francis La Flesche and Jerome Rothenberg

Sweat is a style of the body. John Tranter. NoAM *Fr.* Crying in Early Infancy.

Sweat is leaven for the earth. Wole Soyinka. PBMAP *Fr.* Shuttle in the Crypt, The.

Sweat Song. Peter Blue Cloud. VoR

Sweater, The. Gregory Orr. TRP

Sweaters, The. Lucia Maria Perillo. UnSA

Sweating between his fingers, the agricultural man. Hunger of the Suffering Man, The. Syl Cheney-Coker. PBMAP

Sweating in the midnight snow. First Day of Spring, The. Pedro Juan Pietri. PueRic

Sweating It Out on Winding Stair Mountain. Jim Barnes. CDW

Swedenborg's Skull. Vernon Watkins. FaBoTw

Swedes. Edward Thomas. HarvBoo; RB

Sweeney Agonistes. T. S. Eliot. APT-1
  Two Songs from *Sweeny Agonistes.* UnPo
  "Well here again that don't apply." FaBoVe

Sweeney Among the Nightingales. T. S. Eliot. APT-1; FaBoMo; HAP; HarvBoo; HeIP-4; NAAL-2v2; NAEL-5v2; NAEL-6v2; NOBA; NOBE; NPeEn; NoAM; NoP-4; OBMV; OxBA; OxBEV; PoPoPo; TFi; WeW-3

Sweeney Astray. *Unknown.*
  My Dark Night Has Come Round Again. WoPoe, *tr. by* Seamus Heaney
  Trees of the Forest, The. WoPoe, *tr. by* Austin Clarke

Sweeney Erect. T. S. Eliot. OxBTC; VGW

Sweeney Redivivus. Seamus Heaney.
  Artist, An. PoetW
  Cleric, The. ModIr
  First Kingdom, The. PoetW
  "I stirred wet sand and gathered myself." NoAM
  On the Road. TOF
  "Royal roads were cow paths, The." PoetW

Sweep away. Rosen. JDP, *tr. by* Yoel Hoffmann

Sweep Me through Your Many-Chambered Heart. Diane Ackerman. NIL-7; NIP-4

Sweep the house. Dead Baby, The. William Carlos Williams. NAAL-2v2

Sweep the house clean. Love Song. William Carlos Williams. MoAmPo; SAmP

Sweep the mind. Field, The. Mary Barnard. APT-2

Sweep thy faint strings, Musician. Song of the Shadows, The. Walter De la Mare. MoBrPo

Sweeper collects dry leaves with his broom, The. Vasco [*or* Vasko] Popa. PoSu, *tr. by* Anne Pennington *Fr.* Raw Flesh.

Sweeper of Ways, The. Howard Nemerov. HCAP

Sweeper said Karanje had a temple, The. Karanje Village. Alun Lewis. TCAWP

Sweepers, The. William Whitehead. ECEV; NOEC

Sweeping. Leslie Monsour. FFC

Sweeping past the florist's came the baby and the girl. Girl and Baby Florist Sidewalk Pram Nineteen Seventy Something. Kenneth Koch. NoP-4

Sweet after showers, ambrosial air. Tennyson. EBVV; NAEL-6v2 *Fr.* In Memoriam A. H. H.

Sweet age of blest illusion! blooming boys. Written on Seeing Her Two Sons at Play. Henrietta O'Neill. ECWP

Sweet Amarillis, by a spring's. Upon Mistress Elizabeth Wheeler under the Name of Amarillis. Robert Herrick. CaPo

Sweet and calm the breezes stealing. Sabbath Bells. Josephine D. Henderson Heard. CBWP-4

Sweet and lovely, dimly in my dreams. Oriole at Dawn, An. Li Meng-yang. CoBLCP, *tr. by* Jonathan Chaves

Sweet and Low. Tennyson. ChAP *Fr.* Princess, The.

Sweet and low, sweet and low. Tennyson. FHYEP; NAEL-5v2; NAEL-6v2; SCGP *Fr.* Princess, The.

Sweet and pleasant Sonnet, entitled: My mind to me a kingdom is, A. Sir Edward Dyer. *See* My Mind to Me a Kingdom Is

Sweet-and-Twenty. William Shakespeare. *See* Twelfth Night

Sweet antidote to sorrow, toil and strife. To a Segar. Samuel Low. OBAL

Sweet apple reddens on a high branch, The. Sappho. SaLy, *tr. by* Diane Rayor

Sweet are the thoughts that savo[u]r of content. Robert Greene. CTC; PoToHe; UnPo *Fr.* Farewell to Folly.

Sweet are the ways of death to weary feet. Euripides. OBEV, *tr. by* John Byrne Leicester Warren, Lord de Tabley *Fr.* Medea.

Sweet are the whispers of yon pine that makes. Theocritus. AWP *Fr.* Idylls.

Sweet Armida tooke this charge on hand, The. Torquato Tasso. OBVE *Fr.*

Godfrey of Bulloigne; or, The Recoverie of Jerusalem [Gerusalemme Liberata].

Sweet as the tender fragrance that survives. Delia. Henry Wadsworth Longfellow. TCAPo

Sweet Auburn! loveliest village of the plain. Oliver Goldsmith. CABP; ECEV; FHYEP; MakPoe; NAEL-7v1; NOBE; NoP-4; OxAEP-1; TFi; TreFP *Fr.* Deserted Village, The.

Sweet Auburn! parent of the blissful hour. Oliver Goldsmith. EBEV *Fr.* Deserted Village, The.

Sweet baked apple dappled cinnamon speckled sin of mine. Love Child—a Black Aesthetic. Everett Hoagland. BPo

Sweet Be'mi'ster, that bist a-bound. Be'mi'ster. William Barnes. EBVV

Sweet, be not proud of those two eyes. To Dianeme. Robert Herrick. BASC; BeJo; CaPo; GTBS-P; NOBE; NOSC; OBEV

Sweet beat, I have gone prowling. Song. W. D. Snodgrass. MoAmPo

Sweet beats of jazz impaled on slivers of wind. Walking Parker Home. Bob Kaufman. NAAAL

Sweet beguilings. Cheat, The. Joseph Beaumont. NOSC

Sweet Betsey from Pike. *Unknown.* OBAL; OxBoLi
(Good-by, you big lummux, I'm glad you backed out!) (LL) APN-2
(Oh, don't you remember Sweet Betsey from Pike.) APN-2; TCAPo

Sweet bird, that sing'st away the early howres [*or* hours]. To a Nightingale. William Drummond, of Hawthornden. OWoS

Sweet Bread. Frank X. Walker. SpirFl

Sweet-Briar in Rose. "Michael Field." VWP

Sweet Brown Rice and Red Bones. Lamont B. Steptoe. SpirFl

Sweet Bye and Bye. Ogden Nash. ReLy

Sweet Catullus's all-but-island, olive-silvery Sirmio! (LL) Frater Ave Atque Vale. Tennyson. EBVV; GTBS-P; HAP; NAEL-5v2; NAEL-6v2; NoP-4; OxBSP

Sweet Chance, that led my steps abroad. Great Time, A. William Henry Davies. MoBrPo

Sweet cheat gone, The. (LL) Ghost, The. Walter De la Mare. EnLoPo; MoBrPo; NOBE; OxBTC

Sweet children amid the apple boughs. On the Picture of a Child. Henrietta Cordelia Ray. CBWP-3

Sweet Content. Thomas Dekker. *See* Pleasant Comedy of Patient Grissell [*or* Grissel *or* Grissill], The

Sweet Corrall lips, where Nature's treasure lies. Richard Barnfield [*or* Barnefield]. CAGL *Fr.* Cynthia, with Certain[e] Sonnets.

Sweet country life, to such unknown. Country Life, to the Honored Mr. Endymion Porter[, Groome of the Bed-Chamber to His Maj.], The. Robert Herrick. BeJo

Sweet Cupid, Ripen Her Desire. William Corkine. OxBSP

Sweet cyder is a great thing. Great Things. Thomas Hardy. NOBE

Sweet Daddy. Patricia Smith.
"So Motown taught me all about men. Men worshipped." UnSA

Sweet daughter of a rough and stormy sire. Ode to Spring. Anna Laetitia Barbauld. OxAEP-1

Sweet day, so cool, so calm, so bright. Virtue [*or* Vertue]. George Herbert. AWP; AmFaPo; BASC; ClHu; FSCP; GeHe; HAP; HeIP-4; MeLP; NAEL-5v1; NAEL-6v1; NAEL-7v1; NOBE; NOCV; NOSC; NoP-4; OBEV; OPOU; OxBEV; PAI; PeECV; PoE; PoRA; SCGP; SoSe-8; TFi; TreFP

Sweet, deep sense of mystery filled the wood, A. In Cool, Green Haunts. Mahlon Leonard Fisher. WeW-3

Sweet Disorder in the Dress, A. Harry Hooton. NOBAu

Sweet disorder in the dress[e], A. Delight in Disorder. Robert Herrick. BASC; BeJo; CABP; CaPo; CavPo; ClHu; EBEV; EnLoPo; ErotSp; HAP; HeIP-4; InPK-6; NAEL-5v1; NAEL-6v1; NAEL-7v1; NIL-7; NIP-4; NOBE; NOSC; NPeEn; NoP-4; OBEV; OxAEP-1; OxBEV; PBRV; PeLV; PoE; PoRA; SCGP; TFi; TRP; WeW-3

Sweet Dog! now cold and stiff in death. Georgia Bailey Parrington. VerBaPo *Fr.* Elegy to a Dissected Puppy, An.

Sweet Dreams. Ogden Nash. OTCP

Sweet Dreams. Christian Wiman. AmPoNex

Sweet dreams form a shade. William Blake. FHYEP; OBCP *Fr.* Songs of Innocence.

Sweet earth, he ran and changed his shoes to go. Arrangements with Earth for Three Dead Friends. James Wright (1927–80). NIL-7; NIP-4

Sweet Echo, sweetest Nymph, that livest unseen. John Milton. OBEV *Fr.* Comus; a Masque Presented at Ludlow Castle.

Sweet elfin music comes to me. Dream of Elfland, A. Henrietta Cordelia Ray. CBWP-3

Sweet enthusiast, on a rock reclin'd, The. Power of Love, The. Charlotte Dacre. NOBRP

Sweet especial rural scene. (LL) Binsey Poplars (Felled 1879). Gerard Manley Hopkins. EBVV; NAEL-5v2; NAEL-6v2; NoAM; PAI; RB

Sweet Ethel. Linda Piper. BlSi

Sweet, exclude me[e] not, nor be divided. Thomas Campion. BASC

Sweet flattery! then she loves but me alone. (LL) William Shakespeare. HeIP-4; OxAEP-1 *Fr.* Sonnets.

Sweet flocks, whose soft enamel's wing. Flying Fowl, and Creeping Things, Praise Ye the Lord. Isaac Watts. ChIV-1

Sweet fore-warning?, A. (LL) Hester. Charles Lamb. GTBS-P; OBEV

Sweet friend, when you and I are gone. Patience with the Living. Margaret Elizabeth Munson Sangster. PoToHe

Sweet Galatea's beauty, and my love. (LL) John Gay. NAEL-5v1; NAEL-6v1 *Fr.* Acis and Galatea.

Sweet gentle angel, not that I aspire. To Miss M———, Written by Moonlight, July 18, 1782. Sir Samuel Egerton Brydges. Son

Sweet Georgia Brown. Kenneth Casey. ReLy

Sweet gifts, by me found something less than sweet. Sweet Gifts. Baldomero Garcilaso de la Vega. SpanPo, *tr. by* Edwin Morgan

Sweet, harmles[s] livers [*or* lives]! (on whose holy leisure). Shepherds [*or* Shepheards], The. Henry Vaughan. ChIV-2; ESCV

Sweet heart, / A morning, climbing in its brass. Letter from an Island. John Malcolm Brinnin. TAP

Sweet-Heart I come unto thee. No ring, no Wedding. *Unknown.* BASC

Sweet Highland Girl, a very shower. To the Highland Girl of Inversneyde. William Wordsworth. GTBS-P

Sweet Iesus of thy mercie, our pitifull praiers heare. Hymne of the Daie of Judgment, The. Lady Elizabeth Tyrwhit. EMWP

Sweet in goodly fellowship. There's No Lust like to Poetry. *Unknown.* AWP, *tr. by* John Addington Symonds

Sweet in her green dell the flower of beauty slumbers. Song. George Darley. OBEV

Sweet in your antique body, not yet young. To a Child. Wilfred Owen. Son

Sweet infancy! Rapture, The. Thomas Traherne. GeHe; NOSC

Sweet is the death that taketh end by love. (LL) "Love, That Doth Reign and Live Within My Thought." Henry Howard, Earl of Surrey. GSo; NAEL-6v1; NAEL-7v1; NoP-4

"Sweet is the fruit," say. Cillactor. GrAn

Sweet is the scholar's life. Scholar's Life, The. *Unknown.* NOIV, *tr. by* Thomas Kinsella

Sweet is the whispering of that pine tree, goatherd. Theocritus. *See* Sweet are the whispers of yon pine that makes

Sweet is your antique body, not yet young. Sonnet, to a Child. Wilfred Owen. NOxBChV

Sweet it is to be a child. "Tabitha." FaBoVe

Sweet jesus bleeding asshole no they cant. W. D. Snodgrass. BodElec *Fr.* Führer Bunker, The.

Sweet Jesus, let her save you, let her take. Prayer. Dorianne Laux. OPRER

Sweet jesus, superman. Note, Passed to Superman. Lucille Clifton. ReTh

Sweet joy befall thee! (LL) William Blake. FHYEP; NAEL-5v2; OxAEP-2; OxBSP *Fr.* Songs of Innocence.

Sweet Killen Hill. Tom MacIntyre. *See* On Sweet Killen Hill

Sweet lad, tender lad. Imitation of the Arabic. Alexander Sergeyevich Pushkin. CAGL, *tr. by* Michael Green

Sweet, Let Me Go! *Unknown.* OxBSP

Sweet Levinsky. Allen Ginsberg. NBLV

Sweet little bell. Church Bell in the Night, The. *Unknown.* NOIV, *tr. by* Kuno Meyer

Sweet Lorraine. Mitchell Parish. ReLy

Sweet Love dead. (LL) Evening, An. William Allingham. EnLoPo; NOBVV

Sweet Love, mine only treasure. Where His Lady Keeps His Heart. "A. W." CTC

Sweet love renew thy force. William Shakespeare. SCGP *Fr.* Sonnets.

Sweet lovely infant, innocently gay. Oh My Own Little Daughter, Four Years Old. *Unknown.* ECWP

Sweet Lovers love the spring. (LL) William Shakespeare. AWP; GTBS-P; NAEL-5v1; NOBE; NoSic; OBEV; RB; SCGP; TFi; TTTS *Fr.* As You Like It.

Sweet Lullaby, A. Nicholas Breton. *See* Cradle Song: "Come, little babe."

Sweet Lydia, take this mask, and shroud. Mask for Lydia, A. Thomas Randolph. BeJo

Sweet Maid. Bhartrihari. WoPoe, *tr. by* Barbara Stoler Miller

Sweet maid, if thou wouldst charm my sight. Persian Song of Hafiz, A. Hafiz [*or* Hafez]. AWP, *tr. by* Sir William Jones

Sweet maid, you perform a singular feat. Sweet Maid. Bhartrihari. WoPoe, *tr. by* Barbara Stoler Miller

Sweet Marie-Anne, she thought. Paris Latin Quarter. Femi Osofisan. NAfrP

Sweet marmalade of kisses new gathered. Dissert, A. Margaret Lucas Cavendish, Duchess of Newcastle. PEW

Sweet / May / again. (LL) Locust Tree in Flower, The. William Carlos Williams. Spl; TTTS

Sweet Meat Has Sour Sauce. William Cowper. ECEV; NOEC; OBSV

Sweet mermaid of the incomparable eyes. Mermaid, The. Ben King. OBAL

Sweet molasses. Sonya Brooks. InTrad

Sweet monster you hold death in your beak. Meetings. Paul Éluard. AF, *tr. by* Lloyd Alexander

Sweet mother, I cannot weave. Sappho. SaLy, *tr. by* Diane Rayor

Sweet Mother! rare in gifts of tenderness! To My Mother. Henrietta Cordelia Ray. CBWP-3

Sweet Mountains—Ye tell Me no lie. Emily Dickinson. NALW

Sweet mouth that offers for a taste, The. Sonnet 82. Luis de Góngora y Argote. BLPSL, *tr. by* Rene de Costa, Rigas Kappatos and Eleni Paidoussi

Sweet Mouth, That Send'st a Musky-Rosed Breath. Joshua Sylvester. EnLoPo

Sweet Muse, Descend. Isaac Watts. NOBE

Sweet Music's Power. John Fletcher. *See* King Henry VIII

Sweet my musings used to be. Mot eran dous miei cossir. Arnaut Daniel. AWP, *tr. by* Harriet Waters Preston

Sweet nature, give me holy dreams. At Nature's Shrine. Henrietta Cordelia Ray. CBWP-3

Sweet Nicarete, who served Athene's shuttle. Nicarchos. GrAn

Sweet "No! no!" with a sweet smile beneath, A. Love-Lesson, A. Clément Marot. AWP, *tr. by* Leigh Hunt

Sweet Nosegay, A, or Pleasant Posy. Isabella Whitney. WPE

Sweet nurslings of the vernal skies. Flowers of the Field. John Keble. SacPr

Sweet nymph, come to thy lover. *Unknown.* NoSic

Sweet peace, where dost thou dwell? I humbly crave. Peace. George Herbert. AWP; ESCV; GeHe; NOCV; NOSC; TreFP

Sweet Peas. John Keats. FHYEP *Fr.* I Stood Tip-Toe upon a Little Hill.

Sweet Peril. George Macdonald. ITBLP

Sweet Phosphor tricks to a smile the brow of heaven. All's Right with the World. Gerald Massey. EBVV

Sweet poet of the woods, a long adieu! On the Departure of the Nightingale. Charlotte Smith. RWP; WoRP

Sweet Poetess! as pensive oft I stray. To Mrs. Charlotte Smith. Martha Hanson. CenSon

Sweet Polly Oliver. *Unknown.* FaBoWar

Sweet Potato. Shinkichi Takahashi. ZenPo, *tr. by* Takashi Ikemoto and Lucien Stryk

Sweet Reader, Flanneled and Tulled. Olena Kalytiak Davis. BAP-01; NAPBL

Sweet Red Peppers, Sun-Drieds, the Hearts of Artichokes. Martha Silano. AmPoNex

Sweet Reliquaries, The. Delmira Agustini. TANSG, *tr. by* Mark McCaffrey

Sweet Rivers of Redeeming Love. John A. Granade. AH

Sweet rose [*or* Sweit rois] of virtue [*or* vertew] and of gentleness [*or* gentilnes]. To a Lady[e]. William Dunbar. EBEV; OBEV; OxBS; PeLV

Sweet run ends with the shutdown, The. At Summer's End. Jean Janzen. GeoHom

Sweet, sacred hill! on whose fair brow. Mount of Olives. Henry Vaughan. GeHe

Sweet Saturday afternoons with nothing to do and it's spring-turning-into-. Dolce Far Niente. Fidelito Cortes. ReBoTo

Sweet Sensibility! thou soothing power. Hannah More. ECWP *Fr.* Sensibility; a Poetical Epistle.

Sweet serene sky[e]-like Flower. To Lucasta: The Rose. Richard Lovelace. BeJo

Sweet she was, as kind a love. She Smiled like a Holiday. *Unknown.* OxBoLi

Sweet Silence after Bells! Christopher John Brennan. NOBAu

Sweet silver trumpets / Jesus! (LL) When Sue Wears Red. Langston Hughes. APT-2; NAAAL; TTY

Sweet smiling, and sweet spoken. (LL) To Sally. John Quincy Adams. APN-1; AWP; OBAL

Sweet smiling village, loveliest of the lawn. Oliver Goldsmith. NOIV *Fr.* Deserted Village, The.

Sweet soul, which now with heavenly songs dost tell. To the Marquess of Piscat's Soul. Henry Constable. NoSic

Sweet Soule of goodnesse, in whoe Saintlike brest. Double Acrostich on Mrs Svsanna Blvnt, A. Thomas Jordan. NPeEn

Sweet sounds, oh, beautiful music, do not cease! On Hearing a Symphony of Beethoven. Edna St. Vincent Millay. MoAmPo

Sweet sparrow, my lover's pet. Catullus. ErotSp, *tr. by* Sam Hamill

Sweet Spirit, comfort me! (LL) His Litany to the Holy Spirit. Robert Herrick. BASC; BeJo; NOSC; PeECV

Sweet spouse, you must presently troop and be gone. Imitation of Martial, Book II Ep, An 105. "Captain H——" NOEC

Sweet Spring, thou turn'st with all thy goodly train. Spring Bereaved 2. William Drummond, of Hawthornden. OBEV

Sweet spring, while others hail thy op'ning flowers. Farewell, for Two Years, to England, A. A Poem. Helen Maria Williams. RWP

Sweet springtime showers. Buson. SoOfWa, *tr. by* Sam Hamill

Sweet stream, that dost with equal pace. On His Mistress Drown'd. Thomas Spratt. EnLoPo

Sweet stream, that winds through [*or* thro'] yonder glade. To a Young Lady. William Cowper. GTBS-P; SacPr

Sweet Suffolk owl, so trimly dight. Sweet Suffolk Owl. *Unknown.* EBEV; NPeEn

Sweet summer flowers were braided in her hair. Maniac, The. Agnes Strickland. CenSon

Sweet sweet sweet sweet sweet tea. Susie Asado. Gertrude Stein. APT-1; NoAM; TAP

Sweet Talk. Ferreira Gullar. TCLAP, *tr. by* Renato Rezende

Sweet then the ploughman's slumbers, hale and young. Robert Bloomfield. ECEV *Fr.* Winter.

Sweet, thou art pale. Three Enemies, The. Christina Georgina Rossetti. SacPr; TrCP

Sweet, though short, our. Silver Flask, The. John Montague. CIP-2; PNI

Sweet-tied-tight-in-the-middle. His Praises. Swidi-Nonkamfela Mhlongo. PeSAV, *tr. by* Elizabeth Gunner

Sweet to the chilled frame, nerves soothed were so sore shaken. (LL) After War. Ivor Gurney. HarvBoo; OxBSP

Sweet Trinity (The Golden Vanity), The. *Unknown. See* Golden Vanity, The

Sweet upland, to whose walks, with fond repair. To Hampstead. Leigh Hunt. CenSon

Sweet voice of the Garb. Suibne Geilt. NOIV

Sweet waft their rounds those tuneful brothers five. Balsham Bells. Kenrick Prescot. NOEC

Sweet warrio[u]r, when shall I have peace with you? Edmund Spenser. OxBSo *Fr.* Amoretti.

Sweet Was the Song. *Unknown.* NOCV

Sweet was the sound, when oft at evening's close. Oliver Goldsmith. NPeEn *Fr.* Deserted Village, The.

Sweet were the day[e]s, when thou didst lodge with Lot. Decay. George Herbert. ESCV; SCGP

Sweet western wind, whose luck it is. To the Western Wind. Robert Herrick. CaPo; OBEV

Sweet Will. Philip Levine. LCAP-2; VCAP

Sweet William. "Ern Malley." BMAP

Sweet William he married [him] a wife. Wife Wrapt in Wether's Skin, The. *Unknown.* ESPB

Sweet William's Farewell to Black-Eyed [*or* Black-Ey'd] Susan. John Gay. BoLoP; NOEC

(Black-Eyed Susan.) GTBS-P

Sweet William's Ghost. *Unknown.* AWP; ESPB

Sweet William's gone over seas. Lord William; or, Lord Lundy. *Unknown.* ESPB

Sweet william, silverweed, sally-my-handsome. Spell for Sleeping, A. Alastair Reid. NOxBChV

Sweet William would [*or* he would] a wooing ride. Fair Margaret and Sweet William. *Unknown.* ESPB

Sweet William's Ghost *or* Sweet William and May Margaret. *Unknown.* AWP; ESPB

Sweet Willie's ta'en him o'er the faem. Sweet Willie. *Unknown.* OxBB

Sweet Willie was a widow's son. Willie and Lady Margerie [*or* Maisry]. *Unknown.* ESPB; OxBB

Sweet, winsome May, coy, pensive fay. May. Henrietta Cordelia Ray. CBWP-3

Sweet words that take. Sweet Words on Race. Langston Hughes. LTA

Sweetchile / dem will say dat. Revo Lyric. Kendel Hippolyte. WaCA

Sweet[e] Thames! [*or* Themmes] run[ne] softly, till I end my song. (LL) Edmund Spenser. AWP; EBEV; GTBS-P; HAP; NPeEn; NoSic; OBEV; OxAEP-1; OxBEV; SCGP; TFi; WoPoe

Sweeter Far than the Harp, More Gold than Gold. "Michael Field." OBMV; PeVV

Sweeter than sour apples flesh to boys. Ted Berrigan. FTOS *Fr.* Sonnets, The.

Sweetest love, I do not go[e]. Song. John Donne. AWP; BoLoP; ESCV; FHYEP; HeIP-4; MeLP; NAEL-7v1; NOBE; NoSic; PAI; TFi

Sweetest love return[e] again[e]. Mary Sidney Wroth, Countess of Montgomery. NAEL-6v1; NAEL-7v1 *Fr.* Pamphilia to Amphilanthus.

Sweetest notes among the human heart-strings, The. Love Unexpressed. Constance Fenimore Woolson. APN-2

Sweetest of sweets, I thank you: when displeasure. Church-Music[k]. George Herbert. AmFaPo; ESCV; GeHe; OxBSP

Sweetest Saviour, if my soul. Dialogue, A. George Herbert. FSCP; GeHe; NOSC; OBEV

Sweetest Thing, The. *Unknown.* TTY, *tr. by* Ulli Beier

Sweetgrass. Maurice Kenny. HATNAP

Sweetheart, I love you. Mean to Me. Fred E. Ahlert. ReLy

Sweetly breathed morning. Morning Thesis. Christiania Whitehead. NeBl

Sweetly-favored face, The. Canzonetta: Of His Lady in Absence. Giacomino Pugliesi. AWP; EaItPo, *tr. by* Dante Gabriel Rossetti

Sweetly hath Dorcas of Lycaenis learnt. Meleager. GrAn

Sweetly (my Dearest) I left thee asleep. John Saffin. SCAP

Sweetness. *Unknown.* BIrV, *tr. by* John Montague

Sweetness and wit, they are [*or* they're] but mummy, possessed. (LL) Love's Alchemy [*or* Alchemie]. John Donne. BASC; ESCV; NAEL-5v1; NAEL-6v1; NAEL-7v1; NoP-4; PoE

Sweetness of England, The. Elizabeth Barrett Browning. OxAEP-2 *Fr.* Aurora Leigh.

Sweetness of poverty like this, The. Aspiration. Mário de Andrade. TTY, *tr. by* John Nist

Swell'd with our late successes on the foe. Dryden. EBEV *Fr.* Annus Mirabilis.

Swell me a bowl with lusty wine. Ben Jonson. BeJo *Fr.* Poetaster, The.

Swell the Anthem, Raise the Song. Nathan Strong. AH

Swellfish eaten / He chants nembutsu. Tan Taigi. ZenPo, *tr. by* Takashi Ikemoto and Lucien Stryk

Swells in their cove, and smothers their sweet song. (LL) Seals at High Island. Richard Murphy. BiHa; CIP-2; ModIr; PBCIP

Swells then thy feeling heart, and streams thine eye. Dead Beggar, an Elegy Addressed to a Lady, The. Charlotte Smith. BWW

Swept all my pride away, and trembling I forgave! (LL) Forgiveness. John Greenleaf Whittier. GSo; TrCP

Swept Away. László Kálnoky. IQMS, *tr. by* Kenneth McRobbie and Zita McRobbie

Swept by light the feet of that multitude seemed. Splendor in the Wind. Raúl Zurita. TCLAP, *tr. by* Jack Schmitt

Swept into limbo is the host. Ballad of Religion and Marriage, A. Amy Levy. NPeEn; VWP; ViWPN

"Swerve to the left, son Roger," he said. Judgement of God, The. William Morris. PeVV

Swerving east, from rich industrial shadows. Here. Philip Larkin. NPeEn; PoE

Swet Jesus. Friar Michael of Kildare. NOIV

Swete Jesu, king of blisse. *Unknown.* MiEL

Swete sone, reu on me. *Unknown.* MiEL

Swich fyn hath, lo, this Troilus for love! Geoffrey Chaucer. NOCV; SacPr *Fr.* Troilus and Criseyde [*or* Criseide].

Swift. Thomas Caulfield Irwin.
    "It was a dim October day." BIrV

Swift as a spirit hastening to his task. Shelley. NAEL-5v2; NAEL-6v2; NOBRP

Swift cloud, swift light, now dark, now bright, across the landscape played. Idyl of Harvest Time, An. John Townsend Trowbridge. APN-2

Swift cold and deep. (LL) Charon's Cosmology. Charles Simic. HCAP; PoPoPo

Swift fleet the billowy clouds along the sky. Charlotte Smith. BoWoP; WPE *Fr.* Montalbert.

Swift Floods. Kata Szidónia Petröczy [*or* Petröczi]. WPOW, *tr. by* Laura Schiff

Swift has sailed into his rest. Swift's Epitaph. W. B. Yeats. OBVE

Swift is't in pace, light poiz'd, to look in clear. Description of a New England Spring. John Josselyn. SCAP

Swift Is That Falcon. *Unknown.* CoBCP, *tr. by* Burton Watson

Swift Love, Sweet Motor. Hildegarde Flanner. WPE

Swift red flesh, a winter king, The. Hart Crane. MoAmPo; NAAL-5; OxBA *Fr.* Bridge, The.

Swift's Epitaph. W. B. Yeats. OBVE

Swift shot the curlew 'thwart the rising blast. Ode on Lord Macartney's Embassy to China. William Shepherd. NOEC

Swift stream in the high mountains, dropping dental, lateral, A. River That Flows through Our Land, The. Jeremy Cronin. PeSAV

Swift things are beautiful. Swift Things Are Beautiful. Elizabeth Jane Coatsworth. ChAP

Swift through the yielding air I glide. Lark, The. *Unknown.* NOSC; OWoS

Swift to the western bounds of this wide land. On the Completion of the Pacific Telegraph. Jones Very. TAP

Swifter than hail. Akiko Yosano. OHMPJ

Swiftly Arose. Walt Whitman. TrCP *Fr.* Song of Myself.

Swiftly re-light the flame, "H. D." NALW *Fr.* Tribute to the Angels.

Swiftly riding past the willows. Tune: "Pure Serene Music" En Route to Po-shan. Hsin Ch'i-chi. ColAnChi, *tr. by* Jiaosheng Wang

Swiftly the years, beyond recall. New Corn. Ch'ien T'ao. ChiP, *tr. by* Arthur Waley

Swiftly walk o'er the western wave. To Night. Shelley. AWP; FHYEP; NAEL-5v2; NAEL-6v2; PoRA; TFi

Swifts. Ted Hughes. OWoS

Swifts. Philippe Jaccottet. VCWP, *tr. by* Derek Mahon

Swifts. Glyn Jones. AngWePo

Swifts at Evening. Jeffrey Harrison. UrbNat

Swifts turn in the heights of the air. Distances. Philippe Jaccottet. VCWP, *tr. by* Derek Mahon

Swim like a fish toward Rome. (LL) Cleopatra to the Asp. Ted Hughes. EBEV; RACG

Swim Right Up to Me. Katherine Pierpoint. MFPA

Swimmer. Gladys Cardiff. CDW

Swimmer. Robert Francis. APT-2; WeW-3

Swimmer, The. Brendan Kennelly. PBCIP

Swimmer's Moment, The. Margaret Avison. NOBC

Swimmers, The. Allen Tate. APT-2; FuPo; MoAmPo; NOBA; NoAM

Swimming By Night. James Merrill. ColAP; HarvBoo; VGW

Swimming Chenango Lake. Charles Tomlinson. FaBoMo; NoAM

Swimming in the Flood. John Burnside. EmeKit

Swimming Lesson. Wyatt Townley. SpudSo

Swimming Pool. Myra Cohn Livingston. NOxBChV

Swimming Pool Ghost, The. Gillian Ferguson. MFPA

Swimming Upstream. Aimée Grunberger. PoCoUp

Swimming with Seiger. Rick Agran. AmPoNex

Swinburne, old Swinburn, silly old Swinburne. Sister Swallow to Swinburne. Mary Holtby. UV

Swine gobble dead men's flesh. Han-shan. SuSp

Swineherd. Eiléan Ní Chuilleanáin. BIrV; CIP-2; EmeKit; FaBoWP; NPeEn; WPOW

Swing. Ode to Singer. Paul Van Ostaijen. TuT, *tr. by* Peter Van de Kamp

Swing, The. Robert Louis Stevenson. ChAP; NOxBChV; NTCP; TLR

Swing dat hammer—hunh—. Southern Road. Sterling Allen Brown. APT-2; BPo

Swing Low, Sweet Chariot. *Unknown.* UnPo

Swing Shift Blues. Alan Dugan. BodElec

Swing Song, A. William Allingham. OTCP; TLR

Swing, swing. Swing Song, A. William Allingham. OTCP; TLR

Swing up into the apple-tree. (LL) T. S. Eliot. FaBoCh; GTBS-P; NoAM; WeW-3 *Fr.* Landscapes.

Swinging. *Unknown.* OxNR

Swinging on a Star. Jimmy Van Heusen. ReLy

Swinging on the First Pitch. Dabney Stuart. MoASP

Swinging on the hanger. George Swede. HA

Swirled where I lay down to rest. (LL) Zaydee. Philip Levine. NNaP; TaR

Swirling spring. Young Girl. Ricarda Huch. WPOW, *tr. by* Janine Canan and Deirdre Lashgari

Swirling, swirling—aloeswood-scented smoke. Young Noble at Night's End; a Song. Li Ho. SuSp, *tr. by* Maureen Robertson

Switch. Sean O Riordain. ModIr, *tr. by* Patrick Crotty

Switch Blade; or, John's Other Wife, The. Jonathan Williams. NeAP

Switch on the Night. Ray Bradbury. OBSP

Switzer's Wife, The. Felicia Dorothea Hemans. RWP

Switzerland. Matthew Arnold.
    Dream, A. GTBS-P
    Isolation: To Marguerite. NAEL-6v2
    (To Marguerite.) CABP; NoP-4; PoPoPo
    To Marguerite—Continued. GTBS-P; NAEL-6v2; NPeEn; OxBEV; SoSe-8
    "Was it a dream? We sailed, I thought we sailed." GTBS-P
    "We were apart; yet, day by day." NAEL-6v2
    "Yes! in the sea of life enisled." GTBS-P; NAEL-6v2; NPeEn; OxBEV; SoSe-8

Switzerland upon, A. Child's Birthday, A. Henry Rago. IllVoic

Swollen bottle gourd, A. Shohaku. JDP, *tr. by* Yoel Hoffmann

Swollen river sang through the green hole, The. Arthur Rimbaud. OBWP *Fr.* Eighteen-Seventy.

Swoon of noon, a trance of tide, A. In a Bye-Canal. Herman Melville. APN-2; NCAP

Sword, A. Karin Boye. WPOW, *tr. by* Joanna Bankier

Sword, The. Abu Bakr. TTY, *tr. by* A. J. Arberry

Sword and the Sickle, The. William Blake. FaBoEE *Fr.* Gnomic Verses.

Sword in length a reaping-hook amain. King Harald's Trance. George Meredith. EBNV; PeVV

Sword is a cold bride. Yuk!, The. Michael Foley. PNI *Fr.* True Life Love Stories.

Sword of God doth ever well, The. To Generall Cromwell. "Eliza." EMWP

Sword of Robert Lee, The. Abram Joseph Ryan. CBCWP

Sword of Surprise, The. Gilbert Keith Chesterton. MoBrPo; SacPr

Sword sang [*or* sung] on the barren heath, The. William Blake. FaBoEE *Fr.* Gnomic Verses.

Swordfishtrombone. Tom Waits. PFTM-2

Swung torch scatters seeds, The. Night Piece. "Ern Malley." BMAP

Syama Mother's lap a-climbing. Najrul Islām. SinGod, *tr. by* Rachel Fell McDermott

Syama wakes on the cremation grounds.   Najrul Islām.   SinGod, *tr.* by Rachel Fell McDermott

Sybil, The.   Virgil [*or* Vergil].   OBVE, *tr.* by Gawin [*or* Gavin] Douglas   *Fr.* Aeneid [*or* Eneados, *Aeneis*], The.

Sybil Sibelius! Yes, Belinda Brahms!   Great Women Composers, The.   Gavin Ewart.   OBCoV

Sybilline.   "Ern Malley."   BMAP

Sycamore Canyon Nocturne.   Christopher Buckley.   GeoHom

Sycophantic Fox and the Gullible Raven, The.   Guy Wetmore Carryl.   NBLV; OBCA

Sydney.   Robert Harris.   NOBAu

Sydney and the Bush.   Les A. Murray.   DiPo

Sydney Cove, 1788.   Peter Porter.   NoAM

Sydney Highrise Variations, The.   Les A. Murray.

Flight from Manhattan, The.   BMAP

Sydney Place.   Sean Dunne.

Beans.   ModIr

Bus Station, The.   ModIr

Dead Pianist, The.   ModIr

Lost Wife, The.   ModIr

Mobile, The.   ModIr

Night Sky, The.   ModIr

Old School, The.   ModIr

Poet Upstairs, The.   ModIr

Railings.   ModIr

Tea.   ModIr

Syllables disintegrate ingrate alphabets.   Phyllis Webb.   NOBC   *Fr.* Kropotkin Poems, The.

Syllables shaped around the darkening day's.   Cancer Winter.   Marilyn Hacker.   RA

Syllabling.   Sean O Riordain.   ModIr, *tr.* by Patrick Crotty

Sylphs of the Seasons, The.   Washington Allston.

"And now, in accents deep and low."   APN-1

Sylva.   Abraham Cowley.

To His Mistress.   NOSC; OxAEP-1

Sylvae.   Publius Papinius Statius.

First of December, The.   RomPo, *tr.* by W. G. Shepherd

In Memory of His Father.   RomPo, *tr.* by W. G. Shepherd

Jocular Lines to Plotius Grypus.   RomPo, *tr.* by W. G. Shepherd

Thanksgiving to the Emperor Augustus Germanicus Domitianus.   RomPo, *tr.* by W. G. Shepherd

To Sleep.   RomPo, *tr.* by W. G. Shepherd

Sylvan Delights.   Pope.   NOBE   *Fr.* Pastorals.

Sylvan Revel, A.   Edward Cracroft Lefroy.   AWP   *Fr.* Echoes from Theocritus.

Sylvester's Dying Bed.   Langston Hughes.   NoAM; SAmP; UnPo

(I work up this mornin')   NAAAL

Sylvia.   Samuel Croxall.   NOEC

Sylvia. Do you remember still.   To Sylvia.   Giacomo Leopardi.   NAWM-7v2, *tr.* by Ottavio M. Casale

Sylvia; or, The May Queen.   George Darley.

"View like one of Fairy-land, A."   NOBRP

Sylvia's Death.   Anne Sexton.   LCAP-2; NAAL-2v2; NAAL-5; NALW

SYLVIA the fair, in the bloom of fifteen.   Song.   Dryden.   EBEV

Sylvie and Bruno.   Lewis Carroll.

Mad Gardener's Song, The.   WoPoe

Sylvius, your hands near my mouth are heady flowers.   Marguerite Burnat-Provins.   BoWoP

Sym of Lyntoun, be the ramis horn.   King Berdok.   *Unknown.*   OxBS

Symbols.   Christina Georgina Rossetti.   NALW

Symbols.   W. B. Yeats.   OBMV

Symbols of Gross Experience.   Cecil Day Lewis.   Son   *Fr.* Oh Dreams, Oh Destinations.

Symbols of Transformation.   Ron Padgett.   FTOS

Sympathetic Portrait of a Child.   William Carlos Williams.   APT-1

Sympathies.   Oliver Wendell Holmes.   APN-1   *Fr.* Wind-Clouds and Star-Drifts.

Sympathy.   Paul Laurence Dunbar.   APN-2; GT; NAAAL; NIL-7; NoP-4; SSLK; TCAPo

Sympathy.   Viola Meynell.   LW

Sympathy.   Lizelia Augusta Jenkins Moorer.   CBWP-3

Sympathy.   Henry David Thoreau.   CAGL

Sympathy, A Welcome, A.   John Berryman.   NoP-4

Symphonies.   Herman Melville.   APN-2   *Fr.* Clarel: A Poem and Pilgrimage in the Holy Land.

Symphony from the Balcony.   Jared Angira.   NAfrP

Symphony in Gray Major.   "Rubén Dario."   SpanPo, *tr.* by Denise Levertov

Symphony in Yellow.   Oscar Wilde.   EBVV; MoBrPo; NOBVV; NoAM; OPOU; OxBSP

Symphony No. 2.   Daniil Kharms.   AF, *tr.* by George Gibian

Symphony No. 3, in D Minor.   Jonathan Williams.   VGW   *Fr.* Mahler.

Symptom.   Dorothy Parker.   *See* Symptom Recital

Symptom Recital.   Dorothy Parker.   APT-1

(Symptom.)   LW

Symptoms.   Sophie Hannah.   MFPA

Symptoms of Love.   Robert Graves.   BoLoP

Synagogue in Prague.   Alan Sillitoe.   HP

Synchoresis.   Godfrey Turner.   OBCoV

Synchronized Swimming.   Angela Sorby.   AmPoNex

Syncopation, it has roused the nation to a red, red hot degree.   (That's the Way) Dixieland Started Jazz.   Shelton Brooks.   ReLy

Syne nethir-mare he went quhare Pluto was.   Robert Henryson.   NePenScot   *Fr.* Orpheus and Eurydice.

Syne went thai southwart in the land.   John Barbour.   NePenScot   *Fr.* Bruce, The.

Syng a song of Saxons.   Old-Saxon Fragment.   *Unknown.*   OBCoV

Synge we alle and seye we thus.   *Unknown.*   OHMEL

Synopsis of the Great Welsh Novel.   Harri Webb.   AngWePo; TCAWP

Syntactic and Verbal.   Giulia Niccolai.   CItWP, *tr.* by Cinzia Sartini Blum and Lara Trubowitz

Syntax of the Mind Grips, The.   Quincy Troupe.   NBV

Syren Songs.   George Darley.

Mermaidens' Vesper-Hymn, The.   NAEL-5v2; NAEL-6v2; NPeEn

Sea-Ritual, The.   BIrV

(Siren Chorus.)   BIrV

Syringa.   John Ashbery.   APSN; HCAP; NoAM; VCAP

Syrinx.   Amy Clampitt.   NoP-4

Syrinx.   James Merrill.   HCAP

Syros.   Tomas Tranströmer.   BLT, *tr.* by Leif Sjöberg and May Swenson

System.   Tiziano Rossi.   ItPo, *tr.* by Gayle Ridinger

System.   Robert Louis Stevenson.   PWR

Syvatoslav had no use for comfort.   Memorandum.   Yunna Petrovna [*or* Iunna Pinkhusovna] Moritz [*or* Morits].   TCRusP, *tr.* by Daniel Weissbort

Szondi.   Ferenc Kölcsey.   IQMS, *tr.* by Watson Kirkconnell

T

T.A.P.O.A.F.O.M.   Thomas Sayers Ellis.   BAP-01

T'ai-shan is a holy place, incomparable.   Looking at Mount T'ai.   Tu Fu.   CrYelRi, *tr.* by Sam Hamill

T'ain't No Sin to Dance Around in Your Bones.   Edgar Leslie.   ReLy

T'Ain't No Use.   Burton Lane.   ReLy

T'ao Ch'ien withdrew from all the world.   Tu Fu.   CrYelRi, *tr.* by Sam Hamill   *Fr.* Random Pleasures.

T-Bar.   Patricia K. Page.   NOBC; NoAM

T. E. Lawrence Poems, The.   Gwendolyn MacEwen.   NOBC

T'have hit the wavering form, or given this thing a name! (LL)   Adam Posed.   Anne Finch, Countess of Winchilsea.   ChIV-1; ECWP

T'ien-mu Mountain Ascended in a Dream: A Farewell Song.   Li Po.   SuSp, *tr.* by Wu-Chi Liu

T'ien-t'ai Mountain is tall.   Ballad of Peach Blossom Spring.   Yüan Mei.   CoBLCP, *tr.* by Jonathan Chaves

'T is not to honor thee by verse of mine.   On Michael Angelo.   Washington Allston.   APN-1

T'other eb'ning eb'ryting was still, Oh! babe.   Mister Johnson.   Ben Harney.   OBAL

T. S. Eliot.   W. H. Auden.   OBAL

T. S. Eliot.   Robert Lowell.   NOBA; NoAM

T. S. Eliot is quite at a loss.   Limerick.   W. H. Auden.   PeLi

T'undo, or be undone. (LL)   Ulysses and the Siren [*or* Syren].   Samuel Daniel.   HAP; NAEL-5v1; NAEL-6v1; NOBE; NoP-4; OBEV; OxAEP-1; PoE

T'ung-ch'uan is a beautiful place.   As My Way Passed Through T'ung-ch'uan, I Wished to Visit the Policy Critic of the Right, Mei, but Did Not Know Where to Find Him.   Tai Piao-yüan.   CoBLCP, *tr.* by Jonathan Chaves

T'ung Pass.   Chang Yang-hao.   WoPoe, *tr.* by Sam Hamill

'T was earliest morning in the early spring.   Bird and the Bell, The.   Christopher Pearse Cranch.   APN-1

'T were folly still to hope for higher Heaven. (LL)   Edgar Allan Poe.   OxBA; TAP   *Fr.* Dreams.

Tab, The.   Clark Coolidge.   FTOS

Tabernacle.   D. H. Lawrence.   ChIV-1

Tabernacle Thought, A.   Israel Zangwill.   TrJP

Table, The.   Ray DiPalma.   FTOS

Table and chair were overturned.   Ballade of the Moment After.   Paul Goodman.   BodElec

Table and the Chair, The.   Edward Lear.   ITBLP

Table-Birds.   Kenneth Mackenzie.   BMAP; NOBAu

Table gleams, The.   Yellow Room, The.   Juan Felipe Herrera.   TouFir

Table hurled itself, to our surprise, The.   Lingard and the Stars.   Edwin Arlington Robinson.   OxBSo

Table is spread, the lamp glitters and sighs, The.   Expected Guest, The.   Sidney Keyes.   PoWW

Table Manners.   Frank Gelett Burgess.   OBCA

Table near the band, A.   Music, Maestro, Please!   Herb Magidson.   ReLy

Table Richly Spread, A.   John Milton.   FaBoCh   *Fr.* Paradise Regained [*or* Regain'd].

Table, son, is laid, The.   House, The.   Gabriela Mistral.   BBASP; TCLAP, *tr.* by Doris Dana

Table Talk.   Derek Mahon.   DiPo

Table Talk.   Wallace Stevens.   NoP-4

Table was filled with many objects, The.   "Utopia" The.   Lee Harwood.   SPE

Tableau.   Countee Cullen.   NAAAL

Tableau.   Judith Wright.   CBAP

Tablecloths laid out, for his sons and grandsons, The. (LL)   Cemetery in Punta Arenas.   Enrique Lihn.   TCLAP; VCWP, *tr.* by David Unger

Tables in Pictures.   Diane Ward.   FTOS

Tables Turned, The.   William Wordsworth.   FHYEP; NAEL-5v2; NAEL-6v2; NOBRP; TOF

Tablet II.   Armand Schwerner.   PFTM-2   *Fr.* Tablets, The.

Tablet V.   Armand Schwerner.   PFTM-1

Tablet X.   Armand Schwerner.   PFTM-2   *Fr.* Tablets, The.

Tablet XV.   Armand Schwerner.   PFTM-2   *Fr.* Tablets, The.

Tablet XXVI.   Armand Schwerner.   *Fr.* Tablets, The.

Tablets, The.   Armand Schwerner.
    "Empty holes in the fish-dying-becoming directions."   PFTM-2
    "Probably the song of a temple prostitute, priestess of the second caste."   PFTM-2
    Tablet II.   PFTM-2
    Tablet X.   PFTM-2
    Tablet XV.   PFTM-2
    Tablet XXVI.
    "He is not quite dead."   PFTM-2; WoPoe

Tabloid News.   Blythe Nobleman.   ReTh

Taboo to Boot.   Ogden Nash.   RB

Taches Jaunes, Les.   Théophile Gautier.
    Clarimonde.   AWP
    "With elbow buried in the downy pillow."   AWP

Tacit.   Thom Ward.   AmPoNex

Tact.   Paul Pascal.   WeW-3

Tact.   Edwin Arlington Robinson.   NoAM

Tadhg sat up on his hills.   Senior Members.   Sean Lucy.   CIP-2

Tae be wan o them Kings.   Stars.   George Mackay Brown.   OxBS

Tae titly.   *Unknown.*   FaBoVe; OxNR

Taffy, the topaz-coloured cat.   In Honour of Taffy Topaz.   Christopher Darlington Morley.   WHSW

Taffy was a Welshman, Taffy was a thief.   Mother Goose.   OxNR; RB; ReMoGo

Taffy was born.   *Unknown.*   OxNR

Tag.   Langston Hughes.   APT-2

Taga for Mbaye Dyôb.   Léopold Sédar Senghor.   PFTM-1

Tagging.   Maureen Seaton.   ExTi; IllVoic

Taghore.   Muhammad Al-Ghuzzi.   MAP, *tr.* by John Heath-Stubbs and May Jayyusi

Tagus farewell, that westward with thy streams.   In Spayn.   Sir Thomas Wyatt.   NoSic; OPOU; SCGP

Tahiti.   Louis Johnson.   PeNZ

Tahoe in August.   Robert Hass.   NoP-4

Tahoe Nocturne.   Sherod Santos.   GeoHom

Taiaha Haka Poem.   Apirana Taylor.   PeNZ

Taid's Grave.   Gillian Clarke.   OPOU

Taiga, The.   Ivan Kharabarov.   RusPo, *tr.* by Robert Arthur Douglas Ford

Taiga bore me, The.   Taiga, The.   Ivan Kharabarov.   RusPo, *tr.* by Robert Arthur Douglas Ford

Tail behind, a trunk in front, A.   Elephant, or the Force of Habit, The.   A. E. Housman.   NOBL

Tail of the See, A.   Elizabeth T. Corbett.   OBCA

Taill of the Foxe, That Begylit the Wolf, in the Schadow of the Mone, The.   Robert Henryson.   OxBS

Tailor.   Eleanor Farjeon.   OTCP

Tailor, The.   "S. Ansky."   TrJP, *tr.* by Joseph Leftwich

Tailor, The.   Joseph Leftwich.   TrJP

Tailor Called Sorrow, A.   Betti Alver.   BoWoP, *tr.* by Willis Barnstone and Felix Oinas

Tailor of Bicester.   *Unknown.*   OxNR

Tailor's Wedding, The.   Louis Simpson.   NNaP

Tailpiece.   Max Fatchen.   OTCP

Tails and Heads.   Suzanne Knowles.   RB

Táin, The.   *Unknown.*   NOIV, *tr.* by Thomas Kinsella
    Combat of Ferdia and Cúchulainn.   WoPoe, *tr.* by Thomas Kinsella
    "Ferdia of the hosts."   WoPoe, *tr.* by Thomas Kinsella

Taino.   Jose Angel Figueroa.   PueRic

Taipan.   Kevin Gilbert.   IBA

Taisigh Agat Fein Do Phog.   *Unknown.*   BIrV, *tr.* by Maire Cruise O'Brien

Tak any brid, and put it in a cage.   Geoffrey Chaucer.   OWoS   *Fr.* Canterbury Tales, The.

Tak tyme in tym, or tym will not be tane.   Description of Tyme, A.   Alexander Montgomerie.   OxBEV; OxBS

Tak' Your Auld Cloak about Ye.   *Unknown.*   OxBS

Take a father's admonition, from a heart disturbed.   Father's Testament, A.   Judah ibn Tibbon.   TrJP, *tr.* by Israel Abrahams

Take a hammer to the amphora of soft Euphrates clay.   Jack Gilbert.   Campbell McGrath.   NAPBL

Take a harp.   Bible, *O.T.*   TrJP   *Fr.* Isaiah.

Take a large olive, stone it and then stuff it.   Dish for a Poet, A.   *Unknown.*   OBCP

Take a long view from Mynydd Bach.   Jeremy Hooker.   AngWePo

Take a model of the world so big.   Rescued Year, The.   William Stafford.   ColAP; LCAP-3

Take a note and spin it around spin it around don't.   Genie in the Jar, The.   Nikki Giovanni.   SeSe

Take a pen in your uncertain fingers.   Pen, The.   Muhammad Al-Ghuzzi.   MAP; NAfrP, *tr.* by John Heath-Stubbs and May Jayyusi

Take: A Roman Wedding.   Alice Fulton.   ExTi

Take a sheet of paper.   How to Reach the Sun. . . on a Piece of Paper.   Wes Magee.   NOxBChV

Take a taxi and go fishing.   Future Models May Have Infra-Red Sensors.   Tom Raworth.   Oth

Take a Whiff on Me.   *Unknown.*   NOBA

Take all my loves, my Love, yea, take them all.   William Shakespeare.   HeIP-4; OxAEP-1; SCGP   *Fr.* Sonnets.

Take all of me, pour out my life as wine.   To a Woman.   Helen Hay Whitney.   PoBW

Take all the rest the sun goes round. (LL)   On a Girdle.   Edmund Waller.   AWP; BASC; BeJo; GTBS-P; InPK-6; NAEL-5v1; NOSC; NoP-4; OBEV; PoE; PoRA; SCGP; TFi

Take as a sign of the rising wind the swelling sea.   Aratus.   HePo, *tr.* by Barbara Hughes Fowler   *Fr.* Phaenomena.

Take Away.   Margot Ruddock.   OBMV

Take away the whirlwind of hours.   Siren, The.   Alfonsina Storni.   TANSG, *tr.* by Mark McCaffrey

Take back the heart you with such caution give.   To Lysander.   Aphra Behn.   LW

Take Back Your Mink.   Frank Loesser.   ReLy

Take back your suit.   Song of Faith Forsworn, A.   John Byrne Leicester Warren, 3d Baron De Tabley.   PeVV

Take breath in irregular / measure. (LL)   Denise Levertov.   HeIP-4; InPK-6   *Fr.* Six Variations.

Take care of that face!   That Face.   Mairtin O Direain.   BiHa

Take, cradled Nursling of the mountains, take.   William Wordsworth.   CenSon   *Fr.* River Duddon [A Series of Sonnets], The.

Take Detroit, where boys.   Thinking American.   Hayan Charara.   AmPoNex

Take Down the Fiddle, Karl!   John Shaw Neilson.   CBAP

Take eat take glowing coal eat.   Body and Soul: Poem for Two Readers.   John Taggart.   FTOS

Take fortune as it falls, as one adviseth.   Author, of His Own Fortune, The.   Sir John Harington [*or* Harrington].   FaBoEE

Take, friend, Orthon of Syracuse' advice.   Theocritus.   GrAn

Take from me all my trumpery lest I die. (LL) Apologist's Evening Prayer, The. Clive Staples Lewis. SacPr; TrCP

Take from me my voice and I shall voiceless go. Ballad of a Shadow. Alice Oswald. MFPA

Take, gentle marble, to thy trust. Elegy upon His Tomb in Herndon-Hill Church, Erected by His Wife, Who Speaks, An. James Howell. OBWVE

Take Good Care of Yourself. Mark Wunderlich. NeAmPo; ReTh; WiU

Take hands. Take Hands. Laura Riding Jackson. APT-2

Take heart, monsieur, four-fifths of this province. For Jean Vincent d'Abbadie, Baron St.-Castin. Alden Nowlan. NOBC

Take heart, Ovid. No sentence. Paavo Haavikko. WoPoe, tr. by Anselm Hollo Fr. Fifteen Epigrams in Praise of the Tyrant.

Take heart, Prytherch. Aside. Ronald Stuart Thomas. OxBC

Take heart, the journey's ended. In the Town. Unknown. OBCP, tr. by Eleanor Farjeon

Take heed mine eyes, how you your look[e]s do[e] cast. Mary Sidney Wroth, Countess of Montgomery. BASC; NAEL-7v1; PEW Fr. Pamphilia to Amphilanthus.

Take heed of loving me[e]. Prohibition, The. John Donne. MeLP; NOSC

Take heed of this small child of earth. Poor Children, The. Victor Hugo. AWP, tr. by Algernon Charles Swinburne

Take hence this tuneful trifler's lays! Ode: Written After Reading Some Modern Love-Verses. John Scott of Amwell. ECEV

Take him away, he's dead as they die. Obituary. Kenneth Fearing. IllVoic; VGW

Take home Thy prodigal child, O Lord of Hosts! Birthday Sonnet. Elinor Wylie. MoAmPo

Take in hand the cup of delusion. Drink On. Mary E. Tucker. CBWP-1

Take It from Me. Kenneth O. Hanson. CoAP

Take it from me kiddo. Poem, or Beauty Hurts Mr. Vinal. E. E. Cummings. FaBoA; HarvBoo; MoAmPo; NAAL-2v2; NAAL-5; OBAL; OxBA; PFTM-1; PeLV; TRP

Take it not back! the priceless gift. Invocation to the Muse. Henrietta Cordelia Ray. CBWP-3

Take it to the hoop, "magic" johnson. Poem for "Magic," A. Quincy Troupe. ISC

Take it up like a kite on the wing! (LL) Limerick: "Well, it's partly the shape of the thing." Unknown. KaS; SoSe-8

Take, Lord, this soul of furred unblemished worth. Epitaph for a Good Mouser. Anne Stevenson. Spl

Take me back before everything. (LL) Being Aware. Dennis Cooper. GLP; PmAP

Take me home. "H. D." APT-1; NAAL-5 Fr. Walls Do Not Fall, The.

Take Me in Your Arms, Miss Moneypenny-Wilson. Patrick Barrington. OBCoV

Take me now while it's still early. Hour, The. Juana de Ibarbourou. TCLAP, tr. by Sophie Cabot Black

Take Me Out to the Ball Game. Jack Norworth. OBAL; TCAPo

Take my hand / I'm a stranger in paradise. Stranger in Paradise. George Forrest. ReLy

Take My Hand, Precious Lord. Thomas A. Dorsey. APT-2; ISC

Take My Hand, Precious Lord. Unknown. NAAAL

Take My Life and Let It Be. Frances Ridley Havergal. SacPr

Take my song of love to heart. Unknown. NOIV

Take my spirit to Thee. (LL) Prayers. Henry Charles Beeching. OBEV; SacPr

Take my tunic, woman. Goll Mac Morna Parts from His Wife. Unknown. NOIV, tr. by Thomas Kinsella

Take note, passers-by, of the sharp erosions. Edgar Lee Masters. FaBoEE Fr. Spoon River Anthology.

Take note who stoop. Nicarchus of Alexandria. GrAn

Take, O take the cream away. Breakfast Song in Time of Diet. Stoddard King. OBAL

Take, O Take Those Lips Away. William Shakespeare. AWP; EBEV; EnLoPo; NoSic; OBEV; SCGP; TFi Fr. Measure for Measure.

Take of me what is not my own. Envoi. Kathleen Jessie Raine. NOBE

Take off his hide and feed him to the crows. (LL) On Buying a Horse. Unknown. NBLV; RB

Take off those flimsy nets, Lysidice. Argentarius. GrAn

Take off your clothes, my love! Paulus [or Paulos] Silentiarius. ErotSp, tr. by Sam Hamill

Take off your hat. Pass Office Song. Unknown. PBA; TTY, tr. by Peggy Rutherford

Take, Oh, Take Those Lips Away. John Fletcher. NoP-4

Take I, 4:11:58. Philip Whalen. NeAP

Take 1 green pepper and 2 tomatoes. Pour Commencer. Jon Stallworthy. NoAM

Take One Home for the Kiddies. Philip Larkin. OxBTC

Take sackcloth of the darkest dye. Bible Defence of Slavery. Frances Ellen Watkins Harper. APN-2

Take, take this cosse, atonys, atonys, my hert! Roundel. Charles, Duc d' Orléans. NPeEn

Take telegraph wires, a lonely moor. Telegraph Wires. Ted Hughes. NPeEn

Take that, damn you; and that! Mezzo Forte. William Carlos Williams. SAmP

Take the cloak of all my love. Song for a Jewess. Iwan [or Yvan] Goll. TrJP, tr. by Joseph T. Shipley

Take the Crust. Sadi [or Saadi or Sa'di]. AWP, tr. by L. Cranmer-Byng Fr. Gulistan, The.

Take the Hearts of Children. Sandra Maria Esteves. PueRic

Take the night Myron Stout shut his sure blind eyes. Baby Vallejo. David Rivard. SeSe

Take the world as it is!—with its smiles and its sorrow. Charles Swain. PoToHe Fr. Take the World As It Is.

Take Then, These. Charles Bernstein. FTOS

Take, then your paltry Christ. To the Christians. Francis Lauderdale Adams. ChIV-2; OxBS

Take Therefore That You May Have. "Angelus Silesius." GePo, tr. by George C. Schoolfield Fr. Cherubical Wanderer, The.

Take these who will as may be: I. Permit Me Voyage. James Agee. MoAmPo; YaYoPo

Take this city-filled. Abiquiu. Luis Lopez. GeoH

Take this fruit, these flowers, these branches and leaves. Green. Paul Verlaine. SxFrPo, tr. by Martin Sorrell

Take this hammer, (huh!) carry it to the captain, (huh!). Take this Hammer. Leadbelly. GM

Take this kiss upon the brow! Edgar Allan Poe. NCAP; NOBA; OxBA; TAP; TCAPo

Take this man with an axe. Private, The. Robert Adamson. BMAP

Take this news to the Lakedaimonians, friend. Simonides. See Go tell at Sparta, traveler passing by

Take Thou Our Minds, Dear Lord. William H. Foulkes. AH

Take thou the world and all that will. (LL) Flesh and the Spirit, The. Anne Bradstreet. BASC; ChIV-2; NAAL-2v1; NAAL-3; NOBA; OxBA; OxWW; SCAP; TAP

Take time, my dear, ere Time takes wing. Fading Beauty. Unknown. FaBoEE

Take Time to Live. Thomas Curtis Clark. PoToHe

Take time while time doth last. Song Set by John Farmer. Unknown. CTC; NoSic

Take two hundred soldiers. Hazel. Oliver Reynolds. FaBoWar

Take two photographs. King Kong Meets Wallace Stevens. Michael Ondaatje. NIL-7

Take up the pen: fall into the net of law. Call to Arms. "Lu Hsün." SuSp; WoPoe, tr. by William R. Schultz

Take up the song; forget the epitaph. (LL) To Inez Milholland. Edna St. Vincent Millay. AiP; NALW; WPE

Take what he gives you, even if it's paltry. Take What He Gives You. "Anvari." WoPoe, tr. by Dick Davis

Take Ye Heed, Watch and Pray. Jones Very. ChIV-2

Take yesterday's worries and sort them all out. Worries. Unknown. PoToHe

Take your fill of intimate remorse, perfumed sorrow. Right to Grief, The. Carl Sandburg. IllVoic

Take your first steps in a Walker. Poem for the Children. Carolyn Beard Whitlow. FFC

Take your moon face away. Caminando. Víctor Hernández Cruz. PFTM-2

Take your own kisses; give me mine again. (LL) Kisses. William Strode. FaBoEE; NOSC

Take yourself to the rose-garden, it's the season. Take Yourself to the Rose-Garden. Nedîm. WoPoe, tr. by Walter Andrews, Najaat Black and Mehmet Kalpakli

Taken by storm, she is the girl you will marry. (LL) Courtship. Mark Strand. HCAP; PoPoPo

Taken by surprise. Meeting Bida. Fily-Dabo Sissoko. NegPo, tr. by Ellen Conroy Kennedy

Taken from the. Primitive, The. Haki R. Madhubuti. BPo

Taken in by none but Thee. (LL) To Julia. Robert Herrick. CaPo; NOSC

Takes in / the world / from the heart out. Morning-Glory, The. Raymond Roseliep. HA

Takes one long slow step nearer. (LL) Golden Calf. Norman MacCaig. ChIV-1; OxBS

Taking a Captive / 1984. Barney Bush. HATNAP

Taking a Chance on Love. Ted Fetter. ReLy

Taking a nap. Basho. EH, tr. by Robert Hass

Taking Ford's dictation on Samuel Butler. Ford Madox Ford. Robert Lowell. OxBC

Taking, giving back their lives. Field Hospital, The. Paul Muldoon. CIP-2; PNI

Taking hold, one's astray in nothingness.   Kokai.   ZenPo, *tr. by* Takashi Ikemoto and Lucien Stryk

Taking It Back.   Dixie Salazar.   UnSA

Taking Leave of a Friend.   Li Po.   ChinPo, *tr. by* Yip Wai-lim

Taking Leave of a Friend.   Li Po.   RB, *tr. by* Ezra Pound

Taking Leave of a Friend.   Li Po.   CrYelRi, *tr. by* Sam Hamill

Taking Leave of Two Officials.   Tu Fu.   CrYelRi, *tr. by* Sam Hamill

Taking Notice.   Marilyn Hacker.
  "And I shout at Iva, whine at you. Easily."   VCAP
  "If we talk, we're too tired to make love; if we."   VCAP
  "In the Public Theater lobby, I wait for Marie."   VCAP
  "We work, play, don't cross-reference calendars."   VCAP

Taking of the Koppie, The.   Uys Krige.   FaBoWar; PeSAV

Taking Off My Clothes.   Carolyn Forché.   NIL-7; NoAM

Taking off / my clothes.   Desire.   Connemara Wadsworth.   PasH

Taking stock of what I have and what I haven't.   I Got the Sun in the Morning.   Irving Berlin.   ReLy

Taking Tea with My Father and Mother.   Pam Zinnemann-Hope.   Prnts

Taking the air rifle from my son's hand.   Cain.   Irving Layton.   MoCV

Taking the Census.   Charles Robert Thatcher.   NOBAu

Taking the Ferry at Ta-kao at Dawn.   Yang Wei-chen.   SuSp, *tr. by* Jonathan Chaves

Taking the Hands of Someone You Love.   Robert Bly.   TRP

Taking the Night-Train.   John James Piatt.   APN-2

Taking the Plunge.   John Mole.   NOxBChV

Taking the Soundings on Third Avenue.   David Kherdian.
  "Couple that walked, The."   UrbNat
  "Dogs on a leash."   UrbNat
  "Hawthorne berries, The."   UrbNat
  "In the autumn-come-winter park."   UrbNat
  "Wind rips through the."   UrbNat
  "Wing-set lone seagull, The."   UrbNat

Taking Time to Grow.   Mary Mapes Dodge.   SWaP

Taking Turns.   Norma Farber.   TLR

Taking us by and large, we're a queer lot.   Sisters, The.   Amy Lowell.   NALW

Takings.   Gael Turnbull.   Oth

Taku Skanskan.   Paula Gunn Allen.   HATNAP

Tale.   Jennifer Rankin.   BMAP

Tale, A.   Edward Thomas.   OxBEV

Tale I frame shall be found to tally, The.   Seafarer, The.   *Unknown.*   OBVE, *tr. by* Michael Alexander

Tale is told of long ago, A.   Song of the Yellow Cedar Face, A.   George Clutesi.   HATNAP

Tale of a Friar and A Shoemaker's Wife, a.   Thomas Churchyard.   NoSic

Tale of a Pony, The.   Bret Harte.   OBNV

Tale of Acadie, A.   Henry Wadsworth Longfellow.   APN-1; NoP-4; TCAPo; UV   *Fr.* Evangeline, a Tale of Acadie.

Tale of Bananas, A.   Víctor Hernández Cruz.   PueRic

Tale of Custard the Dragon, The.   Ogden Nash.   ITBLP; MakPoe; OBCA; OTCP; PoRA

Tale of Genji.   Hugh Seidman.   YaYoPo

Tale of Genji, The.   Murasaki Shikibu.
  "Lady Murasaki says."   BoWoP
  "Troubled waters, The/ are frozen fast."   WPOW
  "Warblers are today as long ago, The."   WoPoe, *tr. by* Edward Seidensticker

Tale of Italy, A.   Eloise Bibb.   CBWP-4

Tale of Lord Lovell, The.   *Unknown.*   NOBL; PeLV

Tale of Me, The.   Eiléan Ní Chuilleanáin.   Prnts

Tale of Red-Haired Motele, Mister Inspector, Rabbi Isaiah and Commissar Blokh, The.   Iosif Pavlovich Utkin.   TCRusP, *tr. by* Denis Johnson and Kathy Lewis

Tale of Red-Haired Motl, Mister Inspector, Rabbi Isaiah, and Commissar Blokh, The.   Iosif Pavlovich Utkin.   TCRP, *tr. by* Lubov Yakovleva

Tale of Sigemund, The.   *Unknown.*   AnOE, *tr. by* Charles W. Kennedy   *Fr.* Beowulf.

Tale of Sir Thopas, The.   Geoffrey Chaucer.   NAEL-5v1   *Fr.* Canterbury Tales, The.

Tale of St. Petersburg, A.   Alexander Sergeyevich Pushkin.   WoPoe, *tr. by* D. M. Thomas   *Fr.* Bronze Horseman, The.

Tale of Sunlight, The.   Gary Soto.   NoAM

Tale of the Assyrian Statue.   Mahmoud Al-Buraikan.   MAP, *tr. by* Lena Jayyusi and Naomi Shihab Nye

Tale of the Beginning of Friars and Cloisterers, A.   William Warner.   NoSic   *Fr.* Albion's England.

Tale of the Cyclopses, The.   Nikolai Ivanovich Glazkov.   TCRP, *tr. by* Daniel Weissbort

Tale of the Miser and the Poet, A.   Anne Finch, Countess of Winchilsea.   ECWP

Tale of the Oyster, The.   Cole Porter.   ReLy

Tale of the Sea, A.   William McGonagall.
  "'Twas on the 8th April, on the afternoon of that day."   VerBaPo

Tale of the Upland Mouse and the Burgess Mouse, The.   Robert Henryson.   OBNV
  (Esope, myne authour, makis mentioun.)   NePenScot
  (Two Mice, The.)   NePenScot

Tale of Time.   Robert Penn Warren.   LCAP-2

Talent and Friendship.   Thomas Kinsella.   HarvBoo

Talented Man, The.   Winthrop Mackworth Praed.   CABP; NOBL; PeLV
  (Letter, From a Lady in London to a Lady at Lausanne, A.)   OBCoV

Tales about My Father.   'Abd al-Karim Kassid.   MAP, *tr. by* Lena Jayyusi and Anthony Thwaite

Tales of a Wayside Inn.   Henry Wadsworth Longfellow.
  Birds of Killingworth, The (The Poet's Tale).   OxBA
  "King Solomon, before his palace gate."   APN-1; TCAPo
  (Landlord's Tale: Paul Revere's Ride, The.)   APN-1
  Monk of Casal-Maggiore, The (The Sicilian's Tale).   OxBA
  Paul Revere's Ride [The Landlord's Tale].   AiP; BRP; ChAP; ColAP; EBNV; FaBoTw; HHAm; ITBLP; NOxBCh; OBAL; OBCA; OBNV; PWR; TCAPo; TFi
  Prelude: The Wayside Inn.   APN-1
  ("So through the night rode Paul Revere.")   CA
  Spanish Jew's Tale: Azrael, The.   APN-1; TCAPo
  Spanish Jew's Tale: The Legend of Rabbi Ben Levi, The.   NCAP; TCAPo
  Theologian's Tale: Elizabeth, The.
  "Ships that pass in the night, and speak each other in passing."   PoToHe

Tales of Shatz.   Dannie Abse.   OxBC

Tales of the Hall.   George Crabbe.
  Delay has Danger.   NOBRP
  "Three weeks had past, and Richard rambles now."   NPeEn

Tales of the Islands.   Derek Walcott.   OxBTC

Tali Karng: twilight snake.   Tali Karng: Twilight Snake.   W. Les Russell.   IBA

Taliesin and the Mockers.   Vernon Watkins.   AngWePo

Taliesin 1952.   Ronald Stuart Thomas.   HarvBoo

Taliessin's Song of the Unicorn.   Charles Williams.   FaBoTw

Talin of the Pasta Factory.   Rossana Ombres.   CItWP, *tr. by* Cinzia Sartini Blum and Lara Trubowitz

Talisman, A.   Marianne Craig Moore.   MoAmPo

Talismans.   Maudelle Driskell.   AllShUp

Talk.   Roo Borson.   NIP-4; NOBC

Talk about the shade of the sheltering palms.   Under the Anheuser Bush.   Andrew B. Sterling.   OBAL

Talk all day and then keep silent.   Parrot.   Po Chü-i.   SuSp, *tr. by* Irving Y. Lo

Talk Happiness.   Ella Wheeler Wilcox.   PoToHe

Talk is of boats, sea-legs, the.   Deep.   Patricia Pogson.   Prnts

Talk no more of the lucky escape of the head.   On a Stone Thrown at a Very Great Man, But Which Missed Him.   "Peter Pindar."   NBLV

Talk not of strength, till your heart has known.   *Unknown.*   PoToHe

Talk of old families—last remains.   Death of a Species.   Anthony Conran.   AngWePo

Talk Show, The.   Albert Goldbarth.   IllVoic; ReTh

Talk to me, *javas*, talk to me.   Najrul Islām.   SinGod, *tr. by* Rachel Fell McDermott

Talk to the Peach Tree.   Sipho Sepamla.   PBMAP

Talk with My Cousin Alone, A.   Hone Tuwhare.   PeNZ

Talked to my father again in a dream he seemed happy.   Le Jazz Hot.   Anselm Hollo.   PoM; SeSe

Talker, The.   Benjamin Appel.   TrJP

Talkers in a Dream Doorway.   Judy Grahn.   GLP

Talkin' Trash.   Elena Georgiou.   WiU

Talking.   Miguel Algarin.   PueRic

Talking.   Robert Creeley.   FTOS

Talking about Birds.   *Vietnamese Oral Tradition.*   CaDao, *tr. by* John Balaban

Talking About Things.   Michael Ryan.   YaYoPo

Talking along in this not quite prose way.   Near.   William Stafford.   CoAmPo

Talking Designs.   Liz Sohappy Bahe.   CDW

Talking Drums, The.   Kojo Gyinaye Kyei.   PBA

Talking Dust Bowl.   Woody Guthrie.   APT-2

Talking Fish, The.   Ruth Stone.   BoWoP

Talking for yonks about babies and / washing machines.   Grown-ups.   Geoffrey Holloway.   OTCP

Talking In Bed.   Philip Larkin.   BoLoP; NAEL-5v2; NAEL-6v2; PoetW

Talking of Ezra Pound and long-dead pantos.   Robert Malise Bowyer Nichols.   OBSV   *Fr.* Fisbo.

Talking of poetry, hauling the books.   In a Classroom.   Adrienne Rich.   LoL

Talking of Sharp Things.   Frank Mkalawile Chipasula.   HBAPE

Talking: seven steps, eight falls.   Shishin-Goshin.   ZenPo, tr. by Takashi Ikemoto and Lucien Stryk

Talking to her, he knew it was the end.   Hector.   Valentin Iremonger.   CIP-2

Talking to Jim.   Walta Borawski.   CAGL

Talking to strange men on the subway.   My Mother.   John Wieners.   BB; GLP; PmAP

Talking to the Family.   John A. Stone.   BloBone

Talking to You Afterwards.   Peter Porter.   BMAP

Talking together between the wire grates of a cage. (LL)   My Mother.   John Wieners.   GLP; PmAP

Talking with Soldiers.   Walter James Turner.   MoBrPo

Tall and thin and young and lovely the michael with kaposi's sarcoma goes walking.   D. A. Powell.   AmPoNex

Tall as a foxglove spire, on tiptoe.   Fox Dancing.   Suzanne Knowles.   RB

Tall Buildings.   Munib-ur-Rahman.   OMIP, tr. by Kathleen Grant Jaeger

Tall camels of the spirit, The.   "World Without Objects Is a Sensible Emptiness, A."   Richard Wilbur.   CoAmPo; MoAmPo; NAAL-2v2; NOBA; NoAM

Tall dancer dances, The.   Dancer, The.   Joseph Campbell.   OBMV

Tall Girl, The.   John Crowe Ransom.   OxBSo; Son

Tall grows that pear-tree.   Return from Battle.   Unknown.   ChiP, tr. by Arthur Waley

Tall Hat.   Victor James Daley.   CBAP

Tall man and myself tonight, The.   Grand Army Plaza.   June Jordan.   ISC

Tall Man Executes a Jig, A.   Irving Layton.   MoCV; NOBC; NoAM

Tall marsh fowl stalk through the shallows.   Tu Fu.   CarOv, tr. by Carolyn Kizer   Fr. Meandering River Poems, The.

Tall Nettles.   Edward Thomas.   FaBoTw; FaBoVe; MoBrPo; NPeEn; OxBEV; OxBSP

Tall palm tree sixty feet high, The.   Prayer to the God Thot.   Unknown.   TTY, tr. by Ulli Beier

Tall stately plants with spikes and forks of gold.   Frederick Goddard Tuckerman.   OxBSo

Tall Story for Fred Dibnah.   Geoffrey Summerfield.   OTCP

Tall terrace crumbled long ago, The.   Dragon-Tiger Terrace.   Yang Shih-ch'i.   CoBLCP, tr. by Jonathan Chaves

Tall trees are full of sad wind, The.   Ballad of the Orioles in the Fields.   Ts'ao Chih.   ColAnChi; SuSp, tr. by Hans H. Frankel

Tall unpopular men.   Dedication.   Oliver St. John Gogarty.   OBMV

Tall Walking Woman.   Pat Mora.   OxIBACP

Tall Weeds.   W. S. Rendra.   WoPoe, tr. by Burton Raffel

Tall Wind, The.   K. O. Arvidson.   PeNZ

Tall Wood twins, The.   Les A. Murray.   NewEx

Talla ly li oh / Freedom a come oh!   Freedom a Come Oh!   Unknown.   FaBoVe

Taller To-day.   W. H. Auden.   NPeEn

Taller to-day, we remember similar evenings.   Taller To-day.   W. H. Auden.   NPeEn

Tallulah.   James Matthew Legaré.   APN-2

Tally.   Josephine Miles.   NoAM

Tally Stick, The.   Jarold Ramsey.   NIL-7; NIP-4

Talmud, The.   Simeon Grigoryevich Frug.   TrJP, tr. by Alice Stone Blackwell

Talmud, The.   Unknown.   TrJP

Talmud Student, The.   Hayyim Nahman [or Khayim Nakhman or Chaim Nachman] Bialik.   TrJP, tr. by Helena Frank

Talmudist.   Stanley Burnshaw.   DiPo

Talysarn.   Brenda Chamberlain.   OBWVE

Tam Glen.   Robert Burns.   AWP; OxBS

Tam i' the Kirk.   Violet Jacob.   NePenScot

Tam Lin.   Unknown.   ESPB; NOBE; OBEV; OBNV; OxBB; OxBS

Tam o' Shanter; A Tale.   Robert Burns.   CABP; EBNV; NAEL-5v2; NAEL-6v2; NPeEn; NePenScot; NoP-4; OBNV; OxBS; PeLV

Tam o' the Lin was fu' o' pride.   Tam O' the Lin.   Joanna Baillie.   RWP

Tam o' the linn cam up the gait.   Unknown.   FaBoCh

Tamaki of a Hundred Lovers.   Hirini Melbourne.   PeNZ

Tamaki of a Hundred Lovers.   Merimeri Penfold.   PeNZ, tr. by Margaret Orbell

Tamaracks swing light away.   Swamp.   Roberta Hill Whiteman.   VoR

Tamarind hangs its head, The.   Airy Hall Icongraphy.   Frederick D'Aguiar.   Oth

Tambourine song for Soldiers Going into Battle.   Hind bint Utba.   WPOW, tr. by Bridget Connelly and Deirdre Lashgari

Tambourine Tommy.   Thomas Sayers Ellis.   NAPBL

Tambourines.   Langston Hughes.   SAmP

Tambov wolf is your comrade, A.   Arrow in the Wall.   Andrey [or Andrei] Andreievich Voznesensky [or Voznesenskii].   RusPo, tr. by Robert Arthur Douglas Ford

Tamburlaine the Great.   Christopher Marlowe.
"And ride in triumph through Persepolis?"   FaBoWar
Fair Is Too Foul an Epithet.   EBEV
What Is Beauty?   MakPoe

Tamburlaine the Great, Part 2.   Christopher Marlowe.
"Bastardly boy, sprung from some coward's loins."   FaBoWar
"Blacke is the beauty of the brightest day."   OxBEV
"But now my boys, leave off, and list to me."   FaBoWar
"Now fetch me out the Turkish concubines."   FaBoWar

Tame and Ferocious Animal, A.   Nancy Morejón.   TANSG, tr. by Joy Renjilian-Burgy

Tame Cat.   Ezra Pound.   APT-1; OBAL

Tamed by Miltown we lie on Mother's bed;.   Man And Wife.   Robert Lowell.   BoLoP; CoAmPo; ColAP; NAAL-2v2; VCAP

Tamer and Hawk.   Thom Gunn.   FaBoTw; HarvBoo

Tamer as prey. (LL)   Tamer and Hawk.   Thom Gunn.   FaBoTw; HarvBoo

Tamil, it's true, is the breath of my life.   Tamil.   Gnanakoothan.   OMIP, tr. by A. K. Ramanujan

Taming of the Shrew, The.   William Shakespeare.
"Thy gown? Why, ay. Come, tailor, let us see't."   OBCoV

Tammuz dies on the skyline.   Song in August.   Badr Shakir Al-Sayyab.   MAP, tr. by Lena Jayyusi and Christopher Middleton

Tammy Messer.   Unknown.   FaBoEE

Tamping Ties.   Unknown.   GM

Tan Manhattan.   Andy Razaf.   ReLy

Tan Tien.   Mei-Mei Berssenbrugge.   OpBo

Tanagra! think not I forget.   Walter Savage Landor.   OBEV   Fr. Pericles and Aspasia.

Tangerine.   Johnny Mercer.   ReLy

Tangled Hair.   Lady Izumi.   WoPoe, tr. by Steven D. Carter

Tangled Hair.   Akiko Yosano.
"Thousand lines, A."   WoPoe, tr. by Sanford Goldstein and Seishi Shinoda

Tangled in rocks / and leaves. (LL)   In Cold Storm Light.   Leslie Marmon Silko.   NoAM; VoR

Tangled web indeed we weave, A.   Women's Degrees.   Alfred Denis Godley.   NOBL

Tango.   Ntozake Shange.   GT

Tango'd Love.   J. B. Bernstein.   PasH

Tanka.   Nikolai Stepanovich Gumilyov [or Gumiliov or Gumilev].   TCRP, tr. by Simon Franklin

Tanka.   Lenard D. Moore.   SpirFl

Tanks.   Rhyll McMaster.   CBAP; NOBAu

Tanned blonde, The.   Once-over, The.   Paul Blackburn.   NeAP; PoM

Tannhäuser.   Heinrich Heine.
Best Religion, The.   TrJP, tr. by Emma Lazarus

Tannhauser.   Newman Levy.   OBAL

Tansy buttons, tansy.   Charles Olson.   APT-2; PmAP   Fr. Maximus Poems, The.

Tantalos.   Paulus [or Paulos] Silentiarius.   WoPoe, tr. by Dudley Fitts

Tantramar Revisited, The.   Sir Charles G. D. Roberts.   NOBC

Tantric Praise of the Goddess.   Unknown.   HW, tr. by Jalaja Bonheim

Tao.   Vietnamese Oral Tradition.   CaDao, tr. by John Balaban

Tao and Unfitness at Inistiogue on the River Nore.   Thomas Kinsella.   NPeEn; PBCIP

Tao Te Ching.   Lao Tzu.
"Ancient Masters were profound and subtle, The."   EnlH
"Best be done before the last degree."   WoPoe, tr. by Moss Roberts
"Boundless shaping Power, A."   WoPoe, tr. by Moss Roberts
"Empty your mind of all thoughts."   EnlH
"Every being in the universe."   EnlH
"Good traveler has no fixed plans, A."   EnlH
"Some say that my teaching is nonsense."   EnlH
"Tao that can be told, The."   EnlH
"To understand others is to be knowledgeable."   AmFaPo, tr. by Robert Henricks
"Way as "Way" bespoke is no true lasting way; The."   WoPoe, tr. by Moss Roberts
"When thirty spokes join the wheel-hole."   WoPoe, tr. by Moss Roberts
"Whenever all the world declares fair "fair""   WoPoe, tr. by Moss Roberts

Tao that can be told, The.   Lao Tzu.   EnlH   Fr. Tao Te Ching.

Taoism and Buddhism.   Po Chü-i.   ChiP, tr. by Arthur Waley

Taoist Huang Has Died of Alcoholism, The.   Shen Chou.   CoBLCP; ColAnChi, tr. by Jonathan Chaves

Taoist Song.   Hsi K'ang.   ChiP, tr. by Arthur Waley

Taoist Song.   Wang Yang-ming.   CrYelRi, tr. by Sam Hamill

Taoist Song: "Empty bag of skin filling with desire."   Teng Yu-pin.   CrYelRi, tr. by Sam Hamill

Taoist Song: "Heaven and hell are men's unhappy inventions." Teng Yu-pin. CrYelRi, *tr. by* Sam Hamill

Taoist Song: "In white clouds, in green mountains." Teng Yu-pin. CrYelRi, *tr. by* Sam Hamill

Taormini. John Henry, Cardinal Newman. SacPr

Taos Pueblo Indians: 700 strong according to Bobby's last census. Miguel Algarin. PueRic

Taos Winter. Patty L. Harjo. VoR

Tap. Maggie Hannan. NLP

Tap. Alice Jones. BloBone

Tap-Room, The. Robert Tannahill. NePenScot

Tap Your Troubles Away. Jerry Herman. ReLy

Tape, The. Myra Cohn Livingston. NTCP

Tape Mark. Nanni Balestrini. PFTM-2, *tr. by* Lawrence R. Smith

Taped to the wall of my cell are 47 pictures: 47 black. Idea of Ancestry, The. Etheridge Knight. AF; BPo; CoAmPo; ESEAA; ISC; NAAAL; NIP-4; NNaP; PBCAP; RaBo

Tapered choir, at the late hour of prayer, the. Thomas Warton, the Younger. ECEV *Fr.* Pleasures of Melancholy, The.

Tapers in the great God's hall, The. By Night. Philip Jerome Cleveland. SacPr

Tapes. Thomas Sayers Ellis. AmPoNex

Tapestries. Colleen J. McElroy. NAAAL

Tapestry. Charles Simic. LCAP-2; VCAP

Tapestry of the Heart, The. Jolanda Insana. CItWP, *tr. by* Cinzia Sartini Blum and Lara Trubowitz

Tapestry Weaver, The. Anson G. Chester. ITBLP

Tapping at the window, wind and rain—third watch by now. (LL) Third Month, Night of the Seventeenth, Written While Drunk. Lu Yu. CoBCP; SuSp, *tr. by* Burton Watson

Tapping in on your inner telephone life. Wire Tap. Miguel Algarin. PueRic

Tappster, fille another ale. Drinking Song. *Unknown.* MiEL

Taproot. Debra Kang Dean. NAPBL

Tapu. Arthur Rex Dugard Fairburn. PeNZ

Tar. C. K. Williams. VCAP

Tar paper cabin. Robert Spiess. HA

Tara, Mother / Lift me out by the hair. Kamalākānta Bhattācārya. SinGod, *tr. by* Rachel Fell McDermott

Tara, this is why I call upon You. Tārinī Debī. SinGod, *tr. by* Rachel Fell McDermott

Tara, what more are You planning? Rāmprasād Sen. SinGod, *tr. by* Rachel Fell McDermott

Tara, You are Cintamayi, Full of Thought. Kumār Śambhucandra Rāy. SinGod, *tr. by* Rachel Fell McDermott

Tarahumara Herbs. Alfonso Reyes. TCLAP, *tr. by* Samuel Beckett

Tarantella. Joseph Hilaire Pierre Belloc. FaBoCh; MoBrPo; OBMV; RB; UV

Tarantula, The. Reed Whittemore. CoAP

Tarantula of Love, The. William Fowler.
    "Upon this firthe, as on the sees of love." NePenScot

Tarantula or the Dance of Death. Anthony Hecht. CoAP

Tarantula rattling at the lily's foot, The. O Carib Isle! Hart Crane. APT-2; NoAM; PFTM-1; VGW

Tarantulas on the Lifebuoy. Thomas Lux. LCAP-2

Tardy Epithalamium for E. and N, A. Ralph Pomeroy. GLP

"Tare-an-ages, girls, which o'yees own the child?" (LL) Pharao's Daughter. Michael Moran. BIrV; ChIV-1

Targeted, I know that I can die. Drenching, The. Samuel Hazo. GraLe

Tarn, how delightful wind thy willowed waves. Verses Written at Montauban in France, 1750. Joseph Warton. ECEV

Tarpauling Jacket. *Unknown.* OxBoLi; PeVV

Tarred road simmered in a blue haze. The reservoir was dry, The. Judgement. Ciaran Carson. PBCIP

Tarred rope's end of life burnt through his hands, The. Sunken Sailor. Francis Claiborne Mason. YaYoPo

Tarry a moment, happy feet. Statues, The. Laurence Binyon. OBEV

Tarry Flynn. Patrick Kavanagh. ModIr

Tarry with Me, O My Saviour. Caroline Sprague Smith. AH

Tarrying moon still drips the redness of her blood, A. Midnight. Jacob [*or* Jakov] Fichman. MHP, *tr. by* Ruth Finer Mintz

Tartars led in chains. Prisoner, The. Po Chü-i. ChiP, *tr. by* Arthur Waley

Tartars make their home on saddle horses, The. Song of the Radiant Lady, Replying to a Poem by Wang Chieh-fu. Ou-yang Hsiu. SuSp, *tr. by* Irving Y. Lo

Tartarus. Oliver Wendell Holmes. NCAP

Tarts, The. Mother Goose. LB; OxNR; ReMoGo

Tarye no lenger; toward thyn herytage. Vox Ultima Crucis. John Lydgate. OBEV

Tarzan. Jaime Manrique. WiU

Tashkent Breaks into Bloom. Anna Andreyevna Akhmatova. BoWoP, *tr. by* Richard McKane

Tashlikh. Gerald Stern. TaR

Task, A. Czeslaw Milosz. AF, *tr. by* Czeslaw Milosz

Task, The. William Cowper.
  "Come evening once again, season of peace." NAEL-6v1; NAEL-7v1
  Garden, The.
    "I was a stricken deer, that left the herd." NAEL-5v1; NAEL-6v1; NAEL-7v1; PAI
    ("Morning finds the self-sequestr'd man, The.") PoE
    Stricken Deer, The. NAEL-5v1; NAEL-6v1; NAEL-7v1; PAI
  Sofa, The.
    ("And only there, please highly for their sake.") (LL) NOEC
    Crazy Kate. NAEL-5v1; NAEL-6v1; NAEL-7v1
    Landscape Described, A. NAEL-5v1; NAEL-6v1; NAEL-7v1
  Time-piece, The.
    Against Slavery. NOEC
    Effeminate Englishmen. ECEV
  "Where now the vital energy that moved." NPeEn
  Winter Evening, The.
    Arrival of the Mail. ECEV
    "Just when our drawing-rooms begin to blaze." NOEC; NPeEn; NoP-4
    Reading the Newspaper. ECEV
  Winter Evening, The: A Brown Study. NAEL-6v1; NAEL-7v1
  Winter Morning Walk, The.
    Frosty Morning, A. NOEC
    "Great princes have great playthings. Some have played." FaBoWar
  Winter Walk at Noon, The. NPeEn
    "Night was winter in his roughest mood, The." FHYEP

Task, The. William Cowper. OBGa *Fr.* Task, The.
  "Improvement too, the idol of the age." OBGasC
  "Who loves a garden, loves a greenhouse too." OBGa

Task, The. Denise Levertov. InvLi

Task, The. Subhash Mukhopadhyay. OMIP, *tr. by* Pritish Nandy

Task, The. Ruth Pitter. MoBrPo

Task it was to found the Roman people. (LL) Virgil [*or* Vergil]. NAWM-5v1; NAWM-7v1, *tr. by* Robert Fitzgerald *Fr.* Aeneid [*or* Eneados, *Aeneis*], The.

Task[e] is easier to destroy, than [*or* then] build, The. (LL) Upon His Majesty's [*or* Majesties] Repairing of Paul's. Edmund Waller. BASC; PBRV

Tasmania. Vivian Smith. NOBAu

Tasmanian Scenes. Louisa Meredith. NOBAu

Tassajara, 1969. Diane Di Prima. BB

Taste. Jennifer Maiden. BMAP

Taste. Christopher Smart. ChIV-1; NOCV *Fr.* Hymns for the Amusement of Children.

Taste, The. George Oppen. NNaP *Fr.* Some San Francisco Poems.

Taste for Tomorrow. Jayanta Mahapatra. VCWP

Taste its terror on my hands. (LL) Trout, The. John Montague. ModIr; NoP-4; PBCIP; PNI; PoE

Taste of blood comes, A. Obsession. Léon Damas. NegPo, *tr. by* Ellen Conroy Kennedy

Taste of October on your shoulders, The. To Poetry. Carlos Pellicer. TCLAP, *tr. by* Alexandra Migoya

Taste of pomegranate, The. Persephone. Ziporah Hildebrandt. HW

Taste of soul's desire, The. (LL) God Give to Men. Arna Bontemps. BPo; ColAP

Taste of Wild Cherry, The. Chris Forhan. NAPBL

Tasted, the green cypress is bitter. Empty Purse. Tu Fu. CrYelRi, *tr. by* Sam Hamill

Tasty 'Tanjarines' of Inhambane, The. José Craveirinha. PeSAV, *tr. by* Michael Wolfers

Tatale Swine. Kojo Laing. HBAPE

Tatale there rounding the fat woman that fried it. Tatale Swine. Kojo Laing. HBAPE

Tatar anguish, anguish of the Volga. Tatar Anguish. Anna Barkova. ARWW, *tr. by* Catriona Kelly

Tatar chief forced me to become his wife, A. Ts'ai Yen. WPOW *Fr.* Eighteen Verses Sung to a Tatar Reed Whistle.

Tatar Songs. *Unknown.* EaWin, *tr. by* W. S. Merwin

Tato—Reading at the Nuyorican Poets' Cafe. Miguel Algarin. PmAP

Tattered Kaddish. Adrienne Rich. ColAP

Tattered rain. Wet Pain . . . Tread with Care. Leseko Rampolekeng. NAfrP

Tattered Sack, The. Devara Dasimayya. WoPoe, *tr. by* A. K. Ramanujan

Tattering of rain and then the regin, A. Darkling Summer, Ominous Dusk, Rumorous Rain. Delmore Schwartz. APT-2

Tattle. Godfrey Turner. NOBL

Tatton Parachute Training School. *Unknown.* FaBoWar

Tattoo, The. Muhammad Al-Maghut. MAP, *tr.* by John Heath-Stubbs and May Jayyusi

Tattoo, The. Peter Finch. TCAWP

Tattoo, The. Ania Walwicz. BMAP

Tattoo, Corazon: Ritchie Valens, 1959. David Wojahn. PBCAP *Fr.* Mystery Train: A Sequence.

Tattoo'd man, The. Alan Pizzarelli. HA

Tattoo #47, "Happy Dragon." Paul Allen. ReTh

Tattooed Man, The. Robert Earl Hayden. NoAM

Tattooed on your arm. (LL) I Remember Haifa Being Lovely But. Lyn Lifshin. GotH; UnSA

Tattoos. J. D. McClatchy. BAP-01

Tattoos. Charles Wright. BodElec; HCAP

Taught early that his mother's skin was the sign of error. Mr. Z. M. Carl Holman. SoSe-8

Taurean reaper of the wild apple field. Tattered Kaddish. Adrienne Rich. ColAP

Tauromancy at Memphis. Diogenes Laertius. GrAn, *tr.* by Dudley Fitts

Taut sadness, like old heroes he had imagined. (LL) State Funeral. Thomas McCarthy. CIP-2; ModIr

Tavern, The. Edwin Arlington Robinson. NCAP

Tavern guitar playing a *jota* today. Tavern Guitar Playing a *Jota* Today. Antonio Machado Ruiz. SpanPo, *tr.* by Charles Guenther

Tavern is closed for the night, The. Closed Door, The. Muhammad Al-Faituri [*or* Al-Fituri *or* Al-Fayturi]. MAP, *tr.* by Sargon Boulus and Peter Porter

Tawny are the leaves turned but they still hold. Antique Harvesters. John Crowe Ransom. MoAmPo; OxBA

Tawny-black sky-scurries. David Jones. OBWVE *Fr.* Sleeping Lord, The.

Taxi, The. Amy Lowell. BoWoP; LW; MoAmPo

Taxi-cab whore out at Iver, A. Limerick. Victor Gray. NOBL; PeLi

Taxi Suite. Lew Welch.

After Anacreon. NeAP; PoM

("When I drive cab / I am moved by strange whistles and wear a hat.") BB

Taxidermist, A. Jean Follain. BLT

Taxidermist at the Zoo, The. Ruth Anderson Barnett. UrbNat

Taxidermist is sitting / before the russet breasts, A. Taxidermist, A. Jean Follain. BLT

Taxing. Eileen Myles. BodElec

Taxis, The. Louis MacNeice. EmeKit; NPeEn; OxBTC; PNI

Taxman. George Mackay Brown. NePenScot

Taxonomy. Joy Katz. NeAmPo

Tay Bridge Disaster, The. William McGonagall. VerBaPo

"Beautiful Railway Bridge of the Silv'ry Tay!" UV

Tayis Bank. *Unknown.* FaBoVe

Taylor's Arithmetic from One to Twelve. John Taylor.

"10 Commandments, are the Law Divine." ChIV-1

Tchaikowsky (And Other Russians). Kurt Weill. ReLy

Tchirek River. Tchirek Song (Northern Yueh-Fu). *Unknown.* ChinPo, *tr.* by Yip Wai-lim

Tchirek Song (Northern Yueh-Fu). *Unknown.* ChinPo, *tr.* by Yip Wai-lim

Te Atairangikaahu. Kingi M. Ihaka. PeNZ, *tr.* by Kingi M. Ihaka

Te Deum. Charles Reznikoff. ChIV-1; TrJP

Te Deum, The. *Unknown.* AWP, *tr.* by John Dryden

Te Kaha. Rachel McAlpine. PeNZ

Te Martyrum Candidatus. Lionel Pigot Johnson. OBMV

Te Whetu Plains. Edward Tregear. PeNZ, *tr.* by Alan Myers

Te whit! Te whoo! Te whit! To whit! (LL) Sweet Suffolk Owl. *Unknown.* EBEV; NPeEn

Tea. Ch'u Ch'uang I. OHMPC, *tr.* by Kenneth Rexroth

Tea. Sean Dunne. ModIr *Fr.* Sydney Place.

Tea at the Magdalene. Clara Silva. TANSG, *tr.* by Celeste Kostopulos-Cooperman

Tea at the Palaz of Hoon. Wallace Stevens. APT-1; AmFaPo; FaBoMo; WoPoe

Tea bowls, incense burning—a good feeling here! Wen Cheng-ming. CoBLCP *Fr.* Chung-i Temple, The.

Tea Dance. Wayne Koestenbaum. WiU

Tea flowers. Buson. EH, *tr.* by Robert Hass

Tea for the Emperor arrives on a tray. Princess Parade. Sarah Gorham. FFC

Tea for Two. Irving Caesar. ReLy

Tea for two / And two for tea. W. D. Snodgrass. BodElec *Fr.* Führer Bunker, The.

Tea for Two, before the War. No, No, Nanette. K. Schippers. TuT, *tr.* by Dennis O'Driscoll

Tea garden shows you how, A. Bridge. A. R. Ammons. CoAP; NAAL-2v2

Tea is one, wine another, women third. Women. Trần Tế Xu'o'ng. EaWin; WoPoe, *tr.* by W. S. Merwin and Nguyen Ngoc Bich

Tea-kettle bubbled, the tea things were set, The. Poem on the Supposition of an Advertisement, A; Appearing in a Morning Paper, of the Publication of a Volume of Poems, by a Servant-Maid. Elizabeth Hands. ECWP

Tea-kettle / Hooked in mid-air. Hakuin. ZenPo, *tr.* by Takashi Ikemoto and Lucien Stryk

Tea Making. Antoinette Scudder. PoBW

Tea Mind. Chase Twichell. ExTi

Tea Party. Nancy Vieira Couto. PBCAP

Tea Party, The. Jean Earle. TCAWP

Tea party at Le Cannet, The. Bonnard; a Novel. Richard Howard. CoAP

Tea Poems. George Mackay Brown. OxBC

Tea-rose tea-gown, etc., The. Ezra Pound. ColAP; HarvBoo; MoAmPo; NOBE *Fr.* Hugh Selwyn Mauberley (Life and Contacts).

Tea Shop, The. Ezra Pound. HeIP-4

Tea with the Poets. Sir John Betjeman. PeLV

Teach me, if you can,—forgetfulness! Love's Last Lesson. Letitia [*or* Laetitia] Elizabeth Landon. RWP

Teach me, my God and King. Elixir [*or* Elixer], The. George Herbert. BASC; ESCV; EnlH; FaBoCh; GeHe; NOSC; NoP-4; SacPr

Teach Me Tonight. Sammy Cahn. ReLy

Teach the free man how to praise. (LL) W. H. Auden. AmFaPo; HAP; HeIP-4; MakPoe; MoBrPo; NAEL-6v2; NIL-7; NOBE; NPeEn; NoAM; NoP-4; OxAEP-2; OxBTC; PAI; TFi; TRP; UnPo; WeW-3

Teach the kings sonne, who kings hym self shalbe. Bible, *O.T.* EMWP *Fr.* Psalms.

Teach Us to Mark This, God. Franz Werfel. TrJP, *tr.* by Jacob Sloan

Teach Us to Number Our Days. Rita Dove. ESEAA; NoAM

Teacher, Jimmie's toe is bleedin' Johnny's Pet Superstition. Clara Ann Thompson. CBWP-2

Teacher of tots at Uttoxeter, A. Limerick. Kate McPower. PeLi

Teacher Taught Me, A. Anna Walters. VoR

Teachers of culture hate science but the teachers of science do not hate culture, The. Karl Shapiro. BodElec *Fr.* Bourgeois Poet, The.

Teachers taught her, The. Gertrude Stein. NOxBChV

Teaches the South it is not paradise. (LL) Grasse: The Olive Trees. Richard Wilbur. NAAL-2v2; NOBA; NoAM

Teaching German Literature. Vincent Buckley. OBCoV

Teaching Numbers. Gary Soto. NOxBChV

Teaching Poetry at Votech High, Santa Fe, the Week John Lennon Was Shot. Paula Gunn Allen. ReTh

Teaching the Ape to Write. James Tate. BLT

Teaching the Children. Myra Sklarew. CRP

Teahouse at Hoshioka, A. Liu E. CoBLCP, *tr.* by Jonathan Chaves

Team, The. Suzanne Gardinier. CBAP

Team of Budweiser horses, The. 8-Ball at the Twilite. David Baker. ReTh

Teams, The. Henry Lawson. CBAP

Teamster's Farewell, A. Carl Sandburg. IllVoic

Tear. Linda Hogan. ExTi

Tear. Thomas Kinsella. ModIr; NOIV; NoP-4; OxBEV

Tear, The. Martin Sorescu. VCWP, *tr.* by Seamus Heaney and Joana Russell-Gebbett

Teares I could sonne have brought unto this hearse. Upon a Command to Write on My Father. Gertrude Aston Thimelby. EMWP

Tearing the hairy leeches from his throat. (LL) Thomas Lovell Beddoes. NOBVV; NPeEn; OxBEV; RB *Fr.* Last Man, The.

Tearing Up the Tracks. Christopher Bursk. GM

Tears. Al-Khansa. AWP, *tr.* by R. A. Nicholson

Tears. Elizabeth Barrett Browning. WPE

Tears. Buson. EH, *tr.* by Robert Hass

Tears. "Owen Meredith." EBVV *Fr.* Glenaveril.

Tears. Lizette Woodworth Reese. MoAmPo

Tears. Alena Synková. INSAB

Tears. Edward Thomas. GTBS-P; NAEL-5v2; NAEL-6v2

Tears. *Unknown. See* Weep [*or* Weepe] You No More [Sad Fountains]

Tears. Walt Whitman. APN-1

Tears and love for the gray. (LL) Blue and the Gray, The. Francis Miles Finch. APN-2; CBCWP

Tears at evening?—not infrequent. Inscribed on a Plantain Leaf To Show to a Certain Person. Liu Ling-hsien. CoBCP, *tr.* by Burton Watson

Tears beneath the earth, Heliodora, I give. Meleager. HePo *Fr.* Epigrams.

Tears, ere thy death, for many a one I shed. Tears. Al-Khansa. AWP, *tr.* by R. A. Nicholson

Tears fall in my heart. Tears Fall in My Heart. Paul Verlaine. WoPoe, *tr.* by David Curzon

Tears fall within mine heart. Il Pleut Doucement sur la Ville. Paul Verlaine. AWP, *tr.* by Ernest Dowson

Tears, idle tears, I know not what they mean. Tennyson. AWP; CABP; EBVV; GTBS-P; HAP; NAEL-5v2; NAEL-6v2; NIL-7; NIP-4; NOBE;

NoP-4; OxAEP-2; OxBEV; PoE; PoPoPo; SCGP; TFi; TreFP; UnPo   *Fr.* Princess, The.

Tears in Sleep. Louise Bogan. MakPoe

Tears like a lover wept. (LL) In the Wilderness. Robert Graves. ChIV-2; MoBrPo

Tears of an Affectionate Shepherd Sick for Love, The. Richard Barnfield [*or* Barnefield]. *See* Affectionate Shepherd, The

Tears of Fancy, The. Thomas Watson.
   Go Idle Lines. Son
   I Saw the Object. Son

Tears of Scotland, The. Tobias Smollett. ECEV; NOEC

Tears of the Fatherland, Anno Domini 1636. Andreas Gryphius. GePo, *tr.* by George C. Schoolfield

Tears of the widower, when he sees. Tennyson. CAGL; NAEL-6v2   *Fr.* In Memoriam A. H. H.

Tears of the World. Mu'tamid, King of Seville. AWP, *tr.* by Dulcie L. Smith

Tears! tears! tears! / In the night, in solitude, tears. Tears. Walt Whitman. APN-1

Tears, the firebursts and the vows, The. Cracked Looking Glass. Jean Garrigue. VCAP

Tears wet her gauze kerchief, she cannot sleep. Song of the Rear Palace. Po Chü-i. SuSp, *tr.* by Ronald C. Miao

Teasers, The. William Empson. HarvBoo; OxBTC

Teasing Hsiao-te, My Son. Huang T'ing-chien. SuSp, *tr.* by Michael E. Workman

Teasing Toads, The. Michael Rosen. OTCP

Teatro Amazonas, remnant, the. Talvikki Ansel. YaYoPo   *Fr.* In Fragments, In Streams.

Technical Supplement, A. Thomas Kinsella.
   "Blade licks out and acts, A." BiHa
   "Dark hall. Great green liquid windows, A." BiHa
   "How to put it . . . without offence." BiHa
   "It is hard to beat a good meal." CIP-2
   "Point, greatly enlarged, The." BiHa
   "Veteran smiled and let us pass through, A." BiHa
   "Vital spatterings. Excess." BiHa

Technicalities for Jack Spicer. Philip Whalen. PoM

Technologies. George Starbuck. YaYoPo

Technology of Spring, The. Lynn Emanuel. BodElec

Tecumseh. Charles Mair.
   "I love you better than I love my race." NOBC
   "There was a time on this fair continent." NOBC

Ted & marge had been married eight years. Wasp Sex Myth (Two). Anselm Hollo. PoM

Ted's Bar and Grill. Jim Daniels. ReTh

Ted's studio burnt down, with all his poems. Martial. WoPoe, *tr.* by William Matthews   *Fr.* Epigrams.

Teddy Bear, Teddy Bear. *Unknown.* NTCP

Tee. Reuben Jackson. UnSA

Teed Off. John Nelson. GeoH

Teen Drowns in Rehabilitation Camp Days Before 17th Birthday, Questions Persist. Gaylord Brewer. AmPoNex

Teen idols are the best boys on the block. Teen Idols. Dennis Cooper. WiU

Teenage Interplanetary Vixens Run Wild on Bikini Beach. Allison Joseph. NAPBL

Teenage plankton luminously twitch, A. (LL) Watching the Dance. James Merrill. NIL-7; NIP-4

Teeth. Spike Milligan. OPOU

Teeth. (LL) Teeth and Gums. Mother Goose. NTCP; OxNR; ReMoGo

Teeth and Gums. Mother Goose. NTCP; OxNR; ReMoGo

Teeth are bared, the mouth drawn tight, the face, The. Vera Inber. FaBoWar, *tr.* by Alexander Kaun and Dorothea Prall Radin   *Fr.* Pulkovo Meridian, The.

Teeth Mother Naked at Last, The. Robert Bly. NNaP3
   "But if one of those children came near that we have set / on fire." CDa

Teeth of clogs, carriage wheels, the hooves of horses. Walking in the Country outside T'ai-yüan on a Spring Day. Yang Chi. CoBLCP, *tr.* by Jonathan Chaves

Teeth of flowers, hair of dew. I'm Going to Sleep. Alfonsina Storni. TCLAP, *tr.* by Andrew Rosing

Teeth of flowers, hairnet of dew. I Am Going to Sleep (Suicide Poem). Alfonsina Storni. BoWoP, *tr.* by Aliki Barnstone and Willis Barnstone

Teeth sensitive to the sand. Basho. EH, *tr.* by Robert Hass

Teething. Tom Wayman. CDa

Teevo cheevo cheevio chee. Woodlark, The. Gerard Manley Hopkins. RB

Tefillin. Yona Volach. DTA, *tr.* by Aryeh Cohen and Miriyam Glazer

Teh. has six claims to fame: its numerous hotsprings. Sestina for the Ladies of Tehuántepec. Earle Birney. PeLV

TEHKARIHHOKEN! / Continue to listen! *Unknown.* APN-2   *Fr.* Ancient Rites of the Condoling Council.

Teisa, a Descriptive Poem of the River Tees, Its Towns and Antiquities. Anne Wilson.
   In Praise of Drainage. ECWP

Tel Aviv 1935. Leah Goldberg. FIT, *tr.* by Robert Friend

Tel Zaatar Was the Hill of Thyme. Fawaz Turki.
   "I leave the child to grow up by itself as a beggar from the killing." GraLe

Teleg River. Teleg Song. HSü Ling. ChiP, *tr.* by Arthur Waley

Teleg Song. HSü Ling. ChiP, *tr.* by Arthur Waley

Telegram. Milo De Angelis. NeIt, *tr.* by Lawrence Venuti

Telegrams of Tenderness for Sanaa. Abd al-Aziz Al-Maqalih. MAP, *tr.* by Lena Jayyusi and Christopher Middleton

Telegraph Wires. Ted Hughes. NPeEn

Telemachus with a Transistor. Ruth Dallas. PeNZ

Teleology. May Swenson. VCAP

Telephone, The. "Korney Chukovsky" [*or* Chukovskii]. TCRP, *tr.* by William Jay Smith

Telephone call ran out in the night and glittered over the countryside, A. Homewards. Tomas Tranströmer. WoPoe, *tr.* by Robin Fulton

Telephone Conversation. Wole Soyinka. NoP-4; PBMAP; PoetW; TTY

Telephone Directory. Harry Crosby. SPE

Telephone line goes cold, A. Farm on the Great Plains, The. William Stafford. HAP; VGW

Telephone poles, The. Crossing Kansas by Train. Donald Justice. AiP

Telephoning God. Gary Soto. PBCAP

Telephonist. Janet Frame. WPE

Telescope. Sydney Lea. RA

Telesphere, The. Charles Olson. BodElec   *Fr.* Maximus Poems, The.

Television aerials, Chinese characters. On Roofs of Terry Street. Douglas Dunn. NPeEn; OxBTC

Television as God. Tijan M. Sallah. NAfrP

Tell a wise person, or else keep silent. Holy Longing, The. Goethe. RaBo; WoPoe, *tr.* by Robert Bly

Tell all my mourners. Wake. Langston Hughes. OBAL; OBCoV

Tell, dear Aminta, now 'tis over. Close to Aminta, on the Loss of Her Lover. Sarah Dixon. ECWP

Tell Freedom. Peter Abrahams.
   Me, Colored. PBA

Tell her I love. Poems for My Daughter. Horace Gregory. MoAmPo

Tell Her So. Mrs. Henry Linden. CBWP-4

Tell Her So. *Unknown.* PoToHe

Tell her to find her purse. (LL) Ghost in the Martini, The. Anthony Hecht. DiPo; NoP-4; OxBC

Tell her we still expose our bottoms. Messages. Jack A. Mapanje. HBAPE

Tell Him, O Night. *Unknown.* AWP   *Fr.* Thousand and One Nights, The.

Tell Him So. J. A. Egerton. PWR

Tell him the tale is a lie! Learned Mistress, A. *Unknown.* OBMV, *tr.* by Frank O'Connor

Tell Me. Langston Hughes. APSN; SAmP

Tell me. Rāmprasād Sen. SinGod, *tr.* by Rachel Fell McDermott

Tell me. *Unknown.* WoPoe, *tr.* by Barbara Stoler Miller   *Fr.* Bhagavad-Gita, The.

"Tell me a story." Bedtime Story. Lilian Moore. NTCP

Tell Me a Story. Robert Penn Warren. FuPo; NAAL-5   *Fr.* Audubon: A Vision.

"Tell me a story, father, please." Natives of America, The. Ann Plato. BlSi; TCAPo

Tell Me About It. Ruth Padel. MFPA

Tell me about the good things. How Long Has Trane Been Gone. Joe Corrie. NAAAL

Tell me about the good things. How Long Has Trane Been Gone. Jayne Cortez. ISC

Tell me about yourself they. Word in Edgeways, A. Charles Tomlinson. CABP; NOBL

Tell Me Again. Nigâr Hanim. ItWoWo, *tr.* by Talat Sait Halman and Tâlat S. Halman

Tell me, before the ferryman's return. J. P. Clark Bekederemo. PBMAP   *Fr.* Reed in the Tide, A.

Tell me, can your arts cure this? (LL) Sent to the Master Physician, "Almond Orchard" Shih. Li K'ai-hsien. CoBLCP; ColAnChi, *tr.* by Jonathan Chaves

Tell me, daughter, my pretty daughter. Cossante. Pero Meogo. WoPoe, *tr.* by Yvor Winters

Tell me don't ask me. Down. George Minot. Unle

Tell me, draftsman of the desert. Osip Emilevich Mandelstam [*or* Mandelshtam]. TCRP   *Fr.* Ottave.

Tell me fair Nymph, who justly had design'd.   To Orabella, Marry'd to an Old Man.   Sarah Fyge Egerton.   EMWP

"Tell me, good dog, whose tomb you guard so well."   Tomb of Diogenes, The.   *Unknown.*   AWP, *tr.* by John Addington Symonds

Tell me, good Hobbinoll, what garres thee greete?   Edmund Spenser.   NAEL-5v1; NAEL-6v1; OBEV   *Fr.* Shepheardes [*or* Shepeards *or* Shepherd's] Calender, The.

Tell me herdsman for the sake of Pan.   Erucius [*or* Erycius] of Cyzicus.   GrAn

Tell me I'm beautiful, and bring me flowers.   Eleanor Brown.   NeBl

Tell me if ah seeing right.   Poetry Jump-Up.   John Agard.   NOxBChV

Tell me if I am not glad! (LL)   Lines for an Old Man.   T. S. Eliot.   FaBoTw; RB; RaBo

Tell me if it is too far for you.   Elegy for N. N.   Czeslaw Milosz.   BodElec, *tr.* by Larence Davis

Tell me, is love still a popular suggestion.   I'm a Stranger Here Myself.   Ogden Nash.   ReLy

Tell me, is the rose naked.   Pablo Neruda.   GifTon, *tr.* by William O'Daly   *Fr.* Book of Questions, The.

Tell me lies about Vietnam. (LL)   To Whom It May Concern.   Adrian Mitchell.   FaBoWar; OBWP

Tell me, men with wisdom gifted.   Hiraeth.   *Unknown.*   OBWVE, *tr.* by Aneirin Talfan Davies

Tell me, my heart, how wilt thou do.   Sir Arthur Gorges.   NoSic   *Fr.* Desportes.

Tell me, my patient friends, awaiters of messages.   Speech to a Crowd.   Archibald MacLeish.   MoAmPo

Tell me no more of constancy.   Against Constancy.   John Wilmot, 2d Earl of Rochester.   NOSC; OxAEP-1

Tell me no more of Minds embracing Minds.   No Platonic [*or* Platonique] Love.   William Cartwright.   BeJo; NOSC

Tell me no secret, friend.   Burden, The.   Francesca Yetunde Pereira.   PBA

Tell me not, friend, you are unkind.   Lucasta Replies to Lovelace.   Gilbert Keith Chesterton.   UV

Tell me not here, it needs not saying.   A. E. Housman.   GTBS-P; NOBE; NPeEn; NoAM; OxBEV; OxBTC; SCV

Tell me not in idle jingle.   Psalm of Marriage.   Phoebe Cary.   PWR

Tell me not in joyous numbers.   Stephen Crane.   OBAL

Tell me not, in mournful numbers.   Henry Wadsworth Longfellow.   AH; APN-1; AmFaPo; BRP; ITBLP; NAAL-2v1; NAAL-3; NAAL-5; OBCA; PWR; TAP; TCAPo   *Fr.* Psalm of Life, A.

Tell me not of a face that's fair.   Resolve, The.   Alexander Brome.   NOSC; OBEV

Tell me not, Sweet, I am unkind.   Lines Where Beauty Lingers.   Franklin Pierce Adams.   OBAL

Tell me not, Sweet, I am unkind[e].   To Lucasta, [on] Going to the War[re]s.   Richard Lovelace.   AWP; BASC; BeJo; CABP; CaPo; CavPo; ClHu; EnLoPo; FaBoWar; GTBS-P; HAP; InPK-6; MeLP; NAEL-5v1; NAEL-6v1; NAEL-7v1; NIL-7; NIP-4; NOBE; NOSC; NPeEn; NoP-4; OBEV; OBWP; OxAEP-1; OxBEV; OxBSP; PAI; PBRV; PoE; PoPoPo; PoRA; SCGP; SCV; TFi; UV; WeW-3

Tell me not what too well I know.   On Catullus.   Walter Savage Landor.   OBEV

Tell Me Now.   Wang Chi.   ChiP; FaBoCh, *tr.* by Arthur Waley

Tell me now in what hidden way is.   Ballad[e] of Dead Ladies.   François Villon.   AWP; CTC; OBVE; PoRA, *tr.* by Dante Gabriel Rossetti

'Tell me now, what should a man want."   Tell Me Now.   Wang Chi.   ChiP; FaBoCh, *tr.* by Arthur Waley

Tell me, O Octopus, I begs.   Octopus, The.   Ogden Nash.   RB

Tell me of thy heart's devotion.   Whisper Words of Love to Me.   Lizelia Augusta Jenkins Moorer.   CBWP-3

Tell me, O[h] tell, what kind[e] of thing is wit.   Ode: Of Wit.   Abraham Cowley.   BeJo; MeLP; NAEL-5v1; NAEL-6v1; NAEL-7v1; NOSC

Tell me, shepherd, tell me, pray.   Country Gods.   Cometas.   FaBoCh, *tr.* by T. F. Higham

Tell me, Syama.   Kamalākānta Bhattācārya.   SinGod, *tr.* by Rachel Fell McDermott

Tell me, tell me.   Do It Again.   George Gershwin.   ReLy

Tell me, tell me, smiling child.   Emily Jane Brontë.   NALW

Tell me, tell me, / Unknown stranger.   Galliass, The.   Walter De la Mare.   FaBoTw

Tell me the auld, auld story.   Parrot Cry, The.   Hugh MacDiarmid.   OxBS

Tell me the stories of wanting are flowering.   Promiscuity.   Lisa Fishman.   AmPoNex

Tell me, thou gentle shepherd swain.   Roundelay Between Two Shepherds, A.   Michael Drayton.   NoP-4

Tell me thou safest end of all our woe.   Anne Killigrew.   *See* Tell me thou[gh] safest end of all our woe

'Tell me, thou skilful shepherd's swain."   Michael Drayton.   AEP   *Fr.* Shepherd's Garland, The.

Tell me, thou Star, whose wings of light.   World's Wanderers, The.   Shelley.   TTTS; TreFP

Tell me thou[gh] safest end of all our woe.   On Death.   Anne Killigrew.   BoWoP; ChIV-1

Tell me / Was Venus more beautiful.   Venus Transiens.   Amy Lowell.   APT-1; NAAL-5; NALW

Tell me, what are you doing now, Mind.   Mahendranāth Bhattācārya.   SinGod, *tr.* by Rachel Fell McDermott

Tell me, what binds us to some meaning.   Sentimental Elegy, A.   Arkadii Dragomoschenko.   PFTM-2, *tr.* by Elena Balashova and Lyn Hejinian

Tell me / What can I do?   Kamalākānta Bhattācārya.   SinGod, *tr.* by Rachel Fell McDermott

Tell me what you're doing over here, John Gorham.   John Gorham.   Edwin Arlington Robinson.   MoAmPo

Tell me what you see in it.   Black PIne Tree in an Orange Light.   Sylvia Plath.   BodElec

Tell me whaur, in whit countrie.   Ballat o the Leddies o Langsyne.   François Villon.   OBVE; OxBEV, *tr.* by Tom Scott

Tell me, where doth Whiteness grow.   Whiteness, or Chastity.   Joseph Beaumont.   NOSC

Tell me where, in what country, where.   Ballade.   François Villon.   STV, *tr.* by John Frederick Nims

Tell me where is fancy [*or* Fancie] bred.   William Shakespeare.   NAEL-5v1; NoSic; SCGP; TFi   *Fr.* Merchant of Venice, The.

Tell me, where is your home?   Songs of Ch'ang-kan.   Ts'ui Hao.   CoBCP, *tr.* by Burton Watson

Tell me, why such a foul mood?   Demon in Paradise.   Minuchihri.   ArPe, *tr.* by Omar S. Pound

Tell Me, Wight in the Broom.   *Unknown.*   MiEL; NAEL-5v1; NAEL-6v1 (Sey me, wight in the broom.)   OHMEL

Tell me, woman, your parents, your name, your land. B. Calliteles.   Antipater of Sidon.   HePo   *Fr.* Epigrams.

Tell me, would you like to be my playmate?   Would You Like to Play?   Dezső Kosztolányi.   IQMS, *tr.* by Thomas Kabdebo

Tell me, ye registers of fate.   To the Same.   Charlotte MacCarthy.   PoBW

Tell me, you anti-saints, why glass.   Upon Fairford Windows.   Richard Corbet [*or* Corbett].   BeJo; NOSC

Tell me you Hate; and Flatter me no more.   To J. G.   "Ephelia."   NOSC

Tell me[e] no more how fair[e] she[e] is.   Sonnet.   Henry King, Bishop of Chichester.   EnLoPo; MeLP; OxBEV

Tell the beads of the chromosomes like a rosary.   George Oppen.   AF; APSN; APT-2

Tell the wind.   Small Sins.   Maram Masri.   PoArWo, *tr.* by Amal Amireh

Tell them, because our fathers lied. (LL)   Rudyard Kipling.   FaBoEE; FaBoTw; HarvBoo; NPeEn; PeFWW; WoPoe   *Fr.* Epitaphs of the War [1914–1918].

Tell Them I'm Struggling to Sing with Angels.   David Meltzer.   TaR

Tell them something you can live with.   Cole Porter.   Dionisio D. Martinez.   TouFir

Tell them that brave it most.   Lie, The.   Sir Walter Alexander Raleigh.   SacPr

Tell them what you like. Tell them.   Few Helpful Hints, A.   Peter Sirr.   ModIr

Tell this poem.   Daily Delights.   Hameed Sa'id.   MAP, *tr.* by Lena Jayyusi and Naomi Shihab Nye

Tell this to ladies: how a hero man.   Man without Sense of Direction.   John Crowe Ransom.   OxBA

Tell Us, Josephine.   Ron Padgett.   FTOS

Tell us, Professor.   Imre Madách.   IQMS, *tr.* by Iain MacLeod   *Fr.* Tragedy of Man.

Tell us, streaming lady.   James Liddy.   CIP-2   *Fr.* Love Songs of Corca Bascinn.

Tell Us, Ye Servants of the Lord.   William Staughton.   AH

Tell you a story—an' it's a fac'   Jack the Giant-Killer.   James Whitcomb Riley.   NOxBChV

Tell you? ha! who.   Charles Olson.   NoAM   *Fr.* Maximus Poems, The.

Tell your son, my son.   Message.   Renata Pallottini.   WPOW, *tr.* by Carlos Altschul and Monique Altschul

Telling, The.   Andrew Hudgins.   RA

Telling About Coyote.   Simon J. Ortiz.   STP

(Old Coyote. . . / "If he hadn't looked back")   PFTM-1

Telling Fortunes.   Alice Cary.   SWaP

Telling It.   Nancy Sullivan.   TAP

Telling My Feelings.   Yü Hsüan-chi.   BoWoP, *tr.* by Geoffrey Waters

Telling of the hardships and perils of the voyage. (LL)   Magi, The.   Ramon Guthrie.   GI; PoE

Telling Part, The.   Jackie Kay.   Prnts

Telling the Bees.   Lizette Woodworth Reese.   SWaP

Telling the Bees.   John Greenleaf Whittier.   APN-1; AWP; ColAP; NOBA; NoP-4; TAP; TCAPo

Telling us this is home no more. (LL)　Red Hills of Home.　Chenjerai Hove. HBAPE; NAfrP

Telltale tit.　You Worthless.　*Unknown.*　FaBoVe

Telluric and Magnetic.　César Vallejo.　PFTM-1

Telyric.　Andrei Codrescu.　PmAP

Temeraire, The.　Herman Melville.　APN-2; FaBoWar
　(Gloomy hulls, in armor grim, The.)　GS; NCAP

Temper.　*Unknown.*　PoToHe

Temper (1), The.　George Herbert.　ESCV; GeHe; NOCV
　(How should I praise thee, Lord! how should my rhymes.)　FSCP; NoP-4
　(Temper (I), The.)　NoP-4

Temper (2), The.　George Herbert.　GeHe

Temper my (I), The.　George Herbert.　*See* Temper (1), The

Temper my spirit, O Lord.　Passionate Sword, The.　Jean Starr Untermeyer. TrJP

Temperament.　Martial.　AWP, *tr. by* Joseph Addison

Temperament is related to physique.　Elaine Randell.　Oth　*Fr.* Snoad Hill Poems, The.

Temperaments, The.　Ezra Pound.　BoLoP; NOBA; NoAM; OBCoV; PAI

Temperance Billiards Rooms, The.　P. J. Kavanagh.　OxBTC

Temperature is zero below, The.　Glassworks.　Margit Mikes.　IQMS, *tr. by* Suzanne K. Walther

Tempered, annealed, the hard essence of autumn metals.　Needle and Thread. Pan Chao.　WPOW; WoPoe, *tr. by* Richard Mather and Rob Swigart

Tempered, annealed, the hard essence of autumn metals.　Needle and Thread. Pan Zhao.　WPoS, *tr. by* Richard Mather

Tempest.　Theodore H. Banks, Jr.　YaYoPo

Tempest.　Sekeena Shaben.　PoArWo

Tempest, The.　William Shakespeare.
　Ariel's Song: "Come unto these yellow sands"　CTC; FaBoCh; NOBE; NOSC; NPeEn; NoSic; OBEV; SCGP; SoSe-8; TFi; TTTS
　"Where should this Musick be? I th'aire, or th'earth?"　NPeEn
　Ariel's Song: "Where the bee sucks, there suck I"　NOBE
　(Where the Bee Sucks, There Suck I.)　AWP; CTC; NAEL-5v1; NAEL-6v1; NoP-4; NoSic; OBEV; OxBSP; SCGP; TFi; TTTS
　"Be cheerful, sir:"　EnlH
　"Be not afeard: the isle is full of noises."　OxAEP-1; RB
　"Come unto these yellow sands."　CTC; FaBoCh; NOBE; NOSC; NPeEn; NoSic; OBEV; SCGP; SoSe-8; TFi; TTTS
　"Dost thou forget."　OxAEP-1
　Epilogue.　RB; UV
　Epilogue: "Now my charms are all o'erthrown."　CTC
　Full Fathom Five.　AWP; ClHu; EBEV; FaBoCh; HAP; InPK-6; NAEL-5v1; NAEL-6v1; NoP-4; NoSic; OBEV; OxBEV; OxBSP; PoE; PoPoPo; PoRA; TFi
　"Hast thou, spirit."　OxAEP-1
　Magic.　AWP; EBEV; OxAEP-1; SCV
　"Master, the swabber, the boatswain and I, The."　NOBL; OxBSP
　"Now my charms are all o'erthrown."　CTC
　"Our revels now are ended. These our actors."　RB; UV
　(Sea Dirge, A.)　GTBS-P
　(Sea Song, A.)　NBLV; OBCoV; PeLV
　Song: "Master, the swabber, the boatswain and I, The."　NOBL; OxBSP
　To Dream Again.　OxAEP-1; RB
　"Ye elves of hill(s), brooks, standing lakes, and groves."　AWP; EBEV; OxAEP-1; SCV
　("You doe looke (my son) in a mov'd sort.")　OxBEV

Tempest, The.　William Jay Smith.　MoAmPo

Tempest, The.　Henry Vaughan.　ESCV

Tempest, The.　Marya Alexandrovna Zaturenska.　MoAmPo

Tempest on the plain of Lir.　Storm at Sea.　Rumann, Son of Colman. WoPoe, *tr. by* Frank O'Connor

Tempests pass through the air, as they pile up cloudbank on, The.　Yearning for Winter.　Karl Wilhelm Ramler.　GePo, *tr. by* George C. Schoolfield

Temple, A.　Kenneth Patchen.　SPE

Temple, The.　Robert Herrick.　CaPo

Temple, The.　Po Chü-i.　ChiP; OBMV, *tr. by* Arthur Waley

Temple, The.　Charles Hubert Sisson.　OxBTC

Temple bell / A cloud of cherry flowers.　Basho.　ZenPo, *tr. by* Takashi Ikemoto and Lucien Stryk

Temple bell stops, The.　Basho.　WoPoe, *tr. by* Robert Bly

Temple City Blvd. and Ellis Ln.　Carol Lem.　GeoHom

Temple in / Deep winter grove.　Tan Taigi.　ZenPo, *tr. by* Takashi Ikemoto and Lucien Stryk

Temple Near Quang Tri, Not on the Map.　Bruce Weigl.　CDa

Temple of Artemis at Ephesos, The.　Antipater of Thessalonica.　GrAn, *tr. by* Tony Harrison

Temple of Bequeathed Love, The.　Po Chü-i.　CoBCP, *tr. by* Burton Watson

Temple of Chastity, The.　Mary Robinson.　CenSon; RWP

Temple of Eternal Light.　Muso Soseki.　EaWin, *tr. by* W. S. Merwin

Temple of Hsiang Yü, The.　Li Shan-fu.　SuSp, *tr. by* Irving Y. Lo

Temple of Mars, The.　Geoffrey Chaucer.　NPeEn　*Fr.* Canterbury Tales, The.

Temple of the Animals, The.　Robert Duncan.　NOBA

Temple of the Ocean of Awakening.　Shen Chou.　CoBLCP, *tr. by* Jonathan Chaves

Temple of the Orchid Fragrance Goddess.　Li Ho.　SuSp, *tr. by* Michael Fish

Temple of Venus, The.　Soame Jenyns.　NOEC

Temples of Mount T'ai greeted the sun in the east, The.　Reading the Annals of Emperor Wu of the Han Dynasty.　Wu Wei-yeh.　CoBLCP, *tr. by* Jonathan Chaves

Tempora Mutantur.　James Russell Lowell.　HAP

Temporal.　George Jonas.　NOBC

Temporall Goods.　Robert Herrick.　SacPr

Temporarily in Oxford.　Anne Stevenson.　NoP-4

Temporary City.　Nijole Miliauskaite.　VCWP, *tr. by* Jonas Zdanys

Temporary Heart.　Michael Hannon.　GeoHom

Temporary Language, A.　Larry Eigner.　PmAP

Temporary Situation, A.　David St. John.　BodElec

Temps a Laissié, Le.　Charles, Duc d' Orléans.　WoPoe, *tr. by* Stanley Burnshaw

Tempt Me No More.　Cecil Day Lewis.　MoBrPo; OBMV　*Fr.* Magnetic Mountain, The.

Temptation.　Salwa Al-Neimi.　PoArWo, *tr. by* Subhi Hadidi and Nathalie Handal

Temptation.　Nina Cassian.　AF, *tr. by* Brenda Walker

Temptation.　Arthur Hugh Clough.　PeLV　*Fr.* Dipsychus [and the Spirit].

Temptation.　Robert Herrick.　SacPr

Temptation.　Czeslaw Milosz.　GI

Temptation, The.　Nicole Brossard.　PFTM-2, *tr. by* Barbara Godard　*Fr.* Barbizon, The.

Temptation and Fall of Man, The.　Caedmon.　AnOE, *tr. by* C. W. Kennedy　*Fr.* Genesis.

Temptation of Eve, The.　John Milton.　EBNV　*Fr.* Paradise Lost.

Temptations of Saint Anthony, The.　Phyllis McGinley.　OxBSP

Temptations of St. Antony by His Housekeeper.　Elizabeth Smither.　PeNZ

Temptations still nest in it like basilisks.　Dead Hand.　W. S. Merwin.　InPK-6

Tempted by the Classical on Returning from the Store at Twenty Below Zero. Sydney Lea.　SwNoth

Tempter Disarmed, The.　John Milton.　NOSC　*Fr.* Paradise Lost.

Temujin Becomes Chingis Khan.　*Unknown.*　WoPoe, *tr. by* Paul Kahn　*Fr.* Secret History of the Mongols, The.

Ten bloody years with this quill lying.　Invocation.　Valentin Iremonger.　BIrV

Ten Cents a Dance.　Richard Rodgers.　ReLy

Ten comawndementis I haue broke.　All Ten Commandments I Have Broken. *Unknown.*　SacPr

Ten commandments are between us.　Magdalene.　Marina Ivanovna Tsvetayeva [*or* Tsvetaeva].　GI, *tr. by* Michael M. Naydan

10 Commandments, are the Law Divine.　John Taylor.　ChIV-1　*Fr.* Taylor's Arithmetic from One to Twelve.

Ten Commandments, Seven Deadly Sins, and Five Wits.　*Unknown.*　FaBoEE; MiEL

Ten dancers glide.　Ballad of the Ten Casino Dancers.　Cecília Meireles. BoWoP; TCLAP, *tr. by* James Merrill

Ten Days Leave.　W. D. Snodgrass.　MoAmPo; UnPo

Ten days of wind and rain, depressing darkness!　T'ang Yin.　CoBLCP　*Fr.* Rainstorm Has Dragged On for Ten Days Now.

10 Dead Friends.　Dennis Cooper.　WiU

Ten Definitions of Poetry.　Carl Sandburg.　MoAmPo
　(Poetry is the opening and closing of a door, leaving those who look through to guess about what is seen during a moment.) (LL)　MoAmPo

Ten frozen parsnips hanging in the weather. (LL)　Winter Remembered.　John Crowe Ransom.　HAP; NOBA; OxBA; UnPo; VGW

Ten fussy days running this temple all red tape.　Stephen Berg.　GifTon

Ten heads and twenty hearts! so that this me.　Perhaps.　Sydney Thompson Dobell.　NOBVV

Ten holy nights / Even tea.　Buson.　ZenPo, *tr. by* Takashi Ikemoto and Lucien Stryk

Ten, I kept saying, *I'm only ten.* (LL)　Flash Cards.　Rita Dove.　ESEAA; LoL

Ten ii.　Laurie Duggan.　BMAP

Ten kinds of wolf are gone and twelve of rat.　Names.　William Matthews. PoCoUp

Ten Lines.　Emile Roumer.　NegPo, *tr. by* Ellen Conroy Kennedy

Ten Little Injuns.　Septimus Winner.　OBAL

Ten little nigger boys went out to dine.　*Unknown.*　OxNR

Ten Little Rembrandts.　Theodore Weiss.　NoAM

Ten men will dress in white, The. Hunters of the Deer, The. Dale Zieroth. NOBC

Ten Million Flames of Los Angeles, The. Amy Uyematsu. GeoHom

Ten Mills. Robert Frost.
  Hardship of Accounting, The. FaBoCh; OBAL
  In Divés' Dive. GI; VGW
  Span of Life, The. SoSe-8
  Wrights' Biplane, The. WeW-3

Ten Miscellaneous Poems Written as a Member of the Imperial Retinue on an Inspection Tour of the Frontier—We Reached Hsüan-fu and Then Returned. Yang Shih-ch'i.
  "Forty *li* through Chü-yang Pass." CoBLCP

Ten months after Florimel happen'd to wed. Another True Maid. Matthew Prior. FaBoEE

Ten New Commandments. Robert Greacen. PeLV

Ten O'Clock Scholar, [The]. Mother Goose. LB; OxNR; ReMoGo

Ten o'clock train to New York, The. Winter. Ruth Stone. BoWoP

10:X:57, 45 Years Since the Fall of the Ch'ing Dynasty. Philip Whalen. PoM
  (Forty-five Years Since the Fall of the Ch'ing Dynasty). NeAP

Ten out of ten means you are dead. (LL) Death Is a Matter of Mathematics. Barry Amiel. FaBoWar; PoWW

Ten Patients, and Another. Rafael Campo.
  Jane Doe #2. AmPoNex; WiU
  Kelly. WiU
  Manuel. WiU

Ten Poems on Almond Blossoms. K'ang Hai.
  "When I have chanted my new poems." CoBLCP

Ten Poems on the Tuan-yang Festival. Yang Chi.
  Pitch-Ball. CoBLCP, *tr.* by Jonathan Chaves

Ten Poems Recording Things that Happened at the Ye. Liu K'o-chuang.
  From "Ten Poems Recording Things that Happened at the Year's End" CoBCP

Ten poems written in one month. Valerio Magrelli. NeIt

Ten rains, and then snow, then more snow, then. Ice Skating. Greg Kuzma. InvLad

Ten Scenes at the Hsiao Family Stone Ridge. Yang Shih-ch'i. CoBLCP, *tr.* by Jonathan Chaves

Ten Seconds. Rohan B. Preston. WaCA

Ten Short Poems. Juan Ramón Jiménez.
  "Dawn brings with it, The." SpanPo; WoPoe, *tr.* by James Wright
  "To the bridge of love." SpanPo; WoPoe, *tr.* by James Wright

Ten Songs. W. H. Auden.
  "Carry her over the water." FaBoTw; RB
  Refugee Blues. AmFaPo; HP; OxAEP-2

Ten suns rise in the east, The. Ten Suns Rise in the East, The. Juan Chi. WoPoe, *tr.* by Graham Hartill and Wu Fusheng

10:30. A long and thin. Breathless Storm. Michael Burkard. BodElec

10.30 AM Mass, June 16, 1985. Paul Durcan. BiHa; CIP-2

Ten thousand almond trees by the riverbank. Song of Spring Journeying. Wang Ya. SuSp, *tr.* by Irving Y. Lo

Ten thousand flakes about my window blow. Walter Savage Landor. FaBoEE

Ten Thousand Flowers in Spring, the Moon in Autumn. Wu-Men. EnlH, *tr.* by Stephen Mitchell

Ten thousand pains. (LL) Stormy Night in Autumn. Chu Shu-chen. BoWoP; OHPC, *tr.* by Kenneth Rexroth

Ten Thousand Sutras. Sam Hamill. ErotSp

Ten thousand things are heard when born. On Sound. Wei Ying-wu. SuSp, *tr.* by Irving Y. Lo

Ten thousand things wound my heart when you're before my eyes. In Illness, Dismissing My Singing Girl. Ssu-k'ung Shu. ColAnChi, *tr.* by Burton Watson

Ten thousand years. (LL) Above Pate Valley. Gary Snyder. CoAP; CoAmPo; GeoHom; LCAP-2; NoP-4; TRP

Ten to One to No. Joyce Mansour. SurWo, *tr.* by Mary Beach

Ten Types of Hospital Visitor. Charles Causley. OxBC

Ten Years Ago. Alaric Alexander Watts. TreFP

Ten years ago, beneath the Hotel Astoria. Annus Mirabilis 1989. Elaine Feinstein. HP

Ten years ago as I was a visitor at the wine jar. Song of Picking Mulberry. Ou-yang Hsiu. CoBCP, *tr.* by Burton Watson

Ten years ago it seemed impossible. In Progress. Christina Georgina Rossetti. BoWoP; NAEL-5v2; NAEL-6v2; WPE

Ten years ago you died. Remembering My Wife. Su Tung-p'o (Su Shih). ErotSp, *tr.* by Sam Hamill

Ten Years and More. Miriam Waddington. NOBC

Ten years—dead and living dim and draw apart. Tune: Song of River City. Su Tung-p'o (Su Shih). CoBCP, *tr.* by Burton Watson

Ten years it took. Ten Years It Took. Song Sun. WoPoe, *tr.* by Virginia Olsen Baron and Chung Seuk Park

Ten years of my life, spent at the window or beneath the lamp. Song of Cursive Calligraphy. Hsieh Chin. CoBLCP; ColAnChi, *tr.* by Jonathan Chaves

Ten years of whorehouse joy I'm alone now in the mountains. Ikkyu Sojun. WoPoe, *tr.* by Stephen Berg *Fr.* Four Poems.

Ten years old with my father. Trails. Patrick Williams. PNI

Ten years older in an hour. In the Ward. Robert Lowell. NAAL-2v2

Ten years since we were married, since we stood. Long Finish. Paul Muldoon. HarvBoo

Ten years together without yet a cloud. Firelight. Edwin Arlington Robinson. NoAM

Tenancy, The. Mary Gilmore. CBAP

Tenant at Number 9. John Blight. CBAP

Tenant sits upon his case, The. Kreutzer Sonata, A. "Sasha Chorny" [or Chiornyi]. TCRP, *tr.* by Bernard Meares

Tended by Faustina. Faustina, or Rock Roses. Elizabeth Bishop. FaBoMo

Tender, and averse to killing. (LL) Ode: To Miss Margaret Pulteney. Ambrose Philips. OxAEP-1; UV

Tender Buttons. Gertrude Stein.
  Cloth, A. TCAPo
  Colored Hats. TTTS
  Dog, A. TTTS
  Frightful Release, A. TCAPo
  More. TCAPo
  Mounted Umbrella, A. TCAPo
  New Cup and Saucer, A. TTTS
  Petticoat, A. TTTS
  Purse, A. TCAPo
  Red Roses. TTTS
  Sound, A. TTTS
  Umbrella, An. TTTS

Tender floss of my flesh. Close to Me. Gabriela Mistral. TANSG, *tr.* by Maria Jacketti

Tender-handed stroke a nettle. Written on a Window. Aaron Hill. OxBSP

Tender heart, hairy muscle. Maria Luisa Spaziani. NeIt

Tender-Heartedness. Harry Graham. NBLV; NOxBChV; PeLV *Fr.* Some Ruthless Rhymes.

Tender infant, meek and mild, The. Ballad. Samuel Johnson. OxAEP-1

Tender mulberry leaves fill the basket-racks. Poem Written During a Dream on the Twenty-Third Day of the Intercalary [Month After The] Fourth [Month]. Ch'ien Ch'ien-i [or Ch'ien Ch'ien-yi]. CoBLCP, *tr.* by Jonathan Chaves

Tender mulberry leaves picked so clean. Walking in the Countryside. Wang An-shih. SuSp, *tr.* by Jan W. Walls

Tender, semi- / articulate flickers. For My Mother: Genevieve Jules Creeley. Robert Creeley. PoM; TRP

Tender softness, infant mild. To an Infant Expiring the Second Day of Its Birth. Mehetabel Wright. ECWP; NOEC

Tender winds above the snow. Kyutaro. JDP, *tr.* by Yoel Hoffmann

Tenderitis. Maxine Chernoff. IllVoic

Tenderly. Walter Gross. ReLy

Tenderness. Belinda Zubicueta Carmona. TANSG, *tr.* by Celeste Kostopulos-Cooperman

Tenderness. Stephen Dunn. NIP-4

Tenderness. Aleksei [or Aleksei] Aleksandrovich Surkov. TCRP, *tr.* by Lubov Yakovleva

Tenderness, ache on me, and lay your neck. James Dickey. TAP *Fr.* Zodiac, The.

Tenderness of love is extraordinary, The. Thanksgiving (1974). Stefan Brecht. CLPP

Tending the Graves. Jennifer Strauss. NOBAu

Tendril in the Mesh. William Everson.
  "Daughter of earth and child of the wave be appeased." NoAM

Tendril Love of Africa. Molara Ogundipe-Leslie. HAWP

Tenebrae. Paul Celan. PoetW, *tr.* by John Felstiner

Tenebrae. Paul Celan. PoSu; VCWP

Tenebrae. Austin Clarke. BIrV; CIP-2; NOIV

Tenebrae. David Gascoyne. PeECV

Tenebrae. Geoffrey Hill. HarvBoo

Tenebrae. Juan Ramón Jiménez. SpanPo, *tr.* by Alice Sternberg

Tenebrae. Denise Levertov. NoP-4

Tenebræ. John Banister Tabb. APN-2

Tenebris. Angelina Weld Grimké. APT-1; NAAAL

Tenebris Interlucentem. James Elroy Flecker. MoBrPo

Tengan Osho's Visit to Erin-ji. Muso Soseki. EaWin, *tr.* by W. S. Merwin

Tennessee June. Jorie Graham. HarvBoo

Tennessee Waltz, The. James Haug. OPRER

Tennis. Pierre Drieu la Rochelle. CuPo

Tennis Court Oath, The. John Ashbery. NoAM; TAP

Tennis in the City. Frank Higgins. MoASP

Tennyson. Alan Ansen. CoAP

Tennyson's Poems. Josephine D. Henderson Heard. CBWP-4; SWaP

Tense beat of the drum, The. To a Rabfak Student. Mikhail Arkadyevich [orArkad'evich] Svetlov. TCRP, tr. by Daniel Weissbort

Tenson. Carenza. WPOW, tr. by Bridget Connelly and Doris Earnshaw

Tent marks in Mínan are worn away, The. Var. authors. WoPoe, tr. by Michael Sells Fr. Mu'allaqat, The.

Tent on the Beach: [The Dreamer]. John Greenleaf Whittier.
 "And one there was, a dreamer born." NCAP

Tent stitch is repeated in the blue and red, The. Oh, Nothing. John Ashbery. NAAL-2v2

Tent that is pitched at the base, A. War. Edgar Wallace. OBWP

Tentacled for food. In the Sea of Tears. Naomi Replansky. BrRo

Tentacles, the brazen phiz whose glare, The. Medusa. Amy Clampitt. VCAP

Tenth.9. Roberto Juarroz. PoetW, tr. by Mary Crow

Tenth day of the winter month November, The. Memorandum of Martha Moulsworth, Widow, The. Martha Moulsworth. EMWP; NAEL-7v1

Tenth Satire. Juvenal. Fr. Satires.

Tenth Symphony. John Ashbery. NOBA

10th Untitled Poem. Pedro Juan Pietri. PueRic

Tents, marquees, and baggage-wagons. Camp, The. Mary Robinson. NOBRP

Tenuous and Precarious. Stevie Smith. HarvBoo; OxBTC

Teodoro Luna's Two Kisses. Alberto A. Ríos. PoPoPo

Tepehua Thought-Songs. Unknown. STP, tr. by Charles Boilès

Tequila & chicken. In a Motel on Lake Erie. James Tate. LCAP-2

Terce. W. H. Auden. GI; PoE Fr. Horae Canonicae.

Tercios del Muerte. Gerry Gordon. MiVo

Terence McDiddler. Unknown. OxNR

Terence, This Is Stupid Stuff. A. E. Housman. CABP; HeIP-4; InPK-6; NAEL-5v2; NAEL-6v2; NoAM; NoP-4; TFi
 (Epilogue) MoBrPo

Terentius Neo and wife. Their oval eyes. Portrait of a Married Couple. Margaret Scott. NOBAu

Teresa. Richard Wilbur. NoAM

Teresa of Avila. Elizabeth Jennings. PeECV; TOF

Terezin. Hanuš Hachenburg. INSAB

Terezin. Mif. INSAB

Terezin is full of beauty. It All Depends on How You Look at It. Miroslav Košek. INSAB

Terminal. Thom Gunn. CAGL; OxBEV

Terminal. Karl Shapiro. GM

Terminal. Martin Shea. HA

Terminal Hip. Mac Wellman.
 "Of Power, Money, Cheese, Real Estate, Conboberation, Hoohah." FTOS

Terminally Ill. Anna Swirszczynska. PoSu

Terminus. Ralph Waldo Emerson. APN-1; AWP; NCAP; NOBA; OxBA; TAP; TCAPo

Terminus. Seamus Heaney. PoPoPo

Terminus. Peter Rose. BMAP

Terminus. Edith Wharton. APT-1

Termite, The. Ogden Nash. KaS; OBCA

Terms in Which I Think of Reality, The. Allen Ginsberg. AmFaPo

Terms of all kinds mellow with time, growing. Robert Pinsky. NoAM Fr. Essay on Psychiatrists.

Terms of Appointment. Arthur Rex Dugard Fairburn. PeNZ

Ternarie of Littles, upon a Pipkin of Jellie [or Jelly] Sent to a Lady, A. Robert Herrick. BeJo; FaBoCh

Ternissa. Walter Savage Landor. NOBE

Terpander. Tryphon. GrAn, tr. by Peter Jay

Terpês died among the Spartans, playing. Terpander. Tryphon. GrAn, tr. by Peter Jay

Terpsichore [told] me. Korinna [or Corinna]. SaLy, tr. by Diane Rayor

Terra Australis. James Philip McAuley. NOBAu

Terra Australis. Douglas Stewart. NOBAu

Terra cotta girl, The. In the Counselor's Waiting Room. Bettie M. Sellers. InPK-6

Terrace in the Snow, The. Su Tung-p'o (Su Shih). OHPC, tr. by Kenneth Rexroth

Terrain. A. R. Ammons. CoAmPo; VCAP

Terrapin, The. Elizabeth Smither. PeNZ

Terre Promise. Ernest Christopher Dowson. NOBVV

Terri. Alan Wearne. BMAP Fr. Nightmarkets, The.

Terrible beauty is born, A. (LL) Easter 1916. W. B. Yeats. FaBoMo; HAP; HarvBoo; HeIP-4; NAEL-5v2; NAEL-6v2; NAWM-7v2; NIL-7; NIP-4; NOBE; NOIV; NPeEn; NoAM; NoP-4; OBWP; OxAEP-2; OxBTC; PoE; PoPoPo; TFi

Terrible beds, soft beds, wily, elusive beds. Beds. Charlie Smith. BAP-97

Terrible child-bed hast thou had, my dear, A. William Shakespeare. EBEV; OxAEP-1 Fr. Pericles.

Terrible Door, The. Harold Monro. BoLoP; EnLoPo; FaBoTw

Terrible Infant, A. Frederick Locker-Lampson. OBCoV
 (I recollect a nurse called Ann.) NOxBChV

Terrible is my plight this night. Wolves for Company. Unknown. BIrV

Terrible is the price. Price, The. John Davidson. EBVV

Terrible One, knowing their hearts, The. Cristina Campo. CItWP, tr. by Cinzia Sartini Blum and Lara Trubowitz Fr. Tiger's Absence.

Terrible Path, The. Brian Patten. OTCP

Terrible People, The. Ogden Nash. APT-2

Terrible slowness / overtaking haste. (LL) Tortoise, The. Cid Corman. InPK-6; VGW

Terrible sons of the mighty race, The. Terrible Sons, The. Eleazar ben Kalir. TrJP, tr. by Israel Zangwill

Terrible, the rain. All night, rain. Trace, In Unison. Tess Gallagher. ExTi

Terrible Thought, A. Eliezer Steinbarg. TrJP, tr. by Joseph Leftwich

Terrifying are the attent sleek thrushes on the lawn. Thrushes. Ted Hughes. FaBoMo; TRP

Terror. Denise Levertov. PoE

Terror. "Yehoash." TrJP, tr. by Isidore Goldstick

Terror and stillness and ebon-hued horror, night in its iciness. Midnight. Andreas Gryphius. GePo, tr. by George C. Schoolfield

Terror Conduction. Philip Lamantia. NeAP

Terror for fat burghers on far plains below. (LL) Rocky Acres. Robert Graves. NoAM; UnPo

Terror of Death, The. John Keats. See When I Have Fears [That I May Cease to Be]

Terrorist, The. Sergey Stratanovsky. ItGoST, tr. by J. Kates

Terrorist, He Watches, The. Wislawa Szymborska. PoSu
 (Bomb will go off in the bar at one twenty p.m, The.) AF, tr. by Robert A. Maguire

Terrorist Is Watching, A. Wislawa Szymborska. WoPoe, tr. by Austin Flint

Terrorists of the last. I Am So in Love I Grow a New Hymen. Sandra Cisneros. IllVoic

Terse Elegy for J.V. Cunningham. X. J. Kennedy. DiPo

Tesoro. Valerie Martínez. TouFir

Tess's Lament. Thomas Hardy. FaBoTw; FaBoVe

Tess's Torch Song (I Had a Man). Ted Koehler. ReLy

Test. Nicanor Parra. PFTM-2, tr. by Miller Williams

Test, The. Ralph Waldo Emerson. OBAL

Test of Atlanta 1979, The. June Jordan. ISC

Test of Men, The. Bible, Apocrypha. TrJP Fr. Ecclesiasticus.

Test Paper. Rolfe Humphries. APT-2

Testament. Tudor Arghezi. AF, tr. by Andrei Bantas

Testament. Hayden Carruth. GifTon

Testament. Roland Mathias. AngWePo

Testament. Nizar Qabbani. MAP, tr. by Diana Der Hovanessian and Lena Jayyusi

Testament. Tu Fu. CarOv, tr. by Carolyn Kizer

Testament, The. François Villon.
 "Now I think I hear the laments." NAWM-7v1, tr. by Galway Kinnell

Testament of a Rebel. Breyten Breytenbach. PeSAV, tr. by André Brink

Testament of Beauty, The. Robert Bridges.
 "And yet hath prayer, the heav'n-breathing foliage of faith." OxBTC
 Ethick. OxBTC
 "Sky's unresting cloudland, that with varying play, The." EBEV

Testament of Beauty, Book III, The. Robert Bridges.
 "Art is the true and happy science of the soul." GS

Testament of Cresseid, The. Robert Henryson. NePenScot; OxBS
 "I mend the fyre and beikit me about." EBEV; PoE
 "O ladyis fair of Troy and Grece, attend." NPeEn
 "That samin tyme, of Troy the garnisoun." OxBEV

Testament of Loss. Gloria C. Oden. ESEAA

Testament of Mr. Andro Kennedy, The. William Dunbar. OxBS

Testimonial. Langston Hughes. APT-2

Testimonial. Claudia Rankine. ExTi; NeAmPo

Testimonies. Rosita Kalina. TANSG, tr. by Celeste Kostopulos-Cooperman

Testimonies. Rosita Kalina. MirDau, tr. by Roberta Gordenstein

Testimony. Dan Pagis. PoSu, tr. by Stephen Mitchell

Testimony. Charles Reznikoff.

"Company had advertised for men to unload a steamer across the river, The." ColAP

Testimony. Carolyn M. Rodgers. BPo

Testimony in trials that never got heard. Woman Is Talking to Death, A. Judy Grahn. GLP

Testimony of Light, The. Carolyn Forché. ExTi

Testimony: The United States (1901–10) Recitative/The South. Charles Reznikoff. FTOS

Testing out the door-posts. Gregorio Scalise. ItPo, *tr. by* Gayle Ridinger

Testing the Confucian Ideal. *Vietnamese Oral Tradition.* CaDao, *tr. by* John Balaban

Testing-Tree, The. Stanley Kunitz. APT-2; UnPo

Tête-à-Tête. Edwin Honig. NoAM

Tête-à-Tête. May Probyn. NPeEn; VWP

Tête à Tête; or, Fashionable Pair: an Eclogue, The. Ann Murry. ECWP

Tetélestai. Conrad Potter Aiken. APT-1; MoAmPo

Tethered horse, A. Buson. ChAP; EH, *tr. by* Robert Hass

Tethered Souls, The. Endre Ady. IQMS, *tr. by* Anton N. Nyerges

Tethy's Festival. Samuel Daniel.
 Are They Shadows [That We See]? NoP-4; NOSC
 (Shadows.) NOBE

Texan Rhodes Scholar named Fred, A. Limerick. Lyndon T. Mole. PeLi

Texas. Mei-Mei Berssenbrugge. PmAP

Texas Ranger, The. Margie B. Boswell. AiP

Text, The. Gary Snyder. NAAL-2v2 *Fr.* Myths and Texts.

Text and Commentary. Elke Erb. PFTM-2, *tr. by* Roderick Iverson

Text Book / A case in point, the expert says;. Forensic Medicine. Gieve Patel. OMIP

Text for These Distracted Times, A. Rodney Hall. CBAP

Textbook 10. Helmut Heissenbüttel.
 Lesson 3. PFTM-2, *tr. by* Pierre Joris

Textures. William Stafford. BodElec

Th' Attempt was brave, how happy your success. To Mrs. Manley. By the Author of Agnes de Castro. Catherine Cockburn. EMWP

Th' expense of spirit in a waste of shame. William Shakespeare. *See* Expense of spirit in a waste of shame, The [*or* Th']

Th'o'erflowing of unbounded Wit. *etc.* (LL) Enquiry after Peace. A Fragment. Anne Finch, Countess of Winchilsea. ECWP; PoE

Th Wundrfulness uv th Mountees Our Secret Police. Bill Bissett. NOBC

Thai passit in thare pilgramage. *Unknown.* OxBS *Fr.* Golagros and Gawane.

Thailand Railway. Randolph Stow. CBAP

Thair is nocht ane Winche. *Unknown.* OxBS

Thaïs. Newman Levy. PeLV

Thais, why do you call me old. Martial. PGA

Thalaba the Destroyer. Robert Southey.
 "Cold! cold! 'tis a chilly clime." NOBRP

Thalassa. Louis MacNeice. BIrV; FaBoMo; NOBE; WoPoe

Thames nocturne of blue and gold, The. Impression Du Matin. Oscar Wilde. EBVV; MoBrPo; NAEL-5v2; NAEL-6v2; NoAM

Than a calm spin in a tomb of water. (LL) I Am Root. Claribel Alegría. PoetW; VCWP, *tr. by* Carolyn Forché

Than all men else, than thy self [*or* thyself] only less. (LL) To Ben Jonson. Thomas Carew. BASC; BeJo; CaPo; CavPo; NAEL-5v1; NAEL-6v1; NAEL-7v1; NOSC

Than all the eastern sages knew. (LL) On the Emigration to America [and Peopling the Western Country]. Philip Freneau. ColAP; NAAL-2v1; NAAL-3; NAAL-5; TAP

Than all the flourishing [*or* flour'shing] wreaths by laureates worn. (LL) To My Worthy Friend Master George Sands [*or* Sandys], on His Translation of the Psalms. Thomas Carew. BeJo; CaPo; MeLP

Than blood in the heart. (LL) Night. Louise Bogan. APT-2; NoP-4; UnPo

Than by my threatenings [*or* threat'nings *or* threatnings] rest still innocent. (LL) Apparition, The. John Donne. BASC; ESCV; EnLoPo; FSCP; HeIP-4; NAEL-5v1; NAEL-6v1; NAEL-7v1; NAWM-5v1; NOBE; NOBL; NoSic; OBEV; PoE; SCGP; SCV; SoSe-8; TFi

Than (by yon sunset's wintry glow). E. E. Cummings. VGW

Than could whole seas of craw-fish soup. (LL) To a Young Lady, with Some Lampreys. John Gay. CABP; ECEV; NOEC; OBCoV

Than dare be loved by men of mean degree. (LL) Edmund Spenser. SacPr; Son *Fr.* Amoretti.

Than Dis, on heaps of gold fixing his look. (LL) Christopher Marlowe. EBEV; NPeEn *Fr.* Hero and Leander.

Than go to church with oily Sue and afterwards to bed. (LL) Correspondence between Mr. Harrison in Newcastle and Mr. Sholto Peach Harrison in Hull. Stevie Smith. NBLV; OxBC

Than gold out of that stream. (LL) To His Lady Selvaggia Vergiolesi; Likening His Love to a Search for Gold. Cino da Pistoia. AWP; EaItPo, *tr. by* Dante Gabriel Rossetti

Than, if this noble kyng. John Skelton. PBRV *Fr.* Replycacion, A.

Than, Mau. John Balaban. CDa

Than never to have loved at all. (LL) Tennyson. CABP; CAGL; FHYEP; NAEL-6v2; NAWM-7v2 *Fr.* In Memoriam A. H. H.

Than no illume at all. (LL) Emily Dickinson. APN-2; NCAP

Than none at all. Provide, provide! (LL) Provide, Provide. Robert Frost. APT-1; ChIV-1; HAP; HarvBoo; NAAL-2v2; NOBA; NoAM; NoP-4; PoE; TAP; TFi; TwCP; UnPo; WeW-3; WoPoe

Than on yon gable-ends o' time? (LL) Prows O' Reekie, The. Lewis Spence. NePenScot; OxBS

Than our mountain greenery home! (LL) Mountain Greenery. Richard Rodgers. OBAL; ReLy

Than public faces in private places. (LL) W. H. Auden. FaBoEE; PeLV *Fr.* Shorts [1927–1932].

Than railroads, a soiled red-letter day. (LL) Sitting, The. Medbh McGuckian. CABP; ModIr; PNI

Than rise and bow and speak an idyll. (LL) Dorothy Parker. APT-1; NALW *Fr.* Pig's-Eye View of Literature, A.

Than rule yon isle and be a slave. (LL) Holyhead. September 25, 1727. Jonathan Swift. BIrV; NOIV

Than she fled through the broom. (LL) Broomfield Hill, The. *Unknown.* ESPB; OxBB

Than smiles of other maidens are. (LL) Song. Hartley Coleridge. GTBS-P; OBEV

Than stockit mailins. (LL) Poet's Welcome to His Love-Begotten Daughter [the First Instance that Entitled Him to the Venerable Appellation of Father], A. Robert Burns. NOEC; OxBoLi

Than teach ten thousand stars how not to dance. (LL) You Shall Above All Things Be Glad and Young. E. E. Cummings. ColAP; NOBA; NoAM; OxBA

Than that I lose no more for Stella's sake. (LL) Sir Philip Sidney. NAEL-5v1; NAEL-6v1; NAEL-7v1; NoSic *Fr.* Astrophil and Stella.

Than that it lived at all. Farewell. (LL) Epitaph on Elizabeth, L. H. Ben Jonson. BeJo; FaBoEE; HAP; NAEL-5v1; NAEL-6v1; NIL-7; NIP-4; NOSC; NoP-4; OBEV; PoE; SCGP

Than that, which one day Worms may chance refuse? (LL) Sonnet: "My God, where is that ancient heat towards Thee." George Herbert. ESCV; GeHe; NOSC

Than that which you / Can do! (LL) Charles Olson. NOBA; NoAM; PmAP; PoM *Fr.* Maximus Poems, The.

Than that you should remember and be sad. (LL) Remember [Me]. Christina Georgina Rossetti. AWP; BoLoP; EnLoPo; NOBE; OBEV; OxAEP-2; PoRA; TFi

Than the eyes of a big brown bear. (LL) Dancing Bear, The. Rachel Lyman Field. KaS; NTCP

Than the lovers . . . in the dust . . . in the cool tombs. (LL) Cool Tombs. Carl Sandburg. APT-1; HAP; HeIP-4; MoAmPo; NAAL-2v2; NOBA; NoAM; OxBSP; TAP; TCAPo; TFi

Than the strong man in his wrath. (LL) Elizabeth Barrett Browning. EBVV; OxAEP-2; VWP; ViWPN

Than the two hearts beating each to each! (LL) Meeting At Night. Robert Browning. AWP; BRP; BoLoP; FHYEP; FaBoVe; HeIP-4; ITBLP; NAEL-5v2; NAEL-6v2; NOBE; NOBVV; OBEV; OPOU; OxBEV; OxBSP; PAI; PeVV; PoRA; SCGP; SCV; SoSe-8; TFi; UnPo

Than the wind goin' over my hand. (LL) Sea Love. Charlotte Mew. LW; MoBrPo; OxAEP-2; OxBEV; OxBTC

Than this fair park, from what it was before. (LL) On St. James's Park, as Lately Improved by His Majesty. Edmund Waller. BASC; BeJo; NOSC; OBGa

Than this smart Misery. (LL) Emily Dickinson. APN-2; BoWoP; MoAmPo; TCAPo

Than those that to the earth with many tears they give. (LL) Dead, The. Jones Very. APN-1; HAP; NOBA; NoP-4; OxBA; SacPr; TAP; TCAPo

Than to live not perfected. (LL) His Request to Julia. Robert Herrick. BeJo; CaPo; CavPo; NOSC

Than to say "Abide" and yet shall not obtain. (LL) Sir Thomas Wyatt. BoLoP; EnLoPo

Than when I was a boy. (LL) I Remember, I Remember. Thomas Hood. ITBLP; NOBE; OxAEP-2; OxBEV; TFi; TreFP

Than where I loathed so much. (LL) Discontents in Devon. Robert Herrick. BeJo; CaPo; OxBSP

Than write such hopeless rubbish as thy worst. (LL) Sonnet, A: "Two voices are there: one is of the deep." James Kenneth Stephen. CABP; NOBL; UV

Than you touch with decay. (LL) To Death. Oliver St. John Gogarty. FaBoEE; OBMV

Thanatopsis. William Cullen Bryant. APN-1; AWP; BRP; ColAP; NAAL-2v1; NAAL-3; NAAL-5; NCAP; NOBA; OBEV; OxBA; PWR; TAP; TCAPo; TFi
 "So live, that when thy summons comes to join." PoToHe; TreFP

Thanatos, Thy Praise I Sing. "Michael Field." ViWPN

Thank God. Joseph Rolnik. TrJP, *tr. by* Joseph Leftwich

Thank God. Lousy in Center Field. James Tate. MoASP

Thank God! *Unknown.* PoToHe

Thank God, bless God, all ye who suffer not. Tears. Elizabeth Barrett Browning. WPE

Thank God for All. John Lydgate. SacPr

Thank God for life! Thank God! *Unknown.* PoToHe

Thank God for Little Children. Frances Ellen Watkins Harper. PWR

Thank god he stuck his tongue. Mostly Mick Jagger. Catie Rosemurgy. BAP-97

Thank God, I am content with less! (LL) Dorothy Parker. APT-1; NALW *Fr.* Pig's-Eye View of Literature, A.

Thank God that you are still alive. To the Muse. Nadezhda Elizarovna Maltseva. TCRP, *tr. by* Bernard Meares

Thank God they're all gone. Nazis. Ira Sadoff. LTA; OPRER

Thank Goodness, the moving is over. "When the World Was in Building." Ford Madox Ford. CTC

Thank heav'n! I'm safely landed frae Ostend. To the Memory of Gavin Wilson (Boot, Leg and Arm Maker). George Galloway. NOEC

Thank Heaven! the crisis. For Annie. Edgar Allan Poe. APN-1; ColAP; NOBA; OBEV; OxBA; TCAPo

Thank You. Kenneth Koch. NeAP; PoM

Thank You: A Poem in Seventeen Parts. *Unknown.* STP, *tr. by* Richard Johnny John and Jerome Rothenberg

Thank You Father. Ray Henderson. ReLy

Thank you for attending this tribute to love. Milena Jesenká. Edward Hirsch. BodElec

Thank You, God. Nina Stiles. PoToHe

Thank you, Mr Rason, for the Apples. E. G. Murphy. OBCoV

Thank You, My Fate. Anna Swirszczynska. BLT

Thank you. You are too. (LL) My Erotic Double. John Ashbery. LCAP-2; PoE; VCAP

Thankful Acknowledgment of God's Providence, A. John Cotton. SCAP

Thankful Heart, A. Robert Herrick. *See* Thanksgiving to God for His House, A

Thankful soil manured and winter dressed, The. Shamed by the Creature. Mildmay Fane, 2d Earl of Westmorland. NOSC

Thankfulness. Adelaide Anne Procter. SacPr

Thanking Doctor Jen. Li K'ai-hsien. CoBLCP; ColAnChi, *tr. by* Jonathan Chaves

Thanking Prince Chen-chi for Giving Me a Bronze Seal Engraved with Diagrams of the Five Sacred Mountains. Hsü Chung-hsing. "This metal is engraved with Shang-style markings." CoBLCP

Thankless for favours from on high. On a Similar Occasion for the Year 1792. William Cowper. NOCV

Thankless too for peace. Samuel Taylor Coleridge. FaBoWar *Fr.* Fears in Solitude.

Thanks a Lot, but No Thanks. Adolph Green. ReLy

Thanks and a Plea to Mary. *Unknown.* FaBoVe; MiEL

Thanks Be to God. Janie Alford. PoToHe

Thanks but no. I will do. Dianae Sumus in Fide. Biancamaria Frabotta. CItWP, *tr. by* Cinzia Sartini Blum and Lara Trubowitz

Thanks for Daisen Osho's Visit. Muso Soseki. EaWin, *tr. by* W. S. Merwin

Thanks for the haggis. Could you really spare. Palladas [*or* Pallades]. GrAn

Thanks for the Memory. Ralph Rainger. ReLy

Thanks for your of already some. Age of Correggio and the Carracci, The. Charles Bernstein. BodElec

Thanks in Old Age. Walt Whitman. SAmP

Thanks in Winter. Harri Webb. AngWePo

Thanks Sent to Taihei Osho. Muso Soseki. EaWin, *tr. by* W. S. Merwin

Thanks to a Spanish friend of mine the king of Spain had given me. Spanish Generosity. Max Jacob. CuPo

Thanks to Industrial Essex. Donald Davie. OxBTC

Thanks to life that has given me so much. Here's to Life. Violeta Parra. TCLAP, *tr. by* Joan Baez and James Upton

Thanks to rental movies. Things I can. Insides of Alfred Hitchcock, The. Alejandrino Hufana. ReBoTo

Thanks to Saint Matthew, who had been. Comrade Jesus. Sarah Norcliffe Cleghorn. APT-1

Thanks to the ear. Benediction. James Berry. OPOU

Thanks to the morning light. World-Soul, The. Ralph Waldo Emerson. APN-1; NCAP

Thanks to the Things. Rutger Kopland. VCWP, *tr. by* James Brockway

Thanksgibin' day am now at han' Day befo' Thanksgibin', De. Maggie Pogue Johnson. CBWP-4

Thanksgiving. Martín Espada. PuP-23

Thanksgiving. Steve Hassett. CDa

Thanksgiving. Kenneth Koch. VGW

Thanksgiving. David Abenatar Melo. TrJP, *tr. by* Henry Hart Milman

Thanksgiving. Lizelia Augusta Jenkins Moorer. CBWP-3

Thanksgiving. Liz Rosenberg. PBCAP

Thanksgiving. "Yehoash." TrJP, *tr. by* Isidore Goldstick

Thanksgiving, The. George Herbert. ESCV; GeHe

Thanksgiving at Snake Butte. James Welch. AiP

Thanksgiving Day. Lydia Maria Child. NTCP; WHSW (New-England Boy's Song about Thanksgiving Day, The.) APN-1; ColAP; OBCA; OxIBACP

Thanksgiving Dinner. Aileen Fisher. CA

Thanksgiving for a Habitat. W. H. Auden. Prologue: The Birth of Architecture. "Some thirty inches from my nose." FaBoEE Up There. OxBTC

Thanksgiving (1974). Stefan Brecht. CLPP

Thanksgiving to God for His House, A. Robert Herrick. BASC; BeJo; CavPo; HAP; NOSC; PeECV; PoRA; TrCP (Thankful Heart, A.) PoToHe

Thanksgiving to the Emperor Augustus Germanicus Domitianus. Publius Papinius Statius. RomPo, *tr. by* W. G. Shepherd *Fr.* Sylvae.

Thanksgivings, The. *Unknown.* APN-2, *tr. by* Harriet Maxwell Converse

Thanksgivings for the Beauty of His Providence. Thomas Traherne. FaBoCh

Thankyou Note. Dannie Abse. TCAWP

Thanne woot I wel that it is good ynow. (LL) Geoffrey Chaucer. NAEL-5v1; NAEL-6v1 *Fr.* Canterbury Tales, The.

Thar's More in the Man than Thar Is in the Land. Sidney Lanier. NOBA

Thass a funny title, Mr. Bones. John Berryman. ChIV-2 *Fr.* Dream Songs.

That after Horror—that 'twas us. That after horror that was us. Emily Dickinson. APN-2

That afternoon I had been fishing alone. Dream of Retarded Children, A. Robert Bly. LoL

That all came out jumbled in all the different heads, Napoleon. End of All History, The. Ken Smith. SpudSo

That all these dyings may be life in death. (LL) Mortification. George Herbert. ESCV; FSCP; GeHe; NOSC

That all things should be mine. Amendment. Thomas Traherne. InvLi

That all who taste it are from death restored. (LL) Seek the Lord. Thomas Campion. SacPr; TrCP

That always passes away, and does not end. (LL) Juan Ramón Jiménez. SpanPo; WoPoe, *tr. by* James Wright *Fr.* Ten Short Poems.

That an Immortal binds. (LL) Emily Dickinson. ChIV-2; SacPr

That any thing should be. Axle Song. Mark Van Doren. APT-2

That April Morning. Patricia Lasoen. TuT, *tr. by* Dennis O'Driscoll

That are so wondrous sweet and fair. (LL) Song: "Go[e], lovely rose." Edmund Waller. AWP; BASC; BeJo; BoLoP; CABP; CTC; ClHu; EnLoPo; GTBS-P; HAP; HeIP-4; InPK-6; NAEL-5v1; NAEL-6v1; NAEL-7v1; NIL-7; NOBE; NOSC; NPEEn; NoP-4; OBEV; OxAEP-1; OxBEV; PBRV; PoE; PoPoPo; PoRA; SoSe-8; TFi; UnPo; WeW-3; WoPoe

That are trodden upon are your own or your foes' (LL) James Russell Lowell. NOBA; TCAPo *Fr.* Fable for Critics, A.

That as all parts of it. Posited. James McMichael. GeoHom

That Asiatic striptease girl / who goes in for those. Automedon. GrAn

That asks not happiness, but longs for rest! (LL) To Hope. Helen Maria Williams. CenSon; ECWP; OxBSo

That August afternoon the family. State Funeral. Thomas McCarthy. CIP-2; ModIr

That axe that I hear. Buson. TAL

That bears the coming harvest in its breast. (LL) Zulu Girl, The. Roy Campbell. NoP-4; OBMV; OxAEP-2

That bears the Human soul. (LL) Emily Dickinson. APN-2; BRP; MoAmPo; OBCA; SAmP; SoSe-8; TAP

That bears the zodiac. (LL) Goose Fish, The. Howard Nemerov. HeIP-4; NIL-7; NIP-4; NoAM; NoP-4; PoE

That Been to Me My Lives Light and Saviour. Susan Wheeler. ExTi

That being red, it dyes red soul[e]s to white. (LL) John Donne. EBEV; OxAEP-1; Son; TOF *Fr.* Holy Sonnets.

That bird flying for the first time. Sailor. Vincente Huidobro. TCLAP, *tr. by* David Guss

That bit of filth in dirty walls. Terezin. Hanuš Hachenburg. INSAB

That black forest and the fire in earnest. (LL) Gretel in Darkness. Louise Glück. NoAM; NoP-4

That Black Girl Fulô. Jorge de Lima. TCLAP, *tr. by* Elizabeth Gordon

That blossomed at last, red geranium, and mignonette. (LL) Red Geranium and Godly Mignonette. D. H. Lawrence. GTBS-P; NoAM

That board—you'd racel and rend them with your teeth. (LL) Question, A. John Millington Synge. MoBrPo; NOIV; OBMV; OxBTC; PAI

That boatman am I. (LL) In the Past. Trumbull Stickney. ColAP; NOBA; OxBA

That bony potbellied arrow, wing-pumping along. Cormorant in His Element, The. Amy Clampitt. InPK-6

That bound and tied they fled. Ivano Fermini. ItPo, *tr.* by Gayle Ridinger

That brave Spirit comes agen. (LL) Not Every Day Fit for Verse. Robert Herrick. BeJo; PoRA

That breathes on earth the air of paradise. (LL) Love's Justification. Michelangelo Buonarroti. AWP; OBVE, *tr.* by William Wordsworth

That breeze brought it. Foster Jewell. HA

That brekis thair hairt and nocht the bettir. (LL) Alexander Scott. NPeEn; NePenScot; OxBS; PBRV

That bridge from the city, that was Waimakariri. Mary Ursula Bethell. PeNZ *Fr.* By the River Ashley.

That brings to maddening love, no soothing dream! (LL) Her Address to the Moon. Mary Robinson. CenSon; RWP

That Broad and Spreading Sweet Pear. *Unknown.* CoBCP, *tr.* by Burton Watson

That burns at both its ends. (LL) If. Franklin Pierce Adams. APT-1; OBAL

That by all bodies else obscures her name. (LL) Fulke Greville, 1st Baron Brooke. NPeEn; NoSic *Fr.* Caelica.

That came for the children. (LL) Seven Sorrows, The. Ted Hughes. NAEL-5v2; NAEL-6v2

That Can Not Be Taken Away From It. Carla Harryman. FTOS

That "cannot be done," and you'll do it. (LL) It Couldn't Be Done. Edgar Albert Guest. BRP; ITBLP

That cannot long one fashion entertain. (LL) Michael Drayton. NAEL-5v1; NAEL-6v1; NAEL-7v1; NOSC; Son *Fr.* Idea.

That child I was. Beginning Speech. "Adonis" [*or* "Adunis"]. MAP, *tr.* by John Heath-Stubbs and Lena Jayyusi

That childish thoughts such joys inspire. Thomas Traherne. BASC; ESCV *Fr.* Third Century, The.

That Christmas, unlike others. Gifts. Lenard D. Moore. SpirFl

That civilisation may not sink. Long-Legged Fly. W. B. Yeats. FaBoMo; FaBoTw; NAEL-5v2; NAEL-6v2; NOBE; NPeEn; NoAM; NoP-4; PAI; PoE

That clock is ticking. Marie Lucille. Gwendolyn Brooks. TLR

That Cold Summer. Nin Andrews. BAP-97

That comes into and steadies my soul. (LL) Pangolin, The. Marianne Craig Moore. APT-1; HAP; NOBA; NoAM

That constant Susannah. Susannah. Thulani Davis. GT

That conversation we were always on the edge. Adrienne Rich. BoWoP; NoAM *Fr.* Twenty-one Love Poems.

"That cop was powerful mean." Idiot, The. Dudley Randall. BPo; LTA

That corner of the earth. Aware Aware. Tram Combs. TwCP

That "Craning of the Neck." Isabella Gardner. WPE

That crazed girl improvising her music. Crazed Girl, A. W. B. Yeats. Son

That creepycrawly traversing the stone. Close-ups of Summer. Norman MacCaig. OxBC

That Cypress Boat Is Drifting. *Unknown.* CoBCP, *tr.* by Burton Watson

That Dada Strain. Jerome Rothenberg. FTOS; PFTM-2

That dandy black-and-white gentleman doodling notes. Magpie and Pines. Louis Johnson. PeNZ

That dared attack my Chesterton. (LL) Lion, The. Joseph Hilaire Pierre Belloc. MoBrPo; NBLV; WHSW

That dared attack my Chesterton. (LL) Lines to a Don. Joseph Hilaire Pierre Belloc. MoBrPo; OBSV

That dares profane the cunt I swive! (LL) Ramble in St. James's Park, A. John Wilmot, 2d Earl of Rochester. BASC; PeLV

That dark brown rabbit, lightness in his ears. John Berryman. TwCP *Fr.* Dream Songs.

That Dark Other Mountain. Robert Francis. CRP

That darkesome cave they enter, where they find. Edmund Spenser. OxBEV *Fr.* Faerie Queene, The.

That darkness—is about to pass. (LL) Presentiment. Emily Dickinson. APN-2; HeIP-4; OxBA

That Day. John Leax. TrCP

That Day. Anne Sexton. BoWoP; CoAmPo

That day all the slaves were freed. Brazilian Fazenda. Patricia K. Page. FaBoWP

That day I lost everything. 22.6.1941. Ondra Lysohorsky. AF, *tr.* by Ewald Osers

That day in December I sat down. Miz Rosa Rides the Bus. Angela Jackson. IllVoic

That day in the Interpreter's house, in one of his Significant Rooms. Christiana. Peter Redgrove. OxBC

That day, in the slipping of torsos and straining flanks. Song, The. Lola Ridge. WPE

That day she threw the goose over the roof. Grandma's Man. James Welch. NoAM

That day, so innocent appeared. Picnic Remembered. Robert Penn Warren. NAAL-2v2

That day the albatross. Captain Amasa Delano's Dilemma. Yusef Komunyakaa. BodElec

That day the sails of the ship were torn. Lament for Tadhg Cronin's Children. Aodhagán O Rathaille. ModIr; PBCIP; RB; WoPoe, *tr.* by Michael Hartnett

That day the sunlight lay on the farms. On Heaven. Ford Madox Ford. CTC

That day the / words. That Day. John Leax. TrCP

That day when oats were reaped, and wheat was ripe, and barley ripening. When Oats Were Reaped. Thomas Hardy. OxBTC

That day would skin a fairy. Dying Art, A. Derek Mahon. ModIr

That Dear Little Cat. D'Arcy Wentworth Thompson. NOxBChV

 (And that's the best cure for a little pussy cat.) (LL) NOxBChV

That death in his windows would rise. Leah Goldberg. MHP *Fr.* On Blossoming.

That death might not be casual. Epilogue. Burns Singer. FaBoTw

That death receives you. Amen. Alvaro Mutis. TCLAP, *tr.* by Sophie Cabot Black and Maria Negroni

That desire is quite over. Thinking of Love. Elizabeth Jennings. LW

That dey road no pave. Road of the Dread, The. Lorna Goodison. VCWP

That did invite, but seek another place. (LL) Song: "I prithee spare me, gentle boy." Sir John Suckling. BeJo; CavPo

That does not see you. You must change your life. (LL) Archaic Torso of Apollo. Rainer Maria Rilke. NAWM-7v2; RaBo, *tr.* by Stephen Mitchell

That dolphin-torn, that gong-tormented sea. (LL) Byzantium. W. B. Yeats. EBEV; FaBoMo; HAP; HarvBoo; MoBrPo; NAEL-5v2; NAEL-6v2; NAWM-7v2; NIL-7; NIP-4; NOBE; NoAM; NoP-4; OxBEV; OxBTC; PoE

That doubts as fervently as it believes. (LL) Emily Dickinson. APN-2; FaBoEE

That draws all waters toward / Its live formality. (LL) Looking into History. Richard Wilbur. VCAP; VGW

That dream, her eyes like rocks studded the high. Snow on a Mountain. Dom Moraes. NoP-4

That dried-up arse, Lykainis. Antipater of Thessalonica. GrAn

That drop of sweat which is sliding down my mouth. Esprit d'Escalier. John Wheelwright. APT-2

That each, who seems a separate whole. Tennyson. NAEL-6v2 *Fr.* In Memoriam A. H. H.

That earth shall be forgiven! (LL) Hesperus. John Clare. EBVV; GTBS-P; NOBVV

That eats and drinks of mealand maut. (LL) Hobie [*or* Hobbie] Noble. *Unknown.* ESPB; IBB; OxBB

That eternal spring is hidden. Song of the Soul that Rejoices in Knowing God through Faith. Saint John of the Cross. TOF, *tr.* by K. Kavanaugh and O. Rodrigues

That Eureka of Archimedes out of his bath. Voluptuaries and Others. Margaret Avison. MoCV

That evening. Zoe and the Ghosts. Dieter Weslowski. InvLad

That evening / faces bladed around us. In the Flux. Fadwa Tuqan [*or* Tuquan]. MAP, *tr.* by Patricia Alanah Byrne, Charles Doria and Salma Khadra Jayyusi

That evening Sinda thought she heard the drums. Dream, The. Robert Earl Hayden. ESEAA; NBV

That evening when. Akiko Yosano. OHMPJ

That ever your eyes did see. (LL) Laily Worm and the Machrel of the Sea, The. *Unknown.* ESPB; OxBB; SCGP

That every county in this developed state. Manifest Destiny. Pearse Hutchinson. CIP-2

That every tongue says beauty should look so. (LL) William Shakespeare. NAEL-6v1; NAEL-7v1; OxAEP-1 *Fr.* Sonnets.

That Exploit of Yours. Ford Madox Ford. PeFWW; PoWW

That Face. Ralph Blane. ReLy

That Face. Mairtin O Direain. BiHa

That fall, when we shared a phonograph. Year the Space Age Was Born, The. Floyd Skloot. SwNoth

That Falling. Jane Hirshfield. BodElec

That falls through the clear ether silently. (LL) To One Who Has Been Long in City Pent. John Keats. CenSon; FHYEP

That familiar curving hand. Letter. Sue Hubbard. Prnts

That fateful year I wished for you, flushed. Suicide Year, The. Alice Anderson. AmPoNex

That fellow rides a big horse. Wang Fan-chih. SuSp

That final newsreel of the war. Welcoming Party, A. John Montague. PNI

That finds no object worth its constancy? (LL) To the Moon. Shelley. GTBS-P; OxAEP-2; TTTS

That fine English poet, John Donne. Limerick: "That fine English poet, John Donne." Wendy Cope. PeLi

That fixed the tilt of the wings. (LL) Perfect. Hugh MacDiarmid. NePenScot; NoP-4; OxBEV; RB; WoPoe

That flattering glass, whose smooth face wears. Looking-Glass, A. Thomas Carew. CaPo

That flower unseen, that gem of purest ray. In a Churchyard. Richard Wilbur. HeIP-4

That flowing water! That flowing water! *Unknown.* APN-2, *tr. by* Washington Matthews *Fr.* Mountain Chant, The.

That for seven lustres [*or* lusters] I did never come. To the Reverend Shade of His Religious Father. Robert Herrick. CaPo

That force is lost. Snake Eyes. Imamu Amiri Baraka. VGW

That forming on a cigarette covers the red. (LL) Morning Sun. Louis MacNeice. MoBrPo; TwCP

That fought with us upon Saint Crispin's day. (LL) William Shakespeare. FaBoWar; OxAEP-1 *Fr.* King Henry V.

That frantic error [*or* Frantick Errour] I adore. Apostasy of One and But One Lady, The. Richard Lovelace. CaPo

That free love with bondage bound. (LL) William Blake. ChIV-1; FHYEP; NAEL-5v2; NAEL-6v2; NOBRP; NOEC; PoE *Fr.* Songs of Experience.

That from the seed of men. Psalm. Peter Huchel. AF, *tr. by* Daniel Simko

That ga' me a' my will. (LL) King Henry. *Unknown.* ESPB; OxBB

That gap between the Sunday papers and lunch. (LL) Against Coupling. Fleur Adcock. EmeKit; OxBB

That girl so long ago walked, as they all did, shop girls. Bolt, The. Mary Kinzie. ExTi

That girl wears her hair in a chicken's tail. Across the Field of the Old Corporal. *Vietnamese Oral Tradition.* CaDao, *tr. by* John Balaban

That glitter a cold span above the sea. (LL) Laureate, The. Robert Graves. BIrV; FaBoTw; OBSV

That Glove. Mary E. Tucker. CBWP-1

That God is All, His shadow shows. (LL) Plaint. Ebenezer Elliott. OBEV; SacPr

That God of ours, the Great Geometer. Grace to Be Said at the Supermarket. Howard Nemerov. SoSe-8

That good, my sire, I dedicate to thee. (LL) Dedicatory Sonnet to S. T. Coleridge. Hartley Coleridge. CenSon; Son

That gorgeous kite. Issa. EH, *tr. by* Robert Hass

That great arm-full of yellow flowers. (LL) Evadne. "H. D.". BoWoP; LW

That great blue oak. Basho. SoOfWa, *tr. by* Sam Hamill

That Great Wingless Bird. Adrian C. Louis. UnSA

That grows, at the first touch of day, / Unendurable. (LL) First Light. Thomas Kinsella. BIrV; PoE

That grudging man [can't hurt] you. Korinna [*or* Corinna]. SaLy, *tr. by* Diane Rayor

That had left so much unsaid. (LL) Local Poet, A. John Hewitt. ModIr; PNI

That had moved the congregation so. (LL) Thomas Hardy. InPK-6; MoBrPo; SCV *Fr.* Satires of Circumstance in Fifteen Glimpses.

That had thee here obscure. (LL) Phoebus with Admetus. George Meredith. NOBE; OBEV

That handsaw marks time. Buson. SoOfWa, *tr. by* Sam Hamill

That hanged himself for love. (LL) A. E. Housman. NOBVV; OxBEV

That Harp You Play So Well. Marianne Craig Moore. MoAmPo

That harsh, irregular flame? (LL) Quarrel, The. Stanley Kunitz. APT-2; TaR

That has been hurting her. (LL) Proletarian Portrait. William Carlos Williams. BLT; OBAL; SAmP; TAP

That has no end. (LL) Near the Wall of a House. Yehuda Amichai [*or* Amikhai]. BBASP; PFTM-2, *tr. by* Chana Bloch

That has not been rent. (LL) Crazy Jane Talks with the Bishop. W. B. Yeats. BoLoP; CABP; EBEV; InPK-6; NAEL-5v2; NAEL-6v2; NoAM; NoP-4; OxAEP-2; PAI; PoE; PoPoPo; TOF; TRP

That has transfigured me. (LL) Lamentation of the Old Pensioner, The. W. B. Yeats. HAP; PeVV; TRP; WeW-3

That has yet to enter the language. (LL) Quoof. Paul Muldoon. FaBoVe; NPeEn; PBCIP; PNI

That hath the power over wild beasts. (LL) Ezra Pound. APT-1; PoE; VGW *Fr.* Cantos.

That haughty tyranny of thine. Love Song. Luís De León. TrJP, *tr. by* Thomas Walsh

That he is old and she a shade. (LL) Walter Savage Landor. AWP; CTC; EBEV; FaBoEE; HAP; NAEL-6v2; NOBE; NPeEn; NoP-4; OBEV; OxAEP-2; OxBEV; OxBSP; PoRA; SCGP; TFi; WeW-3; WoPoe *Fr.* Pericles and Aspasia.

That he may sleep upon his hill again? (LL) Abraham Lincoln Walks at Midnight. Nicholas Vachel Lindsay. APT-1; CBCWP; IllVoic; MoAmPo; NOBA; OxBA; TAP; TCAPo; TFi; VGW

That he might just snap again was part of it, blind himself, and, well, you're there. Twilight. Ralph Angel. BodElec

That he slew me to gratify his hatred. (LL) Edgar Lee Masters. APT-1; NoAM *Fr.* Spoon River Anthology.

That he was born it cannot be denied. On a Certain Alderman. John Cunningham. FaBoEE

That he was gone, and I discerned not how. (LL) Dante Alighieri. AWP; EaItPo, *tr. by* Dante Gabriel Rossetti *Fr.* La Vita Nuova.

That he was ugly we have no doubt. Socrates' Death. Michael Jackson. PeNZ

That he will still require some waters to his blood. (LL) Christ's Passion. Abraham Cowley. ChIV-2; SacPr

That heard me whisper. (LL) Other Side of a Mirror, The. Mary Elizabeth Coleridge. BoWoP; NALW; VWP; ViWPN

That heeds no call to die. (LL) Heredity. Thomas Hardy. CTC; EBEV; HarvBoo; RB

That here, obedient to their laws, we lie. (LL) Thermopylae. Simonides. AWP; OBVE; OBWP; WoPoe, *tr. by* William Lisle Bowles

That hick farmer's got my number. *Unknown.* PriapPo, *tr. by* Richard W. Hooper *Fr.* Priapus Poems, The.

That hid the shyest grape. (LL) Monody. Herman Melville. APN-2; NAAL-2v1; NAAL-3; NoP-4; OxBSP; PoE; PoPoPo; TCAPo

That hideous overgrown toad again! Dragon Slaying. Zoltán Jékely. IQMS, *tr. by* George Szirtes

That his daddy once tied up my garter for me! (LL) Dark-Eyed Gentleman, The. Thomas Hardy. MoBrPo; NBLV; UnPo

That his heart trembles and his sight grows dim? (LL) Dante Alighieri. AWP; EaItPo, *tr. by* Dante Gabriel Rossetti *Fr.* La Vita Nuova.

That history is an event. Taku Skanskan. Paula Gunn Allen. HATNAP

That hobnailed goblin, the bobtailed Hob. Country Dance. Dame Edith Sitwell. NoAM

That Holy Thing. George Macdonald. OBEV; SacPr *Fr.* Paul Faber, Surgeon.

That hoop-back man. Compass of the Dying. Laurence Lieberman. IllVoic

That horn chased me. Up on the Spoon. Stanley Crouch. SeSe

That hot September night, we slept in a single bed. Girlfriends. Carol Ann Duffy. HarvBoo

That hour-glass, which there ye see. Hour-Glass, The. Robert Herrick. BeJo; CaPo

That humor now, declines for age drawes on. Thomas Churchyard. PBRV *Fr.* Musicall Consort, A.

That hump of a man bunching chrysanthemums. Old Florist. Theodore Roethke. APT-2; OxBSP

That Hypocrite. *Unknown.* BPo

That I, all else defac'd, not envie Kinges. (LL) Content and Resolute. William Drummond, of Hawthornden. NPeEn; PBRV

That I am clo[a]th[e]d in holy robes for glory. (LL) Huswifery. Edward Taylor. ColAP; ITBLP; InvLi; NAAL-2v1; NAAL-3; NAAL-5; NIP-4; NOBA; NOBE; OxBA; SCAP; SacPr; TAP; TCAPo; TFi

That I am glad to die for love of her. (LL) He Perceives His Rashness in Love, but Has No Choice. Guido Guinicelli. AWP; EaItPo, *tr. by* Dante Gabriel Rossetti

That I am mortal I know and do confess / My span of day. Star-Gazing. Ptolemy. GrAn, *tr. by* Dudley Fitts

That I both night and day. German Language, The. Berthold Viertel. AuPH, *tr. by* Lowell A. Bangerter

That I did always love. Emily Dickinson. SacPr

That I forgot about myself, and got soaking wet. (LL) Catch: On a Wet Day. Franco Sacchetti. AWP; EaItPo, *tr. by* Dante Gabriel Rossetti

That I had alighted there! (LL) Faintheart in a Railway Train. Thomas Hardy. CTC; EnLoPo

That I have been in certain sad places. Song of Reply. Alda Merini. CItWP, *tr. by* Cinzia Sartini Blum and Lara Trubowitz

That I have been looking. Subway Face. Langston Hughes. APT-2

That I have often been in love, deep love. Ode. "Peter Pindar." NOEC

That I love not, without I leave to love. (LL) Sir Philip Sidney. NAEL-5v1; NAEL-6v1; NAEL-7v1 *Fr.* Astrophil and Stella.

That I'm alive to tell you so. (LL) Stella's Birthday ([March 13,] 1727). Jonathan Swift. NoP-4; PoE; SCGP

That I'm lucky. They All Think. Giovanna Pollarolo. TANSG, *tr. by* Marjorie Agosin

That I may fold it round me and in comfort lie. (LL) Embankment, The (The fantasia of a fallen gentleman on a cold, bitter night). Thomas Ernest Hulme. EBEV; FaBoMo; GTBS-P; OPOU; OxBSP; OxBTC

That I might chisel a statue, line on line. Statue, The. Ella Higginson. SWaP

That I might there present it!—Oh! to whom? (LL) Question, The. Shelley. OBEV; OxBEV

That I my Best-Beloved's am; that he is mine. (LL) Francis Quarles. MeLP; NOBE *Fr.* Emblems.

That I revel in this clear dawn stillness. Gratitude to Life. Eugenie Fink. AuPH, *tr. by* Lowell A. Bangerter

That I say: "Lady, I am wholly thine" (LL) Ballata: Of a Continual Death in Love. Guido Cavalcanti. AWP; EaItPo, *tr. by* Dante Gabriel Rossetti

That I shall never find him. (LL) Mad Maid's Song, The. Robert Herrick. AWP; CaPo; EnLoPo; OBEV; RACG

That I shall never find my home. (LL) Mower to the Glowworms [*or* Glow-Worms *or* Glo-Worms], The. Andrew Marvell. AWP; BASC; ESCV;

EnLoPo; FHYEP; FSCP; GeHe; NAEL-5v1; NAEL-6v1; NAEL-7v1; NOBE; NPeEn; NoP-4; OxBoLi; PBRV; PeLV; SCGP; TFi

That I should love, and he should be ingrate. (LL) To One That Asked Me Why I Loved J.G G. "Ephelia." EMWP; NOSC

That I was christened. (LL) David McCord. KaS; OBCA; OBCoV *Fr.* Perambulator Poems, I-VII.

That I was never blest. (LL) Repulse, The. Thomas Stanley. BeJo; MeLP

That I went to warm my self in Lady Betty's Chamber. To Their Excellencies the Lords Justices of Ireland, the Humble Petition of Frances Harris, Who Must Starve, and Die a Maid if It Miscarries. Jonathan Swift. NOEC; OxBEV

That I would like to be. (LL) Grandmither, Think Not I Forget. Willa Sibert Cather. AmFaPo; WPE

That I would not persuaded be. Service Is No Heritage. Nicholas Breton. NoSic

That if I dipped my hand the spawn would clutch it. (LL) Death of a Naturalist. Seamus Heaney. HAP; NoAM; OxBC; OxBEV; WeW-3

That if I stepped out of my body I would break / Into blossom. (LL) Blessing, A. James Wright (1927–80). AmFaPo; InPK-6; NAAL-2v2; NOBA; NoAM; PoE; RaBo; TRP; TwCP; VCAP

That in black ink my love may still shine bright. (LL) William Shakespeare. AWP; HAP; NAEL-5v1; NAEL-6v1; NAEL-7v1; NOBE; NoSic; OxAEP-1; OxBSo; PoRA; RaBo; SCGP; Son; TFi; TreFP; UnPo *Fr.* Sonnets.

That in the manage myself takes delight. (LL) Sir Philip Sidney. NAEL-5v1; NAEL-6v1; NAEL-7v1; NoP-4; PoE *Fr.* Astrophil and Stella.

That insect, without antennae, over its. Crane, The. Charles Tomlinson. MoBrPo

That Is All I Heard. "Yehoash." TrJP, *tr. by* Isidore Goldstick

That is all ye know on earth, and all ye need to know. (LL) Ode on a Grecian Urn. John Keats. AWP; ClHu; EBEV; HAP; HeIP-4; MakPoe; NAEL-5v2; NAEL-6v2; NAWM-7v2; NIP-4; NOBE; NOBRP; OBEV; OxBEV; PoE; SCGP; TFi; TOF; UnPo

That is fit home for Thee! (LL) To the Cuckoo. William Wordsworth. GTBS-P; NOBRP; UV

That is fluent in even the wintriest bronze. (LL) Sense of the Sleight-of-Hand Man, The. Wallace Stevens. HAP; MoAmPo; NOBA; NoAM; TwCP; WeW-3

That is her lover lying there. Illumination. Jeffrey Wainwright. DiPo

That is most difficult. (LL) To a Friend Whose Work Has Come to Nothing. W. B. Yeats. AWP; InPK-6; MoBrPo; OBMV; OxAEP-2; WoPoe

That is no country for old men. The young. Sailing To Byzantium. W. B. Yeats. AmFaPo; CABP; ClHu; GTBS-P; HAP; HarvBoo; HeIP-4; InPK-6; MoBrPo; NAEL-5v2; NAEL-6v2; NAWM-7v2; NIL-7; NIP-4; NOBE; NPeEn; NoAM; OBMV; OWoS; OxBEV; OxBTC; PoE; PoPoPo; PoRA; RaBo; SCGP; SoSe-8; TFi; TOF; UnPo; WeW-3; WoPoe

That is not lovable? (LL) Tzu Yeh. EroLit; WPOW; WoPoe, *tr. by* Chung Ling and Kenneth Rexroth

That is reserved for his kind. (LL) Hyænas [*or* Hyenas], The. Rudyard Kipling. NAEL-5v2; NAEL-6v2; OBSV

That is so heygh, that al ne can I telle! (LL) Geoffrey Chaucer. EBEV; PoE *Fr.* Troilus and Criseyde [*or* Criseide].

That is the dawn fairy. Dawn Fairy, The. Dunya Mikhail. PoArWo, *tr. by* Samira Kawar

That is the glebe and this is the glissando. The future is nothing. Codex. Stephen Rodefer. PmAP

That is the way toward Terezin town. Road to Terezin, The. Ilse Weber. AuPH, *tr. by* Lowell A. Bangerter

That is their quality: not mercy, not mind, not goodness, but the beauty of God. (LL) Birds and Fishes. Robinson Jeffers. NAAL-2v2; NAAL-5; NoP-4

That is what they say, who were broken off from love. Muriel Rukeyser. LCAP-2 *Fr.* Eighth Elegy. Children's Elegy.

That is why we dedicate our books. Books of the Dead, The. Marta Kornblith. MirDau, *tr. by* Roberta Gordenstein

That is, without a doubt, the decisive test. (LL) In Trying Times. Heberto Padilla. AF; PoetW, *tr. by* Andrew Hurley and Alastair Reid

That it is a road. Narihira (Ariwara no Narihira). WoPoe, *tr. by* F. Vos *Fr.* Ise Monogatari, The.

That it is we who are important. (LL) For a Coming Extinction. W. S. Merwin. GifTon; HCAP; NNaP; PoE; VCAP

That it should end in an Albert Pick hotel. At the End of the Affair. Maxine W. Kumin. TAP

That it will never come again. Emily Dickinson. APN-2; NOBA

That Jamestown / Made long ago. (LL) American Heartbreak. Langston Hughes. APT-2; BPo

That Jewish Crusader. Diana Anhalt. MirDau

That Journeys Are Good. Jelaluddin [*or* Jalal al-Din] Rumi. RaBo, *tr. by* Robert Bly

That joy[e]s so ripe, so little keep[e]. (LL) To Amarantha, That She Would Dishevel[l] Her Hair[e]. Richard Lovelace. BeJo; NIL-7; OBEV

That Justice is a blind goddess. Justice. Langston Hughes. BPo

That keep him rich and orphaned and beloved? (LL) Illiterate, The. William Meredith. NoP-4; OxBSo; VCAP

That kill, that kill, that kill. (LL) Elm. Sylvia Plath. NOBA; NoAM; NoP-4

That kindles my mother's fire! (LL) Wife of Usher's Well, The. *Unknown.* AWP; EBEV; ESPB; MakPoe; NAEL-5v1; NAEL-6v1; NAEL-7v1; NOBE; NPeEn; NePenScot; NoP-4; OBEV; OxAEP-1; OxBB; OxBS; RB; SCGP; TFi

That kingfisher jewelling upstream. Kingfisher. Norman MacCaig. NoP-4

That Kings for such a Tomb would wish to die. (LL) On Shakespear[e]. John Milton. MeLP; NAEL-5v1; NOSC; PoE; PoRA; SCGP

That knows—it cannot see. (LL) Emily Dickinson. NAAL-2v1; NAAL-3; TCAPo

That labor / a face to remember in wonder. Sappho. OBVE

That last afternoon. Jack's Last Words. Stephen Kessler. GeoHom

That lately kissed thee. (LL) To Electra. Robert Herrick. CaPo; OBEV

That lay in the house that Jack built. (LL) House That Jack Built, The. Mother Goose. LB; OxBEV; OxBoLi; OxNR; ReMoGo

That lay in the house that Jack built. (LL) House That Jack Built, The. *Unknown.* NBLV; OxBoLi

That lead from Thirty————even to Forty-eight. (LL) Thirty-eight: Addressed to Mrs H—y. Charlotte Smith. ECWP; NALW; PEW; WPOW

That leads me to the Lamb. (LL) William Cowper. ECEV; NOCV; NOEC; PeECV; SCGP; TOF *Fr.* Olney Hymns.

That leaves look[e] pale, dreading the winter's neere [*or* near]. (LL) William Shakespeare. AWP; EnLoPo; GTBS-P; HeIP-4; NAEL-5v1; NAEL-6v1; NAEL-7v1; NOBE; NoSic; OBEV; OxAEP-1; PoRA; SCGP; Son; TFi *Fr.* Sonnets.

That lets Him out again. (LL) Yellow Man, Purple Man. Emily Dickinson. TLR; TTTS

That lies in the house of Bedlam. (LL) Visits to St. Elizabeths. Elizabeth Bishop. CoAP; VGW

That light, reflected, but makes darkness plain. (LL) In Dispraise of the Moon. Mary Elizabeth Coleridge. PEW; ViWPN

That little jukebox right over there. I'd Give a Dollar for a Dime. Eubie Blake. ReLy

That little Negro's married and got a kid. Sister. Langston Hughes. APSN

That little pretty [*or* prettie] bleeding part. To His Savior [*or* Saviour]. The New Years [*or* yeers] Gift. Robert Herrick. ChIV-2; NAEL-6v1

(That liv'd so sweetly) dead, so sweet a Grave! (LL) Music[k]'s Duel[l]. Richard Crashaw. GeHe; NAEL-7v1; NPeEn

That lives for oneness with God? (LL) Mechthild von Magdeburg. EnlH; WPoS

That living there I never could look up. (LL) Glory Trumpeter, The. Derek Walcott. GT; NAEL-5v2; NAEL-6v2; NoP-4; SeSe

That long have watched for light, and wept in vain. (LL) John Codrington Bampfylde. CenSon; NOEC

That Love is all there is. Emily Dickinson. NOBA; TCAPo

That love of mine for him had waxen wings—. Comet, The. Maria Luisa Spaziani. NeIt, *tr. by* Beverly Allen

That love supports his reign. (LL) On a Bed of Guernsey Lilies. Christopher Smart. BBASP; NOEC

That love to her I cast away. (LL) Thomas Carew. BASC; BeJo; CavPo

That Love,—whose power and sovranty we own. Creation of My Lady, The. Francesco Redi. AWP, *tr. by* Sir Edmund William Gosse

That lovely climbing vine, so fresh. Conversation with a Japanese Student. Eleanor Wilner. GifTon

That lovely spot which thou dost see. Upon a Mole in Celia's Bosom. Thomas Carew. CaPo

That lover of a night. Crazy Jane on God. W. B. Yeats. EBEV; OxBTC; RACG

That Lucky Old Sun. Beasley Smith. ReLy

That Lucy's eyes surveyed [*or* survey'd]. (LL) William Wordsworth. AWP; GTBS-P; NAEL-6v2 *Fr.* Lucy.

That made the oleander's leaves tremble. (LL) I-5 Incident. Juan Delgado. AmPoNex; GeoHom

That made the woods of April bright. (LL) Yellow Violet, The. William Cullen Bryant. NAAL-2v1; NAAL-3; TAP

That made them what they were! (LL) Transformations. Thomas Hardy. RB; TRP

That man. Night Song for Two Mystics. Paul Blackburn. NeAP

That Man. Reginald Shepherd. WiU

That man came shouting, I am a chief. Satire. *Unknown.* WoPoe, *tr. by* Sir Arthur Grimble

That man died in Jerusalem. Easter Dawn. Kofi Awoonor. PBMAP

That man entered through my eyes. Dream of the Forgotten Lover. Lucia Fox. BoWoP, *tr. by* R. Maghan

That man, I wish him well. I wish him grass. (LL) Removal from Terry Street, A. Douglas Dunn. FaBoMo; FaBoVe; NPeEn; NoP-4; OxBC

That man is pleasing and worthy of praise who shuns vice and always. Pacifico Massimi. CAGL, *tr. by* James J. Wilhelm *Fr.* Hecateleguim.

That man over there say. Ain't I a Woman? Sojourner Truth. BlSi

That man standing there, who is he? Goethe. WoPoe, *tr. by* James Wright *Fr.* Journey in Winter.

That man walks along weeping. Narration. George Seferis. PoetW, *tr. by* Edmund Keeley and Philip Sherrard

That mandarin did it all on this bed with mirrors. Bed with Mirrors. Gonzalo Rojas. TCLAP, *tr. by* Christopher Maurer

That mans most Noble Passion is to Love. (LL) Call, The. John Hall. MeLP; NOSC

That many friends had opened long ago. (LL) Mr Flood's Party. Edwin Arlington Robinson. APT-1; AWP; AmFaPo; ClHu; ColAP; EBNV; HAP; HeIP-4; MoAmPo; NAAL-2v2; NAAL-5; NIL-7; NIP-4; NOBA; NoAM; NoP-4; OxBA; PoE; PoRA; SoSe-8; TAP; TCAPo; TFi; TRP; UnPo; WeW-3

That March night I remember how we heard. Hare, The. Gillian Clarke. TCAWP

That mare stood in the field. All through the Rains. Gary Snyder. CoAmPo

That marks each of us so differently. (LL) Invocation: "This August night, raccoons." Jane Hirshfield. BodElec; GeoHom

That mayden mylde hir childe dide kepe. *Unknown.* OHMEL

That melancholy that inhabited me once has died. Autumn Leaves Are Virgin Mary. Unsi Al-Haj [*or* Hajj]. MAP, *tr. by* Patricia Alanah Bryne and Salma Khadra Jayyusi

That men weep hearing it, and have no choice. (LL) Dante Alighieri. AWP; CTC; EaItPo, *tr. by* Dante Gabriel Rossetti *Fr.* La Vita Nuova.

That mind—the small one—is soft, like a pullet. Song of the Great Mind. Uri Zvi Greenberg. FIT, *tr. by* Robert Friend

That Moment. Ted Hughes. UV *Fr.* Crow.

That money makethe the man. (LL) Money, Money. *Unknown.* CABP; MiEL

That moon which the sky never saw. Jelaluddin [*or* Jalal al-Din] Rumi. EaWin, *tr. by* Talat Sait Halman and W. S. Merwin

That More Simple Natural Time Tone Distortion. Tom Raworth. Oth

That morn[e] which saw me made a Bride. Upon a Maid That Died [*or* Dyed] the Day She Was Married [*or* Married]. Meleager. AWP; OBVE, *tr. by* Robert Herrick

That Morning. Ted Hughes. HarvBoo

That morning. Man Lying in a Hallway. Huw Jones. TCAWP

That morning, daylight was the same. Approach of War, The. Ellen Hinsey. AmPoNex

That morning early I ran through briars. Nun Takes the Veil, A. Bernard O'Donoghue. ModIr

That morning she stood in the kitchen. Rouge. Ann Townsend. ExTi

That morning the sun trespassed. White Dwarf. Gerry LaFemina. AmPoNex

That morning you found your lights on. Adagio. Gerald William Barrax. GT

That morning you took the wind. Portrait of Woman in Long Black Dress / Aurelia. Juan Felipe Herrera. TouFir

That most ancient Briton of English beasts. (LL) Combe, The. Edward Thomas. GTBS-P; RB

That Mountain Far Away. *Unknown.* CA, *tr. by* Herbert Joseph Spinden

That mountain there. Pilgrimage Song. *Unknown.* WPE, *tr. by* Mary Austin

That mourns its joy and its joy's minister. (LL) Dante Alighieri. AWP; EaItPo, *tr. by* Dante Gabriel Rossetti *Fr.* La Vita Nuova.

That multitude of moulded hands. Jean-Joseph Rabéarivelo [*or* Rebéarivelo]. *See* This multitude of melted hands

That must escape the knife. (LL) Autobiography of a Lungworm. Roy Fuller. NoAM; OxBC

That my face was not handsome. Mirror, The. Dafydd [*or* David] ap Gwilym. WoPoe, *tr. by* Daniel Huws

That my Friends may weep as much as they like. (LL) Epitaph, An: "I was buried near this dyke [*or* Dike]." William Blake. FaBoEE; OBCoV

That my life would be saved by the loss of my dinner?' (LL) Patient Joe; or, The Newcastle Collier. Hannah More. ECWP; WoRP

That my old bitter heart was pierced in this black doom. Grey Eye Weeping, A. Egan [*or* Aodhagán] O'Rahilly [*or* O'Reilly *or* Ó Rathaille]. OBMV, *tr. by* Frank O'Connor

That name: D'VoidofFunk. Sir Nose D'VoidofFunk. Thomas Sayers Ellis. NeAmPo

That Nature Is a Heraclitean Fire and of the Comfort of the Resurrection. Gerard Manley Hopkins. EnlH; FaBoMo; FaBoVe; GTBS-P; PFTM-1; PoE

(Cloud-puffball, torn tufts, tossed pillows flaunt forth, then.) NoP-4

That needed bronze to lock them, bronze or stone. (LL) Substance and Shadow. John Hewitt. ModIr; PNI

That neither fame nor love might wanting be. To Sir Henry Cary. Ben Jonson. NOSC; NoP-4

That never were, nor are, nor e'er shall be. (LL) Against Fruition. Sir John Suckling. BeJo; CaPo

That never yet drowned me. (LL) Our Bog is Dood. Stevie Smith. NAEL-5v2; NAEL-6v2; NBLV; NIL-7; PoE; WeW-3

That nibbles at the soul. (LL) This World Is Not Conclusion. Emily Dickinson. APN-2; NAAL-2v1; NAAL-3; NCAP; TCAPo

That Night. Victor Hugo. SxFrPo, *tr. by* E. H. Blackmore and A. M. Blackmore

That night, all night, he lay on his back. Unguentarium. Elizabeth Garrett. NeBl

That night an eagle swooped down from the skies onto Sophocles' house. Death of Sophocles, The. Anna Andreyevna Akhmatova. PoetW, *tr. by* Max Hayward and Stanley Kunitz

That night at Trafalgar! (LL) Thomas Hardy. FaBoCh; MoBrPo; OBMV *Fr.* Dynasts, The.

That night machines stood in the dark. Instrument. Gerrit Achterberg. TuT, *tr. by* Peter Van de Kamp

That night the house. Lighthouse. Gerard Woodward. EmeKit

That night the moon drifted over the pond. Prediction, The. Mark Strand. LCAP-2; NoP-4; SPE; VCAP

That night, the roof flew, singing. Wave, The. Fatima Lim-Wilson. AmPoNex

That night the whole world mingled. Certain Evening, A. Gilbert Keith Chesterton. OxAEP-2

That night the wind stirred in the forsythia bushes. Crossroads in the Past. John Ashbery. BAP-01

That Night They All Gathered on the Highest Tower. Jovan Hristic. GI, *tr. by* Charles Simic

That night when joy began. W. H. Auden. OxBTC; PAI; SoSe-8 *Fr.* Five Songs.

That night will long delight us, Nealce. Petronius Arbiter. PGA

That night you looked like a little androgyne in your silk tie. Man Who Killed Himself to Avoid August, The. Maureen Seaton. ExTi

That night your great guns, unawares. Channel Firing. Thomas Hardy. CABP; EBEV; HAP; HarvBoo; HeIP-4; NAEL-5v2; NAEL-6v2; NIL-7; NIP-4; NoAM; NoP-4; OxAEP-2; OxBEV; OxBTC; PAI; PeECV; PeFWW; PoE; PoPoPo; PoRA; PoWW; RB; SoSe-8; TFi; UnPo

That no grisly ghost may glide in its shadow. (LL) William Langland. NAEL-5v1; NAEL-6v1; NAEL-7v1 *Fr.* Vision of Piers Plowman, The.

That no man yet could in the bible find. Erat Quaedam Mulier. Lady Mary Cheke. EMWP

That no one hears them among the talk and laughter. (LL) Wolves. Louis MacNeice. NoAM; OxBTC

That no tomorrow shall our beams restore! (LL) William Wordsworth. OxBSo; Son

That none beguiled be by time's quick flowing. Love's Clock. Sir John Suckling. CaPo; NOSC

That none of you can understand? (LL) Where Art Is a Midwife. Tom Paulin. ModIr; NPeEn

That nose is out of drawing. With a gasp. Algernon Charles Swinburne. OxBSo; UV *Fr.* Heptalogia, The.

That note comes clear, like water running clear. Piano Tuner's Wife, The. Karl Shapiro. NoAM

That note you hold, narrowing and rising, shakes. For Sidney Bechet. Philip Larkin. NoP-4

That Nova was a moderate star like our good sun; it stored no doubt a. Nova. Robinson Jeffers. NoAM

That now to them dost all thy substance give. (LL) Lost, The. Jones Very. APN-1; NOBA; NoP-4

That ocean you of late surveyed. To Mr. Newton [on His Return from Ramsgate]. William Cowper. NOEC

That odor in the world? (LL) Mock Orange. Louise Glück. MakPoe; NoAM; PoPoPo; VCAP

That often change doth please a woman's mind. (LL) Divers Doth Use. Sir Thomas Wyatt. NAEL-5v1; OxBEV; Son

That old black magic has me in its spell. That Old Black Magic. Johnny Mercer. ReLy

That Old Devil Called Love. Allan Roberts. ReLy

That old FB eye. FB Eye Blues, The. Richard Wright. APT-2

That Old Feeling. Sammy Fain. ReLy

That "old last act"! / And yet sometimes. Adrienne Rich. NIP-4; NOBA; TAP *Fr.* Two Songs.

That Old Mulemba. Geraldo Bessa Victor. PeSAV, *tr. by* Donald Burness

That Old Sauna High. Anselm Hollo. PoM

That on her lap she casts her humble Eye. On the Blessed Virgins Bashfulnesse. Richard Crashaw. HAP; OxBSP

That once the gentle mind of my dead wife. William Ellery Leonard. APT-1 *Fr.* Two Lives.

That once this life was really mine. Song of Life, A. Franz Werfel. TrJP, *tr. by* Edith Abercrombie Snow

That once was mine! what woman taught you this? (LL) Tennyson. NAEL-5v2; NAEL-6v2 *Fr.* Princess, The.

That one bird, one star. In Praise of Creation. Elizabeth Jennings. PAI

That one long year we moved. We Still Have Basketball, Sara. Lisa Olstein. MoASP

That one might have for an honest living. (LL) Among My Friends. Robert Duncan. CLPP; HarvBoo

That one seems to me to be like the gods, the man whosoever sits facing you and listens nearby to your sweet speech an desirable laughter. Sappho. EroLit, *tr. by* John D. Winkler

That one small boy with a face like pallid cheese. Incendiary. Vernon Scannell. OxBC

That opens and bends closed those leaves. (LL) Swan's Feet, The. Edith Jay Scovell. FaBoWP; OxBTC

That opens and shuts. (LL) Samuel Beckett. ModIr; NOIV

That Orpheus Calliops sonne who stayde the running brooke. Seneca. OBVE *Fr.* Medea.

That our own houses show as strange when we come back in the dawn! (LL) Dykes, The. Rudyard Kipling. HarvBoo; OBWP

That our senses lie and our minds trick us is true, but in general. Advice to Pilgrims. Robinson Jeffers. APT-1

That our thought may take her immediate in its embrace. (LL) Sonnet [*or* Sonetto] 7: "Who is she that comes, makyng turn every man's eye." Guido Cavalcanti. CTC; OBVE, *tr. by* Ezra Pound

That Pain has ceased to mock, to mar. End of "Pain", The. Amanda Ros. VerBaPo

That parts fam'd Trachis from th'Euboic shore. (LL) Sonnet: Suppos'd to Be Written at Lemnos. Thomas Russell. NOBRP; NOEC

That peachtree so frail. *Unknown.* ColAnChi, *tr. by* Jeffrey Riegel *Fr.* Classic of Odes.

That people celebrate it by forgetting its name. (LL) At the Un-National Monument along the Canadian Border. William Stafford. HAP; HeIP-4

That people ought to be. (LL) James Kenneth Stephen. FaBoA; NOBL; NOBVV; OBCoV; PeLV *Fr.* England and America.

That plump little chorus. Sanderlings. Roland Mathias. TCAWP

"That Pobbles are happier without their toes" (LL) Pobble Who Has No Toes, The. Edward Lear. FaBoCh; OTCP

That poem I didn't write. Leah Goldberg. FIT, *tr. by* Robert Friend

That poets are far rarer births than kings. To Elizabeth, Countess of Rutland. Ben Jonson. BeJo; NoP-4

That poets should each other eat. (LL) To a Swallow. Euenos. GrAn; OBVE, *tr. by* John Peale Bishop

That points at him amazed. (LL) Full Moon and Little Frieda. Ted Hughes. HarvBoo; NPeEn; OPOU; OxBC; OxBSP

That posts dwell at times in water and, lifeless themselves. Post Heads. Johanna Kruit. TuT, *tr. by* Eamon Grennan

That pretty girl. Issa. EH, *tr. by* Robert Hass

That Prince, who may doe nothing but what's just. King and No King, A. Robert Herrick. PBRV

That promised corn but ripened into men. (LL) Year 1812, The. Adam Mickiewicz. OBVE; OBWP; WoPoe, *tr. by* Donald Davie

That Pull from the Left. Louise Erdrich. NoAM

That quiet man with the hoe is a beast. Inmate, An. Peter Kocan. NOBAu

That rabbit's foot I carried in my left pocket. Sybilline. "Ern Malley." BMAP

That raddled old queen. Tom Donnelly. PeLi

That ragged / leaking raft held. Ireland. Richard Ryan. CIP-2

That ragged vagabond, snow, brings. Intruder. Alison Bielski. AngWePo

That rain-strewn night in the woods, the chorus, chorus. Chorus. David Wagoner. MiVo

That rank bed. That Rank Bed. Nadine Brummer. Prnts

That reach through nature, molding [*or* moulding] men. (LL) Tennyson. EBVV; FHYEP; NAEL-6v2; NAWM-7v2; NOCV; TOF *Fr.* In Memoriam A. H. H.

That rebellious rodent called Jerry. Bill Greenwell. PeLi

That rides the glorious cherubim. (LL) To Find[e] God. Robert Herrick. BeJo; InvLi; NoP-4

That road / got no people. Sketches. Federico García Lorca. PFTM-1

That romantic star. One. Federico García Lorca. PFTM-1

That romps through the dark. (LL) Canis Major. Robert Frost. KaS; MoAmPo

That Room. John Montague. CIP-2

That rose slowly toward me, watching. (LL) Pike. Ted Hughes. FaBoMo; HAP; HeIP-4; NAEL-5v2; NAEL-6v2; NPeEn; OxBEV; OxBTC; PoE

That row of icicles along the gutter. Beyond Words. Robert Frost. Spl; WeW-3

That runs on and on at its own sweet will. (LL) Sweet Will. Philip Levine. LCAP-2; VCAP

That's a rich man coming. *Unknown.* STP

That's All. Lawrence Joseph. GraLe; PBCAP

That's All. Mother Goose. OxNR; ReMoGo

That's all that I remember. (LL) Incident. Countee Cullen. APT-2; BPo; ChAP; KaS; NAAAL; NAAL-2v2; NAAL-5; NOxBChV; NTCP; NoAM; NoP-4; OBCA; OxIBACP; PoPoPo; SSLK; VGW

That's enough of that, Mr Bones. *Some* lady you make. John Berryman. NAAL-2v2; VCAP *Fr.* Dream Songs.

That's Entertainment. Howard Dietz. ReLy

That's him: head reared above the Babelic ramp. Csontváry. László Nagy. IQMS, *tr. by* George Gömöri and Kenneth McRobbie

That's how billboards give up their promises. Midnight Reports. Lynda Hull. SwNoth

That's how we distinguish a man from a woman, or from. Histories of Bodies. Mariko Nagai. PuP-23

That's it—I love that fawn. Samuel Ha-Nagid. ErotSp, *tr. by* Harris Lenowitz and Jerome Rothenberg

That's Jack. Jack. Charles Henry Ross. NOxBChV; Spl

That's me, arguing for another effort. Appomattox. Terese Svoboda. ExTi

That's me, second from the left. Perpetuum Immobile. Bruce Dawe. CBAP

That's much too difficult. I quit. (LL) Some Opposites. Richard Wilbur. OBCA; OxIBACP

That's my last Duchess painted on the wall. My Last Duchess. Robert Browning. AWP; AmFaPo; CABP; CIHu; EBNV; EBVV; FHYEP; GTBS-P; HAP; HeIP-4; ITBLP; InPK-6; MakPoe; NAEL-5v2; NAWM-7v2; NIL-7; NIP-4; NOBE; NOBVV; NPeEn; NoP-4; OxBEV; PAI; PeVV; PoE; PoPoPo; SCGP; SCV; SoSe-8; TFi; TRP

That's my rime. (LL) Season Song. *Unknown.* RB; WoPoe, *tr. by* Flann O'Brien and Flann O'Brien

That's My Style. Peggy Lee. ReLy

That's My Weakness Now. Sam H. Stept. ReLy

That's not a man in pain. Short Lexicon of Torture in the Eighties, A. Edward Hirsch. VCAP

That's not even it. Recitation. Ellease Southerland. GT

That's Not in My Job Description. Paul Beatty. NeAmPo

That's right, there's a clear spot in me, and in you. Mirrored. Giancarlo Majorino. ItPo, *tr. by* Gayle Ridinger

That's slowish work, Bob. What'st a-been about? William Barnes. PeVV, *tr. by* Hualing Nieh *Fr.* Best Man in the Vield, The.

That's Success! Berton Braley. PoToHe

That's the only image. Wall, A. Charles Simic. HCAP

That's the prison. San Quentin 1968. Robert Peterson. GeoHom

That's the tid i fa la truth. (LL) Derby Ram, The. *Unknown.* OxNR; ReMoGo

That's the trouble around here. Loose Shoes. Charles Bernstein. FTOS

(That's the Way) Dixieland Started Jazz. Shelton Brooks. ReLy

That's the way for Billy and me. (LL) Boy's Song, A. James Hogg. NOxBChV; OBEV; OTCP; OxAEP-2

That's the way it was. (LL) Magic Words. *Unknown.* RaBo; STP, *tr. by* Edward Field

That's the Way, Uh Huh, Uh Huh, I Liked It. Anthony R. Vigil. AmPoNex

That's what I said. (LL) Song of the Mad Prince, The. Walter De la Mare. EBEV; FaBoCh; MakPoe; NOBE; NoAM; OxAEP-2

That's what I tell him. (LL) What I Tell Him. Simon J. Ortiz. CDW; ChAP

That's what I was doing on a Wednesday morning. Keeping Track. Maurya Simon. GeoHom

That's What It's Like. Mikhail Valentinovich Kulchitsky [*or* Kulchitskii]. "I love Russia." TCRP

That's what love is like. The whole river. Crossing Over. William Meredith. NoAM

That's what misery is. Poetry Is a Destructive Force. Wallace Stevens. APT-1; OxBA; RaBo

That's What We'd Do. Mary Mapes Dodge. OBCA

That's what we went for, Holly and I. Carnies. Debra Allbery. PBCAP

That's what young women are made of. (LL) What Are Folks Made Of. Mother Goose. ReMoGo; UV

That's when I saw a whole series of things. Final Manuscript. Giannina Braschi. TANSG, *tr. by* Alan West

That's where Lyle Wilson went, wearing his Mariners. Land of Lincoln. Angela Sorby. AmPoNex

That's why societies usedta throw us away/ or sell us/ or. It's Not so Good to be Born a Girl/ Sometimes. Ntozake Shange. SSLK

That's why the lady is a tramp! (LL) Lady Is a Tramp, The. Richard Rodgers. OBAL; ReLy

That's Why They Call Me "Shine." Cecil Mack. ReLy

That's / your son? the brother. Man's Song, about His Daughter, A. *Unknown.* STP, *tr. by* Armand Schwerner

That's your third sneeze now, my good lamp. Argentarius. GrAn

That sad and joyful dawn. Sonnet: That Sad and Joyful Dawn. Luis de Camões [*or* Camõens]. WoPoe, *tr. by* David Wevill

That sail in cloudless light. Sea Grapes. Derek Walcott. TRP

That sail which leans on light. Sea Grapes. Derek Walcott. PoetW

That samin tyme, of Troy the garnisoun. Robert Henryson. OxBEV *Fr.* Testament of Cresseid, The.

That Saturday at eventide. (LL) High Tide on the Coast of Lincolnshire, 1571, The. Jean Ingelow. EBVV; OxAEP-2

That scalds me now—that scalds me now! (LL) Emily Dickinson. NOCV; SAmP

That sculptor we knew, the passionate-eyed son of a quarryman. Artist, An. Robinson Jeffers. HarvBoo; VGW

That scything wind has cut the rich corn down. John Knox. Iain Crichton Smith. OxBS

That season when the leaf deserts the bole. October 1. Karl Shapiro. MoAmPo

That second time they hunted me. Italian in England, The. Robert Browning. OBNV

That seemed hard frozen: may it happen for you. (LL) Sometimes. Sheenagh Pugh. OPOU; TCAWP

That separate rights are lost in mutual love. (LL) Rights of Woman, The. Anna Laetitia Barbauld. CABP; ECWP; NAEL-6v2; NOEC; NoP-4; PEW; WoRP

That Shadow My Likeness. Walt Whitman. APN-1

That shaman, owl man. Deadly Dance, The. *Unknown.* STP, *tr. by* Edward Kissam

That she adored me as the most. Elegy on Any Lady by George Moore. Max Beerbohm. FaBoEE

That she hath gone to Heaven suddenly. Dante Alighieri. CTC *Fr.* La Vita Nuova.

That she is beautiful is not delight. Augusta Davies Webster. ViWPN *Fr.* Mother and Daughter.

That she sends, milky, to the sea. (LL) Message from Ohanapecosh Glacier. W. M. Ransom. CDW; GifTon

That she that makes me sin, awards me pain. (LL) William Shakespeare. HeIP-4; OxAEP-1 *Fr.* Sonnets.

That she will move from mourning into morning. (LL) Sonnet to My Mother. George Barker. OxBSo; RaBo

That she would grow again. (LL) Countee Cullen. APT-2; MoAmPo; SSLK; VGW *Fr.* Four Epitaphs.

That shede His blode for my redempcion! (LL) *Unknown.* MiEL; NPeEn

That shipwrecked [*or* shipwrackt] vessel which th' Apostle bore. Upon His Majesty's [*or* Majesties] Repairing of Paul's. Edmund Waller. BASC; PBRV

That silent publicizer of unheard-of news. Philodemus. GrAn

That since you would save none of me, I bury some of you. (LL) Funeral[l], The. John Donne. AWP; BoLoP; EBEV; ESCV; EnLoPo; HeIP-4; MeLP; NAEL-5v1; NAEL-6v1; NAEL-7v1; NAWM-5v1; OBEV; PoRA; SCGP; TFi

That Sindhi boy is keen on you. Mrs. Biswas of Maryland on the Phone. Reetika Vazirani. AmPoNex

That sings in the thicket. (LL) Judas Iscariot. Ronald Allison Kells Mason. PeNZ; SacPr

That situates so far. (LL) Emily Dickinson. APN-2; NOBA

That slepen I ne may. (LL) *Unknown.* MiEL; PoE

That slide would be halted. Rollercoaster. Cris Cheek. Oth

That small girl crouched. Eavesdropper, The. Jane O. Wayne. InvLad

That smasher of shams, Bernard Shaw. Limerick. Frank Buckland. PeLi

That snail. Buson. ChAP

That soldier with a machinegun bolted. Two Summers in Moravia. Roger McDonald. CBAP

That some day death who has us all for jest. Augusta Davies Webster. VWP *Fr.* Mother and Daughter.

That sort of place where you stop. Colville 1964. Kendrick Smithyman. PeNZ

That song of his is like a boat with black sails. Listening to a Cricket in the Wainscoting. Robert Bly. InvLad

That spot of blood on the drawing room wall. Conversation in the Drawing Room, The. Weldon Kees. SPE

That spring he was fourteen. By the Rivers. Shirley Kaufman. GifTon

That Spring Night I Spent. Lady Suo. OHPJ, *tr. by* Kenneth Rexroth

That spring was late. We watched the sky. Neighbours. Gillian Clarke. TCAWP

That spurned us—Yesterday! (LL) Emily Dickinson. NOCV; PoBW

That sputter of rain, flipping the hedgerows. Shower, A. Amy Lowell. PoBW

That stand upon the threshold of the new. (LL) Edmund Waller. BASC; BeJo; EBEV; HAP; NOBE; NOCV; NOSC; NPeEn; NoP-4; OBEV; OxBEV; PeECV; PoPoPo; SCGP; SacPr

That star I now see. Star and Sea. William Peskett. PNI

That star the highest seen in heaven's expanse. Dino Frescobaldi. EaltPo, *tr. by* Dante Gabriel Rossetti

That still my Syrinx' lips I kiss. (LL) John Lyly. NPeEn; NoSic; SCGP *Fr.* Midas.

That story which the bold Sir Bedivere. Tennyson. FHYEP; NAEL-5v2; NAEL-6v2 *Fr.* Idylls of the King.

That strange flower, the sun. Gubbinal. Wallace Stevens. NAAL-2v2

That Strangest is of all; yet brought to pass. (LL) Salutation [*or* Salutations], The. Thomas Traherne. ESCV; EnlH; GeHe; NOCV; SacPr

That street washed with violet. Last Trams. Kenneth Slessor. BMAP

That strong god whose touch made Dante tremble. Modern Love. Anne Ridler. SacPr

That substitute teacher in art, you could tell she was strange. Wearing Dad's White Shirt Backwards. Rick Agran. AmPoNex

That sultry afternoon the world went strange. One Tuesday in Summer. James McAuley. BMAP

That summer bird its oft-repeated note. Wryneck's Nest, The. John Clare. CenSon

That summer I did not go crazy. To the Bone. Dorothy Allison. GLP

That summer I went to Woodstock. Woodstock. Jan-Mitchell Sherrill. ReTh

That summer, in a small glass booth. Praise of Italian Chip-Shops. W. N. Herbert. NeBl

That summer in Culpeper, all there was to eat was white. Nineteen. Elizabeth Alexander. GT; InTrad; PoPoPo

That summer the women sat on their porches. Misguided Angels. Gale Renée Walden. ReTh

That summer with a thousand Julys. For the Last Summer. Robert Wrigley. SwNoth

That sun that breathed love's fire into my youth. Dante Alighieri. NAWM-5v1 *Fr.* Divina Commedia.

That surrounds Montecito like the echo of a scream. (LL) In Montecito. Randall Jarrell. CoAP; VGW

That sway from mood to mood the willing mind! (LL) Poet, The. William Cullen Bryant. NAAL-2v1; NAAL-3; NCAP; TAP

That sweet accord is seldom seen. (LL) Honesty. Sir Thomas Wyatt. NoSic; OxBSP

That teacher gave me a new name. . . again. Name Giveaway. Phillip [*or* "Phil"] William George. VoR

That terra-cotta waitress. Villa Restaurant, The. Derek Walcott. WeW-3

That terrible day my heart took a blow that nearly killed. Starlet. Fanny Howe. ExTi

That that mind perceives how to fly alone. Allen Fisher. Oth *Fr.* Emergent Manner.

That that part of me is dripping. *Unknown.* PriapPo, *tr. by* Richard W. Hooper *Fr.* Priapus Poems, The.

That! that! there I was told. Bible, The. Thomas Traherne. PeECV

That the balls of the lover are not larger than the balls of the priest. Christian Karlson Stead. PeNZ *Fr.* Quesada.

That the earth be made safer for men, and more stable. *Unknown.* APN-2 *Fr.* Hardening of the World, and the First Settlement of Men, The.

That the glass would melt in heat. Glass of Water, The. Wallace Stevens. MoAmPo; OxBA; TAP

That the Great Angell-blinding light should shrinke. Giambattista [*or* Giovanni Battista] Marino. SacPr *Fr.* Strage degli innocenti, La.

That the high sheen of death could blot. Midsummer. James Scully. TwCP

That the King enjoys his own again. (LL) King Enjoys His Own Again, The. Martin Parker. FaBoCh; OxBoLi

That the Muses have no more fervent. Person's Tale, The. U. A. Fanthorpe. NoP-4

That the music had somehow got mixed with the whole. (LL) James Russell Lowell. NOBA; TAP; TCAPo *Fr.* Fable for Critics, A.

That the neighborhood might be covered. Larry Eigner. PoM

That the poet "does not number the streaks of the tulip." To Hugh MacDiarmid. Edwin Morgan. FaBoTw

That the proud eagle would have to wife. (LL) Ancients of the World, The. Ronald Stuart Thomas. OPOU; RB

That the right man lay in the dust. (LL) After Goliath. Kingsley Amis. NOBL; OxBTC

That the risen Christ should *be* risen. (LL) Don'ts. D. H. Lawrence. OxBoLi; PeLV

That the Science of Cartography Is Limited. Eavan Boland. HarvBoo; NoP-4; SpudSo

That the Theocritan pick-up has been versed. Rabbiters: A Pastoral, The. John Kinsella. NeBl

That the transactions would end. Beauty and the Beast. Gillian Conoley. BodElec

That the war would be over before they got to you. When You Have Forgotten Sunday: The Love Story. Gwendolyn Brooks. WPOW

That the year would not go well with me. (LL) Omens. *Unknown.* RB; WoPoe, *tr. by* Alexander Carmichael

That then I scorn to change my state with Kings. (LL) William Shakespeare. AWP; AmFaPo; CTC; EBEV; HAP; HeIP-4; ITBLP; InPK-6; NAEL-5v1;

NAEL-6v1; NAEL-7v1; NOBE; NoP-4; NoSic; OBEV; OPOU; OxAEP-1; PoPoPo; SCGP; Son; TFi; WeW-3; WoPoe *Fr.* Sonnets.

That there is falsehood in his looks. Parson's Looks, The. Robert Burns. OxBoLi

That there shall be a day of Dome. (LL) Sea Marke. John Smith. SCAP; TCAPo

That there should never be air. Roses. Barbara Guest. NoP-4

That there was doubt about these things. (LL) Dialogue. Adrienne Rich. NIL-7; TAP

That there was later on. Nothing That Is, The. Ralph Angel. BodElec

That therewith my song is broken. (LL) Sir Philip Sidney. NoSic; PBRV *Fr.* Astrophil and Stella.

That these may be thy Praise, and my Joy too. (LL) Mount of Olives. Henry Vaughan. ESCV; GeHe

That they are brown, no man will dare to say. Her Eyes. Helen Hunt Jackson. PoBW; TCAPo

That they were at the beach—aeolotropic series. Leslie Scalapino.
  "Playing ball—so it's like paradise, not because it's in the past, we're on a." BodElec

That thin little boy. Emigrant's Son, The. Luis Andrade Silva. NAfrP, *tr.* by Don Burness

That thou art blamed shall not be thy defect. William Shakespeare. OxAEP-1; SCGP *Fr.* Sonnets.

That thou find'st none. (LL) Upon the Asse That Bore Our Saviour. Richard Crashaw. ChIV-2; GeHe

That thou hast her, it is not all my grief[e]. William Shakespeare. HeIP-4; OxAEP-1 *Fr.* Sonnets.

That thou hast kept thy love, increased thy will. To the Same [Sir Thomas Roe]. Ben Jonson. BASC

That thou may'st know me[e], and I'll turn[e] my face. (LL) Good Friday [or Goodfriday], 1613. Riding Westward. John Donne. BASC; BBASP; ChIV-2; ESCV; FSCP; MeLP; NAEL-5v1; NAEL-6v1; NAEL-7v1; NOCV; NOSC; NoP-4; PBRV; PeECV; PoE; SacPr; TFi

That thou mayst fit thyself against thy fall. (LL) Church Monuments. George Herbert. BASC; ESCV; GeHe; HAP; NAEL-5v1; NAEL-6v1; NAEL-7v1; NOCV; NOSC; NPeEn; PoE; TRP

That thou mayst injure no man, dove-like be. Prudent Simplicity. Goronwy Owen. FaBoEE, *tr.* by William Cowper

That though thine absence starve me, I wish not thee. (LL) John Donne. NAEL-6v1; NAEL-7v1; NoSic

That throng my hiddenness. (LL) Samuel Beckett. ModIr; NOIV; NoAM

That time I did not save Warsaw, nor Prague later. Natalya [or Natal'ia] Gorbanevskaya [or Gorbanyevskaya or Gorbanevskaia]. TCRusP, *tr.* by Daniel Weissbort

That time / in the sun. When Sun Came to Riverwoman. Leslie Marmon Silko. ReEnLa; VoR

That time my grandmother dragged me. Weakness, The. Toi Derricotte. GT; LTA

That time of drought the embered air. Drought Year. Judith Wright. NoAM

That time of year thou may'st [or maist] in me behold. William Shakespeare. AEP; AWP; BoLoP; CABP; CTC; ClHu; EBEV; GTBS-P; HAP; HeIP-4; InPK-6; NAEL-5v1; NAEL-6v1; NAEL-7v1; NIP-4; NOBE; NoP-4; NoSic; OBEV; OxBSo; PoE; PoRA; SCGP; SoSe-8; Son; TFi; UnPo; WeW-3 *Fr.* Sonnets.

That time of year you may in me behold. Winter Twilight, Glowing Black and Gold, The. Delmore Schwartz. NoAM

That Time of Year Thou Mayst in Me Behold. William Shakespeare. *See* Sonnets

That time stands up vertically. Elegies, or the Stations of the Other Time. Ahmad 'Abd al-Mu'ti Hijazi. MAP, *tr.* by May Jayyusi and Naomi Shihab Nye

That told the history of my lost people. (LL) Belonging. Rafael Campo. AmPoNex; WiU

That tomorrow a new walk is a new walk. (LL) Corsons Inlet. A. R. Ammons. CoAP; ColAP; NAAL-2v2; NAAL-5; NOBA; NoAM; NoP-4; PoE; VCAP

That top-secret flight at night. Lights. Ernesto Cardenal. TCLAP, *tr.* by Jonathan Cohen

That trembles in the ripples. (LL) Li Po. CrYelRi; ErotSp, *tr.* by Sam Hamill *Fr.* Women of Yueh.

That Trinacria was made one part of Italy. To Frederick V, by the Grace of God . . . Bathsua Pell Makin. EMWP

That trumpet tongue which taught a nation. Demagogue, The. Phyllis McGinley. FaBoEE

That tumbled meaning into wind. (LL) Snow Country Weavers. James Welch. CDW; HATNAP

That tunes on Duddon's banks her slender voice. (LL) William Wordsworth. CenSon; Son *Fr.* River Duddon [A Series of Sonnets], The.

"That turn'll get her," I said. Toujours la Politesse. Ezra Pound. OBVE

That unction sweet, which lulls the bleeding breast! (LL) Resolves to Take the Leap of Leucata. Mary Robinson. CenSon; RWP

That Van Gogh's ear, set free. What Is Worth Knowing? Sujata Bhatt. OMIP

That very day. William Wordsworth. NAEL-6v2 *Fr.* Prelude, The; Growth of a Poet's Mind [1850 vers.].

That violence ever after would be obsolete. (LL) Adrienne Rich. PoE; TRP *Fr.* Twenty-one Love Poems.

That Virtue but that body grant to us. (LL) Sir Philip Sidney. NAEL-5v1; NAEL-6v1; NAEL-7v1; NoP-4 *Fr.* Astrophil and Stella.

That virtuous is, when the reward's away. (LL) To Sir Henry Cary. Ben Jonson. NOSC; NoP-4

That wail! 'tis prophecy. Oh, hush! be still. Birth Wail, The. Henrietta Tindal. VWP

That wan and sickly droops upon her breast! (LL) Samuel Taylor Coleridge. CenSon; GSo; Son *Fr.* Effusions.

That wand[e]reth lightly. (LL) George Peele. ChIV-1; NOBE; NPeEn; NoSic; OxBEV; OxBSP; OxBoLi; RB *Fr.* David and [Fair] Bethsabe.

That wants himself[e] is poor[e] indeed. (LL) Grasshopper, The. Richard Lovelace. BASC; BeJo; CaPo; CavPo; EBEV; NAEL-5v1; NAEL-6v1; NAEL-7v1; NOBE; NOSC; NoP-4; OBEV; SCGP; TFi

That war should bankrupts make of merchants is no wonder. Upon the Bankruptcy of a Physician. Henricus Selyns. SCAP

That was a joyous day in Rheims of old. Joan of Arc in Rheims. Felicia Dorothea Hemans. RWP; ViWPN

That Was Before I Met You. P. G. Wodehouse. ReLy

That was enough. You Called Me Corazón. Sandra Cisneros. AmFaPo

That was my very soul that stole to the lips in our kissing. Kiss, The. Plato. STV, *tr.* by John Frederick Nims

That was not a reminder of the end. (LL) Sonnet: Death Warnings. Francisco de Quevedo y Villegas. AWP; OxBEV; WoPoe, *tr.* by John Masefield

That Was Summer. Marci Ridlon. NTCP

That was the best moment of the monk's life. Burning Oneself to Death. Shinkichi Takahashi. ZenPo, *tr.* by Takashi Ikemoto and Lucien Stryk

That was the day they killed the Son of God. Killing, The. Edwin Muir. GI

That was the moment when, without. Short History of the Bourgeoisie. Hans Magnus Enzensberger. VCWP, *tr.* by Hans Magnus Enzensberger and Michael Hamburger

That was the proverb. Let my mistress[e] be. Long and Lazy [or Lazie]. Robert Herrick. FaBoEE

"That was the thrush's last good-night," I thought. Edward Dowden. OxBSo *Fr.* In the Garden.

That was the top of the walk, when he said. Gypsy, The. Ezra Pound. NPeEn

That was the year I drove around all the time. Invention of Pittsburgh, The. Maggie Anderson. PBCAP

That watches and receives. (LL) Tables Turned, The. William Wordsworth. FHYEP; NAEL-5v2; NAEL-6v2; NOBRP; TOF

That we are ruined by the thing we kill. (LL) Australia 1970. Judith Wright. CBAP; HarvBoo; MakPoe; NoAM

That We can show—Today? (LL) Emily Dickinson. APN-2; NOBA; OxBA

That we confront. (LL) George Oppen. AF; APSN; APT-2

That We Head Towards. Stephany Fuller. BPo

That we know you, terrible joy. (LL) Matins. Denise Levertov. FaBoWP; NOBA; NoAM

That we lift, as chaff lifts, toward God. (LL) Mennonites. Julia Kasdorf. NeAmPo; PBCAP

That we may have life. My Father. Felix Mnthali. PBMAP

That we should ever know her perfectly. (LL) Sonnet: A Rapture Concerning His Lady. Guido Cavalcanti. AWP; EaltPo, *tr.* by Dante Gabriel Rossetti

That we with merthe mowe safely singe *Deo gracias!*. (LL) Agincourt Carol, The. *Unknown.* EBEV; NoP-4

That weeps, but not for thee. (LL) A. E. Housman. NOBVV; OxBEV

That weeps. . . as thou must sing. . . alone, aloof. (LL) Elizabeth Barrett Browning. CenSon; OxAEP-2; Son; VWP *Fr.* Sonnets from the Portuguese.

That weren't to be trusted. (LL) Castration. Nigel Jenkins. AngWePo; TCAWP

That what. Dream Thief. Nathaniel Mackey. GT

That when we live no more we may live ever. (LL) To My Dear and Loving Husband. Anne Bradstreet. AmFaPo; BASC; BoWoP; ColAP; ErotSp; HAP; HeIP-4; ITBLP; LW; NAAL-2v1; NAAL-3; NAAL-5; NIL-7; NIP-4; NOBA; NOCV; NOSC; NoP-4; OxBA; OxBEV; OxBSP; OxWW; PEW; PoE; SCAP; SacPr; TAP; TCAPo; TFi; WPE; WeW-3

That which abandoned me. To See Secretary Shu-Yun Off at the Hsieh T'iao Tower at Hsuan-Ch'eng. Li Po. ChinPo, *tr.* by Yip Wai-lim

That which blossoms. Kiko. JDP, *tr.* by Yoel Hoffmann

That which creates a happy life. Happy Life, A. Mildmay Fane, 2d Earl of Westmorland. BeJo

That which her slender waist confined. On a Girdle. Edmund Waller. AWP; BASC; BeJo; GTBS-P; InPK-6; NAEL-5v1; NOSC; NoP-4; OBEV; PoE; PoRA; SCGP; TFi

That which is, being the only answer. Question and Answer. Kathleen Jessie Raine. MoBrPo

That Which Is Enough for Love. Luis Cernuda. CAGL, *tr.* by Rick Lipinski

That Which Is Fugitive, That Which Is Medicinally Sweet or Alterable to Gold, That Which Is Substantiated by Unscientific Means. Valerie Wohlfeld. YaYoPo

That which is in part, finding its whole again throughout the universe. (LL) Tortoise Shout. D. H. Lawrence. NAEL-5v2; NAEL-6v2; PFTM-1

That which my fault has made me, o paint not. Poet to a Painter, A. Aubrey Thomas De Vere. Son

That which ripped an amazed scream. Joseph Brodsky. TCRusP, *tr.* by Bernard Meares *Fr.* Sonnets on the Statue of Mary, Queen of Scots, in the Luxembourg Gardens, Paris.

That which the mouth cannot utter. Stone at the Tip of the Tongue, A. Oumarou Watta. NAfrP

That which then was ours, my love. Don't Ask Me for That Love Again. Faiz Ahmad Faiz. PoetW; VCWP, *tr.* by Agha Shahid Ali

That Which We Call a Rose. Michael Dransfield. CBAP; NOBAu (Black grayed into white a nightmare of bicycling.) BMAP

That which we call reality is that. Corals and Shells. William Bronk. APSN

That which we dare invoke to bless. Tennyson. EBVV; FHYEP; NAEL-6v2; NAWM-7v2; NOCV; SacPr; TOF *Fr.* In Memoriam A. H. H.

That while he lived never thought of death. (LL) Fulke Greville, 1st Baron Brooke. CABP; NOSC; NoSic *Fr.* Caelica.

That whiskey will cook the egg. Bar. Langston Hughes. APSN

That whistles in the wind. (LL) Lucy Gray; or, Solitude. William Wordsworth. NAEL-5v2; NAEL-6v2; NOBRP; OxAEP-2

That white cloud in its contrast. Patrizia Cavalli. NeIt

That Whitsun, I was late getting away. Whitsun Weddings, The. Philip Larkin. FaBoMo; HeIP-4; NoAM; NoP-4; OxAEP-2; OxBTC

That whole morning we were full of joy. Interlude of Joy. George Seferis. PoetW, *tr.* by Edmund Keeley and Philip Sherrard

That will not state—its sting. (LL) Emily Dickinson. NOBA; OxBA; PoRA; SoSe-8; TCAPo

That Willowwood should hold her wandering! (LL) Dante Gabriel Rossetti. NAEL-5v2; NAEL-6v2; OxBSo *Fr.* House of Life, The.

That winged word. (LL) Twenty Years Hence. Walter Savage Landor. NAEL-5v2; NAEL-6v2; NOBVV

That wink of time when I was happy still. Winter Noon. Umberto Saba. STV, *tr.* by John Frederick Nims

That winter, the dead could not be buried. Leningrad Cemetery, Winter of 1941. Sharon Olds. NIL-7; NIP-4

That winter the stairs were always unlit. Confinement. Ann Sansom. NeBl

That with this bright believing band. Impercipient, The. Thomas Hardy. EBVV; NAEL-5v2; NAEL-6v2

"That woman there is almost dead." Rat, The. William Henry Davies. OBWVE; OxBTC

That won my heart in my greener years. (LL) William Cullen Bryant. APN-1; NOBA; OxBA; TCAPo

That wonderous man of Cape Horn. (LL) Limerick: "There was an old man of Cape Horn." Edward Lear. EBEV; PeLi

That would be enough. (LL) What Would I Do White? June Jordan. LTA; UnSA

That would be waving and that would be crying. Waving Adieu, Adieu, Adieu. Wallace Stevens. NoP-4

That wren. Issa. EH, *tr.* by Robert Hass

That year he found himself without a job. Days of 1908. Constantine P. Cavafy. WoPoe, *tr.* by James Merrill

That year no wondering shepherds came. Christmas, the Year One, A.D. Sara Henderson Hay. PoRA

That year of the cloud, when my marriage failed. River Road. Stanley Kunitz. NoAM

That year they fought in the snow. Rostov. George Sutherland Fraser. PoWW

That year we hardly slept, waking like inmates. Getting Out. Cleopatra Mathis. SoSe-8

That yellowed body of the Lord. Vladimir Iul'evich Lvov. TCRP

That you and I, I and you, Anniversary. Davi Walders. MPUn

That you belong to the 'folk,' sonny-boy, had you not better show us. Piece of Advice, A. Gyula Illyés. IQMS, *tr.* by Adam Makkai

"That you two have problems." (LL) Wayman in Love. Tom Wayman. NIL-7; NIP-4; NOBC

That you were gane awa' (LL) Sweet William's Ghost *or* Sweet William and May Margaret. *Unknown.* AWP; ESPB

That you were once unkind befriends me now. William Shakespeare. OxAEP-1 *Fr.* Sonnets.

That your honour's petitioners (dealers in rhymes). To the Right Hon. Henry Pelham. Edward Moore. OBSV

That zephyr every year. Spring Bereaved. William Drummond, of Hawthornden. OBEV

Thatch gate works all right but I never open it. Idle Thoughts. Lu Yu. CoBCP, *tr.* by Burton Watson

Thatched Hut, The. Tu Fu. CrYelRi, *tr.* by Sam Hamill

Thatched hut among the pines, door open near a cliff. Inscribed on a Painting. T'ang Yin. CoBLCP, *tr.* by Jonathan Chaves

Thatcher, The. Brendan Kennelly. CIP-2

Thatcher of Thatchwood went to Thatchet a-thatching, A. *Unknown.* OxNR

That's your freedom—bootleg whiskey. Two Countries. Tadeusz Borowski. AF, *tr.* by Larry Rafferty

Thaw. Margaret Avison. FaBoWP; NOBC

Thaw. Edward Thomas. EBEV; FaBoTw; GTBS-P; MoBrPo; OxAEP-2; OxBEV; OxBSP; OxBTC; Spl

Thaw, The. Marianne Wolfe. GifTon

Thaw out old Dover for the houseless kings? (LL) Great Britain Through the Ice: Or, Premature Patriotism. Charles Tennyson Turner. OxBSo; Son

Thawing. Penny Harter. HA

Thawing earth, The. What We Feared. Judith Ortiz Cofer. PueRic

Thawing ice the garbage blooming out of it. Matsuo Allard. HA

Theaitetos. Callimachus. GrAn, *tr.* by Peter Jay

Theare be great Prince, such as will tell you howe. Samuel Daniel. PBRV *Fr.* Epistle. To Prince Henrie].

These stwonen steps a-zet so true. Stwonen Steps, The. William Barnes. NOBVV

Theater Impressions. Wislawa Szymborska. VCWP

"Theatre." Anne-Marie Albiach. MFP, *tr.* by Martin Sorrell

Theatre. Remco Campert. TuT, *tr.* by Theo Dorgan

Theatrical Venus. George Buchanan. PNI

Thebais [*or* Thebaid]. Publius Papinius Statius.

Book 10. RomPo, *tr.* by Norman Austin and Ruth Morse

"Damp night overwhelmed Phoebus at the western gates." RomPo, *tr.* by Norman Austin and Ruth Morse

Thebes. Honestus. GrAn, *tr.* by Peter Jay

Thee, dear friend, a brother soothes. To Rhea. Ralph Waldo Emerson. APN-1

Thee for my recitative. To a Locomotive in Winter. Walt Whitman. GM; InPK-6; MoAmPo; NAAL-2v1; NAAL-3; NCAP; NoAM; NoP-4; TAP

Thee, God, I come from, to Thee go. Gerard Manley Hopkins. SacPr

Thee Pompey thy past deeds by turns infest. Lucan. OBVE *Fr.* Pharsalia.

Thee, Queen of Shadows!—shall I still invoke. To Fancy. Charlotte Smith. OxBSo

Thee, Sovereign God, our grateful accents praise. Te Deum, The. *Unknown.* AWP, *tr.* by John Dryden

Thee too, modest tressèd maid. Moon. Henry Rowe. OBEV

Thee we adore, O hidden Saviour, thee. Saint Thomas Aquinas. SacPr, *tr.* by F. R. Woodford

Thee will I love, my God and King. Robert Bridges. SacPr

Thee with all mine eyes. (LL) Lover to His Lady, The. Plato. CTC; FaBoEE; NoSic, *tr.* by George Turberville

Theft. Karen Volkman. AmPoNex

Theft of fire, The. Man's worst bargain yet. Palladas [*or* Pallades]. GrAn

Theft's hour—the bus. Late Bus (After a Series of Hold-Ups). Russell Atkins. LTA

Theh Thet Hi Can Wittes Fule-Wis. *Unknown.* HAP

Thei I singe and murthes make. *Unknown.* MiEL

Their adornment for the evening finished now, their bright skin like snow. Tune: "Spring in Jade Pavilion." Li Yü. SuSp, *tr.* by Daniel Bryant

Their ancient, glittering eyes, are gay. (LL) Lapis Lazuli. W. B. Yeats. CABP; EnlH; FaBoMo; FaBoTw; HeIP-4; NAEL-5v2; NAEL-6v2; NAWM-7v2; NOBE; NoAM; NoP-4; TFi

Their Ardour kindles all the Grecian Pow'rs. Homer. OBVE, *tr.* by Alexander Pope *Fr.* Iliad, The.

Their bar-stools have slouched them too early. Slouch. Brendan Cleary. NeBl

Their barbarism did not assuage the grief. Retreat of Ita Cagney, The. Michael Hartnett. CIP-2; PBCIP

Their Beginning. Constantine P. Cavafy. CAGL, *tr.* by Edmund Keeley and Philip Sherrard

Their Behaviour. Dennis Brutus. HBAPE

Their black truck rattled up the dusty hill. Diviners, The. Mary Oliver. WPE

Their bodies lined up against the walls. Waiting for Truth. Susan Griffin. GLP

Their bones in one mad dance. (LL) Horse, The. Philip Levine. CoAP; VCAP

Their bones not even picked for souvenirs. (LL) From Colony to Nation. Irving Layton. NIL-7; NOBC

Their braided arms embrace us. (LL) Jewish Singles Event, The. Stewart Florsheim. GotH; UnSA

Their center blocks out and the ball. Good "D." James McKean. MoASP

Their cheeks were fresh and tender. Civil Song. Pier Paolo Pasolini. VCWP, *tr. by* Norman MacAfee

Their colons fed with mucus, brains with lies. Monologue. Gottfried Benn. AF, *tr. by* Christopher Middleton

Their Cone-like Cabins. Charles G. Ballard. VoR

Their departures hence and die. (LL) Upon the Loss[e] of His Mistresses. Robert Herrick. BASC; BeJo; CaPo; CavPo; NAEL-5v1; NAEL-6v1; NAEL-7v1; NOSC; PoE

Their essences of lilies and of roses. (LL) Thoughts after Ruskin. Elma Mitchell. FaBoWP; NPeEn

Their eyelids are drooping, no tears lie beneath. Weavers. Heinrich Heine. TrJP

Their eyes shining, grave with a perfect pleasure. (LL) Little Dancers, The. Laurence Binyon. MoBrPo; OxBTC

Their faces, safe as an interior. Middle-Aged, The. Adrienne Rich. HCAP; PoPoPo

Their father played the banjo. Rough Boys. Sam Adams. TCAWP

Their feathers were like white silk. Birds from the Mountains, The. Chang Chi. OHMPC, *tr. by* Kenneth Rexroth

Their feet on London, their heads in the grey clouds. Whit Monday. Louis MacNeice. ChIV-1; PeECV

Their fingernails and hair continue to grow. Old, The. Franz Wright. LCAP-2

Their footless dance. Robert Penn Warren. NAAL-5 *Fr.* Audubon: A Vision.

Their footsteps borrow silence from the snow. (LL) Persephone. Michael Longley. NPeEn; PBCIP

Their forces were about three kilometers from our front lines. Bottle of Suze, A. Pablo Picasso. PFTM-1

Their garden has a silent tall stone-wall. Caserta Garden. Richard Wilbur. OBGa

Their ground they stil made good. Homer. OBVE, *tr. by* George Chapman *Fr.* Iliad, The.

Their guilt / is not so very different from ours. Their Behaviour. Dennis Brutus. HBAPE

Their hair, pomaded, faces jaded. Sepia Fashion Show. Maya Angelou. BlSi

Their hands upon their hearts. (LL) A. E. Housman. NAEL-5v2; NAEL-6v2; OBMV

Their Hats Is Always White. Jim Elledge. SwNoth

Their hats to a queen? (LL) Queen of the Blues. Gwendolyn Brooks. NALW; SeSe

Their heels slapped their bumping mules. Merchants from Cathay. William Rose Benét. MoAmPo

Their Height in Heaven comforts not. Emily Dickinson. APN-2

Their hooves through the moonlight. (LL) Herbert Street Revisited. John Montague. CIP-2; ModIr; PBCIP; PNI

Their illicit pleasure has been fulfilled. Their Beginning. Constantine P. Cavafy. CAGL, *tr. by* Edmund Keeley and Philip Sherrard

Their jeans sparkled, cut off. After School, Street Football, Eighth Grade. Dennis Cooper. WiU

Their laughter like a sprinkling of salt. Herring Girls, The. Derick Thomson. NePenScot

Their laughter pelting down on us like trash. (LL) At the Movie: Virginia, 1956. Ellen Bryant Voigt. LTA; NoAM

Their lips upon each other's lips are laid. Speechless: Upon the Marriage of Two Deaf and Dumb Persons. Philip Bourke Marston. EBVV; OxBSo

Their little room grew light with cries. Proper Clay. Mark Van Doren. PoRA

Their Lonely Betters. W. H. Auden. NAEL-5v2; NAEL-6v2; NoAM; OBGa

Their minds are so frail the least squeak upsets them. Dismissing Progress and Its Progenitors. George Reavey. SPE

Their name is Legion, grinning from afar. Athenians' Answer, The. Elizabeth Singer Rowe. BASC

Their necks and their dark heads lifted into a dawn. Loons Mating. David Wagoner. BLT

Their necks make, narrowing the sky. (LL) I Was Sleeping Where the Black Oaks Move. Louise Erdrich. HATNAP; NoP-4; PoPoPo

Their new landlord was a handsome man. On his rounds to collect rent she became. Deserter, A. Charles Reznikoff. TRP

Their ordeal over, now the only trouble. Half a Double Sonnet. Mary Jo Salter. MakPoe

Their out of bounds bedroom. Out of Bounds. Priscilla Borthwick. Prnts

Their own children from death? (LL) Antipater of Sidon. GrAn; PGA; WoPoe, *tr. by* Kenneth Rexroth

Their own deaths offered as a sacrifice to the nation. (LL) Going Out Through the North Gate of Chi. Pao Chao. ColAnChi; SuSp, *tr. by* Daniel Bryant

Their Patients. Robert Pinsky. NoAM *Fr.* Essay on Psychiatrists.

Their Philistinism Considered. Robert Pinsky. NoAM *Fr.* Essay on Psychiatrists.

Their ránsom, théir rescue, ánd first, fást, last friénd. (LL) Lantern Out of Doors, The. Gerard Manley Hopkins. SacPr; TrCP

Their ravish'd spirits did possess. (LL) Ode, upon a Question Moved, Whether

Love Should Continue Forever?, An. Edward Herbert, 1st Baron Herbert of Cherbury. BASC; MeLP; NOBE; OxAEP-1; OxBEV

Their Rectitude Their Beauty. Donald Davie. HarvBoo

Their red lamps make a childlike stab. Billie's Blues. Alfred Corn. CAGL

Their rugs are sodden, their heads are down. Gun Teams. Gilbert Frankau. OxBTC

Their salt wet life erased, eroded, only. Consider the Lillies of the Sea. Anne Porter. APT-2

Their sense is with their senses all mixed in. George Meredith. NAEL-5v2; NAEL-6v2; NoP-4; SCGP *Fr.* Modern Love.

Their Seriousness, with Further Comparisons. Robert Pinsky. NoAM *Fr.* Essay on Psychiatrists.

Their Sex Life. A. R. Ammons. OBCoV

Their shadow dims the sunshine of our day. Birds of Prey. Claude McKay. APT-1

Their shadows grow monstrous. (LL) Poem: "Figures in the fields against the sky!" Antonio Machado Ruiz. AWP; WoPoe, *tr. by* John Dos Passos

Their shoulders you shook. Preacher, The. Al-Mahdi. TTY, *tr. by* A. J. Arberry

Their sleeves like purple orchids. Tu Fu. CarOv, *tr. by* Carolyn Kizer *Fr.* Adviser to the Court.

Their souls became cold. Sappho. SaLy, *tr. by* Diane Rayor

Their souls parchment dry, brittle, they came. Ethiopian Apocalypse of Don, The. Norman Weinstein. WaCA

Their spades grafted through the variably-resistant soil. Geoffrey Hill. EmeKit; PoE *Fr.* Mercian Hymns.

Their Speech, Compared with Wisdom and Poetry. Robert Pinsky. NoAM *Fr.* Essay on Psychiatrists.

Their spinning and experienced bodies. (LL) Soul Train. Allison Joseph. AmPoNex; ExTi

Their squints and stammers disappeared. Children, The. Robert Minhinnick. AngWePo

Their Thing. Léon Damas. NegPo, *tr. by* Ellen Conroy Kennedy

Their Thoughts Cling to Everything They See on the Way. Allen Afterman. NOBAu

Their time past, pulled down. Burning the Christmas Greens. William Carlos Williams. APT-1; ChrPo; NAAL-2v2; NAAL-5; NOBA; NoAM

Their tongues are knives, their forks are hands and feet. Riddle. Adrian Mitchell. FaBoEE; OxBSP

Their voices are thin as lines of rain. Spring Peepers. Joseph Bruchac. PoCoUp

Their voices heard, I stumble suddenly, remembering. One More New Botched Beginning. Stephen Spender. NoAM

Their Wedding Journey. Henry Cuyler Bunner.

"Dear Mother." VerBaPo

Their youth was poor and barren as the land. Banquet. Ruth Bidgood. TCAWP

Theirs is a gesture of sorrow, infinite and taut. Snails. E. D. Blodgett. NOBC

Theirs is the house whose windows—every pane. On the Asylum Road. Charlotte Mew. MoBrPo; VWP

Theirs is yon house that holds the parish poor. George Crabbe. ECEV *Fr.* Village, The.

Theirs was not the peaceful death-bed. Two Smothered Children. Marion Albina Bigelow. VerBaPo

Thekla's Song. Johann Christoph Friedrich von Schiller. AWP *Fr.* Piccolomini, The.

Thelmon and Carmel: An Irregular Poem. Anne Batten Cristall. RWP

Thelonious. Reuben Jackson. ESEAA

Thelonious Monk dies. 17:II:82. David Meltzer. SeSe

Them always fair. (LL) Thomas Hardy. NoAM; OBMV *Fr.* At Casterbridge Fair.

Them and Us. Lucille Clifton. AllShUp

Them and [uz]. Tony Harrison. NoP-4

Them both. (LL) To Our Blessed Lord upon the Choice of His Sepulchre. Richard Crashaw. GeHe; NOSC

Them mounted in magazines. Or stuffed. (LL) How to Write Anglo-Welsh Poetry. John Davies. AngWePo; TCAWP

Them only with / spring. (LL) O Sweet Spontaneous. E. E. Cummings. NAAL-2v2; NAAL-5; NoAM; PAI; RaBo; TCAPo

Them that's got shall get. God Bless the Child. Arthur, Jr. Herzog. ReLy

Them/There. John Ash. HarvBoo

Theme for English B. Langston Hughes. APT-2; ColAP; FaBoA; HCAP; NIL-7; NIP-4; NOBA; NoAM; NoP-4; PoPoPo; SSLK

Theme no poet gladly sung. Prudence. Ralph Waldo Emerson. OBAL

Themselves, they marry, they raise their kind. (LL) Sheep Child, The. James Dickey. EmeKit; HCAP; NOBA; NoAM; TAP; VCAP

Then. Lawrence Joseph. GraLe; PBCAP

Then. Roddy Lumsden. NeBl

Then. Gail Mazur. ExTi

Then. Edwin Muir. OxBEV; PoE

Then. Muriel Rukeyser. GLP; LCAP-2

Then a-drinking we will go. (LL) Henry Fielding. OxBoLi; PeLV *Fr.* Don Quixote in England.

Then a ploughman said, Speak to us of Work. Kahlil Gibran. PoToHe *Fr.* Prophet, The.

Then Achilles. Homer. WoPoe, *tr.* by Christopher Logue *Fr.* Iliad, The.

Then after Eden. New World. Derek Walcott. OxBC

Then all the nations of birds lifted together. Season of Phantasmal Peace, The. Derek Walcott. EmeKit; PoPoPo; PoetW; VCWP

Then / an awakened citron. Ana Istarú. TANSG, *tr.* by Mary Jane Treacy

Then and after were no use to me, nor the desire to make permanent. Grove at Nemi, The. Susan Mitchell. ExTi

Then and Now. Frances Ellen Watkins Harper. PWR

Then and Now. James Laughlin. PmAP

Then and now rivers and mountains have no certain lot. Tune: "Butterflies Lingering over Flowers." Nara Singde. ColAnChi, *tr.* by David McCraw

Then, as if he would have sold. John Donne. PBRV *Fr.* Satire 4.

Then, at 3 A.M. I see her bend. Intensive Care. Carol Muske. PBCAP

Then blank and gone and still, and utterly lost. (LL) Yonnondio. Walt Whitman. NAAL-2v1; NAAL-3

Then[,] blessing all, "Go, children of my care!" Pope. NAEL-6v1; NAEL-7v1; NOEC; NPeEn *Fr.* Dunciad, The.

Then bold Robin Hood to the north he would go. Robin Hood and the Scotchman. *Unknown.* ESPB

Then call me traitor if you must. To Certain Critics. Countee Cullen. BPo

Then call your neighbours in. (LL) Mother Goose. OxNR; ReMoGo

Then came I to the shoreless shore of silence. Conrad Potter Aiken. OxBA *Fr.* Preludes for Memnon; or, Preludes to Attitude.

Then came the cry of "Call all hands on deck!" John Masefield. MoBrPo *Fr.* Dauber.

Then came the year of fires. Years, The. Catherine Davis. FFC

Then came to pass what Merlin spoke of long before. Layamon. NAEL-7v1 *Fr.* Brut, The.

Then cease, like these. (LL) Cemetery, A. Emily Dickinson. MoAmPo; OxBA

Then, certanlye, scho tuke me be the hand. Sir David Lindsay [*or* Lyndsay]. NePenScot *Fr.* Dreme, The.

Then cherish pity, lest you drive an angel from your door. (LL) William Blake. FHYEP; NAEL-5v2; NAEL-6v2; NAWM-7v2; NOBE; NOBRP; NOEC; NPeEn; NoP-4; PeECV; PoE; SCV; TFi; TrCP *Fr.* Songs of Innocence.

Then chiefly lives. (LL) Virtue [*or* Vertue]. George Herbert. AWP; AmFaPo; BASC; CIHu; FSCP; GeHe; HAP; HeIP-4; MeLP; NAEL-5v1; NAEL-6v1; NAEL-7v1; NOBE; NOCV; NOSC; NoP-4; OBEV; OPOU; OxBEV; PAI; PeECV; PoE; PoRA; SCGP; SoSe-8; TFi; TreFP

Then come, dear[e] bridegroom [*or* bridgrome], come away. (LL) As Weary Pilgrim, Now at Rest. Anne Bradstreet. NAAL-2v1; SCAP

Then, day by day, her broidered gown. Earth in Spring, The. Judah Halevi. TrJP, *tr.* by Edward G. King

Then did he to the throng around. Kingdom of Heaven Compared to a Grain of Mustard-Seed, The. Henry Vaughan. ChIV-2

Then do I thinke in deed, that better it is to be private. Sir Philip Sidney. PBRV *Fr.* Countesse of Pembrokes Arcadia, The.

Then draw your curtains, and begin the dawn. (LL) Lark Now Leaves His Watery [*or* Wat'ry] Nest. Sir William Davenant [*or* D'Avenant]. OxBEV; OxBSP; PoRA; TFi

Then drew near unto him all the publicans and sinners. Bible, *N.T.* NAWM-5v1 *Fr.* St. Luke.

Then everyone disappearing into the houses. (LL) TV. Rodney Jones. IllVoic; ReTh

Then, far away, the thudding of the guns. (LL) Death-Bed, The. Siegfried Sassoon. AF; PeFWW

Then fire burned my body to a clear shell. Clear Shell, A. Frances Bellerby. FaBoWP

Then first he form'd th' immense and solid *Shield.* Homer. OBVE, *tr.* by Alexander Pope *Fr.* Iliad, The.

Then first with locks dishevelled and bare. Barnabe Barnes. NPeEn; NoSic *Fr.* Parthenophil and Parthenophe.

Then flashed the living lightning from her eyes. Pope. EroLit *Fr.* Rape of the Lock, The.

Then fled, O brethren, the wicked juba. Ballad of Nat Turner, The. Robert Earl Hayden. BPo; VGW

Then flit[t] not from this heavenly boy[e]. (LL) New Heaven, New War[re]. Robert Southwell. ChIV-2; ESCV; NOBE

Then for / twelve years. Low Volume. Reiner Kunze. PoSu, *tr.* by Michael Hamburger

Then from the teeming Filth, and putrid Heap. Oppian. NPeEn, *tr.* by William Diaper *Fr.* Halieutica.

Then from their poverty they rose. Ordinary Women, The. Wallace Stevens. OxBA

Then Frome (a nobler flood) the Muses doth implore. Michael Drayton. NOSC *Fr.* Polyolbion.

Then gan this crafty couple to devise. Edmund Spenser. NoSic *Fr.* Mother Hubbard's Tale.

Then God said to me, Stop. Tree, The. Frank Gaspar. UrbNat

Then grave Clarissa graceful wav'd her fan. Pope. NPeEn; OxBEV *Fr.* Rape of the Lock, The; an Heroi-Comical Poem.

Then halter up this Cur that is so Curst. (LL) Edward Taylor. NAAL-2v1; NAAL-3 *Fr.* God's Determinations [touching his Elect].

Then hate me when thou wilt; if ever, now. William Shakespeare. AWP; EBEV; NOBE; NoSic; OBEV; OxAEP-1 *Fr.* Sonnets.

Then he went out; and as he went, he wept. (LL) Dante Alighieri. AWP; EaItPo, *tr.* by Dante Gabriel Rossetti *Fr.* La Vita Nuova.

Then Herod, when he saw that he had been tricked by the wise men. Julia Hartwig. GI *Fr.* St. Matthew.

Then hey nonny, hey nonny, nonny! (LL) Thomas Dekker. GTBS-P; HAP; NoSic; RB; SCGP; UnPo *Fr.* Pleasant Comedy of Patient Grissell [*or* Grissel *or* Grissill], The.

Then Hope took hold of a horn of *Deus tu conversus vivificabis nos.* William Langland. NAEL-6v1; NAEL-7v1 *Fr.* Vision of Piers Plowman, The.

Then Hrothgar's minstrel rehearsed the lay. *Unknown.* AnOE, *tr.* by Charles W. Kennedy *Fr.* Beowulf.

Then I am pensive—I hastily walk away fill'd with the bitterest envy. (LL) When I Peruse the Conquer'd Fame. Walt Whitman. APN-1; SAmP

Then—I am ready to go! (LL) Emily Dickinson. PoE; SacPr; TrCP

Then I answered: Yea. (LL) Christina Georgina Rossetti. NoP-4; ViWPN; WPE *Fr.* Old and New Year Ditties.

Then I cried out upon him: Cease. Christina Georgina Rossetti. PeVV *Fr.* Despised and Rejected.

Then I finally understood that the angel. Expulsion. Lisa Sewell. AmPoNex

Then I got on the train, very late. London Welsh v. Bridgend. John Powell Ward. TCAWP

Then I heard the bomber call me in. Little Friend. *Unknown.* WoPoe

Then I'll Be Tired of You. Arthur Schwartz. ReLy

Then I said to the elegant ladies. Sappho. BoWoP

Then I Saw What the Calling Was. Muriel Rukeyser. ColAP; FaBoWP

Then I sign an armmistice, I listen to the voices. Biography. Mariella Bettarini. CItWP, *tr.* by Cinzia Sartini Blum and Lara Trubowitz

Then I stand up on my hassock and say sing that. Pretext. Stephen Rodefer. PmAP

Then I woke up, the shuffle of images still with me. Portishead Suite. Rick Barot. NeAmPo

Then if I think about it. Dario Villa. ItPo, *tr.* by Gayle Ridinger

Then in requite, sweet virgin, love me! (LL) Diaphenia. Henry Constable. GTBS-P; NOBE

Then, in the form of a white rose, the host. Dante Alighieri. NAWM-5v1 *Fr.* Divina Commedia.

Then, in the scale of Pricks, 'tis plain. John Wilkes. EroLit *Fr.* Essay on Woman.

Then in the scalloped leaves of the plane tree. Black Series. Brenda Hillman. BodElec

Then in we went to the garden glorious. Stephen Hawes. OBGa

Then indeed into all our fluttering hearts. Virgil [*or* Vergil]. FaBoWar, *tr.* by Charles Hubert Sisson *Fr.* Aeneid [*or* Eneados, *Aeneis*], The.

Then it is this simple. I felt the unordinary romance of. Dionne Brand. PoBW *Fr.* Hard Against the Soul.

Then it's collar 'im tight. Police Station Ditties. Max Beerbohm. NOBL

Then it was dusk in Illinois, the small boy. First Song. Galway Kinnell. NoP-4; TwCP

Then Jesus was led up by the Spirit into the wilderness to be tempted by the devil. Czeslaw Milosz. GI *Fr.* St. Matthew.

Then Job answered and said. Bible, *O.T.* TrJP *Fr.* Job.

Then Job spoke and cursed his day and chanted and said. Bible, *O.T.* WoPoe, *tr.* by R. P. Scheindlin *Fr.* Job.

Then judge not thou thy fellows what they are. (LL) Sonnet: Of Moderation and Tolerance. Guido Guinicelli. AWP; EaItPo, *tr.* by Dante Gabriel Rossetti

Then lacked I matter, that enfeebled mine. (LL) William Shakespeare. CABP; NoSic; OxAEP-1; SCGP; Son *Fr.* Sonnets.

Then, land!—then, England! oh, the frosty cliffs. Elizabeth Barrett Browning. NAEL-5v2; NAEL-6v2 *Fr.* Aurora Leigh.

Then Laugh. Bertha Adams Backus. PWR; PoToHe

Then leave old regret. Moral Poem, A. James Vincent Cunningham. VGW

Then leave the future to thy sons, / Carolina! (LL) Carolina. Henry Timrod. APN-2; CBCWP

Then Lelex rose, an old experienced man. Ovid. AWP; OBVE *Fr.* Metamorphoses.

Then let us boast of ancestors no more. Daniel Defoe. OBSV *Fr.* True-born Englishman, The.

Then life and all shall cease. (LL) Parental Recollections. Mary Lamb. OxBEV; OxBSP

Then live, my strength, anchor of weary ships. To Grimold, Abbot of St. Gall. Hrabanus Maurus. CAGL, *tr. by* Helen Waddell

Then live with me and be my love. (LL) Cecil Day Lewis. BoLoP; NIP-4; OBMV *Fr.* Two Songs.

Then live with me[e] and be my love. (LL) Passionate Shepherd To His Love, The. Christopher Marlowe. AWP; BoLoP; CTC; ClHu; GTBS-P; HAP; HeIP-4; ITBLP; InPK-6; MakPoe; NAEL-5v1; NAEL-6v1; NAEL-7v1; NBLV; NIL-7; NIP-4; NOBE; NoSic; OBEV; OxAEP-1; OxBEV; PAI; PoE; PoRA; RB; SCV; TFi; TRP; TTTS; WeW-3; WoPoe

Then loudly cried the bold Sir Bedivere. Tennyson. TOF *Fr.* Morte d'Arthur.

Then love is sin, and let me sinful be. (LL) Sir Philip Sidney. NoP-4; NoSic *Fr.* Astrophil and Stella.

Then Lytle turned with an oath—By God it's true! (LL) Oath, The. Allen Tate. FaBoMo; OxBA; VGW

Then Margery [or Marjorie] Milkduck. John Skelton. EBEV; PoE *Fr.* Tunnyng [or Tunning] of Elynour [or Elinor] Rummyng [or Rumming], The.

Then might I see upon a white horse set. Sonnet 14: "Then might I see upon a white horse set." Edmund Spenser. ChIV-2

Then most delighted, when his prey is man. (LL) To the Spider. Thomas Russell. CenSon; Son

Then move not, while my prayers' effect I take. (LL) William Shakespeare. OxAEP-1; SoSe-8; Son *Fr.* Romeo and Juliet.

"Then, must it be." Elizabeth Barrett Browning. NALW *Fr.* Aurora Leigh.

Then must the Jew be mercifull. William Shakespeare. OxBEV *Fr.* Merchant of Venice, The.

Then my father's rain-filled room. *Zuni Oral Tradition.* NAWM-7v2, *tr. by* Ruth L. Bunzel *Fr.* Shalako.

Then Nicholas spoke: "My King, most kind to me." János Arany. IQMS, *tr. by* Watson Kirkconnell *Fr.* Toldi.

Then night was shaken from me. Boethius. MLL *Fr.* Consolation of Philosophy, The ("De Consolacione Philosophie").

Then nobody will buy. (LL) Poem by a Perfectly Furious Academician. Shirley Brooks. NOBVV; PeLV

Then, O blind one, you will see again! (LL) Chorus of the Stars. Nelly Sachs. BBASP; PFTM-1, *tr. by* Michael Roloff

Then one of the twelve, called Judas Iscariot. Bible, *N.T.*. NAWM-5v1 *Fr.* St. Matthew.

Then Oothoon waited silent all the day and all the night. William Blake. NPeEn *Fr.* Visions of the Daughters of Albion.

Then out spake brave Horatius. Thomas Babington Macaulay, 1st Baron Macaulay. CABP; TreFP *Fr.* Lays of Ancient Rome.

Then pallid death at last will with his icy hand. Beauty's Transitoriness. Christian Hofmann von Hofmannswaldau. GePo, *tr. by* George C. Schoolfield

Then pour me the thing in the cup! (LL) Blaming Sons. T'ao Ch'ien [or T'ao Yuan-ming]. CoBCP; ColAnChi, *tr. by* Burton Watson

Then pushed her over the edge into the river. (LL) Traveling Through the Dark. William Stafford. CoAP; ColAP; HAP; HeIP-4; InPK-6; LCAP-2; NoAM; PAI; SoSe-8; TRP; WeW-3

Then rash Patroclus with new fury glows. Homer. FaBoWar, *tr. by* Alexander Pope *Fr.* Iliad, The.

Then rising in his Rage above the Shores. Homer. OBVE, *tr. by* Alexander Pope *Fr.* Iliad, The.

Then rose the King and moved his host by night. Tennyson. PeVV *Fr.* Idylls of the King.

Then Sang Deborah and Barak. Bible, *O.T.* *See* Judges

Then sang Moses and the children of Israel this song. Bible, *O.T.* OBWP *Fr.* Exodus.

Then, say not Man's imperfect, Heaven in fault. John Wilkes. EroLit *Fr.* Essay on Woman.

Then scorn not the limerick either. Limerick. Robert Conquest. PeLi

Then Sense, I fear[e], will be a me[e]re dull Fool[e]. (LL) Imagination. Margaret Lucas Cavendish, Duchess of Newcastle. BASC; NOSC

Then since within this wide great Universe. Edmund Spenser. NPeEn *Fr.* Faerie Queene, The.

Then sit on the lid and laugh. (LL) Then Laugh. Bertha Adams Backus. PWR; PoToHe

Then Sohrab with his sword smote Rustum's helm. Matthew Arnold. OBWP *Fr.* Sohrab and Rustum.

Then spoke the Spirit of the Earth. William Ellery Channing. TCAPo *Fr.* Earth Spirit, The.

Then sprang up first the golden age, which of itself maintained. Ovid. NAEL-5v1; NAEL-6v1; NAEL-7v1, *tr. by* Arthur Golding *Fr.* Metamorphoses.

Then suddenly his brain became the sound. Raymond Tong. NewEx

Then tall Hektor of the shining helm answered her: "All these." Homer. AmFaPo, *tr. by* Richmond Lattimore *Fr.* Iliad, The.

Then tell, O tell, how thou didst murder [or murther] me. (LL) When Thou Must Home. Propertius. AWP; EnLoPo; NPeEn; NoSic; OxAEP-1; OxBEV; OxBSP; PoRA; WoPoe, *tr. by* Thomas Campion

Then the air was a brutal architecture of sugar. Everlasting Quail. Sam Witt. NeAmPo

Then the drawbridge came down, and the thick gates. *Unknown.* WoPoe, *tr. by* Burton Raffel *Fr.* Sir Gawain and the Green Knight.

Then the knee of the wave. "Reclining Figure." Donald Hall. LCAP-2

Then the long sunlight lying on the sea. Insusceptibles, The. Adrienne Rich. CoAmPo; HeIP-4; Son

Then the Lord Answered. Bible, *O.T.* AWP *Fr.* Job.

Then the Lord answered Job out of the whirlwind, and sayd. Bible, *O.T.* AWP; OBVE; WoPoe *Fr.* Job.

Then the Lord answered Job out of the whirlwind. Bible, *O.T.* InvLi, *tr. by* New Revised Standard Version *Fr.* Job.

Then the Lord God spoke and said unto Noah. Caedmon. AnOE, *tr. by* C. W. Kennedy *Fr.* Genesis.

Then the mailman came and. 9.1.59: II. Pablo Picasso. CLPP, *tr. by* Paul Blackburn

Then the Master. Henry Wadsworth Longfellow. NAAL-2v1; NAAL-3 *Fr.* Building of the Ship, The.

Then the mighty Lord Maxfield over the mountains fleeth. *Unknown.* NoSic *Fr.* Scot[t]ish Field[e].

Then the Pharisees went and took counsel how to entangle him in his talk. Desanka Maksimovic. GI *Fr.* St. Matthew.

Then the Provost he uprose. William Edmonstoune [or Edmondstoune] Aytoun. OBWP *Fr.* Edinburgh after Flodden.

Then the son of Weohstan, stalwart in war. *Unknown.* AnOE, *tr. by* Charles W. Kennedy *Fr.* Beowulf.

Then the tall shade, in drooping linens veiled. John Keats. OxBEV *Fr.* Fall of Hyperion; A Dream, The.

Then there is this civilising love of death, by which. Ignorance of Death. William Empson. NoAM

Then there shall be signs in Heaven. Fifteen Days of Judgment, The. Sebastian Evans. NOBVV

Then they moved the whole camp. *Unknown.* WoPoe, *tr. by* Paul Kahn *Fr.* Secret History of the Mongols, The.

Then they paraded Pompey's urn. Jenny Mastoraki. BoWoP

Then they set spur to horse. *Unknown.* WoPoe, *tr. by* Paul Blackburn *Fr.* Poem of the Cid, The.

Then thick as locusts black'ning the ground. Pope. NOEC; NPeEn *Fr.* Dunciad, The.

Then this light flipped in the rowboats. Werner Herzog 68 / Iowa City 88. Ann Lauterbach. ExTi

Then thou alone kingdoms of hearts shouldst owe. (LL) William Shakespeare. OxAEP-1; SCGP *Fr.* Sonnets.

Then, though we[e] do[e] not know, we love. (LL) Hymn: "Lord, when the wise men came from far[r]." Sidney Godolphin. BeJo; HAP; MeLP; NOCV; NPeEn; PeECV; SacPr

Then 'tis at the very best. (LL) Mother Goose. FaBoVe; LB; OxNR

Then to admire some beached whales. Ode to Election Day. Anselm Berrigan. HeMarv

Then to sea, boys, and let her go hang! (LL) William Shakespeare. NOBL; OxBSP *Fr.* Tempest, The.

Then to th' extremest heat of fight he did his valour turn. Homer. FaBoWar, *tr. by* George Chapman *Fr.* Iliad, The.

Then to the bar, all they drew near. Michael Wigglesworth. OBCA *Fr.* Day of Doom, The.

Then Trystan and Gwalchmai went to Arthur. Trystan and Esyllt. *Unknown.* OBWVE, *tr. by* Gwyn Jones

Then turn on the music, Marcia. Rock 'n' Roll. Lesley Frost. AiP

Then up the ladder of the earth I climbed. Pablo Neruda. TCLAP, *tr. by* Nathaniel Tarn *Fr.* Heights of Macchu Picchu, The.

Then up three winding stairs my feet were brought. Philip Freneau. NAAL-2v1; NAAL-3 *Fr.* House of Night, The.

Then very gently the earth grows a mane, swivels maneuvering its. Bucolic. Aimé Césaire. VCWP

Then wake to weep. (LL) Mutability. Shelley. NAEL-5v2; NAEL-6v2; NoP-4

Then was I cast from out my state. George Crabbe. NOBE *Fr.* Sir Eustace Grey.

Then was the dinner served, and the Minister prayed for a blessing. Arthur Hugh Clough. PeLV *Fr.* Bothie of Tober-na-Vuolich, The [A Long-Vacation Pastoral].

Then we all walked under God. God. Boris Abramovich Slutsky [or Slutskii]. TCRP, *tr. by* J. R. Rowland

Then we had just the pink carpet, the drugs kicking in, the flat soda. Mud. Mark Bibbins. WiU

Then we have work to do. (LL)   Jelaluddin [*or* Jalal al-Din] Rumi.   RaBo; WoPoe, *tr. by* Coleman Barks and John Moyne   *Fr.* Three Quatrains.

Then we'll sing of Lydia Pinkham.   Lydia Pinkham.   *Unknown.*   OBCoV

Then, what do you say to the poem of Mizpah?   Dialogue between Father and Daughter.   Robert Browning.   OBCoV

Then what have I to do with thee? (LL)   William Blake.   FHYEP; NAEL-5v2; NAEL-6v2; NOBE   *Fr.* Songs of Experience.

Then what is it I am.   Your Words, My Answers.   Burns Singer.   HarvBoo

Then, what is life? I cried. (LL)   Shelley.   NAEL-5v2; NAEL-6v2; NOBRP

Then why do they sneer at me? (LL)   Jew, The.   Isaac Rosenberg.   ChIV-1; MoBrPo

Then will thou go and leave me here?   Valediction.   Sir Robert Aytoun [*or* Ayton].   NOSC

Then with my white sails and bad luck.   Sibyl.   Robert Adamson.   BMAP

Then you will be practically unconscious without positively having / to go. (LL)   Thoughts about the Person from Porlock.   Stevie Smith.   NAEL-5v2; NAEL-6v2; NoAM; NoP-4

Thence is it, as we all believe.   At Cock-crow.   Prudentius.   MLL, *tr. by* Helen Waddell

Thence passing forth, they shortly do arrive.   Edmund Spenser.   NAEL-6v1; NAEL-7v1; OBGa   *Fr.* Faerie Queene, The.

Thenk, man, of min harde stundes.   *Unknown.*   MiEL

Thenmy of liff decayer of all kynde.   Sir Thomas Wyatt.   FaBoVe

Theocritus.   Oscar Wilde.   NOBE

Theodor Herzl.   Israel Zangwill.   TrJP

Theodore and Honoria, From [Fables Ancient and Modern from] Boccace.   Dryden.
    Disdain Punished.   EBNV; NOSC

Theogenes sent us for Piso's pleasure—.   Antipater of Thessalonica.   GrAn

Theogony.   Hesiod.
    Great Father Eating His Children, The.   RaBo, *tr. by* Richmond Lattimore
    Vision.   WoPoe, *tr. by* Charles Doria

Theologian's Tale: Elizabeth, The.   Henry Wadsworth Longfellow.   *Fr.* Tales of a Wayside Inn.

Theology.   Sherman Alexie.   NeAmPo

Theology.   Paul Laurence Dunbar.   SacPr

Theology.   Ted Hughes.   FaBoMo; NAEL-5v2; NAEL-6v2; NoAM; NoP-4; PAI

Theology and a Patchwork Absolute.   Heather McPherson.   PeNZ

Theology of Jonathan Edwards, The.   Phyllis McGinley.   MoAmPo

Theophia.   Edward Benlowes.
    Pleasures of Retirement, The.   NOSC

Theophilus Thistledown, the successful thistle sifter.   Theophilus Thistledown.   *Unknown.*   OxNR

Theorem.   Walter Conrad Arensberg.   APT-1

Theoretical People.   Paul Hoover.   IllVoic

Theory.   David Huddle.   CDa

Theory, A.   Charles Simic.   ChAP

Theory has it the word came first. But you always.   Nesting of Layer Protocols.   Kit Robinson.   FTOS

Theory of Curve.   Christopher Gilbert.   LTA

Theory of the Flower, The.   Michael Palmer.   HarvBoo

Theory of Tragedy.   Joseph Duemer.   BodElec

Theory on Extinction or what happened to the dinosaurs?   Kenneth Carroll.   AmPoNex; SpirFl

Ther bloweth a cold wynd to-day, to-day.   *Unknown.*   OHMEL

Ther is a chielde, a heuenly childe.   James Ryman.   SacPr

Ther is no rose of swych vertu.   Rose That Bore Jesu, The.   *Unknown.*   NPeEn

Ther once was this ladye from Tyre.   Limerick.   Tim Hopkins.   PeLi

Ther was a lady fair an rear.   Kitchie-Boy, The.   *Unknown.*   ESPB

Therapist's Comment, The.   Jenny Hamlett.   Prnts

Therapy.   Giovanna.   SurWo, *tr. by* Myrna Bell Rochester

Therapy.   John Wright.   BloBone

There.   Etel Adnan.
    "In the green escape of my palace, over a bridge, under a."   PoArWo

There.   Ray Gonzalez.   TouFir

There.   Philip Mead.   BMAP

There.   Caroline Natzler.   Prnts

There a bowl of ambrosia.   Sappho.   SaLy, *tr. by* Diane Rayor

There Actually Stood.   Roy Fuller.   Son   *Fr.* Mythological Sonnets.

There all the golden codgers lay.   News for the Delphic Oracle.   W. B. Yeats.   FaBoMo; NoAM

There all the happy souls that ever were.   Pleasures of Heaven, The.   Ben Jonson.   TreFP

There also stand a num'rous band.   Michael Wigglesworth.   ColAP   *Fr.* Day of Doom, The.

There always is a noise when it is dark!   In the Night.   James Stephens.   OBMV

There ance was a may, and she lo'ed na men.   Werena My Heart Licht I Wad Dee.   Lady Grisel [*or* Grizel *or* Grisell] Baillie.   OBEV

There are a few things yet you haven't heard of.   Imre Madách.   IQMS, *tr. by* Iain MacLeod   *Fr.* Tragedy of Man.

There are abandoned corners of our Exile.   Mathmid, The.   Hayyim Nahman [*or* Khayim Nakhman *or* Chaim Nachman] Bialik.   AWP, *tr. by* Maurice Samuel

There are actually people who revel.   Nikolai Ivanovich Glazkov.   TCRP

There are ads in all the papers.   Military Life, The.   Harold Rome.   ReLy

There are all things reflected here, yet all.   Well, The.   Bernard Raymund.   YaYoPo

There are always questions.   Post Scriptum.   Mark Todd.   GeoH

There are always the poor.   Soliloquy at Potsdam.   Peter Porter.   NOBAu

There are always ties of responsibility.   Transportation.   Karen Alkalay-Gut.   DTA

There are artifacts from every period here.   Tour of Ein Kerem, A.   David Curzon.   GI

There Are Bad Times Just around the Corner.   Noël Coward.   NOBL

There are birds.   Landscape with Yellow Birds.   Shuntaro Tanikawa.   PoetW, *tr. by* Harold Wright

There are blows in life so violent—Don't ask em!   Black Riders, The.   César Vallejo.   RaBo, *tr. by* Robert Bly

There are blows in life so violent—I can't answer!   César Vallejo.   *See* There are blows in life so violent—Don't ask em!

There are bog-people in the foundations.   Foundations, The.   Jennifer Maiden.   BMAP

There are brightest apples on those trees.   Fertile Muck, The.   Irving Layton.   NOBC; NoAM

There are caverns / under our feet.   Shirley Kaufman.   BoWoP

There are cemeteries that are lonely.   Nothing but Death.   Pablo Neruda.   SPE, *tr. by* Robert Bly

There are christs spiked against trees.   There Is Life.   Breyten Breytenbach.   VCWP, *tr. by* Breyten Breytenbach

There are countless tons of rock above his head.   Idris Davies.   TCAWP   *Fr.* Gwalia Deserta.

There are days I have to pretend.   First Person—1981.   D. F. Brown.   CDa

There are days when the dead will have nothing to do with us.   Tending the Graves.   Jennifer Strauss.   NOBAu

There are dealers in pictures named Agnew.   Tom Agnew, Bill Agnew.   Dante Gabriel Rossetti.   FaBoEE

There are ecstatic rituals every do-good deity knows.   Shiva's Prowess.   Maurya Simon.   ErotSp

There are even silences, prosecutors.   Tap.   Maggie Hannan.   NLP

There are exact arrangements.   Mimikòs.   Luigi Fontanella.   NeIt, *tr. by* Michael Palma

There are few moments of silence.   Heartland.   Linda Hogan.   UrbNat

There are few of us now, soon.   For Eli Jacobson.   Kenneth Rexroth.   RaBo

There are few stars north of the Milky Way.   Watching a Lonely Wild Goose at Nightfall.   Hsiao Kang.   CrYelRi, *tr. by* Sam Hamill

There are five thousand of us here.   Estadio Chile.   Víctor Jara.   TCLAP, *tr. by* Joan Jara

There are flowers now, they say, at Alamein.   El Alamein.   John Jarmain.   FaBoWar

There are flowers of Zait in the garden.   *Unknown.*   BoWoP

There are four Graces. Beside the original three.   Statue of Bereniké, A.   Callimachus.   GrAn, *tr. by* Peter Jay

There are four Graces, two Aphrodites, ten Muses.   *Unknown.*   GrAn

There are four kinds of men who'll get no fee from me.   Khosravani.   WoPoe, *tr. by* Dick Davis

There are four men mowing down by the Isar.   Youth Mowing, A.   D. H. Lawrence.   InPK-6; MoBrPo; NoAM

There are four paths.   Four Paths.   Nikolai Ivanovich Glazkov.   TCRP, *tr. by* Daniel Weissbort

There are four vibrators, the world's exactest clocks.   Four Quartz Crystal Clocks.   Marianne Craig Moore.   TwCP

There are great advantages to having been dead.   Gwyneth Lewis.   NeBl

There are great puddles of blood on the world.   Song in the Blood.   Jacques Prévert.   AF, *tr. by* Lawrence Ferlinghetti

There are hearts—stout hearts,—that own no fear.   Eliza Cook.   VerBaPo; VWP   *Fr.* Surgeon's Knife, The.

There are hermit souls that live withdrawn.   House by the Side of the Road, The.   Sam Walter Foss.   BRP; ITBLP

There are hundreds of people in the street.   Anti-Semitic Demonstration, An.   Gail Newman.   GotH

There are in this rude stunning tide.   Happiness.   John Keble.   TreFP

There are just not enough.   Living Space.   Imtiaz Dharker.   NeBl

There are just so many years.   Turning Pro.   Ishmael Reed.   SoSe-8

There are lakes in our region. Inventions. William Scammell. NLP

There are lonely cemeteries. Pablo Neruda. *See* There are cemeteries that are lonely

There are long kilometers. From Now Until Chile. Emma Sepúlveda-Pulvirenti. TANSG, *tr. by* Shaun Griffin

There are lots of fellows think that they're in love. When a Fellow's on the Level with a Girl That's on the Square. George M. Cohan. ReLy

There are loyal hearts, there are spirits brave. Life's Mirror. "Madeline Bridges." PWR; PoToHe

There are many and more. Many and More. Maya Angelou. LW

There are many dead in the brutish desert. First Elegy for the Dead in Cyrenaica. Hamish Henderson. OxBS

There are many dead in the brutish desert, who lie uneasy. End of a Campaign. Hamish Henderson. PoWW

There are many like him there—unsymbolled heap. Grave in Ukraine, A. Saul [*or* Shaul] Tchernichowsky [*or* Tchernichovsky]. TrJP, *tr. by* Robert Mezey, L. V. Snowman and Shula Starkman

There are many minds in circulation. One Life to Live. Kurt Weill. ReLy

There are many monsters that a glassen surface. Octopus, The. James Merrill. CoAP

There are many more Good Fridays. Unkept Good Fridays. Thomas Hardy. GI

There are many sounds which are neither music nor voice. Ear, The. Louis MacNeice. OxBSP

There Are Many Things I Want to Tell You. Indran Amirthanayagam. OpBo

There are many traps in the world. There Are Many Traps in the World. Ferreira Gullar. TCLAP, *tr. by* Renato Rezende

There are many Washingtons. Which Washington? Eve Merriam. NTCP

There are many ways of saying Chinese. Address. Adrienne Su. AmPoNex

There are many ways to die. Robert Penn Warren. CBCWP; MoAmPo *Fr.* Kentucky Mountain Farm.

There are many who say that a dog has his day. Song of the Mischievous Dog, The. Dylan Thomas. OBCoV

There are many winding rivers. Winding Sand. Naresh Guha. OMIP, *tr. by* Lila Ray

There are more functions to a freezing plant. Post Mortem. Wole Soyinka. PoetW

There are more stars in the universe. Size of This Universe, The. Randolph Healy. Oth

There are mountains on this earth. Glistening, The. Deema K. Shehabi. PoArWo

There are Nights. Léon Damas. NegPo, *tr. by* Ellen Conroy Kennedy

There are nights as soft as fur on a foal. Watching Shoah in a Hotel Room in America. Adam Zagajewski. VCWP, *tr. by* Renata Gorcyznski

There are nights with no name. There Are Nights. Léon Damas. NegPo, *tr. by* Ellen Conroy Kennedy

There are no accidents, or so. What Could Hold Us. Heather McHugh. NIP-4

There are no angels　yet. Gabriel. Adrienne Rich. VGW

There are no bolts that do not exactly. Kirkwall Auction Mart. David Scott. NLP

There Are No Doors. Olga Orozco. BLPSL, *tr. by* Rene de Costa, Rigas Kappatos and Eleni Paidoussi

There are no dry bones. Bones of My Father, The. Etheridge Knight. BodElec

There are no handles upon a language. Languages. Carl Sandburg. APT-1; ColAP

There are no leaders to lead us to honour, and yet without leaders we sally. Spies' March, The. Rudyard Kipling. FaBoWar

There are no more shopping days to Christmas. Eve. Howard Nemerov. CRP

There are no pacts. Angelo Lumelli. ItPo, *tr. by* Gayle Ridinger

There Are No People Song. *Navajo Oral Tradition*. TTTS

There are no perfect waves. William Carlos Williams. APT-1

There are no roads but the frost. Old Age Compensation. James Wright (1927–80). NNaP

There are no rocks. Geography: a Song. Howard Moss. OBCoV

There are no signs. The sky is entirely bland. Augury. W. H. Oliver. PeNZ

There are no simple explanations. No Simple Explanations. Jayne Cortez. GT

There are no small ones. Puritans. Elaine Equi. PmAP

There are no stars tonight. My Grandmother's Love Letters. Hart Crane. InPK-6; NOBA; NoAM; NoP-4

There are no trenches dug in the park, not yet. Nightmare at Noon. Stephen Vincent Benét. OxBA

There are no words here. Hooded Legion, The. Gerald McCarthy. CDa

There are notes to lightning in my bedroom. Star Quilt. Roberta Hill Whiteman. CDW; NoAM

There are of course tho' we don't see them. Postscripts 2. Dennis Brutus. HBAPE

There are old drunks among the tenements. Griots Who Know Brer Fox, The. Colleen J. McElroy. NAAAL

There are only so many words. Janet Fisher. MFPA

There are only two things now. New Year's Eve. D. H. Lawrence. BoLoP

There are palm trees in my homeland. Antônio Gonçalves Dias. TTY *Fr.* Song of Exile.

There are people, I know, to be found. Drinking Song. James Kenneth Stephen. NOBL; PeLV

"There are people so dumb," my father said. Plain Talk. William Jay Smith. MoAmPo

There are perfect illustrations. Yury [*or* Iurii] Pavlovich Odarchenko. TCRP

There are, perhaps, whom passion gives a grace. Aged Lover Discourses in the Flat Style, The. James Vincent Cunningham. NoAM

There are pines that are tall enough. Elegy Is Preparing Itself, An. Donald Justice. CRP

There are places in Wales I don't go. Reservoirs. Ronald Stuart Thomas. AngWePo

There are points of silence circling the heart. There Are Points of Silence Circling the Heart. Roberto Juarroz. TCLAP, *tr. by* W. S. Merwin

There are portraits and still-lifes. Paring the Apple. Charles Tomlinson. OxBTC; PoE; TRP

There are ribald interventions. Palinode. "Ern Malley." BMAP

There Are Rivers of Oranges. James Tipton. GeoH

There are rivers of oranges, sweet. There Are Rivers of Oranges. James Tipton. GeoH

There are rock-rooted ranges to dominate. Rex Ingamells. CBAP *Fr.* Memory of Hills.

There are rows of bottles against the glass;. Small-town Gladys. David Campbell. BMAP

There are sea and sky about me. Midnight. Louisa Sarah Bevington. PEW

There are seeds within the tide. City. Joseph Bruchac. CDW

There are seventy times seven kinds of loving. Veterans. George Johnston. NOBC

"There are sixteen lang miles, I'm sure." Bent Sae Brown, The. *Unknown.* ESPB

There are so few photographs of him. Grandfather's Cap, My. David St. John. MoASP

There are so many islands. And Yet. Patricia Goedicke. ExTi

There are so many kinds of awful men. Rondeau Redoublé. Wendy Cope. HarvBoo

There are so many kinds of riches. Best Things in Life Are Free, The. Ray Henderson. ReLy

There are so many photographs of that curve of rocky beach. Imagining Point Dume. Diane Wakoski. GeoHom

There are so many things I want to say to you. My Nightingale. Boris Petrovich Kornilov. TCRP, *tr. by* Bernard Meares

There are some birds in these valleys. Decoys, The. W. H. Auden. PoE

There are some blows in life so hard . . . I don't know! (LL) Black Messengers, The. César Vallejo. PoetW; TCLAP, *tr. by* Rachel Benson

There are some heights in Wessex, shaped as if by a kindly hand. Wessex Heights. Thomas Hardy. EBVV; SCGP

There are some qualities—some incorporate things. Sonnet—Silence. Edgar Allan Poe. ColAP; NOBA; TCAPo

There are some questions one should know by heart. Postscript. Henri Coulette. DiPo

There are spaces. Old Maps and New. Norman MacCaig. OxBC

There are strange hells within the minds war made. Strange Hells. Ivor Gurney. FaBoW; OxBTC; PeFWW

There are strange shadows fostered of the moon. Sonnet. Arthur Davison Ficke. TCAPo

There are strange things done in the midnight sun. Cremation of Sam McGee, The. Robert W. Service. BRP; NOBC; OBCoV; OBNV; TCAPo

There are strange trees in that pale field. Forest of the Dead, The. James Griffyth Fairfax. PoWW

There are sunsets who whisper a good-by. Sunsets. Carl Sandburg. MoAmPo

There are the Alps. What is there to say about them? On the Fly-Leaf of Pound's Cantos. Basil Bunting. FaBoTw; HarvBoo; NoAM; OxBTC

There are things best not set down in books. Road to Patmos, The. John Ennis. PBCIP

There are things to be said. No doubt. Cid Corman. VGW

There are things tonight I've never known. Hilo: First Night Back. Garrett Kaoru Hongo. LoL

There are things which you gave me. Kleptomaniac. Polly Clark. NeBl

There are things you have words for. Two Words; a Wedding. B. P. Nichol. NOBC

There are those fish that swim ever in the dim. Pearl Perch. John Blight. CBAP

There are those to whom place is unimportant. Rose, The. Theodore Roethke. APT-2; NOBA; TRP

There are those who can leave love or take it.   I Fall in Love Too Easily.   Jule Styne.   ReLy

There are those who think.   Prologue from "Legacy."   Patricia Parker.   GLP

There are thow who grow.   Knocker, A.   Zbigniew Herbert.   PoSu, tr. by Czeslaw Milosz

There are three plenties.   Fort of Ard Ruide, The.   *Unknown.*   NOIV

There are three preachers, ever preaching.   Three Preachers, The.   Charles MacKay.   EBVV

There are three suppositions. the first, it's not amiss to number them: there is no more. I shall not name it.   Jacques Roubaud.   PFTM-2, tr. by Rosmarie Waldrop   *Fr.* Some Thing Black.

There are three things which are too wonderful for me.   Bible, *O.T.*   TrJP   *Fr.* Proverbs.

There are three valleys where the warm sun lingers.   Long Harbour, The.   Mary Ursula Bethell.   PeNZ

There are three who await my death.   *Unknown.*   NOIV

There are times for dreaming.   Hours, The.   David Diop.   NegPo, tr. by Ellen Conroy Kennedy

There are times in one's life which one cannot forget.   Mr. Billings of Louisville.   Eugene Field.   NBLV

There are times when everything I touch.   Once You've Been to War.   Walter McDonald.   CDa

There are too many waterfalls here; the crowded streams.   Questions of Travel.   Elizabeth Bishop.   ColAP; HarvBoo; NAAL-2v2; NOBA

There are truths you Americans need to be told.   James Russell Lowell.   OBSV   *Fr.* Fable for Critics, A.

There are twelve months in all the year.   Robin Hood Rescuing Three Squires.   *Unknown.*   ESPB

There are two angels, messengers of light.   Peace and Love.   Ella Wheeler Wilcox.   PWR

There are two bears that near us we should allow to dwell.   Two Bears, The.   Lillian E. Curtis.   VerBaPo

There are two bends in the road, and an unexpected dip.   Pont y Caniedydd.   Alun Llywelyn-Williams.   OBWVE, tr. by Joseph R. Clancy

There are two births: The one when light.   William Cartwright.   *See* Chloe, why wish you that your years

There are two choirs, one poised in space.   Songs of the Valley.   John Koethe.   BAP-01

There are two extremes of love.   One Night Stand.   Kenward Elmslie.   FTOS

There are two kinds of people, soldiers and women.   Postfeminism.   Brenda Shaughnessy.   AmPoNex

There are two Mays.   Emily Dickinson.   NOBA

There are two men.   Two Men.   Andrew Lansdown.   NOBAu

There are two men in the world, who.   Eternal Three, The.   Tove Ditlevsen.   WoPoe, tr. by Martin Allwood, Inga Allwood and John Hollander

There are / two methods.   In the Case of Lobsters.   Petra von Morstein.   BoWoP, tr. by Rosmarie Waldrop

There are two miseries in human life.   Walter Savage Landor.   FaBoEE

There Are Two Worlds.   Larry Levis.   BodElec

There are who say the sonnet's meted maze.   John F. M. Dovaston.   CenSon

There are who separate the eternal light.   One in All, The.   Margaret Fuller.   SWaP

There are wolves in the next room waiting.   Wolves, The.   Allen Tate.   APT-2; NOBA; OxBA

There are women.   Sad Song.   Laura Kasischke.   PuP-23

There are women locked in my joints.   I Walk in the History of My People.   Chrystos.   UnSA

There Are Words.   Gael Turnbull.   Oth

There are words that coast alongside thought.   Valerio Magrelli.   ItPo, tr. by Gayle Ridinger

There aren't many.   Inventory of Places Propitious for Love.   Angel González.   VCWP, tr. by Steven Ford Brown

There as here! (LL)   Epilogue: "At the midnight in the silence of the sleep-time."   Robert Browning.   NAEL-5v2; NAEL-6v2; NOBE

There at the watershed I turned.   Ba Cottage.   Andrew Young.   OxBSP

There be none of Beauty's daughters.   Stanzas for Music.   Byron.   AWP; GTBS-P; HAP; NAEL-5v2; NAEL-6v2; PoRA

There be three hundred different ways and more.   "Owen Meredith."   EBVV   *Fr.* Glenaveril.

[There Douglas] landed Lord Percye. (LL)   Prayer for the Speedy End of Three Great Misfortunes.   *Unknown.*   OBMV, tr. by Frank O'Connor

There between the riverbank.   Angel.   Brad Leithauser.   DiPo

There Blooms No Bud in May.   Walter De la Mare.   MoBrPo

There blows a cold wind today, today.   To Keep the Cold Wind Away.   *Unknown.*   MiEL

There breathes no being but has some pretence.   Poesy.   Oliver Wendell Holmes.   TreFP

There, breathless, with his digging nails he clung.   Byron.   OxAEP-2   *Fr.* Don Juan.

There broke into my cell last night.   Hayim Lenski.   FIT, tr. by Robert Friend

There—but for the clutch of luck—go I.   Death by Heroin of Sid Vicious, The.   Paul Durcan.   NPeEn

There by some wrinkled stones round a leafless tree.   Twelve, The.   Allen Tate.   APT-2; ChIV-2

There, by the curb.   Oil Slick.   Judith Thurman.   SSCS

There calleth me ever a marvelous horn.   Home-Sickness.   Justinus Kerner.   AWP, tr. by James Clarence Mangan

There came a bird out o' a bush.   Lady Isabel and the Elf-Knight.   *Unknown.*   ESPB

There came a Day at Summer's full.   Renunciation.   Emily Dickinson.   APN-2; MoAmPo; NAAL-2v1; NAAL-3; NOBA

There came a dove, an Easter dove.   My Easter Dove.   Henrietta Cordelia Ray.   CBWP-3

There came a ghost to Margret's door.   Sweet William's Ghost *or* Sweet William and May Margaret.   *Unknown.*   AWP; ESPB

There came a knocking at the front door.   Person from Porlock, A.   Ronald Stuart Thomas.   TOF

There came a man across the moor.   Master and Guest.   Mary Elizabeth Coleridge.   VWP; ViWPN

There came a Wind like a Bugle.   Emily Dickinson.   APN-2; NAAL-2v1; NAAL-3; NAWM-7v2; NOBA; OxBA; RB; SAmP

There came an old woman from France.   Old Woman from France, The.   *Unknown.*   ReMoGo

There came from Normandy an old.   Two Lovers, The.   Marie de France.   BoWoP, tr. by Patricia Terry

There came gray stretches of volcanic plains.   In Death Valley.   Edwin Markham.   APN-2

There came this bright young thing.   As for the Quince.   Nuala Ni Dhomhnaill.   BiHa; CIP-2; PBCIP, tr. by Paul Muldoon

There can be no songs for dead children.   Kindertotenlieder.   Michael Longley.   CIP-2

There cedars dark, the osier, and the pine.   Philip Freneau.   NAAL-3   *Fr.* House of Night, The.

There chanced to be a pedlar bold.   Bold Pedlar and Robin Hood, The.   *Unknown.*   ESPB

There chanced to meet together in an inn.   Epigram.   John Taylor.   NOSC

There Charon stands, who rules the dreary Coast.   Virgil [*or* Vergil].   OBVE, tr. by John Dryden   *Fr.* Aeneid [*or* Eneados, *Aeneis*], The.

There Cintheus sat twynklyng upon his harpe stringis.   John Skelton.   NPeEn   *Fr.* Garland [*or* Garlande *or* Garlands] of Laurel[l], The.

There come to me.   Pause.   Octavio Paz.   STV, tr. by John Frederick Nims

There comes a little space between the south.   Depression in Winter.   Jane Kenyon.   LoL

There comes a moment in her veins.   More Lovely than Antiquity.   Witter Bynner.   NoP-4

There comes a moment when to believe is not enough.   Action.   James Oppenheim.   TrJP

There Comes a Time.   Ella Wheeler Wilcox.   PWR

There comes a time to rusticate the numbers.   The way the birds, jug.   Untitled.   Karen Volkman.   NAPBL

There comes a time when everything is laced.   Imagination of Necessity, The.   Andrei Codrescu.   SPE

There comes an hour when begging stops.   Emily Dickinson.   NCAP

There comes Emerson first, whose rich words, every one.   James Russell Lowell.   APN-1; NOBA; OxBA; TAP; TCAPo   *Fr.* Fable for Critics, A.

There comes ———, for instance; to see him's rare sport.   James Russell Lowell.   TCAPo   *Fr.* Fable for Critics, A.

There comes Philothea, her face all aglow.   James Russell Lowell.   TCAPo   *Fr.* Fable for Critics, A.

There comes Poe, with his raven, like fudge.   James Russell Lowell.   APN-1; OxBA; TCAPo   *Fr.* Fable for Critics, A.

There'd an orchestra.   F. Scott Fitzgerald.   AiP   *Fr.* Thousand-and-First Ship.

There'd be, if Adam hadn't sold our stock.   What Might Have Been.   Giuseppe Gioacchino Belli.   WoPoe, tr. by Anthony Burgess

There'd ha'e to be nae warnin' Times ha'e changed.   Prayer for a Second Flood.   Hugh MacDiarmid.   EBEV

There died a myriad.   Ezra Pound.   HarvBoo; MoAmPo; NOBE; NPeEn; PoE; TRP   *Fr.* Hugh Selwyn Mauberley (Life and Contacts).

[There Douglas] landed Lord Percye. (LL)   Northumberland Betray[e]d by Douglas [*or* Dowglas].   *Unknown.*   ESPB; OxBB

There dwelt a fair maid in the West.   James Harris (The Daemon Lover).   *Unknown.*   ESPB

There dwelt a man in fair[e] Westmoreland [*or* Westmerland].   Johnie Armstrong.   *Unknown.*   ESPB

There dwelt an old woman at Exeter.   Woman of Exeter, The.   *Unknown.*   ReMoGo

There existed a person, not a woman or a boy, being in the first part of life.   Semantic Limerick According to Dr. Johnson's Dictionary (Edition of 1765), The.   Gavin Ewart.   OBCoV

There existed an adult male person who had lived a relatively short time. Semantic Limerick According to the Shorter Oxford English Dictionary (1933), The. Gavin Ewart. OBCoV

There exists no proof as. Edmund Clerihew Bentley. NOBL *Fr.* Clerihews.

There fared a mother driven forth. House of Christmas, The. Gilbert Keith Chesterton. ChrPo; MoBrPo; SacPr

There fell red rain of spears athwart the sky. Last Judgment. John Gould Fletcher. AWP

There flourished once a potentate. King of Yvetot, The. Pierre Jean de Béranger. AWP, *tr. by* William Toynbee

There go Adem and Eve—I see. Poems from Subway to Work. Peter Orlovsky. CLPP

There go the grownups. Lazy Thought, A. Eve Merriam. SSCS

There go the storeyed liners. Navigation. Ronald Stuart Thomas. HarvBoo

There God is dwelling too. (LL) William Blake. BBASP; ChAP; FHYEP; InvLi; NAEL-5v2; NAEL-6v2; NOBE; NOBRP; NOEC; NoP-4; OxBEV; PeECV; PoE *Fr.* Songs of Innocence.

There goes a queen! Queen, A. Bella [*or* Izabella] Akhatovna Akhmadulina. TCRusP, *tr. by* Daniel Weissbort

There goes my young intended. He Was Too Good to Me. Richard Rodgers. ReLy

There Goes the Bride. M. Loncar. AmPoNex

There goes the Wapiti. Wapiti, The. Ogden Nash. TLR

There, good night, darling! now, I fain would sleep. (LL) Crazed. Mary E. Tucker. CBWP-1; RACG

There grew two olives, closest of the grove. Homer. OBVE *Fr.* Odyssey.

There grows one in the human brain. (LL) William Blake. FHYEP; NAEL-5v2; NAEL-6v2; NOBRP; NOEC; OxAEP-2; PoE *Fr.* Songs of Experience.

There had been a cricket in the basement. Overture. A. V. Christie. NAPBL

There had been rain in the morning and a chaffinch. All Possession Is Theft. Lauris Edmond. PeNZ

There has been a death in the street. Community. Sally Roberts Jones. AngWePo

There has been a light snow. In a Train. Robert Bly. InvLad; TTTS

There has been more than beginning and end to face. There Has Been More Than Beginning and End to Face. Joan Murray. YaYoPo

There Has to Be a Jail for Ladies. Thomas Merton. VGW

There have been a thousand raggy, draggy dances. Baltimore Buzz. Eubie Blake. ReLy

There have been plates but no appetite. Museum, The. Wislawa Szymborska. PoSu, *tr. by* Magnus F. Krynski

There have been poets that in verse display. To Wordsworth. Hartley Coleridge. Son

There have been times when I have looked at life. Vision. Elizabeth N. Hauer. PoToHe

There have been times when on a city street. On City Streets. Margaret E. Bruner. PoToHe

There have never been men crazier than these. Gregorio Scalise. ItPo, *tr. by* Gayle Ridinger

There he glowed on me. Elizabeth Barrett Browning. NAEL-6v2 *Fr.* Aurora Leigh.

There he goes as usual. If You Hadn't—But You Did. Betty Comden. ReLy

There he goes / Have you ever seen such perfection? Meet the Beat of My Heart. Harry Revel. ReLy

There he moved, cropping the grass at the purple canyon's lip. Horse Thief, The. William Rose Benét. MoAmPo

"There," / He said. John Hancock. Lee Bennett Hopkins. HHAm

There he stood. Lyric Poem. Semyon [*or* Semion] Isaakovich Kirsanov. TCRP, *tr. by* April FitzLyon

There he stood, quite suddenly. Gauguin's White Horse. Vicki Hearne. GS

There he was—having spent. "Yes, But. . ." Theodore Weiss. TAP

There I could never be a boy. Poem. Frank O'Hara. NNaP

There! I have lock'd the door. Real Comfort. Mary Stanley Bunce Dana. SWaP

There I was midsummer skating on a lake. Trendelenburg Position. M. Wyrebek. AmPoNex

There I was sitting on one leg. Daniil Kharms. TCRP

There, I was so interested to hear about it. (LL) Horse Show, The. William Carlos Williams. NOBA; TAP; VGW

There, in some place, some time. Georgy [*or* Georgii Viktorovich] Adamovich. TCRP

There, in that bed so closely curtained round. Written in a Sick Chamber. Samuel Rogers. NOBRP

There, in the corner, staring at his drink. Docker. Seamus Heaney. HeIP-4; NOIV

There in the flower garden. *Unknown.* BoWoP

There in the fragrant pines and the cedars dusk and dim. (LL) Walt Whitman. APN-1; AWP; CBCWP; ColAP; HAP; MoAmPo; NAAL-2v1; NAAL-3; NAAL-5; NCAP; NIL-7; NOBA; NoP-4; OxBA; PAI; PoPoPo; PoRA; SAmP; TAP; TCAPo; TFi *Fr.* Memories of President Lincoln.

There in the hard light. Irish Lake, An. William Robert Rodgers. BIrV

There, in the Promised Land. Child is Born, A. Elina Wechsler. MirDau, *tr. by* Darrell Lockhart

There in the road. (LL) Félix Lope de Vega Carpio. HAP; WoPoe, *tr. by* Geoffrey Hill *Fr.* Pentecost Castle, The.

There Is. Louis Simpson. CoAmPo

There Is a Balm in Gilead. *Unknown.* TCAPo

There is a bareness in the images. Substance and Shadow. John Hewitt. ModIr; PNI

There is a big artist named Val. Dante Gabriel Rossetti. FaBoEE; PeLi

There is a bird in the poplars. Metric Figure. William Carlos Williams. MoAmPo

There is a bird that hangs head-down and cries. Thirst. Genevieve Taggard. APT-2

There is a blue sky. Song, A. Edward Dorn. CoAmPo

There is a boundary in the heart's land. There Is a Boundary. Anna Andreyevna Akhmatova. TCRusP, *tr. by* Daniel Weissbort

There is a brook in the mountains. Mountain Spring, A. Ch'u Ch'uang I. OHMPC, *tr. by* Kenneth Rexroth

There is a change—and I am poor. Complaint, A. William Wordsworth. NOBE

There is a charm in solitude that cheers. Solitude. John Clare. NOBVV; OxBSP

There is a Charm no vulgar mind can reach. On the Luxembourg Gallery. Washington Allston. APN-1

There Is a Charming Land. Adam Oehlenschläger. AWP, *tr. by* Robert Hillyer

There Is a City. "The Jewish Sibyl." TrJP, *tr. by* Bohn *Fr.* Fourth Book of Sibylline Oracles, The.

There is a coal-black Angel. Swamp Angel, The. Herman Melville. APN-2

There is a coldness I do not want. What Is Kept. Linda Gregg. BodElec

There is a creator named God. On the Painter Val Prinsep. Dante Gabriel Rossetti. FaBoEE

There is a creature called God. Limerick. Dante Gabriel Rossetti. PeLi

There is a crying in the world. End of the World. Else Lasker-Schüler. BoWoP, *tr. by* Willis Barnstone and Michael Gillespie

There is a dark tolling in the air. Scattering Flowers. George Hitchcock. CDa

There is a deep brooding. My Arkansas. Maya Angelou. BlSi; NAAAL

There is a dish to hold the sea. John Davidson. MoBrPo *Fr.* New Year's Eve.

There is a drear and lonely tract of hell. Supremacy. Edwin Arlington Robinson. APN-2; NoAM

There is a drought, the farmers have a hard time finding food. Following the Rhymes of Shao-pao Huang's Poem on Being Moved while Visiting the Farmers. Yang Shih-ch'i. CoBLCP; WoPoe, *tr. by* Jonathan Chaves

There is a drunk on Main Avenue, slumped. Song-Maker. Anita Endrezze. HATNAP

There is a face in the honeysuckle—eyes. Man in the Honeysuckle, The. David Campbell. BMAP

There is a faculty or knack, smallish, in the mind that can turn. A. R. Ammons. NoAM *Fr.* Sphere.

There is a fair one. Lute Song, The. Kung Tzu-chen. SuSp, *tr. by* An-yan Tang

There is a faltering crimson by the wall. Day Before Spring, The. Lizette Woodworth Reese. SWaP

"There is a fashion in this land." Knight's Ghost, The. *Unknown.* ESPB

"There is a feast in your father's house." Leesome Brand. *Unknown.* ESPB

There is a flower blossoming out of season. Flower Ensnarer of Psalms. Rossana Ombres. BoWoP, *tr. by* I. L. Salomon

There is a flower I wish to wear. Hearts-Ease. Walter Savage Landor. OxBEV

There is a flower that bees prefer. Purple Clover. Emily Dickinson. MoAmPo

There is a flower that blooms out of season. Ensnaring Flower of Psalms. Rossana Ombres. NeIt, *tr. by* Ruth Feldman

There is a flower, the Lesser Celandine. Lesson, A. William Wordsworth. GTBS-P

There is a fountain fill'd with blood. William Cowper. InPK-6; SacPr *Fr.* Olney Hymns.

There is a fountain, to whose flowery side. Poetical Happiness. Frederick Tennyson. CenSon

There is a friendship that exists between. Dog's Vigil, A. Margaret E. Bruner. PoToHe

There is a garden where lilies. Eutopia. Francis Turner Palgrave. EBVV; OBGa

There is a girl dragging heavy. Ritual Girl. Frank Mkalawile Chipasula. HBAPE

There is a girl you like so you tell her. Courtship. Mark Strand. HCAP; PoPoPo

There is a god in whom I do not believe. God the Eater. Stevie Smith. BWW

There is a God that carves to each his own. (LL) Bible, *O.T.* BASC; NPeEn; NoP-4; PEW, tr. by Mary Sidney Herbert, Countess of Pembroke *Fr.* Psalms.

There is a goddess and I know her. Her hands are not clean. Apotheosis of the Kitchen Goddess II. Teresa Noelle Roberts. HW

There is a golden rule in life. Do As You Would Be Done By. Matilda Caroline Edwards. PWR

There is a great amount of poetry in unconscious. Critics and Connoisseurs. Marianne Craig Moore. APT-1; FaBoWP; NOBA; NoAM; OxBA

There is a great river this side of Stygia. River of Rivers in Connecticut, The. Wallace Stevens. APT-1; FaBoA; HAP; HCAP; NOBA; VGW

There is a greater charm to me. *Unknown.* VerBaPo

There is a green spell stolen from Birmingham;. Death at Winson Green, A. Francis Webb. BMAP

There is a grey thing that lives in the tree-tops. Stephen Crane. APN-2

There is a group of blacks about. Turnabouts. Dyan Newson. IBA

There is a growth that hurts the child. Age, An. Laura Jensen. LCAP-2

There is a hawk that is picking the birds out of our sky. Shiva. Robinson Jeffers. NOBA; NoAM; Son

There is a heaven, for ever, day by day. Theology. Paul Laurence Dunbar. SacPr

There is a heigh-ho in these glowing coals. Heigh-ho on a Winter Afternoon. Donald Davie. OxBTC

There Is a High Place. Edwin Markham. AH

There is a hill and on that hill is a stone. Heart of the World, The. Rabbi Nahman [or Nachman] of Bratzlav. TrJP, tr. by Joseph Leftwich

There is a hit list. Intermission from Sunday. Pedro Juan Pietri. PueRic

There is a hornet in the room. Buried at Springs. James Schuyler. CoAP; PoM

There is a hush now while the hills rise up. Fishing in the Keep of Silence. Linda Gregg. BodElec

There is a joy, which angels well may prize. Social Worship. Bishop Richard Mant. SacPr

There is a joyful night in which we lose. When the Dumb Speak. Robert Bly. NOBA

There is a kind of lace laid over the city, a lightness. Serious Merriment of Women, The. Patricia Goedicke. TAP

There is a knot in the middle of my head. Glimpse, A. John Wieners. FTOS

There is a lady conquering with glances. There Is a Lady. Walther [or Walter] von der Vogelweide. AWP, tr. by Jethro Bithell

There Is a Lady Sweet and Kind. Thomas Ford. EBEV; HeIP-4; NOSC; OBEV

(Passing By.) NOBE

There Is a Lady Sweet and Kind. *Unknown.* NoP-4

There is a land called Lost. Two Chorale-Preludes: On Melodies by Paul Celan. Geoffrey Hill. OxBC

There Is a Land Mine Eye Hath Seen. Gurdon Robins. AH

There is a land of pure delight. Heaven. Isaac Watts. TOF

There is a language before. Mute Prophets. Nicholas Samaras. OPRER

There is a language in a naval log. Edwin John Pratt. MoCV *Fr.* Behind the Log.

There is a Languor of the Life. Emily Dickinson. BoWoP

There is a last, solitary coach about to leave. There Is a Last, Solitary Coach. David Vogel. HP, tr. by A. C. Jacobs

There is a little glass boy. "From Your Depths and Kneeling . . ." Teresa Calderón. TANSG, tr. by Celeste Kostopulos-Cooperman

There is a little lightning in his eyes. Of Robert Frost. Gwendolyn Brooks. NOBA; NoAM

There is a loneliness on city streets. There Is a Loneliness. Margaret E. Bruner. PoToHe

There is a lonely mountain-top. Jephthah's Daughter. "Yehoash." TrJP, tr. by Alter Brody

There is a loud noise of Death. To Dear Daniel. Samuel Greenberg. APT-1

There is a love that tumbles like a stream. Philip Jerome Cleveland. SacPr

There is a magic melting pot. Melting Pot, The. Dudley Randall. BPo; NBV

There is a Maker. Wizards. Alonzo Gonzales Mó. STP, tr. by Allan F. Burns

There is a meadow. Last Light. Robert Kelly. VGW

There is a melody for which I would surrender. Fantasy. Gérard de Nerval. WoPoe, tr. by Geoffrey Wagner

There is a middleaged man, Tim Flanagan. Middleaged Man, The. Louis Simpson. BodElec; NNaP

There is a mole on Ahmad's cheek that draws all those who. Mole, The. Al-Muntafil. RaBo, tr. by Robert Bly

There is a moment blind with light, split by the hum. Icarus in November. Alec Brock Stevenson. FuPo

There is a morn by men unseen. Emily Dickinson. NALW; OxBA

There is a mountain and a wood between us. Separation. Walter Savage Landor. NPeEn

There is a music to this sadness. Tonight I Can Almost Hear the Singing. Silvia Curbelo. TouFir

There Is a Mystery in Human Hearts. *Unknown.* PoToHe

There Is a Mystic Borderland. Helen Field Fischer. PoToHe

There is a nation in my brawny scrotal sac. There is a nation. Lance Jeffers. NBV

There is a pain—so utter. Emily Dickinson. APN-2; BoWoP; NAAL-2v1; NCAP; NOBA

There is a painting by Lucas Cranach. Official Love Story. Linda Gregg. BodElec

There is a painting of it: an eighteenth-century miniature from the Kangra School of India. Painting. Jane Hirshfield. ExTi

There is a parrot imitating spring. Parsley. Rita Dove. ESEAA; HCAP; LoL; NAAAL; NAAL-5; NIL-7; NoAM; NoP-4; PoPoPo; VCAP

There is a path no vulture's eye hath seen. Anne Bradstreet. WPoS *Fr.* Vanity of All Worldly Things, The.

There is a people mighty in its youth. Tribute to America. Shelley. AiP

There is a people of dreams driving. Sea Dreams. Rosita Copioli. CItWP, tr. by Cinzia Sartini Blum and Lara Trubowitz

There is a photograph in my father's. Abbienti. Steven C. Levi. GotH

There is a place at the center of earth. Crossings. Linda Hogan. BodElec

There Is a Place in Distant Seas. Richard, Archbishop Whately. NOBAu

There is a place that some men know. Cross, The. Allen Tate. AWP; ChIV-2; MoAmPo; OxBA

There is a place where Contraries are equally True. William Blake. NOBRP *Fr.* Milton.

There is a pleasure in the pathless woods. Byron. OxAEP-2 *Fr.* Childe Harold's Pilgrimage.

There is a poetaster named Wang. Han-shan. SuSp

There is a poor sneak called Rossetti. On Himself. Dante Gabriel Rossetti. FaBoEE

There is a poor sneak called Rossetti. Dante Gabriel Rossetti. *See* On Himself

There is a precise instant in time. Midway. Robert Desnos. PFTM-1

There is a question. Elegy. Max Winter. NeAmPo

There is a quiet kingdom's strand. Quiet Kingdom, The. Carl Busse. AWP, tr. by Ludwig Lewisohn

There is a quiet spirit in these woods. Spirit of Poetry, The. Henry Wadsworth Longfellow. APN-1

There is a river. No End of No-Story. George Macdonald. NOBVV

There is a sad carnival up the valley. Are They Dancing. Edward Dorn. NeAP; PoM

There is a scud of cloud. Gun Emplacement: Sundown. Jeremy Ingalls. YaYoPo

There is a secret room. Same Gesture, The. John Montague. BIrV; ModIr; PNI

There is a section in my library for death. Tomes. Billy Collins. KGB

There is a ship that sails the sea. When My Ship Comes In. Walter Donaldson. ReLy

There is a sighing in the wood. Silent, The. Jones Very. NCAP

There is a silence of deep gathered eve. Onycha. "Michael Field." ViWPN

There is a silence where hath been no sound. Silence. Thomas Hood. EBEV; GSo; NOBE; OBEV; OxBSo; Son

There is a singer everyone has heard. Oven Bird, The. Robert Frost. APT-1; AWP; GSo; HeIP-4; NAAL-2v2; NAAL-5; NOBA; NoAM; NoP-4; OWoS; OxBA; PoE; Son; TAP; TCAPo

There is a Smile of Love. Smile, The. William Blake. RB

There is a soldier on the battlefield. *Unknown.* BoWoP

There is a solitude in seeing you. Lightning. Witter Bynner. APT-1

There is a song, there is a moaning in the song. Baby at the Bottom of the River. W. S. Rendra. WoPoe, tr. by Harry Aveling

There is a spell, for instance. "H. D.". APT-1 *Fr.* Walls Do Not Fall, The.

There is a sphere, a secret sphere. Inner Realm, The. Priscilla Jane Thompson. CBWP-2

There is a spot where all our hopes. Home. Matilda Caroline Edwards. PWR

There is a stane in yon water. Burd Isabel and Earl Patrick. *Unknown.* ESPB

There is a stone in the air. Peru Eye, the Heart of the Lamp. Clark Coolidge. APSN

There is a story about a hummingbird named isidore. Bird Named Isidore, The. Evelyn Posamentier. GotH

There is a strange, solemn, silent, graceless. David Ferry. FaBoA

There is a stream, I name not its name. Arthur Hugh Clough. FaBoVe *Fr.* Bothie of Tober-na-Vuolich, The [A Long-Vacation Pastoral].

There is a stream which rises. Joseph Bruchac. CDW

There is a street in Cairo, full of sin and shame.   Shari Wag El Burka.   *Unknown.*   FaBoWar

There is a strong wall about me to protect me.   Love Song: "There is a strong wall about me to protect me."   Mary Carolyn Davies.   LW

There is a Supreme God in the ethnological section.   Homage to the British Museum.   William Empson.   FaBoMo; MoBrPo; NPeEn; OxBEV; PoE

There is a sway that comes soon after.   To a Stranger (At the End of a Caboose).   Laura Jensen.   GM

There is a table in the back where she opens.   Waitress.   Jason Shinder.   ReTh

There is a tale.   Simonides.   SaLy, *tr.* by Diane Rayor

There is a tall long-sided dame.   Samuel Butler (1612–80).   OBSV   *Fr.* Hudibras.

There is a temper of atmosphere which prevents rain.   Dennis Phillips.   FTOS   *Fr.* Twenty Questions.

There is a thing which in the light.   Candle, A.   Sir John Suckling.   BASC

There is a tide in the affairs of men.   Rudyard Kipling.   OxBSP   *Fr.* Plain Tales from the Hills.

There is a tide in the affairs of men.   William Shakespeare.   ITBLP   *Fr.* Julius Caesar.

There is a timbre of voice.   Echoes.   Audre Lorde.   NoP-4

There is a time to mount; to humble thee.   Enzo, King of Sardinia.   EaItPo, *tr.* by Dante Gabriel Rossetti

There is a train.   Loco.   Jane Holland.   MFPA

There is a train inside this iris.   Iris.   David St. John.   LCAP-2; MakPoe

There is a tranquil star.   Star, A.   Federico García Lorca.   PFTM-1

There is a tree by day.   Tenebris.   Angelina Weld Grimké.   APT-1; NAAAL

There is a tree native in Turkestan.   Note on Local Flora.   William Empson.   EBEV; FaBoMo; OxAEP-2; OxBEV

There is a tribe of invisible men.   Invisible Men, The.   Nakasuk.   RaBo, *tr.* by Edward Field

There is a truce. . . O lovers, tell.   Truce, The.   Stella Gibbons.   LW

There is a vale which none hath seen.   Rumors from an Aeolian Harp.   Henry David Thoreau.   APN-1

There is a very life in our despair.   Byron.   NOBRP   *Fr.* Childe Harold's Pilgrimage.

There is a vice prevails.   Francesco da Barberini.   EaItPo, *tr.* by Dante Gabriel Rossetti

There is a vice which oft.   Francesco da Barberino.   EaItPo

There is a voice inside the body.   Man Lost by a River, A.   Michael C. Blumenthal.   RaBo

There is a wailing baby under every stone and you walk.   Poem.   Norman McCaig.   SPE

There is a way of seeing that is not seeing.   Trompe L'Œil.   Daryl Hine.   MoCV

There is a / A welcome at the door to which no one comes?   Angel Surrounded by Paysans.   Wallace Stevens.   HCAP; LCAP-2

There is a white cliff, sea-worn, temple-scarred.   Sappho's Leap.   Howard Baker.   APT-2

There is a whole world involved in me.   Martyn Crucefix.   NewEx

There is a willow grows aslant a brook.   William Shakespeare.   OxAEP-1; RB   *Fr.* Hamlet.

There is a window stuffed with hay.   Hay Hotel, The.   Oliver St. John Gogarty.   BIrV

There is a wolf in me . . . fangs pointed for tearing gashes.   Wilderness.   Carl Sandburg.   RaBo

There is a woman in our town.   William Carlos Williams.   PoE   *Fr.* Paterson.

There Is a Woman in This Town.   Patricia Parker.   BlSi

There is a word at heart for the next of death.   Written in Exile.   Kathleen Jessie Raine.   TrCP; WPE

There is a word that never.   Etel Adnan.   PoArWo   *Fr.* Indian Never Had a Horse, The.

There is a Yew-tree, pride of Lorton Vale.   Yew-Trees.   William Wordsworth.   UnPo

There is a Zone whose even Years.   Emily Dickinson.   APN-2; NCAP

There is always a first flinging.   Variations on a Theme.   Anne Wilkinson.   MoCV

There is always a place for you at my table.   There Is Always a Place for You.   Anne Campbell.   PoToHe

There is always a sound.   Linda Zisquit.   DTA   *Fr.* Unopened Letters.

There is always the other one.   Judy Travaillo Variations, The.   Michael Anania.   IllVoic

There is among my thoughts the joyous plan.   Folgore da San Geminiano [*or* Gimignano].   EaItPo, *tr.* by Dante Gabriel Rossetti

There is an aggression of fact.   After Jericho.   Ronald Stuart Thomas.   OxBC

There is an air for which I would disown.   Old Tune, An.   Gérard de Nerval.   AWP, *tr.* by Andrew Lang

There is an ancient forest, its giant trees.   Flower Pot, The.   David Shimoni.   MHP, *tr.* by Ruth Finer Mintz

There is an ancient story.   My Father's Story.   Priscilla Jane Thompson.   CBWP-2

There is an award for this.   I Was Dancing Alone in Binh Dinh Province.   D. F. Brown.   CDa

There is an awful quiet in the air.   Prayer.   Hartley Coleridge.   GSo

There is an egg in the middle of things.   Man Who Loved White Chocolate, The.   Robert Kelly.   PFTM-2

There is an embalmer who operates.   Embalmer.   Rossana Ombres.   NeIt, *tr.* by Ruth Feldman

There is an end of joy and sorrow.   Ilicet.   Algernon Charles Swinburne.   NOBVV

There is an evening coming in.   Going.   Philip Larkin.   WoPoe

There is an eye, there was a tale.   John Berryman.   LCAP-2   *Fr.* Dream Songs.

There Is an Hour of Peaceful Rest.   William Bingham Tappan.   AH

There is an inn, a merry old inn.   Man in the Moon Stayed up To Late, The.   John Ronald Reuel Tolkien.   OBSP

There is an old and very cruel god.   Vicarious Atonement.   Richard Aldington.   MoBrPo

There Is an Old City.   Karl Bulcke.   AWP, *tr.* by Ludwig Lewisohn

There is an old he-wolf named Gambart.   Limerick.   Dante Gabriel Rossetti.   FaBoEE; PeLi

There is another heaven and earth beyond the world of men. (LL)   Conversations in the Mountains.   Li Po.   RaBo; TAL, *tr.* by Robert Payne

There is another Loneliness.   Emily Dickinson.   APN-2

There is, at times, an evening sky.   Vincent Ogé.   George Boyer Vashon.   APN-2

There is Bryant, as quiet, as cool, and as dignified.   James Russell Lowell.   NOBA; TAP   *Fr.* Fable for Critics, A.

There is but one, and that one ever. (LL)   Easter.   George Herbert.   ESCV; FaBoCh; FHYEP; GeHe; NAEL-5v1; NAEL-6v1; NOBE; NOSC; OBEV; OxBEV; PeECV; TrCP

There is Celilo.   She-Who-Watches . . . The Names are Prayer.   Elizabeth Woody.   OPRER

There is comfort in old houses.   Old Houses.   Homer D'Lettuso.   PoToHe

There is death enough in Europe without these.   Dead Ponies.   Brenda Chamberlain.   OBWVE; WPE

There is delight in singing, though none hear.   To Robert Browning.   Walter Savage Landor.   NoP-4

There is downpour, always.   Diesel to Yesterday.   John Tripp.   AngWePo

There is enough.   What We Know.   Raymond R. Patterson.   NBV

There is everything in his eyes.   Dog, The.   Susan Fromberg Schaeffer.   PoCoUp

There is freedom too, a peculiar kind.   Meanwhile, in Rwanda.   Patricia Smith.   SpirFl

There is from the legs in sleep an exhalation of the light, along the tops of the thighs.   Kenneth Irby.   PFTM-2   *Fr.* Three Sets of Three.

There is good news that spring's in the air.   Spring Sentiments.   Chao Yi.   SuSp, *tr.* by Chang Yin-nan

There is great mystery, Simone.   Hair.   Rémy de Gourmont.   AWP, *tr.* by Jethro Bithell

There is Hawthorne, with genius so shrinking and rare.   James Russell Lowell.   NOBA; TAP; TCAPo   *Fr.* Fable for Critics, A.

There is in human closeness a sacred boundary.   Anna Andreyevna Akhmatova.   WPOW

There is in life no blessing like affection.   Bonds of Affection.   Letitia [*or* Laetitia] Elizabeth Landon.   TreFP

There is in this world something.   Sweetest Thing, The.   *Unknown.*   TTY, *tr.* by Ulli Beier

There is, it seems, no poppy seed so old.   Poppy Heads.   Neil Curry.   NLP

There is joy.   Welcome Morning.   Anne Sexton.   PAI

There is Law for Fire.   Seasons of Fire, The.   Billy Marshall-Stoneking.   NOBAu

There Is Life.   Breyten Breytenbach.   VCWP, *tr.* by Breyten Breytenbach

There is life on other planets.   Vyacheslav Kupriyanov [*or* Kuprianov].   TCRP

There is little inspiration.   Tempest.   Sekeena Shaben.   PoArWo

There is Lowell, who's striving Parnassus to climb.   James Russell Lowell.   NOBA; OxBA; TAP; TCAPo   *Fr.* Fable for Critics, A.

There is moonrise under your fingernail—.   Guiffre's Nightmusic.   Thomas McGrath.   SeSe

There is more than glass between the snow and the huge roses. (LL)   Snow.   Louis MacNeice.   CIP-2; FaBoMo; HarvBoo; ModIr; NOBE; NPeEn; NoAM; OPOU; OxAEP-2; OxBEV; OxBSP; OxBTC; PNI

There is, mother, a place in the world called Paris.   Good Sense.   César Vallejo.   PoetW, *tr.* by Clayton Eshleman

There is naught for thee by thy haste to gain.   Created, The.   Jones Very.   APN-1; InvLi; NOCV

There is neither beginning nor end to the imagination.   William Carlos Williams.   CLPP   *Fr.* Kora in Hell.

There is no beauty in New England like the boats.   Product.   George Oppen.   HarvBoo

There is no better way to know us. Modest Proposal, A. Ted Hughes. CABP

There is no bidding me farewell. None. Duo Duo (Li Shizheng). PoetW, *tr. by* Maghiel Van Crevel

There is no chance, no destiny, no fate. Will. Ella Wheeler Wilcox. PoToHe

There is no chapel on the day. Oscar Wilde. EBVV; NoAM *Fr.* Ballad of Reading Gaol, The.

There Is No Country. Julian [*or* Juljan] Tuwim. TrJP, *tr. by* Watson Kirkconnell

There is no death! The stars go down. There Is No Death. John Luckey McCreery. PWR

There is no debauchery worse than thought. Contribution on Pornography, A. Wislawa Szymborska. PoSu, *tr. by* Adam Czerniawski

There is no eighty-eighth storey. Shape of Things, The. Lavinia Greenlaw. MFPA

There is no faith in claret, and it shall. Two Gentlemen That Broke Their Promise of a Meeting. James Shirley. BeJo

There is no faith; the mountain stands within. Faith. Jones Very. SacPr

There is no fire of the crackling boughs. Glenaradale. Walter Chalmers Smith. OBEV; PeVV

There is no form but shape! Rant Block. Michael McClure. SPE

There is no Frigate like a Book. Emily Dickinson. APN-2; BRP; MoAmPo; OBCA; SAmP; SoSe-8; TAP

There Is No God. Arthur Hugh Clough. CABP; NAEL-5v2; NOBE; NOBVV; NPeEn; NoP-4; OxBEV; SacPr *Fr.* Dipsychus [and the Spirit].

"There is no God," the foolish saith. Elizabeth Barrett Browning. SacPr *Fr.* Cry of the Human, The.

"There is no God," the wicked saith. Arthur Hugh Clough. CABP; NAEL-5v2; NOBE; NOBVV; NPeEn; NoP-4; OxBEV; SacPr *Fr.* Dipsychus [and the Spirit].

There is no grammar for the language of the dead. Language of the Dead, The. Thomas McGrath. BodElec

There is no great and no small. Ralph Waldo Emerson. APN-1

There is no happiness on earth! Dialogue No. 5. Dmitry [*or* Dmitrii] Aleksandrovich Prigov. ItGoST, *tr. by* Robert Reid

There is no happy life. Love's Matrimony. William Cavendish, Duke of Newcastle. NOSC

There is no hope. There is no hope. Idea Vilariño. TANSG, *tr. by* Louise B. Popkin

There is no Job but cries to God and hopes. Copy of Verses, A. John Wilson. SCAP

There Is No Land Yet. Laura Riding Jackson. ChIV-1

There is no language but "reconstructed" imaged parentheses back into. Statistics. Barrett Watten. PmAP

There is no language for the present time. Sulking in the Seventies. Kris Hemensley. BMAP

There is no limit to the number of times. From Father to Son. Emyr Humphreys. AngWePo; OBWVE; TCAWP

There is no lord within my heart. Shrine, The. Sara Teasdale. APT-1

There is no magic when we meet. After Love. Sara Teasdale. APT-1

There is no more silence on the plains of the moon. Night After Bushfire. Judith Wright. BMAP

There is no music now in all Arkansas. Variations for Two Pianos. Donald Justice. EmeKit

There Is No Name So Sweet on Earth. George Washington Bethune. AH

There Is No Natural Religion. William Blake. NAEL-6v2

There is no need for me to keep a skull on my desk. Memento Mori. Billy Collins. EmeKit

There is no need for Pain Lord. Breyten Prays for Himself. Breyten Breytenbach. PoetW; VCWP, *tr. by* Denis Hirson

There is no need to personify the wound. Poem for Central America. Hilary Booth. SurWo

There is no needle without piercing point. Death. *Unknown.* RaBo

"There is no one. . ." Edith Södergran. WPoS, *tr. by* Stina Katchadourian

There is no one among men that has not a special failing. Madly Singing in the Mountains. Po Chü-i. BLT; ChiP; WoPoe, *tr. by* Arthur Waley

There is no one here. Matisse: "The Red Studio." W. D. Snodgrass. GS

There is no one in this world who has time. "There is no one. . ." Edith Södergran. WPoS, *tr. by* Stina Katchadourian

There is no one to share my thoughts. (LL) Alone. Chu Shu-chen. BoWoP; OHPC, *tr. by* Kenneth Rexroth

There is no one to teach me the songs that bring the Moon Bird, the fish or any other thing that makes me what I am. Errol West. IBA

There is no other girl, bridegroom, like this. Sappho. SaLy, *tr. by* Diane Rayor

There is no other happiness. (LL) Second Rapture, The. Thomas Carew. BASC; CaPo

There is no other life. (LL) Why Log Truck Drivers Rise Earlier Than Students of Zen. Gary Snyder. GeoHom; LoL; NNaP

There is no outside. Moving Object. Jean Day. FTOS

There is no person lonelier . . . Than he who lies in bed. Visit the Sick. James J. Metcalfe. PoToHe

There is no pigment in blue feathers. Bluebird in Cutleaf Beech. Wendy Wilder Larsen. KGB

There is no place in this dark. Radiant Silhouette II. John Yau. OpBo

There is no place to hide. David Hall. CDa *Fr.* Ambush of the Fourth Platoon, The.

There is no point in work. Work. D. H. Lawrence. OBMV

There is no race of men. Boethius. MLL *Fr.* Consolation of Philosophy, The ("De Consolacione Philosophie").

There is no Raynard fox. Just foxes. Gods, The. Les A. Murray. WoPoe

There Is No Real Peace in the World. Douglas Crase. BodElec

There is no reason for amazement: surely one always knew that cultures decay, and life's end is death. (LL) Purse-Seine, The. Robinson Jeffers. AmFaPo; HAP; NOBA; NoAM; OxBA; WeW-3

There is no rest beside this stream, no love. Peach Blossom Stream. Chou Pang-yen. CrYelRi, *tr. by* Sam Hamill

There is no road here—not even a path. Lake Baskunchak. Andrey Alekseievich Amalrik. TCRP; TCRusP, *tr. by* John Glad

There is no room for pupils any more. (LL) Ballata: Of True and False Singing. *Unknown.* AWP; EaItPo, *tr. by* Dante Gabriel Rossetti

There is no salvation for mankind. Ballad of a Little Lamp. René Depestre. NegPo, *tr. by* Ellen Conroy Kennedy

There is no science of separation. Tristia. Ger Killeen. AmPoNex

There is no sense that I should write a line. To Cynthia. Sir Francis Kynaston. NOSC

There is no Silence in the Earth—so silent. Emily Dickinson. FaBoEE

There is no silence upon the earth or under the earth like the silence under the sea. Silences. Edwin John Pratt. NOBC

There is no such thing as a dada lecture. Tristan Tzara. Edward Hirsch. BodElec

There is no thing in all the world but love. Camel-Rider, The. *Unknown.* AWP, *tr. by* Wilfrid Scawen Blunt

There is no time now for my dream of hawks. (LL) I Have Exhausted the Delighted Range. Michael Hartnett. CIP-2; ModIr

There is no umbrella. To Carlos Drummond de Andrade. Joao Cabral de Melo Neto. TCLAP, *tr. by* Guy Pacitti

There is no whispering of any friend. No Friend Like Music. Daniel Whitehead Hicky. PoToHe

There is no wolf, of course. Where the Wolf Sings. Mary Low. SurWo

There Is No Word for Goodbye. Mary Tallmountain. HATNAP; LoL

There is no word for goodbye. (LL) There Is No Word for Goodbye. Mary Tallmountain. HATNAP; LoL

There Is No Word for Sex in Taglog. Noel Mateo. ReBoTo

There is none. And this means today. Consolation. David Rivard. SwNoth

There is none like the Boy that sold Broom, green Broom. (LL) Broom, Green Broom. *Unknown.* OxBoLi; PoRA

There is none, no none but I. Sir Robert Aytoun [*or* Ayton]. NOSC

There Is Not and There Will Never Be So Much. Gabriella Leto. CItWP, *tr. by* Cinzia Sartini Blum and Lara Trubowitz

There is not in the wide world a valley so sweet. Meeting of the Waters, The. Thomas Moore. NOIV; OxBoLi

There Is Nothin' like a Dame. Oscar Hammerstein, II. OBAL; ReLy

There is nothing. (LL) Day for Anne Frank, A. C. K. Williams. GotH; TaR

There is nothing as sweet as independence. Independence. Adebayo Faleti. PBA, *tr. by* Ulli Beier and Bakare Gbadamosi

There is nothing but water in the holy pools. How Much Is Not True. Kabir. RaBo

There is nothing here. (LL) At the Well. Paul Blackburn. APSN; PFTM-2

There is nothing I can do. Nizar Qabbani. MAP

There is nothing left / "please . . . please" (LL) Two Vietnam Poems: (1966). Bill Knott. PBCAP; SPE

There is nothing more to say. (LL) House on the Hill, The. Edwin Arlington Robinson. APN-2; MakPoe; MoAmPo; NAAL-2v2; NCAP

There is nothing there at the top of the valley. To See if Something Comes Next. Jack Gilbert. BodElec

There is nothing to be afraid of. Nothing at all. (LL) Brother and Sisters. Judith Wright. BMAP; FaBoWP

There is one season of the year. Indian Summer. Olga Fiodorovna Berggolts [*or* Bergholts]. TCRusP, *tr. by* Daniel Weissbort

There is one sin: to call a green leaf grey. Ecclesiastes. Gilbert Keith Chesterton. ChIV-1; MoBrPo; OxBSP

There is one story and one story only. To Juan at the Winter Solstice. Robert Graves. EBEV; FaBoMo; HarvBoo; MoBrPo; NAEL-5v2; NAEL-6v2; NPeEn; NoAM; NoP-4; PoE; RaBo; TwCP

There is only one. Culture. Alfred Kreymborg. APT-1

There Is Only One Almighty. Mariella Bettarini. CItWP, *tr. by* Cinzia Sartini Blum and Lara Trubowitz

There Is Only One of Everything. Margaret Atwood. NOBC

There is only your portrait, drawn in my poem. (LL)   Taoist Huang Has Died of Alcoholism, The.   Shen Chou.   CoBLCP; ColAnChi, tr. by Jonathan Chaves

There is pain in my heart.   Neidhart von Reuental.   GePo

There is pleasure in the wet, wet clay.   Rudyard Kipling.   NOBL   Fr. Naulahka, The.

There Is Power in a Union.   Joe Hill.   HHAm

There is revenge—writing.   To Everyone.   Velemir [or Viktor Vladimirovich] Khlebnikov.   TCRusP, tr. by Kathy Lewis and Bob Perelman

There is sand where the tracks were.   Tearing Up the Tracks.   Christopher Bursk.   GM

There is smoke above the hawks in the hall of the king.   Unknown.   FaBoWar, tr. by Wystan Hugh Auden and Paul B. Taylor   Fr. Treachery of Asmund, The.

There is so little that is close and warm.   Debris of Life and Mind.   Wallace Stevens.   SAmP

There is so much of loneliness.   Unknown.   PoToHe

There is so much pain. (LL)   Ford Madox Ford.   FaBoWar; PeFWW   Fr. Antwerp.

There is some beauty in sorrow.   Placing a $2 Bet for a Man Who Will Never Go to the Horse Races Any More.   Diane Wakoski.   UnPo

There is some goggling and conversation coming from the box.   Outrigger.   Charles Bernstein.   PFTM-2

There is some will talk of lords and knights.   Robin Hood's Delight.   Unknown.   ESPB

There / is someone I can bear.   W. S. Landor.   Marianne Craig Moore.   OBAL

There is something after all of pleasure.   At the Window.   "Rachel" [or "Rahel"].   FIT, tr. by Robert Friend

There is something between us.   Breasts.   Donald Hall.   OBAL

There is something I want to say.   Coming Home.   D. F. Brown.   CDa

There is something in the autumn that is native to my blood.   Vagabond Song, A.   Bliss Carman.   BRP; TCAPo

There is something which I dread.   Fear of Madness, The.   Lucretia Davidson.   TCAPo

There is subtle sad aggression.   Performance Test.   Prageeta Sharma.   HeMarv

There is sun in the mirror, my head in the trees.   Riverbed, The.   Vona Groarke.   MFPA

There is that in me . . . .I do not know what it is . . . .but I know it is in me.   Walt Whitman.   CAGL; ColAP   Fr. Song of Myself.

There is that sound like the wind.   Summer.   John Ashbery.   NAAL-2v2

There Is the Body Lying in State.   Joshua Clover.   AmPoNex

There is the caw of a crow.   Edgar Lee Masters.   OxBA   Fr. Spoon River Anthology.

There is the fire it burns and I am the water I drown.   There Is the Fire.   Valentine Penrose.   SurWo, tr. by Roy Edwards

There is the loneliness of peopled places.   Solitude.   Babette Deutsch.   LW

There is the old pond!   Basho.   NIL-7, tr. by John Thomas Bryan

There is the one who turns.   Chiapas.   Gary Soto.   NoAM

There is the star bloom of the moss.   Forest.   Jean Garrigue.   NOBA

There is the trap that catches noblest spirits, that caught—they say—God, when he walked on earth. (LL)   Shine, Perishing Republic.   Robinson Jeffers.   APT-1; HarvBoo; NAAL-2v2; NAAL-5; NOBA; NoAM; NoP-4; OxBA; PAI; PoPoPo; TAP; TFi; UnPo; VGW

There is the voice of confinement in the pine cone.   There.   Ray Gonzalez.   TouFir

There is the weight of the word.   Letter to Ellen Conroy Kennedy.   Edouard J. Maunick.   NegPo, tr. by Ellen Conroy Kennedy

There is the western gate, Luke Havergal— / Luke Havergal. (LL)   Luke Havergal.   Edwin Arlington Robinson.   APN-2; AWP; MoAmPo; NAAL-2v2; NAAL-5; NOBA; NoAM; TCAPo; TFi; UnPo

There is the woman.   Radio.   Cornelius Eady.   ESEAA

There is this cave.   Jewel, The.   James Wright (1927–80).   CoAP; NAAL-2v2

There is this edge where shadows.   Call It Fear.   Joy Harjo.   NAAL-5

There is too much pain.   Lines Scribbled on an Envelope.   Madeleine L'Engle.   SacPr

There is unfeminine, (but oh, so Female).   Questionnaire.   Susan Saxe.   GLP

There is unknown dust that is near us.   Surprised by Evening.   Robert Bly.   VGW

There is war. (LL)   Poem for the Young White Man Who Asked Me How I, An Intelligent, Well-Read Person Could Believe in the War Between Races.   Lorna Dee Cervantes.   PBCAP; PoPoPo; WPOW

There is Whittier, whose swelling and vehement heart.   James Russell Lowell.   NOBA; OxBA   Fr. Fable for Critics, A.

There Is Wind, There Are Matches.   Gerald Stern.   LCAP-2

There is wind where the rose was.   Autumn.   Walter De la Mare.   NPeEn; OxBTC

There isn't a shadow of doubt.   Limerick.   Unknown.   PeLi

There isn't any death.   Perry Brass.   CAGL

There it all was: the gaslamp, drugstore.   Viktor Aleksandrovich Sosnora.   ItGoST, tr. by Maia Tekses

There it is again.   Arrival.   Gerald McCarthy.   CDa

"There it is!/ You play beside a death-bed like a child."   Elizabeth Barrett Browning.   BrRo   Fr. Aurora Leigh.

There it was, word for word.   Poem That Took the Place of a Mountain, The.   Wallace Stevens.   LCAP-2

There Lackethe Somethynge Style.   Thomas Chatterton.   OxAEP-1   Fr. Aella; a Tragycal Enterlude.

There lasts a wind which I remember, burning.   Street in Agrigento.   Salvatore Quasimodo.   WoPoe, tr. by Denis Devlin

There—leaving out a Man. (LL)   Emily Dickinson.   APN-2; TCAPo

There leeft a may, an a weel-far'd may.   Katharine Jaffray.   Unknown.   ESPB

There leeved a wee man at the fit o yon hill.   Get Up and Bar the Door.   Unknown.   ESPB

There lie the black mountains.   Unknown.   APN-2, tr. by Washington Matthews   Fr. Mountain Chant, The.

There lies a somnolent lake.   In the Past.   Trumbull Stickney.   ColAP; NOBA; OxBA

There lies afar behind a western hill.   Town without a Market, The.   James Elroy Flecker.   MoBrPo

There liv'd a lass in yonder dale.   Katharine Jaffray.   Unknown.   ESPB

There liv'd a man in yonder glen.   Johnie Blunt.   Robert Burns.   OxBB

There liv'd a wife in Whistle Cockpen.   Will Ye Na Can Ye Na Let Me Be.   Unknown.   FaBoVe

There liv'd, as Authors tell, in Days of Yore.   Geoffrey Chaucer.   OBVE   Fr. Canterbury Tales, The.

There livd a laird down into Fife.   Wife Wrapt in Wether's Skin, The.   Unknown.   ESPB

There livd a lord on yon sea-side.   Fair Annie.   Unknown.   ESPB

There lived a carl in Kellyburnbraes.   Kellyburnbraes.   Robert Burns.   OxBB

There lived a certain man and he had three sons . . . (LL)   Western Approaches, The.   Howard Nemerov.   ColAP; HCAP; TAP

There Lived a King.   Sir William Schwenck Gilbert.   OBCoV   Fr. Gondoliers, The.

There lived a king in Thule.   King in Thule, The.   Goethe.   STV, tr. by John Frederick Nims

There lived a soldier in the world.   Paper Soldier.   Bulat Shalvovich Okudzhava.   TCRP, tr. by Albert C. Todd

There lived a wife at Usher's Well.   Wife of Usher's Well, The.   Unknown.   AWP; EBEV; ESPB; MakPoe; NAEL-5v1; NAEL-6v1; NAEL-7v1; NOBE; NPeEn; NePenScot; NoP-4; OBEV; OxAEP-1; OxBB; OxBS; RB; SCGP; TFi

There lived an old man in the Kingdom of Tess.   New Vestments, The.   Edward Lear.   NOBVV

There lived in ancient Scribbletown a wise old writer-man.   Puzzled.   Carolyn Wells.   OBCA

There lived in Gothic days, as legends tell.   Edwin, The Minstrel.   James Beattie.   OxAEP-1

There lives a good-for-nothing cat.   Lazy Pussy, The.   Palmer Cox.   OBCA; OxIBACP

There lives a land beside the western sea.   On the South Coast of Cornwall.   John Gray.   NOBVV

There lives a maid down under yon brae.   Katherine Jaffary.   Unknown.   OxBB

There lives a man in Rynie's land.   Lang Johnny More.   Unknown.   ESPB

There lives in / my childhood street.   Self Portrait 4.   Tove Ditlevsen.   WPOW, tr. by Ann Freeman

There'll be a day when dust flies at the bottom of the sea.   Po Chü-i.   SuSp   Fr. Tune: "Ripples Sifting Sand."

There'll be no more.   Finished.   Kate Llewellyn.   NOBAu

There'll be time enough to sleep. (LL)   Reveille.   A. E. Housman.   CABP; HarvBoo; MoBrPo; NoP-4

There'll come a time when brother speaks with brother.   Alcuin.   MLL

There Love in very presence seemed to be. (LL)   Ballata: Concerning a Shepherd-Maid.   Guido Cavalcanti.   AWP; EaItPo, tr. by Dante Gabriel Rossetti

There lyes all this great erles gold. (LL)   Young [or Younge] Andrew.   Unknown.   ESPB; OxBB

There may be a basement to the Atlantic.   Somebody's Gone.   Charles Henri Ford.   SPE

There may be some places the sun.   Into the Light.   Pattiann Rogers.   PoCoUp

There may be streets that have their sorrow.   Broadway Melody.   Arthur Freed.   ReLy

There may be trouble ahead.   Let's Face the Music and Dance.   Irving Berlin.   ReLy

There may have been a boy.   Last Train, The.   Linda Pastan.   GM

There might be found the flowing grace.   My Welsh Home.   John Morgan.   AngWePo

There mounts in squalls a sort of rusty mire.   Exile's Return, The.   Robert Lowell.   OxBA

There must be one thing that makes you shiver.   Death of Isadora Duncan, The. Dionisio D. Martinez.   TouFir

There Must Be Somethin' Better Than Love.   Dorothy Fields.   ReLy

There, my lad, lie the Articles.   Scene from a Play, Acted at Oxford, Called "Matriculation."   Thomas Moore.   OBSV

There never was.   Song.   Carl Rakosi.   BodElec

There never yet was honest man.   Loving and Beloved.   Sir John Suckling. BeJo; CaPo; CavPo; NAEL-5v1; NAEL-6v1; NAEL-7v1

There never yet was woman made.   Woman's Constancy.   Sir John Suckling. CaPo; CavPo

There now he lives in everlasting joy.   Edmund Spenser.   CAGL   Fr. Faerie Queene, The.

There, O there, where'er I go I'll leave my heart behind me! (LL)   Since First I Saw Your Face.   Unknown.   OBEV; OxBSP

There often wanders one, whom better days.   William Cowper.   NAEL-5v1; NAEL-6v1; NAEL-7v1   Fr. Task, The.

There on Siriu.   Comet.   Federico García Lorca.   PFTM-1

There, on the darkened deathbed, dies the brain.   Sonnnet.   John Masefield. EBEV

There on the horizon.   African Poem.   Agostinho Neto.   PBMAP; PoetW, tr. by W. S. Merwin

There on the sea sails wandered.   Names of Georgian Women, The.   Bella [or Izabella] Akhatovna Akhmadulina.   BoWoP, tr. by Olga Carlisle and Stanley Noyes

There on the sun-hot stone.   Lizard, The.   Lydia Pender.   NOxBChV

There on the top of the down.   June Bracken and Heather.   Tennyson. EnLoPo

There once, on that goat island, I.   Robert Penn Warren.   NOBA   Fr. Tiberius on Capri.

There once the walls.   Tale, A.   Edward Thomas.   OxBEV

There once was a bard of Hong Kong.   Limerick.   Gerard Benson.   OBCoV

There once was a bull named the Duke of Buccleuch.   Duke of Buccleuch, The. J. A. Phelp.   NOBAu

There once was a child who said: "How."   Postscript to Orwell's Animal Farm, A.   Miadesnia.   PeLi

There once was a couple named Mound.   Limerick.   Unknown.   PeLi

There Once was a Cow with a Double Udder.   Cow, The.   Theodore Roethke. OBAL; OBCA

There once was a doctor who said.   Limerick.   Towanbucket.   PeLi

There once was a fellow called Hyde.   Limerick.   E. J. Jackson.   PeLi

There once was a Fellow of Trinity.   Limerick.   Unknown.   PeLi

There once was a Fellow of Wadham / Who approved of the doings of Sodom. Limerick.   Unknown.   PeLi

There once was a flock of wild geese.   Limerick.   B. Semeonoff.   PeLi

There once was a girl from St. Paul.   Limerick.   Unknown.   NIP-4

There once was a girl named Jenny.   Saga of Jenny, The.   Kurt Weill.   ReLy

There once was a judge of Assize.   Limerick.   Unknown.   PeLi

There once was a lady called Lily.   Limerick.   Unknown.   PeLi

There once was a lass of Shalott.   Limerick.   Mary Holtby.   PeLi

There once was a leaf.   Robert Desnos.   MFP, tr. by Martin Sorrell

There once was a leaf with all its lines.   There once was a leaf.   Robert Desnos.   MFP, tr. by Martin Sorrell

There once was a man.   There Once Was a Man.   Jerry Ross.   ReLy

There once was a man [or There was a young man] who said, "Damn!" Limerick.   Maurice Evan Hare.   NOBL; OxBoLi; PeLi

There once was a man who said, "God."   Idealism.   Ronald Arbuthnott Knox. NBLV; OxBEV

There once was a Marquis de Sade.   De Sade.   John Fuller.   NBLV; PeLV

There once was a monarch of Spain.   Limerick.   Unknown.   PeLi

There once was a painter named Scott.   Limerick.   Dante Gabriel Rossetti. PeLi

There once was a person of Chiswick.   Limerick.   J. M. Ross.   PeLi

There once was a plesiosaurus.   Limerick.   Unknown.   PeLi

There Once Was a Puffin.   Florence Page Jaques.   NTCP

There once was a Scot who said: "Evil."   Limerick.   "H. M."   PeLi

There once was a sculptor named Phidias.   Limerick.   Unknown.   PeLi

There Once Was a Spinster of Ealing.   Unknown.   NIP-4

There once was a time.   Unknown.   NOIV

There once was a vicar of Ryhill.   Limerick.   Unknown.   PeLi

There once was a wicked young minister.   Limerick.   Conrad Potter Aiken. OBAL; PeLi

There once was a wise politician.   Limerick.   A. M. Sayers.   PeLi

There once was a witch of Willowby Wood.   Witch of Willowby Wood, The. Rowena Bastin Bennett.   ChAP

There once was a witch of Willowby Wood.   Rowena Bastin Bennett.   ChAP Fr. Witch of Willowby Wood, The.

There once was a writer called James.   Limerick.   R. K. R. Thornton.   PeLi

There once was an artist called Pat.   Limerick.   Margaret Galbreath.   PeLi

There once was an eccentric of Metz.   Limerick.   Leslie Johnson.   PeLi

There once was an eccentric old boffin.   Limerick.   Unknown.   PeLi

There once was monarch called Harry.   Limerick.   Mary Holtby.   PeLi

There once were some people called Sioux.   American Indian, The.   Unknown. NBLV

There once were two Babes in the Wood.   Limerick.   Roger Woddis.   PeLi

There ought to be capital punishment for cars.   Thoughts on Capital Punishment.   Rod McKuen.   InPK-6

There out of hell the Old One bellows.   Unknown.   AnOE, tr. by Charles W. Kennedy   Fr. Christ and Satan.

There reigns a prince, whose hand the sceptre claims.   Joel Barlow.   TCAPo Fr. Vision of Columbus, The.

There rolls the deep where grew the tree.   Tennyson.   HAP; NAEL-6v2; NOBE   Fr. In Memoriam A. H. H.

There runs a road by Merrow Down.   Rudyard Kipling.   NOxBChV   Fr. Just-So Stories.

There runs the wind of spring.   Early Spring.   Hugo von Hofmannsthal. AuPH, tr. by Lowell A. Bangerter

There's a barrel of porter at Tammany Hall.   Song.   Fitz-Greene Halleck. OBAL

There's a barrel-organ caroling across a golden street.   Barrel-Organ, The. Alfred Noyes.   BRP; MoBrPo; PoRA

There's a beautiful woman in the north.   Song.   Li Yen-nien.   CrYelRi, tr. by Sam Hamill

There's a better shine.   Lorine Niedecker.   APT-2

There's a bird perched on my shoulder.   Bird.   Ágnes Nemes Nagy.   BoWoP; PoSu, tr. by Bruce Berlind

There's a black and white photo of Elvis.   Audubon Drive, Memphis.   James Seay.   AllShUp; SwNoth

There's a branch of blossom on shore. (LL)   On the Way to Pa-ling.   Yüan Mei.   CoBLCP; ColAnChi, tr. by Jonathan Chaves

There's a Breathless Hush.   Noel Petty.   UV

There's a breathless hush in the Close tonight.   Vitaï Lampada.   Sir Henry John Newbolt.   FaBoWar; OBWP; UV

There's a Breathless Hush on the Centre Court.   Stanley J. Sharpless.   UV

There's a brief spring in all of us and when it finishes.   To S. T. C. on His 179th Birthday, October 12th, 1951.   Maurice Carpenter.   FaBoTw

There's a bright, golden haze on the meadow.   Oh, What a Beautiful Mornin'! Richard Rodgers.   ReLy

There's a caliche pit not far from here.   Dove at Sundown.   Catherine Bowman.   MoASP

There's a certain beekeeper I've fallen in love with. His hair smells. BZZZZZZZ.   Amy Gerstler.   PmAP

There's a Certain Slant of Light.   Emily Dickinson.   ColAP; PoPoPo

There's a class of men (and women) who are always on their guard.   Men Who Come Behind, The.   Henry Lawson.   NOBAu

There's a combative artist named Whistler.   Limerick.   Dante Gabriel Rossetti. FaBoEE; PeLi

There's a cool in the air.   Friends.   Mikhail Arkadyevich [or Arkad'evich] Svetlov.   TCRP, tr. by Daniel Weissbort

There's a cut-price whore.   Pascoe Polglaze.   PeLi

There's a doctor livin' in your town.   Doctor, Lawyer, Indian Chief.   Paul Francis Webster.   ReLy

There's a fabulous story.   Place Where the Rainbow Ends, The.   Paul Laurence Dunbar.   PWR; SacPr

There's a family nobody likes to meet.   Grumble Family, The.   Unknown. PWR

There's a famous seaside place called Blackpool.   Lion and Albert, The. Marriott Edgar.   OBNV

There's a feeling comes a stealing.   You're a Grand Old Flag.   George M. Cohan.   ReLy

There's a feeling that comes with the daze of joy.   Undertones.   George R. Sims.   NOBVV

There's a fierce gray Bird, with a bending beak.   John Neal.   APN-1   Fr. Battle of Niagara, The.

There's a fortunate priest of St. Paul's.   Limerick.   Douglas Catley.   PeLi

There's a fortune to be made in just about everything.   My Great Great Etc. Uncle Patrick Henry.   James Tate.   OBAL

There's a girl in Rio de Janeiro.   I, Yi, Yi, Yi, Yi (I Like You Very Much). Harry Warren.   ReLy

There's a gleam of the moon on the man on the rim-rock.   My Brother, My Sister.   Jack Davis.   IBA

There's a goblin as green.   Goblin, The.   Jack Prelutsky.   TLR

There's a god on each side.   Unknown.   APN-2, tr. by Washington Matthews Fr. Mountain Chant, The.

There's a good old war-cry sounding, it hangs on every lip.   Waitekauri Every Time!   Edwin Edwards.   PeNZ

There's a Grandfather's Clock in the Hall.   Robert Penn Warren.   NoAM; NoP-4

There's a great camp meeting in the Promised Land. (LL) Walk Together Children. *Unknown.* BPo; NAAAL

There's a green hollow where a river sings. Sleeper of the Valley, The. Arthur Rimbaud. AWP, *tr. by* Ludwig Lewisohn

There's a Hand that Nails Down. Milo De Angelis. ItPo, *tr. by* Gayle Ridinger

There's a heap o' love in the human heart. Human Heart, The. Frank Carleton Nelson. PoToHe

There's a horse on the fridge. Coloring. Mark DeCarteret. AmPoNex

There's a huge hullabaloo in my lotus heart. Mahendranāth Bhattācārya. SinGod, *tr. by* Rachel Fell McDermott

There's a land they call astutely. Okato-Otaia. Sándor Petőfi. IQMS, *tr. by* Anton N. Nyerges

There's a latent queer. Tim Hopkins. PeLi

There's a liddle fact of hishdory vitch few hafe oondershtand. Charles Godfrey Leland. APN-2 *Fr.* Hans Breitmann as a Politician.

There's a life awaiting on a rocky coast. It is Everywhere. Jean Toomer. GT

There's a line of Verlaine's that I'm not going to remember again. Limits (or Good-byes). Jorge Luis Borges. PoetW; TCLAP, *tr. by* Alan Dugan

There's a little fear piercing. Mistaken Identity. Lewis Warsh. BodElec

There's a little low hut by the river side. Picture, A. B. P. Shillaber. TreFP

There's a lodger lives on the first floor. Cornucopia. Christopher Pearse Cranch. APN-1

There's a long-legged girl. Pickin Em Up and Layin Em Down. Maya Angelou. NBLV

There's a Lull in My Life. Mack Gordon. ReLy

There's a man at Crewe. E. O. Parrott. PeLi

There's a man goin''round takin' names. Angel of Death, The. *Unknown.* SacPr

There's a man I know who feigns deafness. Man Who Feigns Deafness, The. Nguyễn Khuyến. WoPoe, *tr. by* Nguyen Ngoc Bich

There's a man, I really believe, compares with. Sappho. STV

There's a man I really believe's in heaven. Sappho. WeW-3

There's a man in my dream. In the Crevices of Night. Gloria Vando. TouFir

There's a Man in My Life. George, Jr. Marion. ReLy

There's a man with a Nose. Ambrose Bierce. APN-2; OBAL *Fr.* Devil's Dictionary, The.

There's a merry brown thrush sitting up in the [*or a*] tree. Brown Thrush, The. Lucy Larcom. OBCA

There's a mouse house. I Wouldn't. John Ciardi. TLR

There's a naked bug at Cold Mountain. Han-shan. WoPoe, *tr. by* Gary Snyder

There's a neat little clock. Clock, The. Mother Goose. ReMoGo

There's a notable family named Stein. Limerick. *Unknown.* NOBL

There's a one-eyed yellow idol to the north of Khatmandu. Green Eye of the Yellow God, The. J. Milton Hayes. EBNV

There's a patch of old snow in a corner. Patch of Old Snow, A. Robert Frost. OxBSP; WeW-3

There's a path that leads to Nowhere. Path that Leads to Nowhere, The. Corinne Roosevelt Robinson. ITBLP

There's a place between two stands of trees where the grass grows uphill. Adrienne Rich. ExTi; LoL *Fr.* Not Somewhere Else, But Here.

There's a place for us. Somewhere. Stephen Sondheim. ReLy

There's a Portuguese person named Howell. Limerick. Dante Gabriel Rossetti. PeLi

There's a pretty fuss and bother both in country and in town. New Song on the Birth of the Prince of Wales, A. John Harkness. NOBVV

There's a publishing party named Ellis. Limerick. Dante Gabriel Rossetti. PeLi

There's a puckle lairds in the auld house. Auld House, The. William Soutar. OxBS

There's a puff—and so good night! (LL) Good Night. Thomas Hood. OTCP; Spl

There's a quaint little place they call Lullaby Town. Lullaby Town. John Irving Diller. ITBLP

There's a reid lowe in yer cheek. Sang. Robert MacLellan. OxBS

There's a Sampson lying, sleeping in the land. Black Sampson, The. Josephine D. Henderson Heard. CBWP-4; SWaP

There's a saying old. Someone to Watch over Me. George Gershwin. ReLy

There's a scandal in the neighborhood. He's a Cousin of Mine. Cecil Mack. ReLy

There's a screen of arabesque between us and them. Arabesque. Ahmed Taha. NAfrP, *tr. by* Clarissa C. Burt

There's a seat right next to me. Brain on Ice. Michael Warr. UnSA

There's a sensitive type in Tom's River. Limerick. *Unknown.* PeLi

There's a serpent, namely, drinking. Social Glass, The. Lizelia Augusta Jenkins Moorer. CBWP-3

There's a shed at the bottom of our garden. Shed, The. Frank Flynn. OTCP

There's a sickness in me. During. Invisible Dreams. Toi Derricotte. PuP-23

There's a Silvery Lining to Every Cloud. Matilda Caroline Edwards. PWR

There's a slow tolling bell in the dark. Limerick. Gavin Ewart. PeLi

There's a small café off the avenue. Wardour Street. Humbert Wolfe. OxBTC

There's a Small Hotel. Richard Rodgers. ReLy

There's a song in the air! Christmas Carol, A. Josiah Gilbert Holland. SacPr

There's a sorry little scrub that is servant unto me. To Samuel, Bishop of Sens In Time of Dearth. Alcuin. MLL, *tr. by* Helen Waddell

There's a tiresome young man of Bay Shore. Limerick. Morris Gilbert Bishop. PeLi

There's a trade you all know well. Overlander, The. *Unknown.* NOBAu

There's a train that runs through Hawthorn. Late Express, The. Barbara Giles. OTCP

There's a tree out in our garden which is very nice to climb. Tree in the Garden, The. Christine Chandler. OTCP

There's a very prim girl called McDrood. Limerick. *Unknown.* PeLi

There's a vile old man. Limeraiku. Ted Pauker. NOBL; PeLi

There's a volcano snow-capped in the air some twenty miles. Resort. George Oppen. FTOS

There's a wanderer, there's a wanderer, his name is Tzu-mei. Seven Songs Written while Living at T'ung-ku in 759. Tu Fu. ColAnChi; SuSp, *tr. by* Geoffrey Waters and Goeffrey Waters

There's a whimsey in my noddle, there's a maggot in my brain. Problem, A. Carolyn Wells. SWaP

There's a whisper down the field where the year has shot her yield. Envoi. Rudyard Kipling. OBEV

There's a woman like a dew-drop, she's so purer than the purest. Robert Browning. OBEV *Fr.* Blot in the 'Scutcheon, A.

There's a woman who resembles a phrase. She has a spot of. Vegetable Calendar. Silvio Giussani. ItPo, *tr. by* Gayle Ridinger

There's a wonderful family called Stein. Limerick. *Unknown.* PeLi

There's a wonderful story. Angel's Message, The. Clara Ann Thompson. CBWP-2

There's a word for what we do. Devotions in Confidence. Margot Schilpp. AmPoNex

There's a yellow rose of Texas that I am going to see. Yellow Rose of Texas, The. *Unknown.* TCAPo

There's always been this dream that reasons, shearing off. Maritime. Reginald Shepherd. AmPoNex

There's an arch in your heart. Isla Mujeres. Lorna Dee Cervantes. TouFir

There's an early memory that I carry around. My Father's Back. Edward Hirsch. VCAP

There's an emerald frog down the loo. Limerick. Ruth Silcock. PeLi

There's an inn in Indiana with a very good clientele. Ladies Who Sing with a Band, The. George, Jr. Marion. ReLy

There's an Irishman, Arthur O'Shaughnessy. On the Poet, Arthur O'Shaughnessy—. Dante Gabriel Rossetti. OBCoV; PeLi

There's an island not so tropical. Spreadin' Rhythm Around. Ted Koehler. ReLy

There's an ordinary woman whom the English call the 'the Queen." English Queen, The. Henry Lawson. NOBAu

There's an Unknown River in Soweto. Zindzi Mandela. NAfrP

There's antimony, arsenic, aluminium, selenium. Elements, The. Tom Lehrer. UV

There's beauty in the azure skies. World Is Full of Beauty, The. Matilda Caroline Edwards. PWR

There's been a Death, in the Opposite House. Emily Dickinson. APN-2; SAmP; SoSe-8

"There's been an accident," they said. Mr. Jones. Harry Graham. UV

There's been an eagle on a nickel. Fact. Langston Hughes. APSN; PFTM-1

There's blood between us, love, my love. Christina Georgina Rossetti. NALW; NoP-4; VWP

There's blues in the night. (LL) Blues in the Night. Johnny Mercer. APT-2; ReLy

There's force to this cold sun, makes beard stubble stand shinily. William Carlos Williams. TCAPo *Fr.* Kora in Hell.

There's heaven above, and night by night. Johannes Agricola in Meditation. Robert Browning. SacPr; TOF

There's Holmes, who is matchless among you for wit. James Russell Lowell. NOBA; TCAPo *Fr.* Fable for Critics, A.

There's holy holy people. Capel Calvin. Idris Davies. AngWePo

There's in my mind a woman. In Mind. Denise Levertov. NAAL-5; NALW

There's just one fellow. I'm Just Wild About Harry. Noble Sissle. ReLy

There's Life in a Mussel; a Meditation. George Farewell. NOEC

"There's light ahead!" Hope ever cries. Hope Deferred. Clara Ann Thompson. CBWP-2

There's lightning in the sky. Dancing with Rex. Beth Cuthand. ReEnLa

There's little coin and less devotion. (LL) Bounty of Our Age, The. Henry Farley. FaBoCh; FaBoEE; NOSC

There's little in taking or giving. Coda. Dorothy Parker. APT-1

There's little joy in life for me.   On the Death of Anne Brontë.   Charlotte Brontë.   VWP; WPE

There's Malichevsky, Rubinstein, Arensky, and Tchaikowsky.   Tchaikowsky (And Other Russians).   Kurt Weill.   ReLy

There's moaning somewhere in the dark.   Voice in Darkness.   Richard Dehmel.   AWP, *tr.* by Margarete Münsterberg

There's more in words than I can teach.   Loving and Liking [Irregular Verses Addressed to A Child].   Dorothy Wordsworth.   SacPr; WoRP

There's much afoot in heaven and earth this year.   Rainy Summer, The.   Alice Thompson Meynell.   OxBSP; OxBTC

There's music in the old bones yet. (LL)   Song for the Clatter-Bones.   Frederick Robert Higgins.   ChIV-1; OBMV

There's my war club.   Hunting Song.   *Unknown.*   STP, *tr.* by Jerome Rothenberg

There's Nae Luck about the House.   Jean Adams.   NePenScot

There's Nae Luck about the House.   William Julius Mickle.   *See* Sailor's Wife, The

There's nane again sae bonnie. (LL)   Bonnie Lesley.   Robert Burns.   CTC; GTBS-P; NOBE; OBEV

There's naught (thou say'st) but one eternal flux.   Edward Young.   NOEC   *Fr.* Night Thoughts.

There's never enough whiskey or rain.   Wishing Africa.   Marilyn Bowering.   NOBC

"There's no a bird in a' this foreste."   Johnie Cock.   *Unknown.*   ESPB

There's No Business Like Show Business.   Irving Berlin.   ReLy

There's no carousing. (LL)   Anacreontic.   Robert Herrick.   CaPo; OxBoLi

There's no comfort inside me, only a small.   Beehive Cell.   Richard Murphy.   CIP-2; OxBSo

There's no excitement, news or anything.   Imre Madách.   IQMS, *tr.* by Iain MacLeod   *Fr.* Tragedy of Man.

There's no helping.   Tune: "New Bounty of Royalty."   Li Yü.   ColAnChi, *tr.* by Jiaosheng Wang

There's no keeping back spring.   Tune: "Magnolia Flower."   Ou-yang Hsiu.   ColAnChi, *tr.* by J. R. Hightower

There's No Lust like to Poetry.   *Unknown.*   AWP, *tr.* by John Addington Symonds

There's no modesty, Todorov.   To a French Structuralist.   David Kirby.   BLT

There's no more to be said. (LL)   On Prince Frederick.   *Unknown.*   FaBoEE; NOBL

There's no occasion for knocking at an out-of-the-way door.   Tune: "Partridge Sky" I Rejoice to Meet a Friend Visting at My Rustic Study.   Ch'iao Lai.   ColAnChi, *tr.* by Jiaosheng Wang

There's no overdoing.   Elegy of Our Times.   Eugenio Montale.   ItPo, *tr.* by Gayle Ridinger

There's No Place to Sleep in This Bed, Tanguy.   Charles Henri Ford.   SPE

There's no poet quite like you, Li Po.   To Li Po on a Spring Day.   Tu Fu.   CrYelRi, *tr.* by Sam Hamill

There's No Rigor Like the Old Rigor 2.   Ira Sadoff.   BodElec

There's no sense in listening to it, except.   Getting the News.   Helen Chasin.   YaYoPo

There's no sense making earnest out of game. (LL)   Geoffrey Chaucer.   NAWM-5v1; NAWM-7v1, *tr.* by Theodore Morrison   *Fr.* Canterbury Tales, The.

There's no such thing as leading apes in hell. (LL)   Married State, A.   Katherine Philips.   BASC; NAEL-7v1

There's No To-Morrow.   Anne Finch (b. 1908).   NIL-7

There's no way out.   In the Suburbs.   Louis Simpson.   TRP

There's no weather over Dikson.   Nonflying Weather.   Robert Ivanovich Rozhdestvensky [*or* Rozhdestvenskii].   TCRP, *tr.* by Albert C. Todd

There's not a chance now that I might recover.   Scar, The.   John Hewitt.   CIP-2; PNI

"There's not a husband whom storms don't benight."   *Unknown.*   GrAn

There's not a joy the world can give like that it takes away.   Stanzas for Music.   Byron.   HAP; NOBRP; NPeEn

There's not a nook within this solemn Pass.   Trosachs, The.   William Wordsworth.   OBEV

There's nothing grieves me, but that age should haste.   Michael Drayton.   NOSC   *Fr.* Idea.

There's nothing happening that you hate.   Leave Them Alone.   Patrick Kavanagh.   OxBSP

There's nothing left for me.   Among My Souvenirs.   Edgar Leslie.   ReLy

There's nothing makes a Greenland Whale.   It Makes a Change.   Mervyn Laurence Peake.   OTCP

There's nothing over there.   After Yes.   James Harms.   AmPoNex

There's nothing truer than fake fruit, let's say.   Edoardo Cacciatore.   ItPo, *tr.* by Gayle Ridinger   *Fr.* Full Powers: Five Warning Signs.

There's nothing very beautiful and nothing very gay.   Little Things.   John Orrick.   PoToHe

There's one called "Wild."   Tubes.   Terry Wolverton.   WiU

There's one Grammarian I know.   Lucilius.   GrAn

There's one I miss. A little questioning maid.   Augusta Davies Webster.   VWP; ViWPN   *Fr.* Mother and Daughter.

There's one thing to think of when you're blue.   Sunny Side Up.   Ray Henderson.   ReLy

There's only this.   Nissim Ezekiel.   OMIP   *Fr.* Hymns in Darkness.

There's our street, let's say.   Sergey Gandlevsky.   ItGoST, *tr.* by Philip Metres

There's parties ad yer meets about.   Albert Chevalier.   UV   *Fr.* Sich a Nice Man Too!

There's pleasure, sure, in being clad in green.   Scene after Hunting at Swallowfield in Berkshire, A.   Sneyd Davies.   NOEC

There's recompense to balm your spirit's ire.   Da Silva Gives the Cue.   Walter Hart Blumenthal.   TrJP

There's silence between one page and another.   Valerio Magrelli.   NeIt

There's snow in every street.   Winter.   John Millington Synge.   NOIV; OBMV; OxBTC

There's so much room in this world, even now.   Solar Loneliness.   "Strannik."   TCRP, *tr.* by April FitzLyon

There's some really good work.   Cream Song, The.   Apirana Ngata.   PeNZ, *tr.* by Margaret Orbell

"There's someone at the door," said gold candlestick.   Green Candles.   Humbert Wolfe.   MoBrPo

There's Someone I Think Of.   *Unknown.*   CoBCP, *tr.* by Burton Watson

There's Somethin'   Adam Small.   PeSAV

There's something about being an Indian.   Something About Being an Indian.   Adrian C. Louis.   UnSA

There's something in the air.   Coming of Spring, The.   Nora Perry.   PWR

"There's something in the air," he said.   Two Voices.   Edmund Charles Blunden.   OBWP; PeFWW

There's something in the air that you can sense.   On Such a Night As This.   Hugh Martin.   ReLy

There's something inside of my heart that cries.   Give Me a Heart to Sing To.   Victor Young.   ReLy

There's something uncertain about the rock.   Land at the World's End, The.   Brian Swann.   PoCoUp

There's something we call a game show with all kinds of dings and glitches.   Tagging.   Maureen Seaton.   ExTi; IllVoic

There's still on the rim of night (having been in it) which is (in night).   Leslie Scalapino.   ExTi   *Fr.* New Time.

There's talk of a New Dawn for Blacks.   New Dawn, The.   Mafika Pascal Gwala.   PeSAV

There's teuch sauchs growin' i' the Reuch Heuch Hauch.   Sauchs in the Reuch Heuch Hauch, The.   Hugh MacDiarmid.   NoAM

There's the place where the ranbow ends. (LL)   Place Where the Rainbow Ends, The.   Paul Laurence Dunbar.   PWR; SacPr

There's the sea, far beyond the yellow hills.   August Moon.   Cesare Pavese.   AF, *tr.* by William Arrowsmith

There's the wonderful love of a beautiful maid.   Love.   *Unknown.*   SoSe-8

There's too much light in my life.   Merk.   Eileen Myles.   WiU

There's where we'll meet and we'll never part no more. (LL)   Carry Me Back to Old Virginny.   James A. Bland.   APN-2; TCAPo

There sandy seems the golden sky.   Cliff Dwelling, A.   Robert Frost.   APT-1

There sat a happy fisherman.   Reed, The.   Mikhail Yuryevich Lermontov.   AWP, *tr.* by J. J. Robbins

There sat down, once, a thing on Henry's heart.   John Berryman.   HAP; HCAP; HarvBoo; NAAL-5; NoP-4; PoE; VCAP   *Fr.* Dream Songs.

There sate the Seniors of the Trojan Race.   Homer.   OBVE, *tr.* by Alexander Pope   *Fr.* Iliad, The.

There, sea and sky are at a mortal war.   Petronius Arbiter.   MLL

There seems no reason he should've died. His hands.   Dead Christ.   Andrew Hudgins.   RA

There seems to be someone / by the bend of the hill.   *Unknown.*   CoBCP, *tr.* by Burton Watson   *Fr.* Nine Songs.

There set out, slowly, for a Different World.   War, A.   Randall Jarrell.   OxBSP

There shall always be the Church and the World.   T. S. Eliot.   SacPr

There she is! There she is!   Ain't She Sweet?   Milton Ager.   ReLy

There she looms on the golden path.   Returning.   Victor Vroomkoning.   TuT, *tr.* by Ruth Hooley

There! She says and.   Game Trail, The.   Mark Todd.   GeoH

There she took her lover to sea.   Long Nook.   John Wieners.   FTOS

There she was, for centuries, the big.   Muse, The.   Eleanor Wilner.   GifTon

There should be two words, dearest, one made up.   Alone.   Carolyn Wells.   PoToHe

There sinks the nebulous star we call the Sun.   Tennyson.   *Fr.* Princess, The.

There smiled the smooth Divine, unused to wound.   Timothy Dwight.   SacPr   *Fr.* Triumph of Infidelity, The.

There, spring lambs jam the sheepfold. In air.   Watercolor of Grantchester Meadows.   Sylvia Plath.   LCAP-2

There stands a lady on a mountain.   Kiss in the Ring.   *Unknown.*   OxBoLi

There stands a lonely pine-tree. Song. Heinrich Heine. TrJP, *tr. by* Emma Lazarus

There stands an over, a strange shaft to see. Oven of Lublin, The. Theodor Kramer. AuPH, *tr. by* Lowell A. Bangerter

There sunk the greatest, nor the worst of men. Byron. NAEL-5v2; NAEL-6v2 *Fr.* Childe Harold's Pilgrimage.

There the ash-tree leaves do vall. Leaves a-Vallen. William Barnes. NOBVV; NPeEn

There the black river, boundary to hell. Southern Road, The. Dudley Randall. GM

There the blue-green gums are a fringe of remote disorder. Envoi. James McAuley. BMAP

There the companions of his fall, o'erwhelmed. John Milton. NOBE *Fr.* Paradise Lost.

There the deer stands with morning on the hilltop. Crystal Moment. Edward Weismiller. YaYoPo

There the most daintie Paradise on ground. Edmund Spenser. EBEV *Fr.* Faerie Queene, The.

"There the Parthenon, & there." Slides. Jennifer Maiden. CBAP

There the true Silence is, self-conscious and alone. (LL) Silence. Thomas Hood. EBEV; GSo; NOBE; OBEV; OxBSo; Son

There the voluptuous nightingales. Shelley. OWoS *Fr.* Prometheus Unbound [A Lyrical Drama in Four Acts].

There, there where those black spruces crowd. Ragged Island. Edna St. Vincent Millay. ColAP; NAAL-2v2; NoP-4

There they are. Blackstone Rangers, The. Gwendolyn Brooks. ESEAA; NoAM

There they are. Anne Sexton. BodElec *Fr.* Furies, The.

There they are again. It's after dark. Black Riviera, The. Mark Jarman. GeoHom

There they are now. Three Sentences for a Dead Swan. James Wright (1927–80). NOBA

There they go. Seed Journey. Gregory Corso. VGW

There they go, down to the fatal ship. Cythera. David Ferry. DiPo; GS

There they go. Slowly they saunter. April in the Old Park. Anna Hajnal. IQMS, *tr. by* Daniel Gerard Hoffman

There they stand, on their ends, the fifty faggots. Fifty Faggots. Edward Thomas. MoBrPo; PeFWW; PoWW

There they were. Seals, The. Pauline Stainer. NeBl

There they were, right before my eyes: it was terrible and at the same. Fable. Eugenio de Andrade. VCWP, *tr. by* Alexis Levitin

There thou shalt find[e] my faults are thine. (LL) Judgement. George Herbert. ESCV; GeHe

There though where they / were regardless. Degree Four. Nathaniel Mackey. ESEAA

There, through the long, long summer hours. June. William Cullen Bryant. TreFP

There to lead my life. (LL) I Have Been a Foster. *Unknown.* EBEV; OxBSP

There, truly they said in this house. *Unknown.* STP, *tr. by* Barbara Tedlock

There, tyrant passion finds a glorious tomb! (LL) Bower of Pleasure, The. Mary Robinson. CenSon; RWP

There u guys go. Astig. Eric Fructuoso. ReBoTo

There used to be a rich old oaf who made. Geoffrey Chaucer. NAWM-5v1; NAWM-7v1, *tr. by* Theodore Morrison *Fr.* Canterbury Tales, The.

There wanders many a lighted star. North Star, The. John Morris-Jones. OBWVE, *tr. by* Anthony Conran

There wanders through the world, a knee. Knee, The. Christian Morgenstern. RB, *tr. by* Lore Segal and W. D. Snodgrass

There was a bad poet named Clough. On Arthur Hugh Clough. Algernon Charles Swinburne. FaBoEE

There was a battle fought of late. To His Mother. John Harington. NoSic

There was a battle in the north. Geordie [An Old Ballad]. *Unknown.* ESPB; OxBB

There was a black cross on the Italian's breast. Italian, The. Mikhail Arkadyevich [*or* Arkad'evich] Svetlov. TCRP, *tr. by* Daniel Weissbort

There Was a Boy. William Wordsworth. RB *Fr.* Prelude, The; Growth of a Poet's Mind [1805 vers.].

There was a boy bedded in bracken. Carol. John Short. FaBoCh; FaBoTw

There was a boy in a village who made. Saw the Cloud Lynx. Samuel Makidemewabe. STP, *tr. by* Howard Norman

There was a boy whose name was Jim. Jim Who Ran Away from His Nurse, and Was Eaten by a Lion. Joseph Hilaire Pierre Belloc. EBNV; NOxBChV; OBSP; OxAEP-2

There was a brave girl of Connecticut. Benjamin. Ogden Nash. PeLi

There was a bridge that Rozinante would not cross. Bridge of Heraclitus, The. George Reavey. BIrV

There Was a Castle. Vivian Lamarque. CItWP, *tr. by* Cinzia Sartini Blum and Lara Trubowitz

There was a cat in Egypt, in Egypt, in Egypt. Cat, The. Rose Fyleman. NOxBChV

There was a certain assistant minister. Record of a Past Affair, A. Li K'aihsien. CoBLCP, *tr. by* Jonathan Chaves

There was a child. Courage, a Tale. Thom Gunn. GLP

There Was a Child Went Forth. Walt Whitman. AWP; NAAL-2v1; NAAL-5; OxBA; SAmP; TAP

There was a collection of schemers. Limerick. Basil Ransome-Davies. PeLi

There was a common wall between the fence of our Elementary School. To Enjoy the Horror. Fawziyya Abu Khalid. PoArWo, *tr. by* Farouk Mustafa

There was a company of young folk living. Geoffrey Chaucer. NAWM-5v1; NAWM-7v1, *tr. by* Theodore Morrison *Fr.* Canterbury Tales, The.

There was a contest. Peaches. Siv Cedering Fox. PBCAP

There Was a Crimson Clash of War. Stephen Crane. UnPo

There was a Crooked Man. Mother Goose. LB; OxBoLi; OxNR; PeLV (Crooked Sixpence, The.) ReMoGo

There was a crooked man, and he went [*or* walked] a crooked mile. There Was a Crooked Man. Mother Goose. LB; OxBoLi; OxNR; PeLV

There was a crusader of Parma. Limerick. *Unknown.* PeLi

There was a dark and awful wood. Wood. Thomas Hornsby Ferril. PoRA

There was a duck egg as green as the evening sky. Ulinda. David Campbell. CBAP

There was a duke's daughter lived in York. Cruel Mother, The. *Unknown.* ESPB

There was a faith-healer of Deal. Limerick. *Unknown.* PeLi

There was a fat lady of Clyde. Limerick. *Unknown.* PeLi

There was a fat man of Bombay. Man of Bombay, The. *Unknown.* ReMoGo

There was a feast that night. Banquet, The. Letitia [*or* Laetitia] Elizabeth Landon. TreFP

There was a French bard who said: "Hell!" Limerick. Towanbucket. PeLi

There was a frost. Frozen Greenhouse, The. Thomas Hardy. OBGa

There was a gallant ship, [and] a gallant ship was she. Golden Vanity, The. *Unknown.* FaBoCh

There was a gather'd stillness in the room. My Mother. William Bell Scott. GSo

There was a girl in our town. *Unknown.* OxNR

There was a gloomy lady. Not a Very Cheerful Song, I'm Afraid. Adrian Mitchell. OTCP

There was a good Canon of Durham. Limerick. William Ralph Inge. PeLi

There was a great battle Saturday morning. Battle of Argoed Llwyfain, The. Taliesin. OBWVE, *tr. by* Anthony Conran

There was a great German Grammarian. Limerick. Thomas Thorneley. PeLi

There was a great Marxist called Lenin. Progress. Robert Conquest. OBCoV

There was a great Marxist called Lenin. Limerick. Ted Pauker. PeLi

There was a guy who. Side 18. Víctor Hernández Cruz. PueRic

There was a hag who kept two chambermaids. Hag and the Slavies, The. Jean de La Fontaine. AWP; OBVE, *tr. by* Edward Marsh

There was a hardware shop in Main Street sold. Didn't He Ramble. James Simmons. PNI

There was a jolly beggar, and a begging he was born. Jolly Beggar, The. James V, King of Scotland. OxBB

There was a jolly miller once. Isaac Bickerstaffe. LB; OxNR *Fr.* Love in a Village.

There was a jury sat at Perth. Earl of Errol, The. *Unknown.* ESPB

There was a kind lady called Gregory. Limerick. James Joyce. FaBoEE; PeLi

There Was a King. *Unknown.* NBLV; OxBoLi

There was a king, and a very great king. Lady Diamond. *Unknown.* ESPB

There was a king met a king. *Unknown.* OxNR

There was a knicht riding frae the east. Riddles Wisely Expounded. *Unknown.* ESPB

There was a knight, an he had a daughter. Erlinton. *Unknown.* ESPB

There was a knight and a lady bright. Broomfield Hill, The. *Unknown.* ESPB; OxBB

There was a knight, in a summer's night. Bonny Birdy, The. *Unknown.* ESPB

There was a lad was born in Kyle. Rantin, Rovin Robin. Robert Burns. OxBS

There was a lady fair and gay. Wife of Usher's Well, The. *Unknown.* ESPB

There was a lady fine and gay. Willie o [*or* of] Winsbury. *Unknown.* ESPB

There was a lady lived in a hall. Two Red Roses across the Moon. William Morris. EBVV; UV

There Was a Lady Loved a Swine. *Unknown.* OxNR

There was a lady of the North Country. Riddles Wisely Expounded. *Unknown.* ESPB

There was a little boy and a little girl. Boy and Girl. Mother Goose. OxNR; ReMoGo

There was a little boy went into a barn. *Unknown.* OxNR

There Was a Little Girl.   Henry Wadsworth Longfellow.   BRP

There Was a Little Girl.   Mother Goose.   OxNR; ReMoGo (Jemima.)   FaBoCh

There was a little girl, she had a little curl.   There Was a Little Girl.   Henry Wadsworth Longfellow.   BRP

There was a little maid, and she was afraid.   *Unknown.*   OxNR

There was a little man.   *Unknown.*   OBCoV

There was a little man.   *Unknown.*   OBCoV   *Fr.* Advertising Rhymes.

There was a little man and he had a little can.   No More Booze.   *Unknown.*   OBAL

There was a little man, / and he wooed a little maid.   Mother Goose.   OxNR; ReMoGo

There was a little one-eyed gunner.   *Unknown.*   OxNR

There was a little rill of water, near the den.   Coyote, The.   Carter Revard.   VoR

There was a little turtle.   Little Turtle, The.   Nicholas Vachel Lindsay.   NOxBChV; NTCP; OBAL; OBCA; OBSP; OxIBACP

There was a little woman, as I've been told.   Hot Codlins.   *Unknown.*   ReMoGo

There was a maid come out of Kent.   Maid of Kent, A.   *Unknown.*   OxBoLi

There was a maid, richly arrayd.   Blancheflour and Jellyflorice.   *Unknown.*   ESPB

There Was a Man.   Dennis Lee.   KaS

There was a man and he had nought.   Mother Goose.   OxNR; ReMoGo

There Was a Man and He Was Mad.   *Unknown.*   RB

There was a man, and his name was Dob.   *Unknown.*   OxNR

There was a man and his shadow.   Shadow, The.   Nathan [*or* Natan] Alterman.   FIT, *tr.* by Robert Friend

There was a man, he went mad.   *Unknown.*   OxNR

There was a man here, Samian born, but he.   Ovid.   NAWM-5v1   *Fr.* Metamorphoses.

There was a man in Arkansaw.   Tuscaloosa Sam.   "Orpheus C. Kerr."   OBAL

There was a man in our town.   Man in Our Town.   *Unknown.*   ReMoGo

There was a man in the land of Ur.   Services.   Carl Rakosi.   ChIV-1

There was a man in The Land of Uz whose name was Job.   Bible, *O.T.*   NAWM-5v1

There was a man lived in the moon.   Aiken Drum.   *Unknown.*   FaBoCh; OxNR

There was a man lived quite near us.   Man with the Wooden Leg, The.   Katherine Mansfield.   FaBoWar

There was a man of Carcassone.   Wife of Carcassone, The.   A. G. Prys-Jones.   TCAWP

There was a man of double deed.   *Unknown.*   OxNR; RB

There was a man of Thessaly.   Alexander's Song.   *Unknown.*   LB

There was a man rode through our town.   *Unknown.*   OxNR

There was a man spent seven years in hell's circles.   Political.   Rita Dove.   FFC

There was a man suspended from a nose.   To a Nose.   Francisco de Quevedo y Villegas.   SpanPo, *tr.* by James Edward Tobin

There was a man who found two leaves.   Fall, The.   Russell Edson.   LCAP-2

There was a man who had no eyes.   *Unknown.*   OxNR

There was a man who married a maid. She laughed as he led her home.   I Love My Love.   Helen Adam.   NeAP; WPOW

There was a man who never was.   There Was a Man.   Dennis Lee.   KaS

There was a man who studied the art of disappearing.   Parable, A.   Li K'ai-hsien.   CoBLCP; ColAnChi, *tr.* by Jonathan Chaves

There was a man who wanted to be an amateur animal. He could.   Amateur, The.   Russell Edson.   LCAP-2

There was a man who watched the river flow.   Cranes of Ibycus, The.   Emma Lazarus.   APN-2

There was a man who won a beautiful woman.   Slighted Lady, The.   Anna Wickham.   LW

There Was a Man with a Tongue of Wood.   Stephen Crane.   MoAmPo   *Fr.* War Is Kind.

There was a man within our tenement.   Oscar Williams.   Son   *Fr.* Variations on a Theme.

"There was a marriage in Cana of Galilee. . . And both."   Bridegroom of Cana, The.   Marjorie Lowry Christie Pickthall.   TrCP

There Was a Monkey.   *Unknown.*   OxNR

There was a monkey climbed a tree.   There Was a Monkey.   *Unknown.*   OxNR

There was a month I called May. When I buried it in papers, passion.   Seasons.   Safaa Fathy.   PoArWo, *tr.* by S. V. Atalla

There was a mountain, over its black roots [the deer].   Papago.   CA

There was a mute noise. The air of wheat when it allows itself.   In the Distance.   Silvio Giussani.   ItPo, *tr.* by Gayle Ridinger

There was a path.   Place.   Robert Creeley.   LCAP-2

There was a pattering in the rafters, mother.   Dialogue.   James McAuley.   BMAP

There was a piper had a cow.   Piper and His Cow, THe.   Mother Goose.   OxNR; ReMoGo

There was a plastic cup of iced coffee.   Red Lipstick on a Straw.   Michael Melo.   ReBoTo

There was a poet whose untimely tomb.   Shelley.   FHYEP; TOF   *Fr.* Alastor; or, The Spirit of Solitude.

There was a Presbyterian cat.   Auld Seceder Cat, The.   *Unknown.*   FaBoCh

There was a Prince, in days of yore.   There Was a Prince.   *Hungarian Oral Tradition.*   IQMS, *tr.* by Joseph Leftwich

There was a professor of Beaulieu.   Materialism.   C. E. M. Joad.   PeLi

There was a Puerto Rican man who.   Man Who Came to the Last Floor, The.   Víctor Hernández Cruz.   PueRic

There was a queen that fell in love with a jolly sailor.   Sailor and the Shark, The.   Paul Fort.   OBMV, *tr.* by Frederick York Powell

There was a Raja, pious-minded, just.   *Unknown.*   TAL   *Fr.* Mahabharata, The.

There was a rash fellow called Weir.   Limerick.   *Unknown.*   PeLi

There was a rat, for want of stairs.   *Unknown.*   OxNR

There was a rich lord, and lived in Forfar.   Bonnie Annie.   *Unknown.*   ESPB

There was a river overhung with trees.   In a Notebook.   James Fenton.   NPeEn

There was a roaring in the wind all night.   William Wordsworth.   EBEV; FHYEP; HAP; NAEL-6v2; NOBE; NOBRP; NOCV; NoP-4; OxAEP-2; TFi

There was a roaring in the wind all night.   William Wordsworth.   ITBLP; WoPoe   *Fr.* Resolution and Independence.

There was a row in the pub.   After the Massacre.   Musaemura Bonus Zimunya.   PeSAV

There was a Saviour.   Dylan Thomas.   ChIV-2; NAEL-6v2

There was a Serpent who had to sing.   Serpent, The.   Theodore Roethke.   NOxBChV

There was a shepherd's dochter [*or* daughter].   Knight and Shepherd's Daughter, The.   *Unknown.*   ESPB

There was a shepherd's son.   Blow the Winds, I-Ho.   *Unknown.*   OxBoLi

There was a sick man of Tobago.   Limerick.   *Unknown.*   PeLi

There was a small boy of Quebec.   Limerick.   Rudyard Kipling.   PeLi

There was a sojourner in Ying who intoned "White Snows."   Li Po.   ColAnChi, *tr.* by Victor H. Mair   *Fr.* Poems in an Old Style.

There was a song.   There Was a Song.   Gerald William Barrax.   GT

There was a sound of revelry by night.   Byron.   EBEV; FaBoWar; OBWP; OxAEP-2; TFi   *Fr.* Childe Harold's Pilgrimage.

There was a speedboat ploughing up Lough Erne.   Enniskillen.   David Morley.   NLP

There was a Stag, did in the Forest lye.   Hunting of a Stag, The.   Margaret Lucas Cavendish, Duchess of Newcastle.   EMWP

There was a stange student from Yale.   *Unknown.*   PeLi

There was a stunted handpost just on the crest.   Near Lanivet, 1872.   Thomas Hardy.   AWP; NoAM

There was a sudden croon of lilies.   Martyrdom of St. Theresa, The.   Alec Derwent Hope.   CBAP

There was a sunlit absence.   Seamus Heaney.   BIrV   *Fr.* Mossbawn.

There was a sunny interlude.   Reasons for the Beginning.   Milo De Angelis.   ItPo, *tr.* by Gayle Ridinger

There was a taed wha thocht sae lang.   Philosophic Taed, The.   William Soutar.   NePenScot

There was a taut dryness all that summer.   Lyric Afterwards, A.   Tom Paulin.   PNI

There was a thing full month old.   *Unknown.*   OxNR

There was a tide-mark on the jetty which.   Landfall, The.   John Blight.   BMAP

There was a time.   To My Daughter.   Keorapetse Kgositsile.   GT

There was a time for discoveries.   Voyage West.   Archibald MacLeish.   APT-1; VGW

There was a time I might have cried.   Muffled Cry, A.   Marjorie Oludhe Macgoye.   HAWP

There was a time, in Esher's peaceful grove.   William Mason.   OBGa   *Fr.* Heroic Epistle to Sir William Chambers, An.

There was a time in former years.   She Hears The Storm.   Thomas Hardy.   NAEL-5v2; NAEL-6v2

There was a time in my life when.   Old Neighborhood, The.   Gerald Costanzo.   OPRER

There was a time on this fair continent.   Charles Mair.   NOBC   *Fr.* Tecumseh.

There was a time, poor phrensied maid.   To a Maniac.   Amelia Alderson Opie.   NOBRP

There was a time! that time the muse bewails.   Verses on Hearing That an Airy and Pleasant Situation, near a Populous and Commercial Town, Was Surrounded with New Buildings.   Maria Logan.   ECWP

There was a time when death was terror.   New Fashions.   George Moses Horton.   OBAL

There was a time when Eucritus and I were going.   Theocritus.   *See* Once on a time did Eucritus and I

There was a time when fanfares. Decampment. Ernst Stadler. PeFWW

There was a time when I could fly. I, Icarus. Alden Nowlan. NOxBChV

There was a time when I thought sweeter than the quiet. Wild Man Comes to the Monastery, The. *Unknown*. RaBo

There was a time when I was very small. Childhood. Jens Baggesen. AWP, *tr. by* Henry Wadsworth Longfellow

There was a time when meadow, grove, and stream. William Wordsworth. AWP; FHYEP; HAP; HeIP-4; NAEL-5v2; NAEL-6v2; NAWM-7v2; NOBE; NOBRP; NPeEn; NoP-4; OBEV; OxBEV; PoE; PoPoPo; SCGP; TFi; TOF; TRP *Fr.* Ode: Intimations of Immortality [from Recollections of Early Childhood].

There was a time when the only worth. There Was a Time When the Only Worth. Dennis Brutus. VCWP

There was a trombonist called Herb. Limerick. Ron Rubin. PeLi

There was a troop of merry gentlemen. Broom of Cowdenknows, The. *Unknown*. ESPB

There was a tumult in the city. Independence Bell—July 4, 1776. *Unknown*. HHAm

There was a weasel lived in the sun. Gallows, The. Edward Thomas. MoBrPo; NoAM; PAI; SCGP; UnPo

There was a wee bit mousikie. Cheetie-Poussie-Cattie, O. *Unknown*. FaBoCh

There was a wee bit wifie. *Unknown*. OxNR

There was a wee cooper who lived in Fife. Wee Cooper of Fife, The. *Unknown*. NePenScot

There was a wee lassie of Ulva. Limerick. David Fisher. PeLi

There was a whispering in my hearth. Miners. Wilfred Owen. MoBrPo; NOBE; OBWVE; OxAEP-2; PeFWW

There was a wicked woman called Malady Festing. Angel Boley. Stevie Smith. EBNV

There was a widow-woman lived in far Scotland. Wife of Usher's Well, The. *Unknown*. ESPB

There was a witch. Two Witches. Charles Reznikoff. OTCP

There was a witch who knitted things. Karla Kuskin. KaS *Fr.* Knitted Things.

There was a woman in Ithaca. Toast. Leonard Nathan. BLT

There was a woman lived in Winston-Salem. I. J. Brittain. VerBaPo *Fr.* Tragedy of Ida Ball Warren and Samuel Christie, The.

There was a woman who had lost her husband. Widow and the Soldier or: The Measure of a Woman's Inconstancy and Lust, The. Phaedrus. RomPo, *tr. by* Eugene O'Connor

There was a wood, a witches' wood. Witches' Wood, The. Mary Elizabeth Coleridge. VWP

There was a young artist called Saint. Limerick. *Unknown*. PeLi

There was a young belle of old Natchez. Requiem. Ogden Nash. KaS; NoP-4

There was a young boy, Jack Horner. Limerick. Fiona Pitt-Kethley. PeLi

There was a young bride named McWing. Limerick. *Unknown*. PeLi

There was a young critic of King's. Limerick. Arthur Clement Hilton. PeLi

There was a young curate called Lloyd. Limerick. Duncan Campbell McGregor. PeLi

There was a young curate of Hants. Limerick. Edmund George Valpy Knox. PeLi

There was a young curate of Kew. Limerick. *Unknown*. PeLi

There was a young curate of Salisbury. Limerick. *Unknown*. PeLi

There was a young faggot called Willy. Limerick. Kenneth Petchenik. PeLi

There was a young fellow called Baker. Limerick. *Unknown*. PeLi

There was a young fellow called Bliss. Limerick. *Unknown*. PeLi

There was a young fellow called Cager. Limerick. *Unknown*. PeLi

There was a young fellow called Chubb. Limerick. *Unknown*. PeLi

There was a young fellow called Clyde. Limerick. *Unknown*. PeLi

There was a young fellow called Crouch. Limerick. Victor Gray. NOBL; PeLi

There was a young fellow called Hall. Limerick. *Unknown*. PeLi

There was a young fellow called Lancelot. Limerick. *Unknown*. PeLi

There was a young fellow called Price. Limerick. *Unknown*. PeLi

There was a young fellow called Shit. Limerick. Victor Gray. PeLi

There was a young fellow called Wyatt. Limerick. *Unknown*. PeLi

There was a young fellow from Tyne. Limerick. *Unknown*. PeLi

There was a young fellow named Cholmondeley. Nomenclaturik. Harry Hearson. OBCoV

There was a young fellow named Fisher. Limerick. *Unknown*. PeLi

There was a young fellow named Fonda. Limerick. Ogden Nash. PeLi

There was a young fellow named Menzies. Limerick. *Unknown*. PeLi

There was a young fellow named Skinner. Limerick. Norman Douglas. PeLi

There was a young fellow named Sydney. Limerick. Don Marquis. PeLi

There was a young fellow of Burma. Limerick. Aldous Leonard Huxley. PeLi

There was a young Fellow of Caius. Limerick. *Unknown*. NOBL

There was a young fellow of Ceuta. Limerick. *Unknown*. PeLi

There was a young Fellow of King's. Limerick. *Unknown*. NOBL

There was a young fellow of Lyme. Limerick. *Unknown*. PeLi

There was a young fellow of Perth. Limerick. *Unknown*. PeLi

There was a young fellow of Trinity. Limerick. *Unknown*. PeLi

There was a young Fellow of Wadham. Limerick. *Unknown*. NOBL

There was a young Fellow of Wadham / Who asked for a ticket to Sodom. Limerick. *Unknown*. PeLi

There was a young fellow went by. Trinity Brethren Attend. Ivor Armstrong Richards. CRP

There was a young genius of Queens' Limerick. Arthur Clement Hilton. PeLi

There was a young girl called Bianca. Limerick. *Unknown*. PeLi

There was a young girl from a Mission. Limerick. A. H. Baynes. PeLi

There was a young girl from Uttoxeter / Who kept hens, but refused to have cocks. It a. Limerick. Alastair Chambre. PeLi

There was a young girl from Uttoxeter / Who made passing oarsmen gape through locks at her. Limerick. L. W. Bailey. PeLi

There was a young girl from Uttoxeter / Who one dreary night had a fox at her. Limerick. George Cowley. PeLi

There was a young girl from Uttoxeter / Who out on a date with two Jocks at a. Limerick. Bob Scott. PeLi

There was a young girl from Uttoxeter / Who sported a tight-fitting baroque sweater. Limerick. Stanley J. Sharpless. PeLi

There was a young girl of Aberystwyth. Limerick. Algernon Charles Swinburne. PeLi

There was a young girl of Australia. Limerick. *Unknown*. PeLi

There was a young girl of Bahari. Limerick. R. P. M. Lehmann. PeLi

There was a young girl of Cape Cod. Limerick. *Unknown*. PeLi

There was a young girl of Darjeeling. Limerick. *Unknown*. PeLi

There was a young girl of East Anglia. Limerick. Aldous Leonard Huxley. PeLi

There was a young girl of La Plata. Limerick. *Unknown*. PeLi

There was a Young Girl of Majorca. Limerick. Edward Lear. PeLi

There was a young girl of Mauritius. Limerick. Victor Gray. PeLi

There was a young girl of old Natchez. Limerick. Ogden Nash. PeLi

There was a young girl of Penzance. Limerick. *Unknown*. PeLi

There was a young girl of Shanghai. Limerick. Bertrand Arthur William Russell, 3d Earl Russell. PeLi

There was a young girl of Siam. Limerick. *Unknown*. PeLi

There was a young girl of St. Cyr. Limerick. *Unknown*. PeLi

There was a young girl of Tralee. Limerick. *Unknown*. PeLi

There was a young girl of Trebarwith. Limerick. R. J. P. Hewison. PeLi

There was a young girl of Uttoxeter / Who noticed that men waved their cocks at her. Limerick. D. Kartun. PeLi

There was a young girl of Uttoxeter / Who worked nine to five as a choc-setter. Limerick. Stanley J. Sharpless. PeLi

There was a young girl whose frigidity. Limerick. *Unknown*. PeLi

There was a young girl with a hernia. Limerick. Heywood Broun. PeLi

There was a young gourmand of John's. Limerick. Arthur Clement Hilton. PeLi

There was a young Jap on a syndicate. Limerick. *Unknown*. PeLi

There was a young Japanese geisha. Limerick. Ron Rubin. PeLi

There was a young lady at court. Limerick. D. H. Cudmore. PeLi

There was a young lady called Alice. Limerick. *Unknown*. PeLi

There was a young lady called Clarice. Limerick. H. A. C. Evans. PeLi

There was a young lady called Dawes. *Unknown*. PeLi

There was a young lady called Etta. Limerick. *Unknown*. PeLi

There was a young lady called Flynn. Limerick. *Unknown*. NOBL

There was a young lady called Gloria. Limerick. *Unknown*. PeLi

There was a young lady called Harris. Limerick. Ogden Nash. PeLi

There was a young lady called Hilda. Limerick. *Unknown*. PeLi

There was a young lady called Kate. Limerick. *Unknown*. PeLi

There was a young lady called Maud. Limerick. *Unknown*. PeLi

There was a young lady called Muffet. Limerick. *Unknown*. PeLi

There was a young lady called Smith. Limerick. *Unknown*. PeLi

There was a young lady called Starky. Limerick. *Unknown*. PeLi

There was a young lady from Gloucester. Sometimes Even Parents Win. John Ciardi. NOxBChV

There was a young lady from Pecking. Limerick. *Unknown*. PeLi

There was a young lady from Ulva. Limerick. Russell Lucas. PeLi

There was a Young Lady in White. Limerick. Edward Lear. PeLi

There was a young lady named Kent. Limerick. *Unknown*. PeLi

There was a young lady named Miller. Austen Baker. PeLi

There was a young lady named [*or called*] Bright. Limerick. Arthur Buller. NOBL; OxBoLi; PeLV; PeLi

There was a young lady of Aenos. Limerick. *Unknown*. PeLi

There was a young lady of Brabant. Limerick. *Unknown*. PeLi

There was a young lady of Chichester. Limerick. *Unknown*. PeLi

There was a young lady of Chiswick. Limerick. *Unknown*. PeLi

There was a young lady of Ealing. Allan M. Laing. PeLi

There was a young lady of Ealing. Limerick. *Unknown*. PeLi

There was a young lady of Ealing / And her lover before her was kneeling. Limerick. Isaac Asimov. PeLi

There was a young lady of fashion. Limerick. *Unknown*. PeLi

There was a young lady of Florence. Limerick. *Unknown*. PeLi

There was a young lady of Joppa. Limerick. *Unknown*. PeLi

There was a young lady of Kew. Limerick. *Unknown*. PeLV

There was a young lady of Leicester. Limerick. Alan Clark. PeLi

There was a young lady of Limerick. Limerick. Andrew Lang. PeLi

There was a young lady of Louth. Limerick. Norman Douglas. PeLi

There was a young lady of Lundy. Limerick. W. F. N. Watson. PeLi

There was a young lady of Nantes. Limerick. S. Littman. PeLi

There Was a Young Lady of Niger. Cosmo Monkhouse. NBLV; TLR

There was a young lady of Nîmes. Limerick. "Little Billee." PeLi

There was a Young Lady of Norway, / Who casually sat in a doorway. Limerick. Edward Lear. PeLi

There was a young lady of Norway / Who hung by her toes in a doorway. Limerick. Algernon Charles Swinburne. PeLi

There was a young Lady of Parma. Limericks, I (v). Edward Lear. OBCoV

There was a young lady of Portugal. Limericks, II (iv). Edward Lear. OBCoV; OxBoLi; PeLV; PeLi

There was a young lady of Rheims. Moonshine. Walter De la Mare. OBCoV

There was a young lady of Riga. Limerick. Cosmo Monkhouse. NIL-7; PeLi

There was a young lady of Riga. *Unknown*. NIL-7

There was a young lady of Ryde, / Who ate some green apples and died. Limerick. *Unknown*. PeLi

There was a young lady of Ryde / Who was carried too far by the tide. Limerick. *Unknown*. PeLi

There was a young lady of Ryde / Whose shoe-strings were seldom untied. Limerick. Edward Lear. OxBoLi; PeLV; PeLi

There was a young lady of Rye. Limerick. *Unknown*. PeLi

There was a young lady of Slough. Limerick. *Unknown*. PeLi

There was a young lady of Spain. Limerick. *Unknown*. PeLi

There was a young lady of station. Limerick. Lewis Carroll. PeLi

There was a young lady of Sweden. Limerick. Edward Lear. EBEV; PeVV

There was a young lady of Tottenham. Limerick. *Unknown*. PeLi; WeW-3

There was a young lady of Trent. Limerick. *Unknown*. PeLi

There was a young lady of Twickenham. Limerick. Oliver Herford. KaS

There was a young lady of Ulva / Who drunkenly said: 'What a hulva.' Limerick. Bill Greenwell. PeLi

There was a young lady of Ulva / Who kept a pet bee in her hand-bag. Limerick. T. Johnston. PeLi

There was a young lady of Ulva / Who said: 'I have granted a culver. Limerick. T. Griffiths. PeLi

There was a young lady of Ulva / Who was famed far and wide for her vulva. Limerick. Gavin Ewart. PeLi

There was a young lady of Ulva / Whose boy-friend said: "Look, I will pulver." Limerick. Stanley J. Sharpless. PeLi

There was a young lady of Ulva / Whose sexual feelings were null. Va. Limerick. Barbara E. Goff. PeLi

There was a young lady of Wantage. Limerick. *Unknown*. PeLi

There was a young lady of Where? Limerick. *Unknown*. PeLi

There was a young lady of Whitby. Limerick. Lewis Carroll. PeLi

There was a young lady . . . tut, tut! Limerick. Stanley J. Sharpless. PeLi

There was a young lady whose bonnet. Edward Lear. EBEV

There was a Young Lady whose chin. Limerick. Edward Lear. PeLi

There was a young lady whose eyes. Limerick. Edward Lear. EBEV; NOBVV

There Was a Young Lady Whose Nose. Edward Lear. EBEV

There was a young lass of Pitlochry. Limerick. *Unknown*. PeLi

There was a young lawyer called Rex. Limerick. *Unknown*. PeLi

There was a young maid of Peru. Limerick. Isaac Asimov. PeLi

There was a young maid who said, "Why." Limerick. *Unknown*. SoSe-8

There was a young maiden from Multerry. Limerick. *Unknown*. PeLi

There was a young maiden of Devon. Limerick. *Unknown*. PeLi

There was a young man from Darjeeling. Limerick. *Unknown*. PeLi

There was a young man named Racine. Limerick. *Unknown*. PeLi

There was a young man of Australia. Limerick. *Unknown*. PeLi

There was a young man of Belgrade. Limerick. Isaac Asimov. PeLi

There was a young man of Bengal. *Unknown*. OxBoLi

There was a young man of Calcutta. Limerick. *Unknown*. PeLi

There was a young man of Cape Horn. Limerick. Algernon Charles Swinburne. PeLi

There was a young man of Cape Race. Limerick. *Unknown*. PeLi

There was a young man of Devizes. Limerick. Archibald Marshall. PeLi

There was a young man of Dumfries. Limerick. *Unknown*. PeLi

There was a young man of Ghent. Limerick. *Unknown*. PeLi

There was a young man of Japan. Limerick. *Unknown*. PeLi

There was a young man of Madras. Limerick. *Unknown*. PeLi

There was a young man of Montrose. Limerick. Arnold Bennett. OxBoLi; PeLi

There was a young man of Nepal. Limerick. *Unknown*. PeLi

There was a young man of Newcastle. Limerick. Terence Melican. PeLi

There was a young man of Ostend. Limerick. E. O. Parrott. PeLi

There was a young man of Porthcawl. Limerick. A. G. Prys-Jones. PeLi

There was a young man of St John's. Limerick. *Unknown*. PeLV

There was a young man of Wood's Hole. Limerick. *Unknown*. PeLi

There was a young man so benighted. Limerick. Frances Parkinson Keyes. PeLi

There was a young man who said: "Ayer." Limerick. *Unknown*. PeLi

There was a young man who said, Damn! Determinism. Maurice Evan Hare. OBCoV

There was a young monarch called Ed. Limerick. *Unknown*. PeLi

There was a young monk from Siberia. Limerick. *Unknown*. PeLi

There was a young outlaw named Hood. Limerick. E. O. Parrott. PeLi

There was a young peasant named Gorse. Limerick. *Unknown*. PeLi

There was a young person called Tate. Limerick. Carolyn Wells. PeLi

There was a Young Person of Ayr. Edward Lear. KaS

There was a young person of Leigh. Limerick. Basil Ransome-Davies. PeLi

There was a young person of Smyrna. Limerick. Edward Lear. OxBoLi; PeLV

There was a young person whose history. Limericks, II (i). Edward Lear. OBCoV

There was a young plumber of Leigh. Limerick. *Unknown*. PeLi

There was a young poet of Kew. Limerick. *Unknown*. PeLi

There was a young poet of Thusis. Limerick. *Unknown*. OxBoLi; PeLi

There was a young priest of Dun Laoghaire. Limerick. *Unknown*. PeLi

There was a young princess, Snow-White. Limerick. Gerard Benson. PeLi

There was a young student called Fred. Limerick. V. R. Ormerod. PeLi

There was a young student called Jones. Limerick. *Unknown*. PeLi

There was a young student of John's. Limerick. *Unknown*. PeLi

There was a young woman, as I've heard tell. Ripperty! Kye! Ahoo! Henry Lawson. CBAP

There was a young woman called Myrtle. Limerick. *Unknown*. PeLi

There was a young woman from Aenos. Young Woman from Aenos, The. *Unknown*. OBAL

There was a young woman named Plunnery. Limerick. Edward Gorey. OBAL

There was a young woman of Dee. Limerick. *Unknown*. PeLi

There was a young woman who said. Limerick. Frances Darwin Cornford. PeLi

There was a youth[e], and a well belovd [or well-belovéd] youth[e]. Bailiff's Daughter of Islington, The. *Unknown*. ESPB; OxBB; OxBoLi

There was aince an auld body o' Sydney. *Unknown*. OBCoV

There was airy music and sport at the fair. Fair at Windgap, The. Austin Clarke. OxBTC

Ther[e] was also a Nonne [or nun], a Prioress[e]. Geoffrey Chaucer. CTC; NPeEn *Fr.* Canterbury Tales, The.

There was always the river or the train. Grandmother Watching at Her Window. W. S. Merwin. VGW

There was an a May and she lo'ed na men. Were Ne My Hearts Light I Wad Dye. Lady Grisel [or Grizel or Grisell] Baillie. EMWP

There was an ancient Grecian boy. Tiger Tale, A. John Bennett. OBCA

There was an ancient sage philosopher. Samuel Butler (1612–80). NOSC *Fr.* Hudibras.

There was an archdeacon who said. Limerick. *Unknown*. OBCoV; OxBoLi

There was an Auchtergaven mouse. Whigmaleerie, A. William Soutar. OxBS

There was an avenue. Pulling the Ivy. Julia Copus. MFPA

There was an old bear that lived near a wood. Bear and the Squirrels, The. Christopher Pearse Cranch. OBCA

There was an old Begum of Frome. Walter De la Mare. PeLi

There was an old Bey of Calcutta. Limerick. *Unknown*. PeLi

There was an old chap who said: "Well." W. Stewart. PeLi

There was an old crow. *Unknown*. OxNR

There was an old cynic who said. Limerick. Allan M. Laing. PeLi

There was an old dame of Toulouse. Limerick. A. M. Sayers. PeLi

There was an old Doctor called Coué. Limerick. Bob Scott. PeLi

There was an old drunk called Hieronymus. Limerick. Ron Rubin. PeLi

There was an old drunkard of Devon. Limerick. Ron Rubin. PeLi

There was an old farmer in Sussex did dwell. Farmer's Curst Wife, The. *Unknown.* ESPB

There was an old fellow called Hugger. Arnold Hyde. PeLi

There was an old fellow named Hewing. Limerick. *Unknown.* PeLi

There was an old fellow of Fife. Limerick. *Unknown.* PeLi

There was an old fellow of Kaber. Limerick. Philip Larkin. OBCoV

There was an old fellow of Kaber. Limerick. Philip Larkin. OBCoV

There was an old fellow of Trinity. Limerick. Arthur Clement Hilton. PeLi

There was an old gossip called Baird. Limerick. Ogden Nash. PeLi

There was an old housewife of Staines. Limerick. E. O. Parrott. PeLi

There Was an Old Lady Named Crockett. William Jay Smith. KaS

There was an old lady of Chertsey. Limericks, II (ii). Edward Lear. OBCoV

There was an old lady of Harrow. Old Lady of Harrow, An. *Unknown.* PeLi

There was an old lady of Leicester. Limerick. Ian T. MacKenzie. PeLi

There was an old Lady of Winchelsea. Limericks, I (ii). Edward Lear. OBCoV

There was an old madam called Rainey. Limerick. *Unknown.* PeLi

There was an old maid of Duluth. Limerick. *Unknown.* PeLi

There was an old man, / And he had a calf. *Unknown.* OxNR

There was an old man and he lived [out] in a wood. Broom, Green Broom. *Unknown.* OxBoLi; PoRA

There was an old man called Dupree. Limerick. "R. I." PeLi

There was an old man from Darjeeling. Old Man from Darjeeling. *Unknown.* NTCP

There was an old man from Peru. *Unknown.* See There was an old man of [or from] Peru / Who dreamt [or dreamed] he was eating his shoe

There was an old man in a Barge. Edward Lear. EBEV

There was an Old Man in a boat. Limerick. Edward Lear. EBEV

There was an Old Man in a tree. Limerick. Edward Lear. PeLi

There Was an Old Man in a Tree. Edward Lear. See Limerick: "There was an Old Man in a tree."

There was an old man in a trunk. Limerick. Ogden Nash. PeLi

There was an old man in a velvet coat. Mother Goose. OxNR; ReMoGo

There was an old man of Bengal. Limerick. "F. Anstey." PeLi

There was an old man of Bohemia. Edward Lear. PAI

There was an old man of Boulogne. Limerick. *Unknown.* PeLi

There Was an Old Man of Boulogne. *Unknown.* See Limerick: "There was an old man of Boulogne."

There was an old man of Calcutta. Arthur. Ogden Nash. NoP-4; PeLi

There was an old man of Cape Horn. Limerick. Edward Lear. EBEV; PeLi

There was an old man of Dunblane. Limerick. Edward Lear. EBEV

There was an old man of Dundee. Limerick. *Unknown.* PeLi

There was an old man of Ibreem. Limerick. Edward Lear. EBEV

There was an old man of Kamschatka. Limerick. Edward Lear. NOBL

There was an old man of Khartoum. Limerick. William Ralph Inge. NOBL; PeLi

There Was an Old Man of Khartoum. William Ralph Inge. See Limerick: "There was an old man of Khartoum."

There was an old man of Lugano. Limerick. Victor Gray. PeLi

There was an Old Man of Nantucket. Old Man of Nantucket, The. *Unknown.* PeLi

There was an old man of [or from] Peru / Who dreamt [or dreamed] he was eating his shoe. Limerick. *Unknown.* SoSe-8

There was an old man of Peru / Who never knew what he should do. Edward Lear. EBEV

There was an old man of Peru / Who watched his wife making a stew. Edward Lear. EBEV

There was an old man of St. Bees. Sir William Schwenck Gilbert. PeLV; PeLi

There was an old man of the Cape. Limerick. Robert Louis Stevenson. PeLi

There was an old man of the coast. Limerick. Edward Lear. PeLi

There was an old man of the East. Edward Lear. EBEV

There was an old man of the West. Edward Lear. EBEV

There was an old man of Thermopylae. Limerick. Edward Lear. EBEV; NOBL; OxAEP-2; PeLi

There was an old man of Tobago. *Unknown.* ReMoGo

There was an old man of Toulouse. Limericks, II (iii). Edward Lear. OBCoV

There was an old man of West Dumpet. Edward Lear. EBEV

There was an old man of Whitehaven. Limerick. Edward Lear. EBEV; NPeEn; OxAEP-2

There was an old man on some rocks. Limerick. Edward Lear. NOBVV; OxBEV; PeLi

There was an old man on the Border. Limerick. Edward Lear. EBEV

There was an Old Man on whose nose. Limerick. Edward Lear. PeLi

There was an old man said, "I fear." Shubble, The. Walter De la Mare. OBCoV

There was an old man who averred. Limerick. *Unknown.* PeLi

There was an Old Man who forgot. Edward Lear. NOxBChV

There was an old man who had a kite for a son. Old Man's Son, An. Russell Edson. LCAP-2

There was an old man who said: "How." Limerick. Edward Lear. PeLi

There was an Old Man who said, "Hush!" Limerick. Edward Lear. KaS; NOBL; OxBoLi; PeLV; PeLi

There was an Old Man who said: 'Well!' Limerick. Edward Lear. PeLi

There was an old man who screamed out. Limerick. Edward Lear. EBEV; NOBVV; NPeEn; OxAEP-2; OxBEV

There was an Old Man who supposed. Limerick. Edward Lear. NAEL-5v2; NAEL-6v2; NOBVV; PeLi

There Was an Old Man Who Supposed. Edward Lear. See Limerick: "There was an Old Man who supposed."

There was an old man whose despair. Limericks, II (v). Edward Lear. OBCoV

There was an old man with a beard. John Clarke. UV

There Was an Old Man With a Beard. Edward Lear. NOBL; NOxBChV; NPeEn; OPOU; PeLV; PeLi; TLR

   (Old Man with a Beard.) NTCP

There was an Old Man with a Beard / Who said: "I demand to be feared." Limerick. Roger Woddis. PeLi

There was an old Member called Bevan. Limerick. Barbara Leigh. PeLi

There was an old mickey called Cassidy. Limerick. Conrad Potter Aiken. PeLi

There was an old miser at [or of] Reading. Limerick. *Unknown.* PeLi

There was an old party of lyme. Limerick. Edward Lear. OxBoLi

There was an old person of Basing. Limerick. Edward Lear. EBEV; NPeEn; OxAEP-2; PAI; PeLi

There was an old person of Blythe. Edward Lear. EBEV

There was an old person of Bow. Limerick. Edward Lear. EBEV; OxAEP-2

There was an old person of Buda. Edward Lear. PAI

There was an old person of Burton. Edward Lear. EBEV

There was an old person of Cassel. Edward Lear. EBEV

There was an Old Person of Cromer. Limerick. Edward Lear. PeLi

There was an old person of Dutton. Edward Lear. EBEV

There was an old person of Fratton. Limerick. *Unknown.* PeLi

There was an Old Person of Hurst. Limerick. Edward Lear. PeLi

There was an old person of Persia. Limerick. William Plomer. PeLi

There was an old person of Prague. Edward Lear. EBEV

There was an old person of Rhodes. Edward Lear. EBEV

There was an old person of Skye. Limerick. Edward Lear. KaS

There was an old person of Slough. Limerick. George Robey. PeLi

There was an old pros. Zelda Chevette. PeLi

There was an old Rabbi of Ur. Dear Sir. Walter De la Mare. OBCoV

There was an old sage of New Delhi. Limerick. Joyce Parr. PeLi

There was an old Scot called McTavish. Limerick. *Unknown.* PeLi

There was an old skinflint of Hitching. Buttons. Walter De la Mare. PeLi

There was an old status quo. Crow and the Fox, The. Reed Whittemore. BodElec

There was an old Welshman called Morgan. Limerick. Ron Rubin. PeLi

There was an old wife and she lived all alone. Old Wife and the Ghost, The. James Reeves. OTCP

There Was an Old Woman. *Unknown.* ReMoGo

There was an old woman / And nothing she had. *Unknown.* OxNR

There was an old woman, and what do you think? Strange Old Woman, A. Mother Goose. FaBoCh; LB; ReMoGo

There was an old [or little woman], as I've heard tell. Old Woman and the Pedlar, The. Mother Goose. OxNR; ReMoGo

There was an old woman called Nothing-at-all. Mother Goose. OxNR

There was an old woman had three cows. *Unknown.* OxNR

There was an old woman had three sons. Three Sons, The. *Unknown.* ReMoGo

There was an old woman, her name was Peg. *Unknown.* OxNR

There was an old woman in Surrey. Old Woman of Surrey. Mother Goose. ReMoGo

There was an old woman lived under a hill. Mother Goose. LB

There was an old woman / Lived under a hill / And if she's not gone. *Unknown.* OxNR

There was an old woman / Lived under a hill / She put a mouse in a bag. Mother Goose. OxNR

There Was an Old Woman Named Piper. William Jay Smith. TLR

There was an old woman of Clare. Cat's Second Song, The. Nancy Willard. FFC

There was an Old Woman of Gloster. Limerick. *Unknown.* PeLi

There was an old woman of Gloucester. Old Woman of Gloucester, The. *Unknown.* ReMoGo

There was an old woman of Harrow. Old Woman of Harrow. *Unknown.* ReMoGo

There was an old woman of Leeds. Old Woman of Leeds, The. *Unknown.* ReMoGo

There was an Old Woman of Lynn. Limerick. *Unknown.* PeLi

There was an old woman sat spinning. That's All. Mother Goose. OxNR; ReMoGo

There was an old woman / Sold puddings and pies. *Unknown.* OxNR

There was an old woman toss[ed] *or* tosso up in a basket [*or* blanket]. Old Woman, Old Woman. Mother Goose. LB; OxNR

There was an old woman tossed [up] in a basket. Old woman, old woman. Mother Goose. ReMoGo

There was an old woman / Went blackberry picking. Berries. Walter De la Mare. MoBrPo

There Was An Old Woman Who Lived in a Shoe. Mother Goose. OxNR; ReMoGo

  (There was an old woman and she lived in a shoe.) OxBoLi

There was an old woman / Who lived in Dundee. *Unknown.* OxNR

There was an old woman who never was wed. Ballad of an Old Woman. Frank A. Collymore. NOxBChV

There was an Orchestra. F. Scott Fitzgerald. AiP *Fr.* Thousand-and-First Ship.

There was an orchestra—Bingo-Bango. F. Scott Fitzgerald. *See* There'd be an orchestra

There was an owl lived in an oak. *Unknown.* OxNR

There was an unwanted child. End, Middle, Beginning. Anne Sexton. PoE

There was ance a may, and she lo'ed na men;. Lady Grisel [*or* Grizel *or* Grisell] Baillie. *See* There ance was a may, and she lo'ed na men

There was another boy, who might have had. Ovid. CAGL, *tr. by* Rolfe Humphries *Fr.* Metamorphoses.

There was Dai Puw. He was no good. On the Farm. Ronald Stuart Thomas. NPeEn; NoP-4; OxBEV; OxBTC; TCAWP

There was Earth inside them, and. Paul Celan. PoetW, *tr. by* John Felstiner

There was earth inside them, and. Paul Celan. PoSu

There was fire & the people were yelling. running crazy. Urban Dream. Víctor Hernández Cruz. NBV

There was Fire in Vancouver. Sinéad Morrissey. MFPA

There was great beauty by the Tree. Eve. Arthur J. Bull. UnPo

There was heard a song on the chiming sea. Song of Emigration. Felicia Dorothea Hemans. VWP

There was movement at the station, for the word had passed around. Man from Snowy River, The. Andrew Barton Paterson. CBAP

There was nae hand there to see! (LL) Ballad of the Were-Wolf, A. Rosamund Marriott Watson. VWP; ViWPN

There was never a sound beside the wood but one. Mowing. Robert Frost. APT-1; ColAP; HarvBoo; ITBLP; NAAL-2v2; NAAL-5; NOBA; OxBA; TRP; VGW

There was no bourgeoisie, the need was not for it. Bourgeoisie. Maksimilian Aleksandrovich Voloshin. TCRP, *tr. by* Albert C. Todd

There was no change in the summer wind. In the Flowering Season. Michael Roberts. FaBoTw

There was no / getting around it. Philosophy. Ray Catina. CDa

There was no good solution. Polish Knot, The. Tomasz Jastrun. AF, *tr. by* Michael March

There was no hole in the universe to fit him. Suicide. Anne Stevenson. FaBoWP

There was no Malady. (LL) They Say That Time Assuages. Emily Dickinson. APN-2; OxBSP

There was no one in him. Everything and Nothing. Jorge Luis Borges. PoetW, *tr. by* Anthony Kerrigan

There was no reason to expect sadness. Wen Cheng-ming. CoBLCP *Fr.* Lines Written on New Year's Day—In the Manner of Liu Hou-ts'un [Liu K'o-chuang (1187–1269)].

There was not loveliness nor fortune there. Shirley Barker. YaYoPo

There was not one who did not think of home. (LL) Conquerors. Henry Treece. OBWVE; TCAWP

There was nothing left for man. Anté Popovski. CarOv, *tr. by* Carolyn Kizer *Fr.* Samuel.

There was once a considerate crocodile. Considerate Crocodile, The. Amos Russel Wells. OBCA; OxIBACP

There was once a hog theater where hogs performed. Performance at Hog Theater, A. Russell Edson. PmAP

There was once a swing in a walnut tree. Walnut Tree, The. David McCord. OBCA

There was once a woman whose father over the years had become an ox. Ox, The. Russell Edson. RaBo

There was once a young man of Oporta. Limerick. Lewis Carroll. PeLi

There was one I recognised in a train. Just a Product of a Certain Situation. Steve Griffiths. AngWePo

There was rain falling as I walked through the quiet streets. Birth-Hour. Lindley Williams Hubbell. YaYoPo

There was rain this morning. Sacrifice. Melanie Hope. WiU

There was set before me a mighty hill. Stephen Crane. APN-2 *Fr.* Black Riders [and Other Lines], The.

There was something I can't bring myself. Poem. Denis Johnson. OPRER

There was still the mark of an O when he got home. (LL) Sightseers, The. Paul Muldoon. BiHa; CIP-2

There was such brilliance lifting off the sea, its aquamarine strip. Denise Riley. Oth *Fr.* Seven Strangely Exciting Lies.

There was such speed in her little body. Bells for John Whiteside's Daughter. John Crowe Ransom. APT-1; ColAP; FuPo; HAP; HarvBoo; HeIP-4; InPK-6; MakPoe; MoAmPo; NAAL-2v2; NIL-7; NIP-4; NOBA; NoAM; NoP-4; OxBA; PAI; PoE; RB; TAP; TFi; UnPo; VGW; WeW-3

There was the buffalo blowing. Composition. Peter Blue Cloud. VoR

There was the chiropodist. Plain Song. Craig Raine. TOF

There was the cottage blazing. Fire! Willy Bal. WoPoe, *tr. by* Yann Lovelock

There was the sky, starless and vast. Night Picnic. Charles Simic. BAP-01

There was the solitary palm, or scattered clumps. In Times and Places. Umberto Piersanti. NeIt, *tr. by* Stephen Sartarelli

There was the sonne of Ampycus of great forecasting wit. Ovid. CTC, *tr. by* Arthur Golding *Fr.* Metamorphoses.

There was the tree the day they planted. Tree, A. Mark Irwin. PoCoUp

There was this gym-teacher. Epigram. Strato [*or* Straton]. GrAn, *tr. by* Teddy Hogge

There was this head had this mouth he kept shooting off. Mouth, The. Ciaran Carson. ModIr; PNI

There was this hidden grin. Grin, A. Ted Hughes. EmeKit

There was this poet. On the Poet Coming of Age. Lorna Dee Cervantes. TouFir

There was this road. Legs, The. Robert Graves. PeLV; RB

There was three kings into the east. John Barleycorn [a Ballad]. Robert Burns. FaBoCh; RB

There was three ladies play'd at the ba' Cruel Brother, The. *Unknown.* ESPB; OxBB

There was time when my fingers could shape the world. Gypsy in the Condemned Cell, A. Mihály Babits. IQMS, *tr. by* Peter Zollman

There was too much, always, then too little. Time. Louise Glück. BAP-01

There was twa sisters in a bow'r [*or* bower]. Twa Sisters, The. *Unknown.* ESPB; OxBS

There was two little boys going to the school. Twa Brothers, The. *Unknown.* EBEV; ESPB; OxBB

There was . . . what?—Pale sunsets, wide expanses. Georgy [*or* Georgii Viktorovich] Adamovich. TCRP

There wasn't much else we could do. Shooting the Dogs. Philip Hodgins. BMAP

There we go in cars, did you guess we wore sandals? Way of Being, A. Barbara Guest. FTOS

There we two, content, happy in being together, speaking little, perhaps not a word. (LL) Glimpse, A. Walt Whitman. APN-1; OxBA; RaBo

There we was, and wanting our tea. Limerick. "P. E. A." PeLi

There we were. Two women, who I think still. 21 East 10th, 2BR, WBF, EIK. Robyn Selman. WiU

There went a warrior's funeral through the night. Peasant Girl of the Rhone, The. Felicia Dorothea Hemans. RWP

There went a widow woman from the outskirts of the city. Cruse of Tears, The. A Russian Legend. Emily Jane Pfeiffer. ViWPN

There went most passionately to life, impellance. Life and Impellance. William Frederick Stevenson. NOBVV

There went out in the dawning light. Pastoral, A. *Unknown.* AWP, *tr. by* John Addington Symonds

There went three children down to the shore. Black Pebble, The. James Reeves. OTCP

There were. There Were Those I Loved. Emperor Gotoba. WoPoe, *tr. by* Howard S. Levy

There were bells on the hill. Till There Was You. Meredith Willson. ReLy

There were bizarre beginnings in old lands for the making of me. Dark Blood. Margaret Abigail Walker. NALW

There were bonfires on the hillsides. Ohakune Fires. Lauris Edmond. PeNZ, *tr. by* Margaret Orbell

There were distinctive. Language of Love. Rae Armantrout. PmAP

There were four of us about that [*or* the] bed. Shameful Death. William Morris. GTBS-P; PeVV

There were ghosts that returned to earth to hear his phrases. Large Red Man Reading. Wallace Stevens. APT-1; HAP; LCAP-2

There were ladies, they lived in a bower. Mary [*or* Marie] Hamilton. *Unknown.* ESPB

There were many *don'ts*: pirates, maidens, deer. In Henry Carlile's *Writing 213.* Martha Silano. AmPoNex

There were never strawberries. Strawberries. Edwin Morgan. BoLoP; NoP-4

There were nine little blackfellas. Kidnappers. Iris Clayton. IBA

There were no antelope on the balcony.   Midnight Special.   Kenneth Patchen.   VGW

There Were No Deer in the Thicket.   David Biespiel.   AmPoNex

There were no leaders, but they were first.   Dog Fox Field.   Les A. Murray.   BMAP

There were no lines of violent diamonds, blinding light.   Madwoman in the Park, The.   Dame Edith Sitwell.   PFTM-1

There were no markets in Watts.   Speaking with Hands.   Luis J. Rodriguez.   UnSA

There were no men and women then at all.   Then.   Edwin Muir.   OxBEV; PoE

There were no poems that year.   For Imelda.   James Simmons.   PNI

There were no undesirables or girls in my set.   Commander Lowell.   Robert Lowell.   VGW

There were once two cats of Kilkenny.   Cats of Kilkenny, The.   Unknown.   ChAP; PeLi; ReMoGo

There were once two young people of taste.   Limerick.   Monica Curtis.   PeLi

There were other forms.   Other Forms of Slaughter.   Catherine Obianuju Acholonu.   HAWP; HBAPE

There were other separations, and so many of them.   Homer.   ModIr, tr. by Michael Longley   Fr. Odyssey.

There were roses, first.   Laszlo.   Frieda Hughes.   NeBl

There were rules.   On Growing Up the Darker Berry.   Harriet Jacobs.   ISC

There were snakes in the.   I Remember Haifa Being Lovely But.   Lyn Lifshin.   GotH; UnSA

There were so many books. she had to separate them to avoid being.   Reading.   Joanne Burns.   BMAP

There were some dirty plates.   Last Words of My English Grandmother, The.   William Carlos Williams.   APT-1; RB; RaBo; SAmP

There were some pines, a canal, a piece of sky.   Landscape with Little Figures.   Donald Justice.   LCAP-2

There Were Some Summers.   Thomas Lux.   LCAP-2

There were the roses, in the rain.   Act, The.   William Carlos Williams.   SAmP; VGW

There were the whales, six of them.   Stranded Whales, The.   Geoffrey Dutton.   CBAP

There Were Those I Loved.   Emperor Gotoba.   WoPoe, tr. by Howard S. Levy

There were three at one table; the pot-bellied judge.   Old Veteran and Napoleon, The.   János Garay.   IQMS, tr. by Watson Kirkconnell

There were three cherry trees once.   Three Cherry Trees, The.   Walter De la Mare.   OBGa

There were three cooks of Colebrook.   Unknown.   OxNR

There were three in the meadow by the brook.   Code, The.   Robert Frost.   OBNV; UnPo

There were three ladies [or maids] lived in a bower [or barn].   Babylon; or, The Bonnie Banks o' Fordie.   Unknown.   ESPB; OxBB

There were three little owls in a wood.   Unknown.   OBCoV; PeLi

There were three ravens [or rauens or crows] sat on a tree.   Three Ravens, The.   Unknown.   ESPB; HeIP-4; InPK-6; NAEL-5v1; OBEV; OxBB; PAI; PoE; SCGP; TFi; UnPo

There were three sailors of Bristol city.   Little Billee.   William Makepeace Thackeray.   FaBoCh; NOBL; OxAEP-2

There were three sisters fair and bright.   Riddling Knight, The.   Unknown.   FaBoCh

There were three sisters in a hall.   Unknown.   OxNR

There were tiny flames in her eyes.   Epitaph on a Living Woman.   Angelina Weld Grimké.   APT-1

There were twa brethren in the North.   Twa Brothers, The.   Unknown.   EBEV; ESPB; OxBB

There were twa knights in fair Scotland.   Twa Knights, The.   Unknown.   ESPB

There were twa sisters [sat] in a bower [or bour or bowr].   Binnorie; or, The Two Sisters.   Unknown.   OBEV; PoE

There were two birds sat on a stone.   Aristotle's Story.   Mother Goose.   OxNR; ReMoGo

There were two conditions.   Pact, The.   P. S. Rege.   OMIP, tr. by Vinay Dharwadker

There were two extra hooks of a worrying nature.   Bargain with the Watchman.   Eva Salzman.   MFPA

There were two royal children.   Unknown.   GePo

There were two sisters sat in a bour.   Cruel Sister, The.   Unknown.   OxBB

There were two sisters, they went playing.   Twa Sisters, The.   Unknown.   ESPB

There were two surprises for us.   At Ynysddu.   Graham Thomas.   AngWePo

There were two thousand queens last night at the Flamingo.   Last Night at the Flamingo.   John Iozia.   CAGL

There were two wrens upon a tree.   Unknown.   OxNR

There weren't any curtains in my parent's house.   Bare Windows.   Martha Rhodes.   ExTi

There, when they thought they saw in well sought Books.   Sir William Davenant [or D'Avenant].   PBRV   Fr. Gondibert Book 2.

There, where a French legionnaire.   In the Footsteps of Genghis Khan.   Jan Barry.   CDa

There where the course is.   At Galway Races.   W. B. Yeats.   WoPoe

There, where the lake into the distance spreads.   Song of Home.   Mida Huber.   AuPH, tr. by Lowell A. Bangerter

There, where the rusty iron lies.   Rooks.   Charles Hamilton Sorley.   MoBrPo

There will be a rusty gun on the wall, sweetheart.   A. E. F.   Carl Sandburg.   MoAmPo

There Will Be a Talking.   Michael Hartnett.   PBCIP

There will be no monograms on our skulls.   Rebellion against the North Side.   Naomi Shihab Nye.   WeW-3

There will be no more cats.   Mort aux Chats.   Peter Porter.   OxBC

There will be no speech from.   No Speech from the Scaffold.   Thom Gunn.   OxBTC

There will be the cough before the silence, then.   Dictum: For a Masque of Deluge.   W. S. Merwin.   YaYoPo

There Will Come Soft Rains.   Sara Teasdale.   APT-1

There Will Never Be Another You.   Harry Warren.   ReLy

There, with ten Rembrandts.   Ten Little Rembrandts.   Theodore Weiss.   NoAM

There, wrapped in his own roars, the lone airman.   Raider, The.   William Robert Rodgers.   MoBrPo

There ye gang, ye daft.   Grace of God and the Meth-Drinker, The.   Sydney Goodsir Smith.   NePenScot

There you are.   Jean-Joseph Rabéarivelo [or Rebéarivelo].   NegPo

There you are again.   To Marie Osmond.   Jack Skelley.   SwNoth

There you go again.   Jeepneyfying.   Noel Mateo.   ReBoTo

There you go, it's everywhere.   Shopping for Midnight.   G. E. Murray.   ReTh

There! You shed a ray.   He Wrote the History Book.   Marianne Craig Moore.   APT-1

There you were in my dreams last night.   Stepfathers.   David Donnell.   NOBC

There you were in your purple vestments.   Miraculous Grass.   Nuala Ni Dhomhnaill.   ModIr, tr. by Seamus Heaney

Thereafter, where that strange creature went. (LL)   Cynewulf.   ASW; WoPoe, tr. by Kevin Crossley-Holland   Fr. Riddles (Exeter Book).

Therefore. (LL)   Susanna and the Elders.   Adelaide Crapsey.   APT-1; TCAPo; WPE

Therefore do thou, stiff-set Northumberland.   Imitation.   Joseph Hilaire Pierre Belloc.   OBCoV

Therefore I Must Tell the Truth.   Torlino.   STP, tr. by Washington Matthews

Therefore John read how that thou wouldst.   Anna Trapnell.   ChIV-2   Fr. Cry of a Stone, A.

Therefore myself is that one only thing.   Christina Georgina Rossetti.   PEW   Fr. Thread of Life, The.

Therefore [or Therfore] that he may raise the Lord throws down. (LL)   Hymn[e] to God My God, In My Sickness[e], A.   John Donne.   BASC; EBEV; ESCV; HeIP-4; MeLP; NAEL-5v1; NAEL-6v1; NAEL-7v1; NOSC; NoP-4; OxAEP-1; PBRV; PoE; SoSe-8; TFi; TOF

Therefore Philippi saw once more the Roman battalions.   Virgil [or Vergil].   APT-2, tr. by Richmond Lattimore   Fr. Georgics.

Therefore release me and depart on your way. (LL)   Whoever You Are Holding Me Now in Hand.   Walt Whitman.   APN-1; CAGL; NAAL-2v1; NAAL-3

Therefore say no more at first. (LL)   Mary Sidney Wroth, Countess of Montgomery.   NAEL-5v1; NAEL-6v1; NAEL-7v1; NoP-4   Fr. Urania.

Therefore We Preserve Life.   Shen Ch'üan.   TrJP, tr. by William C. White

Therefore, We Thank Thee, God.   Reuben Grossman.   TrJP, tr. by L. V. Snowman

Therefore, when thou wouldst pray, or dost thine alms.   Right Use of Prayer, The.   Sir Aubrey De Vere.   SacPr

Therefore, who doeth work rightful to do.   Unknown.   TAL   Fr. Bhagavad-Gita, The.

Therefore your halls, your ancient colleges.   Lines on Cambridge of 1830.   Tennyson.   OxBSo

Thereof be therefore heedful.   Prayer for His Wife and Children, Written in Newgate.   George Wither.   SacPr

There's a fire / in the Architectural!   Big Fire at the Architectural College, The.   Andrey [or Andrei] Andreievich Voznesensky [or Voznesenskii].   CLPP, tr. by Anselm Hollo

There's a green hollow where a river sings.   Arthur Rimbaud.   See Swollen river sang through the green hole, The

There's a whisper down the line at 11.   Skimbleshanks: The Railway Cat.   T. S. Eliot.   NOBL

Theresa of Avila surely had a gold thimble.   Things of This World.   Anna Kamienska.   GI, tr. by David Curzon and Grażyna Drabik

Theresienstadt's Hospital.   Unknown, fr. Terezin Concentration Camp.   INSAB

There. . . you are revealing your secret to me alone.   Secrets.   Ahmad 'Abd al-Mu'ti Hijazi.   MAP, tr. by Sargon Boulus and Peter Porter

Theris, the old man who lived by his fish traps.   Leonidas.   GrAn; PGA; WoPoe, *tr.* by Kenneth Rexroth

Theris the old, the waves that harvested.   Leonidas of Tarentum.   AWP, *tr.* by Andrew Lang   *Fr.* Epigrams.

Theris, thrice-old, who got his living from.   Leonidas of Tarentum.   HePo   *Fr.* Epigrams.

Theris, whose hands were cunning.   Leonidas.   GrAn; PGA

Theris, whose hands were cunning.   *Unknown.*   GrAn

Thermal Stair, The.   William Sydney Graham.   FaBoMo; HarvBoo

Thermopylae.   Simonides.   AWP; OBVE; OBWP; WoPoe, *tr.* by William Lisle Bowles

Thermopylai.   Hegemon.   GrAn, *tr.* by Peter Jay

Thermopylai.   Parmenion of Macedon.   GrAn, *tr.* by Peter Jay

Thermopylai's dead.   Simonides.   SaLy, *tr.* by Diane Rayor

Therof I have a quantyte. (LL)   Chapmen.   *Unknown.*   FaBoVe; MiEL

Theromachos of Crete came to hang up.   Leonidas of Tarentum.   GrAn

THESCRIBESPACKEDCAPITALSACROSSTHEPAGE.   Scribes, The.   Suzanne Noguere.   FFC

These.   William Carlos Williams.   APT-1; MoAmPo; NOBA; OxBA

These accents seem their own defence. (LL)   Some Trees.   John Ashbery.   CoAmPo; HCAP; NAAL-2v2; YaYoPo

These acres, always again lost.   Lost Acres.   Robert Graves.   NoAM

These Americans I see.   13 November 1983.   Lee Cataldi.   BMAP

These apples.   "Paul Dermée."   CuPo

These are amazing: each.   Some Trees.   John Ashbery.   CoAmPo; HCAP; NAAL-2v2; YaYoPo

These are Aristophanes' marvellous plays.   Antipater of Thessalonica.   GrAn

These are calamitous times we're living through.   Modern Times.   Nicanor Parra.   AF, *tr.* by Miller Williams

These are dissenters.   Imre Madách.   IQMS, *tr.* by Iain MacLeod   *Fr.* Tragedy of Man.

These are lilacs.   These are Lilacs.   Nijole Miliauskaite.   VCWP, *tr.* by Jonas Zdanys

These are men! the gaunt, unforesold, the vocal.   Ol' Bunk's Band.   William Carlos Williams.   NOBA

These are my countries, my forests.   Nightsong.   Thamnaret.   WoPoe, *tr.* by Ronald Perry

These are my murmur-laden shells that keep.   On Some Shells Found Inland.   Trumbull Stickney.   APN-2; Son

These are my thoughts on realising.   Anniversary.   John Wain.   TwCP

These are names to haunt our dreams.   Names.   Medora C. Addison.   YaYoPo

These, are not brayed of Tongue. (LL)   Emily Dickinson.   NALW; TRP

These Are Not Brushstrokes.   Cyrus Cassells.   GT

These Are Not Lost.   Richard Metcalf.   PoToHe

These are not roads of shining glass.   My Wife.   Nikolai Ivanovich Glazkov.   TCRP, *tr.* by Daniel Weissbort

These are not the lines that came to me.   Lines Lost Among Trees.   Billy Collins.   BAP-97

These are notes to lightning in my bedroom.   Star Quilt.   Roberta Hill Whiteman.   CDW

These are the absolute top of the line.   Mangosteens.   Daniel Hall.   NoP-4

These are the arrows that kill sleep.   Créide's Lament for Dínertech.   *Unknown.*   NOIV

These are the arrows that murder sleep.   Song of Crede, The.   *Unknown.*   BIrV, *tr.* by Alfred Perceval Graves

These Are the Chosen People.   Robert Nathan.   TrJP

These are the damned circles Dante trod.   Grotesque.   Frederic Manning.   PeFWW

These are the days of our youth, our days of glory and honor.   Days of Our Youth, The.   *Unknown.*   AWP, *tr.* by Wilfrid Scawen Blunt

These are the days whose fingers.   Ninth of Av.   Myra Sklarew.   CRP

These are the desolate, dark weeks.   These.   William Carlos Williams.   MoAmPo; NOBA; OxBA

These are the facts. The uncle, the elder brother, the squire.   Arthur Hugh Clough.   FaBoVe   *Fr.* Amours de Voyage.

These are the fields of light, and laughing air.   Sir Charles G. D. Roberts.   NOBC   *Fr.* Songs of the Common Day.

These are the first citizens of contingency.   Robert Pinsky.   HCAP; NoAM   *Fr.* Essay on Psychiatrists.

These are the first days of fall. The wind.   How To Like It.   Stephen Dobyns.   Unle

These are the gardens of the Desert, these.   William Cullen Bryant.   APN-1; ColAP; ITBLP; NAAL-2v1; NAAL-3; NAAL-5; NCAP; NOBA; OxBA; TAP; TCAPo

These are the green paths trodden by patience.   Rural Mail, The.   John Glassco.   MoCV

These are the holes—only holes.   Elbow in Dumberland, An.   Edwin Torres.   HeMarv

These are the little shoes that died.   Little Shoes That Died, The.   Mary Gilmore.   NOBAu

These are the long weeks. The weeks.   Petition.   Brigit Pegeen Kelly.   ExTi

These are the men from México's boot, the ones.   Penny Men.   Rigoberto González.   GeoHom

These are the middle years.   Middle Years, The.   Anthony Cronin.   CIP-2

These are the Nights that Beetles love.   Emily Dickinson.   NCAP

These are the original monies of the earth.   Cabinet of Seeds Displayed, A.   Howard Nemerov.   CRP

These are the small hours when.   Epithalamion.   Michael Longley.   CIP-2

These Are the Sweet Girls.   Anabel Torres.   TANSG, *tr.* by Celeste Kostopulos-Cooperman

These are / the sweet girls / who go to the matinée.   These Are the Sweet Girls.   Anabel Torres.   TANSG, *tr.* by Celeste Kostopulos-Cooperman

These are the things men seek at dusk.   Dusk.   Helen Welshimer.   PoToHe

These are the things which once possessed.   True Happiness.   Morris Talpalar.   PoToHe

These are the ultimate highlands.   Lines.   Sara Teasdale.   APT-1

These are the voices of the pastors calling.   Old Lutheran Bells at Home, The.   Wallace Stevens.   NoAM

These are thrity carved stones.   Playing the Goldberg Variations on Sunday Morning.   Bill Holm.   MiVo

These are times when their faith in gods.   *From* Florrie Abraham Witness, *December 1972.*   Jack A. Mapanje.   HBAPE

These are what I will remember.   Images of John (1967–92).   Danton R. Remoto.   ReBoTo

These are your lips.   Vasco [*or* Vasko] Popa.   PoSu   *Fr.* Far Within Us.

These, as they change, Almighty Father! these.   James Thomson.   CABP; InvLi; TreFP   *Fr.* Seasons, The.

These baby chicks do not leave their mother.   Paintings of Various Subjects by Fang Jih-sheng: Baby Chicks Following Their Mother.   Pien Kung.   CoBLCP, *tr.* by Jonathan Chaves

These barrows of the century-darkened dead.   Prehistoric Burials.   Siegfried Sassoon.   MoBrPo

These be great cities, new roofs mounting up.   Alcuin.   MLL

These be / Three silent things.   Triad.   Adelaide Crapsey.   APT-1; TCAPo; WPE

These beasts will not do.   Send New Beasts.   Joe Wenderoth.   BodElec

These became part of that child who went forth every day, and who now goes, and will always go forth every day. (LL)   Walt Whitman.   AWP; NAAL-2v1; NAAL-5; OxBA; SAmP; TAP

These berries, with their choices, come to earth.   Aeschyleans, The.   Bernadette Mayer.   FTOS

These birds were born singing for joy.   Another Song of the Same Woman, to Some Partridges, Sent to Her Alive.   Florencia del Pinar.   BoWoP, *tr.* by Julie Allen

These Bones.   T. H. Parry-Williams.   OBWVE, *tr.* by H. Idris Bell

These branches.   Naito Joso.   ZenPo, *tr.* by Takashi Ikemoto and Lucien Stryk

These chaste / words go out.   Any Nest I Can't Sleep in Should Be Burned.   Christopher Davis.   AmPoNex

These cherries are not wine-filled bowls for thirsty birds.   Flowering Cherry, The.   Janet Frame.   PeNZ

These chill pillars of fluted stone.   Winter Homily on the Calton Hill.   Douglas Young.   OxBS

These city streets, the labyrinthine black roads.   Words and Truth.   Yasin Taha Hafiz.   MAP, *tr.* by Sharif Elmusa and Christopher Middleton

These clothes don't fit.   Running Hares.   Tessa Rose Chester.   MFPA

These coastal mountains are as sharp as swords.   Viewing Mountains with His Reverence Hao Ch'u: To My Friends and Relatives in the Capital.   Liu Tsung-yüan.   SuSp, *tr.* by Jan W. Walls

These coloured lights.   Archie Weller.   IBA

These conquered kings pass furiously away.   End of a Year.   Robert Lowell.   HCAP

These Damned Trees Crouch.   Jim Barnes.   CDW

These Days.   Andrew Motion.   DiPo

These Days.   Charles Olson.   APT-2; RaBo

These days.   Sunday Skaters.   Mary Jo Salter.   MoASP

These Days.   William Stafford.   NNaP

These days.   Lifelong farewell.   Idea Vilariño.   TANSG, *tr.* by Louise B. Popkin

These days are too full fraught with diverse dangers.   Alcuin.   MLL

These days I get up with the birches.   Days in White.   Ingeborg Bachmann.   BoWoP

These days steal everything.   Thief Stole This Poem, A.   Allen Ginsberg.   BodElec

These Days the Papers in the Street.   Charles Reznikoff.   VGW

These days, the ubiquitous db.   Limerick.   A. P. Cox.   PeLi

These days, what comes from your mouth.   Non Sequitur.   Margot Schilpp.   AmPoNex

These days you keep on meeting. Seventies, The. Louis Johnson. PeNZ

These decibels / Are a kind of flagellation, an entity of sound. John Ashbery. PmAP   Fr. Skaters, The.

These demonstrations of the one God. Mountains of California: Part 1, The. Al Young. GeoHom

These difficulties—flamboyant tide, modest red berries. Boy Sleeping. Ann Lauterbach. PmAP

These errors loved no less than the saint loves arrows. Elegy V: [Separation of Man from God]. George Barker. FaBoTw

These evenings over the restaurants. Stranger, The. Aleksandr Aleksandrovich Blok. TCRP

These eyes, [deare Lord], once brandons of desire. For the Magdalene. William Drummond, of Hawthornden. ChIV-2

These feeble sounds. Ann Yearsley. ECWP   Fr. Remonstrance in the Platonic Shade. Flourishing on an Height.

These feet and hands, two pelvises, this movement. Upon a Drawing. István Vas. IQMS, tr. by Daniel Gerard Hoffman

These figures moving in my rhyme. Two Figures. N. Scott Momaday. NoP-4

These flat and leathery leaves. Ars Poetica. Jane Hirshfield. BodElec

These flowers are I, poor Fanny Hurd. Voices from Things Growing in a Churchyard. Thomas Hardy. FaBoVe; OxBTC

These Foolish Things (Remind Me of You). James Strachey. ReLy

These foreign laws of God and man. (LL) Laws of God, the Laws of Man, The. A. E. Housman. CAGL; MoBrPo; NOBVV; NPeEn; OBSV

These forty years past, our house and our domain. Tune: "Dance of the Cavalry." Li Yü. SuSp, tr. by Daniel Bryant

These fought in any case. Ezra Pound. HarvBoo; HeIP-4; MoAmPo; NOBE; NPeEn; OBWP; PoE; PoWW; TRP; VGW   Fr. Hugh Selwyn Mauberley (Life and Contacts).

These fresh beauties (we can prove). Why Flowers Change Color. Robert Herrick. HAP

These furies frying thus, yet thus were not content. Admiralls Being Slaine, They Likewise . . . , The. Anne Dowriche. EMWP

These gifts to Aphrodite. Callimachus. HePo   Fr. Epigrams.

These Gothic windows, how they wear me out. Young Glass-Stainer, The. Thomas Hardy. CTC

These grand and fatal movements toward death. Rearmament. Robinson Jeffers. OxBA

These Green-Going-to-Yellow. Marvin Bell. UrbNat

These green painted park benches are. In a Season of Unemployment. Margaret Avison. MoCV; NOBC

These Green Paths. Jeannette Miller. TANSG, tr. by Paula Vega

These have crimes accounted been[e]. (LL) Ben Jonson. BeJo; NPeEn; NoP-4; OxBEV, tr. by Ben Jonson   Fr. Volpone.

These hearts were woven of human joys and cares. Rupert Brooke. PeFWW; SoSe-8   Fr. 1914.

These hills were once mountains. Temporary Heart. Michael Hannon. GeoHom

These hips are big hips. Homage to My Hips. Lucille Clifton. NAAAL

These hollow truncated cones of wicker into mud. Two Varieties of the Bitter Orange. J. L. Jacobs. AmPoNex

These honours, Homer, had been just to thee. (LL) Mr. Pope's Welcome from Greece. John Gay. EBEV; OxAEP-1; OxBoLi

These Horses Came. Ray A. Young Bear. CDW

These I love: hidden plants that grow by the river's edge;. West Creek at Ch'u-chou. Wei Ying-wu. CoBCP, tr. by Burton Watson

These I Singing in Spring. Walt Whitman. APN-1

These, in the day when heaven was falling. Epitaph on an Army of Mercenaries. A. E. Housman. FaBoWar; NAEL-6v2; NPeEn; NoP-4; OxBEV; SCGP; SoSe-8

These just-ripe, perfectly packaged blackberries. Plan, The. Jack Turner. BAP-97

These knacks, my lord, I cannot call to mind. George Gascoigne. SacPr   Fr. Steele Glas, The.

These labor days, when shirking hardly looks like working. Back to Town. John Hollander. NoAM

These laboratories and those picnics. In Hospital. Frank O'Hara. LCAP-2

These labouring wits, like paviours, mend our ways. Edward Young. OBSV   Fr. Epistles to Mr. Pope.

These Lacustrine Cities. John Ashbery. HCAP; PoM; UnPo

These Last Days. Katie Donovan. NeBl

These layers of piled-up skulls. Tower of Skulls, The. Isaac Rosenberg. PeFWW

These lazy spring days. Buson. SoOfWa, tr. by Sam Hamill

These Leaves. William Stafford. NNaP

These lectures afford me a great pleasure. Lectures on Love, The. Edward Hirsch. PuP-23

These light-footed, celebrated cats, created. Tigers of Nanzen-ji, The. Brad Leithauser. DiPo

These lips of Mr. Tunis Flood are cornflower. Postmortem. Maurice Kilwein Guevara. AmPoNex

These little limbs [or limmes]. Salutation [or Salutations], The. Thomas Traherne. ESCV; EnlH; GeHe; NOCV; SacPr

These locks on doors have brought me happiness. Locks. Kenneth Koch. CoAP

These lodge in London in Lent and at other times too. William Langland. NOCV   Fr. Vision of Piers Plowman, The.

These long verandahs seem to be washed clean. Wen Cheng-ming. CoBLCP   Fr. Chung-i Temple, The.

These lovely groves of fountain-trees that shake. Golden Bough. Elinor Wylie. MoAmPo

These lusty plants, complete with blaring sex. Marrows. Louis Johnson. PeNZ

These market-dames, mid-aged, with lips thin-drawn. Thomas Hardy. NoAM; OBMV   Fr. At Casterbridge Fair.

[These] meetings in dreams. Yakamochi (Otomo no Yakamochi). TAL

These men. Tuskegee Airfield. Marilyn Nelson Waniek. ESEAA; GT

These men are on their feet, not all day long. Driftwood and Seacoal. Andrew Crozier. Oth

These men clothed their land with incorruptible. For the Spartan Dead at Plataia. Simonides. GrAn, tr. by Peter Jay

These men died with the wrong names. Dying with the Wrong Name. Sam Hamod. GraLe; UnSA

These men were kings, albeit they were black. Black Majesty. Countee Cullen. VGW

These men? In their dented felt hats. Colors of Desire, The. David Mura. LoL

These messages are secret, the initials. Personal Column. Tom Paulin. PNI

These nights we fear the aspects of the moon. Full Moon: New Guinea. Karl Shapiro. APT-2

These nights when first. August Nights. Jean Janzen. GeoHom

These nights when the wind blows. 0°. Elizabeth Spires. DiPo

These no-man's-lands. Poem-Object. André Breton. PFTM-1

These nymphs that I would perpetuate. Afternoon of a Faun, The. Stéphane Mallarmé. NAWM-7v2, tr. by Henry Weinfield

These old tears in the chopping-bowl. (LL) Peeling Onions. Adrienne Rich. BoWoP; HCAP; TAP

These older towns die. Poema para los Californios Muertos. Lorna Dee Cervantes. PoPoPo

These pages, crumbling under my fingers. Old Photograph Album. Linda Pastan. TaR

These panting damsels, dancing for their lives. Mother's Choice, The. Unknown. OxBoLi

These peaks gather like snowy swords. At Waterfall Temple. Chang K'o-chiu. CrYelRi, tr. by Sam Hamill

These pearls of thought in Persian gulfs were bred. In a Copy of Omar Khayyám. James Russell Lowell. NCAP

These people have not heard your name. In a Cathedral City. Thomas Hardy. EnLoPo

These people, with their illegible diplomas. Metamorphoses. Howard Nemerov. HCAP

These plum buds move one's imagination. Inscribed on a Scroll "Plum Blossoms by the Water." Huang T'ing-chien. SuSp, tr. by Michael E. Workman

These Poems. John Jarmain. FaBoWar

These Poems, She Said. Robert Bringhurst. NOBC

These pools that, though in forests, still reflect. Spring Pools. Robert Frost. APT-1; ColAP; NAAL-2v2; NOBA; NoAM; OxBA

These Purists. William Carlos Williams. OBAL

These Ravens have fed me. (LL) Observation Generall from Their Eating, Etc., The. Roger Williams. SCAP; SacPr

These rioteres three of which I tell. Geoffrey Chaucer. OBNV   Fr. Canterbury Tales, The.

These roads will take you into your own country. Book of the Dead, The. Muriel Rukeyser. APT-2

These Rumours of Hexagonal Rooms in Gone Bee City. David Eggleton. PeNZ

These—saw Visions. Emily Dickinson. SWaP

These sea slugs. Issa. EH, tr. by Robert Hass

These seven houses have learned to face one another. On a Painting by Patient B of the Independence State Hospital for the Insane. Donald Justice. CoAP; CoAmPo; NoAM

These shape the creature that is I. (LL) Long Live the Weeds. Theodore Roethke. NOBA; NoAM

These sheets primeval doctrines yield. On Barclay's Apology for the Quakers. Matthew Green. NOEC

These sibilants aren't the right sound. Sleeplessness. Michelle Boisseau. ExTi

These Six. Sean Lucy. CIP-2

These songs in my ears are enough.   Long Distance.   Max Winter.   NeAmPo

These songs will not stand.   Denis Glover.   PeNZ   *Fr.* Sings Harry.

These souls, my lord, assembled at the bar.   Edward Ward.   NOEC   *Fr.* Journey to Hell, A; or, A Visit Paid to the Devil.

These spectres resting on plastic stools.   Café in Warsaw.   Allen Ginsberg.   HAP

These Strangers, In a Foreign World.   Emily Dickinson.   SAmP

These summer days I carry images of stone.   Phenomenology of Stones, The.   Thomas McCarthy.   PBCIP

These sweeter far than lilies are.   Thanksgivings for the Beauty of His Providence.   Thomas Traherne.   FaBoCh

These tall lilies, color.   Lilies, The.   Richard Emil Braun.   NoAM

These temp'rall goods God (the most Wise) commends.   Temporall Goods.   Robert Herrick.   SacPr

These ten-year-olds all want other names.   Lunch with Girl Scouts.   Sharon Bryan.   ReTh

These—the bright symbols of man's hope and fame.   Stars, The.   Madison Cawein.   APN-2

These Things I Do Remember.   Solomon Ephraim ben, of Lenczicz Aaron.   TrJP, *tr.* by Nina Davis Salaman

These thoughts like wounds from a knife! (LL)   On Failing the Examination.   Meng Chiao.   CoBCP; ColAnChi, *tr.* by Burton Watson

These thousand peaks cut off the flight of birds.   River Snow.   Gary Snyder.   ColAnChi

These to me are beautiful people.   Preference.   Elinor Wylie.   APT-1

These Too Are Our Elders.   Jack A. Mapanje.   HBAPE; NAfrP

These tracings from a world that's dead.   To Violet [with Prewar Poems].   Basil Bunting.   FaBoMo

These Trees Are No Forest of Mourners.   Douglas G. Jones.   NOBC

These Two.   Harriet Monroe.   IllVoic

These two meet for dinner once a week.   Imaginary Translation.   Marilyn Hacker.   DiPo

These two tales I tell of myself and the life I led.   John Hollander.   VCAP   *Fr.* Powers of Thirteen.

These umbered cliffs and gnarls of masonry.   Rome: Building a New Street in the Ancient Quarter.   Thomas Hardy.   Son

These unshaped islands, on the sawyer's bench.   New Zealand.   James Keir Baxter.   NoP-4

These verses weare made By Michaell Drayton Esquier Poett Lawreatt the night before hee dyed.   Michael Drayton.   NPeEn; PBRV

(As I therin noe others face but yours can Veiwe.) (LL)   PBRV

(Soe well I love thee, as without thee.)   NPeEn; PBRV

(Verses Made the Night before He Died.)   NOBE

These walls, so full of monument and bust.   Abbey Church at Bath, The.   Henry Harington.   FaBoEE

These weeping Eyes, those seeing Tears. (LL)   Eyes and Tears.   Andrew Marvell.   FSCP; GeHe

These were the same horses. (LL)   She Had Some Horses.   Joy Harjo.   HATNAP; LoL

These were the sounds that dinned upon his ear.   Dream of Winter.   George Mackay Brown.   FaBoTw

These wings, these lights, this shoal of angels.   Shrimp Boats, Biloxi.   Campbell McGrath.   AmPoNex

These winter days.   Skeleton of Winter.   Joy Harjo.   LoL

These women all.   Women.   ------ Heath.   CTC; NoSic

These women crying in my head.   Three Emily's, The.   Dorothy Livesay.   NALW

These women plunder my husband.   *Unknown.*   WoPoe, *tr.* by David Ray   *Fr.* Gathasaptasati, The.

These wonderful things.   Last World, A.   John Ashbery.   PoM

These wood-shadows, timid, patient.   These wood-shadows.   Philippe Jaccottet.   VCWP, *tr.* by Derek Mahon

These words appall and daunt them all.   Michael Wigglesworth.   NAAL-3   *Fr.* Day of Doom, The.

These words are dedicated to those who died.   Irena Klepfisz.   TaR   *Fr.* Bashert.

These words have no imagination.   Simple Like That.   Wil'um Lee.   InTrad

These words spake Don Henriquez.   Last Words of Don Henriquez, The.   Zalman Schneour.   TrJP, *tr.* by Joseph Leftwich

These words were uttered in a pensive mood.   William Wordsworth.   CenSon

These wreaths, Lais.   Paulus [*or* Paulos] Silentiarius.   GrAn

Theseus: A Trilogy.   Yvor Winters.   NOBA

Theseus and Ariadne.   Robert Graves.   HAP

Thesis.   Edward Dorn.   NOBA

Thespia, bearing a beautiful race, stranger-loving, Muse-beloved.   Korinna [*or* Corinna].   SaLy, *tr.* by Diane Rayor

Thespians at Thermopylae, The.   Norman Cameron.   GTBS-P

They.   Venus Khoury-Ghata.   PoArWo, *tr.* by Lucy McNair

"They."   Siegfried Sassoon.   NAEL-5v2; NAEL-6v2; OBSV; OBWP

(Bishop tells us: "When the boys come back," The.)   NoP-4

They.   Ronald Stuart Thomas.   OxBTC

They agreed that it had been a most / *Unusual* conversation. (LL)   Chocolates.   Louis Simpson.   OBCoV; OxBC

They all came by today.   Garage Sale.   Brian Henry.   AmPoNex

They all came, some wore sentiments.   Other Tradition, The.   John Ashbery.   FTOS; PmAP

They all climbed up on a high board-fence.   Nine Little Goblins, The.   James Whitcomb Riley.   NOxBChV; OBCA

They All Laughed.   George Gershwin.   APT-2; ReLy

They all muddy the water that it may seem deep.   Friedrich Wilhelm Nietzsche.   WoPoe, *tr.* by Ivor Armstrong Richards   *Fr.* Zarathustra.

They all see the same movies.   Powwow.   W. D. Snodgrass.   SoSe-8

They All Think.   Giovanna Pollarolo.   TANSG, *tr.* by Marjorie Agosin

They all took one, and left four in. (LL)   Mother Goose.   OxNR; ReMoGo

They all want to break at some point.   Breaking Points.   Eamon Grennan.   ModIr

They All Want to Play Hamlet.   Carl Sandburg.   NOBA

They all were looking for a king.   George Macdonald.   OBEV; SacPr   *Fr.* Paul Faber, Surgeon.

They also serve who only stand and wait. (LL)   On His Blindness.   John Milton.   AWP; CABP; ChIV-2; GSo; HaP; HeIP-4; ITBLP; InPK-6; NAEL-5v1; NAEL-6v1; NIL-7; NOBE; NOSC; NPeEn; NoP-4; OBEV; OxBSo; PoE; PoPoPo; PoRA; SCGP; SacPr; SoSe-8; TFi; TRP; WeW-3

They amputated / Your hips from my loins.   Pity, A. We Were Such a Good Invention.   Yehuda Amichai [*or* Amikhai].   FIT, *tr.* by Robert Friend

They amputated / Your thighs off my hips.   Pity; We Were Such a Good Invention, A.   Yehuda Amichai [*or* Amikhai].   BoLoP, *tr.* by Assia Gutmann

They and I.   Xavier Villaurrutia.   CAGL, *tr.* by Fanny Arango-Ramos and William Keeth

They and I are civilized. (LL)   Heritage.   Countee Cullen.   APT-2; BPo; ColAP; HeIP-4; MoAMPo; NAAAL; NAAL-2v2; NAAL-5; NoAM; NoP-4; PoPoPo; SSLK; TTY

They answered, 'Mr Toad' (LL)   Kenneth Grahame.   NOBL; NOxBChV   *Fr.* Wind in the Willows, The.

They appeared two but they were one thing only.   Gentleman and the Lady, The.   Vivian Lamarque.   CItWP, *tr.* by Cinzia Sartini Blum and Lara Trubowitz

They applaud at the periods and sigh.   Poet's Shuffle, The.   Calvin Forbes.   GT; LTA

They are a gift I have wanted again.   Horses in Snow.   Roberta Hill Whiteman.   NoAM

They are able, with science, to measure.   C Stands for Civilization.   Kenneth Fearing.   TrJP

They are all dying.   Death as History.   Jay Wright.   ESEAA

They are all gone away.   House on the Hill, The.   Edwin Arlington Robinson.   APN-2; MakPoe; MoAmPo; NAAL-2v2; NCAP

They Are All Gone into the World of Light!   Henry Vaughan.   BASC; CABP; ESCV; GeHe; NAEL-5v1; NAEL-6v1; NAEL-7v1; NOBE; NOSC; NPeEn; NoP-4; PBRV; PeECV; PoPoPo; SCGP; TFi; WoPoe

(Ascension Hymn.)   MeLP; NOCV

(Friends Departed.)   OBEV

They are all outline, uniformly gray.   Those before Us.   Robert Lowell.   LCAP-2

They are as fierce as tigers, rude as bears. (LL)   Common People, The.   Rowland Watkyns.   AngWePo; BASC

They are as light as upper air! (LL)   Garden Seat, The.   Thomas Hardy.   HAP; RB

They are at table.   Last Supper, The.   Jacques Prévert.   CLPP, *tr.* by Lawrence Ferlinghetti

They are bodies left unburied.   Rondeau: "They are bodies left unburied."   Cheryl Clarke.   FFC

They are bringing back the bones of Che Guevara.   Y, The.   Brenda Hillman.   MoASP

They are burning a boat on the beach.   Decommissioning.   Katrina Porteous.   NeBl

They are burying my nanny. A poor.   Nanny Tanya.   Yevgeny [*or* Evgenii] Borisovich Rein.   ItGoST, *tr.* by Judith Hemschemeyer

They are by nature lonely things.   Ideal Angels.   John Robert Colombo.   MoCV

They are Coming.   Filippo Tommaso Marinetti.   PFTM-1

They Are Coming?   Josephine D. Henderson Heard.   CBWP-4

They are creatures lacking malice. (LL)   Geometry Class.   Mark Bibbins.   AmPoNex; WiU

They are cutting down the great plane-trees at the end of the gardens.   Trees Are Down, The.   Charlotte Mew.   BrRo; ChIV-2; MoBrPo; OxAEP-2; TrCP; VWP; WPE; WPOW

They are cutting up into pieces.   It Took One Hundred Years.   Malika O'Lahsen.   HAWP; WoPoe, *tr.* by Eric Sellin

They are dreaming of children. Torrential. Nocturne in the Women's Prison. Maria Beneyto. WPOW, *tr.* by Catherine Rodriguez-Nieto

They are extremely rare. (LL) Frog, The. Joseph Hilaire Pierre Belloc. ChAP; NOxBChV; NTCP

They are fast in their cars. In the Shadow of Fire. Frieda Hughes. NeBl

They are going to some point true and unproven. (LL) Geometry. Rita Dove. HCAP; HeIP-4

They are heard as a choir of seven. Pleiades, The. Mary Barnard. APT-2

They are in the forest. In the Forest. George Bowering. NOBC

They are in their element. (LL) Aquarium du Trocadéro. Duncan Bush. AngWePo; TCAWP

They are lang deid, folk that I used to ken. Elegy. Robert Garioch. NPeEn; NePenScot; OxBS

They are light as flakes of dandruff with scrawny legs. Crabs. Marge Piercy. NBLV

They are like figures held in some glass ball. Children Walking Home from School through Good Neighborhood. Donald Justice. DiPo; NIL-7; NIP-4

They are like those crazy women. At Pegasus. Terrance Hayes. AmPoNex

They are made to stand side by side. Poor Houses, The. Ed Roberson. GT

They are making a crèche at the Saturday morning classes. Crib, The. Robert Finch. OBCP

They are more delicate even than shrubs and they run. Ox Looks at Man, An. Carlos Drummond de Andrade. PoetW; TCLAP, *tr.* by Mark Strand

They are moving inwards; the circle is closing. Man Meeting Himself. Howard Sergeant. SPE

They are my secret food. Children's Letters, The. Dorothy Livesay. NALW; NOBC

They are no lords, no marquesses or dukes. Shrimps. Nguyễn Văn Lạc. WoPoe, *tr.* by Hunh Sanh Thông

They are no trophies of the sun. (LL) Praise for an Urn. Hart Crane. AWP; HAP; MoAmPo; NOBA; NoAM; OxBA; WeW-3

They are not dead, they are not dead! Argonauts, The. D. H. Lawrence. NoAM

They are not here. And we, we are the Others. Absent, The. Edwin Muir. NoAM

They are not long, the weeping and the laughter. Vitae Summa Brevis Spem Nos Vetat Incohare Longam. Ernest Christopher Dowson. AWP; CABP; EBVV; HAP; NOBE; NPeEn; NoP-4; OBEV; OxBEV; OxBSP; PeVV; TFi

They are often. Lattice at "Split." Tina Darragh. FTOS

They are Planning to Cancel the School Milk Program to Fund a Tax Cut for the Middle Class. Liz Rosenberg. InvLad

They are pounded into the earth. It Is This Way with Men. C. K. Williams. RaBo; VCAP

They are rattling breakfast plates in basement kitchens. Morning at the Window. T. S. Eliot. AWP; OxBEV; TCAPo

They are rebuilding / old bridge, the Nagara. Lady Ise. BoWoP, *tr.* by Etsuko Terasaki

They are rhymes rudely strung with intent less. Dedication, A. Adam Lindsay Gordon. CBAP

They are riding away from whatever might have been. Shooting Script, A. Seamus Heaney. BodElec

They are running to arrive. (LL) Rescue, The. Robert Creeley. CRP; VCAP

They are 7 in number, just 7. Seven, The. *Unknown.* RB; WoPoe, *tr.* by Jerome Rothenberg and Jerome K. Rothenberg

They are small enough to find and care for a tiny stone. Her Body. Daniel Halpern. BAP-97

They are so like. Dolls. David St. John. LCAP-2

They are stalking humming birds. It Is a German Honeymoon. Kenneth Rexroth. APT-2

They are still so anthropologically tall here. At the Metro: Old Irrelevant Images. Jack A. Mapanje. PBMAP

They are stones. Words. Catherine Fisher. TCAWP

They are such dear familiar feet that go. Be Patient. "George Klingle." PoToHe

They are taking us beyond Miami. Removal, The. *Unknown.* STP, *tr.* by Frances Densmore

They are taller than their cars. (LL) Do It Yrself. Larry Eigner. NeAP; PoM

They are terribly white. Cyclamens. "Michael Field." NOBVV; VWP; ViWPN

They are the flesh we feed upon come from the depths. Ribbon-Fish, The. Robert Adamson. CBAP

They are the oldest living captive race. Ginkgoes in Fall. Howard Nemerov. HCAP

They Are the Same. Priscilla Jane Thompson. CBWP-2

They are the spit of virtue now. Austin Clarke. NOIV *Fr.* Civil War.

They are there. Dogs on the Cliffs, The. Michael Burkard. BodElec

They are there just the same. Wheels of the Trains, The. W. S. Merwin. GM

They are thin. Women Who Love Angels. Judith Ortiz Cofer. TouFir

They are unholy who are born. Wild Plum. John Orrick. APT-1

They are very small, my neighbors. Minotaur Next Door, The. Greg Pape. PBCAP

They are waiting for it, waiting all their lives. Grass and the Sin, The. Larissa Szporluk. AmPoNex

They are waiting for me somewhere beyond Eden Rock. Eden Rock. Charles Causley. NPeEn; NoP-4

They are weighing the babies again on color television. Video Cuisine. Maxine W. Kumin. NoAM

They Are Wicked. Ernest Sandeen. CRP

They arm themselves with Saracen hauberks. *Unknown.* NAWM-5v1; NAWM-7v1, *tr.* by Frederick Goldin *Fr.* Song of Roland, The.

They arrive. Sirhan Drinks His Coffee in the Cafeteria. Mahmoud Darwish. VCWP, *tr.* by Rana Kabbani

They arrive, always, unexpected. Yiddish Muses, The. Jacqueline Osherow. TaR

They ask her. Shower of Secret Things, The. Nathaniel Mackey. PmAP

They ask me to remember. Why some people be mad at me sometimes. Lucille Clifton. ESEAA

They asked me how I knew. Smoke Gets in Your Eyes. Otto Harbach. ReLy

They asked me to write a poem. Lila's Potatoes. Leland Bardwell. SpudSo

They asked that man for his time. In Trying Times. Heberto Padilla. AF; PoetW, *tr.* by Andrew Hurley and Alastair Reid

They beat me different ways. Beatings. Joan Larkin. WiU

They belong here in their own quenched country. By the Boat House, Oxford. Anne Stevenson. FaBoWP

They bide their time off serpentine. Ancient Monuments. John Ormond. AngWePo; OBWVE

They bowed to him: "O man of God." Prophet, The. "Yehoash." TrJP, *tr.* by Isidore Goldstick

They breathe with the night. Roland Penrose. SPE *Fr.* Road Is Wider than Long, The.

They bring in the knife, they show you. Angels, The. Cleopatra Mathis. ExTi

They bring me gifts, they honour me. If They Honoured Me, Giving Me Their Gifts. "Michael Field." OBMV

They brought a bouquet of thistles. Thistle. Nikolai Alekseievich Zabolotsky [*or* Zabolotskii]. RB, *tr.* by Daniel Weissbort

They brought her to the hospital. Aunt Lil. Paul Zweig. BodElec

They brought him in on a stretcher from the world. Grandfather. Derek Mahon. OxBC; OxBSo

They brought him one morning. Dimitris Tsaloumas. CBAP *Fr.* Rhapsody of Old Men, A.

They brought in the brine-crusted drift-wood. Drift-Wood. Clara Ann Thompson. CBWP-2

They brought me ambrotypes. Edgar Lee Masters. OxBA *Fr.* Spoon River Anthology.

They brought the dead. Gerald McCarthy. CDa *Fr.* War Story.

They brought thy body back to me quite dead. Luca Signorelli to His Son. Eugene Lee-Hamilton. PeVV

They bubble up to the surface of our memory. They. Venus Khoury-Gata. PoArWo, *tr.* by Lucy McNair

They built the front, upon my word. Building of a New Church, The. *Unknown.* HHAm

They buried him in the terrestrial globe. Sergey [*or* Sergei] Sergeievich Orlov. TCRP

They buried him today. My Father Today. Sam Hunt. PeNZ

They burn the radio and listen to the blues. John Tranter. NoAM *Fr.* Crying in Early Infancy.

They burn you. Hitchhikers, The. Diane Wakoski. NoAM

They call all experience of the senses *mystic*, when the experience / is considered. Mystic. D. H. Lawrence. BLT; PAI

They call him the Dog. Brother Ben. John Rybicki. AmPoNex

They call me and I go. Complaint. William Carlos Williams. SAmP

They call me from there. Calling, The. Luis Palés Matos. BLPSL, *tr.* by Rene de Costa, Rigas Kappatos and Eleni Paidoussi

They call me Ghede. The butts. Ghede Poem. Nathaniel Mackey. PmAP

They call, no date. I'll Walk Alone. Sammy Cahn. ReLy

They call thee rich; I deem thee poor. Treasure. Lucilius. AWP, *tr.* by William Cowper

They call this "Black North." Names. Gerald Dawe. PNI

They call you Lady Luck. Luck, Be a Lady. Frank Loesser. APT-2; ReLy

They call your mama girl. Brown Lullaby. Adam Small. PeSAV

They called forth the train whistle at midnight. Nocturno de Washington. Pablo Medina. BodElec

They called her a cat. What They Said. Tanure Ojaide. HBAPE

They called it Annandale—and I was there. How Annandale Went Out. Edwin Arlington Robinson. APT-1; GSo; MoAmPo; NOBA; NoAM; SoSe-8

They called my love a poor blind maid. On a Blind Girl. Baha Ad-din Zuhayr. AWP, *tr. by* E. H. Palmer

They came at night with their flashlights. Minutes of Hasiba, The. Holger Teschke. FaBoWar, *tr. by* Margitt Lehbert

They came back, a well known face. This Beach Can Be Dangerous. Allen Curnow. HarvBoo

They came back from the bush-haunts. Arrivants. Musaemura Bonus Zimunya. HBAPE; NAfrP

They came down from the ridge. Dunbar, 1650. Sidney Keyes. FaBoWar

They came drowned in the afternoon to the blue house on the wharf of brown broadcloth cafes. Epitafio. Ece Ayhan. WoPoe, *tr. by* Murat Nemet-Nejat

They came from the arterial streets. Survivor. Mike Jenkins. TCAWP

They came from the terror and tumult. Exodus. Jaime Torres Bodet. TCLAP, *tr. by* Sonja Karsen

They came hurrying across the mountain highway. Monkeys on Mt. Hiei. Edith Marcombe Shiffert. WPE

They came in to the little town. We Are Going. Oodgeroo of the tribe Noonuccal (Kath Walker). BMAP; CBAP; NOBAu

They came out of the hootch. Search and Destroy. Dale Ritterbusch. CDa

They came out of the sun undetected. Raid, The. William Everson. NoAM

They came running over the perilous sands. 1945. Sir Herbert Read. OxBTC

They came, since there are certain matters, and you gentlemen have / only yourselves to blame. December 14, 1979: A Poetry Reading. Stanislaw Baranczak. AF, *tr. by* Magnus J. Krynski

They came that morning, in gowns of pale green and white. Abstraction. Eleanor Wilner. ExTi

They Came That Night. Léon Damas. NegPo, *tr. by* Ellen Conroy Kennedy

They came that night as the. They Came That Night. Léon Damas. NegPo, *tr. by* Ellen Conroy Kennedy

They Came This Evening. Léon Damas. TTY, *tr. by* Seth L. Wolitz

They Came to Me and Said, "There Is a Child." Muriel Rukeyser. Son *Fr.* Nine Poems for the Unborn Child.

They came to the door because he was small or went to some church. Book of the Dead Man (#58), The. Marvin Bell. OPRER; TaR

They came to the lodge door. Wolf "Aunt." Maurice Kenny. HATNAP

They came with a fury. Flight of the Itzás. Chilam Balam. WoPoe, *tr. by* Christopher Sawyer-Lauçanno

They can shake their boodies but they can't shake *you.* (LL) Blues Don't Change, The. Al Young. ESEAA; GT

They can't plow and harvest. Poverty on the Bank. Mei Yao Ch'en. SuSp, *tr. by* Jonathan Chaves

They Can't Take That Away from Me. George Gershwin. ReLy

They cannot speak who have no words to say. Green Hammock, White Magnolia Tree. Ruth Gilbert. PeNZ

They cannot steal, thou giv'st so much. (LL) To Saxham. Thomas Carew. BASC; BeJo; CavPo

They cared for nothing but the days and hours. Disinherited, The. Charles Spear. PeNZ

They carried a shadow in the soul's place. In the Darkness of the Other. Clara Silva. TANSG, *tr. by* Celeste Kostopulos-Cooperman

They carried her above us. As we walked. Dream of Christopher Columbus, The. Juan Felipe Herrera. TouFir

They carry their long, heavy bosoms inside old sweaters and wear examples. Thrift Shop Ladies. Jennifer M. Pierson. ReTh

They Cast Their Nets in Galilee. William Alexander Percy. AH

They changed her name. Nechama. Shirley Kaufman. LCAP-2

They choke cities like snowstorms. Blonde White Women. Patricia Smith. GT; UnSA

They choose paths. Let Them Choose Paths. Odia Ofeimun. HBAPE

They circle in a dome over Nebraska. (LL) Sunset from Omaha Hotel Window. Carl Sandburg. APT-1; AiP

They circle their rose on my rose tree. (LL) Women and Roses. Robert Browning. NAEL-5v2; NAEL-6v2

They Clapped. Nikki Giovanni. WPOW

They climbed on sketchy ladders towards God. Cathedral Builders. John Ormond. NoP-4; PeECV; TCAWP

They cling to their long-standing fallacies. (LL) Limerick: "Young things who frequent picture-palaces, The." Philip Heseltine. NOBL; PeLi

They Closed Her Eyes. Gustavo Adolfo Bécquer. SpanPo, *tr. by* Muriel Kittel

They Closed Her Eyes. Gustavo Adolfo Bécquer. AWP, *tr. by* John Masefield

They come and are pressed. People of Olives. Nidaa Khoury. DTA, *tr. by* Karen Alkalay-Gut

They come as a boon and a blessing to men. Waverly Pen, The. *Unknown.* OBCoV

They come as couriers of Heaven: their feet. Three Elements, The. Madison Cawein. APN-2

They come back now, those nights my friend and I. Hitting Golfballs off the Bluff. Jeffrey Harrison. MoASP

They come, beset by riddling hail. Thomas Hardy. FaBoWar *Fr.* Dynasts, The.

They come down on their snowmobiles for the last time. End of Human Reign on Bashan Hill, The. Bernadette Mayer. FTOS

They Come Humming. Sharon Chmielarz. MiVo

They come in off the sea peaceable masters. Constable's Clouds for Keats. Stanley Plumly. BodElec

They come in white livery bringing the sun. Robed Heart, The. Elizabeth Spires. ExTi

They come into this room while the quail are crying to huddle up. Reading the Books Our Children Have Written. Dave Jeddie Smith. HCAP

They come like the ghosts of horses, shyly. Pit Ponies, The. Leslie Norris. ChAP

They come, they come, with fife and drum. Palace, The. Charles Stuart Calverley. EBVV

They come to resemble Buddhas. Hamburger. August Kleinzahler. PmAP

They come to you with their descriptions of your soul. Adrienne Rich. HCAP *Fr.* Shooting Script.

They continue. The trains keep on passing. Trains, The. Sarina Helfgott. MirDau, *tr. by* Celeste Kostopulos-Cooperman

They could be reservoirs for water. Angelo Lumelli. ItPo, *tr. by* Gayle Ridinger

They Couldn't Compare to You. Cole Porter. ReLy

They couldn't understand why the drover cried. Drover's Boy, The. Ted Egan. NOBAu

They cross from Glasgow to a black city. Settlers. Tom Paulin. PNI

They cross the frontier as their names cross your pages. New Emigration, The. Kay Boyle. WPE

They cross the yard. Louise Glück. FaBoWP; NALW *Fr.* Dedication to Hunger.

They crucified my Lord, an' He never said a mumbalin' word [*or* / And He never said a mumbaling word]. Crucifixion. *Unknown.* BPo; TAP

They cut off his left arm / and his right arm. National Hero, The. Gojko Djogo. AF, *tr. by* Michael March

They'd eaten every one. (LL) Lewis Carroll. CABP; ChAP; ITBLP; NAEL-5v2; NAEL-6v2; NOBL; NOBVV; NoAM; OBSP; OTCP; OxAEP-2; PeLV; PoRA; TFi *Fr.* Through the Looking-Glass.

They'd latch the screendoors. Sunday Afternoons. Herbert Asquith. NAAAL

They dance the world as. John Cage. APSN *Fr.* Diary: How to Improve the World (You Will Only Make Matters Worse).

They danced by the light of the moon. (LL) Owl and the Pussy-Cat, The. Edward Lear. BRP; CABP; FaBoCh; GTBS-P; NBLV; NOBE; NOxBChV; NPeEn; NTCP; NoP-4; OBCoV; OBSP; OTCP; OWoS; OxBoLi; PeLV; PoRA; TFi; TLR; TTTS; TriCat; WoPoe

They decide to exchange heads. Kinky. Denise Duhamel. AmPoNex

They demanded in loud voices. Rollcall of Bones, The. César Vallejo. AF, *tr. by* Robert Bly

They descended into hell after injustice. Miners. Branko Miljkovic. WoPoe, *tr. by* Charles Simic

They destroyed the famous and wealthy. Ibycus. STV, *tr. by* Diane Rayor

They did not come to claim you back. Helen Todd: My Birthname. Sandra McPherson. LCAP-2; LoL

They did not know. Dawn Dissolves the Monsters. Paul Éluard. AF, *tr. by* Lloyd Alexander

They did not know this face. Job. Elizabeth Sewell. ChIV-1

They did the deed of darkness. You and I Saw Hawks Exchanging the Prey. James Wright (1927–80). NAAL-2v2; NoAM

They did their thing so well. Their Thing. Léon Damas. NegPo, *tr. by* Ellen Conroy Kennedy

They Didn't Get Me. Alma Villanueva. UnSA

They didn't get me. They Didn't Get Me. Alma Villanueva. UnSA

They Didn't Hire Him. Gary Snyder. LCAP-2 *Fr.* Hitch Haiku.

They died, these two. These Two. Harriet Monroe. IllVoic

They dither softly at her bedroom door. Cover Her Face. Thomas Kinsella. CIP-2

They do it with knives. Alistair Paterson. PeNZ *Fr.* Toledo Room, The.

They do me wrong who say I come no more. Opportunity. Walter Malone. PWR

They Do Not Go Gentle. Basil T. Paquet. CDa

They do not live in the world. Animals, The. Edwin Muir. CRP; ChIV-1; EBEV; HeIP-4; MoBrPo

They do not sleep nights. Legend of the Albino Farm. Erin Belieu. NeAmPo

They do not talk of Myrddin on the bridge at Beddgelert. Dinas Emrys. Brian Morris. AngWePo

They do not think whom they souse with spray. (LL) Walt Whitman. CAGL; ColAP; HAP; NoP-4; SAmP *Fr.* Song of Myself.

They do those things so well in France. (LL) Dorothy Parker. APT-1; NALW *Fr.* Pig's-Eye View of Literature, A.

They do zay that a travellen chap. Leane, The. William Barnes. EBVV

They dogged him all one afternoon. On the Way to the Mission. Duncan Campbell Scott. NOBC

They don't build houses like that any more. Verandahs. Robert Francis Brissenden. CBAP; NOBAu

They don't give him a single cent. (LL) Song of Selling Flowers. Tsung Ch'en. CoBLCP; ColAnChi, *tr. by* Jonathan Chaves

They don't have to have that. They Don't Have to Have That Look. David Rattray. WoPoe

They Don't Have to Have That Look. David Rattray. WoPoe

They don't like strangers. Stoney Ridge Dance Hall. Alden Nowlan. MoCV

They don't live long. Basho. EH, *tr. by* Robert Hass

They don't notice. Issa. EH, *tr. by* Robert Hass

They Don't Speak English in Paris. Ogden Nash. OBAL

They Don't Understand a Thing. Vladimir Vladimirovich Mayakovsky [*or* Maiakovskii]. TCRP, *tr. by* Bernard Meares

They don't want to stop. They can't stop. Demographics. Catherine Bowman. ExTi

They done took Cordelia. Stony Lonesome. Langston Hughes. NOBA; SAmP

They dragged you from [the] homeland. Strong Men. Sterling Allen Brown. BPo; TTY

They drank. They ate. They smoked. Igor Khomin. TCRusP, *tr. by* Daniel Weissbort

"They Dream Only of America." John Ashbery. SPE

They drive me mad, those rosy lips, forever prattling. (*fl.* 1st cent. B.C. *or* A.D. 1st cent.) Dioscorides. HePo *Fr.* Epigrams.

They drove to Grado in a borrowed car. Wedding Day, The. V. Penelope Pelizzon. AmPoNex

They drove to the Market with ringing pockets. Hamnavoe Market. George Mackay Brown. EmeKit; NePenScot

They drove us out. Exodus. Horst Bienek. AF

They eat beans mostly, this old yellow pair. Bean Eaters, The. Gwendolyn Brooks. AmFaPo; BlSi; ESEAA; HAP; HHAm; HeIP-4; LCAP-2; NALW; PoE; TAP; TRP; TTY; WeW-3

They eat only metal oatmeal and go barefoot in the spring muds. Their women are. Pontoon. Kit Robinson. FTOS

They Eat Out. Margaret Atwood. NoAM

They end their flight. Buson. EH, *tr. by* Robert Hass

They ended parle, and both addressed for fight. John Milton. OBWP *Fr.* Paradise Lost.

They enter without calling by the false door. Burdens. Laura Riesco. TANSG, *tr. by* Shaun Griffin and Emma Sepúlveda-Pulvirenti

They err who think it glorious to subdue. John Milton. FaBoWar *Fr.* Paradise Regained [*or* Regain'd].

They expanded. McDonald's, New Hartford, NY. Valerie Worth. AiP

They exterminate poets. Bulat Shalvovich Okudzhava. TCRP

They fastened a people to merchant ships. Edouard Glissant. NegPo *Fr.* Indies, The.

They fed the bonfire chips, chair legs. Butane, Kerosene, Gasoline. Ann Townsend. NAPBL

They feed on shadows. Wall of Tomorrow, The. Orkhan Muyassar. MAP, *tr. by* Samuel Hazo and Lena Jayyusi

They feed they Lion and he comes. (LL) They Feed They Lion. Philip Levine. LCAP-2; NNaP; NOBA; NoAM; NoP-4; VCAP

They fell asleep but not for long, for soon. Callimachus. HePo *Fr.* Hecale.

They felt how far beyond the scope. Herman Melville. TCAPo *Fr.* Clarel: A Poem and Pilgrimage in the Holy Land.

They fle from me that sometyme did me seke. Sir Thomas Wyatt. *See* Lover Showeth How He Is Forsaken of Such as He Sometime Enjoyed, The

They Flee From Me. Sir Thomas Wyatt. *See also* Lover Showeth How He Is Forsaken of Such as He Sometime Enjoyed, The

They Flee from Me That Sometime Did Me Seek. Gavin Ewart. OxBC

They fle[e] from me that sometime [*or* sometyme] did me se[e]k[e]. Lover Showeth How He Is Forsaken of Such as He Sometime Enjoyed, The. Sir Thomas Wyatt. ClHu; EnLoPo; HAP; HeIP-4; InPK-6; MakPoe; NAEL-5v1; NPeEn; NoSic; OxBC; OxBEV; PoE; PoRA; SCGP; SCV; TFi; TRP

They flung many quinces toward the chariot. Stesichoros. SaLy, *tr. by* Diane Rayor

They fluttered off like withered souls of men. (LL) Pity of the Leaves, The. Edwin Arlington Robinson. APN-2; MoAmPo

They fold me up into myself. Twilight (Between Dog and Wolf). Olga Orozco. SurWo, *tr. by* Natalie Kenvin

They fought south of the Castle. Fighting South of the Castle. *Unknown.* AWP, *tr. by* Arthur Waley

They fought south of the ramparts. Fighting South of the Ramparts. *Unknown.* ChiP, *tr. by* Arthur Waley

They Fought South of the Wall. *Unknown.* CoBCP; ColAnChi, *tr. by* Burton Watson

They Fought South of the Walls. Li Po. SuSp, *tr. by* Joseph J. Lee

They Fought South of the Walls. *Unknown.* SuSp, *tr. by* Hans H. Frankel
(They Fought South of the Wall.) CoBCP, *tr. by* Burton Watson

They found her unresponsive in the street. Rafael Campo. AmPoNex; WiU *Fr.* Ten Patients, and Another.

They found him in the fields and called him back to music. Bunk Johnson Blowing. Muriel Rukeyser. SeSe

They Found Him Sitting in a Chair. Horace Gregory. MoAmPo

They fuck you up, your mum and dad. This Be The Verse. Philip Larkin. NPeEn; NoAM; PoPoPo; PoetW

They gamble on you. Greyhound, The. Saleem Barakat. MAP, *tr. by* Lena Jayyusi and Naomi Shihab Nye

They gave him a finger, but he took the whole hand. King Saul and I. Yehuda Amichai [*or* Amikhai]. PoSu, *tr. by* Assia Gutmann

They Gave Him Vinegar and Gall (Matt. 27) and Wine Mingled with Myrrh (Mark 15). Francis Quarles. NOSC

They gave it back to me / life. Black Man's Lament, The. Léon Damas. NegPo, *tr. by* Ellen Conroy Kennedy

They gave its splendor to our fall. (LL) Sumach Leaves, The. Jones Very. ColAP; NOBA

They gave me a coat and helmet. Soldier's Ditty, A. Bulat Shalvovich Okudzhava. TCRP, *tr. by* Deming Brown

They gave me in my kindergarten year. Now or Never. Judith Moffett. Son

They gave us the mysterious deep warehouse. Ajax Samples, The. Laura Jensen. LCAP-2

They give a man a taste for death. (LL) A. E. Housman. FaBoEE; NOBVV; OBSV; OxBEV

They give Jacky rights. Mudrooroo Narogin. IBA

They go at it in the backseat of our car. We Take the New Young Couple Out to Dinner. Carol Tufts. PasH

They go by, go by, love, the days and the hours. Teresa de Jesús. WPOW, *tr. by* Maria A. Proser, James Scully and Arlene Scully

They grew in beauty, side by side. Graves of a Household, The. Felicia Dorothea Hemans. NOBRP; RWP; TreFP; WPE

They grow on the sides of the mountain. In Wild Iris Time. Jerry Martien. GeoHom

They grow over the Yangtze, the plum rains. Nisei: Second Generation Japanese-American. James Masao Mitsui. GifTon; OpBo

They had a happy childhood on the banks of the Hudson. Room 5600. Ernesto Cardenal. CLPP, *tr. by* Jonathan Cohen

They had a verb. I Held the Vein, But Death. Dennis Phillips. FTOS

They had begun to whisper. Move. Lucille Clifton. MakPoe; NAAAL

They had come to see the salmon lunging and leaping. Excursion of the Speech and Hearing Class, The. David Wagoner. VCAP

They had crew cuts then, puffed cheeks like kids. Blues for Zoot. Sascha Feinstein. AmPoNex

They had dragged for hours. These Trees Are No Forest of Mourners. Douglas G. Jones. NOBC

They had faces open to whoever passed. Penniless Lovers. Eugenio de Andrade. VCWP, *tr. by* Alexis Levitin

They had made love early in the high bed. Honeycomb, The. Pauline Stainer. NeBl

They had me laid out in a white. April Fools' Day. Yusef Komunyakaa. GT

They had never had one in the house before. Bronzeville Woman in a Red Hat. Gwendolyn Brooks. NALW

They had no other duties. (LL) Epigram: "Within this mindless vault." James Vincent Cunningham. RB; VGW; WoPoe

They had questioned him for hours. Campaign. Ciaran Carson. BiHa; CIP-2; PNI

They had secured their beauty to the dock. Crowd, The. John Masefield. OxBTC

They had stolen my soul away! (LL) Romance. Walter James Turner. MoBrPo; NOBAu; NOBE; NOxBChV; OBMV; PoRA

They had supposed their formula was fixed. White Troops Had Their Orders but the Negroes Looked Like Men. Gwendolyn Brooks. NAAL-5

They hail you as their morning star. Men. Dorothy Parker. APT-1

They Hanged Him, I Said Dismissively. Dennis Brutus. VCWP

They have a little Odor—that to me. Emily Dickinson. TCAPo

They have been driven insane by history. Loyalty. Harvey Shapiro. TaR

They have been gone so long now, your. Mama. Rohan B. Preston. AmPoNex

They have breasts shaped. When I Look at Wifredo Lam's Paintings. Jayne Cortez. SurWo

They have broken every one. (LL) Gone, Gone Again. Edward Thomas. OxAEP-2; PeFWW; PoWW

They have carried the mahogany chair and the cane rocker. Mourning Picture. Adrienne Rich. CoAP

They have chiseled on my stone the words. Edgar Lee Masters. OxBA *Fr.* Spoon River Anthology.

They have closed the prison where they had you. Ringing Words. Mary Kinzie. FFC

They have coarse features, their hands are deft and accustomed to a hammer and nails, to wood and iron. Passion of Our Lord painted by an anonymous hand from the Circle of Rhenish Masters, The. Zbigniew Herbert. GI, *tr. by* Adam Czerniawski

They have crucified their Lord afresh. *Unknown.* MLL *Fr.* Carmina Burana.

They have emptied the heart of Westport. Westport House, Portrush. James Simmons. PBCIP

They have felled him to the ground. Leader, The. J. P. Clark Bekedermo. PBMAP

They have given the orchard back to itself again. Deserted Orchard. Frances Mary Frost. YaYoPo

They have gone / into the green hill, by doors without hinges. Apples. Donald Hall. LCAP-2

They have left bread on the table. Bread. Gabriela Mistral. WPOW, *tr. by* Allan Francovich and Kathleen Weaver

They have lived in each other so long. Demolition, The. Anne Stevenson. OxBSP

They have no graves as yet. (LL) Elegy in a Country Churchyard. Gilbert Keith Chesterton. FaBoWar; MoBrPo; OBWP; OxBSP

They have no word for conscience. Carrier Indians. Ken Belford. NOBC

They have not sown, and feed on bitter fruit. (LL) Black Man Talks of Reaping, A. Arna Bontemps. APT-2; BPo; ColAP; NAAAL; SSLK

They have [*or* They've *or* Th' have] left Thee naked, Lord, O[h] that they had! Upon the Body of Our Blessed Lord, Naked and Bloody. Richard Crashaw. NOSC; PAI

They have put my bed beside the unpainted screen. Last Poem. Po Chü-i. ChiP, *tr. by* Arthur Waley

They have sed. Hospital/Poem. Sonia Sanchez. BPo

They have taken the gable from the roof of clay. Swedes. Edward Thomas. HarvBoo; RB

They have the corner. Women, The. Joseph Ceravolo. FTOS

They have the faces of / no-one. (LL) Animals in That Country, The. Margaret Atwood. NALW; NoAM

They have turned, and say that I am dying. That. I Substitute for the Dead Lecturer. Imamu Amiri Baraka. PoE

They Have Turned the Church Where I Ate God. Gary Gildner. PBCAP

They Have Weighed. Joyce Mansour. SurPaPo, *tr. by* Mary Ann Caws

They have weighed man whitened with chalk. They Have Weighed. Joyce Mansour. SurPaPo, *tr. by* Mary Ann Caws

They have yarns / Of a skyscraper so tall they had to put hinges. Carl Sandburg. MoAmPo *Fr.* People, Yes, The.

They hear and see, and sigh, and then they break. (LL) Lowest Trees Have Tops, The. Sir Edward Dyer. NoSic; OxBSP; RB

They hear Thee not, O God! nor see. Ezekiel. John Greenleaf Whittier. ChIV-1

They heard the south wind sighing. Crocuses, The. Frances Ellen Watkins Harper. BlSi

They heated hatchet blades over gas fires in roadside workshops and. While the Record Plays. Gyula Illyés. PFTM-1

They heaved the stone; they heaped the cairn. Aideen's Grave. Sir Samuel Ferguson. NOIV

They hire you for the silk to line their budgets. Advice from Euterpe. Carter Revard. VoR

They hold their hands over their mouths. Poets Agree to Be Quiet by the Swamp, The. David Wagoner. CoAP; VGW

They hunt chameleon worlds with cameras. Adina. Harold Milton Telemaque. TTY

They Hunt the Night. Kofi Anyidoho. NAfrP

They hunt, the velvet tigers in the jungle. India. Walter James Turner. MoBrPo

They hurry through the forest suitcases in hand. Six Small Fires. Paul Jenkins. OPRER

They in the sea being burnt, they in the burnt ship drowned [*or* drown'd]. (LL) Burnt Ship, A. John Donne. EBVV; FaBoWar; InPK-6; OBWP

They journeyed, / When the darkness of night. Ode. Ibn al-Arabi. AWP, *tr. by* R. A. Nicholson

They just elected me Pope. Poems of the Pope, The. Nicanor Parra. VCWP, *tr. by* Edith Grossman

They Killed Our Longing for Our Homeland. Ernst Waldinger. AuPH, *tr. by* Lowell A. Bangerter

They killed the lad. They Killed the Lad. Robert Ivanovich Rozhdestvensky [*or* Rozhdestvenskii]. TCRusP, *tr. by* Daniel Weissbort

They kneel on the slanting floor. Foot-Washing, The. George Ella Lyon. OxWW

They knew that they were naked, and ashamed. Serpent, The. Jones Very. NCAP

They knew you once, O beautiful and wise. (LL) Conrad Potter Aiken. AWP; NOBA; OxBA; PoRA *Fr.* Discordants.

They Know. Tawfiq Zayyad. MAP, *tr. by* Charles Doria and Sharif Elmusa

They know how to live. They and I. Xavier Villaurrutia. CAGL, *tr. by* Fanny Arango-Ramos and William Keeth

They know me not, but mourn with me. (LL) Tennyson. EBVV; NAEL-6v2 *Fr.* In Memoriam A. H. H.

They know us by our lips. They know the proverb. Cups. Gwen Harwood. EmeKit; HarvBoo

They laid this stone trap. Empty Church, The. Ronald Stuart Thomas. AngWePo; EmeKit

They laugh at me hey farm boy. *Unknown.* ColAnChi, *tr. by* Red Pine

They laughed at one I loved. Innocence. Patrick Kavanagh. ModIr; RB

They lay down by the fire and stretched. Two. Mikhail Arkadyevich [*or* Arkad'evich] Svetlov. TCRP, *tr. by* Daniel Weissbort

They Lay Dying Side by Side. Anna Swirszczynska. PoSu

They lean against the cooling car, backs pressed. Discovery of the Pacific, The. Thom Gunn. HeIP-4

They lean over the path. Orchids. Theodore Roethke. ColAP; HarvBoo; TRP

They learned to turn off the gravity in an auditorium. Childhood Stories. Matthew Rohrer. NAPBL

They leave us—artists, singers, all. When London Calls. Victor James Daley. CBAP

They leave us so to the way we took. In Neglect. Robert Frost. OxBSP; VGW

They left the primrose glistening in its dew. Spring, and the Blind Children. Alfred Noyes. OxBTC

They left their Babylon bare. Destruction of Jerusalem by the Babylonian Hordes, The. Isaac Rosenberg. PeFWW

They licked the platter clean. (LL) Mother Goose. LB; OxNR; ReMoGo

They lie at rest, our blessed dead. Christina Georgina Rossetti. NOBVV

They lie in the Sunday street. Dead, The. Cecil Day Lewis. TwCP

They lie, the men who tell for reasons of their own. Faces in the Street. Henry Lawson. PNI

They lift their skirts like blinds across your eyes. (LL) In Memoriam. Michael Longley. ModIr; PNI

They like to come here. Pleasant sidestreets pave. Visitors, The. Richard Moore. DiPo

They live by the Lakes, an appropriate quarter. On the Lake Poets. Charles Townsend. FaBoEE

They lived out in a women's house. Stephanie Markman. BrRo *Fr.* Rime of the Ancient Feminist, The.

They lived with him, in the same old world. And they're good men, too. (LL) Obituary. Kenneth Fearing. IllVoic; VGW

They'll Carry—Him! (LL) I Can Wade Grief. Emily Dickinson. APN-2; ColAP; HeIP-4; NOBA

They'll not exterminate you now. Georgy [*or* Georgii] Vladimirovich Ivanov. TCRP

They'll soon be flying to Mars, I hear. Progress. Samuel Hoffenstein. OBCoV

They locked us out without a cause—. Glorious Strike of the Builders, The. *Unknown.* FaBoVE

They look at each other dully. Vasco [*or* Vasko] Popa. PoSu, *tr. by* Anne Pennington *Fr.* Quartz Pebble, The.

They look like big dogs badly drawn, drawn wrong. Wolves in the Zoo. Howard Nemerov. NoAM

They look / like newlyweds. Ōshima Ryōta. TTTS

They looked at me all ghosts. Mellisandra. Harriet Rose. BrRo

They looked so good. Young Fenians, The. Padraic Fallon. BIrV

They love me not, who at my table eat. Harvest, The. Jones Very. SacPr

They lured me out of the barracks. Real Chocolate. Stewart Florsheim. GotH

They made impudent inspection of our coast. Rex Ingamells. CBAP *Fr.* Great South Land, The.

They made me a director. Director, The. Edmund George Valpy Knox. OBCoV

They Made Me Erect and Lone. Henry David Thoreau. OxBSP

They made the chamber sweet with flowers and leaves. Pause, A. Christina Georgina Rossetti. VWP

They made the good king pass. King Tut in America. Kwadwo Opoku-Agyemang. NAfrP

They made their grim, sad faces and went out. Death of the Polar Explorers. Gabriel Gbadamosi. HBAPE

They make in the twining tide the motions of birds. Bathers, The. W. S. Merwin. PoE

They make it sound easy: some disjointed. Fradel Schtok. Irena Klepfisz. TaR

They make love in his first language. Las Flores para una Niña Negra. Demetrice A. Worley. SpirFl

They married us when they put. Drafted. Su Wu. OHMPC, *tr. by* Kenneth Rexroth

They may carve monuments yet lack all understanding. (LL) Needle and

Thread. Pan Chao. WPOW; WoPoe, tr. by Richard Mather and Rob Swigart

They may tell you the god is broken. Osiris. Jane Hirshfield. BodElec

They measured you like a cup of meal. This much. Blood Ties. Thelma Seto. TWW

They meet but with unwholesome Springs. William Habington. BeJo Fr. Castara.

They met at the Tagansky subway station. Igor Khomin. TCRusP, tr. by Daniel Weissbort

They met them somewhere at the Polish border. Black Music. Yevgeny [or Evgenii] Borisovich Rein. TCRP, tr. by Lubov Yakovleva

They might not need me—yet they might. Emily Dickinson. PoToHe; Spl

They mock you, my country. To My Country. Ivan Alekseievich Bunin. TCRP, tr. by Simon Franklin

They mount the lonely street. (LL) Lonely Street, The. William Carlos Williams. APT-1; TwCP

They moved like rivers in their mended stockings. Grandmothers, The. Mary Oliver. WPE

They must be shown as about to taste of the tree. Adam and Eve. Charles Hubert Sisson. FaBoTw

They must have buried him away from the lake. Idols. Witter Bynner. APT-1

They must have died like this at Auschwitz. IRT at Rush Hour, The. Christopher Millis. GotH

They must have known that we escaped—if only. Double Crossing. Eva Salzman. MFPA

They must to keep their certainty accuse. Leaders of the Crowd, The. W. B. Yeats. EBEV; MoBrPo; OxAEP-2

They mutilate they torment each other. Voice, A. Tadeusz Rózewicz. BLT, tr. by Czeslaw Milosz

They named it Aultgraat—Ugly Burn. Black Rock of Kiltearn. Andrew Young. FaBoTw; RB

They nearly made it. Bleaklow. Pauline Stainer. NeBl

They never came back to me! (LL) Calico Pie. Edward Lear. FaBoCh; NOxBChV

They never come back, though I loved them well. Ballad of the Bird-Bride. Rosamund Marriott Watson. VWP; ViWPN

They Never Grew Old. Judith Ortiz Cofer. PueRic

They never left / the walled garden of their arms. Waltz Poem of Those in Love and Inseparable Forever. Miguel Hernández. AF, tr. by Timothy Baland

They never read their Hedylos, nor could. Renaissance Drunk, A. George Evans. PmAP

They nicknamed me Mririda. Mririda. Mririda n'Ait Attik. WPOW, tr. by René Euloge, Daniel Halpern and Paula Paley

They nod at me and I at stems. Open. Larry Eigner. NeAP

They only find a medicine for the itch. (LL) No Platonic [or Platonique] Love. William Cartwright. BeJo; NOSC

They operate from pleasure. Juncos. William Stafford. OWoS

They opn our mail petulantly. Th Wundrfulness uv th Mountees Our Secret Police. Bill Bissett. NOBC

They owned their passiveness. (LL) Subalterns, The. Thomas Hardy. MoBrPo; NOBVV; NoAM; PAI

They paper the walls of their world. Recluses, The. Stuart Z. Perkoff. NeAP

They part at the edge of substance. Stele (1–2 c. B.C.). Denise Levertov. BodElec

They parted aff careerin / Fu'blythe that night. (LL) Halloween. Robert Burns. NOBRP; TreFP

They pass by in trains. Shadows. Joy Williams. IBA

They pass like a warning of snow. Insects, The. Nancy Willard. LCAP-2

They pass me by like shadows, crowds on crowds. Street, The. James Russell Lowell. GSo; Son

They pity me. / "Look at him, see." Lonely. André Spire. AWP; TrJP, tr. by Jethro Bithell

They played with the pebble. Vasco [or Vasko] Popa. PoSu, tr. by Anne Pennington Fr. Quartz Pebble, The.

They pointed me out on the highway, and they said. Traveller, The. John Berryman. GM; VGW

They possessed nothing. Inheritors, The. Gary Geddes. NOBC

"They pray for children? Let them!" cried Polyxo. Antipater of Thessalonica. GrAn

They Pray the Best Who Pray and Watch. Edward Hopper. AH

They preen beside puddles. Guide to Urban Birds, A. David B. Axelrod. UrbNat

They pull off his ears. Decomposition with Laughter. Homero [or Umberto] Aridjis. TCLAP, tr. by Jerome Rothenberg

They pushed him straight against the wall. At Sunrise. Rosa Zagnoni Marinoni. PoToHe

They put Us far apart. Emily Dickinson. APN-2

They quite forgot their quarrel. (LL) Mother Goose. LB; NOBL; OxNR; PeLV; ReMoGo

They're a curious lot, Manet's scandalous. Luncheon on the Grass. Carl Phillips. AmFaPo

They're afraid of me. For Medgar Evers. David Ignatow. LTA

They're all gone away. (LL) Polly and Sukey. Mother Goose. LB; OxNR; ReMoGo

They're almost gone. Misconstrued, The. Bruce Berger. GeoH

They're altogether otherworldly now. Grandparents. Robert Lowell. ColAP

They're at it again. Storm. Roger McGough. OTCP

They're bringing them home, now, too late, too early. (LL) Homecoming. Bruce Dawe. BMAP; CBAP; EmeKit

They're Either Too Young or Too Old. Arthur Schwartz. ReLy

They're insignificant when not in use. Stick and Hat. King Lê Thánh–tông. WoPoe, tr. by John S. Major

They're marked men. Their park is like an open prison. Kevin Crossley-Holland. NewEx

They're more beautiful than the angels of heaven. Lennox Island. David McFadden. NOBC

They're nice—one would never dream of going over. Healthy Spot, A. W. H. Auden. AiP

They're only bones the whiteman say. Crowther—Ours. Dyan Newson. IBA

They're only boys / who used to frolic and play. Song of Becoming. Fadwa Tuqan [or Tuquan]. AF, tr. by Naomi Shihab Nye

They're out of sorts in Sunderland. There Are Bad Times Just around the Corner. Noël Coward. NOBL

They're putting Man-Fix on my hair. Wanting Out. Gavin Ewart. SPE

They're richer who diminish their desires. Truly Rich, The. T. Urchard. PWR

They're taking down a tree at the front door. Learning by Doing. Howard Nemerov. HAP; TwCP; WeW-3

They're Tearing Up the Old Graveyard. Kobena Eyi Acquah. NAfrP

They're tearing up the old graveyard. They're Tearing Up the Old Graveyard. Kobena Eyi Acquah. NAfrP

They're the dead ends. You and the Tijuana Mule. Rigoberto González. GeoHom

They're throwing a party upstairs. Party, The. Donald Finkel. OPRER

They're used to carrying it in fine milled gold. Manuscript. Angelina Muñiz Huberman. MirDau, tr. by Aurora Camacho

They're waiting to be murdered. Old Couple. Charles Simic. HCAP; PoPoPo

They're with O'Leary in the grave. (LL) September 1913. W. B. Yeats. GTBS-P; HAP; HarvBoo; NAEL-5v2; NAEL-6v2; NoAM; PoRA

They Receive Instructions Against Chile. Pablo Neruda. AF

They received from on high the divine voice. Cabalists, The. Angelina Muñiz Huberman. MirDau, tr. by Aurora Camacho

They rendezvous each night, at ten. Love Birds. Paul Henry. TCAWP

They Return. Jay Macpherson. NOBC Fr. Way Down, The.

They rise, they walk again. (LL) Heaven of Animals, The. James Dickey. CoAP; ColAP; EmeKit; HeIP-4; NAAL-2v2; NOBA; NoAM; PoE; TAP; TRP; VCAP; WoPoe

They roar / Out of the river tunnels. Rumble, A. Virginia Schonborg. SSCS

They rode north. Blackie Thinks of His Brothers. Stanley Crouch. GT

They rode upon. Ride upon the Death Chariot. Mbuyiseni Oswald Mtshali. PBMAP

They rose up in a twinkling cloud. Stockdoves, The. Andrew Young. NePenScot

They roused him with muffins—they roused him with ice. Lewis Carroll. EBEV; NAEL-5v2; NAEL-6v2; OxAEP-2 Fr. Hunting of the Snark, The.

They rush from Beds with giddy heads. Michael Wigglesworth. TCAPo Fr. Day of Doom, The.

They sadly travelled thus, until they came. Edmund Spenser. EBNV Fr. Faerie Queene, The.

They Said. Lucy Larcom. TCAPo

They said a while ago that the fuzz were coming to take us away. Moment of Truth. Rowley Habib. PeNZ

They said I had to have it. It was an instrument. Will Campbell Displays His Craniotribe. H. J. Van Peenen. BloBone

They said the moon wasn't going to rise no no. August 18. Joanne Kyger. PoM

They said the war was over. Discreet Prayer, A. Dionisio D. Martinez. TouFir

They said there was a woman in the hills. Women Are Not Gentlemen. Harley Matthews. NOBAu

They said to my grandmother: "Please do not be bitter." Bitter Fruit of the Tree. Sterling Allen Brown. NoP-4

They said, "Wait." Well, I waited. Alabama Centennial. Naomi Long Madgett. BPo

They said we were nowhere. Chanson d'Outre Tombe. Philip Whalen. BB

They said, "You are no longer a lad." Battle Won Is Lost. Phillip [or "Phil"] William George. HHAm

They sat down one in front of the other. Genesis (Chapter 7, Verse 5). Manuela Fingueret. MirDau, tr. by Roberta Gordenstein

They sat in even rows. Miss Clement's Second Grade. Maryfrances Cusumano Wagner. UnSA

They saw the young girls twisting their strings, Goulburn Island. Unknown. NOBAu Fr. Goulburn Island Song Cycle.

They saw their mamas put one foot out. Little Girls Posing All Dressed Up. Clarence Major. BodElec

They saw you behind your muzzle much more clearly. To a Farmer Who Hung Five Hawks on His Barbed Wire. David Wagoner. NoAM

They say a child with two mouths is no good. Pantoun for Chinese Women. Shirley Lim. FSt

They say a maiden conceived. Christmas Carols. Patricia Beer. OxBC

They say a man dies. Steve Crow. HATNAP Fr. Songs.

They say a wife and husband, bit by bit. Bridge instead of a Wall, A. Unknown. PoToHe

They say: but cattle near. Christmas. John Frederick Nims. ChrPo

They say dogs killed you. No, Euripides. Adaios of Macedon. GrAn

They say, God wot! On the Death of the Giraffe. Thomas Hood. FaBoEE

They say "he need (present) enemy (plural)" Transformations. Jack Spicer. FTOS

They say I am excitable! How could. King of Owls, The. Louise Erdrich. NoAM

They say I am harsh and haughty. Uncle Sam's Soliloquy. George Sands Johnson. PWR

They say I am robbing myself. Garden of Friendship, The. Frances Sargent Osgood. PoBW

They say I'm a beast. Loose Women. Sandra Cisneros. IllVoic

They say I should feed you. Survivor. Barbara Goldberg. GotH

They say Ideal beauty cannot enter. Hiram Powers' "Greek Slave." Elizabeth Barrett Browning. GS; NALW; ViWPN

They say in my village. Coda. Shafiq Al-Kamali. MAP, tr. by Sargon Boulus and Christopher Middleton

They say, in other days. John Gray. NOBVV

They say, interpret it your own way, Christ is born. (LL) Eclogue for Christmas, An. Louis MacNeice. FaBoMo; NoAM; OBMV

They say into your early life romance came. Sophisticated Lady. Mitchell Parish. ReLy

They say it is waiting for more, the snow. Snow Signs. Charles Tomlinson. NoAM

They say it is you. Conversations with Dr. M. Rachel Loden. GotH

They say it's the iron in the blood that resists transformation. Cannibal Women in the Avocado Jungle of Death. Maureen Seaton. ExTi

They Say It's Wonderful. Irving Berlin. ReLy

They say, little beast, little creator, the elders say. First Prayer for the Hottentotsgod. Breyten Breytenbach. AF, tr. by Denis Hirson

They say my love is going far away. Stone Castle Music. Unknown. CoBCP, tr. by Burton Watson

They Say My Verse Is Sad: No Wonder. A. E. Housman. NoAM; PAI

They Say She Is Lovely. Lőrinc Szabó. IQMS, tr. by Suzanne K. Walther

They Say She Is Veiled. Judy Grahn. HW

They say that an accident. For the Death of a Monk. Muso Soseki. EaWin, tr. by W. S. Merwin

They say that black people. They Say That Black People. . . . Patricia Smith. GT

They say that Byron, though lame. Anacreontic. Austin Clarke. NOIV

They say that every idle word. Idle Words. Walter Savage Landor. OBSV

They say that God lives very high. Child's Thought of God, A. Elizabeth Barrett Browning. InvLi

They say that Hope is happiness. Stanzas for Music. Byron. NAEL-5v2; OxBSP

They say that I was in my youth. Limerick. Unknown. PeLi

They say that in some Gower glen. Bone Prison, The. E. Howard Harries. AngWePo

They say that once it mirrored palace ladies. Well of the King of Wu, The. Kao Ch'i. CoBLCP, tr. by Jonathan Chaves

They say that once Leda found. Sappho. SaLy, tr. by Diane Rayor

They say that plants don't talk, nor do. Rosalía de Castro. BoWoP

They say that poets should keep their tongue in check. Paranoia. Leonard Nolens. TuT, tr. by Michael O'Loughlin

They say that Richard Cory owns. Richard Cory. Paul Simon. InPK-6

They Say that Shadows of Deceased Ghosts. Joshua Sylvester. Son

They Say that the Plants Do Not Speak. Rosalía de Castro. SpanPo, tr. by Kate Flores

They say that the plants do not speak, nor the brooks, nor the birds. They Say that the Plants Do Not Speak. Rosalía de Castro. SpanPo, tr. by Kate Flores

They Say That Time Assuages. Emily Dickinson. APN-2; OxBSP

They say that "Time assuages." They Say That Time Assuages. Emily Dickinson. APN-2; OxBSP

They say the experimental. Nothing. Burns Singer. OxBS

They say the first dream Adam our father had. Adam's Dream. Edwin Muir. NoP-4

They say the jackal and the mole. Love. Kahlil Gibran. GraLe

They say "the lighthouse keeper's world is round." Requiem. Sam Hunt. PeNZ

They say the lion and the lizard keep. Omar Khayyám. EBEV, tr. by Edward Fitzgerald Fr. Rubáiyát of Omar Khayyám [of Naishápúr], The.

They say the men are. Men Are Coming Back! The. Barry Cole. OxBTC

They say the peel is where you get. Skinning. Dan Quisenberry. SpudSo

They say the Phoenix is dying, some say dead. News of the Phoenix. Arthur James Marshall Smith. MoCV

They say the roads to Shu. To See a Friend Off to Shu. Li Po. ChinPo, tr. by Yip Wai-lim

They say the sea is cold, but the sea contains. Whales Weep Not! D. H. Lawrence. NoAM

They say the war is over. But water still. Redeployment. Howard Nemerov. OBWP; PoWW; TrJP

They say there is. Unknown. TAL

They Say There Is a Country. Saul [or Shaul] Tchernichowsky [or Tchernichovsky]. MHP, tr. by Ruth Finer Mintz

They say there is a hollow, safe and still. Frances Ridley Havergal. SacPr Fr. Thoughts of God, The.

They say there is a sweeter air. Carriage from Sweden, A. Marianne Craig Moore. HAP; TwCP

They Say You're Staying in a Mountain Temple. Tu Fu. CoBCP; TTTS, tr. by Burton Watson

They say. . . a drink? I don't believe I would. (LL) You Serve the Best Wines Always, My Dear Sir. Martial. InPK-6; RomPo, tr. by James Vincent Cunningham and J. V. Cunningham

They see Gods wonders that are call'd. Roger Williams. SCAP

They seem hundreds of years away. Breughel. Seamus Heaney. PNI Fr. Mossbawn.

They seem too pale for these cloud-breached days. Clothes, The. Julia Copus. NeBl

They seize the young girls of the western tribes, with their swaying. Unknown. NOBAu Fr. Goulburn Island Song Cycle.

They seized him while his friends were asleep. Last Day. Martinus Nijhoff. TuT, tr. by Desmond Egan

They sell good beer at Haslemere. West Sussex Drinking Song. Joseph Hilaire Pierre Belloc. MoBrPo

They sent him back to her. The letter came. Not to Keep. Robert Frost. OxBA

They sent me a salwar kameez. Presents from My Aunts in Pakistan. Moniza Alvi. MFPA

They sent revolving saucer eyes. Ex-Queen Among the Astronomers, The. Fleur Adcock. FaBoWP; NAEL-6v2; NALW; NoP-4

They served tea in the sandpile, together with. Party, The. Reed Whittemore. CoAP

They set out to bring Beethoven. Bringers of Beethoven, The. Reiner Kunze. PoSu, tr. by Gordon Brotherston and Gisela Brotherston

They set the fish upon the table. Pesci Misti. Leonard [or Lazarus] Aaronson. FaBoTw

They set the slave free, striking off his chains. Slave, The. James Oppenheim. TrJP

They settle out from their curfew. How Things Bear Their Telling. Ann Lauterbach. ExTi

They settled their tent pegs here. Pioneers. Lillian M. Fisher. HHAm

They shall bee upon one day. (LL) Child Waters. Unknown. ESPB; OxBB

They shall find him ware an' wakin', as they found him long ago! (LL) Drake's Drum. Sir Henry John Newbolt. FaBoCh; FaBoWar; OBMV; PoRA; UV

They Shall Know. Kofi Awoonor. VCWP

They Shall Look on Him. "Michael Field." VWP

"They shall never sound in slavery" (LL) Minstrel Boy, The. Sir Thomas More. ChAP; FaBoWar

They shall not return to us, the resolute, the young. Mesopotamia. Rudyard Kipling. HarvBoo; PoWW

They shall see Him in the crimson flush. Pure in Heart Shall See God, The. Frances Ellen Watkins Harper. PWR

They shall sink under water. Cities, The. "Æ" OBMV

They shook the green leaves down. Magic Fox. James Welch. CDW; HATNAP; NoAM

They shorten tedious nights. (LL) Now Winter Nights Enlarge. Thomas Campion. EBEV; NAEL-7v1; NPeEn; NoP-4; OxAEP-1; OxBEV; PBRV

They should have slept, would have. Lynching, The. Thylias Moss. GT

They should let it go by. (LL)   Women.   Louise Bogan.   APT-2; MoAmPo; NALW; NoAM; TwCP; VGW; WPE; WoPoe

They shout out the price of salt harvested from the salt flats.   They Shout Out the Price of Salt.   Ammuvanar.   WoPoe, tr. by George L. III Hart

They showed up for awhile and they died.   Showing.   Liam Rector.   TRP

They shut me up in Prose.   Emily Dickinson.   APN-2; FaBoVe; NALW; NCAP; NOBA; NoP-4

They shut the road through the woods.   Way Through The Woods, The.   Rudyard Kipling.   ChAP; FaBoCh; HarvBoo; NOBE; NOxBChV; NoAM; OBEV; OxAEP-2; OxBTC; SCGP; WHSW; WoPoe

They sing. (LL)   Unknown.   NAEL-5v1; NAEL-7v1

They sing their dearest songs.   During Wind and Rain.   Thomas Hardy.   GTBS-P; HAP; HarvBoo; NAEL-5v2; NAEL-6v2; NIL-7; NPeEn; NoP-4; OxBEV; OxBTC; PeVV; PoE; TFi; TOF; TRP

They sit in a glass egg.   Dead Embryos.   Judit Tóth.   WPOW, tr. by Laura Schiff

They sit in a row.   Fury of Overshoes.   Anne Sexton.   LCAP-2; NIP-4

They sit in a row.   Anne Sexton.   NIL-7   Fr. Furies, The.

They sit in the bright cafe.   Inventing My Parents.   Susan Bartels Ludvigson.   PoSol

They sit under the gumtrees.   Pension Day.   Charmaine Papertalk-Green.   IBA

They sleep, the mountain crags and gullies.   Fragment 58: Night and Sleep.   Alcman.   WoPoe, tr. by Rosanna Warren

They slew by night.   Félix Lope de Vega Carpio.   HAP; WoPoe, tr. by Geoffrey Hill   Fr. Pentecost Castle, The.

They slip on to the bus, hair piled up high.   Young Ones, The.   Elizabeth Jennings.   OxBTC

They slump in booths like rags, not even drunk. (LL)   Drug Store.   Karl Shapiro.   OxBA; TwCP

They smell of Corycian saffron, of a.   Martial.   RomPo, tr. by Peter Whigham

They sneaked into the limbo of time.   Ancestral Faces.   Kwesi Brew.   PBA

They Sometimes Call Me.   Wendy Rose.   CDW

They sought it with thimbles, they sought it with care.   Lewis Carroll.   EBNV; OxAEP-2   Fr. Hunting of the Snark, The.

They sought to put us away like.   They Hunt the Night.   Kofi Anyidoho.   NAfrP

They sound like howling wolves from here.   Song on the Way to Jail.   Kakayek.   STP, tr. by James Koller

They speak not of torment.   Flowers in the Ward.   John Shaw Neilson.   CBAP

They spent my life plotting against me.   Possessions.   Ken Smith.   SPE

They spoke of the horse alive.   Horse, The.   Philip Levine.   CoAP; VCAP

They spoke the loveliest of languages.   History of World Languages.   Dennis Joseph Enright.   OxBC

They sprint eight feet and—.   Ringed Plover by a Water's Edge.   Norman MacCaig.   NoP-4; OxBC

They stack bright pyramids of goods and gather.   Avenue.   Robert Pinsky.   TaR

They stand in the clearing of Kingfisher Flat.   High Embrace, The.   William Everson.   GeoHom

They stand like penitential Augustines.   Gothic Landscape.   Irving Layton.   TrJP

They stand there weeping in the stained daylight.   Fresco: Departure for an Imperialist War.   Thomas McGrath.   AF

They startle dreams and compound the gloom. (LL)   Composed on the Theme "Willows by the Riverside."   Yü Hsüan-chi.   SuSp; WPOW, tr. by Jan W. Walls

They still love you, Elvis. They want your hair, stories about your.   Come Back, Elvis, Come Back to Holyoke.   Mary A. Koncel.   ReTh

They still smell of incense, and their faces are burnt by their crossing / through the Great Dark Places.   Sleep of the Brave, The.   Odysseus Elytis.   AF

They stood—rain pelting at window, shrouded sea.   In the Local Museum.   Walter De la Mare.   HAP

They stood so still the leafless trees.   Spring Landscape.   Augusta Peaux.   TuT, tr. by Tony Curtis

They strike mine eyes, but not my heart. (LL)   Ben Jonson.   BeJo; HAP; NAEL-5v1; NAEL-6v1; NAEL-7v1; NIL-7; NPeEn; NoP-4; PAI; PoPoPo; TFi; WeW-3   Fr. Epicoene; or, The Silent Woman.

They stuck pigs in the throat. Might I not have done.   Work.   Gyula Illyés.   RaBo, tr. by William Jay Smith

They stumbled down their barracks steps.   Playing the Flute for the TMR Class.   Jane Epton Seale.   MiVo

They suck and whisper it in mercury.   Break-up, The.   Abraham Moses Klein.   NOBC

They suffer, and I catch only the surface.   I Am a Cameraman.   Douglas Dunn.   EmeKit

They swallow clouds.   Buson.   EH, tr. by Robert Hass

They swarm in and unpack right.   Bad Birds.   William Trowbridge.   UrbNat

They swore to wipe out the nomads, no thought for themselves.   Song of Lung-hsi.   Ch'en Tao.   CoBCP, tr. by Burton Watson

They take advantage—the soldiers need clothes.   Se Aprovechan.   Irving Feldman.   GS

They take them out in the morning.   Five Men.   Zbigniew Herbert.   PoSu, tr. by Czeslaw Milosz and Peter Dale Scott

They talk of short-lived pleasure—be it so—.   Mutation.   William Cullen Bryant.   NCAP

They taste good to her. (LL)   To a Poor Old Woman.   William Carlos Williams.   BLT; ColAP; OBAL; TAP; TTTS

They tax our policy and call it cowardice.   William Shakespeare.   FaBoWar   Fr. Troilus and Cressida.

They tell me how it was, and how time.   Scars.   William Stafford.   AmFaPo

They Tell Me I Am Lost.   Maurice Kenny.   HATNAP

They tell me I live on a cloud.   Tame and Ferocious Animal, A.   Nancy Morejón.   TANSG, tr. by Joy Renjilian-Burgy

They tell me: "Man." From a Talk.   Yevgeny Aleksandrovich Yevtushenko [or Evtushenko].   CLPP, tr. by Anselm Hollo

They tell me that the Arena in Verona is the most beautifully preserved.   Magnificence.   James Wright (1927–80).   BodElec

They tell me 'tis decided; you depart.   Byron.   NOBRP   Fr. Don Juan.

They tell you to go. And you do. (LL)   Ringing the Bells.   Anne Sexton.   HCAP; PoE; TAP; VGW

They tethered my soul upon a rope.   Tethered Souls, The.   Endre Ady.   IQMS, tr. by Anton N. Nyerges

They that have power to hurt[e], and will do[e] none.   William Shakespeare.   NAEL-5v1; NAEL-6v1; NAEL-7v1; NIL-7; NOBE; NoSic; OBEV; OxAEP-1; OxBEV; OxBSo; PoE; SCGP; SCV; Son; TRP; WoPoe   Fr. Sonnets.

They that in play can do the thing they would.   Robert Bridges.   NoAM   Fr. Growth of Love, The.

They That Sow at Night.   Shin Shalom.   MHP, tr. by Ruth Finer Mintz

They that wash on Monday.   They That Wash on Monday.   Mother Goose.   NBLV

They think / I am stronger than I am.   Naming Power.   Wendy Rose.   OxWW

They thought: Human!   Marina Ivanovna Tsvetayeva [or Tsvetaeva].   TCRusP, tr. by Bob Perelman, Aleksandar Petrov and Shirley Rihner   Fr. Poems to Blok.

They throw in Drummer Hodge, to rest.   Drummer Hodge.   Thomas Hardy.   AWP; EBEV; FaBoWar; GTBS-P; HAP; HarvBoo; NAEL-5v2; NAEL-6v2; NOBVV; NoAM; NoP-4; OBWP; OxAEP-2; PAI; PeFWW; WeW-3

They toke togyder theyr counsell.   Unknown.   PeECV   Fr. Gest of Robyn Hode.

They told me the.   Pistachio Ice Cream.   Annemarie Jacir.   PoArWo

They told me, Francis Hinsley, they told me you were hung.   Evelyn Waugh.   OBCoV   Fr. Loved One, The.

They told me God came to Pius.   In the Dark.   Patrick Williams.   PNI

They told me, Heraclitus, they told me you were dead.   Heraclitus.   William Johnson Cory.   AWP; EBVV; FaBoEE; InPK-6; NOBE; OBEV; OxAEP-2; OxBSP; PoRA; SCGP; UV

They told me, Heraclitus, they told me you were dead.   They Told Me, Heraclitus.   Brian Fore.   UV

They told me, Heraclitus, they told me you were dead.   They Told Me, Heraclitus.   Guy Hanlon.   UV

They told me, when I lived, because my art.   Ancient Revisits, An.   Laura Riding Jackson.   APT-2

They told me you had been to her.   Lewis Carroll.   GTBS-P; NOBVV; NPeEn; OxBoLi; PeLV   Fr. Alice's Adventures in Wonderland.

They told my cousin Rowena not to marry.   Family Secrets.   Toi Derricotte.   SpirFl

They told us / Our mothers told us.   Cornfields in Accra.   Christine Ama Ata Aidoo.   WPOW

They took a tire tool to his head.   Jim Barnes.   HATNAP   Fr. Ex-Deputy Sheriff Remembers the Eastern Oklahoma Murderers, An.

They took all that was child.   Al Wat Kind Is.   Ingrid De Kok.   HAWP

They took me out.   Ku Klux.   Langston Hughes.   BPo

They took my flock away. Should I care? I have nothing to do now.   Saturn Declining.   Sándor Weöres.   IQMS, tr. by Alan Dixon

They took off / and tricolor flags came out of their assholes.   Nungesser und Coli Sind Verreckt.   Benjamin Péret.   AF, tr. by Keith Hollaman

They took quickly, they took hugely.   Marina Ivanovna Tsvetayeva [or Tsvetaeva].   TCRP   Fr. March.

They took quickly, they took hugely.   Marina Ivanovna Tsvetayeva [or Tsvetaeva].   See also O what tears in eyes now

They took their time to die, this dynasty.   Last of the Princes, The.   A. K. Ramanujan.   OxBC

They trod the streets and squares where I now tread.   London Poets.   Amy Levy.   ViWPN

They unfold before the sky.   Doors.   Thérèse Plantier.   BoWoP, tr. by Willis Barnstone and Elene Kolb

They Unite Naked.   Jorge Gaitán Durán.   BLPSL, tr. by Rene de Costa, Rigas Kappatos and Eleni Paidoussi

They used to tell me. Brother, Can You Spare a Dime? Jay Gorney. APT-2; ReLy

They've Come. Alfonsina Storni. BoWoP; WPOW

They've got the whole of death never. Vanished, The. Marie-Claire Bancquart. MFP, *tr. by* Martin Sorrell

They've let me walk with you. Visit, The. Ian Hamilton. NPeEn

They've opened up a road in the jungle and found. 2976. Julia Uceda. BoWoP, *tr. by* Willis Barnstone

They've paid the last respects in sad tobacco. Padraic O'Conaire—Gaelic Storyteller. Frederick Robert Higgins. OBMV

They've put the park bench. Notes for the Park Keeper. Peter Bland. OBGa

They've putten her into prison strang. Sir Aldingar. *Unknown.* ESPB

They've said the art of poetry resembles. Marriage in the Nineties, A. Alfred Corn. WiU

They've taken it apart. Three-Inch Reflector. Caroline Caddy. BMAP

They've taken the great elm down. Neighbor's Elm, The. Robert Ayres. UrbNat

They've taken thee out of the simple soil. Negro Spiritual. Claude McKay. APT-1

They wake with horror, and dare sleep no more. (LL) Dryden. BASC; FaBoWar *Fr. Annus Mirabilis.*

They walk around a corner at the back of town. War of the Roses, The. Michael Dransfield. BMAP

They walked in straitened ways. Old Ladies, The. Colin Ellis. OxBTC

They wander in deep woods, in mournful light. Fields of Sorrow, The. Ausonius. WoPoe, *tr. by* Helen Waddell

They wanted me dead, the bastards. Yury [*or* Iurii] Osipovich Dombrovsky [*or* Dombrovskii*]*. TCRP

They wanted me to tell the truth. What They Wanted. Stephen Dunn. BodElec

They wear. *Unknown.* WoPoe, *tr. by* R. J. Wilkinson and R. O. Winstedt *Fr. Two Pantuns.*

They wear big felt hats. Church Ladies. Nancy Travis. ISC

They wear white scarves and shawls. Madwomen of the Plaza de Mayo, The. Eli W. Mandel. NOBC

They went to sea in a Sieve, the did. Eat Your Heart Out, Edward Lear! Roger Woddis. UV

They went to sea in a sieve, they did. Jumblies, The. Edward Lear. CABP; EBEV; NAEL-5v2; NAEL-6v2; NOxBChV; OxBoLi; PeLV; PeVV; PoRA; TFi; UV

They Went to the Moon Mother. *Unknown.* STP, *tr. by* Barbara Tedlock

They went with axe and rifle, when the trail was still to blaze. Western Wagons. Rosemary Benét. AiP; HHAm

They went with songs to the battle, they were young. Laurence Binyon. FaBoWar *Fr. For the Fallen.*

They wept for the violet-wreathed [lady's]. Simonides. SaLy, *tr. by* Diane Rayor

They were a close family of giant otters. Giant Otters. Jackson Mac Low. FTOS

They Were Alone in the Winter. Luci Tapahonso. ItWoWo

They were alone once more; for them to be. Byron. EBEV *Fr. Don Juan.*

They were always there, at the end of the garden or elsewhere. At Evening. Anthony Thwaite. OxBEV

They were at play, she and her cat. Femme et Chatte. Paul Verlaine. AWP; OBVE

They were beautiful, the old books, beautiful I tell you. Old Books, The. Vernon Scannell. OxBC

They were born together, lived together. Martha and Mary. Gabriela Mistral. GI, *tr. by* Doris Dana

They were both still. Lamentations. Louise Glück. BoWoP; HCAP; VCAP

They were but gourds for earth to drink therefrom. Ikeja, Friday, Four O'Clock. Wole Soyinka. PoetW

They were coming across the prairie, they were galloping hard and fast. Cattle Thief, The. Emily Pauline Johnson. WPOW

They were crushed by a gigantic meteor. Theory on Extinction or what happened to the dinosaurs? Kenneth Carroll. AmPoNex; SpirFl

They were dancing as if. Glass. Takako Uchino Lento. BoWoP, *tr. by the* author

They were difficult to find. It was summer so. Like a Fire in a Fire. Mary Jo Bang. NAPBL

They were gestures out of a movie, I tell you. Hours Musicians Keep, The. Aleda Shirley. SwNoth

They were green paths in the placid time of the needle. These Green Paths. Jeannette Miller. TANSG, *tr. by* Paula Vega

They were introduced in a grave glade. Introduction, The. Louis MacNeice. PNI

They were just meant as covers. My Mother Pieced Quilts. Teresa Palma Acosta. WPOW

They were just playing, lady and cat. Woman and Cat. Paul Verlaine. WoPoe, *tr. by* Felicity Bast

They were kings, after all. Magi, The. Jeffrey Fiskin. GI

They were lovely in the quartz and jasper sand. Starfish. Lorna Dee Cervantes. TouFir

They were not the abandoned ones. Hansel and Gretel. Barbara Noel-Scott. Prnts

They were on location in the hills above a small California town and before. Motion Pictures: 15. Barbara Guest. BodElec

They were once like us, like we were. Rocks Along the Coast, The. Jerry Martien. GeoHom

They were partakers of a strange taste. At the hour when. Deflection Toward the Relative Minor. Forrest Gander. OPRER

They were parted then at last? Winter Song. George Macdonald. NOBVV

They were supposed to be fixed by today, now that they're hardly needed— though they will be again. Screens. Barry Silesky. IllVoic

They were talking on the telephone about a low, drawn out light with blackness to it. Connecting Light. Susan Michie. Prnts

They were the strong nudes of a forgotten. Anagram Born of Madness at Czernowitz, 12 November 1920. Norman Dubie. BodElec

They were twa lovers dear. (LL) Prince Robert. *Unknown.* ESPB; OxBB

They were women then. Alice Walker. WPOW; WWork *Fr.* In These Dissenting Times.

They weren't with me. Samantha. Edward Albee. Unle

They whispered when she passed—gave knowing looks. Sinner, The. Margaret E. Bruner. PoToHe

They Who Are Poor. Attila József. IQMS, *tr. by* Vernon Watkins

They who in folly or mere greed. Where Are the War Poets? Cecil Day Lewis. FaBoMo; NoP-4; OBWP; OxBSP; OxBTC

They Who Prepare My Evening Meal Below. Henry David Thoreau. APN-1

They will be telling you soon who you are. Arsenic. Howard Moss. CoAP

They will be without arms like God. Hummingbirds. Norman Dubie. BodElec; LCAP-2

They will bury that fair body and cover you. Epitaph on a Young Child. Ivor Gurney. FaBoEE

They will come for you in morning. Whispers. Roberta Hill Whiteman. CDW

They will fit, she thinks. Marriage, The. Anne Stevenson. NALW

They will never die on that battlefield. Uccello. Gregory Corso. NeAP; PoM

They will not ask us: have you sinned? Anatoly Steiger. TCRusP, *tr. by* Paul Schmidt

They will not hush, the leaves a-flutter round me, the beech leaves old. (LL) Madness of King Goll, The. W. B. Yeats. NAEL-5v2; NAEL-6v2

They will people your mind. You will never touch their hands. (LL) Imagine the South. George Woodcock. MoCV; NOBC

They will perhaps. Love Poem. Norman Henry Pritchard, II. GT

They will probably come just after the New Year. Three Magi, The. Stanislaw Baranczak. GI

They will tumble down from the rooftops. Judgement Day. Odia Ofeimun. HBAPE

They will wash all my kisses and fingerprints off you. Poem Ended by a Death. Fleur Adcock. NAEL-6v2; NoP-4; PeNZ

They will win, I thought once. Politics. Tom Marshall. NOBC

They without message, having read. Typists. Patricia K. Page. NALW

They won't let railways alone, those yellow flowers. Ragwort. Anne Stevenson. OPOU

They wondered why the fruit had been forbidden. W. H. Auden. ChIV-1; Son *Fr.* Sonnets from China.

They would ask him. Big Bad Art Thing, The. Carter Ratcliff. KGB

They would bar your way in the street. Invaders, The. Bernard Spencer. FaBoWar

They would have invited him gladly. *Unknown.* WoPoe, *tr. by* Paul Blackburn *Fr.* Poem of the Cid, The.

They would leave. Final Solution: Jobs, Leaving. Simon J. Ortiz. PFTM-2

They would like / to put the tick and flea collar. No Hatchet Job. Luz María Umpierre. PueRic

They would say that she of the neck like a duiker's. On Reading an Archeological Article. Molara Ogundipe-Leslie. HBAPE

They wring their hands, their caitiff-hands. Michael Wigglesworth. NAAL-3 *Fr.* Day of Doom, The.

Thick at the schoolgate are the ones. Soul Make a Path Through Shouting. Cyrus Cassells. GT; GifTon; OPRER; UnSA

Thick crust, coarse-grained as limestone rough-cast, A. Churning Day. Seamus Heaney. ModIr

Thick darkness broodeth o'er the world. Past, The. Sarah Helen Whitman. TCAPo

Thick fog. Garden of Shanah. Sara Riwka Erlich. MirDau, *tr. by* Auristela Xavier

Thick, grey and humid, while the marshes sleep. (LL) Marshlands. Emily Pauline Johnson. NOBC; SWaP

Thick-rushing, like an ocean vast. Remembered Music. James Russell Lowell. APN-1

Thick throng the snow-flakes, the evening is dreary. Julia Ward Howe. SWaP *Fr.* Lyrics of the Street.

Thicket of deadly nightshade, The. Latvian Autumn, The. Johannes Bobrowski. PoSu

Thicket's in the thick of what, The. Scared Cows. Douglas Messerli. FTOS

Thicknesses of victor decreased: blanket→sheet→floss. Until no material would do, The. D. A. Powell. NeAmPo

Thief, The. Josephine Jacobsen. WPE

Thief, The. Stanley Kunitz. MoAmPo; VGW

Thief, The. Dorianne Laux. ErotSp; ExTi; PasH

Thief, The. Alden Nowlan. RaBo

Thief and Samaritan. James Keir Baxter. HarvBoo

Thief, and triply so!, A. Diophanes of Myrina. GrAn

Thief became the rabbi, The. Structural Study of Myth, The. Jerome Rothenberg. FTOS; PoM

Thief in the Night, A. Jelaluddin [*or* Jalal al-Din] Rumi. BBASP, *tr.* by Nasrollah Pourjavady and Peter Lamborn Wilson

Thief Stole This Poem, A. Allen Ginsberg. BodElec

Thief, you dare to laugh and even. *Unknown.* PriapPo, *tr.* by Richard W. Hooper *Fr.* Priapus Poems, The.

Thieves, The. Robert Graves. BoLoP; GTBS-P

Thieves and Whores. John Gay. ECEV *Fr.* Trivia; or, The Art of Walking the Streets of London.

Thieves, find some other house, worthy of robbing. Unguarded House, An. Julianus of Egypt. GrAn

Thigh-deep in sedge and marigolds. Other Side, The. Seamus Heaney. CIP-2; PNI

Thin are the night-skirts left behind. Insomnia. Dante Gabriel Rossetti. AWTN

Thin, Black Band, A. Sandor Csoori. VCWP

Thin grass bends on the breezy shore. Night Thoughts While Traveling. Tu Fu. CrYelRi, *tr.* by Sam Hamill

Thin hound's body arched against the snow, The. (LL) Old Countryside. Louise Bogan. HAP; WPE

Thin in beard, and thick in purse. On Tom-o-Combe. *Unknown.* FaBoEE

Thin leaves wave on the *wu-t'ung* tree beside the well. Lonely Night in Early Autumn. Po Chü-i. TAL

Thin lips can make a music. Redivivus. Donald Davidson. FuPo

Thin little leaves of wood fern, ribbed and toothed. Frederick Goddard Tuckerman. APN-2; TAP *Fr.* Sonnets.

Thin Mary sits there. Winter Angel. Ágnes Nemes Nagy. PoSu, *tr.* by Hugh Maxton

Thin mist, A. Fireflies. José Gorostiza. TCLAP, *tr.* by Rachel Benson

Thin mist floats in the desolate void. (LL) Oxhead Temple. Ssu-k'ung Shu. ColAnChi; SuSp, *tr.* by Hellmut Wilhelm

Thin mists—thick clouds—sad all day long. Tune: "Tipsy in the Flower's Shade." Li Ch'ing-chao. SuSp, *tr.* by Eugene Eoyang

Thin Prison, The. Leslie Norris. OTCP

Thin steel in paired lines, forever mated, cuts. North Philadelphia, Trenton, and New York. Richmond Lattimore. APT-2

Thin wet sky, that yellows at the rim, A. Marshlands. Emily Pauline Johnson. NOBC; SWaP

Thin wickedly intricate, The. Dark Area. Russell Atkins. GT

Thin Wire. Leo Vroman. TuT, *tr.* by Desmond Egan

Thine elder that I am, thou must not cling. Sweeter Far than the Harp, More Gold than Gold. "Michael Field." OBMV; PeVV

Thine elders ask, and they will tell it thee. (LL) Give Ear, O Heavens, to That Which I Declare. Henry Ainsworth. AH; ChIV-1

Thine eyes I love, and they, as pitying me. William Shakespeare. OxAEP-1 *Fr.* Sonnets.

Thine eyes shall see the light of distant skies. To Cole, the Painter, Departing for Europe. William Cullen Bryant. AiP; ColAP; TAP; TCAPo

Thine Eyes Still Shined. Ralph Waldo Emerson. ColAP; NOBA

Thine eyes were light; thy lips were life. (LL) Another for the Briar Rose. William Morris. NOBVV; OxBEV

Thine is a strain to read amongst the hills. To [*or* the Poet] Wordsworth. Felicia Dorothea Hemans. BrRo; RWP

Thine Own. Josephine D. Henderson Heard. CBWP-4; SWaP

Thine own reflection in Eternity! (LL) Aspiration. Adah Isaacs Menken. CBWP-1; ViWPN

Thine was a brain of nature's finest mould. Charles Sumner. Henrietta Cordelia Ray. CBWP-3

Thing, The. Theodore Roethke. APT-2

Thing about a shark is—teeth, The. About the Teeth of Sharks. John Ciardi. OBCA; OxIBACP

Thing About Joe Sullivan, The. Roy Fisher. HarvBoo

Thing about playing solitaire, The. Playing Solitaire. Thulani Davis. GT

Thing could barely stand. Yet taken, The. Bull Calf, The. Irving Layton. InPK-6

Thing I hate most is eating, The. Variations on the Edible Tuber. Madeline DeFrees. SpudSo

Thing I must somehow forget. (LL) To His Love. Ivor Gurney. MakPoe; NAEL-5v2; NPeEn; OBWP; PeFWW; PoWW

Thing is in my mind, A. Rinaldo D'Aquino. EaItPo, *tr.* by Dante Gabriel Rossetti

Thing is Violent, The. Gwendolyn MacEwen. MoCV; NOBC

Thing itself was rough and crudely done, The. Knight in the Wood, The. John Byrne Leicester Warren, 3d Baron De Tabley. NOBVV; PeVV

Thing Language. Jack Spicer. APSN *Fr.* Language.

Thing long forgotten. Masaoka Shiki. ZenPo, *tr.* by Takashi Ikemoto and Lucien Stryk

Thing Made Real, The. Ron Loewinsohn. NeAP

Thing must End. I am no boy! I am, The. Sonnet: In Time of Revolt. Rupert Brooke. OBCoV

Thing not done, The. Deutschland. Hugh Maxton. PBCIP

Thing of beauty is a joy forever, A. John Keats. CTC; FHYEP; ITBLP; NAEL-5v2; NAEL-6v2; NIP-4; NOBRP; OPOU; OxAEP-2; OxBEV *Fr.* Endymion: A Poetic Romance.

Thing or Two about Childhood, A. Yury Iofe. TCRusP, *tr.* by John Glad

Thing Poem. Petra von Morstein. BoWoP, *tr.* by Rosmarie Waldrop

Thing that arrests me is, The. Waking in the Dark. Adrienne Rich. FaBoWP

Thing that brought you among my people, The. Homage to John Millington Synge. Mairtin O Direain. NOIV, *tr.* by Thomas Kinsella

Thing that numbs the heart is this, The. Firm Belief. *Unknown.* PoToHe

Thing to do is try for that sweet skin, The. Catch What You Can. Jean Garrigue. VGW

Thing to draw with compasses, The. Circles. Harry Behn. CA

Thing we know of but we do not know, The. (LL) Question, The. Frank Templeton Prince. BoLoP; GTBS-P

Thing which fades, A. *Var. authors.* AWP; BoWoP *Fr.* Kokin Shu.

Things. Geoffrey Holloway. NLP

Things. Donald Justice.
  "Hard, but you can polish it." CRP
  Stone. CRP

Things. W. S. Merwin. HAP

Things. Bob Perelman. PmAP

Things. Louis Simpson. OxBC

Things, The. Conrad Potter Aiken. HAP; WeW-3

Things Are Looking Up. George Gershwin. ReLy

Things begin again. Return. Jewel C. Latimore. BlSi

Things break down in different ways. Entropic Villanelle. Thomas M. [*or* "Tom"] Disch. RA

Things bygone engender nothing but unbearable sorrow. Tune: "Sand Washed by Waves." Li Yü. ColAnChi, *tr.* by Jiaosheng Wang

Things Dead. Marcel Schwob. TrJP, *tr.* by William Brown Meloney

Things exist alone. Moon and Hare. Shinkichi Takahashi. ZenPo, *tr.* by Takashi Ikemoto and Lucien Stryk

Things Experienced upon Withdrawal from Court. Hsieh Chin.
  "Government wine of Peking is sweeter than honey, The." CoBLCP

Things Forbidden. *Unknown.* NoSic

Things glisten. Roof tiles rise. City. Angel González. VCWP, *tr.* by Steven Ford Brown

Things Going out of My Life. Robert Adamson. CBAP

Things going, owing that debt. (LL) On the Debt My Mother Owed to Sears Roebuck. Edward Dorn. CoAmPo; TRP

Things harness me here. I long. Lucy's Letter. James Berry. FaBoVe

Things have an admirable life. Valerio Magrelli. ItPo, *tr.* by Gayle Ridinger

Things have come to a pretty pass. Let's Call the Whole Thing Off. George Gershwin. ReLy

Things he timidly imagined as a schoolboy, The. Passing Through. Constantine P. Cavafy. CAGL, *tr.* by Edmund Keeley and Philip Sherrard

Things I Didn't Know I Loved. Nazim Hikmet. AF; AmFaPo; VCWP

Things I'm told, I could raise your hair, The. Brian [*or* Bryan] Merriman [*or* Merryman]. BIrV, *tr.* by David Marcus *Fr.* Midnight Court, The.

Things I Say Are True, The. Blanca Varela. BoWoP, *tr.* by Donald Yates

Things I used to like, The. It Might As Well Be Spring. Richard Rodgers. ReLy

Things like littlenecks. Spring Night. Hagiwara Sakutaro. PFTM-1

Things live there, held still in glass cases, The. Reflections on a Visit to the Burke Museum, University of Washington, Seattle. Gail Tremblay. HATNAP

Things Lovelier. Humbert Wolfe. TrJP

Things Made by Iron. D. H. Lawrence. Spl

Things may not be as then. (LL) Colonel's Soliloquy, The. Thomas Hardy. FaBoWar; OBWP

Things My Brother and I Could Do. Robert Bly. InvLad

Things of the Blind. Paz Molina. TANSG, *tr.* by Steven F. White

Things of the past may only be lamented, The. Tune: "Ripples Sifting Sand." Li Yü. SuSp, *tr. by* Daniel Bryant

Things of This World. Anna Kamienska. GI, *tr. by* David Curzon and Grażyna Drabik

Things present but as a tale. (LL) One We Knew. Thomas Hardy. NAEL-5v2; NAEL-6v2

Things Seen. Wang Shih-cheng. CoBLCP, *tr. by* Jonathan Chaves

Things Seen on Spring Days. Yüan Mei. CoBLCP, *tr. by* Jonathan Chaves

Things swim. View from the Bathysphere. Peter Rafferty. NLP

Things that are going out of my life remain, The. Things Going out of My Life. Robert Adamson. CBAP

Things That Go Bump in the Night. *Unknown.* NTCP

Things That Happen. William Stafford. NNaP

Things That Happen to You. Alonzo Gonzales Mó. STP, *tr. by* Allan F. Burns

Things that make a life to please, The. Happy Life, A. Martial. OBVE, *tr. by* Sir Richard Fanshawe

Things that Make a Soldier Great, The. Edgar Albert Guest. NIL-7

Things that make the happier life, are these, The. Martial. Epigram XLVII, Book X. Ben Jonson. FaBoEE; OBVE

Things That Matter, The. Edith Nesbit. OxBTC; VWP

Things they did together, no one knew, The. 1904. Frederick Morgan. WeW-3

Things to Come. James Reeves. OxBSP

Things to Do around a Lookout. Gary Snyder. TAP

Things to Do in Holland. Beau Sia. HeMarv

Things to Do in the Bible. Elaine Equi. IllVoic

Things to Do in Valley of the Dolls (The Movie). David Trinidad. WiU

Things turn mortal at twilight. La Naval De Manila: Selim Sot as a Modern Political Observer. Eric Gamalinda. ReBoTo

Things We Did Last Summer, The. Sammy Cahn. ReLy

Things We Dreamt We Died For. Marvin Bell. CoAP

Things which I have seen I now can see no more, The. (LL) William Wordsworth. NAEL-5v2; SCGP; TFi; TOF; TRP *Fr.* Ode: Intimations of Immortality [from Recollections of Early Childhood].

Think a brief while on the most marvellous arts. Lodovico della Vernaccia. EaItPo, *tr. by* Dante Gabriel Rossetti

Think about it. Miracles. Carol Muske. ExTi

Think about St. Joan without. Evolution of Appetite. Kelleen Zubick. OPRER

Think all but one, and me in that one Will. (LL) William Shakespeare. NAEL-5v1; NAEL-6v1; NAEL-7v1 *Fr.* Sonnets.

Think As I Think. Stephen Crane. WeW-3 *Fr.* Black Riders [and Other Lines], The.

"Think as I think," said a man. "Think as I think," said a man. Stephen Crane. KaS

Think Back. Gerry Gomez Pearlberg. WiU

Think back now to that cleft. Power Station, The. James Merrill. CoAmPo

Think Eight. Todd Colby. HeMarv

Think how a peacock in a forest of high trees. Peacock. D. H. Lawrence. TTTS

Think how some excellent, lean torso hugs. Cost, The. Anthony Hecht. OxBC

Think how unspeakably sweet. Asclepiades. ErotSp, *tr. by* Sam Hamill

Think it enough for me to [*or* t'] have had thy love. (LL) John Donne. BoLoP; CABP; EBEV; ESCV; FSCP; MeLP; NAEL-5v1; NAEL-6v1; NAEL-7v1; NPeEn; NoSic; OxAEP-1; SCGP *Fr.* Elegies.

Think not I have not heard. Menses. Edna St. Vincent Millay. APT-1; RACG

Think not, nor for a moment let your mind. Edna St. Vincent Millay. VGW

Think not, O man that dwells herein. Upon the New Building at Appleton. Thomas Fairfax, Baron Fairfax of Cameron. NOSC

Think not this paper comes with vain pretense. Epistle from Mrs. Yonge to Her Husband. Lady Mary Wortley Montagu. NAEL-5v1; NAEL-6v1; NAEL-7v1; NALW; NPeEn; NoP-4

Think Not When You Gather to Zion. Eliza R. Snow. AH

Think, now: if you have found a dead bird. Advice to a Discarded Lover. Fleur Adcock. PeNZ

Think of dress in every light. John Gay. OxBSP *Fr.* Achilles.

Think of him as uninjured, barely disturbed. (LL) Little Exercise. Elizabeth Bishop. CoAP; ColAP; MoAmPo

Think of it in Beijing. Butterfly Effect, The. Harry Humes. BAP-97

Think of me as your friend, I pray. Heart's Anchor, The. William Winter. PoToHe

Think of sweet and chocolate. Anniad, The. Gwendolyn Brooks. BlSi

Think of that only when they think of me. (LL) Firdowsi. OBVE; WoPoe, *tr. by* Basil Bunting

Think of the Buddhist monks. Poet's Heart, The. Richard Jones. GifTon

Think of the children in Baghdad. Karen Alkalay-Gut. DTA *Fr.* Between Bombardments: A Journal.

Think of the shark's tiny brain. In a Museum in the Capital. William Stafford. LCAP-2

Think of the storm roaming the sky uneasily. Little Exercise. Elizabeth Bishop. CoAP; ColAP; MoAmPo

Think of the things that make you happy. Thinking Happiness. Robert E. Farley. PoToHe

Think of this: that under the earth. Deep Mining. Irene McKinney. PBCAP

Think of those naturals who started right off blowing horn. Ambition. Bruce Berger. GeoH

Think of those old, enduring connections. Family Is All There Is, The. Pattiann Rogers. NIP-4

Think of what you're losing. I Won't Dance. Dorothy Fields. ReLy

Think of your age, old man. Homo Erectus, Cerne Abbas. Mercer Simpson. TCAWP

Think of your conception, you'll soon forget. Palladas [*or* Pallades]. GrAn

Think sad thoughts of other days. Song of the Palace of Ch'en. Kuan Hsiu. WoPoe, *tr. by* Jerome P. Seaton

Think'st thou to seduce me then with words that have no meaning? Think'st thou to seduce me then. Thomas Campion. NAEL-5v1; NAEL-6v1; NAEL-7v1; OxAEP-1; OxBSP

Think that this world against the wind of time. Signature for Tempo. Archibald MacLeish. CRP; VGW

Think thou and act; to-morrow thou shalt die. Dante Gabriel Rossetti. GTBS-P; OBEV *Fr.* House of Life, The.

Think upon Death. Hartley Coleridge. Son

Think with your body. Poem. Víctor Hernández Cruz. PueRic

Think you I am not fiend and savage too? To the White Fiends. Claude McKay. NAAAL

Think[e] not 'cause men flattering [*or* flatt'ring] say. To A. L.; Persuasions [*or* Perswasions] to Love. Thomas Carew. CaPo

Thinking. Jorie Graham. BAP-97; ExTi

Thinking about Bill, Dead of AIDS. Miller Williams. NIL-7

Thinking about him. Ono no Komachi. WoPoe, *tr. by* Donald Keene

Thinking American. Hayan Charara. AmPoNex

Thinking around things that edge me into. Crack, The. Clark Coolidge. PmAP

Thinking Happiness. Robert E. Farley. PoToHe

Thinking hard, hunting rhymes, humming by my lamp. Sent to Wen T'ing-yün on a Winter Night. Yü Hsüan-chi. BoWoP, *tr. by* Geoffrey Waters

Thinking he walked on air, he. Ravenna Bridge. Leslie Norris. AngWePo

Thinking he was asking about race, I told him I was black. Origins. Forrest Hamer. GeoHom

Thinking I'd better be prepared when I went. Spit. A. R. Ammons. BodElec

Thinking in terms of one. Counting. Philip Larkin. PoetW

Thinking "In the beginning was the—(*What??*)" What the Lovers in the Old Songs Thought. John Hollander. BAP-01

Thinking myself in a warm country. Six Movements on a Theme. David Ignatow. NNaP

Thinking of a Relation between the Images of Metaphors. Wallace Stevens. SAmP

Thinking of East Mountain. Li Po. CoBCP; TTTS, *tr. by* Burton Watson

Thinking of her had saddened me at first. Celandine. Edward Thomas. OxBTC; TCAWP

Thinking of Holland. Memory of Holland. Hendrik Marsman. TuT, *tr. by* Michael Longley

Thinking of Impoverished Ancients. T'ao Ch'ien [*or* T'ao Yuan-ming]. GifTon, *tr. by* David Hinton

Thinking of Lady Yang at Midnight. *Unknown.* WoPoe, *tr. by* Jean S. Grigsby

Thinking of Li Po. Tu Fu. CrYelRi, *tr. by* Sam Hamill

Thinking of Love. Elizabeth Jennings. LW

Thinking of Mr. D. Thomas Kinsella. NoAM

Thinking of My Brother in Shantung on the Ninth Day of the Ninth Moon. Wang Wei. TAL

Thinking of My Brothers on a Moonlit Night. Tu Fu. TAL

Thinking of My Family on an Autumn Day. Yang Wen-li. WoPoe, *tr. by* Nancy Hodes and Tung Yuan-fang

Thinking of my father. At the Nuclear Rally. Laura Boss. UnSA

Thinking of My Friends at Kou-jung Subprefecture. Yang Chi.
  "Mind and environment—you have quieted both." CoBLCP, *tr. by* Jonathan Chaves

Wu Shan-yang. CoBLCP, *tr. by* Jonathan Chaves

Thinking of My Little Boy. Tu Fu. ColAnChi; WoPoe, *tr. by* David Lattimore

Thinking of My Wife. P'an Yüeh. CoBCP, *tr. by* Burton Watson

Thinking of new ways to kill you. Lily Pond. Vicki Feaver. EmeKit

Thinking of painters, musicians, poets. Orgy. Norman MacCaig. OxBC

Thinking of rain clouds that rose over the city. St. Vincent's. W. S. Merwin. VCAP

Thinking of Tents. Reed Whittemore. TAP

Thinking of "The Autumn Fields." Robert Bly. NNaP

Thinking of the Lost World. Randall Jarrell. NAAL-5; NOBA; NoAM

Thinking of the Past. Po Chü-i. ChiP, tr. by Arthur Waley

Thinking of the Past on an Autumn Night at Tz'u-jen Temple. Wang Shih-chieng. CoBLCP, tr. by Jonathan Chaves

Thinking of the Way Home, a Song. Lo Yin. SuSp, tr. by Geoffrey R. Waters

Thinking of words that would save him, slanting. Finding Them Lost. Howard Moss. CoAP

Thinking of you. Love Notes. Jennifer Strauss. BMAP

Thinking of you, and all that was, and all. Christina Georgina Rossetti. OxBSo Fr. Monna Innominata.

Thinking of You, Hiroshima. Betsy Sholl. PBCAP

Thinking of you, I think of the coureurs de bois. Coureurs de Bois. Douglas Le Pan. MoCV; NOBC

Thinking of you, in autumn night. Autumn Night: A Letter Sent to Ch'iu. Wei Ying-wu. ChinPo, tr. by Yip Wai-lim

Thinking of your vocation, I am filled. To a Friend with a Religious Vocation. Elizabeth Jennings. TOF

Thinking only of their vow that they would crush the Tartars. Turkestan. Ch'en Tao. WoPoe, tr. by Witter Bynner

Thinking the Alps. Michael Davidson. PmAP

Thinking they'd fledged too soon. Bluetits. Ruth Smith. Prnts

Thinking to save all, we cast all away. (LL) Ant, The. Richard Lovelace. BASC; CaPo

Thinking we were safe—insanity! Story of a Hotel Room. Rosemary Tonks. LW; OxBTC

Thinks even her acne. Japanese Figures 2. Unknown. EaWin, tr. by W. S. Merwin

Thinks it's all junk these days, the routine. Elm Tree on Lafayette Street, The. Rod Kessler. OPRER

Thinnest meal on the slightest isle, The. Produce, Produce. Susan Wheeler. KGB

Thinnest Shadow, The. John Ashbery. TTTS

Thinnest sliver of moon, and caterpillars, A. Peony Lover. Lee Ann Roripaugh. AmPoNex

Thir Lenterne Dayis Ar Luvely Lang. William Stewart. OxBS

Thir riveris and thir watteris kepit war. Virgil [or Vergil]. OxBEV, tr. by Gawin [or Gavin] Douglas Fr. Aeneid [or Eneados, Aeneis], The.

Third Avenue in Sunlight. Anthony Hecht. CoAP; VCAP

Third Avenue is a vacant lot with a Desert Air sign. Silent Globe. Debra Gregerman. AmPoNex

Third Body, A. Robert Bly. LoL

Third Century, The. Thomas Traherne.
"Life of sabbaths here beneath!, A." ESCV
News. NOBE; OBEV
"News from a foreign [or forein or forrein] country came." NOBE; OBEV (On News.) ESCV; GeHe
Recovery, The. ESCV
"Sin!/ O only fatal Woe." ESCV
"Sin! wilt thou vanquish me!" ESCV
"That childish thoughts such joys inspire." BASC; ESCV

Third Cycle of Love Poems. George Barker.
Shut the Seven Seas against Us. MoBrPo

Third Day. Thomas Traherne. ChIV-1 Fr. Meditations on the Six Days of the Creation.

Third Day, The. Phillis Levin. BBASP

Third Day of the Third Month at the Meandering River, The. Yu Ch'an. ChinPo, tr. by Yip Wai-lim

Third Degree. Langston Hughes. BPo

Third Dimension, The. Denise Levertov. NeAP

Third Eye, The. Jay Macpherson. MoCV

Third Farming Poem. Brenda Coultas. HeMarv

Third Light, The. Michael Longley. PNI

3rd Light Poem: For Spencer, Beate, & Sebastian Holst—12 June 1962. Jackson Mac Low. PFTM-2

Third Limick. Ogden Nash. PeLi

Third month in T'ientsin, The. Li Po. ChinPo, tr. by Yip Wai-lim

Third Month, Night of the Seventeenth, Written While Drunk. Lu Yu. CoBCP; SuSp, tr. by Burton Watson

Third month, third day, in the air a breath of newness. Song of the Beautiful Ladies. Tu Fu. CoBCP, tr. by Burton Watson

Third movement. Kurt Schwitters. PFTM-1 Fr. Ur Sonata.

Third one crooked the second one leaning, The. Bamboo Garden. Muso Soseki. EaWin, tr. by W. S. Merwin

Third Psalm. Anne Sexton. NALW Fr. O Ye Tongues.

Third Sermon on the Warpland, The. Gwendolyn Brooks. BPo; SeSe

Third Shell, The. David Meltzer. PFTM-2 Fr. Hero/Lil.

Third Shift. Anthony Walton. NAPBL

Third Song. T. Carmi. MHP, tr. by Ruth Finer Mintz Fr. René's Songs.

Third, third, third–the rule I learned. Rule of Thirds, The. Jack Coulehan. BloBone

3rd Untitled Poem. Pedro Juan Pietri. PueRic

Third Warning Sign: An Endless Surprise. Edoardo Cacciatore. ItPo, tr. by Gayle Ridinger Fr. Full Powers: Five Warning Signs.

Third World Calling. Lawrence Ferlinghetti. BB

Third Ypres. Edmund Charles Blunden. PeFWW

Thirsis a youth of the inspired train. Edmund Waller. See Thyrsis, a youth of the inspired train

Thirst. Thurayya Al-Urayyid. PoArWo, tr. by Farouk Mustafa

Thirst. Emily Dickinson. NOCV

Thirst. Arthur Rimbaud. WoPoe, tr. by Michael O'Brien

Thirst. Genevieve Taggard. APT-2

Thirst. Mark Wunderlich. AmPoNex

Thirst for green, because too long deprived, A. Vega. Lawrence Durrell. OxAEP-2

Thirst for the Sea. Magda Portal. TANSG, tr. by Shaun Griffin and Emma Sepúlveda-Pulvirenti

Thirst is no thing and yet it cruel can torment you. "Angelus Silesius." GePo, tr. by George C. Schoolfield Fr. Cherubical Wanderer, The.

Thirstier minstrel drew in me!, A. (LL) George Darley. BIrV; FaBoCh; OBEV Fr. Nepenthe.

Thirsty Earth soaks up the Rain, The. Drinking. Anacreon. BeJo; NOBE; NPeEn; OBEV; OBVE; OxAEP-1; OxBEV; PAI, tr. by Abraham Cowley

Thirsty Island. Jim Tollerud. VoR

13. Edward Fitzgerald. CABP

Thirteen. Ronald Wallace. PBCAP

Thirteen faces waiting to be born. May 1970. Stephen Berg. CDa

13 November 1983. Lee Cataldi. BMAP

Thirteen's no age at all. Thirteen is nothing. Portrait of a Girl with Comic Book. Phyllis McGinley. APT-2

Thirteen Sonnets. Michael Hartnett.
"I saw magic on a green country road." BIrV; PBCIP
Sonnet: "I saw magic on a green country road." BIrV; PBCIP

Thirteen Ways of Looking at a Blackbird. Wallace Stevens. APT-1; HCAP; HeIP-4; InPK-6; NAAL-2v2; NOBA; NoAM; OWoS; PAI; PoE; RB; SAmP; TAP; TCAPo; TFi

Thirteen Ways of Looking at a Hoover. Anthony Conran. TCAWP

Thirteen Years. Erin Mouré. NIL-7

Thirteen years ago, before bulk barns and. Change, The. A. A. Hedge Coke. ReEnLa

Thirteen years / Or haply less, I might have seen, when first. William Wordsworth. OxAEP-2 Fr. Prelude, The; Growth of a Poet's Mind [1805 vers.].

Thirteenth Bard's Song, The. James Hogg. NePenScot Fr. Queen's Wake, The.

13th day of November in that 1917th year, The. In the Paul Guillaume Gallery. Pierre Albert-Birot. CuPo

13th Horse Song of Frank Mitchell, The. María Sabina. PFTM-1

13th Horse Song of Frank Mitchell (White), The. Frank Mitchell. STP

Thirteenth Ode. Sekeena Shaben. PoArWo

Thirtieth Anniversary Report of the Class of '41. Howard Nemerov. HCAP

Thirtieth of November, The. Toward the Solstice. Adrienne Rich. NAAL-2v2

30th Year Dream. Gregory Corso. BodElec

Thirty Bob a Week. John Davidson. CABP; EBEV; EBVV; FaBoTw; NOBE; NOBVV; NPeEn; NePenScot; OxBEV; OxBS; OxBTC

Thirty centimes is all the money I have left. From My Parisian Diary. Mbella Sonne Dipoko. PBMAP

Thirty days hath November. Months of the Year, The. Richard Grafton. MiEL

Thirty days hath September. Mother Goose. OxNR; ReMoGo

Thirty East Forty-Second Street. Alan Davies. FTOS

.38, The. Ted Joans. WeW-3

Thirty-eight: Addressed to Mrs H—y. Charlotte Smith. ECWP; NALW; PEW; WPOW

38 Phoenix Street. Thomas Kinsella. ModIr Fr. One.

Thirty-Eighth Year, The. Lucille Clifton. OxWW

Thirty-eighth year, The. Thirty-Eighth Year, The. Lucille Clifton. OxWW

30 55. Michael Haslam. Oth Fr. Continual Song.

34. Chapter of the Prophet Isaiah, The. Abraham Cowley. ChIV-1

34th Merzgedicht in Memoriam Kurt Schwitters. Jackson Mac Low. PFTM-2

30 Miles from J-Town. Amy Uyematsu. GeoHom

31. Catullus. AmFaPo, tr. by Peter Whigam

Thirty Poems of Longing for People. Chin Nung.
"I get so drunk, I could be called the Earl of Dissipation!" CoBLCP

32 Positions of Love, The. Paul Eluard. PFTM-1 Fr. Immaculate Conception, The.

Thirty-Seven. Jack Marshall. GraLe

Thirty-some years ago, hitchhiking. Memory of Wilmington. Galway Kinnell. OPRER

Thirty Tanka. Tachibana Akemi.
Happiness Is When.
"Happiness is when." WoPoe, tr. by Burton Watson

"Thirty," the doctor said, "three grains, each one." Felo de Se. Thomas Blackburn. OxBTC

Thirty-third Canto. Hans Magnus Enzensberger. PoSu Fr. Sinking of the Titanic, The.

Thirty thousand feet of solid Cumberland. (LL) To the River Duddon. Norman Nicholson. NLP; NoP-4

33. Julia Alvarez.
He: Age Doesn't Matter When You're Both in Love. Son
Mother Asks What I'm Put To. Son
33 Is the Year That Jesus Christ. Son
("Where are the girls who were beautiful?") RA

Thirty-three, goodbye. Happy Birthday. Frank Bidart. HCAP; VCAP

33 Is the Year That Jesus Christ. Julia Alvarez. Son Fr. 33.

32s. 6d. for the chattels of Robert Hod, fugitive, Michaelmas 1230 at York. Alan Halsey. Oth Fr. Robin Hood Book, A.

Thirty-two times I went forth to my life. On My Birthday. Yehuda Amichai [or Amikhai]. MHP, tr. by Ruth Finer Mintz

Thirty white horses upon a red hill. Teeth and Gums. Mother Goose. NTCP; OxNR; ReMoGo

Thirty Years After. János Vajda. IQMS, tr. by Doreen Bell

Thirty years ago: gulls keen in the blue. Woman, A. Robert Pinsky. WeW-3

Thirty years ago, Marseilles lay burning in the sun, one day. Plato's Dog. John A. Scott. BMAP

Thirty years and more. Rankei Doryu. JDP, tr. by Yoel Hoffmann

Thirty Years Rising. Olena Kalytiak Davis. AmPoNex

This admirable gadget, when it is. Gyroscope. Howard Nemerov. NoAM

This ae nighte [or ean night], this ae nighte. Lyke-Wake Dirge, The [or A]. Unknown. EMWP; FaBoCh; HAP; NOBE; NPeEn; OBEV; OxBEV; PeECV; TFi; WeW-3; WoPoe

This afternoon. (LL) Good Luck Gold. Janet S. Wong. NOxBChV; OxIBACP

This afternoon as I sat. Elegy for Jack Bowman. Joseph Bruchac. CDW

This afternoon it rains as never before; and I. Down to the Dregs. César Vallejo. TCLAP, tr. by James Wright and James Wright

This afternoon, my love, speaking to you. In Which She Satisfies a Fear with the Rhetoric of Tears. Sister Juana Inés de la Cruz. BoWoP, tr. by Aliki and Willis Barnstone

This afternoon, my treasure, when I talked with you. Pleaure Given by Suspicion with the Rhetoric of Crying, The. Sister Juana Inés de la Cruz. BLPSL, tr. by Rene de Costa, Rigas Kappatos and Eleni Paidoussi

This afternoon was the colour of water falling through sunlight. September, 1918. Amy Lowell. NAAL-5

This Age. Raymond R. Patterson. NBV

This Alice. Herbert Morris. PoRA

This all happened before. David Lee. GifTon Fr. Driving and Drinking.

This almost bare tree is racing. November through a Giant Copper Beech. Edwin Honig. NoAM

This alone is what I wish for you: knowledge. Rita Dove. NAAAL Fr. Mother Love.

This Amber Sunstream. Mark Van Doren. APT-2

This ancient silver bowl of mine, it tells of good old times. On Lending a Punch-Bowl. Oliver Wendell Holmes. TreFP

This and That. Gareth Owen. OTCP

This angel, who mediates between us. Angel, The. Galway Kinnell. LCAP-2; NoAM

This apotheosis crushes me. Outcries. Hélène d'Oettingen. CuPo

This August night, raccoons. Invocation. Jane Hirshfield. BodElec; GeoHom

This autumn. Basho. EH, tr. by Robert Hass

This autumn day a noble man has died. Lamenting Noble Scholar Chu. Ni Tsan. CoBLCP, tr. by Jonathan Chaves

This autumn scene is worthy of the brush. Kuan Han-ch'ing. SuSp Fr. Tune: "Green Jade Flute."

This autumn the days have been hot. Sitting at Night on the Moon-viewing Terrace. Yang Wan-li. SuSp, tr. by Jonathan Chaves

This autumn will end. Akiko Yosano. OHMPJ

This bamboo I painted a long time ago. I Once Did a Bamboo Painting for Somebody—Now He Wants Me To Do Another. I Have Written This To Answer Him. Hsü Wei. CoBLCP, tr. by Jonathan Chaves

This bank makes welcome citizen and foreigner. Theocritus. GrAn

This Be Our Revenge. Saul [or Shaul] Tchernichowsky [or Tchernichovsky]. TrJP, tr. by Shalom Spiegel

This Be The Verse. Philip Larkin. NPeEn; NoAM; PoPoPo; PoetW

This be where new life commences. Wedding Sonnet. Arthur Zanker. AuPH, tr. by Lowell A. Bangerter

This Beach Can Be Dangerous. Allen Curnow. HarvBoo

This beast which preyed on sheep. Leonidas. GrAn; PGA

This beauteous form assures a piteous mind. (LL) John Donne. BASC; EBEV; HeIP-4; MeLP; NAEL-5v1; NAEL-6v1; NAEL-7v1; NOCV; NOSC; OxAEP-1; PeECV; PoE; Son Fr. Holy Sonnets.

This beauty, is it yours or is it mine? You or I? Ilyas Abu Shabaka. MAP, tr. by Michael Beard and Adnan Haydar

This bed thy center [or centre] is, these walls, thy sphe[a]re. (LL) Sun Rising, The. John Donne. BASC; BoLoP; CABP; ClHu; ESCV; FHYEP; FSCP; HAP; HeIP-4; MeLP; NAEL-5v1; NAEL-6v1; NAEL-7v1; NIL-7; NIP-4; NOBE; NOSC; NoP-4; PAI; PoE; PoPoPo; SCV; TFi; WeW-3

This before Trotsky and Breton. Make-Up. Maurice Kilwein Guevara. TouFir

This began somewhere. Essay on Language. Wanda Coleman. PmAP

This biplane is the shape of human flight. Robert Frost. WeW-3 Fr. Ten Mills.

This bird that a cat sprang loose in the house. More Joy in Heaven. Howard Nemerov. NoAM

This bird was happy once in the high trees. Boethius. MLL Fr. Consolation of Philosophy, The ("De Consolacione Philosophie").

This birthday card. Poem for the Birthday of Huey P. Newton. Sotère Torregian. NBV

This bit of polished marble—this. Bit of Marble, A. Clinton Scollard. APN-2

This black life. Spring Rain. William Hawkins. MoCV

This blessing love gives again into our arms. (LL) After Making Love We Hear Footsteps. Galway Kinnell. ColAP; NAAL-5; NIL-7; NIP-4; NoAM; NoP-4; PasH; RaBo; VCAP

This blue stone. Blue Rock, The. Sojourner Kincaid Rolle. GeoHom

This blue-washed, old, thatched summerhouse. Old Summerhouse, The. Walter De la Mare. GTBS-P

This Body. Michael Cuddihy. GifTon

This Body. Maurina Sherman. GeoHom

This body at night is the sound of the swaying creak of trees as they sink their roots to the river bank. This Body. Maurina Sherman. GeoHom

This body deemed machine—not daemon flesh. Soma. Suzanne Noguere. FFC

This body here feminine that hangs like a distant drop. To a Woman to a Path. Valentine Penrose. SurWo, tr. by Roland Penrose

This body of yours, this glorious flesh. Requiem for Eduard Streltsov. Aleksandr Petrovich Tkachenko. TCRP, tr. by Bradley Jordan

This body won't pollute. Sekioku-Seikyo. ZenPo, tr. by Takashi Ikemoto and Lucien Stryk

This bond of the prelates I pray you revoke. Brian [or Bryan] Merriman [or Merryman]. BIrV, tr. by Arland Ussher Fr. Midnight Court, The.

This bone once moved a hand. Rune-Maker, The. Frederick Feirstein. RA

This book by any yet unread. To My Dear Children. Anne Bradstreet. BASC; NAAL-3

This Book Is for Magda. Lew Welch. BB

This book is my link with father. At the South Pole. Jean Earle. Prnts

This book of Dante's, very sooth to say. Cino da Pistoia. EaItPo, tr. by Dante Gabriel Rossetti

This book says that his form is the same as anarachy in that it is a faculty or. Picasso and Anarchism. Leslie Scalapino. FTOS

This book, this page, this harebell laid to rest. In Our Tenth Year. Simon Armitage. OxBSo

This book was written in order to change the world. Foreword to New Numbers. Christopher Logue. OxBTC

This boy with the eyes of an owl. Cultivation of Orchids, The. Dionisio D. Martinez. TouFir

This brand of soap has the same smell as once in the big. Soap Suds. Louis MacNeice. EmeKit; FaBoMo; ModIr; NAEL-5v2; NAEL-6v2; NOIV; NPeEn; SCV

This Breach of Promise of Marriage! (LL) Sir William Schwenck Gilbert. NAEL-5v2; NAEL-6v2 Fr. Trial by Jury.

This Bread I Break. Dylan Thomas. ChIV-2; FaBoTw; GI; TRP

This Bridge Across. Christopher Gilbert. ESEAA; GT

This bridge of moon on bended knee above us. Paradise. Jill Alexander Essbaum. NAPBL

This bright harvest moon. Basho. SoOfWa, tr. by Sam Hamill

This brilliant boy was stupidly drowned. In Memoriam, J.A.R., Drowned, East London. Guy Butler. PeSAV

This brown woman's voice. Nina Simone. Lance Jeffers. SeSe

This burly son of a bitch. Not Just Yet. Carter Revard. VoR

This butterfly escaped, it seems. Tune: "Tsui-chung T'ien" To the Giant Butterfly. Wang Ho-ch'ing. ColAnChi, tr. by James I. Crump

This came from my counsel. On the Statue of Epaminondas in Thebes. Unknown. GrAn, tr. by Peter Levi

This Can't Be Love. Richard Rodgers. ReLy

This carpenter hadde wedded newe a wyf. Geoffrey Chaucer. NPeEn *Fr.* Canterbury Tales, The.

This cat was bought upon the day. Family Cat, The. Roy Fuller. OxBC

This cattle shed is Heaven now. *Unknown.* GrAn

This cavernous apartment is ours on four months' good will. Five O'Clock Opera. Lavinia Greenlaw. MFPA

This celestial seascape, with white herons got up as angels. Seascape. Elizabeth Bishop. ColAP; FaBoWP; OxBC

This change I feel puzzles me. Like Someone in Love. Jimmy Van Heusen. ReLy

This chapel that you gaze at, these stern tombs. Ruins of Time, The. Luis de Góngora y Argote. WoPoe, *tr. by* Robert Lowell

This Child. Norman Rosten. TrJP

This child is an angel. Angel. Maxine Scates. PBCAP

This Child Is the Mother. Gloria C. Oden. BlSi

This chirping. Sound of Birds at Noon, The. Dahlia Ravikovitch [*or* Ravikovich]. VCWP

This city, Budapest, smells of violets in the spring as do mesdames along the promenade. Gyula Krúdy. IQMS, *tr. by* John Lukacs

This city is made of stone, of blood, and fish. Anchorage. Joy Harjo. HATNAP; LTA; OPRER

This city's architecture is characterised by the colonnades. New Year's Eve. Lavinia Greenlaw. MFPA

This clerk-work, this first January chore. New Diary, A. Dannie Abse. AngWePo; NoAM

This cloak of purple, Leonidas, Xerxes gives you. Imaginary Dialogue. Antiphilus [*or* Antiphilos]. GrAn, *tr. by* Dudley Fitts

This clock. Clock. Valerie Worth. TLR

This Close. Dorianne Laux. ExTi

This cold winter night. Buson. SoOfWa, *tr. by* Sam Hamill

This Compost. Walt Whitman. AWP; MoAmPo; NAAL-2v1; NAAL-3; PFTM-1

This concord tempers then the elements. Boethius. MLL *Fr.* Consolation of Philosophy, The ("De Consolacione Philosophie").

This Condensery: The Complete Writing of Lorine Niedecker, 1985. Lorine Niedecker.

    Fancy Another Day Gone. FTOS

    "Glare from the brass horn makes sun-brown satin fit smoothly the girl by the, The." FTOS

This Consciousness that is aware. Emily Dickinson. NAAL-2v1; NAAL-3

This Corruptible. Elinor Wylie. MoAmPo

This could be. Dinakdakan. Maria Luisa B. Aguilar-Cariño. ReBoTo

This could be Scotland: a crag and far below. Old Folsom Prison. William Matthews. OPRER

This country might have. Right On: White America. Sonia Sanchez. ISC

This Country's Needs. Mrs. Henry Linden. CBWP-4

This crazy man has escaped the world. Wang Chiu-ssu. WoPoe, *tr. by* Jonathan Chaves *Fr.* After Reading the Poems of Master Han Shan.

This creature kneeling / dusted with snow, its teeth. November. Margaret Atwood. NOBC

This crescent's arc is. Kalamu ya Salaam. SpirFl *Fr.* New Orleans Haiku.

This cross is the most sublime. Coventry Cathedral. István Vas. IQMS, *tr. by* George Gömöri and Clive Wilmer

This cross-tree here. Cross-tree, The. Robert Herrick. CavPo; ChIV-2

This Crusty Fragment. Marsden Hartley. APT-1

This Curious Involvement, a Dominant Species. John Seed. Oth

This Dai adjusts his slipping shoulder-straps. David Jones. AngWePo *Fr.* In Parenthesis.

. . . This Damsell was not famous for the place. Arthur Golding. PBRV *Fr.* Ovid's Metamorphoses Book 6.

This dancer's stance slapped solely f'r th'effect. Square. Rob MacKenzie. Oth

This dark autumn. Basho. SoOfWa, *tr. by* Sam Hamill

This dark damnation, this hot unrainbowed rain? (LL) Reading *Paradise Lost* in Protestant Ulster 1984. Seamus Deane. BiHa; PBCIP

This darksome burn, horseback brown. Inversnaid. Gerard Manley Hopkins. FaBoVe; GTBS-P; MoBrPo; NPeEn; NoAM; PeVV; PoRA; RB; SCGP; SacPr; TFi; UnPo

This daughter watching ducks knows. Faraway Places. Walter McDonald. CDa

This Day. Hildegarde Flanner. WPE

This day and age we're living in. As Time Goes By. Herman Hupfeld. ReLy

This day beginning to a creature gave. On Her Own Birthday. Judith Madan. ECWP

This day I saw ane endless muir. Wire, The. Robert Garioch. NePenScot

This day, I think, will be a common day. Help Me Today. Elsie Robinson. PoToHe

This day I will my thankes sure now declare. On the 30th of June to God. Lady Jane Cavendish. EMWP

This day is for Israel light and rejoicing. Sabbath of Rest, A. Isaac Luria. TrJP, *tr. by* Nina Davis Salaman

This day, like all days. Last Chance for the Tarzan Holler. Thylias Moss. ExTi

This day, of all our days, has done. To Penelope, January 2, 1821. Byron. FaBoEE

This day of spring is hot and gold. Spring Day. "Igor Severyanin [*or* Severianin]." TCRP, *tr. by* Bernard Meares

This day's a riddle; for the God that made. Upon the Day of Our Saviour's Nativity. Francis Quarles. NOSC

This day, so many years ago a day. Anniversary with Agave Plants. Margherita Guidacci. CItWP, *tr. by* Cinzia Sartini Blum and Lara Trubowitz

This day the children of Speakthunder. In My Lifetime. James Welch. CDW

This Day, under My Hand. David Malouf. CBAP

This day, whate'er the fates decree. Stella's Birthday ([March 13,] 1727). Jonathan Swift. NoP-4; PoE; SCGP

This day when I lay my hope aside. This Day. Hildegarde Flanner. WPE

This day winding down now. Author's Prologue. Dylan Thomas. ChIV-1

This Dead Relationship. Katherine Pierpoint. EmeKit

This death you have nourished is too orderly. Medbh McGuckian. ModIr *Fr.* Porcelain Bells.

This Decoration. Hayden Carruth. NNaP

This definition poetry doth fit. Thomas Randolph. FaBoEE

This desert is a plateau of light. Language of Fossils, The. Anita Endrezze. HATNAP

This difficult, tedious, painful enterprise. (LL) Lament: "Your dying was a difficult enterprise." Thom Gunn. CAGL; GLP

This dirty—little—Heart. Emily Dickinson. NCAP

This disease is an evil bound upon the day. Sophocles. EroLit, *tr. by* Anne Carson *Fr.* Lovers of Achilles, The.

This divine October afternoon I would like. Pain. Alfonsina Storni. WPOW, *tr. by* Merrilee Antrim

This divine October morning. Sorrow. Alfonsina Storni. TCLAP, *tr. by* Andrew Rosing

This Do in Remembrance of Me. Horatius Bonar.

    "Here, O my Lord, I see Thee face to face." SacPr

This docile one inter. Emily Dickinson. APN-2

This door you might not open, and you did. Bluebeard. Edna St. Vincent Millay. APT-1

This drawing / came / from subtle hands. On the Portrait of a Girl. Erinna. GrAn, *tr. by* Lenore Mayhew

This dread is like a calm. Winter Holding off the Coast of North America. N. Scott Momaday. CDW; ColAP

This dream of water—what does it harbor? I See Chile in My Rearview Mirror. Agha Shahid Ali. NoP-4

This dream was either a prophesy or not. Dream, A. Anna Andreyevna Akhmatova. TCRusP, *tr. by* Daniel Weissbort

This dry night nothing unusual. War Horse, The. Eavan Boland. BIrV; CIP-2; PBCIP

This Durgling was a dual personage. Delivered at the Knighting of Lord Durgling by Great Bruce-Jean. Jean Toomer. GT

This dust was Timas. Dust of Timas, The. Sappho. AWP, *tr. by* E. A. Robinson

This dust was Timas; and they say. *Var. authors.* AWP *Fr.* Variations of Greek Themes.

This early May morn when there is none to wed. (LL) Cherry Trees, The. Edward Thomas. NAEL-5v2; NAEL-6v2; OBWP; PeFWW; Spl

This earth. Bill Neidjie. NOxBChV

This earth flails its environs. Outer Layers of Nervousness, The. Alan Davies. FTOS

This earth gave us. California, 1852. Sharyn Jeanne Skeeter. ISC

This Earth, My Brother. Kofi Awoonor. VCWP

This Earth our mighty Mother is, the Stones. Ovid. NPeEn, *tr. by* John Dryden *Fr.* Metamorphoses.

This earth Pythonax and his brother hides. On Two Brothers. Simonides. AWP, *tr. by* W. H. D. Rouse

This Easter, Arthur Winslow, less than dead. Robert Lowell. TwCP *Fr.* In Memory of Arthur Winslow.

This Edward in the Aprill of his age. Michael Drayton. CAGL *Fr.* Piers Gaveston.

This elderly gentleman. Hat. Tomasz Jastrun. AF, *tr. by* Daniel Bourne

This elderly poet, unpublished for five decades. Ashes, The. Carolyn Kizer. BAP-01

This endless gray-roofed city, and each heart. London Despair. Frances Darwin Cornford. OBMV

This Endris Night. Thys Endris Nyght. *Unknown.* EBEV; NOCV

This England never did, nor never shall. William Shakespeare. OxAEP-1 *Fr.* King John.

This Englishwoman. Stevie Smith. FaBoEE; NALW

This evening I pace chambers where I sought. In the King's Rooms. Timothy Steele. RA

This evening I prepared Wardance Soup. Wardance Soup. Phillip [*or* "Phil"] William George. VoR

This evening stillness. Foster Jewell. HA

This evening, the sturdy Levis. Notice. Steve Kowit. BLT

This Evening When I Spoke to You. Sister Juana Inés de la Cruz. SpanPo, *tr. by* Muriel Kittel

This evening when I spoke to you, my dear. This Evening When I Spoke to You. Sister Juana Inés de la Cruz. SpanPo, *tr. by* Muriel Kittel

This Excellent Machine. John Lehmann. OxBTC

This existence has, without the azure sphere, no reality. Quatrain. Sarmèd the Yahud. TrJP, *tr. by* David Shea

This expanse that spreads its nostrils wide. Shepherd. Avraham Shlonsky. MHP, *tr. by* Ruth Finer Mintz

This fabulous shadow only the sea keeps. (LL) At Melville's Tomb. Hart Crane. APT-2; HAP; HarvBoo; MoAmPo; NAAL-2v2; NAAL-5; NoAM; NoP-4; TAP; UnPo; VGW

This face had no use for light, took none of it. Made Shine. Josephine Miles. NoAM

This fairest lady, who, as well I wot. Sonnet: Death Is Not without but within Him. Cino da Pistoia. AWP; EaItPo, *tr. by* Dante Gabriel Rossetti

This fairest one of all the stars, whose flame. Ballata: One Speaks of the Beginning of His Love. *Unknown.* AWP; EaItPo, *tr. by* Dante Gabriel Rossetti

This fall morning is pretty much. Improvisation for the Stately Dwelling, An. A. R. Ammons. BodElec

This family portrait. Portrait of a Family. Carlos Drummond de Andrade. TCLAP, *tr. by* Virginia de Araújo

This Feast of the Law. *Unknown.* TrJP, *tr. by* Israel Zangwill

This fellow, perfect in men's eyes. Ikuo-Joun. ZenPo, *tr. by* Takashi Ikemoto and Lucien Stryk

This Fevers Me. Richard Eberhart. APT-2

This field-grass brushed our legs. In the Field. Richard Wilbur. NAAL-2v2

This field of stones, he said. In a Christian Churchyard. James Thomson. NOBVV

This final drouth of penitential tears? (LL) John Sutter. Yvor Winters. MoAmPo; NOBA; NoAM

This final scene I'll not see. Choko. JDP, *tr. by* Yoel Hoffmann

This first day of the year. On the Circumcision: New Year's Day. Luke Wadding [*or* Waddinge]. NOIV

This first fallen snow. Basho. SoOfWa, *tr. by* Sam Hamill

This fisher, netted like a fish. On Naucratius, Brother of St. Basil. Gregory of Nazianzus, Saint. GrAn, *tr. by* Robin Skelton

This flat city shortly after dawn. Aimé Césaire. NegPo *Fr.* Return to the Native Land, A.

This flattering glass, whose smooth face wears. On His Mistress Looking in a Glass. Thomas Carew. CaPo

This flesh you have loved. Kenneth Rexroth. APSN; APT-2 *Fr.* Love Poems of Marichiko, The.

This Flock So Small. Anna Nitschmann. AH, *tr. by* Sheema Z. Buehne

This flood thus stained fairer streames. (LL) Bible, *N.T.* NOSC; SacPr, *tr. by* Richard Crashaw *Fr.* St. Luke.

This flying angel's torrent cry. Eastern Tempest. Edmund Charles Blunden. MoBrPo

This, for my soul's peace, have I heard from Thee. *Unknown.* TAL *Fr.* Bhagavad-Gita, The.

This Form of Life Needs Sex. Allen Ginsberg. CLPP; NNaP

This formula for drawing comic rabbits made. (LL) Epitaph on an Unfortunate Artist. Robert Graves. FaBoEE; NOBL; OBCoV

This frightened, horny boy. Romance. Paul Zimmer. ReTh

This frog is more gifted. Swimming Upstream. Aimée Grunberger. PoCoUp

This frontier post brings me sorrow. Wang Ts'an. SuSp *Fr.* Seven Poems of Lament.

This frosty month. Tadatomo. JDP, *tr. by* Yoel Hoffmann

This fucking town's a fucking cuss. Oh! Fucking Halkirk. *Unknown.* FaBoWar

This fugitive between the Earth and Sky. Prelude. Tu Fu. TAL

This furnish'd Ark presents the greedy view. Francis Quarles. ESCV *Fr.* Emblems.

This Garden Being: The Hanging of Books. Clark Coolidge. FTOS

This garden does not take my eyes. Garden, The. James Shirley. BeJo; NOSC

This garden is outlandish. Women's Jail, The. Miriam Waddington. NOBC

This garment I give you. Be Brothers. Ifi Amadiume. HAWP

This gentleman of cultivated virtue. Gardening Chrysanthemums, I Think of [T'ao] Yüan-Ming. Ishikawa Jōzan. WoPoe, *tr. by* Jonathan Chaves

This ghoul-haunted woodland of Weir. (LL) Ulalume [*or* Ulalume—a Ballad]. Edgar Allan Poe. APN-1; AWP; NAAL-2v1; NAAL-5; NCAP; NOBA; OxBA; TAP; TCAPo

This gift, her gold-hemmed saffron gown. Phalaicus. GrAn

This gift of story. Heron-Woman. Marjorie M. Evasco. ReBoTo

This girl / Waits at the corner for. Girl, Boy, Flower, Bicycle. M. K. Joseph. PeNZ

This girlchild was born as usual. Barbie Doll. Marge Piercy. NIL-7; NIP-4

This gives support to insects. Jackson Mac Low. PmAP *Fr.* Pronouns, The—A Collection of 40 Dances—For the Dancers.

This god who has gaped ever since we created him. Lost. Orkhan Muyassar. BBASP; MAP, *tr. by* Samuel Hazo and Lena Jayyusi

This golden head has wit in it. I live. George Meredith. NOBVV *Fr.* Modern Love.

This grandson of fishes holds inside him. Evolution from the Fish. Robert Bly. NOBA; NoAM

This great Grandmother of all creatures bred. Edmund Spenser. NoSic *Fr.* Faerie Queene, The.

This Grizzly. Reg Saner. PoCoUp

This grove is too secret: one thinks of murder. Grove beyond the Barley, The. Alden Nowlan. MoCV

This hand-to-mouth, pert, rapid, nineteenth century. James Russell Lowell. TCAPo *Fr.* Our Own—Progression F.

This handless clock stares boldly from its tower. Clock in the Square, A. Adrienne Rich. HeIP-4

This handwriting wears itself away. Valerio Magrelli. NeIt

This happy place with all delights abounds. James Thomson. UV *Fr.* On Beauty [*or* Beauety].

This hare which scampers into age and death. Dürer's 'Young Hare.' Norah Hill. Prnts

This harpie with dry red curls. Red Dust. Philip Levine. NNaP; NoAM

This has happened before. Mere Pleasure of Flying, The. Jane Duran. MFPA

This has not happened before. (LL) Hollow Thesaurus, The. Roger McDonald. BMAP; CBAP

This haunted heart doesn't fit. Léon Laleau. NegPo, *tr. by* Ellen Conroy Kennedy *Fr.* Black Music.

This having learnt, thou hast attained the summe. John Milton. SCV *Fr.* Paradise Lost.

This he said to american poetry. Eastward Ho! A Succession. David Bromige. FTOS

This He was then. Carpenter, The. Mary Brent Whiteside. TrCP

This heap betrays me: please, Priapus, say. *Unknown.* PriapPo, *tr. by* Richard W. Hooper *Fr.* Priapus Poems, The.

This Heart of Mine. Harry Warren. ReLy

This hermit has his own school of Zen philosophy. (LL) On Receiving My Letter of Termination. Yüan Hung-tao. CoBLCP; ColAnChi, *tr. by* Jonathan Chaves

This high-caught hooded Reason broods upon my wrist. Falcon and the Dove, The. Sir Herbert Read. FaBoMo

This highest scholar in the school of sin. Sir Francis Hubert. NOSC *Fr.* Life and Death of Edward II, The.

This hill has been standing in my heart a long time. Antistrophe. Giacomo Leopardi. WoPoe, *tr. by* Robert Bringhurst

This holy night in open forum. Office Party. Phyllis McGinley. ChrPo; OBSV

This holy season, fit to fast and pray. Edmund Spenser. PoE *Fr.* Amoretti.

This horrible but superb painting. Parable of the Blind, The. William Carlos Williams. LCAP-2; SAmP

This horrible but superb painting. William Carlos Williams. LCAP-2; SAmP *Fr.* Pictures from Brueghel.

This hot day swept away. Basho. SoOfWa, *tr. by* Sam Hamill

This hot summer wind. When the Camel Is Dust it Goes Through the Needle's Eye. Anne Stevenson. Prnts

This hour is made of iron grates where the underground. Michelangelo Coviello. ItPo, *tr. by* Gayle Ridinger *Fr.* Well of Clouds, The.

This hour was set the time for heaven's descent. Twilit Revelation. Léonie Adams. MoAmPo

This Houre Her Vigill. Valentin Iremonger. CIP-2; ModIr; NOIV; OxBTC

This House. Robert Creeley. BodElec

This House. Ray A. Young Bear. CDW

This house has been far out at sea all night. Wind. Ted Hughes. HarvBoo; NAEL-5v2; NAEL-6v2; NoP-4

This house is a wreck said the children. Sad Children's Song, The. Grace Paley. SoSe-8; TaR

This house is closed to neighbors. Wayfarers, The. Yusuf Al-Khal. MAP; PFTM-2, *tr. by* Sargon Boulus and Samuel Hazo

This house is floored with water. Water Below, The. Fleur Adcock. PAI

This house, pitched now. Distances, The. Henry Rago. IllVoic

This *Humanist* Whom No Beliefs Constrained. James Vincent Cunningham. InPK-6

(Epigram: "This *Humanist* Whom No Beliefs Constrained") RB; VGW

This hurt has beat so long. Stillborn. Jane Duran. MFPA

This I admit, Death is terrible to me. Pure Death. Robert Graves. AWP; GTBS-P

This I ask Thee—tell it to me truly, Lord! Sacred Book, The. Zoroaster [*or* Zarathustra]. AWP, *tr. by* A. V. Williams Jackson

This I beheld, or dreamed it in a dream. Opportunity. Edward Rowland Sill. APN-2

This I do, being mad. Siege. Edna St. Vincent Millay. APT-1

This I had not expected. One December Night. Denise Levertov. BodElec

This I know, how love begins to be. Albrecht von Johannsdorf. GePo

This I write, mix ink with tears. Sadi [*or* Saadi *or* Sa'di]. WoPoe, *tr. by* Basil Bunting

This idiotic me is left alone to enjoy this solitude. Questing-for-Spring Arbor. Huang Ching-jen. SuSp, *tr. by* Chang Yin-nan

This, if Japanese, / Would represent grey boulders. Thyme Flowering among Rocks. Richard Wilbur. LCAP-2

This ignorance upon my tongue. On Reading Aloud My Early Poems. John Williams. WeW-3

This image is alive with my longing for you. Robert Glück. WiU   *Fr.* Visit, The.

This indecent procession of the undead. Mannequins. Daniel Mark Epstein. ReTh

This Indian weed, that once did grow. Tobacco. Philip Freneau. TAP

This infant world has taken long to make. Sonnet. George Macdonald. SacPr

This instigates an appetite / Precisely opposite. (LL) Emily Dickinson. APN-2; NOBA

This institution / perhaps one should say enterprise. Marriage. Marianne Craig Moore. APT-1; ColAP; NALW; NOBA

This introspective exile here today. Desmond O'Grady. PBCIP   *Fr.* Lines in a Roman Schoolhouse.

This is a big girl's pink poem. Pink Poem. Jackie Warren-Moore. SpirFl

This is a bridgeless blues. Two Fishing Villages. Ellease Southerland. GT

This is a busy corner. Amy Uyematsu. OpBo

This is a damned inhuman sort of war. Unseen Fire. Ralph Nixon Currey. OBWP; OxBTC; PoWW

This is a day to celebrate can-openers. Cast Off, The. Marge Piercy. NoAM

This is a dream of Winter, sweet as Spring. (LL) Swedes. Edward Thomas. HarvBoo; RB

This is a fearful thing to bear. Horror. Peter Baum. AWP, *tr. by* Jethro Bithell

This is a fine mess. Rāmprasād Sen. SinGod, *tr. by* Rachel Fell McDermott

This is a fine romance! (LL) Fine Romance, A. Dorothy Fields. OBCoV; ReLy

This is a good place for those things to wait. Railway Signals. Sheenagh Pugh. TCAWP

This is a hard life you are living. Album. Josephine Miles. APT-2; ColAP; FaBoWP

This is a hill that holds the church up. Burning Graves at Netherton, The. Roy Fisher. Oth

This is a journey into sight, sound, pain. Jump Black Honey Jump Black. Malkia Amala Cyril. InTrad

This is a litany of lost things. Litany, The. Dana Gioia. BAP-97

This Is a Love. Efraín Huerta. TCLAP, *tr. by* Todd Dampier

This is a love poem to our family. Flowers. Julie Fay. NAPBL

This is a love that began. This Is a Love. Efraín Huerta. TCLAP, *tr. by* Todd Dampier

This is a morning to say something. Morning to Remember, A; or, E Pluribus Unum. Edward Dorn. NoAM

This is a new sort of poem. Buy One Now. Dennis Joseph Enright. NOBL

This is a noon for beggars with whining. Hot Noon in Malabar. Kamala Das. OMIP

This Is a Photograph of Me. Margaret Atwood. NALW; NoAM; NoP-4

This Is a Poem for the Dead. Michael Ryan. YaYoPo

This is a poem like a suitcase. Wedding Preparations in the Country. David St. John. LCAP-2

This is a poem. Take it. Pack it up. Notes to the Reader. Robert Bringhurst. NOBC

This is a poem to my son Peter. Peter Meinke. PBCAP

This is a portrait. Here one can. Grandpapa. Harry Graham. OBCoV

This is a project as overwrought. Changing Address Books. Michael S. Glaser. UnSA

This is a quiet sector of a quiet front. Letter from Aragon, A. John Cornford. OBWP

This is a sailor's grave, while opposite. *Unknown.* GrAn

This is a season of holding back. Drought. Joan I. Siegel. PoCoUp

This is a sight that Wordsworth never knew. View from an Airplane at Night, over California, The. Bruce Bawer. RA

This is a song an epithalamium it is also. Couples. Kate Jennings. BMAP

This is a song for the genius child. Genius Child. Langston Hughes. PoPoPo

This is a song for the speechless. Song. Edward Hirsch. OPRER

This is a spirit poem. This Poem. Shirley Bradley LeFlore. SpirFl

This is a spray the Bird clung to. Misconceptions. Robert Browning. OBEV

This is a story Jung would understand. Candelaria and the Sea Turtle. Gladys Cardiff. HATNAP

This is a story my father told to me. *Tsa'lagi* Council Tree. Gladys Cardiff. HATNAP

This is a straight-forward choice between. Having read up on the subject. Jane Holland. NeBl

This is a strange country. Strange Country. Julie Parson-Nesbitt. MPUn

This is a strange museum. In one square yard see. In a Country Museum. Patricia Beer. FaBoWP

This is a strange seder. Seder, The. Enid Dame. UnSA

This is a symbol of beauty (you continue). "H. D.". NALW   *Fr.* Tribute to the Angels.

This is a tomb, no corpse within. On Lot's Wife Turned to Salt. Agathias. GrAn, *tr. by* Dudley Fitts

This is a wild land, country of my choice. Rocky Acres. Robert Graves. NoAM; UnPo

This is a word we use to plug. Variations on the Word *Love.* Margaret Atwood. LW; NoAM

This is about the summer and the wheels of sleep. Salt Pork, The. Robert Clayton Casto. HeIP-4

This is all that I saw, and all I know of the battle. (LL) Arthur Hugh Clough. EBVV; NPeEn; OxAEP-2; PeVV   *Fr.* Amours de Voyage.

This is all the life there is. Palladas [*or* Pallades]. PGA

This is alone Life, Joy, Empire, and Victory. (LL) Shelley. NAEL-5v2; NAEL-6v2; NOBRP

This Is an African Worm. Margaret Danner. BPo

This is an age-old story. Sinner Kissed an Angel, A. Ray Joseph. ReLy

This is an hour of calm, a quiet hour. Mateja Matevski. CarOv, *tr. by* Carolyn Kizer   *Fr.* Equinox.

This is an old and very cruel god. Vicarious Atonement. Richard Aldington. MoBrPo

This is an open poem. Open Poem. Melinda Goodman. WiU

This is Anacreon's grave. Here lie. Antipater of Sidon. GrAn; WoPoe, *tr. by* Robin Skelton

This is as far from home as you can get. Walk, The. William Scammell. NLP

This is Avram the cello-mender. Son of the Romanovs, A. Louis Simpson. OxBC

This is awkward I apologise. Bird-Woman. Rachel McAlpine. PeNZ

This Is Bad. Gottfried Benn. WoPoe, *tr. by* Harvey Shapiro

This is because I am spiteful. You see, I hate. Cassandra. William Dickey. YaYoPo

This is before electricity. Game after Supper. Margaret Atwood. FaBoWP; LCAP-2

This is before I'd read Nietzsche. Before Kant or Kierkegaard, even before Whitman and Yeats. Gas Station, The. C. K. Williams. VCAP

This is Callaeschrus' empty tomb. Argentarius. GrAn

This is Campidojo, whaur Titus ran. Campidoglio. Robert Garioch. OBVE

This is Charing Cross. Ford Madox Ford. FaBoWar; PeFWW   *Fr.* Antwerp.

This is Claudia Conway RTE News (Colour) Maynooth. (LL) Irish Hierarchy Bans Colour Photography. Paul Durcan. BiHa; PBCIP

This is dedicated to Merry Clayton, Fontella Bass, Vonetta. Black Back-Ups, The. Kate Rushin. ReTh

This is earthquake. Today. Langston Hughes. GLP; VGW

This is Erinna's sweet *oeuvre,* but small. Colophon to a Roll of Erinna's Poems. Asclepiades. GrAn, *tr. by* Lee T. Pearcy

This is eternity. (LL) What Are Years? Marianne Craig Moore. HarvBoo; MoAmPo; NOBA; NoAM; NoP-4; OxBA; SoSe-8

This is far too rich for poetry. Beyond Poetry. Shakuntala Hawoldar. HAWP

This is for *Beasts,* and that for *Men* the *Spring.* (LL) Abraham Cowley. BeJo; HAP; MeLP; OxAEP-1   *Fr.* Mistress, The.

This is for Elsa, also known as Liz. Invocation. Marilyn Hacker. ExTi; PuP-23; WiU

This is for ntozake. Something about You. Jessica Tarahata Hagedorn. PmAP

This is for the brothers—who aint here. For the Brothers Who Aint Here. Ras Baraka. InTrad

This is for the daughter. Cleopatra Mathis. ExTi   *Fr.* Lessons.

This is for the men and women. Isalutu. Askhari. InTrad

This is he . . . (LL) Happy Warrior, The. Sir Herbert Read. FaBoWar; PeFWW

This is he, who, felled by foes. Worship. Ralph Waldo Emerson. APN-1

This is Hill 49, an arena for bad dreams. Tin Woodsman, The. Paulette Jiles. NOBC

This is how he made her fall. Romance. Ann Sansom. MFPA; NeBl

This is how I learned. Wayne Koestenbaum. WiU Fr. Erotic Collectibles.

This is how it's done. Rough Music. Deborah Digges. ExTi

This is how it was. At the Movie: Virginia, 1956. Ellen Bryant Voigt. LTA; NoAM

This is how it was. Lilac preoccupations. Grey Dawn. Julio Herrera y Reissig. TCLAP, tr. by Andrew Rosing

This is how they make rain, the raw. Rain Dance. Susan Wicks. MFPA

This is how you live when you have a cold heart. Lamium. Louise Glück. HarvBoo

This is life fyno. (LL) Fara Diddle Dyno. Thomas Weelkes. FaBoCh; OBCoV

This is in the wind. Unswerving Marine. Carl Rakosi. FTOS

THIS IS IT and so: so long. P.O.E. Lincoln Kirstein. APT-2; PoWW

This is Italian. Here. Gardens of the Villa D'Este, The. Anthony Hecht. ColAP; OBGa

This is joye, this is true pleasure. Verses by the Princess Elizabeth, Given to Lord Harington, of Exton, Her Preceptor. Elizabeth, Queen of Bohemia. EMWP

This Is Just to Say. William Carlos Williams. APT-1; ChAP; HarvBoo; HeIP-4; InPK-6; KaS; NAAL-2v2; NAAL-5; NIL-7; NIP-4; NOBA; NoAM; NoP-4; OPOU; PAI; PoPoPo; TAP; TRP

This is Kypris' place; it ever pleases her. Anyte [or Anytes]. SaLy, tr. by Diane Rayor

This is London! How d'ye like it? (LL) Description of London, A. John Bancks. NOEC; OBCoV

This is made. House Cap. Bernadette Mayer. FTOS

This is my age. Fin-de-Siècle Identikit. Pierre Joris. PFTM-2

This is my cap. Inventory. Günter Eich. AF, tr. by David Young

This is my creed: To do some good. My Creed. Samuel Ellsworth Kiser. PoToHe

This is my curse, Pompous, I pray. Epigram. James Vincent Cunningham. HAP

This is my father. My Wicked Wicked Ways. Sandra Cisneros. ItWoWo

This Is My Father's World. Maltbie Davenport Babcock. AH

This is my home. Husband. Popati Hiranandani. OMIP, tr. by Popati Hiranandani

This is my last affair. (LL) Last Affair: Bessie's Blues Song. Michael S. Harper. ESEAA; HCAP; LCAP-2

This is my letter to the World. This Is My Letter to the World. Emily Dickinson. APN-2; HeIP-4; NAAL-2v1; NAAL-3; NALW; NOBA; NoAM; OxBA; OxWW; SAmP; SCV; TAP; TCAPo; WPE

This is my lyrical foliage. (LL) On Originality. Bill Manhire. HarvBoo; PeNZ

This is my mother's childhood home, my own. This Shade. Susanne Doyle. FFC

This is my mule, a poor long-suffering hack. Palladas [or Pallades]. GrAn

This is my page for English B. (LL) Theme for English B. Langston Hughes. APT-2; ColAP; FaBoA; HCAP; NIL-7; NIP-4; NOBA; NoAM; NoP-4; PoPoPo; SSLK

This is my play's [or playes] last scene, here heavens appoint. John Donne. BASC; EBEV; FaBoVe; MeLP; PAI; Son Fr. Holy Sonnets.

This is my portrait of Joanna—since the split. Seed-Picture, The. Medbh McGuckian. ModIr; PNI

This Is My Rock. David McCord. NTCP; TLR

This is my task: to move five cocoons. Sleep of the Painted Ladies, The. Nancy Willard. LCAP-2

This is my third Cold Food Festival. Rain During the Cold Food Festival. Su Tung-p'o (Su Shih). CrYelRi, tr. by Sam Hamill

This Is My Wine. Ilyas Abu Shabaka. MAP, tr. by Michael Beard and Adnan Haydar

This is my work so. Ann Bell. FaBoVe

This is neither the time nor the place for singing of. Some Walks With You. John Hollander. BodElec

This is newness: every little tawdry. New Year on Dartmoor. Sylvia Plath. FaBoWP

This is no baby skin—. Brown Rosellen. FFC

This Is No Case of Petty Right or Wrong. Edward Thomas. PeFWW; PoWW

This is no joke. She is fat and happy in the U.S.A. The kind of woman. Fat in America. Heid E. Erdrich. AmPoNex

This is no lif, alas, that I do lede. Unknown. MiEL

This is no mountain. Gods Are Here, The. Jean Toomer. APT-2

This is no proper route for middle-age. Stringer's Field. Roy McFadden. PNI

This is no rune nor riddle. "H. D.". APT-1 Fr. Tribute to the Angels.

This is no rune nor symbol. "H. D.". See This is no rune nor riddle

This is no time for a child to be born. Risk of Birth, The. Madeleine L'Engle. SacPr

This is none of I! (LL) Old Woman and the Pedlar, The. Mother Goose. OxNR; ReMoGo

This is not a dance. Large Room with Wood Floor. Clarence Major. GT

This is not a poem but a proem. I want to be in the wide. This is Not a Poem but a Proem. Edward Vincent Swart. PeSAV

This is not a small voice. This is Not a Small Voice. Sonia Sanchez. SpirFl

This is not about romance and dream. C. T. at the Five Spot. Thulani Davis. SeSe

This Is Not Death. Humbert Wolfe. MoBrPo

This is not easy to write about it involves. For All My Brothers and Sisters. Dick Lourie. CDa

This is not exactly what I mean. World and I, The. Laura Riding Jackson. APT-2; ColAP; HarvBoo

This is not first love. Anniversary. Gary Metras. PasH

This is not her, it is the wind. This Is Not Her. Joaquín Pasos. BLPSL, tr. by Rene de Costa, Rigas Kappatos and Eleni Paidoussi

This is not I. I had no body once. Naked Girl and Mirror. Judith Wright. NALW

This is not in German, nor in the tongue. Beethoven's Old Age. István Vas. IQMS, tr. by Daniel Gerard Hoffman

This is not sorrow, this is work: I build. Tomb of Lt. John Learmonth, A.I.F, The. John Streeter Manifold. CBAP

This is not the moon. Narihira (Ariwara no Narihira). OHPJ

This Is Not The Place Where I was Born. Miguel Piñero. PueRic

This is not what I meant to keep. Souvenir. Naomi Long Madgett. NBV

This is not winter: where is the crisp air. California Winter. Edward Rowland Sill. APN-2

This is not yet my poem. Poem of Alienation. Antonio Jacinto. PBMAP; PeSAV, tr. by Michael Wolfers

This is not you? These phrases are not you? Conrad Potter Aiken. MoAmPo Fr. Preludes for Memnon; or, Preludes to Attitude.

This Is of Two Worlds. Christopher Dewdney. NOBC

This is one of those Tuesdays. Temporal. George Jonas. NOBC

This is one poem. Chowa. JDP, tr. by Yoel Hoffmann

This is only a most piteous pretense of sleep! (LL) Beside the Bed. Charlotte Mew. BWW; MoBrPo; OxBSP; WPE

This is our last dance together. There Will Never Be Another You. Harry Warren. ReLy

This is our lot if we live so long and labour unto the end. Old Men, The. Rudyard Kipling. OBSV

This is Pioneer Village. The sun. Pioneer Village. Ruth Silcock. PeLi

This is plenty. This is more than enough. (LL) September Song. Geoffrey Hill. FaBoWar; HP; HarvBoo; NAEL-5v2; NAEL-6v2; NPeEn; NoAM; NoP-4; OBWP; OxBEV

This is prettiest of all, it is very pretty. (LL) Pretty. Stevie Smith. NAEL-5v2; NAEL-6v2; NoAM; NoP-4

This is really the story of a / sista. House of Desire, The. Sherley Anne Williams. BlSi

This is Scotch William Wallace. William Wallace. Francis Lauderdale Adams. OxBS

This is so far asea from the plateau. Marikudo in Kalibo, 1979. Dominador I. Ilio. ReBoTo

This is Tarsus, one place like anyplace else. Francine's Room. Louise Erdrich. NoAM

This is that dream i wake from. Powell (officer charged with the beating of rodney king). Lucille Clifton. RACG

This is Thaumareta's picture, and how well it captures. Nossis. GrAn

This is the anniversary of the day. Wedding Anniversary. Margaret E. Bruner. PoToHe

This Is the Army, Mr. Jones. Irving Berlin. ReLy

This is the barrow of grizzled Maronis, on which you see. Antipater of Sidon. HePo Fr. Epigrams.

This is the beauty of being alone. Stray Animals. James Tate. NoAM

This is the black sea-brute bulling through wave-wrack. Leviathan. W. S. Merwin. CoAmPo; ChIV-1; NOBA; NoAM

This is the bricklayer; hear the thud. Sanctuary. Elinor Wylie. BoWoP; MoAmPo

This is the camping ground. Struggle-Road Dance. Ahmos, II Zu-Bolton. ISC

This is the Chapel: here, my son. Clifton Chapel. Sir Henry John Newbolt. OBEV

This is the child in a buff-colored coat with a foxtail collar. Grossdaadi's Funeral. Julia Kasdorf. NeAmPo

This is the city of great doges hidden. Edgar Lee Masters. TCAPo Fr. Chicago.

This is the city of three leaves. Tripoli. Nadia Tuéni. PoArWo

This is the creature there has never been. Rainer Maria Rilke. OBVE *Fr.* Sonnets to Orpheus.

This is the cripples' hour on Seventh Avenue. Seventh Avenue. Muriel Rukeyser. NoAM

This is the curse. Write. (LL) Curse for a Nation, A. Elizabeth Barrett Browning. NALW; ViWPN; WPE; WPOW

This is the damsel by whom love is bought. Dino Frescobaldi. EaItPo, *tr. by* Dante Gabriel Rossetti

This is the day His hour of life draws near. Allen Tate. ChrPo; NAAL-2v2; Son *Fr.* Sonnets at Christmas.

This is the day the circus comes. Rachel Lyman Field. OBCA *Fr.* Circus Garland, A.

This is the day, the cock has crowed. Good Friday. Kathleen Jessie Raine. BBASP

This is the day, which down the void abysm. Shelley. FHYEP *Fr.* Prometheus Unbound [A Lyrical Drama in Four Acts].

This is the dead fiddle. Look where the wood. Dead Fiddle, The. Humbert Wolfe. TrJP

This is the debt I pay. Debt, The. Paul Laurence Dunbar. ColAP

This is the desk I sit at. That Day. Anne Sexton. BoWoP; CoAmPo

This is The Dust. Pneumoconiosis. Duncan Bush. AngWePo; TCAWP

This is the dust of Timias. Sappho. PGA

This is the easy time, there is nothing doing. Wintering. Sylvia Plath. NALW

This is the eldest daughter. Legacy. Stephanie Sugioka. FSt

This is the end of him, here he lies. Epitaph. Amy Levy. NOBVV; NPeEn; PEW; TrJP

This is the face of him, whose quick resource. On Seeing a Little Child Spin a Coin of Alexander the Great. Charles Tennyson Turner. NOBVV

This is the farmer sowing his corn. This is the House that Jack Built. Mother Goose. NPeEn

This is the female form. Walt Whitman. ErotSp *Fr.* I Sing the Body Electric.

This is the festival; we will inter hope. Tyrant, The. Faiz Ahmad Faiz. AF, *tr. by* Naomi Lazard

This is the field where the battle did not happen. At the Un-National Monument along the Canadian Border. William Stafford. HAP; HeIP-4

This is the field you did not come to, this. To the Lost Child. Brigit Pegeen Kelly. YaYoPo

This is the first poem. First Poem, The. Mark Van Doren. APT-2

This is the flat with its absence of curtains. In Residence: A Worst Case View. Sean O'Brien. OBCoV

This is the forest primeval. The murmuring pines and the hemlocks. Henry Wadsworth Longfellow. APN-1; NoP-4; TCAPo; UV *Fr.* Evangeline, a Tale of Acadie.

This is the form my passion takes. Form of Passion, A. David McFadden. NOBC

This is the garden:colours come and go. Sonnet IV. E. E. Cummings. ChIV-1; MoAmPo

This is the gay cliff of the nineteenth century. Brooklyn Heights. John Wain. OxBTC

This is the gift I thank Medusa for. (LL) Muse as Medusa, The. May Sarton. HW; NALW

This is the grave of Eusthenes the wise. Theocritus. GrAn

This is the grave of grey-haired Maronis. Antipater of Sidon. GrAn

This is the grave of Mike O'Day. On Mike O'Day. *Unknown.* FaBoEE

This is the green wherein a river chants. Sleeper in the Valley, The. Arthur Rimbaud. OBWP; WoPoe, *tr. by* William Jay Smith

This is the hall of broken limbs. Guide to the Other Gallery. Dana Gioia. RA

This Is the Hay That No Man Planted. Elizabeth Jane Coatsworth. OBCA

This is the heat that seeks the flaw in everything. Tennessee June. Jorie Graham. HarvBoo

This is the highest learning. Turn from Self. George Macdonald. PWR

This is the horror that, night after night. Gerald Louis Gould. OxBTC

This is the hour of magic, when the Moon. Hour of Magic, The. William Henry Davies. MoBrPo

This is the hour of reckoning. Mistake, The. Sami Mahdi. MAP, *tr. by* May Jayyusi

This is the hour that we must mourn. Tenebrae. Austin Clarke. BIrV; CIP-2; NOIV

This is the house destroyed by Jack. Berlin Wall Tune, The. Joseph Brodsky. AF, *tr. by* Joseph Brodsky

This is the house of Bedlam. Visits to St. Elizabeths. Elizabeth Bishop. CoAP; VGW

This is the House that Jack built. William Hone. NOBRP

This is the house that Jack built. House That Jack Built, The. Mother Goose. LB; OxBEV; OxBoLi; OxNR; ReMoGo

This is the house where Jesse White. Lowery Cot. Leonard Alfred George Strong. MoBrPo

This is the huge dream of us that we are heroes. Flowers of Politics, I, The. Michael McClure. NeAP

This Is the Key. *Unknown.* FaBoCh; OxBoLi
(Key of the kingdom, The.) OTCP
(This is the key of the Kingdom.) OxNR

This is the key to my happiness. Key, The. Richard Jones. GifTon

This is the knife with a handle of horn. House That Jack Built, The. *Unknown.* NBLV; OxBoLi

This is the lair of the landlady. Landlady, The. Margaret Atwood. NALW

This is the landscape of the Cambrian age. Coastline. Elaine Feinstein. BrRo

This is the lay of Ike. John Berryman. LCAP-2 *Fr.* Dream Songs.

This Is the Life. Louis MacNeice. NoAM

This is the light of the mind, cold and planetary. Moon and the Yew Tree, The. Sylvia Plath. BBASP; CoAP; FaBoMo; FaBoWP; VGW; WPE; WPOW

This is *The Making of America in Five Panels.* Empire Builders. Archibald MacLeish. OxBA

This is THE MAN—all shaven and shorn. William Hone. OBCoV *Fr.* Political House that Jack Built, The.

This Is the Map. Rodger Kamenetz. TaR

This is the meal pleasantly set . . . .this is the meat and drink for natural hunger. Walt Whitman. CAGL *Fr.* Song of Myself.

This is the metre Colombian. Metre Colombian, The. *Unknown.* UV

This is the midnight—let no star. Storm Cone, The. Rudyard Kipling. NoAM; OxBTC

This is the Month, and this the happy morn. John Milton. BASC; ChrPo; MeLP; NAEL-5v1; NAEL-6v1; NAEL-7v1; NOCV; NoP-4; PBRV; SCGP

This is the month sunrise skies. Lucy Larcom. TCAPo *Fr.* November.

This is the month the nightingale, clod-brown. Nightingale, The. John Clare. EBVV

This is the most audacious landscape. The gangster's. Alloy. Muriel Rukeyser. NoAM

This is the night mail crossing the border. Night Mail, The. W. H. Auden. OxBTC

This is the oldest book. Ordovician Fossil Algae. Lindley Williams Hubbell. APT-2

This is the one moment. Don't Worry 'Bout Me. Ted Koehler. ReLy

This is the one song everyone. Margaret Atwood. HAP; NIL-7; NIP-4; WeW-3 *Fr.* Songs of the Transformed.

This is the only thing as large as that. I regret I am not the physical giant. Realism. Tom Mandel. PmAP

This is the part where after a few minutes. Rapt. Irene McKinney. PBCAP

This is the perfect moment of love. Portrait of the Painter Hans Theo Richter and His Wife Gisela in Dresden, 1933. Tony Curtis. TCAWP

This is the place. Notes towards a Poem That Can Never Be Written. Margaret Atwood. NOBC

This is the place: be still for a while, my high-pressure steamboat! Nauvoo. Bayard Taylor. OBAL

This Is the Place to Wait. Horace Gregory. MoAmPo *Fr.* Passion of M'Phail, The.

This is the place / Where far from the unholy populace. In a Meadow. John Swinnerton Phillimore. OBEV

This is the poetry reading. Before the Poetry Reading. Louis Simpson. OxBC

This is the prettiest [or Prittiest] motion. To a Lady That Desired Me I Would Bear My Part with Her in a Song. Richard Lovelace. CaPo

This is the right gift for a poet. Empress Receives the Head of a Taiping Rebel, The. Sarah Gorham. FFC

This is the road I tread today. Death of Moses, The. *Unknown.* TrJP, *tr. by* Alice Lucas

This is the rotten-breathed forest. Raul Bopp. TCLAP, *tr. by* Renato Rezende *Fr.* Black Snake.

This is the sadness of the sea. Sadness of the Sea, The. William Carlos Williams. ColAP

This is the second month of the year I turn thirty-seven. February. Lisa Lewis. BodElec

This is the shame of the woman whose hand hides. Shame. Vern Rutsala. OPRER

This Is the Shape of the Leaf. Conrad Potter Aiken. NOBA; OxBA *Fr.* Priapus and the Pool.

This is the ship of pearl, which poets feign. Oliver Wendell Holmes. APN-1; ColAP; ITBLP; NAAL-3; NCAP; NOBA; NoP-4; TCAPo; TFi *Fr.* Autocrat of the Breakfast Table, The.

This is the silence of astounded souls. (LL) Crossing the Water. Sylvia Plath. HCAP; RB

This is the sin against the Holy Ghost. Unpardonable Sin, The. Nicholas Vachel Lindsay. ChIV-2

This is the skull of a hard-working man. Serapion of Alexandria. GrAn

This is the solid-looking quagmire.   Liberal, or Innocent by Definition.   James Philip McAuley.   NOBAu

This is the song for a soldier.   Come Back Clean.   Ella Wheeler Wilcox.   VerBaPo

This is the song of a dadaist.   Chanson Dada.   Tristan Tzara.   PFTM-1

This is the song of Kuk-ook, the bad boy.   Song of Kuk-ook, the Bad Boy, The.   *Eskimo Oral Tradition.*   TTTS

This is the song of Mehitabel.   Don Marquis.   APT-1; OBCoV   *Fr.* Archy and Mehitabel.

This is the sort of place you might arrive at after a long journey.   Ferns and the Night.   John Ash.   HarvBoo

This is the south. I look for evidence.   New Orleans.   Joy Harjo.   HATNAP

This is the spot where Jack Johnson.   Boxing Day.   Yusef Komunyakaa.   ISC

This is the spread of wings.   "H. D.".   WoPoe   *Fr.* Helen in Egypt.

This is the State above the Law.   Death-Bed, A.   Rudyard Kipling.   OxBEV; PoWW

This is the story of a man and woman.   Listen. This is the Noise of Myth.   Eavan Boland.   ModIr

This is the story of the men who stole chicken soup after it was.   If Chickens Could Talk.   Víctor Hernández Cruz.   PueRic

This is the sweet work of Erinna, not much, of course.   Asclepiades.   HePo   *Fr.* Epigrams.

This is the tale of the man.   Ticonderoga: A Legend of the West Highlands.   Robert Louis Stevenson.   EBNV; OBNV

This is the taste of the.   Islandis.   Víctor Hernández Cruz.   TouFir

This is the terminal: the light.   At the San Francisco Airport.   Yvor Winters.   AiP; HeIP-4; InPK-6; NIL-7; NIP-4; NOBA

This is the time lean woods shall spend.   Sundown.   Léonie Adams.   MoAmPo

This is the time of year.   Armadillo, The.   Elizabeth Bishop.   APT-2; ColAP; HCAP; NAAL-2v2; NAAL-5; NIL-7; NOBA; NoAM; NoP-4; TAP; VCAP; VGW

This is the time of year.   William Carlos Williams.   SAmP

This is the time of year / the lengthening dark appears.   In Lakeview Cemetery.   Christian Wiman.   AmPoNex

This is the tomb of great Megistias.   On His Friend Megistias, Who Died at Thermopylai.   Simonides.   GrAn, *tr.* by Peter Jay

This is the tree of earthly delights.   Tree of Earthly Delights.   Nancy Morejón.   TANSG, *tr.* by Joy Renjilian-Burgy

This is the twentieth century.   First on TV, A.   David Ignatow.   RaBo

This is the urgency: Live!   Second Sermon on the Warpland, The.   Gwendolyn Brooks.   BPo; NOBA

This is the voice of high midsummer's heat.   Mowing, The.   Sir Charles G. D. Roberts.   NOBC

This is the voice of mine own steadfast will. (LL)   Sister of Mercy, The.   Constance Naden.   VWP; ViWPN

This / is the way.   Way, The.   Catherine Obianuju Acholonu.   NAfrP

This is the way.   Overture.   Linda Pastan.   MiVo

This is the way it is. We see.   Ingmar Bergman's "Seventh Seal."   Robert Duncan.   PoE

This is the way of it, wide world over.   Way of It, The.   Ella Wheeler Wilcox.   LW

This is the way that autumn came to the trees.   When Autumn Came.   Faiz Ahmad Faiz.   PoetW, *tr.* by Naomi Lazard

This is the way the farmers ride.   *Unknown.*   LB

This is the way the gentlemen ride.   *Unknown.*   LB

This is the way the ladies ride.   Mother Goose.   LB; OxNR; ReMoGo

This is the way to start a sentence about starting a sentence. Here is the.   Wait.   Charles Bernstein.   PmAP

This is the weather of change.   Turning Thirty, I Contemplate Students Bicycling Home.   Rita Dove.   ESEAA

This is the weather the cuckoo likes.   Weathers [*or* Weather].   Thomas Hardy.   FaBoCh; MoBrPo; OBMV; RB

This is the Wheel of Dreams.   Carriers of the Dream Wheel.   N. Scott Momaday.   CDW; ColAP

This is the wind, the wind in a field of corn.   Wind.   James Fenton.   NAEL-5v2; NAEL-6v2

This is the world.   Map.   Linda Hogan.   ExTi

This is the world we wanted.   Gretel in Darkness.   Louise Glück.   NoAM; NoP-4

This is the year that squatters evict landlords.   Imagine the Angels of Bread.   Martín Espada.   TouFir

This is the young man, two cars ahead.   Accident, The.   Liz Rosenberg.   PBCAP

This is thi.   Tom Leonard.   NPeEn; NePenScot   *Fr.* Unrelated Incidents.

This is This.   Un-Now.   Daniil Kharms.   TCRP, *tr.* by Bradley Jordan

This is thy hour O Soul, thy free flight into the wordless.   Clear Midnight, A.   Walt Whitman.   AWTN; HAP; OxBSP; SAmP; Spl

This is time's.   Dandelion.   Neil Curry.   NLP

This is to say, my dear Augusta.   King William's Dispatch to Queen Augusta.   Coventry Patmore.   FaBoEE

This is too good for words. I lie here naked.   Fritz.   Gerald Stern.   MiVo

This is too tall, dark wave of soul.   Rodin's "Gates of Hell."   Jane Greer.   FFC

This is what I think.   Gochu.   JDP, *tr.* by Yoel Hoffmann

This is what it was like? God on a donkey.   Palms, The.   David Knight.   MoCV

This is what the afternoons of our first youth were like.   Memory.   Roque Dalton.   BLPSL, *tr.* by Rene de Costa, Rigas Kappatos and Eleni Paidoussi

This is what the professor wrote home, listen.   Substituted Poem of Laureate Quynh, The.   *Unknown.*   EaWin, *tr.* by W. S. Merwin and Nguyen Ngoc Bich

This is what the war ended up being about.   Corporal Charles Chungtu, U. S. M. C.   Bryan Alec Floyd.   CDa

This Is What the Watchbird Sings, Who Perches in the Lovetree.   Bruce Boyd.   NeAP

This is what will happen.   Keeping Track of the Serpents.   Víctor Hernández Cruz.   TouFir

This is what you are to me. (LL)   Conrad Potter Aiken.   NOBA; OxBA   *Fr.* Priapus and the Pool.

This is where he sought God.   Llanrhaeadr Ym Mochnant.   Ronald Stuart Thomas.   AngWePo

This is where I learned it. After pounding.   Two Poems.   Rosario Castellanos.   PFTM-2, *tr.* by Magda Bogin

This is where I once saw a deaf girl playing in a field.   Deaf Girl Playing.   James Tate.   LCAP-2

This is where I work. I live a little further to the east.   Thirty East Forty-Second Street.   Alan Davies.   FTOS

This is where stacking pays off.   Patrols.   D. F. Brown.   CDa

This is where the People take tea.   In a Chain-Store Cafeteria.   Paul Grano.   NOBAu

This is where the serpent lives, the bodiless.   Wallace Stevens.   PoE   *Fr.* Auroras of Autumn, The.

This is where the warrior from Ibokun came.   Edouard J. Maunick.   NegPo   *Fr.* As Far as Yoruba Land.

This is where they begin.   Assembling the Dead at Dachau.   Barbara Helfgott Hyett.   GotH

This is Willy Walker, and that's Tam Sim.   *Unknown.*   OxNR

This is your growing seed. Woman, rejoice. (LL)   Annunciation.   Primo Levi.   AF; GI

This is your hour—creep upon it!   This Is Your Hour.   Herbert Kaufman.   PoToHe

This island, garlanded with wild woods.   Archilochus.   OBVE

This Island Liv'd in Peace full many a Day.   Ruine of this Island, The.   Margaret Lucas Cavendish, Duchess of Newcastle.   EMWP

This isn't Italy where even.   Elsewhere.   Lynn Emanuel.   BodElec

This isn't right and I'm not going to throw it. (LL)   Football.   Louis Jenkins.   MoASP; RaBo

This isn't the wind in the willows.   Music in the Age of Iron.   Alberto Blanco.   CLPP, *tr.* by Julian Palley

This Italian square.   Dancers at the Moy.   Paul Muldoon.   BIrV

This itch of scribbling has no end, no ease.   Author's Quietus, The.   Henry Carey.   FaBoVe

This jar of roses and carnations on the window-sill.   Decoration.   Mary Ursula Bethell.   PeNZ

This Journey.   Ingrid Jonker.   BoWoP, *tr.* by Jack Cope and William Plomer

This juxtaposition of events without.   Ken Edwards.   Oth   *Fr.* Five Nocturnes, after Derek Jarman.

This keeps my hands.   Bracelets.   William Strode.   NOSC

This kind o' sogerin' ain't a mite like our October trainin'   James Russell Lowell.   OxBA   *Fr.* Biglow Papers, The.

This kiss.   Mary.   Lucille Clifton.   BBASP

This knave came in where he knew she'd be.   Cynewulf.   EroLit, *tr.* by Michael Alexander   *Fr.* Riddles (Exeter Book).

This knife is as long as my wife in the pool.   Cuauhtemoc.   Frank Lima.   BodElec

This kyng lay at Camylot upon Krystmasse.   *Unknown.*   PoE   *Fr.* Sir Gawain and the Green Knight.

This laboring through what is still undone.   Swan, The.   Rainer Maria Rilke.   NAWM-7v2; OWoS, *tr.* by Stephen Mitchell

This labour passed, by Bridewell all descend.   Pope.   FHYEP   *Fr.* Dunciad, The.

This labour will be welcome, honoured Friend! (LL)   William Wordsworth.   FHYEP; NAEL-6v2   *Fr.* Prelude, The; Growth of a Poet's Mind [1850 vers.].

This ladies' room fluorescence will not be ignored.   Midnight Vapor Light Breakdown.   Betsy Sholl.   LTA

This lady and her beautiful window.   This Lady and Her Beautiful Window.   Michel Deguy.   PFTM-2, *tr.* by Clayton Eshleman

This lady in her wheel chair has been left. Sea World. Eric Berlin. OPRER

This lady of the West Country? (LL) Epitaph, An: "Here lies a most beautiful lady." Walter De la Mare. MoBrPo; OBEV; RB

This Land. Ian Mudie. NOBAu

This land is my block and my people. Song of Devotion to the Forest. David Henderson. GT

This land like a mirror turns you inward. Dark Pines under Water. Gwendolyn MacEwen. NOBC

This Land's No Joy. Nguyễn Chí Thiện. VCWP, tr. by Huynh Sanh Thông

This lassitude. (LL) Nocturnal Visits. Claribel Alegría. TANSG; VCWP, tr. by Darwin Flakoll

This last night of nights. Ranseki. JDP, tr. by Yoel Hoffmann

This Last Pain. William Empson. EBEV; FaBoMo; GTBS-P; HarvBoo; MoBrPo; NPeEn; NoAM

This lay, a favorite of mine. Honeysuckle (Chevrefoil). Marie de France. BoWoP, tr. by Patricia Terry

This legend is told of me. Actaeon. Rayner Heppenstall. FaBoTw

This let me further add, that nature knows. Ovid. OBVE Fr. Metamorphoses.

This Life. Rita Dove. GT

This Life a Theater. Palladas [or Pallades]. NIP-4, tr. by Robert Bland

This life a theatre we well may call. This Life a Theater. Palladas [or Pallades]. NIP-4, tr. by Robert Bland

This life is most jolly. (LL) William Shakespeare. AWP; GTBS-P; NAEL-5v1; NOBE; NoSic; OBEV; SCGP Fr. As You Like It.

This life's a play, said Shakespeare; they're the truest words he spoke. I'm Mighty Glad I'm Living and That's All. George M. Cohan. ReLy

This life, which seems so fair. Madrigal. William Drummond, of Hawthornden. NOSC

This Lime-Tree Bower My Prison. Samuel Taylor Coleridge. FHYEP; HeIP-4; NAEL-5v2; NAEL-6v2; OBGa; OxAEP-2; PoE; TOF

This little attraction takes up no room and deals with only. Weighing-machine, The. Pierre McOrlan. MFP, tr. by Martin Sorrell

This little Babe so few days olde. Robert Southwell. See Come to your heaven, you [or yowe] heavenly choirs [or quires]

This little book a poet. Poet, The. Arseny [or Arsenii] Aleksandrovich Tarkovsky [or Tarkovskii]. TCRP, tr. by Peter Norman

This little courtyard—the wind is pure. Wen Cheng-ming. CoBLCP Fr. Chung-i Temple, The.

This little girl. She Will Gather Roses. Unknown. OxIBACP

This little Grave embraces. Epitaph on the Duke of Buckingham. Unknown. BASC; NPeEn; PBRV

This Little House Is Sugar. Langston Hughes. NTCP

This little house swallows. Ray A. Young Bear. STP

This little pig had a rub-a-dub. Unknown. OxNR

This Little Pig Went to Market. Mother Goose. LB; OxBEV; OxNR; ReMoGo

This little Pipkin fits this little Jellie. (LL) Ternarie of Littles, upon a Pipkin of Jellie [or Jelly] Sent to a Lady, A. Robert Herrick. BeJo; FaBoCh

This little residence is far from any village. Hermit Li's Herb Garden Retreat at T'ung-ch'uan. Hsü Pen. CoBLCP, tr. by Jonathan Chaves

This little rill that, from the springs. Rivulet, The. William Cullen Bryant. APN-1

This little, silent, gloomy monument. Epitaph on the Tombstone of a Child, the Last of Seven That Died Before. Aphra Behn. CABP; NOSC; OxBSo

This little stone, dear Sabinos. Unknown. PGA

This little time the breath and bulk of being. James Agee. APT-2

This Living Hand, Now Warm and Capable. John Keats. AmFaPo; BoLoP; InPK-6; TRP

(This Living Hand.) FHYEP; HAP; NoP-4; OxBSP; PoPoPo

(To Fanny Brawne.) NOBE; WoPoe

This loneliness. Gary Hotham. HA

This lonely hill has always been so dear. Infinite, The. Giacomo Leopardi. NAWM-7v2, tr. by Ottavio M. Casale

This lonely oak. Oak, The. Aleksandr Semionovich Kushner. TCRusP, tr. by Daniel Weissbort

This long valley caught. Pomegranate. Jean Janzen. GeoHom

This longed-for morning here is our sacrifice / to Zeus the finisher, and Artemis goddess of childbirth. Crinagoras. GrAn

This, Lord, was an anxious brother, and. Funeral Oration for a Mouse. Alan Dugan. HAP

This loud morning / sensed a small cry in. Third World Calling. Lawrence Ferlinghetti. BB

This love, I canna' bear it. Love's Pains. John Clare. NOBVV

This love puts all humanity from me. Thomas Hardy. TOF Fr. She, to Him.

This loved Philology. (LL) Emily Dickinson. APN-2; ChIV-2; NAAL-2v1; NAAL-3; NALW; TCAPo

This lovely day will lengthen into ev'ning. I'll Remember April. Don Raye. ReLy

This lovely flower fell to seed. Countee Cullen. APT-2; MoAmPo; SSLK; VGW Fr. Four Epitaphs.

This lovely, sweet, and beauteous Fairy Queen. Pastime of the Queen of Fairies, The. Margaret Lucas Cavendish, Duchess of Newcastle. BASC; NAEL-6v1

This Lunar Beauty. W. H. Auden. MoBrPo; NPeEn; OBMV; OxBTC; RB

This Lydian earth covers Amyntor, Philip's son. Anyte [or Anytes]. SaLy, tr. by Diane Rayor

This mad carnival of loving. Heinrich Heine. TrJP Fr. To Angélique.

This Mahādeva is a great white dog. Walking with the God. Gwyneth Lewis. HarvBoo

This makes my arm your prisoner; that, my heart. (LL) Upon a Ribbon [or Ribband]. Thomas Carew. BeJo; CaPo; NOSC; PoE

This Man. G. S. Shivarudrappa. OMIP, tr. by A. K. Ramanujan

This man charmed newcomers. Pindar. Plato. GrAn, tr. by Peter Jay

This man escaped the dirty fates. Flyer's Fall. Wallace Stevens. SAmP

This man has lived his life in his own fields. Old Man of Verona, The. Claudian. MLL, tr. by Helen Waddell

This man is o so. Item. E. E. Cummings. MoAmPo

This man knew out the secret ways of love. Of Jacopo del Sellaio. Ezra Pound. APT-1

'This man loved me'—then rise and trip away. (LL) Walter Savage Landor. EnLoPo; OBEV Fr. Ianthe.

This man measures my waste like substance abuse. High Speed. Debra Gregerman. AmPoNex

This man of leisure for twenty years. Wen Cheng-ming. CoBLCP Fr. Improvised on Horseback to Say Good-bye to Those Who Are Seeing Me Off.

This man's metallic; at a sudden blow. "George Eliot." LW Fr. Felix Holt: The Radical.

This man: this no-thing: vile: this brutish slave. Bianor. GrAn

This Man Was Strong. Cecil Day Lewis. Son

This man, who his own fatherland forgets. He Is My Countryman. Antoni Slonimski. TrJP, tr. by Frances Notley

This Manes alive once was a slave; now dead. Anyte [or Anytes]. SaLy, tr. by Diane Rayor

This mangled tentacle of the huge scolopendra. Antipater of Sidon. GrAn

This mania of knowing I am an angel. Exile. Alejandra Pizarnik. TCLAP, tr. by Frank Graziano and María Rosa Fort

This many are the days. Zuni Oral Tradition. NAWM-7v2, tr. by Ruth L. Bunzel Fr. Shalako.

This mast, new-shaved, through whom I rive the ropes. Choosing a Mast. Roy Campbell. FaBoTw; NoP-4

This matted and glossy photo of Yesenin. James [or Jim] Harrison. BodElec Fr. Letters to Yesenin.

This meal-white snow. Snow. Walter De la Mare. OxAEP-2

This Measure. Léonie Adams. MoAmPo

This memory of my mother stays with me. Remembrance. Margaret E. Bruner. PoToHe

This menopause of mine. Bloody Pause. "Astra." BrRo

This metal is engraved with Shang-style markings. Hsü Chung-hsing. CoBLCP Fr. Thanking Prince Chen-chi for Giving Me a Bronze Seal Engraved with Diagrams of the Five Sacred Mountains.

This midnight breathing. House Divided, A. Michael Ondaatje. MoCV

This midnight brings a moonless. Is This All That Remains of Love? Yusuf Al-Sa'igh. MAP, tr. by Diana Der Hovanessian and Salma Khadra Jayyusi

This midnight dream whispered to me. Dream about Our Master, William Shakespeare, The. Hyam Plutzik. RB

This might have been a place for sleep. Thistledown. Harold Monro. OxBTC

This moment, this minute. My Shining Hour. Johnny Mercer. ReLy

This Moment Yearning and Thoughtful. Walt Whitman. APN-1

This monument will outlast metal and I made it. Horace. CTC; WoPoe, tr. by Ezra Pound Fr. Odes.

This morn a young squire shall be made a knight. On Knighthood. Folgore da San Geminiano [or Gimignano]. AWP, tr. by John Addington Symonds

This morn ere yet had rung the matin peal. On a Frightful Dream. John Codrington Bampfylde. CenSon; NOEC

This morning. Introit. Paul Murray. BBASP

This morning. At the Shore. Mary Oliver. PoCoUp

This Morning. Michael Rosen. NOxBChV

This Morning. Muriel Rukeyser. BoWoP

This Morning. Kristina Rungano. HAWP; NAfrP

This morning. Suck, The. John Wieners. FTOS

This morning a cat got. Dad and the Cat and the Tree. Kit Wright. OTCP

This morning at the Luxembourg, this autumn at the Luxembourg. Luxembourg 1939. Léopold Sédar Senghor. PBMAP

This morning, between two branches of a tree. Dependencies, The. Howard Nemerov. VCAP

This morning, dear mother, as soon as 'twas light. Christopher Anstey. ECEV *Fr.* New Bath Guide, The.

This morning, flew up the lane. John Crowe Ransom. *See* This morning, there flew up the lane

This morning gathering wood. Sunday Evening. Sam Hunt. PeNZ

This morning I can't seem to get out of bed. Han Yü. CoBCP *Fr.* Autumn Thoughts.

This morning I clipped my fingernails. Michael Lassell. GLP *Fr.* Times Square Poems.

This morning I fight against the silence. Against the Silences to Come. Ron Loewinsohn. PoM

This morning I heard persistent and angry blows on a carpet. In the Yard of the Policlinic. Vladimir Holan. AF, *tr. by* C. G. Hanzlicek

This morning I visited the place where we lay. This Morning. Kristina Rungano. HAWP; NAfrP

This morning I wanted to bring you roses. Roses of Saadi, The. Marceline Desbordes-Valmore. WPOW, *tr. by* Deirdre Lashgari

This morning I will not. Kakinomoto no Hitomaro. OHPJ

This morning I woke / to an impatient scratching on the window. Apricot Tree. Magda Isanos. BoWoP

This morning in a car off Sunset the sky. Entity of Its Word, An. Sam Pereira. BodElec

This morning, it is raining. Rain. Danton R. Remoto. ReBoTo

This morning it was cold in my office study. Sent to the Taoist Holy Man of Ch'üan-chiao. Wei Ying-wu. CoBCP, *tr. by* Burton Watson

This morning my father looks out of the window, rubs his nose. This Morning. Michael Rosen. NOxBChV

This morning of the small snow. Charles Olson. NoAM *Fr.* Maximus Poems, The.

This Morning Our Boat Left. *Unknown.* OHMPC, *tr. by* Kenneth Rexroth

This morning's rainbow. O. Mabson Southard. HA

This morning she bought green 'methi' Another Woman. Imtiaz Dharker. EmeKit

This morning / the hawk / rose up. Hawk. Mary Oliver. NAAL-5; OWoS

This morning the hibiscus is in bloom, so I stayed in bed late. Will. L. S. Asekoff. KGB

This morning, the memory of you. Inertia. Vivienne Finch. BrRo

This morning, there flew up the lane. Lady Lost. John Crowe Ransom. MoAmPo

This morning/ there is a woman giving a sermon/ Her voice trembles over the. On the uptown lexington avenue express: Martin Luther King Day 1995. Duriel Harris. SpirFl

This morning, timely rapt [*or* wrapt] with holy fire. On Lucy, Countess[e] of Bedford. Ben Jonson. BASC; BeJo; NAEL-7v1; NOSC

This Morning Tom Child, the Painter, Died. Samuel Sewall. SCAP

This morning view / is very plain: thou art. Our Father. James Schuyler. ChIV-2

This morning we escort Sharon. Going Home. Patricia Pogson. NLP

This morning we find dead earthworms in the dining room again. First Trimester, The. Campbell McGrath. NeAmPo; UrbNat

This morning we found him. Bushed. Charles Lillard. NOBC

This morning we shall spend a few minutes. Money. Howard Nemerov. OxBC; VCAP; WeW-3

This morning, when a woman walks home. On the Otis Redding Bridge. Judson Mitcham. SwNoth

This morning, when I heard the crows. Crows, The. David McCord. MoAmPo

This morning while waiting for you to wake. INRI. Melanie Hope. WiU

This morning with a blue flame burning. Poem for Trapped Things, A. John Wieners. BB; GLP; NeAP; PmAP; PoM

This mossy [*or* mossie] bank they pressed [*or* press'd *or* prest]. Pastoral[l] Dialogue, A. Thomas Carew. CaPo

This most afflicts me, that departing hence. John Milton. PeECV *Fr.* Paradise Lost.

This moth caught in the room tonight. Lying Awake. W. D. Snodgrass. MoAmPo

This moth saw brightness. Issa. EH, *tr. by* Robert Hass

This motley piece to you I send. Matthew Green. NoP-4 *Fr.* Spleen, The.

This motor won't start. Electroconvulsive Therapy. Elspeth Cameron Ritchie. BloBone

This mound the Achaeans reared—Achilles' tomb. Epitaph on Achilles. *Unknown.* AWP, *tr. by* William M. Hardinge

"This mountain of release is such that the." Dante Alighieri. EnlH *Fr.* Divina Commedia.

This mountain's secret is the son of Euphorion of Athens. Aeschylus. GrAn

This much I have: an urban space. . . Impressive. Asphalt Musings. Carl Hancock Rux. HeMarv

This much, O heaven—if I should brood or rave. Prayer in Darkness, A. Gilbert Keith Chesterton. MoBrPo

This much-praised general made such a cock of things. General's Plaque, The. Ho Xuan Hong. FaBoWar, *tr. by* Graeme Wilson

This multitude of melted hands. Cactus. Jean-Joseph Rabéarivelo [*or* Rebéarivelo]. NegPo, *tr. by* Ellen Conroy Kennedy

This music has lasted since the world began. Aegean, The. Maria Luisa Spaziani. NeIt, *tr. by* Beverly Allen

This music is the country you lost. Flamenco Guitar. Ruth L. Schwartz. WiU

This must be. Joseki. JDP, *tr. by* Yoel Hoffmann

This must have been a pretty garden once. (LL) Time. Mary Ursula Bethell. FaBoWP; OBGa

"This must have been her bedroom, Mr. Choi." Counting the Children. Dana Gioia. RA

This mutilated tree gives. Rivers. Giuseppe Ungaretti. PeFWW, *tr. by* Jon Silkin

This new and gorgeous garment, majesty. William Shakespeare. OxAEP-1 *Fr.* King Henry IV, Pt. II.

This new Daks suit, greeny-brown. Metamorphosis. Peter Porter. OxBTC

This New Day. Vail Read. AH

This new day the eyes of children. This New Day. Vail Read. AH

This new kind of metal will not suffer. Christianite. William Stafford. NoAM

This new year scarce would serve me, so farewell. (LL) Upon Dr. Davies's British Grammar. James Howell. AngWePo; OBWVE

This Newly Created World. *Unknown.* AiP

This Night. N. Revathi Devi. OMIP

This night cast iron over flat land. Unreal Song of the Old, The. James Koller. PoM

This night is pure and clear as thrice refinèd silver. Fountains. Sacheverell Sitwell. MoBrPo

This night presents a play, which publick rage. Prologue to Hugh Kelly's *A Word to the Wise*. Samuel Johnson. EBEV; NPeEn; OxAEP-1

This Night Sees Ireland [*or* Eire] Desolate. Aindrais MacMarcuis. BIrV, *tr. by* Robin Flower

This night shall thy soul be required of thee. Scorpion. Stevie Smith. EBEV; FaBoWP; NPeEn; OxAEP-2; PeECV; PoE

This night there are no limits to what may be given. Jelaluddin [*or* Jalal al-Din] Rumi. WoPoe, *tr. by* Coleman Barks and John Moyne

This night tonight is cold. Janet Campbell (Seònaid Chaimbeul). EMWP

This, no song of an ingénue. Ballade at Thirty-Five. Dorothy Parker. APT-1

This noiseless ball and top so round. Philocles. Leonidas of Tarentum. AWP, *tr. by* F. A. Wright

This notebook in which he used to sketch. Milk. Maurice Riordan. ModIr

This, O my stomach, is a painting. American Heritage. Robert Sward. OBAL

This ocean, humiliating in its disguises. Jack Spicer. APSN *Fr.* Language.

This Octopus Exploits Women. James Fenton. NoAM

This old village. Basho. EH, *tr. by* Robert Hass

This Old Woman. Mongane Wally Serote. NAfrP

This old woman, stalking up the street. This Old Woman. Mongane Wally Serote. NAfrP

This old year sank so weak, defenseless. New Year's Eve 1917. Karl Kraus. AuPH, *tr. by* Lowell A. Bangerter

This on thy posy-ring I've writ. Posy Ring, The. Clément Marot. AWP, *tr. by* Ford Madox Ford

This one lie down on grass. Astrologer Predicts at Mary's Birth, The. Lucille Clifton. NALW

This one remaining rebel / is the sparrow-camel. (LL) He "Digesteth Harde Yron." Marianne Craig Moore. APT-1; NoAM; OWoS

This one request I make to him that sits the clouds above. Love and Debt Alike Troublesome. Sir John Suckling. CavPo

This One's on Me. Phyllis Gotlieb. MoCV; NOBC

This one, said the sculptor, is the last of the biblical figures. David. Linda Pastan. CRP

This one shows me standing by the Delaware. Tashlikh. Gerald Stern. TaR

This one steps into an outsize pair of wings. Poem for a Younger Son. William Scammell. NLP

This one was no philanthropist. For the Grave of a Peace-Loving Man. Hans Magnus Enzensberger. VCWP, *tr. by* Hans Magnus Enzensberger and Michael Hamburger

This one was put in a jacket. Counting the Mad. Donald Justice. CoAmPo; NIP-4; NoP-4; PAI; TRP; UnPo

This onion-dome holds all intricacies. Greenwich Observatory. Sidney Keyes. MoBrPo

This only grant me, that my means may lie [*or* lye]. Of Myself [*or* My Self]. Abraham Cowley. BASC

This [*or* that] is the end / of Solomon Grundy. (LL) Solomon Grundy. Mother Goose. LB; NBLV; OTCP; OxBoLi; OxNR; PeLV; ReMoGo

This oriental country, year after year. Fan from Korea, A. Chu Yün-ming. CoBLCP; ColAnChi, *tr. by* Jonathan Chaves

This page will be no less a riddle. John 1:14 (1969). Jorge Luis Borges. GI, *tr. by* Norman Thomas Di Giovanni

This pair of skin gloves is sixty-six years old. Skins. Judith Wright. BMAP

This palace was once magnificent. At Ch'ang-men Palace. Li Po. CrYelRi, *tr. by* Sam Hamill

This pale winter the wisteria looks like an empty. Wisteria. Eloise Klein Healy. GeoHom

This Pardoner had hair as yellow as wax. Geoffrey Chaucer. SCV *Fr.* Canterbury Tales, The.

This phalanx of pines, these demi-fountains. Martial. Thom Gunn. OBGa, *tr. by* Peter Porter

This phantasm. Okyo. JDP, *tr. by* Yoel Hoffmann

This phantom who is always with me. Phantom. Tawfiq [*or* Taufiq] Sayigh. MAP, *tr. by* Thomas G. Ezzy and Anne Royal

This picnic table's carefully etched. Eighties Meditation. Kay Murphy. SwNoth

This piece of Lydian earth holds Amyntor. Antipater of Sidon. GrAn

This pig got in the barn. *Unknown.* OxNR

This pines. This That and Then. Douglas Messerli. FTOS

This place has no nakedness. Wilderness. Faye George. PoCoUp

This Place in the Ways. Muriel Rukeyser. AiP

This place is cold. Three Poems for the Indian Steelworkers. Joseph Bruchac. CDW

This place is the Cyprian's for she has ever the fancy. Anyte [*or* Anytes]. GrAn

This place moves from me. Poem before Departure. Jean Burden. WPE

This place of wild land. Beyond the World. Muso Soseki. EaWin, *tr. by* W. S. Merwin

This place (quoth she) they say's enchanted. Samuel Butler (1612–80). NOBL *Fr.* Hudibras.

This Place Rumord to Have Been Sodom. Robert Duncan. CAGL; NOBA; NeAP; PoM

This place's quality is not its former nature. Judith Wright. HarvBoo *Fr.* Shadow of Fire: Ghazals, The.

This place up in Charlotte called Chuck's where I. Waiting on Elvis, 1956. Joyce Carol Oates. AllShUp; SwNoth

This *plat* is a true Ratatouille. Ratatouille. Gina Berkeley. PeLi

This Plot, which fail'd for want of common Sense. Dryden. NPeEn *Fr.* Absalom and Achitophel.

This ploughman dead in battle slept out of doors. Private, A. Edward Thomas. GTBS-P; PeFWW; TCAWP

This Poem. Ruth Forman. SpirFl

This Poem. Barbara Leslie Jordan. ExTi

This Poem. Shirley Bradley LeFlore. SpirFl

This Poem. Constance Urdang. PBCAP

This poem by Rupert Brookeborough. Written Answer, A. Tom Paulin. ModIr

This poem I write to teach the reader. Writing in England Now. Philip O'Connor. OxBTC

This poem is a letter to tell you that I. Transformations. Joy Harjo. HATNAP

This poem is about the strength and sadness of potatoes. Potatoes. David Donnell. NIP-4; NOBC; SpudSo

This poem is being written in the dark. Poem Composed During a Brownout. Fidelito Cortes. ReBoTo

This poem is concerned with language on a very plain level. Paradoxes and Oxymorons. John Ashbery. FTOS; HeIP-4; NoAM; PmAP; PoPoPo

This Poem Is Dedicated to Brother Andries Raditsela. Nise Malange. PeSAV

This Poem Is for Bear. Gary Snyder. NOBA; PFTM-2 *Fr.* Myths and Texts.

This Poem Is for Deer. Gary Snyder. GeoHom; NOBA *Fr.* Myths and Texts.

This poem should have started. Between Acts. Janice Lowe. InTrad

This poet describes carbon paper, how it lies flat. Salad Days. Susan Musgrave. NoAM

This pool, the quiet sky. March Evening. Leonard Alfred George Strong. MoBrPo

This Poor Man. W. J. Gruffydd. OBWVE, *tr. by* Gwyn Jones

This poring over your *Grand Cyrus*. On A Romantic Lady. Mary Monck. ECWP; NOEC; RACG

This portrait captures Thaumareta's form—it renders. Nossis. SaLy, *tr. by* Diane Rayor

This portrait which I treasure so. Epigram: Likeness, The. Martial. RomPo, *tr. by* Brian Hill

This Prayer I Make. William Wordsworth. PoToHe

This precarious peak commands a view. Trip to Yüeh-lu Temple, A. Li Tung-yang. CoBLCP, *tr. by* Jonathan Chaves

This present that constantly fails. Demand. Piera Oppezzo. CItWP, *tr. by* Cinzia Sartini Blum and Lara Trubowitz

This prince of a former dynasty. Little Landscape by Chao Ch'ien-li, A. Yü Chi. CoBLCP, *tr. by* Jonathan Chaves

This profound piety is my own country. My Country. Jaime Torres Bodet. TCLAP, *tr. by* Sonja Karsen

This proud scepter which now severed. *Unknown.* PriapPo, *tr. by* Richard W. Hooper *Fr.* Priapus Poems, The.

This purple cloud of grief within my heart. Old Love Butchered (Colorado Springs and Huachuca). Lance Jeffers. NBV

This queen of prey (now prey to you). Lady with a Falcon on Her Fist, A. Richard Lovelace. CaPo

This *quidam* gives that *quidam* for *one* round. Philodemus. GrAn

This Quiet Dust. John Hall Wheelock. MoAmPo

This quiet Dust was Gentlemen and Ladies. Cemetery, A. Emily Dickinson. MoAmPo; OxBA

This quiet morning light. To Mark Anthony in Heaven. William Carlos Williams. NOBA; SAmP; TCAPo

This quiet mound beneath. Corporal Pym. Walter De la Mare. FaBoEE

This quiet roof, bestirred with pigeon plumes. Graveyard by the Sea, The. Paul Valéry. STV, *tr. by* John Frederick Nims

This, quoth the Eskimo master. Latter-day Geography Lesson. Ronald Allison Kells Mason. PeNZ

This Railway Station. Allan M. Laing. UV

This rather tall Indian man shot me in a dream. Action-Packed Sonnet. Prageeta Sharma. HeMarv

This ration card, once shocking pink. Ration Card, The. Liz Sohappy Bahe. CDW

This reckless flight, where is this bound to take us? Imre Madách. IQMS, *tr. by* Iain MacLeod *Fr.* Tragedy of Man.

This red / Italian hand. For My Daughter. John Logan. CRP

This rehabilitation system! (LL) Solitary Confinement. Robert Walker. IBA; NOBAu

This reverend shadow cast that setting sun. Upon Bishop Andrewes's [*or* Andrewes His] Picture before His Sermons. Richard Crashaw. NOSC

This ritzy vista includes the money. Love Poem. John Forbes. BMAP

This River. Annette Allen. MPUn

This road. Basho. EH; NIL-7, *tr. by* Robert Hass

This road our blithe-heart elders knew. Lyric on the Lyric, A. Lizette Woodworth Reese. APN-2

This rock-hewn seat in a favourite corner. His Favourite Seat. Deborah Randall. NeBl

This Room and Everything in It. Li-Young Lee. IllVoic; NAAL-5; OpBo

This room is reserved for wandering Jews. For the Wandering Jews. Philip Schultz. TaR

This rose tree is not made to bear. Envy. Charles Lamb. WoRP

This rudely sculptured porter-pot. Undying Thirst. Antipater of Sidon. AWP, *tr. by* Robert Bland

This ruined temple. Basho. SoOfWa, *tr. by* Sam Hamill

This Runner. Francis Webb. CBAP

This rust-infested cage with worn-out brakes. Lines on a Van's Dereliction. Douglas Houston. TCAWP

This sacred urn holds the ashes of the Queen of Navarre. Jane Seymour. EMWP *Fr.* Hecatodistichon.

This sad world we inhabit. *Unknown.* NOIV *Fr.* Calendar of Oengus, The.

This said, divine Talthybius he call'd, and bad him haste. Homer. FaBoWar, *tr. by* George Chapman *Fr.* Iliad, The.

This said, he reacht to take his sonne. Homer. OBVE, *tr. by* George Chapman *Fr.* Iliad, The.

This said, he turned about his steed. Samuel Butler (1612–80). OxBoLi *Fr.* Hudibras.

This said, she twirled the thread on an ugly spool. Seneca. RomPo, *tr. by* J. P. Sullivan *Fr.* Apocolocyntosis.

This said, the restles generall through the darke. Christopher Marlowe. PBRV *Fr.* Lucan's Pharsalia Book 1.

This salt. Ode to Salt. Pablo Neruda. TCLAP, *tr. by* Margaret Sayers Peden

This same moon hangs over Fu-chou. Moonlit Night. Tu Fu. CrYelRi, *tr. by* Sam Hamill

This savage wish on certain days. Léon Laleau. NegPo, *tr. by* Ellen Conroy Kennedy *Fr.* Black Music.

This sea will never die, neither will it ever grow old. Middle of the World. D. H. Lawrence. HAP; NoAM; WoPoe

This seems, in a world where love must take its chances. Mona Van Duyn. HAP *Fr.* Footnotes to "The Autobiography of Bertrand Russell."

This sense of space. Jeannette Miller. TANSG, *tr. by* Paula Vega

This sense of space, mine, familiar. This sense of space. Jeannette Miller. TANSG, *tr. by* Paula Vega

This sentence have I left behind. Nameless Epitaph, A. Matthew Arnold. FaBoEE

This Shade. Susanne Doyle. FFC

This shade-bestowing pear-tree, thou. *Unknown*. AWP, *tr.* by Allen Upward *Fr.* Shi King.

This shadow at my shoulder doesn't shed. Climbing. Jennifer Maiden. BMAP; CBAP

This she? no, this is Diomed's Cressida. William Shakespeare. OxAEP-1 *Fr.* Troilus and Cressida.

This sheepskin coat may be worn out. Wearing a Worn-Out Coat. Chin Nung. CoBLCP, *tr.* by Jonathan Chaves

This shining that us showers. *Unknown*. WoPoe, *tr.* by Tony Harrison *Fr.* Doomsday, the Mysteries.

This shop in a little road I know is like a grubby sweet left. Hairdresser's, The. Pierre McOrlan. MFP, *tr.* by Martin Sorrell

This short straight sword. Prelude. Ronald Allison Kells Mason. PeNZ

This silence at the sea's edge, so late in the afternoon. About Time. Laurens Vancrevel. TuT, *tr.* by Anne Kennedy

This silken wreath, which circles in mine arm. Upon a Ribbon [*or* Ribband]. Thomas Carew. BeJo; CaPo; NOSC; PoE

This silver thing I send you for your birthday. Crinagoras. GrAn

This silver was not carved but mesmerized. Satyr by Diodorus, A. Plato the Younger. GrAn, *tr.* by G. R. H. Wright

This singing / is a kind of dying. Anne Sexton. BodElec *Fr.* Furies, The.

This skirt's in the style. Hsüeh T'ao. WoPoe, *tr.* by Jeanne Larsen *Fr.* Trying on New-Made Clothes: Three Poems.

This sky is to be opened. Hermetic Bird. Philip Lamantia. VGW

This slow one. (LL) Tortoise-Shell. D. H. Lawrence. FaBoVe; NAEL-5v2; NAEL-6v2; OxAEP-2

This small. Magnet. Valerie Worth. KaS

This small repast, with her I love. Contentment, to a Friend. Charlotte MacCarthy. PoBW

This Smoking World. Graham Lee Hemminger. NBLV

This soft October. Reserved Sacrament. James Schuyler. BodElec

This solitary fretwork. Final Tree. Gabriela Mistral. TCLAP, *tr.* by Doris Dana

This Solitude of Cataracts. Wallace Stevens. LCAP-2

This song of late autumn. Autumn. Itsik [*or* Itzik *or* Itzig] Manger. TrJP

This southern rain nourishes the mossy stones. Tu Fu. SuSp *Fr.* Rain, Four Poems.

This space so clear and blue. Windows. Frank O'Hara. BodElec

This sparrow / who comes to sit at my window. Sparrow, The. William Carlos Williams. LCAP-2; VGW

This speech all Troyans did applaud, who from their traces losde. Homer. OBVE, *tr.* by George Chapman *Fr.* Iliad, The.

This spiritual man left the world behind. Sent To Be Inscribed on the Temple of P'u-jun (Universal Fructification) at Lou-fu Mountain. Yü Chi. CoBLCP, *tr.* by Jonathan Chaves

This spoke, a huge wave tooke him by the head. Homer. OBVE *Fr.* Odyssey.

This spoonful of chocolate tapioca. Thinking of the Lost World. Randall Jarrell. NAAL-5; NOBA; NoAM

This spring as it comes bursts up in bonfires green. Enkindled Spring, The. D. H. Lawrence. NoAM

This spring is going, too. New Music, A. Haniel Long. APT-1

This spring rain. William J. Higginson. HA

This spring, the sky is leaking. Finding Serenity. Yüan Mei. CoBLCP, *tr.* by Jonathan Chaves

This Spud's for You. William Matthews. SpudSo

This squalid dome of soot-obscuréd glass. This Railway Station. Allan M. Laing. UV

This stalk of day-old bread. Three-Course Meal for the New Year, A. Myra Sklarew. TaR

This star is only an augury of the morning. And in the 51st Year of That Century, While My Brother Cried in the Trench, While My Enemy Glared from the Cave. Hyam Plutzik. RB

This still mountain night is not still. Earth Screaming. Esther Iverem. GT

This stone. Stone Hammer Poem. Robert Kroetsch. NOBC

This Stone. *Unknown*. AWP, *tr.* by Goldwin Smith

This stone incorporates three gods:/ the head is unmistakably goat-horned Pan's. Philodemus. GrAn

This stone, with not unpardonable pride. Epitaph. John Sparrow. OBCoV

This story ends with me still rowing. (LL) Rowing. Anne Sexton. BoWoP; LCAP-2

This story is not true. Stesichoros. SaLy, *tr.* by Diane Rayor

This story's strange, but altogether true. "R. B." SCAP

This story was told to me by another traveller. Margaret Atwood. NALW *Fr.* Circe / Mud Poems.

This Strange Calculation of Roots. Edouard J. Maunick. NegPo, *tr.* by Teo Savory

This strange sea-going craze began. Ovid. WoPoe, *tr.* by Derek Mahon *Fr.* Amores.

This strange thing must have crept. Fork. Charles Simic. ChAP; ColAP; HCAP; LCAP-2; PoPoPo; TRP; WeW-3

This string upon my harp was best beloved. Harmonics. William Vaughn Moody. APN-2; AmFaPo

This stripper is dancing. 'Round Killar. Eric Dyer. BloBone

This stupid world. Issa. EH, *tr.* by Robert Hass

This Summer and Last. Thomas Hardy. OxBTC

This summer I caught handfuls of wind. Handfuls of Wind. Laila Halaby. PoArWo

This summer, most friends out of town. Missoula Softball Tournament. Richard Hugo. MoASP

This summer, reading the history of the Jews of Spain. Crypto-Jews, The. Robin Becker. ExTi; OPRER; TaR

This summer's burning heat. Juan Chi. CoBCP *Fr.* Singing of Thoughts.

This Summer's Sky. Bertolt Brecht. PoSu, *tr.* by Michael Hamburger

This Sun. John Rybicki. AmPoNex

This Sun Is Hot. *Unknown*. BPo

This Sun on this Rubble. Dennis Brutus. PBMAP

This sun was mine and yours; we shared it. Our Sun. George Seferis. AF

This sun wears a live chemise of blood. Recital. Muhammad 'Afifi Matar. MAP, *tr.* by Ferial Ghazoul and Desmond O'Grady

This sunday morning breaks blue clear, in st paul de vence. In Jimmy's Garden. Quincy Troupe. GT

This sunken-eyed moment wobbling. Christmas in Biafra (1969). Chinua Achebe. ChrPo

This suspense is killing me. Love Me or Leave Me. Walter Donaldson. ReLy

This tale is doon, and God save al the route [*or* rowte]! (LL) Geoffrey Chaucer. NAEL-6v1; NAEL-7v1; NAWM-5v1; OxBoLi; PeLV *Fr.* Canterbury Tales, The.

This tells of wolf and lamb who drank. Wolf and the Lamb, The. Marie de France. NAEL-7v1, *tr.* by Harriet Spiegel

This terror in whose thrall I am. Interrogation. Qasim Haddad. MAP, *tr.* by Lena Jayyusi and Christopher Middleton

This That and Then. Douglas Messerli. FTOS

This that I give you now. Bread. Stanley Burnshaw. APT-2; TrJP

This that I swear. (LL) Vow, The. Anthony Hecht. CoAmPo; InPK-6; TaR

This that is washed with weed and pebblestone. Figurehead, The. Léonie Adams. APT-2; WPE

This that you see, this colorful pretense. On Her Portrait. Sister Juana Inés de la Cruz. WoPoe, *tr.* by Robert Mezey

This the house of Circe, queen of charms. Circe. John Byrne Leicester Warren, 3d Baron De Tabley. NOBVV

This, the last ornament among the peers. Joseph Hilaire Pierre Belloc. OBSV

This, the twentieth day of March. Letter to Three Irish Poets, A. Michael Longley. BIrV

This then buddy is the blue routine. My Buddy. Richard Hugo. SeSe

This, then, is the grave of my son. Nettles, The. Thomas Hardy. OxBSP

This they know well: the Goddess yet abides. In Her Praise. Robert Graves. BIrV

This thin-lipped king with his helmeted head. To President Bush at the Start of the Gulf War. Robert Bly. RaBo

This thing happens in mid-summer. Purest Rage, The. Charles Baxter. SwNoth

This thing the night flashes. Little Testament. Eugenio Montale. PoetW, *tr.* by Robert Lowell

This, this is he; softly a while. John Milton. UnPo *Fr.* Samson Agonistes.

This, this is what I love, and what is this? George Macdonald. SacPr

This Time. Steve Denning. CDa

This time his father takes him. Father's Day. Gloria Vando. TouFir

This time, I have left my body behind me, crying. Trying to Pray. James Wright (1927–80). BBASP

This time I'll show up. Hunting Song. *Unknown*. STP, *tr.* by Jerome Rothenberg

This time, I mean it. Little Tumescence, A. Jonathan Williams. NeAP; PoM

This time I've realized the essence. Rāmprasād Sen. SinGod, *tr.* by Rachel Fell McDermott

This time I won't permit the blue. Patrizia Cavalli. NeIt; VCWP, *tr.* by Judith Baumel

This time / in the darkness. Stuntman. Lionel Kearns. MoCV

This time, Kali. Rāmprasād Sen. SinGod, *tr.* by Rachel Fell McDermott

This time no one's looking for love. Twilight at a Little Harbor. Chairil Anwar. PoetW, *tr.* by Burton Raffel

This time of pause is as though. Shag Rock. "Paul Henderson." PeNZ

This time of year The North goes by, bird. Chair in the Meadow, The. William Stafford. BodElec

This time the dead man will see them in Hell. (LL) Book of the Dead Man (#58), The. Marvin Bell. OPRER; TaR

This time there was no beak. Pile of Feathers. Gerald Stern. LoL

This to the crown and blessing of my life. Letter to Daphnis, A. Anne Finch, Countess of Winchilsea. EMWP; EnLoPo; LW; MakPoe; NALW; PEW

This Tokyo. Gary Snyder. NeAP

This tomb Damis built for his courageous horse. Anyte [or Anytes]. HePo Fr. Epigrams.

This tombstone heavy with grief announces. Philetas. GrAn

This too is an experience of the soul. Isis Wanderer. Kathleen Jessie Raine. NALW; OxBS

This too is one of them. (LL) Old Man's Lazy, The. Peter Blue Cloud. HATNAP; LTA

This, Too, Shall Pass Away. A. L. Alexander. PoToHe

This Tooth. Lee Bennett Hopkins. TLR

This torch, still burning in my hand. From the Greek Anthology. Crinagoras. PGA, tr. by Kenneth Rexroth

This torment of love. Describes Rationally the Irrational Effects of Love. Sister Juana Inés de la Cruz. SpanPo, tr. by Samuel Beckett

This town has docks where channel boats come sidling. Arrivals, Departures. Philip Larkin. MoBrPo

This Train. Unknown. OxBoLi

This train is bound for glory, this train. This Train. Unknown. OxBoLi

This tranquil vault, assuming files of doves. Graves by the Sea, The. Paul Valéry. WoPoe, tr. by John Finlay

This treasure is the best, of all those gifts the grain. Upon the Birth of a Young and Highly Desired Son. Christian Weise. GePo, tr. by George C. Schoolfield

This tree is God's challah. God's Body. Sara Klugman. HW

This Troilus in armes gan hir streyne. Geoffrey Chaucer. EroLit Fr. Troilus and Criseyde [or Criseide].

This Troilus [or Troylus], with blisse [or Blysse] of that supprysed [or supprised]. Geoffrey Chaucer. EBEV; PoE Fr. Troilus and Criseyde [or Criseide].

This truth-telling is well enough. Visited. Fleur Adcock. PeNZ

This tuft that thrives on saline nothingness. Air Plant, The. Hart Crane. MoAmPo; PAI

This tumultuous life is nothing for me but the sound of a. Michelangelo Coviello. ItPo, tr. by Gayle Ridinger Fr. Caravaggio.

This Tzu-hsia of Hsi-ho. Inkstone Inscription for the Blind Scholar Ho Yung-kuang, An. Chin Nung. CoBLCP, tr. by Jonathan Chaves

This Unimportant Morning. Lawrence Durrell. BoLoP; OxBTC

This unphilosophic sight. To a Lady's Countenance. Elinor Wylie. NALW

This urge, wrestle, resurrection of dry sticks. Cuttings. Theodore Roethke. APT-2; HCAP; LCAP-2; NAAL-2v2; NAAL-5; NOBA; NoAM; OBGa; TAP; TRP; UnPo; VCAP

This used to be a dam. Damside. Margaret Atwood. LCAP-2

This vale—my daily haunt—is a delight. Shepherds and Flocks. Victor Hugo. SxFrPo, tr. by E. H. Blackmore and A. M. Blackmore

This vale of teargas. Unlawful Assembly. Dennis Joseph Enright. OxBTC

This Version of Love. Dorothy Hewett. BMAP; CBAP

This version of the starving artist. Bela. Gerald Stern. BodElec

This very day, a little while ago, you lived. Dead on the War Path. Unknown. FaBoWar, tr. by Herbert J. Spinden and H. J. Spinden

This victim from a lukewarm pigs' redoubt. Unknown. PriapPo, tr. by Richard W. Hooper Fr. Priapus Poems, The.

This virginal long-living lovely day. Stéphane Mallarmé. SxFrPo, tr. by E. H. Blackmore and A. M. Blackmore

This vision of a face, radiant and full of beauty. Marbod of Rennes. CAGL; EroLit, tr. by John Boswell Fr. Unyielding Youth, The.

This voice an older friend has kept. Isaiah by Kerosene Lantern Light. Robert Harris. ChIV-1; NOBAu

This wall-paper has lines that rise. Missing My Daughter. Stephen Spender. GTBS-P

This war's dead heroes, who has seen them? Heroes. Kathleen Jessie Raine. FaBoWar

This warl's a tap-room owre and owre. Tap-Room, The. Robert Tannahill. NePenScot

This warning, Gallus, for thy love I send. Propertius. AWP, tr. by F. A. Wright Fr. Elegies.

This was a city once, that's now a copse. Lament for Troy. Hugh, Primate of Orleans. MLL, tr. by Helen Waddell

This was a dream. (LL) Emily Dickinson. APN-2; NAAL-2v1; NAAL-3; NALW; NCAP; NOBA; NoAM; OxBA

This was a Poet—It is That. Emily Dickinson. APN-2; NAAL-2v1; NAAL-3; NAAL-5; NCAP; NOBA; TCAPo

This was a private crime; but you shall hear. Juvenal. BASC, tr. by John Dryden Fr. Satires.

This was a time, when only the dead. Introduction. Anna Andreyevna Akhmatova. PFTM-1

This was as far as I had got. David Wright. PeSAV Fr. Peripatetic Letter to Isabella Fey, A.

This was Mr Bleaney's room. He stayed. Mr Bleaney. Philip Larkin. NPeEn; OxBC; OxBEV; PoE; PoPoPo; TRP; UV

"This was Mr. Strugnell's room," she'll say. Mr. Strugnell. Wendy Cope. UV

This was not experience. Painted Cup, The. Michael Palmer. FTOS

This was not to be expected. Seaman, 1941. Molly Holden. FaBoWP

This was our first line of defense. It held. Ferniehirst Castle. Richard Hugo. NoAM

This was the brown bull of Cuailnge. Unknown. NOIV, tr. by Thomas Kinsella Fr. How the Bulls Were Begotten.

This was the eerie mine of souls. Orpheus, Eurydice, Hermes. Rainer Maria Rilke. WoPoe, tr. by Franz Wright

This was the first Thanksgiving with my wife's family. Thanksgiving. Martín Espada. PuP-23

This was the moment when Before. BC:AD. U. A. Fanthorpe. OBCP; OxBEV

This was the salty taste of glory. Wallace Stevens. FaBoWar Fr. Phases.

This was the surplus childhood, held as cheap! Sunderland Children, The. Alice Thompson Meynell. NALW

This was the table. Its surface, its legs. Ghost, The. Ágnes Nemes Nagy. PoSu, tr. by Bruce Berlind

This was the woman; what now of the man? George Meredith. NAEL-6v2; Son Fr. Modern Love.

This was the young Camonus; this his face. Martial. RomPo, tr. by Brian Hill

This water droplet, charity of the air. Man Seeking Experience Enquires His Way of a Drop of Water, The. Ted Hughes. OxAEP-2

This watery vague how vast! This misty globe. On the Bay. Richard Watson Gilder. APN-2

This way I salute you. City Johannesburg. Mongane Wally Serote. NAfrP

This way of writing I observed by some. Satire. Unknown. BASC

This way, that way? Polar Cub. Judith Nicholls. NOxBChV

This way, this way, come and hear. John Fletcher. NOSC Fr. Little French Lawyer, The.

This wedding in Lawrence. Blanca's Red Lips. Gloria Vando. TouFir

This wet evening, in a lost age. (LL) Mountain over Aberdare, The. Alun Lewis. AngWePo; TCAWP

This wet sack, wavering slackness. Macduff. Charles Tomlinson. OxBC

This while we are abroad. Ode Written in the Peak[e], An. Michael Drayton. NOSC

This wild team rushes at a savage pace. If I Have to Yield My Bones. Milán Füst. IQMS, tr. by Paul Tabori

This will be the last ditch to fall. Capital. John Tripp. AngWePo

This will go too, this curve of shore. Slate Quay: Felinheli. Peter Gruffydd. AngWePo

This will really try you. Mamma! Frank Horne. BPo

This wind begun to knead the Grass. Emily Dickinson. See Wind begun to knead the Grass, The

This wind is easy, the moon pleasant. Song: Green Water, Singing Girl. Li Ho. CrYelRi, tr. by Sam Hamill

This Wind That Loiters. Odysseus Elytis. WoPoe, tr. by Edmund Keeley and Philip Sherrard

This wine is really awful. Quality of Wine. Hayden Carruth. BodElec

This wine-press is call'd war on earth. William Blake. EBEV Fr. Milton.

This wingtip feather from a hook-beaked eagle. Crinagoras. GrAn

This winter. Sohoku. JDP, tr. by Yoel Hoffmann

This winter's morning, turning the other way. Turning. Robert Finch. MoCV

This wit was with experience bought. Mirror for Detractors, A. Esther Lewis. ECWP

This woman cannot live more than one year. Where I? Robinson Jeffers. OxBSo

This woman is getting on her last bus. Poem for Jacqueline Hill. Unknown. BrRo

This woman vomiten [or vomiting] her. Present. Sonia Sanchez. WPOW

This wondrous art in the human realm. To a Pyrotechnist. Chao Meng-fu. CoBLCP; ColAnChi, tr. by Jonathan Chaves

This world. Lal Ded [or Lalla]. WPoS

This World. Sarah Morgan Bryan Piatt. NCAP

This world a hunting is. Madrigal. William Drummond, of Hawthornden. OxBSP

This world a vale of soul-making. In Cemeteries. Dennis Joseph Enright. OxBC

This world and this life are so scattered, they try me. Zu fragmentarisch ist Welt und Leben. Heinrich Heine. AWP, tr. by Charles Godfrey Leland

This World fares as a Fantasy. John Gower.
   "Of fantasye is all oure fare." SacPr

This World Is All a Fleeting Show. Thomas Moore. SacPr

This world / is amazingly flat. Natalya [or Natal'ia] Gorbanevskaya [or Gorbanyevskaya orGorbanevskaia]. BoWoP

This world is gradually becoming a place. John Berryman. NOBA; NoAM *Fr.* Dream Songs.

This World is not Conclusion. This World Is Not Conclusion. Emily Dickinson. APN-2; NAAL-2v1; NAAL-3; NCAP; TCAPo

This world of dew. Issa. SoOfWa, *tr. by* Sam Hamill

This world of ours. Sami Mansei. OHMPJ

This world of ours. *Unknown.* OHMPJ

This world's a dream, so why. Rising Drunk on a Spring Day. Li Po. CrYelRi, *tr. by* Sam Hamill

This world's dead weight and cycle on your back. (LL) Night Sweat. Robert Lowell. HarvBoo; NAAL-2v2; TAP; VGW

This world's just mad enough to have been made. Creation Myth on a Moebius Band. Howard Nemerov. OBCoV

This worthy lymytour, this noble Frere. Geoffrey Chaucer. PoE *Fr.* Canterbury Tales, The.

This would be a bewildering way unless we had a guide. William Langland. NAEL-6v1; NAEL-7v1 *Fr.* Vision of Piers Plowman, The.

This would not be the war we fought in. See, the foliage. Adrienne Rich. FaBoWP; HCAP *Fr.* Shooting Script.

This year. These Green-Going-to-Yellow. Marvin Bell. UrbNat

This year again the bruise-colored oak. Seeing the Bones. Maxine W. Kumin. NoAM

This year, before it ends, holds out time as a weight to us. This Year, before It Ends. Eve Langley. NOBAu

This year I want. Jakura. JDP, *tr. by* Yoel Hoffmann

This year, maybe, do you think I can graduate? Deferred. Langston Hughes. APSN; APT-2

This year, / Next year. *Unknown.* OxNR

This year on, forever. Issa. SoOfWa, *tr. by* Sam Hamill

This Year's Drive to Appomattox. Eleanor Ross Taylor. CBCWP

"This year she has changed greatly"—meaning you. Change. Robert Graves. OxBTC

This year, the twenty-ninth of the twelfth. Nampo Jomyo. JDP, *tr. by* Yoel Hoffmann

This year the wheels of cars. My Uncle Mohammed at Mecca, 1981. Naomi Shihab Nye. GraLe

This year we are making. Margaret Atwood. PoetW *Fr.* Four Small Elegies.

This Yonder Night I Sawe a Sighte. *Unknown.* MiEL

This, you were sure, whatever happened. Pair of Shoes, A. Theodore Weiss. NoAM

This young boy on my hands at middle age. Teasing Hsiao-te, My Son. Huang T'ing-chien. SuSp, *tr. by* Michael E. Workman

This young mandarin had undoubted genius. Lament for Hsieh T'iao. Shen Yüeh. SuSp, *tr. by* Lenore Mayhew

This Zone, this Breastband & girlish frock. Artemis. Perses. GrAn, *tr. by* Peter Whigham

This? it's my Lounge Lizard look, very. Up. Bill Kushner. GLP; ReTh

Thise olde gentil Brito[u]ns in hir dayes. Geoffrey Chaucer. NAEL-5v1; NAEL-6v1 *Fr.* Canterbury Tales, The.

Thise riotoures thre of whiche I telle. Geoffrey Chaucer. *See* These rioteres three of which I tell

Thistle. Nikolai Alekseievich Zabolotsky [*or* Zabolotskii]. RB, *tr. by* Daniel Weissbort

Thistle rises and forever will, The. (LL) Hugh MacDiarmid. NAEL-5v2; NAEL-6v2 *Fr.* Drunk Man Looks at the Thistle, A.

Thistle's Grown aboon the Rose, The. Allan Cunningham. NePenScot

Thistledown. Denis Glover. PeNZ *Fr.* Sings Harry.

Thistledown. James Merrill. UnPo

Thistledown. Harold Monro. OxBTC

Thistledown blows over the poisoned fields. Martyred Earth, The. Ewart Milne. BIrV

Thistledown's flying Though the winds are all still, The. Autumn. John Clare. BBASP; HAP; WeW-3

Thistles. Ted Hughes. FaBoVe; NPeEn; NoAM; OxBSP; OxBTC; SoSe-8

Thistles. Shinkichi Takahashi. ZenPo, *tr. by* Takashi Ikemoto and Lucien Stryk

Thistles bloomed in the vast moonlit. Thistles. Shinkichi Takahashi. ZenPo, *tr. by* Takashi Ikemoto and Lucien Stryk

Thistles climb the thatch, The. Forever. Clearances, The. Iain Crichton Smith. NePenScot

Tho' grief and fondness in my breast rebel. Samuel Johnson. NPeEn *Fr.* London: A Poem in Imitation of the Third Satire of Juvenal.

Tho hevede erthe of erthe erthe inoh. (LL) *Unknown.* HAP; MiEL

Tho' I'm no Catholic. Catholic Bells, The. William Carlos Williams. NOBA; OxBA; SAmP

Tho' I my party long have chose. Christopher Smart. NOCV *Fr.* Hymns for the Amusement of Children.

Tho' ill at ease, a stranger and alone. Thoughts on Pausing at a Cottage near the Paukataук River. Sarah Kemble Knight. SCAP

Tho' men say thou bring'st the Spring. (LL) Swallow, The. Abraham Cowley. EBEV; OBEV; OxAEP-1

Tho' ne'er another trow me. (LL) Robert Graham. GTBS-P; OBEV

Tho' the days are long. I'll See You in My Dreams. Isham Jones. ReLy

Tho they in flames bright as your eyes expire. (LL) Hester Wyat. EMWP; FaBoVe

Tho when as chearelesse night ycovered had. Edmund Spenser. NAEL-6v1; NAEL-7v1 *Fr.* Faerie Queene, The.

Tho when they came to the sea coast, they found. Edmund Spenser. PBRV *Fr.* Faerie Queene Book 5, The.

Thocht Polibus, pisander, and with them. Sonet. Alexander Montgomerie. NePenScot

Thocht raging stormes movis us to schaik. Reid in the Loch Sayis, The. *Unknown.* OxBS

Thocht that this warld be verie strange. Solace in Age. Sir Richard Maitland. OxBS

Thogh brutal beestes be irrational. Cock and the Fox, The. Robert Henryson. NAEL-7v1

Thomalin, since Thirsil nothing has to leave thee. To Thomalin. Phineas Fletcher. NOSC

Thomas and Beulah. Rita Dove.
  Dusting. NAAL-5
  Event, The. NAAL-5
  "Ever since they'd left the Tennessee ridge." NAAL-5
  "Every day a wilderness—no." NAAL-5
  "In the city, under the saw-toothed leaves of an oak." NAAL-5
  Straw Hat. NAAL-5

Thomas Carlyle. Dorothy Parker. APT-1; NALW *Fr.* Pig's-Eye View of Literature, A.

Thomas Cromwell. *Unknown.* ESPB

Thomas Dudley, Ah! Old Must Dye. *Unknown.* SCAP

Thomas Gray's View of Nature. William Mason. NOEC *Fr.* English Garden, The.

Thomas Hardy. Walter De la Mare. NoAM

Thomas Hardy. Norman Dubie. LCAP-2

Thomas Hardy and A. E. Housman. Max Beerbohm. NBLV

Thomas Hobbes of Malmesbury thought. Limerick. Peter Alexander. PeLi

Thomas Iron-Eyes. Marnie Walsh. WPOW

Thomas Jefferson. Lorine Niedecker. HarvBoo

Thomas lay on the Huntlie bank. Thomas the Rhymer [*or* Rimer]. *Unknown.* FaBoCh; NOBE; OBEV; OxBB

Thomas Logge. Walter De la Mare. FaBoEE

Thomas MacDonagh. Francis Ledwidge. *See* Lament for Thomas MacDonagh

Thomas Müntzer. Jeffrey Wainwright. HarvBoo

Thomas o Yonderdale. *Unknown.* ESPB

Thomas Stuart was a lord. Lord Thomas Stuart. *Unknown.* ESPB

Thomas the Rhymer. *Unknown.* FaBoCh; NOBE; OBEV; OxBB; PAI; PoE; RB; TFi
  (Thomas Rhymer [and the Queen of Elfland].) ESPB; HAP; NPeEn
  (Thomas the Rimer.) InPK-6
  (Thomas Rymer.) ESPB; NePenScot
  (True Thomas.) OxBS

Thomas, the vagrant piper's son. Louis Untermeyer. MoAmPo *Fr.* Mother Goose Up-to-Date.

Thompson's Lunch Room—Grand Central Station. Amy Lowell. APT-1

Thonah! Thonah! / There is a voice above. *Unknown.* APN-2; TCAPo, *tr. by* Washington Matthews *Fr.* Mountain Chant, The.

Thoreau. Timothy Liu. AmPoNex; GifTon; OPRER

Thoreau, / grabbing on, hard. Distances to the Friend, The. Jonathan Williams. NeAP

Thorn, A. *Unknown.* ReMoGo

Thorn, The. William Wordsworth.
  "Before you up the mountain go." VerBaPo

Thorn Leaves in March. W. S. Merwin. TwCP

Thorn Merchant's Mistress, The. Yusef Komunyakaa. RACG

Thorn Vine on the Wall. *Unknown.* CoBCP, *tr. by* Burton Watson

Thorny Gaps Suddenly Moving. Fatma Kandil. PoArWo, *tr. by* Khaled Mattawa

Thorow. Susan Howe. APSN

Thos the damselle spake, and dyed. (LL) Thomas Chatterton. HAP; NOBE; SCGP *Fr.* Aella; a Tragycal Enterlude.

Those ancient Greeks. Unexpected Manna. Gary H. Holthaus. GifTon

Those animals that follow us in dream. Xochitepec. Malcolm Lowry. NOBC

Those are my best days, when I shake with fear. (LL) John Donne. BASC; ChIV-2; NAEL-7v1; NOSC; Son *Fr.* Holy Sonnets.

Those are the features, those the smiles. Lines, / Written on Seeing My

Husband's Picture, painted when he was young: "Those are the features, those the smiles."   Anna Sawyer.   ECWP; LW

Those autumns my parents slept.   Dream of Glass Bangles, A.   Agha Shahid Ali.   OpBo

Those Beauteous Maids.   Moses Ibn Ezra.   TrJP, *tr.* by Solomon Solis-Cohen

Those before Us.   Robert Lowell.   LCAP-2

Those Being Eaten by America.   Robert Bly.   CoAP

Those black silk pajamas.   Black Silk Pajamas.   Danton R. Remoto.   ReBoTo

Those blessed structures, plot and rhyme.   Epilogue: "Those blessed structures, plot and rhyme."   Robert Lowell.   HCAP; NAAL-2v2; NAAL-5; PoetW; VCAP

"Those boy-scouts practicing again!" (LL)   King of China's Daughter, The.   Dame Edith Sitwell.   FaBoMo; MoBrPo

Those Cambridge generations, Russell's, Keynes'   On Bertrand Russell's "Portraits from Memory."   Donald Davie.   FaBoTw

Those camellias.   Clement Hoyt.   HA

Those charming eyes within whose starry sphere.   On the Death of Catarina de Attayda.   Luis de Camões [*or* Camõens].   AWP, *tr.* by R. F. Burton

Those clever rats no longer will invade. (LL)   Broken Lampstand, The.   Wu Wei-yeh.   CoBLCP; ColAnChi, *tr.* by Jonathan Chaves

Those corner winds.   Martin Shea.   HA

Those dabbing hens I ferociously love.   Cock before Dawn.   Norman MacCaig.   OxBC

Those dark mountains face to face.   Dark Mountains.   Milton Lockyer.   CBAP, *tr.* by Frank Wordick

Those days are now.   William Wordsworth.   OxAEP-2   *Fr.* Prelude, The; Growth of a Poet's Mind [1805 vers.].

Those days we slept in a trumpet.   Music for Brass.   Günter Grass.   AF, *tr.* by Christopher Middleton

Those days when it was all right.   Letter to E. Franklin Frazier.   Imamu Amiri Baraka.   BPo

Those dew-moist roses and that bushy thyme.   Theocritus.   GrAn

Those doors through my soul knock about.   Memory of My Private Childhood.   Eunice Odio.   TCLAP, *tr.* by Suzanne Jill Levine

Those dreams that on the silent night intrude.   On Dreams.   Jonathan Swift.   BIrV

Those—dying then.   Emily Dickinson.   APN-2; NCAP

Those eyes that [*or* which] set my fancy on a fire.   Conquest [*or* His Lady's Might].   Philippe Desportes.   AWP; NoSic

Those falling blossoms.   Moritake.   SoOfWa, *tr.* by Sam Hamill

Those famous men of old, the Ogres.   Ogres and Pygmies.   Robert Graves.   FaBoMo; NoAM

Those first days, making love above your father's study.   My Funny Valentine.   Chris Greenhalgh.   NeBl

Those Flapjacks of Brown's.   Bert Leston Taylor.   OBAL

Those folds / leak point of the exit. (LL)   Environs.   Larry Eigner.   FTOS; NeAP

Those four black girls blown up.   American History.   Michael S. Harper.   BPo; ESEAA; HCAP; NAAL-5; NoAM; PoPoPo

Those gone are day by day remote.   *Unknown.*   ChinPo, *tr.* by Yip Wai-lim

Those great sea-horses bare their teeth and laugh at the dawn. (LL)   High Talk.   W. B. Yeats.   FaBoVe; RaBo

Those great sweeps of snow that stop suddenly six feet from the house.   Snowbanks North of the House.   Robert Bly.   AiP; BodElec; LCAP-2; RaBo

Those groans men use.   Mutes, The.   Denise Levertov.   ErotSp; NALW; NOBA

Those hands, which heav'n like to a curtain spread.   Crucified.   Francis Quarles.   NOSC

Those hands which you so clapt [*or* clapped], go now and wring.   Upon the Lines and Life of the Famous Scenic Poet, Master William Shakespeare.   Hugh Holland.   AngWePo; OBWVE

Those in the vegetable rain retain.   Stories of Snow.   Patricia K. Page.   NOBC; NoP-4

Those lesser rivals flee. (LL)   At Ithaca.   "H. D."   ColAP; VGW

Those lions / had stood there.   Stalingrad Theater.   Mikhail Kuz'mich Lukonin.   TCRP, *tr.* by Albert C. Todd

Those lips that Love's own hand did make.   William Shakespeare.   Son   *Fr.* Sonnets.

Those long black tresses.   Fujiwara no Teika.   WoPoe, *tr.* by Steven D. Carter

Those long days measured by my little feet.   "George Eliot."   NOBVV   *Fr.* Brother and Sister.

Those long uneven lines.   MCMXIV.   Philip Larkin.   EBEV; FaBoWar; HarvBoo; NAEL-5v2; NAEL-6v2; NoAM; NoP-4; OBWP; OxAEP-2

Those lumbering horses in the steady plough.   Horses.   Edwin Muir.   FaBoCh

Those many children running in your space.   Children, The.   Qasim Haddad.   MAP, *tr.* by Charles Doria and Sharif Elmusa

Those men who love the *crwth* and harp.   Song and Poetry.   *Unknown.*   OBWVE, *tr.* by Gwyn Jones

Those men with dollars on the mind.   Gamble.   Linda Hogan.   HATNAP

Those moon-gilded dancers.   Gay, The.   "Æ"   OBMV

Those mornings were thick with Benedictine incense.   1965.   Frankie Paino.   AmPoNex

Those most assailed trees.   Macrocarpas.   Michael Jackson.   PeNZ

Those neck-pointing out full bodylength and calling.   Gulls.   Jorie Graham.   BAP-01

Those nymphs, I want to capture them.   Afternoon of a Faun, The.   Stéphane Mallarmé.   WoPoe, *tr.* by Louis Simpson

Those of Pure Origin.   Roy Fuller.   FaBoMo

Those old tunes take me back. I used to go.   Her Dancing Days.   Anna Adams.   BrRo

Those Others.   Ian Wedde.   PeNZ

Those Paperweights with Snow Inside.   Molly Peacock.   RA

Those people were a kind of solution. (LL)   Waiting for the Barbarians.   Constantine P. Cavafy.   AF; BLT

Those perennial apparitions.   Cormorants.   John Kinsella.   OWoS

Those petty [*or* pretty] wrongs that liberty commits.   William Shakespeare.   OxAEP-1   *Fr.* Sonnets.

Those poor, arthritically swollen knees.   With Her.   Czeslaw Milosz.   GI

Those questions, sister.   Stranglehold of English Lit, The.   Felix Mnthali.   PBMAP

Those quiet little feet in the reflected room.   Cesare Greppi.   ItPo, *tr.* by Gayle Ridinger

Those Rainy Mornings.   Frank Mkalawile Chipasula.   HBAPE

Those ravens black that rested.   Heavy-hearted.   Judah Al-Harizi.   TrJP

Those reckless hosts rush to the wells.   Elegy.   Baruch of Worms.   TrJP

Those red men you offended were my brothers.   In My First Hard Springtime.   James Welch.   CDW

Those rivers run from that land.   Song.   Robert Creeley.   VGW

Those ships which left.   Saigyo.   AWP

Those snooty boys in all their purple drag!   Epigram.   Strato [*or* Straton].   GrAn, *tr.* by Tony Harrison

Those speckled trout we glimpsed in a pool last year.   Two Fish.   Katha Pollitt.   DiPo; NIL-7; NIP-4

Those spirits which we Animal do call.   Of the Animal Spirits.   Margaret Lucas Cavendish, Duchess of Newcastle.   PEW

Those sultry nights we used to pass outdoors.   Amos Niven Wilder.   YaYoPo   *Fr.* Battle-Retrospect.

Those that can give, open their hands this day.   New Year's Sacrifice: To Lucinda, A.   Thomas Carew.   CaPo

Those transparent Dacca gauzes.   Dacca Gauzes, The.   Agha Shahid Ali.   NIL-7; NoP-4

Those Troublesome Disguises.   Jonathan Williams.   NeAP

Those trumpeting / petals. (LL)   Iris.   William Carlos Williams.   LCAP-2; WeW-3

Those two are gone who walked upright on two legs.   Leopard in Eden, The.   Gail White.   FFC

Those Two Boys.   Franklin Pierce Adams.   OBCoV; TrJP

Those upon whom Almighty doth intend.   Edward Taylor.   SCAP   *Fr.* God's Determinations [touching his Elect].

Those verses surfaced thirty years ago.   Postscript, 1984.   John Hewitt.   BiHa

Those Walks We Took.   David Wright.   NLP

Those walks we took I shall not take.   Those Walks We Took.   David Wright.   NLP

Those we love die like birds.   Lament: "Those we love die like birds."   Mai Sayigh.   MAP, *tr.* by Charles Doria and Salma Khadra Jayyusi

Those We Love the Best.   Ella Wheeler Wilcox.   PoToHe

Those were the days.   Energy in Sweden.   Kenneth Koch.   NoP-4

Those Were the Days.   Charles Strouse.   ReLy

Those Which Were Pomp and Delight.   Pedro Calderón de la Barca.   WoPoe, *tr.* by Katherine Washburn

Those who.   Petty Bourgeoisie, The.   Roque Dalton.   TCLAP, *tr.* by Richard Schaaf

Those who are beautiful.   Robert Kelly.   APSN

Those who Carry.   Anna Kamienska.   GI, *tr.* by David Curzon and Grażyna Drabik

Those who carry grand pianos / to the tenth floor.   Those Who Carry.   Anna Kamienska.   GI, *tr.* by David Curzon and Grażyna Drabik

Those Who Died for Their Country.   *Unknown.*   CoBCP, *tr.* by Burton Watson   *Fr.* Nine Songs.

Those Who Do Not Dance.   Gabriela Mistral.   WPoS, *tr.* by Maria Giachetti

Those who fling off, toss head.   Meeting Together of Poles & Latitudes: In Prospect.   Margaret Avison.   NOBC

Those who give ear to the heart of the night.   Nocturne.   "Rubén Dario."   SpanPo, *tr.* by Kate Flores

Those who have not been chosen for any higher call.   From the Admonitions of St. Theresa of Avila.   István Vas.   IQMS, *tr.* by George Szirtes

Those Who Lost Everything.   David Diop.   PBA, *tr.* by Langston Hughes

Those Who Love. Cyprian Norwid. WoPoe, *tr.* by Jerzy Peterkiewicz, Burns Singer and Jon Stallworthy

Those Who Love. Sara Teasdale. LW

Those who love the most. Those Who Love. Sara Teasdale. LW

Those who loved freedom. One Kind of Freedom Speaks. Erich Fried. AF, *tr.* by Georg Rapp

Those Who Make Paths. Catherine Fisher. TCAWP

"Those who realize true wisdom." *Unknown.* EnlH *Fr.* Bhagavad-Gita, The.

Those who speak know nothing. Lao Tzŭ. Po Chü-i. BLT; ChiP, *tr.* by Arthur Waley

Those who've been to war love maps. Maps. Bruce Guernsey. IllVoic

Those who would not accept went past. Natalya [*or* Natal'ia] Krandievskaya [*or* Krandievskaia]. TCRP

Those whose houses were burned. Margaret Atwood. PoetW *Fr.* Four Small Elegies.

Those Winter Sundays. Robert Earl Hayden. APT-2; AmFaPo; ChAP; ColAP; ESEAA; HAP; HCAP; ISC; InPK-6; LCAP-2; MakPoe; NAAL-5; NIL-7; NIP-4; NoAM; NoP-4; PoPoPo; RaBo; SSLK; SoSe-8; TFi; UnPo; WeW-3

Those with experience look for a special kind. Going for Peaches, Fredericksburg, Texas. Naomi Shihab Nye. GraLe

Those Women. *Unknown.* WoPoe, *tr.* by Martha Ann Selby *Fr.* Gathasaptasati, The.

Those words, said the lady, are the worst there could be. *Unknown.* EroLit *Fr.* Sir Gawain and the Green Knight.

Those years, I was a green-youthed wanderer. Arriving in Lo-yang Again. Shao Yung. CoBCP, *tr.* by Burton Watson

Thou art alone, fond lover. (LL) Evening Darkens Over, The. Robert Bridges. HAP; NOBVV; SCGP

Thou art gone, and for ever! (LL) Sir Walter Scott. GTBS-P; NOBRP; NPeEn; OxAEP-2; SCGP *Fr.* Lady of the Lake, The.

Thou Art Indeed Just, Lord. Gerard Manley Hopkins. AWP; EBVV; GTBS-P; HAP; InPK-6; InvLi; MoBrPo; NAEL-5v2; NAEL-6v2; NOBE; NOBVV; NoAM; NoP-4; PAI; PeECV; SCGP; SacPr; TFi; TOF; UnPo

(Justus Quidem Tu Es, Domine.) EBEV; OxAEP-2

Thou art love's victim; and must die. Richard Crashaw. EroLit *Fr.* Hymn to the Name and Hono[u]r of the Admirable Saint[e] Teresa, A.

Thou art my pennon that will not go down. (LL) Canzone: To Love and to His Lady. Guido Delle Colonne. AWP; EaItPo, *tr.* by Dante Gabriel Rossetti

Thou art not dead, my Prote! thou art flown. To Prote. Simmias of Thebes. AWP, *tr.* by John Addington Symonds

Thou art not near me, but I see Thine eyes. I Love Thee. Josephine D. Henderson Heard. CBWP-4

Thou art not, Penshurst, built to envious show. Ben Jonson. AWP; BASC; BeJo; CABP; NAEL-6v1; NAEL-7v1; NOSC; NoP-4; OxBEV; PBRV; TFi

Thou art not so black[,] as my heart. Jet Ring Sent, A. John Donne. OxBSP

Thou Art, O God. Thomas Moore. PWR

Thou Art, O God, the God of Might. Emily Swan Perkins. AH

Thou Art the Sky. Rabindranath Tagore. OBMV *Fr.* Gitanjali.

Thou art the star for which all evening waits. Aldebaran at Dusk. George Sterling. TCAPo

Thou Art the Tree of Life. Edward Taylor. AH

Thou Art the Way. George Washington Doane. AH

Thou art the Way. "I Am the Way." Alice Thompson Meynell. NOBVV; OBMV; OxBSP

Thou art the worn memorial, Baker Street. (LL) Metropolitan Railway, The. Sir John Betjeman. EBEV; OxAEP-2; OxBTC

Thou art; there is no stay but in Thy love. Rock, The. Jones Very. InvLi

Thou art to all lost love the best. To the Willow-Tree. Robert Herrick. CaPo; OBEV; SCGP

Thou art too hard for me in Love. Love. George Herbert. PeECV

Thou art weary, weary, weary. Witch's Chant, A. James Hogg. NOBRP

Thou as laborious, as thy master king. Nicolas Boileau-Despéaux. OBGa, *tr.* by John Ozell *Fr.* Epistle to My Gardener.

Thou, att whose feete I waste mie soule in sighes. To Mie Tirante. George Darley. Son

Thou barren waste; unprofitable strand. Standish O'Grady. NOBC *Fr.* Emigrant, The.

Thou bearst the bottle, I the bag (oh Lord). Bottle, The. Ralph Knevet. ChIV-2

Thou beauteous off-spring of a syre as fair. On a Sunbeam. Thomas Heyrick. NOSC

Thou Beautiful Sabbath. *Unknown.* TrJP, *tr.* by Isidore Myers

Thou bid'st me come away. To Death. Robert Herrick. BeJo

Thou bidest wall nor floor, Lord! (LL) Hurricane, The. Hart Crane. MoAmPo; OxBA; TrCP

Thou bleedest, my poor Heart! and thy distress. Samuel Taylor Coleridge. CenSon; GSo; Son *Fr.* Effusions.

Thou Blind Man's Mark. Sir Philip Sidney. HeIP-4; NAEL-5v1; NAEL-6v1; NAEL-7v1; SCGP; Son

(Desire.) NOBE

Thou blind man's mark, thou fool's self-chosen snare. Thou Blind Man's Mark. Sir Philip Sidney. HeIP-4; NAEL-5v1; NAEL-6v1; NAEL-7v1; SCGP; Son

Thou blossom bright with autumn dew. To the Fringed Gentian. William Cullen Bryant. APN-1; AWP; TAP

Thou, born to sip the lake or spring. On a Honey Bee [*or* To a Honey Bee]. Philip Freneau. TAP

Thou breath of things unseen! (LL) Lord of My Heart's Elation. Bliss Carman. AH; NOBC

Thou brimming river, full, how full. Detroit River. Constance Fenimore Woolson. APN-2

Thou call'st me madman, but I call thee blockhead. (LL) To Flaxman. William Blake. FaBoEE; OxBoLi

Thou canst not die whilst any zeal abound. Samuel Daniel. NoSic; Son *Fr.* To Delia.

Thou canst not prove that thou art body alone. Ancient Sage, The. Tennyson. SacPr

Thou comest! all is said without a word. Elizabeth Barrett Browning. BWW; CenSon *Fr.* Sonnets from the Portuguese.

Thou comest, Autumn, heralded by the rain. Autumn. Henry Wadsworth Longfellow. APN-1

Thou comest, much wept for: such a breeze. Tennyson. EBVV; PeECV *Fr.* In Memoriam A. H. H.

Thou cursed cock, with thy perpetual noise. On a Cock at Rochester. Sir Charles Sedley. FaBoEE; NOSC; NPeEn; OBCoV

Thou daughter of the royal line. Ninth Canticle, The. George Wither. ChIV-1

Thou dearest object of my fondest love. Ardelia to Flavia, an Epistle. Charlotte Lennox. PoBW

Thou Didst Delight My Eyes. Robert Bridges. MoBrPo

Thou didst it unto him. (LL) Sheep and the Goat, The. George Macdonald. EBVV; SacPr

Thou dost establish—and our hearts receive—. John Addington Symonds. CAGL *Fr.* Love and Death: A Symphony.

Thou dost not heed my lay. (LL) Mother to Her Waking Infant, A. Joanna Baillie. ECWP; NOEC; NoP-4; WoRP

Thou dost reign on high. O Come to My Heart, Lord Jesus. Emily E.S. Elliott. SacPr

Thou dravest love from thee, who dravest Me. (LL) Hound of Heaven, The. Francis Thompson. CABP; ChIV-2; InvLi; MoBrPo; NAEL-5v2; NAEL-6v2; OBMV; SacPr; TFi

Thou dread'st and hop'st Thou know'st not what. (LL) Adriani Morientis ad Animam Suam. Emperor Hadrian. OBVE; OxBSP, *tr.* by Matthew Prior

Thou, Earth, calm empire of a happy soul. Shelley. PeECV *Fr.* Prometheus Unbound [A Lyrical Drama in Four Acts].

Thou ermined judge, pull off that sable cap! *Unknown.* CAGL *Fr.* Don Leon.

Thou fair-hair'd [*or* fair-haired] angel of the evening. To the Evening Star. William Blake. NAEL-5v2; NAEL-6v2; NOEC; NPeEn; PoE; TFi

Thou false to him, thou fiend to me. (LL) Byron. BoLoP; NPeEn; OxBSP

Thou first and worst disturber of man's rest. (LL) On a Cock at Rochester. Sir Charles Sedley. FaBoEE; NOSC; NPeEn; OBCoV

Thou flimsy, showy, melancholy weed. (LL) To the Poppy. Anna Seward. CenSon; ECWP; WoRP

Thou fool who treatest with the sword, and not. Liberty to M. le Diplomate. Sydney Thompson Dobell. OxBSo

Thou foolish bird, of feathers proud. On a Peacock. Thomas Heyrick. OWoS

Thou Gaia Art I. Heide Göttner-Abendroth. HW

Thou gav'st me leave to kiss. Chop-Cherry. Robert Herrick. EnLoPo

Thou Grace Divine, Encircling All. Eliza Scudder. AH

Thou Great God. *Unknown.* PBA, *tr.* by A. C. Jordan

Thou green and blooming, cool and shaded hill. Petrarch. AWP *Fr.* Sonnets to Laura.

Thou grimmest far o grusome tykes. To a Hedgehog. Samuel Thompson. BIrV

Thou happy, happy elf! Parental Ode to My Son, Aged Three Years and Five Months, A. Thomas Hood. OBCoV

Thou hast a charmed cup, O Fame! Woman and Fame. Felicia Dorothea Hemans. VWP; ViWPN

Thou hast a sister by the mother's side. William Shakespeare. OxAEP-1 *Fr.* Antony and Cleopatra.

Thou hast been where the rocks of coral grow. Diver, The. Felicia Dorothea Hemans. TreFP

Thou hast been wrong'd, I think old age. Old Age. Caroline Clive. VWP

Thou hast begun well, Roe, which stand well too. To Sir Thomas Roe. Ben Jonson. BASC

Thou hast come safe to port. Lament for Hathimoda, Abbess of Gandesheim. *Unknown.* MLL, *tr.* by Helen Waddell

Thou Hast Diamonds. Heinrich Heine. TrJP, *tr.* by Emma Lazarus *Fr.* Homeward Bound.

Thou hast done well, perhaps. Dark Side, The. Adelaide Anne Procter. SacPr

Thou hast filled me a golden cup. To Christina Rossetti. Dora Greenwell. VWP

Thou hast known them all before! (LL) To My Old Schoolmaster. John Greenleaf Whittier. ColAP; NOBA

Thou hast loved and thou hast suffer'd! To a Wandering Female Singer. Felicia Dorothea Hemans. VWP; ViWPN

Thou hast made me, and shall thy work[e] decay? John Donne. EBEV; GSo; InvLi; MeLP; NAEL-5v1; NAEL-6v1; NAEL-7v1; NOBE; NOCV; NOSC; NoP-4; OxAEP-1; SCGP; Son *Fr.* Holy Sonnets.

Thou hast not left the rough-barked tree to grow. I Was Sick and in Prison. Jones Very. ColAP; NOBA; SacPr

Thou hast thy calling to some palace-floor. Elizabeth Barrett Browning. CenSon; OxAEP-2; Son; VWP *Fr.* Sonnets from the Portuguese.

Thou hast thy record in the monarch's hall. Memorial of Mary, The. Felicia Dorothea Hemans. CenSon

Thou heavenly quivering beneath the deathlike above! To a Lark in War-Time. Franz Werfel. TrJP, *tr.* by Edith Abercrombie Snow

Thou hermit, haunter of the lonely glen. Sand Martin, The. John Clare. NPeEn

Thou hidden love of God, whose height. Hymn. John Wesley. NOEC

Thou hide thy face? (LL) Speak. James Wright (1927–80). HAP; NoP-4; TAP

Thou ill-formed offspring of my feeble brain. Author to Her Book, The. Anne Bradstreet. BASC; ColAP; EMWP; InPK-6; MakPoe; NAAL-2v1; NAAL-3; NAAL-5; NALW; NOBA; NoP-4; OxBA; PoE; SCAP; TAP; TCAPo

Thou in the garden, in paradise. (LL) To Amanda Walking in the Garden. N. Hookes. NOSC; OBGa

Thou inmost, ultimate. To the Body. Alice Thompson Meynell. PeVV

Thou Joy of my Life. Sidney Godolphin. OxBEV

Thou king of terrors with thy gastly eyes. Fig for Thee, Oh! Death, A. Edward Taylor. NAAL-2v1; NAAL-3

Thou king of wele and blisse. William Herebert. MiEL

Thou know'st, my Julia, that it is thy turn. To Julia, the Flaminica Dialis, or Queen-Priest. Robert Herrick. CaPo

Thou knowest, love, I know that thou dost know. Love's Entreaty. Michelangelo Buonarroti. AWP, *tr.* by John Addington Symonds

Thou knowest my praise of nature most sincere. William Cowper. NAEL-5v1; NAEL-6v1; NAEL-7v1 *Fr.* Task, The.

Thou knowest that toads and snakes and loathly worms. Shelley. PoE *Fr.* Prometheus Unbound [A Lyrical Drama in Four Acts].

Thou knowst I lov'd thee well. Martin Parker. PBRV *Fr.* Cupid's Wrongs Vindicated.

Thou large-brained woman and large-hearted man. To George Sand: A Desire. Elizabeth Barrett Browning. BoWoP; NAEL-5v2; NAEL-6v2; NALW; PoBW; VWP

Thou leadest, O God! All's well with Thy troopers that follow. (LL) Wild Ride, The. Louise Imogen Guiney. ColAP; RACG; TCAPo

Thou leanest to the shell of night. James Joyce. EBEV

Thou, little sandpiper, and I? (LL) Sandpiper, The. Celia Laighton Thaxter. OBCA; PWR

Thou Long Disowned, Reviled, Oppressed. Eliza Scudder. AH

Thou, Lord, Hast Been Our Sure Defense. John Hopkins. AH

Thou Lord of Hosts, Whose Guiding Hand. Octavius Brooks Frothingham. AH

Thou lovely sorceress of the witching night. To the Moon. Anna Maria Jones. CenSon

Thou Lovest Me. Josephine D. Henderson Heard. CBWP-4

Thou'lt fight, if any man call Thebe whore. To Sergius. Sir Charles Sedley. FaBoEE

Thou mastering me. Gerard Manley Hopkins. FaBoMo; NOBE; NoAM; OxAEP-2; OxBEV; PeECV

Thou mastering me. Gerard Manley Hopkins. NPeEn *Fr.* Wreck of the Deutschland, The.

Thou may'st love on through love's eternity. (LL) Elizabeth Barrett Browning. BWW; CTC; CenSon; GSo; HeIP-4; LW; OBEV; OxAEP-2; OxBSo; SoSe-8 *Fr.* Sonnets from the Portuguese.

Thou mighty gulf, insatiate cormorant. John Marston. NoSic; SCGP *Fr.* Scourge of Villainy [or Villanie], The.

Thou mighty Mars, the god of soldiers brave. Epitaph on Sir Philip Sidney, An. James I, King of England. Son

Thou monstrous gilt and rainbow-tinted thing. New Organ, The. Josephine D. Henderson Heard. CBWP-4

Thou must be true thyself. Be True [or Be True Thyself]. Horatius Bonar. PWR

Thou need'st not flutter from thy half-built nest. Robin, The. Jones Very. Son

Thou noblest monument of Albion's isle! Written at Stonehenge. Thomas Warton, the Younger. Son

Thou One in All, Thou All in One. Seth Curtis Beach. AH

Thou only Good! Eternal All! Samuel Davies. SacPr

Thou our health, our glory Thou. In Honour of the Holy Spirit. Hildebert. MLL, *tr.* by Helen Waddell

Thou, paw-paw-paw; thou, glurd; thou, spotted. Adam's Task. John Hollander. NIL-7; NIP-4; NoP-4; WoPoe

Thou Pleiad of the lyric world. Adelina Patti. Adah Isaacs Menken. CBWP-1

Thou poisonous laurel leaf, that in the soil. Sonnet. Frances Anne [or "Fanny"] Kemble. SWaP

Thou priest that art behind the screen. Ipsissimus. Eugene Lee-Hamilton. PeVV

Thou readest, but each lettered word can give. Eye and Ear, The. Jones Very. APN-1

Thou retir'st to endless rest. (LL) Grasshopper, The. Abraham Cowley. AWP; BASC; BeJo; NOSC; OBVE; OxAEP-1

Thou's welcome, Wean! Mischanter fa' me. Poet's Welcome to His Love-Begotten Daughter [the First Instance that Entitled Him to the Venerable Appellation of Father], A. Robert Burns. NOEC; OxBoLi

Thou sai'st I swore I lov'd thee best. Variety, The. John Dancer. NOSC

Thou saist [or sayest] Love['s] dart. To Oenone. Robert Herrick. CaPo

Thou say'st [or saist] my lines are hard. To My Ill Reader. Robert Herrick. CaPo

Thou Seemest Like a flower. Heinrich Heine. *See* E'en as a lovely flower

Thou seest me, Lucia, this year droop[e]. Crutches. Robert Herrick. CaPo

Thou seest, we are not all alone unhappie. William Shakespeare. OxBEV *Fr.* As You Like It.

Thou shalt be judge how I do spend my time [or tyme]. (LL) Sir Thomas Wyatt. NPeEn; NoSic; OBSV; OBVE; SCGP *Fr.* Satires.

Thou shalt die. Unknown. MLL

Thou shalt have one God only; who. Latest Decalogue, The. Arthur Hugh Clough. CABP; ChIV-1; EBEV; EBVV; FaBoEE; GTBS-P; HAP; NAEL-5v2; NAEL-6v2; NOBE; NOBVV; NPeEn; NoP-4; OBSV; OxBEV; PAI; PeECV; SCGP; SacPr; TFi; WeW-3; WoPoe

Thou Shalt Not. Malka Heifetz-Tussman. AWP, *tr.* by Marcia Falk

Thou shalt not laugh in this leaf, Muse, nor they. John Donne. OBSV *Fr.* Satires.

Thou shalt the mountain move; be strong in me. Mountain, The. Jones Very. NCAP

Thou show'st thy beauty unto all the men. Wasted. Mary Elizabeth Coleridge. ViWPN

Thou silent herald of Time's silent flight! To the Sun-Dial. John Quincy Adams. APN-1

Thou silver deity of secret night. Hymn to the Moon. Lady Mary Wortley Montagu. ECWP

Thou sleepest fast and I with woeful heart. Sir Thomas Wyatt. OxBSP

Thou snowy farm[e] with thy five tenements! Elinda's [or Ellinda's] Glove. Richard Lovelace. CaPo; NOSC

Thou sorrow, venom elfe. Upon a Spider Catching a Fly. Edward Taylor. NOBA; NoP-4; OxBA; OxBEV; PeECV; SCAP; TAP; TCAPo

Thou still unravished [or unravish'd] bride of quietness. Ode on a Grecian Urn. John Keats. AWP; BRP; ClHu; EBEV; HAP; HeIP-4; MakPoe; NAEL-5v2; NAEL-6v2; NAWM-7v2; NIL-7; NIP-4; NOBE; NOBRP; OBEV; OxBEV; PoE; SCGP; TFi; TOF; UnPo

Thou strainest through the mountain fern. Fragment, A. Robert Louis Stevenson. NOBVV

Thou stranger, which for Rome in Rome here seekest. Joachim Du Bellay. OBVE, *tr.* by Edmund Spenser *Fr.* Ruins of Rome.

Thou swear'st thou'lt drink no more; kind Heaven send. To Julius. Martial. FaBoEE, *tr.* by Sir Charles Sedley

Thou sweetly-smelling fresh red rose. Dialogue: Lover and Lady. Ciullo d'Alcamo. AWP; EaItPo, *tr.* by Dante Gabriel Rossetti

Thou Swell. Richard Rodgers. ReLy

Thou that art by Fates degree. New Canaans Genius; Epilogus. Thomas Morton. SCAP

Thou that art wise, let wisdom minister. Sonnet: He Craves Interpreting of a Dream of His. Dante da Maiano. AWP; EaItPo, *tr.* by Dante Gabriel Rossetti

Thou that canst sing so high, canst reach so low. (LL) Answer to Master [or Mr.] Ben Jonson's Ode, to Persuade Him Not to Leave the Stage, An. Thomas Randolph. BASC; BeJo

Thou that from the heavens art. Goethe. AWP *Fr.* Wanderer's Night-Songs.

Thou that loved once now loves no more. Answer, The. Sir Robert Aytoun [or Ayton]. NOSC

Thou, that where Freedom's sacred fountains play. Sonnet to France On Her Present Exertions. Anna Laetitia Barbauld. RWP

Thou thing of years departed! Image in Lava, The. Felicia Dorothea Hemans. CABP; NOBRP

Thou, to whom my name bears witness. Be Not Silent. David ben Meshullam. TrJP

Thou, to whom the World unknown. Ode to Fear. William Collins. NOEC; SCGP

Thou, sail on, O Ship of State! Henry Wadsworth Longfellow. PWR Fr. Building of the Ship, The.

Thou two-faced year, Mother of Change and Fate. 1492. Emma Lazarus. APN-2; SWaP; WPE

Thou tyrant, whom I will not name. Wedlock; a Satire. Hetty Wright. ECWP; NOEC

Thou vexed Atlantic, who hast lately seen. To Mrs. Hayley, On her Voyage to America. 1784. William Hayley. CenSon

Thou visor'd, vast, unspeakable show and lesson! (LL) Broadway. Walt Whitman. NAAL-2v1; NAAL-3

Thou walkest with me as the spirit-light. Mathilde Blind. ViWPN Fr. Love in Exile.

Thou wast all that [or that all] to me, love. To One in Paradise. Edgar Allan Poe. BoLoP; OBEV; OxBA; TAP

Thou water turn'st to Wine (faire friend of Life). To Our Lord, upon the Water Made Wine. Richard Crashaw. GeHe

Thou well hast heard that Rollo had two sons. Fazio degli Uberti. EaItPo, tr. by Dante Gabriel Rossetti

Thou Were My Ain Thing, An. Allan Ramsay. OxAEP-1

Thou wert the morning star among the living. To Stella. Plato. EnLoPo; FaBoEE; OBVE

Thou which art I, ('tis nothing to be so[e]). John Donne. NAEL-6v1; NAEL-7v1; NoSic

Thou who art clothed in silk, who drawest on. Man Is a Weaver. Moses Ibn Ezra. TrJP, tr. by Emma Lazarus

Thou who art thrown at by the great (shepherd) boys. Zebra, The. Unknown. PeSAV, tr. by W. H. I. Bleek

Thou Who Createdst Everything. Unknown. NOCV, tr. by Donald Davie

Thou who didst hang upon a barren tree. Long Barren. Christina Georgina Rossetti. TrCP; ViWPN

Thou who dost all my worldly thoughts employ. Verses Written on Her Deathbed at Bath to Her Husband in London. Mary Monck. ECWP; LW

Thou who hast slept all night upon the storm. To the Man-of-War Bird. Walt Whitman. APN-1

Thou who never canst err, for Thyself art the Way. Night Journey. Alfred Noyes. SacPr

Thou who wilt not love, do[e] this. Upon Some Women. Robert Herrick. BeJo; CaPo

Thou, who with all the poet's genuine rage. Richard Polwhele. NOBRP Fr. Unsex'd Females, The.

Thou, who wouldst wear the name. Poet, The. William Cullen Bryant. NAAL-2v1; NAAL-3; NCAP; TAP

Thou! whom Prosperity has always led. To a Querulous Acquaintance. Charlotte Smith. BWW

Thou, Whom rich and poor adore. Offer, An. Arthur Guiterman. TrJP

Thou, whom the former precepts have. Superliminare. George Herbert. ESCV; NOSC

Thou whose chaste song simplicity inspires. To Mrs. Smith, Occasioned by the First of Her Sonnets. William Hayley. Son

Thou, whose diviner soul hath caused [or caus'd] thee now. To Mr. Tilman after He Had Taken Orders. John Donne. EBEV

Thou! whose impassion'd face. Picture of Sappho, The. Caroline Elizabeth Norton. VWP

Thou, whose sad heart, and weeping head lyes low. Easter-Day. Henry Vaughan. ESCV; PeECV

Thou, whose sweet youth and early hopes enhance. Perirrhanterium. George Herbert. ESCV

Thou, whose sweet youth and early hopes inhance. George Herbert. ESCV

"Thou wilt forget me." "Love has no such word." Spring and Autumn. William James Linton. EBVV

Thou with thy Savior sent in endless bliss. (LL) In Memory of My Dear Grandchild Anne Bradstreet Who Deceased June 20, 1669, Being Three Years and Seven Months Old. Anne Bradstreet. BoWoP; NAAL-2v1; NAAL-3; TrCP

Thou wolt fursake me thrien ere the cok him crowe. (LL) Judas. Unknown. MiEL; PoE

Thou wommon boute fere. Devout Man Prays to His Relations, The. William Herebert. MiEL

Thou worshipest the shadow upon earth. (LL) Sonnet to Heavenly Beauty, A. Joachim Du Bellay. AWP; CTC, tr. by Andrew Lang

Thou wouldst not part thy spoil. To "A Certain Rich Man." Alice Thompson Meynell. ChIV-2

Thou wretched man, whom I discover, born. George Chapman. NOSC Fr. Euthymiae Raptus; or, The Teares of Peace.

Thou wretched thing of blood. John Webster. OxBEV Fr. Duchess of Malfi, The.

Thou wringest, with thy invisible hand, the foam. Wind, The. Thomas Holley Chivers. APN-1

Thou youngest virgin-daughter of the skies. To the Pious Memory of the Accomplished [or Accomplisht] Young Lady, Mrs. Anne Killigrew, [Excellent in the Two Sister-Arts of Poesie and Painting]. Dryden. NAEL-5v1

Thou, Zion, old and suffering. David Levi. TrJP Fr. Bible, The.

Though a seeker since my birth. Garland of Precepts, A. Phyllis McGinley. NBLV

Though all men should desert you. In a Late Hour. James McAuley. BMAP

Though all of you consort now underground. (LL) In Memoriam Francis Ledwidge. Seamus Heaney. CIP-2; NoAM

Though All the Fates Should Prove Unkind. Henry David Thoreau. HAP; TCAPo

Though all the lower world should ransacked be. Chapter IV. Elizabeth Singer Rowe. PEW

Though all thy gestures and discourses be. Innocent Ill, The. Abraham Cowley. BASC

Though / Already / Perhaps / However. One Size Fits All: a Critical Essay. David Lehman. OBCoV

Though Amaryllis Dance in Green. Unknown. NAEL-5v1

Though ask'd, I know not how she would resist. (LL) Charles Cotton. BoLoP; EnLoPo Fr. Resolution in Four Sonnets, of a Poetical Question Put to Me by a Friend, Concerning Four Rural Sisters.

Though authors are a dreadful clan. I Missed His Book, but I Read His Name. John Updike. OBAL

Though beauty be the mark of praise. Elegy, An. Ben Jonson. BeJo; NoP-4; OBEV

Though buds still speak in hints. Field-Glasses. Andrew Young. GTBS-P; RB

Though Caesar falling, shew'd no sign of fear. Caesar and Brutus. Anne Finch, Countess of Winchilsea. EMWP

Though clerical errors are fun. Limerick. Unknown. PeLi

Though Clock, / To tell how night draw[e]s hence, I've none. His Grange, or Private Wealth. Robert Herrick. BASC; BeJo; CaPo; CavPo

Though countless as the Grains of Sand. Boethius. OBVE Fr. Consolation of Philosophy, The ("De Consolacione Philosophie").

Though cruel seas like mountains fill the bay. Apple Island. Robert Graves. EmeKit

Though day is just breaking. Angling, a Day. Galway Kinnell. MoASP

Though days do gain upon the night. Vierzide Chairs, The. William Barnes. NOBVV

Though dusty wits dare scorn astrology. Sir Philip Sidney. Son Fr. Astrophil and Stella.

Though Earth has full many a beautiful spot. Land Which No Mortal May Know, The. Bernard Barton. PWR

Though every thing we see or hear may raise. My Observation at Sea. Mildmay Fane, 2d Earl of Westmorland. BeJo

Though Fatherland Be Vast. Allen Eastman Cross. AH

Though forts of adamant shall ring you round. Enemy in the Fortress, The. Marbod of Rennes. MLL, tr. by Helen Waddell

Though frost and snow locked [or lock'd] from mine eyes. To Saxham. Thomas Carew. BASC; BeJo; CavPo

Though giving pleasure to many. Roger McGough. NewEx

Though good things answer many good intents. Crosses. Robert Herrick. CaPo

Though he is dead now and his miracle. Robert Wilson. Michael Collier. OPRER

Though he looks almost exactly the way. Peace Studies. Lynne McMahon. ExTi

Though her lips are redder than the raspberries. (LL) Berry Picking. Irving Layton. HeIP-4; MoCV; NIP-4; NoP-4

Though her mother told her / Not to go a-bathing. Leda and the Swan. Oliver St. John Gogarty. EBNV; HAP

Though here no towering mountain-steep. Our Island Home. Charles Timothy Brooks. APN-1

Though his plan, when he gave her a buzz. Limerick. Unknown. PeLi

Though his wit and talent did not fail. Trial of Renard, The. Unknown. NAWM-7v1, tr. by Patricia Terry

Though I am dark. Unknown. BoWoP

Though I am Laila of the Persian romance. Princess Zeb-un-Nissa. BoWoP

Though I am young, and cannot tell. Ben Jonson. NOBE Fr. Sad Shepherd, The.

Though I be strange, sweet friend, be thou not so. Court lady Addresses Her Lover, A. Edward de Vere, 17th Earl of Oxford. NoSic

Though I get home how late, how late! Return, The. Emily Dickinson. MoAmPo

Though I go to you.　Ono no Komachi.　WoPoe, *tr. by* Helen Craig McCullough

Though I have touched her flesh of moons.　Modern Craft.　Hart Crane.　CAGL

Though I hum not a psalm's old wonted air.　I Am a Son of the German Language.　Ernst Waldinger.　AuPH, *tr. by* Lowell A. Bangerter

Though I know that we meet ev'ry night.　With a Song in My Heart.　Richard Rodgers.　ReLy

Though I look like you.　Hand Me Down Blues.　Calvin Forbes.　GT

Though I'm in Kyoto.　Basho.　EnlH

Though I'm just a wood Priapus.　*Unknown.*　PriapPo, *tr. by* Richard W. Hooper　*Fr.* Priapus Poems, The.

Though I'm left without a penny.　Never Gonna Dance.　Dorothy Fields.　ReLy

Though I must live here, and by force.　To My Mistress[e] in My Absence.　Thomas Carew.　CaPo; NOSC

Though I sang in my chains like the sea. (LL)　Fern Hill.　Dylan Thomas.　AmFaPo; AngWePo; CABP; ChAP; ClHu; GTBS-P; HAP; HarvBoo; HeIP-4; InPK-6; MoBrPo; NAEL-5v2; NAEL-6v2; NIL-7; NIP-4; NOBE; NoAM; NoP-4; OBWVE; OxBTC; PAI; PoE; PoPoPo; PoRA; SoSe-8; TCAWP; TFi; TRP; TwCP

Though I should be maligned by those.　Prayer for Strength.　Margaret E. Bruner.　PoToHe

Though I Should Seek.　Henry Ustic Onderdonk.　AH

Though I tarry on the road.　Isaibo.　JDP, *tr. by* Yoel Hoffmann

Though I Thy Mithridates Were.　James Joyce.　NoAM

Though I've a Clever Head.　*Unknown.*　HAP

Though I with strange desire.　Kisses Desired.　William Drummond, of Hawthornden.　EnLoPo

Though I would take comfort against sorrow.　Bible, *O.T.*　TrJP　*Fr.* Jeremiah.

Though in my heart.　Lady Otomo no Sakanoé.　ArkPo, *tr. by* Edwin A. Cranston

Though in them he heard the weird symmetry.　It Didn't Begin with Horned Owls Hooting at Noon.　Kevin Stein.　IllVoic

Though it be cold, hard, foul, from loving man / With[h]old thee. (LL)　Sepulchre.　George Herbert.　ESCV; MiEL

Though it contain no place for me. (LL)　Let Me Enjoy.　Thomas Hardy.　AWP; NoAM

Though it is not cold.　Little Travel Story, A.　David Oliveira.　GeoHom

Though it may look like (*Write* it!) like disaster. (LL)　One Art.　Elizabeth Bishop.　APT-2; AmFaPo; DiPo; HAP; HarvBoo; MakPoe; NAAL-2v2; NAAL-5; NALW; NoAM; NoP-4; PoE; PoPoPo; PoetW; SoSe-8; VCAP

Though it's a fickle age.　Ain't Misbehavin'　Harry Brooks.　ReLy

Though it's true we were young girls when we met.　For Jan, in Bar Maria.　Carolyn Kizer.　VGW

Though it seems so late. (LL)　Leaves.　Sam Hamod.　GraLe; UnSA

Though it seems superhuman, but at last.　Forgive, But Do Not Forget.　Ernst Waldinger.　AuPH, *tr. by* Lowell A. Bangerter

Though its map is drenched with watery names.　Moon, The.　Martha Silano.　AmPoNex

Though jealous exclusion may tremble to own us.　Envoy.　May Kendall.　ViWPN

Though leaves are many, the root is one.　Coming of Wisdom with Time, The.　W. B. Yeats.　FaBoEE; HarvBoo; PAI; SoSe-8

Though life be dead, and my joys gone. (LL)　As Time One Day by Me Did Pass.　Henry Vaughan.　ESCV; GeHe; MeLP

Though loath to grieve.　Ode, Inscribed to W.H. Channing.　Ralph Waldo Emerson.　APN-1; HAP; NAAL-2v1; NAAL-3; NOBA; OxBA; TAP; TCAPo

Though love's my daily and my nightly theme.　To Emma, Extempore; Hyaena, off Gambia, June 4, 1779.　Edward Thompson.　NOEC

Though many men had passed the ford, not one.　Fight with a Water-Spirit.　Norman Cameron.　OxBSo

Though marriage by some folks.　My Three Wives.　*Unknown, after* Etienne Pasquier.　FaBoEE

Though Mine Eye Sleep Not.　*Unknown.*　TrJP, *tr. by* Theodor H. Gaster　*Fr.* Dead Sea Scrolls, The.

Though most of the crewmen are whites.　On Board Starship *Enterprise.*　*Unknown.*　PeLi

Though my dwelling be small.　Tosui Unkei.　JDP, *tr. by* Yoel Hoffmann

Though my eyes are dim (LL)　Old Song Ended, An.　Dante Gabriel Rossetti.　BoLoP; EBVV

Though my position is of low degree.　Porter's Love Song to a Chambermaid, A.　James P. Johnson.　ReLy

Though my small incomes never can afford.　Jane Colman Turell.　TCAPo　*Fr.* Invitation Into the Country, In Imitation of Horace, An.

Though my stomach is still in Alabama pig / pens. (LL)　King: April 4, 1968.　Gerald William Barrax.　ESEAA; GT

Though My Thoughts.　Francis Daniel Pastorius.　AH, *tr. by* Sheema Z. Buehne

Though my wanderings are many.　Suibne Geilt.　NOIV

Though naked trees seem dead to sight.　Hopeless Desire Soon Withers and Dies.　"A. W."　NoSic

Though naughty flesh will multiply.　No Mean City.　Patrick MacDonogh.　BIrV; OxBSP

Though never claimed by us within my hearing. (LL)　Swimmers, The.　Allen Tate.　APT-2; FuPo; MoAmPo; NOBA; NoAM

Though never in the wards of the hospital for / Disabled servicemen at Erskine.　Warriors.　Douglas Dunn.　OxBC

Though night after night.　Takuan.　ZenPo, *tr. by* Takashi Ikemoto and Lucien Stryk

Though no blossoms cluster.　Mrs. Mary Furman Weston Byrd.　Mary Weston Fordham.　CBWP-2

Though now and then your problems fall.　When in Rome (I Do As the Romans Do).　Cy Coleman.　ReLy

Though now you are bereft and ways seem black.　For One Lately Bereft.　Margaret E. Bruner.　PoToHe

Though of white marble and dressed straight.　Crinagoras.　GrAn

Though on the day your hard blue eyes met mine.　Heritage.　Dorothea MacKellar.　NOBAu

Though our thoughts often, we ourselves.　Charles Reznikoff.　APT-2

Though pinched with cold, asks never.—Kate is crazed!— (LL)　William Cowper.　NAEL-5v1; NAEL-6v1; NAEL-7v1　*Fr.* Task, The.

Though poverty's no stain.　Anna Petrovna Bunina.　ARWW, *tr. by* Sibelan Forrester

Though prejudice perhaps my mind befogs.　I Think I Know No Finer Things than Dogs.　Hally Carrington Brent.　ITBLP

Though, Priapus, you're stuck with a well-stiffened cock.　*Unknown.*　PriapPo, *tr. by* Richard W. Hooper　*Fr.* Priapus Poems, The.

Though regions far [*or* farr] divided.　Song.　Aurelian Townshend [*or* Townsend].　NOSC

Though riders be thrown in black disgrace.　*Unknown.*　BIrV

Though set like dough, they shall be drawn like bread. (LL)　In Christ Church, Bristol, on Thomas Turner, Twice Master of the Company of Bakers.　Francis, Lord Jeffrey Jeffrey.　FaBoEE; NBLV

Though seven times, or seventy times seven.　Women of Jericho, The.　Phyllis McGinley.　ChIV-1

Though Shakespeare asks us, "What's in a name?"　Thomas Hood.　NOBVV　*Fr.* Miss Kilmansegg and Her Precious Leg.

Though short her strain nor sung with mighty boast.　Erinna.　Antipater of Sidon.　AWP, *tr. by* A. J. Butler

Though sick, I rise at dawn.　Poem for Mr. Li in Early Spring.　Tu Fu.　CrYelRi, *tr. by* Sam Hamill

Though since thy first sad entrance by Just Abel's blood.　Death.　Henry Vaughan.　AngWePo

Though Sir James (God's-a-Formula) Jeans.　Limerick.　R. J. P. Hewison.　PeLi

Though skilled in Latin and in Greek.　To a New England Poet.　Philip Freneau.　NAAL-2v1; NAAL-3

Though stands low on the mountain.　Autumn Aspens: Cumbres Pass.　Reg Saner.　PoCoUp

Though starlings imitate me.　Michael Henry.　NewEx

Though still she kept the form and voice of Mentor. (LL)　Homer.　NAWM-5v1; NAWM-7v1, *tr. by* Robert Fitzgerald

Though storms and tempest mark thy gloomy reign.　Written in a Winter's Morning.　Mrs. B. Finch.　CenSon

Though sun rubbed honey slow.　By the Nape.　Sandra Alcosser.　ExTi

Though Tennyson the Poet King.　James Madison Bell.　CBCWP　*Fr.* Poem Entitled the Day and the War, A.

Though that was not what Berkeley meant at all. (LL)　Fountain, The.　Donald Davie.　GTBS-P; NoP-4; OxBTC

Though the Clerk of the Weather insist.　Pebbles.　Herman Melville.　NCAP

Though the cunning of the Indian and the Zulu's thirst for blood.　Claflin's Alumni.　Lizelia Augusta Jenkins Moorer.　CBWP-3

Though the great song return no more.　Nineteenth Century and After, The.　W. B. Yeats.　FaBoEE

Though the limerick can not be deaded.　Limerick.　*Unknown.*　PeLi

Though the little clouds ran southward still, the quiet autumnal.　Autumn Evening.　Robinson Jeffers.　ChAP

Though the mills of God grind slowly, yet they grind exceeding small.　Retribution.　Friedrich von Logau.　PoToHe, *tr. by* Henry Wadsworth Longfellow

Though the New Teacher Is a Trifle Odd.　Richard Moore.　Son　*Fr.* Word from the Hills.

Though the nuns had dubbed us Crusaders.　Hurley High.　Paul Zarzyski.　SwNoth

Though the purity.　*Unknown.*　OHPJ

Though the road lead nowhere.　Song of Degrees, A.　Howard Nemerov.　TaR

Though the road turn at last.　Prisoners.　Denise Levertov.　NoAM; VCAP

Though the time seemed. Brken Promises. Sibby Anderson-Thompkins. InTrad

Though the walkers walk alone. Path, The. Konstantin Iakovlevich Vanshenkin. TCRusP, *tr. by* Daniel Weissbort

Though the war has been over for years and nothing is / dropping out. Again. Thomas Brush. CDa

Though the willows bent down to shelter us where we played. Doll. Josephine Miles. NALW

Though the world fall apart, surely ye shall prevail. (LL) Carthusians. Ernest Christopher Dowson. NAEL-5v2; NAEL-6v2

Though the world has slipped and gone. Lullaby. Dame Edith Sitwell. NALW

Though then I smile, and speake no words at all. (LL) To His Lovely Mistresses. Robert Herrick. CTC; CaPo

Though there are distances between us. Desert Warfare. Michael Longley. CIP-2

Though there are wild dogs. Orpheus and Eurydice. Geoffrey Hill. TRP

Though thou hast passed thy summer standing, stay. Epithalamion: or, a Song. Ben Jonson. BeJo

Though thou, indeed, hast quite forgotten ruth. Ballata: Of a Continual Death in Love. Guido Cavalcanti. AWP; EaItPo, *tr. by* Dante Gabriel Rossetti

Though thousands traipse round Wordsworth's Lakeland shrine. Remains. Tony Harrison. FaBoVe

"Though three men dwell on Flannan Isle." Flannan Isle. Wilfrid Wilson Gibson. PoRA

Though to good breeding she made no pretence. On a Gentleman Marrying His Cook. Colin Ellis. FaBoEE

Though to strangers' approach. Paired Lives. William Robert Rodgers. CIP-2

Though to the vilest things beneath the moon. Arthur Hugh Clough. OxBSo *Fr.* Blank Misgivings of a Creature Moving About in Worlds Not Realized.

Though to think / Rejoiceth me. Love Song. Margot Ruddock. OBMV

Though Truth and Falsehood be. John Donne. NOBE *Fr.* Satires.

Though truth be gold in any mould, and talents all for use. Morgan Llwyd. AngWePo *Fr.* 1648.

Though unable to imagine. Mezuzah. Alan Shapiro. TaR

Though we lived in the same lane. Answering Li Ying Who Showed Me His Poems about Summer Fishing. Yü Hsüan-chi. BoWoP, *tr. by* Geoffrey Waters

Though we thought it, Doña Carolina did not die. Dream of Husbands, A. Alberto A. Ríos. NoAM

Though with no lily [*or* lilie], stay with me! (LL) Cock-crowing. Henry Vaughan. BASC; ESCV; GeHe; NAEL-7v1; NPeEn; PBRV

Though Ye Suppose. John Skelton. OxBSP

Though you are a continent and two seasons away. Cape Coast Castle Revisted. Jo Ann Hall-Evans. BlSi

Though you are sedentary always, though. Crinagoras. GrAn

Though you be absent here, I needs must say. Abraham Cowley. BeJo; HAP; MeLP; OxAEP-1 *Fr.* Mistress, The.

Though you can tell me. Herman von Lingg. OHPJ

Though you do anything, he thinks no ill. (LL) William Shakespeare. CAGL; HAP; NoSic; OBEV *Fr.* Sonnets.

Though you fled the Capital for the woods. Remembering Priest Quang Tri. Doan Van Kham. WoPoe, *tr. by* Nguyen Ngoc Bich

Though you have never possessed me. Three Moments in Paris. Mina Loy. PFTM-1

Though you in your hermitage. To My Father Norman Alone in the Blue Mountains. Jack Lindsay. NOBAu

Though you'll forgive, I think, my sweet. Postscript to a Pettiness. Arthur Seymour John Tessimond. OxBSP

Though you made me think. *Var. authors.* WoPoe, *tr. by* Helen Craig McCullough *Fr.* Kokin Shu.

Though you my resolution still accuse. Epistle to Clemena, Occasioned by an Argument She Had Maintained Against the Author. Elizabeth Thomas. ECWP

Though you rule the dead, under the earth, who never smile. Julianus of Egypt. GrAn

Though you've decided that our love is wrong. Guilty. Harry Akst. ReLy

Though your dreams may seem normal and right. Limerick. J. C. B. Date. PeLi

Thoughe I seem straunge sweete freende be thou not so. Anne Vavasour Field. EMWP

Thought. Fazil Hüsnü Daglarca. CRP

Thought. D. H. Lawrence. OxBEV

Thought. Ahmad Nadeem Qasmi. WoPoe, *tr. by* Raja Changez Sultan

Thought. Walt Whitman. HHAm

Thought, A. Mikhail Yuryevich Lermontov. AWP, *tr. by* Max Eastman

Thought, A. Abram Joseph Ryan. PWR

Thought, The. Edward Herbert, 1st Baron Herbert of Cherbury. AngWePo

Thought, The. William Brighty Rands. OBEV

Thought about holy skirts—to tune of *"Wheels are growing on rose-".* Holy Skirts. Else Von Freytag-Loringhoven. PFTM-1

Thought about *my* place in the long war, A. Gambier. Joe Osterhaus. AmPoNex; NAPBL

Thought at Walden, A. Henrietta Cordelia Ray. CBWP-3

Thought beneath so slight a film, The. Emily Dickinson. OxBA; TCAPo

Thought bounded / rigid edges glued. Crossing. Diane Ward. FTOS

Thought Eternal, The. Goethe. AWP, *tr. by* Ludwig Lewisohn

Thought flashed 'cross a kindly mind, A. Kindly Deed, A. Priscilla Jane Thompson. CBWP-2

Thought for a Lonely Death-Bed, A. Elizabeth Barrett Browning. ViWPN

Thought-Fox, The. Ted Hughes. FaBoMo; HeIP-4; MakPoe; NPeEn; NoAM; SCV

  (I imagine this midnight moment's forest.) NoP-4

Thought from an Italian Poet. Felicia Dorothea Hemans. RWP

Thought from Propertius, A. W. B. Yeats. OxBSP

Thought from Ruddigore, A. Sir William Schwenck Gilbert. OBCoV *Fr.* Ruddigore.

Thought i'd / never grow old. Michael McClintock. HA

Thought I heard the wind. Spring at Fort Okanogan. Ramona Wilson. VoR

Thought in a Garden, A. John Hughes. ECEV

Thought o' Mary Morison, The. (LL) Mary Morison. Robert Burns. GTBS-P; NePenScot; OBEV; OxBS

Thought of a Briton on the Subjugation of Switzerland. William Wordsworth. *See* Thought[s] of a Briton on the Subjugation of Switzerland

Thought of a dear friend: 1:54 a.m. Captain's Log. Todd Colby. HeMarv

Thought of Death, A. Thomas Flatman. NOSC

Thought of Lake Ontario, A. Henrietta Cordelia Ray. CBWP-3

Thought of mother haunts my memory, The. Mother. Kristina Rungano. HAWP

Thought of our past years in me doth breed, The. William Wordsworth. SacPr *Fr.* Ode: Intimations of Immortality [from Recollections of Early Childhood].

Thought of what America would be like, The. Cantico del Sole. Ezra Pound. OBAL

Thought of writing came to me today, The. W. H. Auden. NOBL *Fr.* Letter to Lord Byron.

Thought on Human Life, A. *Unknown.* OxBSP

Thought on June 26. Raymond Mazisi Kunene. PBMAP

Thought's End. Léonie Adams. MoAmPo

Thought's [*or* Wit's] Forge and Furnace, Mangle-Press [*or* fire-blast, meaning's press] and Screw. (LL) On Donne's Poetry. Samuel Taylor Coleridge. NAEL-5v2; NAEL-6v2; PAI; UV

Thought went up my mind today, A. Emily Dickinson. TCAPo

Thought you killed me. Letter. William Daniel Ehrhart. CDa

Thoughtless wits shall frequent forfeits pay, The. John Gay. ECEV *Fr.* Trivia; or, The Art of Walking the Streets of London.

Thoughts. Michael Benedikt. CoAmPo

Thoughts. Maggie Pogue Johnson. CBWP-4

Thoughts. Amanda Ros. VerBaPo

Thoughts about Sari's Jump. Devorah Amir. DTA, *tr. by* Miriyam Glazer

Thoughts about the Person from Porlock. Stevie Smith. NAEL-5v2; NAEL-6v2; NoAM; NoP-4

Thoughts after Ruskin. Elma Mitchell. FaBoWP; NPeEn

Thoughts and Recollections. Duo Duo (Li Shizheng).

  "Sound of gunfire—dilutes the bloody terror of revolution, The." AF, *tr. by* Gregory Lee

  When the People Stand Up out of the Hard Cheese. AF, *tr. by* Gregory Lee

Thoughts are broken in my memory, The. Dante Alighieri. AWP; EaItPo, *tr. by* Dante Gabriel Rossetti *Fr.* La Vita Nuova.

Thoughts arise endlessly. Daichi. ZenPo, *tr. by* Takashi Ikemoto and Lucien Stryk

Thoughts Before Dawn. John Balaban. CDa

Thoughts Breathing in a Blizzard. "Antler." PoCoUp

Thoughts came to him like long lines of freight, The. Yehuda Amichai [*or* Amikhai]. FIT, *tr. by* Robert Friend

Thoughts During an Air Raid. Stephen Spender. MoBrPo

Thoughts in a Black Taxi. Sinéad Morrissey. MFPA

Thoughts in a Garden. Andrew Marvell. *See* Garden, The

Thoughts in Early Autumn: Thirty Rhymes Sent to Lu-wang. P'i Jih-hsiu. SuSp, *tr. by* Irving Y. Lo

Thoughts in Exile. Su Tung-p'o (Su Shih). OHPC, *tr. by* Kenneth Rexroth

Thoughts in Midnight Hours. Fanny Crosby. SWaP

Thoughts in Separation. Alice Thompson Meynell. OxBSo

Thoughts in the Library. Mihály Vörösmarty. IQMS, *tr. by* Hymen H. Hart

Thought[s] of a Briton on the Subjugation of Switzerland. William Wordsworth. UV

  (England and Switzerland 1802.) GTBS-P

(Thought of a Briton on the Subjugation of Switzerland.)   CABP

Thoughts of a dry brain in a dry season. (LL)   Gerontion.   T. S. Eliot.   APT-1; ColAP; EBEV; GTBS-P; HAP; NAAL-2v2; NAAL-5; NOBA; NPeEn; NoAM; OxAEP-2; OxBA; PAI; TAP; TCAPo; TFi

Thoughts of a Young Girl.   John Ashbery.   CoAmPo; TAP; VGW

Thoughts of Boyhood.   John Lloyd.   AngWePo

Thoughts of God, The.   Frances Ridley Havergal.

"They say there is a hollow, safe and still."   SacPr

Thoughts of Jack Kerouac—& Other Things.   Peter Olds.   PeNZ

Thoughts of Phena.   Thomas Hardy.   EBVV; HarvBoo; NOBVV; NPeEn; NoP-4; OxBTC

Thoughts on Capital Punishment.   Rod McKuen.   InPK-6

Thoughts on Happiness.   Francis Homfray.   AngWePo

Thoughts on Historical Sites: Wang Chao-chün.   Tu Fu.   SuSp, tr. by Irving Lo

Thoughts on Innocence.   Olga Nolla.   TANSG, tr. by Paula Vega

Thoughts on my sick-bed.   Dorothy Wordsworth.   PEW

Thoughts on One's Head.   William Meredith.   HAP; VCAP

Thoughts on Pausing at a Cottage near the Paukataug River.   Sarah Kemble Knight.   SCAP

Thoughts on Schoolchildren.   Ahmad Shauqi.   MAP, tr. by M. Mustafa Badawi and John Heath-Stubbs

Thoughts on T'ien-chin Bridge.   Shao Yung.   CoBCP, tr. by Burton Watson

Thoughts on the First Day of Autumn, Sent to Su Tzu-mei.   Ou-yang Hsiu.   SuSp, tr. by Irving Y. Lo

Thoughts on the Sight of the Moon.   Sarah Kemble Knight.   SCAP

Thoughts on the Works of Providence.   Phillis Wheatley.   InvLi; NAAL-2v1; NAAL-3; NAAL-5

(Arise, my soul, on wings enraptur'd, rise.)   ColAP

Thoughts on the Works of Providence.   Phillis Wheatley.

"As reason's pow'rs by day our God disclose."   SacPr

Thoughts South of the Yangtze.   Yü Hu.   CoBCP, tr. by Burton Watson

Thoughts that burned and glowed within, The. (LL)   Fire of Drift-Wood, The.   Henry Wadsworth Longfellow.   APN-1; ITBLP; MakPoe; NAAL-2v1; NAAL-3; NCAP; NOBA; OxBA; TAP

Thoughts that do often lie too deep for tears. (LL)   William Wordsworth.   AWP; FHYEP; HAP; HeIP-4; NAEL-6v2; NAWM-7v2; NOBE; NOBRP; NPeEn; NoP-4; OBEV; OxBEV; PoE; PoPoPo

Thoughts While Reading.   Chu Hsi.   OHPC, tr. by Kenneth Rexroth

Thoughts While Studying at Hanlin Academy Sent to My Colleagues at the Chi-hsien Academy.   Li Po.   SuSp, tr. by Joseph J. Lee

Thoughts While Walking.   Rachel Wetzsteon.   ExTi

Thousand-and-First Ship.   F. Scott Fitzgerald.

"There'd be an orchestra."   AiP

There was an Orchestra.   AiP

("There was an orchestra—Bingo-Bango.")   OTCP

Thousand and more negro children, A.   Kwela for Tomorrow.   Rui Knopfli.   PeSAV, tr. by the author

Thousand and One Nights, The.   Unknown.

Abu Nowas for the Barmacides.   AWP

Birds.   AWP

"Child, who went gathering the flowers of death."   AWP

Dates.   AWP

Death ("Once he will miss, twice he will miss").   AWP

"Early dew woos the half-opened flowers, An."   AWP

"Enter and learn the story of the rulers."   AWP

"God is praise and glory."   AWP

Haroun Al-Rachid for Heart's-Life.   AWP

Haroun's Favorite Song.   AWP

Her Rival for Aziza.   AWP

"I passed a tomb among green shades."   AWP

Inscriptions at the City of Brass.   AWP

Love ("Love was before the light began").   AWP

"Love was before the light began."   AWP

"My beauty is not wine to me."   AWP

"Once he will miss, twice he will miss."   AWP

Psalm of Battle.   AWP

"Since earth has put you away, O sons of Barmak."   AWP

Sleeper, The.   AWP

"Sleeper, the palm-trees drink the breathless noon."   AWP

Song of the Narcissus, The.   AWP

Tell Him, O Night.   AWP

To Lighten My Darkness.   AWP

Tumadir al-Khansa for Her Brother.   AWP

Wazir Dandan for Prince Sharkan, The.   AWP

"We grow to the sound of the wind."   AWP

"Weep! Weep! Weep!"   AWP

"Wild pigeon of the leaves."   AWP

"Wise to have gone so early to reward."   AWP

Thousand apples you might put in your theories.   Sonnet.   Bernadette Mayer.   PmAP

Thousand bees were tensing, A.   Arbor 1937, The.   Susan Stewart.   ExTi

Thousand Chinese Dinners, A.   Robert Mezey.

"From a thousand Chinese dinners, one cookie:"   RaBo

Thousand days great Beelzebub and Pope his son and fool, A.   Morgan Llwyd.   AngWePo   Fr. 1648.

Thousand doves, A.   Unknown.   WoPoe, tr. by R. J. Wilkinson and R. O. Winstedt   Fr. Two Pantuns.

Thousand goblets at the farewell feast, A.   To Tzu-an.   Yü Hsüan-chi.   SuSp, tr. by Jan W. Walls

Thousand guileless sheep have bled, A.   Song from the Bride of Smithfield.   Sylvia Townsend Warner.   MoBrPo

Thousand Hairy Savages, A.   Spike Milligan.   NBLV

Thousand Islands, The.   Charles Sangster.   NOBC   Fr. St. Lawrence and the Saguenay.

Thousand Killed, A.   Bernard Spencer.   FaBoWar; OBWP

Thousand lines, A.   Akiko Yosano.   WoPoe, tr. by Sanford Goldstein and Seishi Shinoda   Fr. Tangled Hair.

Thousand Martyrs I Have Made, A.   Aphra Behn.   NPeEn

(Thousand Martyrs, A.)   NoP-4

Thousand men then came thronging together, A.   William Langland.   NOCV   Fr. Vision of Piers Plowman, The.

Thousand miles and two world wars, A.   Phoenix.   Elizabeth Kay.   Prnts

Thousand miles of pure river water, A.   On the Road to Pyongyang—An Improvisation.   Liu E.   CoBLCP, tr. by Jonathan Chaves

Thousand mountains—no bird's flight, A.   River Snow.   Liu Tsung-yüan.   ChinPo, tr. by Yip Wai-lim

Thousand strands, A.   Yosano Akiko.   ErotSp, tr. by Sam Hamill

Thousand strands of willow at spring river's bend, A.   Willow Branches.   Liu Yu Hsi.   SuSp, tr. by Dell R. Hales

Thousand streets of London gray, The.   Sheep and the Goat, The.   George Macdonald.   EBVV; SacPr

Thousand things, and yet nothing, The.   Thinking of Impoverished Ancients.   T'ao Ch'ien [or T'ao Yuan-ming].   GifTon, tr. by David Hinton

Thousand times a day, A. (LL)   Of the Birth and Bringing Up of Desire.   Edward de Vere, 17th Earl of Oxford.   FaBoEE; NoSic; SCGP

Thousand times I have sat in resurant windows, A.   There Is Wind, There Are Matches.   Gerald Stern.   LCAP-2

Thousand times travelling over these fields, A.   Millennium.   Patricia Beer.   HarvBoo

Thousand years ago I loved you, A.   Joy Williams.   IBA

Thousand years from now, A.   Extermination of the Jews, The.   Marvin Bell.   GotH; TaR

Thousand years I was sick with darkness, A.   Sun.   Omer Hillel.   MHP, tr. by Ruth Finer Mintz

Thousand years now had his breed, A.   Edwin John Pratt.   MoCV   Fr. Cachalot, The.

Thousand years, with God (the Scriptures say), A.   On the Life of Man.   Francis Quarles.   ChIV-2

Thousand years, you said, A.   Var. authors.   BoLoP   Fr. Manyo Shu, Part 4 of 4.

Thousands and thousands of hushed years ago.   Silence.   James Whitcomb Riley.   GSo

Thousands arrive when a bird's about to fly.   Gwyneth Lewis.   NeBl

Thousands may enter through the gates of death. (LL)   Epistle to a Lady, An.   Mary Leapor.   BWW; CABP; ECWP; NOEC

Thousands of flowers, thousands of petals.   Yang Chi.   CoBLCP   Fr. Spring Days in My Home Town.

Thousands of images have suddenly brightened in the emptiness.   Untitled.   Duo Duo (Li Shizheng).   AF, tr. by Gregory Lee

Thousands of miles away—the Fu-sang tree.   Saying Goodbye to a Monk from Japan.   Hsü Pen.   CoBLCP, tr. by Jonathan Chaves

Thousands of mountains, tens of thousands of mountains.   Miscellaneous Poems Written in the Snow.   Wang T'ing-hsiang.   CoBLCP, tr. by Jonathan Chaves

Thousands of women hold me.   Snapshots of the Chameleon Woman.   Perla Schwartz.   TANSG, tr. by Celeste Kostopulos-Cooperman

Thow art pretty but unconstant.   Lines in the Corner of a Manuscript.   Unknown.   FaBoVe

Thracian filly, why do you.   Anacreon.   SaLy, tr. by Diane Rayor

Thracian page-boy / mastered, A.   Dioscorides.   GrAn

Thracian poet's song gets trees, rocks, The.   Ovid.   WoPoe, tr. by Charles Boer   Fr. Metamorphoses.

Thracian Wonder, The.   John Webster.

Art Thou Gone in Haste?   OxBoLi

Thrall.   Carolyn Kizer.   GifTon

Thrash away, you'll hev to rattle. James Russell Lowell. OxBA　*Fr.* Biglow Papers, The.

Thrasher in the Willow by the Lake, The. Robert Pack. ColAP

Thrashing Doves, The. Jack Kerouac. PmAP

Thraso. Samuel Rowlands. NoSic

Thrawn water? Aye, owre thrawn to be aye thrawn! By Wauchopeside. Hugh MacDiarmid. EBEV; OxAEP-2

Thre Prestis of Peblis, The. John, of Stobo Reid.
"In Peblis town sum tyme, as I heard tell." OxBS

Thread. Catherine Lucy Czerkawska. LW

Thread of Life, The. Christina Georgina Rossetti.
Aloof. NOBE; OBEV
"Irresponsive silence of the land, The." NOBE; OBEV
"Therefore myself is that one only thing." PEW
"Thus am I mine own prison. Everything." PEW
(Verse I.) PEW
Verse II. PEW
Verse III. PEW

Thread of red ants, A. Ants. Yusuf Al-Sa'igh. MAP, *tr. by* Diana Der Hovanessian and Salma Khadra Jayyusi

Thread of silver marks along the sand, A. Lost Continent, The. Jenny Joseph. BrRo

Thread suns / above the grey-black wilderness. Thread suns. Paul Celan. BBASP; OBVE; VCWP, *tr. by* Michael Hamburger

Thread the Needle. *Unknown.* FaBoVe

Thread the needle thread the needle. Thread the Needle. *Unknown.* FaBoVe

Thread the nerves through the right holes. Resurrection Song. Thomas Lovell Beddoes. FaBoEE

Thread to bind the heart of man!, A. (LL) Eve-Song. Mary Gilmore. CBAP; LW

Threading the Miles. Alfred Encarnacion. OpBo

Threading the palm, a web of little lines. Signs. Gjertrud Schnackenberg. InPK-6; VCAP

Threads of rain weave lambent light. To the Tune "Yellow Oriole." Yang Shen. CoBLCP, *tr. by* Jonathan Chaves

Threads our hands in blindness spin, The. Overruled. John Greenleaf Whittier. NCAP

Threadsuns. Paul Celan. PoetW, *tr. by* John Felstiner

Threat'ning clouds of yesternight, The. While the Choir Sang. Priscilla Jane Thompson. CBWP-2

Threat of the Sick. Breyten Breytenbach. PoetW, *tr. by* Denis Hirson

III. Danielle Collobert. MFP, *tr. by* Martin Sorrell

3. Hsüeh T'ao. WoPoe, *tr. by* Jeanne Larsen *Fr.* Trying on New-Made Clothes: Three Poems.

Three. Carolyn Kizer. NALW *Fr.* Pro Femina.

Three, The. Nikolaus Lenau. AuPH, *tr. by* Winthrop H. Root

Three A.M. Eternal. Reginald Shepherd. WiU

Three a.m. smoke rises from underground. Poe Story, A. Anthony Butts. AmPoNex

Three Aldis, not one of them dim. Limerick. Joyce Johnson. PeLi

Three Amoretti. Rick Barot. NeAmPo

Three ancient men in Bethlehem's cave. Mystic Magi, The. Robert Stephen Hawker. OBCP

Three and away. (LL) Mother Goose. OxNR; ReMoGo

Three and seventy years. Ingo. JDP, *tr. by* Yoel Hoffmann

Three Angels. "Bob Dylan." RaBo

Three Animals. Ron Padgett. TTTS

Three Ballate. Angelo [*or* Andrea] Poliziano. AWP, *tr. by* John Addington Symonds

Three blind mice, see how they run! Mother Goose. LB; OxBEV; OxNR; ReMoGo

Three blue king. Feasting with Etang a Hundred Times Around. Al Robles. ReBoTo

Three bold brothers of merrie Scotland. Henry Martyn. *Unknown.* ESPB

Three boots from Great Lakes stumble arm-in-arm. Tattoos. J. D. McClatchy. BAP-01

Three Bushes, The. W. B. Yeats. EBNV

Three Butchers, The. *Unknown.* PeVV

Three Cantos. Ezra Pound. *Fr.* Quia Pauper Amavi.

Three Captains, The. *Unknown.* AWP, *tr. by* Andrew Lang

Three-Card Monte. Malena Mörling. AmPoNex

Three Cherry Trees, The. Walter De la Mare. OBGa

Three chestnuts for morning, four at night. Tune: "Sheep on Mountain Slope." Ch'iao Chi. SuSp, *tr. by* Wayne Schlepp

Three Children. Mother Goose. LB; NOBL; OxNR; ReMoGo

Three children sliding on the ice. Three Children. Mother Goose. LB; NOBL; OxNR; ReMoGo

Three college sophs, and three pert templars came. Pope. FHYEP *Fr.* Dunciad, The.

Three-Coloured Banner. János Pilinszky. PoSu, *tr. by* Peter Jay

Three Companions, The. W. H. Auden. *See* Five Songs

Three 'coons come at his garbage. He be cross. John Berryman. LCAP-2 *Fr.* Dream Songs.

Three-Course Meal for the New Year, A. Myra Sklarew. TaR

Three crests against the saffron sky. Twilight on Tweed. Andrew Lang. EBVV

Three crooked cripples went through Cripplegate. Mother Goose. OxNR

Three cups of wine a prudent man may take. Benefits and Abuse of Alcohol, The. Eubulus. NBLV, *tr. by* Richard Cumberland

Three dark maids, I loved them when. Villancico. *Unknown.* AWP, *tr. by* Thomas Walsh

Three Darks Come Down Together. Robert Francis. CRP

Three Dawns. Jean-Joseph Rabéarivelo [*or* Rebéarivelo]. NegPo, *tr. by* Ellen Conroy Kennedy

Three days. I Starve My Belly for a Sublime Purpose. Anna Swirszczynska. BLT

Three days after the lightning hit it / or the beat, check this, I can play around it. Some Nets. B. P. Nichol. FTOS

Three days before he died the hospital called me. Tongues. Philip Martin. NOBAu

Three days of rain: indoors. Rainpoem. Michael Dransfield. CBAP

Three days of rest. Sun is in Capricorn, The. Joyce Mansour. HAWP, *tr. by* Carol Cosman

Three Days/out of Franklin. Víctor Hernández Cruz. PueRic

Three days we had. First Thanksgiving. Myra Cohn Livingston. HHAm

Three Dimensions. José Craveirinha. PBMAP

Three Dispositions Regarding One Woman. Sa'di Yusuf. MAP, *tr. by* Sargon Boulus and Naomi Shihab Nye

Three Dreams at Chiang-ling. Yüan Chên. SuSp, *tr. by* William H. Nienhauser

Three Dreams in Chiang-ling. Yuan Chen. CrYelRi, *tr. by* Sam Hamill

Three drunks, a leg on one quite gone, bereft. My Iambic Pentameter Lines. Robert Crawford. InPK-6

Three Easters. Alberta Turner. LCAP-2

Three Elements, The. Madison Cawein. APN-2

Three Emily's, The. Dorothy Livesay. NALW

Three Enemies, The. Christina Georgina Rossetti. SacPr; TrCP

Three Epigrams. Paul Ramsey. CRP

Three Epigrams. Theodore Roethke. NBLV
"Behold the critic, pitched like the *castrati*." OBCoV
"He left his pants upon a chair." OBCoV
Mistake, The. OBCoV
Pipling. OBCoV

Three Epigrams. Jonathan Swift. FaBoEE
(Cudgeled Husband, The.) NBLV

Three Epitaphs on John Hewet and Sarah Drew. Pope. NIP-4
Epitaph on the Stanton-Harcourt Lovers. FaBoEE
"Here lie two poor lovers, who had the mishap." FaBoEE

Three Evenings in a Life. Adelaide Anne Procter. VWP

Three excellent qualities in narration. *Unknown.* BIrV, *tr. by* Thomas Kinsella *Fr.* Triads of Ireland, The.

Three Excerpts. André Breton. PFTM-1 *Fr.* Manifesto of Surrealism (1924).

Three-Faced, The. Robert Graves. FaBoEE

Three faces. . . / mirrored in the muddy streams of living. For Andy Goodman—Michael Schwerner—and James Chaney. Margaret Abigail Walker. BPo

Three Fates, The. Rosemary Dobson. BMAP; BoWoP

Three fellows were marching over the Rhine. Hostess' Daughter, The. Ludwig Uhland. AWP, *tr. by* Margarete Münsterberg

Three Fishers [Went Sailing], The. Charles Kingsley. EBVV; PWR

3.5: Carthaginian Peace, The. Horace. MLL, *tr. by* Helen Waddell *Fr.* Odes.

Three Floors. Stanley Kunitz. LoL

Three floors up, I fall. Living Near the Plaza of Thieves. Leslie Ullman. PBCAP

Three flutes, two oboes, English horn, violins. Guide to the Symphony. Weldon Kees. VGW

Three-fold terror of love; a fallen flare, The. Mother of God, The. W. B. Yeats. BBASP; ChIV-2; ChrPo

Three folds in cloth, yet there is but the one cloth. To the Holy Trinity. *Unknown.* NOIV, *tr. by* Thomas Kinsella

Three for Bear. Aimé Césaire. PFTM-1

Three for Children. Thom Gunn.
Aquarium, The. NOxBChV
Cannibal. NOxBChV
"Dolphins play, The." NOxBChV

"Shark, with your mouth tucked under." NOxBChV

Three for the Road. E. San Juan, Jr. ReBoTo

Three Found Poems. Laurie Duggan.
  Hearts (1983). BMAP
  "It is essential that the U. S. A. standard of hygiene and inspection." BMAP

Three Found Poems. George Hitchcock. OBAL

Three Fragments. Bertolt Brecht. PFTM-1

Three Friends. *Unknown.* BoWoP; PBA, *tr.* by Ulli Beier

Three friends were with him at the Élysée. That Night. Victor Hugo. SxFrPo, *tr.* by E. H. Blackmore and A. M. Blackmore

Three Gates of Gold. Beth Day. PoToHe

Three Ghostesses. *Unknown.* OBCoV; OxNR
  (Three Little Ghostesses.) NOxBChV

Three grey boys tracked us to an old house. In One Battle. Imamu Amiri Baraka. BPo

Three grey geese in a green field grazing. *Unknown.* OxNR

Three Gypsies. Shalin Hai-Jew. UnSA

Three Gypsies, The. Nikolaus Lenau. AuPH, *tr.* by Winthrop H. Root

Three Gypsy Songs. *Unknown.*
  "It's you puts the green sprig in my hatband." WoPoe, *tr.* by Anselm Hollo
  "Moon shines on valley." WoPoe, *tr.* by Anselm Hollo
  "See the great vultures." WoPoe, *tr.* by Anselm Hollo

Three-handed Fugue. Phyllis Gotlieb. NOBC

Three-headed hydra of family, The. Galya, Mother, and My Daughter Anna. Yevgeny [*or* Evgenii] Borisovich Rein. TCRP, *tr.* by Bernard Meares

Three Holy Kings, The. Rainer Maria Rilke. ChrPo, *tr.* by Edward Snow

Three hours ago he blundered up the trench. Working Party, A. Siegfried Sassoon. AF; PeFWW

Three hours of peace and soothing rest of brain. (LL) Evening Lull, An. Walt Whitman. NAAL-2v1; NAAL-3

Three Hours; or, The Vigil of Love. Sarah Josepha Buell Hale.
  First Hour.
    "Blessing on the printer's art!, A." SWaP

Three Houses. Padraic Fallon.
  Gurteen. ModIr
  "I had no gift for it." ModIr

Three Hunchbacks, The. *Unknown.* NAWM-7v1, *tr.* by Ned Dubin

300,000,000. What Happened Here Before. Gary Snyder. NNaP

324. An Elegy for W.C.W., The Lovely Man. John Berryman. *See* Dream Songs

Three images of dying stick in my mind like morbid transfers. Bruce Beaver. NOBAu *Fr.* Letters to Live Poets.

Three-Inch Reflector. Caroline Caddy. BMAP

Three Jolly Pigeons, The. Oliver Goldsmith. *See* She Stoops to Conquer

Three Kalis appeared in Daksinesvar. Śyāmāpad Basu Rāy. SinGod, *tr.* by Rachel Fell McDermott

Three Kinds of Life Answerable to the Three Powers of the Soul. John Davies. SacPr

Three Kinds of Pleasures. Robert Bly. AiP

Three kings. Bethlehem. Marina Ivanovna Tsvetayeva [*or* Tsvetaeva]. GI, *tr.* by Nina Kossman

Three Kings, The. Henry Wadsworth Longfellow. ChIV-2; ChrPo

Three Kings came riding from far away. Three Kings, The. Henry Wadsworth Longfellow. ChIV-2; ChrPo

Three kings embark on a long journey. Starlight. Freda Downie. FaBoWP

Three Kings of Bethlehem, The. Attila József. IQMS, *tr.* by Istvan Fekete

Three Kings of Orient. John Henry, Jr. Hopkins. *See* We Three Kings of Orient Are

Three kings stood before the manger. Gifts, The. John Heath-Stubbs. OxBC

Three Ladies, The. Robert Creeley. NeAP

Three Ladies of London, The. Robert Wilson.
  Simplicity's Song. CTC
  "Simplicity sings it and 'sperience doth prove." CTC

Three landlords, stupid ones; cut each in two. Recipe for a Warsaw Novel. Cyprian Norwid. WoPoe, *tr.* by Jerzy Peterkiewicz, Burns Singer and Jon Stallworthy

Three limbs, three seasons smashed; well, one to go. John Berryman. HCAP *Fr.* Dream Songs.

Three lines of "clerk script" calligraphy. Chin Nung. CoBLCP *Fr.* Inscribed on a Lichen-Covered Wall in My Hut.

Three little children sitting on the sand. All, All a-Lonely. *Unknown.* OxBoLi

Three little ghostesses. Three Ghostesses. *Unknown.* OBCoV; OxNR

Three Little Girls. Kate Greenaway. NOxBChV

Three little girls were sitting on a rail. Three Little Girls. Kate Greenaway. NOxBChV

Three little kittens [they] lost their mittens. Three Little Kittens, The. Eliza Lee Cabot Follen. LB; OBCA; OxIBACP; OxNR

Three little maidens they have slain. Song. Maurice Maeterlinck. AWP, *tr.* by Jethro Bithell

Three little unexpected children. Triplets. Arthur Schwartz. ReLy

Three Little Words. Harry Ruby. ReLy

Three Love Poems. Norman Cameron. FaBoTw; GTBS-P
  "All day my sheep have mingled with yours." OxBS
  From a Woman to a Greedy Lover. FaBoEE
  In the Queen's Room. OxBTC
  "In the smoky outhouses of the court of love." OxBTC
  Shepherdess. OxBS
  "What is this recompense you'd have from me?" FaBoEE

Three lovely notes he whistled, too soft to be heard. Unknown Bird, The. Edward Thomas. RB

Three lovely sisters working were. Parcæ, The; or, Three Dainty Destinies: The Armilet. Robert Herrick. CaPo

Three Magi, The. Stanislaw Baranczak. GI

Three Marys at Castle Howard, in 1812 and 1837, The. Ebenezer Elliott. SacPr

Three men are fully clothed, long sleeves, The. Edward Hopper's Nighthawks, 1942. Joyce Carol Oates. PoSol

Three men came talking up the road. Night Piece. John Streeter Manifold. MoBrPo

Three men coming down the winter hill, The. Winter Landscape. John Berryman. GS; HarvBoo; MoAmPo; TwCP

Three Men in a Tent. Marilyn Nelson Waniek. ESEAA

Three men / laughing. Little Crisis Framed in My Window. Christopher Davis. AmPoNex

Three Men of Gotham. Thomas Love Peacock. FaBoCh; OBEV; OxAEP-2

Three merry men, and three merry men. George Peele. NoSic *Fr.* Old Wives' [*or* Wife's] Tale, The.

Three Messages. Aleksandr Aleksandrovich Blok.
  "Black raven in the snowy dusk." TCRP

Three Mirrors, The. Edwin Muir. NoAM

Three Modes of History and Culture. Imamu Amiri Baraka. ESEAA; PmAP

Three Moments in Paris. Mina Loy. PFTM-1

Three Movements. W. B. Yeats. FaBoEE

Three Movements and a Coda. Imamu Amiri Baraka. NAAAL

Three Musicians, The. Aubrey Beardsley. NOBVV; PeVV

3.9: Dialogue between Horace and Lydia, A ("Donec gratus eram"). Horace. OBVE, *tr.* by Robert Herrick *Fr.* Odes.

Three O'Clock Love Song. Michael S. Harper. GT

Three Observations on Belief. Tarin Towers. AmPoNex

"Three Observations on the Zombie Culture." Dolores Kendrick.
  26th Person, The. GT
  "Twenty-five people." GT

Three Octets. Osip Emilevich Mandelstam [*or* Mandelshtam]. RusPo, *tr.* by Robert Arthur Douglas Ford

Three Odes of Horace. Horace.
  Solvitur Acris Hiems. WoPoe, *tr.* by Louis MacNeice
  "Winter to Spring: the west wind melts the frozen rancour." WoPoe, *tr.* by Louis MacNeice

Three of us afloat in the meadow by the swing. Pirate Story. Robert Louis Stevenson. NOxBChV

Three of us went to the top of the city. Poem from the Empire State. June Jordan. BPo

Three old ladies in an apple tree. Ballad of Old Women & of How They Are Constrained To Simulate Youth In Order To Avoid Shocking the Young. Norman Talbot. NOBAu

Three or four hours unconscious there. (LL) Milk for the Cat. Harold Monro. MoBrPo; OBMV

Three outas from the [High] bleak Karoo. Christmas Carol. D. J. Opperman. PeSAV, *tr.* by Anthony Delius

Three Pagoda Dragon Pond. To the Tune "Chiu-ch'üan tzu." Wu Chen. CoBLCP, *tr.* by Jonathan Chaves

Three pairs of dimpled arms, as white as snow. Angels in the House, The. *Unknown.* TreFP

Three Phases of Africa. Francis Ernest Kobina Parkes. PBA

Three pink Hampstead intellectuals. Tea with the Poets. Sir John Betjeman. PeLV

Three places most loved I have left. Saint Columcille [*or* Columba]. NOIV

Three Pleas. Henry Treece. PoWW

3 poems. Aleksei Eliseievich Kruchyonykh [*or* Kruchionykh *or* Kruchenykh]. PFTM-1 *Fr.* Pomade.

Three Poems. Michael Lassell. WiU

Three Poems. Michelangelo Buonarroti. AWP, *tr.* by George Santayana

Three Poems about Children. Austin Clarke. CIP-2

Three Poems for the Indian Steelworkers. Joseph Bruchac. CDW

Three poems from Rediscovery (1964). Kofi Awoonor.

"Call her, call her for me, that girl." PBMAP
Lovers' Song. PBMAP
Three Poems in Memory of Mamá (Grandmother). Judith Ortiz Cofer.
"Before there is a breeze again." ExTi
Cold as Heaven. ExTi
Three Poems 1989. Larry Eigner. PFTM-2
Three Poems of the Atomic Bomb. Dame Edith Sitwell.
"Bound to my heart as Ixion to the wheel." MoBrPo
Dirge for the New Sunrise. MoBrPo
Three Poems on Ch'ang-sha. Yang Shih-ch'i. CoBLCP, tr. by Jonathan Chaves
Three Poems on Friendship. Hafiz [or Hafez].
"Desire's destroyed my life; what gifts have I." WoPoe, tr. by Dick Davis
"Each friend turned out to be an enemy." WoPoe, tr. by Dick Davis
"My friend, hold back your heart from enemies." WoPoe, tr. by Dick Davis
Three Poems to the tune "Lo-mei Feng." Ma Chih-yüan. CoBLCP, tr. by Jonathan Chaves
Three Poems to the Tune "Ssu-k'uai yü" Ma Chih-yüan. CoBLCP, tr. by Jonathan Chaves
Three poets, in three distant ages born. Lines Printed under the Engraved Portrait of Milton [In Tonson's Folio of the "Paradise Lost"]. Dryden. InPK-6; OxAEP-1
Three Portraits. George Hitchcock. VGW
Three Posthumous Poems. W. H. Auden. CAGL
"At break of dawn." CAGL
Glad. CAGL
"Hugerl, for a decade now." CAGL
Minnelied. CAGL
"When one is lonely (and You)." CAGL
Three practical farmers from back of the dale. Shepherds' Carol. Norman Nicholson. OBCP
Three Preachers, The. Charles MacKay. EBVV
Three Presidents. Robert Bly. LCAP-2
Three Puddocks, The. William Soutar. FaBoVe
Three/Quarters Time. Nikki Giovanni. CA
Three Quatrains. Edwin Arlington Robinson. NCAP
Three Quatrains. Jelaluddin [or Jalal al-Din] Rumi.
"Let the lover be disgraceful, crazy," RaBo
"Never too many fish in a swift creek," RaBo
"Night full of talking that hurts, A." RaBo; WoPoe, tr. by Coleman Barks and John Moyne
Three Ravens, The. Unknown. ESPB; HeIP-4; InPK-6; NAEL-5v1; OBEV; OxBB; PAI; PoE; SCGP; TFi; UnPO
(There were three Ravens sat on a tree.) NoP-4
Three Riddles from The Exeter Book. Cynewulf. PeLV, tr. by Kevin Crossley-Holland Fr. Riddles (Exeter Book).
Three Rioters, The. Geoffrey Chaucer. EBNV Fr. Canterbury Tales, The.
Three rivers join in the wilds of Chu. Sailing Down the Han. Wang Wei. CrYelRi, tr. by Sam Hamill
Three roads were shadowy and the sky over. Vanessa Vanessa. Ewart Milne. BIrV
Three rocks, a few burnt pines, an abandoned chapel. George Seferis. WoPoe, tr. by Edmund Keeley and Philip Sherrard Fr. Mythistorima.
Three rompers run together, hand in hand. To ———. Wilfred Owen. OxBSo
Three Roses, The. Walter Savage Landor. NAEL-5v2; NAEL-6v2
Three rounded flanks I loved. Unknown. NOIV
Three Sailors, The. William Makepeace Thackeray. See Little Billee
Three sang of love together: one with lips. Triad, A. Christina Georgina Rossetti. NAEL-5v2; NAEL-6v2; NALW
Three Sayings from Highlands, North Carolina. Jonathan Williams. OBAL
Three scribblers whose names end in Bert. Limerick. C. Vita-Finzi. PeLi
Three Seamstresses, The. Isaac Leibush [or Yitskhok Leybush] Peretz [or Perets]. TrJP, tr. by Joseph Leftwich
Three Seasons. Francis Sparshott. NOBC
Three Sentences for a Dead Swan. James Wright (1927–80). NOBA
Three Sets of Three. Kenneth Irby.
"There is from the legs in sleep an exhalation of the light, along the tops of the thighs." PFTM-2
3.7. Horace. OBVE, tr. by George Stepney Fr. Odes.
Three Silences. Rachel Hadas. RA
Three Sisters. Walter De la Mare. FaBoEE
Three Sisters, The. Arthur Davison Ficke. TCAPo
3.6. Ovid. OBVE, tr. by Christopher Marlowe Fr. Elegies.
Three Songs. Hart Crane. NAAL-2v2 Fr. Bridge, The.
Three Songs. Thom Gunn.
Baby Song. AmFaPo; RB

"From the private ease of Mother's womb." AmFaPo; RB
Three Songs. Rachel Wetzsteon. RA
Three Songs. Rachel Wetzsteon. RA
Three Songs for the Lute. Robert Graves.
Hedges Freaked With Snow. OxBTC
In Her Only Way. OxBSP
"No argument, no anger, no remorse." OxBTC
"When her need for you dies." OxBSP
Three Songs from the Haida. Unknown.
Bear's Song, The. AWP, tr. by Constance Lindsay Skinner
"Beautiful is she, this woman." AWP, tr. by Constance Lindsay Skinner
"I have taken the woman of beauty." AWP, tr. by Constance Lindsay Skinner
Love Song: "Beautiful is she, this woman." AWP, tr. by Constance Lindsay Skinner
"O good sun." AWP, tr. by Constance Lindsay Skinner
Song for Fine Weather. AWP, tr. by Constance Lindsay Skinner
Three Songs from the Temple. Don Domanski. NOBC
Three Songs of Love and Hate. Fay Zwicky.
"I have prayed for the end of his breath." BMAP
Stone Dolphin, The. BMAP
Three Songs of Mad Coyote. Unknown. STP, tr. by Herbert J. Spinden
Three Songs of Mary. Madeleine L'Engle.
"Angel came to me, An." OBCP
O Simplicitas. OBCP
Three Sonnets for Iva. Marilyn Hacker. GLP
Three Sons, The. Unknown. ReMoGo
Three sortes of teares doe from myne eies distraine. William Alabaster. ESCV Fr. Divine Meditations.
Three Spring Notations on Bipeds. Carl Sandburg. AWP
Three Stages. Christina Georgina Rossetti.
"I looked for that which is not, nor can be." NOBE
Pause of Thought, A. NOBE
Three Stanzas. Goethe. WoPoe, tr. by James Wright Fr. Journey in Winter.
Three Star Final. Conrad Potter Aiken. OxBA
Three Stars. Robert Desnos. SurPaPo, tr. by Mary Ann Caws
Three-Step Waterfall. Muso Soseki. EaWin, tr. by W. S. Merwin
Three strange men came to the inn. Lady Comes to an Inn, A. Elizabeth Jane Coatsworth. MoAmPo
Three Straws. Unknown. ReMoGo
Three students sit with a pair of whores. Life. "Sasha Chorny" [or Chiornyi]. TCRP, tr. by Bernard Meares
Three Summers since I chose a maid. Farmer's Bride, The. Charlotte Mew. BWW; BoLoP; EBNV; FaBoWP; MoBrPo; NALW; OxBTC; WPE
Three sunrises. Gabi. Maria Luisa B. Aguilar-Cariño. ReBoTo
Three Swedish Spells. Unknown.
"Dave rode across a bridge." WoPoe, tr. by Siv Cedering Fox
"I read for wolftooth and bearclaw." WoPoe, tr. by Siv Cedering Fox
Spell, A. WoPoe, tr. by Siv Cedering Fox
Spell against Predatory Animals. WoPoe, tr. by Siv Cedering Fox
Spell against Twisting an Ankle. WoPoe, tr. by Siv Cedering Fox
"When meeting a bear, say." WoPoe, tr. by Siv Cedering Fox
3.10: Extremum Tanain. Horace. AWP, tr. by Austin Dobson Fr. Odes.
Three Tests for Darwin Duke. Jane Holland. MFPA
Three that end the same way. St. Anzas VI. B. P. Nichol. FTOS
Three then came forward out of darkness, one. Road, The. Conrad Potter Aiken. MoAmPo; PAI
Three thing[e]s there be[e] that prosper up apace. Sir Walter Ra[u]le[i]gh to His Son[ne]. Sir Walter Ralegh. NAEL-5v1; NAEL-6v1; NAEL-7v1; NPeEn; NoSic; OxBSo; RB; Son; WoPoe
Three Things. Joseph Auslander. TrJP
Three Things. W. B. Yeats. OBMV
Three things come without seeking. Three Things Come Without Seeking. Unknown. NePenScot, tr. by Iain Crichton Smith
Three Things Enchanted Him. Anna Andreyevna Akhmatova. AiP, tr. by Max Hayward and Stanley Kunitz
Three things filled this day for me. Three Things. Joseph Auslander. TrJP
Three things make earth unquiet. Servant When He Reigneth, A. Rudyard Kipling. ChIV-1
Three things there be in man's opinion dear[e]. Fulke Greville, 1st Baron Brooke. NOCV; NOSC; NoSic Fr. Caelica.
Three Things to Remember. William Blake. OWoS; OxBoLi Fr. Auguries of Innocence.
3.13. Ovid. OBVE, tr. by Christopher Marlowe Fr. Elegies.
3.13: To the Fountain[s] of Bandusia ("O fons Bandusiae"). Horace. AWP, tr. by Eugene Field Fr. Odes.
3.30: This Monument Will Outlast (Exegi monumentum aere perennius). Horace. CTC; WoPoe, tr. by Ezra Pound Fr. Odes.

Three Tides. Brendan Kennelly. ModIr *Fr.* Cromwell.

Three times a night it woke you. Coal Train. Jay Parini. GM

Three times down. I'm still on the mountain. (LL) Sourdough Mountain Lookout. Philip Whalen. BB; NeAP; PoM

Three times he crossed our way where with me went. Old Man Pondered. John Crowe Ransom. MoAmPo

Three times I saw him face to face. Antinous. Mikhail Alekseievich Kuzmin. CAGL, *tr.* by Michael Green

Three times the carline grain'd and rifted. Lucky Spence's Last Advice. Allan Ramsay. NePenScot

Three times to the world's end I went. Edge, The. Rosemary Dobson. NOBAu

Three Tiny Songs. Cid Corman.
"I have come far to have found nothing." VGW

Three To's and an Oi. Heather McHugh. ExTi

Three-Toed Sloth, The. Fleur Adcock. OBCoV

Three turkeys fair their last have breathed. Melancholy Lay, A. Marjory Fleming. FaBoCh; NBLV

3.28: Holiday ("Festo quid potius die"). Horace. AWP, *tr.* by Louis Untermeyer *Fr.* Odes.

3.23: To Phidyle ("Caelo supinas si tuleris"). Horace. AWP, *tr.* by Austin Dobson *Fr.* Odes.

3.22: Pine Tree for Diana, The ("Montium custos nemorumque"). Horace. AWP *Fr.* Odes.

Three Undated Fragments. John Keats.
O Grant. ChIV-2
"O grant that like to Peter I." ChIV-2

Three Variations. Boris Leonidovich Pasternak. TrJP, *tr.* by Babette Deutsch

Three Visions of Imperial Rome. John Addington Symonds.
"It is a night of summer: overhead." CAGL
Midnight at Baiae. CAGL

Three Ways to Screw Up on Your Way to The Doings Three Ways. *Unknown.* STP, *tr.* by Richard Johnny John and Jerome Rothenberg

Three wee bit puddocks. Three Puddocks, The. William Soutar. FaBoVe

Three weeks gone and the combatants gone. Vergissmeinicht. Keith Douglas. FaBoMo; FaBoWar; GTBS-P; HarvBoo; NAEL-5v2; NAEL-6v2; NPeEn; NoAM; NoP-4; OBWP; OxBEV; OxBTC; PoWW; RB; SoSe-8; WoPoe

Three weeks had past, and Richard rambles now. Delay Has Danger. George Crabbe. NOBRP

Three weeks had past, and Richard rambles now. George Crabbe. NPeEn *Fr.* Tales of the Hall.

Three weeks past my father's death. After-Image. Linda Bierds. ExTi

Three wise men looked equivocally, The. Magi, The. Ramon Guthrie. GI; PoE

Three wise men of Gotham. Mother Goose. OxNR; ReMoGo; Spl

Three Wise Old Women. Elizabeth T. Corbett. NOxBChV; OBCA; OBSP

Three wise old women were they, were they. Three Wise Old Women. Elizabeth T. Corbett. NOxBChV; OBCA; OBSP

Three wonderful people called Ley. Limerick. Tim Hopkins. PeLi

Three wonderful people called Wick. Limerick. A. M. Sayers. PeLi

Three Woodchoppers. Robert Francis. TRP

Three woodchoppers walk up the road. Three Woodchoppers. Robert Francis. TRP

Three words in my dictionary. Three Little Words. Harry Ruby. ReLy

Three Written Poems, Unconnected. Marianne Vitale. HeMarv

Three xlvii. Laurie Duggan. BMAP

Three-year-old Archianax. Poseidippus. GrAn

Three years ago I left these city walls. Returning to Yin-ch'eng Early in the Year *Ting-ch'ou* (1277). Tai Piao-yüan. CoBLCP, *tr.* by Jonathan Chaves

Three Years from Sorrento. Dorothy Belle Flanagan. YaYoPo

Three years she grew in sun and shower. William Wordsworth. GTBS-P; HAP; NAEL-6v2 *Fr.* Lucy.

Three Young Rats. *Unknown.* OxBoLi; OxNR

Threes. Carl Sandburg. OxBA

Threissa, someone's knocking at the door. Procuress, The. Herodas. HePo, *tr.* by Barbara Hughes Fowler

Threnody for Sunrise. Richard Cecil. BodElec

Threnody for Sunset. Richard Cecil. BodElec

Threnody: "South-wind brings, The." Ralph Waldo Emerson. APN-1; TCAPo

Threnody: "What, what, what / What's the news from Swat?" George Thomas Lanigan. NBLV

Threre are long lines that. Queue. Rashidah Ismaili. HAWP

Threshed corn lay piled like grit of ivory. Barn, The. Seamus Heaney. HAP

Thresher's Labour, The. Stephen Duck.
"Soon as the harvest hath laid bare the plains." NOEC

Threshing Machine, The. Alice Thompson Meynell. WPE

Threshold, The. Fu'ad [*or* Fuad] Rifqa [*or* Rifka]. MAP, *tr.* by Sargon Boulus and Samuel Hazo

Thresholds of Identity. Lionel Abrahams. PeSAV

Thrice, and above, blest (my soul's [*or* soules] half[e]) art thou. Country Life: To His Brother, M. Tho: Herrick. Robert Herrick. CaPo

Thrice bless'd are they, who feel their loneliness. Melchizedek. John Henry, Cardinal Newman. SacPr

Thrice blessed Three in One. (LL) L'Envoy. George Herbert. BASC; ESCV

Thrice Blest the Man. John Barnard. AH

Thrice-cruel maid, may Heaven frown on thee. Elusive Maid, The. Abraham Ibn-Chasdai. TrJP, *tr.* by J. Chotzner

Thrice happy authors, who with little skill. Charles Jenner. NOEC *Fr.* Eclogue IV: The Poet.

Thrice he came. Malacoda. Samuel Beckett. CIP-2

Thrice the Brinded Cat Hath Mewed. William Shakespeare. RB *Fr.* Macbeth.

Thrice Toss[e] These Oaken Ashes in the Air [*or* Ayre]. Thomas Campion. EBEV; EnLoPo; FaBoCh; HAP; OxBSP; OxBSo; PoRA; SCGP; TFi; WeW-3
(Love-Charms.) NOBE

Thrice Welcome First and Best of Days. Isaac Chanler. AH

Thrid Vertical Poetry. Roberto Juarroz.
"Lamp lit, A." VCWP

Thrift. Cornelius Eady. LTA

Thrift alone for meaning ceases. We Forego Mimicry. Ray DiPalma. FTOS

Thrift Shop Ladies. Jennifer M. Pierson. ReTh

Thro elm and maple and syringa branches. Commencement. Constance Carrier. WPE

Throat, The. Wild Flower. Maurice Kenny. PoCoUp

Throat puckered like crepe. My Body. Joan Larkin. WiU

Throat Song: The Whirling Earth. Wendy Rose. HATNAP

Throbbings. Jamil. B. Holway. GraLe, *tr.* by George Dimitri Selim

Throbs the Night with Mystic Silence. Hayyim Nahman [*or* Khayim Nakhman *or* Chaim Nachman] Bialik. TrJP, *tr.* by Bertha Beinkinstadt

Throbs with vain pangs, here will I love to rest. (LL) Written in Autumn. Mary Tighe. CenSon; OxBSo

Throe upon the features, A. Emily Dickinson. TCAPo

Thrombosis Trombone. Thomas Lux. BodElec

Throned in splendor, deathless, O Aphrodite. Sappho. NAWM-7v1, *tr.* by Richmond Lattimore

Throned, yet adoring! (LL) Day of Judg[e]ment, The; an Ode. Isaac Watts. ECEV; HAP; NOBE; NOEC; OBEV; OxBEV

Thronging the heart. Residues: Thronging the Heart. Gael Turnbull. Oth

Through a dull tract of woe, of dread. My Birthday. George Crabbe. OxBSP

Through a few splinters of. Han-shan Te-ch'ing. WoPoe, *tr.* by James M. Cryer *Fr.* Mountain Living.

Through a Glass Eye, Lightly. Carolyn Kizer. BoWoP

Through a hospital window. In a Hospital Garden. Randall Jarrell. OBGa

Through a red prairie. (LL) Last Quatrain of the Ballad of Emmett Till, The. Gwendolyn Brooks. ESEAA; LCAP-2; NAAL-5; WPE

Through a two-way telescope of time. Aerolingual Poet of Prey. Eugene B. Redmond. SpirFl

Through a Window-Light. Sofiya Parnok. ARWW, *tr.* by Catriona Kelly

Through all the employments of life. John Gay. PeLV *Fr.* Begger's Opera.

Through all the evening. Borderlands. Louise Imogen Guiney. TCAPo

Through all the fates of earth, through every spell that works on man its spleen. To Ausonius. Paulinus of Nola. CAGL, *tr.* by Jack Lindsay

Through all the pomp of kingdoms still he shines. Homer. NOSC, *tr.* by George Chapman *Fr.* Iliad, The.

Through All Your Abstract Reasoning. Brian Patten. FaBoTw

Through Alpine meadows soft-suffused. Stanzas From the Grande Chartreuse. Matthew Arnold. NAEL-6v2

Through Alpine meadows soft-suffused. Matthew Arnold. EBVV; NAEL-5v2; PoE

Through and through the inspired leaves. Book-Worms, The. Robert Burns. FaBoEE

Through bars he looks, longing for freedom. Sunshine Prisoner "470". Stephen Clayton. IBA

Through bitterest toil you follow me still. (LL) At Ch'ang-ku, Reading: To Show to My Man Pa. Li Ho. CoBCP; ColAnChi, *tr.* by Burton Watson

Through bruised reeds my boat thrusts. Safaddan. Ruth Bidgood. TCAWP

Through brute nature upward rising. Winged Sphinx. Margaret Fuller. TCAPo

Through cigar smoke, through. Through the Smoke. István Vas. IQMS, *tr.* by George Szirtes

Through clouds of fire and clouds of blood. At Day's End. Hayyim Nahman [*or* Khayim Nakhman *or* Chaim Nachman] Bialik. MHP, *tr.* by Ruth Finer Mintz

Through Clouds, Their Whispers. Martha Rhodes. NAPBL

Through congoed leaves of. Kalamu ya Salaam. SpirFl *Fr.* New Orleans Haiku.

Through deir dus' (LL) Memphis Blues. Sterling Allen Brown. APT-2; NAAAL

Through different streets that are all alike we walk down toward the docks. Night Meeting. Thomas McGrath. BodElec

Through Eden took their solitary way. (LL) John Milton. NAWM-5v1; NAWM-7v1 *Fr.* Paradise Lost.

Through every night we hate. Mothers, Daughters. Shirley Kaufman. BoWoP

Through fear of sharp and bitter pain. King's Last Farewell to the World, The. *Unknown.* BASC

Through frost and snow and sunlight. Brian Patten. NewEx

Through frost and snow locked from mine eyes. To Saxham. Thomas Carew. CaPo

Through frozen rice fields. Basho. SoOfWa, *tr. by* Sam Hamill

Through glades and glooms! Oh fair! Oh, sad! Collins. Lionel Pigot Johnson. OxAEP-2

Through high still air. (LL) Mid-August at Sourdough Mountain Lookout. Gary Snyder. ColAP; HAP; InPK-6; LoL; NoP-4; TAP; VCAP

Through infinite immensity. (LL) Emily Jane Brontë. NAEL-5v2; NAEL-6v2

Through it / over young women's abdomens tense. Stethoscope, The. Dannie Abse. BloBone

Through lane or black archway. Austin Clarke. ModIr; NoAM

Through lenses the world opens. Microscope. Gwyn Thomas. OBWVE, *tr. by* Joseph P. Clancy

Through life's dull road, so dim and dirty. On My Thirty-third Birthday. Byron. FaBoEE

Through me come into the city full of pain. Dante Alighieri. WoPoe, *tr. by* Armand Schwerner *Fr.* Divina Commedia.

Through miles of green cornfields that lusty. Constance Fenimore Woolson. SWaP *Fr.* Two Women.

Through mud, fouled nuts, black grime. Removing the Plate of the Pump on the Hydraulic System of the Backhoe. Gary Snyder. LoL

Through my window, asphalt rooftops, cyclone. Letter Home from Brooklyn. Enid Shomer. UrbNat

Through Nurseryland. *Unknown.* OTCP

Through paths of pleasant thought I ran. Reason and Faith. Cecil Frances Alexander. SacPr

Through pearly deeps of sky, cloud-mountains rose. Sky Picture. Henrietta Cordelia Ray. CBWP-3

Through Persia raving. CXXXIX. Pita Amor. TANSG, *tr. by* Shaun Griffin and Emma Sepúlveda-Pulvirenti

Through random doors we wandered. Exits and Entrances. Naomi Long Madgett. BlSi

Through reedy banks. Nima, The. Jorge Isaacs. TrJP, *tr. by* Alice Jane McVan

Through Ruddy Orchards. Mary Oliver. SoSe-8; WPE

Through salt marsh, grassy channel where the shark's. Tide Turning. John Frederick Nims. DiPo; IllVoic

Through seas of dreams and seas of phantasies. Nirvâna. Sidney Lanier. NCAP

Through sere trees and beheaded. August Rain, after Haying. Jane Kenyon. ExTi

Through snow / Lights of homes. Buson. ZenPo, *tr. by* Takashi Ikemoto and Lucien Stryk

Through space, in the cold. Determination of Time. Alena N´dvorníková. SurWo

Through springtime walks, with flowers perfumed. Song. Anne Batten Cristall. ECWP; RWP

Through storm and wind. *Unknown.* OxNR

Through storms you reach them and from storms are free. Enviable Isles, The. Herman Melville. NCAP

Through summer air. Flight. Jorge Guillén. BLT, *tr. by* Reginald Gibbons

Through tall bamboo the mossy path. Spring Homecoming. Tu Fu. CrYelRi, *tr. by* Sam Hamill

Through that ever-reluctant element. (LL) On Portents. Robert Graves. FaBoMo; HarvBoo

Through that pure *Virgin-Shrine*. Henry Vaughan. BASC; ChIV-2; EBEV; ESCV; GeHe; MeLP; NAEL-5v1; NAEL-7v1; NOBE; NOCV; OBEV; OBWVE; OxAEP-1; OxBEV; SCGP; TFi; TOF

Through that window—all else being extinct. Room, The. Conrad Potter Aiken. APT-1; MoAmPo; NOBA

Through the ample open door of the peaceful country barn. Farm Picture, A. Walt Whitman. BLT; TRP

Through the bending twigs of the coral grove. (LL) Coral Grove, The. James Gates Percival. APN-1; ColAP

Through the black, rushing smoke-bursts. Matthew Arnold. NOBE; OBEV *Fr.* Empedocles on Etna.

Through the bound cable strands, the arching path. Hart Crane. NAAL-5 *Fr.* Bridge, The.

Through the broad bright land. (LL) Song of the Ungirt Runners, The. Charles Hamilton Sorley. MoBrPo; OBEV

Through the bruised unbalanced waves? (LL) Late Night Ode. Horace. WiU; WoPoe, *tr. by* J. D. McClatchy

Through the cambered flesh of clover and wild carrot. (LL) Flitting, The. Medbh McGuckian. PBCIP; PNI

Through the cheap iron gate and its mythic. Night Shift, after Drinking Dinner, Container Corporation of America, 1972. Kevin Stein. IllVoic

Through the clotted street and down. Nocturne. Ellen Bryant Voigt. UrbNat

Through the corridor walks a blind man. Blind Man, The. Yaroslav [*or* Iaroslav] Vasilevich Smelyakov [*or* Smeliakov]. TCRP, *tr. by* Simon Franklin

Through the cracks. Ray A. Young Bear. STP

Through the crawl space. Tattoo #47, "Happy Dragon." Paul Allen. ReTh

Through the dark city. Great Figure, The. William Carlos Williams. AiP; HeIP-4; InPK-6; NoAM; SAmP; TTTS

Through the Dark Sod—as Education. Emily Dickinson. NALW

Through the Dark the Dreamers Came. Earl Bowman Marlatt. AH

Through the deep night a magic mist led me. Magic Mist, A. Owen Roe O'Sullivan. NOIV, *tr. by* Thomas Kinsella

Through the deep shadows of the darkening years. Charlotte Brontë. Paul Hamilton Hayne. APN-2

Through the dusky purple glimmer. Anita and Giovanni. Henrietta Cordelia Ray. CBWP-3

Through the Forest Have I Gone. William Shakespeare. CTC *Fr.* Midsummer Night's Dream, A.

Through the forest the boy wends all day long. Boy and the Flute, The. Bjørnstjerne Bjørnson. AWP, *tr. by* Sir Edmund William Gosse

Through the front gate. *Unknown.* ColAnChi, *tr. by* Jeanne Larsen *Fr.* Midnight Songs.

Through the garbled signals. Heirlooms. Geoffrey Philp. WaCA

Through the green grass. Cantiga de Amigo. Pero Meogo. WoPoe, *tr. by* Keith Bosley

Through the hole in the hut's wall. Deserter, The. Ai. BodElec

Through the host with this the goddess ran. Homer. FaBoWar, *tr. by* George Chapman *Fr.* Iliad, The.

Through the House. William Shakespeare. CTC *Fr.* Midsummer Night's Dream, A.

Through the house what busy joy. First Tooth, The. Charles Lamb. WoRP

Through the lands low-lying, fast and free. Moonlight Ride, A. Harriet Hamilton King. VWP

Through the laurel branches. Casida of the Dark Doves. Federico García Lorca. WoPoe, *tr. by* Edwin Honig

Through the lit crystal of the cup. (LL) Autumn. Roy Campbell. GTBS-P; MoBrPo; OBMV; OxBTC

Through the Long Night. Edward Carpenter. CAGL *Fr.* Towards Democracy.

Through the Looking-Glass. Lewis Carroll.
  Humpty Dumpty's Poetic Recitation. EBEV; NOBVV; NPeEn
  (Humpty Dumpty's Recitation.) OBSP; PeVV
  (Humpty Dumpty's Song.) GTBS-P; OBCoV; OxBoLi; PeLV
  "I'll tell thee everything I can." FaBoCh; NAEL-5v2; NAEL-6v2; NOBE; NOBL; NoAM; NoP-4; PeLV; TFi; UV
  "In winter, when the fields are white." EBEV; NOBVV; NPeEn
  Jabberwocky. AmFaPo; BRP; CABP; ChAP; ClHu; EBEV; EBVV; HeIP-4; ITBLP; InPK-6; NAEL-5v2; NAEL-6v2; NBLV; NOBE; NOBL; NOBVV; NOxBChV; NTCP; NoAM; NoP-4; OBSP; OxAEP-2; OxBEV; PeLV; PeVV; PoRA; RB; TFi; TRP; TTTS; UV
  "Sun was shining on the sea, The." CABP; ChAP; ITBLP; NAEL-5v2; NAEL-6v2; NOBL; NOBVV; NoAM; OBSP; OTCP; OxAEP-2; PeLV; PoRA; TFi
  "To the Looking-Glass world it was Alice that said." UV
  "'Twas brillig, and the slithy toves." AmFaPo; BRP; CABP; ChAP; ClHu; EBEV; EBVV; HeIP-4; ITBLP; InPK-6; NAEL-5v2; NAEL-6v2; NBLV; NOBE; NOBL; NOBVV; NOxBChV; NTCP; NoAM; NoP-4; OBSP; OxAEP-2; OxBEV; PeLV; PeVV; PoRA; RB; TFi; TRP; TTTS; UV
  Walrus and the Carpenter, The. CABP; ChAP; ITBLP; NAEL-5v2; NAEL-6v2; NOBL; NOBVV; NoAM; OBSP; OTCP; OxAEP-2; PeLV; PoRA; TFi
  Welcome Queen Alice. UV
  (White Knight's Ballad, The.) HAP
  White Knight's Song, The. FaBoCh; NAEL-5v2; NAEL-6v2; NOBE; NOBL; NoAM; NoP-4; PeLV; TFi; UV
  (A-Sitting on a Gate.) PoRA

Through the Metidja to Abd-el-Kadr. Robert Browning. WoPoe

Through the narrow aisles of pain. (LL) Solitude. Ella Wheeler Wilcox. BRP; PWR; SWaP; TCAPo

Through the night on fire with my blood. She Speaks the Morning's Filigree. Philip Lamantia. VGW

Through the open French window the warm sun. Still-Life. Elizabeth Daryush. FaBoWP; NPeEn; OxBEV; WPE

Through the orange glow of taillights, I crossed. In the Black Camaro. David Bottoms. ReTh

Through the rain forests, up a long river. Deceptive Grin of the Gravel Porters, The. Gavin Ewart. FaBoMo

Through the screened window. Double Helix. Sean Thomas Dougherty. AmPoNex

Through the slits of my eyes a perambulator passes. Sun, The. Hugo Ball. PFTM-1

Through the slow succeeding ages. Only Way, The. W. N. Ewer. FaBoWar

Through the small holes. Cor Van den Heuvel. HA

Through the small opening in the boarded wall. Autobiographical Response from a Provincial Wasteland (in Reply to a New Year's Greeting Sent with a Bouquet). Elizaveta Shakhova. ARWW, tr. by Catriona Kelly

Through the Smoke. István Vas. IQMS, tr. by George Szirtes

Through the soft evening air enwinding all. Italian Music in Dakota. Walt Whitman. APN-1

Through the strait gate of passion. Paradise Re-entered. D. H. Lawrence. ChIV-2

Through the strait pass of suffering. Emily Dickinson. TOF

Through the supermarket aisles I push a cart. Shopping. Agi Mishol. DTA, tr. by Tsipi Keller

Through the tobacco haze. Blew It. Michael Castro. SeSe

Through the vast crowded wards, thousands came round. Freedom. Anthony Thwaite. OxBSo

Through the viridian (and black of the burnt match). Virgo Descending. Charles Wright. ColAP; LCAP-2; TRP

Through the wall. Martin Shea. HA

Through the white thin bone of a hare. (LL) Collarbone [or Collar-Bone] of a Hare, The. W. B. Yeats. OxAEP-2; OxBTC; RB

Through the wide, grey loft window. Village Life, A. Derek Walcott. GT

Through the Window. Vladislav Felitsianovich Khodasevich. TCRP, tr. by Yakov Hornstein

Through the windy valley. Yün Shou-p'ing. CoBLCP Fr. Inscribed on a Painting by Shih-ku.

Through the years of happiness and hardships. Blockade Swallow, The. Olga Fiodorovna Berggolts [or Bergholts]. TCRusP, tr. by Daniel Weissbort

Through These Halls. Judy Jordan. AmPoNex

Through These Pale Cold Days. Isaac Rosenberg. TrJP

Through this my strong and new misaventure. Guido Cavalcanti. EaItPo, tr. by Dante Gabriel Rossetti

Through this toilsome world, alas! I Shall Not Pass This Way Again. Unknown. ChAP

Through this window, thin rivers. Housework. Joan Larkin. WiU

Through Time's Segments. István Vas. IQMS, tr. by Daniel Gerard Hoffman

Through torrid entrances, past icy poles. To Shakespeare. Hart Crane. Son

Through traffic, honking and off-course, direction veering. Coming to You. Daphne Marlatt. PoBW

Through tranquil years they watched the changes. Clearing for the Plough. Ernest G. Moll. NOBAu

Through Vienna's woods an echo glides. Schubert. Michael Klieba. AuPH, tr. by Lowell A. Bangerter

Through Warmth and Light of Summer Skies. Austin Faricy. AH

Through weathered wood dark. Kalamu ya Salaam. SpirFl Fr. New Orleans Haiku.

Through what long heaviness, assayed in what strange fire. Carthusians. Ernest Christopher Dowson. NAEL-5v2; NAEL-6v2

Through what obscure, half-comprehending night. Candlemas Day. Sister Mary Madeleva. CRP

Through which one may not put one's hands to touch. (LL) Prisms. Laura Riding Jackson. APT-2; ColAP

Through wild and tangled forests. On the Mississippi. Hamlin Garland. APN-2

Through Willing Heart and Helping Hand. Frederick Lucian Hosmer. AH

Through winter-time we call on spring. Wheel, The. W. B. Yeats. GTBS-P

Through woods, Mme Une Telle, a trifle ill. Autumn Chapter in a Novel. Thom Gunn. FaBoMo; OxBTC

Through years and years. Day We Buried Our Bully, The. Mbuyiseni Oswald Mtshali. PeSAV

Through You. Edwin Honig. TAP

Through your love words became clear. Word "Silk," The. Thomas McCarthy. CIP-2

Throughe a forest as I can ryde. Crow and Pie. Unknown. ESPB

Throughout a garden greene and gay. Rose of England, The. Unknown. ESPB

Throughout the field I find no grain. Winter in Durnover Field. Thomas Hardy. MoBrPo

Throughout the whole world, experts say. Limerick. Unknown. PeLi

Throughout the world, if it were sought. Honesty. Sir Thomas Wyatt. NoSic; OxBSP

Throw away thy rod. Discipline. George Herbert. FHYEP; FSCP; GeHe; MeLP; NAEL-5v1; NAEL-6v1; NAEL-7v1; NOBE; NOCV; NoP-4; OBEV; OxAEP-1; PAI

Throw Hannibal on the scales, how many pounds. Juvenal. OBVE, tr. by Robert Lowell Fr. Satires.

Throw him into the river. Kasenduaxtc. STP

Throw me a quince. Unknown. ColAnChi, tr. by Jeffrey Riegel Fr. Classic of Odes.

Throw on rouge and powder, watch the governor pass! Su Tung-p'o (Su Shih). CoBCP Fr. Along the Road to Stone Lake.

Throw open the window. Our Sunday Rest. "Don Aminado." TCRusP, tr. by John Glad

Throw the raincoat under us! (LL) Hops. Boris Leonidovich Pasternak. BoLoP; TTTS

Throw Yourself Like Seed. Miguel de Unamuno. RaBo, tr. by Robert Bly

Throwing a bomb is bad. Ethics for Everyman. Roger Woddis. NOBL

Throwing her arms around her dear father. Anyte [or Anytes]. SaLy, tr. by Diane Rayor

Throwing her arms around her father. Anyte [or Anytes]. GrAn

Throwing Out at / of (Com)pare (Dis)pair, A. Tina Darragh. FTOS

Throwing Out My Father's Dictionary. Moniza Alvi. Prnts

Throwing Out the Flowers. Gwendolyn Brooks. ColAP Fr. Notes from the Childhood and the Girlhood.

Throwing the Beads. Sean Dunne. BiHa

Thrown from the world. (LL) Revelation in the Mother Lode. George Evans. AF; PmAP

Thrown in the moon-glade by the palm. (LL) Herman Melville. APN-1; NCAP Fr. Clarel: A Poem and Pilgrimage in the Holy Land.

Thrown off-center. Theory of Curve. Christopher Gilbert. LTA

Thrush before Dawn, A. Alice Thompson Meynell. MoBrPo; WPE

Thrush in the syringa sings, A. Basil Bunting. HarvBoo; WoPoe

Thrush is singing on the walnut tree, A. Die Zauberflöte. Rosamund Marriott Watson. ViWPN

Thrush is tapping a stone, A. Dawn. Gordon Bottomley. MoBrPo

Thrush, linnet, stare and wren. In Glencullen. John Millington Synge. OBMV

Thrushes. Ted Hughes. FaBoMo; TRP

Thrushes flying under the lake. Nightingales singing underground. Pewter. Jack Gilbert. BodElec

Thrust & Parry. Greg Delanty. BiHa

Thrust and Riposte. Eugenio Montale. PeFWW, tr. by Gavin Ewart

Thrust of the dragon's tight bone, The. Dream Feast (Three Poems), The. Anita Endrezze. VoR

Thrust upon by a softly-swinging wind. (LL) Weather-Cock Points South, The. Amy Lowell. APT-1; NALW; NoP-4

Thrusting its armoury of hot delight. Descartes and the Stove. Charles Tomlinson. FaBoMo

Thule, the period of cosmography. Unknown. NPeEn

Thulène is dead, my lord. I saw his funeral. Sonnet Addressed to Henry III on the Death of Thulène, the King's Fool. Jean Passerat. WoPoe, tr. by Richmond Lattimore

Thumb. Philip Dacey. KaS

Thumb bold. Unknown. OxNR

Thumb he. Unknown. OxNR

Thumb, loose tooth of a horse. Bestiary for the Fingers of My Right Hand. Charles Simic. LCAP-2

Thumbikin, Thumbikin, broke the barn. Unknown. OxNR

Thumbing Old Magazines. Gerald Vizenor. VoR

Thumbkin says, I'll dance. Unknown. OxNR

"Thumbs in the thumb-place." Mitten Song, The. Marie Louise Allen. NTCP

Thumping heart, The. Hospital Interiors. Giovanni Raboni. ItPo, tr. by Gayle Ridinger

Thunder. Fu Hsüan. OHMPC, tr. by Kenneth Rexroth

Thunder. Wang Chiu-ssu. CoBLCP, tr. by Jonathan Chaves

Thunder & the flaw of their great quarrel, The. John Berryman. VCAP Fr. Dream Songs.

Thunder blossoms gorgeously above our heads. Storm Ending. Jean Toomer. APT-2

Thunder Can Break. Christopher Okigbo. HBAPE

Thunder clouds are sweeping, shrouding. Russian Cradle Song, A. David Nomberg. TrJP, tr. by Alter Brody

Thunder has nested in the grass all night. Child Frightened by a Thunderstorm. Ted Kooser. KaS

Thunder in the southern mountains, the third month of the year. Thunder. Wang Chiu-ssu. CoBLCP, tr. by Jonathan Chaves

Thunder moved in sleep. Seven Days. J. R. Rowland. PAI

Thunder mutters louder and more loud, The. John Clare. NOBVV; NPeEn

Thunder. My heart trembles. Thunder. Fu Hsüan. OHMPC, tr. by Kenneth Rexroth

Thunder of the Rain God. House in Taos, A. Langston Hughes. APT-2

Thunder, Perfect Mind, The. *Unknown.* "I was sent forth from the power." PFTM-1

Thunder, rain falling, falling. Inscribed on a Painting. Hsü Wei. CoBLCP, tr. by Jonathan Chaves

Thunder roars past creeks and mountains. Picking Tea: A Ballad. Kao Ch'i. SuSp, tr. by Irving Y. Lo

Thunder Storm. Mary F. Johnson. CenSon

Thunder Storm. George Keithley. PasH

Thunder-Storm, A. Emily Dickinson. APN-2; HAP; NAAL-2v1; NCAP; WeW-3

Thunder storm passing. Foster Jewell. HA

Thunder, The: Perfect Mind. Nag Hammadi Library. "Look upon me." HW "Sent from the Power." WPoS

Thunder / Voices of drowned. Tan Taigi. ZenPo, tr. by Takashi Ikemoto and Lucien Stryk

Thunderbolt—eyes wide, A. Mumon-Ekai. ZenPo, tr. by Takashi Ikemoto and Lucien Stryk

Thundered in her skull for evermore! (LL) In the Children's Hospital. Hugh MacDiarmid. NAEL-5v2; NAEL-6v2; PAI

Thundering drums and cannons. Sacrifice. Christopher Okigbo. PBMAP

Thundering sea, why in savage storm did you plunge. Leonidas of Tarentum. HePo Fr. Epigrams.

Thunderous vapours! / water-spout with lion's teeth. War. Patrice Kayo. PBMAP

Thunders over you all. (LL) Potpourri from a Surrey Garden. Sir John Betjeman. NOBL; NPeEn

Thunderstorm. Pavel Davydovich Kogan. TCRP, tr. by Daniel Weissbort

Thunderstorm. Sam Mitchell. NOBAu, tr. by George von Brandenstein

Thunderstorm, A. Archibald Lampman. NOBC

Thunderstorm breaks up, The. Prince Shiki. SoOfWa, tr. by Sam Hamill

Thunderstorm in South Dakota. Kay Boyle. WPE

Thunderstorm in Town, A. Thomas Hardy. BoLoP; EnLoPo; OxBSP

Thung joo Kwa yaa na povi sah. Gia's Song. Nora Naranjo-Morse. ReEnLa

Thurn, A. John Berryman. NOBA

Thursday. Víctor Hernández Cruz. PueRic

Thursday. Miklós Radnóti. IQMS, tr. by John Wain

Thursday. William Carlos Williams. APT-1

Thursday Before New Yeares Day (Being on the Satterdy) the Maide, by Councell of On, She Trustid Well, Excussid Herself on This Wise to Milord, The. Marie Collyn. EMWP

Thus Achelous ends; his audience hear. Ovid. NOSC, tr. by John Dryden Fr. Metamorphoses.

Thus all men's pleas the Judge with ease. Michael Wigglesworth. NAAL-3 Fr. Day of Doom, The.

Thus all that day, they spent in divers talke. Sir John Harington [or Harrington]. PBRV Fr. Ariosto's Orlando Furioso Book 34.

Thus all the year I mourn. (LL) I Walked [or Walkt] the Other Day to Spend My Hour. Henry Vaughan. BASC; ESCV; FSCP; GeHe; NAEL-6v1

Thus am I mine own prison. Everything. Christina Georgina Rossetti. PEW Fr. Thread of Life, The.

Thus at the panting Dove a Falcon flies. Homer. OBVE, tr. by Alexander Pope Fr. Iliad, The.

Thus been they parted, Arthur on his way. Edmund Spenser. OBNV Fr. Faerie Queene, The.

Thus began / Outrage from lifeless things; but Discord first. John Milton. NAEL-5v1; NAEL-6v1; NAWM-7v1 Fr. Paradise Lost.

Thus Bonny-Boots the Birthday Celebrated. *Unknown.* NPeEn

Thus briefly sketched [or sketch'd] the sacred rights of man. On Mr. Paine's Rights of Man. Philip Freneau. NAAL-2v1; NAAL-3; NAAL-5

Thus by himself compelled to live each day. George Crabbe. NOBE Fr. Borough, The.

Thus, by turns, the leaders suffered the wounds of war. Lucan. RomPo, tr. by Jane Wilson Joyce Fr. Civil War.

Thus charg'd he; nor Argicides denied. Homer. OBVE Fr. Odyssey.

Thus Crosslegged on Round Pillow Sat in Space. Allen Ginsberg. NNaP

Thus departed Hiawatha. (LL) Hiawatha's Photographing. Lewis Carroll. NOBL; PeLV

Thus did a nameless and immortal hand. On a Bas-relief of Pelops and Hippodameia. Mary Elizabeth Coleridge. ViWPN

Thus did this ancient poet look. (LL) Robert Greene. CTC; NoSic; SCGP Fr. Greene's Vision.

Thus dullness, the safe opiate of the mind. On Dullness. Pope. OxBSP

Thus ebbs and flows the current of her sorrow. William Shakespeare. NoSic Fr. Rape of Lucrece, The.

Thus / Egyptians roam about, as roam hippo-. December 31. Ahmed Taha. NAfrP, tr. by Clarissa C. Burt

Thus every dream secretly and small inscribes its letters. Dreams Are Also Wounds. Breyten Breytenbach. VCWP, tr. by André Brink

Thus every one before the Throne. Michael Wigglesworth. TCAPo Fr. Day of Doom, The.

Thus far I did come laden with my sin. John Bunyan. SacPr Fr. Pilgrim's Progress, The.

Thus far, O Friend! have we, though leaving much. William Wordsworth. FHYEP; NAEL-6v2 Fr. Prelude, The; Growth of a Poet's Mind [1850 vers.].

Thus far was right, the rest belongs to Heav'n. (LL) Pope. FHYEP; NAEL-6v1; NAEL-7v1; OxAEP-1; PoE; TFi

Thus far, with rough and all-unable pen. William Shakespeare. CTC Fr. King Henry V.

Thus fareth many and many an one (LL) Complaint of the Fair Armoress [or Armouress], The. François Villon. AWP; CTC; OBVE, tr. by Algernon Charles Swinburne

Thus fell the King, who yet surviv'd the state. Virgil [or Vergil]. OBVE, tr. by Sir John Denham Fr. Aeneid [or Eneados, Aeneis], The.

Thus feverish fancies floated in my brain. *Unknown.* CAGL Fr. Don Leon.

Thus Freud deposed about our infant state. In the Beginning. Howard Nemerov. BodElec

Thus glory hath her being! thus she stands. Glory and Enduring Fame. William Gilmore Simms. Son

Thus God the Heav'n created, thus the Earth. John Milton. PeECV Fr. Paradise Lost.

Thus hath his death raised up this soul of mine. (LL) Fulke Greville, 1st Baron Brooke. CABP; NOSC; NoSic Fr. Caelica.

Thus have I rolled my life throughout. Muso Soseki. JDP, tr. by Yoel Hoffmann

Thus having been, that thou shouldst cease to be. (LL) To Wordsworth. Shelley. CenSon; FHYEP; NAEL-5v2; NAEL-6v2; NPeEn; NoP-4; Son

Thus he addressed the cornfield. Before a Cornfield. Gottfried Benn. WoPoe, tr. by Harvey Shapiro

Thus he doth find of all mankind. Michael Wigglesworth. NAAL-3 Fr. Day of Doom, The.

Thus . . . / He now begins his wakefulness. State of Butterfly. Ahmed Taha. NAfrP, tr. by Clarissa C. Burt

Thus I awoke, as God's my witness, when I lived in Cornhill. William Langland. NAEL-6v1; NAEL-7v1 Fr. Vision of Piers Plowman, The.

Thus I awoke, God knows, when I lived in Cornhill. William Langland. WoPoe, tr. by George Economou Fr. Vision of Piers Plowman, The.

Thus I come to you. Author Unknown. William Montgomerie. OxBS

Thus I complain my grevous hevynesse. *Unknown.* MiEL

Thus I have written this poem on a jet seat in mid Heaven. (LL) Kral Majales. Allen Ginsberg. PFTM-2; PoM

Thus I resolve, and time hath taught me so. Thus I Resolve. Thomas Campion. OxBSP

Thus I stand like the Turk, with his doxies around. John Gay. PeLV Fr. Begger's Opera.

Thus in alternate uproar and sad peace. John Keats. FHYEP Fr. Hyperion.

Thus is his cheek the map of days outworn. William Shakespeare. SCGP Fr. Sonnets.

Thus laykes this lorde by lynde-wodes eves. *Unknown.* EBEV Fr. Sir Gawain and the Green Knight.

Thus man by his own strength to Heaven would soar. Dryden. NOCV Fr. Religio Laici.

Thus mayest thou ever, evermore rejoice. (LL) Dejection: An Ode. Samuel Taylor Coleridge. FHYEP; HeIP-4; NAEL-5v2; NAEL-6v2; NAWM-7v2; NOBE; NOBRP; NoP-4; OxAEP-2; PoE; PoPoPo; TFi; TOF

Thus more and more the kingdoms are extended. First Stone of the New Castle, The. *Unknown.* PeSAV, tr. by H. C. V. Leibbrandt

Thus much he prayed, and thence away he went. Ludovico Ariosto. NoSic Fr. Orlando Furioso.

Thus Neptune rous'd these men. Homer. FaBoWar, tr. by George Chapman Fr. Iliad, The.

Thus now I leave my love in fortunes {handes / bandes}. Sir Walter Ralegh. PBRV Fr. Fortune hath taken the away my love.

Thus o'er his art indignant Rubens reared. Rubens. Washington Allston. APN-1

Thus / people, huddled in a trench. Ballad about Friendship, A. Semyon [or Semion] Petrovich Gudzenko. TCRP, tr. by Gordon McVay

Thus reader, by our astrologick art. Almanac Verse. *Unknown.* SCAP

Thus said The Lord in the Vault above the Cherubim. Last Chantey, The. Rudyard Kipling. FaBoCh; MoBrPo

Thus said the rushing raven. Croon on Hennacliff, A. Robert Stephen Hawker. NOBVV

Thus saith the great god Thoth. *Unknown.* AWP Fr. Book of the Dead.

Thus saith the Ruler of the Skies. Passion and Exaltation of Christ, The. Isaac Watts. NOCV

Thus saying, from her husband's hand her hand. John Milton. *See* To whom thus also th' Angel last repli'd

Thus saying, from her side the fatal Key. John Milton. EBEV *Fr.* Paradise Lost.

Thus saying rose / The monarch, and prevented all reply. John Milton. NOSC *Fr.* Paradise Lost.

Thus set them *ope*. (LL) I Am the Door [*or* Doore]. Richard Crashaw. GeHe; NAEL-5v1; NAEL-6v1; NAEL-7v1

Thus shall I use me. (LL) Pastime. Henry VIII, King of England. CTC; EBEV; NoSic

Thus shall they lie, and wail, and cry. Michael Wigglesworth. NAAL-3 *Fr.* Day of Doom, The.

Thus she had lain. Africa. Maya Angelou. NIL-7; NIP-4

Thus should have been our travels. Over 2000 Illustrations and a Complete Concordance. Elizabeth Bishop. APT-2; HCAP; HarvBoo; LCAP-2; NAAL-2v2; NoAM; PoetW; VCAP

Thus spake an old Chinese mandarin. Limerick. *Unknown.* PeLi

Thus Spake the Saviour. Jeremy Belknap. AH

Thus spoke the lady underneath the tree. Colonel Fantock. Dame Edith Sitwell. MoBrPo; OBMV

Thus spring begins: old. Issa. SoOfWa, *tr. by* Sam Hamill

Thus talking hand in hand alone they pass'd. John Milton. EBEV *Fr.* Paradise Lost.

Thus the Mayne Glideth. Robert Browning. OBEV *Fr.* Paracelsus.

THUS THE RIDE OF SIN. (LL) Stephen Crane. APN-2; NAAL-2v2; NoP-4; TAP *Fr.* Black Riders [and Other Lines], The.

Thus the tale ended. (LL) Skeleton in Armor [*or* Armour], The. Henry Wadsworth Longfellow. APN-1; AWP; TreFP

Thus, therefore, he who feels the fiery dart. Lucretius. EroLit, *tr. by* John Dryden *Fr.* De Rerum Natura (On the Nature of Things).

Thus they in Heav'n, above the starry Sphear. John Milton. EBEV *Fr.* Paradise Lost.

Thus think, then drink Tobacco. (LL) Religious Use of [Taking] Tobacco, A. Robert Wisdome. OBCoV; SCGP

Thus to Glaucus spake / Divine Sarpedon, since he did not find. Homer. NPeEn; OBVE, *tr. by* Sir John Denham *Fr.* Iliad, The.

Thus was my love, thus was my Ganymed. Richard Barnfield [*or* Barnefield]. CAGL *Fr.* Cynthia, with Certain[e] Sonnets.

Thus was this place, / A happy rural seat of various view. John Milton. PeECV *Fr.* Paradise Lost.

Thus with imagin'd wing our swift scene flies. William Shakespeare. EBEV; OxAEP-1 *Fr.* King Henry V.

Thus with myself: how fares it, Friends, with you? (LL) Christina Georgina Rossetti. NAEL-5v2; NAEL-6v2 *Fr.* Later Life: A Double Sonnet of Sonnets.

Thus you will I praise now, o transiency, you who earth's time hold in mastery. Praise of Transitoriness. Hans Leifhelm. AuPH, *tr. by* Lowell A. Bangerter

Thwack of an ax, The. Buson. SoOfWa, *tr. by* Sam Hamill

Thwarted. Priscilla Jane Thompson. CBWP-2

Thwarted. Tu Fu. CarOv, *tr. by* Carolyn Kizer

Thwarted, old friend! Here we are, baulked again! Thwarted. Tu Fu. CarOv, *tr. by* Carolyn Kizer

Thweet Poethy! let me lithp forthwith. Smitten Purist, The. James Whitcomb Riley. VerBaPo

Thy after shock, Manassas, share. (LL) March into Virginia, The. Herman Melville. HAP; NAAL-2v1; NCAP; PoE; TAP

Thy arms with bracelets I will deck. Homage. Gustave Kahn. TrJP, *tr. by* Jethro Bithell

Thy ax shall harm it not. (LL) Woodman, Spare That Tree. George Pope Morris. BRP; PWR; TCAPo

Thy azure robe, I did behold. Julia's Petticoat. Robert Herrick. BeJo; CaPo

Thy banks, O Barrow, sure must be. Written by the Barrow Side, Where She Was Sent to Wash Linen. Ellen Taylor. ECWP

Thy beauty haunts me heart and soul. Moon, The. William Henry Davies. MoBrPo

Thy Best. Henry Cole. PWR; PoToHe

Thy best its best, Please God, thy best is best. (LL) Cardinal Newman. Christina Georgina Rossetti. NAEL-5v2; NAEL-6v2

Thy Better Self. Jones Very. TCAPo

Thy blessing on the boys—for time has come. Prayer. Haim [*or* Chaim *or* Khayim] Guri [*or* Gouri]. TrJP, *tr. by* Ruth H. Lask

Thy bosom is endeared with all hearts. William Shakespeare. NOBE; OBEV *Fr.* Sonnets.

Thy braes were bonny, Yarrow stream. Braes of Yarrow, The. John Logan. GTBS-P; SCGP

"Thy breath is far sweeter than honey." Far Sweeter than Honey. Abraham Ibn Ezra. TrJP, *tr. by* Israel Abrahams

Thy Brother's Blood. Jones Very. APN-1; NOBA; TAP

Thy cheek is pale with thought, but not from woe. Sonnet, to the Same. Byron. OxBSo

Thy Church has long been becoming the Fossil of a Faith. James Thomson. SacPr *Fr.* Doom of a City, The.

Thy country, Wilberforce, with just disdain. To William Wilberforce, Esq. William Cowper. Son

Thy curate's place, thy fruitful wife. Jonathan Swift. UV *Fr.* Parson's Case, The.

Thy dawn, O Ra, opens the new horizon. *Unknown.* AWP *Fr.* Book of the Dead.

Thy eyes and eyebrows I could spare. *Unknown.* FaBoEE

Thy fabulous provinces belong. (LL) Philomela. John Crowe Ransom. APT-1; FuPo; NAAL-2v2; NOBA; NoAM; OBAL; OBSV; OxBA

Thy Faithful Sons. Eleazar. TrJP

Thy fingers make early flowers of. E. E. Cummings. MoAmPo; NAAL-2v2

Thy flattering picture, Phryne, is like thee. Phryne. John Donne. FaBoEE

Thy flesh to earth, thy soul to God. General B. F. Butler. Ambrose Bierce. CBCWP

Thy flow'r afloat, goolden zummer clote! (LL) Clote (Water-Lily), The. William Barnes. FaBoVe; NPeEn

Thy foes had girt thee with their dread array. Last Banquet of Antony and Cleopatra, The. Felicia Dorothea Hemans. RWP

Thy forests, Windsor! and thy green retreats. Pope. NOEC; OxAEP-1 *Fr.* Windsor-Forest [*or* Windsor Forest].

Thy friend, whom thy deserts to thee enchain[e]. To Mr. C.B. John Donne. ESCV

Thy Garden. Don Allen Johnson. AWP, *tr. by* Dulcie L. Smith

Thy garden, orchard, fields. Francis Daniel Pastorius. SCAP

Thy Genius, Colebrooke, faithless to his charge. To Colebrooke Dale. Anna Seward. ECWP

Thy gentle charms a tenfold power to please. (LL) To Oxford. Thomas Russell. CenSon; Son

Thy glass will show thee how thy beauties wear. William Shakespeare. HeIP-4 *Fr.* Sonnets.

Thy Glory then I'le make my fruits and Crop. (LL) Edward Taylor. NOSC; SCAP *Fr.* Preparatory Meditations Before My Approach to the Lord's Supper.

Thy God, thy life, thy Cure. (LL) Peace. Henry Vaughan. AWP; EBEV; ESCV; FSCP; FaBoCh; GeHe; HAP; NOBE; NOCV; OBEV; OxAEP-1; OxBEV; PoE; SCGP; TFi; TOF; TrCP; WeW-3

Thy going smileth in me over. Encounter. August Stramm. PFTM-1

Thy gown? Why, ay. Come, tailor, let us see't. William Shakespeare. OBCoV *Fr.* Taming of the Shrew, The.

Thy grace, dear Lord's my golden wrack I find. Edward Taylor. SCAP *Fr.* Preparatory Meditations Before My Approach to the Lord's Supper.

Thy Heart. *Unknown.* OBCoV

Thy heart is in the upper world, where fleet the chamois bounds. Chamois Hunter's Love, The. Felicia Dorothea Hemans. RWP; VWP

Thy hue, dear pledge, is pure and bright. To a Lock of Hair. Sir Walter Scott. GTBS-P

Thy human frame, my glorious Lord, I spy. Edward Taylor. ChIV-1 *Fr.* Preparatory Meditations Before My Approach to the Lord's Supper.

Thy husband to a banquet goes with me. Ovid. NoSic *Fr.* Elegies.

Thy image, wavering, agonizing. Osip Emilevich Mandelstam [*or* Mandelshtam]. TCRP

Thy joys that I might see! (LL) Hierusalem. *Unknown.* NOBE; PeECV; SCGP; SacPr; TOF

Thy life be[e] written, and not read. (LL) Elegy upon the Death of His Own Father, An. Richard Corbet [*or* Corbett]. BeJo; NOSC

Thy life has touched the edges of my life. My Spirit's Complement. Henrietta Cordelia Ray. CBWP-3

Thy life hath touched the edges of my life. Henrietta Cordelia Ray. *See* Thy life has touched the edges of my life

Thy love thou sentest oft to me. Contrast, A. James Russell Lowell. NCAP

Thy lovely saints do bring Thee love. Christina Georgina Rossetti. SacPr *Fr.* Christ Our All in All.

Thy Loving Kindness, Lord, I Sing. George Barrell Cheever. AH

Thy mansion is the Christian's heart. William Cowper. ChIV-2 *Fr.* Olney Hymns.

Thy Mercies, Lord, to Heaven Reach. William Kethe. AH

Thy mercy, Lord, Lord now thy mercy show. Bible, *O.T.* EMWP; PEW, *tr. by* Mary Sidney Herbert, Countess of Pembroke *Fr.* Psalms.

Thy mercy on Thy People, Lord! (LL) Recessional. Rudyard Kipling. AWP; BRP; CABP; InvLi; MoBrPo; NAEL-6v2; NOBE; NOBVV; NPeEn; NoAM; NoP-4; OBEV; OxAEP-2; OxBEV; PWR; SCGP; TFi; UV; UnPo

Thy mind which voluntary doubts molest. Lines Contributed to Hawkesworth's "The Rival." Samuel Johnson. NPeEn

Thy Mother Was like a Vine. Bible, *O.T.* TrJP *Fr.* Ezekiel.

Thy nags (the leanest things alive). Epigram. Matthew Prior. FaBoEE

Thy nature, and Thy name is Love. (LL) Wrestling Jacob. Charles Wesley. NOBE; NOCV; NOEC; OBEV; OxAEP-1; PeECV; TOF

Thy nearness our forgiving cure. (LL) Broken Dark, The. Robert Earl Hayden. AWTN; GT

Thy nights moan into my days. Psalms of Love. Peter Baum. AWP, tr. by Jethro Bithell

Thy Otway's sorrows, and lament his fate! (LL) To the River Arun. Charlotte Smith. CenSon; RWP

Thy place is changed; thou art the same. (LL) Tennyson. EBVV; NAEL-6v2 Fr. In Memoriam A. H. H.

Thy Praise, O God, in Zion Waits. Jacob Kimball. AH

Thy praise, O Lord, will I proclaim. Palms and Myrtles. Eleazar ben Kalir. TrJP, tr. by Alice Lucas

Thy praise or dispraise is to me alike. To Fool or Knave. Ben Jonson. FaBoEE; NoP-4

Thy pride upon a ring? (LL) "Michael Field." VWP; ViWPN

Thy restless feet now cannot go. Christ Crucified. Richard Crashaw. OBEV

Thy sacred dew: protect them with thine influence. (LL) To the Evening Star. William Blake. NAEL-5v2; NAEL-6v2; NOEC; NPeEn; PoE; TFi

Thy sacred law, O God. On God's Law. Francis Quarles. ChIV-1

Thy sheep with thee. (LL) And do they so? Henry Vaughan. BASC; ESCV; GeHe; MeLP; SacPr

Thy sins [or sinnes] and hairs [or haires] may no man equal[l] call. Licentious Person, A. John Donne. PeLV

Thy sleep makes ridiculous. (LL) Humble-Bee, The. Ralph Waldo Emerson. APN-1; NCAP; NOBA; OxBA

Thy sooty godhead I desire. To Vulcan. Robert Herrick. CaPo

Thy soul within such silent pomp did keep. Quiet Soul, A. John Oldham. OBEV

Thy spirit ere our fatal loss. Tennyson. CAGL Fr. In Memoriam A. H. H.

Thy stricken daughter, now, O Lord, prepares. Hymn for the Eve of the New Year. Abraham Gerondi. TrJP, tr. by Solomon Solis-Cohen

Thy summer's day was long, but couldst thou think. 1802. Mary Tighe. CenSon

Thy summer voice, Musketaquit. Two Rivers. Ralph Waldo Emerson. APN-1; NCAP; NOBA; OxBA; PoE

Thy sword within the scabbard keep. Dryden. OxBSP Fr. Secular Masque, The.

Thy tablet glimmers to the dawn. (LL) Tennyson. NAEL-6v2; PeECV; SCGP Fr. In Memoriam A. H. H.

Thy thoughts, dear Keats, are like fresh-gathered leaves. To Keats: On Reading His Sonnet Written in Chaucer. John Hamilton Reynolds. Son

Thy throne, to Thee the rent in happiness. (LL) Edward Taylor. NAAL-2v1; NAAL-3; NAAL-5 Fr. Preparatory Meditations Before My Approach to the Lord's Supper.

Thy trivial harp will never please. Ralph Waldo Emerson. NCAP; OxBA Fr. Merlin.

Thy various works, imperial queen, we see. On Imagination. Phillis Wheatley. BlSi; NAAAL; OxWW; RWP

Thy victory is in the heart. Victoria. Henry Van Dyke. SacPr

Thy voice is on the rolling air. Tennyson. EBVV; FHYEP; HeIP-4; NAEL-6v2 Fr. In Memoriam A. H. H.

Thy Way, Not Mine. Horatius Bonar. SacPr

Thy weary feet have pressed once more thy native soil. Welcome Home. Josephine D. Henderson Heard. CBWP-4

Thy woes and weep / No more. (LL) Comfort to a Youth That Had Lost His Love. Robert Herrick. NOBE; OBEV

Thy words are compounded of sweet-smelling myrrh. Words Wherein Stinging Bees Lurk. Judah Halevi. TrJP, tr. by Nina Davis Salaman

Thy worn out heart will break at last, / My Mary! (LL) To Mary. William Cowper. EnLoPo; NOEC; UV

Thy Wrath, slay Sin, and in thy Love mee bench. (LL) Edward Taylor. OxBA; SacPr Fr. Preparatory Meditations Before My Approach to the Lord's Supper.

Thyestes. Seneca.
  "Climb at court for me that will." OBVE, tr. by Andrew Marvell
  "Let him that will, ascend the tottering seat." OBVE, tr. by Sir Matthew Hale
  "Let who so lyst with mighty mace to raygne." OBVE, tr. by Jasper Heywood
  "O yee, whome lorde of lande and waters wyde." OBVE, tr. by Jasper Heywood
  "Stand [or Stond] who so list upon the slipper top[pe]." NPeEn; NoSic; OBVE; OxBEV, tr. by Sir Thomas Wyatt
  "Upon the slippery tops of human[e] state." BASC; OBVE, tr. by Abraham Cowley

Thyme Flowering among Rocks. Richard Wilbur. LCAP-2

Thyrsis. Matthew Arnold. FHYEP; NAEL-5v2; NAEL-6v2; NOBE; OBEV

Thyrsis. Edward Cracroft Lefroy. AWP Fr. Echoes from Theocritus.

Thyrsis, a youth of the inspired train. Story of Phoebus and Daphne Applied, [etc.], The. Edmund Waller. NAEL-5v1; NOSC

Thyrsis, sleep'st thou? Holla! Let not sorrow stay us. Thyrsis, Sleep'st Thou? Unknown. NoSic; OxBSP

Thys Endris Nyght. Unknown. EBEV; NOCV

Thyself remov'd, thy power to sooth me left. (LL) William Cowper. NOEC; OxAEP-1

Ti. Melvin B. Tolson. APT-2 Fr. Libretto for the Republic of Liberia.

Ti-ch'ü Song Words. Unknown. CoBCP, tr. by Burton Watson

Tía Olivia Serves Wallace Stevens a Cuban Egg. Richard Blanco. NAPBL

Tiara. Mark Doty. MakPoe

Tiberius on Capri. Robert Penn Warren.
  "All is nothing, nothing all." NOBA
  "There once, on that goat island, I." NOBA

Tichborne's Elegy. Chidiock Tichborne [or Tichbourne]. AmFaPo; HAP; HeIP-4; NoP-4; NoSic; PoPoPo; TFi
  (Elegy: "My Prime of Youth Is But a Frost of Cares") EBEV; NOBE; SCGP; WeW-3
  (Elegy.) NIL-7
  (Elegy for Himself.) RB
  (Elegy, Written with His Own Hand in the Tower before His Execution.) InPK-6
  (My prime of youth is but a froste of cares.) PBRV
  (On the Eve of His Execution.) WoPoe
  (Written the Night before His Execution.) SCV

Ticker. Amy Fusselman. HeMarv

Ticking minutes shed their sound, The. Consolations Before an Affair, Upper West Side. Noelle Kocot. BAP-01

Tickle Rhyme, The. Ian Serraillier. NTCP; Spl

Tickled, / my thoughts wander. Celebration for My Mother. Wendy Rose. CDW

Tickling me with his whiskers. (LL) Mr. McGregor's Garden. Medbh McGuckian. CIP-2; PNI

Tickly, tickly, on your knee. Unknown. OxNR

Ticonderoga: A Legend of the West Highlands. Robert Louis Stevenson. EBNV; OBNV

Tidal River, The. Edith Jay Scovell. HarvBoo Fr. Water Images.

Tiddle liddle lightum. Unknown. OxNR

Tide be runnin' the great world over. Sea Love. Charlotte Mew. LW; MoBrPo; OxAEP-2; OxBEV; OxBTC

Tide gone out for good, The. Death of Irish, The. Aidan Carl Mathews. PBCIP

Tide in the River, The. Eleanor Farjeon. NOxBChV

Tide Line Garden. W. S. Merwin. BodElec

Tide of Battle Turns, The. Homer. NAWM-7v1, tr. by Robert Fagles Fr. Iliad, The.

Tide-Reach. Roland Mathias.
  Laus Deo. AngWePo
  "Water is hard in the well, The." AngWePo

Tide Rises, the Tide Falls, The. Henry Wadsworth Longfellow. APN-1; ITBLP; NOBA; OxBA; PAI; PoE; PoPoPo; PoRA; TAP

Tide Turning. John Frederick Nims. DiPo; IllVoic

Tidepool, A. Cor Van den Heuvel. HA

Tides. Helen Hunt Jackson. LW

Tides, The. Paul Blackburn. PoM

Tides, The. William Cullen Bryant. TAP

Tides, The. Michael Klein. WiU

Tides Run up the Wairau, The. Eileen Duggan. PeNZ

Tides shape the sides of the agate mountain. On Visiting My Son, Port Angeles, Washington. Duane Niatum. CDW

Tidewash. . . Memories. Lament of the Flutes. Christopher Okigbo. PBA

Tidings I bring you, for to tell. Unknown. MiEL

Tidings. Czeslaw Milosz. BodElec, tr. by Lillian Vallee

Tie. Greg Delanty. BiHa

Tie, The. William Heyen. GM

Tie a bandage over his eyes. Rebel, A. John Gould Fletcher. MoAmPo

Tie one end of a rope fast over a beam. Receipt to Cure a Love Fit, A. Unknown. NOEC

Tie the Strings to my Life, My Lord. Emily Dickinson. PoE; SacPr; TrCP

Tie your own noose if you want to be. Advice of an Efficiency Expert, The. Augustus Young. CIP-2

Tier upon tier of storied buildings, decorated pavilions. Kuan Yün-shih. SuSp, tr. by Richard John Lynn Fr. Medley of Southern and Northern Tunes—Scenic Tour of West Lake.

Ties. Raymond Souster. MoCV

Tig. Unknown. FaBoVe

Tiger. Alec Derwent Hope. OxBC; RB

Tiger. Claude McKay. BPo

Tiger, The. Joseph Hilaire Pierre Belloc. MoBrPo

Tiger, The. Marie Laurencin. CuPo

Tiger, The. Peter Niblett. OTCP

Tiger behind the bars of his cage growls, The. Tiger, The. Peter Niblett. OTCP

Tiger Christ unsheathed his sword. For the One Who Would Take Man's Life in His Hands. Delmore Schwartz. MoAmPo; VGW

Tiger comes to mind, A. The twilight here. Other Tiger, The. Jorge Luis Borges. TCLAP, *tr. by* Norman Thomas Di Giovanni

Tiger in the tiger-pit, The. Lines for an Old Man. T. S. Eliot. FaBoTw; RB; RaBo

Tiger in the Zoo, A. Leslie Norris. OTCP

Tiger Lady. Miguel Algarin. PueRic

Tiger Lady. Yusef Komunyakaa. CDa

Tiger-Lilies. "Michael Field." ViWPN

Tiger Lily. Alfred Kreymborg. APT-1

Tiger, on the other hand, is kittenish and mild, The. Tiger, The. Joseph Hilaire Pierre Belloc. MoBrPo

Tiger's Absence. Cristina Campo.

   "Ah that the Tiger." CItWP, *tr. by* Cinzia Sartini Blum and Lara Trubowitz

   Canon 4. CItWP, *tr. by* Cinzia Sartini Blum and Lara Trubowitz

   "Terrible One, knowing their hearts, The." CItWP, *tr. by* Cinzia Sartini Blum and Lara Trubowitz

Tiger shouted, "You don't mean peace, but war!," The. (LL) Legend of Versailles, A. Melvin B. Tolson. BPo; NAAAL

"Tiger, strolling at my side." Triumph of Sensibility. Sylvia Townsend Warner. MoBrPo

Tiger Tale, A. John Bennett. OBCA

Tiger Valley. Muso Soseki. EaWin, *tr. by* W. S. Merwin

Tigers of Nanzen-ji, The. Brad Leithauser. DiPo

Tight Corners. David Bromige.

   "He thought it humanity's lot for ever to be persuading a huge rock up a mountainside." FTOS

Tight scrimmage of blankets in the dark. Ward Two. Francis Webb. CBAP

Tighten. Hadewijch II. WPoS

Tightly coiled, like a snake it sits. Love. Anna Andreyevna Akhmatova. TCRP, *tr. by* Daniel Weissbort

Tightness and the nilness round that space, The. From the Frontier of Writing. Seamus Heaney. CABP; ModIr; PoPoPo; PoetW

Tihei Mauriora I called. Sad Joke on a Marae. Apirana Taylor. PeNZ

Til Death Do Us Part. Kalamu ya Salaam. SpirFl *Fr.* New Orleans Haiku.

Tilden Park. Alison Deming. UrbNat

Tile is loose for splendid feet, A. Stepping Out. Michael Brownstein. FTOS

Tiles. Witter Bynner. APT-1; TCAPo

Till a moment ago we were "Mister" and "Miss." My Darling, My Darling. Frank Loesser. ReLy

Till all my widowed race be run. (LL) Tennyson. EBVV; PeECV *Fr.* In Memoriam A. H. H.

Till all their sweets are gone, and all again refuse them. (LL) Woman's Constancy. Sir John Suckling. CaPo; CavPo

Till all was tranquil as a summer sea. (LL) William Wordsworth. AWP; OxBEV *Fr.* Prelude, The; Growth of a Poet's Mind [1850 vers.].

Till both our heads were in his aureole. (LL) Dante Gabriel Rossetti. NAEL-5v2; NAEL-6v2; OxBSo *Fr.* House of Life, The.

Till bright as blood the peachstone showed. (LL) Peachstone. Dannie Abse. AngWePo; OxBC; WeW-3

'Till cheerless on their path the night descends. (LL) Languid, and sad, and slow. William Lisle Bowles. CenSon; NAEL-6v2

Till cherry-ripe themselves do[e] cry. (LL) Cherry-Ripe. Thomas Campion. BASC; HeIP-4; InPK-6; NAEL-5v1; NAEL-6v1; NAEL-7v1; NOSC; NPeEn; PAI; PBRV; PoE; SCGP; TFi

Till Christ again turn wanderer and child. (LL) Christmas Eve under Hooker's Statue. Robert Lowell. CoAmPo; OxBA

Till Christ ("Till Christ, quhome I am haldin for to lufe"). Unknown. OxBS *Fr.* Gude and Godlie Ballatis, The.

Till Death Do Us Part. Leila Miccolis. BoWoP, *tr. by* Willis Barnstone and Nelson Cerqueira

Till dreadful[l] death do [c]ease my doleful[l] state? (LL) Sir Thomas Wyatt. NoSic; OBVE; OxBEV; PBRV

Till earth restores her sons to heaven again. (LL) I Was Sick and in Prison. Jones Very. ColAP; NOBA; SacPr

Till eight days like any happy fly. Course of a Life, The. Yehuda Amichai [*or* Amikhai]. BBASP, *tr. by* Chana Bloch

Till Eulenspiegel. "Eduard Georgievich Bagritzky" [*or* Bagritsky]. TCRP, *tr. by* Vera Dunham

Till ev'n his beams sing, and my music[k] shine. (LL) Christmas. George Herbert. ChrPo; GeHe; NOSC; PeECV; TOF; TrCP

Till Evening. Jakov [*or* Jacob] Steinberg. FIT, *tr. by* Robert Friend

Till God calls you away. (LL) Unquiet Grave, The. *Unknown.* CABP; ESPB; HAP; HeIP-4; NoP-4; OxBB; RB; TFi; WeW-3; WoPoe

Till human voices wake us, and we drown. (LL) T. S. Eliot. APT-1; AWP; AmFaPo; ClHu; ColAP; EBEV; HAP; HarvBoo; HeIP-4; InPK-6; MakPoe; MoAmPo; NAAL-2v1; NAAL-5; NAEL-5v2; NAEL-6v2; NAWM-7v2; NIL-7; NOBA; NOBE; NPeEn; NoAM; NoP-4; OxAEP-2; OxBEV; OxBTC; PoE; PoPoPo; PoRA; SoSe-8; TAP; TCAPo; TFi; TRP; TwCP; WeW-3; WoPoe

Till I reach heaven [*or* heav'n] and, much more, thee. (LL) Affliction (4). George Herbert. ESCV; GeHe; NOSC

Till I shall come again, let this suffice. Panegyric to Sir Lewis Pemberton, A. Robert Herrick. CaPo

Till I think the Milky Way has tumbled from the ninth height of /Heaven Heaven. (LL) Viewing the Waterfall at Mount Lu. Li Po. CoBCP; ColAnChi; TTTS, *tr. by* Burton Watson

'Till in the rising tide the exhausted sufferer dies. (LL) Written on the Sea Shore.—October, 1784. Charlotte Smith. CenSon; RWP

Till in thy perfect love I ever live & move. (LL) In Him We Live [& Move & Have Our Being]. Jones Very. APN-1; OxBA

Till it could come no more. (LL) At the Seaside [*or* Sea-Side]. Robert Louis Stevenson. NTCP; TLR; WHSW

Till life divine re-animates his dust. (LL) On the Death of the Rev. Mr. George Whitefield, 1770. Phillis Wheatley. NAAL-2v1; NAAL-3; NAAL-5

Till life's last hour, with Phaon's self decays! (LL) Describes Phaon. Mary Robinson. CenSon; RWP

Till Love and Fame to nothingness do sink. (LL) When I Have Fears [That I May Cease to Be]. John Keats. AWP; CABP; CenSon; EBEV; GSo; HAP; HeIP-4; NAEL-5v2; NAEL-6v2; NIL-7; NIP-4; NoP-4; OBEV; PoE; PoPoPo; PoRA; SCGP; Son; TFi; UnPo; WoPoe

Till my bad angel fire my good one out. (LL) William Shakespeare. EBEV; HeIP-4; NAEL-5v1; NAEL-6v1; NAEL-7v1; NIL-7; NIP-4; OxBSo; Son *Fr.* Sonnets.

Till my feet, cloven too, take hold on hell? (LL) World, The. Christina Georgina Rossetti. BoWoP; NALW; PEW; ViWPN

Till my gestures enlarged, wide over the darkening land. (LL) Feeding Ducks. Norman MacCaig. HarvBoo; OxBS

Till now. Ryoto. JDP, *tr. by* Yoel Hoffmann

Till now the doubtful dusk reveal'd. Tennyson. GTBS-P *Fr.* In Memoriam A. H. H.

Till now your indiscretion sets us free. Emilia [*or* Aemelia] Lanier [*or* Lanyer]. BoWoP *Fr.* Salve Deus Rex Judaeorum.

Till souls and bodies both may meet. (LL) To My Mistress[e] in My Absence. Thomas Carew. CaPo; NOSC

Till that her blush taught me my shame to see. (LL) Sir Philip Sidney. NAEL-5v1; NAEL-6v1; NAEL-7v1; NoSic *Fr.* Astrophil and Stella.

Till that we meet again. (LL) To His Lady. Henry VIII, King of England. CTC; EBEV; NoSic

Till the Clouds Roll By. P. G. Wodehouse. ReLy

Till the day-spring breaks forth again from high. (LL) Bird, The. Henry Vaughan. ESCV; GeHe; OBEV; PoE

Till the good morning star. *Unknown.* GrAn

Till the gossamer thread you fling catch somewhere, O my soul. (LL) Walt Whitman. APN-1; AWP; HAP; HeIP-4; ITBLP; InPK-6; MoAmPo; NAAL-2v1; NAAL-3; NAAL-5; NCAP; NIL-7; NOBA; OxBA; OxBSP; PAI; PoE; PoPoPo; SAmP; SCV; TAP; TCAPo; TFi; WoPoe

Till the lamp flickers, and the memory fails. (LL) Holy Tide, The. Frederick Tennyson. OBEV; SacPr

Till the rough-gem moon. Lady Otomo no Sakanoé. ArkPo, *tr. by* Edwin A. Cranston

Till the slow daylight pale. Sun-Flower, The. Dora Greenwell. EroLit; VWP; WPE

Till the white winged Reapers come! (LL) Seed Growing Secretly, The. Henry Vaughan. ChIV-2; ESCV; GeHe

Till There Was You. Meredith Willson. ReLy

Till they are incandescent. (LL) Her Lips Are Copper Wire. Jean Toomer. APT-2; GT; NoAM

Till thy wished smile thy mother's pangs o'erpay. (LL) To a Little Invisible Being Who Is Expected Soon to Become Visible. Anna Laetitia Barbauld. ECWP; NAEL-6v2; WoRP

Till to the leech thy water I have shown. (LL) To Dante Alighieri: He Interprets Dante Alighieri's Dream. Dante da Maiano. AWP; EaItPo, *tr. by* Dante Gabriel Rossetti

Till twelve years' [*or* yeres'] age, how Christ His childhood spent. Christ[e]'s Childhood[e]. Robert Southwell. ChIV-2

Till up in the morning the sun shall arise. (LL) Moon, The. Robert Louis Stevenson. PWR; TLR

Till we[e] shall meet and never part. (LL) Henry King, Bishop of Chichester. HAP; MeLP; NAEL-6v1; SCGP

Tiller of the Soil. Avraham Shlonsky. MHP, *tr. by* Ruth Finer Mintz

Tillers of the earth have few idle months;. Watching the Reapers. Po Chü-i. ChiP, *tr. by* Arthur Waley

Tilling the field. Buson. EH, *tr.* by Robert Hass

Tilly. James Joyce. RB

Tilt, The. Kim Roberts. AmPoNex *Fr.* Constellation Frigidaire, The.

Tilth. Robert Graves. FaBoEE; OBSV

Tim Finnegan [*or* Finnigin *or* Finigan] liv'd in Walkin [*or* lived in Walker] Street. Finnegan's Wake. *Unknown.* NBLV

Tim tryeth truth convicting all that strive. T. Street. SCAP

Timber, The. Henry Vaughan. GeHe; OBEV

Time. Yehuda Amichai [*or* Amikhai].

  "Radius of the bomb was twelve inches." FaBoWar, *tr.* by Benjamin Harshav and Barbara Harshav

  "What is it? An airplane at dawn. No." FaBoWar, *tr.* by Benjamin Harshav

Time. Mary Ursula Bethell. FaBoWP; OBGa

Time. Bhartrihari. AWP, *tr.* by Paul Elmer More

Time. Tom Clark. BodElec

Time. Robert Creeley. BodElec

Time. Robert Creeley. LCAP-2

Time. Louise Glück. BAP-01

Time. George Herbert. NAEL-5v1; NAEL-6v1; NAEL-7v1

Time. Ralph Hodgson. GTBS-P

Time. Dulce Maria Loynaz. TANSG, *tr.* by Alan West

Time. Jasper Mayne. OBEV

Time. Adelia Prado. TANSG, *tr.* by Ellen Watson

Time. William Stafford. Son

Time after time. J. W. Hackett. HA

Time After Time. Jule Styne. ReLy

Time again subdues her. (LL) Wives in the Sere. Thomas Hardy. NOBE; NOBVV

Time Allotted, The. Ingeborg Bachmann. PFTM-2, *tr.* by Jerome Rothenberg

Time and again. Theology and a Patchwork Absolute. Heather McPherson. PeNZ

Time and again I've longed for adventure. All the Things You Are. Jerome Kern. ReLy

Time and again, time and again I tie. Edge, The. Louise Glück. HarvBoo

Time and again we're cut down to size. Martin Sorrell. NewEx

Time and Grief. William Lisle Bowles. OBEV

  ("O Time! who know'st a lenient hand to lay") GSo

Time and Love, I. William Shakespeare. *See* Sonnets

Time and Love, II. William Shakespeare. *See* Sonnets

Time and Music. Janet Lewis. FFC

Time & prayer fitting, I, the god. Perses. GrAn

Time and the Garden. Yvor Winters. APT-2; HarvBoo; MoAmPo; NoAM; VGW

Time and the mortal will stand never fast. Sonnet. Luis de Camões [*or* Camõens]. AWP, *tr.* by Richard Garnett

Time, and thy charms, thou fanciest will redeem. To a Young Lady, Purposing to Marry a Man of Immoral Character in the Hope of his Reformation. Anna Seward. CenSon

Time & time again the laughter after the footsteps. Jungle, The. Diane Di Prima. PoM

Time between us stretches out, The. Black Winter. Frank Stewart. CDa

Time brought me many another friend. Not Yet. Mary Elizabeth Coleridge. PoBW

Time Bum. Jordan Davis. HeMarv

Time came for him to be released, The. Exile. Stephen Dobyns. OPRER

Time can [*or* will] say nothing but I told you so. Villanelle. W. H. Auden. MoBrPo

Time cannot break the bird's wing from the bird. To a Young Poet. Edna St. Vincent Millay. OxBSP

Time comes when a majority of those you remember, A. Titanic, The. Witter Bynner. APT-1

Time comes when you no longer can say: my God, A. Your Shoulders Hold Up the World. Carlos Drummond de Andrade. PoetW, *tr.* by Mark Strand

Time, cruel time, come and subdue that brow. Samuel Daniel. SCGP *Fr.* To Delia.

Time does not bring relief; you all have lied. Edna St. Vincent Millay. HarvBoo; HeIP-4; LW; OxBSo

Time draws near the birth of Christ, The. Tennyson. EBVV; FHYEP; NAEL-6v2; NAWM-7v2; NOCV; SoSe-8 *Fr.* In Memoriam A. H. H.

Time draws near the birth of Christ, The. Tennyson. ChrPo; EBVV; NAEL-6v2 *Fr.* In Memoriam A. H. H.

Time drops in decay. Moods, The. W. B. Yeats. CTC

Time ends when vision sees its lapse in / liberty. Beata l'Alma. Sir Herbert Read. FaBoMo

Time flies by like a great whale. Ted Berrigan. FTOS *Fr.* Sonnets, The.

Time flies, hope flags, life plies a wearied wing. Christina Georgina Rossetti. OxBSo *Fr.* Monna Innominata.

Time flits away, time flits away, lady. Variation on Ronsard. Thomas Sturge Moore. OBMV

Time for a walk. Muso Soseki. EaWin, *tr.* by W. S. Merwin

Time for Dejection. Hamda Khamees. PoArWo, *tr.* by Joseph T. Zeidan

Time for Guns, A. Darryl Holmes. InTrad

Time for summer clothes and wine-tasting. Tune: "Six Toughies"—Written after the Roses Have Faded. Chou Pang-yen. SuSp, *tr.* by James J. Y. Liu

Time for the wood, the clay. Kept. Louise Bogan. APT-2

Time for toil has passed, and night has come, The. Bringing Our Sheaves with Us. Elizabeth Akers. TreFP

Time goes, you say? Ah, no! Paradox of Time, The. Pierre de Ronsard. AWP, *tr.* by Austin Dobson

Time has an end, they say. "H. D.". NOBA; VGW *Fr.* Good Frend.

Time has been that these wild solitudes, The. Winter Piece, A. William Cullen Bryant. APN-1; ColAP; OxBA

Time has been, when yet the muse was young, The. Byron. FHYEP *Fr.* English Bards and Scotch Reviewers.

Time has brought about great changes. Scraps of Time. Mrs. Henry Linden. CBWP-4

Time has come, the clock says time has come, The. Conrad Potter Aiken. OxBA *Fr.* Preludes for Memnon; or, Preludes to Attitude.

Time has come to devote myself to my hiker's stick, The. On Receiving My Letter of Termination. Yüan Hung-tao. CoBLCP; ColAnChi, *tr.* by Jonathan Chaves

Time has no spectacle more stern and strange. Lower New York. George Cabot Lodge. APN-2

Time has not laid. Plait of Hair, The. Alice V. Stuart. PoBW

Time has not quenched your beauty. Much of your bygone prime. Rufinus. HePo, *tr.* by Barbara Hughes Fowler

Time has pulled up a chair, dashed. Ron Mason. Hone Tuwhare. PeNZ

Time has wrinkled your face. Léon Laleau. NegPo, *tr.* by Ellen Conroy Kennedy *Fr.* Black Music.

Time Heals All Wounds—But One. Vernon Rowe. BloBone

Time heals ev'rything. Time Heals Everything. Jerry Herman. ReLy

Time heals not: it extends a sorrow's scope. Epigram. James Vincent Cunningham. VGW; WoPoe

Time, Hope, and Memory. Thomas Hood. TreFP

Time I dropped your almost body down, The. Lost Baby Poem, The. Lucille Clifton. AmFaPo; BlSi; ESEAA; ISC; WPE

Time I've Lost in Wooing, The. Thomas Moore. AmFaPo; NAEL-5v2; NAEL-6v2; NOBRP; PeLV

Time I went to church I sat, The. Mr. Rockefeller's Hat. Helen Smith Bevington. OBAL

Time in the Rock [or, Preludes to Definition]. Conrad Potter Aiken. VGW

Time is, The. Anger. Robert Creeley. PFTM-2

Time is a thing. Epilogue. Stephen Spender. MoBrPo

Time is after dinner, The. Cigarettes. Boarder, The. Louis Simpson. InPK-6

Time is at an end, The. Ox-Bow. Donald Davie. DiPo

Time is come I must depart[e], The. Aucthour Maketh Her Wyll and Testament, The. Isabella Whitney. BWW; EMWP; NoP-4

Time is divided into. Time Is the Mercy of Eternity. Kenneth Rexroth. VGW

Time is hunger, space is cold. Great Prayer. Alfonso Cortes. TCLAP, *tr.* by Thomas Merton

Time is mainly a fiction here. There are. New Guinea Time. Louis Johnson. PeNZ

Time is my debtor for my years untold. (LL) Long Time a Child. Hartley Coleridge. CenSon; NPeEn; OxBSo; Son

Time is not remote when I, The. Jonathan Swift. EBEV; NOBE; NOBL; NOIV; NPeEn; OxAEP-1; OxBEV; PeLV *Fr.* Verses on the Death of Dr. Swift, D.S.P.D.

Time is passing now, The. Holiday, The. Stevie Smith. BWW

Time is ripe and I repent, The. Oengus Céile Dé. NOIV

Time Is Running Out. Oodgeroo of the tribe Noonuccal (Kath Walker). IBA

Time Is Swiftly Rolling On, The. Berryman Hicks. AH

Time is the feather'd thing. Time. Jasper Mayne. OBEV

Time Is the Mercy of Eternity. Kenneth Rexroth. VGW

Time is the root of all this earth. Time. Bhartrihari. AWP, *tr.* by Paul Elmer More

Time it takes, The. Lorraine Ellis Harr. HA

Time like the receptions of a child's piano. Reconciliation, The. Archibald MacLeish. MoAmPo

Time may come, when to remember, A. Fatherland in the Heights. Gyula Illyés. IQMS, *tr.* by Vernon Watkins

Time Now Please. Adriann Roland Holst. TuT, *tr.* by Paula Meehan

Time of Change, A. Egan [*or* Aodhagán] O'Rahilly [*or* O'Reilly *or* Ó Rathaille]. BIrV, *tr.* by Eavan Boland

  (After the Irish of Egan O'Rahilly.) PBCIP

Time of Cherries, A. Suzanne Burrows. Prnts

Time of day: a dim dream, probably. Yards of Sarajevo, The. Richard Hugo. AF

Time of fear, a time of dread, A. Sándor Petőfi. IQMS, tr. by George F. Cushing

Time of Fish Dying. Gabriela Melinescu. BoWoP, tr. by Stavros Deligiorgis

Time of green spring winds returns, The. Springtime South of the Yangtze. Li Po. CrYelRi, tr. by Sam Hamill

Time of loving and fluttering has not yet come, The. Land Stretching Up to the Sky, A. Nada El-Hage. PoArWo, tr. by Nathalie El-Hani

Time of Man, The. Phyllis Webb. MoCV

Time of Martyrdom, The. David Diop. NegPo, tr. by Ellen Conroy Kennedy

Time of naked spears, A. Death Certificate. Rui Knopfli. PeSAV, tr. by the author

Time of Roses. Thomas Hood. OBEV
    (Ballad: Time of Roses.) OBEV; OxAEP-2
    (Time of Roses.) OBEV

Time of Turtles. Grace Perry. NOBAu

Time of vigils comes, alas to blight, The. Verse of Darkness, The. Jenő Dsida. IQMS, tr. by Watson Kirkconnell

Time of Waiting. Geoffrey Dutton. CBAP

Time of Waiting in Amsterdam. Ingrid Jonker. BoWoP, tr. by Jack Cope and William Plomer

Time of white violets; and on the slopes. Convent in '45, The. Maria Luisa Spaziani. NeIt, tr. by Beverly Allen

Time on My Hands. Vincent Youmans. ReLy

Time on Target. William Daniel Ehrhart. CDa

Time only/. Opting for Early Retirement. Tom Leonard. Oth

Time Out. Maurice Riordan. EmeKit; ModIr

Time Passing, Beloved. Donald Davie. BoLoP; HarvBoo; NoP-4

Time Past, A. Denise Levertov. NoAM

Time-piece, The. William Cowper. Fr. Task, The.

Time, Please. Adriann Roland Holst. TuT, tr. by Sean Dunne

Time present and time past. T. S. Eliot. APT-1; HarvBoo; MoAmPo; NAAL-2v2; NAAL-5; PoE Fr. Four Quartets.

Times Presses Me. Lee Ranaldo. HeMarv

Time promises, should I in that confide? Quatrain. Ilyas Farhat. MAP, tr. by John Heath-Stubbs and Salma Khadra Jayyusi

Time quietly compiling us like sheaves. Seferis. Lawrence Durrell. EBEV

Time, Real and Imaginary. Samuel Taylor Coleridge. NOBE; OBEV; OxBSP

Time Recover'd. Thomas Stanley. OBVE

Time Reminded Me. Julia Uceda. BoWoP, tr. by Willis Barnstone

Time's Betrayal. Herman Melville. NCAP

Time's Changes. James Bramston. NOEC Fr. Art of Politics, The.

Time's come up pearls—let us wander. Sándor Weöres. IQMS, tr. by Adam Makkai and Donald E. Morse

Time's Dedication. Delmore Schwartz. VGW

Time's fingers bend us slowly. Crates. PGA

Time's fool, but not heaven's: yet hope not for any return. Time's Fool. Ruth Pitter. MoBrPo; OxBTC; PoRA; WPE

Time's Hand Is Kind. Margaret E. Bruner. PoToHe

Time's noblest offspring is the last. (LL) On the Prospect of Planting Arts and Learning in America. George Berkeley. AiP; NOEC; OxBEV

Time's Whirligig, Or, The Blue-New-Made-Gentleman Mounted. Humphrey Willis. NOSC

Time's winged chariot (poets say). To His Not-so-coy Mistress. Wynford Vaughan-Thomas. NOBL

Time-Servers. Judah Halevi. TrJP, tr. by Solomon Solis-Cohen

Time shall come, when free as seas or wind, The. Pope. ECEV Fr. Windsor-Forest [or Windsor Forest].

Time Signature. Linda Andrews. MiVo

"Time stands still." Unbeseechable, The. Frances Darwin Cornford. MoBrPo

Time stands still, with gazing on her face! Unknown. EnLoPo

Time stays, they said. We go. Ancient Ones, The: Betátakin. Janet Lewis. APT-2

Time stood still. Grandmother, The. Claribel Alegría. TANSG, tr. by Darwin Flakoll

Time Swept Up. Vasco [or Vasko] Popa. PoSu, tr. by Anne Pennington Fr. Raw Flesh.

Time, Temperature. Jim Daniels. LTA

Time that brings [or bringes] all things to light. Epitaph. Thomas Morton. NOSC; SCAP

Time, that gives to music life. Time and Music. Janet Lewis. FFC

Time that is moved by little fidget wheels. Five Bells. Kenneth Slessor. CBAP; NOBAu; PoRA

Time that's forever on his track returning. Spring Time. John Milton. MLL, tr. by Helen Waddell

Time the Hanlin scholar was south of the River, The. Reading the Collected Works of Li Po and Tu Fu: A Colophon. Po Chü-i. SuSp, tr. by Irving Y. Lo

Time ticks away the centre of my pride. Empty Glen, The. R. Crombie Saunders. OxBS

Time To Be Up, Marie, Young Sleepyhead. Pierre de Ronsard. STV, tr. by John Frederick Nims

Time to Die, The. Matilda Caroline Edwards. PWR

Time to draw the left foot back and let it. Water Eased of Its Cliffs by Falling. Alberta Turner. LCAP-2

Time to go. Roshu. JDP, tr. by Yoel Hoffmann

Time to love, and a time to hate; a time of war, and a time of peace, A. (LL) Bible, O.T. NAWM-5v1; OBVE Fr. Ecclesiastes.

Time to Myself. Paulette Jiles. NOBC

"Time to put off the world and go somewhere." Beggar to Beggar Cried. W. B. Yeats. NoAM; OxAEP-2

Time to Shine. Hamda Khamees. PoArWo, tr. by Joseph T. Zeidan

Time to tell you things are well, A. Snow Country Weavers. James Welch. CDW; HATNAP

Time to Tickle a Lizard, The. Lizard, The. Theodore Roethke. NOxBChV

Time topples Statyllios like a doddery oak. Time topples Statyllios like a doddery oak. Myrinos. GrAn, tr. by Tony Harrison

Time Travel. Nick Piombino. FTOS

Time Traveler's Potlatch. Philip Lamantia. CLPP

Time was, a [wealthy] Englishman would join. James Cawthorn. ECEV; NOEC Fr. Of Taste; an Essay.

Time was, and that was termed the time of Gold. Joseph Hall. OBSV Fr. Virgidemiarum.

Time was away and she was here. (LL) Meeting Point. Louis MacNeice. ModIr; NPeEn; PNI

Time was away and somewhere else. Meeting Point. Louis MacNeice. ModIr; NPeEn; PNI

Time was, ere yet in these degenerate days. Byron. FHYEP Fr. English Bards and Scotch Reviewers.

Time was God judged. In the Days of Socrates. Friedrich Hölderlin. PFTM-1

Time was, I sat upon a lofty stool. Literary Reminiscences. Thomas Hood. OxBSo

Time was, I shrank from what was right. Sensitiveness. John Henry, Cardinal Newman. TrCP

Time was I was a plowman driving. Plowman. Sidney Keyes. PoRA

Time was the apple Adam ate. Original Sequence. Philip Booth. ChIV-1

Time was upon / The wing, to flie away. Upon Time. Robert Herrick. BeJo

Time was when his half million drew. Bewick Finzer. Edwin Arlington Robinson. MoAmPo; NAAL-2v2

Time was when I was weapon and warrior. Cynewulf. AnOE, tr. by Charles W. Kennedy Fr. Riddles (Exeter Book).

Time was when once upon a time, such toys. Epigram. Glaukos. GrAn, tr. by Peter Jay

Time was, when we were sow'd, and just began. Ovid. NPeEn, tr. by John Dryden Fr. Metamorphoses.

Time wasted and time spent. Times, The. Charles Madge. OBMV

Time We Climbed Snake Mountain, The. Leslie Marmon Silko. VoR

Time, while it beauty's pow'r impairs. To a Friend, Fearful of Being Forgotten in Absence. Eliza Cobbe, Lady Tuite. PoBW

Time will say nothing but I told you so. If I Could Tell You. W. H. Auden. HarvBoo

Time Will Surely Come, The. Robert T. Daniel. AH

Time Wins. Benoy Majumdar. OMIP, tr. by Jyotirmoy Dutta

Time with his scythe honed fine. Hay Fever. Alec Derwent Hope. NoAM

Time with Stevie Wonder in It. Christopher Gilbert. SwNoth

Time, wouldst thou hurt us? Never shall we grow old. Double Fortress, The. Alfred Noyes. SacPr

Time, You Old Gypsy Man. Ralph Hodgson. MoBrPo

Time, you thief, who love to get. Max Beerbohm. UV

Time you won your town the race, The. To an Athlete Dying Young. A. E. Housman. ChAP; HAP; HeIP-4; InPK-6; MoBrPo; NAEL-5v2; NAEL-6v2; NIP-4; NoAM; NoP-4; PoE; PoRA; SCGP; SoSe-8; TFi; TRP; UnPo; WeW-3

Time Zones. Jane Duran. MFPA

Timely blossom, infant fair. To Miss Charlotte Pulteney in Her Mother's Arms. Ambrose Philips. NOEC

Timer. Tony Harrison. EmeKit; HarvBoo Fr. School of Eloquence, The.

Times. Weatherly. SeSe

Times, The. Charles Churchill.
    Against Sodomy. ECEV
    "Go where we will, at ev'ry time and place." ECEV
    "Is a son born into this world of woe?" OBSV

Times, The. Charles Madge. OBMV

Times are good, there's no cruel government, The.   Along the River, Seeing the Home of Absconded Farmers. Kao Ch'i.   CoBLCP, *tr. by* Jonathan Chaves

Times are torn asunder, The.   Rogen.   JDP, *tr. by* Yoel Hoffmann

Times / at all. (LL)   For Saundra.   Nikki Giovanni.   BPo; NAAAL; TTY

Times come round again, The.   To a Military Rifle, 1942.   Yvor Winters.   MoAmPo

Times followed one another. Came a morn.   Elizabeth Barrett Browning.   NAEL-6v2 *Fr.* Aurora Leigh.

Times Go by Turns.   Richard Verstegan [*or* Verstegen].   SacPr

Times Gone By.   János Vajda.   IQMS, *tr. by* Jess Perlman

Times have changed.   Anything Goes.   Cole Porter.   APT-1; OBAL; ReLy

Times Like This.   Richard Jones.   GifTon

Times [*or* Tymes] Go[e] By Turn[e]s.   Robert Southwell.   ChIV-1; NoSic

Times she'll sit quiet by the hearth, and times.   Woodcutter's Wife, The.   William Rose Benét.   AWP

Times Square.   Alter Brody.   TaR

Times Square Poems.   Michael Lassell.

  Dino.   GLP

  Going Rate, The.   GLP

  "His name is Jason, he's."   GLP

  How to Find Love in an Instant.   GLP

  "Sit as close to the stage as possible."   GLP

  Stud.   GLP

  "This morning I clipped my fingernails."   GLP

Times Square Water Music.   Amy Clampitt.   UrbNat

Times wherein old Pompion was a Saint, The.   New-Englands Crisis.   Benjamin Tompson.   SCAP

Timid Gazelle, The.   Kasmuneh.   TrJP

"Timid grace sits trembling in her eye, A."   Charles Lamb.   GSo

Timid Lover.   Countee Cullen.   ColAP

Timidly, still half asleep, it has blossomed.   Purple Peach Tree, The.   Su Tung-p'o (Su Shih).   OHPC, *tr. by* Kenneth Rexroth

Timing.   Anne Rouse.   NeBl

Timokritos was bold in war. This is his grave.   Anacreon.   GrAn

Timoleon.   Herman Melville.   APN-2

Timon, for you exist no more.   Callimachus.   HePo *Fr.* Epigrams.

Timon of Athens.   William Shakespeare.

  "Here lie I, Timon."   AWP

  "O blessed breeding sun! draw from the earth."   OxAEP-1

  "Put up thy gold: go on,—here's gold,—go on."   OxAEP-1

  Timon's Epitaph.   AWP

  "Warr'st thou 'gainst Athens?"   EBEV

Timon's Epitaph.   William Shakespeare.   AWP *Fr.* Timon of Athens.

Timon's Villa.   Pope.   NOEC; NPeEn; OxBEV *Fr.* Epistle IV, to Richard Boyle, Earl of Burlington.

Timor Mortis conturbat me. (LL)   Lament for the Makaris.   William Dunbar.   EBEV; HAP; MakPoe; NePenScot; OxBS

Timor mortis conturbat me. (LL)   *Unknown.*   NoP-4; SacPr

Timoshenko.   Sidney Keyes.   OBWP

Timothy.   Timothy Steele.   InPK-6; RA

Timothy Titus took two ties.   *Unknown.*   OxNR

Timothy Winters.   Charles Causley.   PeECV; RB

Tin bath once brimmed with daughters, The.   Things.   Geoffrey Holloway.   NLP

Tin Frog, The.   Russell Hoban.   Spl

  (I have hopped, when properly wound up, the whole length.)   Spl

Tin Roof Blues.   Sterling Allen Brown.   NAAAL

Tin-roofed shacks, The.   Ruby Red's Migrant Camp.   Wilma Elizabeth McDaniel.   GeoHom

Tin shack, where my baby sleeps on his back.   Everything: Eloy, Arizona, 1956.   Ai.   BodElec

Tin Wash Dish, The.   Les A. Murray.   BMAP

Tin Woodsman, The.   Paulette Jiles.   NOBC

Tina and Seth met in the midst of an overcrowded militarism.   Histoire.   Harry Mathews.   NIP-4; PmAP

Tina speaks to her friend on the phone.   Motor Oil Queen.   Cheryl Burke.   WiU

Tind friends, I pray extuse me.   New Baby, The.   Fred Emerson Brooks.   VerBaPo

Tinder.   Seamus Heaney.   OxAEP-2

Tinder, The.   Thomas Carew.   CaPo

Tinfoil.   Joyce Mansour.   MFP, *tr. by* Martin Sorrell

Tingle.   Getting Warm.   Rae Armantrout.   FTOS

Tinian.   Friedrich Hölderlin.

  "Pleasant to wander."   WoPoe, *tr. by* David Gascoyne

Tinker, Come Bring Your Solder.   Mary Mapes Dodge.   SWaP

Tinker, come bring your solder.   Tinker, Come Bring Your Solder.   Mary Mapes Dodge.   SWaP

Tinker's Wife.   Patrick Kavanagh.   CIP-2; NoAM

Tinker, / Tailor.   *Unknown.*   OxNR

Tinkle of chimes, The.   Tom Tico.   HA

Tinkling treble, / Rolling bass.   Dream Boogie: Variation.   Langston Hughes.   APSN

Tinsel Marie; The Coora Flower.   Gwendolyn Brooks.   ESEAA *Fr.* Children Going Home.

Tint I cannot take—is best, The.   Emily Dickinson.   APN-2; MoAmPo

Tintype of a Private in the Fifteenth Georgia Infantry.   Paul Horgan.   CBCWP

Tiny baby, you're ugly.   King D. Kuka.   VoR

Tiny Bird, A.   *Vietnamese Oral Tradition.*   CaDao, *tr. by* John Balaban

Tiny bird with red feathers, A.   Tiny Bird, A.   *Vietnamese Oral Tradition.*   CaDao, *tr. by* John Balaban

Tiny children.   Love Song.   Yityangu Ejong.   CBAP, *tr. by* Frank Wordick

Tiny dew reinvigorates the tiny grass, The.   Margherita Guidacci.   CItWP, *tr. by* Cinzia Sartini Blum and Lara Trubowitz *Fr.* Meditations and Maxims.

Tiny Erotion, borne away / By a gnat had this to say.   Lucilius.   GrAn

Tiny fish.   Idyl.   John James.   Oth

Tiny fish.   Alan Pizzarelli.   HA

Tiny fish enjoy themselves, The.   Little Fish.   D. H. Lawrence.   OxBTC; RB; Spl; TTTS

Tiny green birds skate over the surface of the room.   Saturday Night in the Parthenon.   Kenneth Patchen.   SPE

Tiny joys, joys like a lizard's tail.   "Rachel" [*or* "Rahel"].   FIT, *tr. by* Robert Friend

Tiny little pine tree, still shorter than the fence, A.   Poem on a Little Pine, A.   Hsieh Chin.   CoBLCP, *tr. by* Jonathan Chaves

Tiny moon as small and white as a single jasmine flower, A.   White Blossom, A.   D. H. Lawrence.   MoBrPo

Tiny new emotions, The.   Poem.   Tom Clark.   CoAmPo

Tiny petals of the mountain ash [*or* mountain-ash], The. (LL)   Frederick Goddard Tuckerman.   APN-2; NOBA; OxBSo; TAP *Fr.* Sonnets.

Tiny snow of the stunningly cold black day.   In the Snowfall.   Gwerfyl Mechain.   BoWoP, *tr. by* Willis Barnstone

Tiny sun, A.   In the Ashtray.   Vasco [*or* Vasko] Popa.   VCWP, *tr. by* Anne Pennington

Tip, The.   Albert Goldbarth.   HCAP

Tip, The.   Belle Waring.   PBCAP

Tip for Saturday, A.   Francis Webb.   BMAP

Tip their mouths open to the sky.   Small Vases from Hebron, The.   Naomi Shihab Nye.   PoArWo

Tip-Toe Tail.   Dixie Willson.   NTCP

Tipperary.   Desmond O'Grady.   BiHa

Tipping down from above the clouds at Athens.   Athens and Jerusalem.   Rose Drachler.   TaR

Tips waves up big dipper fires.   Wonderful.   Ania Walwicz.   BMAP

Tiptoe on wall-top, head in.   Wild Cherry.   Nigel Jenkins.   TCAWP

Tire tracks words lost in lost snow today.   Generic Elbows.   Bernadette Mayer.   FTOS

Tired.   Basho.   EH, *tr. by* Robert Hass

Tired.   Fenton Johnson.   APT-1; NAAAL; PAI; TCAPo; TTY

Tired.   Allan Roberts.   ReLy

Tired and thirsty, weary of the way.   After the Hunt.   Detlev, Freiherr von Liliencron.   AWP, *tr. by* Ludwig Lewisohn

Tired and Unhappy, You Think of Houses.   Delmore Schwartz.   APT-2; MoAmPo

Tired as I Can Be.   *Unknown.*   FaBoVe

Tired Hunter, The.   Gabriel Preil.   FIT, *tr. by* Robert Friend

Tired i count the ways in which it determines my life.   ISM, The.   Wanda Coleman.   PmAP

Tired Lizi Tired.   Lindiwe Mabuza.   HAWP

Tired Man, The.   Suliaman El-Hadi.   SpirFl

Tired nature's sweet restorer, balmy Sleep!   Edward Young.   NOEC; OxAEP-1 *Fr.* Night Thoughts.

Tired Night, A.   Tu Fu.   SuSp, *tr. by* Jan W. Walls

Tired of all things—with even hope put by.   Valley, The.   Alphonse Marie Louis de Lamartine.   SxFrPo, *tr. by* E. H. Blackmore and A. M. Blackmore

Tired of chewing.   Street Funeral.   Irving Layton.   NIL-7

Tired of him and forgets. (LL)   Turn of Privacy, The.   Rick Noguchi.   AmPoNex; NeAmPo

Tired of my writing brush, I gazed out the window.   Night Duty in the Palace, Dreaming of a Hsien-yu Temple.   Po Chü-i.   CrYelRi, *tr. by* Sam Hamill

Tired of the life I lead.   Tired.   Allan Roberts.   ReLy

Tired of Towns.   Andrew Lang.   EBVV

Tired of waiting for me.   Tongues in My Mouth.   Demetrice A. Worley.   SpirFl

Tired of walking in the red dust. Retreat of Sun Ching-hsiang, The. Chang Yü. CoBLCP, *tr.* by Jonathan Chaves

Tired of women. Cristina Peri Rossi. TANSG, *tr.* by Diana P. Decker *Fr.* Evohé.

Tired [*or* Tir'd, *or* Tir'd] with all these, for restful death I cry. William Shakespeare. AWP; CTC; EBEV; HAP; NOBE; NoSic; OxAEP-1; TFi; WeW-3 *Fr.* Sonnets.

Tired river took shelter in the shade, The. Calm, The. Dulce Maria Loynaz. TANSG, *tr.* by Alan West

Tired Tim. Walter De la Mare. NTCP

Tired with books and rolling on the bed. New River Head, a Fragment, The. E. Dower. NOEC

Tired with dull grief, grown old before my day. 1916 Seen from 1921. Edmund Charles Blunden. NoP-4; PeFWW

Tired with its dogs and doves. Summer Band Concert. Vivian Smith. CBAP

Tired with too long a chase, though stout. On the Death of Squire Christopher. John Wigson. OxBSP

Tired Woman, The. Anna Wickham. MoBrPo

Tired Worker, The. Claude McKay. BPo

Tireder than usual I got up. Personal. Peter Rafferty. NLP

Tireless Sculptor, The. Henrietta Cordelia Ray. CBWP-3; SWaP

Tires chew into the soft. Mud Season. Mark Todd. GeoH

Tires Stacked in the Hallways of Civilization. Martín Espada. InvLad

Tiresias. Austin Clarke.
   "My mother wept loudly." CIP-2
   "Strolling one day, beyond the Kalends, on Mount Cyllene." ModIr

Tirocinium; or, A Review of Schools. William Cowper.
   "Father, who designs his babe a priest, The." OBSV
   "To you, then, tenants of life's middle state." OBSV
   "Would you your son should be a sot or dunce." OBSV

Tiruppavai, The. Andal.
   "O sister of wealth." WPoS

Tiruppavai, The. Andal.
   "O you who guard over." WPoS

Tiruppavai, The. Andal.
   "We rose before dawn." WPoS

Tirzah. Jacob Cohen. MHP, *tr.* by Ruth Finer Mintz

'Tis a dull sight. Old Song. Edward Fitzgerald. OBEV; OxAEP-2

'Tis a fair tree, the almond tree; there spring. Death in the Flower. Letitia [*or* Laetitia] Elizabeth Landon. RWP

'Tis a lesson you should heed. Try, Try Again. T. H. Palmer. ChAP; ITBLP

'Tis a Little Journey. *Unknown.* PoToHe

'Tis a Little Thing. Sir Thomas N. Talfourd. TreFP

'Tis a little thing. Friend, A. Sir Thomas N. Talfourd. PoToHe

'Tis a moon-tinted primrose, with a well. Another. Thomas Lovell Beddoes. Son

'Tis a new life—thoughts move not as they did. New Birth, The. Jones Very. APN-1; NCAP; NOBA; SacPr

'Tis a sad land, that in one day. Death. Henry Vaughan. ChIV-1

'Tis a stern and startling thing to think. Thomas Hood. NOBVV *Fr.* Miss Kilmansegg and Her Precious Leg.

'Tis a strange mystery, the power of words! Power of Words, The. Letitia [*or* Laetitia] Elizabeth Landon. VWP

'Tis a time for much rejoicing. Emancipation. Priscilla Jane Thompson. CBWP-2

'Tis affection but dissembled. Song. Sidney Godolphin. BeJo

'Tis all that Heav'n allows. (LL) Love And Life. John Wilmot, 2d Earl of Rochester. BoLoP; EnLoPo; HAP; NOBE; NPeEn; OBEV; OxBEV

'Tis all the way to Toe-town. Foot Soldiers. John Banister Tabb. OBAL

'Tis an act of the priest to give patience a test. Matrimony. John Williams. NOEC

'Tis an old dial, dark with many a stain. Sundial, The. Austin Dobson. OBGa

'Tis April again in my garden, again the grey stone-wall. To Francis Jammes. Robert Bridges. NPeEn; OxBSo

'Tis better to be vile than vile esteem'd. William Shakespeare. CAGL; NoSic; OxAEP-1; SCGP *Fr.* Sonnets.

Tis braul I cudgel, ranters, Quakers braul. Claudius Gilbert. John Wilson. SCAP

'Tis but a phantom of the weary brain. Life for a Life. Mary E. Tucker. CBWP-1

'Tis Christmas weather, and a country house. George Meredith. NAEL-5v2; NAEL-6v2; NOBVV *Fr.* Modern Love.

'Tis customary as we part. Emily Dickinson. LW

'Tis dead night round about: Horror [*or* Horrour] doth creep[e]. Lamp[e], The. Henry Vaughan. ChIV-2; ESCV

'Tis dead of night; storms rend the troubled air. Sonnet. Mary Locke. ECWP

'Tis death! and peace, indeed, is here. Youth and Calm. Matthew Arnold. FHYEP

'Tis done! Dread Winter spreads his latest glooms. James Thomson. OxAEP-1 *Fr.* Seasons, The.

'Tis dreadful! Aisle of a Temple, The. William Congreve. OxAEP-1

'Tis easy to be true[!]. (LL) Song to Celia. Sir Charles Sedley. GTBS-P; OxBEV

'Tis eight o'clock,—a clear March night. Idiot Boy, The. William Wordsworth. NOBRP; OBNV

'Tis evening, the black snail has got on his track. Evening. John Clare. NOBVV

'Tis fine to see the Old World, and travel up and down. America for Me. Henry Van Dyke. ChAP

'Tis first the true and then the beautiful. Precedence. Horatius Bonar. SacPr

'Tis folly to be wise. (LL) Ode on a Distant Prospect of Eton College. Thomas Gray. GTBS-P; NAEL-5v1; NAEL-6v1; NAEL-7v1; NOBE; NOEC; NoP-4; OxAEP-1; PoE; SCGP

'Tis goodbye then to last night. Soraidh Slan Don Oidhche Areir. Niall Mor MacMuireadach. BIrV, *tr.* by Maire Cruise O'Brien

'Tis grown almost a danger to speak true. Epistle. To Katharine, Lady Aubigny. Ben Jonson. BeJo

'Tis hard to say, if greater want of skill. Pope. NAEL-5v1; NAEL-6v1; NAEL-7v1; TFi

'Tis hard we should be by the men despised. Mary Lee, Lady Chudleigh. ECWP

'Tis his one hope: all else that round his life. Infatuation. Frederick Goddard Tuckerman. NCAP

'Tis, in good truth, a most wonderful thing. Sir William Davenant [*or* D'Avenant]. NOSC

'Tis in the spirit that attire. Christopher Smart. NOCV *Fr.* Hymns for the Amusement of Children.

'Tis known, at least it should be, that throughout. Byron. NOBL; NOBRP; OBNV; OBSV

'Tis late and cold; stir up the fire. John Fletcher. OxAEP-1 *Fr.* Lover's Progress, The.

'Tis Lent, the holy time of fast and prayer. Easter Light, The. Clara Ann Thompson. CBWP-2

'Tis light to love thee living, girl, when hope is full and fair. Thomas Tod Stoddart. NOBRP *Fr.* Death-Wake, The; or, Lunacy.

'Tis little I— could care for Pearls. Emily Dickinson. WPoS

'Tis made by Nothing now again[e]. (LL) And He Answered Them Nothing. Richard Crashaw. ChIV-2; SacPr

'Tis madness to give physic to the dead. William Habington. BeJo *Fr.* Castara.

'Tis May, and yet the skies are overcast. Lines Written on a Very Boisterous Day in May, 1844. John Clare. OxBSP

'Tis men who say that through all hurt and pain. Augusta Davies Webster. VWP; ViWPN *Fr.* Mother and Daughter.

'Tis Midnight. *Unknown.* NTCP

'Tis midnight! and pale Melancholy stands. Written at the Couch of a Dying Parent. Eliza Cook. CenSon

'Tis Midnight, and the setting sun. 'Tis Midnight. *Unknown.* NTCP

'Tis mute, the word they went to hear on high Dodona mountain. Oracles, The. A. E. Housman. HAP

'Tis near the morning watch, the dim lamp burns. Morning Watch, The. Jones Very. APN-1

'Tis near the time. I'm glad 'tis getting late. Achsa W. Sprague. SWaP *Fr.* Poet, The.

'Tis never or but seldom[e] known[e]. Power and Peace. Robert Herrick. CaPo

'Tis night; the mercenary tyrants sleep. Robert Southey. CenSon

"'Tis no sin for a man to labour in his vocation." Ballad of Villon and Fat Madge, The. François Villon. OBVE

'Tis not a coat of gray or shepherd's life. To John Donne. Sir Henry Wotton. NoSic

'Tis not by brooding on delight. Marcus Curtius. Oliver St. John Gogarty. OBMV

Tis not enough for one that is a wife. Chorus. Elizabeth Cary, Countess of Falkland. EMWP

'Tis not ev'ry day that I. Not Every Day Fit for Verse. Robert Herrick. BeJo; PoRA

'Tis not for man to trifle: life is brief. Only One Life. *Unknown.* TreFP

'Tis not for the unfeeling, the falsely refined. Farmer of Tilsbury Vale, The. William Wordsworth. EBEV

'Tis not how long we have to live. Anacreontic. John Thelwall. NOBRP

'Tis not how witty, nor how free. Upon Kind[e] and True Love. Aurelian Townshend [*or* Townsend]. MeLP; NOSC

'Tis not I pity the flowers are about to die. Tu Fu. SuSp *Fr.* Strolling along the Riverbank, Looking for Flowers.

'Tis not on the face displayed. Bedlamite, The. Thomas Mozeen. NOEC

'Tis not that Dying hurts us so. Emily Dickinson. APN-2; BoWoP

'Tis not that I am weary grown. Upon [His] Leaving His Mistress. John Wilmot, 2d Earl of Rochester. BASC; EnLoPo; NBLV; NOSC

'Tis not the gaudy stream of rosy flame. Self-Consciousness Makes All Changes Happy; Ode. Jonathan Richardson. NOEC

'Tis now clear[e] day: I see a rose. Henry Vaughan. ChIV-2; ESCV; GeHe

'Tis now, since I sat[e] down before. Love's Siege. Sir John Suckling. CaPo; NPeEn

"'Tis Now, Since I Sate Down Before." Sir John Suckling. *See* Love's Siege

'Tis now the hour of mirth, the hour of love. Maria Gowen Brooks. APN-1 *Fr.* Zophiël [or, the Bride of Seven].

'Tis of a gallant Yankee ship that flew the stripes and stars. Yankee Man-of-War, The. *Unknown.* TCAPo

'Tis of just a cabin home. Whispering Wind. Catherine Braan Layne. PWR

'Tis on October thirty-first. Hallowe'en. Lizelia Augusta Jenkins Moorer. CBWP-3

'Tis one good part I'd lie withal. (LL) Ben Jonson. NAEL-6v1; NAEL-7v1 *Fr.* Celebration of Charis in Ten Lyric[k] Pieces [or Peeces], A.

'Tis Opposites—entice. Emily Dickinson. PoE

'Tis raging noon; and vertical, the sun. James Thomson. EBEV *Fr.* Seasons, The.

'Tis said. Heavenly Questions. Ch'u Yüan. ColAnChi, *tr.* by Victor H. Mair

'Tis said, as Cupid danced [or danc't] among. How Roses Came Red. Robert Herrick. CaPo; SoSe-8

'Tis said but a name is friendship. Lines to Mrs. Isabel Peace. Mary Weston Fordham. CBWP-2

'Tis said that faith declines; believe it not;. Faith, Hope, and Charity Are the Prospects of Manhood. Leigh Hunt. ChIV-2

'Tis said that to the brow of yon fair hill. Tradition of Oker Hill in Darley Dale, Derbyshire, A. William Wordsworth. OxBSo

'Tis said the Gods lower down that chain above. George Alsop. SCAP

'Tis said there were no thought of hell. Heaven and Hell. Francis Thompson. OxBSP; SacPr

'Tis so appalling—it exhilirates. Emily Dickinson. PoE

'Tis so much joy! 'Tis so much joy! Emily Dickinson. NOCV

'Tis spring, warm glows the south. Birds' Nests. John Clare. OxBSP

'Tis still observ'd, that Fame ne'er sings. Fame. Robert Herrick. FaBoEE

Tis strang. Dialogue betwixt Man, and Nature, A. Margaret Lucas Cavendish, Duchess of Newcastle. PBRV

'Tis strange how much is mark'd on memory. History of the Lyre, A. Letitia [or Laetitia] Elizabeth Landon. VWP

'Tis strange how my head runs on! 'tis a puzzle to understand. City Clerk, The. Thomas Ashe. EBVV

'Tis strange how the newspapers honour. Limerick. Eugene Field. PeLi

Tis strange my Theseus, that these lovers speake of. William Shakespeare. OxBEV *Fr.* Midsummer Night's Dream, A.

'Tis strange she should confess it, though it be true. (LL) Self[e] Accuser, A. John Donne. FaBoEE; PeLV

'Tis strange that he Unborn, ere he saw Light. Some Experimental Passages of My Life, with Reflections upon Jacob's Words, Few and Evil Have the Days of the Years of My Life Been. Elizabeth Tipper. EMWP

'Tis strange to think, if we could fling aside. Mask of Gaiety, The. Letitia [or Laetitia] Elizabeth Landon. VWP

'Tis such a new and gracious miracle. (LL) Dante Alighieri. AWP; EaItPo, *tr.* by Dante Gabriel Rossetti *Fr.* La Vita Nuova.

'Tis summer eve, when heaven's ethereal bow. Thomas Campbell. TreFP *Fr.* Pleasures of Hope, The.

'Tis summer time on Bredon. Summer Time on Bredon. Hugh Kingsmill. NOBL; UV

'Tis the cur-dog of Britain and spaniel of Spain. (LL) Character of Sir Robert Walpole, The. Jonathan Swift. FaBoEE; PoE

'Tis the gift to be simple, 'tis the gift to be free. Simple Gifts. *Unknown.* AH

'Tis the great art of life to manage well. John Armstrong. NOEC *Fr.* Art of Preserving Health, The.

'Tis the human touch in this world that counts. Human Touch, The. Spencer Michael Free. PoToHe

'Tis the Last Rose of Summer. Thomas Moore. NOIV
  (Last Rose of Summer, The.) OxBoLi

Tis the middle of the night by the castle clock. Samuel Taylor Coleridge. FHYEP; NAEL-5v2; NAEL-6v2; NOBRP *Fr.* Christabel.

"'Tis the Octoroon ball! And the halls are alight!" Ballade des Belles Milatraisses. Rosalie Jonas. BlSi

'Tis the practice of the great. (LL) Song, A: "Lying is an occupation." Laetitia Pilkington. PEW; WPE

'Tis the season when Nature awakes from her sleep. Easter; or, Spring-Time. Lizelia Augusta Jenkins Moorer. CBWP-3

'Tis the summer prime, when the noiseless air. Elizabeth Oakes-Smith. SWaP *Fr.* Sinless Child, The.

'Tis the voice of the Lobster: I heard him /declare declare. Lewis Carroll. NOBL; OBCoV; PeLV; UV *Fr.* Alice's Adventures in Wonderland.

'Tis the voice of the [or a] sluggard; I heard him complain. Sluggard, The. Isaac Watts. ECEV; HAP; NOEC; OxBEV; OxBoLi; UV

'Tis the week before Christmas and every night. For the Children or the Grown-ups? *Unknown.* OBCP

'Tis the year's midnight, and it is the day's. Nocturnal[l] upon Saint Lucy's [or S. Lucy's or S. Lucies] Day, Being the Shortest Day, A. John Donne. BASC; CABP; EBEV; ESCV; FHYEP; MeLP; NAEL-5v1; NAEL-6v1; NAEL-7v1; NOBE; NOSC; NoP-4; OxAEP-1; PoE; SCGP; TFi

Tis thy time to choose a lover. (LL) Horace. AWP; OBVE *Fr.* Odes.

'Tis Timarion. Meleager. GrAn

'Tis time this heart should be unmoved. On This Day I Complete My Thirty-sixth Year. Byron. CAGL; FHYEP; NAEL-6v2; NPeEn; NoP-4; OBWP; PoE

'Tis time to conclude. Conclusion of a Letter to the Rev. Mr. C——, The. Mary Barber. CABP; ECWP

'Tis to pen anthems for an angels choir. (LL) Gratulatory to Mr. Ben Johnson for His Adopting of Him to Be His Son, A. Thomas Randolph. BeJo; NPeEn

'Tis to yourself I speak; you cannot know. Yourself. Jones Very. APN-1; NOBA; OxBA; Son

'Tis true, dear[e] Ben, thy just chastizing [or chastising] hand. To Ben Jonson. Thomas Carew. BASC; BeJo; CaPo; CavPo; NAEL-5v1; NAEL-6v1; NAEL-7v1; NOSC

'Tis true I weepe, I sigh, I wring my hands. Eleanora Wyatt Finch. EMWP

'Tis true our life is but a long dis-ease. Song. Katherine Philips. OxBSP

'Tis true—then why should I repine. In Sickness. Jonathan Swift. NOEC

'Tis true, 'tis day, what though it be? Break[e] of Day. John Donne. NAEL-5v1; NAEL-6v1; NAEL-7v1; SoSe-8

'Tis true—yet 'tis no pity that 'tis true. James Kirke Paulding. APN-1 *Fr.* Backwoodsman, The.

'Tis very hard when men forsake. Jack Hall. Thomas Hood. NOBRP

'Tis very sure God walks in mine. (LL) My Garden. Thomas Edward Brown. InPK-6; OBEV; OBGa; UV

'Tis want of sense that makes us poor. (LL) On Leaping over the Moon. Thomas Traherne. GeHe; NAEL-5v1

'Tis war again, and I am glad 'tis so. Dryden. FaBoWar *Fr.* Conquest of Granada, The.

'Tis well, 'tis something; we may stand. Tennyson. EBVV *Fr.* In Memoriam A. H. H.

'Tis Well to Wake the Theme of Love. Eliza Cook. VWP

'Tis well to woo, 'tis well to wed. Building upon the Sand. Eliza Cook. TreFP

'Tis well you think me truly one of those. To John Keats. Leigh Hunt. CenSon; Son

'Tis Winter Now. Samuel Longfellow. AH

'Tis winter that no Christmas tree can dress. Christmas. Hans Just. AuPH, *tr.* by Lowell A. Bangerter

'Tis woman that seduces all mankind! John Gay. PeLV *Fr.* Begger's Opera.

'Tis wretchedness too much to be cast down. Sir Francis Hubert. ChIV-1 *Fr.* Egypt's Favorite.

Tishah B'Ov / 1952. David Meltzer. TaR

Tísica. Diana García. TouFir

Tisza, The. Sándor Petőfi. IQMS, *tr.* by Watson Kirkconnell

Tit, tat, toe. Baby Verse, A. *Unknown.* OxNR

Tita's Poem. Aurora Levins Morales. PueRic

Titan! to whose immortal eyes. Prometheus. Byron. NOBE; OxAEP-2

Titanic, The. Witter Bynner. APT-1

Titanic, The. Edwin John Pratt.
  Final Moments, The. NOBC
  "Fo'c'sle had gone under the creep, The." NOBC

Titanic, The. *Unknown.* APT-1

Titans, The. Betti Alver. BoWoP, *tr.* by Willis Barnstone and Felix Oinas

Tithe [or Tythe]: To the Bride, The. Robert Herrick. CaPo

Tithonus. Tennyson. CABP; HAP; NAEL-5v2; NAEL-6v2; NAWM-7v2; NOBE; NOBVV; NPeEn; NoP-4; OxBEV; PAI; PoE; SCGP

Title conveyed, seal set. Clause for a Covenant. Constance Carrier. APT-2

Title divine—is mine! Emily Dickinson. APN-2; NALW; NOBA; TCAPo

Title of This Poem Was Lost, The. Pedro Juan Pietri. PueRic

Titty cum tawtay. *Unknown.* OxNR

Titty wainscott n' all th'droppin's. Elder Dubb. Edwin Torres. HeMarv

Titus and Berenice. John Heath-Stubbs. GTBS-P

Titus the brave and valorous gallant. Sir John Davies. NoSic *Fr.* Epigrams.

Titwillow. Sir William Schwenck Gilbert. NoP-4

Tizzy Boost. Bruce Andrews.
  "Appetizers'" FTOS

Tjanting. Ron Silliman.
  ("Not this.") FTOS

"Not this. / What then?" PmAP

Tlanusi' Yi, the Leech Place. Gladys Cardiff. CDW

Tlingit Concrete Poem. Nora Dauenhauer. NIP-4

TM. Ulli Freer. Oth

To. To Linda. Guillaume Apollinaire. CuPo

To. Herman Melville. NCAP

To. William Carlos Williams. OBAL

To —. "Shu Ting." CarOv, *tr.* by Carolyn Kizer and Y. H. Zhao

To ———? Richard Dehmel. AWP, *tr.* by Jethro Bithell

To A. A. A. (Akhmatova). Osip Emilevich Mandelstam [*or* Mandelshtam]. TCRP, *tr.* by Bernard Meares

To a Beautiful Pear Tree. James Wright (1927–80). HAP

To a Beauty, White, Pure, and Constant. Abu Bakr ibn Abd al-Malik Ibn Quzman. WoPoe, *tr.* by Leticia Garza-Falcón and Christopher Middleton

To a Bed of Tulips. Robert Herrick. CaPo

To a Bereaved Mother. John Quincy Adams. SacPr

To a Blockhead. Pope. *See* Another [Epigram]

To a Boon Companion. Oliver St. John Gogarty. OBMV

To a Boy. Nancy Morejón. TANSG, *tr.* by Joy Renjilian-Burgy

To a Boy-Poet of the Decadence. Sir Owen Seaman. PeLV

To a Brother Official. Tu Fu. CarOv, *tr.* by Carolyn Kizer *Fr.* Adviser to the Court.

To a Bull Moose. Eugene O'Neill. UV

To a Calvinist in Bali. Edna St. Vincent Millay. NoAM

To a Cape Ann Schooner. John Greenleaf Whittier. OxBSo

To a Captious Critic. Paul Laurence Dunbar. BPo

To a Cat. John Keats. CenSon; FaBoCh; OxBSo; TriCat

To a Caty-did. Philip Freneau. TAP

To a Certain Cantatrice. Walt Whitman. AmFaPo

To a Certain Civilian. Walt Whitman. CBCWP; FaBoWar

To a Certain Most Certainly Certain Critic. David McCord. OBAL

To "A Certain Rich Man." Alice Thompson Meynell. ChIV-2

To a Chameleon. Marianne Craig Moore. APT-1

To a Child. Wilfred Owen. Son

To a Child. Judith Wright. BMAP

To a Child Born in Time of Small War. Helen Sorrells. WPE

To a Child in Death. Charlotte Mew. ChIV-2; MoBrPo

To a Child [of] Five Years Old. Nathaniel Cotton. ECEV

To a Child of Quality [Five Years Old, the Author Supposed Forty]. Matthew Prior. NOBE; NOEC; OBEV; OxBEV

To a Child Running with Outstretched Arms in Canyon de Chelly. N. Scott Momaday. CDW; HATNAP

To a Child Trapped in a Barber Shop. Philip Levine. InPK-6; NOBA; NoAM; PAI; TAP; VGW

To a Child [Written in Her Album]. William Wordsworth. OxBSP; Spl (Written in an Album.) Spl

To a Christmas Two-Year-Old. Luci Shaw. TrCP

To a Cloud. Ida Schwarz. AuPH, *tr.* by Lowell A. Bangerter

To a Coal Miner in Madrid, New Mexico. Luis Lopez. GeoH

To a Common Prostitute. Walt Whitman. MoAmPo

To a Comrade in Arms. Alun Lewis. FaBoTw; MoBrPo

To a Conscript of 1940. Sir Herbert Read. OBWP; PoWW

To a Covetous Churl. Edward May. FaBoEE

To a Crucifix. Anna Wickham. MoBrPo

To a Cuckoo at Coolanlough. Medbh McGuckian. PBCIP

To a Daisy. Alice Thompson Meynell. MoBrPo; SacPr; Son; VWP

To a Dark Girl. Gwendolyn B. Bennett. BlSi; ColAP; NAAAL

To a Daughter at Fourteen Forsaking the Violin. Carole Oles. WeW-3

To a Daughter Leaving Home. Linda Pastan. ItWoWo; NIL-7; NIP-4

To a Dead Friend. Agnes Mary Frances Robinson. PoBW

To a Dead Lady. Antonio Cisneros. TCLAP, *tr.* by Maureen Ahern and David Tipton

To a Deceased Friend. Priscilla Jane Thompson. CBWP-2

To a Departed Spirit. Felicia Dorothea Hemans. RWP

To a Distant Friend. William Wordsworth. GTBS-P (Speak!) OBEV (To a Distant Friend.) GTBS-P

To a Dog Injured in the Street. William Carlos Williams. LCAP-2; SAmP

To a Face in a Crowd. Robert Penn Warren. FuPo

To a Fair Lady Playing with a Snake. Edmund Waller. CABP; EBEV; NOSC; PoE

To a Fallen Walnut Tree. Dávid Baróti Szabó. IQMS, *tr.* by Watson Kirkconnell

To a Farmer Who Hung Five Hawks on His Barbed Wire. David Wagoner. NoAM

To a Fat Lady Seen from the Train. Frances Darwin Cornford. FaBoWP; MoBrPo; OBMV; OxBEV; UV; WeW-3

To a Field Mouse. Robert Burns. *See* To a Mouse; On Turning Her up in Her Nest, with the Plough, November, 1785

To a Fish. Leigh Hunt. NBLV; NPeEn; PeLV; SCGP *Fr.* Fish, the Man, and the Spirit, The.

To a Fly, Taken out of a Bowl of Punch. "Peter Pindar." NOEC

To a French Structuralist. David Kirby. BLT

To a Friend. Matthew Arnold. NAEL-5v2; NAEL-6v2; Son

To a Friend. William Lisle Bowles. CenSon; Son

To a Friend. Hartley Coleridge. CenSon (Friendship.) OBEV

To a Friend. Joseph Rodman Drake. APN-1

To a Friend. Ben Jonson. BeJo

To a Friend. Li Po. CrYelRi, *tr.* by Sam Hamill

To a Friend. Boris Leonidovich Pasternak. TCRP, *tr.* by Yakov Hornstein

To a Friend. Charlotte Smith. RWP

To a Friend and Fellow Poet. Hugh MacDiarmid. NePenScot

To a Friend Concerning Several Ladies. William Carlos Williams. VGW

To a Friend, Fearful of Being Forgotten in Absence. Eliza Cobbe, Lady Tuite. PoBW

To a Friend in Love during the Riots. William Parsons. NOEC

To a Friend, Inviting Him to a Meeting upon Promise. William Habington. BeJo *Fr.* Castara.

To a Friend, on Her Examination for the Doctorate in English. James Vincent Cunningham. VGW

To a Friend on her Marriage. Jane West. "Married, poor soul! your empire's over." ECWP

To a Friend's Child. Aliki Barnstone. BoWoP

To a Friend, Using the Same Rhymes of a Peom He Sent Me. Liu Ya-tzu. SuSp, *tr.* by Wu-Chi Liu

To a Friend, Who Gave the Author a Reading Glass. Elizabeth Moody. PoBW

To a Friend Who Sent Me Some Roses. John Keats. CenSon

To a Friend, Who Thinks Sensibility a Misfortune. Anna Seward. CenSon

To a Friend Who Wouldn't Bother to Strain His Noodleboard Because Even So It Is Hard to Go Hunting When Your Rifle Is Blunt and Love Is Soft as an Old Blanket. Jacob Glatshteyn. PFTM-1

To a Friend Whose Work Has Come to Nothing. W. B. Yeats. AWP; InPK-6; MoBrPo; OBMV; OxAEP-2; WoPoe

To a Friend Whose Work Has Come to Triumph. Anne Sexton. InPK-6

To a Friend with a Religious Vocation. Elizabeth Jennings. TOF

To a Gardener. Robert Louis Stevenson. OBGa

To a Gentleman and Lady on the Death of the Lady's Brother and Sister, and a Child of the Name Avis, Aged One Year. Phillis Wheatley. BlSi

To a Gentleman that Courted Several Ladies. *Poets of the Tixall Circle.* EMWP

To a Gentleman, Who Desired Proper Materials for a Monody. *Unknown.* NOEC

To a Gentleman Who Disordered a Lady's Handerchief, and Immediately Cut His Thumb. Elizabeth Teft. ECWP

To a Gentleman Who Invited Me to Go A-Fishing. Elizabeth Moody. ECWP

To a Gentlewoman Objecting to Him His Grey Hairs. Robert Herrick. BeJo; CaPo

To a Golden-Haired Girl in a Louisiana Town. Nicholas Vachel Lindsay. MoAmPo

To a Golden Heart, Worn round His Neck. Goethe. AWP, *tr.* by Margaret Fuller Ossoli

To a Gone Era. Irma McClaurin. BlSi

To a Goose [*or* Gosse]. Robert Southey. CenSon; NOBL; PeLV; Son

To a Gravel Walk. William Mason. OBGa

To a Guest. Vladislav Felitsianovich Khodasevich. TCRP, *tr.* by Michael Frayn

To a Guest. Tu Fu. CrYelRi, *tr.* by Sam Hamill

To A. H. James M. Whitfield. APN-2

To A.H.B. Margaret Witter Fuller. PoBW

To a Haggis. Robert Burns. FaBoVe; NePenScot (Address to a Haggis.) AmFaPo

To a Hedgehog. Samuel Thompson. BIrV

To a Hermit in the Mountains. Hsü Pen. CoBLCP; ColAnChi, *tr.* by Jonathan Chaves

To a Hermit Thrush. Adelaide Crapsey. APT-1

To a Hero Dead at al-Safra. Ibn Unaib Uthatha. WPOW, *tr.* by Bridget Connelly and Deirdre Lashgari

To a Hooligan Girl. Lajos Kassák. IQMS, *tr.* by Michael Kitka

To a Hunchback. Ibn al-Rumi. ArPe, *tr.* by Omar S. Pound

To a Jilt. Martin Donisthorpe Armstrong. FaBoEE

To A. L.; Persuasions [*or* Perswasions] to Love. Thomas Carew. CaPo

To a Lady. John Gay. OBEV

To a Lady. Pope. *See* Epistle [II,] to a Lady[: Of the Characters of Women]

To a Lady. Francisco de Terrazas. BLPSL, *tr.* by Rene de Costa, Rigas Kappatos and Eleni Paidoussi

To a Lady Asking Him How Long He Would Love Her. Sir George Etherege. OBEV

To a Lady Combing Her Hair. Juan de, Count of Villamediana Tassis y Peralta. BLPSL, *tr.* by Rene de Costa, Rigas Kappatos and Eleni Paidoussi

To a Lady Friend. William Henry Davies. MoBrPo

To a Lady in a Garden. Edmund Waller. BeJo; NPeEn

To a Lady Making Love. Lady Mary Wortley Montagu. LW

To a Lady on Her Passion for Old China. John Gay. SCGP

To a Lady on Reading Sherlock "Upon Death." Philip Dormer Stanhope, 4th Earl of Chesterfield. *See* Verses Written in a Lady's Sherlock "Upon Death."

To a Lady on the Death of Her Husband. Phillis Wheatley. TAP

To a Lady on the Rise of Morn. Anne Batten Cristall. RWP

To a Lady's Countenance. Elinor Wylie. NALW

To a Lady: She Refusing to Continue a Dispute with Me, and Leaving Me in the Argument. Matthew Prior. NoP-4

To a Lady That Desired I Would Love Her. Thomas Carew. BASC; BeJo; CaPo; CavPo; MeLP; SCGP

To a Lady That Desired Me I Would Bear My Part with Her in a Song. Richard Lovelace. CaPo

To a Lady That Forbade to Love before Company. Sir John Suckling. CaPo

To a Lady Upon a Looking-Glass Sent. James Shirley. BeJo

To a Lady, Who Commanded Me to Send Her an Account in Verse. Mary Barber.
    "How I succeed, you kindly ask." ECWP

To a Lady, Who Desired Me Not To Be in Love with Her. John, Baron Cutts Cutts. NOSC

To a Lady, Who Was a Great Talker. Elizabeth Moody. PoBW

To a Lady, with a Guitar. Shelley. *See* With a Guitar, to Jane

To a Lady, with a Present of a Fan. Charles Brandling. NOEC

To a Lady with Child that Asked [*or* Ask'd] an Old Shirt. Richard Lovelace. BASC; NOSC

To a Lady[e]. William Dunbar. EBEV; OBEV; OxBS; PeLV

To a Lark in War-Time. Franz Werfel. TrJP, *tr.* by Edith Abercrombie Snow

To a Lily. James Matthew Legaré. APN-2

To a Little Colored Boy. Priscilla Jane Thompson. CBWP-2

To a Little Girl, One Year Old, in a Ruined Fortress. Robert Penn Warren.
    ("And us, and all, the hands and sing: redeem, redeem!") (LL) FuPo
    ("Should rejoice.") (LL) FuPo
    ("Sirocco, shakes, The.") (LL) FuPo
    ("White goose by palm tree, palm ragged, among stones the.") FuPo
    ("World.") (LL) FuPo

To a Little Invisible Being Who Is Expected Soon to Become Visible. Anna Laetitia Barbauld. ECWP; NAEL-6v2; WoRP

To a Living Author. *Unknown.* NBLV

To a Llangollen Rose, the Day after It Had Been Given by Miss Ponsonby. Matilda Barbara Betham-Edwards. CenSon

To a Lock of Hair. Sir Walter Scott. GTBS-P

To a Locomotive in Winter. Walt Whitman. GM; InPK-6; MoAmPo; NAAL-2v1; NAAL-3; NCAP; NoAM; NoP-4; TAP

To a Lofty Beauty, from Her Poor Kinsman. Hartley Coleridge. OxAEP-2

To a Louse [On Seeing One on a Lady's Bonnet at Church]. Robert Burns. FaBoVe; NAEL-5v2; NAEL-6v2; NOBRP; NOEC; NePenScot; OxBS

To a Loved One. Mary Weston Fordham. CBWP-2

To a Loved One of Other Days. Matilda Caroline Edwards. PWR

To a Man Dying on His Feet. William Carlos Williams. APT-1

To a man eating a pear. Please Say Something. Taeko Tomioka. WPOW

To a Man Who is Rob Southland. Nia Francisco. HATNAP

To a Maniac. Amelia Alderson Opie. NOBRP

To a Mathematician. Jan Kochanowski. WoPoe, *tr.* by Jerzy Peterkiewicz and Burns Singer

To a melody of prayer. Hakuni. JDP, *tr.* by Yoel Hoffmann

To a' men living be it kend. Rising of the Session, The. Robert Fergusson. OxBS

To a Military Rifle, 1942. Yvor Winters. MoAmPo

To a Millionaire. Archibald Lampman. NOBC

To a Mistress Dying. Sir William Davenant [*or* D'Avenant]. *See* Lover and Philosopher

To a Moth that Drinketh of the Ripe October. Emily Jane Pfeiffer. ViWPN

To a mountain village. Spring in a Mountain Village. Noin. WoPoe, *tr.* by Steven D. Carter

To a Mouse; On Turning Her up in Her Nest, with the Plough, November, 1785. Robert Burns. BRP; CABP; FaBoVe; HAP; HeIP-4; NAEL-5v2; NAEL-6v2; NOEC; NPeEn; NePenScot; NoP-4; OxAEP-2; OxBEV; OxBS; PoE; SCGP; TFi; UV
    (To a Field Mouse.) GTBS-P

To a Mousse. W. N. Herbert. NeBl

To a Musician. George Wither. SacPr

To a New Daughter-in-Law. *Unknown.* PoToHe

To a New England Poet. Philip Freneau. NAAL-2v1; NAAL-3

To a new world on Tuesday shifts my song. Folgore da San Geminiano [*or* Gimignano]. EaItPo, *tr.* by Dante Gabriel Rossetti

To a Nightingale. William Drummond, of Hawthornden. OWoS

To a Nightingale. Charlotte Smith. CenSon; OxBSo; RWP

To a Noisy Politician. Philip Freneau. TAP

To a Nose. Francisco de Quevedo y Villegas. SpanPo, *tr.* by James Edward Tobin

To a Nosegay in Pancharilla's Breast. Soame Jenyns. ECEV

To a Nun. John Ormond. EBEV; FaBoTw; NoP-4

To a Pair of Legs. Francisco de Terrazas. BLPSL, *tr.* by Rene de Costa, Rigas Kappatos and Eleni Paidoussi

To a Persian Boy in the Bazaar at Smyrna. Bayard Taylor. CAGL

To a Pessimist. Ronald Arbuthnott Knox. OBCoV

To a Piano. Mary Elizabeth Coleridge. OxBSo

To a Plagiarist. Moses Ibn Ezra. TrJP, *tr.* by Solomon Solis-Cohen

To a Poet. Ágnes Nemes Nagy. PoSu, *tr.* by Bruce Berlind

To a Poet a Thousand Years Hence. James Elroy Flecker. MoBrPo; PoRA

To a Poet a Thousand Years Hence. John Heath-Stubbs. OxBC

To a Poet, Who Would Have Me Praise Certain Bad Poets, Imitators of His and Mine. W. B. Yeats. CTC; FaBoEE

To a Poor Old Woman. William Carlos Williams. BLT; ColAP; OBAL; TAP; TTTS

To a Portrait Painter who Desired Him to Sit. Po Chü-i. ChiP, *tr.* by Arthur Waley

To a President. Witter Bynner. OBAL

To a President. Walt Whitman. NAAL-2v1; NAAL-3

To a Pretty Girl. Israel Zangwill. TrJP

To a Print of Queen Victoria. James Keir Baxter. OxBC

To a Proud Beauty. "Ephelia." PEW

To a Publisher. . . Cut-out. Imamu Amiri Baraka. NeAP

To a Pyrotechnist. Chao Meng-fu. CoBLCP; ColAnChi, *tr.* by Jonathan Chaves

To a Querulous Acquaintance. Charlotte Smith. BWW

To a Rabfak Student. Mikhail Arkadyevich [*or* Arkad'evich] Svetlov. TCRP, *tr.* by Daniel Weissbort

To a Randy Old Woman. Horace. EroLit, *tr.* by *Unknown* *Fr.* Epodes.

To a Red-headed Do-good Waitress. Alan Dugan. Son

To a Rejected Sonnet. William Ewart Gladstone. CenSon

To a Reviewer Who Admired My Book. John Ciardi. OBAL

To a Rich Man. Phineas Fletcher. *See* Against a Rich Man Despising Poverty

To a Sad Daughter. Michael Ondaatje. NoAM

To a School-Boy at Eton, Yes and No. Mary Savage. ECWP

To a Schoolboy. *Unknown.* RB, *tr.* by Anne Pennington

To a Sea Eagle. Hugh MacDiarmid. MoBrPo

To a Segar. Samuel Low. OBAL

To a Shade. W. B. Yeats. NAEL-5v2; NAEL-6v2

To a Sick Friend. Hannah Wallis. ECWP

To a Sigh. Mary Robinson. CenSon; RWP

To a Skylark. Shelley. BRP; FHYEP; GTBS-P; HAP; NAEL-5v2; NAEL-6v2; NOBRP; NoP-4; OBEV; OWoS; OxAEP-2; SCGP; TFi
    (Ode to a Skylark.) NOBE

To a Snail. Marianne Craig Moore. APT-1; FaBoMo; FaBoWP; NAAL-2v2; NALW; PoPoPo

To a Snowflake. Francis Thompson. MoBrPo; SacPr

To a soft, oleaginous mutta. (LL) Arthur. Ogden Nash. NoP-4; PeLi

To a Solitary Disciple. William Carlos Williams. VGW

To a Song of Sappho Discovered in Egypt. Leonora Speyer. APT-1

To a Sparrow. William Carlos Williams. OWoS

To a Squirrel at Kyle-Na-No. W. B. Yeats. ChAP

To a Steam Roller. Marianne Craig Moore. APT-1; BoWoP; FaBoMo; MoAmPo; OxBA; VGW
    (Illustration, The.) PoPoPo

To a Stranger. Edward Carpenter. CAGL *Fr.* Towards Democracy.

To a Stranger. Walt Whitman. APN-1; NOBA; SAmP

To a Stranger (At the End of a Caboose). Laura Jensen. GM

To a Swallow. Euenos. GrAn; OBVE, *tr.* by John Peale Bishop

To a Talkative Guest. Po Chü-i. ChiP, *tr.* by Arthur Waley

To a Teacher of French. Donald Davie. OxBC

To a Thesaurus. Franklin Pierce Adams. NBLV

To a Traitor. *Unknown.* WoPoe, *tr.* by Willard Trask

To a Traveler. Lionel Pigot Johnson. MoBrPo

To a Traveler. Su Tung-p'o (Su Shih). OHPC, *tr.* by Kenneth Rexroth

To a Troubled Friend. James Wright (1927–80). Son

To a Very Young Gentleman at a Dancing-School. Elizabeth Singer Rowe. EMWP

To a Very Young Lady. Edmund Waller. SCGP

To a Vine-clad Telegraph Pole. Louis Untermeyer. MoAmPo

To a Violet. Susan Evance. CenSon

To a Wandering Female Singer. Felicia Dorothea Hemans. VWP; ViWPN

To a Wanton. William Habington. NOSC

To a War Correspondent. Star Black. KGB

To a Waterfowl. William Cullen Bryant. APN-1; AWP; ColAP; ITBLP; NAAL-2v1; NAAL-3; NAAL-5; NCAP; NOBA; NoP-4; OWoS; OxBA; PWR; SoSe-8; TAP; TFi

To a Waterfowl. Donald Hall. BodElec; OBAL

To a Western Boy. Walt Whitman. APN-1

To a wild mountain, whose bare summit hides. Fragment Descriptive of the Miseries of War. Charlotte Smith. ECWP

To a Woman. Helen Hay Whitney. PoBW

To a woman that I knew. Her Eyes. John Crowe Ransom. OBAL

To a Woman to a Path. Valentine Penrose. SurWo, tr. by Roland Penrose

To a Worm. Mikha'il Nu'aima [or Nuaymah]. MAP, tr. by Sargon Boulus and Thomas G. Ezzy

To a Young Ass. Samuel Taylor Coleridge. OxAEP-2 Fr. Effusions.

To a Young Girl. W. B. Yeats. EBEV

To a Young Heir. Samuel Johnson. See Short Song of Congratulation [or To a Young Heir], A

To a Young Lady. William Cowper. GTBS-P; SacPr

To a Young Lady, Purposing to Marry a Man of Immoral Character in the Hope of his Reformation. Anna Seward. CenSon

To a Young Lady That Desired a Verse of My Being Servant One Day and Mistress Another. Elizabeth Tipper. EMWP; NOSC Fr. Pilgrim's Viaticum; or, The Destitute, But Not Forlorn.

To a Young Lady, with Some Lampreys. John Gay. CABP; ECEV; NOEC; OBCoV

To a Young Poet. Valery [or Valerii] Yakovlevich [or Iakovlevich] Bryusov [or Briusov]. TCRP, tr. by April FitzLyon

To a Young Poet. Edna St. Vincent Millay. OxBSP

To a Young Widow. Po Chü-i. CrYelRi, tr. by Sam Hamill

To a Young Writer. Yvor Winters. APT-2

To Abbot Min the Compassionate. Tu Fu. CrYelRi, tr. by Sam Hamill

To accept this vale. One Strategy for Loving the World. Mona Van Duyn. ExTi

To Adelhard, Archbishop of Canterbury. Alcuin. MLL, tr. by Helen Waddell

To Adhiambo. Gabriel Okara. PBA
   (Adhiambo.) PBMAP

To after-Times thy Wit. (LL) To the Virginian Voyage. Michael Drayton. AiP; BASC; HAP; NAEL-5v1; NOBE; NOSC; OBEV; SCGP

To Ailsa Rock. John Keats. CenSon

To air the ditty, / And to earth I. (LL) Fancy's Knell. A. E. Housman. FaBoCh; PoRA

To Alchemists. Ben Jonson. BASC

To Alexis in Answer to His Poem Against Fruition. Aphra Behn. LW; NOSC
   (After fruition ne'er to be concerned.) (LL) PEW

To Alfred Gwyer. Joseph Gwyer. VerBaPo

To Algebra God is inclined. Limerick. J. C. B. Date. PeLi

To All Brothers. Sonia Sanchez. BPo

To all my length. (LL) To Earthward. Robert Frost. APT-1; MoAmPo; NOBA; NoAM; NoP-4; OxBA; RaBo; TAP; TRP

To all the lists of Clay! (LL) Choice. Emily Dickinson. NAAL-2v1; NAAL-3

To all things light gives force; God dwells Himself in light. "Angelus Silesius." GePo, tr. by George C. Schoolfield Fr. Cherubical Wanderer, The.

To all things there is an appointed time, and a time to everie purpose under the heaven. Bible, O.T. See To everything there is a season

To All Us Sansei Who Wanted to Be Westside. Amy Uyematsu. GeoHom

To All Virtuous Ladies in General. Aemilia Bassano Lanyer. BASC

To all you ladies now at Bath. Farewell to Bath. Lady Mary Wortley Montagu. WPE

To all you ladies now at land. Song Written at Sea in the First Dutch War (1665), the Night before an Engagement. Charles Sackville, 6th Earl of Dorset. EnLoPo; NOBE; OBEV; OBWP; OxAEP-1

To Allen Ginsberg & Co. Luciana Frezza. CItWP, tr. by Cinzia Sartini Blum and Lara Trubowitz

To allow himself to be properly held. Man Who Closed Shop, The. Stephen Dunn. NIP-4

To Almystrea. Mary Lee, Lady Chudleigh. EMWP

To Almystrea, on her Divine Works. Elizabeth Thomas. ECWP; EMWP

To Althea, from Prison. Richard Lovelace. AWP; BASC; BeJo; CaPo; CavPo; GTBS-P; HAP; ITBLP; MeLP; NAEL-5v1; NAEL-6v1; NAEL-7v1; NIL-7; NOBE; NOSC; NPeEn; NoP-4; OBEV; OxBEV; PBRV; PoE; PoRA; SCGP; TFi

To Amanda Walking in the Garden. N. Hookes. NOSC; OBGa

To Amarantha, That She Would Dishevel[l] Her Hair[e]. Richard Lovelace. BeJo; NIL-7; OBEV
   (Amarantha sweet and fair.) CABP; CavPo; NoP-4
   (Song: To Amarantha, That She Would Dishevel Her Hair.) CABP; CaPo; NOSC; PoE
   (Song.) CavPo
   (To Amarantha, That She Would Dishevel Her Hair.) NoP-4

To America. James Weldon Johnson. APT-1

To Amine. James Clarence Mangan. OBEV

To Amoret. Henry Vaughan. EnLoPo

To Amoret Gone from Him. Henry Vaughan. BeJo; EnLoPo; MeLP

To Amoret, of the Difference 'twixt Him and Other Lovers, and What True Love Is. Henry Vaughan. BeJo

To Amoret, Walking in a Starry Evening. Henry Vaughan. BeJo

To amuse His Royal Majesty he will change water into wine. Žito the Magician. Miroslav Holub. PoSu; WoPoe, tr. by Ian Milner and George Theiner

To Amuse Myself. Li Po. SuSp, tr. by Joseph J. Lee

To Amy. J. Gordon. OBAL

To an admiring Bog! (LL) Emily Dickinson. APN-2; AmFaPo; BoWoP; ChAP; HeIP-4; NALW; NBLV; NOBA; OBCA; OBCoV; OTCP; OxBSP; OxIBACP; PoPoPo; SAmP; TAP; TCAPo; WPE

To an American Painter Departing for Europe. William Cullen Bryant. See To Cole, the Painter, Departing for Europe

To an American Poet Just Dead. Richard Wilbur. HCAP; NBLV

"To an Amiable Child." Babette Deutsch. APT-2

To an Ancient Tune. Chu Tun-ju. CrYelRi, tr. by Sam Hamill

To an Ancient Tune. Unknown. CrYelRi, tr. by Sam Hamill

To an Ancient Tune. Yao K'uan. CrYelRi, tr. by Sam Hamill

To an Angel in the House. John Sparrow. OBCoV

To an Angry Bee. John Clare. CenSon

To an Angry God. X. J. Kennedy. CRP

To an Anti-Semite. Carl Rakosi. APT-2

To an Artful Theatre Manager. Lorenzo Da Ponte. TrJP, tr. by John Mazzinghi Fr. Il Capriccio Dramatico.

To an Artist, to Take Heart. Louise Bogan. PAI; TRP

To an Athlete Dying Young. A. E. Housman. ChAP; HAP; HeIP-4; InPK-6; MoBrPo; NAEL-5v2; NAEL-6v2; NIP-4; NoAM; NoP-4; PoE; PoRA; SCGP; SoSe-8; TFi; TRP; UnPo; WeW-3

To an Author. Philip Freneau. ColAP; NOBA; OxBA

To an Author who Loved Truth More than Fame. Bessie Rayner Parkes. VWP

To an Elderly Virgin. Mael Isu O Brolchain. NOIV, tr. by Thomas Kinsella

To an Enemy. Maxwell Bodenheim. TrJP

To an English Boy: "Beautiful boy, flower fair." Hilary. EroLit, tr. by John Boswell

To an English Boy: "Hail, fair youth, who seeks no bribe." Hilary. CAGL, tr. by John Boswell

To an Ethiopian Child. Diana Helen Melhem. GraLe

To an Exeter City Cocktail Waitress. Jon Veinberg. GeoHom

To an Hour-Glass. John Clare. CenSon

To an Imaginary Father. Wendy Rose. CDW

To an Inconstant One. Sir Robert Aytoun [or Ayton]. OBEV

To an Indian Poet. Patty L. Harjo. VoR

To an Infant. Mary Weston Fordham. CBWP-2

To an Infant Expiring the Second Day of Its Birth. Mehetabel Wright. ECWP; NOEC

To an Intra-Mural Rat. Marianne Craig Moore. APT-1

To an Isle in the Water. W. B. Yeats. TTTS

To An Old Black Woman, Homeless and Indistinct. Gwendolyn Brooks. ESEAA

To an Old Friend. Nadia Hazboun Reimer. PoArWo

To an Old Gentlewoman That Painted Her Face. George Turberville. OxBSP

To an Old Jaundiced Woman. William Carlos Williams. APT-1

To an Old Lady. William Empson. FaBoTw; GTBS-P; NOBE; NoAM; OxAEP-2; OxBEV

To an Old Philosopher in Rome. Wallace Stevens. APT-1; ColAP; EnlH; NOBA; NoAM

To an Old Tune. Hsin Ch'i-chi. OHMPC, tr. by Kenneth Rexroth

To an Old Tune. Lu Kuei Meng. OHMPC, tr. by Kenneth Rexroth

To an Unborn Infant. Isabella Kelly. ECWP

To an Unborn Pauper Child. Thomas Hardy. GTBS-P

To An Undiscerning Critic. Sir Arthur Conan Doyle. OBCoV

To an Unknown Poet. Carolyn Kizer. OPRER

To Ancestry. John Thelwall. CenSon

To-and-Fro of Saint Theresa. Alfonso Reyes. WoPoe, tr. by Samuel Beckett

To Angélique. Heinrich Heine.

"This mad carnival of loving." TrJP

To Anita. Sonia Sanchez. ISC

To Anna Matilda. Robert Merry. NOBRP

To Anne Frank. Rosita Kalina. MirDau, *tr.* by Roberta Gordenstein

To Annie. Mary E. Tucker. CBWP-1

To Another Housewife. Judith Wright. NALW

To Answer Your Question. Bruce Berger. MiVo

To Antenor. Katherine Philips. EMWP

To Anthea. Robert Herrick. CaPo

To Anthea Lying in Bed. Robert Herrick. BeJo

To Anthea, Who May Command Him Anything. Robert Herrick. BASC; CaPo; GTBS-P; NOBE; NOSC; OBEV; OxBEV

To Any Member of My Generation. George Barker. Son

To Any Reader. Robert Louis Stevenson.

"As from the house your mother sees." NePenScot

To any watch they keep? (LL) Neither Out Far Nor In Deep. Robert Frost. APT-1; HAP; NAAL-2v2; NOBA; NoAM; NoP-4; TAP; TRP; WeW-3; WoPoe

To Aphrodite these wreaths. Kallirrhoê: A Dedication. Agathias. GrAn, *tr.* by Dudley Fitts

To Ararat; all men are Noah's sons. (LL) Still, Citizen Sparrow. Richard Wilbur. ColAP; NoAM; TRP

To Archaeanassa, on whose furrow'd brow. On Archaeanassa. Plato. AWP, *tr.* by Thomas Stanley

To Archinus. Callimachus. AWP, *tr.* by F. A. Wright

To Aristius Fuscus. Horace. OBVE *Fr.* Odes.

To Aristogoras. Meleager. CAGL, *tr.* by Daryl Hine

To Arno of Salzburg. Alcuin. MLL, *tr.* by Helen Waddell

To Artemisia.—'Tis to her we sing. Mary Leapor. PEW *Fr.* Essay on Friendship.

To Arthur de Noé Walker. Walter Savage Landor. OxBSo

To ascend? How? Song of a Man in the Dark. "Adonis" [*or* "Adunis"]. VCWP, *tr.* by Samuel Hazo

To Ashtaroth and Bel. Saul [*or* Shaul] Tchernichowsky [*or* Tchernichovsky]. TrJP, *tr.* by L. V. Snowman

To ask the hard question is simple. Question, The. W. H. Auden. OxAEP-2

To Aspasia. Susanna Highmore Duncombe. PoBW

To Astarte. *Unknown.* GrAn, *tr.* by Guy Davenport

To Atlas in the Attic. Julie Agoos. YaYoPo

To Aunt Rose. Allen Ginsberg. CLPP; ColAP; NAAL-2v2; NoAM; PAI; PmAP; PoE; TaR; VGW

To Aurelius. Catullus. CAGL, *tr.* by Eugene O'Connor

To Aurelius and Furius. Catullus. CAGL, *tr.* by Eugene O'Connor

To Aurora. Sir William Alexander, Earl of Stirling. *See* Aurora

To Ausonius. Paulinus of Nola. CAGL, *tr.* by Jack Lindsay

To Austria. Erika Mitterer. AuPH, *tr.* by Lowell A. Bangerter

To Autumn. William Blake. NAEL-5v2; NAEL-6v2

To Autumn. John Keats. AWP; ClHu; EBEV; FHYEP; HAP; HeIP-4; ITBLP; InPK-6; MakPoe; NAEL-5v2; NAEL-6v2; NAWM-7v2; NIL-7; NiP-4; NOBE; NOBRP; NPeEn; OBEV; OxAEP-2; OxBEV; PAI; PoE; RB; RaBo; SCGP; SCV; SoSe-8; TFi; TRP; UnPo; WeW-3

(Ode to Autumn.) GTBS-P

(Season of mists and mellow fruitfulness!) CABP; NoP-4; PoPoPo

To avoid matrimonial disasters. Limerick. Martin Fagg. PeLi

To B.C. Sir John Suckling. CaPo

To B. P. Aleksandr Semionovich Kushner. TCRusP, *tr.* by Daniel Weissbort

To B.R. Haydon, with a Sonnet Written on Seeing the Elgin Marbles. John Keats. CenSon

To Babylon. Mother Goose. *See* How many miles to Babylon?

To banish the less, I find my chief relief. (LL) Prison in Windsor Castle. Henry Howard, Earl of Surrey. NoSic; SCGP

To banish the less I find my chief relief. (LL) Henry Howard, Earl of Surrey. NAEL-5v1; NAEL-6v1; NAEL-7v1 *Fr.* Windsor Castle.

To Barba. Edward May. FaBoEE

To Bary Jade. Charles Follen Adams. OBAL

To Bayard Taylor. Sidney Lanier. NCAP

To be. Orange Tree, The. Ben Belitt. APT-2

To Be. Marvin Bell. BodElec

To be a Jew in the Twentieth Century. Muriel Rukeyser. NALW; TaR; TrJP *Fr.* Letter to the Front.

To be a mistress. Kiyoko Tsuda. BoWoP

To be a Negro in a day like this. At the Closed Gate of Justice. James David Corrothers. NAAAL

To be a nurse is. To Be a Nurse. A. H. Lawrence. PoToHe

To be a Pilgrim. (LL) John Bunyan. EBEV; NOCV; OxBEV *Fr.* Pilgrim's Progress, The.

To Be a Pilgrim. Robert Conquest. OxBC

To be a poet and not know the trade. Sanctity. Patrick Kavanagh. BIrV; NOIV; NoP-4

To be a poet is to be vanquished. Ars Poetica. Victor Van Vriesland. TrJP, *tr.* by Adriaan J. Barnouw

To Be a Slave of Intensity. Kabir. RaBo, *tr.* by Robert Bly

To be a stranger in a strange land. Thinking of My Brother in Shantung on the Ninth Day of the Ninth Moon. Wang Wei. TAL

To be a whore, despite of grace. Madrigal. Charles Cotton. FaBoEE

To be a woman. To Be a Woman. Shakuntala Hawoldar. HAWP

To be able to see every side of every question. Edgar Lee Masters. APT-1; FaBoEE; NOBA; OBSV; OxBA; PoE *Fr.* Spoon River Anthology.

To be alone in a strange place in spring. Child, The. Judith Wright. BMAP

To be always carrying. Immigrants. Debra Kang Dean. NAPBL

To be an orphan. Orphan, The. *Unknown.* ChiP, *tr.* by Arthur Waley

To be announced. Nicolás Guillén. PFTM-1 *Fr.* Daily Daily, The.

2 B BLK. Val Ferdinand. NBV

To be blessed, throat, eye and knucklebone. (LL) Truth the Dead Know, The. Anne Sexton. ColAP; LCAP-2; MoAmPo; NoAM; NoP-4; TAP; VCAP

To be born! (LL) Eclogue: "Men talking, The." George Oppen. APT-2; FTOS

To be born is to want—is it that simple? Hated Rats, The. Nguyen Binh Khiem. WoPoe, *tr.* by Nguyen Ngoc Bich

To be but to be a crow with claws vicious enough. Barbarian. Mohammed Khaïr-Eddine. PFTM-2, *tr.* by Pierre Joris

To be carried. If I Yes. Olga Broumas. GifTon

To Be Carved on a Stone at Thoor Ballylee. W. B. Yeats. FaBoEE; NoAM; NoP-4

To be caught / out of the dullness of self by such alien thought? (LL) Down from the Country. John Blight. BMAP; CBAP

To Be Engraven on a Dial. Samuel Sewall. SCAP

To be famous is not in good taste. Boris Leonidovich Pasternak. TCRP

To be famous isn't decent, there's. To Be Famous Isn't Decent. Boris Leonidovich Pasternak. TCRusP, *tr.* by Kathy Lewis and Bob Perelman

To be in a place for spring and not have lived its winter. Vincent O'Sullivan. PeNZ *Fr.* Brother Jonathan, Brother Kafka.

To be in any form, what is that? Walt Whitman. CAGL *Fr.* Song of Myself.

To Be in Love. Gwendolyn Brooks. GT

To be in my life, it is your duty. Guest, The. Sheenagh Pugh. TCAWP

To be in the book. To figure in the book of questions, to be part of it. Edmond Jabès. PFTM-1, *tr.* by Rosmarie Waldrop *Fr.* Book of Questions, The.

To be Long Gone . . . (LL) Long Gone. Sterling Allen Brown. APT-2; BPo; NAAAL

To be long silent was my thought. *Unknown.* GePo

To be lost evermore in the main. (LL) Tennyson. EBNV; OBWP *Fr.* Revenge, The.

To be mistaken in old age and not to be afraid. Aleksey [*or* Aleksei] Petrovich Tsvetkov. TCRP

To be my own Messiah to the. Rows of Cold Trees, The. Yvor Winters. NOBA

To Be of Use. Marge Piercy. WWork

To be or not to be. Brian G. Gilmore. SpirFl

To be / or not to be / That is not the question. I Want to Be Bad. Ray Henderson. ReLy

To be or not to be! That is the question. Byron. OBCoV *Fr.* Don Juan.

To be or not to be, that is the question. Arthur's Anthology of English Poetry. Laurence David Lerner. PeLV

To be, or not to be, that is the question. William Shakespeare. OxAEP-1; OxBEV; TreFP; UV *Fr.* Hamlet.

To be pleased and to please. (LL) Why Do You Feel Differently. Gertrude Stein. ItWoWo; PFTM-1

To be put on the train and kissed and given my ticket. Observation Car. Alec Derwent Hope. NoAM

To Be Read above the Castle-Gate, When His Princely Highness Rode in to His Marriage Bed. Simon Dach. GePo, *tr.* by George C. Schoolfield

To Be Recited to Flossie on Her Birthday. William Carlos Williams. VGW

To Be Said at the Seder. Karl Wolfskehl. TrJP, *tr.* by Ernst Morowitz and Carol North Valhope

To Be Said Over and Over Again. György Petri. VCWP, *tr.* by George Gömöri and Clive Wilmer

To be seventeen again. To Be Seventeen Again. Violeta Parra. TANSG, *tr.* by Shaun Griffin and Emma Sepúlveda-Pulvirenti

To be simply like thin flesh without skin. Declaration of Hate. Efraín Huerta. TCLAP, *tr.* by Todd Dampier

To be so held by brittleness, shapeliness. Soul Says. Jorie Graham. PoPoPo

To be soldiers together and allies. Franco Buffoni. ItPo, *tr.* by Gayle Ridinger

To be stabbed on a lonely hill. (LL) Prophets for a New Day. Margaret Abigail Walker. BPo; NAAAL

To Be Sung on the Fourth of July. Wyatt Prunty. RA

To Be Sung on the Water. Louise Bogan. VGW

To be ten and skinny. Exodus. Anita Endrezze. CDW

To be thought an outcast in my beloved country. Inna L'vovna Lisnyanskaya [or Lisnianskaia]. ItGoST, tr. by Judith Hemschemeyer

To be undone! (LL) His Reward. Sir Thomas Wyatt. InPK-6; NoSic

To Be with the Dead. Manuel González Prada. SpanPo, tr. by Kate Flores

To be with the dead. To Be with the Dead. Manuel González Prada. SpanPo, tr. by Kate Flores

To be woo'd and married at a'! (LL) Song: Woo'd and married and a' Joanna Baillie. NAEL-6v2; NoP-4

To be Young, Gifted, and Black. Weldon J., Jr. Irvine. ISC

To be your beadsman now that was your knight. (LL) George Peele. NIP-4; NPeEn; NoP-4; OxBEV; SCGP; TFi Fr. Polyhymnia.

To be your Valentine. (LL) William Shakespeare. EnLoPo; NoSic Fr. Hamlet.

To bear, to nurse, to rear. Jean Ingelow. TreFP Fr. Songs of Seven.

To bear your life you need accompaniment. In Your Own Sweet Time. Alane Rollings. IllVoic

To Beat or Not to Beat. Nina Iskrenko. TCRP, tr. by John High and Katya Olmsted

To beat real iron out, to work the bellows. (LL) Forge, The. Seamus Heaney. NAEL-5v2; NAEL-6v2; NoP-4; OxAEP-2

To become a man, it's little to be born. Mikhail Davidovich Lvov. TCRP

To become a tree. Antonio Porta. ItPo, tr. by Gayle Ridinger Fr. Essences.

To Become an Archer. José Garcia Villa. KaS

To become an archer. To Become an Archer. José Garcia Villa. KaS

"To bed! To bed!" / Says Sleepy-head. Come, Let's to Bed. Unknown. ReMoGo

To Beethoven. Sidney Lanier. NCAP

To Begin. Fran Winant. BrRo

To begin I cut fine silk of Ch'i. Song of Regret. Pan Chieh-yû. CoBCP, tr. by Burton Watson

To begin with something not already caught. How Late Desire Looks. Katrina Roberts. NAPBL

To begin with something not already caught. How Late Desire Looks. Katrina Roberts. NAPBL

To believe it. (LL) To a Dog Injured in the Street. William Carlos Williams. LCAP-2; SAmP

To Belinda. Goethe. STV, tr. by John Frederick Nims

To Belshazzar. Byron. ChIV-1

To Ben, at the Lake. Cilla McQueen. PeNZ

To Ben Jonson. Thomas Carew. BASC; BeJo; CaPo; CavPo; NAEL-5v1; NAEL-6v1; NAEL-7v1; NOSC

To Beth On Her Forty-Second Birthday. Jane Chambers. PoBW

To better the condition of humanity. Our Club Work. Mrs. Henry Linden. CBWP-4

To Black Women. Gwendolyn Brooks. IllVoic

To Blossoms. Robert Herrick. BeJo; CaPo; GTBS-P; NAEL-5v1; NAEL-6v1; NOSC; OBEV; SCGP; TreFP

To Boccaccio. Thomas Russell. OxBSo

To borrow from the song: In Spain. Long Live the Potato: Viva la Papa! Angela de Hoyos. SpudSo

To braid the locks of the dark. Night Hair. Raquel Chalfi. DTA, tr. by Karen Alkalay-Gut

To brave and to know the unknown. Unknown, The. John Davidson. MoBrPo

To break earth's sleep at all? (LL) Futility. Wilfred Owen. FaBoMo; GTBS-P; HarvBoo; MoBrPo; NAEL-5v2; NAEL-6v2; NPeEn; NoAM; NoP-4; OBWP; PAI; PeFWW; RB; TCAWP

To breakfast on a light-blue tablecloth, smelling of milk. Gyula Krúdy. IQMS, tr. by John Lukacs

To breathe and stretch one's arms again. Slow Song for Mark Rothko. John Taggart. PFTM-2

To Breisach, Taken by That Supremely Celebrated Hero, Bernhard, Duke of Saxony. Georg Rudolph Weckherlin. GePo, tr. by George C. Schoolfield

To bring one chrysanthemum. Beside a Chrysanthemum. So Chong-Ju. VCWP, tr. by David R. McCann

To Bring the Dead to Life. Robert Graves. MoBrPo

To bring the honey to the wind. (LL) Tragic Mary Queen of Scots, The. "Michael \QUOTE/Field. EnLoPo; LW; OBMV

To bring them to my brother King Iamye. (LL) Sir Andrew Barton. Unknown. ESPB; OxBB

To bring them to my brother King Iamye. (LL) Sir Andrew Bart[t]on. Unknown. ESPB; OxBB

To broaden into boundless day. (LL) Tennyson. EBVV; FHYEP; HAP; NAEL-6v2; NAWM-7v2; PeECV; TOF Fr. In Memoriam A. H. H.

To Brooklyn Bridge. Hart Crane. AiP; AmFaPo; ChIV-1; ClHu; ColAP; FaBoA; HarvBoo; MakPoe; MoAmPo; NAAL-5; NOBA; NoP-4; OxBA; PoE; PoPoPo; TFi; TRP Fr. Bridge, The.

To build something human with it. (LL) Night Vision. Lucille Clifton. BodElec; GifTon; UnSA

To Buonaparte. Unknown. NOBRP

To burn in this immense torpidity. (LL) Mummy Invokes His Soul, The. "Michael Field." NPeEn; OxBSo; VWP

To burst into fulfillment's desolate attic. (LL) Deceptions. Philip Larkin. GTBS-P; HarvBoo; OxAEP-2

To Caelia. Richard Duke. NOSC

To Caelia. Unknown. FaBoEE

To call, in the harsh morning, sleep-stupid faces through the daily gate. (LL) Birmingham. Louis MacNeice. MoBrPo; OxAEP-2

To call it a wet dream would be too barren. Nocturne, Aubade, and Vesper. James Wright (1927–80). BodElec

To calm the anxious breast, to close the streaming eye. (LL) To Sleep. Charlotte Smith. CenSon; NAEL-6v2; RWP; Son; WPE

To Captain Hungry. Ben Jonson. FaBoWar

To Carlos Drummond de Andrade. Joao Cabral de Melo Neto. TCLAP, tr. by Guy Pacitti

To Carry the Child. Stevie Smith. NoAM

To Castara, Being to Take a Journey. William Habington. NOSC

To Castara ("Do[e] not Their profane orgies hear[e]."). William Habington. BeJo Fr. Castara.

To Castara ("Give me a heart where no impure"). William Habington. BeJo Fr. Castara.

To Castara, upon an Embrace. William Habington. BeJo; NPeEn Fr. Castara.

To Castara, upon Beautie. William Habington. BeJo Fr. Castara.

To catch the spirit in its wayward flight. Self-Mastery. Henrietta Cordelia Ray. CBWP-3; SWaP

To Cattraeth's vale in glitt'ring row. Aneirin. OBVE Fr. Gododdin, The.

To Catulinus That He Cannot Write Him an Epithalamium Because of the Enemy Hosts. Apollinaris Sidonius. MLL, tr. by Helen Waddell

To cause accord or to ag[g]re[e]. Sir Thomas Wyatt. SCGP

To caves the sleeping maid. (LL) William Blake. FHYEP; NOBRP Fr. Songs of Experience.

To celebrate the need of comrades. (LL) In Paths Untrodden. Walt Whitman. APN-1; CAGL; NOBA; OxBA; TCAPo

To Celia. Ben Jonson. See Song: To Celia

To Celia. Ben Jonson. See Volpone

To Celia. Sir Charles Sedley. See Song to Celia

To Celia Pleading Want of Merit. Thomas Stanley. MeLP; NOSC

(To Celia Pleading Want of Merit.) MeLP; NOSC

To Celia, upon Love's Ubiquity. Thomas Carew. CavPo

To Celinda. Elizabeth Singer Rowe. BASC; PEW

To Censorious Courtling. Ben Jonson. NOSC

To Certain Critics. Countee Cullen. BPo

To Ch'eng Fei-t'ao. Wu Chia-chi. CoBLCP, tr. by Jonathan Chaves

To Charles Burney. Frances [or Fanny], Mme D'Arblay Burney. ECWP

To Charles Diodati. John Milton. OxBSo, tr. by William Cowper

To Charles Roux, of Switzerland. Nathaniel Parker Willis. APN-1

To Charlotte Cushman. Eliza Cook. VWP

To Charlotte Pulteney. Ambrose Philips. See To Miss Charlotte Pulteney in Her Mother's Arms

To Charlotte von Stein. Goethe. STV, tr. by John Frederick Nims

To Chatterton. John Keats. CenSon

To "Chick." Frank Horne. BPo Fr. Letters [or Notes] Found near a Suicide.

To Chin Nung. Cheng Hsieh. CoBLCP, tr. by Jonathan Chaves

To Chloe. Martin Joseph Prandstetter. AuPH, tr. by Lowell A. Bangerter

To Chloe, Who Wished Herself Young Enough for Me. William Cartwright. BeJo; NOSC; OxAEP-1

(There are two births: The one when light.) PoToHe

(To Chloe, who for His Sake Wished Herself Younger.) OBEV

To Chloris. William Drummond, of Hawthornden. OxBSP

To Chloris. Sir Charles Sedley. See Mulberry Garden, The

To Chloris, upon a Favour Received. Edmund Waller. OxBSP

To Christ. William Alabaster. NoSic; OxBSo

To Christ Crucified. Miguel de Guevara. SpanPo, tr. by Ian Fletcher

To Christ Our Lord. Galway Kinnell. HeIP-4; TwCP

To Christina Rossetti. "Michael Field." VWP

To Christina Rossetti. Dora Greenwell. VWP

To Christopher North. Tennyson. FaBoEE; PeLV

To circle their wagons? (LL) Why Do So Few Blacks Study Creative Writing? Cornelius Eady. GT; LTA

To civilize with graver notes our wits again. (LL) Ode to Master [or Mr.] Anthony Stafford to Hasten Him into the Country, An. Thomas Randolph. BASC; BeJo; NOBE; NOSC; OBEV

To claim, at a dead party, to have spotted a grackle. Lying. Richard Wilbur. DiPo; HCAP; MakPoe; PeVV

To claim my attention and consume me. (LL) When My Grandmother Said "Pussy." Carole Bernstein. AmPoNex; UnSA

To clarify and allow. Reason, The. Eric Pankey. GI

To clearer light, vouchsaf'd to me! (LL) William Cowper. ChIV-2; TrCP *Fr.* Olney Hymns.

To cleave a running stream with a sword. Written in Behalf of My Wife. Li Po. SuSp, *tr.* by Joseph J. Lee

To Clemena. Elizabeth Thomas. PoBW

To Clement Edmonds, on His *Caesar's Commentaries* Observed, and Translated. Ben Jonson. NOSC

To Clements' Ferry. Josephine D. Henderson Heard. CBWP-4; SWaP

To Cleon's Eyes. Martha Sansom. ECWP

To Cleone. Elizabeth Singer Rowe. PoBW

To climb and descend steps. Walker in Prague. Vitězslau Nezval. AF, *tr.* by Ewald Osers

To climb these stairs again, bearing a tray. Kaleidoscope, The. Douglas Dunn. OxBSo

To climb[e] to thee. (LL) Pearl, The. Matth. 13:45. George Herbert. BASC; ChIV-2; EBEV; ESCV; FHYEP; FSCP; GeHe; HAP; NOCV; NOSC; OxBEV

To Clio, from Rome. John Dyer. NOEC

To Cloe. George Granville [*or* Grenville], Baron Lansdowne. FaBoEE; NBLV; OxBEV

(Cloe.) OxBSP

To Cloe. Hildebrand Jacob. NOEC

To Cloe. Martial. AWP; NBLV, *tr.* by Thomas Moore

To Cloris. Sir Charles Sedley. BoLoP

To Close. William Carlos Williams. SAmP

To clothe the fiery thought. Ralph Waldo Emerson. OxBA; OxBSP; Spl; TCAPo *Fr.* Quatrains.

To Coelia. Charles Cotton. OBEV

To Cole, the Painter, Departing for Europe. William Cullen Bryant. AiP; ColAP; TAP; TCAPo

(Sonnet—To an American Painter Departing for Europe.) NAAL-2v1; NAAL-3

(To an American Painter Departing for Europe.) APN-1

To Colebrooke Dale. Anna Seward. ECWP

To Colindra. Elizabeth Thomas. LW

To Colman Returning. *Unknown.* BIrV, *tr.* by Helen Waddell

To Columbus. "Rubén Dario." TTY, *tr.* by Lysander Kemp

To come back from the sweet South, to the North. Italia, Io Ti Saluto! Christina Georgina Rossetti. VWP; WPE

To come vor evermwore. (LL) Wife A-Lost, The. William Barnes. BoLoP; EBVV; EnLoPo; HAP; OBEV; SCGP

To Conscripts. Alice Thompson Meynell. SacPr

To consecrate the flicker, not the flame. (LL) George Crabbe. Edwin Arlington Robinson. APN-2; MoAmPo; NAAL-2v2; NOBA; NoP-4; OxBA; TAP

To Cordelia. Joseph Stansbury. NOBC

To Cotton Mather, from a Quaker. Thomas Maule. TCAPo

To course across more kindly waters now. Dante Alighieri. NAWM-7v1, *tr.* by Allen Mandelbaum *Fr.* Divine Comedy, The (Mandelbaum Translation).

To cover your shame. Mr. White Discoverer. Amelia Blossom Pegram. HAWP

To covet fetters, though they golden bee. (LL) Edmund Spenser. NAEL-5v1; NAEL-6v1; PAI; Son *Fr.* Amoretti.

To Critic[k]s. Robert Herrick. CaPo

To crown her head, and bosom[e] fill. (LL) Gallery, The. Andrew Marvell. BASC; ESCV; MeLP; NoP-4; PBRV; PoE

To Crown[e] It. Robert Herrick. CaPo

To cry or see one cry is rather embarrassing to see: between crying and. Water of Tears, The. Francis Ponge. AF, *tr.* by Beth Archer

To cultivate in ev'ry noble mind. To the Rev. Dr. Thomas Amory. Phillis Wheatley. SacPr

To Cupid. Joanna Baillie. LW

To cure myself of wanting Cuban songs. My Voice. Rafael Campo. AmPoNex

To cure the mind's wrong bias, Spleen. Matthew Green. ECEV; NPeEn *Fr.* Spleen, The.

To curse is not the office given me. What I Believe. Alma Johanna Koenig. AuPH, *tr.* by Lowell A. Bangerter

To Cynthia. Sir Francis Kynaston. NOSC

To Cynthia, on Concealment of Her Beauty. Sir Francis Kynaston. MeLP; NOBE

To Cynthia on Her Being an Incendiary. Sir Francis Kynaston. HAP

To Cyriack Skinner. John Milton. GTBS-P; OBEV; Son

(Sonnet.) NOSC; OxAEP-1

(Cyriack, Whose Grandsire.) NoP-4

To D'Annunzio: Lines from the Sea. Robert Malise Bowyer Nichols. OBMV

To Daffodils [*or* Daffadills]. Robert Herrick. AWP; BASC; BeJo; CaPo; FaBoCh; GTBS-P; NOBE; NOSC; NoP-4; OBEV; OxAEP-1; PoRA; SCGP; TFi; TTTS; TreFP; UnPo

To Daisies, Not to Shut So Soon[e]. Robert Herrick. BeJo; CaPo; OBEV; OxBSP

To Dame—Augustin nun on her curious gum-work. Jane Barker. EMWP

To Damon. To Inquire of Him if He Cou'd Tell Me by the Style, Who Writ Me a Copy of Verses that Came to Me in an Unknown Hand. Aphra Behn. EMWP

To Dante. Vittorio Alfieri. AWP

To Dante Alighieri. Guido Cavalcanti. AWP; EaItPo, *tr.* by Dante Gabriel Rossetti

To Dante Alighieri (He Commends the Work of Dante's Life). Giovanni Quirino. AWP; EaItPo, *tr.* by Dante Gabriel Rossetti

To Dante Alighieri: He Conceives of Some Compensation in Death. Cino da Pistoia. AWP; EaItPo, *tr.* by Dante Gabriel Rossetti

To Dante Alighieri: He Interprets Dante Alighieri's Dream. Dante da Maiano. AWP; EaItPo, *tr.* by Dante Gabriel Rossetti

To Dante Alighieri: He Interprets Dante's Dream. Cino da Pistoia. AWP; EaItPo, *tr.* by Dante Gabriel Rossetti

To Dante Alighieri: He Mistrusts the Love of Lapo Gianni. Guido Cavalcanti. AWP; EaItPo, *tr.* by Dante Gabriel Rossetti

To Dante Alighieri: He Reports, in a Feigned Vision, the Successful Issue of Lapo Gianni's Love. Guido Cavalcanti. AWP, *tr.* by Dante Gabriel Rossetti

To Dante in Paradise, after Fiammetta's Death. Giovanni Boccaccio. AWP; EaItPo, *tr.* by Dante Gabriel Rossetti *Fr.* Sonnets.

To Dante [*or* Sonnet: Guido Cavalcanti to Dante Alighieri]. Guido Cavalcanti. AWP; OBVE, *tr.* by Percy Bysshe Shelley

To Daphne and Virginia. William Carlos Williams. APT-1

To David, about His Education. Howard Nemerov. HCAP

To-Day. Lessie M. Drown. PWR

To-day. On Christmas Day to My Heart. Clement Paman. ChrPo; NOSC

To-day a rude brief recitative. Song for All Seas, All Ships. Walt Whitman. APN-1

To-Day a Shepherd. Saint Theresa [*or* Teresa] of Avila. AWP, *tr.* by Arthur Symons

To-day, all day, I rode upon the Down. Wilfrid Scawen Blunt. EnLoPo *Fr.* Love Sonnets of Proteus, The.

To-Day I Leave Mrs. Brown's Lodgings. Sir Walter Scott. FaBoEE

To-day / Is the feast day of Saint Anne. Madwoman of Cork, The. Patrick Galvin. BiHa

To Day it self's too Late, the Wise liv'd Yesterday. (LL) Procrastination. Martial. AWP; FaBoEE; OBVE, *tr.* by Abraham Cowley

To-day's house makes to-morrow's road. Survival, The. Edmund Charles Blunden. OBEV; OBMV

To-day the lot caved in upon me. Page from a Diary. Desmond O'Grady. NoAM

To-day there have been lovely things. Vision. May Thielgaard Watts. LW

To-day they laid him in the earth's cold colour. For Angus MacLeod. Iain Crichton Smith. OxBS

To Dean-bourn, a Rude River in Devon, by Which Sometimes He Lived. Robert Herrick. BeJo; CaPo; PBRV

(Dean Bourn, a Rude River in Devon, by Which Sometimes He Lived.) CavPo

To Dear Daniel. Samuel Greenberg. APT-1

To Death. Johann Wilhelm Ludwig Gleim. GePo, *tr.* by George C. Schoolfield

To Death. Oliver St. John Gogarty. FaBoEE; OBMV

To Death. Robert Herrick. BeJo

To Death. Mary Tighe. CenSon

To Death. Anne Finch, Countess of Winchilsea. NoP-4

To Death, from the Genie of My Poetry. Delmira Agustini. TANSG, *tr.* by Mark McCaffrey

To Death, of His Lady. François Villon. AWP, *tr.* by Dante Gabriel Rossetti

To Delia. Samuel Daniel.

"And yet I cannot reprehend the flight." OBEV

"Beauty, sweet love, is like the morning dew." NOBE; NoSic; OBEV

Beauty, Time and Love. NOBE; OBEV

"But love whilst that thou mayst be loved again." NoP-4; NoSic

Care-Charmer Sleep. GTBS-P; NAEL-5v1; NAEL-7v1; NIP-4; NOBE; NPeEn; NoSic; OxAEP-1; OxBEV; OxBSo; SCGP; Son; TFi

("Care-charmer Sleep, son of the sable Night") GSo

"Care-charmer Sleep[e], son[ne] of the sable night." GTBS-P; NAEL-5v1; NAEL-7v1; NIP-4; NOBE; NPeEn; NoSic; OxAEP-1; OxBEV; OxBSo; SCGP; Son; TFi

("Fair is my Love and cruel as she's fair") GSo

(46.) CABP; NAEL-6v1

Half-blown Rose, The. NoSic; SCGP

"I must not grieve my love, whose eyes would read." OBEV

("Let others sing of Knights and Paladines") GSo

("Let others sing of knights and paladins.") CABP; NoP-4

"Let others sing of knights and paladins [or palladines]." NAEL-7v1; NOBE; NoSic; OBEV; SCGP

("Let others sing of Knights and Palladines;") PBRV

"Look, Delia, how we [e]steem the half-blown rose." NoSic; SCGP

("Look, Delia, How we 'steem the half-blown rose.") NoP-4

Most Unloving One, The. OBEV

"My spotless love hovers, with purest wings." OBEV

(Sonnet 33: 'When men shall find thy flower') AEP; NAEL-6v1; NAEL-7v1

(45.) CABP; NAEL-6v1

Sonnet: "Beauty, sweet love, is like the morning dew" NOBE; NoSic; OBEV

Sonnet: "Let others sing of knights and paladin[e]s" NAEL-7v1; NOBE; NoSic; OBEV; SCGP

Sonnet: "When men shall find thy flower, thy glory, pass" NAEL-5v1; NOBE; NoSic; OBEV; SCGP; Son

"Thou canst not die whilst any zeal abound." NoSic; Son

"Time, cruel time, come and subdue that brow." SCGP

"Unto the boundless Ocean of thy beauty." NoP-4

"When men shall find thy flower [or flow'r], thy glory, pass." NAEL-5v1; NOBE; NoSic; OBEV; SCGP; Son

("When men shall find thy flower, thy glory pass.") AEP; NoP-4

("When winter snowes upon thy sable haires.") PBRV

"When winter snows upon thy sable hairs." CTC; NoSic; Son

Why Should I Sing in Verse. Son

To Della Crusca. The Pen. Hannah Cowley. NOBRP

To demolish it. All Splendor on Earth. Karin Kiwus. BoWoP, tr. by Almut McAuley

To Dennis Brutus. Kofi Awoonor. HBAPE

To depart while seated or standing is all one. Koho Kennichi. JDP, tr. by Yoel Hoffmann

To Dependence. Charlotte Smith. CenSon

To Derek Mahon. Michael Longley. See Letter to Derek Mahon

To desire. There is no guilt in love. (LL) Numbers, Letters. Imamu Amiri Baraka. BPo; NOBA; PFTM-2

To Detraction I Present My Poesie. John Marston. NoSic Fr. Scourge of Villainy [or Villanie], The.

To Dian, Queen of Earth, and Heaven, and Hell. (LL) To Homer. John Keats. EBEV; NAEL-5v2; NAEL-6v2; NoP-4; Son

To Diana. Elisaveta Kulman. ARWW, tr. by Catriona Kelly

To Dianeme. Robert Herrick. BASC; BeJo; CaPo; GTBS-P; NOBE; NOSC; OBEV

(Show me thy feet, show me thy legs, thy thighs.) CavPo

To die. Not About Death. Bulat Shalvovich Okudzhava. RusPo, tr. by Robert Arthur Douglas Ford

To Die. Sándor Weöres. IQMS, tr. by Edwin Morgan

To die along the gales of eve. (LL) Song of a Spirit. Ann Radcliffe. ECWP; RWP

To die and know it. This is the Black Widow, death. (LL) Mr. Edwards and the Spider. Robert Lowell. CoAP; ColAP; FaBoMo; HarvBoo; HeIP-4; NAAL-2v2; NAAL-5; NOBA; NoP-4; TFi; TwCP

To die be given us, or attain! Matthew Arnold. FHYEP

To die, but far away. Roberto Juarroz. VCWP Fr. Ninth Vertical Poetry.

To die like thirsting larks. Agony. Giuseppe Ungaretti. PeFWW, tr. by Charles Tomlinson

To Diodorus, Dorotheus, Callicrates et al. Meleager. CAGL, tr. by Daryl Hine

To dip, alas, into some unseemlier world. (LL) Old Mansion. John Crowe Ransom. FuPo; HeIP-4; NOBA; OxBA

To disappear. (LL) Trip to Four or Five Towns, A. John Logan. CoAP; NNaP

To Disgrace of Price. (LL) Emily Dickinson. APN-2; NAAL-2v1; NAAL-3; NALW; NCAP; NoP-4; TCAPo

To Disraeli. Shirley Brooks. NOBL

To distant men, who must go there, or die. (LL) Sea-Shore. Ralph Waldo Emerson. APN-1; ColAP; OxBA

To distant service my heart is well accustomed. Silver Spoon, The. Po Chü-i. ChiP, tr. by Arthur Waley

To dive for the nimbus on the sea-floor. Nimbus. Douglas Le Pan. MoCV

To Dives. Joseph Hilaire Pierre Belloc. ChIV-2; OBSV

To do all I'd want to do. (LL) Lover's Prize, A. Beatrice [or Beatritz or Beatriz], Countess de Die [or Dia]. EroLit; NAWM-7v1, tr. by Peter Dronke

To do as Adam did. Ronald Johnson. FTOS Fr. Ark.

To do celestial chores. (LL) Countee Cullen. APT-2; HeIP-4; InPK-6; NIL-7; NIP-4; OBAL; SSLK; TAP; TRP Fr. Four Epitaphs.

To do less would be nothing but dishonesty. (LL) Peter. Marianne Craig Moore. APT-1; NAAL-2v2; NoP-4; OxBA

To do something very common, in my own way. (LL) Valediction Forbidding Mourning, A. Adrienne Rich. NAAL-2v2; NAAL-5; NoAM; NoP-4

To do the wronged [or wrong'd] Corinna right for thee. (LL) Imperfect Enjoyment, The. John Wilmot, 2d Earl of Rochester. BASC; BoLoP; NAEL-7v1

To do with love. (LL) This Room and Everything in It. Li-Young Lee. IllVoic; NAAL-5; OpBo

To do without what blood remained these wounds. (LL) A Terre. Wilfred Owen. FaBoWar; OxBTC; PAI; PeFWW; PoWW

To—do without you altogether. (LL) To Cloe. Martial. AWP; NBLV, tr. by Thomas Moore

To doat upon me ever! (LL) Unknown. GTBS-P; OBEV; OxBSP

To Dr. Arbuthnot. Pope. See Epistle to Dr. Arbuthnot

To Doctor Bale. Barnabe Googe. NoSic

To Doctor Empiric[k]. Ben Jonson. FaBoEE; NoP-4; WoPoeH

To Dr. Jonathan Swift. Pope. OxAEP-1 Fr. Dunciad, The.

To Dr. Moore, in Anser to a Poetical Epistle Written by Him in Wales. Helen Maria Williams. ECWP; WoRP

To Dr. Swift on His Birthday, 30th November 1721. Esther Johnson. EnLoPo

To doggerel now I turn my pen. Letter to Miss E.B. at Bath. Mary Savage. ECWP

To Don Juan Baz. Mary E. Tucker. CBWP-1

To Dora W[ordsworth]. Charles Lamb. OxBSo

To Dorothy. Marvin Bell. InvLad; VCAP

To Dr. F. B. on His Book of Chess[e]. Richard Lovelace. CaPo

To draw down Gods, and lift the soul to Heaven! (LL) To the Fragment of a Statue of Hercules, Commonly Called the Torso. Samuel Rogers. CenSon; GS

To draw no envy, Shakespeare, on thy name. Ben Jonson. BASC; BeJo; HAP; HeIP-4; NAEL-6v1; NAEL-7v1; NOSC; NoP-4; OxAEP-1; PoPoPo

To Dream Again. William Shakespeare. OxAEP-1; RB Fr. Tempest, The.

To Dreams. Mary Julia Young. CenSon

To drift with every passion till my soul. Hélas! Oscar Wilde. CAGL; MoBrPo; NAEL-5v2; NAEL-6v2; Son

To Drink. Jane Hirshfield. PasH

To Drink. Philippe Soupault. SurPaPo, tr. by Mary Ann Caws and Patricia Terry

To drink and frolic with the water-borne moon. (LL) Autumn Cove. Li Po. CoBCP; ColAnChi; TTTS, tr. by Burton Watson

To drive Paul out of any lumber camp. Paul's Wife. Robert Frost. EBNV

To drown the ancient sorrows. Mountain Drinking Song. Li Po. CrYelRi, tr. by Sam Hamill

To dwell a weeping hermit there! (LL) How Sleep the Brave. William Collins. CABP; NOBE; OBEV; OxAEP-1; TFi

To Dwell Together in Unity. Bible, O.T. See Psalms

To E. Fitzgerald. Tennyson. NOBVV; NPeEn

To E. S. Salomon. Ambrose Bierce. CBCWP

To Each His Own. Ray Evans. ReLy

To Earthward. Robert Frost. APT-1; MoAmPo; NOBA; NoAM; NoP-4; OxBA; RaBo; TAP; TRP

To ease his rumbling stomach our Kriton sniffs. On Kriton the Miser. Lucilius. GrAn, tr. by Dudley Fitts

To Easter Island and the presences. Introduction: My Themes. Pablo Neruda. GifTon, tr. by William O'Daly

To eat mutton cold and cut blocks with a razor. (LL) Oliver Goldsmith. FaBoEE; NOEC; NPeEn; OxBEV Fr. Retaliation.

To eat the world's due, by the grave and thee. (LL) William Shakespeare. CTC; HeIP-4; NAEL-6v1; NAEL-7v1 Fr. Sonnets.

To Echo. Anna Maria Jones. CenSon

To Edom. Heinrich Heine. TrJP

To Edward Alleyn. Ben Jonson. NOSC

To Edward FitzGerald. Robert Browning. NAEL-5v2; NAEL-6v2; OxBSP

To Edward Lawrence. John Milton. See To Mr. Lawrence

To Edward Thomas. Alun Lewis. PoWW

To Electra. Robert Herrick. CaPo; OBEV

To Elinda. Richard Lovelace. CavPo

(If in me anger, or disdain.) CavPo

(To Elinda.) CavPo

((To voice your worth enough) strook dumb.) (LL) CavPo

To Elizabeth Barrett Browning. Bessie Rayner Parkes. VWP

To Elizabeth Barrett Browning, in 1851. Dora Greenwell. PoBW; VWP

To Elizabeth Barrett Browning, in 1861. Dora Greenwell. PoBW; VWP

To Elizabeth, Countess of Rutland. Ben Jonson. BeJo; NoP-4

To Elsie. William Carlos Williams. APT-1; AmFaPo; NAAL-2v2; NAAL-5; NOBA; OxBA; PoE; PoPoPo

To embalm thy father's corse; What? will he die? (LL) John Donne. ESCV; FSCP; NoSic *Fr.* Elegies.

To embrace you forever. (LL) Kenneth Rexroth. APSN; APT-2 *Fr.* Love Poems of Marichiko, The.

To emerge from a woman is to become separate. To Emerge from a Woman Is to Become Separate. Homero [*or* Umberto] Aridjis. TCLAP, *tr. by* W. S. Merwin

To Emily Dickinson. Hart Crane. ColAP; NIL-7; NIP-4; NOBA; NoAM; NoP-4; Son; TAP

To Emily Dickinson. Yvor Winters. Son

To Emma, Extempore; Hyaena, off Gambia, June 4, 1779. Edward Thompson. NOEC

To End Her Fear. John Freeman. OBMV

To English Connoisseurs. William Blake. OxBoLi

To Enjoy the Horror. Fawziyya Abu Khalid. PoArWo, *tr. by* Farouk Mustafa

To Epicles. Antipater of Thessalonica. GrAn, *tr. by* Tony Harrison

To Eros. Wilfred Owen. CAGL

To Eros. Alfonsina Storni. TANSG, *tr. by* Mark McCaffrey

To err is human, I heard you say. Was That the Human Thing to Do? Joe Young. ReLy

To Etna's scorching sands my Phaon flies! Sappho's Conjectures. Mary Robinson. CenSon; RWP

To Eva. Jacqueline Osherow. TaR

To Evening. William Collins. *See* Ode to Evening

To Everlasting Oblivion. John Marston. NoSic; SCGP *Fr.* Scourge of Villainy [*or* Villanie], The.

To every heart which the sweet pain doth move. Dante Alighieri. AWP; EaltPo, *tr. by* Dante Gabriel Rossetti *Fr.* La Vita Nuova.

To every hill crest. Wanderer's Night Song. Goethe. WoPoe, *tr. by* Peter Viereck

To every man. Treehouse, The. James A. Emanuel. BPo

To every woman a happy ending. (LL) Barbie Doll. Marge Piercy. NIL-7; NIP-4

To Everyone. Velemir [*or* Viktor Vladimirovich] Khlebnikov. TCRusP, *tr. by* Kathy Lewis and Bob Perelman

To Everything There Is a Season. Bible, *O.T.* NAWM-5v1; OBVE *Fr.* Ecclesiastes.

To Evoke Posterity. Robert Graves. HarvBoo; NPeEn

To excuse oneself from table. It Being Forbidden. Martha Rhodes. KGB; NAPBL

To experiment on my heart? (LL) Kenneth Rexroth. APSN; APT-2 *Fr.* Love Poems of Marichiko, The.

To explain the nature of fishes in craft of verse. *Unknown.* EBEV, *tr. by* Gavin Bone *Fr.* Physiologus.

To explore the nature of rain I opened the door because inside the workings of language clear vision is impossible. Rosmarie Waldrop. PmAP *Fr.* Inserting the Mirror.

To extol[l] thee. (LL) Praise (2). George Herbert. ChIV-1; ESCV

To F——. Edgar Allan Poe. APN-1

To F. C. Mortimer Collins. NOBVV

To fair Fidele's grassy tomb. Fidele, A. William Collins. NOEC

To fall, like an apple, no mind. In the Emptied Rest Home. Bella [*or* Izabella] Akhatovna Akhmadulina. BoWoP, *tr. by* Olga Carlisle and Jean Valentine

To Fancy. Martha Hanson. CenSon

To Fancy. Charlotte Smith. OxBSo

To Fannie. Mary E. Tucker. CBWP-1

To Fanny. John Keats. *See* I Cry Your Mercy, Pity, Love—Ay, Love!

To Fanny Brawne. John Keats. *See* This Living Hand, Now Warm and Capable

To Fat Boy, the Bomb. Henry Braun. BodElec

To Father. Yury [*or* Iurii] Kuznetsov. TCRP, *tr. by* Sarah W. Bliumis

To Father. Mary E. Tucker. CBWP-1

To Favonius. Edmund Bolton. NoSic

To fear himself, and love all human kind. (LL) Hymn to Intellectual Beauty. Shelley. FHYEP; HAP; HeIP-4; NAEL-5v2; NAEL-6v2; NOBRP; NoP-4; PoE; TOF

To feed ez they hev fed me. (LL) James Russell Lowell. APN-1; NCAP *Fr.* Biglow Papers, The.

To feed on that, which to disused [*or* disus'd] tast[e]s seem[e]s tough. (LL) John Donne. FSCP; MeLP; OxAEP-1; PBRV *Fr.* Elegies.

To feel and speak the astonishing beauty of things—earth, stone and. Beauty of Things, The. Robinson Jeffers. APT-1

To fend for the bony goats and the crying children. (LL) Village, The. Marina Gashe. HAWP; PBA

To Ferencz Liszt. Mihály Vörösmarty. IQMS, *tr. by* Alan Dixon

To fertilize some other ground. (LL) Floating Island at Hawkshead. Dorothy Wordsworth. NPeEn; PEW

To fiddle-faddle in a minor key. (LL) Ambrose Bierce. APN-2; OBAL *Fr.* Devil's Dictionary, The.

To fight aloud, is very brave. Emily Dickinson. WPE

To fill the catalogue of human woes. (LL) Ode: "I hate that drum's discordant sound." John Scott of Amwell. NIP-4; NOEC; OxAEP-1; PAI

To fill the paste that's a-kneading. (LL) Robert Herrick. BeJo; OBCP

To fill up half the *Orb* of Round *Eternity.* (LL) Muse, The. Abraham Cowley. CABP; PBRV

To finally know. Onitsura. SoOfWa, *tr. by* Sam Hamill

To finally pull the plug on the word machine. Poem for Writers, A. Lee Harwood. Oth

To find a style that made writing impossible. (LL) Shifting Colors. Robert Lowell. BodElec; HCAP

To find beyond death / Bridgeport, Ohio. (LL) In Response to a Rumor that the Oldest Whorehouse in Wheeling, West Virginia, Has Been Condemned. James Wright (1927–80). CoAP; NNaP; NoAM; VCAP

To find out the temperature, she tosses a cup of water into the air. Alakanak Break-Up. Mei-Mei Berssenbrugge. PmAP

To find that he is not alone. (LL) Poem for Easter. Robert Kelly. ErotSp; VGW

To find the Western path. Morning. William Blake. FaBoCh; WoPoe

To find they have flown away? (LL) Wild Swans at Coole, The. W. B. Yeats. HeIP-4; MoBrPo; NAEL-5v2; NAEL-6v2; NPeEn; NoAM; NoP-4; OWoS; PoPoPo; SCGP; SoSe-8; TFi; UnPo

To find[e] God. Robert Herrick. BeJo; InvLi; NoP-4

To find[e] out *death* but missest *life* at hand. (LL) Vanity [*or* Vanitie] (1). George Herbert. BASC; FSCP; GeHe; NOSC; NoP-4

To Fine Lady Would-Be. Ben Jonson. FaBoEE; NOSC; NoP-4; OxBSP

To Flaxman. William Blake. FaBoEE; OxBoLi

To flee from memory. Emily Dickinson. FaBoEE

To fling my arms wide. Dream Variation[s]. Langston Hughes. APT-2; HAP; ISC; ITBLP; NAAAL; NAAL-2v2; NOBA; NoP-4; SAmP; SSLK

To float in the space between. (LL) Idea of Ancestry, The. Etheridge Knight. AF; BPo; CoAmPo; ESEAA; ISC; NAAAL; NIP-4; NNaP; PBCAP; RaBo

To float.—The swimmer floats, the lover sleeps. (LL) Swimmer. Robert Francis. APT-2; WeW-3

To Flood Stage Again. James Wright (1927–80). NOBA

To Flossie. William Carlos Williams. SAmP

To flourish amid the incessant hell. Small Kulak Landowner. Innokenty Fiodorovich Annensky. TCRP, *tr. by* Daniel Weissbort and Lubov Yakovleva

To fly high hardly fills the belly. Cicada. Li Shang-yin. SuSp, *tr. by* Eugene Eoyang

To fly off, a ripe pear in a storm. Definition of the Soul. Boris Leonidovich Pasternak. TrJP, *tr. by* Babette Deutsch

To fold up silks, may wrap up wit. (LL) Fancy, A. Thomas Carew. BeJo; NOSC

To follow, to seek, to be with her dear dead son. (LL) Come Up from the Fields Father. Walt Whitman. APN-1; CBCWP; FaBoWar; HHAm; MoAmPo; OBWP; OxBA; SAmP; UnPo

To Fool or Knave. Ben Jonson. FaBoEE; NoP-4

To Ford Madox Ford in Heaven. William Carlos Williams. ColAP; NOBA

To forget. Isabel Meyrelles. SurWo, *tr. by* Jean R. Longland

To Forget Me. Theodore Weiss. CoAP

To Forget the Image. Michel Deguy. PFTM-2, *tr. by* Clayton Eshleman

To Forget? Lőrinc Szabó. IQMS, *tr. by* Watson Kirkconnell *Fr.* Cricket Music.

To forgive Enemies H[ayley] does pretend. On Hayley. William Blake. FaBoEE

To Fortune. Robert Herrick. CavPo; OxBSP

To Fortune. James Thomson. GTBS-P

To frame her cloudy prison for the soul! (LL) Autumn. Thomas Hood. OBEV; OxAEP-2

To Francis Beaumont. Ben Jonson. BeJo

To Francis Jammes. Robert Bridges. NPeEn; OxBSo

To Frankfort I on *Schobbas* came. Heinrich Heine. TrJP, *tr. by* Emma Lazarus *Fr.* Tannhäuser.

To Frederick V, by the Grace of God . . . Bathsua Pell Makin. EMWP

To free the ball the chief now turns his mind. Thomas Mathison. NOEC *Fr.* Goff; an Heroi-comical Poem, The.

To Freedom. Joseph Hucks. CenSon

To Freedom. Ágnes Nemes Nagy. PoSu, *tr. by* Bruce Berlind

To freight cars in the air. William Carlos Williams. InPK-6 *Fr.* Descent of Winter, The.

To freighted ships[,] baffled in wind and blast. (LL) "H. D.". APT-1; MoAmPo; NOBA; TAP *Fr.* Let Zeus Record.

To Friends Behind a Frontier. Tomas Tranströmer. WoPoe, *tr. by* Robin Fulton

To Friends Who Have Also Considered Suicide. Phyllis Webb. NOBC

To Friendship. Charlotte Smith. RWP

To Frighten a Storm. Gladys Cardiff. CDW

To G. *Unknown*. EroLit, *tr. by* John Boswell

To G. H. B. James Bayard Taylor. Son

To G., her singular rose. To G. *Unknown*. EroLit, *tr. by* John Boswell

To gallop in grand review. Red Guard. Maksimilian Aleksandrovich Voloshin. TCRP, *tr. by* Albert C. Todd

To gallop off to town post-haste. Friar Lubin. Clément Marot. AWP, *tr. by* Henry Wadsworth Longfellow

To gather flowers Sappha went. Apron of Flowers, The. Robert Herrick. CaPo

To gather Paradise. (LL) Emily Dickinson. APN-2; EnlH; HeIP-4; NALW; NAWM-7v2; NCAP; NOBA; NoAM; OxBA; TCAPo

To gaze with envy on their gloomy rest. (LL) Pressed by the Moon, Mute Arbitress of Tides. Charlotte Smith. CenSon; NALW

To gem the vanquished heart he scorned to save. (LL) To the Muses. Mary Robinson. CenSon; RWP

To Generall Cromwell. "Eliza." EMWP

To Genevieve Taggard Who Called Me Traitor in a Poem. Max Eastman. APT-1

To gentle, pleasant strains. Ted Berrigan. BodElec

To George Romney, Esq. William Cowper. OxBSo

(Romney! expert infallible to trace.) CenSon

To George Sand: A Desire. Elizabeth Barrett Browning. BoWoP; NAEL-5v2; NAEL-6v2; NALW; PoBW; VWP

To George Sand: A Recognition. Elizabeth Barrett Browning. BoWoP; NAEL-5v2; NAEL-6v2; NALW; PEW; PoBW; VWP

To George Sand on her Interview with Elizabeth Barrett Browning. Isa Blagden. VWP

To Germany. Charles Hamilton Sorley. MoBrPo

To Germany. Georg Rudolph Weckherlin. GePo, *tr. by* George C. Schoolfield

To Geron. Hildebrand Jacob. NOEC

To get a fix on it. What Is Happening Now? Hubert Witheford. PeNZ

To get betimes in Boston town I rose this morning early. Boston Ballad [1854], A. Walt Whitman. OBAL

To Get Clear. J. P. Ward. AngWePo

To get into it / As it lies. Shirt. Charles Simic. HCAP

To get out of this and go back home! Return, The. T'ao Ch'ien [*or* T'ao Yuan-ming]. ColAnChi, *tr. by* J. R. Hightower

To get recruits for Pain, I use. Cupid. Bernard O'Dowd. NOBAu

To Giovan Battista Buoninsegni. Angelo [*or* Andrea] Poliziano. CAGL, *tr. by* James J. Wilhelm *Fr.* Greek Epigrams.

To give a cup of water; yet its draught. 'Tis a Little Thing. Sir Thomas N. Talfourd. TreFP

To give employment to the artisan. (LL) Lord Finchley. Joseph Hilaire Pierre Belloc. FaBoEE; NBLV; NOBL; NoAM; OxAEP-2; OxBoLi; PeLV

To give it away, give it up, before they take it from us. Montezuma. Diane Di Prima. BB

To give me its bright plumes, they shot a jay. Flaw, A. "Michael Field." VWP; ViWPN

To Give One's Life. Mary Carolyn Davies. PoToHe

To give one's life through eighty years is harder. To Give One's Life. Mary Carolyn Davies. PoToHe

To give the people a break. Why God Invented the Cold. Catie Rosemurgy. AmPoNex

To give to romantic passersby. (LL) Li Po. CrYelRi; ErotSp, *tr. by* Sam Hamill *Fr.* Women of Yueh.

To give up everything. Huck Finn at Ninety, Dying in a Chicago Boarding House Room. James Schevill. TAP

To give us comfort through the lonely dark. (LL) Douglass. Paul Laurence Dunbar. CBCWP; GSo; NAAAL; Son

To glad the heart and save from harm. (LL) Lament of the Flowers, The. Jones Very. APN-1; ColAP; NOBA; OxBA

To Glaukos, and to Nereus. Lucianus [*or* Lucian]. GrAn

To Gluttony and Guzzling, that fastidious gourmet. Leonidas of Tarentum. HePo *Fr.* Epigrams.

To go back where we came from. (LL) Belle Isle, 1949. Philip Levine. ColAP; VCAP

To go home and wear shorts forever. Dream of Wearing Shorts Forever, The. Les A. Murray. EmeKit

To Go Through Life Is to Walk Across a Field. S. J. Marks. BodElec

To Go to Lvov. Adam Zagajewski. AmFaPo, *tr. by* Renata Gorcynski

To go to Lvov. Which station. To Go to Lvov. Adam Zagajewski. AmFaPo, *tr. by* Renata Gorcynski

To Go with Shih K'o's Painting of an Old Man Tasting Vinegar. Huang T'ing-chien. CoBCP; ColAnChi, *tr. by* Burton Watson

To go with the old grey Widow-maker! (LL) Rudyard Kipling. HAP; HarvBoo; PoRA; RACG *Fr.* Puck of Pook's Hill.

To God. Ivor Gurney. OxBEV

To God. Robert Herrick. CavPo; ChIV-2; SacPr

To God alone, the only donour. Francis Daniel Pastorius. SCAP

To God: an Anthem, Sung in the Chapel at White-Hall, Before the King. Robert Herrick. ChIV-1

To God be the glory, great things he hath done! Fanny Crosby. SacPr

To God Our Strength Shout Joyfully. Henry Ainsworth. AH

To God the highest glory. Song of the Angels. Lizelia Augusta Jenkins Moorer. CBWP-3

To God the Holy Ghost. Henry Constable. NoSic

To God the praise be. Sufi, The. Kahlil Gibran. GraLe, *tr. by* Andrew Ghareeb

To God: to illuminate all men. Beginning with Skid Road. Psalm III. Allen Ginsberg. ChIV-1

To goldenhaired Phoibos whom Leto bore. Sappho. SaLy, *tr. by* Diane Rayor

To Grandmother on Her Going. Gail Tremblay. HATNAP

To grass it comes. Shikaku. JDP, *tr. by* Yoel Hoffmann

To grass, or leaf, or fruit, or wall. Snail, The. Vincent Bourne. NPeEn; OBVE, *tr. by* William Cowper

To Greet a Letter-Carrier. William Carlos Williams. OBAL; SAmP

To greet you. You will understand. (LL) To a Poet a Thousand Years Hence. James Elroy Flecker. MoBrPo; PoRA

To Grimold, Abbot of St. Gall. Hrabanus Maurus. CAGL, *tr. by* Helen Waddell

To Groves. Robert Herrick. CaPo

To H. John Wieners. FTOS

To ———: "Had I a man's fair form, then might my sighs." John Keats. CenSon; OxAEP-2

To Hampstead. Leigh Hunt. CenSon

To hang all old strange things, let his wife beware. (LL) Antiquary. John Donne. EBEV; NOSC

To hang his pants on while he slept. (LL) Museum Piece. Richard Wilbur. FaBoMo; InPK-6; NIL-7; NIP-4; TAP; TRP

To happiest end address. (LL) In Pilgrim Life Our Rest. Edwin Sandys. AH; ChIV-1

To have been a little ill. Convalescence. Noël Coward. TTTS

To have been held down in a park. Rimbaud Having a Bath. Robert Adamson. BMAP

To have been loved once by someone—surely. When the Sun Went Down. John Ashbery. NAAL-2v2

To have been one. Aspects of Eve. Linda Pastan. CRP

To Have Done with the Judgment of God. Antonin Artaud.
  "I learned yesterday." PFTM-2, *tr. by* Clayton Eshleman and Norman Glass

To have escaped Hitler and come to this. To the Parents of a Childhood Friend, a Suicide. Judith Baumel. TaR

To have found two women with natures like this! (LL) Marrying Again. Mei Yao Ch'en. CoBCP; ColAnChi, *tr. by* Burton Watson

To have it out or not? that is the question. "C. A. W." UV

To have known him, to have loved him. Monody. Herman Melville. APN-2; NAAL-2v1; NAAL-3; NoP-4; OxBSP; PoE; PoPoPo; TCAPo

To have lived [*or* liv'd] eminent in a degree. Upon the Death of My Ever Desired Friend Doctor [*or* Dr] Donne Dean of Paul's. Henry King, Bishop of Chichester. BASC

To have reached. Tiger Lily. Alfred Kreymborg. APT-1

To have / red mouth and green shanks. Moorhen. William Logan. DiPo

To have seen you exactly, once. Art of Translation, The. Adrienne Rich. BodElec

To have to go to bed by day? (LL) Bed in Summer. Robert Louis Stevenson. BRP; NBLV; OTCP

To have white bouquets. Pearl. Irène Hamoir. SurWo, *tr. by* Myrna Bell Rochester

To Have without Holding. Marge Piercy. NIL-7; NIP-4

To have you at home when all have gone. Mother. Beryl Philp-Carmichael (Yungha-Dhu). IBA

To hawks we're a woodland insect. Complicated Shadows. Stephen Corey. PasH

To Haydn. Thomas Holcroft. NOEC

To heal you Hieronymus I had brought you. Bear's Blood. Ileana Malancioui. BoWoP, *tr. by* Stavros Deligiorgis

To hear a dripping water tap in a house. Betweens. Norman McCaig. SPE

To hear all night the goods trains coming and leaving. (LL) Spilt Milk. Sarah Maguire. EmeKit; LW; MFPA

To hear the unlucky wife of Bicci cough. Dante Alighieri. EaItPo, *tr. by* Dante Gabriel Rossetti

To hear with eyes belongs to love's find wit. (LL) William Shakespeare. NoSic; Son *Fr.* Sonnets.

To Heaven. Robert Herrick. ChIV-2; HAP; InvLi; NAEL-5v1; NAEL-6v1; NAEL-7v1; NOCV; NOSC; NPeEn; SCGP; SacPr; TRP; UnPo

To Heaven. Ben Jonson. BASC; BeJo; ChIV-2; HAP; InvLi; NAEL-5v1; NAEL-6v1; NAEL-7v1; NOCV; NOSC; NPeEn; SCGP; SacPr; TRP; UnPo

To Helen. Edgar Allan Poe. APN-1; AWP; BRP; BoLoP; ClHu; ColAP;

HAP; HeIP-4; NAAL-2v1; NAAL-3; NAAL-5; NIP-4; NOBA; NOBE; NoP-4; OBEV; OxBA; PoE; PoPoPo; PoRA; TAP; TCAPo; TFi; WeW-3

To Helen. Winthrop Mackworth Praed. NOBVV

To Helen in a Huff. Nathaniel Parker Willis. OBAL

To Helen of Troy (N.Y.). Peter Viereck. WeW-3

To Helene. George Darley. NOBRP

To Hell and Back, with Cake. Safiya Henderson-Holmes. UnSA

To hell, my love, with you! (LL) Indian Summer. Dorothy Parker. NIL-7; NIP-4

To Hell with Commonsense. Patrick Kavanagh. FaBoTw

To Hell with It. Frank O'Hara. NeAP

To hell with the wind! Nampo Jomyo. JDP, tr. by Yoel Hoffmann

"To hell with ye!" says she. (LL) Brewer's Man, The. Leonard Alfred George Strong. OBCoV; PeLV

To Henry Church. Wallace Stevens. ColAP; NOBA Fr. Notes toward a Supreme Fiction.

To Henry Constable and Henry Keir. Alexander Montgomerie. OxBS

To Henry Darnley, King of Scots. George Buchanan. NePenScot, tr. by Robert Crawford

To Henry James. Robert Louis Stevenson. OBCoV

To Henry Wright of Mobberley, Esq. on Buying the Picture of Father Malebranche. John Byrom. NOEC

To Her Far Away. Nikolaus Lenau. AuPH, tr. by Alexander Gode

To Her Father, with Some Verses. Anne Bradstreet. NAAL-3; NAAL-5; NALW

To her friends, said the Bright one, in chatter. Limerick. Arthur Buller. PeLi

To her gardener, a lady named Liliom. Limerick. Unknown. PeLi

To Her Husband, on New Year's Day 1651. Gertrude Aston Thimelby. EMWP

To Her in Absence; a Ship. Thomas Carew. CaPo

To her let us garlands bring. (LL) William Shakespeare. NoSic; SCGP Fr. Two Gentlemen of Verona, The.

To Her Love. Edward May. FaBoEE

To Her Lover's Complaint. Jane Barker. NPeEn; OxBSP

To Her Modest Mirth-Making Friend, Mr Robert Dover. Sibella Cole Dover. EMWP

To Her of Whom They Dream. Paul Éluard. AF, tr. by Lloyd Alexander

To Her Sea-faring Lover. Unknown. OBEV

To herald in another year. January. Henrietta Cordelia Ray. CBWP-3

To Hermes. Alfred Corn. CAGL; WiU

To Hersa. Forceythe Willson. APN-2

To hide her ordure, claws the cat. Quarrelsome Bishop, A. Walter Savage Landor. FaBoEE

To Hilda Dancing. John Bingham Morton. OBCoV

To him are opening Paradise. (LL) Thomas Gray. GTBS-P; NOEC Fr. Ode on the Pleasure Arising from Vicissitude.

To him who in the love of Nature holds. William Cullen Bryant. APN-1; AWP; BRP; ColAP; NAAL-2v1; NAAL-3; NAAL-5; NCAP; NOBA; OBEV; OxBA; PWR; TAP; TCAPo; TFi

To Him Who Is Feared. Eleazar ben Kalir. TrJP, tr. by Lady Katie Magnus

To Himself. Catullus. AWP, tr. by William Ellery Leonard

To Himself. Paul Fleming. GePo, tr. by George C. Schoolfield

To Himself. Andreas Gryphius. GePo, tr. by George C. Schoolfield

To Himself. Giacomo Leopardi. NAWM-7v2, tr. by Ottavio M. Casale

To His Book. Robert Herrick. OxBSP

To His Book's End. Robert Herrick. NAEL-6v1; NAEL-7v1

To his book's end this last line he'd have placed. To His Book's End. Robert Herrick. CaPo; NAEL-5v1

To His Book[e]. Robert Herrick. BASC; CaPo; NOSC

To His Book[e]. Robert Herrick. NOSC

To His Book[e]. Martial. AWP; OBVE, tr. by Robert Herrick

To His Books. Edmund Spenser. NAEL-6v1; NAEL-7v1 Fr. Shepheardes [or Shepeards or Shepherd's] Calender, The.

To His Books. Henry Vaughan. BASC

To his bride said a numbskull named Clarence. Limerick. Unknown. PeLi

To his Brother Hsing-chien. Po Chü-i. ChiP, tr. by Arthur Waley

To his club-footed child said Lord Stipple. Limerick. Edward Gorey. OBCoV; PeLi

To His Conscience. Robert Herrick. BeJo; ChIV-1; NAEL-5v1

To his cottage again. (LL) Despairing Lover, The. William Walsh. FaBoCh; NBLV; NOBL; OxBoLi; PeLV

To His Coy Love, A Canzonet. Michael Drayton. NOSC; PBRV

To His Coy Mistress. Sir Robert Aytoun [or Ayton]. OBEV

To His Coy Mistress. Andrew Marvell. AWP; AmFaPo; BASC; BoLoP; CABP; ClHu; EBEV; ESCV; EnLoPo; EroLit; ErotSp; FHYEP; FSCP; GeHe; HAP; HeIP-4; InPkK-6; MeLP; NAEL-5v1; NAEL-6v1; NAEL-7v1; NIL-7; NIP-4; NOBE; NOSC; NPeEn; NoP-4; OBEV; OxAEP-1; OxBEV; PBRV; PoE; PoPoPo; PoRA; SCGP; SCV; TFi; TRP; UV; WoPoe

To His Darrest Freind. John Steward of Baldynneis [or Stewart of Baldynnis]. OxBS

To His Dead Body. Siegfried Sassoon. NoAM

To His Dying Brother, Master William Herrick. Robert Herrick. CaPo; CavPo; NOSC

To His Ever-Loving God. Robert Herrick. OxBEV

To His Excellency General Washington. Phillis Wheatley. NAAAL; NAAL-2v1; NAAL-3; NAAL-5; WPE

To His Excellency Joseph Dudley. John Saffin. SCAP

To his extreme annoyance, tempted him. (LL) On Lady Poltagrue, A Public Peril. Joseph Hilaire Pierre Belloc. MoBrPo; OBCoV

To His False Mistress. Catullus. OxBSP, tr. by William Walsh Fr. Carmina.

To His Father on Praising the Honest Life of the Peasant. Parvin E'tesami. WPOW, tr. by Deirdre Lashgari

To His Forsaken Mistress. Sir Robert Aytoun [or Ayton]. OBEV

To His Friend. George Turberville. AEP; CTC

(To His Friend.) AEP; CTC

To His Friend in Absence. Walafrid Strabo. CAGL, tr. by Helen Waddell

To His Friend in Elysium. Joachim Du Bellay. AWP, tr. by Andrew Lang

To His Friend Master R.L., In Praise of Music and Poetry. Richard Barnfield [or Barnefield]. Son

To His Friend, on the Untunable Times. Robert Herrick. CaPo

To His Friend P. of Courting, Traveling, Dicing, and Tennis. George Turberville. NoSic

To his genius victims fall. (LL) Namby-Pamby; or, A Panegyric on the New Versification. Henry Carey. NOEC; OBSV

To His Honored Friend Thomas Stanley Esquire, Upon His Elegant Poems. James Shirley. BeJo

To His Honoured and Most Ingenious Friend Mr. Charles Cotton. Robert Herrick. CaPo; NOSC

To His Importunate Mistress. Peter De Vries. NBLV; NIL-7; NIP-4

To His Importunate Mistress. Paul Griffin. UV

To His Inconstant Mistress. Thomas Carew. See To My Inconstant Mistress [or Mistris]

To his kennel in the dark. (LL) Hunchback in the Park, The. Dylan Thomas. AngWePo; EBEV; FaBoTw; MoBrPo; NAEL-5v2; NAEL-6v2; NoAM; NoP-4; OxBEV; TCAWP; TwCP

To His Kinsman, Master Thomas Herrick, Who Desired to Be in His Book. Robert Herrick. CaPo

To His Kinswoman, Mrs. Penelope Wheeler. Robert Herrick. CaPo

To His Lady. Henry VIII, King of England. CTC; EBEV; NoSic

To His Lady Selvaggia Vergiolesi; Likening His Love to a Search for Gold. Cino da Pistoia. AWP; EaItPo, tr. by Dante Gabriel Rossetti

To His Love. Ivor Gurney. MakPoe; NAEL-5v2; NPeEn; OBWP; PeFWW; PoWW

To His Love. William Shakespeare. See Sonnets

To His Love. Unknown. NoP-4

To his Love that sent him a Ring wherein was gravde, / Let Reason rule. George Turberville. PBRV

(Let Reason rule the harts that she hath wonne.) (LL) PBRV

(To his Love that sent him a Ring wherein was gravde, / Let Reason rule.) PBRV

To His Love When He Had Obtained Her. Sir Walter Ralegh. NoSic

To His Lovely Mistresses. Robert Herrick. CTC; CaPo

To His Lute. William Drummond, of Hawthornden. GTBS-P; NOSC; SCGP; Son

("My lute, be as thou wert when thou didst grow") GSo

To His Maistres [or Mistress]. Alexander Montgomerie. OxBS

To His Mistress. Abraham Cowley. NOSC; OxAEP-1 Fr. Sylva.

To His Mistress. John Wilmot, 2d Earl of Rochester. OBEV

To His Mistress. James Shirley. BeJo

To His Mistress Desiring to Travel with Him as His Page. John Donne. See Elegies

To His Mistress Going to Bed. John Donne. BASC; BoLoP; FSCP; NAEL-6v1; NAEL-7v1; NoP-4; NoSic; PBRV; PoE Fr. Elegies.

To His Mistress in Absence. Torquato Tasso. AWP, tr. by Thomas Stanley

To His Mistress[es]. Robert Herrick. CaPo; ErotSp

To His Mistris Going to Bed. John Donne. See Elegies

To His Mother. John Harington. NoSic

To His Not-so-coy Mistress. Wynford Vaughan-Thomas. NOBL

To His Pandora, from England. Alexander Craig. Son

To His Peculiar Friend Master Thomas Shapcott, Lawyer. Robert Herrick. NOSC

To his Queen said the circumspect Burleigh. Limerick. A. Cinna. PeLi

To his retired friend, an Invitation to Brecknock. Henry Vaughan.

"Town believes thee lost, and didst thou see, The." PBRV

To His Savior [or Saviour]. The New Years [or yeers] Gift. Robert Herrick. ChIV-2; NAEL-6v1

To His Saviour. Robert Herrick. SacPr

To His Saviour, a Child; a Present, by a Child. Robert Herrick. BeJo; ChIV-2; PeECV; TrCP

To His Scribe Adam. Geoffrey Chaucer. *See* Chaucer's Wordes unto Adam, his Owne Scriveyn

To His Sleeping Mistress. John Fletcher. NOSC

To His Son. Sir Walter Ralegh. *See* Sir Walter Ra[u]le[i]gh to His Son[ne]

To His Son Benedict Hoskyns. John Hoskyns [*or* Hoskins]. NOSC

To His Son Bennet. John Hoskyns [*or* Hoskins]. FaBoEE

To His Son [*or* Sonne], Vincent Corbet[t]. Richard Corbet [*or* Corbett]. BeJo; FaBoCh; NOSC; OxAEP-1

To his two little girls. (LL) Star-Fix. Marilyn Nelson Waniek. ESEAA; LTA

To His Watch. Gerard Manley Hopkins. MoBrPo

To His Watch, When He Could Not Sleep. Edward Herbert, 1st Baron Herbert of Cherbury. NOBE

To His Wife. Ausonius. AWP, *tr. by* Terrot Reaveley Glober

To His Wife. Ch'in Chia. ChiP, *tr. by* Arthur Waley

To His Wife. Su Wu. ChiP, *tr. by* Arthur Waley

To His Wife. Fyodor [*or* Feodor] Ivanovich Tyutchev. OxBEV, *tr. by* Henry Gifford and Charles Tomlinson

To His Wife, for Striking Her Dog. Sir John Harington [*or* Harrington]. OxBSP

To his wife said the lynx-eyed detective. Limerick. Langford Reed. PeLi

To His Young Mistress. Pierre de Ronsard. AWP, *tr. by* Andrew Lang

To H.N. David Mura. UnSA

To hold a shadow in your hands the longest time. Battle at the Edge of the Falls. César Moro. BLPSL, *tr. by* Rene de Costa, Rigas Kappatos and Eleni Paidoussi

To hold an avalanche off. (LL) Man With Night Sweats, The. Thom Gunn. CABP; HarvBoo; PoPoPo

To Homer. John Keats. EBEV; NAEL-5v2; NAEL-6v2; NoP-4; Son

To honor the return of sparkling sun. Sonnet 15. Louise Labé. BoWoP, *tr. by* Willis Barnstone

To Honora Sneyd. Anna Seward. CenSon; ECWP; PoBW

To honour all their deaths, who for her bleed. (LL) Sir Philip Sidney. NAEL-5v1; NAEL-6v1; NAEL-7v1; NIL-7; NIP-4; Son *Fr.* Astrophil and Stella.

To Hope. Charlotte Smith. RWP

To Hope. Mihály Csokonai Vitéz. IQMS, *tr. by* Watson Kirkconnell

To Hope. Helen Maria Williams. CenSon; ECWP; OxBSo

To house the Hag, you must doe this. Another to Bring in the Witch. Robert Herrick. BeJo

To Hsiao Shih-ying. Hsieh Chin. CoBLCP, *tr. by* Jonathan Chaves

To Hsü Shih-t'ing. Hsü Wei. CoBLCP, *tr. by* Jonathan Chaves

To Hsuan-Ch'eng, Past Hsin-Lin-P'u, Toward Pan-Ch'iao. Hsieh T'iao. ChinPo, *tr. by* Yip Wai-lim

To Hugh MacDiarmid. Edwin Morgan. FaBoTw

To Human Skin. Cheryl Savageau. TWW

To Hungarian Youth. Dávid Baróti Szabó. IQMS, *tr. by* Matthew Mead

To Hunt. William Blake. OxBoLi

To hurt the Negro and avoid the Jew. University. Karl Shapiro. APT-2; OxBA

To ———: "I fear thy kisses, gentle maiden." Shelley. GTBS-P

To I. Lavrenteyava. Natalya [*or* Natal'ia] Gorbanevskaya [*or* Gorbanyevskaya *or* Gorbanevskaia]. BoWoP, *tr. by* Daniel Weissbort

To Ianthe. John Lyle Donaghy. NOBE

(Past Ruin'd Ilion.) AWP

(To Ianthe.) NOBE

(Verse: "Past ruin'd [*or* ruined] Ilion Helen lives.") OBEV

To Ianthe. Walter Savage Landor. *See* Ianthe

To Ibn Zaidun. Wallāda. WPOW, *tr. by* Deirdre Lashgari and James Monroe

To ignorance revealed. (LL) Emily Dickinson. InPK-6; NCAP

To Il y a. Hélène d'Oettingen. CuPo

To Imagination. Emily Jane Brontë. VWP

To indicate is to / turn off in a world. Data. Joseph Ceravolo. BodElec

To Inez Milholland. Edna St. Vincent Millay. AiP; NALW; WPE

To infancy, O Lord, again I come. Return, The. Thomas Traherne. GeHe

To Insure Survival. Simon J. Ortiz. CDW

To Intellectual Detachment. Allen Tate. FuPo

To interpose them oft, is not unwise. (LL) To Mr. Lawrence. John Milton. AWP; GTBS-P; OBEV; PoE

To invent, and practise this one way, to annihilate all three. (LL) Will, The. John Donne. EBEV; NoSic

To Ireland in the Coming Times. W. B. Yeats. NOIV; NoAM

To Iron-Founders and Others. Gordon Bottomley. OBEV; OBMV

To Isa Sleeping. Thomas Holley Chivers. APN-1

To it, O jazzmen. (LL) Jazz Fantasia. Carl Sandburg. AiP; MoAmPo

To Italy. Giacomo Leopardi. AWP, *tr. by* Romilda Rendel

To J. G. "Ephelia." NOSC

To J—Y Colonna. Gérard de Nerval. WoPoe, *tr. by* Richard Sieburth

To James. Frank Horne. BPo *Fr.* Letters [*or* Notes] Found near a Suicide.

To Jane. Shelley. *See* To Jane: The keen stars were twinkling

To Jane: The Invitation. Shelley. GTBS-P; NAEL-5v2; NAEL-6v2; NPeEn (Invitation, The.) OBEV

To Jane: The keen stars were twinkling. Shelley. NAEL-6v2 (To Jane.) FHYEP

To János Arany. Sándor Petőfi. IQMS, *tr. by* Madeline Mason

To János Arany in Answer to His Poem "Cosmopolitan Poetry." Gyula Reviczky. IQMS, *tr. by* Madeline Mason

To Jerusalem, 1990. Myra Shapiro. OPRER

To Jesus on His Birthday. Edna St. Vincent Millay. ChIV-2; HeIP-4; TrCP

To J.G. on the News of His Marriage. "Ephelia." LW

To John Ashbery on Szymanowski's Birthday. Frank O'Hara. BodElec

To John Clare. John Clare. Son

To John Donne. Ben Jonson. BeJo; NAEL-5v1; NAEL-6v1; NAEL-7v13 (Who shall doubt, Donne, where I a poet be.) NoP-4

To John Donne. Sir Henry Wotton. NOSC; NoSic

To John I ow'd great obligation. Epigram. Matthew Prior. FaBoEE; OBVE; OxBEV

To John Keats. Leigh Hunt. CenSon; Son

To John Keats. Amy Lowell. Son

To John Keats, Poet, at Spring Time. Countee Cullen. NAAAL (To John Keats, Poet, at Spring Time.) NAAAL

To John Lamb, Esq.: Of the South-Sea House. Charles Lamb. Son

To John Reed. Max Eastman. APT-1

To join [*or* joyn] with them, who here confer. His Offering, with the Rest, at the Sepulcher. Robert Herrick. ChIV-2

To Josh Gibson (Legendary Slugger of the Old Negro Baseball League). George, Jr. Mosby. ISC

To Juan at the Winter Solstice. Robert Graves. EBEV; FaBoMo; HarvBoo; MoBrPo; NAEL-5v2; NAEL-6v2; NPeEn; NoAM; NoP-4; PoE; RaBo; TwCP

To Judge Faolain, Dead Long Enough: A Summons. Linda McCarriston. LoL

To Julia. Robert Herrick. CaPo; NOSC

To Julia de Burgos. Julia de Burgos. BoWoP; TCLAP, *tr. by* Grace Schulman

To Julia, the Flaminica Dialis, or Queen-Priest. Robert Herrick. CaPo

To Julius. Martial. FaBoEE, *tr. by* Sir Charles Sedley

To jump his mortal coil. (LL) Elegy on Thomas Hood. Martin Fagg. NOBL; UV

To just such golden ones as these. (LL) O All Down within the Pretty Meadow. Kenneth Patchen. HAP; WeW-3

To justify—Despair. (LL) Emily Dickinson. APN-2; NAAL-2v1; NAAL-3; NAAL-5; NOBA; SAmP; TCAPo

To justify the Dream. (LL) Emily Dickinson. APN-2; MoAmPo; NIL-7; NIP-4; NoP-4; TCAPo

To justify your faith at last. (LL) Any Husband to Many a Wife. Emily Jane Pfeiffer. VWP; ViWPN

To Juventius. Catullus. CAGL, *tr. by* Frank O. Copley

To Kachalov's Dog. Sergey [*or* Sergei] Aleksandrovich Yesenin [*or* Essenin]. TCRP, *tr. by* Daniel Weissbort

To Keats: On Reading His Sonnet Written in Chaucer. John Hamilton Reynolds. Son

To Keep a True Lent. Robert Herrick. SacPr; TrCP

To keep him with us, feasts are not enough. Bartók. László Nagy. IQMS, *tr. by* Adam Makkai

To keep my health! Resolve. Charlotte Perkins Stetson Gilman. PoToHe

To Keep My Love Alive. Richard Rodgers. ReLy

To keep our metaphysics warm. (LL) Whispers of Immortality. T. S. Eliot. APT-1; CTC; NOBA; NoAM; OBMV; OxAEP-2

To Keep the Cold Wind Away. *Unknown.* MiEL (There blows a colde wynd todaye, todaye.) SacPr

To Keep the Memory of Charlotte Forten Grimké. Angelina Weld Grimké. BlSi

To keep the memory of our arms alive. (LL) To my Friend G.N. from Wrest. Thomas Carew. BeJo; CaPo

To keep things whole. (LL) Keeping Things Whole. Mark Strand. CoAP; HCAP; HeIP-4; LCAP-2; PoPoPo; TAP; VCAP

To keep your marriage brimming. Word to Husbands, A. Ogden Nash. OBCoV

To Kengai Osho of Engaku-ji. Muso Soseki. EaWin, *tr. by* W. S. Merwin

To Kill a Deer. Carol Frost. MoASP

To kill a language is to kill a people. Frost is All Over, The. Pearse Hutchinson. PBCIP

To kill its enemies and cheat its friends. International Conference. Colin Ellis. FaBoEE

To Kill Stray Dogs. Mark Todd. GeoH

To kindle fire so that flame.　What Man Can Do on This Planet.　László Kálnoky.　IQMS, *tr. by* George Gömöri

To Kiss a Forehead Is to Erase Worry.　Marina Ivanovna Tsvetayeva [*or* Tsvetaeva].　TCRusP, *tr. by* John Glad

To Kiss God's Rod; Occasioned upon a Child's Sickness.　Mildmay Fane, 2d Earl of Westmorland.　BeJo

To kiss upon thy lips a stainless fame. (LL)　To George Sand: A Desire.　Elizabeth Barrett Browning.　BoWoP; NAEL-5v2; NAEL-6v2; NALW; PoBW; VWP

To know he still is warm tho' I am cold. (LL)　After Death.　Christina Georgina Rossetti.　NAEL-5v2; NAEL-6v2; NALW

To know just how He suffered—would be dear.　Emily Dickinson.　NCAP

To Know Me?　Jolanda Insana.　CItWP, *tr. by* Cinzia Sartini Blum and Lara Trubowitz

To know there are rhododendrons on the slopes of the Himalayas.　Nearer.　Judith Herzberg.　BoWoP, *tr. by* Shirley Kaufman

To / know whether or not art is contemporary.　John Cage.　APSN　*Fr.* Diary: How to Improve the World (You Will Only Make Matters Worse).

To know who I am / why I came there / what and why I am and made to happen. (LL)　Hôtel Transylvanie.　Frank O'Hara.　NeAP; PoM

To Kolya Otrada.　Mikhail Kuz'mich Lukonin.　TCRP, *tr. by* Albert C. Todd

To Kosciusko.　John Keats.　CenSon

To Krishna Haunting the Hills.　Andal.　BoWoP, *tr. by* Willis Barnstone

To Kyris.　Strato [*or* Straton].　GrAn, *tr. by* Teddy Hogge

To L. H. B.　Katherine Mansfield.　FaBoWar

To Ladies' Eyes.　Thomas Moore.　OxBoLi

To Lady Anne Fitzpatrick, When about Five Years Old, with a Present of Shells, 1772.　Horace Walpole, 4th Earl of Orford.　NOEC

To Lady Elizabeth Foster, from Georgiana, Duchess of Devonshire, When She Was Apprehensive of Losing Her Eyesight–1796.　Georgiana Cavendish, Duchess of Devonshire.　PoBW

To Lake Aghmoogenegamook.　American Traveller, The.　"Orpheus C. Kerr."　OBAL

To Lallie.　Amy Levy.　PoBW; ViWPN

To Larr [*or* Lar].　Robert Herrick.　CaPo

To Laura.　Henrietta Cordelia Ray.　CBWP-3

To Laura, on the French Fleet Parading before Plymouth.　Ann Thomas.　ECWP

To Laurels.　Robert Herrick.　CaPo

To lay its fingers on the little heads. (LL)　Naming Day, A.　Odia Ofeimun.　HBAPE; PBMAP

To lazy to be ambitious.　Ryokan.　EnlH

To lead back to splendour. (LL)　Ezra Pound.　APSN; APT-1; PFTM-2　*Fr.* Cantos.

To learn how to die.　*Unknown.*　SoOfWa, *tr. by* Sam Hamill

To Learn How to Speak.　Jeremy Cronin.　PeSAV

To learn that.　Stunned by Freedom.　Eva Svankmajerová.　SurWo, *tr. by* Katerina Pinosová

To learn the scriptures is easy.　Lal Ded [*or* Lalla].　WPoS

To learn the Transport by the Pain.　Emily Dickinson.　NOCV

To leave a light for them when they should come. (LL)　Insusceptibles, The.　Adrienne Rich.　CoAmPo; HeIP-4; Son

To leave my boots. (LL)　Our Photograph[s].　Frederick Locker-Lampson.　NBLV; NOBL; PeLV

To leave the earth was my wish, and no will stayed my rising.　Temple, A.　Kenneth Patchen.　SPE

To leave the world and serve God.　La Compiuta Donzella (The Accomplished Maiden).　WPOW

To leave yet to stay, and by staying to leave.　Sonnet 61.　Félix Lope de Vega Carpio.　BLPSL, *tr. by* Rene de Costa, Rigas Kappatos and Eleni Paidoussi

To Leigh Hunt, Esq.　John Keats.　Son

To let me[e] live, O[h] love and hate mee too. (LL)　Prohibition, The.　John Donne.　MeLP; NOSC

To let the warm Love in! (LL)　Ode to Psyche.　John Keats.　FHYEP; NAEL-5v2; NAEL-6v2; NOBE; NOBRP; NoP-4; OBEV; OxAEP-2; PoE; TFi; TOF

To let them dream they are not dead. (LL)　Pallor.　Agnes Mary Frances Robinson.　NOBVV; VWP

To let them feel they're not quite as nice as they might be. (LL)　English Are So Nice!, The.　D. H. Lawrence.　NoP-4; PoPoPo; RaBo

To ———: "Let those with cost deck their ill-fashioned clay."　Thomas Rymer.　OxBSP

To Leven Water.　Tobias Smollett.　OBEV

To Levine on the Day of Atonement.　Robert Mezey.　TaR

To Li Chien.　Po Chü-i.　AWP; ChiP, *tr. by* Arthur Waley

To Li Po.　Tu Fu.　TAL

To Li Po.　'Aisha bint Ahmad al-Qurtubiyya.　SuSp, *tr. by* Eugene Eoyang

To Li Po on a Spring Day.　Tu Fu.　CrYelRi, *tr. by* Sam Hamill

To Li Po on a Spring Day.　Tu Fu.　TAL

To Li Po on a Winter Day.　Tu Fu.　CrYelRi, *tr. by* Sam Hamill

To liberate my people from its yoke! (LL)　Enslaved.　Claude McKay.　BPo; NAAAL

To Liberty.　Ágnes Nemes Nagy.　IQMS, *tr. by* Ila Egon

To Liberty.　Mary Robinson.　OxBSo

To Licinius.　Horace.　AWP, *tr. by* William Cowper　*Fr.* Odes.

To lie on these beaches for another summer.　Late August on the Lido.　John Hollander.　YaYoPo

To Life.　Lizette Woodworth Reese.　TCAPo

To Life Eternal, I could love. (LL)　Julia's Petticoat.　Robert Herrick.　BeJo; CaPo

To Life I Said Yes.　Chaim Grade.　TrJP, *tr. by* Joseph Leftwich

To lift her over the threshold, and let her in at the door. (LL)　Witch, The.　Mary Elizabeth Coleridge.　BrRo; CABP; NALW; PoBW; VWP; ViWPN; WPE

To Light.　Linda Hogan.　HATNAP

To light him to bed. (LL)　No Shop Does the Bird Use.　Elizabeth Jane Coatsworth.　OBCA; OxIBACP

To light the dark.　Litany.　Elise Paschen.　FFC

To light young poets' hearts.　Cephalus.　GrAn

To Lighten My Darkness.　*Unknown.*　AWP　*Fr.* Thousand and One Nights, The.

To Linda.　Guillaume Apollinaire.　CuPo

To Lindsay.　Allen Ginsberg.　CoAmPo

To Liu Yü-hsi.　Po Chü-i.　ChiP, *tr. by* Arthur Waley

To live and die for thee. (LL)　To Anthea, Who May Command Him Anything.　Robert Herrick.　BASC; CaPo; GTBS-P; NOBE; NOSC; OBEV; OxBEV

To live and not to be thine own.　Thine Own.　Josephine D. Henderson Heard.　CBWP-4; SWaP

To live in court among the crew is care.　To His Friend P. of Courting, Traveling, Dicing, and Tennis.　George Turberville.　NoSic

To live in hell, and heaven to behold.　Henry Constable.　Son　*Fr.* Diana.

To live in mankind, far, far more . . . than to live in a name. (LL)　Eagle That Is Forgotten, The.　Nicholas Vachel Lindsay.　APT-1; AWP; MoAmPo; NOBA; OxBA

To live in Wales.　Welsh Wordscape, A.　Peter Finch.　AngWePo

To live in Wales is to be conscious.　Welsh Landscape.　Ronald Stuart Thomas.　FaBoMo; NoP-4; TCAWP

To Live Merrily, and To Trust to Good Verses.　Robert Herrick.　AWP; BASC; BeJo; CaPo; CavPo; NOSC

To live one's life is no stroll in the park. (LL)　Hamlet.　Boris Leonidovich Pasternak.　GI; WoPoe, *tr. by* Nina Kossman

To live's a gift, to dye's a debt that we.　Porch, The.　Philip Pain.　SCAP

To live with him, and sing in endles[s] morn of light[!]. (LL)　John Milton.　GTBS-P; HeIP-4; NOBE; OBEV; SCGP; SacPr

To live with thee and be thy Love. (LL)　Nymph's [*or* Nimphs] Reply to the Shepherd [*or* Sheepheard], The.　Sir Walter Ralegh.　AmFaPo; CTC; ClHu; HAP; HeIP-4; InPK-6; NAEL-5v1; NAEL-6v1; NAEL-7v1; NBLV; NIL-7; NIP-4; NOBE; NPeEn; NoP-4; NoSic; PAI; PoE; PoPoPo; RACG; RB; SCGP; TFi; TRP; WeW-3

To live within a cave—it is most good.　Salve!　Thomas Edward Brown.　OBEV

To live without him: liked [*or* lik'd] it not, and died [*or* di'd]. (LL)　Upon the Death of Sir Albert Morton's Wife.　Sir Henry Wotton.　BASC; BoLoP; EnLoPo; FaBoEE; NPeEn; OBEV; OxBEV; PBRV; WeW-3

To living virtues turns the deadly vices.　George Chapman.　OxBSo　*Fr.* Coronet for His Mistress Philosophy, A.

To Lizbie Browne.　Thomas Hardy.　FaBoVe; NOBVV; OxAEP-2

To ———: "Lo! dreary Winter, howling o'er the waste."　Ann Yearsley.　CenSon

To London once my stepps [*or* steps] I bent.　London Lickpenny.　*Unknown.*　OBSV

To look at the moon. (LL)　Funeral Rites.　Seamus Heaney.　BiHa; ModIr; PBCIP; PoetW

To look at the river made of time and water.　Ars Poetica.　Jorge Luis Borges.　TCLAP, *tr. by* W. S. Merwin

To look like everyone else. (LL)　Tapestry.　Charles Simic.　LCAP-2; VCAP

To Look Out Once from High Windows.　Sinéad Morrissey.　MFPA

To look up slowly.　Nearing Long Moons.　J. L. Jacobs.　AmPoNex

To look yet not find.　To Look Yet Not Find.　Debby Barben.　IBA

To loosen with all ten fingers held wide and limber.　Moss-Gathering.　Theodore Roethke.　BLT; VGW

To Lord Byron.　Gyula Juhász.　IQMS, *tr. by* John Gordon Nichols

To Lord, nor Lady, nor faire England. (LL)　Fair Flower of Northumberland, The.　*Unknown.*　ESPB; OxBB

To lose a lodging, yet to find the sky.　To a Dead Friend.　Agnes Mary Frances Robinson.　PoBW

To lose one's faith—surpass.　Emily Dickinson.　TCAPo

To Love.　Edward Gardner.　CenSon

To Love. Boris Leonidovich Pasternak. TCRusP, *tr. by* Bogdan Boychuk and Mark Rudman

To Love a Stranger. Sibby Anderson-Thompkins. InTrad

To Love a Woman. Ed. Hoornik. TuT, *tr. by* Mary E. O'Donnell

To love a woman is to escape from death. To Love a Woman. Ed. Hoornik. TuT, *tr. by* Mary E. O'Donnell

To Love and Fate an equal Sacrifice. (LL) Exequies, The. Thomas Stanley. BeJo; MeLP

To Love and to Remember. Christina Georgina Rossetti. Son *Fr.* Later Life: A Double Sonnet of Sonnets.

To love me also in silence with thy soul. (LL) Elizabeth Barrett Browning. CenSon; NAEL-5v2; NAEL-6v2; OxBSo *Fr.* Sonnets from the Portuguese.

To love November, a turned joy. Late in Fall. Ramona Wilson. VoR

To love so much as she'll deserve. (LL) Sir John Suckling. BeJo; MeLP

To love so well the world that we may believe, in the end, in God. (LL) Masts at Dawn. Robert Penn Warren. NAAL-2v2; NoP-4; VCAP

To love some one more dearly ev'ry day. My Task. Maude Louise Ray. PWR

To love somebody. Kasa no Iratsume. OHMPJ

To love somebody / Who doesn't love you. Kasa no Iratsume. WPOW

To love that well which thou must leave ere long. (LL) William Shakespeare. AEP; AWP; BoLoP; CABP; CTC; ClHu; EBEV; GTBS-P; HAP; HeIP-4; InPK-6; NAEL-5v1; NAEL-6v1; NAEL-7v1; NIP-4; NOBE; NoP-4; NoSic; OBEV; OxBSo; PoE; PoRA; SCGP; SoSe-8; Son; TFi; UnPo; WeW-3 *Fr.* Sonnets.

To love, to go in endless thunder. To Love. Boris Leonidovich Pasternak. TCRusP, *tr. by* Bogdan Boychuk and Mark Rudman

To love, to love, to love, to love always, with all. I Love, You Love. "Rubén Dario." BLPSL, *tr. by* Rene de Costa, Rigas Kappatos and Eleni Paidoussi

To love you in shadow as in the light. Glass, The. Edwin Morgan. HarvBoo

To love your country. Prelude. Marilyn Chin. LoL

To Lucasta. Richard Lovelace. CaPo; CavPo; NOSC

(And 'tis both her corse and tomb.) (LL) CavPo

To Lucasta, from Prison. Richard Lovelace. BASC; BeJo; CaPo; CavPo

To *Lucasta, Going Beyond the Seas*. Richard Lovelace. *See* If to be absent were to be

To Lucasta: Her Reserved Looks. Richard Lovelace. CaPo

To Lucasta, [on] Going beyond the Seas. Richard Lovelace. BeJo; CaPo; GTBS-P; MeLP; OBEV; OxAEP-1

(Song: To Lucasta, Going beyond the Seas.) NOSC

(Song.) CavPo

(To *Lucasta, Going Beyond the Seas*.) CavPo

To Lucasta, [on] Going to the War[re]s. Richard Lovelace. AWP; BASC; BeJo; CABP; CaPo; CavPo; ClHu; EnLoPo; FaBoWar; GTBS-P; HAP; InPK-6; MeLP; NAEL-5v1; NAEL-6v1; NAEL-7v1; NIL-7; NIP-4; NOBE; NOSC; NPeEn; NoP-4; OBEV; OBWP; OxAEP-1; OxBEV; OxBSP; PAI; PBRV; PoE; PoPoPo; PoRA; SCGP; SCV; TFi; UV; WeW-3

To Lucasta: The Rose. Richard Lovelace. BeJo

(Ode.) CavPo

(Sweet, serene, sky-like flower.) CavPo

To Lucia Playing on Her Lute, Another. Samuel Pordage. NOSC

To Lucy, Countess[e] of Bedford, with Mr. Donnes Satire's [*or* Satyres]. Ben Jonson. BeJo; NAEL-6v1; NAEL-7v1

(LUCY, you brightnesse of our spheare, who are.) PBRV

(To Lucy, Countesse of Bedford, with Mr. Donnes Satyres.) PBRV

To lull the dog across a bloodless river. (LL) Climbing. Jennifer Maiden. BMAP; CBAP

To Lydia. Horace. *See* Odes

To Lysander. Aphra Behn. LW

To Lysander. Judith Madan. ECWP

To Madam Bhen. "Ephelia." EMWP

To Maecenas. Horace. AWP; OBVE, *tr. by* John Dryden *Fr.* Odes.

To Mæcenas. Phillis Wheatley. NAAAL; NAAL-5

To make a bit of music. Ode: In a Few Hours. Hans Lodeizen. TuT, *tr. by* Eamon Grennan

To make a final conquest of all me. Fair Singer, The. Andrew Marvell. EnLoPo; FSCP; MeLP; NOBE; NoP-4; SCGP

To Make a Poem in Prison. Etheridge Knight. AF

To make a poet black, and bid him sing! (LL) Yet Do I Marvel. Countee Cullen. APT-2; AmFaPo; BPo; InvLi; NAAAL; NAAL-2v2; NAAL-5; NIL-7; NoAM; SSLK; Son; TAP; TTY

To make a prairie it takes a clover and one bee. Emily Dickinson. BoWoP; HeIP-4; NBLV; OBCA; OxBA; TCAPo

To make a start. William Carlos Williams. NOBA; NoAM *Fr.* Paterson.

To Make a Talisman. Olga Orozco. TCLAP, *tr. by* Stephen Tapscott

To make a third she joined the former two. (LL) Lines Printed under the Engraved Portrait of Milton [In Tonson's Folio of the "Paradise Lost"]. Dryden. InPK-6; OxAEP-1

To Make Birds Sing. Vladimir Alekseievich Soloukhin. TCRP, *tr. by* Daniel Weissbort

To make it into history. (LL) It Took One Hundred Years. Malika O'Lahsen. HAWP; WoPoe, *tr. by* Eric Sellin

To make me *deaf*, and mend my *sight*. (LL) Stella's Birthday, 1725. Jonathan Swift. CABP; NOEC

To make me do the thing I will, I won't. Human Animal, The. Jane Mayhall. TAP

To make my grave. (LL) Cross-tree, The. Robert Herrick. CavPo; ChIV-2

To make my love an Immortality. (LL) Sonnet: "She took the dappled partridge flecked [*or* fleckt] with blood." Tennyson. NAEL-5v2; NAEL-6v2

To make One's Toilette—after Death. Emily Dickinson. TCAPo

To make peace with her own monstrous nature. (LL) Patience. Elaine Feinstein. BrRo; FaBoWP

To make quick way I'll leap o'er heavy blocks. Dryden. OBSV *Fr.* Absalom and Achitophel, Part 2.

To make seas. (LL) Mawu of the Waters. Abena Busia. HAWP; NAfrP

To make some bread you must have dough. One, Two, Three—Gough! Eve Merriam. NTCP

To make such feastesses! (LL) Three Ghostesses. *Unknown.* OBCoV; OxNR

To make that curve of the water. Curve of the Water. Hilda Morley. PmAP

To make the cherry red! (LL) Nevertheless. Marianne Craig Moore. HarvBoo; NAAL-2v2; NoP-4; OxBA; SoSe-8

To make the child in your own image is a capital crime. Karl Shapiro. BodElec *Fr.* Bourgeois Poet, The.

To make the vapor bath. That Old Sauna High. Anselm Hollo. PoM

To make this condiment, your poet begs. Salad, A. Sydney Goodsir Smith. NBLV

To make your candles last for aye. Mother Goose. OxNR; ReMoGo

To Mal Waldron and everyone and I stopped breathing. (LL) Day Lady Died, The. Frank O'Hara. HCAP; LCAP-2; NAAL-2v2; NOBA; NeAP; NoAM; NoP-4; PAI; PFTM-2; PmAP; PoE; PoM; RaBo; SwNoth; TRP; VCAP

To many a flute of Arcady. (LL) Tennyson. CAGL; NAEL-6v2; NAWM-7v2 *Fr.* In Memoriam A. H. H.

To Marcus Aurelius. Zbigniew Herbert. VCWP, *tr. by* Czeslaw Miosz and Peter Dale Scott

To Margot Heinemann. John Cornford. *See* Huesca

To Marguerite. Matthew Arnold. *See* Switzerland

To Marguerite—Continued. Matthew Arnold. GTBS-P; NAEL-6v2; NPeEn; OxBEV; SoSe-8 *Fr.* Switzerland.

To Maria Gisborne in England, from Italy. Shelley. NOBE *Fr.* Letter to Maria Gisborne.

To Marie Osmond. Jack Skelley. SwNoth

To Marina. Sarah Fyge Egerton. ECWP

To Marina. Kenneth Koch. NoAM

To Mark Anthony in Heaven. William Carlos Williams. NOBA; SAmP; TCAPo

To market, to market, to buy a fat pig. *Unknown.* LB; OxNR; ReMoGo

To market, to market / To buy a plum bun. Mother Goose. OxNR

To Mars, a Prayer for Peace. Janus Pannonius. IQMS, *tr. by* Anthony Barrett

To Mary. John Clare. EnLoPo

To Mary. William Cowper. EnLoPo; NOEC; UV

(My Mary.) OBEV

(To the Same.) GTBS-P

To Mary. Mary E. Tucker. CBWP-1

To Mary. Charles Wolfe. OBEV

(Song: To Mary.) OxAEP-2

To Mary: 'It Is the Evening Hour.' John Clare. BoLoP

(Mary.) EnLoPo

To Mary, Lady Wroth. Ben Jonson. NOSC

To Mary Pickford—Moving Picture Actress. Nicholas Vachel Lindsay. IllVoic

To Mary Unwin. William Cowper. CenSon; GTBS-P; OBEV

To Marygolds. Robert Herrick. NAEL-5v1

(Give way, an ye be ravished by the sun.) NAEL-6v1; NAEL-7v1

(Give way, and be ye ravish'd by the sun.) CavPo

To mask a King in weeds. (LL) Ralph Waldo Emerson. OxBA; OxBSP; Spl; TCAPo *Fr.* Quatrains.

To Master Davenant for Absence. Sir John Suckling. CaPo

To M. Denham, on His Prospective Poem. Robert Herrick. BeJo

To M. Henry Lawes, the Excellent Composer[,] of his Lyrics. Robert Herrick. CaPo

To Mastres Margery Wentworthe. John Skelton. *See* Garland [*or* Garlande *or* Garlands] of Laurel[l], The

To Match the Prince of Lang-yeh's Poem in the Old Style. Wang Seng-ta. CoBCP, *tr. by* Burton Watson

To Max Jacob. Rosanna Warren. DiPo

To May. Jane West. CenSon

To me, fair[e] Friend, you never can be old. William Shakespeare. GTBS-P; HeIP-4; NoSic; OBEV; OxAEP-1; SCGP *Fr.* Sonnets.

To me he seems like a god. Sappho. BoWoP

To me how wildly pleasing is that scene. Gypsy's Evening Blaze, The. John Clare. CenSon

To me it seems. Sappho. SaLy, *tr. by* Diane Rayor

To me, *lion* was sun on a wing. Eve Names the Animals. Susan Donnelly. NIL-7

To me, Muscovites are sweethearts out of old stories. Bulat Shalvovich Okudzhava. ItGoST, *tr. by* Ronnie Apter and Mark Herman

To me nothing seems as splendid nor as praiseworthy. *Unknown.* GePo

To me, one silly task is like another. Cassandra. Louise Bogan. APT-2; HAP; MoAmPo; NALW; VGW

To me. Somewhere they are building. My Lady Carries Stones. Nick Piombino. FTOS

To me that man seems like a god in heaven. 51. Catullus. NAWM-7v1, *tr. by* Charles Martin

To me the sound of falling rain. Sounds. Lindley Williams Hubbell. APT-2

To me there is more relevance in your single flight. Welsh Homer. Cliff James. AngWePo

To me, to love is no go. Music That Makes Me Dance. Jule Styne. ReLy

To me—who since childhood went on my way. Time. Adelia Prado. TANSG, *tr. by* Ellen Watson

To me, whom in their lays the shepherds call. Inscription for a Grotto. Mark Akenside. NOEC; OBGa

To me you are infinitely distant. Ten Lines. Emile Roumer. NegPo, *tr. by* Ellen Conroy Kennedy

To Meadows [*or* Meddowes]. Robert Herrick. AWP; BASC; CaPo; NOBE; NOSC; NPeEn; OBEV; PBRV

To Meath of the pastures. Drover, A. Padraic Colum. AWP; MoBrPo; OBMV; RB

To meet a bad lad on the African waste. African Lion, The. A. E. Housman. NOxBChV

To meet so enabled a Man! (LL) Emily Dickinson. NAWM-7v2; NOCV; SacPr

To meet the fountain of true life I run. Longing. Judah Halevi. TrJP, *tr. by* Nina Davis Salaman

To meet the Judgment Day. (LL) Wants of Man, The. John Quincy Adams. APN-1; OBAL

To Melancholy. Susan Evance. CenSon

To Melancholy. Anne Finch, Countess of Winchilsea. WPE

To Melancholy. Written on the Banks of the Arun, October 1785. Charlotte Smith. CenSon; RWP

To Memory. Mary Elizabeth Coleridge. ViWPN

To Men. Anna Wickham. MoBrPo

To Meng Hao-jan. Li Po. ColAnChi, *tr. by* Stephen Owen

To Mercy, Pity, Peace and Love. William Blake. BBASP; ChAP; FHYEP; InvLi; NAEL-5v2; NAEL-6v2; NOBE; NOBRP; NOEC; NoP-4; OxBEV; PeECV; PoE *Fr.* Songs of Innocence.

To merely uncover the depths of love. Travelogue. Lewis Warsh. BodElec

To Mertill Who Desired Her to Speak to Clorinda of His Love. Elizabeth Taylor. EMWP

To Michal. Lucille Clifton. ExTi

To Mie Tirante. George Darley. Son

To Minerva. Thomas Hood. NBLV; NOBL; OxBoLi; PeLV

To Mira, On the Care of her Infant. Ann Yearsley.
"Mira, as they dear Edward's senses grow." ECWP

To Miss———. Thomas Moore. OxBSP

To Miss A[——]a M[——]a Tra[——]s; an Epistle from Scotland. Charlotte Brereton. ECWP

To Miss B. John Clare. NOBVV

To Miss C—on Being Desired To Attempt Writing a Comedy. Charlotte Smith. RWP

To Miss Charlotte Pulteney in Her Mother's Arms. Ambrose Philips. NOEC
(To Charlotte Pulteney.) GTBS-P

To Miss Eleanor Ambrose on the Occasion of Her Wearing an Orange Lily at a Ball in Dublin Castle on July the 12th. Philip Dormer Stanhope, 4th Earl of Chesterfield. EnLoPo

To Miss Kitty Phillips. Edward Lovibond. ECEV

To Miss Laetitia Van Lewen. Constantia Grierson. ECWP; WPE

To Miss M———, Written by Moonlight, July 18, 1782. Sir Samuel Egerton Brydges. Son

To Miss Sophia Headle. Dorothea Primrose Campbell. PoBW

To Mr. C——ge. Anna Laetitia Barbauld. *See* To Mr. S. T. Coleridge

To Mr. Gay, Who Wrote Him a Congratulatory Letter on the Finishing His House. Pope. NOEC; NPeEn; OBGa

To Mr. Hayley, on Receiving Some Elegant Lines from Him. Charlotte Smith. RWP

To Mr. Henry Lawes, Who Had Then Newly Set a Song of Mine in the Year 1635. Edmund Waller. BeJo; CTC

To Mr. Lawrence. John Milton. AWP; GTBS-P; OBEV; PoE
(*Lawrence* of vertuous Father vertuous Son.) PBRV
(Sonnet.) NOSC; OxAEP-1
(To Edward Lawrence.) PBRV

To Mr. Murray. Byron. UV

To Mr. R. W. John Donne. ESCV

To Mr. Roland Woodward. John Donne. ESCV

To Mr. S. T. Coleridge. Anna Laetitia Barbauld. CABP; NOEC; NoP-4; WoRP
(To Mr. C——ge.) ECWP
(To Mr [S.T.] C[olerid]ge.) NOBRP

To Mr Thomas Griffith at the University of Glasgow. Jane Brereton.
"You, friend, who whilom tossed the ball." ECWP

To Mr. Tilman after He Had Taken Orders. John Donne. EBEV

To Mrs. G. Charlotte Smith. RWP

To Mistress Katherine Bradshaw, the Lovely, That Crowned Him with Laurel. Robert Herrick. CaPo

To Mrs. M. B. on Her Birth-Day. Pope. EnLoPo

To Mistress Margery Wentworth. John Skelton. EBEV; EnLoPo; NOBE; OBEV *Fr.* Garland [*or* Garlande *or* Garlands] of Laurel[l], The.

To Mrs. Norton. Frances Anne [*or* "Fanny"] Kemble. VWP

To Mistress [*or* Maystres] Isabell Pennell. John Skelton. NOBE; NPeEn; NoSic; OBEV; OxBoLi; SCGP; TTTS *Fr.* Garland [*or* Garlande *or* Garlands] of Laurel[l], The.

To Mistress [*or* Maystres] Margaret Hussey. John Skelton. EBEV; EnLoPo; NAEL-5v1; NAEL-6v1; NBLV; NOBE; NoP-4; NoSic; OBEV; OxBEV; PeLV; PoE; PoRA; SCGP; SCV; TFi *Fr.* Garland [*or* Garlande *or* Garlands] of Laurel[l], The.

To Mrs Thrale [on Her Thirty-fifth Birthday]. Samuel Johnson. FaBoEE

To Mrs. Will H. Low. Robert Louis Stevenson. NOBVV; NPeEn

To mock the barbarous triumphs of despair! (LL) Sappho Discovers her Passion. Mary Robinson. CenSon; RWP

To mock the riddle corpses round Bapaume. (LL) Blighters. Siegfried Sassoon. FaBoTw; NoAM; OxBEV; OxBSP; PoWW

To Modigliani to Prove to Him That I Am a Poet. Max Jacob. TrJP, *tr. by* Wallace Fowlie

To Monsieur de la Mothe le Vayer. Molière. AWP, *tr. by* Austin Dobson

To Morfydd. Lionel Pigot Johnson. MoBrPo; OBMV

To Morning. William Blake. OxAEP-3

To-Morrow. Félix Lope de Vega Carpio. AWP, *tr. by* Henry Wadsworth Longfellow

To-morrow. John Masefield. MoBrPo

To-morrow shall be my dancing day. *Unknown.* ChrPo; OxBoLi *Fr.* My Dancing Day.

To mortal eyes, you, Hope, do seem. To Hope. Mihály Csokonai Vitéz. IQMS, *tr. by* Watson Kirkconnell

To mortal men Peace giveth these good things. Peace on Earth. Bacchylides. AWP, *tr. by* John Addington Symonds

To Mother. Lessie M. Brown. PWR

To Mother. Frank Horne. BPo *Fr.* Letters [*or* Notes] Found near a Suicide.

To Mother. Keorapetse Kgositsile. GT

To Mother. S. Usha. OMIP, *tr. by* A. K. Ramanujan

To Mother and Steve. Mari E. Evans. BPo

To Mother Fairie. Alice Cary. OBCA

To Mother Luddwels Cave and Spring. Martha, Lady Giffard. EMWP

To Mr. Alexander Ross. James Beattie. OxBS

To Mr. ———, an Unlettered Poet, on Genius Unimproved. Ann Yearsley. NOEC

To Mr. Blanchard, the Celebrated Aeronaut in America. Philip Freneau. APN-1

To Mr. C.B. John Donne. ESCV

To Mr. C., St. James's Place, London, October 22nd. Pope. OxBSP

To Mr. Cyriack Skinner upon His Blindness. John Milton. NOSC; NPeEn; PeECV; Son
(Sonnet.) OxAEP-1

To Mr. George Herbert. John Donne. OBVE

To Mr. Gray. Thomas Warton, the Younger. Son

To Mr. H. Lawes On His Airs. John Milton. AWP
(Harry, whose tuneful and well-measured song.) NoP-4
(Sonnet: To Mr. H. Lawes, on His Air[e]s.) NOSC

To Mr. Henry Cary, On the Publication of his Sonnets. Anna Seward. CenSon

To Mr. Henry Lawes. Katherine Philips. NoP-4; WPE

To Mr. Hobbes [*or* Hobs]. Abraham Cowley. BASC; BeJo
(Ode to Mr. Hobbes.) OxAEP-1

To Mr. Maunder Maunder, Professional Poet. Genevieve Taggard. APT-2

To Mr. Newton [on His Return from Ramsgate]. William Cowper. NOEC

To Mr. Opie, On His Having Painted for Me the Picture of Mrs Twis. Amelia Alderson Opie. RWP

To Mr. Punchinello. *Unknown.* OxNR

To Mr. W. B., at the Birth of His First Child. William Cartwright. BeJo

To Mr. William Long, On His Recovery from a Dangerous Illness, 1785. William Hayley. Son

To Mr. Wren, My Valentine Six Year Old. Jane Holt. ECWP

To Mrs B. from a Lady Who Had a Desire to See Her, and Who Complains on the Ingratitude of Her Fugitive Lover. *Unknown.* EMWP

To Mrs. Charlotte Smith. Martha Hanson. CenSon

To Mrs. Francis-Arabella Kelly. Mary Barber. ECWP

To Mrs. Hayley, On her Voyage to America. 1784. William Hayley. CenSon

To Mrs. K———, On Her Sending Me an English Christmas Plum-Cake at Paris. Helen Maria Williams. WoRP

To Mrs M. A. at Parting. Katherine Philips. NAEL-6v1; NAEL-7v1

To Mrs. M.A. Upon Absence. Katherine Philips. PoBW

To Mrs. Manley. By the Author of Agnes de Castro. Catherine Cockburn. EMWP

To Mrs. Manley, upon Her Tragedy Call'd The Royal Mischief. Mary Pix. EMWP

To Mrs.———, on the Death of Her Husband. Hannah Wallis. ECWP

To Mrs S. F. on Her Poems. Mary Pix. EMWP

To Mrs. Smith, Occasioned by the First of Her Sonnets. William Hayley. Son

To Mrs. W. on Her Excellent Verses. Aphra Behn. EMWP

To Ms. Ann. Lucille Clifton. ESEAA

To muddy death . . . (LL) William Shakespeare. OxAEP-1; RB *Fr.* Hamlet.

To muse on uncle Jim. (LL) Uncle Jim. Countee Cullen. GT; NAAL-2v2

To Music. Robert Herrick. CaPo

To Music: A Song. Robert Herrick. CaPo

To Music Bent Is My Retired Mind. Thomas Campion. NOCV; PeECV

To Music, to Becalm a Sweet-sick Youth. Robert Herrick. CaPo

To Music, to Becalm His Fever. Robert Herrick. BeJo; CaPo; OBEV

To ———: "Music, when soft voices die." Shelley. AWP; FHYEP; GTBS-P; HeIP-4; NAEL-5v2; NAEL-6v2; NOBE; OBEV; OxAEP-2; OxBEV; OxBSP; TFi

To mute and to material things. Sir Walter Scott. OBEV *Fr.* Marmion.

To my affections what a slave am I? Verses by my Mother in Her Own Hand. Amy Hammond. EMWP

To My Body. Nancy Sullivan. TAP

To My Bones. Zoltán Jékely. IQMS, *tr. by* George Szirtes

To My Book. Ben Jonson. BeJo; FaBoVe; NAEL-5v1; NAEL-6v1; NAEL-7v1

To My Books. Caroline Elizabeth Norton. CenSon

To My Brother. Mary Bryan. CenSon

To My Brother at St. John's College in Cambridge. Elizabeth Tollet. ECWP

To My Brother Hanson. W. S. Merwin. NAAL-2v2

To My Brother: Killed: Hammont Wood: October, 1918. Louise Bogan. AiP

To My Brother Miguel. César Vallejo. PoetW; TCLAP, *tr. by* John Knoepfle and James Wright

To My Brothers. John Keats. Son

To My Brothers. Käthe Leichter. AuPH, *tr. by* Lowell A. Bangerter

To My Child. "Barry Cornwall." CenSon

To My Children. Karen Gershon. ItWoWo

To My Cosen Mrs. Ellinor Evins. George Alsop. SCAP

To My Country. Ivan Alekseievich Bunin. TCRP, *tr. by* Simon Franklin

To My Cousin, Ching-yuan, Twelfth Month, 403. T'ao Ch'ien [*or* T'ao Yuan-ming]. CrYelRi, *tr. by* Sam Hamill

To My Cousin Mary, for Mending My Tobacco Pouch. Francis Scott Key. OBAL

To My Craft. Ágnes Nemes Nagy. IQMS, *tr. by* Hugh Maxton

To My Daughter. Vadim Leonidovich Andreyev [*or* Andreiev]. TCRP, *tr. by* Belinda Brindle

To My Daughter. N. Balamani Amma. OMIP, *tr. by* N. Balamani Amma

To My Daughter. Keorapetse Kgositsile. GT

To My Daughter. James Michie. OxBSP

To My Daughter. Margit Mikes. IQMS, *tr. by* Suzanne K. Walther

To My Daughter Catherine on Ashwednesday 1645, Finding Her Weeping at Prayers, Because I Would Not Consent to Her Fasting. Katherine Thimelby Aston. EMWP

To My Dead Brother. Clara Ann Thompson. CBWP-2

To My Dear and Loving Husband. Anne Bradstreet. AmFaPo; BASC; BoWoP; ColAP; ErotSp; HAP; HeIP-4; ITBLP; LW; NAAL-2v1; NAAL-3; NAAL-5; NIL-7; NIP-4; NOBA; NOCV; NOSC; NoP-4; OxBA; OxBEV; OxBSP; OxWW; PEW; PoE; SCAP; SacPr; TAP; TCAPo; TFi; WPE; WeW-3

To My Dear and Most Worthy Friend, Mr. Isaac Walton. Charles Cotton. NPeEn

To My Dear Children. Anne Bradstreet. BASC; NAAL-3

To My Dear Friend Mr Congreve [on His Comedy Called "The Double-Dealer"]. Dryden. EBEV; NPeEn; OxAEP-1

To my dear wife. Last Will and Testament, A. John Winstanley. FaBoVe; OBSV

To My Distant Beloved. Alois Jeitteles. TrJP, *tr. by* the Reverend Dr. Troutbeck

To My Dog, Swan. Dezső Kosztolányi. IQMS, *tr. by* Lydia Pasternak-Slater

To My Eldest Brother, With the British Army in Portugal. Felicia Dorothea Hemans. RWP

To My Excellent Lucasia, On Our Friendship. Katherine Philips. BASC; LW; MeLP; NALW; NOSC; NPeEn; NoP-4; OxBEV; PBRV; PEW; PoBW; WPE; WPOW

To My Father. John Berryman. PoPoPo

To My Father. Tony Curtis. AngWePo; TCAWP

To My Father. William Sydney Graham. FaBoTw

To My Father. Henrietta Cordelia Ray. BlSi; CBWP-3; Son

To My Father Norman Alone in the Blue Mountains. Jack Lindsay. NOBAu

To My First White Hairs. Wole Soyinka. OPOU

To my firstborn land, in the south. Firstborn Land, The. Ingeborg Bachmann. BoWoP, *tr. by* Daniel Huws

To My Friend. Anne Campbell. PoToHe

To my Friend G.N. from Wrest. Thomas Carew. BeJo; CaPo

To my Friend, Jerina. Lucille Clifton. ESEAA

To My Friend Mrs.——, on Her Holding an Argument in Favour of the Natural Equality of Both the Sexes. Clara Reeve.
    "Sacred Heliconian spring, The." ECWP

To My Friend (With an Identity Disc). Wilfred Owen. CAGL

To My Friends. Yuly [*or* Iulii] Markovich Daniel. TCRP, *tr. by* Arthur Boyars and David Burg

To My Friends. Nikolai Ivanovich Glazkov. TCRP, *tr. by* Daniel Weissbort

To My Friends. Johann Christoph Friedrich von Schiller. AWP, *tr. by* James Clarence Mangan

To My Friends Against Poetry. Jane Barker. BASC

To My Generation. Benyamin [*or* Benjamin] Galai. TrJP, *tr. by* Jacob Sonntag

To My God in His Sickness. Philip Levine. NNaP

To My Heavenly Charmer. Martha Sansom. LW

To My Honoured [*or* Honour'd] Kinsman, John Driden [of Chesterton in the County of Huntingdon, Esquire]. Dryden.
    "No porter guards the passage of your door." EBEV

To My Honoured Patron Humphery Davie. Benjamin Tompson. SCAP

To My Husband. "Eliza." EMWP; LW; PBRV

To My Ill Reader. Robert Herrick. CaPo

To My Ill-Wishers. Nikolai Ivanovich Glazkov. TCRP, *tr. by* Daniel Weissbort

To My Inconstant Mistress [*or* Mistris]. Thomas Carew. BeJo; EnLoPo; MeLP; NOBE; TFi
    (Song.) CaPo; CavPo; NoP-4
    (To His Inconstant Mistress.) OBEV
    (When thou, poor Excommunicate.) CavPo; NoP-4

To My Infant Daughter. Yvor Winters. IllVoic; VGW; WoPoe
    "Alas, that I should be." VGW; WoPoe

To My Ingenious and Worthy Friend William Lowndes, Esq. John Gay. OBSV

To My Ingenuous Friend, R. W. Henry Vaughan. BeJo

To my jumbled shadows. I Present Myself to the World. Amina Said. PoArWo, *tr. by* Lucy McNair

To My Lady. E. S. Miller. Son

To My Lady Morland at Tunbridge. Aphra Behn. PoBW

To My Least Favorite Reviewer. Howard Nemerov. OBCoV

To My Little Girl. Shakuntala Hawoldar. HAWP

To my Lord Biron's Tune of—Adieu Phillis. Katherine Philips. *See* Song: "'Tis true our life is but a long dis-ease."

To My Love. "The Amorous Lady." ECWP

To My Lucasia, in Defence of Declared Friendship. Katherine Philips. MeLP

To My Lyre. Eliza Cook. VWP

To My Mere English Censurer. Ben Jonson. BeJo

To My Mistress Sitting by a River's Side; an Eddy. Thomas Carew. BeJo; CaPo

To My Mistress[e] in My Absence. Thomas Carew. CaPo; NOSC

To My More Than Meritorious Wife. John Wilmot, 2d Earl of Rochester. OxBSP

To my most dearely-loved friend Henery Reynolds Esquire, of Poets and Poesie. Michael Drayton. PBRV
    (And so my deare friend, for this time adue.) (LL) PBRV
    (First Steps Up Parnassus.) NOBE
    (My dearely loved friend how oft have we.) PBRV
    (To my most dearely-loved friend Henery Reynolds Esquire, of Poets and Poesie.) PBRV

To My Most Honord Cosen, Mrs Somerset on the Unjust Censure Past Upon My Poore Marcelia. Frances Boothby. EMWP
To My Mother. Anna Adams. Prnts
To My Mother. George Barker. See Sonnet to My Mother
To My Mother. Simeon Dumdum. ReBoTo
To My Mother. Mary Weston Fordham. CBWP-2
To My Mother. Samuel Hazo. GraLe
To My Mother. Heinrich Heine. AWP
  (Sonnet to My Mother, A.) TrJP, tr. by Emma Lazarus
To My Mother. Edgar Allan Poe. OxBA
To My Mother. Henrietta Cordelia Ray. CBWP-3
To my mother, / and to my mother's monument. Message. Rosario Ferré. TANSG
To My Mountain. Kathleen Jessie Raine. OxBS
To My Much Esteemed Friend on Her Play Call'd Fatal-Friendship. Lady Sarah Piers. EMWP
To My Muse. Agnes Mary Frances Robinson. VWP
To My Nephew, J. B. Clement Barksdale. OxBSP
To My Niece, A.M., with a New Pair of Shoes. Unknown. ECWP
To My Niece Dorothy, a Sleepless Baby. Dorothy Wordsworth. See Cottager to Her Infant, (By My Sister), The
To My Noble Friend Master William Browne: Of the Evil Time. Michael Drayton. CABP
To My Noble Kinsman, Thomas Stanley, Esquire, on His Lyric Poems Composed by Master John Gamble. Richard Lovelace. CaPo
To My Old Schoolmaster. John Greenleaf Whittier. ColAP; NOBA
To My Own Face. Caroline Lindsay. VWP
To My Own Heart. Maria Jane Jewsbury. VWP
To My Pen. Mary Julia Young. CenSon
To My People. Edwin Seaver. TrJP
To my people it's as though he gave them a sacrifice. Eadwacer. Unknown. WPE
To my prowd foe thus, sister, humblie saye. Virgil [or Vergil]. OBVE, tr. by Henry Howard, Earl of Surrey Fr. Aeneid [or Eneados, Aeneis], The.
To my revenge and to her desperate fears. Bubble; a Song, The. Robert Herrick. CaPo
To My Reverend Dear Brother, M. Samuel Stone. John Cotton. SCAP
To My Rival. Thomas Carew. OxBSo
To My Rival. "Ephelia." LW
To My Sister. Olga Fiodorovna Berggolts [or Bergholts]. BoWoP; TCRusP, tr. by Daniel Weissbort
To My Sister. William Wordsworth. MakPoe
To My Soldier Son. Zseni Várnai. IQMS, tr. by Peter Zollman
To My Son. George Barker.
  "My darkling child the stars have obeyed." TwCP
To My Son. Margaret Johnston Grafflin. PoToHe
To My Son Parker, Asleep in the Next Room. Bob Kaufman. TwCP; VGW
To My Soul. Jean Valentine. YaYoPo
To my trew love and able. Unknown. MiEL
To my true king I offered free from stain. Jacobite's Epitaph, A. Thomas Babington Macaulay, 1st Baron Macaulay. NOBE; OBEV
To My Truly Valiant, Learned Friend, Who in His Book Resolved the Art Gladiatory into the Mathematics. Richard Lovelace. CaPo
To My Twin Sister Who Died at Birth. Kathleene West. GifTon
To my twin who lives in a cruel country. Dual Site, The. Michael Hamburger. TwCP
To My Venerable Friend, the President of the Royal Academy. Washington Allston. APN-1
To my wash-stand. Louis Zukofsky. APT-2 Fr. 29 Songs.
To My Wife. James Vincent Cunningham. VCAP
To My Worthy Friend Master George Sands [or Sandys], on His Translation of the Psalms. Thomas Carew. BeJo; CaPo; MeLP
To My Worthy Friend Mr. Peter Lely [or Lilly]. Richard Lovelace. BASC; CaPo; CavPo; GS; NOSC
To My Worthy Friend, Mr. James Bayley. Nicholas Noyes. SCAP
To My Young Lover. Jane Barker. BASC; LW
To My Younger Brother. Tu Fu. CrYelRi, tr. by Sam Hamill
To Myself. Abba Kovner. AF, tr. by Shirley Kaufman
To Myself. Kenneth Slessor. BMAP
To Napoleon. Dániel Berzsenyi. IQMS, tr. by Adam Makkai
To Nature. Samuel Taylor Coleridge. OxBSo
To Nature. Emily Jane Pfeiffer.
  "If we be fools of chance, indeed, and tend." ViWPN
  "O Nature! thou whom I have thought to love." ViWPN
To Nature, in her shop one day, at work compounding simples. Filling an Order. John Townsend Trowbridge. OBAL
To Ned. Herman Melville. APN-2; NAAL-2v1; NAAL-3; NOBA; TCAPo
To New York. Léopold Sédar Senghor. PoetW; WoPoe, tr. by Melvin Dixon

To New York. Léopold Sédar Senghor. PBA
  (New York.) PBMAP
  (New York.) At first I was confused by your beauty, those tall long-legged golden girls.) NegPo, tr. by Ellen Conroy Kennedy
To Night. Thomas Lovell Beddoes. CenSon; Son
To Night. Shelley. AWP; FHYEP; NAEL-5v2; NAEL-6v2; PoRA; TFi
  (Night.) OBEV
  (To the Night.) GTBS-P
To Night. Charlotte Smith. NAEL-6v2
To Night. Joseph Blanco White. EBEV; GSo; OBEV; OxAEP-2; Son
  (Mysterious night, when the first man but knew.) CenSon
  (Night and Death.) CenSon
To-night I do not come to conquer thee. Anguish. Stéphane Mallarmé. AWP, tr. by Arthur Symons
To-night is a midnight meeting, and the Earl is in the chair. George R. Sims. UV Fr. Two Women.
To Night, the Mother of Sleep and Death. John Addington Symonds. Son
To-night the very horses springing by. Winter Evening. Archibald Lampman. NIL-7; NOBC
To no believable blue I turn my eyes. Sylvia Townsend Warner. OxBSo Fr. Astrophysics.
To nothing fitter can I Thee compare. Michael Drayton. SCGP; Son Fr. Idea.
To Novella, on her saying deridingly, that a Lady of great Merit, and fine Address, was bred in the Old Way. Mary Barber. NIL-7
To Nysus. Sir Charles Sedley. FaBoEE; OBSV
To———: "O thou unknown disturber of my rest." Mary Bryan. CenSon
To———: "O timeless guest!—so soon returned art thou." Mary Bryan. CenSon
To obtain the value. 2 Pages, 122 Words on Music and Dance. John Cage. APT-2
To Odelia. James Shirley. BeJo
To O.E.A E. A. Claude McKay. BPo; GT
To Oenone. Robert Herrick. CaPo; OBEV
To Old Age. Walt Whitman. Spl
To Olga. Alena Synková. INSAB
To Olive. Lord Alfred Bruce Douglas. OBEV
To Olivia. Francis Thompson. MoBrPo
To One Afflicted with Adolescence. Anna Cascella. CItWP, tr. by Cinzia Sartini Blum and Lara Trubowitz
To One Black, and Not Very Handsome, Who Expected Commendation. Edward Herbert, 1st Baron Herbert of Cherbury. NOSC
To one full sound and silently. Man with Three Friends, The. Dora Greenwell. SacPr
To One in Bedlam. Ernest Christopher Dowson. GSo; MoBrPo; OBMV; Son
To one in love with solitude and song. (LL) Echoes. Emma Lazarus. APN-2; GSo
To One in Paradise. Edgar Allan Poe. BoLoP; OBEV; OxBA; TAP
  (Thou wast that all to me, love.) NCAP
To one it is a piece of ground. What is a Garden? Reginald Arkell. OBGa
To one kneeling down no word came. In a Country Church. Ronald Stuart Thomas. FaBoMo; HarvBoo; TOF
To One Loved Whollly Within Wisdom. Genevieve Taggard. APT-2
To One Married to an Old Man. Edmund Waller. FaBoEE; OxBSP
To One Persuading a Lady to Marriage. Katherine Philips. See Answer to Another Persuading a Lady to Marriage, An
To one pure image of regret. (LL) Tennyson. EBVV; FHYEP; TreFP Fr. In Memoriam A. H. H.
To One That Asked Me Why I Loved J.G G. "Ephelia." EMWP; LW; NOSC; PEW
To one that persuades me to leave the Muses. Elizabeth Singer Rowe.
  "Forgo the charming Muses! No, in spite." PEW
To One Who Died in a Garret in Cardiff. Huw Menai. AngWePo
To One Who Had Censured His Public Exposition of Dante. Giovanni Boccaccio. AWP; EaItPo, tr. by Dante Gabriel Rossetti Fr. Sonnets.
To One Who Has Been Long in City Pent. John Keats. CenSon; FHYEP
To One Who Quotes and Detracts. Walter Savage Landor. FaBoEE
To One Who Said I Must Not Love. Sarah Fyge Egerton. ECWP
To One Who Sleepeth. Mary E. Tucker. CBWP-1
To One Who Would Make a Confession. Wilfrid Scawen Blunt. GSo
To———: "One word is too often profaned." Shelley. BoLoP; GTBS-P; NOBE; OBEV; OxAEP-2; TFi
To Open. Antonio Porta. PFTM-2, tr. by Paul Vangelisti
To [or the Poet] Wordsworth. Felicia Dorothea Hemans. BrRo; RWP
To Orabella, Marry'd to an Old Man. Sarah Fyge Egerton. EMWP
To Orestes. Elizabeth Singer Rowe. PEW
To Osbert Sitwell. Cyril Connolly. OBCoV

To other eyes and ears you are a great. Bernard O'Dowd. CBAP *Fr.* Bush, The.

To Our Blessed Lady. Henry Constable. NoSic

To Our Blessed Lord upon the Choice of His Sepulchre. Richard Crashaw. GeHe; NOSC

   (Upon Our Saviour's Tomb[e] Wherein Never Man Was Laid.) ChIV-2; NPeEn

To Our Daughter. Jennifer Armitage. BrRo

To our homes, to our labours. We Must Return. Agostinho Neto. PeSAV, *tr. by* Michael Wolfers

To our house in the street down town. (LL) Samuel Brown. Phoebe Cary. APN-2; OBAL

To our Lord, upon the Water Made Wine. Richard Crashaw. GeHe

To our mother, maimed. American Rain. Marilyn Chin. OpBo

To our theme. The man who has stood on the Acropolis. Byron. OBSV *Fr.* Don Juan.

To Ovid. Elena Ignatova. ItGoST, *tr. by* Sibelan Forrester

To Oxford. Thomas Russell. CenSon; Son

To; Oxon. Marey Waller. EMWP

To P. J. (2 Yrs Old Who Sed Write a Poem for Me in Portland, Oregon). Sonia Sanchez. CA; OxIBACP

   (To P.J.) NOxBChV

To Paint a Water Lily. Ted Hughes. CABP

To paint the summer morning. (LL) London's Summer Morning. Mary Robinson. ECWP; RWP; WoRP

To Pál Ányos. Ábrahám Barcsay. IQMS, *tr. by* Adam Makkai

To Pallas, Theris, cunning of hand, dedicated. Leonidas of Tarentum. HePo *Fr.* Epigrams.

To Pallas, three girls, all of an age, skilled as the spider. Antipater of Sidon. HePo *Fr.* Epigrams.

To Pan the forest-ranger, Gelo the hunter. Philip of Thessalonica. GrAn

To Pan three brothers hung up these tools of the trade. Antipater of Sidon. HePo *Fr.* Epigrams.

To Pandora. Alexander Craig. Son

To Paris that was once her owne though now it be not so. Ovid. OBVE *Fr.* Heroides.

To part no more forever. (LL) Michael Wigglesworth. ColAP; NAAL-3 *Fr.* Day of Doom, The.

To pass all men's believing. (LL) Immorality, An. Ezra Pound. MoAmPo; NOBA; OBAL; TCAPo

To pass the hours away. (LL) Cows. James Reeves. NOxBChV; NTCP

To Patriarch Sun at Hua-yang Grotto. Li Te-yü. ColAnChi, *tr. by* Edward H. Schafer

To Peace. Richard Watson Dixon. OxAEP-2

To Peace. Suzanne Gardinier. AmPoNex

To Penelope, January 2, 1821. Byron. FaBoEE

To Penshurst. Ben Jonson. AWP; BASC; BeJo; CABP; NAEL-6v1; NAEL-7v1; NOSC; NoP-4; OxBEV; PBRV; TFi

To Percy Shelley. Leigh Hunt. CenSon; Son

To Perilla. Robert Herrick. BeJo; CaPo; NOSC; SCGP

To perish—of Delight. (LL) Emily Dickinson. APN-2; SAmP; TCAPo

To perish, or to live? (LL) Final Inch, The. Emily Dickinson. APN-2; NCAP; PoE

To Persecuted Foreigners. Penina Moise. SWaP

To Persephone. Harold Vinal. YaYoPo

To Pertinax Cob. Ben Jonson. BeJo

To Pete Atkin: A Letter from Paris. Clive James.
   "Weather's cleared, The. We're filming at Versailles." OBSV

To Peter, Bishop of Poitiers, Who Withstood William of Aquitaine and Died in Exile. Hildebert. MLL, *tr. by* Helen Waddell

To Petronius Arbiter. Oliver St. John Gogarty. OBMV

To Phaon. Mary Robinson. CenSon; RWP

To Phil Dow, in Oregon. Robert Hass. BodElec

To Philaster. Sarah Fyge Egerton. ECWP

To Philomela. Benjamin Colman. SCAP

To Phryne. Owen Felltham [*or* Feltham]. NOSC

To Phyllis. Edmund Waller. BeJo

To Phyllis to Love and Live with Him. Robert Herrick. CaPo

To Phylocles, Inviting Him to Friendship. "Ephelia." NOSC; WPE

To Pi Ssu Yao. Tu Fu. BLT; OHPC, *tr. by* Kenneth Rexroth

To pile like Thunder to its close. Emily Dickinson. APN-2; NCAP

To Piso, on Epicurus' Birthday. Philodemus. GrAn, *tr. by* William Moebius

To P.J. Sonia Sanchez. *See* To P. J. (2 Yrs Old Who Sed Write a Poem for Me in Portland, Oregon)

To plant in the soft earth of my yard. (LL) Eleven A.M. on My Day Off, My Sister Phones Desperate for a Babysitter. Sharon Hashimoto. FSt; OpBo

To Play Pianissimo. Lola Haskins. MiVo

To play the school games with the others. (LL) Picnic, The. John Logan. CoAmPo; TRP

To pluck the sun down into the dead sea. (LL) And, the last day being come, Man stood alone. Trumbull Stickney. APN-2; NoP-4

To Poetry. Carlos Pellicer. TCLAP, *tr. by* Alexandra Migoya

To Poets. George Darley. Son

To Poets. Walter Savage Landor. FaBoEE

To point a moral, or adorn a tale. (LL) Samuel Johnson. FaBoWar; OBWP; OxBEV *Fr.* Vanity of Human Wishes, The; The Tenth Satire of Juvenal Imitated.

To poll their tops that seek such change and gape for joy. (LL) Doubt of Future Foes. Queen of England Elizabeth I. CTC; NAEL-5v1; NAEL-6v1; NAEL-7v1; NALW; NoSic; WPE

To popularize the mule, its neat exterior. Labors of Hercules, The. Marianne Craig Moore. OxBA

To practice for Eternity. (LL) Bearded Oaks. Robert Penn Warren. APT-2; ColAP; FuPo; MoAmPo; NAAL-2v2; NAAL-5; NOBA; NoAM; NoP-4; PAI; PoE; TAP; TwCP

To practice more than heavenly power permits. (LL) Christopher Marlowe. NAEL-5v1; NAEL-7v1

To praise the blue whale's crystal jet. Whale, His Bulwark, The. Derek Walcott. OxBC; TTY

To pray you open your whole self. Eagle Poem. Joy Harjo. HATNAP; WeW-3

To prepare the body. Ikebana. Cathy Song. YaYoPo

To President bush at the Start of the Gulf War. Robert Bly. RaBo

To Priapos. *Unknown.* GrAn, *tr. by* Guy Davenport

To prink me up and make me higher placed. George Gascoigne. Son *Fr.* Gascoigne's Memories.

To print our poems the propulsive cause. Fame Makes Us Forward. Robert Herrick. CaPo

To Professor Byrd Prillerman. Maggie Pogue Johnson. CBWP-4

To Prote. Simmias of Thebes. AWP, *tr. by* John Addington Symonds

To prove himself no plagiary, Moore. On J. M. S. Gent. Pope. FaBoEE

To pull the metal splinter from my palm. Gift, The. Li-Young Lee. BodElec; LoL; OpBo; RaBo; UnSA

To pull yourself up by your own roots; to eat the last meal in / your old neighborhood. (LL) Adrienne Rich. FaBoWP; HCAP *Fr.* Shooting Script.

To Purity and Truth. *Unknown.* TrJP, *tr. by* William C. White

To push my boat into the river. (LL) Kofi Awoonor. PBMAP; VCWP *Fr.* Night of My Blood (1971).

To put off a decision. No Easy Harbour. Anne Hartigan. CIP-2

To put on shoes and be sophisticated. Ode to Language. Robert Kelly. PFTM-2; SeSe

To put out the word, whore, thou dost me woo. To a Friend. Ben Jonson. BeJo

To put the black well-fashioned yewship. Alexander MacDonald. NePenScot, *tr. by* Hugh MacDiarmid *Fr.* Clanranald's Galley.

To Pyrrha. Horace. AWP, *tr. by* Milton *Fr.* Odes.

To Queen Elizabeth. Mary Sidney Herbert, Countess of Pembroke. *See* To the Thrice-Sacred Queen Elizabeth

To Queen Elizabeth. Jane Seager. EMWP

To R. B. Gerard Manley Hopkins. GTBS-P; OxAEP-2

To R. Hudson. Alexander Montgomerie. OxBS

To R. K. James Kenneth Stephen. FaBoEE; NBLV; NOBL; PeLV; UV

To Raja Rao. Czeslaw Milosz. TOF

To range, deep-wrapt, along a heavenly height. To Bayard Taylor. Sidney Lanier. NCAP

To read it well: that is, to understand. (LL) To the Reader. Ben Jonson. BASC; BeJo; NoP-4; PoE

To read my book[e], the virgin shy [*or* shie]. To His Book[e]. Martial. AWP; OBVE, *tr. by* Robert Herrick

To read our few poets. Ode. Hugh Maxton. PBCIP

To Remain. Constantine P. Cavafy. BoLoP, *tr. by* Stephen Spender and Nikos Stangos

To remember is not always to go back to what was. Time Reminded Me. Julia Uceda. BoWoP, *tr. by* Willis Barnstone

To remember with tears! (LL) Four Ducks on a Pond. William Allingham. NOBVV; NOIV; OxAEP-2

To rend me and redeem. (LL) Bone-Flower Elegy. Robert Earl Hayden. APT-2; NoAM

To replay agonies was the necessary terror. Daughter-Mother-Maya-Seeta. Reetika Vazirani. NAPBL

To reply, in face of a bad season. Ill Wind, The. Jay Macpherson. MoCV

To Restore a Dead Child. Edwin Honig.
   1925. NoAM
   "Sometimes while I sleep." NoAM

To Retiredness. Mildmay Fane, 2d Earl of Westmorland. BeJo; NOSC

To Retirement. Luís De León. TrJP, *tr.* by Thomas Walsh

To Return to the Urges Unconscious of their Beginnings. Pham Tien Duat. AmFaPo, *tr.* by Kevin Bowen and Ngo Vinh Hai

To Rev. Thaddeus Saltus. Mary Weston Fordham. CBWP-2

To Rhea. Ralph Waldo Emerson. APN-1

To Richard Wagner. Sidney Lanier. APN-2; NCAP *Fr.* Street Cries.

To riddle me that. (LL) Riddle: "Land was white, The." *Unknown.* FaBoVe; OxNR

To Ride. Paul Éluard. TTTS, *tr.* by Kenneth Koch

To Robbers furious, and to Lovers tame. Translation of Du Bellay's *Epigram on a Dog.* Samuel Johnson. FaBoEE

To Robert Baron. Arthur Johnston. NePenScot, *tr.* by Robert Crawford

To Robert Browning. Walter Savage Landor. NoP-4

To Robert Louis Stevenson. William Ernest Henley. MoBrPo

To Robert Lowell and Osip Mandelstam. Frederick Seidel. BodElec

To Robert Nichols. Robert Graves. PeFWW

To Robin Redbreast. Robert Herrick. PoE

To roll his mare among the trampled lilies. (LL) Zebras, The. Roy Campbell. MoBrPo; OxBSo

To Rome Entombed in Her Ruins. Francisco de Quevedo y Villegas. SpanPo, *tr.* by Kate Flores

To Roosevelt. "Rubén Dario." PFTM-1; TCLAP, *tr.* by Lysander Kemp

To Rosamond. Geoffrey Chaucer. *See* To Rosamounde

To Rosamounde. Geoffrey Chaucer. PoE

(Madame, ye been of alle beautee shrine.) NoP-4

(To Rosamond.) NoP-4

To Rosania (now Mrs Montague) Being With Her, 25th September 1652. Katherine Philips. PoBW

To Rose. Roberta Hill. ReEnLa

To Roses in the Bosom[e] of Castara. William Habington. BeJo; EnLoPo; MeLP; NOSC; OBEV; SCGP *Fr.* Castara.

To row aboot his corse. (LL) Under the Greenwood Tree. Hugh MacDiarmid. FaBoWar; OBVE

To Russia. Vladimir Vladimirovich Nabokov. TCRP, *tr.* by Vladimir Nabokov

To S.C. Robert Louis Stevenson. NePenScot; PeVV

To S. R. Crockett. Robert Louis Stevenson. *See* Blows the Wind Today

To S. T. C. on His 179th Birthday, October 12th, 1951. Maurice Carpenter. FaBoTw

To safeguard man from wrongs, there nothing must. Distrust. Robert Herrick. CaPo

To sail the entire length of a body. Brief Lessons in Eroticism 1. Gioconda Belli. ErotSp; TANSG, *tr.* by Steven F. White

To Saint Margaret. Henry Constable. NoSic

To Saint Mary Magdalen. Henry Constable. NoSic; Son

To Sallie, Walking. Sterling Allen Brown. GT

To Sally. John Quincy Adams. APN-1; AWP; OBAL

To Sally. Horace. *See* Odes

To Samuel, Bishop of Sens In Time of Dearth. Alcuin. MLL, *tr.* by Helen Waddell

To Satch. Samuel Allen. ISC; MoASP; PAI; TTY

To save lives. (LL) Conception. Josephine Miles. ColAP; FaBoWP

To save the [or th'] *Athenian* walls from ruin bare. (LL) When the Assault Was Intended to the City. John Milton. GTBS-P; OxBSo; SCGP; Son

To Saxham. Thomas Carew. BASC; BeJo; CaPo; CavPo

To scare myself with my own desert places. (LL) Desert Places. Robert Frost. APT-1; HarvBoo; InPK-6; MoAmPo; NAAL-2v2; NAAL-5; NOBA; NoAM; OxBA; PoE; RB; SoSe-8; TAP; TRP; UnPo

To School! Stevie Smith. FaBoEE

To Science. Edgar Allan Poe. *See* Sonnet—To Science

To Scilla. Sir Charles Sedley. FaBoEE

To scream for help through a horn. (LL) February in Sydney. Yusef Komunyakaa. ESEAA; NAAAL

To scug his deadly sin. (LL) Young Benjie. *Unknown.* ESPB; OxBB

To Secretary Lu Ch'ien of Jen City. Li Po. SuSp, *tr.* by Joseph J. Lee

To See a Friend Off. Wang Wei. ChinPo, *tr.* by Yip Wai-lim

To See a Friend Off to Shu. Li Po. ChinPo, *tr.* by Yip Wai-lim

To see a strange [or quaint] outlandish fowl. Bounty of Our Age, The. Henry Farley. FaBoCh; FaBoEE; NOSC

To see a woman long oppressed by fear. Hayden Carruth. ErotSp *Fr.* Sonnets.

To see a World in a Grain of Sand. William Blake. EBEV; EnlH; FaBoCh; InPK-6; KaS; NPeEn; OxAEP-2; OxBEV; OxBoLi; PeECV; TFi1 *Fr.* Auguries of Innocence.

To see both blended in one flood. Upon the Infant Martyrs. Richard Crashaw. GeHe; NPeEn; PAI

To see herself tonight. (LL) Brown Girl Dead, A. Countee Cullen. GT; TAP

To See if Something Comes Next. Jack Gilbert. BodElec

To See Meng Hao-Jan Off to Yang-Chou. Li Po. ChinPo, *tr.* by Yip Wai-lim

To see my father. Golden State. Frank Bidart. NoAM

To see my lady joyful in her place. (LL) Of His Lady in Heaven. Jacopo da Lentino. AWP; EaItPo, *tr.* by Dante Gabriel Rossetti

To See Ol' Booker T. Maggie Pogue Johnson. CBWP-4

To See Secretary Shu-Yun Off at the Hsieh T'iao Tower at Hsuan-Ch'eng. Li Po. ChinPo, *tr.* by Yip Wai-lim

To see such dainty ghosts as you appear. On Meeting a Gentlewoman in the Dark. *Unknown.* FaBoEE

To see the abysses of the human heart. (LL) Heart's Abysses, The. Walter Savage Landor. FaBoEE; OBSV

To see the cherry hung with snow. (LL) A. E. Housman. AWP; ChAP; ClHu; HAP; InPK-6; MakPoe; MoBrPo; NAEL-6v2; NoAM; NoP-4; OxBTC; PoE; PoPoPo; RB; SCGP; SoSe-8; TFi; WeW-3

To See the Cross at Christmas. Roger Cooper. TrCP

To see the green returning. Giacomino Pugliesi. EaItPo, *tr.* by Dante Gabriel Rossetti

To See the Hours of Fever. Gustavo Adolfo Bécquer. SpanPo, *tr.* by John Crow

To see the hours of fever. To See the Hours of Fever. Gustavo Adolfo Bécquer. SpanPo, *tr.* by John Crow

To see the house you were born in. I Stopped in Tupelo, Elvis. Van K. Brock. AllShUp

To see the land I love. (LL) Night Journey. Theodore Roethke. AmFaPo; GM; KaS

To see the lark, delighted, dare. Bernard [or Bernart] de Ventadour [or Ventadorn]. STV

To see the Moscow-bound express withdraw. Poetry of Motion, The. Raymond Garlick. AngWePo

To see them go by drowning in the river. Eli, Eli. Judith Wright. BMAP; CBAP; GI

To see them so: fleshed, fair, erected indivisible. (LL) Imaginary Iceberg, The. Elizabeth Bishop. FaBoWP; MoAmPo

To see those eyes. Philadelphia: Spring, 1985. Sonia Sanchez. ESEAA

To see what my black hen doth lay. (LL) Black Hen, The. Mother Goose. LB; ReMoGo

To see you living and the fountains run. (LL) Napoli Again. Richard Hugo. AF; LCAP-2

To seek a place with less inclement weather. (LL) Two Fish. Katha Pollitt. DiPo; NIL-7; NIP-4

To seek new lechery in Death. (LL) Epitaph on M. H., An. Charles Cotton. EBEV; FaBoEE; NPeEn

To seek our way of thinking. Light in One's Blood, The. Gemino H. Abad. ReBoTo

To Send Away Melancholy. Huang Tsun-hsien. SuSp, *tr.* by An-yan Tang

To Send to Li Tan and Yüan Hsi. Wei Ying-wu. CoBCP, *tr.* by Burton Watson

To Send to Tu Fu as a Joke. Li Po. ColAnChi, *tr.* by Elling O. Eide

To Sergius. Sir Charles Sedley. FaBoEE

To set before the king? (LL) Mother Goose. OxBEV; OxNR

To set things right? (LL) Earnest Liberal's Lament, The. Ernest Hemingway. OBAL; OBSV

To Sextus. Martial. FaBoEE, *tr.* by Sir Charles Sedley

To shade and fiber, milk and memory. (LL) James Merrill. HCAP; LCAP-2; NAAL-2v2; NoAM; NoP-4; VCAP *Fr.* Book of Ephraim, The.

To shadows and delusions here. (LL) Indian Burying Ground, The. Philip Freneau. ColAP; HAP; NAAL-2v1; NAAL-3; NOBA; NoP-4; OxBA; TAP; TCAPo; TFi

To shaggy Pan, and all the Wood-Nymphs fair. Shepherd's Gift, A. Anyte [or Anytes]. AWP, *tr.* by John William Burgon

To Shakespeare. Nina Nikolaevna Berberova. TCRusP, *tr.* by John Glad

To Shakespeare. Hart Crane. Son

To Shakespeare. Thomas Edwards. Son

To Shakespeare. Frances Anne [or "Fanny"] Kemble. Son; SWaP

To shew their sharpnesse. (LL) Homer. NPeEn; OBVE *Fr.* Iliad, The.

To shock-haired Pan and the nymphs who protect the cow-byres. Anyte [or Anytes]. GrAn

To shove this chair away from here. To Sit, to Stand, to Kill, to Die. Attila József. AF, *tr.* by John Batki

To Show How Humble. *Unknown.* AH

To show that still she lives. (LL) Harp That Once through Tara's Halls, The. Thomas Moore. CABP; NAEL-5v2; NAEL-6v2

To show the laboring [or lab'ring] bosom's deep intent. To S.M., a Young African Painter, on Seeing His Works. Phillis Wheatley. BlSi; MakPoe; NAAL-2v1; NAAL-3; NAAL-5

To Show to My Sons. Lu Yu. ColAnChi, *tr.* by Burton Watson

(In death I know well enough all things end in emptiness.) CoBCP, *tr.* by Burton Watson

To shred them: a narrow labor, and simply toss. Destruction of Letters. Babette Deutsch. WPE

To shun the heaven that leads men to this hell! (LL) William Shakespeare. AWP; EBEV; ErotSp; HAP; HeIP-4; NAEL-5v1; NAEL-6v1; NAEL-7v1;

NIL-7; NIP-4; NOBE; NoSic; OBEV; OxAEP-1; OxBEV; PAI; PoE; SCGP; SCV; Son; TFi; UnPo; WoPoe　*Fr.* Sonnets.

To Sickness. Ben Jonson. BeJo

To Sidmouth and Castlereagh. Shelley.　*See* Similes for Two Political Characters of 1819

To sigh, and sing at liberty—like thee! (LL)　To a Nightingale. Charlotte Smith. CenSon; OxBSo; RWP

To Silence. Thomas Lovell Beddoes.　Son

To Silence. Alice Thompson Meynell.　VWP

To Simplicity. Samuel Taylor Coleridge. CenSon　*Fr.* Sonnets Attempted in the Manner of Contemporary Writers.

To simulate the burning of the heart. Patrizia Cavalli. NeIt; VCWP, *tr. by* Judith Baumel

To Simulate the Burning of the Heart, the Humiliation. Patrizia Cavalli. CItWP, *tr. by* Cinzia Sartini Blum and Lara Trubowitz

To sin's a vice in nature, and we find. Daniel Defoe. OBSV　*Fr.* More Reformation.

To sin, unshamed, to lose, unthinking. Russia. Aleksandr Aleksandrovich Blok. AWP, *tr. by* Babette Deutsch and Avrahm Yarmolinsky

To sing of wars, of captain[e]s, and of kings. Anne Bradstreet. BASC; BoWoP; EMWP; NAAL-2v1; NAAL-3; NAAL-5; NALW; NOBA; NoP-4; OxBA; PEW; PoE; SCAP; TAP; TCAPo; WPE

To sing with the loudest voice. (LL)　On the Tattered Edges. Amina Said. HAWP; NAfrP, *tr. by* Eric Sellin

To sing you / one song. Pruzzian Elegy. Johannes Bobrowski. AF

To Siôn Lloyd: the Mother's Advice to Her Heir. Catherin Owen Llwyd. EMWP

To Sir Francis Brian. Sir Thomas Wyatt. NoSic　*Fr.* Satires.

To Sir H. W. at His Going Ambassador to Venice. John Donne. MeLP

To Sir Henry Cary. Ben Jonson. NOSC; NoP-4

To Sir Henry Goodyere. Ben Jonson. NOSC

To Sir Henry Newton, upon His Re-edifying the Church of Charleton in Kent. Thomas Philipott. NOSC

To Sir Henry [*or* Henrie] Savile [upon His Translation of Tacitus]. Ben Jonson. BASC

To Sir Henry Vane the Younger. John Milton. PBRV; Son

To Sir Henry Wotton. John Donne. NoSic; OxAEP-1

To Sir Horace Vere. Ben Jonson. BeJo

To Sir Hudson Lowe. Thomas Moore. OBSV

To Sir Humphry Mackworth. Thomas Yalden.
"Miner thus through perils digs his way, The." ECEV

To Sir John Wentworth, Upon His Curiosities and Courteous Entertainment at Summerly in Lovingland. Mildmay Fane, 2d Earl of Westmorland. OBGa

To Sir Philip Sidney's Soul. Henry Constable.　*See* On the Death of Sir Philip Sidney

To Sir Robert Wroth. Ben Jonson. BeJo

To Sir Thomas Roe. Ben Jonson. BASC

To Sir Toby. Philip Freneau. NAAL-2v1; NAAL-3; NoP-4; TAP

To sit on the moon. (LL)　Witches' Ride, The. Karla Kuskin. NOxBChV; OxIBACP; TLR

To sit on the veranda of a hotel in Jerusalem. Letter. Yehuda Amichai [*or* Amikhai]. VCWP

To sit people on gas-stove jets. Mother-in-Law of the Marquis de Sade, The. Jennifer Maiden. NOBAu

To sit silent. Otomo no Tabito. TAL

To Sit, to Stand, to Kill, to Die. Attila József. AF, *tr. by* John Batki

To sit upon her belly warm. Jack Frost. Fay Zwicky. BMAP

To Sleep. Giovanni Della Casa. AWP, *tr. by* John Addington Symonds

To Sleep. Lord Alfred Bruce Douglas. GSo

To Sleep. John Fletcher.　*See* Tragedy of Valentinian, The

To Sleep. John Keats. NIP-4; OBEV; OxBSo; Son
(Sonnet to Sleep.) NAEL-5v2; NAEL-6v2

To Sleep. Sir Philip Sidney.　*See* Astrophil and Stella

To Sleep. Charlotte Smith. CenSon; NAEL-6v2; RWP; Son; WPE

To Sleep. Publius Papinius Statius. RomPo, *tr. by* W. G. Shepherd　*Fr.* Sylvae.

To Sleep. William Wordsworth. GTBS-P; Son

To sleep alone. (LL)　Lady Izumi. BoWoP; WoPoe, *tr. by* Willis Barnstone

To sleep easy all night.　*Unknown.*　OxNR

To Sleep I give my powers away. Tennyson. NAEL-6v2　*Fr.* In Memoriam A. H. H.

To———, Sleeping. Adah Isaacs Menken. PoBW

To slice through Buddhas, Patriarchs. Daito.　ZenPo, *tr. by* Takashi Ikemoto and Lucien Stryk

To S.M., a Young African Painter, on Seeing His Works. Phillis Wheatley. BlSi; MakPoe; NAAL-2v1; NAAL-3; NAAL-5
(To show the lab'ring bosom's deep intent.) ColAP; NAAAL; NoP-4

Tō So-kin of Rakuyō, ancient friend, Chancellor of Gen.　Exile's Letter. Li Po.　CTC; FaBoMo; OxBA, *tr. by* Ezra Pound

To So-Kin of Rakuyo, ancient friend, Chancellor of Gen.　Exile's Letter. Rihaku.　APT-1, *tr. by* Ezra Pound

To Solitude. Alice Cary.　APN-2

To Solitude. Mihály Csokonai Vitéz.　IQMS, *tr. by* Edmund Charles Blunden

To Some Supposed Brothers. Essex Hemphill.　GLP
(XXI.)　NAAAL

To Someone Who Insisted I Look up Someone. X. J. Kennedy.　OBCoV

To Somes / from incarceration, Taunton State Hospital, 1972.　Children of the Working Class. John Weiners.　BB

To Song. Olga Fiodorovna Berggolts [*or* Bergholts]. BoWoP, *tr. by* Daniel Weissbort

To soothe my Lady's dreams. (LL)　Song: "Linnet in the rocky dells, The." Emily Jane Brontë.　HAP; RACG

To Soulfolk. Margaret Goss Burroughs.　BlSi

To sound of trumpet rather than of horn. Guido Cavalcanti.　EaItPo, *tr. by* Dante Gabriel Rossetti

To spare my sack of coals. (LL)　Winter. John Millington Synge.　NOIV; OBMV; OxBTC

To speak in a flat voice. Speak. James Wright (1927–80).　HAP; NoP-4; TAP

To speak in summer in a lecture hall. Lecture Hall. Patrick Kavanagh. FaBoTw

To Speak of My Influences. Jean Garrigue.　LW

To Speak of Woe That Is in Marriage. Robert Lowell.　NAAL-2v2; NoAM

To speak out clean. Telling It. Nancy Sullivan.　TAP

To speak the truth, although believed too late. (LL)　Upon the Saying That My Verses Were Made by Another. Anne Killigrew.　BASC; CABP; EMWP; NALW; PEW; WPE

To Spencer. George Turberville.　NoSic

To spend uncounted years of pain. Arthur Hugh Clough.　NOBVV; OxBSP

To Spenser. John Hamilton Reynolds.　Son

To spider in our dirt-filled eyes. (LL)　Osip Mandelstam.　Seamus Deane. BiHa; PBCIP

To spoil the first impression. (LL)　To His Saviour, a Child; a Present, by a Child. Robert Herrick.　BeJo; ChIV-2; PeECV; TrCP

To spread the azure canopy of heaven. William Henry Drummond.　OxBSo

To Spring. William Blake. NAEL-5v2; NAEL-6v2; NOEC; OBEV; SCGP

To Spring. Mihály Fazekas. IQMS, *tr. by* Watson Kirkconnell

To Spring. Charlotte Smith. BWW; RWP; WPE

To St. Augustine. "Angelus Silesius." GePo, *tr. by* George C. Schoolfield　*Fr.* Cherubical Wanderer, The.

To St John Baptist. Henry Constable. ChIV-2; NoSic

To St Mary Magdalen. Henry Constable. ChIV-2; NoSic; PBRV
(Sweete Saynt: Thow better canst declare to me.)　PBRV

To St. Michael the Archangel. Henry Constable. ChIV-2

To St. Peter and St. Paul. Henry Constable. NoSic; Son

To stain the stiff dishonoured shroud. (LL)　Sweeney Among the Nightingales. T. S. Eliot. APT-1; FaBoMo; HAP; HarvBoo; HeIP-4; NAAL-2v2; NAEL-5v2; NAEL-6v2; NOBA; NOBE; NPeEn; NoAM; NoP-4; OBMV; OxBA; OxBEV; PoPoPo; TFi; WeW-3

To stand here in the wings of Europe.　On a Return from Egypt. Keith Douglas. NoP-4

To stand on common ground.　Common Ground, A. Denise Levertov. PoM

To stand on the parcel of land where the saint.　Simone Weil: In Assisi. Edward Hirsch. BBASP

To stare at nothing is to learn by heart.　Night, The Porch, The. Mark Strand. KGB

To start somewhere.　Weather They Were Written In, The. Kathy Fagan. PuP-23

To state each horror.　From the Monkey House and Other Cages: Monkey II. Irena Klepfisz. GLP

To stave off disaster, or bring the devil to heel.　Tapu. Arthur Rex Dugard Fairburn. PeNZ

To stay our minds on and be staid. (LL)　Choose Something like a Star. Robert Frost. APT-1; MoAmPo

To stay the season of a mind. (LL)　Massacre, October '66. Wole Soyinka. AF; PBMAP

To Stella. Hester Mulso. ECWP

To Stella. Plato. EnLoPo; FaBoEE; OBVE
(Morning and Evening Star.)　AWP

To Stella. Jonathan Swift. NOEC

To strengthen whilst one stands. (LL)　Christina Georgina Rossetti. EBEV; NAEL-5v2; NAEL-6v2; NALW; NOBVV; NOxBChV; OBNV; OxAEP-2; OxBEV; VWP; ViWPN

To Strephon. Sarah Dixon. ECWP

To strive, to seek, to find, and not to yield. (LL)　Ulysses. Tennyson. AWP; AmFaPo; CABP; ClHu; EBEV; FHYEP; HAP; HeIP-4; InPK-6; MakPoe;

NAEL-5v2; NAEL-6v2; NAWM-7v2; NIL-7; NIP-4; NOBE; NOBVV; NPeEn; NoP-4; OxAEP-2; OxBEV; PoE; PoPoPo; PoRA; SCGP; SCV; SoSe-8; TFi; TRP; UnPo; WeW-3

To strongly, wrongly, vainly love thee still. (LL) Love and Death. Byron. CAGL; EBEV; NOBE

To stub an oar on a rock where none should be. Basking Shark. Norman MacCaig. NePenScot

To Subprefect Chang. Wang Wei. SuSp, tr. by Irving Y. Lo

To such a state have I been brought by your mischief, my Lesbia. 75. Catullus. NAWM-7v1, tr. by Charles Martin

To suffer for this land, to live for it and aid. Encouragement. János Batsányi. IQMS, tr. by Matthew Mead

To sulk upon my mother's breast. (LL) William Blake. FHYEP; NAEL-5v2; NAEL-6v2; OxAEP-2; OxBEV; OxBSP; PoPoPo; RB Fr. Songs of Experience.

To Sultan Murad II. James Clarence Mangan. NOIV

To sup with thee thou didst me home invite. Invitation, The. Robert Herrick. CaPo

To survive things have to be blunted. Blunting, The. Richard Eberhart. BodElec

To survive? (LL) Anchorage. Joy Harjo. HATNAP; LTA; OPRER

To S.V. György Petri. VCWP, tr. by George Gömöri and Clive Wilmer

To swap my poems for squeaky English. (LL) Pity the Man Who English Lacks. Michael Hartnett. CIP-2; PBCIP

To swerve from village chapel to a town's. Visitor's Book, 8, The. John Davies. TCAWP

To Swim, to Believe. Maxine W. Kumin. MoASP

To Sycamores. Robert Herrick. CaPo

To Sylvia. Giacomo Leopardi. NAWM-7v2, tr. by Ottavio M. Casale

To T.A.R.H. Stephen Spender. CAGL

To T. H., a Lady Resembling My Mistress. Thomas Carew. CaPo

To-ta Ti-om. Peter Blue Cloud. HATNAP

To take a Part of mine. (LL) Polwart on the Green. Allan Ramsay. NOEC; NPeEn; OxBEV

To take a woman in your arms. It's Easy. Lee Cataldi. BMAP

To take the darkness in. Crowdoll. L. S. Asekoff. BodElec

To take the field. (LL) Bit of Brass, A. Padraic Fallon. ModIr; NPeEn

To take the only way to be forgiven. (LL) On the Benefactions in the Late Frost. Pope. NOEC; OxBSP

To take the wrong road. Little Infinite Poem. Federico García Lorca. RaBo, tr. by Robert Bly

To take us sick, that sound would not take thee? (LL) Pursuit[e], The. Henry Vaughan. AngWePo; GeHe; NOSC; SacPr; TrCP

To talk about trees. (LL) Adrienne Rich. ExTi; LoL Fr. Not Somewhere Else, But Here.

To talk alone, at the threshold, with already-gone, has-been, to-be- / announced. To be your own legend. Notebook, Two. Edmond Jabès. AF, tr. by Rosmarie Waldrop

To talk to each other. (LL) Little. Dorothy Aldis. NTCP; WHSW

To Tan-Ch'iu. Li Po. AWP; ChiP, tr. by Arthur Waley

To Tan Ch'iu. Li Po. TAL

To Tarshish. Shimon Halkin. MHP, tr. by Ruth Finer Mintz

To taste terrain their heirs need not draw near. (LL) Singing Bones, The. Randolph Stow. BMAP; CBAP

"To tedious Hell this body with its muddy feet in my mind!" (LL) Menses. Edna St. Vincent Millay. APT-1; RACG

To Telembrotos. Antipater of Thessalonica. GrAn, tr. by Alistair Elliot

To tell each point he nameth with a kiss. (LL) William Browne (1591–1643). NOBE; OBEV Fr. Inner Temple Masque, The.

To tell me, out of the body, out of the body travel. (LL) For Esther. Stanley Plumly. GM; LCAP-2

To tell of Prodigies, and cause affright. (LL) Virgil [or Vergil]. NPeEn; OBVE, tr. by John Dryden Fr. Aeneid [or Eneados, Aeneis], The.

To tell strange feats of deamons, here I am. To the Much Honoured R. F. Esq. Richard Chamberlain. SCAP

To tell the world my proper name. Ralph Erskine. SacPr Fr. Believer's Riddle, The.

To tell what others were, came down? (LL) Epicurean Ode, An. John Hall. MeLP; NOSC; NPeEn

To tell you from the start, I have lost him whose hand and eye are gentle. He Whose Hand and Eye Are Gentle. Unknown. OBWVE, tr. by Kenneth Hurlstone Jackson

To Thaliarchus ("Thou seest the hills"). Horace. OBVE, tr. by Sir Richard Fanshawe Fr. Odes.

To that deliberate progress. (LL) Considering the Snail. Thom Gunn. NAEL-5v2; NAEL-6v2; OxBEV; TwCP

To that I am on my way running. (LL) Song for a Young Girl's Puberty Ceremony. Unknown. ChAP; ItWoWo, tr. by Frances Densmore

To that invisible element which claimed. Invisible Element, The. István Vas. IQMS, tr. by George Szirtes

To that place day doth unyoke! (LL) John Fletcher. NOBE; OBEV Fr. Faithful Shepherdess, The.

To that sweet thief which sourly robs from me. (LL) William Shakespeare. HeIP-4; NAEL-5v1; NAEL-6v1; NAEL-7v1; NoSic; OxAEP-1; PoE; SCGP; UnPo Fr. Sonnets.

To the Accuser Who Is the God of This World. William Blake. See Gates of Paradise, The

To the Age's Insanities. Marie Ponsot. VGW

To the Air of a Pibroch. Duncan Ban MacIntyre. NePenScot, tr. by Iain Crichton Smith Fr. Last Farewell to the Hills.

To the Almighty on his radiant throne. Anne Finch, Countess of Winchilsea. ChIV-1 Fr. Pindaric Poem, A.

To the Angel Spirit of the Most Excellent Sir Philip Sidney. Mary Sidney Herbert, Countess of Pembroke. NAEL-7v1

(To the Angel Spirit of the Most Excellent Sir Philip Sidney.) NAEL-7v1

To the Anxious Mother. Valente Goenha Malangatana. PBA; PBMAP, tr. by Dorothy Guedes and Philippa Rumsey

To the apostles of history. Aleksey [or Aleksei] Petrovich Tsvetkov. TCRusP

To the Archbishop of Tuam. Unknown. FaBoEE

To the Archdeacon. George Farewell. NOEC

To the arms of brown people. (LL) Black Hair. Gary Soto. MoASP; UnSA

To the audience hall the worthy banished minister was recalled. Master Chia. Li Shang-yin. ColAnChi, tr. by James J. Y. Liu

To the Author of Agnes de Castro. Delariviere Manley. EMWP

To the Author of Clarissa. Thomas Edwards. Son

To the Autumnal Moon. Samuel Taylor Coleridge. CenSon Fr. Effusions.

To the Avon River above Stratford, Canada. James Reaney. MoCV

To the banks of the Moldau River. How They Made the Golem. John Robert Colombo. MoCV

To the Banquet of the Earth. Martial Sinda. NegPo, tr. by Ellen Conroy Kennedy

To The Barbarian. Else Lasker-Schüler. PFTM-1

To the Bartholdi Statue. Ambrose Bierce. APN-2

To the Bat. Ann Radcliffe. CenSon

To the Beloved. Alice Thompson Meynell. VWP

To the Beloved Grown Past Youth. Amin Nakhla. MAP, tr. by Matthew Sorenson

To the Best, and Most Accomplished Couple. Henry Vaughan. PeECV

To the Blessed Sacrament. Henry Constable. NoSic

To the Blessed Virgin. William Alabaster. NoSic

To the Body. Alice Thompson Meynell. PeVV

To the Body. Coventry Patmore. CABP Fr. Unknown Eros, The.

To the Bone. Dorothy Allison. GLP

To the boy who comes in summer the country. Goat God, The. Cesare Pavese. WoPoe, tr. by William Arrowsmith

To the bridge of love. Juan Ramón Jiménez. SpanPo; WoPoe, tr. by James Wright Fr. Ten Short Poems.

To the Building Trade. Matthew Sweeney. ModIr

To the Cambro-Britons, and their Harp, his Ballad of Agincourt. Michael Drayton. See Battle of Agincourt, The

To the capital / Snow-clouds forming. Basho. ZenPo, tr. by Takashi Ikemoto and Lucien Stryk

To the Child Elis. Georg Trakl. WoPoe, tr. by Robert Firmage

To the Child That Never Was. Emma Sepúlveda-Pulvirenti. TANSG, tr. by Shaun Griffin

To the Children. Gabriela Mistral. SpanPo, tr. by Kate Flores

To the Christians. Francis Lauderdale Adams. ChIV-2; OxBS

To the City of London [or In Honour of the City of London]. William Dunbar. EBEV; OBEV

(Above all rivers thy river hath renown.) OPOU

To the Cloud Juggler. Hart Crane. HarvBoo

To the Clouds. Susan Evance. CenSon

To the Conference. Mrs. Henry Linden. CBWP-4

To the Countess of A— Written on the Anniversary of Her Marriage. Charlotte Smith. RWP

To the Countess of Bedford. John Donne. NOSC

To The Countess of Salisbury. John Donne. PeECV

To the Countesse of Bedford. John Donne. MeLP

To the cove of my breasts your forehead will return. Ana Istarú. TANSG, tr. by Shaun Griffin and Emma Sepúlveda-Pulirenti

To the Creator of My Bones. Anna Hajnal. IQMS, tr. by Jeannette Nichols

To the Critic. Michael Drayton. See Idea

To the Critics. Priscilla Pointon.

"I never tasted the Pierian spring." ECWP

On Her Blindness. ECWP

To the Cuckoo. Michael Bruce. OBEV

(Ode: To the Cuckoo.) NOEC

To the Cuckoo. F. H. Townsend. UV

To the Cuckoo. William Wordsworth. GTBS-P; NOBRP; UV

To the Curlew. Helen Maria Williams. CenSon; WoRP

To the Daisy. William Wordsworth. GTBS-P

To the Dandelion. James Russell Lowell. NAAL-2v1; NAAL-3
   "Dear common flower, that grow'st beside the way." NAAL-2v1

To the Day-Dreamer. Mihály Vörösmarty. IQMS, *tr.* by Hymen H. Hart and Watson Kirkconnell

To the Days. Adrienne Rich. AmFaPo; LoL *Fr.* Not Somewhere Else, But Here.

To the Dead. Frank Bidart. MakPoe

To the Dead Cardinal of Westminster. Francis Thompson. PeVV

To the Dear Lord. Christine Busta. AuPH, *tr.* by Lowell A. Bangerter

To the Death of Mirrors. Nancy Joyce Peters. SurWo

To the Detracter. Robert Herrick. PBRV

To the Diaspora. Gwendolyn Brooks. NAAL-5; NIL-7

To the dim light and the large circle of shade. Of the Lady Pietra degli Scrovigni. Dante Alighieri. AWP; EaItPo; MakPoe; NPeEn; OBVE, *tr.* by Dante Gabriel Rossetti

To the Distant One. Po Chü-i. TAL

To the Dregs. Betsy Sholl. ExTi

To the Eagle. Mary Weston Fordham. CBWP-2

To the Earl of Egremont. Charlotte Smith. RWP

To the Earl of Oxford, Late Lord Treasurer. Jonathan Swift. FaBoWar; OBVE

To the Earl of Warwick, on the Death of Mr. Addison. Thomas Tickell. NOEC; OxAEP-1

To the East and to the West. Walt Whitman. APN-1

To the eastern grove where a spring rises. Replying to a Poem by the Monk Ling-yi at the New Spring. Liu Ch'ang-ch'ing. SuSp, *tr.* by William H. Nienhauser

To the Echo of Tihany. Mihály Csokonai Vitéz. IQMS, *tr.* by Adam Makkai

To the Editor of Mr. Pope's Works. Thomas Edwards. Son

To the Eminent Scholar and Meddler. Kofi Awoonor. HBAPE

To the Emperor. Theodore Prodromos. WoPoe, *tr.* by Jack Lindsay

To the Emperor's Messenger. Muso Soseki. EaWin, *tr.* by W. S. Merwin

To the end, to the end they remain. (LL) For the Fallen. Laurence Binyon. NOBE; NPeEn; OBEV; OBWP; OxBTC

To the Enemies. Vladimir Holan. AF, *tr.* by C. G. Hanzlicek

To the Eolian Harp. Mary Robinson. CenSon; RWP

To the Etruscan Poets. Richard Wilbur. OxBC

To the Evening. John Codrington Bampfylde. NOEC

To the Evening Star. William Blake. NAEL-5v2; NAEL-6v2; NOEC; NPeEn; PoE; TFi
   (Thou fair-hair'd angel of the evening.) GSo; NoP-4

To the Evening Star. Thomas Campbell. GTBS-P; NePenScot

To the Evening Star: Central Minnesota. James Wright (1927–80). NAAL-5

To the Excellent Mrs. Anne Owen. Katherine Philips. NOSC

To the Excellent Orinda. "Philo-Philippa." BASC

To the Excellent Pattern of Beauty and Virtue, Lady Elizabeth, Countess of Ormonde. James Shirley. BeJo

To the Fair Clarinda [*or* Clorinda], Who Made Love to Me, Imagined [*or* Imagin'd] More Than Woman. Aphra Behn. BASC; CABP; EMWP; NALW; NIL-7; NoP-4; PEW; PoBW

To the fancy of Arthur O'Shaughnessy. (LL) On the Poet, Arthur O'Shaughnessy—. Dante Gabriel Rossetti. OBCoV; PeLi

To the Far Corners of Fractured Worlds. Susan Griffin. GifTon

To the Fates. Friedrich Hölderlin. NAWM-7v2, *tr.* by Christopher Middleton

To the Father through the features of men's faces. (LL) As Kingfishers Catch Fire. Gerard Manley Hopkins. EBEV; EBVV; EnlH; FaBoMo; MoBrPo; NAEL-5v2; NAEL-6v2; NOBVV; NOCV; NPeEn; NoP-4; OxAEP-2; PoE; RB

To the Fifteen of Piazzale Loreto. Salvatore Quasimodo. AF, *tr.* by Jack Bevan

To the Filial Son, Ts'ui. Hsü Pen. CoBLCP, *tr.* by Jonathan Chaves

To the Film Industry in Crisis. Frank O'Hara. NOBA; OBAL

To the First of August. Ann Plato. BlSi

To the First Slave Ship. Lydia Huntley Sigourney. ColAP

To the Foot from Its Child. Pablo Neruda. RB, *tr.* by Alastair Reid

To the Fortuneteller Hsüeh T'ieh-yai. Hsieh Chin. CoBLCP, *tr.* by Jonathan Chaves

To the Four Courts, Please. James Stephens. BIrV; MoBrPo; UnPo

To the Fragment of a Statue of Hercules, Commonly Called the Torso. Samuel Rogers. CenSon; GS

To the free skies unpent and glad and strong. (LL) To a Locomotive in Winter. Walt Whitman. GM; InPK-6; MoAmPo; NAAL-2v1; NAAL-3; NCAP; NoAM; NoP-4; TAP

To the French of the Second Empire. Arthur Rimbaud. OBWP, *tr.* by Robert Lowell *Fr.* Eighteen-Seventy.

To the Fringed Gentian. William Cullen Bryant. APN-1; AWP; TAP

To the Garden the World. Walt Whitman. ChIV-1

To the Gardener at Nuneham. Horace Walpole, 4th Earl of Orford. FaBoEE

To the Gardin att O: [Owthorpe] 7:th. Lucy Hutchinson. EMWP

To the Generous Reader. Robert Herrick. CaPo

To the Gentlewoman of Llanarth Hall. Evan Thomas. OBWVE, *tr.* by Gwyn Jones

To the German People. Friedrich Hölderlin. WoPoe, *tr.* by Robert Bly

To the ghostly garden to the laurel mute. Autumn Garden. Dino Campana. STV, *tr.* by John Frederick Nims

To the God of Duality, only with metaphors. In Xóchitl in Cuícatl. Ernesto Cardenal. PFTM-2, *tr.* by Carlos Altschul and Monique Altschul

To the God of Fond Desire. James Thomson. EnLoPo

To the God of Love. Edmund George Valpy Knox. NOBL

To the Gods the Shades Flavinus of the Cavalry Regiment. David Wright. NLP

To the Good Thief. Saunders Lewis. OBWVE, *tr.* by Gwyn Morgan

To the grace of the make-believe bed. (LL) Ted Berrigan. FTOS; PFTM-2 *Fr.* Sonnets, The.

To the Grasshopper. Richard Lovelace. *See* Grasshopper, The

To the Grasshopper and the Cricket. Leigh Hunt. CenSon; GSo; OxBSo; Son (Grasshopper and the Cricket, The.) OxAEP-2

To the Great City of Moscow, as He Was Leaving June 25, 1636. Paul Fleming. GePo, *tr.* by George C. Schoolfield

To the Greek Anthologists. George Rostrevor Hamilton. FaBoEE

To the hall, to the hall. Leveller's Rant, The. Alexander Brome. BASC

To the Hand. W. S. Merwin. SPE

To the Harbormaster. Frank O'Hara. CRP; CoAP; NAAL-2v2; PoM; VCAP

To the Harvest Moon. William Stanley Roscoe. CenSon

To the head bobbing in the gunsight. Line. Milo De Angelis. NeIt, *tr.* by Lawrence Venuti

To the Heart. Tadeusz Rózewicz. PoSu, *tr.* by Victor Contoski

To the heart's weeping, which forgets her not. (LL) Ballata: Of His Lady among Other Ladies. Guido Cavalcanti. AWP; EaItPo; *tr.* by Dante Gabriel Rossetti

To the Heavens above us. Astrologer's Song, An. Rudyard Kipling. MoBrPo

To the High Court of Parliament. Geoffrey Hill. OxBEV

To the highest bidder. Highest Bidder, The. Witter Bynner. TCAPo

To the Highland Girl of Inversneyde. William Wordsworth. GTBS-P

To the Holy Goste my goodes I bequeth. *Unknown.* MiEL

To the Holy Spirit. Yvor Winters. MoAmPo; VGW

To the Holy Trinity. *Unknown.* NOIV, *tr.* by Thomas Kinsella

To the Hon. Mrs. C——e. Jane West. ECWP

To the Hungarian Nation. Matthew Arnold. OxBSo

To the Hungarian People. János Edrosi Sylvester. IQMS, *tr.* by Adam Makkai

To the Hungarians: "Oh you, once mighty Hungary, gone to seed." Dániel Berzsenyi. IQMS, *tr.* by Adam Makkai

To the Hungarians: "Seas of Sorrow boil with a rage, Magyar, The." Dániel Berzsenyi. IQMS, *tr.* by Adam Makkai

To the Immortal[l] Memory [*or* Memorie] and Friendship of That Noble Pair[e], Sir Lucius Cary and Sir H. [*or* Henry] Morison. Ben Jonson. BASC; BeJo; CABP; NAEL-5v1; NAEL-6v1; NAEL-7v1; NOBE; NOSC; NoP-4; PBRV
   (Noble Nature, The.) GTBS-P; TreFP
   (Part of an Ode, A.) OBEV

To the Infant Martyrs. Richard Crashaw. ChIV-2; GeHe; NAEL-5v1; NAEL-6v1; NAEL-7v1; OxBSP; PAI
   (Go, smiling souls, your new-built cages break.) NoP-4

To the Innkeeper at Five Rivers, Sun Pen. Chang Yü. CoBLCP, *tr.* by Jonathan Chaves

To the Insect of the Gossamer. Charlotte Smith. OxBSo

To the interior, limbs folded. Nocturne. Valerie Martínez. TouFir

To the King. Robert Herrick. CavPo

To the King and Queen[e], upon Their Unhappy Distances. Robert Herrick. BASC

To the King, at His Entrance into Saxham: By Master John Crofts. Thomas Carew. CaPo

To the King, on His Navy. Edmund Waller. BeJo

To the King's Most Excellent Majesty. Phillis Wheatley. TAP

To the King, upon His Com[m]ing with His Army into the West. Robert Herrick. BeJo; CaPo
   (To the King.) CavPo
   (Welcome, most welcome to our vows and us.) CavPo

To the King, Upon His Welcome to Hampton Court. Robert Herrick. BeJo

To the King / You are the corner-stone the builders. *Unknown.* ASW, *tr.* by Kevin Crossley-Holland *Fr.* Christ 1.

To the Kinges Most Excellent Majestye. Lady Anne Harris Southwell. EMWP

To the Lacedemonians.　Allen Tate.　NAAL-2v2; NoAM

To the Ladies.　Mary Lee, Lady Chudleigh.　CABP; ECWP; NALW; NIL-7; NOEC; PEW; WPE; WPOW

To the Lady Anne, Countess of Dorset.　Emilia [or Aemelia] Lanier [or Lanyer].

"To you I dedicate this work of grace."　NOSC

To the Lady Arabella.　Emilia [or Aemelia] Lanier [or Lanyer].　NOSC

To the Lady in the Chemisette with Black Buttons.　Nathaniel Parker Willis.　OBAL

To The Lady Lucie, Countesse of Bedford.　Samuel Daniel.　PBRV

To the Lady Margaret, Countess [or Countesse] of Cumberland.　Samuel Daniel.　NOSC

To the Lady Margaret Ley.　John Milton.　GTBS-P; OBEV

To the Lady May.　Aurelian Townshend [or Townsend].　OxBEV

To the Lady Portrayed by Margaret Dumont.　John Hollander.　OBAL

To the Laggards.　Joseph Bovshover.　TrJP, tr. by Joseph Bovshover

To the Late William Jerdan.　Eliza Cook.　VWP

To the Latin Lover I Left at the Candy Store.　Magdalena Gomez.　PueRic

To the Learned and Reverend Mr. Cotton Mather, on His Excellent Magnalia.　Grindall Rawson.　SCAP

To the legion of the lost ones, to the cohort of the damned.　Gentlemen-Rankers.　Rudyard Kipling.　FaBoWar; NOBVV

To the lights and the long street curving. (LL)　Soho Hospital for Women, The.　Fleur Adcock.　NAEL-6v2; NoP-4

To the Looking-Glass world it was Alice that said.　Lewis Carroll.　UV　Fr. Through the Looking-Glass.

To the Lord.　Richard von Schaukal.　AuPH, tr. by Lowell A. Bangerter

To the Lord General Cromwell.　John Milton.　NAEL-5v1; NAEL-6v1; NOSC; SCGP; Son

(Cromwell, our chief of men, who through a cloud.)　GSo; NoP-4; PBRV; PoPoPo

(To the Lord General Cromwell, on the Proposals of Certain Ministers at the Committee for the Propagation of the Gospel.)　GSo

(To the Lord Generall Cromwell May 1652.)　PBRV

To the Lord Love.　"Michael Field."　OBMV

To the Lords of Convention 'twas Claver'se who spoke.　Sir Walter Scott.　FaBoCh; OxBS; OxBoLi; UV　Fr. Doom of Devorgoil, The.

To the Lost Child.　Brigit Pegeen Kelly.　YaYoPo

To the Maiden in the East.　Henry David Thoreau.　OxBA

To the Man after the Harrow.　Patrick Kavanagh.　CIP-2; GTBS-P; ModIr

To the Man Inside.　Carl Rakosi.　BodElec

To the Man-of-War Bird.　Walt Whitman.　APN-1

To the Man Saying "Come on Seis" at Hollywood Park.　David Hayward.　MoASP

To the Marchesana of Pescara.　Michelangelo Buonarroti.　See Love's Justification

To the Marquess of Piscat's Soul.　Henry Constable.　NoSic

To the Marquis of Graham on His Marriage.　Unknown.　OBSV

To the Memory of G. N. Obolduyev.　Yelena [or Elena] Blaginina.　TCRP, tr. by Vera Dunham

To the Memory of Gavin Wilson (Boot, Leg and Arm Maker).　George Galloway.　NOEC

To the Memory of J. Horace Kimball.　"Ada" (Sarah Louisa Forten).　BlSi

To the Memory of John Keats.　John Clare.　CenSon

To the Memory of Mr Oldham.　Dryden.　AWP; BASC; EBEV; HAP; InPK-6; NAEL-6v1; NAEL-7v1; NIL-7; NIP-4; NOBE; NOSC; NPeEn; NoP-4; OxAEP-1; OxBEV; PAI; PoE; PoPoPo; SCGP; TFi; TRP

To the Memory of My Beloved, the Author Mr [or Master] William Shakespeare [And What He Hath Left Us].　Ben Jonson.　BASC; BeJo; HAP; HeIP-4; NAEL-6v1; NAEL-7v1; NOSC; NoP-4; OxAEP-1; PoPoPo

"I, therefore, will begin. Soul of the age!"　NOBE

To the Memory of My Dear and Ever Honored Father Thomas Dudley Esq. Who Deceased July 31, 1653, and of His Age 77.　Anne Bradstreet.　NAAL-2v1; NAAL-3

To the Memory of Sir Isaac Newton.　James Thomson.

"All—intellectual eye, our solar round."　NOEC

To the Memory of the Brave Americans.　Philip Freneau.　AiP

To the Memory of the Learned and Reverend, Mr. Jonathan Mitchell.　Francis Drake.　SCAP

To the Men of Kent (October, 1803).　William Wordsworth.　OBWP

To the Merchantis of Edinburgh.　William Dunbar.　OxBS

To the Mercy Killers.　Dudley Randall.　SoSe-8

To the mind's briefer and more desert place. (LL)　Twelve, The.　Allen Tate.　APT-2; ChIV-2

To the mini-skirted customs official who with sibyl-dove eyes.　Edoardo Sanguineti.　ItPo, tr. by Gayle Ridinger　Fr. Reisebilder.

To the Minister Liu.　Yü Hsüan-chi.　BoWoP, tr. by Geoffrey Waters

To the moaning and the groaning of the bells. (LL)　Bells, The.　Edgar Allan Poe.　APN-1; BRP; ChAP; ITBLP; OBAL; OBCA; TAP; TCAPo; TFi; TreFP

To the Mock-Bird.　Mary Weston Fordham.　CBWP-2

To the Mocking-Bird.　Richard Henry Wilde.　APN-1

To the Moment Last Past.　William Habington.　OxBSo

To the Monk Dúc Son at Thanh-phong Monastery.　Trăn Thái-Tông, King.　AWTN, tr. by Hunh Sanh Thông

To the Monk Wu-hsia on the Occasion of His Editing the Lotus Sutra.　Mo Shih-lung.　CoBLCP; ColAnChi, tr. by Jonathan Chaves

To the Moon.　Paul Fleming.　GePo, tr. by George C. Schoolfield

To the Moon.　Goethe.　STV, tr. by John Frederick Nims

To the Moon.　Anna Maria Jones.　CenSon

To the Moon.　Giacomo Leopardi.　TTTS, tr. by Kenneth Koch

To the Moon.　Pierre de Ronsard.　AWP, tr. by Andrew Lang

To the Moon.　Shelley.　GTBS-P; OxAEP-2; TTTS

To The Moon.　Charlotte Smith.　BWW; CenSon; RWP; Son

To The Moon.　Dávid Baróti Szabó.　IQMS, tr. by Adam Makkai

To the Moon.　Helen Maria Williams.　NoP-4

(Glitt'ring colors of the day are fled, The.)　CenSon

To the Moon.　Yvor Winters.　APT-2

To the Moon and Back.　William Plomer.　OBCoV

To the Moore River Settlement we now go.　Archie Weller.　IBA

To the mooring of starting out, that day so long ago. (LL)　Soonest Mended.　John Ashbery.　HCAP; NAAL-2v2; NAAL-5; PoetW; VCAP

To the Most Beautiful Lady, the Lady Bridget Manners.　Barnabe Barnes.　EnLoPo

To the Most Excellent and Learned Shepherd, Colin Clout.　William Smith.　Son　Fr. Chloris [or the Complaint of the Passionate Despised Shepheard].

To the Most Excellently Accomplished Mrs. Katherine Philips.　Henry Vaughan.　CABP

To the Most Fair and Lovely Mistress Anne Soame, Now Lady Abdie.　Robert Herrick.　CaPo; NOBE; NOSC

To the Most Illustrious and Most Hopeful[l] Prince, Charles, Prince of Wales.　Robert Herrick.　BASC

To the Most Virtuous Mistress Pot, Who Many Times Entertained Him.　Robert Herrick.　CaPo

To the Mothers.　Ernst Toller.　TrJP, tr. by E. Ellis Roberts

To the Much Honoured R. F. Esq.　Richard Chamberlain.　SCAP

To the much-tossed Ulysses, never done.　Ulysses.　Robert Graves.　FaBoTw; NoAM

To the Muse.　Jean Adams.　ECWP

To the Muse.　Denise Levertov.　APSN

To the Muse.　Nadezhda Elizarovna Maltseva.　TCRP, tr. by Bernard Meares

To the Muse.　Robert Louis Stevenson.　EBEV

To the Muse.　Philip Whalen.　PoM

To the Muse.　James Wright (1927–80).　NAAL-2v2; NNaP

To the Muses.　William Blake.　HAP; HeIP-4; NAEL-5v2; NAEL-6v2; NOBE; NOEC; OBEV; SCGP

(From Poetical Sketches.)　NoP-4

To the Muses.　Mary Robinson.　CenSon; RWP

To the Mutable Fair.　Edmund Waller.　BeJo

To the Naiad of the Arun.　Charlotte Smith.　CenSon; RWP

To the Name Above Every Name, the Name of Iesvs a Hymn.　Richard Crashaw.　FSCP

(And break before thee.) (LL)　FSCP

(On the Name of Jesus.)　ESCV

(To the Name Above Every Name, the Name of Iesvs a Hymn.)　FSCP

To the Natural World: at 37.　Genevieve Taggard.　APT-2

To the New Owner.　Lucile Hargrove Reynolds.　PoToHe

To the new wick / Of freedom's torch.　My Thread.　Dovid [or David] Hofshteyn [or Hofstein].　TrJP, tr. by Joseph Leftwich

To the New World.　Claudia Keelan.　BodElec

To the New Year.　Priscilla Jane Thompson.　CBWP-2

To the New Year [For the Countess of Carlisle].　Thomas Carew.　CaPo

To the New Yeere [or Year].　Michael Drayton.　NOSC

To the Newborn.　Judit Tóth.　WPOW, tr. by Laura Schiff

To the Night.　Shelley.　See To Night

To the Nightingale.　Fulbert of Chartres.　MLL, tr. by Helen Waddell

To the Nightingale.　John Milton.　OWoS

(O Nightingale, That on Yon Bloomy Spray.)　SCGP

(To the Nightingale.)　OWoS

To the Nightingale.　Anne Finch, Countess of Winchilsea.　ECWP; NALW; WPE

To the Noble Sir Francis Drake.　Thomas Beedome.　OxBSP

To the Noblest and Best of Ladies, the Countess of Denbigh.　Richard Crashaw.　GeHe; MeLP; NAEL-6v1; NAEL-7v1

(Letter from Mr Crashaw to the Countess of Denbigh, Against Irresolution and Delay in Matters of Religion, A.)　NOSC

(Letter to the Countess of Denbigh.) NOSC

(TO The Noblest and best of Ladyes, the Countesse of Denbigh. Perswading her to Resolution in Religion, and to render her selfe without further delay into the Communion of the Catholick Church.) PBRV

(What heav'n-intreated HEART is This?) PBRV

To the north, the cold and its broken jasmine. Island in the Earth. Sara de Ibáñez. TCLAP, tr. by Inés Probert

To the Oak. "Shu Ting." CarOv, tr. by Carolyn Kizer and Y. H. Zhao

To the Oaks of Glencree. John Millington Synge. MoBrPo; NOIV

To the Ocean. Thomas Hood. CenSon

To the Ocean. S. J. Marks. BodElec

To the ocean now I fly. John Milton. OBEV; OxAEP-1 Fr. Comus; a Masque Presented at Ludlow Castle.

To the old, long life and treasure. Ben Jonson. OxBSP Fr. Gypsies Metamorphosed, The.

To the one and only beautiful girl in the world! (LL) Most Beautiful Girl in the World, The. Richard Rodgers. OBAL; ReLy

To the One of Fictive Music. Wallace Stevens. APT-1; MoAmPo; NoP-4; TCAPo

To the Onlookers. William Heyen. GotH

To the Owl. Thomas Russell. CenSon

To the palaces of the Han. Wang Chao-chün. Tai Shu-lun. SuSp, tr. by William H. Nienhauser

To the Palmetto State, in the year seventy three. Southern Work of Dr. and Mrs. L. M. Dunton. Lizelia Augusta Jenkins Moorer. CBWP-3

To the Parents of a Childhood Friend, a Suicide. Judith Baumel. TaR

To the Parted One. Goethe. AWP, tr. by Christopher Pearse Cranch

To the Pending Year. Walt Whitman. OxBSP

To the People of England, the humble Petition. Petition of the Orangemen of Ireland, The. Thomas Moore. NOIV

To the Phiz an Ode. Allan Ramsay. NePenScot

To the Pious Memory of C. W. Esquire. Henry Vaughan. PeECV

To the Pious Memory of the Accomplished [or Accomplisht] Young Lady, Mrs. Anne Killigrew, [Excellent in the Two Sister-Arts of Poesie and Painting]. Dryden. NAEL-5v1

(Ode to the Pious Memory of the Accomplished Young Lady, Mrs. Anne Killigrew.) OBEV

(To the Pious Memory of the Accomplished Young Lady Mrs. Anne Killigrew.) CABP

To the placid supreme in the sweep of his reign. (LL) Man-of-War Hawk, The. Herman Melville. APN-2; OWoS

To The Poets. Ábrahám Barcsay. IQMS, tr. by Adam Makkai

To the Poets. Unknown. PeNZ

To the Poets in New York. James Wright (1927–80). NAAL-2v2

To the Poets: To Make Much of the World. George Oppen. BodElec

To the Police Officer Who Refused to Sit in the Same Room as My Son because He's a "Gang Banger." Luis J. Rodriguez. IllVoic

To the Poor. Anna Laetitia Barbauld. ECWP; NoP-4

To the Poppy. Anna Seward. CenSon; ECWP; WoRP

To the Powers of Desolation. Genevieve Taggard. APT-2

To the Principal and Professors of the University of St Andrews, on their Superb Treat to Dr Samuel Johnson. Robert Fergusson. NePenScot

To the Queen. Henry Stuart [or Stewart], Lord Darnley. OxBS

To the Queen of Inconstancy, Regina Collier, in Antwerp. Katherine Philips. PEW

To the Queen of the British Government. Mrs. Henry Linden. CBWP-4

To the Queen's Most Excellent Majesty. Aemilia Bassano Lanyer. NAEL-7v1 Fr. Salve Deus Rex Judaeorum.

To the Queen[e], Entertain[e]d at Night by the Countess[e] of Anglesey. Sir William Davenant [or D'Avenant]. MeLP; NOSC

To the railroad tracks at the bottom of summer. Dog-God. Robin Becker. ExTi

To the Reader. Charles Baudelaire. NAWM-7v2, tr. by Robert Lowell

To the Reader. Charles Baudelaire. SxFrPo, tr. by James McGowan

To the Reader. Charles Baudelaire. WoPoe, tr. by Stanley Kunitz

To the Reader. Ben Jonson. BASC; BeJo; NoP-4; PoE

To the Reader. Elizabeth Jane Leon. EMWP

To the Reader. Denise Levertov. PoM; VGW

To the Reader. Urian Oakes. SCAP

To the Reader. Rowland Watkyns. BASC

To the Reader, in Vindication of This Book. Elizabeth Bradford. EMWP

To the Reader of Master William Davenant's Play [The Wits]. Thomas Carew. CaPo

To the Reader of These Sonnets. Michael Drayton. NAEL-5v1; NAEL-6v1; NAEL-7v1; NOSC; Son Fr. Idea.

To the Readers. Maria Luisa Spaziani. CItWP, tr. by Cinzia Sartini Blum and Lara Trubowitz

To the readers of our New First Unexpected. D. Burliuk. PFTM-1 Fr. Slap in the Face of Public Taste, A.

To the Readers Who Write to Me. Daria Menicanti. CItWP, tr. by Cinzia Sartini Blum and Lara Trubowitz

To the real work, to / "What is to be done" (LL) I Went Into the Maverick Bar. Gary Snyder. HCAP; NAAL-2v2; PoE; VCAP

To the real world of her kitchen. (LL) Changeling, The. Judith Ortiz Cofer. NIL-7; TouFir

To the Red Lory. John Shaw Neilson. NOBAu

To the Redbreast. John Codrington Bampfylde. Son

To the rest of us. (LL) Riot Act, April 29, 1992. Ai. ESEAA; NIL-7

To the Retired Scholar Chang. Ni Tsan. CoBLCP, tr. by Jonathan Chaves

To the Rev'd Mr. Jno. Sparhawk on the Birth of his Son. Samuel Sewall. SCAP

To the Rev. Dr. Thomas Amory. Phillis Wheatley. SacPr

To the Revd. Mr. ——— on His Drinking Sea-Water. John Winstanley. NOEC

To the Rev. F. D. Maurice. Tennyson. GTBS-P; NOBVV; PeECV

To the Rev. Mr. Powell. Christopher Smart. OBWVE

To the Reverend Shade of His Religious Father. Robert Herrick. CaPo

(That for seven Lusters I did never come.) CavPo; PBRV

To the Rev. [or Reverend] W. L. Bowles. Samuel Taylor Coleridge. Son Fr. Effusions.

To the right. Well, The. Padma Sachdev. OMIP, tr. by Iqbal Masud

To the Right Hon. and Right Revd. Fredrick, Earl of Bristol, Bishop of Derry, Etc., Etc. Ann Yearsley. RWP

To the Right Hon. Henry Pelham. Edward Moore. OBSV

To the Right Honorable, the Lady Mary, Countess of Pembroke. Samuel Daniel. NAEL-6v1

To the Right Honorable the Lord Windsor. Perdam Sapientiam Sapientum. William Habington. ChIV-2

To the Right Honourable Mildmay, Earl of Westmorland. Robert Herrick. BeJo

To the Right Honourable William, Earl of Dartmouth. Phillis Wheatley.
"No more, America, in mournful strain." WPOW
"Should you, my lord, while you pursue my song." BPo; TTY

To the Right Honourable William, Earl of Dartmouth, His Majesty's Principal Secretary of State for North America. Phillis Wheatley. NAAAL; NAAL-5; NALW

To the Right Worshipful Lady Her Most Dear Mother, the Lady Prudentia Munda, the True Pattern of Piety and Virtue, C. M. Wisheth Increase of Happiness. "Constantia Munda." EMWP

To the Right Worshipfull, My Singular Good Frend, Master Gabriell Harvey, Doctor of the Lawes. Edmund Spenser. NoSic Fr. Commendatory Sonnets.

To the Right Worshipfull, My Singular Good Friend, Master Gabriel Harvey, Doctor of the Lawes. Edmund Spenser. NoSic

To the River Arun. Charlotte Smith. CenSon; RWP

To the River Cherwell. William Lisle Bowles. CenSon

To the River Duddon. Norman Nicholson. NLP; NoP-4

To the River Itchin, near Winton. William Lisle Bowles. CenSon; NAEL-6v2; OxBSo

To the River Otter. Samuel Taylor Coleridge. See Sonnet to the River Otter

To the River Tweed. William Lisle Bowles. See Tweed Visited, The

To the River Wensbeck. William Lisle Bowles. CenSon

To the Roaring Wind. Wallace Stevens. TCAPo

To the Rose upon the Rood of Time. W. B. Yeats. NoAM

To the Royal Society. Abraham Cowley. BASC; BeJo

To the Rulers. Howard Nemerov. OxBC

To the sagging wharf. Summer's Dream, A. Elizabeth Bishop. OxBC

To the Same. William Cowper. See To Mary

To the Same. Leigh Hunt. CenSon

To the Same. Charlotte MacCarthy. PoBW

To the Same [Celia]. Ben Jonson. BeJo; EroLit; NOSC, tr. by Ben Jonson Fr. Volpone.

To the Same; Enquiring Why I Wept. Mary Masters. PoBW

To the Same [My Dear Sister, Mrs S.]: The Tears. William Hammond. NOSC

To the Same Purpose. Thomas Traherne. NoP-4

(To the same purpose: he, not long before.) NoP-4

To the Same [Sir Thomas Roe]. Ben Jonson. BASC

To the scaffold. (LL) Tommorow. Amal Dunqul. MAP; NAfrP, tr. by Sharif Elmusa and Thomas G. Ezzy

To the scullery, and down to the back room. (LL) Ancestor. Thomas Kinsella. BIrV; ModIr; NOIV; NPeEn; OxBEV; PBCIP; PoE

To the Second Person. John Skelton.
"O benign Jesu, my sovereign Lord and King." SCGP

To the Senegalese veterans of war. Et Cetera. Léon Damas. NegPo, tr. by Ellen Conroy Kennedy

To the Shade of Burns. Charlotte Smith. NoP-4

To the Shade of Po Chü-I. William Carlos Williams. HarvBoo

To the ship I carried statues. I Carried Statues. Ágnes Nemes Nagy. BoWoP; PoSu

To the side of the road. (LL) Old Flame, The. Robert Lowell. BoLoP; NOBA; NoAM; PAI

To the side of their own lives. (LL) Afternoons. Philip Larkin. NPeEn; OxBEV; PoetW

To the Singing Girl Named Luu. Nguyễn Khuyến. WoPoe, tr. by Nguyen Ngoc Bich

To the singing, to the drums. (LL) Eagle-Feather Fan, The. N. Scott Momaday. CDW; NoP-4

To the sky. Irving Feldman. TaR

To the sky. (LL) Draft of a Reparations Agreement. Dan Pagis. HP; PoSu; WoPoe, tr. by Stephen Mitchell

To the Skylark. William Wordsworth. GTBS-P

To the Snake. Denise Levertov. NAAL-5; PAI

To the Sour Reader. Robert Herrick. See To the Sour[e] Reader

To the Sour[e] Reader. Robert Herrick. NBLV; NoP-4

To the South. Maurice Thompson. CBCWP

To the South Downs. Charlotte Smith. CenSon

   (Ah, hills beloved!—where once, an happy child.) RWP

To the south-east—three thousand leagues—. Civilization. Yüan Chieh. ChiP, tr. by Arthur Waley

To the south there is a dragon living in a mountain pool. Tu Fu. CoBCP Fr. Seven Songs Written During the Ch'ien-yüan Era.

To the Spider. Thomas Russell. CenSon; Son

To the Spirit of Keats. James Russell Lowell. Son

To the Stars. Andreas Gryphius. GePo, tr. by George C. Schoolfield

To the state of West Virginia. Story of Lovers Leap, The. Maggie Pogue Johnson. CBWP-4

To the States. Walt Whitman. TCAPo

To the States, To Identify the 16th, 17th, or 18th Presidentiad. Walt Whitman. CTC; NAAL-2v1; NAAL-3; RaBo

To the statistical Sparta of the champs. (LL) On Hurricane Jackson. Alan Dugan. CoAP; PAI; TRP

To the Statue on the Capitol. John James Piatt. APN-2; GS

To the still dwelling. (LL) A. E. Housman. FaBoTw; SCV

To the Stone-Cutters. Robinson Jeffers. ColAP; MoAmPo; NAAL-2v2; NAAL-5; NOBA; OxBA; PAI; PoRA

To the Stork. Mihály Tompa. IQMS, tr. by Yakov Hornstein

To the Strawberry. Helen Maria Williams. CenSon; OxBSo; RWP

To the Street Piano. John Davidson.

   "All the day I worked and played." EBVV

   Labourer's Wife, A. EBVV

To the strenuous work of vanishing. (LL) Heroin. Bob Hicok. AmPoNex; BAP-97

To the Sun. Tom Sleigh. UrbNat

To the Sun. Saul [or Shaul] Tchernichowsky [or Tchernichovsky].

   "I have been to my God like the iris and the anemone." MHP

   "Images of a faded world possessed me, I cannot flee!" MHP

   "Or the image-kingdom's idol of the past generation." MHP

To the Sun-Dial. John Quincy Adams. APN-1

To the sunk sun, the far, surrendered sea. (LL) Ebbtide at Sundown. "Michael Field." OxBSo; VWP

To the Superhuman Adelmund, When She Would Undo the Kiss Already Done. Philipp von Zesen. GePo, tr. by George C. Schoolfield

To the Supreme Being. Michelangelo Buonarroti. AWP

To The Supreme Commander, Sirian Forces. Day on the Planet, A. Brian Morse. NOxBChV

To the Swallow. Euenus. OBVE, tr. by William Cowper

To the Swallow. Pamphilus. GrAn, tr. by Dennis Schmitz

To the table down at Mory's, to the place where Louis dwells. Whiffenpoof Song. Ted B. Galloway. TCAPo

To the Terrestrial Globe. Sir William Schwenck Gilbert. NBLV

To the Thawing Wind. Robert Frost. OxBA

To the Thoughtful Reader. William Meredith. NoAM

To the Thrice-Sacred Queen Elizabeth. Mary Sidney Herbert, Countess of Pembroke. NALW; NoP-4

   (To Queen Elizabeth.) PBRV

To the thunder of bells a voice calls for blood! Bells, The. Saul [or Shaul] Tchernichowsky [or Tchernichovsky]. MHP, tr. by Ruth Finer Mintz

To the Torrid Zone. Helen Maria Williams. See Sonnet 6. To the Torrid Zone

To the Translator. Sir Walter Ralegh. PBRV

To the triple goddess of Amarynthus. Theodoridas. GrAn

To the Tune "A Floating Cloud Crosses Enchanted Mountain." Huang O [or Huang Ho]. BoWoP; WoPoe, tr. by Chung Ling and Kenneth Rexroth

To the Tune "A Spray of Flowers" (Not Giving In to Old Age). Kuan Han-ch'ing. WoPoe, tr. by Stephen Owen

To the Tune "Bamboo at West Lake." Shen Chou. CoBLCP, tr. by Jonathan Chaves

To the Tune: Beautiful Barbarian. Li Po. CrYelRi, tr. by Sam Hamill

To the Tune: Beautiful Barbarian. Unknown. CrYelRi, tr. by Sam Hamill

To the Tune: Beautiful Barbarian. Wei Chuang. CrYelRi, tr. by Sam Hamill

To the Tune: Beautiful Lady Yu. Li Yu. CrYelRi, tr. by Sam Hamill

To the Tune: Boat of Stars. Li Ch'ing-chao. See Boat of Stars

To the Tune: Bodhisattva's Headdress. Li Ch'ing-chao. CrYelRi, tr. by Sam Hamill

To the Tune: Butterflies Love Flowers. Li Ch'ing-chao. See Butterflies Love Flowers

To the Tune, "Ch'ing-p'ing Yüeh." Yang Shen. CoBLCP, tr. by Jonathan Chaves

To the Tune "Chao-chün's Sorrow." Yang Shen. CoBLCP, tr. by Jonathan Chaves

To the Tune "Chiang ch'eng tzu." Yang Shen. CoBLCP, tr. by Jonathan Chaves

To the Tune "Child at Play." Yang Shen. CoBLCP, tr. by Jonathan Chaves

To the Tune "Chiu-ch'üan tzu." Wu Chen. CoBLCP, tr. by Jonathan Chaves

To the Tune: Drunk in Flower Shadows. Li Ch'ing-chao. CrYelRi, tr. by Sam Hamill

To the Tune: Eternal Joy. Li Ch'ing-chao. CrYelRi, tr. by Sam Hamill

To the Tune "Flowers in the Rain." Yang Shen. CoBLCP, tr. by Jonathan Chaves

To the Tune "Glittering Sword Hilts." Liu Yu Hsi. OHMPC, tr. by Kenneth Rexroth

To the Tune: Happiness Approaches. Li Ch'ing-chao. CrYelRi, tr. by Sam Hamill

To the Tune "Heavenly Immortal." Yang Shen. CoBLCP, tr. by Jonathan Chaves

To the Tune "I Paint My Lips Red." Li Ch'ing-chao. BoWoP, tr. by Chung Ling and Kenneth Rexroth

   (Flirtation.) WoPoe

To the Tune: In the Hills. Hsueh Chao-yun. CrYelRi, tr. by Sam Hamill

To the Tune "Intoxicated with Shadows of Flowers." Yü Ch'ing-tsêng. EroLit, tr. by Chung Ling and Kenneth Rexroth

To the Tune: Lips Painted Red. Li Ch'ing-chao. CrYelRi, tr. by Sam Hamill

To the Tune: Magnolia Blossoms. Li Ch'ing-chao. CrYelRi, tr. by Sam Hamill

To the Tune "Meeting Happiness." Li Yü. WoPoe, tr. by Arthur Sze

To the Tune "Moon Over West River." Yang Shen. CoBLCP; ColAnChi, tr. by Jonathan Chaves

To the Tune "Nan-hsiang-tzu." Shen Chou. CoBLCP, tr. by Jonathan Chaves

To the Tune "New Moon." Yang Shen. CoBLCP, tr. by Jonathan Chaves

To the Tune of The Coventry Carol. Stevie Smith. FaBoTw; WoPoe

To the Tune: Partridge Sky. Li Ch'ing-chao. CrYelRi, tr. by Sam Hamill

To the Tune "Partridge Sky." Yang Shen. CoBLCP, tr. by Jonathan Chaves

To the Tune: Plum Blossoms. Li Ch'ing-chao. See Plum Blossoms

To the Tune, "Plum Blossoms Fall and Scatter." Li Ch'ing-chao. OHPC, tr. by Kenneth Rexroth

To the Tune "Red Embroidered Shoes." Huang O [or Huang Ho]. WPOW

To the Tune: Sands of the Washing Stream. Li Ch'ing-chao. CrYelRi, tr. by Sam Hamill

To the Tune "Shui hsien-tzu." Ma Chih-yüan. CoBLCP, tr. by Jonathan Chaves

To the tune "Soaring Clouds." Huang O [or Huang Ho]. BoWoP; EroLit; WPOW

To the Tune "Song of the Plum Blossom at the River Town." Yang Shen. CoBLCP, tr. by Jonathan Chaves

To the Tune: Southern Song. Wen T'ing-yün. CrYelRi, tr. by Sam Hamill

To the Tune: Spring at Wu Ling. Li Ch'ing-chao. See Spring at Wu Ling

To the Tune "Spring at Wu Ling." Li Ch'ing-chao. OHMPC, tr. by Kenneth Rexroth

To the Tune "Spring in Tien Is Fine." Yang Shen. CoBLCP, tr. by Jonathan Chaves

To the Tune "Stopping My Horse to Listen." Yang Shen. CoBLCP, tr. by Jonathan Chaves

To the Tune "T'ien ching sha." Ma Chih-yüan.

   Autumn Thoughts. CoBLCP, tr. by Jonathan Chaves

   "Withered vines, old tree." CoBLCP, tr. by Jonathan Chaves

To the Tune "The Drunken Young Lord." Unknown. WoPoe, tr. by C. H. Kwock and Vincent McHugh

To the Tune "The Fair Maid of Yu." Chiang Chieh. OHMPC, tr. by Kenneth Rexroth

To the Tune "The Fall of a Little Wild Goose." Huang O [or Huang Ho]. WPOW

To the Tune "The Joy of Peace and Brightness." Wu Tsao. BoWoP

To the Tune "The Phoenix Hairpin." T'ang Wan. WPOW

To the Tune "The River Is Red." Ch'iu Chin. AiP; BoWoP; ItWoWo, tr. by Chung Ling and Kenneth Rexroth

To the Tune "The Southerner." Yang Shen. CoBLCP, tr. by Jonathan Chaves

To the Tune: The Water Clock. Wen T'ing-yün. CrYelRi, tr. by Sam Hamill

To the Tune: The Wine Spring: "Eternal autumn rain—evening sounds." Li Hsun. CrYelRi; ErotSp, tr. by Sam Hamill

To the Tune: The Wine Spring: "Rain falls on fallen flowers." Li Hsun. CrYelRi; ErotSp, tr. by Sam Hamill

To the Tune "Yellow Oriole." Yang Shen. CoBLCP, tr. by Jonathan Chaves

To the Unborn and Waiting Children. Lucille Clifton. InPK-6

To the Unconstant Cynthia: a Song. Sir Robert Howard. NOSC

To the University. Alicia D'Anvers. NOSC Fr. Academia; or The Humours of the University of Oxford.

To the University of Cambridge, in New-England. Phillis Wheatley. NAAAL; NAAL-2v1; NAAL-3; NAAL-5; TAP; TCAPo

To the Unnamed Buddhist Nun Who Burned Herself to Death on the Night of June 3, 1966. Diane Di Prima. BB

To the Victims of Mauthausen. Maria Luisa Spaziani. CItWP, tr. by Cinzia Sartini Blum and Lara Trubowitz

(To the Virgin). Maria De' Medici. WPoS, tr. by Laura Anna Stortoni

To the Virgin Mary. Andreas Gryphius. WoPoe, tr. by Christopher Benfey

To the Virginian Voyage. Michael Drayton. AiP; BASC; HAP; NAEL-5v1; NOBE; NOSC; OBEV; SCGP

  (Ode. To the Virginian Voyage.) NAEL-6v1; NAEL-7v1

  (You brave heroic minds.) CABP

  (You brave Heroique Minds.) PBRV

To the Virgins, to Make Much of Time. Robert Herrick. AWP; BASC; BeJo; BoLoP; CaPo; CavPo; ClHu; EnLoPo; HAP; HeIP-4; ITBLP; InPK-6; NAEL-5v1; NAEL-6v1; NAEL-7v1; NBLV; NIL-7; NIP-4; NOBE; NOSC; NPeEn; NoP-4; OBEV; OxAEP-1; OxBEV; PAI; PoE; PoPoPo; SCGP; SCV; SoSe-8; TFi; UV

  (Counsel to Girls.) GTBS-P

To the Virgins, to Make the Most of Time. Gavin Ewart. OBCoV

To the Virtuosos. William Shenstone. ECEV

To the Visions of Fancy. Ann Radcliffe. CenSon

To the Water Nymphs, Drinking at the Fountain. Robert Herrick. BeJo; CaPo; NAEL-5v1; NAEL-6v1

To the Waters of the Chia-ling. Yüan Chên. SuSp, tr. by William H. Nienhauser

To the West Wind. Marianne von Willemer. AuPH, tr. by Aurelia G. Scott

To the Western Wind. Judah Halevi. TrJP, tr. by Solomon Solis-Cohen

To the Western Wind. Robert Herrick. CaPo; OBEV

To the Western World. Louis Simpson. CoAP; CoAmPo; NOBA; TAP; TRP

To the Wheel of Progress. Mrs. Henry Linden. CBWP-4

To the White Bird of the Tropic. Helen Maria Williams. CenSon

To the white clouds at the end of the east I'll look for you! (LL) They Say You're Staying in a Mountain Temple. Tu Fu. CoBCP; TTTS, tr. by Burton Watson

To the White Fiends. Claude McKay. NAAAL

To the white-mantled maidens. Korinna [or Corinna]. WPOW

To the willow. Basho. ZenPo, tr. by Takashi Ikemoto and Lucien Stryk

To the Willow-Tree. Robert Herrick. CaPo; OBEV; SCGP

To the wind she says, 'They have eaten me alive' (LL) In The Park. Gwen Harwood. BMAP; CBAP; NIL-7

To the Winds. Ann Radcliffe. RWP

To the Wine Treasurer of the Circuit Mess. Horace [or Horatio] Smith. UV

To the Winter Aphrodite. "Michael Field." VWP

To the Wissahiccon. Frances Anne [or "Fanny"] Kemble. APN-1

To the Wooden Hermit. Han Yü. SuSp, tr. by Kenneth O. Hanson

To the World [A Farewell for a Gentlewoman, Virtuous and Noble]. Ben Jonson. BeJo

To the World: the Perfection of Love. William Habington. BeJo Fr. Castara.

To the World We Must Appear. Heinrich Heine. WoPoe, tr. by Francis C. Golffing

To the world we must appear. To the World We Must Appear. Heinrich Heine. WoPoe, tr. by Francis C. Golffing

To the Writers' Worship in Zomba. Felix Mnthali. PeSAV

To the young man I would say. I'm Older than You, Please Listen. Arthur Rex Dugard Fairburn. PeNZ

To thee, dear Paris, Lord of my Desires. Paraphrase on Oenone to Paris, A. Aphra Behn. EMWP

To Thee, Eternal Soul, Be Praise. Richard Watson Gilder. AH

To thee, fair freedom! I retire. Written at [or in] an Inn at Henley. William Shenstone. AWP; NOBE; NOEC; OBEV; OxAEP-1; OxBEV

To thee, my way in epigrams seems new. To My Mere English Censurer. Ben Jonson. BeJo

To Thee, O God. Abiel Holmes. AH

To Thee, O God, the Shepherd Kings. John Gardiner Calkins Brainard. AH

To thee obeyeth all the East as far as Ganges goes. Ovid. OBVE Fr. Metamorphoses.

To thee—rude warrior, who, we once admired. Susanna Centlivre. ECWP Fr. Epistle to the King of Sweden, An.

To Thee the Tuneful Anthem Soars. Mather Byles. AH

To Thee, Then, Let All Beings Bend. Nathaniel Evans. AH

To thee, whose cautious step and specious air. Annabella Plumptre. ECWP; NOEC Fr. Ode to Moderation.

To Their Excellencies the Lords Justices of Ireland, the Humble Petition of Frances Harris, Who Must Starve, and Die a Maid if It Miscarries. Jonathan Swift. NOEC; OxBEV

To their long home the greatest princes go. Upon a Funeral. Sir John Beaumont. NOSC

To Their Most Excellent Majesty of Great Brittaines Monarchy. Mary Fage. EMWP

To their ssh of vapors and their vowel ooo. (LL) January of a Gnat, The. Carl Rakosi. APT-2; FTOS

To them who crossed the flood. Inscription. Herman Melville. UnPo

To them, yes, every pane! (LL) On the Asylum Road. Charlotte Mew. MoBrPo; VWP

To Theodorus et al. Rhianos. CAGL, tr. by Daryl Hine

To these bare fields, built at today's expense. (LL) Pyrography. John Ashbery. HarvBoo; PoM; VCAP

To these whom death again did wed. Epitaph Upon Husband and Wife Who Died and Were Buried Together, An. Richard Crashaw. EBEV; NOBE; OBEV; OxAEP-1

To Thine Eternal Arms, O God. Thomas Wentworth Higginson. AH

To think a poor man's bones should lie unblessed. (LL) George Crabbe. NAEL-5v1; NAEL-7v1; NOEC; PoE Fr. Village, The.

To think of you is blue as if strolling. Azure Because of You. Eduardo Carranza. BLPSL, tr. by Rene de Costa, Rigas Kappatos and Eleni Paidoussi

To think so many battles have been fought. Surplice, The. David Scott. NLP

To think that this meaningless thing was ever a rose. Summer Is Ended. Christina Georgina Rossetti. NOBVV; NPeEn; OxBEV

To think the face we love shall ever die. Etruscan Tombs. Agnes Mary Frances Robinson. PeVV

To think to know the country and not know. Hillside Thaw, A. Robert Frost. AmFaPo

To This Book. Martin Opitz. GePo, tr. by George C. Schoolfield

To this, great hector said. Homer. FaBoWar, tr. by George Chapman Fr. Iliad, The.

To this grove of dying poplars. Autumn. Gabriela Mistral. SpanPo, tr. by Muriel Kittel

To this sweet and pretty air. Art of Love, The. Arnaut Daniel. NAWM-7v1, tr. by Frederick Goldin

To Thomalin. Phineas Fletcher. NOSC

To Thomas Palmer [on His Book "The Sprite of Trees and Herbs"]. Ben Jonson. NoSic

To Those Born Later. Bertolt Brecht. AF

To those fair isles where crimson sunsets burn. Toussaint L'Ouverture. Henrietta Cordelia Ray. CBWP-3; SWaP

To those fixed on white. People. Jean Toomer. GT

To those who Dwell in Realms of day. (LL) William Blake. EBEV; FaBoCh; OxAEP-2; OxBoLi; PeECV; TFi

To those who have fashioned it. (LL) "H. D.". APT-1; HarvBoo Fr. Flowering of the Rod, The.

To Those Who Have Gone Home Tired. William Daniel Ehrhart. CDa

To those who have tried and seemingly have failed. Courage to Live. Grace Noll Crowell. PoToHe

To ———: "Three rompers run together, hand in hand." Wilfred Owen. OxBSo

To throw that faint thin line upon the shore! (LL) George Meredith. EBEV; EnLoPo; GSo; GTBS-P; HAP; NAEL-6v2; NOBE; NOBVV; NPeEn; NoP-4; OxAEP-2; OxBEV; PoE; SCGP; Son; TFi Fr. Modern Love.

To Thyrza. Byron. CAGL

To Time. Mary Julia Young. CenSon

To Time Past. Anna Seward. RWP Fr. Llangollen Vale.

To tinge his verse as with his own heart's blood. (LL) Poet and Botanist. Constance Naden. VWP; ViWPN

To Tirzah. William Blake. FHYEP; NAEL-5v2; NAEL-6v2; NOBE Fr. Songs of Experience.

To Toussaint L'Ouverture. William Wordsworth. CenSon; InPK-6; NOBE; PoRA

To Trace from Hebrew. Ece Ayhan. PFTM-2, tr. by Murat Nemet-Nejat

To travel high summer. Sierra Cup. Reg Saner. PoCoUp

To travel like a bird, lightly to view. Cecil Day Lewis. GTBS-P Fr. O Dreams, O Destinations.

To tread those blest paths which before I writ. (LL) Passionate Man[']s

Pilgrimage, The. Sir Walter Ralegh. ChIV-2; NOBE; NPeEn; NoSic; OxBEV; PeECV; PoE; PoRA; RB; SCGP; TFi

To tremble in prayer and trepidation. Revelation, The. Stanley Crouch. SeSe

To Try to Find. Wang Kuo-wei. SuSp, tr. by Irving Y. Lo

To try to find my heart, it's hard enough. To Try to Find. Wang Kuo-wei. SuSp, tr. by Irving Y. Lo

To Tu Fu. Li Po. TAL

To Tu Fu from Shantung. Li Po. CrYelRi, tr. by Sam Hamill

To turn a stone. High Noon at Los Alamos. Eleanor Wilner. NoP-4

To Turn Back. John Haines. CoAmPo; TRP

To Turn from Love. Sarah Webster Fabio. BlSi

To turn my volume o'er nor find. How to Read Me. Walter Savage Landor. NOBVV

To ———: "'Twas eve; the broadly shining sun." Edward Coote [or Coate] Pinkney. APN-1

To Two Bereaved. Thomas Ashe. NOBVV

To Tyranny. John Thelwall. CenSon

To Tzu-an. Yü Hsüan-chi. BoWoP, tr. by Geoffrey Waters

To Tzu-an. Yü Hsüan-chi. SuSp, tr. by Jan W. Walls

To——— Ulalume: A Ballad. Edgar Allan Poe. See Ulalume [or Ulalume—a Ballad]

To understand others is to be knowledgeable. Lao Tzu. AmFaPo, tr. by Robert Henricks Fr. Tao Te Ching.

To Urania. Joseph Brodsky. AF, tr. by Joseph Brodsky

To Urania. Benjamin Colman. SCAP

To Usward. Gwendolyn B. Bennett. BlSi

To Vahine (Painted by Gaugin). Enrique Molina. BLPSL, tr. by Rene de Costa, Rigas Kappatos and Eleni Paidoussi

To ———: "Vainly my heart had with thy sorceries striven." Sarah Helen Whitman. APN-1; TCAPo

To Valenton: Impressions circa 1947. Liliane Richman. TWW

To Varus. Catullus. AWP, tr. by Walter Savage Landor Fr. Carmina.

To veil the saintly face. Counterfable of Orpheus. Marie-Claire Bancquart. MFP, tr. by Martin Sorrell

To Venus. Horace. AWP; OBVE Fr. Odes.

To Vera, Who Asked a Song. Edith Nesbit. PoBW

To Vernon Lee. Amy Levy. VWP

To very few, or else to none. (LL) His Content in the Country. Robert Herrick. CaPo; CavPo

To vex thy soul with these unjust alarms. To Orestes. Elizabeth Singer Rowe. PEW

To Violet [with Prewar Poems]. Basil Bunting. FaBoMo

To Violets. Robert Herrick. CaPo; OBEV

To Virgil [or Vergil]. Tennyson. AWP; GTBS-P; NAEL-6v2

To Virgins. Robert Herrick. CaPo

To Vittoria Colonna. Michelangelo Buonarroti. AWP, tr. by Henry Wadsworth Longfellow

To Vulcan. Robert Herrick. CaPo

To W. L. Esq. While He Sung a Song to Purcell's Music. Samuel Taylor Coleridge. CenSon

(To W. L. Esq. While He Sung a Song to Purcell's Music.) CenSon

To W. L. G. on Reading His "Chosen Queen." Charlotte Forten. BlSi

To W. P. George Santayana. TCAPo

To W. R. William Ernest Henley. See Madam Life's a Piece in Bloom

To W. S. M. Arthur W. Monroe. APN-2

To wake up and discover. Well-beloved, The. John Montague. BiHa

To Waken an Old Lady. William Carlos Williams. HAP; InPK-6; PAI; SoSe-8; WeW-3

To Wales once more, though not on holiday now. Louis MacNeice. ModIr Fr. Autumn Sequel.

To walk in the sun. Curfew Breakers, The. Samuel Chimsoro. NAfrP

To walk with sober step, to raise the eyebrow. Joachim Du Bellay. WoPoe, tr. by Denis Devlin Fr. Regrets.

To Walker Evans. James Agee. APT-2

To Waning Day, To the Wide Round of Shadow. Dante Alighieri. STV, tr. by John Frederick Nims

To want is there to be where I am not. Sower, The. Jones Very. SacPr

To warm life passing singing with the grace. Ants. Ramón López Velarde. TCLAP, tr. by Samuel Beckett

To wash the stain ingrain and to make me clean again. (LL) What Would I Give? Christina Georgina Rossetti. NPeEn; OxBSP

To water and eternity. (LL) Across the Swamp. Olav H. Hauge. RaBo; WoPoe, tr. by Robert Bly

To We Who Were Saved by the Stars. Lorna Dee Cervantes. TouFir

To weep there! (LL) William Shakespeare. CTC; NOBE; NoSic; TFi Fr. Twelfth Night.

To weep thine ashes am I come. Lament for Aquileia Destroyed, and Never to be Built Again. Paulinus of Aquileia. MLL, tr. by Helen Waddell

To Wei Pa, a Retired Scholar. Tu Fu. OHPC, tr. by Kenneth Rexroth

To welcome the new-livery'd year. (LL) On a Bank [or Banck] as I Sat[e] [a-]Fishing; a Description of the Spring. Sir Henry Wotton. AmFaPo; BASC; NOSC

To western woods and lonely plains. On the Emigration to America [and Peopling the Western Country]. Philip Freneau. ColAP; NAAL-2v1; NAAL-3; NAAL-5; TAP

To what intent or purpose was Man made. As Concerning Man. Alexander Radcliffe. NOSC; OBSV

To what purpose, April, do you return again? Spring. Edna St. Vincent Millay. APT-1; BoWoP; MoAmPo; NoP-4

To What Strangers, What Welcome. James Vincent Cunningham. APT-2; NoAM

To which I have attuned my breathing for so many years. (LL) Anniversary. Judith Ortiz Cofer. PueRic; TouFir

To Whistler, American. Ezra Pound. AiP; FaBoA; NAAL-2v2

To Whittier. Josephine D. Henderson Heard. CBWP-4

To whoever is not listening to the sea. Poet's Obligation. Pablo Neruda. PoetW; VCWP, tr. by Alastair Reid

To Whom. Peter Klappert. YaYoPo

To Whom Else. George Barker. HarvBoo

To Whom Else Can We Fly? Giles Fletcher, the Younger. SacPr

To Whom Else? Robert Graves. FaBoMo

To whom I owe the leaping delight. Dedication to My Wife, A. T. S. Eliot. BoLoP

To Whom It May Concern. Adrian Mitchell. FaBoWar; OBWP

To Whom it may concern. Judith Johnson Sherwin. YaYoPo

To whom should I speak today? Dispute over Suicide, A. Unknown. TTY, tr. by T. Eric Peet

To whom the Father, without Cloud, serene. John Milton. PeECV Fr. Paradise Lost.

To whom the fiend with fear abasht repli'd. John Milton. PeECV Fr. Paradise Regained [or Regain'd].

To whom the Tempter impudent replied. John Milton. ChIV-2 Fr. Paradise Regained [or Regain'd].

To whom the wingèd hierarch replied. John Milton. NOSC Fr. Paradise Lost.

To whom thus also th' Angel last repli'd. John Milton. OxAEP-1; PeECV Fr. Paradise Lost.

To whom with healing words Adam replied. John Milton. NOSC Fr. Paradise Lost.

To whose chest I give my five senses. Man Who Offers Me His Chest, The. Hala Mohammad. PoArWo, tr. by Cornelia Al-Khaled

To William Camden. Ben Jonson. AWP; BASC; BeJo; NAEL-5v1; NAEL-6v1; NAEL-7v1; NOSC; NPeEn

To William Carlos Williams. Galway Kinnell. NoAM

To William Drummond of Hawthornden. Mary, of Morpeth Oxlie. EMWP

To William Hayley, Esq.: In Reply to His Solicitation to Write with Him in a Literary Work. William Cowper. Son

To William Roe. Ben Jonson. BeJo; NOSC

To William Simpson, Ochiltree. Robert Burns. OxBS

To William (Whom We Have Missed). P. G. Wodehouse. NOBL

To William Wilberforce, Esq. William Cowper. Son

To William Wordsworth. Samuel Taylor Coleridge. FHYEP; NAEL-5v2; NAEL-6v2

To William Wordsworth from Virginia. Julia Randall. WPE

To windward midnight glowed, iridium sheen. Ice. Alan Gould. NOBAu

To Winter. Amelia Alderson Opie. CenSon

To winter-ground thy corse. (LL) William Shakespeare. EBEV; RB Fr. Cymbeline.

To wipe his pretty nose. (LL) Unknown. OxNR; ReMoGo

To wish to climb a ladder to the loft. James Keir Baxter. PeNZ Fr. Autumn Testament.

To wit, the lever said. News. Lorine Niedecker. PFTM-1

To — With the Following Poem. Tennyson. NOBRP

To witless agony. (LL) Open House. Theodore Roethke. NOBA; NoAM

To witness, to / enter this. Blue. William Heyen. GotH

To Women. Richard Hugo. NIP-4

To Women, as Far as I'm Concerned. D. H. Lawrence. NPeEn; OxBSP; RaBo

To women in contemporary voice and dislocation. Re-reading Jane. Anne Stevenson. NALW

To wonder at their Maker, not to serve. (LL) Pope. NOEC; NPeEn Fr. Dunciad, The.

To wood and field. (LL) Snow-Flakes. Henry Wadsworth Longfellow. APN-1; ITBLP; NCAP; NOBA; NoP-4; TAP; TCAPo; UnPo

To Wordsworth. John Clare. Son

To Wordsworth. Hartley Coleridge. Son

To Wordsworth. Shelley. CenSon; FHYEP; NAEL-5v2; NAEL-6v2; NPeEn; NoP-4; Son

To work away in art's traditional measure. Sonnet. Goethe. STV, *tr. by* John Frederick Nims

To World War Two. Kenneth Koch. BAP-01

To wound myself upon the sharp edges of the night? (LL) Taxi, The. Amy Lowell. BoWoP; LW; MoAmPo

To wrestle with the angel—Art. (LL) Art. Herman Melville. AmFaPo; APN-2; ColAP; NAAL-2v1; NAAL-3; NCAP; NOBA

To write of Sol in his exaltation. Robert Copland. NoSic *Fr.* High Way to the Spital House, The.

To write the country. Diana Helen Melhem. PoArWo *Fr.* Country.

To write threescore: this is the second of our reign [*or* raigne]. (LL) Anniversary [*or* Anniversarie], The. John Donne. BASC; BoLoP; ESCV; FHYEP; FSCP; HAP; MeLP; NOBE; NoP-4; NoSic; SCGP; TFi; WeW-3

To W.S.—On his Wonderful Toys. Walter Davies. NOxBChV

To yet more boastful visions of despair. (LL) Recalling War. Robert Graves. AF; HarvBoo; NoAM; OBWP; PeFWW; PoWW

To yield the sin her everlasting doom. (LL) Fulke Greville, 1st Baron Brooke. ChIV-1; NoSic; PeECV *Fr.* Caelica.

To You. Frank Horne. BPo *Fr.* Letters [*or* Notes] Found near a Suicide.

To You. Huda Na'mani. MAP, *tr. by* Lena Jayyusi

To You. Elolongue Epanya Yondo. NegPo, *tr. by* Ellen Conroy Kennedy

To you and to me? (LL) Bride, The. Bella [*or* Izabela] Akhatovna Akhmadulina. BoWoP; MPUn

To you, dere herte, variant and mutable. Unknown. MiEL

To you, fine wine in gold cup. Pao Chao. ChinPo, *tr. by* Yip Wai-lim *Fr.* Weary Road, The.

To you gave Sense, Good-humour, and a Poet. (LL) Epistle [II,] to a Lady[: Of the Characters of Women]. Pope. NAEL-5v1; NAEL-6v1; NAEL-7v1; NOEC

To you gave Sense, Good-humour, and a Poet. (LL) Pope. NAEL-5v1; NOEC

To you I dedicate this work of grace. Emilia [*or* Aemelia] Lanier [*or* Lanyer]. NOSC *Fr.* To the Lady Anne, Countess of Dorset.

To you, Kypris, Lysidike. Asclepiades. GrAn

To you, my friends, to you, my dear ones. Inna L'vovna Lisnyanskaya [*or* Lisnianskaia]. TCRP

To you [*or* yow], my purse [*or* purs], and to non [*or no or* noon] other wight. Complaint of Chaucer to His Empty Purse, The. Geoffrey Chaucer. MiEL; NAEL-5v1; SCGP

To you that lyfe possess grete troubles do befall. Emma Foxe. EMWP

To you, then, tenants of life's middle state. William Cowper. OBSV *Fr.* Tirocinium; or, A Review of Schools.

To you this fragrant oil, sweets to the sweet. Gift, A. Unknown. GrAn, *tr. by* Guy Davenport

To you, troop so fleet. Hymn to the Winds. Joachim Du Bellay. AWP, *tr. by* Andrew Lang

To your judgement which will be just. (LL) Epistle to a Patron, An. Frank Templeton Prince. HarvBoo; OxBEV

To your mistaken shrine, to your false idol Honour! (LL) Trail All Your Pikes. Anne Finch, Countess of Winchilsea. OPOU; WPE

To your owne bents dispose you: you'le be found. William Shakespeare. FaBoVe *Fr.* Winter's Tale, The.

To Your Question. Duane Niatum. CDW

To your question: why are my private parts. Unknown. RomPo, *tr. by* Eugene O'Connor *Fr.* Priapean Corpus, The.

To Youth. Josephine D. Henderson Heard. CBWP-4

To youth alone the mad, impassioned measure. Eternal Controversy, The. Dean B. Lyman, Jr. YaYoPo

To youths, who hurry thus away. On a Painted Woman. Shelley. NBLV

To Yuan Chen. Po Chü-i. CrYelRi, *tr. by* Sam Hamill

To Yung-erh—Imitating a Work by Master Jade Stream. Li Tung-yang. CoBLCP, *tr. by* Jonathan Chaves

To Yvor Winters, 1955. Thom Gunn. GTBS-P

To Zion. Judah Halevi. AWP, *tr. by* Maurice Samuel

Toad. Norman MacCaig. HarvBoo

Toad. Shinkichi Takahashi. ZenPo, *tr. by* Takashi Ikemoto and Lucien Stryk

Toad, A. Elizabeth Akers Allen. OBCA

Toad! It looks like, The. Issa. EH, *tr. by* Robert Hass

Toad the power mower caught, A. Death of a Toad, The. Richard Wilbur. NAAL-2v2; NAAL-5; NoAM

Toadeater, The. Robert Burns. FaBoEE

Toadfish. Stephen Perry. MiVo

Toads. Philip Larkin. NOBL; NoAM; OxAEP-2; OxBTC; PAI; PoE; SoSe-8

Toads mate. Toads Mate and Father Cleans the Pool. Myrna Peña Reyes. FSt

Toads Mate and Father Cleans the Pool. Myrna Peña Reyes. FSt

Toads Revisited. Philip Larkin. NOBL; OxAEP-2

Toady toady min yoself. Digging Sing, A. Unknown. FaBoVe

Toast. Stéphane Mallarmé. WoPoe, *tr. by* Frederick Morgan

Toast. Stéphane Mallarmé. SxFrPo, *tr. by* E. H. Blackmore and A. M. Blackmore

Toast. Thomas McCarthy. PBCIP

Toast. Leonard Nathan. BLT

Toast to the Cook, A. Bernard Cooper. Unle

Toast to 2,000, A. Richard Percival Lister. OBCoV

Toaster, The. William Jay Smith. NOxBChV; OTCP

Toasting my back I lean on the sunny rail. (LL) Thinking of My Little Boy. Tu Fu. ColAnChi; WoPoe, *tr. by* David Lattimore

Tobacco. Philip Freneau. TAP

Tobacco crumbs, vases and rings. (LL) Bean Eaters, The. Gwendolyn Brooks. AmFaPo; BlSi; ESEAA; HAP; HHAm; HeIP-4; LCAP-2; NALW; PoE; TAP; TRP; TTY; WeW-3

Tobacco is a filthy weed. Unknown. FaBoEE

Tobacco stains from your beautiful fingers, The. And I wish I did not feel like your mother. (LL) Rendezvous. Edna St. Vincent Millay. APT-1; NALW

Tobacco Warehouse Blues. Houston A. Baker, Jr. SeSe

Tobera. Jeff Tagami. OpBo

Tobias and the Angel. John Gray. NOBVV

Tobias, journeying to Ecbatane. Tobias and the Angel. John Gray. NOBVV

Tobit. Bible, Apocrypha.

   Blessed Is God. TrJP, *tr. by* D. C. Simpson

Toccata of Galuppi's, A. Robert Browning. EBVV; FaBoVe; GTBS-P; HAP; NAEL-5v2; NAEL-6v2; NOBE; NOBVV; UV

   (Oh Galuppi, Baldassare, this is very sad to find!) NoP-4

Today. John Kendrick Bangs. PoToHe

Today. As Soon As It's Here It's Gone But So What. Emilie Buchwald. MiVo

Today. Thomas Carlyle. PWR

Today. Ethel Romig Fuller. PoToHe

Today. Langston Hughes. GLP; VGW

Today. Today We Will Not Be Invisible Nor Silent. Victoria Lena Manyarrows. UnSA

Today. Moritake. JDP, *tr. by* Yoel Hoffmann

Today. Frank O'Hara. TTTS

Today. Bowl, The. Barbara Smith. WWork

Today. Sunday. Primus St. John. ISC

Today. Sarcophagus. Pauline Stainer. NeBl

Today. Jones Very. TAP

Today a brown duck with a green head. Allen Fisher. Oth *Fr.* Stepping Out.

Today a field of pumpkins. Sassafras. Barbara Guest. FTOS

Today, all at once, when the thread of my vision snapped. Elegy for Hassan Nasir. Faiz Ahmad Faiz. CarOv, *tr. by* Carolyn Kizer

Today, as at my glass I stood. To Mrs. Francis-Arabella Kelly. Mary Barber. ECWP

Today as I hang out the wash I see them again, a code. Geese, The. Jorie Graham. HCAP

Today as in the past, who is the master of these rivers and mountains? Tune: "Butterflies Lingering over Flowers"—Leaving the Border. Na-lan Hsing-te. SuSp, *tr. by* An-yan Tang

Today as the news from Selma and Saigon. Monet's "Waterlilies." Robert Earl Hayden. AmFaPo; GT

Today, as usual, the mind goes hunting for a word. Once Again the Mind. Faiz Ahmad Faiz. AF, *tr. by* Naomi Lazard

Today at the Publix with my daughters. Song for the Sugar Cane. Virgil Suárez. AmPoNex

Today before a goblet of wine I was shamed. Drunk Too Soon. Yüan Chên. SuSp, *tr. by* Dell R. Hales

Today beneath Benignant Skies. Denis Wortman. AH

Today, Braddock Avenue's a parade. Technology of Spring, The. Lynn Emanuel. BodElec

Today— but before today too—. Love Says. Daria Menicanti. CItWP, *tr. by* Cinzia Sartini Blum and Lara Trubowitz

Today, Cheng, I touched your face. Prisoner, The. Keith Douglas. HarvBoo

Today, dear heart, but just today. Her Answer. John Bennett. ITBLP

Today delight's fair ship. Today Delight's Fair Ship. Félix Lope de Vega Carpio. SpanPo, *tr. by* William M. Davis

Today Eurydice played. You All Know the Story of the Two Lovers. Carlota Caulfield. TANSG, *tr. by* Chris Allen

Today even those fireflies have become. Elegy for Mangochi Fishermen, An. Jack A. Mapanje. PBMAP

Today, everything takes. At the Vietnam War Memorial, Washington, D. C. Robert Dana. CDa

Today has it all, sunshine. Gwyn Williams. OBWVE *Fr.* Aspects of Now.

Today I am a farmer in the fields. Wang Chiu-ssu. CoBLCP *Fr.* Robber of Kuan-shan, The.

Today I Am a Homicide in the North of the City. Wanda Coleman. NAAAL

Today I am modest like an animal. Esther Raab. FIT, *tr. by* Robert Friend

Today I am walking alone in a bare place. Late November in a Field. James Wright (1927–80). NAAL-2v2; NNaP

Today I am walking in woods. Beginning, A. Richard Jones. IllVoic

Today I asked the money changer. Sergey [*or* Sergei] Aleksandrovich Yesenin [*or* Essenin]. TCRP

Today I bring you cold chrysanthemums. Between Seasons. Li-Young Lee. TRP

Today I chopped back irises. Clearing Away. Andrew Taylor. BMAP

Today I cleared out the kitchen with Dougie so Hedley could sand the kitchen floor. Day in the Life, A. Stef Pixner. BrRo

Today I'd like to climb the difference. Hades in Manganese. Clayton Eshleman. APSN

Today, I dedicate this to you: you are long. Every Day, Matilde. Pablo Neruda. GifTon, *tr. by* William O'Daly

Today I don't know what to do with the Earth. Voyages. Jules Supervielle. MFP, *tr. by* Martin Sorrell

Today I drove through a cloud of leaves. Hands in the Wind. Ted Kooser. UrbNat

Today I followed my servant, Hestia, down the dusty path. Learning to Walk Alone. Judith Ortiz Cofer. PueRic

Today I found the right fruit for my prime. Kumquat for John Keats, A. Tony Harrison. NoP-4

Today I get this letter from you and the sun. Tom Clark. PmAP; SPE *Fr.* You.

Today I hate that I was born. Desert Cry, A. Magdalena Gomez. PueRic

Today I have drunk the sun through every pore. Intact Pitcher. Yolanda Bedregal. TANSG, *tr. by* Carolyne Wright

Today I have turned thirty-two. For My Birthday. Attila József. IQMS, *tr. by* Istvan Fekete

Today I learned the *coora* flower. Coora Flower, The. Gwendolyn Brooks. ESEAA; IllVoic; NAAL-5; NIL-7; NoP-4 *Fr.* Children Going Home.

Today I like life much less. César Vallejo. TCLAP, *tr. by* Clayton Eshleman

Today I'll wear a cool summer coat. My Soul's Wardrobe. Sharon Dolin. PoCoUp

Today I'm going into town to give away what's left. What's Left. Jack Myers. BodElec

Today I'm your queen. Sonnet for July. Rosemerry Wahtola Trommer. GeoH

Today I met you, son of a Spanish exile. Jane Duran. Prnts *Fr.* Silences from the Spanish Civil War.

Today I picked up. Seven Stones. Marjorie Agosin. TANSG, *tr. by* Cola Franzen

Today I put on. Saint Patrick's Breastplate. *Unknown.* NOIV

Today I put on summer. Michikaze. JDP, *tr. by* Yoel Hoffmann

Today I sat before the cliff. *Unknown.* CoBCP

Today I saw a picture of the cancer cells. Cancer Cells, The. Richard Eberhart. HAP

Today I saw a place no one has seen. Iron Heaven. Betti Alver. BoWoP, *tr. by* Willis Barnstone and Felix Oinas

Today I saw a thing of arresting poignant beauty. Snow in October. Alice Moore Dunbar-Nelson. BlSi

Today I saw a woman plowing a furrow. Sister. Gabriela Mistral. BoWoP, *tr. by* Langston Hughes

Today I saw a woman wrapped in rags. At the Slackening of the Tide. James Wright (1927–80). UnPo; VGW

Today I saw black men. Men, The. E. Ethelbert Miller. UnSA

Today I stopped / I call my niece to tell her I'm through. Healing Logic, A. M. Wyrebek. AmPoNex

Today I think. Digging. Edward Thomas. MoBrPo; OxBTC

Today I've felt the. Embrace. Dulce Maria Loynaz. TANSG, *tr. by* Alan West

Today I wake having swung, naked, in London. Here and There. Ann Lauterbach. PmAP

Today I was caught alone in a summer storm. Judith Wright. HarvBoo *Fr.* Shadow of Fire: Ghazals, The.

Today I watched a woman by the water. Levee: Letter to No One, The. Lorna Dee Cervantes. TouFir

Today / I will b. Epitaph for Willie or Little Black Poet with No Future. Sibby Anderson-Thompkins. InTrad

Today I woke up again. Panorama 2. Romelia Alarcón de Folgar. TANSG, *tr. by* Alison Ridley

Today, if the breath of breeze. Any Lover to Any Beloved. Faiz Ahmad Faiz. WoPoe, *tr. by* Naomi Lazard

Today in hazy San Francisco, I face seaward. We Are Americans Now, We Live in the Tundra. Marilyn Chin. FSt; NIL-7; OPRER; UnSA

Today, in the war-torn state, the nightly news. Nightly News, The. Daniel Anderson. AmPoNex

Today is a day like any other. Watch of Time. Magda Portal. TANSG, *tr. by* Shaun Griffin and Emma Sepúlveda-Pulvirenti

Today Is a Day of Great Joy. Víctor Hernández Cruz. LoL; PueRic; TTY

Today is a holiday in the Western heart. Today Is Armistice, a Holiday. Delmore Schwartz. TrJP

Today Is Armistice, a Holiday. Delmore Schwartz. TrJP

Today is everybody's favorite day of the week. Everybody. Mark Levine. AmPoNex

Today Is Friday. Ramon Guthrie. PoE

Today Is Not Like They Said. Kirk Hall. NBV

Today Is Not the Day. Audre Lorde. AfrBLW

Today is Sunday. In Memoriam. Léopold Sédar Senghor. PoetW, *tr. by* Melvin Dixon

Today is the day. Kimpo. JDP, *tr. by* Yoel Hoffmann

Today is the end of religion's work. Tosui Unkei. JDP, *tr. by* Yoel Hoffmann

Today Is the First Day of the Rest of My Life. David Shire. ReLy

Today is your. April Fool Birthday Poem for Grandpa. Diane Di Prima. CLPP

Today it rains all over the world and we are two. Angel in the Deluge. Rosario Murillo. CLPP, *tr. by* Alejandro Murguía

Today it's going to cost us twenty dollars. How Things Work. Gary Soto. NoAM

Today, lonely for my father, I saw. My Father's Wedding. Robert Bly. NoAM; RaBo

Today / must have been Sunday. Eden After Dark. Richard Shelton. CDa

Today my mother and sisters. They've Come. Alfonsina Storni. BoWoP; WPOW

Today, my poetry has exacted a confession from me. (LL) Manifesto on Ars Poetica. Frank Mkalawile Chipasula. HBAPE; NAfrP

Today no-one has come to inquire. Agape. César Vallejo. TCLAP, *tr. by* Gordon Brotherston and Edward Dorn

Today on a sandy road. On a Recollected Road. Amir Gilbo'a. MHP, *tr. by* Ruth Finer Mintz

Today Rakan, riding an iron horse. Rakan-Keinan. ZenPo, *tr. by* Takashi Ikemoto and Lucien Stryk

Today's Market-in-the-Loop finds the poet. Commerce and the Man. Ricardo M. de Ungria. ReBoTo

Today's Meditation. Antonio Machado. AF, *tr. by* Robert Bly

Today's News. Elizabeth Alexander. ISC; InTrad

Today's sadness is different from yesterday's. Sad Sestina. Robin Becker. BodElec

Today's white fog won't rise above the tree-tops. Judith Wright. HarvBoo *Fr.* Shadow of Fire: Ghazals, The.

Today she parades her shape like swellings of song. Portrait of a Pregnant Woman. Bobi Jones. OBWVE, *tr. by* Joseph P. Clancy

Today, should you let fall a glass it would. Tramontana at Lerici. Charles Tomlinson. GTBS-P

Today, the angel of dread, invisible. Angel of Dread, The. Miklós Radnóti. PFTM-1

Today the ghetto knows a different fear. Fear. Eva Picková. INSAB; ItWoWo

Today the Grandpa Dug Potatoes. Opal Whitely. SpudSo

Today the grandpa dug potatoes in the field. Today the Grandpa Dug Potatoes. Opal Whitely. SpudSo

Today the grave is bright for me. Tennyson. NAWM-7v2 *Fr.* In Memoriam A. H. H.

Today the leaves cry, hanging on branches swept by wind. Course of a Particular, The. Wallace Stevens. APT-1; HCAP

Today the sixth of june. Nigeria in the Year 1999. Catherine Obianuju Acholonu. HBAPE

Today the skies are clear and blue. Now. *Unknown.* PWR

Today the sky above Mount Hiei, too. Shogo. JDP, *tr. by* Yoel Hoffmann

Today the snow is drifting. Snow. Philip Levine. ColAP; UrbNat

Today the sunlight is the paint on lead soldiers. Toyland. Roy Fisher. HarvBoo; NPeEn

Today / the Valley. No Trespassing (Private Beach). Katayoon Zandvakili. AmPoNex

Today, then, is the day. Fusen. JDP, *tr. by* Yoel Hoffmann

Today,/ there came a breeze thin as the needle of a syringe. J. Kitchener Davies. OBWVE *Fr.* Sound of the Wind That Is Blowing, The.

Today there've been moments. For a Daughter Gone Away. Brendan Galvin. GM

Today / to be a Jew in Israel. Dvora. Denyse Kirsch. GotH

Today too. Frank K. Robinson. HA

Today too. Tanko (d. 1735). JDP, *tr. by* Yoel Hoffmann

Today, Tuesday, I decided to move on. Malcolm Mooney's Land. William Sydney Graham. NPeEn; NePenScot

Today Tutu Is Beating the Same Burru As Me. Lebert Bethune. GT

Today Was a Bad Day Like TB. Chrystos. UnSA

Today was a day of fragments.   Mouvance.   Sue Standing.   UrbNat

Today we have marking of folders.   Yesterday.   Marking of Folders.   Anne Anderton.   UV

Today we have naming of parts.   Yesterday.   Henry Reed.   AmFaPo; FaBoWar; MoBrPo; NAEL-6v2; NOBE; NoP-4; OxBEV; OxBTC; PAI; PoPoPo; PoRA; RaBo; SoSe-8; TFi; UV; UnPo   Fr. Lessons of the War.

Today We Will Not Be Invisible Nor Silent.   Victoria Lena Manyarrows.   UnSA

Today we woke up to a revolution of snow.   Snow Day.   Billy Collins.   BAP-01

Today, whatever may annoy.   Today.   John Kendrick Bangs.   PoToHe

Today when I came underneath the spell.   Lőrinc Szabó.   IQMS, tr. by John Gordon Nichols   Fr. Cricket Music.

"Today will be the day of what we both said" (LL)   West-Running Brook.   Robert Frost.   APT-1; MoAmPo; NOBA; NoP-4

Today, you span the far mountains.   Driving to Katoomba.   Merlinda Bobis.   ReBoTo

Today you were supposed to come.   I Waited for Chuang Hsüan-yüan But He Never Came.   Mo Shih-lung.   CoBLCP, tr. by Jonathan Chaves

Todd.   Stewart Conn.   NePenScot

Toe'osh; a Laguna Coyote Story.   Leslie Marmon Silko.   CDW; NoAM; VoR

Toe sticking out from under the hem, The.   On a Fifteenth-Century Flemish Angel.   David Ray.   CRP

Toe tipe.   Unknown.   OxNR

Toe, trip and go.   Unknown.   OxNR

Toe upon [or after] toe, a snowing flesh.   Nude Descending a Staircase.   X. J. Kennedy.   NIP-4; OxBSP

Toe upon toe, a snowing flesh.   X. J. Kennedy.   See Toe upon [or after] toe, a snowing flesh

Together.   Maxine W. Kumin.   BoWoP

Together.   Ludwig Lewisohn.   PoToHe; TrJP

Together Again.   Victor Vroomkoning.   TuT, tr. by Anne Kennedy

Together Again.   Victor Vroomkoning.   TuT, tr. by James Simmons

Together, babe, we could have had the world sewn up.   Olive Senior.   NewEx

Together eternity and death threaten me.   Patrizia Cavalli.   NeIt

Together, fourteen years older.   In the Cathedral.   Patricia Beer.   OxBC

Together in infinite shade.   Too Much Coffee.   Edwin Arlington Robinson.   MoAmPo

Together in this grave lie Benjamin Pantier, attorney at law.   Edgar Lee Masters.   APT-1   Fr. Spoon River Anthology.

Together twists their threads, and yet draws hers the longer. (LL)   Dialogue betwixt Time and a Pilgrim[e], A.   Aurelian Townshend [or Townsend].   NOBE; NPeEn; OxBEV

Together, we will not get through this. (LL)   My Life.   Joe Wenderoth.   BodElec; NAPBL

Together Wherever We Go.   Stephen Sondheim.   ReLy

Together with my stones.   Shibboleth.   Paul Celan.   PoetW, tr. by Michael Hamburger

Together with that which was spilled in battle.   Servile Blood.   Vasily [or Vasilii Dmitrievich] Fyodorov [or Fiodorov].   TCRP, tr. by Lubov Yakovleva

Toil.   Avraham Shlonsky.   MHP, tr. by Ruth Finer Mintz

"Toil! toil! toil!"   Wandering Jew, The.   Eloise Bibb.   CBWP-4

Toilet, The.   Pope.   ECEV; NOBE; OxAEP-1; OxBEV   Fr. Rape of the Lock, The; an Heroi-Comical Poem.

Toilette, The.   John Gay.   ECEV

Toiling in Town now is "horrid."   In Town.   Austin Dobson.   MakPoe

Toishan Song, A.   Unknown.   WoPoe, tr. by Gary Gach and C. H. Kwock

Token.   Alison Bielski.   AngWePo

Token, A.   Robert Creeley.   VGW

Token, The.   Frank Templeton Prince.   FaBoTw; OxBTC

Token Woman, The.   Marge Piercy.   NALW

Token woman gleams like a gold molar in a toothless mouth, The.   Token Woman, The.   Marge Piercy.   NALW

Toki-no-Ge (Satori Poem).   Muso Soseki.   EaWin, tr. by W. S. Merwin

Toldi.   János Arany.
  Canto 1.
    "As on an autumn night a herdman's fire."   IQMS, tr. by Watson Kirkconnell
  Canto 5.
    "Day to the reedy marsh had closed her eye."   IQMS, tr. by Watson Kirkconnell
  Canto 6.
    "As if a nest of hornets rose to sting."   IQMS, tr. by Watson Kirkconnell
  Canto 8.
    "My brother's done for, by all human law."   IQMS, tr. by Watson Kirkconnell
  Canto 11.

  "River seemed a broad stream, fenced with folk, The."   IQMS, tr. by Watson Kirkconnell
  Canto 12.
    "Then Nicholas spoke: "My King, most kind to me""   IQMS, tr. by Watson Kirkconnell

Toledo.   Roy Campbell.   MoBrPo

Toledo Room, The.   Alistair Paterson.
  "They do it with knives."   PeNZ

Tolerance of Crows, The.   Charles Donnelly.   CIP-2

Toll for the brave!   On the Loss of the Royal George.   William Cowper.   EBEV; NOBE

Toll the bell, fellow.   Red Cow Is Dead, The.   Elwyn Brooks White.   NBLV

Tolling from St. Patrick's, The.   Burial of an Irish President.   Austin Clarke.   BIrV

Tollund Man.   Hugo Claus.   TuT, tr. by Peter Van de Kamp

Tollund Man, The.   Hugo Claus.   PFTM-2, tr. by Theo Hermans

Tollund Man, The.   Seamus Heaney.   BIrV; CABP; CIP-2; EBEV; FaBoMo; ModIr; NPeEn; PBCIP; PNI; WoPoe

Toltec, The.   Ana Castillo.   IllVoic

Toltecs were wise, The.   Unknown.   CA

Tom.   James Schuyler.   GLP

Tom Agnew, Bill Agnew.   Dante Gabriel Rossetti.   FaBoEE

Tom Bowling.   Charles Dibdin.   See Poor Tom

Tom Brown's two little Indian boys.   Unknown.   OxNR

Tom-Cat, The.   Don Marquis.   PoRA

Tom Child had often painted Death.   This Morning Tom Child, the Painter, Died.   Samuel Sewall.   SCAP

Tom Deadlight.   Herman Melville.   APN-2; NCAP

Tom Farley.   Colin Thiele.   NOBAu

Tom Fool at Jamaica.   Marianne Craig Moore.   APT-1

Tom—garlanded with squat and surly steel.   Tom's Garland: Upon the Unemployed.   Gerard Manley Hopkins.   Son

Tom, He Was a Piper's Son.   Unknown.   OxNR

Tom o' Bedlam.   Unknown.   FaBoCh; PoRA

Tom o' Bedlam's Song.   Unknown.   BASC; EBEV; FaBoCh; NPeEn; NoP-4; OxBoLi; PoRA; TFi
  (Loving Mad Tom.)   HAP; NOBE; WeW-3
  (Mad Tom's Song.)   RB

Tom Passey's Child.   Maggie Hannan.   NLP

Tom Potts.   Unknown.   ESPB

Tom Punsibi's Letter to Dean Swift.   Thomas Sheridan.   NPeEn

Tom's Garland: Upon the Unemployed.   Gerard Manley Hopkins.   Son

Tom's sickness did his morals mend.   Epigram.   Matthew Prior.   FaBoEE

Tom Sucklebat, in dressing-gown, without his teeth.   Administrator, An.   Geoffrey Grigson.   FaBoEE

Tom the Porter.   John Byrom.   NOEC

Tom Thumbkin.   Unknown.   OxNR

Tom, Tom, the piper's son.   Mother Goose.   LB; OxNR

Tom used spit for lubricant and fucked me.   David Trinidad.   WiU   Fr. Eighteen to Twenty-One.

Tom Wedgwood Tells.   Brian W. Aldiss.   NOBL

Tom, will you let me love you in your restaurant?   Litany.   Carolyn Creedon.   BodElec

Tomarata.   Kendrick Smithyman.   PeNZ

Tomás.   Luis Lopez.   GeoH

Tomato Ketchup.   Unknown.   See On Tomato Ketchup

Tomb.   Stéphane Mallarmé.   SxFrPo, tr. by E. H. Blackmore and A. M. Blackmore

Tomb/ A hollow hateful world.   Sacheverell Sitwell.   OBMV

Tomb, bend / To autum wind—.   Basho.   ZenPo, tr. by Takashi Ikemoto and Lucien Stryk

Tomb, but his fisherman's union. (LL)   Leonidas.   GrAn; PGA; WoPoe, tr. by Kenneth Rexroth

Tomb—just a canal-bank seat for the passer-by. (LL)   Lines Written on a Seat on the Grand Canal, Dublin.   Patrick Kavanagh.   BIrV; NOIV

Tomb of an Ancestor.   Allen Curnow.
  "Oldest of us burst into tears and cried, The."   PeNZ

Tomb of Charles Baudelaire, The.   Stéphane Mallarmé.   SxFrPo, tr. by E. H. Blackmore and A. M. Blackmore

Tomb of Crethon, The.   Leonidas of Tarentum.   AWP, tr. by John Hermann Merivale

Tomb of Diogenes, The.   Unknown.   AWP, tr. by John Addington Symonds

Tomb of Edgar Allan Poe, The.   Stéphane Mallarmé.   SxFrPo, tr. by E. H. Blackmore and A. M. Blackmore

Tomb of Edgar Poe, The.   Stéphane Mallarmé.   NAWM-7v2, tr. by Henry Weinfield

Tomb of Hegeso, The.   Mihály Babits.   IQMS, tr. by Watson Kirkconnell

Tomb of Heracles, The.   James McAuley.   BMAP   *Fr.* Hero and the Hydra, The.

Tomb of Ibykos, The.   *Unknown.*   GrAn, *tr. by* Peter Jay

Tomb of Ilaria Giunigi, The.   Edith Wharton.   APN-2

Tomb of Lt. John Learmonth, A.I.F, The.   John Streeter Manifold.   CBAP

Tomb of Sir Lawrence Tanfield obiit 30 Ap. 1625 erected by Lady Tanfield 1628.   Lady Elizabeth Tanfield.   *See* Epitaph for Sir Lawrence Tanfield

Tomb of the Imagination.   Miguel Hernández.   AF, *tr. by* Tom Jones

Tomb of the Kings, The.   Anne Hébert.   WoPoe, *tr. by* A., Jr. Poulin

Tomb of the Kings, The.   Anne Hébert.   BoWoP, *tr. by* Aliki and Willis Barnstone

Tomb of the Singing Girl Ch'iung-i, The.   Hsü Pen.   CoBLCP, *tr. by* Jonathan Chaves

Tomb on the Shore, A.   Asclepiades.   GrAn, *tr. by* Alan Marshfield

Tomb on the Thracian approaches of Olympus holds, A.   On the Tomb of Orpheus.   Damagetus.   GrAn, *tr. by* John Heath-Stubbs and Carol A. Whiteside

Tombs of the Hetaerae.   Rainer Maria Rilke.   PFTM-1

Tombstone told when she died, The.   Dylan Thomas.   OxBTC

Tomcat born on railroad.   Autobiography.   Tom Weatherly.   NBV

Tomes.   Billy Collins.   KGB

Tommies in the Train.   D. H. Lawrence.   PoWW

Tommorow.   Amal Dunqul.   MAP; NAfrP, *tr. by* Sharif Elmusa and Thomas G. Ezzy

Tommy.   Rudyard Kipling.   CABP; EBEV; FaBoWar; MoBrPo; NoP-4; OBWP; OxAEP-2; OxBTC; PeVV; UV

Tommy is three and when he's bad.   Red Roses.   Anne Sexton.   EmeKit

Tommy kept a chandler's shop.   *Unknown.*   OxNR

Tommy O'Linn was a Scotsman born.   *Unknown.*   OxNR

Tommy's Dead.   Sydney Thompson Dobell.   PeVV

Tommy's tears and Mary's fears.   Fears and Tears.   *Unknown.*   ReMoGo

Tommy Tibule.   *Unknown.*   OxNR

Tommy Tittlemouse.   Mother Goose.   OxNR; ReMoGo

Tommy Trot, a man of law.   *Unknown.*   OxNR

Tommy Tucker.   Mother Goose.   LB; OxNR; ReMoGo

Tomorrow.   Anna Laetitia Barbauld.   ECWP; PEW

Tomorrow.   John Collins.   GTBS-P

Tomorrow.   Langston Hughes.   APSN

Tomorrow.   John Henry Mackay.   CAGL, *tr. by* Hubert Kennedy

Tomorrow.   E. Ethelbert Miller.   ISC

Tomorrow.   Tomorrow.   E. Ethelbert Miller.   ISC

Tomorrow again will shine the sun.   Tomorrow.   John Henry Mackay.   CAGL, *tr. by* Hubert Kennedy

Tomorrow, and Tomorrow, and Tomorrow.   William Shakespeare.   SoSe-8   *Fr.* Macbeth.

"Tomorrow, friend, will be another day."   Faith for Tomorrow.   Thomas Curtis Clark.   PoToHe

Tomorrow I shall.   Elaine Randell.   Oth

Tomorrow I shall wake to welcome him. (LL)   Geoffrey Hill.   NOCV; OxBSo; WoPoe, *tr. by* Geoffrey Hill   *Fr.* Lachrimae; or Seven Tears Figured in Seven Passionate Pavans.

Tomorrow I was.   Akahito.   OHPJ

Tomorrow Is Another Day.   Walter Jurmann.   ReLy

Tomorrow is saint valentine's day.   William Shakespeare.   EnLoPo; NoSic   *Fr.* Hamlet.

Tomorrow, Julia, I betimes must rise.   Perfume, The.   Robert Herrick.   CaPo

Tomorrow morning I will take a shower.   Valerio Magrelli.   NeIt

Tomorrow [*or* To morrow] to fresh woods, and pastures new. (LL)   John Milton.   AWP; AmFaPo; BASC; CABP; ClHu; EBEV; FHYEP; GTBS-P; HAP; MakPoe; NAEL-6v1; NAEL-7v1; NIL-7; NOBE; NOSC; NPeEn; NoP-4; OBEV; OxAEP-1; OxBTC; PAI; PBRV; PoPoPo; SCGP; TFi; UnPo

Tomorrow, since I have so few.   Rooster.   James Tate.   LCAP-2

Tomorrow the Past Comes.   Ion Caraion.   AF, *tr. by* Marguerite Dorian

Tomorrow, the twentieth, we celebrate.   To Piso, on Epicurus' Birthday.   Philodemus.   GrAn, *tr. by* William Moebius

Tomorrow the wind will have fallen.   Epitaph of a Sailor.   Antiphilus [*or* Antiphilos].   GrAn, *tr. by* Dudley Fitts

Tomorrow / they will clothe me in ashes at dawn.   Shadow of Days to Come.   Alejandra Piznarnick.   TANSG, *tr. by* Susan Bassnett

Tomorrow, Tomorrow.   Derek Walcott.   PoetW

Tomorrow we'll be good.   Bad Blood.   U Tam'si Tchicaya.   NegPo, *tr. by* Ellen Conroy Kennedy

Tomorrow, We'll Dance in America.   James Harms.   AmPoNex

Tomorrow we part.   Tune: "Song of the Southern Country."   Chu Yi-tsun.   SuSp, *tr. by* Irving Y. Lo

Tomorrow, when the meadows grow.   Victor Hugo.   SxFrPo, *tr. by* E. H. Blackmore and A. M. Blackmore

Tomorrow will be Monday. (LL)   Mother Goose.   LB; OxNR; ReMoGo

Tomorrow will be Tuesday.   Survival 2.   Chiqui Vicioso.   TANSG, *tr. by* Emma Jane Robinett

Tomorrow you will live, you always cry.   Procrastination.   Martial.   AWP; FaBoEE; OBVE, *tr. by* Abraham Cowley

Tomorrow / you will walk toward other evenings.   History.   Heberto Padilla.   AF, *tr. by* Alastair Reid

Tomorrows.   James Merrill.   OBAL

Tomorrows reactivate somnolence.   Of Promises and Prophecy.   Steve Chimombo.   HBAPE

Tompkins Square Park's a mess of shopping carts.   Given in Person Only.   Mark Wunderlich.   WiU

Tone-deaf old person of Tring, A.   Limerick.   *Unknown.*   PeLi

Tone of Voice, The.   *Unknown.*   PoToHe

Tone Poem.   Oliver Reynolds.

  Bestiary.   TCAWP

  Eous.   TCAWP

  "Python-coils of leg and trunk."   TCAWP

  "'Undress me! Undress me!' you said."   TCAWP

Tongs.   Mother Goose.   LB; OxNR; ReMoGo

Tongue, The.   Georgy [*or* Georgii] Nikolaevich Obolduyev [*or* Obolduev].   TCRP, *tr. by* Vera Dunham

Tongue, The.   Phillips Burrows Strong.   PoToHe

Tongue, call out.   Rāmprasād Sen.   SinGod, *tr. by* Rachel Fell McDermott

Tongue lashing.   Tonguing.   Greg S. Tate.   ISC

Tongue shapes and molds sound.   Speech, The.   Not Sense.   Gail Tremblay.   WeW-3

Tongue that mothered such a metaphor, The.   Hogwash.   Robert Francis.   LCAP-2; NIL-7; NIP-4; TRP

Tongue Tied.   Jaime Jacinto.   ReBoTo

Tongue-tied in Black and White.   Michael S. Harper.   ESEAA; HCAP

Tongue we all, bards Welsh, Ta! (LL)   Cywydd o Fawl.   Harri Webb.   AngWePo; TCAWP

Tongueless man gets his land took, The. (LL)   Tony Harrison.   HarvBoo; NAEL-5v2; NAEL-6v2   *Fr.* School of Eloquence, The.

Tongues.   Philip Martin.   NOBAu

Tongues and tasks of her children's children, The. (LL)   My Grandmother.   Karl Shapiro.   TaR; VGW

Tongues in My Mouth.   Demetrice A. Worley.   SpirFl

Tongues we use for talking.   Tailpiece.   Max Fatchen.   OTCP

Tonguing.   Greg S. Tate.   ISC

Tonight.   Regina DeCormier-Shekejian.   SpudSo

Tonight, a beautiful redhead.   Undertaker's Daughter Feels Neglect, The.   Thylias Moss.   ESEAA

Tonight a blackout. Twenty years ago.   Christmas Eve under Hooker's Statue.   Robert Lowell.   CoAmPo; OxBA

Tonight a half-moon.   O-mei Mountain Moon.   Li Po.   CrYelRi, *tr. by* Sam Hamill

Tonight a man with AIDS called.   Grief.   Ruth L. Schwartz.   AmPoNex

Tonight, after a rain.   Longing for Eternal Life, The.   Liz Rosenberg.   PBCAP

Tonight and forever I shall be yours so says the oleo king.   Some Stories of the Beauty Wapiti.   Ebbe Borregaard.   NeAP

Tonight at *Antony and Cleopatra.*   Between the Acts.   Elise Paschen.   IllVoic

Tonight at Eight.   Sheldon Harnick.   ReLy

Tonight, grave sir, both my poor[e] house and I.   Inviting a Friend to Supper.   Ben Jonson.   AWP; BASC; BeJo; NAEL-6v1; NAEL-7v1; NOBE; NOSC; NPeEn; NoP-4; OxBoLi; PAI; PBRV; PeLV

Tonight / he is understanding Canada.   Understanding Canada.   Peter Sirr.   PBCIP

Tonight he's playing the Black Orchid.   Black Orchid.   David Jauss.   SeSe

Tonight—I am alone in the night.   Marina Ivanovna Tsvetayeva [*or* Tsvetaeva].   AWTN, *tr. by* Elaine Feinstein   *Fr.* Insomnia.

Tonight I Can Almost Hear the Singing.   Silvia Curbelo.   TouFir

Tonight I Can Write the Saddest Lines.   Pablo Neruda.   BoLoP; PoetW; TCLAP, *tr. by* W. S. Merwin

Tonight I disentangle.   Wakepick I.   Kristjana Gunnars.   NOBC

Tonight I do the bidding of a ghost.   House by the Sea, The.   Elizabeth Stoddard.   SWaP

Tonight I have a date.   Serenade for Two Poplars, A.   Esther Raab.   FIT, *tr. by* Robert Friend and Shimon Sandbank

Tonight I hunger so.   Wave-Won.   Emily Pauline Johnson.   SWaP

Tonight I light the candles of my eyes in the lee.   Rhyme for Halloween, A.   Maurice Kilwein Guevara.   TouFir

Tonight I'll walk the razor along your throat.   Punk Pantoum.   Pamela Stewart.   ReTh

Tonight, I look, thunderstruck.   Note on my Son's Face, A.   Toi Derricotte.   ISC

Tonight I'm downhearted.   Are You Lonesome Tonight?   Lou Handman.   ReLy

Tonight I resurrected from the dead. Turn and Turn About. Eva Gerlach. TuT, *tr.* by Eamon Grennan

Tonight I Thank the Potato. Robert Stewart. SpudSo

Tonight I've watched. Sappho. AWTN, *tr.* by Mary Barnard

Tonight I walk home through the park. Recovery. M. Wyrebek. AmPoNex

Tonight I want to say something wonderful. For the Sleepwalkers. Edward Hirsch. IllVoic

Tonight I watch my father's hair. Two Postures beside a Fire. James Wright (1927–80). HCAP; HeIP-4

Tonight in the cold I know most of the living are waiting. Elegy for the Nightbound. Anthony Cronin. PBCIP

Tonight in the hills there was a light. Hawktree. Dave Jeddie Smith. HCAP

Tonight, moon over Fu-chou. Moonlit Night. Tu Fu. ChinPo, *tr.* by Yip Wai-lim

Tonight my children hunch. "It Out-Herods Herod. Pray You, Avoid It." Anthony Hecht. AF; CoAP; NIP-4; NOBA; NoAM; OxBC

Tonight, on holiday in Oxford, Bach's Magnificat. Magnificat! Michael S. Glaser. OPRER

Tonight, on the deck, the lights. Two Stories. Charles Wright. LCAP-2

Tonight our cat, Tahi, who lately lost. Buried Stream, The. James Keir Baxter. HarvBoo; OxBC

Tonight our heaven is an estuary. Pearls. Alan Gould. NOBAu

Tonight, Sally and I are making stuffed / grapeleaves. Leaves. Sam Hamod. GraLe; UnSA

Tonight she is sitting by a window. Old Woman, The. Iain Crichton Smith. WoPoe

Tonight the Famous Psychiatrist. Louis Simpson. OxBC

Tonight the moon hovers in the sky. Modern English. Jeffery Conway. WiU

Tonight the moon is high, to summon all. Elegy. William Bell. FaBoTw

Tonight the moths. Tyranny of Moths. Gerald Vizenor. VoR

Tonight the newspapers report. Fall of Da Nang, The. Gerald McCarthy. CDa

Tonight the tenement smells of oysters. Ecstasy of St Saviour's Avenue, The. Neil Rollinson. EmeKit

Tonight the wind gnaws. Christmas Landscape. Laurie Lee. OBCP

Tonight the winds begin to rise. Tennyson. EBVV; GTBS-P; NAEL-6v2; NAWM-7v2; NOBE; PeECV   *Fr.* In Memoriam A. H. H.

Tonight the workmen. Distance. David Wojahn. YaYoPo

Tonight they need to be both host and stranger. Familiar Story. Alan Shapiro. DiPo; NIP-4

Tonight ungathered let us leave. Tennyson. ChrPo; EBVV; FHYEP; NAEL-6v2   *Fr.* In Memoriam A. H. H.

Tonight, we make up our own legends. Beginning of Things, The. Fatima Lim-Wilson. ReBoTo

Tonight we wait for the alarm. Karen Alkalay-Gut. DTA   *Fr.* Between Bombardments: A Journal.

Tonight, what sort of night. Song of the Viet Boatman. *Unknown.* ColAnChi, *tr.* by Anne Birrell

Tonight when I knelt down next to our cat, Zooey. Wild Gratitude. Edward Hirsch. IllVoic

Tonight when the hoar frost falls on the wood. Christmas in the Wood. Frances Mary Frost. TrCP

Tonight / when the moon comes out. Proposition. Nicolás Guillén. TTY, *tr.* by Langston Hughes

Tonight when the sea runs like a sore. Voyage to Labrador. W.S. Merwin. GS

Tonight with Bold Desire. Amelia Rosselli. CItWP, *tr.* by Cinzia Sartini Blum and Lara Trubowitz

Tonight with wine being poured. Jelaluddin [*or* Jalal al-Din] Rumi. RaBo   *Fr.* Four Quatrains.

Tonight, within my heart! (LL) My Little Dreams. Georgia Douglas Johnson. BlSi; NAAAL

Tonight words fall away from me like shed clothing. Last Poem. Margaret Atwood. LCAP-2

Tonight you too / Are rushed. Issa. ZenPo, *tr.* by Takashi Ikemoto and Lucien Stryk

Tonight, you will not tire. All-Night Diner, The. Markham Johnson. ReTh

Tonight. . . wishing. Michael McClintock. HA

Tonite. Alan Pizzarelli. HA

Tonite I walked out of my red apartment door on East tenth street's. Allen Ginsberg. HCAP; NoAM

Tonite, thriller was. Beware: Do Not Read This Poem. Ishmael Reed. BPo; NIP-4; PAI

Tonite, *thriller* was / abt an ol woman, so vain she. Ishmael Reed. *See* Tonite, thriller was

Tony's father left the family. Tony Went to the Bodega but He Didn't Buy Anything. Martín Espada. PueRic

Tony/ To be casual and have the wish to heal. Jack Spicer. PoM   *Fr.* Holy Grail, The.

Tony Went to the Bodega but He Didn't Buy Anything. Martín Espada. PueRic

Tony White. Richard Murphy. BiHa

Too Bad. Gig Ryan. NOBAu

Too Bright a Day. Norman MacCaig. GTBS-P

Too Close for Comfort. Jerry Bock. ReLy

Too crossover, too, love. (LL) Avalanche. Quincy Troupe. PFTM-2; SpirFl

"Too." Darkly he rose, and then I slept. (LL) True Account of Talking to the Sun at Fire Island, A. Frank O'Hara. AmFaPo; EmeKit; HCAP; NNaP; RB; TTTS

Too Darn Hot. Cole Porter. ReLy

Too far for you to see. Welsh Hill Country, The. Ronald Stuart Thomas. AngWePo

Too foraging to blue-print or deploy! Naomi. Gwendolyn Brooks. NAAL-2v2

Too fragile to endure the heat of a long summer day. Su Tung-p'o (Su Shih). SuSp, *tr.* by Irving Y. Lo   *Fr.* On Chao Ch'ang's Flower Paintings in Wang Po-yang's Collection.

Too frail to soar—a feeble thing. Sparrow's Fall, The. Frances Ellen Watkins Harper. PWR

Too green the springing April grass. Spring in New Hampshire. Claude McKay. BPo; ChAP

Too happy Time dissolves itself. Emily Dickinson. APN-2; NOBA

Too heavy! (LL) Guarded Wound, The. Adelaide Crapsey. APT-1; WPE

Too immense for imagination, just big enough for boredom. Wonderful Whale, The. Eve Merriam. YaYoPo

Too Late. James Vincent Cunningham. *See* Five Epigrams

Too Late. Nora Perry. PoToHe

Too-Late Born, The. Archibald MacLeish. MoAmPo; OxBA

(Silent Slain, The.) PeFWW

Too Late for a Husband. *Unknown.* WoPoe, *tr.* by Nguyen Ngoc Bich

Too late for love, too late for joy. Christina Georgina Rossetti. OBEV; WPE   *Fr.* Prince's Progress, The.

Too lazy even to move a feather fan. Summer Days in the Mountains. Li Po. CrYelRi, *tr.* by Sam Hamill

Too lazy to wave the white plume fan. Summer Day in the Mountains. Li Po. CoBCP, *tr.* by Burton Watson

Too Lazy to Write Poetry. Chu Yün-ming. CoBLCP, *tr.* by Jonathan Chaves

Too little. Door, The. Charles Tomlinson. OxBEV

Too Long I Followed. William Drummond, of Hawthornden. Son   *Fr.* Urania, or Spiritual Poems.

Too long outside your door I have shivered. Terrible Door, The. Harold Monro. BoLoP; EnLoPo; FaBoTw

Too Many Daves. "Dr. Seuss." OBCA; OxIBACP

Too many echoes. Returning Home. "Shu Ting." CarOv, *tr.* by Carolyn Kizer and Y. H. Zhao

Too Many Names. Pablo Neruda. VCWP, *tr.* by Alastair Reid

Too many nights. Apology. Elizabeth Spires. FFC

Too many of the dead, some I knew well. In the Backs. Frances Darwin Cornford. BrRo

Too Many Rings Around Rosie. Irving Caesar. ReLy

Too many summers out of the way of a trowel. Lawn Roller, The. Robert Layzer. OBGa

Too many waves to mark two more or three. (LL) Old Woman. Iain Crichton Smith. FaBoTw; HarvBoo; NePenScot; OxBEV; OxBTC

Too Marvelous for Words. Johnny Mercer. ReLy

Too Much Coffee. Edwin Arlington Robinson. MoAmPo

Too much good luck no less than misery. Joy May Kill. Michelangelo Buonarroti. AWP, *tr.* by John Addington Symonds

Too much have I been a mere man. Self-Transformation. Willem Kloos. TuT, *tr.* by Desmond Egan

Too Much Heat, Too Much Work. Tu Fu. CarOv, *tr.* by Carolyn Kizer   *Fr.* Banishment.

Too much history. Town on the Ten Dollar Note, The. Laurie Duggan. BMAP

Too much of Europe, here transplanted o'er. Joel Barlow. APN-1   *Fr.* Columbiad, The.

Too much to ask. Too Much to Ask. Jien (Former Chief Priest). WoPoe, *tr.* by Howard S. Levy

Too much to drink these days, late getting up each morning. Late Rising on Spring Days. Wei Chuang. CoBCP, *tr.* by Burton Watson

Too nearly join'd to sickness, toils, and pains. Philip Freneau. TCAPo   *Fr.* House of Night, The.

Too old for you as you for me. (LL) To Chloe, Who Wished Herself Young Enough for Me. William Cartwright. BeJo; NOSC; OxAEP-1

Too old to carry arms and fight like the others—. Report from the Besieged City. Zbigniew Herbert. AF, *tr.* by John Carpenter

Too proud to sue! too tender to resign! (LL) To Phaon. Mary Robinson. CenSon; RWP

Too quickly. . . And more quickly every time. (LL) Insert, The. R. L. Barth. CDa; InPK-6

Too sad is the grief in my heart. Elegy for His Daughter Ellen. Goronwy Owen. OBWVE, *tr. by* George Borrow

Too solemn for day, too sweet for night. William Sidney Walker. OBEV

Too soon. (LL) May Swenson. APT-2; GM

Too soon, alas! too soon I plunged into the world with tone and clang. Désilusion. Lady Jane Francesca Wilde. VWP

Too soon put up for the wind that blew it down. City. Michael Smith. PBCIP

Too soon! Too soon! (LL) Lawrence Ferlinghetti. HeIP-4; PoM; TAP

Too sound for waking and for dreams too deep. (LL) Not for That City. Charlotte Mew. ChIV-2; HarvBoo; MoBrPo; VWP

Too tart the fruit it brought! (LL) Shut Out That Moon. Thomas Hardy. NOBE; NoAM

Too tight, it is running over. Fence Wire. James Dickey. VGW

Too tremulously fine! (LL) Kiss, The. Charlotte Dacre. CABP; NOBRP

Too volatile, am I? too voluble? too much a word-person? Ghazal of the Better-Unbegun. Heather McHugh. ExTi

Too weak am I to pray, as some have prayed. Preparation. William Johnson Cory. OxBSo

Too-well-done. Nursery Song. Anna Wickham. NOxBChV

Too wide the earth, mine eyes no more behold thee. Written in Absence. Alcuin. MLL, *tr. by* Helen Waddell

Too Wonderful. Bible, O.T. TrJP *Fr.* Proverbs.

Too young for congregating in the praying corner at church. At Fifty. Vivian Shipley. ExTi

Too young to have known the meaning of sorrow. Silent at Her Window. Wang Ch'ang-ling. ColAnChi; CrYelRi, *tr. by* Sam Hamill

Took his farewell journey to the Promised Land. (LL) Casey Jones. *Unknown.* OxBoLi; PeLV

Took / Two snowdrops to fall off the world. Potter. Michael O'Reilly. BloBone

Tool of Fate, The. "Yehoash." TrJP, *tr. by* Isidore Goldstick

Toot once, strum once. Kuan Han-ch'ing. SuSp *Fr.* Tune: "Song of Great Virtue"—Winter.

Toot, Toot, Tootsie! (Good-bye). Ted Fiorito. ReLy

Tooth, The. Rebekah Carmichael. ECWP

Toothpuller Who Wanted to Turn a Mouth into a Grinding Machine, The. Francisco de Quevedo y Villegas. WoPoe, *tr. by* Willis Barnstone

Top Hat, White Tie, and Tails. Irving Berlin. ReLy

Top of the World, The. Yves Bonnefoy. VCWP, *tr. by* John Naughton

Topcliffe's horses shake. John Logan. CRP *Fr.* Death of Southwell, The.

Topeka. . . Junction City. At the Train Museum. Linda Pastan. GM

Toper who spies in the distance, A. Limerick. Leslie Johnson. PeLi

Tophet. Thomas Gray. ChIV-1; FaBoEE; NOEC; OxBSP

Topics. James Merrill.
   Casual Wear. NIP-4
   "Your average tourist: Fifty. 2.3." NIP-4

Toplight hammered down by shadowless noon. Alfred Corn. NAAL-2v2; VCAP *Fr.* Call in the Midst of the Crowd, A.

Topophilia. Mary Ruefle. BAP-97

Topos. Jane Miller. GifTon

Topple down[e] headlong. (LL) William Shakespeare. OxAEP-1; OxBEV *Fr.* King Lear.

Topple the house down, wind. Nocturne. Lizette Woodworth Reese. PoBW

Toppled wine-cup, A. Bits of Reminiscence. "Shu Ting." CarOv; VCWP, *tr. by* Carolyn Kizer and Y. H. Zhao

Toppling down as the sunset sky grows distant. At an Inn in Yü-kan. Liu Ch'ang-ch'ing. SuSp, *tr. by* William H. Nienhauser

Tops were sign enough, The. Potato Blight. David Lindley. NLP

Toque de queda: Curfew in Lawrence. Martín Espada. PueRic

Tor House. William Everson. APT-2

Tor House. Robinson Jeffers. APT-1

Torah Braids. Tamara Kamenszain. MirDau, *tr. by* Roberta Gordenstein

Torch, The. Walt Whitman. SAmP
   (Call in the midst of the crowd, A.) ColAP

Torch I carry is handsome, The. Guess I'll Hang My Tears Out to Dry. Jule Styne. ReLy

Tore us down to the human. (LL) Blackbottom. Toi Derricotte. GT; LTA; PBCAP

Tormented Mystic. Al-Tijani Yusuf Bashir. MAP, *tr. by* Patricia Alanah Byrne and Matthew Sorenson

Tormented with incessant pains. To Stella. Jonathan Swift. NOEC

Torn Apart. Pam Tjanara-Williams. IBA

Torn between griefs, which grief shall I lament. Sophocles. APT-1; OBVE, *tr. by* Ezra Pound *Fr.* Women of Trachis.

Torn by screaming steel. (LL) Winter Warfare. Edgell Rickword. FaBoWar; OBWP; OxBTC; PeFWW; PoWW

Torn feet and cursed earth. Buna. Primo Levi. AF, *tr. by* Ruth Feldman

Torn hillside with its crooked hands, The. Description of Some Confederate Soldiers, A. Randall Jarrell. CBCWP

Torn into light, you woke wriggling. How Much Earth. Philip Levine. NNaP

Tornado Soup. A. K. Redwing. VoR

Tornados. Thylias Moss. GT; MakPoe

Toroddle, toroddle, toroll. (LL) Oliver Goldsmith. BIrV; NOIV *Fr.* She Stoops to Conquer.

Toronto Board of Trade Goes Abroad. Earle Birney. PeLV

Torque. David Rivard. PBCAP

Torrent, The. Edwin Arlington Robinson. APN-2

Torrent Cuts Off the Poet's Path, A. Antiphilus [*or* Antiphilos]. GrAn

Torrent / of cobalt bullets, A. Lacrimas or There Is a Need to Scream. K. Curtis Lyle. NBV

Torrent of light and river of the air. Galaxy, The. Henry Wadsworth Longfellow. OxBSo

Torrismond. Thomas Lovell Beddoes.
   (How Many Times [Do I Love Thee, Dear]?) NAEL-5v2
   Song: "How many times do I love thee, dear?." NAEL-6v2

Torso / Passages 18, The. Robert Duncan. CAGL; HarvBoo; PmAP

Tortoise, The. Cid Corman. InPK-6; VGW

Tortoise and Badger. Cheryl Clarke. FFC

Tortoise-Shell. D. H. Lawrence. FaBoVe; NAEL-5v2; NAEL-6v2; OxAEP-2

Tortoise Shout. D. H. Lawrence. NAEL-5v2; NAEL-6v2; PFTM-1

Torture. Margaret Atwood. PoE

Torture Chamber. Enrique Lihn. PoetW; VCWP, *tr. by* Mary Crow

Torture chamber is not like anything, The. Footnote to the Amnesty Report on Torture. Margaret Atwood. NoAM

Torture scene developed under a glass bell, The. Heirloom. Leonard Cohen. NOBC

Torture, that we pray it may be mild. Beanstalk, Meditated Later, The. Judith Wright. NoAM

Tortured, The. May Sarton. FFC

Tortured body, lie at rest alone. Unknown Man in the Morgue. Merrill Moore. MoAmPo

Tortured mullet served the Roman's pride, The. On a Vase of Gold-Fish. Charles Tennyson Turner. NOBVV; NPeEn

Tory Pledges. Thomas Moore. OBSV

Toss not my soul, O Love, 'twixt hope and fear. *Unknown.* NoSic

Toss the bouquet. (LL) Atomic Bride. Thomas Sayers Ellis. BAP-97; NeAmPo

Toss your gay heads. At April. Angelina Weld Grimké. BlSi; GT

Tossed midst life's terrific storms. Song. Anne Batten Cristall. RWP

Tossed on the stormy waves of time. "I Was a Stranger and Ye Took Me In." Mary E. Tucker. CBWP-1

Tossed [*or* Toss'd] in a troubled sea of griefs, I float. To Her in Absence; a Ship. Thomas Carew. CaPo

Tossing a crimson ball. Anacreon. SaLy, *tr. by* Diane Rayor

Tossing his mane of snows in wildest eddies and tangles. Earliest Spring. William Dean Howells. OBEV

Total Eclipse. Michael J. Rosen. DiPo

Total failure—Master Han Shan, A. Wang Chiu-ssu. CoBLCP *Fr.* Miscellaneous Poems on Living in the Woods—In the Manner of Han Shan.

Total Influence of Outcome of the Matter: The Sun, The. Marge Piercy. WPOW

Totalled. Peter McDonald. PNI

Totally conscious, and appropos of nothing, he comes to see me. Jelaluddin [*or* Jalal al-Din] Rumi. EnlH

Totem. Eamon Grennan. ModIr

Totem. Léopold Sédar Senghor. PoetW, *tr. by* Melvin Dixon

Totem, The. Léopold Sédar Senghor. NegPo, *tr. by* Ellen Conroy Kennedy

Totems. Christine Ama Ata Aidoo. HAWP

Totting up the takings, quick Death can / reckon much faster than the businessman. Palladas [*or* Pallades]. GrAn

Tou Wan Speaks to Her Husband Liu Sheng. Rita Dove. ESEAA

Toucan, The. Pyke, Jr. Johnson. NTCP

Touch. Eugene Gloria. ReBoTo

Touch. Thom Gunn. HarvBoo

Touch. Octavio Paz. BoLoP, *tr. by* Charles Tomlinson

Touch but thy lyre, my Harry, and I hear. To M. Henry Lawes, the Excellent Composer[,] of his Lyrics. Robert Herrick. CaPo

Touch, cup / the lips. Leontius Scholasticus [*or* Leontius Referendarius]. GrAn

Touch,—for there is a Spirit in the woods. (LL) Nutting. William Wordsworth. NAEL-5v2; NAEL-6v2; NOBRP; RB

Touch Him! Samuel Bamford. NOBRP

Touch It. Robert Mezey. GeoHom

Touch it: it won't shrink like an eyeball. Life, A. Sylvia Plath. NOBA

Touch it to your cheek and it's soft. Peach. Rose Rauter. KaS

Touch me. Unconditionals #3. Viki Akiwumi. InTrad

Touch Me. Stanley Kunitz. APT-2; NoP-4

Touch me, touch me. Grass Fingers. Angelina Weld Grimké. APT-1

Touch of cold in the autumn night, A. Autumn. Thomas Ernest Hulme. FaBoMo; NPeEn

Touch of Human Hands, The. Thomas Curtis Clark. PoToHe

Touch of red left on your lip, A. Out Early One Morning, I Met an Old Acquaintance. Shen Yüeh. CoBCP, tr. by Burton Watson

Touch of red left on your lip, A. Out Early One Morning, I Met an Old Acquaintance. Wang Seng-ta. CoBCP, tr. by Burton Watson

Touch of the Master's Hand, The. Myra Brooks Welch. PoToHe

Touch of Your Lips, The. Ray Noble. ReLy

Touch *them* with gold, *they'll turn to what you please*. (LL) Epigram: "Midas, they say, possessed the art of old." "Peter Pindar." NIL-7; NIP-4

Touch Thou Mine Eyes. Marion Franklin Ham. AH

Touch was all. Memo. Leslie Ullman. YaYoPo

Touch wood, be humble, never dare to say. Touch Wood. Helen Foley. LW

Touché. Jessie Redmond Fauset. BlSi

Touched. Olga Broumas. GifTon

Touched. Elizabeth Dodd. AmPoNex

Touched with a Feeling of Our Infirmities. Cecil Frances Alexander. SacPr

Touches belonging to the ascent of the brother. Evening Walk, An. J. H. Prynne. PFTM-2

Touching and melting. / Nowhere. (LL) Night Dances, The. Sylvia Plath. AmFaPo; LCAP-2

Touching Each Other's Surfaces. Carol Jane Bangs. NIP-4

Touching Ezekiel his workman's hand. Jesus. James Philip McAuley. CBAP; ChIV-2

Touching the ashes of my father. Bob Boldman. HA

Touching the tulips was a shyness. Tulips. Medbh McGuckian. PNI

Touching You Underwater. Stephen J. Lyons. PasH

Touching your goodness, I am, I am like a man. Illiterate, The. William Meredith. NoP-4; OxBSo; VCAP

Touchingly alike, old man, old dog. Difference, The. Elizabeth Delmore. NLP

Touchstone, The. Kalonymos ben Kalonymos. TrJP, tr. by J. Chotzner

Tougaloo Blues. Kelly Norman Ellis. SpirFl

Tough Captain Spud and his First Mate, Spade. Captain Spud and His First Mate, Spade. John Ciardi. OBCA

Tough Guy of London, The. Kojo Gyinaye Kyei. EmeKit

Tough hair like dead. Vacant Lot. Yvor Winters. APT-2

Tough hand closes gently on the load, The. Man Carrying Bale. Harold Monro. MoBrPo

Toughest gal I ever did see. Kissie Lee. Margaret Abigail Walker. BlSi; NALW

Toujours la Politesse. Ezra Pound. OBVE

Tour Guide: La Maison des Esclaves. Melvin Dixon. ESEAA

Tour of Duty. David Huddle. Son
("Training I received did not apply be.") CDa
"What did those girls say when you walked the strip." CDa
Words. CDa

Tour of Ein Kerem, A. David Curzon. GI

Tour to the Glaciers of Savoy, A. "Eliza."
Epistle to John Walker, Esq., An. ECWP
"When we parted with you at Geneve." ECWP

Tourism in the Late 20th Century. Silvia Curbelo. BodElec

Tourist. Muhammad Al-Maghut. MAP, tr. by John Heath-Stubbs and May Jayyusi

Tourist, The. Jane Schapiro. GotH

Tourist, as he views the place, The. Taliesin Williams. AngWePo Fr. Cardiff Castle.

Tourist came in from Orbitville, A. Southbound on the Freeway. May Swenson. NTCP

Tourist Country. William Stafford. NoAM

Tourist Death. Archibald MacLeish. NAAL-2v2

Tourist from Syracuse, The. Donald Justice. NoAM; TwCP; VCAP

Tourist, spare the avid glance. Attic Landscape, The. Herman Melville. NCAP; NOBA; OBAL

Tourist Weather. Silvia Curbelo. TouFir

Tourists. Yehuda Amichai [or Amikhai]. PoSu, tr. by Glenda Abramson and Tudor Parfitt

Tourists. Howard Moss. NoP-4; OBCoV; PeLV

Tourists, Potatoes, and Genocide. Rush Rankin. SpudSo

Tourists / Wonder. Edible World, The. David Bromige. FTOS

Tournament, The. Angelo Politziano.
"Splendor and pride I celebrate." WoPoe, tr. by Guy Davenport

Tournament of Tottenham, The. Unknown. OxBoLi

Touro Synagogue. Ruth Whitman. TaR

Toussaint L'Ouverture. Henrietta Cordelia Ray. CBWP-3; SWaP

Toussaint, the most unhappy man of men! To Toussaint L'Ouverture. William Wordsworth. CenSon; InPK-6; NOBE; PoRA

Tovu-Vavohu. Manuela Fingueret. MirDau, tr. by Roberta Gordenstein

Tow Head on his skateboard. Skateboard. Thom Gunn. MoASP

Tow'rds the lofty walls of Balbi, lo! Durand of Blonden hies. Durand of Blonden. Ludwig Uhland. AWP, tr. by James Clarence Mangan

Toward a Poetics. Onwuchekwa Jemie. PBMAP

Toward calm and shady places. Frances Densmore. APT-1 Fr. Chippewa Music.

Toward Ch'ang-an. Tune: "Merriment Before the Palace Hall." Chang K'o-chiu. ChinPo, tr. by Yip Wai-lim

Toward Eternal Peace. Karl Kraus. AuPH, tr. by Lowell A. Bangerter

Toward evening it ends. Day's overtures. Rain Near Heart Lake. Reg Saner. PoCoUp

Toward evening, the weather turns cold. Night Rain beneath the City Walls of P'i-chou. Yang Shih-ch'i. CoBLCP, tr. by Jonathan Chaves

Toward Guinea: For Larry Neal, 1937–1981. Houston A. Baker, Jr. ISC

Toward morning, slipping the pistol under my arm. Vadim Antonov. TCRP Fr. Vindication.

Toward morning the sun strolled in the forest. Isaac. Amir Gilbo'a. MHP, tr. by Ruth Finer Mintz

Toward Myself. Leah Goldberg. FIT, tr. by Robert Friend

Toward sunset, at a great height. (LL) Heart of Autumn. Robert Penn Warren. APT-2; ColAP; FuPo

Toward that same church, which he forgot. (LL) Sometimes a Man Stands Up During Supper. Rainer Maria Rilke. BBASP; RaBo, tr. by Robert Bly

Toward the city's bright towers. (LL) It Was Fever That Made the World. Jim Powell. NIP-4; SwNoth

Toward the Corner. Laura Riding Jackson. NOxBChV

Toward the dawn. Blanche Edith Baughan. PeNZ Fr. Maui's Fish.

Toward the end of her life she said that the. Berthe Morisot. Anne Waldman. PmAP

Toward the end of my flight. Dream about a Piano, A. Yury [or Iurii] Davydovich Levitansky [or Levitanskii]. TCRP, tr. by Sophie Lund

Toward the Jurassic Age. Claribel Alegría. TCLAP, tr. by Carolyn Forché

Toward the laughter we no longer. To Mother. Keorapetse Kgositsile. GT

"Toward the person who has died." Dying Away. William Meredith. NoAM

Toward the Solstice. Adrienne Rich. NAAL-2v2

Toward the substation in the testing wind. Geoffrey Nutter. BAP-97 Fr. Summer Evening, A.

Toward what force on the beach. Coastal. Valerie Martínez. AmPoNex

Toward which all hungers leap, all pleasures pass. (LL) Baroque Wall-Fountain in the Villa Sciarra, A. Richard Wilbur. ColAP; GS; NAAL-2v2; NoP-4; OBGa; TwCP; VCAP

Toward Winter. Unknown. NOIV; WoPoe, tr. by Thomas Kinsella

Toward world's end, through the bare. Magi, The. Louise Glück. GI; HarvBoo

Towards a Beginning. Silvio Giussani. ItPo, tr. by Gayle Ridinger

Towards Abraham's Bosom. Amelia Blossom Pegram. HAWP

Towards Curing AIDS. Rafael Campo. BloBone; NeAmPo

Towards dawn / taxis / idle, The. Girandole. Gustaf Sobin. APSN

Towards Delhi. Kunwar Narain. OMIP, tr. by Vinay Dahrwadker

Towards Democracy. Edward Carpenter.
"O faithful eyes, day after day as I see and know you—unswerving faithful and beautiful—going about your ordinary work unnoticed." CAGL
Summer Heat. CAGL
"Sun burning down on back and loins, penetrating the skin, bathing their flanks in sweat." CAGL
Through the Long Night. CAGL
To a Stranger. CAGL
"You, proud curve-lipped youth, with brown sensitive face." CAGL

Towards evening time. Conductor, The. Dezső Kosztolányi. IQMS, tr. by Leslie A. Kery

Towards Lillers. Ivor Gurney. NAEL-5v2; NAEL-6v2; NoP-4

Towards nightfall when the wind. Winter Mask. Allen Tate. OxBA

Towards Springtime. Ágnes Nemes Nagy. IQMS, tr. by Ila Egon

Towards Sunset at Camino Cielo. Maurina Sherman. GeoHom

Towards the altar sober-paced I went. John Keats. TOF Fr. Fall of Hyperion; A Dream, The.

Towards the end he sailed into an extraordinary mildness. Herman Melville. W. H. Auden. OxBA

Towards the Land of the Composer. Francis Webb. BMAP

Towards the Last Spike. Edwin John Pratt.
  Gathering, The. MoCV
  "Oatmeal was in their blood and in their names." MoCV
  "On the North Shore a reptile lay asleep." MoCV; NOBC
  Precambrian [or Pre-Cambrian] Shield, The. MoCV; NOBC

Towards the Mind. Milo De Angelis. ItPo, tr. by Gayle Ridinger

Towards the New Millennium. Zoltán Jékely. IQMS, tr. by George Szirtes

Towards the songs' pretended sea. (LL) Legacy. Imamu Amiri Baraka. ColAP; NOBA; NoAM

Towards the Vanishing Point. David Lehman. PmAP

Towards your hand. Dandelion. Frigyes Karinthy. IQMS, tr. by Peter Zollman

Towboat is freckled with rust. What's it doing here so far / inland?, The. Sketch in October. Tomas Tranströmer. VCWP, tr. by Robin Fulton

Tower. David Biespiel. NAPBL

Tower. Deborah Woodard. CDa

Tower, The. W. B. Yeats. NoAM; PoE; SCGP

Tower, no ivy, I. The wind was powerless, A. Hecuba's Testament. Rosario Castellanos. STV, tr. by John Frederick Nims

Tower of Babel, The. Guillaume de Salluste Du Bartas. NoSic, tr. by Joshua Sylvester Fr. Divine Weeks and Works, The.

Tower of Babel, The. Laurance Wieder. ChIV-1

Tower of Refuge is our God, A! Ein feste Burg ist unser Gott. Martin Luther. CTC, tr. by M. Woolsey Stryker

Tower of Skulls, The. Isaac Rosenberg. PeFWW

Tower steep at sky's brink and. Upper-Austrian Landscape. Paula von Preradovic. AuPH, tr. by Lowell A. Bangerter

Towering Alps, the haughty Appenine, The. Philip Freneau. TCAPo Fr. House of Night, The.

Towering is that southern mountain. Unknown. ColAnChi, tr. by Jeffrey Riegel Fr. Classic of Odes.

Towering, thick, its straight trunk soars. Old Pine, An. Wang An-shih. SuSp, tr. by Jan W. Walls

Towers, The. José María Eguren. TCLAP, tr. by Iver Lofving

Towery city and branchy between towers. Duns Scotus's Oxford. Gerard Manley Hopkins. CABP; EBEV; GTBS-P; NAEL-5v2; NAEL-6v2; NoAM; OBMV; OxAEP-2; PeECV

Town. Marie-Claire Bancquart. MFP, tr. by Martin Sorrell

Town a Bird Sanctuary, The. Jan Eijkelboom. TuT, tr. by Peter Van de Kamp

Town again, trailing your legs and crying!, The. (LL) Wild Swans. Edna St. Vincent Millay. HarvBoo; MoAmPo; OWoS; UnPo

Town barberpole. Nicholas Virgilio. HA

Town believes thee lost, and didst thou see, The. Henry Vaughan. PBRV Fr. To his retired friend, an Invitation to Brecknock.

Town, / branches over the river. Kaunas 1941. Johannes Bobrowski. AF

Town Called Providence, Its Fate, The. Benjamin Tompson. SCAP

Town Clerk, The. Mark DeCarteret. AmPoNex

Town clock's face, The. Nicholas Virgilio. HA

Town does not exist, The. Starry Night, The. Anne Sexton. ColAP; NAAL-5; NoAM; PoE; VCAP

Town Dump, The. Howard Nemerov. NIL-7

Town Eclogue, A. "Peter Pindar." OBCoV Fr. Bozzy and Piozzi.

Town Eclogues. Lady Mary Wortley Montagu. ECEV
  "Ill fates pursue me, may I never find." ECEV

Town Garden, A. Tony Lucas. OBGa

Town hall squatting / on its elephant legs, / come again. (LL) Freedom Fighter. Antigone Kefala. BMAP; ItWoWo

Town has opened to the sun, The. Bombardment. D. H. Lawrence. FaBoWar

Town History, 1917. David Huddle. PBCAP

Town I was born in was destroyed by shells, The. Yehuda Amichai [or Amikhai]. PoSu Fr. Patriotic Songs.

Town is old and very steep, The. Ken. Charlotte Mew. VWP

Town is still, The. Bombing. Paul Rodenko. TuT, tr. by Mary E. O'Donnell

Town is tilted toward the stream, The. Sunday Dreamer's Guide to Yarrow, Missouri, A. Jim Barnes. HATNAP

Town less, A. Sherley Anne Williams. GeoHom Fr. Iconography of Childhood, The.

Town lies in the valley, A. Silent Town, The. Richard Dehmel. AWP, tr. by Jethro Bithell

Town-Meeting, A.M., The. John Trumbull. TCAPo Fr. M'Fingal.

Town might abort, A. How the Death of a City Is Never More than the Sum of the Deaths of Those Who Inhabit Its Spaces. Victor Coleman. NOBC

Town of Hill, The. Donald Hall. TAP

Town of Passage, The. Unknown. OxBoLi

Town on the Ten Dollar Note, The. Laurie Duggan. BMAP

Town or poem, I don't care how it looks. Old woman. White Center. Richard Hugo. NAAL-2v2

Town remembers no such plenty, The. Lancashire Winter. Tony Connor. OxBTC

Town's aflame with summer heat, The. Tokuo. ZenPo, tr. by Takashi Ikemoto and Lucien Stryk

Town the wealthy come to, not overly, The. Jeffers Country. Sherod Santos. GeoHom

Town visitor's easy talk flows in an endless stream, The. To a Talkative Guest. Po Chü-i. ChiP, tr. by Arthur Waley

Town was proud of the town's gardens, The. Flowers. Dennis Joseph Enright. OBGa

Town wasn't much, The. Jungle Warfare. Jack Spicer. APSN

Town where I was born is surrounded by hills, The. Town Where I Was Born, The. John Barnie. TCAWP

Town without a Market, The. James Elroy Flecker. MoBrPo

Toy, The. Brancusi's Golden Bird. Mina Loy. APT-1; HarvBoo

Toy Horse, The. Valentin Iremonger. NOIV

Toy-Maker, The. Russell Edson. PmAP

Toy-maker made a toy wife and a toy child. He made a toy house and some toy years, A. Toy-Maker, The. Russell Edson. PmAP

Toy of the Titans. Ebenezer Elliott. Son Fr. Year of Seeds, The.

Toyland. Roy Fisher. HarvBoo; NPeEn

Toys. Gemino H. Abad. ReBoTo

Toys. Carl Phillips. ReTh

Toys, The. Samuel Hazo. GraLe

Toys, The. Coventry Patmore. EBEV; EBVV; NOBVV; OBEV; OxAEP-2; PoToHe; SoSe-8 Fr. Unknown Eros, The.

Toys and rose The zoo body zigzags. How Spring Comes. Alice Notley. PmAP

Toys Talk of the World, The. Katharine Pyle. NOxBChV; OBCA

"Tra la la la—See me dance the polka." Neptune—Polka. Dame Edith Sitwell. NOBE

Tra - ta - ta - tum! Main Street. "Demyan [or Dem'ian] Bedny" [or Bednyi]. TCRP, tr. by Daniel Weissbort and Lubov Yakovleva

Trace, In Unison. Tess Gallagher. ExTi

Traceless, no more need to hide. Suian. ZenPo, tr. by Takashi Ikemoto and Lucien Stryk

Traces/Renown/Shades/Urns/Life(s)/Epoch/Zenith. Habib Tengour. PFTM-2, tr. by Pierre Joris Fr. Empedocles' Sandal.

Traces. Then things themselves are not names. Notes About My Face. Michael Burkard. BAP-01

Tracing of an Evening. David Shapiro. PmAP

Track. Tomas Tranströmer. RB; SPE, tr. by Robert Bly
  (Tracks.) BLT, tr. by Robert Bly
  (Night, two o'clock: moonlight. The train has stopped.) BLT, tr. by Robert Bly
  (2 AM: moonlight. The train has stopped.) SPE, tr. by Robert Bly

Track is my companion, The. Prelude. Laury Wells. IBA

Track of a broad rattler, dragged over dust at dawn, The. Catch, The. Brewster Ghiselin. HAP

Tracking Rabbits: Night. Jim Barnes. CDW

Tracking the Siuslaw Man. Jim Barnes. HATNAP

Tracks. John Montague. CIP-2

Tracks. Tomas Tranströmer. See Track

Tracks and the traces, The. Ernie Dingo. IBA

Tracks of rain and light linger in. Romance Moderne. William Carlos Williams. APT-1

Tract. William Carlos Williams. MoAmPo; NOBA; NoAM; PAI; SAmP; TAP; TwCP; VGW

Tractatus. Derek Mahon. ModIr; OxBSP

Tractor. Ted Hughes. OxAEP-2

Tractor stands frozen—an agony, The. Tractor. Ted Hughes. OxAEP-2

Trade Winds. John Masefield. FaBoCh; OBMV

Trader I am to the African shore, A. Sweet Meat Has Sour Sauce. William Cowper. ECEV; NOEC; OBSV

Trader, untie the long stern-cables. Argentarius. GrAn

Traders in Beauty and Delight. Abu Dulama. ArPe, tr. by Omar S. Pound

Tradition. William Wordsworth. CenSon Fr. River Duddon [A Series of Sonnets], The.

Tradition and Change. Nora Naranjo-Morse. ReTh

Tradition of Oker Hill in Darley Dale, Derbyshire, A. William Wordsworth. OxBSo

Traditional. Traditional Post-Modern Neo-HooDoo Afra-Centric Sister in a Purple Head Rag Mourning Death and Cooking. Michelle T. Clinton. SpirFl

Traditional Funeral Songs. Unknown. BoWoP, tr. by Willis Barnstone and Elene Kolb

Traditional Tune. Muriel Rukeyser. TaR

Traditional Women's Song of Algeria. *Unknown.* BoWoP, tr. by Willis Barnstone

Traditions. Seamus Heaney. FaBoMo

Traduits de la Nuit. Jean-Joseph Rabéarivelo [*or* Rebéarivelo].
"Hide of the black cow is stretched, The." PBMAP
"Black glassmaker, The." PBMAP

Traffic jamming at. New York City. Michael Castro. UrbNat

Traffic Lights. Lina Kasdaglis. BoWoP, tr. by Edmund Keeley and Mary Keeley

Traffic Misdirector. Pedro Juan Pietri. PueRic

Traffic's been worse than ever this year, The. Flyover Elegies. Gwyneth Lewis. MFPA

Trafique Is Earth's Great Atlas. George Alsop. SCAP

Tragedy. "Æ" MoBrPo

Tragedy, A. Théophile Julius Henry Marzials. VerBaPo

Tragedy, A. Tom Masson. OBAL

Tragedy, Colette said, is that one, The. After 65. Richard Howard. BAP-01

Tragedy of a Shepherd. Mark Akenside. *See* Inscription: "Whoe'er thou art whose path, in summer lies."

Tragedy of Dido, The. Christopher Marlowe.
"What is't, sweet wag, I should deny thy youth?" CAGL

Tragedy of Ida Ball Warren and Samuel Christie, The. I. J. Brittain.
"There was a woman lived in Winston-Salem." VerBaPo

Tragedy of Man. Imre Madách.
"Adam, I think I'm going to be a mother." IQMS, tr. by Iain MacLeod
"And you, Lucifer, standing there aloof." IQMS, tr. by Iain MacLeod
"Be strong, brother!" IQMS, tr. by Iain MacLeod
"I'm tired of these grim wastes of snow and ice." IQMS, tr. by Iain MacLeod
"It's hard to say, John, but I need some money." IQMS, tr. by Iain MacLeod
"It's kind of you to let me come alone." IQMS, tr. by Iain MacLeod
"Let them be! Get out!" IQMS, tr. by Iain MacLeod
"Now, this is it, the toilsome journey's end." IQMS, tr. by Iain MacLeod
"Tell us, Professor." IQMS, tr. by Iain MacLeod
"There are a few things yet you haven't heard of." IQMS, tr. by Iain MacLeod
"There's no excitement, news or anything." IQMS, tr. by Iain MacLeod
"These are dissenters." IQMS, tr. by Iain MacLeod
"This reckless flight, where is this bound to take us?" IQMS, tr. by Iain MacLeod
"Very ground dissolves beneath my feet, The." IQMS, tr. by Iain MacLeod
"You see the fellow with the scarlet sash?" IQMS, tr. by Iain MacLeod

Tragedy of Valentinian, The. John Fletcher.
Care-charming Sleep [Thou Easer of All Woes]. OxBSP; SCGP
God Lyaeus, Ever Young. OBEV
Hear, Ye Ladies [That Despise]. NOBE; OBEV
(Love's Emblems.) BoLoP; NOBE; NOSC
(Sleep Song.) NOSC
(Song to Sleep.) OxBoLi
(To Sleep.) PoRA

Tragic Hero. Eleanor Brown. MFPA

Tragic Love. Walter James Turner. OBMV

Tragic Mary Queen of Scots, The. "Michael Field." EnLoPo; LW; OBMV

Tragic Mary Queen of Scots, II, The. "Michael Field." OBMV

Tragicall Epigram, A. Sir John Harington [*or* Harrington]. PBRV

Trail All Your Pikes. Anne Finch, Countess of Winchilsea. OPOU; WPE

Trail among the Pines, A. Lin Pu. SuSp, tr. by Irving Y. Lo

Trail Breakers. James Henry Daugherty.
"Pack train, stage coach, pony express, climb over the mountain passes." HHAm

Trail climbs in zig-zags, The. Trail up Wu Gorge, The. Sun Yün-feng. BoWoP

Trail Crew Camp at Bear Valley. 9000 Feet. Gary Snyder. HCAP

Trail up Wu Gorge, The. Sun Yün-feng. BoWoP

Trail you down the hall—issue. Disembodied Voices of Women, The. Craig Arnold. NAPBL

Trailing a wake of heady odors, what slim. Horace. WoPoe, tr. by Stephen Sandy Fr. Odes.

Trailing her father, bearing his hand axe. Goose. Richard Emil Braun. NoAM

Trailing my stick I go down to the garden edge. Poem without a Category. Gensei. EnlH, tr. by Burton Watson

Trailing pen draws out a seismograph, The. Cryptogram, The. David Lindley. NLP

Trails. Patrick Williams. PNI

Trails of it like trout-streaks skid. Morning Light at Wanship, Utah. Dave Jeddie Smith. BodElec

Train. Donald Justice. GM

Train. Ken Smith. SPE
(In the dark.) SPE

Train. Jennifer Snyder. BodElec

Train, The. Alan Brownjohn. OxBTC

Train, The. *Unknown.* TTY, tr. by D. F. van der Merwe

Train: Abstraction. Genevieve Taggard. WPE

Train has come to rest and ceased its creaking, The. La Máquina a Houston. Edward Dorn. PoM

Train has just come to a stop, The. South. Blaise Cendrars. BLT, tr. by Monique Chefdor

Train has stopped for no apparent reason, The. En Route. Duncan Campbell Scott. NOBC

Train in the Desert—1916. Christopher Buckley. GM

Train is A-Comin' *Unknown.* CA

Train is a-comin', oh yes. Train is A-Comin' *Unknown.* CA

Train is right on time, The. From the Provinces. Ben Scammell. NLP

Train Journey. Judith Wright. NoP-4

Train moves through the Guadarrama, The. Rainbow at Night. Antonio Machado. AF, BLT tr. by Robert Bly

Train Passage. Karen Propp. GotH

Train Ride. John Wheelwright. VGW

Train Rising Out of the Sea. John Ashbery. ColAP

Train's french horn sighs, sheds a few tears, The. To I. Lavrentevaya. Natalya [*or* Natal'ia] Gorbanevskaya [*or* Gorbanyevskaya *or* Gorbanevskaia]. BoWoP, tr. by Daniel Weissbort

Train she rides is sixteen coaches long. David Wojahn. GM; PBCAP Fr. Mystery Train: A Sequence.

Train shot through the dark, The. Return. Seamus Deane. BIrV; PBCIP; PNI

Train sneaks through farm country, The. Example, An. M. Wyrebek. AmPoNex

Train Song. Fiona Kidman. PeNZ

Train Stops at Healy Fork, The. John Haines. BLT

Train tears along, I'm on my way, The. Lapiade, Opus 3. Ödön Palasovszky. IQMS, tr. by Kenneth McRobbie

Train that carried me there was a chip, The. Chip City. Linda France. MFPA

Train, The! The twelve o'clock for paradise. Harold Monro. MoBrPo Fr. Week-End.

Train Tune. Louise Bogan. GM

Train was going downwards very slowly, The. Dream, A. Evan Jones. NOBAu

Train whistles punctual as a clock, The. English-Speaking Persons Will Find Translations. Michael S. Glaser. UnSA

Train will come tomorrow year, The. Train, The. Alan Brownjohn. OxBTC

Train Wreck, 1890: My Grandmother Lies Down with the Dead. T. R. Hummer. GM

Trained tenderly by Heaven and Earth. Contrast, A. Menella Bute Smedley. VWP

Training. Herrera S. Demetrio. TTY, tr. by Dudley Fitts

Trainor, the Druggist. Edgar Lee Masters. APT-1; IllVoic Fr. Spoon River Anthology.

Trainride, Vienna—Bonn. Margaret Atwood. LCAP-2

Trains. Amal Dunqul. MAP, tr. by Sharif Elmusa and Thomas G. Ezzy

Trains. William Scammell. NLP

Trains, The. Sarina Helfgott. MirDau, tr. by Celeste Kostopulos-Cooperman

Trains, The. William Heyen. GotH

Trains go towards the fast bridge where in the darkness the. Towards a Beginning. Silvio Giussani. ItPo, tr. by Gayle Ridinger

Trains Made of Stone. Ray A. Young Bear. CDW

Trains ran through the eleven, The. Dance of the Elephants, The. Michael S. Harper. LCAP-2

Trains!, The, Trains hugged by the tunnels, The. Invitation to a Voyage. Max Jacob. CuPo

Trains travel on a two-railed course. Trains. Amal Dunqul. MAP, tr. by Sharif Elmusa and Thomas G. Ezzy

Trainwrecked Soldiers. John Frederick Nims. GM

Traitor. Allison Joseph. IllVoic

Traitor's skull, we shall drink out of it, The. To a Traitor. *Unknown.* WoPoe, tr. by Willard Trask

Trakl. Norman Dubie. BodElec

Tram bore along, my eyes, The. Marked Ones, The. Gyula Illyés. IQMS, tr. by John Brander and John Wilkinson

Tram That Lost Its Way, The. Nikolai Stepanovich Gumilyov [*or* Gumiliov *or* Gumilev]. TCRP, tr. by Yakov Hornstein

Tramontana at Lerici. Charles Tomlinson. GTBS-P

Tramp. Frank Mkalawile Chipasula. HBAPE; PeSAV

Tramp. Richard Hughes. MoBrPo

Trampling. Miguel Algarin. PueRic

Trampwoman's Tragedy, A.   Thomas Hardy.   NAEL-5v2; NAEL-6v2; OBNV

Trams.   Dame Edith Sitwell.   NOxBChV

Tramstop swarms with schooligans, their brand, A.   Election Eve, with Cat.   Alex Skovron.   BMAP

Tramway climbs from Merthyr to Dowlais, The.   Deluge 1939, The.   Saunders Lewis.   OBWVE, tr. by Gwyn Morgan

Trance.   "H. D.".   APT-1

Trance Event.   Robert Desnos.   PFTM-1

Trane / must have.   Silent Prophet, The.   Norman Jordan.   NBV

Trane. / Trane. / History Love Scream Oh.   Am/Trak.   Imamu Amiri Baraka.   PmAP

Trang Tu's legendary wife is very much the modern woman.   Woman's Heart, A.   Vietnamese Oral Tradition.   CaDao, tr. by John Balaban

Tranquil Miracle, The.   Lőrinc Szabó.   IQMS, tr. by Watson Kirkconnell   Fr. Cricket Music.

Tranquil Night.   Luís De León.   SpanPo, tr. by Edwin Morgan

Tranquil, vacant is the river, girdled by the setting sun.   Crossing South of Li-chou, A.   Wen T'ing-yün.   SuSp, tr. by William R. Schultz

Tranquility as his breath, his eye a camera.   Observation Car and Cigar.   William Stafford.   LCAP-2

Transaction.   A. R. Ammons.   HCAP

Transcanadian.   Robert Hedin.   GifTon

Transcendent beauty molders midst the earth!   Elegy on a Young Lady.   Anne Batten Cristall.   RWP

Transfiguration.   Djuna Barnes.   SPE

Transfiguration.   Ralph Chubb.   CAGL

Transfiguration.   Jack Hirschman.   CLPP

Transfiguration.   John Wright.   BloBone

Transfiguration, The.   Robert Herrick.   CaPo

Transfiguration, The.   Edwin Muir.   ChIV-2; OxBS

Transfiguration of Beauty, The.   Michelangelo Buonarroti.   AWP, tr. by John Addington Symonds

Transfiguration of the Rain.   Jorge Carrera Andrade.   TCLAP, tr. by Michael Surman

Transfigured Night.   Ralph Gustafson.   MoCV

Transformable Prophecy.   Angela Jackson.   IllVoic

Transformation.   Jeni Couzyn.   HAWP

Transformation.   Adria Klinger.   PasH

Transformation.   Karl Kraus.   AuPH, tr. by Lowell A. Bangerter

Transformation and Escape.   Gregory Corso.   PFTM-2

Transformations.   Thomas Hardy.   RB; TRP

Transformations.   Joy Harjo.   HATNAP

Transformations.   Orkhan Muyassar.   MAP, tr. by Samuel Hazo and Lena Jayyusi

Transformations.   Tadeusz Rózewicz.   ChAP, tr. by Czeslaw Milosz

Transformations.   Jack Spicer.   FTOS

Transformations of Livy.   Zbigniew Herbert.   PoetW, tr. by John Carpenter and Bogdana Carpenter

Transgressing the Real.   Robert Duncan.   APSN   Fr. Passages.

Transience.   John Armstrong.   NOEC   Fr. Art of Preserving Health, The.

Transient Hotel Sky at the Hour of Sleep.   Martín Espada.   ReTh

Transient Servitude.   Haroldo de Campos.   "De sol a sol."   PFTM-2, tr. by Edwin Morgan

Transit.   Margaret Avison.   FaBoWP

Transit.   Prageeta Sharma.   HeMarv

Transit.   Richard Wilbur.   DiPo; LCAP-2; NIL-7

Transition #2.   Sabah As-Sabah.   InTrad

Transits.   Sharan Strange.   InTrad

Translated from the American.   Sherman Alexie.   UnSA

Translation.   Roy Fuller.   NOBE; OxBTC

Translation.   Carolyn Kizer.   CarOv

Translation.   Rika Lesser.   KGB

Translation.   Howard Nemerov.   CRP

Translation.   Nicholas Samaras.   YaYoPo

Translation by Mark Willhardt.   William Dunbar.   RACG

Translation from Petrarch, A.   Petrarch.   MoBrPo, tr. by J. M. Synge   Fr. Sonnets to Laura.

Translation from Walter von der Vogelweide, A.   Walther [or Walter] von der Vogelweide.   MoBrPo, tr. by J. M. Synge

Translation of a South American Ode.   Oliver Goldsmith.   NOIV

Translation of Du Bellay's Epigram on a Dog.   Samuel Johnson.   FaBoEE

Translation of Lines by Benserade.   Isaac de Benserade.   FaBoEE; WoPoe, tr. by Samuel Johnson

Translation of "Pax Bello Potior."   Unknown.   NOBRP, tr. by Unknown

Translations.   Adrienne Rich.   WPOW

Translations from Martial.   Robert Louis Stevenson.   OBGa

Translations from the English.   George Starbuck.   VGW

Translator to Translated.   Ezra Pound.   FaBoEE

Translator tried to lay bare, The.   Lesson in Translation, A.   Gabriel Preil.   FIT, tr. by Robert Friend

Translucent green on the wall, a dance of leaves.   Green Afternoon, The.   Henry Rago.   VGW

Translucent Mechanics, The.   George Oppen.   NNaP   Fr. Some San Francisco Poems.

Transmigration.   Bruce Berger.   GeoH

Transmutation.   Julia de Burgos.   TANSG, tr. by Heather Rosario Sievert

Transparent Life, The.   Luigi Fontanella.   NeIt, tr. by W. S. Di Piero

Transplanting rice / He pisses.   Yayu.   ZenPo, tr. by Takashi Ikemoto and Lucien Stryk

Transportation.   Karen Alkalay-Gut.   DTA

Transposition of Clermont, The.   Les A. Murray.   EmeKit

Transubstantiation.   Gary Geddes.   NOBC

Trap Door.   Vítězslau Nezval.   PFTM-1

Trapped.   Adelaide Crapsey.   APT-1

Trapped in a dismal marsh, he told his troops.   All Except Hannibal.   Robert Graves.   EmeKit

Trappers have collected their rabbit traps, The.   Meeting Trappers on the Road in Heavy Snow.   Li K'ai-hsien.   CoBLCP, tr. by Jonathan Chaves

Trapping fairies in West Virginia.   Trapping Fairies.   Frank Gelett Burgess.   OBCoV

Trash.   Kenneth Irby.   PFTM-2

Trash.   Linda Smukler.   WiU

Trashmen Shaking Hands with Hubert Humphrey at the Opening of Apache Plaza Shopping Center, Suburban Minneapolis, August 1963, The.   David Wojahn.   PBCAP   Fr. Mystery Train: A Sequence.

Trauma.   Brad Leithauser.   InPK-6

Traumerei.   David Shapiro.   BodElec

Travail of Passion, The.   W. B. Yeats.   TrCP

Travel.   Julio Cortázar.   TCLAP, tr. by Paul Blackburn

Travel.   Edna St. Vincent Millay.   OBCA

Travel.   Robert Louis Stevenson.   FaBoCh; OTCP

Travel: After a Death.   Jane Kenyon.   FFC

Travel any road.   Tale of Red-Haired Motl, Mister Inspector, Rabbi Isaiah, and Commissar Blokh, The.   Iosif Pavlovich Utkin.   TCRP, tr. by Lubov Yakovleva

Travel Notes.   John Riley.   Oth

Travel Song.   Hugo von Hofmannsthal.   TrJP, tr. by Charles Wharton Stork

Travel through evenings without memories with memories.   Goran's Whispers.   Nathalie Handal.   PoArWo

Travel with Grief—Goodbye to Joy.   Nguyễn Chí Thiện.   VCWP, tr. by Huynh Sanh Thông

Traveler.   Valerie Martínez.   TouFir

Traveler.   Antonio Porta.   ItPo, tr. by Gayle Ridinger

Traveler, The.   Ho Hsun.   OHMPC, tr. by Kenneth Rexroth

Traveler, The.   Nicholas Vachel Lindsay.   MoAmPo

Traveler, The.   Duane Niatum.   HATNAP

Traveler, a traveler, Tzu-mei his name, A.   Tu Fu.   CoBCP   Fr. Seven Songs Written During the Ch'ien-yüan Era.

Traveler at Night Writes His Thoughts, A.   Tu Fu.   CoBCP, tr. by Burton Watson

Traveler, don't ridicule this farming house as too small.   Fan Ch'eng-ta.   SuSp, tr. by Wu-Chi Liu   Fr. Four Songs in Imitation of Wang Chien.

Traveler endures countless tribulations, A.   Climbing Stone Drum Mountain.   Hsieh Ling-yün.   CrYelRi, tr. by Sam Hamill

Traveler has come from south of the Yangtze, A.   Traveler's Moon, The.   Po Chü-i.   CoBCP, tr. by Burton Watson

Traveler, I've been through a thousand changes, A.   Chin Nung.   CoBLCP   Fr. On New Year's Eve of the Year Hsin-wei (1751), Drinking Alone and Sadly Chanting Poems, I Remembered My Aged Wife Who Is Living at Twisting River.

Traveler in the wilds, do not.   Leonidas.   PGA

Traveler, rest. The time of man runs on.   In Blue-Stocking Hollow.   Donald Davidson.   FuPo

Traveler's heart has a hundred thoughts already, The.   At Parting.   Ho Sun.   CoBCP, tr. by Burton Watson

Traveler's homesickness, sad and lonely.   Thinking of the Past on an Autumn Night at Tz'u-jen Temple.   Wang Shih-chieng.   CoBLCP, tr. by Jonathan Chaves

Traveler's Life, A.   Sung Fang-hu.   CrYelRi, tr. by Sam Hamill

Traveler's Moon, A.   Po Chü-i.   SuSp, tr. by Chiang Yee

Traveler's Moon, The.   Po Chü-i.   CoBCP, tr. by Burton Watson

Traveler's Pavilion.   Tu Fu.   CrYelRi, tr. by Sam Hamill

Traveler's Thoughts.   Tu Hsün-ho.   CoBCP, tr. by Burton Watson

Traveler's thoughts stretch on forever, A.   Climbing Stone Drum Mountain Above the Shores of Shang-shu.   Hsieh Ling-yün.   SuSp, tr. by Francis Westbrook

Traveler tires of nights on the water, A. Entering the Mouth of P'eng-li Lake. Hsieh Ling-yün. SuSp, *tr.* by Francis Westbrook

Traveler who wants to stay, The. Inscribed on the Wall at the Temple of the Auspicious Talisman. Tao-chi. CoBLCP, *tr.* by Jonathan Chaves

Traveler will rise at midnight, The. Presented to Wang Wen-hsi. Ho Ching-ming. CoBLCP, *tr.* by Jonathan Chaves

Traveler with his heavy heart, The. Traveler, The. Ho Hsun. OHMPC, *tr.* by Kenneth Rexroth

Travelers. Josephine Miles. KaS

Travelers long on the road. At the Point. Robert Mezey. GeoHom

Travelers perhaps, / but I am not sure of finding. Nuclear Umbrella. Heberto Padilla. AF, *tr.* by Alastair Reid

Traveling as a Family. Carlos Drummond de Andrade. TCLAP, *tr.* by Virginia de Araújo

Traveling at Break of Day. Huang Ching-jen. SuSp, *tr.* by Chang Yin-nan

Traveling at Night. Tu Fu. WoPoe, *tr.* by Greg Whincup

Traveling Boy. William Meredith. YaYoPo

Traveling by Boat. Wang T'ing-hsiang.
"At Arrow Rapids, the water splashes foam." CoBLCP

Traveling by Boat at Shun-ch'ang. Hsü Chung-hsing. CoBLCP, *tr.* by Jonathan Chaves

Traveling Early through a Snowy Valley. Yü Chi. CoBLCP, *tr.* by Jonathan Chaves

Traveling Highway 101. California Dreaming. Carol Lem. GeoHom

Traveling merchant west of the river, A. Tune: "Eternal Longing." *Unknown.* SuSp, *tr.* by Hellmut Wilhelm

Traveling / old armor. Ransetsu. ZenPo, *tr.* by Takashi Ikemoto and Lucien Stryk

Traveling Onion, The. Naomi Shihab Nye. LoL

Traveling this high. Basho. SoOfWa, *tr.* by Sam Hamill

Traveling Through the Dark. William Stafford. CoAP; CoAmPo; ColAP; HAP; HeIP-4; InPK-6; LCAP-2; NoAM; PAI; SoSe-8; TRP; WeW-3

Traveling to Town. Duane Big Eagle. AiP

Traveling Valise. Marjorie Agosin. MirDau, *tr.* by Laura Nakazawa

Traveling with too much baggage is not a good idea. Maria Luisa Spaziani. NeIt   *Fr.* Star of Free Will, The.

Traveller, A. J. R. Rowland. CBAP

Traveller, The. Guillaume Apollinaire. WoPoe, *tr.* by Rachel Blau

Traveller, The. John Berryman. GM; VGW

Traveller, The. C. J. Dennis. NOBAu

TRAVELLER came from across the seas, A. Taoism and Buddhism. Po Chü-i. ChiP, *tr.* by Arthur Waley

Traveller on the Flaminian Way. Martial. RomPo, *tr.* by Olive Pitt-Kethley

Traveller, on this ridge a leafless, barkless tree. Philip V, King of Macedon. GrAn

Travel[l]er; or, A Prospect of Society, The. Oliver Goldsmith.
Britain. NOEC; NPeEn
"Creations mildest charms are there combined." NOEC; NPeEn
"My soul . . . , turn we to survey." FHYEP
On Freedom and Ambition. NOIV
"Remote, unfriended, melancholy, slow." BIrV
"Ye powers of truth, that bid my soul aspire." NOIV

Travel[l]er's Curse after Misdirection[, The]. Robert Graves. MoBrPo; NBLV; OBCoV

Traveller's Song. Hugo von Hofmannsthal. WoPoe, *tr.* by Robert Bly

Traveller take heed for journeys undertaken in the dark of the year. October Journey. Margaret Walker Alexander. GT

Traveller to Timbuktu, A. Limerick. *Unknown.* PeLi

Traveller, traveller. Jules Supervielle. MFP, *tr.* by Martin Sorrell

Traveller, traveller, accept you must go back. Traveller, traveller. Jules Supervielle. MFP, *tr.* by Martin Sorrell

Traveller who walks a temperate zone, A. Against Romanticism. Kingsley Amis. NoAM

Traveller, you must set out. Wole Soyinka. PBMAP   *Fr.* Idanre and Other Poems (1967).

Travellers, The. Eva Gore-Booth. PoBW

Travellers came, after the long day's ride, The. Blinkered Mind, The. Amy Witting. NOBAu

Travellers have seen it, uncovered. Lost City. Harold Farmer. PeSAV

Travelling. Simon J. Ortiz. NAAL-5   *Fr.* Poems from the Veterans Hospital.

Travelling, a man met a tiger, so . . . Good Taste. Christopher Logue. OBSP

Travelling Northward. Tu Fu. BLT; OHPC, *tr.* by Kenneth Rexroth

Travelling Post Office, The. Andrew Barton Paterson. CBAP; NOBAu

Travelling through the Dark. William Stafford. *See* Traveling Through the Dark

Travelling to Gleis-Binario. Andrew Taylor.
Goethe and Brentano. BMAP
"Of course they had servants, dressed for dinner." BMAP

Travelling, / where darkness hauls the world. Tanks. Rhyll McMaster. CBAP; NOBAu

Travelogue. Peter Reading.
"Camping Provencial. Notices: (1)." PeLV

Travelogue. Lewis Warsh. BodElec

Travelogue for Exiles. Karl Shapiro. MoAmPo; TrJP

Travelors poor Tombes thes. avoide and flee. When Hee Was Come to the Other Side of the Contrye, of the Gergesenes, There Mett Him Two: Possessed with Devils Coming Out of the Tombes. Eleanor Touchet Davies. EMWP

Travels in Clouds, seeks Manna, where none is. (LL) Henry Vaughan. ChIV-2; ESCV; GeHe

Travels in the South. Simon J. Ortiz. UnSA

Travels of a Latter-Day Benjamin of Tudela. Yehuda Amichai [*or* Amikhai]. "I am a solitary man, not a democracy." PoSu

Travels with the Band-Aid Army. Lance Henson. VoR

Traversed with streetlights on the plain. (LL) Chances "R." Allen Ginsberg. CAGL; HCAP

Travois of the Nameless. Sotère Torregian. NBV

Treacherous rain and perilous bridge made me fear for my life. Sent to Lo-t'ien for Thinking of Me after the Rainfall. Yüan Chên. SuSp, *tr.* by Angela Jung Palandri

Treacherous sea, The. (LL) Fife Tune. John Streeter Manifold. CBAP; FaBoWar; NBLV; NOBAu

Treachery of Asmund, The. *Unknown.*
"There is smoke above the hawks in the hall of the king." FaBoWar, *tr.* by Wystan Hugh Auden and Paul B. Taylor

Tread lightly here, for here, 'tis said. Epitaph on a Robin Redbreast, An. Samuel Rogers. FaBoEE

Tread lightly, she is near. Requiescat. Oscar Wilde. EBVV; MoBrPo; PeVV

Tread lightly, Stranger! Meleager. GrAn

Tread not the earth where lies her youthful form. Mrs. E. Cohrs Brown. Mary Weston Fordham. CBWP-2

Tread soft, for if you wake this knight alone. Epitaph on the Monument of Sir William Strode. William Strode. NOSC

Tread softly! all the earth is holy ground. Christina Georgina Rossetti. WPoS   *Fr.* Later Life: A Double Sonnet of Sonnets.

Tread softly because you tread on my dreams. (LL) He Wishes for the Cloths of Heaven. W. B. Yeats. ChAP; MoBrPo; NoAM; OBEV

Tread softly; bid a solemn music sound. Epitaph. John Bingham Morton. FaBoEE

Tread softly here! Go reverently and slow! Vimy Ridge. John Oxenham. SacPr

Treading the path to nobler ends. Love's Farewell. Edmund Waller. OxBSo

Treadmill prisoner of that century, The. Scene with Figure. Babette Deutsch. TrJP

Treason doth never prosper [*or* Treason never prospers]; what's the reason? Of Treason. Sir John Harington [*or* Harrington]. FaBoEE; InPK-6; NPeEn; NoSic; OBCoV; OxBEV; OxBoLi; SoSe-8

Treason's Choice. Philip Hammial. BMAP

Treasure. Lucilius. AWP, *tr.* by William Cowper

Treasure, The. U Tam'si Tchicaya. PFTM-2, *tr.* by Pierre Joris

Treasure at the heart of the rose, The. Rose, The. Gabriela Mistral. WPoS, *tr.* by Langston Hughes

Treasure I sought. My Treasure. John Oxenham. SacPr

Treasure Island. Robert Louis Stevenson.
"Fifteen men on the Dead Man's Chest." NOBVV; NPeEn
Pirate Ditty. NOBVV; NPeEn

Treasure Lies In the Cornerstone, The. "Angelus Silesius." GePo, *tr.* by George C. Schoolfield   *Fr.* Cherubical Wanderer, The.

Treasure not so the forlorn days. Behind the Line. Edmund Charles Blunden. OxBEV

Treasures. Claire Richcreek Thomas. PoToHe

Treasures and Glories of Life, The. Manuel González Prada. SpanPo, *tr.* by Kate Flores

Treasures and glories of life, The. Treasures and Glories of Life, The. Manuel González Prada. SpanPo, *tr.* by Kate Flores

Treated shabbily / by fleas, by flies. Issa. ZenPo, *tr.* by Takashi Ikemoto and Lucien Stryk

Treaties. A. R. Ammons. HCAP

Treating Sheep Ailments. John Dyer. ECEV   *Fr.* Fleece, The.

Treatise of Monarchy, A. Fulke Greville, 1st Baron Brooke.
Of Nobility.
"For as the harmony which sense admires." NOSC
Of Peace.
"Peace is the next in order, first in end." NOSC

Treatise of Religion, A. Fulke Greville, 1st Baron Brooke.
"What is the chain which draws us back again." SacPr

Treaty of Human Learning, A. Fulke Greville, 1st Baron Brooke.

"Mind of man is this world's true dimension, The." NOSC

Treblinka. Michael Hamburger. HP

Tree. Zulaykha Abu-Risha. PoArWo, *tr. by* Clarissa C. Burt

Tree. Kevin Gilbert. IBA

Tree. Andrew Hudgins. InvLad

Tree, A. Mark Irwin. PoCoUp

Tree, The. Dorothy Auchterlonie. NOBAu

Tree, The. Ilya Grigoryevich Ehrenburg [*or* Erenburg]. TrJP, *tr. by* Babette Deutsch

Tree, The. Frank Gaspar. UrbNat

Tree, The. Alfred Kreymborg. APT-1

Tree, The. Ezra Pound. HarvBoo

Tree, The. Joel Sloman. VGW

Tree and the Lady, The. Thomas Hardy. MoBrPo

Tree ascending there. O pure transcension, A. Rainer Maria Rilke. TOF *Fr.* Sonnets to Orpheus.

Tree at My Window. Robert Frost. APT-1; MoAmPo; NoAM; OxBA; TAP

Tree by the river, The. Tree of Fire. "Adonis" [*or* "Adunis"]. VCWP, *tr. by* Samuel Hazo

Tree enters and says with a bow, A. Lesson, The. Miroslav Holub. PoSu, *tr. by* Ian Milner and Jarmila Milner

Tree Falling in a Vacant Forest, The. Linda Gregg. ExTi

Tree grew inside my head, A. Tree Within, A. Octavio Paz. TCLAP, *tr. by* Eliot Weinberger

Tree grew under your hand one day, The. Lines for a Painter. Anthony Cronin. PBCIP

Tree has entered my hands, The. Girl, A. Ezra Pound. MoAmPo; NOxBChV

Tree in December. Melville Cane. MoAmPo

Tree in the courtyard turns color suddenly, The. Thoughts on the First Day of Autumn, Sent to Su Tzu-mei. Ou-yang Hsiu. SuSp, *tr. by* Irving Y. Lo

Tree in the Garden, The. Christine Chandler. OTCP

Tree in wind rings glass-like, bell-like, gay. Month-Verses. Ludwig Goldscheider. AuPH, *tr. by* Lowell A. Bangerter

Tree in Winter. Emily Dickinson. NOxBChV

Tree is happy because it is scarcely sentient, The. Fatality. "Rubén Darío." TCLAP, *tr. by* Lysander Kemp

Tree is stripped, The. Form in Void. Ikkyu Sojun. ZenPo, *tr. by* Takashi Ikemoto and Lucien Stryk

Tree let your arms fall. No Ordinary Sun. Hone Tuwhare. PeNZ

Tree Marriage. William Meredith. GLP

Tree nymphs, daughters of River, ambrosial. Moiro. SaLy, *tr. by* Diane Rayor

Tree of Diana. Alejandra Piznarnick.

"I gave the surge of myself to the dawn." TANSG, *tr. by* Susan Bassnett

Tree of Earthly Delights. Nancy Morejón. TANSG, *tr. by* Joy Renjilian-Burgy

Tree of Fire. "Adonis" [*or* "Adunis"]. VCWP, *tr. by* Samuel Hazo

Tree of intense, The. Ode to the Watermelon. Pablo Neruda. SPE, *tr. by* Robert Bly

Tree of Knowledge, The. Edwin Emanuel Bradford.

Equality. VerBaPo

"In a sense a bee may be." VerBaPo

Tree of Knowledge, The. Abraham Cowley. ChIV-1

Tree of Knowledge, The. Lizelia Augusta Jenkins Moorer. CBWP-3

Tree of knowledge was the tree of reason, The. Contraband. Denise Levertov. BLT

Tree of life my soul hath seen, The. Christ the Apple-Tree. *Unknown.* TCAPo

Tree of nothing matters grew red leaves then dropped them confetti-like, The. Triptych. Jim Elledge. IllVoic

Tree of roses. The water crashed headlong. Peter Levi. TOF

Tree Old Woman. Samuel Makidemewabe. STP, *tr. by* Howard Norman

Tree Party. Louis MacNeice. OxBTC

Tree-planting Man. / Stay. (LL) Young Heroes. Gwendolyn Brooks. BPo; NAAAL

Tree rows in orchards are capable of patterns. What, The. Lyn Hejinian. FTOS *Fr.* My Life.

Tree's leaves may be ever so good, A. Leaves Compared with Flowers. Robert Frost. NOBA

Tree Sings to the Stream, The. Leah Goldberg. MHP, *tr. by* Ruth Finer Mintz *Fr.* Songs of the Stream.

Tree still bends over the lake, The. Winter. Sheila Wingfield. EnLoPo; LW

Tree Stillness. Karen L. Mitchell. GT

Tree Telling of Orpheus, A. Denise Levertov. APSN; MiVo

Tree, the close willow, swayed, The. (LL) Visitant, The. Theodore Roethke. PoE; RB; TRP; UnPo

Tree the intact, The. Some Lapland Views. Christian Dotremont. PFTM-2, *tr. by* Pierre Joris

Tree the tempest with a crash of wood, The. On a Tree Fallen across the Road. Robert Frost. RB

Tree Toad. *Unknown.* NTCP

Tree toad loved a she-toad, A. Tree Toad. *Unknown.* NTCP

Tree-topped Hill. *Unknown.* NOEC

Tree was shaken from the inside, The. Not Falling. Lynne McMahon. ExTi

Tree we plant will, when its boughs are grown, The. *Unknown.* CAGL *Fr.* Don Leon.

Tree Within, A. Octavio Paz. TCLAP, *tr. by* Eliot Weinberger

Treefrog winks without springing. Drawings of the Song Animals. Duane Niatum. HATNAP

Treehouse, The. James A. Emanuel. BPo

Trees. Fleur Adcock. OBGa

Trees. Joyce Kilmer. APT-1; BRP; ChAP; ITBLP; TCAPo; UV

Trees. Ágnes Nemes Nagy. PoSu, *tr. by* Bruce Berlind

Trees. Cheryl Savageau. TWW

Trees, The. Philip Larkin. HarvBoo; NoAM; NoP-4; OPOU

Trees, The. Bill Manhire. PeNZ

Trees, The. Adrienne Rich. CoAP; EmeKit; NOBA; WPE

Trees and Evening Sky. N. Scott Momaday. CDW

Trees / and the wind. Hand, The. Brian Fawcett. NOBC

Trees are a'ivied, the leaves they are green, The. Bonnie Laddie's Lang a-Grouwin', The. *Unknown.* OxBS

Trees are ancient, thick with patterns of moss, The. Hsü Chung-hsing. CoBLCP *Fr.* Following the Rhymes of Magistrate Liu's Poems on Entertaining Two Assistant Premiers at Pine-Snow Temple.

Trees are brilliant with flowers, The. Spring Walk to the Pavilion of Good Crops and Peace. Ou-yang Hsiu. OHPC, *tr. by* Kenneth Rexroth

Trees are cages for them: water holds its breath. Stars and Planets. Norman MacCaig. OPOU; OxBSP

Trees are coming into leaf, The. Trees, The. Philip Larkin. HarvBoo; NoAM; NoP-4; OPOU

Trees are Down, The. Charlotte Mew. BrRo; ChIV-2; MoBrPo; OxAEP-2; TrCP; VWP; WPE; WPOW

TREES ARE ELEPHANTS' HEADS, THE. Michael McClure. PFTM-2 *Fr.* Ghost Tantras.

Trees are hopelessly overstylized, the sycamores, The. Self-Portrait, Jackson. James Kimbrell. NAPBL

Trees are in their autumn beauty, The. Wild Swans at Coole, The. W. B. Yeats. HeIP-4; MoBrPo; NAEL-5v2; NAEL-6v2; NPeEn; NoAM; NoP-4; OWoS; PoPoPo; SCGP; SoSe-8; TFi; UnPo

Trees are never the same, The. Return, The. Thomas McGrath. GifTon

Trees are tall, but the moon small, The. Hide and Seek. Robert Graves. KaS; NTCP

Trees are tracing in the waning haze, The. Evening. Victor Van Vriesland. TrJP, *tr. by* Adriaan J. Barnouw

Trees are uncurling their first, The. Married Love. Liz Rosenberg. NIL-7

Trees are very high in the wan signal-beam, for whose slow, The. David Jones. TCAWP *Fr.* In Parenthesis.

Trees at Night. Helene Johnson. BlSi

Trees' black hair electric, The. February Evening in Boston, 1971. Denise Levertov. TaR

Trees both in hills and plaines, in plenty be. William Wood. SCAP

Trees can't tell the two of them apart, The. (LL) Field and Forest. Randall Jarrell. LCAP-2; VGW

Trees descend, image of love, The. Edith Jay Scovell. HarvBoo *Fr.* Water Images.

Trees, drowned in the gray snow. Idea of Russia, The. Viktor Krivulin. TCRusP, *tr. by* Anna Barker and Daniel Weissbort

Trees, Effigies, Moving Objects. Allen Curnow. PeNZ

Trees full of snipers, the new kind, The. War. Lorine Niedecker. FTOS

Trees Green the Quiet Sun. Larry Eigner. PmAP

Trees growing—right in front of my window. Pruning Trees. Po Chü-i. ChiP, *tr. by* Arthur Waley

Trees in groves / Kine in droves. Saadi. Ralph Waldo Emerson. APN-1; OxBA

Trees in the Garden. D. H. Lawrence. MoBrPo

Trees in the old days used to stand. Carentan O Carentan. Louis Simpson. CoAP; NOBA; OBWP; PoE; RB; WoPoe

Trees in the wood lifeless. Little Sunlight, A. Shinkichi Takahashi. ZenPo, *tr. by* Takashi Ikemoto and Lucien Stryk

Trees inside are moving out into the forest, The. Trees, The. Adrienne Rich. CoAP; EmeKit; NOBA; WPE

Trees, late in the season, bare. Trees, Late in the Season. Willem Kloos. TuT, *tr. by* Desmond Egan

Trees, like great jade elephants, The. John Gould Fletcher. MoAmPo *Fr.* Irradiations.

Trees like Tassels—hit—and swung, The. Emily Dickinson. NCAP

Trees make their mark on the sky, The. Palms. June Sylvester. PasH

Trees of Life, The. Jones Very. NOBA

Trees of the Forest, The. *Unknown.* WoPoe, *tr. by* Austin Clarke *Fr.* Sweeney Astray.

Trees shading trees, mist-smoke weaves. Tune: "Beautiful Barbarians." Li Po. ChinPo, *tr. by* Yip Wai-lim

Trees So High, The. *Unknown.* OxBoLi

Trees stand clerically straight, The. Ivanovs, The. Nikolai Alekseievich Zabolotsky [*or* Zabolotskii]. TCRP, *tr. by* Daniel Weissbort

Trees surround a wide pool, the moon casts many shadows. Night Chill. Li Shang-yin. SuSp, *tr. by* Eugene Eoyang

Trees that Change Our Lives. Gary Soto. PasH

Trees were forbidden me, The. Edouard J. Maunick. NegPo *Fr.* As Far as Yoruba Land.

Trees were hung with marzipan, The. Such Sweet Sorrow. Elizabeth Delmore. NLP

Trees were like bubblyjocks, The. Sunny Gale. Hugh MacDiarmid. FaBoVe

Trees were moving. Emilio Villa. ItPo, *tr. by* Gayle Ridinger *Fr.* Words.

Trees were taller than the night, The. Robber, The. Walter James Turner. MoBrPo

Trellie. Lance Jeffers. NBV

Trellis, shorn of grapes, The. Song of an Autumn Night. Chao Meng-fu. CoBLCP, *tr. by* Jonathan Chaves

Tremble, oh my gravemound. Basho. SoOfWa, *tr. by* Sam Hamill

Trembling, across the plain my course I held. Philip Freneau. TCAPo *Fr.* House of Night, The.

Trembling and sobbing. Free Fire Zone. Igor Bobrowsky. CDa

Trembling before Thine Awful Throne. Augustus Lucas Hillhouse. AH

Trembling I write my dream, and recollect. Philip Freneau. NAAL-2v1; NAAL-3; TCAPo *Fr.* House of Night, The.

Trembling November winds. Nocturnal Sounds. Kattie M. Cumbo. BlSi

Trembling old men are stamm'ring. Lines on Carmen Sylva. Emma Lazarus. TrJP

Trembling, sand-dollar. Grunion. Wendy Rose. CDW

Trembling the spectres glide, and plaintive vent. Homer. OBVE *Fr.* Odyssey.

Trembling train clings to the leaning wall, The. Moonrise in the Rockies. Ella Higginson. SWaP

Trembling with engines, gulping oil, the river. Anthony Cronin. PBCIP *Fr.* R.M.S. *Titanic.*

Tremor, The. Jack Hirschman. BodElec

Tremulous word, a lingering hand, the burning, A. Taking the Night-Train. John James Piatt. APN-2

Trench Idyll. Richard Aldington. PeFWW

Trench Poets. Edgell Rickword. FaBoWar

Trenches, The. Frederic Manning. NOBAu; PoWW

Trenches: St Eloi. Thomas Ernest Hulme. PeFWW

Trendelenburg Position. M. Wyrebek. AmPoNex

Trepidation of the Druids. William Wordsworth. Son *Fr.* Ecclesiastical Sonnets.

Trespasser in my own house. Portrait. Constance Urdang. OPRER

Trespasses. Nujoum Al-Ghanim.

"I don't know how I lost my amulets." PoArWo, *tr. by* Clarissa C. Burt

Tretis of the Tua Mariit Wemen and the Wedo, The. William Dunbar. OxBS

"Bot of ane bowrd in to bed I sall yow breif yit." EBEV

Tri, tre, tre, tre, tri-tre-tre-tree! (LL) Mother Goose. LB; OxNR; ReMoGo

Triad. Adelaide Crapsey. APT-1; TCAPo; WPE

Triad, A. Christina Georgina Rossetti. NAEL-5v2; NAEL-6v2; NALW

Triads of Ireland, The. *Unknown.*

"Three excellent qualities in narration." BIrV, *tr. by* Thomas Kinsella

Triage. Lisel Mueller. IllVoic

Triage. Margot Schilpp. AmPoNex

Triage. Larissa Szporluk. NeAmPo

Trial. Ruth Padel. MFPA

Trial, A. Murder. Yury [*or* Iurii] Timofeievich Galanskov. TCRusP, *tr. by* Olive Dehn

Trial, The. Zbigniew Herbert. PoetW, *tr. by* John Carpenter and Bogdana Carpenter

Trial, The. Zbigniew Herbert. AF, *tr. by* John Carpenter

Trial and Error. Phyllis McGinley. PeLV

Trial by Jury. Sir William Schwenck Gilbert.

When I, Good Friends, Was Called to the Bar. NAEL-5v2; NAEL-6v2

Trial of Renard, The. *Unknown.* NAWM-7v1, *tr. by* Patricia Terry

Trials of a Tourist. Anne Tibble. NBLV

Trials that the Saviour bore have paved the golden way, The. Benefits of Sorrow. Lizelia Augusta Jenkins Moorer. CBWP-3

Triangular Legs. Sir Alan Patrick Herbert. NBLV

Tribal Chant. Carol Lee Sanchez. ReEnLa

Tribal Marks. Saundra Sharp. SpirFl

Tribal Memories. Robert Duncan. APSN; NOBA *Fr.* Passages.

Tribe forsook you, The. Nightmare 1. Abdul Maqsoud Abdul Karim. NAfrP, *tr. by* Clarissa C. Burt

Tribes of Ching—that's not my home. Wang Ts'an. CoBCP *Fr.* Seven Sorrows.

Tribunal, The. Chris Wallace-Crabbe. ChIV-2

Tribune's Visitation, The. David Jones.

"I have a word to say to you as men and as a man speaking to." TCAWP

Tributary. Leonard Nolens. TuT, *tr. by* Michael O'Loughlin

Tributary Stream. William Wordsworth. CenSon *Fr.* River Duddon [A Series of Sonnets], The.

Tribute. Eloise Bibb. CBWP-4

Tribute, The. Coventry Patmore. EBEV *Fr.* Angel in the House, The.

Tribute on the Passing of a Very Real Person. *Unknown.* PoToHe

Tribute to a Lost Steamer. Mary Weston Fordham. CBWP-2

Tribute to America. Shelley. AiP

Tribute to Capt. F. W. Dawson. Mary Weston Fordham. CBWP-2

Tribute to Matthew Arnold in a Moment of Self-Abuse, A. Richard Shepherd. PeLi

Tribute to the Angels. "H. D.".

"Ah (you say), this is Holy Wisdom." NALW; NoAM

"And the point in the spectrum." APT-1; NALW

"And yet in some very subtle way," NALW

"Bitter, bitter jewel." NALW

"But nearer than Guardian Angel." NALW

"Every hour, every moment." NALW; NoAM

"Hermes Trismegistus." NALW

"I can not invent it," NALW

"I had been thinking of Gabriel," NALW

"I John saw. I testify." NALW

"In the field-furrow." APT-1

"Invisible, indivisible Spirit." APT-1; BoWoP

"New sensation, A." APT-1

"Not in our time, O Lord." NOBA

"Now polish the crucible." NALW

"O swiftly, re-light the flame." NALW

"O yes—you understand, I say." NALW

"Of the no need." NALW

"One of us said, how odd," NALW

"She carried a book, either to imply." NALW

"So she must have been pleased with us," NALW

"Some call that deep-deep bell." NALW

"Swiftly re-light the flame," NALW

"This is a symbol of beauty (you continue)," NALW

"This is no rune nor riddle." APT-1

("This is no rune nor symbol.") NALW

"We have seen her / the world over." APT-1; CRP; HW; NALW; PFTM-1; VGW

"We see her hand in her lap." APT-1

"What is the jewel colour?" NALW

"Your walls do not fall, he said." NALW

Tribute to the Bride and Groom, A. Priscilla Jane Thompson. CBWP-2

Tribute to Wyatt. Henry Howard, Earl of Surrey. PeECV

(Earth his bones, the heavens possess his ghost, The.) (LL) NAEL-7v1; NoP-4

(Epitaph on Sir Thomas Wyatt.) NAEL-5v1; NAEL-6v1

(Excellent Epitaph of Sir Thomas Wyatt, An.) NoSic

(Tribute to Wyatt.) PeECV

(Wyatt resteth here, that quick could never rest.) NoP-4; PeECV

Trick, The. John Mole. NOxBChV

Trick, The. Mark Wunderlich. WiU

Trick, he said, is to look not at all, The. Beekeeper. Barbara J. Orton. NeAmPo

Trick is, to live your days, The. Advice to My Son. Peter Meinke. PAI

Trick or Treat. John Frederick Nims. IllVoic

Trick that everyone abhors, A. Rebecca, Who Slammed Doors for Fun and Perished Miserably. Joseph Hilaire Pierre Belloc. NOBL

Trickle Drops. Walt Whitman. APN-1; NAAL-2v1; NAAL-3; NAAL-5

Trickle of sand on the grave's edge, A. Ad Infinitum. Joan Aronsten. NOBAu

Trickling. Anita Virgil. HA

Tricks. Daniil Kharms. TCRP, *tr. by* Bradley Jordan

Tricks for the Barmaid. Roddy Lumsden. NeBl

Tricks With Mirrors. Margaret Atwood. NIP-4

Trickster 1 (for Winston Rodney). Kwame Dawes. WaCA

Trickster 2 (for Lee "Scratch" Perry). Kwame Dawes. WaCA

Trickster 4 (for Sister Patra). Kwame Dawes. WaCA

Tricky Margaret.   Mary Macleod (Màiri Nighean Alasdair Ruaidh).   EMWP

Trico's Song.   John Lyly.   NoSic   *Fr.* Alexander and Campaspe.

Trident, in nightmare, The.   Peace Plan: Meditation on the 9 Stages of "Peacemaking" as Tribute to Senator Claiborne Pell: 1997.   Michael S. Harper.   PuP-23

Tries a nosedive, kamikaze.   Baby Random.   Belle Waring.   PBCAP

Trifle for Trafalgar Day, A.   Ted Pauker.   NOBL

Trifles.   George Farquhar.   OBCoV

Trifling song you shall hear, A.   Trifles.   George Farquhar.   OBCoV

Trilce.   César Vallejo.
    "I sdrive to ddddeflect at a blow the blow."   PFTM-1
    Trilce.   PFTM-1

Trilce.   César Vallejo.   PFTM-1   *Fr.* Trilce.

Trilogy for X.   Louis MacNeice.
    And Love Hung Still.   CIP-2; MoBrPo
    "And love hung still as crystal over the bed."   CIP-2; MoBrPo
    For X.   BoLoP; EnLoPo
    "When clerks and navvies fondle."   BoLoP; EnLoPo

Trilogy of Passion.   Goethe.   STV, *tr. by* John Frederick Nims

Trim's Song: The Fair Kitchen-Maid.   Sir Richard Steele.   OxBSP   *Fr.* Funeral, The.

Trim the lamp; polish the lens; draw, one by one, rare.   Geoffrey Hill.   FaBoMo   *Fr.* Mercian Hymns.

Trim, thou are right!—'Tis sure that I.   Death in the Kitchen.   Thomas Hood.   NPeEn

Trinity.   Gerrit Achterberg.   TuT, *tr. by* Dennis O'Driscoll

Trinity.   "Michael Field."   VWP

Trinity, The.   William Langland.   SacPr   *Fr.* Vision of Piers Plowman, The.

Trinity Brethren Attend.   Ivor Armstrong Richards.   CRP

Trinity Place.   Phyllis McGinley.   MoAmPo; OxBSP; SoSe-8

Trinity Sunday.   George Herbert.   OxBSP

Trinity, The. Amen. (LL)   Upon a Dead Man's Head.   John Skelton.   HAP; SCGP; WoPoe

Trio.   Kimberly Ann Collins.   InTrad

Trio for Two Cats and a Trombone.   Dame Edith Sitwell.   NAEL-5v2; NAEL-6v2   *Fr.* Façade.

Trio of Triolets, A.   Gerard Manley Hopkins.
    Child is Father to the Man, The.   NOBVV
    (Triolet.)   NOBL

Triolet.   Wendy Cope.   OBCoV

Triolet.   Gerard Manley Hopkins.   *See* Child Is Father to the Man, The

Triolet.   Gerard Manley Hopkins.   *See* Trio of Triolets, A

Triolet Against Sisters.   Phyllis McGinley.   KaS; OBCA; OxIBACP

Triolet: "When first we met we did not guess."   Robert Bridges.   OxBSP

Trip on Mount T'ai-P'ing.   K'ung Chih-kuei.   ChinPo, *tr. by* Yip Wai-lim

Trip Through the Mind Jail, A.   Raul Salinas.   FaBoA

Trip to a Mountain Village, A.   Li K'ai-hsien.   CoBLCP, *tr. by* Jonathan Chaves

Trip to Four or Five Towns, A.   John Logan.   CoAP; NNaP
    (Gold-coloured skin of my Lebanese friends, The.)   CoAmPo

Trip to Hua-yang Mountain, A.   Tao-chi.   CoBLCP, *tr. by* Jonathan Chaves

Trip to Mountain West Village, A.   Lu Yu.   CoBCP, *tr. by* Burton Watson

Trip to Paris and Belgium, A.   Dante Gabriel Rossetti.
    Antwerp to Ghent.   NPeEn; PeVV
    Boulogne to Amiens and Paris.   PeVV
    "Constant keeping-past of shaken trees."   NPeEn; PeVV
    "Strong extreme speed, that the brain burries with."   PeVV
    "We are upon the Scheldt. We know we move."   NPeEn; PeVV

Trip to Stone Man Peak, A.   Yang Wan-li.   SuSp, *tr. by* Jonathan Chaves

Trip to the Village of the River of White Sand, A.   Tao-chi.   CoBLCP, *tr. by* Jonathan Chaves

Trip to Yüeh-lu Temple, A.   Li Tung-yang.   CoBLCP, *tr. by* Jonathan Chaves

Trip upon trenchers, and dance upon dishes.   Mother Goose.   NOBL; OxNR; ReMoGo

Trip west, The.   Vague Poem.   Elizabeth Bishop.   BAP-01

Tripart.   Gayl Jones.   BlSi

Triphammer Bridge.   A. R. Ammons.   ColAP; NAAL-2v2; NOBA

Triple Benison, The.   Henrietta Cordelia Ray.   CBWP-3

Triple Feature.   Denise Levertov.   NoP-4

Triple Fool, The.   John Donne.   FSCP; NOSC; SoSe-8
    (I am two fooles, I know.)   PBRV
    (Triple Foole, The.)   PBRV

Triple Overtime.   Lucinda Roy.   GT

Triple Trouble.   Assotto Saint.   GLP

Triplets.   Arthur Schwartz.   ReLy

Tripoli.   Peter A. Sanders.   FaBoWar

Tripoli.   Nadia Tuéni.   PoArWo

Trippers and askers surround me.   Walt Whitman.   CAGL; ColAP; EnlH; NAWM-7v2; UnPo   *Fr.* Song of Myself.

Trips.   Nikki Giovanni.   CA

Triptych.   Jim Elledge.   IllVoic

Triptych.   Beatrix Gates.   WiU
    Cathy.   WiU
    "Charlie said he wanted to die."   WiU
    Homeless.   WiU
    "Morning sun outside D'Agostino's, a young man bends."   WiU
    Ron.   WiU
    "Well, since I became a lesbian."   WiU

Triptych.   Christopher Pilling.   NLP

Triptych.   D. A. Powell.   WiU

Tristan and Isolde.   Richard Wagner (1813–83).
    "Smile his lips, A."   EroLit, *tr. by* Alfred Forman

Tristan da Cunha.   Roy Campbell.   MoBrPo

Tristan da Cunha.   Ian D. Colvin.   PeSAV

Tristan had no choice.   Heinrich von Veldeke.   GePo

Tristan Tzara.   Edward Hirsch.   BodElec

Tristia.   Ger Killeen.   AmPoNex

Tristia.   Osip Emilevich Mandelshtam [*or* Mandelshtam].   WoPoe, *tr. by* James Greene

Tristia.   Osip Emilevich Mandelshtam [*or* Mandelshtam].
    "No matter how I concealed them, even the."   PFTM-1
    Tristia.   PFTM-1

Tristia.   Osip Emilevich Mandelshtam [*or* Mandelshtam].   PFTM-1   *Fr.* Tristia.

Tristia.   Ovid.
    Book 1.   RomPo, *tr. by* Peter Green
    "Back from the sea now, back to their sources shall deep rivers."   RomPo, *tr. by* Peter Green
    "Dipped now in Ocean, the She-Bear's stellar guardian."   RomPo, *tr. by* Peter Green
    "Every letter you've read in this whole book was written."   RomPo, *tr. by* Peter Green
    "Friend, henceforth to be reckoned the foremost among my comrades."   RomPo, *tr. by* Peter Green
    "I have (may I always keep!) blonde Minerva's protection: my vessel."   RomPo, *tr. by* Peter Green
    "If you're one who keeps a bust made in my likeness."   RomPo, *tr. by* Peter Green
    "Little book—no, I don't begrudge you—you're off to the City."   RomPo, *tr. by* Peter Green
    "Nagging reminders: the black ghost-melancholy vision."   RomPo, *tr. by* Peter Green
    "Not so dear was Lyde to the Clarian poet, not so truly."   RomPo, *tr. by* Peter Green
    "You gods of sea and sky—what's left me now but prayer?"   RomPo, *tr. by* Peter Green
    "You who are reading this work without malice, may you."   RomPo, *tr. by* Peter Green
    Book 3.
    "Friend of the arts and artists, scholar, generous patron."   WoPoe, *tr. by* David R. Slavitt
    Book 5.
    "I have been looking these pages over, my dearest wife."   WoPoe, *tr. by* David R. Slavitt

Tristia.   Charles Hubert Sisson.   HarvBoo

Tristitia Ante.   Maurice Gilliams.   TuT, *tr. by* Sean Dunne

Tristium.   Ovid.
    "And here I wish my soul died with my breath."   OBVE
    "And on this day, which poets unto thee."   OBVE

Tristram lies sick to death.   Tristram's End.   Laurence Binyon.   OBMV

Tristram of Lyonesse.   Algernon Charles Swinburne.
    King Mark, Tristram, and Palamede.   EBNV
    "On the mid stairs, between the light and dark."   EBNV

Tristram's End.   Laurence Binyon.   OBMV

Tristrem and the Hunters.   Thomas of Erceldoune.   OxBS   *Fr.* Sir Tristrem.

Trit trot to market to buy a penny doll.   *Unknown.*   OxNR

Triumph, The.   Ben Jonson.   *See* Celebration of Charis in Ten Lyric[k] Pieces [*or* Peeces], A

Triumph, The.   William Gilmore Simms.   Son

Triumph! How strange, how strong had triumph come.   Third Ypres.   Edmund Charles Blunden.   PeFWW

Triumph—may be of several kinds.   Emily Dickinson.   TCAPo

Triumph! My Jesus has! Triumph! His empire gained!   15th Kühl-Psalm, The.   Quirinus Kuhlmann.   GePo, *tr. by* George C. Schoolfield

Triumph of Bacchus and Ariadne.   Lorenzo de' Medici.   CTC, *tr. by* Richard Aldington   *Fr.* Carnival Songs.

Triumph of Charis, The. Ben Jonson. *See* Celebration of Charis in Ten Lyric[k] Pieces [*or* Peeces], A

Triumph of Death, The. William Shakespeare. *See* Sonnets

Triumph of Dullness, The. Pope. NAEL-6v1; NAEL-7v1; NOEC; NPeEn *Fr.* Dunciad, The.

Triumph of Dullness [*or* Dulness], The. Pope. *See also* Dunciad, The

Triumph of Infidelity, The. Timothy Dwight.

  Here stood Hypocrisy, in sober brown. NOCV

    Smooth Divine, The. SacPr

      "There smiled the smooth Divine, unused to wound." SacPr

  "Here stood Hypocrisy, in sober brown." NOCV

Triumph of Life, The. Shelley. NAEL-5v2; NAEL-6v2; NOBRP

  "As in that trance of wondrous thought I lay." NPeEn

  "Struck to the heart by this sad pageantry." OxBEV

Triumph of Love. John Hall Wheelock. MoAmPo

Triumph of Peace, The. James Shirley.

  Song to the Masquers. OxBSP

  "Why do you dwell so long in clouds." OxBSP

Triumph of Sensibility. Sylvia Townsend Warner. MoBrPo

Triumph of Superstition, The. Raphael and Ianthe. Anne Batten Cristall. RWP

Triumph of the Church, The. Phineas Fletcher. SacPr *Fr.* Purple Island, The.

Triumph of the Whale, The. Charles Lamb.

  "Io! Paean! Io! sing." OxAEP-2

Triumph of Time, The. Algernon Charles Swinburne.

  "I will go back to the great sweet mother." NAEL-5v2; NAEL-6v2

Triumph of Vice, The. Pope. NOBE; NPeEn; OBSV *Fr.* Epilogue to the Satires, in Two Dialogues.

Triumph or the tomb, The. (LL) Charleston. Henry Timrod. APN-2; CBCWP; ColAP; NOBA; OxBA; TAP; TCAPo

Triumphal March. "Rubén Dario." SpanPo, *tr. by* Charles Guenther

Triumphal March. T. S. Eliot. OBWP *Fr.* Coriolan.

Triumphant Demons stand, and Angels start. Heart's Abysses, The. Walter Savage Landor. FaBoEE; OBSV

Triumphing chariots, statues, crowns of bay. William Drummond, of Hawthornden. NOSC *Fr.* Urania, or Spiritual Poems.

Triumphing over Death, and Chance, and thee O Time. (LL) On Time. John Milton. OBEV; SCGP; SacPr

Triumphs of Nature, The. Samuel Boyse.

  "Next to the fair ascent our steps we traced." OBGa

  Triumphs of Nature, The. OBGa

Triumphs of the Gout, The. Gilbert West.

  "Lives there on Earth to whom I am unknown." ECEV

Triumvirate, The. Elizabeth Thomas. ECWP

Triune, shaping, restless power. Sistrum. Margaret Fuller. APN-1

Trivia; or, The Art of Walking the Streets of London. John Gay.

  "Be sure observe where brown Ostrea stands." OxBEV

  "If clothed in black you tread the busy town." ECEV

  (Of the Weather.) NPeEn

  Pickpockets. ECEV

  Thieves and Whores. ECEV

  "Thoughtless wits shall frequent forfeits pay, The." ECEV

  "Where Lincoln's Inn, wide space, is railed around." ECEV

  "Where the mob gathers, swiftly shoot along." ECEV

  "Who can the various city frauds recite." ECEV

  "Winter my theme confines; whose nitry wind." ECEV; NOEC

  Winter Sports. ECEV; NOEC

Troades. Seneca.

  After Death Nothing Is. EBEV; OBVE, *tr. by* John Wilmot, 2d Earl of Rochester

  (Seneca's Troas. Act 2. Chorus.) OxBEV, *tr. by* John Wilmot, 2d Earl of Rochester

Trŏchĕe trīps frŏm lōng tŏ shōrt. Metrical Feet. Samuel Taylor Coleridge. FHYEP; NIL-7; NIP-4

Troika, The. Louis Simpson. NOBA

Troilus and Cressida. William Shakespeare.

  "And is it true that I must go from Troy?" OxAEP-1

  "Have you seen my cousin?" OxAEP-1

  "Peace, you ungracious clamours! peace, rude sounds!" OxAEP-1

  "They tax our policy and call it cowardice." FaBoWar

  "This she? no, this is Diomed's Cressida." OxAEP-1

  "What! are my deeds forgot?" OxAEP-1

  "You are for dreams and slumbers, brother priest." OxAEP-1

Troilus and Criseyde [*or* Criseide]. Geoffrey Chaucer.

  Complaint of Troilus, The. NOBE; OBEV

  Conclusion. WoPoe, *tr. by* Burton Raffel and Selden Rodman

  "Double sorwe of Troilus to tellen, The." MakPoe

  ("Go, litel boke, go, litel myn tragedye.") NPeEn

"Go, little book, my little tragedy." WoPoe, *tr. by* Burton Raffel and Selden Rodman

("If no love is, O God, what feele I so?") NoP-4

"If no love is, O God, what fele I so." AWP

Love Unfeigned. NOBE; OBEV

"O Paleys [*or* palace], whylom [*or* whilom] croune [*or* crown] of houses all[e]." NOBE; OBEV

"O younge [*or* yonge] fres[s]he folkes, he or she." NOBE; OBEV

Song of Troylus, The. AWP

"Swich fyn hath, lo, this Troilus for love!" NOCV; SacPr

"This Troilus in armes gan hir streyne." EroLit

"This Troilus [*or* Troylus], with blisse [*or* Blysse] of that supprysed [*or* supprised]." EBEV; PoE

(Troilus's Song.) NAEL-7v1

"Whan they unto the paleys were yoemen." PoE

"Wrath, as I bigan yow for to seye, The." OxBEV

Troilus's Song. Geoffrey Chaucer. *See* Troilus and Criseyde [*or* Criseide]

Trois Petits Tours et Puis . . . Marie Ponsot. ExTi

Trojan Women. Seneca. RomPo, *tr. by* Anthony James Boyle

Troll's Nosegay, The. Robert Graves. OxBSo; Son

Troll to her Children, The. Jane Yolen. OTCP

Trolley Song, The. Hugh Martin. ReLy

Trolls, The. Louis MacNeice.

  ("In the misty night humming to themselves like morons.") AF

Trombone Solo. Stoddard King. NBLV

Trompe L'Œil. Daryl Hine. MoCV

Trompe l'oeil. Tracy Ryan. NeBl

Trompe L'Oeil in Winter. Mary Ann Samyn. AmPoNex

Troop home to silent grots and caves. George Darley. NAEL-5v2; NAEL-6v2; NPeEn *Fr.* Syren Songs.

Troop ship, The. Isaac Rosenberg. OxBEV; PoWW

Troop ship whistles once; I still waver, The. Colonial Troops Transport, The. *Vietnamese Oral Tradition.* CaDao, *tr. by* John Balaban

Troop Train. Aleksandr Petrovich Mezhirov. TCRP, *tr. by* Deming Brown

Troop Train. Karl Shapiro. APT-2; OxBA

Troops brought enough suffering to the people, The. On Hearing That the Sea-Barbarians Are About To Attack Hu-chou—Expressing My Feelings to Tzu-yü. Tsung Ch'en. CoBLCP, *tr. by* Jonathan Chaves

Troops exulting sate in order round, The. Homer. OBVE, *tr. by* Alexander Pope *Fr.* Iliad, The.

Troopship, The. Lionel Pigot Johnson. EBVV

Troparion. Kassiane. WPoS, *tr. by* Liana Sakelliou

Trope Market. Jackson Mac Low. PmAP

Trophies of pain I've gathered. whose sorrow. For H.D. Diane Di Prima. PmAP

Trophy Homes. Bruce Berger. GeoH

Tropic green days, red. Kalamu ya Salaam. SpirFl *Fr.* New Orleans Haiku.

Tropical Afternoon. "Rubén Dario." TCLAP, *tr. by* Lysander Kemp

Tropical nights. Boston Beguine, The. Sheldon Harnick. ReLy

Tropicalia. Margaret Haley. YaYoPo

"Tropicals." René Maran. NegPo, *tr. by* Ellen Conroy Kennedy

Tropics in New York, The. Claude McKay. APT-1; GT; MakPoe; NoAM; TTY

Tropics vanish, and meseems that I, The. Robert Louis Stevenson. NePenScot; PeVV

Tropics, why did you give me. Wishes. Carlos Pellicer. TCLAP, *tr. by* Donald Justice

Tropisms on John Berryman. Gerald Vizenor. VoR

Trosachs, The. William Wordsworth. OBEV

Trot, and a canter, a gallop, and over, A. *Unknown.* OxNR

Troth. Michael Davidson. FTOS

Trotsky in Mexico. Dmitry [*or* Dmitrii] Vasil'evich Bobyshev. ItGoST, *tr. by* Michael Van Walleghen

Trotsky's dead. My strays. Letters from an Exile. Valerie Duff. OPRER

Troubadour. Peter Sirr. BiHa

Troubadour Love. Olga Nolla. TANSG, *tr. by* Paula Vega

Trouble. (LL) *Var. authors.* AWP; TAL, *tr. by* Wilfred Scawen Blunt and Lady Anne Blunt *Fr.* Mu'allaqat, The.

Trouble has done her good. Charity. Connie Bensley. FaBoWP

Trouble in Mind. Richard M. Jones. NAAAL

Trouble Is a Man. Alec Wilder. ReLy

Trouble / Mellows to a golden note. (LL) Trumpet Player. Langston Hughes. NAAL-2v2; TTY

Trouble, not of clouds, or weeping rain, A. On the Departure of Sir Walter Scott from Abbotsford, for Naples. William Wordsworth. EBEV

Trouble of a book is first to be, The. Troubles of a Book, The. Laura Riding Jackson. HarvBoo

Trouble was they left her too much alone, The. Poemectomy. John Dickson. IllVoic

Trouble was too much, The. Indian Love Song. Lew Blockcolski. VoR

Trouble with General Sherman, The. Limerick. Basil Ransome-Davies. PeLi

Trouble with home-made armour, The. Children in Armour. Geoffrey Adkins. FaBoWar

Trouble with you is, The. Denunciation; or, Unfrock'd Again. Philip Whalen. NeAP

Trouble with you is, The. Love in a Warm Room in Winter. James Wright (1927–80). OBAL

Trouble with you is you're not, The. How the Last Act Begins. Chana Bloch. ExTi

Troubled Awakening. Magdalena Gomez. PueRic

Troubled midnight and the noon's repose, The. (LL) La Figlia Che Piange. T. S. Eliot. APT-1; FaBoTw; HarvBoo; HeIP-4; OxBEV; OxBTC; TCAPo; UnPo; VGW

Troubled tale that fills me with grief, A. (LL) Song on Enduring the Cold. Ts'ao Ts'ao. CoBCP; ColAnChi, tr. by Burton Watson

Troubled waters, The/ are frozen fast. Murasaki Shikibu. WPOW Fr. Tale of Genji, The.

Troubles of a Book, The. Laura Riding Jackson. HarvBoo

Troubles of the Day. William Barnes. GTBS-P

Troubles with the Soul at Morning Calisthenics. Anna Swirszczynska. BLT

Trousers of Wind. Unknown. PBA; TTY, tr. by Sylvia Pankhurst

Trousseau. Vona Groarke. MFPA

Trout, The. Daryl Hine. CoAP

Trout, The. John Montague. ModIr; NoP-4; PBCIP; PNI; PoE

Trout Fisher. George Mackay Brown. OxBC

Trout Quintet, The. Frank O'Hara. BodElec

Troy. Agathias. GrAn, tr. by Ezra Pound

Troy. Edwin Muir. HarvBoo

Tru's god Lizi. Tired Lizi Tired. Lindiwe Mabuza. HAWP

Truant, A. Mike Jenkins. TCAWP

Truant, The. Edwin John Pratt. NOBC

Truant! You love me not–the reason this. We Can Love But Once. Charlotte Dacre. RWP

Truants, The. Walter De la Mare. MoBrPo

Truce. Paul Muldoon. FaBoWar; PBCIP; PNI

Truce, The. Stella Gibbons. LW

Truce, gentle love, a parley now I crave. Michael Drayton. NoSic Fr. Idea.

Truck, The. John A. Stone. BloBone

Trucker, The. Will Dyson. NOBAu

Trucker leans on his horn down below, A. Work Song. Robyn Selman. TaR

Truckin' Ted Koehler. ReLy

True Account of Talking to the Sun at Fire Island, A. Frank O'Hara. AmFaPo; EmeKit; HCAP; NNaP; RB; TTTS

True and earthy prayer / of salami, The. (LL) Salami. Philip Levine. NNaP; NOBA; TAP; TRP

True, and yet true that I must Stella love. (LL) Sir Philip Sidney. NAEL-5v1; NAEL-6v1; NAEL-7v1; NoSic; Son Fr. Astrophil and Stella.

True Arab knows how to catch a fly in his hands, A. Blood. Naomi Shihab Nye. GraLe

True Beauty, The. Thomas Carew. GTBS-P Fr. Disdain Returned.

True Blue Lou. Sam Coslow. ReLy

True-blue the salmon—from his sally. No Place Like Home. Llawdden. OBWVE, tr. by Gwyn Jones

True-born Englishman, The. Daniel Defoe.
"Breed's described, The: Now, Satire, if you can." OBSV
"In their religion they are so unev'n." OBSV
"Labouring poor, in spite of double pay, The." NOBL
"Then let us boast of ancestors no more." OBSV
"Wherever God erects a house of prayer." NOBL; OBSV

True Brahmin, in the morning meadows wet. Ralph Waldo Emerson. OxBA Fr. Quatrains.

True Bride, The. Amy Gerstler. PmAP

True Confession of George Barker, The. George Barker.
"I sent a letter to my love." FaBoTw

True daughters of Lilith, night demons. Summer Night. Hayyim Nahman [or Khayim Nakhman or Chaim Nachman] Bialik. FIT, tr. by Robert Friend

True, Debby was pure as Weber Bread. Two Timer. Juan Delgado. TouFir

True Descenders. James Kimbrell. AmPoNex; NAPBL

True Dream, A. Elizabeth Barrett Browning. NALW

True ease in writing comes from Art, not Chance. Pope. HAP; InPK-6 Fr. Essay on Criticism, An.

True Effigies of a Certain Squire: Inscribed to Clemena, The. Elizabeth Thomas. ECWP

True Encounter, The. Edna St. Vincent Millay. OxBSP

True Facts of the Case, The. Anthony Euwer. OBAL; PeLi

True faith discovered was, The. Wisdom. W. B. Yeats. TrCP

True feelings come from my innermost heart. On a Painting "Ancient Trees and Flowing Stream." Yün Shou-p'ing. CoBLCP, tr. by Jonathan Chaves

True Friend, The. Ann Plato. SWaP

True Genius. Robert Lloyd. NOEC Fr. Shakespeare; an Epistle to David Garrick, Esq.

True genius, but true woman! dost deny. To George Sand: A Recognition. Elizabeth Barrett Browning. BoWoP; NAEL-5v2; NAEL-6v2; NALW; PEW; PoBW; VWP

True Happiness. Morris Talpalar. PoToHe

True happiness had no localities. Happiness. Robert Pollok. TreFP

True, / he just / lets his glass / set there. (LL) Neighbor. Langston Hughes. APSN; PFTM-1

True-hearted, whole-hearted, faithful and loyal. Frances Ridley Havergal. SacPr

True Heroism. Unknown. ITBLP

True Hymn, A. George Herbert. GeHe; NOCV

True Import of Present Dialogue, Black vs, The Negro. Nikki Giovanni. BPo

True Knight [or True Knighthood], The. Stephen Hawes. OBEV Fr. Pastime of Pleasure, The.

True Knowledge. Bishop Richard Mant. SacPr

True Knowledge. William Wilkie. ECEV Fr. Grasshopper and the Glowworm, The.

True Life Love Stories. Michael Foley.
"Ah no, ah no, they weren't all gross and slow." PNI
"Sois sage, ô ma doleur. . . I don't." PNI
"Sword is a cold bride. Yuk!, The." PNI

True Love. Phoebe Cary. PoToHe

True Love. Sharon Olds. BodElec

True Love. William Shakespeare. See Sonnets
Let Me Not to the Marriage of True Minds. William Shakespeare. See Sonnets

True Love. Unknown. AWP, tr. by Jethro Bithell

True Love, A. Nicholas Grimald. OBEV

True love, come O come to me. True Love. Unknown. AWP, tr. by Jethro Bithell

True love doth pass away! (LL) Song: "My silks and fine array." William Blake. RACG; SCGP

True love in every moment praises God. Mechthild von Magdeburg. WPoS

True Love in this differs from gold and clay. Shelley. FHYEP Fr. Epipsychidion.

True Lover, The. A. E. Housman. EBNV

True Maid, A. Matthew Prior. FaBoEE; NAEL-5v1; NAEL-6v1; NAEL-7v1; NIP-4; NOEC; NPeEn; PeLV

True Man, A. Attila József. IQMS, tr. by Edwin Morgan

True Measure of Life, The. Philip James Bailey. TreFP Fr. Country Town, A.

True name is not the one that gilds portals, illustrates proceedings, The. Hidden Name. Victor Segalen. BBASP, tr. by Nathaniel Tarn

True obedience. Onitsura. SoOfWa, tr. by Sam Hamill

True or False. Catullus. AWP, tr. by Walter Savage Landor Fr. Carmina.

True Power doth grow on; and her rights are these. (LL) 1801. William Wordsworth. CenSon; Son

True Relation of their Practice at Oxford Town when there an Act is, A. Alicia D'Anvers. EMWP Fr. Oxford-Act, The.

True Son of God, Eternal Light. P. J. Cormican. AH

True Story, A. Marvin Bell. BodElec

True Story Ending in False Hope, A. Pearse Hutchinson. PBCIP

True Story of Snow White, The. Bruce Bennett. ReTh

True storyteller is a, The. Unknown. CA

True Tale, A. Mary Chandler. ECWP

True Tale of Robin Hood, A. Unknown. ESPB

True Thomas. Unknown. See also Thomas the Rhymer [or Rimer]

True Thomas lay o'er yond grassy [or on Huntlie] bank. Thomas the Rhymer. Unknown. FaBoCh; NOBE; OBEV; OxBB; PAI; PoE; RB; TFi

True Thomas on earth was never seen. (LL) Thomas the Rhymer. Unknown. FaBoCh; NOBE; OBEV; OxBB; PAI; PoE; RB; TFi

True to myself am I, and false to all. True to myself am I, and false to all. Mary Elizabeth Coleridge. ViWPN; VWP

True to our God, true to our native land. (LL) Lift Every [or Ev'ry] Voice and Sing. James Weldon Johnson. APT-1; TCAPo

True to the Best. Benjamin Keech. PoToHe

True Use of Music, The. Charles Wesley. SacPr

True we are two grown men. True We Are Two Grown Men. Ed Roberson. GT

True Western Summer. Hildegarde Flanner. APT-2

True wit is Nature to advantage dressed. Pope. HAP Fr. Essay on Criticism, An.

Truganinny. Wendy Rose. HATNAP

Truisms, The. Louis MacNeice. NOBE; OBSV; PNI

Truly. Ingeborg Bachmann. PoSu

Truly alone muley. Times. Weatherly. SeSe

Truly Great. William Henry Davies. OBMV

Truly Great, The. Stephen Spender. *See* I Think Continually of Those Who Were Truly Great

Truly, I live in dark times! To Those Born Later. Bertolt Brecht. AF

Truly in the east / The white bean. Song to Promote Growth. *Unknown.* OBVE, *tr. by* Washington Matthews

Truly it was morning, and few to equal it. Levivot. Saul [*or* Shaul] Tchernichowsky [*or* Tchernichovsky]. MHP, *tr. by* Ruth Finer Mintz

Truly my Satan thou art but a dunce. William Blake. HAP; PeECV; PoE; WeW-3 *Fr.* Gates of Paradise, The.

Truly now. *Unknown.* WoPoe, *tr. by* Dennis Tedlock *Fr.* Popul Vuh, The.

Truly Rich, The. T. Urchard. PWR

Trumpet, The. Ilya Grigoryevich Ehrenburg [*or* Erenburg]. TCRP; TrJP, *tr. by* Yakov Hornstein

Trumpet, The. Felicia Dorothea Hemans. TreFP

Trumpet, The. Edward Thomas. MoBrPo

Trumpet call and grand white stars. Christ. *Unknown.* GrAn, *tr. by* Guy Davenport

Trumpet of Judgement, The. Victor Hugo. SxFrPo, *tr. by* E. H. Blackmore and A. M. Blackmore

Trumpet of Liberty, The. John Taylor. NOEC

Trumpet of Liberty, The. *Unknown.* NOBRP

Trumpet Player. Langston Hughes. NAAL-2v2; TTY

Trumpet's loud clangor, The. Dryden. FaBoWar *Fr.* Song for St Cecilia's Day, 1687, A.

Trumpet's voice hath roused the land, The. Trumpet, The. Felicia Dorothea Hemans. TreFP

Trumpet's voice, loud and authoritative, The. Reasons for Attendance. Philip Larkin. PoPoPo

Trumpet, Shout, Carry! Velemir [*or* Viktor Vladimirovich] Khlebnikov. TCRusP, *tr. by* Kathy Lewis and Bob Perelman

Trumpeter of Fyvie, The. *Unknown.* OxBB (Andrew Lammie.) ESPB

Trumpets. Georg Trakl. PeFWW, *tr. by* David McDuff

Trumpets, The. Jorge de Lima. TCLAP, *tr. by* Luiz Fernández García

Trumpets, trams, cars backfiring, screeching brakes. Days of April '43. George Seferis. PoetW, *tr. by* Edmund Keeley and Philip Sherrard

Trundled from / the strangeness of the sea. Sea-Elephant, The. William Carlos Williams. SAmP

Trunks of birches, like scrolls. A. Velichansky. TCRusP, *tr. by* Daniel Weissbort

Truro. Rose Solari. AmPoNex

Trust. Lizette Woodworth Reese. SWaP

Trust in Me. *Unknown.* AH

Trust me, I have not earned your dear rebuke. Christina Georgina Rossetti. OxBSo *Fr.* Monna Innominata.

Trust me. The world is run on a shoestring. Hard Times. John Ashbery. NoAM

Trust never to another's hand. Elfrida. László Arany. IQMS, *tr. by* Watson Kirkconnell

Trust not that thing called woman: she is worse. Rodomontade on His Cruel Mistress, A. John Wilmot, 2d Earl of Rochester. OxBSP

Trust Thou Thy Love. John Ruskin. OBEV

Trust thrust first tinder kindling grown. Burnt Sienna. Norman Henry Pritchard, II. GT

"Trust us," the Voices said. (LL) Lovely Shall Be Choosers, The. Robert Frost. MoAmPo; NOBA; OxBA; PoE

Trusted the servile womb to breed free men? (LL) Advice to Young Ladies. Alec Derwent Hope. NoAM; NoP-4

Trustful curator has left me alone, The. Museum of Man. Earle Birney. OxBC

Trusting Jesus. Frances Ridley Havergal. SacPr

Truth. "Æ" MoBrPo

Truth. Geoffrey Chaucer. AWP; NAEL-5v1; NoP-4
 (And Trouthe shal delivere, it is no drede.) (LL) NoP-4; SacPr
 (And Truthe shall deliver, it is no dread.) (LL) MiEL; SCGP
 (Flee fro the prees and dwelle with soothfastnesse.) NAEL-6v1; NAEL-7v1; NoP-4; SacPr
 (Fly fro the presse, and dwell with sothfastnesse.) TreFP
 (Good Counsail.) TreFP
 (Truth.) AWP; NAEL-5v1; NoP-4

Truth. William Cowper.

Search for True Religion, The. John Donne. *See* Satires

Truth. Eileen Duggan. PeNZ

Truth. Josephine D. Henderson Heard. CBWP-4

Truth. Claude McKay. BPo

Truth. Jean Valentine. BodElec

Truth. Barrie Wade. OTCP

Truth, The. William Henry Davies. FaBoTw

Truth, The. Randall Jarrell. OxBC

Truth, The. Ted Joans. TTY

Truth, The. Frankie Paino. AmPoNex

Truth About God, The. Anne Carson.
 "Best way to insult God, The." BodElec
 By God. BodElec
 Flexion of God. BodElec
 God Coup, The. BodElec
 God Fit, The. BodElec
 "God had no name." BodElec
 "God is a grand heart cut." BodElec
 God's Handiwork. BodElec
 God's Name. BodElec
 God's Work. BodElec
 "I have a friend who is red hot with pain." BodElec
 "Moonlight in the kitchen is a sign of God." BodElec
 My Religion. BodElec
 "My religion makes no sense." BodElec
 "Sometimes by night I don't know why." BodElec
 "Sometimes God will drop a fit on you." BodElec

Truth About Karen, The. Kenneth Carroll. ISC

Truth about My Sister and Me, The. Anita Endrezze. CDW

Truth about truth is elusive, The. Limerick. *Unknown.* PeLi

Truth at Last. Edward Rowland Sill. APN-2

Truth at Last, The. Fred Chappell. WoPoe

Truth embodied in the Buddhas. Yoel Hoffman. JDP, *tr. by* Yoel Hoffmann

Truth Hall. Muso Soseki. EaWin, *tr. by* W. S. Merwin

Truth Has Perished. Ulma Seligman. TrJP, *tr. by* Joseph Leftwich

Truth I do not stretch or shove, The. Dog, The. Ogden Nash. Spl

Truth I pursued, as Fancy sketch'd the way. Samuel Taylor Coleridge. FaBoEE

Truth in Poetry. George Crabbe. FHYEP *Fr.* Village, The.

"Truth in the cups" men say, dear youth. Theocritus. CAGL, *tr. by* W. Douglas P. Hill *Fr.* Idylls.

Truth Is, The. Linda Hogan. HATNAP; ItWoWo; LTA

Truth is a native, naked beauty; but. Roger Williams. SCAP

Truth—is as old as God. Emily Dickinson. MoAmPo

"Truth Is Blind, The." David Gascoyne. SPE
 (Light fell from the window and the day was done, The.) SPE
 (Truth is Blind, The.) SPE

Truth is, I envy them. Tornados. Thylias Moss. GT; MakPoe

Truth is I loved it, The. Addiction. Sheryl St. Germain. IllVoic

Truth is love and love is truth. Mendacity. Alfred Edgar Coppard. OBMV

Truth is not precision but evidence. Lyn Hejinian. PFTM-2 *Fr.* Oxota.

Truth is that there comes a time, The. Sad Strains of a Gay Waltz. Wallace Stevens. OxBA

Truth Like the Belly of a Woman Turning, The. Gary Snyder. NNaP

Truth-loving Persians do not dwell upon. Persian Version, The. Robert Graves. NOBL; NoAM; NoP-4; OBWP; WeW-3

Truth of truth was being missed, The. The one who was thinking. Pieces O'six—XVIII. Jackson Mac Low. FTOS

Truth Put It. Marianne Vitale. HeMarv

Truth Suppressed, The. Lizelia Augusta Jenkins Moorer. CBWP-3

Truth the Dead Know, The. Anne Sexton. ColAP; LCAP-2; MoAmPo; NoAM; NoP-4; TAP; VCAP

Truth? A pebble of quartz? For once, then, something. (LL) For Once, Then, Something. Robert Frost. APT-1; NOBA; NoAM

Truthful James to the Editor. Bret Harte. APN-2

Try a Little Tenderness. Jimmy Campbell. ReLy

Try hard to stay well. (LL) *Unknown.* SuSp; WoPoe, *tr. by* Charles O. Hartman

Try our Rubber Girl-Friend (air-inflatable). Limerick. *Unknown.* PeLi

Try Smiling. *Unknown.* PWR

Try to avoid inhaling the laden air. (LL) Lovers of the Poor, The. Gwendolyn Brooks. ESEAA; IllVoic; LCAP-2; LTA; NAAL-2v2; NOBA; NoAM

Try to cover your shivering shoulders in rags of the oldest. Try to Cover Your Shivering Shoulders. Irina Ratushinskaya [*or* Ratushinskaia]. AF

Try to keep them, poet. When They Come Alive. Constantine P. Cavafy. CAGL, *tr. by* Edmund Keeley and Philip Sherrard

Try to see the spring here. Letter. Sarah Ruden. AmPoNex

Try to think that love's not around. Angel Eyes. Matt Dennis. ReLy

Try Tropic. Genevieve Taggard. APT-2; MoAmPo

Try, try again. (LL)   Try, Try Again.   T. H. Palmer.   ChAP; ITBLP

Trying Again.   Dahlia Ravikovitch [*or* Ravikovich].   VCWP

Trying on a hat in the shop.   Dangerous Hats.   Richard Garcia.   TouFir

Trying on New-Made Clothes: Three Poems.   Hsüeh T'ao.
   "In your astral palace, I."   WoPoe, *tr. by* Jeanne Larsen
   "Nine humors split and woven, The."   WoPoe, *tr. by* Jeanne Larsen
   "This skirt's in the style."   WoPoe, *tr. by* Jeanne Larsen

Trying so hard.   Sunbathing.   Nancy Travis.   ISC

Trying to bite off her tongue. (LL)   After the Fall of Saigon.   Yusef
   Komunyakaa.   AF; CDa

Trying to chop mother down is like.   She Went to Stay.   Robert Creeley.
   OBAL

Trying to forget him.   Alexis Rotella.   HA

Trying to open locked doors with a sword, threading.   Sojourn in the Whale.
   Marianne Craig Moore.   NALW

Trying to Pray.   James Wright (1927–80).   BBASP

Trying to sleep by the lake.   Waiting for the End of the War.   Thomas Brush.
   CDa

Trying to speak means flailing with.   Winged Words.   Rachel Hadas.   FFC

Trying to Talk with a Man.   Adrienne Rich.   HCAP

Trying to understand the words.   Bird-Language.   W. H. Auden.   OWoS

Tryst.   Olga Broumas.   WiU

Tryst.   John Hewitt.   BiHa

Tryst.   Sunanda Tripathy.   OMIP, *tr. by* Jagannath Prasad Das

Tryst, The.   Harriet Prescott Spofford.   SWaP

Tryst, The.   John Banister Tabb.   OBAL

Tryst, The.   Mary E. Tucker.   CBWP-1

Tryst, The.   *Unknown*.   OBWVE, *tr. by* Joseph P. Clancy

Tryst [*or* Trysting Place], The.   William Soutar.   EBEV; NPeEn; NePenScot;
   OxBS
   (Trysting Place, The.)   BoLoP

Trystan and Esyllt.   *Unknown*.   OBWVE, *tr. by* Gwyn Jones

Trysting, A.   Richard Dehmel.   AWP, *tr. by* Jethro Bithell

Trysting Bush, The.   Joanna Baillie.   WPE
   (Scotch Song, A.)   RWP

Trysting Place, The.   William Soutar.   *See* Tryst [*or* Trysting Place], The

Ts'ai Chi'h.   Ezra Pound.   NoP-4

Tsa'lagi Council Tree.   Gladys Cardiff.   HATNAP

Tsar! Send out a shot!   Velemir [*or* Viktor Vladimirovich] Khlebnikov.   TCRP
   Fr. Washerwoman.

Tselkov: An Interpretation.   Lev Vladimir Loseff [*or* Losev].   TCRP, *tr. by*
   Walter Arndt

Tsiek tsiek and again tsiek tsiek.   Mu-Lan.   *Unknown*.   WoPoe, *tr. by* Hans H.
   Frankel

Tsitsa.   Kofi Anyidoho.   NAfrP

Tsu Mei is early dead.   Chang Yu.   Reading the Poems of an Absent Friend.
   Ou-yang Hsiu.   OHPC, *tr. by* Kenneth Rexroth

Tsuneko—Psychiatric Medications Clinic.   Susan Kolodny.   OPRER

Ttest.   Lee Ranaldo.   HeMarv

Tu / cson's of blackmens.   Ron Welburn.   NBV

Tu Do Street.   Yusef Komunyakaa.   LTA; SwNoth

Tu-lu, Tu-lu, evil waters running muddy.   Tu-lu Poem.   Yang Wei-chen.
   CoBLCP, *tr. by* Jonathan Chaves

"Tu Non Se' in Terra, Si Come Tu Credi."   Kathleen Jessie Raine.   WPE

Tua Mariit Wemen and the Wedo, The.   William Dunbar.
   "Deid is now that dyvour and dollin in erd."   RACG
   Widow Has Buried Her Second Husband, The.   RACG

Tub with no bottom, A.   Buson.   EH, *tr. by* Robert Hass

Tube.   W.C.W. Watching Presley's Second Appearance on The Ed Sullivan
   Show: Mercy Hospital, Newark, 1956.   David Wojahn.   AllShUp;
   SwNoth

Tube Ride to Martha's.   Matthew Sweeney.   ModIr

Tube Time.   Eve Merriam.   TLR

Tubes.   Terry Wolverton.   WiU

Tubman Strong.   Darryl Holmes.   InTrad

Tubs of / memory.   Roof Garden.   James Schuyler.   OBGa

Tuckanuck, I.   George Cabot Lodge.   APN-2

Tuckett. Bill Tuckett. Telegraph operator, Hall's Creek.   Morse.   Les A.
   Murray.   NoP-4

Tudor indeed is gone and every rose.   Ezra Pound.   FaBoTw; WoPoe   *Fr.*
   Cantos.

Tuesday Night Affair.   Sandra Turner Bond.   ISC

Tuesday; or, the Ditty.   John Gay.   NOEC   *Fr.* Shepherd's Week, The.

Tuesday Shaman.   Maurice Kilwein Guevara.   TouFir

Tuesday, torrential downpours blackened.   ArabInnocents.   Joanna Kadi.
   PoArWo

Tuft of Flowers, The.   Robert Frost.   APT-1; AWP; MoAmPo; NAAL-2v2;
   OxBA

Tuft of Kelp, The.   Herman Melville.   APN-2; FaBoEE

Tug with bright streets at lonely lights like his. (LL)   Flying at Night.   Ted
   Kooser.   InPK-6; PBCAP

Tugela River.   William Plomer.   PeSAV

Tugged Hand, The.   William Henry Davies.   TCAWP

Tuglik's Song.   Tuglik.   WoPoe, *tr. by* Stephen Berg

Tugs my divining rod with the habit some call hope. (LL)   Buried Stream, The.
   James Keir Baxter.   HarvBoo; OxBC

Tulip.   Penny Harter.   TWW

Tulip.   Humbert Wolfe.   MoBrPo

Tulip Bed, The.   William Carlos Williams.   OBGa

Tulip, just opened, had offered to hold, A.   Butterfly's Dream, The.   Hannah
   Flagg Gould.   SWaP

Tulip or turnip, rosebud or rhubarb.   Tulip or Turnip.   Duke Ellington.   ReLy

Tulip shits on the lawn, The.   Flower Piece.   Gerhard Rühm.   PFTM-2, *tr. by*
   Rosmarie Waldrop

Tulip Time in Sing Sing.   P. G. Wodehouse.   ReLy

Tulip Tree.   Sacheverell Sitwell.   MoBrPo

Tulips.   Medbh McGuckian.   PNI

Tulips.   Sylvia Plath.   HAP; NoP-4; PAI; WPE; WeW-3

Tulips.   Mieke Tillema.   TuT, *tr. by* Joan McBreen

Tulips are too excitable, it is winter here, The.   Tulips.   Sylvia Plath.   HAP;
   NoP-4; PAI; WPE; WeW-3

Tulips I do not love, they seem.   Tulips.   Mieke Tillema.   TuT, *tr. by* Joan
   McBreen

Tulips, like Americans.   Considering Tulips.   Mieke Tillema.   TuT, *tr. by*
   Medbh McGuckian

Tullochgorum.   John Skinner.   OxBS

Tully, the queen of beauty's boast.   Molly Moor.   George Farewell.   NOEC

Tullynoe: Tête-à-Tête in the Parish Priest's Parlour.   Paul Durcan.   ModIr;
   NPeEn; OBCoV

Tumadir al-Khansa for Her Brother.   *Unknown*.   AWP   *Fr.* Thousand and One
   Nights, The.

Tumble me down, and I will sit.   To Fortune.   Robert Herrick.   CavPo;
   OxBSP

Tumbled out of heaven.   Blue Day Journey, The.   Gwyn Jones.   OBWVE

Tumbling Dice.   Rachel Loden.   SwNoth

Tumbling in big solitary drops.   Sexual Water.   Pablo Neruda.   PFTM-1

Tumult in a Syrian town had place, A.   Sadi [*or* Saadi *or* Sa'di].   AWP, *tr. by*
   Sir Edward Arnold   *Fr.* Gulistan, The.

Tumult in the street!, A.   *Unknown*.   GrAn

Tumult of death, dizziness hath seized me, The.   Elegy (for Himself).   Moses
   Rimos of Majorca.   TrJP, *tr. by* Israel Abrahams

Tumult of my fretted mind, The.   Self-Analysis.   Anna Wickham.   MoBrPo

Tumult, weeping, many new ghosts.   Snow Storm.   Tu Fu.   BLT; OHPC, *tr.
   by* Kenneth Rexroth

Tumultuous sea, whose wrath and foam are spent.   Eumares.   Asclepiades.
   AWP, *tr. by* Richard Garnett

Tunbridge Wells.   John Wilmot, 2d Earl of Rochester.   OBSV

Tundra, The.   John Haines.   CoAmPo

Tundra is a living, The.   Tundra, The.   John Haines.   CoAmPo

Tune.   Robert Kelly.   FTOS

Tune, A.   Arthur Symons.   BoLoP

Tune: "A Riverside Town."   Su Tung-p'o (Su Shih).   ColAnChi, *tr. by*
   Jiaosheng Wang

Tune: "A Thousand Autumns."   Huang T'ing-chien.   ColAnChi, *tr. by* J. R.
   Hightower

Tune: "Airing Inmost Feelings."   Li Ch'ing-chao.   ColAnChi, *tr. by* Jiaosheng
   Wang

Tune: "Always Having Fun."   Su Tung-p'o (Su Shih).   ColAnChi, *tr. by* J. R.
   Hightower

Tune: "As If in a Dream."   Nara Singde.   ColAnChi, *tr. by* David McCraw

Tune: "As in a Dream; a Song."   Li Ch'ing-chao.   BoWoP; SuSp, *tr. by*
   Eugene Eoyang

Tune: "As in a Dream; a Song."   Su Tung-p'o (Su Shih).   SuSp, *tr. by* Irving
   Y. Lo

Tune: "Autumn Waters"—Listening to Rain.   Na-lan Hsing-te.   SuSp, *tr. by*
   Bruce Carpenter

Tune: "Bean Leaves Yellow."   Lu Yu.   SuSp, *tr. by* James J. Y. Liu

Tune: "Beating Silk Floss."   Li Yü.   ColAnChi, *tr. by* Jiaosheng Wang

Tune: "Beautiful Barbarians."   Li Po.   ChinPo, *tr. by* Yip Wai-lim

Tune: "Beautiful Barbarians."   Wen T'ing-yün.   ChinPo, *tr. by* Yip Wai-lim

Tune: "Beautiful Lady Yü, The."   Chou Pang-yen.
   "About to leave, yet by the lamplight she lingers."   SuSp
   "Sparse fence, winding path, a small farmhouse."   SuSp

Tune: "Beautiful Lady Yü, The."   Li Yü.   SuSp, *tr. by* Eugene Eoyang

Tune: "Beautiful Lady Yü, The"—Spring Sorrow. Ch'en Liang. SuSp, tr. by Hellmut Wilhelm

Tune: "Beauty Yu." Li Yü. ChinPo, tr. by Yip Wai-lim

Tune becomes a flower, The. Georgy [or Georgii] Vladimirovich Ivanov. TCRP

Tune: "Bells in the Rain." Liu Yung. ChinPo, tr. by Yip Wai-lim

Tune: "Bells Ringing in the Rain." Liu Yung. ColAnChi, tr. by Jiaosheng Wang

Tune: "Big String of Words A"—The Great Wall. Na-lan Hsing-te. SuSp, tr. by Lenore Mayhew

Tune: "Butterflies." Kuan Yün-shih. SuSp, tr. by Richard John Lynn Fr. Medley of Southern and Northern Tunes—Scenic Tour of West Lake.

Tune: "Butterflies Lingering over Flowers." Kung Tzu-chen. SuSp, tr. by Irving Y. Lo

Tune: "Butterflies Lingering over Flowers." Nara Singde. ColAnChi, tr. by David McCraw

Tune: "Butterflies Lingering over Flowers." Ou-yang Hsiu. SuSp, tr. by Eugene Eoyang

Tune: "Butterflies Lingering over Flowers." Ou-yang Hsiu. SuSp, tr. by Jerome P. Seaton

Tune: "Butterflies Lingering over Flowers." Su Tung-p'o (Su Shih). ColAnChi, tr. by Jiaosheng Wang

Tune: "Butterflies Lingering over Flowers." Wang Kuo-wei. SuSp, tr. by Ching-i Tu

Tune: "Butterflies Lingering over Flowers." Yen Chi-tao. SuSp, tr. by An-yan Tang

Tune: "Butterflies Lingering over Flowers"—Leaving the Border. Na-lan Hsing-te. SuSp, tr. by An-yan Tang

Tune: "Calming Windswept Waves." Su Tung-p'o (Su Shih). ColAnChi, tr. by Jiaosheng Wang

Tune: "Casket of Pearls, A." Li Yü. SuSp, tr. by Daniel Bryant

Tune: "Celebration in the Eastern Plain"—Replying to a Lyric Song by the Senior Poet Ma Chih-yüan. Unknown. SuSp, tr. by Sherwin S. S. Fu

Tune: "Ch'ing-P'ing Song." Huang T'ing-chien. ChinPo, tr. by Yip Wai-lim

Tune: "Charm of Nien-nu." Chiang K'uei. SuSp, tr. by James J. Y. Liu

Tune: "Charm of Nien-nu, The." Chu Tun-ju. SuSp, tr. by Irving Y. Lo

Tune: "Charm of Nien-nu, The." Li Ch'ing-chao. SuSp, tr. by Eugene Eoyang

Tune: "Charming Nien-Nu." Su Tung-p'o (Su Shih). ChinPo, tr. by Yip Wai-lim

Tune: "Chilly East Wind." Kuan Yün-shih. SuSp, tr. by Richard John Lynn Fr. Medley of Southern and Northern Tunes—Scenic Tour of West Lake.

Tune: "Chrysanthemums Fresh." Liu Yung. SuSp, tr. by James J. Y. Liu

Tune: "Clear River, a Prelude"—Lovesickness. Hsü Tsai-ssu. SuSp, tr. by Sherwin S. S. Fu

Tune: "Coda." Kuan Yün-shih. SuSp, tr. by Richard John Lynn Fr. Medley of Southern and Northern Tunes—Scenic Tour of West Lake.

Tune: "Courtyard Full of Fragrance." Ch'in Kuan. SuSp, tr. by James J. Y. Liu

Tune: "Courtyard Full of Fragrance, The." Huang T'ing-chien. ColAnChi, tr. by J. R. Hightower

Tune: "Crows Crying at Night." Li Yü. SuSp, tr. by Daniel Bryant

Tune: Crows Crying at Night. Li Yü. CoBCP, tr. by Burton Watson

Tune: "Dance of the Cavalry." Li Yü. SuSp, tr. by Daniel Bryant

Tune: "Decorous and Pretty." Kung Tzu-chen. SuSp, tr. by An-yan Tang

Tune: "Decorous and Pretty"—Respectfully Offered to Circuit Inspector Kao. Liu Chih. SuSp, tr. by Richard John Lynn

Tune: Deva-like Barbarian. Li Yü. CoBCP, tr. by Burton Watson

Tune: "Deva-like Barbarian." Li Yü. SuSp, tr. by Daniel Bryant

Tune: "Deva-like Barbarian." Unknown. SuSp, tr. by Hellmut Wilhelm

Tune: Deva-like Barbarian. Wei Chuang. CoBCP, tr. by Burton Watson

Tune: "Deva-like Barbarian." Wei Chuang. SuSp, tr. by Lois M. Fusek

Tune: Deva-like Barbarian. Wen T'ing-yün. CoBCP, tr. by Burton Watson

Tune: "Deva-like Barbarian"—Ta-po-ti. Mao Tse-tung [or Mao Zedong]. SuSp, tr. by Eugene Eoyang

Tune: "Dim Fragrance"—Plum Blossoms. Chiang K'uei. SuSp, tr. by An-yan Tang

Tune: "Distant Red Window." Chou Pang-yen. SuSp, tr. by Irving Y. Lo

Tune: "Dream Song." Li Ch'ing-chao. ChinPo, tr. by Yip Wai-lim

Tune: "Dreaming of Southland" Thinking of Someone. Liu Shih. ColAnChi, tr. by Kang-i Sun Chang

Tune: Dreaming of the South. Wen T'ing-yün. CoBCP, tr. by Burton Watson

Tune: "Dreaming of the South." Wen T'ing-yün. SuSp, tr. by William R. Schultz

Tune: Drunk among the Flowers. Mao Wen-hsi. CoBCP, tr. by Burton Watson

Tune: "Drunk in Fairyland." Ou-yang Hsiu. ColAnChi, tr. by J. R. Hightower

Tune: "Drunk in the East Wind." Lu Chih. ChinPo, tr. by Yip Wai-lim

Tune: "Echoing Heaven's Everlastingness." Li Ching. SuSp, tr. by Daniel Bryant

Tune: "Echoing Heaven's Everlastingness." Wang Kuo-wei. SuSp, tr. by Ching-i Tu

Tune: "Eight-beat Barbarian Tune." Sun Kuang-hsien. SuSp, tr. by Hellmut Wilhelm

Tune: "Eight Beats of a Kan-chou Song." Liu Yung. ColAnChi; SuSp, tr. by James J. Y. Liu

Tune: "Eternal Longing." Unknown. SuSp, tr. by Hellmut Wilhelm

Tune: Eternal Longing. Unknown. ColAnChi, tr. by Elling O. Eide Fr. Four Tz'u from Tun-huang.

Tune: Eternal Longing. Unknown. ColAnChi, tr. by Burton Watson Fr. Four Tz'u from Tun-huang.

Tune: "Fisherman's Pride." Li Ch'ing-chao. ColAnChi, tr. by Jiaosheng Wang

Tune: Flirtatious Laughter. Wei Ying-wu. CoBCP, tr. by Burton Watson

Tune: "Flower unlike Flower." Po Chü-i. SuSp, tr. by Eugene Eoyang

Tune: "Four Pieces of Jade." Kuan Han-ch'ing. ChinPo, tr. by Yip Wai-lim

Tune: "Four Pieces of Jade"—Idle Leisure. Kuan Han-ch'ing. SuSp, tr. by Jerome Seaton

Tune: "Four Pieces of Jade"—Retirement. Ma Chih-yüan. SuSp, tr. by Sherwin S. S. Fu

Tune: "Fragrance Fills the Courtyard." Su Tung-p'o (Su Shih). ColAnChi, tr. by J. R. Hightower

Tune: "Full Court of Fragrance." Yao Sui. ChinPo, tr. by Yip Wai-lim

Tune: "Full Moon in the Human World"—Spring Evening: Replying to a Song. Unknown. SuSp, tr. by Sherwin S. S. Fu

Tune: "Full River Red." Hsin Ch'i-chi. SuSp, tr. by Irving Y. Lo

Tune: "Full River Red"—A Four-season Song on the Hardships and Joys of Farming Life. Cheng Hsieh. SuSp, tr. by Irving Y. Lo

Tune: "Full River Red"—A Reply to Kuo Mo-jo. Mao Tse-tung [or Mao Zedong]. SuSp, tr. by Eugene Eoyang

Tune: "Gathering Mulberry Leaves." Ou-yang Hsiu. ColAnChi, tr. by J. R. Hightower

Tune: Gazing at the South. Li Yü. CoBCP, tr. by Burton Watson

Tune: "Gazing at the South." Li Yü. SuSp, tr. by Daniel Bryant

Tune: "Going Up Small Pavilion." Kuan Yün-shih. SuSp, tr. by Richard John Lynn Fr. Medley of Southern and Northern Tunes—Scenic Tour of West Lake.

Tune: "Green Jade Cup." Kung Tzu-chen. SuSp, tr. by An-yan Tang

Tune: "Green Jade Cup"—Lantern Festival. Hsin Ch'i-chi. SuSp, tr. by Irving Y. Lo

Tune: "Green Jade Flute." Kuan Han-ch'ing.

  "Fear, as I see the spring go." SuSp

  "Lightly she turns back her long red sleeves." SuSp

  "This autumn scene is worthy of the brush." SuSp

  "Wind sifts through the curtain." SuSp

Tune: "Greeting the Immortal Guest." Yün-k'an Tzu. SuSp, tr. by Jerome P. Seaton

Tune: "Groping for Fish." Hsin Ch'i-chi. SuSp, tr. by Irving Y. Lo

Tune: "Hairpin Phoenix." Lu Yu. ChinPo, tr. by Yip Wai-lim

Tune: "Happily Flitting Oriole." Wu Li. ColAnChi, tr. by Jonathan Chaves

Tune: "Happiness Approaches." Ch'in Kuan. ColAnChi, tr. by Jiaosheng Wang

Tune: "Happy Events Approaching." Ch'in Kuan. SuSp, tr. by James J. Y. Liu

Tune: "Happy Events Approaching." Chu Tun-ju. SuSp, tr. by James J. Y. Liu

Tune: "Happy Events Approaching." Kuan Yün-shih. SuSp, tr. by Richard John Lynn Fr. Medley of Southern and Northern Tunes—Scenic Tour of West Lake.

Tune: "Heaven-Cleansed Sands." Ma Chih-yüan. ColAnChi, tr. by Victor H. Mair

Tune: "Hung Hsiu-hsieh" To a Flea. Yang Na. ColAnChi, tr. by James I. Crump

Tune: "Immortal at the Magpie Bridge." Lu Yu. SuSp, tr. by James J. Y. Liu

Tune: Immortal at the River. Su Tung-p'o (Su Shih). CoBCP

Tune: "Immortal at the River." Su Tung-p'o (Su Shih). SuSp, tr. by Michael E. Workman

Tune: "Immortal at the River." Wang Kuo-wei. SuSp, tr. by Ching-i Tu and Ching-i Tu

Tune: "Immortal at the River"—Ascending a Little Tower at Night. Ch'en Yü-yi. SuSp, tr. by James J. Y. Liu

Tune: "Immortal at the River"—Winter Willow. Na-lan Hsing-te. SuSp, tr. by Irving Y. Lo

Tune: "Immortal at the Riverbank." Ch'en Yü-yi. ColAnChi, tr. by Jiaosheng Wang

Tune: "Immortal by the River." Su Tung-p'o (Su Shih). ChinPo, tr. by Yip Wai-lim

Tune: "Immortal by the River." Su Tung-p'o (Su Shih). ColAnChi, tr. by J. R. Hightower

Tune: "Immortal's Auspicious Crane, An"—On Plum Blossoms. Hsin Ch'i-chi. SuSp, tr. by Irving Y. Lo

Tune: "Intoxication in the East Wind." Kuan Han-ch'ing.
  "Grief: I've grieved as a solitary phoenix grieves." SuSp
  "Heaven in the South, earth Northward." SuSp
Tune: "Intoxication in the East Wind" Autumn Scenery. Lu Chih. SuSp, tr. by Sherwin S. S. Fu
Tune is cowboy, The; the words, sentimental crap. D-Y Bar. James Welch. CDW
Tune: "Jade Butterflies." Liu Yung. SuSp, tr. by Jerome P. Seaton
Tune: "Joy All Under Heaven"—Sunset on the Western Hill. Hsü Tsai-ssu. SuSp, tr. by Sherwin S. S. Fu
Tune: "Joy at Meeting." Li Yü. SuSp, tr. by Eugene Eoyang
Tune: "Joy in Spring's Coming"—Seven Songs. Unknown. SuSp, tr. by Wayne Schlepp
Tune: "Joy of Encounter." Li Yü. ColAnChi, tr. by Jiaosheng Wang
Tune: "Joy of Eternal Union." Li Ch'ing-chao. ColAnChi, tr. by Jiaosheng Wang
Tune: "Joy of Eternal Union"—Passing the Seven-league Shallows. Su Tung-p'o (Su Shih). SuSp, tr. by Irving Y. Lo
Tune: "Joy of Returning to the Fields." Huang T'ing-chien. ColAnChi, tr. by J. R. Hightower
Tune: Lotus-leaf Cup. Wei Chuang. CoBCP, tr. by Burton Watson
Tune: "Lotus-leaf Cup." Wen T'ing-yün. SuSp, tr. by William R. Schultz
Tune: "Magnolia Blossoms, Abbreviated." Chu Tun-ju. SuSp, tr. by James J. Y. Liu
Tune: "Magnolia Blossoms, Abbreviated." Li Ch'ing-chao. SuSp, tr. by Eugene Eoyang
Tune: "Magnolia Blossoms, Slow"—Traveling on the Yangtze. Chiang Ch'un-lin. SuSp, tr. by Bruce Carpenter
Tune: "Magnolia Flower." Ou-yang Hsiu. ColAnChi, tr. by J. R. Hightower
Tune: "Magnolia Flowers." Jiaosheng Wang. ColAnChi
Tune: "Magpie on the Branch." Feng Yen-ssu. SuSp, tr. by Daniel Bryant
Tune: Magpie on the Branch. Unknown. CoBCP; ColAnChi, tr. by Burton Watson Fr. Four Tz'u from Tun-huang.
Tune: "Manifold Little Hills." Li Ch'ing-chao. SuSp, tr. by Eugene Eoyang
Tune: "Memories of the South." Li Yü. ColAnChi, tr. by Jiaosheng Wang
Tune: "Memories of the South." Liu Yu Hsi. ColAnChi, tr. by Jiaosheng Wang
Tune: "Memories of the South." Po Chü-i. ColAnChi, tr. by Jiaosheng Wang
Tune: "Merriment Before the Palace Hall." Chang K'o-chiu. ChinPo, tr. by Yip Wai-lim
Tune: "Midnight Music." Liu Yung. SuSp, tr. by James J. Y. Liu
Tune: "Moon of the Western River." Hsin Ch'i-chi. ChinPo, tr. by Yip Wai-lim
Tune: "Moth Fluttering Against Lamp." Kuan Yün-shih. SuSp, tr. by Richard John Lynn Fr. Medley of Southern and Northern Tunes—Scenic Tour of West Lake.
Tune: "Mountain Hawthorns." Wang An-shih. SuSp, tr. by James J. Y. Liu
Tune: "Mountain Hawthorns." Yen Chi-tao. SuSp, tr. by James J. Y. Liu
Tune: "New Bounty of Royalty." Li Yü. ColAnChi, tr. by Jiaosheng Wang
Tune: "Nien-nu Is Charming." Chu Tun-ju. ColAnChi, tr. by J. R. Hightower
Tune of non-being, A. Daido Ichi'i. JDP, tr. by Yoel Hoffmann
Tune: "On the Trail of Sweet Incense." Li Ch'ing-chao. ColAnChi, tr. by Jiaosheng Wang
Tune: "Overtures"—On Myself. Ch'iao Chi. SuSp, tr. by Sherwin S. S. Fu
Tune: "Pacifying the Western Barbarians." Wen T'ing-yün. SuSp, tr. by William R. Schultz
Tune: Palace of Night Revels. Chou Pang-yen. CoBCP, tr. by Burton Watson
Tune: "Pale-golden Willows." Chiang K'uei. SuSp, tr. by Chiang Yee
Tune: "Partridge Sky." Huang T'ing-chien. SuSp, tr. by James J. Y. Liu
Tune: "Partridge Sky." Li Ch'ing-chao. ColAnChi, tr. by Jiaosheng Wang
Tune: "Partridge Sky." Su Tung-p'o (Su Shih). ColAnChi, tr. by Jiaosheng Wang
Tune: Partridge Sky. Su Tung-p'o (Su Shih). CoBCP, tr. by Burton Watson
Tune: Partridge Sky" At Po-shan Monastery. Hsin Ch'i-chi. ColAnChi, tr. by Jiaosheng Wang
Tune: "Partridge Sky" For a Friend. Hsin Ch'i-chi. ColAnChi, tr. by Jiaosheng Wang
Tune: "Partridge Sky" I Rejoice to Meet a Friend Visting at My Rustic Study. Ch'iao Lai. ColAnChi, tr. by Jiaosheng Wang
Tune: "Partridge Sky"—Parting Sorrows. Na-lan Hsing-te. SuSp, tr. by William Golightly
Tune: "Partridge Sky"—Puppet Theater. Ku T'ai-ch'ing. SuSp, tr. by Irving Y. Lo
Tune: "Partridge Sky"—Written at the Po-shan Monastery. Hsin Ch'i-chi. SuSp, tr. by Irving Y. Lo
Tune: "Paying Homage at the Golden Gate." Sun Kuang-hsien. SuSp, tr. by Hellmut Wilhelm
Tune: "Perfumed Garden." Ch'in Kuan. ColAnChi, tr. by Jiaosheng Wang
Tune: Phoenix Hairpin. Lu Yu. CoBCP, tr. by Burton Watson

Tune: "Phoenix Hairpin." Lu Yu. SuSp, tr. by James J. Y. Liu
Tune: "Phoenix Hairpin"—Crab Apple. Ku T'ai-ch'ing. SuSp, tr. by Irving Y. Lo
Tune: "Picking Mulberry Seeds" Written on a Wall en route to Po-shan. Hsin Ch'i-chi. ColAnChi, tr. by Jiaosheng Wang
Tune: "Pleasure in Front of the Hall." Lu Chih.
  "Be a loafer / Wash off the dust of fame and gain in the vast waves." SuSp
  "Wine in the cup is heavy." SuSp
Tune: "Pleasure of Returning to the Fields: A Prelude." Huang T'ing-chien. SuSp, tr. by James J. Y. Liu
Tune: "Po Pu-tuan" Fat Couple. Wang Ho-ch'ing. ColAnChi, tr. by James I. Crump
Tune: "Po Pu-tuan" Long-Haired Little Dog. Wang Ho-ch'ing. ColAnChi, tr. by James I. Crump
Tune: "Pomegranate Blossoms." Kuan Yün-shih. SuSp, tr. by Richard John Lynn Fr. Medley of Southern and Northern Tunes—Scenic Tour of West Lake.
Tune: "Prelude to Allure Goddesses." Liu Yung. SuSp, tr. by Jerome P. Seaton
Tune: Prelude to Water Music. Su Tung-p'o (Su Shih). CoBCP, tr. by Burton Watson
Tune: "Prelude to Water Music." Su Tung-p'o (Su Shih). SuSp, tr. by Eugene Eoyang
Tune: "Prince Lan-Ling." Chou Pang-yen. ChinPo, tr. by Yip Wai-lim
Tune: "Prince of Lan-ling" (Lan-ling Wang)—on Willows. Chou Pang-yen. SuSp, tr. by Irving Y. Lo
Tune: "Pure Serene Music." Chang Yen. ColAnChi, tr. by Jiaosheng Wang
Tune: "Pure Serene Music." Huang T'ing-chien. SuSp, tr. by James J. Y. Liu
Tune: "Pure Serene Music." Li Ch'ing-chao. SuSp
Tune: "Pure Serene Music." Li Yü. ColAnChi, tr. by Jiaosheng Wang
Tune: Pure Serene Music. Li Yü. CoBCP, tr. by Burton Watson
Tune: "Pure Serene Music." Li Yü. SuSp, tr. by Daniel Bryant
Tune: "Pure Serene Music" En Route to Po-shan. Hsin Ch'i-chi. ColAnChi, tr. by Jiaosheng Wang
Tune: "Pure Serene Music" Rural Life. Hsin Ch'i-chi. ColAnChi, tr. by Jiaosheng Wang
Tune: "Rapt with Wine, Loudly Singing; Joy in Spring's Coming." Kuan Yün-shih. ColAnChi; SuSp, tr. by Richard John Lynn
Tune: "Red Embroidered Slippers"—Spring Night. Unknown. SuSp, tr. by Sherwin S. S. Fu
Tune: "Remembering the Lady of Ch'in—At the Mouth of Dragon Pool." Na-lan Hsing-te. SuSp, tr. by Lenore Mayhew
Tune: "Remembering the Lady of Ch'in"—Loushan Pass. Mao Tse-tung [or Mao Zedong]. SuSp, tr. by Eugene Eoyang
Tune: "Remembering the Prince." Na-lan Hsing-te. SuSp, tr. by William Golightly
Tune: Ripples Sifting Sand. Li Yü. CoBCP, tr. by Burton Watson
Tune: "Ripples Sifting Sand." Li Yü. SuSp, tr. by Daniel Bryant
Tune: "Ripples Sifting Sand." Liu Yu Hsi. SuSp, tr. by Daniel Bryant
Tune: "Ripples Sifting Sand." Po Chü-i.
  "How can the tide of the river be compared to your love?" SuSp
  "There'll be a day when dust flies at the bottom of the sea." SuSp
Tune: "Ripples Sifting Sand: A Song." Li Yü. SuSp, tr. by Daniel Bryant
Tune: "Ripples Sifting Sand"—Accompanying My Husband on a Spring Outing to Stone Pavilion. Ku T'ai-ch'ing. SuSp, tr. by Irving Y. Lo
Tune: "River Messages." Wen T'ing-yün. SuSp, tr. by William R. Schultz
Tune: "River Town." Su Tung-p'o (Su Shih). ColAnChi, tr. by J. R. Hightower
Tune: "Rouged Lips." Ch'in Kuan. ColAnChi, tr. by Jiaosheng Wang
Tune: "Rouged Lips." Li Ch'ing-chao. ColAnChi, tr. by Jiaosheng Wang
Tune: "Rouged Lips." Wang Kuo-wei. ColAnChi, tr. by Jiaosheng Wang
Tune: "Rouged Lips" Rain Just Over on the Night of the Lantern Preview. Wu Wen-ying. ColAnChi, tr. by Jiaosheng Wang
Tune's image holding in the line, The. (LL) Louis Zukofsky. APT-2; VGW
Tune: "Sailing at Night"—A Song Sequence. Ma Chih-yüan. SuSp, tr. by Sherwin S. S. Fu
Tune: "San-fan Yü-lou Jen." Unknown. ColAnChi, tr. by James I. Crump
Tune: "Sand of Silk-Washing Brook." Ch'in Kuan. ColAnChi, tr. by Jiaosheng Wang
Tune: "Sand of Silk-Washing Brook." Wang Kuo-wei. ColAnChi, tr. by Jiaosheng Wang
Tune: "Sand of Silk-Washing Brook." Yen Shu. ColAnChi, tr. by Jiaosheng Wang
Tune: "Sand of Silk-Washing Brook" A Reminiscence. Wu Wen-ying. ColAnChi, tr. by Jiaosheng Wang
Tune: "Sand of Silk-Washing Brook" In Memoriam. Nara Singde. ColAnChi, tr. by Jiaosheng Wang
Tune: "Sand of Silk-washing Stream." Li Ch'ing-chao.
  "In the little courtyard, by the side window." SuSp

"Mild and peaceful spring glow, Cold Food Day." SuSp

Tune: "Sand of Silk-washing Stream." Li Ching. SuSp, *tr.* by Daniel Bryant

Tune: Sand of Silk-washing Stream. Su Tung-p'o (Su Shih). CoBCP, *tr.* by Burton Watson

Tune: Sand of Silk-washing Stream. Su Tung-p'o (Su Shih). CoBCP, *tr.* by Burton Watson

Tune: "Sand of Silk-washing Stream." Wang An-shih. SuSp, *tr.* by James J. Y. Liu

Tune: "Sand of Silk-washing Stream." Wang Kuo-wei. SuSp, *tr.* by Ching-i Tu

Tune: "Sand of Silk-washing Stream." Wei Chuang. SuSp, *tr.* by Lois Fusek

Tune: "Sand of Silk-washing Stream." Wu Wei-yeh. SuSp, *tr.* by Irving Y. Lo

Tune: Sand of Silk-washing Stream ("Flutter, flutter, on clothes and cap, jujube flowers fall"). Su Tung-p'o (Su Shih). CoBCP, *tr.* by Burton Watson *Fr.* Along the Road to Stone Lake.

Tune: Sand of Silk-washing Stream ("Layer on layer of hemp leaves, jute leaves shining"). Su Tung-p'o (Su Shih). CoBCP, *tr.* by Burton Watson *Fr.* Along the Road to Stone Lake.

Tune: Sand of Silk-washing Stream ("Soft grasses, a plain of sedge fresh with passing rain"). Su Tung-p'o (Su Shih). CoBCP, *tr.* by Burton Watson *Fr.* Along the Road to Stone Lake.

Tune: Sand of Silk-washing Stream ("Throw on rouge and powder, watch the governor pass!"). Su Tung-p'o (Su Shih). CoBCP *Fr.* Along the Road to Stone Lake.

Tune: "Sand Washed by Waves." Li Yü. ColAnChi, *tr.* by Jiaosheng Wang

Tune: "Sheep on Mountain Slope." Ch'iao Chi. SuSp, *tr.* by Wayne Schlepp

Tune: "Sheep on Mountain Slope"—Boudoir Thoughts. *Unknown.* SuSp, *tr.* by Hellmut Wilhelm

Tune: "Sheep on Mountain Slope"—Lamenting the Times. Tseng Jui.
"Cock's crow means profit, The." SuSp
"Great success need not be proud." SuSp

Tune: "Sheep on the Mountain Slope." Chang Yang-hao. ChinPo, *tr.* by Yip Wai-lim

Tune: "Sheep on the Mountain Slope." Liu Chih. ChinPo, *tr.* by Yip Wai-lim

Tune: "Shua Hai-erh" Country Cousin at the Theater. Tu Shan-fu. ColAnChi, *tr.* by James I. Crump

Tune: "Six Toughies"—Written after the Roses Have Faded. Chou Pang-yen. SuSp, *tr.* by James J. Y. Liu

Tune: "Sky-clear Sand"—Autumn Thoughts. Ma Chih-yüan. SuSp, *tr.* by Sherwin S. S. Fu

Tune: "Sky-Pure Sand." Ma Chih-yüan. ChinPo, *tr.* by Yip Wai-lim

Tune: "Slow Chant." Ma Chih-yüan. SuSp, *tr.* by Sherwin S. S. Fu

Tune: "Slow Chant"—Kao-tsu's Homecoming. Sui Ching-ch'en. SuSp, *tr.* by Sherwin S. S. Fu

Tune: "Slow Song of Chu Ying-t'ai"—Late Spring. Hsin Ch'i-chi. SuSp, *tr.* by Irving Y. Lo

Tune: "Song of a Dandy." Sun Kuang-hsien. SuSp, *tr.* by Hellmut Wilhelm

Tune: "Song of Clear River." Ma Chih-yüan. ChinPo, *tr.* by Yip Wai-lim

Tune: "Song of Dandy"—Hunting in Autumn. Na-lan Hsing-te. SuSp, *tr.* by Bruce Carpenter

Tune: "Song of Divination." Chu Yi-tsun. SuSp, *tr.* by Irving Y. Lo

Tune: "Song of Divination." Su Tung-p'o (Su Shih). SuSp, *tr.* by Eugene Eoyang

Tune: "Song of Divination"—On the Plum Tree. Lu Yu. SuSp, *tr.* by James J. Y. Liu

Tune: "Song of Divination"—On the Plum Tree, after a Poem by Lu Yu. Mao Tse-tung [*or* Mao Zedong]. SuSp, *tr.* by Eugene Eoyang

Tune: "Song of Divination" Using Quotations from *Chuang-tzu.* Hsin Ch'i-chi. SuSp, *tr.* by Irving Y. Lo

Tune: "Song of Flirtatious Laughter." Wei Ying-wu. SuSp, *tr.* by Hellmut Wilhelm

Tune: "Song of Great Virtue"—Spring. Kuan Han-ch'ing. SuSp, *tr.* by Jerome P. Seaton

Tune: "Song of Great Virtue"—Winter. Kuan Han-ch'ing.
"Snow powder, flowery." SuSp
"Toot once, strum once." SuSp

Tune: Song of Picking Mulberry. Li Ch'ing-chao. CoBCP, *tr.* by Burton Watson

Tune: "Song of Picking Mulberry." Li Ch'ing-chao. SuSp, *tr.* by Eugene Eoyang

Tune: "Song of Picking Mulberry." Wang Kuo-wei. SuSp, *tr.* by Ching-i Tu

Tune: "Song of Picking Mulberry." Wang Kuo-wei. SuSp, *tr.* by Ching-i Tu

Tune: "Song of Picking Mulberry" Double-Ninth Festival. Mao Tse-tung [*or* Mao Zedong]. SuSp, *tr.* by Eugene Eoyang

Tune: "Song of Picking Mulberry"—Recollections of West Lake. Ou-yang Hsiu. SuSp, *tr.* by Jerome P. Seaton

Tune: "Song of Plucking Cassia." Ch'iao Chi. SuSp, *tr.* by Sherwin S. S. Fu

Tune: Song of River City. Su Tung-p'o (Su Shih). CoBCP, *tr.* by Burton Watson

Tune: "Song of River City"—On a Kite. Wu Wei-yeh. SuSp, *tr.* by Irving Y. Lo

Tune: "Song of River Goddess"—Moorinig My Boat at Fen-shui at Night. Huang Shu. SuSp, *tr.* by James J. Y. Liu

Tune: "Song of Shou-yang." Kuan Yün-shih. SuSp, *tr.* by Richard John Lynn

Tune: "Song of Shou-yang." Ma Chih-yüan.
"Lovesickness— / What is the cure?" SuSp
"Voice are still / The moon's bright." SuSp

Tune: "Song of the Lunar Palace." Lu Chih. SuSp, *tr.* by Hellmut Wilhelm

Tune: "Song of the Lunar Palace"—Sending Off Spring. Kuan Yün-shih. SuSp, *tr.* by Richard John Lynn

Tune: "Song of the Southern Country." Chu Yi-tsun. SuSp, *tr.* by Irving Y. Lo

Tune: "Song of the Southern Country." Li Hsün. SuSp, *tr.* by Edward Schafer

Tune: "Song of the Southern Country"—Presented to a Courtesan. Hsin Ch'i-chi. SuSp, *tr.* by Irving Y. Lo

Tune: "Song of the Southern Country"—Spring Thoughts at Pearl River. Chu Yi-tsun. SuSp, *tr.* by Irving Y. Lo

Tune: "Song of the Wine Spring." P'an Lang. SuSp, *tr.* by James J. Y. Liu

Tune: Song of Tzu-yeh. Li Yü. CoBCP, *tr.* by Burton Watson

Tune: "Song of Tzu-yeh." Li Yü. SuSp, *tr.* by Daniel Bryant

Tune: "Southern Song, A." Li Ch'ing-chao. SuSp, *tr.* by Eugene Eoyang

Tune: "Southern Song, A." Wen T'ing-yün. SuSp, *tr.* by William R. Schultz

Tune: "Sparse Shadows"—Plum Blossoms. Chiang K'uei. SuSp, *tr.* by An-yan Tang

Tune: "Sprig of Flowers, A"—Not Bowing to Old Age. Kuan Han-ch'ing. SuSp, *tr.* by Jerome P. Seaton

Tune: "Sprig of Flowers, A"—Written for My "Ugly Studio." Chung Ssu-ch'eng. SuSp, *tr.* by Sherwin S. S. Fu

Tune: Spring at Wu Ling. Li Ch'ing-chao. ColAnChi, *tr.* by Jiaosheng Wang

Tune: "Spring at Wu-ling." Li Ch'ing-chao. SuSp, *tr.* by Eugene Eoyang

Tune: "Spring in Ch'in's Garden." Hsin Ch'i-chi. SuSp, *tr.* by Irving Y. Lo

Tune: "Spring in Ch'in's Garden." Mao Tse-tung [*or* Mao Zedong]. SuSp, *tr.* by Eugene Eoyang

Tune: "Spring in Jade Pavilion." Li Yü. SuSp, *tr.* by Daniel Bryant

Tune: "Spring in Jade Pavilion." Yen Shu. SuSp, *tr.* by An-yan Tang

Tune: "Spring in the Ch'in Garden." Hsin Ch'i-chi. ColAnChi, *tr.* by J. R. Hightower

Tune: "Spring in the Jade House." Yen Shu. ColAnChi, *tr.* by J. R. Hightower

Tune: "Spring in the Painted Hall." Ch'in Kuan. ColAnChi, *tr.* by Jiaosheng Wang

Tune: "Squabbling Quails." Kuan Yün-shih. SuSp, *tr.* by Richard John Lynn *Fr.* Medley of Southern and Northern Tunes—Scenic Tour of West Lake.

Tune: "Stretch of Cloud over Mount Wu, A." Li Hsün. SuSp, *tr.* by Hellmut Wilhelm

Tune: "Sumuche Dancers." Fan Chung-yen. ColAnChi, *tr.* by J. R. Hightower

Tune: "Tartar Tune of Eighteen Beats." *Unknown.* SuSp, *tr.* by Sherwin S. S. Fu

Tune: Telling of Innermost Feelings. Ku Hsiung. CoBCP, *tr.* by Burton Watson

Tune: "Telling of Innermost Feelings." Ku Hsiung. SuSp, *tr.* by James J. Y. Liu

Tune: Telling of Innermost Feelings. Li Ch'ing-chao. CoBCP, *tr.* by Burton Watson

Tune: "Telling of Innermost Feelings." Li Ch'ing-chao. SuSp, *tr.* by Eugene Eoyang

Tune: "Telling of Innermost Feelings." Lu Yu. SuSp, *tr.* by James J. Y. Liu

Tune: "Telling of Innermost Feelings." Wen T'ing-yün. SuSp, *tr.* by William R. Schultz

Tune: "Telling of Innermost Feelings"—Wandering in Spring. Ch'en Tzu-lung. SuSp, *tr.* by Bruce Carpenter

Tune: "The Beauty of Yü" Li Yü. ColAnChi, *tr.* by Jiaosheng Wang

Tune: "The Bodhisattva Foreigner." Wei Chuang. ColAnChi, *tr.* by John Timothy Wixted

Tune: "The Bodhisattva's Golden Headdress." Hsin Ch'i-chi. ColAnChi, *tr.* by Jiaosheng Wang

Tune: "The Charm of a Maiden Singer;" Spring Thoughts. Jiaosheng Wang. ColAnChi

Tune: "The Charm of Nien-nu"—Kunlun Mountains. Mao Tse-tung [*or* Mao Zedong]. SuSp, *tr.* by Eugene Eoyang

Tune: "The Crow's Nocturnal Cry." Li Yü. ColAnChi, *tr.* by Jiaosheng Wang

Tune: "The Dark Clouds of Ch'u" Visiting the Rainy Crag Alone. Hsin Ch'i-chi. ColAnChi, *tr.* by Jiaosheng Wang

Tune: "The Diviner." Li Chih-yi. ColAnChi, *tr.* by Victor H. Mair

Tune: The Fisherman. Li Yü. CoBCP, *tr.* by Burton Watson

Tune the old cow died of, The. Tune the Old Cow Died of, The. Norman Nicholson. EmeKit

Tune: The Taoist Priestess. Wei Chuang. CoBCP, *tr.* by Burton Watson

Tune: "Thinking of the Imperial Capital." Wei Chuang. ColAnChi, *tr.* by John Timothy Wixted

Tune thy music[ke] to thy heart [*or* hart]. Heart's Music. Thomas Campion. OBEV

Tune: "Tipsy in the Flower's Shade." Li Ch'ing-chao. SuSp, *tr. by* Eugene Eoyang

Tune: "Traveler Welcoming the Immortal." Chang K'o-chiu. ChinPo, *tr. by* Yip Wai-lim

Tune: "Treading on Fragrant Grass." Yen Shu. ColAnChi, *tr. by* Jiaosheng Wang

Tune: Treading on Grass. Ou-yang Hsiu. CoBCP, *tr. by* Burton Watson

Tune: "Treading on Grass." Ou-yang Hsiu. SuSp, *tr. by* An-yan Tang

Tune: "Treading on Grass." Yen Shu. SuSp, *tr. by* James J. Y. Liu

Tune: "Trimming the Silver Lamp." Fan Chung-yen. ColAnChi, *tr. by* J. R. Hightower

Tune: "Tsui-chung T'ien" To the Giant Butterfly. Wang Ho-ch'ing. ColAnChi, *tr. by* James I. Crump

Tune: Ugly Rogue. Hsin Ch'i-chi. CoBCP, *tr. by* Burton Watson

Tune: "Unbroken." Chang K'o-chiu. ChinPo, *tr. by* Yip Wai-lim

Tune: "Vast Virtue." Kuan Han-ch'ing. ChinPo, *tr. by* Yip Wai-lim

Tune: "Walk on the Imperial Street." Fan Chung-yen. ChinPo, *tr. by* Yip Wai-lim

Tune: "Wanderings of a Youth." Liu Yung. SuSp, *tr. by* Jerome P. Seaton

Tune: "Water Dragon's Chant" After Chang Chi-fu's Lyric on the Willow Catkin. Su Tung-p'o (Su Shih). SuSp, *tr. by* James J. Y. Liu

Tune: "Water Dragon's Chant"—Loathsome Spring. Ch'en Liang. SuSp, *tr. by* Hellmut Wilhelm

Tune: "Water Mode Song." Su Tung-p'o (Su Shih). ColAnChi, *tr. by* J. R. Hightower

Tune: "Wild Geese Have Come Down; Song of Victory." *Unknown.* SuSp, *tr. by* Sherwin S. S. Fu

Tune: "Wild Geese Have Come Down; Song of Victory"—Idle Leisure. Teng Yu-pin. SuSp, *tr. by* Hellmut Wilhelm

Tune: "Willow Branches." *Unknown.* SuSp, *tr. by* Hellmut Wilhelm

Tune: "Winds of Falling Plums." Ma Chih-yüan. ChinPo, *tr. by* Yip Wai-lim

Tune: "Wu-t'ung Leaves"—Written in Jest at a Banquet. Lu Chih. SuSp, *tr. by* Hellmut Wilhelm

Tune: "Wu Yeh-erh" Twitting the Teller of Tall Tales. *Unknown.* ColAnChi, *tr. by* James I. Crump

Tuned to 104.6 on the FM. Household Gods. Jim Elledge. SwNoth

Tuneful Hipponax rests him here. Epitaph of Hipponax. Theocritus. FaBoEE, *tr. by* Charles Stuart Calverley

Tuneful poet, Britain's glory. Mutual Congratulations of the Poets Anna Seward and Hayley, The. Richard Porson. FaBoEE; OBSV

Tung-ling melons—men say that long ago. Juan Chi. CoBCP *Fr.* Singing of Thoughts.

Tungeei, that was her native name. Captain Cook. *Aborigine Oral Tradition.* NOBAu, *tr. by* Percy Mumbulla

TUNING MYSELF BY MORNING COFFEE. May Morn. Michael McClure. SPE

Tunnel, The. Hart Crane. MoAmPo; NAAL-5; OxBA *Fr.* Bridge, The.

Tunnel, The. Nicanor Parra. TCLAP, *tr. by* W. S. Merwin

Tunnel, The. Mark Strand. HeIP-4; TwCP

Tunnyng [*or* Tunning] of Elynour [*or* Elinor] Rummyng [*or* Rumming], The. John Skelton.

  "Some have no money." NAEL-7v1

  "Then Margery [*or* Marjorie] Milkduck." EBEV; PoE

Tunstall Forest. Donald Davie. OxBEV

Turbulence and Tongue. Anthony Barnett. Oth

Turbulent Water, The. *Unknown.* TAL

Turf-Carrier [*or* Turf Carrier] on Aranmore. John Hewitt. PoRA

Turf Song. Sterling Plumpp. GT

Turf-Stacks. Louis MacNeice. OBMV

  (Turf-Stacks.) OBMV

Turgid itch and the perfume of death. Fear and the Monkey. William S. Burroughs. PFTM-2

Turkestan. Ch'en Tao. WoPoe, *tr. by* Witter Bynner

Turkey, The. Nikolai Stepanovich Gumilyov [*or* Gumiliov *or* Gumilev]. TCRP, *tr. by* Simon Franklin

Turkey in the Corn. Woody Guthrie. KaS

Turkey in the Straw. *Unknown.* TCAPo

Turkey is dancing near the rocks, A. *Unknown.* STP

Turkeys. John Clare. FaBoVe; OWoS

Turkeys in August. Gray Jacobik. UrbNat

Turkeys Observed. Seamus Heaney. OWoS

Turkeys wade the close to catch the bees, The. Turkeys. John Clare. OWoS

Turkish. Belly-dancer. Sexy tricks. Automedon. EroLit, *tr. by* Kenneth McLeish

Turkish Carpet, The. Paul Durcan. CIP-2

Turkish Love Songs. *Unknown.* BoWoP, *tr. by* Reza Baraheni and Zahra-Soltan Shokoohtaezeh

Turmoil, The. Sorley MacLean (Somhairle MacGill-Eain). HarvBoo

Turn. Andrée Chedid. PoArWo, *tr. by* Lucy McNair

Turn, The. Robert Creeley. FTOS; LCAP-2

Turn (a Poem in 4 Parts). Ken Belford. NOBC

Turn again, turn again, turn once again. Carrousel Tune. Tennessee Williams. NBLV; OBAL

Turn and Turn About. Eva Gerlach. TuT, *tr. by* Eamon Grennan

Turn Back, O Man. Clifford Bax. NOCV

Turn back, Uma. Kamalākānta Bhattācārya. SinGod, *tr. by* Rachel Fell McDermott

Turn'd to that dirt from whence he sprung. (LL) Satirical Elegy on the Death of a Late Famous General, A. Jonathan Swift. NBLV; NPeEn; OBSV; PoE

Turn from Self. George Macdonald. PWR

Turn from that road's beguiling ease; return. Sea's Wash in the Hollow of the Heart, The. Denise Levertov. LW

Turn, good wooden horses, round. Wooden Horses. Paul Verlaine. NAWM-7v2, *tr. by* Carlyle Ferren MacIntyre

Turn in the world and bear the day to me. (LL) Turn on Your Side and Bear the Day to Me. George Barker. HarvBoo; OxBTC

Turn inside out turn me. Request. Shuntaro Tanikawa. VCWP, *tr. by* Harold Wright

Turn inward on the brain. What the Emanation of Casey Jones Said to the Medium. Arthur James Marshall Smith. MoCV

Turn me every which way, three-cornered God. Lucky Strikes. Ron Padgett. FTOS

Turn Me to My Yellow Leaves. William Stanley Braithwaite. NAAAL

Turn not to the prophet's page, O Son! For the Holy Family by Michelangelo. Dante Gabriel Rossetti. SacPr

Turn of noontide has begun, The. Half-Way Pause, A. Dante Gabriel Rossetti. NOBVV; OxBEV

Turn of Privacy, The. Rick Noguchi. AmPoNex; NeAmPo

Turn off that charm. Remind Me. Dorothy Fields. ReLy

Turn on my tongue, O Spanish verse; confirm. Ewigkeit. Jorge Luis Borges. WoPoe, *tr. by* Richard Wilbur

Turn On the Heat. Ray Henderson. ReLy

Turn on the prudent Ant thy heedless eyes. Paraphrase. Samuel Johnson. ChIV-1

Turn on the tap for straight and silver water in the sink. Seven Activities for a Young Child. Alan Brownjohn. OTCP

Turn on your left side, back to your right again. Crinagoras. GrAn

Turn on Your Side and Bear the Day to Me. George Barker. HarvBoo; OxBTC

"Turn to me in the darkness." Titus and Berenice. John Heath-Stubbs. GTBS-P

Turn to right, turn to left. Witches' Spells. Madeleine Edmondson. NTCP

Turn to yon vale beneath, whose tangled shade. Bower of Pleasure, The. Mary Robinson. CenSon; RWP

Turn towards the end, be a leaf dying. Jakov [*or* Jacob] Steinberg. FIT, *tr. by* Robert Friend

Turn, turn, my wheel! Turn round and round. Henry Wadsworth Longfellow. APN-1

Turn, turn thy beauteous face away. Francis Beaumont. NOSC *Fr.* Love's Cure.

Turn, Turn, Unhappy Souls, Return. Henry Alline. AH

"Turn, Willie Macintosh." Willie Macintosh. *Unknown.* ESPB; OxBoLi

Turnabout. Linda Pastan. NIP-4

Turnabouts. Dyan Newson. IBA

Turncoat, The. Imamu Amiri Baraka. NeAP; PoE

Turncoat, The. Priscilla Jane Thompson. CBWP-2

Turned down the gas in the hall. (LL) Death in Leamington. Sir John Betjeman. MakPoe; NoP-4; OxAEP-2; RB

Turned into a weapon. (LL) Objection to Being Stepped On, The. Robert Frost. NBLV; OBCoV

Turned into a white blade, which fell. (LL) Hawk. Mary Oliver. NAAL-5; OWoS

Turning. Robert Finch. MoCV

Turning, The. Philip Levine. VGW

Turning a stone house into seven figures. Elixir. Richard Murphy. BiHa

Turning and turning in the widening gyre. Second Coming, The. W. B. Yeats. BIrV; CABP; ChIV-2; ClHu; FaBoMo; GI; GTBS-P; HAP; HarvBoo; HeIP-4; InPK-6; MoBrPo; NAAL-3; NAEL-5v2; NAEL-6v2; NIL-7; NIP-4; NOBE; NoAM; NoP-4; OxAEP-2; OxBEV; OxBTC; PoE; PoPoPo; RaBo; SCV; SoSe-8; TFi; TRP; UnPo; WoPoe

Turning Away from Lies. Robert Bly. LCAP-2

Turning darkness into light. (LL) Pangur Bán. *Unknown.* FaBoCh; RB

Turning Fifty. Thomas William Shapcott. BMAP

Turning, following the arrows through. House of Madam Juju, The. Mieko Kanai. BoWoP, *tr. by* Christopher Drake.

Turning into. Robert Duncan. SPE

Turning it over, considering, like a madman. John Berryman. NoAM *Fr.* Dream Songs.

Turning my chariot I yoke my horses and go. *Unknown.* ChiP *Fr.* Seventeen Old Poems.

Turning of the car. Luigi Fontanella. NeIt

Turning of the Year, The. Delaina Thomas. OpBo

Turning Pro. Ishmael Reed. SoSe-8

Turning Thirty, I Contemplate Students Bicycling Home. Rita Dove. ESEAA

Turning to sponge a flank. Eureka. Maureen Duffy. PoBW

Turning to you, my name—. Recognized Futures. Lisa Suhair Majaj. UnSA

Turning Year, The. Su Tung-p'o (Su Shih). OHPC, *tr. by* Kenneth Rexroth

Turning your back, you button your blouse. That's new. Changing What We Mean. Eloise Klein Healy. WiU

Turnip Vendor, The. Samuel Johnson. OxNR

(Epigram.) PeLV

Turns. Tony Harrison. NAEL-6v2 *Fr.* School of Eloquence, The.

Turns at the Dance. Diana García. TouFir

Turns in the waking west and goes to sleep. (LL) Hart Crane. MoAmPo; NOBA; NoAM; OxBA *Fr.* Bridge, The.

Turnstile, The. William Barnes. NOBVV; NPeEn; OxBEV

Turnstone turned rover, A. Upon Learning That a Bird Exists Called the Turnstone. John Updike. PeLV

Turnus and the Courser. Virgil [*or* Vergil]. OBVE, *tr. by* Gawin [*or* Gavin] Douglas *Fr.* Aeneid [*or* Eneados, *Aeneis*], The.

Turnus and the Stone. Virgil [*or* Vergil]. OBVE, *tr. by* John Dryden *Fr.* Aeneid [*or* Eneados, *Aeneis*], The.

Turnus and the Wanton Courser. Virgil [*or* Vergil]. OBVE, *tr. by* John Dryden *Fr.* Aeneid [*or* Eneados, *Aeneis*], The.

Turnus Summons His Allies, Aeneas Is "Perturbit wyth Gret Thochtis." Virgil [*or* Vergil]. OBVE, *tr. by* Gawin [*or* Gavin] Douglas *Fr.* Aeneid [*or* Eneados, *Aeneis*], The.

Turo, Rescuer of the Sun and Moon. *Unknown.*

"One son of God, The." WoPoe, *tr. by* Keith Bosley

Turtle. Peter Blue Cloud. HATNAP

Turtle, The. William Carlos Williams. EmeKit; RaBo; SAmP

Turtle Blessing. Penny Harter. TWW

Turtle Dove, The. Geoffrey Hill. FaBoTw; OxBEV

Turtle-Dove, The. *Unknown.* OxBoLi

Turtle Head Stupa. Muso Soseki. EaWin, *tr. by* W. S. Merwin

Turtle lives 'twixt plated decks, The. Ogden Nash. NoP-4; OBAL; SoSe-8; TAP

Turtle's Song, The. *Unknown.* BPo

Turtle Soup. Marilyn Chin. LoL

Turtles Hatching. Mark O'Connor. NOBAu

Turvy-Topsy. Paul Groves. TCAWP

Tuscaloosa Sam. "Orpheus C. Kerr." OBAL

Tuscan cypresses. Cypresses. D. H. Lawrence. NAEL-5v2; NAEL-6v2

Tuscan Olives. Agnes Mary Frances Robinson. VWP

Tuscan, that wanderest through the realms of gloom. Dante. Henry Wadsworth Longfellow. NCAP

Tuskegee Airfield. Marilyn Nelson Waniek. ESEAA; GT

Tuskegee Experiment. Mohammed Sadiq. SeSe

Tusks that clashed in mighty brawls, The. On the Vanity of Earthly Greatness. Arthur Guiterman. APT-1; HeIP-4; OBCA; PAI; TrJP

Tuslag. T. A. Robertson. OxBS

Tut-tut! give back the flags—how can you care. Confederate Flags, The. Ambrose Bierce. CBCWP

Tutelar of the Place, The. David Jones.

"Queen of the differentiated sites, administratrix of the." AngWePo; TCAWP

Tuti's Ice Cream. Chairil Anwar. PoetW, *tr. by* Burton Raffel

Tutivillus, the Devil. *Unknown.* EBEV

Tutor not thyself in science: go to masters for perfection. Good Counsel. *Unknown.* NOIV, *tr. by* James Clarence Mangan

Tutor who tooted a flute, A. Limerick. Carolyn Wells. PeLi; SoSe-8

Tutto è Sciolto. James Joyce. OBMV

TV. John Forbes. CBAP

(T.V.) BMAP

T.V. John Forbes. *See* TV

TV. Rodney Jones. IllVoic; ReTh

TV in Black and White. Gary Soto. ReTh

TV set, stirring itself, confides, The. Visitor's Book, 9, The. John Davies. TCAWP

Twa bonny [*or* bony] lads were Sandy and Jockie. Sandy and Jockie. Robert Burns. OxBSP

Twa Books, The. Allan Ramsay. OxBS

Twa Brothers, The. *Unknown.* EBEV; ESPB; OxBB

Twa Corbies, The. *Unknown.* AWP; ESPB; FaBoCh; GTBS-P; HAP; InPK-6; NPeEn; NePenScot; OBEV; OWoS; OxBEV; OxBS; PAI; RB; SCGP; UnPo

(Two Ravens, The.) SoSe-8

Twa Knights, The. *Unknown.* ESPB

Twa Magicians, The. *Unknown.* ESPB; OxBB

(Two Magicians, The.) OxBoLi

Twa Sisters, The. *Unknown.* ESPB; OxBS

Twain that were foes, while Mary lived, are fled. His Lady's Death. Pierre de Ronsard. AWP, *tr. by* Andrew Lang

'Twas a battle of States. Battle of Gettysburg, The. Edgar Lee Masters. CBCWP

'Twas a cloudless morn and the sun shone bright. Cherokee, The. Mary Weston Fordham. CBWP-2

'Twas a new feeling—something more. Did Not. Thomas Moore. BoLoP; PeLV

'Twas a night like this. Little White Lies. Walter Donaldson. ReLy

'Twas a night of dreadful horror. Night of Death, The. Frances Ellen Watkins Harper. PWR

Twas a pause in the hip hop. Club House. Janice Lowe. InTrad

'Twas a summer evening. Robert Southey. *See* It was a summer [*or* summer's] evening

'Twas a Sunday morning, quite serene the air. City Eclogue. "W. J." NOEC

'Twas a tough task, believe it, thus to tame. Upon Dr. Davies's British Grammar. James Howell. AngWePo; OBWVE

'Twas all on board a ship down in a southern sea. Golden Vanity, The. *Unknown.* FaBoCh

'Twas all unlike your great and gracious ways. (LL) Coventry Patmore. NOBE; OBEV *Fr.* Unknown Eros, The.

'Twas at the royal feast, for Persia won. Alexander's Feast; or, The Power of Music [*or* Musique]. Dryden. GTBS-P; NAEL-5v1; NAEL-6v1; NAEL-7v1; NOBE; PeECV; TFi

'Twas at the silent, solemn hour. William and Margaret. David Mallet. NOEC; OxAEP-1

'Twas at the solemn hour of night. Dr. Johnson's Ghost. Elizabeth Moody. ECWP

'Twas August, and the fierce sun overhead. East London. Matthew Arnold. SCGP

'Twas battered and scarred, and the auctioneer. Touch of the Master's Hand, The. Myra Brooks Welch. PoToHe

'Twas brillig, and the slithy toves. Lewis Carroll. AmFaPo; BRP; CABP; ChAP; ClHu; EBEV; EBVV; HeIP-4; ITBLP; InPK-6; NAEL-5v2; NAEL-6v2; NBLV; NOBE; NOBL; NOBVV; NOxBChV; NTCP; NoAM; NoP-4; OBSP; OxAEP-2; OxBEV; PeLV; PeVV; PoRA; RB; TFi; TRP; TTTS; UV *Fr.* Through the Looking-Glass.

'Twas but a dream! I saw the stag leap free. Arabella Stuart. Felicia Dorothea Hemans. RWP

'Twas Christmas Eve and bitter cold. Dark Christmas on Wildwood Road, The. Morris Gilbert Bishop. ChrPo

'Twas Christmas Eve, the month was May. Tragedy, A. Tom Masson. OBAL

'Twas early on a May morning. Lady Isabel. *Unknown.* ESPB

'Twas enough to make a man stare. (LL) Mother Goose. NOBL; OxNR

'Twas eve in sunny Italy. Tale of Italy, A. Eloise Bibb. CBWP-2

'Twas eve; the broadly shining sun. To ———. Edward Coote [*or* Coate] Pinkney. APN-1

'Twas ever thus from childhood's hour! Disaster. Charles Stuart Calverley. NBLV

'Twas fancy first made Celia fair. Fancy. Jonathan Smedley. OxBSP

'Twas fifty quatrains: and from unknown strands. Fifty Quatrains. "Michael Field." VWP

'Twas Fultah Fisher's boarding-house. Ballad of Fisher's Boardinghouse, The. Rudyard Kipling. PoRA

'Twas going to snow—'twas snowing! Curse his luck! Drove-Road, The. Wilfrid Wilson Gibson. OxBTC

'Twas here my summer paused. Emily Dickinson. APN-2

'Twas in a Paris café that first I found him. Just a Gigolo. Julius Brammer. ReLy, *tr. by* Irving Caesar and Leonello Casucci

'Twas in heaven pronounced, and 'twas muttered in hell. Riddle, A. Catherine Maria Fanshawe. NOBRP; OxBEV

'Twas in the mazes of a wood. Savage of Aveyron, The. Mary Robinson. RWP

'Twas in the month of December, and in the year 1883. William McGonagall. PeVV

'Twas in the spring of '72. April Fool, The. Eugene Field. PWR

'Twas in the town of Jacksboro in the spring [*or* year] of seventy-three. Buffalo Skinners, The. *Unknown.* RB

'Twas just this time, last year, I died. Emily Dickinson. PoE

'Twas late, and the gay company was gone. Declaration, The. Nathaniel Parker Willis. OBAL

'Twas like a Maelstrom, with a notch. Final Inch, The. Emily Dickinson.
  APN-2; NCAP; PoE

'Twas mercy brought me from my *Pagan* land. On Being Brought from Africa
  to America. Phillis Wheatley. NAAL-2v1; NAAL-3; NAAL-5; NALW;
  NOBA; NOEC; OxBEV; RWP; SacPr; TAP; TTY; WPE

'Twas midnight—every mortal eye was closed. Helmets; a Fragment, The.
  Thomas Penrose. NOEC

'Twas my pleasure to walk in the river meadows. Brian [*or* Bryan] Merriman
  [*or* Merryman]. NOIV

'Twas night; and Flavia, to her room retired. Soliloquy of a Beauty in the
  Country. George Lyttelton. ECEV

'Twas nobly thought, and worthy-still. Poetical Question concerning the
  Jacobites, sent to the Athenians, A. Elizabeth Singer Rowe. BASC

'Twas not as lonesome as it might have been. Cricket Kept the House, The.
  Edith Matilda Thomas. OBCA

'Twas not for some calm blessing to receive. Her Muffe. Richard Lovelace.
  PBRV

"'Twas not so in my time," surly Grumio exclaims. Epigram. Samuel Bishop.
  NOEC

'Twas on a Holy Thursday, their innocent faces clean. William Blake.
  FHYEP; NAEL-5v2; NAEL-6v2; NAWM-7v2; NOBE; NOBRP; NOEC;
  NPeEn; NoP-4; PeECV; PoE; SCV; TFi; TrCP *Fr.* Songs of Innocence.

'Twas on a lofty vase's side. Ode on the Death of a Favourite [*or* Favorite]
  Cat, Drowned in a Tub [*or* Bowl] of Gold Fishes. Thomas Gray. ClHu;
  EBEV; ECEV; FHYEP; NAEL-5v1; NAEL-6v1; NAEL-7v1; NBLV;
  NOBE; NOBL; NOEC; OBCoV; OxBEV; PeLV; PoE; TFi

Twas on a Monday morning. Charlie is my Darling. James Hogg.
  NePenScot

'Twas on a night, an evening bright. Proud Lady Margaret. *Unknown.* ESPB

'Twas on a summer noon, in Stainsford mead. My Ox Duke. John Dyer.
  NOEC; NPeEn

'Twas on an evening fair I went to take the air. Willie's Fatal Visit. *Unknown.*
  ESPB

'Twas on the 8th April, on the afternoon of that day. William McGonagall.
  VerBaPo *Fr.* Tale of the Sea, A.

'Twas on the shores that round our coast. Yarn of the *Nancy Bell*, The. Sir
  William Schwenck Gilbert. EBNV; FaBoCh; NOBL; TFi; UV

'Twas once *look[e] up*, 'tis now *look[e] down[e]* to Heaven. (LL) On the
  Blessed Virgins Bashfulnesse. Richard Crashaw. HAP; OxBSP

'Twas once upon a time, when Jenny Wren was young. When Jenny Wren Was
  Young. *Unknown.* ReMoGo

'Twas Rollog, and the Minim Potes. *Unknown.* UV

'Twas said of Greece two thousand years ago. Colonial Nomenclature. John
  Dunmore Lang. NOBAu

'Twas so, I saw thy birth: that drowsy [*or* drowsie] lake. Shower [*or* Showre],
  The. Henry Vaughan. ESCV; GeHe

'Twas spring, and dawn returning breathed new-born. Idyll of the Rose.
  Ausonius. AWP, *tr. by* John Addington Symonds

'Twas such a big surprise to see you. Welcome to My Dream. Johnny Burke.
  ReLy

'Twas Summer and the sun was mounted high. Ruined Cottage, The. William
  Wordsworth. NAEL-6v2; NoP-4

'Twas Sunday morning, quite serene the air. City Eclogue, A. "W. J."
  NOEC

'Twas sunset's hallow'd time—and such an eve. James Kirke Paulding. APN-
  1 *Fr.* Backwoodsman, The.

'Twas sunset's hour, the glorious day. Exile's Reverie, The. Mary Weston
  Fordham. CBWP-2

'Twas sure a luckless planet. Out of Luck. Abraham Ibn Ezra. TrJP, *tr. by*
  Solomon Solis-Cohen

'Twas the angel of death that to us downward flew. In Memoriam of E. B.
  Clark. Lizelia Augusta Jenkins Moorer. CBWP-3

'Twas the angel of Eden, to Adam he said. Dedication Day Poem. Lizelia
  Augusta Jenkins Moorer. CBWP-3

'Twas the dream of a God. Ireland. Dora Sigerson Shorter. OBEV

'Twas the horse thief, Andy Regan, that was hunted like a dog. Father Riley's
  Horse. Andrew Barton Paterson. NOBAu

'Twas the night before Christmas. Visit from St Nicholas, A. Clement Clarke
  Moore. APN-1; AiP; BRP; ChAP; ChrPo; NTCP; OBAL; OBCA; OBCP;
  OxIBACP; TCAPo; TFi

'Twas the old [*or* ould] flute still whistling [*or* whistlin'] "The Protestant Boys"
  (LL) Old [*or* Ould] Orange Flute, The. *Unknown.* OBCoV; OxBoLi

'Twas the sight of my Bridey's hand, chewed. Cork Examiner, December 4,
  1846: More Starvation, The. Anna Mortál. SpudSo

'Twas the voice of the Wanderer, I heard her exclaim. Wanderer, The. Stevie
  Smith. NALW

'Twas thereupon. Arch, The. Herman Melville. NCAP

'Twas warm—at first—like Us. Emily Dickinson. APN-2; NAWM-7v2;
  NCAP; SoSe-8

'Twas when bright Cynthia with her silver car. Night-Piece; or, Modern
  Philosophy, A. Christopher Smart. NOEC

'Twas when Tacita hushed the noisy world. Dream, The. "Brian Bendo."
  NOEC

'Twas when the friendly shade of night. To Clarissa. Robert Nugent. NOEC

'Twas When the Seas Were Roaring. John Gay. HAP *Fr.* What D'Ye-Call-It,
  The.

'Twas when the spousal time of May. Coventry Patmore. OxAEP-2 *Fr.*
  Angel in the House, The.

'Twas whispered in Heaven, 'twas muttered in Hell. Enigma. Catherine Maria
  Fanshawe. OBCoV

'Twas yesterday; 'twas long ago. Where Home Was. Augusta Davies
  Webster. ViWPN

Twasinta's Seminoles; Or Rape of Florida. Albery Allson Whitman.
  "Have I not seen the hills of Candahar." APN-2
  "Is manhood less because man's face is black?" APN-2

Twats in the Ops Room. *Unknown.* FaBoWar

Tweed and Till. *Unknown.* FaBoCh; NPeEn; OxBSP
  (Says Tweed tae Till.) FaBoVe
  (Two Rivers, The.) OBEV

Tweed Visited, The. William Lisle Bowles. Son
  (To the River Tweed.) CenSon

Tweedledee and Tweedledoom. Ogden Nash. OBCoV

Tweedledum and Tweedledee. Mother Goose. LB; NOBL; OxNR; PeLV;
  ReMoGo

12th Dance—Getting Leather by Language—21 February 1964. Jackson Mac
  Low. PmAP *Fr.* Pronouns, The—A Collection of 40 Dances—For the
  Dancers.

Twelfth day of Christmas, The. Twelve Days of Christmas, The. *Unknown.*
  ChrPo; OxBoLi

Twelfth Floor West. Marilyn Hacker. ExTi

12th Horse Song of Frank Mitchell (Blue), The. Frank Mitchell. APSN; STP,
  tr. by Jerome Rothenberg

12th Horse-Song of Frank Mitchell (Blue), The. Jerome Rothenberg. FTOS

Twelfth Morning; or What You Will. Elizabeth Bishop. APT-2

Twelfth Night. Phyllis McGinley. APT-2

Twelfth Night. Peter Scupham. OBCP

Twelfth Night. William Shakespeare.
  (Carpe Diem.) GTBS-P
  Clown's Song, The. CTC; NOBE; NoSic; TFi
  (Come Away, Come Away, Death.) NoP-4
  (Come Away, Death.) PoRA
  (Dirge of Love.) GTBS-P
  (Dirge.) OBEV
  (Feste's Song.) NBLV; OxBoLi
  "I see you what you are: you are too proud." OxAEP-1
  ("If Musicke be the food of Love, play on.") OxBEV
  ("O Mistris mine where are you roming?") OxBEV
  O[h] Mistress Mine. AEP; AWP; BoLoP; CTC; ClHu; HAP; NAEL-5v1;
    NAEL-6v1; NBLV; NOBE; NoP-4; NoSic; OxBSP; OxBoLi; PoRA; SCGP;
    TFi; WoPoe
  "O[h] mistress mine, where are you roaming?" AEP; AWP; BoLoP; CTC;
    ClHu; HAP; NAEL-5v1; NAEL-6v1; NBLV; NOBE; NoP-4; NoSic;
    OxBSP; OxBoLi; PoRA; SCGP; TFi; WoPoe
  "Once more, Cesario." SCV
  Song: "When that I was and a little tiny boy." EBEV; FaBoCh; NOBE;
    NoSic; OxAEP-1; PoRA; SCGP; TFi
  (Sweet-and-Twenty.) OBEV; PoE
  (When That I Was and a Little Tiny Boy.) NoP-4

Twelfth Night. Elinor Wylie. ChrPo; SacPr

Twelfth of July, the voice of Ulster speaking, The. Twelfth of July, The.
  Patrick Kavanagh. ModIr

Twelfth Song of the Holy Young Men. *Unknown.* APN-2, *tr. by* Washington
  Matthews *Fr.* Mountain Chant, The.

Twelfth Song of the Thunder. *Unknown.* APN-2; AWP, *tr. by* Washington
  Matthews *Fr.* Mountain Chant, The.

Twelve. Rossana Ombres. NeIt, *tr. by* Ruth Feldman

Twelve, The. Aleksandr Aleksandrovich Blok. TCRP
  "Black Night. / White snow." AWP
  "Making tracks." WoPoe, *tr. by* Anselm Hollo

Twelve, The. Allen Tate. APT-2; ChIV-2

Twelve Articles. Jonathan Swift. NBLV; OBCoV

Twelve Bar Bessie. Jackie Kay. NeBl

Twelve children, twelve gray geese in starched. Handbell Choir, The. Jane
  Flanders. PBCAP

Twelve Days of Christmas, The. *Unknown.* ChrPo; OxBoLi; OxNR
  (On the first day of Christmas.) LB

12 East Scott Street. Elise Paschen. IllVoic

Twelve Faces of the Emerald. Dan Pagis. WoPoe, *tr. by* Stephen Mitchell

Twelve good friends. Peter and John. Elinor Wylie. MakPoe; MoAmPo

Twelve herds of oxen, no less flockes of sheepe. Homer. CTC *Fr.* Odyssey.

Twelve hours after the Allies arrive. Women Bathing at Bergen-Belsen. Enid Shomer. GotH

Twelve Lines about the Burning Bush. "Melech Ravitch." BBASP, *tr. by* Ruth Whitman

Twelve Miscellaneous Poems on the Fang Garden. Chang Yü. CoBLCP, *tr. by* Jonathan Chaves

Twelve O'Clock. Carolyn Kizer. ExTi

Twelve o'clock. / Along the reaches of the street. Rhapsody on a Windy Night. T. S. Eliot. HeIP-4; PoE

12 O'Clock News. Elizabeth Bishop. OxBC

Twelve pears hanging high. Mother Goose. OxNR; ReMoGo

Twelve people, most of us strangers, stand in a room. Eating the Pig. Donald Hall. BodElec

12 second poem. Trasi Johnson. InTrad

Twelve Songs. W. H. Auden.

    Fish In The Unruffled Lakes. BoLoP; MoBrPo

    "O for doors to be open and an invite with gilded edges." PeLV

    "Over the heather the wet wind blows." FaBoWar

    Roman Wall Blues. FaBoWar

    Song of the Beggars. PeLV

    Song: "Stop all the clocks, cut off the telephone." CAGL; MoBrPo; OPOU; RB

    (Stop all the clocks.) NIL-7

    ("Travellers in their last distress.") (LL) NPeEn

Twelve-year-old looks fetching in his prime, A. Strato [*or* Straton]. CAGL, *tr. by* Daryl Hine

Twelve years ago I made a mock. School and Schoolfellows. Winthrop Mackworth Praed. OxAEP-2

Twenties 27. Jackson Mac Low. PmAP

Twenties 26. Jackson Mac Low. PmAP

20th Century, The. Lesley Dauer. NAPBL

Twentieth-Century Blues. Kenneth Fearing. IllVoic

Twentieth Century Fresco. Sándor Weöres. IQMS, *tr. by* Adam Makkai

Twentieth-Century Love. George M. Cohan. ReLy

26th Person, The. Dolores Kendrick. GT *Fr.* "Three Observations on the Zombie Culture."

Twentieth year is well-nigh past, The. To Mary. William Cowper. EnLoPo; NOEC; UV

XX. Craig Arnold. NAPBL

20. Barbara Guest. PoM

Twenty Below. Robert Arthur Douglas Ford. NOBC

Twenty Billion Light Years of Loneliness. Shuntaro Tanikawa. PoetW, *tr. by* Harold Wright

28. Philip Levine. GeoHom

Twenty-eight Characters Sent to Tung-ts'un on the Subject of the Poems He Burned. Cheng Hsieh. CoBLCP, *tr. by* Jonathan Chaves

Twenty-eight Indian Patriarchs. Patriarch Peaks. Muso Soseki. EaWin, *tr. by* W. S. Merwin

Twenty-Eight Poems Inscribed on T'ien-kuan Mountain. Chao Meng-fu. CoBLCP, *tr. by* Jonathan Chaves

Twenty-eight young men bathe by the shore. Walt Whitman. CAGL; ColAP; HAP; NoP-4; SAmP *Fr.* Song of Myself.

Twenty-first Day of the Seventh Month. Henry Vaughan. CoBLCP, *tr. by* Jonathan Chaves

Twenty-First. Night. Monday. Anna Andreyevna Akhmatova. RaBo, *tr. by* Jane Kenyon

21th: and last booke of the Ocean to Scinthia, The. Sir Walter Ralegh. PBRV *Fr.* Ocean's Love to Cynthia, The.

Twenty-first, The. Night. Monday. Poem. Anna Andreyevna Akhmatova. RusPo, *tr. by* Robert Arthur Douglas Ford

25. Lawrence Ferlinghetti. CLPP

2500 years Before Proust. Time. Tom Clark. BodElec

25:I:68. Philip Whalen. PoM

Twenty-Five Laments for Iraq. Robert Minhinnick. HarvBoo

25 Mesostics Re and Not Re Mark Tobey. John Cage. PmAP

Twenty-five people. Dolores Kendrick. GT *Fr.* "Three Observations on the Zombie Culture."

Twenty-five years ago I lied. Broken Silence. Louis M. Abbey. BloBone

XXIV. Essex Hemphill. NAAAL *Fr.* Conditions.

Twenty-four hours can go so fast. Some Other Time. Leonard Bernstein. ReLy

Twenty-four Logics in Memory of Lee Hickman. Michael Palmer. BodElec

Twenty-four Years. Dylan Thomas. OxBEV; OxBSP

Twenty Golden Years Ago. James Clarence Mangan. NOBVV; OxBEV

Twenty Grand (Saturday Night on the Block), The. Naomi Long Madgett. NBV

Twenty lines of. Susan Howe. PmAP *Fr.* Speeches at the Barriers.

Twenty little engines. Twenty Little Engines. James Keir Baxter. NOxBChV

Twenty lost years have stol'n their hours away. Alone in an Inn at Southampton, April the 25th, 1737. Aaron Hill. NOEC

Twenty men crossing a bridge. Metaphors of a Magnifico. Wallace Stevens. TCAPo

Twenty months out of the womb. Standing in the Doorway, I Watch the Young Child Sleep. Sharon Hashimoto. FSt; OpBo

29 Poems. Louis Zukofsky.

    "Blue light is the night harbor-slip." PoE

    Cars Once Steel and Green, Now Old. VGW

    "Cocktails / and signs of." APT-2

    Ferry. APT-2

    "Gleams a green lamp." APT-2

    "Not much more than being." APT-2; PoE

    "Red varnish / Warm flitch." APT-2

    Two Dedications: Tibor Serly. APT-2

29-77-02. Artur Miedzyrzecki. PoSu, *tr. by* Stanislaw Baranczak

29 Songs. Louis Zukofsky.

    In Arizona. TRP

    "In that this happening." APT-2

    "To my wash-stand." APT-2

Twenty-ninth Canto. Hans Magnus Enzensberger. PoSu *Fr.* Sinking of the Titanic, The.

21. Lawrence Ferlinghetti. CLPP

XXI. Essex Hemphill. *See* To Some Supposed Brothers

21 East 10th, 2BR, WBF, EIK. Robyn Selman. WiU

Twenty-one Love Poems. Adrienne Rich. GLP

    "Can it be growing colder when I begin." NAAL-2v2

    "Dark lintels, the blue and foreign stones, The." NALW; NoAM

    "Every peak is a crater. This is the law of volcanoes." NAAL-2v2; NALW; NoAM

    Floating Poem, Unnumbered, The. EroLit; NALW; NoAM

    "I come home from you through the early light of spring." BoWoP

    "I wake up in your bed. I know I have been dreaming." ErotSp; NAAL-2v2; NoAM; TRP

    "No one's fated or doomed to love anyone." PoBW

    "Rain on the West Side Highway." NAAL-2v2

    "Sleeping, turning in turn like planets." TRP

    "That conversation we were always on the edge." BoWoP; NoAM

    "Whatever happens with us, your body." EroLit; NALW; NoAM

    "Your small hands, precisely equal to my own." PoE; TRP

Twenty-one Sonnets. Christian Karlson Stead.

    "Rain, and a flurry of wind shaking the pear's white blossom." PeNZ

Twenty Poems in Imitation of Han-shan and Shih-te. Wang An-shih.

    "Once I was a cow, a horse." CoBCP

Twenty Questions. Dennis Phillips.

    Five. FTOS

    "There is a temper of atmosphere which prevents rain." FTOS

27 July 1830. Georgy [*or* Georgii] Arkadevich Shengeli. TCRP, *tr. by* Daniel Weissbort

27th Dance—Walking—22 March 1964. Jackson Mac Low. FTOS *Fr.* Pronouns, The—A Collection of 40 Dances—For the Dancers.

Twenty-Six Nonsense Rhymes. Edward Lear. RB

Twenty-Six Ways of Looking at a Blackman. Raymond R. Patterson. ESEAA

Twenty sparrows / on. William Carlos Williams. SAmP

Twenty-third Flight. Earle Birney. HeIP-4; OxBC

23rd Psalm, The. Bobby McFerrin. HW

23rd Street Runs into Heaven. Kenneth Patchen. APT-2

23. Gavin Selerie. Oth *Fr.* Roxy.

XXII. Essex Hemphill. NAAAL *Fr.* Conditions.

20-200 on 737. Heather McHugh. NIP-4

22.6.1941. Ondra Lysohorsky. AF, *tr. by* Ewald Osers

Twenty-two Quatrains on Receiving the Obituary Notice for my Son Shih-Chü. T'ang Hsien-tsu.

    "My son, you loved telling the story of Prince Nata." CoBLCP; ColAnChi, *tr. by* Jonathan Chaves

Twenty Views of Wang-ch'uan. Wang Wei. CoBCP, *tr. by* Burton Watson

Twenty-Year Marriage. Ai. BoWoP; GT; NoAM

Twenty Years. Đỗ Tấn Xuân. WoPoe, *tr. by* Nguyen Ngoc Bich

Twenty years a pilgrim. Seiken-Chiju. ZenPo, *tr. by* Takashi Ikemoto and Lucien Stryk

Twenty Years After. János Vajda. IQMS, *tr. by* Neville Masterman

Twenty years ago today, your death changed. Speaking Through White: For My Mother. Kyoko Mori. UnSA

Twenty years are gone. Palinode. Oliver St. John Gogarty. OBMV

Twenty Years From Auschwitz, Bergen-Belsen and Other Camps. Luisa Futuransky. MirDau, *tr. by* Celeste Kostopulos-Cooperman

Twenty Years Hence.   Walter Savage Landor.   NAEL-5v2; NAEL-6v2; NOBVV

Twenty years / I tamed an ant.   Aleksandr Makarov [or Makarov-Krotkov]. TCRP

20 Years of Grant Applications and State College Jobs.   Christopher Buckley. GeoHom

Twenty years on the road of love.   Nizar Qabbani.   MAP   Fr. Painting with Words.

Twentyseven bums give a prostitute the once.   E. E. Cummings.   OBAL

'Twer May, but ev'ry leaf wer dry.   Wife a-Prais'd, A.   William Barnes. EBVV

'Twere blessed to have seen. (LL)   Emily Dickinson.   APN-2; BoWoP; NAAL-3; NCAP; NOBA

'Twere well your judgments but in plays did range.   Dryden.   OBSV   Fr. Spanish Friar [or Fryar], The.

Twice.   Christina Georgina Rossetti.   NOBE; OBEV; TOF; TrCP; VWP

Twice forty months in wedlock I did stay.   On the Death of My First and Dearest Child[e], Hector Philip[p]s.   Katherine Philips.   NAEL-6v1; NAEL-7v1

Twice having seen your shingled heads adorable.   Evening on Lesbos.   Edna St. Vincent Millay.   PoBW

Twice I ended up in a forest.   Woods, The.   Sa'di Yusuf.   MAP, tr. by Sargon Boulus and Naomi Shihab Nye

Twice I have written you that I am unhappy.   Letter to Her Father, A.   Inibsarri.   BoWoP, tr. by Willis Barnstone

Twice in my quickly disappearing forties.   Year's End.   Marilyn Hacker.   WiU

Twice or thrice had I loved thee.   Air[e] and Angels.   John Donne.   BASC; ESCV; MeLP; NAEL-5v1; NAEL-6v1; NAEL-7v1

Twice Shy.   Seamus Heaney.   TwCP

Twice, three times.   Paavo Haavikko.   WoPoe, tr. by Anselm Hollo   Fr. Fifteen Epigrams in Praise of the Tyrant.

Twice Times Then Is Now.   Ibn Hazm al-Andalusi.   ArPe; OBVE; WoPoe, tr. by Omar Pound and Omar S. Pound

Twicknam [or Twickenham] Garden.   John Donne.   BASC; EBEV; ESCV; EnLoPo; MeLP; OBGa; PoE; SCGP

Twig of willow. (LL)   Counting-out Rhyme.   Edna St. Vincent Millay.   InPK-6; NOxBChV; OxIBACP; SoSe-8; TTTS

Twigs stiffen.   Sense.   Rae Armantrout.   FTOS

Twilight.   Ralph Angel.   BodElec

Twilight.   Louisa Sarah Bevington.   PEW

Twilight.   Ch'en Yün.   WoPoe, tr. by Henry Hart

Twilight.   Louisa S. Guggenberger.   WoPoe

Twilight.   Heinrich Heine.   AWP, tr. by Louis Untermeyer

Twilight.   Vladislav Felitsianovich Khodasevich.   TCRP, tr. by Michael Frayn

Twilight.   D. H. Lawrence.   OBMV

Twilight.   Amy Levy.   VWP

Twilight.   John Masefield.   OxBTC

Twilight.   Philippe Soupault.   SurPaPo, tr. by Mary Ann Caws and Patricia Terry

Twilight.   Margit Szécsi.   IQMS, tr. by Agnes Arany-Makkai

Twilight.   Fujiwara No Toshinari.   OHMPJ

Twilight.   Cor Van den Heuvel.   HA

Twilight.   Anita Virgil.   HA

Twilight at a Little Harbor.   Chairil Anwar.   PoetW, tr. by Burton Raffel

Twilight (Between Dog and Wolf).   Olga Orozco.   SurWo, tr. by Natalie Kenvin

Twilight. By now the genial sea of dusk.   Half Past Four, October.   Anna Hajnal.   BoWoP, tr. by Daniel Hoffman

Twilight by the plantation.   John Moat.   NewEx

Twilight Comes.   Hayden Carruth.   NNaP

Twilight Comes.   Wang Wei.   OHMPC, tr. by Kenneth Rexroth

Twilight comes down the mountains to.   Night in the Villa by the River.   Tu Fu.   TAL

Twilight comes over the monastery Garden.   Twilight Comes.   Wang Wei.   OHMPC, tr. by Kenneth Rexroth

Twilight falls; I soften the dusting feathers, The.   Sappho.   James Wright (1927–80).   NoAM

Twilight has already descended upon a thousand trees.   On the Twenty-fourth of the Third Month, in the Year Ting-wei Sailed across Lake T'ai from Behind the Mountain.   Wu Wei-yeh.   SuSp, tr. by Chang Yin-nan

Twilight heavens are flushed with gathering light, The.   Red Sunsets, 1883, The.   Mathilde Blind.   ViWPN

Twilight in Middle March, A.   Francis Ledwidge.   BIrV

Twilight in the Library.   John Tripp.   TCAWP

Twilight in the River Pavilion.   Chiang Shih-ch'üan.   OHMPC, tr. by Kenneth Rexroth

Twilight in West Virginia: Six O'Clock Mine Report.   Irene McKinney.   PBCAP

Twilight is here, soft breezes bow the grass.   In Exile.   Emma Lazarus.   APN-2

Twilight is spacious, near things in it seem far.   Miracles.   Conrad Potter Aiken.   MoAmPo; TCAPo

Twilight it is, and the far woods are dim, and the rooks cry.   Twilight.   John Masefield.   OxBTC

Twilight Musings.   Mary Weston Fordham.   CBWP-2

Twilight of eternal day, The. (LL)   Tennyson.   CABP; EBVV; HAP; HeIP-4; NAEL-6v2; NAWM-7v2; NOCV; PeECV; SCGP; SCV   Fr. In Memoriam A. H. H.

Twilight of the Outward Life.   Hugo von Hofmannsthal.   WoPoe, tr. by Peter Viereck

Twilight of Vanity.   Vyacheslav Kupriyanov [or Kuprianov].   TCRP, tr. by Albert C. Todd

Twilight on Tweed.   Andrew Lang.   EBVV

Twilight on Union Street.   Donald Davidson.   FuPo

Twilight over the field is blurred.   Edge, The.   Andrey [or Andrei] Andreievich Voznesensky [or Voznesenskii].   RusPo, tr. by Robert Arthur Douglas Ford

Twilight Polka Dots.   Barbara Guest.   PmAP

(Lake was filled with distinguished fish purchased, The.)   NoP-4

Twilight's Last Gleaming.   Arthur W. Monks.   NIP-4

Twilight Seduction.   Yusef Komunyakaa.   SeSe

Twilight Shadows round Me Fall, The.   Ernest Edwin Ryden.   AH

Twilight Time.   Floyd Skloot.   MiVo

Twilight Under Pine Ridge.   Robert Mezey.   GeoHom

Twilight was turning to darkness outside.   Vladislav Felitsianovich Khodasevich.   TCRP

Twilights.   James Wright (1927–80).   LCAP-2

Twilit Revelation.   Léonie Adams.   MoAmPo

'Twill learn of things divine, and first of thee to sing. (LL)   On the Death of Mr. Crashaw.   Abraham Cowley.   BASC; BeJo; MeLP

'Twill soon be sunrise. Down the valley waiting.   Lakeward.   Trumbull Stickney.   APN-2

'"Twill take some getting." "Sir, I think 'twill so."   Man and Dog.   Edward Thomas.   PeFWW

Twin Barrel Bucky: A Kingston 12 Dub, The.   Brian Meeks.   WaCA

Twin Flames.   James Broughton.   PasH

Twin memory, we all seek it.   David St. John.   GeoHom   Fr. Of the Remembered.

Twin stars through my purpling pane.   Dusk.   Angelina Weld Grimké.   APT-1

Twin streaks twice higher than cumulus.   Vapor Trails.   Gary Snyder.   NAAL-2v2

Twined together and, as is customary.   Never Such Love.   Robert Graves.   BoLoP

Twining her fingers through.   Satyr, Cunninlinguent: To Herman Melville.   Charles Martin.   RA

Twinkle, twinkle— (LL)   Lewis Carroll.   NOBL; UV   Fr. Alice's Adventures in Wonderland.

Twinkle, twinkle, little star.   Star, The.   Jane Taylor.   NOBRP; NOxBChV; NTCP; OTCP; OxBEV; OxNR; UV

Twinkle Twinkle Little Star.   Jane Taylor.   See Star, The

Twins.   Robert Graves.   FaBoEE; OBCoV

Twins, The.   Robert Browning.   FaBoVe

Twins, The.   Henry Sambrooke Leigh.   OxIBACP

Twins, The.   Karl Shapiro.   MoAmPo; TrJP

Twins, The.   James Stephens.   RaBo

Twins, The.   Mona Van Duyn.   VCAP

Twirling.   Jane Flanders.   ItWoWo; PBCAP

Twirling an angry necklace on her fingers under.   Between.   Christian Karlson Stead.   PoetW

Twirling your blue skirts, travelling the sward.   Blue Girls.   John Crowe Ransom.   APT-1; ColAP; MoAmPo; NoAM; NoP-4; RB; TAP; VGW; WeW-3

Twirls on the tips of a carnation.   Oriental Ballerina, The.   Rita Dove.   NAAAL

Twist, The.   Alfred B. Spellman.   ISC

Twist about, turn about.   Unknown.   OxNR

Twist of cloth on the flat stones, A.   Desmond O'Grady.   PBCIP   Fr. Dark Edge of Europe, The.

Twister Twisting Twine.   John Wallis.   OxNR

Twisting, circling, the green path slants.   Cheng-tao Temple.   Tai Piao-yüan.   CoBLCP, tr. by Jonathan Chaves

Twisting inland.   Michael McClintock.   HA

Twisting tendril, A.   Richard Wright.   APT-2

Twitch nervously about. (LL)   Two Postures beside a Fire.   James Wright (1927–80).   HCAP; HeIP-4

Twitched in her belly, or he raised a fist.   Figlio Maggiore.   Robert Fitzgerald.   NoP-4

Twitching in the cactus. Deathwatch. Michael S. Harper. NAAAL; NAAL-5

Twittingpan seized my arm, though I'd have gone. Encounter, The. Edgell Rickword. OxBTC

'Twixt Carrowbrough Edge and Settlingstones. Old Skinflint. Wilfrid Wilson Gibson. OBMV

'Twixt Cup and Lip. Mark Hollis. NBLV

Twixt devil and deep sea, man hacks his caves. Arachne. William Empson. OBMV

'Twixt East and West a giant shape she grew. Sonnet on the Crimean War. William Forster. CBAP

'Twixt failure and success the point's so fine. C. C. Cameron. PoToHe *Fr.* Success.

'Twixt handkerchief and nose. Rub, A. John Banister Tabb. OBAL

Twixt Kings and Subjects ther[e]'s this mighty odds. Difference Betwixt King and Subjects, The. Robert Herrick. BASC

Twixt the Girthhead and Langwoodend. Lads of Wamphray, The. *Unknown.* ESPB; IBB

'Twixt Tweedledum and Tweedledee! (LL) Epigram on the Feuds between Handel and Bononcini. John Byrom. FaBoEE; NOBL; NOEC

'Twixt women's love, and men's will ever be[e]. (LL) Air[e] and Angels. John Donne. BASC; ESCV; MeLP; NAEL-5v1; NAEL-6v1; NAEL-7v1

Two, The. Hugo von Hofmannsthal. AWP, *tr. by* Ludwig Lewisohn

Two, The. Hugo von Hofmannsthal. AuPH, *tr. by* Lowell A. Bangerter

Two African Breasts. Nizar Qabbani. MAP, *tr. by* Diana Der Hovanessian and Lena Jayyusi

Two Ajaxes Compared to Oxen, The. Homer. OBVE, *tr. by* George Chapman *Fr.* Iliad, The.

Two aldermen, three lawyers, five physicians. Of a Zealous Lady. Sir John Harington [*or* Harrington]. FaBoEE

2 a.m.: moonlight. The train has stopped. Track. Tomas Tranströmer. RB; SPE, *tr. by* Robert Bly

Two and One. Richard Chess. TaR

Two Angels, The. Sharif Elmusa. GraLe

Two Apes of Brueghel, The. Wislawa Szymborska. WoPoe, *tr. by* Sharon Olds

Two Appeals to John Harralson, Agent. *Unknown.* OBAL

Two April Mornings, The. William Wordsworth. EBEV; GTBS-P; NAEL-5v2; NAEL-6v2

Two Armies. Stephen Spender. OBWP; OxBTC

Two armies covered hill and plain. Music in Camp. John Reuben Thompson. CBCWP

Two Artists, The. Constance Naden. VWP; ViWPN

Two autumns. (LL) Buson. ChAP; EH, *tr. by* Robert Hass

Two Backgrounds. Edith Wharton. APN-2

Two basins, one rising from the other. Roman Fountain. Rainer Maria Rilke. GS, *tr. by* Edward Snow

Two battered at the Red Lamp Hitting the bars. Journey, The. Emmy Bridgwater. SurWo

Two battles, hundreds of years ago. After the Fifth of June. Yusuf Al-Khal. MAP, *tr. by* May Jayyusi and Naomi Shihab Nye

Two Bears, The. Lillian E. Curtis. VerBaPo

Two birds, one of them mortal, the other immortal. *Unknown.* EnlH *Fr.* Upanishads, The.

Two-blood passion man. Sounds of a Dreamer. James Berry. WaCA

Two bodies have I. *Unknown.* OxNR

Two bodies that unite naked. They Unite Naked. Jorge Gaitán Durán. BLPSL, *tr. by* Rene de Costa, Rigas Kappatos and Eleni Paidoussi

Two Boys, The. Mary Lamb. WoRP

Two boys uncoached are tossing a poem together. Catch. Robert Francis. InPK-6; RaBo

Two boys, whose birth beyond all question springs. Charles Churchill. OBSV *Fr.* Prophecy of Famine, The.

Two bronzes, but they were passing bronze before. Two Wrestlers. Robert Francis. MoASP

Two Brothers in a Field of Absence. Cynthia MacDonald. NIP-4

Two brothers once, of merry mood. Obey Your Parents. William Bingham Tappan. VerBaPo

Two brothers we are. *Unknown.* OxNR

Two Bulls, The. *Unknown.* NOIV, *tr. by* Thomas Kinsella *Fr.* How the Bulls Were Begotten.

Two campers (King Lear and his clown?). Outward Bound. James Simmons. CIP-2

Two carousing hawk moths, their wings like nervous silk. Inna L'vovna Lisnyanskaya [*or* Lisnianskaia]. ItGoST, *tr. by* Judith Hemschemeyer

Two cars, three loos, a swimming pool. Whiteman Blues, The. Lionel Abrahams. PeSAV

Two Cats / One up a tree. Diamond Cut Diamond. Ewart Milne. FaBoCh

Two cats together. This and That. Gareth Owen. OTCP

Two Centuries in One Day. Eloise Klein Healy. GeoHom

Two Cherokee Songs of Friendship. *Unknown.* APN-2, *tr. by* Samuel L. Mitchill

Two children, dressed in court costume. Old Picture, An. Howard Nemerov. OxBSP

Two children move shells from Tay Ninh. Night on the Kho Bha Dinh. Steve Denning. CDa

Two Chorale-Preludes: On Melodies by Paul Celan. Geoffrey Hill. OxBC

Two Christs were at Golgotha. Early Lynching. Carl Sandburg. ChIV-2; MoAmPo

Two Cigarettes in the Dark. Lew Pollack. ReLy

Two coffees in the Español, the last. Conrad Potter Aiken. APT-1; NoAM *Fr.* Preludes for Memnon; or, Preludes to Attitude.

Two Comical Folk. Mother Goose. OxNR; ReMoGo

Two cops who are really famous actors. In Your Dream after Falling in Love. Richard Hugo. BodElec

Two Countries. Tadeusz Borowski. AF, *tr. by* Larry Rafferty

Two Countries. José Martí. TCLAP, *tr. by* Elinore Randall

Two Countries. José Martí. TTY, *tr. by* Mona Hinton

Two Couples. Debra Bruce. FFC

Two crones were giving a whipping to a drunkard in the fog. Drunken Merchant, The. Milán Füst. IQMS, *tr. by* Jess Perlman

Two crows walk down the road. Pasolini. Robert Glück. WiU

Two Cures for Love. Wendy Cope. OBCoV

Two dayes now in that sea he sayled has. Edmund Spenser. NoSic *Fr.* Faerie Queene, The.

Two days ago they were playing the piano. Malvolio in San Francisco. Jack Gilbert. YaYoPo

Two days' rain. The minute it stops, I'm out. EFT. Roberta Swann. PoCoUp

Two dead divers hauled up in their bell, The. Alison Brackenbury. DiPo

Two Decisions. Vernon Watkins. OxBTC

Two Dedications. Gwendolyn Brooks.

　Chicago Picasso, The. BPo

　"Does man love Art? Man visits Art, but squirms." BPo

　(Two Dedications.) NAAAL

Two Dedications. Gwendolyn Brooks. *See* Two Dedications

Two Dedications: Tibor Serly. Louis Zukofsky. APT-2 *Fr.* 29 Poems.

Two dogs stuck together. The male lifts one leg. Brief Entanglements. Richard Garcia. TouFir

Two Dreams, The. Giovanni Boccaccio. OBGa, *tr. by* Algernon Charles Swinburne

Two Drinking Songs. José Juan Tablada.

　I Built My Hut. AWP, *tr. by* Arthur Waley

　"I built my hut near where people live." AWP, *tr. by* Arthur Waley

Two Drops. Zbigniew Herbert. RB, *tr. by* Czeslaw Milosz

Two earnest young fellows named Wright. Limerick. Basil Ransome-Davies. PeLi

Two Ember Days in Alabama. Andrew Hudgins. RA

Two Englishmen. Douglas Stewart. CBAP

Two evils, monstrous either one apart. Winter Remembered. John Crowe Ransom. HAP; NOBA; OxBA; UnPo; VGW

Two eyes, the cathedral's spires look black. One Tourist's Cologne. Hal Colebatch. NOBAu

Two-Faced Too. *Unknown.* OBWVE, *tr. by* Glyn Jones

Two Fawns That Didn't See the Light This Spring. Gary Snyder. HCAP

Two feet deep. Ajo Lily. Peggy Shumaker. PoCoUp

Two Figures. N. Scott Momaday. NoP-4

Two figures face each other. Greeting Shekinah. Lynn Gottlieb. HW

Two figures in deep water. Walking to Bellrock. Michael Ondaatje. NOBC

Two Figures in Dense Violet Night. Wallace Stevens. MoAmPo

Two figures there beneath the dome, walking with similar pace. St. Sophia. John Fuller. DiPo

Two Fires, The. Judith Wright. MoBrPo

Two Fish. Katha Pollitt. DiPo; NIL-7; NIP-4

Two Fish by a Willow Embankment. Hsü Wei. CoBLCP, *tr. by* Jonathan Chaves

Two Fishermen. Stanley Moss. CoAP

Two Fishing Villages. Ellease Southerland. GT

Two floods I read of; water, and of wine. On the Two Great Floods. Francis Quarles. ChIV-1

Two flowers in a letter. Kenneth Rexroth. APSN *Fr.* Love Poems of Marichiko, The.

Two foals sleep back to back, The. Absent Ones, The. Maxine W. Kumin. PAI

Two foot-companions once in deep discourse—. Nimmers, The. John Byrom. OxAEP-1

Two forms move among the dead, high sleep. Owl in the Sarcophagus, The. Wallace Stevens. FaBoMo

Two forms of darkness are there. One is Night.   Doubt.   Mary Elizabeth Coleridge.   NALW; ViWPN

Two freezing winters, and one summer's heat.   From a Sick Poetess to Mrs St George on Her Feeding the Swans.   *Poets of the Tixall Circle.*   EMWP

Two friends at the close of summer.   Why She Says No.   Ellen Bryant Voigt.   FaBoWP

Two friends took a trip together to Stone Man Peak.   Trip to Stone Man Peak, A.   Yang Wan-li.   SuSp, *tr. by* Jonathan Chaves

Two from Israel.   Dom Moraes.
   "Altermann, sipping wine, reads with a look."   NoP-4

Two Gardens.   Walter De la Mare.   OBGa

Two gardens see!—this, of enchanted flowers.   Two Gardens.   Walter De la Mare.   OBGa

Two Generations.   Leonard Alfred George Strong.   OBMV

Two Gentlemen of Verona, The.   William Shakespeare.
   My Thoughts Do Harbour.   CTC
   (Silvia.)   OBEV
   Who Is Silvia [*or* Sylvia]?   NoSic; SCGP

Two Gentlemen That Broke Their Promise of a Meeting.   James Shirley.   BeJo

Two Gifts.   *Unknown.*   BoWoP, *tr. by* Willis Barnstone

Two Girls.   Suzanne Gardinier.   KGB; NeAmPo

Two girls on a ditch bank.   Fishing.   Paula McLain.   AmPoNex

Two Girls Singing.   Iain Crichton Smith.   NePenScot

Two girls walk to the river bank.   La Llorona.   Juan Delgado.   GeoHom

Two Graces.   *Unknown.*
   Child's Grace, A.   FaBoCh
   "Hurly, hurly, roon the table."   FaBoCh
   "Some hae meat that canna eat."   FaBoCh

Two Grandmas.   Stanley H. Barkan.   UnSA

Two Gray Kits.   *Unknown.*   ReMoGo

Two green-webbed chairs.   Children Playing Checkers at the Edge of the Forest.   Adrienne Rich.   LCAP-2; WeW-3

Two Guitars.   Víctor Hernández Cruz.   PueRic; TouFir

Two guitars were left in a room all alone.   Two Guitars.   Víctor Hernández Cruz.   PueRic; TouFir

Two hands lie still, the hairy and the white.   Love for a Hand.   Karl Shapiro.   CoAP

Two Hands on the Water.   Zuhur Dixon.   MAP, *tr. by* Patricia Alanah Byrne and Salma Khadra Jayyusi

Two hands upon the breast.   Labor and Rest.   Dinah Maria Mulock.   TreFP

Two Hangovers.   James Wright (1927–80).   LCAP-2
   "I slouch in bed."   EmeKit
   I Try to Waken and Greet the World Once Again.   EmeKit
   "In a pine tree, / A few yards from my window sill."   EmeKit

Two Headmistresses.   *Unknown.*   *See* Miss Buss and Miss Beale

Two Hearts Divided.   R. Williams Parry.   OBWVE, *tr. by* Joseph P. Clancy

Two hearts: two blades of grass I braid together.   Weaving Love-Knots 2.   Hsüeh T'ao.   BoWoP, *tr. by* Carolyn Kizer

Two Historians.   J. E. Thorold Rogers.   *See* On the Historians Freeman and Stubbs

Two hollow eyes follow a cat's crie.   Mac Wellman.   FTOS   *Fr.* Hollowness.

Two homecomings sustained my life.   Homecomings.   Pablo Neruda.   GifTon, *tr. by* William O'Daly

Two Hookers.   A. K. Redwing.   VoR

Two Hoppers.   John Updike.   PoSol

Two Horses and a Dog.   James Galvin.   GifTon

Two horses in yellow light.   August.   Adrienne Rich.   NNaP

Two Houses.   Edward Thomas.   FaBoCh

Two hulks on Hudson's stormy bosom lie.   Philip Freneau.   TCAPo   *Fr.* British Prison Ship, The.

Two Hundred and Nineteenth Chorus.   Jack Kerouac.   NeAP   *Fr.* Mexico City Blues.

Two Hundred and Sixty-Five Words.   Sophie Hannah.   HarvBoo

Two Hundred and Twenty-Eighth Chorus.   Jack Kerouac.   NeAP; PmAP   *Fr.* Mexico City Blues.

211th Chorus.   Jack Kerouac.   NeAP; PFTM-2; PmAP; PoM   *Fr.* Mexico City Blues.

Two hundred men and eighteen killed.   James Henry.   NOBVV

209 Canal.   Richard Howard.   TAP

270 The birches are worn out by mirrors.   My Final Agonies.   Benjamin Péret.   PFTM-1

230th Chorus.   Jack Kerouac.   NeAP   *Fr.* Mexico City Blues.

225th Chorus.   Jack Kerouac.   NeAP   *Fr.* Mexico City Blues.

221st Chorus.   Jack Kerouac.   NeAP   *Fr.* Mexico City Blues.

229th Chorus.   Jack Kerouac.   PoM   *Fr.* Mexico City Blues.

Two Men, Two Grapefruits.   Donna Masini.   KGB

Two in a Room.   Viktor Krivulin.   TCRusP, *tr. by* Anna Barker and Daniel Weissbort

Two in August.   John Crowe Ransom.   AWP; OxBA

Two in Bed.   Abram Bunn Ross.   NTCP

Two in the Campagna.   Robert Browning.   EBEV; EBVV; FHYEP; GTBS-P; NAEL-5v2; NAEL-6v2; NOBE; NOBVV; NPeEn; NoP-4; OxAEP-2; OxBEV; PoE; SCGP; TFi; TOF

Two infants vis-à-vis.   Bleecker Street.   Jean Garrigue.   TAP

Two Infinities.   Edward Dowden.   GSo

Two Invocations of Death.   Kathleen Jessie Raine.
   "Death, I repent."   OxBTC
   "From a place I came."   OxBTC
   Invocation of Death.   OxBTC

Two Irish yews, prickly green, poisonous.   Gate Lodge.   Richard Murphy.   PBCIP

Two jays came down my street.   Jays, The.   John Heath-Stubbs.   NOxBChV

Two Kinds of People.   Ella Wheeler Wilcox.   PoToHe

Two Kinds of Welsh Bards.   Endre Ady.   IQMS, *tr. by* Neville Masterman

Two ladies to the summit of my mind.   Sonnet: Of Beauty and Duty.   Dante Alighieri.   AWP; EaItPo, *tr. by* Dante Gabriel Rossetti

Two ladies walked on the soft green grass.   Dream of Comparison, A.   Stevie Smith.   BWW

Two Laments.   *Unknown.*   ChiP, *tr. by* Arthur Waley

Two lands at last connected.   Ode to the Severn Bridge.   Harri Webb.   TCAWP

Two leaps the water from its race.   Mill, A.   William Allingham.   FaBoEE; OxBSP

Two legs sat upon three legs.   Riddle.   Mother Goose.   LB; NTCP; OxNR

Two liddle niggers all dressed in white.   Raise a "Rucus" To-Night.   *Unknown.*   BPo; TAP

Two-line epigram is perfect, A.   Step.   Cyrillus.   GrAn

Two Lines from Paul Celan.   Mark Halperin.   GifTon

Two Lips.   Thomas Hardy.   BoLoP

Two little creatures.   Monkeys.   Padraic Colum.   OxBTC

Two little dicky birds.   *Unknown.*   LB; OxNR

Two little dogs / Sat by the fire.   *Unknown.*   OxNR

Two Little Girls.   Fawziyya Abu Khalid.   PoArWo, *tr. by* Farouk Mustafa

Two little girls, one fair, one dark.   Lost Children, The.   Randall Jarrell.   CoAP; TAP

Two Little Kittens.   *Unknown.*   OBCA

Two little princesses, The.   Palace Cook's Tale.   Joan Aiken.   NOxBChV

Two Lives.   William Ellery Leonard.   Son
   "In the brown grasses slanting with the wind."   APT-1
   Indian Summer.   APT-1
   "That once the gentle mind of my dead wife."   APT-1

Two long had lov'd, and now the nymph desir'd.   There's No To-Morrow.   Anne Finch (b. 1908).   NIL-7

Two Look at Two.   Robert Frost.   MoAmPo

Two Lovers, The.   Marie de France.   BoWoP, *tr. by* Patricia Terry

Two lovers face one another.   Slow Curtain.   John Wheelwright.   APT-2

Two lovers in an Irish wood at dusk.   Story.   Eavan Boland.   HarvBoo

Two lovers to a midnight meadow came.   Amateurs of Heaven, The.   Howard Nemerov.   SoSe-8

Two Loves.   Lord Alfred Bruce Douglas.   CAGL

Two Loves Found Refuge.   Francis Saltus Saltus.
   "Two loves found refuge in my happy heart."   VerBaPo

Two loves I have of comfort and despair.   William Shakespeare.   EBEV; HeIP-4; NAEL-5v1; NAEL-6v1; NAEL-7v1; NIL-7; NIP-4; OxBSo; Son   *Fr.* Sonnets.

Two Lyrics.   Lorenzo de' Medici.   AWP, *tr. by* John Addington Symonds

Two Magicians, The.   *Unknown.*   OxBoLi

Two magpies under the cypresses, The.   What Birds Were There.   William Everson.   NoAM

Two Masks Unearthed in Bulgaria.   William Meredith.   BodElec

Two Meditations.   Rosario Castellanos.   PFTM-2, *tr. by* Julian Pulley

Two Meetings, The.   Eugene Field.   PWR

Two Men.   Andrew Lansdown.   NOBAu

Two men appear on a tractor.   Poem about the Future.   Hans Magnus Enzensberger.   PoSu

Two men embrace on the billboard, their faces.   Simplify Your Combination Therapy.   Mark Wunderlich.   NAPBL

Two men filched pumpkins from the grocery display.   Theft.   Karen Volkman.   AmPoNex

Two men sat roasting in their blue suits, The.   Inspiration.   James Tate.   BodElec

Two men smiled into each other's eyes, The. (LL)   Episode of Hands.   Hart Crane.   CAGL; NIL-7

Two Men, Two Grapefruits.   Donna Masini.   KGB

Two men were dragging a cart through the woods.   Duke and I 2, The.   Charles Ducal.   TuT, *tr. by* Desmond Egan

Two Mesostics Re Merce Cunningham.   John Cage.   PFTM-2

Two Mice, The. Robert Henryson. *See* Tale of the Upland Mouse and the Burgess Mouse, The

Two middle-aged ladies from Fordham. Limerick. *Unknown.* PeLi

Two minutes long it pitches through some bar. Elvis Presley. Thom Gunn. AllShUp

Two minutes' silence was cut to one, The. Armistice Day '77, Honiton. John Tripp. TCAWP

2: Moderation. Horace. PoToHe, *tr. by* William Cowper *Fr.* Odes.

Two Monkeys, The. John Gay. OBCoV

Two Months Married. Aidan Carl Mathews. PBCIP

2 Months Rent Due and 1 Bag of Rice. Luci Beach. ReEnLa

Two More about a Crow, in the Manner of Zukofsky. *Unknown.* STP, *tr. by* Richard Johnny John and Jerome Rothenberg

Two Mothers, The. Rhonda Samuel Napurrurla. IBA

Two mothers both sit down near the fire at evening, The. Two Mothers, The. Rhonda Samuel Napurrurla. IBA

Two moving figures flow together: see. Reflection. Elisabeth Eybers. PeSAV, *tr. by* the author

Two mules stand in front of the brick wall of a warehouse. Mule Team and Poster. Donald Justice. VCAP

Two Musicians, The. Henrietta Cordelia Ray. CBWP-3

Two Mysteries, The. Mary Mapes Dodge. PWR; TrCP

Two nails, The. (LL) Mirror, The. Michael Davitt. BiHa; CIP-2; PBCIP, *tr. by* Paul Muldoon

Two Names. Betty Scott Stam. SacPr

Two, naturally, we are two. Shepherd. Sheila Kohler. Unle

Two-natured, loving my world. Comb and the Mirror, The. Elizabeth Spires. FFC

Two Neighbours, The. George Campbell Hay. OxBS

Two nights in Manchester: nothing much to do. Mr. Cooper. Anthony Thwaite. OxBTC

Two Noble Kinsmen, The. John Fletcher.
  Bridal Song, A: "Roses, their sharp spines being gone." NOBE; NOSC; NoSic
  (Dirge of the Three Queens.) OBEV
  "Roses, their sharp spines being gone." NOBE; NOSC; NoSic

Two nudists of Dover. Third Limick. Ogden Nash. PeLi

Two o'clock on a Saturday afternoon in November. Matinee. Susan Clements. UnSA

2 o'clock: strong moonlight, few stars. (LL) Track. Tomas Tranströmer. RB; SPE, *tr. by* Robert Bly

Two, of course there are two. Death and Co. Sylvia Plath. CoAmPo; EmeKit; LCAP-2

Two of far nobler shape erect and tall. John Milton. PeECV *Fr.* Paradise Lost.

Two of Napoleon's grenadiers. Grenadiers, The. Heinrich Heine. FaBoWar, *tr. by Unknown*

Two of the Festivals of Death. João Cabral de Melo Neto. TCLAP, *tr. by* W. S. Merwin

Two of Them, The. Hugo von Hofmannsthal. STV, *tr. by* John Frederick Nims

Two of us sharing a single pair of shoes, The. (LL) Fêng Mêng-lung. ColAnChi; WoPoe, *tr. by* Richard W. Bodman *Fr.* Mountain Songs.

Two of Us Together, Each of Us Alone, The. Yehuda Amichai [*or* Amikhai]. FIT, *tr. by* Robert Friend

Two Old Crows. Nicholas Vachel Lindsay. OBAL

Two old dancing shoes my grandfather. Genius. Philip Levine. NoAM

Two Old Kings, The. John Byrne Leicester Warren, 3d Baron De Tabley. OBEV

Two Old Ladies. Siegfried Sassoon. OxBTC

Two on one moped, leather-coated. Old in Overijssel. René Van Riessen. TuT, *tr. by* Robert Greacen

2.1. Ovid. OBVE, *tr. by* Christopher Marlowe *Fr.* Elegies.

Two or Three; a Recipe [*or* Receipt] to Make a Cuckold. Pope. BoLoP; FaBoEE

Two or three minutes—two or three hours. Minutes of Gold. *Unknown.* PoToHe

Two or three visits, and two or three bows. Two or Three; a Recipe [*or* Receipt] to Make a Cuckold. Pope. BoLoP; FaBoEE

Two Pages of Szondi, The. János Arany. IQMS, *tr. by* Adam Makkai

2 Pages, 122 Words on Music and Dance. John Cage. APT-2

Two Pantuns. *Unknown.*
  "They wear." WoPoe, *tr. by* R. J. Wilkinson and R. O. Winstedt
  "Thousand doves, A." WoPoe, *tr. by* R. J. Wilkinson and R. O. Winstedt

Two Parents, The. Hugh MacDiarmid. FaBoTw; OxBTC

Two passive and two active—you'd imagine. Two Plus Two. Strato [*or* Straton]. GrAn, *tr. by* Teddy Hogge

Two Performing Elephants. D. H. Lawrence. RB

Two Pigeons. *Unknown.* OxNR; ReMoGo

Two pilgrims, broiling in the sun. Beware of Dogmas. Ebenezer Elliott. FaBoEE

Two playwrights called Beaumont and Fletcher. Limerick. Fiona Pitt-Kethley. PeLi

Two plum trees, The. Buson. EH, *tr. by* R. H. Blyth

Two Plus Two. Strato [*or* Straton]. GrAn, *tr. by* Teddy Hogge

Two Poems. Rosario Castellanos. PFTM-2, *tr. by* Magda Bogin

Two Poems. Aleksandr Soprovsky [*or* Soprovskii].
  "Notes from the house of the dead." TCRP

Two Poems. Andrey [*or* Andrei] Andreievich Voznesensky [*or* Voznesenskii]. VCWP, *tr. by* Patricia Blake and William Jay Smith

Two Poems, The. Kahlil Gibran. GraLe

Two Poems about President Harding. James Wright (1927–80). CoAP

Two Poems for Black Relocation Centers. Etheridge Knight. NNaP
  "Flukum couldn't stand the strain. Flukum." ESEAA
  Poem for Black Relocation Centers, A. ESEAA

Two Poems on Insect Painting by Candidate Yin. Su Tung-p'o (Su Shih).
  "Its rancid saliva can't fill up a shell." SuSp, *tr. by* Irving Y. Lo
  "Its savage eyes, at whom do they glare?" SuSp, *tr. by* Irving Y. Lo
  On a Snail. SuSp, *tr. by* Irving Y. Lo
  On a Toad. SuSp, *tr. by* Irving Y. Lo

Two Poems on Night. Tu Fu. SuSp, *tr. by* Jan Walls

Two Poems on the Catholic Bavarians. Edgar Bowers. CRP

Two Poems on the Eretrians Taken Prisoner by the Persians. Plato.
  "Leaving behind for ever the thundering Aegean." GrAn
  "We are Eretrians from Euboia." GrAn

2 Poems on the Same Theme. Michael Burkard. BodElec

Two Poems Presented to the Gentleman in the Office of Palace Writers Ku Yen-hsien. Lu Chi.
  "Off at dawn to service in the walled and storied palace." CoBCP

Two Poems to the Tune "Chin-tzu ching" The Sutra in Gold Characters. Ma Chih-yüan. CoBLCP, *tr. by* Jonathan Chaves

Two Poems to the Tune "Hsiao-t'iao hung." Ni Tsan. CoBLCP, *tr. by* Jonathan Chaves

Two Poems to the Tune "Jen-yüeh yüan." Ni Tsan. CoBLCP, *tr. by* Jonathan Chaves

Two Poems to the Tune "Po pu tuan." Ma Chih-yüan. CoBLCP, *tr. by* Jonathan Chaves

Two Postures beside a Fire. James Wright (1927–80). HCAP; HeIP-4

Two Prayers. Andrew Gillies. PoToHe
  (Two Prayers.) PoToHe

Two Prison Poems. Ho Chi Minh. PoetW, *tr. by* Burton Raffel

Two purple pigeons circle a London square. Exiled Heart, The. Maurice Lindsay. OxBS

Two Pursuits. Christina Georgina Rossetti. WPE

Two Quartz Pebbles. Vasco [*or* Vasko] Popa. PoSu, *tr. by* Anne Pennington *Fr.* Quartz Pebble, The.

Two Questions, The. Alice Thompson Meynell. WPE

Two Ramages for Old Masters. Robert Bly. BodElec

Two Ravens, The. *Unknown.* *See* Twa Corbies, The

Two Red Roses across the Moon. William Morris. EBVV; UV

Two Rivers. Ralph Waldo Emerson. APN-1; NCAP; NOBA; OxBA; PoE

Two Rivers. Hilary Llewellyn-Williams. AngWePo; TCAWP

Two Rivers, The. *Unknown.* *See* Tweed and Till

Two roads diverged in a yellow wood. Road Not Taken, The. Robert Frost. APT-1; AiP; ChAP; FaBoCh; HAP; HarvBoo; HeIP-4; ITBLP; MoAmPo; NAAL-2v2; NAAL-5; NIL-7; NIP-4; NoAM; NoP-4; OxBA; PoPoPo; SAmP; SoSe-8; TAP; TCAPo; TFi; TRP; TwCP

Two roses I gave the therapist. Two and One. Richard Chess. TaR

Two rows of cabbages. In the Ambulance. Wilfrid Wilson Gibson. FaBoWar

TWO's a couple. Four on a Sidewalk. *Unknown.* CA

Two scenes lie before us. In the first. Nouns of Assemblage. Stephen Dobyns. BodElec

Two Seabirds. *Unknown.* WoPoe, *tr. by* John Updike *Fr.* Wanderer and the Seafarer, The.

Two seas our eyes beheld—one dark, one light. From Green Mountain. William Reed Huntington. APN-2

Two Seconds. Marie-Dominique Massoni. SurWo, *tr. by* Myrna Bell Rochester

Two separate divided silences. Dante Gabriel Rossetti. BoLoP *Fr.* House of Life, The.

Two Shadows. Elizabeth Spires. DiPo

Two shadows now, north from the translucent. Alba, With a Refrain from the Provençal. *Unknown.* WoPoe, *tr. by* Tim Reynolds

Two shall be born, the whole wide world apart. Fate. Susan Marr Spalding. PoToHe

Two shall be born the whole world wide apart. Fate. Carolyn Wells. SWaP

Two Shapes. Arthur Gregor. TAP

Two she-camels spied on a goat. Limerick. *Unknown*. PeLi

Two silhouettes. Story, A. Yusuf Al-Sa'igh. MAP, *tr. by* Diana Der Hovanessian and Salma Khadra Jayyusi

Two Sisters, The. *Aborigine Oral Tradition*. NOBAu, *tr. by* Manoowa

Two sisters who had no brother. Brotherless Sisters. *Unknown*. WoPoe, *tr. by* Charles Simic

Two Sleepy People. Hoagy Carmichael. ReLy

Two Smothered Children. Marion Albina Bigelow. VerBaPo

Two snails are on their way. Song of the snails on their way to a funeral. Jacques Prévert. MFP, *tr. by* Martin Sorrell

Two Soldier's Songs. *Unknown*. ChiP, *tr. by* Arthur Waley

Two soluble aspirins spore in this glass, their mycelia. Spilt Milk. Sarah Maguire. EmeKit; LW; MFPA

Two songs. Louisa Sarah Bevington.
"Deep, and silent, and wide." PEW
With the Tide: A Cry of Weakness. PEW

Two Songs. Cecil Day Lewis. NoP-4

Two Songs. Cecil Day Lewis. HAP; NoAM
"Come, live with me and be my love." BoLoP; NIP-4; OBMV
"I've heard them lilting at loom and belting." OBMV
Song: "Come, live with me and be my love." BoLoP; NIP-4; OBMV

Two Songs. Adrienne Rich. EmeKit; NIL-7
"Sex, as they harshly call it." NIP-4; NOBA; TAP
"That "old last act"! / And yet sometimes." NIP-4; NOBA; TAP
Two Songs. NIP-4; NOBA; TAP

Two Songs. Adrienne Rich. NIP-4; NOBA; TAP *Fr.* Two Songs.

Two Songs. Marina Ivanovna Tsvetayeva [*or* Tsvetaeva].
"Yesterday he could still look in my eyes, yet." TCRP

Two Songs About a Dead Person or a Mole—Whichever It Was. Richard Johnny John. PFTM-1 *Fr.* Songs from the Society of the Mystic Animals.

Two Songs about Flowers & Where I Was Walking. *Unknown*. STP, *tr. by* Johnny John and Jerome Rothenberg

Two Songs from a Play. W. B. Yeats. FaBoTw; HAP; NOBE; PoE *Fr.* Resurrection, The.

Two Songs from *Sweeny Agonistes*. T. S. Eliot. UnPo *Fr.* Sweeney Agonistes.

Two Songs of a Fool. W. B. Yeats. RB

Two Songs of Advent. Yvor Winters. APT-2

Two Songs of Peace. Yehuda Amichai [*or* Amikhai]. AF, *tr. by* Assia Gutmann

Two Songs on the Economy of Abundance. James Agee. MoAmPo

Two Sonnets. John Ashbery. VGW

Two Sonnets. Charles Hamilton Sorley. MoBrPo
"Saints have adored the lofty soul of you." PeFWW
"Such, such is Death: no triumph: no defeat." PeFWW

Two Sonnets on Fame. John Keats.
"Fame, like a wayward girl, will still be coy." CenSon
On Fame. CenSon

Two Sons. Laoiseach Mac an Bhaird. NOIV

Two sons are gone. Later Still. Philip Levine. ColAP

Two Souls. Marjorie Lowry Christie Pickthall. NOBC

Two spiral stairs we climb to bed together. Philip Gross. NewEx

Two Spring Charms. *Unknown*. WoPoe, *tr. by* James Wright

Two Springs. Li Ch'ing-chao. BoWoP; OHPC, *tr. by* Kenneth Rexroth

Two Standards. Elise Paschen. OPRER; ReEnLa

Two Stars, The. William Henry Davies. MoBrPo

Two statesmen met by moonlight. What the Moon Saw. Nicholas Vachel Lindsay. FaBoEE; OxBSP

Two Statues. Pauline Hawkesworth. Prnts

Two sticks and an apple. London Bells. *Unknown*. OPOU

Two Stories. Charles Wright. LCAP-2

Two stories high above Saturn St. For My Mother. Doris Brett. NOBAu

Two Strange Worlds. Francesca Yetunde Pereira. PBA

Two Strangers, The. Manuel A. Viray. ReBoTo

Two Streams, The. Oliver Wendell Holmes. APN-1

Two streams: one dry, one poured all night by our beds. Interrogation, The. Li-Young Lee. PoPoPo

Two strong impulses: One. Jelaluddin [*or* Jalal al-Din] Rumi. RaBo *Fr.* Four Quatrains.

Two Studies in Idealism: Short Survey of American and Human History. Robert Penn Warren. CBCWP

Two Suffering Men. Eugene Hirsch. BloBone

Two Summers in Moravia. Roger McDonald. CBAP

Two summers? Epochs, then, of ice. Return to Harmony 3. Agha Shahid Ali. BAP-97

Two survived the flood. Stones and Bones. Christopher Reid. NPeEn

Two Swedish Riddles. *Unknown*.
"Father's sickle is hanging." WoPoe, *tr. by* Siv Cedering Fox
Nettle. WoPoe, *tr. by* Siv Cedering Fox
New Moon, The. WoPoe, *tr. by* Siv Cedering Fox
"Old green witch, An." WoPoe, *tr. by* Siv Cedering Fox

Two sweeter babes you nare did see. *Unknown*. FaBoEE

Two sweethearts courted happily for quite a while. Some of These Days. Shelton Brooks. ReLy

Two swimmers wrestled on the spar. Emily Dickinson. TCAPo

Two Tales of Clumsy. Gjertrud Schnackenberg.
"When Clumsy harks the gladsome ting-a-lings." NoAM

Two telephones all morning giving each other hell. Cash Positive. Peter McDonald. PNI

Two that could not have lived their single lives. Two in August. John Crowe Ransom. AWP; OxBA

Two that through windy nights kept company. Two Neighbours, The. George Campbell Hay. OxBS

Two things I have asked of Thee. Bible, *O.T.* TrJP *Fr.* Proverbs.

Two Thoughts of Death. Christina Georgina Rossetti. ViWPN

Two thousand feet above the torrent's clattering sibilance. Night Out, A. Douglas Houston. TCAWP

2976. Julia Uceda. BoWoP, *tr. by* Willis Barnstone

Two thousand years ago the Master Tsuang Tsi. Dream of Tsuang Tsi, The. Lőrinc Szabó. IQMS, *tr. by* Adam Makkai

Two Tile Beaks. Maria Amalia Fonte Boa. BoWoP, *tr. by* Willis Barnstone and Nelson Cerqueira

Two Timer. Juan Delgado. TouFir

Two Tokyos. Shuntaro Tanikawa. PoetW, *tr. by* Harold Wright

Two Tongue-Pointing (Satirical) Songs. *Unknown*. NOBAu

Two top-knots not yet plaited into one. Going to the Mountains with a Little Dancing Girl, Aged Fifteen. Po Chü-i. ChiP, *tr. by* Arthur Waley

Two Tramps in Mud Time. Robert Frost. APT-1; MoAmPo; NAAL-2v2; NoAM; SAmP

Two Translations from Kabir. Robert Bly.
"Are you looking for me? I am in the next seat!" WoPoe
Breath, The. WoPoe
(NOTL.) EnlH

Two Trees. Grace Schulman. ExTi

Two Trinities. Kenneth Mackenzie. CBAP

Two Truths. Helen Hunt Jackson. LW

Two / Two cigarettes in the dark. Two Cigarettes in the Dark. Lew Pollack. ReLy

2 Variations: All About Love. Philip Whalen. NeAP

Two Variations on a Theme. Carl Rakosi. APT-2

Two Variations on a Theme by Kobayashi. Larry Levis. BodElec

Two Varieties of the Bitter Orange. J. L. Jacobs. AmPoNex

Two Vast Enjoyments Commemorated. John Danforth. SCAP

Two Vietnam Poems: (1966). Bill Knott. PBCAP; SPE
((End) of Summer (1966).) SPE

Two Views of Two Ghost Towns. Charles Tomlinson. NoAM

Two Villages. Grace Paley. FaBoWar

Two Voices. Edmund Charles Blunden. OBWP; PeFWW

Two Voices. Diana Der Hovanessian. TWW

Two voices are there: one is of the deep. Sonnet, A. James Kenneth Stephen. CABP; NOBL; UV

Two Voices are there; one is of the sea. Thought[s] of a Briton on the Subjugation of Switzerland. William Wordsworth. UV

Two ways I love Thee, selfishly. Rabi'a al-Adawiyya. TOF

Two weeks across a strange sea. Katori Maru, October 1920. James Masao Mitsui. OpBo

Two went to pray? o rather say. Two Went Up into the Temple To Pray. Richard Crashaw. ChIV-2; HAP

Two Went Up into the Temple To Pray. Richard Crashaw. ChIV-2; HAP

Two were silent in a sunless church, The. Her Dilemma. Thomas Hardy. NOBVV

Two wild duck of the upland spaces. Duck. John Lyle Donaghy. BIrV

Two Witches. Robert Frost.
"I stayed [*or* staid] the night for shelter at a farm." APT-1; NOBA; NoAM; PoE
Witch of Coös, The. APT-1; NOBA; NoAM; PoE

Two Witches. Charles Reznikoff. OTCP

Two Women. George R. Sims.
"To-night is a midnight meeting, and the Earl is in the chair." UV

Two Women. Constance Fenimore Woolson.
One. SWaP
Other, The. SWaP

"Through miles of green cornfields that lusty." SWaP

"West from the Capital's crowded throng." SWaP

Two Women Knitting. Mrinal Pande. OMIP, tr. by Mrinal Pande

Two women on the lone wet strand. Watchers, The. William Stanley Braithwaite. NAAAL

Two women, seventies, hold hands. Day Trip. Carole Satyamurti. OPOU

Two women sit at a table by a window. Light breaks. After Twenty Years. Adrienne Rich. TRP

Two women sit in the shade away from the hot sun. Pansy Rose Napaljarri. IBA

Two Words; a Wedding. B. P. Nichol. NOBC

Two words from China: "Ku li"—bitter strength. Ku Li. "Robin Hyde." PeNZ

Two workmen were carrying a sheet of asbestos. Christo's. Paul Muldoon. CIP-2

Two Worlds. Richard Watson Gilder. GS

Two Worlds. Julia Older. TWW

Two Wrestlers. Robert Francis. MoASP

Two X. E. E. Cummings. FaBoMo

Two-Year-Old Has Had a Motherless Week, The. Karl Shapiro. WeW-3

Two years I've been in the Eastern Capital. For Li Po. Tu Fu. SuSp, tr. by Eugene Eoyang

Two Years Later. John Wieners. PmAP; PoM; RaBo

Two years now since I last came. Arriving at Hangchou. Yüan Mei. CoBLCP, tr. by Jonathan Chaves

Two years now since my second marriage. Year Wu-tzu [1048], The, First Month, Night of the Twenty-sixth: A Dream. Mei Yao Ch'en. SuSp, tr. by Jonathan Chaves

Two years we spent. Woods, The. Derek Mahon. NOIV; PBCIP

Two young guys. Tremor, The. Jack Hirschman. BodElec

Two young ones fed, bathèd, zippered, read to and sung to. Time Out. Maurice Riordan. EmeKit; ModIr

'Twould ring the bells of Heaven. Bells of Heaven, The. Ralph Hodgson. MoBrPo; NOBE; OBEV; OxBSP

Tyger, Tyger. Isabel Meyrelles. SurWo, tr. by Penelope Rosemont

Tyger Tyger [or Tyger! Tyger! or Tiger! Tiger!] burning bright. William Blake. AWP; BBASP; BRP; ChAP; ClHu; FaBoCh; HAP; HeIP-4; ITBLP; InPK-6; MakPoe; NAEL-6v2; NAWM-7v2; NIL-7; NIP-4; NOBE; NOBRP; NOEC; NOxBChV; NPeEn; NoP-4; OBEV; OPOU; OxBEV; PeECV; PoE; PoPoPo; PoRA; RB; SCGP; SCV; SoSe-8; TFi; TTTS; UnPo; WHSW Fr. Songs of Experience.

Tying my heart to her by those rich chain[e]s. (LL) Aemilia Bassano Lanyer. BASC; CABP; NAEL-7v1; NoP-4; PBRV

Tying Up for the Night at Maple River Bridge. Chang Chi. CoBCP, tr. by Burton Watson

Tyler scuffs oak leaves to frisk. Nothing Happened. Belle Waring. PBCAP

Tyler was no Whig at all & after his term's end. Jackson Mac Low. APSN Fr. Presidents of the United States of America, The.

Tyndarus attempting too kis a fayre lasse with a long nose. Of Tyndarus, That Frumped a Gentlewoman. Unknown. BIrV, tr. by Richard Stanyhurst

Type of the antique Rome! Rich reliquary. Coliseum, The. Edgar Allan Poe. APN-1; NOBA

Typing the Letters. John A. Scott. BMAP

Typists. Patricia K. Page. NALW

Tyr'd with all these for restfull death I cry. William Shakespeare. See Tired [or Tyr'd, or Tir'd] with all these, for restful death I cry

Tyrannic Love. Dryden.

Epilogue to Tyrannic[k] Love. OBCoV

"Hold, are you mad? you damned [or damn'd] confounded dog." OBCoV

Tyranny of Choice. Elizabeth Garrett. NeBl

Tyranny of fuel, The. Up & down, round & round, merrygoround. Acrospirical Meanderings in a Tongue of the Time. Chris Torrance. Oth

Tyranny of Love, The. Mary Robinson. CenSon; RWP

Tyranny of Moths. Gerald Vizenor. VoR

Tyrant, The. Faiz Ahmad Faiz. AF, tr. by Naomi Lazard

Tyrant in Sleep, Naught Differeth from a Common Man, A. Timothy Kendall. NoSic

Tyrant inspires small poems, The. Paavo Haavikko. WoPoe, tr. by Anselm Hollo Fr. Fifteen Epigrams in Praise of the Tyrant.

Tyrant, why [or whie] swell'st thou thus. BASC; PBRV, tr. by Mary Sidney Herbert, Countess of Pembroke Fr. Psalms.

Tyre brought me up, who born in thee had been. Of Himself. Meleager. AWP, tr. by Richard Garnett

Tyre of the farther West! be thou too warned. John Keble. SacPr Fr. Lyra Apostolica.

Tyrian dye why do you wear. Abraham Cowley. NOSC; OxAEP-1 Fr. Sylva.

Tywater. Richard Wilbur. CoAmPo; TRP

Tzu-yeh Song. Li Po. CoBCP, tr. by Burton Watson

Tzu Yeh Songs. Unknown.

"All night I could not sleep." BoWoP

"At the time when blossoms." BoWoP

"Cool breezes—I sleep by the open window." CoBCP

"Fragrance comes from the scent I wear, The." CoBCP

"Hems gathered up, sash not yet tied." CoBCP

"I heard my love was going to Yang-chou." BoWoP

"I will carry my coat and not put on my belt." BoWoP

"In the hottest time, when all is still and windless." CoBCP

("Nights are long and I cannot sleep.") CoBCP, tr. by Burton Watson

"Out the southern gate at sundown." CoBCP

"When ice on the pond is three feet thick." CoBCP

Tzu-yeh Songs of the Four Seasons. Unknown.

Spring. SuSp

"Before jade pavilions the new moon dims." SuSp

"Bewitching the blossoms of the spring grove." SuSp

"Luminous winds flicker in the moonrise." SuSp

"Plum flowers all fallen and gone." SuSp

"Spring breeze stirs a springtime heart." SuSp

"Young swallows trill their new tune." SuSp

Summer. SuSp, tr. by Michael E. Workman

U

U feel that way sometimes. Mixed Sketches. Haki R. Madhubuti. BPo; TAP

"u", 'je', 'r', 'r', "im", "a", "finally." Douglas Oliver. Oth

U Name This One. Carolyn M. Rodgers. BlSi

U r n / u r n / u r n. Garden Poem. Ian Hamilton Finlay. OBGa

U. S. A. Rosemary Benét.

"So we march into the present." HHAm

U. S. 1946 King's X. Robert Frost. NIP-4

U.S. Sailor with the Japanese Skull, The. Winfield Townley Scott. APT-2

UBI AMOR IBI OCULUS EST. (LL) Ezra Pound. APSN; APT-1; VGW Fr. Cantos.

Ubi Sunt Qui Ante Nos Fuerunt? Unknown. EBEV; PoE

(Wher beth they biforn us weren.) OHMEL

(Where beth they beforen us weren?) WeW-3

(Where beth they biforen us weren?) HAP; MiEL

Uccello. Gregory Corso. NeAP; PoM

Udude. Pol N Ndu. PBMAP

Ugliest little boy. Life of Lincoln West, The. Gwendolyn Brooks. NoAM

Ugly as a jackass. Tune: "Po Pu-tuan" Long-Haired Little Dog. Wang Ho-ch'ing. ColAnChi, tr. by James I. Crump

Ugly Child, The. Elizabeth Jennings. NOxBChV

Ugly creatures, ugly grunting creatures. Suffering. Miroslav Holub. PoSu, tr. by Ian Milner and George Theiner

Ugly Girl, The. Nikolai Alekseievich Zabolotsky [or Zabolotskii]. TCRP, tr. by Daniel Weissbort

Ugly Heart, The. Martha Anthony. InTrad

Ugly old man, An. No Great Matter. David Lawson. VGW

Ugly season of putrifying buzzards, An. Emilio Villa. ItPo, tr. by Gayle Ridinger Fr. Words.

Ugly your uproar at my side. Unknown. EMWP

Ugolino. Dante Alighieri. OxBEV, tr. by Seamus Heaney Fr. Divina Commedia.

Uguisu has not come, The. Akiko Yosano. OHMPJ

Uguisu on the flowering plum, The. Unknown. OHMPJ

Uguisu sing in the blossoming trees. Kenneth Rexroth. APT-2 Fr. Love Poems of Marichiko, The.

Uguisu sleeps in the bamboo grove, The. Kenneth Rexroth. APSN Fr. Love Poems of Marichiko, The.

Uh huh, uh huh, my jefitos. That's the Way, Uh Huh, Uh Huh, I Liked It. Anthony R. Vigil. AmPoNex

Ujamaa. Wole Soyinka. PBMAP Fr. Shuttle in the Crypt, The.

Ulalume [or Ulalume—a Ballad]. Edgar Allan Poe. APN-1; AWP; NAAL-2v1; NAAL-5; NCAP; NOBA; OxBA; TAP; TCAPo

(To——— Ulalume: A Ballad.) NAAL-3

Ulcerated tooth keeps me awake, there is. Letters from a Father. Mona Van Duyn. NoP-4

Ulinda. David Campbell. CBAP

Ulisses and the Syren. Samuel Daniel. See Ulysses and the Siren [or Syren]

Ulrich von Hutten's Song. Ulrich von Hutten. GePo, tr. by Catherine Winkworth

Ulster Names. John Hewitt. BiHa

Ulster Twilight, An. Seamus Heaney. CIP-2; PBCIP

Ulster Unionist Walks the Streets of London, An. Tom Paulin. PNI

Ultima Ratio. Friedrich Georg Jünger. WoPoe, *tr.* by Les A. Murray

Ultima Ratio Reagan. Howard Nemerov. AF

Ultima Ratio Regum. Stephen Spender. FaBoWar; OBWP; PoWW

Ultimate. Gilbert Keith Chesterton. SacPr

Ultimate, The. George Washington and the Loss of His Teeth. Diane Wakoski. PFTM-2

Ultimate Antientropy, The. Theodore Weiss. NoAM

Ultimate Argument. Ion Caraion. AF, *tr.* by Marguerite Dorian

Ultimate Distance, The. Fu'ad [*or* Fuad] Rifqa [*or* Rifka]. MAP, *tr.* by Sargon Boulus and Samuel Hazo

Ultimate Poem, The. Emmett Williams.
 "Art was our bones." PFTM-2
 Rose is a Rose is a Rose is a Rose is a Rose. PFTM-2
 Rose is a Violin is a Codpiece. PFTM-2
 "Violin devil image on." PFTM-2
 What. PFTM-2

Ultimate Tao is nameless, The. Presented to the Taoist Paragon Mao. Cheng Huan. ColAnChi, *tr.* by Edward H. Schafer

Ultimately it does not matter how he died—. Mozart's Death. Richard Foerster. MiVo

Ultimately the air. From Disaster. George Oppen. APT-2

Ultimatum: Kid to Kid. Langston Hughes. NOxBChV

Ultrasound. Maria Luisa Spaziani. CItWP, *tr.* by Cinzia Sartini Blum and Lara Trubowitz

Ulumbo, a Cat. Rutger Kopland. VCWP, *tr.* by James Brockway

Ulysses. Gwendolyn Brooks.
 "At home we pray every morning, we." OxWW
 Religion. OxWW

Ulysses. Robert Graves. FaBoTw; NoAM

Ulysses. James Joyce.
 "Bronze by gold heard the hoofirons, steelyringing." PFTM-1

Ulysses. Robert Lowell. NAAL-2v2

Ulysses. Umberto Saba. WoPoe, *tr.* by Stephen Sartarelli

Ulysses. Tennyson. AWP; AmFaPo; CABP; ClHu; EBEV; FHYEP; HAP; HeIP-4; InPK-6; MakPoe; NAEL-5v2; NAEL-6v2; NAWM-7v2; NIL-7; NIP-4; NOBE; NOBVV; NPeEn; NoP-4; OxAEP-2; OxBEV; PoE; PoPoPo; PoRA; SCGP; SCV; SoSe-8; TFi; TRP; UnPo; WeW-3

Ulysses and the Siren [*or* Syren]. Samuel Daniel. HAP; NAEL-5v1; NAEL-6v1; NOBE; NoP-4; OBEV; OxAEP-1; PoE
 (Come worthy Greeke, Ulisses come.) OxBEV
 (Ulisses and the Syren.) OxBEV

Ulysses Embroidered. Miriam Waddington. NIL-7

Ulysses Insults over the Cyclops. Homer. NOSC, *tr.* by George Chapman *Fr.* Odyssey.

Ulysses Invokes the Dead. Homer. NOSC, *tr.* by George Chapman *Fr.* Odyssey.

Ulysses Reunited with Penelope. Homer. NOSC; OBVE, *tr.* by George Chapman *Fr.* Odyssey.

Um Hakeem. Salah Niyazi [*or* Niazi]. MAP, *tr.* by Charles Doria and Lena Jayyusi

Uma Worshipping Shiva (On a Kangra miniature). Elsa Cross. TANSG, *tr.* by Patricia Dubrava

Umber was painting of a lion [*or* Lyon] fierce. Upon Umber: Epigram. Robert Herrick. CaPo

Umberto / Always worked hard. In the Winter. Sir Osbert Sitwell. OBGa

Umbilical Cord. Ellyn Maybe. AmPoNex

Umbrella, An. Gertrude Stein. TTTS *Fr.* Tender Buttons.

Umbrella / And a raincoat, An. Conversation. Buson. NTCP

Umpteen hundred and eternity. (LL) Carol for the Last Christmas Eve. Norman Nicholson. NOxBChV; OBCP

Un-American Investigators. Langston Hughes. BPo; HHAm

Un-American Women, The. John Tranter. BMAP

U.N. Environmental Sabbath Program. *Unknown.*
 "Great Spirit." FHYEP
 "Great Spirit, whose dry lands thirst, help us to find." FHYEP
 "We have forgotten who we are." FHYEP
 "We join with the earth and with each other." FHYEP

Un Extraño. Tess Gallagher. ExTi

Un is okay. Zen Americana. Paula Gunn Allen. PoPoPo

Un-Now. Daniil Kharms. TCRP, *tr.* by Bradley Jordan

Un pneumatic cross avec suctiondiscs topped avec thistle-tire. . . s'il vous plaît. (LL) Café du Dôme. Else Von Freytag-Loringhoven. APT-1; SurPaPo

Un-red deer, The. Un-Red Deer, The. Charles Hubert Sisson. HarvBoo

Una Bhan. Tomas Mac Coisdealbhaigh. NOIV, *tr.* by Thomas Kinsella

Una fair, my flower of the amber tresses. Una Bhan. Tomas Mac Coisdealbhaigh. NOIV, *tr.* by Thomas Kinsella

Unable. Raymond Roseliep. HA

Unable, Father, Still, to Disavow. Richard Moore. Son *Fr.* Word from the Hills.

Unable to move. Karen Alkalay-Gut. DTA *Fr.* Between Bombardments: A Journal.

Unable to sleep, or pray, I stand. Ice Storm. Robert Earl Hayden. APT-2; ESEAA

Unaccompanied Suite. Barbara Winder. MiVo

Unanimity Has Been Achieved, Not a Dot Less for Its Accidentalness. Bob Kaufman. NAAAL

Unanswerable Apology for the Rich, An. Mary Barber. ECWP

Unanswered. Yannis Ritsos. AF, *tr.* by Edmund Keeley

Unarmed Combat. Henry Reed. NAEL-6v2 *Fr.* Lessons of the War.

Unaswered Letter. Tess Gallagher. NIP-4

Unavoidable violence. What We Learned. Fanny Howe. FTOS

Unawakend, unwilling / to sleep or wake. (LL) Robert Duncan. APSN; NOBA *Fr.* Passages.

Unawakened, sweet / women. (LL) Belly Dancer. Diane Wakoski. NALW; NoAM

Unaware of illusion or enlightenment. Genko. ZenPo, *tr.* by Takashi Ikemoto and Lucien Stryk

Unaware of the dangers above the small neighborhood pond. On Transportation. Benjamin Paloff. UrbNat

Unbelief. Phoebe Cary. SacPr

Unbeliever, The. Elizabeth Bishop. NAAL-2v2; NAAL-5; NoAM

Unbending Prayer. René Char. AF

Unbeseechable, The. Frances Darwin Cornford. MoBrPo

Unborn. John Le Gay Brereton. NOBAu

Unborn Child, An. Derek Mahon. CABP; PNI; WoPoe

Unbosoming. "Michael Field." VWP

Unbounded is thy range; with varied style. William Collins. NOBE *Fr.* Ode on the Popular Superstitions of the Highlands of Scotland, An.

Unbridled licentiousness with no holds barred. Reading Pornography in Old Age. Howard Nemerov. NoAM

Uncalled. Madison Cawein. TCAPo

Uncarved Block professes no activity, The. Inscribed on the Painting "Pleasures of the Lute by the River." Lin Hung. SuSp, *tr.* by Irving Y. Lo

Uncertain-aged Miss Thereabouts. Smithereens. Dante Gabriel Rossetti. NOBVV

Uncertain Battle, The. David Gascoyne. PoWW

Uncertain Oneiromancy. Denise Levertov. MakPoe

Uncertain which, in ocean or in air. (LL) John Milton. NIL-7; NIP-4 *Fr.* Paradise Lost.

Uncertainty of the Poet, The. Wendy Cope. OPOU

Uncessant minutes, whil'st you move you tell. To His Watch, When He Could Not Sleep. Edward Herbert, 1st Baron Herbert of Cherbury. NOBE

Unchangeable, The. William Shakespeare. *See* Sonnets

Unchangeable indeclinable in gold currency in words. Poem Stalin, The. Adriano Spatola. PFTM-2, *tr.* by Paul Vangelisti

Unchanged from what they were when I was young. (LL) I shall go back. Edna St. Vincent Millay. MoAmPo; UnPo

Unchanged within, to see all changed without. Duty Surviving Self-Love. Samuel Taylor Coleridge. NPeEn

Unchanging, The. Sara Teasdale. APT-1

Unchristian Jacobin whoever. Ode to a Jacobin. *Unknown.* UV

Uncircumcised, The. (LL) Poor Christian Looks at the Ghetto, A. Czeslaw Milosz. HP; PoSu; VCWP

Uncivil sickness, hast thou no regard. Henry Constable. OxBSo *Fr.* Diana.

Uncle. Julia Kasdorf. PBCAP

Uncle. Philip Levine. NNaP

Uncle Alfred's Long Jump. Gareth Owen. OBSP

Uncle an' Aunt. William Barnes. NOBVV

Uncle Ananias. Edwin Arlington Robinson. MoAmPo; NIP-4

Uncle Bill had been there. Almost Going. David Huddle. PBCAP

Uncle Charles: A Home Movie. J. Bernlef. TuT, *tr.* by Peter Van de Kamp

Uncle Devereux would blend to the one color. (LL) My Last Afternoon with Uncle Devereux Winslow. Robert Lowell. NAAL-2v2; NoP-4; VGW

Uncle Dog; the Poet at 9. Robert Sward. CoAP; VGW

Uncle Harry at the La Brea Tar Pits. Ruth Whitman. TaR

Uncle Henry. W. H. Auden. NOBL; PeLV

Uncle Hussein mails his underwear. Holy Water. Hayan Charara. AmPoNex

Uncle Ike's Holiday. Priscilla Jane Thompson. CBWP-2

Uncle Iv Surveys His Domain from His Rocker. Jonathan Williams. NBLV; OBAL

Uncle Jim. Countee Cullen. GT; NAAL-2v2

Uncle Jimmie's Yarn. Priscilla Jane Thompson. CBWP-2

Uncle Rube on the Race Problem. Clara Ann Thompson. CBWP-2

Uncle Rube's Defense. Clara Ann Thompson. CBWP-2

Uncle Rube to the Young People. Clara Ann Thompson. CBWP-2

Uncle's First Rabbit. Lorna Dee Cervantes. NoAM

Uncle Sam's Soliloquy. George Sands Johnson. PWR

Uncle Seagram. Gwendolyn Brooks. *See* Children Going Home

Uncle Tom. Langston Hughes. SAmP

Uncle Yair, against a white ceramic wall in my mother's kitchen. Nightingale of Uncle Yair, The. Devorah Amir. DTA, *tr.* by Linda Zisquit

Unclean spirits cry out in the body, The. Guest Ellen at the Supper for Street People, The. David Ferry. NIP-4

Unclean, unclean: my Lord, undone, all vile. Edward Taylor. NAAL-2v1; NAAL-3 *Fr.* Preparatory Meditations Before My Approach to the Lord's Supper.

Unclenched, armless, silk and rough love that breaks all rocks. (LL) There Was a Saviour. Dylan Thomas. ChIV-2; NAEL-6v2

Uncles. Nikky Finney. ISC

Uncloistered Virtue. John Milton. NOSC *Fr.* Paradise Lost.

Unconcerned, The. Thomas Flatman. FaBoCh; NOSC

Unconcerned, The: Song. Thomas Flatman. *See* Unconcerned, The

Unconditionals #3. Viki Akiwumi. InTrad

Unconscious Came a Beauty. May Swenson. APT-2; VCAP

Unconsciously. Ken Edwards. Oth

Uncontrollable mystery on the bestial floor, The. (LL) Magi, The. W. B. Yeats. ChIV-2; GI; HAP; HarvBoo; InPK-6; NPeEn; NoAM; OxAEP-2; PoE; TRP; TrCP

Uncountable tiny pebbles. On the Beach. Jane Hirshfield. ExTi

Uncounted are counting, The. Report from an Unappointed Committee. William Stafford. CDa

Uncurl the sheet of vellum and there. Skin. Mary Leader. NAPBL

"Und now Ladies und Gentlemun, *Der Peedles!*" David Wojahn. PBCAP *Fr.* Mystery Train: A Sequence.

Undated dreams: the sea at Heringsdorf. Dreams in German. "David Martin." NOBAu

Undead, The. Richard Wilbur. CoAP; CoAmPo; OxBC

Undefined Tenderness, An. Joel Oppenheimer. VGW

Undenominational. Sir John Betjeman. SacPr

Under. Raymond Roseliep. HA

Under. Sir John Collings Squire. FaBoTw

Under a Blossoming Plum Tree. David Biespiel. NAPBL

Under a burning tropic sun. Color Sergeant, The. James Weldon Johnson. GT

Under a ceiling high Christmas tree. Filipino Boogie. Jessica Tarahata Hagedorn. UnSA

Under a Certain Little Star. Wislawa Szymborska. PoetW; VCWP, *tr.* by Magnus J. Krynski and Robert A. Maguire

Under a dung-cake. Fable. D. J. Opperman. PeSAV, *tr.* by Jack Cope

Under a futile Torah. Both Your Mothers. Jerzy Ficowski. HP; PoSu, *tr.* by Keith Bosley

Under a Hat Rim. Carl Sandburg. APT-1

Under a hill. *Unknown.* OxNR

Under a hillock, in a field. Judge, The. Yaroslav [*or* Iaroslav] Vasilevich Smelyakov [*or* Smeliakov]. TCRP, *tr.* by Simon Franklin and Albert C. Todd

Under a Lady's Picture. Edmund Waller. EnLoPo

Under a low sky. Silence. William Carlos Williams. SAmP

Under a night sky growing bright with stars. (LL) Lufthansa. John Tranter. BMAP; NOBAu

Under a rain of blows, the heart. Heart Escaping. László Kálnoky. IQMS, *tr.* by Kenneth McRobbie and Zita McRobbie

Under a ruined mill. (LL) Old Woman, The. Joseph Campbell. AWP; MoBrPo; OxBTC; PoToHe

Under a sky, in a garden, there are serious women and beautiful men, were talking. Sailed. Aaron Shurin. FTOS

Under a sky studded with asterisks. On the Night in Question. Patricia Goedicke. TAP

Under a splintered mast. Talisman, A. Marianne Craig Moore. MoAmPo

Under a spreading chestnut tree. Village Blacksmith, The. Henry Wadsworth Longfellow. APN-1; AiP; BRP; OBAL; OBCA; OxIBACP; PWR; UV

Under a starry sky I was taking a walk. Temptation. Czeslaw Milosz. GI

Under a swaying. El Dorado. Richard Ryan. BIrV

Under a tent of stars a lonely man. Romance to Night, A. Georg Trakl. AF, *tr.* by Daniel Simko

Under a white coverlet of snow. January. John Heath-Stubbs. OBCP

Under a winter's moon. (LL) Song of the Rabbits Outside the Tavern, The. Elizabeth Jane Coatsworth. OBCA; OxIBACP; SoSe-8

Under an Impure Star. Armanda Guiducci. CItWP, *tr.* by Cinzia Sartini Blum and Lara Trubowitz

Under an upside-down. World That Lightning Makes, The. Samuel Hazo. GraLe

Under apparel, apparel lies. One Self. Laura Riding Jackson. HarvBoo

Under Ben Bulben. W. B. Yeats. HAP; NAEL-5v2; NAEL-6v2; NoAM; NoP-4; OxBTC

"Cast a cold eye." FaBoEE

"Irish poets, learn your trade." OxAEP-2

"Under bare Ben Bulben's head." WeW-3

Under black yews that protect them. Owls. Charles Baudelaire. OWoS, *tr.* by Richard Howard

Under bright city lights. Underground. Conrad Kent Rivers. SeSe

Under bright moonlight. Illusions. Tzu Yeh. CrYelRi, *tr.* by Sam Hamill

Under Cancer. John Hollander. CoAP

Under cherry trees / There are. Issa. ZenPo, *tr.* by Takashi Ikemoto and Lucien Stryk

Under clouds birds sail. Fishermen from Ma Yuan. "Lucebert." TuT, *tr.* by Peter Van de Kamp

Under Cover. Abbie Huston Evans. APT-1

Under every cathedral. Invention of Fire, The. Andrew Taylor. CBAP

Under God's violent unsleeping eye. Difference. T. Harri Jones. OBWVE

Under great yellow flags and banners of the ancient cold. Shadow of Cain, The. Dame Edith Sitwell. OxBTC

Under Her Crib. Marcia Pelletiere. OPRER

Under her gown the girl is. Only Daughter, The. Laura Riding Jackson. FuPo

Under her solemn fillet saw the scorn. (LL) Days. Ralph Waldo Emerson. APN-1; ColAP; HAP; HeIP-4; NAAL-2v1; NAAL-3; NCAP; NOBA; NoP-4; OxBA; OxBSP; PoE; TAP; TCAPo; TFi

Under his Cross[e]. (LL) Hymn[e] to God the Father, A. Ben Jonson. BeJo; InvLi; NOSC; OxAEP-1; SacPr; TrCP

Under his persistent look I closed my eyes. Student who sat facing me on the Osaka express, A. Lindley Williams Hubbell. APT-2

Under House Arrest. Dennis Brutus. AF

Under it out toward the island. (LL) Henry's Understanding. John Berryman. NOBA; NoAM; WoPoe

Under its mattresses of vines. (LL) Vacancy in the Park. Wallace Stevens. LCAP-2; SAmP

Under its spreading bankruptcy. Splendid Bankrupt, The. Arthur A. Sykes. UV

Under Leafy Bowers. Judah Al-Harizi. TrJP

Under ledges. Foster Jewell. HA

Under Milk Wood. Dylan Thomas.

Johnnie Crack and Flossie Snail. OTCP

Under My Breath. Anne Waldman. BodElec

Under my feet the moon. Brimming Water. Tu Fu. OHPC, *tr.* by Kenneth Rexroth

Under my house. Issa. EH, *tr.* by Robert Hass

Under my skin there lives a caged beast. Dancer. Martinus Nijhoff. TuT, *tr.* by Desmond Egan

Under my window-ledge the waters race. Coole Park and Ballylee, 1931. W. B. Yeats. GTBS-P; NOIV; NoAM; OBGa; OBMV

Under pressure Mick tells me one. Blue Days. Rita Dove. ExTi

Under Sedation. Alec Derwent Hope. BMAP

Under silver wing. Crossing Nation. Allen Ginsberg. AiP

Under Sirius. W. H. Auden. FaBoMo

Under Sorrow's Sign. Gofraidh Fionn O'Dalaigh. BIrV, *tr.* by John Montague

Under Stars. Tess Gallagher. InPK-6

Under striped flutter of awnings, they have come. Renoir. Rosanna Warren. GS

Under that tamarind tree. Martyred Tamarind, The. Alberto Ferreira Gomes. NAfrP, *tr.* by Gerald M. Moser

Under thatched eaves people are quiet. Tune: "Immortal at the Magpie Bridge"—On Hearing the Cuckoo at Night. Lu Yu. SuSp, *tr.* by James J. Y. Liu

Under the afterglow. Tune: "Winds of Falling Plums." Ma Chih-yüan. ChinPo, *tr.* by Yip Wai-lim

Under the almond tree. In Kensington Gardens. Arthur Symons. EnLoPo

Under the Anheuser Bush. Andrew B. Sterling. OBAL

Under the Apple Tree. Diana Rivera. InvLad

Under the arch of life, where love and death. Dante Gabriel Rossetti. OBEV *Fr.* House of Life, The.

Under the blossom that hangs on the bough. (LL) William Shakespeare. AWP; CTC; NAEL-5v1; NBLV; NoSic; OBEV; OxBSP; SCGP; TFi; TTTS *Fr.* Tempest, The.

Under the boardwalk. Alan Pizzarelli. HA

Under the Bram Bush. *Unknown.* FaBoVe

Under the bronze crown. Baroque Wall-Fountain in the Villa Sciarra, A. Richard Wilbur. ColAP; GS; NAAL-2v2; NoP-4; OBGa; TwCP; VCAP

Under the centre of the sky. Death Song. *Unknown.* APN-2, *tr.* by Henry Rowe Schoolcraft

Under the cloudy cliff, near the temple door. On Basho's "Frog." Sengai Gibon. ZenPo, *tr.* by Takashi Ikemoto and Lucien Stryk

Under the cobbled bridge the white swans float. Swans on the River Ayr. Mary Oliver. UrbNat

Under the concrete benches. Weed Puller. Theodore Roethke. HCAP; NAAL-2v2

Under the cypresses the air is still. Life of Intimate Fleeing, A. Robert Kelly. FTOS

Under the day's crust a half-eaten child. Pied Piper, The. John Ashbery. YaYoPo

Under the death of winter's leaves he lies. Metho Drinker. Judith Wright. BMAP

Under: The Dragon. (LL) Louis Zukofsky. APT-2; PoE *Fr.* 29 Poems.

Under the Drooping Willow Tree. *Unknown.* OxBoLi

Under the dusty print of hobnailed boot. Country Press. Rosemary Dobson. FaBoWP; NOBAu

Under the easy glide of water. Spell. Anuradha Mahapatra. OMIP, *tr. by* Jyotirmoy Dutta

Under the eaves, their back burned by the sun as hot as fire. Fan Ch'eng-ta. SuSp, *tr. by* Irving Y. Lo *Fr.* Seasonal Poems on Fields and Gardens.

Under the Edge of February. Jayne Cortez. BlSi

Under the Eildon Tree. Sydney Goodsir Smith.
  "Here I ligg, Sydney Slugabed Godless Smith." OxBS
  Slugabed. OxBS

Under the evening moon. Issa. EH, *tr. by* Robert Hass

Under the evening moon. Avedik Issahakian. ChAP

Under the Eyes. Tom Paulin. CIP-2; PNI

Under the fire escape, crouched, one knee in cinders. Desk, The. David Bottoms. WeW-3

Under the forest, where the day is dark. Manzanita, The. Yvor Winters. VGW

Under the French horns of a November afternoon. Man in Blue, A. James Schuyler. FTOS; PmAP

Under the fucking truck, chum. Generals Ride in Cars. *Unknown.* FaBoWar

Under the great cold lakes, under the midmost. Midland. Mark Van Doren. APT-2

Under the green lamp-light her letter there. Letter of a Mother. Robert Penn Warren. MoAmPo

Under the Greenwood Tree. Hugh MacDiarmid. FaBoWar; OBVE

Under the Greenwood Tree. William Shakespeare. *See* As You Like It

Under the harsh light, scolded by the Book. Exorcism. Dorothy Nimmo. Prnts

Under the Heaven of Our Holy Ruler. Su Tung-p'o (Su Shih). CoBCP, *tr. by* Burton Watson

Under the hemlocks Fancy came. On the Concord River. Henrietta Cordelia Ray. CBWP-3

Under the Hill. Daryl Hine. MakPoe; MoCV

Under the hills and veins of water. Last Letter to Pablo. Pat Lowther. NOBC

Under the hive-like dome the stooping haunted readers. British Museum Reading Room, The. Louis MacNeice. MoBrPo; NOBE

Under the Ice. Stewart Conn. NePenScot

Under the ice with its bouldery death's faces. Bread Hot from the Oven, The. John Thompson. NOBC

Under the image of Buddha. Issa. EH, *tr. by* Robert Hass

Under the Leaves Green. *Unknown. See* My Fair Lady

Under the Light, yet under. Emily Dickinson. FaBoVe; NCAP

Under the linden. Walther [*or* Walter] von der Vogelweide. EroLit, *tr. by* Alan Bold

Under the linden. Under the Linden. Walther [*or* Walter] von der Vogelweide. AuPH, *tr. by* Lowell A. Bangerter

Under the Linden Tree. *Unknown.* EroLit, *tr. by* David Parlett *Fr.* Carmina Burana.

Under the Lindens [*or* Lime Tree]. Walther [*or* Walter] von der Vogelweide. CTC
  ("Under the Lime Tree") GePo, *tr. by* Frederick Goldin
  (Under the lime-tree, on the daisied ground.) OBVE, *tr. by* Thomas Lovell Beddoes

Under the Lindentree. Walther [*or* Walter] von der Vogelweide. WoPoe, *tr. by* Michael Benedikt

Under the Locust Blossoms. Frederick Goddard Tuckerman. NOBA

Under the long dark boughs, like jewels red. Cherry Robbers. D. H. Lawrence. MoBrPo

Under the long shadow-on-snow of the pine. (LL) "H. D.". APT-1; NOBA *Fr.* Flowering of the Rod, The.

Under the Maud Moon. Galway Kinnell. NNaP

Under the Microscope. Slavko Mihalic. PoSu, *tr. by* Charles Simic

Under the Mirabeau Bridge the Seine / Flows and [*or* with] our love[s]. Mirabeau Bridge, The. Guillaume Apollinaire. BoLoP; OBVE

Under the Mirabeau Bridge there flows the Seine. Mirabeau Bridge. Guillaume Apollinaire. WoPoe, *tr. by* Richard Wilbur

Under the mountain, as when first I knew. Frederick Goddard Tuckerman. APN-2; HAP; TAP *Fr.* Sonnets.

Under the neon sign he stands. Drive-In, The. R. S. Gwynn. RA

Under the net of our kisses. (LL) Drunk As Drunk. Pablo Neruda. BoLoP; PasH; WoPoe, *tr. by* Christopher Logue

Under the new pond-dam. Looking Before and After. Carter Revard. HATNAP

Under the Ninth Sky. Georg Nikolic. IllVoic

Under the Oak Table. Colleen J. McElroy. GT

Under the oak tree, oak tree. *Unknown.* BoWoP

Under the olives, in whose night they sleep. (LL) Table-Birds. Kenneth Mackenzie. BMAP; NOBAu

Under the parabola of a ball. How to Kill. Keith Douglas. FaBoMo; HarvBoo; NOBE; NPeEn; PoWW; RB

Under the pines I questioned the boy. Looking for a Recluse but Failing to Find Him. Chia Tao. CoBCP; ColAnChi, *tr. by* Burton Watson

Under the Pondweed. *Unknown.* AWP, *tr. by* Helen Waddell *Fr.* Shi King.

Under the Pot. Robert Graves. FaBoEE

Under the rain's broken fingers. (LL) Gary Soto. GeoHom; PBCAP

Under the red Korean banner. Inupiat Christmas Pageant, The. Peggy Shumaker. PBCAP

Under the roof and the roof's shadow turns. Merry-go-round, The. Rainer Maria Rilke. WeW-3, *tr. by* C. F. MacIntyre

Under the roof of the Fountain House. Anna Andreyevna Akhmatova. PFTM-2, *tr. by* Lenore Mayhew and William McNaughton *Fr.* Poem without a Hero.

Under the running tap that are not the hands of a child. (LL) Soap Suds. Louis MacNeice. EmeKit; FaBoMo; ModIr; NAEL-5v2; NAEL-6v2; NOIV; NPeEn; SCV

Under the sagging clotheslines of crepe paper. Best Slow Dancer, The. David Wagoner. NoAM; VCAP

Under the Scorpion's Heart. Margot Schilpp. AmPoNex

Under the Scraggy Fir Tree. Boris Petrovich Kornilov. TCRP, *tr. by* Bernard Meares

Under the separated leaves of shade. Man Meets a Woman in the Street, A. Randall Jarrell. NoP-4

Under the September Peach. Robert Wallace. Son

Under the shadow of the gloomy night. Prologue. Samuel Rowlands. NOSC

Under the sloped snow. As Children Together. Carolyn Forché. NoAM; OxWW

Under the sovereign crests of dead volcanoes. On a Bougainvillaea Vine at the Summer Palace [*or* in Haiti]. Barbara Howes. MoAmPo

Under the Stairs. Frank Ormsby. PBCIP

Under the stars the great wise Worm lay dead;. Fafnir. Alec Derwent Hope. BMAP

Under the sun is nothing new? To the Archdeacon. George Farewell. NOEC

Under the sunrise the mountains. Robert Bringhurst. PoCoUp *Fr.* Dogen.

Under the Surface. Frances Ridley Havergal. SacPr

Under the thin smoke of winter. Evening Bells near a Temple. Ma Chih-yüan. CrYelRi, *tr. by* Sam Hamill

Under the thunder-dark, the cicadas resound. Dark Summer. Louise Bogan. APT-2

Under the too white marmoreal Lincoln Memorial. March 1, The. Robert Lowell. HCAP; PoPoPo; PoetW

Under the Vulture-Tree. David Bottoms. GifTon

Under the water tower at the edge of town. To the Evening Star: Central Minnesota. James Wright (1927–80). NAAL-5

Under the Waterfall. Thomas Hardy. BoLoP; CTC; NAEL-5v2; NAEL-6v2; NoP-4

Under the Waterfall. Karl Kraus. AuPH, *tr. by* Lowell A. Bangerter

Under the wheels of a hearse. (LL) Empty House. Yuan Chen. CrYelRi; ErotSp, *tr. by* Sam Hamill

Under the white silence of the great gumtree avenue. Finished Gentleman, A. Geoffrey Dutton. NOBAu

Under the wide and starry sky. Requiem. Robert Louis Stevenson. BRP; EBVV; MoBrPo; NBLV; NOBE; NOBVV; NePenScot; OBEV; OxBEV; PoRA; SCGP; TFi

Under the Williamsburg Bridge. Galway Kinnell. UrbNat

Under the Willow Shades. Sir William Davenant [*or* D'Avenant]. BoLoP

Under the willow the willow. Recruiting Drive. Charles Causley. OxBTC

Under the Willows. James Russell Lowell.
  "May is a pious fraud of the almanac." APN-1; TCAPo

Under the wind I saw. Under the wind. Jean Daive. MFP, *tr. by* Martin Sorrell

Under the Window: Ouro Prêto. Elizabeth Bishop. VCAP

Under the yew-tree's heavy weight. Les Hiboux. Charles Baudelaire. AWP, *tr. by* Arthur Symons

Under this bright moon. Issa. SoOfWa, *tr. by* Sam Hamill

Under this heap of stones interred lies. Upon Stephen Stoned. Sir John Suckling. ChIV-2

Under this plaque I lie, the famous woman. *Unknown.* GrAn

Under this real estate—squared street on street. Asphodel. David Malouf. CBAP

Under this stone doth lie. Epitaph upon Thomas, Lord Fairfax, An. George, 2d Duke of Buckingham Villiers. NOSC

Under this stone / Lies a Reverend Drone. Epitaph upon That Profound and Learned Casuist, the Late Ordinary of Newgate, An. Thomas [*or* "Tom"] Brown. OBSV

Under this stone, reader, survey. On Sir John Vanbrugh [Architect]. Abel Evans. FaBoEE; NPeEn

Under this stone, what lies? Evergreen, The. John Frederick Nims. APT-2

Under this sun voices on the radio run down. Complete Birth if the Cool, The. C. D. Wright. LCAP-2

Under Voice, The. Jean Valentine. BodElec; ExTi

Under walls white as a birch forest the ferns of paintings grow. In an. Painter. Zbigniew Herbert. AF, *tr. by* John Carpenter

Under what beechen shade, or silent oak. Sonnet; A Still Place. "Barry Cornwall." NOBRP

Under Which Lyre, a Reactionary Tract for the Times. W. H. Auden. MoBrPo; NOBL; PeLV

Under Willows. Christina Georgina Rossetti. VWP

Under yonder beech-tree single on the green-sward. Love in the Valley. George Meredith. EBVV; NOBE; OBEV

Under you, over you, on you. Ah. Robin Blaser. FTOS

Under your love's burden. My Soul Sinks. Hayyim Nahman [*or* Khayim Nakhman *or* Chaim Nachman] Bialik. FIT, *tr. by* Robert Friend

Underdeveloped Country, An. Dennis Joseph Enright. NOBL

Underfoot rotten boards, forest rubble, bones. Remains of an Indian Village. Alfred Wellington Purdy. NOBC

Undergone swamp ticket relative. Twenties 26. Jackson Mac Low. PmAP

Underground. May Kendall. VWP; ViWPN

Underground. Conrad Kent Rivers. SeSe

Underground grower, blind and a common brown, An. Potato. Richard Wilbur. SpudSo

Underground Stream, The. James Dickey. NOBA

Undergrowth's a conveyance of butterflies, The. Hope's Okay. A. R. Ammons. HCAP

Underneath (1). Jorie Graham. BodElec

Underneath (2). Jorie Graham. BodElec

Underneath (3). Jorie Graham. BodElec

Underneath (7). Jorie Graham. BodElec

Underneath an old oak tree. Raven, The. Samuel Taylor Coleridge. NOxBChV

Underneath my lids another eye has opened. From the Prison House. Adrienne Rich. NNaP

Underneath Oblivion. Yannis Ritsos. AF, *tr. by* Minas Savas

Underneath Our Skirts. Katie Donovan. NeBl

Underneath the Archers *or* What's All This about Walter's Willy? Kit Wright. OBCoV

Underneath the photograph. Informant, The. Eiléan Ní Chuilleanáin. ModIr

Underneath this greedy stone. Epitaph on Erotion. Martial. RomPo, *tr. by* Leigh Hunt

Underneath this marble stone / Lie two beauties join'd in one. Epitaph of Pyramus and Thisbe. Abraham Cowley. FaBoEE

Underneath this myrtle shade. Epicure, The. Abraham Cowley. OxAEP-1

Underneath this sable hearse. William Browne (1591–1643). *See* Underneath this sable hearse [*or* herse]

Underneath this sable hearse [*or* herse]. On the Countess Dowager of Pembroke. William Browne (1591–1643). AWP; BASC; HAP; PoRA; TFi

Underneth this Marble Hearse. William Browne (1591–1643). *See* Underneath this sable hearse [*or* herse]

Underpants / Lying limp, shapeless. Transfiguration. John Wright. BloBone

Undersong of terrible holy joy, An. (LL) Old Women, The. George Mackay Brown. NoP-4; OxBS

Understand that they were sitting just inside the door. State of the Nation, The. Kenneth Patchen. CLPP

Understanding. H. W. Bliss. PoToHe

Understanding. *Unknown.* PoToHe

Understanding. István Vas. IQMS, *tr. by* Godfrey Turton

Understanding Canada. Peter Sirr. PBCIP

Understanding Each Other. Linda Noel. ReEnLa

Understanding is all, my mother would tell me. Dreaming Up Mother. Robert Adamson. BMAP

Understanding the *Ramayana*. Sujata Bhatt. HarvBoo

Understory. Pamela Alexander. ExTi

Undertaker's Daughter Feels Neglect, The. Thylias Moss. ESEAA

Undertakers. Robert Johnstone. PNI

Undertaking, The. John Donne. NAEL-5v1; NAEL-6v1; NAEL-7v1; NOBE (Undertaking or Platonic Love, The.) FSCP

Undertaking, The. Louise Glück. FaBoWP

Undertaking or Platonic Love, The. John Donne. *See* Undertaking, The

Undertones. George R. Sims. NOBVV

Underwater eyes, an eel's. Otter, An. Ted Hughes. NoAM

Underwear. Lawrence Ferlinghetti. EmeKit; OBAL

Underwood. Howard Moss. TwCP

Underworld of children becomes the overworld, The. Blue Glass. Fleur Adcock. FaBoWP

Undesirable you may have been, untouchable. September Song. Geoffrey Hill. FaBoWar; HP; HarvBoo; NAEL-5v2; NAEL-6v2; NPeEn; NoAM; NoP-4; OBWP; OxBEV

Undetectable. Justin Chin. WiU

Undine. Nicole Cooley. AmPoNex

Undiscouraged. Friedrich Wilhelm Nietzsche. WoPoe, *tr. by* Robert Bly

Undiscovered Country. James Longenbach. NAPBL

Undo! *Unknown.* NOCV

Undo me; naked, unbidden, at Night's muted birth. (LL) Wole Soyinka. PBMAP; WoPoe *Fr.* Idanre and Other Poems (1967).

Undo thy dore, my spuse dere! *Unknown.* MiEL

Undo Your Heart. *Unknown.* MiEL

'Undress me! Undress me!' you said. Oliver Reynolds. TCAWP *Fr.* Tone Poem.

Undressed. Alexis Rotella. HA

Undressing a maiden called Sue. Limerick. Brian Allgar. PeLi

Undressing for Li Po. Carl Phillips. WiU

Undulating grace. Woman. Alaíde Foppa. TANSG, *tr. by* Celeste Kostopulos-Cooperman

Undying Thirst. Antipater of Sidon. AWP, *tr. by* Robert Bland

Unearthing / my valentine, An. Louis Zukofsky. APSN *Fr.* A.

Unearthly lightning of presage. Epiphany. Robert Fitzgerald. ChrPo

Unearthly sound, The. Baying, The. James Bertolino. UrbNat

Unemployed. Stephen Spender. NOBE

Unemployed and lazy, I wander around the village. Tu Fu. CrYelRi, *tr. by* Sam Hamill *Fr.* Random Pleasures.

Unemployed Mami. Willie Perdomo. InTrad

Unemployed sky above the clouds, The. First Rock and Roll Song of 1970, The. Pedro Juan Pietri. ReTh

Unemployment in our bones, The. Derry. Seamus Deane. CIP-2

Unemployment/Monologue. June Jordan. WPOW

Unending loneliness from which others drink, The. Six Poems of Loneliness. Enrique Lihn. VCWP, *tr. by* David Unger

Unequal Distribution. Samuel Hoffenstein. TrJP

Unequal Fetters, The. Anne Finch, Countess of Winchilsea. OxBEV

Uneven rows of hedges. Paul Verlaine. SxFrPo, *tr. by* Martin Sorrell

Unexpected interest made him flush, The. Episode of Hands. Hart Crane. CAGL; NIL-7

Unexpected Manna. Gary H. Holthaus. GifTon

Unexpected Meeting. "Shu Ting." CarOv, *tr. by* Carolyn Kizer and Y. H. Zhao

Unexpected Meeting. Wislawa Szymborska. VCWP

Unexpected Pleasure, An. *Unknown.* UV

Unexpressed. Adelaide Anne Procter. SacPr

Unfailing Friend, The. Joseph Scriven. SacPr
(What a Friend We Have in Jesus.) TCAPo

Unfair to Men. *Unknown.* OBWVE, *tr. by* Gwyn Jones

Unfair to Women. *Unknown.* OBWVE, *tr. by* Gwyn Jones

Unfaithful Lover, The. Charlotte Dacre. RWP

Unfaithful Shepherdess, The. *Unknown.* GTBS-P
(Faithless Shepherdess, The.) OBEV
(Philon the Shepherd.) NOBE

Unfaithful Wife, The. Federico García Lorca. WoPoe, *tr. by* Michael Hartnett

Unfaithful Wife, The. Federico García Lorca. ErotSp, *tr. by* Sam Hamill

Unfaithful Wife, The. Federico García Lorca. STV, *tr. by* John Frederick Nims

Unfaithful Wife, The. Federico García Lorca. EroLit, *tr. by* Alan Bold

Unfaithful Wife, The. Nuala Ni Dhomhnaill. ModIr, *tr. by* Paul Muldoon

Unfallen Love. John Milton. NOSC *Fr.* Paradise Lost.

Unfettered at last, a traveling monk. Manan. ZenPo, *tr. by* Takashi Ikemoto and Lucien Stryk

Unfinished Exile. Fabio Doplicher. NeIt, *tr. by* Stephen Sartarelli

Unfinished History. Archibald MacLeish. VGW

Unfinished Letter to My Lady. Dániel Berzsenyi. IQMS, *tr. by* Peter Zollman

Unfinished Race, The. Norman Cameron. OxBS; OxBSo

Unfinished Sewing, The. Evdokiya Rostopchina. ARWW, *tr.* by Catriona Kelly

Unfold, unfold! take in his light. Revival, The. Henry Vaughan. InvLi; NOCV

Unfolding moments. Stretched Out in Solitude. Belinda Zubicueta Carmona. TANSG, *tr.* by Celeste Kostopulos-Cooperman

Unforgettable. Irving Gordon. ReLy

Unforgettable / That's what you are. Unforgettable. Irving Gordon. ReLy

Unforgiven, The. Edwin Arlington Robinson. APT-1

Unforgiving as the course of justice. Holding My Beads. Grace Nichols. ItWoWo

Unfortunate admiral! Your poor America. To Columbus. "Rubén Dario." TTY, *tr.* by Lysander Kemp

Unfortunate Coincidence. Dorothy Parker. LW; NoP-4

Unfortunate Damsel, The. Mrs. Fleetwood Habergham. *See* Seeds of Love, The

Unfortunate Gentleman, The. Cornelius Whur.
　"In a dark and trying hour." VerBaPo

Unfortunate human disorder, The. *Unknown.* ColAnChi, *tr.* by Red Pine

Unfortunate lad from Madrid, An. Limerick. *Unknown.* PeLi

Unfortunate Miller, The. Alfred Edgar Coppard. FaBoTw

Unfortunate Miller; or, The Country Lasses Witty Invention, The. *Unknown.* OxBB
　(All of you that desire to hear a jest.) EroLit

Unfortunate Occurrence at Cwm-Cadno, An. A. G. Prys-Jones. AngWePo

Unfriendly friendly universe. Child Dying, The. Edwin Muir. FaBoTw; GTBS-P; PoWW; RB; WoPoe

Unfunny uncles who insist. Exchanging Hats. Elizabeth Bishop. NIL-7

Unfurled gull on the tide, and over the skerry, The. December Day, Hoy Sound. George Mackay Brown. OxBS

Ungag our souls!! Unstrangle our souls!! Unsmother our souls!! "Antler." CLPP *Fr.* Factory.

Ungar and Rolfe. Herman Melville. *Fr.* Clarel: A Poem and Pilgrimage in the Holy Land.

Ungar's Harangue. Herman Melville. TCAPo *Fr.* Clarel: A Poem and Pilgrimage in the Holy Land.

Ungraciously, under. Basho. SoOfWa, *tr.* by Sam Hamill

Ungrateful Country, if thou e'er forget. William Wordsworth. SacPr *Fr.* Ecclesiastical Sonnets.

Ungrateful Jenny. Mother Goose. OxNR

Ungreeted, and shall give its light embrace. (LL) Inscription for the Entrance to a Wood. William Cullen Bryant. APN-1; OxBA; TAP

Unguarded House, An. Julianus of Egypt. GrAn

Unguarded lies the wishing Maid. Song and Musick, Set by Mr. Eccles, and Sung by Mrs. Leveridge. Delariviere Manley. EMWP

Unguentarium. Elizabeth Garrett. NeBl

Unhand me nurse! thou saucy quean! Maternal Despotism; or, The Rights of Infants. Richard Graves. NOEC

Unhappie [*or* Unhappy] Light. Madrigal. William Drummond, of Hawthornden. NOSC

Unhappily I'm married. (LL) Shades of Night, The. A. E. Housman. NBLV; OBCoV; UV

Unhappy about some far off things. Stars Go Over the Lonely Ocean, The. Robinson Jeffers. HarvBoo

Unhappy and at home. (LL) Tollund Man, The. Seamus Heaney. BIrV; CABP; CIP-2; EBEV; FaBoMo; ModIr; NPeEn; PBCIP; PNI; WoPoe

Unhappy at being delayed at the Yangtze. In the Mountains. Wang Po. CrYelRi, *tr.* by Sam Hamill

Unhappy Boston. Paul Revere. AiP

Unhappy country what wings you have. Even here. Eagle Valor, Chicken Mind. Robinson Jeffers. OxBA; OxBSP

Unhappy Diary Days. Gerald Vizenor. VoR

Unhappy Dido burns, and in her rage. Virgil [*or* Vergil]. NAEL-7v1, *tr.* by Henry Howard, Earl of Surrey *Fr.* Aeneid [*or* Eneados, *Aeneis*], The.

Unhappy exile, whom his fates confine, The. Charlotte Smith. BWW

Unhappy fate: that you have died. Song at Graveside. Ewald von Kleist. GePo, *tr.* by George C. Schoolfield

Unhappy he who his inner sphinx one day. Unhappy He. "Rubén Dario." SpanPo, *tr.* by Muna Lee

Unhappy Kukutis in the Potato Patch. Marcelijus Martinaitis. TWW, *tr.* by Laima Sruoginis

Unhappy Love. Sándor Kisfaludy.
　"As the suffering hart confounded." IQMS, *tr.* by Watson Kirkconnell

Unhappy Lover, The. Judah Al-Harizi. TrJP, *tr.* by J. Chotzner

Unhappy men, why do we travel so. Crinagoras. GrAn

Unhappy [*or* Unhappie] Verse, the witness[e] of my unhappy [*or* unhappie] state. Iambicum Trimetrum. Edmund Spenser. BoLoP; EBEV; NPeEn; OBEV

Unhappy pedophiles, cease your inane. *Unknown.* CAGL, *tr.* by Daryl Hine

Unhappy people in a happy world, An. Wallace Stevens. PoE *Fr.* Auroras of Autumn, The.

Unhappy Phaeton's splendidious sire. Virgo, August. John Taylor. NOSC

Unhappy Race, The. Oodgeroo of the tribe Noonuccal (Kath Walker). IBA

Unhappy sex! how hard's our fate. On Sir J—— S—— Saying in a Sarcastic Manner, My Books Would Make Me Mad; an Ode. Elizabeth Thomas. ECWP

Unhappy summer you. This Summer and Last. Thomas Hardy. OxBTC

Unhappy they, who by their duty led. Mary Lee, Lady Chudleigh. PEW *Fr.* Ladies Defence Or, the Bride-Woman's Counsellor Answered, The.

Unhappy wife. George Swede. HA

Unhappy woman's but a slave at large. (LL) Essay on Woman, An. Mary Leapor. BWW; ECWP; NAEL-7v1; NOEC

Unharnessed, the white horse ambles along. Georgy [*or* Georgii] Vladimirovich Ivanov. TCRusP, *tr.* by Daniel Weissbort

Unharvested. Robert Frost. APT-1; SAmP

Unhistorical Events. Bob Kaufman. CLPP

Unholy Missions. Bob Kaufman. TTY

Unholy Sonnets. Mark Jarman.
　"God like a kiss, God like a welcoming." InvLi

Unholy Spring. John Godfrey. FTOS

Unhurried as a snake I saw Time glide. On Time. Richard Hughes. MoBrPo

Unhurt, like him, your charms I'll hear. (LL) Farewell to Worldly Joys, A. Anne Killigrew. BASC; CABP

Uni-Gym, The. Anne Rouse. NeBl

Unicorn, The. Ruth Pitter. MoBrPo

Unicorn, The. Emile Victor Rieu. OBSP

Unicorn, The. Rainer Maria Rilke.
　"Oh this is the animal that never was." TTTS

Unicorn, The. Isaac Rosenberg.
　"Sick. . . Sick. . . I will lie down and die. How." PeFWW

Unicorn's hoofs!, The. Dance Song. *Unknown.* ChiP; FaBoCh, *tr.* by Arthur Waley

Unicorn stood, like a king in a dream, The. Unicorn, The. Emile Victor Rieu. OBSP

Uniformed in grey that so ill-suits. Plagiarist, The. Bruce Berger. GeoH

Unifying Principle, The. A. R. Ammons. NOBA

Unimaginative, The. Madison Cawein. APN-2

Uninscribed Monument on One of the Battlefields of the Wilderness, An. Herman Melville. CBCWP

Uninteresting specimen might still be putting out shoots, for all we know. (LL) Crazy Weather. John Ashbery. ColAP; PoE

Uninvited, The. Dorothy Livesay. NOBC; NoP-4

Union. Emily Dickinson. FaBoA

Union. Annie Foster. NLP

Union, The. Ifi Amadiume. HAWP

Union of Two, The. Haki R. Madhubuti. ISC; SpirFl

Unison, A. William Carlos Williams. NOBA

Unit. Mary Elizabeth Fullerton. NOBAu

United. Paulus [*or* Paulos] Silentiarius. AWP, *tr.* by W. H. D. Rouse

United bolt and screw. Mac Wellman. HeMarv *Fr.* Rat Minaret: Miniaturist-Divan, The.

United Fruit Co. Pablo Neruda. TCLAP, *tr.* by Jack Schmitt

United States. John Keble. SacPr *Fr.* Lyra Apostolica.

United States, The. Goethe. AiP; FaBoA, *tr.* by Robert Bly

United States Constitution, The. Limerick. Peter Alexander. PeLi

United States Prepare for the Permanent Revolution, The. George Hitchcock. SPE

United Way, The. Jack Marshall. GraLe

Unity. Fazil Hüsnü Daglarca. RaBo, *tr.* by Tâlat S. Halman

Unity. Ralph Waldo Emerson. TCAPo

Universal Beauty. Henry Brooke.
　"While ocean thus the latent store bequeaths." ECEV

Universal Favorite, The. Carolyn Wells. NBLV

Universal *is* the particular, The. (LL) Hugh MacDiarmid. NAEL-5v2; NAEL-6v2; NoP-4 *Fr.* In Memoriam James Joyce.

Universal Prayer [Deo Opt. Max.], The. Pope. InvLi
　(Father of all! in every age.) NoP-4
　(Universal Prayer, The.) NoP-4

Universe is forever falling apart, The. Destruction. Shinkichi Takahashi. ZenPo, *tr.* by Takashi Ikemoto and Lucien Stryk

Universe is large: to be eccentric, The. One's Country. Jonathan Griffin. Oth

Universe is Part of Ourselves, The. Robin Blaser. FTOS

Universe is sad, The. Resonance. Ruth Stone. BodElec

Universe—is still, The. (LL) He fumbles at Your Spirit. Emily Dickinson. APN-2; LW; NAAL-2v1; NAAL-3; NCAP; NOCV; TCAPo; TRP

Universe of heated molecules, just above their bodies, The. (LL) Miniaturist, The. Maurice Kilwein Guevara. AmPoNex; TouFir

Universe of the Rose. Chimako Tada. VCWP, *tr. by* Kirsten Vidaeus

Universe, so whole within my mind, The. (LL) Flaw, A. "Michael Field." VWP; ViWPN

University. Karl Shapiro. APT-2; OxBA

University Curriculum. William Price Turner. OxBS

University Examinations in Egypt. Dennis Joseph Enright. OxBTC; TwCP

Unjust, Imperial Heaven's way. Ying from "The Nine Declarations." Chü Yüan. ChinPo, *tr. by* Yip Wai-lim

Unjust steals [*or* stole] the just's umbrella, The. (LL) Rain It Raineth, The. Charles Synge Christopher Bowen, Baron Bowen. NBLV; NTCP

Unjustifiable / Shocking neglect. (LL) No Foundation. John Hollander. OBAL; OBCoV

Unjustly Punished Child. Sharon Olds. PBCAP

Unkept Good Fridays. Thomas Hardy. GI

Unkindness. George Herbert. NOSC

Unknowing, The. Linda Gregg. ExTi

Unknown, The. John Davidson. MoBrPo

Unknown, The. Denise Levertov. NAAL-2v2

Unknown Bird, The. Edward Thomas. RB

Unknown Citizen, The. W. H. Auden. HeIP-4; InPK-6; NBLV; NIP-4; NOBL; OBSV; PAI; PoRA; SoSe-8; TRP; UnPo

Unknown Color, The. Countee Cullen. OBCA

Unknown Eros, The. Coventry Patmore.

    Arbor Vitae. OxBEV; PeVV

    "Creation's and Creator's crowning good." CABP

    Departure. NOBE; OBEV

    Farewell, A. BoLoP; EnLoPo; GTBS-P; NOBE; OBEV

    "It was not like your great and gracious ways." NOBE; OBEV

    (Magna Est Veritas.) GTBS-P; HAP; NOBE; NOBVV; NPeeEn; OBEV; OxBEV; OxBSP

    "My little son, who looked from thoughtful eyes." EBEV; EBVV; NOBVV; OBEV; OxAEP-2; PoToHe; SoSe-8

    To the Body. CABP

    Toys, The. EBEV; EBVV; NOBVV; OBEV; OxAEP-2; PoToHe; SoSe-8

    "With all my will, but much against my heart." BoLoP; EnLoPo; GTBS-P; NOBE; OBEV

    "With honeysuckle, over-sweet, festooned [*or* festoon'd]." OxBEV; PeVV

Unknown faces in the street. Turning, The. Philip Levine. VGW

Unknown Female Corpse. Rudyard Kipling. PoWW *Fr.* Epitaphs of the War [1914–1918].

Unknown Girl in the Maternity Ward. Anne Sexton. NoAM

Unknown God, The. "Æ" MoBrPo

Unknown Land. Rex Ingamells.

    "We who are called Australians have no country." NOBAu

Unknown love/ Is as bitter a thing. *Var. authors.* AWP *Fr.* Manyo Shu, Part 4 of 4.

Unknown Man in the Morgue. Merrill Moore. MoAmPo

Unknown Master of Moulins, The. Cardinal's Dog, The. John Glassco. MoCV

Unknown road still marching, The. (LL) March in the Ranks Hard-Prest, and the Road Unknown, A. Walt Whitman. CBCWP; NAAL-2v1; NAAL-3; OxBA; PAI

Unknown, she was my favorite shape. Unknown, She Was My Favorite Shape. Paul Éluard. NAWM-7v2, *tr. by* Lloyd Alexander

Unknown Shores. Théophile Gautier. WoPoe, *tr. by* D. M. Thomas

Unknown Soldier, The. Alun Lewis. MoBrPo

Unknown Soldiers. Edgar Lee Masters. NoAM; TAP *Fr.* New Spoon River, The.

Unknown unwanted life, The. (LL) Orient Express, The. Randall Jarrell. CoAP; NOBA; PoE

Unknown voice told me, An. Unknown Voice, An. Carlos German Belli. TCLAP, *tr. by* Maureen Ahern and David Tipton

Unknown World, The. György Sárközi. IQMS, *tr. by* Watson Kirkconnell

Unlawful Assembly. Dennis Joseph Enright. OxBTC

Unlearning English. Michael Melo. ReBoTo

Unless God of his goodness grants us a truce. (LL) William Langland. NAEL-6v1; NAEL-7v1 *Fr.* Vision of Piers Plowman, The.

Unless I walk outside these whitethorn hedges. (LL) Innocence. Patrick Kavanagh. ModIr; RB

Unless it trembled with the strings. (LL) Romance. Edgar Allan Poe. APN-1; NCAP; OxBA

Unless they love you. (LL) Cascando. Samuel Beckett. ModIr; NOIV

Unless you can dance through a common bar. Mahsati. WPOW, *tr. by* Deirdre Lashgari

Unless you remind me. Pavlov. Naomi Long Madgett. BPo

Unlike almost everything. Near the Desert Test Sites. Sherod Santos. GeoHom

Unlike are we, unlike, O princely Heart! Elizabeth Barrett Browning. BWW; CABP; CenSon; OBEV; OxAEP-2 *Fr.* Sonnets from the Portuguese.

Unlike flying or astral projection, walking through walls is a. Walking through a Wall. Louis Jenkins. RaBo

Unlike my friend John I like the painting entitled. 2 Poems on the Same Theme. Michael Burkard. BodElec

Unlike my subject now shall be my song. Philip Dormer Stanhope, 4th Earl of Chesterfield. FaBoEE

Unlike the hawk he has no dream of height. Sea Owl. Dave Jeddie Smith. HCAP

Unlike the heroes of each ancient race. Byron. NOBRP *Fr.* Corsair, The.

Unlikely Obbligato of Andersonstown. Kit Wright. OBCoV

Unloading hell behind him step by step. (LL) Rear-Guard, The. Siegfried Sassoon. MoBrPo; NAEL-5v2; NAEL-6v2; NoAM; OBWP; PoWW

Unloved I love, unwept I weep. Reason. Charlotte Brontë. VWP

Unlucky Nicanor, quenched by the grey and deep. Antipater of Thessalonica. GrAn

Unmarked faces / fierce with grief. Falls Funeral. John Montague. CIP-2

Unmarked Stop in Front of Westmond General Store, Westmond, Idaho. Jonathan Johnson. AmPoNex

Unmoved by cricket song of thee or me. (LL) Cricket, The. Frederick Goddard Tuckerman. APN-2; NCAP; NOBA; TCAPo

Unnamable God, you are fathomless. Bible, *O.T. See* Bless the Lord, O my soul. O Lord my God

Unnamed Lake, The. Frederick George Scott. NOBC

Unnatural Light. Peter Meinke. UrbNat

Unnoticed the first of autumn as nights grow longer. First of Autumn, The. Meng Hao Jan. SuSp, *tr. by* Paul W. Kroll

Unnumbered suppliants crowd preferment's gate. Samuel Johnson. OBSV *Fr.* Vanity of Human Wishes, The; The Tenth Satire of Juvenal Imitated.

Uno, dos. Castanet Clicks. Pat Mora. OxIBACP

Unopened Letters. Linda Zisquit.

    "Because passion is the absence we speak." DTA

    "Because passion is the silence we share." DTA

    "There is always a sound." DTA

Unpardonable Sin, The. Nicholas Vachel Lindsay. ChIV-2

Unperson from West Oceania, An. Limerick. C. Vita-Finzi. PeLi

Unperturbed at the battle. Kamalākānta Bhattācārya. SinGod, *tr. by* Rachel Fell McDermott

Unpetal the flower of me. To Life. Lizette Woodworth Reese. TCAPo

Unpleasing to a married ear! (LL) William Shakespeare. HAP; InPK-6; NAEL-5v1; NAEL-6v1; NBLV; NIL-7; NIP-4; NOBE; NoSic; OBEV; PAI; PoRA; SCGP; TFi; UnPo *Fr.* Love's Labour's Lost.

Unplumbed [*or* unplumb'd], salt, estranging sea, The. (LL) Matthew Arnold. GTBS-P; NAEL-6v2; NPeeEn; OxBEV; SoSe-8 *Fr.* Switzerland.

Unpopular man of Cologne, An. Limerick. *Unknown.* PeLi

Unportrayable on the light silk of a small fan. Kuan Yün-shih. SuSp, *tr. by* Richard John Lynn *Fr.* Medley of Southern and Northern Tunes—Scenic Tour of West Lake.

Unpredicted, The. John Heath-Stubbs. BoLoP; OxBC

Unprofitablenes. Henry Vaughan. ESCV; GeHe; NAEL-7v1; NOSC

Unprofitably pleasing, and unsound. Mary Sidney Wroth, Countess of Montgomery. BASC *Fr.* Pamphilia to Amphilanthus.

Unpurged images of day recede, The. Byzantium. W. B. Yeats. EBEV; FaBoMo; HAP; HarvBoo; MoBrPo; NAEL-5v2; NAEL-6v2; NAWM-7v2; NIL-7; NIP-4; NOBE; NoAM; NoP-4; OxBEV; OxBTC; PoE

Unquiet Grave, The. *Unknown.* CABP; ESPB; HAP; HeIP-4; NoP-4; OxBB; RB; TFi; WeW-3; WoPoe

Unraveling Ravel is no longer a secret. Ravel: Bolero. Al Young. SpirFl

Unraveling wins out: I leave my home, The. Leaving. Tiziano Rossi. ItPo, *tr. by* Gayle Ridinger

Unreachable father, when we were first. Matins. Louise Glück. InvLi

Unreal Dwelling: My Years in Volcano, The. Garrett Kaoru Hongo. OpBo

Unreal Song of the Old, The. James Koller. PoM

Unreal tall as a myth. Bear on the Delhi Road, The. Earle Birney. HeIP-4; MoCV; NOBC; NoAM; NoP-4

Unrealities, The. Johann Christoph Friedrich von Schiller. AWP, *tr. by* James Clarence Mangan

Unreasonable lenses refract the. Prairie Houses. Barbara Guest. PmAP

Unreasonable ryche manne, An. Of unsaciable purchasers. Robert Crowley. PBRV

Unreceived Messages. Robert Walker. IBA

Unrecognized, long after he has died. (LL) Counterfeiter, The. Greg Williamson. AmPoNex; RA

Unrecorded Speech. Anna Adams. BrRo

Unreeling itself across the eletric billboard. Hair. Nina Iskrenko. ItGoST, *tr. by* Patrick Henry, John High and Katya Olmsted

Unrelated Incidents. Tom Leonard.

    "This is thi." NPeeEn; NePenScot

Unrelenting Flood. William Matthews. BodElec

Unremarkable at first, this infant. Tom Passey's Child. Maggie Hannan. NLP

Unremarkable Year, The. Roy Fuller. OxBC

Unrepentant. Brandel France de Bravo. OPRER

Unrestricted / unrestrained / uncompromising. Freedom Hair. Raymond Washington. NBV

Unreturning, The. Wilfred Owen. MoBrPo

Unreturning voyage, my friends to me, The. (LL) Godspeed. John Greenleaf Whittier. GSo; Son

Unrhymed, unrhythmical, the chatter goes. At the Party. W. H. Auden. OxBSP

Unrighteous Mammon (Luke 16:9). Ernesto Cardenal. GI, tr. by Robert Pring-Mill

Unripe grapes. People of Grapes. Nidaa Khoury. PoArWo, tr. by Linda Zisquit

Unromantic Awakening, An. Priscilla Jane Thompson. CBWP-2

Unruly Horses. Vladimir Semionovich Vysotsky [or Vysotskii]. TCRP, tr. by Albert C. Todd

Unsagacious Animal, An. David Gascoyne. PeLV

Unsaid. A. R. Ammons. NOBA

Unseals her earth, and lifts love in its shower. (LL) Broken Tower, The. Hart Crane. APT-2; ColAP; MoAmPo; NOBA; NoAM; NoP-4; OxBA; PoPoPo

Unseemly as a marvellous and astral renegade. Queen Anne's Lace. June Jordan. TAP

Unseen Fire. Ralph Nixon Currey. OBWP; OxBTC; PoWW

Unseen Spirits. Nathaniel Parker Willis. APN-1; TreFP

Unsettled, a bird lost from the flock. T'ao Ch'ien [or T'ao Yuan-ming]. SuSp Fr. Drinking Wine.

Unsettled again and hearing Russian spoken. Hearing Russian Spoken. Donald Davie. GTBS-P

Unsettled, unhappy, near the end of April. Lamentations of the Bronze Camels. Li Ho. SuSp, tr. by Irving Y. Lo

Unsex'd Females, The. Richard Polwhele.
  "Alas! in every aspiration bold." NOBRP
  "Thou, who with all the poet's genuine rage." NOBRP

Unsheathing of the great knife of parting, The. (LL) Dead Child Speaks, A. Nelly Sachs. HP; PoSu

Unsnapping. Gary Hotham. HA

Unspeakable. Margaret Avison. NOBC

Unspeakable. Ferenc Faludi. IQMS, tr. by John Gordon Nichols

Unspeakable sorrow! Tune: Gazing at the South. Li Yü. CoBCP, tr. by Burton Watson

Unspoken. Judith Ortiz Cofer. PueRic

Unsquandered, sure and quiet as a root. Emily's Words. Leslie Monsour. FFC

Unstable dream[e] [or dreme], according [or accordyng] to the place. Sir Thomas Wyatt. OxBSo

Unsteady Yellow. Tess Gallagher. InvLad

Unsubdued. Samuel Ellsworth Kiser. PoToHe

Unsung Heroes, The. Paul Laurence Dunbar. BPo; CBCWP

Unsuspected Blackcurrant river rolls. Blackcurrant River. Arthur Rimbaud. SxFrPo, tr. by Martin Sorrell

Unswerving Marine. Carl Rakosi. FTOS

Untie my fatted lamb strange shepherd. Sonnet 188. Félix Lope de Vega Carpio. BLPSL, tr. by Rene de Costa, Rigas Kappatos and Eleni Paidoussi

Untie my tongue. Muse of fiery ABC. Autumn Prelude. Andrey [or Andrei] Andreievich Voznesensky [or Voznesenskii]. RusPo, tr. by Robert Arthur Douglas Ford

Untied of all binding knots. Mistress of My Own Being. Ifi Amadiume. HAWP

Until Eternity. (LL) Emily Dickinson. HAP; HeIP-4; NAAL-2v1; NAAL-3; NAAL-5; NoP-4; OxBA; SAmP; SacPr

Until, gasping with appreciative racism, both together sink into the unrevealed glory of sexism. (LL) Histoire. Harry Mathews. NIP-4; PmAP

Until He Comes. Trasi Johnson. InTrad

Until he comes in sight. (LL) Ostrich Is a Silly Bird, The. Mary Eleanor Wilkins Freeman. OBCA; OxIBACP

Until he died we thought our neighbor dull. Future Debris. Heid E. Erdrich. AmPoNex

Until he named the horse. Naming the Animals. Lisel Mueller. IllVoic

Until his heart will break. (LL) Blue Water. Li Po. CrYelRi; ErotSp, tr. by Sam Hamill

Until I asked her to please stop doing it and was astonished to find that she not only could. My Mother's Lips. C. K. Williams. EmeKit

Until I escaped, and held my old fishing rod again. (LL) Parable, A. Li K'ai-hsien. CoBLCP; ColAnChi, tr. by Jonathan Chaves

Until I fall into coma. (LL) John Berryman. NAAL-2v2; VCAP Fr. Dream Songs.

Until I reach her and am comforted. (LL) Giovanni Boccaccio. AWP; EaItPo, tr. by Dante Gabriel Rossetti Fr. Sonnets.

Until I Saw the Sea. Lilian Moore. NTCP

Until it alights. Lorraine Ellis Harr. HA

Until life goes out. Unknown. OHMPJ

Until Manuel. Life of an Echo, The. Judith Ortiz Cofer. PueRic

Until New Spring or Death. Árpád Tóth. IQMS, tr. by Madeline Mason

Until now the earth has been drawn in the shape of a pear. Grave for New York, A. "Adonis" [or "Adunis"]. MAP, tr. by Alan Brownjohn and Lena Jayyusi

Until only the mountain remains. (LL) Birds have Vanished, The. Li Po. BLT; EnlH, tr. by Sam Hamill

Until Tatum passed. Standing on the Corner. Philip Levine. NNaP

Until that sun, which keeps. Trains Made of Stone. Ray A. Young Bear. CDW

Until the basket overflows with light. (LL) Song for the Sun That Disappeared behind the Rainclouds. Hottentot Oral Tradition. TTTS; TTY, tr. by Ulli Beier

Until the day. I Get a Kick Out of You. Cole Porter. APT-1

Until the day break, and the shadows flee away, turn, my beloved, and be thou like a roe or a young hart upon the mountains of Bether. (LL) Bible, O.T. BoLoP; OBVE Fr. Song of Solomon, The [or The Song of Songs].

Until the Desert knows. Emily Dickinson. NOBA

Until the destruction of language. (LL) Permanently. Kenneth Koch. CoAP; NoP-4; PmAP; PoM

Until the Real Thing Comes. Alberta Nichols. ReLy

Until the sound of the open ocean grows and the voice. (LL) What the End Is For. Jorie Graham. NoP-4; PoPoPo

Until the sun sinks into a green. Anatoly Steiger. TCRusP, tr. by Paul Schmidt

Until the torches deaden at the bedroom door. (LL) Speaking of Poetry. John Peale Bishop. APT-1; OxBA

Until they are truly quartets. (LL) River Road Studio. Barbara Guest. PmAP; PoM

Until they come to London Bridge. (LL) St. Paul's Steeple. Unknown. LB; OxNR

Until they have made themselves warm, poor things! (LL) Mother Goose. OxNR; ReMoGo

Until thine hands clasp girdlewise the waist of the Belov'd. Ode. Sadi [or Saadi or Sa'di]. AWP, tr. by R. A. Nicholson

Until today. On the table. Experiments in the Impersonal. Steve Wilson. AmPoNex

Until we are pure spirit at the end. (LL) Infirmity. Theodore Roethke. CoAP; NAAL-2v2

Until we reach the town of Sleep. (LL) Young Night Thought. Robert Louis Stevenson. OTCP; PWR

Until yesterday I was polite and peaceful. Opinions of the New Student. Regino Pedroso. TTY, tr. by Langston Hughes

Until you can correct and heal yourself. Sadi [or Saadi or Sa'di]. WoPoe, tr. by Dick Davis

Until you change your mind. Pantoumstone for a Dying Breed. Beth Lisick. AmPoNex

Until you have looked at something so long. Makings of Happiness, The. Ronald Wallace. PBCAP

Untimely Thought, An. Thomas Bailey Aldrich. PWR

Untitled. Rachel Tzvia Back. DTA

Untitled. Ian Duhig. NeBI

Untitled. Duo Duo (Li Shizheng). AF, tr. by Gregory Lee

Untitled. John Irving. Unle

Untitled. Juan Ramon Jimenez. MiVo, tr. by Dennis Maloney

Untitled. Bob Kaufman. ISC

Untitled. Tom Leonard. Oth

UNTITLED. John Milton. OxBEV Fr. Paradise Lost.

Untitled. So Chong-Ju. VCWP, tr. by David R. McCann

Untitled. T'ao Ch'ien [or T'ao Yuan-ming]. WoPoe, tr. by David Hinton

UNTITLED. Tennyson. NAEL-5v2; NAEL-6v2 Fr. Maud [A Monodrama].

Untitled. Karen Volkman. AmPoNex; NeAmPo

Untitled. Franz Wright. LCAP-2

Untitled (April '91). Michael Palmer. BodElec

Untitled Blues; After a Photograph by Yevgeni Yevtushenko. Yusef Komunyakaa. ESEAA; GT; UnSA

Untitled (February 2000). Michael Palmer. BAP-01

Untitled: "If it be event, I go towards and not back. I go tower, not floor." Karen Volkman. NAPBL

Untitled: "In the deepest night and a full moon." Merle Woo. FSt

Untitled: "Shrewd star, who crudes our naming: you should be flame." Karen Volkman. NAPBL; NeAmPo

Untitled: "There comes a time to rusticate the numbers. The way the birds, jug." Karen Volkman. NAPBL

Unto a heavenly course decreed. Star Morals. Friedrich Wilhelm Nietzsche. AWP, *tr.* by Ludwig Lewisohn

Unto Adam, His Own Scriveyn. Geoffrey Chaucer. *See* Chaucer's Wordes unto Adam, his Owne Scriveyn

Unto all generations of the faithful heart. (LL) Lee in the Mountains. Donald Davidson. CBCWP; FuPo

Unto all life of mine may die [*or* dy]. (LL) Richard Crashaw. HAP; NAEL-5v1; NAEL-6v1; NAEL-7v1; NOBE; OBEV; WoPoe

Unto empty pockets. (LL) I Am Raftery [*or* Raferty]. Anthony [*or* Antoine] Raftery [*or* Raifteiri]. AWP; WoPoe, *tr.* by Douglas Hyde

Unto God let praise be brought. And It Came to Pass at Midnight. Yannai. TrJP

Unto Jehovah Sing Will I. Henry Ainsworth. AH

Unto my thinking, thou beheld'st all worth. To Dante Alighieri. Guido Cavalcanti. AWP; EaItPo, *tr.* by Dante Gabriel Rossetti

Unto no body my woman saith she had rather a wife be [*or* bee]. Catullus. OBVE; WoPoe, *tr.* by Sir Philip Sidney

Unto Our God Most High We Sing. John Vance Cheney. AH

Unto that hive of beams / And garland-streams. (LL) Star[re], The. George Herbert. ESCV; PeECV

Unto that lowly lovely maid, I wis. Bernardo da Bologna. EaItPo, *tr.* by Dante Gabriel Rossetti

Unto the blithe and lordly fellowship. Folgore da San Geminiano [*or* Gimignano]. AWP; EaItPo, *tr.* by Dante Gabriel Rossetti

Unto the boundless Ocean of thy beauty. Samuel Daniel. NoP-4 *Fr.* To Delia.

Unto the different dawn! (LL) Emily Dickinson. NALW; OxBA

Unto the gates of hell. Song of Esechia, The. John Hall. ChIV-1

Unto the Person Kind there came. Mother Doorstep. Victor James Daley. NOBAu

Unto the queen of the gods, into whose hands are committed. Hymn to Ishtar. Ashur-Nasir-Pal, King of Assyria. HW

Unto the saints with sad complaints. Michael Wigglesworth. NAAL-3 *Fr.* Day of Doom, The.

Unto the silver night. Revelation. Sir Edmund William Gosse. OBEV

Unto the thinking of the thought divine. (LL) George Santayana. APN-2; TCAPo *Fr.* Sonnets.

Unto the Upright Praise. Moses Hayyim, of Padua Luzzatto. "All ye that handle harp and viol." TrJP, *tr.* by Nina Davis Salaman

Unto this place when as the Elfin Knight. Edmund Spenser. NOBE *Fr.* Faerie Queene, The.

Unto this process briefly compiled. John Skelton. NoSic *Fr.* Magnificence.

Unto Thy Favor. Robert Tofte. Son *Fr.* Laura.

Unto Us a Child is Born. William Dunbar. ChIV-2

Unto Us a Son Is Given. Alice Thompson Meynell. SacPr

Untold Want, The. Walt Whitman. MoAmPo

Untouched grandeur in the hinterlands. Life in the Boondocks. A. R. Ammons. HAP

Untouched, the door swings open before us, and—*voilà!*—we're in the produce section. Man I Love and I Shop at Jewel, The. Jim Elledge. IllVoic; ReTh

Untoward. Ann Lauterbach. BodElec

Untrimming the Tree. John N. Morris. ChrPo

Unum est Necessarium. Agnes Mary Frances Robinson. VWP

Unusual Autumn, An. Dahlia Ravikovitch [*or* Ravikovich]. DTA, *tr.* by Chana Bloch

Unusual View of the Town. J. P. Ward. AngWePo

Unuttered Prayer. Josephine D. Henderson Heard. CBWP-4

Unwanted. Edward Field. GLP

Unwatched, the garden bough shall sway. Tennyson. EBVV; FHYEP; GTBS-P; OBGa; PeECV; SCV *Fr.* In Memoriam A. H. H.

Unweary'd watch their list'ning Leaders keep, Th' Homer. OBVE, *tr.* by Alexander Pope *Fr.* Iliad, The.

Unweathered stone beneath a rigid mane. Sonnet: To a Portrait of Hart Crane. Allen Tate. GS

Unwelcome. Mary Elizabeth Coleridge. OBEV; VWP; WPE

Unwelcome child. Child Compassion, The. Margot Ruddock. OBMV

Unwept, unhonour'd [*or* unhonoured], and unsung. (LL) Sir Walter Scott. ITBLP; NePenScot; OxBEV; OxBS; SoSe-8; TFi *Fr.* Lay of the Last Minstrel, The.

Unwind my riddle. Stephen Crane. APN-2

Unworthy, since thou hast decreed. To the Queen of Inconstancy, Regina Collier, in Antwerp. Katherine Philips. PEW

Unwounded by fate. Alabushevo. Viktor Aleksandrovich Nekipelov. TCRP, *tr.* by Albert C. Todd

Unwritten Law. Louise Glück. BodElec

Unwritten whorls on a spire lead a mollusk forward to build its celestial course, its factory, The. Sea. Valerie Wohlfeld. YaYoPo

Unyielding Youth, The. Marbod of Rennes.

"Horace composed an ode about a certain boy." CAGL; EroLit, *tr.* by John Boswell

"This vision of a face, radiant and full of beauty." CAGL; EroLit, *tr.* by John Boswell

Up. Margaret Atwood. NoP-4

Up. Bill Kushner. GLP; ReTh

Up. Nigel Wells. AngWePo

Up again. (LL) What Happened? John Wieners. FTOS; PoM

Up ahead, I know, he felt it stirring in himself already, the glance. Orpheus and Eurydice. Jorie Graham. VCAP

Up and Doing. Douglas Malloch. ITBLP

Up and Down. James Merrill. GLP

Up and Down. William Shakespeare. CTC *Fr.* Midsummer Night's Dream, A.

Up and down I go, my stock. Lawrence Sail. NewEx

Up and down the City Road. Pop Goes the Weasel! W. R. Mardale. OxNR

Up and down the lawn he walks with cycling hands. Gardener, The. Craig Raine. UV

Up and down the one way streets. Zebra. Natasha Trethewey. TWW

Up and down this red clay route. Late Summer News. Dorothy Barresi. SwNoth

Up and swallowed Bryan's Bryaness. (LL) Lion, The. Ogden Nash. TLR; WHSW

Up and up, the Incense-burner Peak! Having Climbed to the Topmost Peak of the Incense-Burner Mountain. Po Chü-i. ChiP, *tr.* by Arthur Waley

Up at a Villa—down in the City. Robert Browning. FHYEP; GTBS-P; NOBE; PoRA

Up at Piccadilly oh! Coachman, The. Mother Goose. OxNR; ReMoGo

Up at the prow, I wash my mouth, dripping water on my robe. Yang Chi. CoBLCP *Fr.* Miscellaneous Impressions of T'an-chou.

Up-Beat. Langston Hughes. APT-2

Up, black, striped and damasked like the chasuble. Skunk, The. Seamus Heaney. NAEL-5v2; NAEL-6v2; NoP-4; OxBC; PoE

Up, boy! arise, and saddle quick. Message, The. Heinrich Heine. AWP, *tr.* by Kate Freiligrath Kroeker

Up close, at the place. J. W. Hackett. NIL-7

Up country, her husband is working late. One Life. Andrew Motion. HarvBoo

Up Early. Kit Robinson. "Intent to consider." FTOS

Up-flaring through your nerves, you know the flash. Lőrinc Szabó. IQMS, *tr.* by Watson Kirkconnell *Fr.* Cricket Music.

Up from out of in under for? (LL) Naughty Preposition, The. Morris Gilbert Bishop. NBLV; PeLV

Up from the bronze, I saw. Roman Fountain. Louise Bogan. APT-2; NoP-4; WPOW

Up from the Egg; the Confessions of a Nuthatch Avoider. Ogden Nash. PoRA

Up from the Grave He Arose. Robert Lowry. SacPr

Up from the meadows rich with corn. Barbara Frietchie. John Greenleaf Whittier. APN-1; AiP; CBCWP; CTC; ColAP; EBNV; HHAm; ITBLP; NCAP; NOBA; OBAL; OBCA; OxIBACP; TFi

Up from the South, at break of day. Sheridan's Ride. Thomas Buchanan Read. APN-2; CBCWP

Up from the trawlers in the fishdock they walk to my house. Morning Call. Richard Murphy. BiHa; ModIr

Up from the valley. August Town. Bob Stewart. WaCA

Up from the valley, ten children working the fields. Woman Who Weeps. Ellen Bryant Voigt. OPRER

Up from thy hidden springs, while to thy praise I sing. (LL) Edward Taylor. ChIV-2; OxBA; SCAP *Fr.* Preparatory Meditations Before My Approach to the Lord's Supper.

Up half-known roads. (LL) Send-Off, The. Wilfred Owen. HarvBoo; MoBrPo; NPeEn; OBWP; OBWVE; OxBEV; OxBTC; PeFWW; PoWW; RB; TCAWP

Up he stands. Rooster, The. Abu'l Qasim As'ad Ibn Bilita. WoPoe, *tr.* by Leticia Garza-Falcón and Christopher Middleton

Up, Helsum Hairt. Alexander Scott. OxBS

Up here a while. Do come. (LL) Lwonesomeness. William Barnes. NOBVV; OxBEV

Up here in the land of the hot dog stand. South America, Take It Away! Harold Rome. ReLy

Up-Hill. Christina Georgina Rossetti. *See* Uphill

Up hill and down dale. *Unknown.* OxNR

Up in a dirty window in a dark room is a star. Pilot, The. Russell Edson. LCAP-2

Up in Mabel's Room. Kenneth Slessor. BMAP

Up in the Air. Allan Ramsay. NOEC; OxBEV

Up in the Air. Greg Williamson. AmPoNex

Up in the air and down! (LL)   Swing, The.   Robert Louis Stevenson.   ChAP; NOxBChV; NTCP; TLR

Up in the heavenly saloon.   Arizona Nature Myth.   James Michie.   FaBoA; NOBL

Up in the hills are bank on bank of blossoming peach and plum trees.   Liu Yu Hsi.   SuSp   Fr. Bamboo Branch Song.

Up in the mornin', out on the job.   That Lucky Old Sun.   Beasley Smith.   ReLy

Up in the Morning Early.   Robert Burns.   OPOU

Up in the North.   Unknown.   OxBoLi

Up into the Clouds Music.   Li Po.   ColAnChi, tr. by Elling O. Eide

Up into the silence the green.   E. E. Cummings.   TTTS

Up Johnie raise in a May morning.   Johnie Cock.   Unknown.   ESPB

Up late.   Gary Hotham.   HA

Up Late.   Arthur Nortje.   PBMAP

Up Madison, down Park.   I Walk a Little Faster.   Cy Coleman.   ReLy

Up my backside a core of charcoal does its slither. I have completed my feast and.   In Front of a Large Number of People.   John Godfrey.   FTOS

Up on the downs the red-eyed kestrels hover.   Up on the Downs.   John Masefield.   NOBE

Up on the mountaintop the chambermaid puts.   Loss.   Judith Herzberg.   TuT, tr. by Joan McBreen

Up on the Roof.   Maura Dooley.   NeBl

Up on the Spoon.   Stanley Crouch.   SeSe

Up on their brooms the Witches stream.   Ride-by-Nights, The.   Walter De la Mare.   ChAP

(Up on Top of a Rainbow) Sweepin' the Clouds Away.   Sam Coslow.   ReLy

Up! quit thy bower.   Joanna Baillie.   NAEL-6v2; NoP-4

Up Rising.   Robert Duncan.   APSN; NNaP   Fr. Passages.

Up rushed a band, with compasses and scales.   Philip Freneau.   NAAL-2v1; NAAL-3   Fr. House of Night, The.

Up stand / six.   Menage, The.   Carl Rakosi.   FTOS

Up street and down street.   Unknown.   OxNR

Up Tail[e]s All.   Robert Herrick.   BeJo

Up tails all! (LL)   Kenneth Grahame.   NOxBChV; NTCP; OTCP; WHSW   Fr. Wind in the Willows, The.

Up the airy mountain.   Fairies, The.   William Allingham.   FaBoCh; NOBE; NOBVV; NOxBChV; OBEV; OTCP; TFi

Up the ash tree climbs the ivy.   Upper Lambourne.   Sir John Betjeman.   FaBoTw

Up the Country.   Henry Lawson.   CBAP

Up the crag.   Weapons.   Anna Wickham.   MoBrPo

Up the dark avenue, leading to no end.   On an Inyanga Road.   Noel H. Brettell.   PeSAV

Up the hill and down the level!   Origin of the Snake, The.   Unknown.   NOxBChV; OxIBACP

Up the hill, / Hurry me not.   Forget Me Not.   Austin Clarke.   CIP-2

Up the hillside beyond the road's.   Glimpses.   Christopher Gilbert.   GT

Up the Noran Water.   Shy Geordie.   Helen B. Cruickshank.   OxBS

Up the ravine the sun was choking with dust. Emotion on the windows from the.   Saturated.   Aaron Shurin.   FTOS

Up the reputable walks of old established trees.   Campus on the Hill, The.   W. D. Snodgrass.   AiP; NoAM; TAP; TwCP

Up the river there's a college.   Tulip Time in Sing Sing.   P. G. Wodehouse.   ReLy

Up the road.   Apple Core.   Clarence Major.   GT

Up the street sex is sold by the piece.   Limerick.   Unknown.   PeLi

Up the wooden hill.   Unknown.   OxNR

Up There.   W. H. Auden.   OxBTC   Fr. Thanksgiving for a Habitat.

Up There.   Ruth Stone.   ExTi

Up there on the mountain road, the fireworks.   Blue Ridge.   Ellen Bryant Voigt.   NoAM

Up there—or down here.   Lorca Variations (XXVIII), The.   Jerome Rothenberg.   PFTM-2

Up they go, yawning.   1915.   Roger McDonald.   NOBAu

Up this green woodland ride let's softly rove.   Nightingale's Nest, The.   John Clare.   NPeEn

Up those Museum steps you came.   To Lallie.   Amy Levy.   PoBW; ViWPN

Up to the bed by the window, where I be lyin'   Old Shepherd's Prayer.   Charlotte Mew.   MoBrPo; OxBTC; WPE

Up to the top of the haunted turf.   Louis Untermeyer.   MoAmPo   Fr. Mother Goose up-to-Date.

Up to those heights where angels rest.   Perfect Orchestra, The.   Henrietta Cordelia Ray.   CBWP-3

Up to thy summit, Lewesdon, to the brow.   William Crowe.   NOEC   Fr. Lewesdon Hill.

Up, Up, Home & Away.   John Forbes.   NOBAu

Up! up! my Friend, and quit your books.   Tables Turned, The.   William Wordsworth.   FHYEP; NAEL-5v2; NAEL-6v2; NOBRP; TOF

Up! Up! the time for sleep is past!   Judah ibn Sabbatai.   TrJP   Fr. Gift of Judah the Woman-Hater, The.

Up yonder on the mountain.   Shepherd's Lament, The.   Goethe.   AWP, tr. by Bayard Taylor

Upanishads, The.   Unknown.
   Brihadaranyaka Upanishad.
   "Golden God, the Self, the immortal Swan, The."   EnlH, tr. by Stephen Mitchell
   Mantreya Upanishad, The.
   "I am I, but also the other."   WoPoe, tr. by Patrick Olivelle
   Mundaka Upanishad.
   "Two birds, one of them mortal, the other immortal."   EnlH

Upchering of the Messe, The.   Luke Sheperd.
   "Who hath not knowne or herd."   PBRV

Upgrade, past snow-tangled bramble, past.   Sila.   Robert Penn Warren.   NoP-4

Upheaval's stone garden.   Indian Peaks, Colorado.   Reg Saner.   PoCoUp

Uphill.   Christina Georgina Rossetti.   CABP; EBVV; HAP; InPK-6; NAEL-5v2; NALW; NOBE; OBEV; PoE; PoRA; SacPr; TFi; TrCP; WPE; WeW-3 (Up-Hill.)   NAEL-6v2; NoP-4; PEW; PoPoPo

Uphold Me.   Karen Gershon.   LW

Upkeep.   Miriam Goodman.   UnSA

Upland.   A. R. Ammons.   NOBA

Upland Shepherd, as reclined he lies, The.   Sea View, The.   Charlotte Smith.   CenSon; ECWP

Upon a bed of humble clay.   Riddle, A.   Thomas Parnell.   ECEV

Upon a Black Twist, Rounding the Arm of the Countess of Carlisle.   Robert Herrick.   CaPo; CavPo

Upon a Booke Written at the Beginning of the Parliament 1640.   Anna Norman Ley.   EMWP

Upon a Bookseller.   John Oldham.   BASC

Upon a Braid of Hair in a Heart.   Henry King, Bishop of Chichester.   EnLoPo

Upon a Brook.   Ku K'uang.   SuSp, tr. by Irving Y. Lo

Upon a child.   Robert Herrick.   OBEV

Upon a Child That Died [or Dyed].   Robert Herrick.   BeJo; CaPo; InPK-6; NoP-4; PAI
   (Epitaph Upon a Child that Died.)   OBEV

Upon a Cloak [or Cloke] Lent Him by Mr. J. Ridsley.   Henry Vaughan.   BASC
   "Here, take again thy sackcloth! and thank heaven."   AngWePo

Upon a cock-horse to market I'll trot.   Unknown.   OxNR

Upon a Command to Write on My Father.   Gertrude Aston Thimelby.   EMWP

Upon a dark, light, gloomy, sunshine day.   Messe of Nonsense, A.   Unknown.   NOSC

Upon a day, came sorrow in to me.   Sonnet: On the 9th of June 1290.   Dante Alighieri.   AWP, tr. by Dante Gabriel Rossetti

Upon a Dead Man's Head.   John Skelton.   HAP; SCGP; WoPoe
   (Upon a Dead Man's Head, that was Sent to Him from an Honorable Gentlewoman for a Token.)   CABP
   (Youre ugly tokyn.)   CABP; OxBEV

Upon a Drawing.   István Vas.   IQMS, tr. by Daniel Gerard Hoffman

Upon a Dying Lady.   W. B. Yeats.   UnPo

Upon a Fool.   John Hoskyns [or Hoskins].   FaBoEE

Upon a Friend's Pet Cat, Being Sick.   John Winstanley.   TriCat

Upon a Funeral.   Sir John Beaumont.   NOSC

Upon a Girl of Seven Years Old.   Pope.   OxBSP

Upon a gloomy night.   St John of the Cross: Songs of the Soul in Rapture.   Roy Campbell.   PeECV

Upon a grassie hillock He was laid.   Giles Fletcher, the Younger.   PeECV   Fr. Christ's Victory and Triumph.

Upon a Great Shower of Snow That Fell on May-Day, 1654.   Thomas Washbourne.   NOCV

Upon a Joynted Ring.   Francellina Stapleton.   EMWP

Upon a lady my love is lente.   Unknown.   MiEL

Upon a little dappled nag, whose mane.   William Tennant.   NOBRP   Fr. Anster Fair.

Upon a lonely desart beach.   Haunted Beach, The.   Mary Robinson.   ECWP; RWP

Upon a Maid.   Robert Herrick.   CaPo

Upon a Maid That Died [or Dyed] the Day She Was Married [or Marryed].   Meleager.   AWP; OBVE, tr. by Robert Herrick

Upon a Maid[e].   Robert Herrick.   CaPo; FaBoCh; FaBoEE; OxBoLi

Upon a Mole in Celia's Bosom.   Thomas Carew.   BeJo; CaPo

Upon a mouth-organ. (LL)   Der Blinde Junge.   Mina Loy.   APT-1; HarvBoo

Upon a Notorious Shrew.   Unknown.   FaBoEE

Upon a Quarter Million.   Lorna Goodison.   WaCA

Upon a Rare Voice.   Owen Feltham [or Feltham].   NOSC

Upon a Ribbon [or Ribband].   Thomas Carew.   BeJo; CaPo; NOSC; PoE

Upon a Rich Country Gentleman.   Unknown.   FaBoEE

Upon a Row of Old Books and Shoes in a Pawnbroker's Window. Suzanne Gardinier. CBAP

Upon a Sacrament. (LL) Emily Dickinson. APN-2; BoWoP; ITBLP; NCAP; NOBA; OxBA

Upon a simmer Sunday morn. Holy Fair, The. Robert Burns. OBSV

Upon a Spider Catching a Fly. Edward Taylor. NOBA; NoP-4; OxBA; OxBEV; PeECV; SCAP; TAP; TCAPo

Upon a stone I sat. I Sat Upon a Stone. Walther [or Walter] von der Vogelweide. AuPH, tr. by Lowell A. Bangerter

Upon a summer Sunday: sweet the sound. Runaways, The. Mark Van Doren. PoRA

Upon a time, before the faery broods. John Keats. FHYEP; NAEL-6v2; NOBRP Fr. Lamia.

Upon a tree there mounted guard. Cock and the Fox, The. Jean de La Fontaine. AWP, tr. by Elizur Wright

Upon a Wasp Chilled [or Child] with Cold. Edward Taylor. NAAL-2v1; NAAL-3; NAAL-5; NOBA; NOCV; OxBEV

Upon a Wheel of Cloud. (LL) Emily Dickinson. NCAP; RB

Upon a Young Mother of Many Children. Robert Herrick. CaPo

Upon an Ingenious Friend, Over-Vain. Thomas Fitzgerald. OxBSP

Upon an obscure night. Obscure Night of the Soul, The. Saint John of the Cross. AWP; OBMV, tr. by Arthur Symons

Upon an old estate from ancient sires descended. Portraits, The. Anna Maria Lenngren. WPOW, tr. by C. W. Stork

Upon an Unhandsome Gentlewoman, who made Love unto him. Richard Corbet [or Corbett]. BASC

Upon Appleton House [To My Lord Fairfax]. Andrew Marvell. BASC; GeHe; NAEL-7v1
  "And now to the ab[b]yss I pass." PBRV
  "At the demolishing, this seat." NOSC
  "From that blest bed the hero came." OBGa
  Garden, A. OBEV
  Garden of Appleton House, The ("When in the east the morning ray"). NOBE
  "Oh thou, that dear and happy isle." OxBoLi
  "See how the flowers, as at parade." OBEV
  "When in the east the morning ray." NOBE

Upon Arch-bishop Laud, Prisoner in the Tower. 1641. Unknown. PBRV

Upon Batt. Robert Herrick. FaBoEE

Upon Ben Jo[h]nson. Robert Herrick. BeJo; CaPo; FaBoEE; NoP-4
  (Here lies Jonson with the rest.) NoP-4

Upon Ben Johnson [or Jonson]. Edmund Waller. BeJo; NOSC

Upon Bishop Andrewes's [or Andrewes His] Picture before His Sermons. Richard Crashaw. NOSC

Upon Bunce: Epigram. Robert Herrick. CaPo

Upon Castara's Absence. William Habington. BeJo Fr. Castara.

Upon Castara's Departure. William Habington. NOSC

Upon Christ's Nativity or Christmas. Rowland Watkyns. OBWVE

Upon Closing the Book. Armanda Guiducci. CItWP, tr. by Cinzia Sartini Blum and Lara Trubowitz

Upon Defacing of Whitehall. Martin Parker. See King Enjoys His Own Again, The

Upon Dr. Davies's British Grammar. James Howell. AngWePo; OBWVE

Upon Drinking in a Bowl. John Wilmot, 2d Earl of Rochester. OxBoLi
  (Bowl, The.) OxAEP-1

Upon Electra. Robert Herrick. BeJo

Upon Fairford Windows. Richard Corbet [or Corbett]. BeJo; NOSC

Upon Finding a Black Woman's Door Sprayed with Swastikas, I Tell Her This Story of Hands. Kevin Stein. SwNoth

Upon Finding Dying: An Introduction, by L. E. Sissman, Remaindered at IS. Louis Edward Sissman. NoP-4

Upon Good-Friday, I will fast while I may. Charm. Unknown. EMWP

Upon Groins: Epigram. Robert Herrick. CaPo

Upon Her Eyes. Robert Herrick. BeJo

Upon Her Feet. Robert Herrick. BeJo; CaPo; OxBSP; PoE

Upon Her Play Being Returned to Her, Stained with Claret. Mary Leapor. ECWP

Upon her soothing breast. Emily Jane Brontë. BoWoP

Upon Her Voice. Robert Herrick. CaPo

Upon Himself. Robert Herrick. OxBSP

Upon Himselfe Being Buried. Robert Herrick. PBRV

Upon his dull ear fell the stern command. Black Draftee from Dixie, The. Carrie Williams Clifford. BlSi

Upon his frustrate and unhopeful quest. Fragment from "The Maladjusted: A Tragedy." Morris Gilbert Bishop. NBLV

Upon [His] Leaving His Mistress. John Wilmot, 2d Earl of Rochester. BASC; EnLoPo; NBLV; NOSC

Upon His Majesty's [or Majesties] Repairing of Paul's. Edmund Waller. BASC; PBRV

Upon His Picture. Thomas Randolph. BASC; BeJo; NOBE

Upon His Sister-in-Law, Mistress Elizabeth Herrick. Robert Herrick. CaPo

Upon His Spaniel[l] Tracie [or Tracy]. Robert Herrick. BeJo

Upon His Taking of Leicester. To the King. Robert Herrick. CavPo

Upon His Unconstant Mistress. Sir Robert Aytoun [or Ayton]. NOSC

Upon His Verses. Robert Herrick. NAEL-5v1; NAEL-6v1; NAEL-7v1

Upon Israel and upon the rabbis. Kaddish. Charles Reznikoff. TaR

Upon Jack and Jill: Epigram. Robert Herrick. CaPo; NAEL-5v1; NAEL-6v1; NAEL-7v1

Upon Julia's Arctics. Bert Leston Taylor. NBLV; OBAL

Upon Julia's Breasts. Robert Herrick. CaPo

Upon Julia's Clothes. Robert Herrick. AWP; BASC; BeJo; CABP; CaPo; CavPo; ClHu; EBEV; EnLoPo; GTBS-P; HAP; HeIP-4; NAEL-5v1; NAEL-6v1; NAEL-7v1; NBLV; NIL-7; NIP-4; NOBE; NOSC; NoP-4; OBEV; OxAEP-1; OxBEV; OxBSP; PAI; PeLV; PoE; PoPoPo; SCGP; TFi; TRP; TTTS; UV; WeW-3; WoPoe

Upon Julia's Clothes. Edmund George Valpy Knox. UV

Upon Julia's Haire Fill'd with Dew. Robert Herrick. PBRV
  (Daunc't by the Streames.) (LL) PBRV
  (Dew sate on Julia's haire.) PBRV
  (Upon Julia's Haire Fill'd with Dew.) PBRV

Upon Julia's Petticoat. Robert Herrick. See Julia's Petticoat

Upon Julia's Ribband. Robert Herrick. CaPo

Upon Julia's Voice. Robert Herrick. InPK-6; NOBE; NPeEn; SoSe-8

Upon Julia['s] Washing Herself in the River. Robert Herrick. CaPo

Upon Kind[e] and True Love. Aurelian Townshend [or Townsend]. MeLP; NOSC

Upon Lazarus His Teares. Richard Crashaw. GeHe

Upon Learning That a Bird Exists Called the Turnstone. John Updike. PeLV

Upon learning that the mother wrote verses. Soirée. Ezra Pound. OBCoV

Upon Leaving the Parole Board Hearing. Conyus. GT

Upon Love. Robert Herrick. BeJo

Upon Love, by Way of Question and Answer. Robert Herrick. CaPo

Upon Love Fondly Refused [or Refus'd] for Conscience's Sake. Thomas Randolph. BeJo

Upon Lulls. Robert Herrick. CaPo

Upon M. Ben Jo[h]nson: Epigram. Robert Herrick. BeJo; CaPo

Upon Master Edmund Spenser. Francis Beaumont. FaBoEE

Upon Master Walter Montagu's Return from Travel. Thomas Carew. CaPo

Upon mica screens, candles flicker deep shadows. Ch'ang-O. Li Shang-yin. ChinPo, tr. by Yip Wai-lim

Upon Mr. Hopton's Death. Henry Halswell. NOSC

Upon Mrs. Anne Bradstreet, Her Poems, Etc. John Rogers. SCAP

Upon Mistress Elizabeth Wheeler under the Name of Amarillis. Robert Herrick. CaPo

Upon Mistresse Susanna Southwell, Her Cheeks. Robert Herrick. BeJo

Upon Mr Thomas Murrays Fall. Sir Robert Aytoun [or Ayton]. NePenScot

Upon my chest the Cross of the Knights' Order. Letter about Horror, A. Milán Füst. IQMS, tr. by Jess Perlman

Upon my darling's beaming eyes. Auf meiner Herzliebsten Äugelein. Heinrich Heine. AWP, tr. by Richard Garnett

Upon My Dear and Loving Husband His Going into England. Anne Bradstreet. AH

Upon My Lady Carlisle's Walking in Hampton Court Garden. Sir John Suckling. BeJo; CaPo; CavPo
  (Didst thou not find the place inspir'd.) CABP; CavPo
  (Didst thou not find the place inspired.) NoP-4

Upon my lap my sovereign sits. Lullaby. Richard Verstegan [or Verstegen]. OBEV; SCGP

Upon My Lord Brohall's Wedding. Sir John Suckling. CaPo

Upon My Lord Chief Justice's Election of My Lady Anne Wentworth [or A.W.] for His Mistress. Thomas Carew. CaPo

Upon My Lord Winchilsea's Converting the Mount in His Garden to a Terrace. Anne Finch, Countess of Winchilsea. OBGa

Upon my return to America, Josephine. Return. Carolyn Forché. BodElec

Upon my Silver Shelf. (LL) It Dropped So Low in My Regard. Emily Dickinson. HAP; HeIP-4; InPK-6; OxBA; OxBSP

Upon my word and honour. (LL) As I Went to Bonner. Unknown. OxBoLi; OxNR; ReMoGo

Upon Nothing. John Wilmot, 2d Earl of Rochester. NOSC; OBSV; OxAEP-1; OxBEV

Upon one day as I did mourn full sore. Elizabeth Melville, Lady Culross. ChIV-1 Fr. Ane Godly Dream.

Upon One of the Maids of Honour to Queen Elizabeth. John Hoskyns [or Hoskins]. FaBoEE

Upon one side there are two spots of red. (LL) Sleeper in the Valley, The. Arthur Rimbaud. OBWP; WoPoe, *tr. by* William Jay Smith

Upon [*or* up on] the mountain my Lord spoke. Every [*or* Ev'ry] Time I Feel the [*or* de] Spirit. *Unknown.* APN-2

Upon our anguish for each other's sake! (LL) Sonnet: "Oh, my belovèd, have you thought of this." Edna St. Vincent Millay. HeIP-4; LW

Upon Our Saviour's Tomb[e] Wherein Never Man Was Laid. Richard Crashaw. *See* To Our Blessed Lord upon the Choice of His Sepulchre

Upon Overhearing Tagalog. Fatima Lim-Wilson. AmPoNex

Upon Pagget. Robert Herrick. CaPo; FaBoCh

Upon Parson Beanes. Robert Herrick. BeJo

Upon Passing the Homestead. Huang T'ing-chien. SuSp, *tr. by* Michael E. Workman

Upon Paul's steeple stands a tree. St. Paul's Steeple. *Unknown.* LB; OxNR

Upon Phillis Walking in a Morning before Sun-Rising. John Cleveland. MeLP

Upon Platonic Love: To Mistress Cicely Crofts, Maid of Honour. Sir Robert Aytoun [*or* Ayton]. NOSC

Upon Prudence Baldwin Her Sickness[e]. Robert Herrick. BASC

Upon Prue [*or* Prew], His Maid. Robert Herrick. BeJo; CaPo; NAEL-5v1; NAEL-6v1; NAEL-7v1; NoP-4; NPeEn; PAI

(In this little urn is laid.) NoP-4

Upon Receipt of a Pound of Coffee in 1863. Mary E. Tucker. CBWP-1

Upon Rook: Epigram. Robert Herrick. CaPo

Upon Scobble [Epigram]. Robert Herrick. BeJo; CaPo; FaBoEE

Upon Seeing the Fireflies. Tu Fu. SuSp, *tr. by* Wu-Chi Liu

Upon Shaving Off One's Beard. John Updike. OxBSP

Upon Showbread [*or* Shewbread]: Epigram. Robert Herrick. CaPo

Upon Sibilla. Robert Herrick. CaPo

(With paste of Almonds, *Syb* her hands doth scoure;) PBRV

Upon Sir Francis Drake's Return from His Voyage about the World, and the Queen's Meeting Him. *Unknown.* FaBoCh

Upon Sir John Lawrence's Bringing Water over the Hills [to My L. Middlesex His House at Witten]. Sir John Suckling. CaPo

Upon som honest[e] thing [*or* thyng] whil[e] that I drinke [*or* drynke]. (LL) Geoffrey Chaucer. NAEL-6v1; NAEL-7v1 *Fr.* Canterbury Tales, The.

Upon Some Alterations in My Mistress, after My Departure into France. Thomas Carew. CaPo

Upon Some Women. Robert Herrick. BeJo; CaPo

Upon Stephen Stoned. Sir John Suckling. ChIV-2

Upon that cruel season when our Lord. Onesto di Boncima. EaItPo, *tr. by* Dante Gabriel Rossetti

Upon that night, when fairies light. Halloween. Robert Burns. NOBRP; TreFP

Upon the arid shoulder. Giacomo Leopardi. WoPoe, *tr. by* John Heath-Stubbs *Fr.* Broom, The; or, The Flower of the Desert.

Upon the Asse That Bore Our Saviour. Richard Crashaw. ChIV-2; GeHe

Upon the Author. By a Known Friend. Benjamin Woodbridge. SCAP

Upon the Bankruptcy of a Physician. Henricus Selyns. SCAP

Upon the beach are thousands of crabs; they are. Crustaceans. Roy Fuller. NoAM

Upon the Birth of a Young and Highly Desired Son. Christian Weise. GePo, *tr. by* George C. Schoolfield

Upon the Body of Our Blessed Lord, Naked and Bloody. Richard Crashaw. NOSC; PAI

(On Our Crucified Lord, Naked and Bloody.) NAEL-6v1; OxBSP; TrCP

Upon the Book and Picture of the Seraphical Saint Teresa. Richard Crashaw. HAP; NOBE; OBEV; WoPoe *Fr.* Flaming Heart, The.

Upon the Circumcision. John Milton. ChIV-2

Upon the Crucifix. William Alabaster. NoSic

Upon the Curtain[e] of Lucasta's Picture [It Was Thus Wrought]. Richard Lovelace. CaPo

Upon the Day of Our Saviour's Nativity. Francis Quarles. NOSC

Upon the Death of G. B. John Cotton. SCAP

Upon the Death of Her Husband. Elizabeth Singer Rowe. ECWP

Upon the Death of His Much Esteemed Friend Mr. Jno Saffin Junr. Grindall Rawson. SCAP

Upon the Death of Mr. King Drowned in the Irish Seas. John Cleveland. HAP

Upon the Death of My Deare and Lovely Daughter J. P. Jane Pulter, Baptized May 1 1625 and Died Oct 8 1646 Aet. 20. Hester Lee Pulter. EMWP

Upon the Death of My Ever Desired Friend Doctor [*or* Dr] Donne Dean of Paul's. Henry King, Bishop of Chichester. BASC

Upon the Death of Sir Albert Morton's Wife. Sir Henry Wotton. BASC; BoLoP; EnLoPo; FaBoEE; NPeEn; OBEV; OxBEV; PBRV; WeW-3

Upon the Decease of Mrs. Anne Griffin. John Fiske. SCAP

Upon the Double Murther of King Charles I. Katherine Philips. BASC; NAEL-7v1

Upon the Duke of Buckingham. *Unknown.* BASC

Upon the earth there are so many treasures. Earth Felicities, Heavens Allowances. Richard Steere. SCAP

Upon the ecstatic diving board the diver. Lone Bather. Abraham Moses Klein. HeIP-4

Upon the eighteenth day of June. Bonny John Seton. *Unknown.* ESPB

Upon the enigmatic, stationary world. (LL) Face of the Horse, The. Nikolai Alekseievich Zabolotsky [*or* Zabolotskii]. RB; TCRP, *tr. by* Daniel Weissbort

Upon the Ensignes of Christes Crucifyinge. William Alabaster. ESCV *Fr.* Divine Meditations.

Upon the Ensigns of Christ's Crucifying. William Alabaster. NoSic

Upon the eyes, the lips, the feet. Extreme Unction. Ernest Christopher Dowson. MoBrPo; OBMV; PeECV; PeVV

Upon the fifth day of November. On Mr. Pricke. *Unknown.* FaBoEE

Upon the grass no longer hangs the dew. Hay making. Joanna Baillie. OxAEP-2

Upon the Grave of a Beggar. Timothy Kendall. NoSic

Upon the graving of her Name upon a Tree in Barnelmes Walks. Katherine Philips. PBRV

Upon the Hill and Grove at Bilbrough. Andrew Marvell. BASC

Upon the Holy Sepulchre. Richard Crashaw. FaBoEE

Upon the house a crooked sign. For Sale or Rent. *Unknown.* PoToHe

Upon the Image of Death. Robert Southwell. NOBE

"Before my face the picture hangs." NoSic

Upon the Imprisonment of His Sacred Majesties that Unparaleld Prince King Charles the First. Hester Lee Pulter. EMWP

Upon the Infant Martyrs. Richard Crashaw. GeHe; NPeEn; PAI

Upon the infinite shore by the sea. Dame Edith Sitwell. BWW *Fr.* Sleeping Beauty, The.

Upon the jade steps white dews grow. Yu Chieh Yuan (Jade Steps Grievance, Yueh-fu). Li Po. ChinPo, *tr. by* Yip Wai-lim

Upon the King's Return from Flanders, 1695. Henry Hall. NOSC

Upon the LD Saying KT Could Be Sad in Her Company. Katherine Thimelby Aston. EMWP

Upon the level field behold. Baseball. Frank Dempster Sherman. OBCA

Upon the Lines and Life of the Famous Scenic Poet, Master William Shakespeare. Hugh Holland. AngWePo; OBWVE

Upon the Loss[e] of His Little Finger. Thomas Randolph. BeJo; NOSC

Upon the Loss[e] of His Mistresses. Robert Herrick. BASC; BeJo; CaPo; CavPo; NAEL-5v1; NAEL-6v1; NAEL-7v1; NOSC; PoE

Upon the lotus flower. Fuso. JDP, *tr. by* Yoel Hoffmann

Upon the man who's buried here. J. E. Thorold Rogers. FaBoEE

Upon the mountain's edge with light touch resting. Sunset, A. Samuel Taylor Coleridge. OxBSP

Upon the mounts of spices. (LL) British [*or* Brittish] Church, The. Henry Vaughan. ESCV; PeECV

Upon the mournful death of our late Soveraign Lord Charles the first, King of England, etc. Rowland Watkyns. BASC

Upon the Much Lamented Death of the Right Honourable, the Lady Elizabeth Langham. Bathsua Pell Makin. EMWP

Upon the Much-to Be Lamented Desease of the Reverend Mr. John Cotton. John Fiske. SCAP

Upon the Necessity and Benefite of Learning Written in the Beginning of a Common Place Booke Belonging to W. B. a Young Scholler. Anna Norman Ley. EMWP

Upon the New Building at Appleton. Thomas Fairfax, Baron Fairfax of Cameron. NOSC

Upon the Nipples of Julia's Breast. Robert Herrick. CaPo; ErotSp; NAEL-5v1; NAEL-6v1; NAEL-7v1; NOSC; PeLV

Upon the [*or* a] Snail. John Bunyan. OxBSP

Upon the patch of earth that clings. Public Aid for Niagara Falls. Morris Gilbert Bishop. NBLV

Upon the Plymouth shore the wild rose blooms. Wild Rose of Plymouth, The. Jones Very. APN-1

Upon the Poet of His Time, Ben Jonson: His Honoured Friend and Father. James Howell. NOSC

Upon the Priory Grove, His Usual Retirement. Henry Vaughan. BeJo

Upon the Same. Robert Herrick. CaPo

Upon the Saying That My Verses Were Made by Another. Anne Killigrew. BASC; CABP; EMWP; NALW; PEW; WPE

Upon the shepherd-boy the summer sun. Sándor Petőfi. IQMS, *tr. by* Watson Kirkconnell *Fr.* Sir John, The Hero.

Upon the sight of lidless eyes in Hell. (LL) Dante Gabriel Rossetti. NAEL-5v2; NAEL-6v2 *Fr.* House of Life, The.

Upon the slippery tops of human[e] state. Seneca. BASC; OBVE, *tr. by* Abraham Cowley *Fr.* Thyestes.

Upon the Springs Issuing out from the Foot of Plimouth Beach. Samuel Sewall. SCAP

Upon the Sudden Restraint of the Earl[e] of Somerset, Then Falling from Favor [or Favour]. Sir Henry Wotton. NOBE; NOSC; NPeEn; OxBEV

(Dazel'd thus, with height of place.) PBRV

(Earle of Somerset.) PBRV

Upon the threshold of the mind? (LL) Tennyson. HAP; NAEL-6v2; NAWM-7v2 Fr. In Memoriam A. H. H.

Upon the Times. Mildmay Fane, 2d Earl of Westmorland. BeJo

Upon the Tomb of the Most Reverend Mr. John Cotton. Benjamin Woodbridge. SCAP

Upon the Troublesome Times. Robert Herrick. CaPo; CavPo

Upon the utmost corners of the warld. In Orknay. William Fowler. OxBS

Upon the walls of Munkács. Exile of Rákóczi, The. Unknown. IQMS, tr. by Watson Kirkconnell

Upon the work of Walter Landor. Dorothy Parker. APT-1; NALW Fr. Pig's-Eye View of Literature, A.

Upon their quivering wings. (LL) Fairyland [or Fairy-Land]. Edgar Allan Poe. APN-1; NAAL-2v1; NAAL-3

Upon this firthe, as on the sees of love. William Fowler. NePenScot Fr. Tarantula of Love, The.

Upon this ground how well grows barrenness. (LL) Of the Reed That the Jews Set in Our Saviour's Hand. William Alabaster. NPeEn; NoSic

Upon this marble bust that is not I. To Inez Milholland. Edna St. Vincent Millay. AiP; NALW; WPE

Upon this place the great Gustavus died. On Gustavus Adolphus, King of Sweden. Sir Thomas Roe. FaBoEE

Upon thy tender limbs! and so good night. (LL) To One Married to an Old Man. Edmund Waller. FaBoEE; OxBSP

Upon Time. Robert Herrick. BeJo

Upon Tyburn tree! (LL) John Gay. NAEL-6v1; NOEC Fr. Begger's Opera.

Upon Umber: Epigram. Robert Herrick. CaPo

Upon Visiting His Lady by Moonlight. "A. W." CTC

Upon Wedlock and Death of Children. Edward Taylor. ColAP; NAAL-2v1; NAAL-3; NAAL-5; SacPr; TCAPo

Upon what terms, with how much left unsaid. (LL) Middle-Aged, The. Adrienne Rich. HCAP; PoPoPo

Upon Your Leaving. Etheridge Knight. NNaP

Upon Your Leaving. Etheridge Knight. See also Cell Song

Upone Tabacco. Sir Robert Aytoun [or Ayton]. OxBS

Upper-Austrian Landscape. Paula von Preradovic. AuPH, tr. by Lowell A. Bangerter

Upper Broadway. Adrienne Rich. HCAP; ItWoWo

Upper Canadian, The. James Reaney. NOBC

Upper Chamber, An. Frances Bannerman. OBEV

Upper Family. Maxwell Bodenheim. OBAL

Upper Lambourne. Sir John Betjeman. FaBoTw

Upper Marlboro. Kenneth Carroll. SpirFl

Upper slopes are busy with the cricket, The. Elegy on the Dust. Thom Gunn. NoAM Fr. Misanthropos.

Upon the First Sight of New England, June 29, 1638. Thomas Tillam. SCAP

(Hail, Holy Land.) AH

Upraised arm, fist clenched, ready to hit, The. Minnie Bruce Pratt. WiU

Uprearing from the thrashed. Where the Deer Go. Dabney Stuart. PoCoUp

Uprightness. Camouflaged Troop-Ship. Amy Lowell. AiP

Uproar in Leuven, insurrection in the Sorbonne. Imitation of Monsieur Beranger. "Naum Korzhavin." TCRP, tr. by Albert C. Todd

Uprooted tree leaves, An. Group Photo from Pretoria Local on the Occasion of a Fourth Anniversary (Never Taken). Jeremy Cronin. PeSAV

Uprose the King of Men with speed. Descent of Odin, The. Thomas Gray. OxAEP-1

Upside Down. Aileen Fisher. OTCP

Upside down Basket, The. Alan Chong Lau. UnSA

Upstairs Jenny crashed her car and became a living corpse, Jake. Charnel Ground, The. Allen Ginsberg. BB; BodElec

Upstairs on the third floor. Bottled [New York]. Helene Johnson. APT-2; BlSi

Upstate. Simon J. Ortiz. LTA

Upstate. Derek Walcott. GT; OPRER

Upstream. Carl Sandburg. MoAmPo

Upstream, against the wind, they pull hundreds of feet of rope. Song of the Boat-Pullers. Pien Kung. CoBLCP, tr. by Jonathan Chaves

Uptown. Allen Ginsberg. TwCP

Upturn. Anne-Marie Fyfe. Prnts

Upupup! The light percussive. Airborne. Elizabeth Garrett. MFPA

Upward, and rarefy [or Rarifie] the air. (LL) Snail [or Snayl], The. Richard Lovelace. BeJo; CaPo; NPeEn

Upward in motion with wet wind. (LL) Wales Visitation. Allen Ginsberg. APSN; BB; ColAP; NNaP; NOBA; VCAP

Upward Look, An. James Merrill. PoPoPo

Ur / mit / mals. Volcanic tuff. Tina Darragh. FTOS

Ur Sonata. Kurt Schwitters.

"Third movement." PFTM-1

Urals post-master, this is your. Ode. Barry MacSweeney. Oth

Urania. Robert Andrews. NOEC

Urania. Burleigh Mutén. HW

Urania. Mary Sidney Wroth, Countess of Montgomery.

("Bear part with me most straight and pleasant tree.") WPE

"Did I boast of liberty?" LW; PEW

(Duke's Song, The.) RACG; WPE

"Here all alone in silence might I mourne." NAEL-7v1

("How do I find my soul's extremest anguish.") OxBSo

("If a clear fountain still keeping a sad course.") RACG; WPE

("Loss, my molester, at last patient be.") PEW; WPE

"Love what art thou? A vain thought." NAEL-5v1; NAEL-6v1; NAEL-7v1; NoP-4

(Pamphilia's Sonnet.) WPE

Song: "Love what art thou? A vain thought." NAEL-5v1; NAEL-6v1; NAEL-7v1; NoP-4

("Unseen, unknown, I here alone complain.") NAEL-6v1; NAEL-7v1

("Wailing a state which can no comfort give.") (LL) NAEL-6v1; NAEL-7v1

Urania, or Spiritual Poems. William Drummond, of Hawthornden.

Madrigal: "Astrea in this time." NOSC

Too Long I Followed. Son

"Triumphing chariots, statues, crowns of bay." NOSC

Urania takes her morning flight. Adventurous Muse, The. Isaac Watts. NOEC

Uranium. Gerry Bostock. IBA

Uranne. Mary Weston Fordham. CBWP-2

Urban. Oliver Davies. AngWePo

Urban Aboriginal. Jack Davis. IBA

Urban Convalescence, An. James Merrill. CoAP; ColAP; NAAL-2v2; NAAL-5; NOBA

Urban Dream. Víctor Hernández Cruz. NBV

Urban Experience: Part One, The. Lew Blockcolski. VoR

Urban Experience: Part Two, The. Lew Blockcolski. VoR

Urban Gallery. Rachel Wetzsteon. AmPoNex; NeAmPo

Urban Guerrilla, An. Allen Curnow. PeNZ Fr. Moro Assassinato.

Urban Love Songs. Wing Tek Lum. OpBo

Urban, or Sylvan, or whatever name. Passive Participle's Petition, The. John Byrom. ECEV

Urban Pastoral. Babette Deutsch. MakPoe

Urban Poem. Douglas Goetsch. AmPoNex; UrbNat

Urban Pollution. John Armstrong. ECEV; NOEC Fr. Art of Preserving Health, The.

Urban Progress. John Dyer. ECEV Fr. Fleece, The.

Urbane man, composed, aware, An. Like Father. Herbert Williams. AngWePo

Urceus Exit. Austin Dobson. OBEV Fr. Rose-Leaves.

Urchin, The. Konstantin Iakovlevich Vanshenkin. TCRP, tr. by Daniel Weissbort

Urchin saw a rose—a dear. Rosebud in the Heather. Goethe. STV, tr. by John Frederick Nims

Urdeath. August Stramm. PFTM-1

Urge him to return! (LL) Huang E. CoBLCP; ColAnChi, tr. by Jonathan Chaves

Urge me no more! nor think, because I seem. Matilda Barbara Betham-Edwards. CenSon

Urge me no more to sing. I am not able. Satire on the Rebellion, A. Alexander Brome. BASC

Urge to wander is, The. Leaving. Rae Armantrout. FTOS

Urgent Letter, An. Hugh Maxton. PBCIP

Urgent letter that I try to write, The. Night Letter. Stanley Kunitz. AF

Urging Her of a Promise. Ben Jonson. NAEL-6v1; NAEL-7v1 Fr. Celebration of Charis in Ten Lyric[k] Pieces [or Peeces], A.

Uriel. Ralph Waldo Emerson. APN-1; NAAL-2v1; NAAL-3; NOBA; OxBA

Uriel. William Force Stead.

How Infinite Are Thy Ways. OBMV

Urine-stained quilt, A. Buson. EH, tr. by Robert Hass

Urn. Shinkichi Takahashi. ZenPo, tr. by Takashi Ikemoto and Lucien Stryk

Urn Burial. Ted Hughes. EBEV

Ursa Major. Federico García Lorca. PFTM-1

Ursula. David Ray. VGW

Urumbula Song, The. Unknown. CBAP, tr. by T. G. H. Strehlow

Us. Anne Sexton. MPUn

Us-folks is purty pore—but Ma. James Whitcomb Riley. VerBaPo *Fr.* Dubious "Old Kriss," A.

Us po' Black boys. Window Shopping. Lamont B. Steptoe. SpirFl

Us Two. Nina Cassian. PoSu, *tr. by* Nina Cassian

Use maketh maistry [*or* mast'ry], this hath been said alway. Of Use. John Heywood. FaBoEE

Use of Poetry, The. Michael Ryan. BodElec

Use your mental eye. Nīlkantha Mukhopādhyāy. SinGod, *tr. by* Rachel Fell McDermott

Used to be, fellows would ask if you were married. Sweaters, The. Lucia Maria Perillo. UnSA

Used to be you could / touch your eyes. Gigabyte Me—How Much RAM in Your Summer of Love? Edwin Torres. HeMarv

Used to hang and brush their bosoms? I feel chilly and grown old. (LL) Toccata of Galuppi's, A. Robert Browning. EBVV; FaBoVe; GTBS-P; HAP; NAEL-5v2; NAEL-6v2; NOBE; NOBVV; UV

Used to long nights, springtime is past. In Remembrance of the Forgotten. "Lu Hsün." SuSp, *tr. by* William R. Schultz

Used together: seasons, books, a piece of music. Kind of Loss, A. Ingeborg Bachmann. PoetW, *tr. by* Mark Anderson

Useless Day. Rosario Castellanos. WPOW, *tr. by* Maureen Ahern

Useless except to a collector, a rich man. (LL) Behaviour of Fish in an Egyptian Tea Garden. Keith Douglas. FaBoMo; RB

Useless to relate how I've strained my eyes. Cast Away. Christopher Pilling. NLP

Useless Valentines / Are better. Valentine, A. Jack Spicer. APSN

Uses of Light, The. Gary Snyder. PAI

Ushers in a drearier day. (LL) Song. Emily Jane Brontë. FaBoCh; NPeEn; OxBSP

Using words this way. Millennial Polka. Alicia Ostriker. ExTi

Usk. T. S. Eliot. FaBoCh; NOCV; PeECV *Fr.* Landscapes.

Usk, The. Charles Hubert Sisson. HarvBoo; NOCV

Usquebaugh. Wendy Cope. UV

Usual exquisite boredom of patrols, The. Hugh Popham. OxBTC

Usual Immigrant Uncle Poem, The. Askold Melnyczuk. OPRER

Usual is there, The. Landscape with Saxophonist. Thylias Moss. ESEAA

Usually it is night. After Edward Hopper. Lawrence Raab. PoSol

Usually / you wake first. Why. Yusuf Al-Sa'igh. MAP, *tr. by* Diana Der Hovanessian and Salma Khadra Jayyusi

Usurers, The. Nicolás Guillén. PFTM-1

Ut pictura . . . The disconcerting lips. Fan, The. Eugenio Montale. AF, *tr. by* William Arrowsmith

Utah. Anne Stevenson. FaBoVe

Ute Mountain. Charles Tomlinson. RB

Utilitarian View of the Monitor's Fight, A. Herman Melville. APN-2; ColAP; NAAL-2v1; NAAL-3; NCAP; UnPo

Utitia'q's Song. *Inuit Oral Tradition.* AWTN, *tr. by* Franz Boas and Brian Swann

Utitia' q's Song. *Unknown.* APN-2, *tr. by* Franz Boas

Utmost grace the Greeks could show, The. Grecian Kindness. John Wilmot, 2d Earl of Rochester. OxBSP

Utopia. Jewel C. Latimore. BPo

"Utopia" The. Lee Harwood. SPE

Utopia Anglicized. Sir William Schwenck Gilbert. OBSV *Fr.* Utopia Limited.

Utopia Limited. Sir William Schwenck Gilbert. Utopia Anglicized. OBSV

Utter aloneness—. Buson. SoOfWa, *tr. by* Sam Hamill

Utter moorland, high, and wide, and flat, An. Fork of the Road, The. William Renton. NOBVV

Utterance. Donald Davidson. FuPo

Utterance. W. S. Merwin. BLT

Uttering cries that are almost human. (LL) American Poetry. Louis Simpson. FaBoA; NOBA; NoAM; TAP

Utterly secret. I know you, black swan. (LL) Music of Colours—White Blossom. Vernon Watkins. AngWePo; TCAWP

Uuuuuuuuuu. Dope. Imamu Amiri Baraka. APSN

V

V. B. Wigglesworth wakes at noon. V. B. Nimble, V. B. Quick. John Updike. NoP-4; OBCoV

V. Father Death Blues. Allen Ginsberg. CLPP

V. Innocentia Veritas Viat Fides Circumdederunt me inimici mei. Sir Thomas Wyatt. NAEL-6v1

V-Letter. Karl Shapiro. IllVoic; NoAM; TrJP

V. N. and C. I, The. Maggie Pogue Johnson. CBWP-4

V's Farmhouse. Lisa Fishman. AmPoNex

V.A. Hospital. Anthony Petrosky. CDa

Vacancy in the Park. Wallace Stevens. LCAP-2; SAmP

Vacancy in which, apparently, A. All is Emptiness, and I Must Spin. Thomas Kinsella. PBCIP

Vacant Lot. Dudley Randall. NoAM

Vacant Lot. Yvor Winters. APT-2

Vacant Lot, The. Gwendolyn Brooks. NAAAL; NAAL-2v2; NOBA; NoAM *Fr.* Street in Bronzeville, A.

Vacant parade grounds swept by the winter wind. Exile. Anthony Hecht. TaR

Vacant shuttles / Weave the wind. I have no ghosts. T. S. Eliot. UV *Fr.* Gerontion.

Vacation. Rita Dove. SpirFl

Vacation. William Stafford. BLT

Vacation, 1969. Dorothy Barresi. SwNoth

Vachel, the stars are out. To Lindsay. Allen Ginsberg. CoAmPo

Vacillation. W. B. Yeats. NoAM

  "Must we part, Von Hügel, though much alike." OBMV

  "My fiftieth year had come and gone." RaBo

Vacuum, The. Howard Nemerov. NIL-7; NIP-4; RB

Vagabond, A. James Tate. NoAM

Vagabond, The. Robert Louis Stevenson. OxAEP-2

Vagabond Song, A. Bliss Carman. BRP; TCAPo

Vagabonds. Langston Hughes. SAmP

Vague Lyric by G. M. Max Beerbohm. FaBoEE

Vague Poem. Elizabeth Bishop. BAP-01

Vaguely I hear the purple roar of the torn-down Third Avenue El. You Are Gorgeous and I'm Coming. Frank O'Hara. NeAP

Vagueness comes over everything, A. Fog. Amy Clampitt. MakPoe

Vaices That Be Gone, The. William Barnes. NOBVV

Vain Advice, The. Catherine Cockburn. LW

Vain and Careless. Robert Graves. NOxBChV

Vain are those joys that erring man provides. World Not Our Rest, The. Maria Frances Cecelia Cowper. ECWP

Vain, frail, short liv'd, and miserable Man. Song of Emptiness to Fill up the Empty Pages Following, A. Michael Wigglesworth. SCAP

Vain old Professor of Greek, A. Limerick. Ron Rubin. PeLi

Vain Wish, A. Philip Bourke Marston. GSo

Vainglory in Snailhorn. Tune: "Fragrance Fills the Courtyard." Su Tung-p'o (Su Shih). ColAnChi, *tr. by* J. R. Hightower

Vainglory on terra firma. Three for the Road. E. San Juan, Jr. ReBoTo

Vainly I dug for a perfect sky. Muso Soseki. ZenPo, *tr. by* Takashi Ikemoto and Lucien Stryk

Vainly in Hell let Pluto domineer. (LL) Andrew Marvell. BASC; NOBL; PeLV

Vainly my heart had with thy sorceries striven. To ———: "Vainly my heart had with thy sorceries striven." Sarah Helen Whitman. APN-1; TCAPo

Vainly you call on the bluebird to deliver your passionate pleas! (LL) Girl of Mount Hua, The. Han Yü. CoBCP; ColAnChi, *tr. by* Burton Watson

Vajdahunyad. Ferenc Kazinczy. IQMS, *tr. by* Watson Kirkconnell

Vala; or The Four Zoas. William Blake.

  "As the seed waits eagerly watching for its flower and fruit." PoE

  (Night II (Enion's Lament).) PoE

  Night VIII (The Eternal Man). PoE

Vale from Carthage. Peter Viereck. MoAmPo; WoPoe

Vale there is, enwrapped [*or* enwrapt] with dreadful[l] shades, A. Vale of Tear[e]s, A. Robert Southwell. NoSic

Valediction. Sir Robert Aytoun [*or* Ayton]. NOSC

Valediction. Clare Rossini. BAP-97

Valediction, A. Ernest Christopher Dowson. BoLoP

Valediction: "Bid me not go where neither suns nor showers [show'rs]." William Cartwright. BeJo

Valediction: Forbidding Mourning, A. John Donne. AmFaPo; BASC; CABP; ESCV; FHYEP; FSCP; HAP; HeIP-4; MeLP; NAEL-5v1; NAEL-6v1; NAEL-7v1; NIL-7; NOBE; NoP-4; NOSC; NPeEn; OxBEV; PAI; PBRV; PoE; PoPoPo; SCGP; SoSe-8; TFi; UnPo; WeW-3

  "Our two soules therefore, which are one." UV

Valediction Forbidding Mourning, A. Adrienne Rich. NAAL-2v2; NAAL-5; NoAM; NoP-4

Valediction (Liverpool Docks), A. John Masefield. OBMV

Valediction of the Book, A. John Donne. NoP-4

Valediction of Weeping, A. John Donne. BASC; ESCV; FHYEP; FSCP; HAP; HeIP-4; MeLP; NAEL-5v1; NAEL-6v1; NAEL-7v1; NOSC; NoP-4; PoE; SCGP; WeW-3

Valediction to My Contemporaries. Horace Gregory. MoAmPo

Valediction to the River Duddon. William Wordsworth. *See* River Duddon [A Series of Sonnets], The

Valediction—To My Father. Eddy Van Vliet. VCWP, *tr. by* John Van Tiel

Valedictory Sonnet to the River Duddon. William Wordsworth. *See* River Duddon [A Series of Sonnets], The

Valentin's Song. Ferdinand Raimund. AuPH, *tr.* by Lowell A. Bangerter

Valentine. Wendy Cope. NoP-4

Valentine. Donald Hall. NTCP

Valentine. Ernest Hemingway. IllVoic; OBAL

Valentine, A. Robert Graves. FuPo

Valentine, A. Jack Spicer. APSN

Valentine, A. Priscilla Jane Thompson. CBWP-2

Valentine, A. Elizabeth Trefusis.
  Valentine, A. LW

Valentine, A. Elizabeth Trefusis. LW *Fr.* Valentine, A.

Valentine, The. Mary Weston Fordham. CBWP-2

Valentine Browne. Egan [or Aodhagán] O'Rahilly [or O'Reilly or Ó Rathaille]. NOIV, *tr.* by Thomas Kinsella

Valentine Delivered by a Raven. Tess Gallagher. ExTi

Valentine for Ben Franklin Who Drives a Truck in California, A. Diane Wakoski. NoAM

Valentine's Day. Kenneth May. SeSe

Valentine to Sherwood Anderson, A. Gertrude Stein. NoAM
  (I knew too that through them I knew too that he was through, I knew too that he threw them.) PFTM-1
  (Idem the Same.) APT-1

Valentino's Hair. Yvonne Sapia. PeVV; TRP

Valiant-for-Truth's Song. John Bunyan. *See* Pilgrim's Progress, The

Valiant's Song. John Bunyan. *See* Pilgrim's Progress, The

Vallejo. Maggie Nelson. HeMarv

Valley, The. Alphonse Marie Louis de Lamartine. SxFrPo, *tr.* by E. H. Blackmore and A. M. Blackmore

Valley, The. Agnes Mary Frances Robinson. VWP

Valley Bleeds with Roman Rust, The. Osip Emilevich Mandelstam [or Mandelshtam]. TCRusP, *tr.* by John Glad

Valley Candle. Wallace Stevens. SAmP

Valley of Dry Bones, The. Bible, *O.T.* WoPoe, *tr.* by David Curzon *Fr.* Ezekiel.

Valley of Unrest, The. Edgar Allan Poe. APN-1; NAAL-2v1; NAAL-3

Valley Prince. Mervyn Morris. WaCA

Valley Spirit never dies, The. Lao Tzu. HW, *tr.* by Arthur Waley

Valley Wind, The. Lu Yün. ChiP, *tr.* by Arthur Waley

Valley with a silver-grayish mist, The. Vision, A. Hugo von Hofmannsthal. TrJP, *tr.* by Charles Wharton Stork

Valleys crack and burn, the exhausted plains, The. Mahratta Ghats, The. Alun Lewis. AngWePo; OBWVE; PoWW; TCAWP

Valse Oubliée. John Heath-Stubbs. OxBTC

Valse Triste. Sándor Weöres. IQMS, *tr.* by W. Arthur Boggs

Valuable. Stevie Smith. OxBTC

Valuably, the tune unwinds us! with, ah! Military Ball, A. Frank O'Hara. BodElec

Value Added in Smashing a German Roach on the Bathroom Door, The. Luis Cabalquinto. ReBoTo

Vampire, The. Rudyard Kipling. NOBVV; OxBEV

Vampire outlaw of the milky way. (LL) I Am a Cowboy in the Boat of Ra. Ishmael Reed. ESEAA; NAAAL; NIL-7; NIP-4

Vampiro Nox. Marianne van Hirtum. SurWo, *tr.* by Guy Flandre and Peter Wood

Vampyre, The. "Owen Meredith."
  "I found a corpse, with golden hair." VerBaPo

Van Dieman's Land. *Unknown.* NOBAu; PeVV

Van Diemen's Land. Allen Afterman. NOBAu

Van Gogh. David Mitchell. PeNZ

Van Gogh, feeling devil-may-care. Limerick. "Pibwob." PeLi

Van Gogh's The Potato Eaters. Peter Cooley. SpudSo

Van Gogh would paint the landscape. In Hayden's Collage. Michael S. Harper. ESEAA; NAAAL

Van Lingle Mungo. Dave Frishberg. ReLy

Van Winkle. Hart Crane. MoAmPo *Fr.* Bridge, The.

Vandals, The. Jenny Mastoraki. BoWoP, *tr.* by Nikos Germanakos

Vandals, The. Alan Michael Parker. NeAmPo

Vandals are dreaming, wolves are dreaming, The. Vandals, Horses. Alan Michael Parker. NAPBL; PuP-23

Vandals, Horses. Alan Michael Parker. NAPBL; PuP-23

Vandals in the Garden. Alan Michael Parker. NAPBL

Vanderdecken. Douglas Livingstone. PeSAV

Vandunk's Four Humours, in Quality and Quantity. Richard Brathwaite [or Brathwait]. NOSC

Vane, young in yeares, but in sage counsell old. To Sir Henry Vane the Younger. John Milton. PBRV; Son

Vanessa Vanessa. Ewart Milne. BIrV

Vanguard of liberty, ye Men of Kent. To the Men of Kent (October, 1803). William Wordsworth. OBWP

Vanished, The. Marie-Claire Bancquart. MFP, *tr.* by Martin Sorrell

Vanished house that for an hour I knew, A. Souvenir. Edwin Arlington Robinson. APT-1; NoAM

Vanished under clearing skies. (LL) On the Spirit of the Heart as Moon-Disk. Kojijū. WPoS; WoPoe, *tr.* by Edwin A. Cranston

Vanished Work. Hans Magnus Enzensberger. VCWP, *tr.* by Hans Magnus Enzensberger and Michael Hamburger

Vanishes in the obscurer town. (LL) Herman Melville. APN-2; NCAP *Fr.* Clarel: A Poem and Pilgrimage in the Holy Land.

Vanishing, The. Lewis Carroll. OxAEP-2 *Fr.* Hunting of the Snark, The.

Vanishing Lung Syndrome. Miroslav Holub. VCWP

Vanishing Point. Gary Metras. PasH

Vanishing Point, The. Peter Davison. DiPo

Vanishing Shadows. Konstantin Dmitrievich Balmont. TCRP, *tr.* by April FitzLyon

Vanitas Vanitatum. John Webster. *See* Devil's Law Case, The

Vanitas Vanitatum. Israel Zangwill. TrJP

Vanitatum Vanitas. Ferenc Kölcsey. IQMS, *tr.* by Watson Kirkconnell

Vanities of Sir Arthur Gorges' Youth, The. Sir Arthur Gorges.
  "Yourself the sun, and I the melting frost." OxBSo

Vanity. Birago Diop. PBMAP; WoPoe, *tr.* by Ulli Beier and Gerald Moore

Vanity. Robert Graves. GTBS-P

Vanity. Anna Wickham. FaBoTw

Vanity [or Vanitie] (1). George Herbert. BASC; FSCP; GeHe; NOSC; NoP-4

Vanity of All Worldly Things, The. Anne Bradstreet. ChIV-1; SCAP
  "There is a path no vulture's eye hath seen." WPoS

Vanity of Existence, The. Philip Freneau. TCAPo

Vanity of External Accomplishments, The. Mary Whateley. ECWP

Vanity of Human Wishes, The; The Tenth Satire of Juvenal Imitated. Samuel Johnson. CABP; EBEV; ECEV; NAEL-6v1; NAEL-7v1; NOEC; NoP-4; OxAEP-1; TFi
  (Charles XII of Sweden.) NOBE
  "Enlarge my Life with Multitude of Days." OxBEV
  "In full-blown Dignity, see Wolsey stand." OxBEV
  "Let Observation with extensive View." MakPoe; OxBEV; UV; WoPoe
  "On what foundation stands the warrior's pride." FaBoWar; OBWP; OxBEV
  (Power of Prayer, The.) NOBE
  Scholar's Life, The. NOBE; NPeEn; OBSV
  ("Unnumber'd Suppliants croud Preferment's Gate.") OxBEV
  "Unnumbered suppliants crowd preferment's gate." OBSV
  "Where then shall Hope and Fear their objects find?" OxBEV

Vanity of men, The. Issa. SoOfWa, *tr.* by Sam Hamill

Vanity of National Grandeur, The. John Thelwall. CenSon

Vanity of Spirit. Henry Vaughan. ESCV; GeHe; NOSC; TOF

Vanity of the Blue Girls, The. John Crowe Ransom. *See* Blue Girls

Vanity of the Bright Young Men, The. John Crowe Ransom. FuPo *Fr.* Sixteen Poems in Eight Pairings.

Vanity of the World, The. Siôn Cent. OBWVE, *tr.* by Joseph P. Clancy

Vanity of vanities, saith the Preacher, vanity of vanities; all is vanity. Bible, *O.T.* NAWM-5v1; TrJP *Fr.* Ecclesiastes.

Vanity, saith the preacher, vanity! Bishop Orders His Tomb at Saint Praxed's Church, The. Robert Browning. CABP; EBVV; FHYEP; HAP; HelP-4; NAEL-5v2; NAEL-6v2; NAWM-7v2; NOBVV; NPeEn; NoP-4; OBAL; PoE; SCGP; TFi

Vanity, vanity, all is vanity. Ha! Original Sin! Ogden Nash. NBLV

Vanna White's Bread Pudding. Michael Pettit. ReTh

Vanquished and weary was my soul in me. Sonnet: A Trance of Love. Cino da Pistoia. AWP; EaItPo, *tr.* by Dante Gabriel Rossetti

Vantage Point, The. Robert Frost. OxBA

Vanzetti. Charles Buckmaster. CBAP

Vapor Trail Reflected in the Frog Pond. Galway Kinnell. OBWP; VCAP; VGW
  (Old watch: Their / thick eyes, The.) AF

Vapor Trails. Gary Snyder. NAAL-2v2

Vaporetto founders in green slush, The. Gorey at the Biennale. Martin Johnston. BMAP

Vaquero. Edward Dorn. NeAP; PoM

Variable. Joshua Sylvester. NOSC

Variables of Green. Robert Graves. FaBoEE

Variant. John Ashbery. BodElec

Variant on the Songs of the East and West Gates. Ts'ao Ts'ao. WoPoe, *tr.* by David Lattimore

Variation 3 (On Love and More). Lello Voce.
  "Your eyes stolen." ItPo, *tr.* by Gayle Ridinger

Variation on Belloc's "Fatigue." Wendy Cope. UV

Variation on Heraclitus. Louis MacNeice. NoAM

Variation on Nekrasov. "Naum Korzhavin." TCRP, *tr. by* Vladimir Lunis and Albert C. Todd.

Variation on Ronsard. Thomas Sturge Moore. OBMV

Variation on the Word *Sleep*. Margaret Atwood. AmFaPo; NOBC

Variations. Randall Jarrell. VGW; WoPoe

Variations. Maurice Scully. Oth

Variations Done for Gerald Van De Wiele. Charles Olson. APT-2; NOBA; NeAP; NoAM

Variations for the Piano. Siv Cedering. MiVo

Variations for Two Pianos. Donald Justice. EmeKit

Variations for Two Voices. Roberta Hill Whiteman. HATNAP

Variations of Greek Themes. *Var. authors.*

  Doricha. AWP; FaBoEE; OBVE; WoPoe, *tr. by* Edwin Arlington Robinson

  Dust of Timas, The. AWP

  Eutychides. OBAL

  Happy Man, A. AWP

  Inscription by the Sea, An. AWP; FaBoEE

  Lais to Aphrodite. FaBoEE

  Mighty Runner, A. OBAL

  Old Story, The. AWP

  Raven, The. AWP; FaBoEE; OBAL

Variations on a Fragment by Trumbull Stickney. John Hollander. NoP-4

Variations on a Poem by Reznikoff. Louis Simpson. BodElec

Variations on a Text by Vallejo. Donald Justice. NoAM; VCAP

Variations on a Theme. Joseph Awad. GraLe

Variations on a Theme. Anne Wilkinson. MoCV

Variations on a Theme. Oscar Williams.

  Spritely Dead, The. Son

Variations on a theme by morning. Cocoa Morning. Bob Kaufman. NBV

Variations on a Theme by William Carlos Williams. Kenneth Koch. NBLV; NIL-7; NIP-4; NoAM; PmAP; PoM

  (I chopped down the house that you had been saving to live.) KaS

  (I chopped down the house that you had been saving to live in next.) NoP-4; PoPoPo

Variations on an Air: After Robert Browning. Gilbert Keith Chesterton. NOBL

Variations on an Air: After W. B. Yeats. Gilbert Keith Chesterton. NOBL

Variations on an Air Composed on Having to Appear in a Pageant as Old King Cole. Gilbert Keith Chesterton. NOBL

  "Me clairvoyant." NOBL; UV

  Old King Cole ("Me clairvoyant"). NOBL; UV

Variations on [*or of*] an Air: After [Algernon Charles] Swinburne. Gilbert Keith Chesterton. NOBL

Variations on the Edible Tuber. Madeline DeFrees. SpudSo

Variations on the Word *Love*. Margaret Atwood. LW; NoAM

Varied theme it utters, A. Eliza Cook. VerBaPo *Fr.* Lines Among the Leaves.

Variety, The. John Dancer. NOSC

Variety Theater Manifesto, The. Filippo Tommaso Marinetti.

  Futurism Wants to Transform the Variety Theater into a Theater of Amazement, Record-setting, and Body-madness. PFTM-1

Various instants I'm not with you. Robert Johnstone. PNI *Fr.* Every Cache.

Various Multitudes Contained by the Loves of My Love, The. Anselm Berrigan. HeMarv

Various nostalgias: rock, scissor, and paper. Towards the Vanishing Point. David Lehman. PmAP

Various Readings of an Illegible Postcard. Christine Hume. AmPoNex

Various the roads of life; in one. Walter Savage Landor. FaBoEE

Varium et Mutabile. Sir Thomas Wyatt. NoSic

  (Is It Possible.) CABP; NoP-4

Varsity Drag, The. Ray Henderson. ReLy

Vary, re-vary; tune and tune again. Variable. Joshua Sylvester. NOSC

Vas en Afrique! Back to Africa! the butcher we used to / patronize in the rue Cadet market. Racists. C. K. Williams. LTA

Vase of peonies. Alexis Rotella. HA

Vase of the Universe, The. Edwin Torres. HeMarv

Vashti. Frances Ellen Watkins Harper. BlSi; NALW

Vasily Tyorkin. Aleksandr Trifonovich Tvardovsky [*or* Tvardovskii].

  Crossing, The. TCRP, *tr. by* April FitzLyon

Vast and grey, the sky. Desolate Field, The. William Carlos Williams. APT-1

Vast bedroom, The. Tracks. John Montague. CIP-2

Vast bodies of philosophy [*or* Philosophie]. To Mr. Hobbes [*or* Hobs]. Abraham Cowley. BASC; BeJo

Vast mild melancholy splendid. Canberra in April. J. R. Rowland. NOBAu

Vast ocean of light, whose rays surround. Ocean of Light. Phineas Fletcher. NOSC

Vast Parnassus never knew thy face, The. To My Muse. Agnes Mary Frances Robinson. VWP

Vast, tremulous. I Sent Thee Late. Louis Zukofsky. APT-2

Vasty hall of death, The. (LL) Requiescat. Matthew Arnold. AWP; FHYEP; NOBE; OBEV; PoRA

Vaticinio. Nanni Cagnone.

  Book Three: On Preparation. ItPo, *tr. by* Gayle Ridinger

  Fifth Book: On Limitation. ItPo, *tr. by* Gayle Ridinger

Vaulting Ambition. William Shakespeare. OxAEP-1 *Fr.* Macbeth.

Vaunting Oak. John Crowe Ransom. OxBA; VGW

Vauxhall was grey she needed blocks of. Robert Sheppard. Oth *Fr.* Empty Diaries/Twentieth Century Blues 24.

Vectors: Forty-five Aphorisms and Ten-second Essays. James Richardson. BAP-01

Vedic Hymns. *Unknown.*

  Indra, the Supreme God. AWP

  Pushan, God of Pasture. AWP

  Rig Veda.

    Creation Hymn. WoPoe, *tr. by* Frederick Morgan

    Dawn Has Arisen, Our Welfare Is Assured. WoPoe, *tr. by* Raimundo Panikkar

    Hymn to Night. WoPoe, *tr. by* Peter Dent and Edwin Gerow

    "May the wind blows sweetness." WoPoe, *tr. by* Raimundo Panikkar

Veering and wheeling free in the open. (LL) Harbor, The. Carl Sandburg. APT-1; ColAP; TAP

Vega. Lawrence Durrell. OxAEP-2

Vega over the rim of the Val Verzasca. John Peck. HarvBoo

Vegetable Air, The. Cathy Song. NoAM

Vegetable Calendar. Silvio Giussani. ItPo, *tr. by* Gayle Ridinger

Vegetable Garden. Lu Yu. CoBCP, *tr. by* Burton Watson

Vegetable Garden, The. Wyatt Prunty. OBGa

Veil. János Pilinszky. IQMS, *tr. by* Peter Jay

Veil. Marjorie Welish. PmAP

Veil, The. Elizabeth Cobbold. CenSon *Fr.* Sonnets of Laura.

Veil not thy mirror, sweet Amine. To Amine. James Clarence Mangan. OBEV

Veil of death hath fallen, The. To a Deceased Friend. Priscilla Jane Thompson. CBWP-2

Veil of haze protects this, A. City Afternoon. John Ashbery. HeIP-4; InPK-6; NIP-4

Veil's removed, the gaudy, flimsy veil, The. Anna Maria Smallpiece. CenSon

Veil thine eyes, O belovèd, my spouse. Bridegroom of Cana, The. Marjorie Lowry Christie Pickthall. TrCP

Veiled in that light amazing. Dispraise of Absalom, The. *Unknown.* BIrV, *tr. by* Robin Flower

Veiled Lady, The. Maura Stanton. BodElec

Veiled Land. Kahlil Gibran. MAP, *tr. by* Michael Beard and Adnan Haydar

Veils of Prayer. Ralph Angel. BodElec

Vein of sapphires, A. Mahadevi. WPoS; WoPoe, *tr. by* Jane Hirshfield

Vein under my skin, A. Butterflies of Anxiety. Najaat Al-Udwany. PoArWo, *tr. by* Moulouk Berry and Ali Farghaly

Veins All Dried Up. Fatma Kandil. PoArWo, *tr. by* Khaled Mattawa

Velasquez took a pliant knife. Castilian. Elinor Wylie. ColAP

Veld Eclogue: The Pioneers, A. Roy Campbell. OBSV

Velocity of Money. Allen Ginsberg. NIL-7

Velocity with which they write—, The. Movie Actors Scribbling Letters Very Fast in Crucial Scenes. Jean Garrigue. TAP

Velvet Blanket. Marlon D. Satchell. InTrad

Velvet ground we now with pleasure tread, The. Abbé Jacques de Lille. OBGa *Fr.* Gardens, The.

Velvet Hand, The. Phyllis McGinley. OBCoV

Velvet Shoes. Elinor Wylie. MoAmPo; PAI; WHSW

Vending Machine. Hans Magnus Enzensberger. PoSu

Vendors of green oranges vendors of immaculate / ducks. Ferryman's Song at Binh Minh. Herbert Krohn. CDa

Venerable Bee, The. Abraham Moses Klein. TrJP

Venerable Mother Toothache. Charm against the Toothache, A. John Heath-Stubbs. TwCP

Venerating Senses Save Us. Jonathan Griffin. Oth

Veneris Venefica Agrestis. Lucio Piccolo. OBVE, *tr. by* Charles Tomlinson

Venetia. Adah Isaacs Menken. CBWP-1

Venetian Air. Thomas Moore. OxBSP

Venetian Interior, 1889. Richard Howard. VCAP

Venetian Night, A. Hugo von Hofmannsthal. AWP, *tr. by* Ludwig Lewisohn

Venetian Nocturne. Agnes Mary Frances Robinson. VWP

Vengeance will sit above our faults; but till. Ode. John Donne. SacPr

Vengeful across the cold November moors. Pity of the Leaves, The. Edwin Arlington Robinson. APN-2; MoAmPo

Veni Coronaberis. Geoffrey Hill. DiPo; NoP-4

Veni Creator. Alice Thompson Meynell. WPE

Veni Creator Spiritus. Charlemagne. AWP; SacPr, *tr. by* John Dryden

Venice. Henry Wadsworth Longfellow. APN-1

Venice. Herman Melville. APN-2

Venice. Arthur Symons. OxBEV

Venice Beach: Brief Song. Dorothy Barresi. SeSe; SwNoth

Venice Recalled. Bruce Boyd. NeAP

Venio ex Oriente. Nuala Ni Dhomhnaill. BiHa

Venipuncture. John Graham-Pole. BloBone

Venison. Karen Chase. NIL-7

Venni-Vach Revisited. Richard Hall.
 "How oft, ere morning lit the eastern steep." AngWePo

Ventriloquist's breath, The. Iron Lung. Lavinia Greenlaw. MFPA

Ventriloquy / is the mother tongue. Attention. Rae Armantrout. PmAP

Venturing Out. *Vietnamese Oral Tradition.* CaDao, *tr. by* John Balaban

Venus. Federico García Lorca. PFTM-1

Venus and Adonis. Bartholomew Griffin. NoSic

Venus and Adonis. Ovid. NAWM-7v1, *tr. by* Allen Mandelbaum *Fr.* Metamorphoses.

Venus and Adonis. William Shakespeare.
 "All swoln with chasing, down Adonis sits." EroLit
 "At this Adonis smiles as in disdain." EBEV
 (Courser and the Jennet, The.) NOBE
 (Death of Adonis, The.) NoSic

Venus and Cupid. Mark Alexander Boyd. *See* Fra Bank to Bank, Fra Wood to Wood I Rin

VENUS, and young Adonis sitting by her. Venus and Adonis. Bartholomew Griffin. NoSic

Venus Attiring the Graces. William Whitehead. ECEV

Venus de Milo. Gottfried Keller. WoPoe, *tr. by* John Peck

Venus de Milo. Charles Marie René Leconte de Lisle. GS, *tr. by Unknown*

Venus Fly Trap, The. Readymade. John Perreault. SPE

Venus glows in the east. Work to Do Toward Town. Gary Snyder. VGW

Venus Hottentot, The. Elizabeth Alexander. ESEAA; InTrad

Venus, let me never see. (LL) Lady Who Offers Her Looking-Glass to Venus, The. Matthew Prior. FaBoEE; NOEC; NPeeEn; OBEV; OxBEV; OxBSP

Venus of Laussel. Patricia Monaghan. HW

Venus of Milo, The. Henrietta Cordelia Ray. CBWP-3

Venus of the Louvre. Emma Lazarus. APN-2; GS

Venus of the Salty Shell. Denis Devlin. BIrV; NOIV

Venus Pudica stands, bent. Where her hand is. Lady at the Castle, The. John Hollander. NoAM

Venus's Looking-Glass. Christina Georgina Rossetti. NALW

Venus, take my votive glass. Lady Who Offers Her Looking-Glass to Venus, The. Matthew Prior. FaBoEE; NOEC; NPeeEn; OBEV; OxBEV; OxBSP

Venus the gleaming goddess. Virgil [*or* Vergil]. NAWM-5v1; NAWM-7v1, *tr. by* Robert Fitzgerald *Fr.* Aeneid [*or* Eneados, *Aeneis*], The.

Venus! to thee, the Lesbian Muse shall sing. Sappho's Prayer to Venus. Mary Robinson. CenSon; RWP

Venus Transiens. Amy Lowell. APT-1; NAAL-5; NALW

Verandahs. Robert Francis Brissenden. CBAP; NOBAu

Verb "To Think," The. Dennis Joseph Enright. OxBC

Verbum caro factum est. *Unknown.* MiEL

Verdant branch was swinging here, A. So Long Ago. Morris Jacob Rosenfeld. TrJP, *tr. by* Elbert Aidline

Verdict of Stone, A. Tanure Ojaide. NAfrP

Verge bore the remnants of his shearings, The. Grandfather's Rockery. David Woo. OpBo

Vergine bella—it is here that I require. Vergine bella. Geoffrey Hill. PoetW

Vergissmeinicht. Keith Douglas. FaBoMo; FaBoWar; GTBS-P; HarvBoo; NAEL-5v2; NAEL-6v2; NPeeEn; NoAM; NoP-4; OBWP; OxBEV; OxBTC; PoWW; RB; SoSe-8; WoPoe

Verifying the Dead. James Welch. CDW

Verily / The sky clears. Sky Clears, The. *Unknown.* OBVE, *tr. by* Frances Densmore

Veritable night, The. Rigamarole. William Carlos Williams. APT-1

Verka the Free. "Mikhail Semionovich Golodny [*or.*" Golodnyi]. TCRP, *tr. by* Simon Franklin

Verlaine. Richard Hovey. APN-2

Verlaine. Edwin Arlington Robinson. APN-2; NAAL-2v2; NCAP

Vermeer. Stephen Mitchell. GI

Vermin. William Matthews. BAP-97

Verminous aeronaut, leaflight turkey, kite. Egyptian Kites. Rex Warner. OWoS

Vermont. Hayden Carruth.
 "Republicans? We've got a few. In fact." GifTon

Vermont. David Huddle. CDa

Vermont Apollinaire. William Corbett. PmAP

Vermont Ballad: Change of Season. Robert Penn Warren. ColAP

Vermont Has a High Suicide Rate. Richard Donze. BloBone

Vermont: Spring Rains. Edward Weismiller. YaYoPo

Vermont Thaw. Robert Penn Warren. BodElec

Vernal breeze returns to refresh, The. Tune: "The Beauty of Yü" Li Yü. ColAnChi, *tr. by* Jiaosheng Wang

Vernal Equinox. Martin Johnston. CBAP

Vernal Equinox. Amy Lowell. APT-1

Vernal Equinox. Ruth Stone. MoAmPo

Verona. James Wright (1927–80). NNaP

Vers de Société. Philip Larkin. PeLV

Versailles. Adrienne Rich. OBGa

Verse, a breeze [']mid blossoms straying. Youth and Age. Samuel Taylor Coleridge. GTBS-P; OBEV

Verse I. Christina Georgina Rossetti. *See* Thread of Life, The

Verse II. Christina Georgina Rossetti. PEW *Fr.* Thread of Life, The.

Verse III. Christina Georgina Rossetti. PEW *Fr.* Thread of Life, The.

Verse makes heroic[k] virtue live. To Mr. Henry Lawes, Who Had Then Newly Set a Song of Mine in the Year 1635. Edmund Waller. BeJo; CTC

Verse may find him who a sermon flies, A. On the Following Work and Its Author. Jonathan Mitchell. SCAP

Verse of Darkness, The. Jenő Dsida. IQMS, *tr. by* Watson Kirkconnell

Verse: "What should we know." Oliver St. John Gogarty. FaBoCh; OBMV; PoRA

Verse Written in the Album of Mademoiselle. Pierre Dalcour. TTY, *tr. by* Langston Hughes

Verses. William Henry. PeSAV

Verses. Lady Mary Wortley Montagu. *See* Verses Addressed to the Imitator of the First Satire of the Second Book of Horace: An Attack on Pope

Verses about a Nightingale and a Poet. "Eduard Georgievich Bagritzky [*or.*" Bagritsky]. TCRP, *tr. by* Vera Dunham

Verses about Music. Elena Ignatova.
 "Italian Marcello, you breathe a much sweeter air." ItGoST, *tr. by* Sibelan Forrester

Verses about the Dog's Inheritance. Nikolai Ivanovich Tryapkin [*or* Triapkin].
 "We've inherited something from our ancestors, the serfs." TCRP

Verses Addressed to a Friend, Just Leaving a Favourite Retirement. Samuel Henley. NOEC

Verses Addressed to the Imitator of the First Satire of the Second Book of Horace. Lady Mary Wortley Montagu.
 "When God created thee, one would believe." ECWP

Verses Addressed to the Imitator of the First Satire of the Second Book of Horace: An Attack on Pope. Lady Mary Wortley Montagu. ECEV (Verses.) CABP

Verses against the Inconsequence of Men's Taste and Strictures. Sister Juana Inés de la Cruz. SpanPo, *tr. by* Muriel Kittel

Verses by my Mother in Her Own Hand. Amy Hammond. EMWP

Verses by the Princess Elizabeth, Given to Lord Harington, of Exton, Her Preceptor. Elizabeth, Queen of Bohemia. EMWP

Verses: "Clean is the autumn wind." Li Po. TAL

Verses Composed on the Eve of His Execution. James Graham, Marquess of Montrose. *See* On Himself, upon Hearing What Was His Sentence

Verses Design'd by Mrs A. Behn to be Sent to a Fair Lady, that Desir'd She Would Absent Herself to Cure Her Love. Left Un. Aphra Behn. PoBW

Verses Designed to Be Sent to Mr. Adams. Elizabeth Frances Amherst. ECWP

Verses Expressing the Feelings of a Lover. Sister Juana Inés de la Cruz. SpanPo, *tr. by* Samuel Beckett

Verses for a First Birthday. George Barker. MoBrPo

Verses for an Album. Charles Lamb. NOBRP

Verses Found in His Bible in the Gatehouse at Westminster. Sir Walter Ralegh. *See* Authours Epitaph, Made by Himself, The

Verses Found in Thomas Dudley's Pocket after His Death. Thomas Dudley. SCAP

Verses from the Shepherd's Hymn. Richard Crashaw. OBEV *Fr.* In the Holy Nativity of Our Lord God.

Verses: "I am monarch of troubles a host." Maria Jane Jewsbury. VWP

Verses: "I am old, sick and lonely." Su Tung-p'o (Su Shih). TAL

Verses in Baretti's Commonplace Book. Samuel Johnson. OxAEP-1

Verses in Italian and French, Written by the Queen of Scots to the Queen of England. Mary Stuart, Queen of Scots. EMWP

Verses Intended to Have Been Prefixed to the Novel of Emmeline, but Then Suppressed. Charlotte Smith. BWW

Verses Inviting Stella to Tea on the Public Fast-Day. Anna Seward. ECWP (Dear Stella, 'mid the pious sorrow.) PEW

(Verses / Inviting Mrs. C—to Tea on a public Fast-day during the American War.) PEW

Verses Left on a Lady's Toilet. Sarah Dixon. ECWP

Verses Made by a Catholic in Praise of Campion That Was Executed at Tyburn for Treason, As Is Made Known by the Proclamation. *Unknown.* NoSic

Verses Made by Sappho, Done from the Greek by Boyleau, and from the French by a Lady of Quality. Sappho. EMWP

Verses Made by Sir Walter Raleigh the Night before he was Beheaded. Sir Walter Ralegh. *See* Passionate Man['[s] Pilgrimage, The

Verses Made for the Women Who Cry Apples, etc. Jonathan Swift. Onyons. BIrV

Verses Made Sometime Since upon. . . the Indian Squa. John Josselyn. SCAP

Verses Made the Night before He Died. Michael Drayton. NOBE

(As I therin noe others face but yours can Veiwe.) (LL) PBRV

(Soe well I love thee, as without thee I.) NPeEn; PBRV

(These verses weare made by Michaell Drayton Esquier Poett Lawreatt the night before hee dyed.) NPeEn; PBRV

Verses Made the Night before He Died [*or* Dyed]. Sir Walter Ralegh. *See* Even Such Is Time

Verses Made the Night before His Beheading. Sir Walter Ralegh. *See* Authours Epitaph, Made by Himself, The

Verses, my love! As soon could I. On the Author's Husband Desiring Her to Write Some Verses. Mary Whateley. ECWP

Verses Occasioned by the Sudden Drying up of St. Patrick's Well. Jonathan Swift.

"Wretched Ierne! with what grief I see." OBSV

Verses of a True Hungarian Patriot, The. *Unknown.* IQMS, *tr. by* René Bonnerjea and Earl M. Herrick

Verses on Blenheim. Martial. AWP, *tr. by* Jonathan Swift

Verses on Daniel Good. *Unknown.* OxBB

Verses on Hearing That an Airy and Pleasant Situation, near a Populous and Commercial Town, Was Surrounded with New Buildings. Maria Logan. ECWP

Verses on Sir Joshua Reynolds's Painted Window at New College, Oxford. Thomas Warton, the Younger. NOEC

Verses on the Death of Dr. Swift, D.S.P.D. Jonathan Swift.

"Behold the fatal day arrive!" PeLV; SCV

"Doctors tender of their fame, The." NOBL

"Here shift the scene, to represent." OxBEV

"My female friends, whose tender hearts." NOBL

"Now Curll his shop from rubbish drains." PeLV

"Perhaps I may allow, the Dean." NOBE; OxBEV; PeLV

"Suppose me dead; and then suppose." NOBE; NOEC; OxBoLi; PeLV

"Time is not remote when I, The." EBEV; NOBE; NOBL; NOIV; NPeEn; OxAEP-1; OxBEV; PeLV

Verses on the Death of Dr. Swift, D.S.P.D., Occasioned by Reading a Maxim in Rochefoucauld. Jonathan Swift. NAEL-6v1; NAEL-7v1; NOEC

Verses on the Prospect of Planting Arts and Learning in America. George Berkeley. *See* On the Prospect of Planting Arts and Learning in America

Verses: "Poor fellow, what is it to you." Sir Charles Hanbury Williams. OBWVE

Verses Put into a Lady's Prayer-Book. John Wilmot, 2d Earl of Rochester. *See* Written in a Lady's Prayer Book

Verses Sent to Mr Bevil Higgons, on His Sickness and Recovery from the Small-pox, in the Year 1693. Catherine Cockburn. EMWP

Verses Supposed to Be Written by Alexander Selkirk during His Solitary Abode on the Island of Juan Fernandez. William Cowper. NOEC

(Solitude of Alexander Selkirk, The.) GTBS-P

Verses to a Lady, on Her Saying She Preferred Commonalty to an Irish Peerage. Lady Sophia Burrell.

"Clock strikes five—the watchman goes, The." ECWP

Verses to Miss———. J. Wilde. NOEC

Verses to Mr. Richardson on his History of Sir Charles Grandison. Anna Williams. ECWP

Verses to my Heart's-Sister. Henrietta Cordelia Ray. CBWP-3

Verses Written at Montauban in France, 1750. Joseph Warton. ECEV

Verses Written by a Gentlewoman upon the Jaylors Conversion. Anne Dowriche. EMWP

Verses Written by Alis Daughter of Gryffydd Son of Iefan When Her Father Asked Her What Sort of Husband She Would Like. Alis Ferch Gruffyd ab Ieuan ap Llewelyn Fychan. EMWP

Verses Written by Mrs. Hutchinson. Lucy Hutchinson. BASC; NOSC

Verses Written during the War, 1756–63. Thomas Osbert Mordaunt.

(To a Lady on Reading Sherlock "Upon Death") NOEC

(Call, The.) OBEV

Sound, Sound the Clarion. EBEV; FaBoEE; NOBE

Verses Written in a Garden. Lady Mary Wortley Montagu. ECWP

Verses Written in a Lady's Sherlock "Upon Death." Philip Dormer Stanhope, 4th Earl of Chesterfield. EBEV

(To a Lady on Reading Sherlock "Upon Death") NOEC

Verses Written in the Chiosk [of the British Palace], at Pera, Overlooking [the City of] Constantinople. Lady Mary Wortley Montagu. ECEV; ECWP

Verses Written in the Spring. Anne Batten Cristall. RWP

Verses Written on Her Death-Bed at Bath to Her Husband in London. Mary Monk. ECWP; LW

Verses Written the Night before His Execution. Sir Walter Ralegh. *See* Even Such Is Time

Verses: "You who come from the old village." Wang Wei. TAL

Versicles on Sign-Posts. Robert Burns.

"Head pure, sinless quite of brain or soul, A." FaBoEE

Versification of a Passage from Penthouse. Andrew Hudgins. AllShUp

Verso Libre. Nick Carbó. NAPBL

Vertical Poetry. Roberto Juarroz.

"Bottom of things is neither life nor death, The." VCWP

Vertigo is my territory. Eagle. Robin Skelton. NOBC

Very apt question struck me, A. Limerick. Sydney Bernard Smith. PeLi

Very bitter weeping that ye made, The. Dante Alighieri. AWP; EaItPo, *tr. by* Dante Gabriel Rossetti *Fr.* La Vita Nuova.

Very brief. Basho. EH, *tr. by* Robert Hass

Very cautiously. Cleaning. Karel Soudijn. TuT, *tr. by* Peter Van de Kamp

Very day one son was drowned, The. Honestus. GrAn

Very dear though it was I have bought you. Michelangelo Buonarroti. WoPoe, *tr. by* W. S. Merwin

Very due that being each one dwells. Narrow Path, The. Norman Henry Pritchard, II. GT

Very empty cubic, blue room. No windows. No door frames. Colors. Fortunato Depero. PFTM-1

Very Fair My Lot. Jacob David Kamzon. TrJP, *tr. by* Sholom J. Kahn

Very few can. Pecan, The Toucan, The. Robert Williams Wood. NBLV

Very few people know where they will die. Deathplace, A. Louis Edward Sissman. NoP-4

Very fine conga of sweat, A. I See Chano Pozo. Jayne Cortez. PmAP

Very floor of our existence as a couple, The. Very Floor of Our Existence, The. June Billings Safford. PasH

Very friendly / prison, A. Tripart. Gayl Jones. BlSi

Very ground dissolves beneath my feet, The. Imre Madách. IQMS, *tr. by* Iain MacLeod *Fr.* Tragedy of Man.

Very handsome gentleman, A. *Unknown.* BoWoP *Fr.* Shih Ching.

Very high this mountain. Muso Soseki. EaWin, *tr. by* W. S. Merwin

Very like a Whale. Ogden Nash. APT-2; HAP; InPK-6

Very little snail, A. What Do I See. Gertrude Stein. ItWoWo; PFTM-1

Very often when you are striving. Would-be Critic, The. Mrs. Henry Linden. CBWP-4

Very Old, The. Ted Kooser. PBCAP

Very old are the woods. All That's Past. Walter De la Mare. NOBE; OBMV; OxBTC

Very Old Man. James Henry. NOBVV; OxBEV

Very pitiful lady, very young, A. Dante Alighieri. AWP; CTC; EaItPo, *tr. by* Dante Gabriel Rossetti *Fr.* La Vita Nuova.

Very Real Story, A. Julio Cortázar. TCLAP, *tr. by* Paul Blackburn

Very Rich Hours, The. Nick Drake. NeBl

Very Sad Conversation at Night, A. Anna Swirszczynska. PoSu

Very small children in patched clothing, The. Study in Aesthetics, The. Ezra Pound. APT-1; NOBA

Very Soft Shoes. Mary Rodgers. ReLy

Very soon the Yankee teachers. Learning to Read. Frances Ellen Watkins Harper. BlSi; NAAAL; NALW

Very Strong Stomach Has Mr. Luke, A. Manuel González Prada. SpanPo, *tr. by* William M. Davis

Very Thought of You, The. Ray Noble. ReLy

Very True Confessions. Sidney Burris. SwNoth

Very Young Man Speaks, A. "Paul Tanaquil." YaYoPo

Vesey, of verse the judge and friend. Florio: A Tale, and The Bas-bleu; or, Conversation. Hannah More. RWP

Vesica Piscis. Coventry Patmore. SacPr

Vesperal. Ernest Christopher Dowson. OBMV

Vespers. W. H. Auden. FaBoMo *Fr.* Horae Canonicae.

Vespers. Louise Glück. HarvBoo

Vespers. Alan Alexander Milne.

"Hush! Hush! Whisper who dares!" UV

Vespers. Emile Ologoudou. PBMAP

Vespertilia. Rosamund Marriott Watson. ViWPN

Vespertilio. Linda Bierds. ExTi

Vessel, The. C. K. Williams. TaR

Vessel with long red banners of the Prophet, A. Plague, The. Nikolai Stepanovich Gumilyov [*or* Gumiliov *or* Gumilev]. TCRP, *tr. by* Simon Franklin

Vessels of mercy, prepared unto glory! Frances Ridley Havergal. SacPr

Vesta. John Greenleaf Whittier. SacPr

Vesta's Father. Julia Kasdorf. PBCAP

Vestal, The. Nathalia Crane. TrJP

Vestal Virgin, The. Eloise Bibb. CBWP-4

Vestiges. Basil Bunting.
("Girls can be sent on / separately if he insists, The.") (LL) PFTM-1
("Salt grass silent of hooves, the lake stinks.") PFTM-1

Vesuvius at Home. (LL) Volcanoes be in Sicily. Emily Dickinson. NALW; OxWW

Vete. Cultures. Gloria Anzaldúa. UnSA

Veteran. Walter McDonald. CDa

Veteran. Lola Ridge. WPE

Veteran Sirens. Edwin Arlington Robinson. NOBA

Veteran smiled and let us pass through, A. Thomas Kinsella. BiHa *Fr.* Technical Supplement, A.

Veterans. George Johnston. NOBC

Veterans, The. Donagh MacDonagh. CIP-2

Veterans of the Wars. Edgar Lee Masters. CBCWP

Vex no man's secret soul--if that can be. Sadi [or Saadi or Sa'di]. AWP, *tr. by* Sir Edwin Arnold *Fr.* Gulistan, The.

Vex th'ill-natur'd fools we cannot please. (LL) To Nysus. Sir Charles Sedley. FaBoEE; OBSV

Via Crucis. Herman Melville. APN-2; NCAP *Fr.* Clarel: A Poem and Pilgrimage in the Holy Land.

Via, et Veritas, et Vita. Alice Thompson Meynell. SacPr

Via Margutta. Maria Luisa Spaziani. PBMAP; NeIt, *tr. by* Beverly Allen

Via Negativa. Ronald Stuart Thomas. InvLi

Viable. A. R. Ammons. TAP

Viaticum. Birago Diop. NegPo, *tr. by* Ellen Conroy Kennedy

Viaticum. Pao Yu. OHMPC, *tr. by* Kenneth Rexroth

Viaticum. U Tam'si Tchicaya. NegPo, *tr. by* Ellen Conroy Kennedy

Vibrant naive Naabeeho women. Modern on the Surface. Nia Francisco. HATNAP

Vicar, The. George Crabbe. OBSV *Fr.* Borough, The.

Vicar, The. Winthrop Mackworth Praed. OBEV; OxAEP-2 *Fr.* Every-Day Characters.

Vicar of Bray, The. *Unknown.* NOBE; NOBL; OBSV; OxBEV; OxBoLi

Vicar of Wakefield, The. Oliver Goldsmith.
Elegy on the Death of a Mad Dog, An. FaBoCh; NBLV; NOEC; NOIV; OBNV; OxAEP-1; TFi
(Song.) AWP; BoLoP; FHYEP; NOBE; NOEC; OxAEP-1
(Woman.) OBEV

Vicarious Atonement. Richard Aldington. MoBrPo

Vice. Anthony Hecht. OBAL

Vice most obscene and unsavoury, A. Limerick. *Unknown.* NOBL; PeLV

Vice now may lift aloft her speckled head. Spoken Extempore on the Death of Mr. Pope. *Unknown.* NOEC

Vice-regal walls dominate the back street. Gym. Richard Murphy. BiHa

Vice's Song, The. John Pickering [or Pikerying]. NoSic *Fr.* Horestes.

Vices of Men, The. Joyce Mansour. SurPaPo, *tr. by* Mary Ann Caws

Vices of the Modern World. Nicanor Parra. CLPP, *tr. by* Jorge Elliott

Vicious Circle. Marsha Prescod. LW

Vickery's Mountain. Edwin Arlington Robinson. MoAmPo

Vicki and Daphne. Cheryl Clarke. WiU

Victim, The. Thom Gunn. SwNoth

Victim Number 48. Mahmoud Darwish. VCWP, *tr. by* Denys Johnson-Davies
(They found in his chest a lamp of roses and a moon.) VCWP, *tr. by* Denys Johnson-Davies

Victims, The. Sharon Olds. NIL-7; SoSe-8

Victims of the demon dance. For All Unwed Mothers. Robert Fleming. ISC

Victoire. Guillaume Apollinaire.
Listen to the sea. PFTM-1

Victor, The. C. W. Longenecker. PWR

Victor, The. Lajos Áprily. IQMS, *tr. by* Watson Kirkconnell

Victor alone you were not—'twas the Age's Soul, that of Freedom. To Napoleon. Dániel Berzsenyi. IQMS, *tr. by* Adam Makkai

Victor Dog, The. James Merrill. NoAM; NoP-4

Victor Garibaldi. Melvin B. Tolson. GT

Victor Record Catalog. David Schubert. APT-2

Victoria. Henry Van Dyke. SacPr

Victoria Market. Francis Brabazon. NOBAu

Victoria Markets Recollected in Tranquility, The. "Furnley Maurice." NOBAu

Victoria's Secret. Charles Martin. RA

Victoria said: "We've no quarrel." Limerick. Frank Richards. PeLi

Victoria Station. Luigi Fontanella. NeIt, *tr. by* Michael Palma

Victoria was bitterly short. Limerick. Cyril Mountjoy. PeLi

Victorian Family Photograph. Kit Wright. OBCoV

Victorian gent said: "This dance," A. Limerick. Frank Richards. PeLi

Victorian Hangman Tells His Love, A. Bruce Dawe. NoAM

Victorian Idyll, A. David Wagoner. NoAM

Victorian mothers instructed their daughters, ahem. Victoria's Secret. Charles Martin. RA

Victorian Paraphrase, A. Horace. NBLV, *tr. by* William Makepeace Thackeray *Fr.* Odes.

Victories of Love, The. Coventry Patmore.
Music of Forefended Spheres, The. NPeEn

Victories of mind, The. War. Ebenezer Elliott. FaBoWar

Victory. Lionel Pigot Johnson. NOBVV

Victory at Guernica, The. Paul Eluard. SurPaPo, *tr. by* Mary Ann Caws

Victory Calypso, Lord's 1950. Egbert Moore. PeLV
(Victory Calypso.) OBCoV

Victory comes late. Emily Dickinson. APN-2; InPK-6; SWaP

Victory Obtained by Blake over the Spaniards, in the Bay of Santa Cruz in the Island of Teneriffe, 1657. Andrew Marvell.
"For Santacruze the glad fleet takes her way." FaBoWar

Victory of Samothrace, The. "Rubén Dario." GS, *tr. by Unknown*

Victory on the Last Green. Thomas Mathison. NOEC *Fr.* Goff; an Heroi-comical Poem, The.

Victory to Yogendra's Wife, Great Illusion! Anthony Sāheb. SinGod, *tr. by* Rachel Fell McDermott

Video Box: 25, The. Edwin Morgan. EmeKit

Video Cuisine. Maxine W. Kumin. NoAM

Video Mama. Jack Ridl. SwNoth

Video Victim. Luis H. Francia. ReBoTo

Vield Path, The. William Barnes. NOBVV

Vienna in Spring. Emmy Klein-Synek. AuPH, *tr. by* Lowell A. Bangerter

Vienna once the town of songs. Vienna in Spring. Emmy Klein-Synek. AuPH, *tr. by* Lowell A. Bangerter

Vier Takte vor K time then before. Pierre Joris. PFTM-2 *Fr.* Winnetou Old.

Vierge Moderne. Edith Södergran. ItWoWo; PFTM-1, *tr. by* Stina Katchadourian

Viernes Santo / Good Friday. Francisco Alarcon. GeoHom

Vierzide Chairs, The. William Barnes. NOBVV

Vies Manquées. Edith Nesbit. VWP

Viet Kong. William Trowbridge. ReTh

Viet Nam Monument. Nicholas Virgilio. HA

Vietnam. Clarence Major. HHAm

Vietnam. Michael McClintock.
"Hamburger Hill." HA

Vietnam Dream. Ron Carter. CDa

Vietnam #4. Clarence Major. NBV

Vietnam war drags on, The. Newscast, The. Ian Hamilton. FaBoWar; NPeEn

View, A. James Schuyler. BodElec

View, A. Mona Van Duyn. VCAP

View, all ye eyes above, this sight which flings. Edward Taylor. NOSC *Fr.* Preparatory Meditations before My Approach to the Lord's Supper.

View Café, The. Jonathan Johnson. AmPoNex

View from a Cab, The. Henry Taylor. NBLV

View from an Airplane at Night, over California, The. Bruce Bawer. RA

View from an Attic Window, The. Howard Nemerov. CoAP; CoAmPo

View from Cortona, A. Richard Hugo. AF

View from far: beside the gate, The. Returning Home. Yüan Mei. CoBLCP, *tr. by* Jonathan Chaves

View from Heron Tower. Wang Chih-huan. CrYelRi, *tr. by* Sam Hamill

View from Skates in Berkeley, The. Quincy Troupe. UnSA

View from the Bathysphere. Peter Rafferty. NLP

View from the Cliffs. Tu Mu. OHMPC, *tr. by* Kenneth Rexroth

View from the Corner. Samuel Allen. SSLK

View from the Kobenzl. Friedrich Torberg. AuPH, *tr. by* Lowell A. Bangerter

View from the Roof, Waverly Place. Cornelius Eady. InvLad

View from the Window, The. Ronald Stuart Thomas. NoP-4

View it, by day, from the back. Movie House. John Updike. PeLV

View like one of Fairy-land, A. George Darley. NOBRP *Fr.* Sylvia; or, The May Queen.

View Mee, Lord. Thomas Campion. SacPr

View of a Pig. Ted Hughes. OxAEP-2; OxBEV; OxBTC; TwCP

View of Christ's Kingdom, A. William Williams.
Marriage in Eden, The. OBWVE, *tr. by* Gwyn Jones and Lewis Saunders

View of Jersey, A. Edward Field. NeAP

View of the Blue Sea. Ts'ao Ts'ao. ChinPo, *tr. by* Yip Wai-lim

View of the Countryside. Wu Wei-yeh. SuSp, *tr. by* Chang Yin-nan

View of the Library of Congress from Paul Laurence Dunbar High School. Thomas Sayers Ellis. GT

View of the Town, A. In an Epistle to a Friend. Thomas Gilbert. Against Homosexuality. NOEC

View of Things, A. Edwin Morgan. HarvBoo

View on Death, A. Roy W. Watson. PWR

View with a Grain of Sand. Wislawa Szymborska. BLT

Viewed in this way / her voice. Elsewhere, Things Tend. Claudia Rankine. AmPoNex

Viewing Mountains with His Reverence Hao Ch'u: To My Friends and Relatives in the Capital. Liu Tsung-yüan. SuSp, tr. by Jan W. Walls

Viewing Mr. Yü's Landscape Painting on the Wall. Wang Chi. SuSp, tr. by Joseph J. Lee

Viewing the Three Lakes. Hsieh T'iao. ChinPo, tr. by Yip Wai-lim

Viewing the Waterfall at Mount Lu. Li Po. CoBCP; ColAnChi; TTTS, tr. by Burton Watson

(Sunlight streaming on Incense Stone kindles violet.) ChAP

Viewless, through heaven's vast vault your course ye steer. To the Winds. Ann Radcliffe. RWP

Views from the High Camp. W.S. Merwin. CoAmPo

Vigil. Richard Dehmel. AWP, tr. by Ludwig Lewisohn

Vigil. Blair Gibb. Prnts

Vigil. Juan Ramón Jiménez. SpanPo, tr. by Willis Barnstone

Vigil. Cecília Meireles. TCLAP, tr. by James Merrill

Vigil. Giuseppe Ungaretti. PeFWW, tr. by Jonathan Griffin

Vigil of Rizpah, The. Felicia Dorothea Hemans. CenSon

Vigil of Venus, The. *Unknown.* AWP

"Goddesse bade the nymphs remove, The." OBVE

"Love he to morrow, who lov'd never." OBVE

Vigil Strange I Kept on the Field One Night. Walt Whitman. APN-1; CAGL; CBCWP; ColAP; HeIP-4; MoAmPo; NAAL-2v1; NAAL-3; NOBA; NoP-4; OBWP; PoE; PoPoPo; TAP; TCAPo

Vigilance. André Breton. NAWM-7v2; SurPaPo, tr. by Jean-Pierre Cauvin and Mary Ann Caws

Vigilante Man. Woody Guthrie. APT-2

Vigilantius, or a Servant of the Lord Found Ready. Cotton Mather. SCAP

Vikings, The. *Unknown.* BIrV, tr. by John Montague

Vilage is a circle, A. Village, A. Roland Jooris. TuT, tr. by Peter Van de Kamp

Vile, and deformed by sin I stand. Human and Divine. Phoebe Cary. SacPr

Vile World. Simon Rae. UV

Villa at the Foot of Mount Chungnan. Wang Wei. ChinPo, tr. by Yip Wai-lim

Villa d'Este. Edwin Denby. OBGa

Villa Restaurant, The. Derek Walcott. WeW-3

Village. Jean Earle. AngWePo

Village. Octavio Paz. TCLAP, tr. by Charles Tomlinson

Village, A. Roland Jooris. TuT, tr. by Peter Van de Kamp

Village, The. George Crabbe.

Poor-House, The. ECEV

Rural Life. NOBE

Truth in Poetry. FHYEP

Village Life. NAEL-5v1; NAEL-7v1; NOEC; PoE

"Village life, and every care that reigns." NAEL-5v1; NAEL-7v1; NOEC; PoE

Village, The. Marina Gashe. HAWP; PBA

Village, The. Oliver Goldsmith. NPeEn *Fr.* Deserted Village, The.

Village, The. Ronald Stuart Thomas. HarvBoo

Village and Factory. Alexander Ilyich Bezymensky [*or* Bezymenskii]. TrJP, tr. by Babette Deutsch

Village Blacksmith, The. Henry Wadsworth Longfellow. APN-1; AiP; BRP; OBAL; OBCA; OxIBACP; PWR; UV

Village chief made the announcement from door to door. Tune: "Slow Chant"—Kao-tsu's Homecoming. Sui Ching-ch'en. SuSp, tr. by Sherwin S. S. Fu

Village Choir, The. *Unknown.* UV

Village Coddled in the Valley, The. George Barker. OxBSP

Village Curate, The. James Hurdis.

Village Fair, The. ECEV

Village festival is really worth seeing, The. Watching a Village Festival. Yang Wan-li. ColAnChi, tr. by Jonathan Chaves

Village is straddled on both sides, The. Eglwys Newydd. John Tripp. AngWePo

Village Life. George Crabbe. NAEL-5v1; NAEL-7v1; NOEC; PoE *Fr.* Village, The.

Village Life, A. Derek Walcott. GT

Village life, and every care that reigns. George Crabbe. NAEL-5v1; NAEL-7v1; NOEC; PoE *Fr.* Village, The.

Village lights in the dusk. Evening Lights on the River. Chiang Shih-ch'üan. OHMPC, tr. by Kenneth Rexroth

Village Maid, The. Mary F. Johnson. CenSon

Village maid was leaving home, with tears her eyes were wet, A. Edgar Smith. ReLy

Village Mystery. Elinor Wylie. APT-1

Village named Little-Plum-Tree, A. Issa. EH, tr. by Robert Hass

Village Night. Gyula Juhász. IQMS, tr. by Anthony Edkins

Village Night. Po Chü-i. CoBCP, tr. by Burton Watson

Village Noon; Mid-Day Bells. Merrill Moore. MoAmPo

Village Notary's Journey to Buda, A. József Gvadányi. On the Dress of the Hungarians. IQMS, tr. by Watson Kirkconnell

Village of Fochriw grunts among the higher hills, The. Idris Davies. AngWePo *Fr.* Gwalia Deserta.

Village Patriarch, The. Ebenezer Elliott.

"Five rivers, like the fingers of a hand." NOBRP

Village Preacher, The. Oliver Goldsmith. *Fr.* Deserted Village, The.

Village Saturday, The. Giacomo Leopardi. NAWM-7v2, tr. by Ottavio M. Casale

Village Spa. Phyllis McGinley. OBCoV

Village! thy butcher's son, the steward now. Ebenezer Elliott. OBSV *Fr.* Splendid Village, The.

Village Tudda, The. Kenneth Patchen. VGW

Village where they ring, A. Basho. TAL

Village with a thousand eaves. Buson. EH, tr. by Robert Hass

Village without bells, A. Basho. EH; NIL-7, tr. by Robert Hass

Village woman brings her five-year-old son, The. Ballad of Selling a Child. Wang Chiu-ssu. CoBLCP; ColAnChi, tr. by Jonathan Chaves

Villagers who gather round. Spiel of [the] Three Mountebanks. John Crowe Ransom. MoAmPo

Villain, The. William Henry Davies. AngWePo; MoBrPo; OxBSP; OxBTC

Villancico. *Unknown.* AWP, tr. by Thomas Walsh

Villanelle VI. Judith Barrington. FFC

Villanelle: "Every day our bodies separate." Marilyn Hacker. MakPoe

Villanelle for the Middle of the Night. Jacqueline Osherow. MakPoe

Villanelle from a Sentence in a Poet's Brief Biography. Jacqueline Osherow. ExTi

Villanelle: "It is the pain, it is the pain, endures." William Empson. EnLoPo; HarvBoo; NoAM; PoE; TRP; UV

Villanelle: "O winter wind, lat grievin be." Margaret Winefride Simpson. OxBS

Villanelle of His Lady's Treasures. Ernest Christopher Dowson. MakPoe

Villanelle of Marguerites. Ernest Christopher Dowson. MoBrPo

Villanelle of the Poet's Road. Ernest Christopher Dowson. OBMV; UnPo

Villanelle: The Psychological Hour. Ezra Pound. CTC; NAAL-2v2

Villanelle: "Time can [*or* will] say nothing but I told you so." W. H. Auden. MoBrPo

Villeggiature. Edith Nesbit. LW; NOBVV; PEW

Villon. Basil Bunting.

"Remember, imbeciles and wits." NPeEn; OxBEV

Villon's Straight Tip to All Cross Coves. William Ernest Henley. AWP; OxAEP-2

Vimalakirti, Vaishali. Vimalakirti. Shinkichi Takahashi. ZenPo, tr. by Takashi Ikemoto and Lucien Stryk

Vimy Ridge. John Oxenham. SacPr

Vincent Corbet[t], farther known[e]. Elegy upon the Death of His Own Father, An. Richard Corbet [*or* Corbett]. BeJo; NOSC

Vincent Ogé. George Boyer Vashon. APN-2

Vincent Watchman was shot. Pay Up or Else. Luci Tapahonso. ReTh

Vindication. Vadim Antonov.

"Toward morning, slipping the pistol under my arm." TCRP

Vine, The. Robert Herrick. BeJo; CaPo; EroLit; NAEL-5v2; NAEL-6v1; NAEL-7v1

(I dream'd this mortal part of mine.) CavPo

(I dreamed this mortal part of mine.) NoP-4

Vine and the Goat, The. Aesop. AWP, tr. by William Ellery Leonard

Vine I see, and though 'tis time to glean, A. Overripe Fruit. Kasmuneh. TrJP

Vine v. Goat. Euenus. GrAn, tr. by Alistair Elliot

Vines, The. John Gray. NOBVV

Vineta. Charles Spear. PeNZ

Vineyard, The. W. S. Merwin. NNaP

Vineyard of My Beloved, The. Priscilla Jane Thompson. CBWP-2

Vintage. Brendan Kennelly. ModIr *Fr.* Cromwell.

Vintage to the Dungeon, The. Richard Lovelace. BeJo; CaPo

Viola's Song. Sir William Davenant [*or* D'Avenant]. *See* Law against Lovers, The

Violante has commanded me to write. Sonnet All of a Sudden, A. Félix Lope de Vega Carpio. SpanPo, *tr. by* Doreen Bell

Violence. Robert Lowell. NoAM

Violence, how smoothly it came. Shadow Train. John Ashbery. LCAP-2

Violent burning for prodigious beauty, A. Michelangelo Buonarroti. CAGL, *tr. by* James M. Saslow

Violent contrariety of men and days; calm. Geoffrey Hill. FaBoWar *Fr.* Mystery of the Charity of Charles Péguy, The.

Violent Space, The. Etheridge Knight. BPo

Violent storm, A. Abiding Mountain. Muso Soseki. EaWin, *tr. by* W. S. Merwin

Violently vulnerable neck, The. (LL) Portraits of Tudor Statesmen. U. A. Fanthorpe. EmeKit; OxBEV

Violet. Arthur Symons.
   At Seventeen. OxBSo

Violet, The. Goethe. STV, *tr. by* John Frederick Nims

Violet, The. Jane Taylor. WoRP

Violet in the deepest green, A. Violet, The. Goethe. STV, *tr. by* John Frederick Nims

Violet loves a sunny bank, The. Proposal. Bayard Taylor. TreFP

Violet Twilights. Edith Södergran. WPOW, *tr. by* Stina Katchadourian

Violets. Virginia Brady Young. HA

Violets blue of the eyes divine, The. Die blauen Veilchen der Äugelein. Heinrich Heine. AWP, *tr. by* James Thomson

Violets, Daffodils. Elizabeth Jane Coatsworth. TLR
   (Nosegay.) OBCA

Violets for Your Furs. Matt Dennis. ReLy

Violets lie darkly blue, The. Grave, A. Herman von Gilm zu Rosenegg. AuPH, *tr. by* Lowell A. Bangerter

Violin Bow and Strings. Innokenty Fiodorovich Annensky. TCRP, *tr. by* Daniel Weissbort and Lubov Yakovleva

Violin devil image on. Emmett Williams. PFTM-2 *Fr.* Ultimate Poem, The.

Violin which is following me, A. Conspiracy. Jack Spicer. APSN

Violinist tamed the birds, The. Inside the Fence: Tule Lake Internment Camp. Kim R. Stafford. GifTon

Violins complain. Autumn Song. Paul Verlaine. WoPoe, *tr. by* Louis Simpson

Violins float in the sky. Europe, Late. Dan Pagis. HP, *tr. by* Stephen Mitchell

Viper, The. Joseph Hilaire Pierre Belloc. NoAM

Viper, The. Nicanor Parra. TCLAP, *tr. by* W. S. Merwin

Viper, The. Ruth Pitter. FaBoTw

Viper Light. Barbara Leslie Jordan. ExTi

Vir nullá non donandus lauru. (LL) Winthrop Mackworth Praed. OBEV; OxAEP-2 *Fr.* Every-Day Characters.

Vire will wind in other shadows. Saint-Lô. Samuel Beckett. NOIV; NPeEn

Virgidemiarum. Joseph Hall.
   "Gentle squire would gladly entertain, A." NoSic
   "Great is the folly of a feeble brain." EBEV
   Olden Days, The. OBSV
   "Pardon, ye glowing ears; need will it out." NoSic
   "Sturdy ploughman doth the soldier see, The." OBSV
   "Time was, and that was termed the time of Gold." OBSV
   "When Gullion died (who knows not Gullion?)." NoSic

Virgidemiarum Book 5. Joseph Hall.
   "Hous-keping's dead, *Saturio:* wot'st thou where?" PBRV

Virgil, who brought great Aeneas to Laurentian lands. Publius Papinius Statius. RomPo, *tr. by* W. G. Shepherd *Fr.* Sylvae.

Virgin, The. Laura Riding Jackson. ChIV-2

Virgin and Child, by Hans Memmeling; in the Academy of Bruges, A. Dante Gabriel Rossetti. CenSon

Virgin at heart, A. Lost Daughter. Magdalena Gomez. PueRic

Virgin Declares Her Beauties, A. Francesco da Barberini. AWP; EaItPo, *tr. by* Dante Gabriel Rossetti

Virgin Forest, The. Aimé Césaire. SurPaPo, *tr. by* Clayton Eshleman and Annette Smith

Virgin is thinking of a child, The. Leonardo's Secret. Robert Bly. NNaP

Virgin Martyr, The. Ada Cambridge. NOBAu

Virgin Martyrs. John Heath-Stubbs. OxBC

Virgin Mary, The. *Unknown.* OBWVE, *tr. by* Joseph P. Clancy

Virgin Mary by the fire, The? (LL) Joseph. Gilbert Keith Chesterton. ChIV-2; ChrPo

Virgin Mary, daughter of your Son. Dante Alighieri. NAWM-7v1, *tr. by* Allen Mandelbaum *Fr.* Divine Comedy, The (Mandelbaum Translation).

Virgin-Mother stood at distance (there), The. Observation. Robert Herrick. ChIV-2

Virgin Mother walked barefoot, The. Begotten of the Spleen. Charles Simic. LCAP-2

Virgin of the vestal flame. Vestal Virgin, The. Eloise Bibb. CBWP-4

Virgin of Troy, the days were well with thee. Studies from the Antique. Emily Jane Pfeiffer. ViWPN

Virgin's Song, The. *Unknown.* NOBE

Virgin, sing the Virgin Huntress. Horace. OBVE, *tr. by* Branwell Brontë *Fr.* Odes.

Virgin Warrior, The. Gwendolyn MacEwen. FaBoWP

Virginal, A. Ezra Pound. ColAP; MoAmPo; NAAL-2v2; NIL-7; NIP-4; NOBA; OxBA; Son; TAP; TCAPo

Virginal, Vibrant, and Beautiful Dawn, The. Stéphane Mallarmé. NAWM-7v2, *tr. by* Henry Weinfield

Virginal, Vivid, Beautiful, Will This Be. Stéphane Mallarmé. WoPoe, *tr. by* Louis Simpson

Virginia. T. S. Eliot. FaBoA; InPK-6 *Fr.* Landscapes.

Virginia Lake. James Keir Baxter. PeNZ

Virginia Portrait. Sterling Allen Brown. GT

Virginia's writing her diary. Bloomsbury Snapshot. Connie Bensley. OBCoV

Virginia Woolf committed suicide in 1941 when the German bombing. Doubt. Fanny Howe. BAP-01

Virginian Arcady. Anne Rouse. NeBl

Virgins, The. Derek Walcott. OxBC; SoSe-8

Virgins are like the fair flower in its lustre. John Gay. NIL-7 *Fr.* Begger's Opera.

Virgins love thee well, The. (LL) Let Him with Kisses of His Mouth. *Unknown.* AH; ChIV-1

Virgins promis'd when I died [*or* dy'd]. Epitaph upon a Child, An. Robert Herrick. FaBoEE

Virgo, August. John Taylor. NOSC

Virgo Descending. Charles Wright. ColAP; LCAP-2; TRP

Virtual Particles. Frank Wilczek. NBLV

Virtual Reality. Charles Bernstein. FTOS

Virtually whole they perceive it and name it Anagallis tenella. Allen Fisher. Oth *Fr.* Emergent Manner.

Virtue. Nicholas Grimald. SCGP
   (Description of Virtue.) NoSic

Virtue alone can never die. but lives to. Hannah Taylor. FaBoVe

Virtue and compassion. No Gain. Muso Soseki. EaWin, *tr. by* W. S. Merwin

Virtue conceal'd within our breast. Jonathan Swift. OBVE

Virtue, dear friends, needs no 'defense." Horace. OBVE *Fr.* Odes.

Virtue may choose the high or low degree. Pope. NOBE; NPeEn; OBSV *Fr.* Epilogue to the Satires, in Two Dialogues.

Virtue of ancestors handed down. Poem in Rhyme-Prose Form. Pan Chieh-yû. CoBCP, *tr. by* Burton Watson

Virtue of Slovenliness, The. Geoffrey Holloway. NLP

Virtue [*or* Vertue]. George Herbert. AWP; AmFaPo; BASC; ClHu; FSCP; GeHe; HAP; HeIP-4; MeLP; NAEL-5v1; NAEL-6v1; NAEL-7v1; NOBE; NOCV; NoP-4; OBEV; OPOU; OxBEV; PAI; PeECV; PoE; PoRA; SCGP; SoSe-8; TFi; TreFP

Virtue's branches wither, virtue pines. Thomas Dekker. NoSic *Fr.* Old Fortunatus.

Virtue's Goal Is God. "Angelus Silesius." GePo, *tr. by* George C. Schoolfield *Fr.* Cherubical Wanderer, The.

Virtue was the sunset creeping in the grass. Lines on a Platonic Friendship. Daryl Hine. IllVoic

Virtues of an amulet / and quick surprise, The. (LL) Warning, The. Robert Creeley. NeAP; TAP; VGW

Virtues of Carnation Milk, The. *Unknown. See* Carnation Milk

Virtuoso, A. Austin Dobson. PeVV

Virtuous Wife, The. Süsskind von Trimberg. TrJP

Virtuous Woman, The. Bible, *O.T.* TrJP *Fr.* Proverbs.

Virus nibbled the delicacy of my father's brain, A. In Hospital-land. Gillian Ferguson. MFPA

Virus². Jackie Kay. MFPA

Viscount Stansgate, or Wedgwood, or Benn. Limerick. Tim Hopkins. PeLi

Visibility. Maura Stanton. BodElec

Visible Baby, The. Peter Redgrove. EmeKit

Visible, invisible. Jellyfish, A. Marianne Craig Moore. OxBSP

Visible sea at a distance from the shore, The. Seamus Heaney. PoetW *Fr.* Squarings.

Visibly here the tide. Wellfleet Harbor. Paul Goodman. CoAP

Vision. Delmira Agustini. TCLAP, *tr. by* Karl Kirchwey

Vision. Delmira Augustini. WPOW, *tr. by* Marti Moody

Vision. Steve Barney. IBA

Vision. Harry Crosby. APT-2

Vision. SPE

Vision. Harry Crosby. SPE *Fr.* Vision.

Vision. James Devaney. NOBAu

Vision. Elizabeth N. Hauer. PoToHe
Vision. Hesiod. WoPoe, *tr. by* Charles Doria *Fr.* Theogony.
Vision. Louis Johnson. PeNZ
Vision. Francis Reginald. MoCV
Vision. Robert Penn Warren. APT-2
Vision. May Thielgaard Watts. LW
Vision. Israel Zangwill. TrJP
Vision, A. John Clare. EBVV; GTBS-P; NAEL-5v2; NAEL-6v2; NOBVV; OxBEV; PoE
Vision, A. Hugo von Hofmannsthal. TrJP, *tr. by* Charles Wharton Stork
Vision, A. Maria Konopnicka. WPOW, *tr. by* Jerzy Peterkiewicz and Burns Singer
Vision, A. Ts'ao Chih. ChiP, *tr. by* Arthur Waley
Vision, A. W. B. Yeats.
  All Souls' Night. OxAEP-2
Vision, The. Muhammad Al-Faituri [*or* Al-Fituri *or* Al-Fayturi]. MAP, *tr. by* Sargon Boulus and Peter Porter
Vision, The. Robert Burns.
  Duan First.
Vision, The. Robert Herrick. CaPo; CavPo; SCGP
  (Methought I saw, as I did dream in bed.) NOSC
Vision, The. Egan [*or* Aodhagán] O'Rahilly [*or* O'Reilly *or* Ó Rathaille]. NOIV
Vision, The. William Taylor. NOEC
Vision (2). Sherman Alexie. UnSA
Vision V. William Browne (1591–1643). *See* Visions
Vision as of crowded city streets, A. Shakespeare. Henry Wadsworth Longfellow. AWP
Vision at Knock. Gerry Murphy. BiHa
Vision by Sweetwater. John Crowe Ransom. FaBoMo; HarvBoo; NOBA; OxBA; RB
Vision from the Blue Window. Ernesto Cardenal. VCWP, *tr. by* Marc Zimmerman
  (From the round window, everything is blue.) VCWP, *tr. by* Marc Zimmerman
Vision from the Ghetto. Raymond Washington. NBV
Vision in long filaments flows. Vision. Francis Reginald. MoCV
Vision of a haloed host, The. Ultimate. Gilbert Keith Chesterton. SacPr
Vision of Beasts, A. John Heath-Stubbs. ChIV-1
Vision of Beauty, A. Ben Jonson. BASC; NOSC *Fr.* New Inn, The.
Vision of Beulah, The ("Thou hearest the nightingale begin the song of spring"). William Blake. NOBE *Fr.* Milton.
Vision of Children, A. Thomas Ashe. EBVV
Vision of Christ that thou dost see, The. William Blake. ChIV-2 *Fr.* Everlasting Gospel, The.
Vision of Columbus, The. Joel Barlow.
  "There reigns a prince, whose hand the sceptre claims." TCAPo
Vision of Connaught in the Thirteenth Century, A. James Clarence Mangan. NOIV
Vision of Eve, The. Henrietta Cordelia Ray. CBWP-3
Vision of Hiroshima. Oscar Hahn. TCLAP, *tr. by* Sandy McKinney
Vision of Judgment, The. Byron. FHYEP; NPeEn; OBSV; OxAEP-2; OxBoLi *Fr.* Vision of Judgment, The.
  "At length with jostling, elbowing, and the aid." OBSV
Vision of Judgment, The. FHYEP; NAEL-6v2; NPeEn; OBSV; OxAEP-2; OxBoLi
Vision of MacConglinne, The. MacConglinne. BIrV
Vision of Moonlight, A. Henrietta Cordelia Ray. CBWP-3
Vision of Myself, A. Hugh MacDiarmid. OxBEV
Vision of Nature, A. William Langland. CTC *Fr.* Vision of Piers Plowman, The.
Vision of Niamh, The. Eva Gore-Booth. PoBW
Vision of Noah, The. May Kendall. VWP
Vision of Piers Plowman, The. William Langland.
  Age of Reason, The. NOCV
  Civil Service, The. NOCV
  Confession of Gluttony. NAEL-6v1; NAEL-7v1
  Dreamer Meets Conscience and Reason. NAEL-6v1; NAEL-7v1
  Entertainment Industry, The. NOCV
  "Envy with heavy heart asked for shrift." NAEL-5v1; NAEL-6v1; NAEL-7v1
  Et Incarnatus Est. NOBE
  Field Full of Folk, The. PoE
  (Field of Folk, The.) NAEL-5v1; NAEL-6v1; NAEL-7v1
  Glutton [*or* Glutton in the Tavern], The. PoE
  (Gluttony in the Ale-house.) NPeEn
  God's Mercy. NOCV
  Good Works. NOCV
  ("In a somur sesoun whan softe was the sonne.") NPeEn
  Incarnation, The. OBEV
  ("Now bygynneth Glotoun for to go to shryfte.") NPeEn
  Piers Plowman Shows the Way to Saint Truth. NAEL-6v1; NAEL-7v1
    "It is a kynde knowyng," quod she, "that kenneth in thine herte" OxBEV
  Plowing of Piers's Half-acre, The. NAEL-6v1; NAEL-7v1
  (Prologue.) EBVV; NPeEn; OxBEV
  "Barones an burgeises and bondemen als." FaBoVe
  Saint Called "Truth," A. NOCV
  "Thus I awoke, God knows, when I lived in Cornhill." WoPoe, *tr. by* George Economou
  Trinity, The. SacPr
  Vision of Nature, A. CTC
  "What for feere of this ferly and of the false Jewes." EBEV
  "Wool-chafed and wet-shoed I went forth after." NAEL-5v1; NAEL-6v1; NAEL-7v1
  "Yet I courbed on my knees and cried hire of grace." EBEV
Vision of Sir Launfal, The. James Russell Lowell.
  Prelude to Part the First. APN-1
Vision of Spring in Winter, A. Algernon Charles Swinburne. NPeEn
Vision of St. Michael and St. John, The. Jeremy Ingalls. YaYoPo
Vision of Sunday in Heaven, A. Victor James Daley. ChIV-2
Vision of the Graces, The. Edmund Spenser. NoSic *Fr.* Faerie Queene, The.
Vision of the Night, The. Philip Freneau. NAAL-2v1; NAAL-3 *Fr.* House of Night, The.
Vision of Truth, A. Sir John Collings Squire. NOBL
Vision of Your Body. Daisy Zamora. LoL, *tr. by* Dinah Livingston
Vision Shadows. Simon J. Ortiz. NAAL-5
Vision Test, The. Mona Van Duyn. FFC
Vision that appeared to me, A [*or* The]. Vision of MacConglinne, The. MacConglinne. BIrV
Vision upon the Fairy Queen, A. Sir Walter Ralegh. *See* Commendatory Verses to Edmund Spenser's Fairy Queen
Vision upon This Concei[p]t of the Faerie [*or* Faery] Queen[e], A. Sir Walter Ralegh. NAEL-5v1; NoSic; SCGP; Son *Fr.* Commendatory Verses to Edmund Spenser's Fairy Queen.
Vision will come—the Truth be revealed—but, The. Vision. Robert Penn Warren. APT-2
Visionary, The. Emily Jane Brontë. BrRo; NOBE; NOBVV; NPeEn; OxBEV; SCGP; SCV
Visionary theme!—a gorgeous shade, A! (LL) Rejects the Influence of Reason. Mary Robinson. CenSon; RWP
Visions. William Browne (1591–1643).
  "Down in a valley, by a forest's side." OxBSo
  Rose, A. OBEV
  (Vision V.) NOSC
Visions. Elsa Cross. TANSG, *tr. by* Patricia Dubrava
Visions. Petrarch. AWP
Visions. William Stafford. NoAM
Visions, The. Petrarch. AWP *Fr.* Sonnets to Laura.
Visions and Interpetations. Li-Young Lee. NIP-4
Visions Appear to her in a Dream. Mary Robinson. CenSon; RWP
Visions of beauty, of light, and of love. Dreams of Beauty. Adah Isaacs Menken. CBWP-1
Visions of Bellay, The. Joachim Du Bellay.
  "I saw the bird that can the sun endure." Son
  "It was the time, when rest, soft sliding downe." AWP; Son
Visions of Jesus. Jerome Rothenberg. APSN
Visions of Mexico While at a Writing Symposium in Port Townsend, Washington. Lorna Dee Cervantes. NoAM
Visions of the Daughters of Albion. William Blake. CABP; NAEL-6v2
  Desire and Jealousy. ECEV
  "Infancy! fearless, lustful, happy, nestling for delight." OxAEP-2
  "Moment of desire! the moment of desire! the virgin, The." ErotSp; OxBEV
  "Then Oothoon waited silent all the day and all the night." NPeEn
  "With what sense is it that the chicken shuns the ravenous hawk?" OxBEV
Visions you never saw, The. Grandfather. Lance Henson. CDW; HATNAP, *tr. by* Lance Henson
Visit. A. R. Ammons. CoAP; TwCP
Visit. Gerald William Barrax. GT
Visit. Léopold Sédar Senghor. PBMAP
Visit, A. Anna Swirszczynska. PoSu
Visit, The. "Badawi al-Jabal." MAP, *tr. by* John Heath-Stubbs and Matthew Sorenson
Visit, The. Ralph Waldo Emerson. APN-1; NOBA
Visit, The. Annie Foster. NLP

Visit, The. Phillip [or "Phil"] William George. VoR

Visit, The. Robert Glück.
    "Famous monk dropped to this knees before a giant image and cried, A." WiU
    "Odd to close my eyes during the day and open them at night." WiU
    "This image is alive with my longing for you." WiU

Visit, The. Ian Hamilton. NPeEn

Visit, The. Ibn Hazm al-Andalusi. WoPoe, tr. by Leticia Garza-Falcón and Christopher Middleton

Visit, The. Mary Leapor. ECWP

Visit, The. Toon Tellegen. TuT, tr. by Peter Van de Kamp

Visit, The. Unknown. ECWP

Visit, Auschwitz, 1971, The. Lisa Ress. GotH

Visit from Mr. Fox, A. Unknown. See Fox, The

Visit from St Nicholas, A. Clement Clarke Moore. APN-1; AiP; BRP; ChAP; ChrPo; NTCP; OBAL; OBCA; OBCP; OxIBACP; TCAPo; TFi
    (Night before Christmas, The.) PWR

Visit in Winter to the Temple of His Mystical Majesty, A. Tu Fu. CarOv, tr. by Carolyn Kizer

Visit of Hope to Sydney Cove, near Botany-Bay. Erasmus Darwin. ECEV; NOEC

Visit of the Gods, The. Samuel Taylor Coleridge. OBVE

Visit the Sick. James J. Metcalfe. PoToHe

Visit to Bridge House, A. Richard Weber. BIrV

Visit to Castletown House, A. Michael Hartnett. BiHa; PBCIP

Visit to Enniskillen, A. Tadhg Dall O'Huiginn. NOIV

Visit to Merlin, The. Edmund Spenser. NAEL-6v1; NAEL-7v1   Fr. Faerie Queene, The.

Visit to the Author's Paternal Seat, A. Richard Polwhele. NOEC   Fr. Influence of Local Attachment, The.

Visit to the Broken Hill Temple, A. Ch'ang Chien. SuSp, tr. by Joseph J. Lee

Visit to the Hermit Ts'ui. Ch'ien Ch'i. OHMPC, tr. by Kenneth Rexroth

Visit to the House of the Poet—Nicaragua, 1987—Homage to Rubén Darío on His Birthday, A. Thomas McGrath. BodElec

Visit to the Monastery of Good Omen. Lu Chi. OHMPC, tr. by Kenneth Rexroth

Visit to the Palace of Venus. Irene Young. HW

Visit to the Village, A. Michael Smith. PBCIP

Visitant, The. Theodore Roethke. PoE; RB; TRP; UnPo

Visitant Eclogue. John Kinsella. NeBl

Visitant to our dumbly human home. Great Moth, The. Robert Gittings. OxBTC

Visitation. John Dronsfield. PeSAV

Visitation. Jaime Jacinto. ReBoTo

Visitation. Adriann Roland Holst. TuT, tr. by Paula Meehan

Visitation, The. Brigit Pegeen Kelly. YaYoPo

Visitation, The. Jan Owen. NOBAu

Visitation Rights. Heather Wishik. GLP

Visitations. Lawrence Durrell. MoBrPo   Fr. Eight Aspects of Melissa.

Visited. Fleur Adcock. PeNZ

Visiting a Recluse on West Mountain and Not Finding Him In. Ch'iu Wei. CoBCP, tr. by Burton Watson

Visiting conductor, A. Simple Story, A. Gwen Harwood. FaBoWP; NOBAu

Visiting Dr Swift. Pope. See On Riding to See Dean Swift in the Mist of the Morning

Visiting Emily Dickinson's Grave with Robert Francis. Robert Bly. LCAP-2

Visiting Father. Juan Delgado. TouFir

Visiting Father and Friends. Allen Ginsberg. TaR

Visiting Hour (Repatriation Hospital). Michael Dransfield. BMAP

Visiting Hsiang-Chi Monastery. Wang Wei. WoPoe, tr. by Eva Shan Chou

Visiting Light. Jean Earle. TCAWP

Visiting My Gravesite: Talbott Churchyard, West Virginia. Irene McKinney. PBCAP

Visiting My Old Hut in Late Spring. Muso Soseki. EaWin, tr. by W. S. Merwin

Visiting New York. Sarah Rosenblatt. AmPoNex

Visiting Pai-an Pavilion. Hsieh Ling-yün. CrYelRi, tr. by Sam Hamill

Visiting the Garden at Monk Wen Ko's Home. Wu Wei-yeh. SuSp, tr. by Chang Yin-nan

Visiting the graves. Issa. EH, tr. by Robert Hass

Visiting the Hermit Cheng. Po Chü-i. TAL

Visiting the Hsi-Lin Temple. Po Chü-i. ChiP, tr. by Arthur Waley

Visiting the Monastery at Lung-men. Tu Fu. CrYelRi, tr. by Sam Hamill

Visiting the Mountain Hermitage of a Monk at Gan-hua Monastery. Wang Wei. CrYelRi, tr. by Sam Hamill

Visiting the Site of One of the First Churches My Grandfather Pastored. T. Crunk. YaYoPo

Visiting the Temple of Accumulated Fragrance. Wang Wei. CoBCP, tr. by Burton Watson

Visiting the West Bank. S. V. Atalla. PoArWo

Visiting Tsan, Abbot of Ta-Yun. Tu Fu. OHPC, tr. by Kenneth Rexroth

Visiting Zomba Plateau. Jack A. Mapanje. NAfrP

Visitor. Aleksandr Aleksandrovich Blok. TCRusP, tr. by Geoffrey Thurley

Visitor. Unknown. OxNR

Visitor, A. Lewis Carroll. OBCoV

Visitor, A. Idea Vilariño. TANSG, tr. by Louise B. Popkin

Visitor, The. Anna Andreyevna Akhmatova. TCRusP, tr. by Daniel Weissbort

Visitor, The. William Henry Davies. OBWVE

Visitor, The. Carolyn Forché. OPOU

Visitor, The. Jack Prelutsky. OTCP

Visitor comes from Hungary as from outer space, A. Commonwealth, Common Poverty. Gloria Vando. TouFir

Visitor in Marl, A. Emily Dickinson. APN-2; TCAPo

Visitor's Parking. Anne Szumigalski. NOBC

Visitor to Warsaw. Portrait of a Jew Old Country Style. Jerome Rothenberg. NNaP

Visitor Who Never Came, The. Nazik Al-Mala'ika. MAP, tr. by Christopher Middleton and Matthew Sorenson

Visitors. Tu Fu. BLT; OHPC, tr. by Kenneth Rexroth

Visitors, The. Richard Moore. DiPo

Visitor's Book, 8, The. John Davies. TCAWP

Visitor's Book, 9, The. John Davies. TCAWP

Visitors, indignant, didactic, pronounce. Thresholds of Identity. Lionel Abrahams. PeSAV

Visitors to the Black Belt. Langston Hughes. NAAL-5

Visits from the Seventh. Sarah Arvio.
    Mirrors. KGB

Visits of condolence is all we get from them. Tourists. Yehuda Amichai [or Amikhai]. PoSu, tr. by Glenda Abramson and Tudor Parfitt

Visits to St. Elizabeths. Elizabeth Bishop. CoAP; VGW

Vista. Faiz Ahmad Faiz. VCWP, tr. by Agha Shahid Ali

Vista. Elizabeth Garrett. NeBl

Visting hours are over. Open Heart. Sekou Sundiata. SpirFl

Visting Malacca. Shirley Lim. FSt

Visting the graves. Basho. EH, tr. by Robert Hass

Vita Nuova. Stanley Kunitz. VGW

Vita Nuova. Oscar Wilde. CAGL

Vitae Summa Brevis Spem Nos Vetat Incohare Longam. Ernest Christopher Dowson. AWP; CABP; EBVV; HAP; NOBE; NPeEn; NoP-4; OBEV; OxBEV; OxBSP; PeVV; TFi
    (Envoy: "They are not long, the weeping and the laughter") MoBrPo; NAEL-5v2; NAEL-6v2; NOBVV; PoRa

Vitaï Lampada. Sir Henry John Newbolt. FaBoWar; OBWP; UV

Vital, arrogant, fatal, dominant X, The. (LL) Motive for Metaphor, The. Wallace Stevens. APT-1; MoAmPo

Vital spark of heavenly [or heav'nly] flame! Ode: The Dying Christian to His Soul. Pope. ChIV-2; SacPr

Vital spatterings. Excess. Thomas Kinsella. BiHa   Fr. Technical Supplement, A.

Vitality. Maria Amalia Fonte Boa. BoWoP, tr. by Willis Barnstone and Nelson Cerqueira

Vitamins and Roughage. Kenneth Rexroth. NoAM

Vitelli rides west toward Fano, the morning sun. Death of Vitellozzo Vitelli, The. Irving Feldman. TwCP

Vitex in swamp ground. Ezra Pound. APT-1

Vivamos, Mea Lesbia, atque Amemus. Catullus. See Carmina

Vive La Différence. Strato [or Straton]. GrAn, tr. by Teddy Hogge

Vive Le Sport. Harri Webb. TCAWP

Vive Noir! Mari E. Evans. NBV

Vivid grass with visible delight, The. Castaways, The. Claude McKay. APT-1

Vivid summers of my kidhood were. James Brown. Linwood M. Ross. InTrad

Vivid transparence that you bring is peace, The. (LL) Wallace Stevens. ColAP; NOBA   Fr. Notes toward a Supreme Fiction.

Vivre L'Orange. Hélène Cixous.
    "I urgency, I begged. Give me your dish, I said, icy." VCAP

Vixen, The. John Clare. RB

Vixen woman, The. Harold Monro. OBMV   Fr. Natural History.

Vixi Puellis Nuper Idoneus. Sir Thomas Wyatt. See Lover Showeth How He Is Forsaken of Such as He Sometime Enjoyed, The

Vlamertinghe. Edmund Charles Blunden. NoP-4; OBWP; PeFWW

Vlaminck's Tie, the Persistent Imaginal. Michael Harlow. PeNZ

Vocable, as rath and bullaun, A. (LL) New Song, A. Seamus Heaney. CABP; CIP-2; FaBoTw

Vocabulary. Ariel Dorfman. AF, *tr.* by Ariel Dorfman

Vocation. Judith Herzberg. WPOW, *tr.* by Manfred Wolf

Vocation. Carol Rumens. DiPo

Vocational Guidance, with Special Reference to the Annunciation of Simone Martini. Richard Howard. BodElec

Voice. Zbigniew Herbert. PoSu, *tr.* by Czeslaw Milosz

Voice. W. S. Merwin. NNaP

Voice. Ann Sansom. NeBl

Voice. Susan Wicks. MFPA

Voice, A. Tadeusz Rózewicz. BLT, *tr.* by Czeslaw Milosz

Voice, A. Lina Tibi. PoArWo, *tr.* by Subhi Hadidi and Nathalie Handal

Voice, A. *Unknown.* CA

Voice, The. Thomas Hardy. BoLoP; EnLoPo; GTBS-P; HAP; HarvBoo; NAEL-5v2; NAEL-6v2; NPeEn; NoAM; NoP-4; OxAEP-2; OxBEV; PAI; PoE; TFi

Voice, The. May Muzaffar. PoArWo, *tr.* by Tahia Abdel Nasser

Voice, The. Theodore Roethke. VGW

Voice and Address. Michael Palmer. FTOS; PmAP

Voice are still / The moon's bright. Ma Chih-yüan. SuSp *Fr.* Tune: "Song of Shou-yang."

Voice, because of its austerity, will often cause dust to rise, The. Recursus. Michael Palmer. APSN

Voice calls me, A. Yaba. JDP, *tr.* by Yoel Hoffmann

Voice changed to a vinyl disc, a black larynx, A. New Release, A. Alice Fulton. AllShUp

Voice cried out in the wilderness, A. Trickster 2 (for Lee "Scratch" Perry). Kwame Dawes. WaCA

Voice for the Sirens, A. Maura Stanton. YaYoPo

Voice from heaven was heard on earth, A. *Unknown.* AnOE, *tr.* by Charles W. Kennedy *Fr.* Andreas.

Voice from the Bush—through Me. Graham Brady. IBA

Voice from the dark is calling me, A. Divorce. Anna Wickham. MoBrPo; NALW

Voice from the Factories, A. Caroline Elizabeth Norton. VWP *Fr.* Voice from the Factories, A.

Voice from the Invisible World, A. Goethe. AWP, *tr.* by James Clarence Mangan

Voice from the Well [of Life Speaks to the Maiden], The. George Peele. NOBE; NoSic *Fr.* Old Wives' [*or* Wife's] Tale, The.

Voice from under the Table, A. Richard Wilbur. HAP; NOBA

Voice in Darkness. Richard Dehmel. AWP, *tr.* by Margarete Münsterberg

Voice in the fall renouncing your world. Transformation. Karl Kraus. AuPH, *tr.* by Lowell A. Bangerter

Voice in the Garden, A. Selima Hill. FaBoWP

Voice is large, the man is small, The. Frog, A. Friedrich von Logau. GePo, *tr.* by George C. Schoolfield

Voice is never enough, The. Maysoun Saqr Al-Qasimi. PoArWo, *tr.* by Subhi Hadidi *Fr.* Morning of Every Sin, The.

Voice of a Dissipated Woman inside a Tomb. Sor Violante do Céu. BoWoP, *tr.* by Willis Barnstone

Voice of America, 1961, The. James Liddy. CIP-2

Voice of Earth Mediums. Philip Lamantia. CLPP

Voice of God, The. Louis I. Newman. PoToHe

Voice of God Is Calling, The. John Haynes Holmes. AH

Voice of Pride: shout of blaring trumpets. Paul Verlaine. SxFrPo, *tr.* by Martin Sorrell

Voice of Spring, The. Felicia Dorothea Hemans. RWP

Voice of the Ancient Bard, The. William Blake. FHYEP *Fr.* Songs of Experience.

Voice of the dead was a living voice to me, The. (LL) In the Valley of Cauteretz. Tennyson. BoLoP; NAEL-5v2; NAEL-6v2; NOBE

Voice of the last cricket, The. Splinter. Carl Sandburg. KaS; OBCA; SoSe-8; Spl

Voice of the Negro, The. Lizelia Augusta Jenkins Moorer. CBWP-3

Voice of the nightingale. Uko. JDP, *tr.* by Yoel Hoffmann

Voice of the season talking to the oxen, The. (LL) You Will Forget. Chenjerai Hove. HBAPE; NAfrP

Voice of the Swallow, Flittering, Calls to Me, The. *Unknown.* WoPoe, *tr.* by John L. Foster

Voice of Things, The. Thomas Hardy. HarvBoo

Voice of water as it flows and falls, The. Lament for Passenger Pigeons. Judith Wright. HarvBoo

Voice on the winds, A. To Morfydd. Lionel Pigot Johnson. MoBrPo; OBMV

Voice out of the Sabbaths, A. Derek Walcott. WeW-3

Voice peals in this end of night, A. Thrush before Dawn, A. Alice Thompson Meynell. MoBrPo; WPE

Voice said: "Follow, follow;" and I rose, A. Two Pursuits. Christina Georgina Rossetti. WPE

Voice said, "Hurl her down, The!" Lovely Shall Be Choosers, The. Robert Frost. MoAmPo; NOBA; OxBA; PoE

Voice said We are at War, The. Second World War, The. Elizabeth Jennings. ItWoWo

Voice [Speaks] from the Well, A. George Peele. FaBoCh; NOBE; OxBoLi *Fr.* Old Wives' [*or* Wife's] Tale, The.

Voice That Beautifies the Land, The. *Unknown.* APN-2; AWP, *tr.* by Washington Matthews *Fr.* Mountain Chant, The.

Voice that beautifies the land, The! *Unknown.*

Voice that breathed o'er Eden, The. Epithalamium. John Keble. NOCV

Voice that came out of her, The. Callas. Edward Field. BodElec

Voice that would reach you, Hunter, must speak, The. To Roosevelt. "Rubén Dario." PFTM-1; TCLAP, *tr.* by Lysander Kemp

Voiceless, The. Oliver Wendell Holmes. APN-1 *Fr.* Autocrat of the Breakfast Table, The.

Voices. Nora Dauenhauer. HATNAP

Voices. Walter De la Mare. UnPo

Voices. Sumaiya El-Sousy. PoArWo, *tr.* by Atef Abu-Seif and Nathalie Handal

Voices. Primo Levi. AF, *tr.* by Ruth Feldman

Voices. Wislawa Szymborska. PoSu, *tr.* by Magnus F. Krynski

Voices, The. Jean-Baptiste Tati-Loutard. PBMAP

Voices are crying an unknown name in the sky. (LL) Epistle to Be Left in the Earth. Archibald MacLeish. APT-1; MoAmPo; NOBA

Voices / are everywhere, The. Pony Farm. Laura Jensen. LCAP-2

Voices at the Window. Sir Philip Sidney. *See* Astrophil and Stella

Voices fade as he walks. Sweet Dreams. Christian Wiman. AmPoNex

Voices from the Other World. James Merrill. TwCP; VCAP

Voices from Things Growing in a Churchyard. Thomas Hardy. FaBoVe; OxBTC

Voices moving about in the quiet house. Falling Asleep. Siegfried Sassoon. MoBrPo; OxBTC

Voices mute for ever, or since yesterday, or just stilled. Voices. Primo Levi. AF, *tr.* by Ruth Feldman

Voices of death are sounding. Death of Antoñito el Camborio. Federico García Lorca. SpanPo, *tr.* by Robert O'Brien

Voices of the Rain. Henrietta Cordelia Ray. CBWP-3

Voices, single row of nights. They Shall Know. Kofi Awoonor. VCWP

Void. G. M. Muktibodh. OMIP; WoPoe, *tr.* by Vinay Dharwadker

Void has collapsed upon the earth, The. Zekkai Chushin. ZenPo, *tr.* by Takashi Ikemoto and Lucien Stryk

Void in Form. Ikkyu Sojun. ZenPo, *tr.* by Takashi Ikemoto and Lucien Stryk

Void inside us, The. Void, The. G. M. Muktibodh. OMIP; WoPoe, *tr.* by Vinay Dharwadker

Void that's highly embraceable, The. Jack Kerouac. NeAP *Fr.* Mexico City Blues.

Volatile Kerryman, The. Owen Roe O'Sullivan. BIrV, *tr.* by Sean O'Riada

Volatile mosquito. Meleager. GrAn

Volcanic Ash. Peter Sears. UrbNat

Volcanic smoke of Mount Aso, The. Afterimages. Shinkichi Takahashi. ZenPo, *tr.* by Takashi Ikemoto and Lucien Stryk

Volcanic tuff. Tina Darragh. FTOS

Volcano. Ivan Van Sertima. CA

Volcano. Derek Walcott. OxBC

Volcano is dark and suddenly thunder, The. Volcano is Dark, The. Malcolm Lowry. CLPP

Volcano rumbles, The. Kilimanjaro. Hélène d'Oettingen. CuPo

Volcanoes, The. José Santos Chocano. TCLAP, *tr.* by Andrew Rosing

Volcanoes be in Sicily. Emily Dickinson. NALW; OxWW

Volga Towns, The. Johannes Bobrowski. PoSu, *tr.* by Matthew Mead and Ruth Mead

Volkswagen parked in the gap, The. Ireland. Paul Muldoon. PBCIP

Volpone. Ben Jonson. NAEL-5v1; NAEL-7v1

   (Carmina V and VII [To the Same].) OBVE

   (Carmina, 5: To Celia.) OBVE

   "Come my Celia, let us prove." AEP; NIL-7; NPeEn; NoP-4; OxBEV; PoPoPo; TFi, *tr.* by Ben Jonson

   "Good morning to the day; and, next, my gold." OxBEV

   "I feare, I shall begin to grow in love." OxBEV

   "Kiss[e] me, sweet: the wary [*or* warie] Lover." BeJo; EroLit; NOSC, *tr.* by Ben Jonson

   Song. To Celia. BeJo; NPeEn; NoP-4; OxBEV, *tr.* by Ben Jonson

   (To Celia.) AWP; OxAEP-1

   To the Same [Celia]. BeJo; EroLit; NOSC, *tr.* by Ben Jonson

Volumes of books, tea and incense. Wen Cheng-ming. CoBLCP *Fr.* Inscribed on a Painting: Cultivating Leisure.

Voluntaries. Ralph Waldo Emerson. APN-1; CBCWP

Volunteer, The. Herbert Asquith. OBWP; OxBTC

(Here lies the clerk who half his life had spent.) FaBoWar
Volunteer, The. *Unknown*. NOEC
Volunteer's Reply to the Poet, The. Roy Campbell. FaBoWar
Volunteer's Thanksgiving, The. Lucy Larcom. OBCA
Volunteers. Hilda Raz. ExTi
Voluptuaries and Others. Margaret Avison. MoCV
Voluspo. *Unknown*. AWP, *tr. by* Henry Adams Bellows *Fr.* Elder Edda, The.
Von Tempsky's Dance. Murray Edmond. PeNZ
Voodoo. Léon Laleau. NegPo, *tr. by* Ellen Conroy Kennedy *Fr.* Black Music.
Voracious Time, uprooting all, consumes it. Seneca. RomPo, *tr. by* Marcus Wilson
Voremost they that dropp'd behind. (LL) Leaves a-Vallen. William Barnes. NOBVV; NPeEn
Vorkuta. Horst Bienek. AF
Vorthy cit, von Vitsunday, A. Mr. and Mrs. Vite's Journey. *Unknown*. NOBL
Vote, The. Ralph Knevet. FaBoWar; NOSC
(Helmett now an hive for Bees becomes, The.) NPeEn
Vote for Lunn. *Unknown*. FaBoVe
Votive Candles. Nick Carbó. NeAmPo
Voucher. Michael Portnoy. HeMarv
Vow. John Updike. PeLV
Vow, A. Allen Ginsberg. OBWP
Vow, The. Anthony Hecht. CoAmPo; InPK-6; TaR
Vow, The. Galway Kinnell. VCAP
Vow for New Year's, A. Mary Carolyn Davies. PoToHe
Vow to Heavenly Venus, A. Joachim Du Bellay. AWP, *tr. by* Andrew Lang
Vowels. Arthur Rimbaud. TTTS, *tr. by* Kenneth Koch
Vowels. Arthur Rimbaud. SxFrPo, *tr. by* Martin Sorrell
Vows. Shirley Kaufman. TaR
Vows are vain. No suppliant breath. Upon Castara's Departure. William Habington. NOSC
Vox Angelica. Timothy Liu. NeAmPo; WiU
Vox Oppressi, to the Lady Phipps. Richard Henchman. SCAP
Vox Pacifica. George Wither.
"*Sun* hath run his course through all the Signes, The." PBRV
Vox Populi. Dryden. NOBE *Fr.* Medal [*or* Medall], The.
Vox Ultima Crucis. John Lydgate. OBEV
(Tarye no longer; toward thyn herytage.) SacPr
"Voy wawm" said the dustman. Hymn to the Sun. Michael Roberts. FaBoCh; OxBTC
Voyage, A. W. H. Auden.
Sphinx, The. OxBSo
Voyage, The. Charles Baudelaire. NAWM-7v2, *tr. by* Charles Henri Ford
Voyage, The. Heinrich Heine. AWP, *tr. by* John Todhunter
Voyage à l'Infini. Walter Conrad Arensberg. APT-1
Voyage Life is longest made at home, The. (LL) Old Man of Verona, The. Claudian. AWP; OBVE, *tr. by* Abraham Cowley
Voyage of Life, The. Thomas Cole.
"As the broad mountain where the shadows flit." APN-1
Voyage of Life, The. Cynewulf. AnOE *Fr.* Christ 2.
Voyage on the Thames, The. Pope. EBEV; EBNV; ECEV; NOBE; NOEC; OxAEP-1 *Fr.* Rape of the Lock, The; an Heroi-Comical Poem.
Voyage to Cythera, A. Charles Baudelaire. WoPoe, *tr. by* Frederick Morgan
Voyage to Cythera, A. Charles Baudelaire. SxFrPo, *tr. by* James McGowan
Voyage to Labrador. W.S. Merwin. GS
Voyage to Marryland, A; or, The Ladies Dressing Room. Mary Evelyn. EMWP
Voyage to the Isle of Love, A. Aphra Behn.
Dream, The. RACG
Voyage to Tintern Abbey, A. Sneyd Davies.
Crooked bank still winds to something new, The. NOEC
Voyage West. Archibald MacLeish. APT-1; VGW
Voyage within you, on the fabled ocean. Terra Australis. James Philip McAuley. NOBAu
Voyager, The. Guillaume Apollinaire. CuPo
Voyager's Song, The. Edward Coote [*or* Coate] Pinkney. APN-1
Voyages. Hart Crane. APT-2; CAGL; NOBA; NoAM; TAP
"Above the fresh ruffles of the surf." ColAP; NAAL-2v2; NAAL-5; OxBA; PoE; VGW; WoPoe
"And yet this great wink of eternity." ColAP; HAP; MoAmPo; OxBA; PoE; RaBo; TRP; UnPo; VGW; WoPoe
"Infinite consanguinity it bears." AmFaPo; ColAP; OxBA
"Meticulous, past midnight in clear rime." ColAP; NAAL-2v2; NAAL-5; PoE
"Where icy and bright dungeons lift." ColAP; HAP; MoAmPo; UnPo

"Whose counted smile of hours and days, suppose." ColAP
Voyages. Jules Supervielle. MFP, *tr. by* Martin Sorrell
Voyaging. Charles Baudelaire. SxFrPo, *tr. by* James McGowan
Voyce of Anne Askewe out of the 54 Psalme of David, Called, Deus in Nomine Tuo, The. Anne Askew. EMWP
Voyelles. Arthur Rimbaud. WoPoe, *tr. by* F. Scott Fitzgerald
Voyeur. David Moolten. BloBone
Voyeur's Dream. Barney Bush. HATNAP
Voz de la Gente. Jimmy Santiago Baca. PmAP
Vuillard: "The Mother and Sister of the Artist." W. D. Snodgrass. CoAP
Vulcan, contrive me such a cup. Upon Drinking in a Bowl. John Wilmot, 2d Earl of Rochester. OxBoLi
Vulcan Forges the Shield of Achilles. Homer. OBVE, *tr. by* Alexander Pope *Fr.* Iliad, The.
Vulcan's Song. John Lyly. EBEV *Fr.* Sapho and Phao.
Vulgar Error, A. J. E. Thorold Rogers. FaBoEE
Vulgar of manner, overfed. Owed to New York. Byron Rufus Newton. NBLV
Vulgar paw-prints on the BMW. Carmel. Dennis Schmitz. GeoHom
Vulgar race of men, like herds that graze, The. Richard Jago. ECEV *Fr.* Edge-Hill; or, The Rural Prospect Delineated and Moralised.
Vulnerary, A. Jonathan Williams. PoM
Vulture. Robinson Jeffers. APT-1; NAAL-2v2; NOBA; NoAM
Vulture. X. J. Kennedy. OWoS
Vulture. Kenneth Rexroth. NNaP *Fr.* Bestiary, A.
Vulture, The. Joseph Hilaire Pierre Belloc. OWoS
Vulture eats between his meals, The. Vulture, The. Joseph Hilaire Pierre Belloc. OWoS
Vulture's very like a sack, The. Vulture. X. J. Kennedy. OWoS
Vultures. Margaret Atwood. LCAP-2; OWoS
Vultures, The. David Diop. PBA; TTY; WoPoe, *tr. by* Ulli Beier and Gerald Moore
(At that time.) NegPo, *tr. by* Ellen Conroy Kennedy
(In those days.) PBMAP
Vultures are being spring-cleaned, The. Building Society Blues. Roger Roughton. SPE
Vultures Grow Impatient, The. Amina Said. HAWP; NAfrP, *tr. by* Eric Sellin
Vultures waft circles. Remnant Ghosts at Dawn. Oliver La Grone. NBV
Vulva Operetta. Jessica Tarahata Hagedorn. ReBoTo

W

W. James Reeves. NOxBChV; NTCP
W. H. Louise Imogen Guiney. APN-2
W. H. *Eheu!* Samuel Taylor Coleridge. FaBoEE
W. L. M. K. Francis Reginald Scott. NOBC
w. resteth here, that quick could never rest. Excellent Epitaffe of Syr Thomas Wyat, An. Henry Howard, Earl of Surrey. NPeEn
W. S. Landor. Marianne Craig Moore. OBAL
W. W. Imamu Amiri Baraka. HeIP-4; NOBA; PAI
Wa-Sissica, the War Song. *Unknown*. APN-2 *Fr.* War Dance.
Waäit till our Sally cooms in, fur thou mun a' sights to tell. Northern Cobbler, The. Tennyson. EBEV
Wabash Cannonball, The. Delmore Brothers. GM
Wad be my queen, wad be my queen. (LL) O [*or* Oh] Wert Thou in the Cauld Blast. Robert Burns. EBEV; FaBoVe; HAP; NOBE; NPeEn; NePenScot; OxAEP-2; OxBS; SCGP
Wadasa Nakamoon, Vietnam Memorial. Ray A. Young Bear. CDa; HATNAP
Wade in the water. New Miz Praise de Lawd, The. Nicole Breedlove. InTrad
Wade / through black jade. Fish, The. Marianne Craig Moore. APT-1; ColAP; FaBoWP; MoAmPo; NAAL-2v2; NoAM; NoP-4; OxBA
Wading through it. Buson. EH, *tr. by* Robert Hass
Wading up Brunigill's rush. October, Isle of Skye. Carter Revard. NoP-4
Wae's me, wae's me! Cauld Lad of Hilton, The *or* The Wandering Spectre. *Unknown*. OxBoLi
Waement the deid. Coronach. Alexander Scott. OxBS
Waes-hael for [the] knight and [the] dame! King Arthur's Waes-hael. Robert Stephen Hawker. OBEV
Wag a leg, wag a leg. *Unknown*. OxNR
Wag ballock wag. *Unknown*. FaBoVe
Wagers. Marilyn Hacker. RA
Wages of sin is death. These words run, The. AIDS, Among Other Things. Peter Kocan. ChIV-2
Waggon-Maker, The. John Masefield. EBEV
Wagner. Rupert Brooke. FaBoTw; NOBL; PeLV
Wagon Full of Thunder. Louis Oliver. HATNAP

Wagon is going to the woods, The.   The woods.   Where Is the Wagon Going?   Meret Oppenheim.   SurWo, *tr. by* Catherine Schelbert

Wagons clang and horses cry.   Song of the War Wagons.   Tu Fu.   CrYelRi, *tr. by* Sam Hamill

Wagtail and Baby.   Thomas Hardy.   PeLV

Wah-dah do, wah-dah-do.   It Don't Mean a Thing (If It Ain't Got That Swing).   *Unknown.*   NAAAL

Wahiawa is still.   Leaving.   Cathy Song.   NoAM

Waiheke 1972—Rocky Bay.   Christina Beer.   PeNZ

Waikato-Taniwha-Rau.   Vincent O'Sullivan.   PeNZ

Wail, for the world's wrong! (LL)   Dirge, A: "Rough wind, that moanest loud."   Shelley.   NAEL-5v2; NOBE; PoRA; SCGP

Wail of Heights, The.   Wafaa' Lamrani.   PoArWo, *tr. by* Richard McKane and Tahia Abdel Nasser

Wail of the Divorced.   Mary E. Tucker.   CBWP-1

Wail of the Waiter, The.   Marcus Clarke.   NOBAu

Wail, wail, Ah for Adonis!   Lament for Adonis.   Bion.   AWP

Wailed for the golden years. (LL)   Shelley.   HeIP-4; NAEL-6v2   *Fr.* Hellas.

Wailing "Don't be cruel" (LL)   On the Elvis Mailing List.   Neal Bowers.   AllShUp; SwNoth

Wailing, wailing, wailing, the wind over land and sea.   Rizpah.   Tennyson.   NPeEn; PeVV

Wailing wind doth not enough despair, The.   Awake.   Mary Elizabeth Coleridge.   ViWPN

Wain upon the northern steep, The.   Astronomy.   A. E. Housman.   NoP-4; OBWP

Wait.   Charles Bernstein.   PmAP

Wait, A.   Catherine Walsh.
    "Old anorak green."   Oth

Wait!   *Unknown.*   WoPoe, *tr. by* Dennis Tedlock   *Fr.* Popul Vuh, The.

Wait a Little!   *Unknown.*   NOCV

Wait a minute, Death.   Rāmprasād Sen.   SinGod, *tr. by* Rachel Fell McDermott

Wait a moment, Death.   Tāpas Rāy.   SinGod, *tr. by* Rachel Fell McDermott

Wait for Me.   Robert Creeley.   NOBA

Wait for me, and I'll come back.   Konstantin Mikhailovich Simonov.   TCRP

Wait here, and I'll be back, though the hours divide.   Three Star Final.   Conrad Potter Aiken.   OxBA

Wait Mister. Which way is home?   Music Swims Back to Me.   Anne Sexton.   ColAP; MiVo; VCAP

Wait. This seems to be the kind of place.   Roman Temple, A.   'Umar Abu Risha.   MAP, *tr. by* Issa Boullata and Thomas G. Ezzy

Wait till the darkness is deep.   Wallāda.   WPOW, *tr. by* Deirdre Lashgari and James Monroe

Wait Till You See Her.   Richard Rodgers.   ReLy

Wait to scatter.   Spring.   Iio Sogi.   WoPoe, *tr. by* Steven D. Carter

Wait until I too hang up my carriage.   Hsieh Chin.   CoBLCP   *Fr.* Parting from Liu Nan-chou.

Waitekauri Every Time!   Edwin Edwards.   PeNZ

Waiter, Please.   *Unknown.*   *See* Limerick: "Epicure, Dining at Crewe, An."

Waitin on Summer.   Ruth Forman.   SpirFl

Waiting.   Jack Cain.   HA

Waiting.   Jane Cooper.   TAP

Waiting.   Robert Creeley.   VGW

Waiting.   William Ernest Henley.   NAEL-5v2; NAEL-6v2; NOBVV; NPeEn   *Fr.* In Hospital.

Waiting.   Arthur Nortje.   HBAPE

Waiting.   Elaine Randell.   Oth   *Fr.* Snoad Hill Poems, The.

Waiting.   James Reeves.   OTCP

Waiting.   Jean Valentine.   YaYoPo

Waiting.   William Carlos Williams.   SAmP

Waiting.   Donald Woods.   CAGL

Waiting Both.   Thomas Hardy.   MoBrPo; OxBoLi; TTTS

Waiting brief for milkmaid mornstar and worldrise. (LL)   Anglo Saxon Street.   Earle Birney.   HeIP-4; NIL-7; NOBC

Waiting for a spirit to trouble the water.   River Steamer, The.   Edith Jay Scovell.   HarvBoo

Waiting for Audience on a Spring Night.   Tu Fu.   OHPC, *tr. by* Kenneth Rexroth

Waiting For Breakfast, While She Brushed Her Hair.   Philip Larkin.   NoAM

Waiting for Death.   Mordecai Gebirtig.   TrJP, *tr. by* Joseph Leftwich

Waiting for Icarus.   Muriel Rukeyser.   LCAP-2; NNaP

Waiting for Robinson.   Roberta Hill Whiteman.   HATNAP

Waiting for sleep at the air roots.   Ivano Fermini.   ItPo, *tr. by* Gayle Ridinger

Waiting for the Barbarians.   Constantine P. Cavafy.   AF; BLT; FaBoWar; WoPoe, *tr. by* Edmund Keeley and Philip Sherrard

Waiting for the Bus.   Dennis Joseph Enright.   OxBTC

Waiting for the elevated train.   Armitage Street.   David Hernandez.   UnSA

Waiting for the end, boys, waiting for the end.   Just a Smack at Auden.   William Empson.   MoBrPo; OBCoV; PeLV; UV; UnPo

Waiting for the End of the War.   Thomas Brush.   CDa

Waiting for the Ferry at Inchŏn.   Liu E.   CoBLCP, *tr. by* Jonathan Chaves

Waiting for the Fire.   Philip Appleman.   CDa

Waiting for the flesh that dies. (LL)   Bull, The.   Ralph Hodgson.   MoBrPo; OBMV; OxBTC

Waiting for the keys.   La Berline Arrêtée Dans la Nuit.   O. V. de L. Milosz.   GifTon, *tr. by* Kenneth Rexroth

Waiting for the Post.   Dorothy Auchterlonie.   CBAP

Waiting for the Storm.   Timothy Steele.   MakPoe

Waiting for Truth.   Susan Griffin.   GLP

Waiting for weeks till the last one is ready to run, they.   Turtles Hatching.   Mark O'Connor.   NOBAu

Waiting for when the sun an hour or less.   In Santa Maria del Popolo.   Thom Gunn.   FaBoMo; GTBS-P; HarvBoo; NPeEn; OxBC; PoE

Waiting for whose hands to pick it up. (LL)   Karl Shapiro.   BodElec; IllVoic   *Fr.* Bourgeois Poet, The.

Waiting for You to Come By.   Simon J. Ortiz.   CDW

Waiting, I rest in the waiting gate.   Lich Gate, The.   Clayton Eshleman.   PmAP

Waiting in Front of the Columnar High School.   Karl Shapiro.   HAP

Waiting is the poem of waiting.   On Arrival.   Richard Howard.   TAP

Waiting Laughters.   Niyi Osundare.
    "And the snake says to the toad."   NAfrP

Waiting like a trap-door spider for a rookie sell-out. Baseball or the name game?   Four Poems for *The St. Louis Sporting News*.   Jack Spicer.   PoM

Waiting Lists, The.   Jackie Kay.   NeBl

Waiting on Elvis, 1956.   Joyce Carol Oates.   AllShUp; SwNoth

Waiting on the silent shelf. (LL)   You, Doctor Martin.   Anne Sexton.   MoAmPo; NAAL-2v2

Waiting room quiet.   Gary Hotham.   HA

Waiting-rooms.   David Vogel.   FIT, *tr. by* Robert Friend

Waiting to Be Fed.   Ray A. Young Bear.   CDW

Waiting to leave all day I hear the words.   Gates, The.   Muriel Rukeyser.   BodElec

Waiting to whimper or for Messiah.   In the Jury Room, in Pain.   Paul Goodman.   BodElec

Waiting, waiting, waiting.   Waiting.   James Reeves.   OTCP

Waiting with lowered voice.   Jacques Dupin.   VCWP, *tr. by* Paul Auster

Waitress.   Jason Shinder.   ReTh

Waitress's Kid, The.   Peggy Shumaker.   PBCAP

Waitresses.   Ranice Henderson Crosby.   WWork

Waits in unhope. (LL)   Thomas Hardy.   HarvBoo; NoAM; SCGP   *Fr.* In Tenebris.

Waka.   Lindley Williams Hubbell.   APT-2

Wake.   Langston Hughes.   OBAL; OBCoV

Wake.   Giuseppe Ungaretti.   WoPoe, *tr. by* George Garrett

Wake all the dead! What ho! What ho!   Sir William Davenant [*or* D'Avenant].   FaBoCh; HAP; SCGP   *Fr.* Law against Lovers, The.

Wake as you will, but wake in me.   To Song.   Olga Fiodorovna Berggolts [*or* Bergholts].   BoWoP, *tr. by* Daniel Weissbort

Wake at the Well, The.   *Unknown.*   MiEL

Wake, baillie, wake! the crafts are out.   Winding-up Time.   Jean Ingelow.   VWP

Wake, child with the flute.   Mirabai [*or* Mira Bai].   BoWoP, *tr. by* Willis Barnstone and Usha Nilsson

Wake, eat, and drink, evacuate, and sleep. (LL)   Human Life.   Matthew Prior.   FaBoEE; OBCoV; OxBEV

Wake for Papa Montero.   Nicolás Guillén.   PFTM-1

Wake! for the sun, who scattered [*or* scatter'd] into flight.   Omar Khayyám.   TRP, *tr. by* Edward Fitzgerald   *Fr.* Rubáiyát of Omar Khayyám [*of* Naishápúr], The.

Wake, friend, from forth thy lethargy; the drum.   Ben Jonson.   FaBoWar   *Fr.* Epistle to a Friend, to Persuade [*or* Perswade] Him to the Wars, [*or* Warres] An.

Wake, Israel, wake! Recall to-day.   Banner of the Jew, The.   Emma Lazarus.   TrJP

Wake me up at eleven, she says. I want to watch the news, she.   Shooting, Killing, Drug Busts, Cover-Ups, Fuck-Ups, Lighter Sides, Weather, and Sports.   Bruce Jackson.   AmPoNex

Wake Not for the World-heard Thunder.   A. E. Housman.   NoAM

Wake, O my soul; awake, and raise.   Hymn, An.   Phineas Fletcher.   NOSC

Wake the serpent not—let he.   Fragment.   Shelley.   SCGP

Wake: the silver dusk returning.   Reveille.   A. E. Housman.   CABP; HarvBoo; MoBrPo; NoP-4

Wake the Song of Jubilee.   Leonard Bacon.   AH

Wake up, dear boy that holds the flute!   Mirabai [*or* Mira Bai].   WPOW, *tr. by* Usha Nilsson

Wake up, my heart, get out of bed.   Priest in the Sabbath Dawn Addresses His Somnolent Mistress, A.   Peter Didsbury.   EmeKit

Wake up, Syama, wake up, Syama!   Najrul Islām.   SinGod, *tr. by* Rachel Fell McDermott

Wake up, wake up, Mother!   Dāśarathi Rāy.   SinGod, *tr. by* Rachel Fell McDermott

Wake up Woman!   Arise to the Day's Toil.   Assumpta Acam-Oturu.   HAWP

Wake with rapt touch thy glowing strings no more! (LL)   Written December 1790.   Anna Seward.   CenSon; Son

Waked [*or* Wak'd] by the Gospel's Powerful Sound.   Samson Occom.   AH; TCAPo

Wakeful in the Township.   Elizabeth Riddell.   NOBAu

Wakeful they lie. (LL)   Counting the Beats.   Robert Graves.   GTBS-P; HAP; HarvBoo; OxAEP-2; OxBTC; WeW-3; WoPoe

Waken, lords and ladies gay.   Hunting Song.   Sir Walter Scott.   GTBS-P; SCGP

Wakening, The.   *Unknown.*   OBEV

Wakepick I.   Kristjana Gunnars.   NOBC

Wakes that boats make, The.   Ways, The.   Louis Zukofsky.   PoE

Waking.   Hugh Maxton.   BIrV; CIP-2

Waking.   Katharine Pyle.   OBCA

Waking.   Tristan Tzara.   AF

Waking, The.   Galway Kinnell.   BodElec

Waking, The.   Theodore Roethke.   APT-2; AmFaPo; CRP; CoAP; HAP; HCAP; HeIP-4; ITBLP; InPK-6; MakPoe; MoAmPo; NAAL-2v2; NAAL-5; NIL-7; NIP-4; NOBA; NoAM; NoP-4; PoPoPo; RaBo; TAP; TFi; TTTS; TwCP; VCAP; WeW-3; WoPoe

Waking alone in a multitude of loves when morning's light.   On the Marriage of a Virgin.   Dylan Thomas.   EnLoPo

Waking at morn, with the accustomed sigh.   On the Death of His Son Vincent.   Leigh Hunt.   NOBVV

Waking at the Middle of Nowhere.   Reg Saner.   PoCoUp

Waking, Child, While You Slept.   Ethel Louisa Mason Anderson.   WPE   *Fr.* Bucolic Eclogues.

Waking Early Sunday Morning.   Robert Lowell.   FaBoMo; HCAP; HarvBoo; NOBA; OxBC; VCAP

Waking from a bad dream, and thrashing out.   Dream Time.   Anthony Thwaite.   DiPo

Waking from a Nap.   Ni Tsan.   CoBLCP, *tr. by* Jonathan Chaves

Waking from a Nap on the Beach.   May Swenson.   NTCP

Waking from Sleep.   Robert Bly.   NOBA; NoP-4; SPE

Waking from violence: the surgeon's probe left in the foot.   For a Friend in Travail.   Adrienne Rich.   NAAL-5

Waking himself.   Sixty-Six.   Philip Booth.   BodElec

Waking in silence and, through tilted blinds.   Window at Key West, A.   Honor Moore.   KGB; WiU

Waking in the Blue.   Robert Lowell.   AmFaPo; CoAP; HCAP; MoAmPo; UnPo

Waking in the Dark.   Dorothy Livesay.   NOBC

Waking in the Dark.   Adrienne Rich.   FaBoWP

Waking intuitively in the rosegray light of rising sun.   Waking Intuitively.   Quintus Catulus.   WoPoe, *tr. by* Janet Lembke

Waking is this easy.   Aubade.   Marilyn Chin.   NIP-4

Waking Jesus sudden riding a scream like a / train.   I Scream You Scream.   Don McKay.   NOBC

Waking, months after I leave the jungle.   Talvikki Ansel.   YaYoPo   *Fr.* In Fragments, In Streams.

Waking, my eyes, and in the night.   Petronius Arbiter.   PGA

Waking on a Summer Morning.   Mary Oliver.   PoCoUp

Waking to find yourself the same.   Thirty-Seven.   Jack Marshall.   GraLe

Waking to the clatter of hot-plate kettle.   Years, The.   John Ennis.   CIP-2

Waking Up.   Yolanda Palis.   ReBoTo

Waking up over the candy store together.   First Early Mornings Together.   Robert Pinsky.   ColAP

Waking up Twice.   Jack Anderson.   PasH

Wakonda! Talako! deathonic turkey gobbling in the soft-footpatch night!   Spontaneous Requiem For the American Indian.   Gregory Corso.   PoM

Walam Olum; or, Red Score [of the Lenâpé], The [*or* The Wallam Olum; The Red Score or Painted History of the Lenni Lenape].   *Unknown.*
  "After the rushing waters had subsided the Lenape of the turtle were close together, in hollow houses, living together there."   APN-2
  "After the Seizer there were ten chiefs, and there was much warfare south and east."   OBVE
  "At first in that place, at all times, above the earth."   APN-2
  "Great land and a wide land was the east land, A."   OBVE; TCAPo
  "Long ago there was a mighty snake, and beings evil to men."   APN-2

Waldeinsamkeit.   Ralph Waldo Emerson.   APN-1; NOBA

Walden.   William Ellery Channing.   APN-1

Walden.   Henry David Thoreau.

Light-Winged Smoke, Icarian Bird.   APN-1; ColAP; NOBA; TAP; TCAPo (Smoke.)   AWP; NoP-4; OxBA

Walden Pond / All those noxious gases rising from it.   Jack Spicer.   VGW   *Fr.* Graphemics.

Waldere 1.   *Unknown.*   AnOE, *tr. by* Charles W. Kennedy

Waldere 1.   *Unknown.*   ASW, *tr. by* Kevin Crossley-Holland

Waldere 2.   *Unknown.*   AnOE, *tr. by* Charles W. Kennedy

Waldere 2.   *Unknown.*   ASW, *tr. by* Kevin Crossley-Holland

Waldere addressed him, the warrior brave.   Waldere 2.   *Unknown.*   AnOE, *tr. by* Charles W. Kennedy

Waldviertel. Lower Austria.   Alma Johanna Koenig.   AuPH, *tr. by* Lowell A. Bangerter

Wales Re-visited.   Harry Guest.   TCAWP

Wales Visitation.   Allen Ginsberg.   APSN; BB; ColAP; NNaP; NOBA; VCAP

Wales, which I have never seen.   For My Ancestors.   Rolfe Humphries.   PoRA

Walk.   Frank Horne.   BPo

Walk.   Brian [*or* Bryan] Merriman [*or* Merryman].   BIrV, *tr. by* Brendan Behan   *Fr.* Midnight Court, The.

Walk, A.   Raymond Carver.   GM

Walk, A.   Hedwig Lachmann.   TrJP, *tr. by* Jethro Bithell

Walk, A.   Rainer Maria Rilke.   RaBo, *tr. by* Robert Bly

Walk, A.   Gary Snyder.   NOBA

Walk, A.   Nikolai Alekseievich Zabolotsky [*or* Zabolotskii].   RB, *tr. by* Daniel Weissbort

Walk, The.   Ethan Gilsdorf.   OPRER

Walk, The.   Thomas Hardy.   NAEL-5v2; NAEL-6v2; NPeEn; OxBEV; PoE

Walk, The.   William Scammell.   NLP

Walk down the path.   *Unknown.*   LB

Walk east. Dawn polishes the sky.   Direction.   Roberta Hill Whiteman.   CDW

Walk fast in snow, in frost walk slow.   Winter Wise.   *Unknown.*   Spl

Walk Home, The.   Reed Whittemore.   CoAmPo

Walk in Central Park, A.   Central Park.   Julian Symons.   PeLV

Walk in Late Summer, A.   Theodore Roethke.   APT-2

Walk in the Country, A.   Su Tung-p'o (Su Shih).   *See* Rhyming with Tzu-yu's "Treading the Green."

Walk in the Country, A.   T'ang Yen-ch'ien.   SuSp, *tr. by* Edward H. Schafer

Walk in the Precepts.   Moses Ibn Ezra.   TrJP, *tr. by* Solomon Solis-Cohen

Walk in the Rain.   Polly Clark.   NeBl

Walk in your sleep beyond Yeppoon.   Assignation with a Somnambulist.   John Streeter Manifold.   CBAP

Walk into the prison, that domed citadel.   My Lessons in the Jail.   Miriam Waddington.   MoCV

Walk on again walk on.   *Unknown.*   ChinPo, *tr. by* Yip Wai-lim

Walk on by how much you were undone.   Think Eight.   Todd Colby.   HeMarv

Walk on the Moon.   N. Scott Momaday.   CRP

Walk onto the dark stage dressed for a funeral.   Members of the Orchestra, The.   Kevin Hart.   NOBAu

Walk out into your country.   Who Shall Die.   James A., Jr. Randall.   BPo

Walk's end.   Martin Shea.   HA

Walk Softly.   *Unknown.*   TCAPo

Walk to the Eastern River Bank, A.   Kao Ch'i.   CoBLCP, *tr. by* Jonathan Chaves

Walk Together Children.   *Unknown.*   BPo; NAAAL

Walk up, walk up, my bonny boys.   R.H. Ellis.   FaBoWar   *Fr.* Ode to St Crispin's Day.

Walk warily! Remember, sister, we are.   Under Sedation.   Alec Derwent Hope.   BMAP

Walk with the Beautiful and with the Grand.   Beautiful, The.   E. H. Burrington.   TreFP

Walk with the sun.   Dream Song.   Lewis Alexander.   WHSW

Walked in his garden in the cool of the evening, waited. (LL)   Intimate Supper.   Peter Redgrove.   FaBoMo; OxBC

Walked with no one.   On the Sunny Side of the Street.   Dorothy Fields.   ReLy

Walken Hwomme at Night.   William Barnes.   NOBVV

Walker, The.   Arturo Giovannitti.   APT-1

Walker, a large two-hundred-fifty pound blackman.   Christmas 1962.   Paul Mariah.   GLP

Walker in Prague.   Vítězslav Nezval.   AF, *tr. by* Ewald Osers

Walker, It Is Your Footsteps.   Antonio Machado Ruiz.   SpanPo, *tr. by* Kate Flores

Walkin' Around.   Pablo Neruda.   *See* Walking Around

Walkin down that long lonesome highway.   Ballad of Winky.   Merrill Markoe.   Unle

Walkin' My Baby Back Home.   Fred E. Ahlert.   ReLy

Walkin' the Dog.   Shelton Brooks.   ReLy

Walking.   Temporary City.   Nijole Miliauskaite.   VCWP, *tr. by* Jonas Zdanys

Walking. Thomas Traherne. EBEV

Walking a cliff with a lamb. Three Easters. Alberta Turner. LCAP-2

Walking against the Wind. Jon Stallworthy. OxBC

Walking alone in a multitude of loves when morning's light. Marriage of a Virgin, The. Dylan Thomas. ChIV-2

Walking along a river bank in an antiquated universe. Pulling in the Reins. Yoshimasu Gōzō. PFTM-2, tr. by Richard Arno

Walking along the Hudson. Donald Petersen. CoAP

Walking along the Sea of Galilee. "Dovid Knut." TCRP; TCRusP, tr. by John Glad

Walking among my own this windy morning. Spring Vacation, The. Derek Mahon. PNI

Walking Around. Pablo Neruda. PoetW, tr. by W. S. Merwin

Walking Around. Pablo Neruda. TCLAP, tr. by Ben Belitt

Walking Around. Pablo Neruda. RaBo; SPE
    (It happens that I am tired of being a man.) VCWP, tr. by W. S. Merwin
    (It just so happens that I'm tired of being a man.) PFTM-1
    (Walkin' Around.) PFTM-1

Walking around in the park. Toads Revisited. Philip Larkin. NOBL; OxAEP-2

Walking around, wasting time. (LL) Issa. EH; NIL-7, tr. by Robert Hass

Walking at last by the tame little edge of the sea. Evening before Rain. Leonard Alfred George Strong. OxBTC

Walking at leisure we watch laurel flowers falling. Walking at Leisure. Wang Wei. TAL

Walking at Night. Philip Salom. BMAP

Walking at Night. Brian Swann. PoCoUp

Walking at night on asphalt campus. Death News. Allen Ginsberg. BB

Walking beside the Kamogawa, Remembering Nansen and Fudo and Gary's Poem. Philip Whalen. BB

Walking Buddha. Barbara Guest. FTOS

Walking by map, I chose unwonted ground. On the Hall at Stowey. Charles Tomlinson. PoE

Walking by the Cliffside Dyeworks. Robert Carnevale. UnSA

Walking by the river, the morning cold. River Walk. John Stuart Williams. AngWePo

Walking by the waters. In my country. Jackie Kay. MFPA; NeBl

Walking down Jalan Thamrin. Robert Francis Brissenden. CBAP

Walking down the Road. Adrienne Rich. NIL-7; NIP-4

Walking early morning light. Jojopan. Art Goodtimes. GeoH

Walking eight hundred. Removal: Last Part. Carroll Arnett. VoR

Walking Fields at Night South of Hampton, Iowa. Steve Gehrke. AmPoNex

Walking home from school one afternoon. Walking Home. Gjertrud Schnackenberg. WeW-3

Walking in a Meadowe Greene. Unknown. BoLoP

Walking in a Swamp. David Wagoner. HAP

Walking in gardens by the sides. Walking in Gardens. Dylan Thomas. OBGa

Walking in the Country outside T'ai-yüan on a Spring Day. Yang Chi. CoBLCP, tr. by Jonathan Chaves

Walking in the Countryside. Wang An-shih. SuSp, tr. by Jan W. Walls

Walking inland, inland, inland. Oxaitoq's Song. Inuit Oral Tradition. ErotSp, tr. by Sam Hamill

Walking into the shadows, walking alone. Lee in the Mountains. Donald Davidson. CBCWP; FuPo

Walking Late. John Montague. CIP-2

Walking-Mort, The. Djuna Barnes. APT-1

Walking north toward the point, I come on a dead seal. Dead Seal [near McClure's Beach], The. Robert Bly. NNaP

Walking often beside the waves' Coleridge. Ronald Stuart Thomas. TOF

Walking on dishes. Buson. SoOfWa, tr. by Sam Hamill

Walking on Water. James Dickey. ChIV-2

Walking out in the late March midnight. Thorn Leaves in March. W. S. Merwin. TwCP

Walking out of the "big E." Before the Stuff Comes Down. Gary Snyder. HeIP-4

Walking Outside the City Walls on the Day of the Cold Food Festival. Pien Kung. CoBLCP, tr. by Jonathan Chaves

Walking Parker Home. Bob Kaufman. NAAAL

Walking Past Paul Blackburn's Apt. on 7th St. Diane Wakoski. TAP

Walking past the Ritz a girl may be sitting on the last step crying. Part of the Effect of the Public Scene Is to Importune the Passing Viewer. Erin Belieu. AmPoNex

Walking Road, The. Richard Hughes. OBMV

Walking south down Broadway. February Ice Years. Melinda Goodman. WiU

Walking swiftly with a dreadful duchess. Infelice. Stevie Smith. LW

Walking the Baby to the Liquor Store. Michael Van Walleghen. IllVoic

Walking the Dog. John Wright. BloBone

Walking the earth in all the changing. Late Summer. Ruth L. Schwartz. AmPoNex

Walking the heaved cement sidewalk down Main Street. Fog-Talk. Philip Booth. BodElec

Walking the Places I've Never Been. Yury [or Iurii] Arabov. TCRP, tr. by John High and Katya Olmsted

Walking the Plateau. Lupenga Mphande. NAfrP

Walking the snow-crust. Anita Virgil. HA

Walking the suburbs in the afternoon. Suburban Dreams. Edwin Muir. OxBTC

Walking the Wide Road. Unknown. CoBCP, tr. by Burton Watson

Walking this field I remember. Premonition, The. Theodore Roethke. HarvBoo

Walking this winter beach alone. Token. Alison Bielski. AngWePo

Walking through a Wall. Louis Jenkins. RaBo

Walking through twisted hollow pathways. Peter Blue Cloud. VoR

Walking through wet wheat an ocean of mercury after. Iain Sinclair. Oth Fr. Ebbing of Kraft, The.

Walking to Bellrock. Michael Ondaatje. NOBC

Walking to-day by a cottage I shed tears. Scazons. Clive Staples Lewis. EBEV

Walking to my room from the park. Weeping, The. Jack Hirschman. BodElec

Walking to Sleep. Richard Wilbur. VCAP

Walking to the Museum. Bone Thoughts on a Dry Day: Chicago. George Starbuck. TwCP

Walking to the Temple of Precious Light. Wen Cheng-ming. CoBLCP, tr. by Jonathan Chaves

Walking to your place for a love feast. Same Inside, The. Anna Swirszczynska. BLT

Walking towards the village. Elaine Randell. Oth Fr. Snoad Hill Poems, The.

Walking up the driftwood beach at day's end. Flood Year. Judith Wright. NoAM

Walking West. William Stafford. RB

Walking westward. So'oku. JDP, tr. by Yoel Hoffmann

Walking westward / you have it all before you. Christian Karlson Stead. PeNZ Fr. Walking Westward.

Walking, when the Lake of the Air is Blue with Spring. J. S. Harry. BMAP

Walking with God. William Cowper. ECEV; NOCV; NOEC; PeECV; SCGP; TOF Fr. Olney Hymns.

Walking with the God. Gwyneth Lewis. HarvBoo

Walking with the river. Bob Boldman. HA

Walking with you and another lady. Dream of Jealousy, A. Seamus Heaney. NoP-4

Walking Wounded. Vernon Scannell. OBWP

Walkways, The. John Ashbery. BodElec

Wall, A. Charles Simic. HCAP

Wall, The. Witter Bynner. APT-1

Wall, The. William Hawkins. MoCV

Wall, The. Zbigniew Herbert. AF, tr. by John Carpenter

Wall, The. Ismail. OMIP, tr. by V. Narayana Rao

Wall, The. Donald Justice. CRP

Wall, The. Eve Merriam. TaR; TrJP

Wall Calendar. Dan Pagis. VCWP, tr. by Tsipi Keller

Wall, Cave, and Pillar Statements, after Asôka. Alan Dugan. CoAP

Wall continues, The. Before the Actual Cold. Ray A. Young Bear. VoR

Wall-Flower, The. Henrik Arnold Thaulov Wergeland. AWP, tr. by Sir Edmund William Gosse

Wall, no! I can't tell whar he lives. Jim Bludso of the Prairie Belle. John Milton Hay. APN-2

Wall of Dreams (2). Ahmed Taha. NAfrP, tr. by Clarissa C. Burt

Wall of Tomorrow, The. Orkhan Muyassar. MAP, tr. by Samuel Hazo and Lena Jayyusi

Wall of Weeping, The. Edmond Fleg. TrJP, tr. by Humbert Wolfe

Wall of woodland overlooks me, A. Unknown. NOIV, tr. by Thomas Kinsella Fr. Four Glosses.

Wallace Stevens says Money is a kind of poetry. So I offer to trade him Tennes-. Money. Bob Perelman. FTOS

Wallace Stevens, what's he done? Rouse for Stevens, A. Theodore Roethke. OBAL

Walled Garden. Dorothy Wellesley, Duchess of Wellington. OBGa

Wallet, a rawhide goatskin, a cane, A. Leonidas. GrAn; PGA

Wallet stolen, so we must end our stay. Note of Thanks, A. Wyatt Prunty. RA

Wallet, the hide of a goat, tough and untanned, a stick, A. Leonidas of Tarentum. HePo Fr. Epigrams.

Walloping Window-Blind, The.   Charles Edward Carryl.   NBLV; OBCA   *Fr.* Davy and the Goblin.

Wallowing in all kind of sin.   Michael Wigglesworth.   ColAP   *Fr.* Day of Doom, The.

Wallowing in this bloody sty.   Drunken Fisherman, The.   Robert Lowell. ChIV-2; NOBA; OxBA; VGW

Wallpaper.   Julia Alvarez.   BodElec

Walls.   Constantine P. Cavafy.   TrJP, *tr.* by Rae Dalven

Walls, The.   Douglas Goetsch.   AmPoNex

Walls are made of rain, The.   The city's walls.   Cant.   Imamu Amiri Baraka. NAAL-2v2

Walls Do Not Fall, The.   "H. D.".   NAAL-2v2
    "Amen."   WPoS
    "Evil was active in the land."   HarvBoo; NAAL-5
    "In me (the worm) clearly."   APT-1
    "Let us, however, recover the Sceptre."   HarvBoo
    "Now my right hand."   APT-1; NAAL-5
    "O heart, small urn."   APT-1
    "O, Sire, is this the path?"   NAAL-5
    "Or anywhere."   NAAL-5
    "Presence was spectrum-blue, The."   APT-1
    "Sirius:"   NAAL-5
    "Splintered the crystal of identity."   NAAL-5
    "Still the walls do not fall."   NAAL-5
    "Take me home."   APT-1; NAAL-5
    "There is a spell, for instance."   APT-1
    "We have seen how the most amiable."   BoWoP
    "When in the company of the gods."   APT-1
    "Yet we, the latter-day twice-born."   APT-1

Walls Do Not Fall, The.   "H. D.".
    "In no wise is the pillar-of-fire."   WPoS

Walls have been shaded for so many years, The.   Soldier Walks under the Trees of the University, The.   Randall Jarrell.   OxBA

Walls of the garden, the first light, The. (LL)   Map of the Western Part of the County of Essex in England, A.   Denise Levertov.   CoAP; NAAL-2v2

Walls of the maelstrom are painted with trees, The.   Poem.   Charles Madge. SPE

Walls, sun and moon dials, home from home. (LL)   West, The.   Michael Longley.   BiHa; PBCIP

Walls surrounding them they never saw, The.   Wall, The.   Donald Justice. CRP

Walls were the colour, The.   Last Link, The.   Iris Clayton.   IBA

Walls. . . iridescent with eyes.   Fifth-Floor Window, The.   Lola Ridge.   APT-1; WPE

Walnut, A.   Mother Goose.   LB; OxNR; ReMoGo

Walnut and Lily.   Douglas Oliver.   Oth

Walnut, peach and plum—hacked down. (LL)   Thoreau.   Timothy Liu. AmPoNex; GifTon; OPRER

Walnut Tree, The.   David McCord.   OBCA

Walrus and the Carpenter, The.   Lewis Carroll.   CABP; ChAP; ITBLP; NAEL-5v2; NAEL-6v2; NOBL; NOBVV; NoAM; OBSP; OTCP; OxAEP-2; PeLV; PoRA; TFi   *Fr.* Through the Looking-Glass.

Walrus stretches forth a wrinkled hand, The.   Kingfisher's Boxing Gloves, The. James Fenton.   NoAM

Walrus Tusk from Alaska, A.   Alfred Corn.   MakPoe

Walsingham; or, the Pupil of Nature.   Mary Robinson.   RWP

Walsingham[e].   *Unknown, sometimes at. to* Sir Walter Ralegh.   *See* As You Came from the Holy Land [of Walsingham]

Walt.   Ted Hughes.   NoP-4

Walt Whitman.   Edward Dahlberg.   APT-2

Walt Whitman.   Edwin Honig.   TAP

Walt Whitman.   Edwin Arlington Robinson.   APN-2; NCAP; OxBA; TCAPo

Walt Whitman, a kosmos, of Manhattan the son.   Walt Whitman.   ColAP; NAWM-7v2; NoP-4; SAmP; SCV   *Fr.* Song of Myself.

Walt Whitman, an American, one of the roughs, a kosmos.   Walt Whitman. CAGL   *Fr.* Song of Myself.

Walt Whitman at Bear Mountain.   Louis Simpson.   CoAmPo; TRP

Walter de la Mare Tells the Listener about Jack and Jill.   Louis Untermeyer. MoAmPo   *Fr.* Mother Goose Up-to-Date.

Walter Lesly.   *Unknown.*   ESPB

Walter Parmer.   Greg Williamson.   RA

Walter Savage Landor.   Dorothy Parker.   APT-1; NALW   *Fr.* Pig's-Eye View of Literature, A.

Waltz.   Dame Edith Sitwell.   BWW

Waltz, The.   Byron.

Waltz against the Mountains.   Thomas Hornsby Ferril.   APT-2; VGW

Waltz for Debby.   Gene Lees.   ReLy

Waltz of the Twenty-Year-Olds, The.   Louis Aragon.   FaBoWar, *tr.* by Malcolm Cowley and Rolfe Humphries

Waltz Poem of Those in Love and Inseparable Forever.   Miguel Hernández. AF, *tr.* by Timothy Baland

Waltzing Matilda.   Andrew Barton Paterson.   CBAP

Waly, Waly [Love Be Bonny].   *Unknown.*   EnLoPo; HAP; NOSC; OBEV; OxBS; TFi
    (Forsaken Bride, The.)   GTBS-P
    (Jamie Douglas.)   ESPB
    (Lord Douglas.)   OxBB

Wan leafs shak' atour us like the snaw, The.   Hugh MacDiarmid.   NAEL-5v2; NAEL-6v2   *Fr.* Drunk Man Looks at the Thistle, A.

Wan / Swan.   Bereaved Swan, The.   Stevie Smith.   FaBoTw

Wanaka, mother of Clutha.   Shag, The.   Eileen Duggan.   PeNZ

Wanda's daddy was a railroadman, she was his little wife.   Wanda's Blues. Jane Cooper.   SeSe

Wander, estranged in body, not in mind. (LL)   To S.C.   Robert Louis Stevenson.   NePenScot; PeVV

Wander, my troubled soul, sigh mid the night thy pain.   Elegy.   Anne Batten Cristall.   RWP

Wander our thoughts above the dark abyss. (LL)   Henry Wadsworth Longfellow.   PWR; TCAPo

Wander through the house in the wee hours.   Moonlight.   Kim Caldwell. ReEnLa

Wanderer, The.   W. H. Auden.   HarvBoo; NoAM; RB; WeW-3; WoPoe
    (Chorus.)   GTBS-P

Wanderer, The.   Christopher John Brennan.
    "When window-lamps had dwindled, then I rose."   CBAP

Wanderer, The.   "Andrey Platonov."   TCRP, *tr.* by Albert C. Todd

Wanderer, The.   Roland Robinson.
    "I reached that waterhole, its mud designed."   CBAP

Wanderer, The.   Stevie Smith.   NALW

Wanderer, The.   *Unknown.*   AnOE; NAWM-5v1, *tr.* by Charles William Kennedy and Charles W. Kennedy

Wanderer, The.   *Unknown.*   WoPoe, *tr.* by Michael Alexander

Wanderer, The.   William Wordsworth.   *Fr.* Excursion, The.

Wanderer, The.   "Yehoash."   TrJP, *tr.* by Isidore Goldstick

Wanderer and the Seafarer, The.   *Unknown.*
    Two Seabirds.   WoPoe, *tr.* by John Updike

Wanderer in the Night of the World, A.   N.V.M. Gonzalez.   ReBoTo

Wanderer's Bouquet.   So Chong-Ju.   WoPoe, *tr.* by David R. McCann

Wanderer's Night Song.   Goethe.   WoPoe, *tr.* by Peter Viereck

Wanderer's Night-Songs.   Goethe.
    "O'er all the hill-tops."   AWP, *tr.* by Robert Bly
    Second Poem the Night-Walker Wrote, The.   AWP, *tr.* by Robert Bly

Wanderer's Song, A.   John Masefield.   MoBrPo

Wanderer, The: A Rococo Study.   William Carlos Williams.
    Paterson—the Strike.   TCAPo

Wanderer was in love with the spring of the year, The.   Song of Woe.   Shen Yüeh.   SuSp, *tr.* by Richard B. Mather

Wanderers, The.   Robert Browning.   OBEV   *Fr.* Paracelsus.

Wanderers, The.   Robert Williams Buchanan.   OxBSo

Wanderers, wanderers we are.   Emigrant Song.   "S. Ansky."   TrJP, *tr.* by Joseph Leftwich

Wandering.   Muso Soseki.   EaWin, *tr.* by W. S. Merwin

Wandering above a sea of glass.   Down on My Luck.   Arthur Rex Dugard Fairburn.   PeNZ

Wandering amid the horrors of the night.   Written When the Mind Was Oppressed.   Anne Batten Cristall.   RWP

Wandering beside rivers, I remember my home.   By Yangtze and Han.   Tu Fu. CrYelRi, *tr.* by Sam Hamill

Wandering by the heave of the town park, wondering.   On the Closing of Millom Ironworks.   Norman Nicholson.   FaBoTw

Wandering Curves.   Keith Waldrop.   PmAP

Wandering Gentleman, The.   *Unknown.*   SuSp, *tr.* by Ronald C. Miao

Wandering has been my way.   Poem for My Brother Returning to My Farm. Tu Fu.   CrYelRi, *tr.* by Sam Hamill

Wandering, in autumn, the woods of boyhood.   Gold Glade.   Robert Penn Warren.   CRP; TRP

Wandering in the still of eve.   Song.   Anne Batten Cristall.   RWP

Wandering Islands, The.   Alec Derwent Hope.   HarvBoo

Wandering Jew, The.   Eloise Bibb.   CBWP-4

Wandering Jew, The.   Robert Mezey.   TaR

Wandering Jew once met a man, A.   Eternal Jew, The.   Jacob Cohen.   TrJP, *tr.* by I. M. Lask

Wandering late by morning seas.   Shelley's Vision.   Herman Melville.   APN-2

Wandering oversea dreamer.   Prayer after World War.   Carl Sandburg.   VGW

Wandering through cold streets tangled like old string. Brussels in Winter. W. H. Auden. OxBTC

Wandering traveler anxious to make the crossing, A. Crossing the Hsiang River at Night. Meng Hao Jan. SuSp, tr. by Daniel Bryant

Wandering tribe called the Siouxs, A. Prevalent Poetry. Charles Follen Adams. PeLi

Wanderings of Oisin, The. W. B. Yeats.
Old Man Stirs the Fire to a Blaze, An. RB

Wanderings on a Heavenly Body. László Kálnoky. IQMS, tr. by Kenneth McRobbie and Zita McRobbie

Wang Chao-chün. Li Shang-yin. SuSp, tr. by Irving Y. Lo

Wang Chao-chün. Tai Shu-lun. SuSp, tr. by William H. Nienhauser

Wangsun, The. Wang Yen-Shou. ChiP, tr. by Arthur Waley

Waning August Moon. Roberta Hill. ReEnLa

Waning Moon, The. Shelley. FHYEP; OxBSP
(Moon, The.) FaBoCh; OBEV

Waning of the Harvest Moon, The. John Wieners. PmAP

Wanna Be White. Charmaine Papertalk-Green. IBA

Wanna hear something really funny? Woman like Me, A. Eileen Myles. GLP

Want of %&$ Want of —+. Anne Szumigalski. FaBoWP

Want of You, The. Ivan Leonard Wright. SoSe-8

Want, predation, sleep. Mary Kinzie. FFC

Want quickens wit: Want's pupils needs must work. Theocritus. AWP; OBVE, tr. by Charles Stuart Calverley Fr. Idylls.

Wanted. Josiah Gilbert Holland. ITBLP; SacPr

Wanted. Mercedes Roffé. TANSG, tr. by Kathryn Kopple

Wanted, wanted: Dolores Haze. Vladimir Vladimirovich Nabokov. APT-2 Fr. Lolita.

Wanting a Mummy. Sandra McPherson. LCAP-2

Wanting a myth for blowing up the gods. Collective Invention, The. Chris Wallace-Crabbe. BMAP

Wanting children a couple once sat. Limerick. G. W. Hanney. PeLi

Wanting Out. Gavin Ewart. SPE

Wanting To. Jan G. Elburg. TuT, tr. by Peter Van de Kamp

Wanting to Die. Anne Sexton. CoAmPo; ColAP; NoAM; TAP; TRP; VCAP

Wanting to say things. My Father's Song. Simon J. Ortiz. HATNAP; NIL-7

Wanting to swim in touch with soft-mouthed life. (LL) Guttural Muse, The. Seamus Heaney. HarvBoo; NOIV

Wanting to welcome the emperor. Wang Chien. SuSp Fr. Palace Poems.

Wanting You. Terra Hunter. PasH

Wanton. Silabhattarika.
("My husband is the same man who first pierced me.") BoWoP, tr. by Willis Barnstone

Wanton troopers riding by, The. Andrew Marvell. BASC; ESCV; GeHe; HeIP-4; NAEL-5v1; NAEL-6v1; NAEL-7v1; RACG

Wanton Wife of Bath, The. Unknown.
"In Bath a wanton wife did dwell." PBRV

Wanton with long delay the gay spring leaping cometh. April, 1885. Robert Bridges. OxBSP; OxBTC

Wanton young lady of Wimley, A. Limerick. Unknown. PeLi

Wants. Philip Larkin. GTBS-P

Wants my son. White Lady. Lucille Clifton. ESEAA

Wants of Man, The. John Quincy Adams. APN-1; OBAL

Wants to be finished waiting in the car. He ate his pear. Alcoholic's Son at Ten, The. Kathleen Peirce. PBCAP

Wapiti, The. Ogden Nash. TLR

War. André Breton. AF, tr. by Mary Ann Caws

War. Michael Brownstein. FTOS

War. Ebenezer Elliott. FaBoWar

War. Miguel Hernández. AF; RaBo

War. Georg Heym. PeFWW, tr. by Patrick Bridgwater

War. Max Jacob. AF, tr. by Michael Brownstein

War. Patrice Kayo. PBMAP

War. Joseph Langland. AiP

War. Lorine Niedecker. FTOS

War. "Georgy [or Georgii] Avdeievich Rayevsky." [or Raevskii]. TCRP, tr. by Albert C. Todd

War. Andrey [or Andrei] Andreievich Voznesensky [or Voznesenskii]. RB, tr. by Vera Dunham and William Jay Smith

War. Edgar Wallace. OBWP

War, A. Randall Jarrell. OxBSP

War, The. Frank O'Hara. BodElec

War (?) in the Desert, A. Unknown. PeSAV

War against the Trees, The. Stanley Kunitz. HAP; PAI

War against War in South Africa. W. T. Stead.
"Now that war is in the air, e'en the parson in his lair." FaBoWar

War and greed stop food. Poem. Hugh Seidman. BodElec

War and Hell. Ernest Crosby.
"Hail to the hero!" FaBoWar
"I am a great inventor, did you but know it." FaBoWar

War-and-Peace. George Buchanan. PNI

War Ballad. Andrey [or Andrei] Andreievich Voznesensky [or Voznesenskii]. WoPoe, tr. by Stanley Moss

War begets Poverty. Edward Fitzgerald. FaBoWar

War between England and the United States! Iterating Sonnet. Leigh Hunt. OxBSo

War Blinded. Douglas Dunn. DiPo; NePenScot; OBWP

War Books. Ivor Gurney. PeFWW

War broke out in autumn at the empty border, The. Yehuda Amichai [or Amikhai]. PoSu Fr. Patriotic Songs.

War canoes were ready. Thirsty Island. Jim Tollerud. VoR

War Cat. Dorothy Leigh Sayers. TriCat

War-chariots rumble. Song of the War-Chariots (Yueh-Fu). Tu Fu. ChinPo, tr. by Yip Wai-lim

War chief danced the old way, The. At the Klamath Berry Festival. William Stafford. InPK-6

War Comes. Zalman Schneour. TrJP, tr. by Joseph Leftwich

War Dance. Miidhu. NOBAu, tr. by George von Brandenstein

War Dance. Unknown. APN-2, tr. by George Catlin
Approaching Dance, The. APN-2
Eh-Ros-ka, the Warrior's Dance. APN-2
Ha-Kon-E-Crase, the Eagle Dance. APN-2
Wa-Sissica, the War Song. APN-2

War Games. Connie Bensley. FaBoWar

War Games. Walter McDonald. CDa

War God's Horse Song, The. Unknown. RB; TTTS, tr. by Louis Watchman

War Has Been Given a Bad Name. Bertolt Brecht. HP; PoSu

War Horse, The. Eavan Boland. BIrV; CIP-2; PBCIP

War in a Mousetrap. Velemir [or Viktor Vladimirovich] Khlebnikov.
"I, to make myself laugh louder and longer." TCRP

War in Fife, The. Sydney Goodsir Smith. NePenScot Fr. Armageddon in Albyn.

War in Spain has ended long ago / Aunt Rose, The. (LL) To Aunt Rose. Allen Ginsberg. CLPP; ColAP; NAAL-2v2; NoAM; PAI; PmAP; PoE; TaR; VGW

War in the Air, The. Howard Nemerov. ColAP; DiPo; VCAP

War is fought by soldiers in machines, The. Apology. Richard Cecil. BodElec

War Is Kind. Stephen Crane.
"Ah, God, the way your little finger moved." APN-2
Candid Man, The. MoAmPo
"Do not weep maiden, for war is kind." APN-2; FaBoWar; NAAL-2v2; NOBA; OBWP; RaBo; TCAPo
"Each small gleam was a voice." APN-2
"Fast rode the knight." NAAL-2v2
(From War is Kind.) NoP-4
"I explain the silvered passing of a ship at night." APN-2; TCAPo
"Little ink more or less!, A." APN-2
"Man said to the universe, A." APN-2; BRP; FaBoEE; NAAL-2v2; OBAL; OBSV; TAP; TCAPo; WeW-3
Newspaper, A. APN-2; NAAL-2v2
Slant of Sun [on Dull Brown Walls], A. NAAL-2v2
There Was a Man with a Tongue of Wood. MoAmPo
Wayfarer, The. APN-2; MoAmPo

War is kind. (LL) Stephen Crane. APN-2; FaBoWar; NAAL-2v2; NOBA; OBWP; RaBo; TCAPo Fr. War Is Kind.

War is no longer declared. Every Day. Ingeborg Bachmann. PoSu, tr. by Daniel Huws

War is not declared any more. Every Day. Ingeborg Bachmann. BoWoP, tr. by Christopher Middleton

War is the angry man waving his desperate. War-and-Peace. George Buchanan. PNI

War is the mistress of enormity. Joshua Sylvester. FaBoWar

War isn't on yet, though all the toys of battle are ready, The. Outdoor Chums in the Forest. Ann Townsend. ExTi

War Lament: "Autumn flowers." Unknown. CrYelRi, tr. by Sam Hamill

War Lament: "Every plant is burnt yellow." Unknown. CrYelRi, tr. by Sam Hamill

War Lord in the Early Evening. Patricia K. Page. NoAM

War Memento (Somewhere in France 1915). Roger Hecht. CRP

War Memories. Xenophanes. WoPoe, tr. by Theodore Blanchard

War Music. Christopher Logue.
"Battle swayed, The." FaBoWar
"Fate's sister, fortune, favours those." FaBoWar

"See how that royal fights." FaBoWar

War of the Roses, The. Michael Dransfield. BMAP

War of words is done, The. Battle. John Davidson. CABP

War on the Periphery. George Johnston. NOBC

War Photographers, The. Frank Ormsby. PNI

War-planes have been at it all day long. No Hands. Gillian Clarke. TCAWP

War pleased me to know of my interest, The. War, The. Frank O'Hara. BodElec

War Poem. Simon J. Ortiz. CDa

War Poem, A. Jennifer Allen. Unle

War Poet. Sidney Keyes. FaBoWar; NoP-4; PoWW

War Poetry. John Philips. NOEC Fr. Blenheim.

War separated, The. Friends, The. Bertolt Brecht. PoSu, tr. by Michael Hamburger

War ships, cold tides. Yün Shou-p'ing. CoBLCP Fr. Seeing off Mr. Yang on His Journey to Wu-wei Prefecture.

War shook the land where Levi dwelt. Field of Glory, The. Edwin Arlington Robinson. MoAmPo

War shows what each man's country is to him. Invasion. Eileen Duggan. PeNZ

War Song, A. Bertrans [or Bertran or Bertrand] de Born. See Song of Battle

War Song of Dinas Vawr, The. Thomas Love Peacock. AWP; CABP; FaBoCh; FaBoWar; HAP; NAEL-5v2; NAEL-6v2; NOBE; NOBRP; NPeEn; OxAEP-2 Fr. Misfortunes of Elphin, The.

War Song of the Basotho, A. Unknown. PeSAV, tr. by Daniel P. Kunene

War Song of the Saracens. James Elroy Flecker. MoBrPo Fr. Hassan.

War Songs. Unknown. APN-2, tr. by Henry Rowe Schoolcraft

War Songs. Unknown. APN-2, tr. by Alfred Longley Riggs

War Stories. Perry Oldham. CDa

War Story. Gerald McCarthy.
   Med Building. CDa

War Story. Jon Stallworthy. OxBC

War the Source of Riches. Unknown. NOBRP

War-Time. William Robert Rodgers. OxBSP

War to end them all, The. Firebell for Peace. Joyce Lee. NOBAu

War Walking Near. Ray A. Young Bear. CDW

War was her life, with want and the wild air. Yorkshire Wife's Saga. Ruth Pitter. NALW

Warbler sings, The. Basho. SoOfWa, tr. by Sam Hamill

Warblers are today as long ago, The. Murasaki Shikibu. WoPoe, tr. by Edward Seidensticker Fr. Tale of Genji, The.

Ward 6. Tanure Ojaide. HBAPE

Ward X. Lola Ridge.
   "Salvation Army lass, The." WPE

Ward, and still in bonds, one day, A. Regeneration. Henry Vaughan. BASC; ChIV-1; ESCV; FSCP; GeHe; MeLP; NAEL-5v1; NAEL-6v1; NAEL-7v1; NoP-4; PoE

Ward has no heart, they say, I deny it. On J. W. Ward. Samuel Rogers. FaBoEE

Ward Two. Francis Webb. CBAP

Wardance. Phillip [or "Phil"] William George. VoR

Wardance Soup. Phillip [or "Phil"] William George. VoR

Warden Said to Me the Other Day, The. Etheridge Knight. LTA; NBV; PBCAP; SoSe-8

Wardour Street. Humbert Wolfe. OxBTC

Wardrobe, a mirror, a chair, A. Entresol. Jaime Sabines. TCLAP, tr. by Claudine-Marie D'Angelo

Wardrobes. Nicolette Golding. Prnts

Ware Collection of Glass Flowers and Fruit, Harvard Museum, The. Mark Doty. HarvBoo

Warehouse-theatre's. Martin Shea. HA

Warheads of mushrooms round the filter-pond. (LL) Geoffrey Hill. NoAM; PoE Fr. Apology for the Revival of Christian Architecture in England, An.

Warhol at Wetlands. John Kinsella. NeBl

Waring. Robert Browning. NPeEn

Warlike Angels, The. Rafael Alberti. AF, tr. by Geoffrey Connell

Warm and friendly and without challenge. (LL) How to Watch Your Brother Die. Michael Lassell. CAGL; GLP; WiU

Warm ashes of the word, The. Cuncta Semper. Rodolfo Di Biasio. NeIt, tr. by Stephen Sartarelli

Warm country of the horizons, The. (LL) African Poem. Agostinho Neto. PBMAP; PoetW, tr. by W. S. Merwin

Warm day for November, and we, A. Towards Sunset at Camino Cielo. Maurina Sherman. GeoHom

Warm hands, warm. Unknown. LB

Warm Invitation, A. Yüan Chiu-ts'ai. WoPoe, tr. by Henry Hart

Warm night fallen night. Condemned. Philippe Soupault. AF, tr. by Eden Paul

Warm night of Mozambique. Let My People Go. Noémia da Sousa. HAWP, tr. by Jacques-Noël Gouat

Warm plantains and chilled light radishes. Rogers in Italy. Frank O'Hara. FTOS

Warm rain and pure wind, The. Alone in the Night. Li Ch'ing-chao. OHPC, tr. by Kenneth Rexroth

Warm rain before dawn. Ruth Yarrow. HA

Warm rain, sunny wind start to break the chill. Li Ch'ing-chao. BoWoP

Warm rains and gentle winds. Butterflies Love Flowers. Li Ch'ing-chao. ErotSp, tr. by Sam Hamill

Warm rosebuds below, The. (LL) World-Soul, The. Ralph Waldo Emerson. APN-1; NCAP

Warm shone the sun, the wind as warmly blew. Hay-Time; or, The Constant Lovers. A Pastoral. Josiah Relph. NOEC

Warm slipperiness of us in the car's backseat. Door Thrown Open to Daisies. Rick Agran. AmPoNex

Warm sun is failing, the bleak wind is wailing, The. Autumn: A Dirge. Shelley. TreFP

Warm to the Cuddly-toy Charm of a Koala Bear. Gavin Ewart. EmeKit

Warm walnut seats crisscross braces. Powwow remnants. Lew Blockcolski. VoR

Warm winds crossed from the eastern coast, The. Boss's Wife, The. Unknown. CBAP

Warmer. Martha Collins. UrbNat

Warmest welcome, at an inn, The. (LL) Written at [or in] an Inn at Henley. William Shenstone. AWP; NOBE; NOEC; OBEV; OxAEP-1; OxBEV

Warming Her Pearls. Carol Ann Duffy. MakPoe; NePenScot; NoP-4; PoBW

Warming up. Morning Sun. Francisco Alarcon. OxIBACP

Warmness. Anabel Torres. TANSG, tr. by Celeste Kostopulos-Cooperman

Warmth of cows, The. Carol, A. Donald Hall. ChrPo

Warmth of the wind-break wall, The. Louise Herlin. MFP, tr. by Martin Sorrell

Warning. Text and Commentary. Elke Erb. PFTM-2, tr. by Roderick Iverson

Warning. Langston Hughes. BPo

Warning. Jenny Joseph. FaBoWP; OxBTC

Warning. Tadeusz Rózewicz. PoSu, tr. by Magnus F. Krynski

Warning. Nikolai Alekseievich Zabolotsky [or Zabolotskii]. TCRusP, tr. by Daniel Weissbort

Warning, A. Grace Paley. TaR

Warning, A. Coventry Patmore. EnLoPo

Warning, A. Unknown. OxNR

Warning, The. Adelaide Crapsey. APT-1; Spl; TCAPo; WPE (Cinquain: A Warning.) WeW-3

Warning, The. Robert Creeley. NeAP; TAP; VGW

Warning, The. Henry Wadsworth Longfellow. APN-1; ChIV-1; NCAP; TCAPo

Warning against the Gypsies, A. John Langhorne. ECEV Fr. Country Justice, The.

Warning: Augmented. Langston Hughes. APT-2

Warning of Winter. Mary Ursula Bethell. FaBoWP; PeNZ

Warning to America, A. Philip Freneau. TAP

Warning to Children. Robert Graves. FaBoCh; NOxBChV; NPeEn; NoP-4; OxBEV

Warning to One. Merrill Moore. MoAmPo

Warning to Travailers Seeking Accomodations at Mr. Devills Inn. Sarah Kemble Knight. SCAP

Warning to Young Bright Sisters / White A.M. Culture 101A. Michelle T. Clinton. InTrad

Warnings. Nicanor Parra. AF, tr. by Miller Williams

Warping bandstand reminds you of the hard rage, The. Return to La Plata, Missouri. Jim Barnes. HATNAP

Warr'st thou 'gainst Athens? William Shakespeare. EBEV Fr. Timon of Athens.

Warring sighs and groans I'll wage thee. (LL) Ae Fond Kiss. Robert Burns. NAEL-5v2; NAEL-6v2; NePenScot; OBEV

Warrior. Frank Mkalawile Chipasula. PeSAV

Warrior Nation Trilogy. Lance Henson. VoR

Warrior so bold and a virgin so bright. Alonzo the Brave and the Fair Imogine. Matthew Gregory Lewis. NOBRP

Warrior! whose image on thy tomb. Effigies, The. Felicia Dorothea Hemans. NOBRP

Warriors. Douglas Dunn. OxBC

Warriors and chiefs! should the shaft or the sword. Song of Saul before His Last Battle. Byron. ChIV-1

Warru. Jack Davis. BMAP

Wars, The. Howard Moss. VCAP

Wars of Imperialism. John Foulcher. NOBAu

Warsong of the Kwakiutl. Unknown. APN-2, tr. by Franz Boas Fr. Songs of the Kwakiutl Indians.

Wartburg, 1521–22, The.   Timothy Steele.   RA

Wartime Dawn, A.   David Gascoyne.   NPeEn

Warum sind denn die Rosen so blass.   Heinrich Heine.   AWP, *tr. by* Richard Garnett

Wary of time O it seizes the soul tonight.   Easter Eve.   Muriel Rukeyser. VGW

Was a bird; and the song was wordless; the singing will never be done. (LL) Everyone Sang.   Siegfried Sassoon.   GTBS-P; MoBrPo; NAEL-5v2; NAEL-6v2; NOBE; NPeEn; NoAM; NoP-4; OBEV; OBWP; OPOU; OxBSP; OxBTC; TrJP

Was almost eighteen years old.   Herbie.   David Alpaugh.   OPRER

Was, at all hazards, to try to copy the Celt! (LL)   Cult of the Celtic, The. Anthony C. Deane.   NOBL; PeLV

Was balanced on the edge of the platform.   Diver, The.   Christopher Merrill. MoASP

Was banging the doors of the shed in the yard. (LL)   Esyllt.   Glyn Jones. AngWePo; OBWVE

Was broken. / He bade a warrior abandon his horse.   Battle of Maldon, The. *Unknown.*   AnOE

Was dirt.   Floor, The.   Yolanda Palis.   ReBoTo

Was Elizabeth Siddal in a bath.   Ophelia.   Christopher Pilling.   NLP

Was Ever Heart Like Mine?   Edward Taylor.   OxBA; SacPr   *Fr.* Preparatory Meditations before My Approach to the Lord's Supper.

Was faithful unto death, and shamed the Devil. (LL)   Lying.   Richard Wilbur. DiPo; HCAP; MakPoe; PeVV

Was for 300 or maybe 400 years. (LL)   Toe'osh; a Laguna Coyote Story. Leslie Marmon Silko.   CDW; NoAM; VoR

Was *From Charybdis into Scylla.* (LL)   Hag and the Slavies, The.   Jean de La Fontaine.   AWP; OBVE, *tr. by* Edward Marsh

Was hardly a Titan. He stood.   Hyperion.   Leslie Norris.   TCAWP

Was he a mining on the flat.   He Done His Level Best.   "Mark Twain."   AiP

Was he English, or French?   Dead Turk, A.   Li Kuang-t'ien.   WoPoe, *tr. by* Kai-yu Hsu

Was He Married?   Stevie Smith.   NoAM

Was heaven sent. (LL)   Little Lyric (of Great Importance).   Langston Hughes. APT-2; NBLV; OBAL; OBCoV

Was here before us, knew we would come, and sees beyond us. (LL)   Adrienne Rich.   NAAL-2v2; NALW; NoAM   *Fr.* Twenty-one Love Poems.

Was I no more than some fairy being.   Last Poem: Goodbye to My Garden. Yuan Mei.   GifTon, *tr. by* Jerome P. Seaton

Was I wrong when I thought.   Thought on June 26.   Raymond Mazisi Kunene. PBMAP

Was, Is, and Yet-To-Be.   Ella Wheeler Wilcox.   PoToHe

Was it a blast to the balls dear brother.   Black Poet Leaps to His Death, A. Etheridge Knight.   BodElec

Was it a dream, or did I see it plain.   Edmund Spenser.   NIP-4; OxBSo   *Fr.* Amoretti.

Was it a dream? We sailed, I thought we sailed.   Matthew Arnold.   GTBS-P *Fr.* Switzerland.

Was it a mountain wavering on the rim.   Hagar.   Rosanna Warren.   ExTi

Was it a phoney coin that let.   Back End of the Horse, The.   Paul Groves. TCAWP

Was it a vision, or a waking dream?   I heard her voice before I saw.   Irish for No, The.   Ciaran Carson.   PNI

Was it because you'd wear.   "To an Amiable Child."   Babette Deutsch. APT-2

Was it D + 10 or D + 12 we caught.   Frank Ormsby.   PNI   *Fr.* Northern Spring, A.

Was it for this.   William Wordsworth.   NPeEn; RB   *Fr.* Prelude, The; Growth of a Poet's Mind [1805 vers.].

Was it for this I uttered prayers.   Grown-up.   Edna St. Vincent Millay. NoAM; PAI

Was it I making plans.   Octavio Paz.   PoetW, *tr. by* Eliot Weinberger   *Fr.* Sunstone.

Was it in Tahiti?   I Remember You.   Johnny Mercer.   ReLy

Was It Not Curious?   Stevie Smith.   OxBEV

Was it perhaps in an imagined frame.   Vision.   Delmira Agustini.   TCLAP, *tr. by* Karl Kirchwey

Was it really you all the time?   Dream Sequence, Part 9.   Naomi Long Madgett.   BPo

Was it some sweet device of faery land.   Charles Lamb.   CenSon

Was it something uncleaved, clean-cut you wanted?   There's No Rigor Like the Old Rigor 2.   Ira Sadoff.   BodElec

Was it the proud full sail[e] of his great verse.   William Shakespeare.   CABP; NoSic; OxAEP-1; SCGP; Son   *Fr.* Sonnets.

Was it wind off the dumps.   Summer Home.   Seamus Heaney.   PBCIP

Was it yesterday.   Haiku.   Sonia Sanchez.   FFC

Was Jesus Chaste? or did he.   William Blake.   ChIV-2   *Fr.* Everlasting Gospel, The.

Was Jesus Humble? or did he.   William Blake.   ChIV-2   *Fr.* Everlasting Gospel, The.

Was just that I was leaving home and my folks were growing old. (LL) Christmas at Sea.   Robert Louis Stevenson.   ChrPo; EBVV; NePenScot; PeVV

Was left all alone / Fa, le, la, la, lal, de. (LL)   Aristotle's Story.   Mother Goose. OxNR; ReMoGo

Was lout, son of lout, by old lout, and was da to a lout! (LL)   Blue Blood. James Stephens.   MoBrPo; OBCoV; OBMV

Was made for him, to tyrannize upon. (LL)   Hunting of the Hare, The. Margaret Lucas Cavendish, Duchess of Newcastle.   BASC; BWW; FaBoVe; NAEL-7v1; NOSC

Was made steward in king Henerys hall. (LL)   Sir Aldingar.   *Unknown.* ESPB; OxBB

Was made the Lady of the May. (LL)   *Var. authors.*   NoSic; OBEV; TTTS   *Fr.* Honourable Entertainment Given to the Queen's Majesty in Progress at Elvetham, 1591, The.

Was Nature always a snob.   Miami Beach.   Howard Moss.   BodElec

Was Nature angry when she formed my clay?   On Viewing Herself in a Glass. Elizabeth Teft.   ECWP

Was never in Scotland hard nor sene.   *Unknown.*   OxBS

Was nevir in Scotland hard nor sene.   *Unknown.*   *See* Was never in Scotland hard nor sene

Was no more than his due who brought good news from Ghent. (LL)   Robert Browning.   EBNV; FHYEP; NAEL-5v2; NAEL-6v2; OBSP; PeVV; UV

Was not the lost dauphin, though handsome was only.   Robert Penn Warren. APT-2; NAAL-5   *Fr.* Audubon: A Vision.

Was nothing else but secret love. (LL)   Secret Love.   John Clare.   FHYEP; PoE; SCGP

Was one that kept his word. (LL)   Because I liked you better.   A. E. Housman. CAGL; NOBVV; NPeEn; OxBEV; OxBTC; PeVV

Was only an etiquette, a habit of speech not spoken.   House Style, The. Elizabeth Macklin.   KGB

Was Physiognomy. (LL)   Emily Dickinson.   NAAL-2v1; NAAL-3; NALW

Was quenched by death, and broken the bruised reed. (LL)   Keats.   Henry Wadsworth Longfellow.   SonP; TAP

Was sitting by the shed. (LL)   Jenny Wren.   Mother Goose.   OxNR; ReMoGo

Was startled there. (LL)   Raiders' Dawn.   Alun Lewis.   AngWePo; NPeEn

Was taken and carried to Canada. (LL)   Bar[']s Fight[, August 28, 1746]. Lucy Terry.   BPo; BlSi

Was that sticky infusion, that rank flavor of blood, that poetry, by which I lived? (LL)   Bear, The.   Galway Kinnell.   CoAP; MakPoe; NNaP; TAP; TRP; VCAP; VGW

Was That the Human Thing to Do?   Joe Young.   ReLy

Was that the year the water froze.   History of My Father's House, The.   Vona Groarke.   MFPA

Was that young faithful heart! (LL)   Casabianca.   Felicia Dorothea Hemans. BRP; NAEL-6v2; NOBRP; NPeEn; RWP; VWP; ViWPN

Was the arrangement made between the two couples legal?   Some Litanies. Michael Benedikt.   CoAP; TwCP

Was the ethereal kind which did not stop. (LL)   Wadasa Nakamoon, Vietnam Memorial.   Ray A. Young Bear.   CDa; HATNAP

Was the forgetful kingdom of death. (LL)   Janet Waking.   John Crowe Ransom.   APT-1; ColAP; FuPo; InPK-6; MoAmPo; NAAL-2v2; NoAM; PoE; RB; TAP

Was the mist becoming rain. (LL)   Lost Heifer, The.   Austin Clarke.   BIrV; ModIr; WoPoe

Was the one he kept sailing home to? (LL)   Odysseus.   W. S. Merwin. NOBA; NoP-4

Was the only thing I had. (LL)   Homecoming.   Langston Hughes.   SAmP; TRP

Was the silkiest day of the young year.   Day He Died, The.   Ted Hughes. OxAEP-2

Was there another Troy for her to burn? (LL)   No Second Troy.   W. B. Yeats. EnLoPo; GTBS-P; HarvBoo; NAEL-5v2; NAEL-6v2; NOBE; NoAM; OxAEP-2; OxBTC; TFi; WeW-3

Was this His coming! I had hoped to see.   Ave Maria, Gratia Plena.   Oscar Wilde.   ChIV-2

Was this the face that launched a thousand ships?   Christopher Marlowe. EBEV   *Fr.* Doctor Faustus.

Was this the thing Van Horne set out / To conquer? (LL)   Edwin John Pratt. MoCV; NOBC   *Fr.* Towards the Last Spike.

Was this Thy Passover.   Christopher.   Sydney E. Jerrold.   SacPr

Was told the mystic name of Love. (LL)   Natura Naturans.   Arthur Hugh Clough.   HAP; NOBVV

Was, 'Wae to my sister, fair Ellen' (LL)   Twa Sisters, The.   *Unknown.* ESPB; OxBS

Was wrapped like *panettone* in Italian tinfoil. (LL)   Sailing Home from Rapallo. Robert Lowell.   HCAP; PoPoPo; PoetW; TAP

Was you at de hall las' night. Leap Yeah Party, De. Maggie Pogue Johnson. CBWP-4

Wash man out of the earth, shear off. Wash. Eiléan Ní Chuilleanáin. BIrV; WPOW

Wash me in the water. *Unknown.* OBCoV *Fr.* Soldiers' Songs of the First World War.

Wash of surf guitar rolls, A. Teenage Interplanetary Vixens Run Wild on Bikini Beach. Allison Joseph. NAPBL

Wash over her, wet light. Woman Death. Hazel Hall. APT-1

Wash the dishes, wipe the dishes. Mother Goose. OxNR

Washday Battles. Geoffrey Summerfield. NOxBChV

Washed ashore. Repulse Bay. Marilyn Chin. OpBo

Washed by the rain, dust and grime are laid;. Starting Early from the Ch'u-ch'êng Inn. Po Chü-i. ChiP; OBVE, *tr. by* Arthur Waley

Washerwoman. Velemir [*or* Viktor Vladimirovich] Khlebnikov.
"Tsar! Send out a shot!" TCRP
"We don't live in castles." TCRP
"Writers of the knife are we!" TCRP

Washerwoman, The. Mary Collier. ECWP; NOEC *Fr.* Woman's Labour; an Epistle to Mr. Stephen Duck, The.

Washerwoman, The. Mary Weston Fordham. CBWP-2

Washerwoman, The. Veronica Volkow. VCWP, *tr. by* Forrest Gander

Washerwoman is a member of the Salvation Army, The. Washerwoman. Carl Sandburg. IllVoic

Washing-Day. Anna Laetitia Barbauld. ECWP; PEW; WoRP

Washing hanging from the lemon tree, The. Five-Day Rain, The. Denise Levertov. NeAP

Washing hangs upon the line, A. Elizabeth Bishop. RB

Washing Kai in the sauna. Bath, The. Gary Snyder. NNaP; PmAP; TAP; VCAP

Washing machine was chuffing, The. Long after Heine. Gwen Harwood. HarvBoo

Washing Stream, The. Li Ch'ing-chao. ErotSp, *tr. by* Sam Hamill
(To the Tune: Sands of the Washing Stream.) CrYelRi

Washing the hoe. Buson. EH, *tr. by* Yoel Hoffmann

Washing the saucepans. Issa. EH, *tr. by* Robert Hass

Washing Your Hair. Lucia Cordell Getsi. IllVoic

Washington Etude. Elizabeth Alexander. NAPBL

Washington Heights, 1959. Michael C. Blumenthal. HCAP

Washington in Love. John Berryman. LCAP-2

Washington Park. Gerald Costanzo. UrbNat

Washington Square Park and a Game of Chess. Christopher Stanard. SpirFl

Washington, the brave, the wise, the good. Inscription at Mount Vernon. *Unknown.* HHAm

Washington was calm, murderous, neo-classical. After I Seized the Pentagon. Robert Hass. YaYoPo

Wasn't this a queer thing? I stood with your mother. Queer Thing, A. Nancy Keesing. NOBAu

Wasn't this the site, asked the historian. House and Land. Allen Curnow. PeNZ

Wasn't your mother a woman? Hennamma. BoWoP

Wasp Sex Myth (One). Anselm Hollo. PoM

Wasp Sex Myth (Two). Anselm Hollo. PoM

WASP Woman Visits a Black Junkie in Prison, A. Etheridge Knight. NBV

Wasps, The. Homer. OBVE, *tr. by* Alexander Pope *Fr.* Iliad, The.

Wasps' Nest, The. George MacBeth [*or* Macbeth]. OxBTC

Wassaile, The. Robert Herrick. PBRV

Wassailing Song. *Unknown.* OBCP

Waste. Harry Graham. OBCoV; UV

Waste Land, The. T. S. Eliot. APT-1; CABP; FaBoMo; HAP; MoAmPo; NAAL-2v2; NAAL-5; NAEL-5v2; NAEL-6v2; NAWM-7v2; NOBA; NOBE; NoAM; NoP-4; OxAEP-2; OxBA; OxBTC; PoE; TAP; TCAPo; TFi; UnPo

Death by Water. NPeEn; OBVE; OxBEV

Fire Sermon, The. HarvBoo

Game of Chess, A. HarvBoo; SCV

"When lovely woman stoops to folly and." UV

Waste Land Limericks. Wendy Cope. FaBoWP; HarvBoo

Waste remains, the waste remains and kills, The. (LL) Missing Dates. William Empson. HAP; HarvBoo; MakPoe; MoBrPo; NOBE; NPeEn; NoAM; OxBEV; PoE; UnPo

Wasted. Mary Elizabeth Coleridge. ViWPN

Wasted Day, A. Frances Darwin Cornford. MoBrPo

Wasted Day, The. Robert Fuller Murray. EBVV

Wasted Days. Oscar Wilde. CAGL

Wasted flow of water hiding, A. Lonely Woman. Jayne Cortez. NBV

Wasted years, the wasted years, The. Henry E. G. Rope. SacPr

Wasteland. Games at the Hour of the Desert. Manuela Fingueret. MirDau, *tr. by* Roberta Gordenstein

Wasting my breath to cry hooly and fairly! (LL) Hooly and Fairly. Joanna Baillie. RACG; WoRP

Wasting Time. Opal Palmer. FaBoVe

Wat a joyful news, Miss Mattie. Colonization in Reverse. Louise Bennett. OBCoV

Wat ye what my Minnie did. Robert Burns. EroLit

Watch. Amanda Dalton. NeBl *Fr.* Room of Leaves.

Watch. Giuseppe Ungaretti. FaBoWar, *tr. by* Patrick Creagh

Watch, The. Frances Darwin Cornford. InPK-6; MoBrPo; OxBTC

Watch, The. May Swenson. HAP

Watch a red setter stretch and sink in cloud. (LL) Broken Home, The. James Merrill. ColAP; HAP; HCAP; NAAL-2v2; NAAL-5; NOBA; NoAM; NoP-4; PoPoPo

Watch and the Dogs, The. Homer. OBVE, *tr. by* Alexander Pope *Fr.* Iliad, The.

Watch any day his nonchalant pauses, see. Watch Any Day. W. H. Auden. FaBoMo
(Free One, A.) OxAEP-2

Watch for a scorpion, my friend, under every stone. Praxilla. SaLy, *tr. by* Diane Rayor

Watch it. That's the body: what goes on. Body, The. William Bronk. VGW

Watch it—you'll bump / Your heads. Issa. ZenPo, *tr. by* Takashi Ikemoto and Lucien Stryk

Watch long enough, and you will see the leaf. Conrad Potter Aiken. OxBA *Fr.* Preludes for Memnon; or, Preludes to Attitude.

Watch me rise and go. (LL) Piute Creek. Gary Snyder. CoAP; CoAmPo; NAAL-2v2; NOBA

Watch of Time. Magda Portal. TANSG, *tr. by* Shaun Griffin and Emma Sepúlveda-Pulvirenti

Watch over me from heaven while within my arms I hold my boy. Angelo [*or* Andrea] Poliziano. CAGL, *tr. by* James J. Wilhelm *Fr.* Greek Epigrams.

Watch people stop by bodies in funeral homes. On the Symbolic Consideration of Hands and the Significance of Death. Miller Williams. InPK-6

Watch the Lights Fade. Robinson Jeffers. NOBA

Watch these elders. They always come at night. These Too Are Our Elders. Jack A. Mapanje. HBAPE; NAfrP

Watch Your Step—I'm Drenched. Adrian Mitchell. RB

Watch Yourself Go By. Strickland W. Gillilan. PoToHe
(Cure for Fault Finding, A.) PWR

Watched by every human love. (LL) Lullaby: "Lay your sleeping head, my love." W. H. Auden. GLP; HAP; HarvBoo; NAEL-5v2; NAEL-6v2; NOBE; NoAM; NoP-4; OxAEP-2; OxBEV; OxBTC; PoE; TFi; UnPo; WeW-3

Watched with the cruel watching of the stars. In Her Prison. Sarah Morgan Bryan Piatt. NCAP

Watched you / & you were turning, turning. Journey, 1966. Anselm Hollo. PmAP

Watcher, The. James Stephens. MoBrPo; OBEV

Watcher, The. Clara Ann Thompson. CBWP-2

Watchers, The. William Stanley Braithwaite. NAAAL

Watchers, The. Charles Spear. PeNZ

Watches beside me in this windy place. (LL) Edna St. Vincent Millay. HAP; OxBSo

Watching a Cloud. Dannie Abse. OxBC

Watching a different sea. July. Marion Lomax. NeBl

Watching a Lonely Wild Goose at Nightfall. Hsiao Kang. CrYelRi, *tr. by* Sam Hamill

Watching a mallard, just beyond. At Present I Am Working as a Security Guard. Edison Dupree. OPRER

Watching a man vomit on the sidewalk. Play It Again, Salmonella. Jeffrey McDaniel. AmPoNex

Watching a thousand smiles. Discovery. Víctor Hernández Cruz. PueRic

Watching a Village Festival. Yang Wan-li. ColAnChi, *tr. by* Jonathan Chaves

Watching alone by the ancient city wall. Thinking of Lady Yang at Midnight. *Unknown.* WoPoe, *tr. by* Jean S. Grigsby

Watching Ants Play Soccer in Central Park. Anthony Piccione. UrbNat

Watching baseball. Baseball Canto. Lawrence Ferlinghetti. MoASP

Watching buzzards. Crazy Boys. Beverly McLoughland. HHAm

Watching for Dolphins. David Constantine. HarvBoo

Watching for the time of day. (LL) Clock-A-Clay. John Clare. EBEV; EBVV; NAEL-5v2; NAEL-6v2

Watching love stories on TV. Gay Love and the Movies. Ralph Pomeroy. CAGL

Watching Rushcutters' bright bayful of masts and coloured keels. Angels' Weather. Bruce Beaver. BMAP

Watching Salmon Jump. Simon J. Ortiz. CDW

Watching Shoah in a Hotel Room in America. Adam Zagajewski. VCWP, *tr. by* Renata Gorcyznski

Watching Television. Robert Bly. CoAP

Watching Tennis. John Heath-Stubbs. OxBSo; Son

Watching the Break of thy great day. (LL) Dawning, The. Henry Vaughan. GeHe; NOCV

Watching the Dance. James Merrill. NIL-7; NIP-4

Watching the dark my spirit rose in flood. Bach and the Sentry. Ivor Gurney. HarvBoo

Watching the Distances. Tu Fu. CrYelRi, *tr. by* Sam Hamill

Watching the famous eruption of the volcano on Heimaey, Iceland. Hans Magnus Enzensberger. PoSu *Fr.* Sinking of the Titanic, The.

Watching the Hearse. Charles Simic. BodElec

Watching the moon. Lady Izumi. HW, *tr. by* Mariko Aratani and Jane Hirshfield

Watching the moon. Lady Izumi. EnlH; WPoS

Watching the Moon with Thoughts of Far Away. Chang Chiu-ling. CoBCP, *tr. by* Burton Watson

Watching the Old Man Die. Arthur James Marshall Smith. MoCV

Watching the Reapers. Po Chü-i. ChiP, *tr. by* Arthur Waley

Watching the shied core. As Bad as a Mile. Philip Larkin. InPK-6; OxBC; OxBEV; OxBSP

Watching the Swinging. Li K'ai-hsien.

"Colorful frames are erected beside the Yellow River, The." CoBLCP; ColAnChi, *tr. by* Jonathan Chaves

Watching the Wheat. John Jones. AngWePo

Watching the Wheat-Reapers. Po Chü-i. SuSp, *tr. by* Irving Lo

Watching the world disappear as if on a journey of no return. (LL) Things I Didn't Know I Loved. Nazim Hikmet. AF; AmFaPo; VCWP

Watching this dawn's mnemonic of old dawning. Sestina in a Cantina. Malcolm Lowry. MoCV

Watching Trains. Joanna Fuhrman. AmPoNex

Watching, watching from the shore. Shipwreck. Rosalie Moore. YaYoPo

Watching You. Simon J. Ortiz. HATNAP

Watchmaker God. Robert Lowell. HCAP; InvLi; SoSe-8

Watchman, The. Charles Kingsley. EBVV

Watchman, The. Abraham Reisen. TrJP, *tr. by* Joseph Leftwich

Watchman, watchman on your height. Watchman, The. Abraham Reisen. TrJP, *tr. by* Joseph Leftwich

Watchman, What of the Night? Bible, *O.T.* AWP *Fr.* Isaiah.

"Watchman, what of the night?" Watchman, The. Charles Kingsley. EBVV

Watchman! What of the night? John Oxenham. SacPr

Water. Ralph Waldo Emerson. OxBSP

Water. Boat's Blueprint, The. Ian Hamilton Finlay. NePenScot

Water. Ted Hughes. OxBSP

Water. Philip Larkin. EmeKit; FaBoMo; OxBSP; PeECV

Water. Robert Lowell. HeIP-4; LCAP-2; NOBA; NoP-4; PoE

Water. Leslie Norris. AngWePo; OBWVE

Water. Gary Snyder. LCAP-2

Water. Ann Taylor. NOxBChV

Water, The. Irene James Napurrurla. IBA

Water and Fire. José Rizal. WoPoe, *tr. by* Nick Joaquín

Water and Light. Noah Blaustein. MoASP

Water and marble and that silentness. Venice. Arthur Symons. OxBSP

Water and nblod for thee I swete. *Unknown.* MiEL

Water and Wine. Friedrich von Logau. GePo, *tr. by* George C. Schoolfield

Water and Worship: An Open-Air Service on the Gatineau River. Margaret Avison. HAP

Water are we, you say, and yourselves fire. Water and Fire. José Rizal. WoPoe, *tr. by* Nick Joaquín

Water Babies, The. Charles Kingsley.
  Young and Old. EBEV; OxAEP-2

Water Below, The. Fleur Adcock. PAI

Water beneath the hills. Kangaroo, The. Pansy Rose Napaljarri. IBA

Water bird, asleep, A. Robun. JDP, *tr. by* Yoel Hoffmann

Water breaking in me like an anointing. (LL) Anointing, An. Thylias Moss. GT; ReTh

Water bubbles! Water bubbles! Rain Man. Drahomira Vandas. SurWo, *tr. by* Guy Ducornet

Water bug is drawing the shadows, The. Water Bug and the Shadows, The. *Unknown.* OBVE, *tr. by* Frances Densmore

Water: City Wildlife and Greenery. Alfred Corn. UrbNat

Water-clock marks dawn, The. Going to the Palace with a Friend at Dawn. Tu Fu. CrYelRi, *tr. by* Sam Hamill

Water closing, The. Together. Maxine W. Kumin. BoWoP

Water, cold, and sweet, and pure. Xenophanes. Louis Zukofsky. APT-2

Water colour country. Here the hills. Tasmania. Vivian Smith. NOBAu

Water-Colour of Venice, A. Lawrence Durrell. MoBrPo

Water country's reeds and rushes, night, covered with frost, The. Farewell to a Friend. Hsüeh T'ao. SuSp, *tr. by* Eric Johnson

Water-drawing rites. Basho. SoOfWa, *tr. by* Sam Hamill

Water Eased of Its Cliffs by Falling. Alberta Turner. LCAP-2

Water-fall, The. Henry Vaughan. *See* Waterfall [*or* Water-Fall], The

Water falls white on the white. Joni Mitchell. Joseph Hutchison. SwNoth

Water, first creature of the gods. Tea Poems. George Mackay Brown. OxBC

Water flooded everywhere. Rebirth. Catriona Stamp. BrRo

Water, for anguish of the solstice,—yea, Dante Gabriel Rossetti. *See* Water, for anguish of the solstice:—nay

Water, for anguish of the solstice:—nay. For A Venetian Pastoral By Giorgone (In the Louvre). Dante Gabriel Rossetti. GS

Water-Front Streets. Langston Hughes. SAmP

Water hollowed the stone, The. Wind and Water and Stone. Octavio Paz. TCLAP, *tr. by* Mark Strand

Water Images. Edith Jay Scovell.
  "So turbid though I am." HarvBoo
  "Stone you let fall in me will not resile, The." HarvBoo
  Stream, The. HarvBoo
  Tidal River, The. HarvBoo
  Well, The. HarvBoo

Water in a shallow container. Zuni Derivations. *Unknown.* STP, *tr. by* Dennis Tedlock

Water in my prison shatters in a prism, The. Trout, The. Daryl Hine. CoAP

Water is hard in the well, The. Roland Mathias. AngWePo *Fr.* Tide-Reach.

Water is Manhattan. Thursday. Víctor Hernández Cruz. PueRic

Water is practical. Mourning Pablo Neruda. Robert Bly. LCAP-2

Water is so clear and so calm, The. Fish Cove. Blaise Cendrars. BLT, *tr. by* Monique Chefdor

Water, is taught by thirst. Emily Dickinson. NCAP

Water Island. Howard Moss. CoAP; NoP-4

Water. / Lakes and rivers. He Na Tye Woman. Paula Gunn Allen. HW

Water-Lilies. John Clare. WoPoe

Water Lilies. Ralph J. Mills, Jr. IllVoic

Water-Lilies. Sara Teasdale. MoAmPo

Water lilies. John Wills. HA

Water lilies bloom on the Great River. Water Lilies Bloom. Emperor Wu of Liang. OHMPC, *tr. by* Kenneth Rexroth

Water lilies of summer are gone. They are no more, The. Autumn. Su Tung-p'o (Su Shih). OHPC, *tr. by* Kenneth Rexroth

Water-lilies on the meadow stream. Water-Lilies. John Clare. WoPoe

Water lily blooms, A. Lily, The. Vadim Sergeievich Shefner. TCRP, *tr. by* Albert C. Todd

Water Maid. Christopher Okigbo. PBMAP

Water-mill, A. Antipater of Thessalonica. GrAn, *tr. by* Alistair Elliot

Water: no matter how much, there is still not enough. Fountains in the Sea. Martin Sorescu. VCWP, *tr. by* Seamus Heaney and Joana Russell-Gebbett

Water of Tears, The. Francis Ponge. AF, *tr. by* Beth Archer

Water of the Flowery Mill (II), The. Jerome Rothenberg. FTOS

Water of the river goes fleeing from itself, The. Futile Flight, Futile Fugue. Dulce Maria Loynaz. TANSG, *tr. by* Alan West

Water on a slope. Man. Archana Varma. OMIP, *tr. by* Aruna Sitesh

Water Ouzel. William H. Matchett. CoAP

Water plunges to devour us. Travel Song. Hugo von Hofmannsthal. TrJP, *tr. by* Charles Wharton Stork

Water pools. John Wills. HA

Water pouring from clouds. *Unknown.* EaWin, *tr. by* J. Moussaieff Masson and W. S. Merwin

Water pours down in order to swallow us. Traveller's Song. Hugo von Hofmannsthal. WoPoe, *tr. by* Robert Bly

Water running past the rocks, small rocks and big rocks. Water, The. Irene James Napurrurla. IBA

Water's breath mingles with reflected mountains. Autumn Day, An—Leisurely Boating on West Lake. Lin Pu. SuSp, *tr. by* Jonathan Chaves

Water's Chant, The. Philip Levine. GeoHom

Water's flowing. Song. *Unknown.* STP, *tr. by* Jerome Rothenberg

Water / Skidding down platforms of stone. Waking on a Summer Morning. Mary Oliver. PoCoUp

Water smokes, the bulrushes, The. Dead Landscape. Attila József. WoPoe, *tr. by* Edwin Morgan

Water Song. Steve Crow. HATNAP

Water Song. Solomon ibn Gabirol. TrJP, *tr. by* Israel Abrahams

Water Song. Michael S. Weaver. ISC

Water Song, The. Glenna Luschei. GeoHom

Water spilled on level ground. Pao Chao. SuSp *Fr.* Weary Road, The.

Water still flows. Illegitimate Things. William Carlos Williams. MoAmPo

Water that can't be muddied, The. Clear Valley. Muso Soseki. EaWin, *tr. by* W. S. Merwin

Water the Horses at a Breach in the Great Wall. *Unknown.* ChinPo, *tr. by* Yip Wai-lim

Water travels a long shot. Water Song. Steve Crow. HATNAP

Water turned to wine, The. (LL) To the Water Nymphs, Drinking at the Fountain. Robert Herrick. BeJo; CaPo; NAEL-5v1; NAEL-6v1

Water turns a long way down over the raw stone, The The. You Are Happy. Margaret Atwood. TRP

Water under the Earth. Robert Bly. NNaP

Water understands / Civilization well, The. Water. Ralph Waldo Emerson. OxBSP

Water veins. Seiju. JDP, *tr. by* Yoel Hoffmann

Water was too cold for us, The. (LL) Water. Robert Lowell. HeIP-4; LCAP-2; NOBA; NoP-4; PoE

Water washed, the water rose, The. Fisherman, The. Goethe. STV, *tr. by* John Frederick Nims

Water, water I desire. Scar[e]-Fire, The. Robert Herrick. HAP

Water Wheel, The. Antonio Machado Ruiz. SpanPo, *tr. by* James Duffy

Water, White Cotton, and the Rich Man. Martín Espada. PueRic

Water Woman. Catherine Obianuju Acholonu. HAWP

Waterbird. May Swenson. NoP-4

Waterbird goes up, A. 5 Poems. Robert Gray. CBAP

Waterborne. Linda Gregerson. BAP-01

Waterbug running by the frogulp. Alan Pizzarelli. HA

Waterchew! Gregory Corso. VGW

Waterclock drips heavy. To the Tune "Song of the Plum Blossom at the River Town." Yang Shen. CoBLCP, *tr. by* Jonathan Chaves

Watercolor of Grantchester Meadows. Sylvia Plath. LCAP-2

Watered by the Strymon and great Hellespont. Antipater of Thessalonica. GrAn

Waterfall. Seamus Heaney. HeIP-4

Waterfall. Gareth Owen. Spl

Waterfall. Greg Williamson. RA

Waterfall, The. John Keble.
Lyra Innocentium. SacPr

Waterfall at Lu-shan. Li Po. CrYelRi, *tr. by* Sam Hamill

Waterfall [*or* Water-Fall], The. Henry Vaughan. AngWePo; ESCV; GeHe; MeLP; NAEL-5v1; NAEL-6v1; NAEL-7v1; NOBE; NOCV; NoP-4; NOSC; OBWVE; OxAEP-1; SacPr
(Water-fall, The.) FSCP; PBRV

Waterford. Medbh McGuckian. BiHa

Waterford crystal smuggled from the Republic into Paisley's turf. Christmas, Belfast. Robert Coles. BloBone

Waterfowl Descending. Sam Witt. NeAmPo

Waterfront Girls, The. Rufinus. GrAn, *tr. by* Alan Marshfield

Watergaw, The. Hugh MacDiarmid. FaBoVe; HarvBoo; NAEL-5v2; NAEL-6v2; NPeEn; NePenScot

Watering Horses at a Long Wall Hole. *Unknown.* ColAnChi, *tr. by* Anne Birrell

Watering place of the long-tailed stars, The. (LL) Burning Shewolf. Vasco [*or* Vasko] Popa. PFTM-2; VCWP, *tr. by* Charles Simic

Watering the New Lawn. Michael S. Smith. PasH

Waterlilies. Alexis Rotella. HA

Waterloo! Waterloo! Waterloo! dismal plain! Victor Hugo. WoPoe, *tr. by* Phillip Holland *Fr.* Expiation.

Watermelon. "Eduard Georgievich Bagritzky." [*or* Bagritsky]. TCRP, *tr. by* Vera Dunham

Watermelons. Charles Simic. OBAL; VCAP

Waters deep, the waters dark, The. Casting. Howard Nemerov. OxBSP

Waters from cold springs. Orchards in July. Zbigniew Machej. BLT

Waters of K'un-ming Pool recalled the achievements of Han times, The. Tu Fu. SuSp *Fr.* Autumn Thoughts.

Waters of Life, The. Humbert Wolfe. MoBrPo

Waters of Lung-t'ou, The. HSü Ling. ChiP, *tr. by* Arthur Waley

Waters of Waiapu, The. Paraire Henare Tomoana. PeNZ, *tr. by* Margaret Orbell

Waters rippled, gleamed and fell, The. At the Cascade. Henrietta Cordelia Ray. CBWP-3

Watershed, The. Alice Thompson Meynell. VWP

Waterside Village. Yün Shou-p'ing. CoBLCP, *tr. by* Jonathan Chaves

Waterwheels in. Ian Hamilton Finlay. KaS

Waterwings. Cathy Song. NoAM

Watery waste the sinful world has grown, A. Judah Halevi. SWaP, *tr. by* Emma Lazarus *Fr.* On the Voyage to Jerusalem.

Watt's dream was the cream of steam engines. Limerick. Bill Greenwell. PeLi

Watteau, a Dream. Emile Nelligan. WoPoe, *tr. by* David Rattray

Watteau was slightly silly to equip. L'Embarquement pour Cythère. John Streeter Manifold. CBAP

Waulking Song: Two. Minnie Bruce Pratt. GLP

Wave. Gregory Orfalea. GraLe

Wave, The. Witter Bynner. APT-1

Wave, The. Fatima Lim-Wilson. AmPoNex

Wave blossoms for my delight, a thousand sheets of snow. Tune: The Fisherman. Li Yü. CoBCP, *tr. by* Burton Watson

Wave of coldness, A. Akiko Yosano. WPOW

Wave over him, and whisper as they wave. (LL) Charlotte Smith. PEW; WPE *Fr.* Beachy Head.

Wave-Won. Emily Pauline Johnson. SWaP

Waved a tanned hand after me. (LL) Walking along the Sea of Galilee. "Dovid Knut." TCRP; TCRusP, *tr. by* John Glad

Wavelength. Jane Holland. NeBl

Wavelets like rippling trees. Painting, *"Mist and Rain on the Spring River,"* by Hsiao Chao, The. Tai Piao-yüan. CoBLCP, *tr. by* Jonathan Chaves

Wavering. Denise Levertov. PmAP

Wavering blue floor. Campagna. John Peck. HarvBoo

Waverley. Sir Walter Scott.
Hie Away, Hie Away. OxAEP-2

Waverly Pen, The. *Unknown.* OBCoV *Fr.* Advertising Rhymes.

Wavers, a candle's shadow, at the end. (LL) Legal Fiction. William Empson. FaBoMo; HarvBoo; NoAM; NoP-4

Waves. *Unknown.* ArPe, *tr. by* Omar S. Pound

Waves bluster up the bay and through the throat. Family Photograph 1939, A. James Keir Baxter. OxBC

Waves claw, The. On The Beach. John Corben. Spl

Waves come—the large fourth wave, The. On the Oregon Coast. Robert Bly. BodElec

Waves forever move, The. Sisters, The. John Banister Tabb. APN-2

Waves know rocks by foam and recklessness, The. Merl. Jean Toomer. GT

Waves, like ridges of plow'd land, are high, The. Sea Similized to Meadows and Pastures: the Mariners, to Shepherds: the Mast, to a May-Pole: the Fish, to Beasts, The. Margaret Lucas Cavendish, Duchess of Newcastle. NoP-4

Waves now fall short, The. O. Mabson Southard. HA

Waves of brooding. (LL) My Arkansas. Maya Angelou. BlSi; NAAAL

Waves surge higher still, The. Elegy: Ise Lamenting the Death of Empress Onshi. Lady Ise. BoWoP, *tr. by* Etsuko Terasaki

Waves, the rough surf, swept me on the shore, The. Antipater of Thessalonica. GrAn

Waves the short two-by-four. Painting Drunken Twilight. George Barlow. GT

Waves want / to be wheels. Surf. Lillian Morrison. NTCP

Waves wash off the peach blossoms. To the Tune "Heavenly Immortal." Yang Shen. CoBLCP, *tr. by* Jonathan Chaves

Waves which have kept me from reaching you, The. (LL) To the Harbormaster. Frank O'Hara. CRP; CoAP; NAAL-2v2; PoM; VCAP

Waving a Bough. Boris Leonidovich Pasternak. TrJP, *tr. by* Babette Deutsch

Waving a gaudy flag it loves and curses. (LL) Desertmartin. Tom Paulin. CIP-2; ModIr; NPeEn; PBCIP; PNI

Waving Adieu, Adieu, Adieu. Wallace Stevens. NoP-4

Waving Her Farewell. Train Station, Vienna XV, 1939. Lisa Ress. GotH

Waving of the Corn, The. Sidney Lanier. APN-2

Wawking of the Fauld, The. Allan Ramsay. OxBS; SCGP *Fr.* Gentle Shepherd, The.

Wax-contoured, in your face a Muse. Philodemus. GrAn

Wax-white. Thompson's Lunch Room—Grand Central Station. Amy Lowell. APT-1

Waxes and wanes. (LL) Lunar Baedeker. Mina Loy. APT-1; VGW

Waxing Poetic on Marvin. Gordon Chambers. InTrad

Waxwings. Robert Francis. APT-2; BLT; LCAP-2; RaBo

Waxwings. Milton Kessler. InvLad

Way, The. Catherine Obianuju Acholonu. NAfrP

Way, The. Robert Creeley. BoLoP; NeAP

Way a crow, The. Dust of Snow. Robert Frost. APT-1; ChAP; OxBA; OxBSP; PAI; SAmP; SoSe-8; TAP; UnPo; WeW-3

Way a Ghost Dissolves, The. Richard Hugo. NAAL-2v2; NoAM; NoP-4

Way a tired Chippewa woman, The. Hush. David St. John. LCAP-2

Way a woman keeps her house, The. Gliding toward the Lamps. Matthew Rohrer. NeAmPo

Way all girl dogs talk French you'd think we, The. Cosmo Dog. Terese Svoboda. Unle

Way April Leads to Autumn, The. Lynne Yamaguchi Fletcher. FSt

Way as "Way" bespoke is no true lasting way; The. Lao Tzu. WoPoe, *tr. by* Moss Roberts *Fr.* Tao Te Ching.

"Way back in eighty-two or three." Dreadful Fate of Naughty Nate, The. John Kendrick Bangs. OBCA

Way down, The. Philip Levine. NOBA

Way down, The. Jay Macpherson.
"Long desired, the dead return." NOBC
They Return. NOBC

Way down, The. Ernest Sandeen. CRP

Way down among Brazilians. Coffee Song (They've Got an Awful Lot of Coffee in Brazil), The. Bob Hilliard. ReLy

Way down Geneva. Red Boots On. Kit Wright. PeLV

Way down Souf whar de lillies grow. To See Ol' Booker T. Maggie Pogue Johnson. CBWP-4

Way down South in Dixie. Song for a Dark Girl. Langston Hughes. NAAAL; NAAL-2v2; NAAL-5; NoP-4; SAmP

Way down upon the Swanee River [or de] Swanee River [or ribber]. Old Folks at Home[, The]. Stephen Collins Foster. APN-2

Way down Yonder in New Orleans. Henry Creamer. ReLy

Way enchased with glass and beads, A. Temple, The. Robert Herrick. CaPo

Way feare with thy projectes, noe false fyre, A. William Alabaster. ESCV Fr. Divine Meditations.

Way her silky garments undulate, The. Charles Baudelaire. SxFrPo, tr. by James McGowan

Way home is close, The. Tune: "Song of the Southern Country." Li Hsün. SuSp, tr. by Edward Schafer

Way I hear it, Chinese fortune cookies, The. Fortune Cookie Blues. Amy Uyematsu. LTA

Way I hear tell Aunt Jennie, The. Caledonia. Colleen J. McElroy. BlSi; NAAAL

Way I must enter, The. Lady Izumi. WPoS

Way I read a Letter's—this, The. Emily Dickinson. WPE

Way is long and dreary, The. Pilgrims, The. Adelaide Anne Procter. SacPr

Way is still clear, as if in dream, The. In the Year Chi-hai (1299), After Returning by Way of Purple Fungus Mountain at Springmouth, I Lamented for Lecture Master Chin. Tai Piao-yüan. CoBLCP, tr. by Jonathan Chaves

Way It Must Be, The. Enrique Molina. TCLAP, tr. by Naomi Lindstrom

Way It Was, The. Lucille Clifton. WPE

Way Lorene and I went back, The. Need Increasing Itself by Rounds. Kathleen Peirce. PBCAP

Way love rests upon coincidence, The. On Leaving the Artists' Colony. Bruce Bawer. RA

Way of Being, A. Barbara Guest. FTOS

Way of Geometry, The. Choice. David Bromige. FTOS

Way of It, The. Ella Wheeler Wilcox. LW

Way of Life, A. Howard Nemerov. NIL-7; NIP-4

Way of Tet, The. Bruce Weigl. AF

Way of the Water, The. Johanna Kruit. TuT, tr. by Peter Van de Kamp

Way of the Water-Hyacinth. Zawgee. AmFaPo, tr. by Lyn Aye

Way of the World, The. William Congreve. NAEL-5v1; NAEL-6v1

Way of the world as it is, The. Alone at Night. Kwon P'il. GifTon, tr. by Sung-Il Lee

Way on back in the reign of Mrs. Duke. Drawing Hands. Greg Williamson. AmPoNex

Way Out, The. Jeni Couzyn. HAWP

Way out is through fire, The. Way Out, The. Jeni Couzyn. HAWP

Way Out of the Wood, The. Thomas Bolt.
"I crossed." YaYoPo

Way Out West. Imamu Amiri Baraka. NeAP

Way's been lost for a thousand years, The. T'ao Ch'ien [or T'ao Yuan-ming]. CoBCP Fr. Drinking Wine.

Way's not for the blind. Tozan-Gyoso. ZenPo, tr. by Takashi Ikemoto and Lucien Stryk

Way sailors sing, The. Nothing of All That. Jan G. Elburg. TuT, tr. by Pat Boran

Way she played the piano, The. October 23, 1983. June Jordan. SeSe

Way the ball, The. Jump Shooter, The. Dennis Trudell. MoASP

Way the Bird Sat, The. Ray A. Young Bear. CDW; VoR

Way the Cards Fall, The. Yusef Komunyakaa. GT

Way the incense gripped, The. Father of My Father. Lawson Fusao Inada. UnSA

Way the water goes is blink blink blink, The. Intruder in a Set Scene. Norman MacCaig. NePenScot

Way the world is not, The. Sonnet. Bill Knott. PBCAP

Way the world works is like this, The. Advice to a First Cousin. Alberto Ríos. NAAL-5; NIL-7

Way they do, the. Loo-wit. Wendy Rose. HATNAP

Way they wait there, The. Rubbish Bags. Victor Vroomkoning. TuT, tr. by Dennis O'Driscoll

Way things move sometimes, The. If You Need a Reason. Silvia Curbelo. BodElec

Way through, The. Denise Levertov. NeAP; PoM

Way through the Woods, The. Rudyard Kipling. ChAP; FaBoCh; HarvBoo; NOBE; NOxBChV; NoAM; OBEV; OxAEP-2; OxBTC; SCGP; WHSW; WoPoe

Way to Do It, The. Mary Mapes Dodge. SWaP

Way to good is never late', The. (LL) Robert Greene. CTC; NoSic; SCGP Fr. Never Too Late.

Way to hump a cow is not, The. E. E. Cummings. NOBA; NoAM; OxBA

Way to Love God, A. Robert Penn Warren. NAAL-2v2

Way to Make a Living, A. James Wright (1927–80). NNaP

Way to the River, The. W. S. Merwin. CoAP

Way to the Temple, The. Wang Wei. CrYelRi, tr. by Sam Hamill

Way was long, the wind was cold, The. Sir Walter Scott. OxAEP-2 Fr. Lay of the Last Minstrel, The.

Way We Were, The. Alan Bergman. ReLy

Way You Look Tonight, The. Dorothy Fields. ReLy

Way you move, The. Futile Poem, A. Remco Campert. TuT, tr. by Theo Dorgan

Way you see it first is through, The. Secret Garden, The. Eleanor Wilner. GifTon

Wayfarer, The. Stephen Crane. APN-2; MoAmPo Fr. War Is Kind.

Wayfarers, The. Yusuf Al-Khal. MAP; PFTM-2, tr. by Sargon Boulus and Samuel Hazo

Wayfarers in the Wilderness. Alexander R. Thompson. AH

Wayle whit as whalles bon, A. Unknown. MiEL

Wayman in Love. Tom Wayman. NIL-7; NIP-4; NOBC

Wayne's College of Beauty, Santa Cruz. David Swanger. GeoHom

Ways, The. Louis Zukofsky. PoE

Ways and whims. DDD. Bruce Andrews. FTOS

Ways of heaven are mysterious, The. Lament. T'ao Ch'ien [or T'ao Yuan-ming]. CrYelRi, tr. by Sam Hamill

Ways off, someone is singing as he walks, A. Fantasie Metropolitan. Janet Holmes. ExTi

Ways we will make love. (LL) Farewell to a Southern Melody, A. Huang O [or Huang Ho]. BoWoP; WoPoe, tr. by Chung Ling and Kenneth Rexroth

Wayside Station, The. Edwin Muir. FaBoTw

Wayward Son, The. Mrs. Henry Linden. CBWP-4

Wayworn: wide sleepless eyes. A night scene enters. Hearing a Startled Bird during Stayover at Chin-Ch'ang Pavilion. Li Shang-yin. ChinPo, tr. by Yip Wai-lim

Wayzgoose, The. Roy Campbell.
"Attend my fable if your ears be clean." OBSV; PeSAV

Wazir Dandan for Prince Sharkan, The. Unknown. AWP Fr. Thousand and One Nights, The.

W.C. Fields in French Light. Rochelle Owens.
"It is for me poetry." PFTM-2

W.C.W. Watching Presley's Second Appearance on The Ed Sullivan Show: Mercy Hospital, Newark, 1956. David Wojahn. AllShUp; SwNoth

Wdn't it be silly to be serious, now. A. R. Ammons. BAP-97 Fr. Strip.

We. Vladimir Timofeievich Kirillov. TCRP, tr. by Albert C. Todd

We. Juliana Spahr.
"Story goes like this: the light, The." NAPBL

We accept no givens: from here on illusion. Furious Clarity, A. Gabriel Zaid. TCLAP, tr. by George McWhirter

We advance! (LL) Dark Symphony. Melvin B. Tolson. ColAP; NAAAL; SSLK

We ain't got nowheres to run to. (LL) Warden Said to Me the Other Day, The. Etheridge Knight. LTA; NBV; PBCAP; SoSe-8

We all assume that Oscar said it. (LL) Dorothy Parker. APT-1; NALW Fr. Pig's-Eye View of Literature, A.

We All Conspire. Mario Benedetti. TCLAP, tr. by Sophie Cabot Black and Maria Negroni

We all expected to see you lame. Pain. Dionisio D. Martinez. OPRER

We all fall down. (LL) Mother Goose. LB; OxNR; ReMoGo

We all go to the bones. Wenberi's Song. Wenberi. CBAP, tr. by A. W. Howitt

We all heard the alarm. The planes were out. Second Dream, The. Jean Valentine. LCAP-2

We all know that things look strange in the night. Stranger. They look. Never-Dead, The. Anna Couani. BMAP

We all know why you have come back home with no. Making Our Clowns Martyrs. Jack A. Mapanje. HBAPE; NAfrP

We all look on with anxious eyes. When Father Carves the Duck. Ernest Vincent Wright. NTCP

We all loved our comrade although he'd done wrong. (LL) Cowboy's Lament, The. Unknown. APN-2; ChAP; FaBoA

We all place a great deal of reliance. Limerick. Unknown. PeLi

We all scream, most of us inside. Screamer Discusses Methods of Screaming, A. James Schevill. TAP

We all sit around and watch him. (LL)   Jimmy Jet and His TV Set.   Shel [or Shelley] Silverstein.   OBCA; OBCoV

We all slept soundly that night.   In the Dresden Gallery.   Yevgeny [or Evgenii] Mikhailovich Vinokurov.   TCRP, tr. by Albert C. Todd

We all walked under God.   God.   Boris Abramovich Slutsky [or Slutskii].   TCRusP, tr. by Daniel Weissbort

We all were watching the quiz on television.   Singular Metamorphosis, A.   Howard Nemerov.   CoAmPo

We already and first of all discern him making this thing other.   David Jones.   PeECV   Fr. Anathemata, The.

We always had to do our work at night.   Before Action.   Leon Gellert.   CBAP

We anchor the boat alongside a hazy island.   Night on the Great River.   Meng Hao Jan.   OHMPC, tr. by Kenneth Rexroth

We and They.   Rudyard Kipling.   NoAM   Fr. Debits and Credits.

We approached the shore. Once more.   Oldest Place, The.   Thomas Kinsella.   PBCIP

We are a crystal zoo.   John Cotton.   NewEx

We are a garden wall'd around.   Church the Garden of Christ, The.   Isaac Watts.   NOCV; PeECV

We are a meadow where the bees hum.   Bedtime.   Denise Levertov.   TwCP

We are a multitude of contradictions.   From Fanon.   Sandra Maria Esteves.   PueRic

We Are a People.   Lance Henson.   VoR

We are a symphony of scissors.   Collage.   Shara McCallum.   NAPBL

We are all / bargaining with heaven.   Gustave Thibon, How Simone Weil Appeared to Me / 4.   Stephanie Strickland.   ExTi

We are all 44 at a fine point in this place.   5th Tuesday.   John Berryman.   BodElec

We are all friends who have lived our childhood.   Second Half of Our Lives, The.   Sarah Rosenblatt.   AmPoNex

We are all in the dumps.   Unknown.   OxNR

"We are all jugs," the potter said; and, when I smiled, he added: "You."   Earthen Jugs.   Gabriela Mistral.   SpanPo, tr. by Kate Flores

We are all mothers.   Liberation.   Abena Busia.   HAWP; PoetW

We are all near to death. But in my friends.   One Who Watches.   Siegfried Sassoon.   TrJP

We Are Americans Now, We Live in the Tundra.   Marilyn Chin.   FSt; NIL-7; OPRER; UnSA

We are apart; the city grows quiet between us.   At Night.   Sara Teasdale.   APT-1

We are approaching sleep: the chestnut blossoms in the mind.   Awakening.   Robert Bly.   CoAmPo

We are as.   Soldiers.   Giuseppe Ungaretti.   PFTM-1

We are as clouds that veil the midnight moon.   Mutability.   Shelley.   NAEL-5v2; NAEL-6v2

We are asleep. (LL)   Dead Still.   Andrey [or Andrei] Andreievich Voznesensky [or Voznesenskii].   BoLoP; PasH, tr. by Richard Wilbur

We are at a party that doesn't love us. Finally the party lets the mask.   Below Freezing.   Tomas Tranströmer.   VCWP, tr. by Robert Bly

We are becalmed in haze.   Copula.   John Cope.   GeoH

We are betrayed by what is false within. (LL)   George Meredith.   EnLoPo; NAEL-6v2; NOBE; OBEV; SCGP   Fr. Modern Love.

We are born with dreams in our hearts.   Immigrants in Our Own Land.   Jimmy Santiago Baca.   AF; UnSA

We are both different.   Enheduanna and Goethe.   Amal Al-Juburi.   PoArWo, tr. by Salih J. Altoma

We are both from the center of the continent.   Lakota Sister / Cherokee Mother.   Victoria Lena Manyarrows.   UnSA

We are breath of drop of rain.   Gods Wrote, The.   Keorapetse Kgositsile.   GT

We are building every day.   Building.   I. E. Dickenga.   PWR

We are buried somewhere near Narva.   Mistake, A.   Aleksandr Arkadevich Galich.   TCRP, tr. by Albert C. Todd

We are burning / in our heads.   Poet Recognizing the Echo of the Voice, A.   Diane Wakoski.   NIP-4

We are but warriors for the working-day.   William Shakespeare.   FaBoWar   Fr. King Henry V.

We are called.   Higashiyama Crematorium, November 6, 1983.   Lynne Yamaguchi Fletcher.   FSt

We are calm . . . And we do not regret.   Stendhal.   Sergey [or Sergei] Nikolaevich Markov.   TCRP, tr. by Lubov Yakovleva

We are children of the sun.   Children of the Sun.   Fenton Johnson.   TCAPo

We are continually bored with the air.   It's in the Egg.   Joe Rosenblatt.   NOBC

We are Diana's virgin-train.   On a Picture Painted by Herself [or Her self], Representing Two Nymphs [or Nimphs] of Diana's, One in a Posture to Hunt, the other Bath[e]ing.   Anne Killigrew.   BASC; NOSC

We are driven to odd attempts; once it would not have occurred to.   Adrienne Rich.   HCAP   Fr. Shooting Script.

We are driving to the interior. (LL)   Arrival at Santos.   Elizabeth Bishop.   FaBoWP; OxBC

We Are Easily Reduced.   HeidiLynn Nilsson.   NeAmPo

We are encircled by large grieving women.   Large Grieving Women.   Slavko Mihalic.   PoSu, tr. by Charles Simic

We Are Equals.   Gwendoline C. Konie.   HAWP

We are Eretrians from Euboia.   Plato.   GrAn   Fr. Two Poems on the Eretrians Taken Prisoner by the Persians.

We are finished, yet still.   My Country Weeps.   Andreas Gryphius.   WoPoe, tr. by John Peck

We are Fred Karno's army.   Unknown.   OBCoV   Fr. Soldiers' Songs of the First World War.

We are girls of differnt ages.   W. H. Auden.   UV   Fr. Dog beneath the Skin, The.

We Are Going.   Fanny Crosby.   SWaP

We Are Going.   Oodgeroo of the tribe Noonuccal (Kath Walker).   BMAP; CBAP; NOBAu

We are going down a long slide.   Shirley Kaufman.   BoWoP

We Are Going to Be Here Now.   Primus St. John.   GT

We are going to see the rabbit.   Alan Brownjohn.   NOxBChV

We Are Going to Shoot at the Heart.   Anna Swirszczynska.   PoSu

We are going, we are going.   We Are Going.   Fanny Crosby.   SWaP

We are growing old together, you and I.   Old Age.   Po Chü-i.   ChiP, tr. by Arthur Waley

We are hounds. We have always been hounds.   Odyssey, The.   Rick Bass.   Unle

We are huddled in a crowd before Kolpino.   Aleksandr Petrovich Mezhirov.   TCRP

We are in Louisiana now.   Exile's Letter (Or: An Essay on Assimilation).   Marilyn Chin.   OpBo

We are in love's land to-day.   Love at Sea.   Algernon Charles Swinburne.   AWP

We are in over your head.   Inside Job, An.   Brendan Galvin.   PoCoUp

We Are in the Fields.   Peter Finch.   AngWePo

We are learning to make fire. (LL)   Habitation.   Margaret Atwood.   BoWoP; FaBoWP; WeW-3

We are left, finally, to decide why.   Snow.   William Virgil Davis.   YaYoPo

We are like the dead.   What the Gypsy Said to Her Children.   Judith Ortiz Cofer.   OxWW; UnSA

We are made of newspaper and smoke.   Urban Poem.   Douglas Goetsch.   AmPoNex; UrbNat

We are making a good world, we are making a good day.   Prayer upon Cutting down the Sacred Tree.   Unknown.   APN-2, tr. by John G. Bourke

We Are Many.   Pablo Neruda.   VCWP, tr. by Alastair Reid

We are men of the new world a tree prompts us to harmony.   Joseph Miezan Bognini.   PBMAP   Fr. Herbe Féconde (1973).

We are near, Lord.   Tenebrae.   Paul Celan.   PoSu; VCWP

We are no other than a moving row.   68.   Edward Fitzgerald.   CABP

We are not.   Ernie Dingo.   IBA

We are not always dependent on memory.   Pavel Grigoryevich Antokolsky.   TCRusP, tr. by Bob Perelman and Shirley Rihner   Fr. Son.

We are not as small as we appear to be.   Bohol's Tarsier Population.   Clovis L. Nazareno.   ReBoTo

We are not near enough to love.   Insincere Wish Addressed to a Beggar, An.   Mary Elizabeth Coleridge.   NOBVV; NPeEn; PEW; VWP

We are nude beneath our costumes.   Metaphysical Paintings, The.   John Perreault.   SPE

We are old friends.   Hunger.   Charles Simic.   NNaP

We are on a primeval river in a reptilian den.   Further Adventures With You.   C. D. Wright.   LCAP-2

We Are on Our Journey Home.   Unknown.   AH

We Are Passing Away.   Matilda Caroline Edwards.   PWR

We are ravenous after our.   Pizza and Pretense.   Nerissa S. Balce.   ReBoTo

We are reading the story of our lives.   Story of Our Lives, The.   Mark Strand.   VCAP

We are sailing on a charming bay.   Tracey Herd.   NeBl   Fr. Mystery of the Missing Century, The.

We are satisfied, if you are; but why did I die? (LL)   Losses.   Randall Jarrell.   AmFaPo; HCAP; LCAP-2; OxBA; TAP; UnPo

We Are Seven.   William Wordsworth.   NAEL-5v2; NAEL-6v2; NOBRP
   "I met a little cottage Girl."   UV

We are sheepskin coats. Burrowing moles: born stupid.   Velemir [or Viktor Vladimirovich] Khlebnikov.   TCRusP, tr. by Kathy Lewis and Bob Perelman   Fr. Laundress, The.

We are sighing, for time is flying.   Class Song of '91.   Eloise Bibb.   CBWP-4

We are slowly / undermined.   Erosion.   Linda Pastan.   NIP-4

We are sorry to inform you.   In Answer to Your Query.   Naomi Lazard.   NBLV

We are standing facing each other.   Margaret Atwood.   PAI

We are standing under the wall. Our youth has been taken off like a.   Wall, The.   Zbigniew Herbert.   AF, tr. by John Carpenter

We are statues of ourselves, stiffened eulogies.　Robert Sheppard.　Oth　*Fr.* Empty Diaries / Twentieth Century Blues 24.

We Are Such Stuff as Dreams.　Petronius Arbiter.　AWP, *tr. by* Howard Mumford Jones

We are talking about the plane.　When They Know.　Ruth L. Schwartz.　AmPoNex

We are talking in bed. You show me snapshots.　Family Man, A.　Maxine W. Kumin.　TAP

We are ten.　My First Riot: Bronx, NYC.　Safiya Henderson-Holmes.　UnSA

We are ten miles from sea, in a parking lot.　Kendall Gulls.　Ricardo Pau-Llosa.　UrbNat

We are the Akhail. Our youth persists.　Laila Boasting.　Laila Akhyaliyya.　BoWoP, *tr. by* Willis Barnstone

We are the birds always charmed by you from the top of these / belvederes.　Postman Cheval.　André Breton.　SPE, *tr. by* David Gascoyne

We are the blues.　Funk Lore.　Imamu Amiri Baraka.　UnSA

We are the clan of willows.　Willow.　Elizabeth Delmore.　NLP

We are the darkness in the heat of the day.　Song.　Dame Edith Sitwell.　BWW

We are the desperate.　Vagabonds.　Langston Hughes.　SAmP

We are the driving ones.　Rainer Maria Rilke.　EnlH　*Fr.* Sonnets to Orpheus.

We are the dwarfed birches.　Dwarf Birches.　Yevgeny Aleksandrovich Yevtushenko [*or* Evtushenko].　TCRusP, *tr. by* Peter Levi and Robin Milner-Gulland

We are the fools of time and terror: Days.　Byron.　AmFaPo　*Fr.* Manfred.

We are the hollow men.　Hollow Men, The.　T. S. Eliot.　APT-1; MoAmPo; NAAL-2v2; NAAL-5; OBMV

We are the last that there are anywhere.　For Easter Island or Another Island.　William Dickey.　YaYoPo

We are the music-makers.　Ode.　Arthur William Edgar O'Shaughnessy.　OBEV

We are the ones you sent to fight a war.　Relative Thing, A.　William Daniel Ehrhart.　CDa

We are the poor children, come out to see the sights.　Carol of the Poor Children, The.　Richard Middleton.　OBCP

We are the silent poets of the night.　1st Poem for Cuba.　Sandra Maria Esteves.　PueRic

We are the smiling comfortable homes.　Homes.　Charlotte Perkins Stetson Gilman.　SWaP

We are the stars which sing.　Song of the Stars, The.　*Unknown.*　APN-2, *tr. by* Charles Godfrey Leland

We are the Vagabonds that sleep.　Ballade of the Outcasts.　Stuart Merrill.　APN-2

We are the Writing on the Wall.　Dolores Kendrick.　FFC

We Are the Young Magicians.　Ruth Forman.　AmPoNex

We are they who come faster than fate.　James Elroy Flecker.　MoBrPo　*Fr.* Hassan.

We are thine, O Love, being in thee and made of thee.　Lascelles Abercrombie.　OBEV　*Fr.* Emblems of Love.

We are things of dry hours and the involuntary plan.　Gwendolyn Brooks.　BPo; FaBoWP; GT; NAAAL; NAAL-2v2; NAAL-5; NoP-4; PoE; PoPoPo; UnPo　*Fr.* Street in Bronzeville, A.

We are this union.　U Tam'si Tchicaya.　PBMAP　*Fr.* L'Arc Musical (1970).

We are tied to Mars' tail. The previous days.　Captain, The.　Blanca Varela.　WPOW, *tr. by* Lynne Alvarez

We are tired of your tiresome imitations of Mayakovsky.　Answer to Voznesensky and Evtushenko.　Frank O'Hara.　LCAP-2; NNaP; PoM

We Are Transmitters.　D. H. Lawrence.　OxBTC

We are travelling west of Alice Springs, and Sam is at the wheel.　West of Alice.　W. E. Harney.　NOBAu

We are truly fed up.　Voice of Earth Mediums.　Philip Lamantia.　CLPP

We are upon the Scheldt. We know we move.　Dante Gabriel Rossetti.　NPeEn; PeVV　*Fr.* Trip to Paris and Belgium, A.

We are very polite to each other.　Unexpected Meeting.　Wislawa Szymborska.　VCWP

We are visitors into.　Meditating on Star Light While Traveling Highway.　Anita Endrezze.　HATNAP

We are walking on a sidewalk.　Numinous, The.　William Heyen.　GotH

We are walking our very public attraction.　History of Sexual Preference, A.　Robin Becker.　BodElec; ExTi

We are waltzing now into the moonlit morning.　Waltz against the Mountains.　Thomas Hornsby Ferril.　APT-2; VGW

We Are Watching, We Are Waiting.　William O. Cushing.　AH

We are wolves.　Wolves.　Vladimir Alekseievich Soloukhin.　TCRP, *tr. by* Daniel Weissbort

We are, you and me.　*Unknown.*　OHMPJ

We are your grandparents.　Thirst.　Arthur Rimbaud.　WoPoe, *tr. by* Michael O'Brien

We artists have strange nerves!　In a Hotel Writing-Room.　John Cowper Powys.　OxBTC

We asked . . . / Keep the pearls in the shells.　We Asked.　Malak' Abd Al-Aziz.　HAWP, *tr. by* Pamela Vittorio

We Assume: On the Death of Our Son, Reuben Masai Harper.　Michael S. Harper.　GT; LCAP-2

We ate our breakfast lying on our backs.　Breakfast.　Wilfrid Wilson Gibson.　FaBoWar; OBMV; OxBTC

We athletes who, with sternest discipline.　Golden Road to Barcelona: 1992, The.　Martin Fagg.　UV

We awaken in Christ's body.　Symeon.　EnlH

We backed the Tetrarch and got drunk together. (LL)　Sporting Acquaintances.　Siegfried Sassoon.　OxBSo; OxBTC

We banished the tyrant-tsars.　Nikolai Ivanovich Tryapkin [*or* Triapkin].　TCRP

We banter / back and forth.　Perfecto Flores.　Jimmy Santiago Baca.　TRP

We Become New.　Marge Piercy.　TAP

We begged him to teach us Spanish.　Piñon Nuts.　Dixie Salazar.　UnSA

We begin kissing.　Nostalgia.　Charles Rossiter.　PasH

We believe books and music.　Anatoly Steiger.　TCRusP, *tr. by* John Glad

We ben chapmen lyght of fote.　Chapmen.　*Unknown.*　FaBoVe; MiEL

We blk blues singers.　For Walter Washington.　Tom Dent.　NBV

We bore down on the ship at sea's edge.　Homer.　WoPoe, *tr. by* Robert Fitzgerald　*Fr.* Odyssey, The.

We borrowed the loan of Kerr's big ass.　Kerr's Ass.　Patrick Kavanagh.　ModIr; NOIV; RB

We both might wonder what you're doing here.　Communion.　Sarah Maguire.　MFPA

We bought from Laotian refugees a cloth.　Absorption of Rock.　Maxine Hong Kingston.　OpBo

We break off a branch of poplar catkins.　All Year Long.　*Unknown.*　OHMPC, *tr. by* Kenneth Rexroth

We Bring No Glittering Treasures.　Harriet C. Phillips.　AH

We broke out of our dream into a clearing.　Stephano Remembers.　James Simmons.　PBCIP; PNI

We brought him home, I was so pleased.　My New Rabbit.　Elizabeth Gould.　OTCP

We brush the other, invisible moon.　Sleep.　Bill Knott.　SPE

We brushed our hair back and our.　Last Refuge, The.　Augustus Young.　BIrV

We brushed the dirt off, held it to the light.　Edwin Morgan.　NePenScot　*Fr.* Sonnets from Scotland.

We built a palace for them, made of bedrooms.　R-and-R Centre: An Incident from the Vietnam War.　Dennis Joseph Enright.　OxBC

We built a ship upon the stairs.　Good Play, A.　Robert Louis Stevenson.　OTCP; PWR

We Bumped off Your Friend the Poet.　Harold Norse.　GLP

We buried Madaza.　From the Outside.　Mafika Pascal Gwala.　NAfrP

We burn cities.　To Fat Boy, the Bomb.　Henry Braun.　BodElec

We bury and dig each other up.　Bury and Dig.　Minnie Bruce Pratt.　PoBW

We bury ourselves to get high.　Smoking in an Open Grave.　David Bottoms.　InPK-6

We but begin to hope to know, having known.　Subject.　Marie Ponsot.　VGW

We call it a grain of sand.　View with a Grain of Sand.　Wislawa Szymborska.　BLT

We Call Them Greasers.　Gloria Anzaldúa.　GLP

We called the statue.　Niyi Osundare.　HBAPE　*Fr.* Moonsongs.

We came back late from visiting.　Konstantin Iakovlevich Vanshenkin.　TCRusP, *tr. by* Daniel Weissbort

We came down above the houses.　Deaths and Engines.　Eiléan Ní Chuilleanáin.　ModIr

We came during those years.　Norman Rosten.　YaYoPo

We came home to the stranger.　Deadly Weapon.　Beatrix Gates.　GLP

We came of age, and were made man and wife.　Mourning for My Wife.　Mei Yao Ch'en.　SuSp, *tr. by* Jonathan Chaves

We came out safe, under the aspens; wanted.　Politicisation of the North Wind, The.　David Morley.　NLP

We came to the edge.　Pretty Woman, A.　Simon J. Ortiz.　CDW

We came to unexpected latitudes.　Sighting the Slave Ship.　Pauline Stainer.　NeBl

We came to visit the cow.　Freedom, New Hampshire.　Galway Kinnell.　LCAP-2

We came where the salmon were so many.　That Morning.　Ted Hughes.　HarvBoo

We can endure the eyes.　At the Jewish Museum.　Linda Pastan.　TaR

We can get you crucified. (LL)　Murderer and Sarapis, The.　Palladas [*or* Pallades].　GrAn; WoPoe, *tr. by* Tony Harrison

We can go by that door a dozen times.　Strong Room of the House, The.　William Bronk.　APSN

We can look into the stove tonight.　Burning Oneself Out.　Adrienne Rich.　BodElec

We Can Love But Once. Charlotte Dacre. RWP

We Can Say That. Tony Curtis. TCAWP

We can string out our lines. Envy. "Naum Korzhavin." TCRP, *tr. by* Vladimir Lunis and Albert C. Todd

We can string words on a line. "Naum Korzhavin." TCRusP, *tr. by* John Glad

We can't complain. Middle-Class Blues. Hans Magnus Enzensberger. VCWP, *tr. by* Hans Magnus Enzensberger and Michael Hamburger

We can't help being thirsty. Jelaluddin [*or* Jalal al-Din] Rumi. LoL

We can't keep it out. It keeps on filling your room. (LL) Virgo Descending. Charles Wright. ColAP; LCAP-2; TRP

We can tell already. Two Months Married. Aidan Carl Mathews. PBCIP

We cannot bear to roast a book. Parental Critic, The. Keith Preston. NBLV

We cannot celebrate with doleful Music. For Both of You, the Divorce Being Final. John Hollander. YaYoPo

We cannot go to the country. Raleigh Was Right. William Carlos Williams. NIL-7; NIP-4; NoAM; RB; WoPoe

We cannot know his legendary head. Archaic Torso of Apollo. Rainer Maria Rilke. NAWM-7v2; RaBo, *tr. by* Stephen Mitchell

We cannot recognize a single face. (LL) Brides Come to Yuba City, The. Chitra Divakaruni. OpBo; UnSA

We cannot tell now. *Unknown.* ArkPo, *tr. by* Helen Craig McCullough

We Cared for Each Other. Heinrich Heine. AWP, *tr. by* John Todhunter

We caroused, we kissed, we existed once upon a time . . . . Poem about Youth and Romanticism, A. "Naum Korzhavin." TCRP, *tr. by* Vladimir Lunis and Albert C. Todd

We carved our names. Elegy. Chang Chi. CrYelRi, *tr. by* Sam Hamill

We caught fireflies. Ruth. Norman J. Loftis. SpirFl

We caught the tread of dancing feet. Harlot's House, The. Oscar Wilde. EBVV; MoBrPo; NAEL-5v2; NAEL-6v2; NoAM

We chanced in passing by that afternoon. Black Cottage, The. Robert Frost. CBCWP; VGW

We charge through the skies of disillusion. Song at the African Middle Class. Molara Ogundipe-Leslie. HBAPE; PBMAP

We clawed through Paris. Sphinxes. Sandra Hochman. YaYoPo

We climb the slopes of life with throbbing heart. Aspiration. Henrietta Cordelia Ray. CBWP-3

We climbed the dark. We. Island, The. George Woodcock. MoCV

We climbed the hill to look over our land. Our Land. Yannis Ritsos. AmFaPo, *tr. by* Edmund Keeley

—We come in peace from the third planet. First Men on Mercury, The. Edwin Morgan. NePenScot; PeLV

We come now to the space which is boy-shaped. At Sixteen. Ann Darr. LW

We come to this country. To be Sung on the Fourth of July. Wyatt Prunty. RA

We come to uncrate the newness of this world. First Things. Lucienne Desnoues. WPOW, *tr. by* Miller Williams

We commit what we do not commit. Homage to Issac Newton. János Pilinszky. IQMS, *tr. by* Peter Jay

We could be here. This is the valley. Small Town with One Road. Gary Soto. SoSe-8

We could count the times we went for a walk. End of the Affair, The. James Simmons. PBCIP

We could have become a silence. (LL) Quick and Bitter. Yehuda Amichai [*or* Amikhai]. BoLoP; VCWP

We could have crossed the road but hesitated. Interrogation, The. Edwin Muir. NPeEn; PoWW

We Could Have Met. Lee Cataldi. BMAP

We could hitch the Horses of Instruction. Comet. Matthew Rohrer. NAPBL

We could not pause, while yet the noontide air. Obsequies of Stuart. John Randolph Thompson. CBCWP

We could point to the poem and say 'that map." John Tranter. BMAP *Fr.* Alphabet Murders, The.

We could say. Imagination in flight: an improvisational duet. Harriet Jacobs. SpirFl

We could stand the world if it were hard all over. (LL) Across the Bay. Donald Davie. CABP; NoAM

We could weep for him. Bodo. Thomas Lux. OPRER

We could wipe away a fly. Jungle Café, The. Gary Soto. NoAM

We count the broken lyres that rest. Oliver Wendell Holmes. APN-1 *Fr.* Autocrat of the Breakfast Table, The.

We crawled and cried and laughed. Autobiography. Mbella Sonne Dipoko. TTY

We crept in the tall grass and slept till noon. (LL) 1916 Seen from 1921. Edmund Charles Blunden. NoP-4; PeFWW

We cross over the distant Ching-men. Crossing Ching-Men to See a Friend Off. Li Po. ChinPo, *tr. by* Yip Wai-lim

We cross the river narrows. Parting. Li Po. CrYelRi, *tr. by* Sam Hamill

We cross the river over dark waves. Rain on the River. Lu Yu. OHMPC, *tr. by* Kenneth Rexroth

We curl into your eyes. Female God, The. Isaac Rosenberg. FaBoTw

We curve along the edge of civilization. Rincón. Sandra M. Castillo. TouFir

We cut grass. Santhal Poems, 1. Bishnu De. OMIP, *tr. by* Samir Dasgupta

We'd all had a bit too much that night when you brought out. Sea-Cucumber, The. Martin Johnston. BMAP

"We'd better leave him in the sump," he said. (LL) Mending Sump. Kenneth Koch. InPK-6; NeAP; NoAM

We'd found the old Boche dug-out, and he knew. Wilfred Owen. EBNV; FaBoWar; PeFWW; PoWW *Fr.* Sentry, The.

We'd gained our first objective hours before. Counter-Attack. Siegfried Sassoon. MoBrPo; OxAEP-2; PeFWW; PoWW

We'd moved out. You'd stayed behind alone. Before the Brain Surgery. Paula Tatarunis. BloBone

We'd rather have the iceberg than the ship. Imaginary Iceberg, The. Elizabeth Bishop. FaBoWP; MoAmPo

We dance in death's face. Kalamu ya Salaam. SpirFl *Fr.* New Orleans Haiku.

We dance round in a ring and suppose. Secret Sits, The. Robert Frost. InPK-6

We deemed the secret lost, the spirit gone. Flaxman. Margaret Fuller. APN-1

We Delighted, My Friend. Léopold Sédar Senghor. PBA; TTY, *tr. by* Miriam Koshl

We descend on horses onto the battleground. Impromptu. Tu Fu. CrYelRi, *tr. by* Sam Hamill

We did it in front of the mirror. We Did It. Yehuda Amichai [*or* Amikhai]. BoLoP, *tr. by* Harold Schimmel

We did kowtow to a blazing sun. Letter to the Immigration Officer. Jan Kemp. PeNZ

We did not flinch but gave our lives to save. Cenotaph at the Isthmos. Simonides. GrAn, *tr. by* Peter Jay

We did not know the first thing about. Thinking about Bill, Dead of AIDS. Miller Williams. NIL-7

We did our duty. We Have Done Our Duty. Yehuda Amichai [*or* Amikhai]. VCWP, *tr. by* Benjamin Harshav

We did our living in the kitchen. Still-Life with Woodstove. William W. Cook. SpirFl

"We did sums at school, Mummy." Halfway Street, Sidcup. Fleur Adcock. Spl

We did the thing that he projected. Joseph Hilaire Pierre Belloc. FaBoWar *Fr.* Modern Traveller, The.

We did things more dulcet, more marionette. Untitled. Karen Volkman. NeAmPo

We didn't deny the obvious. Obvious, The. Jeffrey McDaniel. AmPoNex

We didn't plan our lives this way. Of Potatoes. Trish Reeves. SpudSo

We didn't sleep / Three nights we sat up. What We Did after My Mother's Mastectomy. Lisa Glatt. AmPoNex

We didn't want to be white—or did we? Struggle, The. Toi Derricotte. LTA; PBCAP

We died in Zortman on a Sunday. Renegade Wants Words, The. James Welch. CDW

We dismount; I give you wine. Seeing Someone Off. Wang Wei. CoBCP, *tr. by* Burton Watson

We dissolve—away from daytime, away from the sun. Twilight. Margit Szécsi. IQMS, *tr. by* Agnes Arany-Makkai

We do assemble that a funeral. Elegy in Memory of the Worshipful Major Thomas Leonard Esq, An. Samuel, Jr. Danforth. SCAP

We do not care if you were. Ben Webster: "Did You Call Her Today?" Ron Welburn. SeSe

We Do Not Know How to Say Goodbye. Anna Andreyevna Akhmatova. TCRusP, *tr. by* Daniel Weissbort

We do not need to be reminded. Mahmoud Darwish. MAP *Fr.* Diary of a Palestinian Wound.

We do not play on Graves. Emily Dickinson. NIL-7; NIP-4

We do not wish anything to happen. T. S. Eliot. OxBTC *Fr.* Murder in the Cathedral.

We docked at noon in the port of Veracruz. We wore our Russian furs. Gloria Gervitz. MirDau, *tr. by* Stephen Tapscott *Fr.* Yiskor.

We don't get to choose our century. Aleksandr Semionovich Kushner. TCRP

We don't have much language for tragedy. Autumn. Thomas William Shapcott. CBAP

We don't lack people here on the Northern coast. Amusing Our Daughters. Carolyn Kizer. VCAP; VGW

We don't live in castles. Velemir [*or* Viktor Vladimirovich] Khlebnikov. TCRP *Fr.* Washerwoman.

We / don't know, you know, / we / don't know, do we? / what / counts. (LL) Zürich, the Stork Inn. Paul Celan. BBASP; HP, *tr. by* Michael Hamburger

We drank while half the stars came out for us. Songs We Fought For, The. Walter McDonald. SwNoth

We draw our lives after ourselves in streams. Lynx, The. Charles Edward Eaton. DiPo

We dream—it is good we are dreaming. Emily Dickinson. BoWoP

We dressed each other. Empress Eifuku. OHMPJ; WPOW

We Drink Farewell. Tu Mu. OHMPC, *tr. by* Kenneth Rexroth

We drove past farms, the hills terraced with sheep. Travel: after a Death. Jane Kenyon. FFC

We drove towards the city. Industrial City. Antigone Kefala. BMAP

We dug up a / grave today. August 17, 1970. Don Receveur. CDa

We dust the walls. Aus Einem April. Frank O'Hara. HarvBoo

We eat and drink and laugh and energize. Death's Transfiguration. Israel Zangwill. TrJP

We eat / bread & stewed sausage. Taste. Jennifer Maiden. BMAP

We Encounter Nat King Cole as We Invent the Future. Joy Harjo. ReTh

We entered the city at noon! High bells. The radio on. One Night Stand. Imamu Amiri Baraka. NeAP

We examine today not sacked cities, but sacked lives. Archaeology of Divorce, The. Patricia Storace. FFC

We fail, and white men call us faggots till the end of / the earth. (LL) Poem for Black Hearts, A. Imamu Amiri Baraka. NAAAL; PoM

We fancied he'd share in our cause. Instead. What's In It for Me? Edgar Albert Guest. PoToHe

We fell on the chair. Hilbert's Program. Milo De Angelis. NeIt, *tr. by* Lawrence Venuti

We few, we happy few, we band of brothers. William Shakespeare. UnPo *Fr.* King Henry V.

We filled our ears with so much noise that. Americans in 1933–4–5–6–7–8–, Etc. Merrill Moore. FaBoA

We find in the East Indies stars there be. Of Stars. Margaret Lucas Cavendish, Duchess of Newcastle. NOSC

We finished clearing the last. Above Pate Valley. Gary Snyder. CoAP; CoAmPo; GeoHom; LCAP-2; NoP-4; TRP

We first lay down among flowers. Elegy. Ikkyu Sojun. ErotSp, *tr. by* Sam Hamill

We fish, we fish, we merrily swim. We Fish. Herman Melville. WHSW

We fished up the Atlantic Cable one day between the Barbadoes. Cable Ship, The. Harry Edmund Martinson. RB, *tr. by* Robert Bly

We fled from the sight inland and that night. Columbus Reaches Juana, 1492. Ralph Gustafson. NOBC

We fly forwards. Look Back into the Future. Andrey [*or* Andrei] Andreievich Voznesensky [*or* Voznesenskii]. PFTM-2, *tr. by* Anselm Hollo

We followed her unto the chamber-door. The Lady of the Assembly. WPE *Fr.* Assembly of Ladies, The.

We forced our faces. Being There. Thomas Sayers Ellis. AmPoNex

We forego Mimicry. Ray DiPalma. FTOS

We forget where we came from. Our Jewish. Jews in the Land of Israel. Yehuda Amichai [*or* Amikhai]. PoSu, *tr. by* Warren Bargad

We forgot to clear your grave, so we stood. On the Anniversary Of Your Death. Karen L. Mitchell. GT

We fought in 1917. Strike up the Band. George Gershwin. ReLy

We found a mouse in the chalk quarry today. Anne and the Field-Mouse. Ian Serraillier. NOxBChV

We found dead animals in our sagebrush hills. Dobbin. George Bowering. NOBC

We four. Manifest Destiny. Suheir Hammad. PoArWo

We four lads from Liverpool are. *Unknown*. KaS

We frolic[k], while 'tis May. (LL) Ode on the Spring. Thomas Gray. GTBS-P; NOEC

We from the black sun of fear. Chorus of the Dead. Nelly Sachs. PFTM-1

We fuckin never had a fuckin chance. Armed Forces Day. Steve Hassett. CDa

We gather at the ship's unlit front deck. Mighty Tropicale Orchestra, The. Sean Harvey. SeSe

We gather our bones from many places, look for. Corn Children. Carol Lee Sanchez. HW

We gather where the weeping willow waves. Decoration Day. Josephine D. Henderson Heard. CBWP-4

We gave a helping hand to grass. Helping Hand, A. Miroslav Holub. PoSu, *tr. by* George Theiner

We get to it through troughs and rainbows. Enlli. Christine Evans. TCAWP

We get up at six with him and build a fire. He Considers the Birds of the Air. Karl Kirchwey. GI

We give them chocolate bars. Negotiations. Ray Catina. CDa

We Go. Karl Wolfskehl. TrJP, *tr. by* Ernst Morwitz, Carol North Valhope and Harry Zohn

We go, in winter's biting wind. Diehards, The. Ruth Pitter. OBGa

We go, Miletos, dear fatherland, spurning. Anyte [*or* Anytes]. SaLy, *tr. by* Diane Rayor

We go no more to Calverly's. Calverly's. Edwin Arlington Robinson. APT-1; NoAM

We go on a business trip. H. C. ten Berge. TuT *Fr.* Lusitanian Variant, The.

We go out in the stony midnight. Thomas McGrath. NNaP *Fr.* Letter to an Imaginary Friend.

We go out together into the staring town. We Go Out Together. Kenneth Patchen. MoAmPo

We go over to see the head of a woman. Balance and Beauty. Clarence Major. FTOS

We go through life this way. Valerio Magrelli. ItPo, *tr. by* Gayle Ridinger

We go to the Golden Palace. Golden Palace, The. *Unknown*. ChiP, *tr. by* Arthur Waley

"We gon have / mo room!" (LL) Inconvenience, An. John Raven. BPo; CRP

We got away—for just two nights. To Be a Pilgrim. Robert Conquest. OxBC

We Got Everything We Needed Here and Aint It Something. *Unknown*. STP, *tr. by* Richard Johnny John and Jerome Rothenberg

We got ready and showed our home. Scattered Congregation, The. Tomas Tranströmer. RaBo, *tr. by* Robert Bly

We got sunlight on the sand. There Is Nothin' like a Dame. Oscar Hammerstein, II. OBAL; ReLy

We got them the hard way. Tapes. Thomas Sayers Ellis. AmPoNex

We got this idea. Our Hands in the Garden. Anne Hébert. BoWoP, *tr. by* A. Poulin, Jr.

We gotta. Survival Motion: Notice. Melvin E. Brown. ISC

We gotta make a film of this, Jack. Script Conference. John Hartley Williams. EmeKit

We Greeks have fallen on evil. Palladas [*or* Pallades]. PGA

We greet thee now open this festal morn. Greeting. Henrietta Cordelia Ray. CBWP-3

We greet you now, Diana. To Diana. Elisaveta Kulman. ARWW, *tr. by* Catriona Kelly

We greet you rarest White Heron of One Flight. Greeting to Queen Elizabeth, the Rare White Heron of Single Flight, A. Wiremu Kingi Kerekere. PeNZ, *tr. by* Wiremu Kingi Kerekere

We grow accustomed to the Dark. Emily Dickinson. SAmP

We grow to the sound of the wind. *Unknown*. AWP *Fr.* Thousand and One Nights, The.

We had a bower among the beans. Bower among the Beans, The. Emily Jane Pfeiffer. ViWPN

We had a drinking party. Drinking with Friends amongst the Blooming Peonies. Liu Yu Hsi. OHMPC, *tr. by* Kenneth Rexroth

We had a female Passenger who came. September 1, 1802. William Wordsworth. OxBSo

We had already left him. I walked the ice. Dante Alighieri. OxBEV, *tr. by* Seamus Heaney *Fr.* Divina Commedia.

We had an old door. Virtue of Slovenliness, The. Geoffrey Holloway. NLP

We had as our platoon commander one. Officers and Gentlemen down Under. John Brookes. FaBoWar

We had been flying all day long at one hundred fucking feet. Twats in the Ops Room. *Unknown*. FaBoWar

We had been in the tall grass for hours. At Midsummer. Norman Dubie. NoAM

We had been school-mates,—she and I. Imogene. Eloise Bibb. CBWP-4

We had 'em. This Time. Steve Denning. CDa

We had expected everything but revolt. Nightmare Number Three. Stephen Vincent Benét. MoAmPo

We had gathered for the love-feast on the time appointed. Who Is My Neighbor? Josephine D. Henderson Heard. CBWP-4

We had many problems set us when Coolgardie was a camp. Smiths, The. E. G. Murphy. NOBAu

We had mor than. Words. Vern Rutsala. WeW-3

We had never seen black cockatoos, though in the park. Shadow of War, 1941. Thomas William Shapcott. BMAP

We had our towers too, a large. Yeats at Athenry Perhaps. Padraic Fallon. ModIr

We had ridden long and were still far from the inn. Sleeping on Horseback. Po Chü-i. BLT; ChiP, *tr. by* Arthur Waley

We had sat up all night hearing it roar, the mere. Morning in the Islands. John Hollander. ColAP

We had stayed up all night, my friends and I, under hanging mosque lamps. Filippo Tommaso Marinetti. PFTM-1 *Fr.* Manifesto of Futurism, The.

We had this stuff that Wayne found in the shed. Cro-Kill. Anthony Lawrence. NOBAu

We hammered him to the cross. His fingers grabbed. Soldier Who Crucified Jesus, The. Martinus Nijhoff. TuT, *tr. by* Desmond Egan

We harden like trees, and like rivers are cold. (LL) Lover, The; a Ballad. Lady Mary Wortley Montagu. ECWP; NAEL-5v1; NAEL-6v1; NAEL-7v1; NoP-4; OxBEV; PEW

We hardly had gotten the man's pants down. "We Hardly." Richard Huelsenbeck. PFTM-1

We have a bed, and a baby too. Laborer, The. Richard Dehmel. AWP, *tr. by* Jethro Bithell.

We have a fiction that we live by: it is the river. Waikato-Taniwha-Rau. Vincent O'Sullivan. PeNZ

We have / a map of the universe. Wings. Miroslav Holub. PoSu, *tr. by* Ian Milner and George Theiner

We have a small hand with five fingers. Toil. Avraham Shlonsky. MHP, *tr. by* Ruth Finer Mintz.

We have all been in rooms. Adultery. James Dickey. TAP

We have all seen them circling pastures. Under the Vulture-Tree. David Bottoms. GifTon

We have always heard music. And sometimes I hear this song in my head. Harriet Jacobs. SpirFl

We have an old mother that peevish is grown. Mother Country, The. Benjamin Franklin. AiP

We have ascended to this paradise. Attic, The. Henri Coulette. PoRA

We have been everywhere, suddenly. Universe is Part of Ourselves, The. Robin Blaser. FTOS

We have been helping with the cake. Day before Christmas. Marchette Chute. NTCP

We have been here before, but we are lost. Wet Camp. Alberto Rios. NAAL-5

We have been rewarded with a great intimacy; we are allowed to know. Justice. Ben Marcus. HeMarv

We have been shown. Denise Levertov. CoAmPo; LCAP-2

We have borne good sons to broken men. Miners' Wives. Joe Corrie. OxBS

We Have Chosen a Timely Day. *Unknown.* ColAnChi, *tr. by* Anne Birrell

We have climbed the mountain. Here in Katmandu. Donald Justice. CoAmPo

We Have Come Home. Lenrie Peters. PBMAP

We have come to the edge of the woods. Jacklight. Louise Erdrich. HATNAP; NIL-7; WeW-3

We have come to your shrine to worship. Plea for Mercy, A. Kwesi Brew. PBA; PBMAP; WoPoe

We have disconcerted / The revolutions with our prayers. Resistance. Horst Bienek. AF

We Have Done Our Duty. Yehuda Amichai [*or* Amikhai]. VCWP, *tr. by* Benjamin Harshav

We have done what we wanted. Coming to This. Mark Strand. HCAP; VCAP

We have done with dogma and divinity. After Trinity. John Meade Falkner. OxBTC

We have dropped out of the other schools. Wayne's College of Beauty, Santa Cruz. David Swanger. GeoHom

We have erased each letter. Life As a Book That Has Been Put Down. John Ashbery. FTOS

We Have Even Lost our Tongues! Ifi Amadiume. HAWP

We have floated to the surface of Monet's pond. Frank Ormsby. ModIr *Fr.* Paris Honeymoon, A.

We have for many years been bored. Pen-guin. The Sword-fish, The. Robert Williams Wood. NBLV

We have forgotten how to offer alms. Nikolai Semionovich Tikhonov. TCRP

We have forgotten Paris, and his fate. Helen Grown Old. Janet Lewis. APT-2

We have forgotten who we are. *Unknown.* FHYEP *Fr.* U.N. Environmental Sabbath Program.

We have gone out in boats upon the sea at night. Passage over Water. Robert Duncan. NOBA; NoAM

We have grown a tree of knowledge, "Worthy Claflin" is the name. Tree of Knowledge, The. Lizelia Augusta Jenkins Moorer. CBWP-3

We have heard no nightingales singing. Working Class. Bertram J. Warr. NOBC

We have learned how to bear. (LL) Zone. Louise Bogan. APT-2; WPE

We Have Lived and Loved Together. Charles Jefferys [*or* Jeffries]. ITBLP; PoToHe

We have lived as ectoplasm. Coda. "Ern Malley." BMAP

We have lived like civilized people. Silent Piano, The. Louis Simpson. EmeKit

We have lost the old tongue, and with it. Old Tongue, The. Herbert Williams. AngWePo; TCAWP

We have loved each other in this time twenty years. Unfinished History. Archibald MacLeish. VGW

We have loved the self, each other, and the rounded slope. Epithalamium, An. Joan Murray. YaYoPo

We Have Never Seen the Sky Light Up. Darryl Holmes. InTrad

We have no choice. (LL) Perhaps. . . . "Shu Ting." BLT; CarOv, *tr. by* Carolyn Kizer and Y. H. Zhao

We have no heart for the fishing—we have no hand for the oar. Dykes, The. Rudyard Kipling. HarvBoo; OBWP

We have no prairies. Bogland. Seamus Heaney. HeIP-4; NOIV; NoAM; PBCIP; PNI; PoPoPo; PoetW

We have no time to stand and stare. (LL) Leisure. William Henry Davies. AWP; AngWePo; NOBE; OBEV; OBMV; PoRA; TFi

We have not been happy, my Lord, we have not been too happy. T. S. Eliot. OxBTC *Fr.* Murder in the Cathedral.

We have not forgotten you but here they have you pretend to work. Letter to a Cretan Flute-Maker. Justin Vitiello. UnSA

We have not known thee as we ought. Thomas Benson Pollock. SacPr

We have our moments. In the Madonna Dell' Orto. Peter Rafferty. NLP

We have our problems / too, with you. (LL) High to Low. Langston Hughes. APT-2; HCAP; PoPoPo

We have reached the end of pastime, for always. End of Play. Robert Graves. EBEV

We have scarcely time to tell thee. James McIntyre. VerBaPo *Fr.* English Poets.

We have seen her / the world over. "H. D.". APT-1; CRP; HW; NALW; PFTM-1; VGW *Fr.* Tribute to the Angels.

We have seen how the most amiable. "H. D.". BoWoP *Fr.* Walls Do Not Fall, The.

We have seen sand frothing like the sea. Sand. John Jarmain. FaBoWar

We have served our day. Rudyard Kipling. HarvBoo *Fr.* Epitaphs of the War [1914–1918].

We have slept in. Message on Cape Cod, The. Michael S. Weaver. GT; PBCAP

We have sold our shadow. Geometrical Place. Günter Eich. AF, *tr. by* David Young

We have struck the regions wherein we are keel or reef. Zone. Louise Bogan. APT-2; WPE

We have talent. People call us. To Pi Ssu Yao. Tu Fu. BLT; OHPC, *tr. by* Kenneth Rexroth

We have the body of a woman, an arch over the ground. It Is Not. Valerie Martínez. TouFir

"We have the mauve or the cerise." Shop Talk. Roy Fuller. OxBC

We have the myrtle's breath around us here. Imelda. Felicia Dorothea Hemans. RWP

We have to discard the past. Past. Pablo Neruda. VCWP, *tr. by* Alastair Reid

We have travelled many miles to find this bed. Bed, The. Moniza Alvi. MFPA

We have tried words before—always in vain. Knife, The. Milton Kaplan. TrJP

We have watched again. Among Hawks. Lance Henson. VoR

We have welded the towbar. Meadow, The. Peter Fallon. PBCIP

We haven't spoken of it since the early days. Ashes. Annie Foster. NLP

We hear her in the square. At two o'clock. Speaker in the Square, A. George Buchanan. PNI

We hear too late or not too late. (LL) Christmas Trees. Geoffrey Hill. ChrPo; NOCV

We heard people were standing. Depression. Isabel Joshlin Glaser. HHAm

We heard the thrushes by the shore and sea. In Kerry. John Millington Synge. MoBrPo

We heard they would jump from buildings. What We Heard about the Japanese. Rachel Rose. BAP-01

We held the last stone wall—when day was red—. Dragon's Breath. Hervey Allen. YaYoPo

We him in glory [*or* glorie] call, The Son[ne] of Man. (LL) Son[ne], The. George Herbert. AngWePo; GeHe; PeECV

We hitched up the mare and we buckled her down. Four of July. Robert Newton Peck. CA

We hold a splendid feast today. *Unknown.* CoBCP

"We hold our flat shields, we wear our jerkins of hide." Hymn to the Fallen. *Unknown.* ChiP; FaBoWar; OBWP, *tr. by* Arthur Waley

We hold these truths to be self-evident. Decoy. John Ashbery. PoM

We Hope For Patrons. Kovur Kilar. WoPoe, *tr. by* George L. III Hart

We hug our little destiny again. (LL) Whatever You Say Say Nothing. Seamus Heaney. OBWP; OxBC

We hunted the mad bastard. As It Should Be. Derek Mahon. EmeKit

We hunted the wren for Robin the Bobbin. Hunting the Wren. *Unknown.* FaBoVe

We hustle hard as the rest of the folk me and my baby. Everything Happens to (Monk and) Me. Brenda Marie Osbey. BodElec

We in our wandering. Song of the Open Road, A. *Unknown.* AWP, *tr. by* John Addington Symonds

We invented these trees and mountains, that long gash. Wilderness. Vern Rutsala. UrbNat

We Irish pride ourselves as patriots. Ireland. John Hewitt. CIP-2

We is gathahed hyeah, my brothahs. Ante-Bellum Sermon, An. Paul Laurence Dunbar. APN-2; BPo; NAAAL

We join with the earth and with each other. *Unknown.* FHYEP *Fr.* U.N. Environmental Sabbath Program.

We joined hands. (LL) My Woman's Transparence. Amina Said. HAWP; NAfrP, *tr. by* Eric Sellin

We Just Couldn't Say Good-bye. Harry Woods. ReLy

We keep forgetting the gods. And if we happened to remember. Requiem on Poros. Yannis Ritsos. VCWP, *tr. by* Edmund Keeley

We keep our quilts in closets and do not dance. Mennonites. Julia Kasdorf. NeAmPo; PBCAP

We kept him an hour in the / bottom. Cocker of Snooks, A. Phyllis Gotlieb. NOBC

We kept war in the kitchen. Dream of the Evil Servant. Reetika Vazirani. NAPBL

We kill what we love. What's left. Destiny. Rosario Castellanos. TANSG, *tr. by* George Bogin

We Kiss'd Again with Tears. Tennyson. PoToHe *Fr.* Princess, The.

We kissed at the barrier; and passing through. On the Departure Platform. Thomas Hardy. NOBE; OxBTC

We knew how to order. Just the dash. Gwendolyn Brooks. IllVoic *Fr.* Gay Chaps at the Bar.

We knew no other jobs. During Recess. Giovanna Pollarolo. TANSG, *tr. by* Marjorie Agosin

We knew so much; when her beautiful eyes could lighten. Sagacity. William Rose Benét. MoAmPo

We know as we grow older. Ella Wheeler Wilcox. *See* I know, as my life grows older

We know, Doctor Williams, you and I. Letter to William Carlos Williams, A. George Young. BloBone

We know not what it is, dear, this sleep so deep and still. Two Mysteries, The. Mary Mapes Dodge. PWR; TrCP

We know poetical poetry the common dangers. Basho 2. Cees Nooteboom. TuT, *tr. by* Michael O'Loughlin

We know so little about what matters. Nature of Suffering, The. Amy Gerstler. ExTi

We know that our master has left us for the day. (LL) Waking from Sleep. Robert Bly. NOBA; NoP-4; SPE

We know the cities by their stones. Postcard from Berlin, A. Derek Mahon. BiHa

We know the Rocket's upward whizz. Bonfires, The. Rudyard Kipling. NPeEn

We know the story. Generation. Rae Armantrout. FTOS

We know this is not life. Baize Queens. Jane Holland. NeBl

We know this story: how his daddy died of drink. David Wojahn. PBCAP *Fr.* Mystery Train: A Sequence.

We know what trembles on the scales. Courage. Anna Andreyevna Akhmatova. TCRP, *tr. by* Max Hayward and Stanley Kunitz

We know where deepest lies the snow. Song. Anne Brontë. PEW

We ladies sense it is the cuckoo builds no nest. Liberation. Ruth Stone. BoWoP

We laugh and we well might weep with the Ballads of George R. Sims. (LL) Ballad of George R. Sims, The. Sir John Betjeman. OBCoV; UV

We laughed. Second Class Citizen. Jennifer Lagier. UnSA

We laughed at him our. We Laughed at Him. Chinua Achebe. PFTM-2

We lay red roses on his grave. Paul Laurence Dunbar. Robert Earl Hayden. ESEAA; GT; NoP-4

We learned that you don't shoot. Statement on Our Higher Education. W. M. Ransom. CDW

We learned the Whole of Love. Emily Dickinson. APN-2

We leave the bed where your fingers. Desire. Kim Ports. PasH

We leave the things of earth. Driving in a Snowstorm, King Salmon to Naknek. Richard Dauenhauer. GifTon

We leave the well-beloved place. Tennyson. EBVV; FHYEP; TreFP *Fr.* In Memoriam A. H. H.

We leave thy courts to-day. Farewell to Allen University. Josephine D. Henderson Heard. CBWP-4

We left before I had time. Back Seat of My Mother's Car, The. Julia Copus. MFPA; NeBl

We left the horses in the draw. Season of Loss, A. Jim Barnes. HATNAP

We left the western island to live among strangers. Search, The. John Hewitt. PNI

We let fire rip, we blacken the pale-gold acres. Burning Off. Geoffrey Dutton. NOBAu

We librarians went to Baja last weekend and sat in the sun. Chapter One. Stephanie Brown. BodElec

We lie back to back. Curtains. Suitor, The. Jane Kenyon. InPK-6

We lie before the fire after love. Old Moon With Her Youth In Her Arms. Gale Swiontkowski. PasH

We lie, day creatures, overhearing night. (LL) Sound of Night, The. Maxine W. Kumin. SoSe-8; WPE

We lie one against the other. Seventh Day Seventh Month. Kuan Yun She. OHMPC, *tr. by* Kenneth Rexroth

We lift our legs. Interrogation. Richard Michelson. GotH

We lift the curtain of the past to-day. Lincoln. Henrietta Cordelia Ray. CBWP-3

We like March—his shoes are Purple. Emily Dickinson. TTTS

We, like shades that were first conjured up. And through the Caribbean Sea. Margaret Danner. BPo

We listened to the music. Sunday Visit. Antigone Kefala. BMAP

We / little children in our shifts. Clap Your Hands for Herod. Josef Hanzlik. OBCP, *tr. by* Ian Milner

We live amidst hills of desolate. South Bronx Testimonial. Sandra Maria Esteves. UnSA

We live by not being . . . by being we die. Summary. Jaime Torres Bodet. TCLAP, *tr. by* Sonja Karsen

We live down here. Framing. Michael Davidson. FTOS

We live here to eat. Biological Light. Primus St. John. GifTon

We Live in a Cage. William J. Harris. GT

We Live in a Rickety House. Alexander McLachlan. NOBC

We live in airless space. Tongue, The. Georgy [*or* Georgii] Nikolaevich Obolduyev [*or* Oboldueev]. TCRP, *tr. by* Vera Dunham

We live in deeds, not years; in thoughts, not breaths. Philip James Bailey. PoToHe *Fr.* Country Town, A.

We live in houses of ample weight. Edvard Munch. Charles Wright. HCAP

We live in the egg. Günter Grass. AF

We live in this world. Children of Night. Amos Neufeld. GotH

We live, not feeling the country beneath us. Poem No. 286 (On Stalin). Osip Emilevich Mandelstam [*or* Mandelshtam]. TCRP

We live, not feeling the ground under our feet. Osip Emilevich Mandelstam [*or* Mandelshtam]. *See* We live, not feeling the country beneath us

We live on the third world from the sun. Number three. Nobody tells us. China. Bob Perelman. FTOS; PFTM-2

We live our lives as wanderers. Old Dust. Li Po. CrYelRi, *tr. by* Sam Hamill

We live; we live in squalor. And so? It had to be. André Marie de Chénier. WoPoe, *tr. by* David Curzon and Jeffrey Fiskin

We live, while we see the sun. Pedro Calderón de la Barca. AWP *Fr.* Life Is a Dream.

We lived deep in a land of optative moods. From the Canton of Expectation. Seamus Heaney. CIP-2; ModIr

We lived east of east L.A. / La Puente. La Puente. Elsa Rediva E'der. ReBoTo

We lived next door to the bootlegger, and were lucky. The. Autobiography. Joy Harjo. LTA

We lived one and twenty year. Upon a Notorious Shrew. *Unknown.* FaBoEE

We lived our little drama. Stars Fell on Alabama. Mitchell Parish. ReLy

We'll all be Penelopes then. Spinster Song: African-American Woman Guild. Angela Jackson. IllVoic

We'll Be Together Again. Frankie Laine. ReLy

We'll dance again the saraband! (LL) Witch's Ballad, The. William Bell Scott. NOBVV; OBEV; PeVV; RACG

We'll dance and sing / "Noel Noel." (LL) E. E. Cummings. NTCP; OBCP

We'll Gather Lilacs. Ivor Novello. ReLy

We'll give them to the poor, says John the Red Nose. (LL) Cutty Wren, The. *Unknown.* OxBoLi; UV

"We'll go home by the water," says Brian O'Linn. (LL) Brian O'Linn. *Unknown.* NBLV; RB

We'll Go No More a-Roving. William Ernest Henley. MoBrPo *Fr.* Echoes.

"We'll meet no more as wont!" she said. Not as Wont. Joseph Skipsey. NOBVV

We'll move away still further: into now. (LL) E. E. Cummings. NAAL-2v2; NOBA; OxBA

We'll, placed in Love's triumphant chariot high. William Cavendish, Duke of Newcastle. OxBSP *Fr.* Humorous Lovers, The.

We'll talk about the dead later. Nightingales. Mikhail Aleksandrovich Dudin. TCRP, *tr. by* Albert C. Todd

We'll to the woods and gather may. Alons au bois le may cueillir. Charles, Duc d' Orléans. AWP, *tr. by* W. E. Henley

We'll to the Woods No More. A. E. Housman. PoRA

We'll worship Jesus / When jesus do. When We'll Worship Jesus. Imamu Amiri Baraka. APSN

We look at woods and say. Finder of a Horseshoe, The. Osip Emilevich Mandelstam [*or* Mandelshtam]. TCRP, *tr. by* Bernard Meares

We look up into the stars, stitch in the constellations. Night Bird, The. Larry Kramer. GeoHom

We looked, we loved, and therewith instantly. Pure Death. Robert Graves. GTBS-P

We lose—because we win. Emily Dickinson. HeIP-4

We love each other so deeply. Ev'ry Time We Say Good-bye. Cole Porter. ReLy

We love the daylight. *Unknown.* WoPoe, *tr. by* James Paul *Fr.* Rune Poem, The.

We love the things we love for what they are. (LL) Hyla Brook. Robert Frost. APT-1; TCAPo

We Love the Venerable House. Ralph Waldo Emerson. AH

We love thee, Ann Maria Smith. Editor's Wooing, The. "Orpheus C. Kerr." OBAL

We love to squeeze bananas. Squeezes. Brian Patten. OTCP; Spl

We love with great difficulty. Sing with Your Body. Janice Mirikitani. WPOW

We loved as friends now twenty years and more:. Change, The. Henry King, Bishop of Chichester. NOSC

We loved each other and were ignorant. (LL) After Long Silence. W. B. Yeats. BoLoP; EnLoPo; HeIP-4; NAEL-5v2; NAEL-6v2; OBMV; UnPo

We made a mistake in this song. *Unknown.* STP

We made castles of grass, green halls, enormous stem-lined rooms. Riders, The. Ann Stanford. WPE

We made love. Then she cleaned. Equality. Hal Sirowitz. KGB

We made our high bed in the low chapel. Airing the Chapel. Sylvia Kantaris. LW

We make more fuss of ballads than of blueprints. Engineers' Corner. Wendy Cope. OBCoV

We make our meek adjustments. Chaplinesque. Hart Crane. APT-2; HeIP-4; NAAL-2v2; NAAL-5; NOBA; NoAM; OxBA; VGW

We make ourselves a place apart. Revelation. Robert Frost. ChIV-2

We make the world in which we live. World We Make, The. Alfred Grant Walton. PoToHe

We make three summer months of heat. (LL) Song: "Winter skies are cold and low." Tzu Yeh. CrYelRi; ErotSp, *tr. by* Sam Hamill

We many men from Mauritania see. Blackamoors, The. Rowland Watkyns. AngWePo

We marched, and saw a company of Canadians. Canadians. Ivor Gurney. FaBoTw

We married for acceptance; to stall the nagging. My Second Marriage to My First Husband. Alice Fulton. EmeKit

We may be learning how to tell the truth. Marilyn Hacker. Son *Fr.* La Fontaine de Vaucluse.

We may come out into the October reality, Imagination. Patrick Kavanagh. ModIr *Fr.* Great Hunger, The.

We may live without poetry, music and art. "Owen Meredith." PoToHe

We may sigh o'er the heavy burdens. Burdens of All, The. Frances Ellen Watkins Harper. PWR

We mean to thrash these Prussian Pups. *Unknown.* PoWW

We meet again. Encounter. Marion Strobel. LW

We Meet in the Lives of Animals. Peter Everwine. NNaP

We men and women die! (LL) Life's Trades. Emily Dickinson. RB; TCAPo

We Met. Thomas Haynes Bayly. TreFP

We met. Marriage, A. Ronald Stuart Thomas. TCAWP

We Met. Mary E. Tucker. CBWP-1

We met, a hundred of us met. Vision, The. William Taylor. NOEC

We met, and memory flew to joys and tears. We Met. Mary E. Tucker. CBWP-1

We met at nine. I Remember It Well. Frederick Loewe. ReLy

We met for supper in your flat-bottomed boat. Dream Barker. Jean Valentine. VGW

We met on Charles Bridge, it was snowing. Old Priest, The. Vladimir Holan. PoSu, *tr. by* George Theiner

We met the British in the dead of winter. Meeting the British. Paul Muldoon. BiHa; CIP-2; EmeKit; NoAM; NoP-4; PNI

We met / them. Issues. Christine Ama Ata Aidoo. HAWP

We met—'twas in a crowd— and I thought he / would shun me;. We Met. Thomas Haynes Bayly. TreFP

We met up in Parliament Square by the left-hand lion. No Dice. Annie Foster. NLP

We met upon a crowded street one day. Casual Meeting. Margaret E. Bruner. PoToHe

We met when time to both was young. Dream Fears. Bessie Rayner Parkes. PoBW

We might have died by now. Horse on a Fence. George Evans. PmAP

We might have guessed it would end in argument. Portrait of the Artist, A. Thomas Kinsella. HarvBoo

We might have known it always: music. Die Musik, An. David Malouf. CBAP

We mind not now the merits of our kind. Sir Charles Sedley. OBSV *Fr.* Happy Pair, The.

We miss a Kinsman more. Emily Dickinson. OxBSP

We miss Her, not because We see. Emily Dickinson. SWaP

We more than others have the perfect right. Song of the Moderns. John Gould Fletcher. AWP

We mourn to-day o'er our sister dead. Resting. Josephine D. Henderson Heard. CBWP-4

We move back to my father's home. 12 East Scott Street. Elise Paschen. IllVoic

We move in elephantine row. Express. William Allingham. NOBVV

We moved house. Peacetime. Tom Paulin. FaBoWar

We moved into a house with 6 rooms: the Bedroom. Map Room, The. Joshua Clover. BAP-97; NeAmPo

We moved like fingers. San Francisco Poem. John Logan. NNaP

We murmur the first moonwords: / *Spasibo. Thanks. O.K..* (LL) Adrienne Rich. NIP-4; NOBA; TAP *Fr.* Two Songs.

We must be kind. Don't Let's Be Beastly to the Germans. Noël Coward. ReLy

We Must Be Polite. Carl Sandburg. OxIBACP

"We Must Die because We Have Known Them." Rainer Maria Rilke. RaBo, *tr. by* Stephen Mitchell

We must fulfill this golden time. While We're Young. William Engvick. ReLy

We must have done this thousands of times. Springtime at Twilight. Michael S. Smith. PasH

We must have nurtured multitudes to be left so alone. Epochs. Juan Gelman. TCLAP, *tr. by* Robert Marquez and Elinore Randall

We must leave the handrails and the Ariadne-threads. À l'Ange Avantgardien. Francis Reginald. MoCV

We must look at the harebell as if. Hugh MacDiarmid. NAEL-5v2; NAEL-6v2; NoP-4 *Fr.* In Memoriam James Joyce.

We must not quarrel, whatever we do. Her Word of Reproach. Sarah Morgan Bryan Piatt. NCAP

We must pass like smoke or live within the spirit's fire. Immortality. "Æ" AWP; OBMV

We must read The Kalevala, before we forget. Origin Charm against Uncertain Injuries. Talvikki Ansel. NeAmPo

We must remember again the tribal pride. Saraband. Austin Hummell. AmPoNex

We Must Return. Agostinho Neto. PeSAV, *tr. by* Michael Wolfers

We must see, we must know. Slop Barrel, The. Philip Whalen. PmAP

We'n you see a man in woe. "Hullo!" Sam Walter Foss. VerBaPo

We Need a God Who Bleeds Now. Ntozake Shange. HW

We need no runners here. Booze is law. Harlem, Montana. James Welch. CDW; HATNAP

We never believed in safety. For Jan as the End Draws Near. Carolyn Kizer. GeoHom

We never half believed the stuff. James Wetherell. Edwin Arlington Robinson. MoAmPo

We never knew his head and all the light. Archaic Torso of Apollo. Rainer Maria Rilke. WoPoe, *tr. by* Edward Snow

We never meet, yet we meet day by day. Thoughts in Separation. Alice Thompson Meynell. OxBSo

We Never Said Farewell. Mary Elizabeth Coleridge. OxBSP; WPE

We Never Stopped Crossing Borders. Luis J. Rodriguez. UnSA

We no longer control could drag us back. (LL) July in Washington. Robert Lowell. LCAP-2; NAAL-2v2

We now lament not, but congratulate. John Donne. NOSC *Fr.* Of the Progres[se] of the Soule; the Second Anniversarie.

We of Sparta fought the Argives—equal in number and arms. Chairemon. GrAn

We often pass a night warm and intimate. Sonnet. Feng Chih. WoPoe, *tr. by* Yip Wai-lim

We only know that in the sultry weather. England and America, 1863. Richard Monckton, 1st Baron Houghton Milnes. EBVV

We only live between. For Sheridan. Robert Lowell. HCAP; PoetW

We open the street door. Same Month They Bombed Cambodia, The. Amy Uyematsu. OpBo

We ourselves are aged. Struggle for the Taal, The. Breyten Breytenbach. AF, *tr. by* Denis Hirson

We outgrow love like other things. Emily Dickinson. NOBA; SoSe-8

We owe the ancients something. You have read. Fitz-Greene Halleck. OBAL *Fr.* Fanny.

We oxen are not only good. Leonidas of Alexandria. GrAn

We park and stare. A full sky of the stars. Death of the Sheriff, The. Robert Lowell. MoAmPo

We pass a stranger. He glances. Stranger Not Ourselves, The. William Stafford. NNaP

We pass the flayed carcass of a cow. Man from Changi, The. Graeme Hetherington. NOBAu

We passed a day on Mosel river. Mosel, The. Caroline Clive. PoBW

We passed each other, turned and stopped for half an hour, then went our way. On the Road to the Sea. Charlotte Mew. BrRo; FaBoWP; PoBW

We passed their graves. Peace. Langston Hughes. BPo

We pattern angels, and they us. (LL)   William Habington.   BeJo; NPeEn   *Fr.* Castara.

We peasants tolerate no word.   We Peasants.   Richard Billinger.   AuPH, *tr. by* Lowell A. Bangerter

We Pick Ferns, We Pick Ferns.   *Unknown.*   CoBCP, *tr. by* Burton Watson

We pick off dots like runners, between.   Static, The.   Lewis Warsh.   FTOS

We pick / the bittersweet grapes.   Napa, California.   Ana Castillo.   WPOW

We picked flints.   Tinder.   Seamus Heaney.   OxAEP-2

We pin dates to shadows.   Borders, Cages and Walls.   Homero [*or* Umberto] Aridjis.   PoCoUp, *tr. by* George McWhirter

We poor Agawams.   Mr. Ward of Anagrams Thus.   Nathaniel Ward.   SCAP

We Praise Thee, God, for Harvests Earned.   John Coleman Adams.   AH

We Praise Thee, If One Rescued Soul.   Lydia Huntley Sigourney.   AH

We pray that it will be done / In beauty / In beauty. (LL)   Eagle Poem.   Joy Harjo.   HATNAP; WeW-3

We pray Thee, have mercy on Zion!   Prayer for Redemption.   *Unknown.* TrJP

We pray to life's source, Mary.   Virgin Mary, The.   *Unknown.*   OBWVE, *tr. by* Joseph P. Clancy

We prepare / the meal together.   Soul Food.   Janice Mirikitani.   OpBo

We pressed our faces.   Train Stops at Healy Fork, The.   John Haines.   BLT

We promise letters and send postcards.   Letter Following.   Aidan Carl Mathews.   PBCIP

We pull off.   Apollo.   Elizabeth Alexander.   ExTi

We pulled for you when the wind was against us and the sails were low.   Song of the Galley-Slaves.   Rudyard Kipling.   GTBS-P; HAP; SCGP

We put a prop beneath the sagging bough.   Wild Cherry, The.   Malcolm Lowry.   NoP-4

We put him on the roof and we painted him blue.   Pedalling Man, The. Russell Hoban.   NOxBChV

We put out our hands on the window—cold.   In Time of Need.   William Stafford.   UnPo

We put this water among this meall.   Charm to Destroy the Male Child of the Laird of Parkis.   Isabel Gowdie.   EMWP

We raise de wheat.   Song.   *Unknown.*   BPo; NAAAL; PAI; TAP

We rake the past, down to an ounce of wants.   Squatter in the Foreground. Kenward Elmslie.   FTOS

We ran across the meadow scabbed with cow-dung, past.   Geoffrey Hill.   HAP *Fr.* Mercian Hymns.

We're a couple of swells; we stop at the best hotels.   Couple of Swells, A. Irving Berlin.   OBCoV; ReLy

We're afraid of sun and hope for rain.   Volcanic Ash.   Peter Sears.   UrbNat

We're all Americans, except the Doc.   Mad Negro Soldier Confined at Munich, A.   Robert Lowell.   FaBoMo; OxBC

We're All Dry.   *Unknown.*   NOBL

(We're all dry with drinking on't.)   OxNR

We're babes on Broadway.   Babes on Broadway.   Ralph Freed.   ReLy

We're eager to look like the manufacture of chocolate.   Two Seconds.   Marie-Dominique Massoni.   SurWo, *tr. by* Myrna Bell Rochester

We're 'er Majesty's bold troubleshooter; wherever they send us we goes.   Bold Troubleshooters.   Peter Veale.   NOBL

We're fed up with national colors!   Project: Flag.   Tadeusz Borowski.   AF, *tr. by* Larry Rafferty

We're foot—slog—slog—slog—sloggin' over Africa.   Boots.   Rudyard Kipling.   BRP; MoBrPo

We're French and Indian like the war.   Like the Trails of Ndakinna.   Cheryl Savageau.   TWW

We're gan' tyek hor off, th' morn.   Charlie Douglas.   Katrina Porteous.   NeBl

We're going to the fair at Holstenwall.   Holstenwall.   Sidney Keyes.   FaBoTw

We're here because we're here.   Because We're Here.   *Unknown.*   FaBoWar

We're hoping to be arrested.   Street Demonstration.   Margaret Abigail Walker. BPo

We're low—we're low—we're very, very low.   Song of the Low, The.   Ernest Charles Jones.   NOBVV

"We're married," said Eddie.   Newlyweds, The.   John Updike.   OBCoV

We're married, they say, and you think you have won me.   Bridal Veil, The. Alice Cary.   TCAPo

"We're not amused," said Victoria.   Limerick.   Stanley J. Sharpless.   PeLi

We're off to See the Wizard (The Wonderful Wizard of Oz).   Harold Arlen. ReLy

We're OK.   Gloria Fuertes.   WPOW, *tr. by* Philip Levine

We're patient, prayerful, meek, resigned. (LL)   Another to Urania.   Benjamin Colman.   ChIV-1; SCAP

We're queer folks here.   Just Folks.   Edgar Albert Guest.   ITBLP

We're snug as a bug in a heated house.   Quatrain.   Adriann Roland Holst. TuT, *tr. by* Sean Dunne

We're so fed up with the Southland.   Jump for Joy.   Sid Kuller.   ReLy

We're Staying at the Castlemount, Western Esplanade.   M. R. Peacocke.   NLP

We're turning back the clocks tonight.   Standard Time: Novena for My Father. Dionisio D. Martinez.   TouFir

We're walking down Grant, through Chinatown.   Playing for Time. Christopher Buckley.   SeSe

We're wed to one eternity. (LL)   Invite to Eternity, An.   John Clare.   NAEL-5v2; NAEL-6v2; NOBVV

We're wonderful one times one. (LL)   E. E. Cummings.   SoSe-8; WeW-3

We reach the promised land.   Story of Joshua.   Alicia Ostriker.   ChIV-1

We Reached Out Far.   Perets [*or* Peretz] Markish.   TrJP, *tr. by* Jacob Sonntag

We read and hear about you every day.   To the Rulers.   Howard Nemerov. OxBC

We Read of a People.   *Unknown.*   AH

We Real Cool.   Gwendolyn Brooks.   AmFaPo; ESEAA; HAP; HHAm; HeIP-4; IllVoic; InPK-6; MakPoe; NAAAL; NAAL-5; NALW; PAI; PoE; PoPoPo; RaBo; SoSe-8; TAP; TFi; TRP; TTY; WeW-3

We received thee warmly—kindly—though we knew thou wert a quiz.   William Edmonstoune [*or* Edmondstoune] Aytoun.   OBCoV   *Fr.* American's Apostrophe to Boz, The.

We reconstruct lives in the intensive.   Clan Meeting: Births and Nations: A Blood Song.   Michael S. Harper.   NoAM

We recruits have our commanders to send us off.   Tu Fu.   CoBCP   *Fr.* On the Border, First Series.

We remember you / calling America.   Poetry Concert.   Michael S. Harper. TAP

We remove a hand.   Ted Berrigan.   BodElec

We resided in a Loreto convent in the centre of Dublin city.   Paul Durcan. ModIr   *Fr.* Six Nuns Die in Convent Inferno.

We ride down the coast hwy through the rain.   Great Santa Barbara Oil Disaster OR, The.   Conyus.   NBV

We rigged up a theater behind the storehouse.   Hamlet.   Yevgeny [*or* Evgenii] Mikhailovich Vinokurov.   TCRP, *tr. by* Daniel Weissbort

We Rise on Sun Beams and Fall in the Night.   Allen Ginsberg.   CLPP

We rise up early and.   Anna Speaks of the Childhood of Mary Her Daughter. Lucille Clifton.   NALW

We roam the streets at night, lovers.   Walking at Night.   Philip Salom. BMAP

We rock and grunt, grunt and / shine. (LL)   Song for Ishtar.   Denise Levertov. NALW; NoAM; PoM

We rode a day, from east, from west.   Friends.   Helen Hunt Jackson.   PoBW

We rode at walking pace.   Grenada.   Mikhail Arkadyevich [*or*Arkad'evich] Svetlov.   TCRP, *tr. by* Daniel Weissbort

We rode hard, and brought the cattle from bushy springs.   Proud Riders. Harold Lenoir Davis.   APT-2

We rode summer on ten speeds.   Woolworth's Poem, The.   Quraysh Ali Lansana.   IllVoic

We rode the canals.   Boxing the Fox.   Pearse Hutchinson.   CIP-2

We rose before dawn.   Andal.   WPoS   *Fr.* Tiruppavai, The.

We rose like a phoenix.   Amryl Johnson.   Oth   *Fr.* Rainbow Dragon Trilogy.

We rose to go.   Sunset blazed on the windows. (LL)   Black Cottage, The. Robert Frost.   CBCWP; VGW

We run the dangercourse.   We Walk the Way of the New World.   Haki R. Madhubuti.   BPo; ESEAA

We's invited down to brudder Browns.   Krismas Dinnah.   Maggie Pogue Johnson.   CBWP-4

We said there'd be a celebration.   Bread and Wine.   Nina Cassian.   AWTN, *tr. by* Andrea Deletant and Brenda Walker

We said: there will surely be hawthorn out.   Spring Snow and Tui.   Mary Ursula Bethell.   PeNZ

We sail out of season into an oyster-gray wind.   Crossing the Atlantic.   Anne Sexton.   NoAM

We sailed in the Ark.   New Noah, The.   "Adonis" [*or* "Adunis"].   AF, *tr. by* Abdullah Al-Udhari

We sat across the table.   Friend, The.   Marge Piercy.   NALW

We sat at the hut of the fisher.   Twilight.   Heinrich Heine.   AWP, *tr. by* Louis Untermeyer

We sat / in big / chairs.   56 Westervelt.   Maggie Nelson.   AmPoNex

We sat in the commons, my eyes scrunched against the smoke.   For the New York City Poet Who Informed Me that Few People Live This Way.   Jeff Gundy.   IllVoic

We sat on the cliff-head.   H. Michael Palmer.   BodElec

We sat there, her tiny audience.   Mom Did Marilyn, Dad Did Fred.   Jack Myers.   ReTh

We sat together at one summer's end.   Adam's Curse.   W. B. Yeats.   BIrV; NAEL-5v2; NAEL-6v2; NoAM; NoP-4; WeW-3

We sat together in the trench.   Trench Idyll.   Richard Aldington.   PeFWW

We sat within the farm-house old.   Fire of Drift-Wood, The.   Henry Wadsworth Longfellow.   APN-1; ITBLP; MakPoe; NAAL-2v1; NAAL-3; NCAP; NOBA; OxBA; TAP

We sate down and wept by the waters.   By the Rivers of Babylon We Sat down and Wept.   Byron.   ChIV-1

We saved enough tinfoil. Last Good War—and Afterward, The. Isabel Joshlin Glaser. HHAm

We saw a town by the track in Colorado. Holding the Sky. William Stafford. GM

We saw death at rather close range. Cricket, The. Konstantin Mikhailovich Simonov. TCRP, *tr. by* Lubov Yakovleva

We saw that sky. Blackness. Place of Fire. Johannes Bobrowski. PoSu

We saw the brows of countries, worthy of crowns. Seafarers. Georg Heym. WoPoe, *tr. by* Christopher Benfey

We saw the flames raise the night. Evening Star, The. Pablo Antonio Cuadra. TCLAP, *tr. by* Ann McCarthy de Zavala and Grace Schulman

We saw the swallows gathering in the sky. George Meredith. EnLoPo; GTBS-P; NOBE; NOBVV; OxBEV *Fr.* Modern Love.

We saw the water-flags in flower! (LL) Coventry Patmore. EBEV; OxBSP *Fr.* Angel in the House, The.

We saw thee, oh stranger, and wept! Stranger in Louisiana, The. Felicia Dorothea Hemans. RWP

We say a heart breaks—like. We Say. Reginald Gibbons. BodElec

We say he is dead; ah, the word is too somber. Not Dead, but Sleeping. Clara Ann Thompson. CBWP-2

We say it for an hour, or for years. Good-By. Grace Denio Litchfield. PoToHe

We say, "It rains." An unbelievable age! Hath the Rain a Father? Jones Very. ChIV-1

We say that a loon, most graceful and dark. Woman Gave Me a Red Star to Wear on My Headband, A. Jimmie Durham. HATNAP

We say the sea is lonely; better say. Open Sea, The. William Meredith. CoAP; TAP; UnPo

We scoured the secret places of the creek. Moules à la Marinière. Elizabeth Garrett. MFPA

We see a forest and say. Whoever Finds a Horseshoe. Osip Emilevich Mandelstam [*or* Mandelshtam]. PFTM-1

We see each living thing finally die. Sonnet 7. Louise Labé. BoWoP, *tr. by* Willis Barnstone

We see God clear and high above the town. (LL) Soul's Liberty. Anna Wickham. MoBrPo; OxBSP

We see her hand in her lap. "H. D.". APT-1 *Fr.* Tribute to the Angels.

We see them not—we cannot hear. Are They Not All Ministering Spirits? Robert Stephen Hawker. OxAEP-2

We send our best apologies to you. (LL) Letter to an American Visitor. Alex Comfort. FaBoWar; OxBTC

We send you home to a grave on Stone Tower Mountain. Weeping for Ying Yao. Wang Wei. CoBCP, *tr. by* Burton Watson

We separate the fragments from the whole. (LL) Love in the Classroom. Al Zolynas. BLT; LTA

We set out yesterday upon a winter drive. Alexandre Dumas. TTY *Fr.* Lady of the Pearls, The.

We shall. (LL) Near-Johannesburg Boy, The. Gwendolyn Brooks. ESEAA; IllVoic

We shall arrive, / to see, soon. (LL) Bend in the River. Simon J. Ortiz. HATNAP; PoPoPo

We shall bathe, my love, in an African presence. Léopold Sédar Senghor. NegPo *Fr.* Songs for Signare.

We shall come tomorrow morning, who were not to have her love. Emily Hardcastle, Spinster. John Crowe Ransom. OxBSP

We shall die in transparent Petropolis. Petropolis. Osip Emilevich Mandelstam [*or* Mandelshtam]. PeFWW

We shall die on the battlefield. (LL) Song of War. Kofi Awoonor. PBMAP; PoetW

We shall find out. (LL) Old Fools, The. Philip Larkin. EmeKit; HarvBoo

We shall go mad no doubt and die that way. (LL) Cool Web, The. Robert Graves. AWP; GTBS-P; HarvBoo; NAEL-5v2; NAEL-6v2; NoAM; OxBEV; OxBTC; SCV; WoPoe

We shall have everything we want and there'll be no more dying. Ode to Joy. Frank O'Hara. GLP; NeAP; PmAP

We shall have had a good Friday. (LL) W. H. Auden. GI; PoE *Fr.* Horae Canonicae.

We Shall Know. *Unknown.* PWR

We shall live again. *Unknown.* STP *Fr.* Ghost-Dance Songs.

We shall not always plant while others reap. From the Dark Tower. Countee Cullen. APT-2; BPo; ColAP; MakPoe; NAAL-2v2; Son

We shall not escape Hell, my passionate. Marina Ivanovna Tsvetayeva [*or* Tsvetaeva]. BoWoP

We shall not ever meet them bearded in heaven. On the Death of Friends in Childhood. Donald Justice. CoAMPo; ColAP; InPK-6; LCAP-2

We shall not go up against you. This Be Our Revenge. Saul [*or* Shaul] Tchernichowsky [*or* Tchernichovsky]. TrJP, *tr. by* Shalom Spiegel

We shall not lift our eyes towards the heavens. Song of Earth. Uri Zvi Greenberg. FIT, *tr. by* Robert Friend

We Shall Overcome. Breyten Breytenbach. PeSAV, *tr. by* Ernst Van Heerden

We Shall Overcome. *Unknown.* AH

We shall overcome! September 11, 1973. Emma Sepúlveda-Pulvirenti. TANSG, *tr. by* Shaun Griffin

We shall remember the wheat stalk in the greenness of her youth. Remembrance of Beginnings of Things. Leah Goldberg. MHP, *tr. by* Ruth Finer Mintz

We Shall Return, Luanda. Ngudia Wendel. PBMAP

We shall sleep-out together through the dark. Ararat. Charles Tomlinson. NoP-4

We shall soon give all our attention to you. (LL) Spring Day. John Ashbery. ColAP; NOBA

We shall walk in the snow. (LL) Velvet Shoes. Elinor Wylie. MoAmPo; PAI; WHSW

We share this: that vanishing figure. Illusions. Sally Roberts Jones. AngWePo

We shared not one idea in thirty years. Reformer to His Father, A. James Simmons. BIrV

We shipped him at the Sandwich Isles. Whaler's Pig, The. Edwin James Brady. NOBAu

We should cultivate our different tastes. Cultivation. Mrs. Henry Linden. CBWP-4

We should have seen it coming back. Dark Days, The. Greg Williamson. NeAmPo

We Show You That Death as a Dancer. Hamish Henderson. PoWW

We shut the red judge in a bronze jar. Red Judge, The. D. M. Black. EmeKit

We sing a hymn to Artemis, for it is. Callimachus. HePo, *tr. by* Barbara Hughes Fowler *Fr.* Hymns.

We sing praise of him who died. Thomas Kelly. SacPr

We sirens, since we rigged up stereophonic sound. Sirens, The. Gordon Challis. PeNZ

We sit at the table and that is grace. November and Aunt Jemima. Thylias Moss. TRP

We sit beside the Mississippi. Making Poems; on the road in Minneapolis. Sekou Sundiata. SpirFl

We sit, crookbacked, at the bar. At the Telephone Club. Henri Coulette. CoAP

We sit here, talking of Barea and Lorca. Conversation in Gibraltar 1943. Charles Causley. PoWW

We sit in the darkness. Feeding, The. Lou Lipsitz. CDa

We sit late, watching the dark slowly unfold. September. Ted Hughes. BoLoP

We sit on a green bench in Harrison Railroad Park. Dreams in Harrison Railroad Park. Nellie Wong. OpBo

We sit on barstools. Whitman on the Beach. Mark Bibbins. WiU

We Sit Solitary. *Unknown.* TrJP

We sit together among. Drinking Wine with a Mountain Hermit. Li Po. CrYelRi, *tr. by* Sam Hamill

We sit watching the afternoon summer smell ripely. James Powell on Imagination. Larry Neal. BPo

We slept on the edge of town, in the last building. After Eden. Rachel Tzvia Back. DTA

We slipped, trampled, tripped. Leaving Mother, 1954. John Graham-Pole. BloBone

We smell on certain people as they pass. (LL) Urban Poem. Douglas Goetsch. AmPoNex; UrbNat

We smiled together. Gardens. Neil Curry. OBGa

We sometimes ride, and sometimes walk. Life at Rickings. Frances Seymour, Countess of Hertford. ECWP

We sound like crying bullheads. Voices. Nora Dauenhauer. HATNAP

We sow the fertile seed and then we reap it. Evening Hymn in the Hovels. Francis Lauderdale Adams. OxBS

We speak the language. No. We Can Say That. Tony Curtis. TCAWP

We spend our morning. Memory of Elena, The. Carolyn Forché. LoL; NoAM

We split a pill in two and walked in the Luxembourg Gardens until some gendarmes appeared on the side of a small hill and told us to leave. White Nights. Lewis Warsh. KGB

We spoke / at all. (LL) Night-Blooming Cereus, The. Robert Earl Hayden. APT-2; ESEAA

We spread torn quilts and blankets. Picnic, an Homage to Civil Rights, The. Michael S. Weaver. ISC; LTA; PoPoPo

We stand in the rain in a long line. What Work Is. Philip Levine. EmeKit

We stand naked behind the line. On the Death of Sylvia Plath. Judith Herzberg. WPOW

We stand on the edge of wounds, hugging canned meat. Dream of Rebirth. Roberta Hill Whiteman. CDW

We stand pinned. Zocalo. Michael S. Harper. NBV

We stand together. Last Journey. John Montague. CIP-2; ModIr; PBCIP; PNI

We stars, we stars.   Chorus of the Stars.   Nelly Sachs.   BBASP; PFTM-1, *tr.* by Michael Roloff

We started home, my son and I.   Jaan Kaplinski.   BLT; GifTon; WoPoe, *tr.* by Sam Hamill and Rina Tamm

We started our house midway through the Cultural Revolution.   Building.   Gary Snyder.   BB

We started speaking.   Meeting, The.   Katherine Mansfield.   LW

We startled each other. She was peering.   Goddess, The.   M. R. Peacocke.   NLP

We step out on the green rectangle.   On the Tennis Court at Night.   Galway Kinnell.   MoASP

We Still Have Basketball, Sara.   Lisa Olstein.   MoASP

We stood at the back door.   And the Trains Go On.   Philip Levine.   GM

We stood at the edge.   Jews Speak in Heaven, The.   Gary Catalano.   NOBAu

We stood at the edge of the crowded bar drinking.   Princess, The.   Muhammad Al-As'ad.   MAP, *tr.* by Charles Doria and Lena Jayyusi

We stood by a pond that winter day.   Neutral Tones.   Thomas Hardy.   CABP; EBVV; HAP; HeIP-4; InPK-6; MoBrPo; NAEL-5v2; NAEL-6v2; NOBVV; NPeEn; NoAM; TFi; UnPo

We stood here in the coupledom of us.   Land Love.   Douglas Dunn.   NePenScot

We stood, my mother and I.   Two Statues.   Pauline Hawkesworth.   Prnts

We stood on the rented patio.   Summer Storm.   Dana Gioia.   RA

We stood up before day.   In the Dordogne.   John Peale Bishop.   APT-1; OBWP; PeFWW; PoWW; VGW

We stripped in the first warm spring night.   Belle Isle, 1949.   Philip Levine.   ColAP; VCAP

We strolled at night through the gardens.   Park of the Dead.   Gerrit Komrij.   TuT, *tr.* by Peter Van de Kamp

We study other languages, the signs and mirrors.   Good Omen.   Lewis Warsh.   BodElec

We suffered drought, months without rain.   In Praise of Rain.   Tu Fu.   CrYelRi, *tr.* by Sam Hamill

We Survive! Hirsch [*or* Glik, Hirsh] Glick.   TrJP, *tr.* by Ruth Rubin

We Survived Them.   Anna Swirszczynska.   AF, *tr.* by Czeslaw Milosz

We swam in the rain-filled gully.   Rain Ditch.   Pinkie Gordon Lane.   ISC

We swing ungirded hips.   Song of the Ungirt Runners, The.   Charles Hamilton Sorley.   MoBrPo; OBEV

We take emerald to Bugojno, then the opal route.   Cycles of Donji Vakuf.   Tony Harrison.   FaBoWar

We take long trips.   Jelaluddin [*or* Jalal al-Din] Rumi.   LoL

We take shelter from the monsoon rains.   Baked Oysters Rockefeller.   Marjorie M. Evasco.   ReBoTo

We Take the New Young Couple Out to Dinner.   Carol Tufts.   PasH

We take up the halberds of Wu.   *Unknown.*   CoBCP, *tr.* by Burton Watson   *Fr.* Nine Songs.

We talk of a friend.   Skimming the Ice.   Tom Sexton.   PoCoUp

We talk of light things you and I in this.   Father and Daughter.   Sonia Sanchez.   FFC; GT

We talk of old men who have forgotten their / thoughts.   Errore.   Pier Giorgio Di Cicco.   NOBC

We talked [*or* talk'd] with open heart, and tongue.   Fountain, The.   William Wordsworth.   GTBS-P; OxAEP-2

We talked together in the Yung-shou Temple;.   Letter, The.   Po Chü-i.   ChiP, *tr.* by Arthur Waley

We Thank Thee, Lord.   Calvin W. Laufer.   AH

We, that did nothing study but the way.   Renunciation, A.   Henry King, Bishop of Chichester.   OBEV

We that have done and thought.   Spilt Milk.   W. B. Yeats.   OxBSP

We that with like hearts love, we lovers twain.   Vow to Heavenly Venus, A.   Joachim Du Bellay.   AWP, *tr.* by Andrew Lang

We, the rescued.   Chorus of the Rescued.   Nelly Sachs.   PoSu; WPOW

We the White Witches are, that free.   Masque of the Virtues against Love.   Mary Monck.   ECWP; NOEC

We think of lukewarm water, hope to get in it. (LL)   Gwendolyn Brooks.   BPo; FaBoWP; GT; NAAAL; NAAL-2v2; NAAL-5; NoP-4; PoE; PoPoPo; UnPo   *Fr.* Street in Bronzeville, A.

We think our loved ones pull us under.   On the Waterfront.   Michael Foley.   PNI

We think to create festivals.   Poem.   Antonio Machado Ruiz.   AWP; WoPoe, *tr.* by John Dos Passos

We think we cannot bear the times of cross and need.   Fortune-Bringing Misfortune.   Catharina Regina von Greiffenberg.   AuPH, *tr.* by Lowell A. Bangerter and George C. Schoolfield

We thirst at first—'tis Nature's Act.   Thirst.   Emily Dickinson.   NOCV

We thought at first, this man is a king for sure.   Blue Blood.   James Stephens.   MoBrPo; OBCoV; OBMV

We thought that love was over.   We Just Couldn't Say Good-bye.   Harry Woods.   ReLy

We thought that Winter with his hungry pack.   On the Occurrence of a Spell of Arctic Weather in May, 1858.   Paul Hamilton Hayne.   APN-2

We three are on the cedar-shadowed lawn.   George Meredith.   NOBVV   *Fr.* Modern Love.

We three kings all orient are.   We Three Kings.   *Unknown.*   FaBoVe

We Three Kings of Orient Are.   John Henry, Jr. Hopkins.   AH; ChrPo   (Three Kings of Orient.)   APN-2

We told them the myths about others.   Port, The.   Bernadette Mayer.   FTOS

We too, we too, descending once again.   Too-Late Born, The.   Archibald MacLeish.   MoAMPo; OxBA

—We took our work, and went, you see.   Recreation.   Jane Taylor.   OBCoV; OxBoLi; PEW; WoRP

We took the children down for an hour's outing.   Household Cavalry, Llanstephan.   Sally Roberts Jones.   TCAWP

We took their orders and are dead. (LL)   Inscription for a War.   Alec Derwent Hope.   BMAP; NoP-4

We tore the green tree down.   Verifying the Dead.   James Welch.   CDW

We touch fingertips.   Snow Climbers.   Steve Wiesinger.   PasH

We touched land.   Not That Far.   May Miller.   BISi

We traded six AK-47s.   Movie, The.   Steve Denning.   CDa

We travel like other people, but we return to nowhere. As if travelling.   Mahmoud Darwish.   AF, *tr.* by Abdullah Al-Udhari   *Fr.* Poems after Beirut.

We trust and fear, we question and believe.   Our Limitations.   Oliver Wendell Holmes.   NCAP

We tunnel through your noonday out to you.   Ants, The.   William Empson.   OxBSo

We turn aside from everything.   Birthday Wishes to a Minister of the Gospel.   Lizelia Augusta Jenkins Moorer.   CBWP-3

We turn off the light.   December 15th.   Vera Gherarducci.   CItWP, *tr.* by Cinzia Sartini Blum and Lara Trubowitz

Two are last in Hell: what may we fear[e].   Barley-Break; or, Last in Hell.   Robert Herrick.   CaPo

We Two Boys Together Clinging.   Walt Whitman.   APN-1

We two stood simply friend-like side by side.   Inapprehensiveness.   Robert Browning.   NOBVV

We two were sweethearts.   Just Friends.   John Klenner.   ReLy

We uncountable dread legions of Labor.   We.   Vladimir Timofeievich Kirillov.   TCRP, *tr.* by Albert C. Todd

We used to get intelligence reports.   Time on Target.   William Daniel Ehrhart.   CDa

We used to look for satellites.   Astronomy.   M. L. Williams.   GeoHom

We used to sleep, you remember.   Barn, The.   "Rachel" [*or* "Rahel"].   FIT, *tr.* by Robert Friend

We used to spend the spring together.   Most Beautiful Girl in the World, The.   Richard Rodgers.   OBAL; ReLy

We used to talk of so many things.   Before and after Marriage.   Anne Campbell.   PoToHe

We used to tell each other erotic stories.   Sleepless Nights.   Marilyn Nelson Waniek.   ISC

We've all been invited up to Killisnoo.   *Unknown.*   STP

We've always thought / Knowledge is naught.   Varsity Drag, The.   Ray Henderson.   ReLy

We've been out for an hour.   Fishing with Elvis.   Dabney Stuart.   AllShUp

We've been taught for two thousand years.   Late Twentieth-Century Prayer, A.   Ernest Sandeen.   WeW-3

We've called ourselves adults for ages now.   Goldminers' Waltz, The.   Aleksandr Arkadevich Galich.   TCRusP, *tr.* by Gerry Smith

We've come intil a gey queer time.   Epistle to John Guthrie.   Sydney Goodsir Smith.   OxBS

We've come, the woman calls out, to listen.   Melancholy.   David Keller.   UrbNat

"We've fought before, but this is worse than rape!"   Baobab Fruit Picking; or, Development in Monkey Bay.   Jack A. Mapanje.   PeSAV

We've fought with many men acrost the seas.   Fuzzy-Wuzzy.   Rudyard Kipling.   MoBrPo

We've found this Scott Fitzgerald chap.   Effervescence and Evanescence.   Keith Preston.   OBAL

We've got a new maid called Chrysanthemum.   Limerick.   *Unknown.*   PeLi

We've got as far as poison-gas. (LL)   Christmas: 1924.   Thomas Hardy.   FaBoEE; OBCP

We've got one day here, and not another minute.   New York, New York.   Adolph Green.   ReLy

We've got the cholera in camp—it's worse than forty fights.   Cholera Camp.   Rudyard Kipling.   FaBoWar

We've got this cheese down here to give away.   Capitalist Poem #36.   Campbell McGrath.   NAPBL

We've heard and heard, and finally believe.   Diary, The.   Goethe.   STV, *tr.* by John Frederick Nims

We've inherited something from our ancestors, the serfs. Nikolai Ivanovich Tryapkin [or Triapkin]. TCRP *Fr.* Verses about the Dog's Inheritance.

We've just been introduced. Shall We Dance? Richard Rodgers. ReLy

We've nothing vast to offer you, no deserts. Welshman to Any Tourist, A. Ronald Stuart Thomas. OxBC

We've our business to attend Day's duties. Bending the Bow. Robert Duncan. HarvBoo

We've / poisoned our food, polluted our air. John Cage. APSN *Fr.* Diary: How to Improve the World (You Will Only Make Matters Worse).

We've rented a flat in Ghosh Buildings, Albert Road. Roys, The. Arvind Krishna Mehrotra. OMIP

We've returned to autumn again; summer. Word for Summer, A. George Seferis. AF

We've socially-conscious biography. Limerick. *Unknown.* PeLi

We've Solved the Problem. Bernadette Mayer. FTOS

We've traveled long together. Verses to my Heart's-Sister. Henrietta Cordelia Ray. CBWP-3

We've trod the maze of error round. George Crabbe. OBEV *Fr.* Reflections.

We wade shin-deep in the channel. Jellyfish Eggs. Gregory Orfalea. GraLe

We waited in silence for our children. Death of the Miners or, The Widows of the Earth. Raymond Mazisi Kunene. PeSAV, *tr.* by the author

We wake and watch the sun make bright. Another Sunday Morning. Derek Mahon. CIP-2

We wake; we wake the day. Indian Singing in 20th Century America. Gail Tremblay. HATNAP; LTA; ReEnLa

We Walk the Way of the New World. Haki R. Madhubuti. BPo; ESEAA

We walk towards a land not of our flesh. We Walk Towards a Land. Mahmoud Darwish. VCWP, *tr.* by Rana Kabbani

We walked across a frozen river in Manchuria. Expatriates. David Woo. OpBo

We walked and blinked at sunlight on the snow. Winter Sonnet. Linda Beatrice Brown. GT

We walked [or walk'd] along, while bright and red. Two April Mornings, The. William Wordsworth. EBEV; GTBS-P; NAEL-5v2; NAEL-6v2

We wander in the bleak silence. Automobile, The. Vladislav Felitsianovich Khodasevich. TCRusP, *tr.* by Daniel Weissbort

We wander in the stifling heat. Shadow in Stone. Janice Mirikitani. OpBo

We wander now who marched before. Old Soldier. Padraic Colum. OBMV

We want to work-we must not die! (LL) Fear. Eva Picková. INSAB; ItWoWo

We want what is real. We want what is real. Don't deceive us. *Unknown.* APN-2 *Fr.* Minnetare Songs.

We wanted Li Wing. Lapsus Linguae. Keith Preston. NBLV; OBAL; OBCoV

We watch. Enemies. Charlotte Zolotow. HHAm

We watched from the house. I Was Sleeping Where the Black Oaks Move. Louise Erdrich. HATNAP; NoP-4; PoPoPo

We watched [or watch'd] her breathing thro' the night. Death-Bed, The. Thomas Hood. GTBS-P; NOBE; OBEV; TreFP

We watched our love burn with the lumberyard. Lumberyard, The. Ruth Herschberger. WPE

We Wear the Mask. Paul Laurence Dunbar. APN-2; AmFaPo; ISC; NAAAL; NIL-7; NIP-4; NoP-4; PoPoPo; SSLK; SacPr; TCAPo; TTY; UnPo

We went north / to escape winter. Indian Song: Survival. Leslie Marmon Silko. CDW; VoR

We went on the trolley. Late 20th Century: Spring. Jerry Martien. GeoHom

We went out, early one morning. Out Fishing. Barbara Howes. WPE

We went there on the train. *They had big barges that they towed.* Protocols. Randall Jarrell. LCAP-2; OxBC; VGW

We went to Oldshoremore. Itinerary. Edwin Morgan. HarvBoo; OBCoV

We went to Pumpkin Hour. My Tenth Birthday. Robert Adamson. BMAP

We went to vote in our democracy. Poisonfield. Glyn Maxwell. HarvBoo

We Went Westward o social telepathy at the. Hannah Weiner. FTOS *Fr.* Spoke Aug 19.

We were a people taut for war; the hills. Welsh History. Ronald Stuart Thomas. OBWVE

We were a tribe, a family, a people. Scotland 1941. Edwin Muir. CABP; NePenScot; OxBS

We were a whole army underground. As Hour and Year Collapsed. Joe Wenderoth. BodElec; NAPBL

We were able to notice that each one in a way carried a bundle, they were. Bundles for Them. Gertrude Stein. PFTM-1

We were all drunk, and Acindynus was determined to keep sober. Lucianus [or Lucian]. GrAn

We were all sitting round the table. Christmas Dinner. Michael Rosen. OBCP

We were apart; yet, day by day. Matthew Arnold. NAEL-6v2 *Fr.* Switzerland.

We were aristocrats in Clare. Molly O'Rourke Cleary Explains. Patricia Cleary Miller. SpudSo

We were born / in the time of the first perfected machine guns. Dialectic. Victor Serge. AF, *tr.* by James Brook

We were brought up to believe. Brief Thoughts on Floods. Miroslav Holub. PoSu, *tr.* by Ian Milner and Jarmila Milner

We were building a fort. Stranger, The. Gerald Locklin. OPRER

We were challenged by The Dingoes—they're the pride of Squatter's Gap. Friendly Game of Football, A. Edward Dyson. CBAP

We were children once long ago, dear, you and I. You Never Knew about Me. P. G. Wodehouse. ReLy

We were consigned. Continuous Time. Milo De Angelis. NeIt, *tr.* by Lawrence Venuti

We were crowded in the cabin. Ballad of the Tempest. James Thomas Fields. TreFP

We were doing laundry. November 22, 1983. Sherman Alexie. ReTh

We were drinking coffee (of course) when in walks. Peoria. M. Loncar. NAPBL

We were drinking for free, bumming beers. Class A, Salem, the Rookie League. Gary Fincke. MoASP

We were driving down the Kennedy having a great time guessing old groups. Ice. Maureen Seaton. IllVoic

We were enclosed. Catherine of Siena (A. K. A. Saint Catherine). WPoS *Fr.* Prayer 20.

We were fancydancing, you see. Powwow Polaroid. Sherman Alexie. UnSA

We were finishing the fourth grade as the storm gathered. Beginning, The. Vladimir Nikolaevich Sokolov. TCRP, *tr.* by Simon Franklin

We were forty miles from Albany. E-ri-e, The. *Unknown.* TCAPo

We were gestures of the ocean once. Secret in the Roar, The. Luis H. Francia. ReBoTo

We were good, good and obedient. Sandor Csoori. VCWP, *tr.* by Len Roberts and László Vértes

We were halfway through July. Handsome afternoon! On the Banks of the Duero. Antonio Machado Ruiz. STV, *tr.* by John Frederick Nims

We were having fun, that devil Hermione and I. Asclepiades. EroLit, *tr.* by Kenneth McLeish

We were in the middle of something big. Motel Story. Maggie Nelson. AmPoNex

We were looking for a basement to live in. Memories of Marriage. Enrique Lihn. TCLAP, *tr.* by John Felstiner

We were looking for a paradise, a place. Catch, The. Rebecca Seiferle. ExTi

We were mistaken, I think. Regalia Figure. Carl Phillips. NAPBL

We were nearly. Above the Pool. John Montague. NOIV

We were never invited to his house. My Rich Uncle, Whom I Only Met Three Times. Marge Piercy. UnSA

We were no good as murderers, we were clowns. (LL) Stephano Remembers. James Simmons. PBCIP; PNI

We were not even moving. No one was moving. On the Eve of Our Mutually Assured Destruction. C. D. Wright. LCAP-2

We were not likened to dogs among the Gentiles—They pity a dog. We Were Not Likened to Dogs among the Gentiles. Uri Zvi Greenberg. MHP, *tr.* by Ruth Finer Mintz

We were not raised to look in. You Were Never Miss Brown to Me. Sherley Anne Williams. GT

We were playing on the green together. "Is It Nothing to You?" May Probyn. OBEV; SacPr

We were riding through frozen fields in a wagon at dawn. Encounter. Czeslaw Milosz. BodElec; ChAP; PoetW; WoPoe, *tr.* by Lillian Vallee

We were rumbling o'er Trumpington stones. (LL) Country Clergyman's Trip to Cambridge, The. Thomas Babington Macaulay, 1st Baron Macaulay. OBSV; OxBoLi; PeLV

We were sick of seeing the liners leave. Refugees at Cobh. Sean Dunne. BiHa

We Were Sisters Weren't We. Katie Donovan. BiHa

We were sitting in a small room. Now Winter Nights. Robert Hass. BodElec

We were situated on the approaches to a village. Tenderness. Aleksey [or Aleksei] Aleksandrovich Surkov. TCRP, *tr.* by Lubov Yakovleva

We were so poor I had to take the place of the. Charles Simic. VCAP *Fr.* World Doesn't End, The.

We were the wrecked elect. Fiction-Makers, The. Anne Stevenson. DiPo

We were there, Avinu. While Bouncing the Shema Back and Forth in Shul. Talia N. Bloch. GotH

We Were Three. Claribel Alegría. AF; TCLAP, *tr.* by Carolyn Forché

We were three women, three men. Sorrow of Kodio, The. *Unknown.* PBA, *tr.* by Miriam Koshl

We were together. Yakamochi (Otomo no Yakamochi). OHPJ

We were together since the War began. Rudyard Kipling. HarvBoo; NPeEn; PeFWW *Fr.* Epitaphs of the War [1914–1918].

We were two daughters of one race. Sisters, The. Tennyson. PAI

We were two pretty babes, the youngest she. Childhood Fled. Charles Lamb. CenSon

We were very tired, we were very merry. Recuerdo. Edna St. Vincent Millay. APT-1; ChAP; NAAL-2v2; NAAL-5; NoAM; OxBA; TAP

We were waiting at the station. Parting Kiss, The. Josephine D. Henderson Heard. CBWP-4

We were walking. Rice Will Grow Again. Frank A. Cross. CDa

We were warned about frost, yet all day the summer. Early Frost. Leslie Norris. AngWePo

We were young, we were merry, we were very very wise. Unwelcome. Mary Elizabeth Coleridge. OBEV; VWP; WPE

We weren't waiting for anything to happen. Then. Gail Mazur. ExTi

We whisper in her ear, "You are not true." (LL) Epistemology. Richard Wilbur. CRP; NOBA; NoAM; OxBSP

We who are called Australians have no country. Rex Ingamells. NOBAu Fr. Unknown Land.

We who are here present thank the Great Spirit that we are here to praise Him. Thanksgivings, The. Unknown. APN-2, tr. by Harriet Maxwell Converse

We who are left, how shall we look again. Lament. Wilfrid Wilson Gibson. OxBTC

We who are responsible for living. Without Histories. Blanca Wiethüchter. TANSG, tr. by Shaun Griffin and Emma Sepúlveda-Pulvirenti

We who are strangers now, after our years of easy friendship. Bangla Desh: 3. Faiz Ahmad Faiz. CarOv, tr. by Carolyn Kizer

We who had known the desert's grit and granite. Exodus. Charles Reznikoff. ChIV-1

We who have always looked with tolerant irony. Prayer for the End of the Century, A. Heberto Padilla. VCWP

We Who Have Loved. Corinne Roosevelt Robinson. LW

We who must act as handmaidens. Muse of Water, A. Carolyn Kizer. FFC; VCAP

We who play under the pines. Song of the Rabbits Outside the Tavern, The. Elizabeth Jane Coatsworth. OBCA; OxIBACP; SoSe-8

We who survived the war and took to wife. Thirtieth Anniversary Report of the Class of '41. Howard Nemerov. HCAP

We Who Were Born. Eiluned Lewis. AngWePo

We Who Were Executed. Faiz Ahmad Faiz. PoetW, tr. by Agha Shahid Ali

We who with songs beguile your pilgrimage. James Elroy Flecker. OBMV; OxBTC; UV Fr. Golden Journey to Samarkand, The.

We, whose lungs fill with the sweetness of day. Child of Europe. Czeslaw Milosz. AF, tr. by Jan Darowski

We will be passing the telephone booths soon. Nonplussed. Ken Bolton. BMAP

We will call you Agua like the rivers and cool jugs. Negotiations with a Volcano. Naomi Shihab Nye. GraLe

We will go no more to Shaemus, at the Nip. Shaemus. Conrad Potter Aiken. OxBA

We will go to the wood, says Robin to Bobbin. Unknown. OxNR

We will kill our love. We Are Going to Shoot at the Heart. Anna Swirszczynska. PoSu

We will mention it. We will remember and mention. Alicia Kozameh. MirDau, tr. by David Davis Fr. Saltos Sobre El Exilio.

We Will Not Fear. David Diamond. AH

We will not whisper, we have found the place. Sonnet. Joseph Hilaire Pierre Belloc. MoBrPo

We will return to life. Comanche Ghost Dance: An Impression. Lance Henson. VoR

We will see more passing than any. Nostalgia. Christopher Buckley. SeSe

We will sing a song. Songs from the Great Feast to the Dead. Unknown. APN-2, tr. by Edward William Nelson

We will take it seriously as we open our morning paper. Sonnet to Be Written from Prison. Robert Adamson. CBAP

We wish a drove of weasels transmuted into horses. Unknown. APN-2 Fr. Minnetare Songs.

We wish not the mechanic arts to scan. Power of Women, The. Matilda Barbara Betham-Edwards. ECWP

We wish only to bury our dead. Shorn. Wole Soyinka. PoetW Fr. Funeral in Soweto.

We wish to bury our dead. Now, a funeral. Funeral Sermon, Soweto. Wole Soyinka. VCWP

We with our Fair pitched among the feathery clover. Individualist Speaks, The. Louis MacNeice. OBMV

We woke early. Names in Monterchi: To Rachel. James Wright (1927–80). NNaP

We woke near midnight. Eruption: Pu'u Ō'ō. Garrett Kaoru Hongo. LoL

We Women. Edith Södergran. WPOW, tr. by Samuel Charters

We won't forget the padre in a hurry. Padre, The. Frank Ormsby. BiHa

We wonder what the horoscope did show. Shakespeare. Henrietta Cordelia Ray. CBWP-3

We Wondered about the Mellow Peaches. Jack A. Mapanje. HBAPE

We work here together. Pine Planters, The. Thomas Hardy. FaBoVe

We work, play, don't cross-reference calendars. Marilyn Hacker. VCAP Fr. Taking Notice.

We would awaken in a twilight gloom. Aleksandr Petrovich Mezhirov. TCRP

We would climb the highest dune. With Kit, Age Seven, at the Beach. William Stafford. RaBo

We Would See Jesus. Anna Bartlett Warner. AH

We write them there forever. (LL) Walt Whitman. Edwin Arlington Robinson. APN-2; NCAP; OxBA; TCAPo

We writhe in a star-net. Fish in the Net. János Pilinszky. IQMS, tr. by Adam Makkai

Weak is the sophistry, and vain the art. Describes the Fascinations of Love. Mary Robinson. CenSon; RWP

Weak Monk, The. Stevie Smith. BoWoP; FaBoTw

Weak Poet, The. David Shapiro. BodElec

Weak sun. Rod Willmot. HA

Weak-winged is song. James Russell Lowell. APN-1; CBCWP; NOBA; OBWP

Weak with nice sense, the chaste MIMOSA stands. Erasmus Darwin. NOBRP Fr. Botanic Garden, The.

Weakened by loss of blood Robin's last act was to slash his sword. Alan Halsey. Oth Fr. Robin Hood Book, A.

Weaker the Wine, The. Su Tung-p'o (Su Shih). OHPC, tr. by Kenneth Rexroth

Weakness, The. Toi Derricotte. GT; LTA

Weakness, The. Bernard O'Donoghue. ModIr; NoP-4

Wealth. Ralph Waldo Emerson. APN-1

Wealth. Sadi [or Saadi or Sa'di]. AWP, tr. by Sir Edwin Arnold Fr. Gulistan, The.

Wealth and honor in life were dew on the grass leaf. Su Tung-p'o (Su Shih). WoPoe, tr. by Burton Watson Fr. Roadside Flowers, Three Poems with Introduction.

Wealth came by water to this farmless island. Delos. Bernard Spencer. NoAM

Wealth covers sin—the poor. Epigram. Kassia. WPOW, tr. by Patrick Diehl

Wealth in the deep of the rose, The. Rose, The. Gabriela Mistral. SpanPo, tr. by Kate Flores

Wealth Is Not Happiness. Caroline Elizabeth Norton. TreFP

Wealth unto every man, I see. Worldly Wealth. Rowland Watkyns. FaBoEE

Wealthy Cit, grown old in trade, The. Cit's Country Box, The. Robert Lloyd. NOEC

Weaning of Furniture-Nutrition. Juan Felipe Herrera. BodElec

Weapon, The. Hugh MacDiarmid. RB

Weapon that comes down as still, A. John Pierpont. APN-1 Fr. Word from a Petitioner.

Weapons. Anna Wickham. MoBrPo

Weapons Training. Bruce Dawe. OBCoV

Wear a dress. Answer to a Man's Question, "What Can I Do about Women's Liberation?", An. Susan Griffin. GLP

Wear dark glasses in the rain. Adultery. Carol Ann Duffy. EmeKit

Wear the heart like a home. Confederacy. Elise Paschen. FFC

Wear thou this fresh green garland this one day. Garland for Advancing Years, A. William Bell Scott. GSo

Weare I a Kinge I coulde commande content. Edward de Vere, 17th Earl of Oxford. See Poem: "Were I a king, I could command content."

Weareth the leaden hue seen in the eyes of the blind. (LL) Fragment: December 18, 1847. Henry Wadsworth Longfellow. APN-1; TCAPo

Wearie thoughts doe waite upon me. Nicholas Breton. NPeEn Fr. Solemne Long Enduring Passion, A.

Wearied arm, and broken sword. William Makepeace Thackeray. AiP Fr. Pocahontas.

Wearied, exhausted, dully sleeping. (LL) Spring in New Hampshire. Claude McKay. BPo; ChAP

Wearied of its own turning. Burning Wheel, The. Aldous Leonard Huxley. ChIV-1

Wearily, drearily. In Prison. William Morris. FaBoWar; PeVV

Wearin' o' the Green, The. Unknown. NOIV

Weariness. Mary E. Tucker. CBWP-1

Weariness in the Evening of January Thirty-Second. 'Isam Mahfouz. MAP, tr. by Sargon Boulus and Samuel Hazo

Weariness of life that has no will, The. Everyman. Siegfried Sassoon. MoBrPo

Wearing a Worn-Out Coat. Chin Nung. CoBLCP, tr. by Jonathan Chaves

Wearing Achilles' Armour, Patroclus, along with the Myrmidons, Attacks the Trojans. Homer. OBVE, tr. by Christopher Logue Fr. Iliad, The.

Wearing an overcoat in August heat. Bag Woman. Dudley Randall. NoAM

Wearing Dad's White Shirt Backwards. Rick Agran. AmPoNex

Wearing her yellow rubber slicker. Myrtle. Ted Kooser. InvLad

Wearing my yellow straw hat. My Yellow Straw Hat. Lessie Jones Little. TLR

Wearing of [*or* Wearin' o'] the Green, The. *Unknown.* AWP; OxBoLi

Wearing that same black dress. Women you are accustomed to, The. Lucille Clifton. ErotSp; GT

Wearing worry about money like a hair shirt. Worry about Money. Kathleen Jessie Raine. FaBoTw

Weary already, weary miles to-night. Match with the Moon, A. Dante Gabriel Rossetti. NOBVV; NPeEn; OxBEV

Weary Blues, The. Langston Hughes. ColAP; FaBoA; HarvBoo; ISC; NAAAL; NOBA; NoAM; NoP-4; PoPoPo; SAmP

Weary, I open wide the antique pane. Poetry and the Poet. Henry Cuyler Bunner. OBAL

Weary is he, and sick of the sorrow of war. Soldier Is Home, The. John Shaw Neilson. CBAP

Weary of all this wordy strife. Catholic Love. Charles Wesley. SacPr

Weary on ye, sad waves! On an Island. "Ethna Carbery." WPE

Weary Road, The. Lu Chao-lin. SuSp, *tr. by* Robin D. S. Yates

Weary Road, The. Pao Chao.

    "Do you not see the riverside grass." ChinPo, *tr. by* Yip Wai-lim

    "Do you not see the young men off to war." ChinPo, *tr. by* Yip Wai-lim

    "Have you not seen the grasses on the riverbank?" SuSp

    "Splash water on level ground." ChinPo, *tr. by* Yip Wai-lim

    "To you, fine wine in gold cup." ChinPo, *tr. by* Yip Wai-lim

    "Water spilled on level ground." SuSp

Weary Song to a Slow Sad Tune, A. Li Ch'ing-chao. BoWoP; OHMPC, *tr. by* Kenneth Rexroth

Weary sun, The. Fisherman, The. Yunna Petrovna [*or* Iunna Pinkhusovna] Moritz [*or* Morits]. TCRusP, *tr. by* Daniel Weissbort

Weary the cry of the wind is, weary the sea. Sorrow of Mydath. John Masefield. MoBrPo

Weary traveler, who, all night long, The. Storied Sonnet. Ann Radcliffe. CenSon

Weary way-wanderer, languid and sick at heart. Soldier's Wife, The. Robert Southey. FaBoWar; OxBSP

Weary wild geese who came. Fujiwara no Teika. WoPoe, *tr. by* Steven D. Carter

Weary with reading and with meditation. Storm and Calm: Sent from Embden to M. Edw. Ma. and M. Tho. Ly, The. Nicholas Murford. NOSC

Weary with toil, I haste me to my bed. William Shakespeare. AWTN; CAGL; HeIP-4; NoSic; SCGP *Fr.* Sonnets.

Weary, worn, and sorrow-laden. Storm-Beaten. Clara Ann Thompson. CBWP-2

Weasel, by a person caught, A. Man and the Weasel, The. Phaedrus. AWP, *tr. by* Christopher Smart

Weather. Michael Burkard. BodElec

Weathers [*or* Weather]. Thomas Hardy. FaBoCh; MoBrPo; OBMV; RB

Weather. Archibald MacLeish. *See* Cook County

Weather. Eve Merriam. TLR

Weather. *Unknown.* OTCP

Weather, The. Gavin Ewart. OTCP

Weather buffets our houses in armour all night. Gales. Anne Stevenson. Spl

Weather changeable at dusk and dawn, The. Written on the Lake, Returning from the Retreat at Stone Cliff. Hsieh Ling-yün. CoBCP, *tr. by* Burton Watson

Weather-Cock Points South, The. Amy Lowell. APT-1; NALW; NoP-4

Weather Ear. Norman Nicholson. OxBSP

Weather in my head, The. Degrees. Kevin Young. AmPoNex

Weather in place of God. Tempted by the Classical on Returning from the Store at Twenty below Zero. Sydney Lea. SwNoth

Weather is fright'ning, The. Isn't This a Lovely Day (To Be Caught in the Rain?) Irving Berlin. ReLy

Weather left me raw, The. How to Change a Flat. Leslie Anne McIlroy. AmPoNex

Weather Newly Cleared. Wang Wei. CoBCP, *tr. by* Burton Watson

Weather of Olympus, The. Robert Graves. FaBoEE; OBCoV

Weather of this winter night, my mistress, The. Childlessness. James Merrill. CoAmPo; ColAP

Weather, peddle our goods and die into the future. (LL) Crypto-Jews, The. Robin Becker. ExTi; OPRER; TaR

Weather Report. Brenda Coultas. HeMarv

Weather Report. Charles Tomlinson. HarvBoo

Weather's cast away its cloak, The. Temps a Laissié, Le. Charles, Duc d' Orléans. WoPoe, *tr. by* Stanley Burnshaw

Weather's cleared, The. We're filming at Versailles. Clive James. OBSV *Fr.* To Pete Atkin: A Letter from Paris.

Weather Signs. Aratus. HePo, *tr. by* Barbara Hughes Fowler *Fr.* Phaenomena.

Weather They Were Written In, The. Kathy Fagan. PuP-23

Weather was fine, The. They took away his teeth. John Berryman. HarvBoo *Fr.* Dream Songs.

Weather wonderful—cannot go out in daylight. Honeymoon Postcard. Paul Durcan. OBCoV

Weathercock: My breast is puffed up and my neck is swollen. Cynewulf. *See* I puff my breast out, my neck swells

Weathercock, The: "I puff my breast out, my neck swells." Cynewulf. RB *Fr.* Riddles (Exeter Book).

Weathered bones. Basho. EH, *tr. by* Robert Hass

Weathered raft I saw myself. Song of the Andoumboulou: 12. Nathaniel Mackey. FTOS

Weathered skeleton, A. Basho. SoOfWa, *tr. by* Sam Hamill

Weathering. Fleur Adcock. DiPo

Weathering Out. Rita Dove. ESEAA; LCAP-2; NoAM

Weave for me. Dyeing. Mabel Tobrise. NAfrP

Weave like a web in the air / Divinely superfluous beauty. (LL) Divinely Superfluous Beauty. Robinson Jeffers. HeIP-4; MoAmPo

Weave the warp, and weave the woof. Curse upon Edward, The. Thomas Gray. OBEV

Weave us a song of many threads. Weaver. Sandra Maria Esteves. PueRic

Weaver Bird, The. Kofi Awoonor. HBAPE; PBMAP

Weavers. Heinrich Heine. TrJP

Weavers Song, The. Thomas Deloney. PBRV

Weaving a garland long ago. Anacreon. ErotSp, *tr. by* Sam Hamill

Weaving at the Window. Wang Chien. SuSp, *tr. by* William H. Nienhauser

Weaving Love-Knots. Hsüeh T'ao. BoWoP, *tr. by* Carolyn Kizer

Weaving Love-Knots 2. Hsüeh T'ao. BoWoP, *tr. by* Carolyn Kizer

Weaving the Morning. João Cabral de Melo Neto. TCLAP, *tr. by* Galway Kinnell

Web, The. Gregory O'Donoghue. BIrV

Web, The. Theodore Weiss. CoAP

Web outside the window filled, The. Spider. William Virgil Davis. YaYoPo

Webern. Christopher Pilling. NLP

Webster Ford. Edgar Lee Masters. APT-1 *Fr.* Spoon River Anthology.

Webster was much possessed by death. Whispers of Immortality. T. S. Eliot. APT-1; CTC; NOBA; NoAM; OBMV; OxAEP-2

Weddin' a woo a clog an' a shoe, A. Weddings. *Unknown.* FaBoVe

Wedding. Alice Oswald. MFPA

Wedding. Nikolai Alekseievich Zabolotsky [*or* Zabolotskii]. TCRP, *tr. by* Daniel Weissbort

Wedding, A. James Tate. NoAM

Wedding, The. Conrad Potter Aiken. TAP

Wedding, The. Pavel Nikolaevich Vasilyev [*or* Vasil'ev]. TCRP, *tr. by* David Macduff *Fr.* Salt Riot, The.

Wedding Anniversary. Margaret E. Bruner. PoToHe

Wedding Bells Are Breaking up That Old Gang of Mine. Willie Raskin. ReLy

Wedding Coat, The. Harriet Rose. BrRo

Wedding Day. Seamus Heaney. OxAEP-2

Wedding Day. Mark Levine. AmPoNex; BAP-01

Wedding Day, The. V. Penelope Pelizzon. AmPoNex

Wedding Day at Nagasaki. Rodney Hall. CBAP

Wedding Feast, The. Edgar Lee Masters. ChIV-2

Wedding Gifts. Adrienne Su. NAPBL

Wedding Hymn. Luis de Góngora y Argote. *Fr.* Solitudes, The.

Wedding in Hanover. Lorna Goodison. GT

Wedding in the Courthouse, The. Kathleen Norris. MPUn

Wedding Morn. D. H. Lawrence. MoBrPo

Wedding night / Graciela bled lightly. Graciela. Gary Soto. NoAM

Wedding over, The. Arizona Zipper. HA

Wedding Party. Donald Hall. LCAP-2

Wedding Party. Allison Joseph. AmPoNex; ExTi; MPUn

Wedding Preparations in the Country. David St. John. LCAP-2

Wedding Reception. Melinda Goodman. GLP

Wedding-Ring. Denise Levertov. NIL-7

Wedding Ring, The. Zinaida Nikolayevna [*or* Nikolaevna] Gippius. ARWW, *tr. by* Catriona Kelly

Wedding Song. Patricia Storace. FFC

Wedding Song. *Unknown.* ChiP, *tr. by* Arthur Waley

Wedding Song in honor of R. Solomon ben Matir. Moses Ibn Ezra. "Rejoice, O youth, in the lovely hind." TrJP

Wedding Sonnet. Arthur Zanker. AuPH, *tr. by* Lowell A. Bangerter

Wedding Vow, The. Sharon Olds. MPUn

Weddings. *Unknown.* FaBoVe

Wedlock; a Satire. Hetty Wright. NOEC

Wedlock, a Satire. Mehetabel Wright. ECWP

Wednesday. Marvin Bell. VCAP

Wednesday at North Hatley. Ralph Gustafson. NOBC

Wednesday in Holy Week. Christina Georgina Rossetti. TrCP

Wednesday, January 1, 1701. Samuel Sewall. *See* Once More, Our God, Vouchsafe to Shine!

Wednesday Night Prayer Meeting. Jay Wright. ISC

Wednesday of Holy Week, 1940. Kenneth Rexroth. ChIV-1

Wednesday on a barge. Poems from Saint Pelagia Prison. Philippe Soupault. AF, *tr. by* Eden Paul

wee. (LL) In Just-spring. E. E. Cummings. FaBoVe; HarvBoo; HeIP-4; InPK-6; MoAmPo; NAAL-2v2; NAAL-5; NIL-7; NIP-4; NOxBChV; NoP-4; OxIBACP; PoPoPo; SoSe-8; WeW-3

Wee Cooper of Fife, The. *Unknown.* NePenScot

Wee Falorie Man, The. *Unknown.* FaBoVe

Wee Jamie, a canny young Scot. Limerick. Joyce Johnson. PeLi

Wee jenny wren she lays sixteen, The. Wee Jenny Wren, The. *Unknown.* FaBoVe

Wee leave Creete Country; and our sayls unwrapped uphoysing. Virgil [*or* Vergil]. BIrV; OBVE *Fr.* Aeneid [*or* Eneados, *Aeneis*], The.

We[e] part not with the[e] at this meeting day. (LL) Sir Walter Ra[u]le[i]gh to His Son[ne]. Sir Walter Ralegh. NAEL-5v1; NAEL-6v1; NAEL-7v1; NPeEn; NoSic; OxBSo; RB; Son; WoPoe

Wee, sleeket [*or* sleekit], cow'rin' [*or* cowran], tim'rous beastie. To a Mouse; On Turning Her up in Her Nest, with the Plough, November, 1785. Robert Burns. BRP; CABP; FaBoVe; HAP; HeIP-4; NAEL-5v2; NAEL-6v2; NOEC; NPeEn; NePenScot; NoP-4; OxAEP-2; OxBEV; OxBS; PoE; SCGP; TFi; UV

Wee Tammy Tyrie. *Unknown.* OxNR

Wee Wee Man, The. *Unknown.* EBEV; ESPB; FaBoCh; OxBB

Wee Willie Winkie rins [*or* runs] through the town. Willie Winkie. William Miller. OxBEV; ReMoGo

Weed, The. Genevieve Taggard. APT-2

Weed, moss-weed. Sea Iris. "H. D.". APT-1

Weed Puller. Theodore Roethke. HCAP; NAAL-2v2

Weeding. Michael Hamburger. OBGa

Weeds. James Dickey. BodElec

Weeds as Partial Survivors. Alan Dugan. YaYoPo

Weeds grow shamelessly / on my tongue. Self-Portrait. Cecil Bodker. BoWoP, *tr. by* Nadia Christensen

Weedy creek, A. Making a Door. Dennis Schmitz. LCAP-2

Weedy light through the uncurtained glass, The. Hiatus. Margaret Avison. HAP

Week after her wedding I watch the Kentucky Derby, A. Louisa's Wedding. Tracy Philpot. AmPoNex

Week after our child was born, A. New Mother. Sharon Olds. PasH

Week after week, month after month, in pain. Memorial Poem. Roy Fuller. OxBSP

Week ago I had a fire, A. All in June. William Henry Davies. OxBSP

Week ago, when I had finished, A. Vikram Seth. *Fr.* Golden Gate, The.

Week-End. Harold Monro.

"Train, The! The twelve o'clock for paradise." MoBrPo

Week-End by the Sea. Edgar Lee Masters. MoAmPo

Week-End Indian, The. Anita Endrezze. VoR

Week in the Life of the Ethnically Indeterminate, A. Elena Georgiou. WiU

Week is dealt out like a hand, The. Hope. Randall Jarrell. MoAmPo

Week of Birthdays, A. Mother Goose. *See* Birthdays

Week on the Concord and Merrimack Rivers, A. Henry David Thoreau.

Low-Anchored Cloud. NCAP

(Mist.) AWP; OxBA

Woof of the Sun, Ethereal Gauze. NCAP; TAP

Week-Seek. Jim Tollerud. VoR

Week the first baby died, The. Caustic Soda. Liz Houghton. Prnts

Weekend at Home. John Pook. AngWePo

Weekend Equestrian, The. Michael S. Weaver. GT

Weekend in Palm Springs. Stewart Florsheim. GotH

Weeks after the solstice. Migrants by Night. W. S. Merwin. BodElec

Weeks go by, The. I shelve them. Firstborn. Louise Glück. HarvBoo

Weeks go quickly by, The. Things We Did Last Summer, The. Sammy Cahn. ReLy

Weeksville Women. Elouise Loftin. ISC

We[e]lcome! but yet no entrance, till we bless[e]. Entertainment, or Porch-Verse, at the Marriage of Mr. Henry Northleigh [*or* Hen. Northly] and the Most Witty Mrs. Lettice Yard, The. Robert Herrick. CaPo

Weep, ah weep love's losing, love's with its dwelling place. *Var. authors.* AWP; TAL, *tr. by* Wilfrid Scawen Blunt and Lady Anne Blunt *Fr.* Mu'allaqat, The.

Weep, and weep long, but do not weep for me. To a Troubled Friend. James Wright (1927–80). Son

Weep, Children of Israel. Thomas Moore. ChIV-1

Weep for me, friends, for now that I am hence. Tears of the World. Mu'tamid, King of Seville. AWP, *tr. by* Dulcie L. Smith

Weep, Israel! your tardy meed outpour. Bar Kochba. Emma Lazarus. TrJP

Weep, Lovers, with Love's very self doth weep. Dante Alighieri. AWP; EaItPo, *tr. by* Dante Gabriel Rossetti *Fr.* La Vita Nuova.

Weep No More. John Fletcher. OBEV; OxAEP-1 *Fr.* Queen of Corinth, The.

Weep not because this child hath died so young. On the Death of Mistress Mary Prideaux. William Strode. NOSC

Weep not for little Leonie. Harry Graham. PeLV *Fr.* Some Ruthless Rhymes.

Weep Not My Wanton. Robert Greene. *See* Menaphon

Weep not, nor backward turn your beams. Lover, upon an Accident Necessitating His Departure, Consults with Reason, A. Thomas Carew. CaPo

Weep Not To-Day. Robert Bridges. OBMV

Weep not, weep not. Go down Death. James Weldon Johnson. ISC; SacPr

Weep o'er the mis'ries of a wretched maid. Dying Prostitute, The; an Elegy. Thomas Holcroft. NOEC

Weep [*or* Weepe] with me, all you that read. Epitaph on S. P. [Salomon *or* Salathiel Pavy], a Child of Q[ueen] El[izabeth's] Chapel. Ben Jonson. BeJo; NAEL-5v1; NAEL-6v1; NAEL-7v1; NOSC; OBEV; OxBEV; SCGP; UnPo

Weep [*or* Weepe] You No More [Sad Fountains]. *Unknown.* EBEV; EnLoPo; HAP; NoP-4; NOSC; NoSic; PoE; TFi

(Tears.) WoPoe

(Weepe you no more sad fountaines.) NPeEn; OxBEV

Weep, weep for him, the Man of God. Weep, Children of Israel. Thomas Moore. ChIV-1

Weep! Weep! Weep! *Unknown.* AWP *Fr.* Thousand and One Nights, The.

Weep, weep, ye woodmen! wail. Anthony Munday. CTC *Fr.* Death of Robert, Earl of Huntingdon.

Weep, you may weep, for you may touch them not. (LL) Greater Love. Wilfred Owen. EnLoPo; FaBoMo; GTBS-P; MoBrPo; NoAM; TFi

Weep You No More, Sad Fountains. *Unknown. See* Weep [*or* Weepe] You No More [Sad Fountains]

Weepe for the dead, for they have lost this light. On Himselfe. Robert Herrick. FaBoEE; NOSC

Weep[e] not, my wanton, smile upon my knee. Robert Greene. NoSic; OxAEP-1 *Fr.* Menaphon.

Weeper, The. Richard Crashaw. FSCP *See also* Saint Mary Magdalene or The Weeper

Weepers Tower in Amsterdam, The. Paul Goodman. VGW

Weepies, The. Paul Muldoon. NoAM; PNI

Weeping, The. Jack Hirschman. BodElec

Weeping and Kissing. Sir Edward Sherburne. NOSC

Weeping and wakeful all the night I lie. Rhodanthe. Agathias. AWP, *tr. by* Andrew Lang

Weeping for Hsüeh Tzu-shu. Liu K'o-chuang. CoBCP, *tr. by* Burton Watson

Weeping for the Zen Master Po-yen. Chia Tao. SuSp, *tr. by* Stephen Owen

Weeping for Ying Yao. Wang Wei. WoPoe, *tr. by* Willis Barnstone, Tony Barnstone and Xu Haixin

Weeping for Ying Yao. Wang Wei. CoBCP, *tr. by* Burton Watson

Weeping Headstones of the Isaac Becketts, The. Paul Durcan. PBCIP

Weeping Melpomene assist my lays. Fatal Dream; or, The Unhappy Favourite, The. Emanuel Collins. NOEC

Weeping, murmuring, complaining. Sonnet, A. Oliver Goldsmith. NOIV

Weeping or smiling pearls to Celia's face. (LL) Lips and Eyes. Giambattista [*or* Giovanni Battista] Marino. OBVE; OxBSP, *tr. by* Thomas Carew

Weeping Sinner, Dry Your Tears. Oliver Holden. AH

Weeping: the food he eats. Louis Zukofsky. APSN *Fr.* A.

Weeping Woman. Denise Levertov. AF

Weeps every eye. (LL) Untitled: "Shrewd star, who crudes our naming: you should be flame." Karen Volkman. NAPBL; NeAmPo

Weeps out of western something new. Birth in a Narrow Room, The. Gwendolyn Brooks. BlSi; NoP-4

Weevilly porridge I'm going insane. Weevilly Porridge. Eva Johnson. IBA

Weft of leafless spray, A. November. William Dean Howells. APN-2

Wei-ch'i Chess. Li K'ai-hsien. CoBLCP, *tr. by* Jonathan Chaves

Wei Wind. Confucius.

"Hill-billy, hill-billy come to buy." CTC; OBVE, *tr. by* Ezra Pound

Pedlar. CTC; OBVE, *tr. by* Ezra Pound

Weigh me the fire; or canst thou find. To Find[e] God. Robert Herrick. BeJo; InvLi; NoP-4

Weighing-In, The. Ibn al-Rumi. ArPe, *tr. by* Omar S. Pound

Weighing-machine, The. Pierre McOrlan. MFP, *tr. by* Martin Sorrell

Weighing the Baby. Ethel Lynn Beers. PoToHe

Weighing the ste[a]dfastness and state. Man. Henry Vaughan. ESCV; GeHe; MeLP; NOBE; NOCV; OBEV; SCGP

Weight. Jay Schneiders. OPRER

Weight Belt. Jeffery Conway. WiU

Weight of Sweetness, The. Li-Young Lee. RaBo

Weight of the moment: immeasurable, the weight, The. Taste of Wild Cherry, The. Chris Forhan. NAPBL

Weightless and / "smiling" (LL) In a Season of Unemployment. Margaret Avison. MoCV; NOBC

Weill, gin they arena deid, it's time they were. (LL) Elegy: "They are lang deid, folk that I used to ken." Robert Garioch. NPeEn; NePenScot; OxBS

Wein Geist. Charles Godfrey Leland. APN-2

Weingarten Travel Blessing, The. Unknown. GePo, tr. by Carroll Hightower

Weir Bridge. Padraic Fallon. CIP-2

Weird as Puppets. Paul Verlaine. SxFrPo, tr. by Martin Sorrell

Weird containing stillness of the neighborhood, The. Pause. Eamon Grennan. NIL-7

Weird hour. It's not. Sundial. Gabriel Zaid. TCLAP, tr. by Adrian Hernandez

Weird sister. In Salem. Lucille Clifton. ESEAA; PAI

Weird stuff this. Elizabeth Bletsoe. NewEx

Wel / come back, brother. Huey. Etheridge Knight. NNaP

Wel mended tinker! sans dispute. Of John Bunyan's Life. John James. SCAP

Wel, who shal thise hornes blowe. Unknown. OHMEL

Weland knew fully affliction and woe. Deor's Lament. Unknown. AnOE, tr. by Charles W. Kennedy

Weland, that dauntless man, well learned to bear [or well knew about exile]. Deor. Unknown. ASW

Welcome. Dream on the Same Mattress. Sharif Elmusa. GraLe

Welcome. David Hernandez. UnSA

Welcome, The. Abraham Cowley. BoLoP Fr. Mistress, The.

Welcome, baby, to the world of swords. News of a Baby. Elizabeth Riddell. ItWoWo

Welcome Back, Mr. Knight: Love of My Life. Etheridge Knight. PBCAP; RaBo

Welcome be ye when ye go. Unknown. MiEL

Welcome, brave gallant, with those locks so fair. Periwig, A. Rowland Watkyns. NOSC

Welcome dear book, souls Joy, and food! The feast. H. Scriptures. Henry Vaughan. ChIV-2; ESCV

Welcome, dear dawn of summer's rising sway. May-Day. Aaron Hill. NOEC

Welcome, dear wanderer, once more! Upon Her Play Being Returned to Her, Stained with Claret. Mary Leapor. ECWP

Welcome Eumenides. Eleanor Ross Taylor. NALW

Welcome, great Caesar, welcome now you are. To the King, Upon His Welcome to Hampton Court. Robert Herrick. BeJo

Welcome, grinned Henry, welcome fifty-one! John Berryman. TAP Fr. Dream Songs.

Welcome Home. Josephine D. Henderson Heard. CBWP-4

Welcome, maids of honor. To Violets. Robert Herrick. CaPo; OBEV

Welcome me, if you will. For James Dean. Frank O'Hara. NNaP; NeAP

Welcome Morning. Anne Sexton. PAI

Welcome, most welcome to our Vow[e]s and us. To the King, upon His Com[m]ing with His Army into the West. Robert Herrick. BeJo; CaPo

Welcome, o Supernatural One, o Swimmer. Prayer to the Sockeye Salmon. Unknown. WPoS; WoPoe, tr. by Jane Hirshfield

Welcome, old friend, long-necked bottle. Argentarius. GrAn

Welcome over the Door of an Old Inn. Unknown. PoToHe

Welcome, pale Primrose! starting up between. Primrose, The. John Clare. CenSon

Welcome, proud lady. (LL) Sir Walter Scott. CABP; FaBoCh; NAEL-5v2; NAEL-6v2; NOBRP; NePenScot; OBEV; OxBEV; OxBS; RACG; SCGP; TFi; UnPo Fr. Heart of Midlothian, The.

Welcome Queen Alice. Lewis Carroll. UV Fr. Through the Looking-Glass.

Welcome, Queen Sabbath. Zalman Schneour. TrJP, tr. by Harry H. Fein

Welcome, stranger! glad I greet thee. To Don Juan Baz. Mary E. Tucker. CBWP-1

Welcome sweet and sacred cheer. Banquet, The. George Herbert. ESCV; GeHe

Welcome sweet, and sacred feast; welcome life! Holy Communion, The. Henry Vaughan. ESCV

Welcome, Sweet Rest. Michael Wigglesworth. AH

Welcome the dawn. (LL) Nightingales. Robert Bridges. MoBrPo; NOBE; OBEV; OBMV; SCGP; TFi; UnPo

Welcome the Wrath. Stanley Kunitz. VGW

Welcome them and dance with them. (LL) Fairies Are Dancing All over the World, The. Michael Rumaker. CAGL; GLP

Welcome thou safe retreat! Solum Mihi Superest Sepulchrum. William Habington. ChIV-1; NOSC

Welcome to Hiroshima. Mary Jo Salter. DiPo; NIL-7; NIP-4; RA

Welcome to Hon. Frederick Douglass. Josephine D. Henderson Heard. CBWP-4

Welcome to Ithaca. Rebecca Seiferle. ExTi

Welcome to My Dream. Johnny Burke. ReLy

Welcome to Sack, The. Robert Herrick. BeJo; CaPo

Welcome to Spring. John Lyly. See Alexander and Campaspe

Welcome to the New Consciousness. Leseko Rampolekeng. NAfrP

Welcome to this my college [or colledge], and though late. To His Kinsman, Master Thomas Herrick, Who Desired to Be in His Book. Robert Herrick. CaPo

Welcome to Thomas Mann. Attila József. IQMS, tr. by Vernon Watkins

Welcome to Wales. John Tripp. AngWePo

Welcome to you. Ordinance on Arrival. Naomi Lazard. BLT

Welcome, wild Northeaster! Ode to the Northeast Wind. Charles Kingsley. OxAEP-2

Welcome, woods crowned with sparse remains of green. Autumn. Alphonse Marie Louis de Lamartine. SxFrPo, tr. by E. H. Blackmore and A. M. Blackmore

Welcome, Ye Hopeful Heirs of Heaven. Phoebe Hinsdale Brown. AH

Welcoming Party, A. John Montague. PNI

Welcum, illustrat Ladye, and oure Quene! Alexander Scott. NePenScot Fr. New Yeir Gift to the Quene Mary, quhen scho come first Hame, 1562, Ane.

Wele, herying and worshipe be to Crist [or Christ] that dere us [or ous] boughte. Palm-Sunday Hymn, A. William Herebert. MiEL

Wele, thu art a waried thing. Unknown. MiEL

Welford Wedding, The. Elizabeth Frances Amherst. ECWP

Welkin's wind, way unhindered. Wind, The. Dafydd [or David] ap Gwilym. OBWVE, tr. by Joseph P. Clancy

Well. Country Dog in the City (On a Leash, Which Is Bizarre Enough) Comes Upon an Obedience Class, A. Roy Blount, Jr. Unle

Well, The. Yves Bonnefoy. VCWP, tr. by John Naughton

Well, The. Thomas Edward Brown. NOBVV

Well, The. Howard Phillips Lovecraft. APT-1

Well, The. Jay Macpherson. NoP-4

Well, The. Mother Goose. OxNR; ReMoGo

Well, The. Bernard Raymund. YaYoPo

Well, The. Padma Sachdev. OMIP, tr. by Iqbal Masud

Well, The. Philip Salom. NOBAu

Well, The. Edith Jay Scovell. HarvBoo Fr. Water Images.

Well, alter ego, Time has trudged. Why Do We Live? Israel Zangwill. TrJP

Well and. Trapped. Adelaide Crapsey. APT-1

Well-beloved, The. John Montague. BiHa

Well-buggered boy named Delpasse, A. Limerick. Unknown. PeLi

Well charged, halfway between generations. Poem 2 (for Duckie Simpson of Black Uhuru). Audrey Ingram-Roberts. WaCA

Well clay it's strange at last we've come to it. Spark's Farewell to Its Clay, The. Ronald Allison Kells Mason. PeNZ

Well, dear Mr. Wright, I must send you a line. To Henry Wright of Mobberley, Esq. on Buying the Picture of Father Malebranche. John Byrom. NOEC

Well, Did You Evah? Cole Porter. OBAL

Well-dressed couple haggle, The. Knowingness. John Hughes. PNI

Well, Emily Sparks, your prayers were not wasted. Edgar Lee Masters. APT-1 Fr. Spoon River Anthology.

Well, first of all, just which God do you mean? Another Voice. Victor Hugo. SxFrPo, tr. by E. H. Blackmore and A. M. Blackmore

Well, folks, and how. Archipelago, The. John Ashbery. BodElec

We'll Go No More A-Roving. Byron. See So We'll Go No More A-Roving

Well he came home from the war. Swordfishtrombone. Tom Waits. PFTM-2

Well, Heaven be thanked my first-love failed. Coventry Patmore. EBVV Fr. Angel in the House, The.

Well, her book, anyway. The Kunitz volume. Anna Akhmatova Spends the Night on Miami Beach. John Balaban. GifTon

Well here again that don't apply. T. S. Eliot. FaBoVe Fr. Sweeney Agonistes.

Well, here I am in the Centre Daily Times. News Update. John Balaban. AF; CDa

Well here we are!—and don't you think we're looking quite. Address. Andrew Geddes Bain. PeSAV

Well, honest John, how fare you now at home? To John Clare. John Clare. Son

Well, I forget the rest. (LL) Memorabilia. Robert Browning. FHYEP; NAEL-5v2; NAEL-6v2; NOBVV; NPeEn; NoP-4; OxBEV; PoE; PoPoPo; RB

Well I have and in fact. On Being Asked to Write a Poem against the War in Vietnam. Hayden Carruth. CDa

Well, I may now receive, and die: my sin. John Donne. OBSV Fr. Satires.

Well I never, did you ever. Unknown. FaBoCh

Well I Remember How You Smiled. Walter Savage Landor. NAEL-6v2 Fr. Ianthe.

Well I remember in my boyish hours. Thoughts of Boyhood. John Lloyd. AngWePo

Well, I said to the missus that something pretty odd. Visitant Eclogue. John Kinsella. NeBl

"Well, I took your advice, Doc," said Knopp. Limerick. *Unknown.* PeLi

Well, I was at the dresser. Just How It Happened. Priscilla Jane Thompson. CBWP-2

Well I woke up this mornin' it was Christmas Day. Adrian Henri's Talking after Christmas Blues. Adrian Henri. PeLV

Well, if a King's a lion, at the least. Pope. ECEV; OBSV *Fr.* First Epistle of the First Book of Horace Imitated, The.

Well; if ever I saw such another man since my mother bound my head. Mary the Cook-Maid's Letter to Dr. Sheridan. Jonathan Swift. NPeEn; OxBoLi; PeLV

Well, if it's a sin to like Guinness. Limerick. Cyril Ray. PeLi

Well! If the Bard was weather-wise, who made. Dejection: An Ode. Samuel Taylor Coleridge. FHYEP; HeIP-4; NAEL-5v2; NAEL-6v2; NAWM-7v2; NOBE; NOBRP; NoP-4; OxAEP-2; PoE; PoPoPo; TFi; TOF

Well, *if* you must know all the facts, I was merely reading a pamphlet. Visitor, A. Lewis Carroll. OBCoV

Well, Ignorance, the cause is yet unknown. On Learning. Elizabeth Teft. ECWP

Well is he born, that may behold you ever. (LL) Edmund Spenser. OxBSo; PoE; Son *Fr.* Amoretti.

Well, it isn't the King, after all, my dear creature! Thomas Moore. PeLV *Fr.* Fudge Family in Paris, The.

Well, it really hurts, to think of him going away. London, Greater London (After *Satire III*). John Holloway. WoPoe

Well it's half-past. Nearly Nowhere. Catherine Walsh. Oth

Well, it's partly the shape of the thing. Limerick. *Unknown.* KaS; SoSe-8

Well it's six o'clock in Oakland. Oakland Blues. Ishmael Reed. NAAAL

Well, it was never mine. This Day, under My Hand. David Malouf. CBAP

Well-Known Elizabethan Double Entendre, A. Pamela Alexander. YaYoPo

Well Langston. Message for Langston, A. "Kush." NBV

Well, let's go. Basho. TTTS

Well may my Book come forth like Public [*or* Publique] Day. To the Most Illustrious and Most Hopeful[l] Prince, Charles, Prince of Wales. Robert Herrick. BASC

Well may she speede and fairely finish her intent. (LL) Edmund Spenser. NAEL-6v1; NAEL-7v1 *Fr.* Faerie Queene, The.

Well may that kisse be sweet that's giv'n t' a sleek. Sir Richard Fanshawe. OBVE *Fr.* Il Pastor Fido.

Well may they write, that sit in parlours fine. On His Writing Verses. John Hawthorn. NOEC

Well meaning readers! you that come as friends [*or* freinds]. Richard Crashaw. NAEL-5v1; NAEL-6v1; NAEL-7v1

Well, Menestratus, you ask me what I think. Lucilius. GrAn

Well met Neighbour. Martin Parker.

"Whither away good neighbour." PBRV

"Well met, well met, my own true love." Carpenter's Wife, The. *Unknown.* OxBB

Well might the ancients dream a grove to be. Prospect of a Landscape, Beginning with a Grove, The. Jane Barker. BASC

Well now, look at this unsightly herd. On the Yellow Footprints. Mcavoy Layne. CDa

Well Now, the Virgin. Roy Fuller. Son *Fr.* Mythological Sonnets.

Well of blackness, all defiling. Contents of an Ink-bottle, The. Mary Elizabeth Coleridge. VWP

Well of Clouds, The. Michelangelo Coviello.

"This hour is made of iron grates where the underground." ItPo, *tr. by* Gayle Ridinger

Well of the King of Wu, The. Kao Ch'i. CoBLCP, *tr. by* Jonathan Chaves

Well of Vertew and Flour of Womanheid, The. *Unknown.* OxBS

Well, old spy. Award. Ray Durem. BPo; TTY

Well, on the day I was born. Have You Anything to Say in Your Defense? César Vallejo. PoetW; RaBo, *tr. by* James Wright

Well pleaseth me the sweet time of Easter. Song of Battle. Bertrans [*or* Bertran *or* Bertrand] de Born. AWP, *tr. by* Ezra Pound

Well, read my cheek, and watch my eye. Lines of Life. Letitia [*or* Laetitia] Elizabeth Landon. NOBRP; NPeEn

Well-rested can, The. (LL) Insomnia. Cornelius Eady. AWTN; ESEAA

Well Rising, The. William Stafford. RB

Well-shadow'd landskip, fare ye well. Sir John Suckling. *See* Well-shadowed landscape, fare ye well!

Well-shadowed landscape, fare ye well! Farewell to Love. Sir John Suckling. CaPo

Well, she told me I had an aura. "What?" I said. Sonnet. Hayden Carruth. GifTon

Well, since I became a lesbian. Beatrix Gates. WiU *Fr.* Triptych.

Well, so that is that. Now we must dismantle the tree. W. H. Auden. ChrPo; MoBrPo; OBCP *Fr.* For the Time Being; a Christmas Oratorio.

Well, some may hate and some may scorn. Emily Jane Brontë. *See* Stanzas to———

Well, sometimes it's Heaven, and sometimes it's Hell. Heaven and Hell. Willie Nelson. InPK-6

Well, son de story of my life. Favorite Slave's Story, The. Priscilla Jane Thompson. CBWP-2; RACG

Well, son, I'll tell you. Mother to Son. Langston Hughes. AmFaPo; ChAP; ISC; NAAAL; NAAL-2v2; NAAL-5; NTCP; OBCA; OxIBACP; SAmP; TTY; WoPoe

Well, sure, it's only. I Visit the Twenty-four Coin-op Church of Elvis. Fleda Brown Jackson. AllShUp

Well swam, swan. (LL) Swan, The. *Unknown.* OxNR; ReMoGo

Well, Teddy, I have found you. Lost Teddy Bear, The. Maggie Pogue Johnson. CBWP-4

Well—the links are broken. Woman's Last Word, A. Adelaide Anne Procter. VWP

Well, the war is done. *Unknown.* TCRP

Well then. Shumeekuli, The. Andrew Peynetsa. PFTM-2, *tr. by* Dennis Tedlock

Well then. Dirty Niggers. Jacques Roumain. NegPo, *tr. by* Ellen Conroy Kennedy

Well then, how can I let you go away? (LL) Ah, yes, to your misfortune. Patrizia Cavalli. ICWP, *tr. by* Judith Baumel

Well then; I now do plainly see. Abraham Cowley. BASC; NOBE; NOSC; NoP-4; OBEV; OxAEP-1; PBRV *Fr.* Mistress, The.

Well, then, let's follow. Hakurin. JDP, *tr. by* Yoel Hoffmann

Well, Then Let Slip the Masks. Gillian Eve Hanscombe. PoBW

Well, then, the last day the sharks appeared. Sharks, The. Denise Levertov. NeAP

Well then, the promised [*or* promis'd] hour is come at last. To My Dear Friend Mr Congreve [on His Comedy Called "The Double-Dealer"]. Dryden. EBEV; NPeEn; OxAEP-1

Well there's no end of things to do. Things My Brother and I Could Do. Robert Bly. InvLad

Well they are gone, and here must I remain. This Lime-Tree Bower My Prison. Samuel Taylor Coleridge. FHYEP; HeIP-4; NAEL-5v2; NAEL-6v2; OBGa; OxAEP-2; PoE; TOF

Well they'd made up their minds to be everywhere because why not. Last One, The. W. S. Merwin. LCAP-2; NoAM; VGW

"Well, this is where I go down to the river." Heat. Kenneth Mackenzie. BMAP; CBAP

Well, though it seems. Liddell and Scott. Thomas Hardy. OBCoV; OxBoLi; PeLV

Well, though the bow's unbent, the wound bleeds on. (LL) Petrarch. NAWM-5v1; NAWM-7v1, *tr. by* Morris Gilbert Bishop *Fr.* Sonnets to Laura.

Well, thrill. That's their story. (LL) Freely Espousing. James Schuyler. FTOS; NeAP; NoP-4

Well, to start with. Jonah and the Whale. Gareth Owen. OBSP

Well to that heart might his these absent greetings pour! (LL) Byron. NAEL-5v2; NAEL-6v2 *Fr.* Childe Harold's Pilgrimage.

Well, twirl my turban! Man alive! Mister Five by Five. Don Raye. ReLy

Well-uh Bird, Bird, Bird, Bird is the Word. David Wojahn. PBCAP *Fr.* Mystery Train: A Sequence.

"Well Uncle Ike! This beats me." Uncle Ike's Holiday. Priscilla Jane Thompson. CBWP-2

Well, Wanton Eye. Charles, Duc d' Orléans. HAP

Well Water. Randall Jarrell. InPK-6; NAAL-2v2; NAAL-5; NOBA; OxBSP; VCAP; VGW

Well water. Eight Sandbars on the Takano River. Gary Snyder. NOBA; VGW

Well we can go. Poem for Cocksuckers, A. John Wieners. CAGL

Well, we either do it or we don't, as the pigeon said to. Sunrise with Sea Monster. Charles North. FTOS

Well—we have reached the precipice at last. On the Masquerades. Christopher Pitt. ECEV; NOEC

Well, we went down town a-shopping. Christmas Rush, The. Clara Ann Thompson. CBWP-2

Well, well, I know the wise ones talk and talk. Augusta Davies Webster. BrRo *Fr.* Castaway, A.

Well, well, 'tis true. Plain Dealing. Alexander Brome. NOSC

Well, well, well, well, well, She Loves Me. Sheldon Harnick. ReLy

Well, well, you's cum at las' People's Literary, De. Maggie Pogue Johnson. CBWP-4

Well what's up, que pasa and a big hello. Hip Hop Bop. Jabari Asim. InTrad

Well, when all is said and done. Epilogue. "Æ" MoBrPo

Well, wife, I've found the model church! I worshipped there to-day. Model Church, The. John H. Yates. PWR

Well, World, you have kept faith with me. He Never Expected Much. Thomas Hardy. NAEL-5v2; NAEL-6v2; NoAM; OxBTC; SCV

Well worth Predecessors, and Fathers by name. Ditties Lamentation for the cruelty of this age. *Unknown.* BASC

Well worthy to be magnified are they. Pilgrim Fathers, The. William Wordsworth. AiP

Well-wrought this wall-stone which fate has broken. Ruin, The. *Unknown.* WoPoe, *tr. by* Michael O'Brien

Well ya got trouble, my friend, right here. Ya Got Trouble. Meredith Willson. ReLy

Well You Needn't. Dave Etter. SeSe

"Wellcome, to the Caves of Artá!" Robert Graves. NBLV; NOBL; PeLV

Wellfleet. Timothy Liu. AmPoNex

Wellfleet Harbor. Paul Goodman. CoAP

Wellfleet Whale, The. Stanley Kunitz. DiPo; NoAM

Wellington. Charles Harpur. NOBAu

Wellspring, The. Sharon Olds. BodElec

Wels a Fish that Lives on the Bottom, The. Sarah Kirsch. PFTM-2, *tr. by* Wayne Kvam

Welsh Ballad, A. Edmwnd Prys. OBWVE, *tr. by* Gwyn Williams

Welsh Espionage. Gwyneth Lewis.
  Advice on Adultery. MFPA
  "So this is the man you dreamt I had betrayed." TCAWP

Welsh Hill Country, The. Ronald Stuart Thomas. AngWePo

Welsh History. Ronald Stuart Thomas. OBWVE

Welsh Homer. Cliff James. AngWePo

Welsh Incident. Robert Graves. NOBE; OBSP; OxBEV; OxBTC

Welsh is a mad language; there are no words in it. Language Difficulty. Ann Drysdale. TCAWP

Welsh Landscape. Ronald Stuart Thomas. FaBoMo; NoP-4; TCAWP

Welsh Love Letter. Michael Burn. TCAWP

Welsh Marches, The. A. E. Housman. FaBoTw; SCGP

Welsh Testament, A. Ronald Stuart Thomas. TCAWP

Welsh Valley Cinema, 1930s. Dannie Abse. TCAWP

Welsh Wordscape, A. Peter Finch. AngWePo

Welshman at St. James' Park, A. Ronald Stuart Thomas. AngWePo

Welshman in Exile Speaks, The. T. Harri Jones. AngWePo; OBWVE

Welshman to Any Tourist, A. Ronald Stuart Thomas. OxBC

Welt ist dumm, die Welt ist blind, Die. Heinrich Heine. AWP, *tr. by* James Thomson

Wemen's Wather. T. S. Law. OxBS

Wen, wen, little wen. Against a Wen. *Unknown.* ASW, *tr. by* Kevin Crossley-Holland

Wenberi's Song. Wenberi. CBAP, *tr. by* A. W. Howitt

Wendell Phillips. Henrietta Cordelia Ray. CBWP-3

Wenest thou, usher, with thyn cointise. Schoolboy's Lot, A. *Unknown.* MiEL

Went and dug them up again. (LL) Dorothy Parker. APT-1; NALW *Fr.* Pig's-Eye View of Literature, A.

Went by; but all my grief ageän awoke. (LL) Wind at the Door, The. William Barnes. GTBS-P; OxAEP-2

Went dicing on my bike. African Boog. Allen Fisher. Oth

Went down to the yards. Long Track Blues. Sterling Allen Brown. GM

Went forth to fight, with murderous faces. (LL) London Fete, A. Coventry Patmore. EBVV; HAP; PeVV

Went home and put a bullet through his head. (LL) Richard Cory. Edwin Arlington Robinson. APN-2; ChAP; ColAP; HAP; InPK-6; MoAmPo; NAAL-2v2; NAAL-5; NCAP; NOBA; NoP-4; OxBA; PAI; PoPoPo; PoRA; TAP; TCAPo; TFi

Went into a shoestore to buy a pair of shoes. Sale. Josephine Miles. APT-2; WPE

Went on cutting bread and butter. (LL) Sorrows of Werther, The. William Makepeace Thackeray. NBLV; NOBL; NOBVV; OBCoV; PeLV

Went out last night, had a great big fight. Prove It on Me Blues. Gertrude "Ma" Rainey. NAAAL

Went to dinner with her thursday. Pubescence at 39. Vickie Sears. GLP

Went up a year this evening! Emily Dickinson. HAP; WeW-3

Went with some of my students to work in the People's. Denise Levertov. CDa *Fr.* Staying Alive.

Weping haveth min wonges wet. *Unknown.* MiEL

Wept, to behold a brighter goddess there! (LL) Determines to Follow Phaon. Mary Robinson. CenSon; RWP

Wer ther outher in this toun. *Unknown.* MiEL

Were aesthetically significant, while Elijah's were very plain. (LL) On Certain Wits. Howard Nemerov. HCAP; OxBC

Were all our sins so empty of enjoyment. Muted Screen of Graham Greene, The. Phyllis McGinley. FaBoEE

Were all the peaks of Gwynedd. Welsh Love Letter. Michael Burn. TCAWP

Were Anomaly. (LL) Emily Dickinson. NOBA; TCAPo

Were answerable to Fate alone, not Zeus. (LL) Weather of Olympus, The. Robert Graves. FaBoEE; OBCoV

Were barren as this moorland hill. (LL) Dreary Change, The. Sir Walter Scott. NAEL-5v2; NAEL-6v2

Were becoming less sane. Growing Days, The. Rick Alley. AmPoNex

Were caught in bed by the dawn. (LL) Empress Eifuku. OHMPJ; WPOW

Were fading and all wars were done. (LL) Dark Hills, The. Edwin Arlington Robinson. AiP; HAP; MoAmPo; NoAM

Were half as silent as their pictures! (LL) Winthrop Mackworth Praed. NOBL; PeLV *Fr.* Every-Day Characters.

Were he composer, he would surely write. Portrait of the Boy as Artist. Barbara Howes. MoAmPo

Were heavy, and he headed for the barn. (LL) Parable. Richard Wilbur. HarvBoo; OxBSP

Were I a general of olden times. Mikhail Alekseievich Kuzmin. CAGL, *tr. by* Michael Green

Were I a king, I could command content. Poem. Edward de Vere, 17th Earl of Oxford. NoSic

"Were I as Base as Is the Lowly Plain." Joshua Sylvester. GSo; NoSic; Son (Love's Omnipresence.) GTBS-P
  (Ubique.) OBEV

Were I employ'd a garden to contrive. Samuel Gilbert. OBGa *Fr.* Florist's Vade-Mecum, The.

Were I idiom and. While. Bruce Andrews. FTOS

Were I in Trouble. Robert Frost. OxBSP *Fr.* Five Nocturnes.

Were I invited to a nectar feast. Sylvia. Samuel Croxall. NOEC

Were I laid on Greenland's coast. John Gay. EnLoPo; NAEL-5v1; NAEL-6v1; NPeEn; OxBEV; OxBoLi; PeLV *Fr.* Begger's Opera.

Were I that wandering citizen whose city is the world. English Graves, The. Gilbert Keith Chesterton. FaBoWar

Were I the palm tree which your love returning. E Questo il Nido in Che la Mia Fenice? Alec Derwent Hope. OxBC

Were I to send word. *Unknown.* ArkPo, *tr. by* Helen Craig McCullough

Were I, who to my cost already am. John Wilmot, 2d Earl of Rochester. BASC; NOSC; OBSV; SCV

Were I (who to my cost already am). John Wilmot, 2d Earl of Rochester. CABP; NPeEn; OxBEV; SCV *Fr.* Satire [*or* Satyre *or* Satyr] against [Reason and] Mankind, A.

Were I (who to my cost already am). Satire against Reason and Mankind, A. Grace Buchanan Sherwood. NoP-4

Were it but to pleasure you. (LL) To His Mistress[es]. Robert Herrick. CaPo; ErotSp

Were it not for / Cries in snow. Chiyojo [*or* Chiyo *or* Chiyo-Ni *or* Kaga no Chiyo *or* Fukuda Chiyo-Ni]. ZenPo, *tr. by* Takashi Ikemoto and Lucien Stryk

Were it not for making a living, which is rather a nouiance. (LL) Introspective Reflection. Ogden Nash. NBLV; OBCoV

Were it not strange that by the tideless sea. Travellers, The. Eva Gore-Booth. PoBW

Were it possible to say. Alexandria. Mongane Wally Serote. NAfrP

Were it sweet. Issa. EH, *tr. by* R. H. Blyth

Were it undo that is ido [*or* y-do]. He Is Far. *Unknown.* MiEL

Were left in loneliness behind. (LL) Winter Night, A. William Barnes. NOBE; WoPoe

Were lives of ease, dear Namesake, ours. Martial. RomPo, *tr. by* Peter Whigham

Were lost, if that were addle. (LL) Richard Corbet [*or* Corbett]. BASC; BeJo; NOSC; OxBEV; PBRV; PeLV

Were Na My Heart Licht, I Wad Die. Lady Grisel [*or* Grizel *or* Grisell] Baillie. *See* Werena My Heart Licht I Wad Dee

Were Ne My Hearts Light I Wad Dye. Lady Grisel [*or* Grizel *or* Grisell] Baillie. EMWP

Were not the one dead, turned to their affairs. (LL) "Out, Out—" Robert Frost. APT-1; AmFaPo; ColAP; HAP; HarvBoo; HeIP-4; NAAL-2v2; NAAL-5; OxBA; PAI; RB; SoSe-8; TCAPo; TRP; UnPo; VGW

Were't aught to me I bore the canopy. William Shakespeare. NoSic *Fr.* Sonnets.

Were't not enclos'd within a pale of gold. (LL) On a Seal. Plato. AWP; FaBoEE, *tr. by* Thomas Stanley

Were the last days of our antithesis! (LL) Labyrinth, The. Jorge Luis Borges. PoetW; WoPoe, *tr. by* John Updike

Were there no limits to my lust. To His Importunate Mistress. Paul Griffin. UV

Were there such an end as destination. Leaving. T. Crunk. YaYoPo

Were thrilling in his heart. (LL) Young Johnstone. *Unknown.* ESPB; OxBB

Were toward Eternity. Emily Dickinson. APN-2; AWP; BRP; BoWoP; ClHu; ColAP; HAP; HeIP-4; ITBLP; InPK-6; MoAmPo; NAAL-2v1; NAAL-3; NAAL-5; NALW; NAWM-7v2; NIL-7; NIP-4; NoAM; NoP-4;

OxBA; PAI; PoE; PoPoPo; SAmP; SCV; SoSe-8; TAP; TFi; TRP; UnPo; WPE; WeW-3

Were we not fine. American Indian Art: Form and Tradition. Diane Di Prima. BB

Were ye but constant, Guelfs, in war or peace. Folgore da San Geminiano [*or* Gimignano]. EaItPo, *tr. by* Dante Gabriel Rossetti

Were you a string of beads. the elder daughter of Lady Otomo no Sakanoé. ArkPo, *tr. by* Edwin A. Cranston

Were you apprenticed to a fortune teller? Mikhail Alekseievich Kuzmin. CAGL, *tr. by* Michael Green

Were you ever down, not a cent in your pockets? For Services Rendered. F. G. Butterfield. FaBoWar

Were you there when they crucified my Lord? *Unknown.* AH; APN-2; BPo; NAAAL; SacPr

Were you there when they laid him in the tomb? (LL) *Unknown.* AH; APN-2; BPo; NAAAL

Were yu normal today did yu screw society. Christ I Wudint Know Normal if I Saw It When. Bill Bissett. NOBC

Werena My Heart Licht I Wad Dee. Lady Grisel [*or* Grizel *or* Grisell] Baillie. OBEV

(There was ance a may, and she lo'ed na men;) CABP; LW

(Were Na My Heart Licht, I Wad Die.) CABP

Werner Herzog 68 / Iowa City 88. Ann Lauterbach. ExTi

Wernher von Braun. Tom Lehrer. OBCoV

Wert thou as prone to yield unto my prayer. Lippo Paschi de' Bardi. EaItPo, *tr. by* Dante Gabriel Rossetti

Werther had a love for Charlotte. Sorrows of Werther, The. William Makepeace Thackeray. NBLV; NOBL; NOBVV; OBCoV; PeLV

Wes. Boss Communication. Mari E. Evans. SeSe

Wessex Heights. Thomas Hardy. EBVV; SCGP

West, The. Alphonse Marie Louis de Lamartine. SxFrPo, *tr. by* E. H. Blackmore and A. M. Blackmore

West, The. Michael Longley. BiHa; PBCIP

West ascending Lotus Flower Mountain. Poem No. 19 in the Old Manner. Li Po. CoBCP, *tr. by* Burton Watson

West Cliff. Chu Yi-tsun. SuSp, *tr. by* Chang Yin-nan

West Coast Indian. George Clutesi. HATNAP

West Country, The. Alice Cary. APN-2; SWaP

West-Country Damosel's Complaint, The. *Unknown.* ESPB

West Creek at Ch'u-chou. Wei Ying-wu. CoBCP, *tr. by* Burton Watson

West Forties: Morning, Noon, and Night, The. Louis Edward Sissman. CoAP

West from the Capital's crowded throng. Constance Fenimore Woolson. SWaP *Fr.* Two Women.

West Indian Primer. Elizabeth Alexander. NIL-7

West Kansas full moon. Directions in Our Blood. Barney Bush. HATNAP

West Lake. Kenneth O. Hanson. CoAP

West London. Matthew Arnold. SCGP; Son

(Crouch'd on the pavement close by Belgrave Square.) GSo

West of Alice. W. E. Harney. NOBAu

West of Murray, just off 641. In Memory of the Boys of Dexter, Kentucky. Joe Bolton. AmPoNex

West of my hut, I grow mulberry. Tu Fu. CrYelRi, *tr. by* Sam Hamill *Fr.* Random Pleasures.

West of the bridge. Waterside Village. Yün Shou-p'ing. CoBLCP, *tr. by* Jonathan Chaves

West of the golden sky. Up into the Clouds Music. Li Po. ColAnChi, *tr. by* Elling O. Eide

West of your door, Blue Mountain dreams of melting. Blue Mountain. Roberta Hill Whiteman. VoR

West Paddocks. Arthur Davies. NOBAu

West Pitch at the Falls. Marsden Hartley. APT-1

West provokes the East, The. The iron arm. Ernest Francisco Fenollosa. APN-2 *Fr.* East and West.

West-Running Brook. Robert Frost. APT-1; MoAmPo; NOBA; NoP-4

West Side—corn tortillas for a penny each. Allí por la Calle San Luis. Carmen Tafolla. WWork

West, so they say, is the home of the jay, The. Forty-five Minutes from Broadway. George M. Cohan. ReLy

West Strand Visions. James Simmons. ModIr; PBCIP

West Sussex Drinking Song. Joseph Hilaire Pierre Belloc. MoBrPo

West Texas Rain Journal. Candice Favilla. ExTi

West Wall. W. S. Merwin. RaBo

West West. Bruce Andrews. FTOS

West Willow. Reginald Shepherd. AmPoNex; IllVoic

West Wind. Mary Oliver.
Poem 12. PoCoUp

West Wind, The. John Masefield. CABP; MoBrPo

West wind has come again to the "tower of makeup," The. Cheng Hsieh. CoBLCP *Fr.* Yangchou.

West wind sets the dragon rippling over the flag. Dragon. Ruth Bidgood. AngWePo

Westering. Seamus Heaney. HarvBoo

Western Approaches, The. Howard Nemerov. ColAP; HCAP; TAP

Western Capital is disordered and lawless, The. Seven Sorrows. Wang Ts'an. ColAnChi

Western Capital is in turmoil, The. Wang Ts'an. SuSp *Fr.* Seven Poems of Lament.

Western CIV, 4 and 5. Joan Retallack. FTOS

Western clouds, hill above hill. Ch'iang Village. Tu Fu. CrYelRi, *tr. by* Sam Hamill

Western Course: a cicada's voice singing, The. On the Cicada: In Prison. Lo Pin-wang. ColAnChi, *tr. by* Stephen Owen

Western Emigrant, The. Lydia Huntley Sigourney. SWaP

Western Landscape. Louis MacNeice. ModIr

Western Patriarch's doctrine is transplanted!, The. Dogen. ZenPo, *tr. by* Takashi Ikemoto and Lucien Stryk

Western ranch is just a branch of Nowhere Junction to me, A. Buttons and Bows. Ray Evans. ReLy

Western sun withdraws the shortened day, The. James Thomson. NAEL-6v1; NAEL-7v1 *Fr.* Seasons, The.

Western Trail Cook, 1880. Sharyn Jeanne Skeeter. ISC

Western Wagons. Rosemary Benét. AiP; HHAm

Western Wall, The. Shirley Kaufman. TaR

Western Wind. *Unknown.* BoLoP; CTC; ClHu; EBEV; EnLoPo; FaBoCh; HAP; HeIP-4; InPK-6; NAEL-6v1; NAEL-7v1; NIL-7; NOBE; NoSic; OPOU; OxBSP; SCGP; SoSe-8; TFi; UnPo; WeW-3; WoPoe

(Lover in Winter Plaineth for the Spring, The.) OBEV

(Westron wynde when wyll thow blow.) FaBoVe; NPeEn

(Western wind when wilt thou blow.) KaS

(Westron Wind[e], When Will Thou Blow.) NAEL-5v1; NIP-4; PoE

Western wind has blown but a few days, The. Cranes, The. Po Chü-i. ChiP; OBVE; OWoS, *tr. by* Arthur Waley

Wester[n] wind, when will [*or* wilt] thou blow. Western Wind. *Unknown.* BoLoP; CTC; ClHu; EBEV; EnLoPo; FaBoCh; HAP; HeIP-4; InPK-6; NAEL-6v1; NAEL-7v1; NIL-7; NOBE; NoSic; OPOU; OxBSP; SCGP; SoSe-8; TFi; UnPo; WeW-3; WoPoe

Westgate-on-Sea. Sir John Betjeman. OxBoLi

Westphalian Song. *Unknown.* AWP; OBVE, *tr. by* Samuel Taylor Coleridge

Westport House, Portrush. James Simmons. PBCIP

Westron Wind[e], When Will Thou Blow. *Unknown. See* Western Wind

Westward, hit a low note, for a roarer lost. Strut for Roethke, A. John Berryman. NOBA

Westward over Lotus Mountain. Li Po. *See* Great odes have had no revival, The

Wet. Yusuf Al-Sa'igh. MAP, *tr. by* Diana Der Hovanessian and Salma Khadra Jayyusi

Wet almond-trees, in the rain. Bare Almond-Trees. D. H. Lawrence. FaBoVe

Wet Bodies. Franz Douskey. PasH

Wet Camp. Alberto Rios. NAAL-5

Wet Casements. John Ashbery. NAAL-2v2; PoM

Wet centre is bottomless, The. (LL) Bogland. Seamus Heaney. HeIP-4; NOIV; NoAM; PBCIP; PNI; PoPoPo; PoetW

Wet dawn inks are doing their blue dissolve, The. Winter Trees. Sylvia Plath. HCAP; LCAP-2

Wet Day. James McAuley. BMAP

Wet Day, A. Andrew Young. NePenScot

Wet Earth. Ramón López Velarde. TCLAP, *tr. by* Samuel Beckett

Wet Evening in April. Patrick Kavanagh. OPOU

Wet Feet. Jackie Hardy. NeBl

Wet green velvet scums the swimming pool, A. Frog in the Swimming Pool, The. Debora Greger. NoP-4

Wet Hair: If Now His Mother Should Come. Robert Penn Warren. NoAM *Fr.* Penological Study: Southern Exposure.

Wet leaf that clings to the threshold, A. (LL) Liu Ch'e. Ezra Pound. APT-1; OBVE; VGW

Wet Night, A. Richard Ryan. CIP-2

Wet Pain . . . Tread with Care. Leseko Rampolekeng. NAfrP

Wet sheet and a flowing sea, A. Sea-Song, A. Allan Cunningham. GTBS-P; OxAEP-2

Wet streets, black trees, a gold leaf smacked. Debra Bruce. FFC *Fr.* ("The Light They Make").

Wet streets. It has rained drops big as silver coins. Eighteen. Maria Banus. BoWoP

Wet, this is instantly mud country, and then as suddenly. In the Country of the Black Pig. Christopher Hope. EmeKit

Wet trees hung above the walks, The. Empty House, The. William Dean Howells. APN-2

Wet Weather. Patricia Low. VGW

Wet with morning dew. Basho. SoOfWa, *tr.* by Sam Hamill

Wet your lungs with wine—the dogstar rises. Alcaeus [*or* Alkaios]. SaLy, *tr.* by Diane Rayor

Wetlands out back of the supermarket. Evolution on 38th Street. Jack Brannon. UrbNat

We've yet to cohabit. For some we simply arrive and leave parties. Alan Wearne. BMAP *Fr.* Nightmarkets, The.

Wey, Ned, man! thou luiks sae down-hearted. Wey, Ned, Man! Susanna Blamire. ECWP

(Joe and Ned.) RWP

Wha daur meddle wi' me? Little Jock Elliot. *Unknown.* IBB

Wha Fe Call I' Valerie Bloom. FaBoVe

Wha kens on whatna Bethlehems. Innumerable Christ, The. Hugh MacDiarmid. EBEV; HarvBoo; OxAEP-2; OxBS

Wha lies here? Johnny Dow [*or* Doo]. *Unknown.* FaBoEE

Wha'll buy [my] caller herrin? Caller Herrin' Carolina Oliphant, Baroness Nairne. OxBS; WoRP

Wha Me Mudder Do. Grace Nichols. NOxBChV

Wha wadna be in love. Maggie Lauder. Francis Sempill. NePenScot; OxBS

Wha?? Wha dem say? Dem say dem wan fi know what is reggae? Reggae. Vejay Steede. WaCA

Whale. William Rose Benét. MoAmPo

Whale, The. *Unknown.* CRP, *tr.* by Richard Wilbur *Fr.* Bestiary, The.

Whale, The. *Unknown.* AnOE *Fr.* Physiologus.

Whale, The. *Unknown.* EBEV, *tr.* by Gavin Bone *Fr.* Physiologus.

Whale billows. At Iku's Embarkation for Yuan China. Muso Soseki. EaWin, *tr.* by W. S. Merwin

Whale Breathing: Bartlett Cove, Alaska. Bill Holm. MiVo

Whale, His Bulwark, The. Derek Walcott. OxBC; TTY

Whale hunt, The. Jacques Prévert. MFP, *tr.* by Martin Sorrell

Whale in the Web, The. Bill O'Daly. GifTon

Whale / is a room, The. In a Blind Garden. David Shapiro. ChIV-1

Whale is the greatest beast in all the ocean waste. *Unknown.* CRP, *tr.* by Richard Wilbur *Fr.* Bestiary, The.

Whale Spouting. Takamura Kotaro. WoPoe, *tr.* by James Kirkup and Akiko Takemoto

Whaler's Pig, The. Edwin James Brady. NOBAu

Whaler's Rhyme. *Unknown.* NOBAu

Whales. Morton Marcus. GeoHom

Whales, The. Marguerite Young. WPE

Whales / Bellowing dawn. Gyodai. ZenPo, *tr.* by Takashi Ikemoto and Lucien Stryk

Whales fall slowly to the ocean floor. Joy Addict, The. James Harms. NAPBL; NeAmPo

Whales off Wales, The. X. J. Kennedy. OBCA

Whales. We're going to hunt whales. Whale hunt, The. Jacques Prévert. MFP, *tr.* by Martin Sorrell

Whales Weep Not! D. H. Lawrence. NoAM

Whaling Song, A. John Osborn. TCAPo

Whan bells war rung, an mass was sung. Sweet William's Ghost. *Unknown.* ESPB

Whan Cnut Cyng the Witan wold enfeoff. Beoleopard; or, The Witan's Whail. *Unknown.* OBCoV

Whan I remembre agayn. John Skelton. *See* When I remember again

Whan I thenke on the rode. *Unknown.* OHMEL

Whan I thenke thynges three. *Unknown.* OHMEL

Whan I was come ayeyn into the place. Geoffrey Chaucer. NPeEn *Fr.* Parlement of Foules, The.

Whan netilles in winter bere roses rede. Impossible to Trust Women. *Unknown.* MiEL

Whan said [*or* seyd *or* seyde] was al this miracle, every man. Geoffrey Chaucer. NAEL-5v1 *Fr.* Canterbury Tales, The.

Whan that Aprille with hise shoures soote. Aprilly. Bert Leston Taylor. OBAL

Whan that Aprille [*or* April *or* Aprill] with his[e] shoures [*or* showres] so[o]te. Geoffrey Chaucer. FHYEP; NAEL-6v1; NAEL-7v1; NAWM-5v1; PoE *Fr.* Canterbury Tales, The.

Whan that the Knight [*or* Knyght] had[de] thus his tale yto[o]ld. Geoffrey Chaucer. NAEL-6v1; NAEL-7v1; NAWM-5v1 *Fr.* Canterbury Tales, The.

Whan the nyghtengale syngeth the wodes waxen grene. *Unknown.* OHMEL

Whan the turf is thy tour. *Unknown.* *See* When the turuf [*or* turf] is thy tour [*or* tower]

Whan they cam' first to Yarrow. (LL) Dowie Houms o' Yarrow, The. *Unknown.* OBEV; OxBS

Whan they han goon nat fully half a mile. Geoffrey Chaucer. OxBEV *Fr.* Canterbury Tales, The.

Whan they unto the paleys were yoemen. Geoffrey Chaucer. PoE *Fr.* Troilus and Criseyde [*or* Criseide].

Whanne mine eyhnen misten. *Unknown.* MiEL

Whapmagoostui. Charles Fishman. PoCoUp

Whare the braid planes in dowy murmurs wave. Ghaists; a Kirk-yard Eclogue, The. Robert Fergusson. OxBS

Wharton ("Wharton! the scorn and wonder of our days"). Pope. AWP *Fr.* Epistle to Sir Richard Temple.

What. Emmett Williams. PFTM-2 *Fr.* Ultimate Poem, The.

What a bankruptcy! How. Bertolt Brecht. FaBoA

What a beautiful day for a wedding in May! For Me and My Gal. Edgar Leslie. ReLy

What a charming thing's a battle! (LL) Isaac Bickerstaffe. NOEC; OBCoV *Fr.* Recruiting Serjeant, The.

What a consoling poem this will be if the roadside. Shadows. Richard Jackson. SeSe

What a cost to be pure! did e'er strike your mind. Refining Fire. Lizelia Augusta Jenkins Moorer. CBWP-3

What a dainty life the milkmaid leads! Song. Thomas Nabbes. NOSC

What a dream I had last night! Kamalākānta Bhattācārya. SinGod, *tr.* by Rachel Fell McDermott

What a fine evening is this. Song of the Boatswain of Yüeh. *Unknown.* SuSp, *tr.* by Irving Y. Lo

What a fine hostess! Tune: "Song of the Southern Country"—Presented to a Courtesan. Hsin Ch'i-chi. SuSp, *tr.* by Irving Y. Lo

What a Friend We Have in Cheeses! William Cole. OBAL

What a friend we have in Jesus. Unfailing Friend, The. Joseph Scriven. SacPr

What a girl called "the dailiness of life." Well Water. Randall Jarrell. InPK-6; NAAL-2v2; NAAL-5; NOBA; OxBSP; VCAP; VGW

What a grand time was the war! World War II. Langston Hughes. APT-2; HCAP; PoPoPo

What a great battle you and I have fought. Marriage, The. Anna Wickham. ItWoWo

What a grudge I am bearing the earth. Petrarch. MoBrPo, *tr.* by J. M. Synge *Fr.* Sonnets to Laura.

What a host you are, Mancinus. Martial. OBVE

What a joke! Rāmprasād Sen. SinGod, *tr.* by Rachel Fell McDermott

What a joy to climb into bed. Presidents. Michael Heffernan. EmeKit

What a kingdom you've brought me to! Fear. Devdas Chhotray. OMIP, *tr.* by Jayanta Mahapatra

What a lark! Osen. JDP, *tr.* by Yoel Hoffmann

What a little girl had on her mind was. What a Little Girl Had on Her Mind. Ibaragi Noriko. WoPoe, *tr.* by Ikuko Atsumi and Kenneth Rexroth

What a Little Moonlight Can Do. Joe Heithaus. SeSe

What a lonely town this is for me. Wedding Bells Are Breaking up That Old Gang of Mine. Willie Raskin. ReLy

What a lovely being is a mother! Mother. Hettye Rayburn Ramsey. PWR

What a man, what a moon, what a fish, what a chip, what a block. What a Man, What a Moon. Anna Couani. BMAP

What a mixup, what a mess. Ain't That the Way It Goes? Fred E. Ahlert. ReLy

What a modern age, modern age, modern age. Twentieth-Century Love. George M. Cohan. ReLy

What a moon. Lucien Stryk. IllVoic *Fr.* Issa: A Suite of Haiku.

What a mouth has to do with the opening in a door. I hid a. Meshes. Elizabeth Robinson. AmPoNex

What a Perfect Combination. Irving Caesar. ReLy

What a pox do you mean with your pride and ill-nature. Solitary Canto to Chloris the Disdainful, A. John Smith. NOEC

What a proud dreamhorse pulling(smoothloomingly)through. E. E. Cummings. VGW

What a relief to be speaking again, restored. Comment on My Host, A. Mark Solomon. OPRER

What a shame—the chaos of the city! Evening View from the Bell Tower at P'ing-ch'ang. T'ang Hsien-tsu. CoBLCP, *tr.* by Jonathan Chaves

What a silence, when you are here. What. Relationship. János Pilinszky. IQMS, *tr.* by Peter Jay

What a splish-splash that would be! (LL) Mother Goose. OxNR; ReMoGo

What a strain it is to be evil. (LL) Mask of Evil, The. Bertolt Brecht. PoSu; WoPoe, *tr.* by Hoffman Reynolds Hays

What a strange thing! Issa. EH, *tr.* by Robert Hass

What a strong little sucker you are! First Beating. Lorna Dee Cervantes. TouFir

What a sublime end of one's body, what an enskyment; what a life after death. (LL) Vulture. Robinson Jeffers. APT-1; NAAL-2v2; NOBA; NoAM

What a sweet little day, what a day! Yury [or Iurii] Pavlovich Odarchenko. TCRP

What a thrill. Cut. Sylvia Plath. EmeKit; TAP

What a wall! Play No Ball. Gerard Benson. NOxBChV

What a wonderful bird the frog are! Frog, The. *Unknown.* NBLV; NOxBChV; NTCP; RB

What a wonderful dumb story of America: country boy. Johnny B. Goode. James Seay. SwNoth

What a world / Where lotus flowers. Issa. ZenPo, *tr. by* Takashi Ikemoto and Lucien Stryk

What abou' de Law? Adam Small. PeSAV, *tr. by* Carrol Lasker

What about all this writing? Young Love. William Carlos Williams. APT-1

What about his feelings—. Beginning by Value. Christopher Gilbert. GT

What about that bad short you saw last week. Black People! Imamu Amiri Baraka. BPo

What about that girl in first grade? The one who hopped up on her desk. Mark Rudman. TaR   *Fr.* Rider.

What about the people who came to my father's office. Questions, The. Robert Pinsky. ColAP; NoAM

What absence only can create. Silence Spoken Here. Samuel Hazo. GraLe

What age is this? What times are now? Time's Whirligig, Or, The Blue-New-Made-Gentleman Mounted. Humphrey Willis. NOSC

What ailes Pigmalion? Is it lunacy. Poem, The. Thomas Morton. SCAP

What ails my heart, that in my breast. When We Cannot Sleep. George Wither. SacPr

What ails my senses thus to cheat? London in July. Amy Levy. PoBW

What Am I after All. Walt Whitman. OPOU

What Am I Chasing! Hala Mohammad. PoArWo, *tr. by* Cornelia Al-Khaled

What am I doing reading. Music Appreciation. Floyd Skloot. MiVo

What am I in the place of nourishment. Curse on Uruk, A. Enheduanna. BoWoP, *tr. by* Aliki Barnstone and Willis Barnstone

What am I suppose to do. You Send Me: Bertha Franklin, December 11, 1964. E. Ethelbert Miller. SpirFl

What am I to do with my sister? *Var. authors.* AWP   *Fr.* Manyo Shu, Part 4 of 4.

What am I? Ah, you know it. Constance Naden. VWP   *Fr.* Evolutional Erotics.

What am I? and from whence?—I nothing know. Edward Young. SacPr   *Fr.* Night Thoughts.

What am I? how produced? and for what end? Know Yourself. John Arbuthnot. ECEV

What am I? Nosing here, turning leaves over. Wodwo. Ted Hughes. HarvBoo; NoAM; WoPoe

What an awful dream. Before the Hunger: Megan's Blessing. Margaret Blanchard. SpudSo

What an elusive target. Fights, The. Milton Acorn. MoCV; NOBC

"What an old lady," says my friend. Dogs of New York, The. Lee Meitzen Grue. UrbNat

What are all the hillmen wanting. Keeper of the Midnight Gate, The. George Mackay Brown. OxBC

What are days for? Days. Philip Larkin. EBEV; FaBoMo; NPeEn; OxAEP-2; OxBC; OxBEV; OxBSP; PeECV; PoetW; RB; TOF; WoPoe

What are deep? The ocean and truth. (LL) What Are Heavy? Christina Georgina Rossetti. FaBoEE; Spl

What Are Folks Made Of. Mother Goose. ReMoGo; UV (Natural History.) OxNR

What Are Heavy? Christina Georgina Rossetti. FaBoEE; Spl

What are little boys made of, made of? What Are Folks Made Of. Mother Goose. ReMoGo; UV

What! are my deeds forgot? William Shakespeare. OxAEP-1   *Fr.* Troilus and Cressida.

What are ruins to us. At Lindos. May Sarton. WPE

What are stars, but hieroglyphics of God's glory writ in lightning. Apollo. Thomas Holley Chivers. APN-1

"What are the bugles blowin' for?" said Files-on-Parade. Danny Deever. Rudyard Kipling. BRP; EBVV; FaBoWar; GTBS-P; MoBrPo; NAEL-5v2; NAEL-6v2; NOBE; NOBVV; NPeEn; NoAM; OxBEV; OxBTC; OxBoLi; PeVV; SCGP; SCV; TFi; UnPo

What are the islands to me. Islands, The. "H. D.". MoAmPo; TCAPo

What are the people like there? How do they live? Them / There. John Ash. HarvBoo

What are the Signs of Zodiac. Zodiac. Eleanor Farjeon. OTCP

What are the suburbs made of? Nursery Rhyme. Gavin Ewart. UV

What are these that glow from afar. Christina Georgina Rossetti. SacPr

What are these things thou lovest? Vanity. On Her Vanity. Wilfrid Scawen Blunt. GSo

What are these women up to? They've gone and strung. Deodand, The. Anthony Hecht. DiPo; NoAM

What are they doing now? I imagine Oliver. Running Battle, A. Brendan Kennelly. BiHa

What are to me those honours or renown. Last Words on Greece. Byron. CAGL

What are we first? First, animals; and next. George Meredith. CABP; HAP; NoP-4   *Fr.* Modern Love.

What are we men indeed? Grim torment's habitation. Human Misery. Andreas Gryphius. GePo, *tr. by* George C. Schoolfield

What are We Playing At? Andrée Chedid. BoWoP; HAWP, *tr. by* Mirène Ghossein and Samuel Hazo

What are we *really?* Pain's return address. Misery. Andreas Gryphius. WoPoe, *tr. by* Christopher Benfey

What are we to do with a heaven. Three Songs from the Temple. Don Domanski. NOBC

What are we waiting for, assembled in the forum? Waiting for the Barbarians. Constantine P. Cavafy. AF; BLT

What are we waiting for, gathered in the market-place? Waiting for the Barbarians. Constantine P. Cavafy. FaBoWar, *tr. by* Edmund Keeley

What are we waiting for: packed in the forum? Waiting for the Barbarians. Constantine P. Cavafy. WoPoe, *tr. by* Edmund Keeley and Philip Sherrard

What Are Years? Marianne Craig Moore. HarvBoo; MoAmPo; NOBA; NoAM; NoP-4; OxBA; SoSe-8

What are you able to build with your blocks? Block City. Robert Louis Stevenson. AmFaPo; NTCP

What are you—banded one? (LL) Pool, The. "H. D.". APT-1; HarvBoo

What are you doing away up there. Night Walk. Max Fatchen. OTCP

What are you doing here, ghost, among these urns. Father in the Railway Buffet. U. A. Fanthorpe. FaBoWP

What are you doing here in this strange world that goes on and off. Traffic Lights. Lina Kasdaglis. WoPoe, *tr. by* Edmund Keeley and Mary Keeley

What are you doing in our street among the automobiles, horse? Charles Reznikoff. WoPoe

What are you doing, my lady, my lady. *Unknown.* OxNR

What Are You Doing? Edmund Vance Cooke. PWR

What are you doing? Something Goes By. May Swenson. BodElec

What, are you grown dull now and perplexed? Before the Court. Aleksandr Aleksandrovich Blok. TCRP, *tr. by* Geoffrey Thurley

What are you, Lady?—naught is here. Winthrop Mackworth Praed. NOBL; PeLV   *Fr.* Every-Day Characters.

"What are you looking at?" the farmer said. Evening Primrose, The. Christopher Pearse Cranch. APN-1

What are you saving it for? Asclepiades. PGA

What are you saying to me? Love-Charm Song. *Chippewa Oral Tradition.* NAAL-5

What are you, then, my love, my friend, my father. Quarry, The. Vassar Miller. WPE

What are you thinking, that you speak no word? Thomas Hardy. FaBoWar   *Fr.* Dynasts, The.

What are you thinking? For One Must Want / To Shut the Other's Gaze. Jorie Graham. BodElec

What are you. . . ? they ask, in wonder. Patrick Anderson. NOBC   *Fr.* Poem on Canada.

What are you? what new device, you who hurry in such a random. Richard Crashaw. PBRV   *Fr.* Bulla.

What art thou, frost? and whence are thy keen stores. James Thomson. OxBS   *Fr.* Seasons, The.

What art thou, love? Whence are those charms. Jacob Allestry. NOSC

What art thou, Mignon, child of mystery? Mignon. Henrietta Cordelia Ray. CBWP-3

What Art thou, oh! thou new-found pain? On Desire A Pindarick. Aphra Behn. EMWP

What art thou, Spleen, which ev'ry thing dost ape? Spleen, The. Anne Finch, Countess of Winchilsea. NALW; NOSC

What ash rises high. Testimonies. Rosita Kalina. TANSG, *tr. by* Celeste Kostopulos-Cooperman

What ash rises up haughtily. Testimonies. Rosita Kalina. MirDau, *tr. by* Roberta Gordenstein

What asks the Bard? He prays for naught. After Horace. Alfred Denis Godley. NOBL

What aspect bore the Man who roved or fled. William Wordsworth. CenSon   *Fr.* River Duddon [A Series of Sonnets], The.

What astonishing contact, old man, your hands establish with our own! Hands. Victor Serge. AF, *tr. by* James Brook

What authors lose, their booksellers have won. On Authors and Booksellers [*or* Publishers]. Pope. FaBoEE

What awful pageants crowd the evening sky! Written September 1791, during a Remarkable Thunder Storm, in which the Moon Was Perfectly Clear, While the Tempest Gathered in Various Directions Near the Earth. Charlotte Smith. CenSon

What beauteous form beneath a marble veil. On an Unfinished Statue. George Santayana. APN-2

What Became of Them? *Unknown.* OBCA

What beckoning [*or* beck'ning] ghost, along the moonlight shade. Pope. ECEV; NOBE; NOEC; OBEV; SCGP

What Becomes Us. Sharon Mesmer. HeMarv

What began as an urge to satisfy. Lovers' Duet. Wendy Lee. PasH

What began that bustle in the village. Birth of Moshesh, The. David Granmer T. Bereng. TTY, *tr.* by Jack Cope and Dan Kunene

What bird so sings, yet so does wail? John Lyly. NoSic *Fr.* Alexander and Campaspe.

What bird unknown. Shore Bird. Brewster Ghiselin. APT-2

What Birds Were There. William Everson. NoAM

What bloody man is that? He can report. William Shakespeare. FaBoWar *Fr.* Macbeth.

"What bluid's that on thy coat lap." Edward. *Unknown.* ESPB

What blust'ring noise now interrupts my sleep. William Drummond, of Hawthornden. NOSC *Fr.* Forth Feasting.

What bone shall speak for me? (LL) Meditation on a Bone. Alec Derwent Hope. NoAM; WoPoe

What Booker can prognosticate. King Enjoys His Own Again, The. Martin Parker. FaBoCh; OxBoLi

What *Booker* doth prognosticate. Martin Parker. *See* What Booker can prognosticate

What boots it that thy steps to distant shores. Elizabeth Cobbold. CenSon *Fr.* Sonnets of Laura.

What booty gave the German War? Booty from the German War. Friedrich von Logau. GePo, *tr.* by George C. Schoolfield

What bowery dell with fragrant breath. Ann Radcliffe. RWP *Fr.* Mysteries of Udolpho, The.

What bring[s] you, sailor, home from the sea. Luck. Wilfrid Wilson Gibson. OBMV

What buck last cattle lap form pits. Leaving Rattle Bar. Clark Coolidge. FTOS

What built a world may sure repair a state. (LL) To Mr. Henry Lawes. Katherine Philips. NoP-4; WPE

What bullet killed him? Dead Soldier. Nicolás Guillén. TTY, *tr.* by Langston Hughes

What business, or what hope brings thee to town. To Sextus. Martial. FaBoEE, *tr.* by Sir Charles Sedley

What business, this? What reason should we give. *Unknown.* RomPo, *tr.* by Eugene O'Connor *Fr.* Priapean Corpus, The.

What can a yellow glove mean in a world of motorcars and. Yellow Glove. Naomi Shihab Nye. LoL; PoArWo

What can I do in Poetry. Departure of the Good Daemon, The. Robert Herrick. BASC; NPeEn

What can I do, now there's nothing to say? Night on the Boulevard. Lőrinc Szabó. IQMS, *tr.* by Laurence James

What Can I Do? Horace Logo Traubel. TrJP *Fr.* Chants Communal.

What can I give thee back, O liberal. Elizabeth Barrett Browning. BWW; CenSon; OxAEP-2 *Fr.* Sonnets from the Portuguese.

What can I give you, my lord, my lover. Gift, The. Sara Teasdale. LW

What can I learn from the hummingbird. After the Storm, August. Gail Mazur. ExTi

What can I say at your grave? To Father. Yury [*or* Iurii] Kuznetsov. TCRP, *tr.* by Sarah W. Bliumis

What can I say to you, darling. Poem Without a Single Bird in It, A. Jack Spicer. BodElec

What can I say? I've even forgotten how. Stitches. Debra Kang Dean. NAPBL

What can I send you under the earth. Traditional Funeral Songs. *Unknown.* BoWoP, *tr.* by Willis Barnstone and Elene Kolb

What Can I Tell My Bones? Theodore Roethke. NOBA *Fr.* Meditations of an Old Woman.

What can I tell you? Though your quarry. Paul Muldoon. NewEx

What can melt a traveler's grief? Rhyming a Friend's Poem. Yü Hsüan-chi. BoWoP, *tr.* by Geoffrey Waters

What can the cause be, when the king hath [*or* K. have] given. Epigram. To the Household. 1630, An. Ben Jonson. BeJo; Son

What can the mutineers hear from the hold? Last Look at the Mutineers, A. Matthew Rohrer. AmPoNex

What can we, a small natoin adrift, beg of mighty Britannia? One For Miss Pardo's Travel Diary. Mihály Vörösmarty. IQMS, *tr.* by Adam Makkai

What can we say to our children? (LL) Sad Children's Song, The. Grace Paley. SoSe-8; TaR

What can you expect. Maryam bint Abi Ya'qub al-Ansari. WPOW

What can you see in yonder bay. Thomas Jeffrey Llewelyn Prichard. AngWePo *Fr.* Land Beneath the Sea, The.

What Cannot Be. John Addington Symonds. CAGL

What Cannot Be Kept. Reginald Shepherd. GT

What care I for the leagues o sand. Mither's Lament, The. Sydney Goodsir Smith. OxBS

What care I for whom she be? (LL) George Wither. OxAEP-1; SCGP *Fr.* Fair Virtue, the Mistress of Philarete.

What care I how black I be? *Unknown.* OxNR

What care I, so they stand the same. Merops. Ralph Waldo Emerson. APN-1; OxBA

What Care I Though the World Reprove. *Unknown.* NOSC

What care I who makes the laws of a nation? Let Me Sing and I'm Happy. Irving Berlin. ReLy

What care our Drunken Dames to whom they spread? Juvenal. OxBEV, *tr.* by John Dryden *Fr.* Satires.

What care the Dead, for Chanticleer. Emily Dickinson. APN-2

What cause have we, asham'd to stand. Fruit of Sin, or a Lamentation for England, The. Julea Palmer. EMWP

What celebration showed there be? Horace. AWP, *tr.* by Louis Untermeyer *Fr.* Odes.

What ceremony else? William Shakespeare. EBEV *Fr.* Hamlet.

What chance / Sweet dreamlike chance. I Won't Sell His Love. Fadwa Tuqan [or Tuquan]. AF, *tr.* by Mounah Aikhouri

What changes take place in the course of a year. Course of a Year, The. George Sands Johnson. PWR

What chord did she pluck in my soul. What Chord Did She Pluck. Steve Kowit. BLT

What Christ Said. George Macdonald. SacPr

What clicks and rattles coloured strings of plastic curtains all the afternoon. Denise Riley. Oth *Fr.* Seven Strangely Exciting Lies.

What Color Is Lonely. Carolyn M. Rodgers. BPo

What cometh here from west to east a-wending? Death Song, A. William Morris. NAEL-5v2; NAEL-6v2

What common language to unravel? Paterson: The Falls. William Carlos Williams. APT-1; ColAP

What conscience dictates to be done. Hymn. Pope. SacPr

What conscience, say, is it in thee. To Oenone. Robert Herrick. OBEV

What could be done? The house was full of folks! Inn That Missed Its Chance, The. Amos Russel Wells. TrCP

What Could Happen. Dorianne Laux. BodElec; GeoHom

What could he know of sky and stars, or heaven's all-hidden life. Sadi [*or* Saadi *or* Sa'di]. AWP, *tr.* by Sir Edwin Arnold *Fr.* Gulistan, The.

What Could Hold Us. Heather McHugh. NIP-4

What could I do. Unrepentant. Brandel France de Bravo. OPRER

What could my father do? My Father Went to Funerals. Howard Nelson. RaBo

What could my mother be. What He Said. Cempulappeyanirar. WoPoe, *tr.* by A. K. Ramanujan

What could my sweet Andean Rita of rush and blackberries. Dead Idyll. César Vallejo. BLPSL, *tr.* by Rene de Costa, Rigas Kappatos and Eleni Paidoussi

What could they know of the years of the tortoise and the crane? (LL) Poem on the Wandering Immortal. Kuo P'o. CoBCP; ColAnChi, *tr.* by Burton Watson

What country is it that I see. Affairs of Memory. Teresa Calderón. TANSG, *tr.* by Celeste Kostopulos-Cooperman

What country woman bewitches your mind. Sappho. SaLy, *tr.* by Diane Rayor

What counts in any action. Dario Villa. ItPo, *tr.* by Gayle Ridinger

What creature's this with his short hairs. Character of a Roundhead, The. *Unknown.* NOSC

What creeps in. At general Electric, where they eat their / young. Robert Farr. SpirFl

What crowding thoughts around me wake. To Mrs. K———, On Her Sending Me an English Christmas Plum-Cake at Paris. Helen Maria Williams. WoRP

What crowds by envied power, the wish of all. Juvenal. OBVE, *tr.* by William Gifford *Fr.* Satires.

What cruel laws depress the female kind. Elizabeth Tollet. ECWP; NOEC *Fr.* Hypatia.

What Cunning Can Express. Edward de Vere, 17th Earl of Oxford. NoSic

What D'Ye-Call-It, The. John Gay. 'Twas When the Seas Were Roaring. HAP

What danger is the pilgrim in. John Bunyan. EBEV *Fr.* Pilgrim's Progress, The.

What Danger We Court. Luci Tapahonso. ReEnLa

What dark and terrible shadow is swaying in the wind? Easter at Christmas. Alun Lewis. PoWW

What dawn is it? Aubade. Karl Shapiro. VGW

What day did you come down from that former place. Rejoicing That the Zen Master Pao Has Arrived from Dragon Mountain. Liu Ch'ang-ch'ing. ColAnChi; CoBCP, *tr.* by Burton Watson

What day is it today? The way I live. Extract from a Diary. János Pilinszky. PoSu, *tr.* by Peter Jay

What death? John Webster. OxBEV *Fr.* Duchess of Malfi, The.

What desire lurks. Nanni Cagnone. ItPo, *tr.* by Gayle Ridinger *Fr.* Vaticinio.

What dexterous thousands just within the goal. John Armstrong. ECEV *Fr.* Art of Preserving Health, The.

What did he do except lie. Banneker. Rita Dove. ESEAA; LCAP-2; NAAL-5; NoAM

(What Did I Do to Be So) Black and Blue? Andy Razaf. NAAAL
  (Black and Blue (What Did I Do to Be So Black and Blue?).) ReLy

What did I see in you? King, hero, saint. Lőrinc Szabó. IQMS, *tr.* by John Gordon Nichols *Fr.* Cricket Music.

WHAT DID LEONEL RUGAMA SAY? Report on the Protest in Front of the United States Embassy by the Pino Grande Movement, A. Daisy Zamora. CLPP, *tr.* by Barbara Paschke

What did she know. After Burying Her Son, A Mother Speaks. Mark Pawlak. GifTon

What did that girl on the playground mean. Traitor. Allison Joseph. IllVoic

What did the day bring? Letter from a Coward to a Hero. Robert Penn Warren. MoAmPo

What did the Indians call you? To the Avon River above Stratford, Canada. James Reaney. MoCV

What Did the Nazi Send His Wife? Bertolt Brecht. FaBoWar, *tr.* by *Unknown*

What did the Old Doctor do. 5.8.1942 / In Memory of Janusz Korczak*. Jerzy Ficowski. HP, *tr.* by Keith Bosley

What did they expect of our toil and extreme. War Books. Ivor Gurney. PeFWW

What Did They Have In Mind? Nikolai Ivanovich Glazkov. TCRP, *tr.* by Daniel Weissbort

What did those girls say when you walked the strip. David Huddle. CDa *Fr.* Tour of Duty.

What did we say to each other. Simile. N. Scott Momaday. CDW

What did we wish from you? Fennel. David Lindley. NLP

What did you hear? Advent; a Carol. Patric Dickinson. OBCP

What did you mean when you called me benighted. You are Mad: and I Mean It! Phumzile Zulu. HAWP

What different dooms our birthdays bring! Thomas Hood. OBCoV; OxBoLi; PeLV *Fr.* Miss Kilmansegg and Her Precious Leg.

What dire offence from am'rous causes springs. Pope. EBNV; NOEC *Fr.* Rape of the Lock, The; an Heroi-Comical Poem.

What dire offence from amorous [*or* am'rous] causes springs. Pope. CABP; FHYEP; HAP; NAEL-6v1; NAEL-7v1; NAWM-7v2; NoP-4; OBNV; PeLV

What direction will you take when the universe collapses. you who when you go must go someplace. D. A. Powell. NAPBL

What do caterpillars do? Caterpillars. Aileen Fisher. TLR

What do I care. Pursuit. "H. D.". WPE

"What Do I Care." Sara Teasdale. VGW

What do I expect from tomorrow's day? Vladimir Burich. TCRP

What Do I Have, That You See Out My Friendship? Félix Lope de Vega Carpio. SpanPo, *tr.* by Kate Flores

What do I have, when I contemplate this. Eleanor Brown. NeBl

What Do I Know. Giovanna. SurWo, *tr.* by Myrna Bell Rochester

What Do I Know of Journey. David Meltzer. UnSA

What Do I See. Gertrude Stein. ItWoWo; PFTM-1

What do I stare at—not the colt. White Horse, The. William Henry Davies. OxBTC

What do I want with a thousand stars in broad daylight. U Tam'si Tchicaya. PBMAP *Fr.* Epitomé (1962).

What do I wish? No more than what I have. Out of Horace. James Wright. NOSC

What Do the Birds Think? Alfred Wellington Purdy. MoCV

What do the long years bring us. Retrospection. Henrietta Cordelia Ray. CBWP-3

What do they matter now, the deprivations. Page to Commemorate Colonel Suárez, Victor at Junín, A. Jorge Luis Borges. PoetW, *tr.* by Alastair Reid

What Do They Say. Gary Snyder. NNaP

What do they sing, the last birds. Last Songs. Galway Kinnell. PAI; VCAP

What do they think has happened, the old fools. Old Fools, The. Philip Larkin. EmeKit; HarvBoo

What do we do with the body, do we. As From a Quiver of Arrows. Carl Phillips. WiU

What Do We Geese Wear For Clothes? *Unknown*. OWoS, *tr.* by William DeWitt Snodgrass

What do we know about the efficacy of medicine? Medicine. Wang Shih-chieng. ColAnChi, *tr.* by Richard John Lynn

What do we know of what is behind us? History. Arthur Gregor. TAP

What do we love when we love, my God: the terrible light of life. What Do We Love When We Love? Gonzalo Rojas. BLPSL, *tr.* by Rene de Costa, Rigas Kappatos and Eleni Paidoussi

What do we praise?—Sunsets, and open fires. Test Paper. Rolfe Humphries. APT-2

What do we share with the past? Again for Hephaistos, the Last Time. Richard Howard. GLP

What do we want to give each other as we park under the sign. Chinese Dragons. David Bottoms. GifTon

What Do Women Want? Mary Jo Salter. FFC; RA

What do you aim at? Or have you grown deaf and dumb? Mississippi. Milán Füst. IQMS, *tr.* by István Tótfalusi

What do you call it, bobsled champion, and you, too, Olympic roller-coaster ace. Twentieth-Century Blues. Kenneth Fearing. IllVoic

What Do You Do When It's Spring? John Woods. CoAmPo

What do you expect if you are always. Wet Feet. Jackie Hardy. NeBl

What do you gain, poor Thyrsis, by these tears? Theocritus. GrAn

What do you make of that odd one by the door. Floor Scrapers. Daniel Tobin. NAPBL

"What do you paint, when you paint on a wall?" I Paint What I See. Elwyn Brooks White. NBLV

What do you say to the mother. Ring of Irony, The. Diane Wakoski. NIL-7

What do you see beside the road. Trash. Kenneth Irby. PFTM-2

What do you take. Prayer. Bill Manhire. PeNZ

What do you think of the USA—NRA—TVA? Conga. Leonard Bernstein. ReLy

"What do *you* think?" The question my head. J. D. McClatchy. WiU *Fr.* First Steps.

What do you understand? Ichishi. JDP, *tr.* by Yoel Hoffmann

What Do You Want: A Meaningful Dialogue, or a Satisfactory Talk? Ogden Nash. OBCoV

What do you want from me? Town Clerk, The. Mark DeCarteret. AmPoNex

What do you want to be when you grow up? Vermin. William Matthews. BAP-97

What Do You Want? John Newlove. NOBC

What does a bird in Cross's air. *Unknown*. NOEC *Fr.* Collection of Hymns . . . of the Moravian Brethren, A.

What does a girl do? Girl, that's up to you. (LL) Mythology. Marilyn Hacker. NoAM; ReTh

What does he do with them all, the old king. Elegy for Drowned Children. Bruce Dawe. BMAP; NBAu

What does he think? Question for the Frankfurt School, A. Heberto Padilla. TCLAP, *tr.* by Andrew Hurley and Alastair Reid

What Does It Matter? Noah Barker. PWR

What does it matter? (LL) To Lallie. Amy Levy. PoBW; ViWPN

What does it take to make a day? Day, A. William Leroy Stidger. PoToHe; SoSe-8

What does love look like? Shape of Death, The. May Swenson. APT-2; TAP

What does not change / is the will to change. Kingfishers, The. Charles Olson. APSN; HarvBoo; NAAL-2v2; NOBA; NeAP; PoM; VCAP

What does not exist cannot be. Way of the Water, The. Johanna Kruit. TuT, *tr.* by Peter Van de Kamp

What does not fade? The tower that long had stood. John Armstrong. NOEC *Fr.* Art of Preserving Health, The.

What Does One Do. Roland Jooris. TuT, *tr.* by Peter Van de Kamp

What does she dream of, lingering all alone. "What does she dream of." Charlotte Brontë. PEW

What does she put four whistles beside heated rugs for? Random Generation of English Sentences; or, The Revenge of the Poets. William Jay Smith. OBAL

What does the cloudy future hold. Prophecy, The. József Bajza. IQMS, *tr.* by Judith Kroll

What does the horse give you. Horse. Louise Glück. NALW

What Does the Little Boy Love? Hsieh Chin. CoBLCP, *tr.* by Jonathan Chaves

What does the old man hope from those books like graves. Taghore. Muhammad Al-Ghuzzi. MAP, *tr.* by John Heath-Stubbs and May Jayyusi

What Does the Political Scientist Know? Artur Miedzyrzecki. PoSu, *tr.* by Stanislaw Baranczak

What does the "u" mean in "gradual"? "u", 'je', 'r', 'r', "im", "a", "finally." Douglas Oliver. Oth

What does the world with its lung of ocean breathe. Paul Verlaine at the Grave of Lucien Létinois. Bin Ramke. OPRER

What doest thou here, Elijah? Ghost of Abel, The. William Blake. ChIV-1

What doth this noise of thoughts within my heart. Family [*or* Familie], The. George Herbert. ESCV

What drove young Joseph to interpret dreams. Yehuda Amichai [*or* Amikhai]. FIT, *tr.* by Robert Friend

What eagle can beho[u]ld her sunbright[e] eye. Sir John Davies. NoSic *Fr.* Gulling[e] Sonnets, The.

What ear to our sobbing hearts? (LL) Vanity. Birago Diop. PBMAP; WoPoe, *tr.* by Ulli Beier and Gerald Moore

What earth is like—as round. Worsted Heather. Jody Gladding. YaYoPo

What ecstasies her bosom fire! To a Lady on Her Passion for Old China. John Gay. SCGP

What else can we do. What are We Playing at? Andrée Chedid. BoWoP; HAWP, tr. by Mirène Ghossein and Samuel Hazo

What else could we do, for the doors were guarded. Curfew. Paul Éluard. BoLoP, tr. by Quentin Stevenson

What else have I to spur me into song. (LL) Spur, The. W. B. Yeats. OxAEP-2; WeW-3

What else in this dark world turns true? Astronomer Works Nights: A Parable of Science, The. Bin Ramke. YaYoPo

What end did she meet, O my God, what end? Deep Are the Wells. Dezső Kosztolányi. IQMS, tr. by Egon F. Kunz

What endures? Not the arranged. Still Life. Sharan Strange. GT

What eucharist of air and blood. Wonder Bread. Alice Fulton. ExTi

What ever happened to fair dealing. Class. John Kander. ReLy

What ever 'tis, whose beauty here below. Starre, The. Henry Vaughan. ESCV

What Every Boy Knows. "Antler." GLP

What Every Woman Should Carry. Maura Dooley. NeBl

What eye doth see the heaven but doth admire. Sir John Davies. PeECV Fr. Orchestra; or, A Poem[e] of Da[u]ncing.

What face, in the water. Lament. William Carlos Williams. VGW

What fair pomp have I spied of glittering ladies. What Fair[e] Pomp[e]. Thomas Campion. NoSic; SCGP

What falls before us like snow. Moth. Lance Henson. VoR

What Family? Yü Chi. CoBLCP, tr. by Jonathan Chaves

What fills the whisper and. Hadrian's Lane. Ray DiPalma. FTOS

What fish feel. Basho. EH, tr. by Robert Hass

What foes are there who could not suddenly. Head of Medusa on a Rotella of Michelangelo da Caravaggio, in the Gallery of the Grand Duke of Tuscany, The. Marino Giambattista. GS, tr. by Unknown

What folly to complain. Soliloquy. Ann Yearsley. NOBRP

What fools they are to believe the angels. Imagining Their Own Hymns. Brigit Pegeen Kelly. IllVoic

What for feere of this ferly and of the false Jewes. William Langland. EBEV Fr. Vision of Piers Plowman, The.

What for? Catullus. WoPoe, tr. by Charles Martin

What Frenzy Has of Late Possess'd the Brain. Sir Samuel Garth. NBLV

What Friendship is, Ardelia show. Friendship between Ephelia and Ardelia. Anne Finch, Countess of Winchilsea. BWW; ECWP; NALW; NoP-4; PoBW

What from the founder Aesop fell. Purpose of Fable-writing, The. Phaedrus. AWP, tr. by Christopher Smart

What from this barren being do we reap? Byron. FHYEP; NOBRP Fr. Childe Harold's Pilgrimage.

What full, sad sounds, the noise that you were making. Resurrection of a Mouse. David J. Rothman. GeoH

What gathers in this sky. Elm. Robert Hass. BodElec

What gifts of speech a man may own. Sincere Man, The. Alfred Grant Walton. PoToHe

What gifts shall we bring in worship. Nativity. Craig Powell. NOBAu

What glories would we? Motions of the soul? Renewal, The. Theodore Roethke. VGW

What Glorious Vision. Thomas Cradock. AH

What God Is. Robert Herrick. BeJo; NOSC

What god is proud. Geriatric. Ronald Stuart Thomas. TCAWP

What God never sees. Unknown. OxNR

What Goes around Comes around, or The Proof is in the Pudding. Cheryl Clarke. FFC

What goes on in the pauses. Torture. Margaret Atwood. PoE

What goes on inside those ambulance boxes. Let Me In. Judith Baumel. TaR

What golden gaine made Higginson remove. Reverend Mr, The Higginson. Edward Johnson. SCAP

What good are words I say to you? Time after Time. Jule Styne. ReLy

What good is it to me if long ago. Sonnet 23. Louise Labé. BoWoP, tr. by Willis Barnstone

What good is sitting alone in your room? Cabaret. Fred Ebb. ReLy

What good luck! Issa. EH, tr. by Robert Hass

What grandeur makes a man seem venerable? Sonnet 21. Louise Labé. BoWoP, tr. by Willis Barnstone

What grass not yellowed? Unknown. ChinPo, tr. by Yip Wai-lim

What greater torment ever could have been. Samuel Daniel. CTC Fr. Complaint of Rosamond, The.

What Greece, when learning flourished, only knew. Dryden. NOSC Fr. Silent Woman to the University of Oxford, The.

What guile [or guyle] is this, that those her golden tresses. Edmund Spenser. NAEL-5v1; NAEL-6v1; PAI; Son Fr. Amoretti.

What Gyges so golden has doesn't matter to me. Archilochus. SaLy, tr. by Diane Rayor

What Habacuck once spake, mine eyes. Roger Williams. SCAP

What had become of the young shark? Birth of a Shark, The. David Wevill. TwCP

What had been lost was heavenly. Presence, The. Pier Paolo Pasolini. ItPo, tr. by Gayle Ridinger

What had you been thinking about. Tennis Court Oath, The. John Ashbery. NoAM; TAP

What Happened Here Before. Gary Snyder. APSN; NNaP; PoM

What Happened to a Young man in a Place Where He Turned to Water. Unknown. STP, tr. by Anselm Hollo

What happened to Barabbas. Speculations on the Subject of Barabbas. Zbigniew Herbert. GI, tr. by John Carpenter

What Happened to Miss Frugle. Brian Patten. OBSP

What happened to the iceman after all? Iceman, The. Gordon Challis. PeNZ

What happened to your green hair. For the Stepford Girl Groups. Gwynne Garfinkle. MiVo

What happened? John Wieners. FTOS; PoM

What happened? / The ninth night is over. Kamalākānta Bhattācārya. SinGod, tr. by Rachel Fell McDermott

What Happens. June Jordan. BPo

What Happens. Tadeusz Rózewicz. AF, tr. by Robert A. Maguire

What Happens in Shakzpeare. Alan Brunton. PeNZ

What happens to a dream deferred? Langston Hughes. APSN; APT-2; AiP; GLP; GT; HCAP; HeIP-4; NAAAL; NoP-4; RaBo; SAmP; SSLK Fr. Lenox Avenue Mural.

What happens to laughter. Sándor Petőfi. IQMS, tr. by Peter Zollman Fr. Clouds, The.

What happens / to the leaves after. Roses, Late Summer. Mary Oliver. NIL-7

What happens when an old black man. Thrift. Cornelius Eady. LTA

What happens when the dog sits on a tiger. What Happens. June Jordan. BPo

What Happiness Can Equal Mine. John David. AH

What happy, secret fountain. Dwelling-Place, The. Henry Vaughan. GeHe; MeLP; NOSC; PeECV

What harm have I done to the stars? Without My Friends the Day Is Dark. Moses Ibn Ezra. TrJP, tr. by Solomon Solis-Cohen

What has been brought to a finish. Disturbing the Sallies Forth. Clark Coolidge. FTOS

What / has happened. Here. Robert Creeley. NOBA

What has happened here in Zuveliskes? Silly Spring. Marcelijus Martinaitis. TWW, tr. by Laima Sruoginis

What has happened to Lulu, mother? What Has Happened to Lulu? Charles Causley. KaS; OBSP

What has happened to the stars? What thief, thin-soled. Between the Moon and the Sun. Dave Jeddie Smith. BodElec

What has just happened between the lovers. Waking, The. Galway Kinnell. BodElec

What has poor Woman done, that she must be. Aphra Behn. WPOW Fr. Sir Patient Fancy.

What has that face got to do with that. In Imitation. Larry Eigner. FTOS

What Has This Bugbear Death. Lucretius. CTC, tr. by John Dryden Fr. De Rerum Natura (On the Nature of Things).

What has this Bugbear death to frighten Man. Lucretius. NPeEn, tr. by John Dryden Fr. Against the Fear of Death.

What has to happen for a tree to sing? . . . . Vladimir Alekseievich Soloukhin. TCRusP, tr. by Daniel Weissbort

What has want to give. Envoi. Kathleen Jessie Raine. WPE

What Has Yet to Be Sung. Malkia Amala Cyril. AfrBLW

What haunts me is a farmhouse among trees. Landscape with Figures. Frank Ormsby. PBCIP

What have I done for you. England, My England. William Ernest Henley. MoBrPo; OBEV

"What have I done?" said Christine. Limerick. Unknown. PeLi

What have I got that the others ain't. Honey in the Honeycomb. Vernon Duke. ReLy

What Have I Learned. Gary Snyder. LoL

What have I made. Children, The. Constance Urdang. CoAP

What, have I thus betrayed my liberty? Sir Philip Sidney. NAEL-5v1; NAEL-6v1; NAEL-7v1; NoP-4 Fr. Astrophil and Stella.

What have they done to Klio what have they done to our Muse. Brian Coffey. BiHa Fr. Advent.

What Have We All—a Soliloquy of Essences. Marsden Hartley. APT-1

What have we done to you, death. Lament for a Brother. Al-Khansa. ArPe, tr. by Omar S. Pound

What have we done? What cruel passion moved thee. Dialogue after Enjoyment. Abraham Cowley. BoLoP

What have you got to crow about. Meleager. PGA

What have you seen on the summits, the peaks that plunge their. Charles Brasch. PeNZ *Fr.* Estate, The.

"What have you there?" the great Panjandrum said. Truant, The. Edwin John Pratt. NOBC

What he did with every cent. (LL) Robert Frost. FaBoCh; OBAL *Fr.* Ten Mills.

What he hated was the blood in the corner of the eye. What He Hated. David Shevin. GotH

What he liked in her voice. Narcissus. Gerda Mayer. LW

What He Said. Cempulappeyanirar. WoPoe, *tr. by* A. K. Ramanujan

What He Said. Orerulavanar. WoPoe, *tr. by* A. K. Ramanujan

What heart could have thought you? To a Snowflake. Francis Thompson. MoBrPo; SacPr

What heartache—ne'er a hill! From the Flats. Sidney Lanier. APN-2; NOBA; NoP-4; OxBA

What heaven-entreated [*or* heaven-besiegèd *or* heav'n-beseiged] heart is this? To the Noblest and Best of Ladies, the Countess of Denbigh. Richard Crashaw. GeHe; MeLP; NAEL-6v1; NAEL-7v1

What heavy, dark delirium! Violin Bow and Strings. Innokenty Fiodorovich Annensky. TCRP, *tr. by* Daniel Weissbort and Lubov Yakovleva

What He[e] Suffered. Ben Jonson. NAEL-6v1; NAEL-7v1 *Fr.* Celebration of Charis in Ten Lyric[k] Pieces [*or* Peeces], A.

What Her Friend Said. Kollan Alici. WoPoe, *tr. by* A. K. Ramanujan

What Her Girl-Friend Said. Peruñcattan. WoPoe, *tr. by* A. K. Ramanujan

What Her Girl Friend Said to Him. Kannan. WoPoe, *tr. by* A. K. Ramanujan

What Her Girlfriends Said to Her. Okkur Macatti. BoWoP, *tr. by* A. K. Ramanujan

What here you see in deceiving tints. On Her Portrait. Sister Juana Inés de la Cruz. SpanPo, *tr. by* Kate Flores

What Hiawatha Probably Did. *Unknown.* NBLV

What high rewards by little pain is won. (LL) To St Mary Magdalen. Henry Constable. ChIV-2; NoSic

What ho! my shepherds, sweet it were. Edward Cracroft Lefroy. AWP *Fr.* Echoes from Theocritus.

What homage will be paid to a beauty built to last. Adrienne Rich. NAAL-5 *Fr.* Atlas of the Difficult World, An.

What hope of safety for our realm. On Sympathisers with the American Revolution. Charles Wesley. NOCV

What Horace says is. Eheu Fugaces. "Thomas Ingoldsby." FaBoEE; OxBoLi

What horrid sin condemned the teeming Earth. On Tobacco. Charles Cotton. OBSV

What horror to awake at night. Lorine Niedecker. APT-2

What House Would You Build For Me. Yves Bonnefoy. WoPoe, *tr. by* Galway Kinnell and Richard Pevear

What How? How now? Hath How such hearing found. On How the Cobler. *Unknown.* SCAP

What hue lies in the slit of anger. Outlines. Audre Lorde. GLP

What hurrying human tides, or day or night! Broadway. Walt Whitman. NAAL-2v1; NAAL-3

What I Believe. Alma Johanna Koenig. AuPH, *tr. by* Lowell A. Bangerter

What I did, I won't excuse, except. Unreal Dwelling: My Years in Volcano, The. Garrett Kaoru Hongo. OpBo

What I do is going four to not to. (LL) Martial. OBVE; RomPo, *tr. by* James Vincent Cunningham

What I do to the grass, does to my thoughts and me. (LL) Mower's Song, The. Andrew Marvell. BASC; ESCV; NAEL-5v1; NAEL-6v1; NAEL-7v1; NOSC

What I don't understand is the beauty. Rothko's Yellow. Dean Young. IllVoic

What I Expected. Stephen Spender. MoBrPo; NOBE; NoAM; OxAEP-2

What I fancy, I approve. No Loathsomnesse in Love. Robert Herrick. BeJo

What I give that man, some other woman takes. Hopping Toad Blues. Raymond R. Patterson. SeSe

What I have from 1956 in one instant at the Holiday. Scene from the Movie *Giant.* Tino Villanueva. ReTh

What I "have to do" has nothing to do. Richard Howard. DiPo *Fr.* Ithaca: The Palace at Four A.M.

What I Have Written I Have Written. Peter Porter. BMAP; NOBAu

What I Heard at the Discount Department Store. David Budbill. RaBo; TRP

What I Heard on the Radio Today. Marc J. Straus. BloBone

What I hope (when I hope) is that we'll. To the Dead. Frank Bidart. MakPoe

What I in her am grieved to want. (LL) Elegy, An: "Though beauty be the mark of praise." Ben Jonson. BeJo; NoP-4; OBEV

What I know. Body and Soul. Luciana Notari. CItWP, *tr. by* Cinzia Sartini Blum and Lara Trubowitz

What I Know Now. Linda France. MFPA *Fr.* On the Game.

What I know of you I take. Weight Belt. Jeffery Conway. WiU

What I Learned from My Mother. Julia Kasdorf. AmPoNex; PBCAP

What I learned on this past trip. Clippings. Kimiko Hahn. ExTi

What I Leave to My Son. Du Tû' Lê. WoPoe, *tr. by* Nguyen Ngoc Bich

What I Like. Alice Fulton. WeW-3

What I like about Clive. Edmund Clerihew Bentley. NOBL; PeLV *Fr.* Clerihews.

What I like about the women in Hopper's paintings. For Edward Hopper, from the Floor. Lucia Maria Perillo. ExTi

What I love about dormice is their size. View of Things, A. Edwin Morgan. HarvBoo

What I mean by too much metaphor and smile. (LL) Very like a Whale. Ogden Nash. APT-2; HAP; InPK-6

What I meant to say to her as she reached. Feed the Mexican Back into Her. Cherríe Moraga. GLP

What I need is lots of money. Take I, 4:11:58. Philip Whalen. NeAP

What I really wanted. Aleksandr Semionovich Kushner. TCRP

What I remember about that day. Eviction. Lucille Clifton. NTCP

What I remember didn't happen. Date With Robbe-Grillet, A. Elaine Equi. PeVV; PmAP

What I remember is the ebb and flow of sound. Sound I Listened For, The. Robert Francis. APT-2

What I Saw. Zbigniew Herbert. AF, *tr. by* John Carpenter

What I saw was just one eye. Bird at Dawn, The. Harold Monro. MoBrPo

What I say is when I plan my future. Blue Book 18 Pages 1–4. Steve Benson. FTOS

What I shall leave thee, none can tell. To His Son [*or* Sonne], Vincent Corbet[t]. Richard Corbet [*or* Corbett]. BeJo; FaBoCh; NOSC; OxAEP-1

What I Tell Him. Simon J. Ortiz. CDW; ChAP

What I thought was love. Liar, The. Imamu Amiri Baraka. NOBA

What I took to be a man in a white beard. Blue Skies, White Breasts, Green Trees. Gerald Stern. BodElec

What I walked down to the highway. Another Sunday Morning. Carter Revard. VoR

What I want is to see your face. Jelaluddin [*or* Jalal al-Din] Rumi. ErotSp, *tr. by* Coleman Barks

What I want to remember is a street. Street. Gary Soto. GeoHom

What I was and what I am. (LL) Christ Triumphant. *Unknown.* MiEL; SacPr; WeW-3

What I was doing with my white teeth exposed. Dog, The. Gerald Stern. Unle; WeW-3

What I was reaching for. Under the Scorpion's Heart. Margot Schilpp. AmPoNex

What I wished you before, but harder. (LL) Writer, The. Richard Wilbur. HCAP; NoAM; OxBC; PoPoPo; SoSe-8

What I would not give for this century, were it only to change! Song from the Occupation Time. Ion Caraion. AF, *tr. by* Marguerite Dorian

What I Wouldn't Do. Dorianne Laux. ExTi

What If a Day [*or* a Month or a Year]. Thomas Campion. EBEV

What If a Much of a Which of a Wind. E. E. Cummings. HarvBoo; MoAmPo; NAAL-2v2; NAAL-5; NOBA; OxBA; PoRA

What if I do go armed? she said. Arms and the Woman. Dorothea MacKellar. NOBAu

What if I own more paper clips than I'll ever use in this. James [*or* Jim] Harrison. BodElec *Fr.* Letters to Yesenin.

What if I said I wanted. However. Jane Mead. NAPBL

What if small birds are peppering the sky. It Is Winter, I Know. Merrill Moore. MoAmPo

What if society became so obsessed with the stars. Star-Struck Utopias of 2000. "Antler." PoCoUp

What if the body goes the sense. Image-Nation 3. Robin Blaser. PoM

What if the heart does not pale as the body wanes. Getting Ready. Jack Gilbert. BodElec

What If the Saint Must Die. John Peck. AH

What if the sun comes out. Boy Remembers in the Field. Raymond Knister. NOBC

What if there wasn't a metaphor. Stigmata. Patrick Lane. NOBC

What if this present were the world's last night? John Donne. BASC; EBEV; HeIP-4; MeLP; NAEL-5v1; NAEL-6v1; NAEL-7v1; NOCV; NOSC; OxAEP-1; PeECV; PoE; Son *Fr.* Holy Sonnets.

What if, with my life half over. Id. Harry Clifton. PBCIP

What in all of heaven could have prompted her to go. Hymn to Him, A. Frederick Loewe. ReLy

What in our lives is burnt. August 1914. Isaac Rosenberg. EBEV; HarvBoo; NOBE; NPeEn; OBWP; OxBEV; OxBTC; PeFWW

What, in the Register of Doom, is writ. Bishop Orders His Tomb in St. Praxed's. Morris Gilbert Bishop. OBAL

What influence they cast, and their effects. (LL)　Discourse of Beasts, A. Margaret Lucas Cavendish, Duchess of Newcastle.　BASC; PEW

What Invisible Rat.　Jean-Joseph Rabéarivelo [*or* Rebéarivelo].　NegPo; PBMAP; TTY

What! Irving? thrice welcome, warm heart, and fine brain.　James Russell Lowell.　TAP　*Fr.* Fable for Critics, A.

What is a blk poem & / or what is it.　Food for Thought.　Val Ferdinand.　NBV

What is a communist? One who hath yearnings.　Epigram.　Ebenezer Elliott.　NOBVV

What is a first love worth except to prepare for a second?　John Milton Hay.　FaBoEE

What is a Friend? I'll tell you.　Friend, A.　*Unknown.*　PoToHe

What is a Garden?　Reginald Arkell.　OBGa

What is a good prince? He is the sheepdog who puts the wolves to flight.　De Principe Bono et Malo.　Sir Thomas More.　PBRV

What is a home? A guarded space.　Home, A.　"Susan Coolidge."　SWaP

What is a Jew in solitude?　Yom Kippur 1984.　Adrienne Rich.　GLP; NoAM; TaR

What Is a Jewish Poem?　Myra Sklarew.　CRP

What is a kiss?　Language Event Two.　Robert Desnos.　PFTM-1

What is a kiss[e]? Why this, as some approve.　Kiss[e], A.　Robert Herrick.　CaPo

What is a locust?　Locust, The.　*Unknown.*　RB, *tr. by* A. Marre and Willard R. Trask.

What is a man but a farmer.　Farmer's Song at Can Tho.　Herbert Krohn.　CDa

What is a modern Poet's fate?　Poet's Fate, The.　Thomas Hood.　FaBoEE

What is a sonnet? 'T is [*or* 'Tis] the pearly shell.　Sonnet, The.　Richard Watson Gilder.　APN-2

What is a woman that you forsake her.　Rudyard Kipling.　HAP; HarvBoo; PoRA; RACG　*Fr.* Puck of Pook's Hill.

What is Africa to me.　Heritage.　Countee Cullen.　APT-2; BPo; ColAP; HeIP-4; MoAmPo; NAAAL; NAAL-2v2; NAAL-5; NoAM; NoP-4; PoPoPo; SSLK; TTY

What is Africa to thee?　Africa Thing, The.　Adam David Miller.　NBV

What is ambition? 'Tis a glorious cheat!　Ambition.　Nathaniel Parker Willis.　OBCA

What is ambition? 'tis unrest, defeat!　Ambition.　Henrietta Cordelia Ray.　CBWP-3

What is an antipoet.　Test.　Nicanor Parra.　PFTM-2, *tr. by* Miller Williams

What is an epigram? a dwarfish whole.　What Is an Epigram?　Samuel Taylor Coleridge.　FaBoEE; NIL-7; NIP-4

What is Beautiful.　Jay Wright.　GT

What is beauty, saith my sufferings, then?　Christopher Marlowe.　MakPoe　*Fr.* Tamburlaine the Great.

What Is Beauty?　Christopher Marlowe.　MakPoe　*Fr.* Tamburlaine the Great.

What is beheld through glass seems glass.　Prisms.　Laura Riding Jackson.　APT-2; ColAP

What is better than leaving a bar.　Swing Shift Blues.　Alan Dugan.　BodElec

What Is Black?　Mary O'Neill.　NTCP

What is broken opened.　Human Universe, The.　Valerie Martínez.　TouFir

What is failure? When the maiden.　Failure.　Henrietta Cordelia Ray.　CBWP-3

"What is funny?" you ask, my child.　Anatomy of Humor, The.　Morris Gilbert Bishop.　NBLV

What Is Good?　John Boyle O'Reilly.　PoToHe

What is green in me.　Stepping Westward.　Denise Levertov.　NALW; VGW

What Is Happening Now?　Hubert Witheford.　PeNZ

What is happening to me now that loved faces.　Childhood in Jacksonville, Florida.　Jane Cooper.　ExTi; TAP

What is he buzzing in my ears?　Confessions.　Robert Browning.　GTBS-P; NOBE; NOBVV

What is he, this lordling, that cometh from the fight.　Who is This that Cometh from Edom?　William Herebert.　ChIV-1; MiEL; SacPr

What Is Heaven?　Philip James Bailey.　PWR

What is her vanishing point?　Gwyneth Lewis.　NeBl

What is it about a Great Northern boxcar.　Great Northern.　Dave Etter.　GM

What is it about women in water.　Renoir's Bathers.　Julie Moulds.　AmPoNex

What is it but a dream?　Hakuen.　JDP, *tr. by* Yoel Hoffmann

What is it, fool, in the tall stars you'd find.　Astrologer, The.　Sir Thomas More.　WoPoe, *tr. by* James Vincent Cunningham

What is it makes thy sound unto my ear.　Shell, The.　Thomas Holley Chivers.　TCAPo

What is it men in women do require?　William Blake.　ErotSp; FaBoEE; NoP-4; OxBEV; WoPoe　*Fr.* Several Questions Answered.

What is it now with me.　Fear of Death.　John Ashbery.　FaBoMo; TAP

What is it our mammas bewitches.　Written for My Son, and Spoken by Him at His First Putting on Breeches.　Mary Barber.　CABP; ECEV; ECWP; NOEC

What is it so transforms the boulevard?　Another Spirit Advances.　Jules Romains.　AWP, *tr. by* Joseph T. Shipley

What is it that always rearranges.　Mutability.　Rachel Hadas.　ExTi

What is it that glitters so clear and serene.　Water.　Ann Taylor.　NOxBChV

What is it that love said when it spoke?　Letter.　Dhabya Khamees.　PoArWo, *tr. by* Clarissa C. Burt

What is it that's cover'd so richly with green.　Earth.　Ann Taylor.　NOxBChV

What is it that shoots from the mountains so high.　Fire.　Ann Taylor.　NOxBChV

What is it that winds about over the world.　Air.　Ann Taylor.　NOxBChV

What is it that you say? (LL)　Hospital for Defectives.　Thomas Blackburn.　GTBS-P; OxBTC

What is it, then between us.　From the Boat.　Patricia Goedicke.　ExTi

What is it to grasp.　Grasshoppers.　Roland Mathias.　TCAWP

What is it to grow old?　Growing Old.　Matthew Arnold.　FHYEP; NAEL-5v2; NAEL-6v2; NAEL-7v1; NOBVV; NPeEn

What is it when your man sits on the floor.　Thief, The.　Dorianne Laux.　ErotSp; ExTi; PasH

What is it with these people-swallowing streets.　All of a Sudden.　Teresa de Jesús.　WPOW, *tr. by* Maria A. Proser, James Scully and Arlene Scully

What is it? An airplane at dawn. No.　Yehuda Amichai [*or* Amikhai].　FaBoWar, *tr. by* Benjamin Harshav　*Fr.* Time.

What Is Kept.　Linda Gregg.　BodElec

What is Left and by Now Reduced to Little.　Gabriella Leto.　CItWP, *tr. by* Cinzia Sartini Blum and Lara Trubowitz

What is Man?　Richard Chenevix Trench.　SacPr

What Is Moving.　Shinkichi Takahashi.　ZenPo, *tr. by* Takashi Ikemoto and Lucien Stryk

What is my lady like? thou fain would'st know.　Sonnet.　Frances Anne [*or* "Fanny"] Kemble.　SWaP

What is my whole life? What?　Path Is Long, The.　Nikolai Ivanovich Glazkov.　TCRP, *tr. by* Daniel Weissbort

What Is Not Mine.　Hamda Khamees.　PoArWo, *tr. by* Joseph T. Zeidan

What is not rooted in static.　Bluesman's Blues, A.　Lenard D. Moore.　ISC

What is our innocence?　Marianne Craig Moore.　HarvBoo; MoAmPo; NOBA; NoAM; NoP-4; OxBA; SoSe-8

What is our life on earth?　Remembering Min Ch'e.　Su Tung-p'o (Su Shih).　OHMPC, *tr. by* Kenneth Rexroth

What Is Our Life?　Sir Walter Ralegh.　EBEV; FaBoEE; NAEL-7v1; NoSic; OxBSP; PAI; SCGP; SoSe-8

(All the World's a Stage.)　NOBE

(On the Life of Man.)　NAEL-5v1; NAEL-6v1

What is our life? a play of passion.　What Is Our Life?　Sir Walter Ralegh.　EBEV; FaBoEE; NAEL-7v1; NoSic; OxBSP; PAI; SCGP; SoSe-8

What Is Poetry.　John Ashbery.　HarvBoo; LCAP-2

What is poetry?　Ilya Abu Madi.　GraLe, *tr. by* George Dimitri Selim　*Fr.* Gratitude.

What is pornography? What is dream?　American River Sky Alcohol Father.　Jean Valentine.　ExTi

What is reality?　Self in 1958.　Anne Sexton.　HCAP

What is so strange about a tree alone in an open field?　Hunting Pheasants in a Cornfield.　Robert Bly.　CoAmPo; TRP

What is song's eternity?　Song's Eternity.　John Clare.　FaBoCh

What is't, good prying friend, you say?　Alarm, The.　Hildebrand Jacob.　NOEC

What is't, sweet wag, I should deny thy youth?　Christopher Marlowe.　CAGL　*Fr.* Tragedy of Dido, The.

What is't you mean, that I am thus approached?　Repulse to Alcander, The.　Sarah Fyge Egerton.　ECWP

What Is Terrible.　Roy Fuller.　PoWW

What is that growling! Screeching! Barking!　Spring Cleaning.　Phillip [*or* "Phil"] William George.　VoR

What is that island, say you, stark and black—.　Redwing.　R. P. Blackmur.　APT-2

What is the boy now, who has lost his ball.　Ball Poem, The.　John Berryman.　ChAP; CoAP; MoAmPo; NoAM

What is the cause, why states, that war and win.　Fulke Greville, 1st Baron Brooke.　FaBoWar

What is the chain which draws us back again.　Fulke Greville, 1st Baron Brooke.　SacPr　*Fr.* Treatise of Religion, A.

What is the curse.　Necessity.　Burton Lane.　ReLy

What is the end of fame? 'Tis but to fill.　Byron.　OBCoV　*Fr.* Don Juan.

What Is the Evil Deed.　Vladimir Vladimirovich Nabokov.　TCRP, *tr. by* Vladimir Nabokov

What is the head.　Some Last Questions.　W. S. Merwin.　HCAP; VCAP

"What is the jewel colour?"　"H. D.".　NALW　*Fr.* Tribute to the Angels.

What is the keyboard.　They Come Humming.　Sharon Chmielarz.　MiVo

What is the life.　Careers.　Imamu Amiri Baraka.　TRP

"What is the matter, grandmother dear?"　Grandma's Lost Balance.　Sydney Dayre.　OBCA

What Is the Matter With Me?　*Unknown.*　OHMPC, *tr.* by Kenneth Rexroth

What is the measure then, the magpie in the field.　Measure, The.　Patrick Lane.　NOBC

What is the metre of the dictionary?　Dylan Thomas.　FaBoMo　*Fr.* Altarwise by Owl-Light.

What is the misery in one that turns one with gladness.　Grace Abounding.　A. R. Ammons.　HCAP

What is the name of King Ringang's daughter?　Beauty Rohtraut.　Eduard Friedrich Mörike [*or* Möricke].　AWP; OBVE, *tr.* by George Meredith

What is the name of this street?　Osip Emilevich Mandelstam [*or* Mandelshtam].　TCRP

What is the old year?　'Tis a book.　Old Year, The.　Clarence Thomas Urmy.　PoToHe

What is the opposite of nuts?　Richard Wilbur.　NOxBChV

What is the opposite of *riot*?　Some Opposites.　Richard Wilbur.　OBCA; OxIBACP

What is the person?　Is it hope?　Person, The.　Charles Hubert Sisson.　HarvBoo

What is the purpose of visits to me twice since you've died?　Grandmother.　Grace Cavalieri.　UnSA

"What is the real good?"　What Is Good?　John Boyle O'Reilly.　PoToHe

What is the rhyme for porringer?　Difficult Rhyme, A.　Mother Goose.　OxNR; ReMoGo

What is the summer.　Summer Lost.　Harriet Hamilton King.　VWP

What is the use of the rule insane.　Brian [*or* Bryan] Merriman [*or* Merryman].　BIrV, *tr.* by Arland Ussher　*Fr.* Midnight Court, The.

What is the Word.　Samuel Beckett.　OxBEV

What is the word for "death."　Flowers for Luis Bunuel.　Stuart Z. Perkoff.　NeAP

What is the world, and what is life.　Hymn.　William Williams.　AngWePo

What is the world, O soldiers?　Napoleon.　Walter de la Mare.　FaBoCh; FaBoTw; NOBE; NPeEn; OxBEV; RB; Spl; WoPoe

What is the *World?* A great *Exchange* of ware.　Francis Quarles.　PBRV　*Fr.* Pentelogia.

What is the world? tell, Worldling (if thou know it).　Mundus Qualis.　Joshua Sylvester.　FaBoEE

What is there in my heart that you should sue.　Geoffrey Hill.　NOCV; OxBSo; WoPoe, *tr.* by Geoffrey Hill　*Fr.* Lachrimae; or Seven Tears Figured in Seven Passionate Pavans.

"What is there in the mountains?" you ask—.　Poem Written in Answer to His Majesty's Question: "What Is There in the Mountains?"　T'ao Hung Ching.　ColAnChi, *tr.* by Stephen Owen

What is there left to be said?　Farewell, A.　Arthur Rex Dugard Fairburn.　PeNZ

What is there that we can do or say.　Poem, A.　Ezekiel Mphahlele.　AF

What Is There to Say?　Vernon Duke.　ReLy

What is there to write.　P.S. I Love You.　Johnny Mercer.　ReLy

What is this Death, ye deep read sophists, say?　Philip Freneau.　TCAPo　*Fr.* House of Night, The.

What is this life if, full of care.　Leisure.　William Henry Davies.　AWP; AngWePo; MoBrPo; NOBE; OBEV; OBMV; PoRA; TFi

What is this life, this active guest.　Solemn Meditation, A.　William Shenstone.　NOEC

What is this recompense you'd have from me?　Norman Cameron.　FaBoEE　*Fr.* Three Love Poems.

What is this strange and uncouth thing?　Cross[e], The.　George Herbert.　ESCV

What is this that I have heard?　Dawn Has Yet to Ripple In.　Melville Cane.　MoAmPo

What is this that roareth thus?　Motor Bus.　Alfred Denis Godley.　NOBL

What Is This Thing Called Love?　Cole Porter.　ReLy

What Is This Thing You Earthlings Speak Of. (LL)　Cuchulainn.　Michael O'Loughlin.　BiHa; PBCIP

What is this wonderful thing? Brown and everywhere!　Looking at a Dry Canadian Thistle Brought in from the Snow.　Robert Bly.　NNaP

What is this? said God. The obstinacy.　Echoes.　Ronald Stuart Thomas.　OxAEP-2

What is Thought but Won't Hold Still.　Clark Coolidge.　FTOS

What is thought that is not free?　Free Thought.　Algernon Charles Swinburne.　NPeEn

What Is Time?　James Marsden.　PWR

What is to be born already fidgets in the stem.　Christmas Card, after the Assassinations, A.　Mona Van Duyn.　ChrPo

What is translation? On a platter.　On Translating "Eugene Onegin."　Vladimir Vladimirovich Nabokov.　APT-2

What is true / is what seems.　Moon River.　Joe Wenderoth.　NAPBL

What is true knowledge?—Is it with keen eye.　True Knowledge.　Bishop Richard Mant.　SacPr

What is weaker than a god? It groans hungry.　Rosario Castellanos.　BoWoP

What is whole has no face. What.　Parśvanatha.　Robert Bringhurst.　GifTon

What Is Woman?　Mrs. Henry Linden.　CBWP-4

What Is Worth Knowing?　Sujata Bhatt.　OMIP

What is wrought in the forge of the living and life.　Hafiz [*or* Hafez].　TAL　*Fr.* Odes.

What is your feeling about the revolutionary spirit.　Firebrand.　Harry Crosby.　SPE

What is your plaster Doctor?　Christmas Rhyme: North Tyrone.　*Unknown.*　FaBoVe

What is your substance, whereof are you made.　William Shakespeare.　CTC; EBEV; NoSic; OBEV; OxAEP-1; OxBEV; SCGP　*Fr.* Sonnets.

What isn't water in us must be bone.　Suffering the Sea Change: All My Pretty Ones.　Lucinda Roy.　GT

What it is all about? (LL)　Civilian and Soldier.　Wole Soyinka.　AF; PBMAP; PoetW

What It's Like Living in My Studio Late in Spring.　Wen Cheng-ming.　"Quiet courtyard fills with greenery, The."　CoBLCP

What It's Like to Be a Black Girl (For Those of You Who Aren't).　Patricia Smith.　UnSA

What it showed was always the same.　Night Mirror, The.　John Hollander.　VCAP

What It Takes.　John Godfrey.　FTOS

What it was, and it might serve me in a time when jests are few. (LL)　Rudyard Kipling.　FaBoEE; NPeEn; PeFWW　*Fr.* Epitaphs of the War [1914–1918].

What It Was Like the Night Cary Grant Died.　Eloise Klein Healy.　WiU

What Jenner Said on Hearing in Elysium That Complaints Had Been Made of His Having a Statue [in Trafalgar Square].　Shirley Brooks.　FaBoEE

What Jenny Knows.　Jackie Kay.　NOxBChV

What Johnny Told Me.　John Ciardi.　TLR

What joy hath yon glad wreath of flowers that is.　Garland and the Girdle, The.　Michelangelo Buonarroti.　AWP, *tr.* by John Addington Symonds

What jungles he swung out of into the imagination.　Gorilla Gorilla.　Bruce Dawe.　NoAM

What, keep love in *perspective?*—that old lie.　In Perspective.　Robert Graves.　OxBSP

What killed that kangaroo-doe, slender skeleton.　River Bend.　Judith Wright.　BMAP

What kind of a person would kill Black children?　Test of Atlanta 1979, The.　June Jordan.　ISC

What kind of animal would you get. (LL)　If You.　Robert Creeley.　NOBA; NeAP; NoAM

What kind of Bacchus are you? By the real.　Beer.　Emperor Julian.　GrAn, *tr.* by Peter Jay

What Kind of Fool Am I?　Leslie Bricusse.　ReLy

What kind of love is this when she.　Anniversary Soak.　Paul Groves.　TCAWP

What Kind of Mistress[e] He Would Have.　Robert Herrick.　CaPo; CavPo　(Be the mistress of my choice.)　CavPo

What kind of pain is it.　Wish.　Maggie Nelson.　AmPoNex

What kind of Pushkin am I.　Vsevolod Nekrasov.　ItGoST, *tr.* by Gerald Janecek

What Kind of Times Are These.　Adrienne Rich.　ExTi; LoL　*Fr.* Not Somewhere Else, But Here.

What lady would not love a shepherd swain? (LL)　Robert Greene.　HAP; NoSic; RACG　*Fr.* Greene's Mourning Garment.

What large, dark hands are those at the window.　Love on the Farm.　D. H. Lawrence.　CABP; MoBrPo; NAEL-5v2; NAEL-6v2; NoAM; NoP-4; SCGP

What Larkin bawled to hungry crowds.　Inscription for a Headstone.　Austin Clarke.　BIrV; CIP-2

What leaves us trembling in an empty house.　Shale.　Vona Groarke.　MFPA

What led to the crassness of Custer.　Limerick.　Bill Greenwell.　PeLi

What Length of Verse?　Sir Philip Sidney.　NoP-4; PoE　*Fr.* Arcadia.

What linking of soul to the halcyons of the afternoon!　Aegean Melancholy.　Odysseus Elytis.　VCWP

What lips my lips have kissed.　Edna St. Vincent Millay.　*See* Sonnet: "What lips my lips have kissed, and where, and why."

What lively lad most pleasured me.　Last Confession, A.　W. B. Yeats.　BoLoP; HAP; NIP-4

What'll I Do?　Irving Berlin.　ReLy

What loud wave-motioned hooves awaken.　Blue Horses, The.　James McAuley.　BMAP

What love I when I love Thee, O my God?　George Macdonald.　SacPr

What Love Is.　Ella Wheeler Wilcox.　PWR

What love is this of thine, that cannot be. Edward Taylor. NOCV; SCAP *Fr.* Preparatory Meditations before My Approach to the Lord's Supper.

What lovely things / Thy hand hath made. Scribe, The. Walter De la Mare. FaBoCh; OBMV; TrCP

What Luck. Tadeusz Różewicz. HP, *tr. by* Adam Czerniawski

What luck I can pick. What Luck. Tadeusz Różewicz. HP, *tr. by* Adam Czerniawski

What made the place a landscape of despair. Claus von Stauffenberg. Thom Gunn. OBWP

What made the porter stare so hard? At Devlin's Siding. Barcroft Henry Boake. CBAP

What mak's me so unnimbly ryse. Aurelian Townshend [*or* Townsend]. OxBEV *Fr.* Albion's Triumph.

What Makes a Happy Life. Martial. AWP, *tr. by* Goldwin Smith

What Makes a Home? *Unknown.* PoToHe

What makes a knave a child of God. Samuel Butler (1612–80). NOBL; OBSV *Fr.* Hudibras.

What makes a plenteous harvest. Virgil [*or* Vergil]. AWP *Fr.* Georgics.

What makes all subjects discontent. Samuel Butler (1612–80). FaBoEE

What makes life worth the living. Giving and Forgiving. Thomas Grant Springer. PoToHe

What makes me disinclined. Pretences. Ibn Rashiq. TTY, *tr. by* A. J. Arberry

What makes me write my dearest Freind you aske. Hester Wyat. EMWP; FaBoVe

What makes my bed seem hard seeing it is soft? Ovid. AWP, *tr. by* Christopher Marlowe *Fr.* Elegies.

What makes the gopher leave his hole. Eagle and Me, The. Harold Arlen. ReLy

What makes us rove that starlit corridor. Science Fiction. Kingsley Amis. NoAM

What Maks Makems. Tom Pickard. Oth

What Man Can Do on This Planet. László Kálnoky. IQMS, *tr. by* George Gömöri

What man has made of man? (LL) Lines Written in Early Spring. William Wordsworth. FHYEP; NAEL-5v2; NAEL-6v2; NOBRP; PAI; SacPr

What man is he, that boasts of fleshly might. Edmund Spenser. FHYEP *Fr.* Faerie Queene, The.

What man is he that yearneth. Sophocles. AWP *Fr.* Oedipus at Colonus.

What man so wise, what earthly wit so ware. Edmund Spenser. FHYEP *Fr.* Faerie Queene, The.

What, many times I musing ask'd, is Man. What is Man? Richard Chenevix Trench. SacPr

What marked the river's flow. "Stephany." NBV

What masque of what old wind-withered New-Year. For Spring by Sandro Botticelli. Dante Gabriel Rossetti. GS

What matter if I live on. Issa. JDP, *tr. by* Yoel Hoffmann

What Matters. Teresa Porzecanski. MirDau, *tr. by* Roberta Gordenstein

What matters here is (can a fish live). Nanni Balestrini. PFTM-2, *tr. by* Lawrence R. Smith *Fr.* Instinct of Self-Preservation, The.

What matters is the renewing and long running kinship. Union of Two, The. Haki R. Madhubuti. ISC; SpirFl

What mean these dreams, and hideous forms that rise. Philip Freneau. NOBA

What mean these loud aerial cracks I hear? *Unknown.* NOEC *Fr.* Bedlam; a Poem on His Majesty's Happy Escape from His German Dominions.

What mean these showy and these sounding signs. Joseph Fawcett. NOEC *Fr.* Art of War, The.

What mean those Amorous Curles of Jet? In Imitation of Horace. Aphra Behn. NOSC

What meanes this silence of Harvardine quils. Supplement, A. Benjamin Tompson. SCAP

What meanes this strangeness now of late. Sir Robert Aytoun [*or* Ayton]. *See* What means this strangeness now of late

What meanest thou, my fortune. *Unknown.* EnLoPo

What meaneth this, that Christ an hymne did singe. William Alabaster. ESCV *Fr.* Divine Meditations.

What means my God? Why dost present to me. Man's Natural Infirmity. John Day. InvLi

What means the mist opaque that veils these eyes. Reproaches Phaon. Mary Robinson. CenSon

What means this host of advancing. Advance of Education, The. Josephine D. Henderson Heard. CBWP-4

What means this stately tablature. To My Noble Kinsman, Thomas Stanley, Esquire, on His Lyric Poems Composed by Master John Gamble. Richard Lovelace. CaPo

What means this strangeness now of late. Song. Sir Robert Aytoun [*or* Ayton]. NOSC

What means this vast assemblage here. Dedication Day. Maggie Pogue Johnson. CBWP-4

What means this watery "canop" bout thy bed. On King Richard the Third, Who Lies Buried under Leicester Bridge. Sir John Suckling. CaPo

What meant our careful parents so to wear. Philippians 1.23. Francis Quarles. ChIV-2

What measure fate to him shall mete. Coventry Patmore. EnLoPo *Fr.* Angel in the House, The.

What memory keeps fresh, frames unspoken. Small Joys. May Sarton. FFC

What men are they who haunt these fatal glooms. James Thomson. EBVV *Fr.* City of Dreadful Night, The.

What Mérida looked like the first time you were there. Things That Happen to You. Alonzo Gonzales Mó. STP, *tr. by* Allan F. Burns

What metaphor could possibly convey. Signs on the Table, The. Amanda Berenguer. TANSG, *tr. by* Louise B. Popkin

What Michaelmas collision'f penis-waggle existentialism, eugenics. Category Mistakes in Biochemistry. Rob MacKenzie. Oth

What Might Have Been. Giuseppe Gioacchino Belli. WoPoe, *tr. by* Anthony Burgess

What more could I, a young man, want. (LL) Eating Alone. Li-Young Lee. NAAL-5; TRP; WeW-3

What more variety of pleasures can. Everard Guilpin. PBRV *Fr.* Skialetheia Satire 5.

What more? Where is the third Calixt. Ballad of the Lords of Old Time. François Villon. AWP; PeVV, *tr. by* Algernon Charles Swinburne

What moves that lonely man is not the boom. Hermit, The. William Henry Davies. MoBrPo

What Mr. Cogito Thinks about Hell. Zbigniew Herbert. VCWP; WoPoe, *tr. by* John Carpenter and Bogdana Carpenter

What must a man do in this house. Blues for the Nightowl. Elton Glaser. PBCAP

What must be studied. The winter trees. Trees. Ágnes Nemes Nagy. PoSu, *tr. by* Bruce Berlind

What must they have grown to now. Sean Dunne. ModIr *Fr.* Sydney Place.

What must you do? Writing a Curriculum Vitae. Wislawa Szymborska. PoSu, *tr. by* Grazyna Drabik

What My Child Learns of the Sea. Audre Lorde. GT

What my hand follows on your body. Beneath My Hand and Eye the Distant Hills, Your Body. Gary Snyder. NAAL-5

What, my Lord, shall I do with. Stanza: "What, my Lord, shall I do with." *Unknown.* WoPoe, *tr. by* Lewis Turco

What mystery pervades a well! Emily Dickinson. NAAL-2v1; NAAL-3; NCAP

What name do I have for you? Just Walking Around. John Ashbery. NAAL-2v2

What nedeth these thretning wordes and wasted wynde? Sir Thomas Wyatt. OBVE

What need you, being come to sense. September 1913. W. B. Yeats. GTBS-P; HAP; HarvBoo; NAEL-5v2; NAEL-6v2; NoAM; PoRA

What needeth feignèd lovès for to seek? (LL) Geoffrey Chaucer. NOBE; OBEV *Fr.* Troilus and Criseyde [*or* Criseide].

What needs complaints. Comfort to a Youth That Had Lost His Love. Robert Herrick. NOBE; OBEV

What needs my *Shakespear[e]* for his honour'd [*or* honoured *or* honored] Bones. On Shakespear[e]. John Milton. MeLP; NAEL-5v1; NOSC; PoE; PoRA; SCGP

What needs to be fed? On the Nature of Food. Alberta Turner. LCAP-2

What needst *thou* ask, or *I* reply? Sydney Owenson, Lady Morgan. RWP *Fr.* Lay of an Irish Harp, or Metrical Fragments, The.

What needst thou have more covering than [*or* then] a man? (LL) John Donne. BASC; BoLoP; FSCP; NAEL-6v1; NAEL-7v1; NoP-4; NoSic; PBRV; PoE *Fr.* Elegies.

What, never filled? Be thy lips screwed so fast. Isaiah 66.11. Francis Quarles. ChIV-1

What new responsibilities are we hatching now. Green Ice. Vivienne Finch. BrRo

What News. Walter Savage Landor. BoLoP

What! no more favours? Not a ribbon more. To a Lady That Forbade to Love before Company. Sir John Suckling. CaPo

What noble courage must their hearts have fired. Oliver, the Younger Goldsmith. NOBC *Fr.* Rising Village, The.

What none, that dare in hand to take a pen. Injured Prince Vindicated, or, A Scurrilous and Detracting Pamphlet Answered, An. Elinor James. BASC

What nonsense they talk who complain of a War. War the Source of Riches. *Unknown.* NOBRP

What now avails to gain a woman's heart. Mortified Genius, The. James Graeme. NOEC

What now / what now dumb nigger damn near dead. Another Poem for Me (after Recovering from an O.D.). Etheridge Knight. NNaP

What nudity is beautiful as this. Portrait of a Machine. Louis Untermeyer. MoAmPo

What numerous votaries 'neath thy shadowy wing. To the Evening. John Codrington Bampfylde. NOEC

What nymph should I admire or trust. Question to Lisetta, The. Matthew Prior. OBEV

What of her glass without her? The blank gray. Dante Gabriel Rossetti. Son Fr. House of Life, The.

What of it, that the realms of this epoch. Animal Howl, The. "M. J." TrJP, tr. by A. Glanz-Leyeles

What of the beauty that these hands have held. Since There's No Help . . . R. P. Blackmur. APT-2

What of the faith and fire within us. Men Who March Away. Thomas Hardy. OBWP; PoWW

What of this house with massive walls. Widows' House, The. Sarah Orne Jewett. APN-2

"What of vile dust?" the preacher said. Praise of Dust, The. Gilbert Keith Chesterton. MoBrPo

What offspring other men have got. Upon His Verses. Robert Herrick. NAEL-5v1; NAEL-6v1; NAEL-7v1

What on Earth deserves our Trust? Epitaph on her Son H. P. at St. Syth's Church. Katherine Philips. MakPoe

What on this wide earth. Potato, The. Lillian E. Curtis. VerBaPo

What one art thou, thus in torn weed yclad? Virtue. Nicholas Grimald. SCGP

What one wants from a letter is not an answer. Giving Way. Johanna Kruit. TuT, tr. by Medbh McGuckian

What others doth discourage and dismay. To His Coy Mistress. Sir Robert Aytoun [or Ayton]. NOSC

What pain, to wake and miss you! Quite Forsaken. D. H. Lawrence. SCGP

What painter has not with a careless smutch. Accident in Art. Richard Hovey. APN-2

What pangs did he merit—so simple, without misdeed ? Death of a Ram. Sedulius Scottus. NOIV

What part of my holiest and most beautiful feelings. Benedetto Varchi. CAGL, tr. by James J. Wilhelm

What! Parted! Not even a kiss? Limerick. "X. A. M." PeLi

What passing-bells for these who die as cattle? Anthem for Doomed Youth. Wilfred Owen. AF; CABP; CAGL; ClHu; EBEV; FaBoMo; FaBoWar; GSo; GTBS-P; HAP; HarvBoo; HeIP-4; InPK-6; MoBrPo; NAEL-5v2; NAEL-6v2; NOBE; NPeEn; NoAM; NoP-4; OBEV; OBWP; OxBEV; OxBTC; PoE; PoPoPo; SCV; SoSe-8; Son; TCAWP; TFi; WeW-3

What peer of France would let him duchess rove. John Gay. ECEV Fr. Epistle to the Right Honourable William Pulteney, Esq.

What people they were! Their boxers the strongest! Bertolt Brecht. FaBoA

What pictures now shall wanton fancy bring? On Winter. Mary Leapor. PEW

What place have the bells come flying from? Flying Bells. Yüan Mei. CoBLCP, tr. by Jonathan Chaves

What plant is not faded? Two Soldier's Songs. Unknown. ChiP, tr. by Arthur Waley

What pleases me in my old age. Tune: "Charm of Nien-nu, The." Chu Tun-ju. SuSp, tr. by Irving Y. Lo

What pleasure can a bannish'd creature have. Mary Sidney Wroth, Countess of Montgomery. EMWP Fr. Pamphilia to Amphilanthus.

What pleasure can this gaudy world afford? Consideratus Considerandus. John Saffin. SCAP

What pleasure have great princes. Quiet Life, The. William Byrd. NoSic

What pleasure in such vehement commotion. Boethius. MLL Fr. Consolation of Philosophy, The ("De Consolacione Philosophie").

What plucky sperm invented Mrs. Gale? New World Symphony, A. Kit Wright. NBLV; PeLV

What potions have I drunk of Siren tears. William Shakespeare. OxAEP-1 Fr. Sonnets.

What powerful Spirit lives within! Hymn upon St. Bartholomew's Day, An. Thomas Traherne. SacPr

What price happiness? Wrap Your Troubles in Dreams. Ted Koehler. ReLy

What profit to Darius of his reign? Unknown. MLL Fr. Carmina Burana.

What Profit? Immanuel di Roma. TrJP, tr. by J. Chotzner

What pull did that leaping flame. Snow Maiden, The. Bella [or Izabella] Akhatovna Akhmadulina. TCRusP, tr. by Daniel Weissbort

What rage is this? What furo[u]r of what kind [or kynd]? Sir Thomas Wyatt. EnLoPo

What rain! / Our sail is drenched. Mikhail Alekseievich Kuzmin. TCRP

What Really Goes on in the College of Cardinals. Unknown. CAGL, tr. by James J. Wilhelm

What reason first imposed thee, gentle name. Family Name, The. Charles Lamb. CenSon; Son

What regiment d'you belong to. Brothers. Giuseppe Ungaretti. PeFWW, tr. by Jonathan Griffin

What remained of our meetings? Aleksey [or Aleksei] Petrovich Tsvetkov. TCRP

What remains in the hands. Kamal Sabti. MAP Fr. Jungles.

What remains of summer. Cold, The. Lance Henson. CDW

What remains of the suicide's voice is the last conversation. Elegy. Edgar Silex. NAPBL

What rhymes are thine which I have ta'en from thee. Cino da Pistoia. EaItPo, tr. by Dante Gabriel Rossetti

What rhythm add to stillness / what applause? (LL) Practice of Magical Evocation, The. Diane Di Prima. PmAP; PoM

What rich profusion here. Manoah Bodman. APN-1 Fr. Oration on Death, An.

What Rider Spurs Him from the Darkening East. Edna St. Vincent Millay. TrCP; WPE

What rituals are in Benares? Sonnet around Stephanie. Lee Ann Brown. BAP-01

What ruse of vision. Bear, The. N. Scott Momaday. CDW; HATNAP

What's a patriot, Dad? Lessons. Jan Barry. CDa

What's become of those small black signs, image and suggestion. Inn of Angels, The. Giampiero Neri. ItPo, tr. by Gayle Ridinger

What's become of Waring. Waring. Robert Browning. NPeEn

"What's beyond making love?" A true question. Green Place, A. Honor Moore. FFC

What's de Use ob Wukin in de Summer Time at All. Maggie Pogue Johnson. CBWP-4

What's death, more than departure? The dead go. To Castara, Being to Take a Journey. William Habington. NOSC

What's fame? A fancied life in others' breath. Pope. FHYEP Fr. Essay on Man, An.

What's going on here? Flypaper. Theodore Weiss. BodElec

What's going on in my garden? Who can explain. Unknown. PriapPo, tr. by Richard W. Hooper Fr. Priapus Poems, The.

What's going to be the end for both of us—God? Twelve Lines about the Burning Bush. "Melech Ravitch." BBASP, tr. by Ruth Whitman

What's Going to Happen to the Tots? Noël Coward. NBLV

What's Good for the Soul is Good for Sales. Richard Wilbur. NBLV Fr. Flippancies.

What's happened to your beautiful dress. Orbit. Gig Ryan. BMAP

What's he that, in yon gilded coach elate. Remonstrance, A. John Gerrard. NOEC

What's his offense? Two Variations on a Theme. Carl Rakosi. APT-2

What's in a Name? Christina Georgina Rossetti. FaBoVe

What's in a name? What's in a name? Fame. Josephine D. Henderson Heard. CBWP-4

What's In It for Me? Edgar Albert Guest. PoToHe

What's in the brain that ink may character. William Shakespeare. TreFP Fr. Sonnets.

What's in the braine that Inck may character. William Shakespeare. See What's in the brain that ink may character

What's in the Cupboard? Unknown. OxNR

What's in there? Unknown. OxNR

What's It For. Pamela Stewart. ExTi

What's it like? You take it from me. Capper Kaplinski at the North Side Cue Club. Hayden Carruth. MoASP

What's Left. Jack Myers. BodElec

What's left but this to say of any war? (LL) Vale from Carthage. Peter Viereck. MoAmPo; WoPoe

What's left for me to say? God. Olga Popova. ItGoST, tr. by J. Kates

What's left for us in light that dazzles, friends. Music for This Time. Ernst Waldinger. AuPH, tr. by Lowell A. Bangerter

What's left now is what happened long before. Thirty Years After. János Vajda. IQMS, tr. by Doreen Bell

What's Left of You. Daria Menicanti. CItWP, tr. by Cinzia Sartini Blum and Lara Trubowitz

What's left of you hanging in the rooms. What's Left of You. Daria Menicanti. CItWP, tr. by Cinzia Sartini Blum and Lara Trubowitz

What's Mo' Temptin' to de Palate? Maggie Pogue Johnson. CBWP-4

What's my sweetheart?—A laundress is she. Jeannette. Otto Julius Bierbaum. AWP, tr. by Jethro Bithell

What's My Thought Like? Thomas Moore. FaBoEE

What's new? Prophet's Lantern, The. David Lehman. KGB

What's new? I'm still in Illinois. Letter to Friends East and West. Albert Goldbarth. IllVoic

What's Not in the Heart. Abba Kovner. AF, tr. by Shirley Kaufman

What's on this May morning in the hills? Ascension Thursday. Saunders Lewis. OBWVE, tr. by Gwyn Morgan

What's playing at the Roxy? Frank Loesser. See When you see a guy reach for stars in the sky

What's poetic. In Defence of Poetry. Mafika Pascal Gwala. PeSAV

What's so drastic in the Germans. By Fire or Flood. David Lindley. NLP

What's So Funny 'bout Peace, Love and Understanding. Robert Long. SwNoth

What's sweeter than at the end of a summer's day. Thanksgiving. Kenneth Koch. VGW

What's That. Anne Sexton. LCAP-2

What's that approaching like dust like poverty. Ballad. Charles Simic. LCAP-2

What's that bird, Mr Long? Geoffrey Lehmann. BMAP *Fr.* Ross's Poems.

What's that in which good housewives take delight. *Unknown.* EroLit *Fr.* Kitty's Atalantis for the year 1766.

What's That Smell in the Kitchen? Marge Piercy. NBLV; NIL-7; NIP-4

What's that that hirples at my side? Rudyard Kipling. PoRA *Fr.* Light That Failed, The.

What's that we see from far? the spring of Day. Nuptiall Song, or Epithalamie, on Sir Clipseby Crew and His Lady, A. Robert Herrick. BeJo; CaPo

What's that you're telling me? Love Charm, The. *Unknown.* STP, *tr. by* Jerome Rothenberg

"What's that?" the boy asks his mother, pointing to the flag. Giulia Niccolai. ItPo, *tr. by* Gayle Ridinger *Fr.* Frisbees '88.

What's the best thing in the world? Best, The. Elizabeth Barrett Browning. OxBEV; OxBSP

What's the best thing in the world? Best Thing in the World, The. Elizabeth Barrett Browning. VWP

What's the difference if I'm aged. *Unknown.* PriapPo, *tr. by* Richard W. Hooper *Fr.* Priapus Poems, The.

What's the fault of the poor mind? Kamalākānta Bhattācārya. SinGod, *tr. by* Rachel Fell McDermott

What's the fault of the poor mind? Rāmprasād Sen. SinGod, *tr. by* Rachel Fell McDermott

What's the lord's vast wealth. Issa. SoOfWa, *tr. by* Sam Hamill

What's the matter. Dickery Dean. Dennis Lee. TLR

"What's the matter, old chap?" "Well, I came." Limerick. Joyce Johnson. PeLi

What's the merriest burial ground? Sándor Petőfi. IQMS, *tr. by* Peter Zollman *Fr.* Clouds, The.

What's the name of this game we're playing? Stop! You're Breakin' My Heart. Ted Koehler. ReLy

What's the name of this town. I Arrived in that Town, Everyone Greeted Me and I Recognized No One. When I Was Going to Read My Verses, the Devil, Hidden behind a Tree, Called Out to Me Sarcastically and Filled My Hands with Newspaper Clippings. J. V. Foix. PFTM-1

What's the news, my bold. What's the News? William Sydney Graham. FaBoWar

What's the news of the day. Balloon, The. Mother Goose. OxNR; ReMoGo

What's the News? William Sydney Graham. FaBoWar

What's the news? Sweet Bye and Bye. Ogden Nash. ReLy

What's the plaint against me, watchman? *Unknown.* PriapPo, *tr. by* Richard W. Hooper *Fr.* Priapus Poems, The.

What's the Railroad to Me? Henry David Thoreau. GM; HHAm; TAP

What's the text today for reading. Morning. Louisa Sarah Bevington. PEW

What's the use. As Long As I Live. Ted Koehler. ReLy

What's the weather on about? Weather, The. Gavin Ewart. OTCP

What's this morn's bright eye to me. Morning Hymn. Joseph Beaumont. SacPr

What's this? A dish for fat lips. Shape of the Fire, The. Theodore Roethke. LCAP-2; VCAP

What's this? What does the anger of the gods ordain? *Unknown.* PriapPo, *tr. by* Richard W. Hooper *Fr.* Priapus Poems, The.

What's worse than this past century? Anna Andreyevna Akhmatova. BoWoP

What's wrong with American literature? Question and Answer. William Carlos Williams. HarvBoo

What's Your Story, Morning Glory. Mary Lou Williams. ReLy

What sacrifice so great! Mother's Love, A. Josephine D. Henderson Heard. CBWP-4

What saies my brother? William Shakespeare. OxBEV *Fr.* Measure for Measure.

What! Salomon! such words from you. To E. S. Salomon. Ambrose Bierce. CBCWP

What saved us? what for? (LL) "H. D.". AF; APT-1; HarvBoo; NAAL-5; NPeEn; NoP-4; OBWP *Fr.* Walls Do Not Fall, The.

What say. John Godfrey. FTOS

What say the Bells of San Blas. Bells of San Blas, The. Henry Wadsworth Longfellow. APN-1; OxBA

What say you, critic, now you have become. Camelus Saltat. George Meredith. OxBSo

What Schoolmasters Say. Martin Seymour-Smith. OxBTC

What scrap is this, you thrust upon me now? Count of Senlis at His Toilet, The. John Byrne Leicester Warren, 3d Baron De Tabley. PeVV

What seas what shores what grey rocks and what islands. Marina. T. S. Eliot.

APT-1; CABP; FaBoMo; GTBS-P; HeIP-4; NAEL-5v2; NAEL-6v2; NOBE; NOCV; NPeEn; OxBEV; PoE; TOF

What Secret Cravings of the Blood. Nelly Sachs. PoSu, *tr. by* Michael Hamburger

What seemed to have bothered him the most, after it was done. False Arrest. Cornelius Eady. LTA

What seems to us for us is true. Coventry Patmore. FaBoEE *Fr.* Angel in the House, The.

What Seeps In. Devorah Amir. DTA, *tr. by* Miriyam Glazer

What seer is this. Ode on the Twentieth Century. Henrietta Cordelia Ray. CBWP-3

What serious students with their busied brains. Epigram LXVII: Time, the Interpreter. Hugh Crompton. NOSC

What serves for one will serve for t' other. (LL) Horace Walpole, 4th Earl of Orford. FaBoEE; NOEC

What shakes the eye but the invisible? Decision, The. Theodore Roethke. CRP; VGW

What shall (alas) become of me? (LL) John Lyly. NoSic; PoRA *Fr.* Alexander and Campaspe.

What shall he have that killed the deer? William Shakespeare. NoSic *Fr.* As You Like It.

What shall I compare them to. Plum Blossoms on Solitary Hill. Wang An-shih. SuSp, *tr. by* Jan W. Walls

What shall I do to be for ever known. Motto, The. Abraham Cowley. BeJo; NOSC

What shall I do with all the days and hours. Frances Anne [*or* "Fanny"] Kemble. PoToHe *Fr.* Absence.

What shall I do with this absurdity. W. B. Yeats. NoAM; PoE; SCGP

What Shall I Do? Frances Anne [*or* "Fanny"] Kemble. PoToHe *Fr.* Absence.

What shall I do? not to be Rich or Great. In Emulation of Mr Cowleys Poem Call'd The Motto. Mary Astell. EMWP; NOSC

What shall I give my children? who are poor. Gwendolyn Brooks. BPo; Son *Fr.* Womanhood, The.

What Shall I Give? Edward Thomas. FaBoCh

What shall I say, because talk I must? Yellow Flower, The. William Carlos Williams. HAP; HarvBoo

What shall I say, my Lord? With what begin? Edward Taylor. ChIV-2; HAP *Fr.* Preparatory Meditations before My Approach to the Lord's Supper.

What shall I say to you, Sankari? Mahendranāth Bhattācārya. SinGod, *tr. by* Rachel Fell McDermott

What shall I teach in the vivid afternoon. Going to School. Karl Shapiro. TrJP

What shall I wear to sleep in alone? Akiko Yosano. WoPoe, *tr. by* Janine Beichman *Fr.* Channel Boat, The.

What shall the world do with its children? Romans Angry about the Inner World. Robert Bly. NOBA

What shall we add now? He is dead. Died. Elizabeth Barrett Browning. NOBVV

What shall we be, sweet, you and I. These Bones. T. H. Parry-Williams. OBWVE, *tr. by* H. Idris Bell

What shall we count to cool our angry pride? Count Ten. Bonaro W. Overstreet. PoToHe

What shall we do for Love these days? Lascelles Abercrombie. MoBrPo *Fr.* Emblems of Love.

What shall we do for the striking seamen? *Unknown.* HHAm

What shall we do for timber? Kilcash. *Unknown.* BIrV; OBMV, *tr. by* Frank O'Connor

What shall we do--what shall we think--what shall we say? Conrad Potter Aiken. FaBoMo *Fr.* Preludes for Memnon; or, Preludes to Attitude.

What shall we do? (LL) Loneliness. Amjad Nasir. BBASP; MAP, *tr. by* Charles Doria and May Jayyusi

What shall we know we don't know. Somebody Died. Robert Creeley. LCAP-2

What shall we say to the lovers of freedom. Wallace Stevens. FaBoWar *Fr.* Phases.

What she and I had between us once, America. John Hollander. VCAP *Fr.* Powers of Thirteen.

What she remembers. Mother of the Groom. Seamus Heaney. OxBSP; PAI

What She Said. Maturai Eruttalan Centamputan. BoLoP; WoPoe, *tr. by* A. K. Ramanujan

What She Said. Kaccipettu Nannakaiyar. WoPoe

What She Said. Kallatanar. WoPoe, *tr. by* A. K. Ramanujan

What She Said. Mamalatan. WoPoe, *tr. by* A. K. Ramanujan

What She Said. Patumanār. AWTN, *tr. by* A. K. Ramanujan

What she said to her companion. Bihari. WoPoe, *tr. by* Krishna P. Bahadur *Fr.* Satasai, The.

What She Said to Her Girl-Friend. Maturaikkataiayattar Makan Vennakan. WoPoe, *tr. by* A. K. Ramanujan

What Ship Is This? Samuel Hauser. AH

What should be said of him cannot be said. Dante. Michelangelo Buonarroti. AWP, *tr.* by Henry Wadsworth Longfellow

What should be the title of a king. Too, how also to include. What happened when. James Sherry. FTOS *Fr.* In Case.

What should happen is. Side 21. Víctor Hernández Cruz. PueRic

What should I do! Unhappy Kukutis in the Potato Patch. Marcelijus Martinaitis. TWW, *tr.* by Laima Sruoginis

What Should I Say. Sir Thomas Wyatt. NoSic; SCGP *See also* Farewell: "What should I say."

What should I tell them? Richard Wilbur. CRP *Fr.* Mind-Reader, The.

What should one. Picture of J. T. in a Prospect of Stone, The. Charles Tomlinson. NPeEn

What should [*or* shulde] I say[e]. Farewell. Sir Thomas Wyatt. NOBE

What should there be in Christ to give offense? William Alabaster. OxBEV

What should we be without the sexual myth. Men Made Out of Words. Wallace Stevens. APT-1; NOBA; OxBSP; TAP; VGW

What should we know. Verse. Oliver St. John Gogarty. FaBoCh; OBMV; PoRA

What sign do you make, O Swan, with your curved neck. Swans, The. "Rubén Dario." SpanPo, *tr.* by Doreen Bell

What silences we keep, year after year. Too Late. Nora Perry. PoToHe

What sin was mine, sweet, silent boy-god, Sleep. Sleep. Publius Papinius Statius. AWP, *tr.* by W. H. Fyfe

What since August, when the sound. Natural History. Richard Howard. TAP

What siren zooming is sounding our coming. Exiles, The. W. H. Auden. OxBTC

What smoldering senses in death's sick delay. Dante Gabriel Rossetti. NOBVV; Son *Fr.* House of Life, The.

What so beyond all madness[e] is the elf. Cupid Far Gone. Richard Lovelace. CaPo

What Soft—Cherubic Creatures. Emily Dickinson. APN-2; HAP; MoAmPo; NALW; TCAPo; WPE

What somehow echo through the clanging of the town bells. Gyula Krúdy. IQMS, *tr.* by John Lukacs

What Song the Syrens Sang. Eleanor Brown. MFPA

What song will ever be so sorrowful. Angelo [*or* Andrea] Poliziano. CAGL, *tr.* by Elizabeth Basset Welles *Fr.* Favola di Orfeo.

What songs should rise, how constant, how divine! (LL) Thoughts on the Works of Providence. Phillis Wheatley. InvLi; NAAL-2v1; NAAL-3; NAAL-5

What soon enough we would know? (LL) Bearer of Evil Tidings, The. Robert Frost. NoAM; SAmP

What soothes the angry snail? Eine Kleine Snailmusik. May Sarton. NBLV

What sort of thing is our family wealth? Reading. P'i Jih-hsiu. SuSp, *tr.* by William H. Nienhauser

What soul hath struck its need of melody. Incompleteness. Henrietta Cordelia Ray. CBWP-3

What sound awakened me, I wonder. Deserter, The. A. E. Housman. OBMV

What sound awoke me? Dragon Skate. Gladys Cardiff. CDW

What sower walked over earth. Sunflower. Rolf Jacobsen. RaBo, *tr.* by Robert Bly

What spells racoon to me. Lucille Clifton. NAAAL

What sphinx of cement and aluminum bashed open their skulls. Allen Ginsberg. CLPP; NeAP; TAP *Fr.* Howl.

What spirit can lift you up, to that immortal praise. Michael Drayton. PBRV *Fr.* Poly-Olbion Song 6.

What Splendid Rays. Christian Gregor. AH

What started out as a study in naturalism. How to Live in the Elegy. Tracy Philpot. AmPoNex

What starts with f and ends with u-c-k? starts. World of Expectations, The. Albert Goldbarth. HCAP

What stays specific in age when much else fades. Has Faded in Part But Magnificent Also Late for RC / Mirrors. Robert Grenier. PmAP

What, still alive at twenty–two. Poem, after A. E. Housman. Hugh Kingsmill. NOBL; UV

What strange pleasure do they get who'd / wipe whole worlds out. This Book is for Magda. Lew Welch. BB

What strange unusual prodigy is here, On the Strange Apparitions at Christ's Death. Henry Colman. ChIV-2

What Strikes My Eye. Wang Shih-chieng. SuSp, *tr.* by Richard John Lynn

What substance had Euridice. Kathleen Jessie Raine. NALW

What sugred termes, what all-perswading arte. Richard Lynche. Son *Fr.* Diella.

What suits with Sappho, Phoebus suits with thee! (LL) Her Last Appeal to Phaon. Mary Robinson. CenSon; RWP

What summer proposes is simply happiness. Tahoe in August. Robert Hass. NoP-4

What sunken splendor in the Eastern skies. To the Statue on the Capitol. John James Piatt. APN-2

What sweet relief the showers to thirsty plants we see. True Love, A. Nicholas Grimald. OBEV

What syllable are you seeking. To the Roaring Wind. Wallace Stevens. TCAPo

What taints thy shade—or doth the year decay? Addressed to a Beech Tree. Christian Carstairs. ECWP

What thanks do you get for it all? They wither. (LL) Samuel Hoffenstein. OBCoV; TrJP *Fr.* Poems in Praise of Practically Nothing.

What that street is called—you can read it on the sign. What That Street Is Called. Yelena [*or* Elena] Shwarts [*or* Shvarts]. VCWP, *tr.* by Michael Molnar

What the billboard. Elvis for the Ages, An. Lynne McMahon. AllShUp

What the Birds Said. John Greenleaf Whittier. APN-1; NOBA

What the Body Told. Rafael Campo. AmPoNex; BloBone; NeAmPo; WiU

What the Bullet Sang. Bret Harte. APN-2; OBEV

What the Chairman Told Tom. Basil Bunting. EmeKit; NoP-4; OxBTC

What the devil is his gripe. Owl. So Chong-Ju. WoPoe, *tr.* by Kevin O'Rourke

What the Doctor Said. Raymond Carver. EmeKit

What the Dog Perhaps Hears. Lisel Mueller. MiVo

What the Donkey Saw. U. A. Fanthorpe. OBCP

What the Emanation of Casey Jones Said to the Medium. Arthur James Marshall Smith. MoCV

What the End Is For. Jorie Graham. NoP-4; PoPoPo

What the eye sees is a dream of sight. To the Hand. W. S. Merwin. SPE

What the goddamn hell are you talking about, boy. How I Wrote It. David Dooley. TRP

What the Gypsy Said to Her Children. Judith Ortiz Cofer. OxWW; UnSA

What the Informant Said to Franz Boas in 1920. *Unknown.* STP, *tr.* by Armand Schwerner

What the Japanese Perhaps Heard. Rachel Rose. BAP-01

What the King Has. Ethel Romig Fuller. PoToHe

What the Light Was Like. Amy Clampitt. FaBoWP

What the Living Do. Marie Howe. ExTi

What the Lovers in the Old Songs Thought. John Hollander. BAP-01

What the Men Talk about When the Women Leave the Room. Dionisio D. Martinez. "Room itself. The women. The absence of women, The." NoP-4

What the Moon Saw. Nicholas Vachel Lindsay. FaBoEE; OxBSP

What the Motorcycle Said. Mona Van Duyn. NIL-7; NIP-4

What the mouth sings, the soul must learn to forgive. What the Water Knows. Sam Hamill. BodElec

What the Music Wants. Gustaf Sobin. PmAP

What the Orderly Dog Saw. Ford Madox Ford. CTC

What the people learn out of lifting and hauling and waiting and losing. Carl Sandburg. OBAL *Fr.* People, Yes, The.

What the Serpent Said to Adam. Archibald MacLeish. ChIV-1 *Fr.* Songs for Eve.

What the Sonnet Is. Eugene Lee-Hamilton. GSo; Son

What the swift mind beholds at every turn. (LL) Edna St. Vincent Millay. FaBoWP; MoAmPo; OxBA

What the Thrush Said. John Keats. *See* O Thou Whose Face Hath Felt the Winter's Wind

What the Train Ran Over. Lucy Larcom. SWaP

What the vandals will do. After the Poem Who Knows. Alan Michael Parker. NAPBL

What the Water Knows. Sam Hamill. BodElec

What the Women Told Me. E. Ethelbert Miller. GT

What their number is, be pined [*or* pin'd]. (LL) Ben Jonson. BeJo; EroLit; NOSC, *tr.* by Ben Jonson *Fr.* Volpone.

What then remains, but, waiving each extreme. Dryden. BASC *Fr.* Religio Laici.

What there is of it. Poem With Two Seasons Right Now. S. J. Marks. BodElec

What there's been of winter moves away. Buddy Holly. David Wojahn. SwNoth

What these can only memorize and mumble. (LL) Grandeur of Ghosts. Siegfried Sassoon. MoBrPo; OBMV

What they are doing is turning. Turn (a Poem in 4 Parts). Ken Belford. NOBC

What they are doing makes their garden feel like a big room. Scissors Ceremony, The. Michael Longley. EmeKit

What they conceal. (LL) Ralph Waldo Emerson. NCAP; OxBA *Fr.* Merlin.

What They Do to You in Distant Places. Marvin Bell. MoASP

What they eats in Rome. (LL) When in Rome. Mari E. Evans. ESEAA; SoSe-8

What they felt then: isn't it / sweeter than every secret. Mary at Peace with the Risen Lord. Rainer Maria Rilke. GI

What they had in common went beyond the I'm cool-are-you. Alice Fulton. AllShUp *Fr.* Give: A Sequence Reimagining Daphne & Apollo.

What they really say is, let them die, / and the children too. (LL) So Mexicans Are Taking Jobs from Americans. Jimmy Santiago Baca. LTA; UnSA

What They Said. Tanure Ojaide. HBAPE

What *they* think is it's the twists and turns of politics. Electra. György Petri. VCWP, *tr. by* George Gömöri and Clive Wilmer

What they undertook to do. Gratitude to the Unknown Instructors. W. B. Yeats. EnlH

What They Wanted. Stephen Dunn. BodElec

What thing did I love that walks the street. Contemporary Muse, The. Edgell Rickword. OBSV

What thing is that, nor felt nor seen. Riddle: On a Kiss, A. William Strode. NOSC

What thing shall be held up to woman's beauty? Lascelles Abercrombie. MoBrPo *Fr.* Emblems of Love.

What Things Are Called. Erich Fried. AF, *tr. by* Georg Rapp

What Think You I Take My Pen in Hand? Walt Whitman. APN-1

What this driver knew of touch. Touch. Eugene Gloria. ReBoTo

What tho', Valclusa, the fond Bard be fled. Sonnet to Valclusa. Thomas Russell. NOBRP

What Thomas an Buile Said in a Pub. James Stephens. MoBrPo; PoRA (What Tomas Said in a Pub.) NoAM; PAI

What thou lovest well remains. Ezra Pound. FaBoTw; NOBE; OxBA; RaBo; WoPoe *Fr.* Cantos.

What Thou Lovest Well Remains American. Richard Hugo. NAAL-2v2

What though, for showing truth to flatter'd [*or* flattered] state. Written on the Day That Mr. Leigh Hunt Left Prison. John Keats. CenSon; Son

What though the rosebuds from my cheek. Departed Youth. Hannah Cowley. CABP; ECWP

What though they conquer us? Witter Bynner. NoP-4 *Fr.* Chinese Drawings.

What though, Valclusa, the fond Bard be fled. Thomas Russell. *See* What tho', Valclusa, the fond Bard be fled

What though your eyes be stars, your hair be night. To One Black, and Not Very Handsome, Who Expected Commendation. Edward Herbert, 1st Baron Herbert of Cherbury. NOSC

What thoughts I have of you tonight, Walt Whitman. Supermarket in California, A. Allen Ginsberg. CAGL; CoAP; HAP; HCAP; HeIP-4; InPK-6; NAAL-5; NAAL-2v2; NAAL-5; NIL-7; NOBA; NeAP; NoAM; PmAP; PoM; ReTh; TAP; TFi; TwCP; UnPo; WeW-3

What time I was your one best bet. Horace. *See* While, Lydia, I was lov'd of thee

What time of night it is. J. P. Clark Bekedermo. PBMAP *Fr.* Reed in the Tide, A.

What time the gifted lady took. Dorothy Parker. APT-1; NALW *Fr.* Pig's-Eye View of Literature, A.

What times are these. Leaf, Treeless for Bertolt Brecht, A. Paul Celan. AF, *tr. by* Michael Hamburger

What to do with a day. Satisfaction Coal Company, The. Rita Dove. LCAP-2

What to do with salvias? In the Park. Peter Jones. OBGa

What to make of them, the professors. Autumnal Sketch, An. August Kleinzahler. PmAP

What to say when the spider / Say when the spider what. Elegy in a Spider's Web. Laura Riding Jackson. PFTM-1

What to start with? Finding a Horseshoe. Osip Emilevich Mandelstam [*or* Mandelshtam]. RusPo, *tr. by* Robert Arthur Douglas Ford

What told us that the day was over? Canciones. Kenneth Zamora Damacion. OPRER

What Tomas Said in a Pub. James Stephens. *See* What Thomas an Buile Said in a Pub

What torments must the virgin prove. Song, A. Charlotte Lennox. ECWP

What treasure greater than a friend. Santob [*or* Shem-Tob] De Carrion. TrJP *Fr.* Proverbios Morales.

What trifling coil do we poor mortals keep. Human Life. Matthew Prior. FaBoEE; OBCoV; OxBEV

What troubles you, wild sleepyhead? Narcissus to Echo. Edgar Bogardus. YaYoPo

What true man would vie with others for a hairbreadth's gain? (LL) Confiscating Salt. Wang An-shih. CoBCP; ColAnChi, *tr. by* Burton Watson

What use for words at all? (LL) Mahadevi. WPoS; WoPoe, *tr. by* Jane Hirshfield

What use to suffer in labor, give birth to children, if she. Diotimus. HePo *Fr.* Epigrams.

What used to be. Change, The. Samuel Chimsoro. NAfrP

What value to me the seven kinds of treasures. Longing for His Son, Furuhi.

Yamanoé [*or* Yamanoué] no Okura. WoPoe, *tr. by* Helen Craig McCullough

What various hindrances we meet. William Cowper. NOCV *Fr.* Olney Hymns.

What varying sounds from yon gray pinnacles. Church Bells, The. Bishop Richard Mant. SacPr

What Viet Nam means to me. Long Reality, The. Haki R. Madhubuti. NAAAL

What voice. Basho. EH, *tr. by* Robert Hass

What Voice at Moth-Hour. Robert Penn Warren. DiPo

What voice is this, thou evening gale! Song. Joanna Baillie. RWP; WoRP

"What voice, what harp, are those we hear." Minstrel, The. Goethe. AWP, *tr. by* James Clarence Mangan

What was he doing, the great god Pan. Musical Instrument, A. Elizabeth Barrett Browning. CABP; EBVV; NAEL-5v2; NAEL-6v2; NPeEn; NoP-4; OBEV; PEW; PoE; PoPoPo; VWP; ViWPN; WPE

What was her beauty in our first estate. She. Richard Wilbur. CoAmPo; NIL-7

What was her blondness like, I can't remember. Gyula Juhász. IQMS, *tr. by* Adam Makkai

What was his creed? H. N. Fifer. PoToHe *Fr.* He Lived a Life.

What was i doing anyway. On extending the olive branch to my own self. Harriet Jacobs. SpirFl

What was Inez supposed to do for. Rape. Jayne Cortez. GT; PmAP

What was it brought you, Seligenstadter. Memling. Roland Mathias. AngWePo

What was it called. Custer Lives in Humbolt County. Janet Campbell Hale. VoR

What was it drove me to insist on sleds. Snow-Day. Judith Baumel. KGB

What was it like, that country house? Country Villa. Jean Garrigue. TAP

What was it / that caught in our throats that day. Greek Room, The. James W. Thompson. BPo

What was it you remember—the summer mornings. To Any Member of My Generation. George Barker. Son

What was it? What was it? Woman as Market. Muriel Rukeyser. NoAM

What Was Life. Idea Vilariño. TANSG, *tr. by* Louise B. Popkin

What Was Not Conceivable. Fatima Mahmoud. PoArWo, *tr. by* Khaled Mattawa

What Was Solomon's Mind? Geoffrey Scott. OBMV

What was that sound we heard. Why Must You Know? John Wheelwright. APT-2; VGW

What was the nub of wonder? Was it. Questions of Swimming, 1935. Peter Davison. DiPo

What was the use of not leaving it there where it would hang what. Gertrude Stein. TCAPo *Fr.* Tender Buttons.

What way does the Wind come? What way does he go? Address to a Child during a Boisterous Winter Evening. Dorothy Wordsworth. WoRP

What we below could not see, Winter pass. (LL) Thaw. Edward Thomas. EBEV; FaBoTw; GTBS-P; MoBrPo; OxAEP-2; OxBEV; OxBSP; OxBTC; Spl

What We Can. Ray A. Young Bear. VoR

What we charge upon. Eat them for us. *Unknown*. APN-2 *Fr.* Minnetare Songs.

What we come round to. Epitaph for the Western Intelligentsia. Richard Allen. NOBAu

What We Did after My Mother's Mastectomy. Lisa Glatt. AmPoNex

What we do best is breed. Christening, A. Donald Davie. OxBC

What we don't forget is what we don't say. Anger Sweetened. Molly Peacock. FFC

What We Feared. Judith Ortiz Cofer. PueRic

What we have lost. Duriel Harris. SpirFl

What We Heard about the Japanese. Rachel Rose. BAP-01

What We Know. Raymond R. Patterson. NBV

What We Learned. Fanny Howe. FTOS

What We Leave Behind. Elmaz Abinader. PoArWo

What we live / before the light is turned off. Quotidian, The. Claudia Rankine. AmPoNex

What We Lost. Eavan Boland. HarvBoo

What we love, can't see. Geology, A. Brenda Hillman. GeoHom

What we mistook for flight. Reunion. T. Crunk. YaYoPo

What we must accept as we journey through the world. Lament for the Evanescence of Life, A. Yamanoé [*or* Yamanoué] no Okura. WoPoe, *tr. by* Helen Craig McCullough

What we reminded you of you are already forgetting. David Constantine. NewEx

What We Teach at Claflin. Lizelia Augusta Jenkins Moorer. CBWP-3

What we think. Returning Fire. D. F. Brown. CDa

What we to-day prize and most fondly cherish. Instability. Henrietta Cordelia Ray. CBWP-3

What we've come for is the Comet. Comet and Treefrog. Jarold Ramsey. PoCoUp

What we, when face to face we see. Arthur Hugh Clough. ChIV-2; SacPr

What weak remonstrance!—how I joy to find. Elizabeth Cobbold. CenSon *Fr.* Sonnets of Laura.

What well-heeled knuckle-head, straight from the unisex. Old Malediction, An. Horace. NoAM; OBCoV; WoPoe, *tr.* by Anthony Hecht

What went ye out to see? a shaken reed? John. Jones Very. ChIV-2

What were the secrets that we didn't tell? In 1969. Katharyn Howd Machan. SwNoth

What were they like as schoolboys? Long on themes. Poets. X. J. Kennedy. OPRER

What Were They Like? Denise Levertov. HeIP-4; NAAL-5; NIP-4; OBWP; PAI; VGW; WPE

What were they talking about? Ah yes, the end! Hans Magnus Enzensberger. PoSu *Fr.* Sinking of the Titanic, The.

What were those strolling fops and dandies. By the North Sea. Aleksandr Aleksandrovich Blok. TCRP, *tr.* by Geoffrey Thurley

What were we playing? Was it prisoner's base? Running. Richard Wilbur. CoAP; MoASP

What Were You Patching? Ruth Lisa Schechter. UnSA

What wert thou, Rome, unbroken, when thy ruin. Rome. Hildebert. MLL, *tr.* by Helen Waddell

What, what, what / What's the news from Swat? Threnody. George Thomas Lanigan. NBLV

What, why didest thou wink when thou a wyf toke? *Unknown.* MiEL

What Wild Dawns There Were. Denise Levertov. NOBA

What Will Be Your Destiny? Caroline Gilman. SWaP *Fr.* Oracles for Youth.

What will become of these, the drab, the harsh. Final reductions. M. R. Peacocke. NLP

What will become of us, Nathalie. You in my memory, I in. Farewell. Enrique Lihn. BLPSL, *tr.* by Rene de Costa, Rigas Kappatos and Eleni Paidoussi

What Will Come of This? Jenő Dsida. IQMS, *tr.* by Adam Makkai

What will our father bring to us. Rondo for the Poet's Children. Jean-Joseph Rabéarivelo [*or* Rebéarivelo]. NegPo, *tr.* by Ellen Conroy Kennedy

What will see us through, a certain calm. Elizabethan & Nova Scotian Music. Charles North. PmAP

What will survive of us is love. (LL) Arundel Tomb, An. Philip Larkin. NoP-4; OxAEP-2

What will they give me, when journey's done? Journey's End. Humbert Wolfe. TrJP

What will we do. Poem for Nana. June Jordan. BlSi

What will you find at the edge of the world? Landscape. Eve Merriam. KaS

What winter floods, what showers of spring. Emily Jane Brontë. NOBVV; OxBEV

What wisdom and beauty his Sermon on the Mount. Gloss to Matthew V 27–28. Alec Derwent Hope. GI

What witchlike spell weaves here its deep design. Anna Hempstead Branch. APT-1; NALW *Fr.* Sonnets from a Lock Box.

What with the Italian. Portrait of Silverio Franconetti. Federico García Lorca. SpanPo, *tr.* by Rachel Benson and Robert O'Brien

What! without feeling? Don't we make pretense. Two Vast Enjoyments Commemorated. John Danforth. SCAP

What Women Are Not. *Unknown.* MiEL

What wond'rous projects formed the fickle fair? Nunnery, The. Anna Williams. ECWP

What wonder, Percy, that with jealous rage. To Percy Shelley. Leigh Hunt. CenSon; Son

What wonder strikes the curious, while he views. Ants, The. John Clare. OxBSo

What Wondrous Love Is This. Alex Means. AH

What words are these have fallen from me? Tennyson. EBEV; NAWM-7v2 *Fr.* In Memoriam A. H. H.

What Words Have Passed. John Milton. TrCP *Fr.* Paradise Lost.

What words must rush in. Cesare Greppi. ItPo, *tr.* by Gayle Ridinger

What Work Is. Philip Levine. EmeKit

What works best / is the mile walk down Sleepy Hollow. Right of Way. Barry Sternlieb. GM

What would earth do without her blessed boobs. Yes, What? Robert Francis. LCAP-2

What Would I Do White? June Jordan. LTA; UnSA

What would I do with these strange tears in a cold night? Strange Tears. Liu Ya-tzu. SuSp, *tr.* by Wu-Chi Liu

What would I do without this world faceless incurious. Samuel Beckett. ModIr; NOIV; NoAM

What Would I Give? Christina Georgina Rossetti. NPeEn; OxBSP

What would I have you do? I'll tell you, kinsman. Advice to a Reckless Youth. Ben Johnson. TreFP

What would it be like. Sacred Grove, A. Fran Winant. BrRo

What would Jung make of such levitation? My Son Shows Me a Photograph of Michael Jordan Performing a Slam Dunk. Louis Phillips. ReTh

What would she put in it? If She Only Had One Minute. Kay Ryan. ExTi

What would this Man? Now upward will he soar. Pope. HeIP-4 *Fr.* Essay on Man, An.

What would we do in this world of ours. Dreams Ahead, The. Edwin Carlile Litsey. PoToHe

What would we talk about before? I ask; what of, when we had. When We Meet Again. Giovanna Pollarolo. TANSG, *tr.* by Marjorie Agosin

What would you buy? (LL) Dream-Pedlary. Thomas Lovell Beddoes. HAP; NOBE; OBEV; OxAEP-2

What Would You Fight For? D. H. Lawrence. OxBSP

What would you have? Your gentleness shall force. William Shakespeare. OxAEP-1 *Fr.* As You Like It.

What wouldst thou have? a King, a Lord, a Knight. Anabaptist, The. Rowland Watkyns. BASC

What year is this? Who can truthfully say? This Age. Raymond R. Patterson. NBV

What Yo' Gwine to [*or* t'] Do When Yo' [*or* de] Lamp Burn Down? *Unknown.* APN-2; BPo

'What you are stepping westward?'—'Yea.' Stepping Westward. William Wordsworth. SCGP

What You Can't See. Karen Chase. SeSe

What you could not see in a face. (LL) William Allingham. NOBVV; NPeEn; OxBEV

What you darkly see you cannot state. Chronicle in Verse, Vienna 1945. Paula von Preradovic. AuPH, *tr.* by Lowell A. Bangerter

What you did to the blues. Blues for Bird. Linda France. NeBl

What you don't trust to stone. Eternal Moment. Sándor Weöres. IQMS, *tr.* by Edwin Morgan

What You Find in the Woods. James Longenbach. NAPBL

What you give me is. Love Poem. Denise Levertov. NIL-7

What You Goin' to Do When the Rent Comes 'Round? Andrew B. Sterling. OBAL

What you have heard is true. Colonel, The. Carolyn Forché. MakPoe; OBWP; SoSe-8

What you love in me. Woman, The. Shakuntala Hawoldar. HAWP

What you may cluster 'round the knees of space. To the Cloud Juggler. Hart Crane. HarvBoo

What you mean to say about the film is that. Over Coffee. Bob Hicok. AmPoNex

What you need to know. Magic Carpet, The. Maurice Kilwein Guevara. TouFir

What you're reading (if you're reading me) are the effects. Edoardo Sanguineti. ItPo, *tr.* by Gayle Ridinger *Fr.* Scartabello.

What you see here is a colorful illusion. She Attempts to Refute the Praises That Truth, Which She Calls Passion, Inscribed on a Portrait of the Poet. Sister Juana Inés de la Cruz. BoWoP

What You Should Know to Be a Poet. Gary Snyder. APSN; NNaP; PFTM-2; PoM

What you want is for the tiger to eat me. Side 22. Víctor Hernández Cruz. PueRic

What young Raw Muisted Beau Bred at his Glass. Horace. NPeEn, *tr.* by Allan Ramsay

What your look meant then. (LL) Watergaw, The. Hugh MacDiarmid. FaBoVe; HarvBoo; NAEL-5v2; NAEL-6v2; NPeEn; NePenScot

What? Langston Hughes. NBLV; OBAL

What? Glom: Labrador, 110 pounds. Karen Shepard. Unle

What? / a rhythm. Paul Niger. NegPo *Fr.* Initiations.

What? an English sparrow sing? Did You Ever Hear an English Sparrow Sing? Bertha Johnston. ITBLP

WhatCHU care. Whitey, Baby. James A. Emanuel. NBV

Whate'er Has Been. Sidney Lanier. Son

Whate'er is Born of Mortal Birth. William Blake. FHYEP; NAEL-5v2; NAEL-6v2; NOBE *Fr.* Songs of Experience.

Whate'er my darkness be. Tenebræ. John Banister Tabb. APN-2

Whate'er thou art, where'er thy footsteps stray. This, Too, Shall Pass Away. A. L. Alexander. PoToHe

Whate'er thy Countrymen have done. Written in the Beginning of Mezeray's History of France. Matthew Prior. NOBE

Whate'er we leave to God, God does. Henry David Thoreau. APN-1; ColAP; NCAP; NOBA; OxBA

Whatever Became of: Freud? Edward Field. BodElec

Whatever city or country road. Double Elegy. Michael S. Harper. ESEAA; NoAM

Whatever clime we travel or explore. Evan Evans. AngWePo *Fr.* Love of Our Country, The.

Whatever constitutes. Act of Love, The. Robert Creeley. HAP

Whatever else be lost among the years. Eternal Values. Grace Noll Crowell. PoToHe

Whatever exists is now. What Is Not Mine. Hamda Khamees. PoArWo, *tr. by* Joseph T. Zeidan

Whatever force insatiable death has, how much power. On the Death of the Noble and Gentle Woman, Lady Joanna Kelley. Elizabeth Jane Leon. EMWP

Whatever God's divine / Decree. To Kiss God's Rod; Occasioned upon a Child's Sickness. Mildmay Fane, 2d Earl of Westmorland. BeJo

Whatever good is naturally done. Sonnet: Of Love, in Honor of His Mistress Becchina. Cecco Angiolieri, da Siena. AWP; EaItPo, *tr. by* Dante Gabriel Rossetti

Whatever Happened to Conway Twitty? Tim Thorne. BMAP

WHATEVER happened to the elephant. Hurrah for Thunder. Christopher Okigbo. HBAPE

Whatever Happened? Philip Larkin. OxBSo; Son

Whatever happens with us, your body. Adrienne Rich. EroLit; NALW; NoAM *Fr.* Twenty-one Love Poems.

Whatever I find if I search will be wrong. Other, The. Ruth Fainlight. BrRo

Whatever I said and whatever you said. Husband and Wife. Arthur Guiterman. PoToHe

Whatever I was able to acquire in my life by way of acts visible to all, that is, to win my own transparency, I owe to a kind of special courage Poetry gave me: to be wind for the kite and kite for the wind, even when the sky is missing. Odysseus Elytis. GifTon, *tr. by* Olga Broumas *Fr.* Anoint the Ariston.

Whatever Is—Is Best. Ella Wheeler Wilcox. PWR
   (We know as we grow older.) PoToHe

Whatever it is, I shouldn't hesitate. *Unknown.* PriapPo, *tr. by* Richard W. Hooper *Fr.* Priapus Poems, The.

Whatever it is, it must have. American Poetry. Louis Simpson. FaBoA; NOBA; NoAM; TAP

Whatever it is, it's a passion. Love in America. Marianne Craig Moore. AiP; NIL-7

Whatever it was is lost to memory. Widower, The. Joseph Awad. GraLe

Whatever it was she had so fiercely fought. Karl Shapiro. ChIV-1 *Fr.* Adam and Eve.

Whatever it was: the grains of the glacier caked in the boot-cleats. Adrienne Rich. FaBoWP; HCAP *Fr.* Shooting Script.

Whatever lives must meet its end. Drinking Alone in the Rainy Season. T'ao Ch'ien [*or* T'ao Yuan-ming]. CrYelRi, *tr. by* Sam Hamill

Whatever Lola Wants (Lola Gets). Jerry Ross. ReLy

Whatever the bird is, is perfect in the bird. Birds. Judith Wright. NoP-4

Whatever the cost. *Unknown.* ArkPo, *tr. by* Helen Craig McCullough

Whatever they wanted for their sons. Déjà Vu. Shirley Kaufman. DTA

Whatever was else or less. Road, The. Robert Creeley. BodElec

Whatever we do, whether we light. Dilemma. David Ignatow. VGW

Whatever went wrong, that week, was more than weather. Hairline Fracture, A. Amy Clampitt. NoAM

Whatever while the thought comes over me. Dante Alighieri. AWP; EaItPo, *tr. by* Dante Gabriel Rossetti *Fr.* La Vita Nuova.

Whatever Will Be, Will Be (Que Sera, Sera). Jay Livingston. ReLy

Whatever will rhyme with Summer. Summer. Sir John Betjeman. PeLi

Whatever wisdom sleep with thee. (LL) Tennyson. CABP; FHYEP; NAEL-6v2 *Fr.* In Memoriam A. H. H.

Whatever you can do. Goethe. RaBo

Whatever you have to say, leave. These Days. Charles Olson. APT-2; RaBo

Whatever You Say Say Nothing. Seamus Heaney. OBWP; OxBC

Whatever you've given me, whiteface glass. I don't love you. Imamu Amiri Baraka. NAAAL

Whatever You Want. Angel González. VCWP, *tr. by* Steven Ford Brown

Whatever your eye alights on this morning is yours. Years of Indiscretion. John Ashbery. NOBA

Whatif. Shel [*or* Shelley] Silverstein. OTCP

Whatsume'er the failings on his part. Charles Dickens. FaBoVe *Fr.* Great Expectations.

Whaur green abune the banks the links stretch oot. Planticru, The. Robert Rendall. OxBS

Whaur yon broken brig hings owre. Song. William Soutar. OxBS

Wheat. Diane Glancy. CRP

Wheat cock up their shoulders and turn away, The. Pulling in the Nets. C. Mikal Oness. GeoHom

Wheat has been quickly harvested, The. Compassion for the Farmers. Li K'ai-hsien. CoBLCP, *tr. by* Jonathan Chaves

Wheat-miners. "Michael Field." ViWPN

Wheatfield under Clouded Sky. Campbell McGrath. NeAmPo

Wheel. Michael Palmer. BodElec

Wheel, The. Aimé Césaire. NegPo, *tr. by* Clayton Eshleman and Denis Kelly

Wheel, The. Robert Earl Hayden. BPo

Wheel, The. Edwin Muir. NoAM

Wheel, The. Molly Peacock. RA

Wheel, The. W. B. Yeats. GTBS-P

Wheel is the most beautiful discovery of man and the only one, The. Wheel, The. Aimé Césaire. NegPo, *tr. by* Clayton Eshleman and Denis Kelly

Wheel of Fortune, The. Thom Gunn. OxBC

Wheel of the quivering Meat, the. Jack Kerouac. NeAP; PFTM-2; PmAP; PoM *Fr.* Mexico City Blues.

Wheel Revolves, The. Kenneth Rexroth. NoAM

Wheelbarrow, The. Russell Edson. LCAP-2

Wheelchair Butterfly, The. James Tate. LCAP-2; NoAM

Wheels are growing on rose-bushes. Affectionate. Else Von Freytag-Loringhoven. PFTM-1

Wheels hurry onward, onward, The. Cartload of Shoes, A. Abraham Sutskever [*or* Sutzkever]. HP, *tr. by* David G. Roskies

Wheels line up, pretty right, right, The. Cattle Loading. Gordon Mackay-Warna. NOBAu, *tr. by* George von Brandenstein

Wheels of the Trains, The. W. S. Merwin. GM

Wheels within Wheels. Seamus Heaney. ModIr

Wheesht, Wheesht. Hugh MacDiarmid. HAP; InPK-6; OxAEP-2

Whelming the dwellings of men, and the toils of the slow-/ footed oxen. Charles Kingsley. PeVV *Fr.* Andromeda.

When. Dame Edith Sitwell. PFTM-1 *Fr.* Façade.

When. Tsurayuki. OHMPJ

When a Beau Goes In. Gavin Ewart. OBWP; OxBTC

When a Beautiful Woman Gets on the Jutiapa Bus. Belle Waring. EmeKit; PBCAP

When a brass sun staggers above the sky. Tramp. Richard Hughes. MoBrPo

When a chile gets to be thirteen. Mystery. Langston Hughes. APT-2

When a clatter came. Sounds of the Day. Norman MacCaig. RB

When a crowd of cares. Aneirin. NePenScot, *tr. by* Joseph P. Clancy *Fr.* Gododdin, The.

When a daffadill [*or* daffodil] I see. Divination by a Daffadill [*or* Daffodil]. Robert Herrick. CaPo

When a daughter tries suicide. Risk, The. Anne Sexton. BoWoP

When a disciple asked of Lu Chü how. Sage in Unison, The. Harold Stewart. NOBAu

When a dream gets kicked around. (LL) Langston Hughes. APSN; APT-2; SSLK *Fr.* Lenox Avenue Mural.

When a dream is born in you. Pinch of Salt, A. Robert Graves. MoBrPo

When a Fellow's on the Level with a Girl That's on the Square. George M. Cohan. ReLy

When a felon's not engaged in his employment. Sir William Schwenck Gilbert. NOBL; PeLV *Fr.* Pirates of Penzance, The.

When a feverish groom in Armenia. Limerick. Morris Gilbert Bishop. PeLi

When a Friend Dies. Marge Piercy. HeIP-4

When a friend said to Leda: "Come on." Limerick. Peter Alexander. PeLi

When a friend starts on a journey of a thousand miles. End of the Year, The. Su Tung-p'o (Su Shih). OHPC, *tr. by* Kenneth Rexroth

When a friend told a typist called Eve. Limerick. Gordon Harper. PeLi

When a girl meets a boy. How about You. Ralph Freed. ReLy

When a girl's in love with someone. Who? Otto Harbach. ReLy

When a green fox looks. Fox. David Campbell. CBAP

When a guy calls your jazz show. You and Them. Patty Seyburn. AmPoNex

When a half-crazed woman stepped aboard. Madame Butterfly. David Moolten. BloBone

When a heavy cart. Buson. SoOfWa, *tr. by* Sam Hamill

When a man dies. Anna Andreyevna Akhmatova. TCRP

When a man hath no freedom to fight for at home. Stanzas. Byron. FaBoEE; NBLV; NoP-4; OxAEP-2; PAI; TRP

When a man is in love. Language. Nizar Qabbani. MAP, *tr. by* Diana Der Hovanessian and Lena Jayyusi

When a man's too old even to toss off, he. Limerick. Robert Conquest. PeLi

When a man turns homeward through the moonfall. When a Man Turns Homeward. Daniel Whitehead Hicky. PoToHe

When a man walks in the forest and lifts his voice there. Song of My People-Forest, People-Sea. Uri Zvi Greenberg. FIT, *tr. by* Robert Friend

When a Negro comes in question you may watch the Southern press. Southern Press, The. Lizelia Augusta Jenkins Moorer. CBWP-3

When a new child comes. At Terezin. Teddy. INSAB

When a new world is born, the old. Rattle. Peter Blue Cloud. HATNAP

When a parasol is cooled in the crystal garden. International Chainpoem. *Unknown.* SPE

When a poet is weak. Weak Poet, The. David Shapiro. BodElec

When a sighing begins. Chansons d'Automne. Paul Verlaine. AWP, *tr. by* Arthur Symons

When a stream ran across my path. Herb-Garden, The. Charles Hubert Sisson. HarvBoo

When a twister a-twisting will twist him a twist. Twister Twisting Twine. John Wallis. OxNR

When a whale rolls ashore. Life Forms. Robin Becker. BodElec

When a Woman Feels Alone. May Sarton. HW

When A Woman Gets Blue. Norman Jordan. ISC; NBV

When a woman looks up at you with a twist about her eyes. Made to Order Smile, The. Paul Laurence Dunbar. GT

When Abraham Lincoln was shoveled into the tombs. Cool Tombs. Carl Sandburg. APT-1; HAP; HeIP-4; MoAmPo; NAAL-2v2; NOBA; NoAM; OxBSP; TAP; TCAPo; TFi

When Adam delf [or dalf] and Eve span. Pointless Pride of Man, The. Unknown. FaBoVe; NPeEN

When Adam found his rib was gone. Lady's-Maid's Song, The. John Hollander. TwCP

When Adam walked in Eden young. A. E. Housman. ChIV-1

When, after muchos años. Wild West Workshop Poem. Anselm Hollo. PmAP

When, after storms that woodlands rue. Requiem[:] for Soldiers Lost in Ocean Transports, A. Herman Melville. APN-2

When age hath made me what I am not now. Upon His Picture. Thomas Randolph. BASC; BeJo; NOBE

When age once snows upon your heart. (LL) Cupid's Call. James Shirley. BeJo; NOSC

When air's chill north his noisome frosts shall blow. Hesiod. NOSC, tr. by George Chapman Fr. Georgics of Heisod, The.

When alarm bells rang. Where Is the Guard? Ahmad al-Safi Al-Najafi. MAP, tr. by Sharif Elmusa and Thomas G. Ezzy

When Alexander entred phrygian land. E. D. in Commendation of the Author and His Choise. "E. D." EMWP

When Alexander Pope strolled in the city. Mr. Pope. Allen Tate. APT-2; ColAP; FuPo; NOBA; NoAM; TwCP; VGW

When Alkibié married. Archilochus. GrAn

When all about me memories arise. For My Mother. David Diop. NegPo, tr. by Ellen Conroy Kennedy

When all Birds els[e] do of their music[k] fail[e]. Money Makes the Mirth. Robert Herrick. CaPo

When all else fails. After Fighting for Hours. Kate Gleason. BAP-97

When all have forsaken me here. Lord's Arrival, The. Endre Ady. IQMS, tr. by Anton N. Nyerges

When all her robes are gone. (LL) Madrigal: "My Love in her attire doth show her wit." Unknown. BoLoP; GTBS-P; HeIP-4; NAEL-5v1; NAEL-6v1; NIP-4; NOBE; OBEV; OxBSP; TFi

When All Is Done. Paul Laurence Dunbar. SacPr; TCAPo

When all is over and you march for home. Spoils. Robert Graves. HAP; Son; WeW-3

When all is ruin once again. (LL) To Be Carved on a Stone at Thoor Ballylee. W. B. Yeats. FaBoEE; NoAM; NoP-4

When All My Five and Country Senses See. Dylan Thomas. MoBrPo; NoAM; Son

When all / My waterfall. Her Time. Theodore Roethke. NAAL-2v2

When all my words were said. Imposed. Digby Mackworth Dolben. EBVV

When all now dead shall reappear[e]. (LL) Poetry Perpetuates the Poet. Robert Herrick. BeJo; FaBoEE

When all of us wore smaller shoes. Ancient Lights. Austin Clarke. BIrV

When all the altar lights were dead. Resurrection. Alfred Noyes. SacPr

When all the others were away at Mass. Seamus Heaney. BLT; PNI Fr. Clearances.

When all the witches were haled to the stake and burned. King Duffus. Sylvia Townsend Warner. FaBoWP

When all the women in the transport. Pigtail. Tadeusz Rózewicz. HP; PoSu

When all the world is a hopeless jumble. Over the Rainbow. Harold Arlen. ReLy

When all the World's a Riddle, why not I? (LL) Elizabeth Tipper. EMWP; NOSC Fr. Pilgrim's Viaticum; or, The Destitute, But Not Forlorn.

When all the world would keep a matter hid. Fabulists, The. Rudyard Kipling. OxBEV

When all this All doth pass from age to age. Fulke Greville, 1st Baron Brooke. EBVV; NoSic Fr. Caelica.

"When all this is over," said the swineherd. Swineherd. Eiléan Ní Chuilleanáin. BIrV; CIP-2; EmeKit; FaBoWP; NPeEn; WPOW

When All Thy Mercies. Joseph Addison. SacPr

When all was quiet and serene, a storm broke out at the dead. Riot, A. Mrs. Henry Linden. CBWP-4

When all within is dark. From Thee to Thee. Solomon ibn Gabirol. TrJP, tr. by Israel Abrahams

When all your world of beauty's [or Beautie's] gone. (LL) To Dianeme. Robert Herrick. BASC; BeJo; CaPo; GTBS-P; NOBE; NOSC; OBEV

When Alysandyr Our King Was Dede. Unknown. See Death of Alexander, The

When America closes for the night. Promises. Richard Shelton. GifTon

When an amorous youth from Atlantis. Limerick. C. Vita-Finzi. PeLi

When an archer is shooting for nothing. Need to Win, The. Chuang Tzu. BLT, tr. by Thomas Merton

When an early Autumn walks the land. Early Autumn. Ralph Burns. ReLy

When an irresistible force such as you. Something's Gotta Give. Johnny Mercer. ReLy

When an obstinate fellow of Fife. Limerick. Allan M. Laing. PeLi

When and where did you first. Sexual Privacy of Women on Welfare. Pinkie Gordon Lane. BlSi

When anger spreads in the breast. Sappho. SaLy, tr. by Diane Rayor

When any mortal (even the most odd). E. E. Cummings. FaBoEE

When Aphrodite saw the Aphrodite of Knidos. Unknown. GrAn

When approached by a person from Porlock. Limerick. Richard Leighton Greene. PeLi

When April & dew brings primroses here. Anecdote of Love, An. John Clare. NOBVV

When are the children all happy and gay? Christmas Times. Maggie Pogue Johnson. CBWP-4

When as [or Whenas] a public[k] ruin[e] bears down All. (LL) To His Book[e]. Robert Herrick. BASC; CaPo

When as I do record. Unknown. EBEV

When as the prince of Angels puffed with pride. To St. Michael the Archangel. Henry Constable. ChIV-2

When As the Rye Reach to the Chin. George Peele. See Old Wives' [or Wife's] Tale, The

When as the sheriff of Nottingham. Robin Hood and the Golden Arrow. Unknown. ESPB

When asked for a sample of his work. Dream of Completion, The. Shirley Kaufman. LCAP-2

When asked her opinion. Cowboy Film. Tom Matthews. PNI

When Asked to Lie down on the Altar. Eleanor Wilner. TaR

When at break of day at a riverside. Piano and Drums. Gabriel Okara. NIP-4; PBA; TTY

When at Collatium this false lord arrived. William Shakespeare. NoSic Fr. Rape of Lucrece, The.

When at last he was well enough to take the sun. Leg in a Plaster Cast, A. Muriel Rukeyser. MoAmPo

When / At the close of war. I Say, Mr. A. Samuel Allen. SeSe

When at the first I took my pen in hand. John Bunyan. FaBoVe Fr. Author's Apology for His Book, The.

When Athens all the Graecian state did guide. Dryden. NOSC Fr. Oedipus.

When August and the sultry summer's drouth. Valley, The. Agnes Mary Frances Robinson. VWP

When August was finally done, his. My Heart. Laura Kasischke. AmPoNex

When Autumn Came. Faiz Ahmad Faiz. PoetW, tr. by Naomi Lazard

When autumn comes, my orchard trees alone. Art and Life. Agnes Mary Frances Robinson. OxBSo; VWP

When autumn rains flatten sycamore leaves. Gary Soto. NoAM Fr. Elements of San Joaquin, The.

When autumn winds blow. Togyu. JDP, tr. by Yoel Hoffmann

When avarice enslaves the mind. Negro Boy, The. David Samwell. AngWePo

When awful darkness and silence reign. Dong with a Luminous Nose, The. Edward Lear. EBNV; EBVV; NOBVV; NOxBChV; OxAEP-2; OxBEV

When Baby's cries grew hard to bear. L'Enfant Glacé. Harry Graham. NBLV; OBCoV; PeLV

When Bad Angels Love Women. Julie Moulds. AmPoNex

When Barbarians overran the city. Thatched Hut, The. Tu Fu. CrYelRi, tr. by Sam Hamill

When beauty breaks and falls asunder. Juan's Song. Louise Bogan. NoP-4

When beechen buds begin to swell. Yellow Violet, The. William Cullen Bryant. NAAL-2v1; NAAL-3; TAP

When before those eyes, my life and light. Gaspara Stampa. BoWoP

When Bells stop ringing—Church—begins. Emily Dickinson. APN-2

When Bibo thought fit from the world to retreat. Epigram. Matthew Prior. FaBoEE

When Bill was a lad he was terribly bad. Those Two Boys. Franklin Pierce Adams. OBCoV; TrJP

When Bird died, I didn't mind. Filling the Gap. Lawson Fusao Inada. OpBo

When bird passes on. Masahide. ZenPo, tr. by Takashi Ikemoto and Lucien Stryk

When birds break open the sky, a smell of snow. Winter Burn. Roberta Hill Whiteman. VoR

When Bishop Berkeley said "there was no matter." Byron. NOBRP Fr. Don Juan.

When Black People Are. Alfred B. Spellman. BPo

When blessed Marie [or Mary] wip'd her Saviours [or Saviour's] feet. Mary [or Marie] Magdalene. George Herbert. ESCV; SacPr

When bold Leander sought his distant fair. On Leander's Swimming over the Hellespont to Hero. Thomas Warton, the Younger. FaBoEE

When bored by the drone of the wedlocked pair. Sacred and Profane Love, or, There's Nothing New under the Moon Either. Peter De Vries. NBLV; OBCoV

When both hands of the town clock stood at twelve. Village Noon; Mid-Day Bells. Merrill Moore. MoAmPo

When boyhood's fire was in my blood. Nation Once Again, A. Thomas Osborne Davis. NOIV

When boys played women's parts, you'd think the stage. Epilogue to "The Parson's Wedding." Thomas Killigrew. NOSC

When breezes are soft and skies are fair. William Cullen Bryant. APN-1; ITBLP; NOBA; OxBA; TCAPo Fr. Green River.

When bright Orion glitters in the skies. Mary Collier. ECWP; NOEC Fr. Woman's Labour; an Epistle to Mr. Stephen Duck, The.

When Britain first, at heaven's command. James Thomson. GTBS-P; NOEC; OBWP; TreFP Fr. Alfred: A Masque.

When Britain really ruled the waves. Sir William Schwenck Gilbert. NAEL-5v2; NAEL-6v2 Fr. Iolanthe.

When buck fever struck. You Don't Know What Happened When You Froze. Talvikki Ansel. NeAmPo

When by its magic lantern Spleen. Matthew Green. OxAEP-1 Fr. Spleen, The.

When by me in the dusk my child sits down. John Berryman. ColAP Fr. Homage to Mistress Bradstreet.

When by mistake you miss. Your Own Image. Michael Ryan. YaYoPo

When by the labour of my 'ands. Half-Ballad of Waterval. Rudyard Kipling. FaBoWar; PeSAV

When by thy scorn[e], O murderess[e] [or murd'ress or murdress], I am dead. Apparition, The. John Donne. BASC; ESCV; EnLoPo; FSCP; HeIP-4; NAEL-5v1; NAEL-6v1; NAEL-7v1; NAWM-5v1; NOBE; NOBL; NoSic; OBEV; PoE; SCGP; SCV; SoSe-8; TFi

When by Zeus relenting the mandate was revoked. Phoebus with Admetus. George Meredith. NOBE; OBEV

When Caesar saw his army prone to war. Lucan. NoSic Fr. Pharsalia.

When calabashes held petrol and men. J. P. Clark Bekederemo. PBMAP Fr. Casualties (1970).

When Canaan did with milk and honey flow. (LL) On Death. Anne Killigrew. BoWoP; ChIV-1

When Catrin was a small child. Foghorns. Gillian Clarke. TCAWP

When cats like him submit to fate. Anne Francis. ECWP Fr. Elegy on a Favorite Cat, An.

When cats run home and light is come. Owl, The. Tennyson. FaBoCh

When Celia frowns, I vow and swear. Verses Left on a Lady's Toilet. Sarah Dixon. ECWP

When chapman [or chapmen] billies leave the street. Tam o' Shanter; A Tale. Robert Burns. CABP; EBNV; NAEL-5v2; NAEL-6v2; NPeEn; NePenScot; NoP-4; OBNV; OxBS; PeLV

When Chicken Man Came Home to Roost. Frank A. Cross. CDa

When children play the livelong day. Children in Slavery. Eliza Lee Cabot Follen. SWaP

When children slap their father's face. Robert Desnos. PFTM-1

When chill November's surly blast. Robert Burns. TreFP

When Christ came from the shadows by the stream. Wherefore the Scars of Christ's Passion Remained in the Body of His Resurrection. Theodulf of Orleans. MLL, tr. by Helen Waddell

When Christ from Heaven comes down straightway. For the Company Underground. Francis MacNamara. NOBAu

When Christ with care and pangs of death opprest. Christs Sleeping Friends. Robert Southwell. ESCV

When civil fury [or dudgeon] first grew high. Samuel Butler (1612–80). BASC; CABP; EBEV; NAEL-5v1; NAEL-6v1; NAEL-7v1 Fr. Hudibras.

When Cleomira disbelieves. Force of Love, The. Samuel Jones. NOEC; NPeEn

When clerks and navvies fondle. Louis MacNeice. BoLoP; EnLoPo Fr. Trilogy for X.

When Clifford wasn't back to camp by nine. After the Wilderness. Andrew Hudgins. CBCWP

When clouds appear like rocks and towers. Unknown. OxNR

When clouds conceal your skies. Close Your Eyes and See. Mikhail Naimy. GraLe, tr. by J.R. Perry

When Clumsy harks the gladsome ting-a-lings. Gjertrud Schnackenberg. NoAM Fr. Two Tales of Clumsy.

When, Coelia, must my old day set. To Coelia. Charles Cotton. OBEV

When consummate the day hangs before you. Three Variations. Boris Leonidovich Pasternak. TrJP, tr. by Babette Deutsch

When Cousin Sam come down vrom Lon'on. Sam'el Down vrom Lon'on. William Barnes. PeVV

When Cromwell "slighted" Kenilworth. State of Preservation. Celeste Turner Wright. FFC

When Cytherea slipped her wily sash off. Antiphanes. GrAn

When Dad and Mother discovered one another. Come Fly with Me. Jimmy Van Heusen. ReLy

When Daddy and Mum got quite plastered. Unknown. OBCoV; PeLi

When Daddy Cums from Wuk. Maggie Pogue Johnson. CBWP-4

When Daffodils Begin to Peer. William Shakespeare. FaBoCh; NoP-4; NoSic; OxAEP-1; OxBSP; SCGP; TFi; UV Fr. Winter's Tale, The.

When Daisies Pied. William Shakespeare. See Love's Labour's Lost

When daisies pied and violets Blue. William Shakespeare. HAP; InPK-6; NAEL-5v1; NAEL-6v1; NBLV; NIL-7; NIP-4; NOBE; NoSic; OBEV; PAI; PoRA; SCGP; TFi; UnPo Fr. Love's Labour's Lost.

When Daniel Boone goes by, at night. Daniel Boone. Stephen Vincent Benét. APT-2; KaS

When darkness is darkest, and sorrow most sorrow. (LL) Window Just over the Street, The. Alice Cary. PoBW; SWaP

When Dasies pied, and Violets blew. William Shakespeare. See When daisies pied and violets Blue

When day begins to darken. Tu Fu. CarOv, tr. by Carolyn Kizer Fr. Adviser to the Court.

When day declining sheds a milder gleam. Naturalist's Summer-Evening Walk, The. Gilbert White. NOEC

When, dearest friend, thy verse doth re-inspire. On Mr. Shirley's Poems. Thomas Stanley. BeJo

When, dearest, I but think on [or of] thee. Song. Sir John Suckling. OBEV

When Death Came. Adam Zagajewski. VCWP, tr. by Renata Gorcyznski

When death crawls by night. Panama. Patrick Sylvain. InTrad

When Death to Either Shall Come. Robert Bridges. OBEV

When descends on the Atlantic. Seaweed. Henry Wadsworth Longfellow. APN-1; ColAP; OxBA; TAP

When despair for the world grows in me. Peace of Wild Things, The. Wendell Berry. VGW

When Dey 'Listed Colored Soldiers. Paul Laurence Dunbar. BPo; CBCWP

When Diana, late at night. Unknown. WoPoe, tr. by Richmond Lattimore Fr. Carmina Burana.

When did I cease to be. Salute to Icheke. Okogbule Wonodi. PBMAP

When did my head become an ancient cow's sacred head? Takahashi Mutsuo. PFTM-2, tr. by Hiroaki Sato Fr. Self-Portraits.

When did she know, when did she know it. Lucille Clifton. ExTi

"When did the world begin and how?" Answers, The. Robert Clairmont. OTCP

When did we drift into each other's arms. Envoi: Waking after Snow. David Baker. PasH

When did you start your tricks. Mosquito, The. D. H. Lawrence. NPeEn; RB

When Dido found Aeneas would not come. Note on the Latin Gerunds, A. Richard Porson. FaBoEE

When Dinah's careless eye was grown too lavish. On Dinah. Francis Quarles. ChIV-1

When dis ya bass-line drop. One Song. Geoffrey Philp. WaCA

When do I see thee most, beloved one? Dante Gabriel Rossetti. EBVV; GTBS-P; NAEL-5v2; NAEL-6v2 Fr. House of Life, The.

When Dobbin and Robin, unharnessed from the plow. Circus-Postered Barn, The. Elizabeth Jane Coatsworth. MoAmPo

When does it end? When does a new poem. Peter Levi. TOF

When does the soul leave the body? For My Mother. Ellen Bryant Voigt. NIP-4

When doome of Peeres and Judges fore-appointed. Tragicall Epigram, A. Sir John Harington [or Harrington]. PBRV

When down the crowded aisle my wandering eyes. Eyeing the Eyes of One's Mistress. Ebenezer Jones. NOBVV

When down the deep-six I'll be stored. Who'll Ferry Love to the Yonder Shore. László Nagy. IQMS, tr. by Adam Makkai

When e'er we enter life's open field. Ambition. Maggie Pogue Johnson. CBWP-4

When Earth's last picture is painted, and the tubes are twisted and dried. L'Envoi. Rudyard Kipling. BRP; PWR

When Eddie had his second birthday. Eddie and the Birthday. Michael Rosen. NOxBChV

When Egypt said, "Exterminate." Retribution. Lizelia Augusta Jenkins Moorer. CBWP-3

When Eliot died it made him seem human. New Year's Eve Poem 1965. Peter Levi. OxAEP-2

When England's multitudes observed with frowns. Bungaloid Growth. Colin Ellis. FaBoEE

When Eve did with the snake dispute. Woman's Wish, The. Matthew Prior. FaBoEE

When Eve first saw the glistering day. Song with Words. James Agee. ChIV-1; MoAmPo

When Eve upon the first of men. Reflection, A. Thomas Hood. FaBoEE; PAI

When evenen sheades o' trees do hide. Vaices That Be Gone, The. William Barnes. NOBVV

When evening comes. *Var. authors.* AWP *Fr.* Manyo Shu, Part 4 of 4.

When every one to pleasing pastime hies. Mary Sidney Wroth, Countess of Montgomery. BASC; PBRV; WPE *Fr.* Pamphilia to Amphilanthus.

When everything but love was spent. Winter Tenement. Malcolm Cowley. APT-2

When Evil-Doing Comes Like Falling Rain. Bertolt Brecht. AF, *tr.* by John Willett

When Faith and Love which parted from thee never. Sonnet: On the Religious Memorie of Mrs. Catherine Thomason My Christian Freind Deceas'd Decem. 1646. John Milton. ChIV-2

When famas go on a trip, when they pass the night in a. Travel. Julio Cortázar. TCLAP, *tr.* by Paul Blackburn

When far-spent night persuades each mortal eye. Sir Philip Sidney. NoSic; PoE; Son *Fr.* Astrophil and Stella.

When Fat Women Fear Famine. Brenda J. Moossy. PoArWo

When Father Carves the Duck. Ernest Vincent Wright. NTCP

When Fergus drew his favourite blade. William Malveisin. NePenScot, *tr.* by Mick Imlah *Fr.* Fergus of Galloway: Knight of King Arthur.

When fierce Pizarro's legions flew. Revenge of America, The. Joseph Warton. ECEV

When fire and drink were a shelter. Essence Is Not in the Living, The. Mairtin O Direain. BiHa, *tr.* by Tomás MacSiomóin and Douglas Sealy

When First. Edward Thomas. NoAM

When first Apollo got my brain with childe. Author to His Book, The. George Alsop. SCAP

When first, descending from the moorlands. William Wordsworth. EBEV; NAEL-6v2; NOBE; SCV

When first described imperfectly. Erections. Erin Belieu. ExTi

When first Eudoxos cut his lovely hair. Euphorion. GrAn

When first, fair mistress, I did see your face. To B.C. Sir John Suckling. CaPo

When first I came here I had hope. When First. Edward Thomas. NoAM

When first I learned the ABC of love. John Davies of Hereford. OxBSo *Fr.* Wit's Pilgrimage.

When first I saw true beauty, and thy joys. Mount of Olives. Henry Vaughan. ESCV; GeHe

When first I saw you in the curious street. German Prisoners. Joseph Lee. FaBoWar

When first I took to cutlass, blunderbuss and gun. Ballad of O'Bruadir, The. Frederick Robert Higgins. OBMV

When first I walked here I hobbled. Seekonk Woods, The. Galway Kinnell. NoAM

When first I was courtin' sweet Rosie O'Grady. Irish Song [Rosie O'Grady]. Noël Coward. NBLV; OBCoV

When first mine eyes beheld your princely name. Michael Drayton. NoSic *Fr.* England's Heroical Epistles.

When first my lines [*or* verse] of heavenly [*or* heav'nly] joy[e]s made mention. Jordan (2). George Herbert. BASC; CABP; ESCV; FSCP; GeHe; NAEL-5v1; NAEL-6v1; NAEL-7v1; NOSC; OBWVE; PBRV; SacPr

When first the college rolls receive his name. Samuel Johnson. NOBE; NPeEn; OBSV *Fr.* Vanity of Human Wishes, The; The Tenth Satire of Juvenal Imitated.

When first the fiery-mantled sun. Ode to Winter. Thomas Campbell. GTBS-P

When first the unflowering Fern-forest. Darwinism. Agnes Mary Frances Robinson. VWP

When first the world grew dark to me. Cross-Road Epitaph, A. Amy Levy. VWP

When first this canvas felt Giorgione's hand. On the Concert. Trumbull Stickney. APN-2

When first thou didst entice to thee my heart. Affliction (1). George Herbert. BASC; ESCV; FHYEP; FSCP; GeHe; MeLP; NAEL-5v1; NAEL-6v1; NAEL-7v1; NOBE; NOSC; NoP-4

When first thou didst even from the grave. Disorder and Frailty. Henry Vaughan. ChIV-1

When first thou on me, Lord, wrought'st thy sweet print. Ebb and Flow, The. Edward Taylor. InvLi; SCAP

When first thy eies unveil, give thy soul leave. Rules and Lessons. Henry Vaughan. ESCV

When first thy sweet and gracious eye. Glance, The. George Herbert. ESCV

When first under fire an' you're wishful to duck. Rudyard Kipling. FaBoWar *Fr.* Young British Soldier, The.

When first we met we did not guess. Triolet. Robert Bridges. OxBSP

When fishes flew and forests walked. Donkey, The. Gilbert Keith Chesterton. ChIV-2; GI; InPK-6; MoBrPo; OBEV; RB

When five year old Pito fell out the sixth floor. Lil' Pito. Sandra Maria Esteves. PueRic

When fivepence a solid meal cannot supply. Volunteer, The. *Unknown.* NOEC

When flighting time is on, I go. Birdcatcher, The. Ralph Hodgson. MoBrPo

When for the Thorns with which I long, too long. Coronet, The. Andrew Marvell. BASC; ESCV; FHYEP; FSCP; GeHe; MeLP; NAEL-5v1; NAEL-6v1; NAEL-7v1; NOCV; NOSC; NoP-4; PBRV; PoE; SCGP; SacPr; TOF

When for Weeks the Sea is Flat. Rick Noguchi. MoASP

When forehead full of torments hot and red. Arthur Rimbaud. AWP, *tr.* by T. Sturge Moore *Fr.* Illuminations.

When Fortune's shield protects thee, then beware. Fortune's Treachery. Judah Halevi. TrJP, *tr.* by Solomon Solis-Cohen

When forty winters shall besiege thy brow. William Shakespeare. HeIP-4; NoSic; SCGP; Son *Fr.* Sonnets.

When forty years come round. At Forty. Yevgeny Aleksandrovich Yevtushenko [*or* Evtushenko]. RusPo, *tr.* by Robert Arthur Douglas Ford

When foxes eat the last gold grape. Escape. Elinor Wylie. MoAmPo

When Francus comes to solace with his whore. In Francum. Sir John Davies. FaBoEE

When Frank was drowning in the River Po. About the Shipwrecked Frandus. Janus Pannonius. IQMS, *tr.* by Iain MacLeod

When Freedom, from her mountain height. American Flag, The. Joseph Rodman Drake. APN-1; BRP

When from afar these mountain tops I view. Sonnet of the Mountain, The. Mellin de Saint-Gelais. AWP, *tr.* by Austin Dobson

When from our better selves we have too long. William Wordsworth. AmFaPo *Fr.* Prelude, The; Growth of a Poet's Mind [1805 vers.].

When from remote lands the wind rose. Spinning. May Muzaffar. PoArWo, *tr.* by Tahia Abdel Nasser

When from the frigid North into the woods. Times Gone By. János Vajda. IQMS, *tr.* by Jess Perlman

When from the gates of Paradise fair Eve. Vision of Eve, The. Henrietta Cordelia Ray. CBWP-3

When from the other world you. Stepping Out with Edvard Munch. Elma Van Haren. TuT, *tr.* by Anne Kennedy

When from the pallid sky the sun descends. James Thomson. OxBS *Fr.* Seasons, The.

When from the Vallais we had turned, and clomb. William Wordsworth. TOF *Fr.* Prelude, The; Growth of a Poet's Mind [1850 vers.].

When from the virile grave. Stepping Out with Edvard Munch. Elma Van Haren. TuT, *tr.* by Medbh McGuckian

When from the world, I shall be tane. To My Husband. "Eliza." EMWP; LW; PBRV

When frost and dew have caused a hundred plants to wither. In Imitation of T'ao P'eng-tse. Wei Ying-wu. SuSp, *tr.* by Irving Y. Lo

When frost will not suffer to dike and to hedge. Thomas Tusser. NoSic *Fr.* Five Hundred Points of Good Husbandry.

When Gabriel (no blest spirit more kind or fair). Abraham Cowley. NOSC *Fr.* Davideis.

When gathering shells cast upwards by the waves. Chrysalis, A. Emily Jane Pfeiffer. ViWPN

When Gauguin was visiting Fiji. Limerick. Victor Gray. NOBL

When geometric diagrams and digits. "Novalis." WoPoe, *tr.* by Robert Bly

When getting my nose in a book. Study of Reading Habits, A. Philip Larkin. InPK-6; NOBL; OBCoV

When glowing Phoebus quits the weeping earth. Mary Tighe. CenSon

When God at first made man. Pulley, The. George Herbert. AWP; BASC; BBASP; ChIV-1; FHYEP; FSCP; GeHe; HAP; HeIP-4; InPK-6; InvLi; NAEL-5v1; NAEL-6v1; NAEL-7v1; NOBE; NOCV; NOSC; NoP-4; OBEV; OxAEP-1; PAI; SCGP; TFi

When God created thee, one would believe. Lady Mary Wortley Montagu. ECWP *Fr.* Verses Addressed to the Imitator of the First Satire of the Second Book of Horace.

When God Descends with Men to Dwell. Hosea, I Ballou. AH

When God gave you to me. Nizar Qabbani. MAP

When God had finished Master Messerin. Sonnet: Of the Making of Master Messerin. Rustico Di Filippo. AWP; EaItPo, *tr.* by Dante Gabriel Rossetti

When God Lets My Body Be. E. E. Cummings. MoAmPo; NOBA

When God makes a great Man he intends all others to crush him. Arthur Hugh Clough. OBSV *Fr.* Amours de Voyage.

When God's parachute failed. Religion Back Home. William Stafford. OBAL

When God was learning to draw the human face. Two Masks Unearthed in Bulgaria. William Meredith. BodElec

When Goldie the golden eagle escaped from the Zoo. Goldie Sapiens. P. J. Kavanagh. OBCoV

When good King Arthur ruled this [*or* the] land. King Arthur. Mother Goose. LB; OxNR

When good St. David, as old writs record.   In Honour of St. David's Day.
  Unknown.   OBWVE

When Grandmamma fell off the boat.   Indifference.   Harry Graham.   NBLV

When grapes turn.   Jelaluddin [*or* Jalal al-Din] Rumi.   EnlH

When great Nature sighs, we hear the winds.   Breath of Nature, The.   Chuang
  Tzu.   BBASP, *tr. by* Thomas Merton

When groping farms are lanterned up.   Country God, A.   Edmund Charles
  Blunden.   MoBrPo

When Gullion died (who knows not Gullion?)   Joseph Hall.   NoSic   *Fr.*
  Virgidemiarum.

When Gwen heard at last.   In Memoriam.   W. J. Gruffydd.   OBWVE, *tr. by* R.
  Gerallt Jones

When hands are joined and head bows in the dark. (LL)   Penal Law.   Austin
  Clarke.   BoLoP; GTBS-P; ModIr; NOIV; OxBEV; PAI

When, hardly moving, you decorate night's hush.   Waters of Life, The.
  Humbert Wolfe.   MoBrPo

When have I known a boy.   Girl on the Land, The.   Alice Thompson Meynell.
  VWP

When he appears a block away, you know.   Man Who Tried to Rape You, The.
  Erin Belieu.   AmPoNex

When He Believed Himself to Be a Young Girl Lifting the Skin of the Water.
  Juan Felipe Herrera.   TouFir

When he breathed his last breath it was he.   Moment of My Father's Death,
  The.   Sharon Olds.   NIP-4

When he brings home a whale.   Naughty Boy.   Robert Creeley.   HeIP-4;
  NOBA; NoAM

When he came home Mother said he looked.   My Father's Martial Art.
  Stephen Shu Ning Liu.   InPK-6

When he came out, into the world.   Born Tying Knots.   Samuel
  Makidemewabe.   STP, *tr. by* Howard Norman

When he comes home at night.   Wasp Sex Myth (One).   Anselm Hollo.   PoM

When he comes up to the bedroom.   Palladas [*or* Pallades].   GrAn

When he dances latin.   El Jibarito Moderno.   Miguel Algarin.   PueRic

When he did read how did we flock to hear.   Thomas Vaughan.   AngWePo
  Fr. On The Death of an Oxford Proctor.

When he entered.   Marxist to Liberals, A.   David Lindley.   NLP

When he finally put.   Kiss, The.   Marie Howe.   ExTi

When he found Laertes alone on the tidy terrace, home.   Homer.   ModIr, *tr.
  by* Michael Longley   *Fr.* Odyssey.

When he gives me a light he has to kneel down.   Sarah Kirsch.   PFTM-2, *tr.
  by* Wayne Kvam   *Fr.* Kite-Flying.

When he got into bed.   Damon & Pythias.   Robert Creeley.   LCAP-2

When he got up that morning everything was different.   Journey, A.   Edward
  Field.   BLT

When he grew pale, and his voice trembled.   Memory, A.   Marceline
  Desbordes-Valmore.   WoPoe, *tr. by* Louis Simpson

When he had made sure there were no survivors in his house.   Homer.   ModIr;
  NPeEn   *Fr.* Odyssey.

When he is ready he is raised and carried.   Glass King, The.   Eavan Boland.
  CIP-2

When he lends [*or* leads] any poet[s] about the town. (LL)   Sir John Suckling.
  BASC; BeJo; CABP; CaPo

When he likened the cemetery to a herd of sheep.   Flute, The.   Oktay Rifat.
  WoPoe, *tr. by* Talat Sait Halman

When he looked at her, he invariably felt.   Looking at Her.   Alan Brownjohn.
  OxBSo

When he looks at me.   Frog.   Issa.   WoPoe, *tr. by* Conrad Totman

When He Met Julia, He Greeterd Her Thus.   Bálint Balassi.   IQMS, *tr. by*
  Adam Makkai

When he pushed his bush of black hair off his brow.   Sicilian Cyclamens.   D.
  H. Lawrence.   NoAM

When he raped a young maid in a train.   Limerick.   *Unknown.*   PeLi

When he reaches for a photo of old times.   Traveler.   Antonio Porta.   ItPo, *tr.
  by* Gayle Ridinger

When he reads.   Avatars.   V. Indira Bhavani.   OMIP, *tr. by* Martha Ann Selby

When he said *Mary,* she did not at once.   Contemplations of Mary.   Roy
  McFadden.   PNI

When he sailed into the harbor.   Korinna [*or* Corinna].   BoWoP, *tr. by* Willis
  Barnstone

When he saw her.   *Unknown.*   TOF

When He Says So We Dance in All Directions—Wow!   *Unknown.*   STP, *tr. by*
  Richard Johnny John and Jerome Rothenberg

When he sets out across ranges of winter sea. (LL)   Islandman.   Brenda
  Chamberlain.   AngWePo; OBWVE

When he shuts the door against his day-to-day, "June, I'm home."   Man I Love
  and I Have a Typical Evening the Night Richard M. Nixon Dies, The.   Jim
  Elledge.   ReTh

When he sit, he sit on what he ain't got—almost. (LL)   Frog, The.   *Unknown.*
  NBLV; NOxBChV; NTCP; RB

When he surrendered his eyes to the dream, this lad.   Dream, A.   Muhammad
  Al-Ghuzzi.   MAP, *tr. by* John Heath-Stubbs and May Jayyusi

When he the nation's heart had won.   Presidents, The.   Lizelia Augusta Jenkins
  Moorer.   CBWP-3

When he trades in tea—it's right nearby.   Song of the Merchant's Wife.   Yang
  Shih-ch'i.   CoBLCP, *tr. by* Jonathan Chaves

When he walked through town, the wing-shot bird he'd hidden.   Author of
  American Ornithology Sketches a Bird, Now Extinct, The.   David
  Wagoner.   BLT

When he was barely five.   Boyhood of Christ, The.   Columba, Saint.   NOIV

When he was dead. (LL)   Comic Adventures of Old Mother Hubbard and Her
  Dog, The.   Sarah Catherine Martin.   OxNR; ReMoGo

When he was eight years old he had become.   Words and Monsters.   Vernon
  Scannell.   OxBC

When he was far away from those evenings.   Franco Buffoni.   ItPo, *tr. by*
  Gayle Ridinger

When he was shot he toppled to the ground.   Shot Who? Jim Lane!   Merrill
  Moore.   MoAmPo

When he was starting out, still green.   Counterfeiter, The.   Greg Williamson.
  AmPoNex; RA

When he was young and gift-strong. (LL)   John Berryman.   NOBA; NoAM
  Fr. Dream Songs.

When he was young, he broke horses.   Passion Drinker, The.   Anita Endrezze.
  VoR

When he wasn't working, on his days off, his father liked to spend his.   Light.
  Peter Markus.   AmPoNex

When He Went Away.   Marcelle Ferry.   SurWo, *tr. by* Myrna Bell Rochester

When he who adores thee has left but the name.   Pro Patria Mori.   Thomas
  Moore.   GTBS-P; OxAEP-2

When he, who is the unforgiven.   Unforgiven, The.   Edwin Arlington
  Robinson.   APT-1

When he whose empire is in clouds saw Hector bent to wage.   Homer.   NOSC,
  tr. by George Chapman   *Fr.* Iliad, The.

When He Would Have His Verses Read.   Robert Herrick.   BASC; BeJo; CaPo;
  CavPo; NOBE; NOSC; SCGP

When Heaven in mercy gives thy prayers return.   Hezekiah's Display.   John
  Keble.   ChIV-1

When Hee Was Come to the Other Side of the Contrye, of the Gergesenes,
  There Mett Him Two: Possessed with Devils Coming Out of the Tombes.
  Eleanor Touchet Davies.   EMWP

When Helen first saw wrinkles in her face.   Walter Savage Landor.   EnLoPo
  Fr. Ianthe.

When Henri Toussaints.   Henri Toussaints.   Cheryl Savageau.   TWW

When Henry was a baby.   Black Henry.   Tejumola Ologboni.   NBV

When Her Father a Widower Asked What She Would Say to His Intention of
  Marrying a Young Girl.   Alis Ferch Gruffyd ab Ieuan ap Lleywelyn
  Fychan.   EMWP

When her need for you dies.   In Her Only Way.   Robert Graves.   OxBSP   *Fr.*
  Three Songs for the Lute.

When *Hercules* did use to spin.   Weavers Song, The.   Thomas Deloney.
  PBRV

When Hermocrates the Miser lay in bed.   Lucilius.   GrAn

When Hilda does the Highland reel.   To Hilda Dancing.   John Bingham
  Morton.   OBCoV

When His Excellency Prince Norodom Chantaraingsey.   Dead Soldiers.   James
  Fenton.   AF; FaBoWar; NoAM; NoP-4; OBWP

When his hour for death had come.   Osceola.   Walt Whitman.   NAAL-2v1;
  NAAL-3

When hit come ter de question er de female vote.   Brother Baptis' on Woman
  Suffrage.   Rosalie Jonas.   BlSi

When home we return, after youth has been spending.   When Home We Return.
  Susanna Blamire.   ECWP

When I a verse shall make.   His Prayer to Ben Jonson.   Robert Herrick.
  BASC; BeJo; CaPo; NAEL-5v1; NAEL-6v1; NAEL-7v1; NOSC; NoP-4;
  OxBSP; OxBoLi; PeLV

When I Admire the Greatness.   Jacob Steendam.   AH

When I admit neglect of Gissing.   Dorothy Parker.   APT-1   *Fr.* Pig's-Eye
  View of Literature, A.

When I am alone.   Fisherman's Wife, The.   Amy Lowell.   BoWoP

When I am alone I am happy.   Waiting.   William Carlos Williams.   SAmP

When I am an old woman I shall wear purple.   Warning.   Jenny Joseph.
  FaBoWP; OxBTC

When I am bored I climb the attic stairs.   We're Staying at the Castlemount,
  Western Esplanade.   M. R. Peacocke.   NLP

When I Am Dead.   Emma Alice Browne.   TreFP

When I Am Dead.   George MacBeth [*or* Macbeth].   OxBTC

When I Am Dead.   *Unknown.*   OxBoLi

When I am dead, and Doctors know not why.   Damp[e], The.   John Donne.
  NOSC

When I am dead and gone. (LL)   A. E. Housman.   MoBrPo; UnPo; WeW-3

When I am dead and over me bright April. I Shall Not Care. Sara Teasdale. APT-1; MoAmPo; TCAPo; UnPo

When I am dead and thou wouldst try. *Unknown*. NOSC

When I am dead, even then. Then. Muriel Rukeyser. GLP; LCAP-2

When I am dead, I hope it may be said. On His Books. Joseph Hilaire Pierre Belloc. FaBoEE; MoBrPo; NBLV; OxBoLi; WeW-3

When I am dead and I want you to dress me. When I Am Dead. *Unknown*. OxBoLi

When I am dead, my dearest. Song. Christina Georgina Rossetti. AWP; BoLoP; CABP; EBEV; NAEL-5v2; NAEL-6v2; NOBE; NOBVV; NPeEn; NoP-4; OBEV; OxAEP-2; PoRA; SCV; VWP; ViWPN; WPE

When I am gone. Epitaph, An. Josephine D. Henderson Heard. CBWP-4

When I am gone. Kizan. JDP, *tr. by* Yoel Hoffmann

When I am gone. Ute Mountain. Charles Tomlinson. RB

When I am grown to man's estate. Looking Forward. Robert Louis Stevenson. NBLV

When I am grown up I shall go and stoop digging clams. *Unknown*. APN-2, *tr. by* Franz Boas *Fr.* Songs of the Kwakiutl Indians.

When I am hungry. Mahadevi. WPoS

When I am living in the Midlands. South Country, The. Joseph Hilaire Pierre Belloc. MoBrPo; OxAEP-2

When I am lonely. Ryozan. OHPJ

When I Am 19 I Was a Medic. D. F. Brown. CDa

When I am no one. (LL) Wish for a Young Wife. Theodore Roethke. NAAL-2v2; NAAL-5; NoAM; NoP-4; OxBSP; TAP

When I am old. Denis Glover. PeNZ *Fr.* Sings Harry.

When I am riding round the ring no longer. Circus-Rider to Ringmaster. Thomas Hardy. RACG

When I am sad and weary. Celia Celia. Adrian Mitchell. FaBoEE; OPOU

When I am sitting at my desk I have feelings. Boat, A. Jordan Davis. HeMarv

When I am the sky. Cancion. Denise Levertov. NALW; PoM

When I am very earnestly digging. Pause. Mary Ursula Bethell. PeNZ

When I am walking with the children, and a girl. Father, The. Donald Finkel. PAI

When I Am with You. Ghazi Al-Gosaibi. MAP, *tr. by* Charles Doria and Sharif Elmusa

When I arrived some clansmen had already come. Wood-Cutter, The. Lupenga Mphande. HBAPE

When I ask Daddy. Ask Mummy Ask Daddy. John Agard. OTCP

When I ask what things they fear. Fears of the Eighth Grade. Toi Derricotte. GT

When I asked for fish in the restaurant facing the Ohio River. Carl Sandburg. PoE *Fr.* Whiffs of the Ohio River at Cincinnati.

When I asked him about. Slave Ritual. Carolyn M. Rodgers. ISC

When I asked the very old man. Quotations. George Oppen. NNaP

When I Awoke. Raymond R. Patterson. NBV

When I awoke with cold. Coffee. James Vincent Cunningham. MoAmPo; VGW

When I become Jack Johnson. (LL) Dream of the Ring: The Great Jack Johnson, A. George Barlow. ESEAA; MoASP

When I beheld the Poet blind, yet bold. On Mr Milton's "Paradise Lost." Andrew Marvell. BASC; CABP; FSCP; NOSC

When I behold a forest spread. Robert Herrick. *See* When I behold a forrest spread

When I behold a forrest spread. Art above Nature, to Julia. Robert Herrick. BeJo; NOSC

When I behold Becchina in a rage. Sonnet. Cecco Angiolieri, da Siena. AWP; EaltPo, *tr. by* Dante Gabriel Rossetti

When I behold how black, immortal ink. Silet. Ezra Pound. MoAmPo; Son

When I behold the havoc and the spoil. George Wither. NOSC *Fr.* Collection of Emblemes, Ancient and Moderne, A.

When I behold the skies aloft. Coventry Patmore. NAEL-6v2 *Fr.* Angel in the House, The.

When I bethink me on that speech whilere. Edmund Spenser. *See* When I bethinke me on that speech whyleare

When I bethinke me on that speech whyleare. Edmund Spenser. NPeEn; NoSic *Fr.* Faerie Queene, The.

When I bethought me well, under the restless sun. Henry Howard, Earl of Surrey. ChIV-1 *Fr.* Paraphrase of Part of the Book of Ecclesiates, A.

When I bid my wad—forty bucks—on a helmet. Space Memorabilia Auction, Superior Stamp and Coin, Beverly Hills, California. Joel Brouwer. AmPoNex

When i blow open green bottles. Nighttrains. Jayne Cortez. PFTM-2

When I bought bubble gum. Why We Bombed Haiphong. Jonathan Holden. ReTh

When I brood on Germany in the night. Night Thoughts. Heinrich Heine. WoPoe, *tr. by* Mark Rudman

When I built upon sand. Foundations. Leopold Staff. PoSu, *tr. by* Adam Czerniawski

When I burn up without a trace. Igor Moiseievich Irtenev. TCRP

When I but hear her sing, I fare. Upon a Rare Voice. Owen Felltham [*or* Feltham]. NOSC

When I Buy Pictures. Marianne Craig Moore. APT-1; ColAP; OxBA

When I called the children from play. For the Father of Sandro Gulotta. Janet Lewis. APT-2

When I Came Back. Bogomil Gjuzel. CarOv, *tr. by* Carolyn Kizer

When I Came from Colchis. W. S. Merwin. VGW

When I came in that night I found. Surprise in the Peninsula, A. Fleur Adcock. EmeKit

When I came into the world the war was endin'. End of the War, The. Ioan Alexandru. FaBoWar, *tr. by* Brenda Walker

When I came to show you my summer cottage. Summer. Josephine Miles. FaBoWP; WPE

When I cannot sleep, I stroke you. Manon Reassures Her Lover. Martha Elizabeth. PasH

When I carefully consider the curious habits of dogs. Meditatio. Ezra Pound. FaBoCh; OBAL

When I carry my little son in the cold. Poem. Thomas McGrath. GifTon

When I come back to my father's house. Galway Kinnell. RaBo *Fr.* Memories of My Father.

When I come down to sleep death's endless night. My City. James Weldon Johnson. NAAAL

When I consider everything that grows. William Shakespeare. AWP; NAEL-5v1; NAEL-6v1; NAEL-7v1; NoSic; SCGP; Son *Fr.* Sonnets.

When I consider Life and its few years. Tears. Lizette Woodworth Reese. MoAmPo

When I consider the many hours spent. Lament of a Subwayite. Eugene O'Neill. UV

When I contemplate all alone. Tennyson. NAEL-6v2 *Fr.* In Memoriam A. H. H.

When I contemplate o'er me. Night Serene, The. Luís De León. TrJP, *tr. by* Thomas Walsh

When I couldn't he always discussed things. Action Would Kill It / A Gamble. Robert Adamson. BMAP; CBAP

When I crack an egg. Best Meals of My Life, The. Joseph Duemer. SpudSo

When I'd finished my bath. Whirlwind. Ravji Patel. OMIP, *tr. by* Hansa Jhaveri

When I'd read that long love poem. On Reading a Love Poem. Kedarnath Singh. OMIP, *tr. by* Vinay Dharwadker

When I die. Lover of Rain in an Inkwell, The. Ghada Al-Samman. PoArWo, *tr. by* Miriam Cooke and Richard McKane

When I die. Hyakuri. JDP, *tr. by* Yoel Hoffmann

When I / die / I'm sure. Rebel, The. Mari E. Evans. CRP

When I die tomorrow. For Some Future Day. Hans Andreus. TuT, *tr. by* Peter Van de Kamp

When I Died on My Birthday. Kate Clark Spencer. Unle

When I died they washed me out of the turret with a hose. (LL) Death of the Ball Turret Gunner, The. Randall Jarrell. ClHu; ColAP; HAP; HarvBoo; HeIP-4; InPK-6; LCAP-2; MoAmPo; NAAL-2v2; NAAL-5; NIL-7; NIP-4; NOBA; NoAM; NoP-4; OBWP; OxBA; PAI; PoE; PoPoPo; PoWW; RB; SoSe-8; TAP; TFi; UnPo; VCAP; VGW

When I discover that the substance of the beautiful is a certain rhythm. George Santayana. TCAPo *Fr.* Normal Madness.

"When I do count the clock that tells the time." William Shakespeare. *See* Sonnets

When I do it, I remember how it was with us. Making Love to Myself. James L. White. GLP

When I don't feel well, I wander among. Sandro Penna. CAGL, *tr. by* John McRae

When I draw the magnificent Dutch girl. Rembrandt—Self Portrait. Gregory Corso. BB

When I Drink I Become the Joy of Faggots. Dorothy Allison. GLP

When I drive cab / I am moved by strange whistles and wear a hat. Lew Welch. NeAP; PoM *Fr.* Taxi Suite.

When I enter through the hatch of memory. Growing up Haunted. Marge Piercy. TaR

When I face north a lost Cree. Returned to Say. William Stafford. CoAmPo

When I fall asleep, and even during sleep. Baudelaire. Delmore Schwartz. TwCP; VGW

When I Fall in Love. Edward Heyman. ReLy

When I feel like a drag queen. Inner Bloke. Joanne Limburg. NeBl

When I find myself among a laughing tribe. Emergency Kit. Tanure Ojaide. EmeKit

When I find that my troubles are too much. Midnight Trolleybus. Bulat Shalvovich Okudzhava. TCRP, *tr. by* Albert C. Todd

When I first came here I had hope. When I First Came Here. Edward Thomas. SCGP

When I first came to London, I rambled about.   Seeker, The.   Matthew Green.   ECEV

When I first learned how to write poetry.   Shown to My Son Yü.   Lu Yu.   SuSp, *tr.* by Irving Y. Lo

When I first opened my eyes.   Autobiography.   Janet Dubé.   BrRo

When I first saw a woman after childbirth.   Ishtar.   Judith Wright.   NALW; NoAM

When I First Saw Snow.   Gregory Djanikian.   UnSA

When I first saw you break through.   Drowned Sailor, The.   Judith Ortiz Cofer.   PueRic

When I first sharpened a.   Poem for George Miles.   Dennis Cooper.   WiU

When I first was brought to light.   Eleanora Wyatt Finch.   EMWP

When I form a fist.   Fists.   Peter Finch.   TCAWP

When I found her in the bathing pool.   Bihari.   ErotSp, *tr.* by Sam Hamill

"When I found where we had crashed, in the snow."   He Said.   Jean Valentine.   TAP

When I gathered flowers.   Kakinomoto no Hitomaro.   OHMPJ

When I gaze at the sun.   Moment Please, A.   Samuel Allen.   PAI; SSLK

When I gaze upon the sky.   Reflection from Sea and Sky.   Walter Savage Landor.   FaBoEE

When I get home from a day's shopping in a city street.   Edna's Hymn.   Barry Humphries.   NOBAu

When I get in Illinois.   Can't You Line It?   *Unknown.*   NAAAL

When I get nervous, it's so hard not to.   Have You Ever Faked an Orgasm?   Molly Peacock.   RA

When I get there, I hope they forgive me if the knot I tie is the wrong knot. (LL)   Hawaii Dantesca.   Charles Wright.   HCAP; LCAP-2

When I go.   After Grave Deliberation.   Elizabeth Flynn.   NBLV

When I go away from you.   Taxi, The.   Amy Lowell.   BoWoP; LW; MoAmPo

When I go down to Wales for the long bank holiday.   I'r Hen Iaith a'i Chaneuon.   Ian Duhig.   ModIr

When I go / Guard my tomb well.   Issa.   ZenPo, *tr.* by Takashi Ikemoto and Lucien Stryk

When I go out, I switch off the light.   Precepts for City Living.   Vladimir Burich.   TCRusP, *tr.* by Daniel Weissbort

When I go[e] musing all alone.   Robert Burton.   NOSC   *Fr.* Anatomy of Melancholy, The.

When I, Good Friends, Was Called to the Bar.   Sir William Schwenck Gilbert.   NAEL-5v2; NAEL-6v2   *Fr.* Trial by Jury.

When I got back to base.   I Am Sad.   Le Ngoc Hiep.   WoPoe, *tr.* by John Balaban and T. L. Nguyen

When I got there the dead opossum looked like.   Behaving Like a Jew.   Gerald Stern.   BodElec; InvLad; LoL; TaR

When I got to the airport I rushed up to the desk.   Race, The.   Sharon Olds.   InvLad; RaBo

When I got up this mornin', I heard the old Southern whistle blow.   Southern Blues, The.   Big Bill Broonzy.   GM

When I grew up I went away to work.   Whores.   Margaret Abigail Walker.   NALW

When I Grow Up.   Hugo Williams.   EmeKit

When I Grow Up.   William Wise.   ChAP

When I grow up, I plan to keep.   Plans.   Maxine W. Kumin.   TLR

When I grow up I want to have a bad leg.   When I Grow Up.   Hugo Williams.   EmeKit

When I had firmly answered "No."   Last Ride Together (from Her Point of View), The.   James Kenneth Stephen.   UnPo

When I had journeyed half our life's way.   Dante Alighieri.   NAWM-7v1, *tr.* by Allen Mandelbaum   *Fr.* Divine Comedy, The (Mandelbaum Translation).

When I had learned enough to fail every test.   My Flute.   Herbert Krohn.   CDa

When I had met my love the twentieth time.   Her Merriment.   William Henry Davies.   EnLoPo

When I had money, money, O!   Money.   William Henry Davies.   OBEV; OBMV

When I had reached the base.   Across the Jarbok.   Gerrit Achterberg.   TuT, *tr.* by Dennis O'Driscoll

When I had spread it all on linen cloth.   Wife's Tale, The.   Seamus Heaney.   CIP-2

When I have a wife at home? (LL)   Soldier, Won't You Marry Me?   *Unknown.*   OxBoLi; PeLV

When I have borne in memory what has tamed.   England, 1802, V.   William Wordsworth.   GTBS-P; OBEV

When I have chanted my new poems.   K'ang Hai.   CoBLCP   *Fr.* Ten Poems on Almond Blossoms.

When I have crossed [*or* crost] the bar. (LL)   Crossing the Bar.   Tennyson.   BRP; ChIV-2; ClHu; EBVV; HeIP-4; ITBLP; NAEL-5v2; NAEL-6v2; NOBE; NOBVV; NoP-4; OBEV; PWR; PeECV; PoRA; SacPr; SoSe-8; TFi; TrCP

When I Have Fears [That I May Cease to Be].   John Keats.   AWP; CABP; CenSon; EBEV; GSo; HAP; HeIP-4; NAEL-5v2; NAEL-6v2; NIL-7; NIP-4; NoP-4; OBEV; PoE; PoPoPo; PoRA; SCGP; Son; TFi; UnPo; WoPoe (Terror of Death, The.)   GTBS-P

When I have gone. (LL)   Oblivion.   Ellis Ayitey Komey.   PBA; PBMAP

When I have heard small talk about great men.   Grandeur of Ghosts.   Siegfried Sassoon.   MoBrPo; OBMV

When I have lost my temper I have lost my reason, too.   Temper.   *Unknown.*   PoToHe

When I have lost the power to feel the pang.   Strangeness of Heart.   Siegfried Sassoon.   TrJP

When I have seen by Time's fell hand defac'd [*or* defaced].   William Shakespeare.   AWP; EnLoPo; HAP; HeIP-4; NOBE; NoSic; OxAEP-1; PoE; PoRA; SCGP; Son; TreFP   *Fr.* Sonnets.

When I Have Time.   *Unknown.*   PWR

When I hear laughter from a tavern door.   Wilfrid Scawen Blunt.   OBMV   *Fr.* Esther [a Young Man's Tragedy].

When I hear that serenade in blue.   Serenade in Blue.   Harry Warren.   ReLy

When I hear the guttural throatcall.   Nightsweats.   Richard Tayson.   AmPoNex; WiU

When I Heard at the Close of the Day.   Walt Whitman.   APN-1; NAAL-2v1; NAAL-3; NoAM; OxBA; PoE

When I Heard the Learn'd Astronomer.   Walt Whitman.   BRP; ChAP; ColAP; HAP; MoAmPo; NAAL-2v1; NAAL-3; NAAL-5; NoP-4; OxBA; PAI; PoPoPo; SoSe-8; TAP; WeW-3

When I hoked there, I would find.   Terminus.   Seamus Heaney.   PoPoPo

When I hug you tight at bedtime.   Unspoken.   Judith Ortiz Cofer.   PueRic

When I Know the Power of my Black Hand.   Lance Jeffers.   ISC

When I landed in the republic of conscience.   From the Republic of Conscience.   Seamus Heaney.   BodElec

When I last rade down Ettrick. (LL)   Ettrick.   Lady John Scott.   LW; SoSe-8; WPE

When I lay dis body down. (LL)   I Know Moon-Rise [*or* Moonrise].   *Unknown.*   APN-2; UnPo

When I lay me down to sleep.   Insomnia the Gem of the Ocean.   John Updike.   NBLV

When I lean down to stir the bathwater.   Jane Duran.   NewEx

When I leap through the flung open windows of your dance.   Picadilly or Paradise.   John Yau.   BodElec

When I Leapt over Tower Bridge.   Sir John Collings Squire.   UV

When I leave.   Tesshu.   JDP, *tr.* by Yoel Hoffman

When I leave the world.   Konkan.   JDP, *tr.* by Yoel Hoffmann

When I left her door I thought / she'd try to stop me.   Humiliation.   Kaifi A'Zmi.   OMIP, *tr.* by Mumtaz Jahan

When I left my girl.   Kakinomoto no Hitomaro.   OHPJ

When I lie down to die.   Valentin Petrovich Katayev [*or* Kataev].   TCRP

When I lie down to sleep dream the Wishing Well it rings.   I Am a Victim of Telephone.   Allen Ginsberg.   NBLV

When I lie where shades of darkness.   Fare Well.   Walter De la Mare.   GTBS-P; NOBE; NoP-4; OBEV; OxBEV

When I lift your letter out of the mailbox.   Correspondence.   Judith Ortiz Cofer.   PueRic

When I listen for the sound of.   Patrizia Cavalli.   ItPo, *tr.* by Gayle Ridinger

When I lived down in Devonshire.   Autobiographical Fragment.   Kingsley Amis.   OBCoV

When I lived in Milan the Duomo was thirty years younger.   Duomo, The.   Maria Luisa Spaziani.   NeIt, *tr.* by Beverly Allen

When I look at her.   *Unknown.*   OHMPJ

When I look at my elder sister now.   Elder Sister, The.   Sharon Olds.   NIL-7; NIP-4

When I look at the falling leaves.   Poem.   Marina Ivanovna Tsvetayeva [*or* Tsvetaeva].   RusPo, *tr.* by Robert Arthur Douglas Ford

When I Look at Wifredo Lam's Paintings.   Jayne Cortez.   SurWo

When I look back upon my former race.   Path of the Just, The.   John Henry, Cardinal Newman.   SacPr

When I look back upon my life nigh spent.   Prayer, A.   George Macdonald.   SacPr

When I look in the mirror.   Hysteria.   Chu Shu-chen.   OHPC, *tr.* by Kenneth Rexroth

When I look in the mirror.   Hopelessness.   Li Ch'ing-chao.   BLT, *tr.* by Kenneth Rexroth

When I looked into your eyes.   Chinoiseries.   Amy Lowell.   PoRA

When I looked under the hedge.   Basho.   EH, *tr.* by Robert Hass

When I looked up, the black man was there.   Pride.   Jackie Kay.   NeBl

When I Lost Slum Life.   Sipho Sepamla.   PeSAV

When I love (as some have told).   Hymn to the Graces, A.   Robert Herrick.   NOSC

When I loved you, I can't but allow.   Thomas Moore.   EnLoPo; OxBSP

When I'm a little older.   My Plan.   Marchette Chute.   WHSW

When I'm eating this I want food. I mean what I say because.   Realism.   Carla Harryman.   PmAP

When I'm far out in drink, your musical box.   To My Daughter.   James Michie.   OxBSP

When I'm killed, don't think of me.   When I'm Killed.   Robert Graves.   FaBoWar

When I'm Not Near the Girl I Love.   Burton Lane.   ReLy

When I'm not playing solitaire.   Don't Get around Much Anymore.   Duke Ellington.   ReLy

When I'm walking through the park.   Oh! What It Seemed to Be.   Bennie Benjamin.   ReLy

When I make love to you.   For Willyce.   Patricia Parker.   PoBW

When I meet a monk.   Motto.   Yüan Mei.   WoPoe, tr. by Jerome P. Seaton

When I meet the morning beam.   Immortal Part, The.   A. E. Housman.   MoBrPo; SCGP; SoSe-8; UnPo

When I move your body.   Anatomy Lesson.   Jack Coulehan.   BloBone

When I must come to you, O my God, I pray.   Prayer to Go to Paradise with the Donkeys, A.   Francis Jammes.   RB; WoPoe, tr. by Richard Wilbur

When I open my legs to let you seek.   Return, The.   Molly Peacock.   PasH; RA

When I parted from my Good.   Friedrich von Hausen.   GePo

When I Passed in the Afternoon.   Laura Riesco.   TANSG, tr. by Shaun Griffin and Emma Sepúlveda-Pulvirenti

When I pause, anemones fall on the month of December.   Year's End.   Frank Lima.   BodElec

When I pay close attention to my senses I become immobile.   Starfish Waving to Me from the Sand.   Matthew Rohrer.   NAPBL

When I perceive your blond and graceful head.   Sonnet 10.   Louise Labé.   BoWoP

When I Peruse the Conquer'd Fame.   Walt Whitman.   APN-1; SAmP

When I pick up my koto.   Unknown.   OHMPJ

When I play on my fiddle in Dooney.   Fiddler of Dooney, The.   W. B. Yeats.   EBVV; FaBoCh; NBLV; OxAEP-2

When I play roulette.   I May Be Wrong (But I Think You're Wonderful).   Henry Sullivan.   ReLy

When I, poor Lais, with my crown.   Lais to Aphrodite.   Edwin Arlington Robinson.   FaBoEE

When I, poor Lais, with my crown.   Var. authors.   FaBoEE   Fr. Variations of Greek Themes.

When I put her out, once, by the garbage pail.   Geranium, The.   Theodore Roethke.   CoAP; EmeKit; UnPo; WeW-3

When I put myself out on a saucer.   Cannibalism.   Diana Chang.   WPOW

When I ran, it rained.   Late in the afternoon.   Between the Wars.   Robert Hass.   VCAP

When I ran to snatch the wires off our roof.   Powerline Incarnation, The.   Les A. Murray.   CBAP

When I reached his place.   It Was All Very Tidy.   Robert Graves.   NPeEn; OxBTC; RB

When I Read Shakespeare.   D. H. Lawrence.   NoAM; OBCoV; Son

When I Read the Book.   Walt Whitman.   NAAL-2v1; NAAL-3

When I recall that place.   Is It Not Strange?   Elizabeth Delmore.   NLP

When I recall you—as I often do.   Eleanor Brown.   NeBl

When I recall you whom the henchmen sent.   Memorials, The.   Ernst Waldinger.   AuPH, tr. by Lowell A. Bangerter

When I Recovered from an Illness after Returning Home To Live in Retirement, I Was Invited by My Friends to Join a Song-Lyric Club.   Li K'ai-hsien.   CoBLCP, tr. by Jonathan Chaves

When I remember again.   John Skelton.   FaBoCh   Fr. Phyllyp Sparowe [or Philip Sparrow].

When I return from the land of exile and silence.   Poem of Return.   Jofre Rocha.   NAfrP; PBMAP, tr. by Don Burness

When I returned from lovers' lane.   Kimono, The.   James Merrill.   ColAP

When I returned to my home town.   Race.   Karen Gershon.   HP

When I returned to the hive I was one.   Lost Bee, The.   Phillis Levin.   RA

When I revolve in my remembrance.   Epitaph of Sir Griffith ap Rhys, The.   Unknown.   AngWePo

When I right the overturned ash can.   My Father's Singing.   Marc J. Sheehan.   MiVo

When I rolled three 7's.   Situation.   Langston Hughes.   APSN; OBAL

When I said "You have grown thin."   Meeting after Separation.   "Marula."   BoWoP, tr. by Tambimuttu and G. V. Vaiyda

When I sailed out of Baltimore.   Child's Pet, A.   William Henry Davies.   RB

When I saw my mother's head on the cold pillow.   Keine Lazarovitch, 1870–1959.   Irving Layton.   NIP-4

When I saw that clumsy crow.   Night Crow.   Theodore Roethke.   InPK-6; NAAL-5; OxBSP; VGW

When I saw the dark clouds, I wept.   Clouds, The.   Mirabai [or Mira Bai].   EnlH

When I saw the grapefruit drying, cherry [or cherries] in each centre lying.   Reproof Deserved; or after the Lecture.   Sir John Betjeman.   OBCoV

When I saw the world had died away / the plants, the human race and all.   Three Fragments.   Bertolt Brecht.   PFTM-1

When I saw your head bow, I knew I had beaten you.   Last Word, The.   Peter Davison.   InPK-6

When I say I believe that women have a soul and that its substance contains two.   Lawn of Excluded Middle.   Rosmarie Waldrop.   FTOS

When I see a couple of kids.   High Windows.   Philip Larkin.   FaBoMo; HarvBoo; NAEL-5v2; NAEL-6v2; NoAM; PoPoPo; PoetW

When I See Another's Pain.   Mani Leib [or Leyb].   TrJP, tr. by Joseph Leftwich

When I see birches bend to left and right.   Birches.   Robert Frost.   APT-1; AmFaPo; FaBoVe; HarvBoo; HeIP-4; ITBLP; MoAmPo; NAAL-2v2; NAAL-5; NoAM; NoP-4; OxBA; PAI; PoPoPo; PoRA; RB; SAmP; SoSe-8; TAP; TCAPo; TFi; TRP

When I see blosmes springe.   Unknown.   MiEL

When I see buildings in a town together.   Mr. Frost Goes South to Boston.   Firman Houghton.   UV

When I see how high it is.   So Beautiful Is the Tree of Night.   Pauline Hanson.   TAP

When I see lobster pots the sea has mangled.   Wrecked Creeves.   Katrina Porteous.   NeBl

When I See on Rood.   Unknown.   OxBSP

When I see the first.   Yakamochi (Otomo no Yakamochi).   OHPJ

When I see the lark a-moving [or stir her wings for joy].   Lark, The.   Bernard [or Bernart] de Ventadour [or Ventadorn].   CTC

When I see the lark stir her wings for joy.   Can Vei La Lauzeta Mover.   Bernard [or Bernart] de Ventadour [or Ventadorn].   APSN, tr. by Paul Blackburn

When I see the red maple.   All the People Who Are Now Red Trees.   Martín Espada.   TouFir

When I see the searchlights splitting the moonlight.   Searchlights.   Kenneth Mackenzie.   BMAP

When I see this end.   Burn this Sari.   A. Jayaprabha.   OMIP

When I / see you / climb the walls.   Pressure.   Anne Waldman.   PoM

When I see Your Face, the stones start spinning!   Jelaluddin [or Jalal al-Din] Rumi.   ErotSp, tr. by Coleman Barks

When I Set Out for Lyonnesse.   Thomas Hardy.   EBVV; MoBrPo; RB

When I shall be without regret.   Epitaph.   James Vincent Cunningham.   InPK-6

When I show up.   Song.   Unknown.   STP, tr. by Jerome Rothenberg

When I sit in the Churchyard at Stoke.   Limerick.   A. M. Sayers.   PeLi

When I Sleep, Then I See Clearly.   J. V. Foix.   PFTM-1

When I solidly do ponder.   Francis Daniel Pastorius.   SCAP

When I some antique jar behold.   To a Lady.   John Gay.   OBEV

When I speak now.   Volcano.   Ivan Van Sertima.   CA

When I spread out my hand here today.   Sitting by a Bush in Broad Daylight.   Robert Frost.   ChIV-1

When I squeeze through the narrow sluice of grief.   Descent.   Robyn Selman.   TaR

When I stand in the center of that man's madness.   Reflection by a Mailbox.   Stanley Kunitz.   TrJP

When I stand on the shore, I wonder where you are.   Villanelle VI.   Judith Barrington.   FFC

When I stand with these three.   Hostages, The.   Muriel Rukeyser.   AF

When I start my fast driving.   Unknown.   EroLit   Fr. Experiences as a taxi-driver in Venezuela.

When I started wanting.   Tzu Yeh.   ColAnChi; WoPoe, tr. by Jeanne Larsen

When I stepped homeward to my hill.   Home-coming.   Léonie Adams.   MoAmPo

When I still barely rose above the ground.   Marina Kudimova.   TCRP

When I strip, / stop walking / and drop into sleep.   Anne-Marie Kegels.   BoWoP

When I survey [or survay] the bright.   William Habington.   BASC; BeJo; MeLP; NOBE; NPeEn; OBEV; OxBEV; SCGP   Fr. Castara.

When I survey the wondrous cross.   Hymn.   Isaac Watts.   OxAEP-1; SacPr

When I take my girl to the swimming party.   One Girl at the Boys Party, The.   Sharon Olds.   InPK-6

When I Take My Sugar to Tea.   Pierre Norman.   ReLy

When I take you out tonight with me.   Surrey with the Fringe on Top, The.   Richard Rodgers.   ReLy

When I taught you.   To a Daughter Leaving Home.   Linda Pastan.   ItWoWo; NIL-7; NIP-4

When I Think about America Sometimes (I Think of Ralph Kramden).   Dorothy Barresi.   ExTi; ReTh

When I Think about Why.   Unknown.   WoPoe, tr. by Virginia Olsen Baron and Chung Seuk Park

When I think how far the onion has traveled.   Traveling Onion, The.   Naomi Shihab Nye.   LoL

When I think of death. Bop Lyrics. Allen Ginsberg. OBAL

When I think of me. Ontology. Rutger Kopland. TuT, *tr. by* Seamus Deane

When I think of my youth I feel sorry not for myself. Mind-Body Problem. Katha Pollitt. KGB

When I think of the house. Summer. David Oliveira. GeoHom

When I think of the long history of the self. Whole Self, The. Naomi Shihab Nye. GraLe; PoArWo

When I think of those mothers giving up. After Reading Reznikoff. Kate Daniels. ExTi

When I think of Tom. Hello, Young Lovers. Richard Rodgers. ReLy

When I think of you. Lady Izumi. ErotSp, *tr. by* Sam Hamill

When I think of your tail-bone, the tart sweetness. Lifelong. Sharon Olds. ExTi

When I think that you're the one girl I adore. Thank You Father. Ray Henderson. ReLy

When I think you gone, abruptly. Black Mood. Rosalía de Castro. WeW-3

When I think you're somewhere yonder. Black Mood. Rosalía de Castro. STV, *tr. by* John Frederick Nims

When I thought about him. Resist Confinement. Joette Harland-Watts. InTrad

When I thought about you, some tears came to mind. Some Tears. Kees Ouwens. TuT, *tr. by* Peter Van de Kamp

When I thought of this Duchess affair. Limerick. *Unknown.* PeLi

When I through all my many poems look. To the Most Virtuous Mistress Pot, Who Many Times Entertained Him. Robert Herrick. CaPo

When I too long have looked upon your face. Edna St. Vincent Millay. HeIP-4

When I / took my. Watch, The. May Swenson. HAP

When I tread the earth, I fear to hurt the ground. Meng Chiao. SuSp *Fr.* Apricots Die Young.

When I try makin' money. I Never Felt Better. Hugh Martin. ReLy

When I try to get the habit of doing what I should. My Heart Is a Hobo. Johnny Burke. ReLy

When I turn the ceiling light on. Self-Portrait. Gerald Stern. TaR

When I turned to look back. Shinkichi Takahashi. ZenPo, *tr. by* Takashi Ikemoto and Lucien Stryk

When I used to stay at my brother's. Weather. Michael Burkard. BodElec

When I Vexed You. Robert Browning. OxBSP *Fr.* Ferishtah's Fancies.

When I visited this shrine of truth. Pavillion-Where-the-Crane-Came, The. Chao Meng-fu. CoBLCP, *tr. by* Jonathan Chaves

When I wake alone in a drone of planes. Gulf. Marion Lomax. NeBl

When I wake now it's below ocherous, saw-ridged. Fall River. David Rivard. PBCAP

When I walk, or look from my window. Crimea. Vladimir Vladimirovich Mayakovsky [*or* Maiakovskii]. RusPo, *tr. by* Robert Arthur Douglas Ford

When I walk the path this morning. Homeplace, The. Lenard D. Moore. GT

When I was a baby. Meditations on Stevie. Gordon Chambers. InTrad

When I was a baby. Good Luck Gold. Janet S. Wong. NOxBChV; OxIBACP

When I was a bachelor / I lived by myself. Mother Goose. LB; ReMoGo

When I was a bachelor [*or* bach'lor *or* batchelor] I lived all alone [*or* early and young *or* by myself *or* young and gay]. Foggy, Foggy Dew, The. *Unknown.* OxBoLi; PeLV

When I was a beggarly boy. Aladdin. James Russell Lowell. TCAPo

When I was a blonde I. First Corinthians at the Crossroads. Bruce Dawe. NoAM

When I was a boy, a relative. Way to Make a Living, A. James Wright (1927–80). NNaP

When I was a boy desiring the title of man. George. Dudley Randall. BPo; CoAmPo; NoAM

When I was a boy I saw the world I was in. Old-Time Childhood in Kentucky. Robert Penn Warren. AiP

When I was a boy, I used to go to bed. Remorse for Time, The. Howard Nemerov. Son

When I was a boy they came in blackness. Lascars, The. Peter Thomas. AngWePo

When I was a child. King: April 4, 1968. Gerald William Barrax. ESEAA; GT

When I was a child. Truth about My Sister and Me, The. Anita Endrezze. CDW

When I was a child. Autobiographia Literaria. Frank O'Hara. NNaP; NOBA; TTTS

When I was a child. Message of the Rain, The. Norman H. Russell. ChAP

When I was a child and the soft flesh was forming. Song for Gwydion. Ronald Stuart Thomas. HarvBoo

When I was a child and thought as a child, I put. Wandering Jew, The. Robert Mezey. TaR

When I was a child, hawthorn. Hawthorn at Digiff. Ruth Bidgood. TCAWP

When I was a child I knew red miners. Childhood. Margaret Abigail Walker. NoP-4; Son; WPOW

When I was a child I saw. To a Child. Judith Wright. BMAP

When I was a chile we used to play. Children's Rhymes. Langston Hughes. BPo

When I was a connoisseuse of slugs. Connoisseuse of Slugs, The. Sharon Olds. LW

When I was a girl. Two Gifts. *Unknown.* BoWoP, *tr. by* Willis Barnstone

When I was a girl by Nilus stream. Witch, The. Adelaide Crapsey. APT-1

When I was a good and quick little girl. *Unknown.* BoWoP

When I was a greenhorn and young. Song. Charles Kingsley. NOBVV

When I was a kid in summer. Some One Liked Me when I Was Twelve. Peter Orlovsky. GLP

When I was a kid, still in short trousers. Three Tests for Darwin Duke. Jane Holland. MFPA

When I was a lad and so was my dad. *Unknown.* OxNR

When I was a little boy / I had but little wit. *Unknown.* OxNR

When I was a little boy / I lived by myself. *Unknown.* OxNR

When I was a little boy, / I washed [*or* wash'd] my / mammy's [*or* Mother's] dishes. When I Was a Little Boy. *Unknown.* OxNR

When I was a little boy / My mammy kept me in. *Unknown.* OxNR

When I was a little girl. Growing up Italian. Maria Gillan. UnSA

When I was a little girl, / about seven years old. Mother Goose. OxNR; ReMoGo

When I was a little maid. Little Maid, The. Anna Maria Wells. OBCA

When I was a medical student. Origin of Music, The. Dannie Abse. BloBone

When I was a young man courting the girls. September Song. Kurt Weill. ReLy

When I was alive, I wandered in the streets of the Capital;. Bearer's Song. Miu Hsi. ChiP, *tr. by* Arthur Waley

When I was almost forty. Golden Bells. Po Chü-i. BLT; ChiP, *tr. by* Arthur Waley

When I was arranging letters into words. Semyon [*or* Semion] Izrailevich Lipkin. TCRP

When I was as high as that. Memory, A. Leonard Alfred George Strong. NOBL

When I Was at My Most Beautiful. Ibaragi Noriko. ItWoWo, *tr. by* Aoyami Miyuki and Leza Lowitz

When I was born. Day's Ration, The. Ralph Waldo Emerson. APN-1

When I was born. (LL) Wonder. Thomas Traherne. BASC; ESCV; GeHe; HAP; NAEL-5v1; NAEL-6v1; NAEL-7v1; NPeEn; NoP-4; OxBEV; PoE; TOF

When I was born a million stars. With Me. Oscar Williams. YaYoPo

When I was born I was hardened and human. Train. Jennifer Snyder. BodElec

When I was born in a world of sin. G. K. Chesterton on His Birth. A. E. Housman. NBLV

When I was born in the large house by the sea. Poem of a Distant Childhood. Noémia da Sousa. HAWP, *tr. by* Allan Francovich and Kathleen Weaver

When I was born on Amman Hill. Collier, The. Vernon Watkins. FaBoTw; OBWVE; TCAWP

When I was born, one of the crooked. Seven-Sided Poem. Carlos Drummond de Andrade. PoetW; TCLAP; VCWP, *tr. by* Elizabeth Bishop

When I was born they christened me plain Samuel Johnson Brown. That's Why They Call Me "Shine." Cecil Mack. ReLy

When I was born, you waited. Jane Kenyon. ExTi; LoL *Fr.* Having It Out With Melancholy.

When I was bound apprentice, in famous Lincolnshire. Lincolnshire Poacher, The. *Unknown.* OxBoLi; PeLV

When I was but thirteen or so. Romance. Walter James Turner. MoBrPo; NOBAu; NOBE; NOxBChV; OBMV; PoRA

When I Was Christened. David McCord. KaS; OBCA; OBCoV *Fr.* Perambulator Poems, I-VII.

When I was dead, my spirit turned. At Home. Christina Georgina Rossetti. VWP

When I was down beside the sea. At the Seaside [*or* Sea-Side]. Robert Louis Stevenson. NTCP; TLR; WHSW

When I was dropped out of my mother. Wingless. Sándor Weöres. IQMS, *tr. by* Adam Makkai and Donald E. Morse

When I was eight I listened to stories of love. Tapestries. Colleen J. McElroy. NAAAL

When I was fair and young, then favour graced me. When I Was Fair and Young. Queen of England Elizabeth I. CTC; NIL-7; NIP-4; NoSic; PoRA

When I was farthest away from my children. My Aunt and the Sun. Michael Burkard. BodElec

When I was fifteen I stood. Potato Escape, A. Robley, Jr. Wilson. SpudSo

When I was five, we lived in Tesuque. Cherries. Joe Lamb. RaBo

When I was five yeras old. Gwendolyn Brooks. ESEAA *Fr.* Children Going Home.

When I was forced from Stella ever dear. Sir Philip Sidney. NAEL-5v1; NAEL-6v1; NAEL-7v1 *Fr.* Astrophil and Stella.

When I was forty the stocktaker came. On My Fortieth Birthday. John Tripp. AngWePo

When I was four my father went to Scotland. Truth, The. Randall Jarrell. OxBC

When I Was Growing Up. Nellie Wong. OxWW; UnSA

When I was in fifth grade. Day 1: Portrait of the Artisit, Small-kid Time. R. Zamora-Linmark. ReBoTo

When I was in high school, I wanted to be an actress. Soap Bubbles. Chrystos. ReTh

When I was just a little girl. Whatever Will Be, Will Be (Que Sera, Sera). Jay Livingston. ReLy

When I was just a tiny tot, with tousled head. Raggedy Ann. Anne Caldwell. ReLy

When I was little and brown. Welcome. David Hernandez. UnSA

When I was little and he was riled. James Merrill. OxBSo *Fr.* Five Old Favorites.

When I was made the magistrate. Magistrate. Chŏng Ch'ŏl. WoPoe, *tr. by* Graeme Wilson

When I was marked for suffering, Love forswore. Sonnet. Miguel de Cervantes Saavedra. AWP, *tr. by* Sir Edmund William Gosse

When I was no one yet. Song: Boundless Space. Sándor Weöres. WoPoe, *tr. by* William Jay Smith

When I was on Night Line. Ego. Philip Booth. TwCP

When I was once in Baltimore. Sheep. William Henry Davies. MoBrPo; NPeEn; RB

When I was one-and-twenty. A. E. Housman. ChAP; HeIP-4; ITBLP; InPK-6; MoBrPo; NAEL-5v2; NAEL-6v2; NoAM; PoE; TFi

When I was only semen in a gland. James Keir Baxter. PeNZ *Fr.* Pig Island Letters.

When I Was Prettiest in My Life. Ibaragi Noriko. WoPoe, *tr. by* Naoshi Koriyama and Edward Lueders

When I was Saul, and sat among the cloaks. St. Paul. Thomas Merton. ChIV-2

When I was seventeen. It Was a Very Good Year. Ervin Drake. ReLy

When I was seventeen. Just How Crazy Brenda Is. Melinda Goodman. GLP

When I was sick and lay a-bed. Land of Counterpane, The. Robert Louis Stevenson. ChAP; EBEV; NBLV; NTCP; PWR; TLR; WHSW

When I was six years old. Cuz' mama played jazz. Daniel Gray-Kontar. SpirFl

When I was small. Clean. Ann Turner. SSCS

When I was small and they talked about love I laughed. Child's Story, The. Elizabeth Jennings. HarvBoo

When I was still a child. Poem. Lesbia Harford. NOBAu

When I was ten. Dora Weeks. GotH

When I was ten. American Son. Mitsuye Yamada. UnSA

When I was ten my mother, having sold. Year of the Foxes, The. David Malouf. NOBAu

When I was thirteen. Tarzan. Jaime Manrique. WiU

When I was three I had a friend. When I Was Three. Richard Edwards [*or* Edwardes]. Spl

When I was three, I told a lie. Stincher, The. Jackie Kay. NOxBChV

When I was twenty I walked past. Trees that Change Our Lives. Gary Soto. PasH

When I was twenty inches long. New-Born Baby's Song, The. Frances Darwin Cornford. NIL-7

When I was very young. Traveling to Town. Duane Big Eagle. AiP

When I was very young. Little Girl Blue. Lorenz Hart. APT-2

When I was very young. Charles Upton. CLPP *Fr.* Panic Grass.

When I was very young indeed. Little Cavalier, A. Lucy Larcom. SWaP

When I Was Well into Being Savored. Joanne Kyger. PoM

When I Was Young. Alun Llywelyn-Williams. OBWVE, *tr. by* Gwyn Williams

When I was young. Sarah Pelham. FaBoVe

When I was young, a questing child. Spectator, The. Evan J. Thomas. AngWePo

When I was young and full of faith. Hesitating Veteran, The. Ambrose Bierce. CBCWP

When I was young and had no money to spend. Growing Old (2). Yüan Mei. WoPoe, *tr. by* Arthur Waley

When I was young and in my prime. T'ao Ch'ien [*or* T'ao Yuan-ming]. SuSp

When I was young and simple. I Never Do Anything Twice (Madam's Song). Stephen Sondheim. ReLy

When I was young and used to wander. Hubert's Museum. Louis Simpson. OxBC

When I was young and wanted to see the sights. On His Queerness. Christopher Isherwood. OxBTC

When I was young, I did not fit into the common mold. T'ao Ch'ien [*or* T'ao Yuan-ming]. SuSp *Fr.* On Returning to My Garden and Field.

When I was young I learnt fencing. Regret. Yuan Chi. ChiP, *tr. by* Arthur Waley

When I was young I little Thought. *Unknown.* EMWP

When I was young I scribbled, boasting, on my wall. Summing-up, The. Stanley Kunitz. OBAL

When I Was Young, I Stopped by a Wine Shop in Chi-men and Wrote This Poem, Inscribed It and Signed It, "Written by Lien the Eighteenth." The People of That District Have Since Taken It to Be a Poem of [the God] Lü Tung-pin! Yü Chi. CoBLCP, *tr. by* Jonathan Chaves

When I was young I studied hard and thirsted after knowledge. Chain Store Daisy. Harold Rome. ReLy

When I was young, I was out of tune with the herd. Returning to the Fields. Ch'ien T'ao. ChiP, *tr. by* Arthur Waley

When I was young, I went to school. One Furrow, The. Ronald Stuart Thomas. OxBC

When I was young, just starting at our game. To My Least Favorite Reviewer. Howard Nemerov. OBCoV

When I was young, my graying father frowned. To the Emperor. Theodore Prodromos. WoPoe, *tr. by* Jack Lindsay

When I was young, my world was disharmonious. Returning to My Fields and Gardens. T'ao Ch'ien [*or* T'ao Yuan-ming]. CrYelRi, *tr. by* Sam Hamill

When I was young, not knowing the taste of grief. Tune: Ugly Rogue. Hsin Ch'i-chi. CoBCP, *tr. by* Burton Watson

When I was young, throughout the hot season. Satire on Paying Calls in August. Ch'êng Hsiao. ChiP, *tr. by* Arthur Waley

When I was young, unapt for use of man. Prayer yo Hymen. *Unknown.* NOSC

When I was young, writing was my one sport. Day Dreams. Tso Ssu. ChiP, *tr. by* Arthur Waley

When I was younger. Pastoral. William Carlos Williams. APT-1; OxBA; SAmP

When I watch my two boys, Walter and Robert, at play. I Am as Happy as a Queen on Her Throne. Mrs. Henry Linden. CBWP-4

When I Watch the Living Meet. A. E. Housman. HarvBoo; MoBrPo; NOBVV; NPeEn; NoP-4; SCGP

When I watch you. Miss Rosie. Lucille Clifton. BISi; ESEAA; TwCP

When I went into my garden, I found. Sister Bertken [*or* Bertke]. BoWoP

When I went into my room, at mid-morning. Man and Bat. D. H. Lawrence. RB

When I went out. Akahito. OHPJ

When I Went Out. Karla Kuskin. NTCP

When I went out in. Kōkō Emperor. OHPJ

When I went out to kill myself, I caught. Saint Judas. James Wright (1927–80). CoAmPo; GI; LCAP-2; NOBA; PAI

When I went with you. *Unknown.* OHMPJ

When I wer still a bwoy, an' mother's pride. False Friends-like. William Barnes. NOBVV; NPeEn; OxBSo

When I were just a little lad, right small. Pulling the Chain. Simon Rae. UV

When I will rise up to the heights beyond the clouds. Path, The. "Valery Frantsevich Pereleshin." TCRP, *tr. by* Albert C. Todd

When I wiped you from. Foolishness. Nizar Qabbani. MAP, *tr. by* Diana Der Hovanessian and Lena Jayyusi

When I Woke. Lindsay Patterson. PAI

When I worked in the mill. If I Loved You. Richard Rodgers. ReLy

When I Would Die. Josephine D. Henderson Heard. CBWP-4

When I would image her features. George Meredith. NOBVV

When I would sing of crooked streams and fields. Song, The. Jones Very. APN-1

When I wrote of the women in their dances and wildness, it was a mask. Poem as Mask, The. Muriel Rukeyser. APT-2; NAAL-5; NALW

When Ibn Batutta, Arabian traveller. Ballad of the Dogs. Lars Gustafsson. WoPoe, *tr. by* Philip Martin

When ice on the pond is three feet thick. *Unknown.* CoBCP *Fr.* Tzu Yeh Songs.

When icicles by silver eaves. Winter Fairyland in Vermont. Francis P. Osgood. WeW-3

When icicles hang by the wall. William Shakespeare. ClHu; GTBS-P; HAP; MakPoe; NAEL-5v1; NAEL-6v1; NIL-7; NIP-4; NoP-4; OBEV; OxBEV; PAI; SCGP; TFi; TRP; UnPo; WeW-3 *Fr.* Love's Labour's Lost.

When idle in a poor Welsh mining valley. Rebel's Progress. Tom Earley. OBWVE

When ignorance possessed the shools. William Wilkie. ECEV *Fr.* Grasshopper and the Glowworm, The.

When in a snap the hinge. Upon Closing the Book. Armanda Guiducci. CItWP, *tr. by* Cinzia Sartini Blum and Lara Trubowitz

When in Banaras. Lepers Cry. Peter Orlovsky. GLP

When in danger or in doubt. Sound Advice. *Unknown.* NBLV

"When in disgrace with Fortune and men's eyes." William Shakespeare. *See* Sonnets

When, in my effervescent youth. Who'd Be a Hero (Fictional)? Morris Gilbert Bishop. OBAL

When, in my fond embraces fast confined. To My Love. "The Amorous Lady." ECWP

When in my pilgrimage I reach. When in My Pilgrimage. *Unknown.* ChIV-2

When in nineteen-thirty-seven, Etta Moten, sweetheart. Convert, The. Margaret Danner. BPo

When, in our turn, we show to them a Man. (LL) Christ in the Universe. Alice Thompson Meynell. MoBrPo; NOBE; OxAEP-2; VWP

When in Rome. Mari E. Evans. ESEAA; SoSe-8

When in Rome (I Do As the Romans Do). Cy Coleman. ReLy

When, in that final week. Evil Days, The. Boris Leonidovich Pasternak. GI, *tr. by* Nina Kossman

When in the chronicle of wasted time. William Shakespeare. AWP; CTC; EnLoPo; FaBoCh; NAEL-5v1; NAEL-6v1; NAEL-7v1; NOBE; NoSic; OBEV; OxAEP-1; PoRA; SCGP; Son; WoPoe *Fr.* Sonnets

When in the company of the gods. "H. D." APT-1 *Fr.* Walls Do Not Fall, The.

When in the dusk a summer day had died. Tisza, The. Sándor Petőfi. IQMS, *tr. by* Watson Kirkconnell

When in the east the morning ray. Andrew Marvell. NOBE *Fr.* Upon Appleton House [To My Lord Fairfax].

When in the empty city a siren blasts through the stop-go then gone the. Ear Training. Sekou Sundiata. SpirFl

When, in the gloomy mansion of the dead. Foresees her Death. Mary Robinson. CenSon; RWP

When in the heat of the first night of summer. My Belovèd Compares Herself to a Pint of Stout. Paul Durcan. EmeKit

When in the mask of night there shone that cut. Landing on the Moon. May Swenson. TAP

When in the night I await her coming. Muse, The. Anna Andreyevna Akhmatova. WoPoe, *tr. by* Stanley Burnshaw

When in the skillfully welded chest. Simonides. SaLy, *tr. by* Diane Rayor

When in the sun the hot red acres smoulder. Zulu Girl, The. Roy Campbell. NoP-4; OBMV; OxAEP-2

When in the throes of suicide. Anna Andreyevna Akhmatova. PoetW, *tr. by* Max Hayward and Stanley Kunitz

When in the wrought chest. Danae and Perseus. Simonides. WoPoe, *tr. by* Richmond Lattimore

When in your gardens entrance you provide. Rene Rapin. OBGa, *tr. by* John, the Younger Evelyn *Fr.* Of Gardens.

When Indian sweat was suddenly soaked dry by the sun. Black Ore. René Depestre. NegPo, *tr. by* Ellen Conroy Kennedy

When infant Reason first exerts her sway. On Education, December 1789. Elizabeth Bentley. WoRP

When Ireland was bloody and leaderless. Limerick. Gina Berkeley. PeLi

When Isaac watched his father strain back. Abraham's Madness. Bink Noll. ChIV-1

When Israel Came Forth out of Egypt. Bible, *O.T.* TrJP *Fr.* Psalms.

When Israel, of the Lord Beloved. Sir Walter Scott. ChIV-1

When Israel's Daughters mourn'd their past Offences. Epigram in a Maid of Honour's Prayer-Book. Pope. FaBoEE

When Israel's ruler on the royal bed. Christopher Smart. ChIV-1

When Israel sate by Babel's stream and wept. Lute of Afric's Tribe, The. Albery Allson Whitman. APN-2

When Israel Was in Egypt's Land. *Unknown. See* Go Down, Moses

When Israel was in Egypt's land. Let My People Go. *Unknown.* APN-2

When it all comes true. Quiet Thing, A. Fred Ebb. ReLy

When it comes back to teach you. Joy. Thomas Centolella. GifTon

When it comes—just so! Musho Josho. JDP, *tr. by* Yoel Hoffmann

When It Happened. Hilda Schiff. HP

When it is finally ours, this freedom, this liberty, this beautiful. Frederick Douglass. Robert Earl Hayden. CBWP; ESEAA; HCAP; ISC; NAAAL; NIL-7; NIP-4; PoPoPo; Son; TTY; VCAP

When it is not yet day. Looking for Mushrooms at Sunrise. W. S. Merwin. NOBA

When it is past—the golden moment—gone! Lost Opportunities. Henrietta Cordelia Ray. CBWP-3

When it makes a man mad all the days of his life? (LL) Song: "I peeled bits of straw and I got switches too." John Clare. NAEL-5v2; NAEL-6v2

When it rain five days an' de skies turned dark as night. Backwater Blues. Bessie Smith. NAAAL

When it rains I dance alone. When I Sleep, Then I See Clearly. J. V. Foix. PFTM-1

When it's cold and raining. Jelaluddin [*or* Jalal al-Din] Rumi. EnlH

When it's hot. Summer. Frank Asch. NTCP

When it's ninety in the shade. Drive a Tractor. *Unknown.* NBLV

When it's time. Listening. Aileen Fisher. NTCP

When it's time for the Sacrifice. Bible Lesson. Harvey Shapiro. TaR

When it was I first encountered you. Mikhail Alekseievich Kuzmin. CAGL, *tr. by* Michael Green

When J——— bawls out to the Chair for a Toast. (LL) Jinny the Just. Matthew Prior. NOBE; NOEC; OBEV

When Jacob from the land of Canaan down. Exodus from Egypt, The. Ezechiel of Alexandria. TrJP, *tr. by* E. H. Gifford

When Jacob rolled the stone off the well. Biblical Meditations. Yehuda Amichai [*or* Amikhai]. WoPoe, *tr. by* Benjamin Harshav and Barbara Harshav

When Jael crept in to see Sisera. Limerick. Bill Greenwell. PeLi

When Jane felt well enough for me to leave her. Porcelain Couple, The. Donald Hall. BAP-97

When Janis Joplin died. Fans. Baron Wormser. SwNoth

When Jenny Wren Was Young. *Unknown.* ReMoGo

When Jesus came to Golgotha they hanged Him on a tree. Indifference. Geoffrey Anketell Studdert-Kennedy. TrCP

When Jesus was leaving this sin-accursed land. Whoso Gives Freely, Shall Freely Receive! Josephine D. Henderson Heard. CBWP-4

When Jill complain[e]s to Jack for want of meat[e]. Upon Jack and Jill: Epigram. Robert Herrick. CaPo; NAEL-5v1; NAEL-6v1; NAEL-7v1

When John Donne dropped to sleep all around him slept. Elegies. Hugh Maxton. PBCIP

When John Henry was a little babe [*or* fellow]. *Unknown. See* John Henry was a lil [*or* little] baby

When John Henry was a little boy. *Unknown. See* John Henry was a lil [*or* little] baby

When Johnny comes marching home again. When Johnny Comes Marching Home. Patrick Sarsfield Gilmore. CBCWP; HHAm

(And we'll all feel gay when Johnny comes marching home.) (LL) TCAPo

When Joseph was an old man. Cherry-Tree Carol, The. *Unknown.* SacPr

When joy surprises me, I ripen. Quatrains for Joy. Muhammad Al-Ghuzzi. MAP; NAfrP, *tr. by* John Heath-Stubbs and May Jayyusi

When Judas, his betrayer. Zbigniew Herbert. GI *Fr.* St. Matthew.

When Judas writes the history of solitude. Sacrifice, The. Frank Bidart. GLP; VCAP

When Julius Fabricius, Sub-Prefect of the Weald. Land, The. Rudyard Kipling. MoBrPo

When June came back from Spain in '66. Les Fils (Sons). Beverly Matherne. TWW

When, just as they are. Void in Form. Ikkyu Sojun. ZenPo, *tr. by* Takashi Ikemoto and Lucien Stryk

When Keats was at work on *Endymion.* Limerick. Victor Gray. PeLi

When Kennedy. Arthur Thinks on Kennedy. Myra Cohn Livingston. HHAm

When Kukutis falls asleep. Kukutis's Sinful Spirit. Marcelijus Martinaitis. TWW, *tr. by* Laima Sruoginis

When lads have done with labor. A. E. Housman and a Few Friends. Humbert Wolfe. UV

When lads were home from labour. Fancy's Knell. A. E. Housman. FaBoCh; PoRA

When Lalement and de Brébeuf, brave souls. Brébeuf and His Brethren. Francis Reginald Scott. NOBC

When land is gone and money spent. *Unknown.* OxNR

When last I heard your nimble fingers play. To Lucia Playing on Her Lute, Another. Samuel Pordage. NOSC

When last I saw thee, I did not[t] thee see. Mary Sidney Wroth, Countess of Montgomery. PEW *Fr.* Pamphilia to Amphilanthus.

When Last We Parted. Catherine Maria Fanshawe. LW

When late (grave Palmer) these thy graffs [*or* grafts] and flowers. To Thomas Palmer [on His Book "The Sprite of Trees and Herbs"]. Ben Jonson. NoSic

When late I attempted your pity to move. Expostulation, An. Isaac Bickerstaffe. OBCoV

When late the trees were stript by winter pale. On Bathing. Thomas Warton, the Younger. OxBSo

When latest Autumn spreads her evening veil. To Melancholy. Written on the Banks of the Arun, October 1785. Charlotte Smith. CenSon; RWP

When lavish Phoebus pours out melted gold. Edward Benlowes. NOSC *Fr.* Theophia.

When Lazarus came back from the dead. Limerick. *Unknown.* PeLi

When Lazarus left his charnel-cave. Tennyson. EBVV; FHYEP; PeECV; TOF *Fr.* In Memoriam A. H. H.

When Learning's Triumph o'er her barb'rous [*or* barbarous] Foes. Samuel Johnson. EBEV; NAEL-5v1; NAEL-6v1; NAEL-7v1; NOEC; OxAEP-1

When leaves fall and cold winds come. (LL) Lines: "When the lamp is shattered [*or* shatter'd]." Shelley. NAEL-5v2; OBEV; OxBEV

When leaves, in evenen winds, do vlee. Jay a-Pass'd. William Barnes. NOBVV

When leaving the primrose, bayberry dunes, seaward. Constant, The. A. R. Ammons. HAP; WeW-3

When legislators keep the law. Latter-Day Warnings. Oliver Wendell Holmes. NCAP

When Lesbia first I saw so heavenly fair. Lesbia. William Congreve. OxBSP

When Letty had scarce pass'd her third glad year. Letty's Globe. Charles Tennyson Turner. NOBVV; NPeEn; OBEV; OxBEV; OxBSo; PeVV

When Life his lusty course began. Goblet, The. Bayard Taylor. TreFP

When Life's realities the Soul perceives. Anna Seward. CenSon

When light burns from the sea. Buddha of Sōkkuram, The. Shirley Kaufman. GifTon

When light bursts in at the window. Blind Man, The. Fazil Abdulovich Iskander. ItGoST, tr. by Avril Pyman

When Light returns to face the Earth anew. Friedrich Hölderlin. WoPoe, tr. by David Rattray Fr. Seasons, The.

When like the rising day. Gerald Griffin. OBEV Fr. Eileen Aroon.

When Lilacs Last in the Dooryard Bloom'd. Walt Whitman. APN-1; AWP; CBCWP; ColAP; HAP; MoAmPo; NAAL-2v1; NAAL-3; NAAL-5; NCAP; NIL-7; NOBA; NoP-4; OxBA; PAI; PoPoPo; PoRA; SAmP; TAP; TCAPo; TFi Fr. Memories of President Lincoln.

When lions mate they disappear for days. Honeymoon. Alice R. Friman. MPUn

When little Fred went to bed. Little Fred. Unknown. ReMoGo

When little girls begin to walk. To My Niece, A.M., with a New Pair of Shoes. Unknown. ECWP

When little heads weary have gone to their bed. Plumppuppets, The. Christopher Darlington Morley. ChAP

When little matchsticks of rain become earth of drenched fields, an. Frog, The. Francis Ponge. BLT, tr. by Beth Archer

When little things would irk me, and I grow. Morning Prayer. Unknown. PoToHe

When living is a pain. (LL) Dryden. BoLoP; EnLoPo; HAP; NOBE Fr. Spanish Friar [or Fryar], The.

WHEN, lo, by break of morning. Unknown. NoSic

When London Calls. Victor James Daley. CBAP

When Londons fatal bills were blown abroad. Marlburyes Fate. Benjamin Tompson. SCAP

When Loneliness is a Man. Yusef Komunyakaa. AWTN

When lonely feelings chill the meadows of your mind. You Must Believe in Spring. Jacques Demy. ReLy, tr. by Alan Bergman, Marilyn Bergman and Michel Legrand

When longing for you. Ono no Komachi. ArkPo, tr. by Helen Craig McCullough

When, looking on the present face of things. October, 1803. William Wordsworth. CenSon

When loose-strife, in flower, line. When to Slap a Woman. Paul Violi. PmAP

When, Lord, I seeke to shew thy praises, then. Edward Taylor. TCAPo Fr. Preparatory Meditations before My Approach to the Lord's Supper.

When Louis came home to the flat. Meet Me in St. Louis, Louis. Andrew B. Sterling. OBAL

When love gushed out. Incontinence. Susan Hahn. IllVoic

When love is a shimmering curtain. On Diverse Deviations. Maya Angelou. BlSi

When Love is fled, and I grow old. (LL) Why I Write Not of Love. Ben Jonson. BeJo; OxBSP

When love is gone. (LL) Night Has a Thousand Eyes, The. Francis William Bourdillon. BRP; BoLoP; OBEV; OxBSP; PoToHe

When Love its utmost vigour does imploy. Lucretius. NPeEn; OxBEV, tr. by John Dryden Fr. De Rerum Natura (On the Nature of Things).

When Love Meets Love. Thomas Edward Brown. UnPo

When love on time and measure makes his ground. False Love. John Lilliat. EBEV

When Love's Perished. Dambudzo Marechera. NAfrP

When love was structured, so was verse—both fit. Good Old Days, The. Barbara Fried. NBLV

When Love with unconfinèd wings. To Althea, from Prison. Richard Lovelace. AWP; BASC; BeJo; CaPo; CavPo; GTBS-P; HAP; ITBLP; MeLP; NAEL-5v1; NAEL-6v1; NAEL-7v1; NIL-7; NOBE; NOSC; NPeEn; NoP-4; OBEV; OxBEV; PBRV; PoE; PoRA; SCGP; TFi

When Lovely Woman. Phoebe Cary. APN-2; UV

When lovely woman stoops to folly. When Lovely Woman. Mary Demetriadis. UV

When lovely woman stoops to folly and. T. S. Eliot. UV Fr. Waste Land, The.

When lovers' lips from kissing disunite. Charles Tennyson Turner. CenSon

When low and heavy sky weighs like a lid. Spleen LXXVIII. Charles Baudelaire. SxFrPo, tr. by James McGowan

When Lucifer was lowliest in Heaven. Two Names. Betty Scott Stam. SacPr

When Lucy draws her mantle around her face. Guido Guinicelli. EaItPo, tr. by Dante Gabriel Rossetti

When ma baby shouts in church. Lena Lovelace. Melvin B. Tolson. GT

When Ma Rainey. Ma Rainey. Sterling Allen Brown. APT-2

When Maggy Gangs Away. James Hogg. CABP

When Magritte died. Homage to René Magritte. George Melly. SPE

When maidens such as Hester die. Hester. Charles Lamb. GTBS-P; OBEV

When maize stands more than ten feet high. Hey, Boys! Up Go We! Unknown. NOBAu

When Malindy Sings. Paul Laurence Dunbar. APN-2; ISC; NAAAL

When man becomes more faithful to man. Communion II. U Tam'si Tchicaya. NegPo, tr. by Ellen Conroy Kennedy

When man in the bush with God may meet? (LL) Good-bye. Ralph Waldo Emerson. PWR; PoToHe; TAP

When many years we'd been apart. Reminiscence. Wallace Irwin. NOBL

When Mark Deloach Ruled the World. Dominique Parker. SpirFl

When Mary on her wedding day. Sister Gone. William Barnes. OxBEV

When Mary Rand. Uncle Alfred's Long Jump. Gareth Owen. OBSP

When May entered the Black Current off Kinkazan Island. Whale Spouting. Takamura Kotaro. WoPoe, tr. by James Kirkup and Akiko Takemoto

When meeting a bear, say. Unknown. WoPoe, tr. by Siv Cedering Fox Fr. Three Swedish Spells.

When men a dangerous disease did 'scape. To Doctor Empiric[k]. Ben Jonson. FaBoEE; WoPoe

When men are belligerent or crude. Spunk Talking. Anne Rouse. MFPA; NeBl

When men are laid away. Inscription for a Graveyard. Yvor Winters. CRP

When men discovered freedom first. Ash and the Oak, The. Louis Simpson. CoAmPo

When men shall find thy flower [or flow'r], thy glory, pass. Samuel Daniel. NAEL-5v1; NOBE; NoSic; OBEV; SCGP; Son Fr. To Delia.

When men straighten their shoulders and go by. Nocturne: The Eternal. Xavier Villaurrutia. GifTon, tr. by Eliot Weinberger

When men were all asleep the snow came flying. London Snow. Robert Bridges. EBEV; EBVV; GTBS-P; MoBrPo; NOBE; NOBVV; NoAM; OxAEP-2; OxBTC; TFi

When mice with wings can wear a human face. (LL) Bat, The. Theodore Roethke. APT-2; ChAP; OBCA; PAI

When Mickey Mantle died. Players. E. Ethelbert Miller. SpirFl

When midnight comes a host of dogs and men. Badger. John Clare. FHYEP; HAP; NPeEn; PAI; SCGP

When midst the summer-roses the warm bees. Calder Campbell. CenSon

When Milton sees his "late espoused saint." Confessional Poetry. Tony Harrison. DiPo

When mine eynen misteth. All too late. Unknown. EBEV

When Missus O'Leary's cow kicked the lantern. Put the Blame on Mame. Doris Fisher. ReLy

When Mrs Gorm (Aunt Eloise). Opportunity. Harry Graham. OBCoV; PeLV

When morning came. Brother, The. Peter Everwine. NNaP

When morning gilds the skies. Unknown. SacPr, tr. by Edward Caswall

When morning has come, all the chief priests and elders of the people. Bible, N.T. NAWM-5v1 Fr. St. Matthew.

When morning is breaking and darkness has fled. We Are Passing Away. Matilda Caroline Edwards. PWR

When Morrice views his prostrate peas. On a Fine Crop of Peas Being Spoiled by a Storm. Henry Jones. OBGa

When Moses an' his soldiers. He's Jus' de Same Today. Unknown. InvLi

When Moses in Horeb struck the rock. On Certain Wits. Howard Nemerov. HCAP; OxBC

When mother divorced you, we were glad. She took it and. Victims, The. Sharon Olds. NIL-7; SoSe-8

When mothers weep and fathers richly proud. Confirmation, The. Karl Shapiro. APT-2

When mountain rocks and leafy trees. Nature's Lineaments. Robert Graves. FaBoTw; RB

When Mr. Dennis does well play. Julia A. Moore. VerBaPo Fr. Grand Rapids Cricket Club, The.

When mum, who never quit the Party. Left Rites. Hylda Sims. Prnts

When music, heav'nly maid, was young. Passions; an Ode for [or to] Music, The. William Collins. GTBS-P

When "Music, Heavenly Maid," was very young. Music. Christopher Pearse Cranch. APN-1

When my arms wrap you round I press. He Remembers Forgotten Beauty. W. B. Yeats. CTC

When my blood flows calm as a purling river. Communism. Ella Wheeler Wilcox. SWaP

When my breast labors with oppressive care, Paraphrase of the Latter part of the Sixth Chapter of St. Matthew, A. James Thomson. ChIV-2

When my brother hogs. Blanket Hog. Paul B. Janeczko. TLR

When my brother Tommy. Two in Bed. Abram Bunn Ross. NTCP

When my cat preens in dusty sunlight. Elegy Residence on Earth. Robert Hass. BodElec

When my cousin Josie played the piano. On Fourteen Maple Street. Barbara Winder. MiVo

When my devotions could not pierce. Denial [l]. George Herbert. BASC; ESCV; FSCP; GeHe; NAEL-5v1; NAEL-6v1; NAEL-7v1; NOBE; NPeEn; NoP-4; PBRV; TOF

When My Dog Died. Freya Littledale. NTCP

When my ex-wife found magnetic north. Beginning of the End, The. Roddy Lumsden. NeBl

When my eyes rove in search of recognition. Sentimental Education. Rachel Hadas. RA

When my father. My Father's House. Sam Cornish. AllShUp

When my father breathed. Not Yet. Lawrence Joseph. GraLe

When my father died I saw a narrow valley. Strawberries. W. S. Merwin. AmFaPo; NoP-4

When my father dozes off beside me I become my father. Sang Yi. PFTM-1 Fr. Crow's-Eye View.

When my father had been dead a week. White Apples. Donald Hall. LoL; TAP

When my grandfather Louie came here, from Chicago. World above Suffering, A. Albert Goldbarth. TaR

When my grandfather stepped from the boat. Gallery. Albert Goldbarth. TaR

When my grandmother left the races with Mr. Hughes. Mr. Hughes. David Campbell. CBAP

When My Grandmother Said "Pussy." Carole Bernstein. AmPoNex; UnSA

When my grave is broke up again[e]. Relic, The. John Donne. BASC; FHYEP; FSCP; HAP; HeIP-4; NAEL-6v1; NAEL-7v1; NOBE; NOSC; NoP-4; TFi

When my hair was first in bangs. Ballad of Long Bank, The. Li Po. WoPoe, tr. by Elling O. Eide

When my heart asked for a way free, it was led into this lightless room. Killarney Clary. GeoHom

When my heart becomes heavy with acute pain of life. On Such A Day. Song-Jook Park. FSt

When my heart settles. Romance of Love. Unknown. BLPSL, tr. by Rene de Costa, Rigas Kappatos and Eleni Paidoussi

When my house was bare of skins and pots of meal. Hungry Master and Hungry Cat. Shamaqmaq, Abu. TriCat

When my husband. Ten Years and More. Miriam Waddington. NOBC

When my last sunset is under a cloud. When I Am Dead. Emma Alice Browne. TreFP

When my life was thrifty, thrifty. Shearing, The. Unknown. OBWVE, tr. by Glyn Jones

When my love swear[e]s that she is made of truth. William Shakespeare. AWP; AmFaPo; EBEV; HeIP-4; NAEL-5v1; NAEL-7v1; NPeEn; NoSic; OxAEP-1; OxBEV; PAI; SoSe-8 Fr. Sonnets.

When my lover touches me, what I feel in my body. Louise Glück. LW Fr. Marathon.

When my mother died I was very young. William Blake. FHYEP; HeIP-4; InPK-6; NAEL-5v2; NAEL-6v2; NAWM-7v2; NOEC; OxAEP-2; PAI; PoE; SCGP; SoSe-8; TFi Fr. Songs of Innocence.

When my mother finally left her body. Legacy. Joan Larkin. WiU

When my o'erlay was white as the foam o' the lin. Song (Poverty Parts Good Company, for an Old Scotch Air). Joanna Baillie. RWP

When my older brother. Rain, The. Zbigniew Herbert. PoetW, tr. by John Carpenter and Bogdana Carpenter

When My Poems were Lost. Raymond Mazisi Kunene. PeSAV, tr. by the author

When, my quiet scientific friend. Divorce and Mr. Circe. David Gewanter. NAPBL

When my sensational moments are no more. E. E. Cummings. Son

When My Ship Comes In. Walter Donaldson. ReLy

When my sister died, I cried a great deal. Successive Deaths. Adelia Prado. TANSG, tr. by Ellen Watson

When my son was born, the moon was not bright. Meng Chiao. SuSp Fr. Apricots Die Young.

When my stomach bulges, I hurl wild whoops. Bill Greenwell. NewEx

When my thought goes out to you, it is perfumed. Autumn Verses. "Rubén Dario." BLPSL, tr. by Rene de Costa, Rigas Kappatos and Eleni Paidoussi

When my time comes. Me. Chairil Anwar. PoetW, tr. by Burton Raffel

When my wife disappeared. Missing. Moniza Alvi. NeBl

When my wife left home. Yakamochi (Otomo no Yakamochi). ErotSp, tr. by Sam Hamill

When my words were wheat. Words. Mahmoud Darwish. VCWP, tr. by Rana Kabbani

When my young brother was killed. War. Joseph Langland. AiP

When Natalia Ginzburg died, the papers of her region declared. Poem for Natalia Ginzburg. Anita Helle. OPRER

When Nature, at our awaking, sometimes proposes to us. Prairie, The. Francis Ponge. AF, tr. by Beth Archer

When Nature bids thee from the world retire. Philip Freneau. TCAPo Fr. House of Night, The.

When Nature bids us leave to live, 'tis late. To William Roe. Ben Jonson. NOSC

When Nature dreamt of making bores. Epigram: On Sir Roger Phillimore. Unknown. NBLV

When Nature made her chief work, Stella's eyes. Sir Philip Sidney. NAEL-5v1; NAEL-6v1; NAEL-7v1; NIL-7; NIP-4; Son Fr. Astrophil and Stella.

When nature rises on its hind legs. Mushrooms. Yury [or Iurii] Kuznetsov. TCRP, tr. by Lubov Yakovleva

When Negro Teeth Speak. Ouologuem Yambo. PBMAP

When neither can hinder the other. (LL) Dryden. NAEL-5v1; NAEL-6v1; NAEL-7v1; NIL-7; NIP-4 Fr. Marriage à la Mode.

When news came that your mother'd. Kin. Michael S. Harper. LCAP-2

When next we met, she bade me turn. Apostasy. Aus of Kuraiza. TrJP, tr. by Hartwig Hirschfeld

When night drifts along the streets of the city. Solitaire. Amy Lowell. MoAmPo; TCAPo

When night finally fades, when false dreams cease to be worshipped. Gutenberg Inscription. Mihály Vörösmarty. IQMS, tr. by Peter Zollman

When Night is almost done. Emily Dickinson. AWTN

When night's black mantle could most darknes[s] prove. Mary Sidney Wroth, Countess of Montgomery. BASC; CABP; MakPoe; NAEL-5v1; NAEL-6v1; NAEL-7v1; Son Fr. Pamphilia to Amphilanthus.

When night shadows slipped across the plain, I saw a man. Nation Wrapped in Stone, A. Roberta Hill Whiteman. BoWoP; CDW

When night stirred at sea. Planter's Daughter, The. Austin Clarke. CIP-2; ModIr; NPeEn; OxBEV; OxBTC

When night-time bars me in. Snowdrops. Margiad Evans. OBWVE

When Noah left the Ark, the animals. Kingfisher, The. John Heath-Stubbs. NOxBChV

When Noah sailed the wet and blue. Noah. Gerda Mayer. OTCP

When none of this interests me I distort my jaw. Each Sentence Is Into the Fast. Joe Wenderoth. BodElec

When nothing is happening. How Everything Happens. May Swenson. APT-2; HAP

When o'er the wold the heedless lamb. Song. Thomas Holcroft. NOEC

When Oats Were Reaped. Thomas Hardy. OxBTC

When ocean breezes blow the moon. Inscribed on the Painting, Solitary Crane, in the Collection of Jao Shih-ying. Yü Chi. CoBLCP, tr. by Jonathan Chaves

When ocean-clouds over inland hills. Misgivings. Herman Melville. APN-2; NAAL-2v1; NAAL-3; NCAP; NOBA; OxBA; TCAPo

When of thy loves, and happy heavenly dreams. Lines. Frances Anne [or "Fanny"] Kemble. VWP

When old corruption first begun. William Blake. RB Fr. Island in the Moon, An.

When Old Tai goes down below. Old Tai's Wine Shop. Li Po. WoPoe, tr. by Elling O. Eide

When on a summer dawn the birds start calling. Silence. Stefan Brecht. CLPP

When on life's ocean first I spread my sail. On Hearing of the Intention of a Gentleman to Purchase the Poet's Freedom. George Moses Horton. APN-1; NAAAL

When on my bed the moonlight falls. Tennyson. NAEL-6v2; PeECV; SCGP Fr. In Memoriam A. H. H.

When on my sick bed I languish. Thought of Death, A. Thomas Flatman. NOSC

When on my time of living I reflect. My Thirty Years. Juan Fransico Manzano. TTY, tr. by Oliver Cobarn and Ursula Lehrburger

When on some balmy-breathing night of Spring. Glow-Worm, The. Charlotte Smith. BWW

When on the high bluff discovering. From the North Saskatchewan. Eli W. Mandel. NOBC

When on the Marge of Evening. Louise Imogen Guiney. ColAP

When, on withering into life, smoke. On Fire. David Morley. NLP

When once the scourging prophet, with his cry. Disused Temple, The. Norman Cameron. OxBS; OxBTC

When once the soul is ready to depart, sir. Sadi [or Saadi or Sa'di]. WoPoe, tr. by Dick Davis

When once they find her flower, her glory, pass. (LL) Samuel Daniel. NoP-4; NoSic Fr. To Delia.

When one dreams of another. Three Dreams at Chiang-ling. Yüan Chên. SuSp, tr. by William H. Nienhauser

When One Has Lived a Long Time Alone. Galway Kinnell. LoL

When One Is Feeling One's Way. Lawrence Joseph. KGB

When one is lonely (and You). W. H. Auden. CAGL *Fr.* Three Posthumous Poems.

When One Loves Tensely. Don Marquis. NBLV

When one of the old, little stars doth fall from its place. Sidera Cadentia. Ford Madox Ford. OxBSP

When one or other rambles. Francis Daniel Pastorius. SCAP

When one was on the cursed tree to die. They Gave Him Vinegar and Gall (Matt. 27) and Wine Mingled with Myrrh (Mark 15). Francis Quarles. NOSC

When Orion straddled his apex of sky. White Land, The. Roberta Hill Whiteman. HATNAP

When Orpheus sent down to the regions below. Power of Music, The. Thomas Lisle. NOBL

When Orpheus turned. Orpheus. Linda Pastan. MiVo

When Oscar came to join his God. Oscar Wilde. Algernon Charles Swinburne. PeVV

When other fair ones [*or* ladies] to the shades [*or* groves] go down. On Certain Ladies. Pope. FaBoEE

When other lips and other eyes. Self-Evident. James Robinson Planché. OBCoV

When Othman's sword, as Paleologue's, is broken. Constantinople. Amin Al-Rihani. GraLe

When our backs are turned. To the Onlookers. William Heyen. GotH

When our beasts low in their stalls. James Philip McAuley. ChIV-1 *Fr.* Family of Love, The.

When our brother Fire was having his dog's day. Brother Fire. Louis MacNeice. AF; NOBE; NoAM

When our cars touched. Jump Cabling. Linda Pastan. InPK-6

When our children cried in the shadow of the gallows. Nathan [*or* Natan] Alterman. TrJP *Fr.* From All Peoples.

When our circus finally collapsed the train stopped on thin rails seven. Decisions, The. Rick Bursky. ReTh

When our dean took a pious young spinster. Limerick. Victor Gray. NOBL; PeLi

When Our Earthly Sun Is Setting. Edwin H. Nevin. AH

When our heads are bowed with woe. Hymn. Henry Hart Milman. SacPr

When our sovereign. Builders. Dmitry [*or* Dmitrii] Borisovich Kedrin. TCRP, *tr. by* Albert C. Todd

When our tears are dry on the shore. Rediscovery. Kofi Awoonor. TTY

When our two souls stand up erect and strong. Elizabeth Barrett Browning. BWW; BoWoP; CenSon; LW; NAEL-5v2; NAEL-6v2; NALW; NOBE; OBEV; WPE *Fr.* Sonnets from the Portuguese.

When our wild day is wiped like a tear. Red Ridinghood. Nathan [*or* Natan] Alterman. MHP, *tr. by* Ruth Finer Mintz

When our women go crazy, they're scared they won't be. When Our Women Go Crazy. Julia Kasdorf. NeAmPo; PBCAP

When out at Shellbrook, round by stile and tree. Shellbrook. William Barnes. OxBEV

When out of bed my love doth spring. Upon Electra. Robert Herrick. BeJo

When out of the woods He came. (LL) Ballad of Trees and the Master, A. Sidney Lanier. APN-2; ChIV-2; ColAP; ITBLP; NOBA; OxBA; TCAPo

When o'er the flowery, sharp pasture's. Flowers by the Sea. William Carlos Williams. APT-1; MoAmPo; NoAM; RB; TAP

When Oxford gave thee two degrees in art. Epitaph. Mrs. Boughton. EMWP

When pails empty the last brightness. O You among Women. Frederick Robert Higgins. BIrV

When Pallas and golden-sandaled Hera saw Maeonis. Rufinus. HePo, *tr. by* Barbara Hughes Fowler

When Parliament passed the Onion Act of 1707. Postmodern Maturity. Tony Towle. KGB

When Parnell's Irish in the House. Wilfred Owen's Photographs. Ted Hughes. OxBC

When passing from nature to being. Vladimir Holan. PFTM-2, *tr. by* Clayton Eshleman, Frantisek Galan and Michael Heim *Fr.* Night with Hamlet, A.

When Patty, lovely Patty, graced the crowd. Robert Dodsley. ECEV *Fr.* Agriculture.

When Paul Bunyan was ill we sent. When Paul Bunyan Was Ill. Willie Reader. KaS

When pavements were blown up, exposing wires. Epilogue to a Human Drama. Stephen Spender. AF

When peace, like a river, attendeth my way. It Is Well with My Soul. Horatio G. Spafford. SacPr

When pears hang green on the garden wall. NOTL. Max Beerbohm. UV

When Pegotty found Barkis was willing. Limerick. Douglas Catley. PeLi

When pensive on that portraiture I gaze. Sonnet on a Family Picture. Thomas Edwards. CenSon; NOEC

When people ask. Rose Furuya Hawkins. FSt *Fr.* Proud Upon an Alien Shore.

When people choose. Life's Will. Abu al-Qasim Al-Shabbi. MAP, *tr. by* Sargon Boulus and Christopher Middleton

When People Rise from Cheese, Statement #1. Duo Duo (Li Shizheng). PFTM-2, *tr. by* John Rosenwald

When people see the man of Cold Mountain. *Unknown.* CoBCP

When people were being killed. Air Raid. Sachiko Yoshihara. GifTon, *tr. by* Naoshi Koriyama and Edward Lueders

When Petula Clark sang "Downtown," I wished I. Meet the Supremes. David Trinidad. SwNoth

When Phoebe formed a wanton smile. Sonnet. William Collins. EnLoPo; OxBSP

When Phoebus had melted the sickles of ice. Robin Hood and the Ranger. *Unknown.* ESPB

When pigeons returned. Absent, The. May Muzaffar. PoArWo, *tr. by* Tahia Abdel Nasser

When pimps out of loneliness cry. Sliver of Sermon. Langston Hughes. APT-2

When plum / Blooms—. Issa. ZenPo, *tr. by* Takashi Ikemoto and Lucien Stryk

When poetry walked the live, spring wood. Kingcups. Sacheverell Sitwell. MoBrPo

When poets print their works, the scribbling crew. To My Ingenious and Worthy Friend William Lowndes, Esq. John Gay. OBSV

When Polly lived back in the old deep woods. Stranger. Elizabeth Madox Roberts. MoAmPo

When poppies tear themselves away. Silence. Slavko Janevski. WoPoe, *tr. by* Charles Simic

When President John Quincy. John Quincy Adams. Rosemary Benét. OBCA

When President Reagan visited Baltimore. Glass Canyons. David Romtvedt. UrbNat

When—presto—turf and trees are green. Bernard [*or* Bernart] de Ventadour [*or* Ventadorn]. STV

When primroses are out in Spring. Days Too Short. William Henry Davies. MoBrPo

When print on paper tells, in the time's affairs. To Genevieve Taggard Who Called Me Traitor in a Poem. Max Eastman. APT-1

When Prodike seemed / alone I begged for it. Prodike. Rufinus. GrAn, *tr. by* Alan Marshfield

When Psyche, Who Is Life, Descends among the Shades. Osip Emilevich Mandelstam [*or* Mandelshtam]. WoPoe, *tr. by* James Greene

On Pym. William Drummond, of Hawthornden. NOSC

When quacks with pills political would dope us. Canopus. Bert Leston Taylor. NOBL

When raging [*or* ragyng] love with extreme pain [*or* payne]. When Raging Love. Henry Howard, Earl of Surrey. NoSic (Consolation.) EBEV; EnLoPo; NOBE

When Reedisdale and Wise William. Redesdale and Wise William. *Unknown.* ESPB

When relatives came from out of town. Blackbottom. Toi Derricotte. GT; LTA; PBCAP

When Reuben Pantier ran away and threw me. Edgar Lee Masters. HAP *Fr.* Spoon River Anthology.

When rising from the bed of death. Joseph Addison. TOF

When roads are covered with ice. Popryshchin. Nikolai Alekseievich Zabolotsky [*or* Zabolotskii]. TCRusP, *tr. by* Daniel Weissbort

When roaring gloom surged inward and you cried. To His Dead Body. Siegfried Sassoon. NoAM

When Robert Graves got involved. Robert Graves. Gavin Ewart. NoAM

When Robin Hood, and his merry men all. Robin Hood and the Valiant Knight. *Unknown.* ESPB

When Robin Hood and Little John. Robin Hood's Death. *Unknown.* ESPB

When Robin Hood in the green-wood livd. Robin Hood Rescuing Will Stutly. *Unknown.* ESPB

When Robin Hood was about eighteen [*or* twenty] years old. Robin Hood and Little John. *Unknown.* ESPB

When Ron and Lisa split up, she took a job. From Now On. James Harms. AmPoNex

When rosy plumelets tuft the larch. Tennyson. FHYEP; NAEL-6v2 *Fr.* In Memoriam A. H. H.

When round the earth the Father's hands. Rest. George Macdonald. SacPr

When rule and era passed away. Herman Melville. APN-2 *Fr.* Clarel: A Poem and Pilgrimage in the Holy Land.

When Russian prose went into the camps. Prosaics. Boris Abramovich Slutsky [*or* Slutskii]. TCRP, *tr. by* J. R. Rowland

When Ruth was left half desolate. Ruth [or, The Influences of Nature]. William Wordsworth. GTBS-P

When Sam goes back in memory. Sam. Walter De la Mare. MoBrPo

When science starts to be interpretive. Self-Protection. D. H. Lawrence. NoP-4

When seasons' images pass out of sight and mind. Friedrich Hölderlin. WoPoe, *tr. by* David Rattray *Fr.* Seasons, The.

When sedentary and when peripatetic. (LL) Bear, The. Robert Frost. MoAmPo; NoAM

When sent to certain death—we sing. Before the Attack. Semyon [*or* Semion] Petrovich Gudzenko. TCRP, *tr. by* Gordon McVay

When serpents bargain for the right to squirm. E. E. Cummings. TwCP

When seven years were come and gane. Sweet William's Ghost. *Unknown.* ESPB

When shall I behold again the cold limbed bare breasted. Return. Archibald MacLeish. APT-1

When shall I see the half-moon sink again. End of Another Home Holiday. D. H. Lawrence. EBEV; FaBoMo; OxAEP-2

When shall I see the white thorn leaves agen. Yellowhammer, The. John Clare. NOBVV

When Shall My Pilgrimage, Jesus My Saviour, Be Ended? Andrew Rudman. AH, *tr. by* Ernest Edwin Ryden

When Shall We All Meet Again? *Unknown.* AH

When shall we be married. *Unknown.* OxNR

When shawes beene sheene, and shrads [*or* shradds] fyll [*or* full] fayre. Robin Hood and Guy of Gisborne. *Unknown.* ESPB

When she and I. Gas Station Attendant. Brian G. Gilmore. SpirFl

When she and I hid. In the Secret House of Night. Jorge Teillier. BLPSL, *tr. by* Rene de Costa, Rigas Kappatos and Eleni Paidoussi

When she approached you on the street. Admonition. Tzu Yeh. CrYelRi, *tr. by* Sam Hamill

When she asked me to keep an eye on her things. Bewley's Oriental Café, Westmoreland Street. Paul Durcan. CIP-2

When she begins to comprehend it. (LL) To a Child of Quality [Five Years Old, the Author Supposed Forty]. Matthew Prior. NOBE; NOEC; OBEV; OxBEV

When she came to visit me, I turned my face to the wall. Pediatrics. Carol Muske. PBCAP

When she cannot be sure. Woman Alone, A. Denise Levertov. BodElec; WPOW

When she died no face turned pale, no lips trembled. Elegy for a Woman of No Importance. Nazik Al-Mala'ika. ItWoWo, *tr. by* Chris Knipp, Mohammed Sadiq and Mohammad Sadiq

When she dreams, she dreams. Mission Poem. Tarin Towers. AmPoNex; PuP-23

When she fed the / child. Feeding, The. Joel Oppenheimer. NeAP

When she is embraced and open to most men. (LL) John Donne. BASC; FSCP; MeLP; NAEL-5v1; NAEL-6v1; NOSC; OxBSo; PeECV; PoE; Son *Fr.* Holy Sonnets.

When She Laughs. Judith Sornberger. HW

When she married years ago. Italian Garden, The. William Carlos Williams. OBGa

When She Plays upon the Harp or Lute. Moses Ibn Ezra. TrJP, *tr. by* Solomon Solis-Cohen

When she rises in the morning. Gloire de Dijon. D. H. Lawrence. EnLoPo; NoAM; PAI

When she showed me her photograph. Marjorie Agosin. TANSG, *tr. by* Celeste Kostopulos-Cooperman

When she snoozes. Lullaby for Suzanne. Michael Stillman. TLR

When she tells him about the lump in her breast. In a Duplex near the San Andreas Fault. Dionisio D. Martinez. NoP-4

When she walks by here. Sonnet. Petrarch. WoPoe, *tr. by* Nicholas Kilmer

When She Was Born. Robert Tofte. Son *Fr.* Laura.

When She Was Here, Li Bo. Peter Williams. InPK-6

When she was little. Poem for Flora. Nikki Giovanni. BPo

When she was tied to the stake. (LL) Lamkin. *Unknown.* ESPB; NPeEn; OxBB

When she was young and dancing. Jane Austen at the Window. Patricia Beer. FaBoWP

When shearing comes, lay down your drums. Whaler's Rhyme. *Unknown.* NOBAu

When Sherman's March was over. Iris. Herman Melville. NCAP

When sickness struck me I had thoughts that. Evening. Khalil Mutran. MAP, *tr. by* Issa Boullata and Thomas G. Ezzy

When Simon received the high idea which, for my sake, put his. Petrarch. NAWM-7v1, *tr. by* Robert M. Durling *Fr.* Sonnets to Laura.

When / Sir / Beelzebub called for his syllabub in the hotel in Hell. Dame Edith Sitwell. BoWoP; FaBoMo; FaBoWP; MoBrPo; NALW; OBCoV; OxBTC *Fr.* Façade.

When Sir [*or* Sr] Joshua Reynolds died. Sir Joshua Reynolds. William Blake. FaBoEE; OxBoLi; PeLV

When Sister sent Joe to the nurse's office. God's Blessing. Len Roberts. BodElec

When skies are gentle, breezes bland. Land, The. Victoria Mary Sackville-West. OBGa

When Skies are Low and Days are Dark. N. M. Bodecker. OTCP

When skies were dark. Great Day. Vincent Youmans. ReLy

When skilful traders first set up. After the Small Pox. Mary Jones. PEW

When slaves their liberties require. Phillis's Resolution. William Walsh. OxBSP

When sleep comes down to seal the weary eyes. (LL) Ere Sleep Comes down to Soothe the Weary Eyes. Paul Laurence Dunbar. APN-2; ColAP; NAAAL

When Slow October Changes Color. Umberto Piersanti. NeIt, *tr. by* Stephen Sartarelli

When smoke stood up from Ludlow. A. E. Housman. MoBrPo; SCGP

When snow like sheep lay in the fold. In Memory of Jane Fraser [*or* Frazer]. Geoffrey Hill. NAEL-5v2; NAEL-6v2; NIL-7; NoAM; OxBTC

When soft Irene like a. Asclepiades. GrAn

When Sol had loosed his weary teams. Juggy's Christening. *Unknown.* NOEC

When some beloved voice that was to you. Substitution. Elizabeth Barrett Browning. SacPr

When some beloveds, 'neath whose eyelids lay. Bereavement. Elizabeth Barrett Browning. SacPr; WPE

When some boys. Some Boys. Chuck Ortleb. GLP

When somebody loves you. All the Way. Sammy Cahn. ReLy

When someone cries, after making love spills. My God, Why Are You Crying? Molly Peacock. PasH

When someone hangs up, having said. Business Life, The. David Ignatow. NNaP

When Something Happens. James A. Randall, Jr. BPo; SSLK

When sorrow and sleep both bind him. *Unknown.* WoPoe, *tr. by* John Updike *Fr.* Wanderer and the Seafarer, The.

When sorrow (using mine own fire's might). Sir Philip Sidney. NAEL-6v1; NAEL-7v1 *Fr.* Astrophil and Stella.

When sorrows had begirt me round. For Deliverance from a Fever. Anne Bradstreet. NAAL-2v1; NAAL-3; NALW

When soul and body feed, one sees. On a Theme from Nicolas of Cusa. Clive Staples Lewis. SacPr

When Spanky goes. Basketball. Nikki Giovanni. NOxBChV

When splendent Sol, which riseth in the East. Rachel Speght. BASC; EMWP; WPE *Fr.* Dream[e], The [*or* A].

When Spoon River became a ganglion. Edgar Lee Masters. NoAM; TAP *Fr.* New Spoon River, The.

When spring doves come I'll make a stew! (LL) Su Tung-p'o (Su Shih). CoBCP; ColAnChi, *tr. by* Burton Watson *Fr.* Eastern Slope.

When spring returns with western gales. Whaling Song, A. John Osborn. TCAPo

When stars are hid in the western wave, dimmed at dawn. Cynewulf. WoPoe, *tr. by* Frank Kuenstler *Fr.* Phoenix, The.

When Statesmen gravely say, "We must be realistic." W. H. Auden. OBCoV *Fr.* Shorts [1939–1947].

When storms arise. Hymn. Paul Laurence Dunbar. SacPr

When storms blow loud, 't is sweet to watch at ease. Lucretius. AWP, *tr. by* W. H. Mallock *Fr.* De Rerum Natura (On the Nature of Things).

When storms swoop down from the far heights. Storm from the Far Heights. Sándor Weöres. IQMS, *tr. by* Adam Makkai and Donald E. Morse

When suddenly I am old, and start to wear purple. (LL) Warning. Jenny Joseph. FaBoWP; OxBTC

When suddenly in the middle of a life arrives a word never before pronounced. Word, A. Alvaro Mutis. TCLAP, *tr. by* Sophie Cabot Black and Maria Negroni

When suddenly, you're hit with good health. Patrizia Cavalli. ItPo

When Sue Wears Red. Langston Hughes. APT-2; NAAAL; TTY

When summer ended. Emplumada. Lorna Dee Cervantes. NoAM; PBCAP

When summer's heat hath done his part. Aestas. Joshua Sylvester. NOSC

When summer smiled, and birds on every spray. Written, Originally Extempore, on Seeing a Mad Heifer Run through the Village. Elizabeth Hands. ECWP

When summoned. Takuchi. JDP, *tr. by* Yoel Hoffmann

When Sun Came to Riverwoman. Leslie Marmon Silko. ReEnLa; VoR

When Sun Doth Rise. Roger Williams. AH

When sun goes home. Taking Turns. Norma Farber. TLR

When Sunday came and old Katis' Katisje's Patchwork Dress. Pauline Smith. PeSAV

When Sunny Gets Blue. Marvin Fisher. ReLy

When supper time is almost come. Milking Time. Elizabeth Madox Roberts. OBCA

When Susan's work was done, she'd [*or* she would] sit. Old Susan. Walter De la Mare. MoBrPo

When Suzy Was. Kelvin Corcoran. Oth

When swallows come I'm sick with wine.   Tune: "Red Embroidered Slippers"—Spring Night.   *Unknown.*   SuSp, *tr. by* Sherwin S. S. Fu

When swallows lay their eggs in snow.   Fool's Song.   Thomas Holcroft.   NOEC

When sweet Echo met Narcissus.   Echo and Narcissus.   Gerda Mayer.   PeLV

When swelling buds their od'rous foliage shed.   John Philips.   OxAEP-1   *Fr.* Cyder.

When swimming and croquet are in full sway, dolor.   Dolor.   Josephine Miles.   FaBoWP

When Sydney and the Bush first met.   Sydney and the Bush.   Les A. Murray.   DiPo

When tenderness.   Silence.   Eugenio de Andrade.   VCWP, *tr. by* Alexis Levitin

When that humble-headed elder, the sea, gave his wide.   End of the Picnic.   Francis Webb.   BMAP; NOBAu

When That I Was and a Little Tiny Boy.   William Shakespeare.   *See* Twelfth Night

When that Master Masons twelve gathered presently.   Wife of Master Mason Clement, The.   *Hungarian Oral Tradition.*   IQMS, *tr. by* Adam Makkai

"When that my sweet son was thirty winter old,"   'O, My Heart Is Woe'   *Unknown.*   ChIV-2

When that repentant tears hath cleansed clear from ill.   Henry Howard, Earl of Surrey.   ChIV-1   *Fr.* Paraphrase of Part of the Book of Ecclesiates, A.

When that shall fade, my verse distills your truth. (LL)   William Shakespeare.   AWP; OBEV; PoE; SCGP   *Fr.* Sonnets.

When that the fields put on their gay attire.   To the Redbreast.   John Codrington Bampfylde.   Son

When that with tragic rapture Moses stood on the edge and ledge.   When That with Tragic Rapture Moses Stood.   Cynthia Ozick.   TaR

When the African Arts.   At Home in Dakar.   Margaret Danner.   BlSi

When the alcoholic passed the crucial point.   Point of No Return.   Robert Graves.   BIrV

When the ancients painted swans and tigers.   On Seeing a Painting of Plants and Insects by Chü-ning.   Mei Yao Ch'en.   SuSp, *tr. by* Jonathan Chaves

When the Assault Was Intended to the City.   John Milton.   GTBS-P; OxBSo; SCGP; Son

(Sonnet.)   OxAEP-1

When the autumn's breezes.   Mr. Edward Fordham.   Mary Weston Fordham.   CBWP-2

When the bad angel loves.   When Bad Angels Love Women.   Julie Moulds.   AmPoNex

When the badger glimmered away.   Badgers, The.   Seamus Heaney.   ModIr

When the bare branch responds to leaf and light.   Spain.   Dorothy Livesay.   NOBC

When the battle was over.   César Vallejo.   RB, *tr. by* Robert Bly   *Fr.* España, Aparta de me Este Caliz.

When the bells justle in the tower.   A. E. Housman.   NOBVV; OxBEV

When the bird of sleep.   Insomnia.   Abu Amir Ibn al-Hammarah.   WoPoe, *tr. by* Cola Franzen

When the birds sang.   *Unknown.*   BoWoP

When the black herds of the rain were grazing.   Lost Heifer, The.   Austin Clarke.   BIrV; ModIr; WoPoe

When the blasts of winter appear[?]. (LL)   William Blake.   FHYEP; FaBoCh; OxAEP-2   *Fr.* Songs of Experience.

When the bleak winds of winter.   Remember the Poor.   Matilda Caroline Edwards.   PWR

When the blind is raised.   Ashikaga Tadayoshi's Palace.   Muso Soseki.   EaWin, *tr. by* W. S. Merwin

When the body becomes Your mirror.   Mahadevi.   WPoS

When the bomb pulverizes our earth.   Bomb of Annihilation, The.   Ilya Abu Madi.   GraLe, *tr. by* George Dimitri Selim

When the bones are no longer curious.   Overture for Bubble-Gum and Flute.   Alistair Paterson.   PeNZ

When the bones walk out of me.   Never.   George Reavey.   BIrV

When the boy's head, full of red torment.   Lice-Seekers.   Arthur Rimbaud.   SxFrPo, *tr. by* Martin Sorrell

When the breath of twilight blows to flame the misty skies.   By the Margin of the Great Deep.   "Æ"   OBEV

When the breeze of a joyful dawn blew free.   Recollections of The Arabian Nights.   Tennyson.   OBGa

When the Bright Consort first stepped out of Han palace.   Song of the Radiant Lady.   Wang An-shih.   SuSp, *tr. by* Jan W. Walls

When the bronze annals of the oak-tree close. (LL)   Advice to a Prophet.   Richard Wilbur.   HarvBoo; MoAmPo; NoP-4; OBWP; OxBC; PoE; TwCP; VCAP

When the buds began to burst.   Three Roses, The.   Walter Savage Landor.   NAEL-5v2; NAEL-6v2

When the burnt flesh is finally at rest.   Annotations of Auschwitz.   Peter Porter.   HP

When the bush warbler.   Shoha.   SoOfWa, *tr. by* Sam Hamill

When the call comes, be calm.   How to Watch Your Brother Die.   Michael Lassell.   CAGL; GLP; WiU

When the Camel Is Dust it Goes through the Needle's Eye.   Anne Stevenson.   Prnts

When the car spun from the road and your neck broke.   Death and the Sun.   Derek Mahon.   BiHa

When the census is taken, of course.   Taking the Census.   Charles Robert Thatcher.   NOBAu

When the census man called upon Gail.   Limerick.   George McWilliam.   PeLi

When the Century Dragged.   Robert Penn Warren.   MoAmPo   *Fr.* Infant Boy at Midcentury.

When the charms of spring awaken, awaken, awaken.   Listen to the Mocking Bird.   Septimus Winner.   TCAPo

When the children are asleep and our old bed.   Hell To Pay.   Susanne Doyle.   FFC

When the chilled dough of his flesh went in an oven.   Tony Harrison.   NAEL-5v2; NAEL-6v2   *Fr.* School of Eloquence, The.

When the city snores in blood-shot eyes.   Rooftop Piper.   David Hernandez.   IllVoic

When the Clapper hits the Bell. (LL)   Belmans Song, A.   Thomas Ravenscroft.   NPeEn; PBRV

When the clapper hits the bell? (LL)   Bellman's Song, The.   *Unknown.*   EBEV; SCGP

When the clouds are upon the hills.   *Unknown.*   OxNR

When the clouds' swoln bosoms echo back the shouts of the many and strong.   Thomas Hardy.   ChIV-1; NoAM; OxBTC   *Fr.* In Tenebris.

When the cock crows.   Lazy Man, The.   *Unknown.*   WoPoe, *tr. by* Ulli Beier and Bakare Gbadamosi

When the cold comes.   Where? When? Which?   Langston Hughes.   BPo

When the cold wind visits you from the corners of the earth.   To Li Po.   Tu Fu.   TAL

When the Corsican Chief, with a view to degrade.   To Buonaparte.   *Unknown.*   NOBRP

When the crickets.   Louis Zukofsky.   APT-2

When the cry goes up.   Sergey [*or* Sergei] Chudakov.   TCRusP, *tr. by* Daniel Weissbort

When the dark is wise to us, what is memory.   Small Hours.   David Barber.   AmPoNex

When the dark months have run out.   Rhyme-Prose on the Snow.   Hsieh Hui-lien.   CoBCP, *tr. by* Burton Watson

When the dawn comes.   *Var. authors.*   AWP   *Fr.* Kokin Shu.

When the day fades away into twilight.   Time on My Hands.   Vincent Youmans.   ReLy

When the daylight came Enkidu got up and cried to Gilgamesh, "O my brother, such a dream I had last night."   *Unknown.*   CAGL, *tr. by* N. K. Sandars   *Fr.* Epic of Gilgamesh, The.

When the Days Shall Grow Long.   Hayyim Nahman [*or* Khayim Nakhman *or* Chaim Nachman] Bialik.   TrJP, *tr. by* A. M. Klein

When the dead man itches, he thinks he has picked up a splinter.   Book of the Dead Man #43, The.   Marvin Bell.   GifTon

When the deep-piled winter snow / melted on her roof.   Antipater of Thessalonica.   GrAn

When the dew is on the grass.   *Unknown.*   OxNR

When the doctor came from Chin-t'an.   Weeping for Hsüeh Tzu-shu.   Liu K'o-chuang.   CoBCP, *tr. by* Burton Watson

When the doctor runs out of words and still.   Body Mutinies, The.   Lucia Maria Perillo.   IllVoic

When the dogstar is aglow.   Garden Calendar.   N. M. Bodecker.   TLR

When the door between the worlds opened.   Red Water.   Dana Levin.   AmPoNex

When the dream departs leaving.   Poem.   Salah Fa'iq.   MAP, *tr. by* Patricia Alanah Byrne and Salma Khadra Jayyusi

When the Dumb Speak.   Robert Bly.   NOBA

When the eager squadrons of day are faint and disbanded.   Cult of the Celtic, The.   Anthony C. Deane.   NOBL; PeLV

When the eagle soared clear through a dawn distilling of emerald.   Crow and the Birds.   Ted Hughes.   HarvBoo

When the earth with spring returning buds again.   To the Nightingale.   Fulbert of Chartres.   MLL, *tr. by* Helen Waddell

When the echo of the last footstep dies.   Song.   Eli W. Mandel.   MoCV

When the enthusiasm / of our time.   Before the Scales, Tomorrow.   Otto René Castillo.   AF, *tr. by* Barbara Paschke

When the Euxine goddess with astonished eyes.   André Marie de Chénier.   WoPoe, *tr. by* Paul Schmidt   *Fr.* Hermes.

When the Eye of Day Is Shut.   A. E. Housman.   NOBVV; NPeEn

When the Fairies.   Edward Dorn.   NeAP

When the Famous Black Poet speaks.   Passing.   Carl Phillips.   PoPoPo

When the far south glittered.   Pilgrimage.   Austin Clarke.   CIP-2

When the feet of the rain tread a dance on the roofs.   Gipsy-Night.   Richard Hughes.   OBWVE

When the female railway clerk. Nissim Ezekiel. OBCoV *Fr.* Poems in the Greek Anthology Mode.

When the fields catch flower. April. Vidame de Chartres. AWP, *tr. by* Algernon Charles Swinburne

When the fierce north wind with his airy forces. Day of Judg[e]ment, The; an Ode. Isaac Watts. ECEV; HAP; NOBE; NOEC; OBEV; OxBEV

When the fifth month comes. Lady Ise. BoWoP

When the fighters slow down, moving towards each other. Late Round. Kim Addonizio. MoASP

When the fires found their way up over the Laguna hills. Good Water. Patty Seyburn. AmPoNex

When the first patches of snow. Execution of Memory, The. Jerzy Ficowski. HP, *tr. by* Keith Bosley

When the Five Prominent Poets. Josephine Jacobsen. TAP

When the flaming lute-thronged angelic door is wide. Travail of Passion, The. W. B. Yeats. TrCP

When the flower droops and the leaf wilts. Lotus. Hsü Wei. SuSp, *tr. by* Irving Y. Lo

When the flowers turn to husks. Cells Breathe in the Emptiness. Galway Kinnell. VGW

When the flush of a new-born sun fell first on Eden's green and gold. Conundrum of the Workshops, The. Rudyard Kipling. MoBrPo

When the Flyin' Scot. Uncle Henry. W. H. Auden. NOBL; PeLV

When the foreman whistled. Field Poem. Gary Soto. PBCAP

When the forests have been destroyed their darkness remains. Asians Dying, The. W. S. Merwin. CoAP; HCAP; NOBA; PoPoPo; VCAP

When the four quarters shall. Jay Macpherson. NOBC *Fr.* Ark, The.

When the French, to their shame. Zaragoza Clubs. SWaP, *tr. by* Luis A. Torres *Fr.* Homenajes de Gratitud.

When the frost is on the punkin and the fodder's in the shock. When the Frost Is on the Punkin. James Whitcomb Riley. APN-2; BRP; ITBLP; OBAL

When the Frosts Cover Them. Rosalía de Castro. SpanPo, *tr. by* Muriel Kittel

When the gardener has gone this garden. In a Garden. Elizabeth Jennings. NOCV

When the gibbons howl one is sure it's dawn. Journeying by Stream: Following Chin-chu Torrent I Cross the Mountains. Hsieh Ling-yün. SuSp, *tr. by* Francis Westbrook

When the god, needing something, decided to become a swan. Leda. Rainer Maria Rilke. RaBo, *tr. by* Robert Bly

When the god of the river. Ovid. WoPoe, *tr. by* Thom Gunn *Fr.* Metamorphoses.

When the Gods Put on Meter. Cal Bedient. BAP-01

When the Grain Is Golden and the Wind Is Chilly, Then It Is the Time to Harvest. Nick Carbó. NeAmPo

When the grass in Yen is still jade thread. Spring Thoughts. Li Po. WoPoe, *tr. by* Elling O. Eide

When the great acacias spread upon the sky. In the Courtyard of the Servants. Ferenc Jankovich. IQMS, *tr. by* Madeline Mason

When the great bell / Booms over the Portland stone urn, and. City. Sir John Betjeman. HarvBoo

When the Great Bird soars. Great Bird, The. Li Po. CrYelRi, *tr. by* Sam Hamill

When the great universe hung nebulous. "Egoisme à Deux." Louisa Sarah Bevington. NOBVV; VWP

When the Greek sea. Sometimes, as a Child. Olga Broumas. YaYoPo

When the green grass rose in the spring. On the Bright Side. Carter Revard. VoR

When the Green Woods Laugh. William Blake. NBLV *Fr.* Songs of Innocence.

When the gunner spoke in his sleep the hut was still. Gunner, The. Francis Webb. BMAP; CBAP

When the half-body dies its frightful death. Resurrection of the Right Side. Muriel Rukeyser. LCAP-2

When the heart bursts into flame. Jelaluddin [*or* Jalal al-Din] Rumi. EaWin, *tr. by* Talat Sait Halman and W. S. Merwin

When the heart's feeling. Song. Thomas Moore. OxBSP

When the Heavenly Jewel reign period was about to end and the Iranian wished to rebel. Iranian Whirling Girls. Yüan Chên. ColAnChi, *tr. by* Victor H. Mair

When the heavens with stars are gleaming. For Who? Mary Weston Fordham. CBWP-2

When the hermit made an end. Tennyson. PeVV *Fr.* Idylls of the King.

When the horny god saw someone. *Unknown.* PriapPo, *tr. by* Richard W. Hooper *Fr.* Priapus Poems, The.

When the horny god was feted. *Unknown.* PriapPo, *tr. by* Richard W. Hooper *Fr.* Priapus Poems, The.

When the hounds of spring are on winter's traces. Algernon Charles Swinburne. AWP; CTC; EBVV; HAP; NAEL-5v2; NAEL-6v2; NOBE; OBEV; OxBEV; PoE; SCGP; TFi; WeW-3 *Fr.* Atalanta in Calydon.

When the hysterical vision strikes. Baroque Exterior. "Ern Malley." BMAP

When the ice fell through, there was plenty of time. Midnight Run. Jonathan Johnson. AmPoNex

When the immutable accidents of birth. God Hunger. Michael Ryan. BodElec

When the iron me mows. Defiant Farewell. Josef Luitpold. AuPH, *tr. by* Lowell A. Bangerter

When the judge with his wife having sport. Limerick. *Unknown.* PeLi

When the king of Yueh returned. Remembering Ancient Days in Yueh. Li Po. CrYelRi, *tr. by* Sam Hamill

When the Kingdom Comes. Jill Alexander Essbaum. NAPBL

When the knight had finished, no one, young or old. Geoffrey Chaucer. NAWM-5v1; NAWM-7v1, *tr. by* Theodore Morrison *Fr.* Canterbury Tales, The.

When the Kye Comes Hame. James Hogg. OxBS

When the lad for longing sighs. A. E. Housman. MoBrPo

When the lamp is shattered [*or* shatter'd]. Lines. Shelley. NAEL-5v2; OBEV; OxBEV

When the land of El Kanesie awakens. Animism. Birago Diop. NegPo, *tr. by* Ellen Conroy Kennedy

When the last bus leaves, moths stream toward lights. Depot in Rapid City. Roberta Hill Whiteman. BoWoP

When the last day comes. Last Day, The. Kevin Hart. BMAP

When the last Flavius, drunk with fury, tore. Juvenal. OBVE *Fr.* Satires.

When the last greyness dwells throughout the air. *Unknown.* EaItPo, *tr. by* Dante Gabriel Rossetti

When the last mine closed. Sinking of Clay City, The. Robert Wrigley. GifTon

When the last newspaper is printed and the ink is faded and dried. Freedom in Peril. "Sagittarius." UV

When the Light Falls. Stanley Kunitz. MoAmPo

When the literary journal. Poet, The. Gerrit Komrij. TuT

When the little blue-bird. Let's Do It, Let's Fall in Love. Cole Porter. OBAL; PeLV; ReLy; UV

When the loneliness of the tomb went down into the marketplace. Mona Sa'udi. WPOW

When the Lord climbed. *Unknown.* MLL

When the Lord fashioned man, the Lord his God. Mother, The. Catulle Mendès. TrJP, *tr. by* W. J. Robertson

When the lover. Vow, The. Galway Kinnell. VCAP

When the M-16 rifle had a stoppage. Guns. Mcavoy Layne. CDa

When the man comes home he takes off his hat. Small Light, A. Cathy Song. TRP

When the man in the window seat. Experts, The. Jack Myers. BodElec

When the master. Hut in Harmony. Muso Soseki. EaWin, *tr. by* W. S. Merwin

When the master sits at ease. Friend Cato. Anna Wickham. MoBrPo

When the Master was calling the roll. Anseo. Paul Muldoon. CIP-2; ModIr; NPeEn; PNI

When the mellow moon begins to beam. Man I Love, The. George Gershwin. ReLy

When the Midnight Choo-Choo Leaves for Alabam' Irving Berlin. ReLy

When the mind is at peace. Layman P'ang. EnlH

When the mists have rolled in splendor. We Shall Know. *Unknown.* PWR

When the monuments to our past. When the Monuments. Funso Aiyejina. NAfrP

When the moon comes up. Moon Rises, The. Federico García Lorca. TTTS, *tr. by* William Bryant Logan

When the Moon is in the River of Heaven. Ou-yang Hsiu. OHPC, *tr. by* Kenneth Rexroth

When the moon's splendour shines in naked heaven. To His Friend in Absence. Walafrid Strabo. CAGL, *tr. by* Helen Waddell

When the moon sails out. Moon Sails Out, The. Federico García Lorca. AmFaPo, *tr. by* Robert Bly

When the moon was full they came to the water. Moon Fishing. Lisel Mueller. CoAP

When the moon wraps the earth in silvery light. Blind Musician, The. 'Ali Mahmud Taha. *tr. by* Issa Boullata and Thomas G. Ezzy

When the morning hymn. Wonder-Teacher, The. Cynthia Ozick. TaR

When the morning was waking over the war. Among Those Killed in the Dawn Raid Was a Man Aged a Hundred. Dylan Thomas. OxBSo; Son

When the mosquito death approaches. (LL) How to Kill. Keith Douglas. FaBoMo; HarvBoo; NOBE; NPeEn; PoWW; RB

When the mouse died at night. Mouse, The. Jean Garrigue. TwCP

When the mouse died, there was a sort of pity. Death of a Whale. John Blight. BMAP; CBAP

When the movie ends and the lights come on, the audience is puzzled. Corpse and Mirror III. John Yau. ReTh

When the movies were 35¢. Imitation of Life. Michael S. Weaver. UnSA

When the müne was shinin' clearly. (LL) Mile an' a Bittock, A. Robert Louis Stevenson. NOBVV; OxBEV

When the neat white. Duck. Valerie Worth. NTCP

When the NEHI Strawberry pop bottle cap. NEHI Strawberry down-and-Away. Luis Lopez. GeoH

When the new teacher said. How the New Teacher Got Her Nickname. Brian Patten. NOxBChV

When the Night and Morning Meet. Dora Greenwell. EBVV

When the night has already turned. At This Juncture. Blanca Wiethüchter. TANSG, tr. by Shaun Griffin and Emma Sepúlveda-Pulvirenti

When the night her visions is weaving. Harp of David, The. "Yehoash." TrJP, tr. by Alter Brody

When the nightegale singes. Unknown. MiEL

When the nightingale in the leaves. Love Song. Jaufré Rudel. NAWM-7v1, tr. by Roy Rosenstein and George Wolf

When the nightingale to his mate. Ezra Pound. APT-1; OBVE; VGW; WeW-3 Fr. Langue d'Oc.

When the Norn Mother saw the Whirlwind Hour. Edwin Markham. MoAmPo

When the old flaming prophet climbed the sky. On a Virtuous Young Gentlewoman That Died Suddenly. William Cartwright. HAP

When the old, long-preserved wine stands at the repast. Five Arabic Verses in Praise of Wine. Unknown. TrJP, tr. by Hartwig Hirschfeld

When the only sound in the empty street. Love for Sale. Cole Porter. ReLy

When the Orient is lit by the great light. Vittoria da Colonna, Marchesa di Pescara. WPOW

When the Osages captured you at the stream. I Will Bring You Twin Grays. Marla Big Boy. ReEnLa

When the ox-horn sounds in the buried hills. Second Psalm: The Signals. W. S. Merwin. GifTon

When the pale moon hides and the wild wind wails. Wolf, The. Georgia Roberts Durston. TLR

When the Parachute Does Not Open. Yevgeny [or Evgenii] Mikhailovich Vinokurov. TCRusP, tr. by Daniel Weissbort

When the peach ripens to a rosy bloom. Morning-Glory, The. Sarah Helen Whitman. ColAP

When the pen that motto drew. (LL) Emily Jane Brontë. NOBVV; NoP-4; PoE

When the People Stand up out of the Hard Cheese. Duo Duo (Li Shizheng). AF, tr. by Gregory Lee Fr. Thoughts and Recollections.

When the pequi fruit blossomed. Mehinaku Girl in Seclusion, A. Cathy Song. OpBo

When the Pilgrims. First Thanksgiving, The. Jack Prelutsky. NTCP

When the pistol muzzle oozing blue vapour. Ted Hughes. UV Fr. Crow.

When the place was green with the shaky grass. Where the Lilies Used to Spring. David Gray. OxBS

When the plunging hoofs were gone. (LL) Listeners, The. Walter De la Mare. AWP; ClHu; HAP; HeIP-4; InPK-6; MoBrPo; NOBE; NOxBChV; NoAM; NoP-4; OBEV; OBMV; OBSP; OxAEP-2; PoRA; SoSe-8; TFi

When the pods went pop on the broom, green broom. Runnable Stag, A. John Davidson. EBNV; HAP; OBEV; OxBTC

When the Portuguese arrived. Portuguese Mistake. Oswald de Andrade. TCLAP, tr. by Flavia Vidal

When the Portuguese came in. Guerillas. Seamus Deane. BiHa

When the power of Han decayed. Lamentation, The. Ts'ai Yen. SuSp, tr. by Yi-T'ung Wang

When the Present has latched its postern behind my tremulous stay. Afterwards. Thomas Hardy. EBEV; GTBS-P; HarvBoo; MoBrPo; NOBE; NoP-4; OxAEP-2; OxBEV; PoPoPo; TFi; TOF; WoPoe

When the priest made his entrance on the altar on the stroke of 10:30. 10:30 A.M. Mass, June 16, 1985. Paul Durcan. BiHa; CIP-2

When the prime mover of my many sighs. To Vittoria Colonna. Michelangelo Buonarroti. AWP, tr. by Henry Wadsworth Longfellow

When the Prince, who was terribly smit. Limerick. Joyce Johnson. PeLi

When the professor tells his class. Dennis Cooper. ReTh; WiU Fr. Some Adventures of John Kennedy Jr.

When the radiant morn of creation broke. Song of the Stars. William Cullen Bryant. TreFP

When the rain an the breeze an the storm an the sun. Quaco Sam. Unknown. FaBoVe

When the rain of God falls down. Rain. Dunya Mikhail. PoArWo, tr. by Nathalie Handal and Samira Kawar

When the Rain Raineth. Unknown. RB

When the rain smell comes with the wind. (LL) Love Poem. Leslie Marmon Silko. UnPo; VoR

When the rains are in season and the wind sets fair. Tune: "Shua Hai-erh" Country Cousin at the Theater. Tu Shan-fu. ColAnChi, tr. by James I. Crump

When the rains began. Prophetess, The. Dorothy Livesay. MoCV

When the rattlesnake bit, I lay. Poisoned Man, The. James Dickey. PAI

When the Red, Red Robin Comes Bob, Bob, Bobbin' Along. Harry Woods. ReLy

When the Regime commanded that books with harmful knowledge. Burning of the Books, The. Bertolt Brecht. PoSu, tr. by John Willeh

When the returning sun begins to smile. James Dance. NOEC Fr. Cricket; an Heroic Poem.

When the rice fields lie fallow. Harmony in the Kingdom. Vietnamese Oral Tradition. CaDao, tr. by John Balaban

When the rich pass proudly by. Poem. Wang Fan-chih. CrYelRi, tr. by Sam Hamill

When the Rooms. Johannes Bobrowski. PoSu, tr. by Matthew Mead and Ruth Mead

When the rooms are deserted. When the Rooms. Johannes Bobrowski. PoSu, tr. by Matthew Mead and Ruth Mead

When the rooster jumps up on the windowsill. Cuba, 1962. Ai. ESEAA

When the ruff [or ruffe] is set elsewhere? (LL) Kisses Loathesome. Robert Herrick. CaPo; OxBSP

When the Sabbath was declining, just at twilight's mystic hour. In Memoriam. Susan Eugenia Bennett. Mary Weston Fordham. CBWP-2

When the sad ruins of that face. Question and Answer, The. Thomas Beedome. NOSC

When the Saints Go Marchin' [or Marching] In. Unknown. TCAPo

When the sea is as grey as her eyes. Soft White. Lee Harwood. SPE

When the Second World War began. Charles Reznikoff. HP Fr. Holocaust.

When the Secretary gave up his office. Mountain Residence of Secretary Cheng Ching-ssu, The. Hsü Pen. CoBLCP, tr. by Jonathan Chaves

When the Seed of Thy Word Is Cast. Cotton Mather. AH

When the Septentrion of the First Heaven. Dante Alighieri. NAWM-5v1 Fr. Divina Commedia.

When the Sex War ended with the slaughter of the Grandmothers. Song. W. H. Auden. PeLV

When the shade threatened with the fatal decree. Stéphane Mallarmé. SxFrPo, tr. by E. H. Blackmore and A. M. Blackmore

When the sheen on tall summer grass is pale. Gazelles, The. Thomas Sturge Moore. OBMV

When the sheep are in the fauld, and the kye [or cows] at hame. Auld Robin Gray. Lady Anne Lindsay. ECWP; GTBS-P; LW; NOEC; OBEV; OxBEV; PeSAV; WPE

When the shimmer of the moonlight now descends. Summer Night, The. Friedrich Gottlieb Klopstock. GePo, tr. by George C. Schoolfield

When the shoals of plankton. Shooting Whales. Mark Strand. ColAP

When the shoe strings break. Blues, The. Langston Hughes. TLR

When the sky darkens. Veils of Prayer. Ralph Angel. BodElec

When the snake bit. Snake. Dannie Abse. NoAM

When the snow falls near the panes. Winter Evening, A. Georg Trakl. AuPH, tr. by Lowell A. Bangerter

When the snow falls the flakes. Dance, The. William Carlos Williams. NAAL-2v2; NAAL-5

When the Snow is on the Ground. Unknown. ReMoGo

When the soul sought refuge in the place of rest. Self-Discipline. "Æ" MoBrPo

When the southeastern wall was first put in. Paintings on My Wall Have Been Damaged by the Weather, The. T'ang Hsien-tsu. CoBLCP, tr. by Jonathan Chaves

When the spent sun throws up its rays on cloud. Acceptance. Robert Frost. GSo; OxBA

When the spider dropped down from the ceiling. Grandmother Came down to Visit Us, The. Joseph Bruchac. CDW

When the stern god. Mythic Fragment. Louise Glück. NoAM

When the stone fall that morning out of the johncrow sky. Stone. Edward Kamau Brathwaite. PFTM-2; WaCA

When the storm passed away. Room for All. Timothy Holmes. PeSAV

When the storm thickens, when the combat burns. Anna Laetitia Barbauld. ECWP Fr. Corsica.

When the storms of life are raging. Stand by Me. Charles A. Tindley. InvLi; NAAAL

"When the Students Resisted, a Minor Clash Ensued." David Knight. MoCV

When the sultry air is ripped by a wind. Hope for a Miracle. György Sárközi. IQMS, tr. by Roy Fuller

When the Summer fields are mown. Aftermath. Henry Wadsworth Longfellow. APN-1; NAAL-2v1; NAAL-3; NOBA; PoPoPo; TAP

When the Sun Comes Out. Ted Koehler. ReLy

When the sun comes up we work. Ground-Thumping Song. Unknown. CoBCP; ColAnChi, tr. by Burton Watson

When the sun decides. You Stand There Fishing. Angie Estes. GeoHom

When the sun is high in the afternoon sky. In the Wee Small Hours of the Morning. Bob Hilliard. ReLy

When the sun is hot, it is burning. Drought. J.G. Mocoancoeng. WoPoe, tr. by Philip Bryant and Mongane Wally Serote

When the sun rose I was still lying in bed. Hearing the Early Oriole. Po Chü-i. ChiP, *tr.* by Arthur Waley

When the sun routinely sets. Waning August Moon. Roberta Hill. ReEnLa

When the sun's whiteness closes around us. Map, The. Gary Soto. NoAM

When the sun sets, the sky is inky dark. Elegy for Myself. Ki Joon. GifTon, *tr.* by Sung-Il Lee

When the Sun Shines More Years Than Fear. Janet Frame. PeNZ

When the sun shouts and people abound. Summer Holiday. Robinson Jeffers. MoAmPo; OxBA

When the sun shuts down her cantina. Dry World. Dieter Weslowski. InvLad

When the sun strikes a tall dead tree. Baalbeck. Nadia Tuéni. PoArWo

When the sun was a child's breath above the Earth. D. Jeffrey McDaniel. NeAmPo

When the Sun Went Down. John Ashbery. NAAL-2v2

When the swans turned my sister into a swan. Black Swan, The. Randall Jarrell. PoE

When the swift-rolling brook, swollen deep. Storm-Wind, The. William Barnes. NOBE

When the son of sixty comes nigh his head. Firdowsi. OBVE; WoPoe, *tr.* by Basil Bunting

When the swordsman fell in Kurosawa's *Seven Samurai*. Heroic Simile. Robert Hass. VCAP

When the synchrotron was being built. Almagest, Last Letter to Zakarias. Siv Cedering Fox. PBCAP

When the tea is brought at five o'clock. Milk for the Cat. Harold Monro. MoBrPo; OBMV

When the third summer freed us from restraint. William Wordsworth. NAEL-6v2 *Fr.* Prelude, The; Growth of a Poet's Mind [1850 vers.]

When the throb of her voice was cut off, I drove. On Re-recording Mozart. Susan Wicks. OxBSo

When the tide smothers you. On Saying Goodbye to the Lady in Green. 'Ali 'Abdallah Khalifa. MAP, *tr.* by Alistair Elliot and Lena Jayyusi

When the Tom-Tom Beats. Jacques Roumain. NegPo, *tr.* by Langston Hughes

When the towered galleys of Wang Chün came down from Yi-chou. Sorrowing for the Past at Western Pass Mountain. Liu Yu Hsi. SuSp, *tr.* by Daniel Bryant

When the train came shrieking down. What the Train Ran Over. Lucy Larcom. SWaP

When the Tree Bares. Conrad Potter Aiken. MoAmPo

When the Troops Were Returning from Milan. Niccolò degli Albizzi. *See* Prolonged Sonnet

When the trumpet blared everything. United Fruit Co. Pablo Neruda. TCLAP, *tr.* by Jack Schmitt

When the turuf [*or* turf] is thy tour [*or* tower]. Grave, The. *Unknown.* MiEL

When the tyrant is young. Everyone waits. Paavo Haavikko. WoPoe, *tr.* by Anselm Hollo *Fr.* Fifteen Epigrams in Praise of the Tyrant.

When the universe goes up in flame. Lament for the Willows outside the City Walls, A. Yün Shou-p'ing. CoBLCP, *tr.* by Jonathan Chaves

When the verdict / was read. After the Verdict. Tony Medina. SpirFl

When the village daylight dimmed. Oleg Grigorevich Chukhonstev. TCRP

When the voices of children are heard on the green. William Blake. AWP; FHYEP; NAEL-5v2; NAEL-6v2; PeLV; RACG; SCGP *Fr.* Songs of Innocence.

When the voices of children are heard on the green / And whisperings [*or* whisprings] are in the dale. William Blake. FHYEP *Fr.* Songs of Experience.

When the wafer dissolves on my tongue, won-. Devolution. Molly Peacock. FFC

When the wall between her and ghost. Family Conference. John Montague. ModIr

When the War Is Over. W. S. Merwin. OxBSP

When the warl's couped soon' as a peerie. Moonstruck. Hugh MacDiarmid. NAEL-5v2; NAEL-6v2

When the warm zummer breeze do blow over the hill. Shep'erd Bwoy, The. William Barnes. EBVV

When the water fell. Flooded Mind. Norman MacCaig. OxBC

When the water's calm. Song. *Unknown.* STP, *tr.* by Jerome Rothenberg

When the weather suits you not. Try Smiling. *Unknown.* PWR

When the white flame in us is gone. Dust. Rupert Brooke. MoBrPo; OxBTC

When the white flame of verses. Garden of Theophrastus, The. Peter Huchel. AF, *tr.* by Daniel Simko

When the white waters fill the spring embankments. Wild Geese on the Lake. Shen Yüeh. SuSp, *tr.* by Richard B. Mather

When the white wave of a glory that is hardly I. Sinfonia Domestica. Jean Starr Untermeyer. MoAmPo

When the whole city is asleep. Tryst. Sunanda Tripathy. OMIP, *tr.* by Jagannath Prasad Das

"When the Wild Goose Finds Food He Calls His Comrades"—*I Ching*. Jan Kemp. PeNZ

When the wild turnip. Issa. SoOfWa, *tr.* by Sam Hamill

When the wind. Michel Deguy. BBASP, *tr.* by Clayton Eshelman and Clayton Eshleman

When the Wind and Dark Waves Come. David J. Rothman. GeoH

When the wind blows. *Unknown.* OxNR

When the wind invades the treetops. Urban Gallery. Rachel Wetzsteon. AmPoNex; NeAmPo

When the wind is asleep and the weather set fair. *Unknown.* ASW *Fr.* Phoenix, The.

When the wind is in the east. Mother Goose. FaBoVe; LB; OxNR

When the wind works against us in the dark. Storm Fear. Robert Frost. APT-1; ColAP; OxBA; TCAPo

When the winter chrysanthemums go. Basho. EH, *tr.* by Robert Hass

When the wintry winds are blowing. California, Here I Come. Joseph Meyer. ReLy

When the Wise Woman wears the crown. Let Wisdom Wear the Crown: Hymn for Gaia. Elsa Gidlow. HW

When the words rustle no more. Stillness. James Elroy Flecker. MoBrPo

When the world ends. Dance, The. Cornelius Eady. GT

When the world ends. Transformable Prophecy. Angela Jackson. IllVoic

When the world finally ends. Baseball. Paul Hoover. MoASP

When the World Is Burning. Ebenezer Jones. OBEV

When the world's folk, one day of freedom. Labourer, The. Iolo Goch. OBWVE, *tr.* by Gwyn Williams

When the world takes over for us. Lear. William Carlos Williams. NAAL-2v2; NAAL-5; NOBA

When the world turns completely upside down. Elinor Wylie. FaBoWP; NAAL-2v2; NALW; OxBA; WPE

"When the World Was in Building." Ford Madox Ford. CTC

When the yellow bird's note was almost stopped. Rejoicing at the Arrival of Chi'en Hsiung. Po Chü-i. AWP, *tr.* by Arthur Waley

When the young brown-haired. Camps, The. Hayden Carruth. GifTon

When the young girls rolled into one. Patriot's Day. Steve Hassett. CDa

When the young have grown tired. For Thomas Moore. James Simmons. BiHa; PBCIP

When Thee (O holy sacrificed Lamb). To the Blessed Sacrament. Henry Constable. NoSic

When their eyes opened, it was more than morning. Making Camp. David Wagoner. VCAP

When their lordships asked Bacon. Edmund Clerihew Bentley. OBCoV *Fr.* Clerihews.

When there are so many we shall have to mourn. In Memory of Sigmund Freud. W. H. Auden. HAP; NoAM; OxBA

When there comes a flower to the stingless nettle. Blue Jacket, The. Marion Angus. NePenScot

When there is no more life. Triage. Larissa Szporluk. NeAmPo

When there is too much to say. Silent as Roses. Gillian Ferguson. NeBl

When there's a hint of spring, and the first crocus. Why Is This Night Different from All Other Nights? Nadine Brummer. Prnts

When there's no one about in the Quad. (LL) Idealism. Ronald Arbuthnott Knox. NBLV; OxBEV

When these graven lines you see. Happy Man, A. Carphyllides. AWP, *tr.* by E. A. Robinson

When these graven lines you see. *Var. authors.* AWP *Fr.* Variations of Greek Themes.

When they are half-undressed. (LL) Saginaw Song, The. Theodore Roethke. NBLV; RB

When they ask us to visualize. In Dreams. Patricia Pogson. NLP

When they bare the iron hand. (LL) Martyr, The. Herman Melville. CBCWP; ColAP; NCAP; TAP; TCAPo

When they begin the beguine. Begin the Beguine. Cole Porter. ReLy

When they bowed. Understanding the *Ramayana*. Sujata Bhatt. HarvBoo

When they brought us a pear jacket. Yury [*or* Iurii] Osipovich Dombrovsky [*or* Dombrovskii]. TCRP

When they brought you down. For Harper, Killed in Action. Walter McDonald. CDa

When they came to that blue harbour. Home. Vincent O'Sullivan. PeNZ

When they came to the tomb. Third Day, The. Phillis Levin. BBASP

When they cast our words. Intellectual, The. Yury [*or* Iurii] Timofeievich Galanskov. TCRusP, *tr.* by Olive Dehn

When They Come Alive. Constantine P. Cavafy. CAGL, *tr.* by Edmund Keeley and Philip Sherrard

When they confess that they have lost the penial bone. God Bless America. John Fuller. OBSV; PeLV

When they cry: / "Man overboard." Sergey [*or* Sergei] Chudakov. TCRP

When they entered through the back door. Morning They Shot Tony Lopez, Barber and Pusher Who Went Too Far, 1958, The. Gary Soto. PBCAP

When they finally found us. At Muktinath. Chitra Divakaruni. FSt

When they go to death—they are singing. Before the Attack. Semyon [or Semion] Petrovich Gudzenko. TCRusP, tr. by Denis Johnson and Shirley Rihner

When they grab my leg. First Problem. Aimé Césaire. NegPo, tr. by Ellen Conroy Kennedy

When they had won the war. Inner Part, The. Louis Simpson. RaBo

When they have eyes for me it's like Heaven. (LL) Malest Cornifici Tuo Catullo. Allen Ginsberg. BB; NeAP

When They Have Lost. Cecil Day Lewis. MoBrPo

When they hear. Children's Children. Sterling Allen Brown. APT-2

When they in throngs a safe retirement seek. William Diaper. OBVE Fr. Halieutica.

When they kiss. Former Love, a Lover of Form, A. Carol Muske. BodElec

When They Know. Ruth L. Schwartz. AmPoNex

When they mourn you over there. Tell Me about It. Ruth Padel. MFPA

When they moved into the house it was winter. Gardener. Dom Moraes. OBGa

When they needed a foreign part. Partial Accounts. William Meredith. GLP

When they plow their fields. Patacara. WPoS

When they ran over her. Passing Remark. Tawfiq Zayyad. MAP, tr. by Charles Doria and Sharif Elmusa

When they're done kicking, their hair is a mess! (LL) On the Cold Food Festival, Entertaining at the Southern Estate—the Guests Were Li Chiu-ho, Ma Nan-yeh, Wei Tung-kao, Li Hu-ch'uan, Huang K'ung-ts'un, Li Lung-t'ang, and Hu Hu-shan. Li K'ai-hsien. CoBLCP; ColAnChi, tr. by Jonathan Chaves

When they removed the bandages. Judgment. Eleanor Wilner. ExTi

When They Robbed Me of My Name. Nora Strejilevich. MirDau, tr. by Celeste Kostopulos-Cooperman

When they said Carrickfergus I could hear. Singer's House, The. Seamus Heaney. EBEV

When they said the time to hide was mine. Rabbit, The. Elizabeth Madox Roberts. OBCA; OxIBACP

When they sailed out of Amsterdam. Flying Dutchman, The. Ian D. Colvin. PeSAV

When they saw off Dai Evan's da. Kingsley Amis. NOBL Fr. Evans Country, The.

When they say Don't I know you? Art of Disappearing, The. Naomi Shihab Nye. LoL

When they say to me: "Alexandria." Mikhail Alekseievich Kuzmin. TCRP

When they sent the robot camera down. Robot Camera. Robert Johnstone. PNI

When they shot you. For F. M. Who Did Not Get Killed Yesterday on 57th Street. Malena Mörling. AmPoNex

When they smile and they smile. Yoruba Love. Molara Ogundipe-Leslie. HAWP

When / they speak of my death. Notes for a Poem from the Middle Passage of Years. Lamont B. Steptoe. SpirFl

When they stop poems. Today Is a Day of Great Joy. Víctor Hernández Cruz. LoL; PueRic; TTY

When they stop / they, suddenly, / are gravel. (LL) Ringed Plover by a Water's Edge. Norman MacCaig. NoP-4; OxBC

When They Told Me I Felt the Cold. Gustavo Adolfo Bécquer. SpanPo, tr. by Doreen Bell

When they took us to the shower I saw. Death Camp. Irena Klepfisz. GLP; TaR

When they use elbow or arm boards to. Louis Zukofsky. APSN Fr. A.

When they were wild. Birth. Louise Erdrich. NoP-4

When they woke me. Coming Back. Joseph Bruchac. CDW

When Thickly Beat the Storms of Life. Gurdon Robins. AH

When thin-strewn memory I look through. Miss Loo. Walter De la Mare. OxBTC

When things go wrong it's rather tame. Blame the Vicar. Sir John Betjeman. SacPr

When thirty spokes join the wheel-hole. Lao Tzu. WoPoe, tr. by Moss Roberts Fr. Tao Te Ching.

When this crystal shall present. To a Lady Upon a Looking-Glass Sent. James Shirley. BeJo

When this fly lived, she used to play. Fly That Flew into My Mistress'[s] Eye, A. Thomas Carew. CaPo

When, this incredible thing, the principal of the junior high. Women Who Cook. Anita Skeen. GLP

When this is the thing you put on. Armor. James Dickey. CoAP

When this man, Manes, lived, he was a slave. Anyte [or Anytes]. See Alive, this man was Manes, a common slave

When this world began. Somebody Loves Me. Ballard MacDonald. ReLy

When this yokel comes maundering. Plot against the Giant, The. Wallace Stevens. OxBA; SAmP

When those renowned noble peers of Greece. Edmund Spenser. PoE Fr. Amoretti.

When thou and I are dead, my dear. Inseparable. Philip Bourke Marston. BoLoP

When thou art dead, and all thy wretched crew? (LL) Written on the Day That Mr. Leigh Hunt Left Prison. John Keats. CenSon; Son

When thou art done thy toil, anew art born. Settler, The. Jones Very. SacPr

When thou art old there's grief enough for thee. (LL) Robert Greene. NoSic; OxAEP-1 Fr. Menaphon.

When thou dost take this sacred book into thy hand. On the Bible. Thomas Traherne. ChIV-1

When thou hast spent the ling[e]ring day in pleasure and delight. Gascoigne's [or Gascoygnes] Good-Night. George Gascoigne. NOCV; NoSic

When thou must home to shades of underground [or under ground]. When Thou Must Home. Propertius. AWP; CABP; EnLoPo; NPeEn; NoSic; OxAEP-1; OxBEV; OxBSP; PoRA; WoPoe, tr. by Thomas Campion

When thou, poor[e] excommunicate. To My Inconstant Mistress [or Mistris]. Thomas Carew. BeJo; EnLoPo; MeLP; NOBE; TFi

When thou shalt be dispos'd to set me light. William Shakespeare. OxAEP-1 Fr. Sonnets.

When thou taught'st Cambridge, and King Edward Greek. (LL) On the Detraction Which Followed upon My Writing Certain Treatises. John Milton. OxBSo; PoE; Son

When thou the choice of Nature's wealth hast scanned. To Sir John Wentworth, Upon His Curiosities and Courteous Entertainment at Summerly in Lovingland. Mildmay Fane, 2d Earl of Westmorland. OBGa

When thou thy youth shalt view. To Phryne. Owen Felltham [or Feltham]. NOSC

When thou to my true-love [or true love] com'st. Westphalian Song. Unknown. AWP; OBVE, tr. by Samuel Taylor Coleridge

WHEN Thraso meets his friend, he swears by God. Thraso. Samuel Rowlands. NoSic

When through the North a fire shall rush. Day of Judgement. Henry Vaughan. ChIV-2

When thy beauty appears. Song. Thomas Parnell. OBEV; OxAEP-1

When thy bright beams, my Lord, do strike mine eye. Edward Taylor. NAAL-2v1; NAAL-3; NAAL-5; TCAPo Fr. Preparatory Meditations before My Approach to the Lord's Supper.

When Thy Heart with Joy O'erflowing. Theodore Chickering Williams. AH

When time has made you wrinkled, sore and slow. Long Way after Ronsard, A. James Simmons. PBCIP

When time—irreversible—begins to doze. Patrizia Vicinelli. ItPo, tr. by Gayle Ridinger

When to Her Lute Corinna [or Corrina] Sings. Thomas Campion. NAEL-5v1; NAEL-7v1; NoP-4; NoSic; PoE

When to Love's influence woman yields. Elizabeth Trefusis. LW Fr. Valentine, A.

When, to my deadly [or deadlie] pleasure. Sir Philip Sidney. EnLoPo; NPeEn

When to my eyes. Midnight. Henry Vaughan. ChIV-2; ESCV

When to my House you come dear Dean. Tom Punsibi's Letter to Dean Swift. Thomas Sheridan. NPeEn

When to my lone soft bed at eve returning. Povre Ame Amoureuse. Louise Labé. AWP, tr. by Robert Bridges

When to Slap a Woman. Paul Violi. PmAP

When to the common rest that crowns our days. Ages, The. William Cullen Bryant. APN-1

When to the music of Byrd or Tallis. King's College Chapel. Charles Causley. PeECV; TOF

"When to the sessions of sweet silent thought." William Shakespeare. See Sonnets

When to thy haunts two kindred spirits flee. (LL) O Solitude! If I Must with Thee Dwell. John Keats. AmFaPo; CenSon

When Tom and Elizabeth took the farm. Magpies, The. Denis Glover. PeNZ

When Tomorrow Is Too Long. Tanure Ojaide. HBAPE

When Torrid Rhymes with Forehead. Ray DiPalma. FTOS

When, towards morning, faces. New Year's Letter in Warsaw, A. Andrey [or Andrei] Andreievich Voznesensky [or Voznesenskii]. TCRusP, tr. by Daniel Weissbort

When trembling voice brings forth that I do Stella love. (LL) Sir Philip Sidney. NAEL-5v1; NAEL-6v1; NAEL-7v1; NoSic; Son Fr. Astrophil and Stella.

When trouble comes your soul to try. Friend Who Just Stands By, The. Bertye Young Williams. PoToHe

When troubles get me. Touch of Your Lips, The. Ray Noble. ReLy

When trout swim down Great Ormond Street. Conrad Potter Aiken. NOBA; NoAM Fr. Priapus and the Pool.

When true lovers meet in Mayfair, so the legends tell. Nightingale Sang in Berkeley Square, A. Manning Sherwin. ReLy

When Two Are Parted. Heinrich Heine. AWP, tr. by Louis Untermeyer

When two Evangelists shall seem to vary. On The Gospel. Francis Quarles. ChIV-2

When two lovers love each other well. Young Bearwell. *Unknown.* ESPB

When two plates of earth scrape along each other. Quake Theory. Sharon Olds. PBCAP

When two strong men stand face to face, though they come from the ends of the earth! (LL) Ballad of East and West, The. Rudyard Kipling. EBNV; OBNV

When two who love are parted. When Two Are Parted. Heinrich Heine. AWP, *tr. by* Louis Untermeyer

When twofold silence was the song of love. (LL) Dante Gabriel Rossetti. GSo; HAP; NAEL-5v2; NAEL-6v2; NoP-4 *Fr.* House of Life, The.

When tyrants' crests and tombs of brass are spent. (LL) William Shakespeare. AWP; CTC; EBEV; HAP; NAEL-5v1; NAEL-6v1; NAEL-7v1; NoSic; OxAEP-1; SCGP *Fr.* Sonnets.

When Ulysses braved the wine-dark sea. Making the Move. Paul Muldoon. NoAM

When unborn, my mother minced. Raw Fish and Vegetables. Shinkichi Takahashi. ZenPo, *tr. by* Takashi Ikemoto and Lucien Stryk

When vain desire at last and vain regret. Dante Gabriel Rossetti. GSo; NAEL-5v2; NAEL-6v2 *Fr.* House of Life, The.

When Venus first did see. Adonis. *Unknown.* NPeEn; NoSic, *tr. by* Theocritus

When Venus her Adonis found. Death of Adonis, The. Theocritus. NPeEn; OBVE *tr. by* Philip Ayres

When Vice triumphant holds her sov'reign sway. Byron. FHYEP *Fr.* English Bards and Scotch Reviewers.

When vile men jeer because my skin is brown. Colour Bar. Oodgeroo of the tribe Noonuccal (Kath Walker). IBA

When Vulcan forged the bolts of Jove. Origins of Naval Artillery. Thomas Dibdin. FaBoWar

When war's red banner trailed along the sky. Robert G. Shaw. Henrietta Cordelia Ray. BlSi; CBWP-3; Son

When / Water forgets. Fire. Fazil Hüsnü Daglarca. CRP

When waves invade the yellowing wheat. Composed While under Arrest. Mikhail Yuryevich Lermontov. AWP, *tr. by* Max Eastman

When We Are Apart. Yuan Chen. CrYelRi, *tr. by* Sam Hamill

When we are dead, and now no more. To My Ingenuous Friend, R. W. Henry Vaughan. BeJo

When we are dead, some Hunting-boy will pass. Statue, The. Joseph Hilaire Pierre Belloc. OxAEP-2

When we are old and these rejoicing veins. Edna St. Vincent Millay. VGW

When we are shadows watching over shadows. Two Shadows. Elizabeth Spires. DiPo

When we as strangers sought. At an Inn. Thomas Hardy. NOBVV

When we assemble here to worship God. Walk Softly. *Unknown.* TCAPo

When we came down from the country, we were strangers to the sea. Down from the Country. John Blight. BMAP; CBAP

When We Cannot Sleep. George Wither. SacPr

When we carried you, Siân, that winter day. Burial Path. Ruth Bidgood. AngWePo

When we caught lice in third grade. Squaring the Names. Diana García. TouFir

When we climbed the slopes of the cutting. Railway Children, The. Seamus Heaney. OPOU

When we come to that dark house. Dame Edith Sitwell. OBMV *Fr.* Sleeping Beauty, The.

When we could have met. The elder daughter of Lady Otomo no Sakanoé. ArkPo, *tr. by* Edwin A. Cranston

When we decided on the Japanese. Choose Your Garden. Erin Belieu. ExTi

When we do trace out nature's laws. James McIntyre. VerBaPo *Fr.* Potato Bug Exterminators.

When we drove up to the curb the woman. On Earth. Olga Broumas. BodElec

When we entered the bazaars. Fall, The. Malak' Abd Al-Aziz. HAWP, *tr. by* Pamela Vittorio

When we fell apart in the Badlands and lay still. In the Badlands. David Wagoner. UnPo

When we first met and loved, I did not build. Elizabeth Barrett Browning. CenSon *Fr.* Sonnets from the Portuguese.

When we [first] moved here, pulled. Oregon Message, An. William Stafford. CoAP

When we first rade down Ettrick. Ettrick. Lady John Scott. LW; SoSe-8; WPE

When we for age could neither read nor write. Edmund Waller. BASC; BeJo; EBEV; HAP; NOSC; NPeEn; NoP-4; OxBEV; PeECV; PoPoPo; SCGP; SacPr

When we fought the Yankees and annihilation was near. Jubilation T. Compone. Johnny Mercer. OBAL; OBCoV

When we found your father's *Playboys.* First Sex. Richard Tayson. WiU

When we fuck, stars don't peer down: they can't. Housebound. Amy Gerstler. ExTi

When we go out into the fields of learning. Fields of Learning. Josephine Miles. NoAM

When we go to the temple, let's see Aphrodite's. Nossis. SaLy, *tr. by* Diane Rayor

When we have come this long way. Anniversary Poem for the Cheyennes Who Fell at Sand Creek. Lance Henson. VoR

When we heard of a lady who. Serenades in Virginia. Andrew Hudgins. CBCWP

When we in kind embracements had agre'd [agreed]. *Unknown.* Son *Fr.* Zepheria.

When we know we are on the way out. Only with Radiance. Margit Szécsi. IQMS, *tr. by* Kenneth McRobbie

When we launched life. You Tell Us What to Do. Faiz Ahmad Faiz. PoetW; VCWP, *tr. by* Agha Shahid Ali

When we learn. It Is the Season. Josephine Jacobsen. TAP

When We'll Worship Jesus. Imamu Amiri Baraka. APSN

When We Look Up. Denise Levertov. TaR *Fr.* During the Eichmann Trial.

When We Meet Again. Giovanna Pollarolo. TANSG, *tr. by* Marjorie Agosin

When we met first and loved, I did not build. Elizabeth Barrett Browning. CenSon *Fr.* Sonnets from the Portuguese.

When we, my love, are gone to dust. Song of Dust, A. John Byrne Leicester Warren, 3d Baron De Tabley. EnLoPo

When we parted with you at Geneve. "Eliza." ECWP *Fr.* Tour to the Glaciers of Savoy, A.

When we reach the field. Celebration: Birth of a Colt. Linda Hogan. HATNAP

When we rested between marches, I read Aristophanes. Virgin Warrior, The. Gwendolyn MacEwen. FaBoWP

When we return to Russia . . . . Georgy [*or* Georgii Viktorovich] Adamovich. TCRP

When we saw human dignity. Easter 1984. Les A. Murray. ChIV-2

When we shuddered and took into ourselves. Whole Story, The. William Stafford. NNaP

When we sigh about our trouble. Good Medicine. *Unknown.* PWR

When we speak of freedom. On the Way Back. Bogomil Gjuzel. CarOv, *tr. by* Carolyn Kizer

When we speak to each other our voices are a little gruff. (LL) Gwendolyn Brooks. ESEAA; VGW *Fr.* Womanhood, The.

When we stand on the tops of Things. Emily Dickinson. PoE

When we start breaking up in the wet darkness. Consolations of Philosophy. Derek Mahon. BIrV; CIP-2; HarvBoo

When we swept through farmer Nguyen's hamlet. Farmer Nguyen. William Daniel Ehrhart. CDa

When We That Now Ha' Childern Wer Childern. William Barnes. NOBVV

When we took my mother. Remission. Katherine Frost. Prnts

When We Two Parted. Byron. BoLoP; FHYEP; GTBS-P; NAEL-5v2; NAEL-6v2; NOBE; NoP-4; OBEV; PoPoPo; SCGP; TFi; UV

When We Two Parted. John C. Desmond. UV

When we were by ourselves. Mewl. Zulaykha Abu-Risha. PoArWo, *tr. by* Clarissa C. Burt

When we were charming *Backfisch.* Friendship. Katherine Mansfield. PoBW

When We Were Children. Alexander the Wild. WoPoe, *tr. by* David Ferry

When we were children old Nurse used to say. Quiet House, The. Charlotte Mew. BrRo; EBEV; HarvBoo; NALW; NPeEn

When we were farm-boys, years ago. Recollections of "Lalla Rookh." John Townsend Trowbridge. APN-2; OBAL

When we were idlers with the loitering rills. To a Friend. Hartley Coleridge. CenSon

When we were in trouble. My Dad. Beryl Philp-Carmichael (Yungha-Dhu). IBA

When we were silly sisters seven. Fair Mary of Wallington. *Unknown.* ESPB

When we were small, folks taught us these precepts. Breaking the Precepts. Yasin Taha Hafiz. MAP, *tr. by* Sharif Elmusa and Christopher Middleton

When We Were Very Silly. John Bingham Morton.
   Hush, Hush. UV
   Someone Asked the Publisher. UV

When we were young and immortal. Communal Living. Alice Jones. BloBone

When we were young we'd lie outside at night. Lunar Eclipse. Tracy Ryan. NeBl

When we would reach the anguish of the dead. Near an Old Prison. Frances Darwin Cornford. OBMV

When we weary with the long day's care. To Imagination. Emily Jane Brontë. VWP

When well we speak, & nothing do that's good. Chewing [of] the Cud, The. Robert Herrick. ChIV-1

When wert thou born, Desire? Of the Birth and Bringing up of Desire. Edward de Vere, 17th Earl of Oxford. FaBoEE; NoSic; SCGP

When Westwall Downes [or Westwell Downs] I gan to tread. On Westwall Downes [or On Westwell Downs]. William Strode. NOSC; NPeEn

When, when, and whenever death closes our eyelids. Ezra Pound. APT-1; NPeEn; OBMV   *Fr.* Homage to Sextus Propertius.

When whispering strains do softly steal. In Commendation of Music. William Strode. OBEV

When white dew descends on the hundred grasses. Han Yü. CoBCP *Fr.* Autumn Thoughts.

When, wild and high, the uproar swells. Cornelius Mathews. APN-1 *Fr.* Poems on Man in His Various Aspects under the American Republic.

When Wild Confusion Wrecks the Air. Mather Byles. AH

When will I be home? I don't Know. When Will I Be Home? Li Shang-yin. OHMPC, *tr. by* Kenneth Rexroth

When will men again. Leaping Laughers, The. George Barker. OBMV

When will my May come, that I may embrace thee? Richard Barnfield [or Barnefield]. CAGL *Fr.* Affectionate Shepherd [or Shephearde], The.

When will the bell ring, and end this weariness? Last Lesson of the Afternoon. D. H. Lawrence. NoAM

When will the flowers grow there? I cannot tell. No Help. Sarah Morgan Bryan Piatt. NCAP

When will ye think of me, my friends? Parting Song, A. Felicia Dorothea Hemans. VWP

When will you ever finish using words? Job 18, 2. José Emilio Pacheco. TCLAP, *tr. by* Alastair Reid

When will you ever, Peace, wild wooddove, shy wings shut. Peace. Gerard Manley Hopkins. GTBS-P; OxBSP; TrCP

"When will you marry me, William." West-Country Damosel's Complaint, The. *Unknown.* ESPB

When Willie Mae went down to the barber shop. Choosing the Blues. Angela Jackson. ISC

When willing nymphs and swains unite. Judgement of Tiresias, The. Hildebrand Jacob. NOEC

When Wilt Thou Save the People? Ebenezer Elliott. OxAEP-2

When Wilt Thou Teach the People? D. H. Lawrence. OBSV

When wilt thou wake, O Mother, wake and see. Sleep-Worker, The. Thomas Hardy. OxBSo

When window-lamps had dwindled, then I rose. Christopher John Brennan. CBAP *Fr.* Wanderer, The.

When winds are raging. Hymn. Harriet Beecher Stowe. AH

When winds rage and the sky is high, gibbons cry mournfully. Climbing the Heights. Tu Fu. SuSp, *tr. by* Wu-Chi Liu

When winds that move not its calm surface sweep. Ocean, The. Moschus. AWP; OBVE

When wine runs low, it is not worth the sparing. Joshua Sylvester. FaBoEE

When Winter's royal robes of white. Parting Hymn, A. Charlotte L. Forten Grimke. BlSi; NAAAL

When Winter snows upon thy sable hairs. (LL) Samuel Daniel. NAEL-5v1; NOBE; NoSic; OBEV; SCGP; Son *Fr.* To Delia.

When winter was half over. Another Sarah. Anne Porter. TTTS

When wintry tempests agitate the deep. To Melancholy. Susan Evance. CenSon

When, with a pain he desires to explain to his servitors, Baby. Rudyard Kipling. NoAM *Fr.* Land and Sea Tales.

When with a serious musing I behold. George Wither. NOSC; SacPr *Fr.* Collection of Emblemes, Ancient and Moderne, A.

When with eyes closed as in an opium dream. Parfum Exotique. Charles Baudelaire. AWP, *tr. by* Arthur Symons

When, with his children clad in animal-skins. Conscience. Victor Hugo. SxFrPo, *tr. by* E. H. Blackmore and A. M. Blackmore

When with May the air is sweet. Love, Whose Month Was Ever May. Ulrich von Liechtenstein. AWP, *tr. by* Jethro Bithell

When with much pains this boasted learning's got. Charles Churchill. OBSV *Fr.* Author, The.

When with the Virgin morning thou dost rise. Matins [or Mattens], or Morning Prayer. Robert Herrick. BASC; CaPo

When within my arms I hold you. Aurelia. Robert Malise Bowyer Nichols. OBMV

When without tears I looke on Christ, I see. William Alabaster. ESCV *Fr.* Divine Meditations.

When woods are odorous at eve. Wood Carols. Henrietta Cordelia Ray. CBWP-3

When working blackguards come to blows. Song. Ebenezer Elliott. EBEV

When world is water and all is flood, God said. Noah's Ark. Marguerite Young. WPE

When World War II was declared. Can't Tell. Nellie Wong. ItWoWo; LTA; OpBo

When, wounded sore, the stricken soul. Touched with a Feeling of Our Infirmities. Cecil Frances Alexander. SacPr

When Yahweh spoke to me, when I saw His name. Battle, The. Abraham Abulafia. WoPoe, *tr. by* Stanley Moss

When Yankies, skill'd in martial rule. John Trumbull. TCAPo *Fr.* M'Fingal.

When years go by, when. Letters to an Unknown Woman. Nicanor Parra. BLPSL, *tr. by* Rene de Costa, Rigas Kappatos and Eleni Paidoussi

When yet a Child, I read great *Virgil* o'er. Dream, The; An Epistle to Mr. Dryden. Elizabeth Thomas. EMWP

When Yon Full Moon. William Henry Davies. MoBrPo

When you and I go down. Harold Monro. OBMV *Fr.* Midnight Lamentation.

When you and I have play'd the little hour. Reunited. Sir Gilbert Parker. OBEV

When you and I on the Palos Verdes cliff. Shane O'Neill's Cairn. Robinson Jeffers. NOBA; NoAM

When you and I shall to our earth return. To Strephon. Sarah Dixon. ECWP

When You and I Were Young, Maggie. George W. Johnson. TCAPo

When you and my true lover meet. Lady's Third Song, The. W. B. Yeats. FaBoTw

When you are called on to perform a duty. Do Your Best. Mrs. Henry Linden. CBWP-4

When you are caught breathless in an empty station. Horace Gregory. MoAmPo *Fr.* Passion of M'Phail, The.

When You Are Grown, Amanda Rose. Laura Boss. OPRER

When You Are Old. W. B. Yeats. AWP; AmFaPo; BoLoP; CTC; ClHu; EBVV; HeIP-4; MoBrPo; NAEL-5v2; NAEL-6v2; NAWM-7v2; NOBVV; NoAM; NoP-4; OBEV; OxBEV; OxBTC; TFi; WoPoe

When you are old, at evening candle-lit. Pierre de Ronsard. WoPoe, *tr. by* Humbert Wolfe *Fr.* Sonnets to Helen.

When you are very old, at evening. Of His Lady's Old Age. Pierre de Ronsard. AWP; CTC, *tr. by* Andrew Lang

When you are walking by yourself. Kick a Little Stone. Dorothy Aldis. TLR

When you are wrapped in happy sleep. Stolen Visit, A. Rosa Mulholland. PoBW

When you bared your china. Party Favour. Daniel David Moses. HATNAP

When you broke from me. Lady Izumi. BoWoP, *tr. by* Willis Barnstone

When you came and you talked and you read with your. To William Carlos Williams. Galway Kinnell. NoAM

When you came, you were like red wine and honey. Decade, [A]. Amy Lowell. MoAmPo; NALW; PasH; PoBW

When you climb. Water Song, The. Glenna Luschei. GeoHom

When you come and sleep with me. When You Come Sleep with Me. Yona Volach. DTA, *tr. by* Miriyam Glazer

When you come, as you soon must, to the streets of our city. Advice to a Prophet. Richard Wilbur. HarvBoo; MoAmPo; NoP-4; OBWP; OxBC; PoE; TwCP; VCAP

When you come out of that. Jalapeña Gypsies. Jay Wright. NBV

When You Come Past My Window. "Shu Ting." CarOv, *tr. by* Carolyn Kizer and Y. H. Zhao

When You Come Sleep with Me. Yona Volach. DTA, *tr. by* Miriyam Glazer

When you come to our country. Crown and Country. Jackie Kay. MFPA

When you come to smoke. Cigarette Case. Stephen Kessler. GeoHom

When you come to visit. My Native Costume. Martín Espada. TouFir

When you consider the radiance, that it does not withhold. City Limits, The. A. R. Ammons. HCAP; NAAL-2v2; NOBA; NoAM; NoP-4; PoPoPo; VCAP

When you contemplate the waters. Kyokusai. JDP, *tr. by* Yoel Hoffmann

When you destroy a blade of grass. To Iron-Founders and Others. Gordon Bottomley. OBEV; OBMV

When you die you'll lie dead, no memory of you. Sappho. SaLy, *tr. by* Diane Rayor

When you died, it was time to light the first. Candle in a Glass, A. Marge Piercy. TaR

When you disappeared. For Kelly, Missing in Action. Walter McDonald. CDa

When you discover. For Those Whom the Gods Love Less. Denise Levertov. BodElec

When you discovered. Dance Lesson, A. A. Van Jordan. SpirFl

When you don't have it. Souvenirs. Jessica Tarahata Hagedorn. ReBoTo

When you enter Chin-hua Mountain. Tsung Ch'en. CoBLCP *Fr.* Sent to Yü Te-fu upon His Receipt of an Official Commission to the Two Che's.

When you feel like saying something. Most Vital Thing in Life, The. Grenville Kleiser. PoToHe; SoSe-8

When you first feel the ground under your feet. Walking in a Swamp. David Wagoner. HAP

When you first rub up against God's own skin. Ars Poetica about Ultimates. Tram Combs. TwCP

When you get the nomination, the award, the promotion. For Those Dead, Our Dead. Ernesto Cardenal. PoetW, *tr. by* Jonathan Cohen

When you get there, do not greet them. Tommorow. Amal Dunqul. MAP; NAfrP, *tr. by* Sharif Elmusa and Thomas G. Ezzy

When you go away the wind clicks around to the north. When You Go Away. W. S. Merwin. LCAP-2

When you go out at early morn. Serving Maid, The. Arthur Joseph Munby. NOBVV

When you go ten miles away. Viaticum. Pao Yu. OHMPC, *tr.* by Kenneth Rexroth

When you go to the tyrant. Keep your head on a platter. Paavo Haavikko. WoPoe, *tr.* by Anselm Hollo *Fr.* Fifteen Epigrams in Praise of the Tyrant.

When you got up this morning the sun. Gary Soto. NoAM *Fr.* Elements of San Joaquin, The.

When you grow up, are no more children. Parent to Children. Robert Graves. OxAEP-2

When you have both. (LL) Toads. Philip Larkin. NOBL; NoAM; OxAEP-2; OxBTC; PAI; PoE; SoSe-8

When You Have Emptied Our Calabashes. Iyamide Hazeley. NAfrP

When You Have Forgotten Sunday: The Love Story. Gwendolyn Brooks. BPo; WPOW

  (And when you have forgotten the bright bedclothes on a.) NAAAL

When you have money, buy me a ring. Whatever You Want. Angel González. VCWP, *tr.* by Steven Ford Brown

When you have nothing more to say, just drive. Peninsula, The. Seamus Heaney. HarvBoo

When you have tidied all things for the night. Solitude. Harold Monro. MoBrPo

When you have wearied of the valiant spires of this country town. Oxford Canal. James Elroy Flecker. OxBTC

When you hear me say "darling" or "dear." Who besides You. Bart Howard. ReLy

When you hear me singing. Margaret Atwood. NIP-4 *Fr.* Songs of the Transformed.

When you imagine trumpet-faced musicians. Homage to Literature. Muriel Rukeyser. SeSe

When you kiss me, moths flutter in my mouth. Beija-Flor. Diane Ackerman. NIP-4

When You Laugh. Ingrid Jonker. WPOW, *tr.* by Elizabeth Jones

When You Leave. Juan Delgado. TouFir

When you lie. Paul Celan. VCWP, *tr.* by Michael Hamburger

When you lie sleeping by my side. Marina. Eugenio Montejo. BLPSL, *tr.* by Rene de Costa, Rigas Kappatos and Eleni Paidoussi

When you live in Jerusalem you begin. Stones. Shirley Kaufman. DTA

When you look at me. Colorstruck. Askhari. InTrad

When you look at me as if to say. Species. Charles Boyle. EmeKit

When you look at this memorial. Epitaph from Athens. *Unknown.* GrAn, *tr.* by Peter Jay

When you look down from the airplane you see lines. Field and Forest. Randall Jarrell. LCAP-2; VGW

When you look life in the face. Round About. Ogden Nash. ReLy

When you look on my grave. *Unknown.* FaBoEE

When you lost touch with lovers' bare skin. John Donne. James Simmons. CIP-2

When you love, or speak of it. Aphra Behn. BoWoP

When you loved me. Look How Rich We are Together. Micere Githae Mugo. HAWP

When you lunch in a town which has recently known war. Lunch in Nablus City Park. Naomi Shihab Nye. GraLe

When you meet a young boy, be direct. Addaeus. CAGL, *tr.* by Daryl Hine

When you plunged. Otter, The. Seamus Heaney. NoAM; PNI

When you're awake, the things you think. Where or When. Richard Rodgers. ReLy

When you're away I sleep a lot. Method, The. J. D. McClatchy. MakPoe

When you're both alive and dead. Bunan. ZenPo, *tr.* by Takashi Ikemoto and Lucien Stryk

When You're Feeling Kind of Bonkers. Richard Tipping. OBCoV

When you're lying awake with a dismal headache, and repose is taboo'd by anxiety. Sir William Schwenck Gilbert. NOBL; OBCoV; OxBoLi; PeLV; PoRA *Fr.* Iolanthe.

When you're not looking. (LL) May Swenson. GLP; PoBW

When you're out in smart society. Well, Did You Evah? Cole Porter. OBAL

When you're sad and down in the dumps. Say "Cheese!" Tommy Wolf. ReLy

When you're tired and worn at the close of day. Confide in a Friend. *Unknown.* PoToHe

When you reach to touch the markings. Indian Rock, Bainbridge Island, Washington. Duane Niatum. CDW

When You Read This Poem. Pinkie Gordon Lane. BlSi

When you said the Shema Yisroel that meant something different each time. Eliahu. Tamara Kamenszain. MirDau, *tr.* by Roberta Gordenstein

When you sang the clear water of your mother's womb. To an Ethiopian Child. Diana Helen Melhem. GraLe

When you say, "Quick, I'm going to come," Martial. EroLit, *tr.* by James Michie

When you scuttled the ship, the shore was still in sight. Meditation of a Mariner. Dorothy Auchterlonie. CBAP

When you see a guy reach for stars in the sky. Guys and Dolls. Frank Loesser. OBAL

When you see a ragged urchin. Boys Make Men. *Unknown.* PWR

When you see millions of the mouthless dead. Sonnet. Charles Hamilton Sorley. FaBoWar; NPeEn; OBWP; OxBSo; PeFWW; PoWW

When you see them. Breath. Mark Strand. HCAP

When you seek variety. Tan Manhattan. Andy Razaf. ReLy

When you send out invitations, don't ask me. Palladas [*or* Pallades]. OBVE, *tr.* by Tony Harrison

When you set out for Afrika. To the Diaspora. Gwendolyn Brooks. NAAL-5; NIL-7

When you set out for Ithaka. Ithaka. Constantine P. Cavafy. WoPoe, *tr.* by Edmund Keeley and Philip Sherrard

When you set up a mirror on the western side of Easter Island, it runs backward. Behavior of Mirrors on Easter Island, The. Julio Cortázar. TCLAP, *tr.* by Paul Blackburn

When You Shake Loose Your Hair. Francisco de Quevedo y Villegas. *See* On Lisi's Golden Hair

When you shake loose your hair from all controlling. On Lisi's Golden Hair. Francisco de Quevedo y Villegas. WoPoe, *tr.* by Roy Campbell

When you shall see me in the toils of Time. Thomas Hardy. OxBTC *Fr.* She, to Him.

When you sit happy in your own fair house. Alcuin. MLL

When you speak about ice, do you mean live ice. About Ice. Malcolm Lowry. OxBSo

When you speak to me I feel my blood sliding. Note Folded Thirteen Ways. Richard Garcia. TouFir

When you stop to consider. Dog Days. Derek Mahon. OPOU

When you studied the sea it seemed to carry. Langston. Frederick D'Aguiar. Oth

When you suddenly. Godlike. Anselm Hollo. PmAP

When you swim in the surf off Seal Rocks, and your family. Family. Josephine Miles. FaBoWP

When you tell me that you were unpopular as a child. Goethe. WoPoe, *tr.* by David Ferry *Fr.* Roman Elegies, The.

When you, that at this moment are to me. Edna St. Vincent Millay. AmFaPo

When you think of the distances. Distances, The. W. S. Merwin. NOBA

When you think of the hosts without no. Cautionary Limerick. *Unknown.* NBLV

When you think of your country. Firewing. Breyten Breytenbach. VCWP, *tr.* by Ernst Van Heerden

When you think you've hit the bottom. You Mustn't Feel Discouraged. Adolph Green. ReLy

When you tried to tell me. Baseball. Linda Pastan. MoASP

When you tug at the rip cord. When the Parachute Does Not Open. Yevgeny [*or* Evgenii] Mikhailovich Vinokurov. TCRusP, *tr.* by Daniel Weissbort

When you turn at the road's. Cain the Immortal. Yusuf Al-Khal. MAP; PFTM-2, *tr.* by Sargon Boulus and Samuel Hazo

When you've laughed out loud and said a friendly. Nossis. SaLy, *tr.* by Diane Rayor

When you've shouted "Rule Britania," when you've sung "God Save the Queen." Absent-Minded Beggar, The. Rudyard Kipling. FaBoWar

When you wake up from sleeping with women. Studying Horses. Robert Kelly. APSN

When you walk through a storm. You'll Never Walk Alone. Richard Rodgers. ReLy

When you walked here. Dumbfounding, The. Margaret Avison. NOBC

When you wardance, sometimes you must. Wardance. Phillip [*or* "Phil"] William George. VoR

When you wear a cloudy collar and a shirt that isn't white. When Your Pants Begin to Go. Henry Lawson. NOBAu

When you were a holy priest. Marvellous Grass. Nuala Ni Dhomhnaill. PBCIP, *tr.* by Michael Hartnett

When you were a tadpole and I was a fish. Evolution. Langdon Smith. BRP

When you were alive, at least. Dead Friend, The. Agnes Mary Frances Robinson. VWP

When you were alive, we often dreamed together. Three Dreams in Chiang-ling. Yuan Chen. CrYelRi, *tr.* by Sam Hamill

When you were born, all the poets I knew. Poem for My Sons. Minnie Bruce Pratt. WiU

When you were down here JC and walked this earth. Memo to J. C. Maureen Watson. IBA

When you were drunk you could always whip Joe Louis. My Right Hand Don't Leave Me No More. Carter Revard. HATNAP

When you were here in wonderful Detroit. Goodbye David Tamunoemi West. Margaret Danner. BPo

When you were there, and you, and you. Dining-Room Tea. Rupert Brooke. MoBrPo

When You Will Walk in the Field. Leah Goldberg. TrJP, *tr. by* Simon Halkin

When You Wish Upon a Star That Turns into a Plane. James Harms. SwNoth

When you woke [up] among them. After Grief. Stanley Plumly. LCAP-2

When you wrote your letter it was April. Response. Mary Ursula Bethell. FaBoWP; PeNZ

When Young Hearts Break. Heinrich Heine. AWP, *tr. by* Louis Untermeyer

When young I scribbled, boasting, on my wall. Summing-up, The. Stanley Kunitz. OBAL

When young I was awed by authority. Italics. Anselm Hollo. PmAP

When Young Melissa Sweeps. Nancy Byrd Turner. NTCP

When your capitalist boss takes his toll. Limerick. Dominic Fitzpatrick. PeLi

When Your Cheap Divorce Is Granted. "Orpheus C. Kerr." OBAL

When your client's hopping mad. Advertising Agency Song, The. *Unknown*. NBLV

When your face dawned. Yevgeny Aleksandrovich Yevtushenko [*or* Evtushenko]. TCRP

When your hour was rung at last. Rendez-vous Manqué dans la Rue Racine. John Millington Synge. BIrV

When your life is tumbling downhill head over heels. New Year March: A Declaration, The. Yuly [*or* Iulii] Markovich Daniel. TCRP, *tr. by* Arthur Boyars and David Burg

When your lips seek my lips they bring. Isolation. Arthur Symons. OxBSP

When your lobster was lifted out of the tank. Something Else. Paul Muldoon. ModIr

When your longing spans the earth. Thirst. Thurayya Al-Urayyid. PoArWo, *tr. by* Farouk Mustafa

When Your Lover Has Gone. E. A. Swan. ReLy

When Your Pants Begin to Go. Henry Lawson. NOBAu

When your teeth decay you cannot. I Get up at Dawn. Lu Yu. OHPC, *tr. by* Kenneth Rexroth

When your water reaches me. Land of Mirrors, The. Amira El-Zein. PoArWo, *tr. by* Husain Haddawy

When youth and charms have ta'en their wanton flight. Advice to Sophronia. Mary Leapor. ECWP

When youthful faith hath fled. Lines. John Gibson Lockhart. OBEV

When Yü-k'o painted bamboo. Su Tung-p'o (Su Shih). ColAnChi, *tr. by* Burton Watson

When Yuba Plays the Rumba on the Tuba. Herman Hupfeld. ReLy

Whenas galoshed my Julia goes. Upon Julia's Arctics. Bert Leston Taylor. OBAL

Whenas in furs my Julia goes. Upon Julia's Clothes. Edmund George Valpy Knox. UV

Whenas in silks my Julia goes. Upon Julia's Clothes. Robert Herrick. AWP; BASC; BeJo; CABP; CaPo; CavPo; ClHu; EBEV; EnLoPo; GTBS-P; HAP; HeIP-4; NAEL-5v1; NAEL-6v1; NAEL-7v1; NBLV; NIL-7; NIP-4; NOBE; NOSC; NoP-4; OBEV; OxAEP-1; OxBEV; OxBSP; PAI; PeLV; PoE; PoPoPo; SCGP; TFi; TRP; TTTS; UV; WeW-3; WoPoe

Whenas [*or* When as] man's life, the light of human[e] lust. Fulke Greville, 1st Baron Brooke. CABP; NOSC; NoSic *Fr.* Caelica.

Whenas [*or* When as] the Rye [*or* Rie] reach to the chin. George Peele. EnLoPo; FaBoCh; FaBoVe; NPeEn; NoSic; OxBEV; OxBoLi; TFi *Fr.* Old Wives' [*or* Wife's] Tale, The.

Whence and Whither. Hayyim Nahman [*or* Khayim Nakhman *or* Chaim Nachman] Bialik. TrJP, *tr. by* Helena Frank

"Whence are you, learning's son?" End of Clonmacnois, The. *Unknown*. CIP-2; WoPoe, *tr. by* Frank O'Connor

Whence came his feet into my field, and why? He and I. Dante Gabriel Rossetti. OxBSo

Whence come [*or* came] ye, Cherubs? from the moon? Chanting Cherubs, The [A Group by Greenough]. Richard Henry Dana. APN-1

Whence come you, all of you so sorrowful? Sonnet: To Certain Ladies; When Beatrice Was Lamenting Her Father's Death. Dante Alighieri. AWP; EaItPo, *tr. by* Dante Gabriel Rossetti

Whence comes those many-colored birds. Birds of Passage, The. Jones Very. NCAP

Whence did all that fury come? Stick of Incense, A. W. B. Yeats. ChIV-2

Whence Had They Come? W. B. Yeats. BoLoP

Whence have you fallen, have you fallen? Haida Cradle-Song. *Unknown*. TCAPo

Whence let us go to. Nicest Phantasies Are Shared, The. Brian Coffey. CIP-2

Whence that low voice?—A whisper from the heart. William Wordsworth. CenSon *Fr.* River Duddon [A Series of Sonnets], The.

Whence this impatience fluttering in my breast! Urania. Robert Andrews. NOEC

Whenceness of the Which. *Unknown*. UV

Whene'er a noble deed is wrought. Santa Filomena. Henry Wadsworth Longfellow. FaBoWar

Whene'er bitter foe attack thee. Advice to Hotheads. Samuel ben Elhanan Isaac, of Padua Archevolti. TrJP, *tr. by* A. B. Rhine

Whene'er I come where ladies are. Coventry Patmore. EBVV; NOBVV *Fr.* Angel in the House, The.

Whene'er I look into your eyes. I Love But Thee. Heinrich Heine. AWP, *tr. by* Louis Untermeyer

Whene'er I recollect the happy time. Frances Anne [*or* "Fanny"] Kemble. CenSon

Whene'er I take my walks abroad. Praise for Mercies Spiritual and Temporal. Isaac Watts. NOEC

Whene'er, in morning airs, I walk abroad. My Shadow's Stature. John James Piatt. APN-2

Whene'er the old exchange of profit rings. Francis Quarles. BASC; NOSC *Fr.* Emblems.

Whene'er the waist makes too much haste. Girdle, A. William Strode. NOSC

Whene'er with haggard eyes I view. George Canning. NOEC; OBCoV *Fr.* Rovers, The.

Whenever a butterfly. Lesson of Silence, A. Tymoteusz Karpowicz. PoSu, *tr. by* Czeslaw Milosz

Whenever a fellow called Rex. Limerick. *Unknown*. NOBL

Whenever all the world declares fair "fair." Lao Tzu. WoPoe, *tr. by* Moss Roberts *Fr.* Tao Te Ching.

Whenever Auntie moves around. Auntie's Skirts. Robert Louis Stevenson. WHSW

Whenever, Chloe, I begin. Song. Philip Dormer Stanhope, 4th Earl of Chesterfield. NOEC

Whenever he got in a fury, a. Limerick. *Unknown*. PeLi

Whenever he observes me purchasing. Sextus the Usurer. Martial. AWP, *tr. by* Kirby Flower Smith

Whenever I go by there nowadays. Tavern, The. Edwin Arlington Robinson. NCAP

Whenever I have, in all humility, moved. Whenever I Have. "Furnley Maurice." NOBAu

Whenever I kissed her. Compromise. Akhtar-ul-Iman. OMIP; WoPoe, *tr. by* Vinay Dharwadker and C. M. Naim

Whenever I listen to Billie Holliday, I am reminded. 1974: My Story in a Late Style of Fire. Larry Levis. BodElec

Whenever I live, like simple. Dmitry [*or* Dmitrii] Aleksandrovich Prigov. TCRP

Whenever I looked in the mirror. Inna L'vovna Lisnyanskaya [*or* Lisnianskaia]. ItGoST, *tr. by* Judith Hemschemeyer

Whenever I Make a New Poem. Lew Welch. BB

Whenever I pause. Noise of the Village, The. *Unknown*. OBVE, *tr. by* Frances Densmore

Whenever I plunge my arm, like this. Under the Waterfall. Thomas Hardy. BoLoP; CTC; NAEL-5v2; NAEL-6v2; NoP-4

Whenever I see him. Waking in the Dark. Dorothy Livesay. NOBC

Whenever I walk to Suffern along the Erie track. House with Nobody in It, The. Joyce Kilmer. ChAP

Whenever Jesus appears at the murky well. French Generals, The. Robert Bly. BAP-01

Whenever Mr. Edwards spake. Theology of Jonathan Edwards, The. Phyllis McGinley. MoAmPo

Whenever my mood. Title of This Poem Was Lost, The. Pedro Juan Pietri. PueRic

Whenever Richard Cory went down town. Richard Cory. Edwin Arlington Robinson. APN-2; ChAP; ColAP; HAP; InPK-6; MoAmPo; NAAL-2v2; NAAL-5; NCAP; NOBA; NoP-4; OxBA; PAI; PoPoPo; PoRA; TAP; TCAPo; TFi

Whenever skies look gray to me. I Concentrate on You. Cole Porter. ReLy

Whenever the moon and stars are set. Windy Nights. Robert Louis Stevenson. KaS; OTCP; PoRA

Whenever the moon faintly shines. (LL) On Love. Hsü Tsai-ssu. CrYelRi; ErotSp, *tr. by* Sam Hamill

Whenever they come from Kansas. Coming from Kansas. Myra Cohn Livingston. NOxBChV

Whenever troublous hours I find. Happiness amidst Troubles. Immanuel di Roma. TrJP, *tr. by* J. Chotzner

Whenever war is spoken of. Great War, The. Vernon Scannell. OBWP

Whenever we wake. Beautiful Signor. Cyrus Cassells. WiU

Whenever you drink all night you make. Martial. FaBoEE

Whenever You're Cornered, the Only Way Out Is to Fight. Merle Woo. FSt

Whenever you see the hearse go by. Be Merry. *Unknown*. RB

Whenever you take a step. Horizon, The. Kevin Hart. NOBAu

Whenever your American Way of Life is raised to the sky. America, America. K. Nisar Ahmad. OMIP, *tr. by* A. K. Ramanujan

Whenne mine eynen misteth. All Too Late. *Unknown*. EBEV

Whenneso will wit overstieth. *Unknown.* MiEL

Wher beth they biforn us weren. *Unknown. See* Where beeth they biforen us weren

Where. Issa. EH, *tr. by* Robert Hass

Where. Aleksandr Ivanovich Vvedensky [*or*Vvedenskii]. TCRP, *tr. by* Robin Milner-Gull and Robin Milner-Gulland

Where a bullet of sense *ought* to hit. (LL) Pastoral Ballad by John Bull, A. Thomas Moore. BIrV; OBSV

Where a great road has its start. Shaman's Song. *Hungarian Oral Tradition.* IQMS, *tr. by* Adam Makkai

Where a Roman consul once judged a foreign people. Notre Dame. Osip Emilevich Mandelstam [*or* Mandelshtam]. TCRusP, *tr. by* John Glad

Where a Roman judged a foreign people. Notre Dame. Osip Emilevich Mandelstam [*or* Mandelshtam]. OBVE, *tr. by* James Greene

Where a young man lands hatless from the air. (LL) Death of King George V. Sir John Betjeman. NOBE; OxBEV; OxBoLi

Where all Manhattan that I've seen must disappear. (LL) My Sad Self. Allen Ginsberg. UnPo; VCAP

Where All Were Good to Me, God Knows. Glyn Jones. TCAWP

Where all who know may drown. (LL) Man against the Sky, The. Edwin Arlington Robinson. OxBA; TCAPo

Where am I. Mary's Plea. Daisy Utemorrah. IBA

Where am I now? And what. Song in Passing, A. Yvor Winters. CRP; VGW

Where am I, O awesome friend? Yitzhak Lamdan. TrJP *Fr.* For the Sun Declined.

Where am I, or how came I here, hath death. On Lazarus Raised from Death. Henry Colman. ChIV-2

Where among the blue clouds. Wen Cheng-ming. CoBLCP

Where ancient music weaves its shapes. Warning. Nikolai Alekseievich Zabolotsky [*or* Zabolotskii]. TCRusP, *tr. by* Daniel Weissbort

Where angels turned into honeysuckle & poured nectar into my mouth. Backyard. Diane Di Prima. PmAP

Where antique woods o'erhang the mountain's crest. Contemns Philosophy. Mary Robinson. CenSon; RWP

Where are all the fussy waders. Mud-Flat. Willem Jan Otten. TuT, *tr. by* Seán Lysaght

Where are Elmer, Herman, Bert, Tom and Charley. Edgar Lee Masters. ColAP; IllVoic; NOBA; NoAM; OxBA; TAP *Fr.* Spoon River Anthology.

Where are my first-born, said the brown land, sighing. First-born, The. Jack Davis. BMAP; IBA

Where are our horses. Viktor Aleksandrovich Sosnora. TCRusP, *tr. by* Daniel Weissbort

Where are the bay-leaves, Thestylis, and the charms. Theocritus. AWP, *tr. by* Charles Stuart Calverley *Fr.* Idylls.

Where are the birth-places of the heroes? Alpheios. GrAn

Where are the braves, the faces like autumn fruit. Indian Reservation: Caughnawaga. Abraham Moses Klein. NOBC; NoP-4

Where are the cabalists, the insidious committees. Cities of the Plain. Edgar Lee Masters. TCAPo

Where Are the Hebrew Children? Peter Cartwright. AH

Where are the horses of the sun? Charioteer of Delphi, The. James Merrill. GS

Where are the Men Chased Away by that Mad Wind? Alda do Espirito Santo. HAWP, *tr. by* Jacques-Noël Gouat

Where Are the Men Seized in this Wind of Madness? Alda do Espirito Santo. PBMAP; TTY; WPOW, *tr. by* Alan Ryder

Where are the passions they essayed. Ballade of Dead Actors. William Ernest Henley. EBVV; OBMV

Where are the people as beautiful as poems. Black Angel, The. Henri Coulette. CoAP

Where are the poems gone, of our first days? Some Time After. Anne Ridler. SacPr

Where are the ribbons I tie my hair with? Ballade of Lost Objects. Phyllis McGinley. CRP; NBLV; PoRA

Where are the tearful smiles of youthful Spring. Written in Ill Health at the Close of Spring. Susan Evance. CenSon

Where Are the War Poets? Cecil Day Lewis. FaBoMo; NoP-4; OBWP; OxBSP; OxBTC

Where Are the Waters of Childhood? Mark Strand. EmeKit; HCAP; LCAP-2; VCAP; WeW-3

Where are the women who, *entre deux guerres*. Ballad of Ladies Lost and Found. Marilyn Hacker. FFC; VCAP

Where are they going, the crowds that pass in the street? Returning to the Port of Authority: A Picaresque. Constance Urdang. PBCAP

Where are they gone, the old familiar faces? Old Familiar Faces, The. Charles Lamb. NOBRP; OxBEV

Where are they? So the World Changes. Kofi Awoonor. VCWP

Where are they? I have never missed before. Leaves. "Michael Field." VWP

Where are those Songs? Micere Githae Mugo. HAWP; PoetW

Where are we going? where are we going. Song of Slaves in the Desert. John Greenleaf Whittier. APN-1; OxBA

Where Are You. Benjamin Péret. SurPaPo, *tr. by* Rachel Stella

"Where are you coming from, Lomey Carter." Old Christmas Morning. Roy Helton. MoAmPo

Where are you, glory of old? Lost deep in the night of the shadows? Flight of Zalán, The. Mihály Vörösmarty. IQMS, *tr. by* Watson Kirkconnell

Where Are You Going, Maiden. Félix Lope de Vega Carpio. SpanPo, *tr. by* W. S. Merwin

Where Are You Going, My Pretty Maid. *Unknown.* NBLV

Where are you going through the streets of Rome. Roman Evening. Pier Paolo Pasolini. CLPP

Where are you going to, Hywel and Blodwen. Hywel and Blodwen. Idris Davies. AngWePo

"Where are you going [to], my pretty maid?" Milk Maid, The. Mother Goose. LB; OxNR; ReMoGo

Where are you going to-night, to-night. John Evereldown. Edwin Arlington Robinson. APN-2; NCAP; OxBA

Where are you going? asked Manny the Mayor. Jig Tune: Not for Love. Thomas McGrath. VGW

Where are you going? To Scarborough Fair? Scarborough Fair. *Unknown.* OxBoLi; PeLV

Where Are You? Harold Adamson. ReLy

Where Are You? Carole Satyamurti. Prnts

Where are your ancient waves, O river. Home-Coming. Albert Ehrenstein. TrJP, *tr. by* Babette Deutsch and Avrahm Yarmolinsky

Where are your fabled Doric beauty, the fringe. Ruins of Corinth, The. Antipater of Sidon. GrAn, *tr. by* Peter Jay

Where are your heroes, my little black ones. Poem for Black Boys. Nikki Giovanni. BPo

Where Art Is a Midwife. Tom Paulin. ModIr; NPeEn

Where art thou, Muse, that thou forget'st so long. William Shakespeare. TreFP *Fr.* Sonnets.

Where art thou, my beloved Son. Affliction of Margaret, The. William Wordsworth. GTBS-P; RACG

Where, as a lordly dream. Bridge, The. John Banister Tabb. APN-2

Where Be You [*or* Ye] Going, You [*or* Ye] Devon Maid? John Keats. FHYEP

Where beeth they biforen us weren. Ubi Sunt Qui Ante Nos Fuerunt? *Unknown.* EBEV; PoE

Where Blind Sorrow Is Taught to See. Suzanne Gardinier. AmPoNex

Where both he and I are the hunters. (LL) My Father's Wedding. Robert Bly. NoAM; RaBo

Where brown children are at play under pollarded willows. Trumpets. Georg Trakl. PeFWW, *tr. by* David McDuff

Where can I go. Captive's Song. *Unknown.* APN-2, *tr. by* Fannie Reed Giffen

Where Can I Hide in January. Osip Emilevich Mandelstam [*or* Mandelshtam]. TCRusP, *tr. by* John Glad

Where can we buy wine? We ask. Mooring Our Boat at Tan-yang Harbor. Kao Ch'i. CoBLCP, *tr. by* Jonathan Chaves

Where Cape Delgado strikes the sea. Edwin John Pratt. MoCV *Fr.* Cachalot, The.

Where Carpos wandered and died, I will fall headlong. Nonnus. CAGL, *tr. by* W. H. D. Rouse *Fr.* Dionysiaca.

Where convex and concave. To the Creator of My Bones. Anna Hajnal. IQMS, *tr. by* Jeannette Nichols

Where cool'd by rills and curtain'd round by woods. Erasmus Darwin. NOBRP *Fr.* Botanic Garden, The.

Where Cross the Crowded Ways of Life. Frank Mason North. AH

Where Cumbria's mountains in the north arise. James Plumptre. NOEC *Fr.* Prologue to "The Lakers; a Comic Opera."

Where deep in the night I hear a voice. (LL) Butcher Shop. Charles Simic. AF; InPK-5; LCAP-2; NNaP

"Where did I come from, Mother, and why?" Christmas Lullaby for a New-Born Child. Yvonne Gregory. NOxBChV

Where did I see this region before with its bleak earth. Baffling Picture. Lajos Kassák. IQMS, *tr. by* Edwin Morgan

Where did it roll in from, that sea of light. In Two Fields. Waldo Williams. OBWVE, *tr. by* Gwyn Jones

Where did these enormous children come from. Parents' Pantoum. Carolyn Kizer. MakPoe

Where did this tiger come from? Ballad of the Ferocious Tiger. Hsü Pen. CoBLCP, *tr. by* Jonathan Chaves

Where did you borrow that last sigh. Sir William Berkeley. OxBSP *Fr.* Lost Lady, The.

Where did you come from, baby dear? George Macdonald. ITBLP; WHSW *Fr.* At the Back of the North Wind.

Where did you get your bodies? Dialogue, The. Vladimir Burich. TCRP, *tr. by* Katya Olmstead

Where did your underwear wander. Sleepwalking Soho. Stuart Dybek. IllVoic

Where dips the rocky highland. Stolen Child, The. W. B. Yeats. NAEL-5v2; NAEL-6v2; NoP-4

Where Do I Come From? Gustavo Adolfo Bécquer. SpanPo, *tr.* by Edward F. Gahan

Where do I get this landscape? Two river-roads. Harpers Ferry. Adrienne Rich. BodElec

Where do I sit. Tea at the Magdalene. Clara Silva. TANSG, *tr.* by Celeste Kostopulos-Cooperman

Where do I stand and where do you? Seems like. Edoardo Cacciatore. ItPo, *tr.* by Gayle Ridinger *Fr.* Full Powers: Five Warning Signs.

Where Do School Days End? Josephine D. Henderson Heard. CBWP-4

Where do these trees come from. Emaciated Teeth. Fatma Kandil. PoArWo, *tr.* by Khaled Mattawa

Where do we live? Variations for Two Voices. Roberta Hill Whiteman. HATNAP

Where Does My Sadness Come From? Kao Ch'i. CoBLCP, *tr.* by Jonathan Chaves

Where does Spring return? Tune: "Ch'ing-P'ing Song." Huang T'ing-chien. ChinPo, *tr.* by Yip Wai-lim

Where does the stream carry my small face? Leah Goldberg. MHP, *tr.* by Ruth Finer Mintz *Fr.* Songs of the Stream.

Where does this poem come from? Edouard J. Maunick. NegPo *Fr.* As Far as Yoruba Land.

Where dost [*or* do'st] thou careless[e] lie. Ode To Himself, An. Ben Jonson. BASC; BeJo; CABP; HAP; NOBE; NOSC; NPeEn; NoP-4; OxAEP-1; PBRV; SCGP

Where dost thou lie, great Nimrod of the West! Richard Henry Wilde. APN-1 *Fr.* Hesperia.

Where down the blind are driven. (LL) Eros Turannos. Edwin Arlington Robinson. APT-1; AmFaPo; HAP; HeIP-4; MoAmPo; NAAL-2v2; NOBA; NoAM; NoP-4; OxBA; PoE; PoPoPo; TAP; TCAPo; TFi; TRP; WoPoe

Where drowsy sound of college-chimes. Cambridge in the Long. Amy Levy. ViWPN

Where dwell the lovely, wild white womenfolk. White Women, The. Mary Elizabeth Coleridge. BrRo; NALW; ViWPN

Where-e'er My Flatt'ring Passions Rove. Isaac Watts. NOCV

Where e're they met, or parting place has been. (LL) Lovers How They Come and Part. Robert Herrick. OxBSP; OxBoLi

Where ends our chancel in a vaulted space. George Crabbe. OBSV *Fr.* Borough, The.

Where Engels Fears to Tread. Cyril Connolly.
"Come on Percy, my pillion-proud, be." OBCoV
"It was late last night when my lord came home." OBCoV
"M is for Marx." OBCoV
"Something is going to go, baby." OBCoV

Where England's Damon used [*or* us'd] to keep. Pastoral on the King's Death, The; [Written in 1648]. Alexander Brome. NOSC

Where'er thy navy spreads her canvas wings. To the King, on His Navy. Edmund Waller. BeJo

Where'er you find "the cooling western breeze." Pope. OBCoV *Fr.* Essay on Criticism, An.

Where Everybody is King. Tanure Ojaide. NAfrP

Where fair Sabrina's wand'ring currents flow. William Somervile [*or* Somerville]. NOEC *Fr.* Bowling-Green, The.

Where fancy paints with nature's simplest hues. Ode on Truth: Addressed to George Dyer. Anne Batten Cristall. RWP

Where Fire Burns. Gladys Cardiff. HATNAP

Where Fishermen Can't Swim. Matthew Sweeney. BiHa

Where folds the central lotus. William Yeats in Limbo. Sidney Keyes. MoBrPo

Where / from / here. 2 B BLK. Val Ferdinand. NBV

Where from the watch towers. Bay Poem. Lance Henson. VoR

Where gentle Thames through stately channels glides. Playhouse, The. Joseph Addison. ECEV

Where glide my thoughts, rash inclinations stay. Reflection, The. Elizabeth Singer Rowe. EMWP

Where Go the Boats? Robert Louis Stevenson. FaBoCh; NOxBChV; NTCP; TLR; WHSW

Where good and evil dwell. Crickety Creek. Arkady Kutilov. TCRP, *tr.* by Bradley Jordan

Where *Grief* and *Mis'ery* can be join'd with *Verse.* (LL) Abraham Cowley. EBEV; OBEV

Where had I heard this wind before. Bereft. Robert Frost. APT-1; MoAmPo; OxBA; SoSe-8

Where hae ye been a' the day. *Unknown.* OxNR

Where harmless robin dwells with gentle thrush. (LL) Happy Were He. Robert Devereux, 2d Earl of Essex. NoSic; OxBSP

Where has he of race divine. Euripides. AWP *Fr.* Cyclops, The.

Where has she come from, this lady. Lady of Chaos. 'Ali Ja'far Al-Allaq. MAP, *tr.* by Sharif Elmusa and Thomas G. Ezzy

Where has spring returned to? Tune: "Pure Serene Music." Huang T'ing-chien. SuSp, *tr.* by James J. Y. Liu

Where has tenderness gone, he asked the mirror. Malcolm Lowry. FaBoTw; NoP-4; OxBTC *Fr.* Cantinas, The.

Where has the lustre of your eyes descended? To the Day-Dreamer. Mihály Vörösmarty. IQMS, *tr.* by Hymen H. Hart and Watson Kirkconnell

Where have all the flowers gone?—long time passing. Where Have All the Flowers Gone? Pete Seeger. NoP-4

Where have I wander'd, London, from thy haunts? Charles Lloyd. NOBRP *Fr.* Desultory Thoughts in London.

Where have these hands been. Musician. Louise Bogan. APT-2

Where have you been all the day, Billy boy, Billy boy? *Unknown.* OxNR

Where Have You Been Dear? Karla Kuskin. NTCP

Where have you been this long time. Axle Song. Mairtin O Direain. BiHa

Where have you disappeared to, horses with the trembling top-knots. In Memory of the Funeral Horses. Zoltán Jékely. IQMS, *tr.* by George Gömöri and Adam Makkai

Where have you gone blue middle of a decade? the gates creak. a sigh is so vastly different. Ode. D. A. Powell. NAPBL

Where Have You Gone, Little Boy. Patty L. Harjo. VoR

Where Have You Gone? Mari E. Evans. BPo; TTY

Where have you hidden away? Spiritual Canticle. Saint John of the Cross. SpanPo; STV, *tr.* by John Frederick Nims

Where he stood and where. Jew. James A. Randall, Jr. BPo

Where her house stood, she goes on living. Woman, A. Gabriela Mistral. TCLAP, *tr.* by Doris Dana

Where her poor Werter—and his sorrows sleep! (LL) By the Same. Charlotte Smith. CenSon; RWP

Where high-country evergreens grown taller. Morning Snowfield. Reg Saner. PoCoUp

Where His Lady Keeps His Heart. "A. W." CTC

Where Home Was. Augusta Davies Webster. ViWPN

Where Hope Lives. Carol Bell. GeoH

Where I cling. (LL) Last Leaf, The. Oliver Wendell Holmes. BRP; ITBLP; NAAL-2v1; NAAL-3; PWR; TCAPo

Where I come from the language is water. World is everything, The. Ann Sansom. NeBl

Where I could think of no thoroughfare. Robert Frost. OxBSP *Fr.* Five Nocturnes.

Where I gaze. Tune: "Jade Butterflies." Liu Yung. SuSp, *tr.* by Jerome P. Seaton

Where I go are flowers blooming. Les Planches-en-Montagnes. Michael Roberts. OBMV

Where I had heard / there would be room for me. (LL) Grandmother, a Caribbean Indian, Described by My Father. Yvonne Sapia. NIL-7; UnSA

Where I Live. Wanda Coleman. GeoHom

Where I Live. Wesley McNair. TRP

Where I live is like an island. Confession, A. Jenő Dsida. IQMS, *tr.* by George Gömöri and Clive Wilmer

Where I live, there are more. Scarecrows. James Kirkup. NOxBChV

Where I made One—turn down an empty Glass! (LL) Omar Khayyám. AWP; EBVV; HAP; NAEL-5v2; NAEL-6v2; NoP-4; TRP, *tr.* by Edward Fitzgerald

Where I may not remove nor be removed. (LL) William Shakespeare. FaBoWar; OxAEP-1; SCGP *Fr.* Sonnets.

Where I Sat. Richard Michelson. GotH

Where I Saw the Snake. Mark Van Doren. APT-2

Where I shall need no glass. (LL) They Are All Gone into the World of Light! Henry Vaughan. BASC; CABP; ESCV; GeHe; NAEL-5v1; NAEL-6v1; NAEL-7v1; NOBE; NOSC; NPeEn; NoP-4; PBRV; PeECV; PoPoPo; SCGP; TFi; WoPoe

Where I work. Small Secrets. John Montague. ModIr

Where I? Robinson Jeffers. OxBSo

Where icy and bright dungeons lift. Hart Crane. ColAP; HAP; MoAmPo; UnPo *Fr.* Voyages.

Where if you glance behind. James Dean. Rae Desmond Jones. BMAP

Where ignorant armies clash by night. (LL) Dover Beach. Matthew Arnold. AWP; AmFaPo; BRP; CABP; ClHu; EBVV; GTBS-P; HAP; HeIP-4; ITBLP; InPK-6; MakPoe; NAEL-5v2; NAEL-6v2; NIL-7; NIP-4; NOBE; NOBVV; NPeEn; NoP-4; OxBEV; PAI; PeVV; PoE; PoPoPo; PoRA; SCGP; SCV; TFi; TOF; WoPoe

Where in blind files. Song. Eavan Boland. CIP-2

Where in the summer-warm woodlands with the sweet wind. Iphione. Thomas Caulfield Irwin. EnLoPo

Where in the world is Helen gone. Gone Ladies. François Villon. WoPoe, *tr.* by Christopher Logue

Where, in what bubbly land, below. Ballade of Dead Gentlemen. Clive Staples Lewis. OBCoV

Where in what ever-blissfully watered gardens, upon what trees. Rainer Maria Rilke. OBVE *Fr.* Sonnets to Orpheus.

Where Innocent Bright-Eyed Daisies Are. Christina Georgina Rossetti. Spl

Where is a foot worthy to walk a garden, Jelaluddin [*or* Jalal-al-Din] Rumi. RaBo *Fr.* Four Quatrains.

Where is all the bright company gone. Song. Dame Edith Sitwell. NALW

Where is all, there all should be. (LL) Invitation, The. George Herbert. ChIV-1; ESCV

Where is another sweet as my sweet. Letter, The. Tennyson. TTTS

Where is David? Oh God's people. In Which Roosevelt Is Compared to Saul. Nicholas Vachel Lindsay. ChIV-1

Where is dew? Where is sand? Where the moon? Where a star? Judith. Gertrud Kolmar. AF, *tr. by* David Kipp

Where is he now, I wonder? Friendship. Anatoly Steiger. TCRusP, *tr. by* Paul Schmidt

Where is he, the wood pecker? Woodpecker, The. Ni Tsan. CoBLCP, *tr. by* Jonathan Chaves

Where Is He? Mother Goose. OxNR

Where is India or even one body. World, The. Donald Revell. BodElec

Where is it now? Look, there it flies in merry sport. Swallow's Flight, The. Louis Levy. TrJP, *tr. by* Martin S. Alwood and Sanford Kaufman

Where is Japanese Poetry? Fujii Sadakazu.
Small Dream. PFTM-2, *tr. by* Christopher Drake
Wolf. PFTM-2, *tr. by* Christopher Drake

Where is my bay? Bring it, Thestylis. Where are my charms? Theocritus. *See* Maid, where's my lawrel? Oh my rageing soul!

Where is my boy, my boy. Edgar Lee Masters. APT-1 *Fr.* Spoon River Anthology.

Where is my Chief, my Master, this bleak night, *mavrone!* O'Hussey's Ode to the Maguire. Eochadh [*or* Eochy] O'Hussey [*or* O'Heughusa]. CABP; NOIV, *tr. by* James Clarence Mangan

Where Is My Country? Nellie Wong. UnSA

Where is my lover and my friend? Elegiac Ballad, An. Hannah Cowley. ECWP

Where is my ruined life, and where the fame. Hafiz [*or* Hafez]. AWP; TAL *Fr.* Odes.

Where is neither faith nor wonder. (LL) Song with Words. James Agee. ChIV-1; MoAmPo

"Where is now Elijah's God?" Martyr's Death, A. Menahem ben Jacob. TrJP

Where Is Our Holy Church? Edwin H. Wilson. AH

Where is poor Jesus gone? Jesus. Francis Lauderdale Adams. OxBS

Where is Praxiteles where. Rufinus. GrAn

Where is Talcott Parsons Now? Sophie Hannah. MFPA

Where is Tangwen now, where Nest, where is Gwenllian. Fragment: Where Is Tangwen Now? Glyn Jones. TCAWP

Where is that baleful maid. Betty Barnes, the Book-Burner. Rosamund Marriott Watson. ViWPN

Where is that gate for grief which, long ago. Jan Kochanowski. WoPoe, *tr. by* Stanislaw Barańczak and Seamus Heaney *Fr.* Laments, The.

Where is that homeland, on which Árpád's blood. Zrínyi's Song. Ferenc Kölcsey. IQMS, *tr. by* Watson Kirkconnell

Where is that old "feast of reconciliation"? One for the "Ancient Gypsy." Gyula Juhász. IQMS, *tr. by* Adam Makkai

Where is that sugar, Hammond. Early Evening Quarrel. Langston Hughes. SAmP; UnPo

Where Is the Angel? Denise Levertov. PmAP

Where is the arbiter of a thousand languages? When My Poems were Lost. Raymond Mazisi Kunene. PeSAV, *tr. by* the author

Where is the dragon's cave? Kanzan-Shigyo. ZenPo, *tr. by* Takashi Ikemoto and Lucien Stryk

Where is the duke my father with his power? William Shakespeare. OxAEP-1 *Fr.* King Richard III.

Where is the gallant race that rose. Thomas Mercer. OxBS *Fr.* Arthur's Seat.

Where is the grave of Sir Arthur O'Kellyn? Knight's Tomb, The. Samuel Taylor Coleridge. FaBoCh; NPeEn; RB

Where Is the Guard? Ahmad al-Safi Al-Najafi. MAP, *tr. by* Sharif Elmusa and Thomas G. Ezzy

Where is the hand to trace. With a Coin from Syracuse. Oliver St. John Gogarty. OBMV

Where is the home for me? Euripides. AWP, *tr. by* Gilbert Murray *Fr.* Bacchae.

Where is the Jack that built the house. Château Jackson. Louis MacNeice. OxBEV

Where is the Jim Crow section. Merry-Go-Round. Langston Hughes. AmFaPo; PAI; SAmP

Where Is the Life That Late I Led? Cole Porter. ReLy

Where is the man who has been tried and found strong and sound? Degenerate Age, A. Solomon ibn Gabirol. TrJP, *tr. by* Emma Lazarus

Where is the nightingale. "H. D." APT-1; MoAmPo *Fr.* Songs from Cyprus.

Where is the nymph, whose azure eye. Song. Thomas Moore. EnLoPo

Where is the promise of my years. Infelix. Adah Isaacs Menken. CBWP-1; TCAPo

Where is the restaurant cat? Grand Canyon, The. Jean Garrigue. APT-2

Where is the sky born? Climate and Lyre. Radovan Pavlovski. CarOv, *tr. by* Carolyn Kizer

Where is the summer with her golden sun? Ancient Greek Song of Exile. Felicia Dorothea Hemans. RWP

Where is the Temple of Teeming Fragrance? Passing the Temple of Teeming Fragrance. Wang Wei. ChinPo, *tr. by* Yip Wai-lim

Where Is the Wagon Going? Meret Oppenheim. SurWo, *tr. by* Catherine Schelbert

Where is the wonder. Wish You Were Here. Harold Rome. ReLy

Where is the wonder to not know? Clark Coolidge. PFTM-2 *Fr.* Crystal Text, The.

Where is the world we roved, Ned Bunn? To Ned. Herman Melville. APN-2; NAAL-2v1; NAAL-3; NOBA; TCAPo

Where is the world? not about. Merchant Marine. Josephine Miles. TAP; VGW

Where is there an end of it, the soundless wailing. T. S. Eliot. AmFaPo *Fr.* Four Quartets.

Where is this beautiful song being sung. Hearing a Song from My Boat. Chang Yü. CoBLCP, *tr. by* Jonathan Chaves

Where is this stupendous stranger. Christopher Smart. ChrPo; NOCV; NPeEn; OxBEV; SacPr *Fr.* Hymns and Spiritual Songs for the Fasts and Festivals of the Church of England.

Where is your famous beauty. Antipater of Thessalonica. PGA

Where Israel's tents do shine so bright. (LL) Mock on, Mock on, Voltaire, Rousseau. William Blake. ChIV-1; HAP; NAEL-5v2; NAEL-6v2; NAWM-7v2; NPeEn; NoP-4; OxBSP; PeECV; PoE; SCGP; TFi

Where It Ends. William Bronk. APSN

Where it goes on Here not anywhere. Prayers, The. Brian Coffey. Oth

Where it says snow. Errata. Charles Simic. NNaP

Where it should have been there were only memories. House. Laura Mullen. ExTi

Where it will break at last. (LL) Indian Serenade, The. Shelley. AWP; OBEV; RaBo; TTTS; TreFP

Where Josh makes faces, grinning at me. (LL) David Wojahn. AllShUp; PBCAP *Fr.* Mystery Train: A Sequence.

Where joy has been forgot and hope has fled. (LL) Hafiz [*or* Hafez]. AWP; TAL *Fr.* Odes.

Where Knock Is Open Wide. Theodore Roethke. HAP; VGW

Where Leftover Misery Goes. Alice Notley. BAP-01

Where Lie All the Slain. Harry Morris. CRP

Where lies the city of the Holy Grail. City of the Grail, The. Henry E. G. Rope. SacPr

Where lies the Land to which yon Ship must go? Sonnet. William Wordsworth. CenSon

Where Lies the Truth? Has Man in Wisdom's Creed. William Wordsworth. TrCP

Where, like a pillow on a bed. Ecstasy, The. John Donne. BASC; BoLoP; CABP; FHYEP; FSCP; HAP; NAEL-5v1; NAEL-6v1; NAEL-7v1; NOBE; NoP-4; OBEV; OxBEV; PoE; TFi; TOF

Where, like the prophet, thou shalt find thy God. (LL) To the Right Honourable William, Earl of Dartmouth, His Majesty's Principal Secretary of State for North America. Phillis Wheatley. NAAAL; NAAL-5; NALW

Where Lincoln's Inn, wide space, is railed around. John Gay. ECEV *Fr.* Trivia; or, The Art of Walking the Streets of London.

Where Liver Eatin' Johnson lies. Old Trail Town, Cody, Wyoming. John Garmon. AMV-80

Where lives the man that never yet did heare. Sir John Davies. NoSic; OxBEV *Fr.* Orchestra; or, A Poem[e] of Da[u]ncing.

Where London's column, pointing at the skies. Pope. NPeEn *Fr.* Epistle III, to Allen Lord Bathurst.

Where long the shadows of the wind had rolled. Sheaves, The. Edwin Arlington Robinson. APT-1; AWP; HAP; MoAmPo; NOBA; NoAM; OxBA; SoSe-8; TAP

Where marble stood and fell. Reflection in a Green Arena. Gregory Corso. VGW

Where met our bards of old, the glorious throng. Felicia Dorothea Hemans. RWP *Fr.* Siege of Valencia, The.

Where metalled road invades light thinning air. Sándor Weöres. OBVE *Fr.* Lost Parasol, The.

Where Mountain Lion Lay [*or* Laid] down with Deer. Leslie Marmon Silko. TRP; VoR; WPOW

Where My Books Go. W. B. Yeats. OBEV

Where my grandfather is is in the ground. Mi Abuelo. Alberto A. Ríos. NIL-7; PoPoPo

Where my Sun-flower wishes to go. (LL) William Blake. AWP; EBEV; FHYEP; HAP; NAEL-6v2; NIP-4; NOBRP; NOEC; NPeEn; NoP-4; PoE; PoPoPo; RB; SCGP; TFi; TOF; UnPo; WeW-3 *Fr.* Songs of Experience.

Where neither King nor shepheard want comes neare. Homer. CTC *Fr.* Odyssey.

Where no one can see us dreaming. (LL) Blue Room, The. Richard Rodgers. OBAL; ReLy

Where not so long ago the breezes stirred. Fall of Rock, A. William Plomer. PeSAV

Where Nothing Dwelt but Beasts of Prey. Isaac Watts. AH

Where Now Are the Hebrew Children? *Unknown.* AH

Where now is the young Adam, sultry in his Aiden? Nocturne. John Crowe Ransom. APT-1

Where now the vital energy that moved. William Cowper. NPeEn *Fr.* Task, The.

Where now these mingled ruins lie. Stanzas Occasioned by the Ruins of a Country Inn. Philip Freneau. OxBA

Where, O! where's the chain to fling. Letitia [or Laetitia] Elizabeth Landon. NOBRP *Fr.* Golden Violet, The.

Where of old, responsive. Echoes. John Banister Tabb. APN-2

Where olive leaves are twinkling in every wind that blew. Damsel of Peru, The. William Cullen Bryant. APN-1

Where on earth. Question of Time, The. William Peskett. PNI

Where once my ancestors grubbed for the fern's root. Ancestors. Rowley Habib. PeNZ

Where once we danced, where once we sang. Ancient to Ancients, An. Thomas Hardy. GTBS-P; OxBTC; SCGP

Where once you could win over grasping boys. Glaucus. CAGL, *tr.* by Daryl Hine

Where one needs one's brains all the time. (LL) Lake Isle, The. Ezra Pound. OBCoV; OxBSP

Where or When. Richard Rodgers. ReLy

Where or When. Philip Whalen. PoM

Where others love, and praise my Verses; still. To the Detracter. Robert Herrick. PBRV

Where oxen do low and apples do grow. Thomas D'Urfey [or Durfey]. NOEC *Fr.* Bath; or, The Western Lass, The.

Where people have dined you find refuse and tin. Potter of Jaen, The. Ilya Grigoryevich Ehrenburg [or Erenburg]. TCRP, *tr.* by Cathy Porter

Where pomelo hangs down lovely fruit. Pomelo, The. *Unknown.* WoPoe, *tr.* by Anne Birrell

Where praise already is is the only place Grief. Rainer Maria Rilke. RaBo *Fr.* Sonnets to Orpheus.

Where rest not England's dead. (LL) England's Dead. Felicia Dorothea Hemans. NAEL-6v2; NoP-4

Where run your colts at pasture? White Horses. Rudyard Kipling. PeVV

Where's an old woman to go when the years. Riddle, The. "H. E. H." PoToHe

Where's Brude? Where's Brude? Columba's Song. Edwin Morgan. HarvBoo

Where's my hairbrush? Where's the belt? Sizing. Heather McHugh. ExTi

Where's that boy with the bugle? If He Walked into My Life. Jerry Herman. ReLy

Where's that careless chambermaid? Lulu's Back in Town. Harry Warren. ReLy

Where's the peck of pickled pepper Peter Piper picked? (LL) Mother Goose. LB; OTCP; OxNR; ReMoGo

Where's the public good in what you write. Palladas [or Pallades]. GrAn

Where San Juan and Chacabuco intersect. Houses like Angels. Jorge Luis Borges. TCLAP, *tr.* by Robert Fitzgerald

Where Seed Falls. Essex Hemphill. GT

Where seek out Tyranny? One Sentence on Tyranny. Gyula Illyés. IQMS, *tr.* by Adam Makkai, Károly Nagy and Vernon Watkins

Where, selfwrung, selfstrung, sheathe-and shelterless, thóughts agáinst thoughts ín groans grínd. (LL) Spelt from Sibyl's Leaves. Gerard Manley Hopkins. FaBoMo; NOBVV; NPeEn; OxBEV; OxBSo; TOF

Where shall Celia fly for shelter. Song. Christopher Smart. EnLoPo

Where shall I find, in all this fleeting earth. Thought from an Italian Poet. Felicia Dorothea Hemans. RWP

"Where shall I gang, my ain true love?" Duke of Athole's Nurse, The. *Unknown.* ESPB

Where shall I lead the flocks to-day? Where the Flocks Shall Be Led. Adah Isaacs Menken. CBWP-1

Where shall the eyes a darkness find. Huw Menai. OBWVE *Fr.* Back in the Return.

Where shall the lover rest. Sir Walter Scott. GTBS-P *Fr.* Marmion.

Where shall we go? where shall we go? June Fugue. Thomas William Shapcott. NOBAu

Where she lived the close remained the best. Way a Ghost Dissolves, The. Richard Hugo. NAAL-2v2; NoAM; NoP-4

Where she, of all the plains of Britain that doth bear. Michael Drayton. NOSC *Fr.* Polyolbion.

Where should this Musick be? I'th'aire, or th'earth? William Shakespeare. NPeEn *Fr.* Tempest, The.

Where silent, unrefractive whiteness lies. (LL) Stories of Snow. Patricia K. Page. NOBC; NoP-4

Where some murdered man must be. (LL) Sea-Side Cave, The. Alice Cary. APN-2; ColAP

Where Somnus' temple rises from a ground. Laudanum. *Unknown.* NOEC

Where sunless rivers weep. Dream Land. Christina Georgina Rossetti. BrRo

Where Sydney Cove her lucid bosom swells. Visit of Hope to Sydney Cove, near Botany-Bay. Erasmus Darwin. ECEV; NOEC

Where tadpoles are never allowed to grow into frogs! (LL) On Being Asked to Write a Poem for 1979. Jack A. Mapanje. AF; PBMAP

Where the afternoon sun blears the city. O My Invisible Estate. Bruce Smith. Son

Where the Bee Sucks. William Shakespeare. AWP; CTC; NAEL-5v1; NBLV; NoSic; OBEV; OxBSP; SCGP; TFi; TTTS *Fr.* Tempest, The.

Where the bishop groans to view him. (LL) Rich and Poor; or, Saint and Sinner. Thomas Love Peacock. NOBE; NOBL; OBSV; OxBEV; PeLV

Where the blood pours out the dead come to the feast. (LL) In Memoriam. Martin Johnston. BMAP; NOBAu

Where the Boul' Mich' meets the Rue. Paris. Miklós Radnóti. IQMS, *tr.* by Zsuzsanna Ozsváth and Frederick Turner

Where the cars razored past on the blue highway. Pastorale. Michael Hofmann. HarvBoo

Where the cedar leaf divides the sky. Passage. Hart Crane. NOBA; PoE

Where the Cedars. Jacob Glatstein [or Glatsteyn]. TrJP, *tr.* by Joseph Leftwich

Where the city's ceaseless crowd moves on the livelong day. Sparkles from the Wheel. Walt Whitman. NAAL-2v1; NAAL-3; SAmP

Where the Corrib river chops through the Claddagh. Last Galway Hooker, The. Richard Murphy. PBCIP

Where the coyote called. Foster Jewell. HA

Where the dawn has that *particular* laughter. (LL) You Also, Gaius Valerius Catullus. Archibald MacLeish. NoAM; TAP

Where the Dead Men Lie. Barcroft Henry Boake. CBAP

Where the Deer Go. Dabney Stuart. PoCoUp

Where the dire Circle keeps its station. Hannah More. ECWP *Fr.* Bas Bleu, The; or, Conversation.

Where the eternal snow. Austrian Song. Anton Wildgans. AuPH, *tr.* by Lowell A. Bangerter

Where the Flocks Shall Be Led. Adah Isaacs Menken. CBWP-1

Where the flowers and trees grow dense. Tune: "Ripples Sifting Sand"— Accompanying My Husband on a Spring Outing to Stone Pavilion. Ku T'ai-ch'ing. SuSp, *tr.* by Irving Y. Lo

Where the flowers lean to their shadows on the wall. Shadows of Chrysanthemums. Edith Jay Scovell. HarvBoo

Where the forest breaks. Tune: "Partridge Sky." Su Tung-p'o (Su Shih). ColAnChi, *tr.* by Jiaosheng Wang

Where the Fu-sang tree grows. Song of Heavenly Ascent. Ts'ao Chih. SuSp, *tr.* by Ronald C. Miao

Where the good God sits to spangle through. (LL) Lady, Lady. Anne Spencer. BlSi; NAAAL

Where the Great Northern plunged in. Wreck of the Great Northern, The. Robert Hedin. GM

Where the Heart Is. Ntozake Shange. GT

Where the Light. Giuseppe Ungaretti. WoPoe, *tr.* by Denis Devlin

Where the Lilies Used to Grow. David Gray. OxBS

Where the living with effort go. White Ship, The. Geoffrey Hill. OxBC

Where the lizard ran to its little prey. Range in the Desert, The. Randall Jarrell. NOBA; PoWW

Where the Mississippi meets the Amazon. Ntozake Shange. ISC

Where the mist has torn. Niu Hsi-chi. EaWin

Where the mob gathers, swiftly shoot along. John Gay. ECEV *Fr.* Trivia; or, The Art of Walking the Streets of London.

Where the Moosatockmaguntic. Ballad of Hiram Hover, The. Bayard Taylor. OBAL

Where the mountain hare has lain. (LL) Memory. W. B. Yeats. BIrV; PoE

Where the Nightmare Begins. Tanure Ojaide. NAfrP

Where the noisy flowers are deepest, a storied building. Tune: "Water Dragon's Chant"—Loathsome Spring. Ch'en Liang. SuSp, *tr.* by Hellmut Wilhelm

Where the old trees reign with their forward dark. Provinces. C. D. Wright. LCAP-2

Where the path opened. In Duffryn Woods. John Stuart Williams. AngWePo

Where the Picnic Was. Thomas Hardy. OxBTC

Where the pipe ends he had fixed the long trough. Windmill at Mandanthanunguna. Pambardu. NOBAu, *tr.* by George von Brandenstein

Where—the place of concatenations. Nostoi. Rodolfo Di Biasio. NeIt, *tr.* by Stephen Sartarelli

Where the plovers cry. Lady Otomo no Sakanoé. ArkPo, *tr.* by Edwin A. Cranston

Where the pools are bright and deep. Boy's Song, A. James Hogg. NOxBChV; OBEV; OTCP; OxAEP-2

Where the quiet-coloured [*or* colored] end of evening smiles. Love among the Ruins. Robert Browning. FHYEP; HAP; NAEL-5v2; NAEL-6v2; NOBE; OBEV; SCGP

Where the racing Wairau slows, homesick for its snowshed. Cloudy Bay. Eileen Duggan. PeNZ

Where the Rainbow Ends. Robert Lowell. HCAP; MoAmPo; PoetW

Where the Rainbow Ends. Richard Rive. PBA; TTY

Where the Red Lion flaring o'er the way. Description of an Author's Bedchamber, A. Oliver Goldsmith. BIrV

Where the remote *Bermudas* ride. Bermudas. Andrew Marvell. AWP; BASC; ESCV; FHYEP; FaBoCh; GeHe; NAEL-5v1; NAEL-6v1; NAEL-7v1; NOBE; NOCV; NOSC; NPeEn; NoP-4; OBEV; PBRV; PeECV; PoE; RB; SCGP; TFi; WoPoe

Where the residents are ghosts or images of the dead. (LL) Homer. ModIr; NPeEn *Fr.* Odyssey.

Where the river cleaves. For the Drunk. Carole Oles. OPRER

Where the river gets swift. Detailed History of the Western World. Joe Wenderoth. AmPoNex

Where the road turns to water. Cross Country. Rod Moran. NOBAu

Where the rue de la Verrerie. St Merri district, The. Robert Desnos. MFP, *tr.* by Martin Sorrell

Where the sea gulls sleep or indeed where they fly. Ballet of the Fifth Year, The. Delmore Schwartz. APT-2; OxBA; TwCP

Where the Slow Fig's Purple Sloth. Robert Penn Warren. APT-2

Where the slow river. Leda. "H. D.". NAAL-2v2

Where the Song Went Where She Went & What Happened When They Met. *Unknown.* STP, *tr.* by Richard Johnny John and Jerome Rothenberg

Where the still sunshine falls. Moor Girl's Well, The. Rosamund Marriott Watson. ViWPN

Where the stream ox-bowed. Sap. Robert Minhinnick. AngWePo

Where the stream winds pine winds linger. Jade Flower Palace. Tu Fu. ColAnChi, *tr.* by David Lattimore

Where the Sun Ends. Peter Davison. ChIV-1

Where the sun rises. *Unknown.* APN-2, *tr.* by Washington Matthews *Fr.* Mountain Chant, The.

Where the sun was always setting on the play. (LL) Long Garden, The. Patrick Kavanagh. HarvBoo; OBGa

Where the swan drifts upon a darkening flood. (LL) Coole Park and Ballylee, 1931. W. B. Yeats. GTBS-P; NOIV; NoAM; OBGa; OBMV

Where the thistle lifts a purple crown. Daisy. Francis Thompson. AWP; MoBrPo; OBEV

Where the Three Roads Meet. Palladas [*or* Pallades]. WoPoe, *tr.* by Anselm Hollo

Where the waves break. (LL) Signature for Tempo. Archibald MacLeish. CRP; VGW

Where the weather is not water. Mexican Fire Breather, A. Juan Delgado. TouFir

Where the Weather Suits My Clothes. John Godfrey. PmAP

Where the wheel of light is turned. Pole Star for This Year. Archibald MacLeish. OxBA

Where the wheel turned the water / gently shirred. (LL) Event, The. Rita Dove. ESEAA; NoAM

Where the Wicked Cease from Troubling, and the Weary Are at Rest. Henry Hart Milman. SacPr

Where the wife is scouring the frying pan. Land of Little Sticks, 1945. James Tate. BodElec; LCAP-2

Where the wild woods and pathless forests frown. Charlotte Smith. CenSon

Where the wind. Footprints on the Glacier. W. S. Merwin. NoAM

Where the wind glitters. (LL) Suddenly. Robin Blaser. FTOS; PoM

Where the wings of a sunny Dome expand. America. Herman Melville. APN-2

Where the Wolf Sings. Mary Low. SurWo

Where the young river, from its wild ravine. Emigrant's Cabin, The. Thomas Pringle. PeSAV

Where then shall hope and fear their objects find? Additional Poem, An. John Ashbery. FaBoMo

Where then shall Hope and Fear their objects find? Samuel Johnson. OxBEV *Fr.* Vanity of Human Wishes, The; The Tenth Satire of Juvenal Imitated.

Where there are humans / you'll find flies. Issa. ZenPo, *tr.* by Takashi Ikemoto and Lucien Stryk

Where there is personal liking we go. Marianne Craig Moore. NOBA; OxBA *Fr.* Part of a Novel, Part of a Poem, Part of a Play.

Where there was some hole. Ruskie's Boy. Víctor Hernández Cruz. PueRic

Where they are, where my lute and drum have fallen? (LL) La Chute. Charles Olson. InPK-6; PAI

Where they come from. (LL) These Days. Charles Olson. APT-2; RaBo

Where they who worshipped idol gods have been. (LL) Eagles, The. Jones Very. TAP; TCAPo

Where they will bury me. Temporarily in Oxford. Anne Stevenson. NoP-4

Where things began to happen and I knew it. (LL) Ground Swell. Mark Jarman. GeoHom; MoASP

Where this is freedom: free to follow each desire. Freedom. Friedrich von Logau. GePo, *tr.* by George C. Schoolfield

Where, to me, is the loss. No Newspapers. Mary Elizabeth Coleridge. NPeEn

Where to store furs and how to treat the hair. (LL) Edna St. Vincent Millay. APT-1; HeIP-4

Where to? what next? (LL) Carl Sandburg. MoAmPo; NOBA; NoAM; OxBA *Fr.* People, Yes, The.

Where tongues were loud and hearts were light. Ancre at Hamel: Afterwards, The. Edmund Charles Blunden. PeFWW

Where tossing in grey sheets you weep. Loba as Eve. Diane Di Prima. HW

Where true love is not given. (LL) Dead Love. Elizabeth Siddal. LW; NOBVV

Where unincarnate spirits purely aspire! (LL) To George Sand: A Recognition. Elizabeth Barrett Browning. BoWoP; NAEL-5v2; NAEL-6v2; NALW; PEW; PoBW; VWP

Where Venta's Norman castle still appears. On King Arthur's Round Table, at Winchester. Thomas Warton, the Younger. Son

Where voices vanish into dream. Elected Silence. Siegfried Sassoon. MoBrPo

Where was it one first heard of the truth? The the. (LL) Man on the Dump, The. Wallace Stevens. APT-1; HAP; NAWM-7v2; NoAM

Where we are the flowers in our clocks flare up their feathers ring the. Great Lament of my Obscurity Three, The. Tristan Tzara. PFTM-1

Where we had stood. Wilpena Pound. Charles Buckmaster. BMAP

Where we live, the teakettle whistles out. Now. William Stafford. NNaP

Where we made the fire. Where the Picnic Was. Thomas Hardy. OxBTC

Where we stood, saying I. (LL) In Those Years. Adrienne Rich. ExTi; LoL

Where we went in the boat was a long bay. Mediterranean, The. Allen Tate. APT-2; FaBoMo; FuPo; HAP; MoAmPo; VGW; WoPoe

Where were the greenhouses going. Big Wind. Theodore Roethke. ColAP; HarvBoo; TRP; VGW

Where were you bound for, unknown man. Journey, The. Igor Bobrowsky. CDa

Where were you in the marriage season? Too Late for a Husband. *Unknown.* WoPoe, *tr.* by Nguyen Ngoc Bich

Where were you in winters of snow. For Lost and Found Brothers. Naomi Shihab Nye. GraLe

Where were you then? Story, A. Margaret Avison. MoCV

Where When Was. Reginald Shepherd. GT

Where, where are my masters? My Masters. Sandor Csoori. VCWP, *tr.* by Len Roberts

Where, where are now the great reports. Fuimus Fumus. Joshua Sylvester. FaBoEE

Where, where but here have Pride and Truth. On Hearing That the Students of Our New University Have Joined the Agitation against Immoral Literature. W. B. Yeats. NoAM

Where wil you have your vertuous names safe laid. Samuel Daniel. NPeEn *Fr.* Musophilus; or, Defence of All Learning.

Where will I go? Nezahualcoyotl. WoPoe, *tr.* by Thelma D. Sullivan

Where will the locust, pine and. Twenty Years from Auschwitz, Bergen-Belsen and Other Camps. Luisa Futuransky. MirDau, *tr.* by Celeste Kostopulos-Cooperman

Where Will You Be? Patricia Parker. AfrBLW; GLP

Where will your strange pilgrimage take you next? Saying Good-Bye to Feng the Hermit. Mo Shih-lung. CoBLCP, *tr.* by Jonathan Chaves

Where, without bloodshed, can there be. Long Feud. Louis Untermeyer. MoAmPo

Where would you look for blessing who are caught. And No Help Came. Peter Porter. BMAP

Where yon proud turrets crown the rock. Bleeding Nun, The. *Unknown.* NOBRP

Where yonder ridgy mountains bound the scene. Anne Grant. RWP *Fr.* Highlanders, The.

Where you are. Peony Afternoon. So Chong-Ju. VCWP, *tr.* by David R. McCann

Where you are it will not be snowing. December 25, 1991. Rose Solari. AmPoNex

Where you going? / (Getting berries. Think I'll try a little farther.). Getting Berries. *Unknown.* STP, *tr.* by Franz Boas

Where you going? / (Going to get firewood.). Getting Firewood. *Unknown.* STP, *tr. by* Franz Boas

Where you have fallen, you stay. On the Wall of a KZ-Lager. János Pilinszky. AF; HP; PoSu

Where your skin / is your passport. (LL) Untitled Blues; after a Photograph by Yevgeni Yevtushenko. Yusef Komunyakaa. ESEAA; GT; UnSA

Where? What? and turn away. (LL) Sketch, A. Christina Georgina Rossetti. GTBS-P; VWP

Where? When? Which? Langston Hughes. BPo

Whereas galoshed my Julia goes. Upon Julia's Arctics. Bert Leston Taylor. NBLV

Whereas he's bravely judged by the illiterate. Hungarian Writer, The. János Batsányi. IQMS, *tr. by* Adam Makkai

Whereas it minds its own business. Emancipation Proclamation. William Heyen. PoCoUp

Wherefore I marvel greatly of myself. The Lady of the Arbour. OBGa *Fr.* Flower and the Leaf, The.

Wherefore the Scars of Christ's Passion Remained in the Body of His Resurrection. Theodulf of Orleans. MLL, *tr. by* Helen Waddell

Wherein Consists the High Estate. Ebenezer Dayton. AH

Wherein the mighty trust! (LL) Image in Lava, The. Felicia Dorothea Hemans. CABP; NOBRP

Wherein to play your violin with grace. (LL) Gwendolyn Brooks. InPK-6; NIL-7; NIP-4 *Fr.* Womanhood, The.

Wherelings whenlings / (daughters of if but offspring of hopefear). E. E. Cummings. HAP; WeW-3

Whereso'er you are, my heart shall truly love you. (LL) "Were I as Base as Is the Lowly Plain." Joshua Sylvester. GSo; NoSic; Son

Whereso'er I turn mine eyes. God Everywhere. Abraham Ibn Ezra. TrJP, *tr. by* D. E. de L

Wheresoe'er I turn my View. Lines on Thomas Warton's Poems. Samuel Johnson. FaBoEE

Whereto should I express. To His Lady. Henry VIII, King of England. CTC; EBEV; NoSic

Wherever are the lowly, the suffering, and the poor. Najrul Islām. SinGod, *tr. by* Rachel Fell McDermott

Wherever God erects a house of prayer. Daniel Defoe. NOBL; OBSV *Fr.* True-born Englishman, The.

Wherever I go (these). Poem against the State (Of Things): 1975. June Jordan. ISC

Wherever I go to find. Pigeons. Bert Meyers. SPE

Wherever Kenji Takezo goes. When for Weeks the Sea is Flat. Rick Noguchi. MoASP

Wherever Summer is a country still. Friedrich Hölderlin. WoPoe, *tr. by* David Rattray *Fr.* Seasons, The.

Wherever that may be? (LL) Questions of Travel. Elizabeth Bishop. ColAP; HarvBoo; NAAL-2v2; NOBA

Wherever there's a woman in any Bengali home. Mā Bāsantī Cakrabarttī. SinGod, *tr. by* Rachel Fell McDermott

Wherever we go. Together Wherever We Go. Stephen Sondheim. ReLy

Wherever we looked the land would hold us up. (LL) One Home. William Stafford. CoAP; VGW

Wherever we remove. (LL) God's Residence. Emily Dickinson. SAmP; WPoS

Wherever we turn in the storm of roses. In the Storm of Roses. Ingeborg Bachmann. AF, *tr. by* Mark Anderson

Wherever you are. Woman with Flaxen Hair in Norfolk Heard, A. Robert Kelly. PmAP

Wherever you are, dig deeply! Undiscouraged. Friedrich Wilhelm Nietzsche. WoPoe, *tr. by* Robert Bly

Wherewith this lady speeds it on its way. (LL) Sonnet: Of the Eyes of a Certain Mandetta. Guido Cavalcanti. AWP; EaItPo, *tr. by* Dante Gabriel Rossetti

Whether all grace have fail'd I scarce may scan. Onesto di Boncima. EaItPo, *tr. by* Dante Gabriel Rossetti

Whether astringent. Chiyojo [*or* Chiyo *or* Chiyo-Ni *or* Kaga no Chiyo *or* Fukuda Chiyo-Ni]. NIL-7, *tr. by* Daniel C. Buchanan

Whether at doomsday tell, ye reverend wise. Quaerè. George Farewell. NOEC; NPeEn; OBCoV

Whether by sea or river or in mountains. Night Talk in a Dream Chamber. Ikkyu Sojun. ErotSp, *tr. by* Sam Hamill

Whether day my spirit's yearning. Thought Eternal, The. Goethe. AWP, *tr. by* Ludwig Lewisohn

Whether his mouth be open or shut. (LL) T. S. Eliot. NBLV; OBAL; OBCoV; PeLV; UV *Fr.* Five-Finger Exercises.

Whether I find thee bright with fair. Changeful Beauty. *Unknown.* EnLoPo, *tr. by* Andrew Lang

Whether I live or fail. (LL) V-Letter. Karl Shapiro. IllVoic; NoAM; TrJP

Whether I see you now. *Unknown.* ErotSp, *tr. by* Sam Hamill

Whether I sit or lie. Ukihashi. WPOW

Whether it be new or old! (LL) William Stevenson. HeIP-4; NAEL-5v1; NAEL-6v1, *tr. by* John Still *Fr.* Gammer Gurton's Needle.

Whether it is fiction or not. (LL) Synopsis of the Great Welsh Novel. Harri Webb. AngWePo; TCAWP

Whether it is from Eden's sacred plan. Hartwell Gardens. A. of Aylesbury Merrick. OBGa

Whether it rose up as a small brown bird. Questions about Poetry since Auschwitz. Tadeusz Rózewicz. AF, *tr. by* Robert A. Maguire

Whether on Ida's shady brow. To the Muses. William Blake. HAP; HeIP-4; NAEL-5v2; NAEL-6v2; NOBE; NOEC; OBEV; SCGP

Whether one is eminent or humble depends on Fate. Juan Chi. ColAnChi *Fr.* Songs of My Soul.

Whether one paints five Helens. Ultimate Antientropy, The. Theodore Weiss. NoAM

Whether or Not. D. H. Lawrence. MoBrPo

Whether or not a paradise. Soa. JDP, *tr. by* Yoel Hoffmann

Whether or not I shall fly. And I Speak of Cosmic Things. Vsevolod Nekrasov. TCRusP, *tr. by* Daniel Weissbort

Whether that soul which now comes up to you. Hymn to the Saints, and to Marquis Hamilton[, An]. John Donne. NOSC

Whether the sensitive plant, or that. Shelley. NPeEn *Fr.* Sensitive Plant, The.

Whether the Turkish new moon minded be. Sir Philip Sidney. NoSic; PoE *Fr.* Astrophil and Stella.

Whether the weather be fine. Weather. *Unknown.* OTCP

Whether they are drunk or sober. Some People Are about Jam. Sandra Maria Esteves. PueRic

Whether they work together or apart. (LL) Tuft of Flowers, The. Robert Frost. APT-1; AWP; MoAmPo; NAAL-2v2; OxBA

Whether thou getst them green, or lets them seed. (LL) Upon Wedlock and Death of Children. Edward Taylor. ColAP; NAAL-2v1; NAAL-3; NAAL-5; SacPr; TCAPo

Whether thou smile or frown, thou beauteous face. Charles Lloyd. CenSon

Whether to Ceaser he was friend or foe? Upon the Death of G. B. John Cotton. SCAP

Whether to Ceaser hee was friend, or foe. (LL) Bacon's Epitaph, Made by His Man. John Cotton. SCAP; TCAPo

Whether to cry or whether to be proud. Till Evening. Jakov [*or* Jacob] Steinberg. FIT, *tr. by* Robert Friend

Whether what we sense of this world. Metonymy as an Approach to a Real World. William Bronk. APSN; VGW

Whether White or Black be best. Verses Made Sometime Since upon. . . the Indian Squa. John Josselyn. SCAP

Whether you are a citizen or stranger coming from elsewhere. Epitaph from Athens. *Unknown.* GrAn, *tr. by* Richmond Lattimore

Whether you are here or yonder. More Than You Know. Vincent Youmans. ReLy

Whether you say it, think it, know it. Ted Hughes. NoAM *Fr.* Stations.

Whi / te boys gone. Val Ferdinand. NBV

Which blamed the living man. (LL) Growing Old. Matthew Arnold. FHYEP; NAEL-5v2; NAEL-6v2; NOBVV; NPeEn

Which breathes its thanks in rough, but timid strains. (LL) On Mrs. Montagu. Ann Yearsley. ECWP; RWP

Which but expressions be of inward evils. (LL) Fulke Greville, 1st Baron Brooke. NPeEn; Son *Fr.* Caelica.

Which carries the feathered grass a long way down the upbreathing air. (LL) Adrienne Rich. ErotSp; NAAL-2v2; NoAM; TRP *Fr.* Twenty-one Love Poems.

Which caused her thus to send thee out of door. (LL) Author to Her Book, The. Anne Bradstreet. BASC; ColAP; EMWP; InPK-6; MakPoe; NAAL-2v1; NAAL-3; NAAL-5; NALW; NOBA; NoP-4; OxBA; PoE; SCAP; TAP; TCAPo

Which Claus of Innsbruck cast in bronze for me! (LL) My Last Duchess. Robert Browning. AWP; AmFaPo; CABP; ClHu; EBNV; EBVV; FHYEP; GTBS-P; HAP; HeIP-4; ITBLP; InPK-6; MakPoe; NAEL-5v2; NAWM-7v2; NIL-7; NIP-4; NOBE; NOBVV; NPeEn; NoP-4; OxBEV; PAI; PeVV; PoE; PoPoPo; SCGP; SCV; SoSe-8; TFi; TRP

Which Contains a Fantasy Satisfied with a Love Befitting It. Sister Juana Inés de la Cruz. ErotSp, *tr. by* Alan S. Trueblood

Which cover lightly, gentle earth. (LL) On My First Daughter. Ben Jonson. BASC; BeJo; EBEV; FaBoEE; NAEL-5v1; NAEL-6v1; NAEL-7v1; NOBE; NOSC; NoP-4; PoE

Which dark green oaks his noontide leisure shields. (LL) Solitude. John Clare. NOBVV; OxBSP

Which Earth grants all her kind. (LL) She Hears the Storm. Thomas Hardy. NAEL-5v2; NAEL-6v2

Which everyone has sat except a man. (LL) E. E. Cummings. FaBoEE; InPK-6; NBLV; OBAL

Which faith had dictated, and angels trod. (LL) On Exodus 3: 14: "I am that I am." Matthew Prior. ChIV-1; NOCV

Which form of you should I imitate to be called yous? Shipwreck.

Biancamaria Frabotta. CItWP, *tr.* by Cinzia Sartini Blum and Lara Trubowitz

Which goes with Bridge, and Women and Champagne. (LL)   On a General Election.   Joseph Hilaire Pierre Belloc.   FaBoEE; NOBE; NOBL; NPeEn; OBSV; OxBEV; OxBTC

Which He from Heaven doth bring[e]. (LL)   New Prince, New Pomp[e].   Robert Southwell.   ChrPo; ESCV; NOBE; NOCV; NoSic; SacPr; TrCP

Which heaves but with the heaving deep. (LL)   Tennyson.   EBEV; EBVV; FHYEP; HeIP-4; NAEL-6v2; NAWM-7v2; NOBE; NPeEn; OxBEV; PeECV   *Fr.* In Memoriam A. H. H.

Which his own lanthorn throws up from himself. (LL)   To Percy Shelley.   Leigh Hunt.   CenSon; Son

Which I am afraid to put on. (LL)   Empire of Dreams.   Charles Simic.   BLT; LCAP-2; VCAP

Which I have loved long since, and lost awhile. (LL)   Pillar of the Cloud, The.   John Henry, Cardinal Newman.   ChIV-1; InvLi; NPeEn; SacPr

Which I was given because.   Lines on Roger Hilton's Watch.   William Sydney Graham.   NPeEn

Which I wish to remark.   Plain Language from Truthful James.   Bret Harte.   APN-2; CTC; EBNV; NOBL; OBAL; OBCoV; PeLV; UV

Which I wish to remark.   Heathen Pass-ee, The.   Arthur Clement Hilton.   NOBL; UV

Which I wish to say is this.   Gertrude Stein.   NoP-4

Which is a proud, and yet a wretched thing. (LL)   Sir John Davies.   NOBE; WoPoe   *Fr.* Nosce Teipsum.

Which is also the case when our women are crazy. (LL)   When Our Women Go Crazy.   Julia Kasdorf.   NeAmPo; PBCAP

Which is in me / like a hill. (LL)   Hill, The.   Robert Creeley.   CRP; RaBo; TRP

Which is not going to go wasted on me which is why I'm telling you about it. (LL)   Having a Coke with You.   Frank O'Hara.   GLP; VCAP

Which is not thought, but the airless stare.   Light.   Marianne Boruch.   PoSol

Which is the cosiest voice.   Gray Thrums.   Clara Doty Bates.   OBCA

Which is the reason my Damon that although.   Sonnet 12.   Francesco de Aldana.   BLPSL, *tr.* by Rene de Costa, Rigas Kappatos and Eleni Paidoussi

Which is the storehouse rich of Nature sweet. (LL)   Pastime of the Queen of Fairies, The.   Margaret Lucas Cavendish, Duchess of Newcastle.   BASC; NAEL-6v1

Which is, to keep that hid. (LL)   Undertaking, The.   John Donne.   NAEL-5v1; NAEL-6v1; NAEL-7v1; NOBE

Which is worse.   *Unknown.*   WoPoe, *tr.* by Helen Craig McCullough and William H. McCullough   *Fr.* Eiga Monogatari, The.

Which is you, old two-in-one?   Archibald MacLeish.   ChIV-1   *Fr.* Songs for Eve.

(Which is your luck.) (LL)   Ballad of Billie Potts, The.   Robert Penn Warren.   FuPo; NOBA; OxBA

Which it is not my style.   Truthful James to the Editor.   Bret Harte.   APN-2

Which look for death as for a blessed thing. (LL)   Dante Alighieri.   AWP; EaItPo, *tr.* by Dante Gabriel Rossetti   *Fr.* La Vita Nuova.

Which made poor Simon whistle. (LL)   Simple Simon.   Mother Goose.   LB; OTCP; OxNR; ReMoGo

Which men who change can never know. (LL)   Coventry Patmore.   NOBVV; OxBSP   *Fr.* Angel in the House, The.

Which might be fair to tell but which I hide. (LL)   Of England, and of Its Marvels.   Fazio degli Uberti.   AWP; EaItPo, *tr.* by Dante Gabriel Rossetti

Which more and more to heaven [*or* heav'n] do grow. (LL)   Bible, *O.T.*   BASC; NOCV, *tr.* by Mary Sidney Herbert, Countess of Pembroke   *Fr.* Psalms.

Which mortals dream of, but which angels know. (LL)   John Pierpont.   APN-1; TreFP   *Fr.* Airs of Palestine.

Which must soon come—as I cannot forget. (LL)   14-Year-Old Convalescent Cat in the Winter, A.   Gavin Ewart.   OPOU; OxBSP

Which my God feels as blood [*or* bloud]; but I, as wine. (LL)   Agony [*or* Agonie], The.   George Herbert.   ESCV; GeHe

Which needs the badge of honor must display. (LL)   To Dante Alighieri: He Mistrusts the Love of Lapo Gianni.   Guido Cavalcanti.   AWP; EaItPo, *tr.* by Dante Gabriel Rossetti

Which nobody can deny. (LL)   Sweet Meat Has Sour Sauce.   William Cowper.   ECEV; NOEC; OBSV

Which now the angels sing! (LL)   It Came upon the Midnight Clear.   Edmund Hamilton Sears.   AH; APN-1; ChrPo; SacPr; TCAPo

Which of the seven deadly sins is worst?   Greed.   Giuseppe Gioacchino Belli.   WoPoe, *tr.* by Anthony Burgess

Which of thy names I take, not only bears.   To Sir Horace Vere.   Ben Jonson.   BeJo

Which of you / is going to take my body?   Song of Starvation.   *Unknown.*   STP, *tr.* by Jerome Rothenberg

Which One Is Genuine?   Charles Baudelaire.   RaBo, *tr.* by Robert Bly

Which One Is the Grown-up?   Haiku.   Liz Rosenberg.   InvLad

Which only breeds your beauty's overthrow. (LL)   I Saw My Lady Weep.   *Unknown.*   EnLoPo; NoSic

Which otherwise had only venial been. (LL)   To My Young Lover.   Jane Barker.   BASC; LW

Which Religion Vouchsafes.   Jane Miller.   GifTon

Which road, which road did you take.   Exaltation.   Franz Werfel.   TrJP, *tr.* by Edith Abercrombie Snow

Which Road?   William Barnes.   NOBVV

Which teaches that all has less value than half. (LL)   James Russell Lowell.   NOBA; TAP   *Fr.* Fable for Critics, A.

Which the Chicken, Which the Egg?   Ogden Nash.   APT-2

Which the same I am free to maintain. (LL)   Plain Language from Truthful James.   Bret Harte.   APN-2; CTC; EBNV; NOBL; OBAL; OBCoV; PeLV; UV

Which the same I am free to maintain. (LL)   Heathen Pass-ee, The.   Arthur Clement Hilton.   NOBL; UV

Which they and all the sullen world have lost. (LL)   L'Amitie: To Mrs. Mary [*or* M.] Awbrey.   Katherine Philips.   NIL-7; NOSC

Which they that know the rest, know more than I. (LL)   Answer, The.   George Herbert.   FaBoVe; NPeEn

Which things being so, as we said when we studied.   Louis MacNeice.   *Fr.* Autumn Journal.

Which those who never loved, can never know! (LL)   Her Confirmed Despair.   Mary Robinson.   CenSon; RWP

Which thou in Pearles did'st lend. (LL)   On the Wounds of Our Crucified Lord.   Richard Crashaw.   NAEL-5v1; NAEL-6v1; NAEL-7v1

Which thus presents and thus records true life. (LL)   Elizabeth Barrett Browning.   FaBoWar; NAEL-5v2; NAEL-6v2; NALW; NoP-4; PeVV   *Fr.* Aurora Leigh.

Which to heare, vouchsafe, O dearest dred a-while, The. (LL)   Edmund Spenser.   FHYEP; NAEL-5v1; NAEL-7v1   *Fr.* Faerie Queene, The.

Which used to lead something into somewhere. (LL)   E. E. Cummings.   NIL-7; NIP-4; PoE

Which Washington?   Eve Merriam.   NTCP

Which way he went?   Rondelet.   May Probyn.   VWP

Which we prefer to the alternative. (LL)   Invocation: "This is for Elsa, also known as Liz."   Marilyn Hacker.   ExTi; PuP-23; WiU

Whichever one of you throwing a party at home.   *Unknown.*   PriapPo, *tr.* by Richard W. Hooper   *Fr.* Priapus Poems, The.

Whichway.   Ron Welburn.   NBV

Whiffenpoof Song.   Ted B. Galloway.   TCAPo

Whiffs of the Ohio River at Cincinnati.   Carl Sandburg.

"When I asked for fish in the restaurant facing the Ohio River."   PoE

Whig's the first letter of his odious name.   Acrostic on Wharton, An.   *Unknown.*   OBSV

Whigmaleerie, A.   William Soutar.   OxBS

Whil'st Alexis lay prest [*or* press'd].   Dryden.   NPeEn; PeLV   *Fr.* Marriage à la Mode.

While.   Bruce Andrews.   FTOS

While a child I longed to be staunch in virtue.   Passing through My Shih-ning Estate.   Hsieh Ling-yün.   SuSp, *tr.* by Francis Westbrook

While a thousand fine projects are planned ev'ry day.   Song, A.   *Unknown.*   NOEC

While Adam slept, from him his Eve arose.   Epigram.   *Unknown.*   FaBoEE

While ago, A.   Promise, The.   Heberto Padilla.   TCLAP, *tr.* by Alexander Coleman and Alastair Reid

While all about us peal the loud, sweet *Te Deums* of the Canterbury bells. (LL)   Madonna of the Evening Flowers.   Amy Lowell.   NAAL-5; NALW

While an intrinsic ardor prompts to write.   To the University of Cambridge, in New-England.   Phillis Wheatley.   NAAAL; NAAL-2v1; NAAL-3; NAAL-5; TAP; TCAPo

While apparition is the instant of illumination and of being touched.   Suicide with Squirtgun.   Tom Clark.   PmAP

While as I lived no house I had.   Upon the Grave of a Beggar.   Timothy Kendall.   NoSic

While battles rage and cannons roar.   Drill's the Thing.   *Unknown.*   FaBoWar

While biding our time. (LL)   Cycle.   Bobbi Sykes.   BMAP; IBA

While boats list in port.   Mother and I.   Shinkichi Takahashi.   ZenPo, *tr.* by Takashi Ikemoto and Lucien Stryk

While Bouncing the Shema Back and Forth in Shul.   Talia N. Bloch.   GotH

While breaking the big rock.   Stone Giant.   Joseph Bruchac.   CDW

While bringing Apollo the pick of the Etruscan plunder.   Simonides.   GrAn

While Bustopher Jones wears white spats! (LL)   Bustopher Jones: The Cat about Town.   T. S. Eliot.   OBCoV; TriCat

While Butler, needy wretch, was yet alive.   On the Setting up of Mr. Butler's Monument in Westminster Abbey.   Samuel Wesley.   NBLV; NOEC; OxBSP

While by the rosebed gay you stood, and revelled in the multitude.   One among the Roses.   Edmund Charles Blunden.   OBGa

While coming to the feast I found. Léonie Adams. *See* In coming to the feast I found

While daylight lasts, I'm reading in my books. Pleasures of Darkness, The. Ahmad al-Safi Al-Najafi. MAP, *tr.* by John Heath-Stubbs and Salma Khadra Jayyusi

While Delia shines at hurlothrumbo. Widow and Virgin Sisters, The. William Broome. ECEV

While driving, Kukutis exclaims. Kukutis's Trip on the Samogitian Highway. Marcelijus Martinaitis. TWW, *tr.* by Laima Sruoginis

While driving north, lost. I Was Looking for the University. Clarence Major. GT

While drunk, I seek merriment. Tune: "Moon of the Western River." Hsin Ch'i-chi. ChinPo, *tr.* by Yip Wai-lim

While Dubliner leopold bloom sought solace. Limerick. Gerard Benson. PeLi

While Eve waited. Sleep of Adam, The. John Hejduk. ChIV-1

While everything external / dies away in the far off. As the Human Village Prepares for Its Fate. Tom Clark. BodElec

While from the dizzy precipice I gaze. Her Reflections on the Leucadian Rock before She Perishes. Mary Robinson. CenSon; RWP

While gazing round this dear ramshackle one. Other People's Glasshouses. Ruth Pitter. OBGa

While gentlefolks strut in their silver and satins. Bartleme Fair. George Alexander Stevens. NOEC

While God is marching on. (LL) Battle Hymn [*or* Battle-Hymn] of the Republic, The. Julia Ward Howe. AH; APN-1; BRP; CBCWP; HHAm; NOBA; NOCV; OBWP; PWR; SCV; SWaP; TAP; TCAPo; TFi; WPE

While going the road to sweet Athy. Johnny, I Hardly Knew Ye. *Unknown.* BIrV; FaBoWar; NPeEn; OxBoLi

While greasy [*or* greasie] Joan[e] doth keel[e] the pot. (LL) William Shakespeare. ClHu; GTBS-P; HAP; MakPoe; NAEL-5v1; NAEL-6v1; NIL-7; NIP-4; NoP-4; OBEV; OxBEV; PAI; SCGP; TFi; TRP; UnPo; WeW-3 *Fr.* Love's Labour's Lost.

While half the globe away the highest peak of Everest. Disproportionate. Timothy Geiger. AmPoNex

While he lives, let him alone. (LL) Artist, An. Robinson Jeffers. HarvBoo; VGW

While he slept, I poured salt in his ears. Judith Recalls Holofernes. Maura Stanton. YaYoPo

While her fond heart against the deed rebels. Widow's Remarriage, The. Mary F. Johnson. CenSon

While her husband spent his afternoons napping. Spirit Papers. Teresa D. Cader. ExTi

While His Body's Vigor Is Whole. Bhartrihari. WoPoe, *tr.* by Barbara Stoler Miller

While Holroyd may boast of her beautiful bottom. On Seeing a Tapestry Chair-Bottom Beautifully Worked by His Daughter for Mrs Holroyd. Richard Owen Cambridge. ECEV

While Homer and Whitman roared in the pines? (LL) Edgar Lee Masters. ColAP; MoAmPo; NOBA; NoAM; OxBA; TAP; TCAPo *Fr.* Spoon River Anthology.

While homeward bound I thought about. Plans Gone up in Smoke. Sándor Petőfi. IQMS, *tr.* by Leslie A. Kery

While I am praying. Prayer for a Thief. Phil DuPlessis. PeSAV, *tr.* by the author

While I Am Young. Silas Ballou. AH

While I asked myself. *Unknown.* ArkPo, *tr.* by Helen Craig McCullough

While I believe that what Im doing depends essentially upon. Real Estate. David Antin. FTOS

While I droop here. (LL) I Am a Parcel of Vain Strivings Tied. Henry David Thoreau. APN-1; ColAP; TAP; TCAPo

While I examine my hands. (LL) Leap, The. James Dickey. NIL-7; NIP-4

While I fled. (LL) Intimates. D. H. Lawrence. BoLoP; NBLV; OxBSP; RaBo

While I incessantly pursue. To a Worm. Mikha'il Nu'aima [*or* Nuaymah]. MAP, *tr.* by Sargon Boulus and Thomas G. Ezzy

While I Listen to Thy Voice. Edmund Waller. BeJo

While I, not less an-hungered, gaze and sing. (LL) Art and Life. Agnes Mary Frances Robinson. OxBSo; VWP

While I recline / At ease beneath. Cotton Boll, The. Henry Timrod. APN-2

While I sit at the door. Eve. Christina Georgina Rossetti. ChIV-1; GTBS-P; NALW; NIL-7; NIP-4

While I sit down scribbling herring verses. Artist and a Wailing Mother, An. Freddy Macha. NAfrP

While I Slept. Robert Francis. APT-2; KaS

While I slept it was all over. Pipe, The. Shinkichi Takahashi. ZenPo, *tr.* by Takashi Ikemoto and Lucien Stryk

While I slept, while I slept and the night grew colder. While I Slept. Robert Francis. APT-2; KaS

While I stood here, in the open, lost in myself. Milkweed. James Wright (1927–80). ColAP; LCAP-2; NOBA; RaBo

While I stuffed wrapping paper. Louie the Tailor. Gary Pacernick [*or* Pacernik]. GotH

While I thoughtfully intone my poem by the autumnal riverbank. (LL) Solitary Falcon above the Buddha Hall of the Monastery of Universal Purity, A. Mei Yao Ch'en. SuSp; WoPoe, *tr.* by Jonathan Chaves

While I walk on. Masahide. JDP, *tr.* by Yoel Hoffmann

While I was building neat. It Is Dangerous to Read Newspapers. Margaret Atwood. HeIP-4; OBWP

While I was musing on my theme. Chiyojo [*or* Chiyo *or* Chiyo-Ni *or* Kaga no Chiyo *or* Fukuda Chiyo-Ni]. AWTN, *tr.* by Asatarō Miyamori

While I was walking, wondering, "Do I, don't I?" Deaf-Mutes. Nikolai Ivanovich Glazkov. TCRP, *tr.* by Daniel Weissbort

While I watch the Christmas blaze. Reminder, The. Thomas Hardy. ChAP; OBCP

While I watch the yellow wheat. Watching the Wheat. John Jones. AngWePo

While in long exile far from you I roam. To Dr. Moore, in Answer to a Poetical Epistle Written by Him in Wales. Helen Maria Williams. ECWP; WoRP

While in my simple gospel creed. Tartarus. Oliver Wendell Holmes. NCAP

While in the mask of night there shone that cut. Landing on the Moon. May Swenson. TAP

While in the park I sing, the listning deer. At Penshurst. Edmund Waller. BeJo

While in this garden *Proserpine* was taking hir pastime. Ovid. NPeEn, *tr.* by Arthur Golding *Fr.* Metamorphoses.

While it's still dark. Magdalenas, Las. Judith Ortiz Cofer. TouFir

While It Was Raining. Wen Cheng-ming. CoBLCP, *tr.* by Jonathan Chaves

While Jove's planet rises yonder, silent over Africa. (LL) Home-Thoughts, from the Sea. Robert Browning. NAEL-5v2; NAEL-6v2; SCGP

While joy gave clouds the light of stars. Villain, The. William Henry Davies. AngWePo; MoBrPo; OxBSP; OxBTC

While joy reanimates the fields. Song on Leaving the Country Early in the Spring. Anne Batten Cristall. RWP

While ladling butter from alternate tubs. On the Historians Freeman and Stubbs. J. E. Thorold Rogers. FaBoEE

While later that night they flurried in, A. Sarah Arvio. KGB *Fr.* Visits from the Seventh.

While leanest beasts in pastures feed. Supreme Fortune Falls Soonest. Robert Herrick. CaPo

While Love, his arrows broke, retires forlorn. (LL) Temple of Chastity, The. Mary Robinson. CenSon; RWP

While, Lydia, I was lov'd of thee. Horace. OBVE, *tr.* by Robert Herrick *Fr.* Odes.

While Many a Merry Tale. Samuel Johnson. UV

While maudlin Whigs deplored [*or* deplor'd] their Cato's Fate. On a Lady Who P-ssed [*or* P———st] at the Tragedy of Cato. Pope. OxBSP

While my father prospered. While My Father. Giovanna Pollarolo. TANSG, *tr.* by Marjorie Agosin

While my father walked through mud. 1905. David Ignatow. TaR

While my hair was still cut straight across my forehead. River Merchant's Wife, The: A Letter. Li Po. APT-1; AWP; BoLoP; ClHu; HAP; HeIP-4; InPK-6; MoAmPo; NAAL-2v2; NIP-4; NOBA; NOBE; NoAM; NPeEn; OBMV; OBVE; OxBA; RB; RaBo; TAP; TFi; TRP; TTTS; TwCP; UnPo; WeW-3, *tr.* by Ezra Pound

While my hair was still cut straight across my forehead. River-Merchant's Wife, The: A Letter. Ezra Pound. AmFaPo; ColAP; HarvBoo; NAAL-5; NIL-7; NoP-4; PoPoPo; RACG; TCAPo

While my sad Muse the darkest Covert Sought. Congratulatory Poem to Her Sacred Majesty Queen Mary, Upon Her Arrival in England, A. Aphra Behn. EMWP

While my wife at my side lies slumbering, and the wars are over long. Artilleryman's Vision, The. Walt Whitman. CBCWP

While neighbouring cities waste the fleeting hours. Anna Seward. NOEC *Fr.* Colebrook Dale.

While Northward the hot sun was sinking o'er the trees. Psalm. Robert Bridges. FaBoTw

While now upon the win' do zwell. Bells ov Alderburnham, The. William Barnes. EBVV

While o'er Our Guilty Land, O Lord. Samuel Davies. AH

While o'er the Deep Thy Servants Sail. George Burgess. AH

While ocean thus the latent store bequeaths. Henry Brooke. ECEV *Fr.* Universal Beauty.

While one sere leaf, that parting autumn yields. Anna Seward. WoRP *Fr.* Sonnets.

While passing through a. No Deposit Returns. Carlos Cumpian. ReTh

While playing at the woodland's edge. Terrible Path, The. Brian Patten. OTCP

While pleasure reigns unrivalled on this shore. Boston in Distress. *Unknown.* NOEC

While preaching. Now be still, and I'll begin. (LL) Geoffrey Chaucer. NAWM-5v1; NAWM-7v1, *tr.* by Theodore Morrison *Fr.* Canterbury Tales, The.

While rain, with eve in partnership. Beyond the Last Lamp. Thomas Hardy. NOBE

While round the arméd bands. Execution of King Charles, The. Andrew Marvell. PoRA

While she sleeps. (LL) While I Slept. Robert Francis. APT-2; KaS

While shepherds watched their flocks by night. Carol. "Saki." UV

While Shepherds Watched [Their Flocks by Night]. Nahum Tate. ChrPo; NOCV; NOSC; SacPr; UV

While shines the sun, the storm even then. In Bonds. Alice Cary. SWaP

While Sidney Bechet was. Tuskegee Experiment. Mohammed Sadiq. SeSe

While smoking her cigarette down to the very end. (LL) Great Palaces of Versailles, The. Rita Dove. ESEAA; NoAM

While snow fell carelessly. Crack, The. Denise Levertov. NALW

While snows the window-panes bedim. December. John Clare. OBCP

While some "rap" over this turmoil. Rhetoric of Langston Hughes, The. Margaret Danner. BlSi

While something hummed along the river. From the Sun Itself. Roberta Hill Whiteman. HATNAP

While soon the "garden's flaunting flowers" decay. Sonnet on Reading the Poem upon the Mountain Daisy, by Mr. Burns. Helen Maria Williams. ECWP

While still young, / I didn't know I was aging. Tune: "Tartar Tune of Eighteen Beats." *Unknown.* SuSp, *tr.* by Sherwin S. S. Fu

While strolling through the hills one day. Tannhauser. Newman Levy. OBAL

While summer roses all their glory yield. To the Poppy. Anna Seward. CenSon; ECWP; WoRP

While summer-suns o'er the gay prospect played. Thomas Warton, the Younger. CenSon

While sun and sea—and I, and I. Island, The. Randall Jarrell. HarvBoo

While sunk in deepest solitude and woe. Sorrow. Laetitia Pilkington. ECWP

While sweet breezes were stroking the young poplars. Requiescat. Leo Ross. TuT, *tr.* by Eamon Grennan

While Tate recites the catalog of ships. (LL) Gambier. Joe Osterhaus. AmPoNex; NAPBL

While that futile old gentleman dozed. (LL) Limerick: "There was an Old Man who supposed." Edward Lear. NAEL-5v2; NAEL-6v2; NOBVV; PeLi

While that my soul repairs to her devotion. Church Monuments. George Herbert. BASC; ESCV; GeHe; HAP; NAEL-5v1; NAEL-6v1; NAEL-7v1; NOCV; NOSC; NPeEn; PoE; TRP

While that the sun with his beams hot. Unfaithful Shepherdess, The. *Unknown.* GTBS-P

While the Billy Boils. David McKee Wright. PeNZ, *tr.* by Margaret Orbell

While the blue noon above us arches. Annihilation. Conrad Potter Aiken. MoAmPo

While the bombers, southward flocking, set Italian cities rocking. Croaked the Eagle: "Nevermore." "Sagittarius." UV

While the Choir Sang. Priscilla Jane Thompson. CBWP-2

While the city of Troy gave itself up to lamentation, the Achaeans withdrew to the Hellespont. Homer. CAGL, *tr.* by Emile Victor Rieu *Fr.* Iliad, The.

While the Constabulary covered the mob. Summer nineteen sixty nine. Seamus Heaney. CIP-2

While the dead. Seminar for Backward Pupils. Günter Eich. AF, *tr.* by David Young

While the earth is still turning, while there is still bright light. François Villon. Bulat Shalvovich Okudzhava. TCRusP, *tr.* by Denis Johnson, Aleksandar Petrov and Shirley Rihner

While the earth still turns, while the. François Villon. Bulat Shalvovich Okudzhava. TCRP, *tr.* by Deming Brown

While the far farewell music thins and fails. Departure. Thomas Hardy. Son

While the farmers all bow down to the Inspector of Fields. (LL) Buddhist Monk Cut and Burned His Own Flesh to Make the Rains Stop—A Man From His Native Place Asked Me to Write a Poem to Send to Him, A. Hsü Wei. CoBLCP; ColAnChi, *tr.* by Jonathan Chaves

While the fish of fire curves its arc. Siesta. Antonio Machado Ruiz. SpanPo, *tr.* by Kate Flores

While the guests order. Clement Hoyt. HA

While the hum and the hurry. Under a Hat Rim. Carl Sandburg. APT-1

While the innocents were being massacred who says. Who Says. Julia Hartwig. GI, *tr.* by Stanislaw Baranczak

While the long grain is softening. Early in the Morning. Li-Young Lee. LoL

While the milder Fates consent. Lyric to Mirth, A. Robert Herrick. CaPo

While the moths are coming down. (LL) Labasheedy (The Silken Bed). Nuala Ni Dhomhnaill. CABP; CIP-2, *tr.* by the author

While the people pressed upon him to hear the word of God. Czeslaw Milosz. GI *Fr.* St. Luke.

While the Record Plays. Gyula Illyés. PFTM-1

While the river banks are quarreling. Agon. Branko Miljkovic. WoPoe, *tr.* by Charles Simic

While the south rains, the north. Sled Burial, Dream Ceremony. James Dickey. NoP-4

While the Sun Still Spends His Fabulous Money. Kenneth Patchen. CLPP

While the Tragedy's afoot. Colophon. Oliver St. John Gogarty. OBMV

While the years draw nigh when the clattering typewriter is a burden. Evil Days, The. Dennis Joseph Enright. OBCoV

While There Is Still the Color of a Rose. Baldomero Garcilaso de la Vega. SpanPo, *tr.* by Edwin Morgan

While these cold nights freeze me dead. (LL) Shall I Come, Sweet Love. Thomas Campion. EBEV; HAP; OxAEP-1; OxBoLi

While they met with the real estate brokers. Beach, The. Douglas Goetsch. AmPoNex

While thirteen moons saw smoothly run. Stanzas Subjoined to the Yearly Bill of Mortality of the Parish of All Saints, Northampton; for the Year 1787. William Cowper. NOCV

While this America settles in the mould of its vulgarity, heavily thickening to empire. Shine, Perishing Republic. Robinson Jeffers. APT-1; HarvBoo; NAAL-2v2; NAAL-5; NOBA; NoAM; NoP-4; OxBA; PAI; PoPoPo; TAP; TFi; UnPo; VGW

While this kind of consolation and exhortation. Surplus. Abigail Child. FTOS

While this was singing, Ovid young in love. George Chapman. NoSic *Fr.* Ovid's Banquet of Sense.

While those disintegrated by exocet. Shot of War, A. J. S. Harry. BMAP

While thou hast gode and getest gode. *Unknown.* MiEL

While Thracians shal with arrowes war, Iaziges with bowe. Ovid. OBVE *Fr.* Invective against Ibis.

While through our air thy kindling course was run. Cold Meteorite, The. William Reed Huntington. APN-2

While thus he spake, th'Angelic Squadron bright. John Milton. SCV *Fr.* Paradise Lost.

While thus he thought, a monst'rous wave up-bore. Homer. OBVE *Fr.* Odyssey.

While thus I wander'd, step by step led on. William Wordsworth. OxAEP-1 *Fr.* Prelude, The; Growth of a Poet's Mind [1805 vers.].

While Titian was grinding rose madder. Limerick. *Unknown.* NOBL

While to you we true children of Liberty pray. Humble Petition of the British Jacobins to their Brethren of France, The. *Unknown.* NOBRP

While unquiet, *Juvenal,* you haunt. Martial. RomPo, *tr.* by Peter Whigham

While upon the journey of life. Mask, The. Patty L. Harjo. VoR

While venal crowds for worthless men engage. Elegy on the Death of Mr Sterne. Miles Peter Andrews. NOBRP

While visiting Arundel Castle. Limerick. Victor Gray. NOBL

While vulgar souls their vulgar love pursue. Cloe to Artimesa. *Unknown.* ECWP; PoBW

While walking down a strange street. Streetcar That Lost Its Way, The. Nikolai Stepanovich Gumilyov [*or* Gumiliov *or* Gumilev]. TCRusP, *tr.* by Denis Johnson and Kathy Lewis

While walking toward housewife wheeling baby. Street Instructions at the Crotch. Edward Field. CAGL

While we lie tumbling in the hay. (LL) William Shakespeare. FaBoCh; NoP-4; NoSic; OxAEP-1; OxBSP; SCGP; TFi; UV *Fr.* Winter's Tale, The.

While We Lowly Bow before Thee. Daniel C. Colesworthy. AH

While We're Young. William Engvick. ReLy

While we shall be merry and sing. (LL) Gaberlunzie Man, The. *Unknown.* OxBB; OxBS

While We Slept. David Wolff. TrJP

While we slept, these formal gardens. Snowfall on a College Garden. Cecil Day Lewis. OBGa

While We Spend Our Lives Ironing. Marianne van Hirtum. SurWo, *tr.* by Guy Flandre and Peter Wood

While we wait. Michael McClintock. HA

While we wandered (thus it is I dream!), A. Gray Nights. Ernest Christopher Dowson. Son

While we were marching through Georgia. (LL) Marching through Georgia. Henry Clay Work. APN-2; CBCWP

While we were visiting David's grave. Despair. Denise Levertov. NNaP

While we were walking under the top. Poem. John Ashbery. SPE

While with a feeling skill I paint my hell. (LL) Sir Philip Sidney. NAEL-5v1; NAEL-6v1; NAEL-7v1 *Fr.* Astrophil and Stella.

While with false pride, and narrow jealousy. On the Use of New and Old Words in Poetry. Anna Seward. Son

While ye relume me with your nightly aid! (LL) On Dreams, October 15, 1782. Sir Samuel Egerton Brydges. CenSon; Son

While yet it was the Empire of the Night.   On the Birth-Day of Queen Katherine.   Anne Killigrew.   EMWP

While yet Rolfe's foot in stirrup stood.   Herman Melville.   APN-2   *Fr.* Clarel: A Poem and Pilgrimage in the Holy Land.

While yet the grapes were green, thou didst refuse me.   Grapes.   *Unknown.* AWP, *tr. by* Alma Strettell

"While yet we wait for spring, and from the dry."   Robert Bridges.   GSo

While you acknowledge no wrongheaded wish to lay waste.   *Unknown.* PriapPo, *tr. by* Richard W. Hooper   *Fr.* Priapus Poems, The.

While you are sleeping.   Counting.   Mark Bibbins.   WiU

While you clambered up ahead.   Climbing Gannett.   Roberta Hill Whiteman.   HATNAP

While you, my lord, the rural shades admire.   Joseph Addison.   NOEC

While you're a white-hot youth, emit the rays.   Richard Wilbur.   NBLV   *Fr.* Flippancies.

While you're alive I'm hopeful, rustic guard.   *Unknown.*   PriapPo, *tr. by* Richard W. Hooper   *Fr.* Priapus Poems, The.

While you're alive it's shameful to put yourself into.   Disbelief in Yourself Is Indispensable.   Yevgeny Aleksandrovich Yevtushenko [*or* Evtushenko]. TCRP, *tr. by* Albert C. Todd

While you that in your sorrow disavow.   Christmas Sonnet, A.   Edwin Arlington Robinson.   ChrPo

While you walk the water's edge.   Beach Glass.   Amy Clampitt.   FaBoWP; NoAM; NoP-4; VCAP

While your hands mold a form.   Craftsmanship.   Nikolai Nikolaevich Ushakov. TCRP, *tr. by* John Glad

Whiles someone did chant this lovely lay, The.   Edmund Spenser.   OBVE   *Fr.* Faerie Queene, The.

Whilom ther was dwellynge in my contree.   Geoffrey Chaucer.   PoE   *Fr.* Canterbury Tales, The.

Whilst all ages run. (LL)   Hymn: "Now the day is over."   Sabine Baring-Gould.   SacPr; WHSW

Whilst dear Sophia plans some pictured strife.   Winter in Wales, A.   Hester Lynch Salusbury Thrale [*later* Mrs. Piozzi].   CABP

Whilst happy I triumphant stood.   On a Juniper Tree, Cut down to Make Busks.   Aphra Behn.   BASC

Whilst human kind / Throughout the lands lay miserably crushed.   Beyond Religion.   Lucretius.   AWP, *tr. by* William Ellery Leonard

Whilst in her prime and bloom of years.   On a Female Rope-Dancer.   *Unknown.*   NOEC

Whilst in this cold and blust'ring clime.   To My Dear and Most Worthy Friend, Mr. Isaac Walton.   Charles Cotton.   NPeEn

Whilst in This World I Stay.   Philip Pain.   AH

Whilst maudlin Whigs deplore their Cato's fate.   Epigram.   Nicholas Rowe.   ECEV

Whilst my heart bleeding writes that deadlie wound.   Written upon the death of the most Noble Prince Henrie.   Sir Arthur Gorges.   PBRV

Whilst my soul's eye beheld no light.   Dialogue betwixt God and the Soul, A.   Sir Henry Wotton.   MeLP; PeECV; SacPr

Whilst on Septimius' panting Breast.   Catullus.   *See* Phyllis Corydon clutched to him

Whilst on the beach I stood, my courage fainted.   Written the First Morning of the Author's Bathing at Teignmouth for the Head-Ache.   Jane Cave.   ECWP

Whilst sitting with my fanny on the desk.   For I Have Taught the Japanese.   Lucia Maria Perillo.   ExTi

Whilst the red spittle of the grape-shot sings.   Evil.   Arthur Rimbaud.   FaBoWar, *tr. by* Norman Cameron

Whilst thine the victor is, and free. (LL)   Aphra Behn.   BASC; NALW; NOBE; NOSC; NPeEn; NoP-4; OBEV; OxAEP-1; OxBEV; PEW; WPE; WeW-3   *Fr.* Abdelazer.

Whilst thirst of praise, and vain desire of fame.   Lady's Resolve, The.   Lady Mary Wortley Montagu.   BoWoP; OxBSP

Whilst thou art far away, I am at peace.   Siena.   Lily Thicknesse.   LW

Whilst thus my pen strives to eternize thee.   Michael Drayton.   Son   *Fr.* Idea.

Whilst Titian was mixing rose madder.   Limerick.   *Unknown.*   PeLi

Whilst what I write I do not see.   Abraham Cowley.   CABP   *Fr.* Mistress, The.

Whilst yet to prove.   Farewell to Love.   John Donne.   BASC

Whilst Youth and Error led my wand'ring mind.   Samuel Daniel.   AEP   *Fr.* Delia.

Whim of Time, A.   Stephen Spender.   MoBrPo

Whimper of Awakening Passion.   Ebenezer Jones.   NOBVV

Whins are blythesome on the knowe, The.   New Spring, A.   Albert D. Mackie.   OxBS

Whip, The.   Robert Creeley.   NeAP; PFTM-2; PoE; PoM

Whip-the-World.   Hugh MacDiarmid.   FaBoVe

Whipping, The.   Robert Earl Hayden.   PAI; PoE; SSLK; SoSe-8

Whipping, The.   Samuel F. Reynolds.   SpirFl

Whipping fishtails beneath the microscope, The.   Night Watch in the Laboratory.   Ann Townsend.   NAPBL

Whippoorwill Calls, The.   Beverly McLoughland.   HHAm

Whippoorwill in the Woods, A.   Amy Clampitt.   OWoS

Whirl, snow, on the blackbird's chatter.   Eager Spring.   Gordon Bottomley.   MoBrPo

Whirl up, sea.   Oread.   "H. D."   APT-1; AWP; ColAP; HeIP-4; MoAmPo; NAAL-2v2; NAAL-5; NALW; NOBA; NPeEn; NoAM; OxBA; PoPoPo; TAP; TCAPo

Whirl Wind Must, The.   George Oppen.   BodElec

Whirled by the three passions, one's eyes go blind.   Ungo Kiyo.   ZenPo, *tr. by* Takashi Ikemoto and Lucien Stryk

Whirling along its living freight, it came.   Christopher Pearse Cranch.   APN-1; GM   *Fr.* Seven Wonders of the World.

Whirling Round the Sun.   Suzanne Noguere.   FFC

Whirlpool, The.   *Unknown.*   PoToHe

Whirls and stands still: the moon comes: terrain. (LL)   Terrain.   A. R. Ammons.   CoAmPo; VCAP

Whirlwind.   Ravji Patel.   OMIP, *tr. by* Hansa Jhaveri

Whirlwind.   David Rokeah [*or* Rokeakh].   MHP, *tr. by* Ruth Finer Mintz

Whirlwinds / nearly always.   Whirlwinds.   Fily-Dabo Sissoko.   NegPo, *tr. by* Ellen Conroy Kennedy

Whirlwinds of hot autumn dust.   Dust World.   Adrian C. Louis.   UnSA

Whiskers Meets Polly.   Michael Stillman.   TLR

Whiskey on your breath, The.   My Papa's Waltz.   Theodore Roethke.   APT-2; AmFaPo; ClHu; ColAP; HAP; HCAP; InPk-6; LCAP-2; NAAL-2v2; NAAL-5; NBLV; NIL-7; NIP-4; NOBA; NOxBChV; NoAM; NoP-4; PAI; PoE; PoPoPo; RaBo; TAP; TFi; TRP; VGW

Whisky Lovers.   *Vietnamese Oral Tradition.*   CaDao, *tr. by* John Balaban

Whisper.   Mona Fayad.   PoArWo

Whisper.   John Banister Tabb.   APN-2

Whisper, The.   Eugene Gloria.   OpBo

Whisper flies to the empty sleeve, A.   Sequel of Appomattox.   Donald Davidson.   CBCWP; FuPo

Whisper in the Dark.   Sándor Weöres.   IQMS, *tr. by* Edwin Morgan

Whisper is a sibilant thing, A.   Whisper.   Mona Fayad.   PoArWo

Whisper it.   And, Yes, Those Spiritual Matters.   Christopher Gilbert.   ESEAA

Whisper of the wind in, The.   Theocritus.   WoPoe, *tr. by* William Carlos Williams   *Fr.* Idylls.

Whisper of yellow globes.   Her Lips Are Copper Wire.   Jean Toomer.   APT-2; GT; NoAM

Whisper Words of Love to Me.   Lizelia Augusta Jenkins Moorer.   CBWP-3

Whispered.   Jiri Orten.   AF, *tr. by* Lyn Coffin

Whispered, "Darling, you have saved me! curfew will not ring tonight." (LL)   Curfew Must Not Ring Tonight [*or* To-Night].   Rose Hartwick Thorpe.   APN-2; BRP; SWaP

Whisperer, The.   Mark Van Doren.   MoAmPo

Whispering to each handhold, "I'll be back."   After Arguing against the Contention That Art Must Come from Discontent.   William Stafford.   NoAM

Whispering Wind.   Catherine Braan Layne.   PWR

Whispering worshipping. (LL)   Mice in the Hay.   Leslie Norris.   NOxBChV; OBCP

Whispers.   Roberta Hill Whiteman.   CDW

Whispers antiphonal in azure swing. (LL)   Hart Crane.   APT-2; NAAL-2v2

Whispers of Immortality.   T. S. Eliot.   APT-1; CTC; NOBA; NoAM; OBMV; OxAEP-2

Whistle.   Janet Holmes.   ExTi

Whistle, The.   Charles Murray.   OxBS

Whistle, and I'll Come to You, My Lad.   Robert Burns.   OxAEP-2; OxBoLi

Whistle, Daughter, Whistle.   *Unknown.*   OxNR; ReMoGo

Whistle howls, the wheels click along, The. (LL)   David Wojahn.   GM; PBCAP   *Fr.* Mystery Train: A Sequence.

Whistle o'er the Lave o't.   Robert Burns.   OxBS

Whistle of a blackbird, envious of the crackling of a fire, ends by, The.   Landscape Heard, A.   Filippo Tommaso Marinetti.   PFTM-1

Whistle / of the bright, The.   Belfast Lough.   *Unknown.*   BIrV, *tr. by* John Montague

Whistlecraft.   John Hookham Frere.   "And certainly they say, for fine behaving."   OBCoV

Whistling arrow flies less eagerly, The.   Luis de Góngora y Argote.   WoPoe, *tr. by* Robert Lowell

Whistling bellows of his furnace, The.   Philip of Thessalonica.   GrAn

Whistling fury of the frozen northern tempests.   Winter's Approach.   Ábrahám Barcsay.   IQMS, *tr. by* Thomas Kabdebo

Whistling in January.   David J. Rothman.   GeoH

Whistling knot of highway, A.   Interchange.   Ted Kooser.   UrbNat

Whit Monday.   Elizaveta Kuzmina-Karavayeva.   "I too have encompassed a lot: a mother thrice—."   TCRP

Whit Monday. Louis MacNeice. ChIV-1; PeECV

White. Grace Nichols. Oth

White, a shingled path. Icos. Charles Tomlinson. GTBS-P

White against a ruddy cliff you stand, chalcedony on sard. (LL) Cameo, The. Edna St. Vincent Millay. MoAmPo; UnPo; WPE

White an' Blue. William Barnes. GTBS-P

White and Black Bones, The. Konrad Bayer. PFTM-2, *tr. by* Malcolm Green

White and blue, an outspread fan. Environs of Vanholt I. Charles Spear. PeNZ

White and curved as a shell she lies. Discoverer. James Michie. DiPo

White and red. Still Life. Francis Sullivan. CRP

White and shapeless mass—, A. (LL) Waning Moon, The. Shelley. FHYEP; OxBSP

White ants, white ants and the little ribs. (LL) Snow. Charles Wright. ColAP; LCAP-2

White Apples. Donald Hall. LoL; TAP

White as coal-ash pressed. Queen of Heaven Mausoleum. Dennis Schmitz. LCAP-2

White as her hand fair Julia threw. Snow-Ball, The. Soame Jenyns. OBVE

White as I can, though not as thee. (LL) Andrew Marvell. BASC; ESCV; GeHe; HeIP-4; NAAL-5v1; NAAL-6v1; NAAL-7v1; RACG

White ash amid funereal cypresses. (LL) Helen. "H. D.". APT-1; BoWoP; ColAP; FaBoWP; MoAmPo; NAAL-2v2; NAAL-5; NALW; NIL-7; NOBA; NoAM; NoP-4; PAI; TAP

White Asparagus. Sujata Bhatt. HarvBoo

White Banners. Sung Sammun. WoPoe, *tr. by* Jean S. Grigsby

White bars from the window. Antonio Porta. ItPo, *tr. by* Gayle Ridinger   *Fr.* Essences.

White Bear. Joy Harjo. NAAL-5

White billows and huge waves block the river crossing. Kept Waiting in the Boat at Chiu-K'ou Ten Days by an Adverse Wind. Po Chü-i. ChiP, *tr. by* Arthur Waley

White Bird, The. Rosamund Marriott Watson. VWP

White Bird, The. Wilfred Watson. MoCV

White bird featherless. Riddle. *Unknown.* FaBoVe; OxBEV; OxNR

White birds over the grey river. Another Spring. Tu Fu. BLT; OHPC, *tr. by* Kenneth Rexroth

White Blossom, A. D. H. Lawrence. MoBrPo

White blossom, white, white shell; the Nazarene. Music of Colours—White Blossom. Vernon Watkins. AngWePo; TCAWP

White blossoms of the pear. Buson. EH, *tr. by* Robert Hass

White bones scattered. Crossing the Yellow River: June 12. Yüan Hao-wen. SuSp, *tr. by* Stephen West

White brick steps were steep and off-level, The. My Father at the North Street Boarding House. James Kimbrell. AmPoNex

White buck come in. Anadarko John. Carroll Arnett. VoR

White butterfly / Darting among pinks. Masaoka Shiki. ZenPo, *tr. by* Takashi Ikemoto and Lucien Stryk

White Candles. BonniLee. GotH

White carcases / of, The. Liberty. Emile Ologoudou. PBMAP

White Cat of Trenarren, The. Alfred Leslie Rowse. OxBTC

White Center. Richard Hugo. NAAL-2v2

White chocolate jar full of petals, the. Chez Jane. Frank O'Hara. CoAP; ColAP; NOBA; NeAP; NoAM; PoE

White Christmas. Irving Berlin. ReLy

White Christmas. William Robert Rodgers. MoBrPo

White chrysanthemums, The. (LL) Ōshima Ryōta. OHPJ; TTTS

White City, The. Claude McKay. APT-1; BPo; NoAM; RaBo; TAP

White Claw, The. Alfonsina Storni. TCLAP, *tr. by* Andrew Rosing

White cloth spread. Towards Abraham's Bosom. Amelia Blossom Pegram. HAWP

White cloud passed over the land, The. Final Painting, The. Lee Harwood. SPE

White clouds are mindless, they never come to rest, The. Nesting among Clouds. Yang Chi. CoBLCP, *tr. by* Jonathan Chaves

White clouds beyond the sky, The. Mushroom Gatherer Deep in the Mountains among the White Clouds, A. Hsü Wei. CoBLCP, *tr. by* Jonathan Chaves

White clouds encircle the waist of the hills like a belt. Written on a Landscape Painting in an Album. Shen Chou. ColAnChi, *tr. by* Daniel Bryant

White clouds, I cannot see their end. Ch'ang-an. Ho Ching-ming. CoBLCP, *tr. by* Jonathan Chaves

White clouds, like a belt, wind around the waist of the mountains. Inscribed on a Painting. Shen Chou. SuSp, *tr. by* Daniel Bryant

White clouds like a scarf enfold the mountain's waist. Shen Chou. CoBLCP

White Clover. Marvin Bell. InvLad; VCAP

White cock in my courtyard. Elegy for a White Cock. Mei Yao Ch'en. SuSp, *tr. by* Jonathan Chaves

White cock's tail / Tosses in the wind, The. Ploughing on Sunday. Wallace Stevens. RB; TTTS

White Conduit House. William Woty. NOEC

White cormorants shaped like houses stare down at you, The. Party at Hydra. Irving Layton. HeIP-4

White Crane. Dean Young. IllVoic

White Crane Hill. Su Tung-p'o (Su Shih). CoBCP; ColAnChi; GifTon, *tr. by* Burton Watson

White cup shrivels round the golden heart, The. (LL) Dante Gabriel Rossetti. EBVV; NoP-4   *Fr.* House of Life, The.

White cups white. Turkish Love Songs. *Unknown.* BoWoP, *tr. by* Reza Baraheni and Zahra-Soltan Shokoohtaezeh

White curtains of infinite fatigue. And the Seventh Dream Is the Dream of Isis. David Gascoyne. SPE

White dawn. Stillness. When the rippling began. Tree Telling of Orpheus, A. Denise Levertov. APSN; MiVo

White day, black river. Predicter of Famine, The. William Carlos Williams. APT-1; VGW

White Days. Reginald Shepherd. GT

White decorators interested in art. Nights of 1964–66: The Old Reliable. Marilyn Hacker. VCAP

White Deer, The. Jay Wright. ESEAA

White Devil, The. John Webster.
  Call for the Robin-Redbreast and the Wren. EBEV; FaBoCh; HAP; NOSC; NPeEn; OxAEP-1; OxBEV; PoRA; RB; SCGP; TFi
  (Dirge, A.) NOBE; OBEV; WoPoe
  (Land Dirge, A.) GTBS-P

White dew. Buson. EH, *tr. by* Robert Hass

White Dou o Truth. Ineffable Dou, The. Sydney Goodsir Smith. OxBS

White Dress. Yuan Chen. CrYelRi, *tr. by* Sam Hamill

White Dress, The. Marya Alexandrovna Zaturenska. MoAmPo

White drops of dew, The. Kasa no Iratsume. ArkPo, *tr. by* Edwin A. Cranston

White dusk moved ahead of them. Image of City. Lance Henson. VoR

White Dust, The. Wilfrid Wilson Gibson. MoBrPo

White Dwarf. Gerry LaFemina. AmPoNex

White Earth. Gerald Vizenor. HATNAP

White-faced, white-suited, as big as the full moon in the tropical sky. Man in the Moon, The. Alvin Greenberg. OPRER

White Feather Legion, The. T. W. H. Crosland. FaBoWar

White fellow, you are the unhappy race. Unhappy Race, The. Oodgeroo of the tribe Noonuccal (Kath Walker). IBA

White Fields. James Stephens. OTCP

White fingers of the sexton sleep heavy upon us. Concert in the Old School Garret. *Unknown, fr. Terezin Concentration Camp.* INSAB

White Fish in Reeds. Joseph Ceravolo. BodElec

White Fisher, The. *Unknown.* ESPB

White floating clouds. Clouds like the plains come and water the earth. *Unknown.* APN-2, *tr. by* Matilda Coxe Stevenson

White flour, earth-flesh, a cold fleece on the mountain. Snowfall, The. Gwerfyl Mechain. OBWVE, *tr. by* Kenneth Hurlstone Jackson

White flowers. Penny Harter. HA

White fog lifting and falling on mountain-brow. Wales Visitation. Allen Ginsberg. APSN; BB; ColAP; NNaP; NOBA; VCAP

"White folks is white," says Uncle Jim. Uncle Jim. Countee Cullen. GT; NAAL-2v2

White Foolscap / Book of Cordelia. Susan Howe. PmAP

White for nothing. (LL) Lawd, Dese Colored Chillum. Ruby C. Saunders. BlSi; LTA

White founts falling in the courts of the sun. Lepanto. Gilbert Keith Chesterton. EBNV; FaBoWar; MoBrPo; OBMV; OBNV; RB

White foxes howl at mountain wind beneath the moon. Ravine on a Cold Evening. Li Ho. ColAnChi; SuSp, *tr. by* Maureen Robertson

White Fury of the Spring, The. Lizette Woodworth Reese. APT-1

White Gloves. William Plomer. PeSAV

White Goddess, The. Robert Graves. HarvBoo; MoBrPo; NAAL-5v2; NAAL-6v2; NoP-4

White Great Nimble Cat, A. Sir Philip Sidney. TriCat

White-habited, the mystic Swan. Swan, The. Jay Macpherson. NoP-4

White hair fallen from my father's beard, A. (LL) Heirloom. Abraham Moses Klein. NIL-7; NOBC; TrJP

White hair shrouds both my temples. Blaming Sons. T'ao Ch'ien [*or* T'ao Yuan-ming]. CoBCP; ColAnChi, *tr. by* Burton Watson

White hair tossed, a black cape flecked with snow. (LL) Richard Murphy. ModIr; NOIV; PBCIP   *Fr.* Battle of Aughrim, The.

White Hairs. Jamal Isfahani. ArPe, *tr. by* Omar S. Pound

White hairs cover my temples. Blaming Sons. Ch'ien T'ao. ChiP, *tr. by* Arthur Waley

White Hare, The. Lilian Bowes-Lyon. OxBTC

White Heart of God, The. Jack Gilbert. BodElec

White Heliotrope. Arthur Symons. BoLoP; EBEV; NPeEn; PeVV

White hill-side is prickled with antlers, The. Knole. Charles Hubert Sisson. NOCV

White Hope. Ishmael Reed. ISC

White horse. John Wills. HA

White Horse, The. William Henry Davies. OxBTC

White Horse, The. D. H. Lawrence. KaS; TTTS

White Horse of Westbury, The. Charles Tennyson Turner. EBEV; PeVV

White Horses. Rudyard Kipling. PeVV

White horses, tails high, rise from the cedar. E Uni Que A The Hi A Tho, Father. Roberta Hill Whiteman. VoR

White-hot midday in the Snake Park, A. In the Snake Park. William Plomer. OxBTC

White House, A. Rossana Ombres. NeIt, tr. by Robert McCracken and Pietro Pedace

White House, The. Claude McKay. ISC; NAAAL; NIP-4

White House Blues. Unknown. APT-1

White house in front of the park, A. White House, A. Rossana Ombres. NeIt, tr. by Robert McCracken and Pietro Pedace

White hummocks here are rounded to a thigh. Early Summer Sea-Tryst. Frederick Thomas Bennett Macartney. CBAP

White hunter is nearly crazy, A. White Hunter, A. Gertrude Stein. PFTM-1

White ignorant hollow of his face, The. (LL) Father and Son. Stanley Kunitz. AF; TaR; TwCP, tr. by Jack Bevan

White in the moon the long road lies. A. E. Housman. AWP

White iris beautifies me, The. (LL) In the Carolinas. Wallace Stevens. SAmP; VGW

White is the sail and lonely. Sail, A. Mikhail Yuryevich Lermontov. AWP, tr. by Max Eastman

White Island. Robert Herrick. BeJo; NOSC; TOF
  (In this world, the isle of dreams.) NoP-4
  (White Island: Or Place of the Blest, The.) NPeEn

White Isle of Leuce, The. Sir Herbert Read. FaBoTw

White Knight's Ballad, The. Lewis Carroll. See Through the Looking-Glass

White Knight's Song, The. Lewis Carroll. FaBoCh; NAEL-5v2; NAEL-6v2; NOBE; NOBL; NoAM; NoP-4; PeLV; TFi; UV Fr. Through the Looking-Glass.

White Lady. Lucille Clifton. ESEAA

White Lady, The. Rosamund Marriott Watson. VWP; ViWPN

White Land, The. Roberta Hill Whiteman. HATNAP

White lather on black soap. Black Soap. Sandra McPherson. VCAP

White Lies. Natasha Trethewey. TWW

White light, receive me your sojourner; O milky way. Elegy of the Wind. Christopher Okigbo. VCWP

White light's wet glaze on asphalt city floor. Studying the Signs. Allen Ginsberg. FTOS

White lighthouse in the hard flat, A. Edward Hopper's "Lighthouse at Two Lights." Tony Quagliano. PoSol

White Lilies, The. Louise Glück. PoPoPo

White lotus. Buson. WoPoe; ZenPo, tr. by Takashi Ikemoto and Lucien Stryk

White low sun, low thunderclouds; and back, A. White Low Sun. . . , A. Marina Ivanovna Tsvetayeva [or Tsvetaeva]. AF; PeFWW, tr. by David McDuff

White man drew a small circle in the sand, The. Circles. Carl Sandburg. HHAm

White man is a tiger at my throat, The. Tiger. Claude McKay. BPo

White man killed my father, The. Time of Martyrdom, The. David Diop. NegPo, tr. by Ellen Conroy Kennedy

White Man Pressed the Locks, The. James C. Kilgore. InPK-6

White Man Problem, The. Jim Everett. IBA

White Man's Foot, The. Henry Wadsworth Longfellow. Fr. Song of Hiawatha, The.

White man's soul, it thirsts for gain, The. Indian's Retort, The. Jones Very. NCAP

White man's vision. Errol West. IBA

White-maned, wide-throated, the heavy-shouldered children of the wind leap at the sea-cliff. Granite and Cypress. Robinson Jeffers. APT-1

White mares lashed to the sulky carriages. In Ohio. James Wright (1927–80). NNaP

White mares of the moon rush along the sky, The. Night Clouds. Amy Lowell. MoAmPo

White men are behind this night's door. Echoes of the Murder of Emmett Till. Ira B. Jones. InTrad

White men handed papers to my mother. Eviction. Michelle T. Clinton. ISC

White metal tubes contain. Planes Landing. Jamie Grant. NOBAu

White moon gleams through scudding / Clouds, The. Sorrow. Chu Shu-chen. BoWoP; OHMPC, tr. by Kenneth Rexroth

White moon is rising, The. Moon Is Rising, The. Unknown. TAL

White moon, perfect, The. About the Men. Adele Ne Jame. PoArWo

White Moonglow, The. Paul Verlaine. NAWM-7v2, tr. by Carlyle Ferren MacIntyre

White moons like midnight's in the morning sun. Autumn Mushrooms. Kenneth Mackenzie. CBAP

White moth to the closing vine, The. Gipsy Trail, The. Rudyard Kipling. PoRA

White Mouses Petition to Lamira the Right Honble the Lady Anne Tufton Now Countess of Salisbury, The. Anne Finch, Countess of Winchilsea. PoBW

White Night. Mary Oliver. AWTN

White Night. Boris Leonidovich Pasternak. RusPo, tr. by Robert Arthur Douglas Ford

White night, the moon an unstrung bow. Two Poems on Night. Tu Fu. SuSp, tr. by Jan Walls

White Nights. Lewis Warsh. KGB

White Nile Elegy. Khaled Mattawa. NAPBL

White Notes. Donald Justice. LCAP-2

White on White. Eugenio de Andrade.
  "Friend is sometimes desert, A." VCWP

White on White. Maria Luisa Spaziani. NeIt, tr. by Beverly Allen

White on white's a flatness. Nikolay Novikov. TCRusP, tr. by Daniel Weissbort

White one?, The. (LL) Wings, The. Denise Levertov. APSN; NALW

White orchid. Raymond Roseliep. HA

White Oxen. Louis Simpson. NoAM

White Paper. V. Narayana Rao. OMIP, tr. by V. Narayana Rao

White Peacock, The. Dmitry [or Dmitrii] Vasil'evich Bobyshev. ItGoST, tr. by Michael Van Walleghen

White Peacock, The. Alice Notley. FTOS

White pearls. Pearls. Léopold Sédar Senghor. VCWP, tr. by Melvin Dixon

White pebbles jut from the river-stream. In the Hills. Wang Wei. TAL

White peonies blooming along the porch. Peonies at Dusk. Jane Kenyon. LoL

White Petticoats. Chana Bloch. MPUn

"White phosphorous, white phosphorous." Overheard over S. E. Asia. Denise Levertov. BoWoP

White Phosphorus. Alice Notley. FTOS

White Poetess. Musaemura Bonus Zimunya. PeSAV

White Porch, The. Cathy Song. NAAL-5; YaYoPo

White Port and Lemon Juice. Yusef Komunyakaa. ISC

White reeds grow on chilly sands. Shipboard Song. Yüan Chüeh. ColAnChi, tr. by John Timothy Wixted

White reflection retreats to western hills. On and on: An Ancient Song (Yueh-Fu). Li Ho. ChinPo, tr. by Yip Wai-lim

White Rose, A. John Boyle O'Reilly. OBEV

White rose in red rose-garden. Algernon Charles Swinburne. See Glad, but not flush'd with gladness

White Rose is a quiet horse. Four Horses, The. James Reeves. TLR

White Roses. John Ashbery. TAP

White Roses. David Biespiel. AmPoNex

White sagebrush desert, The. Noon. O Pioneers! John Peale Bishop. VGW

White Serpent. Nelly Sachs. BoWoP, tr. by Michael Hamburger

White sheep, white sheep, on a blue hill. Riddle. Unknown. FaBoVe

White sheet on the tail-gate of a truck, A. Karl Shapiro. HAP; OBWP; OxBA

White Ship, The. Geoffrey Hill. OxBC

White Ship, The. Dante Gabriel Rossetti. OBNV

White-sided flowers are thrusting up on the hillside. Hawaii Dantesca. Charles Wright. HCAP; LCAP-2

White silence on the water pulls me in and under. And I know it. Mute Swan, The. Constance Merritt. AmPoNex

White sky is exactly the same white, The. Before the Beginning: Maybe God and a Silk Flower Concubine Perhaps. Pattiann Rogers. PuP-23

White sky, over the hemlocks bowed with snow. Buck in the Snow, The. Edna St. Vincent Millay. ColAP; NALW; NoP-4

White Solitude. Leopoldo Lugones. TCLAP, tr. by Julie Schumacher

White southern businessman needed, The. New Windows. Claudia Rankine. GT

White spider, The. Geraldine Clinton Little. HA

White Stallion, The. Abu-I-Salt Umayyah. WoPoe, tr. by Cola Franzen

White Stallion / (The Runaway), The. Guy Owen. KaS

White Star, The. Minnie Bruce Pratt. ExTi

White stone lady on the grass, The. White Lady, The. Rosamund Marriott Watson. VWP; ViWPN

White Stone Slope. Yang Shih-ch'i. CoBLCP, tr. by Jonathan Chaves Fr. Intendant Yao Shan Has Requested Six Poems on Living in the Mountains, The.

White substitute teacher, A. View of the Library of Congress from Paul Laurence Dunbar High School. Thomas Sayers Ellis. GT

White sun. Zebra. Judith Thurman. SSCS

White sun ends with the mountains. Ascend the Heron Tower. Wang Chih-huan. ChinPo, tr. by Yip Wai-lim

White sun is hidden in the mountains, The. View from Heron Tower. Wang Chih-huan. CrYelRi, tr. by Sam Hamill

White sun leaning on the mountain disappears, The. Climbing the Stork Pavilion. Wang Chih-huan. ColAnChi, tr. by Richard W. Bodman

White swan of cities, slumbering in thy nest. Venice. Henry Wadsworth Longfellow. APN-1

White-Tailed Hornet, The. Robert Frost. OxBA

White teeth smiling. Tsangyang Gyatso. WoPoe, tr. by Brian Cutillo and Rick Fields Fr. Love-Poems of the Sixth Dalai Lama.

White though ye be, yet, lillies, know. How Lillies Came White. Robert Herrick. BeJo; CaPo

White Thought, The. Stevie Smith. Spl

White Tiger, The. Ronald Stuart Thomas. AngWePo

White Tiger Leaps, The. Sarah Gorham. FFC Fr. Notes from a Chinese Love Manual.

White to the neck he glides and plunges. Fencing School. John Streeter Manifold. CBAP

White Troops Had Their Orders but the Negroes Looked Like Men. Gwendolyn Brooks. NAAL-5

White undervest nestling on black trousers. Walnut and Lily. Douglas Oliver. Oth

White unicorn?, A. (LL) Black Poet, White Critic. Dudley Randall. BPo; CoAmPo

White Venus limpid wandering in the sky. Sonnet 5. Louise Labé. BoWoP, tr. by Aliki and Willis Barnstone

White violet, The. Sea Violet. "H. D.". APT-1; NoP-4

White violets again and lyre orchestras. Philodemus. GrAn

White violets flower. Meleager. GrAn

White Was I. Félix Lope de Vega Carpio. SpanPo, tr. by Kate Flores

White waters twist and turn among crumbling embankments. In the Evening, Walking in the Western Fields. Chang Yü. CoBLCP, tr. by Jonathan Chaves

White Wedding Slippers. Anna Swirszczynska. AF, tr. by Czeslaw Milosz

White well, A. Incantation. Elinor Wylie. APT-1

White, White. David Morley. NLP

White, white gulls wheel inland, The. Midnight Harvest, A. Rosamund Marriott Watson. ViWPN

White wing brushing the building, A. (LL) Owl and the Lightning, The. Martín Espada. TouFir; UrbNat

White Witch, The. James Weldon Johnson. APT-1

White woman. Circular Fate. Askhari. InTrad

White woman across the aisle from me says, "Look", The. On the Amtrak from Boston to New York City. Sherman Alexie. PoPoPo

White Women, The. Mary Elizabeth Coleridge. BrRo; NALW; ViWPN (Where dwell the lovely, wild white women folk.) PEW; VWP

White World. "H. D." WPoS (Whole White World, The.) APT-1

White world after a urine-yellow sundown. Visiting Hour (Repatriation Hospital). Michael Dransfield. BMAP

White yuppies in santa monica go through their attics. History as Trash. Michelle T. Clinton. SpirFl

Whitebait, The. Basho. EH, tr. by Robert Hass

Whitehall Stairs. Aaron Hill. NOEC

Whitelight, keenair, someone. To John Ashbery on Szymanowski's Birthday. Frank O'Hara. BodElec

Whiteman Blues, The. Lionel Abrahams. PeSAV

Whiteman dressed in your fancy clothes. Who Owns Darling Street? Frank Doolan. IBA

Whiteman Is the Judge, The. Frank Doolan. IBA

Whiteness, hear me universal whiteness! Some Lines on My Mother's Illness. Yunna Petrovna [or Iunna Pinkhusovna] Moritz [or Morits]. TCRP, tr. by Bernard Meares

Whiteness, or Chastity. Joseph Beaumont. NOSC

Whiter than a mountain glacier. White Peacock, The. Dmitry [or Dmitrii] Vasil'evich Bobyshev. ItGoST, tr. by Michael Van Walleghen

Whiter / than the crust. Wind Sleepers, The. "H. D.". WPE

Whites alone upon the jury in a number of the states. Injustice of the Courts. Lizelia Augusta Jenkins Moorer. CBWP-3

Whites had taught him how to rip, The. Sam Smiley. Sterling Allen Brown. NAAAL

Whitewash. Léon Damas. NegPo, tr. by Ellen Conroy Kennedy

Whitey, Baby. James A. Emanuel. NBV

Whither away good neighbour. Martin Parker. PBRV Fr. Well met Neighbour.

WHITHER away so fast. Unknown. NoSic

Whither, I dread to think—but he is gone. (LL) Byron. NAEL-5v2; NAEL-6v2; NOBRP

Whither I kneel or stand or sit in prayer. At Communion. Madeleine L'Engle. TrCP

Whither, 'midst falling dew. To a Waterfowl. William Cullen Bryant. APN-1; AWP; ColAP; ITBLP; NAAL-2v1; NAAL-3; NAAL-5; NCAP; NOBA; NoP-4; OWoS; OxBA; PWR; SoSe-8; TAP; TFi

Whither, O city, are your profits and your gilded shrines. Troy. Agathias. GrAn, tr. by Ezra Pound

Whither, O splendid ship, thy white sails crowding. Passer-by, A. Robert Bridges. MoBrPo; OBEV; OxBTC; SCGP

Whither, O, whither art thou fled. Search, The. George Herbert. ESCV

Whither, O whither didst thou fly. Eclipse, The. Henry Vaughan. OxBSP

Whither, oh! whither wilt thou wing thy way? Flight of the Spirit. Felicia Dorothea Hemans. Son

Whither shall I, the fair maiden, flee from Sorrow? Sorrow. Unknown. AWP, tr. by W. R. S. Ralston

Whither some great, supreme, o'er-ruling Power. George Canning. NOBRP

Whither? Wilhelm Müller. AWP, tr. by Henry Wadsworth Longfellow Fr. Beautiful Maid of the Mill, The.

Whither? Say, whither shall I fly. Frozen Zone; or, Julia Disdainful, The. Robert Herrick. CaPo

Whitman. Larry Levis. ReTh

Whitman on the Beach. Mark Bibbins. WiU

Whitman thought he could live with animals, they were. Small Acts. Thomas Centolella. GifTon

Whitsun Weddings, The. Philip Larkin. FaBoMo; HeIP-4; NoAM; NoP-4; OxAEP-2; OxBTC

Whitsunday. George Herbert. GeHe

Whittier. James Russell Lowell. NOBA; OxBA Fr. Fable for Critics, A.

Who. Moyshe-Leyb [or Moishe-Leib or Leyb] Halpern. TrJP, tr. by Joseph Leftwich

Who. Edwin Honig. TAP

Who. Tim Seibles. ISC

Who a Mother Is. Roy W. Watson. PWR

Who affirms that crystals are alive? Snow. John Davidson. NPeEn; NePenScot

Who am I, Lord? Just an impostor. Elizaveta Kuzmina-Karavayeva. TCRP

Who Am I? Dietrich Bonhoeffer. HP, tr. by Reginald H. Fuller

Who am I? I am a lady faithful to the ways. Lady of the Ferry Inn. Gwerfyl Mechain. BoWoP, tr. by Willis Barnstone

Who am I? Only one of the commonest common people. Out of the Darkness. Voltairine de Cleyre. SWaP

Who am I? They often tell me. Who Am I? Dietrich Bonhoeffer. HP, tr. by Reginald H. Fuller

Who among you has begun his days. Poet. 'Ali Ja'far Al-Allaq. MAP, tr. by Sharif Elmusa and Thomas G. Ezzy

Who and Each. Ron Padgett. PmAP

Who and what am I then? Whence do I come? György Bessenyei to Himself. György Bessenyei. IQMS, tr. by Watson Kirkconnell

Who and Where. Marvin Bell.

"Who I am is a short person with small feet." InvLad

Who are a little wise, the best fools be. (LL) Triple Fool, The. John Donne. FSCP; NOSC; SoSe-8

Who are my friends / the sick / the weak / the poor in spirit. Nicanor Parra. GI Fr. New Sermons and Preachings of the Christ of Elqui (1979).

Who Are My People? Rosa Zagnoni Marinoni. PoToHe

Who are these figures in the street? Smiling Through. Reed Whittemore. BodElec

Who are these from the strange, ineffable places. Arabia. John Meade Falkner. OxBTC

Who are these people at the bridge to meet me? They are the villagers. Bee Meeting, The. Sylvia Plath. HCAP; HarvBoo; NALW; WPE

Who are these? Why sit they here in twilight? Mental Cases. Wilfred Owen. FaBoMo; NoAM; PeFWW

Who are they now? since the Bathurst ground. From a Republican Grave: Daniel Henry Deniehy, 1828–1865. Philip Mead. NOBAu

Who are they talking to in the big temple? Temple, The. Charles Hubert Sisson. OxBTC

Who are they to be in their skin. Subway Witnesses, The. Lorenzo Thomas. GT

Who are we here? Intra-Political. Margaret Avison. MoCV

'Who are we waiting for?' 'Soup burnt?' ' . . Eight—' Feckless Dinner-Party, The. Walter De la Mare. FaBoTw

Who are wretched. (LL) Hummingbirds. Norman Dubie. BodElec; LCAP-2

Who are you. Nizar Qabbani. MAP

Who are you, coming without flash and standing high. Bedrooms. Sandra McPherson. ExTi

Who are you, listening to me, who are you. Poem for Half White College Students. Imamu Amiri Baraka. BPo; TAP; UnPo

"Who are you, Sea Lady." Santorin. James Elroy Flecker. FaBoTw; OBMV

"Who are you that so strangely woke." Princess of Scotland, The. Rachel Annand Taylor. NePenScot

Who are you, whose pitiful bones. Leonidas of Tarentum. GrAn

Who Are You? "Adonis" [or "Adunis"]. MAP, tr. by John Heath-Stubbs and Lena Jayyusi

Who are you? You and I. Tennessee Williams. GLP

Who are you? and with whom do you sleep here? (LL) James Vincent Cunningham. HAP; TRP; VCAP

Who art as black as hell, as dark as night. (LL) William Shakespeare. EBEV; NAEL-5v1; NAEL-6v1; NAEL-7v1; OxAEP-1 Fr. Sonnets.

Who asked the sun to set in the evening? Just because I Am. Malkia Amala Cyril. InTrad

Who asks forgiveness. Sin. Ben Scammell. NLP

Who Be Kind To. Allen Ginsberg. NNaP

Who beckons the green ivy up. Miracle, The. Walter De la Mare. UnPo

Who besides You. Bart Howard. ReLy

Who bought a mountain and became a hermit there? Chin Nung. CoBLCP Fr. I Discuss the Past and Not the Present. What Men of Today Are Worth Discussing? May the Men of the Past Not Blame Me for My Discussion of Them.

Who broke the laws of God, and man and metre. (LL) On Peter Robinson. Francis, Lord Jeffrey Jeffrey. FaBoEE; NBLV

Who builds a church within his heart. Church in the Heart, The. Morris Abel Beer. PoToHe

Who Burns for the Perfection of Paper. Martín Espada. InvLad

Who But the Lord? Langston Hughes. BPo

Who call him spurious and shoddy. Dorothy Parker. APT-1 Fr. Pig's-Eye View of Literature, A.

"Who called?" I said, and the words. Echo. Walter De la Mare. OBMV

Who calls her two-faced? Faces, she has three. Three-Faced, The. Robert Graves. FaBoEE

Who calls? Welcome Eumenides. Eleanor Ross Taylor. NALW

Who came whirling out of the North. Of the Scythians. Katha Pollitt. DiPo

Who can bear / The wail of a young orphan? Rabbi Yussel Luksh of Chelm. Jacob Glatstein [or Glatsteyn]. TrJP, tr. by Nathan Halper

Who can believe with common sense. Epigram on Fasting. Jonathan Swift. OBVE

Who can describe the waves of Mother Syama's world? Kamalākānta Bhattācārya. SinGod, tr. by Rachel Fell McDermott

Who can doubt, Rice, to which eternal place. On Mr. Rice the Manciple of Christ Church in Oxford. Richard Corbet [or Corbett]. NOSC

Who can forget the attitude of mothering? Rita Dove. NAAAL Fr. Mother Love.

Who can grasp for the first time. New Music. Gwen Harwood. CBAP

Who Can I Turn To (When Nobody Needs Me?). Leslie Bricusse. ReLy

Who Can I Turn To? William Engvick. ReLy

Who can keep a blazing fire tied in a cotton cloth? Lex Hixon. HW

Who can live in heart so glad. Nicholas Breton. NoSic Fr. Passionate Shepherd, The.

Who can open the door. Overture. Zuhur Dixon. MAP, tr. by Patricia Alanah Byrne and Salma Khadra Jayyusi

Who can remember back to the first poets. Makers, The. Howard Nemerov. DiPo

Who can say. Song. Tennyson. FaBoCh

Who can say what love is? But Beautiful. Jimmy Van Heusen. ReLy

Who can say? It is silent now. (LL) What Were They Like? Denise Levertov. HeIP-4; NIP-4; OBWP; PAI; VGW; WPE

Who can support the anguish of love? Ode. Ibn al-Arabi. AWP, tr. by R. A. Nicholson

Who can tell the difference between the state. Grace. Laura Kasischke. NAPBL

Who can the various city frauds recite. John Gay. ECEV Fr. Trivia; or, The Art of Walking the Streets of London.

Who can understand Kali? Rāmprasād Sen. SinGod, tr. by Rachel Fell McDermott

Who Can Understand This? László Mécs. IQMS, tr. by Kenneth Thomas

Who cannot guess God's presence out of sight. (LL) Elizabeth Barrett Browning. CenSon; Son; WPE Fr. Sonnets from the Portuguese.

Who Cares? George Gershwin. ReLy

Who carved Love / and placed him by. Statue of Eros, A. Zenodotus. GrAn, tr. by Peter Jay

Who claims one needs wine to dispel grief? Tune: "Autumn Waters"—Listening to Rain. Na-lan Hsing-te. SuSp, tr. by Bruce Carpenter

Who collects the pain. "Stephany." NBV

Who come in the night whispering. Two Girls. Suzanne Gardinier. KGB; NeAmPo

Who comes here? / A grenadier. Grenadier, The. Unknown. OxNR

Who comes? Two Tongue-Pointing (Satirical) Songs. Unknown. NOBAu

Who could believe it? A twin-bladed arrrow. On the Bird Which Still Flew,

Though Its Head Was Severed. Janus Pannonius. IQMS, tr. by Anthony Barrett

Who could believe it? O, the fates are fickle. Unknown. PriapPo, tr. by Richard W. Hooper Fr. Priapus Poems, The.

Who could dispute his choice. Net and the Sword, The. Douglas Le Pan. NOBC

Who could have baked my entire heart's desire. Sylvia Kantaris. NewEx

Who could help but long for the gardens of home? (LL) Spring Night in Lo-Yang—Hearing a Flute. Li Po. CoBCP; TTTS, tr. by Burton Watson

Who could outbalance poised. To the High Court of Parliament. Geoffrey Hill. OxBEV

Who could tire of the long shadows. February Days. May Sarton. APT-2

Who counts himself as nobly born. Nobly Born, The. Frances Ellen Watkins Harper. PWR

Who crieth: "Woe"? who: "Alas"? Bible, O.T. TrJP Fr. Proverbs.

Who crossed cold Lethe, thought it Rubicon. (LL) Fording the River. Seamus Deane. PBCIP; PNI

Who crowd the press with hourly trash. (LL) Jonathan Swift. HAP; SCV Fr. On Poetry: a Rhapsody.

Who'd Be a Hero (Fictional)? Morris Gilbert Bishop. OBAL

Who'd believe me if. Third Dimension, The. Denise Levertov. NeAP

Who'd Want to Be a Man? Gregory Orr. BodElec

Who dare pull down a crown, tear up a tomb? (LL) Upon the Double Murther of King Charles I. Katherine Philips. BASC; NAEL-7v1

Who dares approach the lion's. Daigu. ZenPo, tr. by Takashi Ikemoto and Lucien Stryk

Who dares deny the burning truth of the sun? Virgil [or Vergil]. WoPoe, tr. by David R. Slavitt Fr. Georgics.

Who dares to drop the pin destruction of our silence. Can You Change a Shilling? Toni Del Renzio. SPE

Who dat a-knockin' at the door below. What You Goin' to Do When the Rent Comes 'Round? Andrew B. Sterling. OBAL

Who deem epigrams mere trifles. Martial. RomPo, tr. by Peter Whigham

Who died on the wires, and hung there, one of two. Ivor Gurney. HarvBoo; NAEL-5v2; NAEL-6v2; NPeEn; NoP-4; OBWP; PeFWW; PoWW Fr. Silent One, The.

Who dissect away the wings and the haggard heart from the dove. (LL) Letter to Alex Comfort. Dannie Abse. FaBoTw; TwCP

Who do what we are born to do. (LL) Tiger. Alec Derwent Hope. OxBC; RB

Who does not love the spring deserves no lovers. Georgian Spring. Roy Campbell. OBSV

Who Does Not Love True Poetry. Henry Clay Hall. PoToHe

Who does not sit in the seat of the scoffer. Blessed Is the Man. Marianne Craig Moore. ChIV-1

Who does not wish ever to judge aright. Hog, the Sheep and Goat, Carrying to a Fair, The. Anne Finch, Countess of Winchilsea. ECWP

Who doesn't. Who. Tim Seibles. ISC

Who doesn't come through the door / to get home? (LL) Song: "My heart, my dove, my snail, my sail, my." Cynthia Zarin. NIL-7; NoP-4

. . . who doesn't have the money to buy himself an island. Hôtel Fraternité. Hans Magnus Enzensberger. CLPP, tr. by Jerome Rothenberg

Who doubts? The laws fell down from heaven's height. Joseph Hall. OBSV Fr. Virgidemiarum.

Who Drags the Fiery Artist Down? Clarence Day. NBLV

Who dreamed [or dream'd] that beauty passes like a dream? Rose of the World, The. W. B. Yeats. MoBrPo; NAEL-5v2; NAEL-6v2

Who dwelleth in that secret place. Rest. George Macdonald. SacPr

Who Eats Who? Allen Ginsberg. BodElec

Who else will care for me. Tune: "Sand of Silk-Washing Brook" In Memoriam. Nara Singde. ColAnChi, tr. by Jiaosheng Wang

Who ere she[e] be[e]. Richard Crashaw. BASC; BoLoP; EBEV; MeLP; NOSC; OBEV; OxAEP-1

Who even dead, yet hath his mind entire! Ezra Pound. APT-1; PoE; VGW Fr. Cantos.

Who ever again will be able to say. Patrizia Cavalli. ItPo, tr. by Gayle Ridinger

Who ever hath her wish, thou hast thy Will. William Shakespeare. See Whoever hath her wish, thou hast thy Will

Who ever knew the heavens menace so? William Shakespeare. OxAEP-1 Fr. Julius Caesar.

Who eye pass who eye. Dreadtalk. Frederick D'Aguiar. WaCA

Who fed me from her gentle breast. My Mother. Jane Taylor. ITBLP

Who fired France for Mary without spot. (LL) Duns Scotus's Oxford. Gerard Manley Hopkins. CABP; EBEV; GTBS-P; NAEL-5v2; NAEL-6v2; NoAM; OBMV; OxAEP-2; PeECV

Who first of Christian warriors now did chance. Torquato Tasso. FaBoWar, tr. by G. Grinnell-Milne Fr. Jerusalem Delivered.

Who first reform'd our stage with justest law[e]s. Elegy on Ben Jonson, An. John Cleveland. MeLP

Who first said "false as dreams?" Not one who saw. Dreams. Henry Timrod. APN-2

Who flogged you and threw you out. Slave Girl, The. Rufinus. GrAn, *tr. by* Alan Marshfield

Who forced the Muse to this alliance? On Professor Drennan's Verse. Roy Campbell. GTBS-P

Who forked me like compost from my country? Who spat. Answers on a Postcard. David Morley. NLP

Who fought for Uncle Sam! (LL) Colored Soldiers, The. Paul Laurence Dunbar. APN-2; CBCWP; NAAAL

Who fought their way from night to day and struggled up to God. (LL) Unsung Heroes, The. Paul Laurence Dunbar. BPo; CBCWP

Who gives him the Bath? New Knighthood, The. Rudyard Kipling. UV

Who gives this woman to this man? Epithalamium for a Niece. Norman Nicholson. NLP

Who goes there! hankering, gross, mystical, nude? Walt Whitman. CAGL; ColAP *Fr.* Song of Myself.

Who goes there? God knows. I'm nobody. How should I answer? Etosion achthos aroures. Robert Bridges. OxBEV

Who goes to join the men of Agincourt. (LL) Volunteer, The. Herbert Asquith. OBWP; OxBTC

Who Goes with Fergus? W. B. Yeats. FaBoCh; InPK-6; NAEL-5v2; NAEL-6v2; NOBE; NOBVV; NoAM; PeVV; PoE; PoRA; TRP

Who got used to making it through murdered sons. (LL) For de Lawd. Lucille Clifton. TAP; TwCP

Who had always been so careful while her mistress lived. (LL) Aunt Helen. T. S. Eliot. NPeEn; OBAL

Who had the girl turning handsprings. You're Lookin' at Me. Bobby Troup. ReLy

Who has a face sees. Shed the Fear. Anselm Hollo. PmAP

Who has but dighted his tricks in a bed. This Is What the Watchbird Sings, Who Perches in the Lovetree. Bruce Boyd. NeAP

Who has ever stopped to think of the divinity of Lamont Cranston? In Memory of Radio. Imamu Amiri Baraka. BB; NAAAL; NAAL-2v2; NeAP; PoM

Who has not been sleeping on an inspired day? The mind of the day sleeps us. That Can Not Be Taken Away from It. Carla Harryman. FTOS

Who has not found the Heaven—below. God's Residence. Emily Dickinson. SAmP; WPoS

Who has not seen their lover. Avenue, The. Frances Darwin Cornford. LW

Who has not waked to list the busy sounds. London's Summer Morning. Mary Robinson. ECWP; RWP; WoRP

Who Has Not Walked upon the Shore. Robert Bridges. SCGP

Who Has Our Redeemer Heard. Stephen Collins Foster. AH

Who Has Seen the Wind? Christina Georgina Rossetti. ITBLP; NTCP; SacPr; TLR; WHSW

(Wind, The.) ChIV-2

Who has strangled the tired voice. Appeal. Noémia da Sousa. PBMAP; TTY; WPOW

Who has told you what discoveries. Basics. James Dickey. BodElec

Who hast the red pavilion of my heart? (LL) Arab Love-Song, An. Francis Thompson. AWP; MoBrPo

Who hath beheld the goddess face to face. Poetry. Madison Cawein. APN-2

Who hath desired the Sea?—the sight of salt water unbounded. Sea and the Hills, The. Rudyard Kipling. SCGP

Who hath his Maker's nod. (LL) Henry David Thoreau. APN-1; ColAP; NCAP; NOBA; OxBA

Who hath not knowne or herd. Luke Sheperd. PBRV *Fr.* Upcheringe of the Messe, The.

Who hath not sent out ships to sea? Ship That Went Down, The. Adah Isaacs Menken. CBWP-1

Who hath prophetic vision sees. Prophecy of a Ten Ton Cheese. James McIntyre. VerBaPo

Who hath that conning by wisdam or prudence. *Unknown.* MiEL

Who have been lonely once. Careless Love. Stanley Kunitz. FaBoWar

Who have not yet bruised you. (LL) Advice to a First Cousin. Alberto Rios. NAAL-5; NIL-7

Who have twice come in from the cold? (LL) Dejection. Derek Mahon. PBCIP; WoPoe

Who heard the silly sailor-folk and gave them back their sea! (LL) Last Chantey, The. Rudyard Kipling. FaBoCh; MoBrPo

Who here before me by this waterfall. Under the Waterfall. Karl Kraus. AuPH, *tr. by* Lowell A. Bangerter

Who Here Can Cast His Eyes Abroad. Abiel Holmes. AH

Who hired him. (LL) Idiot, The. Dudley Randall. BPo; LTA

Who hung these shields here still all shiny. Antipater of Sidon. GrAn

Who hunts so late 'neath evening skies. Julia Ward Howe. SWaP *Fr.* Lyrics of the Street.

Who I am is a short person with small feet. Marvin Bell. InvLad *Fr.* Who and Where.

Who I break my head against. First Claims Poem. Víctor Hernández Cruz. NBV

Who I Think You Are. Elizabeth Alexander. FFC; RA

Who in each act that act have done. (LL) Strangers, The. Jones Very. APN-1; OxBA

Who, in his own time, resumed the dark, the straw. (LL) Outlaw, The. Seamus Heaney. NIL-7; OxBC

Who in One Lifetime. Muriel Rukeyser. NALW

Who, in such depths of misery, plunge the fair? (LL) Natural Child, The. Helen Leigh. ECWP; WoRP

Who, in the brief, incredible northern spring. Let Him Return. Leona Hill. PoToHe

Who, in the garden-pony carrying skeps. Horses. Dorothy Wellesley, Duchess of Wellington. OBMV; OxBTC

Who, in the public library, one evening after rain. Public Library. Dannie Abse. OxBC

Who in the waters of this reedy lake. Diodorus Zonas. GrAn

Who in them loved [*or* lov'd] and sought thy face! (LL) Book, The. Henry Vaughan. AngWePo; BASC; GeHe; InvLi; PBRV

Who invited him in? What was he doing here. Dirty Little Accuser, The. Norman Cameron. OxBS

Who is a friend? Who is a foe? Gripe. Lincoln Kirstein. PoWW

Who is a mother some one exclaimed? Who a Mother Is. Roy W. Watson. PWR

Who Is a Poet. Tadeusz Rózewicz. VCWP

Who is, as if he weren't and ne'er had even come. "Angelus Silesius." GePo, *tr. by* George C. Schoolfield *Fr.* Cherubical Wanderer, The.

Who is black. (LL) Kali. Lucille Clifton. HW; NAAAL

Who is faultless, and doesn't exist. (LL) Eve to Her Daughters. Judith Wright. NALW; NoP-4

Who is he, this regretful man. Days of Rain. Li Ho. CrYelRi, *tr. by* Sam Hamill

Who is it calling by the darkened river. Voices. Walter De la Mare. UnPo

Who is it hides my sandals when I'm trying to get dressed? Late for Breakfast. Mary Dawson. TLR

Who is it sings the gypsies' song to-night. Serenade. Rosamund Marriott Watson. ViWPN

Who Is It Talks of Ebony? Manmohan Ghose. OBMV

Who is it that rides through the forest so fast? Goethe. *See* O who rides by night thro' the woodland so wild?

Who is it that this dark[e] night. Sir Philip Sidney. NAEL-6v1; NAEL-7v1; NoSic; OxAEP-1 *Fr.* Astrophil and Stella.

Who is like unto thee who teachest knowledge. Hymn of Unity. *Unknown.* TrJP, *tr. by* H. M. Adler

Who is more sweet than any words can show. (LL) Dante Alighieri. AWP; EaItPo, *tr. by* Dante Gabriel Rossetti *Fr.* La Vita Nuova.

Who Is My Brother? Pinkie Gordon Lane. BlSi

Who is my father in this world, in this house. Irish Cliffs of Moher, The. Wallace Stevens. NOBA; RaBo; TOF; VGW

Who Is My Neighbor? Josephine D. Henderson Heard. CBWP-4

Who is not a stranger still. Stephany Fuller. BPo

Who is on the Lord's side? Frances Ridley Havergal. SacPr

Who is she coming, whom all gaze upon. Sonnet: A Rapture Concerning His Lady. Guido Cavalcanti. AWP; EaItPo, *tr. by* Dante Gabriel Rossetti

Who is she that comes, makyng turn every man's eye. Sonnet [*or* Sonetto] 7. Guido Cavalcanti. CTC; OBVE, *tr. by* Ezra Pound

Who is she whose-feet-go-clattering-the-hard-ground? Choice. Flavien Ranaivo. NegPo, *tr. by* Ellen Conroy Kennedy

Who is Silvia? What a shame. Does That Answer Your Question, Mr Shakespeare? Stanley J. Sharpless. PeLV

Who is Silvia? what is she. William Shakespeare. NoSic; SCGP *Fr.* Two Gentlemen of Verona, The.

Who is so proud. Rachel Lyman Field. OBCA *Fr.* Circus Garland, A.

Who is that blond child laughing as he runs after his colored marbles? Pierre Albert-Birot. CuPo

Who is that BRAHMA? What that Soul of Souls? *Unknown.* TAL *Fr.* Bhagavad-Gita, The.

Who is that running away. C. C. Rider. Lucille Clifton. GT

Who is that Syama woman. Rāmprasād Sen. SinGod, *tr. by* Rachel Fell McDermott

Who is the author of Disaster? John Winthrop, "Reasons to be Considered for . . . the Intended Plantation in New England," 1629. Nicole Cooley. NeAmPo

Who is the East? Yellow Man, Purple Man. Emily Dickinson. TLR; TTTS

Who is the man that stands against this bridge. For Danton. Charles Tomlinson. HarvBoo

Who is the mighty master that can trace. To Haydn. Thomas Holcroft. NOEC

Who is the Poet? He who sings. For Adelaide. Bessie Rayner Parkes. VWP

Who is the runner in the skies. Runner in the Skies, The. James Oppenheim. TrJP

Who is there still remembers. Bertolt Brecht. FaBoA, *tr.* by Frank Jellinek *Fr.* Late Lamented Fame of the Giant City of New York.

Who is there? Me. Marichiko. OHMPJ

Who is there? Me. Kenneth Rexroth. APSN *Fr.* Love Poems of Marichiko, The.

Who is this. Kamalākānta Bhattācārya. SinGod, *tr.* by Rachel Fell McDermott

Who is this. Peter Damian. MLL

Who is this. Raghunāth Rāy. SinGod, *tr.* by Rachel Fell McDermott

Who is this, all alone? Whose woman is She. Mahārājādhirāja Māhtābcānd. SinGod, *tr.* by Rachel Fell McDermott

Who is this black. Dāśarathi Rāy. SinGod, *tr.* by Rachel Fell McDermott

Who is this coming towards you. Ghost, The. Iain Crichton Smith. NOxBChV

Who is this enchantress. Kamalākānta Bhattācārya. SinGod, *tr.* by Rachel Fell McDermott

Who is this I hear?—Lo, this is I, thine heart. Dispute of the Heart and Body of François Villon, The. François Villon. AWP; OBVE, *tr.* by Algernon Charles Swinburne

Who is this King of glory? The Lord of hosts, he is the King of glory. Selah. (LL) Bible, *O.T.* AWP; TrJP, *tr.* by Christopher Smart *Fr.* Psalms.

Who is this Man. Genesis XXIV. Arthur Hugh Clough. ChIV-1

Who is this Moses? who made him, we say. Soliloquy of One of the Spies Left in the Wilderness, A. Gerard Manley Hopkins. TrCP

Who is this that comes in splendour, coming from the blazing East? Airy Christ, The. Stevie Smith. ChIV-2; NOCV

Who is This that Cometh from Edom? William Herebert. ChIV-1; MiEL; SacPr

Who is this that darkeneth counsel by words without knowledge? Bible, *O.T.* AWP *Fr.* Job.

Who Is This Who Howls and Mutters? Stevie Smith. OxBC

Who is this whose feet. Swan's Feet, The. Edith Jay Scovell. FaBoWP; OxBTC

Who is this? An almoner. Almoner, An. "Michael Field." VWP

Who is, who is the rider there. Who. Moyshe-Leyb [*or* Moishe-Leib *or* Leyb] Halpern. TrJP, *tr.* by Joseph Leftwich

Who Killed Cock Robin. Mother Goose. OxNR; ReMoGo; UV

(Heve hes Cock Robin.) OxBoLi

(Who did kill Cock Robbin?) NPeEn

Who killed Cock Robin? Coroner's Inquest. W. D. Snodgrass. OxBEV

Who killed the last fighter [*or* commando]? Dead Witness, The. Buland Al-Haidari [*or* Al-Haydari]. MAP, *tr.* by Patricia Alanah Byrne and Salma Khadra Jayyusi

"Who knocks at my door, so late in the night?" Pilgrims in Mexico. *Unknown.* OBCP

'Who knocks?' "I, who was beautiful." Ghost, The. Walter De la Mare. EnLoPo; MoBrPo; NOBE; OxBTC

Who knows, but beasts, as they do lie. Discourse of Beasts, A. Margaret Lucas Cavendish, Duchess of Newcastle. BASC; PEW

Who knows if they sing in their webs. Ability to Make a Face Like a Spider While Singing Blues: Junior Wells, The. Sandra McPherson. SeSe

Who knows the precise moment when the stream. Kenny Fries. AmPoNex *Fr.* Healing Notebooks, The.

Who knows this or that? Limits. Ralph Waldo Emerson. APN-1; OxBSP

Who knows what fame is! Pushkin. Anna Andreyevna Akhmatova. TCRP, *tr.* by Daniel Weissbort

Who knows what the moonlight means? Magic Composer. Gilbert Sorrentino. FTOS

Who knows what would happen if you stopped? By Forced Marches. Michael Hofmann. HarvBoo

Who knows when love has had its day. Strato [*or* Straton]. GrAn

Who Knows Where. Detlev, Freiherr von Liliencron. AWP, *tr.* by Ludwig Lewisohn

Who knows whether the sea heals or corrodes? Plague of Dead Sharks. Alan Dugan. NoAM

Who knows why the sea. Can This Be Love? Paul James. ReLy

Who knows why we talk of death. Drowning of the Facts of a Life, The. Michael S. Harper. ESEAA

Who Knows? Harold Rome. ReLy

Who Knows? José Santos Chocano. TCLAP, *tr.* by Andrew Rosing

Who knows? This Africa so richly blest. Who Knows? A. L. Milner-Brown. PBA; TTY

Who lay in a ditch, his mouth full of dying fires. (LL) Hamnavoe Market. George Mackay Brown. EmeKit; NePenScot

Who least, hath some; who most hath never all. (LL) Times [*or* Tymes] Go[e] By Turn[e]s. Robert Southwell. ChIV-1; NoSic

Who Likes the Idea of Guide Cats? Gavin Ewart. NOxBChV

Who list his wealth and ease retain. *V. Innocentia Veritas Viat Fides Circumdederunt me inimici mei.* Sir Thomas Wyatt. NAEL-7v1; NoSic

Who list the Romane greatnes forth to figure. Joachim Du Bellay. OBVE *Fr.* Ruins of Rome.

Who lists to see, what ever nature, arte. Edmund Spenser. PBRV *Fr.* Ruines of Rome: by Bellay.

Who lit the furnace of the mammoth's heart? Francis Thompson. MoBrPo *Fr.* Ode to the Setting Sun.

Who live in troubled regions. (LL) Storm Warnings. Adrienne Rich. AiP; NAAL-2v2; NAAL-5; NIL-7; NIP-4; YaYoPo

Who lived here when the stones were green. Syl Cheney-Coker. PBMAP *Fr.* Blood in the Desert's Eyes, The.

Who lives where beggars rarely speed. My Mary. John Clare. NOBRP

Who liveth alone longeth for mercy. Wanderer, The. *Unknown.* WoPoe, *tr.* by Michael Alexander

Who'll Ferry Love to the Yonder Shore. László Nagy. IQMS, *tr.* by Adam Makkai

Who looked upon her awful brow. Ambrose Bierce. APN-2 *Fr.* Devil's Dictionary, The.

Who looking back upon his troubled years. Disillusion. Bessie B. Decker. PoToHe

Who, looking on our grief, hath often grieved. (LL) Dante Alighieri. AWP; EaItPo, *tr.* by Dante Gabriel Rossetti *Fr.* La Vita Nuova.

Who looks after you kids while you work? Who Looks after Your Kids? Kirsten Emmott. BloBone

Who loves a garden, loves a greenhouse too. William Cowper. OBGa *Fr.* Task, The.

Who Loves the Rain. Frances Shaw. PoToHe

Who lowers the unseen hat from on high. Mac Wellman. HeMarv *Fr.* Rat Minaret: Miniaturist-Divan, The.

"Who made God, daddy?" Question Time. Jack Lindsay. NOBAu

Who made honey long ago. (LL) Forefathers. Edmund Charles Blunden. NOBE; NoP-4; OBEV; OBMV; OxBTC

Who made the world, sir? Ants. Alfred Kreymborg. APT-1

Who made the world? Summer Day, The. Mary Oliver. AmFaPo

Who, maiden, makes this river flow? Medicine Song of an Indian Lover. *Unknown.* APN-2, *tr.* by Charles Fenno Hoffman

Who make up a heaven of our misery. (LL) William Blake. FHYEP; NAEL-5v2; NAEL-6v2; NAWM-7v2; NOEC; RB *Fr.* Songs of Experience.

Who makes strong winds be still, gentles the sea. Night Prayer, A. Alcuin. MLL, *tr.* by Helen Waddell

Who masquerades behind the winds? Moods. Leyb [*or* Leib] Kvitko [*or* Kwitko]. TrJP, *tr.* by Joseph Leftwich

Who, mid the grasses of the field. Dante. William Cullen Bryant. APN-1

Who, minter of medallions. Reading a Medal. Terence Tiller. FaBoTw; GTBS-P

Who needs a raft that can invade the stars? Inscribed on a Painting. Yün Shou-p'ing. CoBLCP, *tr.* by Jonathan Chaves

Who Needs Two. James McManus.

"Commercials exaggerate." IllVoic

Who never asked. Let's Hear It for Goliath. Jon Dressel. AngWePo; TCAWP

Who never held up anybody. (LL) Shooting of John Dillinger outside the Biograph Theater July 22, 1934, The. David Wagoner. CoAP; RB

Who never wept knows laughter but a jest. Compensation. E. M. Brainard. PoToHe

Who, now, can speak of gods. Gods, The. Dennis Lee. NOBC

Who of little Love—know how to starve. (LL) Emily Dickinson. APN-2; InPK-6; SWaP

Who of those who step into the stream. Mikhail Aizenberg. ItGoST, *tr.* by J. Kates

Who oft as he saunter'd the streets curv'd with his arm the shoulder of his friend, while the arm of his friend rested upon him also. (LL) Recorders Ages Hence. Walt Whitman. HeIP-4; MoAmPo; SAmP

Who often found their way to pleasant meadows. Elegy for Minor Poets. Louis MacNeice. CABP; PNI

Who on yon throne of Azure sits. Retirement. Henry Vaughan. GeHe

Who on your breast pillows his head now. Lost Jewel, A. Robert Graves. EnLoPo

Who once said all his say, when he was young! (LL) Egan O Rahilly. *Unknown.* EBEV; OBMV, *tr.* by James Stephens

Who, or why, or which, or what. A[h]kond of Swat, The. Edward Lear. FaBoCh; PeLi

Who Owns Darling Street? Frank Doolan. IBA

Who Owns the Night and Lease Stars. Reginald Shepherd. AmPoNex

Who owns these cattle, Corydon? Theocritus. AWP, *tr.* by Charles Stuart Calverley *Fr.* Idylls.

Who owns these scrawny little feet? *Death.* Examination at the Womb-Door. Ted Hughes. NAEL-5v2; NAEL-6v2; NoP-4; OxBC

Who owns this body of mine? Starved. Laura Riding Jackson. FuPo

Who painted you, the non-speaker. Portrait of a Stupid Teacher of Rhetoric. *Unknown.* GrAn, *tr.* by Peter Jay

Who peered from the invisible world. Seven Forbidden Words. Michael Palmer. HarvBoo

Who perished in the cause of Right. (LL) Death of Lincoln, The. William Cullen Bryant. NAAL-2v1; TAP

Who Placed, Amidst the Tracts of Ash. Antonio Machado Ruiz. SpanPo, *tr.* by Kate Flores

Who plainly say, *My God, My King.* (LL) Jordan (1). George Herbert. BASC; FHYEP; FSCP; GeHe; HAP; MeLP; NAEL-5v1; NAEL-6v1; NAEL-7v1; NOCV; NOSC; NoP-4; OxBEV; PeECV; PoE; TFi; TrCP; WoPoe

Who prop, thou ask'st, in these bad days, my mind? To a Friend. Matthew Arnold. NAEL-5v2; NAEL-6v2; Son

Who purchases this garment—Sire—buys death. (LL) Anna Hempstead Branch. APT-1; NALW   *Fr.* Sonnets from a Lock Box.

Who pure as light and chaste as origin has stayed. "Angelus Silesius." GePo, *tr.* by George C. Schoolfield   *Fr.* Cherubical Wanderer, The.

Who really respects the earthworm. Earthworm, The. Harry Edmund Martinson. RB; RaBo, *tr.* by Robert Bly

Who redes this boke of imagerie. *Unknown.* MiEL

Who Remains Standing? Andrée Chedid. HAWP; WoPoe, *tr.* by Mirène Ghossein and Samuel Haze

Who resolves to go astray. (LL) Written in an Ovid. Matthew Prior. FaBoEE; OBCoV

Who rides at night, who rides so late? Invisible King, The. Goethe. RaBo, *tr.* by Robert Bly

Who rideth through the driving rain. King's Son, The. Thomas Boyd. OBMV

Who rules the world with iron rod? Tall Hat. Victor James Daley. CBAP

Who Runs America? Allen Ginsberg. FaBoA

Who's going to read that? Satire 1. Persius. RomPo, *tr.* by Richard Emil Braun

Who's got the last laugh now? (LL) They All Laughed. George Gershwin. APT-2; ReLy

Who's killed the leaves? Leaves. Ted Hughes. OxBC

Who's most afraid of death? Thou. E. E. Cummings. PoE; VGW

Who's on first? Why That Abbott and Costello Vaudeville Mess Never Worked with Black People. Paul Beatty. AmPoNex

Who's on first? The dust descends as. Whose Language. Charles Bernstein. PmAP

Who's Sorry Now? Harry Ruby. ReLy

Who's that coming down the street? Yes, Sir! That's My Baby. Walter Donaldson. ReLy

Who's that knocking on my ring, says the chin. Selima Hill. NewEx

Who's that knocking on the window. Innocent's Song. Charles Causley. GTBS-P; OBCP

Who's that mysterious rider. Horseman on the Skyline, The. Henry Lawson. CBAP

Who's that ringing at my door bell? *Unknown.* FaBoCh; OxNR

"Who's that tickling my back?" said the wall. Tickle Rhyme, The. Ian Serraillier. NTCP; Spl

Who's That? James Kirkup. OTCP

Who's that? Epitaph: Tristran Tzara. Philippe Soupault. SurPaPo, *tr.* by Mary Ann Caws and Patricia Terry

Who's the Dover-based day tripper. Trifle for Trafalgar Day, A. Ted Pauker. NOBL

Who's the jew where is he she it that looms up in your face. Who's the Jew. David Meltzer. TaR

Who's the most important man this country ever knew? Barney Google. Billy Rose. OBAL

Who's therefore true, because her truth kills me[e]. (LL) Twicknam [or Twickenham] Garden. John Donne. BASC; EBEV; ESCV; EnLoPo; MeLP; OBGa; PoE; SCGP

Who's Who. W. H. Auden. MoBrPo; NoAM; Son

Who said / If you took the name All-Destroyer. Giriścandra Ghos. SinGod, *tr.* by Rachel Fell McDermott

Who said, "Peacock Pie?" Song of the Mad Prince, The. Walter De la Mare. EBEV; FaBoCh; MakPoe; NOBE; NoAM; OxAEP-2

Who said to the trout. Pisces. Ronald Stuart Thomas. CABP; OxBC

Who saw nothing. (LL) Joyce Mansour. BoWoP; HAWP; WoPoe, *tr.* by Willis Barnstone

Who saw the petals. Secret Song, The. Margaret Wise Brown. OBCA

Who say[e]s that fictions on[e]ly and false hair. Jordan (1). George Herbert. BASC; FHYEP; FSCP; GeHe; HAP; MeLP; NAEL-5v1; NAEL-6v1; NAEL-7v1; NOCV; NOSC; NoP-4; OxBEV; PeECV; PoE; TFi; TrCP; WoPoe

Who Says. Julia Hartwig. GI, *tr.* by Stanislaw Baranczak

Who Says a Painting Must Look Like Life? Su Tung-p'o (Su Shih). ColAnChi, *tr.* by Burton Watson

Who says a woman's work isn't high art? Woman's Work. Julia Alvarez. RA

Who Says That Drought Was Here? Niyi Osundare. HBAPE; NAfrP

Who says that Giles and Joan at discord be? On Giles and Joan. Ben Jonson. NAEL-5v1; NAEL-6v1; NAEL-7v1; NOBL

Who says that it's by my desire. People Hide Their Love. Emperor Wu of Han [or Wu Ti or Ou-ty or Liu Ch'e or Liu Ch'u]. ChiP, *tr.* by Arthur Waley

Who says that sadness can be cast away for long? Tune: "Magpie on the Branch." Feng Yen-ssu. SuSp, *tr.* by Daniel Bryant

Who says that the dead do not think of us? In Broad Daylight I Dream of My Dead Wife. Mei Yao Ch'en. OHPC, *tr.* by Kenneth Rexroth

Who Says the River is Wide? *Unknown.* CoBCP, *tr.* by Burton Watson

Who Says Words With My Mouth. Jelaluddin [or Jalal al-Din] Rumi. AmFaPo, *tr.* by Coleman Barks and John Moyne

Who says you have no sheep? Herdsman's Song. *Unknown.* ChiP, *tr.* by Arthur Waley

Who says you're like one of the dog days? Shall I Compare Thee to a Summer's Day? Howard Moss. InPK-6

Who see, as I copy and copy and copy. (LL) Meditation by the Xerox Machine. Doris Safie. GraLe; PoArWo

Who see no friend in God—in Satan's host no foes. (LL) Doubt. Mary Elizabeth Coleridge. NALW; ViWPN

Who seeks wisdom in words. Silences. David Mitchell. PeNZ

Who sees him walk the street, can scarce forbear. Marvellous Martin. Charles Harpur. CBAP

Who sees the cross at Christmas? To See the Cross at Christmas. Roger Cooper. TrCP

Who sees, will spew; who smells, be poisoned. (LL) Beautiful Young Nymph Going to Bed, A. Jonathan Swift. ECEV; EroLit; NOEC; NPeEn; OxBEV

Who / SELF, / The World. Job's Epitaph. Joshua Sylvester. ChIV-1

Who sent Jack Barrett there. (LL) Story of Uriah, The. Rudyard Kipling. NOBVV; OxBEV; PeVV; SCV

Who Shall Deliver Me? Christina Georgina Rossetti. SacPr; TOF

Who Shall Die. James A. Randall, Jr. BPo

Who shall doubt, Donne, where [or whe'er] I a poet be[e]. To John Donne. Ben Jonson. BeJo

Who shall have my fair [or faire or fayre] lady? My Fair Lady. *Unknown.* EnLoPo

Who shall I have for friends. Fujiwara No Okikaze. OHMPJ

Who shall invoke when we are gone. Tragic Love. Walter James Turner. OBMV

Who shall open the closed book? Introitus. János Pilinszky. IQMS, *tr.* by Ted Hughes

Who shall speak for the people? Carl Sandburg. OxBA   *Fr.* People, Yes, The.

Who shall tell what did befall. Wealth. Ralph Waldo Emerson. APN-1

Who she was. Back Far Enough, down Deep Enough. Constance Urdang. PBCAP

Who shot the snake? beat it to death on the road? In Memoriam S. L. Akintola. David Knight. MoCV

Who showed me. To Flossie. William Carlos Williams. SAmP

Who sleeps at night? No one is sleeping. Marina Ivanovna Tsvetaeva [or Tsvetaeva]. AWTN, *tr.* by Elaine Feinstein   *Fr.* Insomnia.

Who smoke-snorts toasts o' My Lady Nicotine. Variations on an Air: After Robert Browning. Gilbert Keith Chesterton. NOBL

Who so list to hount[e] I know[e] where is an hynde. Sir Thomas Wyatt. *See* Whoso list to hunt, I know where is an hind

Who speaks of the strong currents. White Asparagus. Sujata Bhatt. HarvBoo

Who speaks the sound of an echo? Tree-Leaf Woman. WPoS

Who spoke out for the dumb and the down-trodden then! (LL) James Russell Lowell. NOBA; OxBA   *Fr.* Fable for Critics, A.

Who spurs on the road when the day is done. Erl-King. Goethe. WoPoe, *tr.* by John Frederick Nims

Who still says that drought was here? (LL) Who Says That Drought Was Here? Niyi Osundare. HBAPE; NAfrP

Who straight, *Your suit is granted*, said, and died. (LL) Redemption. George Herbert. BASC; CABP; ESCV; FSCP; GeHe; HAP; InPK-6; MeLP; NAEL-5v1; NAEL-6v1; NAEL-7v1; NOBE; NOCV; NOSC; NPeEn; NoP-4; OxBEV; OxBSo; PBRV; PeECV; PoE; PoPoPo; SCGP; SCV; SoSe-8; TFi; TrCP; WeW-3

Who strolls so late, for mugs a bait. French Lisette: A Ballad of Maida Vale. William Plomer. OBCoV

"Who stuffed that white owl?" No one spoke in the shop. Owl-Critic, The. James Thomas Fields. OBAL

Who subdues? And who is subdued? This story is told. Ana Maria Shúa. MirDau, *tr.* by Rhonda Buchanan   *Fr.* Golem and Rabbi.

Who sure intended him to stretch a rope. (LL)   Boss, The.   James Russell Lowell.   NCAP; OBAL

Who swept away my gilded fall.   Leah Goldberg.   MHP, *tr. by* Ruth Finer Mintz   *Fr.* Songs of the Stream.

Who swerves from innocence, who makes divorce.   William Wordsworth.   CenSon   *Fr.* River Duddon [A Series of Sonnets], The.

Who take today and jerk it out of joint.   Young Africans.   Gwendolyn Brooks.   NoAM

Who taught me betimes to love working and reading. (LL)   Sluggard, The.   Isaac Watts.   ECEV; HAP; NOEC; OxBEV; OxBoLi; UV

Who taught thee conflict with the pow'rs of night.   On the Death of a Young Gentleman.   Phillis Wheatley.   SacPr

"Who, tell me, shepherd, owns these rows of plants?"   Cometas.   GrAn

Who then has strangled the weary voice.   Call.   Noémia da Sousa.   HAWP, *tr. by* Jacques-Noël Gouat

Who think you comes there?   *Unknown.*   APN-2   *Fr.* Ghost-Dance Songs.

Who thinks of June's first rose to-day?   June, 1915.   Charlotte Mew.   OxAEP-2

Who thought in high midsummer.   Boethius.   MLL   *Fr.* Consolation of Philosophy, The ("De Consolacione Philosophie").

Who told you.   Plan, The.   Rae Armantrout.   BAP-01

Who Translates a Poet Badly.   Manuel González Prada.   SpanPo, *tr. by* William M. Davis

Who travels [*or* trauels] by the wearie wandring way.   Edmund Spenser.   OxAEP-1   *Fr.* Faerie Queene, The.

Who trusteth in hilarity.   Marianne Vitale.   HeMarv   *Fr.* On Justifying Cuckoo La Goose.

Who, trusting his mind, could praise the man of Lindos, Kleoboulos.   Simonides.   SaLy, *tr. by* Diane Rayor

Who utters of his father aught but praise.   Cecco Angiolieri, da Siena.   EaItPo, *tr. by* Dante Gabriel Rossetti

Who wait in long lines for money. (LL)   Curriculum Vitae.   Lawrence Joseph.   GraLe; PBCAP

Who wants to think of us as five? Five keen-nosed grey-maned black-.   Aleksei Eliseievich Kruchyonykh [*or* Kruchionykh *or* Kruchenykh].   PFTM-1   *Fr.* Sahara to America, the.

Who was a man. (LL)   Malcolm X.   Gwendolyn Brooks.   IllVoic; TTY

Who was asking for it.   Boys, the Broom Handle, the Retarded Girl, The.   Alicia Ostriker.   ExTi

Who was born, not of a virgin but a real woman.   Jah Son / Another Way.   Kendel Hippolyte.   WaCA

Who was helpless back in Prague.   Man Proposes, God Disposes.   Bachner.   INSAB

Who was it came.   Daniel Gerard Hoffman.   CoAP

Who Was It, Tell Me.   Heinrich Heine.   TrJP, *tr. by* Richard Garnett (Sag' Mir Wer Einst die Uhren Erfund.)   AWP

Who was it that took away my voice?   Silence.   Bella [*or* Izabella] Akhatovna Akhmadulina.   BoWoP, *tr. by* Daniel Halpern

Who was it who held me on her knee?   Mother.   Josephine D. Henderson Heard.   CBWP-4

Who was Mary Shelley?   Lorine Niedecker.   APSN

Who was my grandmother?   La Sombra of Who I Am.   Michaela Raen.   PoArWo

Who was neither ingenious, sober, nor kind. (LL)   Epitaph: "Here lies the body of Richard Hind."   Francis, Lord Jeffrey Jeffrey.   FaBoEE; OxBoLi

Who was responsible for the very first arms deal.   Peace.   Michael Longley.   BiHa; CIP-2; PBCIP; PNI

Who was that woman sleeping.   Courtesan to Her Lover, A.   Kshetrayya.   WoPoe, *tr. by* V. Narayana Rao, A. K. Ramanujan and David Shulman

Who was the sun, and he sole faithful planet. (LL)   Old Witherington.   Dudley Randall.   NBV; NoAM

Who was this girl.   Looking at Pictures to Be Put Away.   Gary Snyder.   NNaP

Who watches on the mountain with the dead.   Vigil of Rizpah, The.   Felicia Dorothea Hemans.   CenSon

Who wd. cope in this Quick.   Web, The.   Gregory O'Donoghue.   BIrV

Who weds a sot to get his cot.   Proverbial Advice on Marriage.   *Unknown.*   NBLV

Who weep now anywhere in the world.   Solemn Hour.   Rainer Maria Rilke.   TrJP, *tr. by* C. F. MacIntyre

Who Were before Me.   John Drinkwater.   OBMV

Who were the builders? Question not the silence.   Nameless Doon [*or* Dun], The.   William Larminie.   BIrV

"Who were you, shipwrecked stranger?"   Leontichos found.   Callimachus.   GrAn

Who, who and who?   Dark Lord of Savaiki, The.   Alistair Campbell.   PeNZ

Who, who, who will be the next man to entrust his girl to a friend?   Ezra Pound.   FaBoMo   *Fr.* Homage to Sextus Propertius.

Who will believe me later, when I say.   Last of the Courtyard, The.   Emily Grosholz.   FFC

Who Will Buy a Poem?   Mahon O'Heffernan.   NOIV

Who Will Buy Me an Orange?   José Gorostiza.   TCLAP, *tr. by* Rachel Benson

Who will find her beautiful / if you do not? (LL)   Song at midnight.   Lucille Clifton.   ErotSp; UnSA

Who will go drive with Fergus now.   Who Goes with Fergus?   W. B. Yeats.   FaBoCh; InPK-6; NAEL-5v2; NAEL-6v2; NOBE; NOBVV; NoAM; PeVV; PoE; PoRA; TRP

Who will in fairest book of Nature know.   Sir Philip Sidney.   NAEL-5v1; NAEL-6v1; NAEL-7v1; NoP-4; NoSic; PoE   *Fr.* Astrophil and Stella.

Who Will Know Us?   Gary Soto.   GM

Who will last? And what? The wind will stay.   Abraham Sutskever [*or* Sutzkever].   BBASP, *tr. by* Cynthia Ozick   *Fr.* Poems from a Diary.

Who Will Live in Our Houses When We Die?   Michael C. Blumenthal.   NoAM

Who will remember, now I write? (LL)   Solum Mihi Superest Sepulchrum.   William Habington.   ChIV-1; NOSC

Who will remember, passing through this Gate.   On Passing the New Menin Gate.   Siegfried Sassoon.   NAEL-5v2; NAEL-6v2; NoAM; NoP-4; OBMV; PoWW; Son

Who Will Show Us Any Good?   Lady Jane Francesca Wilde.   VWP

Who will show us where.   At the Doors.   "Der Nistor."   TrJP, *tr. by* Joseph Leftwich

Who Will Throw the First Stone?   Clara Silva.   TANSG, *tr. by* Celeste Kostopulos-Cooperman

Who with salt tears this last farewel [*or* farewell] did take. (LL)   Before the Birth of One of Her Children.   Anne Bradstreet.   AmFaPo; BoWoP; EMWP; NAAL-2v1; NAAL-3; NAAL-5; NOBA; PAI; PeECV; SacPr; WPE; WPOW

Who won't praise green. Each minute to caress each minute blade of spring. Green slice us open.   D. A. Powell.   NAPBL; NeAmPo

Who won: the Babylonian system.   Election.   Oswald de Andrade.   TCLAP, *tr. by* Flavia Vidal

Who works harder on earth.   Pablo Neruda.   GifTon, *tr. by* William O'Daly   *Fr.* Book of Questions, The.

Who wot now that is heer / Wher he shal be another yeer?   *Unknown.*   *See* Another year it may betide

Who would be / A merman bold.   Merman, The.   Tennyson.   UV

Who would care to pass his life away.   Lotos Eating.   Mortimer Collins.   NOBVV

Who would divorce her lover with a phone.   Marilyn Hacker.   NIL-7

Who would have loved you in a day or two. (LL)   Edna St. Vincent Millay.   APT-1; NAAL-2v2; NAAL-5

Who Would Have Thought It.   Marie Luise Kaschnitz.   PFTM-2, *tr. by* Lisel Mueller

Who would have thought it Sir, actually putting ME in a WRITING!   Peter Reading.   FaBoVe

Who would have thought she'd end that way? (LL)   Mourning Poem for the Queen of Sunday.   Robert Earl Hayden.   HCAP; NAAAL; NoAM; NoP-4; PoPoPo

Who would have thought that a disease of the ordinary world.   Hsü Chung-hsing.   CoBLCP   *Fr.* Inquiring about the Health of Li Te-hua.

Who would hold fortune's wheel and turn it round. (LL)   Sonnet: To the Lady Pietra degli Scrovigni.   Dante Alighieri.   AWP; EaItPo, *tr. by* Dante Gabriel Rossetti

Who would I show it to.   Elegy.   W. S. Merwin.   HCAP

Who would know the depths of autumn sorrow? (LL)   My Man Pa Replies.   Li Ho.   CoBCP; ColAnChi, *tr. by* Burton Watson

Who Would List.   *Unknown.*   CTC, *tr. by* Andrew Lang   *Fr.* Aucassin and Nicolette.

Who would live in others' breath?   Epitaph: Iohannis Sande.   Thomas Bastard.   FaBoEE

Who would not be.   Laureate, The.   William Edmonstoune [*or* Edmondstoune] Aytoun.   UV

Who would not live long. (LL)   Shield of Achilles, The.   W. H. Auden.   EBEV; FaBoMo; GTBS-P; HAP; NAEL-5v2; NAEL-6v2; NOBE; NOCV; NPeEn; NoAM; NoP-4; OxAEP-2; OxBEV; PeECV; PoE; WeW-3

Who would not sing in May. (LL)   Crazy Woman, The.   Gwendolyn Brooks.   ItWoWo; NALW

Who would not weep, if Atticus were he? (LL)   Pope.   AWP; EBEV; InPK-6; NOBE; OxBEV; TOF; TRP   *Fr.* Epistle to Dr. Arbuthnot.

Who would perish of excess. (LL)   Promises like Pie-Crust.   Christina Georgina Rossetti.   NAEL-6v2; NOBVV; NPeEn

Who would true Valour see.   John Bunyan.   EBEV; NOCV; OxBEV   *Fr.* Pilgrim's Progress, The.

Who would want to die defending Firestone Tire.   Firestone.   David Rivard.   PBCAP

Who would / who could.   Now Ain't That Love?   Carolyn M. Rodgers.   BPo

Who writ for many. Benedicite. (LL)   On Himselfe.   Robert Herrick.   FaBoEE; NOSC

Who writes the words and music.   Dames.   Harry Warren.   ReLy

Who wrote.   In Memoriam Charles Reznikoff.   George Oppen.   APT-2

Who wrote *Who wrote Icon Basilike?* On ["Who Wrote Icon Basilike" by Dr.] Christopher Wordsworth, Master of Trinity. Benjamin Hall Kennedy. FaBoEE; OBCoV

Who? Otto Harbach. ReLy

Who? Czeslaw Milosz. BodElec *Fr.* Lithuania, after Fifty-Two Years.

Whoe doesn't love / roses, and who. Hummingbird Pauses at the Trumpet Vine. Mary Oliver. NAAL-5

Whoe'er has gone through London Street. Butcher, A. Thomas Hood. PeLV

Whoe'er he be that to a taste aspires. James Bramston. NOEC *Fr.* Man of Taste, The.

Whoe'er our stage examines, must excuse. Prologue on the Old Winchester Playhouse over the Old Butchers' Shambles. Thomas Warton, the Younger. ECEV

Whoe'er sighs most, is cruellest, and hastes the other's death. (LL) Valediction: of Weeping, A. John Donne. BASC; ESCV; FHYEP; FSCP; HAP; HeIP-4; MeLP; NAEL-5v1; NAEL-6v1; NAEL-7v1; NOSC; NoP-4; PoE; SCGP; WeW-3

Whoe'er thou art whose path, in summer lies. Inscription. Mark Akenside. NOEC

Whoever comes to shroud me, do not harm. John Donne. *See* Whoever [*or* Who ever] comes to shroud me, do not harm[e]

Whoever despises the clitoris despises the penis. Muriel Rukeyser. APSN; APT-2; GLP; LCAP-2; PFTM-2

Whoever Finds a Horseshoe. Osip Emilevich Mandelstam [*or* Mandelshtam]. PFTM-1

Whoever has a mind to abundance of Trouble. Mary Evelyn. EMWP

Whoever Has Become All Divine. "Angelus Silesius". GePo, *tr. by* George C. Schoolfield *Fr.* Cherubical Wanderer, The.

Whoever has Cold Mountain's poems. *Unknown.* ColAnChi, *tr. by* Red Pine

Whoever has not choked on a word. Truly. Ingeborg Bachmann. PoSu

Whoever hath her wish, thou hast thy Will. William Shakespeare. NAEL-5v1; NAEL-6v1; NAEL-7v1 *Fr.* Sonnets.

Whoever hath washed his hands of living. Sadi [*or* Saadi *or* Sa'di]. AWP, *tr. by* Sir Edwin Arnold *Fr.* Gulistan, The.

Whoever heard of a black cowboy? Nat Love: Black Cowboy. Lee Bennett Hopkins. HHAm

Whoever hurts my favor with my lady. Heinrich von Veldeke. GePo

Whoever lives true life, will love true love. Elizabeth Barrett Browning. OxAEP-2 *Fr.* Aurora Leigh.

Whoever looks on life will see. James Cawthorn. ECEV *Fr.* Wit and Learning.

Whoever looks round sees Eternity there. (LL) Autumn. John Clare. BBASP; HAP; WeW-3

Whoever loves, if he do not propose. John Donne. BASC *Fr.* Elegies.

Whoever [*or* Who ever] comes to shroud me, do not harm[e]. Funeral[l], The. John Donne. AWP; BoLoP; EBEV; ESCV; EnLoPo; HeIP-4; MeLP; NAEL-5v1; NAEL-6v1; NAEL-7v1; NAWM-5v1; OBEV; PoRA; SCGP; TFi

Whoever passes by my tomb, know. Callimachus. HePo *Fr.* Epigrams.

Whoever reads my poems. *Unknown.* ColAnChi, *tr. by* Red Pine

Whoever's seen them carries them in marble. One Hundred Eighty. Giusi Busceti. ItPo, *tr. by* Gayle Ridinger

Whoever said a good man was hard to find. My Handy Man. Andy Razaf. ReLy

Whoever said I can't fly? Female of the Species. Maureen Watson. IBA

Whoever then are you? Whose wretched bones are these. Leonidas of Tarentum. HePo *Fr.* Epigrams.

Whoever to finding fault inclines. St. George Tucker. OBAL

Whoever trusts power and plays potent lord. Seneca. RomPo, *tr. by* Anthony James Boyle

Whoever water drinks, writes wretched poetry. Water and Wine. Friedrich von Logau. GePo, *tr. by* George C. Schoolfield

Whoever weeps somewhere out in the world. Silent Hour. Rainer Maria Rilke. AWP, *tr. by* Jessie Lemont

Whoever without money is in love. Of Why He Is Unhanged. Cecco Angiolieri, da Siena. EaItPo, *tr. by* Dante Gabriel Rossetti

Whoever you are, go out into the evening. Initiation. Rainer Maria Rilke. TrJP, *tr. by* C. F. MacIntyre

Whoever You Are Holding Me Now in Hand. Walt Whitman. APN-1; CAGL; NAAL-2v1; NAAL-3

Whoever you are: in the evening step out. Entrance. Rainer Maria Rilke. AmFaPo, *tr. by* Edward Snow

Whoever you are, we too lie in drifts at your feet. (LL) As I Ebb'd with the Ocean of Life. Walt Whitman. APN-1; NAAL-2v1; NAAL-3; NAAL-5; NOBA; TAP; TCAPo

Whole afternoon field inside me from one stem of reed, A. Answers from the Elements. Jelaluddin [*or* Jalal al-Din] Rumi. BBASP, *tr. by* Coleman Barks and John Moyne

Whole afternoon glistening, The. October Observed, Hudson Falls, New York in Bill's Back Yard. Richard Elman. PoCoUp

Whole Armour of God, The. Charles Wesley. NOCV

Whole-breasted as billows that break on a bank—unwilling! Cassandra. Elena Chizhova. ARWW, *tr. by* Catriona Kelly

Whole city seductively lit up, The. Tatiana Shcherbina. ItGoST, *tr. by* J. Kates

Whole day long, under the walking sun, The. Sleeping Giant, The. Donald Hall. PAI; TwCP

Whole Duty of a Poem, The. Arthur Guiterman. PoToHe

Whole Duty of Children. Robert Louis Stevenson. NBLV

Whole, full, flirtatious span of it, The. (LL) Black Lace Fan My Mother Gave Me, The. Eavan Boland. BiHa; HarvBoo; ModIr; NPeEn

Whole green sky is dying, The. The last tree flares. On a Line from Valéry. Carolyn Kizer. FFC; GifTon

Whole health resides with peace. Description of Elysium. James Agee. YaYoPo

Whole landscape drifted away to the north, The. Window on the North, A. Robert Arthur Douglas Ford. MoCV

Whole landscape flushes on a sudden at a sound, The. (LL) Cuckoo, The. Gerard Manley Hopkins. MoBrPo; OxBSP; RB; TTTS

Whole lifetime assigned to me, A. Lifetime. Narayan Surve. OMIP, *tr. by* Vinay Dharwadker

Whole Mess. . . Almost, The. Gregory Corso. BB

Whole nation, some seven hundred scattered, The. Architect Monk, The. Laurence Lieberman. BodElec

Whole New Scene, A. John Fuller. NOxBChV

Whole night long, A. Vigil. Giuseppe Ungaretti. PeFWW, *tr. by* Jonathan Griffin

Whole night through, A. Watch. Giuseppe Ungaretti. FaBoWar, *tr. by* Patrick Creagh

Whole point seems to be the idea of giving / away the giver, The. (LL) Charnel Ground, The. Allen Ginsberg. BB; BodElec

Whole process is a lie, The. Ivy Crown, The. William Carlos Williams. NAAL-2v2; NoAM

Whole Question, The. Robert Penn Warren. BodElec

Whole Self, The. Naomi Shihab Nye. GraLe; PoArWo

Whole Story, The. William Stafford. NNaP

Whole Truth So Help Me God—Also Known as the Gettin' Rid of Nigguz Business. Lorena M. Craighead. InTrad

Whole two weeks after The Million Man March and still, if you'd ask me, this is all I could say about it, A. Richard Rykard. SpirFl

Whole universe is full of God, The. Yunus Emre. EaWin, *tr. by* Talat Sait Halman and W. S. Merwin

Whole valley has been under for centuries, The. Only the deacon. After the Flood. Maurice Kilwein Guevara. NAPBL

Whole western sky is lemon yellow, The. Tenebrae. Juan Ramón Jiménez. SpanPo, *tr. by* Alice Sternberg

Whole white world is ours, The. White World. "H. D." WPoS

Whole Works, The. Federico García Lorca. PFTM-1

Whole world is clear and empty, The. No End Point. Muso Soseki. EaWin, *tr. by* W. S. Merwin

Whole world is coming, The. *Unknown.* NAAL-5; TCAPo *Fr.* Ghost-Dance Songs.

Whole world now is but the minister, The. Robert Bridges. Son *Fr.* Growth of Love, The.

Wholes. Larry Eigner. PmAP

Wholesome. William Meredith. TAP

Whom have We next? (His syntax is. Reckoning. Fay Zwicky. NOBAu

Whom I thought I should never see more. (LL) Bailiff's Daughter of Islington, The. *Unknown.* ESPB; OxBB; OxBoLi

Whom if ye please, I care for other none! (LL) Edmund Spenser. EBEV; NAEL-5v1; PoE; Son *Fr.* Amoretti.

Whom it is eating to the bone. (LL) Childlessness. James Merrill. CoAmPo; ColAP

Whom none but Beetles—know. (LL) Aurora. Emily Dickinson. APN-2; NCAP

Whom Shall One Teach. Bible, *O.T.* TrJP *Fr.* Isaiah.

Whom weave ye in. Rolfe and the Palm. Herman Melville. NCAP

Whom when I saw assembled in such wise. Virgil [*or* Vergil]. PoE *Fr.* Aeneid [*or* Eneados, *Aeneis*], The.

Whoops! *Unknown.* NTCP

Whoosh of rush hour traffic washes through my head, The. Swifts at Evening. Jeffrey Harrison. UrbNat

Whore and monk, we sleep. Basho. SoOfWa, *tr. by* Sam Hamill

Whore that rides in us abides, The. *Unknown.* SCAP

Whores. Margaret Abigail Walker. NALW

Whorl inside my head buzzes, The. Terminus. Peter Rose. BMAP

Whose accent no farewell can know. (LL) Hart Crane. ColAP; HAP; MoAmPo; UnPo *Fr.* Voyages.

Whose baggage from land to land is despair. Palladas [*or* Pallades]. GrAn; WoPoe, *tr. by* Frank Kuenstler

Whose boat will lift when the cloudburst happens. (LL)   From the Canton of Expectation.   Seamus Heaney.   CIP-2; ModIr

Whose brest hath marble beene to me. (LL)   William Habington.   BeJo; EnLoPo; MeLP; NOSC; OBEV; SCGP   Fr. Castara.

Whose broken window is a cry of art.   Boy Breaking Glass.   Gwendolyn Brooks.   AiP; ESEAA; NAAL-2v2; NoAM; NoP-4

Whose candles light the tulip tree?   Tulip Tree.   Sacheverell Sitwell.   MoBrPo

Whose cherry tree did young George chop?   Mingled Yarns.   X. J. Kennedy.   OBCA

Whose counted smile of hours and days, suppose.   Hart Crane.   ColAP   Fr. Voyages.

Whose day shall never die [or dy] in Night. (LL)   Epitaph Upon Husband and Wife Who Died and Were Buried Together, An.   Richard Crashaw.   EBEV; NOBE; OBEV; OxAEP-1

Whose disappointment broke into a rainbow of tears. (LL)   These Lacustrine Cities.   John Ashbery.   HCAP; PoM; UnPo

Whose dog am I?   Good Day's Work, A.   Naomi Replansky.   WWork

Whose Doom to whom? (LL)   Emily Dickinson.   APN-2; NCAP

Whose fault is it that your tree can't be seen.   In Central Park.   Moyshe-Leyb [or Moishe-Leib or Leyb] Halpern.   WoPoe, tr. by John Hollander

Whose feet are so deep in the sand. (LL)   Yves Tanguy.   David Gascoyne.   NoP-4; SPE

Whose fire from which I came, has now grown cold? (LL)   One Flesh.   Elizabeth Jennings.   FaBoWP; LW; NoP-4; OxAEP-2; OxBTC; Prnts

Whose fish, fish. (LL)   Nature's Lineaments.   Robert Graves.   FaBoTw; RB

Whose fruitlesse worke is broken with least wynd. (LL)   Edmund Spenser.   NoP-4; PBRV

Whose green adventure is to run to seed. (LL)   Remembering the 'Thirties.   Donald Davie.   HarvBoo; NoP-4; OxBTC

Whose Hand.   Unknown.   TrJP, tr. by Arthur Davis

"Whose heart" 'might be lost?' 'Whose mask is this?'   "Who has a mask."   White Phosphorus.   Alice Notley.   FTOS

Whose home is in the straw.   Brave Sparrow.   Michael Collier.   UrbNat

Whose is that long white box in the grove, what have they accomplished, why am I cold. (LL)   Bee Meeting, The.   Sylvia Plath.   HCAP; HarvBoo; NALW; WPE

Whose is the river, Excellency, whose the fish.   Geographers, The.   Karl Shapiro.   OxBA

Whose is this horrifying face.   David Gascoyne.   ChIV-2; NoP-4; OBWP; PeECV   Fr. Miserere.

Whose jade-flute is this, notes flying invisibly.   Hearing the Flute in the City of Loyang in a Spring Night.   Li Po.   ChinPo, tr. by Yip Wai-lim

Whose Language.   Charles Bernstein.   PmAP

Whose laughter plays like summer lightning there. (LL)   Cattle Show.   Hugh MacDiarmid.   FaBoMo; HAP; MoBrPo; OBMV; OxBEV; OxBTC

Whose like this age can scarcely yield another. (LL)   If Ever Hapless Woman Had a Cause.   Mary Sidney Herbert, Countess of Pembroke.   MakPoe; WPE

Whose little pigs are these, these, these?   Unknown.   OxNR

Whose love is given over-well.   Partial Comfort.   Dorothy Parker.   OBAL

Whose Lyre throbs only to the touch of Love! (LL)   Laments the Volatility of Phaon.   Mary Robinson.   CenSon; RWP

Whose modest tresses were bound up for thee! (LL)   To Spring.   William Blake.   NAEL-5v2; NAEL-6v2; NOEC; OBEV; SCGP

Whose [or Who's] hat was in his hand. (LL)   Ballad: "I put my hat upon my head."   Samuel Johnson.   NOBL; OxAEP-1; UV

Whose page is blanker than the raining skies. (LL)   On the Edge.   Philip Levine.   CoAP; TAP

Whose scales turn aside the sun's sword by their polish. (LL)   Egyptian Pulled Glass Bottle in the Shape of a Fish, An.   Marianne Craig Moore.   APT-1; NALW

Whose Scene?   Ruth Stone.   BoWoP

Whose shadow is less given to change than he. (LL)   Upon His Picture.   Thomas Randolph.   BASC; BeJo; NOBE

Whose songs shall never be heard. (LL)   Spectral Lovers.   John Crowe Ransom.   APT-1; HeIP-4

Whose spittle only could restore the blind. (LL)   Easter-Day.   Henry Vaughan.   ESCV; PeECV

Whose sweetheart is very drunk?   Chinook Songs.   Unknown.   APN-2, tr. by Franz Boas

Whose the hand unloosed Clearista's zone.   Meleager.   GrAn

Whose very beard is flesh, and mouth is horn[e]. (LL)   On the Card[e]s, and Dice.   Sir Walter Ralegh.   ChIV-2; RB

Whose wagon is perilously rapt. (LL)   Santa Fe Trail.   Barbara Guest.   FTOS; NeAP; PoM

Whose Window?   Alison Brackenbury.   DiPo

Whose woods these are I think I know.   Stopping by Woods on a Snowy Evening.   Robert Frost.   APT-1; BRP; ChAP; ClHu; ColAP; FaBoCh; HAP; HarvBoo; HeIP-4; ITBLP; InPK-6; MoAmPo; NAAL-2v2; NAAL-5;

NIL-7; NIP-4; NOBA; NTCP; NoAM; NoP-4; OBCA; OxBA; PAI; PoE; PoPoPo; PoRA; RB; SAmP; SCV; SoSe-8; TAP; TFi; TOF; TRP; TTTS

Whoso abandons peace for war-seeking.   Bonaggiunta Urbiciani.   EaItPo, tr. by Dante Gabriel Rossetti

Whoso answers my questions.   Bayard Taylor.   APN-2   Fr. Echo Club, The.

Whoso Gives Freely, Shall Freely Receive!   Josephine D. Henderson Heard.   CBWP-4

Whoso List to Hunt.   Sir Thomas Wyatt.   BoLoP; CABP; EBEV; HAP; NAEL-5v1; NAEL-6v1; NAEL-7v1; NoSic; OBVE; OxBSo; PoE; SCGP; TFi; WoPoe

    (Who so list to hount[e] I know[e] where is an hynde.)   NPeEn; OxBEV; PBRV

Whoso list to hunt, I know where is an hind.   Whoso List to Hunt.   Sir Thomas Wyatt.   BoLoP; CABP; EBEV; HAP; NAEL-5v1; NAEL-6v1; NAEL-7v1; NoSic; OBVE; OxBSo; PoE; SCGP; TFi; WoPoe

Whoso saw on rode.   Unknown.   OHMEL

Whoso thou art that passest by this place.   Epitaph of Maister Win Drowned in the Sea, An.   George Turberville.   FaBoEE

Whoso Would See This Song of Heavenly Choice.   John Wilson.   AH

Whosoever steals a rosebud.   Unknown.   PriapPo, tr. by Richard W. Hooper   Fr. Priapus Poems, The.

"Whu's aw thae fflag-poles ffur in Princess Street?"   Heard in the Cougate.   Robert Garioch.   OxBTC

Whud's like a flee. (LL)   Moonstruck.   Hugh MacDiarmid.   NAEL-5v2; NAEL-6v2

Whuh folks, whuh folks; don' wuk muh brown too hahd!   Scotty Has His Say.   Sterling Allen Brown.   APT-2

Whummil Bore, The.   Unknown.   ESPB

Whut do i keer ef de white-folks do 'buse us!   Uncle Rube's Defense.   Clara Ann Thompson.   CBWP-2

Whut you say, dah? huh, uh! chile.   Cabin Tale, A.   Paul Laurence Dunbar.   NAAAL

Why.   Yusuf Al-Sa'igh.   MAP, tr. by Diana Der Hovanessian and Salma Khadra Jayyusi

Why.   Andrey [or Andrei] Andreievich Voznesensky [or Voznesenskii].   RusPo, tr. by Robert Arthur Douglas Ford

Why a Boy.   Justin Chin.   WiU

Why all the racket, you chattering birds?   Epigram.   Unknown.   GrAn, tr. by Thomas Meyer

Why all these sidelong looks, you shameless tarts?   Unknown.   PriapPo, tr. by Richard W. Hooper   Fr. Priapus Poems, The.

Why am I a Negro? Oh, why am I black?   Slave's Lament, The.   Massillon Coicou.   NegPo, tr. by Ellen Conroy Kennedy

Why am I always so depressed?   Unknown.   CoBCP

Why am I not as they? (LL)   Lineage.   Margaret Abigail Walker.   BlSi; ItWoWo; NALW; OxWW; WWork

Why am I so afraid.   I Am Afraid of Fire.   Anna Swirszczynska.   AF, tr. by Czeslaw Milosz

Why are candles brightly burning.   Christmas Tree, The.   Lizelia Augusta Jenkins Moorer.   CBWP-3

Why Are Daddies So Mean?   Jane Chambers.   GLP

Why are epics.   Note on the Iliad.   Raymond Garlick.   AngWePo; TCAWP

Why are my songs so simple.   So Simple.   Mark Van Doren.   APT-2

Why are our ancestors.   Ancestors.   Dudley Randall.   BPo

Why are people gay.   Love Is Sweeping the Country.   George Gershwin.   ReLy

Why are the things that have no death.   Irony.   Louis Untermeyer.   TrJP

Why Are Those Who Are Loved So Dull and Leaden?   Patrizia Valduga.   CItWP, tr. by Cinzia Sartini Blum and Lara Trubowitz

Why are we[e] by all creatures waited on?   John Donne.   BASC; NOCV; PoE; TrCP   Fr. Holy Sonnets.

Why are you adrift, like a boat, in the midst of a river.   Your Thwarts in Pieces, Your Mooring Rope Cut.   Unknown.   WoPoe, tr. by Erica Reiner

Why are you silent, poets of Israel?   Public Outcry.   Karen Alkalay-Gut.   DTA

Why are you standing there, Mother.   Wintermelons.   Marian Yee.   FSt

Why are you taking me this way? Where does this road go? Tell me.   Unanswered.   Yannis Ritsos.   AF, tr. by Edmund Keeley

Why are your eyes as big as saucers—big as saucers?   Man in the Street.   Robert Penn Warren.   OBAL

Why are your lilies so tall and pure.   Cry of a People.   Mary [or Mollie] Evelyn Moore Davis.   SWaP

Why art thou changed? O Phaon! tell me why?   To Phaon.   Mary Robinson.   CenSon; RWP

Why / as the tips of the petals curl and darken does.   Adagio at Twilight.   John Carter.   PasH

Why blow'st thou not, thou wintry wind.   All Saints' Day.   John Keble.   SacPr

Why boast, O arrogant, imperious man.   On Mrs. Montagu.   Ann Yearsley.   ECWP; RWP

Why bother with the world? Ryushu Shutaku. ZenPo, *tr. by* Takashi Ikemoto and Lucien Stryk

Why Brownlee Left. Paul Muldoon. DiPo; EmeKit; NPeEn; NoP-4; OxBSo; PBCIP

Why, by an ingrained habit, deviate. With the Grain. Donald Davie. NoAM

Why call it dead, wi' life a-vled. All Still. William Barnes. NOBVV

Why call the miser miserable? as. Byron. UnPo *Fr. Don Juan.*

Why, Cambria did I quit thy shore. Edward Williams. AngWePo *Fr.* Stanzas Written in London in 1773.

Why came I so untimely forth. To a Very Young Lady. Edmund Waller. SCGP

Why can't I be the girl that I want to be? Femininity. Jay Livingston. ReLy

Why can't I forget like I should? Memories of You. Andy Razaf. ReLy

Why can't we all be like that bird? [*or* that wise old bird?] (LL) Wise Old Owl, A. Edward Hersey Richards. LB; OxNR

Why cannot we eat enough for a week. Envying the Pelican. Richard Weber. CIP-2

Why, Celia, is your spreading waist. Edward Moore. ECEV *Fr.* Poet and His Patron, The.

Why cherish thus the senseless thing? That Glove. Mary E. Tucker. CBWP-1

Why Come Ye Not to Court. John Skelton.
"Such a prelate, I trow." OBSV

Why confer on us the piercing vision. To Charlotte von Stein. Goethe. STV, *tr. by* John Frederick Nims

Why, Corydon, the silence and that frequent frown? Titus Calpurnius Siculus. RomPo, *tr. by* Guy Lee *Fr.* Eclogues.

Why, country Pan, sitting still. Anyte [*or* Anytes]. GrAn

Why Damon, why, why, why so pressing? Song. Mary Lee, Lady Chudleigh. LW

Why, Damon, with the forward day. Dying Man in His Garden, The. George Sewell. GTBS-P

Why did Ben Jonson. Mute Swans. Neil Curry. NLP

Why did Hagar weep over Ishmael when he thirsted. Yitzhak Lamdan. MHP *Fr.* In the Khamsin.

Why Did I Laugh Tonight? John Keats. CenSon; NAEL-6v2
("Why did I laugh to-night? No voice will tell.") GSo

Why did I wander. Isn't It a Pity? George Gershwin. ReLy

Why did I wrong my judgement so. Upon His Unconstant Mistress. Sir Robert Aytoun [*or* Ayton]. NOSC

Why did Massenet compose *Thaïs?* Greetings from the Chateau. James Schuyler. FTOS

Why did my parents send me to the schools. Sir John Davies. ChIV-1 *Fr.* Of Human Knowledge.

Why did [*or* do] I write? what sin to me unknown. Pope. EBEV; TOF *Fr.* Epistle to Dr. Arbuthnot.

Why did our blessed Savior please to break. On the Holy Scriptures. Francis Quarles. ChIV-2

Why did she seek out the mountains. Heading for the Heights. Merryn Williams. Prnts

Why Did Stingy Thomas. William M. Davis. SpanPo

Why did the children. Carl Sandburg. OBAL *Fr.* People, Yes, The.

Why did the clerk drag his fingertips. Great Helmsman, The. David Woo. OpBo

WHY DID THE MAID WEEP? (LL) Stephen Crane. APN-2; NoP-4; TAP *Fr.* Black Riders [and Other Lines], The.

Why did the sun his beams conceal. Crucifixion, The. Mary Weston Fordham. CBWP-2

Why did the wild pink break? Issa. EH, *tr. by* Robert Hass

Why did you choose me for your wife, Joseph? Asenath. Diana Hume George. ChIV-1

Why did you come. "H. D." PFTM-2 *Fr.* Hermetic Definition.

Why did you come / to trouble my decline? Red Rose and a Beggar. "H. D." APSN

Why did you come, with your enkindled eyes. Why? Mary Webb. LW

Why did you give no hint that night. Going, The. Thomas Hardy. EBEV; HarvBoo; NOBE; OxAEP-2; PAI; SCGP; UnPo

Why did you go. E. E. Cummings. VGW

Why did you hate to be by yourself. As to Being Alone. James Oppenheim. TrJP

Why did you keep me waiting? (LL) After the Last Dynasty. Stanley Kunitz. InvLad; TAP

Why did you reproach him. Protest. Amal Al-Juburi. PoArWo, *tr. by* Salih J. Altoma

Why did you stay away. Way the Cards Fall, The. Yusef Komunyakaa. GT

Why did your spirit. Jay Macpherson. NOBC *Fr.* Ark, The.

Why didn't the first philosopher want to go on living. Theory of Tragedy. Joseph Duemer. BodElec

Why didn't we think of clothes before? Dennis Joseph Enright. OBCoV *Fr.* Paradise Illustrated.

Why didst thou promise such a beauteous day. William Shakespeare. HeIP-4; OxAEP-1 *Fr.* Sonnets.

Why, disease, dost thou molest. To Sickness. Ben Jonson. BeJo

Why do boys' dicksies for a soft cunny yearn and the girls *vice versa?* Difficult and Weighty Question, A. Janus Pannonius. IQMS, *tr. by* Adam Makkai

Why do I allow my heart. Fools Fall in Love. Irving Berlin. ReLy

Why do I curse the jazz of this hotel? Jazz of This Hotel, The. Nicholas Vachel Lindsay. SeSe

Why do I deny manna to another? Sather Gate Illumination. Allen Ginsberg. NeAP

Why do I do just as you say. It Had to Be You. Isham Jones. ReLy

Why do I draw this coole releeving ayer. Barnabe Barnes. PBRV *Fr.* Parthenophil and Parthenophe.

Why I follow you. Sunset. Joseph Ceravolo. FTOS

Why do I hate that lone green dell? Emily Jane Brontë. VWP

Why do I just wither and forget all resistance. Nearness of You, The. Ned Washington. ReLy

Why do I languish thus, drooping and dull. Dulness[e]. George Herbert. ESCV

Why do I live to loathe the cheerful day. Laments her Early Misfortunes. Mary Robinson. CenSon; RWP

Why Do I Live? George Linnaeus Banks. PWR; PoToHe

"Why do I love" You, Sir? Emily Dickinson. APN-2; LW

Why Do I Love You? Roy Croft. *See* Love

Why do I love? Go ask the Glorious Sun. To One That Asked Me Why I Loved J. G. G. "Ephelia." EMWP; NOSC

Why do I post my love letters. Why Don't You Talk to Me? Alistair Campbell. PeNZ

Why do I use my paper, ink, and pen. Verses Made by a Catholic in Praise of Campion That Was Executed at Tyburn for Treason, As Is Made Known by the Proclamation. *Unknown.* NoSic

Why do I weep? to leave the vine. Bride's Farewell, The. Felicia Dorothea Hemans. TreFP

Why do I write today? Apology. William Carlos Williams. OxBA; SAmP

Why do lampreys swim from Riga back. Why. Andrey [*or* Andrei] Andreievich Voznesensky [*or* Voznesenskii]. RusPo, *tr. by* Robert Arthur Douglas Ford

Why do people sit in darkness as regards the Negro race? Truth Suppressed, The. Lizelia Augusta Jenkins Moorer. CBWP-3

Why Do So Few Blacks Study Creative Writing? Cornelius Eady. GT; LTA

Why do the Gentiles tumult, and the Nations. Bible, *O.T. See* Why do the heathen rage

Why do the Graces now desert the Muse? Walter Savage Landor. FaBoEE

Why do the heathen rage. Bible, *O.T.* NAAL-2v1 *Fr.* Psalms.

Why do the houses stand. Song. George Macdonald. NePenScot

Why do the lilies goggle their tongues at me. Grotesque. Amy Lowell. BoWoP

Why do these elders always exploit our disbelief? (LL) These Too Are Our Elders. Jack A. Mapanje. HBAPE; NAfrP

Why do these prudes fear Prakrit poetry. *Unknown.* GifTon, *tr. by* David Ray

Why do they come? What do they seek. On a Replica of the Parthenon. Donald Davidson. FuPo

Why do they stare. On Killing a Tax Collector. Murragh O'Daly. WoPoe, *tr. by* Richard O'Connell

Why do they think up stories that link my name with yours? People Will Say We're in Love. Richard Rodgers. ReLy

Why do we draw the chains tight across thousands of miles? Suitcases, The. 'Abd al-Karim Kassid. MAP, *tr. by* Lena Jayyusi and Anthony Thwaite

Why do we fear words? Love Song for Words. Nazik Al-Mala'ika. MAP, *tr. by* Christopher Middleton and Matthew Sorenson

Why do we in worries waste our lives, and torture. Marcus Manilius. RomPo, *tr. by* Eugene O'Connor *Fr.* Astronomica, The.

Why Do We Live? Israel Zangwill. TrJP

Why do we love her?—that she gave us birth? This World. Sarah Morgan Bryan Piatt. NCAP

Why Do We Mourn Departing Friends? Isaac Watts. AH

Why do we waste so much time in arguing? Sushi. Paul Muldoon. CABP; CIP-2

Why do you cry out, why do I like to hear you. Sound of Breaking. Conrad Potter Aiken. AWP

Why do you dig like long-clawed scavengers. Verlaine. Edwin Arlington Robinson. APN-2; NAAL-2v2; NCAP

Why do you dwell so long in clouds. James Shirley. OxBSP *Fr.* Triumph of Peace, The.

Why do you feel differently about a very little snail and a big one. Why Do You Feel Differently. Gertrude Stein. ItWoWo; PFTM-1

Why do you frown on me, you puritans. Petronius Arbiter. PGA

Why do you heave apart my stone? Gregory of Nazianzus, Saint. GrAn

Why do you hide, O dryads! when we seek. Chant for Reapers. Wilfrid Thorley. OBEV

Why do you lie with your legs ungainly huddled. Dug-Out, The. Siegfried Sassoon. MoBrPo

Why do you rack the ore? The cornerstone alone. "Angelus Silesius." GePo, *tr.* by George C. Schoolfield *Fr.* Cherubical Wanderer, The.

Why do you rush through the field in trains. Fat White Woman Speaks, The. Gilbert Keith Chesterton. OBCoV; UV

'Why do you shrink away, and start and stare?' At the Convent Gate. Charlotte Mew. VWP

Why do you stare so stupidly? Kukutis's Sermon to the Pigs. Marcelijus Martinaitis. TWW, *tr.* by Laima Sruoginis

Why do you, Summer Garden, press close to my lips. Summer Garden, The. Elena Ignatova. ItGoST, *tr.* by Sibelan Forrester

Why do you talk so much. For Robert Frost. Galway Kinnell. NOBA; VGW

"Why do / You thus devise." Susanna and the Elders. Adelaide Crapsey. APT-1; TCAPo; WPE

Why do you visit me, white moths, so often? Georg Heym. PeFWW

Why Do You Want to Be English? Peter Finch. Oth

Why do you wrap your wisdom in a multitude of words? Sister Mary Madeleva. CRP *Fr.* Concerning Death.

Why doe I quake my down-fall to reporte? Michael Drayton. CAGL *Fr.* Piers Gaveston.

Why does a cauliflower so much resemble a brain? Binary. Chris Wallace-Crabbe. OBCoV

Why does he keep bruising against me my dead father why still. Sestina with Refrain. Thomas William Shapcott. CBAP

Why Does It Snow? Laura Elizabeth Richards. NOxBChV; OBCA

Why does she lie to me. December. Miriam Van hee. TuT, *tr.* by Joan McBreen

Why does that pine tree stand. Chŏng Ch'ŏl. WoPoe, *tr.* by Kevin O'Rourke *Fr.* Snow Falling in the Pine Forest: Two Poems.

Why does the sea burn? Why do the hills cry? Zaydee. Philip Levine. NNaP; TaR

Why does the sea moan evermore? By the Sea. Christina Georgina Rossetti. NOBVV; NPeEn

Why does the thin grey strand. Sorrow. D. H. Lawrence. GTBS-P; NPeEn; OBMV

Why [*or* Quhy] does [*or* dois] your brand sae [*or* so] drop wi' blude [*or* drap wi bluid]. Edward [*or* Edward, Edward]. *Unknown.* ClHu; EBEV; ESPB; HAP; InPK-6; NAEL-5v1; NOBE; OBEV; OxBB; OxBEV; OxBS; PAI; PoRA; SCGP; SoSe-8; TFi; TRP

"Why doesn't somebody buy *me* false ears?" From the Joke Shop. Roy Fuller. OxBC

Why don't I write in the language of air? Mona Sa'udi. WPOW

Why Don't I? O. F. Diaz-Duque. ReTh

Why don't people leave off being lovable. Elemental. D. H. Lawrence. NoP-4

Why don't we rock the casket here in the moonlight? Pale Blue Casket, The. Oliver Pitcher. TTY

Why don't we say goodbye right now. Early Afterlife, An. Linda Pastan. ExTi

Why don't you / go down Old Hannah. Ol' Hannah. Doc Reese. PFTM-1

Why don't you shock the whole town and ride down. Dear Rosario. Maria Elena Caballero-Robb. ReBoTo

Why Don't You Talk to Me? Alistair Campbell. PeNZ

Why dost not speak? William Shakespeare. OxAEP-1 *Fr.* Coriolanus.

Why dost thou beat thy breast and rend thine hair. Robert Southey. CenSon

Why dost thou haste away. Sir Philip Sidney. NoSic *Fr.* Arcadia.

Why dost thou hate return instead of love. Ditty. Edward Herbert, 1st Baron Herbert of Cherbury. NOSC

Why dost thou shade thy lovely face? O why. To His Mistress. John Wilmot, 2d Earl of Rochester. OBEV

Why dost thou shade thy lovely face? O[h] why. Francis Quarles. BASC; MeLP; NOSC; OxAEP-1; SacPr *Fr.* Emblems.

Why dost thou so explore. Homer. OBVE *Fr.* Iliad, The.

Why dost thou sound, my dear[e] Aurelian. In Answer of an Elegiacal[l] Letter, Upon the Death of the King of Sweden [from Aurelian Townsend, Inviting Me to Write on That Subject]. Thomas Carew. BeJo

Why each is striving, from of old. Destiny. Sir Edwin Arnold. NOBVV; OxBSP

Why Flowers Change Color. Robert Herrick. HAP

Why from the danger did mine eyes not start. Sonnet: Of His Pain from a New Love. Guido Cavalcanti. AWP; EaItPo, *tr.* by Dante Gabriel Rossetti

Why give signs of life? No Sign of Life. Jorge Teillier. TCLAP, *tr.* by Carolyne Wright

Why go further? One might conceivably rectify the rhythm. William Carlos Williams. TCAPo *Fr.* Kora in Hell.

Why go toward the palaces of description. Painter Asks, The. John Yau. BodElec

Why God Invented the Cold. Catie Rosemurgy. AmPoNex

Why has our poetry eschewed. Food and Drink. Louis Untermeyer. MoAmPo

Why has Spring one syllable less. What's in a Name? Christina Georgina Rossetti. FaBoVe

Why hast thou nothing in thy face? Eros. Robert Bridges. CABP; NOBE

Why have crowds as magnets drawn. Why We Meet. Lizelia Augusta Jenkins Moorer. CBWP-3

Why have such scores of lovely, gifted girls. Slice of Wedding Cake, A. Robert Graves. BoLoP; NAEL-5v2; NAEL-6v2; NOBE; OxBTC

Why Have They Moved Me. Carlos German Belli. TCLAP, *tr.* by Maureen Ahern and David Tipton *Fr.* O Hada Cibernetica.

Why have ye no reuthe on my child? Mary Suffers with Her Son. *Unknown.* MiEL

Why have you made life so intolerable. To God. Ivor Gurney. OxBEV

Why Have You No Ruth? *Unknown.* OxBSP

Why have you risen, to stand with naked feet. With the Dawn. Thomas Caulfield Irwin. BIrV; EnLoPo

Why, having won her, do I woo? Coventry Patmore. OBEV; OxAEP-2; SacPr *Fr.* Angel in the House, The.

Why, he aimed the car right at that girl! Oracular Degeneration. Karl Kirchwey. KGB

Why He Had to Go. Justin Chin. AmPoNex

Why he turned them inside outside. (LL) George A. Strong. OBCoV; PeLV; UV *Fr.* Song of Milkanwatha, The.

Why He Was There. Edwin Arlington Robinson. APT-1; NOBA; OxBSo

Why, Hyllus, do you deny to me today. Martial. RomPo, *tr.* by Mollie Barger

Why I Am a Liberal. Robert Browning. Son

Why I Am Not a Buddhist. Molly Peacock. ExTi

Why I Am Not a Painter. Frank O'Hara. CoAmPo; HCAP; NOBA; NeAP; NoAM; NoP-4; PoE; PoM; PoPoPo; VCAP

Why I Believe in Angels. Rick Mulkey. AmPoNex

Why I Choose Black Men for My Lovers. La Loca. CLPP

Why I Didn't Go to Delphi. James Welch. CDW

Why I Don't Speak Italian. Arthur L. Clements. UnSA

Why I Forgive My Younger Self Her Transgressions. Ruth L. Schwartz. NeAmPo

Why I Like Movies. Patricia Jones. BlSi

Why I Often Allude to Osiris. Ishmael Reed. GT

Why I sit sighing here ask me no more. Upon the Imprisonment of His Sacred Majesties that Unparaleld Prince King Charles the First. Hester Lee Pulter. EMWP

Why I Skip My High School Reunions. Craig Arnold. AmPoNex

Why I tie [*or* tye] about my wrist. Bracelet to Julia, The. Robert Herrick. BASC; OBEV

Why I Voted the Socialist Ticket. Nicholas Vachel Lindsay. MoAmPo

Why I Write Not of Love. Ben Jonson. BeJo; OxBSP

(Some act of *Love's* bound to reherse.) PBRV

Why, if Becchina's heart were diamond. Sonnet: Of Becchina, the Shoemaker's Daughter. Cecco Angiolieri, da Siena. AWP; EaItPo, *tr.* by Dante Gabriel Rossetti

Why, if this interval of being can be spent serenely. Rainer Maria Rilke. EnlH *Fr.* Duino Elegies.

Why in all the many races of the country where we live. Why Negroes Don't Unite. Lizelia Augusta Jenkins Moorer. CBWP-3

Why interrupt. Foreign Land. Greta Knutson. SurWo, *tr.* by Penelope Rosemont

Why is a pump like Viscount Castlereagh? What's My Thought Like? Thomas Moore. FaBoEE

Why is everything I do in my life like a boomerang? Boomerang. John Perreault. SPE

Why Is God Love, Jack? Allen Ginsberg. FTOS

(Because I lay my / head on pillows.) CLPP

Why is it. Lover's Meeting. Ray Mathew. CBAP

Why is it I can't sleep tonight? Bucket, The. Rose Romano. UnSA

Why is it in my middle-aged dream. Black and White. Shirley Lim. UnSA

Why is it modern books are little read. Martial. RomPo, *tr.* by Olive Pitt-Kethley

Why is it not enough, to want death's certain peace? Lamentation during His Most Painful Illness. Simon Dach. GePo, *tr.* by Ingrid Waløe-Engel

Why is it that women. Pure Pop. Allison Joseph. NeAmPo

Why Is It This Way, Almighty God? Violeta Parra. TANSG, *tr.* by Shaun Griffin and Emma Sepúlveda-Pulvirenti

Why Is It? Lizelia Augusta Jenkins Moorer. CBWP-3

Why is my verse so barren of new pride. William Shakespeare. EBEV; NoSic; OxAEP-1 *Fr.* Sonnets.

Why is the cuckoo's melody preferred. Wren, The. John Clare. CenSon

Why is the floor, Chrysilla. Irenaeus Referendarius. GrAn

Why is the snow pale blue? Irina Ratushinskaya [or Ratushinskaia]. TCRP

Why is the word pretty so underrated? Pretty. Stevie Smith. NAEL-5v2; NAEL-6v2; NoAM; NoP-4

Why Is This Night Different from All Other Nights? Nadine Brummer. Prnts

Why / is what i ask myself. Hag Riding. Lucille Clifton. ExTi

Why Isn't It All More Marked. Kay Ryan. ExTi

Why, it's but the motion of eyes and brows! Yuishun. ZenPo, tr. by Takashi Ikemoto and Lucien Stryk

Why, Jack, how now? I hear strange stories. Epistle to My Friend J. B., An. Robert Dodsley. NOEC

Why lean over the fire, and who is this. In the Secret House. Christopher Middleton. FaBoMo

Why, let the strucken deer go weep. William Shakespeare. NoSic Fr. Hamlet.

Why Linger Yet upon the Strand? Louis FitzGerald Benson. AH

Why Log Truck Drivers Rise Earlier Than Students of Zen. Gary Snyder. GeoHom; LoL; NNaP

"Why look at me like that?" Nocturne by Ben Shahn. Ronald Stuart Thomas. OxAEP-2

Why look back at the old roads again? Drugs and buggery flourished. My grief took root. Nostalgia. Stephen Berg. OPRER

Why looks your Grace so heavily today? William Shakespeare. OxAEP-1 Fr. King Richard III.

Why, Lord. Mark Van Doren. AH

Why 'm i. 4 Or 5 Tadpoles. Kusano Shimpei. PFTM-1

Why, Madam, must I tell this idle tale? True Tale, A. Mary Chandler. ECWP

Why make it doubt—it hurts it so. Emily Dickinson. NALW

Why make it so short? Have you lost your old liking. Brevity. Friedrich Hölderlin. NAWM-7v2, tr. by Christopher Middleton

Why, Man of Morals, tell me why? (LL) Drinking. Anacreon. BeJo; NOBE; NPeEn; OBEV; OBVE; OxAEP-1; OxBEV; PAI, tr. by Abraham Cowley

Why Mira Can't Go Back to Her Old House. Mirabai [or Mira Bai]. EnlH, tr. by Robert Bly

   (Colors of the Dark One have penetrated Mira's body; all the, The.) WPoS, tr. by Robert Bly

Why mourns my beauteous friend, bereft? To Urania. Benjamin Colman. SCAP

Why muse wee thus to see the wheeles run cross. Town Called Providence, Its Fate, The. Benjamin Tompson. SCAP

Why must I be hurt? Pain. Elsie Robinson. PoToHe

Why must that slight man. Walk, The. Ethan Gilsdorf. OPRER

Why Must the Show Go On? Noël Coward. ReLy

Why Must You Know? John Wheelwright. APT-2; VGW

Why must you play chess with your friends all day? Poem Expressing My Wife's Response to One I Sent Her, A. Li K'ai-hsien. CoBLCP, tr. by Jonathan Chaves

Why my legs. In the Gloom on the Left. Joyce Mansour. PFTM-2, tr. by Molly Bendall

Why'n't you bring me. To Greet a Letter-Carrier. William Carlos Williams. OBAL; SAmP

Why Negroes Don't Unite. Lizelia Augusta Jenkins Moorer. CBWP-3

Why no! I never thought other than. Via Negativa. Ronald Stuart Thomas. InvLi

Why not merely the despaired of. Cascando. Samuel Beckett. ModIr; NOIV

Why not simply moonlight on a swirling leaf? Death, Dark Agent. Jotie T'Hooft. TuT, tr. by Seán Lysaght

Why not violate sense and say. W. S. Di Piero. PoCoUp

Why of the sheep do you not learn peace? Answer to the Parson, An. William Blake. FaBoEE; NBLV; OxBoLi; WoPoe

Why puts our grand-dame [or Grandame] Nature on. On the Unusual Cold and Rainy [or Rainie] Weather in the Summer, 1648. Robert Heath. NOSC

Why reclining, interrogating? why myself and all drowsing? To the States, to Identify the 16th, 17th, or 18th Presidentiad. Walt Whitman. CTC; NAAL-2v1; NAAL-3; RaBo

Why remember that I am a poet. Protest. Romelia Alarcón de Folgar. TANSG, tr. by Alison Ridley

Why repeat? I heard you the first time. Carl Sandburg. OBAL Fr. People, Yes, The.

Why, Rome was naked once, a bastard smudge. Humble Beginnings. Thomas Lovell Beddoes. NOBVV

Why, rustic Pan, sitting in the lone shady wood. Anyte [or Anytes]. SaLy, tr. by Diane Rayor

Why's/ Wise. Imamu Amiri Baraka.
   Wise 1. PFTM-1
   Wise 3. FTOS

Why say the idiot is not. Locus, The. Cid Corman. VGW

Why seraphim like lutanists arranged. Evening without Angels. Wallace Stevens. VGW

Why She Hurries Out, Then Home. Martha Rhodes. OPRER

Why She Says No. Ellen Bryant Voigt. FaBoWP

Why she should trouble her young. I Have Two Sons and the One I Love Best Is Robert. Paula Tatarunis. BloBone

Why sholde I noght as wel eek telle yow al. Geoffrey Chaucer. NPeEn Fr. Canterbury Tales, The.

Why should a foolish marriage vow. Dryden. NAEL-5v1; NAEL-6v1; NAEL-7v1; NIL-7; NIP-4 Fr. Marriage à la Mode.

Why should a woman who is healthy and strong. Many a New Day. Richard Rodgers. ReLy

Why should I be ashamed. Letter to a Friend. Marjorie Oludhe Macgoye. HAWP

Why should I be eaten by love. James A. Randall, Jr. BPo

Why should I blame her that she filled my days. No Second Troy. W. B. Yeats. EnLoPo; GTBS-P; HarvBoo; NAEL-5v2; NAEL-6v2; NOBE; NoAM; OxAEP-2; OxBTC; TFi; WeW-3

Why should I bother to pry into yours? (LL) Shih-hou Pointed Out to Me That from Ancient Times There Had Never Been a Poem on the Subject of Lice. Mei Yao Ch'en. CoBCP; ColAnChi, tr. by Burton Watson

Why should I call Thee Lord, Who art my God? After Communion. Christina Georgina Rossetti. SacPr; WPoS

Why should I confine myself. Ghetto. Guy Tirolien. NegPo, tr. by Ellen Conroy Kennedy

Why should I fear in evil days. John Quincy Adams. SacPr

Why should I fear the spirits of the dead? Written at Netley Abbey. Susan Evance. CenSon

Why should I feel discouraged. His Eye Is on the Sparrow. C. D. Martin. TCAPo

Why should I find Him here. Christ in the Clay-Pit. Jack R. Clemo. GTBS-P

Why Should I Grieve? Moses Ibn Ezra. TrJP, tr. by Solomon Solis-Cohen

Why should I have raced my boat home from town at dusk? Returning Home at Dusk from Town, on the Fifteenth of the Seventh Month. Shen Chou. SuSp, tr. by Irving Y. Lo

Why should I have returned? Noah's Raven. W. S. Merwin. ChIV-1; HCAP

Why should I heed their railings? What's a prude? Marriage Prospect, A. William Hurrell Mallock. NOBVV

Why should I hesitate? Karai. JDP, tr. by Yoel Hoffmann

Why should I keep holiday. Compensation. Ralph Waldo Emerson. APN-1; TAP

Why should I let the toad work. Toads. Philip Larkin. NOBL; NoAM; OxAEP-2; OxBTC; PAI; PoE; SoSe-8

Why Should I Murmur. Hartley Coleridge. Son

Why should I praise thee, blissful Aphrodite? "Michael Field." ViWPN

Why should I seek for love or study it? Ribh Considers Christian Love Insufficient. W. B. Yeats. BBASP; RaBo

Why Should I Sing in Verse. Samuel Daniel. Son Fr. To Delia.

Why should I sit alone, eyes closed. Rāmrenu Mukhopādhyāy. SinGod, tr. by Rachel Fell McDermott

Why should I speak of motherhood? Pulse. Jane Holland. MFPA

Why should I still pour out my intense desire. Michelangelo Buonarroti. CAGL, tr. by James M. Saslow

Why should I tarry here, to be but one. Above the Tree. Elizabeth Stoddard. SWaP

Why Should I Wander Sadly. Süsskind von Trimberg. TrJP

Why should it be my loneliness. Tell Me. Langston Hughes. APSN; SAmP

Why should my bells, which chime thy praise, when thou. Edward Taylor. ChIV-2 Fr. Preparatory Meditations before My Approach to the Lord's Supper.

Why should scribblers discompose. Walter Savage Landor. See Why should the scribblers discompose

Why Should the American Negro Be Proud? Maggie Pogue Johnson. CBWP-4

Why should the arabs come to my window. Write Off. Breyten Breytenbach. PoetW, tr. by Denis Hirson

Why should the scribblers discompose. Scribblers, The. Walter Savage Landor. OBSV

Why should the tiny harp be chained to themes. Powers of the Sonnet. Ebenezer Elliott. CenSon

Why should this a desert be? William Shakespeare. CTC Fr. As You Like It.

Why should this Negro insolently stride. August. Elinor Wylie. APT-1; MoAmPo

Why Should Vain Mortals Tremble. Nathaniel Niles. AH

Why should we not, as well, desire death. Francis Quarles. PeECV Fr. Divine Fancies.

Why should you [or shouldst thou] swear I am forsworn. Scrutiny [or Scrutinie], The. Richard Lovelace. BeJo; BoLoP; CaPo; EnLoPo; MeLP

Why should you try to crush me? Resentment. Richard Aldington. PeFWW

Why should your fair eyes with such sovereign grace. Michael Drayton. SCGP *Fr.* Idea.

Why Shouldn't It Happen to Us? Alberta Nichols. ReLy

Why sing sadly sad daughter of Pandion. To the Swallow. Pamphilus. GrAn, *tr. by* Dennis Schmitz

Why, sir, as to that—I did not know it was time for the. Pique at Parting, A. Sarah Morgan Bryan Piatt. NCAP

Why so desolate? Is Your Town Nineveh? Marianne Craig Moore. APT-1

"Why so droopy?" did I hear you say? Horace. EroLit, *tr. by Unknown* *Fr.* Epodes.

Why So Many of Them Die. Susan Wallbank. BrRo

Why so pale and wan, fond lover? Sir John Suckling. AWP; BASC; BeJo; BoLoP; CaPo; CavPo; ClHu; EnLoPo; GTBS-P; HAP; HeIP-4; ITBLP; NAEL-5v1; NAEL-6v1; NAEL-7v1; NBLV; NIL-7; NIP-4; NOBE; NPeEn; NoP-4; OBEV; OxAEP-1; OxBEV; PAI; PoE; PoRA; TFi; UnPo *Fr.* Aglaura.

Why solitary crow? He in his feathers. Solitary crow. Norman MacCaig. NoP-4

Why some people be mad at me sometimes. Lucille Clifton. ESEAA

Why speak not they of comrades that went under? (LL) Spring Offensive. Wilfred Owen. GTBS-P; PeFWW

Why speak of memory and death. Two Views of Two Ghost Towns. Charles Tomlinson. NoAM

Why speak of the use. Hayden Carruth. VGW

Why stand aghast. He Hath Need of Rest. Josephine D. Henderson Heard. CBWP-4

Why Tell Me What to Do? Chandidas. WoPoe, *tr. by* Tony Barnstone

Why Ten Men? Rodger Kamenetz. TaR

Why That Abbott and Costello Vaudeville Mess Never Worked with Black People. Paul Beatty. AmPoNex

Why That's Bob Hope. William Hathaway. ReTh

Why the hell do you grumble and blame tourism. Progressive Man's Indignation, A. Dimitris Tsaloumas. BMAP

Why the laughter, witless female? *Unknown.* PriapPo, *tr. by* Richard W. Hooper *Fr.* Priapus Poems, The.

Why the Old Woman Limps. Lupenga Mphande. HBAPE

Why the sea? Pointless Journey. Yolanda Bedregal. TANSG, *tr. by* Carolyne Wright

Why the Stone Remains Silent. William Kloefkorn. GifTon

Why the unbroken spiral, Virtuoso. Apple Peeler. Robert Francis. LCAP-2

Why the Wind Comes. Hirini Melbourne. PeNZ

Why the wooden chair begins. Affair With a Chair, An. Christopher Pilling. NLP

Why There Are Children. Leslie Ullman. YaYoPo

Why, there are maidens of heroic touch. "George Eliot." LW *Fr.* Felix Holt, the Radical.

Why There Are No Unicorns. Judith Ortiz Cofer. PueRic

Why this desperation to move heaven and earth. Palladas [*or* Pallades]. GrAn

Why this man gelded Martial[l] I muse. Raderus. John Donne. PeLV

Why throbs my heart when he appears? Self-Examination, The. *Unknown.* ECWP

Why, through each aching vein, with lazy pace. Her Passion Increases. Mary Robinson. CenSon; RWP

Why trouble you religion's sacred stream. New Illiterate Lay-Teachers, The. Rowland Watkyns. BASC

Why Try to Change Me Now? Cy Coleman. ReLy

Why try to recontruct with words. In the Body. Ferreira Gullar. TCLAP, *tr. by* Renato Rezende

Why utter the names of gods or stars. Other, The. Rosario Castellanos. TCLAP, *tr. by* Maureen Ahern

Why wait we for the torches' lights? Let Us Drink. Alcaeus [*or* Alkaios]. AWP, *tr. by* John Hermann Merivale

Why Was I Born? Jerome Kern. ReLy

Why was it that the thunder voice of Fate. Robert Gould Shaw. Paul Laurence Dunbar. CBCWP; PoPoPo; Son

Why was the airman taking such pains? Airman, The. Aleksandr Semionovich Kushner. TCRusP, *tr. by* Daniel Weissbort

Why We Are Forgiven. Bruce Weigl. BodElec

Why We Are Late. Josephine Miles. NALW

Why We Bombed Haiphong. Jonathan Holden. ReTh

Why We Fear the Amish. Robin Becker. BodElec

Why We Meet. Lizelia Augusta Jenkins Moorer. CBWP-3

Why We Play Basketball. Sherman Alexie. MoASP

Why weep on the hairless skull of tedium. Desire as Light as a Shuttle. Joyce Mansour. HAWP, *tr. by* Mary Beach

Why weep ye by the tide, ladie? Jock of Hazeldean. Sir Walter Scott. GTBS-P; NAEL-5v2; NAEL-6v2; NOBRP; OxBS

Why were you born when the snow was falling? Dirge, A. Christina Georgina Rossetti. EBVV; NOBVV; OxBEV; SCGP

Why were you not like the tree Trung Quan? What Things Are Called. Erich Fried. AF, *tr. by* Georg Rapp

Why, what a particularly pure young man this pure young man must be! (LL) Sir William Schwenck Gilbert. NAEL-5v2; NAEL-6v2; NBLV *Fr.* Patience.

Why, when I gaze on Phaon's beauteous eyes. Sappho Discovers her Passion. Mary Robinson. CenSon; RWP

Why, who makes much of a miracle? Miracles. Walt Whitman. SAmP

Why Why Should I the World Be Minding. Thomas Smith. AiP

Why will Delia thus retire. Receipt to Cure [*or* for] the Vapours, A. Lady Mary Wortley Montagu. ECWP; NOEC; NPeEn; OxBEV; PEW

Why, William, on that old grey [*or* gray] stone. Expostulation and Reply. William Wordsworth. FHYEP; NAEL-5v2; NAEL-6v2; NOBRP

Why won't Eve eat of the fruit? Eve Oh Eve. Taslima Nasrin. VCWP

Why worry when skies are gray? Let's Have Another Cup of Coffee. Irving Berlin. ReLy

Why, you ask, do painted gonads. *Unknown.* PriapPo, *tr. by* Richard W. Hooper *Fr.* Priapus Poems, The.

Why you no rhythm. Stall Me Out. Paul Beatty. AmPoNex

Why Your Grandfather Stopped Playing the Viola. Alice Wirth Gray. MiVo

Why? Melba Joyce Boyd. BlSi

Why? Wassily Kandinsky [*or* Kandinskii]. TCRP, *tr. by* Albert C. Todd

Why? Myra Cohn Livingston. CA

Why? Mary Webb. LW

"Why?" Because all I haply can and do. Why I Am a Liberal. Robert Browning. Son

Whylom [*or* Whilom] ther was dwellyng[e] at Oxenford[e]. Geoffrey Chaucer. NAEL-6v1; NAEL-7v1; NAWM-5v1; OxBoLi; PeLV *Fr.* Canterbury Tales, The.

Wi' a scunner in't. (LL) Scunner. Hugh MacDiarmid. FaBoTw; NePenScot

Wi da lentenin days ida first o da Voar. Tuslag. T. A. Robertson. OxBS

Wi' Jock of Hazeldean. (LL) Jock of Hazeldean. Sir Walter Scott. GTBS-P; NAEL-5v2; NAEL-6v2; NOBRP; OxBS

Wich deceased of thier emocion on a past excursion day. (LL) "Wellcome, to the Caves of Artá!" Robert Graves. NBLV; NOBL; PeLV

Wichita Vortex Sutra, Part I. Allen Ginsberg. FTOS

(For me O dear! on Zero Street.) (LL) FTOS

Wicked and the base do compass round, The. Fear Not: For They That Be With Us. Jones Very. ChIV-1

Wicked Clamor, The. Tuvia Rivner. MHP, *tr. by* Ruth Finer Mintz

Wicked clamor, my ear grows deaf, The. Wicked Clamor, The. Tuvia Rivner. MHP, *tr. by* Ruth Finer Mintz

Wicked Neighbor, The. "Zelda." WPOW, *tr. by* Hannah Hoffman

Wicked Who Would Do Me Harm, The. *Unknown.* RB, *tr. by* A. Carmichael

Wicked Women. *Vietnamese Oral Tradition.* CaDao, *tr. by* John Balaban

Wickedness of Peter Shannon, The. Alden Nowlan. MoCV

Wicker Basket, A. Robert Creeley. HAP; NoAM

Wicker chair / In pinetree's shade. Masaoka Shiki. ZenPo, *tr. by* Takashi Ikemoto and Lucien Stryk

Wickson Plums. William Corbett. PmAP

Wid my Banjo on my knee. (LL) Oh! Susanna. Stephen Collins Foster. OBAL; TCAPo

Wide Empty Landscape with a Death in the Foreground. N. Scott Momaday. CDW

Wide-eyed child in love with maps and plans, The. Voyaging. Charles Baudelaire. SxFrPo, *tr. by* James McGowan

Wide, ho? Ezra Pound. OBVE

Wide is our mouth and. Need Is Our Name. Luci Shaw. TrCP

Wide Land, The. A. R. Ammons. TwCP

Wide open are the gates of Heaven. Great Arbiter of Fate, The. Ch'u Yüan. SuSp, *tr. by* Wu-Chi Liu

Wide Open Are Thy Loving Hands. Bernard of Clairvaux. AH, *tr. by* Charles P. Krauth

Wide Walls. *Unknown.* PoToHe

Wide wide Yangtze, dragons in deep pools, The. Merchant's Joy, The. Lu Yu. CoBCP; ColAnChi, *tr. by* Burton Watson

Widening Spell of the Leaves, The. Larry Levis. PBCAP

Wider than winter. Carmen Ancillae. John Hollander. YaYoPo

Widespread Implications. A. R. Ammons. BodElec

Widgeon. Seamus Heaney. NPeEn

Widow, A. Ted Kooser. PBCAP

Widow, The. W. S. Merwin. UnPo; VGW

Widow, The. Robert Southey. NOBRP; NOEC; UV

Widow and the Soldier or: The Measure of a Woman's Inconstancy and Lust, The. Phaedrus. RomPo, *tr. by* Eugene O'Connor

Widow and Virgin Sisters, The. William Broome. ECEV

Widow at Windsor, The.   Rudyard Kipling.   NAEL-5v2; NAEL-6v2; NoAM

Widow Bird, A.   Shelley.   GTBS-P   Fr. Charles the First.

Widow bird sate mourning for her love, A.   Shelley.   GTBS-P   Fr. Charles the First.

Widow (conscious that time's on the wing).   Limerick.   Stanley J. Sharpless. PeLi

Widow Has Buried Her Second Husband, The.   William Dunbar.   RACG   Fr. Tua Mariit Wemen and the Wedo, The.

Widow in her late seventies, A.   Amsterdam Chronicle.   Rein Bloem.   TuT, tr. by John Hughes

Widow refuses sleep, for sleep pretends, The.   Exile.   Ellen Bryant Voigt. AWTN

Widow's Curse, The.   Unknown.   NOIV, tr. by Thomas Kinsella

Widow's Hymn, A.   George Wither.   OBEV

Widow's Lament.   Unknown.   BoWoP, tr. by Arthur Waley   Fr. Shih Ching.

Widow's Lament in Springtime, The.   William Carlos Williams.   APT-1; HAP; NAAL-2v2; NAAL-5; NOBA; NoAM; PoE; SAmP; SoSe-8; TAP; TCAPo

Widow's Remarriage, The.   Mary F. Johnson.   CenSon

Widow's Tears [or Widdowes Teares]: or, Dirge of Dorcas, The.   Robert Herrick.   ChIV-2

Widower.   Julia Copus.   NeBl

Widower.   David Ray.   SpudSo

Widower, The.   Joseph Awad.   GraLe

Widower, The.   Royall Tyler.   OBAL

Widower in the Country, The.   Les A. Murray.   DiPo

Widower's Courtship, The.   Elizabeth Hands.   WoRP

Widows.   Edgar Lee Masters.   MoAmPo

Widows' House, The.   Sarah Orne Jewett.   APN-2

Widow's Song, The.   Edward Coote [or Coate] Pinkney.   APN-1

Widsith.   Unknown.

   Widsith, the Minstrel.   AnOE

Widsith spoke, his word-hoard unlocked.   Unknown.   AnOE   Fr. Widsith.

Width, a shining peace, under the night, A. (LL)   Rupert Brooke.   PeFWW; SoSe-8   Fr. 1914.

Width of a cube spans defensive rapture.   Defensive Rapture.   Barbara Guest. FTOS

Wie langsam kriechet sie dahin.   Heinrich Heine.   AWP, tr. by Richard Monckton Milnes

Wiederkehr.   Rita Dove.   BodElec

Wife, The.   Robert Creeley.   VGW

Wife a-Lost, The.   William Barnes.   BoLoP; EBVV; EnLoPo; HAP; OBEV; SCGP

Wife a-Prais'd, A.   William Barnes.   EBVV

Wife and children. (LL)   Poem on Losing One's Teeth.   Han Yü.   GifTon; SuSp, tr. by Kenneth O. Hanson

Wife and servant are the same.   To the Ladies.   Mary Lee, Lady Chudleigh. CABP; ECWP; NALW; NIL-7; NOEC; PEW; WPE; WPOW

Wife—at Daybreak I shall be, A.   Emily Dickinson.   TCAPo

Wife in London, A.   Thomas Hardy.   NOBVV; OBWP

Wife is like a blade of grass, A.   Jean-Joseph Rabéarivelo [or Rebéarivelo]. NegPo

Wife of All Ages, The.   Edith Nesbit.   VWP

Wife of Asdrubal, The.   Felicia Dorothea Hemans.   ViWPN

Wife of Bath, The.   Geoffrey Chaucer.   NAWM-7v1, tr. by Theodore Morrison   Fr. Canterbury Tales, The.

Wife of Bath: Prologue, The.   Geoffrey Chaucer.   NAWM-7v1, tr. by Theodore Morrison   Fr. Canterbury Tales, The.

Wife of Bath's Prologue, The.   Geoffrey Chaucer.   FHYEP; NAEL-5v1; NAEL-6v1; NAEL-7v1   Fr. Canterbury Tales, The.

Wife of Bath's Tale, The.   Geoffrey Chaucer.   FHYEP; NAEL-5v1; NAEL-6v1; NAEL-7v1   Fr. Canterbury Tales, The.

Wife of Carcassone, The.   A. G. Prys-Jones.   TCAWP

Wife of Llew, The.   Francis Ledwidge.   MakPoe

Wife of Master Mason Clement, The.   Hungarian Oral Tradition.   IQMS, tr. by Adam Makkai

Wife of the Husband.   Micere Githae Mugo.   HAWP

Wife of Usher's Well, The.   Unknown.   AWP; EBEV; ESPB; MakPoe; NAEL-5v1; NAEL-6v1; NAEL-7v1; NOBE; NPeEn; NePenScot; NoP-4; OBEV; OxAEP-1; OxBB; OxBS; RB; SCGP; TFi

Wife's Complaint, The.   Unknown.   BoLoP, tr. by Michael Alexander

Wife's Lament.   Unknown.   PoE, tr. by Kemp Malone

Wife's Lament, The.   Unknown.   WPE, tr. by Ann Stanford
   (I make this song sadly about myself.)   BoWoP, tr. by Willis Barnstone and Elene Kolb
   (I sing this song about myself, full sad.)   NoP-4
   (Song I sing of sorrow unceasing, A.)   AnOE, tr. by Charles W. Kennedy

Wife's Lament, The.   Unknown.   AnOE

Wife's Tale, The.   Seamus Heaney.   CIP-2

Wife's Thoughts, The.   Hsü Kan.   CoBCP, tr. by Burton Watson

Wife Speaks, The.   Mary Stanley.   PeNZ

Wife Speaks, The.   Elizabeth Stoddard.   SWaP

Wife to a Friend, A.   Kshetrayya.   WoPoe, tr. by V. Narayana Rao, A. K. Ramanujan and David Shulman

Wife to Husband.   Fleur Adcock.   PeNZ

Wife to Husband.   John Harington.   NoSic

Wife was sitting at her reel ae night, A.   Strange Visitor, The.   Unknown. FaBoCh

Wife Who Smashed Television Gets Jail.   Paul Durcan.   CABP; CIP-2

Wife-Woman, The.   Anne Spencer.   NAAAL

Wife Wrapt [or Wrapped] in Wether's Skin, The.   Unknown.   ESPB

Wife's Complaint, The.   Unknown.   See Wife's Lament, The

Wig, rouge, honey, wax, teeth.   Lucilius.   GrAn

Wiglaf.   Marisa De Los Santos.   NAPBL

Wigs and Beards.   Robert Graves.   NOBL

Wilberforce.   Josephine D. Henderson Heard.   CBWP-4

Wild, The.   Wendell Berry.   VGW

Wild air, world-mothering air.   Blessed Virgin Compared to the Air We Breathe, The.   Gerard Manley Hopkins.   NOBVV; PeVV

Wild Ass.   Padraic Colum.   MoBrPo

Wild (at Our First) Beasts Uttered Human Words.   E. E. Cummings.   FaBoMo

Wild Bees.   James Keir Baxter.   NoP-4

Wild bird 'bode in the tame bird's tether, The.   White Bird, The.   Rosamund Marriott Watson.   VWP

Wild bird singer, sing on.   Sand Creek.   Charles G. Ballard.   UnPo; VoR

Wild bird, whose warble, liquid sweet.   Tennyson.   NAEL-6v2   Fr. In Memoriam A. H. H.

Wild birds on the roof are bitterly complaining to man, The.   Seeking Spring Beyond the city.   Su Tung-p'o (Su Shih).   TAL

Wild Boar and the Ram, The.   John Gay.   NOEC; NPeEn   Fr. Fables.

Wild Carthage held her, Rome.   Puritan Lady, A.   Lizette Woodworth Reese. MoAmPo

Wild Cat, A.   Su'ad al-Mubarak Al-Sabah.   MAP, tr. by John Heath-Stubbs and May Jayyusi

Wild-cat come-upon.   First English Wildcat, The.   Colin Simms.   Oth

Wild Cherry.   Nigel Jenkins.   TCAWP

Wild Cherry, The.   Malcolm Lowry.   NoP-4

Wild clefting, you I sing; mountains.   Night.   Georg Trakl.   PeFWW, tr. by R. S. Furness, David McDuff and Jon Silkin

Wild Common, The.   D. H. Lawrence.   NoAM

Wild Crab.   Mary Ellen Solt.   BoWoP

Wild Dog Rose, The.   John Montague.   BIrV; CIP-2; PBCIP; PoE

Wild Dreams, The.   Unknown.   NAWM-7v1, tr. by Ned Dubin

Wild Dreams of Summer What Is Your Grief.   George Barker.   OxBTC

Wild ducks / float with the north wind.   Sun Children.   Leslie Marmon Silko. VoR

Wild-eared, / singing. (LL)   Sunday Greens.   Rita Dove.   GT; LCAP-2

Wild-eyed team with horned and swaying heads, The.   Team, The.   Suzanne Gardinier.   CBAP

Wild fields of Ocean, piling heap on heap.   Mid-Ocean.   Emily Jane Pfeiffer. ViWPN

Wild Flower.   Maurice Kenny.   PoCoUp

Wild Flower Man, The.   Lu Yu.   OHPC, tr. by Kenneth Rexroth

Wild flowers and grass grow on.   In the Mountain Village.   Wang Hung Kung. OHMPC, tr. by Kenneth Rexroth

Wild for Love.   Delmira Agustini.   TANSG, tr. by Mark McCaffrey

Wild gander leads his flock through the cool night, The.   Walt Whitman. ColAP   Fr. Song of Myself.

Wild Gardens Overlooked by Night Lights.   Barbara Guest.   FTOS; PmAP

Wild Geese.   Mary Oliver.   BLT

Wild Geese, The.   Wendell Berry.   TRP

Wild geese cry.   Masaoka Shiki.   OHMPJ

Wild geese / Fellow travelers.   Lady Chine-Jo.   ZenPo, tr. by Takashi Ikemoto and Lucien Stryk

Wild Geese Flying.   Barbara Howes.   OWoS

Wild geese go north of the passes.   Variant on the Songs of the East and West Gates.   Ts'ao Ts'ao.   WoPoe, tr. by David Lattimore

Wild Geese on the Lake.   Shen Yüeh.   SuSp, tr. by Richard B. Mather

Wild geese waking in the March wind.   Withdrawal Letter.   Jim Carroll. PmAP

Wild Glee from Elsewhere.   Joyce Mansour.   SurWo

Wild Goat, The.   Claude McKay.   RACG

Wild goat on the hill, A.   Saleem Barakat.   MAP, tr. by Lena Jayyusi and Naomi Shihab Nye   Fr. Crane, The.

Wild goose, broken-legged on the sandbank.   Boat-pullers, The.   Mei Yao Ch'en.   SuSp, tr. by Jonathan Chaves

Wild Goose, Wild Goose.   Issa.   OHPJ; TTTS, tr. by Kenneth Rexroth

Wild grass, miles on end. Bearers' Song. T'ao Ch'ien [*or* T'ao Yuan-ming]. ChinPo, *tr. by* Yip Wai-lim

Wild Gratitude. Edward Hirsch. IllVoic

Wild Honey. Francis Webb. NOBAu

Wild Honey Suckle, The. Philip Freneau. ColAP; ITBLP; NAAL-2v1; NAAL-3; NOBA; OxBA; TAP; TCAPo

Wild honey to cold cells. (LL) Rainy Summer, The. Alice Thompson Meynell. OxBSP; OxBTC

Wild horses running in the hills. Tsangyang Gyatso. WoPoe, *tr. by* Brian Cutillo and Rick Fields *Fr.* Love-Poems of the Sixth Dalai Lama.

Wild Hyacinth. Joan I. Siegel. PoCoUp

Wild Iris, The. Louise Glück. ColAP

Wild Iron. Allen Curnow. RB

Wild is the foaming sea! The surges roar! Phaon Forsakes Her. Mary Robinson. CenSon; RWP

Wild Life Studies. James Fenton.
  Of Bison Men. PeLV
  Wild Ones[, The]. PeLV

Wild Man Comes to the Monastery, The. *Unknown.* RaBo

Wild man of Ssu-ming Mountain. Li Po. CoBCP *Fr.* Facing Wine with Memories of Lord Ho.

Wild midst the teeming buds of opening May. Morning, Rosamonde. Anne Batten Cristall. ECWP; RWP

Wild Nature. Charles Newton. NOEC *Fr.* Stanzas.

Wild Negro Bill. *Unknown.* BPo; NAAAL

Wild Night, A. Julia Ward Howe. ColAP

Wild Night at Treweithan. Gwyn Williams. AngWePo; TCAWP

Wild Nights—Wild Nights! Emily Dickinson. APN-2; EroLit; ErotSp; HeIP-4; NAAL-2v1; NAAL-3; NALW; NIP-4; NOBA; NoAM; OxBA; PoBW; RaBo; TAP; TCAPo; WPE

Wild Oats. Norman MacCaig. NPeEn; NePenScot; OxBTC

Wild Old Wicked Man, The. W. B. Yeats. RaBo

Wild Ones[, The]. James Fenton. PeLV *Fr.* Wild Life Studies.

Wild Party, The. Joseph Moncure March.
  "Gang was there when midnight came, The." APT-2
  "Queenie was a blonde, and her age stood still." OBCoV

Wild patience has taken me this far, A. Integrity. Adrienne Rich. ColAP

Wild Peaches. Elinor Wylie. FaBoWP; NAAL-2v2; NALW; OxBA; WPE
  Puritan Sonnet, IV. BoWoP; MoAmPo

Wild pigeon of the leaves. *Unknown.* AWP *Fr.* Thousand and One Nights, The.

Wild Plum. John Orrick. APT-1

Wild Provoke of the Endurance Sky. Joseph Ceravolo. BodElec

Wild Radishes. John Kinsella. NeBl

Wild raspberries gathered in a silent valley. Wild Raspberries. John Fuller. NPeEn

Wild Ride, The. Louise Imogen Guiney. ColAP; RACG; TCAPo

Wild roadside flowers, blooming in boundless numbers. Su Tung-p'o (Su Shih). WoPoe, *tr. by* Burton Watson *Fr.* Roadside Flowers, Three Poems with Introduction.

Wild Root. Juana de Ibarbourou. TCLAP, *tr. by* Sophie Cabot Black and Maria Negroni

Wild rose bending. David Lloyd. HA

Wild Rose of Plymouth, The. Jones Very. APN-1

Wild roved the Indians once. Grand Rapids. Julia A. Moore. OBAL

Wild Salmon: Stillaguamish Tribal Hatchery. Joan Swift. PoCoUp

Wild sea, A. Basho. EH, *tr. by* Robert Hass

Wild sea— / In the distance, A. Basho. OHPJ

Wild Sleeve. Marjorie Welish. FTOS

Wild Sports of the West. John Montague. CABP

Wild Strawberries. Robert Graves. FaBoCh

Wild Strawberry. Maurice Kenny. HATNAP

Wild Sunflower. Yvor Winters. APT-2

Wild Swan: "My attire is noiseless when I tread the earth." Cynewulf. AnOE, *tr. by* Charles W. Kennedy *Fr.* Riddles (Exeter Book).

Wild Swans. Edna St. Vincent Millay. HarvBoo; MoAmPo; OWoS; UnPo

Wild Swans at Coole, The. W. B. Yeats. HeIP-4; MoBrPo; NAEL-5v2; NAEL-6v2; NPeEn; NoAM; NoP-4; OWoS; PoPoPo; SCGP; SoSe-8; TFi; UnPo

Wild to be wreckage forever. (LL) Cherrylog Road. James Dickey. CoAP; ColAP; HAP; HCAP; NAAL-2v2; NIL-7; NIP-4; TwCP; WeW-3

Wild Turkeys: The Dignity of the Damned. Brigit Pegeen Kelly. ExTi; IllVoic

Wild warblers are warbling in the jungle, The. Meditation Celestial and Terrestrial. Wallace Stevens. APT-1

Wild water-head, what's your reason / for exalting yourself. Torrent Cuts off the Poet's Path, A. Antiphilus [*or* Antiphilos]. GrAn

Wild West Workshop Poem. Anselm Hollo. PmAP

Wild, wild the storm, and the sea high running. Patrolling Barnegat. Walt Whitman. APN-1

Wild Wind. Li Meng-yang. CoBLCP, *tr. by* Jonathan Chaves

Wild wind, chaotic lightning—black clouds are born. Summer Niight. *Unknown.* SuSp, *tr. by* Edward H. Schafer

Wild winds weep, The. Mad Song. William Blake. NAEL-5v2; NAEL-6v2; NOEC; PoE

Wild winter wind, A. Richard Wright. APT-2

Wild with All Regrets. Wilfred Owen. SCGP
  "Yes, there's the orderly. He'll change the sheets." PeFWW

Wild woman of the forests, The. Mirabai [*or* Mira Bai]. WPoS; WoPoe, *tr. by* Jane Hirshfield

Wild World. Cat Stevens. UV

Wildcat was walking. *Unknown.* STP

"Wilde is the easiest," said my master, one. Lőrinc Szabó. IQMS, *tr. by* John Gordon Nichols *Fr.* Cricket Music.

Wilderness. Ilyas Farhat. MAP, *tr. by* John Heath-Stubbs and Salma Khadra Jayyusi

Wilderness. Faye George. PoCoUp

Wilderness. Vern Rutsala. UrbNat

Wilderness. Carl Sandburg. RaBo

Wilderness, The. Sidney Keyes.
  "Red rock wilderness, The." OBWP; PoWW

Wilderness, The. Kathleen Jessie Raine. BoWoP; WPE

Wilderness Gothic. Alfred Wellington Purdy. HeIP-4; MoCV; NOBC; NoP-4

Wilderness, The: but otherwise. Esther K. Comes to America: 1931. Jerome Rothenberg. NNaP

Wildernesse and the solitarie place shall be glad for them, The. Bible, *O.T.* OBVE *Fr.* Isaiah.

Wilderspin. Mary Elizabeth Coleridge. VWP; ViWPN

Wildflower. Stanley Plumly. LCAP-2

Wildflowers. Richard Howard. NoAM

Wildlife. Tracy Philpot. AmPoNex

Wildly and mournfully the Indian drum. American Forest Girl, The. Felicia Dorothea Hemans. RWP

Wildly he wandered on. Shelley. TOF *Fr.* Alastor; or, The Spirit of Solitude.

Wildly he wandered on. William Wordsworth. TOF *Fr.* Prelude, The; Growth of a Poet's Mind [1850 vers.].

Wildness of haggard flights. Nocturne: "Wildness of haggard flights." Roussan Camille. TTY, *tr. by* Seth L. Wolitz

Wildness of your glances pleases me, The. Rama Kam. David Diop. NegPo, *tr. by* Ellen Conroy Kennedy

Wildsisters Bar. Judith Vollmer. SwNoth

Wilfred Owen's Photographs. Ted Hughes. OxBC

Wilful waste brings woeful want. *Unknown.* OxNR

Wilhelm Meister's Apprenticeship. Goethe.
  ("Knowest thou the land where bloom the lemon trees.") AWP, *tr. by* James Elroy Flecker
  ("You know that land, her lemon groves in bloom?") STV, *tr. by* John Frederick Nims

Will. L. S. Asekoff. KGB

Will. Ella Wheeler Wilcox. PoToHe

Will, The. John Donne. EBEV; NoSic

Will a god trust in the world. (LL) Hedgehog. Paul Muldoon. BIrV; NoAM; PBCIP

Will a man come for me? Song of a Marriageable Girl. *Unknown.* WoPoe, *tr. by* Willard Trask

Will a mouth that's muttered its goodbyes. Joseph Brodsky. TCRusP, *tr. by* Bernard Meares *Fr.* Sonnets on the Statue of Mary, Queen of Scots, in the Luxembourg Gardens, Paris.

Will all be Paradise again. (LL) On the Origin of Evil. John Byrom. NOEC; NPeEn

Will and Testament. Isabella Whitney. *See* Aucthour Maketh Her Wyll and Testament, The

Will anyone tell me what Minne is? Walther [*or* Walter] von der Vogelweide. GePo

Will appear as short as one. (LL) On a Fly Drinking out of [*or* from] His Cup. William Oldys. OBEV; OxAEP-1; OxBEV

Will be a hundred years ago. (LL) Thomas Love Peacock. NOBVV; OBEV *Fr.* Gryll Grange.

Will be ground by the grinders of Gambart. (LL) Limerick: "There is an old he-wolf named Gambart." Dante Gabriel Rossetti. FaBoEE; PeLi

Will bury their own, don't worry. (LL) Journey, The. James Wright (1927–80). NAAL-5; NoAM; PoE

Will Campbell Displays His Craniotribe. H. J. Van Peenen. BloBone

Will cave in on him by and by. (LL) Edna St. Vincent Millay. BRP; ColAP; MoAmPo

Will cease to translate silence. One Day I Know the Page. Amina Said. PoArWo, *tr. by* Lucy McNair

Will commit that indiscretion. (LL) Garden, The. Ezra Pound. APT-1; AWP; HeIP-4; MoAmPo; NIL-7; NIP-4; OxBSP; TwCP

Will days, indeed, yet come in forgiveness and grace. When You Will Walk in the Field. Leah Goldberg. TrJP, *tr. by* Simon Halkin

Will dispel a thousand cares? (LL) Sunset. Tu Fu. BLT; OHPC, *tr. by* Kenneth Rexroth

Will dream[e] that hope again, but else would die. (LL) Dream[e], The. John Donne. ESCV; MeLP; OBMV; TOF

Will drown the silence. (LL) Boundaries. José Emilio Pacheco. PoetW; STV; TCLAP, *tr. by* John Frederick Nims

Will feel uneasy. (LL) Mabel Kelly. Turlough Carolan [*or* O'Carolan]. BIrV; CIP-2; OxBEV, *tr. by* Austin Clarke

Will find its symbol, the woman thinks. (LL) History. Rita Dove. ExTi; FFC

Will go on prancing, proud and unafraid. (LL) Aunt Jennifer's Tigers. Adrienne Rich. ColAP; FaBoWP; HeIP-4; InPK-6; NALW; NIL-7; NIP-4; NoAM; NoP-4; OPOU; TRP

Will guide him *in*. (LL) Joy of My Life! While Left Me Here. Henry Vaughan. BASC; GeHe

Will he always love me? Lady Horikawa. BoWoP; OHPJ

Will He No Come Back Again? *Unknown.* OBEV

Will hear all I say and cannot say. (LL) Paula Becker to Clara Westhoff. Adrienne Rich. NAAL-2v2; VCAP

Will hear of as a god. (LL) How We Heard the Name. Alan Dugan. CoAP; NoAM; YaYoPo

Will I! Will You Write Me a Christmas Poem? Lorine Niedecker. FTOS

Will I always be eleven. Untitled. Franz Wright. LCAP-2

Will I cease to be. Lady Izumi. OHPJ

Will I ever get it? (LL) Zizi's Lament. Gregory Corso. BB; NeAP; VGW

Will i hate mirrors? Rebecca. E. Ethelbert Miller. ISC

Will it ever be finished, this house. Oeuvre. Lucien Stryk. IllVoic

Will it last? he says. Snowflake Which Is Now and Hence Forever, The. Archibald MacLeish. NoP-4

Will know where they are by the absence. Emigrants. Jane Griffiths. NeBl

Will lead my steps aright. (LL) To a Waterfowl. William Cullen Bryant. APN-1; AWP; ColAP; ITBLP; NAAL-2v1; NAAL-3; NAAL-5; NCAP; NOBA; NoP-4; OWoS; OxBA; PWR; SoSe-8; TAP; TFi

Will linger, though enjoyed, like joy in memory yet. (LL) Stanzas Written in Dejection, near Naples [*or*—December 1818, near Naples]. Shelley. GTBS-P; NAEL-5v2; NAEL-6v2; NAWM-7v2; PoRA

Will, lost in a sea of trouble. Archilochus. AmFaPo; PGA, *tr. by* Kenneth Rexroth

Will Love again awake. Muse and Poet. Robert Bridges. OBMV

Will make the Gods of humane crimes partake. (LL) Ausonius. NoSic; OBVE

Will make the whole read human and exact. (LL) Devil's Advice to Story-Tellers, The. Robert Graves. NAEL-5v2; NAEL-6v2; NoAM

Will make their answer to the shuttered heart. (LL) Poet's Obligation. Pablo Neruda. PoetW; VCWP, *tr. by* Alastair Reid

Will make your glistering [*or* glist'ring] gold but more to shine. (LL) Anne Bradstreet. BASC; BoWoP; EMWP; NAAL-2v1; NAAL-3; NAAL-5; NALW; NOBA; NoP-4; OxBA; PEW; PoE; SCAP; TAP; TCAPo; WPE

Will mean the resurrection of her eyes. (LL) Her Eyes. Helen Hunt Jackson. PoBW; TCAPo

Will never come back to me. (LL) Break, Break, Break. Tennyson. AWP; BRP; ClHu; FHYEP; GTBS-P; HAP; HeIP-4; NAEL-5v2; NAEL-6v2; NIL-7; NIP-4; NOBE; NOBVV; NoP-4; PWR; PoRA; RB; SoSe-8; TFi; TreFP; WeW-3

Will night already spread her wings and weave. Night-Thoughts. Solomon ibn Gabirol. TrJP, *tr. by* Emma Lazarus

Will no young British bard, on rhyme intent. Edward Davies. AngWePo *Fr.* Chepstow: A Poem.

Will not be there. (LL) That the Science of Cartography Is Limited. Eavan Boland. HarvBoo; NoP-4; SpudSo

Will not contain you. (LL) Did John's Music Kill Him? Alfred B. Spellman. NAAAL; SeSe

Will not respond, choked off by tears of joy. (LL) Flowers, and tall-stalked grasses, and a bee. Ivan Alekseievich Bunin. GI; WoPoe, *tr. by* David Curzon and Vladislav L. Gucrassev

Will-o'-Wisp. Nancy Morejón. TANSG, *tr. by* Joy Renjilian-Burgy

Will of God we must obey, The. Death of King Edward VII, The. *Unknown.* OxBoLi

Will one of you go. Asking Favors. Wilma Elizabeth McDaniel. GeoHom

Will press the life-drops from the heart. (LL) Slave Auction, The. Frances Ellen Watkins Harper. APN-2; BPo; ColAP; ISC; TTY

Will ripple forward and hold the train. (LL) Rescued Year, The. William Stafford. ColAP; LCAP-2

Will rise and bless each future hour. (LL) Mary Savage. ECWP; LW *Fr.* Letter to Miss E.B. on Marriage.

Will snarl—and man can never be alone. (LL) Wolves, The. Allen Tate. APT-2; NOBA; OxBA

Will soon blow down the road all roses go. (LL) June. Francis Ledwidge. BIrV; NOIV

'Will sprawl, now that the heat of day is best. Caliban upon Setebos; or, Natural Theology in the Island. Robert Browning. AWP; EBEV; FHYEP; NAEL-5v2; NAEL-6v2; NOBVV; OxAEP-2; PeVV

Will Stewart and John. *Unknown.* ESPB

Will swarm to hot flowers. (LL) If Hot Flowers Come to the Street. R. Meenakshi. OMIP; WoPoe, *tr. by* Martha Ann Selby

Will tear through you with his tangled. One Night America: A Boy and His Blowtorch. M. Loncar. NAPBL

Will tell you how he wrote, and talked, and spit. (LL) Doctor Johnson. Soame Jenyns. FaBoEE; OBSV

"Will the fire of the heart and the fire of the mind be one." (LL) Heart and Mind. Dame Edith Sitwell. LW; OxBTC; TwCP

Will the lady with locker key 43. Will You Come Out Now? Valerie Sinason. BrRo

Will the machinegunners please step forward? (LL) Poem Some People Will Have to Understand, A. Imamu Amiri Baraka. BPo; GT; NOBA; RaBo

Will the man who gets clean love his neighbor? Soap (II). Jerome Rothenberg. NNaP

Will there be snowfall on lofty Soracte. Winter in Brighton. Mortimer Collins. NPeEn

Will there never come a season. To R. K. James Kenneth Stephen. FaBoEE; NBLV; NOBL; PeLV; UV

Will there really be a "morning"? Morning. Emily Dickinson. OBCA

Will there yet come days of forgiveness and grace. Will There Yet Come. Leah Goldberg. MHP, *tr. by* Ruth Finer Mintz

Will They Always Remember. Tracy Clarke. InTrad

Will They Cry When You're Gone, You Bet. Imamu Amiri Baraka. NAAL-2v2

Will they have children? Will they have more children? Neighbors. James Tate. LCAP-2

Will they never fade or pass! Farmer Remembers the Somme, The. Vance Palmer. NOBAu

Will to be tickled wants; has got the itch. *Unknown.* FaBoEE

Will to Will. Keith Waldrop. PmAP

Will waste, as this flea's death took life from thee. (LL) Flea, The. John Donne. AmFaPo; BASC; BoLoP; EBEV; ESCV; FSCP; InPK-6; NAEL-5v1; NAEL-6v1; NAEL-7v1; NBLV; NIL-7; NIP-4; NoP-4; NoSic; OxAEP-1; PAI; PoE; SCV; TFi

Will Ye Na Can Ye Na Let Me Be. *Unknown.* FaBoVe

Will Ye No Come Back Again? Carolina Oliphant, Baroness Nairne. NePenScot

Will ye that I should sing. Lady of High Degree, A. *Unknown.* AWP, *tr. by* Andrew Lang

Will Yer Write It down for Me? Henry Lawson. CBAP

Will You Be as Hard? Douglas Hyde. OBMV, *tr. by* Augusta, Lady Gregory and Lady Gregory

Will you come a boating, my gay old hag. Gay Old Hag, The. *Unknown.* BIrV

Will You Come Out Now? Valerie Sinason. BrRo

Will You Crucify Your King? "Michael Field." ViWPN

Will you find out the secret. Secret, The. Fanny Carrión de Fierro. TANSG, *tr. by* Sally Cheney Bell

Will you gang wi' me, Leezie Lindsay. Leezie Lindsay. *Unknown.* FaBoCh

Will you have me? Popular Romance, A. Kevin Ireland. PeNZ

Will you heare a tale of Robin Hood. Robin Hood and the Pedlars. *Unknown.* ESPB

Will you heare the Mode of france. Mode of France, The. *Unknown.* PBRV

Will you leave me alone? I implore you! To Russia. Vladimir Vladimirovich Nabokov. TCRP, *tr. by* Vladimir Nabokov

Will you leave the hills of Scotland? Highland Mary. Mary Weston Fordham. CBWP-2

Will you lend me your eyes to look at you? Myopia. Biancamaria Frabotta. CItWP, *tr. by* Cinzia Sartini Blum and Lara Trubowitz

Will you lend me your mare to ride but a mile? *Unknown.* OxNR

Will You Love Me When I'm Old? *Unknown.* ITBLP

Will you marry it, marry it, marry it. (LL) Applicant, The. Sylvia Plath. EmeKit; NAAL-2v2; NOBA; PoPoPo; TwCP

Will you never let us go? (LL) Song of the Galley-Slaves. Rudyard Kipling. GTBS-P; HAP; SCGP

Will you please rush down and see. To Close. William Carlos Williams. SAmP

Will you seek afar off? you surely come back at last. Walt Whitman. ChIV-1 *Fr.* Song for Occupations, A.

Will you sleep forever? Korinna [*or* Corinna]. BoWoP

Will you speak before I am gone? will you prove already too late? (LL) Walt Whitman. CAGL; ColAP; NAWM-7v2 *Fr.* Song of Myself.

Will You Still Be Mine? Matt Dennis. ReLy

Will you take care? Farewell. Adriaan Morriën. TuT, *tr.* by Peter Van de Kamp

Will you turn a deaf ear. Questioner Who Sits So Sly, The. W. H. Auden. OxAEP-2

"Will you walk a little faster?" said a [*or* the] whiting to a [*or* the] snail. Lewis Carroll. NoAM; OxAEP-2; UV *Fr.* Alice's Adventures in Wonderland.

"Will you walk into my parlor?" said the Spider to the Fly. Spider and the Fly, The. Mary Howitt. ITBLP; OTCP; PWR; UV

Will you, wo'n't you, will you, wo'n't you, wo'n't you join the dance? (LL) Lewis Carroll. NoAM; OxAEP-2; UV *Fr.* Alice's Adventures in Wonderland.

Will You Write Me a Christmas Poem? Lorine Niedecker. FTOS

Willesden Gree. Jimmy Pearse. UV

Willets, The. May Swenson. WPE

William. Lesley Dauer. AmPoNex

William and Margaret. David Mallet. NOEC; OxAEP-1

William and Mary, / George and Anne. *Unknown.* OxNR

William Blake. James Thomson. CABP

William Carlos Williams. Cornelius Eady. GT

William / Carlos / Williams / alive! Louis Zukofsky. PFTM-1 *Fr.* Songs of Degrees.

William Dewy, Tranter Reuben, Farmer Ledlow late at plough. Friends Beyond. Thomas Hardy. EBVV; FaBoVe; GTBS-P; NOBVV; OBEV

William Gifford. Walter Savage Landor. FaBoEE; GTBS-P

William has whole buildings inside him. William. Lesley Dauer. AmPoNex

William Lamb's Return from Paris, Asking Me My Wish. Lady Caroline Lamb. RWP *Fr.* Fugitive Pieces and Reminiscences of Lord Byron with Some Original Poetry, Letters and Recollections of Lady Caroline Lamb, ed. I. Nathan.

William Lloyd Garrison. Henrietta Cordelia Ray. CBWP-3

William of Orange was always worried. Plans. Brendan Kennelly. BiHa

William Oliver maker. Ancestors. Raymond Garlick. AngWePo

William Street. Kenneth Slessor. BMAP; CBAP

William Stukeley made his own Stonehenge. Ronald Johnson. OBGa

William the Conqueror, ten sixty-six. *Unknown.* OxNR

William Wallace. Francis Lauderdale Adams. OxBS

William Wordsworth. Sidney Keyes. OxBTC

William Wordsworth. Gavin Ewart. NoAM

William Yeats in Limbo. Sidney Keyes. MoBrPo

Williams: An Essay. Denise Levertov. PmAP

Williams Avenue Zionist Church, The. Russia. William Carlos Williams. VGW

Williamsbridge. Jana Beranová. TuT, *tr.* by Aidan Sharkey

Willie. "Max Adeler." OBCoV

Willie and Earl Richard's Daughter. *Unknown.* ESPB *See* Birth of Robin Hood, The

Willie and Lady Margerie [*or* Maisry]. *Unknown.* ESPB; OxBB

Willie Brew'd [*or* Brewed] a Peck o' Maut. Robert Burns. AWP; OxBS

Willie Macintosh. *Unknown. See also* As I Came in by Fiddich-Side

Willie Macintosh. *Unknown.* ESPB; OxBoLi

(Burning of Auchindown.) OxBB

Willie Metcalf. Edgar Lee Masters. APT-1 *Fr.* Spoon River Anthology.

Willie o Douglas Dale. *Unknown.* ESPB

Willie o [*or* of] Winsbury. *Unknown.* ESPB

Willie poisoned Auntie's tea. Willie the Poisoner. *Unknown.* NTCP

Willie's Fatal Visit. *Unknown.* ESPB

Willie's Lady. *Unknown.* ESPB

Willie's Lyke-Wake. *Unknown.* ESPB

Willie the Weeper. *Unknown.* OBAL

Willie was a widow's son. Willie and Lady Maisry. *Unknown.* ESPB

"Willie, Willie, I'll learn you a wile." Willie's Lyke-Wake. *Unknown.* ESPB

Willie Winkie. William Miller. OxBEV; ReMoGo

Willie's [*or* Willie] has taen him o'er the fame. Willie's Lady. *Unknown.* ESPB

Willing. Paula McLain. AmPoNex

Willing it, my ailment. (LL) No Road. Philip Larkin. EBEV; MoBrPo; OxAEP-2

Willing Mistress, The. Aphra Behn. LW; NALW *Fr.* Dutch Lover, The.

Willingly. Shizan. JDP, *tr.* by Yoel Hoffmann

Willingness. Chairil Anwar. PoetW, *tr.* by Burton Raffel

Willow. Elizabeth Delmore. NLP

Willow. Richard Watson Dixon. *See* Song: "Feathers of the willow, The."

Willow. Li Shang-yin. SuSp, *tr.* by Eugene Eoyang

Willow, The. Tu Fu. OHPC, *tr.* by Kenneth Rexroth

Willow branch, A. Shigenobu. JDP, *tr.* by Yoel Hoffmann

Willow Branch Song. Liu Yu Hsi. SuSp, *tr.* by Daniel Bryant

Willow Branch Songs. Ch'ien Ch'ien-i [*or* Ch'ien Ch'ien-yi].

"Crescent moon hangs on the tip of the willows, A." SuSp

"Must I lament the time that's gone because I've been cast aside?" SuSp

Willow Branches. Liu Yu Hsi. SuSp, *tr.* by Dell R. Hales

Willow by the Eastern Gate. *Unknown.* CoBCP, *tr.* by Burton Watson

Willow Catkins. Hsüeh T'ao. SuSp, *tr.* by Eric W. Johnson

Willow catkins beyond the garden wait for evening tides. Ch'ien Ch'ien-i [*or* Ch'ien Ch'ien-yi]. CoBLCP *Fr.* In Spring of the Year *Ping-shen.*

Willow floss in the swift wind races against the Spring Festival. Tune: "Song of River City"—on a Kite. Wu Wei-yeh. SuSp, *tr.* by Irving Y. Lo

Willow in Spring Wind: A Showing. Jorie Graham. ExTi

Willow leans into the water, The. Serenade for Ilonka. Jenő Dsida. IQMS, *tr.* by Joseph Leftwich

Willow leaves dancing. Eveningsong. Ramona Wilson. VoR

Willow leaves fallen, The. Buson. EH, *tr.* by Robert Hass

Willow Poem. William Carlos Williams. NAAL-2v2

Willow's shadow straight up. Tune: "Prince of Lan-ling" (*Lan-ling Wang*)—on Willows. Chou Pang-yen. SuSp, *tr.* by Irving Y. Lo

Willow shining, The. Knowledge of Light, The. Henry Rago. VGW

Willow Song. Anne Stevenson. NoP-4

Willow tree in fall, A. Senryu. JDP, *tr.* by Yoel Hoffmann

Willowherb. Peter Rafferty. NLP

Willows bend to the sea breeze. Late Spring. Tzu Yeh. CrYelRi, *tr.* by Sam Hamill

Willows cannot hide a bright moon's sorrow. Heard on a Boat. T'an Yüan-ch'un. SuSp, *tr.* by Irving Y. Lo

Willows carried a slow sound, The. Repose of Rivers. Hart Crane. APT-2; AWP; ColAP; MoAmPo; NOBA; OxBA; PoE

Willows droop, The. Winter and Spring Scene, A. Henry David Thoreau. NCAP

Willows of Massachusetts, The. Denise Levertov. NAAL-2v2

Willows shadows hang straight. Tune: "Prince Lan-Ling." Chou Pang-yen. ChinPo, *tr.* by Yip Wai-lim

Willows trail such glory that the birds are struck dumb, The. Spring View. Tran Nhan-tong. WoPoe, *tr.* by Nguyen Ngoc Bich

Willows weave spring sorrow. To the Tune "Yellow Oriole." Yang Shen. CoBLCP, *tr.* by Jonathan Chaves

Willows whisper very, very low, The. Noonday Rest. Mathilde Blind. ViWPN

Willowware Cup. James Merrill. VCAP

Willowwood ("And now love sang: but his was such a song"). Dante Gabriel Rossetti. NAEL-5v2; NAEL-6v2; OxBSo *Fr.* House of Life, The.

Willowwood ("I sat with Love upon a woodside well"). Dante Gabriel Rossetti. CABP; NAEL-5v2; NAEL-6v2; OxBSo *Fr.* House of Life, The.

Willowwood ("O ye, all ye that walk in Willowwood"). Dante Gabriel Rossetti. NAEL-5v2; NAEL-6v2; OxBSo *Fr.* House of Life, The.

Willowwood ("So sang he: and as meeting rose and rose"). Dante Gabriel Rossetti. NAEL-5v2; NAEL-6v2; OxBSo *Fr.* House of Life, The.

Willy boy, Willy boy, / Where are you going? Mother Goose. OxNR; ReMoGo

Willy Drowned in Yarrow. *Unknown.* GTBS-P

Willy Lyons. James Wright (1927–80). HCAP; NNaP; PoE

Willy's rare, and Willy's fair. Rare Willie Drowned in Yarrow; or, The Water o Gamrie. *Unknown.* ESPB

Willy—the moon's in a cloud—Good-night. I am going. He calls. (LL) Rizpah. Tennyson. NPeEn; PeVV

Willy Wet-Leg. D. H. Lawrence. RB

Willy-willy man. Archie Weller. IBA

Willy, Willy Wilkin. Mother Goose. OxNR; ReMoGo

Wilpena Pound. Charles Buckmaster. BMAP

Wilson and Pilcer and Snack stood before the zoo elephant. Elephants Are Different to Different People. Carl Sandburg. MoAmPo

Wilt thou follow me into the wild? Mistress to the Spirit of Her Lover, The. Charlotte Dacre. RWP

Wilt thou forgive that sin[ne] where I begun[ne]. Hymn[e] to God the Father, A. John Donne. AWP; BASC; EBEV; FSCP; HAP; InPK-6; MeLP; NAEL-5v1; NAEL-6v1; NAEL-7v1; NOBE; NOSC; NPeEn; OxBEV; PeECP; PoRA; SCGP; SCV; SacPr; SoSe-8; TFi; TOF

Wilt thou go with me sweet maid. Invite to Eternity, An. John Clare. NAEL-5v2; NAEL-6v2; NOBVV

Wilt thou love God, as he thee? [*or* thee!] then digest. John Donne. TrCP *Fr.* Holy Sonnets.

Wilt Thou not visit me? Prayer, The. Jones Very. APN-1; OxBA; TrCP

Wilt thou seal up the avenues of ill? Ralph Waldo Emerson. APN-1 *Fr.* Quatrains.

Wilt thou then serve the Philistines with that gift. John Milton. EBEV *Fr.* Samson Agonistes.

Wilt thou use turners craft still? ye by my truoth. John Heywood. PBRV *Fr.* Epygrams.

Wiltshire Downs. Andrew Young. GTBS-P; OxBTC

Wily Fox, The. Edward Davies. OBWVE, *t*: *by* Joseph P. Clancy

Wily Napoleon Bonaparte, The. Limerick. Douglas Catley. PeLi

Wily old writer called Maugham, A. Limerick. Martin Fagg. PeLi

Win at First and Lose at Last; or, A New Game at Cards. Laurence Price. OxBoLi

Wind. Dionne Brand. NOxBChV

Wind. James Fenton. NAEL-5v2; NAEL-6v2

Wind. Hsüeh T'ao. ColAnChi, *tr. by* Jeanne Larsen

Wind. Ted Hughes. HarvBoo; NAEL-5v2; NAEL-6v2; NoP-4

Wind. Dana Levin. AmPoNex

Wind. Lizette Woodworth Reese. APT-1

Wind. Gary Soto. NoAM *Fr.* Elements of San Joaquin, The.

Wind. Larry Wiggin. HA

Wind, The. Thomas Holley Chivers. APN-1

Wind, The. Dafydd [*or* David] ap Gwilym. WoPoe, *tr. by* Daniel Huws

Wind, The. Dafydd [*or* David] ap Gwilym. OBWVE, *tr. by* Joseph P. Clancy

Wind, The. Emily Dickinson. APN-2

Wind, The. Boris Leonidovich Pasternak. RusPo, *tr. by* Robert Arthur Douglas Ford

Wind, The. Boris Leonidovich Pasternak. TCRP, *tr. by* Yakov Hornstein

Wind, The. Christina Georgina Rossetti. *See* Who Has Seen the Wind?

Wind, The. Vladimir Alekseievich Soloukhin. TCRusP, *tr. by* Daniel Weissbort

Wind, The. James Stephens. InPK-6; KaS; NoAM; PAI

Wind, The. Sung Yu. ColAnChi, *tr. by* Burton Watson

Wind, The. *Unknown.* FaBoCh; OxNR

Wind. Improvisation. Alfred Kreymborg. APT-1

Wind, 9. Subramania Bharati. OMIP, *tr. by* A. K. Ramanujan

Wind, a rustle of leaves, The. Edge of Autumn, The. Michael Anania. NoAM

Wind and frost on ordinary silk. On a Portrait of a Falcon. Tu Fu. CrYelRi, *tr. by* Sam Hamill

Wind and Glacier Voices. Simon J. Ortiz. HATNAP

Wind and rain see spring off. Tune: "Song of Divination"—On the Plum Tree, after a Poem by Lu Yu. Mao Tse-tung [*or* Mao Zedong]. SuSp, *tr. by* Eugene Eoyang

Wind and Silver. Amy Lowell. BoWoP; HeIP-4; KaS; MoAmPo; PAI; Spl; TCAPo

Wind and the Moon, The. George Macdonald. NOxBChV

Wind and Tree. Paul Muldoon. NPeEn

Wind and Water and Stone. Octavio Paz. TCLAP, *tr. by* Mark Strand

Wind, Ant, History. Özdemir İnce. WoPoe, *tr. by* Talat Sait Halman

Wind appears, The. Barnyard, The. Yvor Winters. APT-2

Wind at the Door, The. William Barnes. GTBS-P; OxAEP-2

Wind: "At times I resort, beyond man's discerning." Cynewulf. AnOE *Fr.* Riddles (Exeter Book).

Wind at war with wind. Warlike Angels, The. Rafael Alberti. AF, *tr. by* Geoffrey Connell

Wind at Your Door, The. Robert David Fitzgerald. NOBAu

Wind begun to knead the Grass, The. Emily Dickinson. NAAL-2v1; NIL-7; WeW-3

Wind begun to rock the Grass, The. Thunder-Storm, A. Emily Dickinson. APN-2; HAP; NAAL-2v1; NCAP; WeW-3

Wind billowing out the seat of my britches, The. Child on Top of a Greenhouse. Theodore Roethke. KaS; LCAP-2; NOxBChV; NoP-4; VGW

Wind / blade cutting in, The. Impressions / of Chicago; for Howlin' Wolf. Quincy Troupe. NAAAL; NBV

Wind blew, a tile fell from the roof, The. Wang An-shih. SuSp *Fr.* In the Style of Han Shan and Shih Te.

Wind Blew like Water. Alice Sadongei. HATNAP

Wind Bloweth Where It Listeth, The. Countee Cullen. GT

"Wind-blown clamour of the barnacle-geese, The" (LL) Beggar to Beggar Cried. W. B. Yeats. NoAM; OxAEP-2

Wind blows a piece of paper to my feet, The. At the Crossroads. Bill Knott. PBCAP

Wind blows and makes the light tremble, The. Inna L'vovna Lisnyanskaya [*or* Lisnianskaia]. ItGoST, *tr. by* Judith Hemschemeyer

Wind blows, and with a little broom, The. Cathleen Sweeping. George Johnston. NOBC

Wind blows High, The. *Unknown.* FaBoVe

Wind blows high above the people's heads. North Wind, The. Frederick Van Eeden. TuT, *tr. by* Michael Longley

Wind blows out of the Gates of the Day, The. W. B. Yeats. RB *Fr.* Land of Heart's Desire, The.

Wind blows the line out from his fishing pole, The. Fisherman. Ou-yang Hsiu. BLT; OHPC, *tr. by* Kenneth Rexroth

Wind came in for several thousand miles all night, The. On an East Wind from the Wars. Alan Dugan. AF

Wind came up out of the sea, A. Daybreak. Henry Wadsworth Longfellow. ITBLP; PWR

Wind can't blow any harder, The. Bottle Creek Blues. Sam Hunt. PeNZ

Wind-Clouds and Star-Drifts. Oliver Wendell Holmes.

  "Snows that glittered on the disk of Mars, The." APN-1

  Sympathies. APN-1

Wind, come softly. Wind, 9. Subramania Bharati. OMIP, *tr. by* A. K. Ramanujan

Wind comes from opposite poles, The. Marriage, The. Mark Strand. NoAM; SPE

Wind comes from the north, The. Suspense. D. H. Lawrence. MoBrPo

Wind comes rushing from the sea, The. One Night at Victoria Beach. Gabriel Okara. PBMAP; PoetW

Wind Debates Asian Immigration, The. Peter Rose. BMAP

Wind disturbing the eave-chimes again. Tune: "San-fan Yü-lou Jen." *Unknown.* ColAnChi, *tr. by* James I. Crump

"Wind doth blow to-day, my love, The." Unquiet Grave, The. *Unknown.* CABP; ESPB; HAP; HeIP-4; NoP-4; OxBB; RB; TFi; WeW-3; WoPoe

Wind fills her embroidery loom with willow catkins, The. Yang Chi. CoBLCP, *tr. by* Jonathan Chaves *Fr.* Paintings of Ladies Engaged in Four Springtime Occupations.

Wind finds the northwest gap, fall comes. Heart of Autumn. Robert Penn Warren. APT-2; ColAP; FuPo

Wind flapped loose, the wind was still, The. Dante Gabriel Rossetti. CABP; EBEV; GTBS-P; HAP; HeIP-4; NAEL-6v2; NOBE; NPeEn; NoP-4; OBEV; OxBEV; SCGP; TFi; UnPo *Fr.* House of Life, The.

Wind / Flies above the sea, The. Wind, The. Vladimir Alekseievich Soloukhin. TCRusP, *tr. by* Daniel Weissbort

Wind frightens my dog, but I bathe in it, The. April Gale. Ivor Gurney. Spl

Wind from off the sea says nothing new, The. Marrow, The. Theodore Roethke. PeECV

Wind from the east, oh Lapwing of the day. Hafiz [*or* Hafez]. AWP; TAL *Fr.* Odes.

Wind from the northwestern quarter is lifting him high above. Hawk's Cry in Autumn, The. Joseph Brodsky. TCRP, *tr. by* Joseph Brodsky and Alan Myers

Wind frustrates itself held, The. Song to the Banyan. Virgil Suárez. AmPoNex

Wind gathers storm clouds, The. Song of the Stormy Petrel. "Maksim Gorky" [*or* Gorkii]. TCRP, *tr. by* Albert C. Todd

Wind, gigantic, wrestles the April leaves. April Wind. Frederick Turner. RA

Wind gives way to calm. J. W. Hackett. HA

Wind had hanged itself on the plane tree, The. Wind, Ant, History. Özdemir İnce. WoPoe, *tr. by* Talat Sait Halman

Wind has all its answers, The. Night Things. Greg Kuzma. InvLad

Wind has at last got into the clock, The. Wind, the Clock, the We, The. Laura Riding Jackson. APT-2; FaBoVe

Wind has blown a corner of your shawl, The. Bright Sunlight. Amy Lowell. APT-1

Wind has blown the rain away and blown, A. E. E. Cummings. HarvBoo; MoAmPo

Wind has died, The. To the Tune: Happiness Approaches. Li Ch'ing-chao. CrYelRi, *tr. by* Sam Hamill

Wind has scattered my city to the sheep, The. Ruins of the City of Hay. Randolph Stow. CBAP

Wind has stopped, The. Harumichi no Tsuraki. OHPJ

Wind has subsided, The. Tune: Spring at Wu Ling. Li Ch'ing-chao. ColAnChi, *tr. by* Jiaosheng Wang

Wind Has Such a Rainy Sound, The. Christina Georgina Rossetti. TLR

Wind, I hear it sighing, The. Emily Jane Brontë. BWW

Wind in the park. Envoi: Washington Square Park. Myra Cohn Livingston. SSCS

Wind in the Tree, The. Frank Templeton Prince. OxBSP

Wind in the Trees, The. Cathy Song. OpBo

Wind in the west / Fallen leaves. Buson. ZenPo, *tr. by* Takashi Ikemoto and Lucien Stryk

Wind in the willow, why do you weep? Wind in the Willow. Marvin Fisher. ReLy

Wind in the Willows, The. Kenneth Grahame.

  Duck's Ditty. NOxBChV; NTCP; OTCP; WHSW

  Song of Mr Toad, The. NOBL; NOxBChV

Wind in your hair. One Final Fling. Kemal Khojandi. ArPe, *tr. by* Omar S. Pound

Wind Increases, The. William Carlos Williams. NAAL-2v2

Wind Invites Wind. Chimako Tada. VCWP, *tr. by* Naoshi Koriyama

Wind Is Blind, The. Alice Thompson Meynell. MoBrPo

Wind is blowing from side to side, The. Old Trees with Hands Sawing the Air. Margit Szécsi. IQMS, *tr.* by Agnes Arany-Makkai

Wind Is Blowing West, The. Joseph Ceravolo. TTTS

Wind is born from the land, The. Wind, The. Sung Yu. ColAnChi, *tr.* by Burton Watson

Wind is cruel. Her clothes are worn and thin, The. Her Husband Asks Her to Buy a Bolt of Silk. Ch'en Tao. OHMPC, *tr.* by Kenneth Rexroth

Wind is east but the hot weather continues, The. American Letter. Archibald MacLeish. OxBA

Wind is everything to them, The. (LL) Marriage, The. Mark Strand. NoAM; SPE

Wind is not nigh. Zone of Death. William Everson. SacPr; VGW

Wind is not right today, The. Bodega, Goodbye. Edwin Honig. NoAM

Wind is passing by, The. (LL) Who Has Seen the Wind? Christina Georgina Rossetti. ITBLP; NTCP; SacPr; TLR; WHSW

Wind is piercing chill, The. Battlefield. Richard Aldington. OBWP

Wind is ruffling the tawny pelt, A. Far Cry from Africa, A. Derek Walcott. AmFaPo; ESEAA; HeIP-4; NAEL-5v2; NAEL-6v2; NIL-7; NoAM; NoP-4; TTY; UnPo

Wind is shaking this house, The. Storm House, The. Elizabeth Jennings. WPE

Wind is thin. *Unknown.* BoWoP *Fr.* Cambridge Songs.

Wind is wild tonight, The. *Unknown.* NOIV

Wind keen, the sky high, the gibbons wailing, The. On Climbing the Heights on the Ninth Day of the Ninth Moon. Tu Fu. TAL

Wind Last Night Blew Down. *Unknown.* WoPoe, *tr.* by Virginia Olsen Baron and Chung Seuk Park

Wind led me here, The. Wind Thoughts. Pinkie Gordon Lane. GT

Wind like an ocean, The. Larry Eigner. PoM

Wind, like the dodo's. (LL) Bedtime Story. George MacBeth [*or* Macbeth]. EmeKit; SoSe-8

Wind may blow the snow about, The. Country Boy in Winter, A. Sarah Orne Jewett. APN-2; ColAP; OBCA

Wind mutters thinly on the sagging wire. Prairie Graveyard. Anne Marriott. NOBC

Wind o' the East dark with rain. Confucius. CTC, *tr.* by Ezra Pound *Fr.* Airs of Pei.

Wind of dawning riffles the young furze, The. Drafts for a Quatrain. Edmund Wilson. OBAL

Wind of Death's imperishable wing?, The. (LL) Dante Gabriel Rossetti. EBVV; GTBS-P; NAEL-5v2; NAEL-6v2 *Fr.* House of Life, The.

Wind of Liberty. Amélia Veiga. HAWP, *tr.* by Julia Kirst

Wind of old cocoa farms, The. Africa Sky. Kojo Laing. HBAPE

Wind of Our Going: Adagio Ma Non Troppo. Patricia Goedicke. MiVo

Wind of the West, that fans with fragrant wing. To the Western Wind. Judah Halevi. TrJP, *tr.* by Solomon Solis-Cohen

Wind on the Corn. Charles Tennyson Turner. EBVV

Wind on the Hills, The. Dora Sigerson Shorter. NOBVV

Wind, one brilliant day, called, The. Wind, One Brilliant Day, The. Antonio Machado Ruiz. RaBo, *tr.* by Robert Bly

Wind / only, The. Song of the Trees. *Unknown.* OBVE, *tr.* by Frances Densmore

Wind. / Outside my suite, wind screams. Stillborn Night. Beth Brant. ReEnLa

Wind over the lake is mild, the moon fair, The. Written at Lakeside Residence. Chiang K'uei. SuSp, *tr.* by Chiang Yee

Wind passes over the lake. Autumn Evening beside the Lake. Li Ch'ing-chao. OHPC, *tr.* by Kenneth Rexroth

Wind piercing, hill bare, hard to find shelter. *Unknown.* OBWVE *Fr.* Winter.

Wind plays with the moon; the moon, with the wind, The. Linked Verses. *Vietnamese Oral Tradition.* CaDao, *tr.* by John Balaban

Wind pours down, The. (LL) Ploughing on Sunday. Wallace Stevens. RB; TTTS

Wind pushed the sun, The. On The Day They Buried My Mother. Miguel Piñero. PueRic

Wind rips through the. David Kherdian. UrbNat *Fr.* Taking the Soundings on Third Avenue.

Wind rocks our tent. The storm. Thunder Storm. George Keithley. PasH

Wind rocks the car. / We sit parked by the river. Like This Together. Adrienne Rich. VGW

Wind runs free across our plains, The. For Adolf Eichmann. Primo Levi. AF, *tr.* by Ruth Feldman

Wind rustles the bamboos, The. Yakamochi (Otomo no Yakamochi). OHPJ

Wind's hand, The. Whole Works, The. Federico García Lorca. PFTM-1

Wind's in the heart of me, a fire's in my heels, A. Wanderer's Song, A. John Masefield. MoBrPo

Wind's Lament, The. John Morris-Jones. OBWVE, *tr.* by Anthony Conran

Wind's on the wold, The. Inscription for an Old Bed. William Morris. OBEV

Wind's Visit, The. Emily Dickinson. APN-2

Wind sal[l] blaw for evermair, The. (LL) Twa Corbies, The. *Unknown.* AWP; ESPB; FaBoCh; GTBS-P; HAP; InPK-6; NPeEn; NePenScot; OBEV; OWoS; OxBEV; OxBS; PAI; RB; SCGP; UnPo

Wind shakes my window frames. October in the Country: [1983]. James Simmons. BiHa; CIP-2

Wind shall lull us yet, The. From the Antique. Christina Georgina Rossetti. EnLoPo

Wind shoves my New Year's Day sun in my face, The. Edoardo Sanguineti. ItPo, *tr.* by Gayle Ridinger *Fr.* Scartabello.

Wind sifts through the curtain. Kuan Han-ch'ing. SuSp *Fr.* Tune: "Green Jade Flute."

Wind sighs through the Flame tree, The. Homesick Bride, The. *Vietnamese Oral Tradition.* CaDao, *tr.* by John Balaban

Wind Sleepers, The. "H. D." WPE

Wind Song. Carl Sandburg. MoAmPo

Wind sounds through the trees. J. W. Hackett. HA

Wind Speaks, The. Alfred Austin. "Flocks of the wandering waves I hold, The." VerBaPo

Wind sprays pale dirt into my mouth, The. Gary Soto. GeoHom; PBCAP

Wind, stirring in the dark foliage, brings, The. God's Harp. Gustav Falke. AWP, *tr.* by Ludwig Lewisohn

Wind stirs lightly as the sun's, The. *Unknown.* WoPoe, *tr.* by David Ferry *Fr.* Cambridge Songs.

Wind stood up, and gave a shout. Wind, The. James Stephens. InPK-6; KaS; NoAM; PAI

Wind subsides—a fragrance, The. Tune: "Spring at Wu-ling." Li Ch'ing-chao. SuSp, *tr.* by Eugene Eoyang

Wind Suffers of Blowing, The. Laura Riding Jackson. NPeEn; RB (Wind Suffers, The.) NoP-4

Wind, surf, rock-cliff, sunlight. Power Quest, Sooke Park. Jarold Ramsey. PoCoUp

Wind sways over my face, The. Stroll to Parfondeval, A. Remco Campert. TuT, *tr.* by Theo Dorgan

Wind sways the blossoms of the rock orchids, The. Listening-to-the-Rain Studio. Chu Yi-tsun. SuSp, *tr.* by Chang Yin-nan

Wind sways the pines, A. Dirge in Woods. George Meredith. NAEL-5v2; NAEL-6v2; OBEV

Wind-swung, pine-shaded gate and moonlit court. To the Monk Dúc Son at Thanh-phong Monastery. Trân Thái-Tông, King. AWTN, *tr.* by Hunh Sanh Thông

Wind takes colour from the trees, The. Winds. Hugh Raymond McCrae. CBAP

Wind—tapped like a tired Man, The. Wind's Visit, The. Emily Dickinson. APN-2; FaBoVe; MoAmPo; TOF

Wind that rolls a heart on the pavement of courtyards, The. Man Condemned to Death, The. Jean Genet. CAGL, *tr.* by David Fisher and Guy Wernham

Wind that rose, A. Emily Dickinson. RB

Wind that scatters, The. Ki no Tsurayuki. WoPoe, *tr.* by Helen Craig McCullough

Wind That Shakes the Rushes, The. John Clare. PoRA

Wind, the Clock, the We, The. Laura Riding Jackson. APT-2; FaBoVe

Wind, the season-climate mixer. Clear and Colder. Robert Frost. OBCoV

Wind the wind the wind blows high, The. Wind Blows High, The. *Unknown.* FaBoVe

Wind Thoughts. Pinkie Gordon Lane. GT

Wind thrashes the maple seed-pods, The. John Ashbery. APSN *Fr.* Skaters, The.

Wind through the box-elder trees, The. Poem against the British. Robert Bly. CoAmPo

Wind today is full of fish, The. Rising Asleep. Penelope Rosemont. SurWo

Wind took up the Northern Things, The. Emily Dickinson. TTTS

Wind Tossed Dragons. Hsieh Ngao. OHMPC, *tr.* by Kenneth Rexroth

Wind Turns, The. Nicole Espagnol. SurWo, *tr.* by Myrna Bell Rochester

Wind visions are honest. Vision Shadows. Simon J. Ortiz. NAAL-5

Wind was a torrent of darkness among the gusty trees, The. Highwayman, The. Alfred Noyes. BRP; ChAP; EBNV; ITBLP; NOxBChV; OBNV; OBSP

Wind was blowing over the moors, The. Charlotte Brontë. "Susan Coolidge." OBCA

Wind was in another country, and, The. Mirage. R. P. Blackmur. APT-2

Wind was not, flat was, but was imminent. Seas Incarnadine. R. P. Blackmur. APT-2

Wind Was There, The. Bravig Imbs. SPE

Wind waves the lotoses in the scented palace by the water, The. For the Dancer of the King of Wu. Li Po. TAL

Wind whines and whines the shingle. On the Beach at Fontana. James Joyce. MoBrPo; OBMV; RB; RaBo

Wind whines the wine-colored telephone lines. Andy Hasselgard. Dave Etter. IllVoic

Wind whips red. Outside. Susan M. Whitmore. SpudSo

Wind will command them with invincible sound, The. (LL) Wallace Stevens. HCAP; PoE *Fr.* Auroras of Autumn, The.

Wind, wind, give me back my feather. Child on the Shore, The. Ursula K. Le Guin. KaS

Wind won't come to draw smiles in the sand of dreams, The. Elegy. Yehuda Amichai [*or* Amikhai]. PFTM-2, *tr.* by Stephen Mitchell

Windblown forest: the slender moon has fallen. Night feast at the Tsos. Tu Fu. ChinPo, *tr.* by Yip Wai-lim

Windfall. William Heyen. PoCoUp

Windharp. John Montague. CIP-2; PNI

Windhover, The. Gerard Manley Hopkins. AmFaPo; CABP; ClHu; EBVV; GTBS-P; HAP; InPK-6; MoBrPo; NAEL-5v2; NAEL-6v2; NIL-7; NOBE; NOBVV; NPeEn; NoAM; NoP-4; OWoS; OxAEP-2; OxBEV; OxBSo; PeECV; PoE; PoPoPo; PoRA; RB; SCGP; SCV; SacPr; TFi; TOF; TRP; UnPo

Windigo. Louise Erdrich. NoAM; PoPoPo

Windigo. Paulette Jiles. NOBC

Winding around the waters of the world. (LL) Far Field, The. Theodore Roethke. ColAP; NAAL-2v2; NoAM *Fr.* North American Sequence.

Winding creek and scattered maple groves, A. Yüan Hao-wen. SuSp *Fr.* Random Verses on Mountain Life.

Winding Sand. Naresh Guha. OMIP, *tr.* by Lila Ray

Winding Up. Derek Walcott. NoAM

Winding-up Time. Jean Ingelow. VWP

Windless city built on decaying granite, loose ends. Thomas McGrath. NNaP *Fr.* Letter to an Imaginary Friend.

Windless northern surge, the sea-gull's scream, The. Incarnate One, The. Edwin Muir. PeECV

Windless summer day. George Swede. HA

Windmill. Gillian Clarke. TCAWP

Windmill At Mandanthanunguna. Pambardu. NOBAu, *tr.* by George von Brandenstein

Windmills of Your Mind, The. Alan Bergman. ReLy

Window. Carl Sandburg. APT-1

Window, The. Dino Campana. STV, *tr.* by John Frederick Nims

Window, The. Raymond Carver. BLT

Window, The. Robert Creeley. FTOS; NOBA; NoAM; PmAP; TAP; VGW

Window, The. Enrique Gonzáles Martínez. TCLAP, *tr.* by Elizabeth Gordon

Window, The. Lynda Hull. ExTi

Window, The. Kay Sage. SurWo

Window at Key West, A. Honor Moore. KGB; WiU

Window-Blind. Denise Levertov. LCAP-2

Window Dressing. William Peskett. PNI

Window-Glance, The. Heinrich Heine. AWP, *tr.* by John Todhunter

Window insulates me from the street, The. Maternity Gown. David Holbrook. OxBTC

Window into the ground, A. Skara Brae. Michael Longley. PBCIP

Window is nailed and boarded, The. Hallaig. Sorley MacLean (Somhairle MacGill-Eain). HarvBoo; NPeEn; NePenScot; WoPoe

Window Just over the Street, The. Alice Cary. PoBW; SWaP

Window Ledge in the Atom Age. Elwyn Brooks White. NBLV; OBAL

Window makes a frame for the sky, The. Collection, The. Zhao Zhenkai. VCWP, *tr.* by Chen Maiping and Bonnie S. McDougall

Window of the little inn shows light, The. Hungarian Winter. Gyula Juhász. IQMS, *tr.* by Jess Perlman

Window on the North, A. Robert Arthur Douglas Ford. MoCV

Window open, the. Hearing. Tree Falling in a Vacant Forest, The. Linda Gregg. ExTi

Window remained as before, The. The cold. Telegram. Milo De Angelis. NeIt, *tr.* by Lawrence Venuti

Window Shopping. Lamont B. Steptoe. SpirFl

Window Sill, The. Robert Graves. EnLoPo

Window was made of ice with bears lumbering across it, The. Bad Dream. Louis MacNeice. NoAM

Window window window pane. Summer Shower. David McCord. TLR

Windows. Guillaume Apollinaire. CuPo

Windows. Frank O'Hara. BodElec

Windows, The. George Herbert. BASC; ESCV; GeHe; MeLP; NAEL-5v1; NAEL-6v1; NAEL-7v1; NOCV; NoP-4; PeECV; PoE; TrCP

Windows, The. Chris Wallace-Crabbe. BMAP

Windows are black tonight, The. The lamp. Prayer. Elaine Feinstein. HarvBoo

Windows in Providence. Aliki Barnstone. BoWoP

Windows of my poetry are wide open on the boulevards and in the shop windows, The. Contrasts. Blaise Cendrars. CuPo

Windows of the church are bright, The. Christmas Thoughts, by a Modern Thinker. William Hurrell Mallock. NOBVV

Windows, rapturous windows! (LL) Dead Color. Charles Wright. HCAP; LCAP-2

Windows slashed. Crystal Night. Lyn Lifshin. GotH

Windows wide through day and night, The. Last Days at Teddington. Thom Gunn. OBGa

Winds. Hugh Raymond McCrae. CBAP

Winds, The. *Unknown.* ReMoGo

Winds are bleak, stars are bright. Victoria Markets Recollected in Tranquility, The. "Furnley Maurice." NOBAu

Winds are dark passages among the stars, The. Turtle. Peter Blue Cloud. HATNAP

Winds' enclosure, Atlantic's premises, The. Hebrides, The. Michael Longley. PBCIP

Winds had hushed at last as by command, The. Sower, The. Mathilde Blind. WPE

Winds of Africa. Dorothy S. Obi. WPOW

Winds of Change, The. Charles G. Ballard. VoR

Winds of doctrine blow both ways at once, The. Conrad Potter Aiken. VGW *Fr.* Letter from Li Po, A.

Winds of Fate, The. Ella Wheeler Wilcox. BRP

Winds on the stems make them creak like manmade things. Stalin. Robert Lowell. HCAP

Winds that drift over the desert. Winds of Africa. Dorothy S. Obi. WPOW

Winds they did blow, The. Squirrel, The. *Unknown.* OxNR

Winds whistle. Tune: "Vast Virtue." Kuan Han-ch'ing. ChinPo, *tr.* by Yip Wai-lim

Winds, Winds, Winds. Sergey [*or* Sergei] Aleksandrovich Yesenin [*or* Essenin]. TCRusP, *tr.* by Nigel Stott

Windshield Wiper. Eve Merriam. KaS

Windsor Castle. Henry Howard, Earl of Surrey.
    Prisoned in Windsor, He Recounteth His Pleasure There Passed. NAEL-5v1; NAEL-6v1; NAEL-7v1

Windsor-Forest [*or* Windsor Forest]. Pope.
    "Here hills and vales, the woodland and the plain." ECEV
    "Here too, 'tis sung, of old Diana stray'd." OxAEP-1
    Hunting and Fishing. ECEV; FHYEP
    Progress. ECEV
    "Thy forests, Windsor! and thy green retreats." NOEC; OxAEP-1

Windy City. Stuart Dybek. IllVoic

Windy evening. Dark Farmhouses. Charles Simic. LCAP-2

Windy fall. Issa. EH, *tr.* by Robert Hass

Windy forest is checkered, The. Banquet at the Tso Family Manor. Tu Fu. OHPC, *tr.* by Kenneth Rexroth

Windy Nights. Rodney Bennett. KaS

Windy Nights. Robert Louis Stevenson. KaS; OTCP; PoRA

Wine. Micah Joseph Lebensohn. TrJP, *tr.* by A. M. Klein

Wine. Nikolai Nikolaevich Ushakov. TCRP, *tr.* by Daniel Weissbort

Wine & bath-house sensualities. *Unknown.* GrAn

Wine and cakes for gentlemen. *Unknown.* OxNR

Wine and Grief. Solomon ibn Gabirol. TrJP, *tr.* by Emma Lazarus

Wine and treacherous proposals. Hedylos. PGA

Wine and Water. Gilbert Keith Chesterton. ChIV-1; MoBrPo *Fr.* Flying Inn, The.

Wine and woman and song. Villanelle of the Poet's Road. Ernest Christopher Dowson. OBMV; UnPo

Wine Bowl. "H. D." NoP-4

Wine comes in at the mouth. Drinking Song, A. W. B. Yeats. BoLoP

Wine Cup and Bright Moon. Shen Chou. SuSp, *tr.* by Irving Y. Lo

Wine cup, you come here. Tune: "Spring in Ch'in's Garden." Hsin Ch'i-chi. SuSp, *tr.* by Irving Y. Lo

Wine destroyed the Centaur, not just you. Philip V of Macedon. Alcaeus [*or* Alkaios]. GrAn, *tr.* by Alistair Elliot

Wine for old Adam, digging in the briars! (LL) Cana. Thomas Merton. ChIV-2; TrCP

Wine, I Say! I'll Drink to Madness! Mary Tighe. RWP

Wine in the cup is heavy. Lu Chih. SuSp *Fr.* Tune: "Pleasure in Front of the Hall."

Wine Is Drunk, The. Gwen Harwood. LW

Wine is gone, The. Geological Hymn. Joseph Ceravolo. PmAP

Wine is love's test. Asclepiades. GrAn

Wine it is that gives life pleasure. In Praise of Wine. *Unknown.* MLL, *tr.* by Helen Waddell

Wine Menagerie, The. Hart Crane. APT-2; NOBA; NoAM; OxBA; VGW

Wine of Love, The. James Thomson. OBEV *Fr.* Sunday up the River.

Wine of parting flowed and flowed, The. Wen Cheng-ming. CoBLCP *Fr.*

Improvised on Horseback to Say Good-bye to Those Who Are Seeing Me Off.

Wine-Press of Los, The. William Blake. EBEV *Fr.* Milton.

Wine presses hard upon spring grief. Tune: "Butterflies Lingering over Flowers." Kung Tzu-chen. SuSp, *tr. by* Irving Y. Lo

Wine's a sov'reign cure for sorrow. Wine, I Say! I'll Drink to Madness! Mary Tighe. RWP

Wine-Songs. Moses Ibn Ezra. TrJP, *tr. by* Solomon Solis-Cohen

Wine still grown in gardens to the south, The. Liebhartstal. Josef Weinheber. AuPH, *tr. by* Lowell A. Bangerter

Wine, the red coals, the flaring gas. At the Cavour. Arthur Symons. NOBVV; NPeEn; OxBSP

Wine, the toasts that could not be refused, The. Hellenistic Period, The. Hedylos. GrAn, *tr. by* Adrian Wright

Winegrower, The. Milán Füst. IQMS, *tr. by* Jess Perlman

Winemaker's Beat-étude, The. Alfred Wellington Purdy. MoCV

Wing and Prayer. Jack Marshall. GeoHom

Wing and thorn remain, etched into my mind. Rewind. Ger Killeen. AmPoNex

Wing of Separation, The. Ibn Darraj al-Andalusi. AWP, *tr. by* J. B. Trend

Wing of the ostrich rejoiceth, The. Bible, *O.T.* OWoS *Fr.* Job.

Wing Road. Eamon Grennan. PBCIP

Wing-set lone seagull, The. David Kherdian. UrbNat *Fr.* Taking the Soundings on Third Avenue.

Wing to wing, they bake. Toys, The. Samuel Hazo. GraLe

Wingaersheek Beach. Marsden Hartley. APT-1

Winged Abyss. Nathaniel Mackey. ESEAA

Winged bull trundles to the wired perimeter, The. Cecil Day Lewis. OxBTC *Fr.* Flight to Italy.

Winged bulletins issued from frontier outposts. Going Out through the North Gate of Chi. Pao Chao. ColAnChi; SuSp, *tr. by* Daniel Bryant

Winged Hats, The. Rudyard Kipling. *Fr.* Puck of Pook's Hill.

Winged Horse, The. Louise Glück. BodElec

Winged in Gold. Euros Bowen. OBWVE, *tr. by* the author

Wingèd lion on top of that column, The. Notes Made in the Piazza San Marco. May Swenson. CoAP

Winged Man. Stephen Vincent Benét. MoAmPo

Winged mimic of the woods! thou motley fool[!]. To the Mocking-Bird. Richard Henry Wilde. APN-1

Winged Sphinx. Margaret Fuller. TCAPo

Winged women was saying. Mary's Dream. Lucille Clifton. NALW

Winged Words. Rachel Hadas. FFC

Wingfoot Lake. Rita Dove. PoPoPo

(On her 36th birthday.) UnSA

Wingless. Sándor Weöres. IQMS, *tr. by* Adam Makkai and Donald E. Morse

Wingless Victory, The. Hervey Allen. YaYoPo

Wings. John Godfrey. PmAP

Wings. Michael Haslam. Oth *Fr.* Continual Song.

Wings. Miroslav Holub. PoSu, *tr. by* Ian Milner and George Theiner

Wings. Mary Oliver. PoCoUp

Wings. Maureen Seaton. FFC

Wings. *Unknown.* HePo, *tr. by* Barbara Hughes Fowler

Wings. Judith Wright. CBAP; NOBAu

Wings, The. Delmira Agustini. TCLAP, *tr. by* Elizabeth Gordon

Wings, The. Denise Levertov. APSN; NALW

Wings and Seeds. Sandra McPherson. LoL

Wings filmed, the threads of knowledge thicken. Jam Trap, The. Charles Tomlinson. MoBrPo

Wings in the Dark. John Gray. NOBVV

Wings of a Wild Goose, The. Chrystos. GLP

Wings of Time are black and white, The. Compensation. Ralph Waldo Emerson. APN-1; NOBA

Wings outstretched, a horned owl. Signatures. Daniel Gerard Hoffman. VGW

Wings tremble, it is the red admiral, The. Red Admiral, The. Charles Hubert Sisson. HarvBoo

Winifreda. *Unknown.* OBEV

Wining at the Eastern Slope tonight. Tune: "Immortal at the River." Su Tung-p'o (Su Shih). SuSp, *tr. by* Michael E. Workman

Wink. Roger Gilbert-Lecomte. PFTM-1

Wink as they will. Wink most when widows wince. (LL) High-Toned Old Christian Woman, A. Wallace Stevens. NAAL-2v2; NAAL-5; NOBA; NoAM; TAP

Wink at it only with thine eyes. To the Wine Treasurer of the Circuit Mess. Horace [*or* Horatio] Smith. UV

Winked too much and were afraid of snakes. Monkeys, The. Marianne Craig Moore. APT-1; NOBA; OxBA

Winkte. Maurice Kenny. GLP

Winners. Katherine Frost. Prnts

Winnetou Old. Pierre Joris.
  "Vier Takte vor K time then before." PFTM-2

Winnie. Gwendolyn Brooks.
  Song of Winnie. ESEAA

Winnings. Garrett Kaoru Hongo. GeoHom; OpBo
  (It's Gardena, late Saturday afternoon / on Vermont Avenue.) UnSA

Wino, always stumbling. Homyo. ZenPo, *tr. by* Takashi Ikemoto and Lucien Stryk

Wino was eating soup, The. Tornado Soup. A. K. Redwing. VoR

Winslow Homer. Winfield Townley Scott. APT-2

Winston Churchill. David Scott. NLP

Wintah Styles, De. Maggie Pogue Johnson. CBWP-4

Winter. Bella [*or* Izabella] Akhatovna Akhmadulina. BoWoP, *tr. by* Barbara Einzig

Winter. Rae Armantrout. FTOS

Winter. Alexander Barclay. PBRV *Fr.* Eclogues.

Winter. Robert Bloomfield.
  Ploughman's Horse, The. ECEV

Winter. John Clare. CenSon

Winter. John Davies. AngWePo

Winter. Walter De la Mare. OBMV

Winter. John Lyle Donaghy. BIrV

Winter. Fan Ch'eng-ta. SuSp, *tr. by* Irving Y. Lo *Fr.* Seasonal Poems on Fields and Gardens.

Winter. Friedrich Hölderlin. WoPoe, *tr. by* David Rattray *Fr.* Seasons, The.

Winter. Hesiod. NOSC, *tr. by* George Chapman *Fr.* Georgics of Heisod, The.

Winter. Richard Hughes. OBMV; OBWVE

Winter. Anne Hunter. CenSon

Winter. Judy Jordan. AmPoNex

Winter. Mother Goose. ReMoGo

Winter. Ngo Chi Lan. EaWin, *tr. by* W. S. Merwin and Nguyen Ngoc Bich

Winter. Marie Ponsot. ExTi

Winter. Ryokan.
  "Late at night, listening to the winter rain." AWTN, *tr. by* John Stevens

Winter. Philip Salom. NOBAu

Winter. William Shakespeare. ClHu; GTBS-P; HAP; MakPoe; NAEL-5v1; NAEL-6v1; NIL-7; NIP-4; NoP-4; OBEV; OxBEV; PAI; SCGP; TFi; TRP; UnPo; WeW-3 *Fr.* Love's Labour's Lost.

Winter. Robert Southey. CenSon; GSo

Winter. Ruth Stone. BoWoP

Winter. John Millington Synge. NOIV; OBMV; OxBTC

Winter. James Thomson. *Fr.* Seasons, The.

Winter. *Unknown.*
  "Wind piercing, hill bare, hard to find shelter." OBWVE

Winter. Sheila Wingfield. EnLoPo; LW

Winter. Judith Wright. HarvBoo *Fr.* Shadow of Fire: Ghazals, The.

Winter, The. Morgan Llwyd. AngWePo *Fr.* 1648.

Winter again. John Wills. HA

Winter alleys are warm. Daddy's Friends. Esther Iverem. GT

Winter and Spring have come and gone. In Mourning for His Dead Wife. P'an Yüeh. OHMPC, *tr. by* Kenneth Rexroth

Winter and Spring Scene, A. Henry David Thoreau. NCAP

Winter and Summer. Stephen Spender. MoBrPo

Winter and summer, whatever the weather. Floor and the Ceiling, The. William Jay Smith. OBCA; OxIBACP

Winter Anemones. Charles Brasch. PeNZ *Fr.* Night Cries, Wakari Hospital.

Winter Angel. Ágnes Nemes Nagy. PoSu, *tr. by* Hugh Maxton

Winter at Gurnard's Head. David Wright. NLP

Winter at Tomi. Ovid. AWP, *tr. by* F. A. Wright

Winter Ball. August Kleinzahler. MoASP

Winter, before the War. Waclaw Potocki. WoPoe, *tr. by* Jerzy Peterkiewicz and Burns Singer

Winter before the War, The. Walter McDonald. CDa

Winter began with. Lake of the Woods, The. Richard Ryan. PBCIP

Winter being over, The. Song. Anne Collins. PEW

Winter Billet. Peter Huchel. PoSu, *tr. by* Michael Hamburger

Wintir birds, The. Migration. Pinkie Gordon Lane. BlSi

Winter burial. Eric Amann. HA

Winter Burn. Roberta Hill Whiteman. VoR

Winter-burning in the fields. (LL) Crows, The. Louise Bogan. FaBoWP; NALW

Winter by Breughel, the hill with hunters. Breughel's Winter. Rutger Kopland. VCWP, *tr. by* James Brockway

Winter Campaign, A. Eochaidh Ó Heóghusa. CABP

Winter comes I walk alone, The. Winters Spring, The. John Clare. NOBVV

Winter Coming On. Martin Bell. FaBoMo; OBVE; OxBTC

Winter Cricket. John Heath-Stubbs. OBCP

Winter crisp and the brittleness of snow. Words for Love. Ted Berrigan. PmAP

Winter Dawn. Tu Fu. BLT; OHPC, *tr. by* Kenneth Rexroth

Winter dawn. Larry Gates. HA

Winter Day, A. Joanna Baillie.
  Morning. ECWP
    "Fam'ly cares call next upon the wife, The." NePenScot

Winter Day, A. Philip Lamantia. CLPP

Winter day is cold and snowy, The. Aleksandr Aleksandrovich Blok. TCRP

Winter Daybreak above Vence, A. James Wright (1927–80). LCAP-2; VCAP

Winter Days. Gareth Owen. OBCP

Winter deepening, the hay all in, The. Sonnet. Richard Wilbur. OxBSo; Son

Winter Drive. James McAuley. BMAP

Winter: East Anglia. Edmund Charles Blunden. OxBTC

Winter Evening. Archibald Lampman. NIL-7; NOBC

Winter evening. Nicholas Virgilio. HA

Winter Evening, A. Georg Trakl. AuPH, *tr. by* Lowell A. Bangerter

Winter Evening Poem. Laura Jensen. LCAP-2

Winter evening settles down, The. T. S. Eliot. OPOU; TCAPo *Fr.* Preludes (I–IV).

Winter Evening: A Brown Study, The. William Cowper. NAEL-6v1; NAEL-7v1 *Fr.* Task, The.

Winter Fairyland in Vermont. Francis P. Osgood. WeW-3

Winter fells. Deathward. John Lyle Donaghy. BlrV

Winter fly, The. Issa. SoOfWa, *tr. by* Sam Hamill

Winter for a moment takes the mind; the snow. Conrad Potter Aiken. APT-1; OxBA *Fr.* Preludes for Memnon; or, Preludes to Attitude.

Winter Forest. Hans Leifhelm. AuPH, *tr. by* Lowell A. Bangerter

Winter fowl, The. Shumpan. JDP, *tr. by* Yoel Hoffmann

Winter Fruit. Juan Delgado. TouFir

Winter Galaxy. Charles Heavysege. NOBC

Winter garden. Basho. EH, *tr. by* Robert Hass

Winter Garden. David Gascoyne. GTBS-P

Winter Garden. Janet Lewis. APT-2

Winter hanging over the dark well, A. Well, The. Jay Macpherson. NoP-4

Winter has come; fierce is the cold. Hot Cake. Shu Hsi. ChiP, *tr. by* Arthur Waley

Winter has moved off. Rhododendrons. Larry Levis. GeoHom

Winter has reached thee once again at last. To Hampstead. Leigh Hunt. CenSon

Winter Holding off the Coast of North America. N. Scott Momaday. CDW; ColAP

Winter Homily on the Calton Hill. Douglas Young. OxBS

Winter ice. Hyakka. JDP, *tr. by* Yoel Hoffmann

Winter in America. Gil Scott-Heron. ISC

Winter in Brighton. Mortimer Collins. NPeEn

Winter in Durnover Field. Thomas Hardy. MoBrPo

Winter in Lower Canada. Standish O'Grady. NOBC *Fr.* Emigrant, The.

Winter in Minneapolis. Richard Ryan. PBCIP

Winter in their cry. (LL) Rachel Lyman Field. ChAP; NTCP; OBCA; OxIBACP

Winter in Wales, A. Hester Lynch Salusbury Thrale [*later* Mrs. Piozzi]. CABP

Winter is come again. The sweet south west. January 1, 1829. Nathaniel Parker Willis. APN-1

Winter is here with his grouch. Limerick. *Unknown.* PeLi

Winter is icumen [*or* icummen] in. Ancient Music. Ezra Pound. HeIP-4; NBLV; OBAL; OBCoV; OxBA; PeLV; TCAPo; UV

Winter is passing, and the bells. Spring in the Students' Quarter. Henry Murger. AWP, *tr. by* Andrew Lang

Winter is settling on the place; the sedge. Virginia Portrait. Sterling Allen Brown. GT

Winter is the king of showmen. Winter Morning. Ogden Nash. OTCP; TLR

Winter (January / February 1978). Larry Eigner. PFTM-2

Winter Lakes, The. Wilfred Campbell. NOBC

Winter Landscape. John Berryman. GS; HarvBoo; MoAmPo; TwCP

Winter Landscape. Luciana Notari. CItWP, *tr. by* Cinzia Sartini Blum and Lara Trubowitz

Winter Landscape. Stephen Spender. MoBrPo

Winter Landscape, A. Mathilde Blind. ViWPN

Winter Lanscape—Halifax. Douglas Lochhead. NIP-4

Winter leeks, The. Basho. EH, *tr. by* Robert Hass

Winter Love. "H. D."
  "So we were together." FaBoWP

Winter Love. Elizabeth Jennings. BoLoP

Winter lull / No talents. Issa. ZenPo, *tr. by* Takashi Ikemoto and Lucien Stryk

Winter Mask. Allen Tate. OxBA

Winter Memories. Henry David Thoreau. OxBA
  (Within the Circuit of This Plodding Life.) ColAP; NOBA

Winter midnight. Otsuji. OHMPJ

Winter Mirror. Judith Mok. TuT, *tr. by* Michael O'Loughlin

Winter Mirror II. Judith Mok. TuT, *tr. by* Michael O'Loughlin

Winter Moon. Langston Hughes. KaS; SAmP

Winter moon. Robert Spiess. HA

Winter moon. Lucien Stryk. IllVoic *Fr.* Issa: A Suite of Haiku.

Winter morning. Getting up in Winter. Emperor Ch'ien-wen of Liang. BLT, *tr. by* Kenneth Rexroth

Winter Morning. Frank Flynn. OTCP

Winter Morning. Ogden Nash. OTCP; TLR

Winter / morning. / Snowflakes. Snow Poem. Roger McGough. Spl

Winter morning sunrise, The. Rising in Winter. Hsiao Kang. OHMPC, *tr. by* Kenneth Rexroth

Winter Morning Walk, The. William Cowper. *Fr.* Task, The.

Winter must be here, The. What We Can. Ray A. Young Bear. VoR

Winter: My Secret. Christina Georgina Rossetti. BrRo; NAEL-5v2; NAEL-6v2; NOBVV; NPeEn; VWP

Winter my theme confines; whose nitry wind. John Gay. ECEV; NOEC *Fr.* Trivia; or, The Art of Walking the Streets of London.

Winter, Never Mind Where. Hyam Plutzik. APT-2

Winter Night. Edna St. Vincent Millay. APT-1

Winter Night. Boris Leonidovich Pasternak. WoPoe, *tr. by* Edwin Morgan

Winter Night. Boris Leonidovich Pasternak. TCRP, *tr. by* Yakov Hornstein

Winter Night. Po Chü-i. ChiP, *tr. by* Arthur Waley

Winter Night. Charles Simic. HCAP

Winter Night. Yüan Mei. OHMPC, *tr. by* Kenneth Rexroth

Winter Night, A. William Barnes. NOBE; WoPoe

Winter Night, A. Priscilla Jane Thompson. CBWP-2

Winter Night, A. James Thomson. NOBE *Fr.* Seasons, The.

Winter Night: Mount Royal. Abraham Moses Klein. NoAM

Winter Nightfall. Robert Bridges. MoBrPo; OBEV; SCGP

Winter Nightfall. Sir John Collings Squire. OxBTC

Winter Nights. Thomas Campion. *See* Now Winter Nights Enlarge

Winter 1967. Lenard D. Moore. ISC

Winter Nocturne: The Hospital. Alter Brody. APT-2

Winter Noon. Umberto Saba. STV, *tr. by* John Frederick Nims

Winter Ocean. John Updike. InPK-6; PAI

Winter Ode to the Old Men of Lummus Park, Miami, Florida, A. Donald Justice. WeW-3

Winter of Thirty-Eight, The. Robert Ivanovich Rozhdestvensky [*or* Rozhdestvenskii]. TCRusP, *tr. by* Daniel Weissbort

Winter Offerings. Frank Ormsby. PNI

Winter [*or* Wynter] Wakeneth All [*or* Al] My Care. *Unknown.* MiEL
  (Winter Wakens All My Care.) HAP

Winter owl banked just in time to pass, The. Questioning Faces. Robert Frost. APT-1

Winter Palace, The. Paavo Haavikko.
  "Bastard Son is born with a tooth in his mouth and hair on his." WoPoe, *tr. by* Anselm Hollo
  First Poem, The. PFTM-2, *tr. by* Anselm Hollo
  Second Poem, The. PFTM-2, *tr. by* Anselm Hollo

Winter Piece, A. William Cullen Bryant. APN-1; ColAP; OxBA

Winter-Piece, A. Ambrose Philips. NOEC; NPeEn

Winter-Piece to a Friend Away, A. John Berryman. NOBA

Winter Poem. Nikki Giovanni. PAI

Winter pushes into my room. I waken. What We Leave Behind. Elmaz Abinader. PoArWo

Winter rain. Basho. EH, *tr. by* Robert Hass

Winter rain. Penny Harter. HA

Winter Rain, The. Jones Very. NCAP

Winter rain on moss. Buson. SoOfWa, *tr. by* Sam Hamill

Winter Regrets. Bill Knott. BodElec

Winter Remembered. John Crowe Ransom. HAP; NOBA; OxBA; UnPo; VGW

Winter Rose, The. Gillian Ferguson. NeBl

Winter's Approach. Ábrahám Barcsay. IQMS, *tr. by* Thomas Kabdebo

Winter's because it is the end. (LL) Illustration. John Ashbery. NAAL-2v2; NAAL-5

Winter's Cold. William Robert Rodgers. EnLoPo

Winter's coming on, The. Sanctuary. Dorothy Hewett. CBAP

Winter's Day, A. Joanna Baillie. WoRP

Winter's End. Dan Pagis. FIT, *tr. by* Robert Friend

Winter's last rain and a light I don't recognize. Impossible, The. Bruce Weigl. BodElec

Winter's Tale, A. D. H. Lawrence. MoBrPo

Winter's Tale, A. Sylvia Plath. FaBoA

Winter's Tale, A. Wyatt Prunty. RA

Winter's Tale, The. William Shakespeare.
"As she liv'd peerless." OxAEP-1
Autolycus as Peddler. NPeEn; NoSic
Autolycus's Song ("Jog on, jog on, the footpath way.") FaBoCh; NoSic
(Autolycus's Song "When daffodils begin to peer.") NOBE
(Autolycus Sings.) NOBE
"Give me those flowers there, Dorcas. Reverend sirs." OxAEP-1
"I have said / She 's adulteress; I have said with whom." OxAEP-1
"If you would seek us." OxAEP-1
(Pedlar's Song, The.) NBLV; OxBoLi; PeLV
"Shepherdess-- / A fair one are you." PoE
(Song: "Jog on, jog on, the footpath way.") OxBSP
"To your owne bents dispose you: you'le be found." FaBoVe
("When Daffadils begin to peere.") NPeEn
When Daffodils Begin to Peer. FaBoCh; NoP-4; NoSic; OxAEP-1; OxBSP; SCGP; TFi; UV

Winter's thunder. Unknown. FaBoVe; LB

Winter Scene. Marguerite Young. WPE

Winter seclusion—. Basho. SoOfWa, tr. by Sam Hamill

Winter shall not find me withered. Stocking Up. Sylvia Kantaris. LW

Winter showers. Basho. SoOfWa, tr. by Sam Hamill

Winter skies are cold and low. Song. Tzu Yeh. CrYelRi; ErotSp, tr. by Sam Hamill

Winter Sky. John Cope. GeoH

Winter Sky. So Chong-Ju. VCWP, tr. by David R. McCann

Winter-sky began to frown, The. Stella at Wood-Park. Jonathan Swift. BIrV

Winter sky past the feeder, The. In the Kitchen before Dinner. Jane Rohrer. BodElec

Winter snowes, all covered is the grounde, The. Alexander Barclay. PBRV Fr. Eclogues.

Winter solitude. Basho. EH, tr. by Robert Hass

Winter solstice. Pentti Saarikoski. VCWP Fr. Dance Floor on the Mountain, The.

Winter Solstice—for Frank. "Asphodel." BrRo

Winter Solstice Poem. Diana Scott. BrRo

Winter Song. George Macdonald. NOBVV

Winter Song. Salah Abd al-Sabur. MAP, tr. by John Heath-Stubbs and Lena Jayyusi

Winter Song. Elizabeth Tollet. ECWP; NOEC

Winter Sonnet. Linda Beatrice Brown. GT

Winter Sonnets, The. Vyacheslav Ivanovich Ivanov. TCRusP, tr. by Mary Jane White

Winter Sports. John Gay. ECEV; NOEC Fr. Trivia; or, The Art of Walking the Streets of London.

Winter Stars. Larry Levis. GeoHom

Winter Storm. Lucien Stryk. UrbNat

Winter storm, The. Basho. EH, tr. by Robert Hass

Winter Storms, The. Sir William Davenant [or D'Avenant]. NOSC

Winter sun, The. Basho. EH, tr. by Makoto Ueda

Winter Sunflowers. Gillian Ferguson. NeBl

Winter Sunrise. Laurence Binyon. NPeEn

Winter Swan. Louise Bogan. APT-2; ColAP; OWoS

Winter Swim. Pimone Triplett. NAPBL

Winter tells me I shall die alone, The. Winter Song. Salah Abd al-Sabur. MAP, tr. by John Heath-Stubbs and Lena Jayyusi

Winter Tenement. Malcolm Cowley. APT-2

Winter, the empty air, outside. Time with Stevie Wonder in It. Christopher Gilbert. SwNoth

Winter, the old drover, has brought. Ponies, Twynyrodyn. Meic Stephens. AngWePo

Winter Time [or Winter-Time]. Robert Louis Stevenson. EBVV; MoBrPo

Winter to Spring: the west wind melts the frozen rancour. Horace. WoPoe, tr. by Louis MacNeice Fr. Three Odes of Horace.

Winter Tragedy, A. James Thomson. ECEV Fr. Seasons, The.

Winter Traveler, The. Henry Kirke White. CenSon

Winter Trees. Ágnes Nemes Nagy. IQMS, tr. by Adam Makkai

Winter Trees. Ágnes Nemes Nagy. IQMS, tr. by Ila Egon

Winter Trees. Ágnes Nemes Nagy. IQMS, tr. by Hugh Maxton

Winter Trees. Sylvia Plath. HCAP; LCAP-2

Winter Tuesday, the city pouring fire, A. Coming Home, Detroit, 1968. Philip Levine. UrbNat

Winter Twilight. Anne Porter. APT-2

Winter Twilight, A. Angelina Weld Grimké. NAAAL

Winter Twilight, A. John Banister Tabb. APN-2

Winter Twilight, Glowing Black and Gold, The. Delmore Schwartz. NoAM

Winter uncovers distances, I find. Wintry Mind, The. Witter Bynner. NoP-4

Winter uses all the blues there are. Blue Winter. Robert Francis. LCAP-2

Winter Verse for His Sister. William Meredith. TAP

Winter Views Serene. George Crabbe. WoPoe Fr. Borough, The.

Winter Visit, A. Dannie Abse. NoAM

Winter Voyage. Anne-Marie Albiach. PFTM-2, tr. by Joseph Simas

Winter Wakens All My Care. Unknown. See Winter [or Wynter] Wakeneth All [or Al] My Care

Winter Walk at Noon, The. William Cowper. NPeEn Fr. Task, The.

Winter Walking. Alfred Wellington Purdy. NoAM

Winter warbler. Buson. EH, tr. by Robert Hass

Winter Warfare. Edgell Rickword. FaBoWar; OBWP; OxBTC; PeFWW; PoWW

Winter was a vestibule, storing brooms. Standard Time. Ira Sadoff. BodElec

Winter Wedding, The. Paul Henry. TCAWP

Winter will bar the swimmer soon. Swimming Chenango Lake. Charles Tomlinson. FaBoMo; NoAM

Winter Will Follow. Richard Watson Dixon. GTBS-P

Winter wind. Robert Spiess. HA

Winter Wise. Unknown. Spl

Winter with the Gulf Stream. Gerard Manley Hopkins. NoAM

Winter withering. Tan Taigi. OxBEV, tr. by Anthony Thwaite

Winter Work. Peter Fallon. CIP-2; PBCIP

Wintering. Alicia Ostriker. ExTi Fr. Mastectomy Poems, The.

Wintering. Sylvia Plath. NALW

Wintering over at the End of the Century. Alvin Greenberg. UrbNat

Winterlong, off La Manche, wind leaning. Gray stones of the gray. Flaubert in Egypt. Robert Penn Warren. NoAM

Wintermelons. Marian Yee. FSt

Winters at home brought wind. Once in a Lifetime, Snow. Les A. Murray. CBAP; NoP-4

Winters close, Springs open, no child stirs, The. John Berryman. NAAL-2v2; NAAL-5; NoP-4 Fr. Homage to Mistress Bradstreet.

Winters Spring, The. John Clare. NOBVV

Wintertime nighs. Thomas Hardy. NOBE

Wintry day / On my horse. Basho. ZenPo, tr. by Takashi Ikemoto and Lucien Stryk

Wintry haw is burning out of season, The. Haw Lantern, The. Seamus Heaney. HarvBoo; MakPoe; NoAM; PNI

Wintry Mind, The. Witter Bynner. NoP-4

Wintry night, the hearth inhales, A. Remembering Carrigskeewaun. Michael Longley. PBCIP

Wintry wind. Basho. EH, tr. by Robert Hass

Wintry winds have ceased to blow, The. Resurrection. George Crabbe. SacPr

Wipe off my tear[e]s with handkerchief[e]s of praise. (LL) Poet[r]ess's Hasty Resolution, The. Margaret Lucas Cavendish, Duchess of Newcastle. BASC; NAEL-7v1

Wiped out by the hugeness of the big electric crane. On All Fours. Benjamin Péret. PFTM-1

Wiping the chrome. Alan Pizzarelli. HA

Wire. Rod Moran. NOBAu

Wire, The. Robert Garioch. NePenScot

Wire Song. Mark Todd. GeoH

Wire Tap. Miguel Algarín. PueRic

Wired In. Lamont B. Steptoe. UnSA

Wirikota Wirikota. For the God of Peyote. Unknown. STP, tr. by Jerome Rothenberg

Wiring appears to be five years old, The. Richard II. Veronica Forrest-Thomson. Oth

Wisconsin Horse, The. Simon J. Ortiz. PFTM-2

Wisconsin Horse hears the geese, The. Simon J. Ortiz. NAAL-5 Fr. Poems from the Veterans Hospital.

Wisdom. William Cowper. ChIV-1 Fr. Olney Hymns.

Wisdom. George Sands Johnson. PWR

Wisdom. Hy Sobiloff. VGW

Wisdom. Sara Teasdale. MoAmPo

Wisdom. W. B. Yeats. TrCP

Wisdom and Spirit of the universe! William Wordsworth. AWP; NOBE; OxBEV Fr. Prelude; Growth of a Poet's Mind, The [1850 vers.].

Wisdom, Aspasia, by thy gentle muse. To Aspasia. Susanna Highmore Duncombe. PoBW

Wisdom has nothing to do with age. Wisdom. Hy Sobiloff. VGW

Wisdom is / sweeter than honey. Makeda (Queen of Sheba). HW; WPoS

Wisdom is vain, and prophesy. (LL)   Conflict of Convictions, The.   Herman Melville.   APN-2; CBCWP; NOBA

Wisdom of AE, The.   Thomas McCarthy.   PBCIP

Wisdom of Life, The.   "Al-Akhtal al-Saghir."   MAP, *tr. by* Issa Boullata and Thomas G. Ezzy

Wisdom of Merlyn, The.   Wilfrid Scawen Blunt.
   "Wouldst thou be wise, O Man? At the knees of a woman begin."   OBMV

Wisdom of the, The.   b.   Charles Bukowski.   BodElec

Wisdom of the World, The.   Siegfried Sassoon.   MoBrPo

Wise 1.   Imamu Amiri Baraka.   PFTM-1   *Fr.* Why's / Wise.

Wise 3.   Imamu Amiri Baraka.   FTOS   *Fr.* Why's / Wise.

Wise 5.   Imamu Amiri Baraka.   BB   *Fr.* Wise / Whys.

Wise Emblem of our Politick World.   Richard Lovelace.   *See* Wise emblem of our politic[k] world.

Wise emblem of our politic[k] world.   Snail [*or* Snayl], The.   Richard Lovelace.   BeJo; CaPo; NPeEn

Wise guys, The.   Kid Stuff.   Frank Horne.   NOxBChV

Wise Men and Shepherds.   Sidney Godolphin.   *See* Hymn: "Lord, when the wise men came from far[r]."

Wise Men Ask the Children the Way, The.   Heinrich Heine.   OBCP, *tr. by* Geoffrey Grigson

Wise men come here to shit.   From a Lavatory Wall.   *Unknown.*   FaBoEE

Wise men have shown.   To Each His Own.   Ray Evans.   ReLy

Wise men in long white togas come forward during the.   Inventions.   Miroslav Holub.   PoSu, *tr. by* George Theiner

Wise men of yesterday, like the shrimp, The.   Shrimp and Her Daughter, The.   Jean de La Fontaine.   WoPoe, *tr. by* Bruce Boone and Robert Glück

Wise men, you have cast me aside.   *Unknown.*   CoBCP

Wise Old Owl, A.   Edward Hersey Richards.   LB; OxNR

Wise Pallas and the immortal Muses own. (LL)   Inscription for a Grotto.   Mark Akenside.   NOEC; OBGa

Wise Rejoice with Ganymede, The.   *Unknown.*   CAGL, *tr. by* John Boswell   *Fr.* Leiden Manuscript, The.

Wise teacher tell me.   Jelaluddin [*or* Jalal al-Din] Rumi.   EaWin, *tr. by* Talat Sait Halman and W. S. Merwin

Wise to have gone so early to reward.   *Unknown.*   AWP   *Fr.* Thousand and One Nights, The.

Wise Triangle, A.   Vasco [*or* Vasko] Popa.   PoSu   *Fr.* Yawn of Yawns, The.

Wise-Unto-Hell Ecclesiast.   Past Thinking of Solomon.   Francis Thompson.   ChIV-1

Wise / Whys.   Imamu Amiri Baraka.
   Wise 5.   BB

Wise-Woman, The.   Agnes Mary Frances Robinson.   VWP

Wisely and well was it said of him, "Hang it all, he's a."   Addition to Kipling's "The Dead King (Edward VII), 1910."   Max Beerbohm.   FaBoEE; OBCoV

Wisely the Hebrews admit no Present tense in their language.   Elegiac Verse 12.   Henry Wadsworth Longfellow.   TCAPo

Wisest men that Nature e'er could boast, The.   Francis Quarles.   ChIV-1   *Fr.* Job Militant.

Wisest of all men lies buried on this spot, The.   Daniel Casper von Lohenstein.   GePo   *Fr.* Arminius.

Wisest scholar of the wight most wise, The.   Sir Philip Sidney.   NoP-4   *Fr.* Astrophil and Stella.

Wisga.   Lew Blockcolski.   VoR

Wish.   Lance Henson.   CDW

Wish.   Maggie Nelson.   AmPoNex

Wish, A.   Olga Fiodorovna Berggolts [*or* Bergholts].   TCRusP, *tr. by* Daniel Weissbort

Wish, A.   Frances Anne [*or* "Fanny"] Kemble.   WPE

Wish, A.   Laurence David Lerner.   OxBTC

Wish, A.   Samuel Rogers.   GTBS-P; NOBE; OBEV; OxAEP-2

Wish, A.   John Millington Synge.   FaBoEE

Wish, The.   Mary Lee, Lady Chudleigh.   LW

Wish, The.   John Clare.
   "And now a garden pland with nicest care."   OBGa

Wish, The.   Abraham Cowley.   BASC; NOBE; NOSC; NoP-4; OBEV; OxAEP-1; PBRV   *Fr.* Mistress, The.

Wish, The.   Thomas Stanley.   AWP

Wish a greater knowledge, then t'attaine.   Christ and Our Selves.   Francis Quarles.   SacPr

Wish, by a Young Lady, The.   Laetitia Pilkington.   PEW

Wish for a Young Wife.   Theodore Roethke.   NAAL-2v2; NAAL-5; NoAM; NoP-4; OxBSP; TAP

Wish Foundation, The.   Carol Muske.   PBCAP

Wish Fulfillment.   Maggie Nelson.   HeMarv

Wish I had a place to walk to.   It's Kind of Lonesome Out Tonight.   Duke Ellington.   ReLy

Wish, that of the living whole, The.   Tennyson.   EBVV; FHYEP; HAP; NAEL-6v2; NAWM-7v2; SacPr; TOF   *Fr.* In Memoriam A. H. H.

Wish You Were Here.   Harold Rome.   ReLy

Wishbone.   Frank X. Walker.   SpirFl

Wishbone, The.   Paul Muldoon.   CIP-2; PBCIP

Wished Sunday's come: mirth brightens ev'ry face.   White Conduit House.   William Woty.   NOEC

Wishes.   A. C. Child.   PoToHe

Wishes.   Patty L. Harjo.   VoR

Wishes.   Philippe Jaccottet.   MFP, *tr. by* Martin Sorrell

Wishes.   Ger Killeen.   AmPoNex

Wishes.   Carlos Pellicer.   TCLAP, *tr. by* Donald Justice

Wishes.   Robert Louis Stevenson.   OBEV
   (Go Little Book.)   MoBrPo

Wishes for Her.   Denis Devlin.   CIP-2; NOIV

Wishes for Sons.   Lucille Clifton.   NAAAL

Wishes for the Supposed Mistress[e].   Richard Crashaw.   *See* Wishes. To His (Supposed) Mistress[e]

Wishes of an Elderly Man[, Wished at a Garden Party, June 1914].   Sir Walter Alexander Raleigh.   FaBoCh; FaBoEE; NBLV; NOBL; OBCoV; PeLV

Wishes. To His (Supposed) Mistress[e].   Richard Crashaw.   BASC; BoLoP; EBEV; MeLP; NOSC; OBEV; OxAEP-1

Wishful Thinking.   Michael C. Blumenthal.   HCAP

Wishful Thinking Is the Master of Reality.   Duo Duo (Li Shizheng).   AF, *tr. by* Gregory Lee

Wishing Africa.   Marilyn Bowering.   NOBC

Wishing Bone Cycle, The.   Jacob Nibenegenesabe.
   "I try to make wishes right."   WoPoe, *tr. by* Howard Norman
   "One time I wanted two moons."   STP

Wishing for roses, I walk through the garden.   Summer Garden.   Anna Andreyevna Akhmatova.   BoWoP, *tr. by* Stephen Stepanchev

Wishing is good time wasted.   Carolina in the Morning.   Walter Donaldson.   ReLy

Wishing Poem.   *Unknown.*   NTCP; OxNR
   (Star Wish.)   OTCP

Wishing to take her son.   Korinna [*or* Corinna].   SaLy, *tr. by* Diane Rayor

Wishing to try retirement, I requested release from duty.   Wen Cheng-ming.   CoBLCP   *Fr.* Improvised on Horseback to Say Good-bye to Those Who Are Seeing Me Off.

Wishon Line, The.   Sherley Anne Williams.   GeoHom

Wisp of spring cloud, A.   Tom Tico.   HA

Wispy autumn clouds.   Robert Spiess.   HA

Wispy cuttings lie in rows, The.   July in Indiana.   Robert Fitzgerald.   AiP

Wisselton, wasselton, who lives here?   Wassailing Song.   *Unknown.*   OBCP

Wistaria.   Witter Bynner.   APT-1

Wistaria-faced Visigoth, The.   Ivano Fermini.   ItPo, *tr. by* Gayle Ridinger

Wisteria.   Eloise Klein Healy.   GeoHom

Wistful, / they speak of / satis- / faction, love.   People, The.   Robert Creeley.   VGW

Wistful vistas are living in objects, The.   Sonnet for the Season.   Art Lange.   PmAP

Wiston Vault.   Katherine Philips.   BASC; NOSC

Wit and Learning.   James Cawthorn.
   "Whoever looks on life will see."   ECEV
   "Wit was a strange unlucky child."   OBCoV

Wit and Wisdom.   Ambrose Philips.   OxAEP-1

Wit's Pilgrimage.   John Davies of Hereford.
   "Give me, fair sweet, the map, well-coloure'd."   OxBSo
   "It is as true as strange, else trial feigns."   OxBSo
   "So shoots a star as doth my mistress glide."   OxBSo
   "Some blaze the precious beauties of their loves."   Son
   "When first I learned the ABC of love."   OxBSo

Wit's queen (if what the poets sing be true).   Upon a Girl of Seven Years Old.   Pope.   OxBSP

Wit that can creep, and pride that licks the dust. (LL)   Pope.   AWP; NOBE; OBSV; OxBEV; SCV   *Fr.* Epistle to Dr. Arbuthnot.

Wit, transported with enditing, A.   Tale of the Miser and the Poet, A.   Anne Finch, Countess of Winchilsea.   ECWP

Wit was a strange unlucky child.   James Cawthorn.   OBCoV   *Fr.* Wit and Learning.

Witch.   Patricia Beer.   OxBC

Witch, The.   Mary Elizabeth Coleridge.   BrRo; CABP; NALW; PoBW; VWP; ViWPN; WPE

Witch, The.   Adelaide Crapsey.   APT-1

Witch, The.   Thomas Middleton.
   Song: "In a maiden-time professed."   OxBSP

Witch, The.   Santal.   RaBo

Witch, The.   Katharine Tynan.   NOBVV

Witch! Leonora Speyer. APT-1

Witch-Bride, The. William Allingham. NOBVV

Witch Doctor. Robert Earl Hayden. NoAM; PAI

Witch Doctor's Magic Flight, The. Smiler Narautjarri. NOBAu, *tr.* by George von Brandenstein

Witch-elms that counterchange the floor. Tennyson. EBVV; NAEL-6v2; OBGa *Fr.* In Memoriam A. H. H.

Witch-Hazel Wood, The. Emily Hiestand. UrbNat

Witch o' Fife, The. James Hogg. NePenScot

Witch of Coös, The. Robert Frost. APT-1; NOBA; NoAM; PoE *Fr.* Two Witches.

Witch of Willowby Wood, The. Rowena Bastin Bennett. ChAP *Fr.* Witch of Willowby Wood, The.

Witch's Ballad, The. William Bell Scott. NOBVV; OBEV; PeVV; RACG

Witch's Chant, A. James Hogg. NOBRP

Witch's Last Ride, The. Emily Jane Pfeiffer. ViWPN

Witch that came (the withered hag), The. Provide, Provide. Robert Frost. APT-1; ChIV-1; HAP; HarvBoo; NAAL-2v2; NOBA; NoAM; NoP-4; PoE; TAP; TFi; TwCP; UnPo; WeW-3; WoPoe

Witch-Wife. Edna St. Vincent Millay. APT-1

Witchcraft. Cy Coleman. ReLy

Witchcraft: New Style. Lascelles Abercrombie. MoBrPo

Witches, The. *Unknown.* FaBoCh

Witches and poets co-embrace like fate. Fatales Poetae. Henry Parrot. FaBoEE

Witches' Charm. Ben Jonson. FaBoCh *Fr.* Masque of Queens, The.

Witches' Charms, The. Ben Jonson. *Fr.* Masque of Queens, The.

Witches' Chasm. Ben Jonson. RB *Fr.* Masque of Queens, The.

Witches' Ride, The. Karla Kuskin. NOxBChV; OxIBACP; TLR

Witches' Spells. Madeleine Edmondson. NTCP

Witches' Wood, The. Mary Elizabeth Coleridge. VWP

With a broken hoe. (LL) Justice Denied in Massachusetts. Edna St. Vincent Millay. AiP; MoAmPo

With a calm and very clear eye. (LL) Pebble, The. Zbigniew Herbert. AmFaPo; PoetW, *tr.* by Czeslaw Milosz and Peter Dale Scott

With a clover in her hand. (LL) Question, The. Frederick Goddard Tuckerman. APN-2; ColAP

With a Coin from Syracuse. Oliver St. John Gogarty. OBMV

With a decent happiness. (LL) Rain, The. Robert Creeley. AmFaPo; CoAP; CoAmPo; ColAP; ErotSp; InvLad; PmAP; PoE; RaBo; TRP; VGW

With a dozen blows the clock betrays the pulse of time. Jean-Baptiste Tati-Loutard. PBMAP *Fr.* Les Racines Congolaises (1968).

With a Fa, la, la, la, la. (LL) Song written at Sea in the First Dutch War (1665), the Night before an Engagement. Charles Sackville, 6th Earl of Dorset. EnLoPo; NOBE; OBEV; OBWP; OxAEP-1

With-a-fountain's shining-shot furls. (LL) Harry Ploughman. Gerard Manley Hopkins. EroLit; FaBoMo

With a garlande of thornes kene. Seven Sins, The. *Unknown.* SacPr

With a gay lady. (LL) London Bridge. Mother Goose. FaBoVe; LB; NPeEn; OxBoLi; OxNR; ReMoGo

With a Green Scarf. Martin Sorescu. VCWP, *tr.* by Michael Hamburger

With a Guitar, to Jane. Shelley. FHYEP

(To a Lady, with a Guitar.) GTBS-P

With a handful of rice! (LL) Gary Snyder. NOBA; PFTM-2 *Fr.* Myths and Texts.

With a handful of weeds I weep in the slanting sun. Boudoir Lament. Yü Hsüan-chi. BoWoP, *tr.* by Geoffrey Waters

With a heavy paw he guards the frontier. Stone Dog, The. King Lê Thánh–tông. WoPoe, *tr.* by Nguyen Ngoc Bich

With a Heigho, maybe Begorrah, and certainly Fiddlededee. (LL) Irish Song [Rosie O'Grady]. Noël Coward. NBLV; OBCoV

With a lantern that wouldn't burn. Draft Horse, The. Robert Frost. APT-1; EmeKit; HeIP-4; PAI; PoE; SAmP; TRP; WoPoe

With a large ax handle tucked in at his waist. Woodcutter's Ax, A. P'i Jih-hsiu. SuSp, *tr.* by William H. Nienhauser

With a Lifting of the Head. Hugh MacDiarmid. MoBrPo

With a light frost, crouched an outrageous bird. (LL) Birdwatchers of America. Anthony Hecht. NOBA; NoAM

With a line and hook. Boy's Summer, A. Paul Laurence Dunbar. CA

With a long stirrup under fern. Craswall. Roland Mathias. OBWVE

With a louder note. (LL) *Var.* authors. AWP; TAL *Fr.* Kokin Shu.

With a lucky charm around his throat. Lucilius. GrAn

With a mermaid crucified to the wheel while she was still beautiful. (LL) Mathios Paskalis among the Roses. George Seferis. PFTM-1; PoetW, *tr.* by Edmund Keeley and Philip Sherrard

With a muff and a cloak and a tippet—poor Anne. (LL) On Lady Anne Hamilton. Richard Brinsley Sheridan. FaBoEE; NPeEn; OBCoV

With a pert moustache and a ready candid smile. Mixer, The. Louis MacNeice. FaBoTw

With a pint of flour and a sheet of bark. Limejuice Tub, The. *Unknown.* NOBAu

With a Presentation Copy of Verses. Martin Bell. PeLV

With a pull-through and the .22. Premeditations. Geoff Page. NOBAu

With a pure colour there is little one can do. Morning Glory. Ruth Pitter. FaBoWP

With a pure note he welcomes the evening moon. Crane, The. Tu Mu. SuSp, *tr.* by John M. Ortinau

With a radish. (LL) Issa. EH; EnlH

With a rank, Arab bloodstain. (LL) Hand of Solo, A. Thomas Kinsella. CIP-2; NOIV

With a rattle we are walking. Between Scylla and Charybdis. Yunna Petrovna [*or* Iunna Pinkhusovna] Moritz [*or* Morits]. ItGoST, *tr.* by Daniel Weissbort

With a Rod No Man Alive. Walther [*or* Walter] von der Vogelweide. AWP, *tr.* by Jethro Bithell

With a runny nose. Buson. SoOfWa, *tr.* by Sam Hamill

With a scribble like yours. Shorthand. Theodore Weiss. BodElec

With a shy pity pouting in the mouth. (LL) A la Promenade. Paul Verlaine. AWP; OBVE, *tr.* by Arthur Symons

With a simple, truly unrebellious pen. Joseph Brodsky. TCRusP, *tr.* by Bernard Meares *Fr.* Sonnets on the Statue of Mary, Queen of Scots, in the Luxembourg Gardens, Paris.

With a single indecorous groan. Penguin Jane Austen, The. Debora Greger. OWoS

With a Song in My Heart. Richard Rodgers. ReLy

With a *stake* in his inside! (LL) Faithless Nelly Gray. Thomas Hood. NOBL; NOBRP; UV

With a thin slice of sky on a hunk of earth. Magic. Aimé Césaire. NegPo, *tr.* by Clayton Eshleman and Denis Kelly

With a thousand nights' dream. Winter Sky. So Chong-Ju. VCWP, *tr.* by David R. McCann

With a thud. (LL) Let's Hear It for Goliath. Jon Dressel. AngWePo; TCAWP

With a violin in the alley grandfather and son disappeared. Beyond Melody. Nathan [*or* Natan] Alterman. MHP, *tr.* by Ruth Finer Mintz

With a warbler for. Basho. SoOfWa, *tr.* by Sam Hamill

With a whirl of thought oppressed. Day of Judgement, The. Jonathan Swift. BIrV; ChIV-1; NOBE; NOEC; NPeEn; OBSV; OxBEV; SCGP

With a woman friend. Buson. SoOfWa, *tr.* by Sam Hamill

With afternoon tea-cakes and scones. (LL) How to Get on in Society. Sir John Betjeman. NOBL; OBSV; OxBTC; UV

With alarmed and startled eyes. (LL) Deep in the Forest. *Unknown.* VGW; WoPoe, *tr.* by James [*or* Jim] Harrison

With all a woman's virtues but the pox. Pope. OBSV *Fr.* First Satire of the Second Book of Horace [Imitated], The.

With all a woman's virtues but the pox. Pope. OBSV *Fr.* Second Satire of the Second Book of Horace Imitated, The.

With all my heart, in truth, and passion strong. Pride of a Jew, The. Judah Halevi. TrJP, *tr.* by Israel Cohen

With All My Heart, Jehovah, I'll Confess. Henry Ainsworth. AH

With all my memories that could not sleep. (LL) Spleen. Ernest Christopher Dowson. MoBrPo; NOBVV

With all my possessions. Love Burned Out the Light. Hala Mohammad. PoArWo, *tr.* by Cornelia Al-Khaled

With all my will, but much against my heart. Coventry Patmore. BoLoP; EnLoPo; GTBS-P; NOBE; OBEV *Fr.* Unknown Eros, The.

With all respect and humble duty. White Mouses Petition to Lamira the Right Honble the Lady Anne Tufton now Countess of Salisbury, The. Anne Finch, Countess of Winchilsea. PoBW

With all that soft old curd. (LL) Elegy on an X-ray Photo of My Skull. Yelena [*or* Elena] Shwarts [*or* Shvarts]. ItGoST; VCWP, *tr.* by Catriona Kelly and Michael Molnar

With all the subtle paints of Fragonard. Flamingos, The. Rainer Maria Rilke. OWoS, *tr.* by Stephen Mitchell

With all these loads of injuries opprest. Dryden. EBEV *Fr.* Absalom and Achitophel.

With an effort Grant swung the great block. Blocking the Pass. Charles Madge. FaBoMo

With angry brow and stately tread. Earthquake of 1886, The. Josephine D. Henderson Heard. CBWP-4

With black crows. (LL) I Drift in the Wind. Ingrid Jonker. HAWP; WPOW, *tr.* by Jack Cope

With black frenzy and seasickness. (LL) Ibycus. PGA, *tr.* by Kenneth Rexroth

With blackest moss the flower-pots [*or* flowerpots]. Mariana. Tennyson. AWP; FHYEP; NAEL-5v2; NAEL-6v2; NOBE; NOBRP; OBEV; OxAEP-2; PeVV; PoE; SCGP; TFi; UnPo

With blameless carriage, I lived [*or* liv'd] here. Epitaph upon a Sober Matron, An. Robert Herrick. CaPo

With bleeding back, from tyrant's lash. Fugitive, The. Priscilla Jane Thompson. CBWP-2

With Bolts of Melody! (LL) Emily Dickinson. APN-2; NAAL-2v1; NAAL-3; NAAL-5; NOBA; NoP-4; TCAPo; TRP

With both knees pressed down on the sill. Through a Window-Light. Sofiya Parnok. ARWW, tr. by Catriona Kelly

With Bridget and with Nell. (LL) Sir John Suckling. BASC; BeJo; CaPo; EBEV; EBNV; NAEL-7v1; NoP-4

With bridles in the evening come. (LL) At Grass. Philip Larkin. HAP; HarvBoo; NPeEn; OxBEV; OxBTC; RB; WeW-3

With broken wing they limped across the sky. Reported Missing. John Clifford Bayliss. PoWW

With bruise of lash or stone. (LL) Simon the Cyrenian Speaks. Countee Cullen. BPo; ChIV-2; HAP; MoAmPo; TTY; TrCP

With burning fervour. Crystal, The. George Barker. OBMV

With camel's hair I clothed my skin. Dream. Richard Watson Dixon. EBEV; NOBVV; OxBEV; PeVV; SCGP

With candour I confess my love. Unknown. BoWoP

With cast–off rags of the past. Crazy Mother, The. Margherita Guidacci. CItWP, tr. by Cinzia Sartini Blum and Lara Trubowitz

With cheerful mind we yield to men. Frances Gray. FaBoVe

With Child. Genevieve Taggard. MoAmPo

With Christ and All His Shining Train. Thomas Prince. AH

With 'Chuck, chuck, chuck, chuck!' (LL) John Skelton. NOBE; NPeEn; NoSic; OBEV; OxBoLi; SCGP; TTTS   Fr. Garland [or Garlande or Garlands] of Laurel[l], The.

With Circes let them dwell that think[e] not so. (LL) Homage to Diana. Sir Walter Ralegh. NPeEn; NoSic

With clinical eye and mind alert. Poet, The. Dale R. Carver. FaBoWar

With closed eyes, full of intimate voices. Poem of My Sleeping Sorrow. Julia de Burgos. TANSG, tr. by Heather Rosario Sievert

With clothes shaken out at Pure Sound Pavilion. Pure Sound Pavilion. Wang Shih-chieng. ColAnChi, tr. by Richard John Lynn

With coat like any mole's, as soft and black. Mole Catcher. Edmund Charles Blunden. OBMV

With company coming. Thanksgiving Dinner. Aileen Fisher. CA

With compassionate hands. Muso Soseki. EaWin, tr. by W. S. Merwin

With conscience cocked to listen for the thunder. Luther. W. H. Auden. PAI

With cords of love God often strove. Michael Wigglesworth. NAAL-3   Fr. Day of Doom, The.

With courage seek the kingdom of the dead. Last Journey, The. Leonidas of Tarentum. AWP, tr. by Charles Merivale

With Dad gone, Mom and I worked. Adolescence—III. Rita Dove. ISC; NAAL-5; NoAM

With darkest thoughts my mind is overcast. Another for Miss Pardo's Album. Mihály Vörösmarty. IQMS, tr. by Paul Tabori

With darkness and the death-hour rounding it. (LL) Elizabeth Barrett Browning. BWW; BoWoP; CenSon; LW; NAEL-5v2; NAEL-6v2; NALW; NOBE; OBEV; WPE   Fr. Sonnets from the Portuguese.

With dawn it comes or does not come. Impossible, The. Abdul Wahab [or 'Abd al-Wahhab] Al-Bayati [or Al-Bayyati]. MAP, tr. by Salma Khadra Jayyusi and Christopher Middleton

With dead shapes of heroes. Evening, The. Georg Trakl. PFTM-1

With death doomed to grapple. Epitaph for William Pitt. Byron. FaBoEE

With deep affection / And recollection. Bells of Shandon, The. Francis Sylvester Mahony. OBEV

With delicate, mad hands, behind his sordid bars. To One in Bedlam. Ernest Christopher Dowson. GSo; MoBrPo; OBMV; Son

With Demo I fell in love, of Paphian origins. Philodemus. GrAn

With deportment learnt from samurai films. Glasnevin Cemetery. Michael O'Loughlin. PBCIP

With dewdrops dripping. Basho. SoOfWa, tr. by Sam Hamill

With difficulty persist here and there on earth. (LL) Another Epitaph on an Army of Mercenaries. Hugh MacDiarmid. FaBoWar; InPK-6; NAEL-5v2; NAEL-6v2; NoAM; NoP-4; OBWP; RB

With divine rhythm the ocean. Rocking. Gabriela Mistral. SpanPo, tr. by Muriel Kittel

With Donne, whose muse on dromedary trots. On Donne's Poetry. Samuel Taylor Coleridge. NAEL-5v2; NAEL-6v2; PAI; UV

With double portion of his father's art. (LL) Dryden. BASC; CABP; FHYEP; HAP; NAEL-5v1; NAEL-6v1; NAEL-7v1; NoP-4; OBSV; OxAEP-1; OxBoLi; PeLV; PoE; TFi

With dull, sea-spent eyes. (LL) Meeting-House Hill. Amy Lowell. APT-1; ColAP; MoAmPo; OxBA; PoRA; TCAPo

With each flowing pastel note, crowds swooned to the unmistakable. Waxing Poetic on Marvin. Gordon Chambers. InTrad

With each recurrence of this glorious morn. Composed in One of the Valleys of Westmoreland, on Easter Sunday. William Wordsworth. ChIV-2

With each subway rereading. New York Newsday: Truth, Justice and Vomit. Paul Beatty. InTrad

With Earth's first Clay They did the Last Man knead. 73. Edward Fitzgerald. CABP

With echoing step the worshippers. Give Me Thy Heart. Adelaide Anne Procter. SacPr

With elbow buried in the downy pillow. Théophile Gautier. AWP   Fr. Taches Jaunes, Les.

With elegies, sad songs, and mourning lays. Sextain. William Drummond, of Hawthornden. NOSC

With endless life are crowned [or crown'd]. (LL) To Live Merrily, and To Trust to Good Verses. Robert Herrick. AWP; BASC; BeJo; CaPo; CavPo; NOSC

With energy to burn. (LL) One of the Boys. James Simmons. ModIr; PNI

With Esther. Wilfrid Scawen Blunt. OBEV; OBMV   Fr. Esther [a Young Man's Tragedy].

With evening. Patio. Jorge Luis Borges. TCLAP, tr. by Robert Fitzgerald

With every note / of the mountain temple. Unknown. BoWoP

With every rolling stone place me in the breach. Place Me in the Breach. Yehuda Karni. TrJP, tr. by Sholom J. Kahn

With everybody's initials on it. (LL) Man Lying on a Wall. Michael Longley. ModIr; NPeEn; PNI

With eyes like a lizard. (LL) Humanities Lecture. William Stafford. NNaP; NoAM

With fairest flowers, / Whilst summer lasts. William Shakespeare. EBEV; RB   Fr. Cymbeline.

With falling Oars they kept the time. (LL) Bermudas. Andrew Marvell. AWP; BASC; ESCV; FHYEP; FaBoCh; GeHe; NAEL-5v1; NAEL-6v1; NAEL-7v1; NOBE; NOCV; NOSC; NPeEn; NoP-4; OBEV; PBRV; PeECV; PoE; RB; SCGP; TFi; WoPoe

With famin upsoaken. (LL) Virgil [or Vergil]. BIrV; OBVE   Fr. Aeneid [or Eneados, Aeneis], The.

With favour and fortune fastidiously blessed [or blest]. Character of Sir Robert Walpole, The. Jonathan Swift. FaBoEE; PoE

With fellow-angels you enjoy it now. (LL) On the Death of Mrs. Bowes. Lady Mary Wortley Montagu. BoWoP; LW

With fiery-lashing. Whirlwind. David Rokeah [or Rokeakh]. MHP, tr. by Ruth Finer Mintz

With fifteen-ninety or sixteen-sixteen. On an Anniversary. John Millington Synge. FaBoEE; NOIV; OBMV

With fifty years not lived but gone, we find. Cloak, The. James McAuley. BMAP

With finger rais'd he points to the prodigal pictures. (LL) My Picture-Gallery. Walt Whitman. NAAL-2v1; NAAL-3

With fingers weary and worn. Song of the Shirt, The. Thomas Hood. BRP; EBVV

With FitzRoy's twenty-two chronometers. Galapagos. Neil Curry. NLP

With fleshless limbs, at rueful length, was laid. (LL) Philip Freneau. NAAL-2v1; NAAL-3   Fr. House of Night, The.

With flint in the bosom and guts in the head. (LL) Stars Have Not Dealt Me, The. A. E. Housman. EBEV; GTBS-P; PoE

With Flute, with Violin. Lőrinc Szabó. IQMS, tr. by Watson Kirkconnell   Fr. Cricket Music.

With focus sharp as Flemish-painted face. Dome of Sunday, The [or A]. Karl Shapiro. CoAP; MoAmPo; NoAM; OxBA

With footstep slow, in furry pall yclad. On Christmas. John Codrington Bampfylde. CenSon

With frantic pain. (LL) Mad Song. William Blake. NAEL-5v2; NAEL-6v2; NOEC; PoE

With Freedom's Seed. Alexander Sergeyevich Pushkin. TTY, tr. by Babette Deutsch

With freedom, while in the front line they went down. (LL) Simonides. GrAn; WoPoe, tr. by Peter Jay

With fruit and flowers the board is decked. At a Dinner Party. Amy Levy. PoBW

With ganial foire. Mr. Molony's Account of the Crystal Palace. William Makepeace Thackeray. PeVV

With gentle fingers. David Vogel. FIT, tr. by Robert Friend

With gently smiling jaws! (LL) Lewis Carroll. ChAP; FaBoCh; FaBoEE; NBLV; NOBL; NOBVV; OxBEV; RB; TFi; TTTS; UV   Fr. Alice's Adventures in Wonderland.

With glad reception our Commander meets. Luis de Camões [or Camõens]. FaBoWar, tr. by Richard Burton   Fr. Lusiads, The.

With glittering fingers, diamond brooch. Heiress, The. Raymond Garlick. TCAWP

With God and His Mercy. Carl Olof Rosenius. AH

With gold unfading, WASHINGTON! be thine. (LL) To His Excellency General Washington. Phillis Wheatley. NAAAL; NAAL-2v1; NAAL-3; NAAL-5; WPE

With golden reins and jade bridle, a neighing horse. Tune: "Song of a Dandy." Sun Kuang-hsien. SuSp, tr. by Hellmut Wilhelm

With golden wine and gardens' fruit. Effulgent Autumn. Georg Trakl. AuPH, *tr.* by Lowell A. Bangerter

With Gorgon's gear and barebill thongs and fangs. (LL) Andromeda. Gerard Manley Hopkins. EBEV; FaBoMo; OxAEP-2; SCGP

With grace she granted. Visit to the Palace of Venus. Irene Young. HW

With green stagnant eyes. Idiot, The. Charles Reznikoff. APT-2

With guilt and grief by half and half. Gegard. Fazil Abdulovich Iskander. ItGoST, *tr.* by Avril Pyman

With guilty hope at every change of moon! (LL) Marriage. Austin Clarke. BIrV; GTBS-P

With hairs, which for the wind to play with, hung. On Lydia Distracted. Philip Ayres. EnLoPo; Son

With half a heart I wander here. In the States. Robert Louis Stevenson. AiP

With hands all reddened and sore. Washerwoman, The. Mary Weston Fordham. CBWP-2

With hands and faces nicely washed. Clever Peter and the Ogress. Katharine Pyle. OBCA

With Happiness Stretched across the Hills. William Blake. NAEL-5v2

With heart at rest I climbed the citadel's. Epilogue. Charles Baudelaire. AWP, *tr.* by Arthur Symons

With hearts of poor men it is so. Poor, The. Emile Verhaeren. AWP, *tr.* by Ludwig Lewisohn

With heavy groans did I approach my friends. Wine and Grief. Solomon ibn Gabirol. TrJP, *tr.* by Emma Lazarus

With Her. Czeslaw Milosz. GI

With her buskins tipped with dew. May's Invocation after a Tardy Spring. Henrietta Cordelia Ray. CBWP-3

With her, her sister went, a warlike maid. Phineas Fletcher. NOSC *Fr.* Purple Island, The.

With her pure nails offering their onyx high. Stéphane Mallarmé. SxFrPo, *tr.* by E. H. Blackmore and A. M. Blackmore

With her shiny black-patent sandals. Juneteenth. Marilyn Nelson. ExTi

With her to lead his life. (LL) King Estmere. *Unknown.* ESPB; OBNV; OxBB

With her would I fly. (LL) To an Isle in the Water. W. B. Yeats. AWP; TTTS

With hindsight, of course, I can see that the hedge. Hedge, The. Gwyneth Lewis. MFPA

With his baby on my knee! (LL) Airly Beacon. Charles Kingsley. EBVV; OBEV

With His Book, of Gardening. Walafrid Strabo. WoPoe, *tr.* by Tim Reynolds

With his head he says no. Dunce, The. Jacques Prévert. MFP, *tr.* by Martin Sorrell

With his heart. Who'd Want to Be a Man? Gregory Orr. BodElec

With his pale Trophees *Death* hath hung his Armes. (LL) Sonnet: "As in a duskie [*or* dusky] and tempestuous night." William Drummond, of Hawthornden. NOSC; OxAEP-1

With his tall tales and 12-string guitar? (LL) Satchmo. Melvin B. Tolson. BPo; NAAAL

With his weapon a shovel. Denis Glover. PeNZ *Fr.* Arawata Bill.

With his white and tousled godly beard. At the Foot of Mount Zion. Endre Ady. IQMS, *tr.* by Leslie A. Kery

With his work, as with a glove, a man feels the universe. Open and Closed Space. Tomas Tranströmer. SPE, *tr.* by Robert Bly

With honeysuckle, over-sweet, festooned [*or* festoon'd]. Coventry Patmore. OxBEV; PeVV *Fr.* Unknown Eros, The.

With Hopeless Love. Moses Ibn Ezra. TrJP, *tr.* by Solomon Solis-Cohen

With horns and [with] hounds, I waken the day. Dryden. NOBE *Fr.* Secular Masque, The.

With how sad steps, O Moon, thou climb'st the sky. William Wordsworth. CenSon

With huge impatience, he inly swelt. Edmund Spenser. NoSic *Fr.* Faerie Queene, The.

With huge, with strangers' eyes. Battle, The. Dan Pagis. FIT, *tr.* by Robert Friend

With human love. (LL) Prayer for My Son, A. W. B. Yeats. EBEV; OxAEP-2; RaBo

With hunched-up shoulders, eyes shut tight. Idiot in the Bath, The. M. Vasalis. TuT, *tr.* by Peter Van de Kamp

With huntis vp, with huntis vp. *Unknown.* NePenScot *Fr.* Gude and Godlie Ballatis, The.

With implements to fly away, / Passing Pomposity? (LL) Emily Dickinson. APN-2; MoAmPo; NOCV

With infinite delight. (LL) Hymn: "Ye golden lamps of heaven, farewell." Philip Doddridge. ECEV; SacPr

With innocent wide penguin eyes, three. Bird-witted. Marianne Craig Moore. APT-1; NAAL-2v2

With its baby rivers and little towns, each with its abbey or its cathedral. England. Marianne Craig Moore. MoAmPo

With its cloud of skirmishers in advance. Army Corps on the March, An. Walt Whitman. AiP; CBCWP

With its five fingers spread. (LL) Delta. Adrienne Rich. HarvBoo; LoL; NIL-7; NIP-4

With its great length of stay. (LL) Within This Book, Called Marguerite. Marjorie Welish. FTOS; PmAP

With its rat's tooth the clock. Alarum, The. Sylvia Townsend Warner. MoBrPo

With its storks and pagoda. (LL) Tête-à-Tête. May Probyn. NPeEn; VWP

With Janice. Kenneth Koch. PmAP

With jewels of my elegant pain. (LL) Race Question, The. Naomi Long Madgett. BPo; LTA

With joy all relics of the past I hail. Old Ruralities: A Regret. Charles Tennyson Turner. EBVV; Son

With joy Britannia sees her fav'rite goose. To the Marquis of Graham on His Marriage. *Unknown.* OBSV

With Joy erst while, (when knotty doubts arose). Upon the Much-to Be Lamented Desease of the Reverend Mr. John Cotton. John Fiske. SCAP

With joy the guardian Angel sees. Samuel's Prayer. John Keble. ChIV-1

With King Cole and his fiddlers three [!]. (LL) Mother Goose. LB; OTCP; OxNR; ReMoGo

With Kit, Age Seven, at the Beach. William Stafford. RaBo

With leaden foot Time creeps along. Absence. Richard Jago. OBEV

With leering looks, bullfac'd, and freckled fair. On Jacob Tonson, His Publisher. Dryden. FaBoEE; OBSV

With lifted feet, hands still. Going down Hill on a Bicycle. Henry Charles Beeching. NOxBChV; OBEV

With Light and With Death. Odysseus Elytis.
"Even when they destroy you it will still be beautiful." GifTon, *tr.* by Olga Broumas

With lightly closed fists and arms partially rais'd. (LL) Runner, The. Walt Whitman. BLT; InPK-6; SAmP

With lilies underfoot and overhead. (LL) Ballata: One Speaks of the Beginning of His Love. *Unknown.* AWP; EaItPo, *tr.* by Dante Gabriel Rossetti

With limb-loosening desire; and her glances are more melting than sleep or death. Alcman. EroLit, *tr.* by David A. Campbell

With lions, tigers, leopards, and their kind. (LL) Greater Cats, The. Victoria Mary Sackville-West. OBMV; OTCP; Spl

With lips of flame and heart of stone. (LL) Impression Du Matin. Oscar Wilde. EBVV; MoBrPo; NAEL-5v2; NAEL-6v2; NoAM

With little here to do or see. To the Daisy. William Wordsworth. GTBS-P

With loitering step and quiet eye. In November. Archibald Lampman. NOBC

With long sobs. Autumn Song. Paul Verlaine. NAWM-7v2, *tr.* by Carlyle Ferren MacIntyre

With longing I am lad. Maid Mars Me, A. *Unknown.* MiEL

With lovers 'twas of old the fashion. To a Young Lady, with Some Lampreys. John Gay. CABP; ECEV; NOEC; OBCoV

With low thunder, with red bushes smooth. Red Rock Ceremonies. Anita Endrezze. CDW; VoR

With luck I'll help her make beneath it. (LL) Design for a Quilt. John Ormond. AngWePo; TCAWP

With lullay, lullay, like a child[e]. John Skelton. NAEL-6v1; NAEL-7v1; NoSic; SCGP *Fr.* Garland [*or* Garlande *or* Garlands] of Laurel[l], The.

With maggots and rotten dust and ages of repose. I lie here and plot the agony of resurrection. (LL) Antrim. Robinson Jeffers. BIrV; NOBA; VGW

With magic in my eyes! (LL) When I Set Out for Lyonnesse. Thomas Hardy. EBVV; MoBrPo; RB

With many a weary step, and many a groan. Homer. UV *Fr.* Odyssey.

With many grievous words touching her death. (LL) Dante Alighieri. AWP; EaItPo, *tr.* by Dante Gabriel Rossetti *Fr.* La Vita Nuova.

With marjoram [*or* margerain] gentle [*or* jentyll]. John Skelton. EBEV; EnLoPo; NOBE; OBEV *Fr.* Garland [*or* Garlande *or* Garlands] of Laurel[l], The.

With me. (LL) Woman. Hira Bansode. ItWoWo; OMIP; WoPoe, *tr.* by Vinay Dharwadker

With Me. Oscar Williams. YaYoPo

With Me My Lover Makes. Cecil Day Lewis. OBMV

With Meaning. John Weiners. BB

With Mercy for the Greedy. Anne Sexton. HCAP; NIL-7; TOF; VCAP

With mighty hand the Holy Lord. Caedmon. AnOE, *tr.* by C. W. Kennedy *Fr.* Genesis.

With morning in the sky. (LL) Emily Dickinson. NAAL-2v1; NAAL-3

With morning tears thy mournful twilight blesses. (LL) Letter from a Girl to Her Own Old Age, A. Alice Thompson Meynell. MoBrPo; VWP

With much ado you fail to tell. Critic, A. Walter Savage Landor. FaBoEE

With Music. Frances Bellerby. FaBoWP

With my back to the wall. Hard Drive. Paul Muldoon. KGB

With my breath I cut my way through the six forests. Lalleswari. WPOW

With my cane. Tantan. JDP, *tr.* by Yoel Hoffmann

With My Crowbar Key. William Stafford. CoAmPo

With my father. Issa. EH, *tr.* by Robert Hass

With my forked branch of Lebanese cedar. Dowser, The. Edwin Morgan. NPeEn; NoP-4

With my girl. Phooie! Robert Garioch. FaBoWar

With my hand over my mouth. (LL) Poem for Trapped Things, A. John Wieners. GLP; NeAP; PmAP; PoM

With my heart I worship. Saint Thomas Aquinas. MLL

With my high starched collar. Trolley Song, The. Hugh Martin. ReLy

With my looks I am bound to look simple or fast I would rather look simple. Magna Est Veritas. Stevie Smith. NPeEn; OxBC; OxBEV

With my many illnesses I meet the spring. First Day of Spring, The. Pien Kung. CoBLCP, *tr.* by Jonathan Chaves

With My Mother, Missing the Train. Helena Nelson. Prnts

With my old man's wrinkled hand. I Guard Your Eyes. Endre Ady. IQMS, *tr.* by Adam Makkai

With my seven-fold inquisitorial eye. Submarine Tombs. Jean-Baptiste Tati-Loutard. PBMAP

With my teeth. No. Not this pig. (LL) Animals Are Passing from Our Lives. Philip Levine. CoAP; ColAP; NOBA; RaBo; TAP

With Names we summon Cosmos out of Chaos. Ode of Signs. Muhammad 'Abd al-Hayy. NAfrP, *tr.* by Alistair Elliot and Matthew Sorenson

With names we summon cosmos out of chaos. Salah 'Abd al-Sabur. MAP, *tr.* by Alistair Elliot and Matthew Sorenson *Fr.* Ode of Signs.

With night full of spring and stars we stand. Young Girls. Raymond Souster. HeIP-4

With no help. Dragon-Gate House. Muso Soseki. EaWin, *tr.* by W. S. Merwin

With no money. Alan Pizzarelli. HA

With no underrobes. Buson. SoOfWa, *tr.* by Sam Hamill

With noiseless steps good goes its way. World, The. Ella Wheeler Wilcox. PWR

With north / over / the barn. (LL) E. E. Cummings. HAP; WeW-3

With not a thought. Tangled Hair. Lady Izumi. WoPoe, *tr.* by Steven D. Carter

With nought to hide or to betray. L'Amitié et l'Amour. John Swanwick [*or* Swanick] Drennan. BIrV

With oh such peculiar branching and over-reaching of wire. St. Saviour's, Aberdeen Park, Highbury, London, N. Sir John Betjeman. SacPr

With old hours all belfry heads. Ding-Donging. Laura Riding Jackson. NoP-4

With old pleasures. (LL) Long River, The. Donald Hall. CoAmPo; LCAP-2

With one arm as long as the other. (LL) Our Lady of Ardboe. Paul Muldoon. BiHa; PBCIP

With one bold stoke. Corporal Who Killed Archimedes, The. Miroslav Holub. PoSu, *tr.* by Ian Milner and Jarmila Milner

With one breath he makes the place green. On Bismillah Khan's Shehnai. Chennavira Kanavi. OMIP, *tr.* by A. K. Ramanujan

With one consuming roar along the shingle. Felixstowe, or, The Last of Her Order. Sir John Betjeman. OxBTC

With one thumb extended he could eclipse the whole. Masaccio's *Expulsion from Paradise*. Julia Copus. MFPA

With one who safeguards Gwynedd. Stallion, The. Tudur Aled. OBWVE, *tr.* by Joseph P. Clancy

With only his feeble lantern. Charon's Cosmology. Charles Simic. HCAP; PoPoPo

With only itself to love. (LL) Elvin's Blues. Michael S. Harper. BPo; LoL

With open shells in seas, on heauenly due. Oister, The. William Drummond, of Hawthornden. NePenScot

With [*or* Wi'] the Scotch lords at his feet. (LL) Sir Patrick Spens [*or* Spence]. *Unknown.* AWP; ClHu; EBEV; ESPB; FaBoCh; HAP; InPK-6; MakPoe; NAEL-5v1; NAEL-6v1; NAEL-7v1; NIP-4; NOBE; NPeEn; NePenScot; OBEV; OBSP; OxBB; OxBEV; OxBS; PoE; RB; SCGP; TFi; UnPo; WeW-3

With other women I beheld my love. Ballata: Of His Lady among Other Ladies. Guido Cavalcanti. AWP; EaItPo, *tr.* by Dante Gabriel Rossetti

With others / from the neighborhood. Shine. Léon Damas. NegPo, *tr.* by Ellen Conroy Kennedy

With our monocles, our frayed pants. Another Planet. Boris Iulianovich Poplavsky [*or* Poplavskii]. TCRP; TCRusP, *tr.* by Emmett Jarrett, Emmet Jarrett, Dick Lourie and Richard Lourie

With our own brown hands. (LL) What the Gypsy Said to Her Children. Judith Ortiz Cofer. OxWW; UnSA

With outward signs, as well as inward life. First Atlantic Telegraph, The. Jones Very. NCAP

With Pantheist energy of will. Venice. Herman Melville. APN-2

With Passion without Compassion. Oscar Hahn. BLPSL, *tr.* by Rene de Costa, Rigas Kappatos and Eleni Paidoussi

With paste of almonds Syb her hands doth scour[e]. Upon Sibilla. Robert Herrick. CaPo

With peace, let tares and acorns be my food. (LL) Country-Mouse, The. Abraham Cowley. NPeEn; OBVE

With peace on earth, good will to men. (LL) Christmas Bells. Henry Wadsworth Longfellow. AH; ChrPo; OBCP

With pinched cheeks hollow and wan. Outcast, The. Josephine D. Henderson Heard. CBWP-4

With plum blossom scent. Basho. SoOfWa, *tr.* by Sam Hamill

With porcupine locks. Katzenjammer Kids, The. James Reaney. MoCV

With powerful Saint Cyprian. Raising the Mediating Center and the Field of Evil with the Twenty-Five Thousand Accounts and the Chant of the Ancients. Eduardo Calderón. PFTM-2, *tr.* by F. Kaye Sharon

With proud thanksgiving, a mother for her children. For the Fallen. Laurence Binyon. NOBE; NPeEn; OBEV; OBWP; OxBTC

With reeds and bird-lime from the desert air. On a Fowler. Isidorus. AWP, *tr.* by William Cowper

With respect to the understanding of what is symbolized. (LL) Money. Howard Nemerov. OxBC; VCAP; WeW-3

With reverence and submission due. Petition from the Chain Gang at Newcastle to Captain Furlong the Superintendent, A. Francis MacNamara. NOBAu

With rhetoric, promising nothing under the sun. (LL) Ecclesiastes. Derek Mahon. BIrV; CIP-2; ChIV-1; ModIr; PNI

With right all my herte now I you grete. *Unknown.* MiEL

With rocks, and stones, and trees. (LL) William Wordsworth. AWP; EnLoPo; FaBoCh; GTBS-P; HAP; HeIP-4; InPK-6; NAEL-6v2; NOBRP; NPeEn; OxBEV; PoRA; SCV; UnPo; WeW-3 *Fr.* Lucy.

With ruder pomp, in more barbaric taste. William Gilmore Simms. APN-1 *Fr.* City of the Silent, The.

With rue my heart is laden. Samuel Hoffenstein. NBLV *Fr.* Mimic Muse, The.

With Rue My Heart Is Laden. A. E. Housman. AWP; HAP; HeIP-4; InPK-6; MoBrPo; NAEL-5v2; NAEL-6v2; NoAM; NoP-4; PoE; PoPoPo; TFi; UnPo

With sails full set, the ship her anchor weighs. Emigravit. Helen Hunt Jackson. SWaP

With sedative voices we joke and spar. Millie's Date. Dannie Abse. BloBone

With serving still. His Reward. Sir Thomas Wyatt. InPK-6; NoSic

With seven matching calfskin cases for his new suits. Home Leave. Barbara Howes. TwCP

With Ships the Sea Was Sprinkled Far and Nigh. William Wordsworth. CenSon; SCGP; WoPoe

With *Sibells* I cannot Devine. Song Composed in Time of the Civill Warr, when the Wicked Did Much Insult over the Godly, A. Anne Collins. EMWP

With sick and famished [*or* famisht] eyes. Longing. George Herbert. ESCV; UV

With silence and tears. (LL) When We Two Parted. Byron. BoLoP; FHYEP; GTBS-P; NAEL-5v2; NAEL-6v2; NOBE; NoP-4; OBEV; PoPoPo; SCGP; TFi; UV

With Silence My Companion. Shuntaro Tanikawa. "I know how worthless this poem will be." PFTM-2, *tr.* by William I. Elliott and Kazuo Kawamura

With silent Melancholy. (LL) Song: "Memory, hither come." William Blake. NAEL-5v2; NAEL-6v2

With Singing Angels hence she posts away. Parthenea, an Elegy. Elizabeth Singer Rowe. PoBW

With sleep-drunken birds. Safe-Conduct. Ingeborg Bachmann. PoSu, *tr.* by Daniel Huws

With snowy light of moon I cannot you compare. Martin Opitz. GePo

With solitude what sorts, that here's not wondrous rife? Michael Drayton. NOSC *Fr.* Polyolbion.

With some surprise, I balance my small female skull in my hands. Small Female Skull. Carol Ann Duffy. EmeKit; HarvBoo

With someone who is not in love with. Being in Love. Marvin Bell. InvLad

With something of angelic light. (LL) Perfect Woman. William Wordsworth. GTBS-P; HeIP-4; OBEV; PWR; SCGP; TFi

With speed the prior body. Bright Receding. Heather Ramsdell. AmPoNex

With stones, then drive away. (LL) Paul Laurence Dunbar. Robert Earl Hayden. ESEAA; GT; NoP-4

With subtle poise he grips his tray. Atlantic City Waiter. Countee Cullen. APT-2

With such a Pulse, with such disorder'd Veins. Epistle from Alexander to Hephaestion in His Sickness, An. Anne Finch, Countess of Winchilsea. EMWP

With such a sound of gently pitying laughter. (LL) My Grandmother's Love Letters. Hart Crane. InPK-6; NOBA; NoAM; NoP-4

With such a throb does blood. Joy of Knowledge. Isidor Schneider. TrJP

With such compelling cause to grieve. Tennyson. EBVV; NAEL-6v2 *Fr.* In Memoriam A. H. H.

With sun on his back and sun on his belly. Pig. Paul Éluard. TTTS, *tr.* by Kenneth Koch

With supping cold plum [*or* pease] porridge. (LL) *Unknown.* LB; OxBoLi; OxNR

With sweet surprise, as when one finds a flower. On Finding the Truth. Jones Very. TrCP

With sweetest milk and sugar first. Andrew Marvell. FaBoCh *Fr.* Nymph Complaining for the Death of Her Faun [*or* Fawn], The.

With swift. Release. Adelaide Crapsey. APT-1

With switch her horse, and hearts with every look. (LL) Cynthia on Horseback. Philip Ayres. EnLoPo; OxBSo

With tall-necked Hesperia and the Medes. Bridge on the Sangarios, A. Agathias. GrAn, *tr.* by Guy Davenport

With tearful eye, how frequent have I seen. Mary Latter. ECWP *Fr.* Soliloquies on Temporal Indigence.

With tears a-flowing I sign. With Tears A-Flowing. *Unknown.* IQMS, *tr.* by John P. Sadler

With tears of recognition never dry. (LL) Coventry Patmore. BoLoP; EnLoPo; GTBS-P; NOBE; OBEV *Fr.* Unknown Eros, The.

With tears thy grief thou dost bemoan. Stanzas. Solomon ibn Gabirol. TrJP, *tr.* by Emma Lazarus

With tender back glistening. Bella Abramovna Dizhur. TCRP

With Tendrils of Poems. Michael McClure. PoM

With Thanks to Eddie Shaw. Janet Lowe. PasH

With that delight the royal captiv[e]'s brought. Lady A. L., My Asylum [in a Great Extremity], The. Richard Lovelace. CaPo

With that he stripped him to the ivory skin. Christopher Marlowe. NOBE *Fr.* Hero and Leander.

With that I saw two swans of goodly hue [*or* hew]. Edmund Spenser. OWoS *Fr.* Prothalamion.

With that low cunning, which in fools supplies. Charles Churchill. NOEC *Fr.* Rosciad, The.

With that mine hand in his he took anon. Geoffrey Chaucer. OBGa *Fr.* Parlement of Foules, The.

With that the Wretched Child expires. (LL) Henry King, Who Chewed Bits of String, and Was Early Cut off in Dreadful Agonies. Joseph Hilaire Pierre Belloc. NBLV; OBCoV; OxAEP-2; PeLV

With the absolute heart of the poem of life butchered out of their own bodies good to eat a thousand years. (LL) Allen Ginsberg. NoAM; PmAP; VCAP *Fr.* Howl.

With the All-Highest's Son, inseparable from Him. (LL) Patmos. Friedrich Hölderlin. OBVE; WoPoe, *tr.* by David Gascoyne

With the awareness of a creature awaiting some kind of collapse. I Usually Look around Me. Iman Mirsal. NAfrP, *tr.* by Clarissa C. Burt

With the blue-dark dome old-starred at night, green boat-lights purring over water, Galilee Shore. Allen Ginsberg. ChIV-2

With the boys busy. Philomena Andronico. William Carlos Williams. FaBoMo

With the bulge and nuzzle of the sea. (LL) When God Lets My Body Be. E. E. Cummings. MoAmPo; NOBA

With the china and tea-leaves. (LL) Modern Secrets. Shirley Lim. OPOU; UnSA

With the clear. Olga Broumas. WiU *Fr.* Caritas.

With the Crescent Moon, with the Evening Star. Hans Leifhelm. AuPH, *tr.* by Lowell A. Bangerter

With the Dawn. Thomas Caulfield Irwin. BIrV; EnLoPo

With the door closed. (LL) Hanging Fire. Audre Lorde. NIL-7; NIP-4; NoAM; NoP-4; PoPoPo; TRP

With the exact length and pace of his father's stride. For a Father. Anthony Cronin. FaBoTw

With the exact security of the hoisting crane. Monument to Birds (Max Ernst). Luiza Neto Jorge. SurWo, *tr.* by Jean R. Longland

With the face goes a mirror. With the Face. Laura Riding Jackson. APT-2

With the fierce rage of winter deep suffused. James Thomson. NOBE *Fr.* Seasons, The.

With the first light of the early morning dawning. *Unknown.* WoPoe, *tr.* by David Ferry *Fr.* Epic of Gilgamesh, The.

With the forks of flowers I eat the meat of morning. Lyric by Nine. *Unknown.* SPE

With the gipsies dancing round me. (LL) Gipsy Laddie, The. *Unknown.* FaBoCh; OxBoLi

With the glitter of attrition. (LL) Sulpicius Lupercus Servasius. PGA; WoPoe, *tr.* by Kenneth Rexroth

With the gods overthrown like that, nobody knew which way to turn. End of Dodona II, The. Yannis Ritsos. VCWP; WoPoe, *tr.* by Edmund Keeley

With the Grain. Donald Davie. NoAM

With the grave's narrowness, though not its peace. (LL) Sick Love. Robert Graves. BoLoP; EBEV; GTBS-P; HAP; HarvBoo; NOBE; NPeeEn; OxAEP-2

With the green lamp of the spirit. Into the Glacier. John Haines. CoAP

With the heart of a child. (LL) I Found Her Out There. Thomas Hardy. NOBE; NoAM; OxAEP-2; PAI; PoE

With the Herring Fishers. Hugh MacDiarmid. CABP

With the hot sand engraving a symbol of light upon time. There Are No Doors. Olga Orozco. BLPSL, *tr.* by Rene de Costa, Rigas Kappatos and Eleni Paidoussi

With the last garden the road. If. Daria Menicanti. CItWP, *tr.* by Cinzia Sartini Blum and Lara Trubowitz

With the last kindness of a foe or friend? (LL) Alun Lewis. AngWePo; OBWVE

With the last lamp. Scott Montgomery. HA

With the lilt of sunlight in their bones. (LL) Hymn to the Sun. Michael Roberts. FaBoCh; OxBTC

With the little figure without hands in the brown-tree clothes. (LL) Homage to Hieronymus Bosch. Thomas MacGreevy [*or* McGreevy]. BIrV; ModIr; SPE

With the map of the winter sky you drew for me. Map of the Winter Sky, The. Margherita Guidacci. CItWP, *tr.* by Cinzia Sartini Blum and Lara Trubowitz

With the men of that old time? (LL) Sequel of Appomattox. Donald Davidson. CBCWP; FuPo

With the night half over. Philodemus. GrAn

With the night, my demon appears. Magdalene (I). Boris Leonidovich Pasternak. GI, *tr.* by Nina Kossman

With the noon conch blown. Buson. SoOfWa, *tr.* by Sam Hamill

With the old kindness, the old distinguished grace. Upon a Dying Lady. W. B. Yeats. UnPo

With the open eyes of their dead fathers. War. Andrey [*or* Andrei] Andreievich Voznesensky [*or* Voznesenskii]. RB, *tr.* by Vera Dunham and William Jay Smith

With the other husks of summer. (LL) Dragonfly, The. Louise Bogan. APT-2; HeIP-4

With the Pawness, lying low, / Lying low. (LL) Flower-fed Buffaloes, The. Nicholas Vachel Lindsay. MoAmPo; NOBA; OBCA; PoE; RB; TRP; VGW

With the persons / on the edge. (LL) Paean to Place. Lorine Niedecker. APSN; APT-2

With the Quangle Wangle Quee. (LL) Quangle Wangle's Hat, The. Edward Lear. EBEV; PeVV

With the richest royalest seed. (LL) Francis Beaumont. NOBE; OBEV; SCGP *Fr.* On the Tombs in Westminster Abbey.

With the same heart, I said, I'll answer thee. Elizabeth Barrett Browning. CenSon *Fr.* Sonnets from the Portuguese.

With the satin stitch. Little Girl. Vivian Lamarque. CItWP, *tr.* by Cinzia Sartini Blum and Lara Trubowitz

With the second drink, at the restaurant. Promise, The. Sharon Olds. ExTi

With the shining fields of mud. (LL) Youth and Age on Beaulieu River, Hants. Sir John Betjeman. FaBoTw; TwCP

With the Ships of Passage. Georg Heym. WoPoe, *tr.* by Peter Viereck

With the slow smokeless burning of decay. (LL) Wood-Pile, The. Robert Frost. APT-1; InPK-6; NAAL-2v2; NAAL-5; NoAM; SAmP; VGW

With the storm moved on the next town. Centipede. Rita Dove. InvLad

With the swinging rainbow on his shoulder. (LL) Legend. Judith Wright. NOBAu; RB

With the thinking of winter. Cook, The. Ray A. Young Bear. CDW

With the Tide: A Cry of Weakness. Louisa Sarah Bevington. PEW *Fr.* Two songs.

With the wasp at the innermost heart of a peach. Scherzo, A. Dora Greenwell. NOBVV; NPeeEn

With the window sliced open. Thirteenth Ode. Sekeena Shaben. PoArWo

With Thee a moment! Then what dreams have play! Desire. "Æ" OBMV

With thee conversing I forget all time. John Milton. UV; WoPoe *Fr.* Paradise Lost.

With thee, men cannot mock us in the clay. (LL) Francis Beaumont. NOBE; OBEV *Fr.* Captain, The.

With thee, O Master, let me live! (LL) O Master, Let Me Walk with Thee. Washington Gladden. AH; PWR

With their bloom, passes. (LL) Quiet. Marjorie Lowry Christie Pickthall. NOBC; SacPr

With their boxing-glove muzzles. Cattle. Peter Skrzynecki. CBAP

With their gifts to a difficult borning. (LL) Manor Garden, The. Sylvia Plath. FaBoWP; HarvBoo; LCAP-2

With their harsh leaves old rhododendrons fill. Mountain Cemetery, The. Edgar Bowers. CoAmPo

With their poor frozen life and shallow banishment. (LL) Scotland's Winter. Edwin Muir. NePenScot; OxBS; OxBTC

With their respective lions. Sea Unicorns and Land Unicorns. Marianne Craig Moore. NALW; PFTM-1

With these green guests around. Who Says That Drought Was Here? Niyi Osundare. HBAPE; NAfrP

With these heaven-assailing spires. New York. "Æ" OBMV

With this ambiguous earth. Christ in the Universe. Alice Thompson Meynell. MoBrPo; NOBE; OxAEP-2; VWP

With this evening lake I hold discourse in the high. Above the Lake. Aleksandr Aleksandrovich Blok. TCRP, *tr. by* Geoffrey Thurley

With this gift of dirty pictures. *Unknown.* PriapPo, *tr. by* Richard W. Hooper *Fr.* Priapus Poems, The.

With this, my derisive voice. (LL) Seven Sides and Seven Syllables. Edouard J. Maunick. CarOv; NegPo; VCWP, *tr. by* Carolyn Kizer

With this rising bath-mist. Issa. SoOfWa, *tr. by* Sam Hamill

With throbbings of noontide. (LL) I Look into My Glass. Thomas Hardy. EBEV; FaBoTw; HAP; HarvBoo; NAEL-5v2; NAEL-6v2; NOBE; NOBVV; NoP-4; OxAEP-2; OxBSP; SCV; WeW-3

With thy rugged, ice-girt shore. Alaska. Mary Weston Fordham. CBWP-2

With Timbrels. Bible, Apocrypha. TrJP *Fr.* Judith.

With time / and space. Poet the Dreamer, The. Norman Jordan. NBV

With toilsome steps I pass through life's dull road. Addressed to ———. Lady Mary Wortley Montagu. ECWP

With too much hope. Life at the Capital. Li Ho. CrYelRi, *tr. by* Sam Hamill

With tossed-aside, bruised fruit. (LL) Adrienne Rich. AmFaPo; LoL *Fr.* Not Somewhere Else, But Here.

With trembling fingers did we weave. Tennyson. EBVV; FHYEP; NAEL-6v2 *Fr.* In Memoriam A. H. H.

With troubled heart and trembling hand I write. In Memory of My Dear Grandchild Anne Bradstreet Who Deceased June 20, 1669, Being Three Years and Seven Months Old. Anne Bradstreet. BoWoP; NAAL-2v1; NAAL-3; TrCP

With true-love showers. (LL) William Shakespeare. EBEV; EnLoPo; NoSic; PoRA; SCGP *Fr.* Hamlet.

With trumpets clap and syphilis. (LL) E. E. Cummings. NoAM; OxBA

With twenty mortal foes. (LL) Song: "Let not the sluggish sleep." William Byrd. OxBSP; SacPr

With two white roses on her breasts. Brown Girl Dead, A. Countee Cullen. GT; TAP

With *u*, with *i*, the overture begins. Lőrinc Szabó. IQMS, *tr. by* Watson Kirkconnell *Fr.* Cricket Music.

With *Usura*. Ezra Pound. APT-1; HarvBoo; NAAL-2v2; NAAL-5; NOBA; PoE *Fr.* Cantos.

With usura hath no man a house of good stone. Canto XLV. Ezra Pound. ColAP

With visionary care. Summer Noon: 1941. Yvor Winters. ColAP

With walking sick, with curtseys lame. Visit, The. Mary Leapor. ECWP

With walloping tails, the whales off Wales. Whales off Wales, The. X. J. Kennedy. OBCA

With Walter and Amati. Gabriel Preil. FIT, *tr. by* Robert Friend

With water warm enough to make me. Black and White Galaxie, The. Michael S. Weaver. UnSA

With what a gentle sound. September. Henrietta Cordelia Ray. CBWP-3

With what attentive courtesy he bent. Guitarist Tunes up, The. Frances Darwin Cornford. SoSe-8

With what Concern I sat and heard your Play. To My Much Esteemed Friend on Her Play Call'd Fatal-Friendship. Lady Sarah Piers. EMWP

With What Courage. Alessandro Ceni. ItPo, *tr. by* Gayle Ridinger

With what, dear bridegroom, can I fairly compare you? Sappho. SaLy, *tr. by* Diane Rayor

With what deep murmurs through time's silent stealth. Waterfall [*or* Water-Fall], The. Henry Vaughan. AngWePo; ESCV; GeHe; MeLP; NAEL-5v1; NAEL-6v1; NAEL-7v1; NOBE; NOCV; NOSC; OBWVE; OxAEP-1; SacPr

With what sense is it that the chicken shuns the ravenous hawk? William Blake. OxBEV *Fr.* Visions of the Daughters of Albion.

With what sharp checks I in myself am shent. Sir Philip Sidney. NAEL-5v1; NAEL-6v1; NAEL-7v1; NoSic *Fr.* Astrophil and Stella.

With what sword shall I. Question and the Answer, The. Muhammad Al-Faituri [*or* Al-Fituri *or* Al-Fayturi]. MAP, *tr. by* Sargon Boulus and Peter Porter

With what voice. Spider. Basho. TTTS

With what you know now about a garden by the sea. Tide Line Garden. W. S. Merwin. BodElec

With Whom Is No Variableness, Neither Shadow of Turning. Arthur Hugh Clough. SacPr

With whom, then, should I sleep? perhaps with thee. With Whom, then, should I Sleep? George Sylvester Viereck. CAGL

With wild hair, you block out your characters. To Chin Nung. Cheng Hsieh. CoBLCP, *tr. by* Jonathan Chaves

With wine and words of love and every vow. Seduced Girl. Hedylos. BoLoP, *tr. by* Louis Untermeyer

With wine glasses. Alexis Rotella. HA

With wings that will not ever. Fumi Saito. WoPoe, *tr. by* Edith Marcombe Shiffert and Yuki Sawa

With woman's form and woman's tricks. To Miss———. Thomas Moore. OxBSP

With words too sad and strange to syllable. (LL) Two in August. John Crowe Ransom. AWP; OxBA

With worms eternally. (LL) To the Oaks of Glencree. John Millington Synge. MoBrPo; NOIV

With wrinkled hide and great frayed ears. Rachel Lyman Field. OBCA *Fr.* Circus Garland, A.

With yellow pears leans over. Half of Life. Friedrich Hölderlin. OBVE

With yellow pears the country. Half of Life, The. Friedrich Hölderlin. NAWM-7v2, *tr. by* Christopher Middleton

With You. David Diop. NegPo, *tr. by* Ellen Conroy Kennedy

With you away—despair! Quatrain. Rudaki. ArPe, *tr. by* Omar S. Pound

With you, fair maid. (LL) Fair Maid of Amsterdam, The. *Unknown.* OxBoLi; PeLV; RB

With you first shown to me. William Barnes. EnLoPo

With you for mast and sail and flag. Narrow Sea, The. Robert Graves. FaBoEE; FaBoMo

With you I begin. David Steinberg. PasH

With you I have refound my name. With You. David Diop. NegPo, *tr. by* Ellen Conroy Kennedy

With you I will roam to the river's nine channels. Yellow River's Earl, The. Ch'u Yüan. WoPoe, *tr. by* Stephen Owen

With your beautiful hair and seemly. *Unknown.* PGA

With your fair eyes a charming light I see. Love, the Light-Giver [*or* To Tommaso de' Cavalieri]. Michelangelo Buonarroti. AWP, *tr. by* John Addington Symonds

With your name, I shall name this homeless year. Oleg Grigorevich Chukhontsev. TCRP

With Your Permission. Mario Benedetti. TCLAP, *tr. by* David Arthur McMurray

With your tall. Tengan Osho's Visit to Erin-ji. Muso Soseki. EaWin, *tr. by* W. S. Merwin

With your teepee and Lucky Strike. And Where Were You. Len Roberts. BodElec

With youthful loss of memory, in my voiceless land. Stanzas. Viktor Korkiya [*or* Korkiia]. TCRP, *tr. by* Vera Dunham

Withal a meagre [*or* meager] man was Aaron Stark. Aaron Stark. Edwin Arlington Robinson. APN-2; MoAmPo; Son

Withdrawal Letter. Jim Carroll. PmAP

Withdrawing all his postal savings. Two Tokyos. Shuntaro Tanikawa. PoetW, *tr. by* Harold Wright

Wither excursive fancy tends thy flight? Newspaper, The. Penina Moise. SWaP

Withered fields, The. Issa. EH, *tr. by* Robert Hass

Withered flowers fill the courtyard. Sorrow in the Harem, A. Wang Ch'ang-ling. OHMPC, *tr. by* Kenneth Rexroth

Withered grass on the plain. Tune: "Song of Dandy"—Hunting in Autumn. Na-lan Hsing-te. SuSp, *tr. by* Bruce Carpenter

Withered grass / under piling. Basho. ZenPo, *tr. by* Takashi Ikemoto and Lucien Stryk

Withered leaves that drift in Russell Square, The. Drilling in Russell Square. Edward Richard Burton Shanks. OBMV

Withered Rose, A. "Yehoash." TrJP, *tr. by* Isidore Goldstick

Withered tree doesn't blossom, The. Kamalākānta Bhattācārya. SinGod, *tr. by* Rachel Fell McDermott

Withered vines cling to the old tree. In Autumn. Ma Chih-yüan. CrYelRi, *tr. by* Sam Hamill

Withered vines, old tree. Ma Chih-yüan. CoBLCP, *tr. by* Jonathan Chaves *Fr.* To the Tune "T'ien ching sha."

Withered vines, old trees, crows at dusk. Tune: "Sky-clear Sand"—Autumn Thoughts. Ma Chih-yüan. SuSp, *tr. by* Sherwin S. S. Fu

Withered wisteria, old tree, darkling crows. Tune: "Heaven-Cleansed Sands." Ma Chih-yüan. ColAnChi, *tr. by* Victor H. Mair

Withered Zen. Muso Soseki. EaWin, *tr. by* W. S. Merwin

Withering plum blossoms by the wayside station. Tune: "Treading on Grass." Ou-yang Hsiu. SuSp, *tr. by* An-yan Tang

Withers benumbed in a world his joy might have helped to illume. (LL) On a Forsaken Lark's Nest. Mathilde Blind. VWP; ViWPN

Within. Philip Booth. PoCoUp

Within. Uncle Tom. Langston Hughes. SAmP

Within a churchyard, on a recent grave. Caged Goldfinch, The. Thomas Hardy. OWoS

Within a copse, I met a shepherd-maid. Ballata: Concerning a Shepherd-Maid. Guido Cavalcanti. AWP; EaItPo, *tr. by* Dante Gabriel Rossetti

Within a dark and cheerless hut. Old Saint's Prayer, The. Priscilla Jane Thompson. CBWP-2

Within a dream. (LL) Vitae Summa Brevis Spem Nos Vetat Incohare Longam. Ernest Christopher Dowson. AWP; CABP; EBVV; HAP; NOBE; NPeEn; NoP-4; OBEV; OxBEV; OxBSP; PeVV; TFi

Within a garden all alone. Mary, the Mother of Jesus. Ada Belle Gardner. PWR

Within a London hospital there lies. His Mother Drinks. Edwin Emanuel Bradford. VerBaPo

Within a native hut, ere stirred the dawn. Nativity. Gladys May Casely Hayford. PBA; TTY

Within an avalanche of glory hallelujah skybreaks. Avalanche. Quincy Troupe. PFTM-2; SpirFl

Within and Without. Elizabeth Jessup Blake. YaYoPo

Within four walls and one window. Excavation, The. Carl Hancock Rux. HeMarv

Within her someone perpares a banquet. Cycle of Months (Menstruation). Shuntaro Tanikawa. PFTM-2, tr. by Harold Wright

Within herself. Uma Worshipping Shiva (On a Kangra miniature). Elsa Cross. TANSG, tr. by Patricia Dubrava

Within his office, smiling. Dove, The. Victor James Daley. NOBAu

Within King's College Chapel, Cambridge. William Wordsworth. GTBS-P Fr. Ecclesiastical Sonnets.

Within my casement came one night. Dawn of Love, The. Henrietta Cordelia Ray. BlSi; CBWP-3

Within my head, aches the perpetual winter. Winter and Summer. Stephen Spender. MoBrPo

Within My Heart. Judah Al-Harizi. TrJP

Within my heart a stab I felt. En las Internas Entrañas. Saint Theresa [or Teresa] of Avila. WPOW, tr. by Father Benedict Zimmerman

Within my heart Love himself made Heliodora. Meleager. HePo Fr. Epigrams.

Within my life, which is continually torn. Within My Life. J. Slauerhoff. TuT, tr. by Desmond Egan

Within that porch, across the way. Cat, The. William Henry Davies. NOBE

Within the Casket of thy Coelick Breast. Acrostick on Mrs. Winifret Griffin, An. John Saffin. SCAP

Within the Circuit of This Plodding Life. Henry David Thoreau. See Winter Memories

Within the covert of a shady grove. Love Sleeping. Plato. AWP; FaBoEE, tr. by Thomas Stanley

Within the dungeon's noxious gloom. Cell, The. John Thelwall. NOEC

Within the flower there lies a seed. Spell of Creation. Kathleen Jessie Raine. FaBoCh; OxBS

Within the gentle heart Love shelters him. Of the Gentle Heart. Guido Guinicelli. AWP; CTC; EaItPo; OBVE, tr. by Dante Gabriel Rossetti

Within the Gorges there is no lack of men. Invitation to Hsiao Ch'u-shih. Po Chü-i. ChiP; OBVE, tr. by Arthur Waley

Within the great grey flapping tent. Auction Sale, The. Henry Reed. MoBrPo

Within the groves of Grongar Hill. (LL) John Dyer. CABP; NOEC; NoP-4; OxAEP-1

Within the lamplight's radius. Needlework. Mimi Khalvati. MFPA

Within the oak a throb of pigeon wings. Twilight in Middle March, A. Francis Ledwidge. BIrV

Within the pain of words. (LL) Heartsong. Khaled Mattawa. BAP-97; NAPBL; NeAmPo

Within the pale blue haze above. Storm, The. Coventry Patmore. EnLoPo

Within the purple graph of the Hokonuis, the dark. Foxes, The. Janet Frame. WPE

Within the sand of what far river lies. Shadows of His Lady. Jacques Tahureau. AWP, tr. by Andrew Lang

Within the Seasons. Peter Blue Cloud. HATNAP
Spring Equinox. ChAP

Within the Shelter of Our Walls. Elinor Lennen. AH

Within the soul's courts is a temple fair. Soul's Courts, The. Henrietta Cordelia Ray. CBWP-3

Within the streams, Pausanias saith. Last Chance, The. Andrew Lang. NOBVV

Within the vast and empty. Kinko. JDP, tr. by Yoel Hoffmann

Within the Veil. Michelle Cliff. NAAAL

Within the wires of the post, unloading the cans of garbage. Prisoners. Randall Jarrell. OxBA

Within these arms for ever swim. (LL) To My Mistress Sitting by a River's Side; an Eddy. Thomas Carew. BeJo; CaPo

Within These Doors Assembled Now. Oliver Holden. AH

Within this black hive to-night. Beehive. Jean Toomer. GT; TTY

Within This Book, Called Marguerite. Marjorie Welish. FTOS; PmAP

Within this mindless vault. Epigram. James Vincent Cunningham. RB; VGW; WoPoe

Within this pleasant wood, beside the lane. Woodland Seat, A. John Clare. CenSon

Within this restless, hurried, modern world. My Voice. Oscar Wilde. EBVV

Within this sober frame expect. Andrew Marvell. BASC; GeHe; NAEL-7v1

Within this vale. Burma-Shave Roadside Signs. Unknown. OBCoV

WITHIN THIS VALE. Unknown. OBCoV Fr. Advertising Rhymes.

Within where the wrapt machines / are praying. (LL) Semblables, The. William Carlos Williams. FaBoMo; NOBA

Within your breast my only native land. (LL) Mad Woman. Su'ad al-Mubarak Al-Sabah. MAP; PoArWo, tr. by John Heath-Stubbs and May Jayyusi

Within your life and mine. Basho. JDP, tr. by Yoel Hoffmann

Without. Bruce Berger. OPRER

Without a jot of ambition left. Ryokan. ZenPo, tr. by Takashi Ikemoto and Lucien Stryk

Without a king, to see the end of time. (LL) On Mr. Paine's Rights of Man. Philip Freneau. NAAL-2v1; NAAL-3; NAAL-5

Without a pang, and so pass by. (LL) By the Sea. Christina Georgina Rossetti. NOBVV; NPeEn

Without a pass. (LL) Child Who Was Shot Dead by Soldiers at Nyanga, The. Ingrid Jonker. HAWP; PeSAV; WoPoe, tr. by Jack Cope, Uys Krige and William Plomer

Without a passion of exceeding love. (LL) Dante Alighieri. AWP; EaItPo, tr. by Dante Gabriel Rossetti Fr. La Vita Nuova.

Without a pickaxe to my name. Graves. Orkhan Muyassar. MAP, tr. by Samuel Hazo and Lena Jayyusi

Without a single sun. Under the Ninth Sky. Georg Nikolic. IllVoic

Without a Song. Vincent Youmans. ReLy

Without a sound. Ransetsu. SoOfWa, tr. by Sam Hamill

Without a stone to mark the spot. To Thyrza. Byron. CAGL

Without a winter coat. Raising the Flag. Gerald Vizenor. VoR

Without an audience or a history. Being an Immigrant. Matilde Salganicoff. MirDau, tr. by Celeste Kostopulos-Cooperman

Without any travelers, and lonely for no one. (LL) Eating Together. Li-Young Lee. IllVoic; InvLad; NAAL-5

Without asking, you borrowed your father's black tie. Tie. Greg Delanty. BiHa

Without Benefit of Declaration. Langston Hughes. TTY

Without Benefit of Tape. Dorothy Livesay. NOBC

Without breaking anything. (LL) Spring is like a perhaps hand. E. E. Cummings. NoP-4; TAP; VGW

Without Ceremony. Vassar Miller. MoAmPo

Without dismaying you at all. (LL) Force of Love, The. Samuel Jones. NOEC; NPeEn

Without doubt man in nature. Natus de Muliere, Brevi Vivens. Emilio Villa. ItPo, tr. by Gayle Ridinger

Without dressmakers to connect. Because of Clothes. Laura Riding Jackson. APT-2

Without e'er a wife? (LL) Tommy Tucker. Mother Goose. LB; OxNR; ReMoGo

Without ever having felt sorry for itself. (LL) Self-Pity. D. H. Lawrence. OxBTC; RB

Without excess no galaxies. Civilities of Lamplight. Charles Tomlinson. OxBC

Without expectation. Summer Oracle. Audre Lorde. BlSi

Without external reference. Two Horses and a Dog. James Galvin. GifTon

Without flocks or cattle or the curved horns. Time of Change, A. Egan [or Aodhagán] O'Rahilly [or O'Reilly or Ó Rathaille]. BIrV, tr. by Eavan Boland

Without Guile. Paul Verlaine. SxFrPo, tr. by Martin Sorrell

Without haste! without rest! Haste Not! Rest Not! Goethe. TreFP, tr. by Unknown

Without Her. Dante Gabriel Rossetti. Son Fr. House of Life, The.

Without her Diadem. (LL) Emily Dickinson. MoAmPo; OxBA

Without Histories. Blanca Wiethüchter. TANSG, tr. by Shaun Griffin and Emma Sepúlveda-Pulvirenti

Without kings and warriors occasional verse fails. On Being Asked to Write a Poem for 1979. Jack A. Mapanje. AF; NAfrP; PBMAP

Without knowing a page / of it / Themselves. (LL) Alice Walker. WPOW; WWork Fr. In These Dissenting Times.

Without me anyway without way I came near without bread. Without Me Anyway. Meret Oppenheim. SurPaPo, tr. by Catherine Schelbert

Without me you can only. Kenneth Rexroth. APSN; APT-2 Fr. Love Poems of Marichiko, The.

Without muscles without slipping. Silvana Colonna. ItPo, tr. by Gayle Ridinger

Without My Friends the Day Is Dark. Moses Ibn Ezra. TrJP, tr. by Solomon Solis-Cohen

Without my having known. Boy Died in My Alley, The. Gwendolyn Brooks. NoAM

Without my knowing it you are the bottom of my mind. You Are at the Bottom of My Mind. Iain Crichton Smith. WoPoe

Without my mother tongue and my country. Identity. Margit Mikes. IQMS, tr. by Suzanne K. Walther

Without obsessions. Obsession. Angelina Muñiz Huberman. MirDau, tr. by Aurora Camacho

Without pleasure. Simonides. SaLy, tr. by Diane Rayor

Without Presumptions. Chris Forhan. NAPBL

Without question, / Without kiss. (LL) Lethe. "H. D.". APT-1; FaBoWP; MoAmPo; PoRA; TCAPo; VGW

Without relief seeking lost love. (LL) Lost Love. Robert Graves. AWP; FaBoCh; MoBrPo

Without seemliness, / without love. (LL) Mutes, The. Denise Levertov. ErotSp; NALW; NOBA

Without so much / as trying to look. You. Carroll Arnett. VoR

Without support and with Support. Commentary Applied to Spiritual Things. Saint John of the Cross. TOF, tr. by K. Kavanaugh and O. Rodrigues

Without that once clear aim, the path of flight. Without That Once Clear Aim. Stephen Spender. Son

Without the decency of shells. Slugs. Gillian Ferguson. MFPA

Without the hall, and close upon the gate. Homer. OBVE, tr. by George Chapman Fr. Odyssey.

Without the Herdsman. Diotimus. AWP, tr. by John William Burgon

Without, the lonely night is sweet with stars. Martyrdom. "Rufus Learsi." TrJP

Without—the power to die. (LL) Fascicle 34 Poem 9. Emily Dickinson. APN-2; HAP; HeIP-4; InPK-6; NAAL-2v1; NAAL-3; NALW; NAWM-7v2; NCAP; NIP-4; NoP-4; OxWW; PoPoPo; SAmP; SWaP; TCAPo; TRP; WPOW; WeW-3

Without this / what is / worth doing. Land. Carroll Arnett. VoR

Without thought. (LL) At the Ball Game. William Carlos Williams. MoASP; NOBA; NoAM; OxBA; PoE

Without thought, without remorse, without shame. Walls. Constantine P. Cavafy. TrJP, tr. by Rae Dalven

Without Title (1). Li Shang-yin. ChinPo, tr. by Yip Wai-lim

Without Title (2). Li Shang-yin. ChinPo, tr. by Yip Wai-lim

Without Villages. Ray Gonzalez. TouFir

Without warning, the idea of the poem. Carpet. Nancy Morejón. TANSG, tr. by Joy Renjilian-Burgy

Without you and your poetry. (LL) Alas! 'Tis Very Sad to Hear. Walter Savage Landor. GTBS-P; WeW-3

Without you, I prefer the nights. Vicki Feaver. NewEx

Witless of my grief was I. Lament of Mary, The. Unknown. IQMS, tr. by Watson Kirkconnell

Witness. Denise Levertov. BLT

Witness. John Montague. CIP-2

Witness. Rachel Wetzsteon. AmPoNex

Witness, The. Rose Drachler. TaR

Witness the sarcophagus of non-Raphael. Earthworker's God is Healed, The. Bernadette Mayer. FTOS

Witness to Death. Richmond Lattimore. VGW

Witnesses. W. S. Merwin. LCAP-2

Wits, like physicians, never can agree. Rover or the Banished Cavaliers, The. Aphra Behn. BWW

Wits; A Session[s] of the Poets, The. Sir John Suckling. BASC; BeJo; CABP; CaPo

Wittler, hittler, or something like that. (LL) Portrait of a House Detective. Hans Magnus Enzensberger. HP; PoSu, tr. by Michael Hamburger

Witty as Horatius Flaccus. On Seeing Francis Jeffrey Riding on a Donkey. Sydney Smith. FaBoEE

Wives, The. Donald Hall. CoAP

Wives in the Sere. Thomas Hardy. NOBE; NOBVV

Wizard. Thomas Campbell. NePenScot Fr. Lochiel's Warning.

Wizard's Chant, The. Unknown. APN-2, tr. by Charles Godfrey Leland and John Dyneley Prince

Wizard's Funeral, The. Richard Watson Dixon. NOBVV; PeVV

Wizards. Alonzo Gonzales Mó. STP, tr. by Allan F. Burns

Wlk'n down regent street i see. Blkfern-jungal. Aileen Corpus. BMAP

Wm. Brazier. Robert Graves. NOBL

Wo'd see Thy Face, and He not by. (LL) No Coming to God without Christ. Robert Herrick. OxBSP; SacPr

Wo, his purple an' linen, too. Dives and Laz'us. Unknown. TTY

Wo man's Voice Must Be Heard, A. Lorena M. Craighead. InTrad

Wo men draped in black. Wo/men. Chiqui Vicioso. TANSG, tr. by Daisy Cocco De Filippis

Wo worth the days! The days I spent. Few Lines to Fill up a Vacant Page, A. John Danforth. SCAP

Wobbly Rock. Lew Welch. PoM

Wodwo. Ted Hughes. HarvBoo; NoAM; WoPoe

Woe indeed, this tumbleweed! Woe Indeed! Ts'ao Chih. ChinPo, tr. by Yip Wai-lim

Woe Is Me! Bible, O.T. TrJP Fr. Micah.

Woe is me, my stolen daughters! (LL) Farewell, The: "Gone, gone,—sold and gone." John Greenleaf Whittier. AWP; NCAP

Woe's me! by dint of all these sighs that come. Dante Alighieri. AWP; EaItPo, tr. by Dante Gabriel Rossetti Fr. La Vita Nuova.

Woe then to the gossips! They show their evil will. Woe Then to the Gossips. Meinloh von Sevelingen. GePo, tr. by J. W. Thomas

Woe, this tumbleweed. Song of Lament, A. Ts'ao Chih. SuSp, tr. by Hans H. Frankel

Woe to England, when the Kings Life is gone! Revelation 5, October 8. Anne Wentworth. EMWP

Woe to him by this world enticed. Child in Prison, A. Gofraidh Fionn O'Dalaigh. NOIV

Woe to him who slanders women. Gerald Fitzgerald, 4th Earl of Desmond. NOIV

Woe! Woe! / Hearken ye! Chant from the Iroquois Book of Rites. Unknown. APN-2, tr. by Horatio Hale

Woe, woe to them, who (by a ball of strife). To the King and Queen[e], upon Their Unhappy Distances. Robert Herrick. BASC

Woe worth thee, woe worth thee, false Scottlande! Earl Bothwell. Unknown. ESPB

Woeful mankind, born to a woeful earth! Voltaire. WoPoe, tr. by Anthony Hecht Fr. Poem Upon the Lisbon Disaster; or, an Inquiry into the Adage, "All Is for the Best."

Woefully Arrayed. John Skelton. ChIV-2; MiEL; SacPr

Woke up and went to sleep. (LL) One Winter Night in August. X. J. Kennedy. OBCA; OBSP; OxIBACP

Woke up crying the blues. Day in the Life of a Poet, A. Quincy Troupe. NBV

Woke up this mornin' I'm Gonna Go Fishin' Peggy Lee. ReLy

Woke up this morning with a / limp. Poem with a Limp. Roger McGough. OBCoV

Woke up to one of those cold. Barrio Beateo. Jesse F. García. UnSA

Wol ze here a wonder thynge. Riddles Wisely Expounded. Unknown. ESPB

Wold clock's feäce is still in pleäce, The. Wold Clock, The. William Barnes. FaBoVe

Wolde God that hyt were so. Unknown. EMWP

Wolde God that it were so. Love Undeclared. Unknown. MiEL

Wolf. Peter Blue Cloud. HATNAP; VoR

Wolf. Fujii Sadakazu. PFTM-2, tr. by Christopher Drake Fr. Where is Japanese Poetry?

Wolf. Kenneth Rexroth. NNaP Fr. Bestiary, A.

Wolf, The. Unsi Al-Haj [or Hajj]. MAP, tr. by Sargon Boulus and Alistair Elliot

Wolf, The. Georgia Roberts Durston. TLR

Wolf and a lamb had come to the same little brook, A. Wolf and the Lamb, The. Phaedrus. RomPo, tr. by Eugene O'Connor

Wolf and the Dog, The. Jean de La Fontaine. OBVE, tr. by Elizur Wright

Wolf and the Lamb, The. Marie de France. NAEL-7v1, tr. by Harriet Spiegel

Wolf and the Lamb, The. Phaedrus. RomPo, tr. by Eugene O'Connor

Wolf and the Sow, The. Marie de France. NAEL-7v1, tr. by Harriet Spiegel

Wolf and the Stork, The. Jean de La Fontaine. OBVE, tr. by Marianne Moore

Wolf "Aunt." Maurice Kenny. HATNAP

Wolf-bait on the bush beside the spring, The. (LL) Frederick Goddard Tuckerman. APN-2; HAP; NOBA; TAP; TCAPo Fr. Sonnets.

Wolf-Boy. David Malouf. CBAP

"Wolf!" cried my cunning heart. True Encounter, The. Edna St. Vincent Millay. OxBSP

Wolf Cub. Sergey [or Sergei] Sergeievich Narovchatov. TCRP, tr. by Lubov Yakovleva

Wolf is still under the blanket, The. Sounds That Arrived, The. Milo De Angelis. NeIt, tr. by Lawrence Venuti

Wolf met a spring, A. Aesop Revised by Archy. Don Marquis. APT-1

Wolf's profile hangs, The. From the Window of the Beverly Wilshire Hotel. Michael McClure. SPE

Wolf speaks, while chewing, The. Wolf Speaks, The. Paul Klee. PFTM-1

Wolf that follows, the fawn that flies, The. (LL) Algernon Charles Swinburne. AWP; CTC; EBVV; HAP; NAEL-5v2; NAEL-6v2; NOBE; OBEV; OxBEV; PoE; SCGP; TFi; WeW-3 Fr. Atalanta in Calydon.

Wolfe Tone. Austin Clarke. CIP-2

Wolfhound. Richard Murphy. NOIV Fr. Battle of Aughrim, The.

Wolfram's Dirge. Thomas Lovell Beddoes. NOBE; OBEV; OxAEP-2 Fr. Death's Jest Book.

Wolsey, or possibly my John of Gaunt. Santa Claus. Christopher Vernon Hassall. OxBTC

Wolves. Louis MacNeice. NoAM; OxBTC

Wolves. Vladimir Alekseievich Soloukhin. TCRP, *tr. by* Daniel Weissbort

Wolves, The. Allen Tate. APT-2; NOBA; OxBA

Wolves can outeat anyone. Wolf and the Stork, The. Jean de La Fontaine. OBVE, *tr. by* Marianne Moore

Wolves for Company. *Unknown.* BIrV

Wolves in the Zoo. Howard Nemerov. NoAM

Woman. Hira Bansode. ItWoWo; OMIP; WoPoe, *tr. by* Vinay Dharwadker

Woman. Alaide Foppa. TANSG, *tr. by* Celeste Kostopulos-Cooperman

Woman. Fu Hsüan. ChiP, *tr. by* Arthur Waley

Woman. Oliver Goldsmith. OBEV *Fr.* Vicar of Wakefield, The.

Woman. Juana de Ibarbourou. TCLAP, *tr. by* Sophie Cabot Black

Woman. Randall Jarrell. NOBA

Woman. Valente Goenha Malangatana. PBA; PBMAP; TTY, *tr. by* Dorothy Guedes and Philippa Rumsey

Woman. Malangatana Ngwenya. PeSAV, *tr. by* Philippa Rumsey

Woman. Siddhalinga Pattanshetti. OMIP, *tr. by* A. K. Ramanujan

Woman. Magda Portal. WPOW, *tr. by* Irene Vegas-Garcia and Kathleen Weaver

Woman. Carl Rakosi. TAP

Woman. Lady Den Sute-Jo. ZenPo, *tr. by* Takashi Ikemoto and Lucien Stryk

Woman. *Unknown.* AWP, *tr. by* H. A. Giles *Fr.* Shi King.

Woman. Ella Wheeler Wilcox. SWaP

Woman. Elolongue Epanya Yondo. NegPo, *tr. by* Ellen Conroy Kennedy

Woman, A. Yasin Taha Hafiz. MAP, *tr. by* Sharif Elmusa and Christopher Middleton

Woman, A. Gabriela Mistral. TCLAP, *tr. by* Doris Dana

Woman, A. Robert Pinsky. WeW-3

Woman, A. Sa'di Yusuf. MAP, *tr. by* Lena Jayyusi and Naomi Shihab Nye

Woman, The. Shakuntala Hawoldar. HAWP

Woman, The. Kristina Rungano. HAWP

Woman, The. Ronald Stuart Thomas. OxBC

Woman! Woman. Elolongue Epanya Yondo. NegPo, *tr. by* Ellen Conroy Kennedy

Woman, 2. Jyotsna Milan. OMIP, *tr. by* Mrinal Pande

Woman 12, A. Hugo Claus. TuT, *tr. by* Peter Van de Kamp

Woman, a pleasing but a short-lived flow'r. Essay on Woman, An. Mary Leapor. BWW; ECWP; NAEL-7v1; NOEC

Woman Alone, A. Denise Levertov. BodElec; WPOW

Woman alone, living. From the Garden of the Women Once Fallen. Lorna Goodison. VCWP

Woman and a man carried along by life, A. Man and a Woman, A. Juan Gelman. BLPSL, *tr. by* Rene de Costa, Rigas Kappatos and Eleni Paidoussi

Woman and Cat. Paul Verlaine. WoPoe, *tr. by* Felicity Bast

Woman and falcons—they are easily tamed. Der von Kürenberg. GePo

Woman and Fame. Felicia Dorothea Hemans. VWP; ViWPN

Woman and the Angel, The. Robert W. Service. ChIV-1

Woman as Market. Muriel Rukeyser. NoAM

Woman asleep. Marie-Claire Bancquart. MFP, *tr. by* Martin Sorrell

Woman at Lit Window. Eamon Grennan. BLT

Woman at the lecture waves her hand, A. Everyone Who Wants to Work Can. Brooke Wiese. OPRER

Woman at the Piano. Marya Alexandrovna Zaturenska. MoAmPo

Woman at the Washington Zoo, The. Randall Jarrell. CoAP; HAP; HCAP; OxBC; TAP; TwCP; UnPo; VCAP

Woman at the Washtub, The. Victor James Daley. NOBAu

Woman Back in the Kitchen, The. Nicholas Lloyd Ingraham. PWR

Woman Bathing. Raymond Carver. PasH

Woman begins to weep, A. (LL) Afterimages. Audre Lorde. LTA; VCAP

Woman / breathing. (LL) Death of Marilyn Monroe, The. Sharon Olds. HeIP-4; ReTh

Woman, caught in a homeland-trap of the Chosen People: you, A. National Thoughts. Yehuda Amichai [*or* Amikhai]. PFTM-2, *tr. by* Stephen Mitchell

Woman coming down the snowy road, A. Grey Woman. Gladys Cardiff. CDW; GifTon

Woman crossed the park and laughed, A. Enveloping Echo, The. Ion Caraion. AF, *tr. by* Marguerite Dorian

Woman Death. Hazel Hall. APT-1

Woman, Don't Be Troublesome. Augustus Young. CIP-2

Woman Dragged by Welsh Corgis. Joan Retallack. FTOS

Woman drest by Age, A. Margaret Lucas Cavendish, Duchess of Newcastle. PEW

Woman eternal my muse, lean toward me. Paul Goodman. BodElec

Woman fears for man, he goes. Abel's Bride. Denise Levertov. FaBoWP; NALW; VGW

Woman Free. Elizabeth Wolstenholme-Elmy.

"Marriage, which might have been a mateship sweet." BrRo

Woman fresh off the train, A. There Goes the Bride. M. Loncar. AmPoNex

Woman from Ch'ang-kan, The. Li Po. CrYelRi, *tr. by* Sam Hamill *Fr.* Women of Yueh.

Woman from the Book of Genesis, A. "Dovid Knut." TCRP; TCRusP, *tr. by* John Glad

Woman Gave Me a Red Star to Wear on My Headband, A. Jimmie Durham. HATNAP

Woman gave me butter now, A. Present of Butter, A. Tadhg Dall O'Huiginn. BIrV, *tr. by* The Earl of Longford

Woman gets all the blame, A. Trouble Is a Man. Alec Wilder. ReLy

Woman grew, with waiting, over-quiet, A. Narrative. Elisabeth Eybers. PeSAV, *tr. by* the author

Woman grows hard and skinny, A. Ride the Turtle's Back. Beth Brant. ItWoWo

Woman Hanging from Lightpole, Illinois Route 136. Lucia Cordell Getsi. IllVoic

Woman Hanging from the Thirteenth Floor Window, The. Joy Harjo. GLP; HATNAP

Woman "heard angels," A. The paper says angels. Talk Show, The. Albert Goldbarth. IllVoic; ReTh

Woman. I choose to walk here. And to draw this circle, A. (LL) Adrienne Rich. NALW; NoAM *Fr.* Twenty-one Love Poems.

Woman I have never seen before, A. Transit. Richard Wilbur. DiPo; LCAP-2; NIL-7

Woman I Know, The. Jeannette Miller. TANSG, *tr. by* Paula Vega

Woman in front of you's black hair blowing over itself. Rodeo Tangent. Kendra Borgmann. MoASP

Woman in Kitchen. Eavan Boland. BiHa

Woman in Love. Paul Éluard. NAWM-7v2, *tr. by* Lloyd Alexander

Woman in middle-life. Lorine Niedecker. APT-2

Woman in my building who skips, The. Alms. Stanley Plumly. BodElec

Woman in My Notebook, The. Lorna Dee Cervantes. WPOW

Woman in my shower crying, A. What Goes around Comes around, or The Proof is in the Pudding. Cheryl Clarke. FFC

Woman in the Film, The. Lesley Dauer. NAPBL

Woman in the pointed hood, The. Village Mystery. Elinor Wylie. APT-1

Woman in the shape of a monster, a. Planetarium. Adrienne Rich. FaBoWP; HCAP; NAAL-2v2; NALW; NIL-7; NIP-4; NOBA; NoAM; VCAP

Woman in whose voice. Nizar Qabbani. MAP

Woman inside an enormous sunhat, A. Close-up. Heather McPherson. PeNZ

Woman inside every woman, The. Why There Are Children. Leslie Ullman. YaYoPo

Woman / is a problem negative. Woman. Siddhalinga Pattanshetti. OMIP, *tr. by* A. K. Ramanujan

Woman is by aptitude. *Unknown.* OBWVE *Fr.* Against Women.

Woman is perfected, the. Edge. Sylvia Plath. FaBoWP; HCAP; NAAL-2v2; NALW; NPeEn; PoE; PoPoPo; TAP; VCAP

Woman is singing in the valley. The shadows falling blot her out, A. Song. Gabriela Mistral. WPoS, *tr. by* Langston Hughes

Woman is sitting reading a prayer, A. For the Far-Out Experimental Writer. Víctor Hernández Cruz. PueRic

Woman Is Talking to Death, A. Judy Grahn. GLP

Woman is using a handkerchief, The. At the Hammersmith Palais. Alan Riddell. NOBAu

Woman Kneeling in the Sorry Jelly, A. Joyce Mansour. HAWP, *tr. by* Albert Herzing

Woman lay dying on a pallet in a gateway, A. Good Lord Saved Her, The. Anna Swirszczynska. PoSu

Woman like Me, A. Eileen Myles. GLP

Woman Looking through a Viewmaster. C. D. Wright. LCAP-2

Woman-love can't touch my heart. *Unknown.* GrAn

Woman making advances publicly, A. Judith Kazantzis. BrRo

Woman Me. Maya Angelou. BlSi; OxWW

Woman measures, A. Jean Daive. MFP, *tr. by* Martin Sorrell

Woman Meets an Old Lover, A. Denise Levertov. BLT

Woman much missed, how you call to me, call to me. Voice, The. Thomas Hardy. BoLoP; EnLoPo; GTBS-P; HAP; HarvBoo; NAEL-5v2; NAEL-6v2; NPeEn; NoAM; NoP-4; OxAEP-2; OxBEV; PAI; PoE; TFi

Woman named Tomorrow, The. Four Preludes on Playthings of the Wind. Carl Sandburg. MoAmPo; NOBA

Woman Née Wu, The. Wu Chia-chi. CoBLCP, *tr. by* Jonathan Chaves

Woman of Color. Constance Merritt. AmPoNex

Woman of Exeter, The. *Unknown.* ReMoGo

Woman of mine with woodfire hair. Free Union. André Breton. NAWM-7v2, *tr. by* Mary Ann Caws

Woman of Three Cows, The. *Unknown.* NOIV; OBCoV, *tr. by* James Clarence Mangan

Woman of Three Minds, The. Thomas Centolella. GifTon

Woman on the Dump, The. Elizabeth Spires. EmeKit

Woman on the subway touches my hand by mistake, and in that. Recognition. Eve Wood. BAP-97

Woman, parents, brothers, even God, A. Those Who Love. Cyprian Norwid. WoPoe, tr. by Jerzy Peterkiewicz, Burns Singer and Jon Stallworthy

Woman Poem. Nikki Giovanni. BlSi

Woman precedes me up the long rope, A. Climbing. Lucille Clifton. GT; LoL

Woman pulls the cart, The. Inscribed on the Painting, Stabbing a Tiger, by Chao Tzu-ang, in the Collection of Scholar Yang. Yang Shih-ch'i. CoBLCP, tr. by Jonathan Chaves

Woman raises her garment, rain, wind, darkness rise, The. Paavo Haavikko. WoPoe, tr. by Anselm Hollo

Woman refugee arms herself with pride and faith. Her Heart Is a Rose Petal and Her Skin Is Granite. Lorene Zarou-Zouzounis. PoArWo

Woman, rest on my brow your balsam hands. Night of Sine. Léopold Sédar Senghor. PBA, tr. by Ellen Conroy Kennedy

Woman, rest on my brow your balsam hands, your hands gentler than / fur. Léopold Sédar Senghor. See Woman, rest on my brow your balsam hands

Woman, rest your balsam hands upon my brow. Léopold Sédar Senghor. See Woman, rest on my brow your balsam hands

Woman's Answer, A. Adelaide Anne Procter. VWP

Woman's Beauty. Lascelles Abercrombie. MoBrPo Fr. Emblems of Love.

Woman's Cause Is Man's, The. Tennyson. NAEL-5v2; NAEL-6v2 Fr. Princess, The.

Woman's Constancy. John Donne. ESCV; NBLV; NOSC (Now thou hast loved me one whole day.) NoP-2

Woman's Constancy. Sir John Suckling. CaPo; CavPo

Woman's deaf, and does not hear, The. (LL) On a Certain Lady at Court. Pope. NOBE; NOEC; OBEV; OxBSP

Woman's Dream, The. Frances Horovitz. BrRo

Woman's face with Nature's own hand painted, A. William Shakespeare. CAGL; HeIP-4; NAEL-5v1; NAEL-6v1; NAEL-7v1; NoP-4; NoSic; OxAEP-1 Fr. Sonnets.

Woman's Future. May Kendall. VWP; ViWPN

Woman's Hard Fate. Unknown. ECWP

Woman's Heart, A. Vietnamese Oral Tradition. CaDao, tr. by John Balaban

Woman's Intuition, A. Victor Young. ReLy

Woman's Labour; an Epistle to Mr. Stephen Duck, The. Mary Collier. Washerwoman, The. ECWP; NOEC

Woman's Last Word, A. Robert Browning. NAEL-5v2; NAEL-6v2; RACG

Woman's Last Word, A. Adelaide Anne Procter. VWP

Woman's like the flatt'ring ocean. John Gay. PeLV Fr. Polly; an Opera.

Woman's Love. Unknown. TreFP

Woman's Love Song. Somali Oral Tradition. ErotSp, tr. by Sam Hamill

Woman's Mourning Song, The. Bell Hooks. ISC

Woman's Prayer, A. Yehuda Karni. MHP, tr. by Ruth Finer Mintz

Woman's Question, A. Lena Lathrop. ITBLP; PoToHe

Woman's Rights. Rebekah Gumpert Hyneman. SWaP

Woman's Ritornelle. Theodor Storm. WoPoe, tr. by James Wright

Woman's Room in Autumn, A. Yüan Hung-tao. CoBLCP, tr. by Jonathan Chaves

Woman's Song. Judith Wright. PAI

Woman's Song, A. Colleen J. McElroy. BlSi

Woman's Song, about Men, A. Unknown. STP, tr. by Armand Schwerner and Paul-Emile Victor

Woman's white body is a song. Song of Songs, The. Heinrich Heine. EroLit, tr. by Louis Untermeyer

Woman's Wish, The. Matthew Prior. FaBoEE

Woman's Work. Julia Alvarez. RA

Woman's worth to the world can never be told. Oh Woman, Blessed Woman! Mrs. Henry Linden. CBWP-4

Woman sat on the mountain, A. Spring. Adelaida Gertsyk. ARWW, tr. by Catriona Kelly

Woman Seed Player. Roberta Hill Whiteman. HATNAP

Woman sits on her porch. Song. Earle Thompson. HATNAP

Woman / Skating. Margaret Atwood. FaBoWP

Woman / sleeps next to me on the earth, A. Night in the Forest. Galway Kinnell. TAP

Woman stood up in front of the table. Her sad hands, The. Miniature. Yannis Ritsos. VCWP, tr. by Edmund Keeley

Woman tells me, A. Story, A. Jane Hirshfield. BLT

Woman That I Knew, The. Vladimir Aleksandrovich Lugovskoy [or Lugovskoi]. TCRP, tr. by Gordon McVay

Woman that kissed him and—pinched his poke—was the lady that's known as Lou, The. (LL) Shooting of Dan McGrew, The. Robert W. Service. BRP; EBNV; PoRA; RB; UV

Woman the world is furnished by your eyes. Vincente Huidobro. BLPSL, tr. by Rene de Costa, Rigas Kappatos and Eleni Paidoussi Fr. Altazor.

Woman there was balancing her baby, A. Past All Understanding. Heather McHugh. ExTi

Woman Thing, The. Audre Lorde. BlSi (Hunters are back, The.) GT; NAAL-5

Woman! thoughtless, giddy creature. Declaimer, The. Henry Baker. NOEC

Woman to Child. Judith Wright. WPE

Woman to Her Lover, A. Christina Walsh. BrRo

Woman to Man. Ai. NoAM

Woman to Man. Judith Wright. BMAP; CBAP; NoP-4; WPE

Woman to man, they lie. In Bloemfontein. Alan Ross. BoLoP

Woman Tung. Wu Chia-chi. CoBLCP, tr. by Jonathan Chaves

Woman Waits for Me, A. Walt Whitman. ErotSp; HeIP-4; NOBA

Woman Walking. William Carlos Williams. ColAP

Woman wants monogamy. General Review of the Sex Situation. Dorothy Parker. NAAL-2v2

Woman was old, and ragged, and gray, The. Somebody's Mother. Unknown. ChAP

Woman Washing. Patricia Bishop. Prnts

Woman watches her husband rubbing his nose, The. Twenty Below. Robert Arthur Douglas Ford. NOBC

Woman went into the same resturant every Tuesday night, A. Sandwiches. David Donnell. NoAM

Woman Who Could Not Live With Her Faulty Heart, The. Margaret Atwood. LCAP-2

Woman who didn't love me, The. (LL) Valentino's Hair. Yvonne Sapia. PeVV; TRP

Woman Who Died in Line, The. Patricia Smith. SpirFl

Woman Who Drank Us Up, The. Lesley Quayle. Prnts

Woman Who Fell from the Sky, The. Joy Harjo. BodElec

Woman who has grown old, The. Crows, The. Louise Bogan. FaBoWP; NALW

Woman who kicked out the back window, The. Stephen Dobyns. BodElec Fr. Great Doubters of History, The.

Woman who looks like my mother sees a man who looks like / me, A. Four Resurrections in the Valley of the Ghosts. Yehuda Amichai [or Amikhai]. VCWP, tr. by Benjamin Harshav

Woman Who Loved to Cook, The. Erica Jong. TAP

Woman who loves, A. Lucille Clifton. NAAAL

Woman Who Married a Caterpillar, The. Unknown. WoPoe, tr. by Armand Schwerner

Woman Who Mistook her Father for an Irishman, The. Nicki Jackowska. Prnts

Woman Who Raised Dogs, The. Lisa D. Chavez. AmPoNex

Woman Who Weeps. Ellen Bryant Voigt. OPRER

Woman Who Wrote Too Much, The. Kay Ryan. ExTi

Woman wired in memories, A. Adrienne Rich. NoP-4

Woman with a burning flame, A. Smothered Fires. Georgia Douglas Johnson. BlSi

Woman with a Past, A. Wilfrid Scawen Blunt. Son Fr. Love Sonnets of Proteus, The.

Woman with broad, rough hands. Woman. Magda Portal. WPOW, tr. by Irene Vegas-Garcia and Kathleen Weaver

Woman with Flaxen Hair in Norfolk Heard, A. Robert Kelly. PmAP

Woman with Flower. Naomi Long Madgett. GT

Woman with no face walked into the light, A. Homage to Hieronymus Bosch. Thomas MacGreevy [or McGreevy]. BIrV; ModIr; SPE

Woman with no feet sits on the porch, The. Interruption of Flight. Lisa Williams. AmPoNex

Woman with the caught too. Plea for a Captive. W. S. Merwin. NoAM

Woman with Whom I Share My Husband, The. Okot P'Bitek. PoetW Fr. Song of Lawino.

Woman wore a floral apron around her neck, The. Floral Apron, The. Marilyn Chin. LoL

Woman working hard and wisely, A. Epigram. Kassia. WPOW, tr. by Patrick Diehl

Woman, you are afraid of the forest. Maria Wine. ItWoWo, tr. by Nadia Christensen

Woman, you'll never credit what. Shepherd's Tale, The. James Kirkup. OBCP

Womanhood, The. Gwendolyn Brooks.
Beverly Hills, Chicago. ESEAA; VGW
Children of the Poor, The. NAAAL; WPE
First Fight. Then Fiddle. InPK-6; NIL-7; NIP-4
"What shall I give my children? who are poor." BPo
"One wants a Teller in a time like this." WPE
Rites for Cousin Vit, The. BPo; HAP; NAAAL; NoP-4; WPE; WeW-3

"Stand off, daughter of the dusk," NALW

Womanhood, The. Elizabeth Garrett. MFPA

Womanisers. John Press. BoLoP

Womankind. Gerald Massey. NOBVV

Womans face with natures owne hand painted, A. William Shakespeare. *See* Woman's face with Nature's own hand painted, A

Womans Labour, an epistle, The. Mary Collier. PEW

Womb. Sonia Sekula. SurWo

Womb, The. Apirana Taylor. PeNZ

Women. Louise Bogan. APT-2; MoAmPo; NALW; NoAM; TwCP; VGW; WPE; WoPoe

Women. William Cartwright. BeJo

Women. ------ Heath. CTC; NoSic

Women. Frances Horovitz. LW

Women. Zakiyya Malallah. PoArWo, *tr. by* Wen Chin Ouyang

Women. Adrienne Rich. TRP

Women. May Swenson. BoWoP; NALW

Women. Trần Tế Xu'o'ng. EaWin; WoPoe, *tr. by* W. S. Merwin and Nguyen Ngoc Bich

Women. Alice Walker. WPOW; WWork *Fr.* In These Dissenting Times.

Women, The. Cyrus Cassells. UnSA

Women, The. Joseph Ceravolo. FTOS

Women all / cause rue. Palladas [*or* Pallades]. GrAn; WoPoe, *tr. by* Tony Harrison

Women all shout after me and mock, The. Palladas [*or* Pallades]. GrAn

Women and Roses. Robert Browning. NAEL-5v2; NAEL-6v2

Women Are Different. Marsha Prescod. LW

Women Are Not Gentlemen. Harley Matthews. NOBAu

Women Are Not Roses. Ana Castillo. IllVoic

Women are walking to town, The. Rainy Season, The. Linda Hogan. HATNAP; TRP

Women, as some men say, unconstant be. Epigram. George Wither. NOSC

Women as women, me had never charmed. *Unknown.* CAGL *Fr.* Don Leon.

Women at the Corners Stand, The. Louis Golding. TrJP

Women at the Crossroad / May Elegba Forever Guard the Right Doors. Opal Palmer Adisa. GT

Women at the Temple. Herodas. HePo, *tr. by* Barbara Hughes Fowler

Women Bathing at Bergen-Belsen. Enid Shomer. GotH

Women ben full of ragerie. Imitation of Chaucer. Pope. OBCoV

Women come to sing are singing, The. Song of Quavering, A. Jerome Rothenberg. FTOS

Women Don't Die on the Front Lines. Belkis Cuza Malé. TANSG, *tr. by* Pamela Carmell

Women Gather, The. Nikki Giovanni. ISC

Women / Have / A / Way / Of / Making. Beautiful Ladies. Mcavoy Layne. CDa

Women have loved before as I love now. Edna St. Vincent Millay. HeIP-4; NALW; NIL-7

Women have no. Women Are Not Roses. Ana Castillo. IllVoic

Women have no wilderness in them. Women. Louise Bogan. APT-2; MoAmPo; NALW; NoAM; TwCP; VGW; WPE; WoPoe

Women he liked, did shovel-bearded Bob. Bob's Lane. Edward Thomas. PoE

Women in Dutch Painting. Eunice De Souza. OMIP

Women know how to wait here. Lines for Marking Time. Roberta Hill Whiteman. BoWoP; CDW

Women Laughing. U. A. Fanthorpe. ItWoWo

Women Must Put off Their Rich Apparel. Joy Katz. NeAmPo

Women of Dan Dance with Swords in Their Hands to Mark the Time When They Were Warriors, The. Audre Lorde. NAAL-2v2; NALW; NoAM

Women of Jericho, The. Phyllis McGinley. ChIV-1

Women of my country, black and barefoot girls. Black Island. Charles Pressoir. NegPo, *tr. by* Ellen Conroy Kennedy

Women of My Land. Frankie Armstrong. BrRo

Women of Nigeria. Night in Nigeria. Ellease Southerland. GT

Women of Rubens, The. Wislawa Szymborska. WPOW, *tr. by* Celina Wieniewska

Women of Rubens, The. Wislawa Szymborska. PoSu; VCWP

Women of the Future. Mary Scott. ECWP

Women of Trachis. Sophocles.
  "Kupris bears trophies away." CTC
  "Torn between griefs, which grief shall I lament." APT-1; OBVE, *tr. by* Ezra Pound

Women of Yueh. Li Po.
  "Gathering lotuses by Yeh River." CrYelRi; ErotSp, *tr. by* Sam Hamill
  "Mirror Lake's waters are moon-clear." CrYelRi; ErotSp, *tr. by* Sam Hamill
  "Southern women have alabaster skin." CrYelRi; ErotSp, *tr. by* Sam Hamill
  "Woman from Ch'ang-kan, The." CrYelRi, *tr. by* Sam Hamill

Women reminded him of lilies and roses. Thoughts after Ruskin. Elma Mitchell. FaBoWP; NPeEn

Women resemble the clouds. Lightening, The. Gabriella Sica. CItWP, *tr. by* Cinzia Sartini Blum and Lara Trubowitz

Women's Degrees. Alfred Denis Godley. NOBL

Women's Jail, The. Miriam Waddington. NOBC

Women's Locker Room. Marilyn Nelson Waniek. LTA

Women's Marseillaise, The. F. E. M. Macaulay. BrRo

Women's Rondo. *Unknown.* NOBAu

Women's Room in Pennsylvania Station, The. Kate Daniels. GM

Women's Rule. Friedrich von Logau. GePo, *tr. by* George C. Schoolfield

Women's Songs. *Unknown.* PeNZ, *tr. by* Margaret Orbell

Women Sing, The. Luvuyo Mkangelwa. NAfrP

Women spend the afternoon squatting on the porch. Another Life. Taslima Nasrin. VCWP, *tr. by* Carolyne Wright

Women Transport Corps. *Unknown.* WPOW, *tr. by* Kai-yu Hsu

Women Watching Basketball. Marisa De Los Santos. NAPBL

Women were first to catch sight of him, The. N. P. van Wyk Louw. PeSAV, *tr. by* Guy Butler *Fr.* Raka.

Women were making clay bowls, The. What the Women Told Me. E. Ethelbert Miller. GT

Women, / What fools we are. Two Strange Worlds. Francesca Yetunde Pereira. PBA

Women Who Cook. Anita Skeen. GLP

Women who do not know me, The. Women Who Hate Me, The. Dorothy Allison. GLP

Women who fan, The. Another Century. David Keplinger. AmPoNex

Women Who Hate Me, The. Dorothy Allison. GLP

Women Who Love Angels. Judith Ortiz Cofer. TouFir

Women Who Love Elvis All Their Lives, The. Fleda Brown Jackson. AllShUp

Women who sing themselves to sleep. Light Sleep. Hazel Hall. APT-1

Women who Speak with Steak Knives. Susan Hampton. BMAP

Women who were mothers told us about it. Portrait of Auntie Blodwen. Elwyn Davies. AngWePo

Women, whoever wishes to know my lord. Gaspara Stampa. BoWoP

Women Wisdom. Larry Mitchell. GLP

Women with hats like the rear ends of pink ducks. To a Waterfowl. Donald Hall. BodElec; OBAL

Women! Women! Zuveliskes's Women Mourn over Kukutis. Marcelijus Martinaitis. TWW, *tr. by* Laima Sruogiens

Women, women, love of women. *Unknown.* MiEL

Women you are accustomed to, The. Lucille Clifton. ErotSp; GT

Won't It Be Fine? Robert Creeley. BAP-97

Won't last half an hour. (LL) *Unknown.* LB; OxNR; ReMoGo

Won't you become too tired, and quit smiling at me when I languish. For Laura. Mihály Vörösmarty. IQMS, *tr. by* Adam Makkai

Won't you celebrate with me. Lucille Clifton. BodElec

Won't You Dad? Kevin Gilbert. IBA

"Won't you look out of your window, Mrs. Gill?" Mocking Fairy, The. Walter De la Mare. MoBrPo

Wond'rous crowd then 'gan aloud, A. Michael Wigglesworth. NAAL-3 *Fr.* Day of Doom, The.

Wonder. Thomas Traherne. BASC; ESCV; GeHe; HAP; NAEL-5v1; NAEL-6v1; NAEL-7v1; NPeEn; NoP-4; OxBEV; PoE; TOF

Wonder, The. Thylias Moss. ChAP

Wonder Bar / Wishing Well. Neon Signs. Langston Hughes. APSN

Wonder Bread. Alice Fulton. ExTi

Wonder Clock, The. Katharine Pyle. OBCA

Wonder—is not precisely Knowing. Emily Dickinson. NCAP

Wonder not if I stay not here. To Master Davenant for Absence. Sir John Suckling. CaPo

Wonder of these! glory of other times! To the Right Honorable, the Lady Mary, Countess of Pembroke. Samuel Daniel. NAEL-6v1

Wonder Stings Me More than the Bee. Alice Fulton.
  Elvis from the Waist Up. AllShUp

Wonder stranger ne'r was known, A. Suffolk Miracle, The. *Unknown.* ESPB

Wonder-Teacher, The. Cynthia Ozick. TaR

Wonderful. Julian S. Cutler. PWR

Wonderful. Ania Walwicz. BMAP

Wonderful are thy works, as my soul overwhelmingly knoweth. Solomon ibn Gabirol. AWP, *tr. by* Israel Zangwill

Wonderful bears that walked my room all night. Bears. Adrienne Rich. PAI

Wonderful bird is the pelican, A. Limerick. Dixon Lanier Merritt. PeLi

Wonderful countenance and royal neck. Dante da Maiano. EaItPo, *tr. by* Dante Gabriel Rossetti

Wonderful grace of Jesus, Greater than all my sin. Haldor Lillenas. SacPr

Wonderful Guy, A. Richard Rodgers. ReLy

Wonderful! / Oh, it's wonderful. Louise. Richard A. Whiting. ReLy

Wonderful Things. Ron Padgett. PmAP

Wonderful, this road to Cold Mountain. Unknown. CoBCP

Wonderful / under cherry blossoms. Lucien Stryk. IllVoic Fr. Issa: A Suite of Haiku.

Wonderful was the long secret night you gave me, my lover. Terminus. Edith Wharton. APT-1

Wonderful Whale, The. Eve Merriam. YaYoPo

Wonderful workings of the world: wonderful, The. Cut the Grass. A. R. Ammons. HAP; TAP; WeW-3

Wondering, aglow / Fourfooted, tiptoe. (LL) Fallow Deer at the Lonely House, The. Thomas Hardy. AWP; OxBSP; RB; TTTS

Wondering which of all the saints. In a Calendar of Saints. Neil Curry. NLP

Wonders. Unknown. NPeEn
    "Andalusian merchant, that returns, The." FaBoCh

Wonders are many and none is more wonderful than man. Glengormley. Derek Mahon. CIP-2

Wonders of Nature. Unknown. OTCP

Wonders of the Peak, The. Charles Cotton.
    Chatsworth. OBGa

Wondrous, I grant, and caught from heaven the flame. Literature and Action. Goronva Camlan. AngWePo

"'Wondrous life!' cried Marvell at Appleton House." Round. Weldon Kees. CoAP

Wondrous light is filling the air, A. Spirit of the Age, The. Christopher Pearse Cranch. APN-1

Wondrous the Merge. James Richard Broughton. GLP

Wondrous this masonry wasted by Fate! Ruin, The. Unknown. AnOE, tr. by Charles W. Kennedy

Woo Not the World. Mu'tamid, King of Seville. AWP, tr. by Dulcie L. Smith

Wood. Thomas Hornsby Ferril. PoRA

Wood. Novella Nikolaevna Matveyeva [or Matveieva]. TCRP, tr. by Deming Brown

Wood and Fire. Khuong Viet. WoPoe, tr. by Huynh Sanh Thong

Wood Carols. Henrietta Cordelia Ray. CBWP-3

Wood-Chuck. Unknown. TLR

Wood-Cutter, The. Lupenga Mphande. HBAPE

Wood-doves are singing along the Perkiomen, The. Thinking of a Relation between the Images of Metaphors. Wallace Stevens. SAmP

Wood Floor Dreams. Lance Henson. VoR

Wood in Sound, A. Shinkichi Takahashi. ZenPo, tr. by Takashi Ikemoto and Lucien Stryk

Wood is bare: a river-mist is steeping, The. Elegy. Robert Bridges. EBVV

Wood is full of shining eyes, The. Magic Wood, The. Henry Treece. SPE

Wood merchant's parlour, The. Pierre McOrlan. MFP, tr. by Martin Sorrell

Wood of Error. Edmund Spenser. See Faerie Queene, The

Wood of my thoughts is on fire, The. Valerio Magrelli. ItPo, tr. by Gayle Ridinger

Wood of the madrone burns with a flame at once / lavender and mossy green, The. He Thanks His Woodpile. Lew Welch. BB

Wood pile. Marlene Mountain. HA

Wood-Pile, The. Robert Frost. APT-1; InPK-6; NAAL-2v2; NAAL-5; NoAM; SAmP; VGW
    (Out walking in the frozen swamp one gray day.) ColAP; NoP-4

Wood Road, The. Edna St. Vincent Millay. APT-1

Wood Song. Sara Teasdale. APT-1

Wood was rather old and dark, The. Little Boy Lost. Stevie Smith. FaBoTw

Wood with bushes broad there was, begrown with bigtree boughs, A. Virgil [or Vergil]. NoSic, tr. by Thomas Phaer \VP/[or Phayer] Fr. Aeneid [or Eneados, Aeneis], The.

Woodcarver of Stendal, The. Sheenagh Pugh. TCAWP

Woodchucks. Maxine W. Kumin. NIL-7; NIP-4

Woodcutter. Song of the Barren Orange Tree. Federico García Lorca. AmFaPo, tr. by W. S. Merwin

Woodcutter on His Way Home, A. Unknown. EaWin, tr. by W. S. Merwin and Nguyen Ngoc Bich

Woodcutter's Ax, A. P'i Jih-hsiu. SuSp, tr. by William H. Nienhauser

Woodcutter's Wife, The. William Rose Benét. AWP

Woodcutter wakes up: mountain moon is low. Tune: "Song of Clear River." Ma Chih-yüan. ChinPo, tr. by Yip Wai-lim

Woodcutting. Gleb Iakovlevich Gorbovsky [or Gorbovskii]. TCRP, tr. by Lubov Yakovleva

Wooden belly iron back. Riddle. Unknown. FaBoVe

Wooden box rattled, A. Moon Shatters on Alabama Avenue, The. Martín Espada. PueRic

Wooden bridge, gaunt willows. Written on the Night of the Twenty-ninth of the First Month. Yün Shou-p'ing. CoBLCP, tr. by Jonathan Chaves

Wooden Chamber, The. Anne Hébert. WPOW, tr. by Birgit Swenson

Wooden Handle, The. Gojko Djogo. AF, tr. by Michael March

Wooden Horse, The. Mary Mapes Dodge. SWaP

Wooden Horse Is Brought into Troy, The. Virgil [or Vergil]. OBVE, tr. by Gawin [or Gavin] Douglas Fr. Aeneid [or Eneados, Aeneis], The.

Wooden Horse then said, The. Jenny Mastoraki. BoWoP

Wooden Horses. Paul Verlaine. NAWM-7v2, tr. by Carlyle Ferren MacIntyre

Wooden Leg. James McIntyre. VerBaPo

Wooden saint, A. Railway Station, The. Jejuri Arun Kolatkar. EmeKit

Wooden spoon, A. Sorting Things Out. Wanda Barford. Prnts

Woodland Cross, The. Endre Ady. IQMS, tr. by Anton N. Nyerges

Woodland flowers lose their vernal color. Tune: "Joy of Encounter." Li Yü. ColAnChi, tr. by Jiaosheng Wang

Woodland God. Johannes Bobrowski. WoPoe, tr. by Rich Ives

Woodland heather is blue in springtime. In Memory of John Keats. Yury [or Iurii] Mikhailovich Kublanovsky [or Kublanovskii]. TCRusP

Woodland Mass, The. Dafydd [or David] ap Gwilym. OBWVE, tr. by Gwyn Williams

Woodland rivulet,—a Poet's death, A. (LL) After Dark Vapours Have Oppressed Our Plains. John Keats. CenSon; NPeEn

Woodland Seat, A. John Clare. CenSon

Woodlands clothe the slender shoots. Song of Summer. Unknown. NAWM-7v1, tr. by Jan Ziolkowski

Woodlark, The. Gerard Manley Hopkins. RB

Woodlot, The. Amy Clampitt. HCAP

Woodman, Spare That Tree. George Pope Morris. BRP; PWR; TCAPo
    (Oak, The.) APN-1

Woodmanship. George Gascoigne. See Gascoigne's Woodmanship

Woodnotes I ("For this present, hard.") Ralph Waldo Emerson. NOBA
    "In unplowed Maine he sought the lumberers' gang." TAP

Woodnotes II ("As sunbeams stream through liberal space.") Ralph Waldo Emerson. NOBA
    "Once again the pine-tree sung." APN-1

Woodpecker. Gerald Bullett. OWoS

Woodpecker, The. Issa. EH, tr. by Robert Hass

Woodpecker, The. Ni Tsan. CoBLCP, tr. by Jonathan Chaves

Woodpecker, The. Elizabeth Madox Roberts. OBCA; TLR

Woodpecker goes beating a little drum, The. Sleep. Charles Simic. CoAP

Woodpecker on. Lucien Stryk. IllVoic Fr. Issa: a Suite of Haiku.

Woodpecker pecked out a little round hole, The. Woodpecker, The. Elizabeth Madox Roberts. OBCA; TLR

Woods, The. Derek Mahon. NOIV; PBCIP

Woods, The. Sa'di Yusuf. MAP, tr. by Sargon Boulus and Naomi Shihab Nye

Woods Are Wild and Were Not Made for Man, The. Petrarch. WoPoe, tr. by Edwin Morgan

Woods Burial. John Peck. PoCoUp

Woods darken, grasses startled by wind. Lu Lun. SuSp Fr. Frontier Songs.

Woods decay, the woods decay and fall, The. Tithonus. Tennyson. CABP; HAP; NAEL-5v2; NAEL-6v2; NAWM-7v2; NOBE; NOBVV; NPeEn; NoP-4; OxBEV; PAI; PoE; SCGP

Woods of Arcady are dead, The. Song of the Happy Shepherd, The. W. B. Yeats. NoAM

Woods reached water and there was immense silence, The. House in Krasnogruda. Czeslaw Milosz. BodElec

Woods sleep bathed in shadow, The. Evensong. Paul Gerhardt. GePo, tr. by Ingrid Waløe-Engel

Woods, the mountain, silent, The. On a Cold Day I Climbed Tiger Hill with Professor Ho. At the Time, the Local Prefect Had Prohibited Pleasure Excursions and Feasts, But the Mountain Was Quiet and Tranquil, So We Stayed All Day. Mo Shih-lung. CoBLCP, tr. by Jonathan Chaves

Woods–oh, solemn are the boundless woods, The. Edith, a Tale of the Woods. Felicia Dorothea Hemans. RWP

Woodspurge, The. Dante Gabriel Rossetti. CABP; EBEV; GTBS-P; HAP; HeIP-4; NAEL-6v2; NOBE; NPeEn; NoP-4; OBEV; OxBEV; SCGP; TFi; UnPo Fr. House of Life, The.

Woodstock. Jan-Mitchell Sherrill. ReTh

Woodtown Manor. John Montague. PBCIP

Woodworker's Ballad. Herbert Edward Palmer. OBEV

Woody Guthrie Visited by Bob Dylan: Brooklyn State Hospital, New York, 1961. David Wojahn. PBCAP; SwNoth Fr. Mystery Train: a Sequence.

Wooed and Married and A' Alexander Ross. OxBS

Woof of the Sun, Ethereal Gauze. Henry David Thoreau. NCAP; TAP Fr. Week on the Concord and Merrimack Rivers, A.

Woof reversed the the fatal shuttles weave, A. Strikers in Hyde Park. Louise Imogen Guiney. APN-2

Wooing in a Dream. Nicholas Breton. See Report Song [in a Dream], A

Wooing of Etain, The. Unknown. BIrV, tr. by John Montague

Wooing Song. Giles Fletcher, the Younger. OBEV *Fr.* Christ's Victory and Triumph.

Wool-chafed and wet-shoed I went forth after. William Langland. NAEL-5v1; NAEL-6v1; NAEL-7v1 *Fr.* Vision of Piers Plowman, The.

Woolly Words. Robert N. Feinstein. NBLV

Woolworth's. Donald Hall. OBCoV

Woolworth's Poem, The. Quraysh Ali Lansana. IllVoic

Woosel cock so black of hue, The. William Shakespeare. CTC *Fr.* Midsummer Night's Dream, A.

Wooyeo Ball, The. *Unknown.* NOBAu

Wops came down to the port, The. City of Beggars, The. Alfred Hayes. FaBoWar

Word. Stephen Spender. PAI

Word, A. Overflow. Nada El-Hage. PoArWo, *tr. by* Nathalie El-Hani

Word, A. She Fans the Word. Sharif Elmusa. GraLe

Word, A. Alvaro Mutis. TCLAP, *tr. by* Sophie Cabot Black and Maria Negroni

Word, The. Margaret Avison. MoCV

Word, The. Jones Very. NCAP

Word a Hunt, A. William Drummond, of Hawthornden. NOBE

Word arrives from far P'ing-yin. Word from My Brothers. Tu Fu. CrYelRi, *tr. by* Sam Hamill

Word at last, The. Koko. ZenPo, *tr. by* Takashi Ikemoto and Lucien Stryk

Word before the Last about Loss, A. Linda Zisquit. DTA

Word-Bird knows that everybody in Britain is frightened to death of *words,* The. Word-Bird, The. Gavin Ewart. PeLV

Word bites like a fish, The. Word. Stephen Spender. PAI

Word by Night. Charles Brasch. PeNZ

Word eats a road, The. Nursery Rhyme in Eight Strophes. Rossana Ombres. CItWP, *tr. by* Cinzia Sartini Blum and Lara Trubowitz

Word Faith means when someone sees, The. Faith. Czeslaw Milosz. RaBo, *tr. by* Renata Gorcynski, Robert Hass and Robert Pinsky

Word for everybody, myself nobody, A. In Flood. Charles Hubert Sisson. HarvBoo

Word for Summer, A. George Seferis. AF

Word for the Hour, A. John Greenleaf Whittier. NCAP

Word from a Petitioner. John Pierpont.
     Ballot, The. APN-1

Word from My Brothers. Tu Fu. CrYelRi, *tr. by* Sam Hamill

Word from the Hills. Richard Moore.
     It Took TV to Civilize Our Village. Son
     Though the New Teacher Is a Trifle Odd. Son
     Unable, Father, Still, to Disavow. Son

Word from the Loki, A. Maurice Riordan. ModIr

Word Gifts for an Australian Critic. Merlinda Bobis. ReBoTo

Word goes round Repins, The. Absolutely Ordinary Rainbow, An. Les A. Murray. CBAP; HarvBoo

Word has come to May Margerie. Jellon Grame. *Unknown.* EBEV; ESPB; OxBB

Word has gane thro a' this land. Bonny Lass of Anglesey, The. *Unknown.* ESPB

Word I had no one left but God. (LL) Bereft. Robert Frost. APT-1; MoAmPo; OxBA; SoSe-8

Word I spoke in anger, The. Quarrel, The. Stanley Kunitz. APT-2; TaR

Word in Edgeways, A. Charles Tomlinson. CABP; NOBL

Word is an Egg, The. Niyi Osundare. NAfrP

Word is dead, A. Emily Dickinson. SAmP; TCAPo

Word is fast asleep, The. Poem. Labhshankar Thacker. OMIP, *tr. by* Sitanshu Yashashchandra

Word is imitative, The. Mummer. Jack Spicer. APSN

Word is the father of the saints, The. Macumba Word. Aimé Césaire. PFTM-1

Word! it cannot fail; it ever speaks, The. Word, The. Jones Very. NCAP

Word iz. Poem for Trish, A. Gavin Moses. InTrad

Word Knows How to Seduce the Flesh, The. Patrizia Valduga. CItWP, *tr. by* Cinzia Sartini Blum and Lara Trubowitz

Word Made Flesh, The. Walter James Turner. OBMV

Word made Flesh is seldom, A. Emily Dickinson. APN-2; ChIV-2; NAAL-2v1; NAAL-3; NALW; TCAPo

Word: Man, A. Washington Allston. APN-1

Word of a snail on the plate of a leaf, The? Couriers, The. Sylvia Plath. LCAP-2

Word of advice about matters and things, A. Written at the White Sulphur Springs. Francis Scott Key. OBAL

Word of Encouragement, A. J. R. Pope. NBLV; NOBL

Word of endless adoration. Christopher Smart. ChrPo *Fr.* Hymns and Spiritual Songs for the Fasts and Festivals of the Church of England.

Word of God, across the Ages. Ferdinand Q. Blanchard. AH

Word of God came unto me, The. In the Garden of the Lord. Helen Keller. SacPr

Word of Mouth. Ted Greenwald.
     "Open mouth open through." FTOS

Word of the Lord by night, The. Boston Hymn. Ralph Waldo Emerson. CBCWP; InvLi; TCAPo

Word of this prodigy might well have stirred. Ovid. NAWM-7v1, *tr. by* Allen Mandelbaum *Fr.* Metamorphoses.

Word outleaps the world, and light is all, The. (LL) Theodore Roethke. APT-2; MoAmPo; NOBA; NoAM

Word over all, beautiful as the sky. Reconciliation. Walt Whitman. APN-1; FaBoWar; HAP; MoAmPo; NAAL-2v1; NAAL-3; NAAL-5; NoP-4; OBWP; OxBA; OxBSP; PAI; WeW-3; WoPoe

Word *Plum,* The. Helen Chasin. NIL-7; NIP-4

Word's gane to the kitchen. Mary Hamilton. *Unknown.* ESPB; NePenScot; NoP-4; SCGP

Word's gone out, and now they spread the main, The. Daniel Defoe. OBWP *Fr.* Spanish Descent, The.

Word "Silk", The. Thomas McCarthy. CIP-2

Word they had spoken, The. *Ancient Sumerian Oral Tradition.* EroLit, *tr. by* Diane Wolkstein *Fr.* Courtship of Inanna and Dumuzi, The.

Word to come lies in a little night, A. Little Night, A. Douglas Oliver. Oth

Word to Husbands, A. Ogden Nash. OBCoV

Word to New England, A. William Bradford. SCAP

Word to the violent has never been sufficient, A. "Word to the Wise Is Enough, A." Raymond R. Patterson. NBV

Word to the West End, A. Thomas Ashe. EBVV

Word to the Wise, A. Octavio Armand. TCLAP, *tr. by* Carol Maier

"Word to the Wise Is Enough, A." Raymond R. Patterson. NBV

WORD was / is / will BE, The. Genesis 2. Etheridge Knight. BodElec

Word went forth, The. Saint Thomas Aquinas. MLL

Wordless, alone I ascend the West Tower. Tune: "Joy of Encounter." Li Yü. ColAnChi, *tr. by* Jiaosheng Wang

Words. Carlos A. Angeles. ReBoTo

Words. W. H. Auden. OxBSP; PeLV *Fr.* Shorts [1939–47].

Words. Samuel Alfred Beadle. TCAPo

Words. Mary Elizabeth Coleridge. ViWPN

Words. Mahmoud Darwish. VCWP, *tr. by* Rana Kabbani

Words. Catherine Fisher. TCAWP

Words. Barbara Guest. FTOS

Words. Nikolai Stepanovich Gumilyov [*or* Gumiliov *or* Gumilev]. TCRP, *tr. by* Simon Franklin

Words. David Huddle. CDa *Fr.* Tour of Duty.

Words. Sylvia Plath. CoAmPo; HCAP; NAAL-2v2; NALW; PoE; VCAP

Words. Adelaide Anne Procter. SacPr

Words. William Robert Rodgers. OxBSP; PNI

Words. Vern Rutsala. WeW-3

Words. "David Samuilovich Samoylov." [*or* Samoilov]. TCRP, *tr. by* Lubov Yakovleva

Words. Wislawa Szymborska. PoSu, *tr. by* Krystof Zarzecki

Words. Emilio Villa.
     "It is world of the back hune wone it is." ItPo
     "Lend me a battle of unavoidable suggestions." ItPo, *tr. by* Gayle Ridinger
     "Trees were moving." ItPo, *tr. by* Gayle Ridinger
     "Ugly season of putrifying buzzards, An." ItPo, *tr. by* Gayle Ridinger

Words, The. Lee Harwood. SPE

Words and Monsters. Vernon Scannell. OxBC

Words and Music. Samuel Beckett.
     Song: "Age is when to a man." BIrV; ModIr

Words and Thoughts. John Clark Pratt. CDa

Words and Truth. Yasin Taha Hafiz. MAP, *tr. by* Sharif Elmusa and Christopher Middleton

Words are a monstrous excrescence. Phrase-Book. Veronica Forrest-Thomson. HarvBoo

Words are but leaves to the tree of mind. Words. Samuel Alfred Beadle. TCAPo

Words are Doric, Doric too the man, The. Theocritus. GrAn

Words are for those with promises to keep. (LL) Their Lonely Betters. W. H. Auden. NAEL-5v2; NAEL-6v2; NoAM; OBGa

Words are hoops. Horses. Witter Bynner. APT-1

Words are lighter than the cloud-foam. Words. Adelaide Anne Procter. SacPr

Words are like leaves; and where they most abound. Pope. ECEV *Fr.* Essay on Criticism, An.

Words are very like: the name is new, The. (LL) George Meredith. NAEL-5v2; NAEL-6v2 *Fr.* Modern Love.

Words can't do. Four Sonnets about Food. Adrienne Su. NAPBL

Words can't ignite them nor. Song of Diamond Eyes, The. Franco Buffoni. ItPo, *tr. by* Gayle Ridinger

Words, dear companions! In my curtained cot. Words. Mary Elizabeth Coleridge. ViWPN

Words escape through gaps. Man Escaped, A. Lewis Warsh. BodElec

Words for Jazz Perhaps. Michael Longley. SeSe

Words for Love. Ted Berrigan. PmAP

Words for My Daughter. John Balaban. RaBo

Words for the Wind. Theodore Roethke. CoAP; NOBA

Words from Confinement. Cesare Pavese. AF, *tr. by* William Arrowsmith

Words from Hell. David Helwig. NOBC

Words from the Goblet of Wisdom. Yüan Mei. CoBLCP, *tr. by* Jonathan Chaves

Words grow shoots in the bin. Throwing Out My Father's Dictionary. Moniza Alvi. Prnts

Words have grown old inside men, The. Words Will Resurrect, The. Jorge de Lima. TTY, *tr. by* John Nist

Words "I love you", The. *Unknown.* ArkPo, *tr. by* Helen Craig McCullough

Words in the Shadow. Victor Hugo. WoPoe, *tr. by* Louis Simpson

Words in Time. Archibald MacLeish. PoRA

Words Is Not Enough. Bob Stewart. WaCA

Words, Korean mums, The. (LL) Korean Mums. James Schuyler. PmAP; VCAP

Words Like Freedom. Langston Hughes. BPo

Words no longer inflect. Iteration. Piera Oppezzo. CItWP, *tr. by* Cinzia Sartini Blum and Lara Trubowitz

Words no longer need. Expect Nothing Else from Me. Rita Joe. ReEnLa

Words of Agur, The. Bible, *O.T.* *Fr.* Proverbs.

Words of an Old Woman. Howard Phelps Putnam. APT-2

Words of Departure. Jorge de Lima. TCLAP, *tr. by* Luiz Fernández García

Words of Evening, The. Yves Bonnefoy. VCWP, *tr. by* Richard Pevear

Words of Oblivion and Peace. Gabriel Preil. FIT, *tr. by* Robert Friend

Words of our day, The. Same Side of the Canoe, The. Alda do Espírito Santo. HAWP, *tr. by* Allan Francovich and Kathleen Weaver

Words of Tayko-mol. William Oandasan. HATNAP

Words of the All-Wise, The. *Unknown.* WoPoe, *tr. by* Wystan Hugh Auden and Paul B. Taylor *Fr.* Elder Edda, The.

Words, one by one. Freedom. Wimal Dissanayake. ChAP

Words scored upon a bone. Meditation on a Bone. Alec Derwent Hope. NoAM; WoPoe

Words she cannot bear to sing. (LL) To the Tune: the Wine Spring: "Rain falls on fallen flowers." Li Hsun. CrYelRi; ErotSp, *tr. by* Sam Hamill

Words Spoken by Pasternak during a Bombing. Bella [*or* Izabella] Akhatovna Akhmadulina. BoWoP, *tr. by* Olga Carlisle and Jean Valentine

Words that come in smoke and go. Notes for Echo Lake 3. Michael Palmer. PmAP

Words to a Song. Ágnes Nemes Nagy. BoWoP, *tr. by* Bruce Berlind

Words to My Mother. Alfonsina Storni. TANSG, *tr. by* Mark McCaffrey

Words unto Adam, His Own Scriveyn. Geoffrey Chaucer. *See* Chaucer's Wordes unto Adam, his Owne Scriveyn

Words Wherein Stinging Bees Lurk. Judah Halevi. TrJP, *tr. by* Nina Davis Salaman

Words which are flowers become fruits which are deeds. (LL) Hymn among the Ruins. Octavio Paz. PFTM-1; TCLAP, *tr. by* William Carlos Williams

Words, Wide Night. Carol Ann Duffy. NePenScot

Words Will Resurrect, The. Jorge de Lima. TTY, *tr. by* John Nist

Words with no connection. (LL) Kenneth Rexroth. APSN; APT-2 *Fr.* Love Poems of Marichiko, The.

Words won't change again. Sad friend, you cannot change, The. (LL) North Haven. Elizabeth Bishop. HCAP; PAI

Words, Words, Words, and Nothing Doing. Heinrich Heine. WoPoe, *tr. by* W. D. Jackson

Words would not have come to write to you. Ruth Dallas. PeNZ *Fr.* Letter to a Chinese Poet.

Wordsworth. Charlotte L. Forten Grimke. TCAPo

Wordsworth I love, his books are like the fields. To Wordsworth. John Clare Son

Wordsworth on Lloyd George. Mary Visick. UV

Wordsworth to the contrary notwithstanding. In Magic Words. Merrill Moore. Son

Wordsworth Unvisited. Hartley Coleridge. *See* He Lived amidst th' Untrodden Ways

Wordsworth upon Helvellyn! Let the cloud. On a Portrait of Wordsworth by B. R. Haydon. Elizabeth Barrett Browning. HeIP-4

Wordsworths: William and Dorothy, The. Thomas Lux. BodElec

Work. Andrei Codrescu. PmAP; SPE

Work. Luciana Frezza. CItWP, *tr. by* Cinzia Sartini Blum and Lara Trubowitz

Work. Gyula Illyés. RaBo, *tr. by* William Jay Smith

(They stuck pigs in the throat.) PFTM-1

Work. D. H. Lawrence. OBMV

Work. Alexander Sergeyevich Pushkin. AWP, *tr. by* Babette Deutsch and Avrahm Yarmolinsky

Work. J. W. Thompson. PoToHe

Work. Henry Van Dyke. SacPr

Work, The. Armand Schwerner. BodElec

Work and Worry. Cheryl J. Fish. GotH

Work for Small Men. Sam Walter Foss. "Despise not any man that lives." PoToHe

Work-in-Progress. Lawrence Ferlinghetti. "And Pablo Neruda / that Chilean omnivore of poetry." BB

Work is heavy, The. I see. To the Shade of Po Chü-I. William Carlos Williams. HarvBoo

Work of pain on earth, The. (LL) On Parting. Edward Coote [*or* Coate] Pinkney. APN-1; TCAPo

Work of the woman, The. Work. Luciana Frezza. CItWP, *tr. by* Cinzia Sartini Blum and Lara Trubowitz

Work out a perfect will. (LL) By the Statue of King Charles [*or* I] at Charing Cross. Lionel Pigot Johnson. MoBrPo; NOBE; OBEV; OBMV; PeVV

Work out. Ten laps. Heartbeats. Melvin Dixon. ESEAA

Work Song. Mark Levine. AmPoNex

Work Song. Robyn Selman. TaR

Work-table, litter, books and standing lamp. Night Sweat. Robert Lowell. HarvBoo; NAAL-2v2; TAP; VGW

Work to Do toward Town. Gary Snyder. VGW

Work We Hate and Dreams We Love. Jimmy Santiago Baca. LoL

Work-week's end and there's enough. Secular. Natasha Trethewey. SpirFl

Work while you work. One Thing at a Time. M. A. Stodart. PoToHe

Work without Hope. Samuel Taylor Coleridge. CenSon; GSo; NAEL-5v2; NAEL-6v2; NOBE; OBEV; OxAEP-2; OxBSo; PAI; Son; WoPoe

Work? / I don't have to work. Necessity. Langston Hughes. APSN; NOBA; RaBo

Workaholic. Nadia Hazboun Reimer. PoArWo

Workbox, The. Thomas Hardy. InPK-6; NAEL-5v2; NAEL-6v2; UnPo

Workday. Linda Hogan. HATNAP

Worked its filthy way out like a tongue. (LL) Welcome to Hiroshima. Mary Jo Salter. DiPo; NIL-7; NIP-4; RA

Worker, The. Nikolai Stepanovich Gumilyov [*or* Gumiliov *or* Gumilev]. TCRP, *tr. by* Simon Franklin

Worker, The. Gerald Massey. EBVV

Worker Dies, A. Clementina Suárez. TANSG, *tr. by* Janet N. Gold

Worker Who, the Human Who, the Abo Who, The. Lionel Fogarty. IBA

Workers. David Hernandez. IllVoic

Workers earn it. Money. Richard Armour. NBLV

Working. Maxine Scates. PBCAP

Working All Night in Springtime. Tu Fu. CarOv, *tr. by* Carolyn Kizer *Fr.* Adviser to the Court.

Working and Waiting. Adah Isaacs Menken. CBWP-1

Working Class. Bertram J. Warr. NOBC

Working class clouds are living together. Clouds. Stanley Moss. BodElec

Working Construction. Eric Chock. OpBo

Working for British Telecom. Ben Scammell. NLP

Working for school clothes. My Room at Aunt Eura's, 1937. Wilma Elizabeth McDaniel. GeoHom

Working for the Government. Wang An-shih. CrYelRi, *tr. by* Sam Hamill

Working Girl. David Marlatt. AmPoNex

Working in Darkness. Thomas McGrath. BodElec

Working Man, The. Ellen Johnston. VWP

Working my way through life's karma. Year *Chi-wei* (Fifteen Fifty Nine), New Year's Day, The. Wen Cheng-ming. CoBLCP, *tr. by* Jonathan Chaves

Working on the Railway. *Unknown.* APN-2

Working Party, A. Siegfried Sassoon. AF; PeFWW

"Working so many hours," said Liddell. (LL) Liddell and Scott. Thomas Hardy. OBCoV; OxBoLi; PeLV

Working Song. Buluguru. CBAP, *tr. by* E. A. Worms

Working week comes to an end, The. Vladimir Uflyand [*or* Ufliand]. TCRusP, *tr. by* Daniel Weissbort

Working with Mother. Myra Cohn Livingston. TLR

Working with one eye closed or heads buried. War Photographers, The. Frank Ormsby. PNI

Working with Tools. A. R. Ammons. TRP

"Workman, what will you make on the bench today?" Carpenter. George Mackay Brown. OxBC

Workmen Photographed inside the Reactor. David Wojahn. IllVoic

Workmen shall not always work; who builds, The. Laborers, The. Jones Very. SacPr

Works and Days. Hesiod.

"Beware of the month Lenaion, bad days." WoPoe, tr. by Richmond Lattimore

Works of Art. Elizabeth Jennings. PeECV

Works of God, The. Moses Ibn Ezra. TrJP, tr. by Solomon Solis-Cohen

Works, the days, uh, The. But Not That One. John Ashbery. LCAP-2

Works without care, defrauds people, is a thief, The. Unknown. STP; WoPoe, tr. by Elvira Abascal and Denise Levertov

World, The. William Bronk. APSN

World, The. Gillian Conoley. BodElec

World, The. Robert Creeley. NoP-4; PmAP; VCAP

World, The. Frederick William Faber. PWR

World, The. George Herbert. GeHe; NOSC

World, The. Kathleen Jessie Raine. OxBTC

World, The. William Brighty Rands. NOxBChV

World, The. Donald Revell. BodElec

World, The. Christina Georgina Rossetti. BoWoP; NALW; PEW; ViWPN

Eternity, The. Henry Vaughan. See World, The (1)

World, The. Ella Wheeler Wilcox. PWR

World a hunting is, The. Word a Hunt, A. William Drummond, of Hawthornden. NOBE

World above Suffering, A. Albert Goldbarth. TaR

World and I, The. Laura Riding Jackson. APT-2; ColAP; HarvBoo

World and the Child, The. James Merrill. MakPoe

World as Meditation, The. Wallace Stevens. HeIP-4; LCAP-2

World begins at a kitchen table, The. No matter what, we must eat to live. Perhaps the World Ends Here. Joy Harjo. MakPoe; ReEnLa

World below the Brine, The. Walt Whitman. APN-1; NoP-4

World broods with warm breast and with ah! Bright wings. (LL) God's Grandeur. Gerard Manley Hopkins. AWP; AmFaPo; BBASP; CABP; ChAP; ClHu; EBVV; EnlH; GSo; HAP; ITBLP; InPK-6; MoBrPo; NAEL-5v2; NAEL-6v2; NIL-7; NIP-4; NOBE; NOBVV; NoAM; OxBEV; OxBSo; PeVV; PoE; PoPoPo; RaBo; SCGP; SacPr; SoSe-8; Son; TFi; TrCP; UnPo; WeW-3

World cheats those who cannot read, The. Mad Poem Addressed to My Nephews and Nieces, A. Po Chü-i. ChiP, tr. by Arthur Waley

World Contracted to a Recognizable Image, The. William Carlos Williams. APT-1

World currently expended figuratively. Ready-Made World. Piera Oppezzo. CItWP, tr. by Cinzia Sartini Blum and Lara Trubowitz

World dances with hate, The. Lamenting the Inevitable. Alicia Ostriker. UnSA

World, Do Not Ask Those Snatched from Death. Nelly Sachs. BBASP, tr. by Matthew Mead and Ruth Mead

World does not close in your eyes; there, The. Braille for Left Hand. Octavio Armand. TCLAP, tr. by Carol Maier

World Doesn't End, The. Charles Simic.

"We were so poor I had to take the place of the." VCAP

World exists again, The. The roses drop their petals. Echoes. Timothy Liu. ReTh

World—feels Dusty, The. Flags Vex a Dying Face. Emily Dickinson. MoAmPo

World for some years, The. Why Must the Show Go On? Noël Coward. ReLy

World goes none the lamer, The. A. E. Housman. PeVV

World / has become divided, The. Charles Olson. APSN; ColAP Fr. Maximus Poems, The.

World has held great Heroes, The. Kenneth Grahame. NOBL; NOxBChV Fr. Wind in the Willows, The.

World I did not wish to enter, A. Necessitarian's Epitaph, A. Thomas Hardy. FaBoEE

World in gloom and splendour passes by, The. To a Millionaire. Archibald Lampman. NOBC

World in Yellow, A. Marcel Duchamp. PFTM-1

World is, The. Denise Levertov. See World is / not with us enough, The

World is a beautiful place, The. 25. Lawrence Ferlinghetti. CLPP

World is a beautiful place, The. Lawrence Ferlinghetti. HHAm Fr. World is a beautiful place, The.

World is a garden, The. A light bathes the world. Grace. Adelia Prado. TCLAP, tr. by Marcia Kirinus

World Is a Wedding, The. Adele Ne Jame. PoArWo

World is all orange-round, The. Walking Road, The. Richard Hughes. OBMV

World is Bitter, The. Alfonsina Storni. TANSG, tr. by Mark McCaffrey

World is but a sorry scene, The. Christopher Smart. ChIV-2 Fr. Hymns and Spiritual Songs for the Fasts and Festivals of the Church of England.

World is charged with the grandeur of God, The. God's Grandeur. Gerard Manley Hopkins. AWP; AmFaPo; BBASP; CABP; ChAP; ClHu; EBVV; EnlH; GSo; HAP; ITBLP; InPK-6; MoBrPo; NAEL-5v2; NAEL-6v2; NIL-

7; NIP-4; NOBE; NOBVV; NoAM; NoP-4; OxBEV; OxBSo; PeVV; PoE; PoPoPo; RaBo; SCGP; SacPr; SoSe-8; Son; TFi; TrCP; UnPo; WeW-3

World is come upon me, I used to keep it a long way off, The. Deserter, The. Stevie Smith. FaBoWP

World is complete, The. Complete Thought I - XXV. Barrett Watten. PFTM-2

World is dull, the world is blind, The. Welt ist dumm, die Welt ist blind, Die. Heinrich Heine. AWP, tr. by James Thomson

World is everything, The. Ann Sansom. NeBl

World is everything that is the case, The. Tractatus. Derek Mahon. ModIr; OxBSP

World Is Full of Beauty, The. Matilda Caroline Edwards. PWR

World is full of cats, The. For My Sister Shura. Sergey [or Sergei] Aleksandrovich Yesenin [or Essenin]. TCRusP, tr. by Nigel Stott

World is full of gladness, The. Lemon Pie. Edgar Albert Guest. OBAL

World is full of mostly invisible things, The. To David, about His Education. Howard Nemerov. HCAP

World Is Full of Remarkable Things, The. LeRoi Jones. SSLK

World is full of those who love to be officials, The. Drinking Wine. Ch'ien Ch'ien-i [or Ch'ien Ch'ien-yi]. SuSp, tr. by Irving Y. Lo

World is large and wide and long, The. Song of an Old Gray Wolf. Unknown. APN-2, tr. by Alfred Kroeber

World is lyrical, The. Dancing on the Ceiling. Richard Rodgers. ReLy

World is made of his voice, The. (LL) Armand Schwerner. PFTM-2; WoPoe Fr. Tablets, The.

World is my dream, says the wise child, ever so wise, The. Karl Shapiro. BodElec Fr. Bourgeois Poet, The.

World is no more than the Beloved's single face, The. Mirza Asadullah Khan Ghalib. EnlH

World Is Not a Pleasant Place to Be, The. Nikki Giovanni. InvLad

World is / not with us enough, The. O Taste and See. Denise Levertov. ChIV-1; TAP

World is only air / shining, granular, transparent things, The. World is Only Air, The. Jan Polkowski. AF, tr. by Michael March

World is right, The. Fit As a Fiddle. Arthur Freed. ReLy

World is Rome; Carnuntum, on the Danube, The. Marcus Antoninus Cui Cognomen Erat Aurelius. Burns Singer. OxBS

World is so full of a number of things, The. Happy Thought. Robert Louis Stevenson. BRP; PWR; Spl

World Is Too Much With Us, The. William Wordsworth. AWP; BRP; CABP; CenSon; ClHu; FHYEP; GSo; GTBS-P; HAP; HeIP-4; InPK-6; NAEL-5v2; NAWM-7v2; NOBE; NOBRP; NoP-4; OBEV; PWR; PoE; PoPoPo; PoRA; RaBo; SCGP; SacPr; SoSe-8; Son; TFi; TRP; WeW-3

World is Turned Upside Down, The. Unknown. NOSC

World is wise, for the world is old, The. World, The. Frederick William Faber. PWR

World Is with Me, The. Thomas Hood. Son

World is young today, The. Song, A. Digby Mackworth Dolben. NOBVV

World, its hopes, and fears, have passed away, The. To the Memory of John Keats. John Clare. CenSon

World laid low, and the wind blew like a dust, The. Epigram. Unknown. FaBoWar; NOIV, tr. by Thomas Kinsella

World map, The. Home. Pauline Kaldas. PoArWo

World might end in crispness, The. Prediction. Michael Lieberman. BloBone

World-Mother's police chief, The. Rāmprasād Sen. SinGod, tr. by Rachel Fell McDermott

World Needs, The. Unknown. PoToHe

World Not Our Rest, The. Maria Frances Cecelia Cowper. ECWP

World now is a single family, The. (LL) Fan from Korea, A. Chu Yün-ming. CoBLCP; ColAnChi, tr. by Jonathan Chaves

World of books amid a world of green, A. Library in a Garden, A. Richard Le Gallienne. OBGa

World of dew, A. Issa. SoOfWa, tr. by Sam Hamill

World of dew, The. On the Death of the Poet's Daughter Sato. Issa. WoPoe, tr. by Conrad Totman

World of dew, The. Issa. EH, tr. by Robert Hass

World of Dreams, The. Philip Salom. NOBAu

World of Expectations, The. Albert Goldbarth. HCAP

World of Fancy. Sami Mahdi. MAP, tr. by May Jayyusi

World of money, promise and disease, A. (LL) Man from Washington, The. James Welch. CDW; HATNAP; NoAM; PoPoPo; RaBo

World of Simon Raven, The. Peter Porter. PeLV

World of trials, A. Issa. SoOfWa, tr. by Sam Hamill

World of worlds as pendents in each ear, A. (LL) Of Many Worlds in This World. Margaret Lucas Cavendish, Duchess of Newcastle. NOSC; NPeEn

World on Sunday. James McAuley. BMAP

World Outside, The. Denise Levertov. CoAmPo; TRP

World Poetry Circuit. Alfred A. Yuson. ReBoTo

World pursues the very track, The. Chaunts of the Brazen Head, The. Winthrop Mackworth Praed. NOBRP

World's a bubble, and the life of man, The. Life of Man, The. Francis Bacon. NoSic

World's a floor, whose swelling heaps retain, The. Deuteronomy 30.19. Francis Quarles. ChIV-1

World's a Floore, whose swelling heapes retaine, The. Francis Quarles. ESCV Fr. Emblems.

World's a garden; pleasures are the flowers, The. Garden, The. Joshua Sylvester. OBGa

World's a popular disease, that reigns, The. Luke 6.25. Francis Quarles. ChIV-2

World's a shoreless ocean, The. Rāmprasād Sen. SinGod, tr. by Rachel Fell McDermott

World's a stage, The. The trifling entrance fee. World's a Stage, The. Joseph Hilaire Pierre Belloc. OBCoV; OxBTC

World's a stranger's room, we meet to part, The. You Gave Me Hyacinths First a Year Ago. Dorothy Hewett. BMAP

World's a theater, the earth a stage, The. Thomas Heywood. NOSC Fr. Apology for Actors, An.

World's a well strung fidle, mans tongue the quill, The. Nathaniel Ward. SCAP

World's an inn; and I her guest, The. On the World. Francis Quarles. HAP

World's at an end, and we come, we come, The. (LL) Sir William Davenant [or D'Avenant]. FaBoCh; HAP; SCGP Fr. Law against Lovers, The.

World's birds gathered for their conference, The. Farid-uddin Attar. WoPoe, tr. by Afkham Darbandi and Dick Davis Fr. Conference of the Birds, The.

World's bright comforter, whose beamsome light, The. Barnabe Barnes. NOCV Fr. Divine Century of Spiritual Sonnets, A.

World's deceitful, and man's life at best, The. On Mortality. Henry Colman. ChIV-1

World's First Face, The. W. S. Rendra. WoPoe, tr. by Burton Raffel

World's gone forward to its latest fair, The. Moor, The. Ralph Hodgson. MoBrPo

World's Great Age, The. Shelley. HeIP-4; NAEL-5v2; NoP-4; PoE Fr. Hellas.

World's great age begins anew, The. Shelley. HeIP-4; NAEL-5v2; NoP-4; PoE Fr. Hellas.

World's Illusion, The. Moses Ibn Ezra. TrJP, tr. by Solomon Solis-Cohen

World's Last Unnamed Poem, The. A. K. Redwing. VoR

World's light shines; shine as it will, The. But Men Loved Darkness[e] Rather Than [or Then] Light. Richard Crashaw. ChIV-2

World's love runs thin, The. To the Tune "The Phoenix Hairpin." T'ang Wan. WPOW

World's Oldest Comedian Is Dead. Iain Sinclair. Oth Fr. Ebbing of Kraft, The.

World's One Hope, The. Bertolt Brecht. AF

World's pottage, the rat's star, The. (LL) With Mercy for the Greedy. Anne Sexton. HCAP; NIL-7; TOF; VCAP

World's too beautiful for human blood, The. Wound seen from afar. Philippe Jaccottet. MFP, tr. by Martin Sorrell

World's Wanderers, The. Shelley. TTTS; TreFP

World's wonder, I liven wenches, The. Cynewulf. WoPoe, tr. by Lewis Turco Fr. Riddles (Exeter Book).

World's wrong, mother, The. Wyndmere, Windemere. Carol Muske. PBCAP

World-Secret. Hugo von Hofmannsthal. TrJP, tr. by Charles Wharton Stork

World should listen then—as I am listening now, The. (LL) To a Skylark. Shelley. BRP; FHYEP; GTBS-P; HAP; NAEL-5v2; NAEL-6v2; NOBRP; NoP-4; OBEV; OWoS; OxAEP-2; SCGP; TFi

World. Some monuments move. (LL) Ancient Monuments. John Ormond. AngWePo; OBWVE

World-Soul, The. Ralph Waldo Emerson. APN-1; NCAP

World State, The. Gilbert Keith Chesterton. SacPr

World stops in the middle of its course, The. Quiet Spaces. Vincente Huidobro. TCLAP, tr. by Stephen Fredman

World, that all contains, is ever moving, The. Fulke Greville, 1st Baron Brooke. NoSic Fr. Caelica.

World that Lightning Makes, The. Samuel Hazo. GraLe

World, The (1). Henry Vaughan. AWP; ChIV-2; EBEV; ESCV; FSCP; HAP; NAEL-5v1; NAEL-6v1; NAEL-7v1; NOBE; NOCV; NOSC; NPeEn; OxAEP-1; OxBEV; PBRV; PeECV; SCGP; SacPr; TFi; TrCP
(Eternity, The.) OBEV

World, the Devil, and Tom Paine, The. Unknown. AH

World to be stuttered after. Paul Celan. PoetW, tr. by John Felstiner

World to Come, A. Bernard Dadié. NegPo, tr. by Ellen Conroy Kennedy

World turns mild; democracy, they say, The. Tempora Mutantur. James Russell Lowell. HAP

World under the sky, The. Gone, A. Larry Eigner. NeAP

World War II. Jeni Couzyn. PeSAV

World War II. Edward Field. GLP

World War II. Langston Hughes. APT-2; HCAP; PoPoPo

World was everything that was the case, The? James Merrill. HCAP Fr. Mirabell: Books of Number.

World was first a private park, The. Fisherman, The. Jay Macpherson. NOBC

World was full of peaceful sounds, The. Last Letter, The. Bertus Aafjes. TuT, tr. by Tony Curtis

World was quiet then, The. My Childhood in Another Part of the World. Rafael Campo. NeAmPo

World was very large, The. Then. Aubade. Louise Glück. BodElec

World We Make, The. Alfred Grant Walton. PoToHe

World Well Lost 4, The. Marc André Raffalovich. CAGL

World Well Lost 18, The. Marc André Raffalovich. CAGL

World Where News Travelled Slowly, A. Lavinia Greenlaw. MFPA

World with all of its thought and action, The. God's Electric Power. Mrs. Henry Linden. CBWP-4

World Without End. Kevin Stein. SwNoth

'World Without Objects Is a Sensible Emptiness,' A." Richard Wilbur. CoAmPo; MoAmPo; NAAL-2v2; NOBA; NoAM

World Without Peculiarity. Wallace Stevens. HCAP

World world world world / and the face grave. Enueg II. Samuel Beckett. NoAM

World, / world you are wonderful. Round Song, A. Rhyll McMaster. CBAP

Worldes bliss ne last no throwe. Unknown. MiEL

Worldes blisse, have good day! Unknown. MiEL

Worldling. Elizabeth Spires. ExTi

Worldly matters again draw my body;. To Li Chien. Po Chü-i. ChiP, tr. by Arthur Waley

Worldly sky / From now on. Issa. ZenPo, tr. by Takashi Ikemoto and Lucien Stryk

Worldly Wealth. Rowland Watkyns. FaBoEE

Worldly wisdom of the foolish man, The. Francis Quarles. ESCV Fr. Emblems.

Worldman, A. Knocking Donkey Fleas off a Poet from the Southside of Chi. Haki R. Madhubuti. SeSe

Worlds are breaking in my head, The. Yves Tanguy. David Gascoyne. NoP-4; SPE

Worlds are drunk and drinking, The. Quaternary. Gottfried Benn. WoPoe, tr. by Teresa Iverson

Worlds are reconciled, The. (LL) Christmas Hymn, A. Richard Wilbur. ChIV-2; ChrPo; OBCP; TrCP

Worlds light shines; shine as it will, The. Bible, N.T.. ChIV-2, tr. by Richard Crashaw Fr. St. John.

Worlds on worlds are rolling ever. Shelley. HeIP-4; NAEL-6v2 Fr. Hellas.

World's Way, The. William Shakespeare. See Sonnets

Worm artist, The. Earth Worm, The. Denise Levertov. NOBA

Worm Either Way. D. H. Lawrence. NoAM

Worm Fed on the Heart of Corinth, A. Isaac Rosenberg. NPeEn; PeFWW; PoWW

Worm tranquil and slobbering, A. Epigram for a Worm. Daria Menicanti. CItWP, tr. by Cinzia Sartini Blum and Lara Trubowitz

Worm unto his love: lo, here's fresh store, The. Coffin-Worm, The. Ruth Pitter. MoBrPo

Worms at Heaven's Gate, The. Wallace Stevens. NoAM

Wormwood. Thomas Kinsella. CIP-2; PBCIP

Wormwood has enchanted me completely. Hayim Lenski. FIT, tr. by Robert Friend

Worn and torn by many fingers. Family Album, A. Alter Brody. TaR

Worn like a hand-me-down. Growing into my name. Harriet Jacobs. SpirFl

Worn Out. Paul Laurence Dunbar. NAAAL

"Worn out of virtue, as the time of year," David and Bathsheba in the Public Garden. Robert Lowell. ChIV-1

Worn-out pop song, a tattered blues, A. Worn-Out Pop Song, A. Jotie T'Hooft. TuT, tr. by Pat Boran

Worn out slightly by carelessness. (LL) Far from kingdoms. Patrizia Cavalli. NeIt; VCWP, tr. by Judith Baumel

Worn-out voice of the clock breaks on the hour, The. Prize for Good Conduct. Kenneth Allott. OBWP

Worn out were the buildings, I. Death of a Farmyard. Geoffrey Grigson. EmeKit

Worn with life's care, love yet was love. (LL) Marriage Ring, The. George Crabbe. BoLoP; EnLoPo; OBEV; OxBEV

Worried. Nguyen Binh Khiem. WoPoe, tr. by Nguyen Ngoc Bich

Worries. Unknown. PoToHe

Worry. Aaron Anstett. AmPoNex

Worry. Unknown. PoToHe

Worry about Money. Kathleen Jessie Raine. FaBoTw

Worry—is like a distant hill. Worry. *Unknown.* PoToHe

Worrying the carcase of an old song. (LL) Welsh Landscape. Ronald Stuart Thomas. FaBoMo; NoP-4; TCAWP

Worschippe ye that loveris bene this May. Spring Song of the Birds. James I, King of Scotland. OBEV

Worse days are coming. Time Allotted, The. Ingeborg Bachmann. PFTM-2, *tr. by* Jerome Rothenberg

Worsening Situation. John Ashbery. NOBA

Worship. Ralph Waldo Emerson. APN-1

Worship. John Greenleaf Whittier. ChIV-2; NOCV

Worshipping at the Great Shrine at Ise. Basho. OHMPJ

Worst Fate Bookes have, when they are once read, The. Common Fate of Books, The. Margaret Lucas Cavendish, Duchess of Newcastle. PBRV

Worst Fear, The. George MacBeth [*or* Macbeth]. OxBSo

Worst of it, The. Craig Reynolds. CAGL

Worst side of it all, The. White Roses. John Ashbery. TAP

Worst was this,—my love was my decay, The. (LL) William Shakespeare. CAGL; OxAEP-1 *Fr.* Sonnets.

Worsted Heather. Jody Gladding. YaYoPo

Worth Dying For. Christina Georgina Rossetti. LW

Worth keeping your foot in the door. Respectable House. Anne Stevenson. NALW

Worthless as was her itinerary to fame. Amelia Rosselli. ItPo, *tr. by* Gayle Ridinger

Worthless Heart, The. Immanuel di Roma. TrJP

Worthless man is a leaking wine-jar, A. Lucianus [*or* Lucian]. GrAn

Worthwhile. Ella Wheeler Wilcox. PoToHe

Worthy art Thou, O Lord of praise! Deliverance from a Fit of Fainting. Anne Bradstreet. TAP

Worthy kyng, quhen he has seyn, The. John Barbour. OxBS *Fr.* Bruce, The.

Worthy object: our lord's Feet, A. (LL) Saint Mary Magdalene or The Weeper. Richard Crashaw. BASC; ChIV-2; GeHe; MeLP

Worthy of a lover have I loved. White Peacock, The. Alice Notley. FTOS

Wotton, my little Bere dwells on a hill. Ad Henricum Wottonem. Thomas Bastard. FaBoEE

Wou' ye hear of William Wallace. Gude Wallace. *Unknown.* ESPB

Would a circling surface vulture. Mahadevi. BoWoP

Would-be Critic, The. Mrs. Henry Linden. CBWP-4

Would be discover'd by the Cry. (LL) Morning Quatrains, The. Charles Cotton. NOSC; PeECV

Would but indulgent Fortune send. Wish, The. Mary Lee, Lady Chudleigh. LW

Would congregate endlessly. (LL) Water. Philip Larkin. EmeKit; FaBoMo; OxBSP; PeECV

Would drop Him—Bone by Bone. (LL) Emily Dickinson. APN-2; BoWoP; NAAL-2v1; NCAP; NOBA

Would equal, if alive. (LL) Braly Street. Gary Soto. GeoHom; UnSA

Would god that deth with cruell darte. Ellin Thorne Songe. Ellin Thorne. EMWP

Would I could cast a sail on the water. Collarbone [*or* Collar-Bone] of a Hare, The. W. B. Yeats. OxAEP-2; OxBTC; RB

Would I have marched with you Martin. Time for Guns, A. Darryl Holmes. InTrad

Would I Might Go Far over Sea. Marie de France. AWP; PoRA, *tr. by* Arthur O'Shaughnessy

Would I might lie like this, without the pain. In Hospital. James Elroy Flecker. OxBTC

Would I were a king of children. Child-King, The. Morris Wintchevsky. TrJP, *tr. by* Alter Brody

Would I were air that thou with heat opprest. Thomas Stanley. FaBoEE

Would it had been the man of our wish! Thomas Hardy. InPK-6 *Fr.* Satires of Circumstance in Fifteen Glimpses.

Would it please you if I strung my tears. Race Question, The. Naomi Long Madgett. BPo; LTA

Would one think that my Chloe ne'er thought it was she. (LL) I Said to My Heart. Charles Mordaunt, Earl of Peterborough. NOEC; OxBEV

Would [*or* Wo'd] ye[e] have fresh cheese and cream? Fresh Cheese and Cream. Robert Herrick. BASC

Would pause with his needle in the air. (LL) Illustrious Ancestors. Denise Levertov. NAAL-2v2; NOBA; PmAP; TaR; VGW

Would plunge them 'neath the wheel of tide. (LL) Ashtabula Disaster, The. Julia A. Moore. OBAL; VerBaPo

Would pulse with all the life there was within. (LL) Battle, The. Louis Simpson. OBWP; PoWW

Would she have been a person. My Mother, If She Had Won Free Dance Lessons. Cornelius Eady. ISC

Would'st thou then have *me* tempt the comic scene. To Miss C—on Being Desired to Attempt Writing a Comedy. Charlotte Smith. RWP

Would that I streamed like water. Like Water down a Slope. Zalman Schneour. TrJP, *tr. by* Harry H. Fein

Would that the structure brave, the manifold music I build. Abt Vogler. Robert Browning. FHYEP; NAEL-5v2; NAEL-6v2; TOF

Would that there had never been swift ships! Callimachus. HePo *Fr.* Epigrams.

Would 'twere underground! (LL) Bereft. Thomas Hardy. BoLoP; NoAM

Would wake and weary and fall asleep. (LL) From the Antique. Christina Georgina Rossetti. OxBEV; PEW

Would with Thee live, and for thee die. (LL) Dialogue betwixt God and the Soul, A. Sir Henry Wotton. MeLP; PeECV; SacPr

Would write a letter with / my scissors mouth. Young Woman's Neo-Aramaic Jewish Persian Blues. Jerome Rothenberg. BoWoP

Would ye, with faultless judgement, learn to plan. Richard Jago. OBGa *Fr.* Edge-Hill.

Would you a favourite novel make. Receipt for Writing a Novel, A. Mary Alcock. ECWP

Would you adopt a strong logical attitude. Synchoresis. Godfrey Turner. OBCoV

Would you be a man in fashion? *Unknown.* NOSC

Would you be an angel. Something of a Departure. Paul Muldoon. PBCIP

Would You Believe It? Bart Howard. ReLy

Would you believe, when you this Monsieur see. On English Monsieur. Ben Jonson. AEP; NBLV; NoP-4

Would you but soon return, and speak it here. (LL) Letter to Daphnis, A. Anne Finch, Countess of Winchilsea. EMWP; EnLoPo; LW; MakPoe; NALW; PEW

Would you care for a smoke or a sherry? Mopev. UV

Would you care to hear the strangest story. Polka Dots and Moonbeams. Johnny Burke. ReLy

Would you come back if I said the earth. Nadia Tuéni. BoWoP

Would you grasp the fruits already? Final Knowledge. Anton Wildgans. AuPH, *tr. by* Lowell A. Bangerter

Would You Have a Young Virgin? John Gay. EnLoPo; NAEL-5v1; NAEL-6v1 *Fr.* Begger's Opera.

Would you have called me a nobody? (LL) Somebody. Tennyson. FaBoEE; NOBL

Would you have freedom from wage slavery? There Is Power in a Union. Joe Hill. HHAm

Would You Hear of an Old-Time [*or* Old-Fashioned] Sea fight? Walt Whitman. SAmP *Fr.* Song of Myself.

Would you know what's soft? I dare. James Shirley. BeJo

Would You Like to Play? Dezsö Kosztolányi. IQMS, *tr. by* Thomas Kabdebo

Would you like to swing on a star. Swinging on a Star. Jimmy Van Heusen. ReLy

Would You Like to Take a Walk? Harry Warren. ReLy

Would you, my friend, in little room express. Martial. OBVE

Would you not be awed by trees. Aging. Richard Beer-Hofmann. AuPH, *tr. by* Naemah Beer-Hofmann

Would you prefer the examples? The pancakes? Or the words? Male, The. Carla Harryman. PmAP

Would You Think? John Wheelwright. APT-2

Would You Wear My Eyes? Bob Kaufman. GT

Would you your son should be a sot or dunce. William Cowper. OBSV *Fr.* Tirocinium; or, A Review of Schools.

Wouldn't it be a change for you and me. Sleepy Time Gal. Raymond B. Egan. ReLy

Wouldn't it be great to get away? Melbourne or the Bush. Philip Mead. BMAP

Wouldn't It Be Luverly? Alan Jay Lerner. ReLy

Wouldn't this old world be better. I Know Something Good about You. Louis C. Shimon. PoToHe

Wouldn't you like to know. Elementary. Jim Tollerud. VoR

Wouldnt think / t look at m. Panther Man. James A. Emanuel. BPo; NBV

Wouldst know the lark? Listener's Guide to the Birds, A. Elwyn Brooks White. OWoS

Wouldst thou be wise, O Man? At the knees of a woman begin. Wilfrid Scawen Blunt. OBMV *Fr.* Wisdom of Merlyn, The.

Wouldst thou hear what man can say. Epitaph on Elizabeth, L. H. Ben Jonson. BeJo; FaBoEE; HAP; NAEL-5v1; NAEL-6v1; NIL-7; NIP-4; NOSC; NoP-4; OBEV; PoE; SCGP

Wouldst thou live long? The only means are these. He Lives Long Who Lives Well. Thomas Randolph. TreFP

Wound. Alaide Foppa. TANSG, *tr. by* Celeste Kostopulos-Cooperman

Wound, A. Brendan Kennelly. BiHa

Wound, The. Louise Glück. NoAM

Wound, The. Thom Gunn. NPeEn

Wound-Dresser, The. Walt Whitman. APN-1; CBCWP; ColAP; NAAL-2v1; NAAL-3; NAAL-5; NOBA; OBWP; TAP; TCAPo

"Bearing the bandages, water and sponge."

Wound-dresser's Dream, The. Pauline Stainer. NeBl

Wound Man, The. D. A. Feinfeld. BloBone

Wound of Love, The. Heinrich von Morungen. NAWM-7v1, tr. by Peter Dronke

Wound seen from afar. Philippe Jaccottet. MFP, tr. by Martin Sorrell

Wound which the dragon had dealt him began, The. *Unknown*. AnOE, tr. by Charles W. Kennedy   Fr. Beowulf.

Wounded Breakfast, The. Russell Edson. LCAP-2

Wounded Cupid, The. Robert Herrick. AWP; OBVE

Wounded Deer Leaps Highest, A. Emily Dickinson. APN-2; AWP; TAP

Wounded hands, the weary human face, The. (LL) E Tenebris. Oscar Wilde. ChIV-2; MoBrPo; NAEL-5v2; NAEL-6v2; OxAEP-2; Son

Wounded Hawk, The. Herbert Edward Palmer. FaBoTw

Wounded horse dies without a whinny. Horse, The. Marie Laurencin. CuPo

Wounded I sing, tormented I indite. Joseph's Coat. George Herbert. ChIV-1; GeHe

Wounded Otter, The. Michael Hartnett. PBCIP

Wounded wilderness of Morris Graves. Lawrence Ferlinghetti. NeAP

Wounds. Michael Longley. ModIr; NPeEn; PBCIP; PNI

Wounds are terrible. The paint is old, The. Dolls Museum in Dublin, The. Eavan Boland. NoP-4

Wounds, as Wells of Life, The. *Unknown*. SacPr

Woven you are of the spring, lovers. Rose of Fire. Antonio Machado Ruiz. SpanPo, tr. by Kate Flores

Wow man I said / when you tipped my chin. Short Note on the Sparseness of the Language. Diane Di Prima. BB

Wow! wow! wow! (LL) Lewis Carroll. FaBoCh; NBLV; UV   Fr. Alice's Adventures in Wonderland.

Woyi, The. Lew Blockcolski. VoR

Wraith-Friend, The. George Barker. OBMV

Wrap it up wrap it up in a mat. (LL) Harvest of War. Catherine Obianuju Acholonu. HAWP; NAfrP

Wrap Me in Blankets of Momentary Winds. Harold Littlebird. VoR

Wrap the light in tendrons and no one. E Questa Vita Un Lampo. Peter Riley. Oth

Wrap their babies in the American flag. Immigrants. Pat Mora. UnSA

Wrap up in a blanket in cold weather and just read. Things to Do around a Lookout. Gary Snyder. TAP

Wrap Your Troubles in Dreams. Ted Koehler. ReLy

Wrapped, surrounded by ten thousand mountains. On the Road to T'ien-t'ai. Yuan Mei. GifTon, tr. by Jerome P. Seaton

Wrapping dumplings in. Basho. SoOfWa, tr. by Sam Hamill

Wrapping the rice cakes. Basho. EH, tr. by Robert Hass

Wrapt in the old miasmal mist. (LL) Hippopotamus, The. T. S. Eliot. AWP; NAEL-5v2; NAEL-6v2; OBMV; PAI; SacPr; TCAPo; VGW

Wrapt [or Wrapped] up, O Lord, in man's degeneration. Fulke Greville, 1st Baron Brooke. NoSic   Fr. Caelica.

Wrath, as I bigan yow for to seye, The. Geoffrey Chaucer. OxBEV   Fr. Troilus and Criseyde [or Criseide].

Wrath of *Peleus* Son, O Muse, resound, The. Homer. OBVE, tr. by John Dryden   Fr. Iliad, The.

Wrath to Sadness. Robert Grenier. PmAP

Wrathful winter, 'proaching on apace, The. Thomas, 1st Earl of Dorset Sackville. NoSic   Fr. Induction to "A Mirror for Magistrates."

Wreath, A. George Herbert. GeHe; NOSC; NPeEn; OxBSP

Wreath, A. Gyula Illyés. IQMS, tr. by William Jay Smith

Wreath, The. Robert Graves. BoLoP

Wreath for Africa, A. Bernard Dadié. NegPo, tr. by Ellen Conroy Kennedy

Wreath-heavy, a child's body. Raising the Dead. Fatima Lim-Wilson. ReBoTo

Wreathe violets white. Heliodora's Brows. Meleager. GrAn, tr. by Peter Whigham

Wreathèd garland of deservèd praise, A. Wreath, A. George Herbert. GeHe; NOSC; NPeEn; OxBSP

Wreaths. Michael Longley.
    Civil Servant, The. BiHa; ModIr
    Greengrocer, The. BiHa; ModIr
    Linen Workers, The. BiHa; CIP-2; ModIr; NPeEn

Wrecche mon, why artou proud. *Unknown*. MiEL

Wreck, The. Felicia Dorothea Hemans. TreFP

Wreck of the Circus Train, The. Hayden Carruth. GM

Wreck of the Deutschland, The. David Annett. PeLi

Wreck of the Deutschland, The. Gerard Manley Hopkins. FaBoMo; NOBE; NoAM; OxAEP-2; OxBEV; PeECV
    "Sister, a sister calling." FaBoVe
    "Thou mastering me." NPeEn

Wreck of the Edmund Fitzgerald, The. Gordon Lightfoot. NoP-4

Wreck of the Great Northern, The. Robert Hedin. GM

Wreck of the *Hesperus*, The. Henry Wadsworth Longfellow. APN-1; BRP; EBNV; OBCA; OBNV; TCAPo; TreFP

Wreck of the Old 97. David Graves George. GM

Wrecked Boat on the River Shore. Chiang Lu. CoBCP, tr. by Burton Watson

Wrecked castaway. Robinson Crusoe Daniel Defoe. Maurice Sagoff. NBLV

Wrecked Creeves. Katrina Porteous. NeBl

Wren, A. Denise Levertov. PoCoUp

Wren, The. John Clare. CenSon

Wren, The. Issa. NTCP, tr. by R. H. Blyth

Wren dropped down on my window sill, A. Little Wren, A. Priscilla Jane Thompson. CBWP-2

Wrestling. Louisa Sarah Bevington. LW; PEW

Wrestling. "Rachel" [or "Rahel."]. FIT, tr. by Robert Friend

Wrestling Jacob. Charles Wesley. NOBE; NOCV; NOEC; OBEV; OxAEP-1; PeECV; TOF

Wretched are the poor in spirit: for what they were on earth. Jorge Luis Borges. GI, tr. by Norman Thomas Di Giovanni   Fr. Apocryphal Gospel, An.

Wretched Catullus, play the fool no more. To Himself. Catullus. AWP, tr. by William Ellery Leonard

Wretched Catullus! You have to stop this nonsense. 8. Catullus. NAWM-7v1, tr. by Charles Martin

Wretched estate of men by fortune blessed. George Chapman. NOSC   Fr. Euthymiae Raptus; or, The Teares of Peace.

Wretched Flavia, on her couch reclined, The. Lady Mary Wortley Montagu. BWW; ECWP; NOEC; WPE   Fr. Six Town Eclogues.

Wretched Ierne! with what grief I see. Jonathan Swift. OBSV   Fr. Verses Occasioned by the Sudden Drying Up of St. Patrick's Well.

Wretched me / I live a rustic live. Alcaeus [or Alkaios]. SaLy, tr. by Diane Rayor

Wretchedness of my former years I have no need to brag, The. After Passing the Examination. Meng Chiao. SuSp, tr. by Irving Y. Lo

Wretten by Me at the Death of My 4th Sonne and 5th Child Perigrene Payler. Mary Carey. EMWP

Wrights' Biplane, The. Robert Frost. WeW-3   Fr. Ten Mills.

Wring the Swan's Neck. Enrique Gonzáles Martínez. TCLAP, tr. by Samuel Beckett

Wrinkled, crabbèd man they picture thee, A. Winter. Robert Southey. OxBSo

Wrinkles. Penny Harter. HA

Wrinkles: like / valleys etched by glaciers. Riding the North Point Ferry. Wing Tek Lum. OpBo

Wrinkles on the brown face, The. Militance of a Photograph in the Passbook of a Bantu under Detention, The. Michael S. Harper. VCAP

Wrinkling Together. Leo Vroman. TuT, tr. by Anne Kennedy

Writ in my psalter. (LL) His Prayer to Ben Jonson. Robert Herrick. BASC; BeJo; CaPo; NAEL-5v1; NAEL-6v1; NAEL-7v1; NOSC; NoP-4; OxBSP; OxBoLi; PeLV

Write it down. Write it. In ordinary ink. Starvation Camp near Jaslo. Wislawa Szymborska. WPOW

Write it. Write. In ordinary ink. Wislawa Szymborska. *See* Write it down. Write it. In ordinary ink

"Write me a sonnet. On the spot," said she. Sonnet Right off the Bat. Félix Lope de Vega Carpio. STV, tr. by John Frederick Nims

Write Off. Breyten Breytenbach. PoetW, tr. by Denis Hirson

Write poems when I'm sober, and sing when I'm drunk. Lazy Cloud's Nest 1. Ali Hsiying. ColAnChi, tr. by Jerome P. Seaton

Write the poem. Pyramids, The. Nick Piombino. FTOS

Write this. We have burned all their villages. Sun. Michael Palmer. APSN; PFTM-2

Write to Sardis, saith the Lord. William Cowper. ChIV-2   Fr. Olney Hymns.

Write to thine eyes? Why, my poor pen. To Fannie. Mary E. Tucker. CBWP-1

Write with color. Be a Painter. Joe Lothamer. GeoH

Write! Write! Help! Help! Barnabe Barnes. Son   Fr. Parthenophil and Parthenophe.

Write write yow Cronicters of Tyme and Fame. George Peele. PBRV   Fr. Anglorum Feriae.

Writer. Joe Wenderoth. BodElec

Writer, The. Richard Wilbur. HCAP; NoAM; OxBC; PoPoPo; SoSe-8

Writer depersonalises his dreamwork, The. Chris Wallace-Crabbe. BMAP   Fr. Sonnets to the Left.

Writers. Robert Lowell.
    Robert Frost. NAAL-2v2; NoAM; PAI; Son

Writers of the knife are we! Velemir [or Viktor Vladimirovich] Khlebnikov. TCRP   Fr. Washerwoman.

Writhing. Stroke. Hugh Seidman. BodElec

Writing. William Allingham. NOBVV

Writing. Andrew Motion. DiPo

Writing. Howard Nemerov. VCAP

Writing a Curriculum Vitae. Wislawa Szymborska. PoSu, tr. by Grazyna Drabik

Writing a letter he said. Buffalo—Isle of Wight Power Cable. Anselm Hollo. PoM

Writing a poem. Believing in the Absurd. Harold Norse. CLPP

Writing about the mysteries. Mysteries, The. Brenda Hillman. ExTi

Writing again. William J. Higginson. HA

Writing Again on the Same Theme. Po Chü-i. CoBCP, tr. by Burton Watson

Writing in a nearly lightless loft. Michael Haslam. Oth Fr. Continual Song.

Writing in England Now. Philip O'Connor. OxBTC

Writing in Prison. Ken Smith. NPeEn

Writing My Feelings. Yüan Mei. CoBLCP, tr. by Jonathan Chaves

Writing of poems, The. First Drift. Ron Padgett. FTOS

Writing on a Tombstone. J. C. Bloem. TuT, tr. by Desmond Egan

Writing Poetry in the Back Garden. Chao Yi. SuSp, tr. by Chang Yin-nan

Writing poetry needs a mind that's nimble and free. Replying to a Poem by Li T'ien-lin. Yang Wan-li. SuSp, tr. by Sherwin S. S. Fu

Writing / Rubbing it out—. Hokushi. ZenPo, tr. by Takashi Ikemoto and Lucien Stryk

Writing shit about new snow. Issa. EH, tr. by Robert Hass

Writing these poems! / Imagine! (LL) Autobiographia Literaria. Frank O'Hara. NNaP; NOBA; TTTS

Writing through the Cantos. John Cage. PmAP

Writing verse on smooth paper with a new Parker pen. Fire. Amiya Chakravarty. OMIP, tr. by Sujit Mukherjee

Writing What I've Seen. Yuan Mei. GifTon, tr. by Jerome P. Seaton

Writing with the sun on my hand. Sun on My Hand, The. Bert Voeten. TuT, tr. by Tony Curtis

Written a Few Hours before the Birth of a Child. Jane Cave. ECWP

Written after Climbing Kaguyama to Survey the Land. Emperor Jomei. WoPoe, tr. by Helen Craig McCullough

Written after Swimming from Sestos to Abydos. Byron. NAEL-5v2; NAEL-6v2; NBLV; NoP-4

Written Answer, A. Tom Paulin. ModIr

Written at a Farm. John Codrington Bampfylde. CenSon

Written at Bamborough Castle. William Lisle Bowles. CenSon

Written at Bignor Park in Sussex, in August, 1799. Charlotte Smith. CenSon

Written at Boppard on the Rhine, August 25, 1842, just before. Henry Wadsworth Longfellow. See Half of my life is gone, and I have let

Written at Hsiang-kuo Temple on the Occasion of Watching Actors in the Hsing-hsiang Garden of the T'ung-t'ien-chieh Tao-ch'ang. Wang An-shih. SuSp, tr. by Jan W. Walls

Written at Killarney. July 29, 1800. Mary Tighe. CenSon

Written at Lakeside Residence. Chiang K'uei. SuSp, tr. by Chiang Yee

Written at Mauve Garden: Pine Wind Terrace. Chu Yi-tsun. SuSp, tr. by Chang Yin-nan

Written at Netley Abbey. Susan Evance. CenSon

Written at [or in] an Inn at Henley. William Shenstone. AWP; NOBE; NOEC; OBEV; OxAEP-1; OxBEV

Written at Random. Lu Yu. SuSp, tr. by Irving Y. Lo

Written at Rossana. November 18, 1799. Mary Tighe. CenSon

Written at Scarborough. August, 1799. Mary Tighe. CenSon

Written at Sea, in the First Dutch War. Charles Sackville, 6th Earl of Dorset. See Song Written at Sea in the First Dutch War (1665), the Night before an Engagement

Written at Stonehenge. Thomas Warton, the Younger. Son

Written at the Close of Spring. Charlotte Smith. See Sonnet Written at the Close of Spring [or Elegiac Sonnet]

Written at the Couch of a Dying Parent. Eliza Cook. CenSon

Written at the Eagle's Nest, Killarney. July 26, 1800. Mary Tighe. CenSon; OxBSo

Written at the End of Master Ho-ching's Collected Works. Chin Nung. CoBLCP, tr. by Jonathan Chaves

Written at the Hotwells, near Bristol. Charles Lloyd. CenSon

Written at the White Sulphur Springs. Francis Scott Key. OBAL

Written at Tinemouth, Northumberland, after a Tempestuous Voyage. William Lisle Bowles. See At Tynemouth Priory, after a Tempestuous Voyage

Written beneath Hui Mountain, When Tsou Liu-yi Comes by for a Visit. Wang Shih-chieng. SuSp, tr. by Richard John Lynn

Written by Desire of a Lady, on an Angry, Petulant Kitchen-Maid. Jane Cave. ECWP

Written by the Barrow Side, Where She Was Sent to Wash Linen. Ellen Taylor. ECWP

Written December 1790. Anna Seward. CenSon; Son

Written, Directed by and Starring. James Simmons. PBCIP

Written during My Stay at White Clouds Monastery on West Lake. Su Man-shu. SuSp, tr. by Wu-Chi Liu

Written for Love of an Ascension—Coltrane. Carolyn M. Rodgers. SeSe

Written for My Neighbor. Shen Yüeh. CoBCP, tr. by Burton Watson

Written for My Neighbor. Wang Seng-ta. CoBCP, tr. by Burton Watson

Written for My Own Amusement. Wang An-shih. CoBCP, tr. by Burton Watson

Written for My Son, and Spoken by Him at His First Putting on Breeches. Mary Barber. CABP; ECEV; ECWP; NOEC

Written for Old Friends in Yang-Jou City While Spending the Night on the Tung-Lu River. Meng Hao Jan. WoPoe, tr. by Greg Whincup

Written for the Pavilion of the Drunken Old Man at Ch'u-chou. Ou-yang Hsiu. CoBCP, tr. by Burton Watson

Written Forty Miles South of a Spreading City. Robert Bly. NNaP

Written Impromptu upon Returning to My Hometown. Ho Ch'e Ch'ang. ColAnChi, tr. by Victor H. Mair

Written in a Blank Leaf of Dugdale's "Monasticon." Thomas Warton, the Younger. Son

Written in a Blank-Paper Book Given to the Author by a Friend. Mary Russell Mitford. PoBW

Written in a Carefree Mood. Lu Yu. CoBCP; ColAnChi, tr. by Burton Watson

Written in a Copy of Swift's Poems, for Wayne Burns. James Wright (1927–80). NOBA

Written in a Lady's Prayer Book. John Wilmot, 2d Earl of Rochester. BoLoP (Verses Put into a Lady's Prayer-Book.) NOSC

Written in a Ruinous Abbey. Susan Evance. CenSon

Written in a Shrubbery towards the Decline of Autumn. Mrs. B. Finch. CenSon

Written in a Sick Chamber. Samuel Rogers. NOBRP

Written in a Winter's Morning. Mrs. B. Finch. CenSon

Written in Absence. Alcuin. MLL, tr. by Helen Waddell

Written in an Album. William Wordsworth. See To a Child [Written in Her Album]

Written in an Ovid. Matthew Prior. FaBoEE; OBCoV

Written in Autumn. Thomas Cole. AiP

Written in Autumn. Mary Tighe. CenSon; OxBSo

Written in Behalf of My Wife. Li Po. SuSp, tr. by Joseph J. Lee

Written in Blood. Tiffany Midge. ReEnLa

Written in Bracing, Gray L.A. Rainlight. Al Young. SpirFl

Written in Butler's Sermons. Matthew Arnold. OxBSo

Written in Devonshire, near the Dart. Anne Batten Cristall. RWP

Written in Early Spring. William Wordsworth. See Lines Written in Early Spring

Written in Exile. Kathleen Jessie Raine. TrCP; WPE

Written in Farm Wood, South Downs, in May 1784. Charlotte Smith. RWP

Written in Her French Psalter. Queen of England Elizabeth I. WPE

Written in Ill Health. Anna Maria Smallpiece. CenSon

Written in Ill Health at the Close of Spring. Susan Evance. CenSon

Written in Ireland. Mary Alcock. ECWP; NOEC

Written in Jest on Elder Stonegate's Eastern Balcony. Liu Tsung-yüan. SuSp, tr. by Jan W. Walls

Written in Juice of Lem[m]on. Abraham Cowley. CABP Fr. Mistress, The.

Written in London, September, 1802. William Wordsworth. SacPr (England, 1802, I.) OBEV (London, MDCCCII.) GTBS-P

Written in March [While Resting on the Bridge at the Foot of Brother's Water]. William Wordsworth. ChAP; NAEL-5v2; NAEL-6v2; NTCP; SCGP; UnPo

Written in Northampton County Asylum. John Clare. See I Am

Written in October. Charlotte Smith. NoP-4

Written in Pencil in the Sealed Railway-Car. Dan Pagis. AF, tr. by Stephen Mitchell

Written in the Beginning of Mezeray's History of France. Matthew Prior. NOBE

Written in the Church-yard at Middleton in Sussex. Charlotte Smith. See Pressed by the Moon, Mute Arbitress of Tides

Written in the Euganean Hills, North Italy. Shelley. GTBS-P

Written in the Mountains. Kuan Hsiu. WoPoe, tr. by Jerome P. Seaton

Written in the Office Precincts. Wang T'ing-hsiang. CoBLCP, tr. by Jonathan Chaves

Written in the Workhouse. Thomas Hood. CenSon

Written in Tintern Abbey, Monmouthshire. Edward Gardner. CenSon

Written in Unbridled Repugnance near Sioux Falls, Alabama—April 30, 1974. A. K. Redwing. VoR

Written on a Cold Evening. Yang Wan-li. ColAnChi, tr. by Jonathan Chaves

Written on a Gloomy Day, in Sickness. Susanna Blamire. ECWP

Written on a Landscape Painting in an Album. Shen Chou. ColAnChi, tr. by Daniel Bryant

Written on a Leaf. *Unknown.* BoWoP, *tr.* by Geoffrey Waters

Written on a Looking-Glass. *Unknown.* FaBoEE

Written on a Painting Entitled "Misty Yangtze and Folded Hills." Su Tung-p'o (Su Shih). CoBCP, *tr.* by Burton Watson

Written on a Wall at Woodstock. Queen of England Elizabeth I. WPE (Oh Fortune, thy wresting wavering state.) CABP; PEW

Written on a Window. Aaron Hill. OxBSP

Written on Lake View Tower. P'an Lang. SuSp, *tr.* by Jonathan Chaves

Written on My Way into Exile. Han Yü. CoBCP, *tr.* by Burton Watson

Written on Parting from Mr. Ying. Ts'ao Chih. CoBCP, *tr.* by Burton Watson

Written on Seeing Her Two Sons at Play. Henrietta O'Neill. ECWP

Written on Seeing the Flowers, and Remembering My Daughter. Kao Ch'i. ColAnChi, *tr.* by F. W. Mote

Written on the Anniversary of Our Father's Death. Hartley Coleridge. Son

Written on the Day That Mr. Leigh Hunt Left Prison. John Keats. CenSon; Son

Written on the Lake, Returning from the Retreat at Stone Cliff. Hsieh Ling-yün. CoBCP, *tr.* by Burton Watson

Written on the Lake While Returning to Stone Cliff Hermitage. Hsieh Ling-yün. CrYelRi, *tr.* by Sam Hamill

Written on the Night of the Twenty-ninth of the First Month. Yün Shou-p'ing. CoBLCP, *tr.* by Jonathan Chaves

Written on the Sea-Shore. Felicia Dorothea Hemans. RWP

Written on the Sea Shore.—October, 1784. Charlotte Smith. CenSon; RWP

Written on the Thirtieth Day, Ninth Month, Second Year of the Ta-li Reign [767]. Tu Fu. SuSp, *tr.* by Irving Y. Lo

Written on the Wall at Chang's Hermitage. Tu Fu. EnlH; OHPC, *tr.* by Kenneth Rexroth

Written on the Wall of Halfway Mountain Temple. Wang An-shih. SuSp, *tr.* by Jan W. Walls

Written on the Wall of Pan-shan Temple. Wang An-shih. CoBCP, *tr.* by Burton Watson

Written on the Walls of His Dungeon. Luís De León. TrJP, *tr.* by Thomas Walsh

Written on Whitsun-Monday, 1795. Matilda Barbara Betham-Edwards. ECWP

Written, Originally Extempore, on Seeing a Mad Heifer Run through the Village. Elizabeth Hands. ECWP

Written September 1791, during a Remarkable Thunder Storm, in which the Moon Was Perfectly Clear, While the Tempest Gathered in Various Directions near the Earth. Charlotte Smith. CenSon

Written the First Morning of the Author's Bathing at Teignmouth for the Head-Ache. Jane Cave. ECWP

Written the Night before His Execution. Chidiock Tichborne [*or* Tichbourne]. *See* Tichborne's Elegy

Written to a near Neighbour in a Tempestuous Night. Henrietta, Lady Luxborough Knight. ECWP

Written to the Tune "The Fisherman's Honor." Li Ch'ing-chao. *See* "Fisherman's Honor, The."

Written upon Returning to the Mountains. Ku K'uang. SuSp, *tr.* by Irving Y. Lo

Written upon the death of the most Noble Prince Henrie. Sir Arthur Gorges. PBRV

Written When Drunk. Chang Yüeh. CoBCP, *tr.* by Burton Watson

Written when Governor of Soochow. Po Chü-i. ChiP, *tr.* by Arthur Waley

Written When the Mind Was Oppressed. Anne Batten Cristall. RWP

Written While Drunk. Ch'ien T'ao. WoPoe, *tr.* by William Acker and Cyril Birch

Written While Lying on My Pillow in the Morning on the Twelfth Day of the Eleventh Month. Fan Ch'eng-ta. SuSp, *tr.* by Wu-Chi Liu

Written While Riding the Long Island Rail Road. May Swenson. GM

Written While Sick. Wen Cheng-ming. CoBLCP, *tr.* by Jonathan Chaves

Written with a Diamond on Her Window at Woodstock. Queen of England Elizabeth I. PEW; WPE

Wrong #. Lee Ranaldo. HeMarv

Wrong Color. Christopher Stanard. SpirFl

Wrong for the early robin still the potato buries its head in the dirt. Sounds of the Resurrected Dead Man's Footsteps #15. Marvin Bell. SpudSo

Wrong! Is it wrong? Well, may be. Alfred Austin. UV Fr. Jameson's Ride.

Wrong me no more. Changed, Yet Constant. Thomas Stanley. BeJo

Wrong Side of the Door, The. Ray DiPalma. FTOS

Wrong Way Will Haunt You, The. Sydney Lea. RA

Wrong? are they wrong? Of course they are. England's Alfred Abroad. Sir Owen Seaman. UV

Wrongs we bear shall be redressed, The. (LL) From America. James M. Whitfield. APN-2; BPo; NAAAL

Wrote about this: all misunderstanding. (LL) One You Wanted to Be Is the One You Are, The. Jean Valentine. BodElec; ExTi

Wrote the clergy: "Our Dear Madame Prynne." Hawthorne Garland, A. Richard Harter Fogle. OBAL

Wryneck's Nest, The. John Clare. CenSon

Wu-Chueh. Tu Fu. ChinPo, *tr.* by Yip Wai-lim

Wu land mulberry leaves grow green. Sent to My Two Little Children in the East of Lu. Li Po. CoBCP, *tr.* by Burton Watson

Wu Shan-yang. Yang Chi. CoBLCP, *tr.* by Jonathan Chaves *Fr.* Thinking of My Friends at Kou-jung Subprefecture.

Wu-t'ung tree a hundred feet tall, A. Inscribed on a Painting of a Wu-t'ung Tree by Myself. Tao-chi. CoBLCP, *tr.* by Jonathan Chaves

Wu Wei grew old and died. Song of the Painting "River and Mountains," by Wu Wei. Ho Ching-ming. CoBLCP, *tr.* by Jonathan Chaves

Wuddup. Gription. Paul Beatty. InTrad

Wulf and Eadwacer. *Unknown.* BoWoP, *tr.* by Willis Barnstone and Elene Kolb

Wulf and Eadwacer: A Woman's Lament. *Unknown.* WoPoe, *tr.* by Jonathan McKeage *See* Eadwacer

Wurarbuti, as aged as his land. Wurarbuti. Archie Weller. IBA

Wurlitzer stirs, all girl, all groan, The. Small Pleasures. Angela Shaw. NeAmPo

Wye below Bredwardine, The. John Powell Ward. TCAWP

Wyll and Testament. Isabella Whitney. *See* Aucthour Maketh Her Wyll and Testament, The

Wyncote, Pennsylvania: A Gloss. Thomas Kinsella. NOIV

Wyndham! 'tis not thy blood, tho' pure it runs. To the Earl of Egremont. Charlotte Smith. RWP

Wyndmere, Windemere. Carol Muske. PBCAP

Wynken, Blynken, and Nod one night. Wynken, Blynken, and Nod. Eugene Field. ChAP; ITBLP; NBLV; NOxBChV; NTCP; OBAL; OBCA; OTCP; OxIBACP; PoRA; TFi

(Dutch Lullaby, A.) APN-2

Wynkyn de Worde. Edmund Clerihew Bentley. OBCoV *Fr.* Clerihews.

Wynter wakeneth al my care. *Unknown.* OHMEL

Wynyard Sailor. Ray Mathew. CBAP

Wystan, you got off to a wrong start. Memo to Auden. Anne Rouse. MFPA

Wyth a gerlond of thornes kene. *Unknown.* *See* With a garlande of thornes kene

Wythop Mill. Annie Foster. NLP

X

X. Daniel Hall. YaYoPo

X. n Valentine. ExTi

X finds gold and leaves his noose for Y. Statilius Flaccus. GrAn

X L E B. Jack Hirschman. CLPP

X-Ray. Dannie Abse. AngWePo; BloBone

X-Ray. Else Von Freytag-Loringhoven. SurPaPo

X-Ray, The. Andrew Elliott. PNI

X-Rays. I. K. Bonset. TuT, *tr.* by Desmond Egan

X shall stand for playmates Ten. Roman Numerals. *Unknown.* OxNR

Xanthippe's strumming, her chatter, her speaking eye, her song. Philodemus. HePo *Fr.* Epigrams.

Xanthippe, singing at her lyre. Philodemus. ErotSp, *tr.* by Sam Hamill

Xantippe. Amy Levy. BrRo

Xenia: Stranger / Guest. David Gewanter. NAPBL

Xenophanes. Ralph Waldo Emerson. APN-1; NOBA

Xenophanes. Louis Zukofsky. APT-2

Xenophon's Song. István Vas. IQMS, *tr.* by George Gömöri and Clive Wilmer

Xmas for the Boys. Gavin Ewart. OBSV

Xochiquetzal. Pauline Stainer. NeBl

Xochitepec. Malcolm Lowry. NOBC

XX. P. Inman. FTOS

XXX. Dulce Maria Loynaz. TANSG, *tr.* by Alan West

Xylographer started to cross the sea, A. Zealless Xylographer, The. Mary Mapes Dodge. OBAL

Y

Y, The. Brenda Hillman. MoASP

Y'All Are Bird Dogs, Aren't You? Mark Richard. Unle

Y'all listen to me. Self Defense. Ai. ESEAA

Y Ddraig Goch. Henry Treece. TCAWP

Y-e-a-h! (LL) Dream Boogie. Langston Hughes. APSN; HCAP; NAAAL; PFTM-1; SSLK

Y. M. C. A, The. Mrs. Henry Linden. CBWP-4

Ya Got Trouble. Meredith Willson. ReLy

Ya say something botherin you. Grandma Talk. Sonya Brooks. InTrad

Ya Se Van Los Pastores. Dudley Fitts. APT-2

Yacht, The. Catullus. AWP; OBVE, *tr. by* John Hookham Frere *Fr.* Carmina.

Yachts, The. William Carlos Williams. APT-1; HeIP-4; MoAmPo; NOBA; NoAM; NoP-4; OxBA; PoE; SAmP; TFi

Yachts on the Nile. Bernard Spencer. NoAM

Yacove Eved was an Israeli. In Search of Yacove Eved. Fawaz Turki. GraLe

Yahrtzeit Light, The. Lyn Lifshin. UnSA

Yahrzeit. Susan Fromberg Schaeffer. TaR

Yak, The. Joseph Hilaire Pierre Belloc. MoBrPo; NBLV; NOBL; NoAM

Yalding, 1912. My father. On Finding an Old Photograph. Wendy Cope. HarvBoo

Yall / out there. Chant for Young / Brothas and Sistuhs, A. Sonia Sanchez. BPo

Yamaha yamaha. Mysterious East. William Cole. OBAL

Yang-Se-Fu. "Yehoash." TrJP, *tr. by* Isidore Goldstick

Yangchou. Cheng Hsieh.
　"West wind has come again to the "tower of makeup", The." CoBLCP

Yangtze River, autumn colors, The. Inscribed on the Painting, "River in Autumn." Ni Tsan. CoBLCP, *tr. by* Jonathan Chaves

Yangtze rushes past the capital, The. View of the Countryside. Wu Wei-yeh. SuSp, *tr. by* Chang Yin-nan

Yankee Doodle. Richard Shuckburg. OBAL; OxNR
　(Yankeys' Return from Camp, The.) OxBoLi

Yankee Doodle. *Unknown.* TCAPo

Yankee Doodle Boy, The. George M. Cohan. ReLy

Yankee Man-of-War, The. *Unknown.* TCAPo

Yankee ship came [*or* comes] down the river, A. Blow, Boys, Blow [*or* Blow, Bullies, Blow]. *Unknown.* FaBoVe

Yankeys' Return from Camp, The. Richard Shuckburg. *See* Yankee Doodle

Yard, littered, the. Cleaning. Rick Alley. AmPoNex

Yardbird's Skull. Owen Dodson. VGW

Yardley Oak. William Cowper. NOEC

Yards of Sarajevo, The. Richard Hugo. AF

Yarn of the *Nancy Bell*, The. Sir William Schwenck Gilbert. CABP; EBNV; FaBoCh; NOBL; TFi; UV

Yarrow Unvisited [1803]. William Wordsworth. GTBS-P; PoRA

Yarrow Visited [September, 1814]. William Wordsworth. GTBS-P

Yawn of Yawns, The. Vasco [*or* Vasko] Popa.
　Petrified Echoes. PoSu, *tr. by* Anne Pennington
　Wise Triangle, A. PoSu
　Yawn of Yawns, The. PoSu

Ye Alps audacious, thro' the heavens that rise. Hasty Pudding, The. Joel Barlow. NAAL-3; NOBA; OBAL; OxBA; TAP; TCAPo

Ye angells bright, pluck from your wings a quill. Edward Taylor. ChIV-2 *Fr.* Preparatory Meditations before My Approach to the Lord's Supper.

Ye are hamburgers. (LL) That Dada Strain. Jerome Rothenberg. FTOS; PFTM-2

Ye are many—they are few. (LL) Shelley. FHYEP; OBSV; OxAEP-2; RB; SCV

"Ye are the Duke of Athol's nurse." Duke of Athole's Nurse, The. *Unknown.* ESPB

Ye are the spirits who preside. Joanna Baillie. ECWP *Fr.* Address to the Muses, An.

Ye ayres and windes, ye elves of hilles. Ovid. OBVE, *tr. by* Arthur Golding *Fr.* Metamorphoses.

Ye banks and braes and streams around. Highland Mary. Robert Burns. AWP; GTBS-P; OBEV

Ye banks and braes o' Bonnie Doon. Banks O' Doon, The. Robert Burns. OxBEV

Ye beauties! O how great the sum. Christopher Smart. *See* Ye beauties! O how great the sun

Ye beauties! O how great the sun. On a Bed of Guernsey Lilies. Christopher Smart. BBASP; NOEC

Ye belles, and ye flirts, and ye pert little things. Song for Ranelagh. William Whitehead. ECEV

Ye Bruthers Dogg. Jon Anderson. NBLV

Ye buds of Brutus' land, courageous youths, now play your parts! For Soldiers. Humphrey [*or* Humfrey] Gifford. FaBoWar; NoSic

Ye captive soules of blindefold Cyprians boate. Thomas Watson. *See* Ye captive soules of blindfold Cyprian's boat

Ye captive soules of blindfold Cyprian's boat. My Love is Past. Thomas Watson. NoSic

Ye cats that at midnight spit love at each other. Appeal to Cats in the Business of Love, An. Thomas Flatman. EnLoPo; HAP; OBCoV

Ye clouds and darkness, hosts of night. Prudentius. SacPr, *tr. by* R. M. Pope

Ye companies of governor-spirits grave. Sidney Lanier. TCAPo

Ye congregation of the tribes. Psalm 58. Christopher Smart. NoP-4

Ye coop us up, and tax our bread. Caged Rats. Ebenezer Elliott. EBEV

Ye daffodilian days, whose fallen towers. Atoning Yesterday, The. Louise Imogen Guiney. SWaP

Ye distant spires, ye antique towers. Ode on a Distant Prospect of Eton College. Thomas Gray. GTBS-P; NAEL-5v1; NAEL-6v1; NAEL-7v1; NOBE; NOEC; NoP-4; OxAEP-1; PoE; SCGP

Ye dogg, O'Toole. Ye Bruthers Dogg. Jon Anderson. NBLV

Ye elms that wave on Malvern Hill. Malvern Hill. Herman Melville. APN-2; CBCWP; ColAP; TAP

Ye elves of hill(s), brooks, standing lakes, and groves. William Shakespeare. AWP; EBEV; OxAEP-1; SCV *Fr.* Tempest, The.

Ye elves of hills, brooks, standing lakes, and groves. Ovid. AWP, *tr. by* William Shakespeare *Fr.* Metamorphoses.

Ye flaming Powers, and winged Warrio[u]rs bright. Upon the Circumcision. John Milton. ChIV-2

Ye flippering soul[e]. Address to the Soul Occasioned by a Rain, An. Edward Taylor. NAAL-2v1; NOBA; OxBA

Ye flowery banks o' bonie Doon. Bonie Doon. Robert Burns. GTBS-P; NoP-4

Ye gallants of Newgate, whose fingers are nice. Newgate's Garland. John Gay. ECEV; PeLV

"Ye gie corn to my horse." Clyde's Water. *Unknown.* ESPB

Ye glorious Jove-born imps how you rejoice. On the Three Children in the Fiery Furnace. Henry Colman. ChIV-1

Ye glowing seraphs, that now breathe above. Friendship in Perfection. Andrew Michael Ramsay. NOEC

Ye Goat-herd Gods. Sir Philip Sidney. HAP; NAEL-5v1; NAEL-6v1; NOBE; NoSic *Fr.* Arcadia.

Yee Gote-heard Gods, that love the grassie mountaines. Sir Philip Sidney. *See* Ye [*or* you] goat-herd gods, that love the grassy mountains

Ye [*or* you] goat-herd gods, that love the grassy mountains. Sir Philip Sidney. HAP; NAEL-5v1; NAEL-6v1; NOBE; NoSic *Fr.* Arcadia.

Ye Goatherd Gods. Sir Philip Sidney. *See* Arcadia

Ye golden lamps of heaven, farewell. Hymn. Philip Doddridge. ECEV; SacPr

"Ye graceful peasant-girls and mountain-maids." Ballata: His Talk with Certain Peasant Girls. Franco Sacchetti. AWP; EaItPo, *tr. by* Dante Gabriel Rossetti

Ye green-rob'd Dryads, oft' at dusky eve. Enthusiast: or, The Lover of Nature, The. Joseph Warton. NOEC

Ye green-robed Dryads, oft at dusky eve. Joseph Warton. ECEV; NOEC *Fr.* Enthusiast, The; or, The Lover of Nature.

Ye haue heard this yarn afore. Peter Reading. EmeKit

Ye have been fresh and green. To Meadows [*or* Meddowes]. Robert Herrick. AWP; BASC; CaPo; NOBE; NOSC; NPeEn; OBEV; PBRV

"Ye have robbed," said he, "ye have slaughtered and made an end." He Fell among Thieves. Sir Henry John Newbolt. EBVV; OBEV; OBWP; OxBTC

Ye Highlands [*or* hielands] and ye Lawlands [*or* lowlands]. Bonny Earl of Murray, The. *Unknown.* ESPB; NOSC; OBEV; OxBB; OxBS; SCGP

Ye holy Angels bright. Richard Baxter. NOCV *Fr.* Psalm of Praise, A.

Ye holy towers that shade the wave-worn steep. Written at Bamborough Castle. William Lisle Bowles. CenSon

Ye humble souls that seek the Lord. Christ's Resurrection and Ascension. Philip Doddridge. NOCV

Ye jovial boys who love the joys. Fornicator, The. A New Song. Robert Burns. NPeEn

Ye know on earth and all ye need to know. (LL) John Keats. AWP; BRP; ClHu; EBEV; HAP; HeIP-4; NAEL-5v2; NIL-7; NIP-4; NOBE; NOBRP; NPeEn; OBEV; PoE; SCGP; TFi; TOF; UnPo

Ye ladies, walking past me piteous-eyed. Sonnet: To the Same Ladies; With Their Answer. Dante Alighieri. AWP; EaItPo, *tr. by* Dante Gabriel Rossetti

Ye learned sisters which have oftentimes. Edmund Spenser. BoLoP; FHYEP; NAEL-6v1; NAEL-7v1; NOBE; NoSic; OBEV; OxAEP-1

Ye living Lamps, by whose dear light. Mower to the Glowworms [*or* Glow-Worms *or* Glo-Worms], The. Andrew Marvell. AWP; BASC; ESCV; EnLoPo; FHYEP; FSCP; GeHe; NAEL-5v1; NAEL-6v1; NAEL-7v1; NOBE; NPeEn; NoP-4; OxBoLi; PBRV; PeLV; SCGP; TFi

Ye maggots, feed on Willie's brains. Epitaph for William Nicol. Robert Burns. FaBoEE

Ye Mariners of England. Thomas Campbell. GTBS-P; NOBE; OBEV; OBWP; OxAEP-2

Ye mariners of Spain. Song of the Galley, The. *Unknown.* AWP, *tr. by* John Gibson Lockhart

"Ye maun gang to your father, Janet." Fair Janet. *Unknown.* ESPB; OxBB

Ye may pass me by with pitying eye. Song of the Imprisoned Bird. Eliza Cook. VWP

Ye merry hearts that love to play. Win at First and Lose at Last; or, A New Game at Cards. Laurence Price. OxBoLi

Ye Mongers Aye Need Masks for Cheatrie. Sydney Goodsir Smith. OxBS

Ye mountain valleys, pitifully groan! Lament for Bion. Moschus. AWP

Ye nymphs! if e'er your eyes were red. On the Lamented Death of Mrs. Throckmorton's Bullfinch. William Cowper. NOEC

Ye nymphs of Solyma! begin the song. Messiah: A Sacred Eclogue in Imitation of Virgil's Pollio. Pope. ChIV-1

Ye nymphs who cultivate the highest mountains of Fife. Midden-Battle between Lady Scotstarvit and the Mistress of Newbarns, The. William Drummond, of Hawthornden. NePenScot, *tr. by* Allan H. MacLaine

Ye [*or* You] should stay longer if we durst. Francis Beaumont. NOSC *Fr.* Masque of the Inner Temple and Gray's Inne, The.

Ye paltry [*or* paultry] underlings of state. On the Irish Club. Jonathan Swift. OBSV

Ye people all in one accord. John Hopkins. SacPr

Ye people of Ireland, both country and city. New Song of Wood's Halfpence, A. Jonathan Swift. OxBoLi

Ye pilgrim-folk, advancing pensively. Dante Alighieri. AWP; CTC; EaItPo, *tr. by* Dante Gabriel Rossetti *Fr.* La Vita Nuova.

Ye plains, where threefold harvests press the ground. Passage of the Mountain of St. Gothard, The. Georgiana Cavendish, Duchess of Devonshire. ECWP; RWP

Ye powers above and heavenly poles. On Button the Grave-Maker. *Unknown.* FaBoEE

Ye powers of truth, that bid my soul aspire. Oliver Goldsmith. NOIV *Fr.* Travel[l]er; or, A Prospect of Society, The.

Ye praise the humble: of the meek ye say. Sonnet. Sir Aubrey De Vere. SacPr

Ye Realms below the Skies. Hosea, II Ballou. AH

Ye remembre the gentylman ryghte nowe. John Skelton. OxBEV *Fr.* Bowge of Courte, The.

Ye sailors bold both great and small. Fishing Lass of Hakin, The. Lewis Morris. AngWePo

Ye saw't floueran in my breist. Mandrake Hert, The. Sydney Goodsir Smith. OxBS

Ye say they all have passed away. Indian Names. Lydia Huntley Sigourney. APN-1; ColAP; SWaP

Ye Scattered Nations. *Unknown.* AH, *tr. by* Thomas Cradock

Ye single folks all, that adorn this gay table. Song for the Single Table on New Year's Day, A. Elizabeth Frances Amherst. ECWP

Ye smarts and belles, whose airs and arts confess. Vanity of External Accomplishments, The. Mary Whateley. ECWP

Ye sons of earth prepare the plough. William Cowper. ChIV-2 *Fr.* Olney Hymns.

Ye Sorrowers. Franz Werfel. TrJP, *tr. by* Ludwig Lewisohn *Fr.* Eternal Road, The.

Ye sorrowing people! who from bondage fly. Fugitive Slaves, The. Jones Very. TAP

Ye stoll awaye and durst no more be seene. (LL) Admonition to Montgomerie. James I, King of England. GTBS-P; OxBS

Ye sylvan Muses, loftier strains recite. Birth of the Squire; an Eclogue, The. John Gay. NAEL-5v1; NAEL-6v1; NOEC

Ye tender young virgins attend to my lay. Perplexity: A Poem. Elizabeth Hands. WoRP

Ye That Pasen by the Weye. *Unknown.* *See also* Jesus to Those Who Pass By

Ye that passen [*or* pasen] by the weye [*or* weiye]. Jesus to Those Who Pass By. *Unknown.* MiEL

Ye tradeful merchants that, with weary toil. Edmund Spenser. HeIP-4; NIP-4; Son *Fr.* Amoretti.

Ye tradefull Merchants that with weary toyle. Edmund Spenser. *See* Ye tradeful merchants that, with weary toil

Ye vales and woods! fair scenes of happier hours. Petrarch. RWP, *tr. by* Charlotte Smith *Fr.* Sonnets to Laura.

Ye virgins that from Cupid's tents. Isabella Whitney. PEW *Fr.* Admonition by the Auctor to all yong Gentilwomen: And to al other Maids being in Love, The.

Ye walls! sole witnesses of happy sighs. Walter Savage Landor. EnLoPo *Fr.* Ianthe.

Ye wastefull woodes bear witness of my woe. Edmund Spenser. MakPoe *Fr.* Shepheardes [*or* Shepeards *or* Shepherd's] Calender, The.

Ye wha are fain to hae your name. Braid Claith. Robert Fergusson. NOEC; OxBEV; OxBS

Ye who amid this feverish world would wear. John Armstrong. ECEV; NOEC *Fr.* Art of Preserving Health, The.

Ye, who in alleys green and leafy bowers. Laments the Volatility of Phaon. Mary Robinson. CenSon; RWP

Ye who intelligent the Third Heaven move. First Canzone of the Convito, The. Dante Alighieri. OBVE, *tr. by* Percy Bysshe Shelley

Ye whose hearts are beating high. Address to Poets. John Keble. SacPr

Ye wild-eyed Muses, sing the Twins of Jove. *Unknown.* AWP, *tr. by* Percy Bysshe Shelley *Fr.* Homeric Hymns.

Yea, and a good cause why thus should I plain. Nicholas Grimald. NoP-4 *Fr.* Funeral Song, Upon the Decease of Annes His Mother, A.

Yea, beds for all who come. (LL) Uphill. Christina Georgina Rossetti. CABP; EBVV; HAP; InPK-6; NAEL-5v2; NALW; NOBE; OBEV; PoE; PoRA; SacPr; TFi; TrCP; WPE; WeW-3

Yea, gold is son of Zeus: no rust. Gold Is the Son of Zeus: Neither Moth nor Worm May Gnaw It. "Michael Field." OBMV

Yea, let me praise my lady whom I love. Sonnet: He Will Praise His Lady. Guido Guinicelli. AWP; EaItPo, *tr. by* Dante Gabriel Rossetti

Yea, they shall sing for love when Christ shall come. (LL) If Only. Christina Georgina Rossetti. SacPr; TrCP

Yea, though I'm sorry for thee. (LL) Youth Mowing, A. D. H. Lawrence. InPK-6; MoBrPo; NoAM

Yeah, I been to juvee, what about it? Rhonda, Age 15, Emergency Room. Letta Neely. WiU

Yeah, man, / I'll help out / with the / memorial for / Trane. Memorial for Trane. Sam Greenlee. SeSe

Yeah. / they hang you up. To All Brothers. Sonia Sanchez. BPo

Yeah Yeah Yeah. Roddy Lumsden. NeBl

Year. Milo De Angelis. NeIt, *tr. by* Lawrence Venuti

Year, The. Coventry Patmore. EBVV

Year about to end, The. Last Day of the Year, The. Su Tung-p'o (Su Shih). OHPC, *tr. by* Kenneth Rexroth

Year after year. Basho. EH, *tr. by* Robert Hass

Year After Year. Bart Howard. ReLy

Year after year. Toki-no-Ge (Satori Poem). Muso Soseki. EaWin, *tr. by* W. S. Merwin

Year after year I have watched. Li Ch'ing-chao. BoWoP; OHMPC

Year after year in the snow. Tune: "Pure Serene Music." Li Ch'ing-chao. SuSp

Year after year the princess lies asleep. Parabola. Alec Derwent Hope. NOBAu

Year after year. . . how many millennia of worldly affairs. Cave of Gold Essence—in Ning-tu, The. T'ang Hsien-tsu. CoBLCP, *tr. by* Jonathan Chaves

Year ago I fell in love with the functional ward, A. Hospital, The. Patrick Kavanagh. BIrV; CABP; CIP-2; EmeKit; ModIr; NPeEn

Year ago today by, A. By the City Gate. Ts'ui Hao. OHMPC, *tr. by* Kenneth Rexroth

Year ago we walked the wood, A. Vies Manquées. Edith Nesbit. VWP

Year ago you came, A. Pietà. James McAuley. BMAP; CBAP

Year at its turn, The. Last Day of the Year (New Year's Eve), The. Annette von Droste-Hülshoff. BoWoP, *tr. by* Willis Barnstone

Year before, this desert, A. Protesting at the Nuclear Test Site. Denise Levertov. PoCoUp

Year by year on his way to the South Sea. (LL) South, The. Wang Chien. AWP; BLT; ChiP, *tr. by* Arthur Waley

Year *Chi-wei* (Fifteen Fifty Nine), New Year's Day, The. Wen Cheng-ming. CoBLCP, *tr. by* Jonathan Chaves

Year dead-ends here, The. Clumsy December. Bird Nests. Angela Shaw. NeAmPo

Year dies fiercely: out of the north the beating storms, The. Year's End. William Everson. NoAM

Year 1812, The. Adam Mickiewicz. OBVE; OBWP; WoPoe, *tr. by* Donald Davie

Year has changed his mantle cold, The. Spring. Charles, Duc d' Orléans. AWP; CTC, *tr. by* Andrew Lang

Year has come to us as though out of hiding, A. Early January. W. S. Merwin. VGW

Year Hsin-hai (Fifteen Fifty One), New Year's Eve: Keeping Watch, The. Wen Cheng-ming. CoBLCP, *tr. by* Jonathan Chaves

Year I returned to my village, the papers, The. Two Variations on a Theme by Kobayashi. Larry Levis. BodElec

Year I Was Diagnosed with a Sacrilegious Heart, The. Martín Espada. TouFir

Year I was sick, The / and you took care of me. Disfortune. Joe Wenderoth. AmPoNex

Year I-mao (Fifteen Fifty Five), New Year's Eve, The. Wen Cheng-ming. CoBLCP, *tr. by* Jonathan Chaves

Year is done, the last act of the vaudeville, The. Midnight Show. Karl Shapiro. OxBA

Year is ending, The. Hankai. JDP, *tr. by* Yoel Hoffmann

Year is sullen, sullen is the day, The. Sullenness. "Michael Field." VWP

Year lays down his mantle cold, The. (LL) Spring. Charles, Duc d' Orléans. AWP; CTC, *tr. by* Andrew Lang

Year 1937, The. Timur Kibirov. TCRP, *tr. by* Vera Dunham

Year of Our Lord two thousand one hundred and seven, The. John Heath-Stubbs. NOBL *Fr.* Ecclesiastical Chronicle, An.

Year of Seeds, The. Ebenezer Elliott.

Give Not Our Blankets, Tax-Fed Squire.   Son
Ralph Leech Believes.   Son
Toy of the Titans.   Son
Year of the Foxes, The.   David Malouf.   NOBAu
Year of the monkey, year of the human wave.   Way of Tet, The.   Bruce Weigl.   AF
Year of the Olive Oil, The.   Charles North.   FTOS
Year of their ultimate squalor, The.   Bio 7.   David Moolten.   BloBone
Year Passes in My Morning Teacup, The.   Marilyn Chin.   GeoHom
Year's at the spring, The.   Robert Browning.   BRP; ITBLP; NTCP; OBEV; PAI; PoToHe; TrCP; UnPo   Fr. Pippa Passes.
Year's Awakening, The.   Thomas Hardy.   OxBTC
Year's End.   Chang K'o-chiu.   CrYelRi, tr. by Sam Hamill
Year's End.   William Everson.   NoAM
Year's End.   Marilyn Hacker.   WiU
Year's End.   Ted Kooser.   PBCAP
Year's End.   Frank Lima.   BodElec
Year's End.   Ellen Bryant Voigt.   NoAM
Year's End.   Richard Wilbur.   CoAP; HeIP-4; NAAL-2v2
Year's end / All corners.   Basho.   ZenPo, tr. by Takashi Ikemoto and Lucien Stryk
Year's end / Still in straw hat.   Basho.   ZenPo, tr. by Takashi Ikemoto and Lucien Stryk
Year's flowers in the grove die in a day, A.   In a Day.   Li Shang-yin.   SuSp, tr. by Eugene Eoyang
Year's Spinning, A.   Elizabeth Barrett Browning.   NAEL-5v2; NAEL-6v2
Year That Trembled and Reel'd beneath Me.   Walt Whitman.   PAI
Year the institutions would not hold, The.   Becoming of Age.   Simon Armitage.   HarvBoo
Year the Space Age Was Born, The.   Floyd Skloot.   SwNoth
Year the white women came like the plague, The.   Feel Free.   Natasha Tarpley.   ISC
Year was as long and dark as a bed, The.   Potato Thief.   Pentti Saarikoski.   VCWP, tr. by Herbert Lomas
Year was tan-wo, it was the fourth month, summer's first, The.   Chia Yi.   ColAnChi; WoPoe, tr. by J. R. Hightower   Fr. Rhymeprose on an Owl.
Year well remembered! Happy who beheld thee!   Year 1812, The.   Adam Mickiewicz.   OBVE; OBWP; WoPoe, tr. by Donald Davie
Year Wu-tzu [1048], First Month, Night of the Twenty-sixth: A Dream, The.   Mei Yao Ch'en.   SuSp, tr. by Jonathan Chaves
Yearbook.   Milo De Angelis.   NeIt, tr. by Lawrence Venuti
Yearning, A.   Arapera Hineira Blank.   PeNZ, tr. by the author
Yearning for Death.   "Novalis."   NAWM-7v2, tr. by Charles E. Passage
Yearning for Winter.   Karl Wilhelm Ramler.   GePo, tr. by George C. Schoolfield
Yearning of Karakashian, The.   Chava Pinchas-Cohen.   DTA, tr. by Miriyam Glazer
Years.   Walter Savage Landor.   OBEV
Years, The.   Catherine Davis.   FFC
Years, The.   John Ennis.   CIP-2
Years ago, alone in her room, my mother cut.   Cartoon Physics, Part 2.   Nick Flynn.   NAPBL
Years ago, at a private school.   Ever-Fixed Mark, An.   Kingsley Amis.   NoAM
Years ago feasting on raw whale by the eastern sea.   Third Month, Night of the Seventeenth, Written While Drunk.   Lu Yu.   CoBCP; SuSp, tr. by Burton Watson
Years ago I came here.   Bonanza Creek.   John E. Smelcer.   PoCoUp
Years ago, I traveled ten thousand miles in search of honor.   Tune: "Telling of Innermost Feelings."   Lu Yu.   SuSp, tr. by James J. Y. Liu
Years ago I was a gardener.   Writing in Prison.   Ken Smith.   NPeEn
Years ago, to the winding banks of this lake in spring.   At the Lake— Remembering My Dead Son, Yü.   Pien Kung.   CoBLCP, tr. by Jonathan Chaves
Years ago, when I heard the words of my elders.   T'ao Ch'ien [or T'ao Yuan-ming].   SuSp
Years ago, when I was young.   Juan Chi.   CoBCP   Fr. Singing of Thoughts.
Years and scars later.   Jacob.   George Garrett.   CRP
Years and years ago, these sounds took sides.   Casting and Gathering.   Seamus Heaney.   NoP-4
Years circling the same circle.   Yield Everything, Force Nothing.   Jean Valentine.   ExTi
Years from Now.   Kim Sowŏl.   WoPoe, tr. by Kevin O'Rourke
Years have gone. It is spring, The.   Kenneth Rexroth.   APSN; VGW
Years have made up my face, The.   Toward Myself.   Leah Goldberg.   FIT, tr. by Robert Friend
Years have piled up, The.   Sugetsu.   JDP, tr. by Yoel Hoffmann
Years have taken from me, The.   Softly I go now, pad pad. (LL)   Pad, Pad.   Stevie Smith.   NPeEn; OxBEV

Years have touched me, The.   Fujiwara No Yoshifusa.   OHMPJ
Years in the blood keep us naked to the bone, The.   Art of Clay, The.   Duane Niatum.   HATNAP
Years keeping that in mind.   Anbun.   ZenPo, tr. by Takashi Ikemoto and Lucien Stryk
Years Later.   Ruth Stone.   BoWoP
Years later, it was, after everything / got hazy in my head.   Mary.   Philip Appleman.   GI
Years, many parti-coloured years.   Years.   Walter Savage Landor.   OBEV
Years of a lifetime do not reach a hundred, The.   Unknown.   ChiP   Fr. Seventeen Old Poems.
Years of Indiscretion.   John Ashbery.   NOBA
Years of manhood had not tinged, The.   Charley du Bignon.   Mary E. Tucker.   CBWP-1
Years of my youth, years of dissipation.   Sergey [or Sergei] Aleksandrovich Yesenin [or Essenin].   TCRP
Years of the Modern.   Walt Whitman.   NCAP
Years pass like donkeys, The.   Ultimate Argument.   Ion Caraion.   AF, tr. by Marguerite Dorian
Years ride out from the world like couriers gone to a throne, The.   Stephen Vincent Benét.   MoAmPo   Fr. John Brown's Body.
Years saw me still Acasto's mansion grace.   Old Cat's Dying Soliloquy, An.   Anna Seward.   ECWP; NOEC; OxBEV
Years they come and go, The.   Ad Finem.   Heinrich Heine.   AWP, tr. by Elizabeth Barrett Browning
Years to come (empty boxcars), The.   Time.   William Stafford.   Son
Years will pass. Neither late nor soon, The.   Last Merchant, The.   Wolf Ehrlich [or Erlikh].   TCRP, tr. by Daniel Weissbort
Years, years ago,— ere yet my dreams.   Winthrop Mackworth Praed.   NOBRP   Fr. Every-Day Characters.
Yeats at Athenry Perhaps.   Padraic Fallon.   ModIr
Ye[e] blushing virgins happy are.   William Habington.   BeJo; EnLoPo; MeLP; NOSC; OBEV; SCGP   Fr. Castara.
Yee Shall Not Misse of a Few Lines in Remembrance of Thomas Hooker.   Edward Johnson.   SCAP
Ye[e] silent shades, whose each tree here.   To Groves.   Robert Herrick.   CaPo
Yeerd she hadde, enclosed al aboute, A.   Geoffrey Chaucer.   OWoS   Fr. Canterbury Tales, The.
Yelling never works, but I'm told.   Serenade.   Angie Estes.   GeoHom
Yellow.   Josephine Jacobsen.   APT-2
Yellow becomes alive.   Yellow.   Josephine Jacobsen.   APT-2
Yellow-belly, yellow-belly, come and take a swim.   Yes, by Golly.   Unknown.   OxBoLi
Yellow Bittern, The.   Cathal Buidhe Mac Giolla Ghunna.   NOIV, tr. by Thomas Kinsella
Yellow Bittern, The.   Cathal Buidhe Mac Giolla Ghunna.   BIrV; CIP-2; NOIV
Yellow Bittern, The.   Tom MacIntyre.   PBCIP
Yellow Bittern, The.   Unknown.   CIP-2, tr. by Tom MacIntyre
Yellow blood on the dunes.   Before the Pacific.   Blanca Varela.   BoWoP, tr. by Willis Barnstone
Yellow / brown woman / fingers smelling always of onions.   I Am Becoming My Mother.   Lorna Goodison.   OPOU
Yellow butterflies / Over the blossoming virgin corn.   Korosta Katzina Song.   Koianimptiwa.   AWP, tr. by Natalie Curtis Burlin
Yellow canary trilled, A.   Jealous Adam.   Itsik [or Itzik or Itzig] Manger.   TrJP, tr. by Jacob Sonntag
Yellow chirper, beaks its cage, The. (LL)   In the Cage.   Robert Lowell.   NOBA; Son
Yellow-coated pomegranate, figs like lizards' necks, A.   Philip of Thessalonica.   GrAn
Yellow coverlet, A.   Song.   Rosanna Warren.   ExTi; MakPoe
Yellow Dog Blues.   William Christopher Handy.   NAAAL
Yellow dusk: messenger fails to appear.   Unknown.   OBVE; OxBEV, tr. by Arthur Waley
Yellow dust drifts down the road to Ch'ang-an.   Song.   Unknown.   CrYelRi, tr. by Sam Hamill
Yellow Eyes, look at me and look for me. Let me see.   Unknown.   APN-2   Fr. Minnetare Songs.
Yellow feather / of a note, A.   Good Morning.   Carl Rakosi.   FTOS
Yellow Flower, The.   William Carlos Williams.   HAP; HarvBoo
Yellow freesia arc like twining arms.   Letter: Blues.   Elizabeth Alexander.   RA
Yellow Glove.   Naomi Shihab Nye.   LoL; PoArWo
Yellow gold's not precious.   Wang Fan-chih.   SuSp
Yellow Gramophone.   Sheila Cussons.   PeSAV, tr. by the author
Yellow Its Color.   Jafar ibn Uthman Al-Mushafi.   WoPoe, tr. by Leticia Garza-Falcón and Christopher Middleton
Yellow leaf, from the darkness, A.   Brooding Grief.   D. H. Lawrence.   PoE

Yellow leaves spiral down through the air.   Record of My Trip to Mount She, A.   Yüan Hung-tao.   CoBLCP, *tr.* by Jonathan Chaves

Yellow leaves swirl.   Indian Summer.   Karen Chamberlain.   GeoH

Yellow Light.   Garrett Kaoru Hongo.   GeoHom; OpBo

Yellow-lit Budweiser signs over oaken bars.   Uptown.   Allen Ginsberg.   TwCP

Yellow Man, Purple Man.   Emily Dickinson.   TLR; TTTS

Yellow november / comes swaying.   Rushing.   Ray A. Young Bear.   CDW

Yellow-oatmeal flowers of the windmill palms.   Eden.   David Woo.   OpBo

Yellow pears slope down.   Halflife.   Friedrich Hölderlin.   WoPoe, *tr.* by Vyt Bakaitis

Yellow River, The.   Nabaneeta Dev Sen.   OMIP, *tr.* by Nabaneeta Dev Sen

Yellow River's Earl, The.   Ch'u Yüan.   WoPoe, *tr.* by Stephen Owen

Yellow River winds along, The.   Autumn Vista.   Li Meng-yang.   CoBLCP, *tr.* by Jonathan Chaves

Yellow Room, The.   Juan Felipe Herrera.   TouFir

Yellow Rose of Texas, The.   *Unknown.*   TCAPo

Yellow sand, white reeds.   Crossing the Frontier.   Li Meng-yang.   CoBLCP, *tr.* by Jonathan Chaves

Yellow Season, The.   William Carlos Williams.   MoAMPo

Yellow silk and wildflower garlands lie on dark sandaloiled skin.   Jayadeva.   WoPoe, *tr.* by Barbara Stoler Miller *Fr.* Gita Govinda, The.

Yellow Spring.   Juan Ramón Jiménez.   SpanPo, *tr.* by Angel Flores

Yellow steam of Petersburg's winter, The.   Petersburg.   Innokenty Fiodorovich Annensky.   TCRP, *tr.* by Daniel Weissbort and Lubov Yakovleva

Yellow Sunflower of Szechwan.   Chang Yü.   SuSP, *tr.* by Irving Y. Lo

Yellow Violet, The.   William Cullen Bryant.   NAAL-2v1; NAAL-3; TAP

Yellow winds blow in from the north.   Seeing Off Commander In Chief Li to Yün-chung.   Li Meng-yang.   CoBLCP, *tr.* by Jonathan Chaves

Yellowhammer, The.   John Clare.   NOBVV

Yellowjacket.   Peter Blue Cloud.   HATNAP

Yellows and creams, The.   Symbols of Transformation.   Ron Padgett.   FTOS

Yellows cast their spells: the evening primrose.   Crepuscule.   Angela Shaw.   NeAmPo

Yemoja, mother of the fishes.   Yemoja.   Baba Ifa Karade.   HW

Yen-chou City Wall Tower.   Tu Fu.   CrYelRi, *tr.* by Sam Hamill

Yeoman of the Guard.   Sir William Schwenck Gilbert.
  Family Fool, The.   NBLV

Yes.   Denise Duhamel.   AmPoNex

Yes.   Brendan Kennelly.   CIP-2

Yes.   Muriel Rukeyser.   MakPoe

Yes. (LL)   What Do I See.   Gertrude Stein.   ItWoWo; PFTM-1

Yes, All-Highest, to God, be sure. (LL)   Death-Bed, A.   Rudyard Kipling.   OxBEV; PoWW

Yes, and chilled with fear and despair. (LL)   Judith of Bethulia.   John Crowe Ransom.   APT-1; FaBoMo; NOBA; NoAM

"Yes, and continue," said Conscience, and I came to the church. (LL)   William Langland.   NAEL-6v1; NAEL-7v1   *Fr.* Vision of Piers Plowman, The.

Yes, artwork is better.   Art.   Théophile Gautier.   WoPoe, *tr.* by Louis Simpson

Yes as alike as entirely.   To My Father.   William Sydney Graham.   FaBoTw

Yes, be like God. I wonder what I thought.   Jack Spicer.   NeAP   *Fr.* Imaginary Elegies.

Yes! Beauty still rebels!   Art, I.   Alfred Noyes.   OBEV

Yes Bees!   JA ZZ : (The "Say What?") IS IS JA LIVES.   Imamu Amiri Baraka.   SpirFl

Yes, Breisach, your decrease is profit yet and prize.   To Breisach, Taken by That Supremely Celebrated Hero, Bernhard, Duke of Saxony.   Georg Rudolph Weckherlin.   GePo, *tr.* by George C. Schoolfield

"Yes, But. . . "   Theodore Weiss.   TAP

Yes! but not his—'tis Death itself there dies. (LL)   My Baptismal Birthday [*or* Birth-Day].   Samuel Taylor Coleridge.   ChIV-2; NOCV

Yes, but the body is made of water. That's.   Bodies of Water.   Greg Williamson.   NAPBL; NeAmPo

Yes, but we must be sure of verities.   Spring Poem, The.   Dave Jeddie Smith.   PoPoPo

Yes, by Golly.   *Unknown.*   OxBoLi

Yes, call me by my pet-name! let me hear.   Elizabeth Barrett Browning.   CenSon   *Fr.* Sonnets from the Portuguese.

Yes, come to my arms, little doves of iron.   Martyrdom of Saint Sebastian, The.   Eugenio Florit.   TCLAP, *tr.* by Peter Fortunato

Yes, contumelious fair, you scorn.   Author Apologizes to a Lady, for His Being a Little Man, The.   Christopher Smart.   BoLoP

Yes, crazy to suppose one could describe them.   Robert Pinsky.   *See* It's crazy to think one could describe them

Yes! e'en in Sleep th' impressions all remain.   George Crabbe.   NPeEn   *Fr.* Borough, The.

Yes! Ethiopia yet shall stretch.   Ethiopia.   Frances Ellen Watkins Harper.   NAAAL

Yes, every poet is a fool.   Epigram.   Matthew Prior.   FaBoEE

Yes, faint was my applause and cold my praise.   To a Friend.   Joseph Rodman Drake.   APN-1

Yes, faith is a goodly anchor.   After the Burial.   James Russell Lowell.   UnPo

Yes, for the multitude of people it's hard to avoid.   Konstantin Konstantinovich Sluchevsky [*or* Sluchevskii].   TCRP

Yes, from the ingrate heart, the street.   Fugitive, The.   Alice Thompson Meynell.   NOCV

"Yes, go on! This is plain talk of plainer feelings now."   John Hollander.   VCAP   *Fr.* Powers of Thirteen.

Yes, God has made me a woman.   My Rights.   "Susan Coolidge."   SWaP

Yes God the desire hangs there unfilled turns into smoke!   Small Secret Book, A.   Michael McClure.   PFTM-2

Yes, he's got her now.   Blues.   John Fuller.   NOBL

Yes, he said, darling, yes, of course you tried.   Appointment, The.   Leonard Alfred George Strong.   OxBTC

Yes, his face really is so terrible.   Sudden Appearance of a Monster at a Window.   Lawrence Raab.   BLT

Yes! hope may with my strong desire keep pace.   Love's Justification.   Michelangelo Buonarroti.   AWP; OBVE, *tr.* by William Wordsworth

Yes, I am in love.   Mibu no Tadami.   OHPJ

Yes, I am not emitting articulate sound.   Barry MacSweeney.   Oth   *Fr.* Pearl.

"Yes," I answered you last night.   Lady's "Yes", The.   Elizabeth Barrett Browning.   ViWPN

Yes, I believe He loved them, too.   Young Workman, The.   Mary Dillingham Frear.   TrCP

Yes, I can hear you, father.   Soup and Slavery.   Myra Schneider.   Prnts

Yes, I'd rather hear Heliodora's voice.   Meleager.   HePo   *Fr.* Epigrams.

Yes, I did not plow, I did not sow.   Aftergrowth.   "Rachel" [*or* "Rahel."].   MHP, *tr.* by Ruth Finer Mintz

Yes, I do feel like a visitor.   Postcards from god (1).   Imtiaz Dharker.   NeBl

Yes, I do see many of us afraid of scraps.   Quilt of Rights.   Sandra McPherson.   LoL

Yes I have dreams where I am rescued by men.   Feminist Poem Number One.   Elizabeth Alexander.   NAPBL

Yes, I have lied, and so must walk my way.   Arthur Hugh Clough.   CenSon   *Fr.* Blank Misgivings of a Creature Moving about in Worlds Not Realized.

Yes, I have lov'd: yet often have I said.   Sappho; or, The Resolve.   Charlotte Dacre.   NOBRP

Yes! I have seen the ancient oak.   Felicia Dorothea Hemans.   CTC   *Fr.* Brereton Omen, The.

Yes, I know, I am not your kin—.   I and You.   Nikolai Stepanovich Gumilyov [*or* Gumiliov *or* Gumilev].   TCRP, *tr.* by Yakov Hornstein

Yes, I know: only the happy man.   Bad Time for Poetry.   Bertolt Brecht.   PoSu, *tr.* by Ralph Manheim and John Willett

Yes, I look at you now, as you in jewels of springtime.   Second Viennese Elegy.   Ferdinand von Saar.   AuPH, *tr.* by Lowell A. Bangerter

Yes, I remember Adlestrop.   Adlestrop.   Edward Thomas.   HAP; HarvBoo; NAEL-5v2; NAEL-6v2; NOBE; NoP-4; OBEV; OxBTC; UV

Yes, I remember that pain precisely.   Blood, The.   Nina Cassian.   WPOW

Yes, I remember Willesden Gree.   Willesden Gree.   Jimmy Pearse.   UV

Yes I saw your look.   Epitaph: André Breton.   Philippe Soupault.   SurPaPo, *tr.* by Mary Ann Caws and Patricia Terry

Yes, I say, I know.   Cante Jondo.   Yusef Komunyakaa.   BodElec

Yes, I think you can count on that, old boy–to-night'll be a thick night. (LL)   Officers' Mess.   Gavin Ewart.   FaBoWar; OxBTC

Yes, I wanted them to levitate.   At the School for the Gifted.   Carol Muske.   ExTi

Yes, I will go, where circling whirlwinds rise.   Resolves to Take the Leap of Leucata.   Mary Robinson.   CenSon; RWP

Yes, in the end they are much of a pair.   Heinrich Heine.   WoPoe, *tr.* by Robert Lowell   *Fr.* Dying in Paris.

Yes! in the sea of life enisled.   Matthew Arnold.   GTBS-P; NAEL-6v2; NPeEn; OxBEV; SoSe-8   *Fr.* Switzerland.

Yes, in the summer of 1773.   Tom Wedgwood Tells.   Brian W. Aldiss.   NOBL

Yes, injured Woman!—rise, assert thy right!   Rights of Woman, The.   Anna Laetitia Barbauld.   CABP; ECWP; NAEL-6v2; NOEC; NoP-4; PEW; WoRP

Yes, it looked dark and dreary.   Three Evenings in a Life.   Adelaide Anne Procter.   VWP

Yes, it's me. I appear thus to myself.   Aleksey [*or* Aleksei] Petrovich Tsvetkov.   TCRP

"Yes, let me go. Yon fields are green."   Request of a Dying Child.   Lydia Huntley Sigourney.   OBCA

Yes! let the rich deride, the proud disdain.   Oliver Goldsmith.   OBSV   *Fr.* Deserted Village, The.

Yes, Lizbie Browne! (LL)   To Lizbie Browne.   Thomas Hardy.   FaBoVe; NOBVV; OxAEP-2

Yes, / Longfellow wrote about me.   Paul Revere Speaks.   Myra Cohn Livingston.   HHAm

Yes, me bredren.   Champion Chant.   Rohan B. Preston.   WaCA

Yes Miss / Put up your pretty little mouth for a kiss. Admonition to the Muse. Geoffrey Taylor. FaBoEE

Yes, my darling, when life's shadows. In Memoriam. Alphonse Campbell Fordham. Mary Weston Fordham. CBWP-2

Yes! my Lesbia! let us prove. Catullus. *See* Lesbia / live with me

Yes, nonsense is a treasure! Lines on Nonsense. Eliza Lee Cabot Follen. SWaP

Yes, oblivion will come. Oblivion. Fanny Carrión de Fierro. TANSG, *tr. by* Sally Cheney Bell

Yes! Oh yes! Salutations. Shanmuga Subbiah. OMIP, *tr. by* T. K. Doraiswamy

Yes, one in a graven silence no birds breaks. (LL) Father and Son. Frederick Robert Higgins. BIrV; OBMV

Yes; or pass quick into the skies. (LL) Fragment on Death, A. François Villon. CTC; PeVV, *tr. by* Algernon Charles Swinburne

Yes, rub some soap upon your feet! Hike on the Downs, A. Sir John Betjeman. OBCoV

"Yes," said the boy, "first come the gum-tree crowds." Boy who Dreamed the Country Night, The. Christopher Koch. NOBAu

Yes, she's a good dog. Dog Parted from Her Master. Hsüeh T'ao. WoPoe, *tr. by* Jeanne Larsen

Yes, Sir! That's My Baby. Walter Donaldson. ReLy

Yes, somehow and somewhere and always. White Feather Legion, The. T. W. H. Crosland. FaBoWar

Yes, Southey, yes, I to the House of Prayer. Rebuke to Robert Southey, A. *Unknown.* ECWP

Yes! Strike Again That Sounding String. James M. Whitfield. NAAAL

Yes, Tadeusz Rozewicz, I too. In Praise of Old Women. Marya Fiamengo. WPOW

Yes! that fair neck, too beautiful by half. Madame d'Albert's Laugh. Clément Marot. AWP, *tr. by* Leigh Hunt

Yes, that's how I was. Judgment Day. Ronald Stuart Thomas. CRP

Yes, That's the Way Things Are. Miroslav Košek. INSAB

Yes, the Agency Can Handle That. Kenneth Fearing. WeW-3

Yes the bottle comes wrapped in bladderwrack. Christmas Present for My Mother. Sue MacIntyre. Prnts

Yes, the porpoises of course, it could. Mayan Glyphs Unread, The. William Bronk. APSN

Yes, the time / yes. Lighthouse of Alexandria, The. Mercedes Roffé. TANSG, *tr. by* Kathryn Kopple

Yes, there are stingy people. *Unknown.* CoBCP

Yes, there is a vault in the ruined castle. Broceliande. Marilyn Hacker. ExTi

Yes, there is holy pleasure in thine eye! Admonition to a Traveller. William Wordsworth. GTBS-P

Yes, there's the orderly. He'll change the sheets. Wilfred Owen. PeFWW *Fr.* Wild with All Regrets.

Yes, these are the dog-days, Fortunatus. Under Sirius. W. H. Auden. FaBoMo

Yes, they are alive and can have those colors. Blessing in Disguise, A. John Ashbery. ColAP; PoM

Yes, they begin out in a willow, I think. Crucifix in a Deathhand. Charles Bukowski. PmAP

Yes, theyll let you play. Poem for Players, A. Al Young. LTA

Yes, this is where I stood that day. Ballad of Hector in Hades. Edwin Muir. HarvBoo; NOBE; NoAM

Yes, this is where she lived before she won. Interview. Sara Henderson Hay. OBCA

Yes: though the brine may from the desert deep. Frederick Goddard Tuckerman. HAP *Fr.* Sonnets.

"Yes, 'tis the time," I cried, "impose the chain." On the Benefactions in the Late Frost. Pope. NOEC; OxBSP

Yes to the dark, uneven body of each tree. Falling in Love after Forty. Ruth L. Schwartz. NeAmPo

Yes, we are fighting at last, it appears. This morning, as usual. Arthur Hugh Clough. EBVV; NPeEn; OxAEP-2; PeVV *Fr.* Amours de Voyage.

Yes we did! (LL) Martin's Blues. Michael S. Harper. HCAP; NAAL-5

Yes, we had gone down to the shore. Songs without Words. John Ashbery. NAAL-2v2

Yes, we'll rally round the flag, boys, we'll rally once again. Battle-Cry of Freedom, The. George Frederick Root. CBCWP

Yes, we'll walk up the Avenue 'till we're there. (LL) Couple of Swells, A. Irving Berlin. OBCoV; ReLy

Yes, we love this land together. Fatherland Song. BjØrnstjerne BjØrnson. AWP, *tr. by* William Ellery Leonard

Yes, What? Robert Francis. LCAP-2

Yes. Whý do we áll, seeing of a soldier, bless him? bléss. Soldier, The. Gerard Manley Hopkins. FaBoWar

Yes, yes, and there is even a photograph. Meditation on a News Item. John Updike. PeLV

Yes, yes, dear love! I am dead! Resurgam. Adah Isaacs Menken. CBWP-1

Yes, yes / it's time. My Spring Thing. Everett Hoagland. BPo

Yes yes / yeah. Brown Skin Girl. Tommy McClennan. FaBoVe

Yes, yes, yes, yes. (LL) Love in America. Marianne Craig Moore. AiP; NIL-7

"Yes, you did, too!" Little Words. Benjamin Keech. PoToHe

Yes you have said enough for the time being. End Is near the Beginning, The. David Gascoyne. SPE

Yes, you must have had the camera. Forest. Priscilla Borthwick. Prnts

Yes, Your Honor, there are rodents. Tires Stacked in the Hallways of Civilization. Martín Espada. InvLad

Yes, yours, my love, is the right human face. Confirmation, The. Edwin Muir. OxBS

Yesterday. Angel González. VCWP, *tr. by* Steven Ford Brown

Yesterday. W. S. Merwin. LCAP-2; RaBo

Yesterday. Mary Weems. SpirFl

Yesterday a Euclid took trees. Bright green. Breaking Green. Michael Ondaatje. NOBC

Yesterday all the past. The language of size. Spain 1937. W. H. Auden. AF; NAEL-5v2; NAEL-6v2; NoP-4; OBWP

Yesterday, all winter. Flemish Beauty. Talvikki Ansel. AmPoNex

Yesterday at ten below. First Winter: Joy. Peggy Shumaker. PBCAP

Yesterday, at the Sessions held in Buckingham. Case at Sessions, A. Walter Savage Landor. OBSV

Yesterday, dreamed He was near me. Antonio Machado Ruiz. STV

Yesterday evening I saw your corpse. Joyce Mansour. WPOW

Yesterday explorers found. Clarence Day. OBCoV *Fr.* Scenes from the Mesozoic.

Yesterday has flown, leaving only its sorrows. Seeing off a Friend. Li Po. CrYelRi, *tr. by* Sam Hamill

Yesterday he could still look in my eyes, yet. Marina Ivanovna Tsvetayeva [*or* Tsvetaeva]. TCRP *Fr.* Two Songs.

Yesterday He Was Nowhere to Be Found. Ted Hughes. NOxBChV

Yesterday his eyes stared into mine. Ancient Song, An. Marina Ivanovna Tsvetayeva [*or* Tsvetaeva]. TCRusP, *tr. by* John Glad

Yesterday I didn't know this place. V.A. Hospital. Anthony Petrosky. CDa

Yesterday I dined with Demetrius, the boys'/ gymnastics teacher, luckiest of men. Gymnastics Teacher, The. Automedon. GrAn

Yesterday, I exposed myself on the train. Indecent Exposure (A True Story). Linwood M. Ross. InTrad

Yesterday I felt this ode. Ode to Laziness. Pablo Neruda. TCLAP, *tr. by* William Carlos Williams

Yesterday I found one left. Survivor, The. Ronald Stuart Thomas. FaBoTw

Yesterday, I have always seen him. I followed him into Paris: here was the entrance. His Promise. Aaron Shurin. FTOS

Yesterday I heard a lover sigh. Toot, Toot, Tootsie! (Good-bye). Ted Fiorito. ReLy

Yesterday I heard that such-a-one was gone. Separation. Po Chü-i. ChiP, *tr. by* Arthur Waley

Yesterday, / I jumped off a moving train. From My Diary. Yaroslav [*or* Iaroslav] Vasilevich Smelyakov [*or*Smeliakov]. TCRP, *tr. by* Simon Franklin

Yesterday I knew no lullaby. Child of Our Time. Eavan Boland. CIP-2

Yesterday I planted garlic. James Keir Baxter. PeNZ *Fr.* Jerusalem Sonnets.

Yesterday I remembered a clear winter day. I remembered. Bridge in the South. Jorge Teillier. TCLAP, *tr. by* Carolyne Wright

Yesterday I wanted to. For Love. Robert Creeley. CoAmPo; NOBA; PmAP; VCAP

Yesterday I was / given flowers. Anthology Poem. Petra von Morstein. BoWoP, *tr. by* Rosmarie Waldrop

Yesterday I went to a cloud observatory. *Unknown.* ColAnChi, *tr. by* Red Pine

Yesterday, in a big market, I made seven thousand dollars. Back through the Looking Glass to This Side. John Ciardi. NBLV

Yesterday in drizzling rain. Tailor Called Sorrow, A. Betti Alver. BoWoP, *tr. by* Willis Barnstone and Felix Oinas

Yesterday in São Paulo they buried. Oswald Dead. Ferreira Gullar. TCLAP, *tr. by* Renato Rezende

Yesterday in the bath Diodes' penis. Strato [*or* Straton]. CAGL, *tr. by* Daryl Hine

Yesterday, it was hibiscus. Shohaku. JDP, *tr. by* Yoel Hoffmann

Yesterday Mrs. Friar phoned. "Mr. Ciardi." Suburban. John Ciardi. NBLV

Yesterday old Nundah's eldest daughter's son. Archie Weller. IBA

Yesterday Reflecting upon Death. Nikolai Alekseievich Zabolotsky [*or* Zabolotskii]. TCRusP, *tr. by* Daniel Weissbort

Yesterday's conversation has been on my mind all day. Consolation. Dimitris Tsaloumas. BMAP

Yesterday's Illusion *or* Remembering the Thirties. Alun Llywelyn-Williams. OBWVE, *tr. by* R. Gerallt Jones

Yesterday's rain is still on the ground. Yesterday's rain. Sergey [or Sergei] Aleksandrovich Yesenin [or Essenin]. CAGL, tr. by Simon Karlinsky

Yesterday she claimed adherence to the mirror. Self-Portrait in the Third Person. Biancamaria Frabotta. CItWP, tr. by Cinzia Sartini Blum and Lara Trubowitz

Yesterday, sitting. Just. Judith Johnson Sherwin. TAP

Yesterday the fields were only grey with scattered snow. Winter's Tale, A. D. H. Lawrence. MoBrPo

Yesterday the gentle. St. Stephen's Day. Patric Dickinson. OBCP

Yesterday the House was Full of Flies. Geoffrey Summerfield. OTCP

YESTERDAY This Day's Madness did prepare. 74. Edward Fitzgerald. CABP

Yesterday was I, sure of purpose. Fox, The. Dafydd [or David] ap Gwilym. NAWM-7v1, tr. by Richard Morgan Loomis

Yesterday was Wednesday all morning. Yesterday. Angel González. VCWP, tr. by Steven Ford Brown

Yesterday when I'd drunk myself to bed / with water (neat). Antipater of Thessalonica. GrAn

Yesterday / When I found. Reticence. May Muzaffar. PoArWo, tr. by Tahia Abdel Nasser

Yesterday you came my way. I Can't Believe That You're in Love with Me. Clarence Gaskill. ReLy

Yesterday you had a song. Answer, An. Perceval Gibbon. PeSAV

Yesterday, / You were but a thought in our minds. Giovanni Azania. Don Mattera. PeSAV

Yesterday? Today? Yayu. JDP, tr. by Yoel Hoffmann

Yesterdays. Otto Harbach. ReLy

Yet a Little While Is the Light With You. Francis Quarles. ChIV-2

Yet am I still inviolate to You. (LL) Michael Drayton. NOBE; SCGP Fr. Idea.

Yet another great truth I record in my verse. Viper, The. Joseph Hilaire Pierre Belloc. NoAM

Yet Another Poem about a Dying Child. Janet Frame. PeNZ

Yet art hath less of instinct than of thought. Criticism. Ebenezer Elliott. CenSon

Yet at last might reach our raddled selves. (LL) Brian Coffey. BiHa; ModIr Fr. Death of Hektor, The.

Yet burnished by its passage, and still warm. (LL) Harvest Bow, The. Seamus Heaney. BiHa; HarvBoo; ModIr; NoAM; PBCIP; PNI

Yet but Three? William Shakespeare. CTC Fr. Midsummer Night's Dream, A.

Yet cannot they, while thou art present, weep. (LL) Dante Alighieri. AWP; EaItPo, tr. by Dante Gabriel Rossetti Fr. La Vita Nuova.

Yet C[h]loe sure was form'd without a Spot—. Pope. AWP; NOBE; OBSV Fr. Epistle [II,] to a Lady[: Of the Characters of Women].

Yet count this quest the holiest of thy days. (LL) Quest of the Ideal, The. Henrietta Cordelia Ray. CBWP-3; SWaP

Yet Dish. Gertrude Stein. "Put a sun in Sunday, Sunday." TCAPo

Yet Do I Marvel. Countee Cullen. APT-2; AmFaPo; BPo; InvLi; NAAAL; NAAL-2v2; NAAL-5; NIL-7; NoAM; SSLK; Son; TAP; TTY

Yet do not be afraid, yet give no post forlorn. To Himself. Paul Fleming. GePo, tr. by George C. Schoolfield

Yet each man kills the thing he loves. Oscar Wilde. OxBEV Fr. Ballad of Reading Gaol, The.

Yet, even 'mid merry boyhood's tricks and scapes. Frederick Goddard Tuckerman. APN-2 Fr. Sonnets.

Yet find not much more anguish? Be content. (LL) Pessimist's Vision, The. Constance Naden. VWP; ViWPN

Yet for one rounded moment I will be. Mortal Lease, The. Edith Wharton. LW

Yet Ha'e I Silence Left. Hugh MacDiarmid. NAEL-5v2; NAEL-6v2 Fr. Drunk Man Looks at the Thistle, A.

Yet ha'e I Silence left, the croon o' a' Hugh MacDiarmid. NAEL-5v2; NAEL-6v2 Fr. Drunk Man Looks at the Thistle, A.

Yet hard / The travail is for such as bend their minds. Unknown. TOF Fr. Bhagavad-Gita, The.

Yet he was there, and all my thirst. And If He Had Been Wrong for Me. Robert Duncan. RaBo

Yet here, tho' amusing the Sight. Samuel Bently. VerBaPo

Yet I courbed on my knees and cried hire of grace. William Langland. EBEV Fr. Vision of Piers Plowman, The.

Yet I know I will enter again and again. (LL) Kenneth Rexroth. APSN; APT-2 Fr. Love Poems of Marichiko, The.

Yet if his Majestie our Sovareigne lord. Unknown. See Guest, The

Yet if his majesty, our sovereign [or sovraign] Lord. Guest, The. Unknown. FaBoCh; PoRA; SacPr; TrCP

Yet if some voice that man could trust. Tennyson. NAEL-6v2 Fr. In Memoriam A. H. H.

Yet is day over long. (LL) Villanelle of the Poet's Road. Ernest Christopher Dowson. OBMV; UnPo

Yet it's neither—you understand now? (LL) Limerick: "Said an erudite sinologue: 'How'." R. J. P. Hewison. OBCoV; PeLi

Yet let me flap this bug with gilded wings. Pope. ECEV Fr. Epistle to Dr. Arbuthnot.

Yet (Let) one smile more, departing, distant sun! November. William Cullen Bryant. APN-1; GSo; Son; TreFP

Yet Listen Now. Amy Carmichael. SacPr

Yet London, empress of the northern clime. Dryden. NAEL-5v1; NAEL-6v1; NAEL-7v1; PeECV Fr. Annus Mirabilis.

Yet love I best of any creature! (LL) Geoffrey Chaucer. NOBE; OBEV Fr. Troilus and Criseyde [or Criseide].

Yet, love, mere love, is beautiful indeed. Elizabeth Barrett Browning. BWW; CTC; CenSon; OxAEP-2 Fr. Sonnets from the Portuguese.

Yet matter must be gravely planned. Robert Lloyd. ECEV Fr. Poetry Professors, The.

Yet more of me. (LL) End of Another Home Holiday. D. H. Lawrence. EBEV; FaBoMo; OxAEP-2

Yet must I love thee, dear, and as thou art. (LL) Wilfrid Scawen Blunt. GSo; Son Fr. Love Sonnets of Proteus, The.

Yet often I think the king of that country. Gospel of Labor, The. Henry Van Dyke. SacPr

Yet on the other side, faine would he start. Giambattista [or Giovanni Battista] Marino. OBVE Fr. Massacre of the Innocents, The.

Yet once again heaven's king, and Earth's great lord. Abraham's Sacrifice of Isaac. Sir John Stradling. NOSC

Yet once an earlier David took. Goliath and David. Robert Graves. FaBoWar

Yet once more, O ye Laurels and once more. John Milton. AWP; AmFaPo; BASC; CABP; ClHu; EBEV; FHYEP; GTBS-P; HAP; MakPoe; NAEL-6v1; NAEL-7v1; NIL-7; NOBE; NOSC; NPeEn; NoP-4; OBEV; OxAEP-1; OxBEV; PAI; PBRV; PoPoPo; SCGP; TFi; UnPo

Yet one more hour, then comes the night. My Drinking Song. Richard Dehmel. AWP, tr. by Ludwig Lewisohn

Yet Ostia boasts of her regeneration. Daniel Defoe. OBSV Fr. Reformation of Manners.

Yet out of that I have written these songs. (LL) Sometimes with One I Love. Walt Whitman. APN-1; OxBSP; SAmP

Yet, paying, is not paid until I die. (LL) To Her Father, with Some Verses. Anne Bradstreet. NAAL-3; NAAL-5; NALW

Yet, Percy, not for this, should he whose eye. To the Same. Leigh Hunt. CenSon

Yet, planter, let humanity prevail. James Grainger. NOEC Fr. Sugar Cane, The.

Yet resurrection is a sense of direction. "H. D.". APT-1 Fr. Flowering of the Rod, The.

Yet Still. Rashidah Ismaili. HAWP; ItWoWo

Yet still I stand by tilth and filth and praise. (LL) Tilth. Robert Graves. FaBoEE; OBSV

Yet that have hearts vexed with unquiet thought. To Spenser. John Hamilton Reynolds. Son

Yet the language so lovely! like the dyes from gas-tar. (LL) When I Read Shakespeare. D. H. Lawrence. NoAM; OBCoV; Son

Yet the sign is on her. (LL) Once-over, The. Paul Blackburn. NeAP; PoM

Yet there belongs a Sweetnesse, softnesse too. On Sanazar's being honoured with six hundred Duckets by the Clarissimi of Venice, for composing an Elegiack Hexastick of the City. A Satyre. Richard Lovelace. PBRV

Yet there is no great problem in the world today. Hugh MacDiarmid. OxBTC Fr. Lament for the Great Music.

Yet they never persuaded your heart. Praxilla. SaLy, tr. by Diane Rayor

Yet this is you. Portrait d'une Femme. Ezra Pound. APT-1; MoAmPo; NAAL-2v2; NAAL-5; NOBA; NoAM; NoP-4; PAI; TAP; TCAPo; TwCP

Yet this little old woman could never keep quiet. (LL) Strange Old Woman, A. Mother Goose. FaBoCh; LB; ReMoGo

Yet-to-be-dismantled elms, the geese, The. (LL) Poem: "About the size of an old-style dollar bill." Elizabeth Bishop. HCAP; NoAM; PoPoPo; PoetW; VCAP

Yet trusting not in mine, but in His strength alone! (LL) First-Day Thoughts. John Greenleaf Whittier. APN-1; TrCP

Yet we, the latter-day twice-born. "H. D." APT-1 Fr. Walls Do Not Fall, The.

Yet we were looking away! (LL) Self-Unseeing, The. Thomas Hardy. EBEV; HAP; MoBrPo; NOBE; NOBVV; OxAEP-2; OxBEV; RB; WeW-3

Yet what a gap in the world, the missing white frost-face of that slim yellow mountain lion! (LL) Mountain Lion. D. H. Lawrence. FaBoVe; OxBTC; RB

Yet, when I muse on what life is, I seem. Continued. Matthew Arnold. Son

Yet will I fear no evil: not even here. Château, The. Henry Reed. NoP-4

Yet will I love her till I die. (LL) There Is a Lady Sweet and Kind. Thomas Ford. EBEV; HeIP-4; NOSC; OBEV

Yet will I serve although I die therefore. (LL) Anthony Munday. HAP; SCGP *Fr.* Fedele and Fortunio.

Yet, yet a moment, one dim ray of light. Pope. NAEL-5v1; NAEL-6v1; NAEL-7v1 *Fr.* Dunciad, The.

Yet you (great lady) mistress of that place. Aemilia Bassano Lanyer. OBGa *Fr.* Description of Cooke-ham [*or* Cookham], The.

Yeti. John Haines. PoCoUp

Yet[t] faith still cries, Love will not[t] falsify [*or* falsefy). (LL) Mary Sidney Wroth, Countess of Montgomery. NAEL-6v1; NAEL-7v1; NOSC; PEW *Fr.* Pamphilia to Amphilanthus.

Yet[t] since: O me[e]: a lover I have been [*or* binn]. (LL) Mary Sidney Wroth, Countess of Montgomery. BASC; CABP; MakPoe; NAEL-5v1; NAEL-6v1; NAEL-7v1; Son *Fr.* Pamphilia to Amphilanthus.

Yeux Glauques. Ezra Pound. MoAmPo *Fr.* Hugh Selwyn Mauberley (Life and Contacts).

Yevtushenko, Voznesensky and I. Dream, A. Charles Tomlinson. OxBC

Yew. Elizabeth Delmore. NLP

Yew Berries. Ruth Padel. MFPA

Yew-Trees. William Wordsworth. UnPo

Yf I had as faire a face as John Williams. Anne Wrigglesworth. EMWP

Yf my deare love were but the childe of state. William Shakespeare. *See* If my dear love were but the child of state

Yf there be any man that can tell me quicklye. Strangman, Honor, *and others.* EMWP

Yf they that keepe what I you leave. Isabella Whitney. BWW *Fr.* Manner of Her Will and What She Left to London and to All Those in It, at Her Departing, The.

Yggdrasill. Paul Muldoon. PBCIP

YgUDuh / ydoan / yunnuhstan. E. E. Cummings. PeLV

Yi surta. Song. Tom Leonard. Oth

Yiddish Muses, The. Jacqueline Osherow. TaR

Yiddish Poets in America. Richard Chess. TaR

Yiddishe Kopf. Allen Ginsberg. BodElec; TaR

Yield. / No Parking. Yield. Ronald Gross. InPK-6

Yield Everything, Force Nothing. Jean Valentine. ExTi

Yielding clod lulls iron off to sleep. Battlefield. August Stramm. PeFWW

Yielding to a love. Ono no Komachi. WoPoe, *tr. by* Helen Craig McCullough

Yillow, yillow, yillow. Metamorphosis. Wallace Stevens. InPK-6; VGW

Ying from "The Nine Declarations." Chü Yüan. ChinPo, *tr. by* Yip Wai-lim

Yippee! she is shooting in the harbor! he is jumping. Blocks. Frank O'Hara. HCAP; LCAP-2; SPE

"Yis, dame," quod he, "tel forth, and I wol heere." (LL) Geoffrey Chaucer. FHYEP; NAEL-5v1; NAEL-6v1; NAEL-7v1 *Fr.* Canterbury Tales, The.

Yiskor. Gloria Gervitz.

"And what were you searching for, in that dream?" MirDau, *tr. by* Stephen Tapscott

"Can you hear me? Under my name I am." MirDau, *tr. by* Stephen Tapscott

"I listen through underground walls like prisoners signaling." MirDau, *tr. by* Stephen Tapscott

"Maybe we are the same darkness the same words." MirDau, *tr. by* Stephen Tapscott

"Nothing you tell me nothing." MirDau, *tr. by* Stephen Tapscott

"She detaches herself from her shadow. She is an old woman and still beautiful." MirDau, *tr. by* Stephen Tapscott

"She is crying." MirDau, *tr. by* Stephen Tapscott

"Silence is a task that will last all her life. It continues." MirDau, *tr. by* Stephen Tapscott

"We docked at noon in the port of Veracruz. We wore our Russian furs." MirDau, *tr. by* Stephen Tapscott

Yit is God a curteis lord. *Unknown.* MiEL

Yo black. I Know You Are, But What Am I? Paul Beatty. InTrad

Yo bust it: a lost generation. Don't Feel No Way. Kevin Powell. InTrad

Yo-ho-ho, and a bottle of rum! (LL) Robert Louis Stevenson. NOBVV; NPeEn *Fr.* Treasure Island.

Yo soy india / pero no soy. Tribal Chant. Carol Lee Sanchez. ReEnLa

Yogi, don't go away. Mirabai [*or* Mira Bai]. BoWoP

Yogi from far-off Beirut, A. Limerick. *Unknown.* PeLi

Yohoheyheyeyheyhahyeyeyhahhehyohoheyheyeyhey-
hahyeyeyhahhehyohoheyheyeyheyyeyeyheyhahyeyeyhahheh. Richard Johnny John. PFTM-1 *Fr.* Songs from the Society of the Mystic Animals.

Yohoweyah. When He Says So We Dance in All Directions—Wow! *Unknown.* STP, *tr. by* Richard Johnny John and Jerome Rothenberg

Yoke Soft and Dear. John C. Kunze. AH

Yoke uneasy on the ox doth sit, The. Philip Ayres. FaBoEE

Yoko. Thom Gunn. NoAM

Yolanda Meets the Wild Boys. Jessica Tarahata Hagedorn. OpBo

Yom Kippur. Israel Zangwill. TrJP

Yom Kippur, 5726. Cynthia Ozick. TaR

Yom Kippur 1984. Adrienne Rich. GLP; NoAM; TaR

Yom Kippur, Taos, New Mexico. Robin Becker. TaR

Yom Kippur: wearing a bride's dress bought in Jerusalem. Prayer. Grace Schulman. PuP-23

Yon black man-of-war hawk that wheels in the light. Man-of-War Hawk, The. Herman Melville. APN-2; OWoS

Yon cottager who weaves at her own door. Simple Faith. William Cowper. FHYEP

Yon Far Country. A. E. Housman. EBEV; HarvBoo; MoBrPo; NOBE; NOBVV; NPeEn; NoAM; OPOU; OxAEP-2; OxBEV; OxBTC; TFi

Yon is the laddie lo'ed to daunder far. Lintie in a Cage. Alice V. Stuart. OxBS

Yon Island Carrions Desperate of Their Bones. William Shakespeare. RB *Fr.* King Henry V.

Yon laddie wi' the gowdan pow. Riddle, A. William Soutar. OxBS

Yon rising Moon that looks for us again. Omar Khayyam. TRP, *tr. by* Edward Fitzgerald *Fr.* Rubáiyát of Omar Khayyám [*of* Naishápúr], The.

Yon silvery billows breaking on the beach. Sonnet's Voice, The. Theodore Watts-Dunton. GSo

Yon spark's a poet, by my troth! Difference, The. Tadhg Dall O'Huiginn. BIrV, *tr. by* Robin Flower

Yon strange blue city crowns a scarpèd steep. Mona Lisa. Edith Wharton. GS

Yond cawcrow's way-out. Two More about a Crow, in the Manner of Zukofsky. *Unknown.* STP, *tr. by* Richard Johnny John and Jerome Rothenberg

Yonder behold a little purling rill. Anne Wilson. ECWP *Fr.* Teisa, a Descriptive Poem of the River Tees, Its Towns and Antiquities.

Yonder, calm as a cloud, Alcott stalks in a dream. James Russell Lowell. TCAPo *Fr.* Fable for Critics, A.

Yonder comes a courteous knight. Baffled Knight, The. *Unknown.* ESPB

Yonder great shadow—that blot on the passionate glare of the desert. Dead of the Wilderness, The. Hayyim Nahman [*or* Khayim Nakhman *or* Chaim Nachman] Bialik. AWP, *tr. by* Maurice Samuel

Yonder on the linden tree there sang a merry little bird. Dietmar, von Aist [*or* Eist]. GePo

Yonder See the Morning Blink. A. E. Housman. NOBVV

Yonder, yonder, / Yonder. (LL) Leaden Echo and the Golden Echo, The. Gerard Manley Hopkins. GTBS-P; MoBrPo; NOBVV; OBMV

Yonder you weep. Jamila. Nazik Al-Mala'ika. WPOW, *tr. by* Kamal Boullata

Yong wyf and an harvest-gos, A. *Unknown.* MiEL

Yonnondio. Walt Whitman. NAAL-2v1; NAAL-3

York Play of the Crucifixion, The. *Unknown.* NAEL-5v1

Yorkshire Wife's Saga. Ruth Pitter. NALW

Yoruba Love. Molara Ogundipe-Leslie. HAWP

Yorunomado sat in. Black Hat, The. Clayton Eshleman. VGW

Yoshino River. *Unknown.* OHMPJ

You. Carroll Arnett. VoR

You. Tom Clark.

("Chords knotted together like insane nouns Dante, The.") SPE

You (II). SPE

You (III). PmAP; SPE

You (IV). SPE

You (I). PmAP; SPE

You. Shakuntala Hawoldar. HAWP

You. D. H. Lawrence. NoAM

You. Nelly Sachs. AF, *tr. by* Matthew Mead

You! Vladimir Vladimirovich Mayakovsky [*or* Maiakovskii]. TCRP, *tr. by* Bernard Meares

You (II). Tom Clark. SPE *Fr.* You.

You (III). Tom Clark. PmAP; SPE *Fr.* You.

You (IV). Tom Clark. SPE *Fr.* You.

You, all-accomplishing. Song to the Creator. Hildegard von Bingen. WPoS, *tr. by* Barbara Newman

You all by yourself fulfilled. *Unknown.* WoPoe, *tr. by* W. S. Merwin *Fr.* Elegy for the Great Inca Atawallpa, The.

You All Know the Story of the Two Lovers. Carlota Caulfield. TANSG, *tr. by* Chris Allen

"You almost home boy. Go on cross that sea!" (LL) My Father's Geography. Michael S. Weaver. GT; PBCAP

You almost trip as you hear. Rufous Hummingbird. Duane Niatum. PoCoUp

You Alone. Su'ad al-Mubarak Al-Sabah. MAP, *tr. by* John Heath-Stubbs and May Jayyusi

You Also, Gaius Valerius Catullus. Archibald MacLeish. NoAM; TAP

You also, our first great. To Whistler, American. Ezra Pound. AiP; FaBoA; NAAL-2v2

You always belonged here. Here. Jane Kenyon. LoL

You always know what to expect. Country House, The. Louis Simpson. NOBA

You always read about it. Cinderella. Anne Sexton. HeIP-4; NAAL-2v2

You always sang at break of day. Wolfram von Eschenbach. GePo

You and I. Henry Alford. ITBLP

You and I. *Unknown.* WoPoe, *tr. by* Stanley Moss

You and I. Tennessee Williams. GLP

You and I and a fat lady. At the Party. Mikhail Alekseievich Kuzmin. CAGL, *tr. by* Simon Karlinsky

You and I and Amyas. William Cornish. NoSic (Knight and the Lady, The.) NOBE

You and I, are we in the same story? Battle of Wills Disguised, A. Marge Piercy. HeIP-4

You and I by this lamp with these. Together. Ludwig Lewisohn. PoToHe; TrJP

You and I / Have so much love. Married Love. Kuan Tao Shêng. PasH; WoPoe, *tr. by* Chung Ling and Kenneth Rexroth

You and I Saw Hawks Exchanging the Prey. James Wright (1927–80). NAAL-2v2; NoAM

You and I will fold the sheets. Rosemary Dobson. ItWoWo; NOBAu *Fr.* Daily Living.

You and I will go to Finegall. *Unknown.* NOIV

You and the Night and the Music. Arthur Schwartz. ReLy

You and the Tijuana Mule. Rigoberto González. GeoHom

You and Them. Patty Seyburn. AmPoNex

You and You, in the Pink. Christopher Pilling. NLP

You and your client continue to walk. Fiona Templeton. FTOS *Fr.* You: The City.

You and your naked sleep. You don't know it. Sleeplessness. Gerardo Diego. BLPSL, *tr. by* Rene de Costa, Rigas Kappatos and Eleni Paidoussi

You and your sisters said i had the head of a thirty year old. Counting Backwards. Evelyn Posamentier. GotH

You, Andrew Marvell. Archibald MacLeish. APT-1; AWP; ColAP; HAP; HeIP-4; MoAmPo; NAAL-2v2; NOBA; NoAM; NoP-4; OxBA; PoRA; SoSe-8; TFi; TRP; TwCP

You answered, when I held you. Look at Me. Kim Ly Bui-Burton. PasH

You appear in a tinny, nickel-and-dime light. The light of turned milk. Bitter Angel. Amy Gerstler. PmAP

You approach. Tango'd Love. J. B. Bernstein. PasH

You approach me carrying a book. Superballs. Tom Clark. SPE

You Are. Mimi Goese. HeMarv

You Are a Daughter of the Lagides. Alvaro Mutis. BLPSL, *tr. by* Rene de Costa, Rigas Kappatos and Eleni Paidoussi

You are a friend then, as I make it out. Ben Jonson Entertains a Man from Stratford. Edwin Arlington Robinson. MoAmPo

You Are a Jew! Delmore Schwartz. TrJP *Fr.* Genesis.

You are a lord, an earl[e], nay more, a man. To the Right Honourable Mildmay, Earl of Westmorland. Robert Herrick. BeJo

You are a man, tonight! Kassacks. Annette M'Baye d'Erneville. HAWP, *tr. by* Brian Baer

You are a picture no artist could paint. I've Got a Feelin' You're Foolin' Arthur Freed. ReLy

You are a stool pigeon and. Martial. NNaP; PGA; WoPoe, *tr. by* Kenneth Rexroth

You are a sunrise. To a Golden-Haired Girl in a Louisiana Town. Nicholas Vachel Lindsay. MoAmPo

You are a tulip seen today. Meditation for His Mistress[e], A. Robert Herrick. CaPo; NOBE; NOSC; OBEV

You are a wild look—out of an egg. Ted Hughes. NoAM *Fr.* Stations.

You are already. Touch. Thom Gunn. HarvBoo

You are already dead when I am told. Dead Stepfather, The. Terry Wolverton. WiU

You are an extended branch of me. You. Shakuntala Hawoldar. HAWP

You are as gold. Song. "H. D.". APT-1; MoAmPo; TCAPo

You Are at the Bottom of My Mind. Iain Crichton Smith. WoPoe

You are beautiful and faded. Lady, A. Amy Lowell. MoAmPo; TCAPo

You are blind like us. Your hurt no man designed. To Germany. Charles Hamilton Sorley. MoBrPo

You are bright, tremendous, wow. Tom Clark. SPE *Fr.* You.

You are clear / O rose, cut in rock. Garden. "H. D.". APT-1; NoAM

You are coming to woo me, but not as of yore. Lips That Touch Liquor. George W. Young. NBLV

You are coming toward us. Aunt Laura Moves toward the Open Grave of Her Father. Joseph De Roche. HeIP-4

You are desolate, fort of kings. *Unknown.* NOIV

You are disdainful and magnificent—. Sonnet to a Negro in Harlem. Helene Johnson. APT-2; NAAAL; NIL-7; NIP-4; SSLK

You Are Distant, You Are Already Leaving. David Constantine. HarvBoo

You are drowning. How Metaphor Can Save Your Life. Myra Sklarew. CRP

You are eighty years old today, ma. To Mother. Lessie M. Drown. PWR

You are facing the harbor and the open sea. North Star. L. S. Asekoff. BodElec

You are falling asleep and I sit looking at you. After Dark. Adrienne Rich. LCAP-2; VGW

You are far away, blocked by passes and mountains. Sent to My Fourth Son, Shao-Wu (to the Tune "Southern Countryside"). Liang Te-sheng. WoPoe, *tr. by* Nancy Hodes and Tung Yuan-fang

You are for dreams and slumbers, brother priest. William Shakespeare. OxAEP-1 *Fr.* Troilus and Cressida.

You are fortunate, dear friends, that you can tell. Vidya. WPOW, *tr. by* Daniel Ingalls

You are from my country. Viaticum. U Tam'si Tchicaya. NegPo, *tr. by* Ellen Conroy Kennedy

You are going to ask: and where are the lilacs? I'm Explaining a Few Things. Pablo Neruda. TCLAP, *tr. by* Nathaniel Tarn

You Are Gorgeous and I'm Coming. Frank O'Hara. NeAP

You are handsome, aren't you. Courtesan to a Young Customer, A. Kshetrayya. WoPoe, *tr. by* V. Narayana Rao, A. K. Ramanujan and David Shulman

You Are Happy. Margaret Atwood. TRP

You Are Here. Carl Phillips. GT

You are here now. Sleeping Fury, The. Louise Bogan. NALW

You *are* him, and think yourself yourself. (LL) Tattoos. Charles Wright. BodElec; HCAP

You are holding my sister in your arms. Father and Daughter. Cathy Song. OpBo

You are holding up a ceiling. Marriage, A. Michael C. Blumenthal. PoPoPo

You are ice and fire. Opal. Amy Lowell. NALW

You are ideal. Amulet. Carl Rakosi. APT-2

You are ill and so I lead you away. Poem. Alfred Wellington Purdy. NOBC

You are impatient, says the oracle. Reading, A. Virginia Hooper. KGB

You are in Camagüey when we arrive. Primos. Sandra M. Castillo. TouFir

You are Jehova, and I am a wanderer. You and I. *Unknown.* WoPoe, *tr. by* Stanley Moss

You are just the kind of man. Exorcism of the Straight / Man / Demon. Aaron Shurin. GLP

You are leaving me. Something to Remember You By. Arthur Schwartz. ReLy

You are less than one-half. Speaker, The. Charles G. Ballard. VoR

You are like a sun of the tropics. Luxury. Donald Justice. HeIP-4

You are like dust along the road. To an Ancient Tune. Yao K'uan. CrYelRi, *tr. by* Sam Hamill

You are lying on the carpet of your bedroom dead. Acts of Love. Edgar Silex. NAPBL

You are Mad: and I Mean It! Phumzile Zulu. HAWP

You are made of almost nothing. Dragonfly, The. Louise Bogan. APT-2; HeIP-4

You are millions, we are multitude. Aleksandr Aleksandrovich Blok. *See* You are the millions, we are multitude

You are Mine said she. (LL) E. E. Cummings. BoLoP; HeIP-4; NBLV; NOBE; OBCoV; PeLV; PoPoPo

You are my candle, and light me to go. (LL) Chant to the Fire-Fly. *Unknown.* APN-2; OxIBACP, *tr. by* Henry Rowe Schoolcraft

You are my companion. Companion, The. Mary Low. SurWo

You are my finest hour. You Are. Mimi Goese. HeMarv

You are my friend. Lorine Niedecker. VGW

You are my stick, my prop. Houseplant. Felicity Napier. BrRo

You are not beautiful, exactly. To Dorothy. Marvin Bell. InvLad; VCAP

You are not dead, no. Love. Juan Ramón Jiménez. SpanPo, *tr. by* Angel Flores

You are not her darling. (LL) Tennyson. NAEL-5v2; NAEL-6v2; PeVV *Fr.* Maud [A Monodrama].

You are not here! the quaint witch Memory sees. Shelley. NOBE *Fr.* Letter to Maria Gisborne.

You are not merry, brother. Why not laugh. Prodigal Son, The. Edwin Arlington Robinson. GI; MoAmPo

You are not nearer God than we. Annunciation. Rainer Maria Rilke. OBVE, *tr. by* James Blair Leishman

You Are Not Poetry. Rosario Castellanos. TCLAP, *tr. by* Maureen Ahern

You are not wanted. Periphery. Ruth Stone. NALW

You are not with me in fleeting moments. Spiritual Wedding. Manuel Bandeira. TCLAP, *tr. by* Candace Slater

You are now / In London, that great sea. Shelley. EBEV *Fr.* Letter to Maria Gisborne.

"You are old, Father William," the young man cried. Old Man's Comforts and How He Gained Them, The. Robert Southey. UV; UnPo

You are one of those clear cold creeks. Creek, The. Roland Robinson. NOBAu

You are only one of many. One of Many. Stevie Smith. OxBC

You are over there, Father Malloy. Edgar Lee Masters. OxBA *Fr.* Spoon River Anthology.

You are pretty Solange. Solange. Rashidah Ismaili. HAWP

You are probably dreaming. Where the Nightmare Begins. Tanure Ojaide. NAfrP

You are proof that it can happen. Tardy Epithalamium for E. and N, A. Ralph Pomeroy. GLP

You are punctual. (LL) Emily Dickinson. MoAmPo; OxBA; SAmP

You are right. In dreams I might well dance. Possession. Marie Ponsot. VGW

You are right. What we call Poetry is the boat. New Poem, A. Robert Duncan. NNaP; PoM

You are sad. It is the same with me. (LL) Nocturne at Bethesda. Arna Bontemps. ChIV-2; NAAAL

You are safe / You are lying in a hammock. Lullaby. Alpay Ulku. AmPoNex

You are saying good-bye to your last. Good-Bye. Joan Larkin. WiU

You are small and intense. To a Child Running with Outstretched Arms in Canyon de Chelly. N. Scott Momaday. CDW; HATNAP

You are so elegant in your robes. Woman's Love Song. *Somali Oral Tradition*. ErotSp, *tr. by* Sam Hamill

You are so small, I. Miss Cho Composes in the Cafeteria. James Tate. WeW-3

You are somewhat slighter. Angela Dominguez, Ever Present. Nancy Morejón. TANSG, *tr. by* Joy Renjilian-Burgy

You are sucha fool / i haveta love you. You are Sucha Fool. Ntozake Shange. ISC

You are the baby in the barn. (LL) Nick and the Candlestick. Sylvia Plath. CoAP; LCAP-2; NALW

You Are the Brave. Raymond R. Patterson. NIP-4

You are the charge of halcyons now, it may be. For the Cenotaph of a Lost Soldier. Theon. GrAn, *tr. by* Dudley Fitts

You are the companion I talk with. Poetry. Xavier Villaurrutia. TCLAP, *tr. by* Dana Stangel

You are the echo when my body calls. One Who Laughs and Laughs and Laughs, The. Unsi Al-Haj [*or* Hajj]. MAP, *tr. by* Sargon Boulus and Alistair Elliot

You are the faintest freckles on the hide. Sonnet. Elinor Wylie. APT-1

You are the fish that hides. Legendary. James McAuley. BMAP

You are the grain. I Think of Housman Who Said the Poem Is a Morbid Secretion, like a Pearl. Judith Kroll. UnPo

You are the kind of beauty. New World, The. Valerie Martínez. TouFir

You are the merry men, dwarfs of soul. Diakka, The. Gerald Massey. NOBVV

You are the millions, we are multitude. Scythians, The. Aleksandr Aleksandrovich Blok. AWP

You are the most beautiful. Martial. PGA

You are the notes, and we are the flute. Jelaluddin [*or* Jalal al-Din] Rumi. EnlH

You / are the One who put. Stars in Apple Cores. Luci Shaw. TrCP

You are the owner of one complete thought. Voice and Address. Michael Palmer. FTOS; PmAP

You are the problem I propose. Metaphysical Amorist, The. James Vincent Cunningham. VGW

You are the salt of the earth. Gail Holst-Warhaft. GI *Fr.* St. Matthew.

You are the sandstorm beneath my skin. Song. Odia Ofeimun. NAfrP

You are tired. Midnight Tennis Match, The. Thomas Lux. MoASP

You are to me the secret of my soul. World Well Lost 18, The. Marc André Raffalovich. CAGL

You Are Too Beautiful. Richard Rodgers. ReLy

You are too naked for touching. Morning. Jeni Couzyn. HAWP

You are too splendid for this city street. (LL) Sonnet to a Negro in Harlem. Helene Johnson. APT-2; NAAAL; NIL-7; NIP-4; SSLK

You are traveling to play basketball. Your team's. In Your Young Dream. Richard Hugo. InPK-6

You are traveling within the boundaries of your time together. Seizing the Day. Judith Ortiz Cofer. PueRic; SwNoth

You are welcome to your country, dear Antonio. John Webster. NAEL-5v1; NAEL-7v1

You are with me Oregon. Oregon. Bob Kaufman. GT

You arrived that bad winter. Solstice. Gerald Dawe. PNI

You ask. Untitled. Rachel Tzvia Back. DTA

You ask for the date. Nizar Qabbani. MAP

You ask how I spend my time. To Tu Fu from Shantung. Li Po. CrYelRi, *tr. by* Sam Hamill

You ask how it is. I will tell you. Blaen Cwrt. Gillian Clarke. AngWePo

You ask how old am I. Twice Times Then Is Now. Ibn Hazm al-Andalusi. ArPe; OBVE; WoPoe, *tr. by* Omar Pound and Omar S. Pound

You ask me, girl, why I withdraw my sword. Macedonius. GrAn

You ask me how Contempt who claims to sleep. Epigram. James Vincent Cunningham. VCAP

You ask me how I became a madman. It happened thus. Madman (Prologue), The. Kahlil Gibran. GraLe; TCAPo

You ask me how it is living in exile, friend. Eavesdropper. Breyten Breytenbach. PeSAV; PoetW, *tr. by* Ernst Van Heerden

You ask me my name? They got lotsa names. Madarika. Vince Gotera. OpBo; ReBoTo

You ask me, Queen, time after time. Kamalākānta Bhattācārya. SinGod, *tr. by* Rachel Fell McDermott

You ask me what I mean. Sujata Bhatt. PFTM-2 *Fr.* Search for My Tongue.

You ask me what I thought about. Kenneth Rexroth. APSN; APT-2 *Fr.* Love Poems of Marichiko, The.

You ask me *What's love?*—Why, that virtue-fed vapour. Address to Lady——, Who Asked What the Passion of Love Was? Charles Morris. NOEC

You ask me what since we must part. Gifts. Juliana Horatia Ewing. LW

You ask me why I'm always teasing you. Pretty Baby. Egbert Van Alstyne. ReLy

You ask my wish—the boon I crave. Lady Caroline Lamb. RWP *Fr.* Fugitive Pieces and Reminiscences of Lord Byron with Some Original Poetry, Letters and Recollections of Lady Caroline Lamb, ed. I. Nathan.

You ask what I have found, and far and wide I go. Curse of Cromwell, The. W. B. Yeats. BIrV

You ask what I think of your new acquisition. Bitcherel. Eleanor Brown. MFPA; NeBl

You ask what our son's profession should be. Our Son's Profession. Ha Thi Thao. WoPoe, *tr. by* Nguyen Ngoc Bich

You ask when I will go back home. Ni Tsan. CoBLCP *Fr.* Following the Rhymes of Yü-chai's Poems on Autumn.

You ask: when to return? Don't know when. Night Rains: A Letter to Go North. Li Shang-yin. ChinPo, *tr. by* Yip Wai-lim

You ask which is better, whether a king or a senate rules. Neither, if, as. Quis Optimus Reipublicae Status. Sir Thomas More. PBRV

You Ask Why. Li Po. EnlH, *tr. by* Sam Hamill

You ask why gold and velvet bind. On a New Duke. *Unknown*. FaBoEE

You ask why I don't hide my filthy charms? *Unknown*. PriapPo, *tr. by* Richard W. Hooper *Fr.* Priapus Poems, The.

You ask why I live. Questions Answered. Li Po. CrYelRi, *tr. by* Sam Hamill

You ask why I make my home in the mountain forest. You Ask Why. Li Po. EnlH, *tr. by* Sam Hamill

You asked, I came. Evil That Men Do, The. Queen Latifah. NAAAL

You asked me once for something really Native. Connuche. Catron Grieves. ReEnLa

You asked me to enter the holy cloister. Banishment from Ur. Enheduanna. BoWoP, *tr. by* J. J. A. van Dijk and W. W. Hallo

You asked me what is the good of reading the Gospels in Greek. Readings. Czeslaw Milosz. GI

You asked neither for glory nor tears. Stanzas against Forgetting. Guillaume Apollinaire. AF, *tr. by* Carolyn Forché

You asked us to hear the softest vocable of wind. Lines for Roethke Twenty Years after His Death. Duane Niatum. HATNAP

You at the Pump. Frank O'Hara. FTOS

You attribute my recovery. Therapy. John Wright. BloBone

You awoke at midnight. Beyond the window. Storm, A. "Nikolai Nikolaevich Morshen." TCRusP, *tr. by* John Glad

You balanced her within a cyclone. Woman Seed Player. Roberta Hill Whiteman. HATNAP

You be tellin' me You Be Black. Open Letter to All Black Poets, An. Samuel F. Reynolds. SpirFl

You beastly child, I wish you had miscarried. Lightly Bound. Stevie Smith. NALW

You beauteous dames, if that my love you see. You Beauteous Dames. Jane Colman Turell. TCAPo

You beautious ladies, great and small. Famous Flower of Serving-Men; or, The Lady Turn'd Serving-Man, The. *Unknown*. ESPB; OxBB

You became / In many acts and quiet observances. My Company. Sir Herbert Read. PoWW

You Begin. Margaret Atwood. NOBC; NoP-4

You believed in your own story. Fairy Tales. "Shu Ting." VCWP

You belong to the tired, modern kind. Kind of Culture, A. Mihály Babits. IQMS, *tr. by* Peter Zollman

You, Benjamin Jones, dead seventeen. You, Benjamin Jones. Jon Dressel. AngWePo

You bet we'll soon forget the one that died. One That Died, The. William Daniel Ehrhart. CDa

You Bet Your Life. Nancy Vieira Couto. PBCAP

You bid me hold my peace. Worn Out. Paul Laurence Dunbar. NAAAL

You bid me write, Sir, I comply. Address to a Bachelor on a Delicate Occasion. Priscilla Pointon. ECWP

You bid my muse not cease to sing. Written to a Near Neighbour in a Tempestuous Night. Henrietta, Lady Luxborough Knight. ECWP

You black bright stars, that shine while daylight lasteth. You Black Bright Stars. Thomas Morley. NoSic

You black-maned, horse-haired, long-faced creature. To the Gentlewoman of Llanarth Hall. Evan Thomas. OBWVE, tr. by Gwyn Jones

You blame me that I do not write. Letter to a Friend. Jon Stallworthy. NoAM

You blessed Soules, who stand before. Dame Clementia Cary. EMWP

You blow on the hair of your child. Vladimir Burich. TCRP

You both are modest. So am I. Farewell. (LL) Ben Jonson. BASC; BeJo

You bound strong sandals on my feet. Song. Sara Teasdale. PoBW

You Brandenburg's support and Prussia's guarantee. On the Entrance of the Castle Bridge. Simon Dach. GePo, tr. by George C. Schoolfield

You brave heroic [or heroique] minds. To the Virginian Voyage. Michael Drayton. AiP; BASC; HAP; NAEL-5v1; NOBE; NOSC; OBEV; SCGP

You breathe by words ten thousand times a day. And to Be Born Is Here an Unnameable Feast. Gonzalo Rojas. TCLAP, tr. by Christopher Maurer

You Bring Me Back. Patti Tana. PasH

You bring me (neighbourly). Gifts. Thelma Tyfield. PoBW

You Bring Out the Mexican in Me. Sandra Cisneros. IllVoic

You bring the child back to its mother. (LL) Sappho. SaLy; WPoS, tr. by Diane Rayor

You built yourself a tower in the wind. Jean-Joseph Rabéarivelo [or Rebéarivelo]. NegPo

You burned the dawn / with the flame of your guitar. Wake for Papa Montero. Nicolás Guillén. PFTM-1

You burst into the world with smiles wide as April. Sleeping with Foxes. Roberta Hill Whiteman. CDW

You but unlock[e], so we each other bless[e]. (LL) To a Lady That Desired I Would Love Her. Thomas Carew. BASC; BeJo; CaPo; CavPo; MeLP; SCGP

You buy some flowers for your table. Samuel Hoffenstein. OBCoV; TrJP Fr. Poems in Praise of Practically Nothing.

You buy yourself a new suit of clothes. Samuel Hoffenstein. OBCoV Fr. Poems in Praise of Practically Nothing.

You call that wine? On Beer. Emperor Julian. PGA, tr. by Kenneth Rexroth

You called me a name on such and such a day—. For T.S.E. Only. Hyam Plutzik. APT-2; TaR

You Called Me Corazón. Sandra Cisneros. AmFaPo

You called me from lakes and hills. Reply to Prefect Liu. T'ao Ch'ien [or T'ao Yuan-ming]. CrYelRi, tr. by Sam Hamill

You Called to Me, Prison Windows. Danièle Amrane. HAWP, tr. by Eric Sellin

You Came a Long Way from St. Louis. Bob Russell. ReLy

You came and did (well); I felt for you. Sappho. SaLy, tr. by Diane Rayor

You came. And you did well to come. Sappho. BoWoP

You Came down from the Mountains. Marcelle Ferry. SurWo, tr. by Myrna Bell Rochester

You came into my life. First Night. Julia H. Ackerman. PasH

You came to gaze upon me. Farewell to Arms, A. Aleksandr Petrovich Mezhirov. TCRP, tr. by Deming Browm

You came to it through wild country, there the sea's voice. House in the Green Well, The. John Hall Wheelock. MoAmPo

You came to me a little while before. Visit, The. Ibn Hazm al-Andalusi. WoPoe, tr. by Leticia Garza-Falcón and Christopher Middleton

You came to rest on a leaf of my body. You Came to Rest. Emilio Adolfo Westphalen. BLPSL, tr. by Rene de Costa, Rigas Kappatos and Eleni Paidoussi

You Came with Shells. June Jordan. NoAM

You can actually hear it in his voice. Leadbelly. Cornelius Eady. ESEAA

You can always spot them, even from high up. From Altitude, the Diamonds. Richard Hugo. MoASP

You can become a shaman. New Indian Medicine. Emma Lee Warrior. HATNAP

You can call me Herbie Jr. or Ashamah. Unemployment / Monologue. June Jordan. WPOW

You can come to terms with anyone. At the Cave. Artur Miedzyrzecki. PoSu, tr. by Stanislaw Baranczak

You can discover for yourself. You Can Discover. Barbara Guest. BodElec

You can feel the muscles and veins rippling in widening and rising circles. Saying Dante Aloud. James Wright (1927–80). InPK-6

You can go now yes go now. Go east or west, go north or. Carl Sandburg. HHAm Fr. People, Yes, The.

You can hang or drown at last. (LL) Short Song of Congratulation [or To a Young Heir], A. Samuel Johnson. EBEV; HAP; InPK-6; NAEL-6v1; NOBE; NOEC; NPeEn; OBCoV; OBSV; OxAEP-1; OxBEV; PeLV; PoE; TFi; UnPo; WoPoe

You Can Have It. Philip Levine. AmFaPo; NoP-4; VCAP

You can hear the silence of it. David Jones. FaBoMo; FaBoWar Fr. In Parenthesis.

You can make this swooped transition on your lips. Ted Berrigan. FTOS Fr. Sonnets, The.

You can no longer. Wreath, A. Gyula Illyés. IQMS, tr. by William Jay Smith

You can say the broken word but cannot speak. Wheel. Michael Palmer. BodElec

You can see all the way to heaven. (LL) Heaven. Cathy Song. NAAL-5; NIL-7; NoAM

You can see from their faces. Photographs of Pioneer Women. Ruth Dallas. PeNZ

You can see her, hair down, sipping a Coke. What a Little Moonlight Can Do. Joe Heithaus. SeSe

You can see the moon's brightness. Shih Te. SuSp

You can see them everywhere in Cuba. Landscapes. Heberto Padilla. VCWP

You can see why men are such monsters. St. Clare's Underwear. Barbara Hamby. ReTh

You can sigh o'er the sad-eyed Armenian. Appeal to My Countrywomen, An. Frances Ellen Watkins Harper. BlSi

You can stop me. There's Somethin' Adam Small. PeSAV

You can't be serious she said. John Cage. APT-2 Fr. Composition in Retrospect.

You can't beat English lawns. Our final hope. Rolling the Lawn. William Empson. HarvBoo; MoBrPo; OBGa

You can't catch the thief, Mind. Mahendranâth Bhattâcârya. SinGod, tr. by Rachel Fell McDermott

You can't do English much. Why Do You Want to Be English? Peter Finch. Oth

You Can't Escape Your Life Record. Manila Koordada. WoPoe

You can't ever imagine the Virgin Mary having vulvitis or thrush. Sonnet: Supernatural Beings. Gavin Ewart. Son

You Can't Get a Man with a Gun. Irving Berlin. ReLy

You can't get rid of it. Hope. Dolores de Iruretagoyena de Humphrey. ReBoTo

You can't just call it a pig. James Dean and the Pig. Joseph Like. ReTh

You Can't Kill a Baby Twice. Dahlia Ravikovitch [or Ravikovich]. VCWP

You can't leave your home. Side 20. Víctor Hernández Cruz. PueRic

You can't look at yourself. Great Sadness, The. Federico García Lorca. PFTM-1

You Can't Make Love by Wireless. P. G. Wodehouse. ReLy

You can't say it that way any more. And "Ut Pictura Poesis" Is Her Name. John Ashbery. VCAP

You can't see it or hear it. Spring Breeze. Ho Hsun. OHMPC, tr. by Kenneth Rexroth

You can't see us in spiritland, and we can't see at all. (LL) Jack Spicer. NeAP; PmAP Fr. Imaginary Elegies.

You can't spend all day staring into the sea, however. War. Michael Brownstein. FTOS

You Can't Stop Me from Lovin' You. Mann Holiner. ReLy

You can't stop people from talking. Say It Isn't So. Irving Berlin. ReLy

You can't take her out for a night on the town. Cathleen. Nuala Ni Dhomhnaill. ModIr, tr. by Paul Muldoon

You can't take with you. Paavo Haavikko. WoPoe, tr. by Anselm Hollo

You can't walk barefoot in the city. Barefoot in the City. Lisa Buscani. AmPoNex

You can't win Love over / by crying. To Telembrotos. Antipater of Thessalonica. GrAn, tr. by Alistair Elliot

You can't write. You can't open a magazine. Two in a Room. Viktor Krivulin. TCRusP, tr. by Anna Barker and Daniel Weissbort

You can talk about. Visitors to the Black Belt. Langston Hughes. NAAL-5

You can talk to me of sin and related matters. (LL) Welshman in Exile Speaks, The. T. Harri Jones. AngWePo; OBWVE

You can tell by the angle. Londonderry Air, The. Nicolas Bentley. OBCoV

You cannot build bridges between the wandering islands. Wandering Islands, The. Alec Derwent Hope. HarvBoo

You cannot do better than eat them yourselves. (LL) Mother Goose. OxNR; ReMoGo

You Cannot Do This. Gwendolyn MacEwen. FaBoWP

You cannot dream. Things Lovelier. Humbert Wolfe. TrJP

You Cannot Go down to the Spring. John Shaw Neilson. CBAP

You cannot hope. British Journalist, The. Humbert Wolfe. FaBoEE; OBCoV; OxBEV; OxBTC

You cannot see mountains and valleys in the clouds. Spyglass Conversations. Unknown. STP, tr. by Frances Densmore

You cannot tell. Daibai. JDP, tr. by Yoel Hoffmann

You cared whether I died or not. Martha Anthony. InTrad

You / catch my breath with your waking. Blues 1. Barry Wallenstein. SeSe

You cathedral, you! Pure astonishment! To Freedom. Ágnes Nemes Nagy. PoSu, *tr. by* Bruce Berlind

You chose the taste of dust. Footnotes. Arkadii Dragomoschenko. ItGoST, *tr. by* Elena Balashova and Lyn Hejinian

You claim his poems are garbage. Balderdash! Poet Defended, A. Paul Ramsey. InPK-6

You clambered into the glass of whisky. Glass. Anne Rouse. NeBl

You climb. Reply to Gen'no Osho's Poem. Muso Soseki. EaWin, *tr. by* W. S. Merwin

You coax the blues right out of the horn. Mame. Jerry Herman. ReLy

You come forth / the color of a stone cliff. To Insure Survival. Simon J. Ortiz. CDW

You come from a line of. Power. Alma Villanueva. ItWoWo

You come from poets, kings, bankrupts, preachers. For My Son. Muriel Rukeyser. TaR

You come from the ages' origin. Going Forth. Andrée Chedid. PoArWo, *tr. by* Lucy McNair

You come late. "H. D.". GifTon *Fr.* Priest.

You come to fetch me from my work tonight. Putting in the Seed. Robert Frost. APT-1; NoAM; OxBA

You come to in the past, dark, where the fires still burn. Train Wreck, 1890: My Grandmother Lies down with the Dead. T. R. Hummer. GM

You come to market—seeking gain, to be sure. Offered to a Man Who Sells Pines. Yü Wu-ling. SuSp, *tr. by* Edward H. Schafer

You Come to Me. Quincy Troupe. NBV

You come to me at night. Bitch, A. Anna Swir. GifTon, *tr. by* Czeslaw Milosz and Leonard Nathan

You come to me from the oldest wound of wind. Breath. Deema K. Shehabi. PoArWo

You come to Paris, you come to play. You Don't Know Paree. Cole Porter. ReLy

You come with the light on your face. Wave, The. Witter Bynner. APT-1

You could be sitting now in a carrel. Late Aubade, A. Richard Wilbur. PAI; SoSe-8

You could call it abandon, but never leisure. Life of the Body, The. Diane Bonds. PoSol

You could draw a straight line from the heels. Man Lying on a Wall. Michael Longley. ModIr; NPeEn; PNI

You could live in a world so solidly blue. (LL) Falling. Lesley Dauer. AmPoNex; NAPBL

You could love here, not the lovely goat. Milltown Union Bar, The. Richard Hugo. NoAM

You could say that the streets flow softly in the night. Los Angeles Nocturne. Xavier Villaurrutia. TCLAP, *tr. by* Rachel Benson

You could see him, walking between the rifles. Crime Was in Granada, The. Antonio Machado Ruiz. SpanPo, *tr. by* Kate Flores

You could turn this way. Basho. EH, *tr. by* Robert Hass

You Couldn't Be Cuter. Dorothy Fields. ReLy

You couldn't bear to grow old, but we grow old. John Berryman. TAP *Fr.* Dream Songs.

You couldn't find a better time to meet me, Marcus. Pacifico Massimi. CAGL, *tr. by* James J. Wilhelm *Fr.* Hecateleguim.

You couldn't pack a Broadwood half a mile. Song of the Banjo, The. Rudyard Kipling. FaBoCh

You coward . . . this baby that I bleed. (LL) Abortion, The. Anne Sexton. LCAP-2; VGW

You cradle mouthless smiling flowers. Winter Sunflowers. Gillian Ferguson. NeBl

You crash over the trees. Storm. "H. D.". APT-1

You crawl around a rim. In Love with Wholes. Alberta Turner. LCAP-2

You crown me king and queen. There is a name. Dedicace. Aleister Crowley. CAGL

You cry, carry on in tones of pity. Philodemus. GrAn

You cry, She's bred in the Old Way. To Novella, on her saying deridingly, that a Lady of great Merit, and fine Address, was bred in the Old Way. Mary Barber. NIL-7

You cry, waking from a nightmare. Little Sleep's-Head Sprouting Hair in the Moonlight. Galway Kinnell. LCAP-2

You Cry, Whine, Peer Strangely at Me. Philodemus. WoPoe, *tr. by* George Economou

You'd almost think it was despair. (LL) Combat, The. Edwin Muir. MoBrPo; NOBE

You'd Be Surprised. Irving Berlin. ReLy

You'd better abandon all idea of feelings altogether. (LL) To Women, as Far as I'm Concerned. D. H. Lawrence. NPeEn; OxBSP; RaBo

You'd know men's hearts up from the dust. Near Perigord. Ezra Pound. APT-1; FaBoMo

You'd know the folly of being comforted. (LL) Folly of Being Comforted, The. W. B. Yeats. HeIP-4; NAEL-5v2; NAEL-6v2

You'd like to kiss your little boy but he doesn't want to. Lady on Streetcar. Sandro Penna. STV, *tr. by* John Frederick Nims

You'd think all these mandarins, big shots. Mandarins Got Their Raise, The. Tu Mo. WoPoe, *tr. by* Nguyen Ngoc Bich

You'd think they'd be with family. Christmas Eve. Sascha Feinstein. SeSe

You'd think they discovered injustice and achieved. Gulls at Cannon Beach. William Stafford. PoCoUp

You'd think this piece of road. How the Elderly Drive. Erin Belieu. AmPoNex

You dance anger chanting. Ballerina. Rosario Ferré. TANSG, *tr. by* Nancy Diaz

You danced a magnetic dance. So Many Feathers. Jayne Cortez. BISi; ISC

You dare not let your eyes meet theirs. Women Are Different. Marsha Prescod. LW

You dark eye, o rest upon me. Prayer. Nikolaus Lenau. AuPH, *tr. by* Winthrop H. Root

You, dead in '92 and '93. Arthur Rimbaud. OBWP, *tr. by* Robert Lowell *Fr.* Eighteen-Seventy.

You delude yourself. Jean-Joseph Rabéarivelo [*or* Rebéarivelo]. NegPo

You did it, didn't you? Passacaglia. Don Hymans. BAP-97

You did late review my lays. To Christopher North. Tennyson. FaBoEE; PeLV

You did not come. Broken Appointment, A. Thomas Hardy. HarvBoo; NAEL-5v2; NAEL-6v2; NOBVV; NoAM

You did not come to the Paris exposition of 1937 on the opening night when I asked you. Kay Boyle. SurPaPo *Fr.* Complaint for Mary and Marcel, A.

You did not find me, you did not. You Did Not Find Me. Rabindranath Tagore. WoPoe, *tr. by* Pratimer Bowes

You did not see Him on the mountain of Transfiguration. To the Good Thief. Saunders Lewis. OBWVE, *tr. by* Gwyn Morgan

You did not walk with me. Walk, The. Thomas Hardy. NAEL-5v2; NAEL-6v2; NPeEn; OxBEV; PoE

You did not want to remember. Late Words for My Sister. Robin Becker. ExTi

You Didn't Fit. Susan Musgrave. NIL-7

You didn't have to travel to become an airplane. Communication of His Thirtieth Birthday. Marvin Bell. CoAP

You died in spring, father, and now the autumn dies. American Sonnets for My Father. Daniela Gioseffi. UnSA

You died nine years ago today. February 11, 1977. Frederick Morgan. DiPo

You died without my knowing. Elegy for My Friend E. Galo. Raymond Mazisi Kunene. PoetW

You died young, uncle, only fifty-two. Profaning the Dead. Carole Bernstein. AmPoNex

You dive in, head for the other side, sure. Pregnant Poets Swim Lake Tarleton, New Hampshire. Barbara Ras. NAPBL

You do look a little ill, now. Alcohol. Franz Wright. LCAP-2

You do not come, and I wait. Fujiwara no Sadaie. OHPJ

You do not do, you do not do. Mommy. Jill Ciment. Unle

You do not do, you do not do. Daddy. Sylvia Plath. BoWoP; CoAP; ColAP; HCAP; HP; HeIP-4; InPK-6; MakPoe; NAAL-2v2; NAAL-5; NALW; NIL-7; NIP-4; NOBA; NoAM; NoP-4; PAI; PoE; PoPoPo; TFi; TwCP; UnPo; VCAP

You do not have to be good. Wild Geese. Mary Oliver. BLT

You do not hear me, Dad. (LL) Child to His Sick Grandfather, A. Joanna Baillie. CABP; ECWP; NOEC; RACG; WoRP

You do not know how hard it is. Intimations of Anxiety. Laila Al-Saih. PoArWo, *tr. by* May Jayyusi and Naomi Shihab Nye

You do not limp. 194 . . . . Mikhail Valentinovich Kulchitsky [*or* Kulchitskii]. TCRP, *tr. by* Daniel Weissbort

You do not move about, but try. Getting Lost in Nazi Germany. Marvin Bell. GotH; TaR

You do peruse the rest? (LL) I.W. To her unconstant Lover. Isabella Whitney. EMWP; PBRV

You do understand I've waited long enough. Complaint: To the Muse. Philip Whalen. BB

You, Doctor Martin. Anne Sexton. MoAmPo; NAAL-2v2

You don't even have any sins! Géza Páskándi. IQMS, *tr. by* Agnes Arany-Makkai *Fr.* Language Memory.

You don't find so many of them on regular days, in normal months. New Year's Season and Its Poetasters, The. Trần Tế Xu'o'ng. WoPoe, *tr. by* Nguyen Ngoc Bich

You don't have more money. (LL) Martial. NNaP; PGA; WoPoe, *tr. by* Kenneth Rexroth

You don't have to be awake. New Year's Morning. Elmaz Abinader. PoArWo

You don't have to go very far. Some Sights Sometimes Seen and Seldom Seen. William Cole. TLR

You don't have to listen to folk stories. I Saw It! Ilya [or Karl] L'vovich Selvinsky [or Sel'vinskii]. TCRusP, tr. by Denis Johnson

You don't have to listen to folktales. I Saw It. Ilya [or Karl] L'vovich Selvinsky [or Sel'vinskii]. TCRP, tr. by Daniel Weissbort

You don't have to understand a nightingale's song. Speech. Leopold Staff. PoSu, tr. by Adam Czerniawski

You Don't Know Paree. Cole Porter. ReLy

You don't know that I felt good. Lorenz Hart. See Sleepless nights, The

You Don't Know What Happened When You Froze. Talvikki Ansel. NeAmPo

You Don't Know What Love Is. Don Raye. ReLy

You don't remember what you did. Intermission from Friday. Pedro Juan Pietri. PueRic

You don't see buffalo skulls very much any more. Something Starting Over. Thomas Hornsby Ferril. APT-2

You Don't Understand Me. Marge Piercy. NALW

You don't want madhouse and the whole thing there. (LL) Let It Go. William Empson. FaBoMo; HarvBoo; NPeEn; OxBEV; OxBSP; OxBTC

You drank the warm breath of your turtledove. Velemir [or Viktor Vladimirovich] Khlebnikov. TCRP, tr. by Gary Kern

You dream someone is leaving you, though he says kindly, It's not that you're cold. Estrangement. Jane Cooper. ExTi

You dreamed it. From my ground. Jay Macpherson. NOBC Fr. Ark, The.

You dreamed of drowning there, but couldn't read. Another Version of an Ocean. Reginald Shepherd. NeAmPo

You dreamt of being a dancer, but frightened. Abused Child. Michael O'Reilly. BloBone

You drifted lazily from the sky. Looking Back. Joanna Kadi. PoArWo

You drink from crystal. Laurie Duggan. BMAP Fr. Epigrams of Martial, The.

You drink to piss it all away. Anacreontic. R. S. Gwynn. RA

You drive in across this bridge they've built. Welcome to Wales. John Tripp. AngWePo

You drive, the road aims for a mountain. View, A. Mona Van Duyn. VCAP

You each guardian Fay shall bless. (LL) Inscription in a Beautiful Retreat Called Fairy Bower. Hannah More. ECWP; NoP-4

You earthly Souls that court a wanton flame. La Belle Confidente. Thomas Stanley. BeJo; MeLP

You eat me, your. Mother Love. Elaine Feinstein. HarvBoo

You eat whatever you can. Potatoes. Robert Peters. SpudSo

You empress of the stars, the heavens' worthy crown. Spring-Joy Praising God; Praise of the Sun. Catharina Regina von Greiffenberg. WPOW, tr. by George C. Schoolfield

You enter the areas beyond veiled light. Sleep Watch. Lance Henson. VoR

You envied the flying birds and stones. Bakhyt Kenjeev. ItGoST, tr. by Nina Kossman

You excellent women, you valiant men. Walther [or Walter] von der Vogelweide. GePo

You expect, Puss-in-Boots. Justice. Agathias. GrAn, tr. by Peter Whigham

You exquisite girl, dressed absurdly deliciously artifically. Sweet Disorder in the Dress, A. Harry Hooton. NOBAu

You, Failed Pronoun. Eleanor Wilner. ExTi

You, Farrell O'Reilly, I feared as a boy. Farrell O'Reilly. Oliver St. John Gogarty. OxBTC

You Fascinate Me So. Cy Coleman. ReLy

You feed us milkfish stew. Milkfish. Eugene Gloria. OpBo

You feel adequate to the demands of this position? You Will Be Hearing from Us Shortly. U. A. Fanthorpe. OBCoV

You feel no love or pity for me. Sergey [or Sergei] Aleksandrovich Yesenin [or Essenin]. TCRP

You fill me up so much. Where the Mississippi meets the Amazon. Ntozake Shange. ISC

You find it ugly, I find it lovely. (LL) William Street. Kenneth Slessor. BMAP; CBAP

You find them in the darker woods. Persistence of Nature in Our Lives, The. Andrew Hudgins. DiPo; WeW-3

You first, shift your attention (that is, if you withdraw). Angelo Lumelli. ItPo, tr. by Gayle Ridinger

You fit into me. Margaret Atwood. InPK-6; NALW; NoAM

You fix a Dagger in my Heart. To the Same; Enquiring Why I Wept. Mary Masters. PoBW

You flawed the tenderest movement of three lives. (LL) Richard Murphy. BiHa; ModIr Fr. Price of Stone, The.

You fled this island in a bark. Verdict of Stone, A. Tanure Ojaide. NAfrP

You . . . flowing through selves / Toward you. (LL) Now That I Am Forever with Child. Audre Lorde. NAAAL; NALW

You fold your clipped wings in your father's house. Departure. Edgar Silex. NAPBL

You follow foreign ways. Two Sons. Laoiseach Mac an Bhaird. NOIV

You follow me as I come and go. Song for My Shadow, A. Kim Pyŏngyŏn. WoPoe, tr. by Richard John Lynn

You fool yourself and live a crazy day. Voice of a Dissipated Woman inside a Tomb. Sor Violante do Céu. BoWoP, tr. by Willis Barnstone

You for eternity, and have no other choice? (LL) Obit. Robert Lowell. HCAP; PoetW; VCAP

You, for My Meditation. Sara de Ibáñez. TCLAP, tr. by Andrew Rosing

You forgot where you lived at. Intermission from Saturday. Pedro Juan Pietri. PueRic

You found it difficult to woo. Daphnis and Chloe. Haniel Long. APT-1

You, friend, who whilom tossed the ball. Jane Brereton. ECWP Fr. To Mr Thomas Griffith at the University of Glasgow.

You gather them in the shade of pine trees. Eating Roasted Matsutake Mushrooms. Ishikawa Jōzan. WoPoe, tr. by Jonathan Chaves

You gave Bithynicus thousands yearly; still. Martial. RomPo, tr. by J. P. Sullivan

You gave me beauty, Cytherea. Lais' Mirror. Julianus of Egypt. GrAn, tr. by Robin Skelton

You Gave Me Hyacinths First a Year Ago. Dorothy Hewett. BMAP

You gaze at me teasingly through the window. Praxilla. BoWoP

You get a wife, you get a house. Cat, The. Ogden Nash. WHSW

You get these thoughts in melancholy Autumn. Together Again. Victor Vroomkoning. TuT, tr. by James Simmons

You Get What You Pay For. Allen Curnow. HarvBoo

You gets no bread with. One Meat Ball. Thomas Lux. ReTh

You give your cheeks a rosy stain. Artificial Beauty. Lucianus [or Lucian]. AWP, tr. by William Cowper

You glow in my heart. Bungler, The. Amy Lowell. LW

You go home one evening tired from work. Turtle Soup. Marilyn Chin. LoL

You go--it seems to me--with a hint. Disconnections. Silvana Colonna. ItPo, tr. by Gayle Ridinger

You Go to My Head. J. Fred Coots. ReLy

You go to my head, the song says: I wouldn't take. Three A.M. Eternal. Reginald Shepherd. WiU

You go up there cocked. Swinging on the First Pitch. Dabney Stuart. MoASP

You gods of sea and sky—what's left me now but prayer? Ovid. RomPo, tr. by Peter Green Fr. Tristia.

You gods, teach her some more humanity. (LL) Divine Mistress, A. Thomas Carew. BeJo; CavPo

You gods! to fold the charmer in my arms. Rapture, The. Henry Baker. NOEC

You golden freedom, both my wish and my desire. Martin Opitz. GePo

You gonna eat that? Birch. Karen Shepard. Unle

You got to walk that lonesome valley. Lonesome Valley. Unknown. APN-2

You Got You Got to Be Told. Elizabeth Brown. IBA

You Gotta Have Your Tips on Fire. Víctor Hernández Cruz. PueRic

You gotta watch / out for the "Ol Liver" (LL) Welcome Back, Mr. Knight: Love of My Life. Etheridge Knight. PBCAP; RaBo

You govern the locks, You open life. Unknown. ASW Fr. Christ 1.

You grow impatient while I focus, fiddle. You Have Shown Me a Strange Image, and We Are Strange Prisoners. Jeni Couzyn. PBCAP

You grow less agile, more compliant. Exile, Representative. Breyten Breytenbach. AF, tr. by Denis Hirson

You Growing. Milton Acorn. NOBC

You gulp, a frog suddenly on my dinner. You Don't Understand Me. Marge Piercy. NALW

You had a skirt with flounces. Another Kind of Skin. Frances Sackett. Prnts

You had better sleep as well. (LL) Nikolai Alekseievich Zabolotsky [or Zabolotskii]. TCRP; WoPoe, tr. by Daniel Weissbort

You had lived long enough to see things 'nicely settled.' (LL) Geoffrey Hill. EmeKit; PoE Fr. Mercian Hymns.

You had two girls—Baptiste. At the Cedars. Duncan Campbell Scott. NOBC

You hang back, call me. Bathing My Mother. Frances Wilson. Prnts

You Hated Spain. Ted Hughes. EmeKit

You have an idea of yourself. Only Fortunate Thing, The. Joe Wenderoth. BodElec

You have anti-freeze in the car, yes. Christmas Card. Ted Hughes. OBCP

You have been my treasure, Rose Pilgrim. Elect. Mary Ursula Bethell. PeNZ

You have called at the gate of the True Vehicle. Saying Good-bye to a Singing Girl Who Has Decided to Become a Nun. Mo Shih-lung. CoBLCP; CoIAnChi; WoPoe, tr. by Jonathan Chaves

You have coats and robes. Unknown. AWP, tr. by H. A. Giles Fr. Shi King.

You have done nothing but listen to songs. Your Work. Jean-Joseph Rabéarivelo [or Rebéarivelo]. NegPo, tr. by Ellen Conroy Kennedy

You have edited a thousand pages of palm-leaf manuscripts. To the Monk Wu-hsia on the Occasion of His Editing the Lotus Sutra. Mo Shih-lung. CoBLCP; ColAnChi, *tr.* by Jonathan Chaves

You have forgotten me well. (LL) When You Have Forgotten Sunday: The Love Story. Gwendolyn Brooks. BPo; WPOW

You have gone, old tooth. My Last Tooth. *Unknown.* VerBaPo

You have heard, I suppose, of the man in the moon. Coolie Chinee, The. Septimus Winner. OBAL

You have heard it said before. Handle for the Flutist, A. Odia Ofeimun. HBAPE

You have heard that it was said. Gail Holst-Warhaft. GI *Fr.* St. Matthew.

You have Hera's eyes Melite. Rufinus. GrAn

You have left the train too early. Meeting Place. Pauline Hawkesworth. Prnts

You Have Lost, They Tell Me, Your Reason. Rosario Ferré. TANSG, *tr.* by Patricia Santoro

You have made God small. Raptor. Ronald Stuart Thomas. EmeKit

You have netted this dawn. Archaeology of Love, The. Richard Murphy. EnLoPo

You have no right to trouble me. Magic Formula. *Unknown.* CA

You have not conquered me—it is the surge. Infidelity. Louis Untermeyer. TrJP

You have nothing to do with me, alas. Lőrinc Szabó. IQMS, *tr.* by Watson Kirkconnell *Fr.* Cricket Music.

You have now come with me, I have now come with you. Poet: A Lying Word. Laura Riding Jackson. HarvBoo

You have oh haven't we every tenacious moment wet revolve trying. You Oh Even. Marianne Vitale. HeMarv

You have only to wait, they will find you. Messengers. Louise Glück. ColAP; HCAP; VCAP

You Have Shown Me a Strange Image, and We Are Strange Prisoners. Jeni Couzyn. PBCAP

You have spoken your holy command over the city. Inanna and the City of Uruk. Enheduanna. BoWoP

You have stolen their souls with your eyes. (LL) Seizing the Day. Judith Ortiz Cofer. PueRic; SwNoth

You have stopped beating the drums. Anno Domini MCMXLVII. Salvatore Quasimodo. GI, *tr.* by Jack Bevan

You have ten seconds. Ten Seconds. Rohan B. Preston. WaCA

You have the cool clear eyes. I Believe in You. Frank Loesser. ReLy

You have the ingredients on hand. Recipe for an Ocean in the Absence of the Sea. Richard Howard. TAP

You have the light of my life, in your clear and pleasing face, and don't see me. Cecco Nuccoli. CAGL, *tr.* by Jill Claretta Robbins

You Have the Lovers. Leonard Cohen. NOBC

You have to be able to hear past the pain, the obvious. Dissidence. Anthony Walton. NAPBL

You have to be healthy to stretch a cord. Saint Vitus's Dance in October 10. Leonard Nolens. TuT, *tr.* by Michael O'Loughlin

You have to begin somewhere. Lonely Tylenol. Peter Gizzi. ReTh

You have to inhabit poetry. Making Poetry. Anne Stevenson. DiPo

You have to learn. The trees in winter. Winter Trees. Ágnes Nemes Nagy. IQMS, *tr.* by Adam Makkai

You have to quit talking. You have to. Quilts. Kathleen Peirce. PBCAP

You Have to Strike Back. Kate Lilley. BMAP

You Have Touched My Skin. Shakuntala Hawoldar. HAWP

You have turned our land into a desolate place. Desolation. Jack Davis. BMAP

You have your hat and coat on and she says she will be right down. Evening Out, The. Ogden Nash. MoAmPo

You have your language too. Wellfleet Whale, The. Stanley Kunitz. DiPo; NoAM

You have your own place to drink. Hail and beware them, when they come. (LL) Newly Discovered "Homeric" Hymn, A. Charles Olson. NeAP; NoAM; PoM

You haven't finished your ape, said mother to father, who had. Ape. Russell Edson. RaBo

You haven't finished your ape, said mother to father, who had monkey hair and blood on his whiskers. Ape. Russell Edson. PmAP

You hear that heroic big land music? Poem. Alice Notley. PmAP

You hear the chain striking the wall. Well, The. Yves Bonnefoy. VCWP, *tr.* by John Naughton

You hear the hollow hoofbeats of. Lost Horseman, The. Endre Ady. IQMS, *tr.* by Anton N. Nyerges

You hear them kids over there laugh this old woman? Lament for the Drowned Country. Mary Durack. NOBAu

You hear? Tomorrow, they say? No Dream. Maria [*or* Mariia] Mikhailovna Shkapskaya [*or* Shkapskaia]. ARWW, *tr.* by Catriona Kelly

You heard it for the first time. Unaccompanied Suite. Barbara Winder. MiVo

You heard the gentleman, with automatic percision, speak the truth. 1933. Kenneth Fearing. APT-2

You Hebrews are too snug in Ur. Joshua at Schechem. Charles Reznikoff. ChIV-1

You held my lotus blossom. To the tune "Soaring Clouds." Huang O [*or* Huang Ho]. BoWoP; EroLit; WPOW

You Held the Black Face. Léopold Sédar Senghor. PBMAP

You Hide. Edith Bruck. BoWoP, *tr.* by Ruth Feldman

You hire a cook, but she can't cook yet. Samuel Hoffenstein. OBCoV *Fr.* Poems in Praise of Practically Nothing.

You Hit the Spot. Mack Gordon. ReLy

You hitch a ride with a cyclist. You sit in back. In Your Racing Dream. Richard Hugo. BodElec

You hitched a thousand miles. August on Sourdough, a Visit from Dick Brewer. Gary Snyder. LoL; NAAL-5

You hold a bunch of roses, Rose. Dionysius Sophistes. GrAn

You hold out to each prisoner like a cup of light? (LL) Heat. Denis Johnson. MakPoe; SwNoth

You hover above the page staring. Like God. Lynn Emanuel. PuP-23

You hungry You thirsty Turn. (LL) Two Girls. Suzanne Gardinier. KGB; NeAmPo

You, hypocrite lecteur! mon semblable! mon frère! (LL) For T.S.E. Only. Hyam Plutzik. APT-2; TaR

You (I). Tom Clark. PmAP; SPE *Fr.* You.

You, I accuse. Michael Dennis Browne. SpudSo *Fr.* Sun Exercises.

You I give no name to / The mysterious things within you / are an untrodden bower. Ahmad al-Mushari Al-'Udwani. BBASP; MAP, *tr.* by Charles Doria and Hilary Kilpatrick *Fr.* Signs.

You I give no name to / The mysterious things within you / are fragrance, light and melody. Ahmad al-Mushari Al-'Udwani. BBASP; MAP, *tr.* by Charles Doria and Hilary Kilpatrick *Fr.* Signs.

You I know is losing you, The. Ivano Fermini. ItPo, *tr.* by Gayle Ridinger

You, I presume, could adroitly and gingerly. Aristophanes. FaBoWar *Fr.* Lysistrata.

You in Anger. James Reeves. OxBTC

You in despair, take heart! Life shall renew. Seer, The. János Batsányi. IQMS, *tr.* by John Fuller

You / in the night. You. Nelly Sachs. AF, *tr.* by Matthew Mead

You, in the old photographs, are always. Fanfare. U. A. Fanthorpe. Prnts

You incongruous old woman of Smyrna! (LL) Limerick. Edward Lear. OxBoLi; PeLV

You inquire gracefully of a man sick at heart. Separation from the Torah. Solomon ibn Gabirol. TOF, *tr.* by David Goldstein

You intend, it seems. *Unknown.* ArkPo, *tr.* by Helen Craig McCullough

You intimidated me. I was thrown into hell without a trial. Denouement. Ruth Stone. BoWoP

You introduced me to my first goddess. In Memoriam Akbar Babool. Wopko Jensma. PeSAV

You jerk me. Ringmaster's Wife. Fatima Lim-Wilson. ReBoTo

You judge a woman. To Some Supposed Brothers. Essex Hemphill. GLP

You keep eating and raising a family. Suite for Marriage, A. David Ignatow. NNaP

You keep me waiting in a truck. Twenty-Year Marriage. Ai. BoWoP; GT; NoAM

You keep watch from this room. Existing. Alejandra Piznarnick. MirDau, *tr.* by Roberta Gordenstein

You kept your hats, a fine assortment. Nest of Hats, A. Annie Foster. NLP

You kept your tools sequestered. Spirit Level, The. David Barber. AmPoNex

You killed the Dalmatian puppy. Dogs, The. Michael S. Weaver. PBCAP

You kissed me once and now I wait for more. Zodiac. Elizabeth Alexander. FFC

You kissed me once by mistake. Make the Man Love Me. Dorothy Fields. ReLy

You knew he. Lying in Small Pieces. Carol Bell. GeoH

You knew I was coming for you, little one. Windigo. Louise Erdrich. NoAM; PoPoPo

You Know. Jean Garrigue. UnPo

You know all those sonnets the ones where I said, I love you, well. Sonnet. Tom Devaney. AmPoNex

You know, dear, that this vicious world. Mrs. Myrick's Lecture. Mary E. Tucker. CBWP-1

You know his destination by the hardness of his sleeve (right). His sleeve. Dinogon. Michael Portnoy. HeMarv

You know how in the zoo most of the polar bears. One Polar Bear, The. Peter Sears. OPRER

You know how the mad come into a room. Beanstalk Country, The. Tennessee Williams. APT-2

You know I have a husband. Faithful Wife, A. Chang Chi. OHMPC, *tr.* by Kenneth Rexroth

You know, I languish here. Anna Andreyevna Akhmatova. TCRP

You Know I Like to Be.　Chrystos.　WiU

You know, I must leave you again and I can't.　Eugenio Montale.　PoetW, *tr. by* William Arrowsmith

You know I've seen a lot of what the world can do.　Vile World.　Simon Rae.　UV

You know I've seen a lot of what the world can do.　Wild World.　Cat Stevens.　UV

You know it's April by the falling-off.　B Negative.　X. J. Kennedy.　CoAmPo

You Know It's Really Cold.　Shirley Williams.　PAI

You know my trouble: story.　Round Midnight.　Clarence Major.　NAAAL

You know, or you don't know, that great Bacon saith.　Byron.　NOBL　*Fr.* Don Juan.

You know Saint Wigbald's—yonder nunnery cell.　How the Abbey of Saint Werewulf Juxta Slingsby Came by Brother Fabian's Manuscript.　Sebastian Evans.　PeVV

You know, she said, they made you.　Dress of Fire, A.　Dahlia Ravikovitch [*or* Ravikovich].　VCWP

You know that he is going to die.　Red Dog, The.　Laura Jensen.　LCAP-2

You know that I know, my lord, that you know.　Michelangelo Buonarroti.　CAGL, *tr. by* James M. Saslow

You know that I love you, sweetheart, but every time I come around.　*Unknown.*　STP　*Fr.* Kiowa "49" Songs.

You know that something's not quite right.　Riding Westward.　John Balaban.　GifTon

You know the feeling.　Laura.　Johnny Mercer.　ReLy

You know the hay's in.　Hay-Making.　Gillian Clarke.　AngWePo

You know the old woman.　Old Woman, The.　Beatrix Potter.　NTCP

You know the risks when you work.　Risks.　Malcolm Glass.　SpudSo

You know the school; you call it old.　Country School.　Allen Curnow.　HarvBoo

You know the way to heaven's door [*or* heavens doore]. (LL)　Church-Music[k].　George Herbert.　AmFaPo; ESCV; GeHe; OxBSP

You know the world how big it is,　Southern Africa.　Nguno Wakolele.　PeSAV

You know there is not much.　To a Friend Concerning Several Ladies.　William Carlos Williams.　VGW

You know, there's a Venture.　Christmas Shopping.　Carter Revard.　UrbNat

You know this: I must lose you again and cannot.　Eugenio Montale.　WoPoe, *tr. by* Dana Gioia　*Fr.* Motets, The.

You know those rose sherbets.　You Know.　Jean Garrigue.　UnPo

You know those windless summer evenings, swollen to stasis.　Cicadas.　Richard Wilbur.　NOBA

You know, Tut, they were wrong.　Next to Tut.　Jon Veinberg.　GeoHom

You know we French stormed [*or* storm'd] Ratisbon.　Incident of the French Camp.　Robert Browning.　OBWP

You know, we looked at, touched carefully, and studied a copy of.　Marginalia.　Stephanie Brown.　AmPoNex

You know we must be lonely, you and I.　Souls.　Paul Wertheimer.　TrJP, *tr. by* Jethro Bithell

You Know What I'm Saying?　Irving Feldman.　BAP-97

You Know Where You Did Despise.　Vincent Voiture.　WoPoe, *tr. by* Alexander Pope

You'l marvel when I tell ye o.　Loudon Hill; or, Drumclog.　*Unknown.*　ESPB

You ladies all of merry England.　Signior Dildo.　John Wilmot, 2d Earl of Rochester.　BASC

You Laughed and Laughed and Laughed.　Gabriel Okara.　PBA

You lay down in your bed.　Dark Existence.　Brenda Hillman.　BodElec

You lay in wait.　Sappho.　BoWoP

You lean against me.　Dancing in Paradise.　Achy Obejas.　WiU

You leaned in your wooden chair.　Gravestone, The.　'Abd al-Karim Kassid.　MAP, *tr. by* Lena Jayyusi and Anthony Thwaite

You leaned your body in the doorway.　Talkers in a Dream Doorway.　Judy Grahn.　GLP

You leaped from the white horses.　Distaff, The.　Erinna.　WPOW, *tr. by* Marylin Arthur

You learn to accommodate yourself to others, to fit into the space left by their.　Avila.　John Yau.　BodElec

You learned Lear's *Nonsense Rhymes* by heart, not rote.　Plea to Boys and Girls, A.　Robert Graves.　GTBS-P; NAEL-5v2; NAEL-6v2

You leave dead friends in.　Will They Cry When You're Gone, You Bet.　Imamu Amiri Baraka.　NAAL-2v2

You leave, I write what happened, type it—onionskin. A romance.　Poem for the End.　Honor Moore.　WiU

You Leave Me Breathless.　Ralph Freed.　ReLy

You left a message on the board.　Visit, The.　Annie Foster.　NLP

You left behind, Eurymedon, an infant child.　Theocritus.　GrAn

You left in the morning. Tonight my heart is in a thousand pieces.　Mourning for Hokuju Rosen.　Buson.　EH, *tr. by* Robert Hass

You left me my lips, and they shape words, even in silence. (LL)　You Took

Away All the Oceans and All the Room.　Osip Emilevich Mandelstam [*or* Mandelshtam].　OPOU; Spl, *tr. by* Clarence Brown

You left me sad and lonely.　You're Driving Me Crazy (What Did I Do?)　Walter Donaldson.　ReLy

You left me when the weary weight of sorrow.　Forgiven.　Margaret Elizabeth Munson Sangster.　PoToHe

You left. One by one there were less of you.　Devotion.　Susan Minot.　Unle

You lie and I concur. You "give."　Martial.　WoPoe, *tr. by* William Matthews　*Fr.* Epigrams.

You lie down in terror of the darkness.　Seek Out Another Heart.　Mikha'il Nu'aima [*or* Nuaymah].　MAP, *tr. by* Sargon Boulus and Thomas G. Ezzy

You lie, snail-like, on your stomach.　Depression.　Wendy Cope.　FaBoWP

You lie with me nightly. In bathrooms I'm there.　Pamela Gillilan.　NewEx

You lights, for which on earth my sight's thirst ne'er is stilled.　To the Stars.　Andreas Gryphius.　GePo, *tr. by* George C. Schoolfield

You like.　Family Romance.　Paul Hoover.　IllVoic

You like it under the trees in autumn.　Motive for Metaphor, The.　Wallace Stevens.　APT-1; MoAmPo

You like not that French novel? Tell me why.　George Meredith.　NOBVV　*Fr.* Modern Love.

You like peaches and cream.　Peaches and Cream.　Mudrooroo Narogin.　BMAP

You like to have contests of size with people.　Contest Snake, The.　Cheng Hsieh.　CoBLCP, *tr. by* Jonathan Chaves

You live in dishonor grave, Dukes and Mighty Princes.　András Szkhárosi Horvát.　IQMS, *tr. by* Adam Makkai　*Fr.* About the Princes.

You live in the thousand rooms.　In My Dream.　A. V. Christie.　AmPoNex

You live in this, and dwell in lovers' eyes. (LL)　William Shakespeare.　AEP; AWP; CABP; CTC; HeIP-4; NAEL-5v1; NAEL-6v1; NAEL-7v1; NIP-4; NOBE; NoP-4; NoSic; OxAEP-1; OxBSo; PAI; PoE; PoRA; SCGP; Son　*Fr.* Sonnets.

You Live on a Drifting Road.　Robert Ivanovich Rozhdestvensky [*or* Rozhdestvenskii].　TCRP, *tr. by* J. R. Rowland

You live under the microscope.　Under the Microscope.　Slavko Mihalic.　PoSu, *tr. by* Charles Simic

You live where green mountains reach almost.　Looking for Master Yung Ts'un near His Hermitage.　Li Po.　CrYelRi, *tr. by* Sam Hamill

You lived and moved among the best society.　W. H. Auden.　OBSV　*Fr.* Letter to Lord Byron.

You lived, you played, you sang with a bitter grin.　Epitaph for Vysotsky.　Andrey [*or* Andrei] Andreievich Voznesensky [*or* Voznesenskii].　TCRP, *tr. by* William Jay Smith

You'll come in. And your voice will be drowned.　Football.　"Nikolai Karpovich Otrada."　TCRP, *tr. by* Daniel Weissbort

You'll dwell in your own houses as you did before.　False Prophet, The.　Ernst Waldinger.　AuPH, *tr. by* Lowell A. Bangerter

You'll ever give / Or get. (LL)　For a Far-out Friend.　Gary Snyder.　BB; NeAP; PoM

You'll find that I'm the sort.　Abner Silver's "Pu-leeze! Mr. Hemingway!"　Ring Lardner.　OBAL

You'll get fucked, thief, for the first time.　*Unknown.*　PriapPo, *tr. by* Richard W. Hooper　*Fr.* Priapus Poems, The.

You'll go to the plaza.　Camoes and the Debt.　Sophia de Mello Breyner Andresen.　BoWoP, *tr. by* Willis Barnstone and Nelson Cerqueira

You'll have to be a little more standoffish.　All er Nothin'　Richard Rodgers.　ReLy

You'll have to rethink the whole question. This.　Whole Question, The.　Robert Penn Warren.　BodElec

You'll learn, should you steal apples in my care.　*Unknown.*　PriapPo, *tr. by* Richard W. Hooper　*Fr.* Priapus Poems, The.

You'll make tea.　Just the Two of Us.　Taeko Tomioka.　WPOW

You'll never know. (LL)　Certain Lady, A.　Dorothy Parker.　NIL-7; NIP-4

You'll Never Know.　Ruby Marion Wray.　PWR

You'll never know how far i stand from you. (LL)　Measure for Measure.　Sipho Sepamla.　AF; PeSAV

You'll never know *how* good you are.　Auto-erotic.　*Unknown.*　PeLi

You'll never sleep tonight.　Insomnia.　Cornelius Eady.　AWTN; ESEAA

You'll never understand *No Road This Way*.　Past Time.　Edith Jay Scovell.　HarvBoo

You'll Never Walk Alone.　Richard Rodgers.　ReLy

You'll [*or* You'le] ask, perhaps, wherefore I stay.　Excuse of Absence, An.　Thomas Carew.　CaPo

You'll ruin your eyesight, lad.　As Old As Then.　Jan Eijkelboom.　TuT, *tr. by* Michael O'Loughlin

You'll see me park my car upon.　Red Light District Nurse, The.　John Fuller.　OBCoV

You load, focus, aim.　Shooting Back.　Thomas Sayers Ellis.　GT

You look at me.　Drop of Dew, A.　Shmuel Halkin.　TrJP, *tr. by* Jacob Sonntag

You look at me, a hut or cage contains.　"H. D."　NOCV　*Fr.* Sagesse.

You look for Rome in Rome, O traveler! To Rome Entombed in Her Ruins. Francisco de Quevedo y Villegas. SpanPo, *tr.* by Kate Flores

You look upon the air. (LL) Late. Louise Bogan. APT-2; VGW

"You love. . .? love. . .? love. . .?" all on an indrawn breath. (LL) George Meredith. NAEL-5v2; NAEL-6v2; NOBVV *Fr.* Modern Love.

You, love, and I. Counting the Beats. Robert Graves. GTBS-P; HAP; HarvBoo; OxAEP-2; OxBTC; WeW-3; WoPoe

You love her, while I love you. *Unknown.* WoPoe, *tr.* by David Ray *Fr.* Gathasaptasati, The.

You love not me? (LL) Broken Appointment, A. Thomas Hardy. HarvBoo; NAEL-5v2; NAEL-6v2; NOBVV; NoAM

You love the hum of well-oiled engine about to turn 200,000. Because You're American. Kevin Stein. ReTh

You love us when we're heroes, home on leave. Glory of Women. Siegfried Sassoon. FaBoWar; NAEL-5v2; NAEL-6v2; NoP-4; OBWP; OxAEP-2; OxBSo; PeFWW

You love? That's high as you shall go. Coventry Patmore. FaBoEE *Fr.* Angel in the House, The.

You loved me not at all, but let it go. Edna St. Vincent Millay. VGW

You loved Menophila when you were rich. Argentarius. GrAn

You loved when all was young. (LL) Charles Kingsley. EBEV; OxAEP-2 *Fr.* Water Babies, The.

You lower my emotions, sealed in their casket. Parting, The. Sara Berkeley. PBCIP

You lumbered along the stadium. My Father's First Baseball Game. Michael S. Weaver. PBCAP

You 'made a virtue of necessity' To Conscripts. Alice Thompson Meynell. SacPr

You Made It Rain. Ruby C. Saunders. BlSi

You Made Me Love You (I Didn't Want to Do It). Joseph McCarthy. ReLy

You made the home where I go home in dream. To My Mother. Anna Adams. Prnts

You made the silence of lilacs swaying. Recognition. Alejandra Piznarnick. TANSG, *tr.* by Susan Bassnett

You madly kiss my lips—I seem to see. Pit, The. Su'ad al-Mubarak Al-Sabah. MAP, *tr.* by John Heath-Stubbs and May Jayyusi

You make it in your mess-tin by the brazier's rosy gleam. Pot of Tea, A. Robert W. Service. PoWW

You Make Me Feel So Young. Mack Gordon. ReLy

You make me think of many men. To an Intra-Mural Rat. Marianne Craig Moore. APT-1

You, Marc Chagall, should be able to tell us. Ascensions, The. William Pillen [*or* Pillin]. RaBo

You marched away and left this town. They're Either Too Young or Too Old. Arthur Schwartz. ReLy

You, Mascolo, came and went, a half hour in all. Redefining "Orthodoxy." Pier Paolo Pasolini. ItPo, *tr.* by Gayle Ridinger

You Masks of the Masquerade. Gustave Kahn. TrJP, *tr.* by Jethro Bithell

You, master of delays. Killing No Murder. Sylvia Townsend Warner. MoBrPo

You may also look absurd with a miserable face. (LL) Dear Female Heart. Stevie Smith. FaBoEE; ItWoWo; NALW

You may ask the world. Memories of Mudland-Meadow. István Sinka. IQMS, *tr.* by Adam Makkai

You may be Dirty Dinky. (LL) Dinky. Theodore Roethke. OBAL; OBCA; OxIBACP

You may be right, divinity. Prayer. Francis Sullivan. CRP

You may be right: "How can I dare to feel?" Rejoinder to a Critic. Donald Davie. CABP; NoP-4

You may brag about your breakfast foods you eat at break of day. Sausage. Edgar Albert Guest. OBAL

You may call, you may call. Bad Kittens, The. Elizabeth Jane Coatsworth. OBCA

You may catch / a butterfly. Ars Poetica. Linda Pastan. NIP-4

You may catch all the others, but you wo——— (LL) Not Me. Shel [*or* Shelley] Silverstein. NBLV; OBCoV

You may confidently. Breathcrystal. Paul Celan. PFTM-2, *tr.* by Pierre Joris

You may for ever [*or* forever] tarry. (LL) To the Virgins, to Make Much of Time. Robert Herrick. AWP; BASC; BeJo; BoLoP; CaPo; CavPo; ClHu; EnLoPo; HAP; HeIP-4; ITBLP; InPK-6; NAEL-5v1; NAEL-6v1; NAEL-7v1; NBLV; NIL-7; NOBE; NOSC; NPeEn; NoP-4; OBEV; OxAEP-1; OxBEV; PAI; PoE; PoPoPo; SCGP; SCV; SoSe-8; TFi; UV

You may get there by candle light. (LL) How many miles to Babylon? Mother Goose. LB; OxBSP; OxNR

You may give over plow, boys. Tommy's Dead. Sydney Thompson Dobell. PeVV

You May Go But This Will Bring You Back. *Unknown.* NAAAL

You may have heard. Sed Non Frustra. Anton Korteweg. TuT, *tr.* by Seamus Deane

You may have sex. Disown. Rae Armantrout. FTOS

You may have troubles manifold. Mother's Joy, A. Ruth Fortney Maxwell. PWR

You may leave and go to Hali-ma-fack. You May Go But This Will Bring You Back. *Unknown.* NAAAL

You may not get a chance. Ploughman. John Tripp. TCAWP

You May Not Love Me. Jimmy Van Heusen. ReLy

You may speak of a grave in a distant land. Reverie, A. Mary Weston Fordham. CBWP-2

You may talk as you please of the joys of Jamaica. Song of the Transportationist, The. *Unknown.* NOBAu

You may talk o' gin and [*or* an'] beer. Gunga Din. Rudyard Kipling. BRP; EBVV; MoBrPo

You may then live in joy perdurably . . . (LL) Stephen Hawes. EBEV; NoSic; OBEV *Fr.* Pastime of Pleasure, The.

You may want to cut them down. You may want to use a knife. Chrysanthemums. Irene McKinney. PBCAP

You may write me down in history. Still I Rise. Maya Angelou. BlSi; NAAAL

"You mean," he said, "a crocodile" (LL) Purist, The. Ogden Nash. KaS; MoAmPo; NBLV; OBCA

You mean Josie with the small eyes? New Verses for June 7, 1951. Jan Hanlo. TuT, *tr.* by Eamon Grennan

You meaner beauties of the night. On His Mistress [*or* Mistris], the Queen of Bohemia. Sir Henry Wotton. BASC; EnLoPo; HAP; MeLP; NOSC; NPeEn; OxBEV; SCGP; TFi

You merit more; nor could [*or* cou'd] my Love do less. (LL) To My Dear Friend Mr Congreve [on His Comedy Called "The Double-Dealer"]. Dryden. EBEV; NPeEn; OxAEP-1

You midst gay crowds reside, I, hid in shades. Esther Lewis. ECWP *Fr.* Letter to a Lady in London, A.

You might as well live. (LL) Dorothy Parker. APT-1; HeIP-4; InPK-6; NAAL-2v2; NALW; NBLV; NoP-4; OBAL; TrJP; UV *Fr.* Some Beautiful Letters.

You might as well think one thing or another. Amelia Rosselli. ItPo, *tr.* by Gayle Ridinger

You might be sleeping next to me. Your head. 152 Into 5, *El Centro Palabra de Fe.* M. L. Williams. GeoHom

You might be surprised right out the window, whistling dixie on the / way. (LL) Poem for Half White College Students. Imamu Amiri Baraka. BPo; TAP; UnPo

You might come here Sunday on a whim. Degrees of Gray in Philipsburg. Richard Hugo. CoAP; NAAL-2v2; NoAM; TRP; VCAP

You might easy know a doffer. *Unknown.* FaBoVe

You might have been a meadowlark making. Standing between Two Ideas. Maurya Simon. InvLad

You might imagine the desert as a rectangle without angles, as a. Desert, II, The. Edmond Jabès. AF, *tr.* by Rosmarie Waldrop

You might not think Toulouse-Lautrec and Mother Teresa. Controlling Factors. Mary Ruefle. ExTi

You might suppose it easy. Boatman, The. Jay Macpherson. MoCV

You, mine, my love. *Unknown.* WoPoe, *tr.* by Ezra Pound and Noel Stock *Fr.* Conversations in Courtship.

You Missed the Earthquake, Bill. Charles Harper Webb. GeoHom

You, mob, / Are about to be transformed. Mob, The. Mcavoy Layne. CDa

You Mock Me Now in Your Youth. Samuel Ha-Nagid. WoPoe, *tr.* by Peter Cole

You modern wits, who call this world a star. To the Same [My Dear Sister, Mrs S.]: The Tears. William Hammond. NOSC

You, Morningtide Star, now are steady-eyed, over the east. Lying Awake. Thomas Hardy. FaBoVe; NPeEn

You must admit it's natural. Clyde Peeling's Reptiland in Allenwood, Pennsylvania. Kevin Young. NeAmPo

You must admit the loss of blood, brother. Missing Link. Sean Lucy. BiHa

You must agree that Rubens was a Fool. To English Connoisseurs. William Blake. OxBoLi

You must answer softly. Answer. Mildred Bowers. YaYoPo

You must be endless in your loving touch of each other, continuance the answers. (LL) Union of Two, The. Haki R. Madhubuti. ISC; SpirFl

You must be proud, if you'll be wise. (LL) To the Ladies. Mary Lee, Lady Chudleigh. CABP; ECWP; NALW; NIL-7; NOEC; PEW; WPE; WPOW

You must be sad; for though it is to Heaven. To Two Bereaved. Thomas Ashe. NOBVV

You Must Believe in Spring. Jacques Demy. ReLy, *tr.* by Alan Bergman, Marilyn Bergman and Michel Legrand

You must change your life fourteen times. Archaic Torsos. David Shapiro. BodElec

You must come to them sideways. Mirrors at 4 A.M. Charles Simic. AWTN

You must dig in black ashes a long time. Pavel Grigoryevich Antokolsky. TCRusP, *tr.* by Bob Perelman and Shirley Rihner *Fr.* Son.

You must find out, for I don't know. (LL) Three Wise Old Women. Elizabeth T. Corbett. NOxBChV; OBCA; OBSP

You must have. House Call to a Man with Parkinson's Disease, A. Michael O'Reilly. BloBone

You Must Have Been a Beautiful Baby. Johnny Mercer. ReLy

You Must Have Been a Sensational Baby. Harold Norse. GLP

You must have been still sleeping, your wife there. Sacred Hearth, The. David Gascoyne. FaBoTw

You must have music first of all. Art of Poetry, The. Paul Verlaine. NAWM-7v2, tr. by Carlyle Ferren MacIntyre

You Must Help Me Gather. Shakuntala Hawoldar. HAWP

You must not hope to arrive. (LL) Tourist from Syracuse, The. Donald Justice. NoAM; TwCP; VCAP

You must not, said the owl to the capercailzie. End of ARt, The. Reiner Kunze. PoSu, tr. by Michael Hamburger

"You must not wonder, though you think it strange." George Gascoigne. See For That He Looked Not upon Her

You must play. Zosan Junku. JDP, tr. by Yoel Hoffmann

You must remember this when I am gone. Sanctuary. Donald Davidson. APT-1; FuPo

You must stand erect but at your ease, a posture. Singing Lesson, The. David Wagoner. NoAM

You must understand how pinched she's been. Fisherman's Wife, The. Jody Gladding. YaYoPo

You must wear them until you are dead. (LL) Limerick: "There was an archdeacon who said." Unknown. OBCoV; OxBoLi

You Mustn't Feel Discouraged. Adolph Green. ReLy

You Mustn't Quit. Unknown. PoToHe

You / my bell-clapper. Christmas Mass for a Little Atheist Jesus. Claude Maillard. BoWoP, tr. by Maxine W. Kumin and Judith Kumin

You, my friend, fallen among thieves. Thief and Samaritan. James Keir Baxter. HarvBoo

You, my Lord, have tarried long in your journey. Lord of the River Hsiang. Ch'u Yüan. SuSp, tr. by Wu-Chi Liu

You, my statue, why do you torment me? Statue, The. Orkhan Muyassar. MAP, tr. by Samuel Hazo and Lena Jayyusi

You need me for sitting. Michael Rosen. NewEx

You need some help. Hired Hand. David Lee. GifTon

You neigh and whinny, seeming to invite. Macedonius. GrAn

You never asked for sunshine. Tubman Strong. Darryl Holmes. InTrad

You never can tell. (LL) Those Two Boys. Franklin Pierce Adams. OBCoV; TrJP

You Never Can Tell. Ella Wheeler Wilcox. PoToHe

You never claimed to be someone special. She Mends an Ancient Wireless. Paul Durcan. PBCIP

You never could tell what my deaf Uncle Arthur heard. And Don't Be Deaf to the Singing Beyond. Carter Revard. HATNAP

You never hear 'the People' now. People, No, The. Vicki Raymond. NOBAu

You Never Knew about Me. P. G. Wodehouse. ReLy

You never know who has your memory. You Gotta Have Your Tips on Fire. Víctor Hernández Cruz. PueRic

You never married, never took a job—you went completely astray! Written at the End of Master Ho-ching's Collected Works. Chin Nung. CoBLCP, tr. by Jonathan Chaves

You never think it will happen to you. Alicia Ostriker. ExTi Fr. Mastectomy Poems, The.

You never thought it would come to this. Playing Basketball with the Viet Cong. Kevin Bowen. MoASP

You never touch. Akiko Yosano. BoWoP, tr. by Geoffrey Bownas

You New Year. Emmy Klein-Synek. AuPH, tr. by Lowell A. Bangerter

You new year that we're now receiving. You New Year. Emmy Klein-Synek. AuPH, tr. by Lowell A. Bangerter

You, no doubt, have heard the story told of Charleston by the sea? Crum Appointment, The. Lizelia Augusta Jenkins Moorer. CBWP-3

You no give me one wacky you can't pass. Dry River. Unknown. FaBoVe

You no sooner attain the great void. Hakuin. ZenPo, tr. by Takashi Ikemoto and Lucien Stryk

You no sooner got out of prison. Evening Walk, The. Nazim Hikmet. AF

You noble diggers all stand up now. Diggers' Song, The. Unknown. PBRV

You noble Diggers all, stand up now, stand up now. Digger's Song, The. Gerrard Winstanley. BASC; NOSC

You noble fountain set in peace and joy's design. Concerning the Wolffsbrunnen near Heidelberg. Martin Opitz. GePo, tr. by George C. Schoolfield

You not alone, when you are still alone. Michael Drayton. OxBSo Fr. Idea.

You nurtured grief until that leap. Waiting for Robinson. Roberta Hill Whiteman. HATNAP

You, Odysseus trainer of the wooden horse of pleasure. Odyssey or "On Absence," The. Chimako Tada. VCWP, tr. by Naoshi Koriyama

You of the same mind, moor-wandering near one. Largo. Paul Celan. PoSu, tr. by Michael Hamburger

You often say my work is coarse. It's true. Martial. CAGL, tr. by J. A. Pott Fr. Epigrams.

You often went to breathe a timeless air. Scholar, The. Frances Darwin Cornford. BrRo

You Oh Even. Marianne Vitale. HeMarv

You: on candy cameo. Me: ate dumb flash. Stage Duo. Kenward Elmslie. FTOS

You, once a belle in Shreveport. Snapshots of a Daughter-in-Law. Adrienne Rich. FaBoWP; HCAP; NAAL-2v2; NALW; NIP-4; NoAM; NoP-4; VCAP

You once smiled a friendly smile. Aboriginal Australia. Jack Davis. IBA

You only come in the tormenting. Suicide. Robert Lowell. PoE

You open P-K4, it thinks, or blinks. Playing the Machine. Howard Nemerov. BodElec

You open the door after a long ride home in the dark. (LL) Refuge at the One Step Down. Belle Waring. PBCAP; SeSe

You or I? Ilyas Abu Shabaka. MAP, tr. by Michael Beard and Adnan Haydar

You ought to know Mr Mistofmeelees! Mr Mistoffelees. T. S. Eliot. NOxBChV

You over there, young man with the guide book red-bound. Home Sweet Home with Variations. Henry Cuyler Bunner. OBAL

"You owe me five shillings," Bells, The. Unknown. ReMoGo

You paint the wild geese as if I could see them crying. For Contemporary Artist Pien Wei-Ch'I. Cheng Hsieh. SuSp

You pass the tomb of Battus' son, well skilled. Callimachus. HePo Fr. Epigrams.

You paused outside. Shelter. R. S. Jones. Unle

You pay for it, for sure, dont let nobody tell you you don. You pay. Minute of Consciousness, The. Imamu Amiri Baraka. APSN

You people / of the future. Screaming My Head Off. Vladimir Vladimirovich Mayakovsky [or Maiakovskii]. PFTM-1

You perpetuate! Roll on, reels of celluloid, as the great earth rolls on! (LL) To the Film Industry in Crisis. Frank O'Hara. NOBA; OBAL

You phone to say birds have gouged. Apples. Patricia Pogson. NLP

You plant like Paul, you water like Apollos. Rev. Nicholas Noyes to the Rev. Cotton Mather, The. Nicholas Noyes. SCAP

You planted life, protecting. Discords. Fabio Doplicher. NeIt, tr. by Dana Gioia

You played and she sang at my wedding. Winter Wedding, The. Paul Henry. TCAWP

You poured down like gold, / Olympian Zeus. Parmenion of Macedon. GrAn

You praise my self-sacrifice, Spoon River. Edgar Lee Masters. APT-1 Fr. Spoon River Anthology.

You praise the firm restraint with which they write. On Some South African Novelists. Roy Campbell. FaBoEE; GTBS-P; InPK-6; MoBrPo; NOBL; OBCoV; OxAEP-2; OxBEV; OxBTC; PeLV

You pray in vain for Carrousel. (LL) Ballad of a Barber, The. Aubrey Beardsley. NOBVV; PAI

You prayer—, you blasphemy, you. Plashes the Fountain. Paul Celan. OBVE, tr. by Michael Hamburger

You prisoners of New South Wales. Convict's Tour to Hell, A. Francis MacNamara. NOBAu

You probably contain a germ. (LL) Germ, The. Ogden Nash. APT-2; RB

You promise heavens free from strife. Mimnermus in Church. William Johnson Cory. NOBE; OBEV

You promised you would never keep. Green Corn Season. Diana García. TouFir

You, proud curve-lipped youth, with brown sensitive face. Edward Carpenter. CAGL Fr. Towards Democracy.

You pursue my figure. Dies Merini. Alda Merini. CItWP, tr. by Cinzia Sartini Blum and Lara Trubowitz

You / Put success in the mouth. Sappho. SaLy, tr. by Diane Rayor

You raise the axe. Anniversary, The. Ai. BodElec

You raise the creases. Earth, The. Christopher Pilling. NLP

You're. Sylvia Plath. FaBoTw; FaBoWP; RB

You're a better man than I am, Gunga Din! (LL) Gunga Din. Rudyard Kipling. BRP; EBVV; MoBrPo

You're a girl. Character. Taslima Nasrin. VCWP

You're a Grand Old Flag. George M. Cohan. ReLy

You're a teeming truce today, my ladybug, red elytra. Unfinished Exile. Fabio Doplicher. NeIt, tr. by Stephen Sartarelli

You're an Old Smoothie. Richard A. Whiting. ReLy

You're angry over naught with me. To Chloe. Martin Joseph Prandstetter. AuPH, tr. by Lowell A. Bangerter

You're as thrilling as a college cheer. You Hit the Spot. Mack Gordon. ReLy

You're clean shaven in this country. Vegetable Air, The. Cathy Song. NoAM

You're clear out of this world. Out of This World. Johnny Mercer. ReLy

You're Driving Me Crazy (What Did I Do?). Walter Donaldson. ReLy

You're excused, my father would say. As We Forgive Those. Eric Pankey. GI

You're fond of details. On Details. Sami Mahdi. MAP, tr. by Charles Doria and May Jayyusi

You're Getting to Be a Habit with Me. Harry Warren. ReLy

You're going by, west of the sun. Marina Ivanovna Tsvetayeva [or Tsvetaeva]. TCRusP, tr. by Bob Perelman, Aleksandar Petrov and Shirley Rihner Fr. Poems to Blok.

You're gone so long / so long. (LL) So Long. Langston Hughes. APSN; APT-2

You're Gonna Lose Your Gal. Joe Young. ReLy

You're here! I hadn't dared to hope. Surprise. Macedonius. GrAn

You're home, Uma! Stay here. Gíríscandra Ghos. SinGod, tr. by Rachel Fell McDermott

You're in Love. Bobby Troup. ReLy

You're in the city, somewhere. I suppose if I stood. Lost Love. Dick Allen. NIP-4

You're jealous if I kiss this girl and that. Constancy. Elsa Gidlow. PoBW

You're just a lonely little river. River, Stay 'way from My Door. Mort Dixon. ReLy

You're Just in Love. Irving Berlin. ReLy

You're Laughing at Me. Irving Berlin. ReLy

You're like a bough, so silky-whispery. Images. Miklós Radnóti. IQMS, tr. by Peter Zollman

You're like a drifting log with iron nails in it. Funeral Song. Hayiaku. STP, tr. by James Koller

You're Lookin' at Me. Bobby Troup. ReLy

You're Lucky to Me. Eubie Blake. ReLy

You're Mine, You! Edward Heyman. ReLy

You're more beautiful than a silvery ball. Sweet Talk. Ferreira Gullar. TCLAP, tr. by Renato Rezende

You're not mine. Visitor, A. Idea Vilariño. TANSG, tr. by Louise B. Popkin

You're now transcribed, and public view. To Mr. W. B., at the Birth of His First Child. William Cartwright. BeJo

You're only a baby. Poor Little Rich Girl. Noël Coward. ReLy

You're out. The house is dead. With me. Sam's Ghazals. Elise Paschen. Unle

You're pressing your fingers against the sky. Falling. Lesley Dauer. AmPoNex; NAPBL

You're right. In the Library. Michael Patrick Hearn. NTCP

You're right, Lais' smile is sweet. Paulus [or Paulos] Silentiarius. PGA

You're right—"the way is narrow." Emily Dickinson. TCAPo

You're saving it? What for? Asclepiades. GrAn

You're sleeping, Zenophila, my tender bloom. I wish. Meleager. HePo Fr. Epigrams.

You're so funny! I'd give you. Kirsten. Ted Berrigan. TTTS

You're so late getting home from the office. Guess Who I Saw Today. Murray Grand. ReLy

You're song. Jelaluddin [or Jalal al-Din] Rumi. LoL

You're sure you heard something break. Something snap. Thrust & Parry. Greg Delanty. BiHa

You're the Cream in My Coffee. Ray Henderson. ReLy

You're the smoothest so and so. You're an Old Smoothie. Richard A. Whiting. ReLy

You're The Top. Cole Porter. NBLV Fr. You're the Top.

You're the Top. Unknown. NBLV

You're the type of guy. Enemy. Beau Sia. HeMarv

You're the woman I love best and forget fastest, my love. Tall Weeds. W. S. Rendra. WoPoe, tr. by Burton Raffel

You're thin again handsome. in our last. D. A. Powell. WiU

You're thinking of children, of their. You're Thinking of Children. Vladimir Holan. PoSu, tr. by Ian Milner and Jarmila Milner

You're tired of this old world at last. Zone. Guillaume Apollinaire. PFTM-1

You're too late, Lycidas. Nyctilus and boy Alcon. Titus Calpurnius Siculus. RomPo, tr. by Guy Lee Fr. Eclogues.

You're too wild. Understanding Each Other. Linda Noel. ReEnLa

You're walking by the tomb of Battiades. On Himself. Callimachus. GrAn, tr. by Peter Jay

You're with your mother now. (LL) What I Heard at the Discount Department Store. David Budbill. RaBo; TRP

You're wondering if I'm lonely. Song. Adrienne Rich. InPK-6

You read the New York Times. Alfred Corning Clark. Robert Lowell. RB

You read with Auden. In Memorium: Robert Hayden. Norman J. Loftis. SpirFl

You, reading over my shoulder, peering beneath. Reader over My Shoulder, The. Robert Graves. NAEL-5v2; NAEL-6v2

You really got thru to me. Allen. Joe Lothamer. GeoH

You recline that magnificent pair of buttocks. To Kyris. Strato [or Straton]. GrAn, tr. by Teddy Hogge

You recommend that the motive, in Chapter 8, should be changed. Yes, the Agency Can Handle That. Kenneth Fearing. WeW-3

You reconnoiter. Following, I swat and sulk. On The Fly. Diana Chang. FSt

You remember the big Gaston, for whom everyone predicted a bad end? Monsieur Gaston. Abraham Moses Klein. MoCV

You remember the joke, right? Letter to Ibrahim. Khaled Mattawa. AmPoNex

You remember the name was Jensen. She seemed old. What Thou Lovest Well Remains American. Richard Hugo. NAAL-2v2

You remember the sun of Auschwitz. Sun of Auschwitz, The. Tadeusz Borowski. AF, tr. by Larry Rafferty

You remember the sun of Auschwitz. Sun of Auschwitz, The. Tadeusz Borowski. HP, tr. by Tadeuszt Pióro

You return on currents and tides. Return of the Banished. Li Po. CrYelRi, tr. by Sam Hamill

You Rise among Truths. 'Abd al-Razzaq 'Abd al-Wahid. MAP, tr. by Diana Der Hovanessian and Lena Jayyusi

You rise in my dreams. Venus of Laussel. Patricia Monaghan. HW

You rise like the phoenix. Reincarnation. Mudrooroo Narogin. IBA

You rocked my cradle, Charidemus, once. Martial. RomPo, tr. by J. P. Sullivan

You rose from our embrace and the small light spread. Hayden Carruth. ErotSp Fr. Sonnets.

You run round the back to be in it again. Good Teachers, The. Carol Ann Duffy. ItWoWo

You ruthless flea, who desecrate my couch. Song of the Flea. Judah Al-Harizi. TrJP

You said, "Come in to the light." Painter of Destinies, A. Molly Bendall. NAPBL

You said good-bye at Yellow Crane Pavilion. Saying Good-bye to Meng Hao-jan at Yellow Crane Pavilion. Li Po. CrYelRi, tr. by Sam Hamill

You said I could talk. Leaking Roof. Gahlia Gwangwa'a. NAfrP

You said: "I'll go to another country, go to another shore." City, The. Constantine P. Cavafy. AmFaPo, tr. by Edmund Keeley and Philip Sherrard

You said, I will go to another land, I will go to another sea. City, The. Constantine P. Cavafy. WoPoe, tr. by Rae Dalven

You said: it's hot tonight. Maurizio Cucchi. ItPo, tr. by Gayle Ridinger

You said it went all the way. Last Words, 1968. Lance Henson. CDW

You said may God go with you, son. May God Go with You, Son. C. Wright. FaBoWar

You said: My father didn't cry. Ancestral Weight. Alfonsina Storni. WPOW, tr. by Marti Moody

You, said the Lionwoman. Flask of Brandy, A. Padraic Fallon. ModIr

You said the sun would rise. Song to Fidel. Ernesto "Che" Guevara. TCLAP, tr. by Gordon Brotherston and Edward Dorn

You said to me: But I will be your comrade. Nudities. André Spire. AWP, tr. by Jethro Bithell

You said to me: / I shall [or would] become your comrade. Nudities. André Spire. TrJP, tr. by Stanley Burnshaw

You said you would kill it this morning. Pheasant. Sylvia Plath. RB

You sang round-dance songs. Farewell. Liz Sohappy Bahe. CDW

You sang, you sang! you mountain brook. Reason for Silence, A. Louise Imogen Guiney. SWaP

You sat with a bottle of beer. After the Death of an Elder Klallam. Duane Niatum. CDW

You saw Big Mama Thornton. Bumblebee, You Saw Big Mama. Jayne Cortez. SurWo

You saw the wind as the breath of God. After the Hurricane. Sinéad Morrissey. MFPA

You say, as I have often given tongue. To a Poet, Who Would Have Me Praise Certain Bad Poets, Imitators of His and Mine. W. B. Yeats. CTC; FaBoEE

You say, but with no touch of scorn. Tennyson. NAEL-6v2; NOCV Fr. In Memoriam A. H. H.

You say, Columbus with his argosies. Trumbull Stickney. APN-2

You say: I am sitting in a room. At a Sunlit Window. Ondra Lysohorsky. AF, tr. by Ewald Osers

You say, I love. Lesson in Natural History, A. Vyacheslav Kupriyanov [or Kuprianov]. TCRusP, tr. by Pamela Davidson

You say my poetry. Complaint to a Court Poet. Rashidi Samarqandi. ArPe, tr. by Omar S. Pound

You say—one shouldn't weep. Recollections of Siberia. Bella [or Izabella] Akhatovna Akhmadulina. RusPo, tr. by Robert Arthur Douglas Ford

You say, *Postumus*, you'll live tomorrow.   Martial.   RomPo, tr. by Peter Whigham

You say sir that yor-life depends.   Gentlewomans Answer to One, that Sayd He Should Dye, if Shee Refuse His Desires, A.   *Unknown.*   EMWP

You say that I take a good deal upon myself.   Monumentum Aere, Etc.   Ezra Pound.   NOBA

"You say that you believe in Democracy for everybody."   Everybody but Me.   Margaret Goss Burroughs.   BlSi

You say there were no people.   There Are No People Song.   *Navajo Oral Tradition.*   TTTS

You say, to me-wards your affection's strong.   Love Me Little, Love Me Long.   Robert Herrick.   CaPo; SCGP

You say "Tomorrow"; a tomorrow which.   Macedonius.   GrAn

You say you had a letter from.   First Letter from Tamara A.   Reiner Kunze.   PoSu, tr. by Ewald Osers

You say you "live inside a full-stop."   Nichita Stanescu.   Brian Turner.   PeNZ

You say you're glad I write—oh, say not so!   Impromptu.   Frances Anne [or "Fanny"] Kemble.   APN-1

You say you want to go home.   Minding You.   Catherine Byron.   Prnts

You scarcely move your foot when out of nowhere spring.   Voices.   Wislawa Szymborska.   PoSu, tr. by Magnus F. Krynski

You scream, waking from a nightmare.   Little Sleep's-Head Sprouting Hair in the Moonlight.   Galway Kinnell.   LCAP-2

You sea! I resign myself to you also—I guess what you mean.   Walt Whitman.   CAGL   Fr. Song of Myself.

You see a pair of laughing eyes.   (Love Is) The Tender Trap.   Sammy Cahn.   ReLy

You see but never know! (LL)   Sing a Song of People.   Lois Lenski.   NOxBChV; OTCP

You see how far Mans wisedom here extends.   John Wilmot, 2d Earl of Rochester.   OxBEV   Fr. Satire [or Satyre or Satyr] against [Reason and] Mankind, A.

You see, I am alive, I am alive. (LL)   Delight Song of Tsoai-Talee, The.   N. Scott Momaday.   CDW; InPK-6

You see me dying trial, gun inna the dance.   Dance Hall: Version.   Geoffrey Philp.   WaCa

You see, my whole life.   Woman Poem.   Nikki Giovanni.   BlSi

You see that forest on the height?   Pastoral.   John Stuart Williams.   TCAWP

You see that high crag.   Archilochus.   SaLy, tr. by Diane Rayor

You see the fellow with the scarlet sash?   Imre Madách.   IQMS, tr. by Iain MacLeod   Fr. Tragedy of Man.

You see, the problem is.   Blue like Death.   James Welch.   CDW

You see the slender spire that peers.   Days of Yore, The.   Douglas Thompson.   TreFP

You see the smoke at Kapunda.   Song: The Railway Train.   *Unknown.*   NOBAu, tr. by George Taplin

You see them vanish in their speeding cars.   Fugue.   Howard Nemerov.   TAP

You see these little scars? That's where my wife.   Iambic Feet Considered as Honorable Scars.   William Meredith.   OxBSP

You see, they have no judgment.   Drowned Children, The.   Louise Glück.   HCAP; VCAP

You See This Body.   Marcie Rendon.   ReEnLa

You see this dog.   Flush or Faunus.   Elizabeth Barrett Browning.   VWP

You see those mothers squabbling there?   Thomas Hardy.   InPK-6; Son   Fr. Satires of Circumstance in Fifteen Glimpses.

You see us in this picture.   Mrs. Biswas Goes through a Photo Album.   Reetika Vazirani.   AmPoNex

You see, we have to be forgiven things.   Paul Verlaine.   SxFrPo, tr. by Martin Sorrell

You see / we haven't changed that much.   Exile.   Amjad Nasir.   MAP, tr. by Charles Doria and May Jayyusi

You see what I am: change me, change me! (LL)   Woman at the Washington Zoo, The.   Randall Jarrell.   CoAP; HAP; HCAP; OxBC; TAP; TwCP; UnPo; VCAP

You see, where'er you look, on earth but vainness' hour.   All Is Vanity.   Andreas Gryphius.   GePo, tr. by George C. Schoolfield

You seek refuge.   Gift, The.   Greg Delanty.   BiHa

You seemed older.   Work and Worry.   Cheryl J. Fish.   GotH

You seldom talked about the Indian side.   Reservation, The.   Susan Clements.   UnSA

You send for her, you tell her to come, you get everything ready.   Impotent Lover, The.   Automedon.   GrAn

You Send Me: Bertha Franklin, December 11, 1964.   E. Ethelbert Miller.   SpirFl

You send me reams of snowy paper.   Leonidas of Alexandria.   GrAn

You Serve the Best Wines Always, My Dear Sir.   Martial.   InPK-6; RomPo, tr. by James Vincent Cunningham and J. V. Cunningham

You Shall above All Things Be Glad and Young.   E. E. Cummings.   ColAP; NOBA; NoAM; OxBA

You shall be true to them, who are false to you. (LL)   John Donne.   BASC;

BoLoP; ESCV; NAEL-5v1; NAEL-6v1; NAEL-7v1; NAWM-5v1; NOSC; SoSe-8

You shall have an apple.   For Baby.   *Unknown.*   ReMoGo

You shall have, for survival.   For Survival.   Andrée Chedid.   HAWP, tr. by Marie Ponsot

You shall listen to all sides and filter them from yourself. (LL)   Walt Whitman.   CAGL; UnPo   Fr. Song of Myself.

You shall love beauty, which is the shadow of God over the Universe.   Decalogue of the Artist.   Gabriela Mistral.   TCLAP, tr. by Doris Dana

You shall never remain in Thermopylae' (LL)   Limerick: "There was an old man of Thermopylae."   Edward Lear.   EBEV; NOBL; OxAEP-2; PeLi

You shall say that I am your sister. I don't know what became of them. (LL)   William Langland.   NAEL-6v1; NAEL-7v1   Fr. Vision of Piers Plowman, The.

You Shall Walk in Peace!   Martial Sinda.   NegPo, tr. by Ellen Conroy Kennedy

You share your mourning with all Moscow. There.   Pavel Grigoryevich Antokolsky.   TCRusP, tr. by Bob Perelman and Shirley Rihner   Fr. Son.

You shepherds who wander this lonely mountainside.   Leonidas of Tarentum.   GrAn

You should be done with blossoming by now.   To a Vine-clad Telegraph Pole.   Louis Untermeyer.   MoAmPo

You should bid me welcome.   Walther [or Walter] von der Vogelweide.   GePo

You should enjoy your suffering.   New Sentience, The.   Alan Davies.   FTOS

You should have asked me in the cradle: oh yes, then.   Fourth Eclogue, The.   Miklós Radnóti.   IQMS, tr. by John Wain

You should have disappeared years ago.   On Third Avenue.   Mina Loy.   APT-1; HarvBoo

"You should have many lovers."   Very Sad Conversation at Night, A.   Anna Swirszczynska.   PoSu

You should have married Seymour Brilkin.   Adventure.   Jule Styne.   ReLy

You should know the kind.   After Estrangement.   Molly Bendall.   AmPoNex

You should see these musical mice.   New Strain.   George Starbuck.   TwCP

You shouldn't be afraid of the dark.   Lullaby for My Dead Child.   Denise Jallais.   BoWoP, tr. by Maxine W. Kumin and Judith Kumin

You shout and hurry through.   Scaffold, The.   Amal Dunqul.   MAP; NAfrP, tr. by Sharif Elmusa and Thomas G. Ezzy

You show me the poems of some woman.   Translations.   Adrienne Rich.   WPOW

You showed your dirty face first in Detroit.   To the Eminent Scholar and Meddler.   Kofi Awoonor.   HBAPE

You shriek, 'Alas, *but I have failed!*' (LL)   Failures.   May Kendall.   VWP; ViWPN

You shun me, Chloë, wild and shy.   Horace.   AWP; OBVE   Fr. Odes.

You sing a hard blues.   Bulosan Listens to a Recording of Robert Johson.   Alfred Encarnacion.   OpBo

You sir have bought yourself a shiny train. (LL)   Wedding Day.   Mark Levine.   AmPoNex; BAP-01

You sit at your high windows, old men.   Old Men, The.   Alexander Javitz.   TrJP

You sit in a chair, touched by nothing, feeling.   In Celebration.   Mark Strand.   NoAM

You sit in the back.   Sorrow Since Sitting Bull, A.   Christopher Gilbert.   ESEAA

You sit in the middle of the bed.   To a Friend's Child.   Aliki Barnstone.   BoWoP

You slapped me.   For my Torturer, Lieutenant D.   Leila Djabali.   HAWP; WPOW, tr. by Anita Barrows

You slapped my face.   Short Poem.   William Carlos Williams.   SAmP

You sleep here, Daphnis, on the leafy ground.   Theocritus.   GrAn

You sleep in a room with bluegreen curtains.   In the Wake of Home.   Adrienne Rich.   LCAP-2

You sleep on one side, your spine.   Enough.   Tracy Ryan.   NeBl

You smiled when we parted.   Who's Sorry Now?   Harry Ruby.   ReLy

You smiled, you spoke, and I believed.   Walter Savage Landor.   BoLoP

You, so bravely plying reds and blues.   To a Portrait Painter who Desired Him to Sit.   Po Chü-i.   ChiP, tr. by Arthur Waley

You so sleepy baby Who you been.   At Work.   Suzanne Gardinier.   AmPoNex

You So Woman.   Ruth Forman.   SpirFl

You sold a slave just yesterday.   Martial.   WoPoe, tr. by William Matthews   Fr. Epigrams.

You, sons of Adam.   Down with Love.   Harold Arlen.   ReLy

You Sort Old Letters.   Robert Penn Warren.   BodElec

You speak of back home.   Scissortails.   Teresa Whitman.   TWW

You spotted snakes [with double tongue].   William Shakespeare.   NOBE; NoSic; PoRA; SCGP   Fr. Midsummer Night's Dream, A.

You staged the ultimate coup de grâce.   Lundys Letter, The.   Gerald Dawe.   BiHa

You Stand.   Ben Cami.   TuT, tr. by Pat Boran

You stand and hold the post of my small house.   Auvaiyar.   WPOW

You stand beside me here, each day and every hour. Yuly [*or* Iulii] Markovich Daniel. TCRP

You stand in your kitchen. Lithuanian Grandmother. Merra Young-Prottengeier. GotH

You stand, leaning on your spade, and rest. You Stand. Ben Cami. TuT, *tr. by* Pat Boran

You stand near the window as lights wink. 23rd Street Runs into Heaven. Kenneth Patchen. APT-2

You stand on a chair with a wrinkled nose. Making for Planet Alice. Deryn Rees-Jones. MFPA

You Stand There Fishing. Angie Estes. GeoHom

You stand waist-high in snakes. Alice. Michael S. Harper. ISC

You start here—Cozumel—it's an island, some people. You Are Here. Carl Phillips. GT

You start it all. You are lovely. To Women. Richard Hugo. NIP-4

You stay far far away. Union, The. Ifi Amadiume. HAWP

You Stepped Out of a Dream. Nacio Herb Brown. ReLy

You stepped through. Archangel. Ai. SeSe

You stood with your back to me. Sundial, The. Douglas Dunn. NPeEn

You stop to watch the Mandarin ducks. Urban Love Songs. Wing Tek Lum. OpBo

You strange, astonished-looking, angle-faced. Leigh Hunt. HAP; NOBL; NBLV; NPeEn; OBEV; OxBSo; PeLV; SCGP   *Fr.* Fish, the Man, and the Spirit, The.

You, stranger, soul-mate. Grief. Siamanto. AF, *tr. by* Peter Balakian

You, stranger, who only sees us happy and free of care. Hunger. Samik. STP, *tr. by* Edward Field

You strike everything down in battle. Inanna and Ishkur. Enheduanna. BoWoP

You strolled in the open, leisurely and alone. To the Poets in New York. James Wright (1927–80). NAAL-2v2

You, student, whistling those elusive bits. Carnal Knowledge. Dannie Abse. BloBone

You stupid men, who do accuse. Verses against the Inconsequence of Men's Taste and Strictures. Sister Juana Inés de la Cruz. SpanPo, *tr. by* Muriel Kittel

You surprise me, crow. Nigot. STP

You sweet soft murderess. *Unknown.* GePo

You take a piece of clay and mold it, shaping it into a human being. Ana Maria Shúa. MirDau, *tr. by* Rhonda Buchanan   *Fr.* Golem and Rabbi.

You take a woman. Trampling. Miguel Algarin. PueRic

You take my hand and. Margaret Atwood. HAP

You take off, he takes off, we take off. Clothes. Wislawa Szymborska. PoSu, *tr. by* Grazyna Drabik

You take the dollar. For One Moment. David Ignatow. NNaP

You take the rest. (LL) Crossed Apple, The. Louise Bogan. HeIP-4; NALW

You talk about disappointment. Being a Monster. Lawrence Raab. OPRER

You talk like / they don't kick. Langston Hughes. APSN; APT-2   *Fr.* Lenox Avenue Mural.

You taught me the land so well. Trees. Cheryl Savageau. TWW

You tell me about the rickety truck. Jamaica, October 18, 1972. Shara McCallum. AmPoNex

You tell me Christ was born nearly twenty centuries ago in a little horse town called Bethlehem. Christ is a Dixie Nigger. Frank Marshall Davis. APT-2

You tell me, fair one, that you ne'er can love. Female Philosopher, The. Charlotte Dacre. NOBRP; RWP

You Tell Me to Sit Quiet. A. C. Jordan. PBA

You tell me you have right on your side? Familiar Oxen. Oumar Ba. PBMAP

You tell me you're promised a lover. Letter of Advice, A. Winthrop Mackworth Praed. NOBL; OxBoLi; PeLV

You Tell on Yourself. *Unknown.* PoToHe

You tell them this. Interview with a Guy Named Fawkes, U.S. Army. Walter McDonald. CDa

You tell us how to heal these wounds. (LL) You Tell Us What to Do. Faiz Ahmad Faiz. PoetW; VCWP, *tr. by* Agha Shahid Ali

You tell what you are by the friends you seek. You Tell on Yourself. *Unknown.* PoToHe

You tender virgins, fairer than the snow with which you play. Edward May. FaBoEE

You tense up like a bow. Silver Clasps. "Paul Dermée." CuPo

You that a stranger in mid-Rome seek Rome. Rome. James Vincent Cunningham. OBVE

You that are jealous and have a wife. *Unknown.* NOIV

You that are sprung of northern stock. To a Calvinist in Bali. Edna St. Vincent Millay. NoAM

You that are weather-wise and pretend to know. Upon a Great Shower of Snow That Fell on May-Day, 1654. Thomas Washbourne. NOCV

You that do search for every purling spring. Sir Philip Sidney. NAEL-5v1; NoSic; OxAEP-1; Son   *Fr.* Astrophil and Stella.

You That Have Been Often Invited. *Unknown.* AH

You that have spent the silent night. Gascoigne's Good-Morrow. George Gascoigne. NOCV; NoSic

You That Love England. Cecil Day Lewis. FaBoMo

You that love Lovers. Jelaluddin [*or* Jalal al-Din] Rumi. ErotSp, *tr. by* Coleman Barks

You that through all the dying summer. Late Wasp, The. Edwin Muir. HarvBoo

You that thus wear a modest countenance. Dante Alighieri. AWP; EaItPo, *tr. by* Dante Gabriel Rossetti   *Fr.* La Vita Nuova.

You that unto your mistress' eyes. Love Deposed. Thomas Stanley. NOSC

You that will a wonder know. In Praise of His Mistress. Thomas Carew. BASC

You that with allegory's curious frame. Sir Philip Sidney. NAEL-7v1; NoSic   *Fr.* Astrophil and Stella.

You, the choice minions of the proud-lipped Nine. To Poets. George Darley. Son

You: The City. Fiona Templeton.
    Act II - Crossing At the Tracks. FTOS

You, the woman; I, the man; this, the world. Character of Love Seen as a Search for the Lost, The. Kenneth Patchen. CLPP; VGW

You then vor me meade up your mind. Walken Hwomme at Night. William Barnes. NOBVV

You there with the sticky fingers. *Unknown.* PriapPo, *tr. by* Richard W. Hooper   *Fr.* Priapus Poems, The.

You think. (LL) Myth. Muriel Rukeyser. APT-2; FaBoWP; NAAL-5; NALW; NIL-7; NNaP

You think Fuseli is not a Great Painter. I'm glad. To Hunt. William Blake. OxBoLi

You think I am happy. Wang Chiu-ssu. CoBLCP   *Fr.* Forced Feelings.

You think I am your servant but you are wrong. Table Talk. Derek Mahon. DiPo

You think I give myself to you? Giving. Nora B. Cunningham. LW

You think it horrible that lust and rage. Spur, The. W. B. Yeats. OxAEP-2; WeW-3

You think that beard has made you wise. Ammianus. GrAn

You think the coldest girls in the world are Eskimos. Turn on the Heat. Ray Henderson. ReLy

You think this cruel? take it for a rule. Pope. NPeEn   *Fr.* Epistle to Dr. Arbuthnot.

You think this is some malarial dream? Vladimir Vladimirovich Mayakovsky [*or* Maiakovskii]. TCRP   *Fr.* Cloud in Trousers, The.

You think: won't fate tap. "Georgy [*or* Georgii] Avdeievich Rayevsky" [*or* Raevskii]. TCRP

You think you can leave the matter to your lips. Kiss. Emanuel Carnevali. APT-2

You think you / need me. Masquerade. Carolyn M. Rodgers. BlSi

You think yourself, perhaps, more than a speck. Another Voice. Victor Hugo. SxFrPo, *tr. by* E. H. Blackmore and A. M. Blackmore

You though! Die and you'll lie dumb in the dirt; nobody care, and none. On a Lady Indifferent to Poetry. Sappho. STV, *tr. by* John Frederick Nims

You thought I had the strength of men. Clever Woman, A. Mary Elizabeth Coleridge. BrRo; VWP; ViWPN

You thunder at my side. Snoring Bedmate, The. *Unknown.* BIrV, *tr. by* John V. Kelleher

You tire of it, this. Self-analysis. Michael Dransfield. BMAP

You, to whom we flow. To the Lord. Richard von Schaukal. AuPH, *tr. by* Lowell A. Bangerter

You told me: "I am not worthy of you." Marguerite Burnat-Provins. BoWoP

You told me, if something is not used it is meaningless, and took my temperature. Rosmarie Waldrop. FTOS; PFTM-2   *Fr.* Reproduction of Profiles, The.

You told me it was / because of me. Lady Izumi. BoWoP; WoPoe, *tr. by* Willis Barnstone

You told me, Maro, whilst you live. Hinted Wish, A. Martial. AWP, *tr. by* Francis Lewis

You told me my grandfather never wept. Ancestral Weight. Alfonsina Storni. WPOW, *tr. by* Marti Moody Kate Flores

You told me, Sir, your teeth were loose. On a Gentleman's Complaining to a Lady That He Could Not Eat Meat. *Unknown.* ECWP

You told me that I was born under a lucky star. "Ivan Venediktovich Elagin." TCRP

You told me you were growing potatoes. Roots: To My Daughter. Virginia R. Terris. SpudSo

You Too. Edmund Vance Cooke. PWR

You too, Clenorides, homesickness drove. *Unknown.* GrAn

You Too Lie down. Dennis Lee. TLR

You, too, perished by a bush with tangled roots. Anyte [*or* Anytes]. SaLy, *tr. by* Diane Rayor

You too. You too. You too. (LL) In a Parlor Containing a Table. Galway Kinnell. NBLV; OxBSP

You Too? Me Too—Why Not? Soda Pop. Robert Hollander. NIL-7; NIP-4

You Took Advantage of Me. Richard Rodgers. ReLy

You Took Away All the Oceans and All the Room. Osip Emilevich Mandelstam [*or* Mandelshtam]. OPOU; Spl, *tr. by* Clarence Brown

You took me, hostile, sullen—. Olga Fiodorovna Berggolts [*or* Bergholts]. TCRP

You took my kisses and you took my love. All of Me. Seymour Simons. ReLy

You took your father. Spanish of Our Out-Loud Dreams, The. Martín Espada. PueRic

You toss now to the left; you toss now to the right. Crinagoras. HePo *Fr.* Epigrams.

You tossed a blanket from the bed. T. S. Eliot. TCAPo *Fr.* Preludes (I–IV).

You Touch Me. Andrena Zawinski. PasH

You trick your thorny rope with little joys. Geometry of the Soul. Fawziyya Abu Khalid. PoArWo, *tr. by* Farouk Mustafa

You try to hush me, and hearten me. Refuge. Gyula Illyés. IQMS, *tr. by* Peter Zollman

You Turn Around. Jordan Davis. HeMarv

You turn towards meteor showers in August. That Falling. Jane Hirshfield. BodElec

You turned down the wrong street. On the Murder of an Ice Cream Man. Hayan Charara. AmPoNex

You Twist Your Death in Nooses. Nikolai Alekseievich Klyuev [*or* Kliuev *or* Klyuev]. TCRusP, *tr. by* John Glad

Two gardeners. New Jersey Boys. Robert Coles. BloBone

You two sit at the table late, each, now and then. After the Dinner Party. Robert Penn Warren. NAAL-5

You understand him not. Christ does not claim. Understanding. István Vas. IQMS, *tr. by* Godfrey Turton

You understand it? How they returned from Culloden. Culloden and After. Iain Crichton Smith. OxBS

You understand the colors on the hillside have faded. Crucifixion. Hayden Carruth. BodElec

You unseen lightning flash, you darkly radiant light. On the Ineffable Inspiration of the Holy Spirit. Catharina Regina von Greiffenberg. WPoS; WoPoe, *tr. by* Michael Hamburger

You used to let me watch to time the eggs. (LL) Tony Harrison. EmeKit; HarvBoo *Fr.* School of Eloquence, The.

You used to say that you wished to know only Catullus. 72. Catullus. NAWM-7v1, *tr. by* Charles Martin

You vanish with early tears. (LL) Tear. Thomas Kinsella. ModIr; NOIV; NoP-4; OxBEV

You've aroused the lilacs and they brew violets. Hoopla. Star Black. KGB

You've Been a Good Old Wagon, but You've Done Broke Down. Ben Harney. OBAL

You've been asking me that question. Blue Clay. Ellease Southerland. GT

You've been blackberrying again. Spin-Cycle. Jane Holland. MFPA

You've been Englished but you won't forget it, never. (LL) England Nil. Anne Rouse. MFPA; NeBl

You've been in Rome a long time, Corydon. It must. Titus Calpurnius Siculus. RomPo, *tr. by* Guy Lee *Fr.* Eclogues.

You've come. Ulysses Embroidered. Miriam Waddington. NIL-7

You've come a long way (they said). En Route. Alan Ross. FaBoWar

You've done taken my blues and gone—. Langston Hughes. *See* You've taken my blues and gone

You've done your duty. Raishi. JDP, *tr. by* Yoel Hoffmann

You've drawn 3 rings around me. Complaint for a Sorcerer. Susy Hare. SurWo

You've enchanted the world. Mahārāja Nandakumār Rāy. SinGod, *tr. by* Rachel Fell McDermott

You've found the place in time—no permanent shade. Making Camp. David Wagoner. PoCoUp

You've got nice knees. Love Song. Gavin Ewart. OxBTC

You've got no time for me. I've Got Your Number. Cy Coleman. ReLy

You've got to give. Glory of Love, The. Billy Hill. ReLy

You've got to hand it to the fairer sex. Are You Makin' Any Money? Herman Hupfeld. ReLy

You've gotta have heart. Jerry Ross. ReLy *Fr.* Damn Yankees.

You've gotten in through the transom. To a Child Trapped in a Barber Shop. Philip Levine. InPK-6; NOBA; NoAM; PAI; TAP; VGW

"You've had your operation, Mrs. Brown." Other Side, The. Roy Fuller. OxBC

You've heard monkeys crying. Basho. EH, *tr. by* Robert Hass

You've lived there long, away from the trappings of office. To a Hermit in the Mountains. Hsü Pen. CoBLCP; ColAnChi, *tr. by* Jonathan Chaves

You've locked so many Blacks away. Whiteman Is the Judge, The. Frank Doolan. IBA

You've lost your religion, the Rabbi said. Debate with the Rabbi. Howard Nemerov. TaR

You've moved to a house backing the outer wall. Looking for Lu Hung-chien but Failing To Find Him. Chiao-jan. CoBCP, *tr. by* Burton Watson

You've never been in a public bath. Bathhouse, The. Boris Abramovich Slutsky [*or* Slutskii]. TCRP, *tr. by* J. R. Rowland

You've not been to the local bathhouse. Bathhouse, The. Boris Abramovich Slutsky [*or* Slutskii]. TCRusP, *tr. by* Daniel Weissbort

You've planted seven wealthy husbands. Agriculture. Martial. WoPoe, *tr. by* Fred Chappell

You've pluck'd [*or* plucked] a curlew, drawn a hen. On an Island. John Millington Synge. BIrV; FaBoVe; MoBrPo; NPeEn; OxBEV; OxBSP; PeVV

You've pulled back, like. Grass Crust, The. Christiania Whitehead. NeBl

You've rocked at many passage rites, at drums. On African Writing. Jack A. Mapanje. HBAPE

You've seen a strawberry. Nevertheless. Marianne Craig Moore. HarvBoo; NAAL-2v2; NoP-4; OxBA; SoSe-8

You've taken my blues and gone. Note on Commercial Theatre. Langston Hughes. NAAL-5

You've Told Me, Maro. Martial. NIL-7; NIP-4, *tr. by* F. Lewis

You vilify me, but I rise above grief. Lament after Her Husband Bishr's Murder. Al-Khirniq. BoWoP, *tr. by* Willis Barnstone

You virgins that did late despair. James Shirley. NOBE *Fr.* Imposture, The.

You wait for a right moment. Sea Without Poets. Branko Miljkovic. WoPoe, *tr. by* Charles Simic

You waited with impatience. Still. Ronald Stuart Thomas. TCAWP

You wake in a Córdoba. Don José Gorostiza Encounters El Cordobés. Jay Wright. ESEAA

You wake me, / Part my thighs, and kiss me. Kenneth Rexroth. APSN *Fr.* Love Poems of Marichiko, The.

You wake up and you don't know who it is there breathing. Region of Unlikeness, The. Jorie Graham. HarvBoo

You wake up filled with dread. Up. Margaret Atwood. NoP-4

You walk for miles beside me. Walk in the Rain. Polly Clark. NeBl

You walk into an ordinary room. Laburnum. Paula Meehan. ModIr

You walk on. Door, A. W. S. Merwin. SPE

You walk on air. Glance. Dhabya Khamees. PoArWo, *tr. by* Clarissa C. Burt

You walk up there in the light. Hyperion's Song of Fate. Friedrich Hölderlin. NAWM-7v2, *tr. by* Christopher Middleton

You walked, all of a sudden, though. In Memory of Gerard Dillon. Michael Longley. BiHa

You walked, all of a sudden, through. In Memory of Gerard Dillon. Michael Longley. PBCIP

You walked dusty dry roads;. Southern Road. Mwatabu Okantah. SeSe

You, Walking Past Me. Marina Ivanovna Tsvetayeva [*or* Tsvetaeva]. AF, *tr. by* Mary Maddock

You wander above in brightness. Friedrich Hölderlin. WoPoe, *tr. by* M. L. Rosenthal *Fr.* Hyperion.

You wandered in the desert waste, athirst. Oasis, An. Agnes Mary Frances Robinson. VWP

You want a guarantee. Testament. Nizar Qabbani. MAP, *tr. by* Diana Der Hovanessian and Lena Jayyusi

You want a soothing life. Traders in Beauty and Delight. Abu Dulama. ArPe, *tr. by* Omar S. Pound

You want biographical news, you want. Biographical News. Daria Menicanti. CItWP, *tr. by* Cinzia Sartini Blum and Lara Trubowitz

You want coins? Roman? Greek? Nice vase? Head of god, goddess. Ali Ben Shufti. Anthony Thwaite. OxBTC

You want corporate woman I get her for you. Lilies of the Field. Anne Rouse. MFPA; NeBl

You want me to call you generous. Martial. RomPo, *tr. by* Dorothea Wender

You want the summer lightning, throw the knives. Ingeborg Bachmann. BoWoP, *tr. by* Daniel Huws

You want this world, smudge of oil on the feather. Ruth. Mary Crockett Hill. AmPoNex

You want to change your name. You're looking. Riddle of Noah, The. Maxine W. Kumin. OPRER

You want to make some honey? Bee. X. J. Kennedy. OBCA; Spl

You want? You're in my way. (LL) Not My Best Side. U. A. Fanthorpe. EmeKit; FaBoWP

You wanton, quiet memory that haunts me all the while. Forgotten. *Unknown, fr. Terezin Concentration Camp.* INSAB

You wear, and the star running down his cheek. (LL) Swimming by Night. James Merrill. ColAP; HarvBoo; VGW

You wear the face. Lady Izumi. BoWoP

You wear the morning like your dress. Song. Joseph Hilaire Pierre Belloc. OBEV

You, weeping wide at war, weep with me now. Coward, The. Eve Merriam. TrJP

You well[-]compacted groves, whose light and shade. Sonnet Made upon the Groves near Merlou [or Merlow] Castle. Edward Herbert, 1st Baron Herbert of Cherbury. NOSC; NPeEn; OxBSo

You went away, I let you. Lover, Come Back to Me! Sigmund Romberg. ReLy

You went downstairs. May Swenson. GLP; PoBW

You went out with the turning tide. Exit Amor. Virginia Hamilton Adair. APT-2

You went to the front like sheep. First World War Poets. Edward Bond. FaBoWar

You went to the verge, you say, and came back safely. Conrad Potter Aiken. FaBoMo; TwCP Fr. Preludes for Memnon; or, Preludes to Attitude.

You were. Praise Song for My Mother. Grace Nichols. Prnts

You were a child, and liked me, yesterday. Arthur Symons. OxBSo Fr. Violet.

You were a fool, Old Man of the Moon. Nguyễn Gia Thiều. WoPoe, tr. by Nguyen Ngoc Bich Fr. Sorrows of an Abandoned Queen.

You were a girl of satin and gauze. Wheel Revolves, The. Kenneth Rexroth. NoAM

You were a haughty beauty, Polly. Private Theatricals. Louise Imogen Guiney. PoBW

You were a kind man and you died in want. (LL) Ford Madox Ford. Robert Lowell. OxBC; TwCP

You were a moral dandy, sir. The font. To Max Jacob. Rosanna Warren. DiPo

You were a pretty boy once, Archestratus, and. Epigram. Philip of Thessalonica. GrAn, tr. by Edith Morgan

You were a sophist. Advice. Gwendolyn B. Bennett. BlSi

You were a swan, you're now a crow. Martial. RomPo, tr. by Olive Pitt-Kethley

You were a tender desire, an insinuating cloud. Luis Cernuda. CAGL, tr. by Rick Lipinski

You were born; must die; were loved; must love. Sonnet. Stephen Spender. MoBrPo; Son

You Were Broken. Giuseppe Ungaretti. STV, tr. by John Frederick Nims

You were dead, but how sleek and darkly calm you were! Dream of William Carlos Williams, A. Robert Bly. BodElec

You were forgiven. Dialogue of the Night of the Roses. Zuhur Dixon. MAP, tr. by Patricia Alanah Byrne and Salma Khadra Jayyusi

You were framed by your dark chestnut hair. Working for British Telecom. Ben Scammell. NLP

You were half-right, I did lie. On Apologies. Valerie Jean. SpirFl

You were made. Creation. Jeni Couzyn. HAWP

You Were Meant for Me. Arthur Freed. ReLy

You were my adored one. Blame It on My Youth. Edward Heyman. ReLy

You were my beginning and again I am with you, here, where I. In Szetejnie. Czeslaw Milosz. BodElec, tr. by Robert Hass

You were my death. Paul Celan. PoetW, tr. by John Felstiner

You were my mother, thorn apple bush. Graves, The. Lorine Niedecker. APT-2

You were my youth, you gave to me. Dedication. N. P. van Wyk Louw. PeSAV, tr. by Hugh Finn

You Were Never Lovelier. Johnny Mercer. ReLy

You Were Never Miss Brown to Me. Sherley Anne Williams. GT

You were never told, Mother, how old Illya was drunk. Czar's Last Christmas Letter: A Barn in the Urals, The. Norman Dubie. NoAM

You were praised, my books. Salutation the Second. Ezra Pound. NOBA; OxBA

You were reading. I was dreaming. Reading, Dreaming, Hiding. Kelly Cherry. FFC

You were separated from me Hori. Space Invaders Machine, The. Pita Sharples. PeNZ, tr. by the author

You were tall and beautiful. First Love. Mary Dorcey. BrRo

You were the light that brightened my life. It's a Blue World. Robert Wright. ReLy

You were the morning star among the living. Aster. Plato. GrAn; WoPoe, tr. by Peter Jay

You were the one for skylights. I opposed. Seamus Heaney. OxBSo Fr. Glanmore Revisited.

You were to be the centre of our dream. Nozizwe. Raymond Mazisi Kunene. PeSAV, tr. by the author

You Were Wearing. Kenneth Koch. AiP; CoAP; NIP-4; NNaP; SPE

You were young--but that was scarcely to your credit. Gerald Louis Gould. OxBTC Fr. Monogamy.

You were your own and not mine and I had not lost you. (LL) Epitaph for a Poet. Homero [or Umberto] Aridjis. PoetW; STV; TCLAP, tr. by John Frederick Nims

You weren't well or really ill yet either. Embrace, The. Mark Doty. AmFaPo

You who. Maram Masri. PoArWo, tr. by Amal Amireh

You who are born in decay. Firefly. Tu Fu. CrYelRi, tr. by Sam Hamill

You who are earth, and cannot rise. William Habington. BeJo Fr. Castara.

You, who are lieutenants in the army. Sebestyén Tinódi. IQMS, tr. by Joseph Leftwich Fr. Call to Lieutenants.

You who are reading this work without malice, may you. Ovid. RomPo, tr. by Peter Green Fr. Tristia.

You who are still and white. Slain. T. W. H. Crosland. OBWP

You who ask where I find the courage. Return to the Tree of Time, A. Vesna Parun. WPOW, tr. by Vasa D. Mihailovich and Ronald Morgan

You, who behold in wonder Rome and all. Rome. Joachim Du Bellay. WoPoe, tr. by Yvor Winters

You who can grant, or can refuse, the pow'r. Sea-Chaplain's Petition to the Lieutenants in the Ward-Room, for the Use of the Quarter-Gallery, A. "J. T." NOEC

You who can see the future. Oracle. Fanny Carrión de Fierro. TANSG, tr. by Sally Cheney Bell

You who come from the old village. Verses. Wang Wei. TAL

You who desired so much—in vain to ask. To Emily Dickinson. Hart Crane. ColAP; NIL-7; NIP-4; NOBA; NoAM; NoP-4; Son; TAP

You Who Dog My Footsteps. Leyb [orLeib] Kvitko [orKwitko]. TrJP, tr. by Joseph Leftwich

You who draw into yourself each depth. Merciful Shore, The. Maria Luisa Spaziani. NeIt, tr. by Beverly Allen

You who / fail. Femina. Daphne Marlatt. NOBC

You who have forgotten yourself in this moving tomb. Short Revelation Concerning Death and Chaos. René Daumal. PFTM-1

You who have spoken words in the earth. Reproach to Dead Poets. Archibald MacLeish. NAAL-2v2

You who hear in scattered rhymes the sound of those sighs with. Petrarch. NAWM-7v1, tr. by Robert M. Durling Fr. Sonnets to Laura.

You who in evenings by the fire. These Poems. John Jarmain. FaBoWar

You, who inconstancy so constantly can squander. To the Moon. Paul Fleming. GePo, tr. by George C. Schoolfield

You who knew nothing, understood everything. Now That I Have Grown up, Mother. Clementina Suárez. TANSG, tr. by Janet N. Gold

You who live secure. Shemà. Primo Levi. AF; FaBoWar; HP, tr. by Ruth Feldman and Ruth Feldman

You who look lovely from the windows. Praxilla. SaLy, tr. by Diane Rayor

You who never took. To My Ill-Wishers. Nikolai Ivanovich Glazkov. TCRP, tr. by Daniel Weissbort

You, who now pass blind-eyed, uncaringly. Royal Procession. Ernst Goll. AuPH, tr. by Lowell A. Bangerter

You Who Occupy Our Land. Maria Manuela Margarido. HAWP; WPOW, tr. by Allan Francovich

You who paints forests all. Fall. Ferdinand von Saar. AuPH, tr. by Lowell A. Bangerter

You who rest your belly on a pair of fat pilings. Trumpet, Shout, Carry! Velemir [or Viktor Vladimirovich] Khlebnikov. TCRusP, tr. by Kathy Lewis and Bob Perelman

You Who Sleep. Philippe Soupault. AF, tr. by Eden Paul

You who smile from the disarmed. Possibility. Tiziano Rossi. ItPo, tr. by Gayle Ridinger

You who snore with your sleeping wife so near. Tristan Corbière. OBVE Fr. Litany of Sleep.

You who stoop, you who weep. Challenge. David Diop. NegPo, tr. by Ellen Conroy Kennedy

You, who thought that my heart would be full of anguish. Song of Reproach. Ferenc Apáti. IQMS, tr. by Adam Makkai

You, who to avoid my manhood. Unknown. PriapPo, tr. by Richard W. Hooper Fr. Priapus Poems, The.

You who visit in turn. Poseidippus. PGA

You who walked like a broken old dream. Negro Tramp. David Diop. NegPo, tr. by Ellen Conroy Kennedy

You who want. Hadewijch II. HW; WPoS

You who were darkness warmed my flesh. Woman to Child. Judith Wright. WPE

You who will die, watch over your life; don't set sail. Epitaph for Cleonicus. Alexander of Pleuron. GrAn

You whom I could not save. Dedication. Czeslaw Milosz. WoPoe

You whom I could not save / Listen to me. Czeslaw Milosz. See You whom I could not save

You whom I disavow, most human one. Pope John XXIII. Ernst Waldinger. AuPH, tr. by Lowell A. Bangerter

You, whose day it is, make it beautiful. Song to Bring Fair Weather. Unknown. WoPoe, tr. by Frances Densmore

You, whose head once gazed at a sky so lofty. To a Fallen Walnut Tree. Dávid Baróti Szabó. IQMS, *tr.* by Watson Kirkconnell

You will always be at some border. We All Conspire. Mario Benedetti. TCLAP, *tr.* by Sophie Cabot Black and Maria Negroni

You will ask: And where are the lilacs? I Explain a Few Things. Pablo Neruda. PoetW, *tr.* by Nathaniel Tarn

You will awaken me at dawn. Saga. Andrey [*or* Andrei] Andreievich Voznesensky [*or* Voznesenskii]. TCRP, *tr.* by Vera Dunham and William Jay Smith

You will be able to see me. (LL) This Is a Photograph of Me. Margaret Atwood. NALW; NoAM; NoP-4

You will be astonished to hear the freedom of Paul. You Will Be Astonished. Michel Deguy. PFTM-2, *tr.* by Clayton Eshleman

You Will Be Hearing from Us Shortly. U. A. Fanthorpe. OBCoV

You will be obscured by a cloud of postures. Nadar. Richard Howard. GS

You will carry this suture. Trauma. Brad Leithauser. InPK-6

You will come into an antique town. Where I Live. Wesley McNair. TRP

You will come to a well on the left side of hell's house. Petelia Tablet, The. *Unknown.* WoPoe, *tr.* by Robert Bringhurst

You Will Die. *Unknown.* AWP, *tr.* by H. A. Giles *Fr.* Shi King.

You will find here a new representation of the universe. Horse Calligram. Guillaume Apollinaire. PFTM-1

You will find my past not spotless. My Future Just Passed. George, Jr. Marion. ReLy

You Will Forget. Chenjerai Hove. HBAPE; NAfrP

You will have smiled, I shall have tossed your hair. (LL) À Quoi Bon Dire. Charlotte Mew. MakPoe; NPeEn; OxBEV; OxBTC; VWP

You will have the road gate open, the front door ajar. In Memory of My Mother. Patrick Kavanagh. BIrV

You will hear the drumming hooves. (LL) Earth and I Gave You Turquoise. N. Scott Momaday. CDW; HATNAP; UnPo

You Will Know When You Get There. Allen Curnow. EmeKit; NoP-4; PeNZ

You will marry that mouth in your mind. (LL) Mission Poem. Tarin Towers. AmPoNex; PuP-23

You will move into its depth. (LL) Hadewijch. BoWoP; WoPoe, *tr.* by Willis Barnstone and Elene Kolb

You will need. Truganinny. Wendy Rose. HATNAP

You will not be able to buy. Child Bride. Garnett Kilberg Cohen. MPUn

You will not be able to stay home, brother. Revolution Will Not Be Televised, The! Gil Scott-Heron. NAAAL

You will not dare to think your own thoughts. Sentence, The. Yuly [*or* Iulii] Markovich Daniel. TCRP, *tr.* by Arthur Boyars and David Burg

You will not tame this sea. Sea and the Man, The. Anna Swirszczynska. BLT

You will not travel. Ultimate Distance, The. Fu'ad [*or* Fuad] Rifqa [*or* Rifka]. MAP, *tr.* by Sargon Boulus and Samuel Hazo

You will remember that strange precipice. Sonnet 4. Pablo Neruda. BLPSL, *tr.* by Rene de Costa, Rigas Kappatos and Eleni Paidoussi

You will remember the kisses, real or imagined. Resurrection. Kenneth Fearing. PoE

You will remember, when the bombs. Paris—Christmas 1938. Edwin Rolfe. APT-2

You will see me in the wolf's footstep. Signs. Silvia Grénier. SurWo, *tr.* by Myrna Bell Rochester

You Will See Your Lord a-Coming. *Unknown.* AH

You will speak of our days in whispers. Eclipse. John Haines. PoCoUp

You wished for a love-letter, Doctor. Love-letter, A. Mary E. Tucker. CBWP-1

You with the beard as red as Barbarossa's. For My Great-Grandfather: A Message Long Overdue. Maxine W. Kumin. UnSA

You with your back to the wall. (LL) Orion. Adrienne Rich. NAAL-2v2; NIP-4; NoAM; NoP-4; WPE

You with your beautiful swaying walk, where. You with Your Beautiful Swaying Walk. Amaru. WoPoe, *tr.* by Henry Heifetz

You, with your rainbow-brows woven of light. Hymn for All Seasons. László Nagy. IQMS, *tr.* by Adam Makkai

You won't be the one to turn away when death. Clay Pipes, The. Cathal Ó Searcaigh. ModIr, *tr.* by Seamus Heaney

You won't find them in places where society goes. Dandelions. Will D. Stanton. SoSe-3

You wonder at that Georgian terrace. Lychees. Medbh McGuckian. PBCIP

You wonder, since I'm wooden front to rear. *Unknown.* PriapPo, *tr.* by Richard W. Hooper *Fr.* Priapus Poems, The.

You wonder who this is! And, why I name. On the Town's Honest Man. Ben Jonson. NOSC

You wonder why Drab sells her love for gold? Epigram. James Vincent Cunningham. APT-2

You wonder why I sail along in uncertainty. Bird-Shooting. Eugenio Montale. ItPo, *tr.* by Gayle Ridinger

You wonder why it is they write of it, sing of it. Up on the Roof. Maura Dooley. NeBl

You words, come, after me! You Words. Ingeborg Bachmann. PoSu, *tr.* by Mark Anderson

You wore blue peddle pushers and polka dot tops. Girl. Kelly Norman Ellis. SpirFl

You worked me well, Mr Thomas. Master, The. Bryn Griffiths. TCAWP

You worry me whoever you are. Badman of the Guest Professor. Ishmael Reed. BPo; SSLK

You Worthless. *Unknown.* FaBoVe

You would always offer me a mug. Big John's Tears Fall to the River. Siobhan Campbell. MFPA

You would have scoffed if we had told you yesterday. To a Child in Death. Charlotte Mew. ChIV-2; MoBrPo

You Would Have Understood Me. Paul Verlaine. BoLoP; MoBrPo; NOBVV; PeVV, *tr.* by Ernest Dowson

You would hoist an old hat on the tines of a fork. Bat on the Road, A. Seamus Heaney. PoE

You would not believe it; I sat. Giving Thanks. Anne K. Smith. PasH

You would not believe, would you. Edgar Lee Masters. APT-1 *Fr.* Spoon River Anthology.

You would not guess it is the voice. Frog Song. Hildegarde Flanner. APT-2

You would not have me roar, or crow. (LL) After Galen. Oliver St. John Gogarty. FaBoEE; OBMV; PoRA

You would not recognize me. Tourist from Syracuse, The. Donald Justice. NoAM; TwCP; VCAP

You would not say to children. Folk Museum, The. Medbh McGuckian. CIP-2

You would rather scream out your anger in a workshop. For an Asian Woman Who Says My Poetry Gives Her a Stomachache. Nellie Wong. FSt

You would shrink back / jump up. July 4, 1984: For Buck. June Jordan. NoAM

You would think that night could lift. Testament of Loss. Gloria C. Oden. ESEAA

You would think the fury of aerial bombardment. Fury of Aerial Bombardment, The. Richard Eberhart. APT-2; FaBoMo; HelP-4; InPK-6; NIL-7; NIP-4; NoAM; NoP-4; OBWP; PAI; PoWW; RB; TAP; TwCP; UnPo; VGW

You wouldn't be so depressed. Jane Kenyon. LoL *Fr.* Having It Out with Melancholy.

You wouldn't believe all this house has cost me. Flitting, The. Medbh McGuckian. PBCIP; PNI

You wouldn't fit in your coffin. You Didn't Fit. Susan Musgrave. NIL-7

You wouldn't have. (LL) E. E. Cummings. OxBSP; WeW-3

You write with ease, to shew your breeding. Clio's Protest. Richard Brinsley Sheridan. FaBoEE

You wrong me, Strephon, when you say. Song. "Ephelia." EMWP

You wrote this from Beirut, two years before. Homage to Faiz Ahmed Faiz. Agha Shahid Ali. OpBo

You, you caribou. Magic Words for Hunting Caribou. *Unknown.* STP, *tr.* by Johnny John and Jerome Rothenberg

You. You dwell in this old house. To the Beloved Grown Past Youth. Amin Nakhla. MAP, *tr.* by Matthew Sorenson

You / You're like a crocus, like a sugar maple. Spring Fever. Rosario Morales. PueRic

You. You running across the field. Orpheus and Eurydice. Jean Valentine. FaBoWP; LCAP-2

You yourself are all the Nine. (LL) Mutual Congratulations of the Poets Anna Seward and Hayley, The. Richard Porson. FaBoEE; OBSV

You yourself must be the seventh. (LL) Seventh, The. Attila József. AF; RB, *tr.* by John Batki

Young Acacia, The. Hayyim Nahman [*or* Khayim Nakhman *or* Chaim Nachman] Bialik. TrJP, *tr.* by Helena Frank

Young Africans. Gwendolyn Brooks. NoAM

Young Allan. *Unknown.* ESPB

Young and Healthy. Harry Warren. ReLy

Young and Old. Charles Kingsley. EBEV; OxAEP-2 *Fr.* Water Babies, The.

"Young and old, rejoice." Neidhart von Reuental. GePo

Young and Radiant, He Is Standing. Allen Eastman Cross. AH

Young and willing to learn (but what?) he was the boy. Razzmatazz. Gilbert Sorrentino. FTOS

Young are quick of speech, The. On Teaching the Young. Yvor Winters. APT-2; MakPoe; NOBA; NoAM

Young at Heart. Carolyn Leigh. ReLy

Young attendants wrapped him in a red, The. Inpatient. Dolores Kendrick. FFC

Young Bearwell. *Unknown.* ESPB

Young Beichan. *Unknown.* ESPB

Young Ben he was a nice young man. Faithless Sally Brown. Thomas Hood. NOBL; OBNV

Young Benjie. *Unknown.* ESPB; OxBB

Young Birch, A. Robert Frost. SAmP

Young bloods come round less often now, The. Horace. *See* Ribald Romeos less and less berattle

Young bride. Sengai Gibon. JDP, *tr. by* Yoel Hoffmann

Young bride and groom of Australia, A. Limerick. *Unknown.* PeLi

Young British Soldier, The. Rudyard Kipling. "When first under fire an' you're wishful to duck." FaBoWar

Young but not youthful he thou lovest not. Rose Leaves When the Rose Is Dead. Marc André Raffalovich. CAGL

Young child of Diodoros's house, A. Diodoros of Sardis. GrAn

Young Chinese gets down, The! Midnight Rocker, Tiananmen Square, May 27, 1989. Edith Rylander. MiVo

Young clerk peruses the court's files, A. Corruption. Freddy Macha. NAfrP

Young Clovis by a happy chance. On a Bashful Shepherd. "Ephelia." PEW

Young Colin Clout, a lad of peerless meed. John Gay. NOEC *Fr.* Shepherd's Week, The.

Young composer, working that summer at an artist's colony, had watched her for a week, The. Story about the Body, A. Robert Hass. RaBo

Young Corydon [*or* Coridon] and Phyllis [*or* Phillis]. On the Happy Corydon and Phyllis. Sir Charles Sedley. BoLoP

Young couple who lived at "The Laurels", A. Limerick. W. F. N. Watson. PeLi

Young Don't Want to Be Born. James Wright (1927–80). BodElec

Young Dove, The. Moses Ibn Ezra. TrJP, *tr. by* Solomon Solis-Cohen

Young Earl of Essex's Victory over the Emperor of Germany, The. *Unknown.* ESPB

Young Elvis. Cornelius Eady. AllShUp

Young Endymion sleeps Endymion's sleep, The. Keats. Henry Wadsworth Longfellow. Son; TAP

Young engine-driver called Hunt, A. Limerick. Victor Gray. NOBL

Young engineer receives a wooden crate marked: *unusual cargo*, A. In the Interest of Possibility. Thom Ward. AmPoNex

Young Fenians, The. Padraic Fallon. BIrV

Young finch asked the old one why he wept, The. Caged Birds. Ignacy Krasicki. WoPoe, *tr. by* Jerzy Peterkiewicz and Burns Singer

Young flirt of Ceylon, A. Ogden Nash. PeLi

Young flowers were whispering in melody. Edgar Allan Poe. NOBA *Fr.* Al Aaraaf.

Young Fools, The. Paul Verlaine. WoPoe, *tr. by* Louis Simpson

Young Gal's Blues. Langston Hughes. NAAL-2v2

Young, gifted, and black. To be Young, Gifted, and Black. Weldon J., Jr. Irvine. ISC

Young Girl. Ricarda Huch. WPOW, *tr. by* Janine Canan and Deirdre Lashgari

Young Girl. Carl Rakosi. APT-2

Young Girl and the Beach, The. Sophia de Mello Breyner Andresen. WPOW, *tr. by* Alexis Levitin

Young girl dancing lifts her face, The. Dancer, The. Walter James Turner. NOBAu; OBMV

Young girl moves like an ear of grain, A. Young Girl and the Beach, The. Sophia de Mello Breyner Andresen. WPOW, *tr. by* Alexis Levitin

Young girl of English nativity, A. Limerick. *Unknown.* PeLi

Young girl, only eleven, A. Mother-in-Law Is Cruel. Cheng Hsieh. CoBLCP, *tr. by* Jonathan Chaves

Young Girl Peeling Apples. Mary Jo Salter. FFC

Young girl stood beside me, The. Orange Tree, The. John Shaw Neilson. CBAP

Young girl who was no good at tennis, A. Limerick. *Unknown.* PeLi

Young Girl with a Pitcher Full of Water, A. David Wagoner. NoAM

Young Girls. Raymond Souster. HeIP-4

Young Glass-Stainer, The. Thomas Hardy. CTC

Young, having risen early, had gone, The. Guardians, The. Geoffrey Hill. NoP-4

Young Hermes, who placed you at the starter's mark? Philip of Thessalonica. GrAn

Young Heroes. Gwendolyn Brooks. BPo; NAAAL

Young Horseman. Lajos Kassák. IQMS, *tr. by* Edwin Morgan

Young Housewife, The. William Carlos Williams. APT-1; ColAP; HeIP-4; NAAL-2v2; NAAL-5; TAP

Young Hunting. *Unknown.* ESPB; OxBB

Young Hunting. *Unknown.* OxBoLi

Young I am, and yet unskill'd. Song for a Girl. Dryden. ErotSp

Young in Fall I said: the birds. Lorine Niedecker. VGW

Young Ionia, The. John Frederick Nims. IllVoic

Young Irish servant in Drogheda, A. Limerick. *Unknown.* PeLi

Young Japanese son was in love with a servant boy, The. Dream Data. Robert Duncan. NeAP

Young Johnnie Jones, he had a cute little boat. Row, Row, Row. William Jerome. ReLy

Young Johnstone. *Unknown.* ESPB; OxBB

Young Joseph's new coat was real nice. Limerick. Cyril Mountjoy. PeLi

Young Juan wandered by the glassy brooks. Byron. OBCoV *Fr.* Don Juan.

Young Keats, a flowering laurel on your brow. (LL) To John Keats. Leigh Hunt. CenSon; Son

Young king must have been terrible to behold, The. Alexander at Thebes. Anna Andreyevna Akhmatova. FaBoWar, *tr. by* Max Hayward and Stanley Kunitz

Young knight, what ever that dost armes professe. Edmund Spenser. FHYEP *Fr.* Faerie Queene, The.

Young Knowledge. "Robin Hyde." PeNZ

Young lady may increase her stock, A. Cillactor. GrAn

Young lady, whose life-style the malicious, A. Limerick. Gavin Ewart. PeLi

Young Lass's Soliloquy, A. Rebekah Carmichael. ECWP

Young Laundryman, The. William Carlos Williams. SAmP

Young Lochinvar. Sir Walter Scott. *See* Marmion

Young lords o' the north country, The. Lady Maisry. *Unknown.* ESPB; OxBB

Young Love. Andrew Marvell. OxAEP-1

Young Love. William Carlos Williams. APT-1

Young Love lies sleeping. Dream-Love. Christina Georgina Rossetti. HAP

Young man, alone, on the high bridge over the Tagus, A. High Bridge above the Tagus River at Toledo, The. William Carlos Williams. CTC

Young man and an aged man of late, A. On a Young Man and an Old Man. Edward May. OxBSP

Young man and I face each other, The. On The Subway. Sharon Olds. LTA

Young Man and the Young Nun, The. Albert D. Mackie. OxBS

Young man, before time flies further away. Advice to a Young Man. *Unknown.* CAGL, *tr. by* James J. Wilhelm

Young man by a girl was desired, A. Limerick. *Unknown.* PeLi

Young man, do not hurl yourself. Crone, The. Karolina Pavlova. ARWW, *tr. by* Catriona Kelly

Young man, hardly more, The. Gettysburg, July 1, 1863. Jane Kenyon. CBCWP

Young man / I love you and life is wonderful, The. Spurt of Blood, The. Antonin Artaud. PFTM-1

Young man is a pitiful wretch, A. Song of Parable, A. *Unknown.* SuSp, *tr. by* Jan W. Walls

Young Man Loves a Maiden, A. Heinrich Heine. NAWM-7v2, *tr. by* Hal Draper

Young man made for the corner, A. Cynewulf. PeLV, *tr. by* Kevin Crossley-Holland *Fr.* Riddles (Exeter Book).

Young Man Naughty's Adventure. Charlotte Brontë. VWP

Young man of alien beauty. Muireadhach Albanach O'Dalaigh. NOIV

Young man once went off to war, A. APO 96225. Larry Rottman. CDa

Young Man's Song, A. William Bell. FaBoTw

Young Man Thinks of Sons, The. Ronald Allison Kells Mason. PeNZ

Young man who lived at Holme Hale, A. Limerick. Ida Thurtle. PeLi

Young Man with a Yellow Hat. Li Ho. SuSp, *tr. by* Michael Fish

Young man with passions quite gingery, A. Limerick. *Unknown.* PeLi

Young Mary, loitering once her garden way. Mary and Gabriel. Rupert Brooke. ChIV-2

Young May Moon, The. Thomas Moore. OBEV; PeLV

Young men always expose themselves to me on Amtrak. Tea Dance. Wayne Koestenbaum. WiU

Young Men Come Less Often—Isn't It So, The? Horace. WoPoe, *tr. by* Robert Fitzgerald

Young men dancing, and the old. Youthful Age. Anacreon. AWP, *tr. by* Thomas Stanley

Young Men Dead. John Peale Bishop. APT-1

Young men give ear to me a while. Maid's Complaint for Want of a Dil Doul, The. *Unknown.* EroLit

Young men of the world, The. Lament. Francis Stewart [*or* "Frank"] Flint. PeFWW

Young men should not write sonnets, if they dream. Sonnet-writing. To F. W. F. Frederick William Faber. CenSon

Young men who frequent picture palaces. Limerick. *Unknown.* PeLV

Young Miracle Stag, The. László Nagy. IQMS, *tr. by* Adam Makkai

Young model undressed before the poet, The. Evening Wind. William Carpenter. PoSol

Young mouse, poor, no experience, A. Jean de La Fontaine. WoPoe, *tr. by* Bruce Boone and Robert Glück

Young Mrs. Snooks was sick of sex. Nursery Rhyme. Kenneth Burke. OBAL

Young Night Thought. Robert Louis Stevenson. OTCP; PWR

Young Noble at Night's End; a Song. Li Ho. SuSp, *tr. by* Maureen Robertson

Young Oedipus learned from the Sphinx. Limerick. Basil Ransome-Davies. PeLi

Young Ones, The. Elizabeth Jennings. OxBTC

Young or Old We Die. Rudaki. ArPe, tr. by Omar S. Pound

Young [or Younge] Andrew. Unknown. ESPB; OxBB

Young Peggy. Unknown. ESPB

Young persons, it is true, admire. True Friend, The. Ann Plato. SWaP

Young Pete. Mihály Vörösmarty. IQMS, tr. by Yakov Hornstein

Young poet comes to me, A. Blind Solo. Michael S. Weaver. UnSA

Young Prince and the Young Princess, The. John Ashbery. CoAmPo

Young Prince of Tyre. "Ern Malley." BMAP

Young Robin of the plain, erst blithest blade. Snaith Marsh; a Yorkshire Pastoral. "Ophelia." ECWP

Young Roger and Dolly. Henry Carey. See Roger and Dolly

Young Roger came tapping at Dolly's window. Roger and Dolly. Henry Carey. NOEC; OxNR

Young Ronald. Unknown. ESPB

Young schizophrenic named Struther, A. Unknown. OBCoV; PeLi

Young Shepherd Bathing His Feet. Peter Clarke. PBA

Young skull which the wind scrapes, which the sand. On the Relative Merit of Friend and Foe, Being Dead. Donald Thompson. FaBoWar

Young skunk. Shu Swamp, Spring. May Swenson. APT-2

Young Sleep, most gentle of gods, by what misdeed. Publius Papinius Statius. RomPo, tr. by W. G. Shepherd Fr. Sylvae.

Young Son, The. John Ashbery. YaYoPo

Young Soul. Imamu Amiri Baraka. BPo

Young sparrows. Issa. SoOfWa, tr. by Sam Hamill

Young Stock. Victoria Mary Sackville-West. OxBTC

Young swallows trill their new tune. Unknown. SuSp Fr. Tzu-yeh Songs of the Four Seasons.

Young Sycamore. William Carlos Williams. APT-1; TAP

Young then, / we were bored already. Epitaph. Eleanor Wilner. ChIV-1

Young things who frequent picture-palaces, The. Limerick. Philip Heseltine. NOBL; PeLi

Young Traveller Is Presented to the Goddess Dulness, A. Pope. NOEC Fr. Dunciad, The.

Young trees the bright green of a moonless night. August Zero. Jane Miller. BodElec

Young unmarried man, with a good name, A. Byron. NOBL Fr. Don Juan.

Young Waters he did dee. (LL) Young Waters. Unknown. ESPB; OxBB

Young Wife, A. D. H. Lawrence. MoBrPo

Young Wife, The. Derek Walcott. DiPo

Young Wife's Lament. Brigit Pegeen Kelly. IllVoic

Young Willie stands in his stable door. Clyde's Waters. Unknown. OxBB

Young Woman at a Window. William Carlos Williams. HHAm

Young Woman from Aenos, The. Unknown. OBAL

Young woman is just sitting on the bed, The. Edward Hopper, "Hotel Room," 1931. Larry Levis. PoSol

Young Woman of Beare, The. Austin Clarke. NoAM
 "Through lane or black archway." ModIr

Young Woman's Complaint about Her Sweetheart, A. Elen Gwdman. EMWP

Young Woman's Neo-Aramaic Jewish Persian Blues. Jerome Rothenberg. BoWoP

Young Woman Who Becomes a Bear set fire in the mountains. Unknown. APN-2, tr. by Washington Matthews Fr. Mountain Chant, The.

Young women are obsessed with beauty, The. Clothes Pit, The. Douglas Dunn. OxBTC

Young women have no orifice that grips. Heterosexual Poem. Strato [or Straton]. GrAn, tr. by Teddy Hogge

Young women, they [or they'll] run like hares on the mountain. Hares on the Mountain. Unknown. PeLV

Young Workman, The. Mary Dillingham Frear. TrCP

Younger, / I felt the dead. Roots. Seamus Deane. PNI

Younger Than Springtime. Richard Rodgers. ReLy

Youngest Daughter, The. Cathy Song. NoAM

Your Absence. Roy Fuller. OxBSo Fr. Cancer Hospital, The.

Your absence has gone through me. Separation. W. S. Merwin. HAP; NoP-4

Your alms are my salary. Torture Chamber. Enrique Lihn. PoetW; VCWP, tr. by Mary Crow

Your Anger. Paz Molina. TANSG, tr. by Steven F. White

Your ankle wrapped in iron, yourself encased. Convict. Edward Vincent Swart. PeSAV

Your appearance is pleasing because it is proper and handsome. Your Appearance is Pleasing. Baudri of Bourgueil. CAGL, tr. by Thomas Stehling

Your arm is gone. D-Day, 1994. Jack Coulehan. BloBone

Your art has brought you great respect. Sent to the Painter, Lu Hsiao-feng. Li K'ai-hsien. CoBLCP, tr. by Jonathan Chaves

Your ashen hair Shulamite. (LL) Death Fugue, A. Paul Celan. CLPP; GifTon; PFTM-2, tr. by Jerome Rothenberg

Your ashen hair Shulamith. (LL) Death Fugue, A. Paul Celan. HP; PoSu; TrJP; VCWP

Your ashen hair Shulamith. (LL) Death Fugue. Paul Celan. AuPH; HP; VCWP; WoPoe, tr. by Michael Hamburger

Your ashes will not stir, even on this high ground. In Carrowdore Churchyard. Derek Mahon. CIP-2; NoP-4; PBCIP; PNI

Your attention, ladies and gentlemen, your attention for one moment. Pilgrim, The. Nicanor Parra. VCWP

Your Attention Please. Peter Porter. OBWP; OxBTC

Your average tourist: Fifty. 2.3. James Merrill. NIP-4 Fr. Topics.

Your baby grows a tooth, then two. Little Tooth, A. Thomas Lux. BodElec

Your Beauty and My Reason. Unknown. NoSic

Your Beauty, ripe and calm, and fresh. Lover and Philosopher. Sir William Davenant [or D'Avenant]. NOBE; OBEV

Your bed's got two wrong sides. Your life's all grouse. Tony Harrison. NAEL-5v2; NAEL-6v2 Fr. School of Eloquence, The.

Your behavior proves how stingy You are, Ma. Mahendranāth Bhattācārya. SinGod, tr. by Rachel Fell McDermott

Your blond hair and autumn sweater. Janna. King D. Kuka. VoR

Your blood does not flow, not even a little. Poem for Diane Wakoski, A. Ray A. Young Bear. CDW

Your body derns. Scunner. Hugh MacDiarmid. FaBoTw; NePenScot

Your Body Glistens From the Bath. Charles Rossiter. PasH

Your body is a garden, a bush of flowers. Jorge Carrera Andrade. BLPSL, tr. by Rene de Costa, Rigas Kappatos and Eleni Paidoussi Fr. Body of the Beloved, The.

Your body is a golden temple. Jorge Carrera Andrade. BLPSL, tr. by Rene de Costa, Rigas Kappatos and Eleni Paidoussi Fr. Body of the Beloved, The.

Your body is bathed eternally. Jorge Carrera Andrade. BLPSL, tr. by Rene de Costa, Rigas Kappatos and Eleni Paidoussi Fr. Body of the Beloved, The.

Your Body Is Stars. Stephen Spender. FaBoTw

Your body tolls the hour. Glass, The. Carolyn Kizer. ErotSp

Your bosom's sweet treasures thus ever disclose! To Miss Kitty Phillips. Edward Lovibond. ECEV

Your bottoms are not purple. Horror Comic. Robert Conquest. OxBTC

Your breasts of shining black satin. Soul of the Black Land, The. Guy Tirolien. NegPo, tr. by Ellen Conroy Kennedy

Your breasts will not fall. Se Praj. ErotSp, tr. by Sam Hamill

Your bum is a gorgeous basket brimming with fruits and meat. (LL) Peasant Declares His Love, The. Emile Roumer. NegPo; TTY, tr. by John Peale Bishop

Your burning blood, your dancing tongue. (LL) Women you are accustomed to, The. Lucille Clifton. ErotSp; GT

Your Character is Your Destiny. Erin Belieu. ExTi

Your charm[e]s I obey [or obay], but[t] love not[t] want of eyes. (LL) Mary Sidney Wroth, Countess of Montgomery. BASC; Son Fr. Pamphilia to Amphilanthus.

Your cheeks flat on the sand. Venus Khoury-Gata. BoWoP

Your chest, hospital gown. My Father's Neck. Robert Bly. BodElec

Your children are not your children. Kahlil Gibran. PoToHe Fr. Prophet, The.

Your clear eye is the one absolutely beautiful thing. Child. Sylvia Plath. HCAP; NAAL-5

Your clear hands call my name. Dead of Winter. Salvatore Quasimodo. WoPoe, tr. by George Garrett

Your coffin looked unreal. Child Burial. Paula Meehan. EmeKit; MakPoe; ModIr

Your comedy I've read, my friend. To a Living Author. Unknown. NBLV

Your compassionate mind. Lover of Mountains. Muso Soseki. EaWin, tr. by W. S. Merwin

Your coulter cuts the soil that erst was sown. Poor Ploughman to a Gentleman for Whom He Had Taken a Little Pains, A. George Turberville. NoSic

Your dandelions dotting half. Grass Widows. Robert B. Shaw. CRP

Your daughter, fifteen, has drunk half a bottle. Father of the Man. David Graham. SwNoth

Your Death and Mine. János Pilinszky. IQMS, tr. by Adam Makkai

Your death has come to me over hundreds of miles away. This Poem Is Dedicated to Brother Andries Raditsela. Nise Malange. PeSAV

Your doctor, Lord. For Dr. and Mrs. Dresser. Margaret Avison. MoCV

Your door is shut against my tightened face. White House, The. Claude McKay. ISC; NAAAL; NIP-4

Your dream: / The letters HIV appear. Hayden Carruth. GifTon Fr. Sleeping Beauty, The.

Your dresses never kept you warm. Jean Rhys. William Scammell. NLP

Your dusky shadow at the window lingers. Morning and Evening. Antoni Slonimski. TrJP, tr. by Watson Kirkconnell

Your dying was a difficult enterprise. Lament. Thom Gunn. CAGL; GLP

Your every day is a pilgrimage. To An Old Black Woman, Homeless and Indistinct. Gwendolyn Brooks. ESEAA

Your eyen two will slay me suddenly. Geoffrey Chaucer. BoLoP; NAEL-5v1; NAEL-6v1; SCGP *Fr.* Mercilse[s] Beaute [*or* Beautée *or* Beauty].

Your Eyes. Muhammad Al-Ghuzzi. MAP, *tr. by* John Heath-Stubbs and May Jayyusi

Your eyes are just. Four-Word Lines. May Swenson. GLP; WPE

Your eyes are like a night of rain. Nizar Qabbani. MAP

Your Eyes Are Mirth. Tom Weatherly. NBV

Your eyes are open. Carious Exposure. Gladys Cardiff. CDW

Your eyes are the eyes of a man in love. For Two Voices. Luis Cernuda. CAGL, *tr. by* Rick Lipinski

Your eyes are tonight so unusually thoughtful and sad. Nikolai Stepanovich Gumilyov [*or* Gumiliov *or* Gumilev]. TCRP, *tr. by* Yakov Hornstein

Your eyes are two palm tree forests in early light. Rain Song. Badr Shakir Al-Sayyab. MAP, *tr. by* Lena Jayyusi and Christopher Middleton

Your eyes don't shine like they used to shine. (I'm Afraid) The Masquerade Is Over. Herb Magidson. ReLy

Your eyes drink of me. Mystery, The. Sara Teasdale. PasH

Your eyes, O my beloved. Your Eyes, O My Beloved. Nelly Sachs. WPoS, *tr. by* Matthew Mead and Ruth Mead

Your eyes stolen. Lello Voce. ItPo, *tr. by* Gayle Ridinger *Fr.* Variation 3 (On Love and More).

Your eyes were ever brown, the colour. On Not Being Your Lover. Medbh McGuckian. PBCIP; PNI

Your eyes were not there. Lonely Night. P. C. Boutens. TuT, *tr. by* Tony Curtis

Your face broods from my table, Suicide. John Berryman. TAP *Fr.* Dream Songs.

Your face did not rot. Lost Pilot, The. James Tate. CoAP; EmeKit; NoAM; OBWP; TwCP; UnPo

Your Face Has No Name. Dacia Maraini. CItWP, *tr. by* Cinzia Sartini Blum and Lara Trubowitz

Your Face Here. Robin S. Chapman. PoCoUp

Your face is all of silver like a halberd. Chagall's Cornflowers. Andrey [*or* Andrei] Andreievich Voznesensky [*or* Voznesenskii]. TCRP, *tr. by* Vera Dunham

Your face is the face of all the others. Face of Love, The. Ingrid Jonker. HAWP, *tr. by* Jack Cope

Your face is the unexplored earth. Flash, A. May Muzaffar. PoArWo, *tr. by* Tahia Abdel Nasser

Your face is written in my soul, and when. Your Face Is Written in My Soul. Baldomero Garcilaso de la Vega. SpanPo, *tr. by* Edwin Morgan

Your face scrapes my sleep tonight. Letter to be Disguised as a Gas Bill. Marge Piercy. WPE

Your face, the beauty of a time long past evokes the perfumed robes in faded hues. Léopold Sédar Senghor. NegPo *Fr.* Songs for Signare.

Your Family. Black and Divided or Chittlins and Caviar. Nicole Breedlove. InTrad

'Your father's gone,' my bald headmaster said. Lesson, The. Edward Lucie-Smith. OxBTC; TwCP

"Your father walks like you." Family Stories. Dacia Maraini. CItWP, *tr. by* Cinzia Sartini Blum and Lara Trubowitz

Your Figure or the War against Fat. Joyce Mansour. SurPaPo, *tr. by* Mary Ann Caws

Your final bed was not adorned with roses. Requiem. Annette M'Baye d'Erneville. HAWP, *tr. by* Brian Baer

Your fine promises. Fujiwara No Mototoshi. OHPJ

Your fingers circle. Adria Klinger. PasH

Your fingers fully awake, it. Alan Brownjohn. NewEx

Your fingers touch me like a bird's wing. Bird of Endless Time, The. James Laughlin. WeW-3

Your fires burnt my forests. Womb, The. Apirana Taylor. PeNZ

Your flatteries are boring. Bassus [*or* Bassos]. PGA

Your foot's on my gown. After. May Probyn. VWP

Your fury explodes. Kali. Elsa Cross. TANSG, *tr. by* Patricia Dubrava

Your ghost will walk, you lover of trees. Robert Browning. FHYEP; SCGP

Your gloves. Small Ode to a Black Cuban Boxer. Nicolás Guillén. TCLAP, *tr. by* Robert Marquez and David Arthur McMurray

Your grace, and falter on the stony path! (LL) Last Days of Alice. Allen Tate. APT-2; FuPo; NAAL-2v2; NOBA; OxBA; UnPo

Your Grave Disfigures Me. Eibhlin Dubh O'Connell. WoPoe, *tr. by* Patrick Galvin *Fr.* Death of Art O'Leary, The.

Your gravity. Force of Gravity, The. Luiza Neto Jorge. SurWo, *tr. by* Jean R. Longland

Your hair. I Have Touched. Patti Tana. PasH

Your hair has turned white. Kakinomoto no Hitomaro. OHPJ

Your hair is drunk again. Descriptive Passages. William Matthews. BodElec

Your Hand Full of Hours. Paul Celan. OBVE; PoetW, *tr. by* Michael Hamburger

Your Hand in Mine. Alaide Foppa. TANSG, *tr. by* Celeste Kostopulos-Cooperman

Your hand is heavy, Night, upon my brow. Wole Soyinka. PBMAP; WoPoe *Fr.* Idanre and Other Poems (1967).

Your handkerchief should be blue. Love Song. *Unknown.* BoWoP, *tr. by* Reza Baraheni and Zahra-Soltan Shokoohtaezeh

Your hands cracked and calloused in summer, bled. Sonnets for Stan Gage (1945–92). Sascha Feinstein. SeSe

Your hands have work in them like the weather. Poems to My Father. Mick North. NLP

Your hands lie open in the long fresh grass,—. Dante Gabriel Rossetti. GSo; HAP; NAEL-5v2; NAEL-6v2; NoP-4 *Fr.* House of Life, The.

Your hands made a tent o'er mine eyes. Whimper of Awakening Passion. Ebenezer Jones. NOBVV

Your hands, my dear, adorable. Chilterns, The. Rupert Brooke. MoBrPo

Your hat blows off. Breezy Delicious Day. Edwin Torres. HeMarv

Your head it waves outside. Poem. Víctor Hernández Cruz. PueRic

Your health, Master Willow. Contrive me a bat. Tree Party. Louis MacNeice. OxBTC

Your hearse pulled by deep summer twilight. Watching the Hearse. Charles Simic. BodElec

Your heart is all you need. To Make a Talisman. Olga Orozco. TCLAP, *tr. by* Stephen Tapscott

Your heart, like an old milk tooth. Heart. Maura Dooley. NeBl

Your heart trembles in the shadows, like a face. When the Tom-Tom Beats. Jacques Roumain. NegPo, *tr. by* Langston Hughes

Your hidden loneliness, Lord. Psalm. Lucian Blaga. PFTM-1

Your hip replacement mended. Orchestration. Jane Mayes. PasH

Your home is deep in the white clouds. Mountain Retreat of a Recluse, The. Chang Yü. CoBLCP, *tr. by* Jonathan Chaves

Your Honor, when my mother stood. To Judge Faolain, Dead Long Enough: A Summons. Linda McCarriston. LoL

Your horse is black your cloak is black. Yscolan. Myrddyn (Merlin). WoPoe, *tr. by* W. S. Merwin

Your house is near the southern tip of the lake. Hermit Feng's Residence on the Lake. Hsü Pen. CoBLCP, *tr. by* Jonathan Chaves

Your house like the upper deck of a ship. Pot. Tiziano Rossi. ItPo, *tr. by* Gayle Ridinger

Your houseplant is a delicate thing. Why So Many of Them Die. Susan Wallbank. BrRo

Your husband gave you a Ring. Lady T-rc----l's Ring. *Unknown.* NOBRP

"Your husband's lying here in the next bed." They Lay Dying Side by Side. Anna Swirszczynska. PoSu

Your husband will be with us at the treat. Ovid. *See* Thy husband to a banquet goes with me

Your husband, your daughters, your son. (LL) Dream, The. Irving Feldman. TaR; VCAP

Your ideas of home life. I Don't Know Exactly. Eva Svankmajerová. SurWo, *tr. by* Katerina Pinosová

Your image is engraved. Nizar Qabbani. MAP

Your image lit in me. (LL) Epigram: "At 12 o'clock in the afternoon." Meleager. GrAn; WoPoe, *tr. by* Peter Whigham

Your image, tormenting and elusive. Osip Emilevich Mandelstam [*or* Mandelshtam]. BBASP, *tr. by* David McDuff

Your integrity now a wall of memory. Change, The. Ellis Ayitey Komey. PBMAP

Your job's to work the surface. Don't. Michele Roberts. NewEx

Your joyful understanding, lady mine. Meo Abbracciavacca. EaItPo, *tr. by* Dante Gabriel Rossetti

Your kindness has painted the singing of the birds. Poem of the Sea and of Her. Carlos Oquendo de Amat. BLPSL, *tr. by* Rene de Costa, Rigas Kappatos and Eleni Paidoussi

Your kink, Heraclea, is sucking off. Argentarius. GrAn

Your laughter is like a burst pomegranate. When You Laugh. Ingrid Jonker. WPOW, *tr. by* Elizabeth Jones

Your leaves bound up compact and fair. To an Author. Philip Freneau. ColAP; NOBA; OxBA

Your leaving brought an end to spring. End to Spring, An. Tzu Yeh. CrYelRi, *tr. by* Sam Hamill

Your legs would be pretty, if you had legs. Portrait of a Nun. Bobi Jones. OBWVE, *tr. by* Joseph P. Clancy

Your letter came.—Glutted the earth & cold. Winter-Piece to a Friend Away, A. John Berryman. NOBA

Your letter unfolds and unfolds forever. Letter Smuggled in a Fish. Yuan Chen. CrYelRi, *tr. by* Sam Hamill

Your letter wrecked my day. My Sister's Letter. Bogomil Gjuzel. CarOv, *tr. by* Carolyn Kizer

Your life hurts me, son. Wound. Alaíde Foppa. TANSG, tr. by Celeste Kostopulos-Cooperman

Your life is a baby not yet born. Maria Luisa Spaziani. NeIt

Your Lily Eyes Said Yes. Manuel González Prada. SpanPo, tr. by Kate Flores

Your lips were like a red and ruby chalice. Midnight Sun. Johnny Mercer. APT-2; ReLy

Your lips were so laughing. Langston Blues. Dudley Randall. SeSe

Your little dog that barked as I came by. To His Wife, for Striking Her Dog. Sir John Harington [or Harrington]. OxBSP

Your little hands. Samuel Hoffenstein. NBLV; OBCoV; TrJP Fr. Love-songs, at Once Tender and Informative.

Your little house stands in a bamboo grove. Sent in Parting to Yen Kung-su. Shen Chou. CoBLCP, tr. by Jonathan Chaves

Your little mind! (LL) Samuel Hoffenstein. NBLV; OBCoV; TrJP Fr. Love-songs, at Once Tender and Informative.

Your lot, O Ovid, the prince of your art. On the Second Tristia of Ovid. Elizabeth Jane Leon. EMWP

Your Love fond fugitive to gain. (LL) Song: "Nothing ades to Loves fond fire." Elizabeth Wilmot, Countess of Rochester. EMWP; LW

Your love is dead, lady, your love is dead. Madrigal. Ronald Stuart Thomas. BoLoP; EnLoPo

Your love lurks in my veins like a bandit. Wild Cat, A. Su'ad al-Mubarak Al-Sabah. MAP, tr. by John Heath-Stubbs and May Jayyusi

Your love's great realm, my separation measures. (LL) Written in Exile. Kathleen Jessie Raine. TrCP; WPE

Your love threw me down. Nizar Qabbani. MAP

Your love turned my body into water. Nur, Empress Jahan. BoWoP

Your lynx-eyes, Asia. Anna Andreyevna Akhmatova. BoWoP

Your machete slices through my jungle. Machete. Rikki Ducornet. SurWo

Your Magnificent Lord. Concerning the Islands Newly Discovered. Joy Katz. NeAmPo

Your man, says the Man, will walk into the bar like this—here his. Bloody Hand. Ciaran Carson. PBCIP

Your marvellous songs. (LL) For Thomas Moore. James Simmons. BiHa; PBCIP

Your master died from drinking too much. Taoist Huang Has Died of Alcoholism, The. Shen Chou. CoBLCP; ColAnChi, tr. by Jonathan Chaves

Your matronly face is. Summer Fires of Mulanje Mountain. Edison Mpina. NAfrP

Your milk was already poisoned. Childhood. Edith Bruck. AF

Your mind and you are our Sargasso Sea. Portrait d'une Femme. Ezra Pound. APT-1; MoAmPo; NAAL-2v2; NAAL-5; NOBA; NoAM; NoP-4; PAI; TAP; TCAPo; TwCP

Your mistress [or mistris], that you follow whores, still taxeth you. Self[e] Accuser, A. John Donne. FaBoEE; PeLV

Your mother is not your mother. When the Kingdom Comes. Jill Alexander Essbaum. NAPBL

Your mother slept through it all. Early Morning Test Light over Nevada, 1955. Robert Vasquez. GeoHom

Your mother, tall as a flower. In the Shakespeare Garden at Northwestern University. Paul Carroll. IllVoic

Your Mozart is not my Mozart anymore. Valediction. Clare Rossini. BAP-97

Your name—a bird on my hand. Marina Ivanovna Tsvetayeva [or Tsvetaeva]. TCRusP, tr. by Bob Perelman, Aleksandar Petrov and Shirley Rihner Fr. Poems to Blok.

Your name, Esther, in your mother's shy campesino voice. Estel. Julia Alvarez. ExTi

Your Name is Gift. Stella P. Chipasula. HAWP

"Your name is Rumplestiltskin!" cried. Rumplestiltskin. Glyn Maxwell. OBCoV

Your name is the Wheel of Progress—a pleasant name indeed. To the Wheel of Progress. Mrs. Henry Linden. CBWP-4

Your names ring clearly. Requiem. Annette Bialik Harchik. GotH

Your Neighbor. H. Howard Biggar. PoToHe

Your neighbor, sir, whose roses you admire. My Neighbor's Reply. Unknown. PoToHe

Your nerves the nerves of a midwife / learning her trade. (LL) Mirror in Which Two Are Seen as One, The. Adrienne Rich. NAAL-2v2; NNaP

Your nights draw nearer. Letter to My Father on the Other Side. Jack Marshall. GraLe

Your nurse could only speak Italian. Sailing Home from Rapallo. Robert Lowell. HCAP; PoPoPo; PoetW; TAP

Your offspring avert their faces from you. (LL) Shemà. Primo Levi. AF; FaBoWar; HP, tr. by Ruth Feldman and Ruth Feldman

Your old hat hurts me, and those black. Dad. Elaine Feinstein. Prnts

Your One Good Dress. Brenda Shaughnessy. AmPoNex

Your own greyhounds bark at your side. Midnight Diner by Edward Hopper, A. David Ray. PoSol

Your own hands are lying. (LL) Taking off My Clothes. Carolyn Forché. NIL-7; NoAM

Your Own Image. Michael Ryan. YaYoPo

Your parents look at you. Parents. Marta Kornblith. MirDau, tr. by Roberta Gordenstein

Your past was bereft of pleasure. Sighing. József Bajza. IQMS, tr. by Watson Kirkconnell

Your penis rolls to the dream. Ana Istarú. TANSG, tr. by Shaun Griffin and Emma Sepúlveda-Pulvirenti

Your perch is the branch. To a Sparrow. William Carlos Williams. OWoS

Your photograph won't do you justice. Letters to a Young Poet. Adrienne Rich. ExTi

Your pinks, your tulips live an hour. To the Gardener at Nuneham. Horace Walpole, 4th Earl of Orford. FaBoEE

Your pleasure, Priapus, is the island coast. Maccius. GrAn

Your Poem. Semyon [or Semion] Isaakovich Kirsanov. "Back then I cut off a lock." TCRP

Your poise! / Your pose! You Couldn't Be Cuter. Dorothy Fields. ReLy

Your poore estates, alone. (LL) To Meadows [or Meddowes]. Robert Herrick. AWP; BASC; CaPo; NOBE; NOSC; NPeEn; OBEV; PBRV

Your Presence. David Diop. PBA; PBMAP, tr. by Ulli Beier

Your presence is requested. Don't Bring Lulu. Ray Henderson. ReLy

Your promises come to me always together with your betrayals, which you have more of than the fox. Cecco Nuccoli. CAGL, tr. by Jill Claretta Robbins

Your punishment is just, you must confess. To a Gentleman Who Disordered a Lady's Handerchief, and Immediately Cut His Thumb. Elizabeth Teft. ECWP

Your Radiola recording of the Amos 'n Andy Show. Only Now I Realize. Luis Lopez. GeoH

Your residence on earth, a floating, nothing but a dream. Lamenting the Taoist Wei Kung-yüan. Chao Meng-fu. CoBLCP, tr. by Jonathan Chaves

Your retreat hardly prompted. Recollection of Gabriela Mistral. Claudia Lars. TCLAP, tr. by Nancy Christoph

Your Rose is Dead. "Michael Field." VWP

Your rosy-fingered prick that used to charm. Strato [or Straton]. CAGL, tr. by Daryl Hine

Your sad tires in a mile-a. (LL) William Shakespeare. FaBoCh; NoSic Fr. Winter's Tale, The.

Your scent is in the room. Jasmine. Claude McKay. APT-1; GT

Your Shoulders Hold up the World. Carlos Drummond de Andrade. PoetW, tr. by Mark Strand

Your silence is leaning toward judgement. Unaswered Letter. Tess Gallagher. NIP-4

Your sins have brought my mind so low. Catullus. ErotSp, tr. by Sam Hamill

Your sister 's play'd you scorn. (LL) Gay Goshawk [or Goss-Hawk], The. Anna Gordon Brown. ESPB; OxBB; WPE

Your slave boy's cock is aching, Naevolus. Martial. CAGL, tr. by Joseph S. Salemi Fr. Epigrams.

Your sleep is a closed almond. Your Sleep. Iwan [or Yvan] Goll. AF, tr. by Paul Zweig

Your sleep is so profound. Aurora. Timothy Steele. DiPo

Your sleep will be. Caterpillar's Lullaby. Jane Yolen. Spl

Your small hands, precisely equal to my own. Adrienne Rich. PoE; TRP Fr. Twenty-one Love Poems.

Your smile, delicate. Woman Me. Maya Angelou. BlSi; OxWW

Your smiles are not, as other womens be [or bee]. To the Lady May. Aurelian Townshend [or Townsend]. OxBEV

Your smiling cheeks, burning clouds. Poem about Fan the Fourth, A. Li K'ai-hsien. CoBLCP, tr. by Jonathan Chaves

Your smiling, or the hope, the thought of it. Simile for Her Smile, A. Richard Wilbur. InPK-6

Your son baby / Respectably as ever, / Joe. (LL) Langston Hughes. APT-2; PoE Fr. Lenox Avenue Mural.

Your son presses against me. Apple Trees, The. Louise Glück. HCAP

Your song caresses. Basho. SoOfWa, tr. by Sam Hamill

Your song is welcome, Melissus, a most welcome gift. Queen's Answer, The. Queen of England Elizabeth I. EMWP

Your soul is a sealed garden. Clair de Lune. Paul Verlaine. AWP, tr. by Arthur Symons

Your soul is like a painter's landscape where. Moonlight. Paul Verlaine. NAWM-7v2, tr. by Carlyle Ferren MacIntyre

Your spouse not laboured-at nor spun. (LL) Habit of Perfection, The. Gerard Manley Hopkins. ChIV-2; MoBrPo; NoAM; OBEV; OBMV; OxAEP-2; PoRA; RB; SacPr; TFi

Your Standard's up, we fix a Conquest there. (LL) To the King, upon His Com[m]ing with His Army into the West. Robert Herrick. BeJo; CaPo

Your stars are muscled like the lion. (LL) Baseball and Writing. Marianne Craig Moore. BoWoP; FaBoA; MoASP

Your starved and ancient Presence O Lord I wait in my room at your Mercy. (LL) Lion for Real, The. Allen Ginsberg. EmeKit; GLP; HCAP; RB

Your step at once.   In the Forest.   Heather Allen.   GifTon

Your stones I shall polish into a mirror.   Jerusalem.   David Rokeah [or Rokeakh].   MHP, tr. by Ruth Finer Mintz

Your Street Again.   Sophie Hannah.   MFPA

Your street at sundown.   Look.   Belle Waring.   ExTi

Your subjects hope, dread Sire.   To the King's Most Excellent Majesty.   Phillis Wheatley.   TAP

Your sweaters.   Your Sweaters.   Herman De Coninck.   TuT, tr. by Eamon Grennan

Your sweet voice is trapped in the drum.   Singing Drum, The.   Frank Mkalawile Chipasula.   NAfrP

Your swim bladder vibrates like a drum—.   Toadfish.   Stephen Perry.   MiVo

Your tears, Niobe.   Hayden Carruth.   VGW

Your tears. You are not worth their merriment. (LL)   Apologia Pro Poemate Meo.   Wilfred Owen.   MoBrPo; NAEL-5v2; NAEL-6v2; PeFWW

Your teeth are loose, your head is bald.   Admonition to Myself, An.   Chao Meng-fu.   CoBLCP; WoPoe, tr. by Jonathan Chaves

Your thighs are appletrees.   Portrait of a Lady.   William Carlos Williams.   HarvBoo; NAAL-2v2; NAAL-5; NOBA; NoAM; OxBA

Your thighs your belly.   Sea Flower.   Mary Dorcey.   BrRo

Your thought.   Cloud in Trousers, A.   Vladimir Vladimirovich Mayakovsky [or Maiakovskii].   TCRusP, tr. by Kathy Lewis and Bob Perelman

Your throat, my hunting partridge, will no longer.   Decoy Partridge, A.   Simmias [or Simias] of Rhodes.   GrAn, tr. by Peter Jay

Your Thwarts in Pieces, Your Mooring Rope Cut.   Unknown.   WoPoe, tr. by Erica Reiner

Your tongue has spent the night.   Dream-Language of Fergus, The.   Medbh McGuckian.   CIP-2

Your tongue like a barefoot walk.   Language.   Marjorie Agosin.   TANSG, tr. by Cola Franzen

Your tongue thrums and moves.   Kenneth Rexroth.   APSN; APT-2   Fr. Love Poems of Marichiko, The.

Your torch flames.   Lady of Largest Heart.   Enheduanna.   HW, tr. by Betty De Shong Meador

"Your touch is abrasive. My blood seethes and smarts."   Occasional Verses.   Marilyn Hacker.   Son

Your tune is a tempest of heat.   July.   Daniel Gray-Kontar.   SpirFl

Your turn came, and you chose to take it.   Winter Solstice—for Frank.   "Asphodel."   BrRo

Your turn now are next. (LL)   Eddie Priest's Barbershop and Notary.   Kevin Young.   AmPoNex; ISC; SpirFl

Your ugly token.   Upon a Dead Man's Head.   John Skelton.   HAP; SCGP; WoPoe

Your upset / or mine? (LL)   Bible Study.   Gloria C. Oden.   ESEAA; GT

Your vividness grants color where.   To Sallie, Walking.   Sterling Allen Brown.   GT

Your voice awakens.   Gong, A.   Odia Ofeimun.   PBMAP

Your voice bleeds bafflement and anger.   'Phoning.   Peter Sirr.   BiHa

Your voice is the color of a robin's breast.   To O.E.A E. A.   Claude McKay.   BPo; GT

Your voice unwrapping.   Haiku.   Sonia Sanchez.   FFC

Your voice watered the doubt of my breast in the sweet wooden booth.   Federico García Lorca.   CAGL, tr. by David William Foster   Fr. Sonetos del Amor Oscuro [Sonnets of Dark Love].

Your volume proves that 'Nothing is worth while."   To a Pessimist.   Ronald Arbuthnott Knox.   OBCoV

Your voluntary love. (LL)   W. H. Auden.   BoLoP; MoBrPo   Fr. Twelve Songs.

Your walk sacerdotal and slow, undulant.   Black Girl Goes By, A.   Emile Roumer.   TTY, tr. by Edna Worthley Underwood

Your walls do not fall, he said.   "H. D."   NALW   Fr. Tribute to the Angels.

Your walls fold gently.   Jerusalem Song.   Lisa Suhair Majaj.   PoArWo

Your way / is turning bad.   Unknown.   STP

Your weight sweetly upon me.   Made Out of Links.   Hilda Morley.   PmAP

Your white house and tranquil garden, I shall leave.   Anna Andreyevna Akhmatova.   TCRP

Your wicked minds requite. (LL)   Babes in the Wood, The.   Unknown.   OBNV; OxAEP-1

Your wife's forty-five.   Gift Horse.   Yusef Komunyakaa.   GT

Your womb is smarter than your head.   Madrigal.   Nicolás Guillén.   CLPP, tr. by Kenneth Rexroth

Your words are mine, at the end. (LL)   Net of Place, The.   Paul Blackburn.   PFTM-2; PmAP

Your words came just when needed.   Accept My Full Heart's Thanks.   Ella Wheeler Wilcox.   PoToHe

Your Words, My Answers.   Burns Singer.   HarvBoo

Your words my friend (right healthful caustics) blame.   Sir Philip Sidney.   NAEL-5v1; NAEL-7v1; NoSic; PoE   Fr. Astrophil and Stella.

Your Work.   Jean-Joseph Rabéarivelo [or Rebéarivelo].   NegPo, tr. by Ellen Conroy Kennedy

Your work, that was done, to be done to be done to be done. (LL)   To the Diaspora.   Gwendolyn Brooks.   NAAL-5; NIL-7

Your young breasts were gleaming.   River, The.   Jacques Prévert.   MFP, tr. by Martin Sorrell

Youre ugly tokyn.   John Skelton.   See Your ugly token

Yours is the face that the earth turns to me.   Love-Poem.   Kathleen Jessie Raine.   LW; MoBrPo

Yours is the only body.   And This Is So.   Joseph H. Ball.   PasH

Yours to absolve of ruin, or make an end. (LL)   Christ Walks in This Infernal District Too.   Malcolm Lowry.   MoCV; NOBC

Yourself.   Jones Very.   APN-1; NOBA; OxBA; Son

Yourself and Myself.   Unknown.   NOIV, tr. by Thomas Kinsella

Yourself the sun, and I the melting frost.   Sir Arthur Gorges.   OxBSo   Fr. Vanities of Sir Arthur Gorges' Youth, The.

Youth.   Aneirin.   WoPoe, tr. by Desmond O'Grady   Fr. Gododdin, The.

Youth.   "Laurence Hope."   WeW-3

Youth.   Georgia Douglas Johnson.   NAAAL

Youth.   David J. Rothman.   GeoH

Youth.   Vernon Rowe.   BloBone

Youth, A.   Stephen Crane.   MoAmPo   Fr. Black Riders [and Other Lines], The.

Youth and a maiden from Costessey, A.   Limerick.   S. C. Turner.   PeLi

Remember Then Thy Creator.   Bible, O.T.   See Ecclesiastes

Youth and Age.   Byron.   See Stanzas for Music

Youth and Age.   Samuel Taylor Coleridge.   GTBS-P; OBEV

Youth and Age.   Mimnermus.   AWP, tr. by John Addington Symonds

Crabbed Age and Youth.   Var. authors.   NoSic; OBEV   Fr. Passionate Pilgrim, The.

Youth and Age.   W. B. Yeats.   FaBoEE

Youth and Age on Beaulieu River, Hants.   Sir John Betjeman.   FaBoTw; TwCP

Youth and Art.   Robert Browning.   CTC; NAEL-5v2; NAEL-6v2; NOBVV; NPeEn

Youth and Calm.   Matthew Arnold.   FHYEP

Youth and Love.   John Gay.   NOBE   Fr. Begger's Opera.

Youth and Maidenhood.   Sarah Williams.   LW

Youth, beauty, virtue, innocence.   Epitaph Upon the Lady Elizabeth, Second Daughter to his Late Majesty, An.   Henry Vaughan.   BeJo

Youth buried you, Captain; as sons for their mother, The.   Anyte [or Anytes].   SaLy, tr. by Diane Rayor

Youth Dreams, The.   Rainer Maria Rilke.   AWP; TrJP, tr. by Ludwig Lewisohn

Youth gone, and beauty gone if ever there.   Christina Georgina Rossetti.   GSo; OxBSo; Son   Fr. Monna Innominata.

Youth, I offer you this silver cup.   Fount, The.   "Rubén Dario."   SpanPo, tr. by William M. Davis

Youth in apparel that glittered, A.   Stephen Crane.   APN-2; NAAL-2v2   Fr. Black Riders [and Other Lines], The.

Youth in Arms.   Harold Monro.   Carrion.   PeFWW

Youth Mowing, A.   D. H. Lawrence.   InPK-6; MoBrPo; NoAM

Youth of a Poet, The.   James Beattie.   NOEC   Fr. Minstrel, The.

Youth of delight, come hither.   William Blake.   FHYEP   Fr. Songs of Experience.

Youth of Han-tan, The; a Song.   Kao Shih.   SuSp, tr. by Joseph J. Lee

Youth of my heart, my beloved one.   Love Song to King Shu-Suen.   Kubatum.   WPOW, tr. by Thorkild Jacobsen

Youth rambles on life's arid mount.   Progress of Poesy, The.   Matthew Arnold.   NOBVV

Youth's a stuff[e] will not endure. (LL)   William Shakespeare.   AEP; AWP; BoLoP; CTC; ClHu; HAP; NAEL-5v1; NAEL-6v1; NBLV; NOBE; NoP-4; NoSic; OxBSP; OxBoLi; PoRA; SCGP; TFi; WoPoe   Fr. Twelfth Night.

Youth's the season made for joys.   Cotillion.   John Gay.   NoP-4

Youth's years how few, age how sure! (LL)   Autumn Wind, The.   Emperor Wu of Han [or Wu Ti or Ou-ty or Liu Ch'e or Liu Ch'u].   ChiP; FaBoCh, tr. by Arthur Waley

Youth shows but half; trust God, see all, nor be afraid. (LL)   Robert Browning.   ITBLP; PoToHe   Fr. Rabbi Ben Ezra.

Youth, That Pursuest.   Richard Monckton, 1st Baron Houghton Milnes.   TreFP

Youth there was, Elpenor was he nam'd, A.   Homer.   OBVE   Fr. Odyssey.

Youth there was possessed of every charm, A.   Story of Inkle and Yarico, The.   Frances Seymour, Countess of Hertford.   ECWP

Youth! Thou Wear'st to Manhood Now.   Sir Walter Scott.   OxBSP

Youth walks up to the white horse, The.   White Horse, The.   D. H. Lawrence.   TTTS

Youth walks up to the white horse, to put its halter on, The.   White Horse, The.   D. H. Lawrence.   KaS

Youth, with proud heart, pure and strong, A.   After-Glow of Pain, The.   Clara Ann Thompson.   CBWP-2

Youth with Red-gold Hair, The. Dame Edith Sitwell. FaBoTw

Youthful Age. Anacreon. AWP, *tr. by* Thomas Stanley

Yow that take pleasure in yowr cruelty. Sonnet 25. Robert Sidney. PBRV

Yow! Yow! Night gibbons cry. Listening to Gibbons at Rock-Pool Creek. Shen Yüeh. ColAnChi, *tr. by* Richard W. Bodman

Yr Iaith. Nigel Jenkins. AngWePo

Yscolan. Myrddyn (Merlin). WoPoe, *tr. by* W. S. Merwin

Yt fell abowght the Lamasse tyde. Battle of Otterburn [*or* Oterborne], The. *Unknown.* ESPB; IBB; OxBS

Yu Chieh Yuan (Jade Steps Grievance, Yueh-fu). Li Po. ChinPo, *tr. by* Yip Wai-lim

Yu teach me. Speak. Benjamin Zephaniah. Oth

Yüan, Ch'ü. Ch'u Yüan. SuSp *Fr.* Li Sao.

Yuba City School. Chitra Divakaruni. GeoHom; LTA; OpBo

Yucca clump / is blooming, The. Yucca Moth, The. A. R. Ammons. NOBA

Yucca Moth, The. A. R. Ammons. NOBA

Yugoslav Cemetery. Celeste Turner Wright. WPE

Yugoslav Story. Susan Hampton. BMAP

Yuh Lookin Good. Carolyn M. Rodgers. BPo

Yun'er's Bell. Yun'er. WoPoe, *tr. by* Constance A. Cook

Yung Wind. Confucius. CTC, *tr. by* Ezra Pound

Sans Equity and sans Poise. WoPoe, *tr. by* Ezra Pound

Yut yee sam see. One to Ten. Janet S. Wong. OxIBACP

Yves Tanguy. David Gascoyne. NoP-4; SPE

Ywis, pole hatchet, she bleared thine eye. (LL) John Skelton. NAEL-6v1; NAEL-7v1; NoSic; SCGP *Fr.* Garland [*or* Garlande *or* Garlands] of Laurel[I], The.

Z

Z is the Zenith from which we decline. Zewhyexary. Thomas M. [*or* "Tom"] Disch. OBCoV

Z was a zany, a silly old [*or* poor harmless] fool. (LL) *Unknown.* LB; OxNR

Z, Y, X, and W, V. *Unknown.* OxNR

Zack Bumstead uster flosserfize. Philosopher, A. Sam Walter Foss. OBAL

Zalman. Seymour Mayne. GotH

Zang Tumb Tuuum. Filippo Tommaso Marinetti.

Correction of proofs + desires in speed. PFTM-1

Zangezi. Velemir [*or* Viktor Vladimirovich] Khlebnikov.

Plane Four. PFTM-1

Zangezi: R, K, L, G—. Velemir [*or* Viktor Vladimirovich] Khlebnikov. PFTM-1

Zapato, El. Richard Garcia. TouFir

Zapolya. Samuel Taylor Coleridge.

Glycine's Song. OBEV

Zarathustra. Friedrich Wilhelm Nietzsche.

Notes. WoPoe, *tr. by* Ivor Armstrong Richards

Zarian was saying: Florence is youth. Water-Colour of Venice, A. Lawrence Durrell. MoBrPo

Zaydee. Philip Levine. NNaP; TaR

Zaynab complained against me. Throbbings. Jamil. B. Holway. GraLe, *tr. by* George Dimitri Selim

Zazen / Fat mosquitoes. Tan Taigi. ZenPo, *tr. by* Takashi Ikemoto and Lucien Stryk

Zazen on Ching-t'ing Mountain. Li Po. CrYelRi, *tr. by* Sam Hamill

Zealless Xylographer, The. Mary Mapes Dodge. OBAL

Zealots of Yearning. David Rokeah [*or* Rokeakh]. TrJP, *tr. by* I. M. Lask

Zealots of Yearning. David Rokeah [*or* Rokeakh]. MHP, *tr. by* Ruth Finer Mintz

Zealous. Joshua Clover. PuP-23

Zealous Admonition to Praise. Catharina Regina von Greiffenberg. GePo, *tr. by* George C. Schoolfield

Zealous flea. Issa. EH, *tr. by* Robert Hass

Zealous locksmith died of late, A. On a Puritanicall Lock-Smith. William Camden. FaBoEE

Zealous Puritan, The. *Unknown.* NOSC

Zebaoth. Else Lasker-Schüler. TrJP, *tr. by* Jethro Bithell

Zebra. Judith Thurman. SSCS

Zebra. Natasha Trethewey. TWW

Zebra, The. Marie Laurencin. CuPo

Zebra, The. *Unknown.* PeSAV, *tr. by* W. H. I. Bleek

Zebra Goes Wild Where the Sidewalk Ends, The. Henry Dumas. GT

Zebras, The. Roy Campbell. MoBrPo; OxBSo

Zechariah. Bible, *O.T.*

I Return unto Zion. TrJP

Open Thy Doors, O Lebanon. AWP

Zeimbekiko. Robin Magowan. SPE

Zeitgehoft. Paul Celan. AmFaPo, *tr. by* Michael Hamburger *Fr.* Zeitgehoft.

Zeke. Leonard Alfred George Strong. MoBrPo

Zella Wheeler! did I evah? Interrupted Reproof, The. Priscilla Jane Thompson. CBWP-2

Zen Americana. Paula Gunn Allen. PoPoPo

Zen Buddhism and Psychoanalysis / Psychoanalysis and Zen Buddhism. Jackson Mac Low. PoM

Zen mind is unperturbed by the envy of moth-browed beauties, A. Addressed to a Koto-player. Su Man-shu. SuSp, *tr. by* Wu-Chi Liu

Zen of Housework, The. Al Zolynas. BLT

Zenith. Sonia Delaunay. CuPo

Zenith. Juan Ramón Jiménez. SpanPo, *tr. by* Kate Flores

Zenith / noon beats out / on its solar anvil / the rays of light. Zenith. Sonia Delaunay. CuPo

Zenonis has a splendid tutor for her son—. Lucilius. GrAn

Zepheria. *Unknown.*

Proud in Thy Love. Son

Zephyr, kindliest of winds. Dioscorides. GrAn

0°. Elizabeth Spires. DiPo

.05. Ishmael Reed. ESEAA

Zero hour. Waiting yet again. James Merrill. HCAP *Fr.* Book of Ephraim, The.

Zero, this spume—a virgin verse. Toast. Stéphane Mallarmé. WoPoe, *tr. by* Frederick Morgan

Zero tolerance is too wet for me. Zero Tolerance. Bruce Andrews. PFTM-2

Zeus and Ganymede. Ovid. CAGL, *tr. by* Rolfe Humphries *Fr.* Metamorphoses.

Zeus as an eagle came to Ganymede. *Unknown.* CAGL, *tr. by* Daryl Hine

Zeus, / Brazen-thunder-hurler. Faun Sees Snow for the First Time, The. Richard Aldington. MoBrPo

Zeus, Father Zeus, you've power over heaven. Archilochus. SaLy, *tr. by* Diane Rayor

Zeus isn't such a raving Casanova. Palladas [*or* Pallades]. GrAn

Zeus lies in Ceres' bosom. Ezra Pound. APT-1; FaBoMo; FaBoTw; HarvBoo; NAAL-2v2; NOBA; NOBE; NoAM; OxBA; RaBo; VGW *Fr.* Cantos.

Zeus paid Danaé in gold: / thus I pay you. Parmenion of Macedon. GrAn

Zeus was once overheard to shout at Hera. Weather of Olympus, The. Robert Graves. FaBoEE; OBCoV

Zeus, whoever Zeus may be, if he. Aeschylus. TOF

Zeus, Zeus himself could not undo these nets. Labyrinth, The. Jorge Luis Borges. PoetW; WoPoe, *tr. by* John Updike

Zewhyexary. Thomas M. [*or* "Tom"] Disch. OBCoV

Zhi, zhi, zhi, zhi, zhi, zhi, zhi, zhi. Battle Song. Shaka, King of the Zulus. PeSAV, *tr. by* Henry Francis Fynn

Zhoukoudian Bride's Harvest. Carolyn Lau. FSt

Zig zag mothers of the gods, The. That Dada Strain. Jerome Rothenberg. FTOS; PFTM-2

Zilver-Weed, The. William Barnes. NOBVV

Zimmer Drunk and Alone, Dreaming of Old Football Games. Paul Zimmer. PBCAP

Zimmer Imagines Heaven. Paul Zimmer. PBCAP

Zimmer in Fall. Paul Zimmer. CA

Zimmer in Grade School. Paul Zimmer. KaS; PBCAP

Zimmer's Head Thudding against the Blackboard. Paul Zimmer. PBCAP

Zimri: "In the first rank of These did Zimri stand." Dryden. HAP *Fr.* Absalom and Achitophel.

Zimri: "Numerous host of dreaming saints succeed." Dryden. *See* Absalom and Achitophel

Zimri: "Some of their chiefs were princes of the land." Dryden. AWP *Fr.* Absalom and Achitophel.

Zimri: The Duke of Buckingham. Dryden. NOBE; OBSV *Fr.* Absalom and Achitophel.

Zing—Boom—Snap. Still-Life. Tatiana Shcherbina. ItGoST, *tr. by* J. Kates

Zing! Went the Strings of My Heart. James F. Hanley. ReLy

Zinnias. Valerie Worth. NTCP

Zinnias, stout and stiff. Zinnias. Valerie Worth. NTCP

Zion me wan go home. *Unknown.* FaBoVe

Zion, or the City of God. John Newton. *See* Glorious Things of Thee Are Spoken

Zion, wilt thou not ask if peace's wing. Ode to Zion. Judah Halevi. TrJP, *tr. by* Nina Davis Salaman

Zionist Marching Song. Naphtali Herz Imber. TrJP, *tr. by* Israel Zangwill

Zip. Richard Rodgers. ReLy

Zippo lighter, A. Off the Back of a Lorry. Tom Paulin. ModIr; PBCIP

Žito the Magician. Miroslav Holub. PoSu; WoPoe, *tr. by* Ian Milner and George Theiner

Zizi's Lament. Gregory Corso. BB; NeAP; VGW

Zocalo. Michael S. Harper. NBV

Zodiac. Elizabeth Alexander. FFC

Zodiac. Eleanor Farjeon. OTCP

Zodiac, The. James Dickey.
"Tenderness, ache on me, and lay your neck." TAP

Zodiac, The. Guillaume de Salluste Du Bartas. NOSC, *tr. by* Joshua Sylvester
Fr. Divine Weeks and Works, The.

Zodiac Song, The. John Ruskin. NOBVV

Zoe and the Ghosts. Dieter Weslowski. InvLad

Zoetropes. Bill Manhire. PeNZ

Zohar. Tom Carey. KGB

Zola. Edwin Arlington Robinson. OxBA

Zombie Jet. Connie Deanovich. AmPoNex

Zone. Guillaume Apollinaire. CuPo

Zone. Guillaume Apollinaire. WoPoe, *tr. by* Samuel Beckett

Zone. Guillaume Apollinaire. PFTM-1

Zone. Louise Bogan. APT-2; WPE

Zone of Death. William Everson. SacPr; VGW

Zong, A. William Barnes. BoLoP

Zonnebeke Road, The. Edmund Charles Blunden. OBWP; PeFWW

Zoo. Polly Clark. NeBl

Zoo. Shuntaro Tanikawa. PoetW, *tr. by* Harold Wright

Zoo, The. Jordan Davis. HeMarv

Zoo, The. Gilbert Sorrentino. NeAP

Zoo is full of cages and it lies, The. Picture Postcard of a Zoo. Oscar Williams. Son

Zoom! Simon Armitage. HarvBoo

Zoom (The Commodores). Thulani Davis. ISC

Zophiël [or, the Bride of Seven]. Maria Gowen Brooks.
Palace of the Gnomes. APN-1

Zosimé was a slave in body only. Damaskius. GrAn

Zounds, gramercy, and rootity-toot! Phyllis McGinley. OBSV *Fr.* Speaking of Television.

Zrínyi's Second Song. Ferenc Kölcsey. IQMS, *tr. by* Adam Makkai

Zrínyi's Song. Ferenc Kölcsey. IQMS, *tr. by* Watson Kirkconnell

Zrínyi, who knew well that his life's end was nearing. Sortie, The. Miklós Zrínyi. IQMS, *tr. by* Thomas Kabdebo

Zrinyiad, The. Miklós Zrínyi.
Invocation: "I, who in times before, with youthful mind." IQMS, *tr. by* Thomas Kabdebo

Zu fragmentarisch ist Welt und Leben. Heinrich Heine. AWP, *tr. by* Charles Godfrey Leland

Zulu Girl, The. Roy Campbell. NoP-4; OBMV; OxAEP-2

Zuni Dancers. Eric Mottram. Oth

Zuni Derivations. *Unknown*. STP, *tr. by* Dennis Tedlock

Zurich, at the Stork. Paul Celan. PoetW, *tr. by* John Felstiner

Zurich Chronicle February 1916. Tristan Tzara. PFTM-1

Zürich, the Stork Inn. Paul Celan. BBASP; HP, *tr. by* Michael Hamburger

Zuveliskes's Women Mourn over Kukutis. Marcelijus Martinaitis. TWW, *tr. by* Laima Sruoginis

AUTHOR INDEX

Arabic, Chinese, and old-style Japanese names in the Author Index are alphabetized, following standard practice, in uninverted form. Pseudonymous names are enclosed in quotation marks.

A

"A., F. P." *See* **Adams, Franklin Pierce**
"A., P. E."
 Limerick: "There we was, and wanting our tea."
A Santa Clara, Abraham
 Moon, The.
Aafjes, Bertus (1914–1992)
 Last Letter, The.
Aal, Katharyn Machan
 Leda's Sister and the Geese.
Aaron, Solomon Ephraim ben, of Lenczicz (d. 1619)
 These Things I Do Remember.
Aaronson, Leonard [*or* Lazarus] (b. 1894)
 Homeward Journey, The.
 Pesci Misti.
Abad, Gemino H.
 Holy Order.
 Jeepney.
 Light in One's Blood, The.
 Toys.
Abbey, Louis M.
 Broken Silence.
Abbott, Deborah
 All Day at Work.
Abbracciavacca, Meo (*fl.* 1250)
 By the long sojourning.
 Your joyful understanding, lady mine.
'Abd al-Hayy, Muhammad (b. 1944)
 Ode of Signs.
'Abd al-Sabur, Salah (1931–81)
 Adam Sign, The.
'Abd al-Wahid, 'Abd al-Razzaq (b. 1932)
 Dreaded Road.
 Reaching Forty.
 You Rise among Truths.
Abd-ar-Rahman I
 Palm Tree, The.
Abdal, Pir Sultan (*fl.* c.1550)
 Ilahi.
'Abdallah, Hasan (b. 1945)
 I Remember Having Loved.
Abdul Karim, Abdul Maqsoud (b. 1956)
 Nightmare 1.
 Nightmare 3.
Abelard, Peter (1079–1142)
 David's Lament for Jonathan.
 Hymn for the Close of the Week.
 More than a brother to me, Jonathan.
Abena, Busia (b. 1953)
 Exiles.
 Illicit Passion.
 Liberation.
 Mawu of the Waters.
Abercrombie, Lascelles (1881–1938)
 All Last Night.
 Epilogue: "What shall we do for Love these days?"
 Epitaph: "Sir, you should notice me: I am the Man."
 Fear, The.
 Hope and Despair.
 Hymn to Love.
 Mary and the Bramble.

 Song: "Balkis was in her marble town."
 Stream's Song, The.
 Witchcraft: New Style.
 Woman's Beauty.
Abi Shaqra, Shauqi (b. 1935)
 Fugue.
 Student, The.
Abid ibn al-Abras (*fl.* 500–550)
 Arab Chieftain to His Young Wife, An.
 Lament for an Arab Encampment.
Abinader, Elmaz (b. 1954)
 Although the Sky.
 Dar a Luz.
 Gentry, The.
 Letters from Home.
 Letters from Home.
 Making It New.
 New Year's Morning.
 On a Summer Night.
 Pigeon Rock: Lebanon.
 What We Leave Behind.
Ablan, Huda (b. 1971)
 Strangers.
Aborigine Oral Tradition
 Captain Cook.
 Mapooram.
 Moon-Bone Song [*or* Cycle].
 Platypus, The.
 Star-Tribes, The.
 Two Sisters, The.
Abrahams, Lionel (b. 1928)
 Thresholds of Identity.
 Whiteman Blues, The.
Abrahams, Maurice
 Rag Time Cowboy Joe.
Abrahams, Peter (b. 1919)
 Lonely Road.
 Me, Colored.
Abse, Dannie (b. 1923)
 Brueghel in Naples.
 Carnal Knowledge.
 Case History.
 Cousin Sidney.
 Doctor, The.
 Down the M4.
 Epithalamion: "Singing, today I married my white girl."
 Florida.
 Footnote Extended, A.
 Hunt the Thimble.
 In the Theatre.
 Inscription on the Flyleaf of a Bible.
 Letter to Alex Comfort.
 Lunch and Afterwards.
 Millie's Date.
 New Diary, A.
 Not Adlestrop.
 Origin of Music, The.
 Pathology of Colours.
 Peachstone.
 Photograph and White Tulips.
 Public Library.
 Return to Cardiff.
 Snake.
 Stethoscope, The.
 Tales of Shatz.
 Thankyou Note.
 Watching a Cloud.
 Welsh Valley Cinema, 1930s.

 Winter Visit, A.
 X-Ray.
Abu Bakr (d. 1116)
 Sword, The.
Abu Dharr (d. 1208)
 Oranges, The.
Abu Dhu'ayb al-Hudhali (d. 649?)
 Lament for Five Sons Lost in a Plague.
Abu Dulama (d. 778)
 Behold My Mother!
 Humorous Verse.
 Traders in Beauty and Delight.
Abu-l-Salt Umayyah (1067–1134)
 White Stallion, The.
Abu Ishaq al-Ilbin (d. 1067)
 Granada (1000 A.D.)
Abu Khalid, Fawziyya (b. 1955)
 Country, A.
 Geometry of the Soul.
 Mother's Inheritance.
 To Enjoy the Horror.
 Two Little Girls.
Abu 'l-Ala al-Ma'Arri (973–1057)
 Aweary Am I.
Abu-l-Hasan Ibn Al-Qabturnuh (*fl.* 12th cent.)
 In Battle.
Abu Madi, Ilya (1890–1957)
 Be a Balm.
 Bomb of Annihilation, The.
 Eat and Drink!
 Holiday Present.
 Human Clay, The.
 Phoenix, The.
 Riddles.
 Silent Tear, The.
 What is poetry?
Abu Nuwas
 Rake, The.
Abu Risha, 'Umar (b. 1910)
 Eagle, An.
 Roman Temple, A.
Abu-Risha, Zulaykha
 Khobayza.
 Marble.
 Mewl.
 Tree.
Abu Sa'id (978–1066)
 I Asked My Love.
Abu Shabaka, Ilyas (1904–47)
 I Love You.
 This Is My Wine.
 You or I?
Abu Zakariya (d. 1249)
 Bubbling Wine.
Abulafia, Abraham (*fl.* c.1250)
 Battle, The.
Acam-Oturu, Assumpta (b. 1953)
 Agony . . . A Resurrection, An.
 Arise to the Day's Toil.
Achebe, Chinua (b. 1930)
 Bull and Egret.
 Christmas in Biafra (1969)
 We Laughed at Him.
Acholonu, Catherine Obianuju
 Dissidents, The.
 Going Home.
 Harvest of War.

Nigeria in the Year 1999.
Other Forms of Slaughter.
Spring's Last Drop, The.
Water Woman.
Way, The.

Achterberg, Gerrit (1905–62)
Across the Jarbok.
Departure.
Instrument.
Pentecost.
Trinity.

Ackerly, W. C.
Prayer of an Unemployed Man.

Ackerman, Diane (b. 1948)
Beija-Flor.
Pumping Iron.
San Francisco Sunrise.
Sweep Me through Your Many-Chambered
　　Heart.

Ackerman, Julia H.
First Night.

Ackland, Valentine (1906–69)
Clock Plods On, The.
Eyes of [or the] body, being blindfold by night,
　　The.
Since the first toss of gale that blew.

Acorn, Milton (b. 1923)
Fights, The.
I've Tasted My Blood.
Knowing I Live in a Dark Age.
On Saint-Urbain Street.
You Growing.

Acosta, Teresa Palma
My Mother Pieced Quilts.

Acquah, Kobena Eyi (b. 1952)
I Want to Go to Keta.
They're Tearing Up the Old Graveyard.

Acton, Helen C.
Beads of spring rain.

"Ada" (Sarah Louisa Forten) (1814–1898?)
Appeal to Women, An.
Lines.
Lines: "From fair Jamaica's fertile plains."
Oh, when this earthly tenement.
Scroll is open, The.
To the Memory of J. Horace Kimball.

Adaios of Macedon
If you see someone beautiful / hammer it out
　　right then.
John spared his patient labouring ox.
They say dogs killed you. No, Euripides.

Adair, Tom (1913–88)
Everything Happens to Me.
Let's Get Away from It All.
Night We Called It a Day, The.
Violets for Your Furs.
Will You Still Be Mine?

Adair, Virginia Hamilton (b. 1913)
Buckroe, After the Season, 1942.
Exit Amor.

**"Adalis, Adelina Efimovna" (Adelina Efimovna
Efron) (b. 1900)**
Conversation at Midnight.

Adam, Helen (b. 1909)
Huntsman, The.
I Love My Love.
Mune Rune.
Shallow-Water Warning.

**Adamovich, Georgy [or Georgii Viktorovich]
(1894–1972)**
Autumn night, in a hotel, the two, An.
One of them said: "One life is much too little"
There, in some place, some time.
There was...what?—Pale sunsets, wide
　　expanses.
When we return to Russia...

Adams, Anna (b. 1926)
Her Dancing Days.
To My Mother.
Unrecorded Speech.

**Adams, Charles Follen ("Yawcob Strauss")
(1842–1918)**
John Barley-Corn, My Foe.
Misplaced Sympathy.

My Infundibuliform Hat.
Prevalent Poetry.
Repartée.
To Bary Jade.

Adams, Francis Lauderdale (1862–93)
Evening Hymn in the Hovels.
Hagar.
Jesus.
To the Christians.
William Wallace.

Adams, Franklin Pierce ("F. P. A.") (1881–1960)
Composed in the Composing Room.
Double Standard, The.
If.
Lines Where Beauty Lingers.
Rich Man, The.
Those Two Boys.
To a Thesaurus.

Adams, Henry
Buddha and Brahma.
Prayer to the Virgin of Chartres.

Adams, Jean (1710–65)
Dream, or the Type of the Rising Sun, A.
On the Phoenix.
There's Nae Luck about the House.
To the Muse.

Adams, John Coleman (1849–1922)
We Praise Thee, God, for Harvests Earned.

Adams, John G. (1810–47)
Heaven Is Here.

Adams, John Quincy (1767–1848)
Lord of all worlds, let thanks and praise.
Send Forth, O God, Thy Light and Truth.
To a Bereaved Mother.
To Sally.
To the Sun-Dial.
Wants of Man, The.
Why should I fear in evil days.

Adams, Lee (b. 1924)
But Alive.
Kids!
Once Upon a Time.
Put on a Happy Face.
Those Were the Days.

Adams, Léonie (1899–1988)
April Mortality.
Bell Tower.
Country Summer.
Death and the Lady.
Figurehead, The.
Fragmentary Stars.
Ghostly Tree.
Grapes Making.
Gull Goes Up, A.
Home-coming.
Horn, The.
Kingdom of Heaven.
Light at Equinox.
Lullaby: "Hush, lullay."
Moon and Spectator, The.
Mount, The.
Night-Piece.
River in the Meadows, The.
Rounds and Garlands Done, The.
Sundown.
This Measure.
Thought's End.
Twilit Revelation.

Adams, Mary (fl. 1676)
Oh London I once more to thee do speak.

Adams, Nehemiah
Saints in Glory, We Together.

Adams, Sam (b. 1934)
Gwbert: Mackerel Fishing.
Hill Fort, Caerleon.
Rough Boys.
Sliding.

Adams, Sarah Flower (1805–48)
Nearer, My God, to Thee.

Adamson, Harold (1906–80)
Everything I Have Is Yours.
I Just Found Out About Love.
It's a Most Unusual Day.
It's Been So Long.
Make with the Feet.

Time on My Hands.
Where Are You?

Adamson, Robert (b. 1944)
Action Would Kill It / A Gamble.
Dead Horse Bay.
Dreaming Up Mother.
Elm Tree in Paddington, An.
Gutting the Salmon.
Home, The Spare Room, The.
My House.
My Tenth Birthday.
O to be in the news again—now as fashion
　　runs.
Passing Through Experiences.
Private, The.
Ribbon-Fish, The.
Rimbaud Having a Bath.
Sail Away.
Sibyl.
Sonnet to Be Written from Prison.
Things Going out of My Life.

Adcock, Fleur (b. 1934)
Advice to a Discarded Lover.
Against Coupling.
Before Sleep.
Below Loughrigg.
Blue Glass.
Dreaming.
Ex-Queen Among the Astronomers, The.
Future Work.
Halfway Street, Sidcup.
Happy Ending.
Message, A.
Net, The.
Note on Propertius I.5.
Immigrant.
Over the Edge.
Poem Ended by a Death.
Soho Hospital for Women, The.
Surprise in the Peninsula, A.
Three-Toed Sloth, The.
Trees.
Visited.
Water Below, The.
Weathering.
Wife to Husband.

Addaeus
When you meet a young boy, be direct.

Addison, Joseph (1672–1719)
Letter from Italy [to the Right Honourable
　　Charles Lord Halifax], A.
Ode: "Spacious firmament on high, The."
Playhouse, The.
Poem to His Grace the Duke of Marlborough,
　　A.
Song: "Oh the charming month of May!"
Soul, The.
When All Thy Mercies.
When rising from the bed of death.

**Addison, Medora C. (Mrs. Charles Read Nutter)
(b. 1890)**
Names.

Addonizio, Kim
Alone in Your House.
At Moss Beach.
Bird.
Broken Sonnets.
China Camp, California.
Conversation in Woodside.
Event.
Late Round.

Ade, George (1866–1944)
Il Janitoro.
Microbe's Serenade, The.
R-E-M-O-R-S-E.

Adelman, Patricia
My Exorcist Mother.

Adiga, M. Gopalakrishna (1918–92)
Do Something, Brother.

Adisa, Opal Palmer
Count Ossie.
Cultural Trip, A.
Discover Me.
Ethiopia Unda a Jamaican Mango Tree.
No, Women Don't Cry.
Rainbow, The.

Women at the Crossroad / (May Elegba
Forever Guard the Right Doors)

Adkins, Geoffrey
Arthur.
Children in Armour.

Adler, Felix (1851–1933)
Hail! the Glorious Golden City.

Adler, Friedrich
By the Waterfall.

Adler, Richard (b. 1921)
Heart.
Hernando's Hideaway.
Hey There.
There Once Was a Man.
Whatever Lola Wants (Lola Gets)

Adnan, Etel (b. 1925)
Beirut-Hell Express, The.
Butterfly came to die, A.
Human race is going to the cemetery, The.
In the green escape of my palace, over a
bridge, under a.
Sometimes, they open a new highway, and let
it roll, open wide.
There is a word that never.

**"Adonis" [or "Adunis"] ('Ali Ahmad Sa'id) (b.
1929)**
Beginning Speech.
Diary of Beirut Under Siege, 1982, The.
Eiffel tower, The.
Elegy for the Time at Hand.
Grave for New York, A.
It came to pass—.
It is my desire moving.
Mihyar, A King!
Mirror for the Twentieth Century, A.
Mirror to Khalida, A.
My passion is full of seeds issuing secretly
from heraclitus and nietzsche.
New Noah, The.
No, my body is neither a pelican nor a water
lily.
Passage, The.
Song, A: "O close of night, I would have you
linger."
Song of a Man in the Dark.
Tree of Fire.
Who Are You?

Ady, Endre (1877–1919)
Adam, Where Art Thou?
Ancient 'Kayán', The.
At the Foot of Mount Zion.
Autumn Slipped Into Paris.
Behold My Treasures, Darling.
Black Piano, The.
Blood and Gold.
Grandson of György Dózsa, The.
Hackney Coach, The.
I Guard Your Eyes.
I Want to Be Loved.
In Front of Good Prince Silence.
Judas and Jesus.
Kinsman of Death, The.
Lady of the White Castle, The.
Lost Horseman, The.
Magyar Fallow, The.
Magyar Messiahs, The.
Matthias' Demented Scholar.
Memories of a Summer Night.
On Elijah's Chariot.
On New Waters.
On the Tisza.
Peacock Takes Its Perch, A.
Poet of the Hortobágy, The.
Prayer After War.
Saint Margaret's Legend.
Song of a Hungarian Jacobin.
Tethered Souls, The.
Two Kinds of Welsh Bards.
Woodland Cross, The.

"Æ" (Russell, George William) (1867–1935)
By the Margin of the Great Deep.
Cities, The.
Continuity.
Desire.
Epilogue: "Well, when all is said and done."

Exiles.
Frolic.
Gay, The.
Germinal.
Great Breath, The.
Holy Hill, A.
Immortality.
Lonely, The.
Mountain Wind, A.
New York.
Outcast[, The].
Pain.
Reconciliation.
Secret, The.
Self-Discipline.
Tragedy.
Truth.
Unknown God, The.

Aeschylus (525–456 B.C.)
Agamemnon.
Chorus: "Great Fortune is a hungry thing."
Eumenides, The.
For Ares, gold-exchanger for the dead.
If I were to tell of our labours, our hard
lodging.
Lament for the Two Brothers Slain by Each
Other's Hand.
Libation Bearers, The.
On the Thessalians Who Fought at Marathon.
Signal Fire, The.
This mountain's secret is the son of Euphorion
of Athens.
Zeus, whoever Zeus may be, if he.

Aesop (6th cent. B.C.)
Ass in the Lion's Skin, The.
Mountain in Labor, The.
Shepherd-Boy and the Wolf, The.
Swan and the Goose, The.
Vine and the Goat, The.

"Aetolus" *See* Alexander of Pleuron

Africa-Bolasco, Karina
Sauna 2.

Afterman, Allen (b. 1941)
Pietà.
Their Thoughts Cling to Everything They See
on the Way.
Van Diemen's Land.

Agard, John (b. 1949)
Ask Mummy Ask Daddy.
For Bob Marley.
Half-caste.
Listen Mr Oxford Don.
Lollipop Lady.
New Shoes.
Palm Tree King.
Poetry Jump-Up.

Agathias (Agathias Scholasticus) (536–82)
Astrologer, The.
Beautiful Melite, in the throes of middle age.
Bridge on the Sangarios, A.
House in Byzantium, A.
It is not wine that makes me reel / Not juice of
grape I crave.
Justice.
Kallirrhoê: A Dedication.
Latrine in a Suburb of Smyrna, A.
Manifesto.
Not Such Your Burden.
On Lot's Wife Turned to Salt.
Partridge.
Plutarch.
Restless and discontent / I lie awake all night
long.
Rhodanthe.
Troy.

Agee, James (1909–55)
Description of Elysium.
In Heavy Mind.
Lyrics.
Not met and marred with the year's whole turn
of grief.
Now stands our love on that still verge of day.
Permit Me Voyage.
Rapid Transit.
So it begins. Adam is in his earth.
Song with Words.

Sonnets.
This little time the breath and bulk of being.
To Walker Evans.
Two Songs on the Economy of Abundance.

Ager, Milton
Ain't She Sweet?
Everything Is Peaches Down in Georgia.
Glad Rag Doll.
Happy Days Are Here Again.
Hard-Hearted Hannah (The Vamp of
Savannah)
Louisville Lou (The Vampin' Lady)
Mamma Goes Where Papa Goes.

Agoos, Julie
Portinaio.
To Atlas in the Attic.

Agosin, Marjorie
Dance, The.
Disappeared Woman V.
Fear.
Fear 2.
Language.
Memorial.
Miriam.
Most Unbelievable Part, The.
Night.
Obedient Girl, The.
Seven Stones.
Traveling Valise.
When she showed me her photograph.

Agran, Rick (b. 1960)
Cakes Continue to Rise.
Door Thrown Open to Daisies.
Swimming with Seiger.
Wearing Dad's White Shirt Backwards.

"Agricola" (*fl.* c.1757)
Daventry Wonder, The.

Aguilar-Cariño, Maria Luisa B.
Dinakdakan.
Familiar.
For the Lover.
Gabi.

Aguilar, Mila D.
Pall Hanging over Manila.
Poem from Sierra Madre.

Agustini, Delmira (1886–1914)
Another Race.
Break, The.
In Fields of Sleepdreaming.
Ineffable, The.
Intruder, The.
Life.
Marble Beads.
Miraculous Ship, The.
Night Came in the Drowsy Living Room, The.
Public Prayer.
Shadow Beds.
Swan, The.
Sweet Reliquaries, The.
To Death, from the Genie of My Poetry.
Vision.
Wild for Love.
Wings, The.

**"Agyeya" (Sachidananda Hirananda Vatsyayan)
(1911–86)**
Hiroshima.

Ahlert, Fred E.
Ain't That the Way It Goes?
I Don't Know Why (I Just Do)
I'll Get By (As Long As I Have You)
I'm Gonna Sit Right Down and Write Myself a
Letter.
Life Is a Song, Let's Sing It Together.
Mean to Me.
Walkin' My Baby Back Home.

Ahmad, K. Nisar (b. 1936)
America, America.

Ai (Florence Anthony) (b. 1947)
Abortion.
Anniversary, The.
Archangel.
Back in the World.
Before You Leave.
Blue Suede Shoes.
Chance.

Charisma.
Child Beater.
Country Midwife: A Day, The.
Cuba, 1962.
Deserter, The.
Disregard.
Endangered Species.
Everything: Eloy, Arizona, 1956.
German Army, Russia, 1943, The.
Good Shepherd: Atlanta, 1981, The.
I Can't Get Started.
Kid, The.
Man with the Saxophone, The.
Mexico, 1940.
Mexico, August 20, 1940.
More.
New Crops for a Free Man.
Paparazzi, The.
Resurrection of Elvis Presley, The.
Riot Act, April 29, 1992.
Russia, 1927.
Salome.
Self Defense.
Twenty-Year Marriage.
Woman to Man.

Ai Ch'ing (b. 1910)
Chilean Cigarette Pack, The.

Ai Shih-te (*fl.* c.17th cent.)
Human Mind, The.

Aichinger, Ilse (b. 1921)
Enumeration.
Glimpse from the Past.
In Which Names.

Aig-Imoukhuede, Frank (b. 1935)
One Wife for One Man.

Aiken, Conrad Potter (1889–1973)
Accomplices, The.
All Lovely Things.
And in the Hanging Gardens.
And in the Human Heart.
Animula Vagula Blandula.
Annihilation.
At a Concert of Music.
But How It Came from Earth.
Chance Meetings.
Dear Uncle Stranger.
Doctors' Row.
Hatteras Calling.
Herman Melville.
Limerick: "It's time to make love. Douse the glim."
Limerick: "Quoth a cow in the marshes of Glynne."
Limerick: "Said a dreadfully literate cat."
Limerick: "Said Isolde to Tristan: "How curious!""
Limerick: "Said Old Father William: "I'm humble""
Limerick: "Scion of Boston society, A."
Limerick: "Sighed a dear little shipboard divinity."
Limerick: "There once was a wicked young minister."
Limerick: "There was an old mickey called Cassidy."
Miracles.
Morning Song.
Music I Heard.
Nameless Ones, The.
Nuit Blanche: North End.
Obituary.
Prelude I: "Winter for a moment takes the mind; the snow."
Prelude II: "Two coffees in the Español, the last."
Prelude LVI: "Rimbaud and Verlaine, precious pair of poets."
Prelude LVII: "One star fell and another as we walked."
Prelude VI: "This is not you? These phrases are not you?"
Prelude VII: "Beloved, let us once more praise the rain."
Prelude XIV: "You went to the verge, you say, and came back safely."
Prelude XIX: "Watch long enough, and you

will see the leaf."
Prelude XLII: "Keep in the heart the journal nature keeps."
Prelude XXIX: "What shall we do--what shall we think--what shall we say?"
Prelude XXVIII: "Time has come, the clock says time has come, The."
Prelude XXXIII: "Then came I to the shoreless shore of silence."
Puppet Dreams, The.
Quarrel, The.
Road, The.
Room, The.
Sea Holly.
Shaemus.
Solitaire.
Sound of Breaking.
South End.
Summer.
Tetélestai.
Things, The.
This Is the Shape of the Leaf.
Three Star Final.
Time in the Rock [or, Preludes to Definition].
Wedding, The.
When the Tree Bares.
When trout swim down Great Ormond Street.
Winds of doctrine blow both ways at once, The.

Aiken, Joan (b. 1924)
Do It Yourself.
John's Song.
Palace Cook's Tale.
Rhyme for Night.

Aikin, John (1747–1822)
Picturesque; a Fragment.

Aini, Leah
Empress of Imagined Fertility, The.
In Their House.
Liquidation.
One Girl's Dance.
Shower.

Ainsworth, Henry (1571–c.1623)
Except the Lord, That He for Us Had Been.
Fire in My Meditation Burned.
Give Ear, O Heavens, to That Which I Declare.
How Long, Jehovah?
I Minded God.
I Spread Out unto Thee My Hands.
In the Distress upon Me.
To God Our Strength Shout Joyfully.
Unto Jehovah Sing Will I.
With All My Heart, Jehovah, I'll Confess.

Aisenberg, Nadya
Leaving Eden.

'Aisha bint Ahmad al-Qurtubiyya (*fl.* late 10th cent.)
I am a lioness.
To Li Po.

Aist [*or* Eist], Dietmar, von (*fl.* 12th cent.)
Bird Was Singing, A.
Gay Summer's Bliss, Good-bye.
How can I hope a wise heart to attain.
Lady Stood, A.
Lady Stood Alone, A.
Parting at Morning.
Yonder on the linden tree there sang a merry little bird.

Aitken, E.
Elaine, pretending it was salt.

Aiyejina, Funso
Dialogue, The.
May Ours Not Be.
When the Monuments.

Aizenberg, Mikhail (b. 1948)
Look what's come to light.
Not in the chimney, but in the gas-pipes.
So where is that guy who left us piles.
Who of those who step into the stream.

Aizenberg, Susan
Art.
Kiss.
Meeting the Angel.

Akahito (Yamabé no Akahito) (d. 736?)
Black jewel like, The.

I passed by the beach.
I wish I were close.
In Waka Bay when.
Mists rise over, The.
On Fujiyama / Under the midsummer moon.
Tomorrow I was.
When I went out.

Akazome Emon (d. 1027)
I should not have waited.
I, who cut off my sorrows.
In my heart's depth.

Akenside, Mark (1721–70)
Amoret.
Complaint, The.
Creative Process, The.
Hymn to Science.
Inscription for a Grotto.
Inscription: "Whoe'er thou art whose path, in summer lies."
Love of Nature.
Poetic Genius.

Akers, Elizabeth
Bringing Our Sheaves with Us.

Akers, Elizabeth Chase *See* **Allen, Elizabeth Akers**

Åkesson, Sonja (1926–77)
Autobiography.
Ears.
Evening Walk.

Akhenaton [*or* Akhnaton] (Amenhotep IV) (d. c.1354 B.C.)
Hymn to the Sun.

Akhmadulina, Bella [*or* Izabella] Akhatovna (b. 1937)
Again September, like the swarm of seasons past.
At Night.
Autumn.
Blizzard.
Bride, The.
Chill, A.
Chills.
Coffee Imp, The.
Dream, A.
Fairy Tale about Rain, A.
Fever.
Fifteen boys, or perhaps even more.
God.
Goodbye.
I Swear.
I was so buoyant.
In the Emptied Rest Home.
Incantation.
Lines Written During a Sleepless Night in Tbilisi.
Lunatics.
Names of Georgian Women, The.
Queen, A.
Recollections of Siberia.
Remembrance of Yalta.
Silence.
Sleepwalkers.
Small Aircraft.
Snow Maiden, The.
Snowfall.
Sound of Rain, The.
St. Bartholomew's Night.
Winter.
Words Spoken by Pasternak during a Bombing.

Akhmatova, Anna Andreyevna (Anna Andreyevna Gorenko) (1889–1966)
1915.
Alexander at Thebes.
Alone.
And people will think this like.
Boris Pasternak.
Cleopatra.
Courage.
Dante.
Death of Sophocles, The.
Dedication.
Don't Frighten Me.
Dream, A.
Epigram: "Could Beatrice have written like Dante."
Epilogue.

Everything Is Plundered.
Fear turns objects over in the darkness.
Guest, The.
He Loved Three Things.
How can you look at the Neva.
I am not one of those who left the land.
I care nothing for battle odes.
I heard a voice, within me, call.
I taught myself to live simply and wisely.
I wrung my hands under my dark veil.
In 1940.
In Memory of M. B.
In the Evening.
In the Looking Glass.
Instead of a Preface.
Introduction.
July 1914.
Land not mine, still, A.
Lot's Wife.
Love.
Muse, The.
One man follows a straight path.
Pavlovsk.
Poem: "Twenty-first, The. Night. Monday."
Pushkin.
Railings of iron.
Reading Hamlet.
Requiem.
Requiem 1935–1940.
Requiem: "No foreign sky protected me."
Round my neck a rosary of fine beads.
Sentence, The.
Sister, I have come to take your place.
Slander.
So, I Remained Alone.
Solitude.
Specter, The.
Such Days as These.
Summer Garden.
Tashkent Breaks into Bloom.
There Is A Boundary.
There is in human closeness a sacred
  boundary.
This cruel age has deflected me.
Three Things Enchanted Him.
Twenty-First. Night. Monday.
Visitor, The.
We Do Not Know How to Say Goodbye.
What's worse than this past century?
When a man dies.
When in the throes of suicide.
You know, I languish here.
Your lynx-eyes, Asia.
Your white house and tranquil garden, I shall
  leave.

Akhtar-ul-Iman (b. 1915)
Compromise.

Aki-No-Bo (d. 1718)
Fourth day, The.

Akiko, Yosano (1878–1942)
Are you still longing.
Spring quickly passes.
Thousand strands, A.

Akiwumi, Viki
Different Ones #6—Future Possibilities (An
  Aids Soliloquy)
Unconditionals #3.

Akjartoq (fl. c.1920)
Old Woman's Song, An.

Akst, Harry
Am I Blue?
Dinah.
Guilty.
Straw Hat in the Rain.
What a Perfect Combination.

Al-Abbas ibn al-Ahnaf (d. 808?)
Love.

Al-Ahmad, Muhammad Sulaiman See "Badawi
  al-Jabal"

**"Al-Akhtal al-Saghir" (Bishara Abdallah al-
  Khuri) (1884–1968)**
Hind and Her Mother.
Wisdom of Life, The.

Al-Allaq, 'Ali Ja'far (b. 1945)
Lady of Chaos.
Poet.

Al-As'ad, Muhammad (b. 1944)
Gardens for the Fire and the Rain.
Princess, The.

Al-Aziz, Malak' Abd (b. 1935)
Fall, The.
We Asked.

Al-Baraduni, 'Abd-Allah (b. 1929)
From Exile to Exile.
His fame stole his real name.

**Al-Bayati [or Al-Bayyati], Abdul Wahab [or
  'Abd al-Wahhab] (b. 1926)**
Birth of Aisha and Her Death, The.
Elegy for Aisha.
Impossible, The.
Luzumiyya.

Al-Buraikan, Mahmoud (b. 1943)
Man of the Stone City.
Tale of the Assyrian Statue.

**Al Faituri [or Al-Fituri or Al-Fayturi]
  Muhammad**
Closed Door, The.
Dervish, The.
I Am a Negro.
Incident.
Knell, The.
Question and the Answer, The.
Scream, A.
Story, The.
Vision, The.

Al-Ghanim, Nujoum
I don't know how I lost my amulets.
Sand in Flames.

Al-Ghuzzi, Muhammad (b. 1949)
Beggar, The.
Dream, A.
Female.
My Sister.
Pen, The.
Quatrains for Joy.
Taghore.
Your Eyes.

Al-Gosaibi, Ghazi (b. 1940)
Octopus.
Silence.
When I Am with You.

Al-Haidari [or Al-Haydari], Buland (b. 1926)
Age of the Rubber Seals.
Dialogue.
Genesis.
Dead Witness, The.

Al-Haj [or Hajj], Unsi (b. 1937)
Autumn Leaves Are Virgin Mary.
Blue Crest of Fondness.
Charlatan, The.
He Knew Joy on Earth.
One Who Laughs and Laughs and Laughs,
  The.
Wolf, The.

Al-Harizi, Judah (fl. early 13th cent.)
Heavy-hearted.
Lightning, The.
Love Song: "Long closed door, oh open it
  again, The."
Lute, The.
Song of the Flea.
Song of the Pen, The.
Sun, The.
Under Leafy Bowers.
Unhappy Lover, The.
Within My Heart.

Al-Hutay'a (600?–662?)
It Is New.

Al-Ifriqi al-Mutayyam (fl. 975)
My Wife Complains I Pray No More.

Al-Jawahiri, Muhammad Mahdi (b. 1900)
Come Down, Darkness.
Lullaby for the Hungry.

Al-Juburi, Amal (b. 1967)
Enheduanna and Goethe.
Protest.

Al-Junaid
Now I have known, O Lord.

Al-Kamali, Shafiq (1930–84)
Coda.
Disposition No. 1.

Harvest, The.

Al-Khal, Yusuf (1917–87)
After the Fifth of June.
Cain the Immortal.
Deserted Well, The.
Wayfarers, The.

Al-Khansa (fl. 7th cent.)
Elegy for Her Brother Sakhr.
In Death's Field.
Lament for a Brother.
Night, The.
On Her Brother.
On Her Brother Sakhr.
Rain to the Tribe.
Sleepless.
Tears.

Al-Khirniq (fl. 6th cent.)
Lament after Her Husband Bishr's Murder.

Al-Khuri, Bishara Abdallah See "Al-Akhtal al-
  Saghir"

Al-Lajjam al-Harrani (fl. 960)
His Banquets Cure Most Ills.

Al-Maghut, Muhammad (b. 1934)
Arab Traveler in a Space Ship, An.
Executioner of Flowers.
From the Threshold to the Sky.
Orphan, The.
Tattoo, The.
Tourist.

Al-Mahdi (d. 1130)
Preacher, The.

Al-Majdhoub, Muhammad al-Mahdi (1921–82)
Birth (al-Maulid)
Rain, The.

Al-Mala'ika, Nazik (b. 1923)
Cholera.
Elegy for a Woman of No Importance.
Five Hymns to Pain.
Jamila.
Lilies for the Prophet.
Love Song for Words.
Song for the Moon.
Visitor Who Never Came, The.

Al-Mansouri, Al-Zahra
Abandonment.
Secrecy of Mirrors, The.

Al-Maqalih, Abd al-Aziz (b. 1939)
Choice.
First Communiqué from One Returning from
  the Zanj Revolt.
Telegrams of Tenderness for Sanaa.

Al-Muntafil
Mole, The.

Al-Mushafi, Jafar ibn Uthman (d. 982)
Yellow Its Color.

Al-Najafi, Ahmad al-Safi (1892–1978)
Moth, The.
Pleasures of Darkness, The.
Ship of Life, The.
Where Is the Guard?

Al-Na'mani, Houda (b. 1930)
Purple Thought, The.
Stone Will Talk, The.

Al-Neimi, Salwa
Dracula.
Paranoia.
Temptation.

Al-Qasim, Samih (b. 1939)
Girl from Rafah.
I feel my limbs.
Sons of War.

Al-Qasimi, Maysoun Saqr (b. 1958)
Cusp of Desire, The.
Dream Recalling a Temptation, A.
I'm not sleeping now.
Salty like my seashores.
Voice is never enough, The.

Al-Rahabi, Sayf (b. 1956)
Entering the Gardens of Doom.

Al-Rasafi, Ma'ruf (1875–1945)
Abyss of Death, The.
Poem to al-Raihani.

Al-Rihani, Amin (1876–1940)
Constantinople.

Hail, Sana'i, the Moon of the Soul.
I Dreamt I Was a Donkey Boy Again.
I ran and still I run away from Thee.
It Was All for Him.
Lilatu Laili.
On the Mediterranean coast, between the
　estuary and Jubail.

Al-Sabah, Su'ad al-Mubarak (b. 1942)
Free Harbor.
Mad Woman.
Pit, The.
Wild Cat, A.
You Alone.

Al-Sa'igh, Yusuf
Ants.
Hair.
Is This All That Remains of Love?
Story, A.
Suddenly.
Wet.
Why.

Al-Saih, Laila
Intimations of Anxiety.
Sea Desires.

Al-Samau'al ibn Adiya (fl. c.550)
Now listen to boasting which leaves the heart
　dazed.
Oh, Would That I Knew.
Oh, Ye Censurers.

Al-Samman, Ghada (b. 1942)
Lover of Blue Writing above the Sea, The.
Lover of Rain in an Inkwell, The.

Al-Sayyab, Badr Shakir (1926–64)
Death and the River.
In the Arab Maghreb.
Jaikur and the City.
Rain Song.
River and Death, The.
Song in August.

Al-Shabbi, Abu al-Qasim (1909–34)
Cupbearer, take your wine away.
Life's Will.

Al-Sharqawi, 'Ali (b. 1948)
I shall knock three times at the door.

Al-Sindi, Fawziyya
Awakening.
Banners of the Heart.

Al-Tayyib, 'Abdallah (b. 1921)
Breaking of the Glass, The.

Al-Tirimmah (660?–725)
In the Heart of the Desert.
Lord of the Throne.

Al-'Udwani, Ahmad al-Mushari (b. 1923)
Answer, An.
I asked the grave-digger, "Do you have"
Mysterious things within you, The.
You I give no name to / The mysterious things
　within you / are an untrodden bower.
You I give no name to / The mysterious things
　within you / are fragrance, light and melody.

Al-Udwany, Najaat (b. 1956)
Boat on the Pacific, A.
Butterflies of Anxiety.
Carthage.

Al-Urayyid, Thurayya
In the Stealth of Stillness.
Thirst.

Al-Wahaybi, Al-Munsif (b. 1929)
Camel, The.
Ceremony.
Desert, The.
In the Arab House.
Man Rises from the Cave of Hira', A.

Al-Wugayyan, Khalifa (b. 1941)
Elegy: "Newspaper appears in the morning,
　The."
Letter to a Bedouin Informer.

Al-Zahawi, Jamil Sidqi (1862–1936)
Both Strangers.

Alabaster, William
AWAY, fear, with thy projects, no false fire.
Beehould a cluster to itt selfe a vine.
Dear, and so worthy both by your desert.
Divine Meditations.

Divine Sonnet, A.
Exaltatio Humanae Naturae.
Haile gracefull morning of eternall Daye.
Incarnatio Est Maximum Dei Donum [or
　Donum Dei].
Jesu, thie love within mee is soe maine.
My soule a world is by Contraccion.
Night, the Starless Night of Passion, The.
Now I have found thee, I will ever more.
Now that the midd day heate doth scorch my
　shame.
O starry Temple of unvalted space.
Of the Reed That the Jews Set in Our
　Saviour's Hand.
Sunne begins uppon my heart to shine, The.
Three sortes of teares doe from myne eies
　distraine.
To Christ.
To the Blessed Virgin.
Upon the Crucifixe.
Upon the Ensignes of Christes Crucifyinge.
Way feare with thy projectes, noe false fyre, A.
What meaneth this, that Christ an hymne did
　singe.
What should there be in Christ to give offense?
When without tears I looke on Christ, I see.

Alabaú, Magali (b. 1945)
Sister.

Alakoye, Adesanya (1943–80)
Eshu.

Alarcon, Francisco
Las calles lloran / Streets Are Crying.
Blues del SIDA / AIDS Blues.
Frontera / Border.
Laughing Tomatoes.
Los árboles son poetas / Trees Are Poets.
Morning Sun.
Viernes Santo / Good Friday.

Albanach, Muireadhach See **O'Dalaigh,
Muireadhach Albanach**

Albanez, Franciso
One Who Is at Home, The.

Albee, Edward
Samantha.

Albert-Birot, Pierre (1876–1967)
Balalaïka.
Bluesky.
City is free of sin, The.
In the Paul Guillaume Gallery.
Who is that blond child laughing as he runs
　after his colored marbles?

Albert, Heinrich (1604–51)
Musical Pumpkin-Hut.

Alberti, Rafael (b. 1902)
Angels of the Ruins, The.
Blue.
Bosch.
Giotto.
Homecoming of Love Amongst Illustrious
　Ruins.
Punishments.
Warlike Angels, The.

Albiach, Anne-Marie (b. 1937)
He accepts the circle, speech and so.
"Theatre"
Winter Voyage.

Albizzi, Niccolò degli (fl. 13th cent.)
Prolonged Sonnet: When the Troops Were
　Returning from Milan.

Albrecht, Abigail
Anacapa.
Below White Cliffs.
Elkhorn Slough.
Passing Piedras Blancas.

Alcaeus [or Alkaios] (b. c.620 B.C.)
And excited the heart of Argive.
Come! Put by Pelops' Isle.
Come tip a few with me.
Come to me, leaving the Peloponnesos.
Drink...with me, Melanippos. Why (think that).
Epigram: "Nicander, ooh, your leg's got hairs!"
Fair Protarchus doesn't want to.
Having done most shameful, unjust things.
Her heart so stricken, Helen.
Hipponax.

I don't understand the conflict of the winds.
I hate Eros. He is loathsome and will not.
I long for the call to council.
Let Us Drink.
Philip at Kynoskephalai.
Philip of Macedon.
Philip V of Macedon.
Storm, The.
Story goes, from evil, The.
Wet your lungs with wine—the dogstar rises.
Wretched me / I live a rustic life.

Alcayaga, Lucila Godoy See **Mistral, Gabriela**

Alcman (fl. 7th cent. B.C.)
All asleep: mountain peaks and chasms.
But often on the mountain peaks when.
Desire Loosening.
Fragment 58: Night and Sleep.
It isn't Aphrodite, but wild Eros.
Love, again sweetly streaming down.
No longer, O honeytongued, holyvoiced
　maidens.
Olympian [Muses], round my mind.
Polydeukes.
With limb-loosening desire; and her glances
　are more melting than sleep or death.

Alcock, Mary (1742?–1798)
Chimney-Sweeper's Complaint, The.
Instructions, Supposed to Be Written in Paris,
　for the Mob in England.
Modern Manners.
Receipt for Writing a Novel, A.
Written in Ireland.

Alcosser, Sandra
By the Nape.
Dancing the Tarantella at the County Farm.
My Number.

Alcott, Amos Bronson (1799–1888)
Sonnet 14: "Not Wordsworth's genius,
　Pestalozzi's love."
Sonnet 18: "Adventurous mariner! in whose
　gray skiff."

Alcott, Louisa May (1832–88)
Lay of a Golden Goose, The.
Little Kingdom I Possess, A.
Our Little Ghost.

Alcox, Anna (b. c.1645)
All you that are to mirth Inclin'd.

Alcuin (c.735–804)
By these, by these same chains, O Rome.
Come, Make an End.
Dedication to St. Michael.
Epitaph for Paulinus of Aquileia and Arno of
　Salzburg.
Epitaph for St. Amand, Bishop of Utrecht.
For His Friends.
In the Refectory.
Inscription in Monastic Refectory.
Lament for the Cuckoo.
Love has pierced my heart with its flame.
Night Prayer, A.
On the Cross.
On the Killing at Lindisfarne.
One goodness ruleth by its single will.
Prayer at Night.
Sailor rescued from his buffeting, The.
There'll come a time when brother speaks with
　brother.
These be great cities, new roofs mounting up.
These days are too full fraught with diverse
　dangers.
To Adelhard, Archbishop of Canterbury.
To Arno of Salzburg.
To Samuel, Bishop of Sens In Time of Dearth.
When you sit happy in your own fair house.
Written in Absence.

Aldana, Francesco de
Sonnet 12.

Alden, Joseph Reed
Sleepy Time Gal.

Aldington, Richard (1892–1962)
After Two Years.
At the British Museum.
Battlefield.
Evening.
Faun Sees Snow for the First Time, The.

Field Manoeuvres.
Images.
In the Trenches.
Possession.
Resentment.
Trench Idyll.
Vicarious Atonement.
Aldis, Dorothy (1896–1966)
Hiding.
Kick a Little Stone.
Little.
No One Heard Him Call.
Aldiss, Brian W. (b. 1925)
Tom Wedgwood Tells.
Aldrich, Henry (1647–1710)
Catch, A.
Aldrich, Thomas Bailey (1836–1907)
At a Reading.
By the Potomac.
Fannie.
Fredericksburg.
Identity.
Lycidas.
Memory.
Song: "Chestnuts shine through the cloven rind, The."
Untimely Thought, An.
Alechinsky, Pierre
Ad Miró.
Alegría, Claribel (b. 1924)
Accounting.
Ars Poetica.
Desire.
Documentary.
Erosion.
From the Bridge.
Grandmother, The.
Have Pity.
I Am Root.
Letter to an Exile.
Loneliness and July Ninth.
Nocturnal Visits.
Savoir Faire.
Search.
Silence.
Small Country.
Summing Up.
Toward the Jurassic Age.
We Were Three.
"Aleichem, Sholom" (Sholem Rabinowich) (1859–1916)
Epitaph: "Here lies a simple Jew."
Sleep, My Child.
Aleixandre, Vicente (1898–1984)
Old Man Is Like Moses, The.
Alepoudelis, Odysseus *See* **Elytis, Odysseus**
Aleshire, Joan (b. 1938)
Double, The.
Aleshkovsky, Yuz [*or* Iosif Efimovich] (b. 1929)
Comrade Stalin.
Alexander, A. L.
This, Too, Shall Pass Away.
Alexander, Alan (b. 1941)
For Raftery.
Gathering Place, The.
Alexander, Cecil Frances (1818–95)
All Things Bright and Beautiful.
Dreams.
Hymn: "Eternal gates lift up their heads, The."
Jesus calls us! O'er the tumult.
Reason and Faith.
Touched with a Feeling of Our Infirmities.
Alexander, Elizabeth (b. 1962)
Affirmative Action Blues (1993)
Apollo.
Aspirin.
Boston Year.
Compass.
Deadwood Dick.
Equinox.
Farewell to You.
Feminist Poem Number One.
Kevin of the N.E. Crew.
Ladders.
Letter: Blues.

Minnesota Fats Describes His Youth.
Narrative: Ali.
Nineteen.
Ode: The sky was a street map with stars.
Overture: Watermelon City.
Painting / (Frida Kahlo)
Passage.
Stravinsky in L.A.
Today's News.
Venus Hottentot, The.
Washington Etude.
West Indian Primer.
Who I Think You Are.
Zodiac.
Alexander, Lewis (1900–1945)
Dream Song.
Alexander, Margaret Walker
Chicago.
Iowa Farmer.
Memory.
October Journey.
People of Unrest.
Alexander, Meena
Her Garden.
Alexander of Pleuron ("Aetolus") (b. c.315 B.C.)
Epitaph for Cleonicus.
Alexander, Pamela
Look Here.
Manners.
Marriage of Sorts, A.
Scherzo.
Soon.
Understory.
Well-Known Elizabethan Double Entendre, A.
Alexander, Paul
Limerick: "Chief Stewardess on a Boeing, The."
Alexander, Peter
Limerick: "Modern composer called Cage, A."
Limerick: "Randy young girl called Miranda, A."
Limerick: "Said Marlowe: Bay City's a drag."
Limerick: "Said Wittgenstein: Don't be misled!"
Limerick: "Sigmund Freud says that one who reflects."
Limerick: "Thomas Hobbes of Malmesbury thought."
Limerick: "United States Constitution, The."
Limerick: "When a friend said to Leda: Come on."
Alexander the Wild (fl. 13th cent.)
Strawberry Picking.
When We Were Children.
Alexander, Will (b. 1948)
Albania and the Death of Enver Hoxha.
Alexander, William, Archbishop of Armagh
Birthday Crown, The.
Alexandru, Ioan
End of the War, The.
Alexie, Sherman (b. 1966)
Crazy Horse Speaks.
Defending Walt Whitman.
Evolution.
Exaggeration of Despair, The.
Father and Farther.
I Would Steal Horses.
November 22, 1983.
Penance.
Powwow Polaroid.
Reservation Love Song.
Theology.
Translated from the American.
Vision (2)
On the Amtrak from Boston to New York City.
Why We Play Basketball.
Alexopoulos, Marion (b. 1948)
Night Flight.
Alfani, Gianni
Guido, that Gianni who, a day agone.
Alfieri, Vittorio (1749–1803)
To Dante.
Alfonso X (1221–1284)
Scorpions, The.
Alford, Henry (1810–71)
Harvest Home.

You and I.
Alford, Janie
Thanks Be to God.
Alfred, King of England (849–99)
Proverbs of Alfred, The.
Alfred, William (b. 1922)
Mary Lifted from the Dead.
Algarin, Miguel
Always Throw the First Punch.
At the Electronic Frontier.
Broadway Opening.
Christmas Eve: Nuyorican Café.
Dante Park.
El Jibarito Moderno.
Happy New Year.
Infections.
Meeting Gaylen's 5th Grade Class.
Nudo de Claridad.
Prologue.
Rosa.
San Francisco.
Talking.
Taos Pueblo Indians: 700 strong according to Bobby's last census.
Tato—Reading at the Nuyorican Poets' Cafe.
Tiger Lady.
Trampling.
Wire Tap.
Ali, Agha Shahid (b. 1949)
Cracked Portraits.
Dacca Gauzes, The.
Desert Landscape.
Dream of Glass Bangles, A.
Homage to Faiz Ahmed Faiz.
Houses.
I See Chile in My Rearview Mirror.
Jogger on Riverside Drive, 5:00 A.M., The.
Postcard from Kashmir.
Return to Harmony 3.
Ali Hsiying
Lazy Cloud's Nest 1.
Lazy Cloud's Nest 2.
Aliger, Margarita Iosifovna (1918–92)
Blue Hour, The.
I live / with a bullet in my heart.
Summer days are noticeably shortening, The.
Alkabez, Solomon Halevi (fl. 16th cent.)
Come, O Friend, to Greet the Bride.
Alkaios *See* **Alcaeus [*or* Alkaios]**
Alkalay-Gut, Karen (b. 1945)
Instead of his leash.
Kitzbuhl Church.
Life Goes On.
Public Outcry.
So we begin to plan.
Some people terrified for their lives cut.
Think of the children in Baghdad.
Tonight we wait for the alarm.
Transportation.
Unable to move.
Allah, Fareedah *See* **Saunders, Ruby C.**
Allan, Lewis (fl. 1939)
Strange Fruit.
Allard, Matsuo
Alone tonight one fish ripples the lake.
Deep in my notebook a lily pad floats away.
Icicle the moon drifting through it, An.
Passing clouds only a stand of aspens is in light.
Silence a droplet of water trickles down a stone, The.
Snow by the window paper flowers gathering dust.
Thawing ice the garbage blooming out of it.
Allbery, Debra
Assembler.
Carnies.
Offering.
Produce.
Allen, Annette
This River.
Allen, Dick (b. 1939)
Lost Love.
Allen, Elizabeth Akers (Elizabeth Chase Akers) (1832–1911)
Endurance.

In the Defences.
Rock Me to Sleep[, Mother].
Street Music.
Toad, A.

Allen, Fergus (b. 1921)
Elegy for Faustina.
Fall, The.

Allen, Graham (b. 1938)
Poem For My Father.

Allen, Grant (1848–99)
Ballade of Evolution, A.

Allen, Heather
In the Forest.

Allen, Hervey (1889–1949)
Dragon's Breath.
Wingless Victory, The.

Allen, Jennifer
War Poem, A.

Allen, Jonathan (1749–1827)
Sinners, Will You Scorn the Message?

Allen, Lillian (b. 1951)
Riddim an' Hardtimes.
Rub a Dub Style inna Regent Park.

Allen, Marie Louise (b. 1911)
Mitten Song, The.

Allen, Paul
Pickup.
Tattoo #47, 'Happy Dragon.'

Allen, Paula Gunn (b. 1939)
Catching One Clear Thought Alive.
Dear World.
He Na Tye Woman.
Kopis'taya.
Meditations on the Moon.
Soundings.
Taku Skanskan.
Teaching Poetry at Votech High, Santa Fe, the
Week John Lennon Was Shot.
Zen Americana.

Allen, Richard (1760–1831)
Epitaph for the Western Intelligentsia.
God of Bethel Heard Her Cries, The.

Allen, Richard (b. 1960)
See! How the Nations Rage Together.

Allen, Samuel ("Paul Vesey") (b. 1917)
Harriet Tubman aka Moses.
I Say, Mr. A.
Moment Please, A.
To Satch.
View from the Corner.

Allen, William S. (1803–79)
Erie Canal, The.

Allerton, Ellen Palmer (1835–93)
Beautiful Things.

Allestry, Jacob (1653–86)
What art thou, love? Whence are those charms.

Alley, Rick (b. 1963)
Canary Man and You, The.
Cleaning.
Dissecting Uncle Sorrow.
Growing Days, The.

Allgar, Brian
Limerick: "Undressing a maiden called Sue."

Alline, Henry (1748–84)
Amazing Sight! The Saviour Stands.
Hard Heart of Mine.
Turn, Turn, Unhappy Souls, Return.

Allingham, William (1824–89)
Across the Sea.
At Ballyshannon, Co. Donegal.
Dream, A [or The].
Evening, An.
Everything passes and vanishes.
Eviction, The.
Express.
Fairies, The.
Four Ducks on a Pond.
In a Spring Grove.
In Snow.
Lord Crashton: The Absentee Landlord.
Mill, A.
No funeral gloom, my dears, when I am gone.
Swing Song, A.
Witch-Bride, The.

Writing.

Allison, Dorothy (b. 1949)
To the Bone.
When I Drink I Become the Joy of Faggots.
Women Who Hate Me, The.

Allison, Drummond (1921–43)
Brass Horse, The.
Dedication: "Had there been peace there never
had been riven."
Funeral Oration, A.
King Lot's Envoys.
No Remedy.

Allott, Kenneth (b. 1912)
Lament for a Cricket Eleven.
Prize for Good Conduct.
Statue, The.

Allston, Washington (1779–1843)
America to Great Britain.
And now, in accents deep and low.
Art.
On a Falling Group in the Last Judgement of
Michael Angelo, in the Cappella Sistina.
On Kean's Hamlet.
On Michael Angelo.
On Rembrant; Occasioned by His Picture of
Jacob's Dream.
On Seeing the Picture of Æolus by Pelegrino
Tibalbi, in the Institute at Bologna.
On the Group of the Three Angels Before the
Tent of Abraham, by Raffaelle, in the
Vatican.
On the Luxembourg Gallery.
On the Statue of an Angel, by Bienaimé, in the
Possession of J.S. Copley Greene, Esq.
Rubens.
To My Venerable Friend, the President of the
Royal Academy.
Word: Man, A.

'Allush, Laila
Path of Affection, The.

Alpaugh, David
Herbie.

Alpheios
Andromache's lament is still in our ears.
Where are the birth-places of the heroes?

Alsop, George (c.1638–c.1680)
Author to His Book, The.
Be just (domestick monarchs) unto them.
Could'st thou (O Earth) live thus obscure, and
now.
Heavens bright lamp, shine forth some of thy
light.
Lines on a Purple Cap Received as a Present
from My Brother.
Poor vaunting earth, gloss'd with uncertain
pride.
'Tis said the Gods lower down that chain
above.
To My Cosen Mrs. Ellinor Evins.
Trafique Is Earth's Great Atlas.

Altamirano, Santiago
Eagle above Us, The.

Alterman, Nathan [or Natan] (1910–70)
Abandoned, The.
Beyond Melody.
Convert Comes to the City, A.
First Smile.
Householder Departs from the City, The.
Introduction: "Joy of the poor knocked on the
door, The."
Maid, The.
Memento of Roads.
Mole, The.
Moon.
Moon.
Red Ridinghood.
Saul.
Shadow, The.
Song to the Wife of His Youth, The.
Spinner, The.
Summer Night.
When our children cried in the shadow of the
gallows.

Altizer, Nell
Sonnet 2: "My own heart let me have. More

pity on."
Sonnet 5: "No, I'll not, carrion, comfort you.
Comfort."

Altman, Arthur
All or Nothing at All.

Altschul, Monique *See* **Altschul, Carlos**

Alurista (b. 1947)
Address.

Alvarez, Julia (b. 1950)
33 Is the Year That Jesus Christ.
Bilingual Sestina.
Estel.
He: Age Doesn't Matter When You're Both in
Love.
How I Learned to Sweep.
Mother Asks What I'm Put To.
Naming the Fabrics.
Redwing Sonnets.
Sonnet 1: "Everything that happens to me
these days."
Sonnet 42: "Sometimes the words are so close
I am."
Wallpaper.
Woman's Work.

Alver, Betti (b. 1906)
Iron Heaven.
Painter in the Lion Cage, The.
Tailor Called Sorrow, A.
Titans, The.

Alvi, Moniza (b. 1954)
Backgrounds.
Bed, The.
Carrying My Wife.
Fish.
Houdini.
Laughing Moon, The.
Man Impregnated.
Missing.
Presents from My Aunts in Pakistan.
Throwing Out My Father's Dictionary.

Ama Ata Aidoo, Christine (b. 1942)
Cornfields in Accra.
For Kinna 2.
Gynae One.
Issues.
Totems.

Amadiume, Ifi (b. 1947?)
4th Witness—The Petty Thieves.
Be Brothers.
Bitter.
Bloody Masculinity.
Creation.
Mistress of My Own Being.
Nok Lady in Terracotta.
Oya Now.
Union, The.
We Have Even Lost our Tongues!

Amalrik, Andrey Alekseievich (1938–80)
Lake Baskunchak.

Amann, Eric
Billboards.
Circus tent, The.
Names of the dead, The.
Night train passes, A.
Quietly dozing.
Snow falling.
Winter burial.

Amano Hachiro (d. 1868)
Lightning flickers.

Amara, Lamea Abbas (b. 1927)
Commandments, The.
San Diego (On a rainy day)

Amarou (fl. 1st? cent.)
Drunken Rose, The.

Amaru (fl. 7th cent.)
Lying in Bed.
Much Too Close.
You with Your Beautiful Swaying Walk.

Ambapali (fl. 4th cent. B.C.)
Black and glossy as a bee and curled was my
hair.

Ambo Oral Tradition
Five Ghost Songs.

Ambrose, Saint (c.340–397)
Eternal, Thou.

Hymn: "Framer of the earth and sky."
O splendour of God's glory bright.
Ameen, Mark (b. 1958)
Monologue of a Dying Beast.
Sonnet No. 21.
Sonnet No. 22.
Amenhotep IV *See* **Akhenaton [*or* Akhnaton]**
Amergin (*fl.* before Christian era)
Amergin's Songs.
Ames, Bernice (b. 1915)
Country of Water.
Amherst, Elizabeth Frances (c.1716–79)
From a Young Woman to an Old Officer Who
Courted Her.
Prize Riddle on Herself When 24, A.
Song for the Single Table on New Year's Day,
A.
Verses Designed to Be Sent to Mr. Adams.
Welford Wedding, The.
Amichai [*or* Amikhai], Yehuda (b. 1924)
All the Generations Before Me.
Almost a Love Poem.
And That Is Your Glory.
Anniversaries of War.
Appendix to the Vision of Peace, An.
Biblical Meditations.
Couplets.
Course of a Life, The.
Death of My Father, The.
Diameter of the Bomb Was Thirty Centimeters,
The.
Don't prepare for tomorrow, enter the narrow
lane.
Elegy.
Even my loves are measured by wars.
Four Resurrections in the Valley of the Ghosts.
Half of the people in the world.
I am a solitary man, not a democracy.
I have nothing to say about the war.
Ibn Gabirol.
Instructions for a Waitress.
Is all this sorrow? I don't know.
Jews in the Land of Israel.
King Saul and I.
Leaves without Trees.
Let the memorial hill remember, instead of me.
Letter.
Like Our Bodies' Imprint.
Lips of the dead once thoughtlessly.
Little Ruth.
Luxury.
Man in His Life, A.
Mayor.
My father fought their war four years or so.
My father was four years at their war.
My Mother Once Told Me.
My Son.
National Thoughts.
Near the Wall of a House.
Not like the cypress.
On My Birthday.
On the Day of Atonement.
Pity, A. We Were Such a Good Invention.
Psalm: "Psalm on the day, A."
Quick And Bitter.
Radius of the bomb was twelve inches.
Savage Memories.
Seven Laments for the War-Dead.
Song of Lies on Sabbath Eve, A.
Summer or Its Ending.
Thoughts came to him like long lines of
freight, The.
Tourists.
Town I was born in was destroyed by shells,
The.
Two of Us Together, Each of Us Alone, The.
Two Songs of Peace.
Two Songs of Peace.
War broke out in autumn at the empty border,
The.
We Did It.
We Have Done Our Duty.
What drove young Joseph to interpret dreams.
What is it? An airplane at dawn. No.
Amiel, Barry
Death Is a Matter of Mathematics.

"Aminado, Don" (Aminado Petrovich
Shpolyansky) (1888–1957)
Honest with Oneself.
Our Sunday Rest.
Amir, Devorah (b. 1948)
After Fall, 1956.
I Have Longings for My Dead.
Nightingale of Uncle Yair, The.
Thoughts about Sari's Jump.
What Seeps In.
Amiri, Akhtar
My home is the mountain.
Amirthanayagam, Indran
Elephants Are in the Yard, The.
So Beautiful.
There Are Many Things I Want to Tell You.
Amis, Kingsley (1922–95)
Aberdarcy: The Main Square.
After Goliath.
Against Romanticism.
Aldport (Mystery Tour)
Alternatives.
Autobiographical Fragment.
Beowulf.
Bookshop Idyll, A.
Brynbwrla.
Dream of Fair Women, A.
Ever-Fixed Mark, An.
Fforestfawr.
Aberdarcy: The Chaucer Road.
Helbatrawss, The.
Langwell.
Last War, The.
Mightier than the Pen.
New Approach Needed.
Note on Wyatt, A.
Nothing to Fear.
Pendydd.
Reborn.
Science Fiction.
Shitty.
Sight Unseen.
Silent Room, The.
St. Asaph's.
Amis, Lewis R. (1856–1904)
Jehovah, God, Who Dwelt of Old.
Ammianus (*fl.* 2d cent.)
Dawn after dawn after dawn / then suddenly
the Dark One.
Dawn after dawn comes on the wine.
Distaste.
Epitaph of Nearchos.
John's efforts to extract a thorn / failed
miserably.
May the soil cover / your interred corpse.
Supper at Apelles'/ was a garden-butcher's
work.
You think that beard has made you wise.
Ammons, Archie Randolph (1926–2001)
Above the Fray Is Only Thin Air.
Apologia pro Vita Sua.
Arc Inside and Out, The.
Auto Mobile.
Bonus.
Bridge.
Cascadilla Falls.
Chasm.
Choice.
City Limits, The.
Clarity.
Classic.
Cleavage.
Coming Right Up.
Confirmers, The.
Conserving the Magnitude of Uselessness.
Constant, The.
Coon Song.
Corsons Inlet.
Coward.
Cut the Grass.
Easter Morning.
Eternal City, The.
First Carolina Said-Song.
Foot-Washing, The.
Garbage has to be the poem of our time
because.

Grace Abounding.
Gravelly Run.
Hardweed Path Going.
He Held Radical Light.
Hope's Okay.
Hymn: "I know if I find you I will have to
leave the earth."
I don't know about you,/ but I'm sick of good
poems.
I was pulling veronica out of the lawn when
this hornet came.
Improvisation for Jerald Bullis, An.
Improvisation for the Stately Dwelling, An.
Laser.
Life in the Boondocks.
Mansion.
Mechanism.
Motion's Holdings.
Mountain Talk.
Needs.
Parting.
Periphery.
Prospecting.
Reflective.
Second Carolina Said-Song.
Silver.
Singing & Doubling Together.
Small Song.
So I Said I Am Ezra.
Spit.
Spring Coming.
Terrain.
Their Sex Life.
There is a faculty or knack, smallish, in the
mind that can turn.
Transaction.
Treaties.
Triphammer Bridge.
Unifying Principle, The.
Unsaid.
Upland.
Viable.
Visit.
Wdn't it be silly to be serious, now.
Wide Land, The.
Widespread Implications.
Working with Tools.
Yucca Moth, The.
Ammuvanar
They Shout Out the Price of Salt.
Amner, John (*fl.* c.1615)
Motet: "Stranger here, as all my fathers were,
A."
Amor, Pita (b. 1920)
CXLII.
CXXX.
CXXXIV.
CXXXIX.
"Amorous Lady, The" (fl. 1733–35)
Letter to My Love—All Alone, Past 12, in the
Dumps, A.
On Being Charged with Writing Incorrectly.
To My Love.
Amrane, Danièle (b. 1931)
You Called to Me, Prison Windows.
Anacreon Anacreontea (*fl.* 6th cent. B.C.)
Again Love struck me like a smith with a
giant.
All Abdéra mourned at the funeral pyre.
Already my temples are grey.
Come, boy, bring us.
Count, if you can, every leaf on every tree.
Dice of Love are, The.
Drinking.
Elegy 2.
Fragment 17.
Fragment 360.
I implore you, deer-shooter.
Lad, glancing like a virgin.
Not / But near another you have a timid.
O Lord, with whom subduer Love.
Ode 3: "Of late, what time the Bear turned
round."
Picture, The.
Roses.
Soaring again from the Leukadian Rock.

Spring.
Thracian filly, why do you.
Timokritos was bold in war. This is his grave.
Tossing a crimson ball.
Weaving a garland long ago.
Youthful Age.

Anacreontea *See* **Anacreon,**

Anania, Michael (b. 1939)
Edge of Autumn, The.
Fall, The.
Interstate 80.
Judy Travaillo Variations, The.
Memorial Day.
On the Conditions of Place.
Riversongs of Arion, The.
Second-Hand Elegy, A.

Anatolius (*fl.* 7th cent.)
Fierce was the wild billow, Dark was the night.

Anawrok, Edgar
Each Time.

Anaximander (b. 610 B.C.)
It is necessary that things.

Anaya, Rudolfo
La Papa.

Anbun
Years keeping that in mind.

Ancient Egyptian Oral Tradition
Poem to the Sun.
Poem to the Sun.

Ancient Sumerian Oral Tradition
Bridegroom, dear to my heart.
Word they had spoken, The.

Andal (*fl.* 10th cent.)
Cuckoo, noisy among the Shenbaka flowers.
O people who live in the world.
O sister of wealth.
O you who guard over.
To Krishna Haunting the Hills.
We rose before dawn.

Andersen, Astrid Hjertenaes (b. 1915)
Before the sun goes down.

Anderson, Alice (b. 1966)
Licking Wounds.
Suicide Year, The.

Anderson, Bill (b. 1928)
Letter from a Black Soldier.
Outbreak.

Anderson, Daniel (b. 1964)
Executive Geochrone.
Nightly News, The.

Anderson, Danny
Domi Solus.

Anderson, Doug
Itinerary.

Anderson, Ethel Louisa Mason (1883–1958)
Afternoon in the Garden.
Waking, Child, While You Slept.

Anderson, Jack (b. 1935)
Waking Up Twice.

Anderson, Jon (b. 1940)
Ye Bruthers Dogg.

Anderson, Judith
Re-member Us.

Anderson, Laurie
Dog Show.
Red Hot.

Anderson, Maggie
Closed Mill.
Country Wisdoms.
Invention of Pittsburgh, The.
Spitting in the Leaves.

Anderson, Maxwell (1888–1959)
It Never Was You.
Lost in the Stars.
September Song.

Anderson, Patrick (1915–79)
Cold Colloquy.
Coming of the White Man, The.
Houses Burning; Quebec.

Anderson, Sherwood (1876–1941)
American Spring Song.
Evening Song.

Anderson-Thompkins, Sibby (b. 1966)
Brken Promises.

Epitaph for Willie or Little Black Poet with No
Future.
Interlude.
To Love a Stranger.

Anderson, William (1762–90)
I'm Naebody Noo.

Anderton, Anne
Marking of Folders.

Andeyek
I know how people get treated when they die.

Andrade, Eugenio de (b. 1923)
Fable.
Friend is sometimes desert, A.
Music.
Penniless Lovers.
Silence.

Andrade, Mário de (1893–1945)
Aspiration.
Inspiration.
Nocturne.
Processions, The.
Rondeau for You.
Sunday.

Andrade, Oswald de (1890–1953)
Babbling.
Election.
Frontier.
Good Luck.
Hierofant.
Portuguese Mistake.

Andresen, Sophia de Mello Breyner (b. 1919)
Camoes and the Debt.
Small Square, The.
Young Girl and the Beach, The.

Andreus, Hans (Johan van der Zant) (1926–77)
Empty Room, The.
For Some Future Day.
Song: "All roocoogirls."

Andrew, Nigel
Limerick: "In childhood it's easy to feel."

Andrew of Wyntoun (c.1350–1425)
Macbeth.

Andrews, Bruce (b. 1948)
AKA.
Appetizers'
Bomb Then, Bomb Now.
DDD.
Gestalt Me Out!
Impatient Heart, The.
Methodology.
Rich little circle south.
Species Means Guilt.
Stalin's Genius.
West West.
While.
Zero Tolerance.

"Andrews, Clement"
Morn's Recompense.

Andrews, Linda
Time Signature.

Andrews, Miles Peter ("Arley") (d. 1814)
Elegy on the Death of Mr Sterne.

Andrews, Nin (b. 1958)
Notes for a Sermon on the Mount.
Poets on Poets.
That Cold Summer.

Andrews, Robert (b. 1766?)
Mercury; on Losing My Pocket Milton at Luss
near Ben Lomond, and Other Mountains.
Urania.

**Andreyev [or Andreiev], Daniil Leonidovich
(1906–59)**
For the Unveiling of a Memorial.
Night winds! Dark mountainous skies.

**Andreyev [or Andreiev], Vadim Leonidovich
(1903–1976)**
Deep scar engraved in the bark's dark silver,
A.
Rebecca.
To My Daughter.

Andros, Dionysius of *See* **Dionysius Sophistes**

Aneirin (*fl.* 6th cent.)
Gorcheanu: The Three Laments.
Lord of Gododdin will be praised in song, A.

Men went to Catraeth, keen their war-band.
Men went to Gododdin, laughter-loving.
To Cattraeth's vale in glitt'ring row.
When a crowd of cares.
Youth.

Angel, Ralph (b. 1951)
Breaking the Rock Down.
Evolving Similarities.
Nothing That Is, The.
Twilight.
Veils of Prayer.

Angela, Frances
Old Stone Age.

Angeles, Carlos A.
Light Invested.
Words.

Angell, Barbara (b. 1945)
Street Music.

Angelou, Maya (b. 1928)
Africa.
Caged Bird.
Come, And Be My Baby.
Life Doesn't Frighten Me.
Many and More.
My Arkansas.
On Diverse Deviations.
Pickin Em Up and Layin Em Down.
Sepia Fashion Show.
Still I Rise.
Woman Me.

"Angelus Silesius" (Johannes Scheffler) (1624–77)
Abomination Of Evil, The.
Belief.
Body, Soul, And Godhead.
Chance And Essence.
Each In His Own.
God is a pure no-thing.
God Is Nothing Physical.
God Is To Me What I Desire.
God, whose love and joy.
I Am As God And God As I.
It Depends on You.
Light Exists In The Fire, The.
Love.
Man Is The Highest Thing.
More Abandoned, The More Divine, The.
One Knows Not What One Is.
Only His Son Is With God.
Rose, The.
Secret Virginity, The.
Sin.
Spiritual Alchemy, The.
Spiritual Ark And The Manna-Vessel, The.
Spiritual Impregnation, The.
Take Therefore That You May Have.
To St. Augustine.
Treasure Lies In the Cornerstone, The.
Virtue's Goal Is God.
Whoever Has Become All Divine.

Anghelaki-Rooke, Katerina (b. 1939)
Body Is the Victory and the Defeat of Dreams,
The.

Angilbert (c.740–814)
Angilbert's Prayer.
Epitaph: "O King, give Angilbert thy rest."

Angira, Jared (b. 1936)
Country of the Dead, The.
Dialogue.
If.
Look in the Past, A.
Manna.
Newscast.
Obbligato from a Public Gallery.
Old Wharf Canto.
Request.
Symphony from the Balcony.

Anguita, Eduardo (1914–92)
Real Moment, The.

Angus, Marion (1870–1946)
Alas! Poor Queen.
Blue Jacket, The.
Doors of Sleep, The.
Invitation.
Mary's Song.

Angwin, Roselle
I offer you four things.

Anhalt, Diana
That Jewish Crusader.

Annand, James King (b. 1908)
Arctic Convoy.
Heron.
I Winna Let On.
Mavis.

Annensky, Innokenty Fiodorovich (1856–1909)
Capitol, The.
It Happened in Vallen-Koski.
One Second.
Petersburg.
Small Kulak Landowner.
Snow.
Violin Bow and Strings.

Annett, David
Wreck of the Deutschland, The.

Ansari, Kwaja Abdullah (1006–1089)
O God, / I have bound myself to you to the exclusion of all else.

Ansen, Alan (b. 1922)
Fatness.
Tennyson.

"Ansky, S." (Solomon Rappoport) (1863–1920)
Emigrant Song.
Tailor, The.

Anstett, Aaron (b. 1968)
Man Saves Own Life.
Pharmacy.
Shift.
Worry.

Anstey, Christopher (1724–1805)
Hearken, Lady Betty, hearken.
This morning, dear mother, as soon as 'twas light.

"Anstey, F." (Thomas Anstey Guthrie) (1856–1934)
Limerick: "There was an old man of Bengal."

Antar [or Antara] (fl. 6th cent.)
Black Night, The.

Anthony, Florence See Ai,

Anthony, George (1873–1950?)
Autumn Evening.

Anthony, Jim
Limerick: "Henley's a special regatta."

Anthony, Martha (b. 1967)
So suddenly.
Ugly Heart, The.
You cared whether I died or not.

ANTIMEDON
Drinking together in the evening we are human.

Antin, David (b. 1932)
David ross called up from syracuse and wanted to know if.
Definitions for Mendy.
Endangered Nouns.
List of the Delusions of the Insane / What They Are Afraid Of, A.
Private Occasion in a Public Place, A.
Real Estate.

Antipater of Sidon (fl. 2d cent. B.C.)
Already prepared in the golden chamber.
Antiodemis, Aphrodite's pet cherub, from a baby.
Aristeides.
Artemeias, surely when you from the nether world's bark.
Bitto gives to Athena.
Erinna.
Erinna's *Distaff*.
Here beside the threshing floor, O hardworking ant.
I, who used to ward off the starlings and that snatcher.
Let the four-clustered ivy flourish about you, Anacreon.
Lysidice, I'm anxious to find out the meaning.
Myriad times, Ptolemy, your father, myriad times.
Never again, Orpheus.
Pindar.
Priapos of the Harbor.
Reporter of the courage of heroes.
Ruins of Corinth, The.

Tell me, woman, your parents, your name, your land. B. Calliteles.
This is Anacreon's grave. Here lie.
This is the barrow of grizzled Maronis, on which you see.
This is the grave of grey-haired Maronis.
This mangled tentacle of the huge scolopendra.
This piece of Lydian earth holds Amyntor.
To Pallas, three girls, all of an age, skilled as the spider.
To Pan three brothers hung up these tools of the trade.
Undying Thirst.
Who hung these shields here still all shiny.

Antipater of Thessalonica
All sea is sea. How mad it is to blame.
Am I to blame the drink or the downpour?
Deserted islands, broken sherds of land.
Don't judge men by their gravestones.
Europa (in Athens) does business / at truly reasonable rates.
Fortune-tellers say I won't last long.
Gipsies tell me my life-line's a short one, The.
Glykon, glory of Asia / born in Pergamum.
Gorgo, a Cretan bitch, on a deer's track.
Homer said everything beautifully, but to call.
I'm not at all scared of the Pleiades setting.
I've Never Feared.
I was Hermocrateia: twenty-nine / children I bore.
In my stars there's three times ten.
In winter on her hearth lighting some coal.
It is morning, Chrysilla. Some time ago the clarion cock.
Italian dust covers a Libyan.
"They pray for children? Let them!" cried Polyxo.
Man who first built up with good strong words, The.
Mentorides, please tell us who.
Neither war, nor cyclones, nor earthquakes.
Phoebus was a herdsman.
Priapus, seeing Cimon's rigid rod.
Priapus seeing Kimon with a stand.
Temple of Artemis at Ephesos, The.
That dried-up arse, Lykainis.
Theogenes sent us for Piso's pleasure—.
These are Aristophanes' marvellous plays.
To Epicles.
To Telembrotos.
Unlucky Nicanor, quenched by the grey and deep.
Water-mill, A.
Watered by the Strymon and great Hellespont.
Waves, the rough surf, swept me on the shore, The.
When the deep-piled winter snow / melted on her roof.
Where is your famous beauty.
Yesterday when I'd drunk myself to bed / with water (neat)

Antiphanes (c.388–c.311 B.C.)
Lost Bride, The.
Man's makeshift days would flash past at the best.
Piddle-paddling race of critics, rhizome-fanciers.
Strange race of critics, A.
When Cytherea slipped her wily sash off.

Antiphilus [or Antiphilos]
Earthquaked, my house collapsed.
Epitaph of a Sailor.
Even then I said.
Gifts to a Lady.
Give me a mattress on the ship's poop some day.
Imaginary Dialogue.
On Diogenes the Cynic.
On the Death of the Ferryman, Glaucus.
Quince Preserved through the Winter, Given to a Lady, A.
Torrent Cuts Off the Poet's Path, A.

Antistius Vetus (Gaius Antistius Vetus) (fl. A.D. c.26)
Priapus the Scarecrow.

"Antler" (b. 1946)
Machines waited for me, The.

Star-Struck Utopias of 2000.
Thoughts Breathing in a Blizzard.
Ungag our souls!! Unstrangle our souls!! Unsmother our souls!!
What Every Boy Knows.

Antoine, Pierre See Motteux, Peter Anthony

Antokolsky, Pavel Grigoryevich (1896–1978)
Ballad of the Wondrous Moment.
From their journeys our dreams return.
Hate!
Hieronymus Bosch.
Paul the First.
Sans Culotte.
We are not always dependent on memory.
You must dig in black ashes a long time.
You share your mourning with all Moscow. There.

Antoninus, Brother See Everson, William

Antonov, Vadim (b. 1942)
Toward morning, slipping the pistol under my arm.

"Anvari" (Awhad ad-Din 'Ali ibn Vahid ad-Din Muhammad Khavarani) (1126?–1190?)
Composing.
Drunkenness.
Hors de Combat.
Take What He Gives You.

Anwar, Chairil (1922–49)
At the Mosque.
Heaven.
Me.
Ordinary Song, An.
Tuti's Ice Cream.
Twilight at a Little Harbor.
Willingness.

Anyidoho, Kofi (b. 1947)
Elegy for the Revolution.
Hero and Thief.
Murmuring.
Our Birth-Cord.
They Hunt the Night.
Tsitsa.

Anyte [or Anytes]
Alive, this man was Manes, a common slave.
And you too perished long ago, by a bush with matted roots.
Behold the horned goat of Bacchos, how lordly.
Big enough for an ox, the cauldron.
Child Myro made this tomb, The.
Children, billy goat, have put crimson reins, The.
Children have put purple, The.
Children have tied you, billy-goat, with bright, The.
Cock, A.
Damis erected this mound for his dead steadfast.
Damis set this up, to commemorate.
Dedication: A Spear.
Ease your weary limbs, stranger, under this elm—.
For her locust, nightingale of the fields, and her cricket that slept.
For the cricket (nightingale of the field) and oak.
I am Hermes. I stand in the crossroads by a windy.
I, Hermes, have been set up.
I, Hermes, stand here by the windy tree-lined.
I mourn for Antibia the virgin.
I mourn maiden Antibia: desiring her, many.
Indeed then, it was your own courage.
Instead of a solemn wedding and marriage-bed.
Instead of bridal bed and holy wedding songs.
Kypris keeps this spot.
Lone Theudotos placed this gift beneath the mountain.
Look at the horned goat of Dionysus.
Lounge in the shade of the luxuriant laurel's.
No longer, as before, plying with whirring wings.
No longer, as before, will you wake at dawn and flap.
No longer shall I exult in the floating seas and arch.

No longer will I fling up my neck, exulting.
Often keening on her daughter's tomb, Kleina.
Often on this her daughter's tomb did Cleina
  grieve.
On a Dolphin.
On this her daughter's tomb.
Ox-sized cauldron, Kleubotos gave, An.
Putting red reins on you, goat, with a
  noseband.
Shepherd's Gift, A.
Sit down in the shade of this fine spreading
  laurel.
Sit, everyone, under the luxuriant laurel.
Stand there, manslaying spear; no longer drip.
Stranger, below the boulder rest your spent
  limbs.
This is Kypris' place; it ever pleases her.
This Lydian earth covers Amyntor, Philip's
  son.
This Manes alive once was a slave; now dead.
This place is the Cyprian's for she has ever the
  fancy.
This tomb Damis built for his courageous
  horse.
Throwing her arms around her dear father.
Throwing her arms around her father.
To shock-haired Pan and the nymphs who
  protect the cow-byres.
We go, Miletos, dear fatherland, spurning.
Why, country Pan, sitting still.
Why, rustic Pan, sitting in the lone shady
  wood.
You, too, perished by a bush with tangled
  roots.
Youth buried you, Captain; as sons for their
  mother, The.
Anzaldúa, Gloria (b. 1946)
  Cultures.
  Horse.
  Interface.
  We Call Them Greasers.
Apache Oral Tradition
  Corn Ceremony.
Apáti, Ferenc (*fl.* early 16th cent.)
  Song of Reproach.
Api
  Another Me.
Apollinaire, Guillaume (1880–1918)
  Bonds.
  Calligram, 15 May 1915.
  Cantor.
  Cavalier's Farewell, The.
  Fete.
  Heart.
  Horse Calligram.
  In this mirror I am enclosed.
  It's Raining.
  Kings who have died.
  Listen to the sea.
  Meadow Saffron.
  Mirabeau Bridge.
  Monday rue Christine.
  My darling little Lou how I love you.
  Post Card.
  Shadow.
  Sighs of the Gunner from Dakar, The.
  Stanzas Against Forgetting.
  To Linda.
  Traveller, The.
  Voyager, The.
  Windows.
  Zone.
Apollinaris Sidonius (c.430–484)
  Invitation to the Dance.
  To Catulinus That He Cannot Write Him an
    Epithalamium Because of the Enemy Hosts.
Apollinarius
  If you insult me in my absence.
Apollonides (*fl.* 6 B.C.)
  Beeman Cliton hews / From the flower fed
    hive.
  Cup clinks out, my friend, The.
  Lacking rich acres, thick grape-crops.
  Snow, clothing sky & mountain.
Apollonius Rhodius (222 B.C.–181 B.C.)
  Argonautica, The.

Apotheker, Alison
  Burning Bush.
Appel, Benjamin (b. 1907)
  Talker, The.
Appel, Karel (b. 1921)
  Mad Talk.
Appleman, Philip (b. 1926)
  Mary.
  Matthew 1:18–25: Now the birth of Jesus
    Christ took place.
  Peace with Honor.
  Waiting for the Fire.
Applewhite, James (b. 1935)
  Prayer for My Son.
Áprily, Lajos (1887–1967)
  Antigone.
  March in Transylvania.
  Night in Kolozsvár.
  Night Song.
  Nostalgia.
  On the Wall of My Age.
  Plea to Old Age.
  Stag of Irisoda, The.
  Victor, The.
Apuleius, Lucius
  I who am Nature, mother of all.
'Aql, Sa'id (b. 1912)
  Dark Beauty.
  Do Not Show Your Love.
  More Beautiful Than Your Eyes.
  My ecstasy is that I have met you.
Arabov, Yury [*or* Iurii] b. 1954
  I'm introducing it as a hunchback.
  Walking the Places I've Never Been.
Aragon, Louis (1897–1982)
  Lilacs and the Roses, The.
  Night at Dunkirk.
  Poem to Shout in the Ruins.
  Richard II Forty.
  Waltz of the Twenty-Year-Olds, The.
Arakida Moritaké (Moritaké) (1473–1549)
  Falling flower, The.
  Haiku: "Fallen flowers rise."
  Haiku: "Falling flower, The."
Arany, János (1817–82)
  As if a nest of hornets rose to sting.
  As on an autumn night a herdman's fire.
  Bards of Wales, The.
  Civilisation.
  Cosmopolitan Poetry.
  Day to the reedy marsh had closed her eye.
  Family Circle.
  Imprisoned Souls.
  Mistress Agnes.
  Mother of King Matthias, The.
  My brother's done for, by all human law.
  Nighingale, The.
  Reply to Petőfi.
  River seemed a broad stream, fenced with folk,
    The.
  Scholar's Cat, The.
  Then Nicholas spoke: 'My King, most kind to
    me'
  Two Pages of Szondi, The.
Arany, László (1844–98)
  Albion, teach me (and not with loud, unsubtle)
  Elfrida.
Aratus (*fl.* 3d cent. B.C.)
  Beneath both the feet of Boötes you may see.
  Proem: "From Zeus let us begin, him we
    mortals never."
  Weather Signs.
Arbiter, Caius Petronius *See* **Petronius Arbiter,**
Arbuthnot, John (1667–1735)
  Epitaph on Colonel Francis Chartres.
  Know Yourself.
Archevolti, Samuel ben Elhanan Isaac, of Padua
  (*fl.* 17th cent.)
  Advice to Hotheads.
Archias
  Desire, get your bow ready / and go quietly
    after / another mark.
  "Get away from Eros!"
Archias of Byzantium (*fl.* c.120 B.C.)
  Not even in death can I.

  Sea Dirge.
Archias of Macedon
  Hektor of Troy.
Archilochus (c.680?–c.640? B.C.)
  Attribute all to the gods: often they raise.
  Be Bold! That's One Way.
  Buffeted by the waves.
  Decks awash, / Mast-top dipping.
  Fireworks on the Grass.
  Fox knows many things, The.
  Glaukos, look: already the deep sea is troubled.
  Heart, my heart churning with fathomless
    cares.
  Here is a fable men tell.
  Hold back completely.
  I am a servant of the War Lord.
  I don't give a damn if some Thracian ape strut.
  I don't like a tall general, swaggering.
  I said, 'Be mine.'
  Ideal General, The.
  If only I might touch Neobule's hand.
  Like Odysseus under the ram.
  May he lose his way on the cold sea.
  Miserable I lie in desire.
  My ash spear is my barley bread.
  My friend, limb-loosening.
  No townsman, Perikles, will blame us for
    groaning.
  Nothing is unexpected or sworn impossible.
  Sergeant to Enyalios.
  She delighted to hold a slip of myrtle.
  Some Thracian exults in an excellent shield.
  Strategy.
  Such passion for love coiled in my heart.
  This island, garlanded with wild woods.
  What Gyges so golden has doesn't matter to
    me.
  When Alkibié married.
  Will, lost in a sea of trouble.
  You see that high crag.
  Zeus, Father Zeus, you've power over heaven.
'Archpoet,' The (c.1130–c.1165)
  Never yet could I endure.
Arcos, René
  Dead, The.
Argensola, de, Lupercio Leonardo
  Damon's Lament for His Clorenda, Yorkshire,
    1654.
Arends, Jan (1925–1974)
  I.
  I Have.
Arensberg, Walter Conrad
  Arithmetical Progression of the Verb 'To Be'
  Axiom.
  Ing.
  Theorem.
  Voyage à l'Infini.
Aretino, Pietro (1492–1556)
  If famous Apelles with his hand of art.
Argentarius (Marcus Argentarius) (*fl.* c.60 B.C.)
  About Menophila's morals there are strange
    rumours.
  Aristomache loved a drink: / The old
    chatterbox was fonder.
  Blackbird, singing on the highest branch / Of
    the oak.
  Come, Gobrys, there are other gods besides the
    Muses.
  Damned bird, why have you ruined my sleep.
  Dead, they'll burn you up with electricity.
  Dead, you will lie under a yard of earth.
  Drunk I observe the golden dance of stars.
  Epigram: "Hetero-sex is best for the man of a
    serious turn of mind."
  Her perfect naked breast.
  Here lie a grasshopper and a / Cicada.
  Here's to Lysidice: pour in ten ladles, boy.
  I can't bear to watch your hips.
  Isias my love, with your scented breath.
  Look at this, golden-horned moon.
  Love Is Not.
  Melissa means honeybee; yes, you're true.
  My name was Pnytagoras; I died by drowning.
  Old Story, The.
  Once I was reading Hesiod.
  Psyllus lies here. Procuring was his trade.

Rather skinny beauty, you'll find, / is Diocleia,
   A.
Take off those flimsy nets, Lysidice.
That's your third sneeze now, my good lamp.
This is Callaeschrus' empty tomb.
Trader, untie the long stern-cables.
Welcome, old friend, long-necked bottle.
You loved Menophila when you were rich.
Your kink, Heraclea, is sucking off.

Arghezi, Tudor
Flowers of Mildew.
Last Hour, The.
Psalm.
Testament.

Aridjis, Homero [or Umberto] (b. 1940)
Borders, Cages and Walls.
Decomposition with Laughter.
Epitaph for a Poet.
Letter from Mexico.
Poem, The.
Rain is Falling, The.
Rivers.
To Emerge from a Woman Is to Become
   Separate.

Arika, Abba *See* **Rab**

Arimaru (d. 1703)
Running shallow.

Ariosto, Ludovico (1474–1533)
Alcyna met them at the outer gate.
Astolfo flies by Chariot to the Moon, where he
   collects Orlando's lost wits.
Blessed angell not a word replies, The.
Go soule, go sweetest soule for ever blest.
Masters go abrod to vew the towne, The.
Medoro's Inscription Book XXIII.
Soon after, he a crystal stream espying.
Thus much he prayed, and thence away he
   went.

Aristodicus of Rhodes (*fl.* **3d cent. B.C.**)
Cricket, you'll sing no more.
On a Pet Grasshopper.

Ariston (*fl.* **3d cent. B.C.**)
If you mice are looking for *food.*

Aristophanes (c.450–c.385 B.C.)
Chorus of Birds.
How the Women Will Stop War.
Lysistrata.
Song of the Clouds.

Aristophanes of Byzantium
On the advice of Praxilla.

Ariwara no Yukihira (815–93)
I must leave you, but.

Arkell, Reginald (1882–1959)
What is a Garden?

Arlen, Harold
Accentuate the Positive.
As Long As I Live.
Between the Devil and the Deep Blue Sea.
Come Rain or Come Shine.
Down with Love.
Eagle and Me, The.
For Every Man There's a Woman.
Fun to be Fooled.
Happiness Is Just a Thing Called Joe.
Happy As the Day Is Long.
Hooray for Love.
I Gotta Right to Sing the Blues.
I've Got the World on a String.
I Wonder What Became of Me.
If I Only Had a Brain (If I Only Had a Heart)
   (If I Only Had the Nerve)
Ill Wind.
It's Only a Paper Moon.
Last Night When We Were Young.
Let's Fall in Love.
Let's Take a Walk Around the Block.
Lydia, the Tattooed Lady.
Man That Got Away, The.
Morning After, The.
My Shining Hour.
One for My Baby (And One More for the
   Road)
Out of This World.
Over the Rainbow.
Sing, My Heart.

Stormy Weather (Keeps Rainin' All the Time)
Tess's Torch Song (I Had a Man)
That Old Black Magic.
We're Off to See the Wizard (The Wonderful
   Wizard of Oz)
When the Sun Comes Out.

"Arley" *See* **Andrews, Miles Peter**

Armand, Octavio
Another Poetics.
Braille for Left Hand.
Poem with Skin.
Sonnet: "I am an honest man."
Word to the Wise, A.

Armantrout, Rae (b. 1947)
Attention.
Disown.
Garden, The.
Generation.
Getting Warm.
Incidence.
Language of Love.
Leaving.
Native.
Necromance.
Plan, The.
Sense.
Winter.

Armitage, Jennifer
To Our Daughter.

Armitage, Simon (b. 1963)
Becoming of Age.
Before You Cut Loose.
Hitcher.
In Our Tenth Year.
Poem: "And if it snowed and snow covered the
   drive."
Robinson's Resignation.
Zoom!

Armour, Richard (b. 1906)
Hiding Place.
Money.
Pachycephalosaurus.

Armstrong, Frankie
Collier Lass, The.
Month of January.
Out of the Darkness.
Women of My Land.

Armstrong, Jeannette
I Study Rocks.

Armstrong, John (1709–79)
Advice to Lovers.
Art of Preserving Health, The.
Causes of Old Age.
Diet.
Madness.
Transience.
Urban Pollution.

Armstrong, Martin Donisthorpe (1882–1974)
To a Jilt.

Arnaout, 'Aisha (b. 1946)
Orbits.
Spinal Cord.

Arnett, Carroll ("Gogisgi") (b. 1927)
Anadarko John.
Drunk.
Land.
Powwow.
Removal: Last Part.
Rock Painting.
Something for Supper.
Story of My Life, The.
You.

Arnheim, Gus
I Cried for You.

Arnold, Bob
No Tool or Rope or Pail.

Arnold, Craig (b. 1967)
Disembodied Voices of Women, The.
Extravagance of Zoos, The.
Locker Room Etiquette.
My Love Is Sick.
Party She Outdid Herself, The.
Why I Skip My High School Reunions.
XX.

Arnold, Denise Y.
Song to the Alpaca.

Arnold, Sir Edwin (1831–1904)
Destiny.

Arnold, George (1834–65)
Beer.

Arnold, Matthew (1822–88)
Atossa.
Balder Dead, *sels.*
Below the Surface-Stream.
Buried Life, The.
Continued.
Dover Beach.
Dream, A.
East London.
Forsaken Merman, The.
Geist's Grave.
Growing Old.
Hymn of Empedocles.
In Harmony with Nature.
Isolation: To Marguerite.
Last Word, The.
Lines Written in Kensington Gardens.
Longing.
Memorial Verses.
Nameless Epitaph, A.
Palladium.
Philomela.
Poet, The.
Progress.
Progress of Poesy, The.
Requiescat.
Resignation.
Rugby Chapel.
Scholar Gypsy, The.
Shakespeare.
Sohrab and Rustum, *sels.*
Sohrab Dead.
Song of Callicles, The.
Strayed Reveller to Ulysses, The.
Stanzas From the Grande Chartreuse.
Thyrsis.
To a Friend.
To Marguerite—Continued.
To the Hungarian Nation.
West London.
Written in Butler's Sermons.
Youth and Calm.

Arodin, Sidney
Lazy River.

Aronsten, Joan (b. 1914)
Ad Infinitum.

Arouet, François Marie *See* **Voltaire**

Arp, Hans [or Jean] (1887–1966)
Great Unrestrained Sadist, The.
Domestic Stones (fragment), The.
Kaspar Is Dead.
Man, The. The Woman.
People.

Arrillaga, Maria
Dream.
Like Raquel.
Mariana II.
Rosa/Filí.

Arrowsmith, Pat (b. 1930)
Christmas Story (1980)
Political Activist Living Alone.

Artaud, Antonin (1896–1948)
All Writing Is Garbage.
I learned yesterday.
Spurt of Blood, The.

Artemidorus (*fl.* **2d cent. B.C.**)
Pastoral Muses once were scattered, The.

Artmann, H. C. (b. 1921)
Ah rosie.
Optician has a Glass Heart, An.

Arturo, Aurelio (1906–74)
Madrigal 3.
Song of the Silent Night.

Arvey, Verna (b. 1910)
All That I Am.

Arvidson, K. O. (b. 1938)
Fish and Chips on the Merry-Go-Round.
Tall Wind, The.

Arvio, Sarah
Mirrors.

"Arzhak, Nikolai" *See* **Daniel, Yuly [or Iulii]**

Markovich
As-Sabah, Sabah (b. 1966)
I'll Never Know No Sunday in This Weekday
   Room.
Jubilee.
Transition #2.
Asalache, Khadambi (b. 1934)
Death of a Chief.
Asbaje, Juana Rumirez de See **Juana Inés de la**
Cruz, Sister
Asch, Frank (b. 1946)
Leaves.
Play.
Summer.
Sunflakes.
Asclepiades (fl. 270 B.C.)
Although she's a girl, Dorkion.
Arkheanassa.
Bitto and Nannion do not.
Colophon to a Roll of Erinna's Poems.
Dear Lamp, she swore by you.
Didyme waved an olive branch at me.
Didyme waved her wand at me.
Dorkion, sweet little tomboy.
Drink, Asklepiades.
Eumares.
Get drunk, my boy, don't weep, you're.
Great is a drink of snow.
Here Lies Archeanassa.
I am not yet twenty-two and I am tired of
   living.
I touched up sexy Hermione.
It is sweet in summer to slake.
Leave the rags, you tiny lusts.
Love has found out how to mix.
Lysidice dedicated to you, Cypris.
Night long and wintry / the Pleiades half set.
Nikarete's face, sweetly moistened.
On a Ring.
Pampered Philainion stabbed me, The.
Playing once with facile.
Snow, hail and smut the sky.
Snow! Hail! Lower! Lightning! Thunder!
Stay, my tendrils, where hung.
Think how unspeakably sweet.
This is the sweet work of Erinna, not much, of
   course.
To you, Kypris, Lysidike.
Tomb on the Shore, A.
We were having fun, that devil Hermione and
   I.
What are you saving it for?
When soft Irene like a.
Wine is love's test.
You're saving it? What for?
Asclepiodotus (fl. 1st cent. B.C.)
Hear in the sea, Thetis, Memnon's alive.
Asei (d. 1752)
Flowers of the grass.
Asekoff, L. S.
Crowdoll.
Invisible Hand.
North Star.
Rounding the Horn.
Starwork.
Will.
Aseyev [or Aseiev], Nikolai Nikolaievich (1899–
1963)
Dark Blue Hussars.
How shall I tell you.
Ash, John (b. 1948)
Desert Song.
Ferns and the Night.
Following a Man.
Monuments, The.
Poor Boy: Portrait of a Painting.
Them/There.
Ashanti, Baron James (fl. 20th cent.)
Just Another Gig.
Ashbery, John (b. 1927)
Additional Poem, An.
And "Ut Pictura Poesis" Is Her Name.
Archipelago, The.
As One Put Drunk into the Packet-Boat.
At North Farm.

Blessing in Disguise, A.
Boy, A.
Brute Image.
Bungalows, The.
Business Personals.
But Not That One.
Cæsura.
Cathedral Is, The.
Chapter 2, Book 35.
City Afternoon.
Civilization and Its Discontents.
Couple in the Next Room, The.
Crazy Weather.
Crossroads in the Past.
De Imagine Mundi.
Decoy.
Definition of Blue.
Down by the Station, Early in the Morning.
Drunken Americans.
Farm Implements and Rutabagas in a
   Landscape.
Faust.
Fear of Death.
For John Clare.
Forgotten Song.
Forties Flick.
Friends.
Glazunoviana.
Grand Abacus.
Hard Times.
Hotel Lautréamont.
How Much Longer Will I Be Able to Inhabit
   the Divine Sepulcher.
Illustration.
Improvement, The.
Instruction Manual, The.
Into the Dusk-Charged Air.
Just Walking Around.
Knocking Around.
Landscapeople.
Last Month.
Last World, A.
Le Livre Est sur la Table.
Leaving the Atocha Station.
Life As a Book That Has Been Put Down.
Limited Liability.
Lost and Found and Lost Again.
Love Poem, A.
Many Wagons Ago.
Märchenbilder.
Meditations of a Parrot.
Melodic Trains.
Mixed Feelings.
Morning Jitters.
My Erotic Double.
My Name Is Dimitri.
My Philosophy of Life.
Myrtle.
Never Seek to Tell Thy Love.
New Constructions.
Oh, Nothing.
Old Complex, The.
On Autumn Lake.
On The Empress's Mind.
One Thing That Can Save America, The.
Ongoing Story, The.
Operators Are Standing By.
Other Tradition, The.
Our Youth.
Painter, The.
Pantoum.
Paradoxes and Oxymorons.
Picture of Little J. A. in a Prospect of Flowers,
   The.
Pied Piper, The.
Poem: "While we were walking under the top."
Problem of Anxiety, The.
Pyrography.
Rain.
Rain Moving In.
Rivers and Mountains.
Self-Portrait in a Convex Mirror.
Shadow Train.
Some Trees.
Songs without Words.
Soonest Mended.
Spring Day.

Statuary.
Street Musicians.
Summer.
Syringa.
Tennis Court Oath, The.
Tenth Symphony.
These Lacustrine Cities.
'They Dream Only of America'
Thinnest Shadow, The.
Thoughts of a Young Girl.
Train Rising Out of the Sea.
Two Sonnets.
Variant.
Walkways, The.
Wet Casements.
What Is Poetry.
When the Sun Went Down.
White Roses.
Worsening Situation.
Years of Indiscretion.
Young Prince and the Young Princess, The.
Young Son, The.
Ashby, Cliff (b. 1918)
Latter Day Psalms.
Stranger in This Land, A.
Ashe, Thomas (1836–89)
City Clerk, The.
Corpse-bearing.
To Two Bereaved.
Vision of Children, A.
Word to the West End, A.
Ashur-Nasir-Pal, King of Assyria (fl. 1000 B.C.)
Hymn to Ishtar.
Asim, Jabari
Dumas.
Harlem Haiku: A Scrapbook.
Hip Hop Bop.
Asimov, Isaac (1920–92)
Limerick: "Industrious young obstetrician,
   An."
Limerick: "On the beach," said John sadly,
   "there's such."
Limerick: "There was a young lady of Ealing /
   And her lover before her was kneeling."
Limerick: "There was a young maid of Peru."
Limerick: "There was a young man of
   Belgrade."
Askew, Anne (1520–46)
Ballad Which Anne Askew Made and Sang
   When She Was in Newgate, The.
Voyce of Anne Askewe out of the 54. Psalme
   of David, Called, Deus in Nomine Tuo, The.
Askhari
Circular Fate.
Colorstruck.
Isalutu.
REcreation.
Aspden, Bryan (b. 1933)
News of the Changes.
"Asphodel" (Pauline Long) (b. 1921)
Full Moon in Malta.
On the Pilgrim's Way in Kent, as It Leads to
   the Coldrum Stones.
Winter Solstice—for Frank.
Asquith, Herbert (1881–1947)
Banking Potatoes.
Birds on a Powerline.
Sunday Afternoons.
Volunteer, The.
Assiba d'Almeida, Irène
Sister, You Cannot Think a Baby Out!
Astell, Mary (1666–1731)
In Emulation of Mr Cowleys Poem Call'd The
   Motto.
Aston, Alasdair (b. 1930)
Everything in the Garden is Lovely.
Aston, Katherine Thimelby (c.1620s–1650s)
To My Daughter Catherine on Ashwednesday
   1645, Finding Her Weeping at Prayers,
   Because I Would Not Consent to Her
   Fasting.
Upon the LD Saying KT Could Be Sad in Her
   Company.
"Astra" (b. 1927)
Bloody Pause.

Daughters.
Now or Never.

Atalla, S. V.
Diaspora.
Visiting the West Bank.

Atimantiyar (*fl.* 3rd cent.)
Nowhere, not among the warriors at their
    festival.

Atkins, Russell (b. 1926)
Dark Area.
Late Bus (After a Series of Hold-Ups)
Lisbon.
Narrative.
New Storefront.
Lakefront, Cleveland.

Atmanam
Next Page.

Ato Tobira (*fl.* 8th cent.)
Only one fleeting.

Atsujin (d. 1836)
Earth and metal.

Attlee, Clement (1883–1967)
Few thought he was even a starter.

Atwood, Margaret (b. 1939)
Against Still Life.
Animals in That Country, The.
At first I was given centuries.
Beauharnois (1)
Beauharnois (3)
Beauharnois, Glengarry (2)
Circle Game, The.
Daguerreotype Taken in Old Age.
Damside.
Death of a Young Son by Drowning.
Disembarking at Quebec.
Dream 2: Brian the Still-Hunter.
Dufferin, Simcoe, Grey (4)
Earth.
Eden Is a Zoo.
Elegy for the Giant Tortoises.
Eventual Proteus.
Explorers, The.
Flowers.
Footnote to the Amnesty Report on Torture.
Four Small Elegies.
Game after Supper.
Habitation.
I made no choice / I decided nothing.
It Is Dangerous to Read Newspapers.
It's the story that counts.
Landcrab I.
Landcrab II.
Landlady, The.
Last Poem.
Marrying the Hangman.
Men with the heads of eagles.
More and More.
Notes towards a Poem That Can Never Be
    Written.
November.
People come from all over to consult me,
    bringing their limbs.
Postcard.
Procedures for Underground.
Puppet of the Wolf, The.
Rat Song.
Robber Bridegroom, The.
Settlers, The.
Siren Song.
Spelling.
There Is Only One of Everything.
They Eat Out.
This Is a Photograph of Me.
This story was told to me by another traveller.
Torture.
Trainride, Vienna—Bonn.
Tricks With Mirrors.
Up.
Variation on the Word *Sleep*.
Variations on the Word *Love*.
Vultures.
We are standing facing each other.
Woman Skating.
Woman Who Could Not Live With Her Faulty
    Heart, The.
You Are Happy.

You Begin.
You Fit into Me.
You take my hand and.

Aubert, Alvin (b. 1930)
Bessie.
Bessie Smith's Funeral.
Opposite of Green, The.

Auchterlonie, Dorothy (b. 1915)
Meditation of a Mariner.
Tree, The.
Waiting for the Post.

Audelay, John (*fl.* 1425)
Seven Gifts of the Holy Ghost, The.

Auden, Wystan Hugh (1907–73)
1929.
A. E. Housman.
Adolescence.
After Christmas.
Alone in a room Pope Gregory whispered his
    name.
Always the Following Wind.
Amor Loci.
Another Time.
Anthem: "Let us praise our Maker, with true
    passion extol Him."
As I Walked Out One Evening.
At the Party.
Atlantis.
Aubade: "At break of dawn."
August 1968.
Ballad of Barnaby, The.
Behold the manly mesomorph.
Bird-Language.
Brussels in Winter.
Calypso.
Carry her over the water.
Cave of Making, The.
Consider.
Cultural Presupposition, The.
Dear, Though the Night Is Gone.
Decoys, The.
Dedication: "Let us honour if we can."
Dedication: "Private faces in public places."
Dog beneath the Skin, The.
Door, The.
Earth, receive an honoured guest.
Edward Lear.
England, my England--you have been my
    tutrix.
Epilogue: 'O where are you going?' said
    reader to rider.
Epitaph on a Tyrant.
Exiles, The.
Fall of Rome, The.
Far from a cultural centre he was used.
Fish in the Unruffled Lakes.
For Christopher Isherwood and Chester
    Kallman.
From "The Prolific and the Devourer"
Gare du Midi.
Give Me a Doctor.
Glad.
Good-Bye to the Mezzogiorno.
Happy New Year, A.
He turned his field into a meeting-place.
Healthy Spot, A.
Henry Adams / Was mortally afraid of
    Madams.
Here war is harmless like a monument.
Herman Melville.
History of Truth, The.
I Cannot Grow.
I like your muse because she's gay and witty.
If I Could Tell You.
In a garden shady this holy lady.
In Memory of Sigmund Freud.
In Memory of W. B. Yeats.
In Praise of Limestone.
It's No Use Raising a Shout.
Jumbled in the Common Box.
Lauds.
Leap Before You Look.
Legend.
Letter, The.
Limerick: "As the poets have mournfully
    sung."

Limerick: "Marquis de Sade and Genet, The."
Limerick: "T. S. Eliot is quite at a loss."
Lost.
Love Feast, The.
Love Song: "For what as easy."
Luke 23:26–38; And as they led him away.
Lullaby: "Din of work is subdued, The."
Lullaby: "Lay your sleeping head, my love."
Luther.
Mad to be had, to be felt and smelled. My lips.
May.
Minnelied.
Miranda.
Miss Gee.
Moon Landing.
More Loving One, The.
Mundus et Infans.
Musée des Beaux Arts.
New Year Greeting, A.
Night Mail, The.
Now through Night's Caressing Grip.
O What Is That Sound [Which So Thrills the
    Ear].
Ode to Terminus.
Ode to the Diencephalon.
On the Circuit.
On This Island.
Ottava Rima would, I know, be proper.
Doggerel by a Senior Citizen.
Our Hunting Fathers.
Oxford.
Passenger Shanty.
Paysage Moralisé.
Petition.
Precious Five.
Prime.
Prologue: "O love, the interest itself in
    thoughtless heaven."
Question, The.
Questioner Who Sits So Sly, The.
Refugee Blues.
Roman Wall Blues.
September 1, 1939.
Shield of Achilles, The.
So an age ended, and its last deliverer died.
Some thirty inches from my nose.
Song: "Deftly, admiral, cast your fly."
Song for St. Cecilia's Day.
Song of the Beggars.
Song of the Master and Boatswain.
Song: "Stop all the clocks, cut off the
    telephone."
Song: "When the Sex War ended with the
    slaughter of the Grandmothers."
Spain 1937.
Sphinx, The.
Starling and a willow-wren, A.
Statesmen.
Strings' Excitement, The.
Summer Night, A.
T. S. Eliot.
Taller To-day.
Terce.
That night when joy began.
Their Lonely Betters.
They wondered why the fruit had been
    forbidden.
This Lunar Beauty.
Thought of writing came to me today, The.
Three Posthumous Poems.
Uncle Henry.
Under Sirius.
Under Which Lyre, a Reactionary Tract for the
    Times.
Unknown Citizen, The.
Up There.
Vespers.
Villanelle: "Time can [*or* will] say nothing but
    I told you so."
Wanderer, The.
Watch Any Day.
We are girls of differnt ages.
Who's Who.
Words.
You lived and moved among the best society.

Aue, Hartmann von (1170–1215)
I go, with your good grace, lords and kinsmen.

I said I would always live for her.
None Is Happy.
Often a friend will greet me thus.

Augustini, Delmira (1886–1914)
Vision.

Aus of Kuraiza (*fl.* 7th cent.)
Apostasy.

Auslander, Joseph (1897–1965)
Elegy: "Fled is the swiftness of all the white-footed ones."
Sunrise Trumpets.
Three Things.

Ausonius (Decimus Magnus Ausonius) (c.310–395)
Echo.
Fields of Sorrow, The.
I am that Dido which thou here do'st see.
I used to tell you, "Frances, we grow old"
Idyll of the Rose.
On the Sicilian strand a hare well wrought.
Since worms and dust must be your fate.
To His Wife.

Austen, Katherine (1628–83)
Dec. 5th 1644 Upon Robin Austins Recovery of the Smal Pox and General Popams Son John Diing of Them.
On the Situation of Highbury.

Austin, Alfred (1835–1913)
And do they wear that lubricating lie.
But the fleet hours pass pitilessly fleeter.
Flocks of the wandering waves I hold, The.
Go away, Death!
Is Life Worth Living?
Jameson's Ride.
Last Night, The.
Wrong! Is it wrong? Well, may be.

Austin, John
Love of Christ, The.

Austin, Louie *See* **Hunter, Albert**

Austin, William
Sepulchrum Domus Mea Est.

Automedon (*fl.* c.6th cent. B.C.)
Gymnastics Teacher, The.
Having dined yesterday on a goat's foot.
Impotent Lover, The.
Nicetes begins with gentle declamation.
Phoebus, accept this dinner that I bring you.
That Asiatic striptease girl / who goes in for those.
Turkish. Belly-dancer. Sexy tricks.

Autumn Maid Tu (Tu Ch'iu-niang) (fl.807)
Robe of Golden Thread, The.

Auvaiyar (*fl.* between 1st and 3d cent.)
Shall I charge like a bull.
You stand and hold the post of my small house.

Ava, Frau (*fl.* c.1160)
I am yours, you are mine.

Avakkumova, Mariya [or Mariia] (b. 1943)
Dead man touched me with his hand, A.
Russia can't be grasped by the mind.

Avery, Richard K. (b. 1934)
And the Cock Begins to Crow.

Avianus
Calf and the Ox, The.

Avicolli, Tommi (b. 1951)
Rape Poem, The.

Avidan, David (b. 1934)
Life of a Dead Dog.
Six Local Poems.

Avila, Teresa de *See* **Teresa de Cepeda Y Ahumada,**

Avis, Nick
Evening star, The.
Freshly fallen snow.

Avison, Margaret (b. 1918)
Civility a Bogey.
Dumbfounding, The.
For Dr. and Mrs. Dresser.
Hiatus.
In a Season of Unemployment.
Intra-Political.
Lament: "Gizzard and some ruby inner parts, A."

Meeting Together of Poles & Latitudes: In Prospect.
Nameless One, A.
New Year's Poem.
Snow.
Story, A.
Swimmer's Moment, The.
Thaw.
Transit.
Unspeakable.
Voluptuaries and Others.
Water and Worship: An Open-Air Service on the Gatineau River.
Word, The.

Awad, Joseph
Autumnal.
First Snow.
For Jude's Lebanon.
Generations.
I Think Continually of Those Who Were Truly Failures.
Lament for Philip Larkin, A.
Man Who Loved Flamenco, The.
Stopping at the Mayflower.
Variations on a Theme.
Widower, The.

Awatere, Arapeta (1910–70)
Lament for Kepa Anaha Ehau.

Awoonor, Kofi (George Williams) (b. 1935)
Agosu if you go tell them.
America.
American Memory of Africa, An.
At the Gates.
Easter Dawn.
First Circle, The.
Lovers' Song.
On Having Been an Experimental Sacred Cow for Four Years, and a Token African on Faculty.
Rediscovery.
Sea Eats the Land at Home, The.
So the World Changes.
Something has happened to me.
Song of War.
Songs of Sorrow.
They Shall Know.
This Earth, My Brother.
To Dennis Brutus.
To the Eminent Scholar and Meddler.
Weaver Bird, The.

Aworinde, Awotunde
If a Suite in Praise of the Yoruba Oracle.

'Awwad, Thérèse (b. 1933)
I found one word.
I Undressed Myself.
My Loneliness.

Axelrod, David B. (b. 1943)
Guide to Urban Birds, A.
Once in a While a Protest Poem.

Ayer, Nat D.
If You Were the Only Girl in the World.

Aygi, Gennady (b. 1934)
Dream: Flight of a Dragonfly.
Dream: Queue for Paraffin.
Going to Sleep in Childhood.
Poppies of This Year.
Rose of Silence.
Rustle of Birches.

Ayhan, Ece
Epitafio.
Geranium and the Child.
Nigger in a Photograph, The.
To Trace from Hebrew.

Ayres, Philip (1638–1712)
Cynthia on Horseback.
Death of Adonis, The.
Describes the Place Where Cynthia Is Sporting Herself.
Epigram on Woman, An.
Ever Present.
Fly, The.
Invites His Nymph to His Cottage.
Invites Poets and Historians to Write in Cynthia's Praise.
On a Fair Beggar.
On Lydia Distracted.

Yoke uneasy on the ox doth sit, The.

Ayres, Robert
Corporeal.
Neighbor's Elm, The.

Aytoun [or Ayton], Sir Robert (1570–1638)
Answer, The.
On the Prince's Death, to the King.
Posy, A: "Dear love, I am resolved with thee to live."
Rejection, The.
Song, A: On His Mistress.
Song: "What means this strangeness now of late."
Sonnet: on Loss.
Sonnet: On the River Tweed.
There is none, no none but I.
To His Coy Mistress.
To His Forsaken Mistress.
Upon His Unconstant Mistress.
Upon Mr Thomas Murrays Fall.
Upon Platonic Love: To Mistress Cicely Crofts, Maid of Honour.
Upone Tabacco.
Valediction.

Aytoun, William Edmonstoune [or Edmondstoune] (1813–65)
Laureate, The.
Morning dawned full darkly, The.
Royal Banquet, The.
Sonnet to Britain.
Then the Provost he uprose.
We received thee warmly—kindly—though we knew thou wert a quiz.

A'yunini
Killer, The.

Azevedo, Kathleen de
Famous Women—Claudette Colbert.

A'Zmi, Kaifi (b. 1924)
Humiliation.

Azmi, Khalil-ur-Rahman (1927–78)
I and I.

B

"B., C. K."
American girl in Versailles, An.

"B., M."
Deportation.

"B., R."
This story's strange, but altogether true.

"B.V." *See* **Thomson, James**

Ba, Oumar (b. 1900?)
Familiar Oxen.
Justice is Done.
Nobility.
Ox-Soldier, The.

Baba Kuhi of Shiraz (948–1050)
In the market, in the cloister—only God I saw.

Babcock, Donald Campbell (b. 1885)
O God, in Whom the Flow of Days.

Babcock, Maltbie Davenport (1858–1901)
Be Strong.
School Days.
This Is My Father's World.

Babits, Mihály (1883–1941)
Against Horace.
Before Easter.
Book of Jonah, The.
Danaïds, The.
Gypsy in the Condemned Cell, A.
Jonah's Prayer.
Kind of Culture, A.
Like a Dog.
Lyric Poet's Epilogue, The.
Memorial.
Psychologia Christiana.
Question at Night.
Tomb of Hegeso, The.

Baca, Jimmy Santiago (b. 1952)
Cloudy Day.
Green Chile.
How We Carry Ourselves.
I Applied for the Board.

Immigrants in Our Own Land.
It Started.
Like an Animal.
Mantanza to Welcome Spring.
Mi Tío Baca el Poeta de Socorro.
Oppression.
Perfecto Flores.
So Mexicans Are Taking Jobs from Americans.
Voz de la Gente.
Work We Hate and Dreams We Love.

Bacchylides (b. 450 B.C.)
Peace on Earth.

Bacharach, Naftali
Poem for the Sefirot as a Wheel of Light, A.

Bachhuber, David
Mozart in a Classroom of Children.

Bachmann, Ingeborg (1926–73)
Curriculum Vitae.
Days in White.
Early Noon.
Every Day.
Every Day.
Exile.
Firstborn Land, The.
Fog Land.
Go, My Thought.
Great Freight, The.
In the Storm of Roses.
Instructed in love.
Invocation of the Great Bear.
Kind of Loss, A.
No Delicacies.
Out of the corpse-warm vestibule of heaven steps the sun.
Paris.
Respite, The.
Safe-Conduct.
Settlement.
Songs from an Island.
Time Allotted, The.
Truly.
You want the summer lightning, throw the knives.
You Words.

Bachner
Little Mouse, The.
Man Proposes, God Disposes.
Yes, That's the Way Things Are.

Bachri, Sutardji Calzoum (b. 1942)
Soldiers.

Back, Rachel Tzvia (b. 1960)
Abu Salim, Healer.
After Eden.
Gaza, Undated.
Notes: From the Wait.
Untitled.

Backus, Bertha Adams
Then Laugh.

Bacmeister, Rhoda Warner (b. 1893)
Galoshes.

Bacon, Anne Cooke (1528?–1610)
A—B—on the Learned Bartholo Sylva.

Bacon, Crystal
Outlook.

Bacon, Francis (1561–1626)
Life of Man, The.

Bacon, Leonard (1802–81)
Hail, Tranquil Hour of Closing Day.
Pilgrim Fathers, The.
Wake the Song of Jubilee.

"Badawi al-Jabal" (Muhammad Sulaiman al-Ahmad) (1907–81)
Beauty.
Dark Mirage.
Immortality.
Visit, The.

Baffo, Giorgio (1694–1768)
Sonnet: "My meditation turns to thinking."

Bagg, Robert (b. 1935)
Ronald Wyn.

Baggesen, Jens (1764–1826)
Childhood.

"Bagritzky [or Bagritsky], Eduard Georgievich" (Eduard Georgievich Dzyubin) (1895–1934)
Black bread and a faithful wife.

He Tries out the Concords Gently.
My Honeyed Languor.
Origin.
Piece of Black Bread, A.
Smugglers.
Till Eulenspiegel.
Verses about a Nightingale and a Poet.
Watermelon.

Baha Ad-din Zuhayr (d. 1258)
On a Blind Girl.

Bahe, Liz Sohappy (b. 1947)
And What of Me?
Farewell: "You sang round-dance songs."
Grandmother Sleeps.
Once Again.
Printed Words.
Ration Card, The.
Talking Designs.

Bai, Mukta (fl. 13th cent.)
I live where darkness / is not.

Baiho (1633–1707)
On Entering His Coffin.

Baika (d. 1843)
People, when you see the smoke.

Baiko (d. 1903)
Plum petals falling.

Baildon, Henry Bellyse (1849–1907)
Moth, A.

Bailey, L. W.
Limerick: "There was a young girl from Uttoxeter / Who made passing oarsmen gape through locks at her."

Bailey, Philip James (1816–1902)
We live in deeds, not years; in thoughts, not breaths.
What Is Heaven?

Bailey, R. V.
Father's Things.

Baillie, Joanna (1762–1857)
Blackcock, The [or The Black Cock].
Child to His Sick Grandfather, A.
Disappointment, A.
Evening.
Fam'ly cares call next upon the wife, The.
Ghost of Edward.
Ghost of Fadon, The.
Hay making.
Hooly and Fairly.
Horse and His Rider, The.
Morning.
Mother to Her Waking Infant, A.
Outlaw's Song, The.
Reverie, A.
Song (Poverty Parts Good Company, For an Old Scotch Air.
Song: "What voice is this, thou evening gale!"
Song: Woo'd and married and a'
Summer's Day, A.
Tam O' the Lin.
To Cupid.
Trysting Bush, The.
Winter's Day, A.
Ye are the spirits who preside.

Baillie, Lady Grisel (1665–1746)
Were Ne My Hearts Light I Wad Dye.

Bain, Andrew Geddes (1797–1864)
Address.
Polyglot Medley.

Bainen (d. 1905)
Now spring has come.

Baird, Martha (1921–81)
Do Not Make Things Too Easy.

Bairyu (d. 1863)
O hydrangea.

Baisei (d. 1745)
Island of Eternity.

Baiseki (d. 1716)
Journey west, The.

Bajza, József (1804–58)
Autumn Song.
Prophecy, The.
Sighing.

Baker, Austen
There was a young lady named Miller.

Baker, David
Someone's Been Sending Me Flowers.

Baker, David (b. 1954)
8-Ball at the Twilite.
Envoi: Waking After Snow.

Baker, Henry (1698–1774)
Declaimer, The.
Love.
Rapture, The.

Baker, Houston A., Jr. (b. 1943)
Of Walter White's Father in the Rain.
Tobacco Warehouse Blues.
Toward Guinea: For Larry Neal, 1937–1981.

Baker, Howard (b. 1905)
Advice to a Man Who Lost a Dog.
Ode to the Sea.
Sappho's Leap.

Baker, Kathleen Leland (b. 1951)
Baby Hilary, Sir Edmund, The.
Honey Moon.

Baker, Thomas (b. 1871)
Lord Stanhope hit upon a novel plan.

Baker, Tony (b. 1954)
Armillaria mellea.
Le passage (Morbihan)
Pavane on Mr Wray's Locations, A.

Bâkî (1526–1600)
Oh Beloved, Since the Origin We Have Been.

Bako (d. 1751)
Looking back at the valley.

Bakusui (1720–83)
Returning / By an unused path—violets.

Bal, Willy (b. 1916)
Fire!

Balaban, John (b. 1943)
After Our War.
Along the Mekong.
Anna Akhmatova Spends the Night on Miami Beach.
April 30, 1975.
Dead for Two Years, Erhart Arranges to Meet Me in a Dream.
Dragonfish, The.
For Miss Tin in Hue.
For Mrs. Cam, Whose Name Means "Printed Silk."
For the Missing in Action.
Graveyard at Bald Eagle Ridge.
Guard at the Binh Thuy Bridge, The.
Heading Out West.
Hurricane.
In Celebration of Spring.
News Update.
Opening Le Ba Khon's Dictionary.
Riding Westward.
Story.
Than, Mau.
Thoughts Before Dawn.
Words for My Daughter.

Balakian, Peter (b. 1951)
End of the Reagan Era, The.
Rock 'n Roll.

Balamani Amma, N. (b. 1909)
To My Daughter.

Balassi, Bálint (1554–94)
For Wine Drinkers.
Having to Part From His Mistress at Dawn.
He Pleads for Forgiveness Before His Intended Marriage.
In Which He Rejoices Over Having Discarded Love.
Soldier's Song.
When He Met Julia, He Greeted Her Thus.

Balbulus, Notker (c.840–912)
Hymn to Holy Women, A.

Balce, Nerissa S.
Pizza and Pretense.

Balderston, Jean (b. 1936)
Anne Steele.

Baldwin, James (1924–87)
Guilt, Desire and Love.
Lover's Question, A.

Baldwin, Thomas (1753–1825)
From Whence Doth This Union Arise?

Baldwin, William (*fl.* 1547–49)
Christ, My Beloved.
Christ to His Spouse [*or* The Beloved to the Spouse].

Balestrini, Nanni (b. 1935)
Tape Mark.
What matters here is (can a fish live)

Balingit, Joann
Quiet Evening, Home Away.

Ball, Angela (b. 1952)
Dance Pianist, The.
Jazz.
Kiss, The.
Man in a Shell, The.

Ball, Caroline Augusta (b. 1825)
Jacket of Gray, The.

Ball, Hugo (1886–1927)
Complete Sound-Poems of Hugo Ball, The.
Flight out of Time.
Sun, The.

Ball, Joseph H.
And This Is So.

Ballagas, Emilio (1908–54)
Nocturne and Elegy.
Of Another Fashion.

Ballantine, James
Castles in the Air.

Ballard, Charles G.
During the Pageant at Medicine Lodge.
Grandma Fire.
Memo.
Now the People Have the Light.
Sand Creek.
Speaker, The.
Spirit Craft, The.
Their Cone-like Cabins.
Winds of Change, The.

Ballou, Hosea, I (1771–1852)
Dear Lord, Behold Thy Servants.
In God's Eternity.
When God Descends with Men to Dwell.

Ballou, Hosea, II (1796–1861)
Ye Realms below the Skies.

Ballou, Silas (1753–1837)
Almighty God in Being Was.
While I Am Young.

Ballowe, James (b. 1933)
Coal Miners, The.
Starved Rock.

Balmont, Konstantin Dmitrievich (1867–1942)
I don't know the wisdom others seem to need.
Vanishing Shadows.

Bamber, Jill
Broken Necklace.

Bamford, Samuel (1788–1872)
Touch Him!

Bampfylde, John Codrington (1754–96)
As when, to one who long hath watched, the morn.
On a Frightful Dream.
On a Wet Summer.
On Christmas.
On Hearing That Torture Was Suppressed throughout the Austrian Dominions.
To the Evening.
To the Redbreast.
Written at a Farm.

Banchs, Enrique (1888–1968)
Mumbling.

Banckes, Elizabeth (*fl.* 1616)
Roysters give Roome, for here comes a Lass.

Bancks, John (1709–51)
Description of London, A.
Fragment, A: "In Cloe's chamber, she and I."

Bancquart, Marie-Claire (b. 1932)
Baroque.
Counterfable of Orpheus.
Curriculum vitae.
Epitaph.
Portrait of Jonah with woman.
Sea.
Town.
Vanished, The.
Woman asleep.

Bancroft, James Henry (1819–44)
Brother, Though from Yonder Sky.

Bandeira, Manuel (1886–1968)
Evocation of Recife.
Interview.
Mozart in Heaven.
Off to Pasárgada.
Poetics.
Portrait.
Rondeau of the Little Horses.
Spiritual Wedding.

Bandele, Asha (b. 1966)
1980–1990: A Poet's Personal Review.
Prayer for the Living, A.

Bang, Mary Jo
Constant Bride, The.
Crossed-Over, Fiend-Snitched, X-ed Out.
Dog Bark, The.
It Says, I Did So.
Like a Fire in a Fire.
Louise in Love.
Star's Whole Secret, The.

Bangs, Carol Jane (b. 1949)
Touching Each Other's Surfaces.

Bangs, Edward *See* **Shuckburg, Richard**

Bangs, John Kendrick (1862–1922)
Blind.
Dreadful Fate of Naughty Nate, The.
Hired Man's Way, The.
I Never Knew a Night So Black.
If.
Little Elf, The.
My Dog.
On File.
Philosophy.
Today.

Bankoku (d. 1748)
Longest winter night, The.

Banks, Jr., Theodore H.
Tempest.

Bannerman, Frances
Upper Chamber, An.

Banning, Lex (b. 1921)
And No Regrets.
Epitaph for a Scientist.
Romancero.

Bansode, Hira (b. 1939)
Woman.

Bantock, Gavin (b. 1939)
Bard.
Dirge: "Body lies under the ground."
Joy.

Banus, Maria (b. 1914)
Eighteen.
Gift Hour.

Banzan (d. 1730)
Farewell.

Baraka, Imamu Amiri (LeRoi Jones) (b. 1934)
After the Ball.
Agony, An. As Now.
Alba.
All is One for Monk.
Am/Trak.
Audubon, Drafted.
Babylon Revisited.
Balboa, the Entertainer.
Ballad of the Morning Streets.
Beautiful Black Women.
Biography.
Black Art.
Black Bourgeoisie.
Black Dada Nihilismus.
Black People!
Cant.
Careers.
Clay.
Cold Term.
Contract. (For The Destruction and Rebuilding of Paterson), A.
Crow Jane.
Cuba Libre.
Das Kapital.
Dope.
Duke's World.
Each Morning.

Evil Nigger Waits for Lightnin'
For Hettie.
For Maulana Karenga & Pharoah Sanders.
Funk Lore.
Hymn for Lanie Poo.
I don't love you.
I Substitute for the Dead Lecturer.
In Memory of Radio.
In One Battle.
Incident.
Invention of Comics, The.
JA ZZ : (The 'Say What?') IS IS JA LIVES
Ka 'Ba.
Kenyatta Listening to Mozart.
Last Word, The.
Leadbelly Gives an Autograph.
Legacy.
Leroy.
Letter to E. Franklin Frazier.
Liar, The.
Look for You Yesterday, Here You Come Today.
Major Bowes' Diary.
Minute of Consciousness, The.
Nation Is Like Ouselves, The.
New Reality Is Better Than a New Movie!, A.
New World, The.
Numbers, Letters.
One Night Stand.
Ostriches and Grandmothers!
Pause of Joe, The.
Poem for Black Hearts, A.
Poem for Deep Thinkers, A.
Poem for Half White College Students.
Poem for Speculative Hipsters, A.
Poem for Willie Best, A.
Poem Some People Will Have to Understand, A.
Political Poem.
Politics of Rich Painters, The.
Preface to a Twenty Volume Suicide Note.
Pressures, The.
Return of the Native.
Sacred Chant for the Return of Black Spirit and Power.
Short Speech to My Friends.
Snake Eyes.
Song Form.
SOS.
State/meant.
Study Peace.
Three Modes of History and Culture.
Three Movements and a Coda.
To a Publisher . . . Cut-out.
Turncoat, The.
W. W.
Way Out West.
When We'll Worship Jesus.
Will They Cry When You're Gone, You Bet.
Wise 1.
Wise 3.
Wise 5.
World Is Full of Remarkable Things, The.
Young Soul.

Baraka, Ras (b. 1969)
After-Word.
Five-0.
For the Brothers Who Aint Here.
I Remember Malcolm.
In the Tradition Too.

Barakat, Saleem (b. 1951)
Cows of Heaven, The.
Dilana and Diram.
Flamingo, The.
Greyhound, The.
Hoopoe Bird, The.
Squirrel, The.

Baranczak, Stanislaw (b. 1946)
December 14, 1979: A Poetry Reading.
February 8, 1980: And No One Has Warned Me.
N. N. Tries to Remember the Words of a Prayer.
Three Magi, The.

Barannikov, Kostya [*or* **Kostia**] (b. 1950)
May there always be sun!

Baratier, David (b. 1970)
American Standard.
Estrella's Prophecies #47.
Fall of Because, The.
She Wants.

'Barba-Jacob, Porfirio' (Miguel Angel Osorio Benítez) (1883–1942)
Song of the Fleeting Day.

Barbauld, Anna Laetitia (1743–1825)
Call, The.
Eighteen Hundred and Eleven.
Life.
Life's 'Good-Morning'
Mouse's Petition, The.
Ode to Spring.
On a Lady's Writing.
On General Paoli and the Corsican Struggle for Liberty.
On the Expected General Rising of the French Nation.
Praise to God, immortal praise.
Rights of Woman, The.
Sonnet to France On Her Present Exertions.
To a Little Invisible Being Who Is Expected Soon to Become Visible.
To Mr. S. T. Coleridge.
To the Poor.
Tomorrow.
Washing-Day.

Barben, Debby (b. 1959)
Do You Know What You're Saying.
Eight Beds, Eight Lockers.
Four White Walls.
To Look Yet Not Find.

Barber, David (b. 1960)
Little Overture.
Nocturne.
Small Hours.
Spirit Level, The.

Barber, Mary (1690?–1757)
Conclusion of a Letter to the Rev. Mr. C——, The.
How I succeed, you kindly ask.
On Seeing an Officer's Widow Distracted.
Stella and Flavia.
To Mrs. Francis-Arabella Kelly.
To Novella, on her saying deridingly, that a Lady of great Merit, and fine Address, was bred in the Old Way.
Unanswerable Apology for the Rich, An.
Written for My Son, and Spoken by Him at His First Putting on Breeches.

Barber, William (b. 1947)
Explanation.
Gay Poet, The.

Barberini, Francesco da (1264–1348)
Of Caution.
There is a vice prevails.
Virgin Declares Her Beauties, A.

Barberino, Francesco da
Now these four things, if thou.
There is a vice which oft.

Barbour, Dave
I Don't Know Enough About You.
It's a Good Day.
Mañana (Is Soon Enough for Me)

Barbour, John (1316?–1395)
Before Bannockburn.
Freedom [or Fredome].
Prologue to the Avowis of Alexander.
Storys to rede ar delitabill.
Syne went thai southwart in the land.

Barclay, Alexander (1475–1552)
Eating in Hall.
Winter.

Barclay, Edwin (d. 1953)
Human Greatness.

Barcsay, Ábrahám (1742–1806)
On Sweet Coffee.
To Pál Ányos.
To The Poets.
Winter's Approach.

Bardoloi, Nirmalprabha (b. 1933)
Dawn.

Bardwell, Leland (b. 1928)
Lila's Potatoes.

Barer, Marshall (1923–98)
Beyond Compare.
Here Come the Dreamers.
On Such a Night As This.
Shall We Join the Ladies?
Very Soft Shoes.

Barford, Wanda
Sorting Things Out.

Bargen, Walter
Potato Conflicts.

Barham, Richard Harris *See* "Ingoldsby, Thomas"

Barham, Richard Harris (1788–1845)
Jackdaw of Rheims, The.

Baring, Anne
Song, The: "Beehive source."

Baring-Gould, Sabine (1834–1906)
Hymn: "Now the day is over."
Onward, Christian Soldiers.

Barkan, Stanley H.
Two Grandmas.

Barker, D. W.
Limerick: "Of attractions the Sabines ain't stinted."
Limerick: "One morning the Monarch said: 'When.'"

Barker, David
Make Your Mark.

Barker, George (b. 1913)
Channel Crossing.
Crystal, The.
Elegy V: [Separation of Man from God].
Epitaph for the Poet.
Gardens of Ravished Psyche, The.
He Comes Among.
How many apples grow on the tree?
I sent a letter to my love.
Images! Venerable as Druidical trees.
In Memory of a Friend.
Leaping Laughers, The.
Memorial Couplets for the Dying Ego.
Morning in Norfolk.
My darkling child the stars have obeyed.
My Joy, My Jockey, My Gabriel.
News of the World II.
News of the World III.
Not in the poet is the poem or.
O Golden Fleece.
O Tender under Her Right Breast.
Oak and the Olive, The.
Resolution of Dependence.
Satan Is on Your Tongue.
Section VI.
Shut the Seven Seas against Us.
Song: "Now this bloody war is over."
Sonnet of Fishes.
Sonnet to My Mother.
Summer Idyll.
Summer Song I.
To Any Member of My Generation.
To Whom Else.
Turn on Your Side and Bear the Day to Me.
Verses for a First Birthday.
Village Coddled in the Valley, The.
Wild Dreams of Summer What Is Your Grief.
Wraith-Friend, The.

Barker, Jane (1652–1727?)
Invitation to my Friends at Cambridge, An.
Necessity of Fate, The.
On the Death of My Dear Friend and Play-Fellow Mrs. E. D. Having Dream'd the Night Before I Heard Thereof that I Had Lost a Pearl.
Prospect of a Landscape, Beginning with a Grove, The.
To Dame—Augustin nun on her curious gum-work.
To Her Lover's Complaint.
To My Friends Against Poetry.
To My Young Lover.

Barker, Noah
What Does It Matter?

Barker, Shirley
There was not loveliness nor fortune there.

Barkley, Alben (1877–1956)
Limerick: "In New Orleans dwelt a young Creole."

Barkova, Anna (1901–1976)
Few Autobiographical Facts, A.
Tatar Anguish.

Barks, Coleman (b. 1937)
Becoming Milton.
So it is.

Barksdale, Clement (1609–87)
To My Nephew, J. B.

Barlow, George (b. 1948)
4½ Months: Halfway Song.
Dream of the Ring: The Great Jack Johnson, A.
In My Father's House.
Mingus Speaks: Found Poems.
Nook.
Painting Drunken Twilight.
Place Where He Arose, The.
Salt.

Barlow, Jane (1857–1917)
Christmas Rede.

Barlow, Joel (1754–1812)
Advice to a Raven in Russia [December, 1812].
Along the Banks.
But now had Hesper from the Hero's sight.
Columbiad, The.
From Mohawk's mouth, far westing with the sun.
From slavery then your rising realms to save.
From sultry Mobile's gulf-indented shore.
Hasty Pudding, The.
He spoke; and silent tow'rd the northern sky.
Judge Me, O God.
Now graceful truce suspends the burning war.
O God of My Salvation, Hear.
There reigns a prince, whose hand the sceptre claims.

Barnard, John (1681–1770)
Nations That Long in Darkness Walked.
Thrice Blest the Man.

Barnard, Mary (b. 1909)
Field, The.
Lethe.
Logging Trestle.
Pleiades, The.
Shoreline.
Solitary, The.
Static.

Barnes, Barnabe (1569–1609)
God's Virtue.
Jove, for Europa[e]s love took[e] shape of bull.
Life of Man, The.
Lovely Maya, Hermes' mother.
Mistress, Behold, in This True-Speaking Glass.
No More Lewd Lays.
O Powers Celestial, with what sophistry.
Sestina: "Then first with locks dishevelled and bare."
Sestine 4.
Soft, lovely, rose-like lips, conjoined with mine.
To the Most Beautiful Lady, the Lady Bridget Manners.
Why do I draw this coole releeving ayer.
Write! Write! Help! Help!

Barnes, Billy (fl. 1957)
Something Cool.

Barnes, Dick
Chuang Tzu and Hui Tzu.

Barnes, Djuna (1892–1982)
Portrait of a Lady Walking.
Transfiguration.
Walking-Mort, The.

Barnes, F. J. (fl. 1909)
I've Got Rings on My Fingers.

Barnes, Jane (b. 1943)
Hot Dog Poem, The.
How to Dress Like a Femmy Dyke.
How to Dress like a Scary Dyke.

Barnes, Jim (b. 1933)
American Heritage Potato, The.
Autobiography, Chapter XLII: Three Days in Louisville.
Autobiography, Chapter XVII: Floating the Big

Piney.
Autobiography: Last Chapter.
Bone Yard.
Camping Out on Rainy Mountain.
Captive Stone, The.
Four Things Choctaw.
Halcyon Days.
Heartland.
La Plata, Missouri: Clear November Night.
Last Look at La Plata, Missouri.
Lying in a Yuma Saloon.
Paiute Ponies.
Return to La Plata, Missouri.
Season of Loss, A.
Summerfield.
Sunday Dreamer's Guide to Yarrow,
    Missouri, A.
Sweating It Out on Winding Stair Mountain.
These Damned Trees Crouch.
Tracking Rabbits: Night.
Tracking the Siuslaw Man.

Barnes, Jo (b. 1941)
Clinic Day.

Barnes, Julians (*fl.* 15th cent.)
Book of Hunting.

Barnes, William (1801–86)
All Still.
Bachelor, The.
Be'mi'ster.
Bells ov Alderburnham, The.
Bit o' Sly Coorten, A.
Brisk Wind, A.
Childhood.
Clote (Water-Lily), The.
Echo, The.
Evenen in the Village.
Evening, and Maidens.
False Friends-like.
Grammer's Shoes.
Hill-Shade, The.
Jay a-Pass'd.
Jenny out from Hwome.
Leane, The.
Leaves a-Vallen.
Light or Sheade.
Lullaby.
Lwonesomeness.
Mater Dolorosa.
Musings.
My Orcha'd in Linden Lea.
Polly Be-en Upzides wi' Tom.
Rwose in the Dark, The.
Sam and Bob.
Sam'el Down vrom Lon'on.
Seasons and Times.
Shellbrook.
Shep'erd Bwoy, The.
Shop o' Meat-Weare.
Sing Again Together.
Sister Gone.
Slow to Come, Quick a-Gone.
Sonnet: "In every dream thy lovely features
    rise."
Storm-Wind, The.
Stwonen Steps, The.
Troubles of the Day.
Turnstile, The.
Uncle an' Aunt.
Vaices That Be Gone, The.
Vield Path, The.
Vierzide Chairs, The.
Walken Hwomme at Night.
When We That Now Ha' Childern Wer
    Childern.
Which Road?
White an' Blue.
Wife A-Lost, The.
Wife a-Prais'd, A.
Wind at the Door, The.
Winter Night, A.
With you first shown to me.
Wold Clock, The.
Zilver-Weed, The.
Zong, A.

Barnett, Anthony (b. 1941)
Critique.

Music of the Spheres.
Turbulence and Tongue.

Barnett, Ruth Anderson
Anorexic, The.
Taxidermist at the Zoo, The.

Barney, Natalie Clifford (1877–1972)
Habit.

Barney, Steve
Black People Cry.
Vision.

Barnfield [or Barnefield], Richard (1574–1629)
Affectionate Shepherd, The.
Beauty and majesty are fallen at odds.
But if thou wilt not pittie my complaint.
Comparison of the Life of Man, A.
Daphnis to Ganymede.
Oh would to God he would but pitty mee.
Scarce had the morning starre hid from the
    light.
Sighing, and sadly sitting by my Love.
Sometimes I wish that I his pillow were.
Sporting at fancie, setting light by love.
Sweet Corrall lips, where Nature's treasure
    lies.
Thus was my love, thus was my Ganymed.
To His Friend Master R.L., In Praise of Music
    and Poetry.
When will my May come, that I may embrace
    thee?

Barnie, John (b. 1941)
I Had Climbed the Long Slope.
Town Where I Was Born, The.

Barnstone, Aliki (b. 1956)
Mating the Goats.
To a Friend's Child.
Windows in Providence.

Barolini, Helen (*fl.* 20th cent.)
Having the Wrong Name for Mr. Wright.

Barot, Rick (b. 1969)
Portishead Suite.
Riffing.
Three Amoretti.

Barras, Jonetta (b. 1950)
Peace.

Barrax, Gerald William (b. 1933)
Adagio.
For a Black Poet.
Domestic Tranquility.
In the Restaurant.
King: April 4, 1968.
Last Letter.
Old Gory, The.
Scuba Diver Recovers the Body of a Drowned
    Child, The.
Singer, The.
Strangers Like Us: Pittsburgh, Raleigh, 1945–
    1985.
There Was A Song.
Visit.

Barreno, Maria Isabella *See* **Marias, The Three**

Barresi, Dorothy (*fl.* 20th cent.)
Back-Up Singer, The.
Called Up: Tinker to Evers to Chance.
How It Comes.
Late Summer News.
Lifting.
Nine of Clubs, Cleveland, Ohio.
Vacation, 1969.
Venice Beach: Brief Song.
When I Think About America Sometimes (I
    Think of Ralph Kramden)

Barrington, Judith
Villanelle VI.

Barrington, Patrick (b. 1908)
I Had a Duck-billed Platypus.
I Had a Hippopotamus.
Take Me in Your Arms, Miss Moneypenny-
    Wilson.

Barrios, Miguel de (1625–1701)
Epitaph: "Daniel and Abigail."

Barris, Harry
Wrap Your Troubles in Dreams.

Barry, Celia
Finding.

Barry, Jan
Floating Petals.

Green Hell, Green Death.
Harvest Moon.
In the Footsteps of Genghis Khan.
Lessons.
Nights in Nha Trang.
Nun in Ninh Hoa, A.

Barry, Lynda
I love my master I love my master.

Barsotti, Charles
Limerick: "Insurance salesman named Flint,
    An."

Bart, Lionel (1930–98)
As Long As He Needs Me.
Fings Ain't Wot They Used t'Be.
Reviewing the Situation.

Barth, John (b. 1930)
Minstrel's Last Lay, The.

Barth, R. L.
Insert, The.
Letter from An Hoc (4), by a Seedbed.
P.O.W.s.
Postscript.

Bartlett, Elizabeth (b. 1913)
Charlotte, Her Book.
Contre Jour.
God Is Dead—Nietzche.
999 Call.
Smile for Daddy.

Barton, Bernard (1784–1849)
Land Which No Mortal May Know, The.

Barton, Joan (b. 1908)
Mistress, The.

Baruch of Worms (*fl.* c.1200)
Elegy: "Those reckless hosts rush to the
    wells."

Bashir, Al-Tijani Yusuf (1912–37)
Memories of the Village School.
Tormented Mystic.

**Bashlachov [or Bashlachev], Aleksandr (1960–
    1988)**
Griboyedov's Waltz.

Basho (Matsuo Basho) (1644–94)
Airing out the robe.
All along this road.
All That Is Left.
All the field hands.
All this foolishness.
Along my journey.
Along the shore.
Among moon gazers.
Ancient pool. Sound.
Ancient silent pond.
Another year gone.
Around existence twine.
As Firmly Cemented Clam-Shells.
As for the hibiscus.
As the sound fades.
At the ancient pond.
Autumn approaches.
Autumn / Even the birds.
Autumn evening.
Autumn moon / Tide foams.
Autumn moonlight.
Autumn wind / Blasting the stones.
Autumnal full moon.
Awake at night.
Awakened at midnight.
Banana tree, The.
Bee, A.
Beginning of art, The.
Behind Ise Shrine.
Beside the road.
Blowing stones.
Breakfast enjoyed.
Bucket of azaleas, A.
Buddha's death-day / Old hands.
Bush warbler.
But for a woodpecker.
By the old temple.
Calm moon, A.
Caterpillar, A.
Cats making love.
Cedar umbrella / Off to Mount Yoshino.
Chestnut by the eaves.
Chilling autumn rains.

Cicada shell, A.
Clear water.
Clouds come and go, The.
Clouds now and then.
Clouds of blossoms.
Clouds of cherry blossoms!
Clouds, The.
Cold night: the wild duck.
Cold rain starting, A.
Come, let's go / snow-viewing.
Come out to view.
Come, see / real flowers.
Cool fall night, A.
Cool it is, and still.
Coolness.
Coolness of melons.
Cormorant fishing / How stirring.
Crane's legs, The.
Crossing half the sky.
Crow, A.
Crow's / Abandoned nest.
Cuckoo cries, A.
Culture's beginnings.
Deep autumn.
Delight, then sorrow.
Don't imitate me.
Dozing on horseback / smoke from tea-fires.
Dragonfly, The.
Dusk.
Each year it is but a peck of rice.
Early fall.
Even in Kyoto.
Even these long days.
Exciting at first.
Exhausted, I sought.
Fall going.
Fall of night.
Farmer's roadside, The.
Felling a tree.
Field of cotton, A.
First cold rain.
First day of spring.
First snow.
First winter rain.
Fish shop.
Fishy smell, A.
Fleas, lice.
Friend sparrow, do not eat, I pray.
From all these trees.
From every direction.
Gathering.
Girl cat / So thin.
Good house.
Gray hairs being plucked.
Group of them, A.
Haiku: "Lightning flashes, The!"
Haiku: "Lightning gleam, A."
Hailstones.
Harvest moon.
Having planted a banana tree.
Heard, not seen.
Heat-lightning streak.
Heat waves shimmering.
Hollyhocks, The.
How admirable!
How cool it feels.
How reluctantly.
How rough a sea.
How very noble!
How wild the sea is.
I don't know.
I'm a wanderer.
I would like to use.
In the fish shop.
In the old stone pool.
It's not like anything.
It would melt.
Jars of octopus, The.
Journey's end / Still alive.
June rain / hollyhocks turning.
Kannon's tiled temple.
Lead my pony.
Life in this world.
Lightning.
Lightning flash.
Lightning-gleam, A.
Lightning in the clouds!

Lonely pond in age-old stillness sleeps, A.
Lonely silence.
Long conversations.
Long rains, The.
Lovely spring night, A.
Many, many things.
Many nights on the road.
Melon / In morning dew.
Midfield.
Midnight frost.
Misty rain.
Monk sips morning tea, A.
Moonlight slanting.
Moor / Point my horse.
More than ever I want to see.
Morning glories, The.
Morning glory also, The.
My summer robes.
No rice—In that hour.
No sign.
Not this human sadness.
Nothing in the cry.
Now I see her face.
O cricket, from your cheery cry.
Oak tree, The.
Old men, white-haired, beside the ancestral
    graves.
Old pond—a frog jumps in, kerplunk, The.
Old pond: / frog-jump-in.
Old pond, / frog jumps in.
Old pond—frogs jumped in—sound of water.
Old pond / Leap-splash.
Old pond, The.
Old pond / The sound, An.
Old-time pond, from off whose shadowed
    depth, An.
On a journey, ill.
On a withered branch.
On Buddha's birthday.
On Buddha's deathday.
On New Year's Day.
On the cow shed.
On the way to the outhouse.
On this road / no one will follow me.
Only for Morning Glories.
Peasant's child, The.
Petal shower, A.
Pine mushroom.
Plates and bowls.
Ploughing the land.
Polished and polished.
Quick-falling dew.
Roadside thistle, eager, The.
Sad beauty?
Sad nodes.
Sea darkening, The.
Searching storehouse eaves.
Seas slowly darken.
Seeing people off.
Seen in plain daylight.
She cat, The.
Shrieking plovers / Calling darkness.
Sick on a journey.
Sick on a journey / Over parched fields.
Sick on my journey.
Sickly.
Singing, flying, singing.
Singing, planting rice.
Skylark.
Smell of autumn / Heart longs.
Snowy morning, A.
Solitary, A.
Some of them with staves.
Spider.
Spring!
Spring going.
Spring moon.
Spring rain.
Spring we don't see, The.
Squid seller's call, The.
Staying at an inn.
Still alive.
Still old pond, The.
Stillness.
Such stillness.
Summer grass.
Summer grasses.

Summer grasses / All that remains.
Summer grasses grow, The.
Taking a nap.
Teeth sensitive to the sand.
Temple bell / A cloud of cherry flowers.
Temple bell stops, The.
That great blue oak.
There is the old pond!
They don't live long.
This autumn.
This bright harvest moon.
This dark autumn.
This first fallen snow.
This hot day swept away.
This old village.
This road.
This ruined temple.
Though I'm in Kyoto.
Through frozen rice fields.
Tired.
To the capital / Snow-clouds forming.
To the willow.
Tomb, bend / To autum wind.
Traveling this high.
Tremble, oh my gravemound.
Ungraciously, under.
Very brief.
Village where they ring, A.
Village without bells, A.
Visting the graves.
Warbler sings, The.
Water-drawing rites.
Weathered bones.
Weathered skeleton, A.
Well, let's go.
Wet with morning dew.
What fish feel.
What voice.
When I looked under the hedge.
When the winter chrysanthemums go.
Whitebait, The.
Whore and monk, we sleep.
Wild sea, A.
Winter garden.
Winter leeks,The.
Winter rain.
Winter seclusion.
Winter showers.
Winter solitude.
Winter storm, The.
Winter sun, The.
Wintry day / On my horse.
Wintry wind.
With a warbler for.
With dewdrops dripping.
With plum blossom scent.
Withered grass / Under piling.
Within your life and mine.
Worshipping at the Great Shrine At Ise.
Wrapping dumplings in.
Wrapping the rice cakes.
Year after year.
Year's end / All corners.
Year's end / Still in straw hat.
You could turn this way.
You've heard monkeys crying.
Your song caresses.

Bass, Franta (1930–44)
    Garden, The.
    Home.
    I am a Jew.
    Illness.
    Old House, The.

Bass, Rick
    Odyssey, The.

Basse [or Bas], William (*fl.* c.1602)
    Angler's Song, The.

Bassui Tokusho (d. 1387)
    Look straight ahead. What's there?

Bassus [or Bassos] (Lollius Bassus) (*fl.* A.D. 1st
cent.)
    I am not going to turn into gold.
    I'm not planning to turn into gold. Somebody
    else.
    I refuse to turn into gold.
    Your flatteries are boring.

Bastard, Thomas (1566–1618)
Ad Henricum Wottonem.
De Naevo in Facie Faustinae.
Epitaph: Iohannis Sande.
In Gaetam.

Basu, Rām (1738–1812)
How are you faring, Uma.
I had a good dream last night.

Basu Rāy, Śyāmāpad
Three Kalis appeared in Daksinesvar.

Basualto, Neftalí Ricardo Reyes *See* **Neruda, Pablo**

Bat-Miriam, Yocheved (b. 1901)
Distance Spills Itself, The.
Like This before You.
Monasteries Lift Gold Domes, The.
Precious stones that my mother.
Sound of the waves in the silence, The.

Bateman, Edgar (1860–1946)
Cockney's Garden, The.
It's a Great Big Shame.

Bateman, Meg
Lightness.

Bates, Charles
Hard-Hearted Hannah (The Vamp of
Savannah)

Bates, Clara Doty (1838–95)
At Grandfather's.
Gray Thrums.

Bates, David (c.1810–1870)
Speak Gently.

Bates, Katharine Lee (1859–1929)
America the Beautiful.
Despised and Rejected.
Even as this Globe Shall Gleam and Disappear.

Bateson, Thomas
I Heard a Noise and Wishèd for a Sight.

Batizi, András (c.1510–50)
Remembrance of Death.

Batsányi, János (1763–1845)
Encouragement.
Hungarian Writer, The.
On the Changes in France.
Rhythm Is Only a Servant.
Seer, The.

Battiss, Walter (1906–82)
Limpopo.

Baudelaire, Charles (1821–67)
Albatross, The.
Autumn Song.
Beauté, La.
Blind, The.
Carcass, A.
Carrion, A.
Cats.
Clock, The.
Correspondences.
Cracked Bell, The.
Damned Women.
Don Juan in Hell.
Élévation.
Epilogue: "With heart at rest I climbed the
citadel's."
Fuses I and II.
Giantess, The.
Gypsies on the Move.
Harmonie du Soir.
Harmony of Evening, The.
Head of Hair.
Her Hair.
Intimate Associations.
Invitation to the Voyage.
Inward Conversation.
Jewels, The.
L'Invitation au Voyage.
Le Balcon.
Les Hiboux.
Litany to Satan.
Meditation.
Owls.
Parfum Exotique.
Peace, Be at Peace, O Thou My Heaviness.
Possessed.
Sed non satiata.
Seven Old Men, The.

Snake that Dances, The.
Song of Autumn I.
Spleen LXXV.
Spleen LXXVI.
Spleen LXXVII.
Spleen LXXVIII.
Swan, The.
To the Reader.
Voyage, The.
Voyage to Cythera, A.
Voyaging.
Way her silky garments undulate, The.
Which One Is Genuine?

Baudri of Bourgueil (1046–1130)
Your Appearance is Pleasing.

Bauer, Grace
Oldies But Goodies.
She Calms the Savage Beast with Her Aubade.
So You Want to Hear the Blues.

Baugh, Edward (b. 1939)
Carpenter's Complaint, The.
Nigger Sweat.

Baughan, Blanche Edith (1870–1958)
Logs, at the door, by the fence; broadcast over
the paddock.
Old Place, The.
Toward the dawn.

Baum, Peter (1869–1916)
Horror.
Psalms of Love.

Baumel, Judith (b. 1956)
Let Me In.
Samuel.
Snow-Day.
To the Parents of a Childhood Friend, a
Suicide.

Bawer, Bruce (b. 1956)
Grand Central Station, 20 December 1987.
On Leaving the Artists' Colony.
View from an Airplane at Night, over
California, The.

Bax, Clifford (1886–1962)
Turn Back, O Man.

Baxter, Charles (b. 1947)
Diptych: Jesus and the Stone.
Dog Kibble: A Villanelle.
Purest Rage, The.

Baxter, Elizabeth
In Your Absence.

Baxter, James Keir (1926–72)
Apple Tree, The.
Ballad of the Stonegut Sugar Works.
Bar Room Conversation.
Bay, The.
Bees that have been hiving above the church
pond, The.
Brother Ass, Brother Ass, you are full of
fancies.
Buried Stream, The.
Colin, you can tell my words are crippled now.
Dark Welcome, The.
Dentist's Window, A.
East Coast Journey.
Evidence at the Witch Trials.
Family Photograph 1939, A.
Firemen, The.
From an old house shaded with macrocarpas.
Haere Ra.
Harry Fat and Uncle Sam.
I am dying now because I do not die.
In Auckland it was the twelve days' garland.
In the Lecture Room.
Lazarus.
Mandrakes for Supper.
Morning and Evening Calm.
New Zealand.
News from a Pacified Area.
Obsequy for Dylan Thomas.
On the Death of Her Body.
Private Conference of Harry Fat, The.
Rata blooms explode, the bow-legged tomcat,
The.
Small grey cloudy louse that nests in my
beard, The.

Spider crouching on the ledge above the sink,
The.
Spring Song of a Civil Servant.
Thief and Samaritan.
To a Print of Queen Victoria.
To wish to climb a ladder to the loft.
Twenty Little Engines.
Virginia Lake.
When I was only semen in a gland.
Wild Bees.
Yesterday I planted garlic.

Baxter, Richard (1615–91)
Good Shepherd, The.
Now it belongs not to my care.
Resolution, The.
Ye holy Angels bright.

Bayer, Konrad (1932–64)
Electrical Hierarchy, The.
White and Black Bones, The.

**"Baylebridge, William" (Charles William
Blocksidge) (1883–1942)**
Quiet moon, immaculate of face, The.

Bayliss, John Clifford (b. 1919)
Apocalypse and Resurrection.
Reported Missing.
Seven Dreams.

Bayly, Thomas Haynes (1797–1839)
Novel of High Life, A.
Out, John.
We Met.

Baynes, A. H.
Limerick: "So obese is my cousin from
Hendon."
Limerick: "There was a young girl from a
Mission."

Baytelman, Shlomit
My Name is Shlomit.

Beach, Luci
2 Months Rent Due and 1 Bag of Rice.

Beach, Seth Curtis (1837–1925)
Mysterious Presence! Source of All.
Thou One in All, Thou All in One.

"Beachcomber" *See* **Morton, John Bingham**

Beadle, Samuel Alfred (1857–1932)
Words.

Beardsley, Aubrey (1872–98)
Ballad of a Barber, The.
Three Musicians, The.

**Beatrice [*or* Beatritz *or* Beatriz], Countess de Die
[*or* Dia] (*fl.* late 12th cent.)**
Handsome friend, charming and kind.
Lately I've felt a grave concern.
Lover's Prize, A.
My true love makes me happy.

Beattie, James (1735–1803)
Edwin, The Minstrel.
Epitaph, An: "Like thee I once have stemm'd
the sea of life."
To Mr. Alexander Ross.
Youth of a Poet, The.

Beatty, Paul (b. 1962)
Doggin the Rockman.
Gription.
I Know You Are, But What Am I?
Independent Study.
New York Newsday: Truth, Justice and Vomit.
Stall Me Out.
That's Not in My Job Description.
Why That Abbott and Costello Vaudeville
Mess Never Worked with Black People.

Beaumont, Francis (1584–1616)
Letter to Ben Jonson, A.
Masque of the Inner Temple and Gray's Inne,
The.
On the Tombs in Westminster Abbey, *sels.*
Upon Master Edmund Spenser.

Beaumont, Francis (1584–1616) *and* **John
Fletcher**
Captain, The, *sels.*
Knight of the Burning Pestle, The, *sels.*
Lore's Cure, *sels.*
Maid's Tragedy, *sels.*
Queen of Corinth, *sels.*

Beaumont, Isobel (b. 1589, d. after 1607)
Poor Bess Turpin, I pytty thy case as farr as I

can.

Beaumont, John (1583–1627)
In Desolation.

Beaumont, Sir John (1583–1627)
Of My Dear Son [or Deare Sonne], Gervase
Beaumont.

Beaumont, John (1583–1627)
Of the Epiphany.

Beaumont, Sir John (1583–1627)
Upon a Funeral.

Beaumont, Sir John (1583–1627)
Description of Love, A.

Beaumont, Joseph (1616–99)
Cheat, The.
Garden, The.
Gentle Check, The.
Gnat, The.
Hourglass, The.
Love's Mystery.
Morning Hymn.
Whiteness, or Chastity.

**Beauveau, Marie-Françoise-Catherine de,
Marquise de Boufflers (1711–86)**
Air: Sentir avec Ardeur.

Beaver, Bruce (b. 1928)
Angels' Weather.
Day 20.
Déjeuner Sur l'Herbe.
Drummer, The.
Entertainer, The.
Folk Song: "O I'm off to Hullaboola where the
climate's never cooler."
Letters to Live Poets.
More than 9 Lives.
Silo Treading.
Three images of dying stick in my mind like
morbid transfers.

Beck, Julian (1925–85)
State Will Be Served Even By Poets, The.

Beck, Thomas (fl. 1780–1820)
Sonnet to Nothing.

Becker, Charlotte
Door-Bell, The.

Becker, Edwin (d. 1925)
Mother's Day.

Becker, Robin
Bath, The.
Crypto-Jews, The.
Dog-God.
Dreaming at the Rexall Drug.
Grief.
History of Sexual Preference, A.
In Pompano Beach, Florida.
Late Words for My Sister.
Life Forms.
Medical Science.
Midlife.
Monarchs of Parque Tranquilidad.
Near Sheridan.
On the Eve of the Warsaw Uprising.
Peter Pan in North America.
Sad Sestina.
Sonnet to the Imagination.
Spiritual Morning.
Story I Like to Tell, The.
Why We Fear the Amish.
Yom Kippur, Taos, New Mexico.

Beckett, Samuel (1906–89)
Alba.
Cascando.
Dieppe.
Echo's Bones.
Enueg I.
Enueg II.
Gnome.
Imagination Dead Imagine.
Malacoda.
My way is in the sand flowing.
Ooftish.
Roundelay: "On all that strand."
Saint-Lô.
Something There.
Song: "Age is when to a man."
What is the Word.
What would I do without this world faceless

incurious.

Beckford, William (1759–1844)
Elegiac Sonnet to a Mopstick.

Beckman, Joshua (b. 1971)
Lament for the Death of a Bullfighter.

Bécquer, Gustavo Adolfo (1836–70)
Arrow Flying Past, An.
As the Breeze that Cools the Blood.
Black Swallows Will Return, The.
Dark in a Corner of the Room.
Darkling Swallows Will Come Again, The.
Gentle Breeze with a Whispered Cry, The.
Great Waves Breaking with a Roar.
I Am Ardent, I Am Brunette.
I Know a Strange, Gigantic Hymn.
I Lay Awake, Wandering in that Limbo.
Into Her Eyes a Tear Crept.
Invisible Atoms of the Air, The.
It Goes Against My Interest to Confess It.
Nameless Spirit.
Sighs Are Air, and Go to the Air.
They Closed Her Eyes.
To See the Hours of Fever.
When They Told Me I Felt the Cold.
Where Do I Come From?

Beddoes, Thomas Lovell (1803–49)
And what's your tune?
Another.
Crocodile, A.
Death Sweet.
Dream-Pedlary.
Fair and bright assembly: never strode, A.
Fantastic Simile, A.
Humble Beginnings.
Hymn: "And many voices marshalled in one
hymn."
Lake, A.
Old Adam, the Carrion Crow.
Phantom-Wooer, The.
Resurrection Song.
Song by Isbrand.
Song: "How many times do I love thee, dear?"
Song on the Water.
Song: "Strew not earth with empty stars."
Sonnet: To Tartar, a Terrier Beauty.
To Night.
To Silence.

Bede, The Venerable (c.672–c.735)
Bede's Death Song.
Hymn: "Hymn of glory let us sing, A."
Prayer of the Venerable Bede.

Bedford, Madeline Ida
Munition Wages.

Bedient, Cal (b. 1935)
When the Gods Put on Meter.

**"Bedny [or Bednyi], Demyan [or Dem'ian]"
(Efim Alekseyevich Pridvorov) (1883–1945)**
Main Street.

Bedregal, Yolanda (b. 1916)
Gestures From My Window.
Intact Pitcher.
Martyrdom.
Night, I Know All About You.
Nocturne of Hope.
Pointless Journey.
Poppies.

Beeching, Henry Charles (1859–1919)
Going Down Hill on a Bicycle.
Knowledge after Death.
Prayers.

Beedome, Thomas (d. 1641?)
Petition, The.
Question and Answer, The.
To the Noble Sir Francis Drake.

Beeks, Clarence King Pleasure
Parker's Mood.

Beer, Christina (b. 1945)
1974—The Sounds.
Fox Glove Song.
Waiheke 1972—Rocky Bay.

Beer-Hofmann, Richard (1866–1945)
Aging.
Evil Man, An!
Jacob's Destiny.
Lullaby for Mirjam.

Beer, Morris Abel (1887?–1936)
Church in the Heart, The.

Beer, Natalie
My Vorarlberg.

Beer, Patricia (b. 1924)
Ballad of the Underpass.
Birthday Poem from Venice.
Christmas Carols.
Christmas Eve.
Christmas Tree, The.
Creed of Mr. Nicholas Culpeper.
Dilemma.
Dream of Hanging, A.
Faithful Wife, The.
Flood, The.
Footbinding.
Gallery Shepherds.
Grave Doubts.
In a Country Museum.
In the Cathedral.
Jane Austen.
Jane Austen at the Window.
John Milton and My Father.
Leaping into the Gulf.
Lemmings.
Letter, The.
Lion Hunts.
Middle Age.
Millennium.
Ninny's Tomb.
Postilion Has Been Struck by Lightning, The.
Witch.

Beerbohm, Max (1872–1956)
Addition to Kipling's "The Dead King
(Edward VII), 1910."
After Hilaire Belloc.
Ballade Tragique à Double Refrain.
Brave Rover.
Chorus of a Song That Might Have Been
Written by Albert Chevalier.
Elegy on Any Lady by George Moore.
Epitaph for G. B. Shaw.
In a Copy of More's (or Shaw's or Wells's or
Plato's or Anybody's) Utopia.
Luncheon, A.
On the Imprint of the First English Edition of
"The Works of Max Beerbohm."
Police Station Ditties.
Prayer, A: "If I popped in at Downing Street."
Same Cottage—But Another Song, of Another
Season.
Sonnet to the "Most Distinguished Chancellor"
that Oxford Has Had.
Thomas Hardy and A. E. Housman.
Time, you thief, who love to get.
Vague Lyric by G. M.
When pears hang green on the garden wall.

Beers, Ethel Lynn (1827–79)
All Quiet along the Potomac Tonight.
Weighing the Baby.

Beeson, Jane
Bald head with the fringe, The.

Beevers, John (1911–75)
Atameros.

Begay, Shonto (b. 1954)
Mother's Lace.

"Beginner, Lord" See **Moore, Egbert**

Begley, T.
Sappho's Gymnasium.

Behar, Ruth
Jewish Cemetery in Guanabacoa, The.
Survivals.

Behn, Aphra (1640–89)
And Forgive Us Our Trespasses.
Angellica's Lament.
Cabal at Nickey Nackey's, The.
Congratulatory Poem to Her Sacred Majesty
Queen Mary, Upon Her Arrival in
England, A.
Defiance, The.
Disappointment, The.
Dream, The.
Epitaph on the Tombstone of a Child, the Last
of Seven That Died Before.
In a cottage by the mountain.

In Imitation of Horace.
Love's Witness.
Not to sigh and to be tender.
Oh, How the Hand the Lover Ought to Prize.
On a Juniper Tree, Cut Down to Make Busks.
On Desire A Pindarick.
On Her Loving Two Equally.
On Mr. Dryden, Renegade.
On the Death of the Late Earl of Rochester.
Paraphrase on Oenone to Paris, A.
Pindaric on the Death of our Late Sovereign: with an Ancient Prophecy on His Present Majority, A.
Rover or The Banished Cavaliers, The.
Silvio's Complaint: A Song, To a Fine Scotch Tune.
Song: "Ah false Amyntas, can that hour."
Song: "All joy to mortals, joy and mirth."
Song: "Curse upon that faithless maid, A."
Song: "I led my Silvia to a grove."
Song: Love Armed [or Arm'd].
Song: "Oh! Love, that stronger art than wine."
Thousand Martyrs I Have Made, A.
To Alexis in Answer to His Poem Against Fruition.
To Damon. To Inquire of Him if He Cou'd Tell Me by the Style, Who Writ Me a Copy of Verses that Came to Me in an Unknown Hand.
To Lysander.
To Mrs. W. on Her Excellent Verses.
To My Lady Morland at Tunbridge.
To the Fair Clarinda [or Clorinda], Who Made Love to Me, Imagined [or Imagin'd] More Than Woman.
Verses Design'd By Mrs A. Behn to be Sent to a Fair Lady, that Desir'd She Would Absent Herself to Cure Her Love.
What has poor Woman done, that she must be.
When you love, or speak of it.

Behn, Harry (1898–1973)
Circles.
New Little Boy, The.

Beissel, Henry (b. 1929)
In the one-two domestic goose one-two one-two step.

Beissel, Johann Conrad (1690–1768)
Sun Now Risen, The.

Bejerano, Maya
From morning slumber a stir a shift a spinning motion of tossing.
I Made a New Memory for You.
In a slick, black bodysuit Job stood before me.
Interlude.
It has all begun with still waters.
Job: I was cast onto a new life cycle.
Noon. 12:45 already.
Oh spare me, spare me.
States of War.
Suddenly I was stabbed from behind.

Bek, Tatiana (b. 1949)
I breathed my fill—and then breathed out.
If a song flies to me from the garden.
Oh life, long as an epic.

Belford, Ken (b. 1946)
Carrier Indians.
Turn (a Poem in 4 Parts)

Belieu, Erin
At St. Sulpice.
Choose Your Garden.
Erections.
How the Elderly Drive.
Legend of the Albino Farm.
Lovely.
Man Who Tried to Rape You, The.
My Field Guide.
Nocturne: My Sister Life.
Part of the Effect of the Public Scene Is to Importune the Passing Viewer.
Radio Nebraska.
Rondeau at the Train Stop.
Sleeping Man Must Be Awakened to Be Killed, A.
Your Character is Your Destiny.

Belitt, Ben (b. 1911)
Kites: Ars Poetica.

Orange Tree, The.

Belknap, Jeremy (1744–98)
Far from Our Friends.
Thus Spake the Saviour.

"Bell, Acton" See **Brontë, Anne**

Bell, Ann
This is my work so.

Bell, Carol
Lying in Small Pieces.
Where Hope Lives.

"Bell, Currer" See **Brontë, Charlotte**

"Bell, Ellis" See **Brontë, Emily Jane**

Bell, James Madison (1826–1902)
Though Tennyson the Poet King.

Bell, Juanita
Indian Children Speak.

Bell, Julian (1908–37)
Redshanks, The.

Bell, Martin (1918–78)
Footnote to Enright's "Apocalypse."
Reason for Refusal.
Senilio Passes, Singing.
Senilio's Weather Saw.
Winter Coming On.
With a Presentation Copy of Verses.

Bell, Marvin (b. 1937)
Being in Love.
Book of the Dead Man #1, The.
Book of the Dead Man #43, The.
Book of the Dead Man #58, The.
Book of the Dead Man #87, The.
Communication of His Thirtieth Birthday.
Dew at the Edge of a Leaf.
Drawn by Stones, by Earth, by Things That Have Been in the Fire.
Extermination of the Jews, The.
Getting Lost in Nazi Germany.
How I Got the Word.
Israeli Navy, The.
Marco Polo.
Mystery of Emily Dickinson, The.
Perfection of Dentistry, The.
Primer about the Flag, A.
Self and the Mulberry, The.
Slow.
Someone Is Probably Dead.
Sounds of the Resurrected Dead Man's Footsteps #15.
Street Fair: The Quartet.
These Green-Going-to-Yellow.
Things We Dreamt We Died For.
To Be.
To Dorothy.
True Story, A.
Wednesday.
What They Do to You in Distant Places.
White Clover.
Who I am is a short person with small feet.

Bell, William (1924–48)
Elegy: "Tonight the moon is high, to summon all."
Young Man's Song, A.

Belleau, Remy [or Remi] (1528–77)
April.

Bellerby, Frances (1899–1975)
Bereft [or Bereaved] Child's First Night.
Clear Shell, A.
Inconclusive Evening, An.

Belli, Carlos German (b. 1928)
Down with the Money-Exchange.
Father, Mother.
My Parents, Know It Well.
Poem: "Our love is not found in our respective."
Segregation #1.
Unknown Voice, An.
Why Have They Moved Me.

Belli, Gioconda (b. 1948)
Birth.
Blood of Others, The.
Brief Lessons in Eroticism 1.
Nicaragua Water Fire.

Belli, Giuseppe Gioacchino (1791–1863)
Greed.
Revenge 1.

What Might Have Been.

Bellinger, Alfred Raymond
Bright as a single poppy in a field.

Bellman, Carl Michael (1740–1795?)
Fredman's Epistle No. 23.

Belloc, Joseph Hilaire Pierre (1870–1953)
A stands for Archibald who told no lies.
Almighty God, Whose Justice Like a Sun.
B stands for Bear. When bears are seen.
Ballade of Hell and of Mrs. Roebeck.
Big Baboon, The.
Bison, The.
But how much more unfortunate are those.
Charles Augustus Fortescue.
Child, Do Not Throw This Book About.
Discovery.
Dreadful Dinotherium he, The.
E stands for egg.
Early Morning, The.
Epitaph on the Favourite Dog of a Politician.
Epitaph on the Politician Himself.
Evenlode, The.
False Heart, The.
Fatigue.
First in his pride the orient sun's display.
Franklin Hyde.
Frog, The.
Ha'nacker Mill.
Henry King, Who Chewed Bits of String, and Was Early Cut Off in Dreadful Agonies.
Her Faith.
Hippopotamus, The.
I am a sundial. Ordinary words.
I am a sundial, turned the wrong way round.
Imitation.
Is there any reward?
Jim Who Ran Away from His Nurse, and Was Eaten by a Lion.
Juliet.
Justice of the Peace, The.
K for the Klondyke, a country of gold.
Lines to a Don.
Lion, The.
Llama, The.
Lord Finchley.
Lord Heygate.
Lord Hippo.
Lord Lucky.
Lord Lundy.
Love and Honour.
Matilda.
Maxim Gun, The.
Night, The.
Noël.
Obiter Dicta.
On a Dead Hostess.
On a General Election.
On a Puritan.
On a Sundial.
On His Books.
On Hygiene.
On Jam.
On Lady Poltagrue, A Public Peril.
On Mundane Acquaintances.
On Noman, a Guest.
Pacifist, The.
Prophet Lost in the Hills at Evening, The.
R the reviewer, reviewing my book.
Rebecca, Who Slammed Doors for Fun and Perished Miserably.
Song: "You wear the morning like your dress."
Sonnet: "We will not whisper, we have found the place."
South Country, The.
Statesman, The.
Statue, The.
Tarantella.
This, the last ornament among the peers.
Tiger, The.
To Dives.
Viper, The.
Vulture, The.
West Sussex Drinking Song.
World's a Stage, The.
Yak, The.

Bely [or Belyi], Andrey [or Andrei] (Boris Nikolaevich Bugayev) (1880–1934)
By-street was bathed in sun, The.

Despair.
Beman, Nathan S. S. (1785–1871)
　Jesus, I Come to Thee.
Ben-Lev, Dina (b. 1964)
　Broken Helix.
　Sensualist Speaks on Faith, A.
Bendall, F. W. D. (1882–1953)
　Outposts.
Bendall, Molly (fl. 20th cent.)
　After Estrangement.
　Book of Sharp Silhouettes, The.
　Conversation with Isadora Duncan.
　Fete on the Lake.
　Matinée Idylls.
　Need for Shoes, The.
　Painter of Destinies, A.
"Bendo, Brian"
　Dream, The.
Benedetti, Mario (b. 1920)
　We All Conspire.
　With Your Permission.
Benedikt, Michael (b. 1937)
　Divine Love.
　European Shoe, The.
　Eye, The.
　Fate in Incognito.
　Some Feelings.
　Some Litanies.
　Thoughts.
Benét, Rosemary and **Stephen Vincent Benét**
　Hernando De Soto.
　John Quincy Adams.
　Nancy Hanks.
　Peregrine White and Virginia Dare.
　So we march into the present.
　Western Wagons.
Benét, Stephen Vincent (1898–1943)
　1935.
　American Names.
　Ballad of William Sycamore, The.
　Congressmen Came Out to See Bull Run, The.
　Cotton Mather.
　Daniel Boone.
　For All Blasphemers.
　For City Spring.
　He was a farmer, he didn't think much of
　　towns.
　Hymn in Columbus Circle.
　Invocation: "American muse, whose strong and
　　diverse heart."
　John Brown's body lies a-mouldering in the
　　grave.
　John Brown's Prayer.
　King David.
　Litany for Dictatorships.
　Love Came By from the Riversmoke.
　Metropolitan Nightmare.
　Nightmare at Noon.
　Nightmare Number Three.
　Nonsense Song, A.
　Rain after a Vaudeville Show.
　So we march into the present.
　Song of the Riders.
　Western Wagons.
　Winged Man.
Benét, Stephen Vincent See **Benét, Rosemary**
Benét, William Rose (1886–1950)
　Brazen Tongue.
　Eternal Masculine.
　Fawn in the Snow, The.
　Horse Thief, The.
　Inscription for a Mirror in a Deserted
　　Dwelling.
　Jesse James.
　Merchants from Cathay.
　Night.
　Sagacity.
　Whale.
　Woodcutter's Wife, The.
Beneyto, Maria (b. 1925)
　Nocturne in the Women's Prison.
Benford, Lawrence (b. 1946)
　Beginning of a Long Poem on Why I Burned
　　the City, The.
Benjacob, Isaac (1801–63)
　Epitaph, An: "Here lies Nachshon, a man of

great renown."
Benjamin, Bennie
　Oh! What It Seemed to Be.
Benjamin, Park (1809–64)
　Press On.
Benlowes, Edward (1603?–76)
　Pleasures of Retirement, The.
Benn, Gottfried
　Before a Cornfield.
　Bunch of Drifter Sons Hollered, A.
　Cycle.
　Fragments.
　Little Aster.
　Man and Woman Go Through the Cancer
　　Ward.
　Monologue.
　Night Café.
　Quaternary.
　This Is Bad.
Bennani, Ben (b. 1946)
　Camel's Bite.
　Letters to Lebanon.
Bennard, George (1873–1958)
　Old Rugged Cross, The.
Bennett, Alan (b. 1934)
　Place-Names of China.
Bennett, Anna Elizabeth (b. 1914)
　Hush Thee, Princeling.
Bennett, Arnold (1867–1931)
　Limerick: "There was a young man of
　　Montrose."
　Love Affair, A.
Bennett, Bruce (b. 1940)
　Experience, The.
　Leader.
　True Story of Snow White, The.
Bennett, Charles
　I live alone where echoes roost.
Bennett, Gwendolyn B. (1902–81)
　Advice.
　Fantasy.
　Hatred.
　Heritage.
　Secret.
　Sonnet—2: "Some things are very dear to me."
　Song: "I am weaving a song of waters."
　To a Dark Girl.
　To Usward.
Bennett, Henry Holcomb (1863–1924)
　Flag Goes By, The.
Bennett, John (1865–1956)
　Her Answer.
　In a Rose Garden.
　Tiger Tale, A.
Bennett, Louise (b. 1919)
　Colonization in Reverse.
　Independance.
Bennett, Rodney
　Windy Nights.
Bennett, Rowena Bastin (b. 1896)
　Gingerbread Man, The.
　Smoke Animals.
　Witch of Willowby Wood, The.
　Witch of Willowby Wood, The.
Bennis, Mohammad (b. 1948)
　Belonging to a New Family.
　Second Coming, The.
Benseki (d. 1728)
　Child of the way.
Benserade, Isaac de (fl. c.1650)
　Translation of Lines by Benserade.
Bensko, John (b. 1949)
　Bones of Lazarus.
　Butterfly Net, The.
　Last Look in the Sambre Canal, A.
Bensley, Connie (b. 1929)
　Bloomsbury Snapshot.
　Charity.
　Desires.
　One's Correspondence.
　War Games.
Benson, Arthur Christopher (1862–1925)
　Ant-Heap, The.
　Phoenix, The.

Benson, Gerard
　Ben Barley.
　Cat and the Pig, The.
　Limerick: "I'm in love with a girl from
　　Uttoxeter."
　Limerick: "'Is it thou?' 'Ay,' cries Fra Lippo
　　Lippi."
　Limerick: "There once was a bard of Hong
　　Kong."
　Limerick: "There was a young princess, Snow-
　　White."
　Limerick: "While Dubliner leopold bloom
　　sought solace."
　Play No Ball.
　Probatioun Officeres Tale, The.
Benson, Leticia R. (b. 1963)
　Asante.
　P Word Poem, The.
Benson, Louis FitzGerald (1855–1930)
　O Love That Lights the Eastern Sky.
　O Risen Lord upon the Throne.
　O Thou Whose Feet Have Climbed Life's Hill.
　Why Linger Yet upon the Strand?
Benson, Robert Hugh (1871–1914)
　Lab Lines.
Benson, Stella (1892–1933)
　Frost.
　Now I Have Nothing.
Benson, Steve
　As sincerely as possible.
　Beaten Track, The.
　Beethoven's Sixth Symphony.
　Blue Book 18 Pages 1–4.
Bentley, Edmund Clerihew (1875–1956)
　After dinner Erasmus.
　Art of Biography, The.
　"Dinner-time?" said Gilbert White.
　George III.
　How vigilant was Spenser.
　I am not Mahomet.
　Intrepid Ricardo, The.
　J. S. Mill.
　Lord Clive.
　"No," said Charles Peace.
　"No, sir," said General Sherman.
　Savonarola.
　Sir Christopher Wren.
　Sir Humphry Davy.
　"Susaddah!" exclaimed Ibsen.
　There exists no proof as.
　When their lordships asked Bacon.
　Wynkyn de Worde.
Bentley, Elizabeth (1767–1839)
　On Education, December 1789.
Bentley, Nelson (d. 1990)
　Iron Man of the Hoh.
Bentley, Nicolas (1907–78)
　Cecil B. De Mille.
　Londonderry Air, The.
　On Lady A———.
Bently, Samuel (fl. 1760s)
　River Dove: a Lyric Pastoral, The.
Benton, Suzanne
　Lilith.
　Second Coming, The.
Benttinen, Ted
　Maritime Pastoral.
Béranger, Pierre Jean de (1780–1857)
　King of Yvetot, The.
Beranová, Jana
　Mother's Mark.
　Williamsbridge.
Berberova, Nina Nikolaevna (b. 1901)
　Eagles & butterflies (and some other things)
　I Remain.
　To Shakespeare.
Berchan (fl. 8th cent.)
　Fort of Rathangan, The.
Berditshev, Isaac of See **Levi-Yitzhok [or Levi-
　Isaac] of Berditchev**
Bereng, David Granmer T.
　Birth of Moshesh, The.
Berenguer, Amanda
　Housework.

Signs on the Table, The.
Beresford, Ann (b. 1919)
Courtship, The.
Berezan, Jennifer
Hail Mother full of grace power is with thee.
Berg, Stephen (b. 1934)
Desnos Reading the Palms of Men on Their
Way to the Gas Chambers.
May 1970.
Nostalgia.
On This Side of the River.
Orpingalik's My Breath: Eskimo Song.
Prayer: "Nobody understands so let the Rabbi."
Ten fussy days running this temple all red tape.
Berger, Bruce (b. 1938)
Ambition.
Ballad of the Bright Angel.
Haunts of the Mirage.
Misconstrued, The.
Photo Safari.
Plagiarist, The.
Salad Days.
Silver-Paced.
Stout Brahms.
To Answer Your Question.
Transmigration.
Trophy Homes.
Without.
Berger, Donald
Dinner in the Sun.
Language Pile, The.
Lincoln Bedroom, The.
Berger, Jacqueline (b. 1960)
Between Worlds.
Getting to Know Her.
Gun, The.
Berggolts [or Bergholts], Olga Fiodorovna (1910–75)
Blockade Swallow, The.
Conversation with a Neighbor.
Don't turn around, don't look back.
Friends repeat: "All means are good."
Indian Summer.
Infidelity.
My Country.
My insatiable memory is like.
Ordeal, The.
To My Sister.
To Song.
Wish, A.
You took me, hostile, sullen.
Bergman, Alan (b. 1925)
Summer Me, Winter Me.
Way We Were, The.
Windmills of Your Mind, The.
Bergman, Alexander (1921–41)
Chronicler, The.
Letter.
Bergman, David (b. 1950)
Blueberry Man.
Bergman, Marilyn (b. 1929)
Summer Me, Winter Me.
Way We Were, The.
Windmills of Your Mind, The.
Bergner, Zekharye Khone See "Ravitch, Melech"
Berke, Judith
Dancing to the Track Singers at the Nightclub.
Fifties Rock Party, 1985.
Berkeley, George (1685–1753)
On the Prospect of Planting Arts and Learning
in America.
Berkeley, Gina
Limerick: "Calculus fit to compute on, A."
Limerick: "Last Christmas, when Puss was in
Boots."
Limerick: "Mr. Rochester's wife's pyromania."
Limerick: "'Princess,' said the Frog, 'Do not
wince.'"
Limerick: "When Ireland was bloody and
leaderless."
Ratatouille.
Berkeley, Sara (b. 1967)
Learning to Count.
Mass is Over, The.
Parting, The.

Berkeley, Sir William (1606?–1677)
Song: "Where did you borrow that last sigh."
Berkson, Bill (b. 1939)
Melting Milk.
Rebecca Cutlet.
Russian New Year.
Berlin, Eric
Sea World.
Berlin, Irving
Alexander's Ragtime Band.
Always.
Blue Skies.
Change Partners.
Cheek to Cheek.
Couple of Swells, A.
Easter Parade.
Fools Fall in Love.
Heat Wave.
How Deep Is the Ocean? (How High Is the
Sky?)
I Got Lost in His Arms.
I Got the Sun in the Morning.
I've Got My Love to Keep Me Warm.
Isn't This a Lovely Day (To Be Caught in the
Rain?)
It's a Lovely Day Today.
Let Me Sing and I'm Happy.
Let's Face the Music and Dance.
Let's Have Another Cup of Coffee.
Little Things in Life, The.
Manhattan Madness.
Oh! How I Hate to Get Up in the Morning.
Pack Up Your Sins and Go to the Devil.
Pretty Girl Is Like a Melody, A.
Puttin' on the Ritz (Original Version)
Puttin' on the Ritz (Revised Version)
Remember.
Say It Isn't So.
Slumming on Park Avenue.
Song Is Ended (But the Melody Lingers On),
The.
Supper Time.
There's No Business Like Show Business.
They Say It's Wonderful.
This Is the Army, Mr. Jones.
Top Hat, White Tie, and Tails.
What'll I Do?
When the Midnight Choo-Choo Leaves for
Alabam'
White Christmas.
You Can't Get a Man with a Gun.
You'd Be Surprised.
You're Just in Love.
You're Laughing at Me.
Berman, Cassia
Deep inside me at my core.
Mother Lakshmi's Poem.
Poem for the Shechina.
Bernard, April
Praise Psalm of the City-Dweller.
See It Does Rise.
Bernard, Artis
Snowfall.
**Bernard [or Bernart] de Ventadour [or
Ventadorn] (c. 1145–1180)**
Can Vei La Lauzeta Mover.
Chantars No Pot Gaire Valer.
Good time of the year, The.
Joy! a heart so overflowing.
Lark, The.
Men, a word of wisdom. Give.
No Marvel Is It.
To see the lark, delighted, dare.
When—presto—turf and trees are green.
Bernard of Clairvaux (1091–1153)
Jesus, Thou Joy of Loving Hearts.
Wide Open Are Thy Loving Hands.
Berners, Dame Juliana (b. 1388?)
Properties of a Good Greyhound, The.
Bernie, Ben (fl. 1925)
Sweet Georgia Brown.
Bernlef, J. (b. 1937)
Beatrice.
Disconcerting Object.
Uncle Charles: A Home Movie.

Bernstein, Carole (b. 1960)
Caught.
Cup of Coffee, The.
Profaning the Dead.
When My Grandmother Said "Pussy"
Bernstein, Charles (Henk Marsman) (b. 1950)
Age of Correggio and the Carracci, The.
By absorption I mean engrossing, engulfing.
Dysraphism.
Freud's Butcher.
From Lines of Swinburne.
Gradation.
Intersection, The.
Kiwi Bird in the Kiwi Tree, The.
Klupzy Girl, The.
Loose Shoes.
Matters of Policy.
Memories.
Of Time and the Line.
Outrigger.
Poem: "Here. Forget."
Take Then, These.
Virtual Reality.
Wait.
Whose Language.
Bernstein, J. B.
Tango'd Love.
Bernstein, Leonard
America.
Conga.
Gee, Officer Krupke.
I Can Cook, Too.
Little Bit in Love, A.
Lonely Town.
Lucky to Be Me.
New York, New York.
Some Other Time.
Bernstein, Marion (fl 1876)
Manly Sports.
Berrigan, Anselm
Advice to a Young Philosopher.
Bloodletting.
Four Minute History of Getting It Together in
Order to Be Fabulous, Briefly, A.
Looking Up My Balance.
Mercy Flight.
Ode to Election Day.
Sabotage.
Short History of Autumn, A.
Various Multitudes Contained by the Loves of
My Love, The.
Berrigan, Daniel (b. 1921)
But God is Silent / Psalm 114.
Crucifix, The.
My Name.
Prayer.
Rehabilitative Report: We Can Still Laugh.
Berrigan, Ted (1934–83)
Academy of the future is opening its doors,
The.
Bean Spasms.
(Clarity! clarity!) a semblance of motion,
omniscience.
Dear Margie, hello. It is 5:15 a.m.
Final Sonnet, A.
Go fly a kite he writes.
It is a human universe: & I.
It is night. You are asleep. And beautiful tears.
Kirsten.
Mud on the first day (night, rather.
Now she guards her chalice in a temple of fear.
& Now the book is closed.
Orange Jews.
Où sont les neiges des neiges?
People of the Future.
Personal Poem #9.
Poem upon the page is as massive as, The.
Real Live.
Sonnet: "My dream a drink with Lonnie
Johnson we discuss the code."
Sonnet I: "His piercing pince-nez. Some dim
frieze."
Sonnet III: "Stronger than alcohol, more great
than song."
Sonnet LV: "Grace to be born and live as
variously as possible."

Sonnet LXX: "Sweeter than sour apples flesh to boys."
Sonnet XXXIV: "Time flies by like a great whale."
Sonnet XXXIV: "Time flies by like a great whale."
Sonnet XXXV: "You can make this swooped transition on your lips."
Sonnet XXXV: "You can make this swooped transition on your lips."
To gentle, pleasant strains.
We remove a hand.
Words for Love.

Berry, David Chapman (b. 1947)
On Reading Poems to a Senior Class at South High.
Sun goes.

Berry, James (b. 1924)
Benediction.
Girls Can We Educate We Dads?
I am cuddle-shaped and freckled.
Lucy's Letter.
One.
Sounds of a Dreamer.
Such a peculiar lot.

Berry, Wendell (b. 1934)
Getting Away: Verses and Choruses for Various Voices.
Let Us Pledge.
Mad Farmer, Flying the Flag of Rough Branch, Secedes from the Union, The.
Music, A.
Old Man Climbs a Tree, The.
Our Christmas Tree.
Peace of Wild Things, The.
Ripening.
Slip, The.
Wild Geese, The.
Wild, The.

Berryman, John (1914–72)
Again, his friend's death made the man sit still.
Alcoholic.
Alcoholic in the 3rd Week of the 3rd Treatment, The.
Also I love him: me he's done no wrong.
American Lights, Seen from Off Abroad.
April Fool's Day, or St. Mary Egypt.
Astronomies and slangs to find you, dear.
At Henry's bier let some thing fall out well.
Ball Poem, The.
Bats have no bankers and they do not drink.
Boston Common.
Canto Amor.
Carpenter's Son, The.
Certainty Before Lunch.
Chilled in this Irish pub I wish my loves.
Deprived of his enemy, shrugged to a standstill.
Dispossessed, The.
Dream Song 8.
Dream Song 14.
Dream Song 26.
Dream Song 29.
Dream Song 45.
Dream Song 55.
Dream Song 61.
Dream Song 255.
Dream Song 384.
Dry Eleven Months.
Elegy for W.C.W., the Lovely Man, An.
Eleven Addresses to the Lord.
4th Song.
4th Weekend.
5th Tuesday.
Gislebertus' Eve.
Go, ill-sped book, and whisper to her or.
Governor your husband lived so long, The.
Grandfather, sleepless in a room upstairs.
Group.
He lay in the middle of the world, and twitcht.
He Resigns.
Henry by Night.
Henry's Confession.
Henry's Fate.
Henry's mind grew blacker the more he thought.

Henry's pelt was put on sundry walls.
Henry's Understanding.
Henry sats in de bar and was odd.
How this woman came by the courage, how she got.
Huffy Henry hid the day.
I am, outside. Incredible panic rules.
I can't get him out of my mind, out of my mind.
I have moved to Dublin to have it out with you.
I'm cross with god who has wrecked this generation.
I'm scared a lonely. Never see my son.
I trundle the bodies, on the iron bars.
I've found out why, that day, that suicide.
Ill lay he long, upon this last return.
Irish have the thickest ankles in the world, The.
King David Dances.
Lauds.
Lay of Ike, The.
Love her he doesn't but the thought he puts.
Master of beauty, craftsman of the snowflake.
Moon and the Night and the Men, The.
Nothing there? nothing up the sky alive.
O all your ages at the mercy of my loves.
Of Suicide.
Parting as Descent.
Phase Four.
Poet's Final Instructions, The.
Professor's Song, A.
Recognition, The.
Sabbath.
Scholars at the Orchid Pavilion, The.
Seedy Henry rose up shy in de world.
So Long? Stevens.
Sole watchman of the flying stars, guard me.
Some good people, daring and subtle voices.
Sometimes the night echoes to prideless wailing.
Song of the Tortured Girl, The.
Sonnet 115: "All we were going strong last night this time."
Sonnets.
Strut for Roethke, A.
Supreme my holdings, greater yet my need.
Sympathy, a Welcome, A.
That dark brown rabbit, lightness in his ears.
That's enough of that, Mr Bones. *Some* lady you make.
This world is gradually becoming a place.
Three 'coons come at his garbage. He be cross.
Three limbs, three seasons smashed; well, one to go.
Thunder & the flaw of their great quarrel, The.
Thurn, A.
To My Father.
Traveller, The.
Turning it over, considering, like a madman.
Washington in Love.
Welcome, grinned Henry, welcome fifty-one!
When by me in the dusk my child sits down.
Winter Landscape.
Winter-Piece to a Friend Away, A.
Winters close, Springs open, no child stirs, The.
You couldn't bear to grow old, but we grow old.
Your face broods from my table, Suicide.

Bersohn, Robert
Dignity of Labor, The.

Berssenbrugge, Mei-Mei (b. 1947)
Alakanak Break-Up.
Chronicle.
Constellation Quilt, The.
Duration of Water.
Jealousy.
Spring Street Bar.
Swan, The.
Tan Tien.
Texas.

Bertken [or Bertke], Sister (Bertha Jacobs) (1427–1514)
Ditty: "I went into my garden to gather some herbs."
When I went into my garden, I found.

Bertolino, James
American Poetry.
Baying, The.
See Willow.
Snail River.

Bertrand, Aloysius (1807–1841)
Mason, The.

Bertrans [or Bertran or Bertrand] de Born (fl. 12th cent.)
In Praise of War.
Perigord pres del muralh, A.
Protestation.
Sirventes.
Song of Battle.

Berwick, Thurso (b. 1919)
Idleset: "Ill's the airt o the Word the day."

Berzsenyi, Dániel (1776–1836)
Approaching Winter, The.
Horace.
Hungary.
My Portion.
Philosophy of Life.
Prayer: "Oh, God, beyond the wit of the genius."
Solitude.
To Napoleon.
To the Hungarians: "Oh you, once mighty Hungary, gone to seed."
To the Hungarians: "Seas of Sorrow boil with a rage, Magyar, The."
Unfinished Letter to My Lady.

Beshenkovskaya [or Beshenkovskaia], Olga (b. 1947)
In a land whose prosperity constantly grows.
Old Russia's slavery rights. Boiler room.
Night.

Bessenyei, György (1747?–1811)
György Bessenyei to Himself.
Morning Splendour of the Tisza, The.

Best, C. F.
Limerick: "Said a pupil of Einstein: 'It's rotten.'"

Betham-Edwards, Matilda Barbara
In a Letter to A.R.C. on Her Wishing to Be Called Anna.
Power of Women, The.
To a Llangollen Rose, the Day after It Had Been Given by Miss Ponsonby.
Urge me no more! nor think, because I seem.
Written on Whitsun-Monday, 1795.

Bethel, Marion (b. 1953)
Reggae Prophecy.

Bethell, Mary Ursula ("Evelyn Hayes") (1874–1945)
9th July, 1932.
Decoration.
Detail.
Discipline.
Elect.
Erica.
Fortune.
Hour is dark. The river comes to its end, The.
Long Harbour, The.
Midnight.
Pause.
Response.
Sauntering home from church we lingered.
Spring Snow and Tui.
That bridge from the city, that was Waimakariri.
Time.
Warning of Winter.

Bethune, George Washington (1805–62)
Jesus, Shepherd of Thy Sheep.
O for the Happy Hour.
There Is No Name So Sweet on Earth.

Bethune, Lebert (b. 1937)
For Singing In Good Mood.
Harlem Freeze Frame.
Today Tutu Is Beating the Same Burru As Me.

Betjeman, Sir John (1906–84)
Advent 1955.
Archaeological Picnic, The.
Arrest of Oscar Wilde at the Cadogan Hotel, The.

Ballad of George R. Sims, The.
Before the Anæsthetic; or, A Real Fright.
Blame the Vicar.
Business Girls.
Christmas.
City.
Death in Leamington.
Death of King George V.
Devonshire Street W.1.
Diary of a Church Mouse.
East Anglian Bathe.
Executive.
False Security.
Felixstowe, or, The Last of Her Order.
Flight from Bootle, The.
Green shutters, shut your shutters! Windyridge.
Hike on the Downs, A.
House of Rest.
How to Get On in Society.
Hunter Trials.
Huxley Hall.
In a Bath Teashop.
In Memory of Basil, Marquess of Dufferin and
  Ava.
In Westminster Abbey.
Incident in the Early Life of Ebenezer Jones,
  Poet, 1828, An.
Inevitable.
Invasion Exercise on the Poultry Farm.
Ireland with Emily.
Licorice Fields at Pontefract, The.
Limerick: "G'uggery G'uggery Nunc."
Longfellow's Visit to Venice.
Lord Cozens Hardy.
Meditation on the A30.
Metropolitan Railway, The.
Middlesex.
My dear deaf father, how I loved him then.
Myfanwy.
NW5 and N6.
Old Land Dog, The.
On Seeing an Old Poet in the Café Royal.
Our Padre.
Parliament Hill Fields.
Potpourri from a Surrey Garden.
Remorse.
Reproof Deserved; or After the Lecture.
Senex.
Shropshire Lad, A.
Slough.
St. Saviour's, Aberdeen Park, Highbury,
  London, N.
Subaltern's Love-Song, A.
Summer.
Sunday Afternoon Service in St. Enodoc
  Church, Cornwall.
Sunday Morning, King's Cambridge.
Tea with the Poets.
Undenominational.
Upper Lambourne.
Westgate-on-Sea.
Youth and Age on Beaulieu River, Hants.
Betsugen (1294–1364)
All night long I think of life's labyrinth.
Bettarini, Mariella (b. 1942)
Biography.
Epilogue (At the Proper Distance)
Fragment for the Mother.
Holm Oak, The.
I Say That the Cricket the Scorpion the
  Grasshopper.
If Nature Bellows.
In That Moment When the Body Drowns.
Let Us Love As We Choose: Water.
My home (did you know?)—my home.
Name, The.
There Is Only One Almighty.
Bevan, Maggie
Confrontation with a Bouquet.
Beveridge, Judith (b. 1956)
Catching Webs.
Dining Out.
Domesticity of Giraffes, The.
In the Park.
Bevington, Helen Smith (b. 1906)
Mrs. Trollope in America.

Mr. Rockefeller's Hat.
Penguins in the Home.
Bevington, Louisa Sarah (1847–1895)
Afternoon.
Am I to Lose You?
Dreamers?
'Egoisme à Deux.'
Measurements.
Midnight.
Morning.
One More Bruised Heart!
Twilight.
With the Tide: A Cry of Weakness.
Wrestling.
Bewe (fl. c.1576)
I Would I Were Actaeon.
Bewick, Elizabeth
Black my beginning.
Beyer, Tony (b. 1948)
Island Waters.
Beznos, Fanny (1907–1940s)
I Go, the Wind Pushing Me Along.
PURITY! PURITY! PURITY!
**Bezymensky [or Bezymenskii], Alexander Ilyich
  (1898–1973)**
About a Hat.
Village and Factory.
Bhāndārī, Śāradā
Ma, You are Brahmani in the world of Brahma.
Menaka says, Hey listen, Mountain King.
Bharati, Subramania (1898–1921)
Wind, 9.
Bhartrihari (fl. c.500)
Apathy Is Ascribed to the Modest Man.
Bald-Headed Man, A.
Bearing the lustre of a full moon.
In former days we'd both agree.
Man May Tear a Jewel, A.
Peace.
She Who Is Always In My Thoughts.
Sweet Maid.
Time.
While His Body's Vigor Is Whole.
Bhatt, Sujata (b. 1956)
Different History, A.
Go To Ahmedabad.
Looking Up.
Muliebrity.
Stinking Rose, The.
Understanding the *Ramayana*.
What Is Worth Knowing?
White Asparagus.
You ask me what I mean.
Bhattācārya, Āśutos
Get up, get up, Mountain: no more sleep for
  you!
Bhattācārya, Kamalākānta (c.1769–1821)
Bee of my mind, The.
Consulting the omens.
Crazy Mind.
Ever-blissful Kali.
External rituals mean nothing.
From her autumn-lotus mouth.
From now on.
Go, my Lord of the Mountains.
Hara came and made off with my Gauri.
Here, Queen of the Mountains.
Hey, Hara, Ganges-Holder.
Hey, Mountain King, Gauri is sulking.
How can that black woman be so beautiful?
How could you have forgotten her.
How will You rescue me, Tara?
I know, I know, Mother.
Is my black Mother Syama really black?
Jaya, tell him that Uma will not be sent.
Kali / Is everything You do misleading?
Kali! / Today in the dark grove.
Kali, what family are You from?
Kali, you have removed all my difficulties.
King of the Mountains is on his way to Hara's
  abode, The.
Mother / You're always finding ways to amuse
  Yourself.
My Gauri / You've come home!
My Uma has come!

Other than Your two red feet, Syama.
Queen asks, The.
So, forgetful Mahadeva.
Stay within yourself, Mind.
Tara, Mother / Lift me out by the hair.
Tell me, Syama.
Tell me / What can I do?
Turn back, Uma.
Unperturbed at the battle.
What a dream I had last night!
What happened? / The ninth night is over.
What's the fault of the poor mind?
Who can describe the waves of Mother
  Syama's world?
Who is this.
Who is this enchantress.
Withered tree doesn't blossom, The.
You ask me, Queen, time after time.
Bhattācārya, Mahendranāth (1843–1908)
Come, brothers, everyone together.
Everyone's flocking to Gajan.
I've gone mad drinking nectar.
Look at all these waves.
Ma, are you really dead?
Oh Ma Kali, for a long time now.
Screening its face amongst lotus stalks.
Tell me, what are you doing now, Mind.
There's a huge hullabaloo in my lotus heart.
What shall I say to You, Sankari?
You can't catch the thief, Mind.
Your behavior proves how stingy You are, Ma.
Bhavani, V. Indira (b. 1942)
Avatars.
**Bialik, Hayyim Nahman [or Khayim Nakhman
  or Chaim Nachman] (1873–1934)**
Alone.
And If the Angel Should Ask.
At Day's End.
At Twilight.
Beneath Thy Wing.
City of Slaughter, The.
Dance of Despair, The.
Dead of the Wilderness, The.
Death of David, The.
Do not.
Graveyard, The.
I Have a Garden.
If Thou Wouldst Know.
If you found my heart's scroll in the dust.
Mathmid, The.
Midnight Prayer.
My Soul Sinks.
Night.
Only a single ray, but suddenly.
Orphanhood.
Pool, The.
Prophet, Go, Flee!
Queen Sabbath.
Should I Be a Rabbi?
Songs of the People.
Stars Are Lit, The.
Stars shine and go out.
Summer is dying in the purple and gold and
  russet.
Summer Night.
Sunset.
Talmud Student, The.
Throbs the Night with Mystic Silence.
When the Days Shall Grow Long.
Whence and Whither.
Young Acacia, The.
Bialoszewski, Miron (b. 1922)
Ballad of Going Down to the Store, A.
Bianor (b. late 1st cent. B.C.)
House fell head-first, quietly crushing all but a
  child, The.
In the clear water by the beach.
Sardis, the old city of Gyges and Alyattes.
This man: this no-thing: vile: this brutish slave.
Bibb, Eloise (Eloise Bibb Thompson) (1878–1927)
Anne Boleyn.
Belshazzer's Feast.
Capt. Smith and Pocahontas.
Catharine of Arragon.
Charmion's Lament.
Class Song of '91.

Destiny.
Early Spring.
Eliza in Uncle Tom's Cabin.
Expulsion of Hagar, The.
Gerarda.
Hermit, The.
Imogene.
In Memoriam Frederick Douglass.
In Memory of Arthur Clement Williams.
Judith.
Leona, dear, twelve months ago.
Lines to Mrs. M. C. Turner.
Lines to the Hon. George L. Knox.
Ode to the Sun.
Offering, An.
Sonnet: "O thou who never harbored fear."
Tale of Italy, A.
Tribute.
Vestal Virgin, The.
Wandering Jew, The.

Bibbins, Mark
Bluebeard.
Counting.
Geometry Class.
Mud.
Pathology of Proximity, The.
Whitman on the Beach.

Bibby, Cyril
Limerick: "Musical maiden from Frome, A."

Bible, Apocrypha
All flesh waxeth old as a garment.
Blessed Is God.
By his commandment hee maketh the snow to
 fall apace.
Dirge: "Her house is become like a man
 dishonored."
Great Mourning.
Jeremie .17.
Judas Maccabeus.
Music.
O Death.
Our Fathers.
Path of Wisdom, The.
Steel Usurps the Forests; Silence Dethrones
 Dialogue.
Test of Men, The.
With Timbrels.

Bible, N.T.
Aa this while, Peter wis doun ablò i the yaird.
And he said, So is the kingdome of God.
And he said, So soule doth magnifie the Lord.
And it came to pass in those days, that there
 went out a decree from Caesar Augustus.
And seeing the multitudes, he went up.
Beatitudes, The.
Blessed be the Paps which Thou hast Sucked.
Feare not, litle flocke, for it is your fathers
 good pleasure to give you the kingdome.
I am the true vine, and my Father is the
 husbandman.
In the beginnin o aa things the Wurd wis there
 ense.
In the end of the sabbath, as it began to dawn
 toward the first day of the week.
John 3; But Men Loved Darknesse Rather than
 Light.
Luke 7; She Began To Wash His Feet with
 Teares and Wipe Them with the Haires of
 Her Head.
Magnificat, The.
No man can serve two masters.
Parable of the Good Seed, The.
Spirit saith, come, The.
Then drew near unto him all the publicans and
 sinners.
Then one of the twelve, called Judas Iscariot.
When morning has come, all the chief priests
 and elders of the people.

Bible, O.T.
Affliction.
All Flesh Is Grass.
And God saw that the wickedness of man was
 great.
And Joseph was brought down to Egypt.
And Noah was six hundred years old when the
 flood of waters.

And the whole earth was of one language, and
 of one speech.
As a Seal upon Thy Heart.
As a servant earnestly desireth the shadow, and
 as an hireling looketh for the reward of his
 work.
As apple tree among the trees of wood.
As Fowlers Lie in Wait.
Balaam's Blessing.
Behold, thou art fair.
Blessed above women / shall Jael the wife of
 Heber the Kenite be.
But Fear Thou Not, O Jacob.
But in the last days it shall come to pass.
Cast thy bread upon the waters.
Comfort ye, comfort ye my people.
Cry of the Daughter of My People, The.
Cursed Be the Day.
David's Lament.
Desolation in Zion.
Drunkard, The.
Each inmost peece in me is thine.
Fear of the Lord, The.
For the Lordes parte is his folke.
For Thus saith The Lord to the men of Judah
 and Jerusalem.
For Zion's Sake.
Genesis.
Give Ear, Ye Heavens.
Give me all the kisses of your mouth.
Go to the Ant [Thou Sluggard].
Gods boundles bownties gods promise ever
 abyding.
Hannah's Song of Thanksgiving.
Hannah's Thanksgiving.
Happy he who has found wisdom.
Happy Is the Man.
Hark! My Beloved!
Hear, O my people, and I will speak.
Hear the Word of the Lord.
How beautiful are thy feet with shoes.
How Beautiful upon the Mountains.
How doth the city sit solitary that was full of
 people.
How lovely are thy tabernacles.
I am come into my garden, my sister, my
 spouse.
I am come into my garden, my sister, my
 spouse.
I Am My Beloved's.
I am the first and I am the last.
I Am the Rose of Sharon.
I have been brought into darkness.
I Return unto Zion.
I Sleep, but My Heart Waketh.
I was drowsy, but my heart was awake. Listen!
I Waste Away.
In the beginning God created the heaven and
 the earth.
In the End of Days.
Inscription on the Liberty Bell.
Israel, My Servant.
It Is Better.
Job.
Job Cries Out.
Jonah's Prayer.
Joseph, being seventeen years old, was feeding
 the flock with his brethren.
Knowest thou the time when the wild goates of
 the rocke bring forth?
Lamentation.
Legacy, The.
Let Me Sing of My Well-beloved.
Let the Day Perish [Wherein I Was Born].
Let us synge unto the Lorde, for he is become
 glorious.
Leviathan.
Messiah, The.
Misery of Jerusalem, The.
Moreover the Lord answered Job, and said.
My beloved spake, and said unto me.
My love has gone down to his garden.
My love is white and ruddy.
My Thoughts Are Not Your Thoughts.
Naomi and Ruth.
Neither Poverty nor Riches.
Not Flesh of Brass.

O Lord, Thou Hast Enticed Me.
O Ye That Would Swallow the Needy.
Oh That I Were in the Wilderness.
On My Bed I Sought Him.
Open Thy Doors, O Lebanon.
Out of the Whirlwind.
Psalms, sels.
Remember Now Thy Creator.
Return, Return, O Shulammite.
Rod of Jesse, The.
Scribes have cast the blame, The.
See, the smelle of my sone is as the smell of a
 feld.
She of the Impudent Face.
Song: "At night on my bed I longed for."
Song: "Come, my beloved."
Song: "I am dark, daughters of Jerusalem."
Song: "I was asleep but my heart stayed
 awake."
Song of Deborah, The.
Song of Solomon, The [or The Song of
 Songs].
Song of the Harlot.
Song of the Suffering Servant, The.
Song of the Well.
Sound of my lover, The.
Then Job spoke and cursed his day and
 chanted and said.
Then Sang Moses.
Then the Lord answered Job out of the
 whirlwind.
Thy Mother Was like a Vine.
To Everything There Is a Season.
Too Wonderful.
Valley of Dry Bones, The.
Vanity of vanities, saith the Preacher, vanity of
 vanities; all is vanity.
Watchman, What of the Night?
Whom Shall One Teach.
Wildernesse and the solitarie place shall be
 glad for them, The.
Wing of the ostrich rejoiceth, The.
Woe Is Me!

Bible, Pseudepigrapha
Enoch.
Seven Metal Mountains.

Bickerstaffe, Isaac (c.1735–c.1812)
Expostulation, An.
There was a jolly miller once.
What a charming thing's a battle!

Bidart, Frank (b. 1939)
Another Life.
Confessional.
Elegy.
Ellen West.
For the Twentieth Century.
Golden State.
Happy Birthday.
Sacrifice, The.
Self-Portrait.
To the Dead.

Bidgood, Ruth (b. 1922)
All Souls'
Banquet.
Burial Path.
Chimneys.
Dragon.
Hawthorn at Digiff.
Little of Distinction.
Old Pump-house, Llanwrtyd Wells.
Safaddan.
Standing Stone.

Bielski, Alison (b. 1925)
Intruder.
Token.

Bienek, Horst (b. 1930)
Exodus.
Our Ashes.
Resistance.
Vorkuta.

Bierbaum, Otto Julius (1865–1910)
Blacksmith Pain.
Jeannette.
Kindly Vision.
Oft in the Silent Night.

Bierce, Ambrose (1842–c.1914)
Alone.

Bierds
Body-Snatcher.
Confederate Flags, The.
Corporal.
Death of Grant, The.
Don't steal. Thou'lt never thus compete.
Egotist.
Elegy: "Cur foretells the knell of parting day, The."
Freedom.
General B. F. Butler.
Gorgon.
Hesitating Veteran, The.
Hypochondriasis.
Lead.
Nose.
Orthography.
Passing Show, The.
Prospect.
Rimer.
Safety-Clutch.
Statesmen, The.
To E. S. Salomon.
To the Bartholdi Statue.

Bierds, Linda
After-Image.
Depth of Field.
Lawrence and Edison in New Jersey: 1923.
Vespertilio.

Biespiel, David (b. 1964)
After the Wedding.
Heat Sours, The.
Lilacs.
There Were No Deer in the Thicket.
Tower.
Under a Blossoming Plum Tree.
White Roses.

Big Boy, Marla
I Will Bring You Twin Grays.

Big Eagle, Duane (b. 1946)
Traveling to Town.

Bigelow, Bob
Hard-Hearted Hannah (The Vamp of Savannah).

Bigelow, Marion Albina (fl. 1850)
Come, lowly ones, and take your places now.
Two Smothered Children.

Bigg, J. Stanyan (1825–65)
Irish Picture, An.

Biggar, H. Howard
Your Neighbor.

Biggs, Carrie
Chair That Is Filled, The.

Bihari
All day she studies her new.
As if to lift my babe-in-arms.
Loveliness beyond words.
What she said to her companion.
When I found her in the bathing pool.

Bilal (fl. c.600)
Muhammedan Call to Prayer.

Bilhana (fl. 11th cent.)
Black Marigolds.
Even now.
Fantasies of a Love-Thief.

Billinger, Richard
Soldier's Betrothed, The.
We Peasants.

Billings, William (1746–1800)
Let Tyrants Shake Their Iron Rod.

Bingen, Hildegard von (1098–1197)
Alleluia-verse for the Virgin.
Antiphon for Divine Wisdom.
Antiphon for the Angels.
Antiphon for the Holy Spirit.
Earth is at the same time mother, The.
Holy Spirit, / giving life to all life.
Hymn to St. Maximinus, A.
I am the one whose praise.
Like the honeycomb dropping honey.
O crimson blood.
Song to the Creator.

Binney, Thomas (1798–1874)
Eternal Light!

Binyon, Laurence (1869–1943)
Beauty.

For the Fallen.
Harebell and Pansy.
House That Was, The.
Hunger.
Invocation to Youth.
Little Dancers, The.
Nothing Is Enough.
Now is the time for the burning of the leaves.
Song, A: "For mercy, courage, kindness, mirth."
Statues, The.
They went with songs to the battle, they were young.
Tristram's End.
Winter Sunrise.

Bion (c.315–255 B.C.)
Dream of Venus, A.
Lament for Adonis.

Biran, Paddy
Paddy Biran's Song.

Bird, Bessie Calhoun (b. 1906)
Proof.

Bird, Dolly (b. 1950)
Can I Say.

Bird, Harold *See* Littlebird, Harold

Birken, Sigmund von (1626–81)
Shepherd-Song.

Birney, Earle (b. 1904)
Anglo Saxon Street.
Bear on the Delhi Road, The.
Bushed.
Can. Hist.
Can. Lit.
Canada: Case History: 1973.
Cartagena de Indias.
David.
El Greco: Espolio.
From the Hazel Bough.
Gray Woods Exploding, The.
Hot Springs.
Christchurch, N. Z.
Irapuato.
Museum of Man.
My Love Is Young.
Charité Espérance et Foi.
Poet-Tree.
Sestina for the Ladies of Tehuántepec.
Sinalóa.
Slug in Woods.
Small Faculty Stag for the Visiting Poet, A.
Toronto Board of Trade Goes Abroad.
Twenty-third Flight.

Bishop, Elizabeth (1911–79)
Armadillo, The.
Arrival at Santos.
At the Fishhouses.
Bight, The.
Brazil, January 1,1502.
Burglar of Babylon, The.
Casabianca.
Cold Spring, A.
Cootchie.
Crusoe in England.
Exchanging Hats.
Faustina, or Rock Roses.
Filling Station.
First Death in Nova Scotia.
Fish, The.
Florida.
From Trollope's Journal.
House Guest.
Imaginary Iceberg, The.
In the Waiting Room.
Insomnia.
Invitation to Miss Marianne Moore.
Large Bad Picture.
Letter to N.Y.
Little Exercise.
Man-Moth, The.
Manners.
Manuelzinho.
Map, The.
Monument, The.
Moose, The.
North Haven.
One Art.

Over 2000 Illustrations and a Complete Concordance.
Pink Dog.
Poem: "About the size of an old-style dollar bill."
Prodigal, The.
Questions of Travel.
Roosters.
Sandpiper.
Seascape.
Sestina: "September rain falls on the house."
Shampoo, The.
Sleeping on the Ceiling.
Some Dreams They Forgot.
Song for the Rainy Season.
Songs for a Colored Singer.
Sonnet: "Caught—the bubble."
Summer's Dream, A.
Twelfth Morning; or What You Will.
12 O'Clock News.
Unbeliever, The.
Under the Window: Ouro Prêto.
Vague Poem.
Visits to St. Elizabeths.
Washing hangs upon the line, A.

Bishop, John Peale (1892–1944)
Always, from My First Boyhood.
Hours, The.
In the Dordogne.
Metamorphoses of M.
O Pioneers!
Recollection, A.
Return, The.
Sleep Brought Me Vision.
Speaking of Poetry.
Young Men Dead.

Bishop, Morris Gilbert (1893–1973)
Adventures of Id, The.
Anatomy of Humor, The.
Bishop Orders His Tomb in St. Praxed's.
Dark Christmas on Wildwood Road, The.
Diogenes.
Fragment from "The Maladjusted: A Tragedy."
Gas and Hot Air.
How to Treat Elves.
Limerick: "At spirit séances in Queen's."
Limerick: "Lady who rules Fort Montgomery, A."
Limerick: "'I have heard,' said a maid from Montclair."
Limerick: "Limerick Is Furtive and Mean, The."
Limerick: "One-day-old baby in Wallabout, A."
Limerick: "Pushing young man in Patchogue, A."
Limerick: "Said a fervent young lady of Hammels."
Limerick: "There's a tiresome young man of Bay Shore."
Limerick: "When a feverish groom in Armenia."
My Friend the Cuckold.
Naughty Preposition, The.
Ozymandias Revisited.
Public Aid for Niagara Falls.
Sales Talk for Annie.
Song of the Pop-Bottlers.
Who'd Be a Hero (Fictional)?

Bishop, Patricia
Like the tides I rise and fall.
Woman Washing.

Bishop, Samuel (1731–95)
Epigram: "'Twas not so in my time, surly Grumio exclaims."
Epigram: "Need from excess—excess from folly growing."

Bissert, Ellen Marie (b. 1947)
Most Beautiful Woman at My Highschool Reunion, The.

Bisset, James (1762?–1832)
Next day they rambled round the town, and swore.

Bissett, Bill (b. 1939)
Christ I Wudint Know Normal if I Saw It When.

Dont Worry Yr Hair.
Th Wundrfulness uv th Mountees Our Secret Police.

Bitar, Walid
Happy Hour.

Bizet, Georges
Dat's Love (Habanera)

Bjørnson, Bjørnstjerne (1832–1910)
Boy and the Flute, The.
Fatherland Song.

Black, D. M. (b. 1941)
For and Against the Environment.
Red Judge, The.

Black Elk (1863–1950)
Everything the Power of the World Does Is Done in a Circle.

Black, Isaac J.
Racist Psychotherapy.

Black, Johnny S.
Paper Doll.

Black, Star
Blank Abandon of Beds, The.
Hoopla.
Lust.
Personals.
Rilke's Letter from Rome.
To a War Correspondent.

Blackburn, John (fl. 1944)
Moonlight in Vermont.

Blackburn, Paul (1926–71)
Assistance, The.
At the Well.
Brooklyn Narcissus.
Continuity, The.
El Camino Verde.
Encounter, The.
Hot Afternoons Have Been in West 15th Street.
Invitation Standing.
Mind returns to it always, The.
Net of Place, The.
Night Song for Two Mystics.
Once-over, The.
Park Poem.
Phone Call to Rutherford.
Problem, The.
17. IV. 71.
Sirventes.
Slogan, The.
Tides, The.

Blackburn, Thomas (1916–77)
Families.
Felo de Se.
Hospital for Defectives.
Lucky Marriage, The.
Oedipus.

Blackley, Barney
Fiery young fellow called Bryant, A.
Limerick: "Most women get married, 'tis true."

Blackmore, Sir Richard (1653–1729)
Digestive System, The.

Blackmore, Richard Doddridge (1825–1900)
Dominus Illuminatio Mea.
Heart of the Night, The.

Blackmur, Richard Palmer (1904–65)
Communiqués from Yalta, The.
Mirage.
One grey and foaming day.
Redwing.
Seas Incarnadine.
Since There's No Help.
Sunt Lacrimae Rerum et Mentem Mortalia Tangunt.

Blaeser, Kimberly M. (fl. 20th cent.)
Certificate of Live Birth.
Rituals, Yours—and Mine.

Blaga, Lucian (1895–1961)
I Will Not Crush the World's Corolla of Wonders.
Psalm.

Blagden, Isa (1816?–1873)
Alice.
To George Sand on Her Interview with Elizabeth Barrett Browning.

Blagg, Teresa
In Bed this Morning.

Blaginina, Yelena [or Elena] (1903–89)
To the Memory of G. N. Obolduyev.

Blair, Eric See Orwell, George

Blair, Robert (1699–1746)
All Impelled Onward Alike.
But see! the well-plumed hearse comes nodding on.
Grave-yard on a Stormy Night, The.
Oft in the lone church-yard at night I've seen.
Peace the End of the Good Man.
Sickly taper / By glimmering through thy low-browed misty vaults, The.

Blake, Elizabeth Jessup
Within and Without.

Blake, Eubie
Baltimore Buzz.
I'd Give a Dollar for a Dime.
I'm Craving for That Kind of Love.
I'm Just Wild About Harry.
Memories of You.
My Handy Man Ain't Handy No More.
Tan Manhattan.
You're Lucky to Me.

Blake, James W. (1862–1935)
Sidewalks of New York, The.

Blake, Marie
Barter.

Blake, William (1757–1827)
All Religions Are One.
Another [Epitaph]: "Here lies John Trot, the Friend of all mankind."
Answer to the Parson, An.
Auguries of Innocence.
Book of Thel, The.
Book of Urizen [or First Book of Urizen], The.
Caverns of the Grave [I've Seen], The.
Cradle Song, A: "Sleep, sleep, beauty bright."
Crystal Cabinet, The.
Epitaph, An: "I was buried near this dyke [or Dike]."
Everlasting Gospel, The, sels.
Gates of Paradise, The, sels.
Ghost of Abel, The.
Gnomic Verses, sels.
Grey Monk, The.
Grown old in Love from Seven till Seven times Seven.
Her Whole Life Is an Epigram.
How Sweet I Roamed [or Roam'd] from Field to Field.
I laid me down upon a bank.
I told my love I told my love.
In a Myrtle [or Mirtle] Shade.
Island in the Moon, An, sels.
Jerusalem; The Emanation of the Giant Albion, sels.
Lacedemonian Instruction.
Long John Brown & Little Mary Bell.
Love's Secret.
Mad Song.
Marriage.
Marriage of Heaven and Hell, The.
Mental Traveller, The.
Merlins Prophecy.
Milton, sels.
Mock On, Mock On, Voltaire, Rousseau.
Morning.
Mr. Cromek [or On Cromek].
Mr Cromek to Mr Stothard.
O Lapwing!
Old Maid Early, An.
On Hayley.
Orator Prigg.
Several Questions Answered, sels.
Sir Joshua Reynolds.
Smile, The.
Soft Snow.
Song: "Fresh from the dewy hill, the merry year."
Song: "Memory, hither come."
Song: "My silks and fine array."
There Is No Natural Religion.
To Autumn.
To English Connoisseurs.

To Flaxman.
To Hunt.
To Morning.
To Spring.
To the Evening Star.
To the Muses.
Vala; or The Four Zoas, sels.
Visions of the Daughters of Albion.
With Happiness Stretched [or stretched] across the Hills.

Blaker, Margaret
Pippa Passes, but I Can't Get Around This Truck.

Blamire, Susanna (1747–94)
Auld Robin Forbes.
Epistle to Her Friends at Gartmore.
From where dark clouds of curling smoke arise.
I've Gotten a Rock, I've Gotten a Reel.
North Country Village, A.
O Donald! Ye Are Just the Man.
O Jenny Dear.
Siller Croun, The.
Wey, Ned, Man!
When Home We Return.
Written on a Gloomy Day, in Sickness.

Blanchard, Edward Laman (1804–45)
Ode to the Human Heart.

Blanchard, Ferdinand Q. (1876–1968)
O Child of Lowly Manger Birth.
Word of God, Across the Ages.

Blanchard, Margaret
Before the Hunger: Megan's Blessing.

Blanco, Alberto (b. 1951)
Music in the Age of Iron.
Poem Seen in a Motel Fan.

Blanco, Richard (b. 1968)
El Malibú.
Last Night in Havana.
Letter to El Flaco on His Birthday.
Shaving.
Silver Sands, The.
Tía Olivia Serves Wallace Stevens a Cuban Egg.

Bland, Edith Nesbit See Nesbit, Edith
Bland, James A. (1854–1911)
Carry Me Back to Old Virginny.
Oh, Dem Golden Slippers!

Bland, Peter (b. 1934)
Notes for the Park Keeper.

Blandiana, Ana (b. 1942)
Couple, The.
I need only fall asleep / to return.

Blanding, Don (1894–1957)
Aloha Oe.

Blane, Ralph (1914–95)
Ev'ry Time.
Have Yourself a Merry Little Christmas.
I Never Felt Better.
Love: "Love can be a moment's madness."
Occasional Man, An.
Spring Isn't Everything.
That Face.
Trolley Song, The.

Blank, Arapera Hineira (b. 1932)
Yearning, A.

Blanvillain, Jean-Marie
(All of a Sudden) My Heart Sings.

Blaser, Robin (b. 1925)
Ah.
Even on Sunday.
Finder, The.
4 Part Geometry Lesson, A.
Herons.
Image-Nation 3.
Image-Nation 13 (the Telephone)
Image-Nation 22.
Image-Nation (the Poēsis)
Poem: "And when I pay death's duty."
Poem by the Charles River.
Poem: "For years I've heard."
Ruler, The.
Suddenly.
Universe Is Part of Ourselves, The.

Blaustein, Noah
Water and Light.

Blessing, Richard
Elegy for Elvis.
Bletsoe, Elizabeth
Weird stuff this.
Blevins, Steven (d. 1994)
New York.
Blight, John (b. 1913)
Coral Reef, The.
Cormorants.
Death of a Whale.
Down from the Country.
Evolution.
Garfish.
Gate's Open, The.
Into the Ark.
Anchor, The.
Landfall, The.
Letter, The.
Mangrove.
Morgan.
Oyster-Eaters, The.
Pearl Perch.
Sun.
Tenant at Number 9.
Blind Harry (c. 1450–93)
Sevint Buik, Lines 1029–92, The.
Blind, Mathilde (1841–96)
Beautiful Beeshareen Boy, The.
Chaunts of Life.
Entangled.
Fantasy, A.
Haunted Streets.
I charge you, O winds of the West, O.
I was again beside my Love in a dream.
I would I were the glow-worm, thou the
  flower.
Manchester by Night.
Many Will Love You.
Message, The.
Motherhood.
Mourning Women.
Noonday Rest.
On a Forsaken Lark's Nest.
Once We Played.
Reapers.
Red Sunsets, 1883, The.
Russian Student's Tale, The.
Scarabæus Sisyphus.
Sower, The.
Thou walkest with me as the spirit-light.
Winter Landscape, A.
Blishen, Edward (b. 1920)
Abroad Thoughts.
Bliss, Daniel (1740–1806)
Epitaph of John Jack.
Bliss, H. W.
Understanding.
Bliss, Philip Paul (1838–76)
Almost Persuaded.
Last Hymn.
Bliss, William
Limerick: "If no Pain were, how judge we of
  Pleasure?"
Blitzstein, Marc (1905–64)
Art for Art's Sake.
Bloch, Chana (b. 1940)
Act One.
How the Last Act Begins.
Puzzle Pieces.
White Petticoats.
Bloch, Jean-Richard (1884–1947)
Idea of a Swimmer.
Bloch, Talia N.
While Bouncing the Shema Back and Forth in
  Shul.
Blockcolski, Lew
After the First Frost.
Flicker, The.
Flint Hills, The.
49 Stomp, The.
Indian Love Song.
Langston Hughes.
My Dream.
Peyote Vision.
Playing Pocahontas.

Powwow remnants.
Reservation Special.
Urban Experience: Part One, The.
Urban Experience: Part Two, The.
Wisga.
Woyi, The.
Blocksidge, Charles William *See* **"Baylebridge,
  William"**
Blodgett, E. D. (b. 1935)
Fossil.
Snails.
Bloem, J. C. (1887–1966)
After Liberation.
Dapper Street.
Honeysuckle.
Sunday.
Writing on a Tombstone.
Bloem, Rein (b. 1932)
Amsterdam Chronicle.
Blok, Aleksandr Aleksandrovich (1880–1921)
Above the Lake.
At first she turned the whole thing to a joke.
Before the Court.
Black Night. / White snow.
Black raven in the snowy dusk.
Blizzard sweeps the streets, A.
By the North Sea.
Factory, The.
Girl was singing in the choir with fervor, A.
Gray Morning.
I want to live.
In the Dunes.
In the Restaurant.
In those far years of inertia.
Kite, The.
Making tracks.
Night: A Street.
Night, street, a lamp, a chemist's window.
Night, the street, the lamp, the drugstore, The.
On Death.
On the Islands.
On the Plain of Kulikovo.
On the Railway.
Poets, The.
Red Glow in the Sky, A.
Russia.
Scythians, The.
Sorcerer sang the spring to sleep, The.
Stranger, The.
Twelve, The.
Visitor.
Winter day is cold and snowy, The.
Blokh, Raisa (1901–43)
Random talk has blown in.
Blood, Benjamin Paul (1832–1919)
Late.
Stop!—Gaze thro' this hushed gallery! The air.
Bloom, Rube
Day In—Day Out.
Don't Worry 'Bout Me.
Give Me the Simple Life.
Good for Nothin' Joe.
Truckin'
Bloom, Valerie (b. 1956)
Sun-a-shine, Rain-a-fall.
Wha Fe Call I'.
Bloomfield, Robert (1766–1823)
Ploughman's Horse, The.
**Bloomgarden [or Bloomgarten or Blumgarden],
  Solomon** *See* **"Yehoash"**
Blount, Annabella (fl. 1700–41)
Cure for Poetry, A.
Blount, Roy, Jr. (b. 1941)
Against Broccoli.
Country Dog in the City (On a Leash, Which
  Is Bizarre Enough) Comes Upon an
  Obedience Class, A.
For the Record.
Gryll's State.
Blue Cloud, Peter (b. 1933)
Bear: A Totem Dance As Seen by Raven.
Composition.
Crazy Horse Monument.
Death Chant.
Hawk Nailed to a Barn Door.

Oche Iron.
Old Man's Lazy, The.
Rattle.
Spring Equinox.
Sweat Song.
To-ta Ti-om.
Turtle.
Walking through twisted hollow pathways.
Within the Seasons.
Wolf.
Yellowjacket.
Blumenthal, Michael C. (b. 1949)
Abandoning Your Car in a Snowstorm:
  Rosslyn, Virginia.
Back from the Word-Processing Course, I Say
  to My Old Typewriter.
Elephants Dying, The.
I Have Lived This Way for Years and Do Not
  Wish to Change.
Inventors.
Litrajure of Everyday Life, The.
Man Lost by a River, A.
Marriage, A.
Washington Heights, 1959.
Who Will Live in Our Houses When We Die?
Wishful Thinking.
Blumenthal, Walter Hart (1883–1969)
Da Silva Gives the Cue.
Blumstein [or Blaustein or Bluwstein], Rahel *See*
  "Rachel"
Blundell, G. J.
Squire Squint, shooting at a pheasant.
Blunden, Edmund Charles (1896–1974)
Almswomen.
Ancre at Hamel: Afterwards, The.
At the Great Wall of China.
Barn, The.
Behind the Line.
Come On, My Lucky Lads.
Concert Party: Busseboom.
Country God, A.
Departure.
Eastern Tempest.
Forefathers.
Giant Puffball, The.
Gouzeaucourt: The Deceitful Calm.
In Festubert.
La Quinque Rue.
Late Light.
Lonely Love.
Midnight Skaters, The.
Mole Catcher.
1916 Seen from 1921.
One among the Roses.
Poor Man's Pig, The.
Preparations for Victory.
Recovery, The.
Report on Experience.
Survival, The.
Third Ypres.
Two Voices.
Vlamertinghe.
Winter: East Anglia.
Zonnebeke Road, The.
Blunt, Wilfrid Scawen (1840–1922)
As to His Choice of Her.
Depreciating Her Beauty.
Farewell, then. It is finished. I forego.
Farewell to Juliet ("I see you, Juliet, still, with
  your straw hat")
Gibraltar.
Honour Dishonoured.
I Will Not Tell the Secrets.
Nocturne: "Moon has gone to her rest, The."
Old Squire, The.
On Her Vanity.
St. Valentine's Day.
Storm in Summer, A.
To One Who Would Make a Confession.
When I hear laughter from a tavern door.
With Esther.
Woman with a Past, A.
Wouldst thou be wise, O Man? At the knees of
  a woman begin.
Bly, Robert (b. 1926)
After the Industrial Revolution, All Things

Happen at Once.
Afternoon Sleep.
Andrew Jackson's Speech.
Anger against Children.
As a Child.
At a March against the Vietnam War.
August Rain.
Awakening.
Breath, The.
But if one of those children came near that we
  have set / on fire.
Christmas Eve Service at Midnight at St.
  Michael's.
Come with Me.
Counting Small-Boned Bodies.
Day We Visited New Orleans, The.
Dead Seal [near McClure's Beach], The.
Dream of Retarded Children, A.
Dream of William Carlos Williams, A.
Driving to Town Late to Mail a Letter.
Driving toward the Lac Qui Parle River.
Evolution from the Fish.
Executive's Death, The.
Exhausted Bug, The.
Extra Joyful Chorus for Those Who Have
  Read This Far, An.
For My Son Noah, Ten Years Old.
French Generals, The.
Gaiety of Form, The.
Great Society, The.
Hollow Tree, A.
Hunting Pheasants in a Cornfield.
In a Train.
Johnson's Cabinet Watched by Ants.
Kneeling Down to Look [or Peer] into a
  Culvert.
Leonardo's Secret.
Listening to a Cricket in the Wainscoting.
Listening to the Köln Concert.
Looking at a Dead Wren in My Hand.
Looking at a Dry Canadian Thistle Brought In
  from the Snow.
Looking at New-Fallen Snow from a Train.
Looking at Some Flowers.
Looking into a Face.
Mourning Pablo Neruda.
My Father's Neck.
My Father's Wedding.
On the Oregon Coast.
Poem against the British.
Poem against the Rich.
Poem in Three Parts.
Possibility of New Poetry, The.
Potato, A.
Prodigal Son, The.
Romans Angry about the Inner World.
Seeing the Eclipse in Maine.
Six Winter Privacy Poems.
Sleet Storm on the Merritt Parkway.
Small Bird's Nest Made of White Reed
  Fiber, A.
Snowbanks North of the House.
Snowfall in the Afternoon.
Solitude Late at Night in the Woods.
Sunday in Glastonbury.
Surprised by Evening.
Taking the Hands of Someone You Love.
Teeth Mother Naked at Last, The.
Things My Brother and I Could Do.
Thinking of "The Autumn Fields."
Those Being Eaten by America.
Three Kinds of Pleasures.
Three Presidents.
To President Bush at the Start of the Gulf War.
Turning Away from Lies.
Two Ramages for Old Masters.
Visiting Emily Dickinson's Grave with Robert
  Francis.
Waking from Sleep.
Watching Television.
Water under the Earth.
When the Dumb Speak.
Written Forty Miles South of a Spreading City.

Blyth, Moira
  First of all people was Adam, The.

Boake, Barcroft Henry (1866–92)
  Allegory, An.
  At Devlin's Siding.
  Digger's Song, The.
  Where the Dead Men Lie.

Bobis, Merlinda
  Driving to Katoomba.
  Word Gifts for an Australian Critic.

Bobrowski, Johannes (1917–65)
  Dead Language.
  Elderblossom.
  In the Torrent.
  Kaunas 1941.
  Latvian Autumn, The.
  Latvian Songs.
  Novgorod: Coming of the Saints.
  Place of Fire.
  Pruzzian Elegy.
  Volga Towns, The.
  When the Rooms.
  Woodland God.

Bobrowsky, Igor
  Free Fire Zone.
  Journey, The.

**Bobyshev, Dmitry [or Dmitrii] Vasil'evich (b.
  1936)**
  Indifference.
  Other World, The.
  Return.
  Trotsky in Mexico.
  White Peacock, The.

Boccaccio, Giovanni (1313–75)
  Inscription for a Portrait of Dante.
  Of Fiammetta Singing.
  Of His Last Sight of Fiammetta.
  Of Three Girls and of Their Talk.
  To Dante in Paradise, after Fiammetta's Death.
  To One Who Had Censured His Public
    Exposition of Dante.
  Two Dreams, The.

Bock, Jerry
  If I Were a Rich Man.
  (I'll Marry) the Very Next Man.
  Little Tin Box.
  Matchmaker.
  She Loves Me.
  Sunrise, Sunset.
  Tonight at Eight.
  Too Close for Comfort.

Bodecker, N. M. (b. 1922)
  Cats and Dogs.
  First Snowflake.
  Garden Calendar.
  Hurry, Hurry, Mary Dear!
  Miss Bitter.
  Mr. 'Gator.
  Mr. Slatter.
  One Year.
  Radish.
  Small Rains.
  Snowman Sniffles.
  When Skies are Low and Days are Dark.

Bodel, Jean (fl. c.1200)
  Les Congés du Lépreux.

Bodenheim, Maxwell (1893–1954)
  Advice to a Forest.
  Death.
  Interlude.
  Old Age.
  Poem: "O men, walk on the hills."
  Poem to Gentiles.
  Rear Porches of an Apartment Building.
  To an Enemy.
  Upper Family.

Bodker, Cecil (b. 1927)
  Calendar.
  Self-Portrait.

Bodman, Manoah (1765–1850)
  What rich profusion here.

**Boethius (Anicius Manlius Severinus Boethius)
  (480–524)**
  Alas, the ignorance of unhappy men.
  All human kind on earth.
  Happy he whose eyes have view'd.
  Happy, too happy was the world.
  Happy Too Much.
  He that hath set his headlong heart.
  He who has made his reckoning with life.
  Heu Quam Precipiti.
  Hither, O captives, hither let you come.
  Huc omnes pariter.
  "Heu Quam Praecipih Mersa Profundo"
  Lib. 2. Metrum 5.
  New Year's Eve.
  O Father, give the spirit power to climb.
  O Maker of the starry world.
  O thou whose pow'r o'er moving worlds
    presides.
  O Thou whose reason guides the universe.
  Songs I wrote when I was young and ardent,
    The.
  Stars hidden by dark clouds.
  Then night was shaken from me.
  There is no race of men.
  This bird was happy once in the high trees.
  This concord tempers then the elements.
  Though countless as the Grains of Sand.
  What pleasure in such vehement commotion.
  Who thought in high midsummer.

Bogan, Louise (1897–1970)
  Alchemist, The.
  Baroque Comment.
  Cartography.
  Cassandra.
  Come, Break with Time.
  Crossed Apple, The.
  Crows, The.
  Dark Summer.
  Decoration.
  Didactic Piece.
  Dragonfly, The.
  Dream, The.
  Evening in the Sanitarium.
  Evening-Star.
  Frightened Man, The.
  Heard by a Girl.
  Henceforth, from the Mind.
  Juan's Song.
  July Dawn.
  Kept.
  Knowledge.
  Last Hill in a Vista.
  Late.
  M., Singing.
  Man Alone.
  Medusa.
  Meeting, The.
  Men Loved Wholly Beyond Wisdom.
  Morning.
  Musician.
  My Voice Not Being Proud.
  Night.
  Old Countryside.
  Roman Fountain.
  Several Voices Out of a Cloud.
  Short Summary.
  Simple Autumnal.
  Single Sonnet.
  Sleeping Fury, The.
  Song for the Last Act.
  Song: "It is not now I learn."
  Statue and Birds.
  Sub Contra.
  Tears in Sleep.
  To an Artist, to Take Heart.
  To Be Sung on the Water.
  To My Brother: Killed: Hammont Wood:
    October, 1918.
  Train Tune.
  Winter Swan.
  Women.
  Zone.

Bogardus, Edgar
  Narcissus to Echo.

Bogen, Don
  All Shook Up.

Bognini, Joseph Miezan (b. 1936)
  Earth and Sky.
  My Days Overgrown.
  Suddenly an old man on the threshold of the
    age.
  We are men of the new world a tree prompts
    us to harmony.

Boiardo, Matteo Maria (1441–94)
Il Canto de li Augei di Frunda in Frunda.
Boileau-Despéaux, Nicolas (1636–1711)
Epistle to My Gardener.
Boisseau, Michelle
Cassiopeia at Noon.
Fog.
Potato.
Sleeplessness.
Boker, George Henry (1823–90)
Ah, lute, how well I know each tone of thee.
As stands a statue on its pedestal.
Awaking of the Poetic Faculty, The.
Blood, blood! The lines of every printed sheet.
Brave comrade, answer! When you joined the war.
Farewell once more,—and yet again farewell!
God to Thee We Humbly Bow.
If she should give me all I ask of her.
Leaden eyelids of wan twilight close, The.
Love Is That Orbit.
My darling's features, painted by the light.
Oh! craven, craven! while my brothers fall.
Bokov, Viktor Fiodorovich (b. 1914)
Commune for Me, The.
Salt.
Bokukei (d. 1869)
Cuckoo, I too.
Bokuo (1384–1455)
For seventy-two years / I've kept the ox well under.
Bokusui (d. 1914)
Parting word?, A.
Bolamba, Antoine-Roger (b. 1913)
Bonguemba.
Esanzo.
Fistful of News, A.
In a Storm.
Portrait.
Boland, Eavan (b. 1944)
Achill Woman, The.
That the Science of Cartography Is Limited.
Anna Liffey.
Black Lace Fan My Mother Gave Me, The.
Child of Our Time.
Distances.
Dolls Museum in Dublin, The.
Emigrant Irish, The.
Famine Road, The.
Fond Memory.
From the Painting "Back from Market" by Chardin.
Glass King, The.
Huguenot Graveyard at the Heart of the City, The.
I Remember.
In Her Own Image.
Irish Childhood in England: 1951, An.
It's a Woman's World.
Journey, The.
Latin Lesson, The.
Listen. This is the Noise of Myth.
Love: "Dark falls on this mid-western town."
Midnight Flowers.
Ode to Suburbia.
Oral Tradition, The.
Pomegranate, The.
Ready for Flight.
Self-Portrait on a Summer Evening.
Song: "Where in blind files."
Story.
War Horse, The.
What We Lost.
Woman in Kitchen.
Bold, Alan (b. 1943)
Malfeasance, The.
Bold, Henry (1627–83)
Song: "Chloris, forbear a while."
Boldman, Bob
Day darkens.
Face wrapping a champagne glass.
Fin, A.
I end in shadow.
I hammer a nail.
I read.

In the doll's.
In the heat.
In the temple.
January first.
Just past sunset.
Leaves blowing into a sentence.
Mist.
Moment in the box of jade, A.
Priest, The.
Sitting.
Touching the ashes of my father.
Walking with the river.
Boleyn, Anne (1507–36)
Defiled Is My Name Full Sore.
Boleyn, George (d. 1536)
O Death, Rock Me Asleep.
Bolger, Dermot (b. 1959)
Dublin Girl, Mountjoy, 1984.
Last night in swirling colour we daced again.
Bolles, Matthew (1769–1838)
Here, Lord, Retired, I Bow in Prayer.
Bolt, Thomas
Glimpse of Terrain.
Meditation in Loudoun County.
Bolton, Edmund (1575?–1633?)
Palinode, A.
To Favonius.
Bolton, Frank
Insult before Gift-Giving.
Bolton, Gillie
Little Red Riding Hood and the Wolf.
Bolton, Guy
Till the Clouds Roll By.
Bolton, Joe (1961–90)
American Tragedy.
Fin de Siècle.
In Memory of the Boys of Dexter, Kentucky.
Lights at Newport Beach, The.
Parthenon at Nashville, The.
Bolton, Ken (b. 1949)
Nonplussed.
Bolton, Ken See also Jenkins, John
Bolton, Sarah Knowles (1841–1916)
His Monument.
Influence.
Now.
Bona, Mary Jo (fl. 20th cent.)
Amazone.
Dream Poem.
Bonaguida, Noffo (fl. 1280)
Spirit of Love, with Love's intelligence, A.
Bonar, Horatius (1808–90)
Be True [or Be True Thyself].
Evening brings all home. For that we wait, The.
Fill thou my life, O Lord my God.
Here, O my Lord, I see Thee face to face.
Hymn: "O Love of God, how strong and true."
Length of Days.
Not what my hands have done.
Precedence.
Thy Way, Not Mine.
Boncho (Nozawa Boncho) (d. 1714)
Each year it is but a peck of rice.
Long, long river, The.
Nightingale / My clogs.
Piled for burning/ Brushwood.
Bond, Edward
First World War Poets.
How We See.
If.
Bond, Julian (b. 1940)
Look at That Gal.
Bond, Sandra Turner (b. 1951)
Tuesday Night Affair.
Bondone, Giotto
Many there are, praisers of Poverty.
Bonds, Diane
Life of the Body, The.
Bone, Edith (1889–1975)
On Myself.
Bonhoeffer, Dietrich
Who Am I?
Bonitaz Nuño, Rubén (b. 1923)
Smoke.

Bonnefoy, Yves (b. 1923)
All, the Nothing, The.
Book, for Growing Old, The.
De Natura Rerum.
Remember the Island Where They Build the Fire.
Stone, A.
Summer Again.
Top of the World, The.
Well, The.
What House Would You Build for Me.
Words of Evening, The.
BonniLee
White Candles.
Bonset, I. K. (1883–1931)
Remembering the Night Fountains.
X-Rays.
Bontemps, Arna (1902–73)
My Heart Has Known Its Winter.
Black Man Talks of Reaping, A.
Blight.
Dark Girl.
God Give to Men.
Miracles.
Nocturne at Bethesda.
Nocturne of the Wharves.
Reconnaissance.
Return, The.
Southern Mansion.
Booth, Hilary (b. 1956)
Our Skin Is Paper.
Poem for Central America.
Preface to I Am Rain.
Booth, Philip (b. 1925)
Bee.
Day the Tide, The.
Deer Isle.
Ego.
First Lesson.
Fog-Talk.
Hard Country.
Marin.
One Man's Wife.
Original Sequence.
Sixty-Six.
Stations.
Stefansson Island.
Within.
Boothby, Frances (fl. c.1669)
To My Most Honord Cosen, Mrs Somerset on the Unjust Censure Past Upon My Poore Marcelia.
Bopp, Raul (1898–1984)
Begins here, the ciphered forest.
I pass the swamp borders.
I wake up.
Sky very blue.
This is the rotten-breathed forest.
Borawski, Walta (b. 1947)
Cheers, Cheers for Old Cha Cha Ass.
English Was Only a Second Language.
Invisible History.
Power of One.
Some of Us Wear Pink Triangles.
Talking to Jim.
Borden, William
Morning Chamber Orchestra Near Piney Crick, Wyoming, 7 A.M., The.
Borges, Jorge Luis (1899–1986)
Ars Poetica.
Baruch Spinoza.
Borges and Myself.
Chess.
Compass.
Conjectural Poem.
Everness.
Everything and Nothing.
Ewigkeit.
From an Apocryphal Gospel.
Golem, The.
Houses like Angels.
Inferno 1, 32.
John 1:14 (1964)
John 1:14 (1969)
John 1:14; And the Word became flesh and dwelt among us.

Juan Lopez and John Ward.
Labyrinth, The.
Limits.
Limits (or Good-byes)
Luke 23:39–43; One of the criminals.
Manuscript Found in a Book of Joseph Conrad.
Matthew 5:1–12; Seeing the crowds, he went
    up on the mountain.
Matthew 25:14–30; "For it will be as when a
    man."
Matthew XXV:30.
Mythical Founding of Buenos Aires, The.
Oedipus and the Riddle.
Other Tiger, The.
Page to Commemorate Colonel Suárez, Victor
    at Junín, A.
Patio.
Poem of the Gifts.
Poem Written in a Copy of Beowulf.
Possession of Yesterday.
Sea, The.
Soldier of Urbina, A.
Spinoza.

Borgmann, Kendra
Rodeo Tangent.

Borisova, Maya
Dry birch tree stood, The.
It's not when they leave.

Born, Anne
End of the Row.
I chuck their chins.

Bornemisza, Péter (1535–1584)
How Woeful It Is for Me.

Borodin, Alexander
And This Is My Beloved.
Baubles, Bangles, and Beads.
Stranger in Paradise.

Borowski, Tadeusz (1922–51)
Farewell to Maria.
Green of the distant meadows, lightly.
Night over Birkenau.
Project: Flag.
Sun of Auschwitz, The.
Two Countries.

Borregaard, Ebbe (b. 1933)
Each Found Himself at the End Of.
Some Stories of the Beauty Wapiti.

Borson, Roo (b. 1952)
After a Death.
Flowers.
Gray Glove.
Jacaranda.
Rain.
Save Us From.
Talk.

Borthwick, Priscilla
Forest.
Out of Bounds.

Boruch, Marianne (b. 1950)
Camouflage.
Light.

Boryu (fl. 18th cent.)
Cloud above lotus / It too.

Bose, Buddhadeva
Frogs.

Bosley, Keith
Bird Sips Water.

Boss, Laura (fl. 20th cent.)
At the Nuclear Rally.
Candy Lady, The.
My Ringless Fingers on the Steering Wheel
    Tell the Story.
When You Are Grown, Amanda Rose.

Bosselaar, Laure-Anne (b. 1943)
Cellar, The.

Bossidy, John Collins (1860–1928)
Boston.

Bostock, Gerry (b. 1942)
Childhood Revisited.
Night Marauders.
Uranium.

Bostok, Janice
Foetus kicks.
Pregnant again.

Boston, B. H.
Apiary.
By All Lights: 1959.
Savage, Our Fathers, The.

Boswell, Margie B. (1875–1952)
Texas Ranger, The.

Bottke, Amy
How to Approach Your Lover's Wife.

Bottomley, Gordon (b. 1874)
Dawn.
Eager Spring.
Eagle Song.
End of the World, The.
To Iron-Founders and Others.

Bottoms, David (b. 1949)
Chinese Dragons.
Desk, The.
Homage to Lester Flatt.
In a U-Haul North of Damascus.
In the Black Camaro.
Sierra Bear.
Smoking in an Open Grave.
Under the Vulture-Tree.

Bottrall, Ronald (b. 1906)
Icarus.

Boughton, Mrs. (b. c.1600, d. after 1650)
Epitaph: "When Oxford gave thee two degrees
    in art."

Boulus, Sargon (b. 1944)
Lighter.
My Father's Dream.
Poem: "I want to know today."
Siege.

Boundzekei-Dongala, Emmanuel
Fantasy under the Moon.

Bourdillon, Francis William (1852–1921)
Night Has a Thousand Eyes, The.

Bourne, Vincent (1695–1747)
Snail, The.

Bourne, W. O.
Heart's Fine Gold, The.

Boutens, P. C. (1870–1943)
Lonely Night.

Bouwers, Lenze L. (b. 1940)
Final Signs, The.

Bovshover, Joseph (1872–1916)
To the Laggards.

Bowden, Samuel (1726?–1771?)
Kite, completed thus, is borne along, The.

**Bowen, Charles Synge Christopher Bowen,
Baron (1835–96)**
Rain It Raineth, The.

Bowen, Euros (b. 1904)
Blackthorn.
Nettles in May.
Winged in Gold.

Bowen, Kevin
Playing Basketball with the Viet Cong.

Bowering, George (b. 1938)
Dobbin.
Envies, The.
Está Muy Caliente.
Grandfather.
Grass, The.
House, The.
I am slowly dying, water evaporating.
In the Forest.
Inside the Tulip.
Moon Shadow.

Bowering, Marilyn (b. 1949)
Russian Asylum.
Seeing Oloalok.
Wishing Africa.

Bowers, Edgar (b. 1924)
Adam's Song to Heaven.
Afternoon at the Beach, An.
Amor Vincit Omnia.
Awakened by some fear, I watch the sky.
Centaur Overheard, The.
I drive home with the books that I will read.
In nameless warmth, sun light in every corner.
Le Rêve.
Mountain Cemetery, The.
Prince, The.

Snow and then rain. The roads are wet. A car.
Stoic: for Laura von Courten, The.
Two Poems on the Catholic Bavarians.

Bowers, Mildred
Answer.

Bowers, Neal
Conversions.
On the Elvis Mailing List.

Bowes-Lyon, Lilian (1895–1949)
Feather, The.
White Hare, The.

Bowie, Walter Russell (1882–1969)
God of the Nations.
O Holy City Seen of John.

Bowles, William Lisle (1762–1854)
At Tynemouth Priory, after a Tempestuous
    Voyage.
Languid, and sad, and slow.
Milton: On the Busts of Milton, in Youth and
    Age.
Netley Abbey.
On the Death of William Linley, esq.
Sonnet 5: "Evening, as slow thy placid shades
    descend."
Time and Grief.
To a Friend.
To the River Cherwell.
To the River Itchin, near Winton.
To the River Wensbeck.
Tweed Visited, The.
Written at Bamborough Castle.

Bowman, Catherine (b. 1957)
Bride wore a gown, The.
Demographics.
Dove at Sundown.
Heart.
Jackie in Cambodia.
My Knicks Are Going to Beat Your Spurs—
    NBA Souvenir Bracelet 1999 for My Long
    Distance Love.
No Sorry.

Bowring, Sir John (1510–55)
In the Cross of Christ I Glory.

Boychuk, Bogdan
Fairy Tale, A.

Boyd, Bruce (b. 1928)
Sanctuary.
This Is What the Watchbird Sings, Who
    Perches in the Lovetree.
Venice Recalled.

Boyd, Elisse (fl. 1952)
Guess Who I Saw Today.

Boyd, Elizabeth (fl. 1727–45)
On the Death of an Infant of Five Days Old.

Boyd, Marion Margaret
Sea Spray.

Boyd, Mark Alexander (1563–1601)
Fra Bank to Bank, Fra Wood to Wood I Rin.

Boyd, Melba Joyce (b. 1950)
Beer Drops.
Sunflowers and Saturdays.
Why?

"Boyd, Nancy" See Millay, Edna St. Vincent

Boyd, Thomas (1898–1935)
King's Son, The.

Boyden, Polly Chase
Mud.

Boye, Karin (1900–1941)
Sword, A.

Boyle, Charles (b. 1951)
Species.

Boyle, Darl Macleod
Curtain, The.

Boyle, Kay (b. 1903)
Complaint for M and M, A.
New Emigration, The.
Ode to a Maintenance Man and His Family.
Thunderstorm in South Dakota.

Boyse, Samuel (1708–49)
On Platonic Love.
Triumphs of Nature, The.

Brabazon, Francis
Victoria Market.

Bracho, Coral (b. 1951)
From Their Eyes Adorned with Vitreous Sands.

On Contact Opens Its Indigo Pit.
On the Facets: The Flashing.
Sediment of Lukewarm and Radiant Rain.

Brackenbury, Alison (b. 1953)
Two dead divers hauled up in their bell, The.
Whose Window?

Brackenridge, Hugh Henry (1748–1816) *and*
Philip Freneau
Rising Glory of America, The.

Bradbury, Ray
Byzantium I Come Not From.
Switch on the Night.

Bradford, Edwin Emanuel (1860–1944)
Equality.
His Mother Drinks.

Bradford, Elizabeth (1663?–1731)
To the Reader, in Vindication of This Book.

Bradford, William (1589?–1657)
And Truly It Is a Most Glorious Thing.
Epitaphium Meum.
Of Boston in New England.
Word to New England, A.

Brading, Tilla
Punt gliding under a chain of smiles, A.

Bradley, George (b. 1953)
E Pur Si Muove.

Bradstreet, Anne (c.1612–72)
Another.
As Spring the Winter Doth Succeed.
As Weary Pilgrim, Now at Rest.
Author to Her Book, The.
Before the Birth of One of Her Children.
Contemplations.
Deliverance from a Fit of Fainting.
Dialogue between Old England and New, A.
Flesh and the Spirit, The.
For Deliverance from a Fever.
Four Seasons of the Year, The.
Here Follows Some Verses upon the Burning
of Our House [July 10th, 1666. Copied Out
of a Loose Paper].
Here lies the pride of Queens, pattern of Kings.
Here sleeps the Queen, this is the royall bed.
I am obnoxious to each carping tongue.
In Honour of that High and Mighty Princess
Queen Elizabeth of Happy Memory.
In Memory of My Dear Grandchild Anne
Bradstreet Who Deceased June 20, 1669,
Being Three Years and Seven Months Old.
In Memory of My Dear Grandchild Elizabeth
Bradstreet Who Deceased August, 1665,
Being a Year and Half Old.
In Reference to Her Children, 23 June, 1659
[*or* 1659].
Letter to Her Husband, Absent upon Public[k]
Employment, A.
Mariner that on smooth waves doth glide, The.
Old Age.
On My Dear Grandchild Simon Bradstreet,
[Who Died on 16th November, 1669, Being
but a Month and One Day Old].
Prologue, The.
Shall I then praise the heavens, the trees, the
earth.
So he that saileth in this world of pleasure.
There is a path no vulture's eye hath seen.
To Her Father, with Some Verses.
To My Dear and Loving Husband.
To My Dear Children.
To the Memory of My Dear and Ever Honored
Father Thomas Dudley Esq. Who Deceased
July 31, 1653, and of His Age 77.
Upon My Dear and Loving Husband His
Going into England.
Vanity of All Worldly Things, The.

Bradstreet, Samuel (c.1633–82)
Almanack for the Year of Our Lord, 1657, An.

Brady, Edwin James (1869–1925)
Whaler's Pig, The.

Brady, Graham
Voice from the Bush—Through Me.

Brady, Nicholas *See* **Tate, Nahum**

Brainard, E. M.
Compensation.

Brainard, Joe (b. 1942)
I Remember.

Brainard, John Gardiner Calkins (1796–1828)
I Saw Two Clouds at Morning.
To Thee, O God, the Shepherd Kings.

Braithwaite, William Stanley (1878–1962)
City Garden, A.
House of Falling Leaves, The.
Quiet Has a Hidden Sound.
Rhapsody.
Rye Bread.
Sic Vita.
Turn Me to My Yellow Leaves.
Watchers, The.

Braley, Berton (1882–1966)
Start Where You Stand.
Success.

Brammer, Julius
Just a Gigolo.

Bramston, James (1694?–1743)
Time's Changes.
Whoe'er he be that to a taste aspires.

Branch, Anna Hempstead (1875–1937)
Around this rod my writhing self might twist.
Connecticut Road Song.
Ere the Golden Bowl Is Broken.
I say that words are men and when we spell.
I used to wonder . . . number was fixed and still.
In the Beginning Was the Word.
Into the void behold my shuddering flight,.
Monk in the Kitchen, The.
What witchlike spell weaves here its deep
design.

Brand, Dionne (b. 1953)
Then it is this simple. I felt the unordinary
romance of.
Wind.

Brandling, Charles (1733–1802)
To a Lady, with a Present of a Fan.

Brannon, Jack
Evolution on 38th Street.

Brant, Beth (b. 1941)
Her Name Is Helen.
Ride the Turtle's Back.
Stillborn Night.

Brant, LeRoy V. (b. 1890)
Green Plumes of Royal Palms.
Oh, Day of Days.

Brasch, Charles (1909–73)
Ambulando.
Home Ground.
Life Mask.
Shoriken.
What have you seen on the summits, the peaks
that plunge their.
Winter Anemones.
Word by Night.

Braschi, Giannina (b. 1954)
Final Manuscript.

Brass, Perry (b. 1947)
I Have This Vision of Madness.
Only Silly Faggots Know.
There Isn't Any Death.

Brathwaite, Edward Kamau (b. 1930)
Blues.
Colombe.
Caliban.
Calypso.
Citadel.
Journeys, The.
Look wha' happen las' week at de Oval!
Making of the Drum, The.
Mmenson.
Naima.
New World a-Comin'.
New Year Letter.
Stone.

Brathwaite [*or* Brathwait], Richard (1588?–1673)
Vandunk's Four Humours, in Quality and
Quantity.

Braun, Felix
How Long?

Braun, Henry
To Fat Boy, the Bomb.

Braun, Richard Emil (b. 1934)
Goose.

Lilies, The.
Seeking an Explanation.

Brautigan, Richard (1935–c.1990)
Boat, A.
Haiku Ambulance.
Surprise.

Braxton, Charlie R. (b. 1961)
Apocalypse.
Arts Are Black, The.

Bray, J. J. (b. 1912)
Execution of Madame du Barry, The.

Braybrook, Patrick
Limerick: "People the Churches love best,
The."

Brecht, Bertolt (1898–1956)
Alabama Song.
Bad Time for Poetry.
Burning of the Books, The.
Changing the Wheel.
Concerning the Infanticide, Marie Farrar.
Contemplating Hell.
First Psalm (Posthumous)
Fishing-Tackle, The.
Friends, The.
From a German War Primer.
God of War, The.
I, the Survivor.
Late Lamented Fame of the Giant City of New
York.
Letter to the Actor Charles Laughton
Concerning the Work on the Play "The Life
of Galileo."
Luke 2:8–20; And in that region there were
shepherds.
Mary.
Mask of Evil, The.
1940.
Of Poor B. B.
On Reading a Recent Greek Poet.
One-Armed Man in the Undergrowth, The.
Solution, The.
This Summer's Sky.
Three Fragments.
To Those Born Later.
War Has Been Given a Bad Name.
What a bankruptcy! How.
What Did the Nazi Send His Wife?
What people they were! Their boxers the
strongest!
When Evil-Doing Comes Like Falling Rain.
World's One Hope, The.

Brecht, Stefan (b. 1924)
Here then is the life-giving activity given to
every man: the sexual / act, vivificator.
Silence.
Silence, 2.
Thanksgiving (1974)

Breckenridge, Jill
General John Cabell Breckinridge.

Breedlove, Nicole (b. 1971)
Black and Divided or Chittlins and Caviar.
New Miz Praise de Lawd, The.

Breeze, Jean Binta (b. 1957)
Dubbed Out.
Eena Mi Corner.
Natural High.
Riddym Ravings (The Mad Woman's Poem)

Breidenbach, Tom
Confessional.

"Breitman, Hans" *See* **Leland, Charles Godfrey**

Bremser, Ray (b. 1934)
Blood.
Let me lay it to you gently, Mr. Gone!

Brennan, Christopher John (1870–1932)
Because She Would Ask Me Why I Loved
Her.
Fire in the Heavens.
Sweet Silence after Bells!
When window-lamps had dwindled, then I
rose.

Brennan, J. Keirn (1873–1948)
Let the Rest of the World Go By.

Brent, Earl (*fl.* 1946)
Angel Eyes.

Brent, Hally Carrington (b. 1943?)
I Think I Know No Finer Things than Dogs.

Brereton, Charlotte (b. c.1720)
To Miss A[——]a M[——]a Tra[——]s; an
   Epistle from Scotland.
Brereton, Jane (1685–1740)
But should some snarling critic chance to view.
On Mr. Nash's Picture at Full Length.
You, friend, who whilom tossed the ball.
Brereton, John Le Gay (1871–1933)
Unborn.
Breton, André (1896–1966)
Dreaming I See You.
Fourier what have they done with your
   keyboard.
Free Union.
Go for Broke.
In the Eyes of the Gods.
"Factory."
Man and Woman Absolutely White, A.
Marquis de Sade, The.
More than Suspect.
Mystery Corset, The.
On the Road to San Romano.
Poem-Object.
Postman Cheval.
Spectral Attitudes, The.
Three Excerpts.
Vigilance.
War.
Breton, André *See also* **Eluard, Paul**
Breton, Nicholas (1542–1626)
Assurance, An.
Chess Play, The.
Cradle Song: "Come, little babe."
I have neither Plummes nor Cherries.
Let mee thinke no more on thee.
Merry Country Lad, The.
Olden Love-making.
Report Song [in a Dream], A.
Service Is No Heritage.
Wearie thoughts doe waite upon me.
Brett, Doris (b. 1953)
For My Mother.
Brett, Lily
I Keep Forgetting.
La Pathétique.
Leaving You.
My Mother's Friend.
Brettell, Noel H. (b. 1908)
African Student.
On an Inyanga Road.
Brew, Kwesi (b. 1928)
Ancestral Faces.
Lonely Traveller, The.
Plea for Mercy, A.
Search, The.
Brewer, Gaylord (b. 1965)
Journals, The.
Mountains.
Teen Drowns in Rehabilitation Camp Days
   Before 17th Birthday, Questions Persist.
Brewster, Elizabeth (b. 1922)
Anti-Love Poems.
Death by Drowning.
Great-Aunt Rebecca.
If I Could Walk Out into the Cold Country.
Brewster, Martha (b. 1710)
Stately Structure of This Earth, The.
Breytenbach, Breyten (b. 1939)
Asylum.
Black City, The.
Breyten Prays for Himself.
Constipation.
Dar es-Salaam: Harbour of Peace.
Dreams Are Also Wounds.
Dung-beetle.
Eavesdropper.
Exile, Representative.
Firewing.
First Prayer for the Hottentotsgod.
Journey.
Lullaby.
Menace of the Sick.
Out There.
Padmapani.
Sleep My Little Love.

Struggle for the Taal, The.
Testament of a Rebel.
There Is Life.
Threat of the Sick.
We Shall Overcome.
Write Off.
Brice, Andrew (1690–1773)
Poet's Terror at the Bailiffs of Exeter, The.
Brickley, Chuck
Autumn rain.
Deserted wharf.
Few flakes appear, A.
Outside the pub.
Puppet, The.
Sheet lightning.
Slipping in the snow.
Spring evening.
Summer evening.
Bricusse, Leslie (b. 1931)
Candy Man, The.
Goldfinger.
What Kind of Fool Am I?
Who Can I Turn To (When Nobody Needs
   Me?)
Bridgeman, Pam (b. 1950)
Cockatoo.
"Bridges, Madeline" (Mary Ainge De Vere) (fl.
  c.1840)
Life's Mirror.
Bridges, Robert (1844–1930)
April, 1885.
Awake, My Heart, to Be Loved.
Elegy on a Lady, Whom Grief for the Death of
   Her Betrothed Killed.
Elegy: "Wood is bare: a river-mist is steeping,
   The."
Eros.
Ethick.
Etosion achthos aroures.
Evening Darkens Over, The.
Garden in September, The.
Ghosts.
I Have Loved Flowers.
I Heard a Linnet Courting.
I Love All Beauteous Things.
I Will Not Let Thee Go.
Johannes Milton, Senex.
London Snow.
Low Barometer.
Man that sees by chance his picture made, A.
Muse and Poet.
My Delight and Thy Delight.
My Lady Pleases Me.
Nightingales.
Noel; Christmas Eve, 1913.
O Weary Pilgrims.
On a Dead Child.
Passer-by, A.
Pater Filio.
Poor Poll.
Psalm: "While Northward the hot sun was
   sinking o'er the trees."
Sky's unresting cloudland, that with varying
   play, The.
Snow Lies Sprinkled on the Beach, The.
Storm is over, the land hushes to rest, The.
Thee will I love, my God and King.
They that in play can do the thing they would.
Thou Didst Delight My Eyes.
To Francis Jammes.
Triolet: "When first we met we did not guess."
Weep Not To-Day.
When Death to Either Shall Come.
Who Has Not Walked upon the Shore.
Whole World Now, The.
Winter Nightfall.
Bridges, Thomas
Squabbling gods the fight forsake, The.
Bridgwater, Emmy (b. 1906)
Back to the First Bar.
Journey, The.
On the Line.
Brierre, Jean (b. 1909)
Harlem.
Briggs, G. W. (1875–1959)
Lord, who hast made me free.

Bringhurst, Robert (b. 1946)
Behind you: the owl, whose eyes.
Deuteronomy.
For the Bones of Josef Mengele, Disinterred
   June 1985.
Notes to the Reader.
Parśvanatha.
Song of Ptahhotep, The.
These Poems, She Said.
Under the sunrise the mountains.
Brinnin, John Malcolm (b. 1916)
Ascension: 1925, The.
Hotel Paradiso e Commerciale.
Letter from an Island.
Nuns at Eve.
Roethke Plain.
Skin Diving in the Virgins.
Brion, Rofel G.
Good Friday.
If Fortune Smiles.
Love Song.
One Morning Beside a Pond.
Brissenden, Robert Francis (b. 1928)
Verandahs.
Walking down Jalan Thamrin.
Bristol, Augusta Cooper (b. 1835)
Crime of the Ages, The.
Night.
Bristow, Paul
Limerick: "General once lived named de
   Gaulle, A."
Brittain, I. J. (fl. 1918)
There was a woman lived in Winston-Salem.
Broaddus, Andrew (1770–1848)
Help Thy Servant.
Brock-Broido, Lucie
Carrowmore.
Her Habit.
Housekeeping.
Domestic Mysticism.
Of the Finished World.
Prescient.
Radiating Naïveté.
Brock, Van K. (b. 1932)
All the Stars Are Foxfire.
I Stopped in Tupelo, Elvis.
Mary's Dream.
Remembering Dresden.
Sphinx.
Brod, Max (b. 1884)
Goldfish on the Writing Desk.
Brode, Anthony (b. 1923)
Breakfast with Gerard Manley Hopkins.
Calypsomania.
Brodrick, Albert (1830–1908)
Epitaph on a Diamond Digger.
Joe's Luck.
On a Government Surveyor.
Shu' Shu' of Delgo.
Brodsky, Joseph
Belfast Tune.
Berlin Wall Tune, The.
Bosnia Tune.
Eclogue IV: Winter.
Elegy.
Hawk's Cry in Autumn, The.
I Sit by the Window.
In my declining years, in a land beyond the
   ocean.
In the Lake District.
Lagoon.
Letters from the Ming Dynasty.
Love Song.
Mary, the Scots are sots in any case.
May 24, 1980.
Nature Morte.
October Tune.
Odysseus to Telemachus.
Part of the field, A. Trumpets sound and two
   men enter.
Roman Elegies.
September came on Tuesday.
Sextet.
Six Years Later.
That which ripped an amazed scream.

To Urania.
Will a mouth that's muttered its goodbyes.
With a simple, truly unrebellious pen.

Brody, Alter (b. 1895)
Cry of the Peoples, The.
Family Album, A.
Ghetto Twilight.
Kartúshkiya-Beróza.
Lamentations.
Times Square.
Winter Nocturne: The Hospital.

Brome, Alexander (1620–66)
Come a *brimmer* (my bullies) drink whole
ones or nothing.
Epithalamy.
Leveller's Rant, The.
New-Courtier, The.
On Sir G. B. his defeat.
Pastoral on the King's Death, The; [Written in
1648].
Plain Dealing.
Resolve, The.
Riddle: "No more, no more, / We are already
pined [pin'd]."
Saints' Encouragement, The.
Satire on the Rebellion, A.

Bromige, David (b. 1933)
Choice.
Eastward Ho! A Succession.
Edible World, The.
He thought it humanity's lot for ever to be
persuading a huge rock up a mountainside.
Lines: "Repressive desublimation."
Log.
Logical Positivist, The.
Point, The.

Bronk, William (1918–1999)
Aspects of the World like Coral Reefs.
At Tikal.
Body, The.
Corals and Shells.
Feeling, The.
I Thought It Was Harry.
Life Supports.
Mayan Glyphs Unread, The.
Metonymy as an Approach to a Real World.
Plainest Narrative, The.
Postcard to Send to Sumer, A.
Strong Room of the House, The.
Where It Ends.
World, The.

Brontë, Anne ("Acton Bell") (1820–49)
Arbour, The.
Captive Dove, The.
Doubter's Prayer, The.
Fragment, A.
He Doeth All Things Well.
Home.
Lines Composed in a Wood on a Windy Day.
Memory.
Night.
Penitent, The.
Song.

Brontë, Charlotte ("Currer Bell") (1816–55)
'Again I find myself alone.'
Autumn day its course has run—The Autumn
evening falls, The.
Diving.
Dream that stole o'er us in the time.
House was still—the room was still, The.
I now had only to retrace.
Is this my tomb, this humble stone.
Like wolf—and black bull or goblin hound.
Lonely Lady, The.
Nurse believed the sick man slept, The.
Obscure and little seen my way.
On the Death of Anne Brontë.
On the Death of Emily Jane Brontë.
Orphan Child, The.
Pilate's Wife's Dream.
Reason.
'What does she dream of.'
Young Man Naughty's Adventure.

Brontë, Emily Jane ("Ellis Bell") (1818–48)
All hushed and still within the house.
Alone I sat; the summer day.

Aye there it is! It wakes tonight.
Come, walk with me.
D. G. C. to J. A.
Day Dream, A.
Death.
Death Scene, A.
F. de Samara to A. G. A.
Fair sinks the summer evening now.
God of Visions.
Had there been falsehood in my breast.
Hope.
How still, how happy! These [or Those] are
words.
I am the only being whose doom.
I know not how it falls on me.
I'm happiest when most away.
If grief for grief can touch thee.
It's over now; I've known it all.
It will not shine again.
Little while, a little while, A.
Long Neglect Has Worn Away.
Love and Friendship.
Mild the mist upon the hill.
Night Wind, The.
No Coward Soul Is Mine.
O come with me, thus ran the song.
O Dream, where art thou now?
Philosopher, The.
Prisoner, The.
Remembrance.
Shall Earth no more inspire thee.
She dried her tears, and they did smile.
Song.
Song: "Linnet in the rocky dells, The."
Spellbound.
Stanzas: "I'll not weep that thou art going to
leave me."
Stanzas: "Often rebuked, yet always back
returning."
Stanzas to———.
Stars.
Sun Has Set, The.
Tell me, tell me, smiling child.
To Imagination.
Upon her soothing breast.
Visionary, The.
What winter floods, what showers of spring.
Why do I hate that lone green dell?
Wind, I hear it sighing, The.

Brooke, Henry (1703?–83)
Jack the Giant Queller; an Antique History.
While ocean thus the latent store bequeaths.

Brooke, L. Leslie (1862–1940)
Johnny Crow's Garden.

Brooke, Rupert (1887–1915)
Busy Heart, The.
Chilterns, The.
Clouds.
Dead, The ("These hearts were woven")
Dining-Room Tea.
Dust.
Great Lover, The.
Heaven.
Hill, The.
Mary and Gabriel.
Old Vicarage, Grantchester, The.
Peace.
Safety.
Second Best.
Soldier, The.
Sonnet: In Time of Revolt.
Sonnet: "Oh! Death will find me, long before I
tire."
Sonnet Reversed.
Success.
Wagner.

Brookes, John
Officers and Gentlemen Down Under.

Brookes, Peter
Limerick: "Isaac Singer (you probably know)"

Brooks, Adrian (b. 1947)
Here is the queen.

Brooks, Brenda (b. 1952)
Anything.

Brooks, Charles Timothy (1813–88)
Lines: Composed at the Old Temples of

Maralipoor.
Our Island Home.

Brooks, Fred Emerson (1850–1923)
Barnyard Melodies.
Foreigners at the Fair.
From thine eyrie, the crag.
New Baby, The.
Stuttering Lover, The.

Brooks, Frederic
General Description of Men and Things in
Cape Town, A.

Brooks, Gwendolyn (1917–2000)
Anniad, The.
Aspect of Love, Alive in the Ice and Fire, An.
Ballad of Rudolph Reed, The.
Bean Eaters, The.
Beverly Hills, Chicago.
Big Bessie Throws Her Son into the Street.
Birth in a Narrow Room, The.
Blackstone Rangers, The.
Boy Breaking Glass.
Boy Died in My Alley, The.
Bronzeville Mother Loiters in Mississippi, A.
Meanwhile, a Mississippi Mother Burns
Bacon.
Bronzeville Woman in a Red Hat.
Chicago *Defender* Sends a Man to Little Rock,
The.
Chicago Picasso, The.
Children of the Poor, The.
Coora Flower, The.
Crazy Woman, The.
Cynthia in the Snow.
"Do Not Be Afraid of No."
First Fight. Then Fiddle.
Gang Girls.
Gay Chaps at the Bar.
Hunchback Girl: She Thinks of Heaven.
Jamal; Nineteen Cows in a Slow Line Walking.
Jessie Mitchell's Mother.
Kitchenette Building.
Kojo: I Am a Black.
Langston Hughes.
Last Quatrain of the Ballad of Emmett Till,
The.
Life for my child is simple, and is good.
Life of Lincoln West, The.
Lovely Love, A.
Lovers of the Poor, The.
Malcolm X.
Marie Lucille.
Maxie Allen.
Medgar Evers.
Mentors.
Merle; Uncle Seagram.
Michael Is Afraid of the Storm.
Vacant Lot, The.
Mother, The.
Mrs. Small.
My Dreams, My Works Must Wait Till after
Hell.
Naomi.
Narcissa.
Near-Johannesburg Boy, The.
Notes from the Childhood and the Girlhood.
Novelle; My Grandmother Is Waiting for Me
to Come Home.
Of De Witt Williams on His Way to Lincoln
Cemetery.
Of Robert Frost.
Old Relative.
One wants a Teller in a time like this.
Parents: People Like Our Marriage Maxie and
Andrew, The.
Penitent Considers Another Coming of
Mary, A.
Pete at the Zoo.
Piano after War.
Pygmies Are Pygmies Still, Though Percht on
Alps.
Preacher, The: Ruminates behind the Sermon.
Primer for Blacks.
Queen of the Blues.
Religion.
Riot.
Rites for Cousin Vit, The.
Sadie and Maud.

Second Sermon on the Warpland, The.
Sermon on the Warpland, The.
Song in the Front Yard, A.
Song of Winnie.
Southeast Corner.
Stand off, daughter of the dusk.
Still Do I Keep My Look, My Identity.
Street in Bronzeville, A.
Sunday Chicken.
Sundays of Satin-Legs Smith, The.
Sunset of the City, A.
Third Sermon on the Warpland, The.
Throwing Out the Flowers.
Tinsel Marie; The Coora Flower.
To an Old Black Woman, Homeless and
    Indistinct.
To Be in Love.
To Black Women.
To the Diaspora.
We Real Cool.
What shall I give my children? who are poor.
When You Have Forgotten Sunday: The Love
    Story.
White Troops Had Their Orders but the
    Negroes Looked Like Men.
Young Africans.
Young Heroes.

Brooks, Harry
    Ain't Misbehavin'

Brooks, Harry *See also* **Waller, Thomas ("Fats")**

Brooks, John Benson
    You Came a Long Way from St. Louis.

Brooks, Jonathan Henderson (1904–45)
    Muse in Late November.

Brooks, Maria Gowen (1795–1845)
    Palace of the Gnomes.

Brooks, Phillips (1835–93)
    Christmas Everywhere.
    O Little Town of Bethlehem.

Brooks, Shelton (1886–1975)
    Darktown Strutter's Ball, The.
    Some of These Days.
    (That's the Way) Dixieland Started Jazz.
    Walkin' the Dog.

Brooks, Shirley (1816–74)
    For A' That and A' That.
    Poem by a Perfectly Furious Academician.
    To Disraeli.
    What Jenner Said on Hearing in Elysium That
        Complaints Had Been Made of His Having a
        Statue [in Trafalgar Square].

Brooks, Sonya (b. 1968)
    Grandma Talk.
    Middle Passage.
    Sweet molasses.

Brooks, William E.
    Pilate Remembers.

Broome, William (1689–1745)
    Rose-Bud, The.
    Widow and Virgin Sisters, The.

Broonzy, Big Bill
    Southern Blues, The.

Brossard, Nicole
    Barbizon Hotel for Women, The.
    Temptation, The.

Brough, Robert Barnabas (1828–60)
    My Lord Tomnoddy.

**Brougham and Vaux, Henry Peter Brougham, 1st
Baron (1778–1868)**
    Orator's Epitaph, The.

Broughton, James
    Twin Flames.

Broughton, James Richard (b. 1913)
    Feathers or Lead?
    Wondrous the Merge.

Broumas, Olga (b. 1949)
    After *The Little Mariner*.
    Artemis.
    Beauty and the Beast.
    Cinderella.
    Erik Satie, accused.
    Etymolgy.
    For Every Heart.
    If I Yes.

Landscape with Leaves and Figure.
Landscape with Next of Kin.
Lumens.
Masseuse, The.
Next to the *Café Chaos*.
On Earth.
Oregon Landscape with Lost Lover.
Pealing, The.
Perpetua.
Photo Genic.
Privacy.
Rapunzel.
Sappho's Gymnasium.
She Loves.
Sometimes, as a Child.
Song / for Sanna.
Touched.
Tryst.
With the clear.

Broun, Heywood
    Limerick: "There was a young girl with a
        hernia."

Brouwer, Joel (b. 1968)
    Conservatory Pond, Central Park, New York,
        New York.
    Space Memorabilia Auction, Superior Stamp
        and Coin, Beverly Hills, California.
    Steve's Commando Paintball, San Adriano,
        California.

Brown, Anna Gordon (1747–1810)
    Gay Goshawk [*or* Goss-Hawk], The.

Brown, Arthur (1947–1982)
    Assassination of Charlie Parker, The.

Brown, Charles Walter (1866–1934)
    If I Should Die To-Night.

Brown, D. F.
    Coming Home.
    Eating the Forest.
    First Person—1981.
    I Was Dancing Alone in Binh Dinh Province.
    Illumination.
    Patrols.
    Returning Fire.
    Still Later There Are War Stories.
    When I Am 19 I Was a Medic.

**Brown, Dorothy (Diorbhail nic a Bhriuthainn)
(c.1620s–late 17th cent.)**
    Song to Alasdair Mac Colla, A.

Brown, Eleanor (b. 1969)
    Beauty and the Prince Formerly Known as
        Beast.
    Bitcherel.
    Jezebel to the Eunuchs.
    Out.
    Probably the most human thing I do.
    Sonnet 43.
    Tell me I'm beautiful, and bring me flowers.
    Tragic Hero.
    What do I have, when I contemplate this.
    What Song the Syrens Sang.
    When I recall you—as I often do.

Brown, Elizabeth
    Spiritual Land.
    You Got You Got to Be Told.

Brown, Ford Madox (fl. 19th cent.)
    Last of England, The.

Brown, George Mackay (b. 1921)
    Beachcomber.
    Carpenter.
    December Day, Hoy Sound.
    Desertion of the Women and Seals, The.
    Dream of Winter.
    Haddock Fishermen.
    Hamnavoe Market.
    Hawk, The.
    Keeper of the Midnight Gate, The.
    Kirkyard.
    Old Fisherman with Guitar.
    Old Women, The.
    Shroud.
    Stars.
    Taxman.
    Tea Poems.
    Trout Fisher.

Brown, Isaac Hinton (1842–89)
    Honest Deacon, The.

Only a Pin.

Brown, James (b. 1928) *and* **Alfred Ellis**
    Say It Loud—I'm Black and I'm Proud.

Brown, John (1800–59)
    Rhapsody, Written at the Lakes in
        Westmorland, A.

Brown, Kurt
    Good Devil, The.

Brown, Lee Ann (b. 1963)
    Sonnet around Stephanie.

Brown, Les
    Sentimental Journey.

Brown, Lew (1893–1958)
    Best Things in Life Are Free, The.
    Birth of the Blues, The.
    Button Up Your Overcoat.
    Don't Bring Lulu.
    (Here Am I) Broken Hearted.
    I Want to Be Bad.
    If I Had a Talking Picture of you.
    It All Depends on You.
    Life Is Just a Bowl of Cherries.
    Magnolia.
    Maybe This Is Love.
    Never Swat a Fly.
    Straw Hat in the Rain.
    Sunny Side Up.
    Thank You Father.
    That Old Feeling.
    Turn On the Heat.
    Varsity Drag, The.
    You're the Cream in My Coffee.

Brown, Linda Beatrice
    Green Arbor, A.
    Winter Sonnet.

Brown, Maimee Lee
    Created Clay.

Brown, Margaret Wise (1910–52)
    Little Black Bug.
    Secret Song, The.

Brown, Melvin E. (b. 1950)
    Survival Motion: Notice.

Brown, Nacio Herb
    All I Do Is Dream of You.
    Broadway Melody.
    Good Morning.
    I've Got a Feelin' You're Foolin'
    Singin' in the Rain.
    You're an Old Smoothie.
    You Stepped Out of a Dream.
    You Were Meant for Me.

Brown, Nathan (1807–86)
    My soul is not at rest. There comes a strange.

Brown, Pamela (b. 1948)
    I Remember Dexedrine. 1970.
    Leaving.

Brown, Phoebe Hinsdale (1783–1861)
    I Love to Steal Awhile Away.
    Welcome, Ye Hopeful Heirs of Heaven.

Brown, Rita Mae (b. 1944)
    Sappho's Reply.

Brown Rosellen (b. 1939)
    Famous Writers School Opens Its Arms in the
        Next Best Thing to Welcome, The.
    Fry says a word.
    I have a neighbor.
    I want to understand light years.
    Storm high.
    This is no baby skin—.

Brown, Solyman (1790–1865?)
    Her lips disclosed to view.

Brown, Stephanie (b. 1961)
    Chapter One.
    Feminine Intuition.
    I Was a Phony Baloney!
    Interview with an Alchemist in the New Age.
    It Took a Village.
    Marginalia.
    Marriage.
    No, No Nostalgia!
    Schadenfreude.

Brown, Sterling Allen (1901–89)
    After Winter.
    Bitter Fruit of the Tree.

Cabaret.
Call Boy.
Children's Children.
Chillen Get Shoes.
Conjured.
Crispus Attucks McCoy.
Tin Roof Blues.
Long Gone.
Long Track Blues.
Ma Rainey.
Memphis Blues.
Odyssey of Big Boy.
Old Lem.
Old Woman Remembers, An.
Riverbank Blues.
Sam Smiley.
Scotty Has His Say.
Sister Lou.
Slim Greer.
Slim in Atlanta.
Slim in Hell.
Southern Cop.
Southern Road.
Sporting Beasley.
Strange Legacies.
Strong Men.
To Sallie, Walking.
Virginia Portrait.

Brown, Steven Ford
After the Vietnam War.

Brown, Stewart (b. 1951)
Let Them Call It Jazz.

Brown, Thomas [or "Tom"] (1663–1704)
Colonels here in solemn manner meet, The.
Doctor Fell.
Epitaph upon That Profound and Learned
Casuist, the Late Ordinary of Newgate, An.
Oaths.
Reader, beneath this turf I lie.

Brown, Thomas Edward (1830–97)
Between Our Folding Lips.
Bristol Channel, The.
Conjergal Rights.
Dartmoor: Sunset at Chagford.
Disguises.
High overhead.
I Bended unto Me.
Indwelling.
Land, Ho!
My Garden.
O Englishwoman on the Pincian.
Pain.
Preparation.
Salve!
Sermon at Clevedon, A.
Well, The.
When Love Meets Love.

Browne, Emma Alice
When I Am Dead.

Browne, Francis Fisher (b. 1843)
Australian Emigrant, The.

Browne, Isaac Hawkins (1705–60)
Blest leaf! whose aromatic gales dispense.
Fire Side, The; a Pastoral Soliloquy.
Letter from a Captain in Country Quarters to
his Corinna in Town, A.

"Browne, Matthew" See **Rands, William Brighty**

Browne, Michael Dennis (b. 1940)
Lamb.
You, I accuse.

Browne, Moses (1704–87)
Shrimp, A! Black thing as widow's crape.
Survey of the Amphitheatre, A.

Browne, Sir Thomas (1605–82)
Colloquy with God, A.
In yellow meadows I take no delight.
O for a toe, such as the funeral pyre.
Signs of Spring.

Browne, William (1591–1643)
Caelia.
Down in a valley, by a forest's side.
[Epitaph] In Obitum M.S., X Maij [or Maii],
1614.
Golden Age: Flower-weaving, The.
Golden Age, The.

Happyer those times were, when the Flaxen
clew.
Love Who Will, for I'll Love None.
Memory.
Morning.
On the Countess Dowager of Pembroke.
Praise of Spenser.
Rose, A.
Shall I tell you whom I love?
Sirens' Song, The.
Song: "For her gait, if she be walking."

Browne, Sir William (1692–1774)
Epigram: "King to Oxford sent a troop of
horse, The."

Brownell, Henry Howard (1820–72)
John Brown's Body.
Suspiria Noctis.

Browning, Elizabeth Barrett (1806–61)
Aurora Leigh.
Bereavement.
Bertha in the Lane.
Best, The.
Best Thing in the World, The.
Bianca among the Nightingales.
Casa Guidi Windows.
Child's Thought of God, A.
Comfort.
Convinced by Sorrow.
Cowper's Grave.
Cry of the Children, The.
Curse for a Nation, A.
Died.
Farewells from Paradise.
Flush or Faunus.
Forced Recruit, The.
Grief.
Hiram Powers' "Greek Slave."
L. E. L.'s Last Question.
Lady's "Yes," The.
Look, The.
Lord Walter's Wife.
Loved Once.
Man's Requirements, A.
Mask, The.
Meaning of the Look, The.
Mother and Poet.
Musical Instrument, A.
My Heart and I.
On a Portrait of Wordsworth by B. R. Haydon.
Only a Curl.
Out in the Fields [with God].
Romance of the Swan's Nest, The.
Runaway Slave at Pilgrim's Point, The.
Sleep, The.
Sonnets from the Portuguese, sels.
Substitution.
Sweetness of England, The.
Tears.
Thought for a Lonely Death-Bed, A.
To George Sand: A Desire.
To George Sand: A Recognition.
True Dream, A.
Year's Spinning, A.

Browning, Robert (1812–89)
Abt Vogler.
Andrea del Sarto.
Any Wife to Any Husband.
Apparent Failure.
Appearances.
Bishop Orders His Tomb at Saint Praxed's
Church, The.
Blot in the 'Scutcheon, A, sels.
Caliban upon Setebos; or, Natural Theology in
the Island.
Childe Roland to the Dark Tower Came.
Christmas-Eve, sels.
Confessions.
Dialogue between Father and Daughter.
Dîs Aliter Visum; or, Le Byron de Nos Jours.
Earth's Immortalities, sels.
Epilogue: "At the midnight in the silence of
the sleep-time."
Epilogue: "On the first of the Feast of Feasts."
Epistle Containing the Strange Medical
Experience of Karshish, the Arab Physician,
An.

Eternity Affirms the Hour.
Evelyn Hope.
Eyes, Calm beside Thee (Lady, Could'st Thou
Know!)
Face, A.
Ferishtah's Fancies, sels.
Fra Lippo Lippi.
Garden Fancies, sels.
Grammarian's Funeral, A.
Guardian-Angel, The.
Home-Thoughts, from Abroad.
Home-Thoughts, from the Sea.
House.
How It Strikes a Contemporary.
How They Brought the Good News from
Ghent to Aix.
Inapprehensiveness.
Incident of the French Camp.
Instans Tyrannus.
Italian in England, The.
James Lee's Wife, sels.
Johannes Agricola in Meditation.
Laboratory, The (Ancien Régime)
Last Ride Together, The.
Life in a Love.
Likeness, A.
Lost Leader, The.
Lost Mistress, The.
Love among the Ruins.
Love in a Life.
May and Death.
Meeting at Night.
Memorabilia.
Misconceptions.
"Moses" of Michael Angelo, The.
My Last Duchess.
Names, The.
Never the Time and the Place.
Now.
Paracelsus, sels.
Parting at Morning.
Patriot, The [An Old Story].
Pauline [A Fragment of a Confession], sels.
Pictor Ignotus.
Pied Piper of Hamelin, The, sels.
Pippa Passes, sels.
Pisgah-Sights. I.
Pisgah-Sights. II.
Prospice.
Rabbi Ben Ezra.
Porphyria's Lover.
Respectability.
Rhyme for a Child Viewing a Naked Venus in
a Painting [of "The Judgement of Paris"].
Ring and the Book, The, sels.
Soliloquy of the Spanish Cloister.
Solomon and Balkis.
Sordello.
Through the Metidja to Abd-el-Kadr.
To Edward FitzGerald.
Toccata of Galuppi's, A.
Twins, The.
Two in the Campagna.
Up at a Villa—Down in the City.
Waring.
Why I Am a Liberal.
Woman's Last Word, A.
Women and Roses.
Youth and Art.

Brownjohn, Alan (b. 1931)
Class Incident from Graves.
Common Sense.
In a Convent Garden.
Looking at Her.
Negotiation.
Of Dancing.
Seven Activities for a Young Child.
Train, The.
Your fingers fully awake, it.

**"Brownjohn, John" (Charles Remington Talbot)
(1851–91)**
School-Master and the Truants, The.

Brownlee, W. S.
Little Miss Muffet.
Said Little Boy Blue.

Brownlie, W. S.
Limerick: "Man in the Land of the

Houyhnhnms, A."

Brownstein, Michael (b. 1943)
Glass Enclosure, The.
Jet Set Melodrama.
Last Spell Cast, The.
Oracle night / the porch is frozen.
Paris Visitation.
Stepping Out.
War.

Bruce, Debra
Plunder.
Prognosis.
Sonnet 2: "Deep in her seventh month, my sister dozes."
Sonnet 4: "Wet streets, black trees, a gold leaf smacked."
Two Couples.

Bruce, George (b. 1909)
My House.
Singers, The.
Sumburgh Heid.

Bruce, Michael (1740–67)
Farewell, ye blooming fields! ye cheerful plains!
To the Cuckoo.

Bruce, Wallace (b. 1844)
Holland Brick, A.

Bruchac, Joseph (b. 1942)
Birdfoot's Grampa.
City.
Coming Back.
Elegy for Jack Bowman.
For a Winnebago Brave.
Frozen Hands.
Grandmother Came Down to Visit Us, The.
Hiking.
Let the Midnight Special.
Poem for Jan.
Prayer: "Let my words."
Second Skins—a Peyote Song.
Spring Peepers.
Stone Giant.
There is a stream which rises.
Three Poems for the Indian Steelworkers.

Bruck, Edith (b. 1932)
Birth.
Childhood.
Pretty Soon.
You Hide.

Brucker, H. P.
Praise Now Your God.

Brummer, Nadine
That Rank Bed.
Why Is This Night Different from All Other Nights?

Brün, Frederike
Chamouni at Sunrise.

Bruna, Carmen (b. 1928)
Moi-Même.

Bruner, Margaret E. (1886–1970?)
Angry Word, An.
Atonement.
Beggar, The.
Beyond the Grave.
Casual Meeting.
Clown, The.
Dog's Vigil, A.
Dreaded Task, The.
For One Lately Bereft.
For One Who Is Serene.
Gift, The.
God's Ways Are Strange.
Good-By.
Greater Gift, The.
If Lincoln Should Return.
Lonely Dog, The.
Midwinter.
Monk and the Peasant, The.
On City Streets.
Plea for Tolerance.
Prayer for Strength.
Rebirth.
Remembrance.
Retaliation.
Selfishness.

Sinner, The.
There Is a Loneliness.
Time's Hand Is Kind.
Wedding Anniversary.

Bruno, Giordano (1548–1600)
Philosophic Flight, The.

Brunton, Alan (b. 1946)
Her voice is like some angel picking at the door.
I say hello to the sunshine.
Oh me / is that the ambulance chasing out of town?
What Happens in Shakzpeare.

Bruschetto, Lodovico *See* **Bryskett, Lodowick [or Lewis]**

Brush, Thomas
Again.
Waiting for the End of the War.

Brutus, Dennis (b. 1924)
At a Funeral.
At Night.
Cold.
Endurance.
Let not this plunder be misconstrued.
Letters to Martha.
Nightsong: City.
Off to Philadelphia in the Morning.
On the Island.
Poems about Prison.
Postscripts 2.
Prayer: "O let me soar on steadfast wing."
Robben Island Sequence.
Sand Wet and Cool, The.
Simple lust is all my woe, A.
Sometimes a mesh of ideas.
Sounds Begin Again, The.
Their Behaviour.
There Was a Time When the Only Worth.
They Hanged Him, I Said Dismissively.
This Sun on this Rubble.
Under House Arrest.

Bryan, Mary (fl. 1815)
Maniac, The.
To My Brother.
To————: "O thou unknown disturber of my rest."
To————: "O timeless guest!—so soon returned art thou."

Bryan, Sharon (b. 1943)
Lunch with Girl Scouts.

Bryant, Frederick, Jr. (b. 1942)
Cathexis.

Bryant, John Frederick (1753–91)
On a Piece of Unwrought Pipeclay.

Bryant, William Cullen (1794–1878)
African Chief, The.
After a Tempest.
Ages, The.
As Shadows Cast by Cloud and Sun.
Autumn Woods.
Conjunction of Jupiter and Venus, The.
Constellations, The.
Crowded Street, The.
Damsel of Peru, The.
Dante.
Death of Lincoln, The.
Death of Slavery, The.
Death of the Flowers, The.
Forest Hymn.
Fountain, The.
Green River.
Hymn to the North Star.
I Cannot Forget with What Fervid Devotion.
Indian at the Burial-Place [or Burying-Place] of His Fathers, An.
Inscription for the Entrance to a Wood.
June.
Meditation on Rhode Island Coal, A.
Midsummer.
Mighty One, before Whose Face.
Mutation.
Night Journey of a River, The.
Not Yet.
November.
O Thou Whose Own Vast Temple Stands.
October.

Oh [*or* O] Fairest of the Rural Maids.
Painted Cup, The.
Poet, The.
Prairies, The.
Return of Youth, The.
Rivulet, The.
Robert of Lincoln.
So live, that when thy summons comes to join.
Song of the Stars.
Summer Wind.
Thanatopsis.
These are the gardens of the Desert, these.
Tides, The.
To a Waterfowl.
To Cole, the Painter, Departing for Europe.
To the Fringed Gentian.
When breezes are soft and skies are fair.
Winter Piece, A.
Yellow Violet, The.

Brydges, Sir Samuel Egerton (1762–1837)
Lines Written Immediately after Parting from a Lady.
No more by cold philosophy confined.
On Dreams, October 15, 1782.
To Miss M————, Written by Moonlight, July 18, 1782.

Bryll, Ernest (b. 1935)
Ballad of the Bayonet, A.
Nike.

Bryskett, Lodowick [or Lewis] (Lodovico Bruschetto) (1546–1612)
Pastoral Eclogue upon the Death of Sir Philip Sidney Knight, A.

Bryusov [or Briusov], Valery [or Valerii] Yakovlevich [or Iakovlevich] (1873–1924)
O, close your pale legs!
Radiant Ranks of Seraphim.
Stonemason, The.
To a Young Poet.

Bu-er, Sun (b. 1124)
Cut brambles long enough.
Late Indian summer's.

Buchanan, George (1506–82)
May Morning.
To Henry Darnley, King of Scots.

Buchanan, George (1904–89)
Conversations with Strangers.
I Suddenly.
Jill's Death.
Lewis Mumford.
Lyle Donaghy, Poet, 1902–1949.
Song for Straphangers.
Speaker in the Square, A.
Theatrical Venus.
War-and-Peace.

Buchanan, Robert Williams (1841–1901)
Wanderers, The.

Buchwald, Emilie
As Soon as It's Here It's Gone but So What.

Buck, Howard
Mort, Le.

Buckham, John Wright (1864–1945)
Hills of God, Break Forth in Singing.
O God, above the Drifting Years.

Buckland, Frank
Limerick: "That smasher of shams, Bernard Shaw."

Buckley, Christopher (b. 1948)
20 Years of Grant Applications and State College Jobs.
Concerning Paradise.
Father, 1952.
Nostalgia.
Playing for Time.
Presocratic, Surfing, Breathing Cosmology Blues, The.
Sycamore Canyon Nocturne.
Train in the Desert—1916.

Buckley, Vincent (1925–88)
Child Is Revenant to the Man, The.
Ghosts, Places, Stories, Questions.
Good Friday and the Present Crucifixion.
In the faint blue light.
Man, a Woman, A.
No New Thing.

Origins.
Parents.
Return of a Popular Statesman.
Teaching German Literature.
Buckmaster, Charles (1951–72)
End to Myth, An.
Seed.
Vanzetti.
Wilpena Pound.
Budapest, Z
Medea speaks: / This is God, children, listen
up well. The.
Budbill, David
What I Heard at the Discount Department
Store.
Buddingh', Cees (b. 1918)
Hyena, The.
Some Biographical Data.
Buddy, Callin
Callin Buddy / Bolden.
Budenz, Julia
Poeta Fui.
Budy, Andrea Hollander
Ellis Island, September 1907.
On High Street.
Buffoni, Franco (b. 1950)
And in the end, the entire earth may answer to
a single name.
And those level fingernails of theirs.
De Pisis—Piacenza Papers.
On Poetry.
Partitions.
Song of Diamond Eyes, The.
To be soldiers together and allies.
When he was far away from those evenings.
Bufu (d. 1792)
Oh, I don't care.
Bugayev, Boris Nikolaevich See **Bely** [or**Belyi**],
Andrey [or **Andrei**]
Bugeja, Michael
Conifer King, The.
Bui-Burton, Kim Ly
Look at Me.
My Love Is Like a Lily.
Poem for R.
Bukowski, Charles (1920–94)
B.
Black Poets, The.
Crucifix in a Deathhand.
Drooling Madness at St. Liz.
Elvis Lives.
I Am Dead but I Know the Dead Are Not Like
This.
Mockingbird, The.
Not Much Singing.
Secret, The.
My Old Man.
Startled into Life Like Fire.
Bulcke, Karl (b. 1875)
There Is an Old City.
Bulfinch, Stephen Greenleaf (1809–70)
Hail to the Sabbath Day.
Bulich, Vera (1898–1954)
From My Diary, 3.
Omnibus, The.
Bulkeley, Peter, the Younger (1643–91)
Like to the Grass That's Green Today.
Bull, Arthur J. (b. 1903)
Eve.
Buller, Arthur (1874–1944)
Limerick: "There was a young lady named [or
called] Bright."
Limerick: "To her friends, said the Bright one,
in chatter."
Bullett, Gerald (b. 1893)
Footnote to Tennyson.
Woodpecker.
Bullock, Michael (b. 1918)
Garden.
Buluguru
Working Song.
Bun-Etsu, Unpo
Sixty-five years.
Bunan (1602–76)
Die while you're alive.

Moon's the same old moon, The.
When you're both alive and dead.
Bungay, George W. (1818?–92)
Creeds of the Bells.
Bunimovich, Yevgeny [or Evgenii] (b. 1954)
Explanatory Note.
Moscow: Summer '86.
Bunin, Ivan Alekseievich (1870–1953)
At the gates of Zion, over Kedron.
Endless downpour; misty wood.
Flax.
Flowers, and tall-stalked grasses, and a bee.
High up on a snowy peak.
It was near midnight when I entered.
Loneliness.
Stone Idol, The.
To My Country.
Bunina, Anna Petrovna (1774–1829)
Conversation between Me and the Women.
From the Seashore.
Though poverty's no stain.
Bunner, Henry Cuyler (1855–96)
Behold the Deeds!
Dear Mother.
Home, Sweet Home, with Variations.
Poetry and the Poet.
Real Romance, A.
Bunting, Basil (1900–85)
Brag, sweet tenor bull.
Chomei at Toyama.
Complaint of the Morpethshire Farmer, The.
Gin the Goodwife Stint.
Grass caught in willow tells the flood's height
that has subsided.
I have been noting events for forty years.
Loaded with mail of linked lies.
Now that sea's over that island.
On the Fly-Leaf of Pound's Cantos.
Orotava Road, The.
Remember, imbeciles and wits.
Riding silk, adrift at noon.
Thrush in the syringa sings, A.
To Violet [with Prewar Poems].
What the Chairman Told Tom.
Bunya no Asayasu (c.900)
In a gust of wind the white dew.
Bunyan, John (1628–88)
Christian Loses His Burden.
Pilgrim Song, The.
Shepherd Boy Sings [in the Valley of
Humiliation], The.
Upon the [or a] Snail.
What danger is the pilgrim in.
When at the first I took my pen in hand.
Bunzan
I crossed from last.
Burbank, Elevena (b. 1956)
I Danced to the Rumble of the Drum.
Burbidge, Thomas (1816–95)
She Bewitched Me.
Burden, Jean (b. 1914)
Poem before Departure.
Burdette, Robert Jones (1844–1914)
Orphan Born.
Soldier, Rest!
Burford, William (b. 1927)
Christmas Tree, A.
Burge, Maureen
Diet, The.
Disillusion.
Burgess, Anthony (b. 1917)
Limerick: "Man from the *Washington Post*, A."
Burgess, Frank Gelett (1866–1951)
Cinq Ans Après.
Limerick: "For hours my wife says
'Goodbye.'"
Limerick: "I wish that my room had a floor."
Low Trick, A.
On Digital Extremities.
Purple Cow, The.
Table Manners.
Trapping Fairies.
Burgess, George (1809–60)
Harvest Dawn Is Near, The.

While o'er the Deep Thy Servants Sail.
Burgess, Helen Chalakee
Rational.
Burgon, John William (1813–88)
Match me such marvel save in Eastern clime.
Burgoyne, John (1722–92)
Dashing White Sergeant, The.
Burich, Vladimir (b. 1932)
Citizen's Way, The.
Dialogue, The.
Precepts for City Living.
What do I expect from tomorrow's day?
You blow on the hair of your child.
Burkard, Michael (b. 1947)
2 Poems on the Same Theme.
Breathless Storm.
Dogs on the Cliffs, The.
Foolish Thing.
I have a silence in the rain.
Meditation Brought About by George Bogin's
Translation of Jules Supervielle's Poem 'The
Sea.'
My Aunt and the Sun.
Notes about My Face.
Personal Histories, The.
Weather.
Burke, Cheryl
Lizzie.
Motor Oil Queen.
Burke, Joe
Little Bit Independent, A.
Burke, Johnny (1908–64)
Ain't It a Shame about Mame.
But Beautiful.
Good Time Charlie.
Here's That Rainy Day.
I've Got a Pocketful of Dreams.
Imagination.
It Could Happen to You.
Like Someone in Love.
Misty.
Moonlight Becomes You.
My Heart Is a Hobo.
Pennies from Heaven.
Personality.
Polka Dots and Moonbeams.
Road to Morocco, The.
Sleigh Ride in July.
Swinging on a Star.
Welcome to My Dream.
You May Not Love Me.
Burke, Kenneth (b. 1897)
Civil Defense.
Frigate Jones, the Pussyfooter.
Know Thyself.
Nursery Rhyme.
Burke, Martin
On the twelfth floor.
Rainy winter evening.
Burke, Sonny
Black Coffee.
Burket, Gail Brook (b. 1905)
From Countless Hearts.
So Touch Our Hearts with Loveliness.
Burleigh, William Henry (1812–71)
Abide Not in the Realm of Dreams.
Lead Us, O Father, in the Paths of Peace.
**Burliuk, D., Aleksandr Kruchenykh, V.
Mayakovsky and Viktor Khlebnikov**
Slap in the Face of Public Taste, A.
**Burlyuk [or Burliuk], David Davidovich (1882–
1967)**
Everyone is young, young, young.
Burn, Michael
For the Common Market.
In Japan.
Welsh Love Letter.
Burnat-Provins, Marguerite (1872–1952)
Fruits you give me are more savory than
others, The.
Sylvius, your hands near my mouth are heady
flowers.
You told me: "I am not worthy of you."
Burnett, Ernie
My Melancholy Baby.

Burnett, W. Hodgson (*fl.* c.1920)
My Shadow.

Burney, Frances [*or* **Fanny**], **Mme D'Arblay** (1752–1840)
To Charles Burney.

Burnham, Deborah
Maintaining the Species.

Burns, Joanne (b. 1945)
How.
Marble surfaces.
Reading.
Revisionism.

Burns, Ralph
Early Autumn.
Fishing in Winter.

Burns, Robert (1759–96)
Address to the Deil.
Address to the Unco Guid, or the Rigidly Righteous.
Address to the Woodlark.
Ae Fond Kiss.
Auld Lang Syne.
Birks of Aberfeldy, The [Composed on the Spot].
Bonie Doon.
Bonnie Lesley.
Book-Worms, The.
Comin[g] thro' [*or* through] the Rye.
Comin' thro' the Rye.
Cotter's Saturday Night [nscribed to Robert Aiken [*or* R. A****], Esq.], The.
De'il's [*or* Deil's] Awa wi' th' [*or* the] Exciseman, The.
Death and Doctor Hornbook [A True Story].
Drinking Song.
Duncan Gray.
Epistle to a Young Friend.
Epitaph for William Nicol.
Epitaph: "Lo worms enjoy the seat of bliss."
Epitaph on a Schoolmaster.
Epitaph on Mr. Burton.
First Six Verses of the Ninetieth Psalm, The.
Flow Gently, Sweet Afton.
For A' That and A' That ['Is there, for honest poverty'].
Fornicator. A New Song, The.
Grace after Dinner.
Grace at Kirkudbright.
Green Grow the Rashes [A Fragment].
Green Sleeves [and Tartan Ties].
Halloween.
Head pure, sinless quite of brain or soul, A.
Highland Harry Back Again.
Highland Mary.
Holy Fair, The.
Holy Willie's Prayer.
Hughie Graham.
I am a Bard of no regard.
I Once Was a Maid.
John Anderson, My Jo.
John Barleycorn [a Ballad].
Johnie Blunt.
Keekin' Glass, The.
Kellyburnbraes.
Kirk's Alarm, The.
Lord Galloway.
Man Was Made to Mourn, a Dirge.
Mary Morison.
Memory.
Morality, thou deadly bane.
My Heart's in the Highlands.
O [*or* Oh] Wert Thou in the Cauld Blast.
On Elphinston's Translation of Martial.
O Were My Love Yon Lilac[k] Fair.
Of A' the Airts [the Wind Can Blaw].
On a Dog of Lord Eglinton's.
On a Noisy Polemic.
On Lord Galloway.
On Mr. Pitt's [*or* Pit's] Hair-Powder Tax.
On W. R———, Esq.
Open the Door to Me, Oh!
Parson's Looks, The.
Patriarch, The.
Poet's Welcome to His Love-Begotten Daughter [the First Instance that Entitled Him to the Venerable Appellation of

Father], A.
Poor Merry-andrew, in the [*or* a] neuk.
Prayer, in the Prospect of Death, A.
Rantin' Dog, the Daddie o't, The.
Rantin Laddie, The.
Rantin, Rovin Robin.
Sandy and Jockie.
Scotch Drink.
Scots Wha Hae.
Second Epistle to Davie.
Silver Tassie, The.
So sung the BARD—and Nansie's waws.
Song: "O my love's [*or* luve's *or* love is *or* luve is] like a red, red rose."
Sonnet upon Sonnets, A.
Such a Parcel of Rogues in a Nation.
Sun had clos'd the winter-day, The.
Tam Glen.
Tam o' Shanter; A Tale.
To a Haggis.
To a Louse [On Seeing One on a Lady's Bonnet at Church].
To a Mouse; On Turning Her up in Her Nest, with the Plough, November, 1785.
To William Simpson, Ochiltree.
Toadeater, The.
Up in the Morning Early.
Wat ye what my Minnie did.
Whistle, and I'll Come to You, My Lad.
Whistle o'er the Lave o't.
Willie Brew'd [*or* Brewed] a Peck o' Maut.
Ye Banks and Braes.

Burnshaw, Stanley (b. 1906)
Bread.
End of the Flower World (A.D. 2300)
House in St. Petersburg.
Strange.
Talmudist.

Burnside, John (b. 1955)
Autobiography.
Dundee.
Swimming in the Flood.

Burr, Amelia Josephine (b. 1878)
Lynmouth Widow, A.

Burrell, Lady Sophia (1750?–1802)
Chloe and Myra.
Clock strikes five—the watchman goes, The.
Picture of a Fine Gentleman, The.
School for Satire, The.

Burrington, E. H. (*fl.* 1830–80)
Beautiful, The.

Burris, Jim (*fl.* 1913)
Ballin' the Jack.

Burris, Sidney (b. 1953)
On Living with a Fat Woman in Heaven.
Very True Confessions.

"Burroughs, Ellen" *See* **Jewett, Sophie**
Burroughs, Margaret Goss (b. 1917)
Black Pride.
Everybody but Me.
Only in This Way.
To Soulfolk.

Burroughs, William S. (1914–97)
Cold Lost Marbles.
Fear and the Monkey.
My Legs Señor.

Burrowes, Elizabeth (b. 1885)
O God, Send Men.

Burrows, Suzanne
Time of Cherries, A.

Bursk, Christopher (b. 1943)
First Aid at 4 A.M.
Lies.
Tearing Up the Tracks.

Bursky, Rick
Decisions, The.

Burstein, Abraham (b. 1893)
Love of Hell, The.

Burt, Bates G. (1878–1948)
O God of Youth.

Burt, Della (b. 1944)
Little Girl's Dream World, A.
On the Death of Lisa Lyman.
Spirit Flowers.

Burton, Henry (1840–1930)
Pass It On.

Burton, Robert (1577–1640)
Authors [*or* Author's] Abstract of Melancholy, The.

Burwell, Cliff
Sweet Lorraine.

Buscani, Lisa (b. 1964)
Barefoot in the City.
Downtime.
Miss Mary Mack.

Busceti, Giusi (b. 1955)
Dissonances.
Eight Phases of Contemplation.
Exhausted Inconsistency Floats Here, An.
One Hundred Eighty.
Suddenly on a day in July.

Busch, Trent (b. 1937)
Heartland.

Bush, Barney (b. 1945)
Autumn Warrior.
Directions in Our Blood.
Her Voice.
Memory Sire, The.
Taking a Captive / 1984.
Voyeur's Dream.

Bush, Duncan (b. 1946)
Aquarium du Trocadéro.
Drainlayer.
Hook, The.
Living in Real Times.
Pneumoconiosis.
Summer 1984.
Sunday the Power Went Off, The.

Buson (Yosa Buson) (1716–83)
Along the roadside.
Apprentice's day off.
Around the small house.
At a roadside shrine.
At the ancient well.
At the old pond.
Autumn breezes.
Autumn evening.
Avoiding fishnet.
Bamboo hat, straw coat.
Bat flits, A.
Bats flitting here and there.
Before the white chrysanthemum.
Behavior of the pigeon, The.
Blossoms on the pear.
Blow of an ax.
Blown from the west.
Brushing flies.
Butterfly.
Buying leeks.
By flowering pear.
By moonlight.
Calligraphy of geese.
Camellia, The.
Camellia tips, The.
Cherry blossoms fallen.
Chrysanthemum growers.
Clinging to the bell.
Coming back.
Conversation.
Coolness.
Cover my head.
Crossing.
Crossing the autumn moor.
Cut the peony.
Darting here and there.
Dawn.
Day slow in going, A.
Deer in rain / Three cries.
Dew on the bramble / Thorns.
Dewy morn / These saucepans.
Dog barking, A.
Early summer rain.
End of spring, The.
Escaped the nets.
Evening cloudburst—, An.
Evening primrose.
Evening wind.
Fallen petals of red plum.
Fallen red blossoms.
Ferry departs, The.
Field of bright mustard.
Field of mustard, A.

Flowers offered to the Buddha.
Flying squirrel, A.
Gleaning the rice field.
Going home.
Goodbye. I willgo.
Green leaves.
Green plum.
Gust of wind, A.
Happy traveler / Mosquito wick.
Harvest moon.
Having reddened the plum blossoms.
He's on the porch.
Head pillowed on arm.
Heavy cart rumbles by, A.
How awkward it looks.
I go.
I go out alone.
In a bitter wind.
In pale moonlight.
In seasonal rain.
In sudden flare / Of the mosquito wick.
In the drained fields.
In the summer rain.
In the white plum blossoms.
Iris, An.
It cried three times.
It pierces through me.
Late evening cow, The.
Leaves some trout.
Light of the moon.
Light winter rain.
Lighting one candle.
Lighting the lantern.
Lightning flash, A.
Lights are going out, The.
Listening to the moon.
Listening to the plovers.
Long hard journey, A.
Mad girl, The.
Makes the eye happy.
Mason's finger, The.
May rains.
Miles of frost / On the lake.
Misty grasses.
Moon in midsky, high.
Moored boat, A.
Morning breeze.
Mountain cuckoo, The.
Mountains of Yoshino / Shedding petals.
Mourning for Hokuju Rosen.
My arm for a pillow.
My old man's ears.
My village / Dragonflies.
New Year's first poem.
Night deepens.
No bridge.
No poem you send.
Nobly, the great priest.
Not a leaf stirring.
Not cherry blossoms.
Not quite dark yet.
Of late the nights.
Old calendar, The.
Old cormorant keeper, The.
Old man, The.
Old well.
On the iris / Kite's.
On the one-ton temple bell.
On these southern roads.
Only the shoots.
Over the vast field of mustard flowers.
Over water / Sharp sickles.
Owner of the field, The.
Peonies scattering.
People visiting all day.
Petals fall, The.
Piercing Chill I Feel, The.
Plum blossoms here and there.
Plum blossoms in bloom.
Plum blossoms scent.
Plum scent / Haloing.
Plum-viewing: "Plum-viewing."
Plums in blossom.
Priestly poverty.
Pure white plum blossoms.
Raftsmen on their floats.
Rain falls on the grass.

Remembering how.
Riding.
Scattering bloom, The.
Short nap.
Short night, The. / Broken, in the shallows.
Short night, The. / Bubbles of crab froth.
Short night, The. / Near the pillow.
Short night, The. / Oi River, The.
Short night, The. / On the hairy caterpillar.
Short night, The. / On the outskirts of the
　village.
Short night, The. / Patrolmen.
Short night, The. / Peony, The.
Short night, The. / Shallow footprints.
Short night, The. / Waves beating in.
Shortcut, A.
Sick man passing.
Sleeping late.
Slung over a screen.
Song of the Yodo River.
Sound of a bell.
Sound of a saw.
Sparrow singing.
Spring rain! And as yet.
Spring Scene.
Spring sea rising, The.
Spring Wind on the Riverbank at Kema.
Straw sandal half sunk.
Such a moon.
Sudden chill, A.
Sudden shower.
Swallows / In eaves of mansions.
Sweet springtime showers.
Tea flowers.
Tears.
Ten holy nights.
Tethered horse, A.
That axe that I hear.
That handsaw marks time.
That snail.
These lazy spring days.
They end their flight.
They swallow clouds.
This cold winter night.
Through snow.
Thwack of an ax, The.
Tilling the field.
Tub with no bottom, A.
Two plum trees, The.
Urine-stained quilt, A.
Utter aloneness—.
Village with a thousand eaves.
Wading through it.
Walking on dishes.
Washing the hoe.
When a heavy cart.
White blossoms of the pear.
White dew.
White lotus.
Willow leaves fallen, The.
Wind in the west.
Winter rain on moss.
Winter warbler.
With a runny nose.
With a woman friend.
With no underrobes.
With the noon conch blown.

Busse, Carl (b. 1872)
In the Night of the Full Moon.
Quiet Kingdom, The.

Busta, Christine (b. 1915)
My Beloved.
Seasons.
To the Dear Lord.

Butler, Charles E. (1909–81)
Darkness, The.
Letter to the Survivors.
Other Places, The.

Butler, Guy (b. 1918)
Great-great-grandmother.
In Memoriam, J. A. R., Drowned, East
　London.
Stranger to Europe.

Butler, Marylin
Listen.

Butler, Samuel (1612–80)
Argument, The.

Arms and the Man.
Ass will with his long ears fray, An.
Authority is a disease, and cure.
Convert's but a fly, that turns about, A.
Devil was more generous than Adam, The.
Far greater numbers have been lost by hopes.
For his religion it was fit.
Great philosopher did choke, A.
Greatest saints and sinners have been made,
　The.
How silly were those sages heretofore.
Hypocrisy will serve as well.
In mathematic[k]s he was greater.
Independent Squire.
Law, The.
Love.
Married man comes nearest to the dead, A.
Metaphysical Sectarian, The.
On William Prynne.
Question then, to state it first, The.
Quoth he, My faith as adamantine.
Quoth he, to bid me not to love.
Sidrophel, the Rosicrucian Conjurer.
Some were for setting up a king.
There is a tall long-sided dame.
This place (quoth she) they say's enchanted.
What makes a knave a child of God.
What makes all subjects discontent.
When civil fury [or dudgeon] first grew high.

Butler, Samuel (1835–1902)
O God! O Montreal!
Prayer, A: "Searcher of souls, you who in
　heaven abide."
Righteous Man, The.
She was too kind, wooed too persistently.

Butler, Tony
Limerick: "As played by the phantoms of
　Shrule."

Butler, William Allen (1825–1907)
Nothing to Wear.

Butterfield, F. G.
For Services Rendered.

Butts, Anthony (b. 1969)
Belle Isle Men, The.
Nature of Braille, The.
Poe Story, A.
Skin.

Butts, Antony
Massenet.

Buxton, Esther W. (fl. c.1910)
Putting the World to Bed.

Buzea, Constanta (b. 1941)
I'm Not Here / Never Was.

Buzzi, Paolo (1874–1956)
Finger-nails.

Buzzuola, Tommaso (fl. 1280)
Even as the moon amid the stars doth shed.

Bye, Reed (b. 1948)
Spring.

Byles, Mather (1706–88)
Great God, How Frail a Thing Is Man.
Great God, Thy Works.
To Thee the Tuneful Anthem Soars.
When Wild Confusion Wrecks the Air.

**Bynner, Witter ("Emanuel Morgan") (1881–
1959)**
All tempest.
Any other time would have done.
But for these apertures.
Defeat.
Donald Evans.
Driftwood.
Drinking Alone with the Moon.
Foreigner, A.
Haskell.
Highest Bidder, The.
Horses.
Idols.
If I were only dafter.
Lightning.
Lovers.
Moon, The.
More Lovely than Antiquity.
Opus 2.
Opus 17.

Sigh, A.
Tiles.
Titanic, The.
To a President.
Wall, The.
Wave, The.
What though they conquer us?
Wintry Mind, The.
Wistaria.

Byok Namkung (*fl.* **20th cent.**)
Grass.

Byrd, William (1543–1623)
Lulla, My Sweet Little Baby.
Quiet Life, The.
Song: "Let not the sluggish sleep."

Byrom, John (1692–1763)
Careless Content.
Christians, awake, salute the happy morn.
Dear Martin Folkes, dear scholar, brother, friend.
Epigram on the Feuds between Handel and Bononcini.
Four Epigrams on the Naturalization Bill.
Hymn: "Christians, awake, salute the happy morn."
Hymn for Christmas Day, A.
Jacobite Toast.
My Spirit Longeth for Thee.
Nimmers, The.
On Clergymen Preaching Politics.
On the Origin of Evil.
On Two Monopolists.
Passive Participle's Petition, The.
To Henry Wright of Mobberley, Esq. on Buying the Picture of Father Malebranche.
Tom the Porter.

Byron, Catherine (b. 1947)
Minding You.
Shipping the Pictures from Belfast.

Byron, George Gordon, 6th Baron (1788–1824)
Alas, the country! how shall tongue or pen.
All Is Vanity, Saith the Preacher.
And now I will convey thee to thy world.
And thou, who never yet of human wrong.
Answer to ——'s Professions of Affection.
Aristomenes.
At length with jostling, elbowing, and the aid.
Beppo; a Venetian Story.
'Bring forth the horse!' The horse was brought.
But I forget.—My pilgrim's shrine is won.
By the Rivers of Babylon We Sat Down and Wept.
Childe Harold's Pilgrimage, *sels.*
Corsair, The, *sels.*
Cornelian, The.
Darkness.
Destruction of Sennacherib, The.
Don Juan, *sels.*
Egeria! sweet creation of some heart.
Elegy: "O [*or* Oh] snatch'd away in beauty's bloom!"
England! with all thy faults I love thee still.
English Bards and Scotch Reviewers, *sels.*
Epistle to Augusta.
Epitaph for William Pitt.
Fare Thee Well.
Giaour, The.
Harp the Monarch Minstrel Swept, The.
Hear, Jehovah! / May the eternal serpent's curse be on him!
If Sometimes in the Haunts of Men.
Jephtha's Daughter.
Kind of change came in my fate, A.
Lachin y Gair.
Last Words on Greece.
Lawyer and the critic but behold, The.
Lines on Hearing That Lady Byron Was Ill.
Lines to Mr Hodgson.
Lines Written beneath a Picture.
Love and Death.
Maid of Athens, Ere We Part.
Manfred, *sels.*
Muse of the many-twinkling feet! whose charms.
Nurse's Dole in the Medea, The.
Oh! thou dead.

Oh! Weep for Those.
On a Carrier Who Died of Drunkenness.
On Jordan's Bank.
On My Thirty-third Birthday.
On This Day I Complete My Thirty-sixth Year.
One Struggle More, and I Am Free.
Or view the Lord of the unerring bow.
Prayer of Nature, The.
Prometheus.
Remember Thee! Remember Thee!
She Walks In Beauty.
So We'll Go No More A-Roving.
Song of Saul before His Last Battle.
Sonnet on Chillon.
Sonnet to Lake Leman.
Sonnet, to the Same.
Spirit Pass'd Before Me, A.
Stanzas for Music.
Stanzas: "When a man hath no freedom to fight for at home."
Stanzas Written on the Road between Florence and Pisa.
There Was a Sound of Revelry by Night.
To Belshazzar.
To Mr. Murray.
To Penelope, January 2, 1821.
To Thyrza.
Vision of Judgment, The.
What from this barren being do we reap?
When We Two Parted.
Written after Swimming from Sestos to Abydos.

Byron, Henry James (1834–84)
Adage: "Gardener's rule applies to youth and age, The."
Rural Simplicity.

C

"C., E." (*fl.* c.1595)
Emaricdulfe.

"C., E. F."
Limerick: "Cryptic philosopher, Kant, The."
Limerick: "I suppose I could try if I chose."

"C., J. E."
Limerick: "Old poet called Omar cried: 'Now,' An."

Caballero-Robb, Maria Elena
Dear Rosario.
Memoranda for Rosario.

Cabalquinto, Luis
Depths of Fields.
Ordinance, The.
Value Added in Smashing a German Roach on the Bathroom Door, The.

Cabico, Regie
Afternoon in Pangasinan with No Electricity, An.
Antonio Banderas in His Underwear.
Art in Architecture.
Check One.
Gameboy.
Mango Poem.

Cable, George Washington (1844–1925)
Belle Layotte.
Criole Candjo.
Dirge of St. Malo, The.
English muskets went bim! bim!, The.
Song of Cayetano's Circus, The.

Cabral de Melo Neto, Joao (b. 1920)
Canefield and the Sea, The.
Emptiness of Being a Man, The.
Like a bullet.
To Carlos Drummond de Andrade.

Cacciatore, Edoardo (b. 1912)
First Warning Sign: Epiphany.
Let's try another hand, let's redo the count.
Second Warning Sign: The Game Heats Up.
Third Warning Sign: An Endless Surprise.
Where do I stand and where do you? Seems like.

Caddel, Richard
Against Numerology.
For Tom.

Caddy, Caroline (b. 1944)
Three-Inch Reflector.

Cader, Teresa D.
Empress Shōtoku Invents Printing in 1770.
Spirit Papers.

Cady, Joseph
After Hearing Heterosexual Poets in October 1974: What It Seems Like to Write a Male Homosexual Love Poem Now.
Starting 1973: What to Do Now that Peace Has Been Announced.

Caedmon (*fl.* c.675 A.D.)
Cædmon's Hymn.
Hymn: "Now we should praise Heaven-kingdom's guard."
Noah's Flood.
Temptation and Fall of Man, The.

Caesar, Irving
Animal Crackers in My Soup.
Crazy Rhythm.
I Want to Be Happy.
Is It True What They Say about Dixie?
Sometimes I'm Happy.
Spanish Jake.
Tea for Two.
Too Many Rings Around Rosie.
What a Perfect Combination.

Cage, John (1912–92)
2 Pages, 122 Words on Music and Dance.
25 Mesostics Re and Not Re Mark Tobey.
Abundance.
Boddhisattva Doctrine: Enter.
The / children have a society of their own.
Continue; I'll discover where you sweat (Kierkegaard)
Daily warmth we, The.
Get it, / she said, so it's unknown which parent.
Hearing of past actions.
Lazy dog (a bomb containing ten), The.
Lecture on Nothing.
Let's Call It The / Collective Consciousness (We've Got).
Mother wrote to say: "Stay."
Since the / Spirit's omnipresent, there's a difference.
Solo for Voice 17 Song with Electronics (Relevant)
They dance the world as.
To / know whether or not art is contemporary.
Two Mesostics Re Merce Cunningham.
We've / poisoned our food, polluted our air.
Writing through the Cantos.
You can't be serIous she said.

Cagnone, Nanni (b. 1939)
Book Three: On Preparation.
Fifth Book: On Limitation.
General names, no other.
It isn't any of this.
It lies—when urged to, it lies.
No place is extreme.

Cahn, Sammy (1913–93)
All the Way.
Call Me Irresponsible.
Come Fly with Me.
Day by Day.
Guess I'll Hang My Tears Out to Dry.
I Fall in Love Too Easily.
I'll Walk Alone.
I Should Care.
It's Magic.
Let It Snow! Let It Snow! Let It Snow!
Love and Marriage.
(Love Is) the Tender Trap.
Put 'Em in a Box, Tie 'Em with a Ribbon (And Throw 'Em in the Deep Blue Sea)
Second Time Around, The.
Teach Me Tonight.
Things We Did Last Summer, The.
Time after Time.
Until the Real Thing Comes.

Cain, Jack
Empty elevator, An.
Empty room.
Someone's newspaper.
Waiting.

Cakrabartī, Nabíncandra
Can you claim to win.

Cakrabarttī, Mā Bāsantī
Ma, if You wore a Benarasi sari.
Wherever there's a woman in any Bengali home.

Calderón de la Barca, Pedro (1600–81)
Dream Called Life, The.
Life Is a Dream.
Those Which Were Pomp and Delight.
We live, while we see the sun.

Calderón, Eduardo
Raising the Mediating Center and the Field of Evil with the Twenty-Five Thousand Accounts and the Chant of the Ancients.

Calderón, Teresa (b. 1955)
Affairs of Memory.
Domestic Blues.
Exile.
From Your Depths and Kneeling.
State of Seige.

Caldwell, Anne
I Know That You Know.
Left All Alone Again Blues.
Raggedy Ann.

Caldwell, E. K.
Love Poem: "Olfactory paradise."

Caldwell, Kim
Moonlight.

Calil, Amina (b. 1970)
Blouse of Felt.

Calisch, Edward N. *See* **Moise, Penina**

Call, Wathen Mark Wilks (1817–90)
Summer Days.

Callimachus (c.300–240 B.C.)
As long as it was still noon and the earth.
At dawn we buried Melanippus. At sunset.
Crethis.
Do not say "Godspeed" to me, wicked heart.
Does Charidas lie beneath you? If you mean.
Eileithyia, once more.
Epigram.
"Goodbye, O sun," said Cleombrotus of Ambracia.
"Goodbye Sun!" said the Ambracian.
Here Philip the father buried.
Here Saon of Akanthos, Dikon's son.
Hesiod's is the theme and his the style.
Hesiod's style and themes: the poet from Soloi.
His Son.
His twelve-year-old / son.
Hymn to Apollo.
Hymn to Artemis.
Hymn to Demeter.
I despise neo-epic verse sagas.
I hate the cyclic poem, nor do I rejoice.
Kallignotos swore to Ionis—no one.
Kallistion the wife of Kritias.
Menoitas of Lyktos.
Mousetrap, The.
News of Your Death.
On Himself.
On the Bath of Pallas.
On the mountain, Epicydes the hunter seeks.
Or rather the sacred fish with the golden faces.
Our guest's wound went unnoticed.
Prologue to the Aetia.
Saon of Acanthus.
Since you are dead, Timon, tell me which.
Sleep cold at someone's.
Somebody told me you were dead.
Someone spoke of your death, Herakleitos. It brought me.
Someone told me, Heracleitus.
Something's there, by Pan there's something hidden.
Sopolis.
South wind does not shed so great a cast, The.
Statue of Bereniké, A.
Stranger was short: let my verse be such, The.
Theaitetos.
These gifts to Aphrodite.
They fell asleep but not for long, for soon.
Timon, for you exist no more.
To Archinus.

"Who were you, shipwrecked stranger?"
Leontichos found.
Whoever passes by my tomb, know.
Would that there had never been swift ships!
You pass the tomb of Battus' son, well skilled.

Calloway, Cab
Minnie, the Moocher.

Calpurnius Siculus, Titus (*fl.* 1st cent. A.D.)
Eclogues, *sels.*

Calverley, Charles Stuart (1831–84)
Ballad: "Auld wife sat at her ivied door, The."
Changed.
Companions.
Contentment.
Disaster.
Dover to Munich.
Flight.
"Forever."
Hic Vir, Hic Est.
In the Gloaming.
Lines on Hearing the Organ.
On the Rhine.
Palace, The.
Peace.
Schoolmaster abroad with His Son, The.

Cambridge, Ada (1844–1926)
Desire.
Fashion.
Future Verdict, The.
Virgin Martyr, The.

Cambridge, Richard Owen (1717–1802)
Fakir, The.
On Seeing a Tapestry Chair-Bottom Beautifully Worked by His Daughter for Mrs Holroyd.

Camden, William (1551–1623)
On a Puritanicall Lock-Smith.

Cameron, C. C.
Don't Give Up.
Success.

Cameron, Mary (Mairi Chamaran, Nighean Fream Challaird) (b. c.1625)
Song of Sorrow, A.

Cameron, Nigel
I have no substance and no form.

Cameron, Norman (b. 1905)
Compassionate Fool, The.
Dirty Little Accuser, The.
Disused Temple, The.
Fight with a Water-Spirit.
Firm of Happiness, Limited, The.
For the Fly-Leaf of a School-Book.
Forgive Me, Sire.
From a Woman to a Greedy Lover.
Green, Green Is El Aghir.
In the Queen's Room.
Meeting My Former Self.
Naked among the Trees.
She and I.
Shepherdess.
Thespians at Thermopylae, The.
Three Love Poems.
Unfinished Race, The.

Cami, Ben (b. 1920)
You Stand.

Camille, Roussan (1915–61)
Nocturne: "Wildness of haggard flights."

Camlan, Goronva (*fl.* c.1846)
Education in Wales.
Lady Charlotte Guest.
Literature and Action.

Camões [or Camõens], Luis de (1524–80)
Babylon and Sion (Goa and Lisbon)
Battle's uncertain work begins; and move.
Do This Favour for Me.
Feats of Arms, and famed heroick Host, The.
Lusiads, The.
On a Shipmate, Pero Moniz, Dying at Sea.
On Revisiting Cintra after the Death of Catarina.
On the Death of Catarina de Attayda.
Rev'rend Father stood inculcating, The.
Sonnet: "Leave me, all sweet refrains my lip hath made."
Sonnet: My Errors My Loves My Unlucky Star.

Sonnet: That Sad and Joyful Dawn.
Sonnet: "Time and the mortal will stand never fast."
With glad reception our Commander meets.

Camp, James (b. 1923)
Female Dancer.

Campana, Dino (1885–1932)
Autumn Garden.
Genoa.
Window, The.

Campanella, Tomasso (1568–1639)
People, The.

Campbell, Alistair (b. 1925)
Against Te Rauparaha.
Bitter Harvest.
Dark Lord of Savaiki, The.
Return, The.
Why Don't You Talk to Me?

Campbell, Anne
Before and After Marriage.
Shabby Old Dad.
There Is Always a Place for You.
To My Friend.

Campbell, Calder
When midst the summer-roses the warm bees.

Campbell, David (1915–79)
Anguish of Ants, The.
Ariel.
Australian Dream, The.
Duchesses.
Fox.
Hear the Bird of Day.
Here, under Pear-trees.
Hotel Marine.
Lovers, The.
Mothers and Daughters.
Mr. Hughes.
Night Sowing.
On Frosty Days.
Pallid Cuckoo.
Small-town Gladys.
Song for the Cattle.
Man in the Honeysuckle, The.
Ulinda.

Campbell, Dorothea Primrose
To Miss Sophia Headle.

Campbell, James Edwin (1867–96)
Mors et Vita.

Campbell, Janet (Seònaid Chaimbeul) (*fl.* c.1645)
This night tonight is cold.

Campbell, Jimmy
Good Night, Sweetheart.
If I Had You.
Try a Little Tenderness.

Campbell, John (1766–1840)
I'm Far from What I Call My Home.

Campbell, Joseph (Seosamh MacCathmhaoil) (1881–1944)
Ad Limina.
Antiquary, The.
Blind Man at the Fair, The.
Dancer, The.
Darkness.
Gombeen, The.
I Am the Mountainy Singer.
Ideal and Reality.
Old Woman, The.

Campbell, Meg (b. 1937)
Journeys.
Maui.

Campbell, Roy (1902–57)
Attend my fable if your ears be clean.
Autumn.
Choosing a Mast.
Fishing Boats in Martigues.
Georgian Spring.
Good Resolution, A.
Hail, mediocrity, beneath whose spell.
Heartbreak Camp.
Here, where relumed by changing seasons, burn.
Horses on the Camargue.
Luis de Camões.
Mass at Dawn.
Maternal Earth stirs redly from beneath.

Next him Jack Squire through his own tear-
    drops sploshes.
On Professor Drennan's Verse.
On Some South African Novelists.
On the Same.
Palm, The.
Serf, The.
Sisters, The.
St John of the Cross: Song of the Soul That Is
    Glad to Know God by Faith.
St John of the Cross: Songs of the Soul in
    Rapture.
Toledo.
Tristan da Cunha.
Veld Eclogue: The Pioneers, A.
Volunteer's Reply to the Poet, The.
Zebras, The.
Zulu Girl, The.

Campbell, Siobhan (b. 1962)
Big John's Tears Fall to the River.
Chairmaker, The.
Constant Welcome, The.
Legacy.

Campbell, Thomas (1774–1844)
Battle of the Baltic.
Freedom and Love.
Hohenlinden.
Jilted Nymph, The.
Last Man, The.
Lord Ullin's Daughter.
Maid of Neidpath, The.
Ode to Winter.
River of Life, The.
Soldier's Dream, The.
'Tis summer eve, when heaven's ethereal bow.
To the Evening Star.
Wizard.
Ye Mariners of England.

Campbell, Wilfred (William Wilfred Campbell)
(1861–1918)
How One Winter Came in the Lake Region.
Indian Summer.
Morning on the Shore.
Winter Lakes, The.

Campbell, William Wilfred *See* **Campbell,**
Wilfred

Campert, Jan (1902–43)
Eighteen Dead, The.

Campert, Remco (b. 1929)
Avignon.
Futile Poem, A.
Message about the Times.
Sign of the Times.
Silver Talk.
Stroll to Parfondeval, A.
Theatre.

Campion, Thomas (1567–1620)
As by the stream[e]s of Babylon [or Babilon].
Author of light, revive my dying spright.
Awake, Awake! [Thou Heavy Sprite].
Blame Not My Cheekes.
Dance, The.
Fain Would I Wed.
Fire, fire, fire, fire!
First Love.
Follow, follow[e] / Though with mischiefe.
Follow Thy Fair Sun[ne] [Unhappy Shadow].
Follow your saint, follow with accents sweet.
Heart's Music.
Hymn in Praise of Neptune, A.
I Care Not for These Ladies.
It Fell on a Summer's [or Sommers] Day [or
    Daie].
Jack and Joan.
Kind Are Her Answers.
Man of Life Upright, The.
Now Winter Nights Enlarge.
O Come Quickly!
Rose-cheeked Laura, Come.
Seek the Lord.
Shall I come, if I swim? wide are the waves,
    you see.
Shall I Come, Sweet Love.
Sleep, Angry Beauty.
Sweet, exclude me[e] not, nor be divided.
There is a garden in her face.

Think'st thou to seduce me then.
Thrice Toss[e] These Oaken Ashes in the Air
    [or Ayre].
Thus I Resolve.
To Music Bent Is My Retired Mind.
View Mee, Lord.
What Fair[e] Pomp[e].
What If a Day [or a Month or a Year].
When to Her Lute Corinna [or Corrina] Sings.

Campo, Cristina (1923–77)
Ah that the Tiger.
At Times I Say: Let's Try to Be Joyous.
Canon 4.
Devout like a Branch.
Indian Summer.
Love, Today My Lip.
Now I Want All My Letters White Again.
White Summer Clothes are Folded Away, The.

Campo, Rafael (b. 1964)
Allegory.
Asylum.
Aunt Toni's Heart.
Battle Hymn of the Republic, The.
Belonging.
El Curandero.
El Día de los Muertos.
For J. W.
Her Final Show.
Jane Doe #2.
Kelly.
Lost in the Hospital.
Lost Plaza Is Everywhere, The.
Manuel.
Medical Student Learns Love and Death, A.
My Childhood in Another Part of the World.
My Voice.
Our Country of Origin.
S. W.
Superman Is Dead.
Towards Curing AIDS
What the Body Told.

Canan, Janine (b. 1942)
Goddesses, The.
Inanna's Chant.
Mother Dawning.
Oh Kali.
Radioactive.

Candī, Andha
Bring Tara quickly, Mountain.

Cane, Melville (b. 1879)
Dawn Has Yet to Ripple In.
Hymn to Night.
Tree in December.

Cangiullo, Francesco (1884–1977)
Detonation.

Cannan, May Wedderburn (1893–1973)
Rouen.

Cannell, Skipwith (1887–1957)
King, The.

Canning, George (1770–1827)
From mental mists to purge a nation's eyes.
Inscription: "For one long term, or e'er her
    trial came."

Canning, George (1770–1827) *and* **John**
Hookham Frere
Friend of Humanity and the Knife Grinder,
    The.

Canning, George (1770–1827) *and* **William**
Gifford (1756–1826)
Progress of Man, The.

Canning, George (1770–1827), George Ellis *and*
John Hookham Frere
Rogero's Song.

Canning, Josiah D. (1816–92)
Indian Gone!, The.

Cannon, Hughie
Bill Bailey, Won't You Please Come Home.

Cannon, Melissa
Sisters, The.

Canton, William (1845–1926)
Day-Dreams.

Cao Bá Quát (1809–53)
On Reading *The Book of Odes*.

Capetanakis, Demetrios (1912–44)
Abel.

Isles of Greece, The.

Capito
Lacking grace / beauty.

Capone, Giovanna (Janet)
In Answer to Their Questions.

Caraion, Ion (1923–86)
Enveloping Echo, The.
Remember.
Song from the Occupation Time.
Tomorrow the Past Comes.
Ultimate Argument.

Carberry, H. D.
It takes a mighty fire.

"Carbery, Ethna" (Anna Johnston MacManus)
(1866–1902)
King of Ireland's Cairn, The.
Love-Talker, The.
On an Island.

Carbó, Nick
Civilizing the Filipino.
I Found Orpheus Levitating.
In Tagalog Ibon Means Bird.
Little Brown Brother.
Robo.
Verso Libre.
Votive Candles.
When the Grain Is Golden and the Wind Is
    Chilly, Then It Is the Time to Harvest.

Carbone, Lisa M.
Flight from the Marriage Bed.

Cardenal, Ernesto (b. 1925)
For me to lose you and for you to lose me, we
    both lose.
For Those Dead, Our Dead.
From those theaters, Claudia, from those
    feasts.
I offer these verses to you, Claudia, because
    you are their mistress.
In Xóchitl in Cuícatl.
León.
Lights.
Like Empty Beer Cans.
Luke 16:1–9; He also said to the disciples.
Mosquito Kingdom.
Prayer for Marilyn Monroe.
Psalm 5.
Room 5600.
Unrighteous Mammon (Luke 16:9)

Cardiff, Gladys (b. 1942)
Candelaria and the Sea Turtle.
Carious Exposure.
Combing.
Dragon Skate.
For His Ring and Watch on the Night Stand.
Grey Woman.
Hunting the Dugong.
It has something to do with final words.
Leaves like Fish.
Long Person.
Making Lists.
Swimmer.
Tlanusi' Yi, the Leech Place.
To Frighten a Storm.
Tsa'lagi Council Tree.
Where Fire Burns.

Carducci, Giosuè (1835–1907)
Petrarch.
Primo Vere.
Snowfall.

Carenza *and* **Iselda** (*fl.* 12th cent.)
Tenson.

Carew, Thomas (1594?–1640?)
Another [Epitaph on the Lady Mary Villiers].
Another [On the Duke of Buckingham].
Beautiful Mistress, A.
Boldness[e] in Love.
Come, then, and mounted on the wings of
    Love.
Comparison, The.
Deposition from Love, A.
Disdain Returned.
Divine Mistress, A.
Elegy upon the Death of the Dean of [St.]
    Paul's, Dr. John Donne, An.
Epitaph on the Lady Mary Villiers.

Carey

Eternity of Love Protested.
Excuse of Absence, An.
Fancy, A.
Fly That Flew into My Mistress'[s] Eye, A.
For a Picture Where a Queen Laments over the
Tomb of a Slain Knight.
Hymeneal Song, on the Nuptials of the Lady
Ann Wentworth and the Lord Lovelace, An.
I will enjoy thee now my Celia, come.
In Answer of an Elegiacal[l] Letter, Upon the
Death of the King of Sweden [from Aurelian
Townsend, Inviting Me to Write on That
Subject].
In Praise of His Mistress.
Ingrateful[l] Beauty Threatened.
Lady's Prayer to Cupid, A.
Looking-Glass, A.
Love's Force.
Lover, upon an Accident Necessitating His
Departure, Consults with Reason, A.
Maria Wentworth.
Mediocrity in Love Rejected.
New Year's Sacrifice: To Lucinda, A.
Now in more subtle wreaths I will entwine.
On His Mistress Looking in a Glass.
On Sight of a Gentlewoman's Face in the
Water.
On the Death of Donne.
On the Marriage of T. K. and C. C.: The
Morning Stormy.
Pastoral[l] Dialogue, A.
Persuasions to Enjoy.
Prayer to the Wind, A.
Rapture, A.
Second Rapture, The.
Secrecy [or Secresie] Protested.
Song, [A]: "Ask[e] me no more where Jove
bestow[e]s."
Song: The Willing Prisoner to His Mistress.
Spring, The.
Tinder, The.
To A. L.; Persuasions [or Perswasions] to
Love.
To a Lady That Desired I Would Love Her.
To Ben Jonson.
To Celia, upon Love's Ubiquity.
To Her in Absence; a Ship.
To my Friend G.N. from Wrest.
To My Inconstant Mistress [or Mistris].
To My Mistress[e] in My Absence.
To My Mistress Sitting by a River's Side; an
Eddy.
To My Rival.
To My Worthy Friend Master George Sands
[or Sandys], on His Translation of the
Psalms.
To Saxham.
To T. H., a Lady Resembling My Mistress.
To the King, at His Entrance into Saxham: By
Master John Crofts.
To the New Year [For the Countess of
Carlisle].
To the Reader of Master William Davenant's
Play [The Wits].
True Beauty, The.
Upon a Mole in Celia's Bosom.
Upon a Ribbon [or Ribband].
Upon Master Walter Montagu's Return from
Travel.
Upon My Lord Chief Justice's Election of My
Lady Anne Wentworth [or A.W.] for His
Mistress.
Upon Some Alterations in My Mistress, after
My Departure into France.

Carey, Henry (1693?–1743)
Author's Quietus, The.
Drinking-Song, A.
Lilliputian Ode on Their Majesties'
Accession, A.
Maid's Husband, The.
Namby-Pamby. A Panegyric on the New
Versification, Address'd to A———
P———, Esq.
Namby-Pamby; or, A Panegyric on the New
Versification.
Roger and Dolly.
Sally in Our Alley.

Carey, Lady Elizabeth (1589–1639)
Mariam.
Carey, Mary (d. after 1680)
Wretten by Me at the Death of My 4th Sonne
and 5th Child Perigrene Payler.
Carey [or Cary], Patrick (c.1623–57)
Fig for the Lower House, A.
Nulla Fides.
Carey, Tom (b. 1951)
Zohar.
Cariaga, Catalina (b. 1958)
Family Tree, The.
Carkesse, James (fl. 1678)
His Rule of Behaviour: If You Are Civil, I Am
Sober.
On the Doctors' Telling Him that till He Left
off Making Verses He Was Not Fit to Be
Discharged.
Carle, Frankie
Oh! What It Seemed to Be.
Carlson, Douglas
Russ Joy Little League.
Carlson, Sir Edward
Scribbled at a Cabinet Meeting.
Carlson, Jim
I need appreciation.
Stand up, be proud.
Carlson, Ron
Max Who Caught a Car.
Carlyle, Thomas (1795–1881)
Morning.
Sower's Song, The.
Today.
Carman, Bliss (William Bliss Carman) (1861–1929)
Lord of My Heart's Elation.
Low Tide on Grand Pré.
More Ancient Mariner, A.
Morning in the Hills.
Northern Vigil, A.
Vagabond Song, A.
Carman, Bliss (1861–1929) and Richard Hovey (1864–1900)
Earth's Lyric.
Carman, William Bliss See Carman, Bliss
Carmi, T. (b. 1925)
First Song.
Second Song.
She Sleeps.
Short Song.
Third Song.
Carmichael, Amy
Do We Not Hear Thy Footfall?
Last Defile, The.
Yet Listen Now.
Carmichael, Hoagy (1899–1981)
Baltimore Oriole.
Doctor, Lawyer, Indian Chief.
Don't Forget to Say No, Baby.
Georgia on My Mind.
Hong Kong Blues.
How Little We Know.
I Get Along Without You Very Well.
Lazy River.
Nearness of You, The.
Rockin' Chair.
Skylark.
Star Dust.
Two Sleepy People.
Carmichael, Rebekah (fl. 1790–1806)
Tooth, The.
Young Lass's Soliloquy, A.
Carmona, Belinda Zubicueta (b. 1955)
Another Day.
Between the Lines.
Daily Task.
Storing Memories.
Stretched Out in Solitude.
Tenderness.
Carnevale, Robert (fl. 20th cent.)
Walking by the Cliffside Dyeworks.
Carnevali, Emanuel (b. 1898)
Almost a God.
Kiss.

Queer Things.
Serenade.
Sermon.
Carolan [or O'Carolan], Turlough (1670–1738)
Gracey Nugent.
Mabel Kelly.
Peggy Browne.
Caroutch, Yvonne (b. 1937)
Child of silence and shadow.
I come to you with the vertigoes of the source.
Limb of forests rises up, The.
Night opens like an almond.
Carpenter, Edward (1844–1929)
Summer Heat.
Through the Long Night.
To a Stranger.
Carpenter, Maurice (b. 1911)
To S. T. C. on His 179th Birthday, October
12th, 1951.
Carpenter, William (b. 1940)
Evening Wind.
Ghosts.
Night Shadows.
Carphyllides
Happy Man, A.
Passer-by, don't blame this memorial.
Carr, Sir John (1732–1807)
Memories of Childhood.
Carr, Leroy (1905–1935)
How Long Blues.
Carr, Mary Jane
Castle in the Fire, The.
Carr, Sally
Easter Outing.
Carranza, Eduardo (1913–85)
Azure because of You.
Carrera Andrade, Jorge (d. 1903)
Clock, The.
Perfect Life, The.
Second Life of My Mother.
Sunday.
Transfiguration of the Rain.
Your body is a garden, a bush of flowers.
Your body is a golden temple.
Your body is bathed eternally.
Carrier, Constance (b. 1908)
At Tripolis.
Clause for a Covenant.
Commencement.
Elegy.
Helianthus.
Laudare.
Point of View, A.
Pro Patria.
Carroll, Harry
I'm Always Chasing Rainbows.
Carroll, Jim (b. 1951)
Heroin.
Maybe I'm Amazed.
Paregoric Babies.
Withdrawal Letter.
Carroll, Kenneth (b. 1959)
DC Nocturne.
Domino Theory (or Snoop Dogg rules the
world), The.
Short Poem.
Something easy for Ultra Black nationalists.
Theory on Extinction or what happened to the
dinosaurs?
Truth about Karen, The.
Upper Marlboro.
Carroll, Lewis (Charles Lutwidge Dodgson) (1832–98)
Alice's Recitation.
Baker's Tale, The.
Brother and Sister.
Crocodile, The.
Duchess's Lullaby, The.
Evidence Read at the Trial of the Knave of
Hearts.
Father William.
Fit the Second: The Bellman's Speech.
Fit the Sixth: The Barrister's Dream.
Hiawatha's Photographing.
Humpty Dumpty's Poetic Recitation.

Hunting of the Snark, The.
Jabberwocky.
Limerick: "His sister named [*or* called] Lucy O'Finner."
Limerick: "There was a young lady of station."
Limerick: "There was a young lady of Whitby."
Limerick: "There was once a young man of Oporta."
Little Birds Are Playing.
Lobster Quadrille, A.
Long Tale, A.
Mad Gardener's Song, The.
Mad Hatter's Song, The.
Poeta Fit, Non Nascitur.
Rules and Regulations.
Song of the Mock Turtle, The.
Sum, A.
Vanishing, The.
Visitor, A.
Walrus and the Carpenter, The.
Welcome Queen Alice.
White Knight's Song, The.

Carroll, Paul (b. 1927)
Father.
In the Shakespeare Garden at Northwestern University.
Ode on a Bicycle on Halsted Street in a Sudden Summer Thunderstorm.
Ode to the Angels Who Move Perpetually toward the Dayspring of Their Youth.

Carruth, Hayden (b. 1921)
Ah, you beast of love.
Called him "Big Joe" yes and Joe Turner it was his name.
Camps, The.
Capper Kaplinski at the North Side Cue Club.
Cows at Night, The.
Crucifixion.
Emergency Haying.
Essay on Death.
Fear and Anger in the Mindless Universe.
Hard Journey, A. Yes.
In filthy Puerto Rico lives a bird with no.
Insomniac Sleeps Well for Once and, The.
Late Sonnet.
Little Citizen, Little Survivor.
Of Distress Being Humiliated by the Classical Chinese Poets.
On Being Asked to Write a Poem against the War in Vietnam.
Once more by the brook the alder leaves.
Our Tense and Wintry Minds.
Paragraph 36.
Quality of Wine.
Republicans? We've got a few. In fact.
Rimrock, Where It Is.
Saturday at the Border.
So be it. I am.
Soft Time of the Year, The.
Sonnet: "Cry, crow."
Sonnet: "To see a woman long oppressed by fear."
Sonnet: "Well, she told me I had an aura. 'What?' I said."
Sonnet: "You rose from our embrace and the small light spread."
Testament.
This Decoration.
Twilight Comes.
Why speak of the use.
Wreck of the Circus Train, The.
Your dream: / The letters HIV appear.
Your tears, Niobe.

Carryl, Charles Edward (1841–1920)
Sleepy Giant, The.
Song of the Camel, The.
Walloping Window-Blind, The.

Carryl, Guy Wetmore (1873–1904)
Ballad: "As I was walkin' the jungle round, a-killin' of tigers an' time."
Domineering Eagle and the Inventive Bratling, The.
Embarrassing Episode of Little Miss Muffet, The.
How a Girl Was Too Reckless of Grammar [by

Far].
Patrician Peacocks and the Overweening Jay, The.
Sycophantic Fox and the Gullible Raven, The.

Carson, Anne
By God.
Flexion of God.
God Coup, The.
God Fit, The.
God's Handiwork.
God's Name.
God's Work.
Longing, a Documentary.
My Religion.

Carson, Ciaran (b. 1948)
Army.
Asylum.
Bagpipe Music.
Belfast Confetti.
Bloody Hand.
Bomb Disposal, The.
Calvin Klein's Obsession.
Campaign.
Car Cemetery, The.
Céilí.
Cocktails.
Dresden.
Hamlet.
Insular Celts, The.
Irish for No, The.
Judgement.
Knee, The.
Mouth, The.
Slate Street School.

Carson, Jo
I Am Asking You to Come Back Home.

Carson, Robert (b. 1945)
Old Sailor Looking at a Container Ship.

Carstairs, Christian (*fl.* 1763–86)
Addressed to a Beech Tree.
Nightingale.
On Loch Leven.
Song, A: "Farewell my Betty, and farewell my Annie."

Carter, Anne Babson
Cobb's Barns.

Carter, Elizabeth (1717–1806)
Dialogue, A.
Ode to Wisdom.
On the Death of Mrs. Rowe.

Carter, John
Adagio at Twilight.

Carter, Martin (b. 1927)
Bitter Wood.

Carter, Ron
Vietnam Dream.

Cartwright, Keith (b. 1960)
ALL-YOU-CAN-EAT / catfish houses.
Delta, The / Itch of cayenne.
In / dreams / diving deeper / than my disbelief.

Cartwright, Peter (1785–1872)
Our Bondage It Shall End.
Where Are the Hebrew Children?

Cartwright, William (1611–43)
Beauty and Denial.
Dream Broke, A.
Falsehood.
New Year's Gift, A.
No Platonic [*or* Platonique] Love.
On a Virtuous Young Gentlewoman That Died Suddenly.
On the Great Frost (1634)
On the Queen's Return from the Low Countries.
Song of Dalliance, A.
To Chloe, Who Wished Herself Young Enough for Me.
To Mr. W. B., at the Birth of His First Child.
Valediction: "Bid me not go where neither suns nor showers [show'rs]."
Women.

Carus, Titus Lucretius *See* **Lucretius**

Caruthers, Mazie V.
Prayer of Any Husband.

Carver, Dale R.
Poet, The.

Carver, Raymond (1939–90)
Catch, The.
Cobweb, The.
Quiet Nights.
Walk, A.
What the Doctor Said.
Window, The.
Woman Bathing.

Cary, Alice (1820–71)
Autumn.
Bridal Veil, The.
In Bonds.
Katrina on the Porch.
Kemp Owyne.
My Creed.
November.
Sea-Side Cave, The.
Telling Fortunes.
To Mother Fairie.
To Solitude.
West Country, The.
Window Just Over the Street, The.

Cary, Dame Clementia (1615–71)
You blessed Soules, who stand before.

Cary, Elizabeth *See* **Falkland, Elizabeth Cary, Countess of**

Cary, Phoebe (1824–71)
Advice Gratis to Certain Women.
Day Is Done, The.
Granny's House.
Harvest Gathering.
Homes for All.
Human and Divine.
Hymn: "How dare I in thy courts appear."
Jacob.
Leak in the Dike, The.
Legend of the Northland, A.
Nearer Home.
Prodigals.
Psalm of Marriage.
Samuel Brown.
Shakespearian Readings.
True Love.
Unbelief.
When Lovely Woman.

Casal, Julián de (1863–93)
My Loves.

Cascella, Anna (b. 1941)
Difficult with You.
Even Your Escape Is a Bit Special.
Forgetfulness Is Not.
In the Deposits of the Heart.
Nomad of the Sky, The.
To One Afflicted with Adolescence.

Casey, Kenneth (*fl.* 1925)
Sweet Georgia Brown.

Casey, Michael (b. 1947)
Learning.
LZ Gator Body Collector, The.
On What the Army Does with Heads.

Casey, Philip (b. 1950)
Casanova on His Deathbed.

Cashdan, Liz
Laughing All the Way.

Cass, Stephen
Limerick: "Psychiatrist fellow from Rye, A."

Cassell, M.
Limerick: "Said Old Nick: 'Mister Lewis and me.'"

Cassells, Cyrus (b. 1957)
Beautiful Signor.
Courtesy, A Trenchant Grace, A.
From the Theater of Wine.
Marathon.
New Song of Solomon, The.
Soul Make a Path through Shouting.
These Are Not Brushstrokes.
Women, The.

Cassian, Nina (b. 1924)
Blood, The.
Bread and Wine.
Capital Punishment.
Ghost.
Hills picking up the / moonlight like.
I Left Those Walls.

Knowledge.
Lady of Miracles.
Like Ana.
Like Gulliver.
Morning Exercises.
Orbits.
Other Life, The.
Part of a Bird.
Rabbit, The.
Sand.
Temptation.
Us Two.

Castel Fiorentino, Terino da (*fl.* 1250)
If, as thou say'st, thy love tormenteth thee.

Castellanos, Rosario (1925–74)
Destiny.
Farewell, The.
Foreign Woman.
Great fish's eyes never shut, The.
Hecuba's Testament.
Meditation on the Threshold.
Nazareth.
O cloud that wants to be the sky's arrow.
Origin.
Other, The.
Palm Tree, A.
Parable of the Unfaithful Wife.
Poetry Is Not You.
Return, The.
Silence around an Ancient Stone.
Speaking of Gabriel.
Two Meditations.
Two Poems.
Useless Day.
What is weaker than a god? It groans hungry.
You Are Not Poetry.

Casterton, Julia
One Flesh.

Castillejo, Cristóbal de (1490–1550)
Some Day, Some Day.

Castillo, Ana (b. 1953)
Me and Baby.
Napa, California.
Toltec, The.
Women Are Not Roses.

Castillo, Otto René (1936–67)
Apolitical Intellectuals.
Before the Scales, Tomorrow.
Distances.

Castillo, Sandra M.
Almendares.
El Apagón.
At the Havana Hilton.
Contra, The.
Cuba.
En el Sol de Mi Barrio.
Letter to Yeni on Peering into Her Life.
Monday Night at Pedro's.
Primos.
Rincón.

Casto, Robert Clayton (b. 1932)
Salt Pork, The.

Caston, Anne
Blowing Eggs.
Burden, The.
Gathering at the River.

Castro, Michael (b. 1945)
Blew It.
New York City.

Castro, Rosalía de (1837–85)
Ailing Woman Felt Her Forces Ebb, The.
As I Composed This Little Book.
Atmosphere Is Incandescent, The.
Bells, The.
Black Mood.
Candescent Lies the Air.
Feeling Her End Would Come with Summer's
    End.
Feet of Spring Are on the Stair, The.
Glowworm Scatters Flashes, A.
He Who Weeps Goes Not Alone.
Hour After Hour, Day After Day.
I in My Bed of Thistles.
I Know Not What I Seek Eternally.
I Love You... Why Do You Hate Me?

I Was Born at Birth of Blossoms.
Justice of Men! I Go in Search of You.
Mild Was the Air.
Now all that sound of laughter, sound of
    singing.
Now that the Sunset of Hope.
Plants don't talk, people say.
Spring Does Not Flow Now, The.
They say that plants don't talk, nor do.
They Say that the Plants Do Not Speak.
When the Frosts Cover Them.

Catalano, Gary (b. 1947)
Australia.
Jews Speak in Heaven, The.

Cataldi, Lee (b. 1942)
13 November 1983.
Advice.
It's Easy.
We Could Have Met.

Cather, Willa Sibert (1876–1947)
Grandmither, Think Not I Forget.
Somewhere, sometime, in an April twilight.
Spanish Johnny.

Catherine of Siena (Saint Catherine) (1347–80)
We were enclosed.

Catina, Ray
Negotiations.
Philosophy.

Catley, Douglas
Limerick: "Boadicea often would goad."
Limerick: "Famed big-hitter in cricket, A."
Limerick: "God brought perfect man to
    fruition."
Limerick: "Good mechanics are all of one
    mind."
Limerick: "Lass of curvacious physique, A."
Limerick: "Prostitute living in London, A."
Limerick: "Scribe, to the vulgar inclined, A."
Limerick: "There's a fortunate priest of St.
    Paul's."
Limerick: "When Pegotty found Barkis was
    willing."
Limerick: "Wily Napoleon Bonaparte, The."

Cato, Nancy (b. 1917)
Independence.

**Catullus (Gaius [*or* Caius] Valerius Catullus)
(87–c.54 B.C.)**
Accept, O Priapus, the moister.
Attis.
By strangers' coasts and waters, many days at
    sea.
Carmina, *sels.*
De Amore Suo.
He is like a god.
He Seems to Me Almost a God.
Ipsithilla, my pet, my favorite dish.
Just now I found a young boy.
Lesbia.
Lesbia's sparrow!
My lovely, sweet Ipsithilla.
My Sweetest Lesbia.
My woman says she'd rather have me.
Odi et Amo.
Sun May Set, The.
Sweet sparrow, my lover's pet.
To Aurelius.
To Aurelius and Furius.
To Himself.
To Juventius.
Unto no body my woman saith she had rather
    a wife be [*or* bee].
What for?
Your sins have brought my mind so low.

Catulus, Quintus (*fl.* 102 B.C.)
Waking Intuitively.

**"Caudwell, Christopher" (Christopher St. John
Sprigg) (1901–37)**
Classic Encounter.
Progress of Poetry, The.

Caulfield, Carlota (b. 1953)
For Albert, the Terrible.
In My Labyrinth (The Minotaur's Game)
Merci Bien, Monsieur.
You All Know the Story of the Two Lovers.

Causley, Charles (b. 1917)
Angel's Song.

Apple-Tree Man, The.
Armistice Day.
At Candlemas.
At Kfar Kana.
At the British War Cemetery, Bayeux.
Autobiography.
Balaam.
Ballad for Katharine of Aragon, A.
Ballad of the Bread Man.
Betjeman, 1984.
Bible Story.
By St. Thomas Water.
Chief Petty Officer.
Colonel Fazackerley.
Conversation in Gibraltar 1943.
Cowboy Song.
Death of a Poet.
Eden Rock.
Figgie Hobbin.
For an Ex-Far East Prisoner of War.
Fox Came into my Garden, A.
HMS *Glory.*
I Am the Great Sun.
I Am the Song.
I Saw a Jolly Hunter.
Infant Song.
Innocent's Song.
King's College Chapel.
Legend.
Loss of an Oil Tanker.
Mary's Song.
Nursery Rhyme of Innocence and Experience.
Old Mrs. Thing-um-e-bob.
On Being Asked to Write a School Hymn.
On the Thirteenth Day of Christmas.
Recruiting Drive.
Sailor's Carol.
Song of Samuel Sweet, The.
Song of the Dying Gunner A.A.1.
Ten Types of Hospital Visitor.
Timothy Winters.
What Has Happened to Lulu?

Cavafy, Constantine P. (1863–1933)
Alexander Jannai.
As Much as You Can.
At the Cafe Door.
City, The.
Comes to Rest.
Days of 1908.
In Despair.
In the Street.
Ithaka.
On the Street.
One Night.
One of the Jews.
Passing Through.
Return.
Supplication.
Their Beginning.
To Remain.
Waiting for the Barbarians.
Walls.
When They Come Alive.

Cavalcanti, Guido (1250–1301)
As thou wert loth to see, before thy feet.
Ballata.
Ballata: Concerning a Shepherd-Maid.
Ballata: In Exile at Sarzana.
Ballata: Of a Continual Death in Love.
Ballata: Of his Lady among other Ladies.
Ballata II: Last Song: From Exile.
Ballata 5: "Light do I see within my Lady's
    eyes."
Being in thought of love, I chanced to see.
Devastating flame of that fierce plague, The.
Encounter, An.
Fountain-head that is so bright to see, The.
Guido, an image of my lady dwells.
I come to thee by daytime constantly.
If I were still that man, worthy to love.
Lady in whom love is manifest—, A.
Lo! I am she who makes the wheel to turn.
Nero, thus much for tidings in thine ear.
O poverty, by thee the soul is wrapp'd.
O sluggish, hard, ingrate, what doest thou?
Sonetto XXXV: To Guido Orlando.
Sonnet: A Rapture concerning his Lady.

Sonnet: He compares all Things with his Lady, and finds them wanting.
Sonnet: He Speaks of a Third Love of His.
Sonnet: Of an ill-favored Lady.
Sonnet: Of His Pain from a New Love.
Sonnet: Of the Eyes of a Certain Mandetta.
Sonnet: On the Detection of a False Friend.
Sonnet: To a Friend who does not pity his Love.
Sonnet: To His Lady Joan, of Florence.
Sonnet [or Sonetto] 7: "Who is she that comes, makyng turn every man's eye."
Through this my strong and new misaventure.
To Dante Alighieri.
To Dante Alighieri: He Mistrusts the Love of Lapo Gianni.
To Dante Alighieri: He Reports, in a Feigned Vision, the Successful Issue of Lapo Gianni's Love.
To Dante [or Sonnet: Guido Cavalcanti to Dante Alighieri].
To sound of trumpet rather than of horn.

Cavalieri, Grace
First, The.
Grandmother.

Cavalli, Patrizia (b. 1949)
Across My Face the Nights Fall.
Ah, yes, to your misfortune.
And to see the city again and to see it again.
Before when you left you would always forget.
But first one must free oneself.
Far from the Kingdoms.
How pointless this straining.
I don't have any seed to cast about the world.
I Go, but Where? Oh Gods!
I Have No Seed to Scatter through the World.
I pretend to wait for you to enlarge the minutes.
I remember little of myself.
If Now You Knocked on My Door.
In that small dark fever of every reawakening.
In the Just Dampened Park.
In the shade of a metaphor.
Inside Your Sea My Boat Was Sailing.
It Will Not Apprehend the Object.
Little of myself do I remember.
Moroccans with the carpets, The.
Now that the time seems all mine.
Of All Distances the Best Possible One.
Of all the huntresses.
Outside, in fact, there wasn't any change.
Outside nothing's really changed.
Rain brings me back, The.
Someone told me.
Stunned I Was Looking for Reasons.
That white cloud in its contrast.
This time I won't permit the blue.
To simulate the burning of the heart.
To Simulate the Burning of the Heart, the Humiliation.
Together eternity and death threaten me.
When I listen for the sound of.
When suddenly, you're hit with good health.
Who ever again you'll be able to say.

Cave, Jane (c.1754–1813)
Ah! why from me art thou for ever flown.
Elegy on a Maiden Name, An.
Poem for Children, A; or, On Cruelty to the Irrational Creation.
Written a Few Hours before the Birth of a Child.
Written by Desire of a Lady, on an Angry, Petulant Kitchen-Maid.
Written the First Morning of the Author's Bathing at Teignmouth for the Head-Ache.

Cavendish, George (1499?–1561?)
Epitaph of Our Late Queen Mary, An.

Cavendish, Lady Jane (1621–69)
Answeare to my Lady Alice Edgertons Songe, of I prethy send mee back my Hart, An.
On my honorable Grandmother, Elizabeth Countess of Shrewbury.
On the 30th of June to God.

Cavendish, Margaret Lucas, Duchess of Newcastle (1623?–73)
Claspe, The.

Common Fate of Books, The.
Courting the Faerie Queen.
Dialogue between Melancholy and Mirth, A.
Dialogue betwixt Man, and Nature, A.
Dialogue betwixt the Body and the Mind, A.
Discourse of Beasts, A.
Discourse of Melancholy, A.
Dissert, A.
Her Descending Down.
Hunting of a Stag, The.
Hunting of the Hare, The.
Imagination.
Landscape, A.
Love, how thou'rt tired out with rhyme!
Mirth and Melancholy.
Nature's Cook.
O do not grieve, Dear Heart, nor shed a tear.
Of Cold Winds.
Of Many Worlds in This World.
Of Stars.
Of the Animal Spirits.
Of the Theme of Love.
Pastime of the Queen of Fairies, The.
Poet[r]ess's Hasty Resolution, The.
Ruine of this Island, The.
Sea Similized to Meadows and Pastures: the Mariners, to Shepherds: the Mast, to a May-Pole: the Fish, to Beasts, The.
Some with sharp swords, to tell O most accursed!
Soul and Body.
Soul's Garment, The.
Woman drest by Age, A.

Cavendish, William, Duke of Newcastle (1592–1676)
Love's Epitaph.
Love's Matrimony.
Love's Sun.
Song: "We'll, placed in Love's triumphant chariot high."

Cavin, Susan (b. 1948)
Christmas with the Holy Family.
Look Away child.

Cawein, Madison (1865–1914)
Beauty.
Caverns.
Dead Cities.
Deserted.
Echo.
Mnemosyne.
Music.
On Reading the Life of Haroun Er Reshid.
Orgie.
Poetry.
Purple Valleys, The.
Rome.
Stars, The.
Three Elements, The.
Uncalled.
Unimaginative, The.

Cawthorn, James (1719–61)
Englishman at the Table, The.
Whoever looks on life will see.
Wit was a strange unlucky child.

Caylely, John (b. 1956)
Four Screen Shots.

Cecco Angiolieri, da Siena (1258–1320)
Dreadful and the desperate hate I bear, The.
I am enamoured, and yet not so much.
I'm caught, like any thrush the nets surprise.
I would like better in the grace to be.
If I'd a sack of florins, and all new.
Let not the inhabitants of Hell despair.
Never so bare and naked was church-stone.
Of Why He Is Unhanged.
Sonnet: He Argues His Case with Death.
Sonnet: He Is Past All Help.
Sonnet: He Rails against Dante, Who Had Censured His Homage to Becchina.
Sonnet: He Will Not Be Too Deeply in Love.
Sonnet: In Absence from Becchina.
Sonnet: Of All He Would Do.
Sonnet: Of Becchina in a Rage.
Sonnet: Of Becchina, the Shoemaker's Daughter.
Sonnet: Of Love, in Honor of His Mistress Becchina.
Sonnet: Of Love in Men and Devils.
Sonnet: Of the 20th of June 1291.
Sonnet: Of Why He Would Be a Scullion.
Sonnet: To Dante Alighieri (He Writes to Dante, Then in Exile at Verona, Defying Him as No Better Than Himself)
Sonnet: To Dante Alighieri on the Last Sonnet of the Vita Nuova.
Who utters of his father aught but praise.

Ceccoli, Marino (fl. 14th cent.)
Oh, and yet I see that I will return to you anyway, and throw myself at your feet and cry a lot over my sins, until my crime will be pardoned.
Sir, I have remained so overcome, that I can no longer suffer your attacks.

Cecil, Mildred, Lady Burleigh (1526–89)
As when at first primitive men were dwelling on the fruitful earth.

Cecil, Richard (fl. 20th cent.)
Apology.
Richard's Blues.
Threnody for Sunrise.
Threnody for Sunset.

Cedering, Siv
Regarding Music.
Variations for the Piano.

"Ceiriog" See Hughes, John Ceiriog

Ceitinn, Seathrum See Keating, Geoffrey

Celan, Paul (1920–70)
Alchemical.
All those sleep shapes.
Aspen Tree.
Breathcrystal.
Corona.
Death Fugue, A.
Etched Away From.
Fugue of Death.
I am the first.
I Hear That The Axe Has Flowered.
Into the Foghorn.
Irish.
Jugs, The.
Language Mesh.
Largo.
Leaf, treeless, A.
Leaf, Treeless for Bertolt Brecht, A.
Leap-Centuries.
Little night.
Mandorla.
Matière de Bretagne.
Night Ray.
Nothingness, for the, The.
Plashes the Fountain.
Poles, The.
Profuse announcement.
Psalm.
Psalm: "No one kneads us again out of earth and clay."
Psalm: "No one moulds us again out of earth and clay."
Shibboleth.
Shot Forth.
Speak You Too.
Tenebrae.
There was Earth inside them, and.
Thread suns.
When you lie.
World to be stuttered after.
You were my death.
Your Hand Full of Hours.
Zeitgehoft.
Zurich, at the Stork.
Zürich, the Stork Inn.

Cempulappeyanirar
What He Said.

Cendrars, Blaise (Frédéric-Louis Sauser-Hall) (1887–1961)
Aleutian Islands.
Back then I was still young.
Contrasts.
Fish Cove.
Frisco-City.
Great Fetishes, The.
Hammock.

Harvest.
Head, The.
Medrano Academy.
My Dance.
Prose of the Trans-Siberian and Little Jean of
    France.
South.

Ceni, Alessandro (b. 1957)
Atrium.
Fragment.
Key and the Tree, The.
Reconciled Flame.
With What Courage.

Centamputan, Maturai Eruttalan
What She Said.

Centlivre, Susanna (1669?–1723)
From the Country, to Mr. Rowe in Town.
To thee—rude warrior, who, we once admired.

Centolella, Thomas (b. 1952)
Joy.
Small Acts.
Woman of Three Minds, The.

Cephalus (Constantinus Cephalus) (fl. 10th cent.)
To light young poets' hearts.

Cepollaro, Biagio (b. 1959)
Requiem in C.

Ceraman Kottampalattut
Great It May Be.

Ceravolo, Joseph (1934–88)
Invisible Autumn.
Caught in the Swamp.
Celebration.
Conception.
Data.
Fill and Illumined.
Geological Hymn.
Grow.
Ho Ho Ho Caribou.
New Realism.
Spring of Work Storm.
Stolen Away.
Sunset.
White Fish in Reeds.
Wild Provoke of the Endurance Sky.
Wind Is Blowing West, The.
Women, The.

Cerealius (Julius Cerealius) (fl. 1st–2d cent.)
Poet went to the Isthmian games, A.

Cerenio, Virginia
13 June 1994.
20 July 1994.
23 October 1992.
Family Photos: Black and White: 1960.
My Mother.

Cernuda, Luis (1903–63)
For Two Voices.
I don't want to return a sad spirit.
I'll Tell You How You Were Born.
If Man Could Name.
Invisible wall, The.
Lover Digresses, The.
Nocturnal, you sword-fight.
Shadow, The.
That Which Is Enough for Love.
You were a tender desire, an insinuating cloud.

Cerruto, Oscar (1912–81)
Love: "Afternoon is offered to us, The."

Cervantes, Lorna Dee (b. 1954)
A un Desconocido.
Archeology.
Beneath the Shadow of the Freeway.
Cannery Town in August.
Como lo Siento.
Emplumada.
First Beating.
Freeway 280.
Interpretation of Dinner by the Uninvited
    Guest, An.
Isla Mujeres.
Levee: Letter to No One, The.
Meeting Mescalito at Oak Hill Cemetery.
On the Poet Coming of Age.
Poem for the Young White Man Who Asked
    Me How I, an Intelligent, Well-Read Person
    Could Believe in the War between Races.

Poema para los Californios Muertos.
Poet Is Served Her Papers, The.
Refugee Ship.
Starfish.
To We Who Were Saved by the Stars.
Uncle's First Rabbit.
Visions of Mexico While at a Writing
    Symposium in Port Townsend, Washington.
Woman in My Notebook, The.

Cervantes Saavedra, Miguel de (1547–1616)
Sonnet: "When I was marked for suffering,
    Love forswore."

Césaire, Aimé (b. 1912)
Automatic Crystal, The.
Beat It Night Dog.
Blank to Fill in on the Visa of Pollen.
Bucolic.
Day and Night.
Different Horizon.
Do Not Have Pity.
First Problem.
I shall not regard my swelled head as a sign of
    real glory.
In Memory of a Black Union Leader.
In Order to Speak.
Islands scars of the water.
Lagoonal Calendar.
Lay of the Rover.
Macumba Word.
Magic.
Miraculous Weapons, The.
Mississippi.
On the Islands of All Winds.
Return to My Native Land.
Since Akkad, Since Elam, Since Sumer.
State of the Union.
Sun Serpent.
This flat city shortly after dawn.
Three for Bear.
Virgin Forest, The.
Wheel, The.

Cesaire, Aime and Rene Depestre
How did you come to develop the concept of
    Negritude?

Cetina, Gutierre de (c.1520–c.57)
Happy Hours that Hurry Away.
In What Region, in What Part of the World.
Madrigal 1.
Madrigal: Eyes of Clear Serenity.

Céu, Sor Violante do (1602?–93)
Voice of a Dissipated Woman inside a Tomb.

Ch'en-hsiang See Acton, Harold

Ch'en Meng-chia (1911–66)
Old White Russian, An.

Ch'en Yün (1886–1910)
Twilight.

Cha, Theresa Hak Kyung (1951–82)
Elitere Lyric Poetry.

Chabbi, Fadhila (b. 1946)
Blind Goddess, The.
Engraving Twenty-Nine.

Chacko, Chemmanam (b. 1926)
Rice.

Chagy, John 1912–90
Haggai.

Chaikin, Miriam (b. 1928)
Light Another Candle.
One-Upmanship.

Chairemon (fl. c.300–c.100 B.C.)
Epitaph: "Athenagoras begot Eubulus—."
We of Sparta fought the Argives—equal in
    number and arms.

Chakrabarti, Nirendranath (b. 1924)
Amalkanti.

Chakravarty, Amiya (1901–86)
Fire.

Chalfi, Raquel
Night Hair.
Reading the I Ching.

Chalkhill, John (fl. c.1600)
Coridon's Song.

Challis, Gordon (b. 1932)
Iceman, The.
Sirens, The.

Chamberlain, Brenda (1912–71)
Dead Ponies.
Islandman.
Lament: "My man is a bone ringèd with
    weed."
Seal Cave.

Chamberlain, Karen
Airlift.
Indian Summer.
Riding the Lion, Riding the Lamb.
Stepping in the Same River.

Chamberlain, Richard (1632–98)
To the Much Honoured R. F. Esq.

Chamberlayne, William (1619–89)
Bad Landlord, The.

Chambers, Gordon
If Only for One Night.
Meditations on Stevie.
Waxing Poetic on Marvin.

Chambers, Jane (1937–83)
To Beth On Her Forty-Second Birthday.
Why Are Daddies So Mean?

Chambre, Alastair
Limerick: "There was a young girl from
    Uttoxeter / Who kept hens, but refused to
    have cocks."

Chan Fang-sheng (fl. c.400)
Folk-Songs.
Sailing Back to the Capital.
Sailing Homeward.
Sailing into the South Lake.

Chandidas (fl. 1375–1450)
Why Tell Me What to Do?

Chandler, Christine
Tree in the Garden, The.

**Chandler, Ellen Louise See Moulton, Louise
Chandler**

Chandler, Mary (1687–1745)
My Own Epitaph.
True Tale, A.

Chang Chi (768–830)
Birds from the Mountains, The.
Coming at Night to a Fisherman's Hut.
Elegy: "We carved our names."
Faithful Wife, A.
Maple Bridge Night Mooring.
Night at Anchor by Maple Bridge.
Night-Mooring at Maple Bridge.
Tying Up for the Night at Maple River Bridge.

Ch'ang Chien (fl. c.749)
Visit to the Broken Hill Temple, A.

Chang Chih-ho (c.742–c.782)
Before dusk on the lake, the moon just full.
Near the rim of Hsi-sai Mountain, white egrets
    fly.
Oh, about the joy of owning a crab hut at
    Sung-chiang!

Chang Chiu-ling (673–740)
Since You Left.
Watching the Moon with Thoughts of Far
    Away.

Chang, Diana (b. 1934)
Cannibalism.
Foreign Ways.
On Being in the Midwest.
On The Fly.

Chang, Edmond Yi-teh (b. 1965)
After the Storm.
Bamboo Elegy: Two.
Near-Sightedness.

Chang Heng (A.D. 78–139)
Bones of Chuang Tzu, The.

Chang K'o-chiu (1265?–1345?)
At Waterfall Temple.
Tune: 'Merriment before the Palace Hall.'
Tune: 'Traveler Welcoming the Immortal.'
Tune: 'Unbroken.'
Year's End.

Ch'ang Kuo Fan (fl. 19th cent.)
On His Thirty-Third Birthday.

**Chang-soo Koh See Ko Changsu (Chang-soo
Koh)**

Chang Tsai
Desecration of the Han Tombs, The.

Chang Yang-hao (1269–1329)
Ch'ü Yüan's 'sorrow.'
T'ung Pass.
Tune: 'Sheep on the Mountain Slope.'

Chang Yen (1248–c.1320)
Tune: 'Pure Serene Music.'

Chang Yü (1333–85)
Four Poems on the Ch'ung-wu Festival.
Four Seasons in the Mountains, The.
Hearing a Song from My Boat.
In a Boat on the Cha River.
In a Book-Box I Found the Lost Manuscript of
     a Poem Sent to Me by the Late Kao [Ch'i].
In the Evening, Walking in the Western Fields.
Lamenting for Kao Ch'ing-ch'iu, Chi-ti.
Merchant's Joy, The.
Mountain Retreat of a Recluse, The.
Painting.
Paintings.
Pavilion for Listening to Fragrance, The.
Presented to a Lady within the Palace.
Quatrain: "At this remote village, I have no
     neighbors."
Reading the Poetry Collection of Lü Fang-
     ch'ing.
Retreat of Liu Kuo-pao, The.
Retreat of Sun Ching-hsiang, The.
Seven Poems on Living in the Mountains:
     Seeing Off.
"Song of Farewell" in the Tartar Mode.
Song of the Old Oak.
Staying Overnight at T'ien-ning Ch'an Temple.
To the Innkeeper at Five Rivers, Sun Pen.
Twelve Miscellaneous Poems on the Fang
     Garden.
Yellow Sunflower of Szechwan.

Chang Yüeh (667–730)
Written When Drunk.

Chanler, Isaac (1700–49)
Awake My Soul, Betimes Awake.
Thrice Welcome First and Best of Days.

Channing, William Ellery (1818–1901)
Barren Moors, The.
Chant to the Fire-fly.
Harbor, The.
Hymn of the Earth.
Murillo's Magdalen.
Then spoke the Spirit of the Earth.
Walden.

Chao, Hsu
Locust Swarm, The.

Ch'ao Li-houa [or Chao Li-hua]
Farewell: "My boat goes west, yours east."

Chao Luan-luan (fl. 8th? cent.)
Creamy Breasts.
Slender Fingers.

Chao Meng-fu (1254–1322)
Admonition to Myself, An.
Eulogy of the Sagely Virtue of His Imperial
     Majesty Emperor Shih-tsu, A.
Fisherman's Lyric.
In the Ancient Manner.
Inscribed on a Landscape by Mi Yüan-hui.
Inscribed on a Wall Painting of Assembled
     Immortals.
Inscribed on Sun An-chih's "Painting of Pines
     and Catalpas."
Inscribed on the Painting "Spring Dawn at
     Peach Blossom Spring" by Scholar Shang
     Te-fu.
Lamenting the Taoist Wei Kung-yüan.
Living in Retirement at Te-ch'ing.
Pavillion-Where-the-Crane-Came, The.
Poem of Prefectural Judge Yang T'ien-jui
     Righting a Wrong.
Song of an Autumn Night.
To a Pyrotechnist.
Twenty-Eight Poems Inscribed on T'ien-kuan
     Mountain.

Chao Shan-ch'ing (fl. c.1320)
Autumn on the Riverbank.

Chao Yi (1727–1814)
In Search of Solitude.
Rising Early in the Morning.
Spring Sentiments.

Strolling in the Countryside.
Writing Poetry in the Back Garden.

Chao Ying-tou (fl. 17th cent.)
Decrees of God, The.

Chapin, Edwin Hubbell (1814–80)
Hark! Hark! with Harps of Gold.
O Thou, Who Didst Ordain the Word.

Chaplin, Saul
Until the Real Thing Comes.

Chapman, Arthur (1873–1935)
Out Where the West Begins.

Chapman, George (1559?–1634)
And, for our tongue, that still is so empayr'd.
Bridal Song: "Now sleep, bind fast the flood of
     air."
But dwell in darkness, for your god is blind.
Corinna Bathes.
Death Described by His True Effects.
Ear's Delight, The.
For words want art and art wants words to
     praise her.
Her look doth promise and her life assure.
Homer and the Brazen Head of Rumour.
Hymn[e] to Our Saviour on the Cross[e], A.
Justice.
Learning ("So Learned Men in Controversies
     Spend").
Love flows not from my liver but her living.
Muses that fame's loose feathers beautify.
Muses that sing love's sensual empery.
Nor riches to the virtues of my love.
Of her removed and soul-infused regard.
Peace Discovers the Poet.
Peace of Death, The.
So her close beauties further blaze her fame.
To living virtues turns the deadly vices.

Chapman, J. Wilbur (1859–1918)
Jesus! What a friend for sinners!
One Day!

Chapman, John Alexander (b. 1875)
Gipsy Queen.

Chapman, Robin S.
Your Face Here.

Chappell, Fred (b. 1936)
Guess Who.
Skin Flick.
Truth at Last, The.

Char, René (b. 1907)
Argument.
Disdained Apparitions.
Leaves of Hypnos No. 128.
Man flees suffocation.
On the Bell Frieze of a Roman Church.
Poet, conserver of the infinite faces of the
     living, The.
Unbending Prayer.

Charach, Ron
Evidence on Film, The.
Labour and Delivery.
MRI.
Question of Vitamins, A.

Charara, Hayan (b. 1972)
Holy Water.
My Father Breaks the Neighbor's Nose.
On the Murder of an Ice Cream Man.
Thinking American.

Charbonel, Monique (1941–71)
It's a Number.

Charig, Philip
Sunny Disposish.

Charlemagne and Hrabanus Maurus
Veni Creator Spiritus.

Charles, Dorthi (b. 1963)
Bang! the starter's gun—.
Concrete Cat.
Getting Dirty.

Charles, J. B. (1910–83)
Polish Girl Standing on a Chair, A.

Charles, Tony
I saw a great building with many storeys piled
     high.

Charry Lara, Fernando (b. 1920)
I Would Have Loved You.

Chartier, Alain (c.1385–c.1433)
I turn you out of doors.

Chartres, Vidame de (fl. 13th cent.)
April.

Chase, Karen (fl. 20th cent.)
Venison.
What You Can't See.

Chase, Naomi Feigelson
Music Mother.

Chase, Newell
My Ideal.

Chasin, Helen (b. 1938)
City Pigeons.
Getting the News.
In Communication with a UFO.
Joy Sonnet in a Random Universe.
Strength.
Word Plum, The.

Chatterton, Thomas (1752–70)
Aella, sels.
Bristowe Tragedie: or, The Dethe of Syr
     Charles Bawdin.
Excelente Balade of Charitie, An.
If Wishing for the Mystic Joys of Love.
Methodist, The.
Resignation.
Sentiment.
Sunday: A Fragment Transcribed from a Ms. in
     Chatterton's Handwriting.

Chattopadhyay, Shakti (b. 1933)
Forgive Me.

Chaucer, Geoffrey (1340?–1400)
Canterbury Tales, The, sels.
Chaucer's Wordes unto Adam, his Owne
     Scriveyn.
Complaint of Chaucer to His Empty Purse,
     The.
Complaint unto Pity, The.
Gentilesse.
Lak of Stedfastnesse.
Legend of Good Women, The, sels.
Merciles[s] Beaute [or Beautée or Beauty].
Parlement of Foules, The, sels.
To Rosamounde.
Troilus and Criseyde [or Crisede], sels.

Chaudhari, Bahinabai (1880–1951)
Naming of Things, The.

Chaudhari, Kirti (b. 1935)
Inertia.

Chavez, Lisa D. (b. 1961)
After the Prom.
Clean Sheets.
Woman Who Raised Dogs, The.

Chazal, Malcolm de
Bicycle rolls on the road, A.

Chedid, Andrée (b. 1921)
For Survival.
Full face.
Future and the Ancestor, The.
Going Forth.
Imagine.
Man-today.
Movement.
Naked Face, The.
Renegade.
Stepping Aside.
Turn.
What are We Playing at?
Who Remains Standing?

Cheek, Cris
Rollercoaster.

Cheever, George Barrell (1807–90)
Blest Be the Wondrous Grace.
Thy Loving Kindness, Lord, I Sing.

Cheke, Lady Mary (c.1527–1616)
Erat Quaedam Mulier.

Chen Huan (776–839)
Presented to the Taoist Paragon Mao.

Ch'en Liang (1143–94)
Tune: "Beautiful Lady Yü, The"—Spring
     Sorrow.
Tune: "Water Dragon's Chant"—Loathsome
     Spring.

Ch'en Lin, Susan
Song: "I watered my horse at the Long Wall
     caves."

Ch'en Shih-tao (1053–1102)
Cold Night.

Ch'en Tao (779–843)
Her Husband Asks Her to Buy a Bolt of Silk.
Song of Lung-hsi.
Turkestan.

Ch'en Tzu-ang (661–702)
As the crescent moon is born from the Western Sea.
Business Men.
I close my door and trace the transformations of nature.
I dwell in seclusion and observe the creative process.
I dwell in the forest nursing a long illness.
Inscription on a Tree atop mount Sacrifice (Ssu Shan) and Sent to Censor Ch'iao.
Kingfishers nest on South Sea islands.
Men in the market pride themselves on their knowledge and craft, The.
Orchids grow through spring and summer.
Song on Climbing the Gate Tower at Yu-chou, A.
Song on Climbing Yu-chou Gate Tower.

Ch'en Tzu-lung (1608–47)
Ballad of the Little Cart, A.
Little Cart, The.
Parable, A.
Tune: "Telling of Innermost Feelings"—Wandering in Spring.

Ch'en Yü-yi (1090–1138)
Enlightment.
Journeying to Hsiang-yi.
Sitting on a Rock by Mountain Stream.
Spring Morning.
Tune: 'Immortal at the Riverbank.'
Tune: "Immortal at the River"—Ascending a Little Tower at Night.

Chen, Yüan
Recalling When I Was Drunk.

Cheney-Coker, Syl
Analysis.
Childhood.
Dead Eyes.
Hunger of the Suffering Man, The.
Letter to a Tormented Playwright.
On Being a Poet in Sierra Leone.
Outsider, The.
Peasants.
Philosopher, The.
Poem for a Guerrilla Leader.
Poem for a Lost Lover.
Poet among Those Who Are Also Poets.
Road to Exile Thinking of Vallejo, The.

Cheney, John Vance (1848–1922)
Unto Our God Most High We Sing.

Ch'êng Hsiao (c. 220–264)
Satire on Paying Calls in August.

Cheng Hsieh (1693–1765)
Collecting Antiques.
Contest Snake, The.
For Contemporary Artist Pien Wei-Ch'I.
Girl from Ch'ang-kan, The.
Inscribed on a Painting.
Mother-in-Law Is Cruel.
Mourning for My Son Jun-erh.
On a Painting of a Knight-Errant.
Poem for My Wet Nurse, A.
Seven Songs.
Small Garden, The.
Song of Surfing on the Bore.
To Chin Nung.
Tune: "Full River Red"—A Four-season Song on the Hardships and Joys of Farming Life.
Twenty-eight Characters Sent to Tung-ts'un on the Subject of the Poems He Burned.
West wind has come again to the "tower of makeup," The.

Ch'eng-kung Sui (231–273)
Rhapsody on Whistling.

Chénier, André Marie de (1762–94)
Elegies.
Happy is he given to sage disciplines.
We live; we live in squalor. And so? It had to be.

When the Euxine goddess with astonished eyes.

Chernoff, Maxine (b. 1952)
Amble.
Black.
Breasts.
How Lies Grow.
Japan.
Lost and Found.
Man Struck Twenty Times by Lightning, The.
Tenderitis.

Cherry, Kelly (b. 1940)
Bride of Quietness, The.
History.
Late Afternoon at the Arboretum.
Love.
Pines Without Peer, The.
Raiment We Put on, The.
Reading, Dreaming, Hiding.

Chess, Richard (b. 1953)
Growing up in a Jewish Neighborhood.
No Music.
Two and One.
Yiddish Poets in America.

Chester, Anson G. (1824–1911)
Tapestry Weaver, The.

Chester, Tessa Rose (b. 1950)
Buttons.
Candle at Canterbury, A.
Running Hares.

Chesterfield, Philip Dormer Stanhope, 4th Earl of (1694–1773)
On Lord Ila's Improvements, near Hounslow Heath.
On Miss Eleanor Ambrose, a Celebrated Beauty in Dublin.
On Mr. Nash's Present of His Own Picture at Full Length.
Song: "Whenever, Chloe, I begin."
To Miss Eleanor Ambrose on the Occasion of Her Wearing an Orange Lily at a Ball in Dublin Castle on July the 12th.
Unlike my subject now shall be my song.
Verses Written in a Lady's Sherlock "Upon Death."

Chesterton, Gilbert Keith (1874–1936)
After W. B. Yeats.
Antichrist, or the Reunion of Christendom; an Ode.
Aristocrat, The.
Ballad of Abbreviations, A.
Ballade D'une Grande Dame.
Ballade of Suicide, A.
Certain Evening, A.
Christmas Carol, A: "God rest you merry gentlemen."
Christmas Carol: "Christ child lay on Mary's lap, The."
Citizenship; Form 8889512, Sub-Section Q.
Convert, The.
Donkey, The.
Ecclesiastes.
Elegy in a Country Churchyard.
English Graves, The.
Fantasia.
Fat White Woman Speaks, The.
Femina contra Mundum.
For a War Memorial.
From a Spanish Cloister.
Geography.
Gold Leaves.
History.
Holy of Holies, The.
House of Christmas, The.
Joseph.
Lepanto.
Lucasta Replies to Lovelace.
Old King Cole ("Me clairvoyant").
Old Song, The.
On Reading "God."
Post-Recessional.
Praise of Dust, The.
Prayer in Darkness, A.
Rolling English Road, The.
Sea Replies to Byron, The.
Secret People, The.

Skeleton, The.
Song against Grocers, The.
Sword of Surprise, The.
Ultimate, The.
Variations on an Air: After Robert Browning.
Variations on an Air: After W. B. Yeats.
Variations on an Air Composed on Having to Appear in a Pageant as Old King Cole.
Variations on [or of] an Air: After [Algernon Charles] Swinburne.
Wine and Water.
World State, The.

Chevalier, Albert (1860–1923)
There's parties ad yer meets about.

Chevallier, C.
Limerick: "Naïve young lady of Bude, A."

Chevette, Zelda
There was an old pros.

Cheyne, Jane *See* **Cavendish, Lady Jane**

Chhotray, Devdas (b. 1946)
Fear.

Chia Tao (779–843)
Evening View as the Snow Clears.
Looking for a Recluse but Failing to Find Him.
Passing by a Mountain Village: Evening.
Sick Cicada.
Spending the Night at a Mountain Temple.
Weeping for the Zen Master Po-yen.

Chia Yi (201–196 B.C.)
Owl, The.
Rhyme-Prose on the Owl.
Year was tan-wo, it was the fourth month, summer's first, The.

Chiang Chieh (fl. 13th cent.)
To the Tune "The Fair Maid of Yu."

Chiang Ch'un-lin (1818–68)
Tune: "Magnolia Blossoms, Slow"—Traveling on the Yangtze.

Chiang K'uei (1155?–1235)
Tune: "Charm of Nien-nu."
Tune: "Dim Fragrance"—Plum Blossoms.
Tune: "Pale-golden Willows."
Tune: "Sparse Shadows"—Plum Blossoms.
Written at Lakeside Residence.

Chiang Lu (fl. 6th cent.)
Wrecked Boat on the River Shore.

Chiang Shih-ch'üan (1725–85)
Evening Lights on the River.
Twilight in the River Pavilion.

Ch'iao Chi (1280–1345)
Love Song: "Orioles and orioles."
Tune: "Overtures"—On Myself.
Tune: "Sheep on Mountain Slope."
Tune: "Song of Plucking Cassia."

Chiao-jan (730–99)
Looking for Lu Hung-chien but Failing to Find Him.

Ch'iao Lai (1640–94)
Tune: 'Partridge Sky' I Rejoice to Meet a Friend Visting at My Rustic Study.

Chiboku (d. 1740)
Running stream, The.

Chichester, Sir Richard of (c.1197–1253)
Day by Day.

Chichibabin, Boris Alekseievich (b. 1923)
Camel.
I'll be finished, if I'll survive—.

Chicken, Edward (1698–1746)
At last the beef appears in sight.

Ch'ien Ch'i (fl. 8th cent.)
Mount T'ai P'ing.
Visit to the Hermit Ts'ui.

Ch'ien Ch'ien-i [or Ch'ien Ch'ien-yi] (1582–1664)
Crescent moon hangs on the tip of the willows, A.
Drinking Wine.
Fishing cove and long lines of fishermen's huts, A.
In Lamplight, Watching My Wife Preparing a Flower Arrangement—Playfully Inscribing Four Poems.
Miscellaneous Feelings at West Lake.
Miscellaneous Poems Written While in Jail.

Must I lament the time that's gone because
   I've been cast aside?
Nightly the watchman's rattle startles my sleep.
No Flowers.
On the Road to Western Hill.
Pavilions of dance, terraces of song.
Poem on Drinking Wine with the Degree-
   Holder Ku.
Poem Written during a Dream on the Twenty-
   Third Day of the Intercalary [Month after
   the] Fourth [Month].
Rebuttal of Tung-p'o's Poem on "Bathing the
   Infant," A.
Spluttering burnt-out lamp blazes in the dusk.
Willow catkins beyond the garden wait for
   evening tides.

Ch'ien T'ao (*fl.* early 11th cent.)
Blaming Sons.
Chill and harsh the year draws to its close;.
I BUILT my hut in a zone of human habitation.
In Praise of Ching K'o.
In the quiet of the morning I heard a knock at
   my door.
Flood.
LONG time ago, A.
Moving House.
New Corn.
On Reading the Seas and Mountains Classic.
Poems after Drinking Wine.
Reading the Book of Hills and Seas.
Returning to the Fields.
Shady, shady the wood in front of the Hall.
Substance, Shadow, and Spirit.
Written While Drunk.

Ch'ien Wen-Ti, Emperor (503–51)
Lo-yang.

Chifu
No mind, no Buddhas, no live beings.

Chigetsu, Lady (*fl.* 17th cent.)
Chirping / Grasshopper.

Chikako (Jusammi Chikako) (*fl.* c.1290–1316)
On this summer night.

Chikamatsu Monzaemon (1653–1725)
Journey, The.

Chikuro (d. 1895)
Butterflies in flight.

Chikusen (1292–1348)
He's part of all, yet all's transcended.

Chilam Balam
Flight of the Itzás.

Child, A. C.
Wishes.

Child, Abigail (b. 1950)
Motive for Mayhem, A.
Squeeze.
Surplus.

Child, Lydia Maria (1802–80)
Thanksgiving Day.

Chimombo, Steve (b. 1945)
Death Song, A.
Derailment: A Delirium.
Four Ways of Dying.
Messengers, The.
Obituary.
Of Promises and Prophecy.

Chimsoro, Samuel (b. 1949)
Change, The.
Curfew Breakers, The.

Chin Ch'ang-hsü (*fl.* 10th cent.)
Spring Grievance.
Spring Sorrow.

Ch'in Chia (*fl.* 2nd cent. A.D.)
Ch'in Chia's Wife's Reply.
To His Wife.

Chin, David
Sleeping Father.
Sterling Williams' Nosebleed.

Chin Ho (1819–85)
Ballad of the Maiden of Lan-ling.

Chin, Justin
Bergamot.
Cocksucker's Blues.
Ex-Boyfriends Named Michael.
Night.

Undetectable.
Why a Boy.
Why He Had to Go.

Ch'in Kuan (1049–1100)
Along the Grand Canal.
Farewell Song.
From a Dream.
Returning from Kuang-ling.
Sleepless.
Song: "Pleading eyebrows, intoxicating eyes!"
Spring Rain.
Tune: 'Happiness Approaches.'
Tune: "Courtyard Full of Fragrance."
Tune: "Happy Events Approaching."
Tune: 'Perfumed Garden.'
Tune: 'Rouged Lips.'
Tune: 'Sand of Silk-Washing Brook.'
Tune: 'Spring in the Painted Hall.'

Chin, Marilyn
Altar.
American Rain.
Aubade: "Waking is this easy."
Autumn Leaves.
Barbarian Suite.
Beijing Spring.
Composed Near the Bay Bridge (after a wild
   party)
Disorder, The.
Elegy for Chloe Nguyen.
Exile's Letter (Or: An Essay on Assimilation)
Floral Apron, The.
How I Got That Name.
Leaving San Francisco.
Prelude.
Repulse Bay.
Turtle Soup.
We Are Americans Now, We Live in the
   Tundra.
Year Passes in My Morning Teacup, The.

Chin Nung (1687–1764)
Evening Scene at Twin Forests.
I get so drunk, I could be called the Earl of
   Dissipation!
I remember when he took me on a trip to this
   place.
In the silences between peals of the bell.
Inkstone Inscription for the Blind Scholar Ho
   Yung-kuang, An.
Inscribed on the Wall of a Rice Cake Shop.
Mooring in the Rain at Sung-ling.
Three lines of "clerk script" calligraphy.
Traveler, I've been through a thousand
   changes, A.
Wearing a Worn-Out Coat.
Who bought a mountain and became a hermit
   there?
Written at the End of Master Ho-ching's
   Collected Works.

Chine (d. 1688)
It lights up.
Sadly I see.

Chine-Jo, Lady (*fl.* late 17th cent.)
Wild geese / Fellow travelers.

Chingono, Julius (b. 1949)
Epitaph, An: "Here lies Stephen Pwanya."

Chinn, Daryl Ngee
Not Translation, Not Poetry.
Skin Color from the Sun.

Chinnov, Igor Vladimirovich (b. 1909)
Black bird on a black and snowy branch, A.
Do you think we might go to hell too?
Gust of memory stirs faded letters, A.
In the land of Schlaraffenland.
Instance of fore-ordained harmony, An.
Sometimes, you give way to sickness.

Chinook Oral Tradition
I won't care / if you desert me.

Chipasula, Frank Mkalawile (b. 1949)
Because the Wind Remembers.
Double Song.
Dusk.
Everything to Declare.
Friend, Ah You Have Changed!
Going Back Patiently.
Love Poem for My Country, A.
Manifesto on Ars Poetica.

My Blood Brother.
My Friendly People.
Ritual Girl.
Singing Drum, The.
Talking of Sharp Things.
Those Rainy Mornings.
Tramp.
Warrior.

Chipasula, Stella P.
I'm My Own Mother, Now.
Your Name is Gift.

Chippewa Oral Tradition
Approach of the Storm, The.
Love-Charm Song.
My Love Has Departed.
Sioux Woman Defends Her Children, The.
Sioux Women Gather up Their Wounded, The.
Song of the Captive Sioux Woman.
Song of the Crows.

Chiri (d. 1716)
First crops.

Chirin (d. 1794)
In earth and sky.

Chisholm, Alison
Contact.

Chisholm, Thomas O.
Great Is Thy Faithfulness.

Chitre, Dilip (b. 1938)
My Father Travels.

Chitsu
No more head shaving.

Ch'iu Chin (1879–1907)
To the Tune "The River Is Red."

Ch'iu Wei (694–789?)
Visiting a Recluse on West Mountain and Not
   Finding Him In.

Chiun (*fl.* 15th cent.)
Nameless / Weed quickening.

Chivers, Thomas Holley (1809–58)
Apollo.
Avalon.
Lily Adair.
Moon of Mobile, The.
Shell, The.
To Isa Sleeping.
Wind, The.

Chiyojo [*or* Chiyo *or* Chiyo-Ni *or* Kaga no Chiyo
   or Fukuda Chiyo-Ni] (1703–75)
After a long winter, giving / each other
   nothing.
Bearing no flowers.
Don't dress for it.
Fawn frolics, A.
From the mind.
Grazing.
Hardly spring, with ice.
In the well-bucket / A morning glory.
Morning glory, The.
Once my parents were older.
Since morning glories.
Were it not for / Cries in snow.
Whether astringent.
While I was musing on my theme.

Chiyoni (d. 1775)
I saw the moon as well.

Chizhova, Elena (b. 1957)
Cassandra.

Chmielarz, Sharon
They Come Humming.

Cho, Pyong-hwa (b. 1921)
One Wintry Day.

Cho Wen-chun (*fl.* 2nd cent.)
Lament: "Hills are white with snow, The."

Cho-yong (c.1050–1100)
Song: "I carouse all night."

Chock, Eric (b. 1950)
Bait, The.
Poem for George Helm: Aloha Week 1980.
Working Construction.

Ch'oe Ch'ung (984–1068)
In the Night.

Chogo (d. 1806)
I long for people.

Choha (d. 1740)
Raging sea, A.

Choko (d. 1731)
This final scene I'll not see.
Cholmondeley-Pennell, Henry (1837–1915)
Night Mail North, The.
Chonaill, Eibhlin Dubh Ni *See* O'Connell, Eibhlin Dubh
Chŏng Ch'ŏl (1536–93)
Magistrate.
Snow falling in the pine forest.
Why does that pine tree stand.
Chora (d. 1776)
Paradise.
Chori (d. 1778)
Leaves never fall.
"Chorny [or Chiornyi], Sasha" (Aleksandr Mikhailovich Glikberg) (1880–1932)
Drunkard's Nocturnes, A.
Kreutzer Sonata, A.
Life.
My Love.
Stylized Donkey, A.
Choshi (d. 1768)
On its way west.
Chosui (d. 1769)
I wait, white clouds.
Chou Pang-yen (1056–1121)
About to leave, yet by the lamplight she lingers.
Peach Blossom Stream.
Sparse fence, winding path, a small farmhouse.
Tune: "Distant Red Window."
Tune: Palace of Night Revels.
Tune: 'Prince Lan-Ling.'
Tune: "Prince of Lan-ling" (*Lan-ling Wang*)— on Willows.
Tune: "Six Toughies"—Written after the Roses Have Faded.
Choudhury, Malay Roy (b. 1939)
Stark Electric Jesus.
Chowa (d. 1715)
This is one poem.
Christensen, Inger (b. 1935)
Alphabet 9, 10.
Men's Voices.
Christie, A. V. (b. 1963)
Belongings.
Coming off a Depression, She Prepares for Venice.
Hollywood Finch, The.
In My Dream.
Overture.
Possible Man, The.
Christine de Pisan (1364–c.1430)
Alone am I, and alone I wish to be.
Alone in Martyrdom.
Christine to Her Son.
Fountain of tears, river of grief.
I am a widow, robed in black, alone.
I'll always dress in black and rave.
Marriage is a lovely thing.
Christopher, Nicholas (b. 1951)
Far from Home.
Midsummer.
Palm Reader, The.
Chrystos (b. 1946)
As I Leave You.
I Bought a New Red.
I Bring You Greetings: How.
I Have Not Signed a Treaty with the United States Government.
I Suck.
I Walk in the History of My People.
Okeydokey Tribe, The.
Old Indian Granny, The.
Portrait of Assimilation.
Real Indian Leans against, The.
Soap Bubbles.
Today Was a Bad Day Like TB.
Wings of a Wild Goose, The.
You Know I Like to Be.
Chu Chen Po (fl. 9th cent.)
Hedgehog.
Rustic Temple Is Hidden, The.
Chu Ch'ing-yü (fl. c.826)
Gathering Lotus.

Great Wall, The.
Palace Poem.
Ch'u Ch'uang I (fl. 8th cent.)
Country House.
Evening in the Garden Clear after Rain.
Mountain Spring, A.
Tea.
Chu Hsi (1130–1200)
Boats Are Afloat, The.
Farm by the Lake, The.
Spring Sun.
Thoughts While Reading.
Chu Hsiang (1904–33)
Pawnshop, The.
Ch'u Kuang-hsi (707–59)
Cowherd, The; a Song.
Farm Routine.
Farmer's Thoughts, A.
Streets of Ch'ang-an, The.
Chu Shu-chen (fl. early 12th cent.)
Alone.
Hysteria.
Lost.
Morning.
Old Anguish, The.
Plaint.
Sorrow.
Spring.
Stormy Night in Autumn.
Chu Tun-ju (1081?–1159?)
To an Ancient Tune.
Tune: "Charm of Nien-nu, The."
Tune: "Happy Events Approaching."
Tune: "Magnolia Blossoms, Abbreviated."
Tune: 'Nien-nu Is Charming.'
Chu Yi-tsun (1629–1709)
Deepening-Green Pavilion.
Inscribed on the Painting of "Garden for Retirement": Pavilion of Sincerity, on Rocky Mountain.
Listening-to-the-Rain Studio.
Majestic Valley.
Tune: "Song of Divination."
Tune: "Song of the Southern Country."
Tune: "Song of the Southern Country"—Spring Thoughts at Pearl River.
West Cliff.
Written at Mauve Garden: Pine Wind Terrace.
Ch'u Yüan (fl. 4th cent. B.C.)
Great Arbiter of Fate, The.
Great Summons, The.
Heavenly Questions.
In the beginning of old.
Lament for Ying, A.
Li Sao, *sels.*
Lord of the River Hsiang.
Nine Songs.
Oftentimes, I grew dejected and sobbed.
Summons of the Soul, The.
Yellow River's Earl, The.
Ying from 'The Nine Declarations.'
Chu Yün-ming (1461–1527)
As I Looked at a Lake, My Thoughts Turned to a Certain Friend.
Clouds are swept into the sunset—a sky beyond the sky.
Drinking.
Fan from Korea, A.
For Several Years I Have Wanted To Grow a Garden, But Have Never Finished One. This Year It Is Already Halfway through Summer, and This Has Made Me Despondent.
Forest Birds (A Woman Speaks)
Improvisations.
Landscape Painted on a Fan—Echoing a Poem by Wen Cheng-ming, A.
Late Spring—Traveling through the Mountains.
Little Landscape, A.
Making Fun of the Well at the Inn below the Mountain.
Miscellaneous Poems Written in My Studio on an Autumn Day.
Painting of the Butterfly Dream by the Master Artist Li Tsai, A.
Remembering My Late Wife.
Shrine of General Pien, The.

Too Lazy to Write Poetry.
Chuang Tzu
Breath of Nature, The.
Cutting up an Ox.
Man Is Born in Tao.
Need to Win, The.
Chubb, Ralph (1892–1960)
Song of My Soul.
Transfiguration.
Chubb, Thomas Caldecot (b. 1899)
Merlin.
Chudakov, Sergey [or Sergei] (b. 1936)
Suicide is a duel with yourself.
When the cry goes up.
When they cry: / "Man overboard."
Chudleigh, Mary Lee, Lady (1656–1710)
Offering: Part One, The.
Resolve, The.
Song: "Why Damon, why, why, why so pressing?"
'Tis hard we should be by the men despised.
To Almystrea.
To the Ladies.
Unhappy they, who by their duty led.
Wish, The.
Chukhonstev, Oleg Grigorevich (b. 1938)
Chaadayev on Basmannaya.
Elegy: "Cross between a bakehouse and a bell tower, A."
Epistle to Baron Delvig.
Farewell to Autumn.
In the Menagerie.
Parrot, The.
When the village daylight dimmed.
With your name, I shall name this homeless year.
"Chukovsky [or Chukovskii], Korney" (Nikolai Vasilyevich Korneichukov) (1882–1969)
Telephone, The.
Chung-ch'ang T'ung (179–220)
Speaking My Mind.
Chung Ssu-ch'eng
Tune: "Sprig of Flowers, A"—Written for My "Ugly Studio."
Chuo Wen-chün (179?–117? B.C.)
Song of Snow-white Heads.
Church, Richard (1893–1972)
Alchemist, The.
Be Frugal.
On Hearing the First Cuckoo.
Churchill, Charles (1731–64)
Against Sodomy.
Character of a Critic.
Dedication: "Health to great Gloucester—from a man unknown."
First (entitled to the place), The.
Gods! with what pride I see the titled slave.
Gotham.
Is a son born into this world of woe?
Oft have I heard thee mourn the wretched lot.
On His Own Poetry.
Pomposo (insolent and loud)
Spectators only on this bustling stage.
Two boys, whose birth beyond all question springs.
When with much pains this boasted learning's got.
Churchyard, Thomas (c.1520–1604)
Tale of a Friar and A Shoemaker's Wife, A.
That humor now, declines for age drawes on.
Chute, Marchette (1909–94)
Day before Christmas.
My Dog.
My Plan.
Ciardi, John (1916–86)
About the Teeth of Sharks.
All about Boys and Girls.
Back through the Looking Glass to This Side.
Ballad of the Icondic.
Captain Spud and His First Mate, Spade.
Censorship.
Dawn of the Space Age.
Elegy Just in Case.
Faces.
Goodnight.

I Wouldn't.
Man Who Sang the Sillies, The.
On Evolution.
On Learning to Adjust to Things.
Plea.
On a Photo of Sgt. Ciardi a Year Later.
Sometimes Even Parents Win.
Stranger in the Pumpkin, The.
To a Reviewer Who Admired My Book.
What Johnny Told Me.
Suburban.

Cibber, Colley (1671–1757)
Blind Boy, The.

Cillactor
Married life for a poor man.
"Sweet is the fruit," say.
Young lady may increase her stock, A.

Ciment, Jill
Mommy.

Cinna, A.
Limerick: "Consistent disciples of Marx."
Limerick: "Did Ophelia ask Hamlet to bed?"
Limerick: "Dr. Johnson, when sober or pissed."
Limerick: "Of all God's jokes none is bluer."
Limerick: "Othello loved Desdemona."
Limerick: "Said Nelson at his most la-di-da-di."
Limerick: "Said the Queen to her favourite ghillie."
Limerick: "To his Queen said the circumspect Burleigh."

Cino da Pistoia (1270–1336)
Albeit my prayers have not so long delay'd.
Among the faults we in that book descry.
Canzone: His Lament for Selvaggia.
Dante, since I from my own native place.
I know not, Dante, in what refuge dwells.
Sonnet: A Trance of Love.
Sonnet: Death is not without but within him.
Sonnet: Of the Grave of Selvaggia, on the Monte della Sambuca.
Sonnet: To Love, In Great Bitterness.
This book of Dante's, very sooth to say.
To Dante Alighieri: He Conceives of Some Compensation in Death.
To Dante Alighieri: He Interprets Dante's Dream.
To His Lady Selvaggia Vergiolesi; Likening His Love to a Search for Gold.
What rhymes are thine which I have ta'en from thee.

Cisneros, Antonio (b. 1942)
Hampton Court.
Karl Marx Died 1883 Aged 65.
Paris Cinquième.
Spider Hangs Too Far from the Ground, The.
To a Dead Lady.

Cisneros, Sandra
Good Hot Dogs.
Heart, My Lovely Hobo.
I Am So in Love I Grow a New Hymen.
Loose Women.
Muddy Kid Comes Home.
My Wicked Wicked Ways.
Poet Reflects On Her Solitary Fate, The.
You Bring Out the Mexican in Me.
You Called Me Corazón.

Citino, David (b. 1947)
Famine.

Ciullo d'Alcamo (fl. c.1175)
Dialogue: Lover and Lady.

Cixous, Hélène (b. 1937)
I urgency, I begged. Give me your dish, I said, icy.

Clairmont, Robert (b. 1902)
Answers, The.
Hero in the Land of Dough, A.

Claman, Elizabeth
Show Biz Parties.

Clampitt, Amy (1920–94)
Baroque Sunburst, A.
Beach Glass.
Beethoven, Opus 111.
Cormorant in His Element, The.
Cure at Porlock, A.

Dancers Exercising.
Easter Morning.
Fog.
Gooseberry Fool.
Hairline Fracture, A.
Imago.
Kingfisher, The.
Medusa.
Meridian.
Procession at Candlemas, A.
Stacking the Straw.
Sun Underfoot among the Sundews, The.
Syrinx.
Times Square Water Music.
What the Light Was Like.
Whippoorwill in the Woods, A.
Woodlot, The.

Clanchy, Kate (b. 1965)
Deadman's Shoes.
For a Wedding.
Foreign.
One Night When We Paused Half-way.
Recognition.

Clancy, Joseph P. (b. 1928)
Miscarriage.

Clare, John (1793–1864)
After Reading in a Letter Proposals for Building a Cottage.
Anecdote of Love, An.
Ants, The.
Autumn.
Badger, The.
Birds' Nest.
Birds' Nests.
Clock-A-Clay.
Death.
Death's Memories.
December.
Eternity of Nature, The.
Evening.
Fallen Elm, The.
Farewell: "Farewell to the bushy clump close to the river."
February.
Field Path.
First Love.
Flitting, The.
Flood, The.
Fragment: "Language has not the power to speak what love indites."
Gipsies: "Gipsies seek wide sheltering woods again, The."
Glad Christmas comes, and every hearth.
God Looks on Nature With a Glorious Eye.
Grasshoppers.
Green Woodpecker's Nest, The.
Gypsy's Evening Blaze, The.
Hares at Play.
Hen's Nest.
Hesperus.
Hymn to the Creator.
I Am.
I Feel I Am.
I've Had Many an Aching Pain.
I wish I was where I would be.
Invite to Eternity, An.
Lament of Swordy Well, The.
Last of April, The.
Lines Written on a Very Boisterous Day in May, 1844.
Little Trotty Wagtail.
Lord, Hear My Prayer.
Love's Emblem.
Love's memories haunt my footsteps still.
Love's Pains.
Loves Lives Beyond the Tomb.
Maple Tree, The.
Married to a Soldier.
Mist in the Meadows.
Mouse's Nest.
My Mary.
Nightingale's Nest, The.
Nightingale, The.
Noon.
Nutting.
Old pond full of flags and fenced around, The.
Old Year, The.

Peasant Poet, The.
Pewits Nest.
Primrose, The.
Rawk o' the autumn, The.
Remember Dear Mary.
Returned Soldier, The.
Rural Scenes.
Sabbath Bells.
Sand Martin, The.
Secret Love.
Shadows.
She Tied up Her Few Things.
Shepherd Boy, The.
Shepherd's Tree, The.
Silver Mist, The.
Sky Lark, The.
Soldier, The.
Solitude.
Song: "I peeled bits of straw and I got switches too."
Song: "I went my Sunday mornings round."
Song: "Mist rauk is hanging, The."
Song's Eternity.
Song: "Soft falls the sweet evening."
Stanzas: "Black absence hides upon the past."
Stanzas: "Passing of a dream, The."
Sudden Shower.
Thunder mutters louder and more loud, The.
To an Angry Bee.
To an Hour-Glass.
To John Clare.
To Mary: 'It Is the Evening Hour.'
To Miss B.
To the Memory of John Keats.
To Wordsworth.
Turkeys.
Vision, A.
Vixen, The.
Water-Lilies.
Wind That Shakes the Rushes, The.
Winter.
Winters Spring, The.
Wish, The.
Woodland Seat, A.
Wren, The.
Wryneck's Nest, The.
Yellowhammer, The.

Clare of Assisi (1193–1253)
Blessing Attributed to Saint Clare, The.

Clare, Sidney (fl. 1934)
On the Good Ship Lollipop.

Clark, Alan
Limerick: "There was a young lady of Leicester."

Clark, Badger See **Clark, Charles Badger, Jr.**

Clark Bekederemo, John Pepper (b. 1935)
Abiku.
Agbor Dancer.
Casualties, The.
Death of a Lady.
Epilogue to Casualties.
Family Procession, A.
New from Ethiopia and the Sudan, The.
Order of the Dead, The.

Clark, Charles Badger, Jr. (Badger Clark) (1883–1957)
Border Affair, A.

Clark, J. (fl. c.1886)
Maxims in Rhyme for the Young.

Clark, Leonard (1905–88)
Ground Elder.
Singing in the Streets.

Clark, Moira
Mushrooms.

Clark, Polly (b. 1968)
Excitement.
Kleptomaniac.
My Life with Horses.
Walk in the Rain.
Zoo.

Clark, Thomas A. (b. 1944)
As I walked out early.
Blessing on the house, A.
Our boat touches the bank.
Shadow extends the tree.

Sit for a while on a stone.

Clark, Thomas Curtis (1879?–1953)
Faith for Tomorrow.
Friends.
I Am Still Rich.
Sons of Promise.
Take Time to Live.
Touch of Human Hands, The.

Clark, Tom (b. 1941)
As the Human Village Prepares for Its Fate.
Baseball and Classicism.
"Before Dawn."
Daily News.
Doors.
Eyeglasses.
Going to School in France or America.
"Like Musical Instruments."
On the Beach.
Poem: "Tiny new emotions, The."
Society.
Sonnet: "Orgasm completely, The."
Suicide with Squirtgun.
Superballs.
Time.
You (I)
You (II)
You (III)
You (IV)

Clarke, Austin (1896–1974)
Anacreontic.
Ancient Lights.
Burial of An Irish President.
Celibacy.
Early Unfinished Sketch.
Envy of Poor Lovers, The.
Fair at Windgap, The.
Forget Me Not.
Her Voice Could Not Be Softer.
Inscription for a Headstone.
Irish-American Dignitary.
Japanese Print.
Jest, The.
Last Republicans, The.
Lost Heifer, The.
Marriage.
Martha Blake.
Martha Blake at Fifty-one.
Maurice was in an Exhibition Hall.
Miss Marnell.
My mother wept loudly.
Night and Morning.
One night he heard heart-breaking sound.
Past the house where he was got.
Penal Law.
Pilgrimage.
Planter's Daughter, The.
Scholar, The.
Sermon on Swift, A.
St Christopher.
Straying Student, The.
Strolling one day, beyond the Kalends, on
    Mount Cyllene.
Strong Wind, A.
Subjection of Women, The.
Tenebrae.
They are the spit of virtue now.
Three Poems about Children.
Through lane or black archway.
Wolfe Tone.
Young Woman of Beare, The.

Clarke, Cheryl (b. 1947)
14th Street Was Gutted in 1968.
Of Althea and Flaxie.
Older American, The.
Make-Up.
Nothing.
Palm Leaf of Mary Magdalene.
Passing.
Poet's Death, A.
Rondeau: "They are bodies left unburied."
Stuck.
Tortoise and Badger.
Vicki and Daphne.
What Goes around Comes around, or The
    Proof is in the Pudding.

Clarke, Gillian (b. 1937)
All afternoon I hope.

Baby-Sitting.
Blaen Cwrt.
Border.
Foghorns.
Hare, The.
Hay-Making.
Lament: "For the green turtle with her pulsing
    burden."
Les Grottes.
Migraine.
Neighbours.
No Hands.
Overheard in County Sligo.
Ram.
St. Thomas's Day.
Suicide on Pentwyn Bridge.
Taid's Grave.
Windmill.

Clarke, Grant
Am I Blue?
Everything Is Peaches Down in Georgia.
Rag Time Cowboy Joe.
Second Hand Rose.

Clarke, James Freeman (1810–88)
Brother, Hast Thou Wandered Far.
Dear Friend, Whose Presence in the House.

Clarke, John
Accounting Cat, The.
Jenny Hit Me.
Story So Far, The.
There was an old man with a beard.

Clarke, Macdonold (1798–1849)
In the Graveyard.

Clarke, Marcus (1846–81)
Wail of the Waiter, The.

Clarke, Peter
In Air.
Play Song.
Young Shepherd Bathing His Feet.

Clarke, Tracy
For Babies Unborn.
Will They Always Remember.

Clarkson, Laurence (1615–67)
Behold, the King of glory now is come.

Clary, Killarney (b. 1953)
Another hot afternoon upstairs after school.
In this wind, the sharp blue cut of the San
    Gabriels flattens against the neon east.
Mr. Dooms would meet us across the Bay
    Bridge at a restaurant that featured 'Dancing
    Waters.'
Restless before the canary, wave of traffic on
    an inhale, I can just barely see on a dark
    blue ground black arabesques.
When my heart asked for a way free, it was led
    into this lightless room.

Claudian (Claudius Claudianus) (c.370–404)
Epitaph: "Fate to beauty still must give."
For France.
Lonely Isle, The.
Old Man of Verona, The.

Claudianus, Claudius See **Claudian**

Claus, Hugo (b. 1929)
Tollund Man, The.
Woman 12, A.

Clausen, Jan (b. 1950)
After Touch.

Clayton, Iris
Black Rat, The.
Kidnappers.
Last Link, The.
River Bidgee.

Clayton, Stephen (b. 1956)
Boom Time.
Good Old Days, The.
Redfern at Night.
Soul Music.
Sunshine Prisoner '470.'

Cleage, Pearl (b. 1948)
Confession.

Cleary, Brendan (b. 1958)
Boys' Own.
Chicken & Sex.
New Rock n Roll, The.
Sealink.

Slouch.

Cleavland, Benjamin (1733–1811)
O Could I Find from Day to Day.

Cleghorn, Sarah Norcliffe (1876–1959)
Comrade Jesus.
Golf Links, The.

Cleland, William (1661?–1689)
Hallo My Fancy.

Clemens, Prudentius Aurelius See **Prudentius**

Clemens, Samuel Langhorne See **"Twain, Mark"**

Clementelli, Elena
Bend of the gulf.
Circle and Obsession of Walls.
I'd Like to Try Telling You of Spring.
Your Hands, My Love.
Moviola.
Subterranean geography.

Clements, Arthur L. (fl. 20th cent.)
Elegy.
Why I Don't Speak Italian.

Clements, Susan (fl. 20th cent)
Deer Cloud.
Matinee.
Reservation, The.
Susans.

Clemmons, Carole C. Gregory (b. 1945)
Freedom Song for the Black Woman, A.
Greater Friendship Baptist Church, The.
Love Letter.
Revelation.

Clemo, Jack R. (b. 1916)
Burnt Bush, The.
Christ in the Clay-Pit.
Growing in Grace.
Mould of Castile.
Neither Shadow of Turning.
On the Death of Karl Barth.

Cleoboulos (d. 6th cent. B.C.)
I am the maiden in bronze set over the tomb of
    Midas.

Clephane, Elizabeth Cecilia (1830–69)
Beneath the cross of Jesus.

Clerk, Sir John, of Penicuik (fl. 15th cent.)
Country Seat, The.
Fane Wald I Luve.

Clerq, J. G. Clemenceau Le See **"Tanaquil, Paul"**

Cleveland, John (1613–58)
Antiplatonic[k], The.
Elegy on Ben Jonson, An.
Epitaph on the Earl of Strafford.
General Eclipse, The.
He that saw hell in his melancholy dream.
How? Providence? and yet a Scottish crew?
King's Disguise, The.
Lord! what a goodly thing is want of shirts.
Nature herself doth Scotchmen beasts confess.
Rebel Scot, The.
Upon Phillis Walking in a Morning before
    Sun-Rising.

Cleveland, Philip Jerome (b. 1903)
By Night.
I Yield Thee Praise.
There is a love that tumbles like a stream.

Clewell, David
Poem for the Man Who Said Shit.

Cleyre, Voltairine de (1866–1912)
Love's Compensation.
Out of the Darkness.

Cliff, Michelle (b. 1946)
History of Costume, A.
Within the Veil.

Clifford, Carrie Williams (1882–1958)
Black Draftee from Dixie, The.

Clifford, John (1836–1923)
Anvil—God's Word, The.

Clifton, Harry (b. 1952)
Death of Thomas Merton.
Distaff Side, The.
Eccles Street, Bloomsday, 1982.
Euclid Avenue.
Id.
Monsoon Girl.
Seamstress, The.

Clifton, Lucille (b. 1936)
1. at nagasaki.

4/30/92 for rodney king.
11/10 Again.
Admonitions.
Anna Speaks of the Childhood of Mary Her
    Daughter.
Astrologer Predicts at Mary's Birth, The.
At Jonestown.
At the Cemetery, Walnut Grove Plantation,
    South Carolina, 1989.
Atlantic is a sea of bones.
Blake.
Bodies broken on, The.
C. C. Rider.
Calming Kali.
Climbing.
Cruelty. Don't talk to me about cruelty.
Cutting Greens.
Dear Jesse Helms.
Death of Crazy Horse, The.
December.
Driving through new england.
Earth is a living thing, The.
Eviction.
For de Lawd.
Fury.
Good Times.
Hag Riding.
Here is another bone to pick with you.
Holy Night.
Homage to My Hips.
How Is He Coming Then.
I am Accused of Tending to the Past.
If I Stand in My Window.
If mama / could see.
In Salem.
In the Inner City.
In White America.
Island Mary.
Kali.
Light / on my mother's tongue.
Listen Children.
Lost Baby Poem, The.
Lost Women, The.
Love Rejected.
Malcolm.
Mary.
Mary's Dream.
Miss Rosie.
Move.
My Dream About the Cows.
My Dream About the Poet.
My Mama Moved among the Days.
Night Vision.
Note, Passed to Superman.
Powell (officer charged with the beating of
    rodney king)
Prayer.
Sam.
Shapeshifter Poems.
She Lived.
Slave Cabin, Sotterly Plantation, Maryland,
    1989.
Slaveship.
Song at midnight.
Song of Mary, A.
Sorrow Song.
Them and Us.
Thirty-Eighth Year, The.
To Michal.
To Ms. Ann.
To my friend, Jerina.
To the Unborn and Waiting Children.
Way It Was, The.
What spells racoon to me.
When did she know, when did she know it.
White Lady.
Why some people be mad at me sometimes.
Wishes for Sons.
Woman who loves, A.
Women you are accustomed to, The.
Won't you celebrate with me.

Clinton, Michelle T. (b. 1954)
Black Rape.
Eviction.
History as Trash.
I Wanna Be Black.
Plan of the Klan.

Traditional Post-Modern Neo-HooDoo Afra-
    Centric Sister in a Purple Head Rag
    Mourning Death and Cooking.
Warning to Young Bright Sisters / White AM.
    Culture 101A.

Clive, Caroline
Mosel, The.
Mother, The.
Old Age.

Clough, Arthur Hugh (1819–61)
Across the Sea, Along the Shore.
Amours de Voyage, sels.
Blank Misgivings of a Creature Moving about
    in Worlds Not Realized, sels.
Bothie of Tober-na-Vuolich, The. [A Long-
    Vacation Pastoral], sels.
Come Home, Come Home!
Darkness.
Dipsychus (and the Spirit), sels.
Duty.
Epi-strauss-ium.
Genesis XXIV.
Here am I yet, another twelvemonth spent.
In Stratis Viarum IV.
Latest Decalogue, The.
Luther, they say, was unwise; he didn't see
    how things were going.
Mary Trevellyn to Miss Roper.
Natura Naturans.
Qua Cursum Ventus.
Questioning Spirit, The.
Revival.
Say Not the Struggle Nought Availeth.
Sic Itur.
Spectator ab Extra, sels.
To spend uncounted years of pain.
What we, when face to face we see.
With Whom Is No Variableness, Neither
    Shadow of Turning.

"Clout, Colin" See **Spenser, Edmund**

Clouts, Sydney (b. 1926)
After the Poem.
Firebowl.
Roy Kloof.

Clover, Joshua
Alas, That Is the Name of Our Town; I Have
    Been Concealing It All This Time.
Archive of Confessions, a Genealogy of
    Confessions, An.
Ceriserie.
El periférico, or Sleep.
Family Romance.
Institute for Social Change, The.
Map Room, The.
There Is the Body Lying in State.
Zealous.

Clutesi, George (b. 1905)
Beast in Man, The.
Ko-Ishin-Mit Goes Fishing.
Song of the Yellow Cedar Face, A.
West Coast Indian.

Cluysenaar, Anne (b. 1936)
Knife reduces a polished oval, The.

Coates, Eric
Sleepy Lagoon.

Coatsworth, Elizabeth Jane (b. 1893)
And Stands There Sighing.
Bad Kittens, The.
Barn, The.
Circus-Postered Barn, The.
Daniel Webster's Horses.
Lady Comes to an Inn, A.
March.
Mouse, The.
No Shop Does the Bird Use.
Nosegay.
Old Mare, The.
On a Night of Snow.
Open Door, The.
Song of the Rabbits Outside the Tavern, The.
Storm, The.
Swallows, The.
Swift Things Are Beautiful.
This Is the Hay That No Man Planted.
Violets, Daffodils.

Cobb, Alice S. (b. 1942)
Angela Davis.

Searching, The.

Cobbe, Eliza See **Tuite, Eliza Cobbe, Lady**

Cobbett, William
Elegy in Newgate.

Cobbing, Bob
Bird Bee.
Hymn to the Sacred Mushroom.

Cobbold, Elizabeth (1767–1824)
On Some Violets Planted in My Garden by a
    Friend.

Coccimiglio, Vic
Night Beach.
St. Francis Speaks to Me at a Young Age.

Cockburn, Alison Rutherford (1713–1794)
Flowers of the Forest, The.

Cockburn, Catherine (1679–1749)
Caution, The.
To Mrs. Manley. By the Author of Agnes de
    Castro.
Vain Advice, The.
Verses Sent to Mr Bevil Higgons, on His
    Sickness and Recovery from the Small-pox,
    in the Year 1693.

Cocteau, Jean (1891–1963)
Cape of Good Hope, The.
Fairy Scene.

Codling, Caroline
Assist me while I wander here.

Codrescu, Andrei (b. 1946)
Against Meaning.
Circle Jerk.
Grammar, A.
Imagination of Necessity, The.
Paper on Humor.
Poetry Paper.
Telyric.
Work.

Coe, Charles
Possibility.

Cofer, Judith Ortiz (b. 1952)
Anniversary.
Campesino's Lament, The.
Changeling, The.
Cold as Heaven.
Correspondence.
Counting.
Dream of Birth, The.
Drowned Sailor, The.
Fever.
Hour of the Siesta, The.
How to Get a Baby.
Idea of Islands, The.
Las Magdalenas.
Learning to Walk Alone.
Lesson of the Sugarcane, The.
Lesson of the Teeth, The.
Letter from Home in Spanish.
Life of an Echo, The.
My Grandfather's Hat.
Old Women.
Photographs of My Father.
Purpose of Nuns, The.
Saint Rose of Lima.
Seizing the Day.
Spring.
They Never Grew Old.
Unspoken.
What the Gypsy Said to Her Children.
What We Feared.
Why There Are No Unicorns.
Women Who Love Angels.

Coffey, Brian (1905–95)
And where no snow had.
Awakening like return to Earth from Moon.
Blooms such as wither at finger-touch.
Cold.
Consider his song.
Headrock.
Homer where born where buried of whom the
    son.
"My son my son" the Blakean figure mourns
    and affirms.
Nicest Phantasies Are Shared, The.
Nightfall, Midwinter, Missouri.
Prayers, The.

Coffin

What have they done to Klio what have they
done to our Muse.

Coffin, C. (1676–1749)
Advent of our God With eager hearts we greet,
The.

Coffman, Lisa (b. 1963)
Cheerleaders.
Courage, or One of Gene Horner's Fiddles.
Girl/Spit.
Likely.

Coghill, Mary
Knowing.

Cohan, George M. (1878–1942)
Down by the Erie Canal.
Forty-five Minutes from Broadway.
Give My Regards to Broadway.
I'm Mighty Glad I'm Living and That's All.
I Want to Hear a Yankee Doodle Tune.
If I'm Going to Die I'm going to Have Some
Fun.
If Washington Should Come to Life.
Life's a Funny Proposition after All.
Mary's a Grand Old Name.
Nothing New Beneath the Sun.
Over There.
So Long, Mary.
Twentieth-Century Love.
When a Fellow's on the Level with a Girl
That's on the Square.
Yankee Doodle Boy, The.
You're a Grand Old Flag.

Cohen, Garnett Kilberg
Child Bride.

Cohen, Jacob (1881–1959)
Eternal Jew, The.
Harp of David, The.
Surely My Soul.
Tirzah.

Cohen, Leonard (b. 1934)
All There Is to Know about Adolph Eichmann.
Bus, The.
Elegy: "Do not look for him."
Genius, The.
Heirloom.
I Have Not Lingered in European Monasteries.
Killers, The.
Kite Is a Victim, A.
Only Tourist in Havana Turns His Thoughts
Homeward, The.
Out of the Land of Heaven.
You Have the Lovers.

Cohen, Marc (b. 1951)
Evensong.

Coicou, Massillon (1865–1908)
Lord's Prayer, The.
Slave's Lament, The.

Coiffait, Carol
Last Apple, The.

Coignard, Gabrielle de (d. 1594)
Prayer: "Fear of death disturbs me constantly,
The."

Cokayne, Sir Aston (1608–84)
Epitaph on a Great Sleeper.

Coke, A. A. Hedge
Change, The.

Cokinos, Christopher
Earth Movers, The.

Colby, Todd
Boy and the Girl, The.
Captain's Log.
Dear, I Love.
Labor Day Picnic Poem.
Think Eight.

Cole, Barry (b. 1936)
Men Are Coming Back!, The.

Cole, George Douglas Howard (1889–1959)
And you'll say a nation totters.

Cole, Henri (b. 1956)
Cabbage Butterfly, The.
40 Days and 40 Nights.
Prince Enters the Forest, The.
Roman Baths at Nîmes, The.

Cole, Henry (1808–82)
Thy Best.

Cole, Joanna (b. 1944)
Happy New Year, Anyway.
Hippopotamus.

Cole, Peter
Isaac: a Poise.

Cole, Thomas (1801–48)
As the broad mountain where the shadows flit.
Dial, The.
I Saw a Cave of Sable Depth Profound.
Lago Maggiore.
Lament of the Forest, The.
Life of Hubert, The.
Lines Suggested by Hearing Music on the
Boston Common at Night.
Painter, A.
To Her Modest Mirth-Making Friend, Mr
Robert Dover.
Written in Autumn.

Cole, William (b. 1919)
Back Yard, July Night.
Marriage Couplet.
Mutual Problem.
Mysterious East.
Oh, Noa, Noa!
Poor Kid.
Some Sights Sometimes Seen and Seldom
Seen.
What a Friend We Have in Cheeses!

Colebatch, Hal (b. 1947)
On the Death of Ludwig Erhard.
One Tourist's Cologne.

Coleman, Cy
Best Is Yet to Come, The.
Hey, Look Me Over.
I'm Gonna Laugh You Right Out of My Life.
I've Got Your Number.
I Walk a Little Faster.
It Amazes Me!
Real Live Girl.
Riviera, The.
Rules of the Road, The.
When in Rome (I Do As the Romans Do)
Why Try to Change Me Now?
Witchcraft.
You Fascinate Me So.

Coleman, Emily Holmes (1899–1974)
Liberator, The.

Coleman, Horace
Black Soldier Remembers, A.
Downed Black Pilot Learns How to Fly, A.
In Ca Mau.
Remembrance of Things Past.
Night Flare Drop, Tan Son Nhut.
OK Corral East Brothers in the Nam.
Poem for a "Divorced" Daughter.

Coleman, Jane
Soap.

Coleman, John (fl. early 17th cent.)
Poor Bess Turpin, I pytty thy case as farr as I
can.

Coleman, Victor (b. 1944)
Day Twenty-three.
How the Death of a City Is Never More than
the Sum of the Deaths of Those Who Inhabit
Its Spaces.

Coleman, Wanda (b. 1946)
African Sleeping Sickness.
American Sonnet (10)
April in Hollywood.
At the Record Hop.
Aunt Jessie.
Be Quiet, Go Away.
Bedtime Story.
Breast Examination.
Brute Strength.
Coffee.
Dog Suicide.
Emmett Till.
Essay on Language.
Cousin Mary.
ISM, The.
Mastectomy.
Prisoner of Los Angeles (2)
Today I Am a Homicide in the North of the
City.

Where I Live.

Coleridge, Hartley (1796–1849)
All nature ministers to Hope. The snow.
Dedicatory Sonnet to S. T. Coleridge.
Early Death.
First Birthday, The.
Full Well I Know.
He Lived amidst th' Untrodden Ways.
How Long I Sailed.
If I have sinned in act, I may repent.
Is love a fancy, or a feeling? No.
Jesus Praying.
"Multum Dilexit."
Long Time a Child.
Night.
November.
Prayer.
She Is Not Fair to Outward View.
She Was a Queen.
Think upon Death.
To a Friend.
To a Lofty Beauty, from Her Poor Kinsman.
To Wordsworth.
Why Should I Murmur.
Written on the Anniversary of Our Father's
Death.

Coleridge, Mary Elizabeth (1861–1907)
Alcestis to Admetus.
At a Friends' Meeting.
Awake.
Bid me remember, O my gracious Lord.
Blue and White.
Broken Friendship.
But in that Sleep of Death what Dreams may
Come?
Clever Woman, A.
Contents of an Ink-bottle, The.
Day-dream, A.
Death.
Devil's Funeral, The.
Doubt.
Fire, the lamp, and I, were alone together, The.
Friends—With a Difference.
Gifts.
Gone.
He Came Unto His Own, and His Own
Received Him Not.
Huguenot, A.
Hush.
I envy not the dead that rest.
I Saw a Stable.
Impromptu.
In Dispraise of the Moon.
In London Town.
Insincere Wish Addressed to a Beggar, An.
Jealousy.
Lady of Trees, The.
Lord of the Winds.
Marriage.
Master and Guest.
Mistaken.
Moment, A.
Mortal Combat.
My True Love Hath My Heart and I Have His.
No Newspapers.
Not Yet.
Nurse's Lament, The.
O Earth, My Mother! Not Upon Thy Breast.
On a Bas-relief of Pelops and Hippodameia.
Only a little shall we speak of thee.
Other Side of a Mirror, The.
Our Lady.
Poison Flower, The.
Pride.
Punctilio.
Regina.
Sadness.
September.
Shadow.
Solo.
Some in a Child Would Live, Some in a Book.
Street Lanterns.
To a Piano.
To Memory.
True to myself am I, and false to all.
Unwelcome.
Wasted.

We Never Said Farewell.
White Women, The.
Wilderspin.
Witch, The.
Witches' Wood, The.
Words.

Coleridge, Samuel Taylor (1772–1834)
And now the Storm-blast came, and he.
Answer to a Child's Question.
Apologia pro Vita Sua.
Burke.
Christabel.
Christmas Carol, A: "Shepherds went their
  hasty way, The."
Cologne.
Constancy to an Ideal Object.
Dejection: An Ode.
Devil's Thoughts, The.
Duty Surviving Self-Love.
Eolian Harp, The.
Epitaph on Himself.
Epitaph: "Stop, Christian passer-by!—Stop,
  child of God."
Fancy in Nubibus.
Fears in Solitude.
Fire, Famine, and Slaughter.
Forbearance.
Frost at Midnight.
Glycine's Song.
Good Great Man, The.
Hexameters[; Paraphrase of Psalm XLVI].
Homeric Hexameter, The.
Hymn before Sunrise, in the Vale of
  Chamouni.
I fear thee, ancient Mariner!
In the Touch of This Bosom There Worketh a
  Spell.
Invocation, An: "Hear, sweet spirit, hear the
  spell."
Knight's Tomb, The.
Koskiusko.
Kubla Khan: or, A Vision in a Dream.
La Fayette.
Love.
Metrical Feet.
Modern Critics.
My Baptismal Birthday [or Birth-Day].
Nightingale, The.
Old Man's Sigh, The. A Sonnet.
On a Discovery Made Too Late.
On a Ruined House in a Romantic Country.
On an Infant Which Died before Baptism.
On Donne's Poetry.
On Imitation.
Pains of Sleep, The.
Pantisocracy.
Pensive at eve on the hard world I mus'd [or
  mused].
Phantom.
Pitt.
Raven, The.
Recollections of Love.
Rime of the Ancient Mariner, The.
Sonnet Composed on a Journey Homeward;
  the Author Having Received Intelligence of
  the Birth of a Son, 20 September 1796.
Sonnet to a Friend Who Asked How I Felt
  When the Nurse First Presented My Infant
  to Me.
Sonnet to the River Otter.
Sonnets Attempted in the Manner of
  Contemporary Writers.
Sunset, A.
Thankless too for peace.
This Lime-Tree Bower My Prison.
Time, Real and Imaginary.
'Tis the middle of night by the castle clock.
To a Young Ass.
To Nature.
To Simplicity.
To the Autumnal Moon.
To the Rev. [or Reverend] W. L. Bowles.
To William Wordsworth.
Truth I pursued, as Fancy sketch'd the way.
Visit of the Gods, The.
W. H. Eheu!
What Is an Epigram?

Work without Hope.
Youth and Age.

Coleridge, Sara (1802–52)
Blest is the tarn which towering cliffs
  o'ershade.
Father! no amaranths e'er shall wreathe my
  brow.
Garden Year, The.
Storm, The.

Coles, Don (b. 1928)
Natalya Nikolayevna Goncharov.
Photograph in a Stockholm Newspaper for
  March 13, 1910.

Coles, Gladys Mary (b. 1942)
Dornier, The.
Heron in the Alyn.
Ithaca-Liverpool.

Coles, Robert
Christmas, Belfast.
Goddam Street, The.
New Jersey Boys.
On Dutch's Death.

Colesworthy, Daniel C. (1810–93)
Be Never Discouraged.
While We Lowly Bow before Thee.

Collier, John (1708–76)
Pluralist and Old Soldier, The.

Collier, Mary (1690?–c.1762)
Washerwoman, The.
Womans Labour, an epistle, The.

Collier, Michael
Brave Sparrow.
North Corridor.
Robert Wilson.

Collins, Anne (fl. c.1653)
Song.
Song Composed in Time of the Civill Warr,
  when the Wicked Did Much Insult over the
  Godly, A.
Song: "My straying thoughts, reduced stay."

Collins, Billy
Death of Allegory, The.
Going Out for Cigarettes.
Lines Lost Among Trees.
Memento Mori.
Snow Day.
Tomes.

Collins, Emanuel (b. 1712?)
Fatal Dream; or, The Unhappy Favourite, The.

Collins, John (1742?–1808)
Tomorrow.

Collins, Kimberly Ann (b. 1964)
I Am Africa.
Sisters.
Trio.

Collins, Martha (b. 1940)
Border, The.
Lies.
Like Her Body the World.
Out of My Own Pocket.
Warmer.

Collins, Mortimer (1827–76)
If.
Lotos Eating.
Positivists, The.
To F. C.
Winter in Brighton.

Collins, William (1721–59)
Fidele, A.
How Sleep the Brave.
Ode Occasioned by the Death of Mr. Thomson.
Ode on the Poetical Character.
Ode on the Popular Superstitions of the
  Highlands of Scotland, An.
Ode to Evening.
Ode to Fear.
Ode to Simplicity.
Passions; an Ode for [or to] Music, The.
Sonnet: "When Phoebe formed a wanton
  smile."
Stormy Hebrides, The.

Collobert, Danielle (1940–78)
As if dead the buried text.

Collop, John (1625–62?)
Praise of a Yellow Skin, The; or An Elizabeth

in Gold.

Collymore, Frank A. (1893–1980)
Ballad of an Old Woman.

Collyn, Marie (b. 1555 or 1556, d. after 1600)
Thursday Before New Yeares Day (Being on
  the Satterdy) the Maide, by Councell of On,
  She Trustid Well, Excussid Herself on This
  Wise to Milord, The.

Colman, Benjamin (1673–1747)
Another to Urania.
God of My Life!
Poem on Elijahs Translation, A.
Quarrel with Fortune, A.
To Philomela.
To Urania.

Colman, George, the Younger (1762–1836)
Cold blows the blast—the night's obscure.
London Rurality.
On Sir Nathaniel Wraxall the Historian.

Colman, Henry (fl. 1640)
On Lazarus Raised From Death.
On Mortality.
On the Inscription Over the Head of Christ on
  the Cross.
On the Strange Apparitions at Christ's Death.
On the Three Children in the Fiery Furnace.

Colombo, John Robert (b. 1936)
How They Made the Golem.
Ideal Angels.

Colonna, Silvana (b. 1942)
But what an idea she'd gotten into her head.
But your imagining was wrong.
Disconnections.
He spins about (laughing) then shows.
Orientation from Afar.
So it tries to reach her inside her mind.
Without muscles without slipping.

**Colonna, Vittoria da, Marchesa di Pescara
(1490–1547)**
As a hungry fledgling, who sees and hears.
As When Some Hungry Fledgling Hears and
  Sees.
I live on this depraved and lonely cliff.
I see in my mind, surrounding God.
When the Orient is lit by the great light.

Colum, Padraic (1881–1972)
Book of Kells, The.
Drover, A.
Interior.
Monkeys.
No Child.
Old Soldier.
Old Woman of the Roads, The.
Plower, The.
Poor Scholar of the 'Forties, A.
River-Mates.
She Moved through the Fair.
Wild Ass.

Columba [or Columcille], Saint (fl. c.543–615)
Boat Song, A.
Boyhood of Christ, The.
Clamour of the wind making music.
Farewell to Ireland.
If I owned all of Alba.
Invocation, An: "My claw is tired of scribing!"
Maker on High, The.
Mary mild, good maiden.
O Son of God, it would be sweet.
On some island I long to be.
St. Columcille the Scribe.
Three places most loved I have left.

Columbo, Russ
Prisoner of Love.

Colvin, Ian D. (1877–1938)
Flying Dutchman, The.
Tristan da Cunha.

Combs, Tram (b. 1924)
Ars Poetica about Ultimates.
Aware Aware.
Just after Noon with Fierce Shears.

Comden, Betty (b. 1917)
Adventure.
All of My Life.
Conga.
I Can Cook, Too.

Cometas

If You Hadn't—But You Did.
Just in Time.
Little Bit in Love, A.
Lonely Town.
Lucky to Be Me.
Make Someone Happy.
New York, New York.
Not Mine.
Party's Over, The.
Some Other Time.
Thanks a Lot, but No Thanks.
You Mustn't Feel Discouraged.

Cometas (*fl.* c.950)
Country Gods.
"Who, tell me, shepherd, owns these rows of plants?"
Phyllis, loving Demophoon.

Comfort, Alex (b. 1920)
Epitaph: "One whom I knew, a student and a poet."
Fear of the Earth.
Letter to an American Visitor.
Notes for My Son.
Song for the Heroes.

Compagni, Dino
No man may mount upon a golden stair.

Comte de Lautréamont
I am filthy. Lice gnaw me. Swine, when they look at me, vomit. The scabs.

Conder, Josiah (1789–1855)
Bread of Heaven, on Thee We Feed.
Day by Day the Manna Fell.

Condon, R. D.
Limerick: "Horsewoman of charm at Uttoxeter, A."

Conforti, Gerard John
On the mountain slope.

Confucius (551–479 B.C.)
Alba.
Efficient Wife's Complaint, The.
Fraternitas.
Great Digest, The.
In the South be drooping trees.
Pedlar.
Sans Equity and sans Poise.
Shao and the South.
Songs of Ch'en.
Songs of Cheng.
Yung Wind.

Congreve, William (1670–1729)
Aisle of a Temple, The.
Doris.
False Though She Be.
Hue and Cry after Fair Amoret, A.
Lesbia.
Music.
Pious Selinda [*or* Celinda].
See, see, she wakes, Sabina wakes!
Way of the World, The.

Conkling, Grace Hazard (b. 1878)
I Will Not Give Thee All My Heart.

Conley, Larry (*fl.* 1930)
Cottage for Sale, A.

Conn, Stewart (b. 1936)
Todd.
Under the Ice.

Connelly, Reginald
Good Night, Sweetheart.
If I Had You.
Try a Little Tenderness.

Connolly, Cyril (1903–74)
Come on Percy, my pillion-proud, be.
It was late last night when my lord came home.
M is for Marx.
On Geoffrey Grigson.
On Himself.
Something is going to go, baby.
To Osbert Sitwell.

Connor, T. W. (b. 1936)
She Was One of the Early Birds.

Connor, Tony (b. 1930)
Apologue.
Lancashire Winter.
Last of the Poet's Car.

Conoley, Gillian
Beauty and the Beast.
Beckon.
Masters, The.
Sky Drank In, The.
World, The.

Conquest, Robert (b. 1917)
Agents, The.
Appalachian Convalescence.
Bagpipes at the Biltmore.
Excerpt from a Report to the Galactic Council.
Generalities.
Guided Missiles Experimental Range.
Horror Comic.
Lake Success.
Limerick: "My demands upon life are quite modest."
Limerick: "Our existence would be that much grimmer ex-."
Limerick: "Then scorn not the limerick either."
Limerick: "When a man's too old even to toss off, he."
Man and Woman.
Progress.
Rokeby Venus, The.
747 (London–Chicago)
To Be a Pilgrim.

Conrad, Con
Continental (You Kiss While You're Dancing), The.

Conran, Anthony (b. 1931)
Death of a Species.
Elegy for Sir Ifor Williams.
Elegy for the Welsh Dead, in the Falkland Islands, 1982.
Fledgling.
Spirit Level.
Thirteen Ways of Looking at a Hoover.

Constable, Henry (1562–1613)
Diaphenia.
Hope, like the hyaena [*or* hyena], coming to be old.
Miracle of the world, I never will deny.
Of his Mistress, upon Occasion of her Walking in a Garden.
On the Death of Sir Philip Sidney.
Resolved to love, unworthy to obtain.
To God the Holy Ghost.
To live in hell, and heaven to behold.
To Our Blessed Lady.
To Saint Margaret.
To Saint Mary Magdalen.
To St. John Baptist.
To St. Michael the Archangel.
To St. Peter and St. Paul.
To the Blessed Sacrament.
To the Marquess of Piscat's Soul.
Uncivil sickness, hast thou no regard.

Constantine, David (b. 1944)
He arrived, towing a crowd, and slept.
Lasithi.
Watching for Dolphins.
What we reminded you of you are already forgetting.
You Are Distant, You Are Already Leaving.

Constantinus Cephalus *See* **Cephalus**

Converse, Florence (b. 1871)
Friendship.

Conway, Hugh (1818–65)
Falkland at Newbury, 1643.

Conway, Jack (1887–1952)
Clothes Make the Man.

Conway, Jeffery
Hangover.
Marlo Thomas in Seven Parts and Epilogue.
Modern English.
Weight Belt.

Conyus (b. 1942)
Confession to Malcolm.
Day in the Life of . . . , A.
Great Santa Barbara Oil Disaster OR, The.
I Rode with Geronimo.
Six Ten Sixty-Nine.
Upon Leaving the Parole Board Hearing.

Coogler, J. Gordon (1865–1901)
Alas! Carolina!
Alas! for the South.
Byron.
God Correctly Understood.
Her charming steel-horse could not miss.
How strange are dreams! I dreamed the other night.
In Memorial.
More Care for the Neck Than for the Intellect.
Mustacheless Bard, A.
O that the lilies and roses were mine.
Pretty Girl, A.

Cook, C. S.
Limerick: "Famous philosopher, Kant, The."
Limerick: "I was brought up on old Aristotle."

Cook, Christopher
For being unfaithful though ever true.

Cook, Ebenezer (c.1670–c.1732)
Sot-Weed Factor, The.

Cook, Eliza (1818–89)
Building upon the Sand.
I plunged my beak in the marbling cheek.
Idiot-Born, The.
Lines: Suggested by the Song of a Nightingale.
"No!"
Many a lip is gaping for drink.
Mouse and the Cake, The.
My Old Straw Hat.
Old Arm-Chair, The.
On Seeing a Bird-Catcher.
Our Father.
Pathetic Lament, A.
Song for the Workers, A.
Song of the Imprisoned Bird.
Song of the Modern Time.
Song of the Rushlight.
Song of the Ugly Maiden.
Surgeon's Knife, The.
There are hearts—stout hearts,—that own no fear.
'Tis Well to Wake the Theme of Love.
To Charlotte Cushman.
To My Lyre.
To the Late William Jerdan.
Varied theme it utters, A.
Written at the Couch of a Dying Parent.

Cook-Lynn, Elizabeth (b. 1830)
Grandfather at the Indian Health Clinic.
Journey.
My Grandmother's Burial Ground.

Cook, Mrs. M. A. W (1806–74)
In Some Way or Other the Lord Will Provide.

Cook, Russell Sturgis (1811–64)
Just as Thou Art.

Cook, Stanley (b. 1922)
Boiling an Egg.
Christmas Tree.

Cook, William W.
Corn, corn, sweet Indian corn.
Seth Bingham.
Spiritual: 'How did you feel when you come out the wilderness?'
Still-Life with Woodstove.

Cooke, Captain Henry (d. 1672)
Song: "Goe turne away those Cruell Eyes."

Cooke, Edmund Vance (1866–1932)
Are You You?
How Did You Die?
Pass.
Plug.
What Are You Doing?
You Too.

Cooke, Philip Pendleton (1816–50)
Florence Vane.
Orthone.

Cooke, Rose Terry (1827–92)
Arachne.
Bluebeard's Closet.
Che Sara Sara.
Hospital Soliloquy, A.
Schemhammphorasch.
Snow-filled Nest, The.

Coolbrith, Ina (1841–1948)
Lines.
Longing.
My Cloth of Gold.

Ownership.

Cooley, Nicole (b. 1966)
Diane Arbus, New York.
Family History, The.
John Winthrop, 'Reasons to be Considered for...the Intended Plantation in New England,' 1629.
Mary Warren's Sampler.
Mother: Dorcas Good, The.
Publick Fast on Account of the Afflicted: March 31, 1692.
Undine.

Cooley, Peter (b. 1940)
Brother Body.
Secret, The.
Sleep of Beasts, The.
Van Gogh's The Potato Eaters.

Coolidge, Clark (b. 1939)
Album—A Runthru.
Brill.
Crack, The.
Disturbing the Sallies Forth.
Glance in White Space.
Hand Further, The.
I came here. I don't know you here.
Jerome in His Study.
Leaving Rattle Bar.
Morning muezzin in orange and a mosquito.
New hunt / the morning bent, A.
Noon Point.
On Induction of the Hand.
Peru Eye, the Heart of the Lamp.
Saturday Night.
Some Glow on the Sill.
Styro.
Tab, The.
This Garden Being: The Hanging of Books.
What is Thought but Won't Hold Still.
Where is the wonder to not know?

"Coolidge, Susan" (Sarah Chauncey Woolsey) (1835–1905)
Charlotte Brontë.
Edenhall.
Home, A.
My Rights.

Cooper, Afua (b. 1957)
Stepping to da Muse/Sic.

Cooper, Bernard
Pet Names.
Toast to the Cook, A.

Cooper, Dennis (b. 1958)
After School, Street Football, Eighth Grade.
Being Aware.
10 Dead Friends.
David Cassidy Then.
Dreamt Up.
Drugs.
In New York.
In School.
My Past.
No God.
Poem for George Miles.
Teen Idols.

Cooper, Jane (b. 1924)
Atom bellies like a cauliflower, The.
Childhood in Jacksonville, Florida.
Circle, a Square, a Triangle and a Ripple of Water, A.
Dispossessions.
El Sueño de la Razón.
Estrangement.
Hotel de Dream.
My Mother in Three Acts.
My Young Mother.
Poem with Capital Letters, A.
Praise.
Rent.
Waiting.
Wanda's Blues.

Cooper, John Gilbert (1723–69)
Elves and Fairies.

Cooper, Katherine Bradley and **Edith** See also **"Field, Michael"**

Cooper, Roger
To See the Cross at Christmas.

Cooper, Wyn
Leaving the Country.
Pollen.

Coots, J. Fred
For All We Know.
Santa Claus Is Comin' to Town.
You Go to My Head.

Cope, John (b. 1934)
Copula.
Dementia.
Solstice for John.
Sunset.
Winter Sky.

Cope, Wendy (b. 1945)
At 3 A.M.
Bloody Men.
Budgie Finds His Voice.
Depression.
Emily Dickinson.
Engineers' Corner.
Exchange of Letters.
Flowers.
I Worry.
Lavatory Attendant, The.
Limerick: "If Eve hadn't eaten the apple."
Limerick: "That fine English poet, John Donne."
Lonely Hearts.
Mr. Strugnell.
Not only marble, but the plastic toys.
On Finding an Old Photograph.
Policeman's Lot, A.
Reading Scheme.
Rondeau Redoublé.
Serious Concerns.
Sisters.
Strugnell's Bargain.
Strugnell's Rubáiyát.
Triolet.
Two Cures for Love.
Uncertainty of the Poet, The.
Usquebaugh.
Valentine.
Variation on Belloc's "Fatigue."
Waste Land Limericks.

Copeland, Benjamin (1855–1940)
Christ's Life Our Code.
Our Fathers' God.

Copenhaver, Laura S. (1868–1940)
Heralds of Christ.

Copioli, Rosita (b. 1948)
Eurydice.
Heart and the Severed Head, The.
Make Your Body a Heart.
Sea Dreams.

Copland, Robert (fl. 1508–47)
To write of Sol in his exaltation.

Coppard, Alfred Edgar (1878–1957)
Apostate, The.
Epitaph: "Like silver dew are the tears of love."
Mendacity.
Unfortunate Miller, The.

Copping, Coral E.
Limerick: "Dad waited while Mum bought the ham."

Copus, Julia (b. 1969)
Art of Interpretation, The.
Back Seat of My Mother's Car, The.
Clothes, The.
Cricketer's Retirement Day, The.
Making of Eve, The.
Masaccio's *Expulsion from Paradise*.
Miss Havisham's Letter.
Pulling the Ivy.
Sea-Polyp, The.
Widower.

Corben, John
Harlech Castle.
In the eggs.
On the Beach.

Corbet [or Corbett], Richard (1582–1635)
Distracted Puritan, The.
Elegy upon the Death of His Own Father, An.
Epitaph on Dr. Donne, Dean of Paul's, An.

Great Tom.
Little lute, when I am gone.
On Mr. Rice the Manciple of Christ Church in Oxford.
On the Lady Arabella.
Proper New Ballad Entitled [or Intituled] The Fairies' [or Faeryes] Farewell, or God-a-Mercy Will, A.
To His Son [or Sonne], Vincent Corbet[t].
Upon an Unhandsome Gentlewoman, who made Love unto him.
Upon Fairford Windows.

Corbett, Elizabeth T. (fl. c.1880)
Misspelled Tail, A.
Tail of the See, A.
Three Wise Old Women.

Corbett, William (b. 1942)
Cold Lunch.
Vermont Apollinaire.
Wickson Plums.

Corbière, Tristan (Edouard Joachim Corbière) (1845–75)
Blindman's Cries, The.
Epitaph: "Of many things adulterate."
Insomnia.
It's getting dark, little thief of starlight!
Old Roscoff.
You who snore with your sleeping wife so near.

Corcadail, Aithbhreac Inghean (fl. 1460)
O rosary that recalled my tear.

Corcoran, Kelvin (b. 1956)
In the Red Book.
Music of the Altai Mountains.
When Suzy Was.

Cording, Robert
Peregrine Falcon, New York City.

Corey, Stephen (b. 1948)
Complicated Shadows.

Corfield, Joy
Morse Lesson.

Corkine, William
Sweet Cupid, Ripen Her Desire.

Cormac, King of Cashel (fl. 9th cent.)
Instructions of King Cormac.

Corman, Cid (b. 1924)
Call it a louse—I'm.
Container, The.
Deceased.
Desk, The.
I have come far to have found nothing.
La Selva.
Locus, The.
There are things to be said. No doubt.
Tortoise, The.

Cormican, P. J. (1858–1945)
True Son of God, Eternal Light.

Corn, Alfred (b. 1943)
Billie's Blues.
Contemporary Culture and the Letter "K."
Darkening Hotel Room.
Fire: The People.
Kimchee in Worcester (Mass.)
Long-Distance Call to Gregg, Who Lived with AIDS as Long as He Could.
Marriage in the Nineties, A.
Naskeag.
Navidad, St. Nicholas Ave.
Older Men.
To Hermes.
Walrus Tusk from Alaska, A.
Water: City Wildlife and Greenery.

Cornford, Adam (b. 1950)
And it came to pass just as they had foretold.

Cornford, Frances Darwin (1886–1960)
All Souls' Night.
At Night.
Autumn Morning at Cambridge.
Avenue, The.
Child's Dream, A.
Childhood.
Coast, The: Norfolk.
Country Bedroom, The.
For M. S. Singing *Fruhlingsglaube* in 1945.
Glimpse, A.

Guitarist Tunes Up, The.
Hills, The.
In the Backs.
Inscription for a Wayside Spring.
Limerick: "How often and often I wish."
Limerick: "There was a young woman who said."
London Despair.
Near an Old Prison.
New-Born Baby's Song, The.
Parting in Wartime.
Recollection, A.
Scholar, The.
She Warns Him.
Summer Beach.
To a Fat Lady Seen from the Train.
Unbeseechable, The.
Wasted Day, A.
Watch, The.

Cornford, John (1915–36)
Full Moon at Tierz; before the Storming of Huesca.
Huesca.
Letter from Aragon, A.

Cornish, Sam (b. 1935)
Brother of the Streets.
Elvis.
Generations 1.
Generations 2.
His Fingers Seem to Sing.
My Father's House.

Cornish, William (c.1465–c.1523)
Pleasure It Is.

"Cornwall, Barry" (Bryan Waller Proctor) (1787–1874)
Address to the Ocean.
For a Fountain.
Leveller, The.
Sonnet; A Still Place.
To My Child.

Corob, Tricia
Either Way.

Corpi, Lucha (b. 1945)
Dark Romance.

Corpus, Aileen (b. 1950)
Blkfern-jungal.

Corrie, Joe (b. 1894)
Image o' God, The.
Miners' Wives.

Corrothers, James David (1869–1917)
At the Closed Gate of Justice.
Indignation Dinner, An.
Me 'n' Dunbar.
Snapping of the Bow, The.

Corso, Gregory (b. 1930)
Birthplace Revisited.
But I Do Not Need Kindness.
Dialogue—2 Dollmakers.
Difference of Zoos, A.
Dream of a Baseball Star.
Dreamed Realization, A.
From Another Room.
Hello.
I Held a Shelley Manuscript.
Love Poem for Three for Kaye & Me.
Mad Yak, The.
Marriage.
Notes after Blacking Out.
Ode to Coit Tower.
Paranoia in Crete.
Paris.
Poets Hitchhiking on the Highway.
Reflection in a Green Arena.
Rembrandt—Self Portrait.
Sea Chanty.
Seed Journey.
Song: "Oh, dear! Oh, me! Oh, my!"
Spontaneous Requiem For the American Indian.
30th Year Dream.
Transformation and Escape.
Uccello.
Waterchew!
Whole Mess . . . Almost, The.
Zizi's Lament.

Cortázar, Julio (1914–84)
Behavior of Mirrors on Easter Island, The.

Lines of the Hand, The.
Normal Behavior of the Famas.
Travel.
Very Real Story, A.

Cortes, Alfonso
Great Prayer.
Space Song.

Cortes, Fidelito
Dolce Far Niente.
Fish 2.
Palace of Fine Arts in San Francisco, The.
Poem Composed During a Brownout.

Cortez, Jayne (b. 1936)
Adupe.
Bumblebee, You Saw Big Mama.
Consultation.
Feathers.
For the Poets.
Give me the Red on the Black of the Bullet (for Claude Reece Jr.)
Grinding Vibrato.
Heavy Headed Dance, The.
How Long Has Trane Been Gone.
I Am New York City.
I'm a Worker.
I See Chano Pozo.
In the Line of Duty.
In the Morning.
Jazz Fan Looks Back.
Lonely Woman.
Make Ifa.
Nighttrains.
No Simple Explanations.
Orange Chiffon.
Orisha.
Phraseology.
Pray for the Lovers.
Rape.
Rising, The.
Sacred Trees.
Say It.
So Long.
So Many Feathers.
Suppression.
Under the Edge of February.
When I Look at Wifredo Lam's Paintings.

Corwin, Norman (b. 1910)
Man unto His Fellow Man.

Cory, David (1872–1966)
Miss You.

Cory, William Johnson (1823–92)
Desiderato.
Deteriora.
Heraclitus.
Hersilia.
Mimnermus in Church.
Parting.
Poor French Sailor's Scottish Sweetheart, A.
Preparation.

Coslett, Coslett (1834–1910)
Pole Star, The.

Coslow, Sam (1902–83)
Cocktails for Two.
(I'm In Love With) The Honorable Mr. So and So.
It's Love Again.
My Old Flame.
True Blue Lou.
(Up on Top of a Rainbow) Sweepin' the Clouds Away.

Cossins, A. C.
Limerick: "Modest young maiden of Rennes, A."

Costanzo, Gerald (b. 1945)
Everything You Own.
In the Aviary.
Jeane Dixon's America.
Old Neighborhood, The.
Washington Park.

Cothi, Lewis Glyn (fl. 1447–86)
Lament for Siôn y Glyn.
On the Death of His Son.

Cott, Jonathan
Isis (Lady of Petals).

Cottle, Joseph (1770–1853)
Industrial Evils.

Cotton, Charles (1630–87)
Alice is tall and upright as a pine.
But, to leave fooling, I assure ye.
Chatsworth.
Epitaph on M. H., An.
Litany: "From a ruler that's a curse."
Madrigal.
Marg'ret of humbler stature by the head.
Morning Quatrains, The.
On Tobacco.
Resolution in Four Sonnets, of a Poetical Question Put to Me by a Friend, Concerning Four Rural Sisters.
Song: Montrose.
To Coelia.
To My Dear and Most Worthy Friend, Mr. Isaac Walton.

Cotton, John (1584–1652)
In Saram.
Thankful Acknowledgment of God's Providence, A.
To My Reverend Dear Brother, M. Samuel Stone.
We are a crystal zoo.

Cotton, John (fl. c.1676)
Bacon's Epitaph, Made by His Man.
Upon the Death of G. B.

Cotton, Nathaniel (1705–80)
On Lord Cobham's Garden.
To a Child [of] Five Years Old.

Couani, Anna (b. 1948)
Map of the World, The.
Never-Dead, The.
Obvious, The.
What a Man, What a Moon.

Coulehan, Jack
Anatomy Lesson.
Azalea Poem, The.
D-Day, 1994.
Dynamizer and the Oscilloclast, The.
I'm Gonna Slap Those Doctors.
Lovesickness: A Medieval Text.
Man with a Hole in His Face, The.
Rule of Thirds, The.

Coulette, Henri (b. 1927)
At the Telephone Club.
Attic, The.
Black Angel, The.
Correspondence.
Family Goldschmitt, The.
Postscript.

Coultas, Brenda
Capitalist Projections.
Dr. Wasserman.
Human Museum, The.
Lecture #1.
Third Farming Poem.
Weather Report.

Courtney, Margaret
Be Kind.

Cousin, Anne R.
In Emmanuel's Land.

Couto, Nancy Vieira
Living in the La Brea Tar Pits.
Lizzie.
Tea Party.
You Bet Your Life.

Couzyn, Jeni (b. 1942)
Creation.
Heartsong.
Morning.
My Father's Hands.
Mystery, The.
Pain, The.
Spell for Birth.
Spell for Jealousy.
Spell to Cure Barrenness.
Spell to Protect Our Love.
Transformation.
Way Out, The.
World War II.
You Have Shown Me a Strange Image, and We Are Strange Prisoners.

Coverdale, Miles (1488–1569)
Let Go the Whore of Babylon.

Of the Resurrection.
Song of the Virgin Mary, The.
Coviello, Michelangelo (b. 1950)
Self-Portrait.
This hour is made of iron grates where the underground.
Coward, Noël (1899–1973)
A. Stands for Absolutely Anything.
Any Part of Piggy.
Bar on the Piccola Marina, A.
Boy Actor, The.
Contours.
Convalescence.
Don't Let's Be Beastly to the Germans.
He Never Did That to Me.
I'll See You Again.
(I'm So) Weary of It All.
I've Been to a Marvelous Party.
I Wonder What Happened to Him.
Irish Song [Rosie O'Grady].
Let's Do It.
London Pride.
Mad About the Boy.
Mad Dogs and Englishmen.
Mr. Irving Berlin.
Never Again.
Nina.
Poor Little Rich Girl.
Regarding yours, dear Mrs Worthington.
Room with a View, A.
Sail Away.
Stately Homes of England, The.
There Are Bad Times Just around the Corner.
What's Going to Happen to the Tots?
Why Must the Show Go On?
Cowdery, Mae V. (b. 1910)
I Sit and Wait for Beauty.
Cowley, Abraham (1618–67)
Against Fruition.
Against Hope.
Age.
Brutus.
Change, The.
Cheer Up, My Mates.
Christ's Passion.
Chronicle; a Ballad, The.
Country-Mouse, The.
Coy Nature (which remain'd, though aged grown)
Davideis, sels.
Destinie.
Dialogue after Enjoyment.
Epicure, The, sels.
Epitaph of Pyramus and Thisbe.
Grasshopper, The.
Honour.
Hymn: To Light.
In Praise of Hope.
Innocent Ill, The.
London Subverted by the Furies.
Love.
Motto, The.
Muse, The.
Ode: Of Wit.
Of Myself [or My Self].
Of Solitude.
On the Death of Mr. Crashaw.
On the Death of Mr. William Hervey [or Harvey], sels.
Platonic[k] Love.
Powers of Darkness.
Reason.
Resurrection, The.
Spring, The.
Supplication, A.
Swallow, The.
34. Chapter of the Prophet Isaiah, The.
To His Mistress.
To Mr. Hobbes [or Hobs].
To the Royal Society.
Tree of Knowledge, The.
Welcome, The.
Wish, The.
Written in Juice of Lem[m]on.
Cowley, George
Limerick: "There was a young girl from

Uttoxeter / Who one dreary night had a fox at her."
Cowley, Hannah ("Anna Matilda") (1743–1809)
Blank Verse Written on the Sea Shore.
Departed Youth.
Elegiac Ballad, An.
Invocation. To Horror.
Ode to Della Crusca.
To Della Crusca. The Pen.
Cowley, Malcolm (1898–1989)
Ernest.
Long Voyage, The.
Winter Tenement.
Cowper, Maria Frances Cecelia (1726–97)
On Viewing Her Sleeping Infant.
World Not Our Rest, The.
Cowper, William (1731–1800)
Against Slavery.
Arrival of the Mail.
Beau's Reply.
Castaway, The.
Winter Evening, The: A Brown Study.
Comparison, A.
Crazy Kate.
Effeminate Englishmen.
Epitaph on a Hare.
Frosty Morning, A.
Future Peace and Glory of the Church, The.
Great princes have great playthings. Some have played.
Just when our drawing-rooms begin to blaze.
Landscape Described, A.
Light Shining out of Darkness.
Lines Written During a Period of Insanity.
Lines Written upon a Window-Shutter at Weston.
Love Constraining to Obedience.
Man on the dubious waves of error toss'd.
Negro's Complaint, The.
Night was winter in his roughest mood, The.
Olney Hymns, sels.
On a Similar Occasion for the Year 1790.
On a Similar Occasion for the Year 1792.
On a Spaniel Called Beau Killing a Young Bird.
On the Lamented Death of Mrs. Throckmorton's Bullfinch.
On the Loss of the *Royal George*.
On the Receipt of My Mother's Picture out of Norfolk [the Gift of My Cousin Ann Bodham].
Poplar Field, The.
Reading the Newspaper.
Shrubbery, The.
Simple Faith.
Stanzas Subjoined to the Yearly Bill of Mortality of the Parish of All Saints, Northampton; for the Year 1787.
Stricken Deer, The.
Sweet Meat Has Sour Sauce.
Task, The.
Tiroeinium, sels.
To a Young Lady.
To George Romney, Esq.
To Mary.
To Mary Unwin.
To Mr. Newton [on His Return from Ramsgate].
To William Hayley, Esq.: In Reply to His Solicitation to Write with Him in a Literary Work.
To William Wilberforce, Esq.
Verses Supposed to Be Written by Alexander Selkirk during His Solitary Abode on the Island of Juan Fernandez.
Winter Walk at Noon, The.
Yardley Oak.
Cox, A. P.
Limerick: "These days, the ubiquitous db."
Cox, Mark
Barbells of the Gods, The.
Cox, Nancy
Singing Alone.
Cox, Palmer (1840–1924)
Brownies' Celebration, The.
Lazy Pussy, The.

Mouse's Lullaby, The.
Cox, Samuel K. (1823–1909)
Lord, Thou Hast Promised.
Coxe, Arthur Cleveland (1818–96)
Father, Who Mak'st Thy Suff'ring Sons.
Saviour, Sprinkle Many Nations.
Coxon, William W.
Flash Colonial Barman, The.
Crabbe, George (1754–1832)
Burough, The, sels.
Condemned Man, The.
Frenzy.
Lady of the Manor, The.
Late Wisdom.
Letter 1.
Lover's Journey, The, sels.
Marriage Ring, The.
Meeting.
My Birthday.
Parish Register, The, sels.
Peter Grimes.
Priest attending, found he spoke at times, The.
Procrastination.
Resurrection.
Tales of the Hall, sels.
Village, The, sels.
Cradock, Thomas (1718–70)
What Glorious Vision.
Craig, Alexander (b. 1923)
To His Pandora, from England.
Craig, John (1512–1600)
O Hear My Prayer, Lord.
O Lord, That Art My God and King.
Craig, Maurice James (b. 1919)
Ballad to a Traditional Refrain.
Craighead, Lorena M. (b. 1968)
Dancin' Our Lives Away.
Whole Truth So Help Me God—Also Known as the Gettin' Rid of Nigguz Business.
Wo/man's Voice Must Be Heard, A.
Craik, Dinah Maria Mulock (1826–87)
Douglas, Douglas, Tender and True.
Friendship.
Cranch, Christopher Pearse (1818–92)
Autumn Rain, The.
Bear and the Squirrels, The.
Bird and the Bell, The.
Bird Language.
Cataract Isle, The.
Cornucopia.
Correspondences.
December.
Evening Primrose, The.
Hours, The.
In the Palais Royal Garden.
Locomotive, The.
Music.
My Old Palette.
Old Cat's Confessions, An.
Photograph, The.
Pines and the Sea, The.
Printing-Press, The.
Spirit of the Age, The.
Crane, Frank
Because You Care.
Crane, Hart (1899–1932)
Above the fresh ruffles of the surf.
Air Plant, The.
And yet this great wink of eternity.
Garden Abstract.
At Melville's Tomb.
Atlantis.
Ave Maria.
Black Tambourine.
Bridge, The.
Broken Tower, The.
C33.
Cape Hatteras.
Capped arbiter of beauty in this street.
Carrier Letter.
Chaplinesque.
Circumstance, The.
Cutty Sark.
Dance, The.
Episode of Hands.

For the Marriage of Faustus and Helen.
Forgetfulness.
Harbor Dawn, The.
Hurricane, The.
Imperator Victus.
In Shadow.
Infinite consanguinity it bears.
Legend.
Meticulous, past midnight in clear rime.
Modern Craft.
Name for All, A.
National Winter Garden.
North Labrador.
O Carib Isle!
Passage.
Power.
Praise for an Urn.
Recitative.
Repose of Rivers.
River, The.
Royal Palm.
Stark Major.
Sunday Morning Apples.
My Grandmother's Love Letters.
Three Songs.
To Brooklyn Bridge.
To Emily Dickinson.
To Shakespeare.
To the Cloud Juggler.
Tunnel, The.
Van Winkle.
Voyages.
Where icy and bright dungeons lift.
Whose counted smile of hours and days,
    suppose.
Wine Menagerie, The.

Crane, Nathalia (b. 1913)
Vestal, The.

Crane, Stephen (1871–1900)
Ah, God, the way your little finger moved.
Behold the Grave of a Wicked Man.
Black Riders, The.
Blades of Grass, The.
Book of Wisdom, The.
Candid Man, The.
Do Not Weep Maiden, for War Is Kind.
Each small gleam was a voice.
Fast rode the knight.
God in Wrath, A.
God lay dead in Heaven.
Heart, The.
I explain the silvered passing of a ship at night.
I Saw a Man Pursuing the Horizon.
I Stood upon a High Place.
I Walked in a Desert.
If I should cast off this tattered coat.
"It Was Wrong to Do This" Said the Angel.
Learned Man [Came to Me Once], A.
Little Birds of the Night.
Little Ink More Or Less!, A.
Livid lightnings flashed in the clouds, The.
Man Adrift on a Slim Spar, A.
Man feared that he might find an assassin, a.
Man Said to the Universe, A.
Many red devils ran from my heart.
Many Workmen.
Naked woman and a dead dwarf, A.
Newspaper, A.
Scaped.
Should the wide world roll away.
Slant of Sun [on Dull Brown Walls], A.
Tell me not in joyous numbers.
There Is a Grey Thing That Lives in the Tree-
    Tops.
There Was a Crimson Clash of War.
There Was a Man with a Tongue of Wood.
There Was Set before Me a Mighty Hill.
Think As I Think.
Unwind my riddle.
Wayfarer, The.
Youth in Apparel That Glittered, A.

Crapsey, Adelaide (1878–1914)
Amaze.
Anguish.
Arbutus.
Fragment.
Guarded Wound, The.

Lonely Death, The.
Moon-Shadows.
Niagara.
Night Winds.
November Night.
On Seeing Weather-Beaten Trees.
Release.
Snow.
Song: "I make my shroud but no one knows."
Sun-Dial, The.
Susanna and the Elders.
To a Hermit Thrush.
Trapped.
Triad.
Warning, The.
Witch, The.

Crase, Douglas (b. 1944)
Astropastoral.
Elegy for New York, The.
If I could raise rivers, I'd raise them.
There Is No Real Peace in the World.

Crashaw, Richard (1613?–1649)
And He Answered Them Nothing.
Bubble, The.
But Men loved Darkness[e] Rather Than [or
    Then] Light.
C[h]aritas Nimia; or, The Dear[e] Bargain.
Christ Crucified.
Christ's Victory.
Come See the Place Where the Lord Lay.
Epitaph Upon Husband and Wife Who Died
    and Were Buried Together, An.
Epithalamium: "Come, virgin tapers of pure
    wax."
Flaming Heart, The.
Howres for the Hours of Matines, The.
Hymn to the Name and Hono[u]r of the
    Admirable Saint[e] Teresa, A.
I Am the Door [or Doore].
In the Holy Nativity of Our Lord God.
Live in these conquering leaves; live all the
    same.
Love's Horoscope.
Love, thou art absolute sole lord.
Luke 10.
Luke 11: Blessed Be the Paps Which Thou
    Hast Sucked.
Music[k]'s Duel[l].
Neither Durst Any Man From That Day Ask
    Him Any More Questions.
O Heart! the equal poise of love's both parts.
O sweet incendiary! shew here thy art.
On Marriage.
On Mr. G. Herberts Booke, The Temple.
On the Baptized Ethiopian.
On the Blessed Virgins Bashfulnesse.
On the Miracle of Loaves.
On the Miracle of Multiplied [or Multiplyed]
    Loaves.
On the Water of Our Lord's Baptism[e].
On the Wounds of Our Crucified Lord.
Saint Mary Magdalene or The Weeper.
Samson to His Delilah.
Shepherds' Hymn, The.
Song: "Lord, when the sense of Thy sweet
    grace."
Thou art love's victim; and must die.
To Our Blessed Lord upon the Choice of His
    Sepulchre.
To Our Lord, upon the Water Made Wine.
To the Infant Martyrs.
To the Noblest and Best of Ladies, the
    Countess of Denbigh.
Two Went Up into the Temple To Pray.
Upon Bishop Andrewes's [or Andrewes His]
    Picture before His Sermons.
Upon Lazarus His Teares.
Upon the Asse That Bore Our Saviour.
Upon the Body of Our Blessed Lord, Naked
    and Bloody.
Upon the Book and Picture of the Seraphical
    Saint Teresa.
Upon the Holy Sepulchre.
Upon the Infant Martyrs.
Weeper, The.
Wishes. To His (Supposed) Mistress[e].

Crates (fl. 450 B.C.)
Time's fingers bend us slowly.

Craveirinha, José (b. 1922)
Ode to a Lost Cargo in a Ship Called Save.
Poem of the Future Citizen.
Seed Is in Me, The.
Tasty 'Tanjarines' of Inhambane, The.
Three Dimensions.

Crawford, Isabella Valancy (1850–87)
Battle, A.
Camp of Souls, The.
Dark Stag, The.
Said the Canoe.

Crawford, Robert (b. 1959)
Downtown Sunday.
My Iambic Pentameter Lines.

Crawford, Roger
Love Song of Tommo Frogley.

Crawford, Vesta Pierce (1899–1983)
Pioneer Woman.

Crawley III, William T. (b. 1966)
Bud.
Poetry for the Goddess.

Creamer, Henry (1879–1930)
After You've Gone.
If I Could Be with You.
Way Down Yonder in New Orleans.

Creedon, Carolyn (b. 1969)
Litany.

Creeley, Robert (b. 1926)
Act of Love, The.
After Lorca.
Again.
Age.
Air: "The Love of a Woman."
All That Is Lovely in Men.
America.
And.
Anger.
Awakening, The.
Ballad of the Despairing Husband.
Be of Good Cheer.
Body.
Bresson's Movies.
Buffalo Evening.
City, The.
Company, The.
Counterpoint, A.
Damon & Pythias.
Death of Venus, The.
Door, The.
Echo.
Edge, The.
En Famille.
Faces, The.
Fancy.
Fathers.
Figures, The.
Fire, The.
Flower, The.
For Friendship.
For Love.
For My Mother: Genevieve Jules Creeley.
For No Clear Reason.
For W. C. W.
Form of Women, A.
Gift of Great Value, A.
Gift, The.
Here.
Heroes.
Hill, The.
House, The.
I Keep to Myself Such Measures.
I Know a Man.
If You.
Immoral Proposition, The.
In a Boat Shed.
Innocence, The.
Invitation, The.
Invoice, The.
Just Friends.
Kind of Act Of, The.
Kore.
Language, The.
Man, The.
Marriage, A.
Mazatlan: Sea.
Memory Gardens.

Memory, The.
Messengers, The.
Moon, The.
Naughty Boy.
Oh No.
Parade.
People, The.
Place.
Place, The.
Pool, The.
Prayer to Hermes.
Quick-Step.
Rain, The.
Rescue, The.
River Wandering Down.
Road, The.
Self-Portrait.
She Went to Stay.
Somebody Died.
Something for Easter.
Somewhere.
Song: "Those rivers run from that land."
Stairway to Heaven.
Statue, The.
Talking.
This House.
Three Ladies, The.
Time.
Token, A.
Turn, The.
Wait for Me.
Waiting.
Warning, The.
Way, The.
Whip, The.
Wicker Basket, A.
Wife, The.
Window, The.
Won't It Be Fine?
World, The.

Cresson, Abigail
Cloak of Laughter.

Crevel, René (1900–35)
Nighttime.

Crew, Louie (b. 1936)
Gay Psalm from Fort Valley, A.

Crinagoras (b. c.70 B.C.)
Back from the west, back from the war,
Marcellus.
Dedication of a Torch.
Eartha my mother's name, now earth.
Epitaph on an Infant.
Forehead without scalp, dry shell without yolk
of eye.
Foul sod covers a bad one here.
Here are grapes ready to turn to wine.
How long in these empty thermals near the
cold.
Linguist parrot flicked his flowery wings, The.
Lucky shepherd, if only on the hill.
On the Death of Cleopatra-Selene.
Roses used to bloom in spring.
Sailing to Italy—fitting out / commissioning—
to see the friends.
This longed-for morning here is our sacrifice /
to Zeus the finisher, and Artemis goddess of
childbirth.
This silver thing I send you for your birthday.
This wingtip feather from a hook-beaked eagle.
Though of white marble and dressed straight.
Though you are sedentary always, though.
Turn on your left side, back to your right
again.
Unhappy men, why do we travel so.
You toss now to the left; you toss now to the
right.

Crist, Richard
Dusty pickup, The.
She has gone.

Cristall, Anne Batten (b. c.1798)
Before Twilight. Eyezion.
Blind Man, The.
Elegy on a Young Lady.
Elegy: "Wander, my troubled soul, sigh mid
the night thy pain."
Enthusiast, The. Arla.

Evening, Gertrude.
Holbain.
Morning, Rosamonde.
Noon. Lysander.
Ode, An.
Ode on Truth: Addressed to George Dyer.
Snow-Fiend, The.
Song: "Balmy comforts that are fled, The."
Song: "Both gloomy and dark was the
shadowy night."
Song: "Come, let us dance and sing."
Song: "Eve descends with radiant streaks,
The."
Song of Arla, Written During Her Enthusiasm,
A.
Song on Leaving the Country Early in the
Spring.
Song: "Through springtime walks, with flowers
perfumed."
Song: "Tossed midst life's terrific storms."
Song: "Wandering in the still of eve."
Thelmon and Carmel: An Irregular Poem.
To a Lady on the Rise of Morn.
Triumph of Superstition, The. Raphael and
Ianthe.
Verses Written in the Spring.
Written in Devonshire, Near the Dart.
Written When the Mind Was Oppressed.

Crites, Lucile (b. 1885)
Folks and Me.

Croft, Julian
D-Zug.
Graffiti.
Greenhalgh's Pub.

Croft, Roy (1919–77)
Love.

Croly, George (1780?–1860)
Aestuary, An.
Domestic Love.
Supplication, A.

Crompton, Hugh (fl. 1657)
Epigram LXVII: Time, the Interpreter.
Epigram VII: Winifred.

Cromwell, Ann See Williams, Ann

Cromwell, Baptina Palavicino (c.1595–1618)
Eternal power from whose allseeing eye.

Cromwell, Elizabeth (fl. late 1630s?)
Sisters Newyearsgift from Elizabeth to Mary a
Happie Mother of Good Children, The.

Cronin, Anthony (b. 1925)
Apology.
Baudelaire in Brussels.
Elegy for the Nightbound.
For a Father.
Lines for a Painter.
Man Who Went Absent from the Native
Literature, The.
Middle Years, The.
On the bog road the blackthorn flowers, the
turf-stacks.
Responsibilities.
Trembling with engines, gulping oil, the river.

Cronin, Jeremy (b. 1949)
Group Photo from Pretoria Local on the
Occasion of a Fourth Anniversary (Never
Taken)
Lullaby: "But who killed Johannes, mama?"
Motho Ke Motho Ka Batho Babang (A Person
Is a Person Because of Other People)
Naval Base (Part III), The.
River That Flows through Our Land, The.
To Learn How to Speak.

Cronwright, Samuel Cron (1863–1936)
Song of the Wagon-whip, A.

Crosby, Ernest (1856–1907)
Hail to the hero!
I am a great inventor, did you but know it.
Military Creed, The.

**Crosby, Fanny (Frances Jane Crosby) (1820–
1915)**
Blessed Assurance.
I Am Thine, O Lord.
Jesus, Keep Me Near the Cross.
Let Me Die on the Prairie.
Mandan Chief, The.

On Hearing a Description of a Prairie.
Thoughts in Midnight Hours.
To God be the glory, great things he hath done!
We Are Going.

Crosby, Harry (1898–1929)
Firebrand.
Telephone Directory.
Photoheliograph (For Lady A.)
Vision.

Crosby, Ranice Henderson (b. 1952)
Waitresses.

Crosland, T. W. H. (1865–1924)
Slain.
White Feather Legion, The.

Cross, Allen Eastman (1864–1942)
Gray Hills Taught Me Patience, The.
Though Fatherland Be Vast.
Young and Radiant, He Is Standing.

Cross, Elsa (b. 1946)
Banyan.
Kali.
Sri Nityananda Mandir (The Temple of
Nityananda)
Uma Worshipping Shiva (On a Kangra
miniature)
Visions.

Cross, Frank A.
Accident, An.
Fifty Gunner, The.
Rice Will Grow Again.
When Chicken Man Came Home to Roost.

Cross, Jr., Frank A.
Gliding Baskets.

Cross, Mary Ann [or Marian] Evans Lewes See
"Eliot, George"

Cross, Zora (b. 1890)
Love Sonnets.

Crossley-Holland, Kevin (b. 1941)
They're marked men. Their park is like an
open prison.

Croswell, William (1804–51)
Lord! Lead the Way the Saviour Went.

Crouch, Stanley (b. 1945)
Blackie Thinks of His Brothers.
Chops Are Flyin.
Like a Blessing.
Revelation, The.
Riding Across John Lee's Finger.
Up on the Spoon.

Crow, Christine
City Park.

Crow, Steve (b. 1949)
El Alamein.
Louisiana.
Revival.
They say a man dies.
Water Song.

Crowe, William (1745–1829)
In evil hour, and with unhallow'd voice.
Up to thy summit, Lewesdon, to the brow.

Crowell, Albert
Joy of Incompleteness, The.

Crowell, Grace Noll (b. 1877)
Common Tasks, The.
Courage to Live.
Definition.
Eternal Values.
I Have Found Such Joy.
I Think That God is Proud.
Prayer for a Day's Walk.

Crowley, Aleister (1875–1947)
Ballad of Passive Paederasty, A.
Dedicace.
Go into the Highways and Hedges, and
Compel Them to Come In.
Rondels.

Crowley, Robert
Of unsaciable purchasers.

Crowne, John (1640?–1703?)
Song: "Kind lovers, love on."

Croxall, Samuel (1690?–1752)
Sylvia.

Crozier, Andrew (b. 1943)
Driftwood and Seacoal.

Heifer, The.
Loopy Dupes.

Crozier, Lorna (b. 1948)
Last Testaments.
Poem for Sigmund.
So This Is Love.

Crucefix, Martyn
There is a whole world involved in me.

Cruceius, Annibal
Fair Ursly, in a merry mood.

Cruickshank, Helen B.
Comfort in Puirtith.
Ponnage Pool, The.
Shy Geordie.

Crummy, Biddy
Poem to Be Said on Hearing the Birds Sing, A.

Crunk, T.
Leaving.
Reunion.
Visiting the Site of One of the First Churches
My Grandfather Pastored.

"Crusca, Della" *See* **Merry, Robert**

Cruz e Sousa, João da (1861–98)
Acrobat of Pain.
Antiphony.
Good Friday.
Sacred Hatred.

Cruz Varela, Maria Elena (b. 1953)
Invocation.
Kaleidoscope.
Love Song for Difficult Times.

Crystal, Catherine Nomura
Embroidery.

Csokor, Franz Theodor
Return Home 1918, The.

Csoori, Sandor (b. 1930)
My Masters.
Postponed Nightmare.
Somebody Consoles Me with a Poem.
Thin, Black Band, A.
We Were Good, Good and Obedient.

Cuadra, Angel (b. 1931)
Brief Letter to Donald Walsh (in memoriam)
In Brief.

Cuadra, Pablo Antonio
Birth of the Sun, The.
Evening Star, The.
Horses in the Lake.
Manuscript in a Bottle.

Cucchi, Maurizio (b. 1945)
Every season has its dead.
Hibernation.
I wouldn't know what it's like to be a pawn.
It's over now, the time for observation, for.
Like the Chinese, I too am going to.
You said: it's hot tonight.

Cuddihy, Michael
Solitude.
This Body.

Cudmore, C. D.
Limerick: "'Active balls?' said an old man of
Stoneham."

Cudmore, D. H.
Limerick: "Ascetic art student named Josh,
An."
Limerick: "Ballistical student named Raffity,
A."
Limerick: "English professor named Brooks,
An."
Limerick: "There was a young lady at court."

Cuevish, Lucario
Before They Made Things Be Alive They
Spoke.

Cullen, Countee (1903–46)
Atlantic City Waiter.
Black Majesty.
Brown Girl Dead, A.
Christus Natus Est.
For a Lady I Know.
For a Mouthy Woman.
For a Poet.
For a Virgin Lady.
For Daughters of Magdalen.
For Hazel Hall, American Poet.

For My Grandmother.
For One Who Gayly Sowed His Oats.
For Paul Laurence Dunbar.
From Life to Love.
From the Dark Tower.
Heritage.
Incident.
Leaves.
Litany of the Dark People, The.
Night Rain.
Only the Polished Skeleton.
Saturday's Child.
Shroud of Color, The.
Simon the Cyrenian Speaks.
Song in Spite of Myself.
Tableau.
Timid Lover.
To Certain Critics.
Uncle Jim.
Unknown Color, The.
Wind Bloweth Where It Listeth, The.
Yet Do I Marvel.

Cullinan, Patrick (b. 1932)
M. François le Vaillant Recalls His Travels to
the Interior Parts of Africa.

**Cumberland, Margaret Russell Clifford,
Countess of (1560–1616)**
Epitaph for Richard Cavendish, Engraved on
his Monument in Hornsey Church.

Cumbie, Richard
New Jersey Turnpike.

Cumbo, Kattie M. (b. 1938)
Black Sister.
Ceremony.
Domestics.
I'm a Dreamer.
Morning after . . . Love, The.
Nocturnal Sounds.

Cumming, Patricia
Midsummer.

Cummings, E. E. (1894–1962)
All ignorance toboggans into know.
All in green went my love riding.
All nearness pauses,while a star can grow.
All which isn't singing is mere talking.
Always before your voice my soul.
Anyone lived in a pretty how town.
As freedom is a breakfastfood.
Being to timelessness as it's to time.
Bigness of cannon, The.
Buy me an ounce and i'll sell you a pound.
Cambridge ladies who live in furnished souls,
The.
Come,gaze with me upon this dome.
Darling!because my blood can sing.
First of all my dreams, The.
For prodigal read generous.
Four III.
God pity me whom (god distinctly has)
Goodby Betty,don't remember me.
Greedy the people, The.
Hist   whist / little ghostthings.
I carry your heart with me(i carry it in)
I like my body when it is with your.
I sing of Olaf glad and big.
I thank You God for most this amazing.
I was sitting in mcsoreley's.   outside it was
New York and beauti– / fully snowing.
I will be / M o ving in the Street of her.
If everything happens that can't be done.
If i have made, my lady.
If i should sleep with a lady called death.
If there are any heavens my mother will (all by
herself) have.
(Im)c-a-t(mo)
Impression.
IN) all those who got.
In heavenly realms of hellas dwelt.
In Just.
It is at moments after I have dreamed.
It may not always be so; and i say.
It's over a(see just)
Item.
L(a.
Ladies and gentlemen this little girl.
Little joe gould has lost his teeth and doesn't

know where.
Little tree / little silent Christmas tree.
Love is a place.
Maggie and Milly and Molly and May.
Man who had fallen among thieves, A.
May i feel said he.
May my heart always be open to little.
Me up at does.
Mr U.
My father moved through dooms of love.
My love / thy hair is one kingdom.
My specialty is living said.
My sweet old etcetera.
Next to of course god america i.
Nine birds(rising / through a gold
moment)climb.
No man,if men are gods; but if gods must.
No thanks, No. 70.
No time ago / or else a life.
Nobody loses all the time.
Noster, The.
Notice the convulsed orange inch of moon.
Now comes the good rain farmers pray
for(and)
Now is a ship / which captain am.
O by the by / has anybody seen.
O pr / gress verily thou art m.
O Sweet Spontaneous.
Out of midsummer's blazing most not night.
Picasso / you give us Things.
Pity this busy monster,manunkind.
Plato told.
Poem, or Beauty Hurts Mr. Vinal.
Politician, A.
Ponder, darling, these busted statues.
Portrait.
Purer than purest pure.
Q:dwo / we know of anything which can.
R-P-O-P-H-E-S-S-A-G-R.
Raise the shade.
Right here the other night something.
Salesman, A.
Season 'tis,my lovely lambs, The.
She being Brand.
Silence / .is / a / looking.
Since feeling is first.
Slightly before the middle of Congressman
Pudd.
Somewhere i have never travelled, gladly
beyond.
Space being(don't forget to remember)Curved.
Spring is like a perhaps hand.
Spring omnipotent goddess thou dost.
Sunset.
Than(by yon sunset's wintry glow)
Thy fingers make early flowers of.
Twentyseven bums give a prostitute the once.
Up into the silence the green.
Way to hump a cow is not, The.
What a proud dreamhorse
pulling(smoothloomingly)through.
What if a much of a which of a wind.
When any mortal(even the most odd)
When god lets my body be.
When my sensational moments are no more.
When serpents bargain for the right to squirm.
Wherelings whenlings / (daughters of if but
offspring of hopefear)
Who's most afraid of death?thou.
Why did you go.
Wild (at our first) beasts uttered human words.
Wind has blown the rain away and blown, A.
YgUDuh / ydoan / yunnuhstan.
You shall above all things be glad and young.

Cummins, Evelyn Atwater (b. 1891)
I Know Not Where the Road Will Lead.

Cumpian, Carlos (b. 1953)
Armadillo Charm.
Estrellitas.
No Deposit Returns.

Cuney, Waring (1906–76)
Conception.
Death Bed, The.
My Lord, What a Morning.
No Images.

Cunningham, Allan (1784–1842)
Hame, Hame, Hame.

Sea-Song, A.
Thistle's Grown aboon the Rose, The.
Cunningham, Ed
  Limerick: "As the natives got ready to serve."
Cunningham, James Vincent (1911–85)
  Aged Lover Discourses in the Flat Style, The.
  Agnosco Veteris Vestigia Flammae.
  All in Due Time.
  And Now You're Ready Who While She Was Here.
  Bride loved old words, and found her pleasure marred.
  Choice.
  Coffee.
  Envoi: "Hear me, whom I betrayed."
  Epigram: "After some years Bohemian came to this."
  Epigram: "And what is love? Misunderstanding, pain."
  Epigram: "Dark thoughts are my companions. I have wined."
  Epigram: "Dear, if unsocial privacies obsess me."
  Epigram: "Good Fortune, when I hailed her recently."
  Epigram: "Here lies my wife. Eternal peace."
  Epigram: "Here lies New Critic who would fox us."
  Epigram: "Homer was poor. His scholars live at ease."
  Epigram: "How we desire desire! Joy of surcease."
  Epigram: "I had gone broke, and got set to come back."
  Epigram: "I who by day am function of the light."
  Epigram: "In whose will is our peace? Thou happiness."
  Epigram: "Life flows to death as rivers to the sea."
  Epigram: "This is my curse, Pompous, I pray."
  Epigram: "Time heals not: it extends a sorrow's scope."
  Epigram: "Within this mindless vault."
  Epigram: "You ask me how Contempt who claims to sleep."
  Epigram: "You wonder why Drab sells her love for gold?"
  Epitaph for Someone or Other.
  Epitaph: "When I shall be without regret."
  For My Contemporaries.
  Friend, on This Scaffold Thomas More Lies Dead.
  History of Ideas.
  I married in my youth a wife.
  In Innocence.
  Interview with Doctor Drink.
  Lip.
  Meditation on Statistical Method.
  Metaphysical Amorist, The.
  Montana Pastoral.
  Moral Poem, A.
  Neaera when I'm there is adamant.
  On a cold night I came through the cold rain.
  Pope from penance purgatorial, The.
  Rome.
  This *Humanist* Whom No Beliefs Constrained.
  To a Friend, on Her Examination for the Doctorate in English.
  To My Wife.
  To What Strangers, What Welcome.
Cunningham, John (1729–73)
  Epigram: "Member of the modern great, A."
  Holiday Gown.
  Miller, The.
  Morning.
  On a Certain Alderman.
Cunningham, Nora B. (*fl.* late 19th–early 20th cent.)
  Giving.
Cunninghame-Graham, Robert *See* **Graham, Robert**
Curbelo, Silvia (b. 1955)
  Among Strangers.
  Bedtime Stories.
  Between Language and Desire.

Dreaming Horse.
Drinking Song.
If You Need a Reason.
Lake Has Swallowed the Whole Sky, The.
Last Call.
Listening to a White Man Play the Blues.
Photograph of My Parents.
Tonight I Can Almost Hear the Singing.
Tourism in the Late 20th Century.
Tourist Weather.
Curnow, Allen (b. 1911)
  Canst Thou Draw Out Leviathan with an Hook.
  Continuum.
  Country School.
  House and Land.
  Landfall in Unknown Seas.
  Oldest of us burst into tears and cried, The.
  On the Road to Erewhon.
  Pacific 1945–1995.
  Polynesia.
  Skeleton of the Great Moa in the Canterbury Museum, Christchurch, The.
  Small Room with Large Windows, A.
  Spectacular Blossom.
  This Beach Can Be Dangerous.
  Trees, Effigies, Moving Objects.
  Urban Guerrilla, An.
  Wild Iron.
  You Get What You Pay For.
  You Will Know When You Get There.
Currey, Ralph Nixon (b. 1907)
  Burial Flags.
  Jersey Cattle.
  Unseen Fire.
Currie, Mary Montgomerie Currie, Baroness *See* **"Fane, Violet"**
Curry, Neil (b. 1937)
  Anne Hathaway Composes Her 18th Sonnet.
  Dandelion.
  Galapagos.
  Gardens.
  In a Calendar of Saints.
  Mute Swans.
  Poppy Heads.
  St Kilda.
  Swallows and Tortoises.
Curtis, Lillian E. (*fl.* 1870)
  Only One Eye.
  Potato, The.
  Two Bears, The.
Curtis, Monica
  Limerick: "There were once two young people of taste."
Curtis, Simon (b. 1943)
  Satie, at the End of Term.
Curtis, Tony (b. 1946)
  Brigitte Bardot in Grangetown.
  Gambit.
  Games with My Daughter.
  Land Army Photographs.
  Neighbour's Pear Tree.
  Pembrokeshire Buzzards.
  Portrait of the Painter Hans Theo Richter and His Wife Gisela in Dresden, 1933.
  Preparations.
  Queen's Tears.
  Soup.
  Spirit of the Place, The.
  To My Father.
  We Can Say That.
Curzon, David (b. 1941)
  Instructions to a Seed.
  Proverbs 6:6.
  Tour of Ein Kerem, A.
Cushing, James (*fl.* 20th cent.)
  Autumn Leaves.
  Every Time We Say Goodbye.
  Lover Man.
Cushing, William O. (1823–1902)
  We Are Watching, We Are Waiting.
Cushman, Stephen (b. 1956)
  Make the Bed.
Cussons, Sheila
  Barn-yard, The.

Yellow Gramophone.
Cussrooee, Biddy
  My Grief on the Sea.
Cust, Henry (1861–1917)
  Non Nobis.
Cuthand, Beth
  Dancing with Rex.
  She Ties Her Bandanna.
Cutler, Julian S.
  Wonderful.
Cutler, William (1812–89)
  One Talent, The.
Cutting, Sewall Sylvester (1813–82)
  God of the World, Thy Glories Shine.
  Gracious Saviour, We Adore Thee.
Cutts, John, Baron Cutts (1661–1707)
  To a Lady, Who Desired Me Not To Be in Love with Her.
Cutts, Simon
  On parquet.
Cynddelw Brydydd Mawr (*fl.* 1155–1200)
  In Praise of Owain Gwynedd.
  Petition for Reconciliation.
  Poem on His Death-Bed.
Cynewulf (*fl.* late 7th cent.)
  Christ 2, *sels.*
  Dream of the Rood, A, *sels.*
  Elene, *sels.*
  Fates of the Apostles, *sels.*
  Juliana, *sels.*
  Riddles, (Exeter Book), *sels.*
Cyril, Malkia Amala (b. 1974)
  Children's Games.
  Jump Black Honey Jump Black.
  Just Because I Am.
  What Has Yet to Be Sung.
Cyrillus
  Two-line epigram is perfect, A. Step.
Czerkawska, Catherine Lucy (b. 1950)
  Thread.

D

"D., H." *See* **Doolittle, Hilda**
da Bologna, Bernardo
  Unto that lowly lovely maid, I wis.
da Pavia, Saladino (*fl.* 1250)
  Fair sir, this love of ours.
Da Ponte, Lorenzo (1749–1837)
  "Giovinette, Che Fate All'Amore."
  To an Artful Theatre Manager.
da Signa, Dello (*fl.* 1250)
  Prohibiting all hope.
da Silva, Adelina (b. 1958)
  Along the Banks of the Charles.
  Return to the Homeland.
da Todi, Jacopone (1228–1306)
  Praise of Diseases.
da Todi, Masolino (*fl.* 1250)
  Man should hold in very dear esteem, A.
Dabney, Ford
  That's Why They Call Me 'Shine.'
Dacey, Philip (b. 1939)
  Drummer, The.
  Jack, Afterwards.
  Musica.
  Musician, The.
  Thumb.
Dach, Simon (1605–59)
  Bonds of Friendship, The.
  Lamentation during His Most Painful Illness.
  On the Entrance of the Castle Bridge.
  To Be Read above the Castle-Gate, When His Princely Highness Rode in to His Marriage Bed.
Dacre, Charlotte ("Rosa Matilda") (1782–c.1841)
  Female Philosopher, The.
  Kiss, The.
  Mistress to the Spirit of Her Lover, The.
  Poor Negro Sadi, The.
  Power of Love, The.
  Sappho; or, The Resolve.

Similie.
Unfaithful Lover, The.
We Can Love But Once.

Dadié, Bernard (b. 1916)
Dry Your Tears, Africa!
Hands.
I Give You Thanks My God.
I Thank You, Lord.
In Memoriam.
Ode to Africa.
World to Come, A.
Wreath for Africa, A.

Dafydd Ab Edmwnd (fl. 1450–80)
Christmas Revel, A.
Cywdd to Morvydd, The.
Duw gwyddiad mai da y gweddai.
Fox, The.
Girl's Hair, A.
Girls of Llanbadarn, The.
In Morfudd's Arms.
May.
Mirror, The.
Penis, The.
Rattle Bag, The.
Ruin, The.
Seagull, The.
Wind, The.
Woodland Mass, The.

Dafydd [or David] Benfras (d. 1257)
From Exile.

Dafydd Nanmor (fl. 1450–80)
Ode to Rhys ap Maredudd of Tywyn.

Daglarca, Fazil Hüsnü (b. 1914)
Fire.
Hollow Echo.
Sultan of the Animals Is the Night, The.
Thought.
Unity.

D'Aguiar, Frederick (b. 1960)
Airy Hall Icongraphy.
Dread.
Dreadtalk.
English Sampler, An.
Langston.
Mama Dot.
Mama Dot Warns Against an Easter Rising.
Now the Two Are One.
Obeah Mama Dot.
Sound Bite.

Dahbur, Ahmad (b. 1946)
Death of the Shoemaker, The.
In Memory of Izziddin al-Qalaq.

Dahlberg, Edward (1900–77)
February Ground.
Walt Whitman.

Daibai (fl. 8th cent.)
My seventy years—a withered.
You cannot tell.

Daichi (1290–1366)
Thoughts arise endlessly.

Daichu
Fiery unicorn snapped, The.

Daido Ichi'i (d. 1370)
Tune of non-being, A.

Daie-Soko (1089–1163)
Life's as we / Find it—death too.

Daigu (1584–1669)
Here none think of wealth or fame.
Who dares approach the lion's.

Daijiu, Nyūdo Saki no Dajō See Kintsune
Daio (1235–1308)
I have had a companion on the road.

Dairin Soto (d. 1568)
My whole life long I've sharpened my sword.

Daisen (fl. 13th cent.)
All things come apart.

Daito (1282–1337)
At last I've broken Unmon's barrier!
To slice through Buddhas, Patriarchs.

Daive, Jean (b. 1941)
I rise from the depths.
Lost in contemplation.
Nomad, A.
She does not move.

Space instead.
Under the wind.
Woman measures, A.

dal Bagno Pisano, Pannuccio (fl. 1250)
My lady, thy delightful high command.

Dalcour, Pierre
Verse Written in the Album of Mademoiselle.

Daldorph, Brian
Spuds.

Dale, Langham (1826–98)
Prejudice against Colour.

Dale, Peter (b. 1938)
Few ever came to help you speak or sell.
I start with a straight back and two points.

Daley, Frank (b. 1940)
Piano, The.

Daley, Victor James (1858–1905)
Dove, The.
Lachesis.
Mother Doorstep.
Tall Hat.
Vision of Sunday in Heaven, A.
When London Calls.
Woman at the Washtub, The.

Dali, Salvador (1904–89)
Art of Picasso, The.
Great Masturbator, The.

dall' Antela, Simone (fl. c.1300)
Prolonged Sonnet: In the Last Days of the
Emperor Henry VII.

Dallago, Carl
Summer Stanzas.

Dallán Forgaill (fl. 6th? cent.)
Poem in Praise of Colum Cille, A.

Dallas, Sir George (1758–1833)
Miss Emily Brittle Sails for India.

Dallas, Ruth (b. 1919)
Autumn Wind.
Clouds on the Sea.
Girl with Pitcher.
In the Giant's Castle.
Milking before Dawn.
Photographs of Pioneer Women.
Telemachus with a Transistor.

D'Almeida, Fernando (b. 1955)
By Forty-Sixth.

Dalton, Amanda (b. 1957)
Almost Bird.
Dad-Baby, The.
How to Disappear.
In Love.
Kitchen Beast.
Nest.

Dalton, John (1709–63)
Agape the sooty collier stands.

Dalton, Roque
Ars Poetica.
From a Revolutionary to J. L. Borges.
Looking for Trouble.
Memory.
My Neighbor.
Petty Bourgeoisie, The.
Soldier's Rest.

Daly, Thomas Augustin (1871–1948)
Mia Carlotta.
Pennsylvania Places.

Damacion, Kenneth Zamora
Canciones.

Damagetus (fl.3d cent.B.C.)
Epitaph of a Sailor.
In the name of the God of strangers, we beg
you.
On the Tomb of Orpheus.

Damas, Léon (b. 1912)
Black Man's Lament, The.
Blues.
Et Cetera.
Hiccups.
Just Like the Legend.
No One Remembers.
Obsession.
Position.
Put Down.
Reality.

S.O.S
Sell Out.
Shine.
Sleepless Night.
So Often.
Their Thing.
There Are Nights.
They Came That Night.
They Came This Evening.
Whitewash.

Damaskius (fl. c.529)
Zosimé was a slave in body only.

Dambroff, Susan
Resistance.

Dame, Enid
On the Road to Damascus, Maryland.
Seder, The.

Damian, Peter (1007–72)
Paradise.
Who is this.

**Damocharis of Kos (Damocharis Grammaticus)
(fl. 6th cent.)**
Lead disc composed of black stuff for marking,
A.

Dana, Mary Stanley Bunce (1810–83)
O Sing to Me of Heaven.
Real Comfort.

Dana, Richard Henry (1787–1879)
Chanting Cherubs, The [A Group by
Greenough].
Daybreak.
Dying Raven, The.
Husband's and Wife's Grave, The.
Pleasure Boat, The [or Pleasure-Boat, The].

Dana, Robert (fl. 20th cent.)
At the Vietnam War Memorial, Washington,
D. C.
Elegy for the Duke.
Mark, The.

Dance, James (1722–74)
When the returning sun begins to smile.

Dancer, John (fl. 1660–1707)
Variety, The.

Danforth, John (1660–1730)
Few Lines to Fill up a Vacant Page, A.
Mercies of the Year, The.
On My Lord Bacon.
Poem upon the Triumphant Translation of . . .
Mrs. Anne Eliot, A.
Profit and Loss: An Elegy upon the Decease of
Mrs. Mary Gerrish.
Two Vast Enjoyments Commemorated.

Danforth, Samuel (1626–74)
Almanac Verse.
Awake yee westerne nymphs, arise and sing.

Danforth, Samuel, Jr. (1666–1727)
Ad Librum.
Elegy in Memory of the Worshipful Major
Thomas Leonard Esq, An.

Dangai
Earth, river, mountain.

Daniel, Arnaut (fl. c.1180–1210)
Art of Love, The.
Autet e bas.
Bel m'es quan lo vens m'alena.
Firm desire which enters, The.
L'Aura Amara.
Mot eran dous miei cossir.
Resolute Desire That Enters, The.

Daniel, George (1616–57)
After a Storm, Going a Hawking.
Landscape, The.
One Desiring Me to Read, But Slept It Out,
Wakening.
Robin, The.

Daniel, H. J. (1818–89)
My Epitaph.

Daniel, Robert T. (1773–1840)
Time Will Surely Come, The.

Daniel, Samuel (1562–1619)
And yet I cannot reprehend the flight.
Are They Shadows [That We See]?
Beauty, Time and Love.
Behold how every man, drawn with delight.

Behold what hap *Pigmalion* had to frame.
But love whilst that thou mayst be loved again.
Care-Charmer Sleep.
Go wailing verse, the infants of my love.
Half-blown Rose, The.
I must not grieve my love, whose eyes would read.
It was upon the twilight of that day.
Lonely Beauty.
Love Is a Sickness.
Most Unloving One, The.
Ode: "Now each creature joys the other."
Place there is, where proudly raised there stands, A.
Poet and Critic.
Poetry in England.
Sacred Religion, mother of form and fear.
Sonnet: "Beauty, sweet love, is like the morning dew."
Sonnet: "Let others sing of knights and paladin[e]s."
Sonnet: "When men shall find thy flower, thy glory, pass."
Sonnet 5: 'Whilst Youth and Error.'
Stonehenge.
Theare be great Prince, such as will tell you howe.
Thou canst not die whilst any zeal abound.
Time, cruel time, come and subdue that brow.
To the Lady Margaret, Countess [*or* Countesse] of Cumberland.
To the Right Honorable, the Lady Mary, Countess of Pembroke.
Ulysses and the Siren [*or* Syren].
Unto the boundless Ocean of thy beauty.
When winter snows upon thy sable hairs.
Why Should I Sing in Verse.

Daniel, Yuly [*or* Iulii] Markovich ("Nikolai Arzhak") (1925–88)
House, A.
New Year March: A Declaration, The.
Sentence, The.
To My Friends.
You stand beside me here, each day and every hour.

Daniells, Roy (b. 1902)
Journey.

Daniels, Jim
Short-Order Cook.
Ted's Bar and Grill.
Time, Temperature.

Daniels, Kate (b. 1953)
After Reading Reznikoff.
Bus Ride.
Ethiopia.
Not Singing.
Prayer to the Muse of Ordinary Life.
Women's Room in Pennsylvania Station, The.

Dankyo-Myorin (*fl.* 13th cent.)
Coming, I clench my hands.

Danner, Margaret (b. 1915)
And through the Caribbean Sea.
At Home in Dakar.
Convert, The.
Garnishing the Aviary.
Goodbye David Tamunoemi West.
Grandson Is a Hoticeberg, A.
Painted Lady, The.
Rhetoric of Langston Hughes, The.
Slave and the Iron Lace, The.
This Is an African Worm.

Dante Alighieri (1265–1321)
Ballata: He Will Gaze upon Beatrice.
Because I find not whom to speak withal.
Canzone: He Beseeches Death for the Life of Beatrice.
Convito, *sels.*
Divine Comedy, The, *sels.*
Guido, I wish that Lapo, thou, and I.
Inferno, *sels.*
King by whose rich grace His servants be, The.
La Vita Nuova, *sels.*
Love and Poetry.
Love, since it is thy will that I return.
New Love and the Gentle Heart.
O Bicci, pretty son of who knows whom.

Of the Lady Pietra degli Scrovigni.
Paradiso, *sels.*
Purgatario, *sels.*
Sestina: "I have reached, alas, the long shadow."
Sonnet: "Guido, I wish that you and Lapo and I."
Sonnet: He rebukes Cino for Fickleness.
Sonnet: Of Beatrice de' Portinari, on All Saints' Day.
Sonnet: Of Beauty and Duty.
Sonnet: On the 9th of June 1290.
Sonnet: To Brunetto Latini.
Sonnet: To Certain Ladies; When Beatrice Was Lamenting Her Father's Death.
Sonnet: To Guido Cavalcanti.
Sonnet: To the Lady Pietra degli Scrovigni.
Sonnet: To the Same Ladies; With Their Answer.
To hear the unlucky wife of Bicci cough.
To Waning Day, To the Wide Round of Shadow.

Dante da Maiano (*fl.* c.1300)
On the last words of what you write to me.
So greatly thy great pleasaunce pleasured me.
Sonnet: He Craves Interpreting of a Dream of His.
To Dante Alighieri: He Interprets Dante Alighieri's Dream.
Wonderful countenance and royal neck.

D'Anvers, Alicia (1688?–1725)
To the University.
True Relation of their Practice at Oxford Town when there an Act is, A.

"Dao, Bei" *See* **Zhenkai, Zhao**

Da'oud, Siham
I Love in White Ink.

D'Aquino, Rinaldo (*fl.* 1240–50)
Now, when it flowereth.
Thing is in my mind, A.

D'Arcos, Joaquim Paço
Re-encounter.

Dare, Joan
Limerick: "Cleric once heard with dismay, A."

d'Arezzo, Fra Guittone (*fl.* 1250)
To the Blessed Virgin Mary.

"Dario, Rubén" (Félix Rubén García Sarmiento) (1867–1916)
Alleluya.
Autumn Verses.
Autumnal.
Doom.
Eheu!
Far Away and Long Ago.
Fatality.
Fount, The.
I Love, You Love.
I Pursue a Form.
I Seek a Form.
It Was a Gentle Air.
Leda.
Marguerite.
Melancholy.
Nicaraguan Triptych.
Nocturne.
Philosophy.
Seashell, The.
Sonatina.
Spring.
Springtime.
Swan, The.
Swans, The.
Symphony in Gray Major.
To Columbus.
To Roosevelt.
Triumphal March.
Tropical Afternoon.
Unhappy He.
Victory of Samothrace, The.

Darley, George (1795–1846)
Fallen Star, The.
Free-booter, The.
Hundred-gated Thebes.
Hurry me Nymphs! O, hurry me.
It Is Not Beauty I Demand.
Mermaidens' Vesper-Hymn, The.

O blest unfabled incense tree.
Pass of Death, The.
Rebellion of the Waters, The.
Sea-Ritual, The.
Song: "Sweet in her green dell the flower of beauty slumbers."
To Helene.
To Mie Tirante.
To Poets.
View like one of Fairy-land, A.

Darnley, Henry Stuart [*or* Stewart], Lord (1545–67)
Gife Langour.
To the Queen.

Darr, Ann (b. 1920)
At Sixteen.
Gift, The.

Darragh, Tina (b. 1950)
Footnote at "Figure of Speech."
Lattice at "Split."
Lattice at/of (Com)pare (Dis)pair.
"Legion" to "Lent" for "R."
"Luteous" to "Lymph" for "F."
Sis Boom Ba.
Throwing Out at / of (Com)pare (Dis)pair, A.
Volcanic tuff.

Daruwalla, Keki N. (b. 1937)
Of Mohenjo Daro at Oxford.

Darwin, Erasmus (1731–1802)
CARYO's sweet smile DIANTHUS proud admires.
Descend, ye hovering sylphs! aerial choirs.
Fair Chunda smiles amid the burning waste.
Kew.
Nightmare.
On DOVE's green brink the fair TREMELLA stood.
Steam Power.
Visit of Hope to Sydney Cove, near Botany-Bay.
Weak with nice sense, the chaste MIMOSA stands.
Where cool'd by rills and curtain'd round by woods.

Darwish, Mahmoud (b. 1942)
Apple for the sea, marble narcissus flower, An.
Bread.
Earth Poem.
Guests on the Sea.
Identity Card.
On Our Last Evening on This Land.
On Wishes.
Poems after Beirut.
Prison.
Psalm 2.
Sirhan Drinks His Coffee in the Cafeteria.
Steps in the Night.
We do not need to be reminded.
We Travel Like Other People.
We Walk Towards a Land.
Words.

Daryush, Elizabeth (1887–1976)
Anger Lay by Me All Night Long.
Children of wealth in your warm nursery.
Forbidden Love.
How on Solemn Fields of Space.
Still-Life.
Subalterns.

Das, Jagannath Prasad (b. 1936)
Corpse, The.

Das, Jibanananda (1899–1954)
In Camp.

Das, Kamala (b. 1934)
Hot Noon in Malabar.
Introduction: "I don't know politics but I know the names."

Dās, Raghunāth (*fl.* late 18th cent.)
Now I'll see whether Siva.

Dāsdatta, Rāmlāl
Because You love cremation grounds.

Dasgupta, Pranabendu (b. 1937)
Man: 1961.

Date, J. C. B.
Limerick: "Though your dreams may seem normal and right."

Limerick: "To Algebra God is inclined."

Dauenhauer, Nora (b. 1927)
How To Make Good Baked Salmon from the River.
Kelp.
Skiing on Russian Christmas.
Tlingit Concrete Poem.
Voices.

Dauenhauer, Richard
Driving in a Snowstorm, King Salmon to Naknek.

Dauer, Lesley (b. 1965)
20th Century, The.
Falling.
Lois at the Hair Salon.
Mammals.
Philip the Store Policeman.
William.
Woman in the Film, The.

Daugherty, James Henry (1889–1974)
Pack train, stage coach, pony express, climb over the mountain passes.

Daumal, René (1908–44)
Clavicles for a Great Poetic Game.
Jesus before Pilate.
Matthew 27:11–24; Now Jesus stood before.
Persephone That Is to Say Double Issue.
Short Revelation Concerning Death and Chaos.

Davenant [or D'Avenant], Sir William (1606–68)
Christian's Reply to the Philosopher, The.
City Morning, The.
Countess of Anglesey lead Captive by the Rebels, at the Disforresting of Pewsam, The.
Endimion Porter and Olivia.
For the Lady Olivia Porter; a Present upon a New Year's Day.
Lark Now Leaves His Watery [or Wat'ry] Nest.
Lover and Philosopher.
O Thou That Sleep'st like Pig in Straw.
Praise and Prayer.
Soldier Going to the Field, The.
There, when they thought they saw in well sought Books.
'Tis, in good truth, a most wonderful thing.
To the Queen[e], Entertain[e]d at Night by the Countess[e] of Anglesey.
Under the Willow Shades.
Wake All the Dead.

Davenport, Robert (fl. 1624–40)
Sacrifice, A.

Davey, Frank (b. 1940)
She'd Say.

Davey, Vicki
Shadow of Life, The.

David ben Meshullam (fl. Middle Ages)
Be Not Silent.

David, John (1761–1841)
What Happiness Can Equal Mine.

David, Mack (1912–93)
Candy.
I'm Just a Lucky So-and-So.
Sinner Kissed an Angel, A.
Sunflower.

Davidman, Joy (b. 1915)
And Pilate Said.
Lament for Evolution.
Night-Piece.

Davidson, Donald (1893–1968)
Descending Chestnut Ridge.
Immigrant, The.
In Blue-Stocking Hollow.
Lee in the Mountains.
Lines for a Tomb.
Lines Written for Allen Tate on His Sixtieth Anniversary.
On a Replica of the Parthenon.
Randall, My Son.
Redivivus.
Refugees.
Sanctuary.
Sequel of Appomattox.
Twilight on Union Street.
Utterance.

Davidson, John (1857–1909)
Ballad of a Nun, A.

Ballad of Hell, A.
Battle.
Contraption,—that's the bizarre, proper slang.
Crystal Palace, The.
Holiday at Hampton Court.
Imagination.
In a Music-Hall.
In Romney Marsh.
Labourer's Wife, A.
London.
Northern Suburb, A.
Price, The.
Runnable Stag, A.
Snow.
Song: "Boat is chafing at our long delay, The."
Thirty Bob a Week.
Unknown, The.

Davidson, L. A.
Beyond stars.
In the dark lobby.
It is growing dark.
On my return.
Silent crowd, The.

Davidson, Lucretia (1808–25)
Charnel Ship, The.
Fear of Madness, The.

Davidson, Michael (b. 1944?)
Century of Hands.
Dream Dream, The.
Et in Leucadia Ego.
Feeling Type and His Friends, The.
Form of Chiasmus; The Chiasmus of Forms, The.
Framing.
Landing of Rochambeau, The.
Sensation Type and His Friends, The.
Thinking the Alps.
Troth.

Davidson, R. R.
Gravy Train, The.

Davie, Donald (1922–95)
Across the Bay.
Barnsley and District.
But this, so feminine?
Christening, A.
Devil on Ice.
Epistle. To Enrique Caracciolo Trejo.
Fountain of Cyanë, The.
Fountain, The.
G. M. B.
Garden Party, The.
Gardens No Emblems.
Hearing Russian Spoken.
Heigh-ho on a Winter Afternoon.
Hill Field, The.
Horae Canonicae.
In California.
In the Stopping Train.
Jacob's Ladder.
Meeting of Cultures, A.
Mushroom Gatherers, The.
On Bertrand Russell's "Portraits from Memory."
Ordinary God.
Ox-Bow.
Priory of St Saviour, Glendalough, The.
Prose for Des Esseintes.
Rejoinder to a Critic.
Remembering the 'Thirties.
Rodez.
Rousseau in His Day.
Thanks to Industrial Essex.
Their Rectitude Their Beauty.
Time Passing, Beloved.
To a Teacher of French.
Tunstall Forest.
With the Grain.

Davies, Alan (b. 1951)
New Sentience, The.
Outer Layers of Nervousness, The.
Personality syndrome, The.
Thirty East Forty-Second Street.

Davies, Arthur
West Paddocks.

Davies, Dudley G. (1891–1981)
At Branwen's Grave.

Carmarthenshire.

Davies, Edward (1718–89)
Chepstow: A Poem.
Will no young British bard, on rhyme intent.
Wily Fox, The.

Davies, Eleanor Touchet (1590–1652)
Gatehouse Salutation, The.
When Hee Was Come to the Other Side of the Contrye, of the Gergesenes, There Mett Him Two: Possessed with Devils Coming Out of the Tombes.

Davies, Elwyn (b. 1912)
Portrait of Auntie Blodwen.

Davies, Frank
Limerick: "Giraffes, yes, even the strongest."

Davies, Gareth Alban (b. 1926)
Dance, The.

Davies, Gloria Evans (b. 1932)
Her Name like the Hours.
Holly Gone.

Davies, Hilary
Beachy Head.

Davies, Hugh Sykes (1909–84)
Music in an Empty House.
Poem: "In the stump of the old tree, where the heart has rotted out."
Poem: "It doesn't look like a finger it looks like a feather of broken glass."

Davies, Idris (1905–53)
Angry Summer 20, The.
Angry Summer 28, The.
Angry Summer, The.
Capel Calvin.
Consider Famous Men, Dai Bach.
Dark gods if all our days.
Do You Remember 1926?
Gwalia Deserta XV.
Gwalia Deserta XXII.
Gwalia Deserta XXVI.
High Summer on the Mountains.
Hywel and Blodwen.
In Gardens in the Rhondda.
Lay Preacher Ponders, The.
Angry Summer, The.
There are countless tons of rock above his head.

Davies, J. Kitchener (1902–52)
Today, / there came a breeze thin as the needle of a syringe.

Davies, Sir John (1569–1626)
Affliction.
Amongst the poets Dacus numbered is.
As when the bright[e] Crulean firmament.
Cosmus hath more discoursing in his head.
Faith (wench) I cannot court thy sprightly eyes.
Fine youth Ciprius is more terse and neat, The.
Gulling[e] Sonnets, The.
I know my soul hath power to know all things.
In Francum.
In Fuscum.
In Librum.
My case is this.
Nosce Teipsum.
On the Deputy of Ireland's Child.
Orchestra; or, A Poem[e] of Da[u]ncing.
Philo the gentleman, the fortune teller.
Praise of Dancing, The.
Reasons drawn from Divinity.
Sacred muse that first[e] made love divine [or devine], The.
Sole heir of virtue, and of beauty both.
Speach of Love persuading men to learn Dancing, The.
Titus the brave and valorous gallant.
What eagle can beho[u]ld her sunbright[e] eye.
What eye doth see the heaven but doth admire.
Where lives the man that never yet did heare.
Why did my parents send me to the schools.

Davies, John (b. 1944)
Acclamation, An.
At the Zoo.
How to Write Anglo-Welsh Poetry.
In Port Talbot.
Intellectual Powers of the Soul, The.
Port Talbot.

Sunny Prestatyn.
Three Kinds of Life Answerable to the Three
  Powers of the Soul.
Visitor's Book, 8, The.
Visitor's Book, 9, The.
Winter.

Davies, John, of Hereford (c.1565–1618)
Against Gaudy-Bragging-Undoughty Daccus.
Against Proud Poor Phryna.
Although we do not all the good we love.
Author Loving These Homely Meats, The.
Give me, fair sweet, the map, well-coloured.
Great Grandame Wales, from whom those
  ancestors.
It is as true as strange, else trial feigns.
Of Kate's Baldness.
Remembrance of My Friend Mr. Thomas
  Morley, A.
So shoots a star as doth my mistress glide.
Some blaze the precious beauties of their
  loves.
When first I learned the ABC of love.

Davies, Mary Carolyn
Let Me Be a Giver.
Love Song: "There is a strong wall about me
  to protect me."
Prayer for Every Day, A.
To Give One's Life.
Vow for New Year's, A.

Davies, Oliver (1881–1960)
Urban.

Davies, Russell (b. 1946)
Book Review.

Davies, Samuel (1723–61)
Eternal Spirit, Source of Light.
Lord, I Am Thine.
One Thing Needful Generally Neglected, The.
Science.
Thou only Good! Eternal All!
While o'er Our Guilty Land, O Lord.

Davies, Sneyd (1709–69)
Crooked bank still winds to something new,
  The.
Scene after Hunting at Swallowfield in
  Berkshire, A.

Davies, T. Glynne (b. 1926)
Caernarfon, 2 July 1969.
Old Man in a Moon Loft.
Sentences While Remembering Hiraethog.

Davies, Walter (1761–1849)
Nightfall.
To W. S.—On his Wonderful Toys.

Davies, William Henry (1871–1940)
All in June.
Ambition.
Bed-Sitting Room, The.
Best Friend, The.
Black Cloud, The.
Bright Day, A.
Cat, The.
Child's Pet, A.
D is for Dog.
Days That Have Been.
Days Too Short.
Dog, The.
Dumb World, The.
Elements, The.
Example, The.
Flirt, The.
Great Time, A.
Greeting, A.
Her Merriment.
Hermit, The.
Hill-Side Park, The.
Hour of Magic, The.
I Am the Poet Davies, William.
Inquest, The.
J is for Jealousy.
Jenny Wren.
Joy and Pleasure.
Kingfisher, The.
Leaves.
Leisure.
Mind's Liberty, The.
Money.
Moon and a Cloud, The.

Moon, The.
Nailsworth Hill.
No Man's Wood.
Rain, The.
Rat, The.
School's Out.
Sea, The.
Sheep.
Sluggard, The.
Songs of Joy.
To a Lady Friend.
Truly Great.
Truth, The.
Tugged Hand, The.
Two Stars, The.
Villain, The.
Visitor, The.
When Yon Full Moon.
White Horse, The.

Davis, Abijah (1763–1817)
Blest Is the Man Whose Tender Breast.

Davis, Benny (fl. 1921)
I'm Nobody's Baby.

Davis, Catherine (b. 1924)
Belongings.
Out of Work, Out of Touch, Out of Sorts.
Years, The.

Davis, Christopher (b. 1960)
Any Nest I Can't Sleep in Should Be Burned.
Little Crisis Framed in My Window.
Murderer, The.
Nod.

Davis, Dick (b. 1945)
Childhood of a Spy.
Christmas Poem, A.

Davis, Frank Marshall (b. 1905)
Arthur Ridgewood, M.D.
Christ is a Dixie Nigger.
Giles Johnson, Ph.D.
Jazz Band.
Robert Whitmore.
Sam Jackson.

Davis, Glover (b. 1939)
August Fires.
Children in the Arbor.
Orphan, The.

Davis, Harold Lenoir (1896–1960)
Proud Riders.

Davis, Jack (b. 1917)
Aboriginal Australia.
Aboriginal Reserve.
Day Flight.
Desolation.
First-born, The.
My Brother, My Sister.
One Hundred and Fifty Years.
Slum Dwelling.
Urban Aboriginal.
Warru.

Davis, Jordan (b. 1970)
Boat, A.
Fire Barns.
He Is Lightning.
Kids on Television Imagine Me, The.
Time Bum.
You Turn Around.
Zoo, The.

Davis, Lydia
Mown Lawn, A.

Davis, Mary [or Mollie] Evelyn Moore
Cry of a People.
Going Out and Coming In.

Davis, Olena Kalytiak
In the Clear Long After.
Moorer Denies Holyfield in Twelve.
New Philosophy of Composition, or, How to
  Ignore the Non-Reasoning Creature Capable
  of *Speeech* Perched Outside Your Bathroom
  Window, A.
Panic of Birds, The.
Small Number, A.
Sweet Reader, Flanneled and Tulled.
Thirty Years Rising.

Davis, Ozora Stearns (1866–1931)
At Length There Dawns the Glorious Day.

Davis, Robert H. (b. 1954)
At the Door of the Native Studies Director.
Black Buoy.
Raven is Two-Faced.
Raven Tells Stories.

Davis, Thadious M. (b. 1944)
Asante Sana, Te Te.
Double Take at Relais de L'Espadon.
It's All the Same.
"Honeysuckle Was the Saddest Odor of All, I
  Think."
Remembering Fannie Lou Hamer.

Davis, Thomas Osborne (1814–45)
Lament for the Death of Eoghan Ruadh
  O'Neill.
Nation Once Again, A.

Davis, Thulani
Boppin' is Safer than Grindin'
C. T. at the Five Spot.
Desire 1.
Playing Solitaire.
Rogue and Jar: 4/27/77.
Susannah.
Zoom (The Commodores)

Davis, William M.
Why Did Stingy Thomas.

Davis, William Virgil
In a Room.
Sleep of the Insomniac, The.
Snow.
Spider.

Davison, Edward (b. 1898)
In This Dark House.

Davison, Peter (b. 1928)
Bed Time.
Birthright, The.
Cross Cut.
Dead Sea, The.
Delphi.
Equinox 1980.
From the Outland.
Gift of Tongues, The.
Last Word, The.
Lunch at the Coq d'Or.
Motley.
Questions of Swimming, 1935.
Star Watcher, The.
Vanishing Point, The.
Where the Sun Ends.

Davitt, Michael (b. 1950)
Counterfeiter, The.
In Memory of Elizabeth Kearney, Blasket-
  Islander.
Mirror, The.
Old People.
Shortening the Road.

Davys, Mary (1674–1732)
Behind the moth-eaten curtain, 'stead of press.

Dawe, Bruce (b. 1930)
Abandonment of Autos.
Americanized.
At Shagger's Funeral.
Beatitudes.
Copy-writer's Dream, The.
Dogs in the Morning Light.
Drifters.
Elegy for Drowned Children.
Family Man, The.
First Corinthians at the Crossroads.
Going.
Gorilla Gorilla.
Happiness Is the Art of Being Broken.
Homecoming.
Homo Suburbiensis.
Morning Becomes Electric.
Not-so-good Earth, The.
On the Death of Ronald Ryan.
Perpetuum Immobile.
Renewal Notice.
Suburban Lovers.
Victorian Hangman Tells His Love, A.
Weapons Training.

Dawe, Gerald (b. 1952)
Likelihood of Snow, The / The Danger of Fire.
Lundys Letter, The.

Names.
Question of Covenants, A.
Seamen's Mission.
Sheltering Places.
Solstice.
Dawes, Kwame (b. 1962)
Black Heart.
Some Tentative Definitions 1.
Some Tentative Definitions 4.
Some Tentative Definitions 7.
Some Tentative Definitions 11.
Trickster 1 (for Winston Rodney)
Trickster 2 (for Lee 'Scratch' Perry)
Trickster 4 (for Sister Patra)
Dawson, Mary
Late for Breakfast.
Dawson, William James (1854–1928)
House of Pride, The.
Day, Clarence (1874–1935)
Egg, The.
Might and Right.
Who Drags the Fiery Artist Down?
Yesterday explorers found.
Day, Jean
From Momentary Work, A Wrench.
Moving Object.
Day, Jeffery (1896–1918)
North Sea.
Day, John (1574–1640)
Man's Natural Infirmity.
Picket before Bull Run, The.
Prayer: "Grant that no Hobgoblins fright me."
Day Lewis, Cecil (1904–72)
Album, The.
Almost Human.
As One Who Wanders into Old Workings.
Can the Mole Take.
Carol, A.
Chiefly to Mind Appears.
Christmas Tree, The.
Come Up, Methuselah.
Conflict, The.
Dead, The.
Departure in the Dark.
Do Not Expect Again a Phoenix Hour.
Emily Brontë.
Failure, A.
Few Things Can More Inflame.
I've heard them lilting at loom and belting.
Maple and Sumach.
My Mother's Sister.
Nabara, The.
Nearing Again the Legendary Isle.
Newsreel.
Now She Is like the White Tree-Rose.
Poem for an Anniversary.
Reconciliation.
Rest from Loving and Be Living.
Sheepdog Trials in Hyde Park.
Snowfall on a College Garden.
Song: "Come, live with me and be my love."
Stand-To, The.
Symbols of Gross Experience.
Tempt Me No More.
This Man Was Strong.
To travel like a bird, lightly to view.
Two Songs.
When They Have Lost.
Where Are the War Poets?
Winged bull trundles to the wired perimeter, The.
With Me My Lover Makes.
You That Love England.
Day, Lucille (b. 1947)
Reject Jell-o.
Dayre, Sydney (fl. 1881)
Grandma's Lost Balance.
Lesson for Mamma, A.
Dayton, Ebenezer (fl. mid–18th cent.)
Wherein Consists the High Estate.
Ddu, Ieuan See **Thomas, John L.**
de Aerenlund, Consuelo
Cuando el tecolote canta, el Indio muere.
De Angelis, Milo (b. 1951)
And Then the Water.

Continuous Time.
Every Metaphor.
Finite Intuition.
Hilbert's Program.
In the Lungs.
July Has Come for the Dead.
Line.
Main Idea, The.
Narrator, The.
Now She Is Unadorned.
On the Way to Mind.
Protect Me, My Talisman.
Reasons for the Beginning.
Rowing in Familiar January.
Sounds That Arrived, The.
Telegram.
There's a Hand that Nails Down.
Towards the Mind.
Year.
Yearbook.
De, Bishnu (b. 1909)
Santhal Poems, 1.
de Burgos, Julia (1914–53)
Ay, Ay, Ay of the Kinky-Haired Negress.
I Have Lost A Verse.
Nothing.
Poem Arrested at Daybreak.
Poem of My Sleeping Sorrow.
Poem to My Death.
Sea and You, The.
To Julia de Burgos.
Transmutation.
de Campos, Haroldo
De sol a sol.
De Carrion, Santob (fl. 14th cent.)
Friend, A.
Resignation.
Self-Defense.
de Carvalho, Ruy Duarte (b. 1941)
I Come from a South.
De Casseres, Benjamin (1873–1945)
Moth-Terror.
De Coninck, Herman (b. 1944)
Ballad of Indolence.
If Only.
Your Sweaters.
de Fierro, Fanny Carrión (b. 1939)
Grain of Sand.
Heart of Time.
Hidden Pleasure.
If Time Waits.
Oblivion.
Only You.
Oracle.
Secret, The.
Speak to Me.
de Folgar, Romelia Alarcón (b. 1920)
Irreverent Epistle to Jesus Christ.
Monday.
Nocturnal.
Panorama.
Panorama 2.
Protest.
de Gillies, Giles
De Puerorum osculis.
De [or Du] Guillet, Pernette (c.1520–1545)
But if he came straight for me.
Non Que Je Veuille Ôter la Liberté.
De Hearn, Nellie
Shut-In, The.
de Jesús, Teresa
Proverbs.
Curfew.
Flag of Chile, The.
De Kok, Ingrid (b. 1951)
Al Wat Kind Is.
Our Sharpeville.
Small Passing.
De la Mare, Walter ("Walter Ramal") (1873–1956)
Alas, Alack!
All but Blind.
All That's Past.
Alone.
Arrogance.

As Lucy Went A-Walking.
At Ease.
At the Keyhole.
Autumn.
Ballad of Christmas, A.
Bards, The.
Berries.
Birthnight: To F, The.
Buttons.
Christmas Eve.
Corporal Pym.
Crazed.
Cupboard, The.
Dear Sir.
Dove, The.
Echo.
Epitaph, An: "Here lies a most beautiful lady."
Faint Music.
Fare Well.
Feckless Dinner-Party, The.
Fly, The.
Galliass, The.
Ghost, The.
Hare, A.
Hi!
Ice.
In the Local Museum.
Iron.
Listeners, The.
Jenny Wren.
John Mouldy.
Last Chapter, The.
Martha.
Miracle, The.
Miss Loo.
Miss T.
Mocking Fairy, The.
Moonlight.
Moonshine.
Motley.
Napoleon.
Ned Vaughan.
Nod.
Old Men, The.
Old Summerhouse, The.
Old Susan.
Owl, The.
Peace.
Pooh!
Portrait, A.
Railway Junction, The.
Reserved.
Ride-by-Nights, The.
Sam.
Scarecrow, The.
Scholars.
Scribe, The.
Shubble, The.
Silver.
Silver Penny, The.
Sleeper, The.
Slim Cunning Hands.
Snow.
Someone [or Some One].
Song of Finis, The.
Song of the Mad Prince, The.
Song of the Shadows, The.
Spotted Flycatcher, The.
Stone, The.
Storm, The.
Stranger, The.
Summer Evening.
Sunk Lyonesse.
Susannah Prout.
There Blooms No Bud in May.
There was an old Begum of Frome.
Thomas Hardy.
Thomas Logge.
Three Cherry Trees, The.
Three Sisters.
Tired Tim.
Truants, The.
Two Gardens.
Voices.
Winter.
De la Tierra, Tatiana (b. 1961)
De Ambiente.

De León, Luís (1528–91)
At the Ascension.
Life of the Blessed, The.
Life Withdrawn, The.
Love Song: "That haughty tyranny of thine."
Night Serene, The.
O Courtesy, O Harborage Most Sweet.
Ode to Francisco Salinas.
On Leaving Prison.
To Retirement.
Tranquil Night.
Written on the Walls of His Dungeon.

de Lille, Abbé Jacques
Gardens, The.

De Los Santos, Marisa
Milagros Mourns the Queen of Scat.
Wiglaf.
Women Watching Basketball.

De' Medici, Maria (1573–1642)
To the Virgin.

De Mello Breyner, Sophia (b. 1919)
Beach.
Day of Sea.
Flute, The.
I Feel the Dead.
Muse.
Small Square, The.

De Paul, Gene
I'll Remember April.
Milkman, Keep Those Bottles Quiet!
Mister Five by Five.
Teach Me Tonight.
You Don't Know What Love Is.

de Portalatin, Aida Cartagena
Black Autumn.
Humble Litany.
Second Elegy.

De Regnier, Henri (b. 1864)
Je ne veux de personne aupres de ma tristesse.
Night.

De Roche, Joseph (b. 1938)
Aunt Laura Moves toward the Open Grave of
Her Father.
Blond.

De Rose, Peter
Deep Purple.

**De Tabley, John Byrne Leicester Warren, 3d
Baron (1835–95)**
Circe.
Count of Senlis at His Toilet, The.
Knight in the Wood, The.
Nuptial Song.
Philoctetes.
Pilgrim Cranes, The.
Power of Interval, The.
Song of Dust, A.
Song of Faith Forsworn, A.
Sonnet: "Record is nothing, and the hero
great."
Study of a Spider, The.
Two Old Kings, The.

De Veaux, Alexis (b. 1948)
Sisters, The.

De Vere, Sir Aubrey (1788–1846)
Children Band, The.
Reality.
Right Use of Prayer, The.
Sonnet: "Ye praise the humble: of the meek ye
say."

De Vere, Aubrey Thomas (1814–1902)
Correggio's Cupolas at Parma.
Implicit Faith.
In Ruin Reconciled.
Poet to a Painter, A.
Serenade: "Softly, O midnight Hours!"
Song: Little Black Rose, The.
Sorrow.

**De Vere, Edward, 17th Earl of Oxford (1550–
1604)**
Court lady Addresses Her Lover, A.
If Women Could Be Fair.
Lively lark stretched forth her wing, The.
Of the Birth and Bringing Up of Desire.
Pains and Gains.
Poem: "Were I a king, I could command

content."
SITTING alone upon my thought, in melancholy
mood.

De Viau, Theophile (1591–1626)
Ode: "Raven croaks before me, A."
Sleep.

de Vries, Hendrik (1896–1989)
My Brother.

De Vries, Peter (b. 1910)
Bacchanal.
Christmas Family Reunion.
Loveliest of Pies.
Poets Have Their Ear to the Ground.
Psychiatrist.
Sacred and Profane Love, or, There's Nothing
New under the Moon Either.
To His Importunate Mistress.

De Vries, Rachel
On Alabama Ave., Paterson, NJ, 1954.

Dean, Debra Kang (b. 1955)
Arrival.
Back to Back.
Immigrants.
In the Way Back.
Stitches.
Taproot.

Deane, Anthony C. (1870–1946)
Cult of the Celtic, The.
Ode: "I sing a song of sixpence, and of rye."

Deane, John F. (b. 1943)
On a Dark Night.

Deane, Seamus (b. 1940)
Brethren, The.
Burial, A.
Derry.
Fording the River.
Guerillas.
History Lessons.
Northern Ireland: Two Comments.
Osip Mandelstam.
Power Cut.
Reading *Paradise Lost* in Protestant Ulster
1984.
Return.
Roots.
Scholar I.
Scholar II.
Schooling, A.

Deanovich, Connie
American Avalon.
Frankenstein.
My Favorite Monk Is.
Natalie gets discovered in her pit by an old,
drunken transient.
Requirements for Suggesting Fats Waller.
Zombie Jet.

Deb, Āśutos (1805–56)
I started a fire with Kali's name.

Debī, Tāriṇī
Tara, this is why I call upon You.

Debravo, Jorge (1938–67)
Beds of Purification.

DeCarteret, Mark (b. 1960)
Coloring.
Town Clerk, The.

Decker, Bessie B.
Disillusion.

DeCormier-Shekejian, Regina
Grandmother.
Left Eye of Odin, The.
Snow.
Tonight.

Deems, Charles F. (1820–93)
I Shall Not Want: In Deserts Wild.

Defoe, Daniel (1660–1731)
Breed's described: Now, Satire, if you can,
The.
In their religion they are so unev'n.
Labouring poor, in spite of double pay, The.
London.
Search all the Christian climes from pole to
pole.
Then let us boast of ancestors no more.
To sin's a vice in nature, and we find.
Wherever God erects a house of prayer.

Word's gone out, and now they spread the
main, The.
Yet Ostia boasts of her regeneration.

DeFoe, Mark
Aviary.
Dream Lover.
Forgetting the Sixties.
Red Salamander—Video Store Parking Lot.

DeFrees, Madeline (b. 1919)
Beetle Light.
Blueprints.
Census of Animal Bodies: Driving Home.
In the Locker Room.
In the middle of Priest Lake.
Variations on the Edible Tuber.

**Degen, Yona [or Iona] (Iosif Lazarevich Degen)
(b. 1925)**
My comrade is in the final agony before death.

Degenaar, Job (b. 1952)
Irish Sheep, The.
Phenomenon, A.

Deguy, Michel (b. 1930)
This Lady and Her Beautiful Window.
To Forget the Image.
When the wind.
You Will Be Astonished.

Deharme, Lise (d. 1979)
Empty Cage, The.
Little Girl of the Black Forest.

Dehmel, Richard (1863–1920)
Before the Storm.
Harvest Song.
Laborer, The.
My Drinking Song.
Silent Town, The.
To ———?
Trysting, A.
Vigil.
Voice in Darkness.

Dehn, Paul (1912–76)
Alternative Endings to an Unwritten Ballad.
Armistice.
At the Dark Hour.
Devil damn thee black, thou cream-faced loon,
The.
Game of Consequences, A.
In a cavern, in a canyon.
Jack and Jill went up the hill / To fetch some
heavy water.
St. Aubin d'Aubigne.

Dei-Anang, Michael (b. 1909)
My Africa.

Dekker, Thomas (1572?–1632?)
Art thou poore yet hast thou golden Slumbers.
Folly's Song.
Fortune and Virtue.
Golden Slumbers.
Happy Heart, The.
O, the Month of May.
Portrait, A.
Priest's Song, A.

Del Medigo, Joseph Solomon (1591–1655)
Epigram: "If men be judged wise."

Del Renzio, Toni
Can You Change a Shilling?

DeLange, Eddie (1904–49)
Darn That Dream.
Shake Down the Stars.
Solitude.

Delanty, Greg (b. 1958)
Gift, The.
Thrust & Parry.
Tie.

Delaunay, Sonia (1885–1979)
Greetings, Blaise Cendrars.
Zenith.

DeLeeuw, Adele
Auction Sale—Household Furnishings.

Deletant, Andrea See Walker, Brenda

Delgado, Juan (b. 1960)
Awakened in a Field.
Campesinos.
Chuparosa.
Con Los Pájaros.

Dandelion.
Flora's Plea to Mary.
I-5 Incident.
La Llorona.
Lame Boy Returns, The.
Letters from School, The.
Mexican Fire Breather, A.
Phone Booth at the Corner, The.
Recommitted.
Two Timer.
Visiting Father.
When You Leave.
Winter Fruit.

Della Casa, Giovanni (1503–56)
To Sleep.

della Vernaccia, Lodovico (fl. 1200)
Think a brief while on the most marvellous
arts.

della Viola, Albertuccio (fl. 1260)
Among the dancers I beheld her dance.

Delle Colonne, Guido (fl. 13th cent.)
Canzone: To Love and to His Lady.

Delmore, Alton (1908–64)
Girl by the River, The.

Delmore Brothers
Wabash Cannonball, The.

Delmore, Elizabeth (b. 1916)
Difference, The.
Is It Not Strange?
Marmalade.
Such Sweet Sorrow.
Willow.
Yew.

Delone, Vadim Nikolaevich (1947–83)
Ballad of Fate.

Deloney, Thomas (1543–1600)
For true report rung in his royall eares.
Long have I lov'd this bonny Lasse.
Our Savior Christ tracing the bordering hills,.
Weavers Song, The.

Delp, Mike
Fishing the Dream.

**Dementyev [or Dement'ev], Andrey Dmitrievich
(b. 1928)**
As long as we feel another's pain.
It's all over...

**Dementyev [or Dement'ev], Nikolai Ivanovich
(1907–35)**
Mother, The.

Demetriadis, Mary
When Lovely Woman.

Demetrio, Herrera S. (b. 1902)
Training.

Deming, Alison
Tilden Park.

Demodocus (fl. 4th? cent. B.C.)
All the Cilicians are bad.
Nasty snake once bit a Cappadocian, A.

Dempster, Roland Tombekai (1910–65)
Africa's Plea.
Is This Africa.

Demy, Jacques
You Must Believe in Spring.

Denby, Edwin (b. 1903)
New York Face, A.
Subway, The.
Villa d'Este.

Denham, Sir John (1615–69)
Cooper's Hill.
Had Cowley ne'er spoke, Killigrew ne'er writ.
Here have I seen the king, when great affairs.
Here should my wonder dwell, and here my
praise.
My eye descending from the Hill, surveys.
O could I flow like thee, and make thy stream.
On Mr. Abraham Cowley, His Death and
Burial amongst the Ancient Poets.
Preface to The Progress of Learning.
Song, A: "Morpheus, the humble god, that
dwells."
Song, A: "Somnus, the humble god, that
dwells."

Denney, Reuel (b. 1915)
Building the Dam.

Death in an ancient country was a simple
passport.
Fixer of Midnight.
Mathematician's Dream, The.
Song: "No use to aim that sextant now."

Denniker, Paul
S'posin'

Denning, Steve
Fire Support Burk.
Kim-San.
Movie, The.
Night on the Kho Bha Dinh.
This Time.

Dennis, C. J. (1876–1938)
Martyred Democrat, The.
Traveller, The.

Dennis, Carl
History.
St. Francis and the Nun.

Dennis, Matt
Angel Eyes.
Everything Happens to Me.
Let's Get Away from It All.
Night We Called It a Day, The.
Violets for Your Furs.
Will You Still Be Mine?

Densmore, Frances
I Am Walking.
I Have Found My Lover.
My Love Has Departed.
Sky Will Resound, The.
Song of Spring, A.
Song of the Butterfly, The.
Sound Is Fading Away, The.

Dent, Tom (b. 1932)
For Cool Papa Bell.
For Walter Washington.
Ray Charles at Mississippi State.

Depero, Fortunato (1892–1960)
Colors.

Depestre, René (b. 1926)
Attibon Legba.
Ballad of a Little Lamp.
Baron-Samedi.
Black Ore.
Cap'tain Zombi.
Chango.
Prelude.
Season of Anger.

Dèr Mouw, J. Adwaita (1863–1919)
Audible Still.
Does Anyone Know This Feeling.
I am Brahman.

"Der Nistor" (Pinhas Kahanovitch) (1884–1956)
At the Doors.

"Dermée, Paul" (Camille Janssen) (1886–1951)
Coffee grinder.
Poem: "Ace of spades."
Poem: "I play tennis with the shells."
Poem: "Is it a plane in the sky."
Silver Clasps.
These apples.

Derricotte, Toi (b. 1941)
1994 Inventory.
Allen Ginsberg.
Black Boys Play the Classics.
Blackbottom.
Bookstore.
Boy at the Paterson Falls.
St. Peter Claver.
Family Secrets.
Fears of the Eighth Grade.
For Black Women Who Are Afraid.
For Sister Sue Ellen and Her Special
Messenger.
Friendship, The.
From a Letter: About Snow.
In an Urban School.
Invisible Dreams.
Minks, The.
Note on my Son's Face, A.
Passing.
Promise, The.
Struggle, The.
Weakness, The.

Derwood, Gene
After Reading St. John the Divine.

Desbordes-Valmore, Marceline (1786–1859)
Intermittent Dream of a Sad Night.
Memory, A.
My Room.
Roses of Sa'adi, The.

Deschamps, Eustache (1346–1410)
Ballade 1.
Ballade 2.
Rondeau: "Fleas, stink, pigs, mold."

**Desmond, Gerald Fitzgerald, 4th Earl of
(Gearold Iarla Mac Gearailt) (d. 1398)**
Against Blame of Woman.
Woe to him who slanders women.

Desmond, John C.
When We Two Parted.

Desnos, Robert (1900–45)
Ars Poetica.
Cuckoo.
Epitaph: "I lived in those times. For a thousand
years."
Hour farther.
I Have So Often Dreamed of You.
I've Dreamed of You So Much.
I've dreamed such dreams of you.
If, like winds.
If You Knew.
Language Event Two.
Last Poem.
Letter to Youki.
Like.
Midway.
Night Watchman of Pont-au-Change, The.
No, Love Is Not Dead.
Obsession.
Oh Pangs of Love!
Sleep Spaces.
St Merri district, The.
There once was a leaf.
Three Stars.
Trance Event.
When children slap their father's face.

Desnoues, Lucienne (b. 1921)
First Things.

Desportes, Philippe (1545–1606)
Conquest [or His Lady's Might].

DeSylva, B. G. (1895–1950)
April Showers.
Best Things in Life Are Free, The.
Birth of the Blues, The.
Button Up Your Overcoat.
California, Here I Come.
Do It Again.
I'll Say She Does.
I Want to Be Bad.
If I Had a Talking Picture of you.
If You Knew Susie (Like I Know Susie)
It All Depends on You.
Look for the Silver Lining.
Magnolia.
Maybe This Is Love.
Never Swat a Fly.
Somebody Loves Me.
Stairway to Paradise.
Sunny Side Up.
Thank You Father.
Turn On the Heat.
Varsity Drag, The.
You're an Old Smoothie.
You're the Cream in My Coffee.

Detsinyi, Ludwig See **"Martin, David"**

Deutsch, Babette (1895–1982)
Barges on the Hudson.
Creatures in the Zoo.
Destruction of Letters.
Homage to the Philosopher.
Paradigm.
Scene with Figure.
Solitude.
Stranger than the Worst.
To an Amiable Child.
Urban Pastoral.

Dev Sen, Nabaneeta (b. 1938)
Yellow River, The.

Devaney, James (b. 1890)
Vision.
Devaney, Tom (b. 1969)
American Pragmatist Fell in Love, The.
Sonnet: "You know all those sonnets the ones where I said, I love you, well."
Devara Dasimayya (fl. 1000)
Tattered Sack, The.
Devi, N. Revathi
This Night.
Devlin, Denis (1908–59)
Ank'hor Vat.
Anteroom: Geneva.
Ascension.
Daphne Stillorgan.
Encounter.
Lancet, The.
Little Elegy.
Lough Derg.
Oteli Asia Palas, Inc.
Renewal by Her Element.
Spires, firm on their monster feet rose light and thin, The.
Venus of the Salty Shell.
Wishes for Her.
Devonshire, Georgiana Cavendish, Duchess of (1757–1806)
Passage of the Mountain of St. Gothard, The.
To Lady Elizabeth Foster, from Georgiana, Duchess of Devonshire, When She Was Apprehensive of Losing Her Eyesight–1796.
Dewdney, Christopher (b. 1951)
August a haze amniotic our dream aether and lens of distance. Tree sentinels in.
Grid Erectile.
Out of Control; the Quarry.
She is liquid darkness occult with desire.
This Is of Two Worlds.
D'Haen, Christine (b. 1923)
Epiphany.
Mole, The.
Dharker, Imtiaz (b. 1954)
Another Woman.
Living Space.
Minority.
Name of god, The.
Namesake.
Postcards from god (1)
Purdah, 1.
Dharwadker, Vinay (b. 1954)
New Delhi, 1974.
Dhasal, Namdeo (b. 1949)
Stone-masons, My Father, and Me.
"Dhoomil" (Sudama Pandeya) (1935–75)
City, Evening, and an Old Man: Me, The.
Dhu 'l-Nún
I die, and yet not dies in me.
Dhu'l-Rumma (696?–736?)
Of All Garments.
di Amici, Ruggieri (fl. 1250)
I play this sweet prelude.
Di Biasio, Rodolfo (b. 1937)
Cuncta Semper.
Nostoi.
Poem of the Dawn and the Night.
Snow Poem.
di Boncima, Onesto (fl. 1250)
Upon that cruel season when our Lord.
Whether all grace have fail'd I scarce may scan.
Di Cicco, Pier Giorgio (b. 1949)
Errore.
Flying Deeper into the Century.
Head Is a Paltry Matter, The.
Male Rage Poem.
Di Filippo, Rustico (1200?–70)
If any one had anything to say.
Master Bertuccio, you are called to account.
Sonnet: Of the Making of Master Messerin.
di Fiorenza, Pucciarello (fl. 1260)
Pass and let pass,—this counsel I would give.
di Marco, Ubaldo (fl. 1250)
My body resting in a haunt of mine.
Di Michele, Mary (b. 1949)
Moon and the Salt Flats, The.

Di Montorio, Antonio (1404–77)
El Ropero.
Di Piero, W. S. (b. 1945)
Near Damascus.
Why not violate sense and say.
Di Prima, Diane (b. 1934)
Abyss.
American Indian Art: Form and Tradition.
April Fool Birthday Poem for Grandpa.
Backyard.
Brief Wyoming Meditation.
Death Poems in September.
Death Sunyata Chant: A Rite for Passing Over.
For H. D.
For the Dead Lecturer.
Fragmented Address to the FBI.
Goodbye Nkrumah.
I Ching.
I Fail as a Dharma Teacher.
If he did not come apart in her hands, he fell.
In Memory of My First Chapatis.
Jungle, The.
Letter to Jeanne (at Tassajara)
Loba Addresses the Goddess, The / or The Poet as Priestess Addresses the Loba-Goddess.
Loba as Eve.
Montezuma.
Notes on the Art of Memory.
On Sitting Down to Write, I Decide Instead to Go to Fred Herko's Concert.
Only war that matters is the war against the imagination, The.
Poem in Praise of My Husband (Taos)
Practice of Magical Evocation, The.
Prophetissa.
Revolutionary Letter #1.
Short Note on the Sparseness of the Language.
Studies in Light.
Tassajara, 1969.
To the Unnamed Buddhist Nun Who Burned Herself to Death on the Night of June 3, 1966.
di Ricco da Messina, Mazzeo (fl. 1250)
I laboured these six years.
If any his own foolishness might see.
Lofty worth and lovely excellence, The.
di Sant' Angelo, Bartolomeo (fl. 13th cent.)
Sonnet: He Jests Concerning His Poverty.
Diamond, David (b. 1915)
We Will Not Fear.
Diaper, William (1686?–1717)
Had mournful Ovid been to Brent condemned.
Happy are you, whom Quantock overlooks.
Lamprey, glowing with uncommon fires, The.
Sex-life of Fish, The.
When they in throngs a safe retirement seek.
Diaz-Duque, O. F.
Why Don't I?
Dib, Mohammed
Language sovereign secret incompatible submerged in the universal wound.
Dibdin, Charles (1745–1814)
Anchorsmiths, The.
Captain Wattle and Miss Roe.
Jolly Young Waterman, The.
Lady's Diary, The.
Poor Tom.
Popular Functionary, A.
Dibdin, Thomas (1771–1841)
Origins of Naval Artillery.
Dickenga, I. E.
Building.
Dickens, Charles (1812–90)
Fine Old English Gentleman; New Version, The.
Joe Gargery's Epitaph on His Father.
Dickey, James (b. 1923)
Adultery.
Armor.
Basics.
Bee, The.
Birth, A.
Bread.
Buckdancer's Choice.

Common Grave, The.
Dog Sleeping on My Feet, A.
Driver, The.
Dusk of Horses, The.
Eagles.
Falling.
Fence Wire.
Firebombing, The.
For the Death of Vince Lombardi.
For the Nightly Ascent of the Hunter Orion over a Forest Clearing.
Gamecock.
Heaven of Animals, The.
Hedge Life.
Hospital Window, The.
Hunting Civil War Relics at Nimblewill Creek.
In the Marble Quarry.
Leap, The.
Lifeguard, The.
Magus, The.
Movement of Fish, The.
Cherrylog Road.
One, The.
Performance, The.
Poisoned Man, The.
Power and Light.
Pursuit from Under.
Sheep Child, The.
Sled Burial, Dream Ceremony.
So long.
Strength of Fields, The.
Tenderness, ache on me, and lay your neck.
Underground Stream, The.
Walking on Water.
Weeds.
Dickey, Ralph (1945–72)
Father.
Leaving Eden.
Mulatto Lullaby.
Dickey, William (b. 1928)
Canonical Hours.
Cassandra.
Death of John Berryman,The.
For Easter Island or Another Island.
Memoranda.
Plot, The.
Dickinson, Emily (1830–86)
Abraham to kill him.
Admirations—and Contempts—of time, The.
Afraid! Of whom am I afraid?
After a hundred years.
After great pain a formal feeling comes.
Ah, Necromancy Sweet!
All Circumstances are the Frame.
Alter! When the Hills do—.
Altered look about the hills, An.
Although I put away his life.
Ample make this Bed.
Apparently with no surprise.
"Arcturus" is his other name.
As if some little Arctic flower.
As imperceptibly as grief.
At Half past Three, a single Bird.
At least—to pray—is left—is left.
Baffled for just a day or two.
Beauty be not caused—It Is.
Because I could not stop for Death.
Bee his burnished Carriage, A.
Bee is not afraid of me, The.
Before I got my eye put out.
Before you thought of Spring.
Behind Me—dips Eternity.
Belshazzar had a Letter.
Bereavement in their death to feel.
Besides the autumn poets sing.
Better—than Music! For I—who heard it.
Between the form of Life and Life.
Bible is an antique Volume, The.
Bird came down the Walk, A.
Bone that has no Marrow, The.
Brain—is wider than the Sky, The.
Brain, within its Groove, The.
Bring me the sunset in a cup.
Bustle in a House, The.
Butterfly upon the Sky, The.
By a departing light.
Civilization—spurns—the Leopard!

Clock stopped, A.
Clock strikes one that just struck two, The.
Clover's simple Flame, The.
Color, Caste, Denomination.
Color of the Grave is Green, The.
Come show thy Durham Breast.
Come slowly—Eden!
Consulting summer's clock.
Could I but ride indefinite.
Could mortal lip divine.
Crumbling is not an instant's Act.
Dare you see a Soul *at the White Heat?*
Day that I was crowned, The.
Death is a Dialogue between.
Death is the supple Suitor.
Did Our Best Moment last.
Did the Harebell loose her girdle.
Difference between Despair, The.
Do People moulder equally.
Drama's Vitallest Expression is the Common
   Day.
Dropped into the Ether Acre.
Drowning is not so pitiful.
Dust is the only Secret.
Dying Tiger—moaned for Drink, A.
Each Life Converges to some Centre.
Earth has many keys, The.
Eden is that Old-Fashioned House.
Elijah's Wagon knew no thill.
Ended, ere it begun.
Essential oils—are wrung.
Everywhere of Silver, An.
Except the Heaven had come so near.
Experiment escorts us last.
Exultation is the going.
"Faith" is a fine invention.
Faith—is the Pierless Bridge.
Fame is a bee.
Fame is a fickle food.
Far from Love the Heavenly Father.
Farthest Thunder that I heard, The.
Finding is the first Act.
Finite—to fail, but infinite to Venture.
First Day's Night had come, The.
Flags Vex a Dying Face.
For each ecstatic instant.
Four Trees—upon a solitary Acre.
Further in Summer than the Birds.
Gentian weaves her fringes, The.
Glass was the Street—in tinsel Peril.
Glee—The great storm is over.
Go not too near a House of Rose.
Go slow, my soul, to feed thyself.
God is a distant—stately Lover.
God is indeed a jealous God.
Good Morning—Midnight.
Great Streets of silence led away.
He ate and drank the precious Words.
He fumbles at Your Spirit.
He preached upon 'Breadth' till it argued him
   narrow.
He Put the Belt Around My Life.
He showed me heights I never saw.
He touched me, so I live to know.
Heart asks Pleasure—first, The.
Heart! We [*or* Heart, we] will forget him!
"Heaven"—is what I cannot reach!
"Heavenly Father"—take to thee.
Her breast is fit for pearls.
Her face was in a bed of hair.
Her—'last Poems.'
Her Losses make our Gains ashamed.
Her Sweet turn to leave the Homestead.
Her sweet Weight on my Heart at Night.
His Feet are shod with Gauze.
His Mansion in the Pool.
"Hope" is the thing with feathers.
How brittle are the Piers.
How happy is the little Stone.
How many times these low feet staggered.
How noteless Men, and Pleiads, stand.
How the old Mountains drip with Sunset.
I am afraid to own a Body.
I am alive—I guess.
I asked no other thing.
I can wade Grief.
I cannot be ashamed.

I cannot dance upon my Toes.
I cannot live with You.
I could bring You Jewels—had I a mind to.
I died for Beauty—but was scarce.
I dreaded that first Robin, so.
I dwell in Possibility.
I felt a Cleaving in my Mind.
I Felt a Funeral in My Brain.
I found the words to every thought.
I gave myself to Him—.
I got so I could take his name.
I had been hungry, all the Years.
I had no time to Hate.
I had not minded—Walls.
I have no Life but this.
I heard a Fly buzz—when I died.
I know some lonely Houses off the Road.
I know that He exists.
I like a look of Agony.
I like to see it lap the Miles.
I'll tell you how the Sun rose.
I'm ceded—I've stopped being Theirs.
I'm Nobody! Who are you?
I'm sorry for the Dead—Today.
I many times thought Peace had come.
I measure every Grief I meet.
I met a King this afternoon!
I never hear the word "escape."
I never lost as much but twice.
I never saw a Moor.
I reason, Earth is short.
I reckon—when I count at all.
I saw no Way. The Heavens were stitched.
I shall keep singing!
I shall know why—when Time is over.
I should have been too glad, I see.
I showed her Heights she never saw.
I stepped from Plank to Plank.
I suppose the time will come.
I taste a liquor never brewed.
I think I was enchanted.
I think that the Root of the Wind is Water.
I think the Hemlock likes to stand.
I think to Live—may be a Bliss.
I took my Power in my Hand.
I took one Draught of Life.
I've known a Heaven, like a Tent.
I've seen a Dying Eye.
I watched the Moon around the House.
I would not paint—a picture.
I Years had been from Home.
If I can stop one Heart from breaking.
If I may have it, when it's dead.
If What we could—were what we would.
If you were coming in the Fall.
Immortal is an ample word.
In this short Life.
In Winter in my Room.
Infinite a sudden Guest, The.
It always felt to me—a wrong.
It ceased to hurt me, though so slow.
It dropped so low—in my regard.
It feels a shame to be Alive.
It is an honorable Thought.
It might be lonelier.
It's easy to invent a Life.
It's like the Light.
It was a quiet way—.
It was not Death, for I stood up.
It was too late for Man.
It would have starved a Gnat.
It would never be Common—more—I said.
Just as He spoke it from his Hands.
Lad of Athens, faithful be.
Last Night that She lived, The.
Let me not thirst with this Hock at my Lip.
Let my first Knowing be of thee.
Light exists in Spring, A.
Lightly stepped a yellow star.
Lightning is a yellow Fork, The.
Like Rain it sounded till it curved.
Little Dog that wags his tail, A.
Little East of Jordan, A.
Little Madness in the Spring, A.
Little Road—not made of Man, A.
Loneliness One dare not sound, The.
Look of thee, what is it like, The.

Loss of something ever felt I, A.
Man may make a Remark, A.
Martyr Poets—did not tell, The.
Me—come! My dazzled face.
Me from Myself—to banish.
Mine—by the Right of the White Election!
Mine Enemy is growing old.
Missing All—prevented Me, The.
Moon is distant from the Sea, The.
Moon upon her fluent Route, The.
More than the Grave is closed to me.
Morning after Woe, The.
Morns are meeker than they were, The.
Mountains grow—unnoticed, The.
Much Madness is divinest Sense.
Murmur of a Bee, The.
Murmuring of Bees, has ceased, The.
Musicians wrestle everywhere.
My Cocoon tightens—Colors tease.
My friend must be a Bird.
My life closed twice before its close.
My Life had stood—a Loaded Gun.
My nosegays are for Captives.
My period had come for Prayer.
My Portion is Defeat—today.
My Triumph lasted till the Drums.
Name—of it—is "Autumn," The.
Nature—sometimes sears a Sapling.
Nature—the Gentlest Mother is.
Nearest Dream recedes—unrealized, The.
Nearness to Tremendousness, A.
No Bobolink—reverse His Singing.
No Brigadier throughout the Year.
No Passenger was known to flee.
No Rack can torture me.
None can experience stint.
Not any higher stands the Grave.
Not "Revelation" 'tis, that waits.
Not probable—The barest Chance.
Of Course—I prayed.
Of nearness to her sundered Things.
Of Paul and Silas it is said.
Oh give it Motion—deck it sweet.
Oh Sumptuous moment.
On a Columnar Self.
On such a night, or such a night.
One Blessing had I than the rest.
One crown that no one seeks.
One Crucifixion is recorded—only.
One need not be a Chamber—to be Haunted.
One of the ones that Midas touched.
One who could repeat the Summer day, The.
Only News I know, The.
Opinion is a flitting thing.
Our journey had advanced.
Our lives are Swiss.
Ourselves we do inter with sweet derision.
Outer—from the Inner, The.
Over and over, like a Tune.
Over the fence.
Pain—expands the Time.
Pain—has an Element of Blank.
Partake as doth the Bee.
Pass to thy Rendezvous of Light.
Pedigree of Honey, The.
Perception of an object costs.
Perhaps I asked too large.
Pit—but Heaven over it, A.
Poets light but Lamps, The.
Popular Heart is a Cannon first, The.
Prayer is the little implement.
Precious—moldering pleasure—'tis, A.
Prison gets to be a friend, A.
Promise This, When You be Dying.
Props assist the House, The.
Province of the Saved, The.
Publication—is the Auction.
Read—Sweet—how others—strove.
Rearrange a "Wife's" affection!
"Remember me" implored the Thief!
Remorse—is Memory—awake.
Renunciation—is a piercing Virtue.
Reportless Subjects, to the Quick.
Riddle we can guess, The.
Saddest noise, the sweetest noise, The.
Safe in their Alabaster Chambers.
Satisfaction—is the Agent.

Savior! I've no one else to tell.
Savior must have been, The.
Severer Service of myself.
Shade upon the mind there passes, A.
She dealt her pretty words like Blades.
She rose to His Requirement—dropt.
Single Screw of Flesh, A.
Sky is low—the Clouds are mean, The.
So much Summer.
So proud she was to die.
So well that I can live without.
Soft Sea washed around the House, A.
Softened by Time's consummate plush.
Solemn thing—it was—I said, A.
Some keep the Sabbath going to Church.
Some one prepared this mighty show.
Some things that fly there be.
Somehow myself survived the Night.
Soul has Bandaged moments, The.
Soul's distinct connection, The.
Soul's Superior instants, The.
Soul selects her own Society, The.
Soul that hath a Guest, The.
Sown in dishonor!
Spider holds a Silver Ball, The.
Spider sewed at Night, A.
Spirit lasts, but in what mode, The.
Split the Lark—and you'll find the Music.
Spring is the Period.
Stimulus beyond the Grave, The.
Strong Draughts of Their Refreshing Minds.
Struck, was I, not yet by Lightning.
Success is counted sweetest.
Sun and Fog contested, The.
Sun kept setting—setting—still, The.
Sunrise runs for Both, The.
Surgeons must be very careful.
Sweet Mountains—Ye tell Me no lie.
Tell all the Truth but tell it slant.
That after horror that was us.
That I did always love.
That it will never come again.
That Love is all there is.
Their Height in Heaven comforts not.
There are two Mays.
There came a Wind like a Bugle.
There comes an hour when begging stops.
There is a Languor of the Life.
There is a morn by men unseen.
There is a pain—so utter.
There is a Zone whose even Years.
There is another Loneliness.
There is no Frigate like a Book.
There is no Silence in the Earth—so silent.
There's a certain Slant of light.
There's been a Death, in the Opposite House.
These are the Nights that Beetles love.
These—saw Visions.
These Strangers, In a Foreign World.
They have a little Odor—that to me.
They might not need me—yet they might.
They put Us far apart.
They say that "Time assuages."
They shut me up in Prose.
This Consciousness that is aware.
This dirty—little—Heart.
This docile one inter.
This is my letter to the World.
This was a Poet—It is That.
This World is not Conclusion.
Those—dying then.
Thought beneath so slight a film, The.
Thought went up my mind today, A.
Throe upon the features, A.
Through the Dark Sod—as Education.
Through the strait pass of suffering.
Tie the Strings to my Life, My Lord.
Tint I cannot take—is best, The.
'Tis customary as we part.
'Tis little I— could care for Pearls.
'Tis not that Dying hurts us so.
'Tis Opposites—entice.
'Tis so appalling—it exhilirates.
'Tis so much joy! 'Tis so much joy!
Title divine—is mine!
To fight aloud, is very brave.
To flee from memory.

To know just how He suffered—would be
    dear.
To learn the Transport by the Pain.
To lose one's faith—surpass.
To make a prairie it takes a clover and one bee.
To make One's Toilette—after Death.
To pile like Thunder to its close.
Too happy Time dissolves itself.
Trees like Tassels—hit—and swung, The.
Triumph—may be of several kinds.
Truth—is as old as God.
'Twas here my summer paused.
'Twas just this time, last year, I died.
'Twas warm—at first—like Us.
Two swimmers wrestled on the spar.
Under the Light, yet under.
Until the Desert knows.
Victory comes late.
Visitor in Marl, A.
Volcanoes be in Sicily.
Water, is taught by thirst.
Way I read a Letter's—this, The.
We do not play on Graves.
We dream—it is good we are dreaming.
We grow accustomed to the Dark.
We learned the Whole of Love.
We like March—his shoes are Purple.
We lose—because we win.
We miss a Kinsman more.
We miss Her, not because We see.
We outgrow love like other things.
Went up a year this evening!
What care the Dead, for Chanticleer.
What mystery pervades a well!
What Soft—Cherubic Creatures.
When Bells stop ringing—Church—begins.
When Night is almost done.
When we stand on the tops of Things.
"Why do I love" You, Sir?
Why make it doubt—it hurts it so.
Wife—at Daybreak I shall be, A.
Wild Nights—Wild Nights!
Wind begun to knead the Grass, The.
Wind—tapped like a tired man, The.
Wind that rose, A.
Wind took up the Northern Things, The.
Wonder—is not precisely Knowing.
Word is dead, A.
Word made Flesh is seldom, A.
Wounded Deer—leaps highest, A.
You're right—"the way is narrow."

Dickinson, Patric (b. 1914)
    Advent; a Carol.
    St. Stephen's Day.
Dickinson, Peter (b. 1927)
    Moses and the Princess.
Dickson, John
    Aragon Ballroom, The.
    Poemectomy.
Dickson, Samuel Henry (1798–1872)
    Song—Written at the North.
Didsbury, Peter (b. 1946)
    Bee, A.
    Hailstone, The.
    Priest in the Sabbath Dawn Addresses His
        Somnolent Mistress, A.
Diego, Gerardo (1896–1987)
    Sleeplessness.
Dietz, Howard (1896–1983)
    Alone Together.
    Blue Grass.
    Dancing in the Dark.
    Haunted Heart.
    I Guess I'll Have to Change My Plan.
    I See Your Face Before Me.
    If There Is Someone Lovelier Than You.
    Rhode Island Is Famous for You.
    Something to Remember You By.
    That's Entertainment.
    Triplets.
    You and the Night and the Music.
Digby, John (1580–1655)
    Grieve Not, Dear Love.
    One Night Away from Day.
    Sooner or Later.
Digges, Deborah
    Akhmatova.

Five Smooth Stones.
Rough Music.
Diller, John Irving
    Lullaby Town.
Dillon, George (b. 1906)
    Hours of the Day, The.
    Snow.
Dimitrova, Blaga (b. 1922)
    Blind woman was more intimate with it, The.
Dingo, Ernie
    Aboriginal achievement.
    Tracks and the traces, The.
    We are not.
Dinka Oral Tradition
    Magnificent Bull, The.
Dīnrām
    Being the child of a Mad Mother.
    From the time of the womb.
    I've given up wanting.
    Ma, I've drunk Your poisoned nectar.
    O Baba! Look at this Cadak tree.
    Out of love for You.
    Renunciation's agonies.
Diodes
    Somebody said when snubbed, "Is Damon so."
Diodoros of Sardis
    Young child of Diodoros's house, A.
Diodorus Zonas (b. 125? B.C.)
    Come tawny bees.
    For Demeter winnowing, for the Hours who
        haunt the furrows.
    From the field's plane tree.
    Pan Asks about Daphnis.
    Pomegranate just splitting, a peach just furry,
        A.
    Spare the mother of acorns, man. Cut down
        some paliurus.
    Who in the waters of this reedy lake.
Diogenes Laertius (fl. A.D. 3rd cent.)
    Nor, by God, shall we neglect.
    Tauromancy at Memphis.
Dionysius
    No wonder I slipped, being soaked.
Dionysius Sophistes (Dionysius of Andros)
    You hold a bunch of roses, Rose.
Diop, Birago (b. 1906)
    Animism.
    Ball.
    Breaths.
    Desert.
    Diptych.
    Kassak.
    Omen.
    Spirits.
    Vanity.
    Viaticum.
Diop, David (1927–60)
    Africa.
    Challenge.
    For a Black Child.
    For My Mother.
    He Who Has Lost All.
    Hours, The.
    Listen Comrades.
    Negro Tramp.
    Rama Kam.
    Renegade, The.
    Suffer, Poor Negro!
    Those Who Lost Everything.
    Time of Martyrdom, The.
    Vultures, The.
    With You.
    Your Presence.
Diophanes of Myrina
    On Love.
    Thief, and triply so!, A.
Dioscorides (fl. 3rd cent. B.C.)
    First fruits from her fruitful bed, The.
    My Downfall.
    Thracian page-boy / mastered, A.
    Zephyr, kindliest of winds.
Dioscorides (fl. 1st cent. B.C. or A.D. 1st cent.)
    Call me Polyxena, the wife of Archelaus.
    Eros, that bane of men, molded soft as
        marrow.

Hiero's former Nurse.
Lamisca, who breathed her last in lamentable pangs of labor.
They drive me mad, those rosy lips, forever prattling.
Diotimus (fl. c.250 B.C.)
Cold Pastoral.
Homing at dusk—the snow falls on them—cattle.
Polyaenus' daughter, Scyllis, came to the wide gates.
What use to suffer in labor, give birth to children, if she.
Without the Herdsman.
DiPalma, Ray (b. 1943)
Annotations Tropes and Lacunae of the Itoku Master.
Bed, The.
Each Moment is Surrounded.
Empire Smoke, Forgeries, Salient and The Ritz.
Fragment.
Hadrian's Lane.
Memory's Wedge.
Motion of the Cypher.
Pink Maniac, A.
Poem for Claude.
Poem: "In danger of which."
Prerogative of Lieder, The.
Rebus Tact.
Rumor's Rooster.
Sheaf Mark.
Table, The.
We Forego Mimicry.
When Torrid Rhymes with Forehead.
Wrong Side of the Door, The.
DiPasquale, Emanuel (b. 1943)
Rain.
Dipoko, Mbella Sonne (b. 1936)
Autobiography.
Exile.
From My Parisian Diary.
Our Life.
Pain.
Poem of Villeneuve St Georges, A.
DiPrima, Chani
Her Eyes a Thousand Times Over.
Disch, Thomas M. [or "Tom"] (b. 1940)
Abecedary.
Agreement of Predicate Pronouns, The.
Ballade of the New God.
Bookmark, A.
Clouds, The.
Convalescing in London.
Entropic Villanelle.
Garage Sale as a Spiritual Exercise, The.
La, La, La!
Poems: "I think that I shall never read."
Rapist's Villanelle, The.
Zewhyexary.
Dissanayake, Wimal (b. 1939)
Freedom.
Ditlevsen, Tove (1918–76)
Eternal Three, The.
Self Portrait 4.
Dittberner-Jax, Norita
Blues for Aunt Ruth.
Divakaruni, Chitra (b. 1956)
At Muktinath.
Brides Come to Yuba City, The.
Childhood.
Founding of Yuba City, The.
Indian Movie, New Jersey.
Indigo.
Leaving Yuba City.
Outside Pisa.
Restroom.
Yuba City School.
Dixon, Henry (1675–1760)
Description of a Good Boy, The.
Dixon, Melvin
Getting Your Rocks Off.
Grandmother: Crossing Jordan.
Heartbeats.
Place, Places.

Tour Guide: La Maison des Esclaves.
Dixon, Mort (1892–1956)
Bye Bye Blackbird.
Great Big Bunch of You, A.
I Found a Million Dollar Baby (In a Five and Ten Cent Store)
Lady in Red, The.
Nagasaki.
River, Stay 'Way from My Door.
Would You Like to Take a Walk?
Dixon, Richard Watson (1833–1900)
Both Less and More.
Dawning.
Dream.
Song: "Feathers of the willow, The."
To Peace.
Winter Will Follow.
Wizard's Funeral, The.
Dixon, Sarah (fl. 1716–45)
Close to Aminta, on the Loss of Her Lover.
Lines Occasioned by the Burning of Some Letters.
Request of Alexis, The.
Returned Heart, The.
Slattern, The.
To Strephon.
Verses Left on a Lady's Toilet.
Dixon, Zuhur (b. 1933)
Dialogue of the Night of the Roses.
Overture.
Season of Beginning and End.
Two Hands on the Water.
Dizhur, Bella Abramovna (b. 1903)
Eve's Monologue.
Here is an island. Here is a house on stilts.
Silence.
With tender back glistening.
Djabali, Leila (b. 1933)
For my Torturer, Lieutenant D.
Djanikian, Gregory (b. 1949)
How I Learned English.
In the Elementary School Choir.
When I First Saw Snow.
Djogo, Gojko (b. 1940)
Black Sheep, The.
National Hero, The.
Wooden Handle, The.
Djoko Damono, Sapardi (b. 1940)
Mask.
Djurberaui
All You Others, Eat.
D'Lettuso, Homer
Old Houses.
Dlugos, Tim (d. 1991)
Gilligan's Island.
Đỗ Tấn Xuân
Twenty Years.
Doan Van Kham (fl. 1090)
Remembering Priest Quang Tri.
Doane, George Washington (1799–1858)
Evening Contemplation.
Fling Out the Banner!
Once More, O Lord.
Thou Art the Way.
Doane, William Croswell (1832–1913)
Ancient of Days.
Preacher's Mistake, The.
Dobbie, Joan (b. 1946)
Forty Three Years After Hitler My Parents Visit Eugene.
Dobell, Sydney Thompson (1824–74)
Ballad of Keith of Ravelston, The.
Chanted Calendar, A.
Liberty to M. le Diplomate.
Perhaps.
Tommy's Dead.
Dobson, Austin (Henry Austin Dobson) (1840–1921)
All passes. Art alone.
Ballad of 'Beau Brocade,' The.
Before Sedan.
Dora versus Rose.
Fame and Friendship.
Garden Song, A.

In After Days.
In Town.
Incognita.
Ladies of St. James's, The.
Sundial, The.
Urceus Exit.
Virtuoso, A.
Dobson, John (fl. c.1746)
Robin; a Pastoral Elegy.
Dobson, Rosemary (b. 1920)
Being Called For.
Bystander, The.
Child with a Cockatoo.
Country Press.
Edge, The.
Eutychus.
Fever, The.
Folding the Sheets.
In a Café.
Three Fates, The.
Dobyns, Stephen (b. 1941)
Allegorical Matters.
Dancing in Vacationland.
Exile.
Freight Cars.
Frenchie.
How to Like It.
Nouns of Assemblage.
Seeing Off a Friend.
Woman who kicked out the back window, The.
Dock, Christopher (d. 1771)
O Children, Would You Cherish?
Docwra, Anne (1624–1710)
Mystery of Profession great, The.
Dodd, Elizabeth (b. 1962)
Dieback.
Like Memory, Caverns.
Lyric: "It doesn't matter / whether / a tree falls."
Touched.
Dodd, Wayne (b. 1930)
Of His Life.
Of Rain and Air.
Doddridge, Philip (1702–51)
Christ's Resurrection and Ascension.
Hark, the glad sound! the Saviour comes.
Hymn: "Ye golden lamps of heaven, farewell."
Live While You Live.
Meditations on the Sepulchre in the Garden.
Dodge, Mary Abigail (Gail Hamilton) (1833–96)
Note.
Dodge, Mary Mapes (1831–1905)
Early to Bed.
Fire in the window.
Letters at School, The.
Mayor of Scuttleton, The.
Moon Came Late, The.
Poor Crow!
Shepherd John.
Someone in the Garden.
Taking Time to Grow.
That's What We'd Do.
Tinker, Come Bring Your Solder.
Two Mysteries, The.
Way To Do It, The.
Wooden Horse, The.
Zealless Xylographer, The.
Dodgson, Charles Lutwidge See **Carroll, Lewis**
Dodsley, Robert (1703–64)
Epistle to My Friend J. B., An.
Progress of Love, The.
Rustic Courtship.
Song: "Man's a poor deluded bubble."
Stolen Kiss, The.
Dodson, Owen (1914–83)
Black Mother Praying.
Confession Stone, The.
Yardbird's Skull.
d'Oettingen, Hélène (d. 1950)
Kilimanjaro.
Outcries.
To Il y a.
Dogen (1200–53)
Coming, going, the waterfowl.
On Non-dependence of Mind.

On the Treasury of the True Dharma Eye.
Western Patriarch's doctrine is transplanted!,
  The.

Dohaku (d. 1675)
Cargoless.

Dokyo Etan (d. 1721)
Here in the shadow of death it is hard.

Dolben, Digby Mackworth (1848–67)
Enough.
He Would Have His Lady Sing.
One night I dreamt that in a gleaming hall.
Sea Song, A.
Song, A: "World is young today, The."

Dolin, Sharon
My Soul's Wardrobe.

Dolmatovsky Yevgeny Aronovich (b. 1915)
Hero.

Domanski, Don (b. 1950)
Deadsong.
Three Songs from the Temple.

Dombrovsky Yury Osipovich (1909–78)
I'm at the bottom again. The baron's there.
They wanted me dead, the bastards.
When they brought us a pear jacket.

Domin, Hilde (b. 1912)
Birthdays.

Domina, Lynn
Pharoah's Army Got Drowned.

Domino, Ruth (b. 1908)
Sparrow in the Dust, A.

Donaghy, John Lyle (b. 1902)
Deathward.
Duck.
Portrait.
Winter.

Donaghy, Michael (b. 1954)
Caliban's Books.

Donald, Christine M. (b. 1950)
Eye for an Eye, An.
I Expect You Think This Huge Dark Coat.

Donaldson, Walter
Because My Baby Don't Mean Maybe Now.
Carolina in the Morning.
How 'Ya Gonna Keep 'Em Down on the
  Farm? (After They've Seen Paree)
It's Been So Long.
Kansas City Kitty.
Little White Lies.
Love Me or Leave Me.
Makin' Whoopee.
My Baby Just Cares for Me.
My Blue Heaven.
Okay, Toots.
One I Love (Belongs to Someone Else), The.
T'ain't No Sin to Dance Around in Your
  Bones.
When My Ship Comes In.
Yes, Sir! That's My Baby.
You're Driving Me Crazy (What Did I Do?)

Donati, Forese
Other night I had a dreadful cough, The.
Right well I know thou'rt Alighieri's son.

Donatus, Saint (829–76)
Land Called Scotia, The.

Dongala, Emmanuel (b. 1941)
Fantasy under the Moon.

Donne, John (1572–1631)
Air[e] and Angels.
And new philosophy calls all in doubt.
Anniversary [or Anniversarie], The.
Annunciation.
Antiquary.
Apparition, The.
At the round earth's imagined corners, blow.
Autumnal[l], The.
Bait[e], The.
Batter my heart, three-personed [or three
  person'd] God; for you.
Blossom [or Blossome], The.
Bracelet, The.
Break[e] of Day.
Broken Heart, The.
Burnt Ship, A.
Calm[e], The.

Canonization, The.
Change.
Comparison, The.
Computation, The.
Confined Love.
Crown, The.
Damp[e], The.
Death be not proud, though some have called
  thee.
Dream[e], The.
Ecstasy, The.
Expiration, The.
Farewell to Love.
Father, The.
Flea, The.
Funeral[l], The.
God grant thee thine own wish, and grant thee
  mine.
Good Friday [or Goodfriday], 1613. Riding
  Westward.
Good-Morrow, The.
Hero and Leander.
Hill of Truth, The.
His Parting from Her.
His Picture.
Holy Ghost, The.
How sits this city, late most populous.
Hymn[e] to Christ, at the Author's Last Going
  into Germany, A.
Hymn[e] to God My God, In My
  Sickness[e], A.
Hymn[e] to God the Father, A.
Hymn to the Saints, and to Marquis Hamilton.
I am a little world made cunningly.
If poisonous [or poysonous] mineral[l]s, and if
  that tree.
Indifferent, The.
Jet Ring Sent, A.
Klockius.
La Corona.
Lame Beggar, A.
Lecture upon the Shadow, A.
Licentious Person, A.
Love's Alchemy [or Alchemie].
Love's Deity [or Deitie].
Love's Growth.
Love's Progress.
Lovers' Infiniteness[e].
Message, The.
Nativity [or Nativitie].
Nature's lay idiot [or ideot], I taught thee to
  love.
Nocturnal[l] upon Saint Lucy's [or S. Lucy's
  or S. Lucies] Day, Being the Shortest
  Day, A.
O might those sigh[e]s and tear[e]s return[e]
  again[e].
Ode: "Vengeance will sit above our faults; but
  till."
Oh, let me not serve so, as those men serve.
Oh my black[e] soul[e]! now thou art
  summoned.
Oh, to vex me, contraries [or contraryes] meet
  in one.
On His Mistress [or Mistris].
Paradox, The.
Perfume, The.
Phryne.
Poet Turned Lawyer, The.
Prohibition, The.
Raderus.
Relic, The.
Resurrection, Imperfect.
Satire 1 [A London Street].
Satire 3 [Religion].
Satire 4.
Satire 5.
Second Anniversary [or Anniversarie], The.
Seek True Religion!
Self[e] Accuser, A.
Show me dear[e] Christ, thy spouse, so bright
  and clear[e].
Since whom[e] I loved [or lov'd or lovd]
  hath paid [or payd] her last debt.
Son, The.
Song: "Go and catch a falling star."
Song: "Sweetest love, I do not go[e]."

Spit in my face ye [or you] Jew[e]s, and pierce
  my side.
Storm at Sea, A.
Storm[e], The.
Sun Rising, The.
Then, as if he would have sold.
This is my play's [or playes] last scene, here
  heavens appoint.
Thou hast made me, and shall thy work[e]
  decay?
To His Mistress Going to Bed.
To Mr. C. B.
To Mr. George Herbert.
To Mr. R. W.
To Mr. Roland Woodward.
To Mr. Tilman after He Had Taken Orders.
To Sir Henry Wotton.
To the Countess of Bedford.
To the Countess of Salisbury.
Triple Fool, The.
Twicknam [or Twickenham] Garden.
Undertaking, The.
Valediction: Forbidding Mourning, A.
Valediction: of Weeping, A.
We now lament not, but congratulate.
What if this present were the world's last
  night?
Why are we[e] by all creatures waited on?
Will, The.
Wilt thou love God, as he thee? [or thee!] then
  digest.
Woman's Constancy.

Donnell, David (b. 1939)
Canadian Prairie's View of Literature, The.
Lakes.
Potatoes.
Sandwiches.
Stepfathers.

Donnelly, Charles (1914–37)
Flowering Bars, The.
Last Poem.
Tolerance of Crows, The.

Donnelly, Susan (b. 1939)
Eve Names the Animals.

Donnelly, Tom (d. 1976)
That raddled old queen.

Donovan, Katie (b. 1962)
Entering the Mare.
First Autumn Night.
Grooming.
These Last Days.
Underneath Our Skirts.
We Were Sisters Weren't We.

Donsui (d. 1729)
Lotus seeds in ten.

Donze, Richard
Vermont Has a High Suicide Rate.

Doolan, Frank
Last Fullblood, The.
Whiteman Is the Judge, The.
Who Owns Darling Street?

Dooley, David (b. 1947)
How I Wrote It.

Dooley, Maura (b. 1957)
At Les Deux Magots.
Dancing at Oakmead Road.
Does It Go Like this?
Heart.
Heat.
History.
Letters from Yorkshire.
Mansize.
No, Go On.
Up on the Roof.
What Every Woman Should Carry.

Doolittle, Hilda ("H. D.") (1886–1961)
Acon.
Adonis.
At Baia.
At Ithaca.
Birds in Snow.
Centaur Song.
Circe.
Egypt.
Epitaph: "So I may say."

Evadne.
Evening.
Eurydice, *sels.*
Flowering of the Rod, The, *sels.*
Fragment 36 [*or* Thirty-Six]: "I know not what to do."
Fragment 113: "Not honey, / not the plunder of the bee."
Garden, The.
Gather for festival.
Good Friend, *sels.*
Halycon, *sels.*
Heat.
Helen.
Helen in Egypt, *sels.*
Helmsman, The.
Hermes of the Ways.
Hippolytus Temporizes.
Holy Satyr.
Islands, The.
Lais.
Leda.
Let Zeus Record, *sels.*
Lethe.
Mid-day.
Moon in Your Hands, The.
Mysteries Remain, The.
Mysteries, The.
Never more will the wind.
Orchard.
Oread.
Pear Tree.
Pool, The.
Priest, *sels.*
Pursuit.
Red Rose and a Beggar.
Sagesse, *sels.*
Sea Iris.
Sea Poppies.
Sea Rose.
Sea Violet.
Shrine, The.
Sigil, *sels.*
Song: "You are as gold."
Storm.
Trance.
Tribute to the Angels, *sels.*
Walls Do Not Fall, The, *sels.*
We see her hand in her lap.
Where is the nightingale.
White World.
Wind Sleepers, The.
Wine Bowl.
Winter Love, *sels.*

Doplicher, Fabio (b. 1938)
Asymmetry of the Universe.
Discords.
Interludes.
Unfinished Exile.

Dorcey, Mary (b. 1950)
First Love.
Night.
Sea Flower.

Dorchester, Katherine Colyear, Countess of (1657–1717)
As Frazier one night at her Post in the Drawing Room stood.

Dorfman, Ariel (b. 1942)
I Just Missed the Bus and I'll Be Late for Work.
Last Waltz in Santiago.
Vocabulary.

Doria, Prinzivalle (*fl.* 12th cent.)
Canzone: Of His Love, with the Figure of a Sudden Storm.

D'Orleans, Charles
Oft in My Thought.
Smiling Mouth, The.

Dormer, Anne, Lady Hungerford (d. 1603)
Lady Hungerford's Meditacions upon the Beades, The.

Dorn, Edward (b. 1929)
Air of June Sings, The.
Are They Dancing.
Biggest Killing, The.
Comforted by Limestone.

For the New Union Dead in Alabama.
From Gloucester Out.
Geranium.
Hide of My Mother, The.
Home on the Range, February 1962.
I met in Mesilla.
Idle Visitation, An.
La Máquina a Houston.
Los Mineros.
Morning to Remember, A; or, E Pluribus Unum.
Mourning Letter, March 29 1963.
On the Debt My Mother Owed to Sears Roebuck.
Rick of Green Wood, The.
Song, A.
Song, The: "So light no one noticed."
Thesis.
Vaquero.
When the Fairies.

Dornin, Christopher L.
In a Building Named for a Governor.

Dorough, Bob
I'm Hip.

Dorr, Julia Caroline Ripley (1825–1913)
Not Mine.

Dorris, Michael (1945–97)
Prey.

Dorsett, Thomas
Survivor, The.

Dorsey, Jimmy
I'm Glad There Is You (In This World of Ordinary People)

Dorsey, Thomas A. (1899–1993)
Take My Hand, Precious Lord.

Dotremont, Christian (1922–1979)
Some Lapland Views.

Doty, Mark (b. 1953)
Almost Blue.
Aubade: Opal and Silver.
Beau: Golden Retrievals.
Days of 1981.
Embrace, The.
Homo Will Not Inherit.
Letter from the Coast, A.
Lilacs in NYC.
Michael's Dream.
My Tattoo.
New Dog.
No.
Tiara.
Ware Collection of Glass Flowers and Fruit, Harvard Museum, The.

Doubiago, Sharon
Out the window, Colombia, out the window.

Double-face
If there is someone above.

Doubleday, Thomas (1790–1870)
Friends, when my latest bed of rest is made.
No walk today;—November's breathings toss.
Poppies, that scattered o'er this arid plain.

Dougherty, Dan
Glad Rag Doll.

Dougherty, Sean Thomas (b. 1965)
Cocoons.
Double Helix.
Long Coats with Deep Pockets.
Puerto Rican Girls of French Hill, The.

Doughty, Charles Montague (1843–1926)
Gauls Sacrifice, The.
Hymn to the Sun.
Roman Emperor Writes, A.

Douglas, Gawin [*or* Gavin] (1474?–1522)
Prolog of the Sevynt Buik, The.
Prolog of the Twelt Buik, The.

Douglas, Keith (1920–44)
Aristocrats.
Behaviour of Fish in an Egyptian Tea Garden.
Cairo Jag.
Deceased, The.
Desert Flowers.
Egypt.
Enfidaville.
Gallantry.
How to Kill.

Knife, The.
Marvel, The.
Offensive, The.
On a Return from Egypt.
Prisoner, The.
Russians.
Simplify Me When I'm Dead.
Soissons.
Vergissmeinicht.

Douglas, Lord Alfred Bruce (1870–1945)
Dead Poet, The.
Green River, The.
Impression de Nuit; London.
Rejected.
To Olive.
To Sleep.
Two Loves.

"Douglas, Marian" (Annie Douglas Green Robinson) (1842–1913)
Ant-Hills.
Snow-Man, The.

Douglas, Norman
Limerick: "There was a young fellow named Skinner."
Limerick: "There was a young lady of Louth."

Douglass, Frederick (c.1817–95)
Parody, A.

Douskey, Franz (b. 1941)
Dog Days and Delta Nights.
Wet Bodies.

Dovaston, John F. M. (1782–1852)
Streamlet! methinks thy lot resembles mine.
There are who say the sonnet's meted maze.

Dove, Angela
Crab.

Dove, Olive
Dragon.

Dove, Rita (b. 1952)
Adolescence—I.
Adolescence—II.
Adolescence—III.
After Reading *Mickey in the Night Kitchen* for the Third Time Before Bed.
Banneker.
Beauty and the Beast.
Bistro Styx, The.
Blue Days.
Canary.
Centipede.
Courtship.
Daystar.
Demeter Mourning.
Demeter's Prayer to Hades.
Demeter, Waiting.
Dusting.
Event, The.
Exit.
Fifth Grade Autobiography.
First Book, The.
Fish in the Stone, The.
Flash Cards.
Genie's Prayer Under the Kitchen Sink.
Geometry.
Götterdämmerung.
Great Palaces of Versailles, The.
History.
Horse and Tree.
House Slave, The.
Hully Gully.
In the Old Neighborhood.
Island Women of Paris, The.
Lady Freedom Among Us.
"Blown Apart By Loss . . . ."
Lint.
Listen to the Sound of My Horn.
Motherhood.
Musician Talks About 'Process,' The.
Ö.
Wingfoot Lake.
Oriental Ballerina, The.
Parsley.
Passage, The.
Pastoral: "Like an otter, but warm."
Persephone Abducted.
Persephone Underground.
Planning the Perfect Evening.

Poem in Which I Refuse Contemplation.
Political.
Rosa.
Satisfaction Coal Company, The.
Secret Garden, The.
Sightseeing.
Small Town.
Alfonzo Prepares to Go Over the Top.
Statistic: The Witness.
Straw Hat.
Sunday Greens.
Teach Us to Number Our Days.
This Life.
Tou Wan Speaks to Her Husband Liu Sheng.
Turning Thirty, I Contemplate Students
  Bicycling Home.
Vacation.
Weathering Out.
Who can forget the attitude of mothering?
Wiederkehr.

Dover, Sibella Cole (*fl.* 1630)
To Her Modest Mirth-Making Friend, Mr
  Robert Dover.

Dow, Philip (b. 1937)
Drunk Last Night with Friends, I Go to Work
  Anyway.

Dow, Robert
How Should I Say This?

Dowden, Edward (1843–1913)
Burdens.
In the Cathedral Close.
Leonardo's "Mona Lisa."
Singer, The.
Two Infinities.

Dowe, Katherine (*fl.* before 1588)
Arise earelie.

Dower, E. (*fl.* c.1738)
New River Head, a Fragment, The.

Dowland, John (1562–1626)
Come Away, Come, Sweet Love.
Dear, If You Change.
Fine knacks for ladies, cheape choise brave
  and new.

Downie, Freda
Great-Grandfather.
Her Garden.
Italians Are Excited, The.
Miss Grant.
Starlight.

Dowriche, Anne (*fl.* 1589–96)
Admiralls Being Slaine, They Likewise . . . ,
  The.
So him at first *De Nance* commanded was to
  kill.
Verses Written by a Gentlewoman upon the
  Jaylors Conversion.

Dowson, Ernest Christopher (1867–1900)
Autumnal.
Carthusians.
Dregs.
Epigram: "Because I am idolatrous and have
  besought."
Exchanges.
Exile.
Extreme Unction.
Flos Lunae.
Gray Nights.
Last Word, A.
Non Sum Qualis Eram Bonae sub Regno
  Cynarae.
O Mors! Quam Amara Est Memoria Tua
  Homini Pacem Habenti In Substantiis Suis.
Spleen.
Terre Promise.
To One in Bedlam.
Valediction, A.
Vesperal.
Villanelle of His Lady's Treasures.
Villanelle of Marguerites.
Villanelle of the Poet's Road.
Vitae Summa Brevis Spem Nos Vetat Incohare
  Longam.
You would have understood me, had you
  waited.

Doyle, Sir Arthur Conan
To An Undiscerning Critic.

Doyle, Sir Francis Hastings (1810–88)
Private of the Buffs; or, The British Soldier in
  China.

Doyle, Kirby (1810–88)
Strange.

Doyle, R. Erica (b. 1968)
Ma Ramon.

Doyle, Susanne
Hell to Pay.
Some Girls.
This Shade.

Doyu (1201–56)
In all my six and fifty years.

Drachler, Rose (b. 1911)
As I Am My Father's.
Athens and Jerusalem.
Evening of the Sixth Day, The.
Prophet, The.
Witness, The.

Dragomoschenko, Arkadii (b. 1946)
Footnotes.
Instructing Clarity in a Confusion.
March Elegy.
Sentimental Elegy, A.

Drake, Ervin (b. 1919)
Friendliest Thing (Two People Can Do), The.
It Was a Very Good Year.
Just for Today.

Drake, Francis (b. 1650, d. after 1668)
To the Memory of the Learned and Reverend,
  Mr. Jonathan Mitchell.

Drake, Joseph Rodman (1795–1820)
American Flag, The.
Bronx.
Mocking-Bird, The.
National Painting, The.
Niagara.
To a Friend.

Drake, Nick (b. 1961)
Foley Artist, The.
Man in the White Suit, The.
Very Rich Hours, The.

Dransfield, Michael (1948–73)
Bum's Rush.
Day at a Time.
Endsight.
Epiderm.
Fix.
Flying.
In the forest, in unexplored.
Loft.
Memoirs of a Velvet Urinal.
Minstrel.
Pas de Deux for Lovers.
Pioneer Lane.
Portrait of the Artist as an Old Man.
Rainpoem.
Self-analysis.
Sky ceases. There is only.
Strange Bird, A.
That Which We Call a Rose.
Visiting Hour (Repatriation Hospital)
War of the Roses, The.

Draycott, Jane
Prince Rupert's Drop, The.

Drayton, Michael (1563–1631)
Another to the River Ankor.
As Love and I.
Battle of Agincourt, The.
Crier, The.
Cupid, I Hate Thee.
England's Heroical Epistles, *sels.*
Heart, The.
His Defence Against the Idle Critic.
Idea, *sels.*
Idea's Mirror, *sels.*
In time the Princess playing with the child.
Like an Adventurous Seafarer Am I.
Methinks I See Some Crooked Mimic Jeer.
Most Excellent Song which Was Solomon's
  The, *sels.*
Muses Elysium X, *sels.*
Noah's Flood, *sels.*
Ode Written in the Peak[e], An.
Other Song of the Faithful, for the Mercies of

God, An.
Our sacred Muse, of Israel's Singer sings.
Piers Gaveston, *sels.*
Polyolbion, *sels.*
Roundelay Between Two Shepherds, A.
Sacrifice to Apollo, The.
Shepherd's Garland, The, *sels.*
Song of Jonah in the Whale's Belly, The.
Song of the Faithful, A.
Sonnet 35: 'Some, misbelieving and profane.'
To His Coy Love, A Canzonet.
To My Noble Friend Master William Browne:
  Of the Evil Time.
To the New Yeere [*or* Year].
To the Virginian Voyage.

Drennan, John Swanwick [*or* Swanick] (1809–93)
Epigram: "Golden casket I designed, A."
Epigram: "Love signed the contract blithe and
  leal."
L'Amitié et l'Amour.
On the Telescopic Moon.

Dressel, Jon (b. 1931)
Dai, Live.
Drouth, The.
Intercity, Swansea-London.
Let's Hear It for Goliath.
You, Benjamin Jones.

Drevniok, Betty
Deep snow.
Snow at dusk.

Drieu la Rochelle, Pierre (1893–1945)
Roundness.
Tennis.

"Drinan, Adam" See MacLeod, Joseph Gordon

Drinkwater, John (1882–1937)
Birthright.
Cottage Song.
Moonlit Apples.
Sun, The.
Who Were before Me.

Driscoll, Louise (b. 1875)
Hold Fast Your Dreams.

Driskell, Maudelle
Talismans.

Driver, C. J. (b. 1941)
Ballad of Hunters, A.
Letter to Breyten Breytenbach from Hong
  Kong.

Drofenko, Sergey [*or* Sergei] (1937–71)
Sketches from History.

Dromgoole, Will Allen (1865–1943)
Building the Bridge.
Old Ladies.

Dronsfield, John (1900–51)
Visitation.

Droste-Hülshoff, Annette von (1797–1848)
Last Day of the Year (New Year's Eve), The.
On the Tower.

Drown, D. A.
Rose by the Wayside, The.

Drown, Lessie M.
To-Day.
To Mother.

Druce, Robert (b. 1929)
Apropos of Garden Statuary: A Disquisition
  upon a Minor Genre.

Druk, Vladimir (b. 1957)
Communal Krakovyak.
Drukascripts.

Drummond de Andrade, Carlos (1902–87)
Dead in Frock Coats, THe.
Diminutive.
Don't Kill Yourself.
Elegy: "I've won (lost) my day."
In the Middle of the Road.
Infancy.
Looking for Poetry.
Motionless Faces.
Ox Looks at Man, An.
Portrait of a Family.
Residue.
Seven-Sided Poem.
Traveling as a Family.
Your Shoulders Hold Up the World.

Drummond, William Henry (1854–1907)
Log Jam, The.
To spread the azure canopy of heaven.
Drummond, William, of Hawthornden (1585–1649)
Against the King.
All Changeth.
Blessednesse of Faithfull Soules by Death, The.
Book, The.
Change Should Breed Change.
Content and Resolute.
Doth then the world go thus, doth all thus move?
Faith Above Reason.
For a Lady's Summons of Non-Entry.
For the Baptiste.
For the Magdalene.
Forth Feasting, sels.
Hymn of the Fairest Fair, The, sels.
If of the dead save good nought should be said.
Invocation: "Pheobus, arise! / And paint the sable skies."
Kisses Desired.
Madrigal: "Ah! silly soul, what wilt thou say."
Madrigal: "Astrea in this time."
Madrigal: "Daedal of my death, A."
Madrigal: "Like the Idalian Queen[e]."
Madrigal: "My thoughts hold mortal[l] strife."
Madrigal: "This life, which seems so fair."
Madrigal: "This world a hunting is."
Madrigal: "Unhappie [or Unhappy] Light."
Mans Knowledge, Ignorance in the Misteries of God.
Midden-Battle between Lady Scotstarvit and the Mistress of Newbarns, The.
Miserable Estate of the World Before the Incarnation of God.
Oister, The.
On Pym.
Saint John Baptist.
Sanquhar, whom this earth could scarce contain.
Sextain: "Sith gone is my delight and only pleasure."
Sextain: "With elegies, sad songs, and mourning lays."
Sleep, Silence' Child.
Sonnet: "Alexis, here she stayed; among these pines."
Sonnet: "As in a duskie [or dusky] and tempestuous night."
Sonnet: "How many times Nights silent Queene her Face."
Sonnet: "I know that all beneath the moon decays."
Sonnet: "Slide soft, fair forth, and make a crystal plain."
Sonnet: "Triumphing chariots, statues, crowns of bay."
Spring Bereaved.
Spring Bereaved 2.
Stolen Pleasure.
To a Nightingale.
To Chloris.
To His Lute.
Too Long I Followed.
Word a Hunt, A.
Drunina, Yuliya [or Iuliia] Vladimirovna (1924–91)
In all ages, always, everywhere, and everywhere.
So many times I've seen hand-to-hand combat.
Dryden, John (1631–1700)
Absalom and Achitophel, sels.
Alexander's Feast; or, The Power of Music [or Musique].
Amboyna; or, The Cruelties of the Dutch to the English Merchants, sels.
Amphitryon, sels.
Annus Mirabilis, sels.
Aureng-Zebe, sels.
Character of a Good Parson, The.
Cymon and Iphigenia, sels.
Evening's Love, An, sels.
Hind and the Panther, The, sels.
Lines Printed under the Engraved Portrait of

Milton [In Tonson's Folio of the "Paradise Lost"].
Love Triumphant, sels.
Mac Flecknoe [or, A Satire upon the True-Blue Protestant Poet T. S.], sels.
Marriage à la Mode, sels.
Medal [or Medall], The, sels.
On Jacob Tonson, His Publisher.
Religio Laici, sels.
Secret Love; or The Maiden Queen, sels.
Secular Masque, The, sels.
Song for a Girl.
Song for St Cecilia's Day, 1687, A.
Song: "SYLVIA the fair, in the bloom of fifteen."
Song to a Fair Young Lady, Going Out of the Town in the Spring.
State of Innocence, The, sels.
Theodore and Honoria, sels.
Threnodia Augustalis, sels.
To My Dear Friend Mr Congreve [on His Comedy Called "The Double-Dealer"].
To the Memory of Mr Oldham.
To the Pious Memory of the Accomplished [or Accomplisht] Young Lady, Mrs. Anne Killigrew, [Excellent in the Two Sister-Arts of Poesie and Painting].
Tyrannic Love, sels.
Dryden, John (1631–1700) and Nahum Tate
Absalom and Achitophel, sels.
Troilus and Cressida, sels.
Drysdale, Ann (b. 1942)
Lament of the White Queen.
Language Difficulty.
Dsida, Jenő (1907–38)
Confession, A.
Maundy Thursday.
Poet's Resurrection, The.
Serenade for Ilonka.
Verse of Darkness, The.
What Will Come of This?
Du Bartas, Guillaume de Salluste (1544–90)
Adam, quoth He, the beauties manifold.
Tower of Babel, The.
Zodiac, The.
Du Bellay, Joachim (1522–60)
Epitaph on a Pet Cat.
Heureux Qui, Comme Ulysse, a Fait un Beau Voyage.
Hope ye, my verses, that posterity.
Hymn to the Winds.
I Saw the Bird That Dares Behold the Sun.
Regrets, sels.
Rome.
Ruins of Rome, sels.
Sonnet to Heavenly Beauty, A.
To His Friend in Elysium.
Visions of Bellay, sels.
Vow to Heavenly Venus, A.
Du Bois, Dorothea (1728–74)
Song: "Scholar first my Love implor'd, A."
Du Maurier, George (1834–96)
Music.
du Perron, E. (1899–1940)
Sick Man, The.
Du Tử Lê Lê Cự Phách
What I Leave to My Son.
Dubé, Janet
Autobiography.
So to Tell the Truth.
Dube, Oswald Basize (b. 1957)
He Was a Man of Jokes outside Office.
Dubie, Norman (b. 1945)
Anagram Born of Madness at Czernowitz, 12 November 1920.
Annual of the Dark Physics, An.
At Midsummer.
Czar's Last Christmas Letter: A Barn in the Urals, The.
Death of the Race Car Driver, The.
Elegy for Wright & Hugo.
Elizabeth's War with the Christmas Bear.
February; the Boy Breughel.
Fox Who Watched for the Midnight Sun, The.
Funeral, The.

Ganges, The.
Hummingbirds.
Lamentations.
Obscure, The.
Peace of Lodi, The.
Poem: "Mule kicked out in the trees, A. An Early."
Sanctuary.
Thomas Hardy.
Trakl.
Dubin, Al (1891–1945)
Cup of Coffee, a Sandwich, and You.
Dames.
Forty-second Street.
Gold Digger's Song (We're in the Money), The.
I'll String Along with You.
I Only Have Eyes for You.
Lullaby of Broadway.
Lulu's Back in Town.
Remember Me?
September in the Rain.
She's a Latin from Manhattan.
Shuffle Off to Buffalo.
You're Getting to Be a Habit with Me.
Young and Healthy.
Dubois, Lady Dorothea (1728–74)
Song: "Scholar first my love implored, A."
DuBois, William Edward Burghardt (1868–1963)
Litany of [or at] Atlanta, A.
Song of the Smoke, The.
Dubrava, Patricia
Miraculous Marriage of Zarife Dominquez.
Ducal, Charles (b. 1952)
Duke and I 2, The.
Duchamp, Marcel (1887–1968)
1914 Box, The.
Cast Shadows.
Deferment.
Electricity Breadthwise.
Speculations.
SURcenSURE.
World in Yellow, A.
Duché, Jacob (1738–98)
Chilled by the Blasts of Adverse Fate.
Great Lord of All, Whose Work of Love.
Duck, Stephen (1705–56)
On Richmond Park.
Soon as the harvest hath laid bare the plains.
Duclaux, Mme *See* **Robinson, Agnes Mary Frances**
Ducornet, Rikki
Dark Star, Black Star.
Machete.
My Special Madness.
Necromancy.
Dudek, Louis (b. 1918)
Coming Suddenly to the Sea.
Dead, The.
García Lorca.
Marine Aquarium, The.
Provincetown.
Dudin, Mikhail Aleksandrovich (b. 1916)
Nightingales.
Dudley, Anne Seymour (b. after 1535, d. 1587)
This sacred urn holds the ashes of the Queen of Navarre.
Dudley, Ellen
Pathologist.
Dudley, Lady Jane Grey (1537–54)
Certaine verses written by the said ladie Jane with a pinne.
Dudley, Michael
At the backyard fence.
Home late.
Lulling me to sleep.
Menstrual cramps.
Dudley, Thomas (1576–1653)
Verses Found in Thomas Dudley's Pocket after His Death.
Dudley, William E. (b. 1887)
City, Lord, Where Thy Dear Life, The.
Duemer, Joseph
Best Meals of My Life, The.

Theory of Tragedy.
Duerden, Richard (b. 1927)
  Dance with Banderillas.
  Moon Is to Blood.
  Musica No. 3.
Dufault, Peter Kane (b. 1923)
  Burden.
  First Night, A.
  Mud Dauber Wasp, The.
Duff, Valerie
  Letters from an Exile.
Dufferin, Helen Selina Blackwood, Countess of (1807–67)
  Charming Woman, The.
  Countess of Dufferin, The.
  Mother's Lament, The.
Duffield, George, Jr. (1818–88)
  Stand Up! Stand Up for Jesus.
Duffy, Carol Ann (b. 1955)
  Adultery.
  Foreign.
  Girlfriends.
  Good Teachers, The.
  Grammar of Light, The.
  Oppenheim's Cup and Saucer.
  In Your Mind.
  Prayer: "Some days, although we cannot pray, a prayer."
  Small Female Skull.
  Stealing.
  Warming Her Pearls.
  Words, Wide Night.
Duffy, Maureen (b. 1933)
  Eureka.
  I Am Beset with a Dream of Fair Woman.
  Semi-Skilled Lover.
Dugan, Alan (b. 1923)
  Actual Vision of Morning's Extrusion.
  Against a Sickness: To the Female Double Principle God.
  American Variation on How Rilke Loved a Princess and Got to Stay in Her Castle.
  Barefoot Homiletics, After Wittgenstein and Boswell.
  Drunken Memories of Anne Sexton.
  Elegy: "I know but will not tell."
  Fabrication of Ancestors.
  Funeral Oration for a Mouse.
  Glad at the Cold (1955)
  How We Heard the Name.
  Internal Migration: On Being on Tour.
  Last Statement for a Last Oracle.
  Let Heroes Account to Love.
  Letter to Eve.
  Love Song: I and Thou.
  Memorial Service for the Invasion Beach Where the Vacation in the Flesh Is Over.
  Memories of Verdun.
  Mirror Perilous, The.
  Nomenclature.
  On a Seven-Day Diary.
  On an East Wind from the Wars.
  On Being a Householder.
  On Hurricane Jackson.
  On the Elk, Unwitnessed.
  On Trees.
  Plague of Dead Sharks.
  Poem for Elliot Carter on His 90th Birthday.
  Portrait from the Infantry.
  Prayer: "God, I need a job because I need money."
  Prison Song.
  Swing Shift Blues.
  To a Red-headed Do-good Waitress.
  Wall, Cave, and Pillar Statements, after Asôka.
  Weeds as Partial Survivors.
Duggan, Eileen (1894–1972)
  Ballad of the Bushman.
  Cloudy Bay.
  Invasion.
  Prophecy.
  Rosa Luxembourg.
  Shag, The.
  Tides Run up the Wairau, The.
  Truth.
Duggan, Laurie (b. 1949)
  Eight xx.

Five. One.
Hearts (1983)
One. One.
One xxxvii.
Qantas Bags.
South Coast Haiku.
Ten ii.
Three xlvii.
Town on the Ten Dollar Note, The.
Duhamel, Denise (b. 1961)
  Art.
  Barbie's Molester.
  Bicentennial Barbie.
  Ego.
  How Much Is This Poem Going to Cost Me?
  I'm Dealing with My Pain.
  Kinky.
  Sex with a Famous Poet.
  Yes.
Duhig, Ian (b. 1954)
  First Second, The.
  Fred.
  From the Irish.
  Fundamentals.
  I prayed to the ghost of Carrie.
  I'r Hen Iaith a'i Chaneuon.
  Reforma Agraria.
  Margin Prayer from an Ancient Psalter.
  Untitled.
Duke, Richard (1658–1711)
  Song, A.
  To Caelia.
Duke, Vernon
  April in Paris.
  Autumn in New York.
  Cabin in the Sky.
  Honey in the Honeycomb.
  I Can't Get Started.
  I Like the Likes of You.
  Love Turned the Light Out.
  Make with the Feet.
  Not a Care in the World.
  Round About.
  Sea-Gull and the Ea-Gull, The.
  Summer Is a-Comin' In.
  Sweet Bye and Bye.
  Taking a Chance on Love.
  What Is There to Say?
Duke, William (1757–1840)
  Hail Our Incarnate God!
Dumas, Alexandre (1802–70)
  We set out yesterday upon a winter drive.
Dumas, Edmund (d. 1884)
  Our School Now Closes Out.
Dumas, Henry (1935–68)
  America.
  Concentration Camp Blues.
  Knees of a Natural Man.
  Island within Island.
  Root Song.
  Zebra Goes Wild Where the Sidewalk Ends, The.
Dumdum, Simeon
  Li Pos of the Polis.
  Some Die of Light.
  To My Mother.
Dunbar-Nelson, Alice Moore (1875–1935)
  April Is on the Way.
  I Sit and Sew.
  Music.
  Snow in October.
  Sonnet: "I had no thought of violets of late."
Dunbar, Paul Laurence (1872–1906)
  Accountability.
  Ante-Bellum Sermon, An.
  Boy's Summer, A.
  Cabin Tale, A.
  Colored Soldiers, The.
  Common Things.
  Companion's Progress, A.
  Compensation.
  Debt, The.
  Dinah Kneading Dough.
  Distinction.
  Douglass.

Ere Sleep Comes Down to Soothe the Weary Eyes.
Frederick Douglass.
Harriet Beecher Stowe.
Haunted Oak, The.
Her Thought and His.
Hymn, A: "Lead gently, Lord, and slow."
Hymn: "When storms arise."
In the Morning.
Little Brown Baby.
Longing.
Made to Order Smile, The.
Misapprehension.
Mystery, The.
Negro Love Song, A.
Night.
Not They Who Soar!
Ode to Ethiopia.
Paradox, The.
Passion and Love.
Philosophy.
Place Where the Rainbow Ends, The.
Poet, The.
Prayer, A: "O Lord, the hard-won miles."
Resignation.
Robert Gould Shaw.
Ships That Pass in the Night.
Signs of the Times.
Slow Through the Dark.
Soliloquy of a Turkey.
Song of Summer.
Spiritual, A.
Summer in the South.
Summer's Night, A.
Sympathy.
Theology.
To a Captious Critic.
Unsung Heroes, The.
We Wear the Mask.
When All Is Done.
When Dey 'Listed Colored Soldiers.
When Malindy Sings.
Worn Out.
Dunbar, William (c.1465–c.1530)
  All Erdly Joy Returns in Pane.
  Amendis to the Telyouris and Sowtaris for the Turnament Maid on Thame, The.
  Ballad of Kynd Kittok, The.
  Ballad of our Lady, *sels.*
  Dance of the Sevin Deidly Synnis, The.
  Done is a battle on the dragon black.
  Golden [*or* Goldyn] Targe, The, *sels.*
  In Praise of Women.
  Lament for the Makaris.
  Magryme, The.
  Man of Valour to His Fair Lady, The.
  Meditatioun in Wyntir.
  O Wretch, Beware.
  Of the Changes of Life.
  Petition of the Gray Horse, Auld Dunbar, The.
  Quod Dunbar to Kennedy.
  Remonstrance to the King.
  Testament of Mr. Andro Kennedy, The.
  To a Lady[e].
  To the City of London [*or* In Honour of the City of London].
  To the Merchantis of Edinburgh.
  Tretis of the Tua Mariit Wemen and the Wedo, The, *sels.*
  Widow Has Buried Her Second Husband, The.
Duncan, Robert (1919–88)
  Achilles' Song.
  African Elegy, An.
  After a Long Illness.
  After a Passage in Baudelaire.
  Among My Friends.
  And If He Had Been Wrong for Me.
  Ark for Lawrence Durrell, An.
  At the Loom.
  Bending the Bow.
  Childhood's Retreat.
  Chords Passages 14.
  Close.
  Coming out of.
  Correspondences.
  Dance, The.
  Dancing Concerning a Form of Women, A.

Dream Data.
Drinking Fountain, The.
Envoy: "Good Night, at last."
Eyesight II.
Feast, The.
Fire, The.
Food for Fire, Food for Thought.
Fourth Song the Night Nurse Sang.
Glimpse, A.
Homage and Lament for Ezra Pound in
    Captivity.
I Am a Most Fleshly Man.
In Blood's Domaine.
Ingmar Bergman's "Seventh Seal."
Letting the Beat Go.
Little Language, A.
Ballad of Mrs. Noah, The.
My Mother Would Be a Falconress.
New Poem, A.
Night Scenes.
Often I Am Permitted to Return to a Meadow.
Owl Is an Only Bird of Poetry, An.
Part-Sequence for Change, A.
Passage Over Water.
Passages 37.
Persephone.
Poem Beginning with a Line by Pindar, A.
Poetry, a Natural Thing.
Preface to the Suite: "Childhood, boyhood,
    young manhood."
Presence of the Dance / The Resolution of the
    Music, The.
Question, The.
Rites of Participation.
Roots and Branches.
Sentinels, The.
Sleep is a Deep and Many Voiced Flood.
Moon, The.
Song of the Borderguard, The.
Songs of an Other.
Strains of Sight.
Structure of Rime XVIII.
Structure of Rime XXIII.
Styx.
Temple of the Animals, The.
This Place Rumord to Have Been Sodom.
Torso / Passages 18, The.
Transgressing the Real.
Tribal Memories.
Turning into.
Up Rising.
Duncombe, Susanna Highmore (1725–1812)
    To Aspasia.
Dunkerley, William Arthur *See* **Oxenham, John**
Dunkin, William (1709?–65)
    Hibernia's Helicon is dry.
Dunn, Carolyn Marie
    Margaret/Haskell Indian School.
Dunn, Douglas (b. 1942)
    After the War.
    Clothes Pit, The.
    Dream of Judgement, A.
    Elegy for the Lost Parish.
    Emblems.
    Estuarial Republic, The.
    Gardeners.
    Glasgow Schoolboys, Running Backwards.
    House Next Door, The.
    I Am a Cameraman.
    In the Grounds.
    Kaleidoscope, The.
    Land Love.
    Landscape with One Figure.
    Modern Love.
    Musical Orchard, The.
    On Roofs of Terry Street.
    Patricians, The.
    Remembering Lunch.
    Removal from Terry Street, A.
    She sat up on her pillows, receiving guests.
    St Kilda's Parliament: 1879–1979.
    Sundial, The.
    Supreme Death.
    War Blinded.
    Warriors.
Dunn, Gwen
    Journey Back to Christmas.

Dunn, J. P. (*fl.* 1917)
    Kansas.
    Ode to Governor Capper, An.
Dunn, Max (b. 1895)
    O, Where Were We Before Time Was.
Dunn, Stephen (b. 1939)
    Because You Mentioned the Spiritual Life.
    Buster's Visitation.
    Competition.
    Criminal.
    Dancing with God.
    Day and Night Handball.
    Guardian Angel, The.
    Impediment.
    Man Who Closed Shop, The.
    Tenderness.
    What They Wanted.
Dunn, Stephen P. (b. 1928)
    Men Talk.
Dunne, Sean (b. 1956)
    Beans.
    Bus Station, The.
    Dead Pianist, The.
    Lost Wife, The.
    Mobile, The.
    Night Sky, The.
    Old School, The.
    Poet Upstairs, The.
    Railings.
    Refugees at Cobh.
    Tea.
    Throwing the Beads.
Dunqul, Amal (1940–82)
    City a Wrecked Ship, The.
    Corner.
    Scaffold, The.
    Tommorow.
    Trains.
Duo Duo (Li Shizheng) (b. 1951)
    At Parting.
    Handicraft—After Marina Tsvetaeva.
    In England.
    Looking Out from Death.
    Morning.
    Night.
    No More Than One Allowed.
    None.
    North Sea.
    When the People Stand Up out of the Hard
        Cheese.
    Untitled.
    When People Rise from Cheese, Statement #1.
    Wishful Thinking Is the Master of Reality.
Dupin, Jacques (b. 1927)
    From a thread in space, endless and unbroken.
        Without unravelling.
    Mineral Kingdom.
DuPlessis, Phil (b. 1944)
    Prayer for a Thief.
Dupree, Edison
    At Present I Am Working as a Security Guard.
Durack, Mary (b. 1913)
    Lament for the Drowned Country.
Duran, Jane
    For the Woman Who Dressed Up to Listen to
        Gigli on the Radio.
    Mere Pleasure of Flying, The.
    Mr Teller the Piano Teacher.
    Pyrenees, The.
    Spanish Peasant Boy.
    Stillborn.
    Time Zones.
    When I lean down to stir the bathwater.
Durand, Oswald (1840–1906)
    Black Man's Son, The.
    Francie-the-Possessed.
Durant, Mrs. Kenneth *See* **Taggard, Genevieve**
Durcan, Paul (b. 1944)
    Around the Corner from Francis Bacon.
    Backside to the Wind.
    Bewley's Oriental Café, Westmoreland Street.
    Birth of a Coachman.
    Death by Heroin of Sid Vicious, The.
    Divorce Referendum, Ireland, 1986, The.
    Going Home to Mayo, Winter, 1949.

    Hat Factory, The.
    Haulier's Wife Meets Jesus on the Road Near
        Moone, The.
    Honeymoon Postcard.
    Ireland 1972.
    Irish Hierarchy Bans Colour Photography.
    Jewish Bride, The.
    Kilfenora Teaboy, The.
    Late Mr Charles Lynch Digresses, The.
    Levite and His Concubine at Gibeah, The.
    Micheál Mac Liammóir.
    My Belovèd Compares Herself to a Pint of
        Stout.
    Pietà's Over, The.
    Raymond of the Rooftops.
    She Mends an Ancient Wireless.
    Sister Agnes Writes to Her Beloved Mother.
    10.30 AM Mass, June 16, 1985.
    Tullynoe: Tête-à-Tête in the Parish Priest's
        Parlour.
    Turkish Carpet, The.
    We resided in a Loreto convent in the centre of
        Dublin city.
    Weeping Headstones of the Isaac Becketts,
        The.
    Wife Who Smashed Television Gets Jail.
Durem, Ray (1915–63)
    Award.
    I Know I'm Not Sufficiently Obscure.
D'Urfey [or Durfey], Thomas (1653–1723)
    Chloe Divine.
    Dialogue, between Crab and Gillian.
    Fisherman's Song, The.
    I'll Sail upon the Dog-Star.
Durham, Jimmie (b. 1940)
    Columbus Day.
    Justiniano Lamé Has Been Killed.
    Middle.
    Woman Gave Me a Red Star to Wear on My
        Headband, A.
Duris (*fl.* c.3rd cent. B.C.)
    Ephesos.
Duroux, Mary
    Dirge for a Hidden Art.
    Lament for a Dialect.
Durrell, Lawrence (b. 1912)
    Acropolis.
    Ballad of the Good Lord Nelson, A.
    Ballad of the Oedipus Complex.
    Delos.
    In Arcadia.
    In the Garden: Villa Cleobolus.
    Lesbos.
    My uncle sleeps in the image of death.
    Mythology.
    Nemea.
    On First Looking into Loeb's Horace.
    Poggio.
    Sarajevo.
    Seferis.
    Strip-tease.
    Swans.
    This Unimportant Morning.
    Vega.
    Visitations.
    Water-Colour of Venice, A.
Durston, Georgia Roberts
    Wolf, The.
Dutton, Anne *See* **King, Anne**
Dutton, Geoffrey (b. 1922)
    Burning Off.
    Finished Gentleman, A.
    Fish Shop Windows.
    Stranded Whales, The.
    Time of Waiting.
Dwight, Timothy (1752–1817)
    As Down a Lone Valley.
    Country Pastor, The.
    Here stood Hypocrisy, in sober brown.
    I Love Thy Kingdom, Lord.
    Shall Man, O God of Light.
    Sing to the Lord Most High.
    Smooth Divine, The.
Dybek, Stuart (b. 1942)
    Benediction.

Brass Knuckles.
Cherry.
Mowing.
My Father's Fights.
My Neighborhood.
Sleepwalking Soho.
Windy City.
Dyer, Sir Edward (c.1540–1607)
I Would It Were Not As It Is.
Lowest Trees Have Tops, The.
My Mind to Me a Kingdom Is.
PROMETHEUS, when first from heaven high.
Dyer, Eric
Painting the Nude.
'Round Killar.
Dyer, John (1699–1758)
Enough of Grongar and the shady dales.
Grongar Hill.
Happy Workhouse and the Good Effects of Industry, The.
I am resolved, this charming day.
My Ox Duke.
Now, I gain the Mountain's Brow.
To Clio, from Rome.
Treating Sheep Ailments.
Dyer, Lady Catherine [or Katherine] (fl. c.1641)
Epitaph on the Monument of Sir William Dyer at Colmworth, 1641.
M. S. Sir Will: Dyer, Kt: Who Put on Immortality Aprill the 29th Anno Domini 1621.
"Dylan, Bob" (Robert Zimmerman) (b. 1941)
Quinn the Eskimo.
Three Angels.
Dyment, Clifford (1914–70)
As a boy with a richness of needs I wandered.
Derbyshire Born, Monmouth Is My Home.
Fox.
Swans, The.
Dyson, Edward (1865–1931)
Friendly Game of Football, A.
Old Whim Horse, The.
Dyson, Will (1880–1938)
Trucker, The.
Dzyubin, Eduard Georgievich See **"Bagritzky [or Bagritsky], Eduard Georgievich"**

E

"E." See **Fullerton, Mary Elizabeth**
"E. D." (fl. 1587)
E. D. in Commendation of the Author and His Choise.
E. D. in Prayse of Mr. W. Fouler Her Friend.
Eady, Cornelius (b. 1954)
April.
Crows in a Strong Wind.
Dance, The.
False Arrest.
Hank Mobley's.
Insomnia.
Jack Johnson Does the Eagle Rock.
Jazz Dancer.
Johnny Laces Up His Red Shoes.
Leadbelly.
Muddy Waters and the Chicago Blues.
My Mother, If She Had Won Free Dance Lessons.
My Mother is a God Fearing Woman.
Radio.
Sherbet.
Song.
Success.
Thrift.
View from the Roof, Waverly Place.
Why Do So Few Blacks Study Creative Writing?
William Carlos Williams.
Young Elvis.
"Eagle, Solomon" See **Squire, Sir John Collings**
Earle, Jean (b. 1909)
At the South Pole.
Backgrounds Observed.
Blondie.

Exits.
Jugged Hare.
May Tree, The.
Old Tips.
Saturday in the '20s, A.
Tea Party, The.
Village.
Visiting Light.
Earley, Tom (b. 1911)
Lark.
Rebel's Progress.
Early, Gerald
Country or Western Music.
Innocency or Not Song X.
"Eastaway, Edward" See **Thomas, Edward**
Eastburn, James Wallis (1797–1819)
O Holy, Holy, Holy, Lord.
Eastman, Max (1883–1969)
To Genevieve Taggard Who Called Me Traitor in a Poem.
To John Reed.
Eaton, Charles Edward (b. 1916)
Lynx, The.
Ebb, Fred (b. 1932)
And All That Jazz.
Cabaret.
Class.
Happy Time, The.
My Coloring Book.
Nowadays.
Quiet Thing, A.
Eberhart, Richard (b. 1904)
Blunting, The.
Brotherhood of Men.
Cancer Cells, The.
Chart Indent.
Dam Neck, Virginia.
Flux.
For a Lamb.
Fury of Aerial Bombardment, The.
Garden God, The.
Gnat on My Paper.
Groundhog, The.
Hard Structure of the World, The.
Hardy Perennial.
Horse Chestnut Tree, The.
I Walked over the Grave of Henry James.
I Went to See Irving Babbitt.
Immortal Picture, The.
La Crosse at Ninety Miles an Hour.
Loon Call, A.
New England Bachelor, A.
New Hampshire, February.
On a Squirrel Crossing the Road in Autumn, in New England.
Rainscapes, Hydrangeas, Roses, and Singing Birds.
Sea-Hawk.
Seals, Terns, Time.
Spider, The.
This Fevers Me.
Ebner-Eschenbach, Marie von (1830–1916)
Epitaph: "In shadows of this willow rests."
Little Song, A.
Echeruo, Michael (b. 1937)
Man and God Distinguished.
Melting Pot.
Eclipse
Cicada.
Eddy, Mary Baker (1821–1910)
O'er Waiting Harp-Strings of the Mind.
Shepherd, Show Me How to Go.
Eddy, Zachary (1815–91)
Floods Swell around Me, Angry, Appalling.
Jesus, Enthroned and Glorified.
E'der, Elsa Rediva
La Puente.
Once We Were Farmers.
Edgar, Christopher (b. 1961)
Cloud of Unknowing, The.
Edgar, Marriott (1880–1951)
Lion and Albert, The.
Edman, Irwin (1896–1954)
Peace.
Edmond, Lauris (b. 1924)
All Possession Is Theft.

Difficult Adjustment, A.
Ghosts II.
Jardin des Colombières.
Latter Day Lysistrata.
Ohakune Fires.
Sums, The.
Edmond, Murray (b. 1949)
House.
Von Tempsky's Dance.
Sprig of Karo, A.
Edmondson, Madeleine
Witches' Spells.
Edson, Russell (b. 1935)
Amateur, The.
Ape.
Automobile, The.
Bringing a Dead Man Back into Life.
Conjugal.
Cottage in the Wood, A.
Counting Sheep.
Darwin Descending.
Death of an Angel, The.
Fall, The.
Feeding the Dog.
In the Forest.
Journey through the Moonlight, A.
Long Picnic, The.
Old Man's Son, An.
Optical Prodigal, The.
Ox, The.
Performance at Hog Theater, A.
Pilot, The.
Toy-Maker, The.
Wheelbarrow, The.
Wounded Breakfast, The.
Edwards, Edwin
Waitekauri Every Time!
Edwards, Gus
By the Light of the Silvery Moon.
Edwards, Ken (b. 1950)
About this time streetlamps flicker up like.
Art of definition—is this, An.
De—um majorettes.
Good Science.
Lexically.
Night falls on single vision zombies everywhere.
Provisionally.
This juxtaposition of events without.
Unconsciously.
Edwards, Matilda Caroline
Do As You Would Be Done By.
Home.
I Love the Night.
Remember the Poor.
There's a Silvery Lining to Every Cloud.
Time to Die, The.
To a Loved One of Other Days.
We Are Passing Away.
World Is Full of Beauty, The.
Edwards [or Edwardes], Richard (1523–66)
Blue Room, The.
Recollections of an Old Spook.
When I Was Three.
Edwards, Thomas (1699–1757)
On the Edition of Mr. Pope's Works with a Commentary and Notes.
Sonnet on a Family Picture.
To Shakespeare.
To the Author of Clarissa.
To the Editor of Mr. Pope's Works.
Tongue-doughty pedant; whose ambitious mind.
Efron, Adelina Efimovna See **"Adalis, Adelina Efimovna"**
Egan, Raymond B. (fl. 1925)
Ain't We Got Fun.
Sleepy Time Gal.
Egan, Ted
Drover's Boy, The.
Egemo, Constance
Silver Poplar at Sunrise.
Egerton, Elizabeth, Lady Brackley (1626–63)
On My Boy Henry.
Egerton, J. A. (b. 1935)
Tell Him So.

Egerton, Sarah Fyge (1670–1723)
Blasphemous wretch! How canst thou think or
say.
Emulation, The.
Liberty, The.
On My Wedding Day.
Repulse to Alcander, The.
To Marina.
To One Who Said I Must Not Love.
To Orabella, Marry'd to an Old Man.
To Philaster.
Eggleton, David (b. 1953)
Painting Mount Taranaki.
These Rumours of Hexagonal Rooms in Gone
Bee City.
Eglington, Charles (b. 1918)
Lourenço Marques.
Eglinton, Edna
Alive, I flourish.
Eguren, José María (1882–1942)
Dead, The.
Girls of the Light, The.
Peregrin, Wandering Hunter of Faces.
Towers, The.
**Ehrenburg [or Erenburg], Ilya Grigoryevich
(1891–1967)**
I lived obscurely and uncertainly.
January 1939.
"Reconnaissance in force"—just three brief
words.
Our Grandsons Will Be Astonished.
Potter of Jaen, The.
Retribution.
Sons of Our Sons, The.
Tree, The.
Trumpet, The.
Ehrenstein, Albert (1884–1950)
Ares.
Home-Coming.
Homer.
Poet and War, The.
Suffering.
Ehret, Terry
Lost Body.
Ehrhart, William Daniel
Blizzard of Sixty-Six, The.
Confirmation, A.
Farmer Nguyen.
Guerrilla War.
Hunting.
Invasion of Grenada, The.
Light that cannot fade, The.
Letter.
Making the Children Behave.
Night Patrol.
One That Died, The.
Relative Thing, A.
Time on Target.
To Those Who Have Gone Home Tired.
Ehrlich [or Erlikh], Wolf (1902–37)
Last Merchant, The.
Louse.
Ehrmann, Max (1872–1945)
Away.
Hate and the Love of the World, The.
I Ponder on Life.
If You Made Gentler the Churlish World.
Mother.
Eian
Joshu's 'Oak in the courtyard.'
Eich, Günter (1907–72)
Geometrical Place.
Inventory.
Old Postcards.
Seminar for Backward Pupils.
Eichendorff, Joseph, Freiherr von (1788–1857)
On My Child's Death.
Eichu (1340–1416)
My eyes eavesdrop on their lashes!
Eifuku, Empress (1271–1342)
We dressed each other.
Eigner, Larry (b. 1927)
Ah, so, yes.
All Intents.
B.

Back to it.
Bare trees / alternate, The.
Dark swimmers, The.
Do It Yrself.
Don't go.
Elysee.
Environs.
Explanation / tangent things.
Fete, A.
Flake diamond of / the sea.
Fleche.
For Sleep.
From the sustaining air.
Gone, A.
How It Comes About.
I have felt it as they've said.
If You Weep, I Think That.
In Imitation.
It Sounded.
Keep Me Still, for I Do Not Want to Dream.
Letter for Duncan.
Live /, Bird Which.
Noise Grimaced.
Open.
Open Air Where.
Passages.
Temporary Language, A.
That the neighborhood might be covered.
Three Poems 1989.
Trees Green   the Quiet Sun.
Wholes.
Wind like an ocean, The.
Winter (January / February 1978)
Eijkelboom, Jan (b. 1926)
A Nos Glorieux Morts.
As Old as Then.
Sometimes.
Town a Bird Sanctuary, The.
Eikei (fl. late 10th cent.)
Autumn has come / To the lonely cottage.
Eimers, Nancy
Morbid.
Night Without Stars, A.
No Moon.
Eiseley, Loren C. (1907–77)
And as for Man.
Eisner, Aleksey [or Aleksei] (1908–84)
Autumn nears. The branches yellow.
Ejong, Yityangu (d. before 1981)
Love Song: "Tiny children."
Ekelof, Gunnar
Absentia Animi.
Alone in the quiet night.
Ayíasma.
Greece.
Hangman.
If You Ask Me.
Leavetaking.
Like Ankle-Rings, This Music.
Marche Funèbre.
Moon, The.
Ekpe, Komi
Abuse Poems: For Kodzo and Others.
El-Hadi, Suliaman
Drama, The.
Tired Man, The.
El-Hage, Nada (b. 1958)
Follow Me.
Journey of the Shadow, The.
Land Stretching Up to the Sky, A.
Overflow.
El-Shafa'i, Ghada
Interlaced Lines for the Same Moment.
Scene for the Mornings Preceding the Fire, A.
El-Sousy, Sumaiya (b. 1974)
Voices.
El-Zein, Amira
Land of Mirrors, The.
Ela, David H. (1831–1907)
Chosen Three, on Mountain Height, The.
**"Elagin, Ivan Venediktovich" (Ivan
Venediktovich Matveyev) (1918–87)**
Amnesty.
Come now, my friend, you must not say.
Has my life been a failure? I wonder—.

I know that a gangster will not murder me.
I like these foreign shores and I have never.
My murderer is no thief.
You told me that I was born under a lucky star.
Elburg, Jan G. (b. 1919)
Nothing of All That.
Wanting To.
Elder, Anne (1918–76)
Carried Away.
Farmer Goes Beserk.
One Foot in the Door.
School Cadets.
Eleazar (fl. Middle Ages)
Thy Faithful Sons.
Elhami, Hussein (fl. 20th cent.)
Lyric in Exile, A.
**Elijah ben Menahem Hazaken, of LeMans (fl.
11th cent.)**
Precepts He Gave His Folk.
**"Eliot, George" (Mary Ann [or Marian] Evans
Lewes Cross) (1727–1805)**
Armgart.
Brother and Sister.
But sudden came the barge's pitch-black prow.
Death of Moses, The.
Felix Holt, the Radical.
How Lisa Loved the King.
I Cannot Choose but Think upon the Time.
In a London Drawingroom.
Our brown canal was endless to my thought.
School Parted Us.
Those long days measured by my little feet.
Eliot, Thomas Stearns (1888–1965)
Animula.
Ash Wednesday [or Ash-Wednesday], sels.
Aunt Helen.
Boston Evening Transcript, The.
Bustopher Jones: The Cat About Town.
Cat Morgan Introduces Himself.
Choruses from the Rock, sels.
Cousin Nancy.
Dedication to My Wife, A.
Eyes That Last I Saw in Tears.
Five-Finger Excercises, sels.
Four Quartets, sels.
Gerontion.
Growltiger's Last Stand.
Gus: The Theatre Cat.
Hippopotamus, The.
Hollow Men, The.
Journey of the Magi.
La Figlia Che Piange.
Landscapes, sels.
Lines for an Old Man.
Love Song of J. Alfred Prufrock, The, sels.
Macavity: The Mystery Cat.
Marina.
Mr Mistofelees.
Murder in the Cathedral, sels.
Naming of Cats, The.
Portrait of a Lady.
Preludes, sels.
Rhapsody on a Windy Night.
Rum Tum Tugger, The.
Skimbleshanks: The Railway Cat.
Song for Simeon, A.
Song of the Jellicles, The.
St. Luke, sels.
St. Matthew, sels.
Sweeney Agonistes, sels.
Sweeney Among the Nightingales.
Sweeney Erect.
Waste Land, The, sels.
Whispers of Immortality.
Eliscu, Edward (1901–98)
Flying Down to Rio.
Great Day.
More Than You Know.
Without a Song.
"Eliza" (fl. 18th cent.)
Epistle to John Walker, Esq., An.
To Generall Cromwell.
To My Husband.
Elizabeth I, Queen of England (1533–1603)
Ah silly pugg wert thou so sore afraid.
Doubt of Future Foes.

Dread of future foes exyle my present Joy, The.
Genus Infoelix Vitae.
On Fortune.
On Monsieur's Departure.
Queen's Answer, The.
Songe Made by Her Majestie and Songe before Her at Her Cominge from White Hall to Powles through Fleete Streete in Anno Domini 1588, A.
When I Was Fair and Young.
Written in Her French Psalter.
Written on a Wall at Woodstock.
Written with a Diamond on Her Window at Woodstock.

Elizabeth, Martha
Manon Reassures Her Lover.
She Teaches Him to Reach Out.

Elizabeth of York, Queen (1465–1503)
My heart is set upon a lusty pin.

Elizabeth, Queen of Bohemia (1596–1660)
Verses by the Princess Elizabeth, Given to Lord Harington, of Exton, Her Preceptor.

Elledge, Jim
Duckling, Swan.
14 Reasons Why I Mention Mario Lanza to the Man I Love Every Chance I Get Tonight.
Household Gods.
Man I Love and I Have a Typical Evening the Night Richard M. Nixon Dies, The.
Man I Love and I Shop at Jewel, The.
Strangers: An Essay.
Their Hats Is Always White.
Triptych.

Ellerton, John (1826–93)
Day Thou Gavest, Lord, Is Ended, The.

Ellington, Duke
Don't Get Around Much Anymore.
I Ain't Got Nothin' But the Blues.
I Didn't Know About You.
I Got It Bad and That Ain't Good.
I'm Beginning to See the Light.
I'm Gonna Go Fishin'.
I'm Just a Lucky So-and-So.
It's Kind of Lonesome Out Tonight.
It Shouldn't Happen to a Dream.
Jump for Joy.
Maybe I Should Change My Ways.
Prelude to a Kiss.
Satin Doll.
Solitude.
Something to Live For.
Sophisticated Lady.
Tulip or Turnip.

Elliot, Alistair (b. 1932)
Latitudes of Home, The.

Elliot, Jane [or Jean] (1727–1805)
Flowers of the Forest, The.

Elliott, Andrew (b. 1961)
Angel.
Here Today.
Love Poem, The.
Stay Behind, The.
X-Ray, The.

Elliott, Charlotte
Just as I Am.

Elliott, Ebenezer (1781–1849)
Battle Song.
Beware of Dogmas.
Caged Rats.
Child, Is Thy Father Dead?
Criticism.
Drone v. Worker.
Epigram: "'Prepare to meet the King of Terrors,' cried."
Epigram: "What is a communist? One who hath yearnings."
Fatal Birth, The.
Five rivers, like the fingers of a hand.
Give Not Our Blankets, Tax-Fed Squire.
Here lies the man who stripp'd Sin bare.
How Different!
In These Days.
John.
On a Rose in December.

Paddy, I have but stol'n your living.
Plaint.
Poet vs. Parson.
Powers of the Sonnet.
Ralph Leech Believes.
Song: "Donought would have everything."
Song: "When working blackguards come to blows."
Spring.
Three Marys at Castle Howard, in 1812 and 1837, The.
Toy of the Titans.
Village! thy butcher's son, the steward now.
War.

Ellis, Alfred *See* **Brown, James**
Ellis, Colin (1895–1969)
Adder's Epigrams.
Bungaloid Growth.
Epitaph, An: "He worshipped at the altar of Romance."
International Conference.
Modern World, The.
New Vicar of Bray, The.
Old Ladies, The.
On a Gentleman Marrying His Cook.

Ellis, Edwin John
At Golgotha I stood alone.

Ellis, Harold (*fl.* 1851)
Limerick: "O sage of the stage, Shaw of Shaws!"

Ellis, John (1698–1791)
Sarah Hazard's Love Letter.

Ellis, Kelly Norman
Girl.
Tougaloo Blues.

Ellis, R. H.
Walk up, walk up, my bonny boys.

Ellis, Robert (1812–75)
Hour of Sleep, The.

Ellis, Thomas Sayers
Atomic Bride.
Being There.
Break of Dawn, The.
Hush Yo Mouf.
Kiss in the Dark, A.
Making Ends Meet.
On Display.
Practice.
Shooting Back.
Sir Nose D'VoidofFunk.
Star Child.
Sticks.
T.A.P.O.A.F.O.M.
Tambourine Tommy.
Tapes.
View of the Library of Congress from Paul Laurence Dunbar High School.

Ellis, Vivian Locke
Spread a Little Happiness.

Elman, Richard (d. 1997)
October Observed, Hudson Falls, New York in Bill's Back Yard.

"Elmo" (*fl.* c.1902?)
Our Ernest.

Elmslie, Kenward
Amazon Club.
Big Bar.
Duo-Tang.
Feathered Dances.
Fruit.
Island Celebration.
Japanese City.
Marbled Chuckle in the Savannahs.
One Night Stand.
Picnic.
Squatter in the Foreground.
Stage Duo.

Elmusa, Sharif (b. 1947)
Bookishness.
Dream on the Same Mattress.
Expatriates.
Father Lullabies the Unborn.
In the Refugee Camp.
She Fans the Word.
Snapshots.

Two Angels, The.

Elsschot, Willem (1882–1960)
Mother.

Elton, W. R.
Hopper: In the Cafe.

Éluard, Paul (Eugène Grindel) (1895–1952)
Curfew.
Dawn Dissolves the Monsters.
Deaf and Blind, The.
Lady Love.
Meetings.
Mirror of a Moment, The.
Nature Was Caught in the Nets of Your Life.
Nazi Song.
November 1936.
On my school notebooks.
Pig.
She Is Always Unwilling to Understand.
To Her of Whom They Dream.
To Ride.
Unknown, She Was My Favorite Shape.
Woman In Love.

Eluard, Paul *and* Andre Breton
32 Positions of Love, The.
Identities.
One good mistress deserves another.
Second Nature.
Victory at Guernica, The.

Elvey, George J.
Come, Ye Thankful People, Come.

Elwood, Thomas
Prayer, A: "O that mine eyes might closed be."

Elytis, Odysseus (Odysseus Alepoudelis) (1911–91)
Aegean Melancholy.
Anniversary.
As Endymion.
Autopsy, The.
Even when they destroy you it will still be beautiful.
I was late in understanding the meaning of humility.
Mad Pomegranate Tree, The.
March toward the Front, The.
Origin of Landscape or the End of Mercy, The.
Sun the First.
This Wind That Loiters.
Whatever I was able to acquire in my life.

Ema Saiko (1787–1861)
Evening Stroll.

Emanuel, James A.
Black Man, 13th Floor.
Emmett Till.
For "Mr. Dudley," a Black Spy.
Negritude.
Negro, The.
Nightmare.
Panther Man.
Treehouse, The.
Whitey, Baby.

Emanuel, Lynn
Corpses, The.
Elsewhere.
Halfway Through the Book I'm Writing.
Homage to Sharon Stone.
In English in a Poem.
Like God.
Outside Room Six.
She.
Sleeping, The.
Technology of Spring, The.

Embury, Emma Catherine (1806–63)
Pilgrim, The.

Emerson, Ralph Waldo (1803–82)
Alphonso of Castile.
Art.
Astræa.
Awed I Behold Once More.
Bacchus.
Blight.
Boston Hymn.
Brahma.
Character.
Chartist's Complaint, The.
Circles.

Climacteric.
Compensation.
Concord Hymn.
Dæmonic and the Celestial Love, The.
Day's Ration, The.
Days.
Dear Brother, Would You Know the Life.
Dirge: "I reached the middle of the mount."
Each and All.
Eros.
Every morn I lift my head.
Experience.
Fable: "Mountain and the squirrel, The."
Fate.
Forbearance.
Forerunners.
Freedom.
Friendship.
Gardener.
Give All to Love.
Good-bye.
Grace.
Guy.
Hamatreya.
Harp, The.
Him strong Genius urged to roam.
History.
Humble-Bee, The.
I have an arrow that will find its mark.
Illusions.
In unplowed Maine he sought the lumberers'
    gang.
Intellect.
Letters.
Limits.
Maia.
Memory.
Merlin.
Merops.
Mithridates.
Musketaquid.
Nature [1836].
Nature [1844].
Nemesis.
Nominalist and Realist.
Ode, Inscribed to W. H. Channing.
Once again the pine-tree sung.
Orator.
Past, The.
Patient Pan, The.
Poet.
Problem, The.
Prudence.
Rhodora, The [On Being Asked Whence Is the
    Flower].
Saadi.
Sea-Shore.
Shakspeare.
Snow-Storm [or Snowstorm], The.
Solution.
Song of Nature.
Sphinx, The.
Spiritual Laws.
Sursum Corda.
Suum Cuique.
Terminus.
Test, The.
Thine Eyes Still Shined.
Threnody: "South-wind brings, The."
To Rhea.
Two Rivers.
Unity.
Uriel.
Visit, The.
Voluntaries.
Waldeinsamkeit.
Water.
We Love the Venerable House.
Wealth.
Woodnotes I ("For this present, hard")
Woodnotes II ("As sunbeams stream through
    liberal space")
World-Soul, The.
Worship.
Xenophanes.

Emmens, Jan (b. 1924)
Lion of Judah, The.

Emmett, Daniel Decatur (1815–1904)
Blue Tail Fly or Jimmy Cracked Corn, The.
Boatman's Dance.
Dixie [or Dixie's Land].

Emmott, Kirsten
Who Looks after Your Kids?

Emperor Ch'ien-wen of Liang
Getting Up in Winter.

Empson, William (1906–84)
Ants, The.
Arachne.
Aubade: "Hours before dawn we were woken
    by the quake."
Bacchus.
Beautiful Train, The.
Camping Out.
Homage to the British Museum.
Ignorance of Death.
Invitation To Juno.
Just a Smack at Auden.
Just a Smack at Auden.
Legal Fiction.
Let It Go.
Missing Dates.
Not your winged lust but his must now change
    suit.
Note on Local Flora.
Rolling the Lawn.
Scales, The.
Success.
Teasers, The.
This Last Pain.
To an Old Lady.
Villanelle: "It is the pain, it is the pain,
    endures."
Waiting for the end, boys, waiting for the end.

Emre, Yunus
Whole universe is full of God, The.

Encarnacion, Alfred (b. 1958)
Bulosan Listens to a Recording of Robert
    Johson.
Seattle, Autumn, 1933.
Threading the Miles.

Endersby, J.
Limerick: "Few people could hope to
    compare."

Endrezze, Anita (b. 1952)
Birdwatching at Fan Lake.
Canto Llano.
Dream Feast (Three Poems), The.
Eclipse.
Exodus.
Girl Who Loved the Sky, The.
Hansel, Gretel and Ruby Redlips.
In the Flight of the Blue Heron: To
    Montezuma.
Language of Fossils, The.
Learning the Spells; a Diptych.
Manifest Destiny.
Meditating on Star Light While Traveling
    Highway.
Notes from an Analyst's Couch.
November Harvest.
Passion Drinker, The.
Raven/Moon.
Red Rock Ceremonies.
Return of the Wolves.
Reviewing Past Lives while Leaf-Burning.
Song-Maker.
Stripper, The.
Sunset at Twin Lake.
Truth about My Sister and Me, The.
Week-End Indian, The.

Engels, John (b. 1931)
Bullhead.

England, Amy (b. 1962)
Art of the Snake Story, The.

Engle, Paul (b. 1908)
Hart Crane.
Look! The air shudders when you breathe it in.
Lord of Each Soul.

English, Mary (1652?–94)
May I with Mary choose the better part.

English, Thomas Dunn (1819–1902)
Ben Bolt.

English, William (1710?–1778)
Cashel of Munster.

Engvick, William (b. 1914)
Crazy in the Heart.
While We're Young.
Who Can I Turn To?

Enheduanna (fl. c.2300 B.C.)
Antiphonal Hymn in Praise of Inanna.
Appeal to the Moongod Nanna-Suen to Throw
    Out Lugalanne.
Banishment from Ur.
Condemning the Moongod Nanna.
Crimes of Lugalanne.
Curse on Uruk, A.
Final Prayer.
Hymn to Inanna, The.
Inanna and An.
Inanna and Ebih.
Inanna and Enlil.
Inanna and Ishkur.
Inanna and the Anunna.
Inanna and the City of Uruk.
Inanna and the Divine Essences.
Lady of Largest Heart.
O lady of all truths bright light going forth.
Restoration of Enheduanna to Her Former
    Station, The.

Enni Ben'en (d. 1280)
All my life I taught Zen to the people.

Ennis, John (b. 1944)
Alice of Daphne, 1799.
Coyne's.
Drink of Spring, A.
Meeting at a Salesyard.
Road to Patmos, The.
Years, The.

Enquist, Anna (b. 1945)
December Offensive.
Invasion.

Enright, Dennis Joseph (b. 1920)
Anecdote from William IV Street.
Apocalypse.
Buy One Now.
Days of Adam were 930 years, The.
Development.
Dreaming in the Shanghai Restaurant.
Evil Days, The.
Flowers.
Guest.
History of World Languages.
In Cemeteries.
Kyoto Garden, A.
Laughing Hyena, after [or by] Hokusai, The.
Midstream.
Monuments of Hiroshima, The.
No Offence.
Poet Wondering What He Is Up To.
Posterity.
R-and-R Centre: An Incident from the Vietnam
    War.
Remembrance Sunday.
"Rich soil," remarked the Landlord.
Royalties.
Since Then.
Underdeveloped Country, An.
University Examinations in Egypt.
Unlawful Assembly.
Verb "To Think," The.
Waiting for the Bus.
Why didn't we think of clothes before?

Enright, Nick
John Keats rose at dawn.

Enryo (d. 1855)
Autumn waters.

Ensei (d. 1725)
Parting gift to my body.

Ensetsu (d. 1743)
Autumn gust.
Many things befell me as I followed Buddha.

Enshi (d. 1900)
All moving things.

Enslin, Theodore (b. 1925)
Fire Poem, The.

Enzensberger, Hans Magnus (b. 1929)
At Thirty-three.

Divorce, The.
For a Senior College Textbook.
For the Grave of a Peace-Loving Man.
Holiday, The.
Hôtel Fraternité.
Last Will and Testament.
Middle-Class Blues.
Poem about the Future.
Poison, The.
Portrait of a House Detective.
Reprieve, The.
Short History of the Bourgeoisie.
Sixteenth Canto.
Song for Those Who Know.
Thirty-third Canto.
Twenty-ninth Canto.
Vanished Work.
Vending Machine.

Enzo, King of Sardinia (1225–1272)
There is a time to mount; to humble thee.

"Ephelia" (Joan Philips) (fl. c.1679)
Advice to His Grace.
First Farewell to J. G.
In the Person of a Lady, to Bajazet, Her Unconstant Gallant.
Maidenhead.
On a Bashful Shepherd.
Song: "You wrong me, Strephon, when you say."
To a Proud Beauty.
To J. G.
To J. G. on the News of His Marriage.
To Madam Bhen.
To My Rival.
To One That Asked Me Why I Loved J. G.
To Phylocles, Inviting Him to Friendship.

Ephraim ben Jacob, Rabbi (1132–1200)
Sacrifice of Isaac, The.

Epictetus
Pleasd with thy Place.

Epshtein, Mikhail Semionovich See "Golodny [or Golodnyi], Mikhail Semionovich"

Epstein, Daniel Mark (b. 1948)
Barrel Organ, The.
Mannequins.
Old Times.

Equena
Before he died.

Equi, Elaine (b. 1953)
Autobiographical Poem.
Being Sick Together.
Bouquet of Objects, A.
Date with Robbe-Grillet, A.
In a Monotonous Dream.
Lesbian Corn.
Puritans.
Things to Do in the Bible.

Eratosthenes (fl. 6th cent.)
Bacchus, receive my offering, not.
Meditation, Followed by Excellent Advice.

Erb, Elke (b. 1938)
Text and Commentary.

Erdélyi, József (1896–1978)
Black Kőrös.
Cherry-Tree.
Sons Changed into Stags, The.
Splendid Stags, The.

Erdman, Ernie
No, No, Nora.
Toot, Toot, Tootsie! (Good-bye)

Erdrich, Heid E. (b. 1963)
Fat in America.
Future Debris.
Hopi Prophet Chooses a Pop.
Quiet Earth, The.

Erdrich, Louise (b. 1954)
Birth.
Butcher's Wife, The.
Captivity.
Dear John Wayne.
Family Reunion.
Fooling God.
Francine's Room.
I Was Sleeping Where the Black Oaks Move.
Immaculate Conception.

Indian Boarding School: The Runaways.
Jacklight.
King of Owls, The.
Lady in the Pink Mustang, The.
Love Medicine, A.
Night Sky.
Old Man Potchikoo.
Owls.
Strange People, The.
That Pull from the Left.
Windigo.

Erickson, C. L.
Light in the Window, The.

Erinna (fl. 3rd cent. B.C.)
Baucis.
Delicate hands fashioned this portrait: good Prometheus.
Distaff, The.
Epitaph on a Betrothed Girl.
Escort fish, Pompilos, sending sailors a fair sailing.
From here an empty echo penetrates to Hades.
Girls / Brides / Tortoise.
I am the grave of Baucis the bride. Passing by.
I'm the tomb of Baukis, a bride; passing the deeply lamented.
On the Portrait of a Girl.
Stele and my Sirens and mournful pitcher that hold.
Stele and my sirens and mournful urn.

Eristi-Aya (c.1790–1745 B.C.)
Letter to Her Mother, A.

Erlich, Sara Riwka
Garden of Shanah.
Jerusalem.

Ernst, John F. (fl. late 18th cent.)
O Jesus Christ, True Light of God.

Ernst, Max (1891–1976)
Hundred Headless Woman, The.

Erskine, John (1879–1951)
Kings and Stars.
Shepherd Speaks, The.

Erskine, Ralph (1685–1752)
Fourfold Exercise for the Believer in His Lodging on Earth, A.
I though from condemnation free.
Mine arms embrace my God, yet I.
My life's a maze of seeming traps.
My life's a pleasure and a pain.
To tell the world my proper name.

Erskine, Thomas Erskine, 1st Baron (1750–1823)
James Alan Park / Came naked stark.
On Scott's Poem "The Field of Waterloo."
On Tom Moore's Translation of Anacreon.

Erucius of Cyzicus (fl. c.30 B.C.)
Even though he lies underground.
Glaukon and Korydon, mountain herdsmen.
How massively, with what a fine stiff rise.
I am Athenian, that was my city.
I, the priest of Rhea, long-haired.
Kleson's goat snorted all night through the dark.
May supple-footed theatre-growing ivy.
Tell me herdsman for the sake of Pan.

Escandor, Virginia E.
Summer Nostalgia.

Eshleman, Clayton (b. 1935)
Black Hat, The.
Deeds Done and Suffered by Light.
Hades in Manganese.
Lich Gate, The.
Notes on a Visit to Le Tuc d'Audoubert.
Our Lady of the Three-Pronged Devil.
Placements I.

Eskimo Oral Tradition
Magic Words.
Song of Kuk-ook, the Bad Boy, The.

Espada, Martín (b. 1955)
All the People Who Are Now Red Trees.
Beloved Spic.
Bully.
Cada Puerco Tiene Su Sábado.
Coca-Cola and Coco Frío.
Cockroaches of Liberation.
Courthouse Graffiti for Two Voices.

Dándole la mano a Mongo.
David Leaves the Saints for Paterson.
Do Not Put Dead Monkeys in the Freezer.
Fidel in Ohio.
Green and Red, Verde y Rojo.
Imagine the Angels of Bread.
Man Who Beat Hemingway, The.
Jeep Driver, The.
La tormenta.
Latin Night at the Pawnshop.
Majeski Plays the Saxophone.
Moon Shatters on Alabama Avenue, The.
My Cockroach Lover.
My Native Costume.
Owl and the Lightning, The.
Pitching the Potatoes.
Prisoners of Saint Lawrence, The.
Savior Is Abducted in Puerto Rico, The.
Shaking Hands with Mongo.
Spanish of Our Out-Loud Dreams, The.
Thanksgiving.
Tires Stacked in the Hallways of Civilization.
Tony Went to the Bodega but He Didn't Buy Anything.
Toque de queda: Curfew in Lawrence.
Transient Hotel Sky at the Hour of Sleep.
Water, White Cotton, and the Rich Man.
Who Burns for the Perfection of Paper.
Year I Was Diagnosed with a Sacrilegious Heart, The.

Espagnol, Nicole (b. 1937)
Conclusion Is Not Drawn, The.
Female Socket.
Heartstopping.
Wind Turns, The.

Espaillat, Rhina P. (b. 1932)
Metrics.

Espinet, Ramabai (b. 1948)
Merchant of Death.

Espirito Santo, Alda do (b. 1926)
Far from the Beach.
Grandma Mariana.
Same Side of the Canoe, The.
Where Are the Men Chased Away by that Mad Wind?
Where Are the Men Seized in this Wind of Madness?

Espy, Willard R. (b. 1910)
My TV Came down with a Chill.

Esrefoğlu (d. 1469)
O My God Do Not Part Me from Thee.

Essbaum, Jill Alexander
In the Beginning.
Paradise.
Post-Communion Striptease.
When the Kingdom Comes.

Essex, Robert Devereux, 2d Earl of (1567–1601)
Happy Were He.

Esson, Louis (Thomas Louis Buvelot Esson) (1879–1943)
Shearer's Wife, The.

Estep, Maggie
I Have to Go Now.

Estes, Angie
Annunciation in an Initial R.
Nocturne.
Now and Again: An Autobiography of Basket.
Serenade.
You Stand There Fishing.

Esteves, Sandra Maria
Ahora.
Celebration of Home Birth: November 15th, 1981, A.
1st Poem for Cuba.
For Fidel Castro.
For Lolita Lebron.
For South Bronx.
From Fanon.
Here.
In the Beginning.
It Is Raining Today.
Lil' Pito.
One Woman.
Some People Are about Jam.
South Bronx Testimonial.

Take the Hearts of Children.
Weaver.

E'tesami, Parvin (1910–41)
To His Father on Praising the Honest Life of the Peasant.

Etherege, Sir George (1653–91)
Song: "Ladies, though to your conquering eyes."
To a Lady Asking Him How Long He Would Love Her.

Etherege, Sir George *See* **Walsh, William**

Etheridge, Ken (1911–81)
Annunciation.

Ethuin, Anne (b. 1921)
Legend.

Etsujin (1656–1739)
First snow / Head clear.

Etter, Dave (b. 1928)
Andy Hasselgard.
Drink and Agriculture.
Elwood Collins: Summer of 1932.
Great Northern.
Monk's Dream.
Riding the Rock Island Through Kansas.
Roma Higgins.
Romp.
Singing in the Toyota.
Stuffy Turkey.
Well You Needn't.

Ettinger, Esther
Believe Me.
Excerpts from the Sabbath Dream Book.
Glass, The.
Micrographic Manuscript, Miniature (1)
Micrographic Manuscript, Miniature (2)

Eubulus (*fl.* 4th cent.)
Benefits and Abuse of Alcohol, The.

Euenos
To a Swallow.
To the Swallow.

Euenus (Euenus the Grammarian, Euenus of Askelon, Euenus of Paros) (*fl.* 5th cent. B.C.)
B kw rm.
If hate is painful and if love's a pain.
Vine *v.* Goat.

Eugenius Vulgarius (*fl.* c.1900 B.C.)
Metrum Parhemiacum Tragicum.

Euodos
Echo: / mimic, / last sip.

Euphorion (b. c.276 B.C.)
Not the wild olive, not the fatal stones.
When first Eudoxos cut his lovely hair.

Euripides (485–406 B.C.)
And Pergamos, / City of the Phrygians.
Chorus of Satyrs, Driving Their Goats.
Chorus: "Sweet are the ways of death to weary feet."
Fragment 652.
Home of Aphrodite, The.
Love Song: "One with eyes the fairest."
Medea.
No more, O my spirit.
O for the Wings of a Dove.
Strength of Fate, The.

Euwer, Anthony (1877–1955)
Limerick: "Ankle's chief end is exposiery, The."
True Facts of the Case, The.

Evald, Johannes (1743–81)
King Christian.

Evance, Susan (*fl.* 1808–1818)
To a Violet.
To Melancholy.
To the Clouds.
Written at Netley Abbey.
Written in a Ruinous Abbey.
Written in Ill Health at the Close of Spring.

Evans, Abbie Huston (b. 1881)
Fringed Gentians.
Juniper.
Martian Landscape.
Old Yellow Shop, The.
Under Cover.

Evans, Abel (1679–1737)
Author's Epitaph, Written by Himself, An.

Keep the commandments, Trapp, and go no further.
On Sir John Vanbrugh [Architect].

Evans, Bill
Waltz for Debby.

Evans, Christine
Callers.
Enlli.
Lucy's Bones.

Evans, David Allan (b. 1940)
Pole Vaulter.
Song of Racquetball.

Evans, Donald (1884–1921)
Dinner at the Hotel de la Tigresse Verte.
En Monocle.
In the Vices.

Evans, Evan (1731–88)
Hall of Ifor Hael, The.
Whatever clime we travel or explore.

Evans, George (b. 1948)
Eye Blade.
Horse on a Fence.
Renaissance Drunk, A.
Revelation in the Mother Lode.

Evans, H. A. C.
Limerick: "There was a young lady called Clarice."

Evans, Margiad (1909–58)
Rain.
Resurrection.
Snowdrops.

Evans, Mari E. (b. 1923)
And the Hotel Room Held Only Him.
And the Old Women Gathered.
Black Jam for Dr. Negro.
Boss Communication.
Daufuskie.
How Will You Call Me, Brother.
I Am a Black Woman.
Marrow of My Bone.
Rebel, The.
Spectrum.
Status Symbol.
To Mother and Steve.
Vive Noir!
When in Rome.
Where Have You Gone?

Evans, Nathaniel (1742–67)
To Thee, Then, Let All Beings Bend.

Evans, Ray (b. 1915)
Buttons and Bows.
Femininity.
Haven't Got a Worry.
Keep It Simple.
Mona Lisa.
Never Let Me Go.
To Each His Own.
Whatever Will Be, Will Be (Que Sera, Sera)

Evans, Redd (*fl.* 1947)
No Moon at All.

Evans, Sebastian (1830–1909)
Fifteen Days of Judgment, The.
How the Abbey of Saint Werewulf Juxta Slingsby Came by Brother Fabian's Manuscript.
Seven Fiddlers, The.

Evasco, Marjorie M.
Baked Oysters Rockefeller.
Dancing a Spell.
Elemental.
Heron-Woman.

Evelyn, Mary (1665–85)
Mundus Muliebris.
Voyage to Marryland, A; or, The Ladies Dressing Room.

Everaerts, Jan Nicolai *See* **"Secundus, Johannes"**

"Everage, Edna" *See* **Humphries, Barry**

Everett, Jim (b. 1942)
Ode to Salted Mutton Birds.
Old Co'es.
Rest Our Spiritual Dead.
White Man Problem, The.

Everhard, Jim (b. 1946)
Curing Homosexuality.

Eversley, Mary
Just to Be Needed.

Everson, Ronald G. (b. 1903)
Cold-Weather Love.
Injured Maple.
Laprairie Hunger Strike.
Letter from Underground.
Old Snapshot.
One-Night Expensive Hotel.
Pauper Woodland.
Stranded in My Ontario.

Everson, William (Brother Antoninus) (1912–1994)
Advent.
Canticle to the Waterbirds, A.
Daughter of earth and child of the wave be appeased.
Flight in the Desert, The.
Gale at Dawn.
High Embrace, The.
Kingfisher Flat.
Making of the Cross, The.
Man-Fate, The.
Muscat Pruning.
Narrows of Birth, The.
Passion Week.
Poet Is Dead, The.
Raid, The.
Rainy Easter.
Runoff.
South Coast, The.
Stone Face Falls.
Tor House.
What Birds Were There.
Year's End.
Zone of Death.

Everwine, Peter (b. 1930)
Brother, The.
Burden of Decision, The.
Clearing, The.
Distance.
Drinking Cold Water.
From the Meadow.
Going.
Gray Poem.
In the End.
Just Before Sleep.
Learning to Speak.
Marsh, New Year's Day, The.
Night.
Perhaps It's as You Say.
Routes.
Someone Knocks.
We Meet in the Lives of Animals.

"Evoe" *See* **Knox, Edmund George Valpy**

Ewart, Gavin (b. 1916)
Black Box, The.
Bofors A. A. Gun, The.
Christmas Message, A.
Deceptive Grin of the Gravel Porters, The.
Dell, The.
Dream of a Slave.
On the Tercentenary of Milton's Death.
Ella Mi Fu Rapita!
Ending.
Exeter Riddle, An.
Fiction: A Message.
Fiction: The House Party.
From V. C. (a Gentleman of Verona)
14-Year-Old Convalescent Cat in the Winter, A.
Great Women Composers, The.
It's Hard to Dislike Ewart.
Jubilate Matteo.
Larkin Automatic Car Wash, The.
Lifelines.
Limerick: "Life is sad and so slow and so cold."
Limerick: "There's a slow tolling bell in the dark."
Limerick: "There was a young lady of Ulva / Who was famed far and wide for her vulva."
Limerick: "Young lady, whose life-style the malicious, A."
Lines: "Other day I was loving a sweet little fruitpie-and-cream, The."

Love Song: "You've got nice knees."
Lovesleep, The.
Miss Twye.
New Poet Arrives, A.
Not Wavell but Browning.
Nursery Rhyme.
Office Friendships.
Officers' Mess.
Old Husband Suspects Adultery, An.
One for the Anthologies.
Owl Writes a Detective Story, The.
Pastoral: "Dominic Francis Xavier Brotherton-Chancery."
Personal Footnote, A.
Poets.
Prayer: "Lord I am not entirely selfish."
Robert Graves.
Semantic Limerick According to Dr. Johnson's Dictionary (Edition of 1765), The.
Semantic Limerick According to the Shorter Oxford English Dictionary (1933), The.
Short Time.
Sonnet: Equality of the Sexes.
Sonnet: Supernatural Beings.
Sonnet: The Last Things.
They Flee from Me That Sometime Did Me Seek.
To the Virgins, to Make the Most of Time.
Wanting Out.
Warm to the Cuddly-toy Charm of a Koala Bear.
Weather, The.
When a Beau Goes In.
Who Likes the Idea of Guide Cats?
William Wordsworth (1770–1850)
Word-Bird, The.
Xmas for the Boys.

Ewer, W. N. (1885–1977)
Chosen People, The.
Only Way, The.

Ewing, Juliana Horatia (1841–85)
Gifts.

Eybers, Elisabeth (b. 1915)
Confrontation with an Artist.
Narrative.
Reflection.
Snail.

Eyen, Jennifer Pierce
New Dream, A (Wuski A-Baw-Tan)

Eyton, Frank
Body and Soul.

Ezechiel of Alexandria (*fl.* 2nd cent. B.C.)
Exodus from Egypt, The.

Ezekiel, Nissim (b. 1924)
Family.
Goodbye Party for Miss Pushpa T. S
I met a man once.
Patriot, The.
Song to be Shouted Out.
There's only this.
When the female railway clerk.

Ezenwa-Ohaeto
I Wan Bi President.

Ezobi, Joseph (*fl.* 12th cent.)
Barren Soul, A.

F

Faber, Frederick William (1814–63)
After-State.
Confessional, The.
Dream of Blue Eyes, A.
Eternal Years, The.
Eternity of God, The.
My God, how wonderful Thou art.
Right Must Win, The.
Shadow of the Rock, The.
Sonnet-writing. To F. W. F.
World, The.

Fabian, Cosi
Liturgy for Lilith.
On reading the new physics—Creation and Cosmology.
Prayer of Dedication.

Qadesha (Sacred Whore)

Fabio, Sarah Webster (1928–79)
All Day We've Longed for Night.
Back into the Garden.
For Louis Armstrong, A Ju-Ju.
To Turn from Love.

Facos, James (b. 1924)
Fable.

Fagan, Kathy
California, *She Replied.*
Desire.
In California.
Moving and St Rage.
Revisionary Instruments 1.
She Attempts to Tell the Truth About True Romance.
Weather They Were Written In, The.

Fage, Mary (*fl.* 1637)
To Their Most Excellent Majesty of Great Brittaines Monarchy.

Fagg, Martin
Elegy on Thomas Hood.
Golden Road to Barcelona: 1992, The.
Limerick: "Dickensian borough of Coketown, The."
Limerick: "Quirky old gent, name of Freud, A."
Limerick: "Salopian student of Greek, A."
Limerick: "To avoid matrimonial disasters."
Limerick: "Wily old writer called Maugham, A."
Mrs Nightingale.

Faigao, Bataan
Balitaw.
Kundiman.

Fain, Sammy
Are You Havin' Any Fun?
I Can Dream, Can't I?
I'll Be Seeing You.
Love Is a Many-Splendored Thing.
Love Is a Random Thing.
Secret Love.
Springtime Cometh, The.
That Old Feeling.
Was That the Human Thing to Do?
Wedding Bells Are Breaking Up That Old Gang of Mine.
When I Take My Sugar to Tea.

Fainlight, Harry
Bride, A.

Fainlight, Ruth (b. 1931)
Another Full Moon.
Archive Film Material.
Handbag.
Other, The.

Fa'iq, Salah (b. 1945)
Poem: "As I traveled from the city."
Poem: "I know / how fascinated we are with clarity."
Poem: "If I speak always of the dead."
Poem: "Nothing is more cruel than to see."
Poem: "When the dream departs leaving."

Fairbridge, Kingsley (1885–1924)
Magwere, Who Waits Wondering.
South African Exhibition, 1907.

Fairburn, Arthur Rex Dugard (1904–57)
Back Street.
Beggar to Burgher.
Cave, The.
Conversation in the Bush.
Diogenes.
Down on My Luck.
Farewell, A: "What is there left to be said?"
Full Fathom Five.
I'm Older than You, Please Listen.
Naked Girl Swimming, A.
Possessor, The.
Tapu.
Terms of Appointment.

Fairchild, B. H.
Body and Soul.
Old Men Playing Basketball.

Fairfax, James Griffyth (1886–1976)
Forest of the Dead, The.

Fairfax, John
My emblem is an arrow.

Fairfax of Cameron, Thomas Fairfax, Baron (1612–71)
On the Fatal Day January 30, 1648.
Shortness of Life.
Upon the New Building at Appleton.

Faiz, Faiz Ahmad (1911–84)
Any Lover to Any Beloved.
Bangla Desh: 1.
Bangla Desh: 2.
Bangla Desh: 3.
Before You Came.
Day Death Comes, The.
Don't Ask Me for That Love Again.
Elegy for Hassan Nasir.
Fragrant Hands.
If I Were Certain.
No Sign of Blood.
Once Again the Mind.
Prison Daybreak, A.
Prison Evening, A.
So Bring the Order for My Execution.
Tyrant, The.
Vista.
We Who Were Executed.
When Autumn Came.
You Tell Us What to Do.

Falckner, Justus (1672–1723)
Rise, Ye Children.

Falconar, Maria (b. 1771?)
Prefatory Epistle, A.

Falconer, William (1732–69)
Amid this fearful trance, a thundering sound.
Ship Is Lost, The.
Ship Sets out, the.

Faleti, Adebayo
Independence.

Falk, Marcia (b. 1946)
Home for Winter.
Sabbath Morning.
Shulamit in Her Dreams.

Falke, Gustav (1853–1916)
God's Harp.
Strand-Thistle.

Falkland, Elizabeth Cary, Countess of (c.1585–1639)
Chorus: "'Tis not enough for one that is a wife."

Falkner, John Meade (1858–1922)
After Trinity.
Arabia.
Christmas Day; the Family Sitting.

Fallon, Padraic (1905–74)
Assumption.
Bit of Brass, A.
Dardanelles 1916.
Flask of Brandy, A.
For Paddy Mac.
Gurteen.
Head, The.
Hedge Schoolmaster, A.
Holy Well.
Kiltartan Legend.
Lakshmi.
Mater Dei.
Odysseus.
Painting of My Father.
Pot Shot.
Weir Bridge.
Yeats at Athenry Perhaps.
Young Fenians, The.

Fallon, Peter (b. 1951)
Airs and Graces.
Herd, The.
Himself.
Meadow, The.
Moons.
My Care.
Spring Song.
Winter Work.

Faludi, Ferenc (1704–79)
Fickle Fortune.
Spring.
Unspeakable.

Fan Ch'eng-ta (1126–93)
Autumn.

Consoling the Yü Farmers.
Farming Family Invites the Guest to Stay
　Overnight, A.
Late Spring.
Pressing for Tax Payment.
Reeling Silk.
Rejoicing the Spirits.
Summer.
Winter.
Written While Lying on My Pillow in the
　Morning on the Twelfth Day of the Eleventh
　Month.

Fan Chung-yen (989–1052)
Tune: 'Sumuche Dancers.'
Tune: 'Trimming the Silver Lamp.'
Tune: 'Walk on the Imperial Street.'

Fan Yun (451–505)
Farewell to Shen Yueh.

"Fane, Violet" (Mary Montgomerie Currie, Baroness Currie) (1843–1905)
At Her Feet.
In an Irish Churchyard.
Siren, The.

Fanning, Roger (b. 1962)
Baudelaire's Ablutions.
In the Barn.
Oink as Taunt.
Parable of the Boy and the Polar Bear.
Space Needle, The.

Fanshawe, Catherine Maria (1765–1834)
Enigma.
Riddle, A: "'Twas in heaven pronounced, and
　'twas muttered in hell."
When Last We Parted.

Fanshawe, Sir Richard (1608–66)
Fall, The.
Golden Age, The.
How I forsook / Elias and Pisa after, and
　betook.
Learn women all from this housewifery.
Ode on His Majesty's Proclamation.
Of Beauty.
Our beauty is to us that which to men.
Rose, A.
Well may that kisse be sweet that's giv'n t' a
　sleek.

Fanthorpe, U. A. (b. 1929)
At the Ferry.
BC:AD.
Door, A.
Fanfare.
Father in the Railway Buffet.
Nativities.
Not My Best Side.
Our Dog Chasing Swifts.
Person's Tale, The.
Portraits of Tudor Statesmen.
Reindeer Report.
Relief of Myopia, The.
Resuscitation Team.
What the Donkey Saw.
Women Laughing.
You Will Be Hearing from Us Shortly.

Farawell, Martin Jude
Everything I Need to Know I Learned in
　Kindergarten.

Farber, Norma (1909–84)
Bow Down, Mountain.
For a Quick Exit.
Manhattan Lullaby.
Taking Turns.

Farewell, George (fl. c.1733)
Adieu to My Landlady, An.
Crunking crane heard high amongst the clouds,
　The.
Molly Moor.
Privy-Love for My Landlady.
Quaerè.
There's Life in a Mussel; a Meditation.
To the Archdeacon.

Farhat, Ilyas (1893–1980)
My Burned Suit.
Quatrain: "I saw that thieves had burgled as
　they do."
Quatrain: "I've learnt to laugh now at

adversity."
Quatrain: "Just life and death make up our
　worldly state."
Quatrain: "My foolish heart keeps beckoning
　to me."
Quatrain: "O gold, a deep contempt for you I
　own."
Quatrain: "Seekers of peace, enough
　hypocrisy!"
Quatrain: "Time promises, should I in that
　confide?"
Salma.
Wilderness.

Faricy, Austin (b. 1911)
Through Warmth and Light of Summer Skies.

Farid-uddin Attar (1119–1202)
Conference of the Birds, The.
Invocation to the Conference of the Birds.
World's birds gathered for their conference,
　The.

Farjeon, Eleanor (1881–1965)
Advice to a Child.
Bedtime.
Cats.
Down! Down!
Good Night.
Keeping Christmas.
Mrs. Peck-Pigeon.
Ned.
Night Will Never Stay, The.
Over the Garden Wall.
Tailor.
Tide in the River, The.
Zodiac.

Farley, Henry (fl. c.1621)
Bounty of Our Age, The.

Farley, Robert E.
Thinking Happiness.

Farmer, Harold (b. 1943)
Lost City.

Farquhar, George (1678–1707)
Song, A.
Trifles.

Farr, Robert
At general Electric, where they eat their/young.

Farrar, John Chipman (1896–1976)
Comparison, A.
Song for a Forgotten Shrine to Pan.

Farrokhzad, Forugh (1935–67)
I'm Sad.
In the land of dwarfs.
O Realm Bejewelled.
On Earth.
Once More.
Someone like No One Else.

Fatchen, Max (b. 1920)
Hullo, Inside.
I Often Meet a Monster.
It's a Bit Rich.
Night Walk.
Tailpiece.

Fathy, Safaa (b. 1958)
Sailor, The.
Seasons.

Faugeres, Margaretta (1771–1801)
Friendship.

Fauset, Jessie Redmond (1888–1961)
Oblivion.
Oriflamme.
Touché.

Faust, Henri
After the Storm.
Six Cranes at Dusk.

Faverey, Hans (b. 1933)
Bit by Bit.
In the Service of the Wheel.

Favilla, Candice
Red Clay.
West Texas Rain Journal.

Fawcett, Brian (b. 1944)
Hand, The.

Fawcett, Joseph (1758?–1804)
Feast of Blood, The.

Fawkes, Francis (1720–77)
Elegy on the Death of Dobbin, the

Butterwoman's Horse, An.

Fay, John
Limerick: "Hopeful old fellow called
　Rousseau, A."

Fay, Julie
Flowers.
Mother of Andromeda, The.
Santorini Daughter.
Stereograph: 1903.

Fayad, Mona
Salma in Wonderland.
Whisper.

Fazekas, Mihály (1776–1828)
' But good Sir, look here' —said he.
To Spring.

Fazio degli Uberti (1326–60)
Canzone: His Portrait of His Lady, Angiola of
　Verona.
Of England, and of Its Marvels.
Thou well hast heard that Rollo had two sons.

Fazli, Nida (b. 1940)
Page from the New Diary, A.

Fearing, Kenneth (1902–61)
American Rhapsody.
Any Man's Advice to His Son.
Art Review.
Beware.
Bryce & Tomlins.
C Stands for Civilization.
Cultural Notes.
Dirge: "1-2-3 was the number he played but
　today the number came 3-2-1."
Escape.
Evening Song.
4 A.M.
Green Light.
How Do I Feel?
Literary.
Love, 20c the First Quarter Mile.
Memo.
Minnie and Mrs. Hoyne.
1933.
Obituary.
People vs. the People, The.
Portrait.
Readings, Forecasts, Personal Guidance.
Reception Good.
Resurrection.
Twentieth-Century Blues.
Yes, the Agency Can Handle That.

Feaver, Vicki
Coat.
Lily Pond.
Without you, I prefer the nights.

Feilding, Frances (1650?–1709)
One the Morening the King was Taken Ill my
　Dreame of Him.

Feinfeld, D. A.
Carmelita.
Wound Man, The.

Feinman, Alvin (b. 1929)
November Sunday Morning.

Feinstein, Elaine (b. 1930)
Annus Mirabilis 1989.
At Seven a Son.
Bathroom.
Calliope in the Labour Ward.
Coastline.
Dad.
Getting Older.
June.
Lais.
Lazarus' Sister.
Magic Apple Tree, The.
Medium, The.
Mother Love.
Patience.
Prayer.

Feinstein, Martin (1892–1934)
Burning Bush.

Feinstein, Robert N. (b. 1915)
Woolly Words.

Feinstein, Sascha
Blues for Zoot.
Blues Villanelle for Sonny Criss.

Christmas Eve.
Singapore, July 4th.
Sonnets for Stan Gage (1945–1992)
Summerhouse Piano.

Feiritear, Piaras (1600–53)
Lay your weapons down, young lady.

Feirstein, Frederick (b. 1940)
Mark Stern.
Mark Stern Wakes Up.
Rune-Maker, A.

Feldman, Alan (b. 1945)
Contemporary American Poetry.

Feldman, Irving (b. 1928)
Death of Vitellozzo Vitelli, The.
Dream, The.
Family History.
Handball Players at Brighton Beach, The.
Of Course, We Would Wish.
Old Men, The.
Pripet Marshes, The.
Simple Outlines, Human Shapes.
Surely They're Just So Large.
Se Aprovechan.
To the Six Million.
You Know What I'm Saying?

Fell, Alison (b. 1944)
And Again.
Significant Fevers.

Fell, Frank
Gifted with vision the snowman would see.

Felltham [or Feltham], Owen (c.1602–68)
On a Hopeful Youth.
On the Duke of Buckingham, Slain by Felton, the 23rd August, 1628.
To Phryne.
Upon a Rare Voice.

Feng Chih (b. c.1905)
Sonnet: "We often pass a night warm and intimate."

Fêng Mêng-lung (c. 1590–1646)
Feeling the Itch.
Fooling Mom.
Love-Poem.
My Old Man's Small.
No Old Lady.
Smart.

Feng Yen-ssu (903–60)
Tune: "Magpie on the Branch."

Fenollosa, Ernest Francisco (1853–1900)
Here let me sit, in this empty, cool, terraced hall.
I remember an ancient Chinese picture kept over there in Daitokuji.
Separated East, The.
Soul of my inner face, face of my race.
West provokes the East, The. The iron arm.

Fenton, Elijah (1683–1730)
Olivia.

Fenton, James (b. 1949)
Ballad of the Shrieking Man, The.
Born Too Soon.
Cambodia.
Dead Soldiers.
For the context of the basidiocarp Singer states.
German Requiem, A.
God, A Poem.
His wife nods, and a secret smile.
In a Notebook.
In Paris with You.
Jerusalem.
Kingfisher's Boxing Gloves, The.
Lines for Translation into Any Language.
Lollipops of the Pomeranian Baroque.
Of Bison Men.
Pitt-Rivers Museum, Oxford, The.
Poem against Catholics.
Possibility, The.
Red Light District Nurse, The.
Skip, The.
This Octopus Exploits Women.
Wild Ones[, The].
Wind.

Ferch Gruffyd ab Ieuan ap Lleywelyn Fychan, Alis (fl. 1540–70)
Verses Written by Alis Daughter of Gryffydd

Son of Iefan When Her Father Asked Her What Sort of Husband She Would Like.
When Her Father a Widower Asked What She Would Say to His Intention of Marrying a Young Girl.

Ferch Gruffydd ab Ieuan ap Llywelyn Fychan, Catrin (fl. 1555)
Praise Poem to Christ, A.

Ferdinand, Val
Blues (in Two Parts), The.
Food for Thought.
2 B BLK.
Whi / te boys gone.

Ferguson, Gillian (b. 1965)
Fear of the Future.
In Hospital-land.
Inhaling His Hair.
Scan.
Silent as Roses.
Slugs.
Swimming Pool Ghost, The.
Winter Rose, The.
Winter Sunflowers.

Ferguson, Sir Samuel (1810–86)
Aideen's Grave.
At the Polo-Ground.
Burial of King Cormac, The.
Lament for the Death of Thomas Davis.

Fergusson, Robert (1750–74)
Auld Reikie! wale o' ilka town.
Braid Claith.
Daft Days, The.
Drinking Song.
Epigram on a Lawyer's Desiring One of the Tribe to Look with Respect to a Gibbet.
Ghaists; a Kirk-yard Eclogue, The.
Hallow-Fair.
My Winsome Dear.
Rising of the Session, The.
Sow of Feeling, The.
To the Principal and Professors of the University of St Andrews, on their Superb Treat to Dr Samuel Johnson.

Ferlinghetti, Lawrence (b. 1919)
And Pablo Neruda / that Chilean omnivore of poetry.
Away above a harborful.
Baseball Canto.
Christ Climbed Down.
Constantly Risking Absurdity.
Cro-Magnons.
Dada would have liked a day like this.
Dark Portrait, A.
Don't Let That Horse.
Frightened / by the sound of my own voice.
He.
I am waiting for my case to come up.
In Golden Gate Park that day.
In Goya's greatest scenes we seem to see.
Lost Parents.
Monet's Lilies Shuddering.
One Thousand Fearful Words for Fidel Castro.
Pennycandystore beyond the El, The.
People Getting Divorced.
Pound at Spoleto.
Retired Ballerinas, Central Park West.
River Still To Be Found, A.
Sarolla's women in their picture hats.
Sea and Ourselves at Cape Ann, The.
Sometime During Eternity.
Starting from San Francisco.
Third World Calling.
Underwear.
World is a beautiful place, The.
Wounded wilderness of Morris Graves, The.

Fermini, Ivano (b. 1948)
Detouring through the rooms were men and fumes.
First unexpected pain is beautiful, The.
It descends rapidly under the twistable vine in the sky.
Moments that hands without a vine...laughter.
Statue, The.
That bound and tied they fled.
Waiting for sleep at the air roots.
Wistaria-faced Visigoth, The.

You I know is losing you, The.

Fernández, Abraham
If You Happy Would Be.

Fernandez, Renaldo
Legacy of a Brother.

Ferraz, Leila (b. 1944)
My Love, I Speak to You of a Love.

Ferré, Rosario (b. 1940)
Ballerina.
I Hear You've Let Go.
Message.
Opprobium.
You Have Lost, They Tell Me, Your Reason.

Ferrell, Anderson
Out.

Ferril, Thomas Hornsby (b. 1896)
Always Begin Where You Are.
Jupiter at Beer Springs.
Morning Star.
Noon.
Something Starting Over.
Waltz against the Mountains.
Wood.

Ferriter, Pierce (fl. c.1653)
Lay Your Arms Aside.

Ferry, David (b. 1924)
Anasazi drink from underground rivers, The.
Cythera.
Embarkation for Cythera, The.
Guest Ellen at the Supper for Street People, The.
He stands against what looks like the other side.
Photographs from a Book: Six Poems.
Picture of Eakins and a couple of other people, A.
Plate 134. By Eakins. 'A cowboy in the West.'
Rereading Old Writing.
There is a strange, solemn, silent, graceless.

Ferry, Marcelle (d. 1992)
Frenzy, Sweet Little Child, You Sleep.
One Seated on the Stones of Cheops, The.
When He Went Away.
You Came Down from the Mountains.

Fet [or Foeth], Afanasi Afanasievich (1820–92)
Morning Song.

Fetherling, Doug (b. 1949)
Elijah Speaking.
Explorers as Seen by the Natives.

Fetter, Ted
Taking a Chance on Love.

Fiacc, Padraic (b. 1924)
British Connection, The.
Enemy Encounter.
First Movement.
Gloss.
Goodbye to Brigid / An Agnus Dei.
Haemorrhage.
Intimate Letter 1973.
Introit.
Poet, The.
Saint Coleman's Song for Flight / An Ite Missa Est.
Soldiers.

Fiamengo, Marya (b. 1926)
In Praise of Old Women.

Fiawoo, F. K.
Soliloquy on Death.

Fichman, Jacob [or Jakov] (1881–1958)
Abishag.
Afternoon Light.
Eve.
In the Old City.
Jerusalem.
Midnight.
Secrets of the Landscape, The.

Ficke, Arthur Davison (1883–1945)
Opus 118.
Opus 131.
Sonnet: "There are strange shadows fostered of the moon."
Three Sisters, The.

Ficowski, Jerzy
Assumption of Miriam from the Street in the

Field *(continued)*
Winter of 1942, The.
Both Your Mothers.
Cogito Ergo.
Execution of Memory, The.
5.8.1942 / In Memory of Janusz Korczak.
Girl of Six from the Ghetto Begging in Smolna
Street in 1942, A.
I Did Not Manage to Save.
I would like just to be silent.
Ovid Twice Exiled.
Pawiak 1943.
Seven Words, The.

Field, Anne Vavasour (b. c.1560, d. after 1622)
Thoughe I seem straunge sweete freende be
thou not so.

Field, Barron (1786–1846)
Kangaroo, The.

Field, Edward (b. 1924)
Both My Grandmothers.
Bride of Frankenstein, The.
Callas.
Curse of the Cat Woman.
Event, An.
Floor Is Dirty, The.
Journey, A.
Lower East Side: The George Bernstein Story.
Notes from a Slave Ship.
Oh, the Gingkos.
Street Instructions at the Crotch.
Unwanted.
View of Jersey, A.
Whatever Became Of: Freud?
World War II.

Field, Eugene (1850–95)
Angel's Visit, The.
April Fool, The.
Duel, The.
Jest 'fore Christmas.
Johnny's Team.
Limerick: "'Tis strange how the newspapers
honour."
Little Boy Blue.
Little Peach, The.
Mr. Billings of Louisville.
Piazza Tragedy, A.
Red.
Sugar-Plum Tree, The.
Two Meetings, The.
Wynken, Blynken, and Nod.

**"Field, Michael" (Katherine Bradley and Edith
Cooper)**
After Mass.
After Soufrière.
Ah, Eros doth not always smite.
Already to mine eyelids' shore.
And on My Eyes Dark Sleep by Night.
Aridity.
As two fair vessels side by side.
Atthis, my darling, thou did'st stray.
Beloved, My Glory in Thee is Not Ceased.
Beloved, Now I Love God First.
Bury Her at Even.
Climbing the hill a coil of snakes.
Come, Gorgo, put the rug in place.
Constancy.
Cyclamens.
Descent from the Cross.
Dying Viper, A.
Ebbtide at Sundown.
Elsewhere.
Embalmment.
Eros.
Fellowship.
Fifty Quatrains.
Flaw, A.
Girl, A.
Goad, The.
Gold Is the Son of Zeus: Neither Moth nor
Worm May Gnaw It.
I Am thy Charge, thy Care!
I love you with my life.
I sing thee with the stock-dove's throat.
If They Honoured Me, Giving Me Their Gifts.
Irises.
It was deep April, and the morn.

L'indifférent.
La Gioconda; Leonardo Da Vinci, The Louvre.
Leaves.
Life Plastic.
Lo, my loved is dying, and the call.
Love rises up some days'
Loved, on a sudden thou didst come to me.
Lovers.
Macrinus against Trees.
Maidenhair.
Maids, not to you my mind doth change.
Mummy Invokes His Soul, The.
Nests in Elms.
Nightfall.
Noon.
Nought to me! So I choose to say.
O Wind, thou hast thy kingdom in the trees.
Onycha.
Palimpsest, A.
Penetration.
Picture, A.
Portrait, A.
Prometheus fashioned man.
Renewal.
Second Thoughts.
She is Singing to Thee, *Domine!*
'Sing to us Sappho!' cried the crowd.
So jealous of your beauty.
Sometimes I do despatch my heart.
Sullenness.
Sweet-Briar in Rose.
Sweeter Far than the Harp, More Gold than
Gold.
Thanatos, Thy Praise I Sing.
They Shall Look on Him.
Tiger-Lilies.
To Christina Rossetti.
To the Lord Love.
To the Winter Aphrodite.
Tragic Mary Queen of Scots, The.
Tragic Mary Queen of Scots, II, The.
Trinity.
Unbosoming.
Wheat-miners.
Why should I praise thee, blissful Aphrodite?
Will You Crucify Your King?
Your Rose is Dead.

Field, Rachel Lyman (1894–1942)
Dancing Bear, The.
Epilogue: "Nothing now to mark the spot."
Equestrienne.
General Store.
Gunga.
Manhattan Lullaby.
Parade.
Performing Seal, The.
Skyscrapers.
Some People.
Something Told the Wild Geese.
Summer Morning, A.

Fielding, Henry (1707–54)
Hunting Song.

Fields, Annie (1834–1915)
Ephemeron.

Fields, Dorothy
Blue Again.
Bojangles of Harlem.
Don't Blame Me.
Fine Romance, A.
Have Feet, Will Dance.
I Can't Give You Anything but Love.
I'm in the Mood for Love.
I'm Livin' in a Great Big Way.
I Won't Dance.
It's All Yours.
Lovely to Look At.
Make the Man Love Me.
Never Gonna Dance.
On the Sunny Side of the Street.
Pick Yourself Up.
Remind Me.
There Must Be Somethin' Better Than Love.
Way You Look Tonight, The.
You Couldn't Be Cuter.

Fields, James Thomas (1817–81)
Alarmed Skipper, The.

Ballad of the Tempest.
Jupiter and Ten.
Owl-Critic, The.

Fields, Julia (b. 1938)
Citizen.
Jolly Fat Widows, The.

Fife, Connie
Dear Webster.

Fifer, H. N.
What was his creed?

Figueroa, Jose Angel (b. 1946)
Boricua.
Confessions from the Last Cloud.
Felipa, La Filosofa de Rincon que Nació a los
98 Años.
Homemade Smiles.
Murdered Luggage.
Pablo Neruda.
Poet Pedro Pietri.
Puerto Rico Made in Japan.
Taino.

Fiksman, David Mironovich *See* **"Knut, Dovid"**

Filicaia, Vincenzo da (1642–1707)
Italy.

Filliou, Robert
Homage in dance, An.

Finch, Anne (b. 1908)
Sapphics for Patience.
Dickinson.
For Grizzel McNaught (1709–1792)
O, love, in your sweet name enough.
Reply From His Coy Mistress, A.
There's No To-Morrow.

Finch, Mrs. B. *(fl. 1805)*
Written in a Shrubbery Towards the Decline of
Autumn.
Written in a Winter's Morning.

Finch, Eleanora Wyatt (late 1590s–1623)
Lady weare those bayes, you may.
'Tis true I weepe, I sigh, I wring my hands.
When I first was brought to light.

Finch, Francis Miles (1827–1907)
Blue and the Gray, The.

Finch, Peter (b. 1947)
Acer.
Fists.
How Callum Innes Paints.
Marks the English Left on the Map.
Reds in the Bed.
Scaring Hens.
Tattoo, The.
We Are in the Fields.
Welsh Wordscape, A.
Why Do You Want to Be English?

Finch, Robert (b. 1900)
Aria Senza da Capo.
Collective Portrait, The.
Crib, The.
Last Visit.
Room.
Silverthorn Bush.
Turning.

Finch, Vivienne
Green Ice.
Inertia.

Fincke, Gary
Class A, Salem, the Rookie League.

Fingueret, Manuela
86 Pasteur Corner.
Eve in Eden.
Games at the Hour of the Desert.
Genesis (Chapter 7, Verse 5)
Jerusalem.
Leviticus (Chapter 7, Verse 2–5)
My Father.
Psalms (Chapter 137, Verse 5–6)
Second Portrait.
Tovu-Vavohu.

Fink, Eugenie
Gratitude to Life.
Mozart.

Finkel, Donald (b. 1929)
Father, The.
Flagpole Sitter, The.

Gesture.
Hands.
Joyful Noise, A.
Letter to My Daughter at the End of Her
 Second Year.
Party, The.

Finlay, Ian Hamilton (b. 1925)
Boat's Blueprint, The.
Cloud's Anchor, The.
Evening—Sail.
Garden Poem.
Great frog race.
Lackblockblackb.
Ruined stone temple by the side of a lake, A.
Waterwheels in.

Finnell, Dennis
Belladonna.
Over *Voice of America*.

Finney, Nikky (b. 1957)
Fishing Among the Learned.
Lobengula: Having a son at 38.
Uncles.

Finnigan, Joan (b. 1925)
Stoop on the log-house is brown with sweet
 rain-rot, The.

Finnin, Olive Mary (b. 1906)
Man from Strathbogie, The.

Fiorentino, Ciuncio (*fl.* 1250)
Lady, with all the pains that I can take.

Fiorito, Ted
No, No, Nora.
Toot, Toot, Tootsie! (Good-bye)

Firdowsi (Abul Kasim Mansur) (940–1020)
Alas for Youth.
Birth of Sohráb, The.
Death of Sohráb, The.
When the sword of sixty comes nigh his head.

Firer, Susan
1956, The Year My Sister, Using Her Ill Health
 Once Again, Blackmailed My Parents into
 an Accordion.
Saxophone Julie.

Fischer, Carl
We'll Be Together Again.

Fischer, Helen Field (b. 1940)
New Leaf, A [*or* The].

Fish, Cheryl J.
Work and Worry.

Fisher, Aileen (b. 1906)
After a Bath.
Cat in the Snow.
Caterpillars.
Fair Exchange.
Houses.
Listening.
Mouse Dinner.
On Mother's Day.
Snowy Benches.
Thanksgiving Dinner.
Upside Down.

Fisher, Aileen *and* Olive Rabe
Martin Luther King.
Pioneers.

Fisher, Allen (b. 1944)
African Boog.
Birdland.
Conga.
Continental Walk.
Diary Theme, The.
Ditchley Portrait, The.
Machynlleth.
Murder One.
Progressions of Spacetime: 1.
Rims of Distinction: 1.
Stepping Out: 1.
Stepping Out: 2.

Fisher, Catherine (b. 1957)
Frozen Tarn.
Severn Bore.
Those Who Make Paths.
Words.

Fisher, David (1794–1886)
Limerick: "There was a wee lassie of Ulva."

Fisher, Doris (b. 1915)
Put the Blame on Mame.

That Old Devil Called Love.
Tired.

Fisher, Janet (b. 1943)
Camp.
Gooseflesh.
It's February But.
Life, A.
Pearls.
There are only so many words.

Fisher, Lillian M.
Child of the Sun.
Pioneers.

Fisher, Mahlon Leonard (b. 1874)
In Cool, Green Haunts.

Fisher, Marvin
Cloudy Morning.
I Keep Going Back to Joe's.
Nothing Ever Changes My Love for You.
When Sunny Gets Blue.
Wind in the Willow.

Fisher, Roy (b. 1930)
As He Came near Death.
Brick-dust in sunlight.
Burning Graves at Netherton, The.
Paraphrases.
Entertainment of War, The.
He paints words with the past.
Least, The.
Memorial Fountain, The.
Occasional Poem 7.1.72.
Rules and Ranges for Ian Tyson.
Sign Illuminated, A.
Supposed Dancer, The.
Thing About Joe Sullivan, The.
Toyland.

Fisher, Salih Michael (b. 1956)
Assumption about the Harlem Brown Baby.
Hometown.

Fishman, Charles
Death March.
Not Only in the Six-Day War.
Whapmagoostui.

Fishman, Lisa (b. 1966)
Diagnosis: My Mother's Breast.
Promiscuity.
V's Farmhouse.

Fisk, Molly
Late Afternoon.
Red River.

Fiske, John (1608–1677)
Upon the Decease of Mrs. Anne Griffin.
Upon the Much-to Be Lamented Desease of
 the Reverend Mr. John Cotton.

Fiskin, Jeffrey
Magi, The.

Fitch, Eleazar Thompson (1791–1871)
By Vows of Love Together Bound.
Lord, at This Closing Hour.

Fitger, Arthur (1840–1900)
Evening Prayer.

Fitts, Dudley (1903–68)
Ya Se Van Los Pastores.

Fitzgerald, Edward (1809–83)
Old Song.
Rubáiyát of Omar Khayyam, The, *sels.*
War begets Poverty.

**Fitzgerald, F. Scott (Francis Scott Key
 Fitzgerald) (1896–1940)**
Obit on Parnassus.
There was an Orchestra.

Fitzgerald, Mary Scott
Rendezvous.

Fitzgerald, Robert (1910–85)
Cobb Would Have Caught It.
Entreaty.
Epiphany.
Et Quidquid Aspiciebam Mors Erat.
Farewell.
Figlio Maggiore.
History.
Horae.
Imprisoned, The.
July in Indiana.
Manuscript with Illumination.

Mise en Scène.
Mutations.
Shore of Life, The.
Song for September.
Souls Lake.
South Side.
Spring Shade.

Fitzgerald, Robert David (1902–87)
1918–1941.
Bog and Candle.
Copernicus.
Edge.
Face of the Waters, The.
Favour.
Grace before Meat.
Rain in my ears: impatiently there raps.
Wind at Your Door, The.

Fitzgerald, Thomas (1695?–1752)
Upon an Ingenious Friend, Over-Vain.

Fitzgerald, Zelda Sayre (1900–48)
I Do Love My Charlie So.
Over the Top with Pershing.

Fitzpatrick, Conal (b. 1951)
Discovering Lasseter.

Fitzpatrick, Dominic
Limerick: "When your capitalist boss takes his
 toll."

Fitzpatrick, Kevin (b. 1949)
Highland, 1955.

Flaccus, Aulus Persius *See* **Persius**

Flaccus, Gaius Valerius (d. c.93–5)
Book 7.

Flaccus, Quintus Horatius *See* **Horace**

Flaischlen, Cäsar (1864–1920)
Most Quietly at Times.

Flanagan, Dorothy Belle
Three Years from Sorrento.

Flanders, Jane (b. 1940)
Big Cars.
Other Lives of the Romantics.
Handbell Choir, The.
House That Fear Built: Warsaw, 1943, The.
Twirling.

Flanders, Michael (1922–75)
Have Some Madeira, M'dear?

Flanner, Hildegarde (1899–1987)
Dumb.
Fern Song.
Frog Song.
Hawk Is a Woman.
Let Us Believe.
Moment.
Sonnets in Quaker Language.
Swift Love, Sweet Motor.
This Day.
True Western Summer.

Flatman, Thomas (1637–88)
Appeal to Cats in the Business of Love, An.
Nudus Redibo.
On Marriage.
Sad Day, The.
Thought of Death, A.
Unconcerned, The.

Flavell [*or* Lavell], Thomas (b. 1906)
County of Mayo, The.

Fleckenstein, Mark
Getting Even.

Flecker, James Elroy (1884–1915)
And how beguile you? Death has no repose.
Ballad of Hampstead Heath, The.
Ballad of the Londoner.
Epilogue: "Away, for we are ready to a man!"
Hassan's Serenade.
In Hospital.
No Coward's Song.
Old Ships, The.
Oxford Canal.
Parrot, The.
Prologue: "We Who with Songs Beguile Your
 Pilgrimage."
Rioupéroux.
Santorin.
Stillness.
Tenebris Interlucentem.

To a Poet a Thousand Years Hence.
Town without a Market, The.
War Song of the Saracens.
Flecknoe, Richard (1600–78)
Ant, The.
Invocation of Silence.
Fleg, Edmond (1874–1964)
Wall of Weeping, The.
Fleischer, Max
Rich Harvest.
Fleischman, Paul (b. 1952)
Fireflies.
Fleming, Marjory (1803–11)
Melancholy Lay, A.
Fleming, Paul (1609–40)
Concerning Himself.
Devotion.
How He Should Like to Be Kissed.
It Is in Vain, the Sorrow.
To Himself.
To the Great City of Moscow, as He Was
    Leaving June 25, 1636.
To the Moon.
Fleming, Robert (b. 1950)
For All Unwed Mothers.
Fletcher, Curley W.
High-loping Cowboy, The.
Fletcher, Giles, the Elder (c.1549–1611)
Are those two stars, her eyes, my life's light
    gone.
Crucify Him!
First did I fear, when first my love began.
I saw, sweet Licia, when the spider ran.
In Time the Strong and Stately Turrets Fall.
Fletcher, Giles, the Younger (1585–1623)
As when the cheerfull Sunne, elamping wide.
Celestial City, The.
Easter Morn.
Mercy Replies to Justice.
Seemèd that Man had them devoured all.
To Whom Else Can We Fly?
Upon a grassie hillock He was laid.
Wooing Song.
Fletcher, John (1579–1625)
Beggar's Bash, sels.
Chances, The, sels.
Elder Brother, The, sels.
Faithful Shepherdess, The, sels.
Fletcher's Lament for his Friend, sels.
Little French Lawyer, The, sels.
Lover's Progress, The, sels.
Mad Lover, The, sels.
Nice Valor, The, sels.
Spanish Curate, The, sels.
Tragedy of Valentinian, The, sels.
Women Pleased, sels.
Fletcher, John See also **Beaumont, Francis**
Fletcher, John (1564–1616) and **William
Shakespeare**
King Henry VIII, sels.
Two Nobel Kinsmen, The, sels.
Fletcher, John Gould (1886–1950)
Before Olympus.
Blue Symphony.
Clipper-Ships.
Green Symphony.
Irradiations.
Last Judgment.
Lincoln.
London Nightfall.
Rebel, A.
Skaters, The.
Song of the Moderns.
Trees, like great jade elephants, The.
Fletcher, Louisa
Land of Beginning Again, The.
Fletcher, Lynne Yamaguchi
After Delivering Your Lunch.
Higashiyama Crematorium, November 6, 1983.
Way April Leads to Autumn, The.
Fletcher, Phineas (1580–1650)
Against a Rich Man Despising Poverty.
Divine Wooer, The.
Dying Husband's Farewell, The.
Hymn, An: "Wake, O my soul; awake, and

raise."
Hymn: "Drop, drop, slow tears, and bathe
    those beauteous feet."
Me Lord? can'st Thou mispend.
Ocean of Light.
Say Muses, say; who now in those rich fields.
Sin, Despair, and Lucifer.
To Thomalin.
With her, her sister went, a warlike maid.
Flint, Francis Stewart [or "Frank"] (1885–1960)
Eau-Forte.
Lament: "Young men of the world, The."
Flint, James (1779–1885)
In Pleasant Lands Have Fallen the Lines.
Florian, Douglas (b. 1950)
First.
Send My Spinach.
Florián, Mario (b. 1917)
Pastora.
Florit, Eugenio (b. 1903)
Elegy for Your Absence.
Martyrdom of Saint Sebastian, The.
Present Evening, The.
Florsheim, Stewart
Business in Germany.
Jewish Singles Event, The.
Real Chocolate.
Weekend in Palm Springs.
Floyd, Bryan Alec
Captain James Leson, U. S. M. C.
Corporal Charles Chungtu, U. S. M. C.
Corporal Kevin Spina, U. S. M. C.
Lance Corporal Purdue Grace, U. S. M. C.
Private First Class Brooks Morgenstein, U. S.
    M. C.
Private Ian Godwin, U. S. M. C.
Private Jack Smith, U. S. M. C.
Sergeant Brandon Just, U. S. M. C.
**Flynn, Desiré (Sheila Desiré Savory Rodd) (b.
1917)**
Collector, The.
From the Rain Forest.
Flynn, Elizabeth (1890–1964)
After Grave Deliberation.
Flynn, Frank
Clothes on the Washing Line.
Shed, The.
Winter Morning.
Flynn, Nick (b. 1960)
Bag of Mice.
Cartoon Physics, Part 1.
Cartoon Physics, Part 2.
Emptying Town.
Fragment (Found Inside My Mother)
God Forgotten.
Foerster, Richard
Bronx Park.
Playland.
Mozart's Death.
Fogarty, Lionel (b. 1958)
Ecology.
No Grudge.
Remember Something Like This.
Shields Strong, Nulla Nullas Alive.
Worker Who, the Human Who, the Abo Who,
    The.
Fogel, Ephim G. (1920–1992)
Shipment to Maidanek.
Fogel, Ephraim
Shipment to Maidanek.
Fogle, Richard Harter (b. 1911)
Hawthorne Garland, A.
Foix, J. V. (1893–1987)
I Arrived in that Town, Everyone Greeted Me
    and I Recognized no One. When I Was
    Going to Read My Verses, the Devil, Hidden
    Behind a Tree, Called Out to Me
    Sarcastically and Filled My Hands with
    Newspaper Clippings.
Sonnet: "Alone, in mourning, wearing an
    archaic black gown."
When I Sleep, Then I See Clearly.
Folcachiero de' Folcachieri (fl. c.1175)
Canzone: He Speaks of His Condition through

Love.
Foley, Helen (1896–1937)
Touch Wood.
Foley, James William (1874–1939)
Drop a Pebble in the Water.
Foley, Kate
Matching Flowers.
My Father, Counting Sheep.
Foley, Michael (b. 1947)
Ah no, ah no, they weren't all gross and slow.
Brothers and Sisters.
Lucky Eugene.
Middle Manager in Paradise, The.
On the Waterfront.
Provincial Adolescence, A.
Sois sage, ô ma doleur . . . I don't.
Sword is a cold bride. Yuk!, The.
Folger, Peleg (1734–89)
Praise Ye the Lord, O Celebrate His Fame.
Follain, Jean (1903–71)
Black Meat.
Buying.
Face the Animal.
Mirror, A.
Music of Spheres.
School and Nature.
Taxidermist, A.
Follen, Eliza Lee Cabot (1787–1860)
Children in Slavery.
For the Fourth of July.
Good Moolly Cow, The.
Lines on Nonsense.
Lord, Deliver, Thou Canst Save.
Three Little Kittens, The.
Fong, Herman (b. 1963)
Asylum.
Fontana, Jennie
Ask many women and they'll claim no
    knowledge, but some.
Fontanella, Luigi (b. 1943)
After the Party.
Father-Sequence.
For Emma.
I'm on a straight path with the sun gone down.
Image of the frozen lake, The.
In The Nighttime Someone.
It's a slow warmth I find once more.
Mimikòs.
Sleeplessness.
Transparent Life, The.
Turning of the car.
Victoria Station.
Fonte Boa, Maria Amalia
Two Tile Beaks.
Vitality.
Foot, Edward Edwin (b. 1828)
Altho' we mourn for one now gone.
Captain scans the ruffled zone, The.
Jane Hollybrand; or, Virtue Rewarded.
Foot, P. W. R.
Limerick: "Cried the maid: "You must marry
    me, Hume!""
Limerick: "Philosopher Berkeley once said,
    The."
Foote, Samuel (1720–77)
Great Panjandrum [Himself], The.
Foppa, Alaide (b. 1932)
First Portrait of My Son.
Nocturne.
Woman.
Wound.
Your Hand in Mine.
Forbes, Calvin (b. 1945)
Blue Monday.
Dark Mirror.
Europe.
Hand Me Down Blues.
Home.
Killer Blues.
Lullaby for Ann-Lucian.
My Father's House.
Picture of a Man.
Poet's Shuffle, The.
Potlicker Blues.
Potter's Wheel, The.

Reading Walt Whitman.

Forbes, Duncan (b. 1947)
Politics of Envy.

Forbes, John (b. 1950)
Age of Plastic, The.
Angel.
Death, an Ode.
Four Heads & How to Do Them.
Love Poem.
Malta.
Monkey's Pride.
Speed, a Pastoral.
TV.
Up, Up, Home & Away.

Forché, Carolyn (b. 1950)
Ancapagari.
As Children Together.
Colonel, The.
Elegy.
Garden Shukkei-en, The.
Kalaloch.
Memory of Elena, The.
Morning Baking, The.
Ourselves or Nothing.
Return.
Reunion.
Skin Canoes.
Taking Off My Clothes.
Testimony of Light, The.
Visitor, The.

Ford, Charles Henri (b. 1913)
Bad Habit, The.
Plaint.
'January wraps up the wound of his arm.'
Overturned Lake, The.
Somebody's Gone.
There's No Place to Sleep in This Bed,
Tanguy.

Ford, Ford Madox (Ford Madox Hueffer) (1873–1939)
For the white-limbed heroes of Hellas ride by
  upon their horses.
"When the World Was in Building."
Old Houses of Flanders, The.
On Heaven.
Sidera Cadentia.
That Exploit of Yours.
This is Charing Cross.
What the Orderly Dog Saw.

Ford, John (1586–1640?)
Dawn.
Love's Martyrs.

Ford, Robert Arthur Douglas (b. 1915)
Back to Dublin.
Earthquake.
Revenge of the Hunted.
Sakhara.
Twenty Below.
Window on the North, A.

Ford, Simon (1619?–1699)
Hail, glorious day; mayst thou be writ in gold.

Ford, Thomas (1580–1648)
There Is a Lady Sweet and Kind.

Ford, William (fl. 20th cent.)
Of Miles Davis.

Fordham, Mary Weston (fl. c.1897)
Alaska.
Atlanta Exposition Ode.
Bells of St. Michael.
Cherokee, The.
Chicago Exposition Ode.
Christ Child, The.
Coming Woman, The.
Creation.
Crucifixion, The.
Death of a Grandparent. Mrs. Jennette
  Bonneau.
Dedicated to the Right Rev'd D. A. Payne.
Dying Girl, The.
Exile's Reverie, The.
For Who?
Grafted Bud, The.
Highland Mary.
In Memoriam. Alphonse Campbell Fordham.
In Memoriam. Susan Eugenia Bennett.

June.
"By the Rivers of Babylon."
Lines to———.
Lines to Florence.
Lines to Mrs. Isabel Peace.
Magnolia.
Maiden and River.
Marriage.
Mother's Recall.
Mr. Edward Fordham.
Mrs. E. Cohrs Brown.
Mrs. Louise B. Weston.
Mrs. Mary Furman Weston Byrd.
Mrs. Rebecca Weston.
Nativity, The.
Nestle-down Cottage.
October.
Ode to Peace.
On Parting with a Friend.
Passing of the Old Year.
Past, The.
Pen, The.
Queenie.
Rally Song.
Requiem: "O, insatiable monster! Could'st thou
  not."
Rev. Samuel Weston.
Reverie, A.
Saxon Legend of Language, The.
Serenade: "Sleep, love sleep."
Shipwreck.
Snow Storm, The.
Snowdrop, The.
Song to Erin.
Sonnet to My First Born.
Stars and Stripes.
Sunset.
To a Loved One.
To an Infant.
To My Mother.
To Rev. Thaddeus Saltus.
To the Eagle.
To the Mock-Bird.
Tribute to a Lost Steamer.
Tribute to Capt. F. W. Dawson.
Twilight Musings.
Uranne.
Valentine, The.
Washerwoman, The.

Fore, Brian
They Told Me, Heraclitus.

Forhan, Chris
Big Jigsaw.
Taste of Wild Cherry, The.
Without Presumptions.

Forman, Ruth (b. 1968)
Abraham Got All the Stars N the Sand.
Green Boots n Lil Honeys.
Kin.
Someone.
This Poem.
Waitin on Summer.
We Are the Young Magicians.
You So Woman.

Forrest, Frederick (fl. c.1766)
St. Anthony and His Pig; a Cantata.

Forrest, George (1915–99)
And This Is My Beloved.
Baubles, Bangles, and Beads.
It's a Blue World.
Strange Music.
Stranger in Paradise.

Forrest-Thomson, Veronica (1947–75)
Lemon and Rosemary.
Michaelmas.
Pfarr-Schmerz (Village-Anguish)
Phrase-Book.
Richard II.
Sonnet: "My love, if I write a song for you."

Forster, Edward Morgan (1879–1970)
I Strove with None.

Forster, William (1818–82)
In New South Wales, as I plainly see.
Love Has Eyes.
Poor of London, The.
Sonnet on the Crimean War.

Forsyth, Sarah
My Christmas; Mum's Christmas.

Fort, Charles
For Martin Luther King.

Fort, Paul (1872–1960)
Ballade: "Pretty maid she died, she died, in
  love-bed as she lay, The."
Pan and the Cherries.
Sailor and the Shark, The.

Forten, Charlotte (1839–1914)
Parting Hymn, A.
Poem: "In the earnest path of duty."
To W. L. G. on Reading His "Chosen Queen."

Forten, Sarah L. See "Ada" (Sarah Louisa
  Forten)

Fortini, Franco (b. 1917)
Italy 1942.
Perhaps the Time of Blood.
Poetry of Roses, The.

Fosdick, Harry Emerson (1878–1969)
Prince of Peace His Banner Spreads, The.

Foss, Sam Walter (1858–1911)
Despise not any man that lives.
House by the Side of the Road, The.
Husband and Heathen.
"Hullo!"
Philosopher, A.

Foster, Annie (b. 1955)
Ashes.
Caterpillar.
Field.
Gap, The.
God and the Holy Stones.
Nest of Hats, A.
No Dice.
Starting School.
Union.
Wythop Mill.

Foster, David (b. 1944)
Alchemists say the Stone turns lead to gold.
Don't give everything.
Seeking heat men become cold, and look for
  meaning.

Foster, Michael
Recruiting Song.

Foster, Stephen Collins (1826–84)
Camptown Races.
Jeanie with the Light Brown Hair.
My Old Kentucky Home[, Good Night!].
Oh! Susanna.
Old Folks at Home[, The].
Who Has Our Redeemer Heard.

Foulcher, John (b. 1952)
After the Flood.
Wars of Imperialism.

Foulkes, William H. (1877–1961)
Take Thou Our Minds, Dear Lord.

Fournier, Rick
Encounter.

Fowler, Andrew (1760–1850)
Awake, My Soul! In Grateful Songs.
O Gracious Jesus, Blessed Lord!

Fowler, Russell T.
In Blanco County.

Fowler, William (1560–1612)
In Orknay.
Ship-broken Men Whom Stormy Seas Sore
  Toss.
Upon this firthe, as on the sees of love.

Fox, Gail (b. 1942)
It Is Her Cousin's Death.
Portrait.
She Lay Wrapped.

Fox, Lucia (b. 1930)
Dream of the Forgotten Lover.

Fox, Siv Cedering (b. 1939)
Almagest, Last Letter to Zakarias.
Grandmother.
In the Evening.
Miss Pimberton Of.
Peaches.

Foxe, Emma (d. 1570)
To you that lyfe possess grete troubles do
  befall.

Foy, James L.
Autopsy.
Frabotta, Biancamaria (b. 1946)
Dianae Sumus in Fide.
Dim Light Splits the Woods in Two Distinct Lines, The.
Erosion of Utopia or Rigor of Patience?
Here dwells the whole and scattered.
It Is True. I Am Not a Poet the Way You Are.
Myopia.
Self-Portrait in the Third Person.
Shipwreck.
Fraire, Isabel (b. 1936)
If night takes the form of a whale and.
Frame, Janet (b. 1925)
Christmas and Death.
Clown, The.
Flowering Cherry, The.
Foxes, The.
Letter.
Place, The.
Telephonist.
When the Sun Shines More Years Than Fear.
Yet Another Poem about a Dying Child.
France de Bravo, Brandel
Unrepentant.
France, Linda (b. 1958)
Blues for Bird.
Body Language.
Chip City.
Eater of Wives, The.
Gentleness of the Very Tall, The.
In Kind.
Mess With It.
Meteorology.
My Muse, the Whore.
New York Spring.
North and South.
What I Know Now.
France, Peter
Death.
France, Ruth *See* **"Henderson, Paul"**
Frances, Emmanuel [*or* Immanuel] ben David (1618–c.1703)
Price of Begging, The.
Frances, Jacob ben David (1615–77)
Song of Hate.
Francescato, Martha Paley (b. 1934)
Parody.
Semen.
Francia, Luis H.
In Gurgle Veritas.
Is there There in dying.
Secret in the Roar, The.
Video Victim.
Francis, Anne (1738–1800)
When cats like him submit to fate.
Francis, Arthur (*fl.* 1922)
Stairway to Paradise.
Francis of Assisi, Saint (1181–1226)
Cantica: Our Lord Christ: Of Order.
Canticle of the Brother Sun, The.
Canticle of the Creatures.
Canticle of the Sun.
Cantico del Sole.
Prayer of St. Francis of Assisi for Peace.
Francis, Robert (b. 1901)
Apple Peeler.
As Easily As Trees.
Base Stealer, The.
Blue Jay [*or* Bluejay].
Blue Winter.
Bouquets.
Boy Riding Forward Backward.
Broken View, A.
By Night.
Catch.
Cold.
Coming and Going.
Curse, The.
Cypresses.
December.
Earthworm.
Everyman/ Preacher or lecher, saint or sot.
Exclusive Blue.

Fair and Unfair.
Fall.
Farm Boy after Summer.
Hogwash.
Hound, The.
Juniper.
Like Ghosts of Eagles.
Mouse Whose Name Is Time, The.
Museum Vase.
Night Train.
Onion Fields.
Pitcher, The.
Rock Climbers, The.
Sheep.
Silent Poem.
Slow.
Sound I Listened For, The.
Swimmer.
That Dark Other Mountain.
Three Darks Come Down Together.
Three Woodchoppers.
Two Wrestlers.
Waxwings.
While I Slept.
Yes, What?
Francis, Samuel Trevor (1834–1925)
O the deep, deep love of Jesus!
Francisco, Nia (b. 1952)
Kayenta Times Yet Dreaming On.
Modern on the Surface.
Roots of Blue Bells.
To a Man Who is Rob Southland.
Francisco, Prince Ioann Shakhovskoy, Archbishop of San *See* **"Strannik"**
Frank, Florence Kiper (b. 1890)
Jewish Conscript, The.
Frankau, Gilbert (1884–1952)
Deserter, The.
Gun Teams.
Franklin, Benjamin (1706–90)
Epitaph: "Body / of / Benjamin Franklin, The."
Mother Country, The.
Franzen, John (b. 1904)
O God of Stars and Distant Space.
Fraser, George Sutherland (1915–80)
Christmas Letter Home.
Lament: "In a dismal air; a light of breaking summer."
Lean Street.
Letter to Anne Ridler.
Rostov.
Fraser, Kathleen (b. 1937)
Re:searches (Fragments, after Anakreon, for Emily Dickinson)
Fraser, Sanford
Looking Out to Sea Again on the Uptown Express.
Frear, Mary Dillingham (b. 1810)
Young Workman, The.
Frederick II, Emperor (1194–1250)
For grief I am about to sing.
Free, Spencer Michael (b. 1856)
Human Touch, The.
Freed, Arthur (1894–1973)
All I Do Is Dream of You.
Broadway Melody.
Fit As a Fiddle.
Good Morning.
I Cried for You.
I've Got a Feelin' You're Foolin'
Singin' in the Rain.
This Heart of Mine.
You Were Meant for Me.
Freed, Florence W.
Private School for Girls, May 14, 1948, New York City, A.
Freed, Ralph (1907–73)
Babes on Broadway.
How About You.
You Leave Me Breathless.
Freeman, Arthur (b. 1938)
Cell of Himself, The.
Freeman, Carol [*or* Carole] (b. 1941)
Christmas Morning I.

Freeman, Enoch W. (1798–1835)
Hither We Come, Our Dearest Lord.
Freeman, James (1759–1835)
Lord of the Worlds Below!
Freeman, Jan
Fifteen.
Freeman, John (1880–1929)
Asylum.
Hounds, The.
To End Her Fear.
Freeman, Mary Eleanor Wilkins (1852–1930)
Blue-eyed Mary.
Marm Grayson's Guests.
Ostrich Is a Silly Bird, The.
Pretty Ambition, A.
Freeman, Robert (1878–1940)
Braving the Wilds All Unexplored *with music*.
Freeman, Stan
Other Half of Me, The.
Freer, Ulli (b. 1947)
Baseline pressure.
TM.
Freeth, John (1731?–1808)
Botany Bay.
Bunker's Hill, or the Soldier's Lamentation.
Cottager's Complaint, on the Intended Bill for Enclosing Sutton-Coldfield, The.
Frémont, John Charles (1813–90)
On Recrossing the Rocky Mountains after Many Years.
French, William Percy (1854–1920)
Mountains of Mourne, The.
Queen's After-Dinner Speech, The.
Freneau, Philip *See* **Brackenridge, Hugh Henry**
Freneau, Philip (1752–1832)
American Soldier, The.
And by that light around the dome appear'd.
And from the woods the late resounding note.
And from within the howls of Death I heard.
And here and there with laurel shrubs between.
At distance far approaching to the tomb.
At last, by chance and guardian fancy led.
Before the hearse Death's chaplain seem'd to go.
But now this man of hell toward me turned.
By Babel's Streams *with music*.
By some sad means, when reason holds no sway.
Columbus to Ferdinand.
Dark was the sky, and not one friendly star.
Dim burnt the lamp, and now the phantom Death.
Epitaph for Jonathan Robbins.
France aids them now, a desperate game I play.
George the Third's Soliloquy.
Hills sink to plains, and man returns to dust.
Hurricane, The.
Indian Burying Ground, The.
Indian Convert, The.
Indian Student; or, Force of Nature, The.
Libera nos, Domine—Deliver Us, O Lord.
Literary Importation.
Meantime from an adjoining chamber came.
Much spoke he of the myrtle and the yew.
No pleasant fruit or blossom gaily smiled.
Nor look'd I back, till to a far off wood.
O'er a dark field I held my dubious way.
On a Honey Bee [*or* To a Honey Bee].
On Mr. Paine's Rights of Man.
On Observing a Large Red-Streak Apple.
On the Civilization of the Western Aboriginal Country.
On the Conflagrations at Washington.
On the Emigration to America [and Peopling the Western Country].
On the Great Western Canal of the State of New York.
On the Religion of Nature.
On the Uniformity and Perfection of Nature.
Pathetic were their words, and well they aimed.
Peace to this awful dome!—when straight I heard.
Poppy there, companion to repose, The.
Primrose there, the violet darkly blue, The.
Rude, from the wide extended Chesapeke.

Sad was his countenance, if we can call.
Stanzas Occasioned by the Ruins of a Country
  Inn *or* On the Ruins of a Country Inn.
Then up three winding stairs my feet were
  brought.
There cedars dark, the osier, and the pine.
To a Caty-did.
To a New England Poet.
To a Noisy Politician.
To an Author.
To Mr. Blanchard, the Celebrated Aeronaut in
  America.
To Sir Toby.
To the Memory of the Brave Americans.
Tobacco.
Too nearly join'd to sickness, toils, and pains.
Towering Alps, the haughty Appenine, The.
Trembling, across the plain my course I held.
Trembling I write my dream, and recollect.
Two hulks on Hudson's stormy bosom lie.
Up rushed a band, with compasses and scales.
Vanity of Existence, The.
Vision of the Night, The.
Warning to America, A.
What is this Death, ye deep read sophists, say?
When Nature bids thee from the world retire.
Wild Honey Suckle, The.

Frere, John Hookham (1769–1846)
And certainly they say, for fine behaving.
Fable, A.
I've often wish'd that I could write a book.

Frere, John Hookham *See* **Canning, George**

Frescobaldi, Dino
That star the highest seen in heaven's expanse.
This is the damsel by whom love is bought.

Frezza, Luciana (b. 1926)
Against the Current.
Eurydice.
Old Dedication.
Places.
Smile, The.
Summer.
To Allen Ginsberg & Co.
Work.

Fried, Barbara (b. 1924)
Good Old Days, The.

Fried, Erich (b. 1921)
Exile.
Measures Taken, The.
My Girlfriends.
One Kind of Freedom Speaks.
What Things Are Called.

Friedman, Sari
Answering Machine Message.
Skin.

Friedmann, Pavel (1921–1944)
Butterfly, The.
Butterfly, The.

Fries, Kenny (b. 1960)
I bed next to you, I feel your heartbeat.
Who knows the precise moment when the
  stream.

Friman, Alice R. (b. 1933)
Honeymoon.

Frishberg, Dave (b. 1933)
Another Song About Paris.
I'm Hip.
Peel Me a Grape.
Van Lingle Mungo.

Fritsch, H. S.
How Old Are You?

Froissart, Jean (c.1337–1410?)
Rondel: "Love, love, what wilt thou with this
  heart of mine?"

Frost, Carol
Consent.
Custom.
To Kill a Deer.

Frost, Frances Mary (1905–59)
Christmas in the Wood.
Deserted Orchard.

Frost, Katherine
Remission.
Winners.

Frost, Lesley (1899–1983)
Rock 'n' Roll.

Frost, Richard (b. 1929)
Night Person, The.

Frost, Robert (1874–1963)
Acceptance.
Acquainted with the Night.
After Apple-Picking.
Aim Was Song, The.
All Revelation.
America Is Hard to See.
Answer, An.
Armful, The.
Away!
Axe-Helve, The.
Bear, The.
Bearer of Evil Tidings, The.
Bereft.
Beyond Words.
Birches.
Black Cottage, The.
Bond and Free.
Boundless Moment, A.
Brook in the City, A.
Brown's Descent; or, The Willy-Nilly.
Cabin in the Clearing, A.
Canis Major.
Choose Something like a Star.
Clear and Colder.
Cliff Dwelling, A.
Code, The.
Come In.
Considerable Speck, A.
Cow in Apple Time, The.
Death of the Hired Man, The.
Demiurge's Laugh, The.
Departmental.
Desert Places.
Design.
Directive.
Draft Horse, The.
Drumlin Woodchuck, A.
Dust of Snow.
Egg and the Machine, The.
Ends.
Fire and Ice.
Fireflies in the Garden.
For Once, Then, Something.
Forgive, O Lord, my little jokes on Thee.
Fountain, a Bottle, a Donkey's Ears and Some
  Books, A.
Freedom of the Moon, The.
From Plane to Plane.
Gathering Leaves.
Gift Outright, The.
Happiness Makes Up in Height for What It
  Lacks in Length.
Hardship of Accounting, The.
Hill Wife, The.
Hillside Thaw, A.
Home Burial.
House Fear.
Hyla Brook.
I Shall Say What Inordinate Love Is.
Immigrants.
Impulse, The.
In Divés' Dive.
In Hardwood Groves.
In Neglect.
In White.
In winter in the woods alone.
Investment, The.
It takes all sorts of in- and outdoor schooling.
Last Word of a Bluebird, The.
Leaf-Treader, A.
Leaves Compared with Flowers.
Limerick: "For Travelers Going Sidereal."
Line-Gang, The.
Lockless Door, The.
Loneliness.
Lost in Heaven.
"Out, Out—."
Lovely Shall Be Choosers, The.
Lucretius versus the Lake Poets.
Luke 16:19–26; "There was a rich man."
Meeting and Passing.
Middleness of the Road, The.
Minor Bird, A.
Mood Apart, A.

Moon Compasses.
Most of It, The.
Mowing.
My November Guest.
Need of Being Versed in Country Things, The.
Neither Out Far Nor In Deep.
Never Again Would Birds' Song Be The Same.
Not to Keep.
Nothing Gold Can Stay.
Objection to Being Stepped On, The.
Oft-Repeated Dream, The.
Old Man's Winter Night, An.
On a Bird Singing in its Sleep.
On a Tree Fallen across the Road.
On the Heart's Beginning to Cloud the Mind.
Once by the Pacific.
One More Brevity.
Onset, The.
Oven Bird, The.
Pan with Us.
Pasture, The.
Patch of Old Snow, A.
Paul's Wife.
Peaceful Shepherd, The.
Prayer in Spring, A.
Pride of Ancestry.
Provide, Provide.
Putting in the Seed.
Questioning Faces.
Range-finding.
Reluctance.
Revelation.
Road Not Taken, The.
Rose Family, The.
Runaway, The.
Sand Dunes.
Secret Sits, The.
Servant to Servants, A.
Silken Tent, The.
Sitting by a Bush in Broad Daylight.
Mending Wall.
Sound of Trees, The.
Span of Life, The.
Spring Pools.
Star in a Stoneboat, A.
Stopping by Woods on a Snowy Evening.
Storm Fear.
Strong Are Saying Nothing, The.
Subverted Flower, The.
To Earthward.
To the Thawing Wind.
Tree at My Window.
Tuft of Flowers, The.
Two Look at Two.
Two Tramps in Mud Time.
U. S. 1946 King's X.
Unharvested.
Vantage Point, The.
Were I in Trouble.
West-Running Brook.
White-Tailed Hornet, The.
Witch of Coös, The.
Wood-Pile, The.
Wrights' Biplane, The.
Young Birch, A.

Frothingham, Nathaniel Langdon (1793–1870)
O God Whose Presence Glows in All.

Frothingham, Octavius Brooks (1822–95)
Thou Lord of Hosts, Whose Guiding Hand.

Fructuoso, Eric
Astig.

Frug, Simeon Grigoryevich (1860–1916)
Sail Peacefully Home.
Talmud, The.

Fu Hsien (239–294)
Ruinous Rains.

Fu Hsüan (d. 278)
Gentle Wind, A.
Pity Me!
Thunder.
Woman.

Fuertes, Gloria (b. 1920)
Human Geography.
I Write Poems.
Interior Landscape.
Love Which Frees.

We're OK.

Fufu (d. 1762)
My companion in the skies.

Fugai (fl. 17th cent.)
Only the Zen-man knows tranquillity.

Fuhaku (1714–1807)
So very still, even.

Fuhrman, Joanna (b. 1972)
Atlantis.
Evidence.
Here, I Say.
Personal Ad.
Watching Trains.

Fujii Sadakazu (b. 1942)
Small Dream.
Wolf.

Fujiwara no Atsutada (d. 961?)
I think of the days.

Fujiwara no Go-Kanesuke (fl. 10th cent.)
River Izumi, The.

Fujiwara no Go-Kyōgoku (fl. late 12th cent.)
Cricket cries, The.

Fujiwara no Kiyosuke (d. 1177)
I may live on until.

Fujiwara no Masatsune (1170–1221)
From Yoshino / Mountain side, the.

Fujiwara no Michinobu (973–95)
In the dawn, although I know.

Fujiwara no Sadaie (1162–1242)
You do not come, and I wait.

Fujiwara no Sadayori (fl. 11th cent.)
As the mists rise in the dawn.

Fujiwara no Teika (1162–1241)
After his tryst.
From the beginning.
I gaze far and long.
I rein in my horse.
Spring night's, The.
Those long black tresses.
Weary wild geese who came.

Fujiwara No Toshinari
In all the world.

Fujiwara no Yasusue
Nothing Whatsoever.

Fujo (d. 1764)
Rise, let us go.

Fukaku (d. 1753)
Empty cicada shell.

Fukyu (d. 1771)
Bright and pleasant, A.

Fulbert of Chartres (c.975–1028)
Abbot John.
To the Nightingale.

Fuller, Cynthia (b. 1948)
My Father's Dreams.

Fuller, Ethel Romig
Today.
What the King Has.

Fuller, John (b. 1937)
Alex at the Barber's.
Blues.
Born Too Soon.
Butterfly, The.
Can-Can.
De Sade.
God Bless America.
Linda.
Poem against Catholics.
Polka.
Red Light District Nurse, The.
Sonata.
St. Sophia.
Statue, The.
Whole New Scene, A.
Wild Raspberries.

Fuller, Margaret (1810–50)
Flaxman.
Jesus a Child His Course Begun.
Let Me Gather from the Earth.
Lines Written in Boston on a Beautiful
   Autumnal Day.
Meditations.
One in All, The.
Sistrum.

Winged Sphinx.

Fuller, Margaret Witter (1872–1954)
To A.H.B.

Fuller, Roy (b. 1912)
Autobiography of a Lungworm.
Autumn 1942.
Christmas Day.
Consolations of Art.
Coptic Socks.
Crustaceans.
Day, The.
Death.
Dedicatory Epistle, with a Book of 1949.
During a Bombardmant by V-Weapons.
Edmond Halley.
Family Cat, The.
Faust's Servant.
From the Joke Shop.
Hittites, The.
How startling to find the portraits of the gods.
Image, The.
In Africa.
Limerick: "How varied the family Sen!"
Memorial Poem.
Metamorphoses.
Middle of a War, The.
Other Side, The.
Outside the Supermarket.
Reading in the Night.
Shop Talk.
Spring 1942.
Suns in a skein, the uncut stones of night.
There Actually Stood.
Those of Pure Origin.
Translation.
Unremarkable Year, The.
Well Now, the Virgin.
What Is Terrible.
Your Absence.

Fuller, Stephany (b. 1947)
In the Silence.
Let Me Be Held When the Longing Comes.
My Love When This Is Past.
That We Head Towards.
Who is not a stranger still.

Fullerton, Mary Elizabeth ("E.") (1868–1946)
Farmer, The.
John 14:1–2.
Man's [a] Sliding Mood, A.
Martyr.
Martyr.
Ninety.
Poetry.
Stupidity.
Unit.

Fulton, Alice (b. 1952)
About Face.
Elvis from the Waist Up.
Give: A Sequence Reimagining Daphne &
   Apollo.
It might mean immersion, that sign.
My Second Marriage to My First Husband.
New Release, A.
News of the Occluded Cyclone.
Some Cool.
Take: A Roman Wedding.
What I Like.
Wonder Bread.

Fumi Saito (b. 1909)
As a landscape in the far distance.
Palm of the hand, The / Is not aware of dying
   as.
With wings that will not ever.

Fumon (1302–69)
Magnificent! Magnificent!

Funk, Wilfred John (1883–1965)
Hospital.

Furber, Douglas
Lambeth Walk.
Me and My Girl.

Furness, William Henry (1802–96)
In the Morning I Will Pray.

Furnival, Christine (b. 1931)
Rhiannon.

Fusen (d. 1777)
Today, then, is the day.

Fuso (d. 1886)
Upon the lotus flower.

Fusselman, Amy
Journal.
Mother Nature.
Puffy Jacket.
Sleeper.
Ticker.

Fussenegger, Gertrud
How Far.

Füst, Milán (1888–1967)
Death of Sagittarius.
Drunken Merchant, The.
Ghost Street.
If I Have to Yield My Bones.
Letter about Horror, A.
Mississippi.
Old Age.
Self-Portrait.
Winegrower, The.

Futuransky, Luisa
Israel Revisited.
Jerusalem, a Whirling Glass.
Jerusalem, Timeless.
More Chagall than Chagall.
Twenty Years From Auschwitz, Bergen-Belsen
   and Other Camps.

Fuwa (d. 1712)
Earth is fragrant, The.

Fuyo-Dokai (1042–1117)
Seventy-six: done.

Fychan, Anne (fl.1688)
On the Seven Bishops.

Fyfe, Anne-Marie
Upturn.

Fyleman, Rose (1877–1957)
Cat, The.
Goblin, The.
(Mice)
Punch and Judy.
Solo with Chorus.

Fynn, Henry Francis (Mbuyazi) (1803–61)
Adieu, to Fortune.

Fyodorov, Vasily (1918–84)
Servile Blood.

G

Gaba, Ntsikana (1780–1821)
Great Hymm.

Gabai, Ilya Iankelevich (1935–73)
For the Last Time on My Native Estate.

**Gaetulicus (Gnaeus Cornelius Lentulus
   Gaetulicus) (fl. A.D. c.26)**
Here, by the seashore, there lies / Archilochus.

Gaffarel, Jacques
Celestial Alphabet Event.

Gahagan, Judy
Colour of the Old Man's Eyes, The.

Gaitán Durán, Jorge (1924–62)
They Unite Naked.

Gaius Valerius Catullus See **Catullus**

Gaki (d. 1927)
One spot, alone.

Galai, Benyamin [or Benjamin] (b. 1921)
Canaan.
Of Those Who Go, Not to Return.
To My Generation.

**Galanskov, Yury [or Iurii] Timofeievich (1939–
   72)**
Bird-cherry was my wife, The.
I am in pain.
Intellectual, The.
It shames one to look.
Last Platform, The.
Murder.
Night is dark, The.

Galassi, Jonathan (b. 1949)
Argument.

Galbreath, Margaret
Limerick: "There once was an artist called
   Pat."

Gale, Norman (b. 1862)
Country Faith, The.
Gal'ed, Zerubavel
Chickory.
Galemire, Julia
Inventing Fables about the Stone.
Galich, Aleksandr Arkadevich (1919–77)
Goldminers' Waltz, The.
Hospital Gypsy Song.
Mistake, A.
Prospectors' Little Waltz, The.
Galindo, David Escobar (b. 1943)
Short Story, A.
Gallagher, Katherine (b. 1935)
Distances.
Girl's Head, A.
Gallagher, Tess (b. 1943)
Black Silk.
Each Bird Walking.
Fresh Stain.
Instructions to the Double.
Little Invitation in a Hushed Voice.
Monologue at the Chinook Bar and Grill.
Not There.
Sea Inside the Sea.
Sudden Journey.
Trace, In Unison.
Un Extraño.
Unanswered Letter.
Under Stars.
Unsteady Yellow.
Valentine Delivered by a Raven.
Gallaudet, Thomas H. (1787–1851)
Jesus, in Sickness and in Pain.
Gallico, Paul (1897–1976)
Application.
Confession.
Galloway, George (b. 1755)
To the Memory of Gavin Wilson (Boot, Leg
and Arm Maker)
Galloway, Ted B. (fl. 1911)
Whiffenpoof Song.
Gallup, Dick (b. 1941)
Backing into the Future.
Galsworthy, John (1867–1933)
Limerick: "Angry young husband called
Bicket, An."
Galt, John (1779–1839) and "Christopher North"
Canadian Boat Song.
Galvin, Brendan (b. 1938)
Bullfrog.
Cougar.
For a Daughter Gone Away.
Inside Job, An.
Knot Hole Gang, The.
Mail from Right Here, The.
Returning a Lawn to the Field It Was.
Running.
Galvin, James (b. 1951)
Independence Day, 1956: A Fairy Tale.
Little Dantesque.
Post-Modernism.
Shadow-Casting.
Station (1)
Station (2)
Station (4)
Two Horses and a Dog.
Galvin, Patrick (b. 1927)
Madwoman of Cork, The.
My Father Spoke with Swans.
Plaisir d'Amour.
Gamalinda, Eric
Denials.
La Naval De Manila: Selim Sot as a Modern
Political Observer.
Lament Beginning w/a Line after Cavafy.
Light Falls Obliquely.
Gambold, John (1711–71)
Mystery of Life, The.
Gammons, Susan E.
Just One Day.
Gander, Forrest (b. 1956)
Deflection Toward the Relative Minor.
Gandersheim, Hroswitha von (c.935–1005)
I bring you a goat.

Gandlevsky, Sergey (b. 1952)
Dear God, allow me to recall my works.
Is it time to change the record? But I'm
dreaming again.
Oh, how the lilacs are this May! Bulging-large
bunches fell.
There's our street, let's say.
Gangemi, Kenneth
Notes on a Moonwatcher.
Gangnus, Aleksandr Rudolfovich (1910–72)
Firing back at my heavy heart.
Gangopadhyay, Sunil (b. 1934)
Calcutta and I.
Gannett, William Channing (1840–1923)
From Heart to Heart.
He Hides within the Lily.
Gannon, Kim (1900–74)
Dreamer's Holiday, A.
Moonlight Cocktail.
Reciprocity.
Gansan (d. 1895)
Blow if you will.
Ganse, Hervey Doddridge (1822–91)
Lord, I Know Thy Grace Is nigh Me.
Garay, János (1812–53)
King Matthias in Gömör.
Old Veteran and Napoleon, The.
García, Diana
Clog of Her Body, The.
Green Corn Season.
La Curandera.
Matter of Control, A.
Orchard of Figs in the Fall, An.
Other Marías.
Serpentine Voices.
Squaring the Names.
Tísica.
Turns at the Dance.
García, Jesse F. (fl. 20th cent.)
Barrio Beateo.
I Ain't Going to Hurry No More.
García Lorca, Federico (1895–1936)
Absence of the Soul.
Ah secret voice of dark love! Ah bleating
without wool! Ah wound! Ah prick of gall,
sunken camellia!
Amparo.
Arrest of Antoñito el Camborio.
At the Poorhouse.
Ballad of Black Grief.
Ballad of One Doomed to Die.
Below.
Casida of Sobbing.
Casida of the Dark Doves.
Comet.
Death of Antoñito el Camborio.
Elegy for Joan the Mad One.
Faithless Wife, The.
Goring and the Death, The.
Great Sadness, The.
Guitar.
In a Corner of the Sky.
Lament for Ignacio Sánchez Mejías.
Little Ballad of the Three Rivers.
Little Infinite Poem.
Little Mute Boy, The.
Memory.
Moon Rises, The.
Moon Sails Out, The.
Mr. Lizard is Crying.
My Little Girl Went to the Sea.
New York.
Night of Sleepless Love.
One.
Poet Asks His Love About the Enchanted City
of Cuenca, The.
Poet Asks His Love to Write to Him, The.
Poet Speaks the Truth, The.
Poet Speaks with Love by Telephone, The.
Portrait of Silverio Franconetti.
Preciosa and the Wind.
Prelude.
Quarrel, The.
Rundown Church (Ballad of the First World
War)

Second Anniversary.
Silly Song.
Six Strings, The.
Sketches.
Sleepwalkers' Ballad.
Sleepwalking Ballad, The.
Somnambulist Ballad.
Song of the Barren Orange Tree.
Song of the Rider.
Song Wants to Be Light, The.
Sonnet of Sweet Complaint.
Sonnet of Sweet Weeping.
Spring Song.
Star, A.
Swath.
Unfaithful Wife, The.
Ursa Major.
Venus.
Whole Works, The.
Garcia, Richard
Book of Dreams, The.
Brief Entanglements.
Dangerous Hats.
Death in Larkspur Canyon, A.
Diver for the NYPD Talks to His Girlfriend, A.
El Zapato.
Elite Syncopations.
Los Amantes.
Nobody Here But Us.
Note Folded Thirteen Ways.
Story of Keys, The.
Garcilaso de la Vega, Baldomero (1503?–1536)
I Came to a Valley in the Wilderness.
Nemoroso.
O waters running pure and crystal clear.
Oh, to my sobs, Galatea, you are harder than a
stone.
One Moment My Hope Rises Up on Wings.
Rough Are the Roads.
Song 3: "Surrounded by the gentle sound."
Sonnet 5.
Sonnet 10.
Sweet Gifts.
While There Is Still the Color of a Rose.
Your Face Is Written in My Soul.
Gardelle, Charlotte (b. 1879)
Air.
Peaceful Sunday.
Rain.
Gardiner, Allen F. (1794–1851)
Natal Hunters, The.
Gardinier, Suzanne (b. 1961)
Admirals (Columbus)
Agricultural Show, Flemington, Victoria, The.
At Work.
Blues.
Democracy.
Ghost of Santo Domingo, The.
Letter to My Mother.
On a Grey-haired Old Lady Knitting at an
Orchestral Concert.
Supremer Sacrifice, The.
Team, The.
To Peace.
Two Girls.
Upon a Row of Old Books and Shoes in a
Pawnbroker's Window.
Where Blind Sorrow Is Taught to See.
Gardner, Ada Belle (d. 1949)
Mary, The Mother of Jesus.
Gardner, Edmund (1752?–1798)
Sonnet Written in Tintern Abbey,
Monmouthshire.
Gardner, Isabella (1915–81)
Cock-a-Hoop.
In the Museum.
Nightmare.
That "Craning of the Neck."
Gardner, John (1933–82)
Feat of Gardening, The.
"Gardons, S. S." *See* Snodgrass, William DeWitt
Garfitt, Roger
Rarest of the esculents, its distribution.
Garioch, Robert (Robert Sutherland) (1909–81)
At Robert Fergusson's Grave, October 1962.

Campidoglio.
Did Ye See Me?
Elegy: "They are lang deid, folk that I used to
    ken."
Embro to the Ploy.
Fair Cop, A.
Heard in the Cougate.
I Was Fair Beat.
Judgment Day.
Maple and the Pine, The.
1941.
On Seein an Aik-Tree Sprent Wi Galls.
Phooie!
Property.
Sanct Christopher II.
Wire, The.

Garland, Hamlin (1860–1940)
Boyish sleep.
Dakota Wheat-Field, A.
Do You Fear the Wind?
Fighting Fire.
Goin' Back T'morrer.
Horses Chawin' Hay.
In August.
Indian Summer.
Mountains Are a Lonely Folk, The.
On the Mississippi.
Plowing: A Memory.
Prairie Fires.

Garlick, Raymond (b. 1926)
Ancestors.
Anthem for Doomed Youth.
Behind the Headlines.
Capitals.
Consider Kyffin.
Dylan Thomas at Tenby.
Heiress, The.
Map Reading.
Note on the Iliad.
Poetry of Motion, The.
Still Life.

Garman, Douglas (fl. 1920–30)
Bury the Great Horse.

Garmon, John
Old Trail Town, Cody, Wyoming.

Garner, Alan (b. 1934)
Summer Solstice.

Garner, Erroll
Misty.

Garnett, Richard (1835–1906)
Fading-Leaf and Fallen-Leaf.

Garnett, Ruth (b. 1954)
Dealing Scraps.

Garrett, Edward Cortez
Bachelors, The.
Grandfather's Mint.

Garrett, Elizabeth (b. 1958)
Airborne.
Anatomy of Departure.
Contrary Motion.
History Goes to Work.
I am the difficult silk that slides from your
    grasp.
Lost Property.
Love's Parallel.
Mimesis.
Miser.
Moules à la Marinière.
Reprieve, The.
Ribes rubrum.
Tyranny of Choice.
Unguentarium.
Vista.
Womanhood, The.

Garrett, George (b. 1929)
Giant Killer.
Jacob.

Garrick, David (1716–79)
Epitaph on Laurence Sterne.
Friend Col and I, both full of whim.
Heart of Oak.
Jupiter and Mercury.
On a Certain Lord Giving Some Thousand
    Pounds for a House.
On Oliver Goldsmith.

On Sir John Hill, M. D., Playwright.
Garrigue, Jean (1914–72)
After Reading "The Country of the Pointed
    Firs."
Amsterdam.
Amsterdam Letter.
Bleecker Street.
Catch What You Can.
Country Villa.
Cracked Looking Glass.
Epitaph for My Cat.
Forest.
From Venice Was That Afternoon.
Grand Canyon, The.
Grenoble Café.
Mouse, The.
Movie Actors Scribbling Letters Very Fast in
    Crucial Scenes.
Now Snow Descends.
Old Haven.
Primer of Plato.
Remember That Country.
Shore.
Song for "Buvez les Vins du Postillion"—
    Advt.
Song in Sligo.
Stranger, The.
To Speak of My Influences.
You Know.

Garrison, Theodosia Pickering (1874–1944)
Closed Door, The.

Garshman, Barbara J.
Keys.

Garth, Sir Samuel (1661–1719)
As bold Mirmillo the grey dawn descries.
Dispensary, The.
What Frenzy Has of Late Possess'd the Brain.

Gasan (1275–1365)
Invaluable is the Soto Way.

Gascoigne, George (1539–77)
De Profundis, sels.
Farewell, A.
For That He Looked Not upon Her.
Fruits of War, sels.
Gascoigne's Good-Morrow.
Gascoigne's [or Gascoygnes] Good-Night.
Gascoigne's Memories, sels.
Gascoigne's Woodmanship.
Gloze Upon This Text, Dominus iis opus
    habet, A.
Green Knight's Farewell to Fancy, The.
Lullaby [or Lullabie] of a Lover, The.
Magnum Vectigal Parsimonia.
Steele Glas, The.

Gascoyne, David
And the Seventh Dream Is the Dream of Isis.
Cage, The.
Cubical Domes, The.
De Profundis.
Ecce Homo.
Elegy: "Friend, whose unnatural early death."
End Is Near the Beginning, The.
Eve.
Ex Nihilo.
Landscape.
Orpheus in the Underworld.
Rex Mundi.
Sacred Hearth, The.
Salvador Dali.
Snow in Europe.
Tenebrae.
Truth Is Blind, The.
Uncertain Battle, The.
Unsagacious Animal, An.
Wartime Dawn, A.
Winter Garden.
Yves Tanguy.

Gashe, Marina
Village, The.

Gaskill, Clarence (1892–1948)
I Can't Believe That You're in Love with Me.
Minnie, the Moocher.
Prisoner of Love.

Gaspar, Frank (b. 1946)
Part of What I Mean.
Tree, The.

Gasztold, Carmen Bernos de
Noah's Prayer.

Gates, Beatrix (b. 1949)
Cathy.
Deadly Weapon.
Homeless.
Ron.
Triptych.

Gates, Larry
At the river-bend.
Crow flies off, The.
Killdeer, The.
Lights are going out, The.
On the jewelweed.
Rowing.
Silent Buddha, The.
Winter dawn.

Gauradas
Dear Echo, do me a favour; it's somewhat.

Gautier, Théophile (1811–72)
Art.
Carmen.
Clarimonde.
Posthumous Coquetry.
Unknown Shores.

Gaxe
I wonder what eagle did to him.

Gay, John (1685–1732)
Achilles, sels.
Acis and Galatea, sels.
Beggar's Opera, sels.
Birth of the Squire; an Eclogue, The.
Cotillion.
Damon and Cupid.
Fables, sels.
I'm like a skiff on the ocean tost.
Molly Mog [or The Fair Maid of the Inn].
Mr. Pope's Welcome from Greece.
My Own Epitaph.
New Song of New Similies, A.
Newgate's Garland.
Ode for the New Year, An.
Polly; an Opera, sels.
She who hath felt a real pain.
Shepherd's Week, The, sels.
Sweet William's Farewell to Black-Eyed [or
    Black-Ey'd] Susan.
To a Lady.
To a Lady on Her Passion for Old China.
To a Young Lady, with Some Lampreys.
To My Ingenious and Worthy Friend William
    Lowndes, Esq.
Toilette, The.
Trivia, or The Art of Walking the Streets of
    London, sels.
Two Monkeys, The.
What D'Ye—Call-It, The, sels.

Gay, Noel (1898–1954)
Lambeth Walk.
Leaning on a Lamppost.
Me and My Girl.

Gazen (d. 1825)
I lean against.

Gbadamosi, Gabriel (b. 1961)
Death of the Polar Explorers.
Reading, The.
Sango's son came down to the river.

**Gearailt, Gearold Iarla Mac See Desmond,
    Gerald Fitzgerald, 4th Earl of**

Gebeyli, Claire (b. 1930)
Beirut.
Man Is Dead, A.

Gebirtig, Mordecai (1877–1942)
Waiting for Death.

Geddes, Alexander (1737–1802)
Epistle to the President of the Scottish Society
    of Antiquaries: On Being Chosen a
    Correspondent Member.

Geddes, Gary (b. 1940)
Inheritors, The.
Transubstantiation.

Gehrke, Steve (b. 1971)
Mouth to Mouth.
Near the Mississippi.
Walking Fields at Night South of Hampton,

Iowa.

Geier, Joan Austin
On Your Twenty-First Birthday.

Geiger, Timothy
Disproportionate.
Dry Spell of Faith, A.
Soundtracks.

Geisel, Theodore Seuss *See* "Seuss, Dr."

Gekko-Sojo
How Zenists carry on.

Gekkutsu-Sei
I set down the emerald lamp.

Gelbtrunk, Aida (d. 1999)
All Illusion Is a Form of Hope.
Coincidence.
Empty House, The.
God said to Abraham.

Gellert, Leon (b. 1892)
Before Action.
House-Mates.

Gelman, Juan (b. 1930)
Epochs.
Eyes.
History.
Man and a Woman, A.

Genet, Jean (1910–86)
Man Condemned to Death, The.

Gengen'ichi (d. 1804)
Morning glory.

Genko (d. 1505)
Unaware of illusion or enlightenment.

Gensei (1623–68)
Distant View from a Grass Hill.
Evening View from Grass Hill.
Poem without a Category.

Gensho (d. 1742)
Graveyard, A.

Gensler, Lewis E.
Love Is Just Around the Corner.

George, David Graves
Wreck of the Old 97.

George, Diana Hume (b. 1948)
Asenath.

George, Don (1909–85)
I Ain't Got Nothin' But the Blues.
I'm Beginning to See the Light.
It's Kind of Lonesome Out Tonight.
It Shouldn't Happen to a Dream.
Tulip or Turnip.

George, Faye
Shagbark.
Wilderness.

George, Phillip [*or* "Phil"] William
America's Wounded Knee.
Battle Won Is Lost.
Favorite Grandson Braid.
First Grade.
Moon of Huckleberries.
Morning Vigil.
Name Giveaway.
Prelude to Memorial Song: 100 Years Later.
Spokane Falls.
Spring Cleaning.
Spruce.
Sunflower Moccasins.
Visit, The.
Wardance.
Wardance Soup.

George, Stefan (1868–1933)
Antichrist, The.
Do Not Ponder Too Much.
Have you his lovely image still in mind.
Invocation and Prelude.
Lord of the Isle, The.
No way too long–no path too steep.
Rapture.
Stanzas Concerning Love.

Georges, Esther Valck
Alley Cat.

Georgiou, Elena
From Where I Stand.
Intimate Mixture.
Space Between, The.
Talkin' Trash.

Week in the Life of the Ethnically
Indeterminate, A.

Gerard, Gertrude
In Arabia.

Gergely, Agnes (b. 1933)
Crazed Man in Concentration Camp.

Gerhardt, Ida G. M. (b. 1905)
Buried Birds, The.
Expectation.
Rejected Gift, The.
Remembrance Day.

Gerhardt, Paul (1607–76)
Commit thy way unto the Lord.
Evensong.
Go out in this dear summertide.
O Sacred Head Now Wounded.

Gerlach, Eva (b. 1948)
Turn and Turn About.

Gerner, Ken
House of Breath.
Prey.

Gerondi, Abraham (*fl.* 13th cent.)
Hymn for the Eve of the New Year.

Gerrard, John (*fl.* c.1769)
Remonstrance, A.

Gershon, Karen (b. 1923)
At a Reception.
Experiments with God.
I Was Not There.
Race.
To My Children.
Uphold Me.

Gershwin, George (1898–1937)
Babbitt and the Bromide, The.
Bidin' My Time.
Blah, Blah, Blah.
But Not for Me.
Do, Do, Do.
Do It Again.
Embraceable You.
Fascinating Rhythm.
Foggy Day (in London Town), A.
How Long Has This Been Going On?
I Got Plenty o' Nuthin'
I Got Rhythm.
Isn't It a Pity?
It Ain't Necessarily So.
Let's Call the Whole Thing Off.
Long Ago (And Far Away)
Love Is Here to Stay.
Love Is Sweeping the Country.
Man I Love, The.
Nice Work If You Can Get It.
Of Thee I Sing.
Oh, Lady, Be Good!
'S Wonderful.
Somebody Loves Me.
Someone to Watch over Me.
Strike Up the Band.
Summertime.
They All Laughed.
They Can't Take That Away from Me.
Things Are Looking Up.
Who Cares?

Gershwin, Ira (1896–1983)
Babbitt and the Bromide, The.
Bidin' My Time.
Blah, Blah, Blah.
But Not for Me.
Do, Do, Do.
Embraceable You.
Fascinating Rhythm.
Foggy Day (in London Town), A.
Fun to be Fooled.
How Long Has This Been Going On?
I Can't Get Started.
I Got Plenty o' Nuthin'
I Got Rhythm.
Isn't It a Pity?
It Ain't Necessarily So.
Let's Call the Whole Thing Off.
Let's Take a Walk Around the Block.
Long Ago (And Far Away)
Love Is Here to Stay.
Love Is Sweeping the Country.

Man I Love, The.
Man That Got Away, The.
My Ship.
Nice Work If You Can Get It.
Of Thee I Sing.
Oh, Lady, Be Good!
One Life to Live.
'S Wonderful.
Saga of Jenny, The.
Someone to Watch over Me.
Strike Up the Band.
Sunny Disposish.
Tchaikowsky (And Other Russians)
They All Laughed.
They Can't Take That Away from Me.
Things Are Looking Up.
Who Cares?

Gerstler, Amy (b. 1956)
Bitter Angel.
BZZZZZZZ.
Fan Letter, A.
Housebound.
Marriage.
Max's Lecture on Canine Buddhism.
Nature of Suffering, The.
Saints.
Sinking Feeling, A.
Siren.
True Bride, The.

Gertsyk, Adelaida (1874–1925)
Silent, draped in the garments of sacrifice.
Spring.

Gervitz, Gloria (b. 1943)
And what were you searching for, in that
dream?
Can you hear me? Under my name I am.
I listen through underground walls like
prisoners signaling.
Life is nothing but time.
Maybe we are the same darkness the same
words.
Nothing you tell me nothing.
She detaches herself from her shadow. She is
an old woman and still beautiful.
She is crying.
Silence is a task that will last all her life. It
continues.
We docked at noon in the port of Veracruz. We
wore our Russian furs.

Gesshu Soko (1618–96)
Inhale, exhale.
Seven seas sucked up together, The.

Getsi, Lucia Cordell
Washing Your Hair.
Woman Hanging from Lightpole, Illinois Route
136.

Getsudo (1285–1361)
I moved across the Dharma-nature.

Getsurei (d. 1919)
Stumble.

Gewanter, David
Divorce and Mr. Circe.
One-Page Novel.
Xenia: Stranger/Guest.

Gezelle, Guido (1830–99)
Ego Flos.
Little Mother.

Ghalib, Mirza Asadullah Khan (1797–1869)
Colors of tulips and roses are not the same,
The.
Even at prayer, our eyes look inward.
For the raindrop, joy is in entering the river.
Freely in Hidden Fire.
Ghazal 5.
Ghazal 12.
Ghazal 15.
Ghazal 21.
Ghazal 25.
Ghazal 34.
I'm Neither the Loosening of Song nor the
Close-Drawn Tent of Music.
Let the ascetics sing of the garden of Paradise.
Not All, Only a Few, Return as the Rose or the
Tulip.
World is no more than the Beloved's single
face, The.

Gheraducci, Vera (b. 1928)
April 5th.
December 15th.
June 30th.
October 27th.
September 22nd.

Ghiberti, Carnino (fl. 1250)
I am afar, but near thee is my heart.

Ghigna, Charles (b. 1946)
Lesson of Night, A.
Park Elms.

Ghiselin, Brewster (b. 1903)
Bath of Aphrodite.
Catch, The.
Food of Birds, The.
Learning the Language.
Net Breaker, The.
Rattler, Alert.
Shore Bird.

Ghos, Giríscandra (1844–1912)
I plaster myself with ashes.
Who said / If you took the name All-
Destroyer.
You're home, Uma! Stay here.

Ghose, Manmohan (1869–1924)
Who Is It Talks of Ebony?

Giacometti, Alberto
Brown Curtain, The.

Gianni, Lapo
Ballad, since Love himself hath fashioned thee.
Love, I demand to have my lady in fee.

Gibb, Blair
Vigil.

Gibb, Robert
Letter to Russel Barron.
Paul Butterfield, Dead at 44.

Gibbon, Perceval (1878–1926)
Answer, An.
Mooimeisjes.

Gibbons, Orlando (1583–1625)
Silver Swan, The.

Gibbons, Reginald (b. 1947)
Affect of Elms, The.
American Trains.
Breath.
Hoppy.
"Luckies."
Ruined Motel, The.
Sparrow.
We Say.

Gibbons, Stella (b. 1902)
Truce, The.

Gibbs, C. Armstrong
Limerick: "Serious young lady from Welwyn, A."

Gibran, Kahlil (1883–1931)
Cobbler in Jerusalem, A.
Crime and Punishment.
Dead Are My People.
Defeat.
Earth.
Fame.
Fox, The.
From the grasp of Pharaoh.
Gravedigger, The.
Heavy-Laden Is My Soul.
Love.
Madman (Prologue), The.
Mannus the Pompeiian to a Greek.
Mary Magdalen.
My soul spoke unto me and counselled me.
On Children.
On Work.
Seven Stages, The.
Song of the Wave.
Sufi, The.
Two Poems, The.
Veiled Land.

Gibson, Douglas
January.

Gibson, Walker (b. 1919)
Advice to Travelers.

Gibson, Wilfrid Wilson (1878–1962)
All Being Well.

Breakfast.
Drove-Road, The.
Flannan Isle.
Henry Turnbull.
Ice, The.
In the Ambulance.
Lament: "We who are left, how shall we look again."
Long Tom.
Luck.
Old Skinflint.
Parrot, The.
Prelude: "As one, at midnight, wakened by the call."
Sight.
Stone, The.
White Dust, The.

Gidlow, Elsa (b. 1898)
Constancy.
Creed for Free Women, A.
Let Wisdom Wear the Crown: Hymn for Gaia.
Philosophy.
Relinquishment.

Gido (1325–88)
Inscription over His Door.

Gier, Jean V.
California Coast.
Examining the I.
First View of the Islands, A.
Going Baroque.

Giffard, Martha, Lady (1638–1722)
Of Sleep.
To Mother Luddwels Cave and Spring.

Gifford, Fannie Stearns (b. 1884)
Moon Folly.

Gifford Humphrey (fl. c.1580)
For Soldiers.
In the Praise of Music.

Gifford, William (1756–1826)
Lo, Della Crusca! In his closet pent.

Gilbart, Thomas (fl. c.1583)
Declaration of the Death of John Lewes, A.

Gilbert, Celia (b. 1932)
Midwives, The.

Gilbert, Christopher (b. 1950)
African Sculpture.
And, Yes, Those Spiritual Matters.
Beginning by Value.
Chosen to Be Water.
Directions, The.
Enclosure.
Glimpses.
Kite-Flying.
Now.
Pushing.
Resonance.
Sorrow Since Sitting Bull, A.
Theory of Curve.
This Bridge Across.
Time with Stevie Wonder in It.

Gilbert, Jack (b. 1925)
Abnormal Is Not Courage, The.
Elephant Hunt in Guadalajara.
Getting Ready.
It Is Clear Why the Angels Come No More.
Malvolio in San Francisco.
Perspective He Would Mutter Going to Bed.
Pewter.
Prospero Listens to the Night.
Revolution, The.
To See if Something Comes Next.
White Heart of God, The.

Gilbert, Kevin (b. 1933)
Celebrators '88.
Gularwundul's Wish.
Kiacatoo.
Mum.
New True Anthem, The.
Peace and the Desert.
Same Old Problem.
Taipan.
Tree.
Won't You Dad?

Gilbert, Lady See **Mulholland, Rosa**

Gilbert-Lecomte, Roger (1907–43)
Preface or The Drama of Absence in an

Eternal Heart.
Son of the Bone Speaks, The.
Wink.

Gilbert, Ruth (b. 1917)
Green Hammock, White Magnolia Tree.
Jacob.

Gilbert, Samuel (d. 1692?)
Florist's Vade-Mecum, The.

Gilbert, Sandra M. (b. 1936)
Ladies' Home Journal, The.
Mafioso.

Gilbert, Thomas (1713?–47)
Against Homosexuality.

Gilbert, Sir William Schwenck (1836–1911)
Captain Reece.
Etiquette.
Ferdinando and Elvira; or, The Gentle Pieman.
Gilbertian Cats.
Gondoliers, The, sels.
H. M. S. Pinafore, sels.
Iolanthe, sels.
Mikado, sels.
Patience, sels.
Pirates of Penzance, sels.
Rival Curates, The.
Ruddigore, sels.
There was an old man of St. Bees.
To the Terrestrial Globe.
Trial by Jury, sels.
Utopia Limited, sels.
Yarn of the Nancy Bell, The.
Yeoman of the Guard, sels.

Gilbo'a, Amir (b. 1917)
Against the Wind.
Birth.
Circle of Weeping, The.
Evening of the Whirlwind.
From All Sides Laughter Shall Strike Them.
If They Show Me a Stone and I Say Stone.
In Darkness.
Isaac.
Moses.
On a Recollected Road.
Song of Blue and Red, A.
Song Yet Song.

Gilder, Richard Watson (1844–1909)
Failure and Success.
Hour in a Studio, An.
On the Bay.
Sonnet, The.
To Thee, Eternal Soul, Be Praise.
Two Worlds.

Gildner, Gary (b. 1938)
Digging for Indians.
4th Base.
High-Class Bananas, The.
House on Buder Street, The.
Nails.
Runner, The.
They Have Turned the Church Where I Ate God.

Giles, Barbara
Late Express, The.
Mrs. Lorris, Who Died of Being Clean.

Giles, Joseph (fl. late 18th cent.)
Leasowes: Or, A Poetical Description of the Late Mr. Shenstone's Rural Retirement, The.

Gilfillan, Robert
Exile's Song, The.

Gilkey, James G. (1889–1964)
O God, in Whose Great Purpose.
Outside the Holy City.

Gill, Gagan (b. 1959)
Girl's Desire Moves Among Her Bangles, The.

Gillan, Maria
Arturo.
Growing Up Italian.
In Memory We Are Walking.
In New Jersey Once.
Public School No. 18: Paterson, New Jersey.

Gillespie, Abraham Lincoln (1895–1950)
Purplexicon of Dissynthegrations, A.
READIE-SOUNDPIECE (after a suggestion of Hilaire Hiler) (synchro-with Orchestrauto maton)

Gillespie, Haven (1888–1975)
Breezin' Along with the Breeze.
Santa Claus Is Comin' to Town.
That Lucky Old Sun.
You Go to My Head.

Gilliams, Maurice (1900–1982)
Autumn.
Tristitia Ante.

Gillilan, Pamela
Looking North.
Mistress, The.
You lie with me nightly. In bathrooms I'm there.

Gillilan, Strickland W. (1869–1954)
Are You There?
Be Hopeful.
Need of Loving.
On the Antiquity of Microbes.
Watch Yourself Go By.

Gillington, Mary C. (1892–1902)
Dead March, A.

Gilm zu Rosenegg, Herman von (1812–64)
All Souls' Day.
Grave, A.
Night.

Gilman, Caroline (1794–1888)
Anna Playing in a Graveyard.
Boat, The.
Dead Sister, The.
What Will Be Your Destiny?

Gilman, Charlotte Perkins Stetson (1860–1935)
Anti-Suffragists, The.
Christian Virtues.
Homes.
Mother's Charge, The.
Resolve.

Gilman, Samuel (1791–1858)
O God, Accept the Sacred Hour.

Gilmore, Brian G. (b. 1962)
Bow to Allah.
Coming to the net.
Elvis.
Gas Station Attendant.
Revolution.
To be or not to be.

Gilmore, Joseph Henry (1834–1918)
He Leadeth Me.

Gilmore, Mary (1865–1902)
Eve-Song.
Fourteen Men.
Harvesters, The.
Heritage.
Little Shoes That Died, The.
Myall in Prison, The.
Nationality.
Saturday Tub, The.
Tenancy, The.

Gilmore, Patrick Sarsfield ("Louis Lambert") (1829–92)
When Johnny Comes Marching Home.

Gilonis, Harry (b. 1956)
Answer to Herrick, An.
Song 9.
Song for Annie.

Gilsdorf, Ethan
Walk, The.

Gilyard, Keith (b. 1952)
Daughter, That Picture of You.
Letter.
On Top of It All.
Portraits of a Moment.

Gimei (d. 1748)
Illness lingers on and on.

"Ginger" *See* **Irwin, Wallace**

Ginger, Aleksandr Samsonovich (1897–1965)
Name, A.

Ginka (d. 1784)
I leap from depths.

Ginko (d. 1790)
See.

Ginsberg, Allen (1926–2000)
After Lalon.
After Yeats.
America.

American Change.
At Apollinaire's Grave.
Back on Times Square, Dreaming of Times Square.
Bayonne Turnpike to Tuscarora.
Blue Angel, The.
Bop Lyrics.
Café in Warsaw.
Caw caw caw crows shriek in the white sun over grave stones.
Chances "R."
Change: *Kyoto-Tokyo Express*, The.
Charnel Ground, The.
Crossing Nation.
Death News.
Death to Van Gogh's Ear!
Dream Record: June 8 1955.
Easter Sunday.
End, The.
First Party at Ken Kesey's with Hell's Angels.
Fourth Floor, Dawn, Up All Night Writing Letters.
Friday the Thirteenth.
Further Proposal, A.
Galilee Shore.
Green Automobile, The.
Grim Skeleton.
Homeless Compleynt.
Homework.
Howl.
I Am a Victim of Telephone.
In Back of the Real.
Is About.
Kaddish.
Kral Majales.
Land O'Lakes, Wisconsin: Vajrayana Seminary.
Last Night in Calcutta.
Lion for Real, The.
Looking over my shoulder.
Malest Cornifici Tuo Catullo.
Memory Gardens.
Mescaline.
Message.
Mugging.
My Alba.
My Sad Self.
No Way Back to the Past.
Not Dead Yet.
On Neal's Ashes.
Please Master.
Poem Rocket.
Prophecy, A.
Psalm III: "To God: to illuminate all men. Beginning with Skid Road."
Pull My Daisy.
Reflections at Lake Louise.
S. F. Southward.
Sather Gate Illumination.
Shrouded Stranger, The.
So I dream nightly of an embarkation.
Studying the Signs.
Sunflower Sutra.
Supermarket in California, A.
Sweet Levinsky.
Terms in Which I Think of Reality, The.
Thief Stole This Poem, A.
This Form of Life Needs Sex.
Thus Crosslegged on Round Pillow Sat in Space.
To Aunt Rose.
To Lindsay.
Tonite I walked out of my red apartment door on East tenth street's dusk.
Uptown.
Velocity of Money.
Visiting Father and Friends.
Vow, A.
Wales Visitation.
We Rise on Sun Beams and Fall in the Night.
Who Be Kind To.
Who Eats Who?
Who Runs America?
Why Is God Love, Jack?
Yiddishe Kopf.

Ginsberg, Arthur
Chief of Medicine, The.

Line Drive.
Stroke.

Ginsberg, Louis (1896–1976)
Biography of an Agnostic.
Clocks.
Hounds of the Soul, The.
Prices.
Roots.
Song: "I know that any weed can tell."
Soon at Last My Sighs and Moans.

Gioia, Dana (b. 1950)
Becoming a Redwood.
California Hills in August.
Counting the Children.
Country Wife, The.
Cruising with the Beach Boys.
Failure.
Guide to the Other Gallery.
In Chandler Country.
In Cheever Country.
Insomnia.
Litany, The.
Lives of the Great Composers.
Los Angeles after the Rain.
Maze Without a Minotaur.
My Confessional Sestina.
Next Poem, The.
Planting a Sequoia.
Prayer.
Summer Storm.
Sunday News, The.

Giorno, John (b. 1936)
Life Is a Killer.
Pornographic Poem.
Scum & Slime.

Gioseffi, Daniela
American Sonnets for My Father.
Bicentennial Anti-Poem for Italian-American Women.

Giovanna
Therapy.
What Do I Know.

Giovanni, Nikki (b. 1943)
Basketball.
Beautiful Black Men.
Concerning One Responsible Negro with Too Much Power.
December of My Springs, The.
Poem (for Langston Hughes), A.
Ego Tripping [(There May Be a Reason Why)].
For Saundra.
Funeral of Martin Luther King, Jr, The.
Genie in the Jar, The.
My Poem.
Kidnap Poem.
Knoxville, Tennessee.
Life I Led, The.
Master Charge Blues.
Mother's Habits.
Mothers.
Nikki-Rosa.
Poem for Aretha.
Poem for Black Boys.
Poem for Flora.
Poem for My Nephew.
Poem for Unwed Mothers.
Springtime.
Stars.
They Clapped.
Three/Quarters Time.
Trips.
True Import of Present Dialogue, The: Black vs. Negro.
Winter Poem.
Woman Poem.
Women Gather, The.
World Is Not a Pleasant Place to Be, The.

Giovannitti, Arturo (1884–1959)
Walker, The.

Gippius, Zinaida Nikolayevna [*or* Nikolaevna] (1869–1945)
Incantation.
Little Demon, The.
Seamstress, The.
She.

Wedding Ring, The.
Giscombe, C. S. (b. 1950)
Bro Duncanson.
(1980)
(1978, Remembering 1962)
(1962 At the Edge of Town)
(Recent Past, The)
Gitoku (d. 1754)
Clear sky.
Gittings, Robert (b. 1911)
Great Moth, The.
Gittins, Diana
I flash for megabucks.
Giudice, Simbuono (fl. 1250)
Often the day had a most joyful morn.
Giun (1253–1333)
All doctrines split asunder.
Giussani, Silvio (b. 1951)
Abel and Abel.
Aridness of Air, The.
Body Politic.
Clothes Without the Monk, The.
Hot and Cold.
In the Distance.
Towards a Beginning.
Vegetable Calendar.
Given, Thomas
Poetical Epistle tae Cullybackey Auld
Nummer.
Song for February, A.
Gizan Zenrai (d. 1878)
I was born into this world.
Gizzi, Peter
Lonely Tylenol.
Gjuzel, Bogomil (b. 1939)
Flood at the International Writer's Workshop.
My Sister's Letter.
On the Way Back.
Professional Poet.
Prostitution.
When I Came Back.
Gladden, Washington (1836–1918)
O Lord of Life.
O Master, Let Me Walk with Thee.
Gladding, Jody
Fisherman's Wife, The.
Locust Shell.
Worsted Heather.
Gladstone, William Ewart (1809–1898)
To a Rejected Sonnet.
Gladwin, Herman (b. 1906)
Dear Miss.
Glancy, Diane
At the Pauwels.
First Reader Santee Training School, 1873,
The.
Johnna at the Windmill.
Kemo Sabe.
Landscape Painting.
Rahab.
Wheat.
Glanz-Leyeles, Aaron See **Leyeles, A.**
Glaser, Elton
Blues for the Nightowl.
Cheap Replicas of the Eiffel Tower.
Confluences at San Francisco.
Coroner.
Revelation: The Movie.
Smoking.
Glaser, Isabel Joshlin
Depression.
Last Good War—and Afterward, The.
Glaser, Michael S.
Changing Address Books.
English-Speaking Persons Will Find
Translations.
Magnificat!
Preparations for Seder.
Glass, Malcolm (b. 1936)
Risks.
Glassco, John (1909–81)
Brummell at Calais.
Cardinal's Dog, The.
Day, The.

Entailed Farm, The.
One Last Word.
Quebec Farmhouse.
Rural Mail, The.
Glatshteyn [or Glatsteyn or Glatstein], Jacob
(1896–1971)
Back to the Ghetto.
Bratzlav Rabbi to His Scribe, The.
Matthew 5:38–48; "You have heard that it was
said, 'An eye.'"
Rabbi Yussel Luksh of Chelm.
To a Friend Who Wouldn't Bother to Strain.
Where the Cedars.
Glatt, Lisa
Amanda.
One Night With a Stranger at 30.
What We Did After My Mother's Mastectomy.
Glaukos
Epigram: "Time was when once upon a time,
such toys."
No, not earth, nor a stone slab.
Pan and the Nymphs.
Where once you could win over grasping boys.
Glazer, Joseph
Drinking with the Nazis.
Glazer, Michele
Star-Spangled.
Glazier, Lyle
On TV.
Glazkov, Nikolai Ivanovich (b. 1918)
Bast Shoe, The.
Boyarina Morozova, The.
Conversation of a Private and the Virgin.
Deaf-Mutes.
Declaration.
Four Paths.
I strolled around the zoo.
Introduction to a Poem.
Khikhimora.
My Wife.
Path Is Long, The.
Poetograd.
Prayer: "Lord, stand up for the Soviets."
Races will disappear.
Raven, The.
Simple Man, A.
Subject for a Story.
Tale of the Cyclopses, The.
There are actually people who revel.
To My Friends.
To My Ill-Wishers.
What Did They Have in Mind?
Gleason, Kate
After Fighting for Hours.
Gleason, Madeline (b. 1913)
Once and Upon.
Gleim, Johann Wilhelm Ludwig (1719–1803)
Anacreon.
To Death.
Glick, Hirsch [or Glik, Hirsh] (1922–44)
We Survive!
Glikberg, Aleksandr Mikhailovich See **"Chorny**
[or Chiornyi], Sasha"
Glissant, Edouard (b. 1928)
Child climbs to the island's highest point, The.
O Sun! O age-old labor mutely mixed with
ocean.
One of them, taking advantage of the crew's
momentary carelessness.
They fastened a people to merchant ships.
Gloria, Eugene (b. 1957)
Aleng Maria.
Assimilation.
In Language.
Milkfish.
Rizal's Ghost.
Touch.
Whisper, The.
Glover, Denis (1912–80)
All of These.
Brightness.
Camp Site.
Home Thoughts.
Magpies, The.
Old Jason, the Argonaut, The.

Once the Days.
Printers.
River Crossing, The.
Song: "If everywhere in the street."
Song: "These songs will not stand."
Song: "When I am old."
Thistledown.
With his weapon a shovel.
Glover, Richard (1712–85)
Admiral Hosier's Ghost.
Glover, Sheilah
Power of the Soul.
Glück, Louise (b. 1943)
All Hallows.
Apple Trees, The.
Aubade: "World was very large, The. Then."
Celestial Music.
Condo.
Cottonmouth Country.
Day Without Night.
Departure.
Descending Figure.
Drowned Children, The.
Edge, The.
Elms.
Eurydice.
Firstborn.
For Jane Myers.
For My Mother.
From the Suburbs.
Garden, The.
Gift, The.
Gratitude.
Gretel in Darkness.
Happiness.
Hawk's Shadow.
Hesitate to Call.
Horse.
Hyacinth.
Illuminations.
Labor Day.
Lamentations.
Lamium.
Legend.
Letters, The.
Magi, The.
Matins.
Messengers.
Mock Orange.
Moonless Night.
Mount Ararat.
Mountain, The.
Mutable Earth.
My Neighbor in the Mirror.
Mythic Fragment.
Nativity Poem.
New Life, The.
Palais des Arts.
Poem: "In the early evening, as now, a man is
bending."
Pond, The.
Queen of Carthage, The.
Racer's Widow, The.
Roman Study.
School Children, The.
Song of Obstacles.
Time.
Undertaking, The.
Unwritten Law.
Vespers.
White Lilies, The.
Wild Iris, The.
Winged Horse, The.
Wound, The.
Glück, Robert
Burroughs.
Famous monk dropped to this knees before a
giant image and cried, A.
Invaders from Mars.
Odd to close my eyes during the day and open
them at night.
Pasolini.
This image is alive with my longing for you.
Glycon
Everything's laughter / everything dust.
Nothing but laughter, nothing.

Gnanakoothan (b. 1938)
Tamil.
Gochikubo
Matsushima.
Gochu (d. 1733)
This is what I think.
Godden, James
Lost.
Godeschalk (805–69)
Sequaire.
Godfrey, John (b. 1945)
Air.
Bath.
In Front of a Large Number of People.
My Mother, Life.
One or More Together.
Our Lady.
Radiant Dog.
Show Me a Rose.
So Let's Look at It Another Way.
Unholy Spring.
What It Takes.
What Say.
Where the Weather Suits My Clothes.
Wings.
Godley, Alfred Denis (1856–1925)
After Horace.
Motor Bus.
Women's Degrees.
Godley, Elizabeth
Ninety-Nine.
Godo (d. 1801)
Chrysanthemums were yellow.
Godolphin, Margaret, Lady (1652–78)
Song: "As F— at her Toliet sat."
Godolphin, Sidney (1610–43)
Chloris, It Is Not Thy Disdain.
Constancy[e].
Elegy on D. D.
Faire Friend, 'tis true, your beauties move.
Hymn: "Lord, when the wise men came from far[r]."
No More Unto My Thoughts Appear.
On Ben Jonson.
Song: "Or love me less, or love me more."
Song: "Noe more unto my thoughts appeare."
Song: "'Tis affection but dissembled."
Thou Joy of my Life.
Godwin, A. (fl. 15th cent.)
Now wolde I fayne sum merthis [or faine some merthes] mak[e].
Goedicke, Patricia (b. 1931)
After the Second Operation.
And Yet.
Daily the Ocean between Us.
From the Boat.
Ground Beneath Us, The.
Imprint of Microscopic Life Found in Arctic Stones.
Interior Music, The.
Lacrimae Rerum.
On the Night in Question.
Serious Merriment of Women, The.
Wind of Our Going: Adagio Ma Non Troppo.
Goese, Mimi
Dive, The.
I slowly crack my joints to ready and steady myself. Sharpen my mind on.
Love Ghost.
You Are.
Goethe, Johann Wolfgang von (1749–1832)
Anacreon's Grave.
Death of a Fly.
Diary, The.
Ecstatic Longing.
Erl-King, The.
Faust, sels.
Fisherman, The.
Found.
Haste Not! Rest Not!
Holy Longing, The.
Hunter's Song at Nightfall, The.
Ill Humor.
Invisible King, The.
Irish Lamentation, An.

Journey in Winter, sels.
King in Thule, The.
King of Thulé, The.
Lay of the Captive Count, The.
May Song.
Meeting, the Departure, The.
Minstrel, The.
Nature and Art.
Permanence in Change.
Prometheus.
Roman Elegies, sels.
Rose, The.
Rosebud in the Heather.
Shepherd's Lament, The.
Song from the Coptic, A.
Song of the Traveler at Evening.
Sonnet: "To work away in art's traditional measure."
Thought Eternal, The.
To a Golden Heart, Worn round His Neck.
To Belinda.
To Charlotte von Stein.
To the Moon.
To the Parted One.
Trilogy of Passion, sels.
United States, The.
Violet, The.
Voice from the Invisible World, A.
Wanderer's Night Songs, sels.
Whatever you can do.
Wilhelm Meister's Apprenticeship, sels.
Goetsch, Douglas (b. 1963)
Beach, The.
Nobody's Hell.
Urban Poem.
Walls, The.
Goetz, E. Ray
For Me and My Gal.
Goff, Barbara E.
Limerick: "There was a young lady of Ulva. Whose sexual feelings were null. Va."
Goffstein, M. B. (b. 1940)
On This Day.
Gofu (d. 1771)
I have not yet grown weary.
Gogarty, Oliver St. John (1878–1957)
After Galen.
Colophon.
Conquest, The.
Death May Be Very Gentle.
Dedication: "Tall unpopular men."
Farrell O'Reilly.
Hay Hotel, The.
Image-Maker, The.
Leda and the Swan.
Marcus Curtius.
Non Dolet.
On First Looking into Krafft-Ebing's Psychopathosexualis [or Psychopathia Sexualis].
On the Use of Jayshus.
Palinode.
Per Iter Tenebricosum.
Plum Tree by the House, The.
Portrait with Background.
Ringsend.
To a Boon Companion.
To Death.
To Petronius Arbiter.
Verse: "What should we know."
With a Coin from Syracuse.
"Gogisgi" See Arnett, Carroll
Gohei (d. 1808)
Lone paulownia leaf, A.
Second month, The.
Gojusan
Seamless.
Gokei (1416–1500)
Fields dying off.
Gold, Artie (b. 1947)
I Don't Have the Energy.
Life.
Goldbarth, Albert (b. 1948)
Book of Human Anomalies, The.
Complete with Starry Night and Bourbon

Shots.
Counterfeit Earth!, The.
Family Grove.
Gallery.
History of Civilization, A.
Letter to Friends East and West.
Meop.
Mishipasinghan, Lumchipamudana, Etc.
People Are Dropping Out of Our Lives.
Seriema Song.
Shoyn Fergéssin: 'I've Forgotten' in Yiddish.
Steerage.
Talk Show, The.
Tip, The.
World Above Suffering, A.
World of Expectations, The.
Goldberg, Barbara
Our Father.
Survivor.
Goldberg, Beckian Fritz
My Bomb.
Once a Shoot of Heaven.
Rebirth.
Swallower.
Goldberg, Israel See "Learsi, Rufus"
Goldberg, Jacqueline (b. 1966)
Luba 1.
Luba 2.
Luba 3.
Goldberg, Leah (1911–70)
Blade of Grass Sings to the River, The.
Blade of Grass Sings to the Stream, The.
Dialogue.
From My Mother's Home.
Girl Sings to the Stream, The.
God Once Commanded Us, A.
Heavenly Jerusalem, Jerusalem of the Earth.
How shall we bring our dying heart up.
In the Jerusalem Hills.
Moon Sings to the Stream, The.
My room is so small.
Not for a long time now has anyone waited for me.
Observation of a Bee.
Of Myself.
Old woman, blue eyed and sun burned.
On This Day.
Our Backs Are to the Cypress.
Prodigal Son, The.
Remembrance of Beginnings of Things.
Scarlet, warm and heavy in black velvet leaves.
Song of the Strange Woman.
Stream Sings to the Stone, The.
Tel Aviv 1935.
That death in his windows would rise.
That poem I didn't write.
Toward Myself.
Tree Sings to the Stream, The.
When You Will Walk in the Field.
Will There Yet Come.
Golding, Arthur
This Damsell was not famous for the place.
Golding, Louis (b. 1895)
"I."
Is It Because of Some Dear Grace.
Jack.
Judaeus Errans.
O Bird, So Lovely.
Quarries in Syracuse.
Women at the Corners Stand, The.
Golding, Nicolette
My Father Makes a Lightbox for Vivienne Westwood.
Wardrobes.
Goldscheider, Ludwig
Conversation with the Moon.
Month-Verses.
Summer Night.
Goldsmith, Kenneth
One pair ridiculous gorilla slippers; 3 pairs of cheap shit sunglasses.
Goldsmith, Oliver (1730?–74)
Captivity, The, sels.
Description of an Author's Bedchamber, A.

Deserted Village, The.
Double Transformation, The.
Epilogue to the Sister, *sels.*
Retaliation, *sels.*
She Stoops to Conquer, *sels.*
Sonnet, A: "Weeping, murmuring,
  complaining."
Translation of a South American Ode.
Traveler, The; or, A Prospect of Society, *sels.*
Vicar of Wakefield, *sels.*
Goldsmith, Oliver, the Younger (1794–1861)
Lonely Settler, The.
Goldsworthy, Peter (b. 1951)
Act Six.
After Babel.
Goll, Claire (1891–1977)
Prayer: "In the bright bay of your morning, O
  God."
Goll, Ernst
Autumn Fullness.
Blossoms.
Royal Procession.
Goll, Iwan [or Yvan] (1891–1950)
Ferry of Lead, The.
Lackawanna Elegy.
Last River, The.
Pear-Tree, The.
Recitative.
Salt Lake, The.
Song for a Jewess.
Your Sleep.
**"Golodny [or Golodnyi], Mikhail Semionovich"
(Mikhail Semionovich Epshtein) (1903–49)**
Judge Gorba.
Stallion, The.
Verka the Free.
Gomes, Alberto Ferreira (b. 1957)
Martyred Tamarind, The.
Gomez, Antonio Enriquez (d. 1662)
Elegy: "I die for Your holy word without
  regret."
Gomez de Avellaneda, Gertrudis (1814–73)
Imitating an Ode by Sapho.
On Leaving Cuba, Her Native Land.
Gomez, Jewelle (b. 1948)
My Chakabuku Mama: A Comic Tale.
Gomez, Magdalena (b. 1954)
Chocolate Confessions.
Desert Cry, A.
Looking Deep.
Lost Daughter.
Making It.
Solo Palabras.
To the Latin Lover I Left at the Candy Store.
Troubled Awakening.
Gomringer, Eugen
Hang and swinging hang and swinging.
Mist.
Gonçalves Dias, Antônio (1823–64)
There are palm trees in my homeland.
Gondlevsky Sergey (b. 1952)
May God grant me the memory to recall my
  life.
Góngora y Argote, Luis de (1561–1627)
Capture of Larache, The.
Deceiver Time.
Fable of Polyphemus and Galatea, *sels.*
Let Me Go Warm.
O Noble and Most High in Beauty, Thou.
On the Armada That Battled against England.
Pride of the Fourth and Liquid Element.
Roistering I'll Chaff.
Rosemary Spray, The.
Ruins of Time, The.
Solitudes, The, *sels.*
Sonnet 82.
Sonnet 103.
Spectre of the Rose, The, *sels.*
Whistling arrow flies less eagerly, The.
Gonzales, Alonzo
Chipmunk can't drag it along.
Chipmunk was standing.
Mole makes his pole redhot.
Gonzáles Martínez, Enrique (1871–1952)
Last Journey.

Like Sister and Brother.
Nectar of Ápan, The.
Pain.
Window, The.
Wring the Swan's Neck.
Gonzales, Ray
Praise the Tortilla, Praise the Menudo, Praise
  the Chorizo.
Gonzales, Rebecca
South Texas Summer Rain.
González, Angel
Before I Could Call Myself Ángel González.
City.
Diatribe against the Dead.
Future, The.
Inventory of Places Propitious for Love.
Whatever You Want.
Yesterday.
Gonzalez, N. V. M. (b. 1915)
Deepest Well in Madras, The.
How the Heart Aches.
I Made Myself a Path.
Wanderer in the Night of the World, A.
González Prada, Manuel (1848–1918)
Cosmos Shows His Power, The.
How Old Is Pilar?
If the Tomb Is Not Oblivion.
Inca's Arrows, The.
Into the Hearth They Are Tossing Logs.
Living and Dying.
Mitayo, The.
Pope.
To Be with the Dead.
Treasures and Glories of Life, The.
Very Strong Stomach Has Mr. Luke, A.
Who Translates a Poet Badly.
Your Lily Eyes Said Yes.
Gonzalez, Ray
Angels of Juárez, Mexico, The.
At the Rio Grande Near the End of the
  Century.
Beyond Having.
Brown Pot.
Cabato.
Calling the White Donkey.
In Peru, the Quechuans Have a Thousand
  Words for Potato.
San Jacinto Plaza.
Savior.
Some Sixties.
Still Life with Endings.
There.
Without Villages.
González, Rigoberto (b. 1970)
Day of the Dead.
Death of the Farm Workers' Cat.
Marías, Old Indian Mothers.
Penny Men.
Perla at the Mexican Border Assembly Line of
  Dolls.
You and the Tijuana Mule.
Goode, Kate Tucker
Failure.
Goode, Starr
Lady of Pazardzik.
Goodge, W. T. (1862–1909)
Bad Break!, A.
Federation.
How We Drove the Trotter.
Goodhart, Al
Fit as a Fiddle.
Goodhue, Sarah (1641–81)
My first, as thy name is Joseph, labour so in
  knowledge to increase.
Goodison, Lorna (b. 1947)
Always Homing Now Soul Toward Light.
Birth Stone.
For Don Drummond.
From the Garden of the Women Once Fallen.
Heartease 3.
I Am Becoming My Mother.
Jah Music.
Jamaica 1980.
Kenscoff.
On Becoming a Tiger.

Road of the Dread, The.
Songs of the Fruits and Sweets of Childhood.
Upon a Quarter Million.
Wedding in Hanover.
Goodland, Giles
More powerful than the government.
Goodman, Benny
Stompin' at the Savoy.
Goodman, Melinda (b. 1957)
Cobwebs.
February Ice Years.
Just How Crazy Brenda Is.
Lullabye for a Butch.
New Comers.
Open Poem.
Wedding Reception.
Goodman, Miriam (*fl.* 20th cent.)
Upkeep.
Goodman, Mitchell (b. 1923)
Coming and Going.
Man and Wife.
Goodman, Paul (1911–72)
April 1962.
Ballade of the Moment After.
Birthday Cake.
Classical Quatrain, A.
Connary, Blodgett, Day, Hapgood.
Gravestone, August 8, 1968, A.
I planned to have a border of lavender.
In the Jury Room, in Pain.
It was good when you were here.
Long Lines: Youth and Age.
Lordly Hudson, The.
Now only praise makes me cry.
Saint Harmony my patroness.
Sentences After *Defence of Poetry.*
Sonnet 21: "I start awake at night afraid of
  death."
Sprayed with strong poison.
Weepers Tower in Amsterdam, The.
Wellfleet Harbor.
Woman eternal my muse, lean toward me.
**Goodrich, Samuel Griswold ("Peter Parley")
(1783?–1860)**
Higglety, Pigglety, Pop!
Goodtimes, Art
Art of Getting Lost, The.
Jojopan.
Learning to Smile.
Roadkill Coyote.
Sartor Resartus.
Googe, Barnabe (1540–94)
Coming Homeward out of Spain.
Epitaph of the Death of Nicholas Grimald, An.
Of Money.
To Doctor Bale.
Gorbanevskaya, Natalya (b. 1936)
And there is nothing at all—neither fear.
And where am I from? From an anecdote.
Curse! Joy! Writing!, A.
Drought, malevolent stepmother.
Here, as in a painting, yellow noon burns [or
  noon burns yellow].
Hold out a handful of snow.
Hurry, take pleasure in the oblique caress of
  rain while the sun shines.
It is time to think.
Like a soldier from Anders's army.
Love, love! What nonsense it is.
Not because of you, not because of me, just
  that.
Savage cold of Russian winters, The.
Square of the Holy Passion, gaze on the
  demonstrators.
Sukhanovo.
That time I did not save Warsaw, nor Prague
  later.
This world / is amazingly flat.
To I. Lavrentevaya.
**Gorbovsky [or Gorbovskii], Gleb Iakovlevich (b.
1931)**
Woodcutting.
Gordon, Adam Lindsay (1833–70)
Dedication, A: "They are rhymes rudely strung
  with intent less."

How We Beat the Favourite.
Question Not.
Rest, and be thankful! On the verge.
Sick Stockrider, The.

Gordon, Gerry
Gas.
Tercios del Muerte.

Gordon, Irving (1915–96)
Be Anything (But Be Mine)
Prelude to a Kiss.
Unforgettable.

Gordon, J. (1865–1901)
To Amy.

Gordon, Joan
Love.

Gordon, Judah Leib (1830–92)
Simhat Torah.

Gordon, Mack (1904–59)
Chattanooga Choo-Choo.
Head Over Heels in Love.
I've Got a Gal in Kalamazoo.
I, Yi, Yi, Yi, Yi (I Like You Very Much)
Love Thy Neighbor.
Mam'selle.
Meet the Beat of My Heart.
Serenade in Blue.
There's a Lull in My Life.
There Will Never Be Another You.
Time on My Hands.
You Hit the Spot.
You Make Me Feel So Young.

Gore-Booth, Eva (1872–1926)
Travellers, The.
Vision of Niamh, The.

Gorenko, Anna Andreyevna See **Akhmatova, Anna Andreyevna**

Gorey, Edward (1925–2000)
Limerick: "As tourists inspected the apse."
Limerick: "Babe, with a cry brief and dismal, The."
Limerick: "Dowager Duchess of Spout, The."
Limerick: "Each night father fills me with dread."
Limerick: "From the bathing machine came a din."
Limerick: "Headstrong young lady of Ealing, A."
Limerick: "Incautious young woman named Venn, An."
Limerick: "Lady, who signs herself 'Vexed,' A."
Limerick: "Some Harvard men, stalwart and hairy."
Limerick: "There was a young woman named Plunnery."
Limerick: "To his club-footed child said Lord Stipple."

Gorges, Sir Arthur (1577–1625)
Her Face, Her Tongue, Her Wit.
Tell me, my heart, how wilt thou do.
Written upon the death of the most Noble Prince Henrie.
Yourself the sun, and I the melting frost.

Gorham, Sarah
Empress Receives the Head of a Taiping Rebel, The.
Princess Parade.
White Tiger Leaps, The.

"Gorky [or Gorkii], Maksim" (Aleksey Maksimovich Peshkov) (1868–1936)
Song of the Stormy Petrel.

Gorman, Leroy
Beyond the laughing billboard girl.
Billboard girl.
Down the billboard girl's bare belly.
For the smell.
Her long paper legs.
I hear her sew.
I shut down the lawnmower.
Loud wind.
My family asleep.
One AM.

Gorney, Jay
Brother, Can You Spare a Dime?

Gorostiza, José (1901–73)
Elegy: "Alone, with harsh marine aloneness."

Filled with myself, walled up in my skin.
Fireflies.
Who Will Buy Me an Orange?

Gorrell, Stuart (fl. 1930)
Georgia on My Mind.

Gorton, Samuel (c.1592–1677)
Serpent with a voyce, so slie and fine, The.

Gosen (d. 1799)
Spring will meet this year.

Goshi (d. 1775)
Returning thanks.

Goshu (d. 1788)
Disgusted with.

Goshuku (d. 1888)
Cuckoo cries, A.

Gosse, Sir Edmund William (1849–1928)
Lying in the Grass.
Revelation.
Sestina: "In fair Provence, the land of lute and rose."

Gotera, Vince (b. 1952)
Dance of the Letters.
First Mango.
Gambling.
Madarika.
Manong Chito Tells Manong Ben about His Dream over Breakfast at the Manilatown Cafe.
Pacific Crossing.

Gotlieb, Phyllis (b. 1926)
Death's Head.
Cocker of Snooks, A.
Late Gothic.
This One's on Me.
Three-handed Fugue.

Gotoba, Emperor (1180–1239)
There Were Those I Loved.

Gottheil, Gustav (1827–1903)
Come, O Sabbath Day.

Gottlieb, Ann (b. 1946)
Meditation on the Feminine Nature of Shekinah, A.

Gottlieb, Lynn
Greeting Shekinah.

Göttner-Abendroth, Heide
Thou Gaia Art I.

Götz, Johann Nikolaus (1721–81)
First Rondeau: After a French Poet of the Fourteenth Century.
Second Rondeau.

Gould, Alan (b. 1949)
Demolisher.
Galaxies.
Ice.
Observed Observer, The.
Pearls.

Gould, Elizabeth (b. 1904)
My New Rabbit.

Gould, Gerald Louis (1885–1936)
This is the horror that, night after night.
You were young—but that was scarcely to your credit.

Gould, Hannah Flagg (1789–1865)
Apprehension.
Butterfly's Dream, The.
Child's Address to the Kentucky Mummy, The.
Day of God! Thou Blessed Day.
Dying Child's Request, The.
Spider, The.

Gould, Janice (b. 1949)
Coyotismo.
Earthquake Weather.
Easter Sunday.
I Learn a Lesson About Our Society.

Gould, Morton
There Must Be Somethin' Better Than Love.

Gould, Roberta
Amateur Drummer.

Goulding, Edmund
Mam'selle.

Gouri, Haim (b. 1923)
Heritage.

Gourmont, Rémy de (1858–1915)
Hair.

Gowar, Mick (b. 1951)
Annabell and the Witches.
Christmas Thank You's.
Rat Trap.

Gowdie, Isabel (fl. 1662)
Charm to Destroy the Male Child of the Laird of Parkis.
For Cadging Fish.
Shapeshifting.

Gower, John (1325–1408)
Address to the King, The, *sels.*
Confessio Amantis, *sels.*
This World Fares as a Fantasy, *sels.*

Gozan (d. 1789)
Snow of yesterday, The.

Gozan (d. 1733)
Blossoms scent the air.

Gōzō, Yoshimasu
Pulling in the Reins.

Gozzano, Guido (1883–1916)
Most Beautiful, The.

Grachova [or Grachiova], Nina (b. 1971)
Of what use to me are the nights full of wine.

Grade, Chaim (b. 1910)
Refugees.
Sodom.
To Life I Said Yes.

Graeme, James (1721–66)
Mortified Genius, The.

Grafflin, Margaret Johnston
To My Son.

Grafton, Richard (d. 1527)
Months of the Year, The.

Graham, David (1808–52)
Father of the Man.
Jesus Never Sleeps.

Graham, Harry ("Col. D. Streamer") (1874–1936)
Breakfast.
Calculating Clara.
Cockney of the North, The.
Compensation.
Englishman's Home, The.
Gourmand, The.
Grandpapa.
Indifference.
It was a winter's morning.
L'Enfant Glacé.
Lord Gorbals.
Mr. Jones.
Necessity.
Stern parent, The.
Tender-Heartedness.
Waste.
Opportunity.

Graham, Jorie (b. 1951)
At Luca Signorelli's Resurrection of the Body.
Breakdancing.
For One Must Want / To Shut the Other's Gaze.
Geese, The.
Guardian Angel of Not Feeling, The.
Gulls.
History.
Mind.
My Garden, My Daylight.
Of Forced Sightes and Trusty Ferefulness.
Of the Ever-Changing Agitation in the Air.
Opulence.
Orpheus and Eurydice.
Over and Over Stitch.
Region of Unlikeness, The.
San Sepolcro.
Soul Says.
Surface, The.
Tennessee June.
Thinking.
Underneath (1)
Underneath (2)
Underneath (3)
Underneath (7)
What the End Is For.
Willow in Spring Wind: A Showing.

Graham, Joyce Anstruther Maxtone See **"Struther, Jan"**

Graham, Matthew (fl. 20th cent.)
After the War; When Coltrane Only Wanted to
Play Dance Tunes.
Greta's Song.

Graham-Pole, John
Candor.
Leaving Mother, 1954.
Pain, The.
Venipuncture.

**Graham, Robert (Robert Cunninghame-
Graham) (1735–99)**
If doughty [or daughty] deeds my lady
please[s].

Graham, Virginia (b. 1912)
Disillusionment.
Ein Complaint.

Graham, William Sydney (1918–86)
Beast in the Space, The.
Children of Greenock, The.
Conscript Goes, The.
Dark Dialogues, The.
Imagine a Forest.
Johann Joachim Quantz's Five Lessons.
Letter V.
Letter VI.
Lines on Roger Hilton's Watch.
Listen. Put on Morning.
Loch Thom.
Malcolm Mooney's Land.
Many without Elegy.
Night's Fall.
Thermal Stair, The.
To My Father.
What's the News?

Grahame, Kenneth (1859–1932)
Duck's Ditty.
Song of Mr Toad, The.

Grahn, Judy (b. 1940)
Ah, Love, You Smell of Petroleum.
Carol, in the Park, Chewing on Straws.
Ella, in a Square Apron, Along Highway 80.
Fortunately the skins.
Funeral Plainsong from a Younger Woman to
an Older Woman, A.
Grand Grand Mother is returning.
History of Lesbianism, A.
I Have Come to Claim Marilyn Monroe's
Body.
In the place where.
She holds things together, collects bail.
Talkers in a Dream Doorway.
They Say She Is Veiled.
Woman Is Talking to Death, A.

Grainger, James (1724–67)
Bryan and Pereene.
Compost.
North-east wind did briskly blow, The.
Of composts shall the Muse disdain to sing?
Slaves.
Solitude: An Ode.

Grammaticus, Damocharis See **Damocharis of
Kos**

Granade, John A. (c.1770–1807)
Come All Ye Mourning Pilgrims.
Sweet Rivers of Redeeming Love.

Grand, Murray
Guess Who I Saw Today.

Grandfather Koori
Massacre Sandhill.
Never Blood So Red.
Song in the Symbol, The.

Grandmaster Flash and **the Furious Five**
Message, The.

Grandsen, K. W. (b. 1925)
Interview, An.

Grano, Paul (b. 1894)
Headlined in Heaven.
In a Chain-Store Cafeteria.

Grant, Anne (1755–1838)
Aged Bard's Wish (Translation of a Gaelic
Poem Composed in the Isle of Skye), The.
Highland Poor, The.
Metrical Translation of the Song of Macgregor
Na Ruara.
Nymph of the Fountain to Charlotte, The.

Grant, Jamie (b. 1949)
Auditor Thinks about Female Nature, An.
Planes Landing.
Skywriting.

Grant, Sir Robert (1779–1838)
O worship the King all glorious above.

**Granville [or Grenville], George, Baron
Lansdowne (1666–1735)**
Cloe.
Impatient with Desire.
Love.
To Cloe.

Grass, Günter (b. 1927)
Gasco.
In the Egg.
Music for Brass.
Saturn.

Grave, John (fl. mid–17th cent.)
If Thou Wilt Hear.

Graves, John Woodcock (1795–1886)
John Peel.

Graves, Richard (1715–1804)
Maternal Despotism; or, The Rights of Infants.

Graves, Robert Ranke (1895–1985)
All Except Hannibal.
Allie.
Angry Samson.
Apple Island.
At First Sight.
Beach, The.
Beauty in Trouble.
Blue-Fly, The.
Broken Girth, The.
Call It a Good Marriage.
Carol of Patience.
Cat Goddesses.
Certain Mercies.
Change.
Christmas Robin, The.
Cloak, The.
Cool Web, The.
Corporal Stare.
Counting the Beats.
Cry Faugh!
Dead Cow Farm.
Devil's Advice to Story-Tellers, The.
Dr. Newman with the crooked pince-nez.
Down, Wanton, Down!
1805.
End of Play.
Epitaph on an Unfortunate Artist.
Escape.
Eugenist, The.
Face in the Mirror, The.
Fallen Tower of Siloam, The.
False Report, A.
Flying Crooked.
Forced Music, A.
Frosty Night, A.
Full Moon.
Galatea and Pygmalion.
Gardener.
General Elliott, The.
Goliath and David.
Grotesques.
Hag-Ridden.
Hedges Freaked With Snow.
Henry and Mary.
Hide and Seek.
I'd Love to Be a Fairy's Child.
I Wonder What It Feels Like to Be Drowned?
In Broken Images.
In Her Only Way.
In Her Praise.
In Perspective.
In Procession.
In the Wilderness.
In Time.
It's a Queer Time.
It Was All Very Tidy.
Lament for Pasiphaë.
Laureate, The.
Legs, The.
Leveller, The.
Lollocks.
Lost Acres.

Lost Jewel, A.
Lost Love.
Love Story, A.
Love Without Hope.
Lovers in Winter.
My Name and I.
Naked and the Nude, The.
Narrow Sea, The.
Nature's Lineaments.
Neglectful Edward.
Never Such Love.
Nobody.
Not at Home.
Ogres and Pygmies.
On Dwelling.
On Portents.
One Hard Look.
Parent to Children.
Persian Version, The.
Pier-Glass, The.
Pinch of Salt, A.
Plea to Boys and Girls, A.
Poets' Corner.
Point of No Return.
Pure Death.
Queen Mother to New Queen.
Quiet Glades of Eden, The.
Reader over My Shoulder, The.
Recalling War.
Reproach to Julia.
Rocky Acres.
Sea Horse, The.
Sergeant-Major Money.
Sharp Ridge, The.
She Is No Liar.
She Tells Her Love While Half Asleep.
Sick Love.
Sir John addressed the Snake-god in his
temple.
Slice of Wedding Cake, A.
Song: Lift-Boy.
Spoils.
Star-Talk.
Straw, The.
Surgical Ward: Men.
Symptoms Of Love.
Theseus and Ariadne.
Thieves, The.
Three-Faced, The.
Tilth.
To Bring the Dead to Life.
To Evoke Posterity.
To Juan at the Winter Solstice.
To Robert Nichols.
To Whom Else?
Travel[l]er's Curse after Misdirection[, The].
Troll's Nosegay, The.
Twins.
Ulysses.
Under the Pot.
Vain and Careless.
Valentine, A.
Vanity.
Variables of Green.
Warning to Children.
Weather of Olympus, The.
Wellcome, to the Caves of Artá!
Welsh Incident.
When I'm Killed.
White Goddess, The.
Wigs and Beards.
Wild Strawberries.
Window Sill, The.
Wm. Brazier.
Wreath, The.

Gray, Sir Alexander (1882–1968)
On a Cat Aging.
Scotland.
Sir Halewyn.

Gray, Alice Wirth
Music in the Meadow.
Why Your Grandfather Stopped Playing the
Viola.

Gray, David (1838–61)
My Epitaph.
Sonnet I: "If it must be; if it must be, O God!"
Sonnet: "October's gold is dim—the forests

rot."
Where the Lilies Used to Spring.
Gray, Frances
With cheerful mind we yield to men.
Gray, John (1866–1934)
Barber, The.
Battledore.
Flying Fish, The.
Les Demoiselles de Sauve.
Mishka.
On the South Coast of Cornwall.
Poem: "Geranium, houseleek, laid in oblong beds."
Spleen.
They say, in other days.
Tobias and the Angel.
Vines, The.
Wings in the Dark.
Gray-Kontar, Daniel
Cuz' mama played jazz.
July.
Not no socialism/communism classical, but some power to the people jazz.
Gray, Robert (b. 1945)
Curriculum Vitae.
Dusk, The.
5 Poems.
Flames and Dangling Wire.
Journey: the North Coast.
Gray, Stephen (b. 1941)
Apollo Café.
Hottentot Venus.
Gray, Thomas (1716–71)
Bard, The [A Pindaric Ode], sels.
Curse upon Edward, The.
Death of Hoel, The.
Descent of Odin, The.
Elegy Written in a Country Churchyard, sels.
Epitaph on Dr. Keene.
Epitaph on Dr. Keene's Wife.
Hymn to Adversity.
Ode on a Distant Prospect of Eton College.
Ode on the Death of a Favourite [or Favorite] Cat, Drowned in a Tub [or Bowl] of Gold Fishes.
Ode on the Pleasure Arising from Vicissitude, sels.
Ode on the Spring.
On Dr. Keene, Bishop of Chester.
On Lord Holland's Seat near Margate, Kent.
Progress of Poesy, The, sels.
Sonnet [on the Death of Mr. Richard West].
Tophet.
Gray, Victor (b. 1926)
All the World's a Stage.
Limerick: "Charlotte Brontë said, 'Wow, sister! What a man!'"
Limerick: "Example of Kant's sterling wit, An."
Limerick: "First chap to fuck little Sophie, The."
Limerick: "I was thrilled when I went to the Zoo."
Limerick: "It's a pity that Casabianca."
Limerick: "Meanwhile, back home at the ranch."
Limerick: "Oedipus said to the Sphinx."
Limerick: "Old East End worker called Jock, An."
Limerick: "One midnight, old D. G. Rossetti."
Limerick: "One morning old Wilfrid Scawen Blunt."
Limerick: "Postmaster-General cried: 'Arsehole!,' The."
Limerick: "Rebuke by the Bishop of London, A."
Limerick: "Said a famous old writer called Fender."
Limerick: "Said a gloomy young fellow called Fart."
Limerick: "Said Arnold to Arthur Hugh Clough."
Limerick: "Said Tennyson: 'Yes, Locksley Hall's."
Limerick: "Said the famous philosopher, Russell."

Limerick: "Sir John Shagbag (Conservative, Nore)"
Limerick: "Taxi-cab whore out at Iver, A."
Limerick: "There was a young fellow called Crouch."
Limerick: "There was a young fellow called Shit."
Limerick: "There was a young girl of Mauritius."
Limerick: "There was an old man of Lugano."
Limerick: "When Gauguin was visiting Fiji."
Limerick: "When Keats was at work on Endymion."
Limerick: "When our dean took a pious young spinster."
Limerick: "While visiting Arundel Castle."
Limerick: "Young engine-driver called Hunt, A."
Greacen, Robert (b. 1920)
Bird, The.
Captain Fox.
Carnival at the River.
Father and Son.
Ten New Commandments.
St. Andrew's Day.
Summer Day, A.
Grealy, Lucy
Murder.
Green, Adolph (b. 1915)
Adventure.
All of My Life.
Conga.
I Can Cook, Too.
If You Hadn't—But You Did.
Just in Time.
Little Bit in Love, A.
Lonely Town.
Lucky to Be Me.
Make Someone Happy.
New York, New York.
Not Mine.
Party's Over, The.
Some Other Time.
Thanks a Lot, but No Thanks.
You Mustn't Feel Discouraged.
Green, Bud (fl. 1928)
Sentimental Journey.
That's My Weakness Now.
Green, D. Rubin
Names and sorrows.
Green, F. Pratt (b. 1903)
Old Couple, The.
Green, Jane
Songs of Divorce.
Green, Johnny
Body and Soul.
Easy Come, Easy Go.
I Cover the Waterfront.
I Wanna Be Loved.
You're Mine, You!
Green, Joseph (1706–80)
Permit Us, Lord, to Consecrate.
Green, Matthew (1696–1737)
On Barclay's Apology for the Quakers.
Seeker, The.
Spleen, The, sels.
Green, Melissa (b. 1954)
More than novelty crooked its finger—silent, austere.
Greenaway, Kate (1846–1901)
Three Little Girls.
Greenberg, Alvin
City Life.
Freight Train, Freight Train.
Man in the Moon, The.
Wintering Over at the End of the Century.
Greenberg, Samuel (1893–1917)
African Desert.
Etching.
Glass Bubbles, The.
God.
Secrecy.
To Dear Daniel.
Greenberg, Uri Zvi (1896–81)
At Your Feet, Jerusalem.

By the Waters of the Sava.
Hour is tired as if it were time for bed, The.
I have never been at the top of wind-played Olympus.
I thirst for water; wine is my need no longer.
In the Covenant's Radiance.
Jerusalem the Dismembered.
Lord! You Saved Me from Ur-Germany as I Fled.
Naming Souls.
Penny for You, A.
Song of Earth.
Song of My People-Forest, People-Sea.
Song of the Great Mind.
Song to Heaven.
We Were Not Likened to Dogs among the Gentiles.
Greene, Albert Gorton (1802–68)
Old Grimes.
Greene, Alice (1858–1920)
Four Roads, The.
Greene, Carl H. (b. 1945)
Excuse, The.
Realist, The.
Something Old, Something New.
Greene, Richard Leighton (1904–83)
Limerick: "When approached by a person from Porlock."
Greene, Robert (1558?–92)
Description of Sir Geoffrey Chaucer, The.
Description of the Shepherd and His Wife, The.
Ideals.
Maesia's Song.
Night Visitor, A.
Palmer's Ode, The.
Palmer, The.
Sephestia's Song to Her Child[e].
Shepherd's Wife's Song, The.
Song: "Sweet are the thoughts that savour of content."
Greenfield, Eloise (b. 1929)
Moochie.
Greenfield, Freddie (b. 1929)
Oh God Forbid.
Greenhalgh, Chris
Big No-No, The.
Man in the Valley of Women, A.
My Funny Valentine.
Night I Met Marilyn, The.
Of Love, Death and the Sea-Squirt.
Greening, Michael
Missing — Believed Drowned.
Greenlaw, Lavinia (b. 1962)
Earliest Known Representation of a Storm in Western Art, The.
Five O'Clock Opera.
Iron Lung.
Love from a Foreign City.
Millefiori.
New Year's Eve.
Shape of Things, The.
World Where News Travelled Slowly, A.
Greenlee, Sam (fl. 20th cent.)
Memorial for Trane.
Greenwald, Ted (b. 1942)
And, Hinges.
Coordinating cities gulls still gull, and, arms binged with wine, as wine.
I Hear a Step.
Open mouth open through.
Privets Come into Season at High Tide.
Greenwell, Anne (1630s–80)
Some Account of Anne Whitehead's Early Experience, as Written by Her Near Thirty Years Ago.
Greenwell, Bill
Christopher Robin Changes Guard with Dylan Thomas.
Limerick: "By Loch Ness they can toss, like confetti."
Limerick: "Filthy young fellow called Lawrence, A."
Limerick: "For his Campbell's Soup screen-prints, society's."

Limerick: "Glib little beer-buff from Troon, A."
Limerick: "In Genesis, Adam's the winner."
Limerick: "No, listen, there's this albatross."
Limerick: "Pop's tops!"
Limerick: "Reason we're asked to endure, The."
Limerick: "Shelley's death—was it really his wish."
Limerick: "There was a young lady of Ulva / Who drunkenly said: 'What a hulva'"
Limerick: "Watt's dream was the cream of steam engines."
Limerick: "What led to the crassness of Custer."
Limerick: "When Jael crept in to see Sisera."
That rebellious rodent called Jerry.
When my stomach bulges, I hurl wild whoops.

Greenwell, Dora (1812–82)
Broken Chain, The.
Christina.
Content.
Demeter and Cora.
Fidelity Rewarded.
Man with Three Friends, The.
Picture, A.
Reconciliation.
Saturday Review, The.
Scherzo, A.
Sun-Flower, The.
To Christina Rossetti.
To Elizabeth Barrett Browning, in 1851.
To Elizabeth Barrett Browning, in 1861.
When the Night and Morning Meet.

Greer, Jane
Rodin's "Gates of Hell."

Greger, Debora (b. 1949)
Frog in the Swimming Pool, The.
Man on the Bed, The.
Notre Dame, Sainte Chapelle, Sacré Coeur by foot—.
Penguin Jane Austen, The.

Gregerman, Debra (b. 1962)
High Speed.
Lullaby.
Silent Globe.
Strictly Speaking.

Gregerson, Linda (b. 1950)
Line Drive Caught by the Grace of God.
Mother Ruin.
Saint's Logic.
Waterborne.

Gregg, Linda (b. 1942)
Adult.
Clapping, The.
Dark Thing Inside the Day, A.
Edge of Something, The.
Fish Tea Rice.
Fishing in the Keep of Silence.
Flower No More Than Itself, A.
Lilith.
Limits of Desire, The.
Night Music.
Not Saying Much.
Official Love Story.
Past Perfect.
Singers Change, the Music Goes on, The.
Stuff.
Tree Falling in a Vacant Forest, The.
Unknowing, The.
What Is Kept.

Gregor, Arthur (b. 1923)
Enough.
History.
Late Last Night.
Likeness, The.
Lyric: "Embodiment of what, The."
Poem: "So many pigeons at Columbus."
Spirits, Dancing.
Two Shapes.

Gregor, Christian (1723–89)
What Splendid Rays.

Gregory, Horace (1898–1982)
Among the shades I heard my father's father.
Ask No Return.
Cage of Voices, The.

Chinese Garden, The.
For You, My Son.
Longface Mahoney Discusses Heaven.
Meek Shall Disinherit the Earth,The.
Poems for My Daughter.
Postman's Bell Is Answered Everywhere, The.
Rehearsal, The.
They Found Him Sitting in a Chair.
This Is the Place to Wait.
Valediction to My Contemporaries.

Gregory, Leona
Silence, an Eloquent Applause.

Gregory, Mrs. Horace *See* **Zaturenska, Marya Alexandrovna**

Gregory of Nazianzus, Saint (c.330–90)
Leave my tomb. Employ your pick.
On Naucratius, Brother of St. Basil.
Why do you heave apart my stone?

Gregory the Great, Saint (540–604)
Behold, the Shade of Night Is Now Receding.

Gregory, Yvonne (b. 1919)
Christmas Lullaby for a New-Born Child.

Greiffenberg, Catharina Regina von (1633–94)
Concerning the Fruit-bringing Autumn Season.
Concerning the Joyous and Splendid Resurrection of Christ.
Fortune-Bringing Misfortune.
I look.
On the Fruit-Providing Autumn Season.
On the Ineffable Inspiration of the Holy Spirit.
Spring Joy Praising God.
Spring-Joy Praising God; Praise of the Sun.
Zealous Admonition to Praise.

Gréki, Anna (1931–67)
Before Your Waking.
Future is for Tomorrow, The.

Grenfell, Joyce (1910–79)
Stately as a Galleon.

Grenfell, Julian (1888–1915)
Into Battle.

Grenier, Robert (b. 1941)
Crow.
Easter Roses.
Has Faded in Part But Magnificent Also Late for RC / Mirrors.
Open the door Oakland.
Sunday Morning.
Wrath to Sadness.

Grénier, Silvia
Salomé.
Signs.

Grennan, Eamon (b. 1941)
Breaking Points.
Conjunctions.
Facts of Life, Ballymoney.
Four Deer.
Incident.
Lizards in Sardinia.
Men Roofing.
Pause.
Potatoes.
Shoreline After Storm.
Soul Music: The Derry Air.
Sunday Morning Through Binoculars.
Totem.
Wing Road.
Woman at Lit Window.

Grenville, R. H.
Praise.

Greppi, Cesare (b. 1936)
Boy's Afraid of the Live Tiger, The.
If it had been possible.
If you dropped me on the table.
Like a handful of leaves.
Rain of hollow malice, A.
Subtle erratic vocation, A.
Those quiet little feet in the reflected room.
What words must rush in.

Greshoff, J. (1888–1971)
Friendship for a Woman of Grace.
I Greet You.

Greville, Fanny [or Frances] Macartney (c.1727–1789)
Miss F[———]ny M[———]t[———]y to Miss P[———]y B[———]s.

Prayer for Indifference, A.

Greville, Fulke, 1st Baron Brooke (1554–1628)
Caelica, *sels.*
Epitaph on Sir Philip Sidney.
Mustapha, *sels.*
Treatise of Monarchy, A, *sels.*
Treatise of Religion, A, *sels.*
Treaty of Human Learning, *sels.*

Grey, Clifford (1887–1941)
Hallelujah!
If You Were the Only Girl in the World.
Spread a Little Happiness.

Grieg, Edvard
Strange Music.

Grier, Eldon (b. 1917)
I Am Almost Asleep.
Kissing Natalia.
More Than Most People.
Mountain Town—Mexico.
My Winter Past.
On the Subject of Waves.
Sensible Is the Label.

Grierson, Constantia (1706?–32)
To Miss Laetitia Van Lewen.

Grieve, Christopher Murray *See* **MacDiarmid, Hugh**

Grieves, Catron
Connuche.
Indian Car.

Griffin, Bartholomew (d. 1602)
Care-Charmer Sleep.
Venus and Adonis.

Griffin, Gerald (1803–40)
When like the rising day.

Griffin, Jonathan
Emperor, The.
Night Sky Hiss.
One's Country.
Venerating Senses Save Us.

Griffin, Paul
Limerick: "I once had a cat called Maria."
New Tarantella.
To His Importunate Mistress.

Griffin, Susan (b. 1943)
Answer to a Man's Question, "What Can I Do About Women's Liberation?," An.
I Like to Think of Harriet Tubman.
I Wake Thinking of Myself as a Man.
Ordinary, as Love.
Our Mother.
Song My.
Song of the Woman with Her Parts Coming Out, The.
To the Far Corners of Fractured Worlds.
Waiting for Truth.

Griffith, Llewelyn Wyn (1890–1977)
Exile: Welsh Service from Daventry.
From his own solitude to the world unheeding.
Office Window.
Silver Jubilee.

Griffiths, Ann (1776–1805)
His left hand, in heat of noonday.
Lo, between the Myrtles Standing.

Griffiths, Bill (b. 1948)
For P—Celtic: found text from Machen.
Fragment 1.
Fragment 4.
Fragment 9.
Fragment 11.
Fragment 12.
Fragment 13.
Fragment 18.
Shepherd's Calendar.
Shepherd's Calendar cont'd.
Ship, The.
South Song.

Griffiths, Bryn (b. 1935)
Dolphins.
Master, The.

Griffiths, Jane (b. 1970)
Emigrants.
Errata.
Lost and Found.
Migration.

Griffiths, Steve (b. 1949)
Getting It Wrong, Again.

Just a Product of a Certain Situation.
Mines in Sepia Tint, The.
Griffiths, T.
Limerick: "Is there really a new Mr. Nixon."
Limerick: "There was a young lady of Ulva /
    Who said: 'I have granted a culver'"
Grigson, Geoffrey (b. 1905)
Above the High.
Administrator, An.
Before a Fall.
By the Road.
Critics and Poets.
Death of a Farmyard.
In the Spring Garden.
Landscape Gardeners, The.
On a Lover of Books.
On the Relinquishment of a Title.
Grillparzer, Franz (1791–1872)
Between Gaeta and Capua.
In Praise of Austria.
Grimald, Nicholas (1519–62)
Funeral Song, Upon the Decease of Annes His
    Mother, A, *sels.*
True Love, A.
Virtue.
Grimberg, Faina (b. 1951)
For a long time I haven't seen such a young
    face.
Grimes, Anne
Alice's Cat, New Year's Eve 1990.
Grimké, Angelina Weld (1880–1958)
At April.
Butterflies.
Caprichosa.
Dawn.
Dusk.
Epitaph on a Living Woman.
For the Candle Light.
Grass Fingers.
Mona Lisa, A.
Rosabel.
Tenebris.
To Keep the Memory of Charlotte Forten
    Grimké.
Winter Twilight, A.
Grimke, Charlotte L. Forten (1837–1914)
Parting Hymn, A.
Wordsworth.
**Grimmelshausen, Hans Jakob Christoffel von
(1621–76)**
Come, balm of night, oh nightingale.
Grindal, Edmund (1519–83)
Give Peace in These Our Days, O Lord.
Grindel, Eugène See **Éluard, Paul**
Grindrod, Cathy
Searching.
Griswold, Alexander V. (1766–1843)
Holy Father, Great Creator.
Groarke, Vona
Family Photograph, The.
History of My Father's House, The.
Riverbed, The.
Shale.
Trousseau.
Grobman, Mikhail
In mass graves the bodies of plants.
Grosholz, Emily
Back Trouble.
Eden.
Last of the Courtyard, The.
Legacies.
Life of a Salesman.
Old Fisherman, The.
On the Ferry, Toward Patras.
Outer Banks, The.
Remembering the Ardèche.
Gross, Philip (b. 1952)
Two spiral stairs we climb to bed together.
Gross, Ronald (b. 1935)
Yield.
Gross, Walter
Tenderly.
Grossman, Allen (b. 1932)
Enough Rain for Agnes Walquist.

Grossman, Reuben (1905–74)
Therefore, We Thank Thee, God.
Grossmith, George
You Can't Make Love by Wireless.
Groves, Paul
Anniversary Soak.
Back End of the Horse, The.
Heroine.
Turvy-Topsy.
Gruber, Abraham L.
My Neighbor's Roses.
Gruber, Johann A. (1694–1763)
Love That's Pure, Itself Disdaining.
Grue, Lee Meitzen
Dogs of New York, The.
Gruffudd ab yr Ynad Coch (*fl.* c.1280)
Lament for Llywelyn ap Gruffudd.
Gruffydd, Owen (1643–1730)
Old, old / To live on, wretched to behold.
Gruffydd, Peter (b. 1935)
Digging Soil.
Slate Quay: Felinheli.
Gruffydd, W. J. (1881–1954)
Gwladys Rhys.
In Memoriam.
This Poor Man.
Grün, Anastasius
In Winter.
Grunberger, Aimée (1954–98)
Old Road, The.
Swimming Upstream.
Grundtvig, Nicolai Frederik Severin (1783–1872)
I Know a Flower So Fair and Fine.
Grunke, Ann Lundberg
Learning to Live with the Piano.
Gryphius, Andreas (1616–64)
All Is Vanity.
Epitaph for Mariana Gryphius, His Brother
    Paul's Little Daughter.
Evening.
Hell.
Human Misery.
Midnight.
Misery.
My Country Weeps.
Not Mine the Years Time Took Away.
On the Birth of Jesus.
Solitude.
Tears of the Fatherland, Anno Domini 1636.
To Himself.
To the Stars.
To the Virgin Mary.
Gu Cheng (1956–93)
Ark.
Bulin is Dead, It Seems.
Bulin Met Bandit.
Discovery.
Forever Parted: Graveyard.
Generation, A.
Guarini, Giovanni Battista (1537–1612)
Claim to Love.
Shepherd Thirsis longed to die, The.
Spring.
Gubanov, Leonid (1946–83)
Palette of Grief.
Guchu (1334–1409)
Men without rank, excrement spatulas.
Gudo (1579–1661)
It's not nature that upholds utility.
**Gudzenko, Semyon [*or* Semion] Petrovich (1922–
53)**
Ballad about Friendship, A.
Before the Attack.
I fought on foot in every quarter.
Not from old age our death will come.
Guérin, Charles (1873–1904)
Partings.
Guernsey, Bruce (b. 1944)
Apple, The.
Louis B. Russell.
Maps.
Guerzo di Montecanti (*fl.* 13th cent.)
He Is Out of Heart with His Time.
Guest, Barbara (b. 1920)
Advance of the Grizzly, The.

Bleat.
Defensive Rapture.
Direction.
Emphasis Falls on Reality, An.
Geese Blood.
Green Revolutions.
Heavy Violets.
Luminous, The.
Motion Pictures: 4.
Motion Pictures: 15.
Nebraska.
Otranto.
Parachutes, My Love, Could Carry Us Higher.
Parade's End.
Piazzas.
Poem: "Disturbing to have a person."
Prairie Houses.
Red Dye.
Red Lilies.
River Road Studio.
Roses.
Santa Fe Trail.
Sassafras.
Sunday Evening.
Twilight Polka Dots.
Walking Buddha.
Way of Being, A.
Wild Gardens Overlooked by Night Lights.
Words.
You Can Discover.
Guest, Edgar Albert (1881–1959)
Equipment.
Home.
It Couldn't Be Done.
Just Folks.
Kindly Neighbor, The.
Lemon Pie.
Let's Be Brave.
Sausage.
Sittin' on the Porch.
Things that Make a Soldier Great, The.
What's In It for Me?
Guest, Harry (b. 1932)
No fragrance yet the fold.
Wales Re-visited.
Guevara, Ernesto 'Che' (1928–67)
Song to Fidel.
Guevara, Maurice Kilwein (b. 1961)
Abuelo, Answers and Questions.
After the Colombian Earthquake.
After the Flood.
Buddy Holly Poem, The.
Doña Josefina Counsels Doña Concepción
    Before Entering Sears.
Easter Revolt Painted on a Tablespoon, The.
Hands of the Old Métis, The.
Long Distance.
Long Woman Bathing, The.
Magic Carpet, The.
Make-Up.
Miniaturist, The.
Once When I Was in the Eighth Grade.
Postmortem.
Reader of This Page.
Rhyme for Halloween, A.
Tuesday Shaman.
Guevara, Miguel de (c.1585–c.1646)
To Christ Crucified.
Guggenberger, Louisa S. (b. 1945)
Afternoon.
Egoisme à Deux.
Love and Language.
Twilight.
Guha, Naresh (b. 1924)
Winding Sand.
Guidacci, Margherita (b. 1921)
Anniversary with Agave Plants.
At Night.
Before Our Encounter.
Crazy Mother, The.
First to feast is love, The. On the scraps of
    love the fever feasts.
It Is like a Shortness of Breath.
Madame X.
Map of the Winter Sky, The.
Spring.

Tiny dew reinvigorates the tiny grass, The.

Guiducci, Armanda (b. 1923)
Brevity of Embraces.
Delivery.
I Look at You So Old.
In Emily's Manner.
Perhaps One Day There Will Be Ways.
Readings.
Under an Impure Star.
Upon Closing the Book.

Guillaume de Poitiers (d. c.1240)
Behold, the Meads.

Guillén, Jorge (1893–1984)
Flight.
I Want to Sleep.

Guillén, Nicolás (b. 1904)
Bars.
Dead Soldier.
Don't Know No English.
Guadalupe, W. I.
Madrigal.
Moon.
My Last Name.
National Police Headquarters.
Proposition.
Sensemayá.
Sightseers in a Courtyard.
Small Ode to a Black Cuban Boxer.
Usurers, The.
Wake for Papa Montero.

Guillory, Dan (b. 1944)
Retinal burn of warm November light.

Guilpin, Everard (b. 1572?)
What more variety of pleasures can.

Guiney, Louise Imogen (1861–1920)
At a Symphony.
Atoning Yesterday, The.
Borderlands.
Deo Optimo Maximo.
Down Stream.
Fog.
Garden Chidings.
In the Reading-Room of the Brtish Museum.
Kings, The.
Knight Errant, The.
Lights of London, The.
Oh, give my youth, my faith, my sword.
Open, Time.
Private Theatricals.
Reason for Silence, A.
Salutation, A.
Strikers in Hyde Park.
Sunday Chimes in the City.
W. H.
When on the Marge of Evening.
Wild Ride, The.

Guinicelli, Guido (fl. 13th cent.)
Among my thoughts I count it wonderful.
He Perceives His Rashness in Love, but Has
  No Choice.
Love and Nobility.
Of the Gentle Heart.
Sonnet: He Will Praise His Lady.
Sonnet: Of Moderation and Tolerance.
When Lucy draws her mantle around her face.

Guiterman, Arthur (1871–1943)
Ancient History.
Anthologistics.
Bears.
Brief Essay on Man.
Everything in Its Place.
Habits of the Hippopotamus.
Heredity.
Husband and Wife.
Little Lost Pup.
Local Note.
Of Courtesy.
Offer, An.
On the Vanity of Earthly Greatness.
Sea-Chill.
Song of Hate for Eels.
Strictly Germ-proof.
Whole Duty of a Poem, The.

Gullar, Ferreira (b. 1930)
In the Body.
Noise.

Oswald Dead.
Poster.
Sweet Talk.
There Are Many Traps in the World.

Gumilyov, Nikolai Stepanovich (1886–1921)
Baby Elephant, A.
Childhood.
First Canzone.
Fragments 1920–1921.
Giraffe, The.
I and You.
I, who could have been the best of poems.
Memory.
Moon at Sea.
No flowers will live in my room.
On polar and on southern seas.
Plague, The.
Porcelain Pavilion, The.
Pre-Memory.
Progeny of Cain, The.
Sixth Sense, The.
Streetcar That Lost Its Way, The.
Tanka.
Tram That Lost Its Way, The.
Turkey, The.
Words.
Worker, The.

Gundy, Jeff (b. 1952)
For the New York City Poet Who Informed Me
  that Few People Live This Way.
Rain.

Gunn, Thom (b. 1929)
Allegory of the Wolf Boy, The.
Aquarium, The.
As Expected.
Autobiography.
Autumn Chapter in a Novel.
Baby Song.
Black Jackets.
Breakfast.
Byrnies, The.
Cannibal.
Carnal Knowledge.
Cherry Tree, The.
Claus von Stauffenberg.
Considering the Snail.
Courage, a Tale.
Discovery of the Pacific, The.
Donahue's Sister.
Elegy on the Dust.
Elvis Presley.
Expression.
Faustus Triumphant.
Feel of Hands, The.
For Signs.
From the Highest Camp.
From the Wave.
Hug, The.
Idea of Trust, The.
In Santa Maria del Popolo.
In the Post Office.
In the Tank.
Innocence.
J Car, The.
Jesus and His Mother.
Lament: "Your dying was a difficult
  enterprise."
Last Days at Teddington.
Last Man, The.
Lebensraum.
Lines for a Book.
Man With Night Sweats, The.
Map of the City, A.
Martial.
Missing, The.
Moly.
My Sad Captains.
No Speech from the Scaffold.
On the Move.
Painkillers.
Pope's Carnations Knew Him.
Reassurance, The.
Serving man. Curled my hair, A.
Skateboard.
Street Song.
Tamer and Hawk.
Terminal.

To Yvor Winters, 1955.
Touch.
Victim, The.
Wheel of Fortune, The.
Wound, The.
Yoko.

Gunnars, Kristjana (b. 1948)
Changeling VIII.
Wakepick I.

Günther, Johann Christian (1695–1723)
Consolation Aria.
Departure Aria.

Gupta, Īśvarcandra (1818–59)
I got some news from Kailasa!

Gurevitch, Zali (b. 1949)
Everyone's dancing where I live.
Line of a Poem.

Guri, Haim
But We Shall Bloom.
His Mother.
Odysseus.
Pictures of the Jews.
Piyyut for Rosh Hashana.
Prayer: "Thy blessing on the boys—for time
  has come."
Requiescat.
Silent Words, The.

Gurney, Ivor (1890–1937)
After War.
April Gale.
Bach and the Sentry.
Ballad of the Three Spectres.
Behind the Line.
Bohemians, The.
Butchers and Tombs.
Canadians.
December 30th.
Epitaph on a Young Child.
Escape, The.
Felling a Tree.
First March.
First Time In.
High Hills, The.
If I Walked Straight Slap.
It Is Near Toussaints'
La Gorgue.
Love Song: "Out of the blackthorn hedges."
Mangel-Bury, The.
Moments.
Not-Returning, The.
Old Dreams.
On the Night.
Possessions.
Requiem: "Pour out your light, O stars."
Silent One, The.
Soaking, The.
Song: "Only the wanderer."
Strange Hells.
To God.
To His Love.
Towards Lillers.
War Books.

Gurr, Robin
Creation.

Gustafson, Ralph (b. 1909)
Armorial.
Columbus Reaches Juana, 1492.
In the Yukon.
Mothy Monologue.
My Love Eats an Apple.
Of Green Steps and Laundry.
Swans of Vadstena, The.
Transfigured Night.
Wednesday at North Hatley.

Gustafsson, Lars
Ballad of the Dogs.

Guthrie, Ramon (1896–1973)
Elegy for Mélusine from the Intensive Care
  Ward.
Homage to Paul Delvaux.
Magi, The.
Red-Headed Intern, Taking Notes.
Scene: A Bedside in the Witches' Kitchen.
Today Is Friday.

Guthrie, Thomas Anstey See "Anstey, F."

Guthrie, Woody (1912–67)
Dust Storm Disaster.
Talking Dust Bowl.
Turkey in the Corn.
Vigilante Man.

Gutiérrez Nájera, Manuel (1859–95)
Non Omnis Moriar.

Gutteridge, Bernard (b. 1916)
Enemy Dead, The.
In September 1939.
Man into a Churchyard.
Shillong.

Guxnawu
Song for the Richest Woman in Wrangell.

Gvadányi, József (1725–1801)
On the Dress of the Hungarians.

Gwala, Mafika Pascal (b. 1946)
From the Outside.
In Defence of Poetry.
My House Is Bugged.
New Dawn, The.
Promise!

Gwangwa'a, Gahlia
Leaking Roof.

Gwdman, Elen (*fl.* 1609)
Young Woman's Complaint about Her
Sweetheart, A.

"Gwenallt" *See* Jones, David Gwenallt

Gwyer, Joseph
Albert Victor loved his mother.
At evening too the dazzled light.
Heap on more grass was his request.
Intoxicating draughts he never does drink.
To Alfred Gwyer.

Gwynn, R. S. (b. 1948)
Among Philistines.
Anacreontic.
Approaching a Significant Birthday, He
Peruses the Norton Anthology of Poetry.
Body Bags.
Classroom at the Mall, The.
Drive-In, The.
Release.
Snow White and the Seven Deadly Sins.

Gyatso, Tsangyang (1683–1706)
I sought my lover at twilight.
Lover met by chance on the road.
White teeth smiling.
Wild horses running in the hills.

Gylys, Beth (b. 1964)
Balloon Heart.
Family Reunion—Aunt Vern's Two Cents.
Fat Chance.

Gyodai (Kato Gyodai) (1732–92)
Inching / From dark to dark.
Slowly / Over cedars.
Whales / Bellowing dawn.

Gyodai, Kato *See* Gyodai

Gyöngyösi, István (1629–1704)
Beauty of Ilona Zrínyi, The.
Day is done; the twilight grows more dark,
The.

H

"H., C. G."
Power of Innocence, The.

"H——, Captain" (*fl.* c.1716)
Imitation of Martial, Book II Ep, An 105.

"H., H." *See* Jackson, Helen Hunt

"H., H. E."
Riddle, The.

Ha Jin
Past, The.

Ha-Nagid, Samuel (993–1056)
First War.
Gazelle, The.
I'd sell my soul for that fawn.
I Look Up to the Sky.
One Who Works and Buys Himself Books.
Prison, The.
Proverbs.
That's it—I love that fawn.

You Mock Me Now in Your Youth.

Ha Thi Thao (b. c.1940)
Our Son's Profession.

Haaff, Katherine Maurine
Good Thoughts.

Haas, Rosamond
Autumn evening.
Building the dollhouse.
Moon at the window.
Rain mixed with sleet.

Haavikko, Paavo (b. 1931)
Bastard Son is born with a tooth in his mouth
and hair on his.
Before you ask for justice. Make sure.
Bowmen, The.
Days become years. Years.
Don't say this to an old idol that's lost its nose.
Don't smile. So you won't become a Buddha.
First Poem, The.
Hades is an even worse place.
How decisively.
I always bow down deep before a small tree
and a great tyrant.
It has been proposed that the stars should be
removed from sight.
Look, life has been constructed this way to
make sure.
One who writes us is now doing four plays a
year, The.
Plant trees. Exactly against this tree.
Precisely the way you divide your small
change between two.
Second Poem, The.
Soul against the state, The.
Take heart, Ovid. No sentence.
Twice, three times.
Tyrant inspires small poems, The.
When the tyrant is young. Everyone waits.
When you go to the tyrant. Keep your head on
a platter.
Woman raises her garment, rain, wind,
darkness rise, The.
You can't take with you.

Habergham, Mrs. Fleetwood
Seeds of Love, The.

Habib, Rowley (Nga Pitiroirangi) (b. 1935)
Ancestors.
Moment of Truth.

Habington, William (1605–54)
Against Them Who Lay Unchastity to the Sex
of Women.
Cogitabo Pro Peccato Meo.
Cupio Dissolvi.
Dialogue between Araphil and Castara, A.
In vain, fair sorceress, thy eyes speak charms.
Nox Nocti Indicat Scientiam.
Perdam Sapientiam Sapientum.
Solum Mihi Superest Sepulchrum.
To a Friend, Inviting Him to a Meeting upon
Promise.
To a Wanton.
To Castara, Being to Take a Journey.
To Castara ("Do[e] not Their profane orgies
hear[e].")
To Castara ("Give me a heart where no
impure")
To Castara, upon an Embrace.
To Castara, upon Beautie.
To Roses in the Bosom[e] of Castara.
To the Moment Last Past.
To the World: the Perfection of Love.
Upon Castara's Absence.
Upon Castara's Departure.

Hachenburg, Hanuš (1929–43)
Terezin.

Hacker, Marilyn (b. 1942)
Almost Aubade.
And I shout at Iva, whine at you. Easily.
Azure striation swirls beyond the stones.
Ballad of Ladies Lost and Found.
Boy, The.
Broceliande.
Cancer Winter.
Canzone: "Consider the three functions of the
tongue."
Canzone: "No better lost than any other

woman."
Coming Downtown.
Conclusion: "Did you love well what very
soon you left?"
Dusk: July.
Eight Days in April.
Elysian Fields.
Feeling and Form.
Fifteen to Eighteen.
Going Back to the River.
If we talk, we're too tired to make love; if we.
Imaginary Translation.
In the Public Theater lobby, I wait for Marie.
Invocation: "This is for Elsa, also known as
Liz."
Mythology.
Nights of 1964–66: The Old Reliable.
1973.
O little one, this longing is the pits.
Occasional Verses.
Rondeau after a Transatlantic Telephone Call.
Runaways Café II.
Rune of the Finland Woman.
Squares and Courtyards.
Three Sonnets for Iva.
Twelfth Floor West.
Villanelle: "Every day our bodies separate."
Wagers.
We may be learning how to tell the truth.
We work, play, don't cross-reference calendars.
Who would divorce her lover with a phone.
Year's End.

Hackett, J. W.
Deep within the stream.
Fleeing sandpipers, The.
Haiku: "Bitter morning, A."
Half of the minnows.
Long line of web, A.
Moon fades into dawn.
Old spider web, An.
Searching on the wind.
Stillness of dawn, The.
Time after time.
Up close, at the place.
Wind gives way to calm.
Wind sounds through the trees.

Hadas, Rachel (b. 1948)
Easter Afternoon.
Falcon.
House Beside the Sea, The.
In the Grove.
Journey Out.
Lair, The.
Mars and Venus.
Moments of Summer.
Mutability.
On That Mountain.
Red Hat, The.
Sentimental Education.
Shells.
Still Life in Garden.
Three Silences.
Winged Words.

Haddad, Qasim (b. 1948)
All of Them.
Book of the defeated man.
Children, The.
Interrogation.
Like the White.

Hadewijch (*fl.* 13th cent.)
Cult of Love, The.
Knowing Love in Herself.
Love has seven names.
Love has subjugated me.
Love's Constancy.
Love's Maturity.
Madness of Love, The.

Hadewijch II (*fl.* 13 cent.)
All things.
If I desire something, I know it not.
Tighten.
You who want.

Hadfield, Charles
My skin shimmers with all the colours.

**Hadrian, Emperor (Publius Aelius Hadrianus)
(A.D. 76–138)**
Adriani Morientis ad Animam Suam.

Emperor Hadrian on his Soul.
Hadrian's Address to His Soul When Dying.

Hadrianus, Publius Aelius *See* **Hadrian, Emperor**

Hafiz [*or* **Hafez**] **(1320–1389)**
Come pass me the cup quickly and hand it on.
Comrades, the morning breaks, the sun is up.
Days of spring are here, The! the eglantine.
Desire's destroyed my life; what gifts have I.
Each friend turned out to be an enemy.
Flower-tinted cheek, the flowery close, A.
From Canaan Joseph shall return, whose face.
Ghazal 24: For Years My Heart Asked Me for
    Jamshid's Cup.
Ghazal: Half-Way Through the Night.
Grievous folly shames my sixtieth year, A.
I cease not from desire till my desire.
I have borne the anguish of love, which ask me
    not to describe.
I said to heaven that glowed above.
Jewel of the secret treasury, The.
Lady that hast my heart within thy hand.
Light of my eyes, there *is* something to be
    said.
Lord Be Praised, The.
Love's hidden pearl is shining yet.
Mirth, Spring, to linger in a garden fair.
Mortal never won to view thee.
My friend, hold back your heart from enemies.
My soul is the veil of his love.
Oft have I said, I say it once more.
Persian Song of Hafiz, A.
Rose has flushed red, the bud has burst, The.
Rose is not the rose unless thou see, The.
Saki, for God's love, come and fill my glass.
What is wrought in the forge of the living and
    life.
Where is my ruined life, and where the fame.
Wind from the east, oh Lapwing of the day.

Hafiz, Yasin Taha (b. 1938)
Breaking the Precepts.
Gazelle, The.
Woman, A.
Words and Truth.

Hafsa bint al-Hajj (d. 1184)
Shall I come there, or you here?

Hagedon, Jessica
Song of Bullets, The.

Hagedorn, Friedrich von (1708–54)
Anacreon.

Hagedorn, Jessica Tarahata (b. 1949)
Filipino Boogie.
Latin Music in New York.
Listen.
Smokey's Getting Old.
Something about You.
Souvenirs.
Vulva Operetta.
Yolanda Meets the Wild Boys.

Hagenau, Reinmar von (*fl.* 12th cent.)
As on the Heather.
Childish Game, A.

Hagiwara Sakutaro (1886–1942)
Chair.
Lover of Love.
So Terrifyingly Melancholy.
Spring Night.

Hahn, Kimiko (b. 1955)
Annotation in Her Last Court Diary.
Boat Down the River of Yellow Silt, A.
Clippings.
Hula Skirt, 1959, The.
Radiator.
Sewing Without Mother: A Zuihitsu.

Hahn, Oscar
Death Is Sitting at the Foot of My Bed.
Gladioli by the Sea.
Man.
No Place Is Here or There.
Vision of Hiroshima.
With Passion without Compassion.

Hahn, Susan
Confession.
Fifth Amendment, The.
For Beauty.
Incontinence.

January Ovaries.
Nijinsky's Dog.
Perennial.

Hai-Jew, Shalin (*fl.* 20th cent.)
Father's Belt.
Kinged.
Three Gypsies.

Haicéad, Pádraigín (c.1600–1654)
On Hearing It Has Been Ordered in the
    Chapterhouse of Ireland That the Friars
    Make No More Songs or Verses.

Haida
Song for Smooth Waters.

"Haida Charlie"
How is it all gonna turn out.

Haines, John (b. 1924)
Awakening.
Cloud Factory, The.
Eclipse.
Evening Change.
Flight, The.
Foreboding.
If the Owl Calls Again.
Into the Glacier.
Nocturnal.
On a Certain Field in Auvers.
Poem Like a Grenade, A.
Roadside Weeds.
Snowbound City, The.
To Turn Back.
Train Stops at Healy Fork, The.
Tundra, The.
Yeti.

Hajnal, Anna (1907–1977)
After Life.
April in the Old Park.
Cyclones.
Deserted Angel, The.
Fear.
Felled Plane Tree, The.
Half Past Four, October.
In Praise of the Body.
Makpelah.
To the Creator of My Bones.

Hakuen (d. 1806)
I wonder where.

Hakuen (d. 1859)
What is it but a dream?

Hakugai (1343–1414)
Last year in a lovely temple in Hirosawa.

Hakuin (1685–1768)
How lacking in permanence the minds of the
    sentient.
Past, present, future: unattainable.
Priceless is one's incantation.
Tea-kettle / Hooked in mid-air.
You no sooner attain the great void.

Hakujubo (d. 1817)
My heart serene.

Hakukin (d. 1817)
Pampas grass, all dry.

Hakuni (d. 1792)
To a melody of prayer.

Hakurin (d. 1897)
Well, then, let's follow.

Hakuro (d. 1766)
Ailing mallard, An.

Hakusai (d. 1792)
Farewell—and though there be.

Hakusen (d. 1820)
Oh, morning glory.

Hakusetsu (d. 1735)
At peace.

Hakuto (d. 1727)
Deutzia blossoms.

Hakuyo
Over the peak spreading clouds.

Halaby, Laila
Handfuls of Wind.
Long Distance.
Refugee.

Haldane, J. B. S. *See* **Haldane, John Burdon
Sanderson**

**Haldane, John Burdon Sanderson (J. B. S.
Haldane) (1892–1964)**
Cancer's a Funny Thing.

Hale, Janet Campbell (b. 1947)
Aaron Nicholas, Almost Ten.
Cinque.
Custer Lives in Humbolt County.
Desmet, Idaho, March 1969.
On a Catholic Childhood.
On Death and Love.
Salad La Raza.
Six Feet Under.

Hale, Sarah Josepha Buell (1788–1879)
Blessing on the printer's art!, A.
Mary's Lamb [*or* Mary and Her Lamb].
Mole and the Eagle, The.
Our Father in Heaven.

Halevi, Judah (1085–1140)
Awake, My Fair.
Distant Dove.
Dove, The.
Earth in Spring, The.
Fortune's Treachery.
God, Whom Shall I Compare to Thee?
Greetings ladies, kith and kin.
Grey Hair, The.
He Cometh.
Heal Me, My God.
Hymn for Atonement Day.
Immortal Israel.
Israel's Duration.
Jerusalem.
Letter to His Friend Isaac, A.
Longing.
Longing for Jerusalem.
Lord, Where Shall I Find Thee?
Love Song: "Let my sweet song be pleasing
    unto Thee."
Love Song: "See'st thou o'er my shoulders
    falling."
Marriage Song.
Meditation on Communion with God.
Mirror, The.
My Heart Is in the East.
My Sweetheart's Dainty Lips.
Ode to Zion.
On Parting with Moses ibn Ezra.
Ophra.
Parting.
Poem in Parts.
Pride of a Jew, The.
Sabbath, My Love.
Song of Loneliness.
Summer.
Time-Servers.
To the Western Wind.
To Zion.
Watery waste the sinful world has grown, A.
Words Wherein Stinging Bees Lurk.

Haley, Margaret
Tropicalia.

Halfe, Louise Bernice
Pähkahkos.

Halkin, Shimon (b. 1898)
Before Your Wonders I Stand, My World.
Here Is Much Burning Anger.
Reward.
Seventy-five Are My Abyssed Forests.
To Tarshish.

Halkin, Shmuel (1897–1960)
Drop of Dew, A.

Hall, Amanda Benjamin (b. 1890)
It Seems That God Bestowed Somehow.
Limerick: "King Richard, in one of his rages."

Hall, Daniel (b. 1952)
Dusting.
Hardy's 'Shelley's Skylark.'
Hermit with Landscape.
Love-Letter-Burning.
Mangosteens.
Short Circuit.
X.

Hall, David
Disgrace.
How is it the stomach knows first.
There is no place to hide.

Hall, Donald (b. 1928)
Airstrip in Essex, 1960, An.
Alligator Bride, The.

Apples.
Black Faced Sheep, The.
Brain Cells, The.
Breasts.
Carol, A.
Christmas Eve in Whitneyville, 1955.
Eating the Pig.
Eighth Inning, The.
Exile.
Fifth Inning, The.
Funeral, The.
Grace, A.
Granite and Grass.
Her Garden.
Je Suis une Table.
Long River, The.
"Reclining Figure."
Matthew 21:18–22; In the morning.
Mount Kearsarge.
My Son, My Executioner.
Names of Horses.
New Hampshire.
O Cheese.
Old Pilot, The.
Ox Cart Man.
Peaches.
Poet at Twenty, A.
Porcelain Couple, The.
Professor Gratt.
Raisin, The.
Sister on the Tracks, A.
Sleeping Giant, The.
Small Fig Tree, A.
Sudden Things.
To a Waterfowl.
Town of Hill, The.
Valentine.
Wedding Party.
White Apples.
Wives, The.
Woolworth's.

Hall-Evans, Jo Ann (b. 1934)
Cape Coast Castle Revisted.
Seduction.

Hall, Hazel (1886–1924)
Light Sleep.
Listening Macaws, The.
Seams.
Woman Death.

Hall, Henry Clay
Who Does Not Love True Poetry.

Hall, John (1529–66)
Job. I.
Numeri XIII.
Praise of Faith, The.
Praise of Godly Love Out of 1 John. 4, The.
Proverb, XXX.
Song of Esechia, The.

Hall, John (1627–56)
Call, The.
Epicurean Ode, An.
On an Hour[e]-Glass[e].
Pastoral[l] Hymn[e], A.
Song: "Distil not poison in mine ears."

Hall, John (b. 1945)
Even as the Wandering Traveler.

Hall, Joseph (1574–1656)
Anthem for the Cathedral of Exeter.
Coxcomb, The.
For Christmas Day.
Gentle squire would gladly entertain, A.
Great is the folly of a feeble brain.
Hous-keping's dead, *Saturio:* wot'st thou
    where?
Olden Days, The.
Pardon, ye glowing ears; need will it out.
Satire VIII.
Sturdy ploughman doth the soldier see, The.
When Gullion died (who knows not Gullion?)
Who doubts? The laws fell down from
    heaven's height.

Hall, Kirk (b. 1944)
Blackgoldblueswoman.
Today Is Not Like They Said.

Hall, Richard (1817–66)
Crickhowel.

How oft, ere morning lit the eastern steep.
Pontypool.

Hall, Rodney (b. 1935)
Black Bagatelles.
Journey.
Mrs. Macintosh.
Owner of My Face, The.
Text for These Distracted Times, A.
Wedding Day at Nagasaki.

Halleck, Fitz-Greene (1790–1867)
At midnight, in his guarded tent.
Fanny was younger once than she is now.
They burnt their last witch in CONNECTICUT.
We owe the ancients something. You have
    read.

Halleck, Fitz-Greene (1790–1867)
Alnwick Castle.
On the Death of Joseph Rodman Drake.
Red Jacket.
Song: "There's a barrel of porter at Tammany
    Hall."

Halleck, Fitz-Greene and Joseph Rodman Drake
National Painting [*or* Paintings], The.

Halloran, Laurence Hynes (1766–1831)
Animal Magnetism; the Pseudo-Philosopher
    Baffled.

Halm, Friedrich
My Heart, I Want to Ask You.

Halperin, Mark (b. 1950)
Two Lines from Paul Celan.

Halpern, Daniel (b. 1945)
Dance, The.
Her Body.

Halpern, Leivick *See* Leivick [*or* Leyvick], H.

Halpern, Moyshe Leyb (1886–1932)
In Central Park.
Long for Home.
My Portrait.
Restless as a Wolf.
Who.

Halsall, Martyn
Return to Ararat.

Halswell, Henry (fl. 1656)
Upon Mr. Hopton's Death.

Ham, Marion Franklin (1867–1956)
As Tranquil Streams.
O Thou Whose Gracious Presence Shone.
Touch Thou Mine Eyes.

Hamadani, Ayn Al-Qozat (1098–1132)
Quatrain.

Hamburger, Michael (b. 1924)
Treblinka.
Between the Lines.
Dual Site, The.
Garden, Wilderness.
Memory.
Weeding.

Hamby, Barbara
St. Clare's Underwear.

Hamei (d. 1837)
Man's end.

Hame'iri, Avigdor (1890–1970)
Passover in Jerusalem.
Purity.

Hamer, Forrest
Allegiance.
Berkeley, Late Spring.
Charlene-N-Booker 4Ever.
Different Strokes Bar, San Francisco, The.
Line Up.
Origins.

Hamill, Gerry (b. 1919)
Limerick: "Fat-tailed Dwarf Lemur, in bed, A."
Limerick: "Gamekeeper of Lady Chatterley,
    The."
Limerick: "Left-wing young lady from
    Wick, A."
Limerick: "'If you're aristocratic,' said
    Nietzsche."
Limerick: "Said Tebbitt: 'I don't understand
    'em'"
Song of the GPO, A.

Hamill, Sam (b. 1942)
Abstract.

Another Duffer.
Gift of Tongues, The.
Reading Seferis.
Ten Thousand Sutras.
What the Water Knows.

Hamilton, Bobb (b. 1928)
Poem to a Nigger Cop.

Hamilton, Cicely (1872–1952)
March of the Women, The.

Hamilton, David Osborne
Ajax.

**Hamilton, George Rostrevor ("George
    Rostrevor") (1888–1967)**
Don's Holiday.
Exchange.
Exile.
No Occupation.
Old Ox, The.
Schoolmaster.
To the Greek Anthologists.

Hamilton, Ian ("Edward Pygge") (b. 1938)
Newscast, The.
Notes for a Revised Sonnet.
Notes for a Sonnet.
Revised Notes for a Sonnet.
Robert Lowell's Notebook.
Visit, The.

Hamilton, Janet (fl. c.1863)
Oor Location.

Hamilton, Lucy
My Father's Words.

Hamilton, Nancy (fl. 1940)
How High the Moon.

Hamilton, Sarah (c.1769–1843)
Farewell to France.
Poppy, The.

Hamlett, Jenny
Therapist's Comment, The.

Hamlisch, Marvin
One.
Way We Were, The.

Hammad, Suheir (b. 1973)
Broken and Beirut.
Manifest Destiny.
Of Woman Torn.

Hammerstein, Oscar, II (1895–1960)
All er Nothin'
All the Things You Are.
Bill.
Can't Help Lovin' Dat Man.
Dat's Love (Habanera)
Don't Ever Leave Me.
Folks Who Live on the Hill, The.
Gentleman Is a Dope, The.
Happy Talk.
Hello, Young Lovers.
I Cain't Say No.
I'll Take Romance.
I've Told Ev'ry Little Star.
If I Loved You.
It Might As Well Be Spring.
June Is Bustin' Out All Over.
Kansas City.
Last Time I Saw Paris, The.
Lover, Come Back to Me!
Make Believe.
Many a New Day.
Mister Snow.
Money Isn't Everything!
My Favorite Things.
Oh, What a Beautiful Mornin'!
Ol' Man River.
People Will Say We're in Love.
Shall We Dance?
Soliloquy.
Some Enchanted Evening.
Song Is You, The.
Sound of Music, The.
Surrey with the Fringe on Top, The.
There Is Nothin' like a Dame.
Who?
Why Was I Born?
Wonderful Guy, A.
You'll Never Walk Alone.
Younger Than Springtime.

Hammial, Philip (b. 1937)
Automobiles of the Asylum.
Jane.
Petit Guignol.
Russians Breathing.
Sadie.
Treason's Choice.

Hammond, Amy (d. 1693)
Verses by my Mother in Her Own Hand.

Hammond, Mary Stewart
GWB in the Rain, The.

Hammond, William (b. 1614?)
On the Same [Death of My Dear Brother, Mr. H.S., Drowned]: The Boat.
To the Same [My Dear Sister, Mrs S.]: The Tears.

Hamod, Sam (b. 1936)
After the Funeral of Assam Hamady.
Dying with the Wrong Name.
Leaves.
Letter.
Libyan/Egyptian Acrobats/Israeli Air Circus.
Lines to My Father.
So we move now.

Hamoir, Irène
Aria.
Pearl.

Hamon (d. 1804)
In stillness, I.

Hampton, Susan (b. 1949)
Crafty Butcher, The.
Fire Station's Delight, The.
In Andrea's Garden.
Women who Speak with Steak Knives.
Yugoslav Story.

Han-ch'ing *See* Kuan Han-ch'ing

Han Kwak (fl. 16th cent.)
Don't Bring Out the Straw Mat.

Han-shan (Cold Mountain) (c.730–c.850)
As for me, I delight in the everyday Way.
As long as I was living in the village.
Birds and their chatter overwhelm me with feeling, The.
Certain scholar named Mr. Wang, A.
Clambering up the Cold Mountain path.
Cold Mountain is a house.
Cold Mountain is full of weird sights.
Cold Mountain Poem No. 158.
Do you have the poems of Han-shan in your house?
Ever since I left home.
From my father and mother I inherited land enough.
Graceful handsome youth, A.
Have I a body or have I none?
His mind is as high as a mountain.
I came once to sit on Cold Mountain.
I climb the road to Cold Mountain.
I live in a little country village.
I look far off at T'ien-t'ai's summit.
I think of all the places I've been.
In the house east of here lives an old woman.
Last night in a dream I returned to my old home.
Last year in the spring when the birds were calling.
Man lives his life in a dust bowl.
My father and mother left me a good living.
My place is on Cold Mountain.
One Budding-Talent Wang.
Parrots dwell in the west country.
People ask about Cold Mountain Way.
People ask the way to Cold Mountain.
Place where I spend my days, The.
Pole your three winged galleons.
Raise girls but not too many.
Reading won't save us from death.
So Han-shan writes you these words.
Someone sits in a mountain gorge.
Storied cliffs were the fortune I cast.
Swine gobble dead men's flesh.
There is a poetaster named Wang.
There's a naked bug at Cold Mountain.
They laugh at me hey farm boy.
Today I sat before the cliff.
Unfortunate human disorder, The.

When people see the man of Cold Mountain.
Whoever has Cold Mountain's poems.
Whoever reads my poems.
Why am I always so depressed?
Wise men, you have cast me aside.
Wonderful, this road to Cold Mountain.
Yes, there are stingy people.
Yesterday I went to a cloud observatory.

Han-shan Te-ch'ing (1546–1623)
Through a few splinters of.

Han Wo (fl. c.902)
Sent to a Ch'an Master.

Han Yongwun (1879–1944)
Artist, The.

Han Yü (786–824)
Amongst the Cliffs.
Autumn Thoughts.
Demoted I Arrive at Lan-t'ien Pass and Show This Poem to My Brother's Grandson Han Hsiang.
Don't shoo the morning flies away.
Girl from Flower Mountain, The.
Girl of Mount Hua, The.
Leaves fall turning turning to the ground.
Mornings the sparrow twitters seeking food.
My ceramic lake in dawn, water settled clear.
Occasional Poem.
Officer at the Rapids, The.
Old men are like little boys.
Poem on Losing One's Teeth.
Pond in a Bowl, The.
Pond in a Jardiniere, A.
Pond shine and sky glow, blue matching blue.
Sentiments at Autumn.
Southern Mountains.
This morning I can't seem to get out of bed.
To the Wooden Hermit.
When white dew descends on the hundred grasses.
Written on My Way into Exile.

Hanaford, Phoebe A. (1829–1921)
Cast Thy Bread upon the Waters.

Handal, Nathalie
Forgetting, Love.
Goran's Whispers.
Sigh, The.

Handlin, Jim
Cold winter morning.
Full autumn moon, A.
Sunset.

Handman, Lou
Are You Lonesome Tonight?

Hands, Elizabeth (fl. c.1789)
Epistle, An.
Favourite Swain, The.
Lob's Courtship.
On an Unsociable Family.
Perplexity: A Poem.
Poem on the Supposition of an Advertisement, A; Appearing in a Morning Paper, of the Publication of a Volume of Poems, by a Servant-Maid.
Poem on the Supposition of the Book Having Been Published and Read, A.
Widower's Courtship, The.
Written, Originally Extempore, on Seeing a Mad Heifer Run through the Village.

Handy, M. P.
Only a Little Thing.

Handy, William Christopher (1873–1958)
Beale Street Blues.
Yellow Dog Blues.

Hanighen, Bernie (fl. 1944)
'Round Midnight.

Hanim, Nigâr (1862–1918)
Tell Me Again.

Hankai (d. 1882)
Year is ending, The.

Hankey, Katherine
I love to tell the story.

Hanley, James F.
Second Hand Rose.
Zing! Went the Strings of My Heart.

Hanlo, Jan (1912–69)
New Verses for June 7, 1951.

Hanlon, Guy
They Told Me, Heraclitus.

Hann, Isaac (1690–1778)
After Reading the Life of Mrs. Catherine Stubbs in Isaac Ambrose's "War with the Devils."

Hannah, Sophie
End of Love, The.
Good Loser, The.
My Enemies.
Narrow for love that must be fitted in.
Norbert Dentressangle Van, The.
Postcard from a Travel Snob.
Symptoms.
Two Hundred and Sixty-Five Words.
Where is Talcott Parsons Now?
Your Street Again.

Hannan, Maggie
Bone Die, The.
Coming Down from Derry Hill.
Drive.
Inmates.
Lamper, The.
Life Model.
Making Conversation.
Seq.
Tap.
Tom Passey's Child.

Hanney, G. W.
Limerick: "Wanting children a couple once sat."

Hannon, Michael (b. 1939)
Beneath Cold Mountain.
Beyond Freedom.
Homeless.
Real Estate.
Subterranean.
Temporary Heart.

Hanri (d. 1835)
My life.

Hans, Marcie
Hurt.

Hanscombe, Gillian Eve
Well, Then Let Slip the Masks.

Hansen, Chadwick (b. 1926)
Creator of Infinities.

Hansen, Ron
Do Not Let Skeezix Go in There: Winslow's Villanelle.

Hanson, Kenneth O. (b. 1922)
Before the Storm.
Take It from Me.
West Lake.

Hanson, Martha (fl. 1809)
How proudly Man usurps the power to reign.
Occasioned by Reading Mrs. M. Robinson's Poems.
To Fancy.
To Mrs. Charlotte Smith.

Hanson, Pauline (b. 1917)
And I Am Old to Know.
From Creature to Ghost.
So Beautiful Is the Tree of Night.

Hanzlicek, C. G.
Feeding Frenzies.
Last Trains, The.
Moment.
On the Road Home.
Sierra Noon.

Hanzlik, Josef (b. 1938)
Clap Your Hands for Herod.

Harata Tangikuku (fl. c.1860–1875)
Invalid's Song.

Haraway, Fran
Midnight Vigil.

Harbach, Otto (1873–1963)
Let's Begin.
Love Nest, The.
Poor Pierrot.
She Didn't Say "Yes."
Smoke Gets in Your Eyes.
Who?
Yesterdays.

Harbaugh, Henry
Jesus, I Live to Thee.

Harburg, E. Y. [*or* "Yip"] (1898–1981)
April in Paris.
Brother, Can You Spare a Dime?
Down with Love.
Eagle and Me, The.
Fun to be Fooled.
Happiness Is Just a Thing Called Joe.
How Are Things in Glocca Morra?
I Like the Likes of You.
If I Only Had a Brain (If I Only Had a Heart)
    (If I Only Had the Nerve)
If This Isn't Love.
It's Only a Paper Moon.
Last Night When We Were Young.
Let's Take a Walk Around the Block.
Lydia, the Tattooed Lady.
Moon About Town.
Necessity.
Old Devil Moon.
Over the Rainbow.
Springtime Cometh, The.
Then I'll Be Tired of You.
We're Off to See the Wizard (The Wonderful
    Wizard of Oz)
What Is There to Say?
When I'm Not Near the Girl I Love.
Harchik, Annette Bialik
Earrings.
Requiem: "Your names ring clearly."
Hardenberg, Friedrich von *See* **"Novalis"**
Harding, Samuel (*fl.* 1640)
Noblest bodies are but gilded clay.
Hardison, O. B., Jr. (b. 1928)
Marina.
Small Talk in a Garden.
Stella Maris.
Hardt, Ernst (1876–1947)
Specter, The.
Hardy, Jackie (b. 1946)
Computer Aided Design: Creation.
Difference, The.
Objection Overruled.
Wet Feet.
Hardy, Thomas (1840–1928)
After a Journey.
After the Fair.
After the Visit.
Afternoon Service at Mellstock.
Afterwards.
Agnosto Theo [To an Unknown God].
Ah, Are You Digging on My Grave?
Albuera.
Ancient to Ancients, An.
Anniversary, An.
At an Inn.
At Castle Boterel.
At the Altar-Rail.
At the Draper's.
August Midnight, An.
Bags of Meat.
Ballad-Singer, The.
Bedridden Peasant, The.
Beeny Cliff.
Bereft.
Beyond the Last Lamp.
Birds at Winter Nightfall.
Broken Appointment, A.
Burghers, The.
By Her Aunt's Grave.
Caged Goldfinch, The.
Cardinal Bembo's Epitaph on Raphael.
Certain sort of bravery, A.
Channel Firing.
Choirmaster's Burial, The.
Christmas: 1924.
Christmas Ghost-Story, A.
Church Romance, A.
Circus-Rider to Ringmaster.
Colonel's Soliloquy, The.
Commonplace Day, A.
Convergence of the Twain, The.
Country Wedding, The.
Dark-Eyed Gentleman, The.
Darkling Thrush, The.
Departure.
Domicilium.

Dream Question, A.
Drummer Hodge.
During Wind and Rain.
Embarcation.
Epitaph for George Moore.
Epitaph: "I never cared for Life: Life cared for
    me."
Epitaph on a Pessimist.
Eve of Waterloo, The.
Exeunt Omnes.
Faintheart in a Railway Train.
Fallow Deer at the Lonely House, The.
First Sight of Her and After.
Five Students, The.
For Life I Had Never Cared Greatly.
Former Beauties.
Friends Beyond.
Frozen Greenhouse, The.
Garden Seat, The.
God-Forgotten.
Going and Staying.
Going, The.
Great Things.
Hap.
Harbour Bridge, The.
Haunter, The.
He Never Expected Much.
Her Dilemma.
Heredity.
His Visitor.
House of Hospitalities, The.
I Am the One.
I Found Her Out There.
I Look into My Glass.
I Looked Up from My Writing.
I Need Not Go.
If It's Ever Spring Again.
Impercipient, The.
In a Cathedral City.
In a Wood.
In Church.
In Death Divided.
In Tenebris.
In the Cemetery.
In the Moonlight.
In the Nuptial Chamber.
In the Restaurant.
In the Room of the Bride-Elect.
In the Servants' Quarters.
In Time of "The Breaking of Nations."
Lausanne: In Gibbon's Old Garden: 11–12
    p.m.
Let Me Enjoy.
Levelled Churchyard, The.
Liddell and Scott.
Lines to a Movement in Mozart's E-Flat
    Symphony.
Long Plighted.
Lying Awake.
Man He Killed, The.
Men Who March Away.
Midnight on the Great Western.
Minute before Meeting, The.
Lodging-House Fuchsias, The.
Mound, The.
My Spirit Will Not Haunt the Mound.
Near Lanivet, 1872.
Necessitarian's Epitaph, A.
Nettles, The.
Neutral Tones.
New Toy, The.
New Year's Eve.
Newcomer's Wife, The.
Night of Trafalgar, The.
O Tim, my own Tim I must call 'ee—I will!
Often When Warring.
Old Furniture.
On a Midsummer Eve.
On an Invitation to the United States.
On Sturminster Foot-Bridge.
On the Departure Platform.
One We Knew.
Oxen, The.
Peace-Offering, The.
Phantom Horsewoman, The.
Pine Planters, The.
Pink Frock, The.

Places.
Placid Man's Epitaph, A.
Poet, A.
Rain on a Grave.
Reminder, The.
Respectable Burgher, The.
Roman Road, The.
Rome: Building a New Street in the Ancient
    Quarter.
Ruined Maid, The.
Sapphic Fragment.
Self-Unseeing, The.
She Hears The Storm.
Shelley's Skylark.
Shut Out That Moon.
Sleep-Worker, The.
Snow in the Suburbs.
Something stands here to peril our advance.
Subalterns, The.
Sunshade, The.
Tess's Lament.
This love puts all humanity from me.
This Summer and Last.
Thoughts of Phena.
Thunderstorm in Town, A.
To an Unborn Pauper Child.
To Lizbie Browne.
Trampwoman's Tragedy, A.
Transformations.
Tree and the Lady, The.
Two Lips.
Under the Waterfall.
Unkept Good Fridays.
Voice of Things, The.
Voice, The.
Voices from Things Growing in a Churchyard.
Wagtail and Baby.
Waiting Both.
Walk, The.
Weathers [*or* Weather].
Wessex Heights.
What are you thinking, that you speak no
    word?
When I Set Out for Lyonnesse.
When Oats Were Reaped.
When the clouds' swoln bosoms echo back the
    shouts of the many and strong.
When you shall see me in the toils of Time.
Where the Picnic Was.
Wife in London, A.
Winter in Durnover Field.
Wintertime nighs.
Wives in the Sere.
Workbox, The.
Year's Awakening, The.
Young Glass-Stainer, The.
Hare, Maurice Evan (1886–1967)
Alfred de Musset.
Determinism.
Limerick: "There once was a man [*or* There
    was a young man] who said, 'Damn!'"
Hare, Patrick (b. 1936)
Deceit in the Park.
Hare, Susy
Complaint for a Sorcerer.
Harechavi, Hedva
1 x 2.
Already Night, Already Day.
And It Is Still That Way.
Harer, Katharine
Lucky 7.
Harford, Lesbia (1891–1927)
Beauty and Terror.
Experience.
I can't feel the sunshine.
I Count the Days Until I See You, Dear.
Poem: "I'm like all lovers, wanting love to
    be."
Poem: "Sometimes I wish that I were Helen-
    fair."
Poem: "When I was still a child."
Hargreaves, William (1881–1941)
Burlington Bertie from Bow.
Harington, Henry (1727–1816)
Abbey Church at Bath, The.
Harington, John (*fl.* c.1550)
Groom of the Chamber's Religion in King

Henry the Eighth's Time, A.
Husband to Wife.
Of the Wars in Ireland.
Sir John Raynsford's Confession.
Sonnet Written upon My Lord Admiral
    Seymour, A.
To His Mother.
Wife to Husband.

Harington [or Harrington], Sir John (1561–1612)
Against an Old Lecher.
Author, of His Own Fortune, The.
Author to His Wife, of a Woman's Eloquence,
    The.
Fair, Rich, and Young.
Of a Zealous Lady.
Of an Heroical Answer of a Great Roman
    Lady to Her Husband.
Of honest Theft. To my good friend Master
    Samuel Daniel.
Of Treason.
Thus all that day, they spent in divers talke.
To His Wife, for Striking Her Dog.
Tragicall Epigram, A.

Harington, Lucy, Countess of Bedford (d. 1627)
Elegy: "Death be not proud, thy hand gave not
    this blow."

Harjo, Joy (b. 1951)
Anchorage.
Autobiography.
Bird.
Call It Fear.
Drowning Horses.
Eagle Poem.
For Alva Benson, and for Those Who Have
    Learned to Speak.
Healing Animal.
I Give You Back.
New Orleans.
Perhaps the World Ends Here.
Postcolonial Tale, A.
Remember.
Resurrection.
She Had Some Horses.
Skeleton of Winter.
Strange Fruit.
Transformations.
We Encounter Nat King Cole as We Invent the
    Future.
White Bear.
Woman Hanging from the Thirteenth Floor
    Window, The.
Woman Who Fell from the Sky, The.

Harjo, Patty L. ("Ya-Ka-Nes") (b. 1947)
Death.
Mask, The.
Taos Winter.
To an Indian Poet.
Where Have You Gone, Little Boy.
Wishes.

Harkness, John
New Song on the Birth of the Prince of
    Wales, A.

Harland-Watts, Joette (b. 1968)
For a Woman's Rights.
Let It Be Known.
Resist Confinement.

Harling, W. Franke
Beyond the Blue Horizon.

Harlow, Michael (b. 1937)
Anima Has a Predilection, The.
Vlaminck's Tie, the Persistent Imaginal.

Harmon, Beatrice E.
Chanson Delice.

Harmon, William (b. 1938)
Bureaucratic Limerick.

Harms, James
After Yes.
As Always.
Dogtown.
Elegy as Evening, as Exodus.
From Now On.
Joy Addict, The.
Los Angeles.
Los Angeles, The Angels.
My Androgynous Years.

My Own Little Piece of Hollywood.
Reel Around the Shadow.
Sky.
Soon.
Tomorrow, We'll Dance in America.
When You Wish Upon a Star That Turns into a
    Plane.

Harmsen van Beek, Fritzi (b. 1927)
Introduction to a Prayer.

Harney, Ben (1872–1938)
Mister Johnson.
You've Been a Good Old Wagon, but You've
    Done Broke Down.

Harney, W. E. (1895–1903)
West of Alice.

Harnick, Sheldon
Ballad of the Shape of Things, The.
Boston Beguine, The.
(I'll Marry) the Very Next Man.
If I Were a Rich Man.
Little Tin Box.
Matchmaker.
She Loves Me.
Someone's Been Sending Me Flowers.
Sunrise, Sunset.
Tonight at Eight.

Harper, Frances Ellen Watkins (1825–1911)
Appeal to My Countrywomen, An.
Aunt Chloe's Politics.
Bible Defence of Slavery.
Burdens of All, The.
Bury Me in a Free Land.
Crocuses, The.
Deliverance.
Double Standard, A.
Eliza Harris.
Ethiopia.
Go Work in My Vineyard.
God Bless Our Native Land.
Grain of Sand, A.
He "Had Not Where to Lay His Head."
Learning to Read.
Lines: "At the Portals of the Future."
Mission of the Flowers, The.
Night of Death, The.
Nobly Born, The.
Nothing and Something.
Oh never on that mountain.
Present Age, The.
Pure in Heart Shall See God, The.
Refiner's Gold, The.
Renewal of Strength.
Slave Auction, The.
Save the Boys.
She's Free!
Slave Mother, The.
Songs for the People.
Sparrow's Fall, The.
Thank God for Little Children.
Then and Now.
Vashti.

Harper, Gordon
Limerick: "When a friend told a typist called
    Eve."

Harper, Michael S. (b. 1938)
Alice.
Alone.
American History.
Archives.
Bandstand.
Br'er Sterling and the Rocker.
Breaded Meat, Breaded Hands.
Clan Meeting: Births and Nations: A Blood
    Song.
Dance of the Elephants, The.
Dear John, Dear Coltrane.
Deathwatch.
Debridement.
Double Elegy.
Drowning of the Facts of a Life, The.
Elvin's Blues.
Eve (Rachel)
Fireplace, The.
For Bud.
Ghost of Soul-making, The.
Goin' to the Territory.

Guerrilla-Cong, The.
Here Where Coltrane Is.
High Modes: Vision as Ritual: Confirmation.
Homage to the Brown Bomber.
Homage to the New World.
In Hayden's Collage.
Grandfather.
Jazz Station.
Kin.
Landfill.
Last Affair: Bessie's Blues Song.
Loon, The.
Makin' Jump Shots.
Martin's Blues.
Militance of a Photograph in the Passbook of a
    Bantu under Detention, The.
Mother Speaks: The Algiers Motel Incident,
    Detroit, A.
Narrative of the Life and Times of John
    Coltrane: Played by Himself, A.
Nightmare Begins Responsibility.
Peace Plan: Meditation on the 9 Stages of
    "Peacemaking" as Tribute to Senator
    Claiborne Pell: 1997.
Poetry Concert.
Reuben, Reuben.
Sandra: At the Beaver Trap.
Song: I Want a Witness.
Studs.
Three O'Clock Love Song.
Tongue-tied in Black and White.
We Assume: On the Death of Our Son, Reuben
    Masai Harper.
Zocalo.

Harpur, Charles (1813–68)
Basket of Summer Fruit, A.
Bush Justice.
Dead city walls may pen us in, but still.
Flight of Wild Ducks, A.
I verse a settler's tale of olden times.
Marvellous Martin.
Wellington.

Harpur, James
I work in the evening, alone and in silence.

Harr, Lorraine Ellis
After the snowfall.
Hot summer wind, A.
Indian summer.
Late snowfall.
On the old scarecrow.
Pale dawn moon, A.
Sparkler goes out, The.
Time it takes, The.
Until it alights.

Harries, E. Howard (1876–1961)
Bone Prison, The.

Harrington, James (1611–77)
Inconstancy.

Harris, Benjamin (c.1640–1720)
Account of the Cruelty of the Papists, An.
God save the King, that King that sav'd the
    land.
Of the French Kings Nativity.

Harris, Duriel (b. 1969)
For My Father.
Landscapes.
On the uptown lexington avenue express:
    Martin Luther King Day 1995.
What we have lost.

Harris, James
Balance.

Harris, June Brown
Home.

Harris, Max (b. 1921)
Martin Buber in the Pub.
Message from a Cross.

Harris, Peter (b. 1955)
Some Songs Women Sing.

Harris, Robert (b. 1951)
Ambition, The.
Call, The.
Isaiah by Kerosene Lantern Light.
Literary Excellence.
Riding Over Belmore Park.
Sydney.

Harris, William J. (b. 1942)
Daddy Poem, A.
Historic Moment, An.
My baby / loves flowers.
Rib Sandwich.
Samantha Is My Negro Cat.
We Live in a Cage.

Harrison, Gregory (b. 1928)
Playground, The.

Harrison, James [or Jim] (b. 1937)
Helen.
I am four years older than you but scarcely an
unwobbling.
I don't have any medals. I feel their lack.
I wanted to feel exalted so I picked up.
It would surely be known for years after as the
day I shot.
Leda's Version.
Lustra. Officially the cold comes from
Manitoba.
Penelope.
Poem: "Form is the woods: the beast."
Returning at Night.
Sound.
This matted and glossy photo of Yesenin.
What if I own more paper clips than I'll ever
use in this.

Harrison, Jeffrey
Birds That Woke Us: An Urban Pastoral, The.
Hitting Golfballs off the Bluff.
Swifts at Evening.

Harrison, Tony (b. 1937)
Them and [uz].
Art and Extinction.
Book Ends.
Breaking the Chain.
Bright Lights of Sarajevo, The.
Call of Nature, The.
Classics Society.
Confessional Poetry.
Continuous.
Cycles of Donji Vakuf.
Durham.
Earthen Lot, The.
Hands, The.
Heartless Art, The.
Heredity.
Kumquat for John Keats, A.
"I've done my bits of mindless aggro too."
Long Distance.
Marked with D.
National Trust.
On Not Being Milton.
Queen's English, The.
Remains.
Study.
Timer.
Turns.

Harrison, William (1685–1713)
In Praise of Laudanum.

Harry, J. S. (b. 1939)
Honesty-Stones.
Poem Films Itself, The.
Shot of War, A.
Walking, when the Lake of the Air is Blue
with Spring.

Harryman, Carla
Allegory.
Magic (or Rousseau)
Male, The.
Matter.
Mothering.
My Story.
Not-France.
Realism.
That Can Not Be Taken Away From It.

Hart, David
Hair on your body, The.

Hart, Joanne
Only Applebaum Can Make a Tree.

Hart, Kevin (b. 1954)
Flemington Racecourse.
Horizon, The.
Last Day, The.
Members of the Orchestra, The.
Story, The.

Hart, Lorenz (1895–1943)
Bewitched, Bothered and Bewildered.
Blue Moon.
Blue Room, The.
Dancing on the Ceiling.
Falling in Love with Love.
Glad to Be Unhappy.
Have You Met Miss Jones?
He Was Too Good to Me.
I Didn't Know What Time It Was.
I've Got Five Dollars.
I Wish I Were in Love Again.
It Never Entered My Mind.
It's Got to Be Love.
Johnny One-Note.
Lady Is a Tramp, The.
Little Girl Blue.
Manhattan.
Most Beautiful Girl in the World, The.
Mountain Greenery.
My Funny Valentine.
My Heart Stood Still.
My Romance.
Nobody's Heart.
Ship Without a Sail, A.
Spring Is Here.
Ten Cents a Dance.
There's a Small Hotel.
This Can't Be Love.
Thou Swell.
To Keep My Love Alive.
Wait Till You See Her.
Where or When.
With a Song in My Heart.
You Are Too Beautiful.
You Took Advantage of Me.
Zip.

Hart-Smith, William (b. 1911)
Boomerang.
Golden Pheasant.
Inca Tupac Upanqui, The.
Nullarbor.

Harte, Bret (Francis Bret Harte) (1836–1902)
Ballad of the Emeu, The.
California Madrigal.
Chicago.
Colenso Rhymes for Orthodox Children.
Further Language from Truthful James.
John Burns of Gettysburg.
Miss Edith's Modest Request.
Mrs. Judge Jenkins[; Being the Only Genuine
Sequel to "Maud Muller"].
Plain Language from Truthful James.
Schemmelfennig.
Second Review of the Grand Army, A.
Society Upon the Stanislaus, The.
Stage-Driver's Story, The.
Tale of a Pony, The.
Truthful James to the Editor.
What the Bullet Sang.

Harte, Francis Bret *See* **Harte, Bret**

Harte, Walter (1709–74)
Enchanted Region; or, Mistaken Pleasures,
The.

Harteis, Richard (b. 1946)
Grace of Animals, The.
Star Trek III.

Harter, Penny
Bitter tea.
Broken bowl.
Cat's whiskers, The.
Clouds.
Grandmother's mirror.
In the mirror.
On the padlock.
Only letting in the cat.
Pine needles.
Sister Death.
Snowflakes.
Thawing.
Tulip.
Turtle Blessing.
White flowers.
Winter rain.
Wrinkles.

Hartigan, Anne (b. 1932)
Advent.

Brazen Image.
No Easy Harbour.
Salt.
St. Bridget's Cross.

**Hartigan, Patrick Joseph ("John O'Brien")
(1879–1952)**
Field of the Cloth of Gold, The.

Hartley, Marsden (1877–1943)
As the Buck Lay Dead.
Fishmonger.
Lapping of waters / thick, upon razorblade.
This Crusty Fragment.
West Pitch at the Falls.
What Have We All—a Soliloquy of Essences.
Wingaersheek Beach.

Hartman, Mary R.
Life's Made up of Little Things.

Hartnett, Michael (b. 1941)
All That Is Left.
All the Death-Room Needs.
All the Same, It Would Make You Laugh.
Chef Yeats, that master of the use of herbs.
Death of an Irishwoman.
Domestic Scene.
Enamoured of the Miniscule.
For My Grandmother, Bridget Halpin.
Gaelic is the conscience of our leaders.
Half afraid to break a promise.
Hartnett, the poet, might as well be dead.
Her eyes were coins of porter and her West.
I Have Exhausted the Delighted Range.
I Have Heard Them Knock.
I Think Sometimes.
Last Vision of Eoghan Rua Ó Súilleabháin,
The.
Man Who Wrote Yeats, the Man Who Wrote
Mozart, The.
Moonsnow '77.
Person as Dreamer: We Talk about the Future,
The.
Pity the Man Who English Lacks.
Possibility That Has Been Overlooked Is the
Future, The.
Retreat of Ita Cagney, The.
Small Farm, A.
Sonnet: "I saw magic on a green country
road."
There Will Be a Talking.
Visit to Castletown House, A.
Wounded Otter, The.

Hartsough, Lewis (1828–1919)
Come, Friends and Neighbors, Come.
Let Me Go Where Saints Are Going.

Hartwig, Julia (b. 1921)
Above Us.
Matthew 2:16–18; Then Herod, when he saw.
Who Says.

Harumichi no Tsuraki (fl. 10th cent.)
Wind has stopped, The.

Harvey, Andrew
Prayer to the Divine Mother, A.

Harvey, Christopher (1597–1663)
Church Festivals.

Harvey, Frederick William (1888–1957)
November.

Harvey, Sean (fl. 20th cent.)
Mighty Tropicale Orchestra, The.

Harwood, Gwen (1920–95)
Andante.
At the Sea's Edge.
Bone Scan.
Carnal Knowledge.
Carnal Knowledge 2.
Clair de Lune.
Cups.
Death Has No Features of His Own.
Father and Child.
Game of Chess, A.
Homage to Ferd. Holthausen.
Hospital Evening.
In the Bistro.
In The Park.
Lion's Bride, The.
Long After Heine.
Mid-Channel.

Naked Vision.
New Music.
Night Thoughts: Baby & Demon.
Nightfall.
Panther and Peacock.
Prize-giving.
Sea Anemones, The.
Second Life of Lazarus, The.
Simple Story, A.
Suburban Sonnet.
Wine Is Drunk, The.

Harwood, Lee (b. 1939)
Czech Dream.
Final Painting, The.
Poem for Writers, A.
Soft White.
"Utopia," The.
Words, The.

Hasford, Gustav
Bedtime Story.

Hashimoto, Sharon (b. 1953)
Eleven A.M. on My Day Off, My Sister
   Phones Desperate for a Babysitter.
Mirror of Matsuyama, The.
Standing in the Doorway, I Watch the Young
   Child Sleep.

Hashin
No sky and no earth at all.

Haskell, Dennis (b. 1947)
Call, The.

Haskell, Jefferson (b. 1807)
My Latest Sun Is Sinking Fast.

Haskins, Lola
Prodigy, The.
To Play Pianissimo.

Hasluck, Nicholas (b. 1942)
All day the bicycles come and go.
Christmas Day. 1696.
Islands.

Hass, Robert (b. 1941)
After I Seized the Pentagon.
Bashō, a Departure.
Between the Wars.
Bookbuying in the Tenderloin.
Concerning the Afterlife, the Indians of Central
   California Had Only the Dimmest Notions.
Elegy Residence on Earth.
Elm.
Heroic Simile.
House.
Image, The.
Interrupted Meditation.
Late Spring.
Letter to a Poet.
Measure.
Meditation at Lagunitas.
Misery and Splendor.
Now Winter Nights.
Pact, A.
Palo Alto: the Marshes.
Pornographer, The.
Privilege of Being.
Return of Robinson Jeffers, The.
San Pedro Road.
Song: "Afternoon cooking in the fall sun."
Spring Rain.
Story about the Body, A.
Tahoe in August.
To Phil Dow, in Oregon.

Hassall, Christopher Vernon (1912–64)
Santa Claus.

Hassett, Steve
Armed Forces Day.
Christmas.
Mother's Day.
Patriot's Day.
Thanksgiving.

Hastings, Beatrice (1879–1943)
Mind Pictures.

Hastings, Thomas (1784–1872)
Hail to the Brightness of Zion's Glad Morning.
Jesus, Merciful and Mild!
Now Be the Gospel Banner.
Now from Labor and from Care.

Hatfield, Edwin Francis (1807–83)
Hallelujah! Praise the Lord.

Hathaway, William (b. 1944)
Why That's Bob Hope.

Hatshepsut, Queen (d. 1468 B.C.)
I have done this with a loving heart for my
   father Amun.
Now my heart turns to and fro.

Hattersley, Geoff (b. 1956)
Death's Boots.
Frank O'Hara Five, Geoffrey Chaucer Nil.
New Mr Barnsley Something, The.
On the Buses with Dostoyevsky.
Remembering Dennis's Eyes.
Singing.

Hatton, Joseph (1840–1907?)
Christmas Bills.

Hatton, Julia Ann (1764–1838)
Swansea Bay.

Hatton, R. (fl. 1631)
Epithalamium: "Hymen hath together tied."

Hauer, Elizabeth N.
Vision.

Haug, James
Pool is a Godless Sport.
Tennessee Waltz, The.

Hauge, Olav H.
Across the Swamp.
I Stand Here, Do You Understand.

Hausen, Friedrich von (d. 1190)
Help! How Minne has deserted me.
I think sometimes about.
My heart and my body want to separate.
She may not accuse me.
When I parted from my Good.

Hauser, Samuel (1833–1914)
What Ship Is This?

Hausman, Gerald
Appaloosa Hail Storm.
September City.

Havergal, Frances Ridley (1836–79)
Afterwards.
Just When Thou Wilt.
One Reality, The.
Perfect Peace.
Take My Life and Let It Be.
They say there is a hollow, safe and still.
True-hearted, whole-hearted, faithful and loyal.
Trusting Jesus.
Under the Surface.
Vessels of mercy, prepared unto glory!
Who is on the Lord's side?

Havey, Elianour (fl. 1658)
Acrostick Eligie on the Death of the No Less
   Prudent than Victorious Prince Oliver Lord
   Protector, An.

"Havhesp, Dewi" *See* **Roberts, David**

Hawes, Stephen (1474–1523)
Epitaph of Graunde [*or* La Graunde] Amoure,
   The.
Pastime of Pleasure, The.
True Knight [*or* True Knighthood], The.

Hawi, Khalil (1925–82)
Bridge, The.
Flute and Wind in the Hermit's Cell.
Magi in Europe, The.

Hawker, Robert Stephen (1804–75)
Are They Not All Ministering Spirits?
Butterfly, The.
Cornish Emigrant's Song, The.
Croon on Hennacliff, A.
King Arthur's Waes-hael.
Land is lonely now, The: Anathema.
Legend of the Hive, A.
Mystic Magi, The.
Poor Man and His Parish Church, The.

Hawkesworth, Pauline
Meeting Place.
Two Statues.

Hawkhead, John
I am a glider on time's thermals.

Hawkhead, Patricia
I am the swift scribble.

Hawkins, Desmond
Night Hawk.

Hawkins, Jane (fl. 1629)
O lett it be for ever told.

Hawkins, Rose Furuya (b. 1944)
Issei Men: The First Generation.
Nisei Daughter: The Second Generation.
Sansei: The Third Generation.

Hawkins, William (b. 1940)
New Light, A.
Spring Rain.
Wall, The.

Hawling, Francis (fl. c.1727–c.1751)
Author Consults a Critic and Sells His
   Manuscript, The.

Hawoldar, Shakuntala (b. 1944)
Beyond Poetry.
Destruction.
I Am Not Just a Body for You.
I Have Gone into My Prison Cell.
It Is Not Just.
To Be a Woman.
To My Little Girl.
Woman, The.
You.
You Have Touched My Skin.
You Must Help Me Gather.

Hawthorn, John (fl. c.1779)
Deathbed, A.
On His Writing Verses.

"Hawthorne, Alice" *See* **Winner, Septimus**

Hawthorne, Nathaniel (1804–64)
I Left My Low amd Humble Home.
Ocean, The.
Oh Could I Raise the Darken'd Veil.

Haxton, Brooks (b. 1950)
Nietzsche Possessed.

Hay, George Campbell (1915–84)
Bizerta.
Flooer o the Gean.
Song: "Day will rise and the sun from
   eastward."
Sonnet: "Beckie, my luve!—What is't, ye twa-
   faced tod?"
Two Neighbours, The.

Hay, John (b. 1915)
Defend Us, Lord, from Every Ill.

Hay, John Milton (1838–1905)
Good Luck and Bad.
Jim Bludso of the Prairie Belle.
Pledge at Spunky Point, The.
What is a first love worth except to prepare for
   a second?

Hay, Sara Henderson (1906–87)
Christmas, the Year One, A.D.
Interview.

Hayati, Bibi (d. 1853)
Before there was a trace of this world of men.
Is this darkness the night of Power, or the
   black falling of your hair?

Hayden, Robert Earl (1913–80)
[American Journal].
Astronauts.
Aunt Jemima of the Ocean Waves.
Ballad of Nat Turner, The.
Ballad of Remembrance, A.
Ballad of Sue Ellen Westerfield, The.
Beginnings.
Bone-Flower Elegy.
Broken Dark, The.
Crispus Attucks.
Diver, The.
Double Feature.
Dream, The.
El-Hajj Malik El-Shabazz.
For a Young Artist.
Frederick Douglass.
Free Fantasia: Tiger Flowers.
Full Moon.
Homage to the Empress of the Blues.
Ice Storm.
In the Mourning Time.
Islands, The.
Letter from Phillis Wheatley, A.
'Mystery Boy' Looks for Kin in Nashville.
Middle Passage.
Monet's "Waterlilies."
Mourning Poem for the Queen of Sunday.
Names.

Night-Blooming Cereus, The.
Night, Death, Mississippi.
O Daedalus, Fly Away Home.
October.
On Lookout Mountain.
Paul Laurence Dunbar.
Perseus.
Plague of Starlings, A.
Point, The.
Road in Kentucky, A.
Runagate Runagate.
Soledad.
Sphinx.
Stars.
Summertime and the Living.
Tattooed Man, The.
Those Winter Sundays.
Wheel, The.
Whipping, The.
Witch Doctor.

Hayes, Alfred (1911–85)
Angel, The.
City of Beggars, The.
Epistle to the Gentiles.
Joe Hill.

"Hayes, Evelyn" *See* Bethell, Mary Ursula

Hayes, J. Milton (1884–1940)
Green Eye of the Yellow God, The.

Hayes, Terrance (b. 1971)
At Pegasus.
Boxcar.
Goliath Poem.

Hayford, Gladys May Casely (Aquah Laluah) (1904–50)
Nativity.
Shadow of Darkness.

Hayford, James (b. 1913)
Mason's Trick.

Hayiaku
Funeral Song.

Hayley, William (1745–1820)
To Mr. William Long, On His Recovery from a Dangerous Illness, 1785.
To Mrs. Hayley, On her Voyage to America. 1784.
To Mrs. Smith, Occasioned by the First of Her Sonnets.

Hayman, Robert (1579?–1631?)
Pleasant Life in Newfoundland, The.
Of the Great and Famous . . . Sir Francis Drake, and of My Little-Little Selfe.
Owen's Bracelet.
Saturn's Three Sons.

Hayne, Paul Hamilton (1830–86)
Charlotte Brontë.
October.
On the Occurrence of a Spell of Arctic Weather in May, 1858.

Haynes, Carol (b. 1897)
Any Wife or Husband.

Hays, Hoffman Reynolds (1904–80)
Case, The.
For One Who Died Young.
January.
Manhattan.
Sacred Children, The.

Hays, Mary (1760–1843)
Ah! let not hope fallacious, airy, wild.

Hayward, Amey (fl. 1699)
Spiritual Meditation upon a Bee, A.

Hayward, Charles W. (1866–1950)
King George V.

Hayward, David
To the Man Saying 'Come on Seis' at Hollywood Park.

Hazeley, Iyamide
Beloved.
Lungi Crossing.
When You Have Emptied Our Calabashes.

Hazo, Samuel (b. 1928)
Child of Our Bodies.
Drenching, The.
Battle News.
For Fawzi in Jerusalem.

Maps for a Son Are Drawn as You Go.
Only the New Branches Bloom.
Pittsburgh in Passing.
Silence Spoken Here.
Some Words for President Wilson.
To My Mother.
Toys, The.
World that Lightning Makes, The.

Headly, Henry (1765–88)
Child of the potent spell and nimble eye.

Healy, Eloise Klein
Artemis in Echo Park.
Changing the Oil.
Changing What We Mean.
City Beneath the City, The.
From Los Angeles Looking South.
Louganis.
Moroni on the Mormon Temple / Angel on the Wall.
Two Centuries in One Day.
What It Was Like the Night Cary Grant Died.
Wisteria.

Healy, Randolph (b. 1956)
Mutability Checkers.
Primula veris.
Size of This Universe, The.

Heaney, Seamus (b. 1939)
Alphabets.
Anahorish.
Annals say: when the monks of Clonmacnoise, The.
Artist, An.
Ash Plant, The.
At a Potato Digging.
Badgers, The.
Barn, The.
Bat on the Road, A.
Be literal a moment. Recollect.
Birthplace, The.
Black water. White waves. Furrows snowcapped.
Blackberry-Picking.
Boat that did not rock or wobble once, A.
Bog Queen.
Bogland.
Broagh.
Cana Revisited.
Casting and Gathering.
Casualty.
Churning Day.
Claritas. The dry-eyed Latin word.
Clearances.
Cleric, The.
Constable Calls, A.
Death of a Naturalist.
Deserted harbour stillness. Every stone.
Digging.
Disappearing Island, The.
Docker.
Dream of Jealousy, A.
Drink of Water, A.
Exposure.
First Kingdom, The.
Follower.
Forge, The.
From the Canton of Expectation.
From the Frontier of Writing.
From the Republic of Conscience.
Funeral Rites.
Grauballe Man, The.
Guttural Muse, The.
Harvest Bow, The.
Haw Lantern, The.
Hazel Stick for Catherine Ann, A.
His Dawn Vision.
I had come to the edge of the water.
I stirred wet sand and gathered myself.
In Memoriam Francis Ledwidge.
In the last minutes he said more to her.
Inishbofin on a Sunday morning.
Iron Spike.
Keeping Going.
Like a convalescent, I took the hand.
Limbo.
Mid-Term Break.
Mossbawn.

Mossbawn Sunlight.
Mother of the Groom.
Mud Vision, The.
My brain dried like spread turf, my stomach.
New Song, A.
On the Road.
Other Side, The.
Otter, The.
Outlaw, The.
Oysters.
Peacock's Feather, A.
Peninsula, The.
Personal Helicon.
Pitchfork, The.
Postcard from North Antrim, A.
Punishment.
Railway Children, The.
Requiem for the Croppies.
Rite of Spring.
Roof it down. Batten down. Dig in.
Scaffolding.
Schoolbag, The.
Seed Cutters, The.
Ship of Death, A.
Shooting Script, A.
Singer's House, The.
Skunk, The.
Skylight, The.
Sloe Gin.
Sofa in the Forties, A.
Song: "Rowan like a lip-sticked girl, A."
Strand at Lough Beg, The.
Summer Home.
Summer nineteen sixty nine.
Summer of Lost Rachel, The.
Terminus.
Tinder.
Tollund Man, The.
Traditions.
Turkeys Observed.
Twice Shy.
Ulster Twilight, An.
Visible sea at a distance from the shore, The.
Waterfall.
Wedding Day.
Westering.
Whatever You Say Say Nothing.
Wheels within Wheels.
When all the others were away at Mass.
Widgeon.
Wife's Tale, The.

Heard, Josephine D. Henderson (b. 1861)
Admiration.
Advance of Education, The.
Assurance.
Bereft.
Birth of Jesus, The.
Birth of Time, The.
Bishop James A. Shorter.
Black Sampson, The.
City by the Sea, The.
Day after Conference, The.
December.
Deception.
Decoration Day.
Do You Think?
Doxology.
Earthquake of 1886, The.
Easter Morn.
Epitaph, An: "When I am gone."
Eternity.
Fame.
Farewell to Allen University.
Forgetfulness!
General Robert Smalls.
Happy Heart, A.
He Comes Not To-night.
He Hath Need of Rest.
Heart-Hungry.
Hope.
Hope Thou in God.
I Love Thee.
I Will Look Up.
In Memory of James M. Rathel.
Judge Not.
Love Letters.
Matin Hymn.

Message to a Loved One Dead, A.
Morn.
Mother.
Mother's Love, A.
Music.
My Canary.
My Grace Is Sufficient.
My Husband's Birthday.
My Mocking Bird.
National Cemetery, Beaufort, South Carolina, The.
New Organ, The.
Night.
On Genessarett.
Out in the Desert.
Outcast, The.
Parting Kiss, The.
Parting, The.
Quarrel, The.
Quarto Centennial, The.
Question, The.
Resting.
Retrospect.
Rev. Andrew Brown, over the Hill to Rest.
Rt. Rev. Richard Allen.
Sabbath Bells.
Slumbering Passion.
Solace.
Sunshine after Cloud.
Tennyson's Poems.
They Are Coming?
Thine Own.
Thou Lovest Me.
To Clements' Ferry.
To Whittier.
To Youth.
Truth.
Unuttered Prayer.
Welcome Home.
Welcome to Hon. Frederick Douglass.
When I Would Die.
Where Do School Days End?
Who Is My Neighbor?
Whoso Gives Freely, Shall Freely Receive!
Wilberforce.

Hearn, Michael Patrick
At Dawn.
In the Library.

Hearne, Betsy
Commuters.

Hearne, Thomas (1678–1735)
On the Tack.

Hearne, Vicki (b. 1946)
Gauguin's White Horse.

Hearson, Harry (fl. c.1940)
Nomenclaturik.

Heath (fl. c.1500)
Women.

Heath, Robert (b. 1931)
On Clarastella walking in Her Garden.
On the Unusual Cold and Rainy [or Rainie] Weather in the Summer, 1648.
Seeing Her Dancing.

Heath-Stubbs, John (b. 1918)
Artorius.
Ballad of Don and Dave and Di, The.
Beggar's Serenade.
Carol for Advent.
Charm against the Toothache, A.
December: Prayer to St. Nicholas.
Epitaph: "Mr. Heath-Stubbs as you must understand."
February.
Footnote to Belloc's "Tarantella."
For the Nativity.
Gifts, The.
History of the Flood, The.
January.
Jays, The.
Kingfisher, The.
Lady's Complaint, The.
Mozart.
Not Being Oedipus.
One.
Poet of Bray, The.
Preliminary Poem.

Raft drifted, The.
Send for Lord Timothy.
Simcox.
Starling, The.
Titus and Berenice.
To a Poet a Thousand Years Hence.
Unpredicted, The.
Valse Oubliée.
Virgin Martyrs.
Vision of Beasts, A.
Watching Tennis.
Winter Cricket.
Year of Our Lord two thousand one hundred and seven, The.

Heber, Reginald (1783–1826)
Brightest and Best of the Sons of the Morning.
By Cool Siloam's Shady Rill.
From Greenland's Icy Mountains.
Holy, Holy, Holy.

Hébert, Anne (b. 1916)
Alchemy of Day, The.
Bread Is Born.
Crown of Happiness.
Great Fountains, The.
Life in the Castle.
Offended.
Our Hands in the Garden.
Skinny Girl, The.
Tomb of the Kings, The.
Wooden Chamber, The.

Hecht, Anthony (b. 1923)
Adam.
Alceste in the Wilderness.
At the Frick.
Avarice.
Behold the Lilies of the Field.
Birdwatchers of America.
Book of Yolek, The.
Christmas Is Coming.
Cost, The.
Death the Painter.
Deodand, The.
Double Sonnet.
Dover Bitch, The.
End of the Weekend, The.
Exile.
Feast of Stephen, The.
Firmness.
From the Grove Press.
Gardens of the Villa D'Este, The.
Ghost in the Martini, The.
Going the Rounds; a Sort of Love Poem.
Goliardic Song.
Hill, A.
House Sparrows.
Illumination.
Improvisations on Aesop.
Jason.
Letter, A.
"It Out-Herods Herod. Pray You, Avoid It."
Lizards and Snakes.
'More Light! More Light!'
Lot of Night Music, A.
Man Who Married Magdalene, The.
Mysteries of Caesar, The.
Naming the Animals.
Paradise Lost, Book V: An Epitome.
Peripeteia.
Pig.
Samuel Sewall.
Sarabande on Attaining the Age of Seventy-Seven.
Sestina d'Inverno.
Still Life.
Tarantula or the Dance of Death.
Third Avenue in Sunlight.
Vice.
Vow, The.

Hecht, Roger (b. 1926)
War Memento (Somewhere in France 1915)

Hedge, Frederic Henry (1805–90)
Mighty Fortress Is Our God, A.
Sovereign and Transforming Grace.

Hedin, Robert
At Betharram.
At the Olive Grove of the Resistance.

Transcanadian.
Wreck of the Great Northern, The.

Hedyla (fl. 3rd cent. A.D.)
Either cockleshells from the Erythraian reef as gifts.

Hedylos (fl. 270? B.C.)
Dedication to Aphrodite, A.
From dawn to dark, and back from dark to dawn.
Hellenistic Period, The.
Let's drink up: with wine, what original.
Musical Wine-Jar, A.
Our prize fish is done!
Seduced Girl.
Wine and treacherous proposals.

Heermann, F. (1585–1647)
Ah, holy Jesus, how hast thou offended.

Heffernan, Michael (b. 1942)
Message, The.
Presidents.
Reading Aquinas.

Heffernan, William (b. 1937)
Kathaleen Ny-Houlahan [or Kathleen-Ni-Houlahan].

Hegemon (fl. c.370 B.C.)
Thermopylai.

Hegesippus (fl. 300 B.C.)
Hang that day with black, that night, sinister, moonless.

Hegley, John
I'm skulking by the scandal and the handle on the door.

Heidbreder, Robert
Copycat.

Heide, Florence Parry (b. 1919)
Rocks.

Heidsieck, Bernard (b. 1928)
Canal Street 33/14.
Canal Street 39/27.

Heifetz-Tussman, Malka (b. 1896)
Thou Shalt Not.

Heimel, Cynthia
Sally.

Hein, Piet
Noble Funerals Arranged.

Hein, Silvio
He's a Cousin of Mine.

Heine, Heinrich (1797–1856)
Ad Finem.
Ah, Death is Like the Long Cool Night.
And When I Lamented.
Anno 1829.
Auf meiner Herzliebsten Äugelein.
Azra, The.
Best Religion, The.
By the Waters of Babylon.
Coffin, The.
Dear Maiden.
Dearest Friend, Thou Art in Love.
Death and Morphine.
Die blauen Veilchen der Äugelein.
Die Lotusblume ängstigt.
Du bist wie eine Blume.
Ein Fichtenbaum steht einsam.
Enfant perdu.
Epilogue: "Like the stalks of wheat in the fields."
Es fällt ein Stern herunter.
Es Stehen Unbeweglich.
Evening Twilight.
Every idle desire has died in my breast.
Farewell: "Linden blossomed, the nightingale sang, The."
Fresco-Sonnets to Christian Sethe.
Grenadiers, The.
Hebrew Melodies, sels.
Heimkehr, Die, sels.
Homeward Bound, sels.
I, a Most Wretched Atlas.
I Love But Thee.
I'm Black and Blue.
I Met by Chance.
I Wept as I Lay Dreaming.
Ich Weiss Nicht Was Soll es Bedeuten.
If, Jerusalem, I Ever Should Forget Thee.

Im Traum sah ich ein Männchen klein und putzig.
Lassie, What Mair Wad You Hae?
Lorelei.
Love's Résumé.
Mädchen mit dem rothen Mündchen.
Maiden Lies in Her Chamber, A.
Mein Herz, Mein Herz Ist Traurig.
Mein Kind, wir waren Kinder.
Mein Liebchen, wir sassen zusammen.
Memory, A.
Message, The.
Mir träumte von einem Königskind.
Mir träumte wieder der alte Traum.
Mond ist aufgegangen, Der.
Mortal, Sneer Not at the Devil.
My Songs Are Poisoned.
My zenith was luckily happier than my night.
New Jewish Hospital at Hamburg, The.
Night by the Sea, A.
Night Thoughts.
North Sea, The, sels.
Oh Lovely Fishermaiden.
Pine Is Standing Lonely, A.
Princess Sabbath.
Proem: "Out of my own great woe."
Revenge—?
Rose, die Lilie, die Taube, die Sonne, Die.
Sag', wo ist dein schönes Liebchen.
Sea Hath Its Pearls, The.
Sea-Sickness.
Silesian Weavers, The.
Solomon.
Song of Songs, The.
Song: "There stands a lonely pine-tree."
Songs to Seraphine.
Sonnet to My Mother, A.
Storm, The.
Tannhäuser, sels.
This mad carnival of loving.
Thou Hast Diamonds.
To Angélique, sels.
To Edom.
To My Mother.
To the World We Must Appear.
Twilight.
Voyage, The.
Warum sind denn die Rosen so blass.
We Cared for Each Other.
Weavers.
Welt ist dumm, die Welt ist blind, Die.
When Two Are Parted.
When Young Hearts Break.
Who Was It, Tell Me.
Wie langsam kriechet sie dahin.
Window-Glance, The.
Wise Men Ask the Children the Way, The.
Words, Words, Words, and Nothing Doing.
Young Man Loves a Maiden, A.
Zu fragmentarisch ist Welt und Leben.

Heissenbüttel, Helmut
Combination II.
Didactic Poem on the Nature of History, A.D. 1954.
Homesick.
Lesson 3.

Heithaus, Joe (fl. 20th cent.)
What a Little Moonlight Can Do.

Hejduk, John
Sleep of Adam, The.

Hejinian, Lyn (b. 1941)
Book 2.
Can one take captives by writing.
In the dark sky there.
Mask of Anger, A.
Moment yellow, just as four years later when, A.
Nights.
No form at all—it's impossible to imagine its being.
Solitude flared out, The.
Tree rows in orchards are capable of patterns. What, The.

Helfgott, Sarina (b. 1928)
Trains, The.

Helle, Anita
Poem for Natalia Ginzburg.

Heller, Binem (b. 1943)
Pesach Has Come to the Ghetto Again.

Heller, Richard
Minister has all his notes in place, The.

Helton, Roy (b. 1886)
Lonesome Water.
Old Christmas Morning.

Helwig, David (b. 1938)
Considerations.
Dead Weasel, A.
Drunken Poem.
For Edward Hicks.
Lot.
Words from Hell.

Hemans, Felicia Dorothea (1793–1835)
Agony in the Garden, The.
American Forest Girl, The.
Ancient Greek Song of Exile.
Arabella Stuart.
Beings of the Mind, The.
Brereton Omen, The, sels.
Bride of the Greek Isle, The.
Bride's Farewell, The.
Bring Flowers.
Casabianca.
Chamois Hunter's Love, The.
Corinne at the Capitol.
Costanza.
Despondency and Aspiration.
Diver, The.
Dreaming Child, The.
Edith, a Tale of the Woods.
Effigies, The.
England's Dead.
Epitaph on Mr W—.
Evening Prayer, at a Girls' School.
Flight of the Spirit.
Gertrude, or Fidelity Till Death.
Grave of a Poetess, The.
Graves of a Household, The.
Homes of England, The.
Hour of Death, The.
Illuminated City, The.
Image in Lava, The.
Imelda.
Indian City, The.
Indian Woman's Death-Song, The.
Joan of Arc in Rheims.
Juana.
Landing of the Pilgrim Fathers [in New England], The.
Last Banquet of Antony and Cleopatra, The.
Last Song of Sappho, The.
Lost Pleiad, The.
Madeline, A Domestic Tale.
Magic Glass, The.
Mary at the Feet of Christ.
Memorial of Mary, The.
Memorial Pillar, The.
Mirror in the Deserted Hall, The.
Mountain Sanctuaries.
New Monthly Magazine, sels.
Night-Blooming Flowers.
Olive Tree, The.
Palm-tree, The.
Parting Song, A.
Pauline.
Peasant Girl of the Rhone, The.
Properzia Rossi.
Queen of Prussia's Tomb, The.
Remembrance of Grasmere, A.
Return, The.
Revellers, The.
Rock of Cader Idris, The.
Sabbath Sonnet.
Second Sight.
Siege of Valencia, The, sels.
Song of Emigration.
Spirit's Mysteries, The.
Stanzas to the Memory of the Late King.
Statue of the Dying Gladiator, The.
Stranger in Louisiana, The.
Stranger's Heart, The.
Switzer's Wife, The.
Thought from an Italian Poet.
To a Departed Spirit.

To a Wandering Female Singer.
To My Eldest Brother, With the British Army in Portugal.
To [or the Poet] Wordsworth.
Trumpet, The.
Vigil of Rizpah, The.
Voice of Spring, The.
Wife of Asdrubal, The.
Woman and Fame.
Wreck, The.
Written on the Sea-Shore.

Hemensley, Kris (b. 1946)
Look! she said you can see.
My poem's in the oven where it.
Place was famed for, The.
Poem by John Thorpe, A.
Sulking in the Seventies.

Hemingway, Ernest (1899–1961)
Age Demanded, The.
Champs d'Honneur.
Earnest Liberal's Lament, The.
Lady Poets With Foot Notes, The.
Neo-Thomist Poem.
Valentine.

Hempel, Amy
Rain.

Hemphill, Essex (1957–95)
Better Days.
Cordon Negro.
Family Jewels.
Homocide.
Isn't It Funny?
Soft Targets.
To Some Supposed Brothers.
Where Seed Falls.
XXII.
XXIV.

Henchman, Richard (c.1655–1725)
In Consort to Wednesday, Jan. 1st. 1701.
Vox Oppressi, to the Lady Phipps.

Henderson, David (b. 1943)
Alvin Cash/Keep on Dancin'
Elvin Jones Gretsch Freak.
Horizon Blues.
Lee Morgan.
Song of Devotion to the Forest.

Henderson, Hamish (b. 1919)
End of a Campaign.
First Elegy for the Dead in Cyrenaica.
Flyting o' Life and Daith, The.
Ninth Elegy: Fort Capuzzo.
Opening of an Offensive.
We Show You That Death as a Dancer.

Henderson-Holmes, Safiya (b. 1952)
Battle, Over and Over Again, The.
'C' ing in Colors: Blue.
'C' ing in Colors: Red.
Failure of an Invention.
Friendly Town #1.
Friendly Town #3.
Goodhousekeeping #17.
My First Riot: Bronx, NYC.
To Hell and Back, with Cake.

"Henderson, Paul" (Ruth France) (1913–67)
Shag Rock.

Henderson, Ray (1896–1970)
Animal Crackers in My Soup.
Best Things in Life Are Free, The.
Birth of the Blues, The.
Button Up Your Overcoat.
Bye Bye Blackbird.
Don't Bring Lulu.
Five Foot Two, Eyes of Blue (Has Anybody Seen My Girl?)
I'm Sitting on Top of the World.
I Want to Be Bad.
If I Had a Talking Picture of you.
It All Depends on You.
Life Is Just a Bowl of Cherries.
Magnolia.
Maybe This Is Love.
Never Swat a Fly.
Sunny Side Up.
Thank You Father.
Turn On the Heat.
Varsity Drag, The.

You're the Cream in My Coffee.

Hendry, J. F. (b. 1912)
Constant North, The.

Henein, Georges
Healthy Remedies.

Henjō Abbot
If the winds of heaven.

Henley, Samuel (1740–1815)
Verses Addressed to a Friend, Just Leaving a Favourite Retirement.

Henley, William Ernest (1849–1903)
All in a Garden Green.
At Queensferry.
Ballade Made in the Hot Weather.
Ballade of Dead Actors.
Before.
Bowl of Roses, A.
Echoes, The, *sels.*
England, My England.
From a Window in Princes Street.
Interior.
Invictus.
Madam Life's A Piece in Bloom.
Moral, The.
On the Way to Kew.
Out of Tune.
Since Those We Love and Those We Hate.
Song of the Sword, *sels.*
To Robert Louis Stevenson.
Villon's Straight Tip to All Cross Coves.
Waiting.
We'll Go No More a-Roving.

Hennamma (*fl.* **late 17th cent.)**
Wasn't your mother a woman?

Hennell, Thomas (1903–45)
Mermaiden, A.
Queen Anne's Musicians.
Shepherd and Shepherdess.

Henniker-Heaton, Peter J.
Post Early for Space.

Henri, Adrian (b. 1932)
Adrian Henri's Talking after Christmas Blues.
Mrs. Albion You've Got a Lovely Daughter.

Henry, Brian (b. 1972)
Discovery.
Garage Sale.
Moraine Lake.
Skin.

Henry, James (1798–1876)
Another and another and another.
My Stearine Candles.
Old Man.
Once on a time a thousand different men.
Out of the Frying Pan into the Fire.
Pain.
Son's a poor, wretched, unfortunate creature, The.
Two hundred men and eighteen killed.
Very Old Man.

Henry, Michael
Though starlings imitate me.

Henry, Paul (b. 1959)
Love Birds.
Winter Wedding, The.

Henry VIII, King of England (1491–1547)
Pastime.
To His Lady.

Henry, William
Verses.

Henryson, Robert (c.1425–c.1506)
Cock and the Fox, The.
I mend the fyre and beikit me about.
O ladyis fair of Troy and Grece, attend.
Preiching of the Swallow, The.
Robin [*or* Robene] and Makyne.
Syne nethir-mare he went quhare Pluto was.
Taill of the Foxe, That Begylit the Wolf, in the Schadow of the Mone, The.
Tale of the Upland Mouse and the Burgess Mouse, The.
Testament of Cresseid, The.
That samin tyme, of Troy the garnisoun.

Henson, Lance (b. 1944)
Among Hawks.
Anniversary Poem for the Cheyennes Who Fell

at Sand Creek.
At Chadwicks Bar and Grill.
Bay Poem.
Between Rivers and Seas.
Buffalo Blood.
Cold, The.
Comanche Ghost Dance: An Impression.
Coyote Fragments.
Crazy Horse: The Last Morning.
Curtain.
Dawn in January.
Day Song.
Epitaph: Snake River.
Flock.
Grandfather.
I Am Singing the Cold Rain.
Image of City.
Last Words, 1968.
Moon at Three A.M.
Moth.
Near Twelve Mile Point.
North.
Old Man Told Me.
Old Story.
Other.
Our Smoke Has Gone Four Ways.
Poem for Carroll, Descendant of Chiefs.
Rain.
Scattered Leaves.
Sitting Alone in Tulsa Three A.M.
Sleep Watch.
Solitary.
Splitting Wood Near Morris, Oklahoma on Robbie and Lesa McMurtry's Farm.
Sundown at Darlington 1878.
Travels with the Band-Aid Army.
Warrior Nation Trilogy.
We Are a People.
Wish.
Wood Floor Dreams.

Henson, Stuart
Grab the beast by the horns.

Heóghusa, Eochaidh Ó
On Maguire's Winter Campaign.
Winter Campaign, A.

Hepburn, Mrs. Patrick *See* **Wickham, Anna**

Heppenstall, Rayner (1911–81)
Actaeon.

Heraclitus of Halicarnassus (*fl.* **c.240 B.C.)**
Soil is freshly dug, the half-faded wreaths of leaves, The.

Herarty, Toeti (b. 1935)
Cyclus.

Herbert, Sir Alan Patrick (1890–1971)
General inspecting the trenches, The.
I Like Them Fluffy.
Less Nonsense.
Lines for a Worthy Person Who Has Drifted by Accident into a Chelsea Revel.
Saturday Night.
Triangular Legs.

Herbert, Audrey
Limerick: "All his life, Mr. George Bernard Shaw."

Herbert, Bill
I do not have a body.

Herbert, Cicely (b. 1937)
Everything Changes.

Herbert, Edward, 1st Baron Herbert of Cherbury (1583–1648)
Breaking from under that thy cloudy veil.
Ditty: "If you refuse me once, and think again."
Ditty: "Why dost thou hate return instead of love."
Elegy over a Tomb.
Epitaph on Sir Philip Sidney Lying in St Paul's without a Monument, to be Fastned upon the Church Door.
In a Glass-Window for Inconstancy.
Inconstancy's the Greatest of Sins.
Kissing.
La Gialletta Gallante, or the Sunburned Exotic Beauty.
Ode, upon a Question Moved, Whether Love

Should Continue Forever?, An.
Platonic Love.
Sonnet Made upon the Groves near Merlou [*or* Merlow] Castle.
Sonnet of Black Beauty.
Thought, The.
To His Watch, When He Could Not Sleep.
To One Black, and Not Very Handsome, Who Expected Commendation.
You well-compacted groves, whose light and shade.

Herbert, George (1593–1633)
Aaron.
Affliction (1).
Affliction (3).
Affliction (4).
Affliction: "Kill me not every [*or* ev'ry] day."
Agony [*or* Agonie], The.
Altar, The.
Anagram.
Answer, The.
Antiphon: "Let all the world in ev'ry corner sing / My God and King."
Artillery [*or* Artillerie].
Bag, The.
Banquet, The.
Bitter-Sweet.
British Church, The.
Bunch of Grapes, The.
Christmas.
Church-Floor[e], The.
Church-Lock and Key.
Church Militant, The, *sels.*
Church Monuments.
Church-Music[k].
Church-Porch, The.
Collar, The.
Complaining.
Confession.
Conscience.
Cross[e], The.
Dawning, The.
Death.
Decay.
Denial[l].
Dialogue, A.
Discipline.
Divinity.
Doomsday.
Dotage.
Dulness[e].
Easter.
Easter Wings.
Elixir [*or* Elixer], The.
Employment (1).
Employment: "He that is weary, let him sit."
Evensong [*or* Even-Song].
Family [*or* Familie], The.
Flower, The.
Forerunners, The.
Frailty.
Glance, The.
Good Friday.
Grace.
Grieve Not the Holy Spirit, etc.
H[oly] Communion, The.
Heaven.
Holy Baptism (1)
Holy Baptism (2)
Hope.
Humility.
Iesu.
Invitation, The.
Jesu.
Jordan (1)
Jordan (2)
Joseph's Coat.
Judge Not the Preacher; for He is Thy Judge.
Judgement.
L'Envoy.
Life.
Longing.
Love.
Love (1)
Love (2)
Love (3)
Man.

Mary [or Marie] Magdalene.
Mattens.
Memoriae Matris Sacrum, *sels.*
Mortification.
O sacred Providence, who from end to end.
Obedience.
Sacrifice, The.
Thanksgiving, The.
Paradise.
Parody [or Parodie], A.
Peace.
Pearl, The. Matth. 13:45.
Perirrhanterium.
Pilgrimage, The.
Posy [or Posie], The.
Praise (2)
Prayer (1): "Prayer the Church's banquet, Angels' age."
Priesthood, The.
Providence.
Pulley, The.
Quidditie [or Quiddity], The.
Quip, The.
Redemption.
Reprisal[l], The.
Search, The.
Sepulchre.
Sin (1)
Sin (2): "O that I could a sin once see!"
Sin's Round.
Sion.
Size, The.
Son[ne], The.
Sonnet: "My God, where is that ancient heat towards Thee."
Sonnet: "Sure Lord, there is enough in thee to dry."
Star[re], The.
Storm, The.
Sunday.
Superliminare.
Temper (1), The.
Temper (2), The.
Time.
Trinity Sunday.
True Hymn, A.
Unkindness.
Vanity [or Vanitie] (1)
Virtue [or Vertue].
Whitsunday.
Windows, The.
World, The.
Wreath, A.

Herbert, Joyce (b. 1923)
Dossers at the Imperial War Museum.
Irish Scullery Maid, The.

Herbert, W. N. (b. 1961)
Baby Poem Industry Poem, The.
Black Wet, The.
Cabaret McGonagall.
Coco-de-Mer.
Praise of Italian Chip-Shops.
Socialist Manifesto for East Balgillo, The.
To a Mousse.

Herbert, Zbigniew (b. 1924)
Abandoned, The.
Apollo and Marsyas.
At the Gate of the Valley.
Biology Teacher.
Damastes (Also Known As Procrustes) Speaks.
Devil, A.
Drawer.
Elegy of Fortinbras.
Envoy of Mr. Cogito, The.
Five Men.
Georg Heym—The Almost Metaphysical Adventure.
Hakeldama.
Hen.
I Would Like to Describe.
Knocker, A.
Longobards, The.
Matthew 27:3–10; When Judas, his betrayer, saw.
Meditations of Mr. Cogito on Redemption.
Mr. Cogito and the Imagination.
Mr. Cogito Meditates on Suffering.

Mr. Cogito Tells about the Temptation of Spinoza.
Our Fear.
Painter.
Pan Cogito on Virtue.
Passion of Our Lord painted by an anonymous hand from the Circle of Rhenish Masters, The.
Pebble, The.
Power of Taste, The.
Rain, The.
Remembering My Father.
Report from the Besieged City.
Return of the Proconsul, The.
Speculations on the Subject of Barabbas.
To Marcus Aurelius.
Transformations of Livy.
Trial, The.
Two Drops.
Voice.
Wall, The.
What I Saw.
What Mr. Cogito Thinks About Hell.

Herd, Tracey (b. 1968)
Bathing Girls, The.
Big Girls.
Bombshell.
Coronach.
Exhibits, The.
Gia.
Hyperion's Bones.
I stopped the car and stepped out onto gravel.
Marilyn Climbs Out of the Pool.
Missing.
On the Glittering Beaches.
Pat Taffe and Arkle.
Pink Rose Rings, The.
Survivors, The.
We are sailing on a charming bay.

Herder, Johann Gottfried von (1744–1803)
Esthonian Bridal Song.
Sir Olaf.

Herebert, William (c.1270–c.1333)
Biseth you in this ilke lif.
Com, Shuppere, Holy Gost, ofsech oure thoughtes.
Crist, buyere of alle icoren.
Devout Man Prays to His Relations, The.
Herodes, thou wikked foe, wharof is thy dredinge?
Heyl, Levedy, see-sterre bright.
Holy moder, that bere Crist.
Holy Wroughte of sterres bright.
Jesu our raunsoun.
My Folk, What Have I Done Thee?
Palm-Sunday Hymn, A.
Steddefast cross, inmong alle other.
Thou king of wele and blisse.
Who is This that Cometh from Edom?

Heredia, José-Maria de (1842–1905)
Flute; a Pastoral, The.
Laborer.

Herford, Oliver (1863–1935)
Bunny Romance, A.
Crocodile, The.
Eve.
Fall of J. W. Beane, The.
I Heard a Bird Sing.
Limerick.
Musical Lion, The.
Platypus, The.
Smile of the Goat, The.
Smile of the Walrus, The.

Herlin, Louise (b. 1925)
Echo of fireplace, An.
Gull inch-perfect over water, The.
Light brush of dawn, A.
Morning space.
Red round sun, The.
Sky has recovered, The.
So many traces.
Warmth of the wind-break wall, The.

Herman, Grace
Clinic, The.

Herman, Jerry (b. 1931)
Before the Parade Passes By.

Hello, Dolly!
I Won't Send Roses.
If He Walked into My Life.
Mame.
Tap Your Troubles Away.
Time Heals Everything.

Herman, Woody
Early Autumn.

Hermocreon (fl. 3rd? cent. B.C.)
Inscription on a Statue.
Nymphs of the surface, whom Hermokreon gave.

Hernández-Ávila, Inés
Presente.

Hernández Cruz, Víctor (b. 1949)
Anonymous.
Areyto.
Art of Hurricanes, The.
Borinkins in Hawaii.
Caminando.
Discovery.
Energy.
Entering Detroit.
Essay on William Carlos Williams, An.
First Claims Poem.
For the Far-Out Experimental Writer.
Going Uptown to Visit Miriam.
If Chickens Could Talk.
Ironing Goatskin.
Islandis.
It's Miller Time.
Keeping Track of the Serpents.
Latin and Soul for Joe Bataan.
Loíza Aldea.
Man Who Came to the Last Floor, The.
Mesa Blanca.
Milagrosa, La.
Mountain Building.
New/Aguas Buenas/Jersey.
Perlas.
Physics of Ochun, The.
Poem: "Greater cities are, The."
Poem: "Think with your body."
Poem: "Your head it waves outside."
Problems With Hurricanes.
Puerta Rica.
Ruskie's Boy.
Scarlet Skirt.
Side 4.
Side 12.
Side 18.
Side 20.
Side 21.
Side 22.
Side 26.
Side 32.
Slick.
Snaps of Immigration.
Spirits.
Swans' Book, The.
Tale of Bananas, A.
Three Days/out of Franklin.
Thursday.
Today Is a Day of Great Joy.
Two Guitars.
Urban Dream.
You Gotta Have Your Tips on Fire.

Hernandez, David (fl. 20th cent.)
Armitage Street.
Martin and My Father.
Pigeons.
Rooftop Piper.
Welcome.
Workers.

Hernández, Miguel (1910–42)
Final Sonnet.
I Go on in the Dark, Lit from Within.
July 18, 1936–July 18, 1938.
Lullaby of the Onion.
Tomb of the Imagination.
Waltz Poem of Those in Love and Inseparable Forever.
War.

Hernton, Calvin C. (b. 1932)
Distant Drum, The.
Long Blues, The.

Poem.

Herodas (*fl.* 3rd cent. B.C.)
Friends in Private.
Procuress, The.
Schoolmaster, The.
Women at the Temple.

Herodicus (*fl.* 2nd cent. B.C.)
Out of Hellas if you please, Aristarchean
   pedants.

Hérold, Vera
Big L, The.

Herpin, Henri
(All of a Sudden) My Heart Sings.

Herrera, Fernando de (1534–97)
Sonnet 32.

Herrera, Juan Felipe
Atavistic: Traces after the Rain.
Cherry Bowl with Blue Revolver: Neo-
   American Landscape.
Dream of Christopher Columbus, The.
Fuselage Installation.
Future Martyr of Supersonic Waves.
Hallucinogenic Bullfighter.
Iowa Blues Bar Spiritual.
Mexican World Mural / 5 x 25.
Poetry of America, The.
Portrait of Woman in Long Black Dress /
   Aurelia.
Resurrection of the Flesh, The.
Weaning of Furniture-Nutrition.
When He Believed Himself to Be a Young Girl
   Lifting the Skin of the Water.
Yellow Room, The.

Herrera y Reissig, Julio (1875–1910)
Grey Dawn.
Heraldic Decoration.
July.
Return, The.
Sadistic Love.
Sorrowful Shadow, The.

Herrick, Robert (1591–1674)
All Things Decay and Die.
Amber Bead, The.
Ambition.
Anacreontic.
Anacreontic[k] Verse.
Another.
Another Charme for Stables.
Another to Bring in the Witch.
Apparition of His Mistress[e] Calling Him to
   Elizium [*or* Elysium], The.
Apron of Flowers, The.
Argument of His Book, The.
Art above Nature, to Julia.
Ass[e], The.
Bad Season Makes the Poet Sad, The.
Barley-Break; or, Last in Hell.
Beggar to Mab, the Fairy [*or* Fairie] Queen,
   The.
Bell-Man, The.
Bellman, The.
Body, The.
Bracelet to Julia, The.
Bubble; a Song, The.
Calling, and Correcting.
Canticle to Apollo, A.
Captived Bee; or, The Little Filcher, The.
Casualties.
Ceremonies for Candlemas[se] Eve.
Ceremonies for Christmas[se].
Ceremony upon Candlemas Eve.
Charme, or an Allay for Love, A.
Charmes.
Cheat of Cupid; or, The Ungentle Guest, The.
Cherry-ripe [*or* Cherrie-ripe].
Chewing [of] the Cud, The.
Chop-Cherry.
Clothes Do But Cheat and Cozen [*or* Cousen]
   Us.
Comfort to a Youth That Had Lost His Love.
Coming of Good Luck, The.
Corinna's Going a-Maying.
Country Life: To His Brother, M. Tho: Herrick.
Country Life, to the Honored Mr. Endymion
   Porter[, Groome of the Bed-Chamber to His
   Maj.], The.

Cross-tree, The.
Crosses.
Cruell Maid, The.
Cruelties.
Crutches.
Curse. A Song, The.
Definition of Beauty, The.
Delight in Disorder.
Departure of the Good Daemon, The.
Difference Betwixt King and Subjects, The.
Dirge of Jephthah's Daughter, The.
Discontents in Devon.
Distrust.
Divination by a Daffadill [*or* Daffodil].
Dream[e]s.
Duty to Tyrants.
End of His Work, The.
Entertainment, or Porch-Verse, at the Marriage
   of Mr. Henry Northleigh [*or* Hen. Northly]
   and the Most Witty Mrs. Lettice Yard, The.
Epitaph upon a Child, An.
Epitaph upon a Sober Matron, An.
Epithalamy to Sir Thomas Southwell and His
   Lady, An.
Evensong.
Eye, The.
Fair[e] Days; or, Dawn[e]s Deceitful[l].
To Blossoms.
Fairy Temple; or, Oberon's Chapel, The.
Fame.
Fame Makes Us Forward.
Farewell Frost; or, Welcome the Spring.
Four[e] Things Make Us Happy Here.
Fresh Cheese and Cream.
Frolic[k], A.
Frozen Zone; or, Julia Disdainful, The.
Funeral[l] Rites of the Rose, The.
God's Mercy.
Gods Anger without Affection.
Gods Keyes.
Gods Presence.
Gods Providence.
Good Friday: Rex Tragicus, or, Christ Going to
   His Cross[e].
Good-Night, or Blessing, The.
Grace for a Child.
Hag, The.
Hell.
Her Bed.
Her Legs.
Epitaph upon a Virgin, An.
His Age, Dedicated to His Peculiar Friend,
   Master John Wickes, under the Name of
   Posthumus.
His Cavalier.
His Content in the Country.
His Creed.
His Desire.
His Farewell [*or* Fare-well] to Sack.
His Grange, or Private Wealth.
His Hope or Sheet-Anchor.
His Litany to the Holy Spirit.
His Offering, with the Rest, at the Sepulcher.
His Own Epitaph.
His Poetry His Pillar.
His Prayer for Absolution.
His Prayer to Ben Jonson [*or* Johnson].
His Request to Julia.
His Return to London.
His Saviour['] s Words, Going to the Cross[e].
His Tears to Thamesis [*or* Thamasis].
His Winding-Sheet.
Hock-Cart, or Harvest Home, The.
Hour-Glass, The.
How Lillies Came White.
How Marigolds Came Yellow.
How Roses Came Red.
How Violets Came Blue.
Hymn to the Graces, A.
Hymne to Love, An.
Upon Love, by Way of Question and Answer.
Ill Government.
Impossibilities to His Friend.
In the Dark None Dainty.
Invitation, The.
Julia's Petticoat.
King and No King, A.

Kiss[e], A.
Kisses Loathesome.
Kissing and Bussing.
Life Is the Body's [*or* Bodies] Light.
Lips Tongueless[e].
Long and Lazy [*or* Lazie].
Love Me Little, Love Me Long.
Love What It Is.
Lovers How They Come and Part.
Lyric[k] for Legacies.
Lyric to Mirth, A.
Mad Maid's Song, The.
Man's Dying-Place Uncertain.
Matins [*or* Mattens], or Morning Prayer.
May-Pole, The.
Maypole, The.
Meditation for His Mistress[e], A.
Moderation.
Money Gets the Mastery [*or* Masterie].
Mount of the Muses, The.
Music.
My Ben.
Neutrality Loathsome.
New-Year's [*or* New-Yeares] Gift Sent to Sir
   Simeon Steward, A.
Night-Piece, to Julia, The.
No Coming to God without Christ.
No Difference in the Dark [*or* i'th'dark].
No Loathsomnesse in Love.
No Lock against Lechery.
Not Every Day Fit for Verse.
Not to Love.
Nothing New.
Nuptiall Song, or Epithalamie, on Sir Clipseby
   Crew and His Lady, A.
Oberon's Feast.
Oberon's Palace.
Observation.
Ode for Him [*or* Ben Jonson], An.
Ode on the Birth of Our Saviour, An.
Ode to Master Endymion Porter, upon His
   Brother's Death, An.
On Himself[e].
Orpheus.
Panegyric to Sir Lewis Pemberton, A.
Parcæ, The; or, Three Dainty Destinies: The
   Armilet.
Perfume, The.
Persecutions Purifie.
Peter-penny, The.
Pillar of Fame, The.
Plaudite, or End of Life, The.
Poet Loves a Mistress, but Not to Marry, The.
Poetry Perpetuates the Poet.
Power and Peace.
Power in the People, The.
Predestination.
Primrose, The.
Rainbow; or Curious Covenant, The.
Request to the Graces, An.
Right Hand, The.
Ring Presented to Julia, A.
Sabbaths.
Salutation.
Scar[e]-Fire, The.
Seest thou those diamonds which she wears.
Shame, No Statist.
Sho[o]e Tying, The.
Silken Snake, The.
Spell, The.
Steam in Sacrifice.
Supreme Fortune Falls Soonest.
Temple, The.
Temporall Goods.
Temptation.
Ternarie of Littles, upon a Pipkin of Jellie [*or*
   Jelly] Sent to a Lady, A.
Thanksgiving to God for His House, A.
Tithe [*or* Tythe]: To the Bride, The.
To a Bed of Tulips.
To a Gentlewoman Objecting to Him His Grey
   Hairs.
To Anthea.
To Anthea Lying in Bed.
To Anthea, Who May Command Him
   Anything.
To Critic[k]s.

To Crown[e] It.
To Daffodils [or Daffadills].
To Daisies, Not to Shut So Soon[e].
To Dean-bourn, a Rude River in Devon, by Which Sometimes He Lived.
To Death.
To Dianeme.
To Electra.
To Find[e] God.
To Fortune.
To God.
To God: an Anthem, Sung in the Chapel at White-Hall, Before the King.
To Groves.
To Heaven.
To His Book.
To his book's end this last line he'd have placed.
To His Conscience.
To His Dying Brother, Master William Herrick.
To His Ever-Loving God.
To His Friend, on the Untunable Times.
To His Honoured and Most Ingenious Friend Mr. Charles Cotton.
To His Kinsman, Master Thomas Herrick, Who Desired to Be in His Book.
To His Kinswoman, Mrs. Penelope Wheeler.
To His Lovely Mistresses.
To His Mistress[es].
To His Peculiar Friend Master Thomas Shapcott, Lawyer.
To His Savior [or Saviour]. The New Years [or yeers] Gift.
To His Saviour.
To His Saviour, a Child; a Present, by a Child.
To Julia.
To Julia, the Flaminica Dialis, or Queen-Priest.
To Keep a True Lent.
To Larr [or Lar].
To Laurels.
To Live Merrily, and to Trust to Good Verses.
To M. Denham, on His Prospective Poem.
To M. Henry Lawes, the Excellent Composer[,] of his Lyrics.
To Marygolds.
To Meadows [or Meddowes].
To Mistress Katherine Bradshaw, the Lovely, That Crowned Him with Laurel.
To Music.
To Music: A Song.
To Music, to Becalm a Sweet-sick Youth.
To Music, to Becalm His Fever.
To My Ill Reader.
To Oenone.
To Perilla.
To Phyllis to Love and Live with Him.
To Robin Redbreast.
To Sycamores.
To the Detracter.
To the Generous Reader.
To the King.
To the King and Queen[e], upon Their Unhappy Distances.
To the King, upon His Com[m]ing with His Army into the West.
To the King, Upon His Welcome to Hampton Court.
To the Most Fair and Lovely Mistress Anne Soame, Now Lady Abdie.
To the Most Illustrious and Most Hopeful[l] Prince, Charles, Prince of Wales.
To the Most Virtuous Mistress Pot, Who Many Times Entertained Him.
To the Reverend Shade of His Religious Father.
To the Right Honourable Mildmay, Earl of Westmorland.
To the Sour[e] Reader.
To the Virgins, to Make Much of Time.
To the Water Nymphs, Drinking at the Fountain.
To the Western Wind.
To the Willow-Tree.
To Violets.
To Virgins.
To Vulcan.
Transfiguration, The.

Up Tail[e]s All.
Upon a Black Twist, Rounding the Arm of the Countess of Carlisle.
Upon a child.
Upon a Child That Died [or Dyed].
Upon a Maid.
Upon a Young Mother of Many Children.
Upon Batt.
Upon Ben Jo[h]nson.
Upon Bunce: Epigram.
Upon Electra.
Upon Groins: Epigram.
Upon Her Eyes.
Upon Her Feet.
Upon Her Voice.
Upon Himself.
Upon Himselfe Being Buried.
Upon His Sister-in-Law, Mistress Elizabeth Herrick.
Upon His Spaniel[l] Tracie [or Tracy].
Upon His Verses.
Upon Jack and Jill: Epigram.
Upon Julia's Breasts.
Upon Julia's Clothes.
Upon Julia's Ribband.
Upon Julia's Voice.
Upon Julia['s] Washing Herself in the River.
Upon Love.
Upon Lulls.
Upon M. Ben Jo[h]nson: Epigram.
Upon Mistress Elizabeth Wheeler under the Name of Amarillis.
Upon Mistresse Susanna Southwell, Her Cheeks.
Upon Pagget.
Upon Parson Beanes.
Upon Prudence Baldwin Her Sickness[e].
Upon Prue [or Prew], His Maid.
Upon Rook: Epigram.
Upon Scobble [Epigram].
Upon Showbread [or Shewbread]: Epigram.
Upon Sibilla.
Upon Some Women.
Upon the Loss[e] of His Mistresses.
Upon the Nipples of Julia's Breast.
Upon the Same.
Upon the Troublesome Times.
Upon Time.
Upon Umber: Epigram.
Vine, The.
Vision, The.
Vision, The.
Wassaile, The.
Welcome to Sack, The.
What God Is.
What Kind of Mistress[e] He Would Have.
Money Makes the Mirth.
When He Would Have His Verses Read.
White Island.
Why Flowers Change Color.
Widow's Tears [or Widdowes Teares]: or, Dirge of Dorcas, The.
Wounded Cupid, The.

Herschberger, Ruth (b. 1917)
Huron, The.
Lumberyard, The.

Hershenson, Miriam
Husbands and Wives.

Hertz, Dalia
Return, The.

Hervey, Christopher (*fl.* mid–18th cent.)
Confusion.

Herzberg, Judith (b. 1934)
Loss.
Morning.
Nearer.
On the Death of Sylvia Plath.
Reunion.
Seagulls.
Vocation.

Herzog, Arthur, Jr. (*fl.* 1941)
God Bless the Child.

Heseltine, Philip
Limerick: "Young things who frequent picture-palaces, The."

Hesiod (*fl.* c.700 B.C.)
Beware of the month Lenaion, bad days.

Great Father Eating His Children, The.
Vision.
Winter.

Hesketh, Phoebe (b. 1909)
Death of a Gardener.
Dilemma.
Love's Advocate.

Hesse, Hermann (1877–1962)
Night.
Spring Song.

Hester, M. L. (b. 1947)
Lightning Rod Salesman, The.

Hetherington, Graeme (b. 1937)
Man from Changi, The.

Hewett, Dorothy (b. 1923)
Anniversary.
In Moncur Street.
Moon-Man.
Sanctuary.
Sunset flames over the city, The.
This Version of Love.
You Gave Me Hyacinths First a Year Ago.

Hewison, R. J. P.
Genius.
Limerick: "Said an erudite sinologue: 'How'"
Limerick: "There was a young girl of Trebarwith."
Limerick: "Though Sir James (God's-a-Formula) Jeans."

Hewitt, John (1907–87)
Because I Paced My Thought.
Calling on Peadar O'Donnell at Dungloe.
Colony, The.
Father's Death, A.
From a Museum Man's Album.
From the Tibetan.
Frontier, The.
How have I served you? I have let you waste.
I Write For.
If I had given you that love and care.
Ireland.
Irishman in Coventry, An.
Local Poet, A.
Once Alien Here.
Once in a seaside town with time to kill.
Postscript, 1984.
Ram's Horn, The.
Scar, The.
Search, The.
St. Stephen's Day.
Substance and Shadow.
Tryst.
Turf-Carrier [or Turf Carrier] on Aranmore.
Ulster Names.

Heyen, William (b. 1940)
Blue.
Crane in Reeds.
Derailment.
Emancipation Proclamation.
For Hermann Heyen.
Mantle.
Numinous, The.
Passover: the Injections.
Riddle: "From Belsen a crate of gold teeth."
Stadium, The.
Tie, The.
To the Onlookers.
Trains, The.
Windfall.

Heym, Georg
Demons of the Cities, The.
Final Vigil.
Seafarers.
War.
Why do you visit me, white moths, so often?
With the Ships of Passage.

Heyman, Edward (1907–81)
Blame It on My Youth.
Body and Soul.
Easy Come, Easy Go.
Ho Hum.
I Cover the Waterfront.
I Wanna Be Loved.
When I Fall in Love.
You're Mine, You!

Heynen, Jim
Clean People, The.

I Think That I Shall Never See.
Heyrick, Thomas (1649–94)
On a Peacock.
On a Sunbeam.
On an Indian Tomineois, the Least of Birds.
Heyward, DuBose (1885–1940)
Jasbo Brown.
Summertime.
Heywood, John (c.1497–1580)
Egles byrde hath spred his wings, The.
Of Use.
On Botching.
Praise of His Lady, A.
Quiet Neighbour, A.
Wilt thou use turners craft still? ye by my trouth.
Heywood, Thomas (1575?–1650)
Author to His Book[e], The.
Epitaph, An: "I was, I am not; smiled, that since did weep."
Good Morrow.
Hibernicus Exul (fl. 8th–9th cent.)
O Christ, receive these souls in thy Mother's house.
Hickey, Emily (1845–1924)
For Richer, For Poorer.
I Think of You as of a Good Life-boat.
Song: "Beloved, it is morn!"
Hicks, Berryman (1778–1839)
Time Is Swiftly Rolling On, The.
Hicky, Daniel Whitehead (b. 1902)
No Friend Like Music.
When a Man Turns Homeward.
Hicok, Bob (b. 1960)
Alzheimer's.
Heroin.
Over Coffee.
Hiebert, Paul Gerhardt (b. 1892)
Farmer and the Farmer's Wife, The.
Hiestand, Emily
Day Lily and the Fox, The.
Moon Winx Motel.
Witch-Hazel Wood, The.
Higgins, Brian (1930–65)
Analogy.
Baedeker for Metaphysicians.
Corrupt Man in the French Pub, The.
Genesis.
Higgins, Frank
Tennis in the City.
Higgins, Frederick Robert (1896–1941)
Ballad of O'Bruadir, The.
Chinese Winter.
Father and Son.
Little Clan, The.
O You among Women.
Old Jockey, The.
Padraic O'Conaire—Gaelic Storyteller.
Song for the Clatter-Bones.
Higginson, Ella (1862–1940)
Dawn.
Dawn on the Willamette.
Dream of Sappho, A.
Eve.
Four-Leaf Clover.
Moonrise in the Rockies.
Opal Sea, The.
Statue, The.
Higginson, Thomas Wentworth (1823–1911)
Past Is Dark with Sin and Shame, The.
To Thine Eternal Arms, O God.
Higginson, William J.
Before the descent.
Ducks land, The.
Evening star.
High tide.
Holding the water.
I look up.
Interstices.
More intricate.
Robin listens, A.
Summer moon.
This spring rain.
Writing again.
Highfill, Mitch
Marginalization of Poetry, The.

Rebis.
Sea Breeze.
Hightower, J. R.
On Reading the Seas and Mountains Classic.
Higo, Aig (b. 1929)
Hidesong.
Ritual Murder.
Hijazi, Ahmad ʿAbd al-Muʿti (b. 1935)
Elegies, or the Stations of the Other Time.
Lonely Woman's Room, The.
Rendezvous in the Cave.
Secrets.
Hikmet, Nazim (1902–63)
About Mount Uludağ.
Angina Pectoris.
Cucumber, The.
Evening Walk, The.
Things I Didn't Know I Loved.
Letters from a Man in Solitary.
Letters from Chankiri Prison.
On Living.
Rubai.
Since I Was Thrown Inside.
Hilal, Dima
Bedouin Eyes.
Different Morning Altogether, A.
Ghaflah—the sin of forgetfulness.
Hilary (fl. c.1125)
To an English Boy: "Beautiful boy, flower fair."
To an English Boy: "Hail, fair youth, who seeks no bribe."
Hilberry, Conrad (b. 1928)
Body and Mind.
Hildebert (1056–1133)
Christian Rome.
For Whitsuntide.
In Honour of the Holy Spirit.
Mood of Vichy, The.
Nor God, nor man, the image thou dost see.
On the Death of Henry the Lion.
Prayer to God the Father.
Rome.
Shepherd cheerfully, The.
Songs you sent me I have read, The.
To Peter, Bishop of Poitiers, Who Withstood William of Aquitaine and Died in Exile.
Hildebrandt, Rosemary C.
O Eve.
Hildebrandt, Ziporah
In Hecate's Garden.
Kali.
Persephone.
Hill, Aaron (1685–1750)
Alone in an Inn at Southampton, April the 25th, 1737.
Garden Window, The.
May-Day.
Modesty.
On a Lady, Preached into the Colic, by One of Her Lovers.
Whitehall Stairs.
Written on a Window.
Hill, Billy (fl. 1936)
Glory of Love, The.
Hill, Geoffrey (b. 1932)
Canticle for Good Friday.
Christmas Trees.
Distant Fury of Battle, The.
Domaine Public.
Eve of St Mark, The.
Funeral Music, *sels*.
Genesis.
Guardians, The.
Hymns to Our Lady of Chartres, *sels*.
Idylls of the King.
Imaginative Life, The.
In Memory of Jane Fraser [*or* Frazer].
In Piam Memoriam.
Lachrimae Amantis.
Lachrimae Verae.
Laurel Axe, The.
Masque of Blackness, The.
Mercian Hymns, *sels*.
Merlin.

Mystery of the Charity of Charles Péguy, The, *sels*.
Orpheus and Eurydice.
Ovid in the Third Reich.
Pastoral, A: "Mobile, immaculate and austere."
Picture of a Nativity.
Pre-Raphaelite Notebook, A.
Quaint Mazes.
Requiem for the Plantagenet Kings.
September Song.
Short History of British India, A.
Song from Armenia, A.
Tenebrae.
To the High Court of Parliament.
Triumph of Love, The, *sels*.
Turtle Dove, The.
Two Chorale-Preludes: On Melodies by Paul Celan.
Veni Coronaberis.
White Ship, The.
Hill, Joe (1879–1914)
Preacher and the Slave, The.
There Is Power in a Union.
Hill, Leona
Let Him Return.
Hill, Mary Crockett (b. 1969)
Abomination.
Bad Karma.
Ruth.
Sleep.
Hill, Norah (b. 1945)
Dürer's "Young Hare."
Hill, Roberta
To Rose.
Waning August Moon.
Hill, Roberta *See* **Whiteman, Roberta Hill**
Hill, Selima (b. 1945)
Being a Wife.
Below Hekla.
Voice in the Garden, A.
Who's that knocking on my ring, says the chin.
Hille, Peter (1854–1904)
Beauty.
Maiden, The.
Hillel, Omer (b. 1926)
Sun.
Hillhouse, Augustus Lucas (1792–1859)
Trembling before Thine Awful Throne.
Hilliard, Bob (1918–71)
Civilization (Bongo, Bongo, Bongo)
Coffee Song (They've Got an Awful Lot of Coffee in Brazil), The.
In the Wee Small Hours of the Morning.
Hillman, Brenda (b. c.1945)
Arroyo, The.
Black Series.
Dark Existence.
Every Life.
Formation of Soils, The.
Geology, A.
Little Furnace.
Male Nipples.
Mysteries, The.
Y, The.
Hillyer, Robert Silliman (1895–1961)
As One Who Bears beneath His Neighbor's Roof.
Assassination, The.
Dead Man's Corner.
Eternal Return, The.
Hills turn hugely in their sleep, The.
Letter to Robert Frost, A.
Moo!
Pastoral: "So soft in the hemlock wood."
Hilton, Arthur Clement (1851–77)
Heathen Pass-ee, The.
Limerick: "There was a young critic of King's."
Limerick: "There was a young genius of Queens'"
Limerick: "There was a young gourmand of John's."
Limerick: "There was an old fellow of Trinity."
Octopus.

Hilton, David (b. 1938)
I Try to Turn in My Jock.
Hilton, John (d. 1657)
Madrigal: "My mistress frowns when she
should play."
Hinckley, Priscilla Baird
New Our Father, The.
Hincks, Elizabeth (fl. 1671)
Some More Scruples Clear'd.
Something about Silence.
Hind bint Utba (fl. early 7th cent.)
Fury against the Moslems at Uhud.
Tambourine song for Soldiers Going into
Battle.
Hind bint Uthatha (fl. early 7th cent.)
To a Hero Dead at al-Safra.
Hindle, Annie (b. c.1847, d. after 1897)
Her Gift.
Hine, Daryl (b. 1936)
Apart from You.
Bewilderment at the Entrance of the Fat Boy
into Eden, A.
Côte de Liesse.
Destruction of Sodom, The.
Fabulary Satire IV.
Here is another poem in a picture.
Letting Go.
Lines on a Platonic Friendship.
Man's Country.
Once when I was coming from art class they
surprised me.
Plain Fare.
Point Grey.
Riddle: "Invisible, chimerical."
Survivors, The.
Trompe L'Œil.
Trout, The.
Under the Hill.
Hines, Nellie Womack
Home.
Hines, P. R.
My Garden.
Hinkson, Katharine Tynan See **Tynan, Katharine**
Hinsey, Ellen
Approach of War, The.
Art of Measuring Light, The.
Body in Youth, The.
Planisféria, Map of the World, Lisbon, 1554.
Roman Arbor, The.
Hippolyte, Kendel (b. 1952)
Antonette's Boogie.
Jah Son / Another Way.
Reggae Cat (for Boston Jack).
Revo Lyric.
So Jah Sey.
Hipponax (fl. 6th cent.B.C.)
Still Waiting for My Winter Coat: A Sequence
of Fragments.
Hiranandani, Popati (b. 1924)
Husband.
Hirsch, Edward (b. 1950)
American Apocalypse.
Ancient Signs.
Art Pepper.
Edward Hopper and the House by the Railroad.
Fast Break.
For the Sleepwalkers.
Husband and Wife.
In Memoriam Paul Celan.
Lectures on Love, The.
Man on a Fire Escape.
Milena Jesenká.
My Father's Back.
My Grandfather's Poems.
Paul Celan: A Grave and Mysterious Sentence.
Short Lexicon of Torture in the Eighties, A.
Simone Weil: In Assisi.
Song: "This is a song for the speechless."
Tristan Tzara.
Wild Gratitude.
Hirsch, Eugene
Two Suffering Men.
Hirsch, Louis A.
Love Nest, The.
Hirschhorn, Norbert
Number Our Days.

Hirschman, Jack (b. 1933)
Headlands.
Painting, The.
Transfiguration.
Tremor, The.
Weeping, The.
X L E B.
Hirshbein, Peretz (b. 1880)
Captive.
I Shall Weep.
Stars Fade.
Hirshfield, Jane
Ars Poetica.
At Night.
Each Happiness Ringed by Lions.
Half-sleeping, / my body pulls toward yours.
In Praise of Coldness.
Invocation: "This August night, raccoons."
Letter to Hugo from Later.
Lives of the Heart,The.
Music Like Water, The.
Not-Yet.
Of Gravity and Angels.
On the Beach.
Osiris.
Painting.
Rain in May.
Story, A.
That Falling.
To Drink.
Hisho See **Ryojin Hisho**
Hitchcock, George
Figures in a Ruined Ballroom.
May All Earth Be Clothed in Light.
One Whose Reproach I Cannot Evade, The.
Scattering Flowers.
Solitaire.
Song of Expectancy.
Three Found Poems.
Three Portraits.
United States Prepare for the Permanent
Revolution, The.
Hitomaro, Kakinomoto no See **Kakinomoto no
Hitomaro**
Hittan of Tayyi
His Children.
Hix, H. L.
Man in Novosibirsk.
Hixon, Lex
My blissful Mother exists fully through every
creature!
Who can keep a blazing fire tied in a cotton
cloth?
Ho Ch'i-fang
Get Drunk.
Ho Ch'e Ch'ang (659–744)
Homecoming.
Written Impromptu upon Returning to My
Hometown.
Ho Chi Minh (1890–1969)
Two Prison Poems.
Ho Ching-ming (1483–1521)
Alone I Stand.
Ballad of the Government Granary Clerk.
Ballad of Yi River.
Bamboo Branch Song.
Ch'ang-an.
Ch'en-hsi County.
Fish in a Painting.
Night of the Fourteenth.
Presented to Wang Wen-hsi.
Rainy Night.
Seeing Off Han Ju-ch'ing as He Returns to the
Land Within the Passes.
Song of the Painting "River and Mountains,"
by Wu Wei.
Ho Hsun (d. 527)
Spring Breeze.
Traveler, The.
Ho Nansorhon (1563–1603)
For My Brother Hagok.
Ho Sun (d. 518)
At Parting.
Ho Thien
Green Beret.

Ho Xuan Hong
General's Plaque, The.
Hồ Xuân Hu'o'ng (fl. 18th–19th cent.)
On Sharing a Husband.
Hoagland, Everett (b. 1942)
Anti-Semanticist, The.
Big Zeb Johnson.
Gorée.
It's a Terrible Thing!
Kinda Blue Miles Davis Died Today.
Love Child—a Black Aesthetic.
My Spring Thing.
Hoban, Russell (b. 1925)
Egg Thoughts.
Friendly Cinnamon Bun, The.
Jigsaw Puzzle.
Old Man Ocean.
Pedalling Man, The.
Tin Frog, The.
Hoberman, Mary Ann (b. 1930)
Bugs.
Combinations.
Folk Who Live in Backward Town, The.
Let's Dress Up.
Hobsbaum, Philip (b. 1932)
Lesson in Love, A.
Hobson, Geary (b. 1941)
Buffalo Poem #1.
Hoby, Elizabeth Cooke (1540–1609)
Elizabeth Hoby, Wife, to Thomas Hoby,
Knight, Her Husband.
Epicedium by Elizabeth Hoby, Their Mother,
on the Death of Her Two Daughters
Elizabeth and Anne, An.
Hoccleve [or Occleve], Thomas (1370?–1450?)
Hoccleve Remembers His Madness.
Lament for Chaucer.
O maister deere and fader reverent!
Hochman, Sandra (b. 1936)
Cannon Hill.
Goldfish Wife, The.
Hairbrush, The.
Manhattan Pastures.
Sphinxes.
Hodes, Aubrey (b. 1927)
Jew Walks in Westminster Abbey, A.
Hodge, Arthur J. (fl. late 19th cent.)
Five Were Foolish.
Hodges, Cyril (1915–74)
Naturalised.
Hodges, Johnny
I'm Beginning to See the Light.
It Shouldn't Happen to a Dream.
Hodgins, Philip (b. 1959)
Death Who.
Making Hay.
Self-Pity.
Shooting the Dogs.
Hodgson, Ralph (1871–1962)
After.
Bells of Heaven, The.
Birdcatcher, The.
Bull, The.
Eve.
Flying Scrolls.
Ghoul Care.
Gipsy Girl, The.
Hammers, The.
House across the Way, The.
Hymn to Moloch.
Late, Last Rook, The.
Moor, The.
Mystery, The.
Reason Has Moons.
Silver Wedding.
Song of Honor [or Honour], The.
Stupidity Street.
Time.
Time, You Old Gypsy Man.
Hodza, Aaron (1924–83)
Slighted Wife, The.
Hoekstra, Han G. (1906–1988)
Cedar, The.
Hoffenstein, Samuel (1890–1947)
Babies Haven't Any Hair.

Birdie McReynolds.
Come, live with me and be my love.
Early bird may catch the worm, The.
I'm Fond of Doctors.
Love-Songs, at Once Tender and Informative.
Lullaby: "Sleep, my little baby, sleep."
Miss Millay Says Something Too.
Now, alas, it is too late.
Only the wholesomest foods you eat.
Progress.
Sheep.
Songs about Life and Brighter Things Yet.
Unequal Distribution.
With rue my heart is laden.
You buy some flowers for your table.
You buy yourself a new suit of clothes.
You hire a cook, but she can't cook yet.
Your little hands.

Hoffman, Al
Fit As a Fiddle.

Hoffman, Balthasar (1686–1775)
Be Glorified Eternally.

Hoffman, Daniel Gerard (b. 1923)
Armada of Thirty Whales, An.
At Provincetown.
Center of Attention, The.
È, the Feasting Florentines.
Ephemeridae.
Exploration.
In the Days of Rin-Tin-Tin.
Lobsterpot Labyrinths.
Seals in Penobscot Bay, The.
Signatures.
Special Train, A.
Who was it came.

Hoffman, O. S.
Five Best Doctors, The.

Hoffman, Sydney
Limerick: "No Portuguese Lady is Nautical."

Hoffmann, Heinrich (1809–94)
Story of Augustus Who Would Not Have Any
    Soup, The.

Hoffmann, Martha
Old Aussee.

Hofmann, Michael (b. 1957)
Ancient Evenings.
By Forced Marches.
Eclogue: "Industry undressing in front of
    Agriculture."
Pastorale.
Postcard from Cuernavaca.

Hofmannsthal, Hugo von (1874–1929)
Ballad of the Outer Life.
Do You See the Town?
Early Spring.
Many Indeed Must Perish in the Keel.
On the Transitory.
On Transitoriness.
Prologue to the Book 'Anatol.'
Ship's Cook, a Captive Sings, The.
Stanzas on Mutability.
Travel Song.
Traveller's Song.
Twilight of the Outward Life.
Two.
Two of Them, The.
Two, The.
Venetian Night, A.
Vision, A.
World-Secret.

Hofmannswaldau, Christian Hofmann von
Beauty's Transitoriness.
Description of Perfect Beauty.
He Loves in Vain.
So sweet, so golden.

Hofshteyn, Dovid (1889–1952)
My Thread.

Hogan, Linda (b. 1947)
Celebration: Birth of a Colt.
Chambered Nautilus.
Crossings.
Eclipse II.
Gamble.
Heartland.
Heritage.

Man in the Moon.
Map.
New Apartment.
Nothing.
Potholes.
Rainy Season, The.
Return: Buffalo.
Seeing through the Sun.
Skin.
Tear.
To Light.
Truth Is, The.
Workday.

Hogan, Michael (b. 1943)
Spring.

Hoge
How long the tree's been barren.

**Hogg, James ("The Ettrick Shepherd") (1770–
1835)**
Boy's Song, A.
Charlie is my Darling.
Kilmeny.
Lock the Door, Lariston.
McLean's Welcome.
Thirteenth Bard's Song, The.
When Maggy Gangs Away.
When the Kye Comes Hame.
Witch o' Fife, The.
Witch's Chant, A.

Hogg, Robert (b. 1942)
Little Falls.

Hoggra, Robert
Poem: "In its going down, the moon."

Hogyoku (d. 1869)
Quick sounds.

Hoin
On the rocky slope, blossoming.

Hoitsu (1760–1828)
Buddha / Cherry flowers.

Hokusai (d. 1849)
Now as a spirit.

Hokushi (1655–1718)
Gone up in flames.
I write, erase, rewrite.
My house gutted.
Sailboats in line.
Writing / Rubbing it out—.

Hokuso (d. 1790)
O sacred spirit.

Holan, Vladimir (1905–80)
Between.
But.
Chicken, The.
Children at Christmas in 1945.
During an Illness.
Epoch.
Glimpsed.
How?
In the Yard of the Policlinic.
Mother.
Old Priest, The.
Reminiscence.
Resurrection.
To the Enemies.
When passing from nature to being.
You're Thinking of Children.

Holbrook, David (b. 1923)
Drought.
Maternity Gown.

Holcroft, Thomas (1745–1809)
Dying Prostitute, The; an Elegy.
Fool's Song.
Gaffer Gray.
On Shakespeare and Voltaire.
Seasons, The.
Song: "When o'er the wold the heedless
    lamb."
To Haydn.

Holden, Jonathan (b. 1941)
How to Play Night Baseball.
Liberace.
Poem for Ed "Whitey" Ford, A.
Saturday Afternoon, October.
Why We Bombed Haiphong.

Holden, Molly (b. 1927)
Giant Decorative Dahlias.

Photograph of Haymaker, 1890.
Seaman, 1941.

Holden, Oliver (1765–1844)
How Sweet Is the Language of Love.
Weeping Sinner, Dry Your Tears.
Within These Doors Assembled Now.

Hölderlin, Friedrich (1770–1843)
All the fruit is ripe, plunged in fire, cooked.
Autumn.
Brevity.
But speech.
Descriptive Poetry.
Half of Life.
Halflife.
Hyperion's Song of Fate.
In the Days of Socrates.
No Pardon.
Oh friend, we arrived too late.
Patmos.
Pleasant to wander.
Ripe, Being Plunged into Fire.
Schicksalslied.
Spring.
Summer.
To the Fates.
To the German People.
Winter.

Holiday, Billie (1915–59)
Fine and Mellow.
God Bless the Child.

Holiner, Mann (1897–1958)
Until the Real Thing Comes.
Why Shouldn't It Happen to Us?
You Can't Stop Me from Lovin' You.

Holland, Henry Scott (1847–1918)
Judge eternal, throned in splendours.

Holland, Hugh (1569–1635)
Epitaph on Prince Henry.
Owen Tudor.
Upon the Lines and Life of the Famous Scenic
    Poet, Master William Shakespeare.

Holland, Jane (b. 1966)
Baize Queens.
Having read up on the subject.
Loco.
Pulse.
Sleep.
Spin-Cycle.
Three Tests for Darwin Duke.
Wavelength.

Holland, Josiah Gilbert (1819–81)
Christmas Carol, A: "There's a song in the
    air!"
Laocöon! thou great embodiment.
Wanted.

Holland, Noy
Alice.

Holland, Sir Richard (c.1420–c.1485)
Douglas and the Bruce's Heart.

Holland, Walter
Christopher Street 1979.
Journal of the Plague Years, A.

Hollander, Frederick
Boys in the Backroom, The.
You Leave Me Breathless.

Hollander, John (b. 1929)
Adam's Task.
After the midwinter marriages—the bride of
    snow.
Appearance and Reality.
At the New Year.
Back to Town.
By the Sound.
Carmen Ancillae.
Comment on an Observation by One of My
    Masters.
Curse, The.
Danish Wit.
Edward Hopper's Seven A.M.
Effet de Neige.
For Both of You, the Divorce Being Final.
Great Bear, The.
Heliogabalus.
Historical Reflections.
Lady at the Castle, The.

Lady's-Maid's Song, The.
Last Words.
Late August on the Lido.
Letter to Jorge Luis Borges: Apropos of the Golem.
Like some ill-fated butterfly, the literalists.
Lion Named Passion, A.
Mad Potter, The.
Morning in the Islands.
Movie-Going.
Night Mirror, The.
Ninth of July, The.
No Foundation.
Old-Fashioned Song, An.
Old Guitar, The.
Owl.
Russian Soul II, The.
Science and Human Behavior.
So we came at last to meet, after the lights were out.
Some Walks With You.
Song at the End of a Meal.
State of Nature, A.
Sunday A.M. Not in Manhattan.
Swan and Shadow.
These two tales I tell of myself and the life I led.
To the Lady Portrayed by Margaret Dumont.
Under Cancer.
Variations on a Fragment by Trumbull Stickney.
What she and I had between us once, America.
What the Lovers in the Old Songs Thought.
"Yes, go on! This is plain talk of plainer feelings now."
Hollander, Robert (b. 1933)
You Too? Me Too—Why Not? Soda Pop.
Hollander, Vicki
Rosh Chodesh Tisheri.
Hollenbeck, Peter
Anorexia.
Höllerer, Walter
'Held Back, Like a Bow Drawn Tight.'
Hollis, Mark (b. 1908)
Careless Talk.
'Twixt Cup and Lip.
Hollo, Anselm (b. 1934)
Amazing Grace.
Buffalo—Isle of Wight Power Cable.
Discovery of LSD a True Story, The.
Dream of Instant Total Representation, The.
Godlike.
Italics.
Journey, 1966.
Le Jazz Hot.
Rain.
Shed the Fear.
That Old Sauna High.
Wasp Sex Myth (One)
Wasp Sex Myth (Two)
Wild West Workshop Poem.
Holloway, Geoffrey
Bash on Basho: Six of the Best.
Ford Castle: The Borders.
Grown-ups.
Hand for Some Others, A.
Hypochondriac.
Indian Rope Trick.
Lovers, The.
Monitors.
Non-Accidental Injury Slides.
Old Man.
Things.
Virtue of Slovenliness, The.
Holloway, John (b. 1920)
London, Greater London (After *Satire III*)
Holloway, Lucy Ariel Williams (b. 1905)
Northboun'
Holloway, Stanley (1890–1982)
Old Sam.
Holm, Bill
Advice.
Blizzard.
Playing the Goldberg Variations on Sunday Morning.

Scott Joplin.
Whale Breathing: Bartlett Cove, Alaska.
Holman, Bob (b. 1948)
Performance Poem.
Poem: "Once when I was little I knelt before an onion."
Holman, Felice (b. 1919)
I Can Fly.
Supermarket.
Holman, Jesse L. (1783–1842)
Lord, in Thy Presence Here.
Holman, M. Carl (b. 1919)
Mr. Z.
Holmes, Abiel (1763–1837)
To Thee, O God.
Who Here Can Cast His Eyes Abroad.
Holmes, Darryl (b. 1958)
Nostalgia.
Time for Guns, A.
Tubman Strong.
We Have Never Seen the Sky Light Up.
Holmes, Georgiana Klingle *See* **"Klingle, George"**
Holmes, Janet
Depressive Episode.
Fantasie Metropolitan.
Whistle.
Holmes, John (1904–62)
Evening Meal in the Twentieth Century.
Four and a Half.
Good Night! Good Night!
Map of My Country, A.
Old Professor, The.
Peace Is the Mind's Old Wilderness.
Holmes, John Haynes (1879–1964)
God of the Nations, Near and Far.
O'er Continent and Ocean.
Voice of God Is Calling, The.
Holmes, Oliver Wendell (1809–94)
Aestivation [an Unpublished Poem, by My Late Latin Tutor].
After-Dinner Poem (Terpsichore), An.
Angel of Peace, Thou Hast Wandered Too Long.
At the "Atlantic" Dinner, December 15, 1874.
Ballad of the Oysterman, The.
Cacoëthes Scribendi.
Chambered Nautilus, The.
Contentment.
Deacon's Masterpiece; or, The Wonderful "One-Hoss Shay," The.
Dorothy Q.
Flaneur, The.
God Bless Our Father-Land.
Height of the Ridiculous, The.
Illustration of a Picture.
Iris, Her Book.
Last Leaf, The.
Latter-Day Warnings.
Limerick: "Reverend Henry Ward Beecher, The."
Living Temple, The.
Lord of All Being, Throned Afar.
Many Things.
My Aunt.
Nearing the Snow-Line.
O Love Divine, That Stooped to Share.
Ode for a Social Meeting.
Old Ironsides.
On Lending a Punch-Bowl.
Our Father! While Our Hearts Unlearn.
Our Limitations.
Peau de Chagrin of State Street, The.
Ploughman, The.
Poesy.
Poet Grows Old, The.
Prelude to a Volume Printed in Raised Letters for the Blind.
Prologue.
Sea Dialogue, A.
Sympathies.
Tartarus.
Two Streams, The.
Voiceless, The.
Holmes, Timothy (b. 1936)
Deep.

Room for All.
Holofcener, Larry
Too Close for Comfort.
Holst-Warhaft, Gail
In the End Is the Body.
John 1:1 and 14.
Matthew 5:13; You are the salt of the earth.
Matthew 5:27–30; You have heard that it was said.
Old Men of Athens, The.
Holt, Jane (fl. 1701–17)
To Mr. Wren, My Valentine Six Year Old.
Holt, Rochelle Lynn
Pleasure of Feeling Inside Your Body, The.
Holtby, Mary
Answer to a Kind Enquiry.
Dawn Chorus.
Limerick: "Said Mars when entangled with Venus."
Limerick: "There once was a lass of Shalott."
Limerick: "There once was monarch called Harry."
Sister Swallow to Swinburne.
Holthaus, Gary H.
Unexpected Manna.
Hölty, Ludwig Heinrich Christoph (1748–76)
Harvest Song.
Holub, Miroslav (b. 1923)
Achilles and the Tortoise.
Brief Thoughts on Cats Growing on Trees.
Brief Thoughts on Cracks.
Brief Thoughts on Floods.
Bullfight.
Corporal Who Killed Archimedes, The.
Death in the Evening.
Fairy Tale.
Fly, The.
Forest, The.
Great and Strong.
Helping Hand, A.
History Lesson, A.
How to Paint a Perfect Christmas.
Immanuel Kant.
In the Miscroscope.
Inventions.
Jewish Cemetery at Olsany, Kafka's Grave, April, Sunny Weather, The.
Lesson, The.
Napoleon.
On the Origin of the Contrary.
Polonius.
Silence.
Suffering.
Vanishing Lung Syndrome.
Wings.
Žito the Magician.
Holway, Jamil B. (1883–1946)
Satan.
Throbbings.
Holyday, Barten (1593–1661)
Bogs, purgatory, wolves and ease, by fame.
Clay, sand, and rock, seem of a diff'rent birth.
Pride cannot see itself by mid-day light.
Holz, Arno (1863–1929)
Buddha.
Leave-Taking, A.
Phantasus.
Roses Red.
Holzer, Remy
Current 'Now, Voyager' Fantasy.
"Home, Cecil" *See* **Webster, Augusta Davies**
Homer (fl. before 700 B.C.)
Iliad, The, *sels.*
Odyssey, The, *sels.*
Homer, Ben
Sentimental Journey.
Homfray, Francis (fl. c.1817)
Thoughts on Happiness.
Homyo
Wino, always stumbling.
Hone, William (1780–1838)
Political House that Jack Built, The.
This is THE MAN—all shaven and shorn.
Honestus (fl. A.D. 40)
I would never marry a young girl or an old

woman.
Thebes.
Very day one son was drowned, The.

Hongo, Garrett Kaoru (b. 1951)
Confession of the Highway / The Hermit
Speaks.
Eruption: Puʻu Ōʻō.
Hilo: First Night Back.
Hongo Store 29 Miles Volcano Hilo, Hawaii,
The.
Legend, The.
Mendocino Rose.
O-Bon: Dance for the Dead.
Off from Swing Shift.
Pier, The.
Porphyry of Elements, A.
Redness: Thinking it Through.
Unreal Dwelling: My Years in Volcano, The.
Winnings.
Yellow Light.

Honig, Edwin (b. 1919)
1925.
Being Somebody.
Bodega, Goodbye.
November through a Giant Copper Beech.
Now, My Usefullness Over.
Tête-à-Tête.
Through You.
Walt Whitman.
Who.

Hood, Thomas (1799–1845)
Autumn.
Born in wealth and wealthily nursed.
Bridge of Sighs, The.
Butcher, A.
Choosing Their Names.
Death-Bed, The.
Death in the Kitchen.
Domestic Asides; or, Truth in Parentheses.
Dust to Dust.
Epicurean Reminiscences of a Sentimentalist.
Fair Ines.
Faithless Nelly Gray.
Faithless Sally Brown.
False Poets and True.
First Attempt in Rhyme, A.
Good Night.
Haunted House, The.
Her Accident.
Her Christening.
Her Death.
Her Education.
Her Precious Leg.
I Remember, I Remember.
Jack Hall.
Literary Reminiscences.
Miss Kilmansegg's Birth.
No!
Nocturnal Sketch, A.
On the Death of the Giraffe.
Our Village—by a Villager.
Parental Ode to My Son, Aged Three Years
and Five Months, A.
Poet's Fate, The.
Poor dear dead have been laid out in vain, The.
Public Dinner, A.
Reflection, A.
Ruth.
Serenade, A.
Silence.
Song of the Shirt, The.
Sonnet to a Sonnet.
Sonnet to Vauxhall.
Time, Hope, and Memory.
To Minerva.
To the Ocean.
World Is with Me, The.
Written in the Workhouse.

Hoofdakker, Rudi van den See **Kopland, Rutger**

Hoogerhuis, Inge
Search, The.

Hooker, Jeremy (b. 1941)
Gull on a Post.
Take a long view from Mynydd Bach.

Hookes, N. (1628–1712)
To Amanda Walking in the Garden.

Hooks, Bell (b. 1952)
Body Inside the Soul, The.
Woman's Mourning Song, The.

Hooper, Patricia
Listening to Mozart at Meadow Brook.

Hooper, Peter (b. 1919)
Pencilled by the Rain.

Hooper, Virginia (b. 1955)
Reading, A.

Hoornik, Ed. (1910–1970)
Pogrom.
To Love a Woman.

Hooton, Harry (1908–61)
Sweet Disorder in the Dress, A.

Hoover, Paul (b. 1946)
Baseball.
California.
Desire.
Family Romance.
Heart's Ease.
Letter to Einstein Beginning Dear Albert.
Poems We Can Understand.
Theoretical People.

Hope, Alec Derwent (b. 1907)
Advice to Young Ladies.
Australia.
Bed, The.
Beware of Ruins.
Beyond Phigalia.
Blason, A.
Brides, The.
Commination, A.
Death of the Bird, The.
Double Looking Glass, The.
E Questo il Nido in Che la Mia Fenice?
Easter Hymn.
Fafnir.
Faustus.
Female Principle, The.
Flower Poem.
Gateway, The.
Gloss to Matthew V 27–28.
Hay Fever.
House of God, The.
Imperial Adam.
Inscription for a War.
Lingam and the Yoni, The.
Lot and His Daughters I.
Lot and His Daughters II.
Luke 24:36–49; As they were saying this,
Jesus.
Martyrdom of St. Theresa, The.
Massacre of the Innocents.
Meditation on a Bone.
Möbius Strip-Tease.
Moschus Moschiferus.
Observation Car.
On an Engraving by Casserius.
On Shakespeare Critics.
Parabola.
Paradise Saved.
Prometheus Unbound.
Return of Persephone, The.
Tiger.
Under Sedation.
Wandering Islands, The.

Hope, Christopher (b. 1944)
Flight of the White South Africans, The.
In the Country of the Black Pig.
Lines on a Boer War Pin-up Girl Seen in the
Falcon Hotel, Bude.

**"Hope, Laurence" (Adela Florence Cory
Nicolson) (1815–1904)**
I Shall Forget.
Youth.

Hope, Melanie
Bare Floors.
INRI.
Only Days.
Sacrifice.
Sixth Grade.

Hopkins, Ellice
Life in Death.

Hopkins, Gerard Manley (1844–89)
Andromeda.

As Kingfishers Catch Fire.
At a Welsh Waterfall.
Binsey Poplars (Felled 1879)
Blessed Virgin Compared to the Air We
Breathe, The.
Bugler's First Communion, The.
Caged Skylark, The.
Candle Indoors, The.
Carrion Comfort.
Child Is Father to the Man, The.
Cuckoo, The.
Duns Scotus's Oxford.
Epithalamion: "Hark, hearer, hear what I do;
lend a thought now, make believe."
Felix Randal.
God's Grandeur.
Habit of Perfection, The.
Hailstorm in May.
Handsome Heart, The.
Harry Ploughman.
He hath abolished the old drouth.
Heaven-Haven.
How Looks the Night?
Hurrahing in Harvest.
I Wake and Feel the Fell of Dark, Not Day.
In Honour of St. Alphonsus Rodriguez.
In the Valley of the Elwy.
Inversnaid.
Lantern Out of Doors, The.
Leaden Echo and the Golden Echo, The.
Let me be to Thee as the circling bird.
May Magnificat, The.
Moonless darkness stands between.
Moonrise.
Mrs. Hopley, on Seeing Her Children Say
Goodnight to Their Father.
My Own Heart Let Me More Have Pity On.
Myself unholy, from myself unholy.
No Worst, There Is None. Pitched Past Pitch of
Grief.
Not of All My Eyes See.
Peace.
Peacock's Eye, The.
Pied Beauty.
Rainbow, The.
Sea and the Skylark, The.
Seven Epigrams, *sels.*
She Schools the Flighty Pupils of Her Eyes.
Soldier, The.
Soliloquy of One of the Spies Left in the
Wilderness, A.
Sonnet: "Patience, hard thing! the hard thing
but to pray."
Spelt from Sibyl's Leaves.
Spring.
Spring and Fall.
Starlight Night, The.
That Nature Is a Heraclitean Fire and of the
Comfort of the Resurrection.
Thee, God, I come from, to Thee go.
Thou Art Indeed Just, Lord.
To His Watch.
To R. B.
Tom's Garland: Upon the Unemployed.
Winter with the Gulf Stream.
Windhover, The.
Woodlark, The.
Wreck of the *Deutschland*, The, *sels.*

Hopkins, John (c.1520–1570)
Thou, Lord, Hast Been Our Sure Defense.
Ye people all in one accord.

Hopkins, John Henry, Jr. (1810–91)
Alleluia! Christ Is Risen Today.
God of Our Fathers, Bless This Our Land.
We Three Kings of Orient Are.

Hopkins, Josiah (1786–1862)
O Turn Ye, O Turn Ye.

Hopkins, Lee Bennett (b. 1938)
En-vi-RON-ment.
Flash.
John Hancock.
Nat Love: Black Cowboy.
Subways Are People.
This Tooth.

Hopkins, Lightnin' (1912–1982)
Death Bells.

Hopkins, Tim (1859–1936)
Limerick: "She was caught, a young girl of Uttoxeter."
Limerick: "Ther once was this ladye from Tyre."
Limerick: "Three wonderful people called Ley."
Limerick: "Viscount Stansgate, or Wedgwood, or Benn."
There's a latent queer.

Hopkinson, Francis (1737–91)
Arise and See the Glorious Sun.
At Length the Busy Day Is Done.
Battle of the Kegs, The.
O'er the Hills.

Hoppe, Anna (1889–1941)
Precious Child, So Sweetly Sleeping.

Hopper, Edward (1818–88)
Jesus Saviour, Pilot Me.
They Pray the Best Who Pray and Watch.

Horace (Quintus Horatius Flaccus) (65–8 B.C.)
Art of Poetry, The, *sels.*
Epistles, *sels.*
Epodes, *sels.*
Good bailiff of my farm, that snug domain.
If, O Maecenas, versed in lore antique.
Ne'er fash your *thumb* what *gods* decree.
Odes, *sels.*
Old Malediction, An.
Satires, *sels.*
What young Raw Muisted Beau Bred at his Glass.
Young Men Come Less Often, The—Isn't It So?

Horan, Robert (b. 1922)
By Hallucination Visited.
Little City.
Prometheus.
Soft Swimmer, Winter Swan.

Horder, John (b. 1936)
Sick Image of My Father Fades, The.

Horgan, Paul (b. 1903)
Now Evening Puts Amen to Day.
Tintype of a Private in the Fifteenth Georgia Infantry.

Horikawa, Lady (*fl.* 12th cent.)
How long will it last?
Will he always love me?

Horne, Frank (b. 1899)
Kid Stuff.
Mamma!
On Seeing Two Brown Boys in a Catholic Church.
Patience.
To James.
To "Chick."
To Mother.
To You.
Walk.

Horne, Nanna Banyiwa (b. 1949)
Messages.
Note to My Liberal Feminist Sister, A.

Horne, Richard Henry [*or* Hengist] (1803–84)
Plough, The.

Horoku (d. 1878)
Mountain temple.

Horovitz, Frances (1938–83)
Do You Not Know that I Need to Touch You.
Loving You.
Messenger, The.
Moon.
Night-Piece.
Woman's Dream, The.
Women.

Horton, George Moses (1797?–1883?)
Creditor to His Proud Debtor, The.
Division of an Estate.
Early Affection.
General Grant—the Hero of the War.
George Moses Horton, Myself.
Lover's Farewell, The.
New Fashions.
On Hearing of the Intention of a Gentleman to Purchase the Poet's Freedom.
On Liberty and Slavery.

Snaps for Dinner, Snaps for Breakfast, and Snaps for Supper.

Horvát, András Szkhárosi (*fl.* early 16th cent.)
Dreadful are the happenings of our evil ages.
Hurry up, Christendom, think about salvation.
You live in dishonor grave, Dukes and Mighty Princes.

Horváth, Ádám Pálóczi (1760–1820)
Dance of the Magyars, The.
Lover Under Suspicion.

Hoshi, Saigyo *See* **Saigyo**

Hoskyns [*or* Hoskins], John (1566–1638)
Absence.
Bellows Maker of Oxford, The.
Epitaph, An: On a Man for Doing Nothing.
Epitaph on Sir Walter Pye.
Epitaph on the Fart in the Parliament House.
Here lies the man that madly slain.
His Own Epitaph, When He Was Sick.
Of the Loss of Time.
On a Contentious Companion.
On a Whore.
On One That Lived Ingloriously.
To His Son Bennet.
Upon a Fool.
Upon One of the Maids of Honour to Queen Elizabeth.

Hosmer, Frederick Lucian (1840–1929)
From Age to Age They Gather.
Hear, Hear, O Ye Nations.
O Beautiful, My Country.
O Day of Light and Gladness.
Through Willing Heart and Helping Hand.

Hoss, E. Embree (1849–1919)
O God, Great Father, Lord, and King.

Hosshin (13th cent.)
Coming, all is clear, no doubt about it.

Hotham, Gary
Coffee.
Distant thunder.
Every night.
Fog.
Home early.
Letting.
Library book, The.
Morning fog.
Morning quiet.
My wife still asleep.
Night comes.
On the ceiling.
Quietly.
Stalled car.
Sun and moon.
Sunset dying.
This loneliness.
Unsnapping.
Up late.
Waiting room quiet.

Hottentot Oral Tradition
Song for the Sun That Disappeared behind the Rainclouds.

Hou (d. 1811)
Encased by winter.

Hough, Graham (b. 1908)
Age of Innocence.

Houghton, Firman
Mr. Frost Goes South to Boston.

Houghton, Liz
Caustic Soda.
Saturday with Dad.

Housman, Alfred Edward (1859–1936)
1887.
African Lion, The.
Along the field as we came by.
As into the Garden Elizabeth Ran.
Astronomy.
Be still, my soul, be still; the arms you bear are brittle.
Because I liked you better.
Bredon Hill.
Carpenter's Son, The.
Could man be drunk for ever.
Crossing Alone the Nighted Ferry.
Deserter, The.
Diffugere Nives.

Easter Hymn.
Eight O'Clock.
Elephant, or the Force of Habit, The.
Epitaph.
Epitaph on an Army of Mercenaries.
Fairies Break Their Dances, The.
Fancy's Knell.
Far in a western brookland.
Farewell to barn and stack and tree.
Fragment of a Greek Tragedy.
Fragment of an English Opera.
From Far, from Eve and Morning.
G. K. Chesterton on His Birth.
Grenadier.
Half-way, for one commandment broken.
Hallelujah!
He would not stay for me; and who can wonder?
Hell Gate.
Her Strong Enchantments Failing.
Ho, everyone that thirsteth.
I Counsel You Beware.
I hoed and trenched and weeded.
I to my perils.
If it chance your eye offend you.
If truth in hearts that perish.
Immortal Part, The.
In midnights of November.
In valleys green and still.
Infant Innocence.
Inhuman Henry.
Is my team plowing?
Isle of Portland, The.
It nods and curtseys and recovers.
Jack and Jill.
Lads in Their Hundreds, The.
Lancer.
Laws of God, the Laws of Man, The.
Loitering with a vacant eye.
Look not in my eyes, for fear.
Loveliest of Trees, the Cherry Now.
March.
Mark 16:19–20; So then the Lord Jesus, after.
My dreams are of a field afar.
New Mistress, The.
Night Is Freezing Fast, The.
Now hollow fires burn out to black.
Oh see how thick the goldcup flowers.
Oh stay at home, my lad, and plough.
Oh, When I Was In Love.
Oh who is that young sinner with the handcuffs on his wrists?
Olive, The.
On moonlit heath and lonesome bank.
On the idle hill of summer.
On Wenlock Edge.
Oracles, The.
Others, I am not the first.
Parta Quies.
Pope, The.
Purple William or The Liar's Doom.
Rainy Pleiads Wester, The.
Reveille.
Shades of Night, The.
Shake hands, we shall never be friends, all's over.
Shot? so quick, so clean an ending?
Sigh that heaves the grasses, The.
Sinner's Rue.
Soldier from the Wars Returning.
Some can gaze and not be sick.
Stars Have Not Dealt Me, The.
Stars, I Have Seen Them Fall.
Tell Me Not Here [It Needs Not Saying].
Terence, This Is Stupid Stuff.
They Say My Verse Is Sad: No Wonder.
To an Athlete Dying Young.
True Lover, The.
Wake Not for the World-heard Thunder.
We'll to the Woods No More.
Welsh Marches, The.
When Adam walked in Eden young.
When I Was One-and-Twenty.
When I Watch the Living Meet.
When smoke stood up from Ludlow.
When the bells justle in the tower.
When the Eye of Day Is Shut.

When the lad for longing sighs.
White in the moon the long road lies.
With Rue My Heart Is Laden.
World goes none the lamer, The.
Yon Far Country.
Yonder See the Morning Blink.

Houston, Douglas (b. 1947)
Lines on a Van's Dereliction.
Night Out, A.

Houston, Libby (b. 1941)
I can lift gravity's stern glower.
Old Woman and the Sandwiches, The.
Story of Canobie Dick, The.

Houston, Peyton (1910–94)
Sonnet Variations.

Hovanessian, Diana Der
Exiles.
Inside Green Eyes, Black Eyes.
Mixed Marriage.
On Commonwealth Avenue and Brattle Street.
Two Voices.

Hove, Chenjerai
Child's Parliament.
Country Life.
Lost Bird.
Migratory Bird.
Other Syllabus, The.
Red Hills of Home.
You Will Forget.

Hovell-Thurlow, Edward, 2nd Baron Thurlow (1781–1829)
May.

Hovey, Richard See also **Carman, Bliss**

Hovey, Richard (1864–1900)
Accident in Art.
At Sea.
Barney McGee.
Eleazar Wheelock.
Evening on the Potomac.
Mocking-Bird, The.
Sea Gypsy, The.
Song by the Shore, A.
Verlaine.

Howard, Anne, Duchess of Arundel (1557–1630)
Good Shepherd's Sorrow for the Death of His Beloved Son, The.

Howard, Bart (b. 1915)
Fly Me to the Moon (In Other Words).
Who Besides You.
Would You Believe It?
Year After Year.

Howard, Ben (b. 1944)
Break.
River's Answer, The.
River Song.

Howard, Frances Minturn
Sampler from Haworth.

Howard-Jones, Stuart (1904–74)
Hibernia.

Howard, Lady Margaret (1515–78)
Now that ye be assemblld heer.
Sueden chance ded mak me mues, The.

Howard, Leonard (1699?–1764)
Humours of the King's Bench Prison, a Ballad, The.

Howard, Richard (b. 1929)
209 Canal.
1915: A Pre-Raphaelite Ending, London.
After 65.
Again for Hephaistos, the Last Time.
At the Monument to Pierre Louÿs.
Author of Christine, The.
Bonnard; a Novel.
Crepuscular.
Far Cry after a Close Call, A.
Giovanni da Fiesole on the Sublime.
Last Words.
Mrs. Eden in Town for the Day.
Nadar.
Natural History.
Nikolaus Mardruz to his Master Ferdinand, Count of Tyrol, 1565.
On Arrival.
Oystering.
Recipe for an Ocean in the Absence of the Sea.

Stanzas in Bloomsbury.
Venetian Interior, 1889.
Vocational Guidance, with Special Reference to the Annunciation of Simone Martini.
Wildflowers.

Howe, Fanny (b. 1940)
Basic Science.
Bathroom.
Doubt.
First Chance Twice.
From a donkey, excuse me, one lesson is given.
My Broken Heart.
Scattered Light.
Seeking Out His Face in a Cup.
Set golden butter out in a dish.
Starlet.
What We Learned.

Howe, Julia Ward (1819–1910)
Battle Hymn [or Battle-Hymn] of the Republic, The.
House of Rest, The.
Kosmos.
Lost Jewel, The.
My Last Dance.
Outside the Party.
Robert E. Lee.
Soul-Hunter, The.
Street Yarn.
Wild Night, A.

Howe, Marie (b. 1950)
Attic, The.
How Some of It Happened.
Kiss, The.
Sixth Grade.
What the Living Do.

Howe, Solomon (1750–1835)
Our Kind Creator.

Howe, Susan (b. 1937)
Age of earth and us all chattering.
Bride's Day.
He plodded away through drifts of ice.
In its first dumb form.
Right or ruth.
Sabbath and sweet spices.
Say that a ballad.
Scattering as Behavior Toward Risk.
Silence Wager Stories.
Thorow.
Twenty lines of.
White Foolscap/Book of Cordelia.

Howe, William Walsham (1823–97)
Funeral Hymn.

Howell, Christopher
Liberty and Ten Years of Return.
Memories of Mess Duty and the War.
Reminder to the Current President, A.

Howell, James (1594–1666)
Elegy upon His Tomb in Herndon-Hill Church, Erected by His Wife, Who Speaks, An.
Upon Dr. Davies's British Grammar.
Upon the Poet of His Time, Ben Jonson: His Honoured Friend and Father.

Howells, William Dean (1837–1920)
Earliest Spring.
Empty House, The.
Forlorn.
November.
Royal Portraits, The.

Howes, Barbara (b. 1914)
Chimera.
Danaë.
Death of a Vermont Farm Woman.
Home Leave.
Letter from the Caribbean, A.
On a Bougainvillaea Vine at the Summer Palace [or in Haiti].
On Galveston Beach.
Out Fishing.
Portrait of the Boy as Artist.
Wild Geese Flying.

Howitt, Mary (1799–1888)
Cry of the Animals, The.
Dying Child, The.
Spider and the Fly, The.

Hoyos, Angela de (b. 1940)
Long Live the Potato: Viva la Papa!

Hoyt, Clement
Down from the bridge rail.
Hair, in my comb's teeth.
Hallowe'en mask, A.
In that empty house.
In that lightning flash.
Leaves moil in the yard.
Pretty matron, The.
Those camellias.
While the guests order.

Hoyu (d. late 17th cent.)
Praise to skies.

Hristic, Jovan (b. 1933)
That Night They All Gathered on the Highest Tower.

Hsi-chün (fl. c.105 B.C.)
Lament of Hsi-chün.
Lost Horizon.

Hsi K'ang (c.223–262)
Sent to the Hsiu-ts'ai on His Entry into the Army.
Taoist Song.

Hsiang Chi (232–202 B.C.) (Hsiang Yü)
Song of Kai-hsia.

Hsiang Ssu (fl. 9th cent.)
Ailing Japanese Monk, The.

Hsiao Kang
Flying Petals.
Pheasant on His Morning Flight, A.
Rising in Winter.
Watching a Lonely Wild Goose at Nightfall.

Hsiao Yen
Spring Song of Tzu-yeh, A.

Hsiao-yün-shih-hai-ya See **Kuan Yün-shih**

Hsieh Chin (1369–1415)
Government wine of Peking is sweeter than honey, The.
I still remember Conch-Shell Slope, west of the River Tzu.
Inscribed on a Painting of Dragons by Ch'en So-weng.
Playful Poem on a Chicken Egg, A.
Poem on a Little Pine, A.
Sandal Mountain.
Song of Cursive Calligraphy.
To Hsiao Shih-ying.
To the Fortuneteller Hsüeh T'ieh-yai.
Wait until I too hang up my carriage.
What Does the Little Boy Love?

Hsieh Hui-lien (397–433)
Fulling Cloth for Clothes.
Rhyme-Prose on the Snow.

Hsieh Ling-yün (385–433)
By T'ing Yang Waterfall.
Climbing a Solitary Islet in the River.
Climbing Stone Drum Mountain.
Climbing Stone Drum Mountain Above the Shores of Shang-shu.
Climbing the Tower by the Pond.
Crossing the Mountain, I Follow the Chin-chu River.
Entering the Mouth of P'eng-li Lake.
Exchange of Poems by Tung-yang Stream, An.
From Chin-Chu Creek, Past the Ridge, Along the Stream.
Journeying by Stream: Following Chin-chu Torrent I Cross the Mountains.
Leaving West Archery Hall at Dusk.
Night: Setting out from Shih-Kuan Pavilion.
On Climbing the Highest Peak of Stone Gate Mountain.
On My Way from South Mountain to North Mountain, I Glance at the Scenery from the Lake.
Passing through My Shih-ning Estate.
Passing White Banks Pavilion.
Replying to a Poem from My Cousin Hui-lien.
Scene from South Hill to North Hill Passing the Lake.
Spending the Night on Stone Gate Mountain.
Visiting Pai-an Pavilion.
Written on the Lake, Returning from the Retreat at Stone Cliff.

Written on the Lake While Returning to Stone Cliff Hermitage.

Hsieh Ngao (*fl.* 13th cent.)
Wind Tossed Dragons.

Hsieh Shang (308–57)
Song of the Thoroughfare.

Hsieh T'iao (464–99)
Ascend the Three Mountains Toward the Evening: Looking Back at the Capital.
Complaint Near the Jade Stairs.
Jade Steps Plaint.
Roaming the East Field.
Song of the Men of Chin-ling.
To Hsuan-Ch'eng, Past Hsin-Lin-P'u, Toward Pan-Ch'iao.
Viewing the Three Lakes.

Hsin Ch'i-chi (1140–1207)
To an Old Tune.
Tune: "Full River Red."
Tune: "Green Jade Cup"—Lantern Festival.
Tune: "Groping for Fish."
Tune: "Immortal's Auspicious Crane, An"—On Plum Blossoms.
Tune: "Moon of the Western River."
Tune: "Partridge Sky"—Written at the Po-shan Monastery.
Tune: "Partridge Sky" At Po-shan Monastery.
Tune: "Partridge Sky" For a Friend.
Tune: "Picking Mulberry Seeds" Written on a Wall en route to Po-shan.
Tune: "Pure Serene Music" En Route to Po-shan.
Tune: "Pure Serene Music" Rural Life.
Tune: "Slow Song of Chu Ying-t'ai"—Late Spring.
Tune: "Song of Divination" Using Quotations from *Chuang-tzu*.
Tune: "Song of the Southern Country"—Presented to a Courtesan.
Tune: "Spring in Ch'in's Garden."
Tune: "Spring in the Ch'in Garden."
Tune: "The Bodhisattva's Golden Headdress."
Tune: "The Dark Clouds of Ch'u" Visiting the Rainy Crag Alone.
Tune: Ugly Rogue.

Hsü Chün-ch'ien (*fl.* 6th cent.)
Beginning of Spring—A Stroll with My Wife.
Sitting Up with My Wife on New Year's Eve.

Hsü Chung-hsing (1517–78)
Cane of Ch'iung Bamboo, The.
How brave the peasant who lives beside the lake.
I shake my robe—and mists disperse, leaving clear autumn sky.
This metal is engraved with Shang-style markings.
Traveling by Boat at Shun-ch'ang.
Trees are ancient, thick with patterns of moss, The.
Who would have thought that a disease of the ordinary world.

Hsu Hsuan (916–91)
Lu-lung Village, Autumn.

Hsü Kan (171–217)
Deepening shadows bring on sorrow, The.
Drifting clouds, distant and vast, The.
Sadly, sadly the season draws to an end.
Steep, steep the lofty mountain peak.
Wife's Thoughts, The.

Hsü Ling (507–583)
Waters of Lung-t'ou, The.
Teleg Song.

Hsü Pen (1335–80)
Ballad of the Ferocious Tiger.
Ballad of the Merchant.
Deserted Estate at South Garden, The.
Five Things Sought For—In the Manner of Han Wo.
Following the Rhymes of Kao Chi-ti's Poem: "We Had Planned to Travel to Cloud Cliff But Couldn't Because of Rain."
Hermit Feng's Residence on the Lake.
Hermit Li's Herb Garden Retreat at T'ung-ch'uan.
In Harmony with Kao "The Second" Ch'i's Poem "On Hearing a P'i-p'a Played Next

Door."
Mountain of green trees and orioles everywhere!
Mountain Residence of Secretary Cheng Ching-ssu, The.
Poem on Buddha's Begging Bowl—For Hui-ku, His Holiness Ming, A.
Saying Goodbye to a Monk from Japan.
To a Hermit in the Mountains.
To the Filial Son, Ts'ui.
Tomb of the Singing Girl Ch'iung-i, The.

Hsü Tsai-ssu (*fl.* c.1300)
On Love.
Tune: "Clear River, a Prelude"—Lovesickness.
Tune: "Joy All Under Heaven"—Sunset on the Western Hill.

Hsü Wei (1521–93)
Abandoning the Plans of Visiting West Lake.
Buddhist Monk Cut and Burned His Own Flesh to Make the Rains Stop—A Man From His Native Place Asked Me to Write a Poem to Send to Him, A.
Colossal. / Like towers and pavilions from the flat plain.
Fifth day of the fifth month.
From Chekiang I Went to Hsin-an and Climbed Even-with-the-Clouds Mountain. On the Way Back There Were Many Beautiful Sights at the Inns Where I Stayed and Yet I Could Not Write One Word of Poetry. When I Got Back to the Main Road I Wrote These Four L.
I Once Did a Bamboo Painting for Somebody—Now He Wants Me to Do Another. I Have Written This to Answer Him.
I Tried to Exchange Two Paintings for Some Grain But Failed.
Inscribed on a Painting.
Inscribed on a Painting of Windy Bamboo, to Be Presented to Tzu-kan.
Inscribed on Paintings for the People of Hangchow.
Kite, A.
Lotus.
Mushroom Gatherer Deep in the Mountains Among the White Clouds, A.
On the Road Through the Wu-i Mountains—Making Fun of Chia-tse for Falling Off His Horse.
Painting of People Strolling through a Pine Forest, A.
Returning from the Seventy-Two Mountains.
Songs of Yen-ching.
To Hsü Shih-t'ing.
Two Fish by a Willow Embankment.

Hsüan-yeh (1654–1722)
Lines in Praise of a Self-Chiming Clock.

Hsüan-ying *See* **Su Man-shu**

Hsueh Chao-yun (900–32)
Oriole Song.
To the Tune: In the Hills.

Hsüeh T'ao (768–831)
1.
2.
3.
Autumn Spring.
Blossoms crowd the branches: too beautiful to endure.
Dog Parted from Her Master.
Farewell to a Friend.
Gazing at Spring.
Listening to a Monk Play the Reed Pipes.
Lotus-Gathering Boat.
Moon, The.
Weaving Love-Knots.
Willow Catkins.
Wind.

Hu Chih-yu (1227–1293)
Love Song: "Lazy flowers brew honey for the bees."

Hu Shih (*fl.* c.1927)
Dream and Poetry.

Huang Ching-jen (1749–83)
Mixed Emotions.
Questing-for-Spring Arbor.

Sentiments on New Year's Eve in the Year Kuei-ssu.
Traveling at Break of Day.

Huang E (1498–1569)
Pearl-teardrops roll and gather.

Huang O [*or* **Huang Ho**] (1498–1569)
Farewell to a Southern Melody, A.
To the Tune "A Floating Cloud Crosses Enchanted Mountain."
To the Tune "Red Embroidered Shoes."
To the Tune "The Fall of a Little Wild Goose."
To the tune 'Soaring Clouds.'

Huang Shu (1131–91)
Tune: "Song of River Goddess"—Mooring My Boat at Fen-shui at Night.

Huang T'ing-chien (1045–1105)
Buffalo Boy.
Clear Bright.
Climbing K'uai Pavilion.
Following the Rhymes of Chang Hsün, in My Study in Late Spring.
Following the Rhymes of Fellow Graduate P'ei Chung-mou.
Following the Rhymes of Wang An-shih's Poem "Inscribed on the Wall of the Temple of Western Great Unity."
Inscribed on a Scroll "Plum Blossoms by the Water."
Living in Exile at Ch'ien-nan.
On a Painting of Ants and Butterflies.
Out in the Snow, Spending the Night at the New Stockade, Extremely Depressed.
Passing Hung-fu Monastery with Yüan-ming: Inscribed in Jest.
Peach and plum blossoms, speechless, keep swaying in the wind.
Short on brains, long on stupidity, the mantis seizes the cicada.
Song of the Clear River.
Teasing Hsiao-te, My Son.
To Go with Shih K'o's Painting of an Old Man Tasting Vinegar.
Tune: "A Thousand Autumns."
Tune: "Ch'ing-P'ing Song."
Tune: "Courtyard Full of Fragrance, The."
Tune: "Joy of Returning to the Fields."
Tune: "Partridge Sky."
Tune: "Pleasure of Returning to the Fields: A Prelude."
Tune: "Pure Serene Music."
Upon Passing the Homestead.

Huang Tsun-hsien (1848–1905)
Recuperating in Chang Villa.
Sent in Lieu of a Letter to Shih-wu, Lan-ku, and Other Friends.
Spending the Night in an Inn at Swatow and Writing about My Feelings, Sent to Liang Shih-wu.
To Send Away Melancholy.

Hubbard, Sue
Letter.

Hubbell, Lindley Williams
Beer Bottles.
Birth-Hour.
Ordovician Fossil Algae.
Sounds.
Student who sat facing me on the Osaka express, A.
Waka.

Hubbell, Patricia (b. 1928)
Owl of the Greenwood.
Shadows.
Streetcleaner's Lament, The.

Huber, Meg
Potato Cellar.

Huber, Mida
Song of Home.

Hubert, Sir Francis (1568 *or* 1569–1629)
Joseph in Carcere.
This highest scholar in the school of sin.

Huch, Ricarda (1864–1947)
Young Girl.

Huchel, Peter (1903–81)
Garden of Theophrastus, The.
In the rush odour of Danish meadows.

King Lear.
Landscape Beyond Warsaw.
Psalm.
Roads.
Winter Billet.

Hucks, Joseph (d. 1800)
To Freedom.

Huddle, David (b. 1942)
Almost Going.
Bac Ha.
Cousin.
Delivering the Times, 1952–1944.
Gregory's House.
Holes Commence Falling.
Miss Florence Jackson.
Music.
My Daddy, Whenever He Went Some Place.
Theory.
Tour of Duty.
Town History, 1917.
Vermont.
Words.

Hudgins, Andrew (b. 1951)
After the Wilderness.
Air, The.
Around the Campfire.
At Chancellorsville.
Buddy.
Burial Detail.
Childhood of the Ancients.
Dead Christ.
Elegy for My Father, Who Is Not Dead.
Hereafter, The.
Persistence of Nature in Our Lives, The.
Praying Drunk.
Rosie.
Serenades in Virginia.
Soldier on the Marsh, A.
Southern Crescent Was on time, The.
Telling, The.
Tree.
Two Ember Days in Alabama.
Versification of a Passage from Penthouse.

Hueffer, Ford Madox *See* **Ford, Ford Madox**

Huelsenbeck, Richard (1892–1974)
"We Hardly."

Huelsenbeck, Richard (1892–1974), Marcel Janko *and* **Tristan Tzara**
L'amiral cherche une maison à louer.

Huerta, Efraín (1914–1982)
Declaration of Hate.
Men of Dawn, The.
This Is a Love.

Hufana, Alejandrino
Contemporary.
Floating Epitaphs, Their Possible Explanations in Poro Point.
From the Raw.
Insides of Alfred Hitchcock, The.

Huff, Robert (b. 1924)
Course, The.

Hugh, Primate of Orleans (1094–1160)
Lament for Troy.

Hughes, Cyril
Limerick: "Remember when you are bemusing."

Hughes, Frieda (b. 1960)
Bird.
Birds.
Different Voice, The.
Foxes.
In the Shadow of Fire.
Kookaburra.
Laszlo.

Hughes, John (1677–1720)
Thought in a Garden, A.

Hughes, John (b. 1962)
Dog Day Lesson.
Knowingness.
Respect for Law and Order, A.

Hughes, John Ceiriog ("Ceiriog") (1832–87)
Epilogue to Alun Mabon.
Mountain Stream, The.

Hughes, Langston (1902–67)
Advice.

American Heartbreak.
Angola Question Mark.
April Rain Song.
Aunt Sue's Stories.
Backlash Blues, The.
Bad Luck Card.
Bad Man.
Bad Morning.
Ballad of the Girl Whose Name Is Mud.
Ballad of the Landlord.
Ballad of the Man Who's Gone.
Bar.
Be-Bop Boys.
Blue Monday.
Blues at Dawn.
Blues, The.
Boogie: 1 A.M.
Brass Spittoons.
Café: 3 A.M.
Casualty.
Catch.
Children's Rhymes.
Chord.
College Formal: Renaissance Casino.
Comment on Curb.
Cross.
Cubes.
Cultural Exchange.
Curious.
Danse Africaine.
Dead in There.
Deferred.
Democracy.
Dinner Guest: Me.
Dive.
Down and Out.
Dream Boogie.
Dream Boogie: Variation.
Dream Variation[s].
Drum.
Early Evening Quarrel.
Easy Boogie.
Ennui.
Esthete in Harlem.
Evil.
Fact.
Feet O' Jesus.
50–50.
Fire.
Florida Road Workers.
Frederick Douglass: 1817–1895.
Gal's Cry for a Dying Lover.
Gauge.
Genius Child.
Request.
Good Morning.
Gypsy Man.
Hard Daddy.
Harlem.
Harlem Sweeties.
Heaven, Heaven, Heaven Is the Place.
High to Low.
Homecoming.
Homesick Blues.
Hope.
House in Taos, A.
I, Too.
In Time of Silver Rain.
Island.
Jam Session.
Jazz Band in a Parisian Cabaret.
Jazzonia.
Juke Box Love Song.
Junior Addict.
Justice.
Ku Klux.
Lady's Boogie.
Let America Be America Again.
Letter.
Letter to the Academy.
Life Is Fine.
Lincoln Monument: Washington.
Little Lyric (of Great Importance)
Little Old Letter.
Little Song.
Lord Has a Child, The.
Lover's Return.

Low to High.
Luck.
Madam and Her Madam.
Madam and the Census Man.
Madam and the Minister.
Madam and the Rent Man.
Madam and the Wrong Visitor.
Madam's Calling Cards.
Madam's Past History.
Madrid—1937.
Mama and Daughter.
Merry-Go-Round.
Minstrel Man.
Miss Blues'es Child.
Morning After.
Mother to Son.
Mulatto.
My People.
Mystery.
Necessity.
Negro Servant.
Negro Speaks of Rivers, The.
Neighbor.
Neon Signs.
Night Funeral in Harlem.
Nightmare Boogie.
Note on Commercial Theatre.
Old Walt.
125th Street.
Passing.
Peace.
Personal.
Piggy-back.
Poem: "I loved my friend."
Preference.
Projection.
Question.
Question and Answer.
Railroad Avenue.
Red Silk Stockings.
Same in Blues.
Saturday Night.
Sea Calm.
Shame on You.
Share-Croppers.
Shepherd's Song at Christmas.
Silhouette.
Sister.
Situation.
Sliver of Sermon.
So Long.
Song for a Dark Girl.
Songs.
Stars.
Still Here.
Stony Lonesome.
Strange Hurt.
Street Song.
Subway Face.
Subway Rush Hour.
Suicide's Note.
Summer Night.
Sunday by the Combination.
Sweet Words on Race.
Sylvester's Dying Bed.
Tag.
Tambourines.
Tell Me.
Testimonial.
Theme for English B.
Third Degree.
This Little House Is Sugar.
Today.
Tomorrow.
Trumpet Player.
Ultimatum: Kid to Kid.
Un-American Investigators.
Uncle Tom.
Up-Beat.
Vagabonds.
Visitors to the Black Belt.
Wake.
Warning: Augmented.
Water-Front Streets.
Weary Blues, The.
What?
When Sue Wears Red.

Where? When? Which?
Who But the Lord?
Winter Moon.
Without Benefit of Declaration.
World War II.
Young Gal's Blues.

Hughes, Richard (1900–76)
Burial of the Spirit of a Young Poet.
Felo de Se.
Gipsy-Night.
Glaucopis.
Image, The.
Invocation to the Muse.
Lover's Reply to Good Advice.
Old Cat Care.
On Time.
Ruin, The.
Sermon, The.
Tramp.
Walking Road, The.
Winter.

Hughes, Selwyn
Got No Shame.
Home on Palm.

Hughes, Ted (1930–98)
All the dreary Sunday morning.
Amulet.
Bear, The.
Bones.
Buzz in the Window.
Cat and Mouse.
Childish Prank, A.
Christmas Card.
Cleopatra to the Asp.
Crow.
Crow and the Birds.
Crow's First Lesson.
Crow's Last Stand.
Crow's Theology.
Crueller than owl or eagle.
Curlews Lift.
Day He Died, The.
Dove, A.
Dove-Breeder, The.
Esther's Tomcat.
Examination at the Womb-Door.
February 17th.
Full Moon and Little Frieda.
God, A.
Grin, A.
Hawk Roosting.
Heptonstall.
Her Husband.
Horses, The.
Howling of Wolves, The.
I can understand the haggard eyes.
I See a Bear.
I suppose you just gape and let your gaspings.
Kreutzer Sonata.
Lake, The.
Lark begins to go up, The.
Leaves.
Like those flailing flames.
Man Seeking Experience Enquires His Way of
a Drop of Water, The.
Matthew 27:45–56; Now from the sixth hour
there was darkness.
Minstrel's Song.
Modest Proposal, A.
Moon-Hops.
My idleness curdles.
New Year's [or Year] Song.
November.
October Robin, An.
October Salmon, An.
Old Age Gets Up.
Orf.
Other, The.
Otter, An.
Out.
Owl's Song.
Pibroch.
Pike.
Relic.
River.
River in March, The.
Roe-Deer.

Roger the Dog.
Rooks love excitement.
Second Glance at a Jaguar.
September.
Seven Sorrows, The.
Six Young Men.
Snowdrop.
Suddenly his poor body.
Swifts.
Telegraph Wires.
That Moment.
That Morning.
Theology.
Thistles.
Thought-Fox, The.
Thrushes.
To Paint a Water Lily.
Tractor.
Urn Burial.
View of a Pig.
Walt.
Water.
Whether you say it, think it, know it.
Wilfred Owen's Photographs.
Wind.
Wodwo.
Yesterday He Was Nowhere to Be Found.
You are a wild look—out of an egg.
You Hated Spain.

Hughes, Thomas (fl. 1818–65)
Cheese for the Archdeacon, A.

Hugo, Richard (1923–82)
Death of the Kapowsin Tavern.
Degrees of Gray in Philipsburg.
Driving Montana.
Elegy: "I expected him to look dead in the
casket."
Ferniehirst Castle.
Freaks at Spurgin Road Field, The.
From Altitude, the Diamonds.
Graves at Elkhorn.
In Your Bad Dream.
In Your Dream after Falling in Love.
In Your Racing Dream.
In Your Young Dream.
Lady in Kicking Horse Reservoir, The.
Letter to Bell from Missoula.
Letter to Birch from Deer Lodge.
Letter to Blessing from Missoula.
Letter to Gale from Ovando.
Letter to Goldbarth from Big Fork.
Letter to Haislip from Hot Springs.
Letter to Hill from St. Ignatius.
Letter to Levertov from Butte.
Letter to Libbey from St. Regis.
Letter to Logan from Milltown.
Letter to Mantsch from Havre.
Letter to Oberg from Pony.
Letter to Reed from Lolo.
Letter to Scanlon from Whitehall.
Letter to Wagoner from Port Townsend.
Letter to Welch from Browning.
Map of Montana in Italy, A.
Milltown Union Bar, The.
Missoula Softball Tournament.
My Buddy.
Napoli Again.
Neighbor.
Open Country.
Places and Ways to Live.
River Now, The.
Salt Water Story.
To Women.
View from Cortona, A.
Way a Ghost Dissolves, The.
What Thou Lovest Well Remains American.
White Center.
Yards of Sarajevo, The.

Hugo, Victor (1802–85)
After the Battle.
After the Voices.
Another Voice.
At the Window in the Dark.
At Villequier.
Be Like the Bird.
Boaz Asleep.
Bridge, The.

Broken Vase, The.
Conscience.
Djinns, The.
Et Nox Facta Est.
Expiation, *sels.*
Genesis of Butterflies, The.
Grandmother, The.
Grave and the Rose, The.
Heard on the Mountain.
I could see, far above my head, a black speck.
Inquisition, The.
Jeanne was holed up (pitch darkness; bread
and water)
More about God (But with Some Reservations)
More Strong Than Time.
Night of the Fourth: A Recollection, The.
Open Windows.
Poor Children, The.
Russia 1812.
Set Him Apart!
Shepherds and Flocks.
Sound, sound forever, trumpet-calls of thought!
Sunset, A.
That Night.
Tomorrow, when the meadows grow.
Trumpet of Judgement, The.
Words in the Shadow.

Huidobro, Vincente (1893–1948)
Ars Poetica.
Blind.
Canto 2 (excerpts)
Canto I (excerpt)
Cow Boy.
Eiffel Tower.
Express.
Here and now I have to dilute myself into
many things.
I am king.
Midnight.
Morning.
New Song.
Poetry Is a Heavenly Crime.
Quiet Spaces.
Sailor.
So you're a windmill.

Hull, Akasha (Gloria) (b. 1944)
Another Rhythm.

Hull, Coral
Flying Kangaroos.

Hull, Lynda
Lost Fugue for Chet.
Midnight Reports.
Night Waitress.
Ornithology.
Red Velvet Jacket.
Window, The.

Hulme, Doris
In grandfather's house I ran up and down.

Hulme, Keri (b. 1947)
He Hola.

Hulme, Thomas Ernest (1883–1917)
Above the Dock.
Autumn.
Conversion.
Embankment, The (The fantasia of a fallen
gentleman on a cold, bitter night)
Image.
Trenches: St Eloi.

Hulü Chin (fl. 6th cent.)
Song of the Tölös.

Hume, Alexander (c.1556–1609)
O perfite light, quhilk schaid away.
Of Gods Omnipotencie.
Of the Day Estivall.

Hume, Christine (b. 1968)
Birthday.
Dialogue of Thunder.
Dirty Money.
Helicopter Wrecked on a Hill.
Various Readings of an Illegible Postcard.

Humes, Harry
Butterfly Effect, The.

Hummell, Austin (b. 1963)
I Never Saw a Goddess Go.
Salt Longing.

Saraband.
Sculpture Garden.
Hummer, T. R. (b. 1950)
Ideal, The.
Poem in the Shape of a Saxophone.
Train Wreck, 1890: My Grandmother Lies
Down with the Dead.
Humphrey, Dolores de Iruretagoyena de
April in Houston.
Hope.
No Immunity.
Humphreys, Emyr (b. 1919)
Ancestor Worship.
Apple Tree and a Pig, An.
From Father to Son.
Humphries, Barry ("Edna Everage") (b. 1934)
Edna's Alphabet.
Edna's Hymn.
Humphries, Rolfe (1894–1969)
Dafydd ap Gwilym Resents the Winter.
Europa.
For My Ancestors.
From the Green Book of Yfan.
Test Paper.
Hungarian Oral Tradition
Blessed Pentecost.
By Three Kinds of Flowers I'm Challenged.
Dead Brother, The.
Dear Child, My Darling Daughter.
Fire Is Laid, The.
Fisherman, Hey!
Hey There, Peacock.
I Chant of the Miracle Stag (Christian Version)
I Chant of the Miracle Stag (Shamanistic
Version)
I Left My Home.
Ilona Budai, The Cruel Mother.
Katie Kádár.
King's Courtyard, The.
Mallard Nests, The.
Rare Is the Wheat-Field in Which There's No
Blemish.
Shaman's Song.
There Was a Prince.
Wife of Master Mason Clement, The.
Hunt, G. W.
Dogs of war are loose and the rugged russian
bear, The.
Hunt, Leigh (1784–1859)
Abou Ben Adhem.
Christmas.
Faith, Hope, and Charity Are the Prospects of
Manhood.
Fish Answers, A.
Fish, the Man, and the Spirit, The.
Iterating Sonnet.
Man's life is warm, glad, sad, 'twixt loves and
graves.
Nile, The.
On Receiving a Crown of Ivy from the Same.
On the Death of His Son Vincent.
One day—'twas on a gentle, autumn noon.
Rondeau: "Jenny kissed [*or* kiss'd] me when
we met."
Story of Rimini, The.
To a Fish.
To Hampstead.
To Hampstead.
To John Keats.
To Percy Shelley.
To the Grasshopper and the Cricket.
To the Same.
Hunt, Sam (b. 1946)
At Castor Bay.
Birth of a Son.
Bottle Creek Blues.
Maintrunk Country Roadsong.
My Father Scything.
My Father Today.
Porirua Friday Night.
Requiem: "They say "the lighthouse keeper's
world is round""
Sunday Evening.
Hunter, Albert (1897–1984) *and* **Louie Austin
(1897–1972)**
Down-Hearted Blues.

Hunter, Anne (1742–1841)
North American Death Song.
Pastoral Song, A.
Winter.
Hunter, Terra
Wanting You.
Hunter, William (1811–77)
Joyfully, Joyfully Onward I Move.
"Go Bring Me," Said the Dying Fair.
Hunter, William Elijah (1839–1913)
Monologue in a Rand Hospital.
**Huntingdon, Lucy Hastings, Countess of (1613–
1679)**
Bowells of the Earth my bowells hide, The.
Huntington, William Reed (1838–1909)
Cold Meteorite, The.
From Green Mountain.
Lowlands.
Hupfeld, Herman (1894–1951)
Are You Makin' Any Money?
As Time Goes By.
Let's Put Out the Lights and Go to Sleep.
When Yuba Plays the Rumba on the Tuba.
Hurdis, James (1763–1801)
Adriano; or, The First of June.
Peasants at Work.
Village Fair, The.
Hurley, Mary Rita
Limerick: "Old Indian chief, Running B'ar,
An."
Hurston, Zora Neale
Faith hasn't got no eyes, but she long-legged.
Husain [*or* Hussein], Rashid (1936–77)
Jerusalem and the Hour.
Lessons in Parsing.
Huss, Avraham (b. 1924)
Command, The.
Green Refrain, The.
Hussein, Hoda (b. 1972)
Childhood.
Male Grownups.
Room of One's Own, A.
Hutchinson, Abby (1829–92)
Kind Words Can Never Die.
Hutchinson, Lucy (b. 1620, d. after 1675)
Another on the Sun Shine.
Argument of the Third Booke, The.
On my Visitt to WS Which I Dreamt of That
Night.
To the Gardin att O: [Owthorpe] 7:th.
Verses Written by Mrs. Hutchinson.
Hutchinson, Pearse (b. 1927)
Amhrán na mBréag.
Be Born a Saint.
Boxing the Fox.
Bright after Dark.
Fleadh Cheoil.
Frost is All Over, The.
Gaeltacht.
Look, No Hands.
Málaga.
Manifest Destiny.
Sometimes Feel.
True Story Ending in False Hope, A.
Hutchison, Joseph
Joni Mitchell.
Hutten, Ulrich von (1488–1523)
Ulrich von Hutten's Song.
Hutton, Virgil (b. 1931)
Dusk over the lake.
Moving shadows, The.
Huxley, Aldous Leonard (1894–1963)
Armour.
Burning Wheel, The.
Christlike is my behaviour.
Fifth Philosopher's Song.
First Philosopher's Song.
Limerick: "There was a young fellow of
Burma."
Limerick: "There was a young girl of East
Anglia."
Second Philosopher's Song.
September.
Hwang Chin-i (c.1500–44)
I Will Cut Out the Middle Watch.

Hyakka (d. 1779)
Late-blooming cherry.
Winter ice.
Hyakuri (d. 1727)
When I die.
Hyde, Abby Bradley (1799–1872)
And Canst Thou, Sinner, Slight.
Dear Saviour, If These Lambs Should Stray.
Hyde, Arnold
There was an old fellow called Hugger.
Hyde, Douglas (1860–1944)
Cold, Sharp Lamentation.
He Meditates on the Life of a Rich Man.
Will You Be as Hard?
Hyde, Lewis
Goldfish in the Charles River.
"Hyde, Robin" (Iris Gulver Wilkinson) (1906–39)
Adolicus; that's a creeper rug, its small.
Close under here, I watched two lovers once.
Cool and certain, their oars will be lifted in
dusk.
Deserted Village, The.
Hares on their forms at dusk were not so still.
Ku Li.
Last Ones, The.
None of it true; for Christ's sake, spill the ink.
Pihsien Road.
Young Knowledge.
Hyde, William deWitt (1858–1917)
Creation's Lord, We Give Thee Thanks.
Hyett, Barbara Helfgott
Assembling the Dead at Dachau.
Hymans, Don (b. 1970)
Passacaglia.
Hyneman, Rebekah Gumpert (1812–75)
No. 5, Judith.
Woman's Rights.
Hywel ab Owain Gwynedd (d. 1170)
Exultation.
Poet's Loves, The.

I

I, Fu *See* **Mei Sheng**
"I, Mary" *See* **Osborn, Mary I.**
"I., R."
Limerick: "There was an old man called
Dupree."
Ibáñez, Sara de (1910–1971)
Empty Page, The.
I Cannot.
Island in the Earth.
Island in the Light.
You, for My Meditation.
Ibaragi Noriko (b. 1926)
What a Little Girl Had on Her Mind.
When I Was at My Most Beautiful.
When I Was Prettiest in My Life.
Ibarbourou, Juana de (1897–1979)
Hour, The.
Life-Hook.
Rainy Night.
Strong Bond, The.
Wild Root.
Woman.
Ibbetson, Julius Caesar (1759–1817)
Sally Birkett's Ale.
Ibn Abithur, Joseph
Sanctification.
Ibn al-Arabi (1165–1240)
My heart is capable of every form.
Ode: "They journeyed / When the darkness of
night."
Ode: "Who can support the anguish of love?"
Oh, her beauty—the tender maid! Its brilliance
gives light.
Ibn al-Hammarah, Abu Amir (*fl.* 12th cent.)
Insomnia.
Ibn al-Rumi (836–96)
Compromise, The.
Slow Giving.
To a Hunchback.

Weighing-In, The.
Ibn Arfa' Ra'suh (*fl.* **11th cent.**)
    Singing Lute, The.
Ibn Billita, Abu'l Qasim As'ad (*fl.* **c.1050**)
    Rooster, The.
Ibn-Chasdai, Abraham (*fl.* **c.1250**)
    Advice to Bores.
    Elusive Maid, The.
    Meek and the Proud, The.
    Poor Scholar, The.
Ibn Darraj al-Andalusi (*fl.* **11th cent.**)
    Wing of Separation, The.
Ibn Ezra, Abraham (**1092–1167**)
    Ages of Man, The.
    Far Sweeter than Honey.
    Freedom.
    God Everywhere.
    God Supreme.
    Law, The.
    Living God, The.
    My Stars.
    Out of Luck.
    Song of Chess, The.
Ibn Ezra, Moses (**c.1070–1138**)
    And Where Are the Graves.
    Beautiful Is the Loved One.
    Beauty of the Stars, The.
    Dying Wife to Her Husband, A.
    Elegy: "In pain she bore the son who her
        embrace."
    Elegy: "My thoughts impelled me to the
        resting-place."
    End of Man Is Death, The.
    Garden of Song, The.
    God That Doest Wondrously.
    Hot Flame of My Grief, The.
    I Went Out into the Garden.
    Joy of Life.
    Man Is a Weaver.
    Men Are Children of This World.
    My Love is Like a Myrtle.
    On My Sorrowful Life.
    Rejoice, O youth, in the lovely hind.
    Sources of My Being, The.
    Splendor of Thine Eyes, The.
    Strange Love.
    Those Beauteous Maids.
    To a Plagiarist.
    Walk in the Precepts.
    When She Plays upon the Harp or Lute.
    Why Should I Grieve?
    Wine-Songs.
    With Hopeless Love.
    Without My Friends the Day Is Dark.
    Works of God, The.
    World's Illusion, The.
    Young Dove, The.
ibn Hariq, Ali (**d.1225**)
    Galley Oars.
Ibn Hazm al-Andalusi (**994–1064**)
    Separation by Death.
    Twice Times Then Is Now.
    Visit, The.
Ibn 'Iyad (**1083–1149**)
    Grainfield.
Ibn Kamal (**d. 1573**)
    How an Old Man Can Regain His Youth
        Through Sexual Potency.
Ibn Quzman, Abu Bakr ibn Abd al-Malik
    (**c.1086–1160**)
    To a Beauty, White, Pure, and Constant.
Ibn Rashiq (**d. 1064**)
    Pretences.
Ibn Sara (**d. 1123**)
    Eggplant.
Ibn Sharaf (**d. 1068**)
    Satire.
Ibn Zaydun (**1003–71**)
    Cordova.
Ibnu 'l-Farid (**c.1181–1235**)
    Let passion's swelling tide my senses drown!
Ibrahim, Hafiz (**1871–1932**)
    Describing a Suit.
Ibsen, Henrik (**1828–1906**)
    In the Orchard.

Ibycus (*fl.* **564 B.C–61 B.C.**)
    Again Love, glancing meltingly.
    And I killed the Molione boys.
    In Spring.
    In the Spring the quince and the.
    On its highest leaves.
    They destroyed the famous and wealthy.
Iché, Laurence
    I Prefer Your Uneasiness Like a Dark Lantern.
    Scissors Strokes by the Clock.
Ichigen
    Joshu exclaimed, "Dog's no Buddha."
    Seventy-eight awkward years.
Ichijitsu, Ōkura
    Snow falls and falls, The.
Ichimu (**d. 1854**)
    Broken dream, A.
Ichishi (**d. 1746**)
    What do you understand?
Ietaka (Fujiwara no Ietaka) (**1158–1237**)
    Old Scent of the Plum Tree.
Ietaka, Fujiwara no *See* **Ietaka**
Ignatova, Elena (**b. 1947**)
    I have encountered a valley, in ragged bast
        matting.
    Italian Marcello, you breathe a much sweeter
        air.
    Summer Garden, The.
    To Ovid.
Ignatow, David (**1914–97**)
    1905.
    Against the Evidence.
    All Quiet.
    Allegory, An.
    And the Same Words.
    Bagel, The.
    Boxing Match, The.
    Business Life, The.
    Crystal Chandeliers.
    Dialogue, A.
    Dilemma.
    Dream, The.
    Each Day.
    East Bronx.
    Elegy: "I must wait for a stranger to knock on
        my door."
    Europe and America.
    First on TV, A.
    For Medgar Evers.
    For One Moment.
    Get the Gasworks.
    Harold.
    He Puts Me to Rest.
    Kaddish.
    Last Night.
    News Report.
    Night at an Airport.
    No Theory.
    Notes for a Lecture.
    Oedipus.
    Pit, The.
    Professional, The.
    Promenade.
    Rescue the Dead.
    Rightful One, The.
    Ritual Three.
    Self-employed.
    Signal, The.
    Simultaneously.
    Six Movements on a Theme.
    Sky Is Blue, The.
    Suburbia.
    Suite for Marriage, A.
    Sunday at the State Hospital.
Ihaka, Kingi M. (**b. 1921**)
    Te Atairangikaahu.
Iio Sogi (Sogi) (**1421–1502**)
    Life in this world.
    Night frost / Pulsing wings.
    Spring.
Ikkyu Sojun (**1394–1481**)
    After ten years in the red-light district.
    Don't worry please please how many times do
        I have to say it.
    Elegy: "We first lay down among flowers."

    Face to Face with My Lover on Daito's
        Anniversary.
    Form in Void.
    In all the kingdom southward.
    My Hand is Lady Mori's Hand.
    My Love's Dark Place Is Fragrant Like
        Narcissus.
    Night Talk in a Dream Chamber.
    Nobody told the flowers to come up nobody.
    Oh green green willow wonderfully red flower.
    Song of the Dream Garden.
    Ten years of whorehouse joy I'm alone now in
        the mountains.
    Void in Form.
Ikuo-Joun
    This fellow, perfect in men's eyes.
Ikuo-Myotan
    Seventy-two years I've hung.
Ilio, Dominador I. (**b. 1913**)
    Children of the Atomic Age.
    Marikudo in Kalibo, 1979.
    Prokosch in Tehran, 1978.
    Site of My Grandfather's House, The.
Illyés, Gyula (**1902–83**)
    Apricot Tree, The.
    Bartók.
    Bondage.
    Faithful Mirror.
    Fatherland in the Heights.
    Horror.
    Logbook of a Lost Caravan.
    Marked Ones, The.
    On Seeing the Reformation Memorial in
        Geneva.
    One Sentence on Tyranny.
    Piece of Advice, A.
    Refuge.
    Sacrifice.
    While the Record Plays.
    Work.
    Wreath, A.
Image, Selwyn (**1849–1930**)
    Meditation for Christmas, A.
Iman, Yusef
    Love Your Enemy.
Imber, Naphtali Herz (**1856–1909**)
    Hatikvah—a Song of Hope.
    Zionist Marching Song.
Imbs, Bravig (**1904–46**)
    Sleep.
    Wind Was There, The.
Immanuel di Roma (**c.1270–1330**)
    Elegy: "Floods of tears well from my deepest
        heart, The."
    Happiness amidst Troubles.
    Love.
    Machberoth.
    My Sweet Gazelle!
    On the Wall.
    Paradise.
    What Profit?
    Worthless Heart, The.
Imr el [*or* ul] Kais [*or* Qais](**520–65**)
    Ode of Imr El-Qais, The.
Inada, Lawson Fusao (**b. 1938**)
    Concentration Constellation.
    F.B.I. swooped in early, The.
    Father of My Father.
    Filling the Gap.
    Fresno Truth, The.
    Great Bassist, The.
    It began as truth, as fact.
    Legend of Home, The.
    Making It Stick.
    Projected Scenario of a Performance to Be
        Given Before the UN.
Inber, Vera (**1890?–1972**)
    Teeth are bared, the mouth drawn tight, the
        face, The.
İnce, Özdemir (**b. 1938**)
    Wind, Ant, History.
Inez, Colette (**b. 1931**)
    Courtyard Noises from the North, Twenty-
        fourth Precinct.
    Digging Potatoes.

Listening to Dvorak's Serenade in E.
Monologue of the Falconer's Wife.

Ingalls, Jeremy (b. 1911)
Apprehension.
For the Intellectuals.
Gun Emplacement: Sundown.
Vision of St. Michael and St. John, The.

Ingamells, Rex (1913–55)
Cook admired the native courage, made.
There are rock-rooted ranges to dominate.
They made impudent inspection of our coast.
We who are called Australians have no
country.

Inge, Charles Cuthbert (b. 1868)
Limerick: "Certain young gourmet of
Crediton, A."

Inge, William Ralph (1860–1954)
Limerick: "There was a good Canon of
Durham."
Limerick: "There was an old man of
Khartoum."

Ingelow, Jean (1820–97)
And didst thou love the race that loved not
thee?
Dappled sky, a world of meadows, A.
Divided.
Echo and the Ferry.
For Exmoor.
Giving in Marriage.
High Tide on the Coast of Lincolnshire, 1571,
The.
Little babe, while burns the west.
Long White Seam, The.
Seven Times Three—Love.
Story, A.
Winding-up Time.

**Ìnghean Uí Domhnaill Bhriain (O'Brien),
Fionnghuala** (*fl.* c.1617)
May your journey, Uaithne, be in the name of
the Holy Spirit.

Inghilfredi, Siciliano (*fl.* 1220)
Hard is it for a man to please all men.

Ingo (d. 1281)
Three and seventy years.

**"Ingoldsby, Thomas" (Richard Harris Barham)
(1788–1845)**
Eheu Fugaces.
Jackdaw of Rheims, The.
Lines Left at Mr Theodore Hook's House in
June, 1834.
Not a Sous Had He Got.

Ingraham, Nicholas Lloyd
She Would Have Roses.
Woman Back in the Kitchen, The.

Ingram, Anne, Viscountess Irwin (c.1696–1764)
Castle Howard, the Seat of the Rt. Hon.
Charles, Earl of Carlisle.
Epistle to Mr. Pope Occasioned by His
Characters of Women, An.
Female mind like a rude fallow lies, A.

Ingram-Roberts, Audrey
Poem 2 (for Duckie Simpson of Black Uhuru)

Inib-sarri (c.1790–45 B.C.)
Letter to Her Father, A.

Inman, P.
Centered.
Colloam.
Field dodd.
Subtracted Words.
XX.

Inman, Will (b. 1923)
Dark brother touches me, The.

Insana, Jolanda (b. 1937)
From wonder to wonder.
I am unable to recapture the allbody poured.
No fear of losing my sanity.
Rooting, The.
Tapestry of the Heart, The.
To Know Me?

Inseki (d. 1765)
I give my name back.

Instone, R. B. S.
Limerick: "How Socratic is Somerset
Maugham!"

Inuit Oral Tradition
Oxaitoq's Song.
Utitia'q's Song.

Iofe, Yury
Olsanski Cemetery, The.
Thing or Two about Childhood, A.

Iolo Goch (c.1320–c.1398)
Labourer, The.

Iozia, John
Fag Art.
Last Night at the Flamingo.

Ippu (d. 1731)
Falling in the wind.

Iqbal, Mohammed (1876–1938)
Make Your Radiant Twining Curls.

Irby, Kenneth (b. 1936)
Heredom.
I met the Angel Sus on the Skin Bridge.
January 1965, Looking on.
Sequence.
Slowly the old stone building walls downtown
dissolve.
There is from the legs in sleep an exhalation of
the light, along the tops of the thighs.
Trash.

Ireland, Kevin (b. 1933)
My First Forty Years.
Popular Romance, A.

Iremonger, Valentin (b. 1918)
Clear View in Summer.
Dog, The.
Hector.
Icarus.
Invocation: "Ten bloody years with this quill
lying."
This Houre Her Vigill.
Toy Horse, The.

Irenaeus Referendarius (*fl.* c.6th cent.)
Eyes filled with speaking fire.
O supercilious delicious Rhodope.
Why is the floor, Chrysilla.

Ironbiter, Suzanne
Song to the Mother of the World.

Irtenev, Igor Moiseievich (b. 1947)
Camelia.
Ditchdigger, The.
When I burn up without a trace.

Irvine, Weldon J., Jr. (b. 1943)
To be Young, Gifted, and Black.

Irving, John
Untitled.

Irving, Minna (b. 1872)
Marching Still.

Irwin, Mark
Autumnal.
Give.
Tree, A.

Irwin, Thomas Caulfield (1823–83)
Iphione.
It was a dim October day.
With the Dawn.

**Irwin, Wallace ("Ginger"; "Hashimura Togo")
(1876–1959)**
Constant Cannibal Maiden, The.
Reminiscence.

**Isaac ben Abun, Simeon ben, of Mainz (*fl.*
c.1020)**
All the Hosts of Heaven.
I Come to Supplicate.

Isaac ben Samuel of Dampière (*fl.* c.1175)
His Hand Shall Cover Us.

Isaacs, Jorge (1837–95)
Nima, The.

Isaibo (d. 1780)
Matsushima.
Though I tarry on the road.

**Isakovsky [*or* Isakovskii], Mikhail Vasilevich
(1900–1973)**
Enemy Had Burned His Cottage Home, The.

Isan (1795–1864)
Autumn hues, The.
For not honoring my parents.

Isanos, Magda (1916–44)
Apricot Tree.

Ise, Lady (d. 939)
Because we suspected / the pillow would say
"I know."
Correspondence: / when I have sad thoughts.
Elegy: Ise Lamenting the Death of Empress
Onshi.
Even in my dreams / I must no longer meet
you.
Flower of waves, A.
Hanging from the branches of a green / willow
tree.
If I consider / My body like the fields.
If it is you, there / in the light boat on the
pond.
Is it your command.
Like a ravaged sea / this bed.
Near a Waterfall at Ryumon.
News of the palace.
Not even in dreams / Can I meet him anymore.
On Seeing the Field Being Singed.
Pillows know, they say.
Seeing the Plum Blossoms by the River.
Seeing the Returning Geese.
They are rebuilding / the old bridge, the
Nagara.
When the fifth month comes.

Ise Tayu (*fl.* 11th cent.)
Clear water of the imperial pond, The.
Farmer's clothes are soaked through and never
dried, The.

Iselda *See* **Carenza**

Isherwood, Christopher (1904–86)
Common Cormorant [*or* Shag], The.
On His Queerness.

Ishigaki, Rin (b. 1920)
Cocoon.
Hands.

Ishikawa Jōzan (1583–1672)
Eating Roasted *Matsutake* Mushrooms.
Gardening Chrysanthemums, I Think of [T'ao]
Yüan-Ming.

Ishkhan, Moushegh (b. 1913)
Armenian Language Is the Home of the
Armenian, The.

Isidorus (d. 450?)
My name is Eteocles. The sea seduced me
from my farm.
Now Endymion dedicates / his cold bed's
failure to the moon.
On a Fowler.

Iskander, Fazil Abdulovich (b. 1929)
Blind Man, The.
Devil and the Shepherd, The.
Gegard.
Once a girl, all April-fresh.
Overtired branches are fragile.

Iskrenko, Nina (b. 1951)
Hair.
How To Live Through This Night (A Dream)
Isn't She Not a Bird.
Polystylistics.
Sex—A Five-Minute Briefing.
To Beat or Not to Beat.

Islām, Najrul (1899–1976)
Don't go back, Ma, don't go back, Mother.
He who has seen my Mother.
Let's be girls, Ma.
Now there'll be a new mantra, Mother.
Oh hey, All-Destroyer.
Syama Mother's lap a-climbing.
Syama wakes on the cremation grounds.
Talk to me, *javas*, talk to me.
Wake up, Syama, wake up, Syama!
Wherever are the lowly, the suffering, and the
poor.

Isler, Elizabeth
Little Things, The.

Ismail (b. 1928)
Wall, The.

Ismail, Donia, El-Amal (b. 1971)
Moment of Mourning, A.

Ismaili, Rashidah (b. 1941)
Bajji.
Lagos.
Queue.

Solange.
Yet Still.

Issa (Kobayashi Issa) (1763–1827)
About the field / Crow moves.
After a long nap.
All the time I pray to Buddha.
As I grow older.
As the great old trees.
As we grow old / What triumph.
Asked how old he was.
At prayer / Bead-swinging.
Autumn evening.
Autumn evening / Knees in arms.
Autumn moon.
Autumn wind / Mountain's shadow.
Autumn wind / The beggar looks.
Bath when you're born.
Bats flying.
Be respectful / Sparrows.
Bedbugs, The.
Before I arrived.
Before this autumn wind.
Blossoming plum!
Blossoms at night.
Borrowing my house / From insects.
Brilliant moon.
Buddha Law / Shining.
Buddha's Nirvana / Beyond flowers.
Changing clothes / But not.
Cherry blossoms? / In these parts.
Children / Don't harm the flea.
Children imitating cormorants.
Climb Mount Fuji.
Closer, closer / to paradise—.
Clouds of mosquitoes / It would be bare.
Crescent moon.
Cricket.
Cries of wild geese.
Crow, The.
Cuckoo's crying / Nothing special to do.
Cuckoo singing.
Cuckoo sings, The.
Cuckoo sings / To me, to the mountain.
Deer licking.
Dew spread / The seeds of hell.
Distant mountains, The.
Don't fly off, nightingale.
Don't kill that fly!
Don't kill that poor fly!
Don't know about the people.
Don't weep, insects / Lovers, stars, themselves.
Don't worry, spiders.
Dragonfly, The.
Dry riverbed, A.
Ducks bobbing on the water.
Even a fleabite.
Even considered.
Even on the smallest islands.
Even with insects.
Evening clears, The.
Evening moon.
Face of the spring moon.
Faint yellow rose, A.
Farmer / Pointing the way.
Fat priest, The.
Fireflies / Entering my house.
First cicada / Life is.
First firefly / Why turn away.
Five yen each / A cup of tea.
Fleas in my hut.
Flies in the temple, The.
Flies swarming / What do they want of.
Flopped on the fan.
Flowering plum, A.
Flying out from.
For you too, my fleas.
For your fleas too.
Frog.
From burweed / Such a butterfly.
From now on.
From one basin.
From that woman.
From the bough.
From the end of the nose.
From the Great Buddha's.
Full moon.
Garden butterfly.

Geese, fresh greens / Wait for you.
Give me a homeland.
Goes out.
Going to Tend Our Family Graves.
Good world, A.
Gratitude for gifts.
Having slept, the cat gets up.
Her row veering off.
Here.
Here in Shinano.
Hey, sparrow!
Holes in the wall, The.
How *much*.
Huge frog and I, A.
I envy.
I'm going out.
I'm going to roll over.
I'm leaving / Now you can make love.
I wish she were here.
If the times were good.
In a dream.
In my hidden house.
In my house / Mice and fireflies.
In my life / As in the twilight.
In spring rain.
In the beggar's tin.
In the cherry blossom's shade.
In the midst of this world.
In the thicket's shade.
In this mountain village.
In this world.
In this world / Even butterflies.
Insects.
Insects on a bough.
It once happened.
Its mother on guard.
January.
Just beyond the gate.
Just by being / I'm here.
Just to say the word.
Kites shriek / Together—.
Last time, I think.
Let's take / The duckweed way.
Like misty moonlight.
Listen / All creeping things.
Lost in bamboo.
Man pulling radishes, The.
Mokuboji Temple.
Moon and the flowers, The.
Moon, plum blossoms.
Moon tonight, The.
Mosquito at my ear.
Mother I never knew.
Mother, I weep.
Mountain cuckoo, The.
My cat.
My dear old village.
My hut / Thatched.
My noontime nap.
My old village lies.
My spring is just this.
Naked.
Napped half the day.
Napping at midday.
Never forget / We walk on hell.
New foal, The.
New year arrived, The.
New Year's Day.
New Year's morning.
Nightingale's song / this morning.
No doubt about it.
No talent.
Noon.
Not knowing.
Not very anxious.
Not yet become a Buddha.
Now we are leaving.
Nursing her child.
O autumn winds.
O flea! whatever you do.
O owl!
O summer snail.
Old dog listens, The.
Old dog, The.
On the Death of the Poet's Daughter Sato.
One bath / After another.
One human being.

One person.
Only one guy and.
Outliving / Them all, all.
Over paddies / At its foot.
Owls are calling / 'Come, come.'
People working fields.
Pheasant cries, The.
Pissing in the snow.
Plumes of pampas grass.
Poor box, A.
Poor quarter, A.
Prostitute's shack, The.
Red morning sky.
Reflected / In the dragonfly's eye—.
Seen.
She's put the child to sleep.
Sheet of rain, A.
Shinano.
Short night / Scarlet flower.
Shush, cicada / Old Whiskers.
Six Ways, The.
Skylarks singing / The farmer.
Snail gets up.
Snow is melting, The.
So many flea bites.
Spring day, The.
Spring rain.
Summer night.
That gorgeous kite.
That pretty girl.
That wren.
These sea slugs.
They don't notice.
This moth saw brightness.
This stupid world.
This world of dew.
This year on, forever.
Thus spring begins: old.
Toad! It looks like, The.
Tonight you too / Are rushed.
Treated shabbily / by fleas, by flies.
Under cherry trees / There are.
Under my house.
Under the evening moon.
Under the image of Buddha.
Under this bright moon.
Vanity of men, The.
Village named Little-Plum-Tree, A.
Visiting the graves.
Washing the saucepans.
Watch it—you'll bump / Your heads.
Were it sweet.
What a strange thing!
What a world / Where lotus flowers.
What good luck!
What matter if I live on.
What's the lord's vast wealth.
When I go / Guard my tomb well.
When plum / Blooms—.
When the wild turnip.
Where.
Where there are humans / you'll find flies.
Why did the wild pink break?
Wild Goose, Wild Goose.
Windy fall.
Winter fly, The.
Winter lull / No talents.
With my father.
With this rising bath-mist.
Withered fields, The.
Woodpecker, The.
World of dew, The.
World of trials, A.
Worldly sky / From now on.
Wren, The.
Writing shit about new snow.
Young sparrows.
Zealous flea.

Issa, Kobayashi *See* **Issa**
Issahakian, Avedik (1875–1957)
Climb Mount Fuji.
Don't kill that fly!
Even with insects—.
For you fleas too.
Under the evening moon.

Issaia, Nana (b. 1934)
Dream.

Sacrifice.
Issho (d. 1688)
From deep in my heart.
Isso (d. 1899)
Cut your price!
Istarú, Ana (b. 1954)
Bodies / tidal waves.
Crescent moon, A.
From where you have come.
Moon became mired on our bed, The.
Then / an awakened citron.
To the cove of my breasts your forehead will return.
Your penis rolls to the dream.
Itaikkunrurkilar
His Legs Strong and Lithe.
Italicus, Catius as Conius Silius (c. 25–c. 101 A.D.)
At the city's heart stood the shrine to Dido's ghost.
Death comes in strange forms and contrasting images.
Furiously along the banks stormed Hannibal.
Give me Maeonian Homer's resonant tongue.
Horses which Titan when discharged for the night, The.
Memories of past struggles were expelled by fear.
Itō Hiromi (b. 1955)
Near Kitami Station on the Odakyū Line.
Ivanov, Georgy [or Georgii] Vladimirovich (1894–1958)
Boiling up over the years.
Covered with a glory that had lost its luster.
Even the graves are not tended in Russia.
Fog. The road I usually wander down.
I imagine everything wrapped in a beatific mist.
I walk and think of various things.
If you want to live, then live...
Not so long ago, the world was complete.
Oh, how fastidious you once were.
Old man shuffles to the fish market, The.
On the boundary of snow and melting.
People.
Quarter century of exile has passed, A.
Should I tell of all the absolute fools.
Spring said nothing to me—it couldn't.
They'll not exterminate you now.
Tune becomes a flower, The.
Unharnessed, the white horse ambles along.
Ivanov, Vyacheslav Ivanovich (1866–1949)
Holy Rose, The.
Russian Mind, The.
Winter Sonnets, The.
Ivanova, Iraida Gustavovna Geinike *See* **Odoyevtseva [or Odoevtseva], Irina**
Ivask, Yury [or Iurii] (1907–86)
Emily Dickinson.
Ode for the Dancing Khlysty.
Shall we forget the shiver.
Iverem, Esther (b. 1960)
Daddy's Friends.
Earth Screaming.
Journalist's Convention 1987.
Keeper.
Murmur.
Ives, George (1867–1950)
With Whom, then, should I Sleep?
Izen, Hirose
As the late night passes.
Izumi, Lady (Izumi Shikibu) (c.974–c.1030)
Although the wind.
Being a person.
From darkness / I go onto the road / of darkness.
From one darkness.
Here in this world / I won't live.
I cannot say.
I go out of darkness / Onto a road of darkness.
I left my hills.
I wish you would come.
If Someone Would Come.
If you have no time.
If you love me.

In My Idleness.
In the Autumn, on Retreat at a Mountain Temple.
In the dusk the path.
It is the time of rain and snow.
Lying down alone.
Lying here alone.
My black hair tangled.
On nights when hail / falls noisily.
On this winter night.
Orange leaves are gone.
Since that night / I cannot know myself.
So forlorn am I.
Someone else / looked at the sky.
Tangled Hair.
Watching the moon.
Way I must enter, The.
When I think of you.
When you broke from me.
Will I cease to be.
You told me it was / because of me.
You wear the face.

J

"J., L. E."
Limerick: "Conception, an Archbishop said, The."
"J., M."
Animal Howl, The.
Funeral, The.
Song of a Jewish Boy.
"J., W."
City Eclogue.
Jaber, 'Enayat
Circle.
Clarity.
Smell.
Solitude.
Jabès, Edmond (b. 1912)
Beginning of the Book, The.
Book of the Living, The.
Book, The.
Desert, II, The.
Desert, The.
Have you seen how a word is born and dies?
Jew answers every question with another question, The.
Notebook, Two.
To be in the book. To figure in the book of questions, to be part of it.
Jaccottet, Philippe (b. 1925)
Dawn.
Daybreak.
Distances.
Don't worry.
Fruit.
Glimpses.
I Rise with an Effort.
Letter of the 26th June.
Reason.
Right at the end of night.
Serenity.
Swifts.
These wood-shadows.
Wishes.
Wound seen from afar.
Jacinto, Antonio (b. 1924)
Letter from a Contract Worker.
Monangamba.
Poem of Alienation.
Jacinto, Jaime
Absence.
Heaven Is Just Another Country.
Visitation.
Jacir, Annemarie
Pistachio Ice Cream.
Jackowska, Nicki (b. 1942)
Family Outing—a Celebration.
Insect Kitchen, The.
Meeting, The.
Sisters, The.
Woman Who Mistook her Father for an Irishman, The.

Jackson, Angela (b. 1951)
Billie in Silk.
Choosing the Blues.
Make/n My Music.
Miz Rosa Rides the Bus.
Ohnedaruth.
Spinster Song: African-American Woman Guild.
Transformable Prophecy.
Jackson, Bruce (b. 1963)
Another Impostor.
In Exchange for Forty Acres.
Riot at Winchell's.
Shooting, Killing, Drug Busts, Cover-Ups, Fuck-Ups, Lighter Sides, Weather, and Sports.
Jackson, David (b. 1931)
Grandmother Jackson.
Jackson, E. J.
Limerick: "There once was a fellow called Hyde."
Jackson, Fleda Brown (b. 1944)
Death of Gladys Presley, The.
Elvis Acts as His Own Pallbearer.
Elvis at the End of History.
Elvis Goes to the Army.
Elvis Reads The Wild Swans at Coole.
Elvis Sings Gospel.
I Visit the Twenty-four Coin-op Church of Elvis.
Women Who Love Elvis All Their Lives, The.
Jackson, Gale (b. 1958)
Alice.
Fugitive Slaves.
Some of Betty's Story Round 1850.
Jackson, Helen Hunt ("H. H."; "Saxe Holm") (1830–85)
Cheyenne Mountain.
Crossed Threads.
Distance.
Dreams.
Emigravit.
Friends.
Grab-Bag.
Her Eyes.
My House Not Made with Hands.
My Lighthouses.
My Strawberry.
October.
October's Bright Blue Weather.
Opportunity.
September [Days Are Here].
Solitude.
Tides.
Two Truths.
Jackson, Laura Riding (1901–91)
All Things.
Ancient Revisits, An.
As Well As Any Other.
Because of Clothes.
Chloe or . . .
City Seems, A.
Dimensions.
Ding-Donging.
Divestment of Beauty.
Elegy in a Spider's Web.
Faith Upon the Waters.
Forgotten Girlhood.
Helen's Burning.
Lucrece and Nara.
Map of Places, The.
Mask, The.
Nothing So Far.
O Vocables of Love.
One Self.
Only Daughter, The.
Poet: A Lying Word.
Poet's Corner, The.
Prisms.
Reasons of Each, The.
Sad Boy, The.
Sea, False Philosophy.
Starved.
Summary for Alastor.
Take Hands.
There Is No Land Yet.

Toward the Corner.
Troubles of a Book, The.
Virgin, The.
Wind Suffers of Blowing, The.
Wind, the Clock, the We, The.
With the Face.
World and I, The.

Jackson, Major L.
Blunts.
Don Pullen at the Zanzibar Blue Jazz Cafe, 1994.
Some Kind of Crazy.

Jackson, Michael (b. 1940)
Macrocarpas.
Mask-Maker.
Moths, The.
Red Flag, The.
Return from Luluabourg.
Socrates' Death.

Jackson, Reuben (b. 1956)
63rd and broadway.
1973.
After the Dance.
Albert James.
Big Chill Variations.
For duke ellington.
For Thurman Thomas.
Jamal's Lamentation.
Lady's Way.
Lonely Affair, A.
Sunday Brunch.
Tee.
Thelonious.

Jackson, Richard
Eight Ball.
Poem That Was Once Called 'Desperate' But Is Now Striving to Become the Perfect Love Poem.
Shadows.

Jackson, Tony
Pretty Baby.

Jacob, Hildebrand (1693–1739)
Alarm, The.
Here Delia's buried at fourscore.
Judgement of Tiresias, The.
Swain, give o'er your fond pretension.
To Cloe.
To Geron.

Jacob, Max (1876–1944)
1914.
Horrible Today, The.
I thought he was bankrupt.
In Honor of the Sardana and the Tenora.
In Search of the Traitor.
Invitation to a Voyage.
Little Poem.
Moon Poem.
Rooster and the Pearl, The.
Spanish Generosity.
To Modigliani to Prove to Him That I Am a Poet.
War.

Jacob, Violet (1863–1946)
Last o' the Tinkler, The.
Pride.
Tam i' the Kirk.

Jacobik, Gray (b. 1944)
Dust Storm.
Turkeys in August.

Jacobs, Bertha See Bertken [or Bertke], Sister
Jacobs, Harriet (b. 1951)
About our hips.
And sometimes i hear this song in my head.
Goree.
Growing into my name.
Imagination in flight: an improvisational duet.
It is not Just.
On extending the olive branch to my own self.
On Growing Up the Darker Berry.

Jacobs, Henry Eyster (1844–1932)
Lord Jesus Christ, We Humbly Pray.

Jacobs, Henry S. (1827–93)
How Goodly Is Thy House.

Jacobs, J. L. (b. 1967)
Nearing Long Moons.

Snakeroot.
Two Varieties of the Bitter Orange.

Jacobs, Leland B. (b. 1907)
Subway Train, The.

Jacobsen, Josephine (b. 1908)
Bush.
Destinations.
Hourglass.
It Is the Season.
Limbo Dancer, The.
Matadors, The.
Only Alice.
Poems for My Cousin.
Primer, The.
Rainy Night at the Writers' Colony.
Reindeer and Engine.
Shade-Seller, The.
Thief, The.
When the Five Prominent Poets.
Yellow.

Jacobsen, Rolf (b. 1907)
Catacombs in San Callisto, The.
Cobalt.
Crust on Fresh Snow.
Express Train.
Gaslight.
Guardian Angel.
Meadowsweet.
Sunflower.

Jacopo da Lentino (fl. 13th cent.)
Canzonetta: He Will Neither Boast nor Lament to His Lady.
Canzonetta: Of His Lady, and of His Making Her Likeness.
Marvellously elate.
Of His Lady in Heaven.
Of His Lady's Face.
Remembering this—how Love.
Sapphire, nor diamond, nor emerald.

Ja'far, Hasab al-Shaikh (b. 1942)
Descent of Abu Nuwas.

Jafri, Ali Sardar (b. 1913)
Morsel.

Jagger, Barbara
Anyway.

Jago, Richard (1715–81)
Absence.
Instructions on landscaping.
Iron Industry in Birmingham, The.
Sage Philosophy.

Jahan, Nur, Empress (d. 1646)
Moon of Id came, The.
Your love turned my body into water.

Jahin, Salah
Quatrains.

Jaimes Freyre, Ricardo (1870?–1933)
Dawn, The.
Eternal Farewell.
Sad Voices, The.

Jakiela, Lori
Personal History of Hands, A.

Jakua (d. 1801)
Cuckoo.

Jakura (d. 1906)
This year I want.

Jakuren (d. 1202)
Hanging raindrops, The.

Jakushitsu (1290–1367)
Refreshing, the wind against the waterfall.

Jallais, Denise
Lullaby for My Dead Child.

Jamal Isfahani (d. 1192)
White Hairs.

"James" See James, Alice Archer Sewall
James, Alice Archer Sewall ("James") (b. c.1870?)
Graffiti.

James, Allston
Honor (1969)

James, Cliff (b. 1943)
Welsh Homer.

James, Clive (b. 1939)
Book of My Enemy Has Been Remaindered, The.

Johnny Weissmuller Dead in Acapulco.
Weather's cleared, The. We're filming at Versailles.

James, David Emrys (1891–1952)
Horizon.

James, Elinor (fl. late 17th cent.)
Injured Prince Vindicated, or, A Scurrilous and Detracting Pamphlet Answered, An.

James, Elmore (1918–1963)
Sunnyland.

James, George (fl. 1616)
Roysters give Roome, for here comes a Lass.

James, Harry
I'm Beginning to See the Light.

James I, King of England (1566–1625)
Admonition to Montgomerie.
Epitaph on Sir Philip Sidney, An.
Lady Cicely Wemyss.
Sonnet on Sir William Alexander's Harsh Verses after the English Fashion, A.

James I, King of Scotland (1394–1437)
Heigh in the hevynnis figure circulere.
King is Quair, The.
Spring Song of the Birds.

James, John (1633–1729)
Of John Bunyan's Life.
On the Decease of the Religious and Honourable Jno Haynes Esqr.

James, John (b. 1939)
Bye Bye Blackbird.
Idyl: "Tiny fish."
Shakin All Over.
Sister Midnight.

James, John (1633–1729) and Robert Wedderburn
Balulalow.

James, Nicholas (fl. c.1742)
May poverty, without offence, approach.

James, Paul
Can't We Be Friends?
Can This Be Love?
Fine and Dandy.

James, Thomas (1593?–1635?)
Lines on His Companions Who Died in the Northern Seas.

James V, King of Scotland (1513–42)
Jolly Beggar, The.

Jami, Nuru'ddin Abdu 'R-Rahman (1414–92)
Even from earthly love thy face avert not.

Jamie, Kathleen (b. 1962)
Flower-sellers, Budapest.
Mr and Mrs Scotland Are Dead.
Queen of Sheba, The.
St Bride's.

Jamieson, Robert Alan
De.

Jamíl (660?–701)
Salsabíl.

Jammes, Francis (1868–1938)
Amsterdam.
Child Reads an Almanac, The.
Five Sorrowful Mysteries, The.
Love.
Prayer to Go to Paradise with the Asses.
Prayer to Go to Paradise with the Donkeys, A.

Jana Bai (fl. 14th cent.)
Cast off all shame.
She was my staff and I am blind.

Jandl, Ernst (b. 1925)
Calypso.
Chanson.
Preliminary Studies for the Frankfurt Readings 1984.

Janeczko, Paul B. (b. 1945)
Blanket Hog.
Mail King.

Janevski, Slavko
Silence.

Jang-hi Lee See Yi Jang'hi (Jang-hi Lee)
Jankovich, Ferenc (1907–71)
In the Courtyard of the Servants.
On the Shores of Szántód.

Janosco, Beatrice
Garden Hose, The.

Janssen, Camille *See* "Dermée, Paul"
Janzen, Jean
  At Summer's End.
  August Nights.
  Claiming the Dust.
  Pomegranate.
Japicx, Gysbert (b. 1603)
  Lovelight.
Jaques, Florence Page (1890–1972)
  There Once Was a Puffin.
Jara, Víctor (1935–73)
  Estadio Chile.
Jaramillo Agudelo, Darío (b. 1947)
  Some Day.
Jarmain, John
  El Alamein.
  Embarkation, 1942.
  Prisoners of War.
  Sand.
  These Poems.
Jarman, Mark (b. 1955)
  Black Riviera, The.
  Cavafy in Redondo.
  God like a kiss, God like a welcoming.
  Ground Swell.
  Psalm: The New Day.
  Supremes, The.
Jarrell, Randall (1914–65)
  Bird of Night, The.
  Author to the Reader, The.
  Bats.
  Black Swan, The.
  Blind Sheep, The.
  Burning the Letters.
  Camp in the Prussian Forest, A.
  Chipmunk's Day, The.
  Cinderella.
  Come to the Stone.
  Country Life, A.
  Dead Wingman, The.
  Death of the Ball Turret Gunner, The.
  Description of Some Confederate Soldiers, A.
  Eighth Air Force.
  Elementary Scene, The.
  Field and Forest.
  Front, A.
  Game at Salzburg, A.
  Girl in a Library, A.
  Gunner.
  Hope.
  House in the Wood, The.
  Hunt in the Black Forest, A.
  In a Hospital Garden.
  In Montecito.
  In Nature There Is Neither Right nor Left nor Wrong.
  In the Camp There Was One Alive.
  Island, The.
  Islands, The.
  Jews at Haifa.
  Jonah.
  Knight, Death, and the Devil, The.
  Lonely Man, The.
  Losses.
  Lost Children, The.
  Lullaby, A: "For wars his life and half a world away."
  Man Meets a Woman in the Street, A.
  Märchen, The.
  Mockingbird, The.
  Nestus Gurley.
  Next Day.
  90 North.
  On the Railway Platform.
  Orient Express, The.
  Pilot from the Carrier, A.
  Pilots, Man Your Planes.
  Player Piano, The.
  Prisoners.
  Protocols.
  Range in the Desert, The.
  Refugees, The.
  Say Good-bye to Big Daddy.
  Second Air Force.
  Seele im Raum.
  Sick Child, A.

  Sick Nought, The.
  Snow-Leopard, The.
  Soldier Walks under the Trees of the University, The.
  Thinking of the Lost World.
  Truth, The.
  Variations.
  War, A.
  Well Water.
  Woman.
  Woman at the Washington Zoo, The.
Jarry, Alfred (1873–1907)
  Passion of Jesus Considered as an Uphill Race, The.
Jarvenpa, Diane
  Polka.
Jarwood, Su
  I am a winged creature, flightless.
Jastrun, Tomasz (b. 1950)
  Hat.
  Polish Knot, The.
  Scrap.
  Seed, The.
Jastrzebska, Maria
  Cracking Walnuts.
Jaufré Rudel (*fl.* mid–12th cent.)
  Love Song.
Jauss, David (b. 1951)
  After the End of the World.
  Black Orchid.
  Last Solo: Charlie Parker, Hotel Stanhope, March 12, 1955.
Javitz, Alexander
  Old Men, The.
Jay, T.E.
  Fir.
Jayadeva (*fl.* 12th cent.)
  Hymn to Vishnu.
  Sandal and garment of yellow and lotus garlands upon his body of blue.
  Song of Krishna: The Fourth Song, Sung with Raga 'Ramakari.'
Jayaprabha, A. (b. 1957)
  Burn this Sari.
Jayyusi, Salma Khadra (b. 1926)
  April Woman.
  Dearest Love.
  In the Casbah.
  On Visiting the M. D. Anderson.
  Scrapping Limits.
  Ship of Love, The.
  Sunken Ship, The.
Jeffers, Lance (1919–85)
  How High the Moon.
  I Do Not Know the Power of My Hand.
  My Blackness Is the Beauty of This Land.
  Nina Simone.
  Old Love Butchered (Colorado Springs and Huachuca)
  There is a nation.
  Trellie.
  When I Know the Power of my Black Hand.
Jeffers, Robinson (1887–1962)
  Advice to Pilgrims.
  Age in Prospect.
  Animals.
  Ante Mortem.
  Antrim.
  Apology for Bad Dreams.
  Artist, An.
  Ascent to the Sierras.
  Autumn Evening.
  Ave Caesar.
  Beaks of Eagles, The.
  Beauty of Things, The.
  Bed by the Window, The.
  Birds.
  Birds and Fishes.
  Birth-Dues.
  Boats in a Fog.
  But I Am Growing Old and Indolent.
  Carmel Point.
  Cassandra.
  Clouds of Evening.
  Compensation.

  Continent's End.
  Credo.
  Cremation.
  Deer Lay Down Their Bones, The.
  Divinely Superfluous Beauty.
  Eagle Valor, Chicken Mind.
  Evening Ebb.
  Eye, The.
  Fawn's Foster-Mother.
  Fire on the Hills.
  For Una.
  Gale in April.
  Granite and Cypress.
  Haunted Country.
  Home.
  Hurt Hawks.
  Inquisitors, The.
  Love the Wild Swan.
  May-June, 1940.
  New Mexican Mountain.
  Night.
  Noon.
  Nova.
  November Surf.
  Original Sin.
  Pelicans.
  Phenomena.
  Place for No Story, The.
  Post Mortem.
  Prescription of Painful Ends.
  Promise of Peace.
  Purse-Seine, The.
  Rearmament.
  Return.
  Rock and Hawk.
  Salmon Fishing.
  Science.
  Shane O'Neill's Cairn.
  Shine, Perishing Republic.
  Shiva.
  Stars Go Over the Lonely Ocean, The.
  Summer Holiday.
  To the Stone-Cutters.
  Tor House.
  Vulture.
  Watch the Lights Fade.
  Where I?
Jefferson, Blind Lemon
  Easy Rider Blues.
  Long Distance Moan.
Jefferys [*or* Jeffries], Charles
  We Have Lived and Loved Together.
Jeffrey, Francis, Lord Jeffrey (1773–1850)
  Epitaph: "Here lies the body of Richard Hind."
  In Christ Church, Bristol, on Thomas Turner, Twice Master of the Company of Bakers.
  On Peter Robinson.
Jeffrey, William (1896–1946)
  Carlyle on Burns.
  Stones.
Jeitteles, Alois (1794–1858)
  To My Distant Beloved.
Jeitteles, Benedict (1762–1813)
  Epitaph for a Judge.
Jékely, Zoltán (1913–1982)
  Dragon Slaying.
  Footballers.
  In Memory of the Funeral Horses.
  In the Church of Marosszentimre.
  Ode to Chaplin.
  To My Bones.
  Towards the New Millennium.
Jekyll, Joseph (1752–1837)
  See, one physician, like a sculler, plies.
Jemie, Onwuchekwa (b. 1940)
  Iroko.
  Toward a Poetics.
Jemmat, Catherine (*fl.* 1750–66)
  Rural Lass, The.
Jên Jui (d. 1949)
  Midnight.
Jenkins, Alan
  Murphy's Law.
Jenkins, Christina (b. 1962)
  Sunday Morning.

Jenkins, Gordon
P.S. I Love You.
Jenkins, John (b. 1949) *and* **Ken Bolton (b. 1949)**
In Ferrara.
Jenkins, Louis (b. 1942)
Appointed Rounds.
Basketball.
Confessional Poem.
Football.
In a Tavern.
Library.
Walking through a Wall.
Jenkins, Mike (b. 1953)
Chartist Meeting.
Diver-Bird.
Martins.
Survivor.
Truant, A.
Jenkins, Nigel (b. 1949)
Ainadamar.
Castration.
Land of Song.
Shirts.
Wild Cherry.
Yr Iaith.
Jenkins, Paul
Six Small Fires.
Jenkinson, Biddy (b. 1929)
Spray.
Jenks, Tudor (1857–1922)
Accommodating Lion, An.
Hard to Bear.
Jenner, Charles (1736–74)
Eclogue IV: The Poet.
Soliloquy in the Suburbs, A.
Jennings, Elizabeth (b. 1926)
After a Time.
Afterthought.
Annuciation, The.
Answers.
At Night.
Child's Story, The.
Christ Seen by Flemish Painters.
Counterpart, The.
Delay.
First Love.
Fountain.
Fragment for the Dark.
I wish, God, for some end I do not will.
In a Garden.
In Praise of Creation.
Interrogator, The.
Letter to Peter Levi, A.
My Grandmother.
One Flesh.
Resurrection, The.
Second World War, The.
Song at the Beginning of Autumn.
Song for a Birth or a Death.
Storm House, The.
Teresa of Avila.
Thinking of Love.
To a Friend with a Religious Vocation.
Ugly Child, The.
Winter Love.
Works of Art.
Young Ones, The.
Jennings, Humphrey (1907–50)
Prose Poem.
Jennings, Kate
Couples.
Just the Two of Us.
Jensen, Laura (b. 1948)
Adoration of the Anchor.
Age, An.
Ajax Samples, The.
As the Window Darkens.
Candles Draw Well after All, The.
Cloud Parade, The.
House Is an Enigma.
Household.
Kitchen.
Kite.
Pony Farm.
Red Dog, The.

To a Stranger (At the End of a Caboose)
Winter Evening Poem.
Jensma, Wopko (b. 1939)
In Memoriam Akbar Babool.
In Memoriam Ben Zwane.
Jenyns, Soame (1704–87)
But let me now my lovely charge remind.
But soon th'endearments of a husband cloy.
Choice, The.
Dare I in such momentous points advise.
Doctor Johnson.
Epitaph on Dr Samuel Johnson.
For love no time has she, or inclination.
In days, my Lord, when mother Time.
Just broke from school, pert, impudent, and
raw.
Let each fair maid, who fears to be disgraced.
Modern Fine Lady, The.
Nor can I for my soul delight.
Now haste, my Muse, pursue thy destined way.
Snow-Ball, The.
Temple of Venus, The.
To a Nosegay in Pancharilla's Breast.
Jerome, William
Row, Row, Row.
Jerrold, Sydney E.
Beggar Maid, The.
Christopher.
Earthly Joy.
Hope.
John in Prison.
Non Te Rapiet Quisquam de Manua Mea.
"Jerry, Bongo" (Robin Small) (b. 1948)
Mabrak.
Jesús, Teresa de
All of a Sudden.
They go by, go by, love, the days and the
hours.
Jevon, Rachel (b. 1627, d. after 1662)
Exultationis Carmen To the Kings Most
Excellent Majesty upon His Most Desired
Return.
Jewell, Foster
Cliff dweller ruins.
Disturbing some brush.
Fall wind in pinyons.
Finding this cavern.
Last screech owl cry.
Mountain shadow.
Nearing the mountain.
Some unknown sound.
Somewhere behind me.
That breeze brought it.
This evening stillness.
Thunder storm passing.
Under ledges.
Where the coyote called.
Jewett, Sarah Orne (1849–1909)
At Home from Church.
Caged Bird, A.
Country Boy in Winter, A.
Widows' House, The.
Jewett, Sophie ("Ellen Burroughs") (1849–1909)
For a Birthday.
Letter, A.
"Jewish Sibyl, The"
There Is a City.
Jewsbury, Maria Jane (1800–33)
Farewell to the Muse, A.
My heart's in the kitchen, my heart is not here.
Summer Eve's Vision, A.
To My Own Heart.
Verses: "I am monarch of troubles a host."
Jien (Former Chief Priest) (1155–1225)
Too Much to Ask.
Jikko (d. 1791)
Family whispers.
Rather than leave behind me.
Jiles, Paulette (b. 1933)
Paper Matches.
Tin Woodsman, The.
Time to Myself.
Windigo.
Jimenez, Juan Ramon
Untitled.

Jiménez, Juan Ramón (1881–1958)
Countryside Sleeps, Trembling, The.
Dawn brings with it, The.
Definitve Journey, The.
Faster, Earth, Faster.
Fleeting Return.
I Am Not I.
Immense Hour.
Love.
Mariner's Ideal Epitaph.
Moon Was Gliding the River, The.
Nightfall. The Coolness of My Watered
Garden.
Oxcarts Are Now on Their Way, The.
Sea Is Enormous, The.
Street Is Waiting for the Night, The.
Sunset.
Tenebrae.
To the bridge of love.
Jiménez, Juan Ramón (1881–1958)
Vigil.
Yellow Spring.
Zenith.
Jinzu
In serving, serve.
Joachim, Paulin (b. 1931)
Burial.
Joad, C. E. M. (1891–1953)
Materialism.
Joans, Ted (b. 1928)
.38, The.
Truth, The.
Jobim, Antonio Carlos
Quiet Nights of Quiet Stars (Corcovado)
Joe, Rita
Expect Nothing Else from Me.
Johannes Barbucollas (fl. c.551)
Don't halt your voyage, sailor, nor drop sail.
Johannsdorf, Albrecht von (fl. 1185–1209)
God's Gifts.
I discovered the sweet lovely lady.
This I know, how love begins to be.
John of Damascus, Saint (c.700–c.760)
Day of Resurrection, The.
John of the Cross, Saint (1542–91)
Christmas Ballad.
Commentary Applied to Spiritual Things.
Dark Night.
I Entered Where I Did Not Know.
I Know Full Well the Water's Flowing Power.
I Live and Do Not Live in Myself.
I live without inhabiting / Myself.
More Stanzas Applied to Spiritual Things.
Not Without Hope Pulsing My Breast.
O Flame of Living Love.
O Living Flame of Love.
Obscure Night of the Soul, The.
One Dismal Night.
Shepherd, Young and Mournful, Grieves
Alone, A.
Song of the Soul that Rejoices in Knowing
God through Faith.
Spiritual Canticle.
Stanzas Concerning an Ecstasy Experienced in
High Contemplation.
Stanzas of the Soul that Suffers with Longing
to See God.
John Paul II, Pope *See* Wojtyla, Karol
John, Richard Johnny, Jerome Rothenberg *and*
Ian Tyson
Two Songs About a Dead Person or a Mole—
Whichever It Was.
Johns, Orrick (1887–1946)
Invitation.
Salon de Vers.
Johnson, A. R.
Joint is Jumpin', The.
Johnson, Amryl (b. 1939)
Oil on Troubled Waters.
Johnson, Ben
Advice to a Reckless Youth.
Johnson, Denis (b. 1949)
Harold's Bowl and Food.
Heat.

Incognito Lounge, The.
Poem: "There was something I can't bring myself."

Johnson, Don Allen ("Mustafa") (b. 1942)
Fountain, The.
I Traveled with Them.
Thy Garden.

Johnson, Edward (1598–1672)
Among These Trooopes of Christs Souldiers, Came . . . Mr. Roger Harlackenden.
Good News from New England.
Mr. Eliot Pastor of the Church of Christ at Roxbury.
Mr. Thomas Shepeard.
Oh King of Saints, how great's thy work, say we.
Onely the Reverend Grave and Godly Mr. Buckly Remaines.
Reverend Mr, The Higginson.
Yee Shall Not Misse of a Few Lines in Remembrance of Thomas Hooker.

Johnson, Emily Pauline ("Tekahionwake") (1886–1913)
Cattle Thief, The.
Joe.
Marshlands.
Ojistoh.
Wave-Won.

Johnson, Esther ("Stella") (1681–1728)
If It Be True.
Jealousy.
To Dr. Swift on His Birthday, 30th November 1721.

Johnson, Eva (c.1950)
Letter to My Mother, A.
Remember?
Right to Be.
Weevilly Porridge.

Johnson, Fenton (1886–1958)
Aunt Hannah Jackson.
Children of the Sun.
Lonely Mother, The.
Minister, The.
My God in Heaven Said to Me.
Singing Hallelujia.
Song of the Whirlwind.
Tired.

Johnson, George Sands (1894?–1951?)
Beyond the Beaten Way.
By the Pasture Bars.
Christmas Rhyme, A.
Course of a Year, The.
Deacon Brown's Conclusion.
I Am Growing Old.
If We Try.
Old Rustic Mill, The.
Uncle Sam's Soliloquy.
Wisdom.

Johnson, George W.
When You and I Were Young, Maggie.

Johnson, Georgia Douglas (1886–1966)
Common Dust.
Heart of a Woman, The.
I Want to Die While You Love Me.
Interracial.
Lost Illusions.
My Little Dreams.
Smothered Fires.
Youth.

Johnson, Halvard (b. 1936)
Berlioz in the Madhouse.
Fringe-Area Reception.

Johnson, Helene (1907–95)
Bottled [New York].
Invocation: "Let me be buried in the rain."
Magalu.
Road, The.
Sonnet to a Negro in Harlem.
Summer Matures.
Trees at Night.

Johnson, J. C.
Guess Who's in Town? (Nobody but That Gal of Mine)
Joint is Jumpin', The.
My Special Friend (Is Back in Town)

Johnson, James P.
Charleston.
If I Could Be with You.
Porter's Love Song to a Chambermaid, A.

Johnson, James Weldon (1871–1938)
Before a Painting.
Brer Rabbit, You's de Cutes' of 'Em All.
Brothers.
Color Sergeant, The.
Creation, The.
Envoy: "If homely virtues draw from me a tune."
Girl of Fifteen.
Go Down Death.
Judgment Day, The.
Lift Every [or Ev'ry] Voice and Sing.
Listen, Lord—[a Prayer].
Mother Night.
My City.
O Black and Unknown Bards.
Sence You Went Away.
Sunset in the Tropics.
To America.
White Witch, The.

Johnson, Jim
Music for the Cows.

Johnson, Jonathan (b. 1967)
Eclipse.
Midnight Run.
Unmarked Stop in Front of Westmond General Store, Westmond, Idaho.
View Café, The.

Johnson, Joyce
Bat that blocks at close of play, The.
Limerick: "Both Keats and Boccaccio tell a."
Limerick: "Exposing his plate to the air."
Limerick: "Old Woman who lived in the Shoe, The."
Limerick: "Simple living was clearly the nub."
Limerick: "Three Aldis, not one of them dim."
Limerick: "Wee Jamie, a canny young Scot."
Limerick: "'What's the matter, old chap?' 'Well, I came'"
Limerick: "When the Prince, who was terribly smit."

Johnson, Leslie
Limerick: "Don't think it will fall to your lot."
Limerick: "If you feel that you're right on your beam ends."
Limerick: "My purpose was purely corrective."
Limerick: "Sardines seem to get out of hand."
Limerick: "There once was an eccentric of Metz."
Limerick: "Toper who spies in the distance, A."
Paradise Lost, Book IV, lines 639—654.

Johnson, Linton Kwesi (b. 1952)
Five Nights of Bleeding.
Mi Revalueshanary Fren.
Reggae Sounds.

Johnson, Lionel Pigot (1867–1902)
Age of a Dream, The.
Burden of Easter Vigil, A.
By the Statue of King Charles [or I] at Charing Cross.
Cadgwith.
Church of a Dream, The.
Collins.
Dark Angel, The.
Lambeth Lyric.
My Own Fate.
Mystic and Cavalier.
Precept of Silence, The.
Roman Stage, The.
Stranger, A.
Te Martyrum Candidatus.
To a Traveler.
To Morfydd.
Trooppship, The.
Victory.

Johnson, Louis (b. 1924)
Bread and a Pension.
Death of the Bosun's Mate.
Here Together Met.
Magpie and Pines.
Marrows.

New Guinea Time.
Seventies, The.
Tahiti.
Vision.

Johnson, Mary F. (d. 1863)
Idiot Girl, The.
Invocation to the Spirit Said to Haunt Wroxall Down.
Second Evening.
Thunder Storm.
Village Maid, The.
Widow's Remarriage, The.

Johnson, Maggie Pogue (b. 1949)
Ambition.
As We Sow We Shall Reap.
Christmas Times.
Dat Mule ob Brudder Wright's.
Day befo' Thanksgibin', De.
Dedicated to Dr. W. H. Sheppard.
Dedication Day.
Dream, A.
I Wish I Was a Grown Up Man.
James Hugo Johnston.
Krismas Dinnah.
Leap Yeah Party, De.
Lost Teddy Bear, The.
Meal Time.
Men Folks ob Today, De.
Negro Has a Chance, The.
Old Maid's Soliloquy.
People's Literary, De.
Poet of Our Race.
Sister Johnson's Speech.
Sometimes.
Story of Lovers Leap, The.
Strawberry, The.
Superstitions.
Thoughts.
To Professor Byrd Prillerman.
To See Ol' Booker T.
V. N. and C. I, The.
What's de Use ob Wukin in de Summer Time at All.
What's Mo' Temptin' to de Palate?
When Daddy Cums from Wuk.
Why Should the American Negro Be Proud?
Wintah Styles, De.

Johnson, Markham
All-Night Diner, The.

Johnson, Michael L.
Old Dog.

Johnson, Pyke, Jr. (1889–1969?)
Toucan, The.

Johnson, Robert (1911–1938)
Hellhound on My Trail.
Love in Vain.
Me and the Devil Blues.
Stones in my Passway.

Johnson, Ronald (b. 1935)
Ark 34, Spire on the Death of L. Z.
Ark 37, Prospero's Songs to Ariel (constructed in the form of a quilt snipped from Roger Tory Peterson's *A Field Guide to Western Birds*)
Ark 44, The Rod of Aaron.
Beam 4.
Beam 7.
Beam 25, A Bicentennial Hymn.
Beam 30, The Garden.
Letters to Walt Whitman.
William Stukeley made his own Stonehenge.

Johnson, Samuel (1709–84)
Anacreon's Dove.
Ballad: "I put my hat upon my head."
Ballad: "If the man who turnips cries."
Ballad: "Tender infant, meek and mild, The."
Comets and Princes.
Epitaph on William Hogarth, An.
Epitaph upon the Celebrated Claudy Phillips, Musician, Who Died Very Poor, An.
Hermit Hoar.
Lines Contributed to Goldsmith's 'The Traveller.'
Lines Contributed to Hawkesworth's 'The Rival.'
Lines on Thomas Warton's Poems.

On the Death of Dr [*or* Mr] Robert Levet [a
  Practiser in Physic].
Paraphrase.
Poverty in London.
Prologue Spoken by Mr[.] Garrick at the
  Opening of the Theatre in Drury Lane, 1747.
Prologue to Hugh Kelly's *A Word to the Wise*.
Short Song of Congratulation [*or* To a Young
  Heir], A.
Tho' grief and fondness in my breast rebel.
To Mrs Thrale [on Her Thirty-fifth Birthday].
Translation of Du Bellay's *Epigram on a Dog*.
Turnip Vendor, The.
Vanity of Human Wishes, The; The Tenth
  Satire of Juvenal Imitated, *sels.*
Verses in Baretti's Commonplace Book.
Where then shall Hope and Fear their objects
  find?
While Many a Merry Tale.

Johnson, Samuel (1822–82)
Father, in Thy Mysterious Presence Kneeling.
I Bless Thee, Lord, for Sorrows Sent.
Life of Ages, Richly Poured.

Johnson, Trasi (b. 1967)
12 second poem.
Until He Comes.

Johnston, Arthur (1587–1641)
Cocktails for Two.
My Old Flame.
Pennies from Heaven.
To Robert Baron.

Johnston, Bertha
Did You Ever Hear an English Sparrow Sing?

Johnston, Charles (d. 1823)
I know thee not, bright creature, ne'er shall
  know.
Spirit of evil, with which the earth is rife.

Johnston, Ellen (1835–1873)
Address to Nature on its Cruelty, An.
Last Sark, The.
Lines: To a Young Gentleman of Surpassing
  Beauty.
Lines to Ellen, the Factory Girl.
Mother's Love, A.
Nelly's Lament for the Pirnhouse Cat.
Working Man, The.

Johnston, George (b. 1913)
Bliss.
Bulge, The.
Cathleen Sweeping.
Noctambule.
Music on the Water.
O Earth, Turn!
Veterans.
War on the Periphery.

Johnston, Martin (b. 1947)
Airport.
Café of Situations, The.
Directions for Dreamfishing.
Drinking Sappho Brand Ouzo.
Gorey at the Biennale.
In Memoriam.
Quantum.
Sea-Cucumber, The.
Vernal Equinox.

Johnston, Patricia
I'll Remember April.

Johnston, T.
Limerick: "There was a young lady of Ulva /
  Who kept a pet bee in her hand-bag."

Johnstone, Philip
High Wood.

Johnstone, Robert (b. 1951)
Eden Says No.
Fruit of Knowledge, The.
He's a high clear forehead.
Not from our dreams, not from our daft cadres.
Robot Camera.
Undertakers.
Various instants I'm not with you.

Jolas, Eugene (1894–1952)
Mater Dolorosa.

Jolobe, J. J. R. (1902–76)
Making of a Servant, The.

Jolson, Al
California, Here I Come.

I'll Say She Does.

Jomei (d. 1766)
Leaves of words.

Jomei, Emperor (593–641)
Written After Climbing Kaguyama to Survey
  the Land.

Jonas, George (b. 1935)
For the Record.
Four Stanzas Written in Anxiety.
Portrait: The Freedom Fighter.
Temporal.

Jonas, Rosalie (1861?–1953)
Ballade des Belles Milatraisses.
Brother Baptis' on Woman Suffrage.

Jones, Alice
Anorexia.
Communal Living.
Tap.

Jones, Anna Maria (1748–1829)
To Echo.
To the Moon.

Jones, Bobi (b. 1929)
Portrait of a Nun.
Portrait of a Pregnant Woman.
Portrait of an Engine Driver.
Spring at Nant Dywelan.

Jones, David (1895–1974)
A, a, a, Domine Deus.
Anathema, *sels.*
In Parenthesis, *sels.*
Mabinog's Liturgy, *sels.*
Sleeping Lord, The, *sels.*
Wall, The, *sels.*

Jones, David Gwenallt ("Gwenallt") (1899–1968)
Cymru.
Earth, The.
Old Woman, An.
Rhydcymerau.

Jones, Douglas G. (b. 1929)
Beautiful Creatures Brief as These.
For Spring.
From Sex, This Sea.
I Thought There Were Limits.
On a Picture of Your House.
Perishing Bird, The.
River; North of Guelph, The.
Soliloquy to Absent Friends.
Summer Is a Poem by Ovid.
These Trees Are No Forest of Mourners.

Jones, Ebenezer (1820–60)
Development of Idiotcy, A.
Eyeing the Eyes of One's Mistress.
High Summer.
When the World Is Burning.
Whimper of Awakening Passion.

Jones, Ellis (1884–1948?)
Eaves.

Jones, Ernest Charles (*fl.* c.1852)
Song of the Low, The.

Jones, Evan (b. 1927)
Dream, A.
Point, The.
Study in Blue.

Jones, Gayl (b. 1949)
Many Die Here.
Satori.
3-31-70.
Tripart.

Jones, Glyn (b. 1905)
Again.
Common Path, The.
Dafydd's Seagull and the West Wind.
Esyllt.
Fragment: Where Is Tangwen Now?
Merthyr.
Morning.
Profile of Rose.
Swifts.
Where All Were Good to Me, God Knows.

Jones, Gwilym R. (b. 1903)
Psalm to the Creatures.

Jones, Gwyn (b. 1951)
Blue Day Journey, The.

Jones, Henry
On a Fine Crop of Peas Being Spoiled by a

Storm.

Jones, Huw (b. 1955)
Man Lying in a Hallway.

Jones, Ira B.
Echoes of the Murder of Emmett Till.
Revolutionary Vision, The.

Jones, Isham
I'll See You in My Dreams.
It Had to Be You.

Jones, Jacquie (b. 1965)
Drugs.

Jones, John (1788–1858)
Now slowly winding from the mountain's
  head.

Jones, John ("Talhaiarn") (1810–69)
Glyndwr's War Song.
Watching the Wheat.

Jones, M. Keel
Election Reflection.

Jones, Mary (d. 1778)
After the Small Pox.
Epistle from Fern Hill.
Epistle to Lady Bowyer, An.
Lass of the Hill, The.
Soliloquy on an Empty Purse.
Stella's Epitaph.

Jones, Patricia (b. 1951)
Birth of Rhythm and Blues, The.
I Done Got So Thirsty That My Mouth Waters
  at the Thought of Rain.
If I Were Rita Hayworth.
Song: "I have so little sorrow."
Why I Like Movies.

Jones, Peter (b. 1929)
In the Formal Garden.
In the Park.

Jones, Peter Thabit (b. 1951)
Modris.

Jones, R. S.
Shelter.

Jones, Rae Desmond (b. 1941)
Age.
Front Window, The.
James Dean.
Shakti.

Jones, Richard
Apology to Andrew.
Beginning, A.
Key, The.
Novel, The.
Poet's Heart, The.
Portrait of My Father and His Grandson.
Song of the Old Man.
Times Like This.

Jones, Richard M. (c. 1889–1945)
Trouble in Mind.

Jones, Rodney (b. 1950)
End of Communism, The.
Blasphemy, A.
Nell.
On the Bearing of Waitresses.
TV.

Jones, Roland
Foam.

Jones, Sally Roberts (b. 1935)
Ann Griffiths.
Another Lazarus.
Community.
Household Cavalry, Llanstephan.
Illusions.
New World.

Jones, Samuel (d. 1732)
Force of Love, The.
Ploughman, in Imitation of Milton, The.
Poverty, in Imitation of Milton.

Jones, T. Gwynn (1871–1944)
Argoed.

Jones, T. Harri (1921–65)
Back?
Bird on a Jaunt.
Cwmchwefri.
Difference.
Llanafan Unrevisited.
Mr Jones as the Transported Poet.

My Grandmother Died in the Early Hours of the Morning.
Rhiannon.
Welshman in Exile Speaks, The.
Jones, Sir William (1746–94)
Epigram: "On parent knees, a naked new-born child."
Hymn to Indra, A.
Hymn to Na'ra'yena, A.
Hymn to Su'rya, A.
Jones, William Basil Tickell
Match Me Such Marvel.
Jong, Erica (b. 1941)
Alcestis on the Poetry Circuit.
Castration of the Pen.
Colder.
How You Get Born.
Parable of the Four-Poster.
Woman Who Loved to Cook, The.
Jonker, Ingrid (1933–65)
Bitterberry Daybreak.
Child Who Was Shot Dead by Soldiers at Nyanga, The.
Dog.
Don't Sleep.
Face of Love, The.
I Am with Those.
I Don't Want Any More Visitors.
I Drift in the Wind.
Pregnant Woman.
This Journey.
Time of Waiting in Amsterdam.
When You Laugh.
Jonson, Ben (1572–1637)
Alchemist, The, *sels.*
And Must I Sing? What Subject Shall I Choose?
Another. In Defense of Their Inconstancy [*or* Inconstancie]. A Song.
Another Lady's [*or* Ladyes] Exception, Present at the Hearing.
Begging Another, on Colour of Mending the Former.
Carol.
Celebration of Charis in Ten Lyric[k] Pieces [*or* Peeces], A, *sels.*
Claiming [*or* Clayming] a Second Kiss[e] by Desert.
Death and Love.
Dinner for the Devil.
Dream[e], The.
Echo's [*or* Eccho's] Song.
Elegy, An: "Though beauty be the mark of praise."
Epicoene; or, The Silent Woman.
Epigram. To the Household. 1630, An.
Epigram. To the Small-Pox, An.
Epistle Answering to One that Asked to Be Sealed of the Tribe of Ben, An.
Epistle to a Friend, to Persuade [*or* Perswade] Him to the Wars, [*or* Warres] An, *sels.*
Epistle. To Katharine, Lady Aubigny.
Epistle to Master John Selden, An.
Epitaph on Elizabeth, L. H.
Epitaph on Master Philip Gray, An.
Epitaph on Master Vincent Corbet[t], An.
Epitaph on S. P. [Salomon *or* Salathiel Pavy], a Child of Q[ueen] El[izabeth's] Chapel.
Epithalamion: or, a Song.
Epode: "Not to know vice at all, and keep[e] true state."
Execration upon Vulcan, An.
Faery Beam upon You, The.
Fit of Rhyme [*or* Rime] against Rhyme [*or* Rime], A.
Help, help all tongues to celebrate this wonder.
Her Man Described by Her Own[e] Dictamen.
Her Triumph.
Here She Was Wont to Go.
His Discourse with Cupid.
His Excuse for Loving.
Hour-Glass [*or* Houre-Glasse], The.
How He Saw Her.
Hymn[e] on the Nativity [*or* Nativitie] of My Saviour, A.
Hymn[e] to God the Father, A.

In the Person of Womankind [A Song Apologetic].
Inviting a Friend to Supper.
It Was a Beauty That I Saw.
Little Shrub Growing By, A.
Martial. Epigram XLVII, Book X.
Masque of Christmas, The.
Musical Strife; in a Pastoral Dialogue, The.
My Picture Left in Scotland.
Nymph's Passion, A.
Ode, An: "High-spirited friend, / I send not balms, nor corsives to your wound."
Ode To Himself, An.
Ode to Himself[e].
Ode. To Sir William Sydney, on His Birthday.
Of Life and Death.
On Don Surly.
On English Monsieur.
On Giles and Joan.
On Groin.
On Gut.
On Lieutenant Shift.
On Lucy, Countess[e] of Bedford.
On My First Daughter.
On My First Son[ne].
On Playwright.
On Poet-Ape.
On Something, that Walk[e]s Somewhere.
On Spies.
On the Famous Voyage, *sels.*
On the Town's Honest Man.
Picture of the Body, The.
Pleasure Reconciled to Virtue.
Pleasures of Heaven, The.
Poetaster, The, *sels.*
Return of Astraea, The.
So White, So Soft, So Sweet.
Song: "If I freely may discover."
Song: "If to your ear it wonder bring."
Song. That Women Are But Men's Shadows.
Song: "To the old, long life and treasure."
Sonnet to the Noble Lady, the Lady Mary Wroth, A.
To a Friend.
To Alchemists.
To Captain Hungry.
To Censorious Courtling.
To Clement Edmonds, on His *Caesar's Commentaries* Observed, and Translated.
To Doctor Empiric[k].
To Edward Alleyn.
To Elizabeth, Countess of Rutland.
To Fine Lady Would-Be.
To Fool or Knave.
To Francis Beaumont.
To Heaven.
To John Donne.
To Lucy, Countess[e] of Bedford, with Mr. Donnes Satire's [*or* Satyres].
To Mary, Lady Wroth.
To My Book.
To My Mere English Censurer.
To Penshurst.
To Pertinax Cob.
To Sickness.
To Sir Henry Cary.
To Sir Henry Goodyere.
To Sir Henry [*or* Henrie] Savile [upon His Translation of Tacitus].
To Sir Horace Vere.
To Sir Robert Wroth.
To Sir Thomas Roe.
To the Immortal[l] Memory [*or* Memorie] and Friendship of That Noble Pair[e], Sir Lucius Cary and Sir H. [*or* Henry] Morison.
To the Memory of My Beloved, the Author Mr [*or* Master] William Shakespeare [And What He Hath Left Us], *sels.*
To the Reader.
To the Same [Sir Thomas Roe].
To the World [A Farewell for a Gentlewoman, Virtuous and Noble].
To Thomas Palmer [on His Book "The Sprite of Trees and Herbs"].
To William Camden.
To William Roe.
Urging Her of a Promise.

Volpone, *sels.*
What He[e] Suffered.
Why I Write Not of Love.
Jooris, Roland (b. 1936)
Village, A.
What Does One Do.
Jordan, A. C. (1906–64)
You Tell Me to Sit Quiet.
Jordan, Barbara Leslie (b. 1915)
Peaceable Kingdom.
This Poem.
Viper Light.
Jordan, Judy (b. 1961)
Sandbar at Moore's Creek.
Through These Halls.
Winter.
Jordan, June (b. 1936)
Cameo No. II.
Clock on Hancock Street.
DeLiza Spend the Day in the City.
Female and the Silence of a Man, The.
For My Mother.
Getting Down to Get Over.
Grand Army Plaza.
In Memoriam: Martin Luther King, Jr.
I Must Become a Menace to My Enemies.
If You Saw a Negro Lady.
Intifada.
July 4, 1984: For Buck.
Mid-Year Report: For Haruko.
My Sadness Sits around Me.
Nobody Riding the Roads Today.
Notes on the Peanut.
October 23, 1983.
Okay "Negroes."
Onesided Dialog.
Poem about Intelligence for My Brothers and Sisters, A.
Poem About My Rights.
Poem Against the State (Of Things): 1975.
Poem for Guatemala.
Poem for My Family: Hazel Griffin and Victor Hernandez Cruz.
Poem for Nana.
Poem from the Empire State.
Poem to My Sister, Ethel Ennis, Who Sang "The Star-spangled Banner" at the Second Inauguration of Richard Milhous Nixon.
Queen Anne's Lace.
Reception, The.
Roman Poem Number Nine.
Second Poem from Nicaragua Libre: War Zone.
Snow, The.
Something Like a Sonnet for Phillis Miracle Wheatley.
Speculations on the Present through the Prism of the Past.
Sunflower Sonnet Number One.
Sunflower Sonnet Number Two.
Test of Atlanta 1979, The.
Unemployment/Monologue.
What Happens.
What Would I Do White?
You Came with Shells.
Jordan, Norman (b. 1938)
Be You.
I Have Seen Them.
July 27.
Poet the Dreamer, The.
Silent Prophet, The.
When a Woman Gets Blue.
Jordan, Thomas (1612?–1685)
Careless Gallant, The.
Double Acrostich on Mrs Svsanna Blvnt, A.
Jorge, Luiza Neto (1939–89)
Another Genealogy.
Fable: "Animal understands itself, The."
Force of Gravity, The.
Monument to Birds (Max Ernst)
Joris, Pierre (b. 1946)
Fin-de-Siècle Identikit.
Vier Takte vor K time then before.
Josefowitz, Natasha
Foreplay.
Music.

Joseki (d. 1779)
This must be.

Joseph, Allison (fl. 20th cent.)
Adolescence.
Chalazion.
In the Bookstore.
Junior High Dance.
Learning to Laugh.
My Father's Heroes.
Numbers.
On Being Told I Don't Speak Like a Black Person.
On Sidewalks, on Streetcorners, as Girls.
Pleasure.
Pure Pop.
Reading Room.
Searching for *Melinda's Magic Moment*.
Soul Train.
Teenage Interplanetary Vixens Run Wild on Bikini Beach.
Traitor.
Wedding Party.

Joseph, Jenny (b. 1932)
Back to Base.
Dog Body and Cat Mind.
Lost Continent, The.
Rose in the Afternoon.
Warning.

Joseph, Lawrence (b. 1948)
Curriculum Vitae.
Do What You Can.
Here.
In the Age of Postcapitalism.
It's Not Me Shouting at No One.
Not Yet.
Sand Nigger.
That's All.
Then.
When One Is Feeling One's Way.

Joseph, M. K. (1914–81)
Distilled Water.
Epilogue to a Poetry Reading.
Girl, Boy, Flower, Bicycle.
Mercury Bay Eclogue.

Joseph, Ray
Sinner Kissed an Angel, A.

Joshi, Umashankar (b. 1911)
Passing through Rajasthan.

Joso *See* **Naito Joso**

Josselyn, John (1630–75)
And the bitter storm augments; the wild winds wage.
Description of a New England Spring.
Verses Made Sometime Since upon . . . the Indian Squa.

Joubert, Jean ((b. 1928)
Brilliant Sky.

Jowa (d. 1785)
Second month.

Joyce, James (1882–1941)
All Day I Hear the Noise of Waters.
Bahnhofstrasse.
Ballad of Persse O'Reilly, The.
Blurb for *Anna Livia Plurabelle*, A.
Bronze by gold heard the hoofirons, steelyringing.
Ecce Puer.
Flood.
Flower Given to My Daughter, A.
Hear, O hear, Iseult la belle! Tristan, sad hero, hear! The Lambeg drum.
Holy Office, The.
Limerick: "There was a kind lady called Gregory."
My Dove, My Beautiful One.
On the Beach at Fontana.
Ondt and the Gracehoper, The.
Post Ulixem Scriptum.
Thou leanest to the shell of night.
Though I Thy Mithridates Were.
Tilly.
Tutto è Sciolto.

József, Attila (1905–37)
Ars Poetica.
Attila József.

Belated Lament.
By the Danube.
City Limits, The.
Dead Landscape.
Encouraging.
For My Birthday.
Freight Trains.
How Long the Lord.
Humans.
Hunger.
I Have Done My Reckoning.
Lullaby: "Sky is letting its blue eyes close, The."
Mother.
Ode: "Here I'm perched on a sheer cliff."
On Mankind.
Seventh, The.
Songs of Innocence.
They Who Are Poor.
Three Kings of Bethlehem, The.
To Sit, to Stand, to Kill, to Die.
True Man, A.
Welcome to Thomas Mann.

Juan Chi (210–63)
Autumn's onset means cooling breezes.
Confucianist is versed in the Six Arts, The.
Deep in the night and unable to sleep.
Elder lives by the side of the river, An.
Hibiscus grows lushly on the grave mounds, The.
In North Ward they do many strange dances.
It is the middle of the night—I cannot sleep.
Long ago, at fourteen or fifteen.
Long ago there was an immortal man.
Lucent dew congeals into frost, The.
Mujin Flowers Blossom on the Rolling Graves, The.
My steps lead me to a junction of three roads.
Singing of Thoughts.
Ten Suns Rise in the East, The.
This summer's burning heat.
Tung-ling melons—men say that long ago.
Whether one is eminent or humble depends on Fate.
Years ago, when I was young.

Juan II, of Castile (1405–54)
Cancion: "O love, I never, never thought."

Juana Inés de la Cruz, Sor (Juana Rumirez de Asbaje) (1651–95)
Describes Rationally the Irrational Effects of Love.
Elusive Shadow of My Substance, Stay.
Fifth Villancico, in Alternating Voices, Written for the Feast of the Nativity in Puebla, 1689, The, *sels*.
First Dream, *sels*.
First Villancico, Written for the Nativity of our Lord, Puebla, 1689, *sels*.
Green Enravishment of Human Life.
Hope.
I Can Neither Hold You Nor Let You Go.
In Acknowledgment of the Praises of European Writers.
In Containing a Thought Satisfied with Chaste Love.
In Which She Satisfies a Fear with the Rhetoric of Tears.
Oh World, Why Do You Thus Pursue Me?
On Her Portrait.
Perpetual Infirmity of Hope.
Pleaure Given by Suspicion with the Rhetoric of Crying, The.
She Attempts to Refute the Praises That Truth, Which She Calls Passion, Inscribed on a Portrait of the Poet.
She Proves the Inconsistency of the Desires and Criticism of Men Who Accuse Women of What They Themselves Cause.
Stay, shade of my shy treasure! Oh, remain.
This Evening When I Spoke to You.
Verses Against the Inconsequence of Men's Taste and Strictures.
Verses Expressing the Feelings of a Lover. Which Contains a Fantasy Satisfied with a Love Befitting It.

Juarroz, Roberto (b. 1925)
Any movement kills something.

Bell is full of wind, The.
Bottom of things is neither life nor death, The.
Emptiness of the day, The.
Every word is a doubt.
Lamp lit, A.
Life Draws a Tree.
Look First at the Air and Its Black Element Which Never Stops.
Prompting of my shadow, The.
Somewhere There's a Man.
Tenth.9.
There Are Points of Silence Circling the Heart.
To die, but far away.

"Judah" (fl. Middle Ages)
Fragrant Thy Memories.

Judah, Daniel ben (fl. c.1350)
Living God, The.

Judah ibn Sabbatai (fl. 12th cent.)
Expensive Wife, The.

Judah ibn Tibbon (1120–1190?)
Father's Testament, A.

Judson, Adoniram (1788–1850)
Come Holy Spirit, Dove Divine.
Our Father, God.

Judson, Sarah (1803–45)
Proclaim the Lofty Praise.

Juhász, Ferenc (b. 1928)
Birth of the Foal.
Boy Changed into a Stag Clamours at the Gate of Secrets, The.
Rainbow-Colored Whale, The.

Juhász, Gyula (1883–1937)
Death of Shakespeare, The.
Hungarian Summer [1918].
Hungarian Winter.
Lost Behind the Back of God.
Magyar Scene Through Magyar Eyes, A.
One for the "Ancient Gypsy."
Song about Kőrösi Csoma.
To Lord Byron.
Village Night.
What Was Her Blondness Like.

Julian, Emperor (Flavius Claudius Julianus; "Julian the Apostate") (332–63)
Beer.
On Beer.

Julianus of Egypt (fl. 5th cent.)
Anastasia, the Graces blossom and you were their flower.
"Drink was the end of you, Anacreon."
Epitaph in Dialogue on the Sceptic Philosopher Pyrrho.
I kept singing this, and I will call it out from the grave.
Julianus Sees a Bronze Statue of Icarus in a Public Bath.
Julianus Sees a Magistrate's Axe.
Julianus Sees the Chair of the Sophist Craterus.
Lais' Mirror.
On a Young Wife.
Though you rule the dead, under the earth, who never smile.
Unguarded House, An.

Julius Cerealius *See* **Cerealius**

Julius Polyaenus
Although your ears must be plentifully occupied.
Hope is what skims time always from our lives.

Juljan *See* **Tuwim, Julian** [*or* **Juljan**]

Jünger, Friedrich Georg (b. 1898)
Ultima Ratio.

Juntoku, Emperor
Royal Dwellings.

Juo
Beyond the snatch of time, my daily life.

Jurmann, Walter
All God's Chillun Got Rhythm.
Tomorrow Is Another Day.

Jussawalla, Adil (b. 1940)
Sea Breeze, Bombay.

Just, Hans
Christmas.
Moon, The.

Justice

Night Walk Through the Burg.

Justice, Donald (b. 1925)
Anonymous Drawing.
Another Song.
Assassination, The.
Beyond the Hunting Woods.
Bus Stop.
But That Is Another Story.
Childhood.
Children Walking Home from School through
Good Neighborhood.
Counting the Mad.
Crossing Kansas by Train.
Dancer's Life, A.
Dreams of Water.
Elegy Is Preparing Itself, An.
Evening of the Mind, The.
Here in Katmandu.
In Bertram's Garden.
In Memory of My Friend the Bassoonist John
Lenox.
In Memory of the Unknown Poet, Robert
Boardman Vaughn.
Incident in a Rose Garden.
Insomnia of Tremayne, The.
Landscape with Little Figures.
Lethargy.
Luxury.
Man Closing Up, The.
Memo from the Desk of X.
Men at Forty.
Mrs. Snow.
Mule Team and Poster.
Ode to a Dressmaker's Dummy.
On a Painting by Patient B of the
Independence State Hospital for the Insane.
On the Death of Friends in Childhood.
Pantoum of the Great Depression.
Poet at Seven, The.
Psalm and Lament.
Snowfall, The.
Sonatina in Yellow.
Stone.
Tourist from Syracuse, The.
Train.
Variations for Two Pianos.
Variations on a Text by Vallejo.
Wall, The.
White Notes.
Winter Ode to the Old Men of Lummus Park,
Miami, Florida, A.

Juvenal (c.50–c.130 A.D.)
Satires, sels.

Juvencus (fl. c.330)
Naught in the world keeps an immortal stay.

K

"K."
How Firm a Foundation.
Jungle Night.

Kabir (c.1488–1512)
Ascetic Dyes His Robes, The.
Between the conscious and the unconscious,
the mind has put up a swing.
Eternity.
Give up erotic games, Kabir.
Guest Is Inside, The.
Hopeful Spiritual Athlete, The.
How Much Is Not True.
I Cherish That Love.
I have been thinking of the difference between
water.
Inside this clay jar there are meadows and
groves and the One who made them.
Knowing Nothing Shuts the Iron Gates.
My friend, this body is His lute. He tightens
the strings and plays its songs.
Simple Purification, The.
Sometimes, everywhere I look.
Swan, tell my your old story.
To Be a Slave of Intensity.

Kaccipettu Nannakaiyar (fl. 3rd cent.)
My lover capable of terrible lies.

Kadi, Joanna
ArabInnocents.

Looking Back.

Kadima-Nzuji, Mukula
Incantations of the Sea: Moando Coast.

Kaen (d. 1772)
Back-yard chrysanthemum, A.

Kaffka, Margit (1880–1918)
Dawn Rhythms.
Litany: "My sweet, beloved companion."

Kafka, Franz (1883–1924)
Before the Law.

Kafka, Helene
Soldier's Song.

Kafu (d. 1784)
If I must die.
Nights grow short.

Kagai (d. 1778)
Barren branches.

Kagami Shiko (1665–1731)
Arid fields / The only life—.
Night snow / Neighbor's cock.
Small fish-boats / After what.

Kagank
It's only whiskey that makes you pity me.

Kageyama, Claire (fl. 20th cent.)
Mama.

Kahal, Irving (1903–42)
I Can Dream, Can't I?
I'll Be Seeing You.
Night Is Young and You're So Beautiful, The.
Wedding Bells Are Breaking Up That Old
Gang of Mine.
When I Take My Sugar to Tea.

Kahaney, Phyllis
Germany, 1981.
Pogrom.

Kahanovitch, Pinhas See "Der Nistor"

Kahclamet, Philip
Crier, The.

Kahf, Mohja
First Thing, The.
On the Death of Nizar Qabbani.
Roc, The.

Kahn, Gustave (1886–1941)
Ain't We Got Fun.
All God's Chillun Got Rhythm.
Carolina in the Morning.
Flying Down to Rio.
Guilty.
Homage.
I'll Say She Does.
I'll See You in My Dreams.
I'm Through with Love.
It Had to Be You.
Love Me or Leave Me.
Makin' Whoopee.
My Baby Just Cares for Me.
No, No, Nora.
Okay, Toots.
One I Love (Belongs to Someone Else), The.
Pilgrim from the East, The.
Pretty Baby.
Song: "O lovely April, rich and bright."
Tomorrow Is Another Day.
Toot, Toot, Tootsie! (Good-bye)
When My Ship Comes In.
Yes, Sir! That's My Baby.
You Masks of the Masquerade.
You Stepped Out of a Dream.

Kahn, Roger Wolfe
Crazy Rhythm.

Kaiga (d. 1718)
Strange—like messengers.

Kaigen
Old master held up fluff, The.

Kaikai (d. 1868)
Round a flame.

Kaisho (d. 1914)
Evening cherry-blossoms.

Kakayek
Song on the Way to Jail.

Kakei (1648–1716)
At the break of dawn.
Morning glory / So pure.

Kakinomoto no Hitomaro (fl. 7th–8th cent.)
Bay of Tsunu, The.

Colored leaves, The.
Gossip grows like weeds.
I sit at home.
In the empty mountains.
Mourning Princess Asuka.
My girl is waiting for me.
My thoughts are with a boat.
On the Eastern horizon.
On the shingle.
Pheasant of the mountain, The.
Plovers cry, The.
Strange old man, A.
This morning I will not.
When I gathered flowers.
When I left my girl.
Your hair has turned white.

Kakkai Patiniyar Naccellaiyar
Many Said.

Kalamaras, George (b. 1956)
Mud.

Kalar, Joseph (1906–72)
Papermill.

Kaldas, Pauline
Home.
Landscapes.
Morning.

Kalia, Mamta
After Eight Years of Marriage.

Kalidasa (fl. c.500)
Even the man who is happy.
High on the Mount of Rama a yaksha dwelt,
who for.
Salutation to the Dawn.
Seasons, The.

Kalina, Rosita (b. 1932)
Cabalistic Rabbis, The.
Dayeinu—they said.
I Am of the Tribe of Yehuda.
Ritual.
Testimonies.
To Anne Frank.

Kalir, Eleazar ben (fl. 7th–8th cent.)
O Hark to the Herald.
Palms and Myrtles.
Prayer for Dew.
Prophet Jeremiah and the Personification of
Israel, The.
Terrible Sons, The.
To Him Who Is Feared.

Kallatanar
What She Said.

Kalmar, Bert (b. 1895) and Harry Ruby
Nevertheless (I'm in Love with You)
Three Little Words.
What a Perfect Combination.
Who's Sorry Now?

Kálnoky, László (1912–1985)
De Profundis.
Hamlet's Lost Monologue.
Heart Escaping.
Meeting.
Remembering.
Svidrigailov's Last Night.
Swept Away.
Wanderings on a Heavenly Body.
What Man Can Do on This Planet.

Kalonymos ben Judah (fl. c.1160)
Although Tormented.

Kalonymos ben Kalonymos (1286–c.1328)
Touchstone, The.

Kalonymos ben Moses of Lucca (fl. c.950)
His Sovereignty.

Kamatari (Fujiwara no Kamatari) (614–69)
Hey! Ho! Hurrah!

Kambala
KYE HO! Wonderful!

Kambar, Chandrashekhar (b. 1938)
Pond Named Ganga, A.

Kamenetz, Rodger (b. 1950)
History of the Invisible.
Missing Jew, The.
This Is the Map.
Why Ten Men?

Kamenszain, Tamara
Eliahu.

Mea Shearim.
Return 2.
Torah Braids.

Kamienska, Anna (1920–86)
Annunciation.
Luke 1:26–38; In the sixth month the angel Gabriel.
Luke 10:38–42; Now as they went on their way.
Matthew 19:16–24; And behold, one came up to him.
On the Cross*.
Prayer That Will Be Answered, A.
Saint Martha.
Things of This World.
Those Who Carry.

Kamzon, Jacob David
Very Fair My Lot.

Kana-jo, Lady
Quivering together / Ears of barley.

Kanai, Mieko (b. 1947)
House of Madam Juju, The.

Kanastoga, Wasabi
El Elvis.

Kanavi, Chennavira (b. 1928)
On Bismillah Khan's Shehnai.

Kandel, Lenore (b. 1932)
First They Slaughtered the Angels.
Spring 61.

Kander, John
And All That Jazz.
Cabaret.
Class.
Happy Time, The.
My Coloring Book.
Nowadays.
Quiet Thing, A.

Kandil, Fatma (b. 1958)
Emaciated Teeth.
Thorny Gaps Suddenly Moving.
Veins All Dried Up.

Kandinsky [or Kandinskii], Wassily (1866–1944)
Chalk and Soot.
Sounds.
Why?

Kando (1825–1904)
It's as if our heads were on fire, the way.

Kane, Julie
Reasons for Loving the Harmonica.

Kane, Paul
Disciples Asleep at Gethsemane.

Kaneko, Lonny
Bailey Gatzert: The First Grade, 1945.

Kaneko Mitsuharu (1895–1975)
Mount Fuji.

Kanemasa (Minamoto Kanemasa) (fl. 12th cent.)
Awaji Island.
Guardian of the gate.

Kanemitsu-Kogun (fl. 19th cent.)
My hands released at last, the cliff soars.

Kanemori (fl. 10th cent.)
Although I hide it.
In the mountain village.

K'ang Hai (1475–1541)
Dreaming of Master Chung-lu.
Listening to the Rain.
Sitting by Myself.
When I have chanted my new poems.

Kanga (d. 1812)
Chill, A.

Kangyu (d. 1861)
It is indeed like that.

Kanik, Orban Veli (1914–50)
Erol Güney's Cat.
I Am Listening to Istanbul.

Kanna (d. 1744)
Autumn breeze.

Kannan
What Her Girl Friend Said to Him.

Kanshu (d. 1772)
Although the autumn moon.

Kantaris, Sylvia (b. 1936)
Airing the Chapel.

Body Language.
Not-loving.
Stocking Up.
Who could have baked my entire heart's desire.

Kanzan-Shigyo
Where is the dragon's cave?

Kao Ch'i (1336–74)
Along the River, Seeing the Home of Absconded Farmers.
Ballad of a Ferocious Tiger.
Ballad of the Deserted Mansion.
Ballad of the Neighborhood Shaman.
Cold Spring.
Going Out to the Country on a Boat Trip, Sheltering from Rain Beneath a Tree.
In the Mountains, Parting from Master Ning as I Return to West Bank.
Lament of a Soldier's Wife.
Lying at Leisure during Rain.
Mooring Our Boat at Tan-yang Harbor.
Moss below the Stairs.
Nodding Off.
Old Cowboy, The.
On a Painting by Hsia Kuei Entitled "Returning in Wind and Snow to a Village Home."
On a Painting of the Radiant Emperor's Night Revels by Candlelight.
Passing By the Battlefield at Feng-k'ou.
Picking Tea: A Ballad.
Returning to Lotus Village.
Seeing Flowers I Remember My Late Daughter, Shu.
Seeking out Hermit Hu.
Silkworm Song of Torchlit Fields.
Song of the Duck Hunters.
Song of the Man of Green Hill, The.
Spring Day—Remembering Living on the River, A.
Sunflower.
Walk to the Eastern River Bank, A.
Well of the King of Wu, The.
Where Does My Sadness Come From?
Written on Seeing the Flowers, and Remembering My Daughter.

Kao Shih (702?–765)
Song of Yen.
Youth of Han-tan, The; a Song.

Kaper, Bronislaw
All God's Chillun Got Rhythm.
Tomorrow Is Another Day.

Kaplan, Milton (b. 1910)
Knife, The.

Kaplinski, Jaan (b. 1941)
My Wife and Children.
Night comes and extinguishes the numbers and the year.
We started home, my son and I.

Kapos, Martha
Pulse, The.

Karade, Baba Ifa
Yemoja.

Karai (d. 1778)
Why should I hesitate?

Karandikar, Vinda (b. 1918)
Knot, The.

Karasumaru-Mitsuhiro (1579–1638)
Beware of gnawing the ideogram of nothingness.

Kari (d. 1770)
How sad: cherry blossoms.

Kariara, Jonathan (b. 1935)
Leopard Lives in a Muu Tree, A.

Karibo, Minji
Superstition.

Karinthy, Frigyes (1887–1938)
Dandelion.
Mene Tekel.
Message in the Bottle,The.
Struggle for Life.

Kariuki, Joseph E. (b. 1931)
New Life.

Karni, Yehuda (1884–1949)
Place Me in the Breach.

Put Me into the Breach.
Woman's Prayer, A.

Karp, Vickie
Harm.

Karpowicz, Tymoteusz (b. 1921)
Dog Which Barked Itself Out, The.
Hunting.
Lesson of Silence, A.
Rifle, The.
Silence.

Karr, Mary
Hubris.

Kartun, D.
Limerick: "There was a young girl of Uttoxeter / Who noticed that men waved their cocks at her."

Kasa no Iratsume, Lady (fl. 8th cent.)
As one hears the cry.
Have I let my love.
I dreamed I held / A sword against my flesh.
I love and fear him.
I shall think of you.
Look at this keepsake.
To love somebody.
White drops of dew, The.

Kaschnitz, Marie Luise (1901–74)
Girl thinks if I can only manage, The.
Humility.
My Ground.
Resurrection.
Who Would Have Thought It.

Kasdaglis, Lina (b. 1928)
Traffic Lights.

Kasdorf, Julia
Dying with Amish Uncles.
Eve's Striptease.
First TV in a Mennonite Family.
Green Market, New York.
Grossdaadi's Funeral.
Leftover Blessings.
Mennonites.
Streak, The.
Uncle.
Vesta's Father.
What I Learned from My Mother.
When Our Women Go Crazy.

Kasei (d. 1859)
Ash I leave behind, The.

Kasenduaxtc
Throw him into the river.

Kasenjo (d. 1776)
Depths of cold.

Kasenni (d. 1729)
Cicada of the night.

Kasischke, Laura
Fatima.
Grace.
My Heart.
Oven.
Pall.
Please.
Sad Song.

Kasmuneh (fl. 12th–13th cent.)
Overripe Fruit.
Timid Gazelle, The.

Kaso Sodon (d. 1428)
Drop of water freezes instantly, A.

Kassák, Lajos (1887–1967)
Baffling Picture.
Dictator, The.
Factory, The.
I Am With You.
Like This.
My Poetry.
Snapshot.
To a Hooligan Girl.
Young Horseman.

Kassan (d. 1818)
Summer.

Kassia (fl. 9th cent.)
Epigram: "Poverty? wealth? seek neither."
Epigram: "Wealth covers sin—the poor."
Epigram: "Woman working hard and wisely, A."

Lord, this woman who fell into many sins. Sticheron for Matins, Wednesday of Holy Week.

Kassiane (b. 804?)
Troparion.

Kassid, 'Abd al-Karim (b. 1945)
Gravestone, The.
Suitcases, The.
Tales about My Father.

Katayev [or Kataev], Valentin Petrovich (1897–1986)
Distrust the pomp of Caesar.
For a long time, not a year, not two.
When I lie down to die.

Katda
My wife went away, left me.

Katene-Horvath, Hera (b. 1912)
In Days Gone By.

Kates, J.
No Altarpiece.

Kato (d. 1908)
Moon departs, The.

Katona, József (1791–1830)
Speak out, speak, well.

Katrovas, Richard (b. 1953)
Black English.
Sky.

Katz, Joy (b. 1963)
Concerning the Islands Newly Discovered.
Falling.
Imperfect Is Our Paradise, The.
Taxonomy.
Women Must Put Off Their Rich Apparel.

Katzin, Olga See **"Sagittarius"**

Kaufman, Bob (b. 1925)
African Dream.
Afterwards, They Shall Dance.
All those ships that never sailed.
Battle Report.
Cocoa Morning.
Geneology.
Grandfather Was Queer, Too.
Heavy Water Blues.
I am a Camera.
Jail Poems.
January 30, 1976: Message to Myself.
Oregon.
Private Sadness.
To My Son Parker, Asleep in the Next Room.
Unanimity Has Been Achieved, Not a Dot Less for Its Accidentalness.
Unhistorical Events.
Unholy Missions.
Untitled.
Walking Parker Home.
Would You Wear My Eyes?

Kaufman, David Samuilovich See **"Samoylov [or Samoilov], David Samuilovich"**

Kaufman, Herbert
This Is Your Hour.

Kaufman, Shirley (b. 1923)
Above Vitebsk.
Accuser, The.
Always She Moves from Me.
Beetle on the Shasta Daylight.
Buddha of Sŏkkuram, The.
By the Rivers.
Déjà Vu.
Dream of Completion, The.
Emperor of China, The.
His Wife.
I see bodies in the morning kneel.
Job's Wife.
Looking at Henry Moore's Elephant Skull Etchings in Jerusalem during the War.
Mothers, Daughters.
Mount of Olives, The.
Nechama.
Next Year, in Jerusalem.
Poem in November.
Roots in the Air.
Security.
Stones.
There are caverns / under our feet.
Vows.

We are going down a long slide.
Western Wall, The.

Kavanagh, P. J. (b. 1931)
Goldie Sapiens.
Praying.
Temperance Billiards Rooms, The.

Kavanagh, Patrick (1905–69)
Art McCooey.
Canal Bank Walk.
Cards are shuffled and the deck, The.
Christmas Childhood, A.
Clay is the word and clay is the flesh.
Come Dance with Kitty Stobling.
Dear Folks.
Elegy for Jim Larkin.
Epic: "I have lived in important places, times."
Father Mat.
Fields were bleached white, The.
He gave himself another year.
Hospital, The.
I Had a Future.
In Memory of My Mother.
Inniskeen Road: July Evening.
Innocence.
Intimate Parnassus.
Is.
Kerr's Ass.
Leave Them Alone.
Lecture Hall.
Lines Written on a Seat on the Grand Canal, Dublin.
Long Garden, The.
Maguire is not afraid of death, the Church will light him a candle.
Memory of Brother Michael.
Memory of my Father.
My father played the melodion.
October.
On Looking into E. V. Rieu's Homer.
One, The.
Poor Paddy Maguire, a fourteen-hour day.
Question to Life.
Sanctity.
Self-slaved, The.
Shancoduff.
Spraying the Potatoes.
Stony Grey Soil.
Tarry Flynn.
Tinker's Wife.
To Hell with Commonsense.
To the Man after the Harrow.
Twelfth of July, The.
We may come out into the October reality, Imagination.
Wet Evening in April.

Kawai Chigetsu-Ni (1632–1736)
Grasshoppers / Chirping in the sleeves.

Kawamura Yoichi
On the Sand Dune.

Kay, Elizabeth
Phoenix.

Kay, Jackie (b. 1961)
Crown and Country.
Dance of the Cherry Blossom.
English Cousin Comes to Scotland.
Even the Trees.
In my country.
Maw Broon Visits a Therapist.
Pounding Rain.
Pride.
Somebody Else.
Stincher, The.
Telling Part, The.
Twelve Bar Bessie.
Virus².
Waiting Lists, The.
What Jenny Knows.

Kaya Shirao (Shiroa) (1738?–1791)
Forty years / How sharp.
Moonlit night / By melon flowers.
Mountain mist / Torches dropped.

Kayacan, Feyyaz (b. 1919)
Division of Labor.

Kayo, Patrice
Song of the Initiate.
War.

Kazakova, Rimma Fiodorovna (b. 1932)
I am growing calmer.

Kazantzis, Judith
Arachne.
Frightened Flier Goes North, The.
In Memory, 1978.
Midwife.
My Dada.
Woman making advances publicly, A.

Kazarnovsky, Yury (1904–56)
Chinese Laundry.

Kazin, Vasily [or Vasilii] Vasilevich (1898–1981)
Accordionist, The.

Kazinczy Ferenc (b.1759–1831)
Boat, The.
Hard and Easy.
Merits of Writers.
Our Tongue.
Soul of a Man, The.
Vajdahunyad.

Keach, Benjamin (d. 1704)
How Glorious Are the Morning Stars.

Kearney, Meg
Nature Poetry.

Kearns, Lionel (b. 1937)
Environment.
Foreign Aid.
Stuntman.

Keary, E. (fl. 1857–88)
Old Age.

Keate, George (1729–97)
Midst the fair range of buildings which, new-reared.

Keating, Geoffrey (Seathrum Ceitinn) (b. 1570)
At the news from Fal's high plain I cannot sleep.
Mourn for Yourself.
O lady full of guile.

Keats, John (1795–1821)
Addressed to Haydon.
After Dark Vapours Have Oppressed Our Plains.
Blue! 'Tis the Life of Heaven, the Domain.
Bright Star.
Dawlish Fair.
Day Is Gone and All Its Sweets Are Gone, The.
Endymion: A Poetic Romance, sels.
Epistle to George Keats, sels.
Eve of St Agnes, The, sels.
Fall of Hyperion; A Dream, The.
Fancy.
Fragment of an Ode to Maia Written on May Day, 1818.
Great Spirits Now on Earth.
Happy Is England! I Could Be Content.
"How Many Bards Gild the Lapses of Time!"
Human Seasons, The.
Hyperion, sels.
I Cry Your Mercy, Pity, Love—Ay, Love!
If by Dull Rhymes Our English Must Be Chained.
In a Drear-nighted December.
In Drear-nighted December.
Keen, Fitful Gusts are Whisp'ring.
La Belle Dame sans Merci [A Ballad].
Lamia.
Lines on the Mermaid Tavern.
Meg Merrilies [or Merrilees].
On Seeing the Elgin Marbles.
Nebuchadnezzar's Dream.
O Grant.
O Solitude! If I Must With Thee Dwell.
O Thou Whose Face Hath Felt the Winter's Wind.
Ode: "Bards of passion and of mirth."
Ode on a Grecian Urn.
Ode on Indolence.
Ode on Melancholy.
Ode to a Nightingale.
Ode to Psyche.
On Fame.
On First Looking into Chapman's Homer.
On Leaving Some Friends at an Early Hour.
On Oxford.

On Sitting Down to Read "King Lear" Once Again.
On the Grasshopper and [the] Cricket.
On the Sea.
Robin Hood.
Saturn.
Sleep and Poetry, *sels.*
Song About Myself, A, *sels.*
Song of the Indian Maid.
Sweet Peas.
To a Cat.
To a Friend Who Sent Me Some Roses.
To Ailsa Rock.
To Autumn.
To B.R. Haydon, with a Sonnet Written on Seeing the Elgin Marbles.
To Chatterton.
To Homer.
To Kosciusko.
To Leigh Hunt, Esq.
To ———: "Had I a man's fair form, then might my sighs."
To My Brothers.
To One Who Has Been Long in City Pent.
To Sleep.
When I Have Fears [That I May Cease to Be].
Where Be You [*or* Ye] Going, You [*or* Ye] Devon Maid?
Why Did I Laugh Tonight?
Written on the Day That Mr. Leigh Hunt Left Prison.

Keble, John (1792–1866)
Address to Poets.
All Saints' Day.
Epithalamium: "Voice that breathed o'er Eden, The."
Fill High the Bowl.
Flowers of the Field.
Happiness.
Hezekiah's Display.
Lyra Innocentium.
Malvern at a Distance.
November.
Rainbow, The.
Samuel's Prayer.
See Lucifer Like Lightning Fall.
Sun of my soul, thou Saviour dear.
United States.

Kedrin, Dmitry [*or* Dmitrii] Borisovich (1907–45)
Builders.

Keech, Benjamin
Discovery.
Little Words.
Love Is Kind.
True to the Best.

Keelan, Claudia
Blue Diamond.
Gravity and Grace.
To the New World.

Kees, Weldon (1914–55)
After the Trial.
Aspects of Robinson.
Beach in August, The.
Coming of the Plague, The.
Conversation in the Drawing Room, The.
For My Daughter.
Guide to the Symphony.
Heat in the Room, The.
If This Room is Our World.
January.
La Vita Nuova.
1926.
Robinson at Home.
Round: "'Wondrous life!' cried Marvell at Appleton House."
Small Prayer.

Keeshig-Tobias, Lenore
I Grew Up.
Mother with Child.

Keesing, Nancy (b. 1923)
Queer Thing, A.
Reverie of a Mum.

Kefala, Antigone
Freedom Fighter.
Industrial City.
Party, The.

Saturday Night.
Sunday Visit.

Kegels, Anne-Marie (b. 1912)
I write to make you suffer.
Nocturnal Heart.
When I strip, / Stop walking / And drop into sleep.

Keido (d. 1750)
Bound homeward under.
Cuckoo's voice, The.

Keith, Joseph Joel
Definitions.

Keithley, George (b. 1935)
First Morning.
Small Moon on the Shoulder of New York.
Thunder Storm.

Keizan (1268–1325)
Border of the realm.

Kekova, Svetlana (b. 1951)
Ants, The.
Everything has come true. The punishment fits the crime.
Having submitted your petition for dismissal.
Sky is covered with stars, like a body with sores, The.

Kelber, Mim
Pledge of Allegiance to the Family of Earth, A.

Kelen, S. K. (b. 1956)
First Circle, The.
Gods Ash Their Cigarettes, The.
Rabbit Shoeshine.

Keller, David
After Supper.
Man Who Knew the Words to 'Louie, Louie,' The.
Melancholy.

Keller, Gottfried (1819–90)
Now Have I Fed and Eaten Up the Rose.
Venus de Milo.

Keller, Helen (1880–1968)
In the Garden of the Lord.

Kello, Esther (1571–1624)
Prayer to God.

Kelly, Aileen
Given Flesh Returns Nothing but Bread, The.

Kelly, Brigit Pegeen
Botticelli's St. Sebastian.
Imagining Their Own Hymns.
Leaving, The.
Petition.
Song: "Listen: there was a goat's head hanging by ropes in a tree."
To the Lost Child.
Visitation, The.
Wild Turkeys: The Dignity of the Damned.
Young Wife's Lament.

Kelly, Isabella (c.1759–1857)
To an Unborn Infant.

Kelly, Robert (b. 1934)
Bittersweet Growing Up the Red Wall.
Book of Persephone, The.
Coming.
In June.
Last Light.
Life of Intimate Fleeing, A.
Looking.
Man Who Loved White Chocolate, The.
Ode to Language.
Poem for Easter.
Rainmakers, The.
Recessional.
Sound, The.
Studying Horses.
Those who are beautiful.
Tune.
Woman with Flaxen Hair in Norfolk Heard, A.

Kelly, Thomas
Head That Once Was Crowned with Thorns, The.
Second Advent, The.
We sing praise of him who died.

Kelpius, Johannes (1673?–1708)
I Love My Jesus Quite Alone.

Kemal Khojandi (d. 1401?)
One Final Fling.

Kemble, Frances Anne [*or* "Fanny"] (1809–93)
Cover me with your everlasting arms.
Faith.
Farewell to Italy.
Impromptu.
Lines.
Noonday Vision, A.
Parting.
Petition, A.
Sonnet: "If there were any power in human love."
Sonnet: "Thou poisonous laurel leaf, that in the soil."
Sonnet: "What is my lady like? thou fain would'st know."
To Mrs. Norton.
To Shakespeare.
To the Wissahiccon.
What Shall I Do?
Whene'er I recollect the happy time.
Wish, A.

Kemp, Anne (*fl.* 1650s)
Contemplation on Bassets Down-Hill by the Most Sacred Adorer of the Muses Mrs. A. K., A.

Kemp, Jan (b. 1949)
Letter to the Immigration Officer.
Poem: "Puriri moth's wing, A."
"When the Wild Goose Finds Food He Calls His Comrades"—*I Ching.*

Ken, Thomas (1637–1711)
Glory to Thee, My God, This Night.
Morning Hymn.
Now.
Priest of Christ, The.

Kendall, Henry Clarence (1839–82)
Bell-Birds.
Beyond Kerguelen.
Christmas Creek.
Last of His Tribe, The.
Mooni.
Orara.

Kendall, May (1861–1943)
Ballad of the Cadger.
Ballad of the Ichthyosaurus.
Church Echoes.
Education's Martyr.
Envoy.
Ether Insatiable.
Failures.
Fossil, A.
In the Toy Shop.
Last Performance, The.
Lay of the Trilobite.
Legend of the Crossing-Sweeper.
Lower Life, The.
Philanthropist and the Jelly-fish, The.
Pure Hypothesis, A.
Sandblast Girl and the Acid Man, The.
Underground.
Vision of Noah, The.
Woman's Future.

Kendall, Timothy (*fl.* 1577)
Desire of Dominion.
Difference Between a King and a Tyrant, The.
Of a Good Prince and an Evil.
Tyrant in Sleep, Naught Differeth from a Common Man, A.
Upon the Grave of a Beggar.

Kendrick, Dolores (b. 1927)
Alone for a Week.
Gethsemane A. D.
Inpatient.
Jenny in Love.
Jenny in Sleep.
Note to the Ophthalmologist.
Sadie Snuffs a Candle.
Sidney, Looking for her Mother.
Solo: The Good Blues.
Sophie, Climbing the Stairs.
26th Person, The.
We are the Writing on the Wall.

Kendrick, Leatha
Simple Thing, A.

Kenjeev, Bakhyt (b. 1950)
And a fool, and a smart one, a miser.

Gone is the sound of my favorite misfortune,
which even yesterday.
You envied the flying birds and stones.

Kenju (d. 1759)
Melting snows, The.

Kennedy, Benjamin Hall (1804–89)
Bad Luck to This Marching.
On ["Who Wrote Icon Basilike" by Dr.]
Christopher Wordsworth, Master of Trinity.

Kennedy, Imogene Elizabeth
One day.

Kennedy, James (1793–1827)
Chased from my calling to this hackneyed
trade.

Kennedy, Laura H.
I am in the most exquisite distress.
Moonburn.

Kennedy, Walter (c.1460–c.1508)
Honour with Age.

Kennedy, X. J. (b. 1929)
Artificer.
B Negative.
Bee.
Brats.
Dirty English Potatoes.
Driving Cross-Country.
Emily Dickinson in Southern California.
Epitaph for a Postal Clerk.
First Confession.
Hangover Mass.
Help!
Hummingbird.
In a Prominent Bar in Secaucus [One Day].
Japanese Beetles.
Joshua.
Keep a Hand on Your Dream.
Landscapes with Set-Screws.
Last Child.
Last Lines.
Last Lines on a Wrestler.
Lighting a Fire.
Little Elegy.
Loneliness of Lincoln, The.
Loose Woman.
Mingled Yarns.
Mother's Nerves.
Nothing in Heaven Functions as It Ought.
Nude Descending a Staircase.
One Winter Night in August.
Poets.
Terse Elegy for J.V. Cunningham.
To an Angry God.
To Someone Who Insisted I Look up Someone.
Vulture.
Whales off Wales, The.

Kennelly, Brendan (b. 1936)
Big Words, The.
Bread.
Dream of a Black Fox.
Horse's Head, The.
In the Sea.
Island, The.
Limerick Train, The.
Master.
My Dark Fathers.
Plans.
Position of Praise, The.
Proof.
Running Battle, A.
Swimmer, The.
Thatcher, The.
Three Tides.
Vintage.
Wound, A.
Yes.

Kenney, Richard (b. 1948)
Apples on Champlain.
Aubade: "Cold snap. Five o'clock."
Battle of Valcour Island, The.
In April.
In Retrospect.
La Brea.
Light.
Perfect Disc of the Moon, The.
Plume.
Sailing.

Sawmill.

Kenny, Maurice (b. 1929)
December.
First Rule.
Legacy.
O Wendy, Arthur.
Reverberation.
Still-Life.
Strawberrying.
Sweetgrass.
They Tell Me I Am Lost.
Wild Flower.
Wild Strawberry.
Winkte.
Wolf "Aunt."

Kenny, Nick
Patty-Poem.

Kent, Walter
Reciprocity.

Kenyon, Jane (1947–95)
August Rain, after Haying.
Bat, The.
Briefly It Enters, and Briefly Speaks.
Depression in Winter.
Dutch Interiors.
February: Thinking of Flowers.
Finding a Long Gray Hair.
From Room to Room.
From the Nursery.
Gettysburg, July 1, 1863.
Having It Out With Melancholy.
Here.
In and Out.
Insomnia at the Solstice.
Let Evening Come.
Often.
Once There Was Light.
Otherwise.
Pardon.
Peonies at Dusk.
Pharaoh.
Potato.
Suggestion from a Friend.
Suitor, The.
Travel: After a Death.

Kenyon, John (1784–1856)
Champagne Rosée.

Kenzheyev [or Kenzheiev], Bakhyt (b. 1950)
Poets have often noticed.

Keplinger, David (b. 1968)
Another Century.
Distance Between Zero and One, The.
Inside: George Gaines at Graterford Prison,
1981.

Keppo
Searching Him took.

Ker, L. (fl. c.1787)
Death of the Gods; an Ode Written in Imitation
of Pindar, The.

Kerekere, Wiremu Kingi (b. 1923)
Greeting to Queen Elizabeth, the Rare White
Heron of Single Flight, A.

Kern, Jerome (fl. 1920)
All the Things You Are.
Bill.
Bill (Original Version)
Bojangles of Harlem.
Bungalow in Quogue.
Can't Help Lovin' Dat Man.
Cleopatterer.
Don't Ever Leave Me.
Fine Romance, A.
Folks Who Live on the Hill, The.
I'm Old-Fashioned.
I've Told Ev'ry Little Star.
I Won't Dance.
In Love In Vain.
It's a Hard, Hard World for a Man.
Land Where the Good Songs Go, The.
Last Time I Saw Paris, The.
Left All Alone Again Blues.
Let's Begin.
Look for the Silver Lining.
Lovely to Look At.
Make Believe.

Napoleon.
Never Gonna Dance.
Pick Yourself Up.
Poor Pierrot.
Raggedy Ann.
Remind Me.
She Didn't Say 'Yes.'
Smoke Gets in Your Eyes.
Song Is You, The.
That Was Before I Met You.
Till the Clouds Roll By.
Tulip Time in Sing Sing.
Way You Look Tonight, The.
Who?
Why Was I Born?
Yesterdays.
You Can't Make Love by Wireless.
You Couldn't Be Cuter.
You Never Knew About Me.
You Were Never Lovelier.

Kerner, Justinus (1786–1862)
Home-Sickness.

Kerouac, Jack (John Kerouac) (1922–69)
And What Do I Owe You, God.
Arms folded.
Birds singing.
Buddha.
Did I create that sky? Yes, for, if it was.
Flies.
How to Meditate.
Hymn.
In my medicine cabinet.
Mexican Loneliness.
Mexico City Blues, sels.
Missing a kick.
My Gang.
Poem.
Sea Shroud, The.
Straining at the padlock.
Thrashing Doves, The.

Kerouac, John See **Kerouac, Jack**

**"Kerr, Orpheus C." (Robert Henry Newell)
(1836–1901)**
American Traveller, The.
Columbia's Agony.
Dear Father, Look Up.
Editor's Wooing, The.
Neutral British Gentleman, The.
O, Be Not Too Hasty, My Dearest.
Rejected "National Hymns," The.
Tuscaloosa Sam.
When Your Cheap Divorce Is Granted.

Kessler, Milton (b. 1930)
Secret Love.
Waxwings.

Kessler, Rod
Elm Tree on Lafayette Street, The.

Kessler, Sharon
Family Secrets.
Names the Dead Speak.

Kessler, Stephen (b. 1947)
Cigarette Case.
Jack's Last Words.
Marty's Mother.

Kethe, William (fl. 16th cent.)
Such as in God the Lord Do Trust.
Thy Mercies, Lord, to Heaven Reach.

Key, Francis Scott (1779–1843)
Lord with glowing heart I'd praise thee.
Star-Spangled Banner, The.
To My Cousin Mary, for Mending My Tobacco
Pouch.
Written at the White Sulphur Springs.

Keyes, Frances Parkinson
Limerick: "There was a young man so
benighted."

Keyes, Sidney (1923–43)
Advice for a Journey.
Death and the Plowman.
Dunbar, 1650.
Early Spring.
Elegy: "April again, and it is a year again."
Europe's Prisoners.
Expected Guest, The.
Gardener, The.

Grail, The.
Greenwich Observatory.
Holstenwall.
Moon is a poor woman, The.
Neutrality.
Plowman.
Red rock wilderness, The.
Timoshenko.
War Poet.
William Wordsworth.
William Yeats in Limbo.

Keyser, Gustave
In the wake.
Rainy summer night.

Kgositsile, Keorapetse (b. 1938)
Acknowledgement.
Air I Hear, The.
For Art Blakey and the Jazz Messengers.
Gods Wrote, The.
In the Mourning.
Mirrors, Without Song.
Song for Ilva Mackay and Mongane.
To Mother.
To My Daughter.

Khaïr-Eddine, Mohammed
Barbarian.
Refusal to Inter.

Khalifa, 'Ali 'Abdallah (b. 1944)
Clover Flower, The.
On Saying Goodbye to the Lady in Green.

Khalvati, Mimi (b. 1944)
Baba Mostafa.
Blue Moon.
Coma.
Knocking on the door.
Needlework.
On Reading Rumi.
One eye crystal, one eye flame, it arrives.
Rubaiyat.
Stone of Patience.

Khamees, Dhabya (b. 1958)
Glance.
Gulf.
Letter.
Loneliness.
Standing Worship.

Khamees, Hamda (b. 1946)
Time for Dejection.
Time to Shine.
What Is Not Mine.

Khan, Akhlaq Mohammad *See* "Shahryar"

Kharabarov, Ivan (1935–70)
Taiga, The.

Kharms, Daniil (1905–42)
Beginning of a Beautiful Day (A Symphony), The.
Death of the Wild Warrior.
Each Tuesday above a roadway.
Event on the Street, An.
From "The Blue Notebook" No. 12.
Khaldeyev, Naldeyev, and Peppermaldeyev.
Symphony No. 2.
There I was sitting on one leg.
Tricks.
Un-Now.

Khavarani, Awhad ad-Din 'Ali ibn Vahid ad-Din Muhammad *See* "Anvari"

Khayr, Abu Sa'id Abul (967–1048)
For men and women soon the day draws near.
His absence is the knife that cuts your throat?
If I've been dead for twenty years or so.
I'm going to tell You something that is true.

Khayyám, Omar (d. 1123)
Ah, with the grape my fading life provide.
And when like her, oh Sákí, you shall pass.
Awake! for morning in the bowl of night.
Book of verses underneath the bough, A.
But leave the Wise to wrangle, and with me.
Come, fill the cup, and in the fire of spring.
For some we loved, the loveliest and the best.
Here with a Loaf of Bread beneath the Bough.
'How sweet is mortal Sovranty!' — think some.
I sometimes think that never blows so red.
Iram indeed is gone with all his rose.

Moving Finger writes; and, having writ, The.
Myself when young did eagerly frequent.
Oh, come with old Khayyám and leave the Wise.
Rubáiyát of Omar Khayyám [of Naishápúr], The.
Some for the Glories of This World; and some.
They say the lion and the lizard keep.
Wake! for the sun, who scattered [*or* scatter'd] into flight.
Yon rising Moon that looks for us again.

Kherdian, David (b. 1931)
Couple that walked, The.
Dogs on a leash.
Hawthorne berries, The.
In the autumn-come-winter park.
Wind rips through the.
Wing-set lone seagull, The.

Khlebnikov, Oleg (b. 1956)
From three sources, / vital sources flowing in dull shades of red.

Khlebnikov, Velemir [*or* Viktor Vladimirovich] (1885–1922)
And so the castles of world trade.
Bo-be-o-bee sang the mouth.
Burning Field, The.
Clan of stony desert women, A.
Feeding the Dove.
Four Poems.
Hey...y! Uh...hm!, covered with sweat.
I need but little! A crust of bread.
I, to make myself laugh louder and longer.
I Went Out.
Iranian Song.
It Has the Unassuming Face of a Burnt-out Candle.
Lone Performer, The.
Lonely Masquerader.
Manifesto of the Presidents of the Terrestrial Globe.
Me and Russia.
Once again, once again.
Once More, Once More.
One Book, The.
Persons, people, and the years.
Plane Four.
She came and spoke low.
Stop Fooling.
Suppose I Make a Timepiece of Humanity.
To Everyone.
Trumpet, Shout, Carry!
Tsar! Send out a shot!
We don't live in castles.
Writers of the knife are we!
Zangezi: R, K, L, G—.

Khlebnikov, Viktor *See* Burliuk, D.

Khodasevich, Vladislav Felitsianovich (1886–1939)
Amidst a smoking desolation.
Automobile, The.
Ballad: "Oh, quietly mad I'd like to be."
Bride, The.
Dactyls.
In Front of the Mirror.
Monkey.
Monkey.
Monument, A.
Monument, The.
Music.
On the Death of My Tomcat Murr.
Plainsong.
Shape ships to seek some shining shore.
Through the Window.
To a Guest.
Twilight.
Twilight was turning to darkness outside.

Kholin, Igor (b. 1929)
Recently in Sokol.

Khomin, Igor
Dike, a flower bed, a bare linden tree, A.
They drank. They ate. They smoked.
They met at the Tagansky subway station.

Khosravani
There are four kinds of men who'll get no fee from me.

Khouri, Khalil (b. 1934)
Ants and the Sun.

Cripple, The.

Khoury-Gata, Venus (b. 1937)
Autumn made colors burn, The.
Because They Hesitated Between Roses and Darkness.
Humbly, He Speaks to His Tools.
It Was a Season Tattooed on the Forehead of the Earth.
They.
Your cheeks flat on the sand.

Khoury, Nidaa (b. 1959)
Death Is Your Salvation.
Last Bullet, The.
People of Figs.
People of Fire.
People of Grapes.
People of Olives.
People of Pomegranates.

Ki Joon
Elegy for Myself.

Ki Lady (*fl.* 8th cent.)
I know the reputation / Of the idle ways.

Ki no Tomonori (*fl.* early 10th cent.)
In the eternal / Light of the spring day.

Ki no Tsurayuki (882–946)
Hue is as rich, The.
No, the human heart.
On a spring hillside.
Out in the marsh reeds.
Wind that scatters, The.

Kiba (d. 1868)
My old body.

Kibai (d. 1788)
My one wish.

Kibirov, Timur (b. 1955)
Year 1937, The.

Kibkarjuk
Song of the Rejected Woman.

Kidman, Fiona (b. 1940)
Guy Fawkes '58.
Train Song.

Kie Tapu
Song by a Woman Accused of Adultery.

Kifu (d. 1898)
Cutting a swath.

Kigen (d. 1736)
Seventy-one!

Kikaku (1661–1707)
Bantam rooster, A.
Above the boat.
Cicada chirp / Fan peddler.
Evening bridge / A thousand hands.
Full autumn moon / On the straw mat.
Her mate devoured.
I begin each day.
In the Emperor's bed.
Leaf / Of the yam.
May he who brings / Flowers tonight.
O Great Buddha.
On Buddha's birthday.
Over the long road.
Riding the wide leaf.
Sacred night / Through masks.
Shrine gate / Through morning mist.
Single yam leaf, A.
Sprinkle water wide / For the sparrow.
Summer airing / Trying on a quilt.

Kiko
Mount Sumeru—my fist!
That which blossoms.

Kilgore, James C. (b. 1928)
White Man Pressed the Locks, The.

Killeen, Ger (b. 1960)
At the Black Edge.
My Father's Angels.
Rewind.
Tristia.
Wishes.

Killigrew, Anne (1660–85)
Alexandreis.
Cloris' Charms Dissolved by Eudora.
Complaint of a Lover, The.
Discontent, The.
Farewell to Worldly Joys, A.

On a Picture Painted by Herself [*or* Her self], Representing Two Nymphs [*or* Nimphs] of Diana's, One in a Posture to Hunt, the other Bath[e]ing.
On Death.
On the Birth-Day of Queen Katherine.
On the Soft and Gentle Motions of Eudora.
Pastoral Dialogue.
Upon the Saying That My Verses Were Made by Another.

Killigrew, Katherine (1542?–1583)
Lady Katherine Killigrew Wrote This Poem about Her Own Death, The.
Mildred, if you take the trouble to send me what I want.

Killigrew, Thomas (1612–83)
Epilogue to "The Parson's Wedding."

Kilmer, Joyce (1886–1918)
House with Nobody in It, The.
Trees.

Kilmer, Nicholas (b. 1941)
In my first gentle days.

Kim, Alison
Sewing Woman.

Kim Ku (1488–1534)
I Spy the Three-Colored Peach Blossom.

Kim Kwangsŏp (1905–77)
Having Died.

Kim, Myung Mi (b. 1957)
Into Such Assembly.
Rose of Sharon, A.

Kim Pyŏngyŏn (1807–63)
Song for My Shadow, A.

Kim Sang-yong
Love Is False.

Kim Sowŏl (1903–34)
Years from Now.

Kim Sujang (c.1680–1730)
Deception.
Moonlight.

Kimball, Harriet McEwen (1834–1912)
Angel of the Rain.
In Reverie.

Kimball, Jacob (1761–1826)
Thy Praise, O God, in Zion Waits.

Kimbrell, James (b. 1967)
Mt. Pisgah.
My Father at the North Street Boarding House.
Rooftop.
Self-Portrait, Jackson.
Slow Night on Texas Street, A.
True Descenders.

Kimpo (d. 1894)
Today is the day.

Kimpu (*fl.* c.1686)
One gulp.

Kin'ei (d. 1778)
Autumn flowers, The.

Kin'u (d. 1817)
How leisurely the cherry.

King, Anne (b. 1621, d. after 1671)
Essay upon Good-Friday, An.

King, Ben (Benjamin Franklin King) (1857–99)
Cultured Girl Again, The.
Hair-Tonic Bottle, The.
Mermaid, The.
Pessimist, The.
Sum of Life, The.

King, Benjamin Franklin *See* **King, Ben**

King, Harriet Hamilton (1840–1920)
Dream Maiden, A.
Moonlight Ride, A.
Summer Lost.

King, Helen
If we give love and sympathy.

King, Henry, Bishop of Chichester (1592–1669)
Change, The.
Contemplation upon Flowers, A.
Double Rock, The.
Exequy, The.
Forfeiture, The.
Renunciation, A.
Sic Vita.

Silence: A Sonnet.
Sonnet: "Go, thou that vainly dost mine eyes invite."
Sonnet: "Tell me[e] no more how fair[e] she[e] is."
Surrender, The.
Upon a Braid of Hair in a Heart.
Upon the Death of My Ever Desired Friend Doctor [*or* Dr] Donne Dean of Paul's.

King, Jane (b. 1952)
Intercity Dub.

King Pleasure *See* **Beeks, Clarence**

King, Stoddard (1889–1933)
Breakfast Song in Time of Diet.
Crime at Its Best.
Difference, The.
Hearth and Home.
Idyll: "He was a selfish shellfish."
Trombone Solo.

King, William (1662–1712)
Beggar Woman, The.
Far from the parlour have your kitchen placed.

Kingsley, Charles (1819–75)
Airly Beacon.
Farewell, A: "My fairest child, I have no song to give you."
Invitation, The.
Last Buccaneer, The.
Ode to the Northeast Wind.
Sands of Dee, The.
Song: "When I was a greenhorn and young."
Three Fishers [Went Sailing], The.
Watchman, The.
Whelming the dwellings of men, and the toils of the slow-/ footed oxen.
Young and Old.

Kingsley, Henry (1830–76)
At Glastonbury.
Magdalene at Michael's gate.

Kingsmill, Hugh (1889–1949)
Poem, after A. E. Housman.
Summer Time on Bredon.

Kingston, Maxine Hong (b. 1940)
Absorption of Rock.
Restaurant.

Kinko (d. 1860)
Within the vast and empty.

Kinnell, Galway (b. 1927)
After Making Love We Hear Footsteps.
Angel, The.
Angling, a Day.
Another Night in the Ruins.
Avenue Bearing the Initial of Christ into the New World, The.
Bear, The.
Black bear sits alone, A.
Blackberry Eating.
Burning.
Cells Breathe in the Emptiness.
Coals go out, The.
Correspondence School Instructor Says Goodbye to His Poetry Students, The.
Crying.
Daybreak.
Dead Shall Be Raised Incorruptible, The.
Duck-chasing.
First Song.
Flower Herding on Mount Monadnock.
For Robert Frost.
For the Lost Generation.
Freedom, New Hampshire.
Getting the Mail.
Gray Heron, The.
Hen Flower, The.
In a Parlor Containing a Table.
In Fields of Summer.
Lackawanna.
Last Gods.
Last Songs.
Lastness.
Little Sleep's-Head Sprouting Hair in the Moonlight.
Man on the Hotel Room Bed, The.
Man Splitting Wood in the Daybreak, The.
Memory of Wilmington.
Night in the Forest.

Oatmeal.
On the Oregon Coast.
On the Tennis Court at Night.
Path among the Stones, The.
Pen, The.
Porcupine, The.
Quick and the Dead, The.
Ruins under the Stars.
Saint Francis and the Sow.
Seekonk Woods, The.
Shroud, The.
Supper after the Last, The.
To Christ Our Lord.
To William Carlos Williams.
Under the Maud Moon.
Under the Williamsburg Bridge.
Vapor Trail Reflected in the Frog Pond.
Vow, The.
Waking, The.
When I come back to my father's house,.
When One Has Lived a Long Time Alone.

Kinsella, John (b. 1963)
Archetypal Chillies.
Bright Cigar-Shaped Object Hovers Over Mount Pleasant, A.
Chess Piece Cornered.
Cormorants.
Fall, The.
Orpheus.
Pig Melons.
Plumburst.
Rabbiters: A Pastoral, The.
Sick Woman.
Visitant Eclogue.
Warhol at Wetlands.
Wild Radishes.

Kinsella, Thomas (b. 1929)
Again in the mirrored dusk the paddles sank.
All is Emptiness, and I Must Spin.
Ancestor.
Another September.
Artists' Letters.
At the Crossroads.
Baggot Street Deserta.
Ballydavid Pier.
Blade licks out and acts, A.
Brotherhood.
Character, indistinct, entered, A.
Chrysalides.
Clarence Mangan.
Country Walk, A.
Cover Her Face.
Dark hall. Great green liquid windows, A.
Death Bed.
Dispossessed, The.
Downstream.
Endymion.
Enough.
First Light.
Folk Wisdom.
Foot of the tower. An angle where the darkness, The.
Furnace, The.
Hand of Solo, A.
Harmonies.
Hen Woman.
His Father's Hands.
How to put it . . . without offence.
I must lie down with them all soon and sleep.
In the Ringwood.
Inside, it is bare but dimly alive.
It is an August evening, in Wicklow.
It is hard to beat a good meal.
Je T'Adore.
Lady of Quality, A.
Laundress, The.
Mirror in February.
Model School, Inchicore.
Monk, The.
1956.
Nuchal, a Fragment.
Old Atheist Pauses by the Sea, An.
Oldest Place, The.
Point, greatly enlarged, The.
Portrait of the Artist, A.
Ritual of Departure.
Route of the Táin, The.

Scylla and Charybdis.
Secret Garden, The.
Soft, To Your Places.
Talent and Friendship.
Tao and Unfitness at Inistiogue on the River Nore.
Tear.
Thinking of Mr. D.
38 Phoenix Street.
Veteran smiled and let us pass through, A.
Vital spatterings. Excess.
Wormwood.
Wyncote, Pennsylvania: A Gloss.

Kintsune (*fl.* 13th cent.)
Flowers whirl away, The.

Kinzie, Mary
Among mosquitoes.
Beautiful Days.
Bolt, The.
Boy.
But her arm—damp, small.
Canicula.
Engraving of Blake, An.
Glinting like water.
Heat-heavy creatures.
In air hard as sand.
Lunar Frost.
Orchard dying, The.
Ringing Words.
Sound Waves.
Summers of Vietnam.
Sun and Moon.
Want, predation, sleep.

Kipling, Rudyard (1865–1936)
Absent-Minded Beggar, The.
Arithmetic on the Frontier.
Astrologer's Song, An.
At His Execution.
Ballad of East and West, The.
Ballad of Fisher's Boardinghouse, The.
Batteries Out of Ammunition.
Beginner, The.
Bombed in London.
Bonfires, The.
Boots.
Bridegroom, The.
Bridge-Guard in the Karroo.
Broken Men, The.
Brown Bess.
Cells.
Cholera Camp.
Christmas in India.
Common Form.
Conundrum of the Workshops, The.
Convoy Escort.
Coward, The.
Dane-Geld.
Danny Deever.
Dead Statesman, A.
Death-Bed, A.
Derelict, The.
Drifter off Tarentum, A.
Dykes, The.
'Eathen, The.
Eddi's Service.
Envoi: "There's a whisper down the field where the year has shot her yield."
Epitaphs of the War [1914–1918], *sels.*
Equality of Sacrifice.
Evarra and His Gods.
Ex-Clerk.
Fabulists, The.
For to Admire.
Ford o' Kabul River.
Fuzzy-Wuzzy.
Galley-Slave, The.
Gallio's Song.
Gentlemen-Rankers.
Gethsemane.
Gipsy Trail, The.
Glory of the Garden, The, *sels.*
Gods of the Copybook Headings, The.
Gunga Din.
Half-Ballad of Waterval.
Heriot's Ford.
Hump, The.
Hyænas [*or* Hyenas], The.

Hymn before Action.
If—.
In the Neolithic Age.
Journalists.
Jungle Book, *sels.*
Kim, *sels.*
King, The.
L'Envoi.
La Nuit Blanche.
Ladies, The.
Land, The.
Land and Sea Tales, *sels.*
Last Chantey, The.
Lie, The.
Limerick: "There was a small boy of Quebec."
Look, You Have Cast Out Love!
Looking Glass, The.
Loot, *sels.*
Mandalay.
McAndrew's Hymn.
Merrow Down.
Mesopotamia.
Morning Song in the Jungle.
My Rival.
Naaman's Song.
Nativity, A.
New Knighthood, The.
Old Men, The.
Pelicans in the Wilderness (A Grave near Halfa)
Puck of Pook's Hill, *sels.*
R.A.F. (Aged Eighteen)
Rabbi's Song, The.
Recessional.
Refined Man, The.
Return, The.
Sacrifice of Er-Heb, The.
Screw-Guns.
Sea and the Hills, The.
Sergeant's Weddin', The.
Servant, A.
Servant When He Reigneth, A.
Sestina of the Tramp-Royal.
Shillin' a Day.
Son, A.
Song of the Banjo, The.
Song of the Galley-Slaves.
Sons of Martha, The.
Spies' March, The.
St. Helena Lullaby, A.
Storm Cone, The.
Story of Uriah, The.
There Is a Tide.
Tommy.
Unknown Female Corpse.
Vampire, The.
Way Through The Woods, The.
We and They.
When first under fire an' you're wishful to duck.
White Horses.
Widow at Windsor, The.

Kipp, Karen
Ditches.
I'm Sending You Saint Francis Preaching to the Birds.
Rat, The.

Kirby, David (b. 1944)
Dear Derrida.
To a French Structuralist.

Kirby, Jeannie
I Wonder.

Kirchwey, Karl (b. 1956)
He Considers the Birds of the Air.
Matthew 8:20; And Jesus said to him.
Oracular Degeneration.

Kirilenko-Voloshin, Maksimilian *See* **Voloshin, Maksimilian Aleksandrovich**

Kirillov, Vladimir Timofeievich (1890–1943)
We.

Kirkland, Hilaire (1941–75)
Clotho, Lachesis, Atropos.
Observations.

Kirkup, James (b. 1923)
Baby's Drinking Song.
Correct Compassion, A.

Scarecrows.
Shepherd's Tale, The.
Who's That?

Kirn, Walter
Envoi: "I left. I'd finished raising you. I walked."

Kirsanov, Semyon [*or* Semion] Isaakovich (1906–72)
Back then I cut off a lock.
I Am White, Darling.
Lyric Poem.
New Heart, The.
Suddenly.

Kirsch, Denyse
Dvora.

Kirsch, Melissa (b. 1974)
Sleep's Underside.

Kirsch, Sarah (b. 1935)
Call.
Dandelions for Chains.
In an Airplane I'm Supposed To.
Legend of Lilja.
Mail.
Mornings.
Pandora's Box.
Pictures.
Renting a Room.
Wels a Fish that Lives on the Bottom, The.

Kirstein, Lincoln (b. 1907)
Double Date.
Foresight.
Gloria.
Gripe.
P.O.E.
Rank.

Kisei (d. 1764)
Nine-month moon.
Since I was born.

Kiser, Samuel Ellsworth (1862–1942)
Bargain Sale, A.
My Creed.
Unsubdued.

Kisfaludy, Károly (1788–1830)
Plowman of Rákos Under the Turks.
Sighing, O greet you and mourn you, O meadow of burial, Mohács.

Kisfaludy, Sándor (1772–1844)
As the suffering hart confounded.
Song: "I have heard the silvery note."

Kishu
Once the goal's reached.

Kiss, József (1843–1921)
Fires.
Make haste slowly, my friend, make haste slowly.
Oh, Why So Late.
Rhyme Is Running Out,The.

Kitahara Hakushū (1885–1942)
Secret Song of the Heretics.

Kiwus, Karin (b. 1942)
All Splendor on Earth.

Kiyoko Tsuda (b. 1920)
To be a mistress.

Kiyowara Fukuyabu (c.900–930)
River-Fog.

Kiyu (d. 1820)
Evening.

Kizan (d. 1786)
Clouds drifting off.

Kizan (d. 1851)
When I am gone.

Kizer, Carolyn (b. 1925)
Afternoon Happiness.
American Beauty, An.
Amusing Our Daughters.
Ashes, The.
Bitch.
Columns and Caryatids.
Election Day, 1984.
Fearful Women.
Food of Love.
For Jan as the End Draws Near.
For Jan, in Bar Maria.
For Sappho/After Sappho.

Glass, The.
Great Blue Heron, The.
Hera, Hung from the Sky.
Horseback.
Ingathering.
Intruder, The.
Lines to Accompany Flowers for Eve.
Muse of Water, A.
On a Line from Valéry.
One.
One to Nothing.
Parents' Pantoum.
Promising Author.
Race Relations.
Reunion.
Semele Recycled.
Summer near the River.
Thrall.
Three.
Through a Glass Eye, Lightly.
To an Unknown Poet.
Translation.
Twelve O'Clock.
Two.

Klaj, Johann (1616–56)
Oh golden life, waken! Fortunate night!
Stroll-Joy.

Klappert, Peter (b. 1942)
Court of Divine Justice, The.
For the Poet Who Said Poets Are Struck by
    Lightning Only Two or Three Times.
In Memory of H. F.
To Whom.

Klauber, Edgar
On Buying a Dog.

Kleban, Edward (*fl.* 1975)
One.

Klee, Paul (1879–1940)
Friend, A.
Happy One, The.
Poem.
Wolf Speaks, The.

Klein, Abraham Moses (1909–72)
Autobiographical.
Baal Shem Tov.
Ballad of the Days of the Messiah.
Biography.
Break-up, The.
For the Sisters of the Hôtel Dieu.
Haggadah.
Heirloom.
In re Solomon Warshawer.
Indian Reservation: Caughnawaga.
Lone Bather.
Monsieur Gaston.
Montreal.
Political Meeting.
Portrait of the Poet as Landscape.
Rabbi Yom-Tob of Mayence Petitions His God.
Rev Owl.
Rocking Chair, The.
Venerable Bee, The.
Winter Night: Mount Royal.

Klein, Michael
Guardian Life.
Letters from the Front.
Range of It, The.
Scenes for an Elegy.
Tides, The.

Klein, Robin
Amanda!

Klein-Synek, Emmy
Vienna in Spring.
You New Year.

Kleinschmidt, Edward (b. 1951)
Cooking to Music.
Orchestrion.

Kleinzahler, August (b. 1949)
Autumnal Sketch, An.
Case in Point, A.
Ebenezer Californicus.
Green Sees Things in Waves.
Hamburger.
Lunatic of Lindley Meadow, The.
Poetics.

Spleen.
Winter Ball.

Kleiser, Grenville (1868–1953)
Most Vital Thing in Life, The.

Kleist, Ewald von (1715–59)
Song at Graveside.

Klemm, Wilhelm
Clearing-Station.

Klenner, John
Just Friends.

Klepfisz, Irena (b. 1941)
Death Camp.
Fradel Schtok.
From the Monkey House and Other Cages:
    Monkey II.
My Mother's Sabbath Days.
Perspectives on the Second World War.
These words are dedicated to those who died.

Klieba, Michael
Schubert.

Klimentov, Andrei Platonovich *See* "Platonov,
    Andrey"

Klinger, Adria
Transformation.
Your fingers circle.

"Klingle, George" (Georgiana Klingle Holmes)
Be Patient.

Klipschutz
Funicello at 50.

Kloefkorn, William
Why the Stone Remains Silent.

Kloepfer, Hans
Late Autumn in Styria.

Kloos, Willem (1859–1938)
Evening.
Self-Transformation.
Sonnet.
Trees, Late in the Season.

Klopstock, Friedrich Gottlieb (1724–1803)
Early Graves, The.
Fredensborg.
Lake of Zurich, The.
Rose Wreaths, The.
Summer Night, The.

Klugman, Elana
She Who Listens.

Klugman, Sara
God's Body.

**Klyuyev [or Kliuev or Klyuev], Nikolai
Alekseievich (1884–1937)**
Can I Tell You My Love with a Portrait.
Conversational Melody, A Good Verse, A.
Fourth Rome, The.
Lenin has the spirit of an Old Believer.
Mother Sabbath.
October, A Copper-Crawed Cock.
Sky Lies Blue—Like a Sea, The.
You Twist Your Death in Nooses.

Knapp, Shepherd (1873–1946)
Lord God of Hosts.
Not Only Where God's Free Winds Blow.

Knevet, Ralph (1601–72)
Bottle, The.
Contrition.
Habitation, The.
Harp, The.
Navigation.
Vote, The.

Knibbe, Hester (b. 1946)
Skater, The.

Knight, David (b. 1926)
Chief of the West, Darkling, The.
In Memoriam S. L. Akintola.
Palms, The.
"When the Students Resisted, a Minor Clash
    Ensued."

Knight, Etheridge (1933–91)
Another Poem for Me (after Recovering from
    an O.D.)
As You Leave Me.
Black Poet Leaps to His Death, A.
Bones of My Father, The.
Cell Song.
Crazy Pigeon.

Dark Prophecy: I Sing of Shine.
Eastern guard tower.
Feeling Fucked/Up Up.
For Black Poets Who Think of Suicide.
For Freckle-Faced Gerald.
For Langston Hughes.
Genesis 2.
Green Grass and Yellow Balloons.
Haiku: "Eastern guard tower."
Hard Rock Returns to Prison from the Hospital
    for the Criminal Insane.
He Sees Through Stone.
Huey.
Idea of Ancestry, The.
It Was a Funky Deal.
My Life, the Quality of Which.
My Uncle Is My Honor and a Guest in My
    House.
Once on a Night in the Delta: A Report From
    Hell.
On the Removal of the Fascist American Right
    from Power.
On the Yard.
On Watching Politicians Perform at Martin
    Luther King's Funeral.
Poem for Black Relocation Centers, A.
Poem for Myself (Or Blues for a Mississippi
    Black Boy), A.
Poem of Attrition, A.
Poem to Galway Kinnell, A.
To Make a Poem in Prison.
Two Poems for Black Relocation Centers.
Upon Your Leaving.
Violent Space, The.
Warden Said to Me the Other Day, The.
WASP Woman Visits a Black Junkie in
    Prison, A.
Welcome Back, Mr. Knight: Love of My Life.

**Knight, Henrietta, Lady Luxborough (1699–
1756)**
Bullfinch in Town, The.
Written to a Near Neighbour in a Tempestuous
    Night.

Knight, Richard Payne (1750–1824)
Landscape, The.

Knight, Sarah Kemble (1666–1727)
Pleasant Delusion of a Sumpteous City.
Resentments Composed because of the Clamor
    of Town Topers Outside My Apartment.
Thoughts on Pausing at a Cottage near the
    Paukataug River.
Thoughts on the Sight of the Moon.
Warning to Travailers Seeking Accomodations
    at Mr. Devills Inn.

Knight, Stephen
Big Parade, The.
Daedalus.
Double Writing.
Eyeball Works, The.
In Case of Monsters.
Mermaid Tank, The.
Surf Motel, The.

Knister, Raymond (1899–1932)
Boy Remembers in the Field.
February's Forgotten Mitts.
Nell.

Knoepfle, John (b. 1923)
Bath.
Confluence.
Dark Spaces: Thoughts on All Souls Day.
Harpe's Head.
Late Winter in Menard County.
Skibbereen the Famine Pit.

Knopfli, Rui (b. 1932)
Death Certificate.
Kwela for Tomorrow.

Knott, Bill
Ant Dodger.
At the Crossroads.
Christmas at the Orphanage.
Comic Look at Damocles, A.
Death.
Feeding the Sun.
Funny Poem.
Goodbye.
Hair Poem.

Monodrama.
Mrs. Frye and the Pencilsharpener.
Poem: "After your death."
Poem: "At your light side trees shy."
(Poem) (Chicago) (The Were-Age)
Poem: "Only response, The."
Save As: Salvation.
Shorts / Excerpts.
Sleep.
Sonnet: "Way the world is not, The."
Two Vietnam Poems: (1966)
Winter Regrets.

Knowles, Herbert (1798–1817)
Lines Written in the Church Yard of
Richmond, Yorkshire.

Knowles, James D. (1798–1838)
O God, though Countless Worlds of Light.

Knowles, Suzanne (b. 1911)
Fox Dancing.
Tails and Heads.

Knox, Edmund George Valpy ("Evoe") (1881–1971)
Director, The.
Limerick: "There was a young curate of
Hants."
To the God of Love.
Upon Julia's Clothes.

Knox, Jennifer L. (b. 1968)
Bright Light of Responsibility, The.

Knox, Ronald Arbuthnott (1888–1957)
Anglican curate in want, An.
Idealism.
Limerick: "Evangelical vicar in want."
O God, for as much as without Thee.
To a Pessimist.

"Knut, Dovid" (David Mironovich Fiksman) (1900–55)
Walking along the Sea of Galilee.
Woman from the Book of Genesis, A.

Knutson, Greta (b. 1899)
Foreign Land.

Ko Changsu (Chang-soo Koh) (b. 1934)
Ocean Liner.

K'o Chun (961–1023)
Springtime South of the Yangtze.

Kocan, Peter (b. 1947)
AIDS, Among Other Things.
Bill.
Cows.
Inmate, An.
Mutineer's Ballad, The.
Sleepers, The.

Kocbek, Edvard (1904–81)
Dialectics.
Game, The.
Hands.
Longing for Jail, A.

Koch, Christopher (b. 1932)
Boy who Dreamed the Country Night, The.
Shelly Beach.

Koch, Kenneth (b. 1925)
Alive for an Instant.
Circus, The.
Down at the Docks.
Energy in Sweden.
Fresh Air.
Geography.
Girl and Baby Florist Sidewalk Pram Nineteen
Seventy Something.
I certainly have lost something.
Locks.
Mending Sump.
New Guide, A.
Permanently.
Poem of the Forty-eight States, A.
Sleeping with Women.
Stones of Time, The.
Supposing that one walks out into the air.
Thank You.
Thanksgiving.
To Marina.
To win the love of women one should first
discover.
To World War Two.
Variations on a Theme by William Carlos

Williams.
With Janice.
You Were Wearing.

Kochanowski, Jan (1530–84)
I'd Buy You, Wisdom.
In Defence of Drunkards.
To a Mathematician.
Where Is That Gate for Grief.

Kochetkov, Aleksandr (1900–1953)
Ballad About a Smoke-Filled Railway
Carriage.

Kocot, Noelle (b. 1969)
Consolations Before an Affair, Upper West
Side.

Kodo (1370–1433)
Serving the Shogun in the capital.

Koehler, Ted (1894–1973)
Animal Crackers in My Soup.
As Long As I Live.
Between the Devil and the Deep Blue Sea.
Don't Worry 'Bout Me.
Good for Nothin' Joe.
Happy As the Day Is Long.
I Gotta Right to Sing the Blues.
I've Got the World on a String.
Ill Wind.
Let's Fall in Love.
Sing, My Heart.
Spreadin' Rhythm Around.
Stop! You're Breakin' My Heart.
Stormy Weather (Keeps Rainin' All the Time)
Tess's Torch Song (I Had a Man)
Truckin'
When the Sun Comes Out.
Wrap Your Troubles in Dreams.

Koehn, Adam (b. 1974)
Divorce.

Koenig, Alma Johanna (1887–1942)
Sad Ode.
Waldviertel. Lower Austria.
What I Believe.

Koertge, Ron (b. 1940)
Lazarus.

Koestenbaum, Phyllis (b. 1930)
Sonnet 37: "I'd decided I initiate most."

Koestenbaum, Wayne
1977.
1980.
1992.
Gaudy Slave Trader.
Tea Dance.

Koethe, John (b. 1945)
From the Porch.
Songs of the Valley.

Kogaku Soko (d. 1548)
My final words are these.

Kogan, Pavel Davydovich (1918–42)
Star.
Thunderstorm.

Kogetsu Sogan (d. 1643)
Katsu!

Koha (d. 1897)
I cast the brush aside.

Kohler, Sheila
Shepherd.

Koho Kennichi (d. 1316)
To depart while seated or standing is all one.

Koianimptiwa
Korosta Katzina Song.

Kojijū (1121–1201)
On the Spirit of the Heart as Moon-Disk.

Koju (d. 1806)
And if I do.

Kokai (1403–69)
Taking hold, one's astray in nothingness.

Kokei Sochin (d. 1597)
For over sixty years.

Koko
Word at last, The.

Kōkō Emperor (fl. 9th cent.)
When I went out in.

Kolatkar, Jejuri Arun (b. 1932)
Alphabet, The.

Low Temple, A.
Railway Station, The.

Kölcsey, Ferenc (1797–1838)
Huszt.
Köcsey.
Libations.
National Anthem.
One For a Keepsake Album.
One For Balassi.
Szondi.
Vanitatum Vanitas.
Zrínyi's Second Song.
Zrínyi's Song.

Kollan, Alici
What Her Friend Said.

Kollar, Sybil
Late Arrivals.
Sunday Matinee.

Koller, James (b. 1936)
I Have Cut an Eagle.
O Dirty Bird Yr Gizzard's Too Big & Full of
Sand.
Some Magic.
Unreal Song of the Old, The.

Kolmar, Gertrud (1894–1943?)
Judith.
Out of the Darkness.
Sacrifice, The.

Kolodinsky, Alison
Midnight.

Kolodny, Susan
Tsuneko—Psychiatric Medications Clinic.

Kombem, Sim (b. 1962)
Another Moment.

Komey, Ellis Ayitey (1927–72)
Change, The.
Oblivion.

Komrij, Gerrit (b. 1944)
Park of the Dead.
Poet, The.

Komunyakaa, Yusef (b. 1947)
After the Fall of Saigon.
April Fools' Day.
Back Then.
Banking Potatoes.
Between Days.
Boat People.
Boxing Day.
Break from the Bush, A.
Cante Jondo.
Captain Amasa Delano's Dilemma.
Chastity Belt.
Dead at Quang Tri, The.
Elegy for Thelonious.
Euphony.
Facing It.
February in Sydney.
Forgive and Live.
Fragging.
Gift Horse.
Hanoi Hanna.
Homage to a Bellhop.
How I See Things.
Instructions for Building Straw Huts.
Jeanne Duval's Confession.
Never Land.
Report from the Skull's Diorama.
Salt.
Seven Deadly Sins.
Slam, Dunk, and Hook.
Smokehouse, The.
Somewhere Near Phu Bai.
Speed Ball.
Starlight Scope Myopia.
Thorn Merchant's Mistress, The.
Tiger Lady.
Tu Do Street.
Twilight Seduction.
Untitled Blues; After a Photograph by Yevgeni
Yevtushenko.
Way the Cards Fall, The.
When Loneliness is a Man.
White Port and Lemon Juice.

Koncel, Mary A.
Come Back, Elvis, Come Back to Holyoke.

Kondo, Tadashi
Autumn light.
Konie, Gwendoline C.
In the Fist of Your Hatred.
We Are Equals.
Konishi Raizan (Raizan) (1654–1716)
Farewell, sire.
For rice-planting women.
Girls planting paddy.
Green, green, green / Herbs splash.
Raizan has died.
Konkan (d. 1801)
When I leave the world.
Konopnicka, Maria (1842–1910)
Vision, A.
Kool, Marga (b. 1949)
Different.
Koordada, Manila (fl. mid 20th cent.)
You Can't Escape Your Life Record.
Kooser, Ted (b. 1939)
Abandoned Farmhouse.
At the End of the Weekend.
At the Office Early.
Child Frightened by a Thunderstorm.
City Limits.
Country School.
Flying at Night.
Genuine Poem, Found on a Blackboard in a
Bowling Alley in Story City, Iowa.
Hands in the Wind.
How to Make Rhubarb Wine.
In the Basement of the Goodwill Store.
Interchange.
Late Lights in Minnesota.
Myrtle.
Selecting a Reader.
Self-Portrait at Thirty-Nine.
Shooting a Farmhouse.
Very Old, The.
Widow, A.
Year's End.
Kopelke, Kendra (b. 1957)
Eager Street.
Kopland, Rutger (Rudi van den Hoofdakker) (b. 1934)
Breughel's Winter.
Natzweiler.
Ontology.
Thanks to the Things.
Ulumbo, a Cat.
Koraku (d. 1837)
Joy of dewdrops, The.
Korican, Leah
City Goddess.
Her Story.
Korinna
Although I was her pupil / Even I reproach
Myrtis.
Are you, happy man, grandson of Kronos.
Are you sleeping endlessly? You never did
before, Korinna.
But I sing the excellence of heroes.
But let one of you hear this.
Daughter of Hyria, land of lovely dances.
I blame even clear-voiced.
I disapprove even of eloquent / Myrtis.
I Korinna am here to sing the courage.
Kithairon sang of cunning Kronos.
Kouretes hid the goddess's, The.
Leaving the [streams] of Ocean.
Mighty Orion conquered.
Of your daughters: Zeus, Father.
Over you, Hermes fights.
Terpsichore [told] me.
That grudging man [can't hurt] you.
Thespia, bearing a beautiful race, stranger-
loving, Muse-beloved.
To the white-mantled maidens.
When he sailed into the harbor.
Will you sleep forever?
Wishing to take her son.
Korkiya [or Korkiia], Viktor b. 1948
Stanzas: "With youthful loss of memory, in my
voiceless land."
Korn, Rachel [or Rokhl] (1898–1982)
Generations.

Keep Hidden from Me.
Kornblith, Marta (1959–97)
Books of the Dead, The.
Mirrors.
Parents.
Korneichukov, Nikolai Vasilyevich See
"Chukovsky [or Chukovskii], Korney"
Kornilov, Boris Petrovich (1907–38)
Continuation of Life.
Drawer of My Writing Desk, The.
High Seas on the Caspian.
My Nightingale.
Under the Scraggy Fir Tree.
Kornilov, Vladimir Nikolaevich (b. 1928)
Announcer, The.
Johnny.
Poorer than X.
Sky, The.
Snow.
Koroneu
Funeral Eva.
Korteweg, Anton (b. 1944)
Sed Non Frustra.
**Korvin-Piotrovsky, Vladimir L'vovich (1891–
1966)**
Farewell, Captain. In bygone days.
**"Korzhavin, Naum" (Naum Moiseievich Mandel)
(b. 1925)**
Envy.
For certain, I did not live thus in this world.
How difficult to live without you!
I could be in Paris or Vienna.
I was never an ascetic.
Imitation of Monsieur Beranger.
Leningrad.
Or did I really fall out of love with my
country?—.
Poem about Youth and Romanticism, A.
Variation on Nekrasov.
We can string words on a line.
Kosai (fl. c.1686)
Autumn ends.
Poor Kosai.
Košek, Miroslav (1932–44)
It All Depends on How You Look at It.
Little Mouse, The.
Man Proposes, God Disposes.
Yes, That's the Way Things Are.
Koseki (d. 1788)
Swear to me, pine.
Kosen (1808–93)
Blind horse trotting up an icy ledge, A.
Koson (d. 1920)
I die.
Kosovic, Ante (1882–1958)
Ah Dalmatia, if only I could send word of your
dear sons.
Kossman, Nina
John 13:21–30; When Jesus had thus said, he
was troubled.
Judas' Reproach.
Pilate's Wife.
Kostelanetz, Richard (b. 1940)
Concentric.
Disintegration.
Koster, Edward B. (1861–1937)
Shoal of Silver Angelfish, A.
Kosztolányi, Dezső (1885–1936)
Conductor, The.
Dark Fates, The.
Dear mum's old picture.
Deep Are the Wells.
Eminent Public Figure.
Funeral Oration.
I am an entry in all kinds of books.
I want to kill myself.
Inks of all colours are filling my dreams.
Like someone who has fallen between the rails.
Marcus Aurelius.
Revolutionary,The.
Society Woman, The.
Song About Benedek Virág.
Song of 'Kornél Esti,' The.
To My Dog, Swan.

Would You Like to Play?
Kouchag, Nahabed (d. 1592)
I Was Suffering Exile.
Kouwenaar, Gerrit (b. 1923)
Elba.
4 Variations On.
Kovner, Abba (b. 1918)
Far, Far a City Lies.
My Sister.
To Myself.
What's Not in the Heart.
Kovur Kilar
We Hope For Patrons.
Kowit, Steve (b. 1938)
Cosmetics Do No Good.
In the Morning.
Notice.
What Chord Did She Pluck.
Koyama, Tina
Currents.
Downtown Seattle in the Fog.
Koyo (d. 1903)
If I must die.
Kozameh, Alicia
It's absorbed, perceived, partially picked up.
The brightness envelops.
Presence. Opposites. Absence. Forces
exercising pressure against.
We will mention it. We will remember and
mention.
Kozan (d. 1747)
How sublime.
Kozan Ichikyo (d. 1360)
Empty-handed I entered the world.
Koziol, Urszula (b. 1935)
Alarum.
Kramer, Alex
Candy.
Kramer, Larry
Brilliant Windows.
Images of the San Francisco Disaster.
Night Bird, The.
Strong Winds Below the Canyons.
Kramer, Lotte
I am chained.
Love Letters.
Non-Emigrant, The.
On Shutting the Door.
Red Cross Telegram, The.
Shoemaker's Wife, The.
Kramer, Samuel Noah See **Wolkstein, Diane**
Kramer, Theodor
Oven of Lublin, The.
Krandievskaya, Natalya (1888–1963)
Those who would not accept went past.
Krasicki, Ignacy (1735–1801)
Caged Birds.
Lamb and the Wolves, The.
Master and the Dog, The.
Krasnikov, Gennady (b. 1951)
Come on, Mama, we'll slake the lime.
Kraus, Karl (1874–1936)
Before a Fountain.
Dying Soldier, The.
Express Train.
Lilacs.
National Folk Hymn.
New Year's Eve 1917.
On the Threshold.
Resurrection.
Toward Eternal Peace.
Transformation.
Under the Waterfall.
Kraushaar, Mark
Free Throw.
Krayer, Stevie
My Mother Dressed for the Wedding.
Kremer, Pem
Choice, Inanna and the Galla.
Epiphany.
Kresh, David
Musical Saw.
Kretzmer, Herbert
Limerick: "Kinky young girl from

Uttoxeter, A."

Kreymborg, Alfred (1883–1966)
Ants.
Culture.
Improvisation.
Tiger Lily.
Tree, The.

Krichevsky [or Krichevskii], Ilya (1963–91)
Exhausted from depression.
Refugees.

Kriebel, Casper (fl. mid–18th cent.)
Now Sleep My Little Child So Dear.

Krige, Uys (b. 1910)
Taking of the Koppie, The.

Kriloff, Ivan Andreevich (1768–1844)
Peasant and the Sheep, The.

Krishnamurti, M. (b. 1912)
Spirit's Odyssey, The.

Krivulin, Viktor (b. 1944)
And the silver age, unattainable.
Crossing the keyboards of the palace.
Glory to caesar! and glory to God in the
  highest!
Guard.
Idea of Russia, The.
Southwest.
Two in a Room.

Krmpotic, Vesna (b. 1932)
December Forest, A.

Kroetsch, Robert (b. 1927)
Stone Hammer Poem.

Krohn, Herbert
Can Tho.
Farmer's Song at Can Tho.
My Flute.
Ferryman's Song at Binh Minh.

Kroll, Judith (b. 1943)
I Think of Housman Who Said the Poem Is a
  Morbid Secretion, like a Pearl.

Kruchyonykh, Aleksei Eliseievich (1886–1968)
Declaration of the Word as Such.
At midnight I noticed on my sheet A.
Pomade.
Sahara to America, The.

Krúdy, Gyula (1878–1933)
This city, Budapest, smells of violets in the
  spring as do mesdames along the
  promenade.
To breakfast on a light-blue tablecloth,
  smelling of milk.
What somehow echo through the clanging of
  the town bells.

Kruit, Johanna (b. 1940)
Birds Leaving.
Giving Way.
House By the Sea.
Landscape.
Post Heads.
Way of the Water, The.

Krynicki, Ryszard (b. 1943)
I Can't Help You.

Krysl, Marilyn
Carpe Diem: Time Piece.
Persephone, to Demeter.

Kryukova, Yelena (b. 1956)
Song of Songs.

Kshemendra (fl. 1150)
Poet should learn with his eyes, A.

Kshetrayya (fl. 17th cent.)
Courtesan to a Young Customer, A.
Courtesan to Her Lover, A.
Dancing-Girl's Song.
Wife to a Friend, A.

Ku Hsiung (fl. c.928)
Tune: "Telling of Innermost Feelings."

Ku K'uang (725?–c.814)
On the River.
Sonny.
Upon a Brook.
Written upon Returning to the Mountains.

Ku T'ai-ch'ing (1799–1876?)
Tune: "Partridge Sky"—Puppet Theater.
Tune: "Phoenix Hairpin"—Crab Apple.
Tune: "Ripples Sifting Sand"—Accompanying

My Husband on a Spring Outing to Stone
  Pavilion.

Kuan Han-ch'ing (Han-ch'ing) (c.1220–c.1300)
Fear, as I see the spring go.
Grief: I've grieved as a solitary phoenix
  grieves.
Heaven in the South, earth Northward.
In the Southern Mode, to the Tune "A Sprig of
  Flowers" The Refusal to Get Old.
Lightly she turns back her long red sleeves.
Snow powder, flowery.
This autumn scene is worthy of the brush.
To the Tune 'A Spray of Flowers' (Not Giving
  In to Old Age)
Toot once, strum once.
Tune: "Four Pieces of Jade."
Tune: "Song of Great Virtue"—Spring.
Tune: "Sprig of Flowers, A"—Not Bowing to
  Old Age.
Tune: "Vast Virtue."
Wind sifts through the curtain.

Kuan Hsiu (832–912)
Bad Government.
Song of the Palace of Ch'en.
Written in the Mountains.

Kuan Tao Shêng (1262–1319)
Married Love.

Kuan Yun She (fl. 13th cent.)
Seventh Day Seventh Month.

Kuan Yün-shih (Hsiao-yün-shih-hai-ya) (1286–1324)
Love Song: "Fondling and snuggling."
Tune: "Butterflies."
Tune: "Chilly East Wind."
Tune: "Coda."
Tune: "Going Up Small Pavilion."
Tune: "Happy Events Approaching."
Tune: "Moth Fluttering Against Lamp."
Tune: "Pomegranate Blossoms."
Tune: "Rapt with Wine, Loudly Singing; Joy in
  Spring's Coming."
Tune: "Song of Shou-yang."
Tune: "Song of the Lunar Palace"—Sending
  Off Spring.
Tune: "Squabbling Quails."

Kubatum (fl. c.2038 B.C.)
Love Song to King Shu-Suen.

Kublanovsky, Yury Mikhailovich
Armor of the Petrograd oak is rusty, but, The.
He who gave weight to the wind.
In Memory of John Keats.
My Russia, mine!

Kuchu
Joshu's word—Nothingness.

Kudimova, Marina (b. 1953)
Outing, The.
When I still barely rose above the ground.

Kuhlmann, Quirinus (1651–89)
15th Kühl-Psalm, The.
From Deepest Need.

Kuka, King D.
Evening.
February Morning.
Gallery of My Heart.
Jackie.
Janna.
My Friend the Wind.
My Song.
Tiny baby, you're ugly.

Kukai (774–835)
Singing Image of Fire.

Kukoku (1328–1407)
Riding backwards this wooden horse.

**Kulchitsky [or Kulchitskii], Mikhail
  Valentinovich (1919–43)**
Dreamer, visionary, green-eyed sluggard!
I love Russia.
Mayakovsky.
194...

Kulik, William
Fictions.
Flexible.
Hi.
Old House Blues.

Kuller, Sid
Jump for Joy.

Kulman, Elisaveta (1808–1825)
To Diana.

Kumar, Sati (b. 1938)
Come Back, Alexander.

Kumbirai, Joseph (1922–86)
Dawn.

Kumin, Maxine W. (b. 1925)
Absent Ones, The.
After Love.
Almost Spring, Driving Home, Reciting
  Hopkins.
At the End of the Affair.
Chain, The.
Credo.
Despair.
Early Thoughts of Winter.
Envelope, The.
Excrement Poem, The.
Family Man, A.
For My Great-Grandfather: A Message Long
  Overdue.
400-Meter Freestyle.
Getting the Message.
Gus Speaks.
Hay.
Height of the Season, The.
Hermit Has a Visitor, The.
How It Is.
In the Absence of Bliss.
In the Root Cellar.
Living Alone with Jesus.
Making the Jam without You.
Morning Swim.
Nuns of Childhood: Two Views, The.
October, Yellowstone Park.
Plans.
Poet Visits Egypt and Israel, The.
Presence, The.
Retrieval System, The.
Riddle of Noah, The.
Seeing the Bones.
Sound of Night, The.
Spree.
To Swim, to Believe.
Together.
Video Cuisine.
Woodchucks.

Kunene, Raymond Mazisi (b. 1930)
"Advice" to a Young Poet.
Death of the Miners or, The Widows of the
  Earth.
Echoes, The.
Elegy.
Elegy for My Friend E. Galo.
Meeting with Vilakazi, the Great Zulu Poet, A.
Nozizwe.
Thought on June 26.
When My Poems were Lost.

K'ung Chih-kuei (448–501)
Trip on Mount T'ai-P'ing.

Kung Tzu-chen (1792–1841)
Lute Song, The.
Miscellanies of the Year Chi-hai.
My Neighbor's Child Cries in the Middle of
  the Night.
Tune: "Butterflies Lingering over Flowers."
Tune: "Decorous and Pretty."
Tune: "Green Jade Cup."

Kung, Wang Hung (fl. 20th cent.)
In the Mountain Village.

Kunitz, Stanley (b. 1905)
Abduction, The.
After the Last Dynasty.
Benediction.
Careless Love.
Catch, The.
Choice of Weapons, A.
Dragonfly, The.
End of Summer.
Father and Son.
Flight of Apollo, The.
For the Word Is Flesh.
He.
Hornworm: Autumn Lamentation.
Hornworm: Summer Reverie.
Illumination, The.

Intimations of Mortality.
Knot, The.
Last Picnic, The.
Layers, The.
Night Letter.
Old Cracked Tune, An.
Passing Through.
Portrait, The.
Quarrel, The.
Quinnapoxet.
Reflection by a Mailbox.
River Road.
Round, The.
Route Six.
Science of the Night, The.
She Wept, She Railed.
Snakes of September, The.
Summing-up, The.
Testing-Tree, The.
Thief, The.
Three Floors.
Touch Me.
Vita Nuova.
War against the Trees, The.
Welcome the Wrath.
Wellfleet Whale, The.
When the Light Falls.

Kunyayev [or Kuniaev], Stanislav Iurievich (b. 1932)
It's hard to understand how one can leave.

Kunze, John C. (c.1745–1807)
Yoke Soft and Dear.

Kunze, Reiner (b. 1933)
Aerial, The.
Brief Curriculum.
Bringers of Beethoven, The.
End of Art, The.
First Letter From Tamara A.
Hymn to a Woman Under Interrogation.
Low Volume.
Need for Censorship, The.
Reply.

Kuo Mo-jo (1892–1978)
Earthquake.

Kuo P'o (276–324)
Kingfishers sport among orchids and begonias.
Poem on the Wandering Immortal.

Kuong Viet (fl. 1050)
Wood and Fire.

Kuppner, Frank (b. 1952)
Architecture is when the sun shines on a
   facade daily.

Kupriyanov [or Kuprianov], Vyacheslav (b. 1939)
Epidemic / Of freedom, An.
Everything gets forgotten.
For a long time he tried to survive.
Lesson in Natural History, A.
There is life on other planets.
Twilight of Vanity.

Kürenberg, Der von (1150–75)
"Late at night I stood on a battlement."
Morning star goes under cover, The.
Woman and falcons—they are easily tamed.

Kurihara, Sadako
Let Us Be Midwives!

Kuroda, Saburoh (1919–80)
Afternoon 3.

Kurup, G. Shankara
Master Carpenter, The.

Kusamaru (d. 1836)
My morning porridge.

Kusano Shimpei (b. 1903)
4 or 5 Tadpoles.
Birthday Party.
Skylarks and Fuji.

"Kush"
Message for Langston, A.

Kushner, Aleksandr Semionovich (b. 1936)
Airman, The.
And if you sleep, and if the sheets are clean.
As Catullus wrote, a man's voice deserts him.
Cypress.
Don't bother about the news!
Envelope looks so peculiar, The.
He who doesn't dance still dances.

Memoirs.
No better fate is given than to die in Rome.
Oak, The.
Picture, A.
Remembering Love.
Rooster, The.
Star burns out over the tree tops, The.
To B. P.
We don't get to choose our century.
What I really wanted.

Kushner, Bill (b. 1931)
Up.

Kushner, Dale M. (fl. 20th cent.)
Grandma in the Shower.

Kushniroff, Aaron (1891–1952)
Die My Shriek.

"Kusikov, Aleksandr Borisovich" (Aleksandr Borisovich Kusikyan) (1896–1977)
Mountain Forest.

Kusikyan, Aleksandr Borisovich See **"Kusikov, Aleksandr Borisovich"**

Kuskin, Karla (b. 1932)
Catherine.
I Woke Up This Morning.
Knitted Things.
Question, The.
Rose on My Cake, The.
When I Went Out.
Where Have You Been Dear?
Witches' Ride, The.

Kusz, Natalie
Retired Greyhound, I.
Retired Greyhound, II.

Kuthaiyir (663?–723?)
At Her Grave.

Kutilov, Arkady (1925–88)
Crickety Creek.

Kuzma, Greg (b. 1944)
Ice Skating.
Night Things.

Kuzmin, Mikhail Alekseievich (1875–1936)
Ah, those lips, kissed by so many.
Antinous.
At noon I must have been conceived.
At the Party.
If they say: "you must suffer both torture and
   burning."
Leaving my house in the morning.
Nine delightful birthmarks.
Not for nothing did we read the theologians.
People see gardens and houses.
Were I a general of olden times.
Were you apprenticed to a fortune teller?
What rain! / Our sail is drenched.
When it was I first encountered you.
When they say to me: "Alexandria."

Kuzmina-Karavayeva, Elizaveta (Mother Maria [or Mat' Mariia]) (1891–1945)
And copper and worn my farthing.
Even in repentance there is pleasure.
Everything has been checked. My inventory is
   ready.
I still kept thinking that I was rich.
I too have encompassed a lot: a mother
   thrice—.
Long-Barrow Princess 2.
Ruth.
Who am I, Lord? Just an impostor.

Kuzminsky [or Kuzminskii], Konstantin Konstantinovich (b. 1940)
I'm cold. I'm destitute and absurd.

Kuznetsov, Yury [or Iurii] (b. 1941)
Atomic Fairy Tale.
Mushrooms.
Should I see a cloud high up in the sky.
To Father.

Kvitko, Leyb (1893–1952)
Moods.
You Who Dog My Footsteps.

Kwakiutl Oral Tradition
Fires run through my body—the pain of loving
   you.

Kwŏn Homun (1532–87)
Nights After Rain When the Moon.

Kwon P'il
Alone at Night.

Kydios
Beware. There are fawns.

Kyei, Kojo Gyinaye (b. c.1930)
African in Louisiana.
Talking Drums, The.
Tough Guy of London, The.

Kyffin, Morris (c.1555–1598)
Adore November's sacred seventeenth day.

Kyger, Joanne (b. 1934)
And with March a Decade in Bolinas.
August 18.
Caption for a Miniature.
Destruction.
Don't Hope to Gain by What Has Preceded.
Every day I burn a stick of incense.
I Have No Strength for Mine.
It's been a long time.
Maze, The.
My Father Died This Spring.
News bulletin from Keith Lampe.
Of All Things for You to Go Away Mad.
Pan as the Son of Penelope.
Philip Whalen's Hat.
Pigs for Circe in May, The.
When I Was Well into Being Savored.

Kyle, Christiane Jacox
Argument, The.
Fire in Early Morning.
Season of Locking-In, The.

Kyme, Anne See **Askew, Anne**

Kynaston, Sir Francis (1587–1642)
To Cynthia.
To Cynthia, on Concealment of Her Beauty.
To Cynthia on Her Being an Incendiary.

Kyo'on (d. 1749)
Last fart, A.

Kyohaku (fl. c.1686)
I am not worthy.

Kyokusai (d. 1874)
When you contemplate the waters.

Kyoshu (d. 1769)
Journey of no return, A.

Kyurin-Eki
Eighty-three years—at last.

Kyutaro (d. 1928)
In heavy snow.
Tender winds above the snow.

L

"L., L. E." See **Landon, Letitia [or Laetitia] Elizabeth**

La Compiuta Donzella (The Accomplished Maiden) (fl. 13th cent.)
To leave the world and serve God.

La Coste, Marie (c.1840–c.1909)
Somebody's Darling.

La Fontaine, Jean de (1621–95)
Aesop's Fable of the Frogs.
Cock and the Fox, The.
Crow and the Fox, The.
Donkey and the Lapdog, The.
Eagle and the Beetle, The.
Fox and the Crow, The.
Hag and the Slavies, The.
Love and Folly.
Man and His Image, The.
Phoebus and Boreas.
Pig, Goat, Sheep.
Rat and the Elephant, The.
Saddled Ass, The.
Shrimp and Her Daughter, The.
Wolf and the Dog, The.
Wolf and the Stork, The.
Young mouse, poor, no experience, A.

La Grone, Oliver (b. 1906)
Lines to the Black Oak.
Remnant Ghosts at Dawn.
Suncoming.

La Loca
Why I Choose Black Men for My Lovers.

Labé, Louise (1524–66)
Bright Venus, Who Across the Heavens Stray.

Elegy 23: "How does it help me if, with flawless art."
Kiss me again, and kiss me still, and kiss.
Long-Felt Desires.
Povre Ame Amoureuse.
Sonnet 1: "Not Ulysses, no, nor any other man."
Sonnet 2: "O handsome chestnut eyes, evasive gaze."
Sonnet 3: "O interminable desires, O futile hope."
Sonnet 4: "From that first flash when awful Love took flame."
Sonnet 5: "White Venus limpid wandering in the sky."
Sonnet 6: "Coming of that limpid star is twice, The."
Sonnet 7: "We see each living thing finally die."
Sonnet 8: "I live, I die, I burn myself and drown."
Sonnet 9: "As soon as I lie down in my soft bed."
Sonnet 10: "When I perceive your blond and graceful head."
Sonnet 11: "O eyes clear with beauty, O tender gaze."
Sonnet 12: "Lute, companion of my calamity."
Sonnet 13: "If I could linger on his lovely chest."
Sonnet 15: "To honor the return of sparkling sun."
Sonnet 17: "I flee the city, temples, and each place."
Sonnet 18: "Kiss me again, re-kiss and kiss me whole."
Sonnet 21: "What grandeur makes a man seem venerable?"
Sonnet 22: "O blazing Sun, how happy you are there."
Sonnet 23: "What good is it to me if long ago."
Sonnet 24: "Don't blame me, ladies, if I've loved. No sneers."
Sonnet XIV.
Sonnet XIX: "After having slain very many beasts."
Sonnet XVI: "After an age when thunderbolts and hail."
Sonnet XX.

Labriola, Gina
Orgy (That Is, Vegetable Market, at Sarno)

Labrunie, Gérard *See* **Nerval, Gérard de**

Lacaussade, Auguste (1817–97)
My lips from this day forgot how to smile.

Lacavaro, Anthony
Advantages of Being a World Class Athlete, The.

Lachmann, Hedwig (1870–1918)
Home-Sickness.
Walk, A.

Lady of the Arbour, The (*fl.* c.1450)
And at the last I cast my mine eye aside.
Flower and the Leaf, The.

Lady of the Assembly, The (*fl.* late 15th cent.)
Assembly of Ladies, The.
Palace of Pleasant Regard, The.

Laederach, Monique (b. 1938)
Penelope.

LaFemina, Gerry (b. 1968)
Her Rose Tattoo.
White Dwarf.

Laforgue, Jules (1860–87)
Clair de Lune.
Complaint on the Oblivion of the Dead.
For the Book of Love.
Mystery of the Three Horns, The.
Sunday Piece.

Lagier, Jennifer (*fl.* 20th cent.)
Second Class Citizen.

Lagrone, Oliver (*fl.* 20th cent.)
I Heard the Byrd.

"Laider" *See* **Mac Coisdealbhaigh, Tomas**

Laila Akhyaliyya (*fl.* late 7th cent.)
Camel.

Laila Boasting.
Lamenting Tauba.

Laine, Frankie (*fl.* 1945)
We'll Be Together Again.

Laing, Allan M. (b. 1887)
Grace for Ice-Cream, A.
Limerick: "It's a nightmare that horrifies hakes."
Limerick: "Said a medical student, unmanned."
Limerick: "There was an old cynic who said."
Limerick: "When an obstinate fellow of Fife."
New Jerusalem, The.
There was a young lady of Ealing.
This Railway Station.

Laing, Kojo
Africa Sky.
Godhorse.
Huge Car with the Sad Voice, The.
I Am the Freshly Dead Husband.
Many Worlds Are Walked Once.
One Hundred Lines for the Coast.
Race on Gathering Bites.
Same Corpse, The.
Senior Lady Sells Garden Eggs.
Steps.
Tatale Swine.

Lake, Paul
Blue Jay.
Crime and Punishment.
In Rough Weather.
Introduction to Poetry.

Lakides, Lucy
Armed Forces.

Lakshminkara (*fl.* 8th cent.)
Lay your head on a block of butter and chop.

Lal Ded [*or* Lalla] (*fl.* 14th cent.)
At the end of a crazy-moon night.
Coursing in emptiness.
I drag a boat over the ocean.
I searched for my Self.
I was passionate.
Impermanence.
On the way to God the difficulties.
Soul, like the moon, The.
This world.
To learn the scriptures is easy.

Laleau, Léon (b. 1892)
Betrayal.
Cannibal.
Legacies.
Sacrifice.
Voodoo.

Lalleswari (*fl.* late 14th cent.)
Good repute is water carried in a sieve.
I set forth hopeful—cotton-blossom Lal.
With my breath I cut my way through the six forests.

Laluah, Aquah *See* **Hayford, Gladys May Casely**

Lamantia, Philip (b. 1927)
Hermetic Bird.
Man Is in Pain.
Morning Light Song.
Romantic Movement, The.
She Speaks the Morning's Filigree.
Terror Conduction.
Time Traveler's Potlatch.
Voice of Earth Mediums.
Winter Day, A.

Lamarque, Vivian (b. 1946)
Gentleman and the Lady, The.
Gentleman in Front, The.
Gentleman in the Heart, The.
I Wanted to Dream the Mailman.
Illegitimate Poem.
Lady of the Last Time, The.
Lady of the Snow, The.
Little Girl.
Looking at the Moon.
Newborn Lover.
Prayer of Mothers Who Unintentionally Failed Their Children.
There Was a Castle.

Lamartine, Alphonse Marie Louis de (1790–1869)
Autumn.

Cedars of Lebanon, The.
Infinite in the Skies, The.
Isolation.
Lake, The.
Lizard, The.
Valley, The.
West, The.

Lamb, Arthur J.
Bird in a Gilded Cage, A.

Lamb, Charles (1775–1834)
Anger.
As When a Child.
Childhood Fled.
David in the Cave of Adullam.
Envy.
Family Name, The.
Farewell to Tobacco, A.
First Tooth, The.
Free Thoughts on Several Eminent Composers.
Gipsy's Malison, The.
Hester.
If from my lips some angry accents fell.
Io! Paean! Io! sing.
Methinks How Dainty Sweet It Were.
Nonsense Verses.
O! I could laugh to hear the midnight wind.
Old Familiar Faces, The.
On an Infant Dying as Soon as Born.
Salome.
"Timid grace sits trembling in her eye, A."
To Dora W[ordsworth].
To John Lamb, Esq.: Of the South-Sea House.
Was it some sweet device of faery land.

Lamb, Elizabeth Searle
Broken kite, sprawled.
Far back under a ledge.
Far shore, The.
Leaving all the morning glories closed.
Lizard inching, A.
Old album, The.
Pausing.
Shimmering beneath the glaze.
Still . . . some echo.

Lamb, Joe
Cherries.

Lamb, Lady Caroline (1785–1828)
By Those Eyes Where Sweet Expression.
Duet.
If Thou Couldst Know What 'Tis to Weep.
Let the harp be mute for ever.
Sing Not for Others, But for Me.
William Lamb's Return from Paris, Asking Me My Wish.

Lamb, Mary (1764–1847)
Anger.
Envy.
First Tooth, The.
Helen.
Parental Recollections.
Two Boys, The.

"Lambert, Louis" *See* **Gilmore, Patrick Sarsfield**

Lamdan, Yitzhak (1899–1954)
Distant soughing of pine forests caresses my ear, The.
How little of God's grace caresses you, Massadah.
Israel.
On roads beyond the camp the Khamsin struck me.
Where am I, O awesome friend?
Why did Hagar weep over Ishmael when he thirsted.

Lamott, Anne
Spoon River Sadie Louise.

Lampadius, Sabina (*fl.* c.377)
As a symbol.

Lampert, David
Poem for Sophie.

Lampman, Archibald (1861–99)
City of the End of Things, The.
Heat.
In November: "Hills and leafless forests slowly yield, The."
In November: "With loitering step and quiet eye."

Thunderstorm, A.
To a Millionaire.
Winter Evening.
Lamport, Felicia (b. 1916)
Eggomania.
Mother, Mother, Are You All There?
Poll Star.
Lamrani, Wafaa' (b. 1960)
I Am Consecrated to the Coming One.
Wail of Heights, The.
Lancaster, Osbert (b. 1908)
Eireann.
French.
English.
Manhattan.
Landesman, Fran (b. 1927)
Ballad of the Sad Young Men, The.
Photographs.
Say 'Cheese!'
Spring Can Really Hang You Up the Most.
Landon, Letitia [or Laetitia] Elizabeth ("L. E. L.") (1802–38)
Airey Force.
Banquet, The.
Bonds of Affection.
Castle of Chillon, The.
Child Screening a Dove from a Hawk, A.
Dancing Girl, The.
Death in the Flower.
Dying Child, The.
Enchanted Island, The.
Experience Too Late.
Farewell, The.
Farewell, The.
Gifts Misused.
Girl at Her Devotions, A.
History of the Lyre, A.
Introduction.
Lady, thy face is very beautiful.
Lines of Life.
Lines Written Under a Picture of a Girl
    Burning a Love-Letter.
Lorenzo.
Love's Last Lesson.
Marriage Vow, The.
Mask of Gaiety, The.
Poet's Lot, The.
Poor, The.
Power of Words, The.
Princess Victoria, The.
Revenge.
Sappho's Song.
Scale Force, Cumberland.
Scenes in London: Piccadilly.
Secrets.
Small Miseries.
Song.
Song: "My heart is like the failing hearth."
Song: "Where, O! where's the chain to fling."
Stanzas on the Death of Mrs Hemans.
Stern Truth.
Landor, Walter Savage (1775–1864)
Above all gifts we most should prize.
Age.
Alas! 'Tis Very Sad to Hear.
Alciphron and Leucippe.
Autumn.
Behold, O Aspasia! I Send You Verses.
Bourbons.
Case at Sessions, A.
Corinna, from Athens, to Tanagra.
Crimean Heroes, The.
Critic, A.
Death of the Day.
Death Stands above Me.
Dirce.
Distribution of Honours for Literature.
Dragon-Fly, The.
Duke of York's Statue, The.
Epigrams must be curt, nor seem.
Exhausted now her sighs, and dry her tears.
For an Epitaph at Fiesole.
Foreign Ruler, A.
Georges, The.
God Scatters Beauty.
Had We Two Met.

Heart's Abysses, The.
Hearts-Ease.
Here lies Landor.
How often, when life's summer day.
How to Read Me.
I Strove With None.
Ianthe.
Ianthe's Troubles.
Idle Words.
Interlude.
Ireland Never Was Contented.
La Promessa Sposa.
Maid's Lament, The.
Memory.
Mother, I Cannot Mind My Wheel.
Neither in idleness consume thy days.
No charm can stay, no medicine can assuage.
Now to Aurora, borne by dappled steeds.
On Catullus.
On Himself.
On Seeing a Hair of Lucretia Borgia.
On the Heights.
Our youth was happy: why repine.
Pigmies and Cranes.
Plays.
Poet! I like not mealy fruit; give me.
Proud word you never spoke, but you will
    speak.
Quarrelsome Bishop, A.
Reflection from Sea and Sky.
Remain, Ah Not in Youth Alone.
Rose Aylmer.
Scentless laurel a broad leaf displays, The.
Scribblers, The.
Sensible Girl's Reply to Moore's, A.
Separation.
Sleepless, with pleasure and expiring fears.
Ten thousand flakes about my window blow.
There are two miseries in human life.
Three Roses, The.
To Arthur de Noé Walker.
To One Who Quotes and Detracts.
To Poets.
To Robert Browning.
Twenty Years Hence.
Various the roads of life; in one.
Well I Remember How You Smiled.
What News.
When Helen first saw wrinkles in her face.
Why do the Graces now desert the Muse?
William Gifford.
Ye walls! sole witnesses of happy sighs.
Years.
Yes; I write verses now and then.
You Smiled, You Spoke, and I Believed.
Lane, Burton (1912–97)
Babes on Broadway.
Come Back to Me.
Everything I Have Is Yours.
Have Feet, Will Dance.
How About You.
How Are Things in Glocca Morra?
I Hear Music.
I Left My Hat in Haiti.
If This Isn't Love.
Lady's in Love with You, The.
Necessity.
Old Devil Moon.
On a Clear Day You Can See Forever.
Stop! You're Breakin' My Heart.
T'Ain't No Use.
When I'm Not Near the Girl I Love.
Lane, Patrick (b. 1939)
At the Edge of the Jungle.
If.
Measure, The.
Passing into Storm.
Stigmata.
Lane, Pinkie Gordon (b. 1937)
Girl at the Window.
Lake Murry.
Midnight Song.
Migration.
Nocturne: "Listening for the sound."
On Being Head of the English Department.
Rain Ditch.
Sexual Privacy of Women on Welfare.

Spring.
When You Read This Poem.
Who Is My Brother?
Wind Thoughts.
Lang, Andrew (1844–1912)
Brahma.
Last Chance, The.
Limerick: "There was a young lady of
    Limerick."
Odyssey, The.
Romance.
Tired of Towns.
Twilight on Tweed.
Lang, John Dunmore (1799–1878)
Colonial Nomenclature.
Lange, Art (b. 1952)
Perugia.
Sonnet for the Season.
Langfield, June Mercer
Full fathom five thy father lies.
Langford, G. W.
Speak Gently.
Langhorne, John (1735–79)
Gypsies.
Poor, The.
Studley Park.
Warning against the Gypsies, A.
Langland, Joseph (b. 1917)
War.
Langland, William (1330–1400)
Age of Reason, The.
Barones an burgeises and bondemen als.
Barones and burgieses and bandemen als.
Civil Service, The.
Confession of Gluttony.
Dreamer Meets Conscience and Reason.
Entertainment Industry, The.
Envy with heavy heart asked for shrift.
Et Incarnatus Est.
Field Full of Folk, The.
Glutton [or Glutton in the Tavern], The.
God's Mercy.
Good Works.
Incarnation, The.
"It is a kynde knowyng," quod she, "that
    kenneth in thine herte."
Piers Plowman Shows the Way to Saint Truth.
Plowing of Piers's Half-acre, The.
Saint Called "Truth," A.
Thus I awoke, God knows, when I lived in
    Cornhill.
Trinity, The.
Vision of Nature, A.
What for feere of this ferly and of the false
    Jewes.
Wool-chafed and wet-shoed I went forth after.
Yet I courbed on my knees and cried hire of
    grace.
Langley, Eve (b. 1908)
Native Born.
This Year, before It Ends.
Langley, R. F.
Jack's Pigeon.
Mariana.
Langton, Stephen (d. 1228)
Hymn to the Holy Spirit.
O Holy Ghost.
Lanier, Emilia (1569–1645)
Description of Cooke-ham, The.
Eves Apologie.
Now Pontius Pilate is to judge the cause.
To the Lady Arabella.
To you I dedicate this work of grace.
Lanier, H. Glenn
O Christ of Bethlehem.
Lanier, Sidney (1842–81)
Ballad of Trees and the Master, A.
Clover.
Crystal, The.
Dying Words of Stonewall Jackson, The.
Evening Song.
From the Flats.
Hymns of the Marshes.
In my sleep I was fain of their fellowship, fain.
Laus Mariae.

Marsh Song—At Sunset.
Marshes of Glynn, The.
Mocking Bird, The.
My Springs.
Nirvâna.
Now comes the Course-of-things, shaped like
  an Ox.
Raven Days, The.
Revenge of Hamish, The.
Song for "The Jacquerie."
Song of the Chattahoochee.
Struggle.
Thar's More in the Man than Thar Is in the
  Land.
To Bayard Taylor.
To Beethoven.
To Richard Wagner.
Waving of the Corn, The.
Whate'er Has Been.

Lanigan, George Thomas (1845–86)
Threnody: "What, what, what / What's the
  news from Swat?"

Lanjewar, Jyoti (b. 1950)
I Never Saw You.

Lankesh, P. (b. 1935)
Mother.

Lansana, Quraysh Ali (b. 1964)
Woolworth's Poem, The.

Lansdown, Andrew (b. 1954)
Behind the Veil.
Golgotha.
Mercy.
Two Men.

"Lantos" *See* Tinódi, Sebestyén

Lanusse, Armand (1812–67)
Epigram: "Do you not wish to renounce the
  Devil?"

Lanyer, Aemilia Bassano (1569–1645)
Author's Dream to the Lady Mary, the
  Countess Dowager of Pembroke, The.
Description of Cooke-ham [or Cookham], The.
Now let me come unto that stately tree.
Our Mother *Eve,* who tasted of the Tree.
Salve Deus Rex Judaeorum.
To All Virtuous Ladies in General.
To the Queen's Most Excellent Majesty.
Yet you (great lady) mistress of that place.

Lao Tzu (c.604–531 B.C.)
Ancient Masters were profound and subtle,
  The.
Best be done before the last degree.
Boundless shaping Power, A.
Empty your mind of all thoughts.
Every being in the universe.
Good traveler has no fixed plans, A.
Some say that my teaching is nonsense.
Tao that can be told, The.
To understand others is to be knowledgeable.
Valley Spirit never dies, The.
Way as 'Way' bespoke is no true lasting way;
  The.
When thirty spokes join the wheel-hole.
Whenever all the world declares fair "fair."

Lara, Alda (b. 1930)
Nights.

Larbaud, Valery (1881–1957)
Images.

Larcom, Lucy (1824–93)
Brown Thrush, The.
Dumpy Ducky.
In the Tree-Top.
Little Cavalier, A.
Spring Whistles.
They Said.
This is the month sunrise skies.
Volunteer's Thanksgiving, The.
What the Train Ran Over.

Lardner, Ring (1885–1933)
Abner Silver's "Pu-leeze! Mr. Hemingway!"
Hail to Thee, Blithe Owl.
Hardly a Man Is Now Alive.
Parodies of Cole Porter's "Night and Day."
Quiescent, a Person Sits Heart and Soul.

Larkin, Joan (b. 1939)
Beatings.

Clifton.
Cold River.
Good-Bye.
Housework.
Inventory.
Legacy.
My Body.
Origins.
Rape.
Rhyme of My Inheritance.

Larkin, Mary Ann (b. 1945)
House of Broughton Street, The.
Riding on a Streetcar with My Father.

Larkin, Philip (1922–85)
Absences.
Afternoons.
Age.
Ambulances.
Annus Mirabilis.
Arrivals, Departures.
Arundel Tomb, An.
As Bad as a Mile.
At Grass.
Aubade: "I work all day, and get half-drunk at
  night."
Card-Players, The.
Church Going.
Coming.
Counting.
Cut Grass.
Days.
Deceptions.
Dedicated, The.
Dockery and Son.
Dublinesque.
Explosion, The.
Faith Healing.
Fiction and the Reading Public.
First Sight.
For Sidney Bechet.
Forget What Did.
Going.
Going, Going.
Here.
High Windows.
Homage to a Government.
Home Is So Sad.
I Remember, I Remember.
If, My Darling.
Limerick: "There was an old fellow of Kaber."
Lines on a Young Lady's Photograph Album.
Love Again.
Love Songs in Age.
Maiden Name.
Matthew 10:1.
MCMXIV.
Money.
Mr Bleaney.
Myxomatosis.
Naturally the Foundation Will Bear Your
  Expenses.
New Year.
Next, Please.
No Road.
North Ship, The.
Nothing to Be Said.
Old Fools, The.
Poetry of Departures.
Posterity.
Reasons for Attendance.
Sad Steps.
Self's the Man.
Seventy Feet Down.
So through that unripe day you bore your head.
Spring.
Study of Reading Habits, A.
Sunny Prestatyn.
Take One Home for the Kiddies.
Talking In Bed.
This Be The Verse.
Toads.
Toads Revisited.
Trees, The.
Vers de Société.
Waiting For Breakfast, While She Brushed Her
  Hair.
Wants.

Water.
Whatever Happened?
Whitsun Weddings, The.

Larminie, William (1885–1930)
Nameless Doon [or Dun], The.

Lars, Claudia (1899–1974)
Recollection of Gabriela Mistral.
Sketch of the Frontier Woman.

Larsen, Lance (b. 1961)
Lips.
Peach.
Red.

Larsen, Wendy Wilder
Bluebird in Cutleaf Beech.
Learning the War.

Lasker-Schüler, Else (1876–1945)
Abraham and Isaac.
Always in the Parting Year.
And Look for God.
Chronica.
End of the World.
Georg Trakl.
George Grosz.
Hagar and Ishmael.
I Have a Blue Piano.
I Know That I Must Die Soon.
Jacob.
Jacob and Esau.
Love's Flight.
Love-Song.
Love Song: "Come to me in the night—we
  shall sleep closely together [or Let us sleep
  entwined]."
My Love-Song.
My People.
O God.
Only for You.
Rock Crumbles, The.
To The Barbarian.
Zebaoth.

Lasoen, Patricia (b. 1948)
That April Morning.

Lassell, Michael (b. 1947)
Brady Street, San Francisco.
Dino.
Going Rate, The.
Going to Europe.
How to Find Love in an Instant.
How to Watch Your Brother Die.
Kissing Ramén.
Stud.
Sunset Stripping: Visiting L.A.
Three Poems.

**Lathbury, Mary Artemisia ("Aunt Mary")
  (1841–1913)**
Break Thou the Bread of Life.
Day Is Dying in the West.

Lathrop, Lena
Woman's Question, A.

**Latimore, Jewel C. (Johari Amini; Johari M.
  Kunjufu) (b. 1935)**
Ceremony.
Promise, The.
Return.
Saint Malcolm.
Utopia.

Latouche, John (1917–56)
Cabin in the Sky.
Honey in the Honeycomb.
Lazy Afternoon.
Love Turned the Light Out.
Maybe I Should Change My Ways.
Not a Care in the World.
Summer Is a-Comin' In.
Taking a Chance on Love.

Latta, Ruth
Hand reaches up, A.

Latter, Mary (1722?–1777)
Now calumnies arise, and black reproach.
Strangers to meek compassion's tender touch.
With tearful eye, how frequent have I seen.

Lattimore, Richmond (1906–84)
Max Schmitt in a Single Scull.
North Philadelphia, Trenton, and New York.
Note on the L and N.

Witness to Death.

Lau, Alan Chong
My Ship Does Not Need a Helmsman.
Upside Down Basket, The.

Lau, Carolyn
Zhoukoudian Bride's Harvest.

Lauder, Marie Maitland (*fl.* 16th cent.)
As phoebus in his spheris hicht.

Laufer, Calvin W. (1874–1938)
We Thank Thee, Lord.

Laughlin, James (b. 1914)
Bird of Endless Time, The.
Inn at Kirchstetten, The.
Kind, The.
Mountain Afterglow, The.
My Ambition.
O Best of All Nights, Return and Return
  Again.
Rhyme.
Step on His Head.
Swarming Bees, The.
Then and Now.

Laurencin, Marie (1885–1956)
Horse, The.
Present, The.
Tiger, The.
Zebra, The.

Lauterbach, Ann (b. 1942)
Boy Sleeping.
Clamor.
Gesture and Flight.
Here and There.
How Things Bear Their Telling.
Meanwhile the Turtle.
Mimetic.
Novelist Speaks, The.
Platonic Subject.
Procedure.
Revelry in Black-and-White.
Untoward.
Werner Herzog 68 / Iowa City 88.

Laux, Dorianne (b. 1952)
Children's Train, The.
China.
Fast Gas.
Finding What's Lost.
Homecoming.
If This Is Paradise.
Lovers, The.
Prayer.
Thief, The.
This Close.
What Could Happen.
What I Wouldn't Do.

Lavant, Christine (b. 1915)
Buy Us a Little Grain.
Do Not Ask.

Lavater, Louis (1867–1953)
Barrier, The.

Lavieri, Jon
Autobiography of John Doe, The.

Lavrin, Aleksandr (b. 1952)
As I remember, barracks still stand.

Lavrov, Leonid (1906–43)
Farewell, I say, farewell to the incomplete.

Law, T. S. (b. 1910)
Wemen's Wather.

Lawless, Emily (1845–1913)
After Aughrim.

Lawrence, A. H.
To Be a Nurse.

Lawrence, Anthony (b. 1957)
Cro-Kill.
Fencing.
Robert Penn Warren's Book.

Lawrence, David Herbert (1885–1930)
Andraitx—Pomegranate Flowers.
Argonauts, The.
Aware.
Bare Almond-Trees.
Bare Fig-trees.
Bat.
Bavarian Gentians.
Blue Jay, The.

Body of God, The.
Bombardment.
Bride, The.
Brooding Grief.
Butterfly.
Cherry Robbers.
Collier's Wife, The.
Cypresses.
Desire Is Dead.
Discord in Childhood.
Don'ts.
Drained Cup, The.
Elemental.
Eloi, Eloi, Lama Sabachthani?
End of Another Home Holiday.
English Are So Nice!, The.
Enkindled Spring, The.
Evening Land, The.
Fatality.
Fate and the Younger Generation.
Figs.
Flowers and Men.
Food of the North.
Gazelle Calf, The.
Giorno dei Morti.
Gloire de Dijon.
Glory.
Grasshopper Is a Burden.
Green.
"Gross, Coarse, Hideous" (Police Description
  of My Pictures)
Hands of God, The.
Healing.
Hills, The.
History.
How Beastly the Bourgeois Is.
Humming-Bird.
Hymn to Priapus.
I Am in a Novel.
I Am like a Rose.
In Trouble and Shame.
Innocent England.
Intimates.
Kangaroo.
Kisses in the Train.
Last Lesson of the Afternoon.
Let There Be Light!
Lightning.
Little Fish.
Living Quetzalcoatl, The.
Lizard.
Lord's Prayer.
Lord Tennyson and Lord Melchett.
Love On the Farm.
Love Thy Neighbour.
Lui et Elle.
Man and Bat.
Man of Tyre, The.
Matthew 6:7–15; "And in praying do not heap
  up empty."
Maximus.
Medlars and Sorb-Apples.
Middle of the World.
Morning Work.
Mosquito Knows, The.
Mosquito, The.
Mountain Lion.
My Name Is Jesus.
Mystic.
New Year's Eve.
O! Start a Revolution.
Paradise Re-entered.
Pax.
Peacock.
Piano.
Proper Pride.
Quetzalcoatl Looks Down on Mexico.
Quite Forsaken.
Race and Battle.
Red Geranium and Godly Mignonette.
Retort to Jesus.
Root of Our Evil, The.
Sea-Weed.
Self-Pity.
Self-Protection.
Shadows.
Ship of Death, The.

Sicilian Cyclamens.
Snake.
Song of a Man Who Has Come Through.
Sorrow.
Spring Morning.
Stand Up!
Storm in the Black Forest.
Suburbs on a Hazy Day.
Suspense.
Swan.
Tabernacle.
Things Made by Iron.
Thought.
To Women, as Far as I'm Concerned.
Tommies in the Train.
Tortoise-Shell.
Tortoise Shout.
Towards the sun, towards the south-west.
Trees in the Garden.
Twilight.
Two Performing Elephants.
We Are Transmitters.
Wedding Morn.
Whales Weep Not!
What Would You Fight For?
When I Read Shakespeare.
When Wilt Thou Teach the People?
Whether or Not.
White Blossom, A.
White Horse, The.
Wild Common, The.
Willy Wet-Leg.
Winter's Tale, A.
Work.
Worm Either Way.
You.
Young Wife, A.
Youth Mowing, A.

Lawrence, Jack (b. 1912)
All or Nothing at All.
Foolin' Myself.
Linda.
Other Half of Me, The.
Sleepy Lagoon.
Tenderly.
What's Your Story, Morning Glory.

Lawrence, Philippa
Hit Men, The.

Lawson, David (b. 1940)
No Great Matter.

Lawson, Henry (1867–1922)
English Queen, The.
Faces in the Street.
Horseman on the Skyline, The.
Men Who Come Behind, The.
Ned's Delicate Way.
Ripperty! Kye! Ahoo!
Teams, The.
Up the Country.
When Your Pants Begin to Go.
Will Yer Write It Down for Me?

Lawson, Mrs. David *See* **Ridge, Lola**

Layamon (*fl.* c.1200)
Arthur's Dream.
Arthur was mortally wounded, grievously
  badly.
Passing of Arthur, The.

Layman P'ang (740–808)
My daily affairs are quite ordinary.
When the mind is at peace.

Layne, Catherine Braan
Whispering Wind.

Layne, Mcavoy
Collect Call.
Gettin' Straight.
On Hats and Things.
Guns.
Intersection in the Sky.
On the Yellow Footprints.
Beautiful Ladies.
Mob, The.

Layton, Irving (b. 1912)
Aubade, An.
Berry Picking.
Birth of Tragedy, The.
Black Huntsmen, The.

Bull Calf, The.
Butterfly on Rock.
Cain.
Cold Green Element, The.
Day Aviva Came to Paris, The.
Fertile Muck, The.
For Mao Tse-tung; a Meditation on Flies and
　Kings.
For Musia's Grandchildren.
From Colony to Nation.
Gothic Landscape.
Grand Finale.
Improved Binoculars, The.
Keine Lazarovitch, 1870–1959.
Party at Hydra.
Street Funeral.
Tall Man Executes a Jig, A.

Layton, J. Turner
After You've Gone.
Way Down Yonder in New Orleans.

Layzer, Robert (b. 1931)
Lawn Roller, The.

Lazard, Naomi (b. 1936)
In Answer to Your Query.
Ordinance on Arrival.

Lazarus, Emma (1849–87)
Banner of the Jew, The.
Bar Kochba.
By the Waters of Babylon.
City Visions.
Cranes of Ibycus, The.
Crowing of the Red Cock, The.
Echoes.
Evening.
1492.
Gifts.
How Long?
In Exile.
In the Jewish Synagogue at Newport.
Kindle the Taper.
Lines on Carmen Sylva.
Long Island Sound.
New Colossus, The.
South, The.
Success.
Venus of the Louvre.

Le Gallienne, Richard (1866–1947)
Beauty Accurst.
Library in a Garden, A.
Song: "She's somewhere in the sunlight
　strong."

Le Guin, Ursula K. (b. 1929)
Child on the Shore, The.
Riding on the Coast Starlight.

Le Ngoc Hiep (1944–70)
I Am Sad.

Lễ, Nguyễn Thú' See Thế Lũ'

Le Pan, Douglas (b. 1914)
Country without a Mythology, A.
Coureurs de Bois.
Incident, An.
Net and the Sword, The.
Nimbus.

Le Sueur, Meridel (b. 1900)
Behold This and Always Love It.

Lê Thánh–tông (King) (1442–97)
Stick and Hat.
Stone Dog, The.

Lea, Sydney
At the Flyfisher's Shack.
Clouded Evening, Late September.
Feud, The.
Insomnia: The Distances.
One White Face in the Place, The.
Telescope.
Tempted by the Classical on Returning from
　the Store at Twenty Below Zero.
Wrong Way Will Haunt You, The.

"Leadbelly" (Huddie Ledbetter) (1888–1949)
Take this Hammer.

Leader, Mary
Impetus.
Madrigal: "How the tenor warbles in April!"
Portrait.
Skin.

Leaf, Ebba M.
Dear Mother.
Her Son.

Leapor, Mary (1722–46)
Advice to Sophronia.
Epistle of Deborah Dough, The.
Epistle to a Lady, An.
Essay on Woman, An.
Headache, The.
In the Kitchen.
Man the Monarch.
Mira's Will.
Mira to Octavia.
On Winter.
Patrons of My Early Song, The.
Portrait of the Artist, A.
Proserpine's Ragout.
Sacrifice: An Epistle to Celia, The.
Soto, a Character.
Strephon to Celia.
To Artemisia.—'Tis to her we sing.
Upon Her Play Being Returned to Her, Stained
　with Claret.
Visit, The.

Lear, Edward (1812–88)
A[h]kond of Swat, The.
Calico Pie.
Children of the Owl and the Pussy-Cat, The.
Cold Are the Crabs.
Courtship of the Yonghy-Bonghy-Bo, The.
Dong with a Luminous Nose, The.
How Pleasant to Know Mr. Lear.
Incidents in the Life of My Uncle Arly.
Jumblies, The.
Limerick.
Limerick: "There once was an old man of
　Lyme."
Limerick: "There was a young lady whose
　eyes."
Limerick: "There was a Young Girl of
　Majorca."
Limerick: "There was a Young Lady of
　Norway / Who casually sat in a doorway."
Limerick: "There was a young lady of Ryde /
　Whose shoe-strings were seldom untied."
Limerick: "There was a young lady of
　Sweden."
Limerick: "There was a Young Lady whose
　chin."
Limerick: "There was a young person of
　Smyrna."
Limerick: "There was an Old Man in a boat."
Limerick: "There was an Old Man in a tree."
Limerick: "There was an old man of Cape
　Horn."
Limerick: "There was an old man of
　Dunblane."
Limerick: "There was an old man of Ibreem."
Limerick: "There was an old man of
　Kamschatka."
Limerick: "There was an old man of the
　coast."
Limerick: "There was an old man of
　Thermopylae."
Limerick: "There was an old man of
　Whitehaven."
Limerick: "There was an old man on some
　rocks."
Limerick: "There was an old man on the
　Border."
Limerick: "There was an Old Man on whose
　nose."
Limerick: "There was an old man who said:
　'How'"
Limerick: "There was an Old Man who said,
　'Hush!'"
Limerick: "There was an Old Man who said:
　'Well!'"
Limerick: "There was an old man who
　screamed out."
Limerick: "There was an Old Man who
　supposed."
Limerick: "There was an old person of
　Basing."
Limerick: "There was an old person of Bow."
Limerick: "There was an Old Person of
　Cromer."

Limerick: "There was an Old Person of Hurst."
Limerick: "There was an old person of Skye."
Limericks, I (ii)
Limericks, I (v)
Limericks, II (i)
Limericks, II (ii)
Limericks, II (iii)
Limericks, II (iv)
Limericks, II (v)
New Vestments, The.
O dear! How disgusting is life!
Owl and the Pussy-Cat, The.
Pelican Chorus, The.
Pobble Who Has No Toes, The.
Quangle Wangle's Hat, The.
Table and the Chair, The.
There was a young lady whose bonnet.
There Was a Young Lady Whose Nose.
There was a Young Person of Ayr.
There was an old man in a Barge.
There was an old man of Bohemia.
There was an old man of Peru / Who never
　knew what he should do.
There was an old man of Peru / Who watched
　his wife making a stew.
There was an old man of the East.
There was an old man of the West.
There was an old man of West Dumpet.
There was an Old Man who forgot.
There Was an Old Man With a Beard.
There was an old person of Blythe.
There was an old person of Buda.
There was an old person of Burton.
There was an old person of Cassel.
There was an old person of Dutton.
There was an old person of Prague.
There was an old person of Rhodes.
Twenty-Six Nonsense Rhymes.

Learmont, John (fl. c.1791)
Poor crawlin' bodies, sair neglectit.

"Learsi, Rufus" (Israel Goldberg) (1887–1938)
Martyrdom.

Leax, John
Fire Burns Low, The.
Her Seventeenth Winter.
Incarnation Poem.
That Day.

Lebensohn, Micah Joseph (1828–52)
Wine.

Lebovitz, Richard
HANDSAWWWWWWWWWWWWWWWWWW.

Leconte de Lisle, Charles Marie René (1818–94)
Hialmar Speaks to the Raven.
Jaguar's Dream, The.
Venus de Milo.

Lecount, David E.
Bridge toll-booth, The.

Ledbetter, Huddie See Leadbelly

Lederer, Katherine
Dream of Mimesis, A.

Ledwidge, Francis (1891–1917)
Fear, A.
June.
Lament for the Poets: 1916.
Lament for Thomas MacDonagh.
Twilight in Middle March, A.
Wife of Llew, The.

Lee, Alfred M. [or "Al"] (b. 1932)
Far Side of Introspection, The.

Lee, Alice
Confession.

Lee, Ann (fl. 1660s)
On the Returne of King Charles 2nd.

Lee, Bert See Weston, R. P.

Lee, David
Benediction.
For Jan, with Love.
Hired Hand.
Jan's Birthday.
This all happened before.

Lee, Dennis (b. 1939)
Billy Batter.
Coat, The.
Coming of Teddy Bears, The.
Dickery Dean.

Gods, The.
I Eat Kids Yum Yum!
Last Cry of the Damp Fly, The.
Often I sit in the sun and brooding over the
    city, always.
There Was a Man.
You Too Lie down.
Lee, Don L. *See* **Madhubuti, Haki R.**
Lee, Eleanor Percy (1820–49)
Forests and Caverns.
Sun-Struck Eagle, The.
Lee-Hamilton, Eugene (1845–1907)
Among the Firs.
Henry I to the Sea.
Idle Charon.
Ipsissimus.
Luca Signorelli to His Son.
Luther to a Bluebottle Fly.
Noon's Dream-Song.
Sunken Gold.
What the Sonnet Is.
Lee, J. H.
Limerick: "Man from Maputo and so on, A."
Lee, Joseph (1862–1937?)
German Prisoners.
Lee, Joyce (b. 1913)
Firebell for Peace.
My Father's Country.
Lee, Kim C. (b. 1967)
Haiku #3.
On South Africa.
Lee, Laurie (b. 1914)
Christmas Landscape.
Invasion Summer.
Milkmaid.
Moment of War, A.
Lee, Li-Young (b. 1957)
Between Seasons.
City in Which I Love You, The.
Cleaving, The.
Dreaming of Hair.
Early in the Morning.
Eating Alone.
Eating Together.
From Blossoms.
Gift, The.
He gossips like my grandmother, this man.
I Ask My Mother to Sing.
Interrogation, The.
Irises.
Mnemonic.
Persimmons.
Story, A.
This Room and Everything in It.
Visions and Interpetations.
Weight of Sweetness, The.
Lee, Nathaniel (1653–93)
Nathaniel Lee to Sir Roger L'Estrange.
Nay, *Clytus*, you that cou'd advise—.
Lee, Peggy (b. 1920)
I Don't Know Enough About You.
I Love Being Here with You.
I'm Gonna Go Fishin'
It's a Good Day.
Mañana (Is Soon Enough for Me)
That's My Style.
Lee, Susan K. C.
Letter from Turtle Beach.
Lee, Wendy
Lovers' Duet.
Sex Has a Way.
Lee, Wil'um
Aunt Martha.
Simple Like That.
Leeflang, Ed (b. 1929)
1945.
Lees, Gene (b. 1928)
Right to Love, The.
Waltz for Debby.
Lees, Joseph (1748–1824)
Jone o' Grinfilt.
Lefevre, Adam
Halftime.
LeFlore, Shirley Bradley
Dream/Eaters.

Rayboy Blk & Bluz.
This Poem.
Lefroy, Edward Cracroft (1855–91)
Cleonicos.
Epitaph of Eusthenes, The.
Flute of Daphnis, The.
Grave of Hipponax, The.
Idler Listening to Socrates Discussing
    Philosophy with His Boy-Friends, An.
Monument of Cleita, The.
Palaestral Study, A.
Sacred Grove, A.
Sylvan Revel, A.
Thyrsis.
Leftwich, Joseph (1892–1983)
Tailor, The.
Legaré, James Matthew (1823–59)
Tallulah.
To a Lily.
Léger, Alexis Saint-Léger *See* **"Perse, St.-John"**
Legrand, Michel
Summer Me, Winter Me.
Windmills of Your Mind, The.
Lehman, David (b. 1948)
Difference Between Pepsi and Coke, The.
First Offense.
One Size Fits All: a Critical Essay.
Prophet's Lantern, The.
Towards the Vanishing Point.
Lehmann, Geoffrey (b. 1940)
Harold's Walk.
Night Flower.
Pigs, The.
Poem for Maurice O'Shea, A.
Pope Alexander VI.
Roses.
Ross's Poems.
Saving the Harvest.
Song for Past Midnight.
What's that bird, Mr Long?
Lehmann, John (1907–87)
This Excellent Machine.
Lehmann, R. P. M.
Limerick: "There was a young girl of Bahari."
Lehrer, Tom (b. 1928)
Alma.
Elements, The.
Wernher von Braun.
Leib [or Leyb], Mani (1883–1953)
Door and Window Bolted Fast.
Hush, Hush.
When I See Another's Pain.
Leichter, Käthe
To My Brothers.
Leifhelm, Hans
Autumn Call.
On the Hoping Life.
Praise of Transitoriness.
Winter Forest.
With the Crescent Moon, with the Evening
    Star.
Leigh, Barbara
Limerick: "There was an old Member called
    Bevan."
Leigh, Carolyn (1926–83)
Best Is Yet to Come, The.
Hey, Look Me Over.
How Little We Know (How Little It Matters)
I've Got Your Number.
I Walk a Little Faster.
It Amazes Me!
Real Live Girl.
Rules of the Road, The.
When in Rome (I Do As the Romans Do)
Witchcraft.
You Fascinate Me So.
Young at Heart.
Leigh, F. *See* **Murray, L.**
Leigh, Helen (*fl.* 1788, d. c.1795)
Lady and the Doctor, The.
Natural Child, The.
Leigh, Henry Sambrooke (1837–83)
Rhymes (?)
Twins, The.

Leigh, Richard (1649?–1728)
Greatness in Little.
On a Fair Lady, Looking in the Glass.
Leighton, Robert (1611–84)
Bunch of Larks, The.
Leipoldt, C. Louis (1880–1947)
Oom Gert's Story.
Leiser, Joseph (b. 1873)
Kol Nidra.
Leithauser, Brad (b. 1953)
Angel.
Buried Graves, The.
Ghost of a Ghost, The.
Haunted, The.
In a Japanese Moss Garden.
In Minako Wada's House.
Old Bachelor Brother.
Tigers of Nanzen-ji, The.
Trauma.
**Leivick [or Leyvick], H. (Leivick Halpern) (1888–
1962)**
Lament at Night.
**Leland, Charles Godfrey ("Hans Breitman")
(1824–1903)**
Ballad by Hans Breitmann.
Breitmann in Paris.
Dere's a liddle fact in hishdory vitch few hafe
    onnershtand.
Hans Breitmann's Party [*or* Barty].
There's a liddle fact of hishdory vitch few hafe
    oondershtand.
Wein Geist.
Leland, John (1554?–1600)
Day Is Past and Gone, The.
Now Behold the Saviour Pleading.
Lem, Carol
California Dreaming.
Office Hour.
So Now You're Chicana.
Temple City Blvd. and Ellis Ln.
Len
Limerick: "Said the Chinese philosopher, Lin."
**Lenau, Nikolaus (Nikolaus Franz Niembsch von
Strehlenau) (1802–50)**
Postillion, The.
Prayer: "You dark eye, o rest upon me."
Three Gypsies, The.
Three, The.
To Her Far Away.
L'Engle, Madeleine (b. 1918)
At Communion.
Lines Scribbled on an Envelope.
O Simplicitas.
Risk of Birth, The.
Lenier, Sue (b. 1957)
Finale.
Lenk, Elisabeth
Automatic Text for Anne Ethuin.
Lennen, Elinor
Within the Shelter of Our Walls.
Lenngren, Anna Maria (1754–1817)
Portraits, The.
Lennon, John (1940–80)
Fat Budgie, The.
Lennox, Charlotte (1729?–1804)
Ardelia to Flavia, an Epistle.
Art of Coquetry, The.
Song, A: "What torments must the virgin
    prove."
Lenski, Hayim (1905–41)
Day turns to evening on the lake.
Incredible splendour—ethereal, delicate!
Light, my light, who commanded, 'Disappear!
Lightly a slight shadow floats on the March
    snows.
Moon's brightness turns a freezing blue, The.
Near the Mill.
There broke into my cell last night.
Wormwood has enchanted me completely.
Lenski, Lois (1893–1974)
Sing a Song of People.
Lenton, Mrs. Babington *See* **Pope, Jessie**
Leon, Elizabeth Jane (1582–1612)
On the Death of the Noble and Gentle Woman,

Lady Joanna Kelley.
On the Flooding of Prague, which Arose from Continuous Rain in the Year 1596.
On the Second Tristia of Ovid.
To the Reader.

Leon, Raphael de (*fl.* 1920s–1930s)
Have you not heard the gossip and the rumour going around.

Leonard, Priscilla
Happiness.

Leonard, Tom (b. 1944)
Evidence, The.
Fathers and Sons.
Jist Ti Let Yi No.
100 Differences Between Poetry and Prose.
Opting for Early Retirement.
Song: "Yi surta."
This is thi.
Untitled.

Leonard, William Ellery (1876–1944)
Indian Summer.
That once the gentle mind of my dead wife.
Two Lives.

Leong, Russell (b. 1950)
Aerogrammes.

Leonidas of Alexandria (d. 450 B.C.)
Menodotis.
We oxen are not only good.
You send me reams of snowy paper.

Leonidas of Tarentum (c.290–c.220 B.C.)
Ambrosia, brought safe.
Antiginides' two daughters, Melo.
Atthis hung up the belt with the pompoms.
By themselves in the twilight.
Cleitagoras.
Cold water falling out of the split rock.
Don't waste yourself, dragging out the life of a vagrant.
Eileithyia, brought safe.
Eros taught Pratalidas his adolescent beauty.
Eurotas said to the goddess of love.
Evening and morning old Platthis kept.
Far from Italy, far from my native Tarentum.
Fisherman, The.
For that goatfucker, goatfooted.
Forever brigands and pirates, the Cretans are never just.
Get out of my hut, you stealthy vermin! Leonidas'
Give me one small smothering of earth.
Gloomy minister of Hades who sail this stream.
Go softly past the graveyard where.
Good hunting, rabbit-catcher and bird-catcher.
His ball, beautiful leaved, and his noisy boxwood rattle.
His poor mother gives Mikythos'.
I am the tomb of Tellen, I contain.
If the tombstone placed over me is small to see and close.
"I'm like a vine supported on a stick."
Last Journey, The.
Night and mist, what bones you have eaten.
Nymphs of water, daughters of Doros.
Old Platthis often thrust away her morning's sleep.
Philocles.
Philokles offers his bouncing.
Remember Euboulos [*or* Eubolus], who lived and died sober?
Sheep-folds, holy spring of the Nymphs.
Silver Eros the ankle bracelet, The.
Silver Love, an anklet, A.
Sōsos the cattleman slew the lion.
Spinning Woman, The.
Spring on the Coast.
Staff and slippers hang here, Kypris, A.
Sudden strong squalls from the sou'-west.
Sun whirls an axle on fire, The.
Theris, the old man who lived by his fish traps.
Theris, thrice-old, who got his living from.
Theris, whose hands were cunning.
Theromachos of Crete came to hang up.
This beast which preyed on sheep.
Thundering sea, why in savage storm did you plunge.

To Gluttony and Guzzling, that fastidious gourmet.
To Pallas, Theris, cunning of hand, dedicated.
Tomb of Crethon, The.
Traveler in the wilds, do not.
Wallet, a rawhide goatskin, a cane, A.
Wallet, the hide of a goat, tough and untanned, a stick, A.
Who are you, whose pitiful bones.
Whoever then are you? Whose wretched bones are these.
You shepherds who wander this lonely mountainside.

Leonovich, Vladimir (b. 1937)
I have to write a page.

Leontius Scholasticus (*fl.* 6th cent.)
Orpheus, dying, not all Music died.
Touch, cup / the lips.

Leopardi, Giacomo (1798–1837)
Antistrophe.
Infinite, The.
Infinito, L'
Remembering Leopardi's Moon.
Saturday Night in the Village.
Sè Stesso, A.
To Himself.
To Italy.
To Sylvia.
To the Moon.
Upon the arid shoulder.
Village Saturday, The.

Lermontov, Mikhail Yuryevich (1814–41)
Borodino.
Composed While under Arrest.
Dagger.
Dream.
Mountain, The.
On the sightless seas of ether.
Reed, The.
Sail, A.
Thought, A.

Lerner, Alan Jay (1918–86)
Almost Like Being in Love.
Camelot.
Come Back to Me.
Heather on the Hill, The.
Hymn to Him, A.
I Could Have Danced All Night.
I Left My Hat in Haiti.
I'm Glad I'm Not Young Any More.
I Remember It Well.
I've Grown Accustomed to Her Face.
If Ever I Would Leave You.
On a Clear Day You Can See Forever.
On the Street Where You Live.
Paris Is Paris Again.
Rain in Spain, The.

Lerner, Laurence David (b. 1925)
Arthur's Anthology of English Poetry.
Raspberries.
Wish, A.

Lerner, Sammy
Is It True What They Say About Dixie?
Spanish Jake.

Lernet-Holenia, Alexander
Asoka's Love Song.

Lersch, Heinrich (1889–1936)
Brothers.

Lesley [*or* Leslie *or* Lesly], George (d. 1701)
Behold, how Sodom swaggers in its Pride.

Leslie, Edgar
Among My Souvenirs.
For Me and My Gal.
Kansas City Kitty.
Little Bit Independent, A.
T'ain't No Sin to Dance Around in Your Bones.

Leslie, Kenneth (1892–1974)
Halibut Cove Harvest.
Silver herring throbbed thick in my seine, The.

Lesser, Rika (b. 1953)
Translation.

Leto, Denise Nico (*fl.* 20th cent.)
For Talking.
Mary Morelle Show, The.

Leto, Gabriella (b. 1930)
Among Myths and Specters of the Future.
Here Where the Path.
If a Privileged Light.
Indeed You Came Home Too Late.
It Wasn't the Love of Others or Mine.
Love Dream Verse.
Ship Waits in the Harbor, The.
Steep Acquisitions Motionless Fears.
There is Not and There Will Never Be So Much.
What is Left and by Now Reduced to Little.

Letters, Francis
Inglorious Milton, The.

Letts, Winifred M. (1882–1971)
Spires of Oxford, The.

Levant, Oscar
Blame It on My Youth.

Levertov, Denise (1923–97)
Abel's Bride.
About Marriage.
Ache of Marriage, The.
Adam's Complaint.
Advent 1966.
Age of Terror.
At the Edge.
Bedtime.
Beyond the End.
By Rail through the Earthly Paradise, Perhaps Bedfordshire.
Caedmon.
Cancion: "When I am the sky."
Cat as Cat, The.
Change, The.
Christmas 1944.
Claritas.
Closed World, The.
Clouds.
Come into Animal Presence.
Common Ground, A.
Contraband.
Crack, The.
Crystal Night.
Dead Butterfly, The.
Death in Mexico.
Despair.
Divorcing.
Dog of Art, The.
Don't You Hear that Whistle Blowin'
Earliest Spring.
Earth Worm, The.
Else a great Prince in prison lies.
Eros at Temple Stream.
Everything flows.
Everything That Acts Is Actual.
Eye Mask.
February Evening in Boston, 1971.
February Evening in New York.
Five-Day Rain, The.
For Those Whom the Gods Love Less.
Fragrance of Life, Odor of Death.
Goddess, The.
Goethe's Blues.
Good Dream, The.
Goodbye to Tolerance.
Grace-Note, The.
Gulf, The.
Gypsy's Window, The.
Hands, The.
Hymn, The.
Hymn to Eros.
Hypocrite Women.
Ikon: The Harrowing of Hell.
Illustrious Ancestors.
In Mind.
In Thai Binh (Peace) Province.
Innocent, The.
Intrusion.
Jacob's Ladder, The.
Last Night's Dream.
Leaving Forever.
Life at War.
Life of Art, The.
Living.
Losing Track.
Love Poem.

Mad Song.
Malice of Innocence, The.
Map of the Western Part of the County of Essex in England, A.
Matins.
Merritt Parkway.
Mutes, The.
Note to Olga (1966), A.
O Taste and See.
Oblique Prayer.
October.
Old Adam, The.
Olga Poems.
One December Night.
Our Bodies.
Overheard.
Overheard over S. E. Asia.
Overland to the Islands.
Partial Resemblance.
Peachtree, The.
People at Night.
Perhaps No Poem at All But All I Can Say and I Cannot Be Silent.
Pleasures.
Poet and Person.
Prisoners.
Protesting at the Nuclear Test Site.
Psalm Concerning the Castle.
Quarry Pool, The.
Quest, The.
Recognition, The.
Relearning the Alphabet.
Reminder, The.
Roasting Potatoes.
Scenes from the Life of the Peppertrees.
Sea's Wash in the Hollow of the Heart, The.
Seeing for a Moment.
Sharks, The.
Shlup, shlup, the dog.
Six Variations.
Son, The.
Song for Ishtar.
Springtime, The.
St. Peter and the Angel.
Stele (1–2 c. B.C.)
Stepping Westward.
Sunday Afternoon.
Task, The.
Tenebrae.
Terror.
Third Dimension, The.
Time Past, A.
To the Muse.
To the Reader.
To the Snake.
Tree Telling of Orpheus, A.
Triple Feature.
Uncertain Oneiromancy.
Unknown, The.
Wavering.
Way Through, The.
Wedding-Ring.
Weeping Woman.
Went with some of my students to work in the People's.
What Were They Like?
What Wild Dawns There Were.
When We Look Up.
Where Is the Angel?
Williams: An Essay.
Willows of Massachusetts, The.
Window-Blind.
Wings, The.
Witness.
Woman Alone, A.
Woman Meets an Old Lover, A.
World Outside, The.
Wren, A.

Levi, David (1816–98)
Thou, Zion, old and suffering.

Levi, Peter (b. 1931)
City built in darkness and cold air, A.
I imagine where God has never been.
In stone settlements when the moon is stone.
New Year's Eve Poem 1965.
Smoke when the sun fell and when it rose.
Tree of roses. The water crashed headlong.

When does it end? When does a new poem.

Levi, Primo (1919–87)
Annunciation.
Buna.
For Adolf Eichmann.
Reveille.
Shemà.
Survivor, The.
Voices.

Levi, Steven C.
Abbienti.

Levi-Yitzhok [or Levi-Isaac] of Berditchev (Isaac of Berditshev) (1740–1809)
Kaddish.

Levien, Michael (b. 1927)
In the Falling Deer's Mouth.

Levin, Bernard
Limerick: "Earnest young leftie named Tariq."
Limerick: "Prince Charles in his Welsh principality."

Levin, Dana (b. 1965)
Field.
Red Water.
Wind.

Levin, Konstantin (1924–84)
Artillery was burying us.

Levin, Phillis (b. 1954)
Citizens and Sky.
Dark Horse.
Lost Bee, The.
Meeting of Friends, A.
Night Coach.
Planting Roses.
Shadow Returns, The.
Third Day, The.

Levine, Mark (b. 1965)
Everybody.
Wedding Day.
Work Song.

Levine, Philip (b. 1928)
Above It All.
And the Trains Go On.
Animals Are Passing from Our Lives.
At the Fillmore.
Autumn.
Baby Villon.
Belief.
Belle Isle, 1949.
Blasting from Heaven.
Clouds.
Coming Home, *Detroit*, 1968.
Death of Saul, The.
Distant Winter, The.
Fox, The.
Gangrene.
Genius.
Heaven.
Horse, The.
How Much Earth.
I Caught a Glimpse.
In the New Sun.
Keep Talking.
Later Still.
Life Ahead, The.
Listen Carefully.
Lost Angel, The.
Milkweed.
My Father with Cigarette Twelve Years Before the Nazis Could Break His Heart.
New Days for Old, Old Days for New.
1933.
Old Testament, The.
On a Drawing by Flavio.
On the Edge.
Poem Circling Hamtramck, Michigan, All Night in Search of You, The.
Rain Downriver.
Red Dust.
Red Shirt, The.
Right Cross, The.
Salami.
Sea We Read About, The.
Sierra Kid.
Simple Truth, The.
Sleepless Night, A.
Smoke.

Snow.
Soloing.
Standing on the Corner.
Sweet Will.
They Feed They Lion.
To a Child Trapped in a Barber Shop.
To My God in His Sickness.
Turning, The.
28.
Uncle.
Water's Chant, The.
Way Down, The.
What Work Is.
You Can Have It.
Zaydee.

Levis, Larry (b. 1946)
Anastasia and Sandman.
Caravaggio: Swirl and Vortex.
Decrescendo.
Edward Hopper, "Hotel Room," 1931.
Family Romance.
Linnets.
Morning After My Death, The.
1974: My Story in a Late Style of Fire.
Oldest Living Thing in L.A., The.
Photograph: Migrant Worker, Parlier, California, 1967.
Picking Grapes in an Abandoned Vineyard.
Poem You Asked For, The.
Poet at Seventeen, The.
Rhododendrons.
There Are Two Worlds.
Two Variations on a Theme by Kobayashi.
Whitman.
Widening Spell of the Leaves, The.
Winter Stars.

Levitansky, Yury Davydovich (b. 1922)
Dream about a Piano, A.

Levy, Amy (1861–89)
At a Dinner Party.
Ballad of Religion and Marriage, A.
Ballade of an Omnibus.
Birch-Tree at Loschwitz, The.
Cambridge in the Long.
Captivity.
Christopher Found.
Cross-Road Epitaph, A.
Epitaph: "This is the end of him, here he lies."
Felo de Se.
First Extra, The.
In the Mile End Road.
London in July.
London Plane-Tree, A.
London Poets.
Magdalen.
March Day in London, A.
Minor Poet, A.
Oh, Is It Love?
Old House, The.
On the Threshold.
Philosophy.
Reminiscence, A.
Run to Death.
Sequel to "A Reminiscence," The.
Sinfonia Eroica.
Straw in the Street.
To Lallie.
To Vernon Lee.
Twilight.
Xantippe.

Levy, Elvira
Gradually.
It Is Still Early.

Levy, Louis (1875–1940)
Swallow's Flight, The.

Levy, Newman (1888–1966)
Rigoletto.
Tannhauser.
Thaïs.

Lewis, Alun (1915–44)
All Day It Has Rained.
Autumn, 1939.
Christmas Holiday.
Dawn on the East Coast.
Easter at Christmas.
Goodbye.

Grey monkeys gibber, ignorant and wise.
In Hospital: Poona (1)
Infantry.
Jungle, The.
Karanje Village.
Mahratta Ghats, The.
Mountain over Aberdare, The.
Peasants, The.
Post-Script: for Gweno.
Raiders' Dawn.
Sentry, The.
Song (On Seeing Dead Bodies Floating Off the
    Cape)
To a Comrade in Arms.
To Edward Thomas.
Unknown Soldier, The.

Lewis, Clive Staples (1898–1963)
After Prayers, Lie Cold.
Apologist's Evening Prayer, The.
Ballade of Dead Gentlemen.
Epitaph, An: "Erected by her sorrowing
    brothers."
Evensong.
Evolutionary Hymn.
Late Passenger, The.
Naked Seed, The.
Nativity, The.
On a Theme from Nicolas of Cusa.
On a Vulgar Error.
Pilgrim's Problem.
Prayer: "Master, they say that when I seem."
Reason.
Save yourself. Run and leave me. I must go
    back.
Scazons.
Sonnet: "Bible says Sennacherib's campaign
    was spoiled, The."
Stephen to Lazarus.

**Lewis, Dominic Bevan Wyndham ("Timothy
    Shy") (1891–1969)**
Ale they drink in Giggleswick, The.
If So the Man You Are.
Lost Chord, The.
Pastoral: "Lumpish trollop, The!"
Sapphics.
Shot at Random, A.

Lewis, Eiluned (1900–1979)
We Who Were Born.

Lewis, Emily
My Dog.

Lewis, Esther (fl. 1747–89)
Advice to a Young Lady Lately Married.
Mirror for Detractors, A.
You midst gay crowds reside, I, hid in shades.

Lewis, Gwyneth (b. 1959)
Advice on Adultery.
And this, too, is love.
Chernobyl Icon.
Drew trips over his shadow by the pool.
Flyover Elegies.
Hedge, The.
Herod's Palace.
It looks like she's drowning.
Last suppers, I fancy, are always wide-screen.
"No" Madonnas, The.
Oxford Booklicker.
Pentecost.
Second time the comet swung by, The.
Six Poems on Nothing.
So this is the man you dreamt I had betrayed.
Sunday Park.
There are great advantages to having been
    dead.
Thousands arrive when a bird's about to fly.
Walking with the God.
What is her vanishing point?

Lewis, Howell Elvet [or Elfed] (1860–1953)
Life's Morning.

Lewis, J. Patrick (b. 1942)
How to Tell a Camel.
Stories.

Lewis, Janet (b. 1889)
Ancient Ones, The: Betátakin.
April Hill, The.
Country Burial.
For the Father of Sandro Gulotta.

Fossil, 1975.
Garden Note I, Los Altos.
Garden Note II, March.
Girl Help.
Grandmother Remembers, A.
Helen Grown Old.
Indians in the Woods, The.
Lullaby: "Lulee, lullay."
Reader, The.
Remembered Morning.
Time and Music.
Winter Garden.

Lewis, Jenny
I'm not in court to be judged.

Lewis, Lisa (b. 1956)
February.
Responsibility.

**Lewis, Matthew Gregory ("Monk" Lewis) (1775–
    1818)**
Alonzo the Brave and the Fair Imogine.

Lewis, Morgan
How High the Moon.

Lewis, Naomi
Footprint on the Air, A.

Lewis, Percy Wyndham (1882–1957)
I would set all things whatsoever front to back.
Song of the Militant Romance, The.

Lewis, Robert
If You Had a Friend.

Lewis, Sam M. (1885–1959)
Dinah.
Five Foot Two, Eyes of Blue (Has Anybody
    Seen My Girl?)
For All We Know.
How 'Ya Gonna Keep 'Em Down on the
    Farm? (After They've Seen Paree)
I'm Sitting on Top of the World.
I Wonder Why She Kept on Saying 'Si-Si-Si-
    Si-Senor.'
Just Friends.
Rock-a-Bye Your Baby with a Dixie Melody.
Street of Dreams.

Lewis, Saunders (b. 1893)
Ascension Thursday.
Deluge 1939, The.
Mary Magdalene.
Pine, The.
To the Good Thief.

Lewisohn, Ludwig (1882–1955)
Heinrich Heine.
Together.

Ley, Anna Norman (b. before 1620, d. 1641)
Upon a Booke Written at the Beginning of the
    Parliament 1640.
Upon the Necessity and Benefite of Learning
    Written in the Beginning of a Common
    Place Booke Belonging to W. B. a Young
    Scholler.

Leyeles, A. (Aaron Glanz-Leyeles) (1889–1966)
Castles.

Lezama Lima, José (1910–76)
Ah, That You Escape.
Call of the Desirous.
Dark Meadow Invites Me, A.
Fragments of the Night, The.
Portrait of José Cemí.
Rhapsody for the Mule.

Li Chih-yi (fl. 1071)
Tune: "The Diviner."

Li Ching (916–61)
Tune: "Echoing Heaven's Everlastingness."
Tune: "Sand of Silk-washing Stream."

Li Ch'ing-chao (1084–1151)
Alone in the Night.
As in a Dream.
Autumn Evening Beside the Lake.
Boat of Stars.
Butterflies Love Flowers.
Clear Bright.
Day of Cold Food, The.
End to Spring, An.
"Fisherman's Honor," The.
Hopelessness.
I let the incense grow cold.
In the little courtyard, by the side window.

Last night thin rain, gusty wind.
Light mist, then dense fog.
Long Melancholy Tune, A.
Lyric to the Tune "Immortal by the River."
Melting in thin mist and heavy clouds.
Mild and peaceful spring glow, Cold Food
    Day.
Mist.
Plum Blossoms.
Poem to the Tune of "Tsui hua yin."
Poem to the Tune of "Yi chian mei."
Quail Sky.
Rattan bed, paper netting. I wake from
    morning sleep.
Red lotus incense fades on / the jewelled
    curtain.
Sky links cloud waves, links dawn fog.
Spring at Wu Ling.
To the Tune: Bodhisattva's Headdress.
To the Tune: Drunk in Flower Shadows.
To the Tune: Eternal Joy.
To the Tune: Happiness Approaches.
To the Tune: "I Paint My Lips Red."
To the Tune: Lips Painted Red.
To the Tune, "Plum Blossoms Fall and
    Scatter."
To the Tune "Spring at Wu Ling."
To the Tune: Magnolia Blossoms.
To the Tune: Partridge Sky.
To the Tune: Partridge Sky.
To the Tune: Sands of the Washing Stream.
Tune: "Airing Inmost Feelings."
Tune: "As in a Dream; a Song."
Tune: "Charm of Nien-nu, The."
Tune: "Dream Song."
Tune: "Fisherman's Pride."
Tune: "Joy of Eternal Union."
Tune: "Magnolia Blossoms, Abbreviated."
Tune: "Magnolia Flowers."
Tune: "Manifold Little Hills."
Tune: "On the Trail of Sweet Incense."
Tune: "Partridge Sky."
Tune: "Pure Serene Music."
Tune: "Rouged Lips."
Tune: "Song of Picking Mulberry."
Tune: "Southern Song, A."
Tune: "Spring at Wu-ling."
Tune: "Telling of Innermost Feelings."
Tune: "The Charm of a Maiden Singer;"
    Spring Thoughts.
Tune: "Tipsy in the Flower's Shade."
Two Springs.
Warm rain, sunny wind start to break the chill.
Washing Stream, The.
Weary Song to a Slow Sad Tune, A.
Year after year I have watched.

Li Chü (fl. mid 20th cent.)
Harvesting Wheat for the Public Share.

Li Ho (791–817)
Arrowhead from the Ancient Battlefield of
    Ch'ang-p'ing, An.
At Ch'ang-ku, Reading: To Show to My Man
    Pa.
Ch'ang-ku.
Cold in the North (After Yueh-Fu)
Country Road, A.
Days of Rain.
Drinking All Night, Sleeping All Day.
Flying Light.
For the Examination at Ho-nan-fu: Songs of
    the Twelve Months.
Grave of Little Su, The.
High the Mount of Wu.
In Protest.
King Ch'in Drinks Wine.
King of Ch'in Drinks Wine, The.
Lament for a Courtesan.
Lamentations of the Bronze Camels.
Last month of the year, grass roots taste sweet.
Life at the Capital.
Lute Player, The.
Master dragon-tamer has fled the world, The.
Melancholic.
My Man Pa Replies.
New Bamboo in the North Garden at Ch'ang-
    ku.
Northland in Cold, The.

Li Hsun

On and On: An Ancient Song (Yueh-Fu)
Ravine on a Cold Evening.
Song: Green Water, Singing Girl.
Song of the Sacred Strings.
Temple of the Orchid Fragrance Goddess.
Young Man with a Yellow Hat.
Young Noble at Night's End; a Song.

Li Hsun (855–930)

To the Tune: The Wine Spring: "Eternal
  autumn rain—evening sounds."
To the Tune: The Wine Spring: "Rain falls on
  fallen flowers."

Li Hsün (855?–930?)

Tune: "Song of the Southern Country."
Tune: "Stretch of Cloud over Mount Wu, A."

Li K'ai-hsien (1502–68)

Colorful frames are erected beside the Yellow
  River, The.
Commiserating with the Poor.
Compassion for the Farmers.
Crossing the ridge, the woodcutter loses his
  way.
Drunk, Climbing to the Peak of Iron Tomb on
  Wei Mountain.
Earthquake covered Shansi and Shensi, The.
Gazing at Ch'ang-po Mountain.
Impromptu Poems.
In the Second Month of Summer, Taking My
  Family to the Villages East of the City.
Jade trees from the rear courtyard of the
  empire of Ch'en.
Meeting Trappers on the Road in Heavy Snow.
Night of the First Full Moon, The.
Night of the Seventeenth, The.
Not a day goes by without someone borrowing
  books from me.
On My Birthday—Sick.
On the Cold Food Festival, Entertaining at the
  Southern Estate—the Guests Were Li Chiu-
  ho, Ma Nan-yeh, Wei Tung-kao, Li Hu-
  ch'uan, Huang K'ung-ts'un, Li Lung-t'ang,
  and Hu Hu-shan.
Parable, A.
Pleasures among the Fields during the Four
  Seasons.
Poem about Fan the Fourth, A.
Poem Expressing My Wife's Response to One
  I Sent Her, A.
Prosperous Villager, The.
Record of a Past Affair, A.
Recording a Weird Happening.
Sent to the Master Physician, "Almond
  Orchard" Shih.
Sent to the Painter, Lu Hsiao-feng.
Songs of the Frontier.
Staying Overnight on the Banks of
  Embroidered River.
Thanking Doctor Jen.
Trip to a Mountain Village, A.
Wei-ch'i Chess.
When I Recovered from an Illness After
  Returning Home To Live in Retirement, I
  Was Invited by My Friends to Join a Song-
  Lyric Club.

Li Kuang-t'ien (1906–68)

Dead Turk, A.

Li Ling

Parting from Su Wu.

Li Meng-yang (1413–1529)

Autumn Vista.
Crossing the Frontier.
Mooring at Hsia-k'ou at Night.
Oriole at Dawn, An.
Seeing Off Commander in Chief Li to Yün-
  chung.
Song of Lin Liang's Painting "Two Horned
  Falcons."
Spring Vista from the Tower of Illuminated
  Distance.
Wild Wind.

Li Mi-an (fl. 16th cent.?)

Half-and-Half Song, The.

Li P'in (fl. late 9th cent.)

Crossing Han River.

Li Po (701–62)

About Tu Fu.

Ages have passed since the stately Odes
  flourished.
Ancient Air.
Ancient Airs.
Ascend the Phoenix Terrace.
At Ch'ang-men Palace.
At Su Terrace Viewing the Past.
At the Sky's End, Thinking of Li Po.
At Yellow Crane Tower Taking Leave of Meng
  Hao-jan.
Autumn Cove.
Awakening from Drunkenness on a Spring
  Day.
Ballad of Long Bank, The.
Barbarian pass is filled with windblown sand,
  The.
Birds have Vanished, The.
Blue Water.
Boating Song.
Bring the Wine!
Calling on a Taoist Priest in Tai-t'ien Mountain
  but Failing to See Him.
Ch'iu-p-u teems with white gibbons.
Clearing at Dawn.
Climbing Phoenix Terrace at Chin-ling.
Conversations in the Mountains.
Crossing Ching-Men to See a Friend Off.
Crows at Dusk.
Drinking Alone in Moonlight.
Drinking Alone in the Moonlight.
Drinking Alone under Moonlight.
Drinking Alone with the Moon.
Drinking Wine with a Mountain Hermit.
Exile's Letter.
Facing Wine with Memories of Lord Ho.
Fall River Song.
Farewell to Yin Shu.
Fighting on the South Frontier.
Fighting South of the Wall.
For Meng Hao-jan.
For the Dancer of the King of Wu.
Furnace fire lights up earth and sky, The.
Gathering lotuses by Yeh River.
Girl of Yueh, The.
Girls of Yueh, The.
Going to Visit a Taoist Recluse on Heaven's
  Mountain Only to Find Him Gone.
Great Bird, The.
Hearing the Flute in the City of Loyang in a
  Spring Night.
How like a bolt of white silk is this water.
If Heaven weren't fond of wine.
In a Village by the River.
In Imitation of Ancient Songs.
In Memory of Ho Chi-chen.
In Praise of a Gold and Silver Painted Scene of
  the Buddha Manifestation in the Pure Land
  of the West, with a Preface.
In Reply When Lesser Officials of Chung-tu
  Brought a Pot of Wine and Two Fish to My
  Inn as Gifts.
In the Mountains on a Summer Day.
In Yüeh Viewing the Past.
Inscribed at Summit Temple.
Inscribed on the Wall of Hsü Hsüan-Ping's
  Retreat.
Jewel Stairs' Grievance, The.
Ku Feng (After the Style of Ancient Poems)
Lament of the Frontier Guard.
Late Bloomer at the Front of My Garden.
Listening to a Flute in Yellow Crane Pavilion.
Listening to a Flute on a Spring Night in Lo-
  yang.
Listening to a Monk from Shu Playing the
  Lute.
Listening to the Lute Played by Monk Chun
  from Shu.
Lonely Wife, The.
Longing for Someone.
Looking for Master Yung Ts'un near His
  Hermitage.
Mirror Lake's waters are moon-clear.
Moon over Mountain Pass.
Moon over the Mountain Pass, The.
Mountain Drinking Song.
My sword at my waist, I climb a high tower.
My white hair of thirty thousand feet.

Night with a Friend, A.
O-mei Mountain Moon.
Old Dust.
Old Style Poem.
Old Tai's Wine Shop.
On Climbing the Phoenix Tower at Chinling.
On Dragon Hill.
On the River.
On Visiting Taoist Recluse of Tai-Tien-Shan
  and Not Finding Him.
One set on the highway to sing.
Parting.
Poem by the Bridge at Ten-shin.
Poem Composed at the Command of the
  Emperor.
Poem No. 19 in the Old Manner.
Pot of wine among the flowers, A.
Presented to Wang Lun.
Questions Answered.
Quiet Night Thoughts.
Remembering Ancient Days in Yueh.
Remembering East Mountain.
Remembering Our Excursion in the Past.
Resentment Near the Jade Steps.
Return of the Banished.
Rhymeprose on the Sword Gallery.
Rising Drunk on a Spring Day.
River Merchant's Wife, The; a Letter.
River Song.
Road to Shu Is Hard, The.
Saying Farewell to a Friend.
Saying Good-bye in a Ch'in-ling Wineshop.
Saying Good-bye to Meng Hao-jan at Yellow
  Crane Pavilion.
Seeing a Friend Off.
Seeing Meng Hao-jan Off to Kuang-ling.
Seeing Off a Friend.
Self-abandonment.
Sent to My Two Little Children in the East of
  Lu.
Separation on the River Kiang.
Sitting Alone in Ching-t'ing Mountain.
Song of Ch'ang-Kan (Yueh-Fu), The.
Song of Hsiang-yang.
Song of War, A.
Southern women have alabaster skin.
Spring Night in Lo-Yang—Hearing a Flute.
Spring Thoughts.
Springtime South of the Yangtze.
Still Night Thoughts.
Suite in the Ch'ing-p'ing Mode, A.
Summer Day in the Mountains.
Summer Days in the Mountains.
Summit Temple, The.
T'ien-mu Mountain Ascended in a Dream: A
  Farewell Song.
Taking Leave of a Friend.
There was a sojourner in Ying who intoned
  "White Snows."
They Fought South of the Walls.
Thinking of East Mountain.
Third month in T'ientsin, The.
Thoughts While Studying at Hanlin Academy
  Sent to My Colleagues at the Chi-hsien
  Academy.
To a Friend.
To Amuse Myself.
To Meng Hao-jan.
To Secretary Lu Ch'ien of Jen City.
To See a Friend Off to Shu.
To See Meng Hao-Jan Off to Yang-Chou.
To See Secretary Shu-Yun Off at the Hsieh
  T'iao Tower at Hsuan-Ch'eng.
To Send to Tu Fu as a Joke.
To Tan-Ch'iu.
To the Tune: Beautiful Barbarian.
To Tu Fu.
To Tu Fu from Shantung.
Tune: "Beautiful Barbarians."
Tzu-yeh Song.
Up into the Clouds Music.
Verses: "Clean is the autumn wind."
Viewing the Waterfall at Mount Lu.
Waterfall at Lu-shan.
Woman from Ch'ang-kan, The.
Written in Behalf of My Wife.
You Ask Why.

Yu Chieh Yuan (Jade Steps Grievance, Yueh-fu)
Zazen on Ching-t'ing Mountain.

Li Shan-fu (*fl.* c.874)
My Detached Villa.
Temple of Hsiang Yü, The.

Li Shang-yin (812–58)
About Geese.
Alone by the Autumn River.
At eight stealing a mirror glance.
Bite back passion. Spring now sets.
Boasting of My Son.
Boudoir Feelings.
Candle Casts Dark Shadows, The.
Ch'ang-O.
Chance to Meet Is Difficult, The.
Cicada.
Evening Comes.
Fallen Flowers.
For Lotus Flower.
From the Heights.
Hearing a Startled Bird During Stayover at Chin-Ch'ang Pavilion.
Her Beauty Is Hidden.
Hibiscus Flowers.
I Wake Up Alone.
In a Day.
Inlaid Lute, The.
Last night's planets and stars, last night's wind.
"Coming" is an empty word, "going" leaves no trace.
Little Peach Blossoms in the Garden.
Master Chia.
Night Chill.
Night Rains: A Letter to Go North.
Old Harem, The.
Phoenix tail on scented silk, flimsy layer on layer.
Poem for My Little Boy.
Richly Painted Zither, The.
Spring Rain.
Wang Chao-chün.
When Will I Be Home?
Willow.
Without Title (1)
Without Title (2)

Li Shen (772–846)
Pitying the Farmer.

Li Te-yü (787–849)
To Patriarch Sun at Hua-yang Grotto.

Li Tung (*fl.* 9th cent.)
For the Monk San-tsang on His Return to the Western Regions.

Li Tung-yang (1447–1511)
Following the Rhymes of Yang T'ing-ho's Poem, "On the Road Back, Accompanying the Imperial Retinue on a Visit to the Tombs of Former Emperors."
Inscribed on the Painting "Meaning of a Poem by Wang Wei."
Long Handscroll of Bamboo by Wang Meng-tuan, The.
On a Painting of Fish Being Caught, A Song.
Song of the Painting "Catching Fish."
To Yung-erh—Imitating a Work by Master Jade Stream.
Trip to Yüeh-lu Temple, A.

Li Yen-nien (c.140–87 B.C.)
Song, A: "In the north there is a lovely woman."
Song: "There's a beautiful woman in the north."

Li Yi (c.749–c.829)
At Night atop Shou-hsiang Citadel, Hearing Tartar Flutes.
Listening to a Flute at Night near the City Wall.
Looking in a Mirror the Day before the Advent of Autumn.

Li Yü (937–78)
One scull in the spring wind, one leaf of a boat.
To the Tune "Meeting Happiness."

Li Yu (937–78)
To the Tune: Beautiful Lady Yu.

Li Yü (937–78)
Tune: "Beautiful Lady Yü, The."

Tune: "Beating Silk Floss."
Tune: "Beauty Yu."
Tune: "Casket of Pearls, A."
Tune: "Crows Crying at Night."
Tune: "Dance of the Cavalry."
Tune: "Deva-like Barbarian."
Tune: "Gazing at the South."
Tune: "Joy at Meeting."
Tune: "Joy of Encounter."
Tune: "Memories of the South."
Tune: "New Bounty of Royalty."
Tune: "Pure Serene Music."
Tune: "Ripples Sifting Sand."
Tune: "Sand Washed by Waves."
Tune: "Song of Tzu-yeh."
Tune: "Spring in Jade Pavilion."
Tune: "The Crow's Nocturnal Cry."
Tune: The Fisherman.

Liagarang
Snails.

Liang Te-sheng (1886–1910)
Sent to My Fourth Son, Shao-Wu (to the Tune "Southern Countryside")

Lichtenstein, Alfred (1889–1914)
Leaving for the Front.

Lickbarrow, Isabella
On Esthwaite Water.
On Sensibility: A Fragment.
On the Slave-Trade.
Patterdale.

Liddy, James (b. 1934)
Donagh MacDonagh.
History.
I know nothing but this scene.
Paean to Eve's Apple.
Strand Hotel, Rosslare, The.
Voice of America, 1961, The.

Lieberman, Elias (1883–1969)
Sholom Aleichem.

Lieberman, Laurence (b. 1935)
Architect Monk, The.
Compass of the Dying.
Coral Reef, The.
God's Measurements.
Lobsters in the Brain Coral.
Organist's Black Carnation, The.

Lieberman, Michael
Los Olivos.
On the Anniversary of My Father's Death.
Prediction.
Regret.

Liechtenstein, Ulrich von (*fl.* 13th cent.)
Love, Whose Month Was Ever May.

Liessin, Abraham (b. 1872)
Spring Nocturne.

Lifshin, Lyn (b. 1944)
After the Anti-Semitic Calls on a Local Talk Station.
Being Jewish in a Small Town.
Bergen-Belsen 1945.
Crystal Night.
Hearing of Reagan's Trip to Bitburg.
I Remember Haifa Being Lovely But.
Seeing the Documentary by the British Liberating Bergen-Belsen.
Yahrtzeit Light, The.

Light, Kate (b. 1960)
Because.
Idea of Love Between Us, The.
My Worst Nightmare.
Safe-T-Man.

Lightfoot, Gordon (b. 1938)
Wreck of the Edmund Fitzgerald, The.

Lihn, Enrique (1929–1988)
Cemetery in Punta Arenas.
Dark Room, The.
Farewell.
Favorite Little Shrine, A.
Goodnight, Achilles.
Memories of Marriage.
Mud.
Of All Despondencies.
Revolution.
Six Poems of Loneliness.
Torture Chamber.

Like, Joseph
James Dean and the Pig.
Postmodern: A Definition.

Liliencron, Detlev, Freiherr von (1844–1909)
After the Hunt.
Autumn.
Who Knows Where.

Lili'u-o-ka-lani, Queen (1838–1917)
Aloha'oe.
Ka Waiapo Lani.
Ku'u Pua I Paoakalani.
Lawn Sprinkler, The.
Sanoe.

Lillard, Charles (b. 1944)
Bushed.
Lobo.

Lillenas, Haldor
Wonderful grace of Jesus, Greater than all my sin.

Lilley, Kate (b. 1960)
Sewing Lesson, The.
You Have to Strike Back.

Lilliat, John (c.1550–c.1599)
False Love.

Lim, Genny (b. 1946)
Children are Colorblind.

Lim, Shirley (b. 1944)
Black and White.
Father from Asia.
I Defy You.
In California with Neruda.
Learning to Love America.
Lost Name Woman.
Modern Secrets.
Monarchs Steering.
Pantoun for Chinese Women.
Riding into California.
Starlight Haven.
Visting Malacca.

Lim-Wilson, Fatima (*fl.* 20th cent.)
Alphabet Soup.
Beginning of Things, The.
Explaining the Origin of My Name.
Raising the Dead.
Ringmaster's Wife.
Upon Overhearing Tagalog.
Wave, The.

Lima, Frank (b. 1938)
Cuauhtemoc.
Hand, The.
Year's End.

Lima, Jorge de (1893–1953)
Distribution of Poetry.
Enormous Hand, The.
Papa John.
Poem of any Virgin.
Stranger, Stranger.
That Black Girl Fulô.
Trumpets, The.
Words of Departure.
Words Will Resurrect, The.

Lima, Maria Eugénia (b. 1935)
Madalena.
Marketwoman of Luanda.
Shoeshine Boy.

Limburg, Joanne (b. 1970)
Barton in the Beans.
Inner Bloke.
Queen of Swords, The.
Return, The.
Seder Night with My Ancestors.

"Limonov, Eduard Veniaminovich" (Eduard Veniaminovich Savenko) (b. 1943)
And it's the summer civil war.
As if a quiet branch drew a line.
Fantastic!
For whisper and orchestra.
I would hold another person in my thoughts.
It is good in May, in marvelous wet May, to be the chairman of the All-Russian Extraordinary Committee in the city of Odessa.
Japanese restaurant is good in autumn—in dank weather—the hot napkins, the warm sake, The.

Lin, Ch'en
Horses at a Breach in the Great Wall.
Lin Hung (*fl.* c.1383)
Drinking Wine.
Inscribed on the Painting "Pleasures of the Lute by the River."
Sailing at Night on Flowing-sand River.
Saying Farewell to Magistrate Ch'en Ta-yu.
Lin Pu (967–1028)
Autumn Day—Leisurely Boating on West Lake, An.
Locust Wood Mallet for Papermaking, A.
Trail among the Pines, A.
Lincoln, Abraham (1809–65)
Gettysburg Address, The.
My Childhood-Home I See Again.
Lindbergh, Anne Morrow (b. 1906)
Even.
Linden, Mrs. Henry (b. 1859)
All We Ask Is Justice.
As Women of Our Race.
Bird Song, The.
Brave Man and Brave Woman.
Church Bells, The.
Count Your Blessings.
Cultivation.
Do Your Best.
Encouragement.
Fall Is Here, The.
For the Good of the Pythian Order.
God's Electric Power.
Golden Jubilee of Wilberforce.
Gossip.
Household of Ruth, The.
I Am as Happy as a Queen on Her Throne.
Last Day of the Year; or, New Year's Eve, The.
Let Us Strive to Do Something.
Life's Golden Sunset.
Lonely World.
Man Is What He Wills to Be.
Marriage Vow.
May.
Missionary, The.
New Year's Morning; or, the First Day of the Year.
October Is Here.
Oh Woman, Blessed Woman!
Orphan Girl, An.
Our Club Work.
Our Noble Booker T. Washington.
Parting Lovers, The.
Paul Laurence Dunbar.
Pay Your Debts.
Prospect of the Future, The.
Riot, A.
Scraps of Time.
Silent Night, The.
Sun of Our Existence, The.
Tell Her So.
This Country's Needs.
To the Conference.
To the Queen of the British Government.
To the Wheel of Progress.
Wayward Son, The.
What Is Woman?
Would-be Critic, The.
Y. M. C. A., The.
Lindley, David (b. 1946)
By Fire or Flood.
Cromwell: The Last Portrait.
Cryptogram, The.
Curly Kale.
Fennel.
Marxist to Liberals, A.
Nearness.
Potato Blight.
Lindon, J. A. (b. 1914)
Limerick issued from Lear, The.
Limerick: "Mr. Alan Jay Lerner (with by-play)"
My Garden.
Lindsay, Caroline (1844–1912)
Love or Fame.
To My Own Face.
Lindsay, Christian (*fl.* 1580s)
Christen Lyndesay to Ro. Hudsone.

Lindsay [*or* Lyndsay], **Sir David** (c.1490–c.1555)
After the Flood.
Deuisioun of the Eirth, The.
My patent pardouns ye may see.
Of the Realme of Scotland.
Squire Meldrum at Carrickfergus.
Lindsay, Jack (b. 1900)
Angry Dusk.
Question Time.
To My Father Norman Alone in the Blue Mountains.
Lindsay, Lady Anne (1750–1825)
Auld Robin Gray.
Lindsay, Maurice (b. 1918)
Exiled Heart, The.
Hurlygush.
Lindsay, Nicholas Vachel (1879–1931)
Abraham Lincoln Walks at Midnight.
Apple-Barrel of Johnny Appleseed, The.
Arts are old, old as the stones, The.
At Mass.
Bryan, Bryan, Bryan, Bryan.
Chinese Nightingale, The.
Congo, The.
Dove of New Snow, The.
Eagle That Is Forgotten, The.
Factory Windows Are Always Broken.
Flower-fed Buffaloes, The.
General William Booth Enters into Heaven.
Ghosts of the Buffaloes, The.
I Heard Immanuel Singing.
In Which Roosevelt Is Compared to Saul.
Indian Summer Day on the Prairie, An.
Jazz of This Hotel, The.
John Brown.
King of Yellow Butterflies, The.
Leaden-eyed, The.
Little Turtle, The.
Moon's the North Wind's Cooky, The.
Mysterious Cat, The.
Rain.
She is madonna in an art.
Simon Legree—A Negro Sermon.
Spider and the Ghost of the Fly, The.
To a Golden-Haired Girl in a Louisiana Town.
To Mary Pickford—Moving Picture Actress.
Traveler, The.
Two Old Crows.
Unpardonable Sin, The.
What the Moon Saw.
Why I Voted the Socialist Ticket.
Lindsay, Ruth Temple
Hunters, The.
Lindsay, Vachel (1879–1931)
Flower-Fed Buffaloes, The.
Lindtová, Anna (1930–44)
Campfire.
Lingg, Herman von (1820–1905)
Though you can tell me.
Link, Harry
These Foolish Things (Remind Me of You)
Link, Lenore M.
Holding Hands.
Linton, William James (*fl.* c.1851)
Epicurean.
Spring and Autumn.
Lion-Face, Dakini
KYE HO! Wonderful!
Lipkin, Semyon [*or* Semion] **Izrailevich** (b. 1911)
Conjunction.
He who appointed weight to the wind.
In the Desert.
When I was arranging letters into words.
Lippman, Matthew (b. 1965)
Hallelujah Terrible.
Lipsitz, Lou (b. 1938)
Bedtime Story.
Feeding, The.
Prospect Beach.
Lipton, James (b. 1946)
Misericordia!
Lisboa, Henriqueta
Beyond the Image.
Camellia.
Echo.

Elegy: "At first the dead."
Idyll: "Lord, forgive me if I do not look for you."
Minor Elegy.
Lisella, Julia
Song of the Third Generation.
Lish, Gordon
Rusty.
Lisick, Beth (b. 1968)
Empress of Sighs.
Pantoumstone for a Dying Breed.
Lisle, Thomas (1709–67)
Power of Music, The.
Lisnyanskaya [*or* Lisnianskaia], **Inna L'vovna** (b. 1928)
To be thought an outcast in my beloved country.
To you, my friends, to you, my dear ones.
Two carousing hawk moths, their wings like nervous silk.
Whenever I looked in the mirror.
Wind blows and makes the light tremble, The.
Lister, Elizabeth H.
Limerick: "Don't thee think, Zurrr, I be zo amazin'"
Limerick: "I consider I really am through."
Lister, Richard Percival (b. 1914)
Lament of an Idle Demon.
Mind Reborn in Streatham Common, A.
Revolutionaries, The.
Toast to 2,000, A.
Litchfield, Grace Denio (1849–1946)
Good-By.
Litsey, Edwin Carlile
Dreams Ahead, The.
"Little Billee"
Limerick: "Devil's no longer a myth, The."
Limerick: "Devil, who plays a deep part, The."
Limerick: "Said an elderly Bishop called Greville."
Limerick: "There was a young lady of Nîmes."
Little, Geraldine Clinton
Fallen horse.
Now ice-covered.
White spider, The.
Little, Janet (1759–1813)
Given to a Lady Who Asked Me to Write a Poem.
Little, Lessie Jones
My Yellow Straw Hat.
Littlebird, Harold (Harold Bird) (b. 1951)
Alone Is the Hunter.
Coming Home in March.
Could I Say I Touched You.
For Drum Hadley.
For the Girls 'cause They Know.
For Tom Numkena, Hopi/Spokane.
Gaa-a-Muna, a Mountain Flower.
Hummingbird.
If You Can Hear My Hooves.
In a Double Rainbow.
Mother / Deer / Lady.
Oh but It Was Good.
Old Moke.
Pennsylvania Winter Indian 1974.
Wrap Me in Blankets of Momentary Winds.
LittleCoon See **Oliver, Louis**
Littledale, Freya
When My Dog Died.
Littlefield, Milton S. (1864–1934)
O Son of Man, Thou Madest Known.
Littleton, Edward (1698?–1734)
Spider, The.
Littman, Jeffery
Limerick: "O Great Queen Whom I idolize."
Littman, S.
Limerick: "There was a young lady of Nantes."
Litvinoff, Emanuel (b. 1915)
If I Forget Thee.
Liu Ch'ang-ch'ing (710?–785?)
At an Inn in Yü-kan.
Encountering a Snowstorm, I Stay with the Recluse of Mount Hibiscus.
Listening to the Washblock in the Moonlight.

On Parting with the Buddhist Pilgrim Ling-Ch'ê.
Rejoicing that the Zen Master Pao Has Arrived from Dragon Mountain.
Replying to a Poem by the Monk Ling-yi at the New Spring.
Saying Goodby to the Monk Ling-ch'e.
Sent to the Taoist of Dragon Mountain, Hsü Fa-leng.
Snow on Lotus Mountain.

Liu Ch'e (140 B.C.–87 B.C.)
Oh the sound of her silk sleeves.

Liu Cheng (d. 217)
Cockfight.
Poem without a Category.

Liu Chi-hsün (fl. c.100 B.C.)
Lament.

Liu Chih (c.1280–c.1335)
Tune: "Decorous and Pretty"—Respectfully Offered to Circuit Inspector Kao.
Tune: 'Sheep on the Mountain Slope.'

Liu Chün (430–64)
In Imitation of Hsü Kan.

Liu E (1857–1909)
Boiling Falls.
House of Red Leaves, The.
I Remember.
New Year's Eve.
On the Fifteenth Day of the Eighth Month: Watching a Rainstorm from a Tower in Seoul.
On the Night of the Sixteenth of the Eighth Month: Watching the Moon from the Deck of the Ship, Aimo-maru in the Black Water Sea.
On the Road to Pyongyang—An Improvisation.
On the Twenty-fourth: Improvisations.
Pleasures of Shinbashi.
Poem on Falling Leaves.
Poems for Yukiko of Tamba.
Teahouse at Hoshioka, A.
Waiting for the Ferry at Inchŏn.

Liu Hsün's Wife
Curtain of the Wedding Bed, The.

Liu K'o-chuang (1187–1269)
From "Ten Poems Recording Things that Happened at the Year's End."
Leaving the City.
Weeping for Hsüeh Tzu-shu.

Liu Ling-hsien (fl. 6th cent.)
Inscribed on a Plantain Leaf to Show to a Certain Person.

Liu Pang (256–195 B.C.)
Song of the Great Wind.

Liu Shih (1618–64)
Tune: 'Dreaming of Southland' Thinking of Someone.

Liu, Stephen Shu Ning (b. 1930)
My Father's Martial Art.

Liu, Timothy
Ariel Singing.
Brooklyn Botanic Garden, The.
Echoes.
Highway 6.
Ikon.
Kindertotenlieder.
Mama.
Poem.
Poem: "Late butterflies gliding through the air—."
Reading Whitman in a Toilet Stall.
Size of It, The.
Strange Fruit.
Sunday.
Thoreau.
Vox Angelica.
Wellfleet.

Liu Tsung-yüan (773–819)
Arriving at North Pond by Stupid Brook on a Morning Walk after the Rain.
Beyond the bamboo fence, cooking fire and smoke.
By an ancient road, abundant thistle plants.
Drinking at Night in the Western Pavilion of the Fa-hua Temple.
Feeling Old Age.
Meditation Hall.
Morning Walk in Autumn to South Valley Passing an Abandoned Village.
On Covering the Bones of Chang Chin, the Hired Man.
Poem to Send to Friends in the Capital, A.
River Snow.
Snowy River.
Viewing Mountains with His Reverence Hao Ch'u: To My Friends and Relatives in the Capital.
Written in Jest on Elder Stonegate's Eastern Balcony.

Liu Ya-tzu (1887–1958)
Beyond the stream at Seta stretches an endless view.
By Flower-and-Moon Pavilion, I stay my carriage.
Cataracts flying down a thousand fathoms roll up a raging billow.
Dragons and Snakes.
Filled with Emotions on the Moon-ferrying Bridge at Arashiyama.
For Guests after Their Visit.
On Hearing the News of the Japanese Surrender.
On the Second Day of the Fifth Month—Written after Drink.
Overjoyed at Soviet Russia's Entry into the War.
Strange Tears.
To a Friend, Using the Same Rhymes of a Peom He Sent Me.

Liu Yin (1249–1282)
Miscellaneous Poem on Rural Life.

Liu Yu Hsi (772–842)
Bamboo Branch Song.
Blacktail Row.
Chin-ling.
Coming Again to Heng-yang, I Mourn for Liu Tsung-yüan.
Drinking with Friends amongst the Blooming Peonies.
Gorges of Wu are hoary and dim in the season of mist and rain, The.
Looking at My Knife-hilt Ring, a Song.
Song of Spring Replying to a Poem by Po Chü-yi, A.
Sorrowing for the Past at Western Pass Mountain.
To the Tune "Glittering Sword Hilts."
Tune: "Ripples Sifting Sand."
Tune: 'Memories of the South.'
Up in the hills are bank on bank of blossoming peach and plum trees.
Willow Branch Song.
Willow Branches.

Liu Yung (fl. c.1034)
Cicada Song.
Lament: "Late autumn, a brief shower."
Song: "After the eating, the drinking, the singing."
Song: "Because spring brings miserable green and painful red."
Song: "It's the wine, this ache, this longing."
Song: "She lowers her fragrant curtain."
Song to the Tune 'Ting Feng Po.'
Tune: 'Bells in the Rain.'
Tune: 'Bells Ringing in the Rain.'
Tune: 'Eight Beats of a Kan-chou Song.'
Tune: "Chrysanthemums Fresh."
Tune: "Jade Butterflies."
Tune: "Midnight Music."
Tune: "Prelude to Allure Goddesses."
Tune: "Wanderings of a Youth."

Livesay, Dorothy (1909–1996)
Arms and the Woman.
Children's Letters, The.
Eve.
Fantasia.
Green Rain.
Leader, The.
Other.
Prophetess, The.
Spain.
Three Emily's, The.
Uninvited, The.
Waking in the Dark.
Without Benefit of Tape.

Livingston, Jay (b. 1915)
Buttons and Bows.
Femininity.
Haven't Got a Worry.
Keep It Simple.
Mona Lisa.
Never Let Me Go.
To Each His Own.
Whatever Will Be, Will Be (Que Sera, Sera)

Livingston, Jerry
It's the Talk of the Town.

Livingston, Joseph A.
I'm Through with Love.

Livingston, Myra Cohn (b. 1926)
4-Way Stop.
12 October.
74th Street.
Arthur Thinks on Kennedy.
Car Wash.
Coming from Kansas.
Cried a man on the Salisbury Plain.
Dark, The.
Doll.
Envoi: Washington Square Park.
Father.
First Thanksgiving.
Invitation.
Lazy Witch.
Lemonade Stand.
Night, The.
Paul Revere Speaks.
Poor.
Swimming Pool.
Tape, The.
Why?
Working with Mother.

Livingstone, Dinah
Stepmother.

Livingstone, Douglas (b. 1932)
Bad Run at King's Rest.
Bateleur.
Lake Morning in Autumn.
On Clouds.
One Time.
Piece of Earth, A.
Sleep of My Lions, The.
Vanderdecken.

Llawdden (fl. c.1460)
No Place Like Home.

Llewellyn, Kate (b. 1940)
Colonel.
Finished.

Llewellyn-Williams, Hilary (b. 1951)
Feeding the Bat.
Little Cloth, The.
Making Babies.
Short Wave.
Two Rivers.

Lloyd, Charles (1775–1839)
Erst when I wandered far from those I loved.
Metaphysical Sonnet.
My pleasant home! where erst when sad and faint.
Oh, I have told thee every secret care.
Oh, she was almost speechless! nor could hold.
Where have I wander'd, London, from thy haunts?
Whether thou smile or frown, thou beauteous face.
Written at the Hotwells, near Bristol.

Lloyd, David (1597–1633)
At the bottom.
Duck feathers.
Longest night, The.
Moonlit sleet.
Over dried grass.
Quietly shaping.
Wild rose bending.

Lloyd, Evan (1734–76)
Helen like the Rose.

Portrait of a Bishop.
Religion and the Lower Classes.
Sons of War sometimes are known, The.
Lloyd, John (1797–1875)
Kingfisher, The.
Thoughts of Boyhood.
Lloyd, Ludovic (fl. 1573–1610)
Flee, stately Juno, Samos fro.
Lloyd, Margaret
Simplest and the Hardest, The.
Lloyd, Robert (1733–64)
Acting, dear Thornton, its perfection draws.
Cit's Country Box, The.
Mark yon round parson, fat and sleek.
Old England has not lost her prayer.
Public Schools.
True Genius.
Yet matter must be gravely planned.
Lluellyn [or Lluelyn], Martin (1616–82)
Epithalamium: To Mistress M. A.
Llwyd, Catherin Owen (d. 1602)
To Siôn Lloyd: the Mother's Advice to Her
Heir.
Llwyd, Huw (c.1568–1630)
Fox's Counsel, The.
Llwyd, Morgan (1619–59)
Awake, O Lord, Awake Thy Saints.
Come Wisdome Sweet.
Excuse, The.
Harvest, The.
Law was ever above kings, The.
Spring, The.
Summer, The.
What? summer now? divisions ring.
Winter, The.
Llwyd, Richard (1752–1835)
Here, still sequestered, Penmon's sacred dome.
Llywelyn ab y Moel (d. 1440)
Battle of Waun Gaseg, The.
Llywelyn Goch ap Meurig Hen (fl. 1360–90)
Lament for Lleucu Llwyd.
Llywelyn-Williams, Alun (b. 1913)
In Berlin, August 1945: Lehrte Bahnhof.
Pont y Caniedydd.
When I Was Young.
Yesterday's Illusion or Remembering the
Thirties.
Lo Pin-Wang (640?–684?)
On the Cicada: In Prison.
Lo Yin (833–909)
Book-burning Pit, The.
Sent to the Ch'an Master Wu-hsiang.
Thinking of the Way Home, a Song.
Lochhead, Douglas (b. 1922)
Winter Lanscape—Halifax.
Lochhead, Liz (b. 1947)
Grim Sisters, The.
Hickie, The.
My Rival's House.
Neckties.
Poem for My Sister.
Riddle-Me-Ree.
Something I'm Not.
Locke, Anne Vaughan (c. 1530–c. 1590)
Sin and Despair Have So Possess'd My Heart.
So Foul Is Sin and Loathsome in Thy Sight.
Locke, Mary (fl. 1786–1816)
Sonnet: "I hate the Spring in parti-coloured
vest."
Sonnet: "'Tis dead of night; storms rend the
troubled air."
Locker-Lampson, Frederick (1821–95)
Mr. Placid's Flirtation.
My Life Is a———.
Old Oak Tree at Hatfield Broadoak, The.
Our Photograph[s].
Terrible Infant, A.
Lockhart, John Gibson (1794–1854)
Lines: "When youthful faith hath fled."
Locklin, Gerald (b. 1941)
Stranger, The.
Lockyer, Milton
Dark Mountains.
Lodeizen, Hans (1924–50)
Its Pliancy.

Ode: In a Few Hours.
Loden, Rachel
Conversations with Dr. M.
Far In.
Tumbling Dice.
Lodge, George Cabot
Fall.
Lower New York.
On an Æolian Harp.
Pastoral: "Slopes of the sun and vine, and thou
dark stream."
Strong saturation of sea! O widely flown.
Tuckanuck, I.
Lodge, Thomas (1558?–1625)
Animal Weather-Forecasting.
I Hope and Fear.
Love Guards [or Guides] the Roses of Thy
Lips.
Minde through thee divines on endlesse things,
The.
No Stars Her Eyes.
O Pleasing Thoughts.
Pluck the Fruit and Taste the Pleasure.
Rosalind's [or Rosalynd's] Madrigal[l].
Rosaline.
Shepherd's Sorrow, Being Disdained in Love,
The.
Loesser, Frank (1910–69)
Adelaide's Lament.
Baby, It's Cold Outside.
Boys in the Backroom, The.
Fugue for Tinhorns.
Guys and Dolls.
I Believe in You.
I Don't Want to Walk Without You.
I Hear Music.
I Wish I Didn't Love You So.
If I Were a Bell.
Lady's in Love with You, The.
Luck, Be a Lady.
Make a Miracle.
Murder, He Says.
My Darling, My Darling.
Once in Love with Amy.
Sand in My Shoes.
Sit Down, You're Rockin' the Boat.
Somebody, Somewhere.
Spring Will Be a Little Late This Year.
Take Back Your Mink.
They're Either Too Young or Too Old.
Two Sleepy People.
Loewe, Frederick
Almost Like Being in Love.
Camelot.
Heather on the Hill, The.
Hymn to Him, A.
I Could Have Danced All Night.
I'm Glad I'm Not Young Any More.
I Remember It Well.
I've Grown Accustomed to Her Face.
If Ever I Would Leave You.
On the Street Where You Live.
Paris Is Paris Again.
Rain in Spain, The.
Loewinsohn, Ron (b. 1937)
Against the Silences to Come.
Insomniac Poem.
Mrs. Loewinsohn etc.
My Sons.
Pastoral: "Death. / The death of a million."
Stillness of the Poem, The.
Thing Made Real, The.
Loftin, Elouise (b. 1950)
Weeksville Women.
Lofting, Hugh (1886–1947)
Picnic.
Loftis, Norman J. (b. 1943)
Big John.
Brief Encounter.
Delirium.
Fights After School.
In Memoriam: Robert Hayden.
Ruth.
Logan, John (1748–88)
Braes of Yarrow, The.
Poem: Tears, Spray and Steam.

Logan, John (1923–1971?)
Century Piece for Poor Heine, A.
For My Daughter.
He told the crowd "The devils."
Picnic, The.
Rescue, The.
Saint, who overlaps.
San Francisco Poem.
Saturday Afternoon at the Movies.
Spring of the Thief.
Topcliffe's horses shake.
Trip to Four or Five Towns, A.
Logan, Maria (fl. c.1793)
Verses on Hearing That an Airy and Pleasant
Situation, near a Populous and Commercial
Town, Was Surrounded with New Buildings.
Logan, William (b. 1950)
Moorhen.
Logau, Friedrich von (1604–55)
Birth is Death, Death is Birth.
Booty from the German War.
Divine Revenge.
Drunkenness.
Faith.
Fools and Wise Men.
Freedom.
French Dress.
Frog, A.
German Language, The.
Old Nobility, The.
One Faith and No Faith.
Our Naughty Time.
Physicians' Fortune, The.
Powerful Servants.
Retribution.
Soul and Body.
Water and Wine.
Women's Rule.
Logghe, Joan
Insomnia Litany.
Madonna of the Peaches.
Mixed Marriage.
Logue, Christopher (b. 1926)
Battle swayed, The.
Epitaph: "I am old."
Fate's sister, fortune, favours those.
Foreword to New Numbers.
Friday. Wet Dusk.
Good Taste.
I Shall Vote Labour.
Rat, O Rat.
See how that royal fights.
Song of the Dead Soldier, The.
Lohenstein, Daniel Casper von (1635–83)
Her Eyes.
Night Thoughts Concerning a Dream.
Sonnet: "Here lies the noble flesh of Spartacus
the knave."
Sonnet: "Light-spring, oh sun, in light our
wedding joys immure."
Sonnet: "Wisest of all men lies buried on this
spot, The."
Loines, Russell Hillard (1874–1922)
On a Magazine Sonnet.
Lok [or Locke], Anne (b. c.1535, d. after 1590)
Anna Dering on Bartolomeo Silva, Doctor of
Turin.
Necessitie and Benefit of Affliction, The.
Lok, Henry (c.1553–1608)
Sundry Christian Passions Contained in Two
Hundred.
Lokhvitskaia, Nadezhda Aleksandrovna See
"Teffi"
Lom, Iain (John MacDonald) (1620?–1716?)
Lament for the State of the Country, A.
Lomas, Herbert
I quake like Satan.
Lomax, Marion (b. 1953)
Amor Diving.
Gruoch.
Gulf.
July.
Kith.
Other Woman, The.
Lombreglia, Ralph
Daisy, Five, Speaks to Sophia, Two.

Loncar, M. (b. 1968)
  As My Cat Eats the Head of a Field Mouse He
    Has Caught.
  Insomniac.
  Kentucky.
  One Night America: A Boy and His
    Blowtorch.
  Peoria.
  Picasso Shag.
  There Goes the Bride.
"Long, Doc" *See* **Long, Doughtry**
Long, Doughtry ("Doc Long")
  Black Love Black Hope.
  Ginger Bread Mama.
  One Time Henry Dreamed the Number.
Long, Haniel (b. 1888)
  Cobweb.
  Daphnis and Chloe.
  Day and Night.
  For Tony, Embarking in Spring.
  In the Dark World.
  Lightning.
  New Music, A.
  Our Spring Needs Shoveling.
Long, Joel (b. 1964)
  Bermuda Triangle.
  Music's Wife.
Long, Pauline *See* **"Asphodel"**
Long, Peter (*fl.* 19th cent.)
  Remember Thy Creator Now.
Long, Robert (b. 1954)
  What's So Funny 'bout Peace, Love and
    Understanding.
Long, Robert Hill
  Conspiracy, The.
Longenbach, James
  Learning Window.
  Undiscovered Country.
  What You Find in the Woods.
Longenecker, C. W.
  Victor, The.
Longfellow, Henry Wadsworth (1807–82)
  Aftermath.
  Afternoon in February.
  Arrow and the Song, The.
  Autumn.
  Belisarius.
  Bells of San Blas, The.
  Birds of Killingworth, The (The Poet's Tale)
  Bridge, The.
  Broken Oar, The.
  Builders, The.
  Building of the Ship, The, *sels.*
  Chaucer.
  Children's Hour, The.
  Christmas Bells.
  Couplet: February 24, 1847.
  Courtship of Miles Standish, The, *sels.*
  Cross of Snow, The.
  Cumberland, The.
  Curfew.
  Dante.
  Day Is Done, The.
  Daybreak.
  Dedication.
  Delia.
  Disasters.
  Divina Commedia, *sels.*
  Elegiac Verse, *sels.*
  Evangeline, *sels.*
  Evening Star, The.
  Excelsior.
  Famine, The.
  Fire of Drift-Wood, The.
  Fragment: August 4, 1856.
  Fragment: December 18, 1847.
  Galaxy, The.
  Galley of Count Arnaldos, The.
  Golden Mile-Stone, The.
  Grave, The.
  Harvest Moon, The.
  Haunted Houses.
  Hiawatha's Wooing.
  Hiawatha: The White Man's Foot.
  Holiest of all holidays are those, The.

Hymn to the Night.
In the Churchyard at Cambridge.
In the Coliseum.
Introduction: "Should you ask me, whence
  these stories?"
It Is Not Always May.
Jewish Cemetery at Newport, The.
Jugurtha.
Keats.
Kéramos.
Killed at the Ford.
Mezzo Cammin.
Michael Angelo: A Fragment, *sels.*
Milton.
Monk of Casal-Maggiore, The (The Sicilian's
  Tale)
Morituri Salutamus, *sels.*
My Lost Youth.
Nature.
Night.
Old Clock on the Stairs, The.
Paul Revere's Ride [The Landlord's Tale].
Picture-Writing.
Poet's Calendar, The.
Poets, The.
Prelude: The Wayside Inn.
Psalm of Life, A.
Rain in Summer.
Rainy Day, The.
Rhyme of Sir Christopher, The.
Ropewalk, The.
Sand of the Desert in an Hour-Glass.
Sandalphon.
Santa Filomena.
Seaweed.
Shakespeare.
Ship of State, The.
Skeleton in Armor [*or* Armour], The.
Slave in the Dismal Swamp, The.
Slave's Dream, The.
Snow-Flakes.
Song of Hiawatha, The, *sels.*
Sound of the Sea, The.
Spanish Jew's Tale: Azrael, The.
Spanish Jew's Tale: The Legend of Rabbi Ben
  Levi, The.
Spirit of Poetry, The.
Tale of Acadie, A.
Tales of a Wayside Inn, *sels.*
Tell Me Not in Mournful Numbers.
Then the Master.
There Was a Little Girl.
Three Kings, The.
Tide Rises, the Tide Falls, The.
Venice.
Village Blacksmith, The.
Warning, The.
Wreck of the *Hesperus*, The.
Longfellow, Samuel (1819–92)
  Again as Evening's Shadow Falls.
  Holy Spirit, Truth Divine.
  O Life That Maketh All Things New.
  'Tis Winter Now.
Longley, Judy
  Famine's End.
Longley, Michael (b. 1939)
  Amish Rug, An.
  Ash Keys.
  Between Hovers.
  Caravan.
  Civil Servant, The.
  Desert Warfare.
  Detour.
  Emily Dickinson.
  Epithalamion: "These are the small hours
    when."
  Fleance.
  Freeze-Up.
  Frozen Rain.
  Ghetto.
  Ghost Town.
  Gorse Fires.
  Greengrocer, The.
  Hebrides, The.
  I flourish between pleasure and pain.
  In Memoriam.
  In Memory of Gerard Dillon.

Kindertotenlieder.
Letter to Derek Mahon.
Letter to Three Irish Poets, A.
Linen Industry, The.
Linen Workers, The.
Man Lying on a Wall.
No Continuing City.
On Slieve Gullion.
Peace.
Persephone.
Remembering Carrigskeewaun.
River and Fountain.
Scissors Ceremony, The.
Self-Heal.
Skara Brae.
Sulpicia.
Swans Mating.
Third Light, The.
West, The.
Words for Jazz Perhaps.
Wounds.
Lönnrot, Elias (1802–84)
  It is my desire, it is my wish.
Lonzano, Menahem ben Judah (d. after 1608)
  Gentleman, The.
Loomis, Charles Battell (1861–1911)
  O-U-G-H.
Lope de Vega Carpio, Félix (1562–1635)
  And you my spent heart's treasure.
  At Dawn the Virgin Is Born.
  Down in the orchard.
  I shall go down.
  Ice and Fires Contend with My Child.
  If You Leave at Daybreak.
  In Santiago.
  Judith.
  Little Carol of the Virgin, A.
  May Song.
  Pentecost Castle, The.
  Seguidillas of the Guadalquivir River.
  Shepherd Who With Your Tender Calls.
  Song of the Virgin Mother, A.
  Sonnet 61.
  Sonnet 188.
  Sonnet All of a Sudden, A.
  Sonnet Right off the Bat.
  Splendidly-shining darkness.
  Strange Shepherd, Set My Bellwether Free.
  Stranger to Love, Whoever Loves Not Thee.
  They slew by night.
  To-Morrow.
  Today Delight's Fair Ship.
  What Do I Have, That You Seek Out My
    Friendship?
  Where Are You Going, Maiden.
  White Was I.
Lopez, Barry
  Desert Reservation.
Lopez, Luis
  Abiquiu.
  Images of San Luis.
  NEHI Strawberry Down-and-Away.
  Only Now I Realize.
  To a Coal Miner in Madrid, New Mexico.
  Tomás.
Lopez-Penha, Abraham Z. (b. 1870)
  Dusk.
Lopez, Tony (b. 1956)
  Dauntless the slug-horn to my lips I set.
  No Transport.
  Path Marked with Breadcrumbs, A.
López Velarde, Ramón (1888–1921)
  Ants.
  Baleful Return.
  In the Dying Afternoon.
  Malefic Return, The.
  My Cousin Agueda [*or* Agatha].
  My Heart, Faithful.
  Provincial Sundays.
  Purple Spot, The.
  Wet Earth.
Lorde, Audre (1934–92)
  Afterimages.
  Beams.
  Between Ourselves.
  Chain.

Coal.
Coniagui Women.
Dahomey.
Day They Eulogized Mahalia, The.
Echoes.
Father Son and Holy Ghost.
Fishing the White Water.
For the Record.
From the House of Yemanjá.
Generation.
Hanging Fire.
Harriet.
Learning to Write.
Litany for Survival, A.
Love Poem.
Movement Song.
Naturally.
New York City 1970.
Night-Blooming Jasmine, The.
Now That I Am Forever with Child.
On a Night of the Full Moon.
Outlines.
Political Relations.
Power.
Prologue.
Question of Climate, A.
Recreation.
Rock Thrown into the Water Does Not Fear
   the Cold, A.
Song for a Thin Sister.
Summer Oracle.
Today Is Not the Day.
What My Child Learns of the Sea.
Woman Thing, The.
Women of Dan Dance with Swords in Their
   Hands to Mark the Time When They Were
   Warriors, The.

Lorenzo, Ange
Sleepy Time Gal.

Loseff [or Losev], Lev Vladimir (b. 1937)
Conversation with a New York Poet.
I know—the Mongol yoke, the years of
   famine.
Petrograd Side, The.
Reading Milosz.
Tselkov: An Interpretation.

Lotaryov, Igor' Vasilievich *See* **"Severyanin [or Severianin], Igor"**

Lothamer, Joe
Allen.
Be a Painter.
October Falls in Black and White.

"Lothrop, Amy" *See* **Warner, Anna Bartlett**

Lothrop, Harriett Mulford (1844–1921)
Little Brown Seed, The.

Louis, Adrian C. (b. 1946)
At the House of Ghosts.
Dust World.
Something About Being an Indian.
Sonny's Purple Heart.
That Great Wingless Bird.

Lourie, Dick (b. 1931)
For All My Brothers and Sisters.

Louw, N. P. van Wyk (b. 1906)
Coming of Raka, The.
Dedication.
Oh Wide and Sad Land.

Love, B.D.
Bryan Ferry.

Love, Monifa Atungaye (b. 1955)
Initiation.

Lovecraft, Howard Phillips (1890–1937)
Alienation.
Well, The.

Lovelace, Richard (1618–58)
Advice to My Best Brother, Colonel Francis
   Lovelace.
Anniversary on the Hymeneals of My Noble
   Kinsman, Thomas Stanley, Esquire, An.
Another.
Ant, The.
Apostasy of One and But One Lady, The.
Black Patch on Lucasta's Face, A.
Cupid Far Gone.
Dual, The.
Elinda's [or Ellinda's] Glove.
Fair Beggar, The.
Falcon, The.
Fly about a Glass[e] of Burnt Claret, A.
Fly Caught in a Cobweb, A.
Fool much bit by fleas put out the light, A.
Grasshopper, The.
Gratiana Dancing [or Dauncing] and [or &]
   Singing.
Her Muffe.
In Allusion to the French Song.
La Bella Bona-Roba.
À La Bourbon.
Lady A. L., My Asylum [in a Great
   Extremity], The.
Lady with a Falcon on Her Fist, A.
Loose Saraband, A.
Love Enthroned.
Love Made in the First Age[: To Chloris].
Lucasta's Fan[ne], with a Looking-Glass[e] in
   It.
Lucasta's World.
Mock Charon, A.
Mock Song, A.
Night.
On Sanazar's being honoured with six hundred
   Duckets by the Clarissimi of Venice, for
   composing an Elegiack Hexastick of The
   City. A Satyre.
Orpheus to Beasts.
Orpheus to Woods.
Painture [or Peinture].
Scrutiny [or Scrutinie], The.
Snail [or Snayl], The.
Song: "In mine one [or own] monument I lie
   [or lye]."
Song: "Strive not, vain Lover, to be fine."
To a Lady That Desired Me I Would Bear My
   Part with Her in a Song.
To a Lady with Child that Asked [or Ask'd] an
   Old Shirt.
To Althea, from Prison.
To Amarantha, That She Would Dishevel[l]
   Her Hair[e].
To Dr. F. B. on His Book of Chess[e].
To Lucasta.
To Lucasta, from Prison.
To Lucasta: Her Reserved Looks.
To Lucasta, [on] Going beyond the Seas.
To Lucasta, [on] Going to the War[re]s.
To Lucasta: The Rose.
To My Noble Kinsman, Thomas Stanley,
   Esquire, on His Lyric Poems Composed by
   Master John Gamble.
To My Truly Valiant, Learned Friend, Who in
   His Book Resolved the Art Gladiatory into
   the Mathematics.
To My Worthy Friend Mr. Peter Lely [or
   Lilly].
Upon the Curtain[e] of Lucasta's Picture [It
   Was Thus Wrought].
Vintage to the Dungeon, The.

Loveman, Robert (1864–1923)
April Rain.

Lovibond, Edward (1724–75)
To Miss Kitty Phillips.

Loving, Pierre (1893–1950)
Black Horse Rider, The.

Low, Denise
California Potatoes.

Low, Mary
Companion, The.
Encounter.
Perchance to Dream.
Q.E.D.
Where the Wolf Sings.

Low, Patricia (b. 1932)
First Day of the Hunting Moon, The.
Wet Weather.

Low, Samuel (b. 1765)
To a Segar.

Lowbury, Edward (b. 1913)
Huntsman, The.
Swan.

Lowe, Janet
With Thanks to Eddie Shaw.

Lowe, Janice (b. 1963)
Between Acts.
Club House.

Lowe, Robert, Viscount Sherbrooke (1811–92)
Commissioner bet me a pony—I won, The.
Gum has no shade, The.
Songs of the Squatters.

Lowell, Amy (1874–1925)
April.
Aubade.
Bright Sunlight.
Bungler, The.
Camouflaged Troop-Ship.
Captured Goddess, The.
Carrefour.
Chinoiseries.
Cyclists, The.
Decade, [A].
Dissonance.
Epitaph on a Young Poet Who Died before
   Having Achieved Success.
Falling Snow.
Fisherman's Wife, The.
Free Fantasia on Japanese Themes.
From One Who Stays.
Grotesque.
Hoar-Frost.
I dug a grave under an oak-tree.
Katydids.
Lady, A.
Letter, The.
Lilacs.
Madonna of the Evening Flowers.
Meeting-House Hill.
New Heavens for Old.
Night Clouds.
Opal.
Painted Ceiling, The.
Patterns.
Pike, The.
Proportion.
Seeing You Stand Once More before My Eyes.
September, 1918.
Shore Grass.
Shower, A.
Sisters, The.
Solitaire.
Spring Longing.
St. Louis.
Taxi, The.
Thompson's Lunch Room—Grand Central
   Station.
To John Keats.
Venus Transiens.
Vernal Equinox.
Weather-Cock Points South, The.
Wind and Silver.

Lowell, James Russell (1819–91)
After the Burial.
Aladdin.
Alcott.
Auspex.
Boss, The.
Bryant.
Channing and Thoreau.
Contrast, A.
Cooper.
Courtin', The.
Darkened Mind, The.
Emerson.
Fable for Critics, A.
First Snowfall [or Snow-Fall], The.
Fountain, The.
God Is Not Dumb.
Hawthorne.
His Throne Is with the Outcast.
Hob Gobbling's Song.
Holmes.
I praise him not.
In a Copy of Omar Khayyám.
In an Album.
Irving.
Letter, A ("This kind o' sogerin' ain't a mite
   like our October trainin' ")
Letter, A ("Thrash away, you'll hev to rattle")
Letter Six—The Pious Editors' Creed.
Lowell.

May is a pious fraud of the almanac.
Memoriae Positum R. G. Shaw.
Misconception, A.
Ode Recited at the Harvard Commemoration
   (July 21, 1865)
Old Joe is gone, who saw hot Percy goad.
Philothea (Lydia Child)
Phoebus.
Poe and Longfellow.
Prelude to Part the First.
Present Crisis, The.
Remembered Music.
Rev. Homer Wilbur's "Festina Lente."
Science and Poetry.
Sixty-Eighth Birthday.
Sonnet.
Street, The.
Tempora Mutantur.
There are truths you Americans need to be
   told.
There comes Poe, with his raven, like Barnaby
   Rudge.
This hand-to-mouth, pert, rapid, nineteenth
   century.
To the Dandelion.
To the Spirit of Keats.
Whittier.

Lowell, Maria White (1821–53)
Opium Fantasy, An.
Rouen, Place de la Pucelle.

Lowell, Robert (1917–77)
After the Convention.
After the Surprising Conversions.
Alfred Corning Clark.
As a Plane Tree by the Water.
At the Altar.
At the Indian Killer's Grave.
Beyond the Alps.
Book of Wisdom, The.
Child's Song.
Children of Light.
Christmas Eve under Hooker's Statue.
Colloquy in Black Rock.
Commander Lowell.
David and Bathsheba in the Public Garden.
Dead in Europe, The.
Death and the Bridge.
Death from Cancer.
Death of the Sheriff, The.
Difficulties, the impossibilities, The.
Dolphin.
Drunken Fisherman, The.
End of a Year.
Epilogue: "Those blessed structures, plot and
   rhyme."
Exile's Return, The.
Eye and Tooth.
Ezra Pound.
Fall 1961.
Falling Asleep over the Aeneid.
Fishnet.
Flaw, The.
For George Santayana.
For John Berryman.
For Sale.
For Sheridan.
For the Union Dead.
Ford Madox Ford.
Grandparents.
Harriet.
History.
Holy Innocents, The.
Home After Three Months Away.
Identification in Belfast (I.R.A. Bombing)
In the Cage.
In the Ward.
Inauguration Day: January 1953.
It Did.
July in Washington.
Katherine's Dream.
Lady Ralegh's Lament.
Last Things, Black Pines at 4 A.M.
Lesson, The.
Mad Negro Soldier Confined at Munich, A.
Man And Wife.
March 1, The.
Memories of West Street and Lepke.

Middle Age.
Mouth of the Hudson, The.
Mr. Edwards and the Spider.
My Last Afternoon with Uncle Devereux
   Winslow.
Near the Ocean.
Neo-Classical Urn, The.
New Year's Day.
Night Sweat.
Nihilist as Hero, The.
Notice.
Obit.
Old Flame, The.
Public Garden, The.
Quaker Graveyard in Nantucket, The.
Reading Myself.
Robert Frost.
Robespierre and Mozart as Stage.
Sailing Home from Rapallo.
Saint-Just 1767–93.
Salem.
Shako, The.
Shifting Colors.
Skunk Hour.
South of Boston, south of Washington.
Stalin.
Suicide.
T. S. Eliot.
Those before Us.
To Speak of Woe That Is in Marriage.
Ulysses.
Violence.
Waking Early Sunday Morning.
Waking in the Blue.
Watchmaker God.
Water.
Where the Rainbow Ends.

Lowenfels, Walter (1897–1976)
Among the Luminals.

Lowry, Malcolm (1909–57)
About Ice.
After Publication of Under the Volcano.
Christ Walks in This Infernal District Too.
Delirium in Vera Cruz.
Epitaph: "Malcolm Lowry."
Eye-Opener.
For *Under the Volcano*.
He Liked the Dead.
Lighthouse Invites the Storm, The.
Salmon Drowns Eagle.
Sestina in a Cantina.
Strange Type.
Volcano is Dark, The.
Wild Cherry, The.
Xochitepec.

Lowry, Robert (1862–99)
Beautiful River.
Up from the Grave He Arose.

Lowther, Pat (1935–75)
Last Letter to Pablo.
Stone Diary, A.

Löwy, Hanuš (1931–44)
Little Mouse, The.
Man Proposes, God Disposes.
Yes, That's the Way Things Are.

Loy, Mina (1882–1966)
Apology of Genius.
Brancusi's Golden Bird.
Der Blinde Junge.
Gertrude Stein.
Jules Pascin.
Love Songs.
Lunar Baedeker.
On Third Avenue.
Poe.
Three Moments in Paris.

Loynaz, Dulce Maria
Calm, The.
Cloud, The.
Embrace.
Futile Flight, Futile Fugue.
I have slept and I awaken . . . Or I haven't
   awakened.
Sea Surrounded.
Snow.
Time.

XXX.

Lu Chao-lin (c.641–680)
Lotuses on the Crooked Pond.
Mount Wu Is High.
Weary Road, The.

Lu Chi (261–303)
Off at dawn to service in the walled and
   storied palace.
Music of Words, The.
Riding Crop, The.
Satisfaction, The.
She Thinks of Her Beloved.
Song of Mount T'ai.
Visit to the Monastery of Good Omen.

Lu Chih (1246?–1309?)
Be a loafer / Wash off the dust of fame and
   gain in the vast waves.
Seventy Years Are Few.
Tune: 'Drunk in the East Wind.'
Tune: "*Wu-t'ung* Leaves"—Written in Jest at a
   Banquet.
Tune: "Intoxication in the East Wind" Autumn
   Scenery.
Tune: "Song of the Lunar Palace."
Wine in the cup is heavy.

"Lu Hsün" (Chou Shu-jen) (1881–1936)
Call to Arms.
Hesitation.
In Remembrance of the Forgotten.
Lamenting Yang Ch'uan.
Self-mockery.
Sending Off O. E. Who Brought an Orchid
   Home to Japan.

Lu Kuei Meng (d. c.881)
Fisherman on a Southern Stream.
Lone Wild Goose, A.
Replying to Hsi-mei's "Thoughts in Early
   Autumn."
To an Old Tune.

Lu Lun (fl. c.770)
Moon blackens, geese fly high.
Select fine arrows and call for falcons.
Woods darken, grasses startled by wind.

Lu Yu (1125–1210)
At Ta-an I Got Sick from Wine and Had to
   Lay Over for Half a Day. Governor Wang
   Invited Me to His Place Again.
Autumn Thoughts.
Blue Rapids.
Boating in Autumn.
Border Mountain Moon.
Evening in the Village.
Farm Families.
Feeling Sorry for Myself.
Harp Song.
Herd-Boy, The.
How I Sailed on the Lake till I Came to the
   Eastern Stream.
I Get Up at Dawn.
I Had Occasion to Tell a Visitor about an Old
   Trip I Took.
I Walk Out into the Country at Night.
Idle Thoughts.
Idleness.
Impressions.
In a Boat on a Summer Evening, I Heard the
   Cry of a Water Bird.
In a Dream.
In a Dream I Traveled among Ten Thousand
   Acres of Lotuses.
In the Country.
Inscribed on My Grass-script Calligraphy
   Written While Drunk.
Insomnia.
It Has Snowed Repeatedly and We Can Count
   On a Good Crop of Wheat and Barley.
Lazy.
Leaving the Monastery Early in the Morning.
Merchant's Joy, The.
Mural, Ch'ien-ming Temple.
My Village Home.
Night Thoughts.
Occasional Poem, An.
Pedlar of Spells, The.
Phoenix Hairpins.
Rain Cleared and the Breeze and Sunshine Are

Superb as I Stroll Outside the Gate, The.
Rain on the River.
Sailing on the Lake to the Ching River.
Sending Tzu-lung Off to a Post in Chi-chou.
Shown to My Son Yü.
Sitting Outdoors.
Sitting Up at Night.
Snug—the robe sewn from coarse cotton.
Sounds of Autumn.
Stone on the Hilltop, The.
Third Month, Night of the Seventeenth,
  Written While Drunk.
To Show to My Sons.
Trip to Mountain West Village, A.
Tune: "Bean Leaves Yellow."
Tune: "Hairpin Phoenix."
Tune: "Immortal at the Magpie Bridge"—On
  Hearing the Cuckoo at Night.
Tune: "Song of Divination"—On the Plum
  Tree.
Tune: "Telling of Innermost Feelings."
Vegetable Garden.
Wild Flower Man, The.
Written at Random.
Written in a Carefree Mood.

Lu Yün (262–303)
For Ku Yen-hsien, A Poem for Him to Give to
  His Wife.
Peacock Flew, A.
Valley Wind, The.

Lucan (Marcus Annaeus Lucanus) (A.D. 39–65)
Civil War, *sels.*
Pharsalia, *sels.*
Speech out of Lucan, A.

Lucanus, Marcus Annaeus *See* **Lucan**

Lucas, Alice (1852–1935)
Prayer before Sleep.

Lucas, Frank Lawrence (1894–1967)
Spain, 1809.

Lucas, Russell
Limerick: "There was a young lady from
  Ulva."

Lucas, Tony (b. 1941)
Town Garden, A.

Luce, Nancy (*fl.* 1860)
Poor little Ada Queetie has departed this life.

"Lucebert" (L. J. Swaanswijk) (b. 1924)
9000 Jackals Swimming to Boston.
Fishermen from Ma Yuan.
I Reel Off.
Rousseau Le Douanier.

Lucianus [*or* Lucian] (b. c.125, d. after 180)
Artificial Beauty.
Beard-wagging stick-waving beggarman
  Cynic, A.
Do tell me, Hermes, what was it like when the
  soul.
Enjoy your fortune as if you were about to die.
For Glaukos, for the Nereids.
For mortals, mortal things. And all things leave
  us.
I am Priapus. I was put here according to
  custom.
I was Kallimachos, age five.
If you really imagine wisdom grows with a
  beard.
To Glaukos, and to Nereus.
We were all drunk, and Acindynus was
  determined to keep sober.
Worthless man is a leaking wine-jar, A.

Lucie-Smith, Edward (b. 1933)
Lesson, The.
Poet in Winter.

Lucilius (d. c.102 B.C.)
Apollophanes married for an alibi.
As a poet put it once, an ant / may seem 'a
  monstrous elephant.'
As thin little Proclus was fanning the fire.
Aulus / is childless.
Bad actors love to play great villains.
Cleombrotus the bruiser.
Crown your Bacchus with lettuce leaves, not
  ivy.
Diophon, seeing / another man.
Doubly unfortunate are those who dwell in

Hell.
Eutychides the thief was in a rare.
Eutychus the painter / Fathered twenty sons.
Final adventure of Skinny Marcus.
Further adventure of Skinny Marcus.
Gently, so as not to rouse / His skinny girl.
Here I am launching my Second Book of
  Epigrams.
Hermogenes is rather short.
HIS GRATEFUL OPPONENTS SET UP THIS STATUE
  OF APIS THE BOXER.
I'm round at Heliodorus' place—.
It's said you take a long time over a bath.
Lazy Marcus once dreamed.
Lean Gaius, Who Was Thinner than a Straw.
Lifted by a little breeze.
Light-fingered Dio takes after the God of
  Thieves.
Lysimachus' cushion caught Antiochus' eye.
Marcus in the armed hoplites' race.
Mean old Hermon.
Miser and the Mouse, The.
My Dad was worried about his brother.
Olympicus, the welter-weight.
On an Old Woman.
On Kriton the Miser.
Orator Flaccus can commit solecisms.
Poor Calpurnius, the most Schweikian soldier
  in the land.
Recent earthquake, A.
Some say you dye your hair, Nikylla.
There's one Grammarian I know.
Tiny Erotion, borne away / By a gnat had this
  to say.
Treasure.
Well, Menestratus, you ask me what I think.
When Hermocrates the Miser lay in bed.
Wig, rouge, honey, wax, teeth.
With a lucky charm around his throat.
Zenonis has a splendid tutor for her son.

Lucretius (Titus Lucretius Carus) (94–55 B.C.)
Address to Venus.
Beyond Religion.
Darling of Gods and Men, beneath the gliding
  stars.
Gods, by right of Nature, must possess, The.
No Single Thing Abides.
Now since the members of the world we view.
Suave Mari Magno.
Thus, therefore, he who feels the fiery dart.
What has this Bugbear death to frighten Man.
When Love its utmost vigour does imploy.

Lucy, Sean (b. 1931)
Friday Evening.
Longshore Intellectual.
Missing Link.
Senior Members.
Supervising Examinations.
These Six.

Ludvigson, Susan Bartels (b. 1942)
Inventing My Parents.

Ludwig, Paula
End of the Year.

Lueders, Edward *See* **Koriyama, Naoshi**

Lugones, Leopoldo (1874–1938)
Gray Waves.
Indulgence.
Rain Psalm.
Slow Delight.
White Solitude.

**Lugovskoy [*or* Lugovskoi], Vladimir
  Aleksandrovich (1901–57)**
Bandit, The.
Bear, The.
Woman That I Knew, The.

Lui Chi (1311–75)
Poet Thinks, A.

Luitpold, Josef
Defiant Farewell.

Lukonin, Mikhail Kuz'mich (1918–76)
My Friends.
Stalingrad Theater.
To Kolya Otrada.

Lum, Wing Tek
Chinese Hot Pot.

Going Home.
Picture of my Mother's Family, A.
Riding the North Point Ferry.
Urban Love Songs.

Lumelli, Angelo (b. 1944)
Candid Camera.
There are no pacts.
They could be reservoirs for water.
You first, shift your attention (that is, if you
  withdraw)

Lumsden, Roddy (b. 1966)
Beginning of the End, The.
ITMA.
Mercy.
Prayer to Be with Mercurial Women.
Show and Tell.
Then.
Tricks for the Barmaid.
Yeah Yeah Yeah.

Lumumba, Patrice Emery (1926–51)
Dawn in the Heart of Africa.

Lupellus
Limerick: "Solipsist with triplets said: Though,
  A."

Luria, Isaac (1534–72)
Sabbath of Rest, A.

Luschei, Glenna
Here.
Arrangement.
Pozo Basket, The.
Water Song, The.

Luswat
Shaman Song.

Luterman, Alison
Justice of the Peace, The.

Luther, Martin (1483–1546)
Away in a Manger.
Ein feste Burg ist unser Gott.
From Depths of Woe I Cry to You.
From Heaven Above to Earth I Come.
In the Very Midst of Life.
Mighty Fortress Is Our God, A.

Luttrell, Henry (1765?–1851)
Have you not seen (you must remember)
London, within thy ample verge.
O death, thy certainty is such.
On a Man Run Over by an Omnibus.

Lux, Thomas (b. 1946)
Barn Fire.
Bodo.
Commercial Leech Farming Today.
Creature Has a Purpose, The.
Farmers.
Flying Noises.
Little Tooth, A.
Midnight Tennis Match, The.
Milkman and His Son, The.
My Grandmother's Funeral.
Night above the Town.
One Meat Ball.
Plague Victims Catapulted over Walls into
  Besieged City.
Solo Native.
Tarantulas on the Lifebuoy.
There Were Some Summers.
Thrombosis Trombone.
Wordsworths: William and Dorothy, The.

Luzi, Mario (b. 1914)
But then an even greater sense of the
  inexpressible.
Postscriptum.
Reflective life separates us from the sources of
  reflection.

Luzzatto, Isaac (*fl.* 16th cent.)
Death, Thou Hast Seized Me.

Luzzatto, Moses Hayyim, of Padua (1707–47)
Chorus: "All ye that handle harp and viol."

Lvov, Mikhail Davidovich (1916–87)
To become a man, it's little to be born.

Lvov, Vladimir Iul'evich (1926–61)
That yellowed body of the Lord.

Ly Ngoc Kieu (Dieu Nhan) (1041–1113)
Birth, old age.

Lyall, Sir Alfred Comyn (1835–1911)
Badminton.

Lydgate, John (1370?–1451?)
Complaint of the Black Knight, The.
Like a Midsummer Rose.
O thow Minstral that cannest so note and pipe.
Thank God for All.
Vox Ultima Crucis.

Lydston, Donna R.
Family, The.

Lyle, K. Curtis (b. 1944)
Lacrimas or There Is a Need to Scream.
Sometimes I Go to Camarillo and Sit in the
Lounge.

Lyles, Peggy
Doe's leap, A.
Moon.
Summer night.
Summer stillness.

Lyly, John (1553–1606)
Cupid and My Campaspe Played.
Daphne.
'Las, how long shall I.
Pan's Syrinx.
Pinch him, pinch him black and blue.
Sapho's Song.
Serving Men's Song, A.
Song of Apollo.
Stand! Who goes there?
Trico's Song.
Vulcan's Song.

Lyman, Abe
I Cried for You.

Lyman Jr., Dean B.
Eternal Controversy, The.

Lynch, Charles (b. 1943)
Ancestral Echoes/Rap Music.

Lynch, Thomas (b. 1948)
Grimalkin.
Maura.

Lynch, Thomas Toke (1818–71)
Lift Up Your Heads, Rejoice!

Lynche, Richard (fl. 1596–1601)
Soon as the Azure-colored Gates.
What Sugared Terms.

Lynde, Benjamin (1666–1745)
Lines Descriptive of Thomson's Island.

Lyon, George Ella (b. 1949)
Foot-Washing, The.

Lyons, Stephen J.
Loving Along Western Rivers.
Remembering.
Touching You Underwater.

Lysohorsky, Ondra (1909–89)
22.6.1941.
At a Sunlit Window.
Ballad of Jan Palach, Student and Heretic.

Lyte, Henry Francis (1793–1847)
Abide With Me.

Lyttelton, George (1709–73)
Soliloquy of a Beauty in the Country.

**Lytton, Edward Robert Bulwer-Lytton, 1st Earl
of** See **"Meredith, Owen"**

M

"M." (fl. c.1776)
On the Frequent Review of the Troops.

"M., H."
Limerick: "There once was a Scot who said:
Evil."

M–rt–n, B–ll (fl. c.1726)
Humble Wish, The.

"M., X. A."
Limerick: "What! Parted! Not even a kiss?"

"Ma" See **Rainey, Gertrude "Ma"**

Ma Chih-yüan (1260?–1334?)
Autumn Thoughts.
Evening Bells near a Temple.
Four Poems to the Tune "Ch'ing-chiang yin."
In Autumn.
Love Song: "Clouds circle the moon."
Lovesickness— / What is the cure?
Three Poems to the tune "Lo-mei Feng."

Three Poems to the Tune "Ssu-k'uai yü."
To the Tune "Shui hsien-tzu."
Tune: 'Heaven-Cleansed Sands.'
Tune: "Four Pieces of Jade"—Retirement.
Tune: "Sailing at Night"—A Song Sequence.
Tune: "Sky-clear Sand"—Autumn Thoughts.
Tune: "Slow Chant."
Tune: 'Sky-Pure Sand.'
Tune: 'Song of Clear River.'
Tune: 'Winds of Falling Plums.'
Two Poems to the Tune "Chin-tzu ching" The
Sutra in Gold Characters.
Two Poems to the Tune "Po pu tuan."
Voice are still / The moon's bright.

Mabutsu (d. 1696)
Snowman's eyes, The.

Mabutsu (d. 1874)
Moon in a barrel.

Mabuza, Lindiwe
Death to the Gold Mine!
Dream Cloud.
Love Song, A.
Summer nineteen seventy.
Tired Lizi Tired.

Mac an Bhaird, Laoiseach (fl. late 16th cent.)
Fond greeting, hillock there, A.
Two Sons.

**Mac Coisdealbhaigh, Tomas ("Laider") (fl. mid–
17th cent.)**
Una Bhan.

Mac Con Brettan, Bláthmac (fl. 8th cent.)
I call you with honest words.

**Mac Con Midhe, Giolla Brighde (fl. mid–13th
cent.)**
Defence of Poetry, A.

Mac Cuarta, Seamas Dall (1650–1733)
Houses of Corr an Chait are cold, The.

**Mac Giolla Ghunna, Cathal Buidhe (c.1680–
1756)**
Yellow Bittern, The.

mac Lenini, Colman
In Praise of a Sword Given Him by His Prince.

Mac Low, Jackson (b. 1922)
Almost Casanova Electricity.
Antic Quatrains.
Asymmetry 205.
1845.
1841 (I)
1841 (II)
1809.
1801.
1817.
1837.
1825.
1829.
59th Light Poem: for La Monte Young and
Marian Zazeela—6 November 1982.
1st Dance—Making Things New—6 February
1964.
Giant Otters.
Giant Philosophical Otters.
Lack of Balance but not Fatal, A.
Mani-Mani Gatha.
Pieces O'six—XVIII.
Pieces O'six—XXIV.
2nd Dance—Seeing Lines—6 February 1964.
2nd Light Poem: For Diane Wakoski.
1789.
1797.
7th Light Poem: For John Cage—17 June
1962.
6th Dance—Doing Things With Pencils—17–
18 February 1964.
3rd Light Poem: For Spencer, Beate, &
Sebastian Holst—12 June 1962.
34th Merzgedicht in Memoriam Kurt
Schwitters.
Trope Market.
12th Dance—Getting Leather by Language—
21 February 1964.
Twenties 26.
Twenties 27.
27th Dance—Walking—22 March 1964.
Zen Buddhism and Psychoanalysis /
Psychoanalysis and Zen Buddhism.

Macarthur, Bessie J. B. (b. 1889)
Nocht o' Mortal Sicht.

**Macartney, Frederick Thomas Bennett (1887–
1980)**
Early Summer Sea-Tryst.
Kyrielle: Party Politics.
No Less than Prisoners.

Macaulay, F. E. M. (fl. c.1904)
Women's Marseillaise, The.

**Macaulay, Thomas Babington Macaulay, 1st
Baron (1800–1859)**
Armada, The, sels.
Battle of Naseby, The.
Country Clergyman's Trip to Cambridge, The.
Dies Iræ.
Horatius [or Horatius at the Bridge].
Jacobite's Epitaph, A.
Lays of Ancient Rome, sels.
Radical War Song, A.

MacBeth [or Macbeth], George (1932–92)
Five-Minute Orlando Macbeth, The.
Bedtime Story.
God of Love, The.
Killing, The.
Land-Mine, The.
Miner's Helmet, The.
Orange Poem, The.
Orlando Commercial, The.
Owl.
Poem of Death, A.
Political Orlando, The.
Scissor-Man.
Snowdrops.
Wasps' Nest, The.
When I Am Dead.
Worst Fear, The.

MacCaig, Norman (b. 1910)
Aspects.
Aunt Julia.
Basking Shark.
Blue Tit on a String of Peanuts.
By Achmelvich Bridge.
Celtic Cross.
Chauvinist.
Climbing Suilven.
Close-ups of Summer.
Cock before Dawn.
Crossing the Border.
Drowned, The.
Ego.
Feeding Ducks.
Fetching Cows.
Flooded Mind.
Golden Calf.
Gone Are the Days.
In My Mind.
Instrument and Agent.
Interruption to a Journey.
Intruder in a Set Scene.
Kingfisher.
Likenesses.
Milne's Bar.
Moorings.
Movements.
No Consolation.
Notations of Ten Summer Minutes.
Nude in a Fountain.
Old Maps and New.
Orgy.
Praise of a Collie.
Return to Scalpay.
Ringed Plover by a Water's Edge.
Sheep Dipping.
Sleeping Compartment.
Sleet.
Small Lochs.
So Many Summers.
Solitary crow.
Sounds of the Day.
Spate in Winter Midnight.
Stars and Planets.
Summer Farm.
Toad.
Too Bright a Day.
Wild Oats.

MacCarthy, Charlotte
Contentment, to a Friend.

To the Same.
MacCathmhaoil, Seosamh *See* **Campbell, Joseph**
Maccius
  I swore, love, by your / dominion, to rest.
  Philistion's a hard bitch:/ in her book
    'penniless lover.'
  Your pleasure, Priapus, is the island coast.
MacConglinne (*fl.* 12th cent.)
  Vision of MacConglinne, The.
MacDiarmid, Hugh (Christopher Murray
  Grieve) (1892–1978)
  All is lithogenesis – or lochia.
  Another Epitaph on an Army of Mercenaries.
  At My Father's Grave.
  Bonnie Broukit Bairn, The.
  British Leftish Poetry, 1930–40.
  By Wauchopeside.
  Caledonian Antisyzygy, The.
  Cattle Show.
  Cloudburst and Soaring Moon.
  Cophetua.
  Crowdieknowe.
  Crystals like Blood.
  Dae what ye wull ye canna parry.
  Dead Liebknecht, The.
  Eemis-Stane, The.
  Empty Vessel.
  Ex Vermibus.
  Facing the Chair.
  Farewell to Dostoevski.
  Fleggit Bride, The.
  Glass of Pure Water, The.
  Great Wheel, The.
  I Heard Christ Sing.
  In the Children's Hospital.
  In the Pantry.
  Innumerable Christ, The.
  Language that but sparely floo'ers, The.
  Let the only consistency.
  Light and Shadow.
  Little White Rose, The.
  Love.
  Moonstruck.
  O wha' the bride that cairries the bunch.
  Of John Davidson.
  Old Wife in High Spirits.
  On a Raised Beach.
  On the Ocean Floor.
  On the Oxford Book of Victorian Verse.
  One of the Principal Causes of War.
  Parley of Beasts.
  Parrot Cry, The.
  Perfect.
  Poetry and Science.
  Prayer for a Second Flood.
  Reflections in a Slum.
  Robber, The.
  Royal Stag, The.
  Sauchs in the Reuch Heuch Hauch, The.
  Scotland Small?
  Scunner.
  Skeleton of the Future, The.
  Spanish War, The.
  Spur of Love, The.
  Storm-Cock's Song, The.
  Sunny Gale.
  To a Friend and Fellow Poet.
  To a Sea Eagle.
  Two Parents, The.
  Under the Greenwood Tree.
  Vision of Myself, A.
  Watergaw, The.
  We must look at the harebell as if.
  Weapon, The.
  Wheesht, Wheesht.
  Whip-the-World.
  With a Lifting of the Head.
  With the Herring Fishers.
  Yet Ha'e I Silence Left.
  Yet there is no great problem in the world
    today.
MacDonagh, Donagh (1912–68)
  Dublin Made Me.
  Going to Mass Last Sunday.
  Hungry Grass, The.
  Just an Old Sweet Song.

Of what a quality is courage made.
  Prothalamium.
  Veterans, The.
Macdonagh, Thomas (1878–1916)
  John-John.
  Man Upright, The.
MacDonald, Alexander (Alasdair MacMhaighstir
  Alasdair) (1700–1770)
  Incitement for Rowing to Sailing-place.
  Month of plants and of honey.
Macdonald, Andrew (1755?–1790)
  Lover's Leap; a Tale, The.
MacDonald, Ballard
  Somebody Loves Me.
MacDonald, Cynthia (b. 1932)
  Two Brothers in a Field of Absence.
Macdonald, George (1824–1905)
  At Aberdeen.
  Baby-Sermon, A.
  Better Things.
  Christmas Carol, A.
  Diary of an Old Soul.
  Dorcas.
  Father's Hymn for the Mother to Sing.
  Hurt of Love, The.
  Lost and Found.
  Mammon Marriage.
  No End of No-Story.
  O Thou of Little Faith!
  Prayer, A: "When I look back upon my life
    nigh spent."
  Professor Noctutus.
  Rest.
  Shall the Dead Praise Thee?
  Sheep and the Goat, The.
  Shortest and Sweetest of Songs, The.
  Song.
  Sonnet: "This infant world has taken long to
    make."
  Sweet Peril.
  That Holy Thing.
  This, this is what I love, and what is this?
  Turn from Self.
  What love I when I love Thee, O my God?
  Where did you come from, baby dear?
  Wind and the Moon, The.
  Winter Song.
MacDonald, John *See* **Lom, Iain**
MacDonogh, Patrick (1902–61)
  Alone and Godless, stopped by the sudden
    edge.
  No Mean City.
  Now the Holy Lamp of Love.
  She Walked Unaware.
Macedonius (*fl.* c.6th cent.)
  Be patient, Morning Star, with Love; though
    close.
  Beauty kissed your mouth, and gave the petals.
  Dedication, A: "Anchored now to Neptune's
    temple floor, this."
  Earth and Goddess of Birth.
  Every year men harvest grapes, not seeing.
  I dreamt I held the laughter-loving girl.
  Praise memory and forgetfulness!
  She who shook and swayed among the chorus.
  You ask me, girl, why I withdraw my sword.
  You neigh and whinny, seeming to invite.
  You're here! I hadn't dared to hope. Surprise.
  You say "Tomorrow"; a tomorrow which.
MacEwen, Gwendolyn (b. 1941)
  Arcanum One.
  Breakfast for Barbarians, A.
  Caravan, The.
  Dark Pines under Water.
  Discovery, The.
  Manzini; Escape Artist.
  Open Secrets.
  Sea Things.
  T. E. Lawrence Poems, The.
  Thing is Violent, The.
  Virgin Warrior, The.
  You Cannot Do This.
MacFayden, H. R. (b. 1877)
  Lone Wild Fowl, The.
MacGabhrain, Aodh *See* **MacGowran, Hugh**

MacGill-Eain, Somhairle *See* **MacLean**
  (Somhairle MacGill-Eain), **Sorley**
MacGill, Patrick (b. 1890)
  Matey.
Macgillivray, Pittendrigh (1856–1938)
  Return, The.
MacGowran, Hugh (Aodh MacGabhrain) (*fl.*
  c.1720)
  Description of an Irish Feast, The.
  O'Rourke's Feast.
Macgoye, Marjorie Oludhe
  August the First; Court Martial. The Mother
    Speaks.
  August the First: The Shadow. Patel Speaks.
  August the First: The Watchman Speaks.
  For Miriam.
  Freedom Song, A.
  Letter to a Friend.
  Mathenge.
  Muffled Cry, A.
  Omera.
MacGreevy [or McGreevy], Thomas (1894–1967)
  Aodh Ruadh O'Domhnaill.
  De Civitate Hominum.
  Homage to Hieronymus Bosch.
  Homage to Jack Yeats.
  Homage to Marcel Proust.
  Nocturne of the Self-evident Presence.
  Recessional.
MacGregor, Mrs., of Glenstrae (*fl.* 1570)
  Lament for MacGregor of Glenstrae.
Macha, Freddy
  Artist and a Wailing Mother, An.
  Corruption.
Machado de Assis, Joaquim Maria (1839–1908)
  Blue Fly.
Machado Ruiz, Antonio (1875–1939)
  Between living and dreaming.
  Breeze Tells Me, Loved One, The.
  But look in your mirror for the other one,.
  Come sing with me in chorus: it's nothing, all
    we know.
  Crime Was in Granada, The.
  Deep Song.
  Denuded Is the Earth.
  Don't trace out your profile.
  Eye You See Isn't, The.
  Good Thing Is, We Know, The.
  Her Street Is Dark.
  Here's another Spaniard! Welcome!
  House of Alvargonzález, The.
  I go on dreaming.
  If I were a poet / of love, I would make.
  In our souls everything.
  Lament of the Virtues and Verses on Account
    of the Death of Don Guido.
  Last Night.
  Look for your other half.
  Look, our Spaniard's yawning.
  Lord, You Have Ripped Away.
  Meditation for this Day.
  Moldering Hulk, The.
  Narcissism / is an ugly fault.
  On the Banks of the Duero.
  Parables, I.
  People Possess Four Things.
  Plaza and the Flaming Orange Trees, The.
  Plaza Has a Tower, The.
  Poem: "Figures in the fields against the sky!"
  Poem: "Frail sound of a tunic trailing, A."
  Poem: "Naked is the earth."
  Poem: "We think to create festivals."
  Portrait.
  Primavera.
  Rose of Fire.
  Siesta.
  Song: "Now the moon is rising."
  Spanish Folk Songs.
  Spring Has Come.
  Summer Night.
  Summer's Night, A.
  Tavern Guitar Playing a *Jota* Today.
  Walker, It Is Your Footsteps.
  Water Wheel, The.
  Who Placed, Amidst the Tracts of Ash.
  Wind, One Brilliant Day, The.

Yesterday, dreamed He was near me.
Machan, Katharyn Howd
  Hazel Tells LaVerne.
  In 1969.
  No, Superman Was Not the Only One.
Machej, Zbigniew (b. 1958)
  Orchards in July.
Machiavelli, Niccolò (1469–1527)
  Opportunity.
MacIntyre, Duncan Ban (1724–1808)
  To the Air of a Pibroch.
MacIntyre, Sue
  Christmas Present for My Mother.
  Letters from the Concertina File 1939–1940.
MacIntyre, Tom (b. 1933)
  Drumlin Prayer.
  On Sweet Killen Hill.
  Yellow Bittern, The.
Mack, Alexander (1679–1735)
  I Am the Lord.
Mack, Cecil
  Charleston.
  He's a Cousin of Mine.
  That's Why They Call Me 'Shine.'
MacKay, Charles (1814–89)
  Clear the Way.
  Louise on the Door-Step.
  Mowers: An Anticipation of the Cholera, 1848, The.
  Poor Man's Sunday Walk, The.
  Three Preachers, The.
MacKay, Isabel Ecclestone (1875–1928)
  Meeting, The.
Mackay, Jessie (1864–1938)
  In Galilee.
Mackay, John Henry (1864–1933)
  Nameless Love, The.
  Tomorrow.
MacKay, Robert (Macaoidh, Rob Donn) (1714–1778)
  Rispond Miser, The.
Mackay-Warna, Gordon
  Cattle Loading.
MacKellar, Dorothea (b. 1885)
  Arms and the Woman.
  Fancy Dress.
  Heritage.
Mackellar, Thomas
  At the door of Mercy Sighing.
MacKenzie, Ian T.
  Limerick: "There was an old lady of Leicester."
Mackenzie, Kenneth (1913–55)
  Autumn Mushrooms.
  Caesura.
  Children Go, The.
  Door swung open, The.
  Earth Buried.
  Fool, The.
  Ginger-flowers.
  God! How I Long for You.
  Heat.
  Hospital—Retrospections, The.
  Searchlights.
  Shall Then Another.
  Sick Men Sleeping.
  Table-Birds.
  Two Trinities.
MacKenzie, Rob (b. 1964)
  Blue Sky in Morning.
  Category Mistakes in Biochemistry.
  Like Pornography.
  Square.
Mackey, Nathaniel (b. 1947)
  Alphabet of Ahtt.
  Degree Four.
  Dream Thief.
  Falso Brilhante.
  Ghede Poem.
  Kiche Manitou.
  Phantom Light of All Our Day, The.
  Shower of Secret Things, The.
  Song of the Andoumboulou.
  Song of the Andoumboulou: 6.

Song of the Andoumboulou: 7.
Song of the Andoumboulou: 12.
Song of the Andoumboulou: 15.
Winged Abyss.
Mackie, Albert D. (b. 1904)
  New Spring, A.
  Young Man and the Young Nun, The.
Mackintosh, Ewart Alan (1893–1917)
  Cha Till Maccruimein (Departure of the 4th Camerons).
  In Memoriam[, Private D. Sutherland].
Macklin, Elizabeth (b. 1952)
  House Style, The.
Maclaurin, John, Lord Dreghorn (1734–96)
  Elegy: "Nor Hammond's love nor Shenstone's was sincere."
MacLean, Sorley (Somhairle MacGill-Eain) (b. 1911)
  Calvary.
  Death Valley.
  Ebb.
  Heroes.
  Highland Woman, A.
  Kinloch Ainort.
  Turmoil, The.
  Hallaig.
MacLeish, Archibald (1892–1983)
  Aeterna Poetae Memoria.
  American Letter.
  Ars Poetica.
  Autumn.
  Brave New World.
  Burying Ground by the Ties.
  Cook County.
  Corporate Entity.
  Critical Observations.
  Eleven.
  Empire Builders.
  End of the World, The.
  Epistle to Be Left in the Earth.
  Ezry.
  Grazing Locomotives.
  Immortal Autumn.
  L'An Trentiesme de Mon Eage.
  Lines for an Interment.
  Memorial Rain.
  Mother Goose's Garland.
  Not Marble nor the Gilded Monuments.
  Old Men in the Leaf Smoke, The.
  Panic.
  Pole Star for This Year.
  Prologue: "And the way goes on in the worn earth."
  Reconciliation, The.
  Reproach to Dead Poets.
  Return.
  Sentiments for a Dedication.
  Signature for Tempo.
  Snowflake Which Is Now and Hence Forever, The.
  Speech to a Crowd.
  Speech to Those Who Say Comrade.
  Too-Late Born, The.
  Tourist Death.
  Unfinished History.
  Voyage West.
  What the Serpent Said to Adam.
  Words in Time.
  You Also, Gaius Valerius Catullus.
  You, Andrew Marvell.
MacLellan, Robert (b. 1907)
  Sang.
MacLeod, Joseph Gordon ("Adam Drinan") (b. 1903)
  Men of the Rocks.
Macleod, Mary (Màiri Nighean Alasdair Ruaidh) (b. c.1615, d. after 1705)
  Blue Song.
  Dirge: "It is harm to me and anguish."
  Tricky Margaret.
MacManus, Anna Johnston See "Carbery, Ethna"
MacMarcuis, Aindrais
  This Night Sees Ireland [or Eire] Desolate.
MacMuireadach, Niall Mor
  Farewell for ever to last night.

Soraidh Slan Don Oidhche Areir.
MacNamara, Francis (b. 1811?)
  Convict's Tour to Hell, A.
  For the Company Underground.
  Petition from the Chain Gang at Newcastle to Captain Furlong the Superintendent, A.
MacNamee, Giolla Brighde (fl. late 13th cent.)
  Childless.
Macneacail, Aonghas (b. 1942)
  Gaelic is alive.
MacNeice, Louis (1907–63)
  And Love Hung Still.
  Apple Blossom.
  Autobiography.
  Autumn Journal, *sels.*
  Bad Dream.
  Bagpipe Music.
  Belfast.
  Birmingham.
  British Museum Reading Room, The.
  Brother Fire.
  Canto XX: "To Wales once more."
  Carrickfergus.
  Charon.
  Château Jackson.
  Christmas Shopping.
  Circe.
  Cradle Song: "Clock's untiring fingers wind the wool of darkness, The."
  Dublin.
  Ear, The.
  Eclogue for Christmas, An.
  Elegy for Minor Poets.
  Evening in Connecticut.
  Figure of Eight.
  For X.
  Goodbye to London.
  House on a Cliff.
  Individualist Speaks, The.
  Introduction, The.
  Leaving Barra.
  Les Sylphides.
  Libertine, The.
  London Rain.
  Mayfly.
  Meeting Point.
  Mixer, The.
  Morning Sun.
  Museums.
  Nature Morte.
  Night Club.
  Nostalgia.
  Nuts in May.
  Once-in-Passing, The.
  Prayer Before Birth.
  Precursors.
  Prognosis.
  Selva Oscura.
  Snow.
  Soap Suds.
  Spring Voices.
  Star-Gazer.
  Streets of Laredo, The.
  Suicide, The.
  Sunday Morning.
  Sunlight on the Garden, The.
  Taxis, The.
  Thalassa.
  This Is the Life.
  Tree Party.
  Truisms, The.
  Variation on Heraclitus.
  Western Landscape.
  Whit Monday.
  Wolves.
MacNutt, F. B. (1873–1949)
  Let all the multitudes of light.
Macoubrie, John (1925–83)
  Boethius at Cavalzero.
Macpherson, James ("Ossian") (1736–96)
  I sit by the mossy fountain; on the top of the hill of winds.
Macpherson, Jay (b. 1931)
  Ark Anatomical.
  Ark Apprehensive.
  Ark Artefact.

Ark Articulate.
Ark Astonished.
Ark Overwhelmed.
Ark Parting.
Ark to Noah.
Beauty of Job's Daughters, The.
Boatman, The.
Fisherman, The.
Go Take the World.
Hail Wedded Love!
Ill Wind, The.
Leviathan.
Lost Soul, A.
Martyrs, The.
Ordinary People in the Last Days.
Swan, The.
They Return.
Third Eye, The.
Well, The.

Macrae, John (Mhurchaidh, Ian Mac) (d. 1780)
Sleep Softly.

MacSweeney, Barry (b. 1948)
Far Cliff Babylon.
Flame Ode.
Ode Long Kesh.
Ode: "Urals post-master, this is your."
Pearl Alone.
Pearl Says.
Shells Her Auburn Hair Did Show, The.

Macuilxochitl (b. c.1435)
Battle Song.

MacWard, Owen Roe (d. 1849) and Hugh O'Donnell
Dark Rosaleen.

Madách, Imre (1823–64)
Adam, I think I'm going to be a mother.
And you, Lucifer, standing there aloof.
Be strong, brother!
I'm tired of these grim wastes of snow and ice.
It's hard to say, John, but I need some money.
It's kind of you to let me come alone.
Let them be! Get out!
Now, this is it, the toilsome journey's end.
Tell us, Professor.
There are a few things yet you haven't heard of.
There's no excitement, news or anything.
These are dissenters.
This reckless flight, where is this bound to take us?
Very ground dissolves beneath my feet, The.
You see the fellow with the scarlet sash?

Madan, Judith (1702–81)
Abelard to Eloisa.
Ode Composed in Sleep, An.
On Her Own Birthday.
To Lysander.

Madani, Rachida (b. 1953)
Here I am Once More.

Madden, Edward (fl. 1909)
By the Light of the Silvery Moon.

Madeira, Paul (fl. 1942)
I'm Glad There Is You (In This World of Ordinary People)

Madeleva, Sister Mary (b. 1887)
Candlemas Day.
Dumb Oxen.
From an Afternoon Caller.
I Ask My Teachers.
O / Holy / Wood.

Madge, Charles (1912–1996)
At War.
Birds of Tin, The.
Blocking the Pass.
Fortune.
Loss.
Lusty Juventus.
Monument, A.
On One Condition.
Poem: "Character of a landscape stands always in a mysterious relation, The."
Poem: "Walls of the maelstrom are painted with trees, The."
Solar Creation.
Times, The.

Madgett, Naomi Long (Naomi Long Witherspoon) (b. 1923)
Alabama Centennial.
Black Woman.
Brothers at the Bar.
Deacon Morgan.
Dream Sequence, Part 9.
Echoes.
Exits and Entrances.
Images.
Midway.
New Day.
Nomen.
Offspring.
Pavlov.
Plea for My Heart's Sake.
Quest.
Race Question, The.
Sally: Twelfth Street.
Simple.
Souvenir.
Star Journey.
Twenty Grand (Saturday Night on the Block), The.
Woman with Flower.

Madhubuti, Haki R. (Don. L. Lee) (b. 1942)
After Her Man Had Left Her for the Sixth Time That Year (An Uncommon Occurrence)
America calling.
Assassination.
B Network, The.
Back Again, Home.
Big Momma.
But He Was Cool; or, He Even Stopped for Green Lights.
Change Is Not Always Progress.
Communication in Whi-te.
Don't Cry, Scream.
Empty Warriors.
Gwendolyn Brooks.
Judy-One.
Killing Memory.
Knocking Donkey Fleas off a Poet from the Southside of Chi.
Loneliness, A.
Long Reality, The.
Magnificent Tomorrows.
Malcolm Spoke / Who Listened?
Man Thinking about Woman.
Men and Birth: the Unexplainable.
Mixed Sketches.
My Brothers.
One Sided Shoot-out.
Poem Looking for a Reader, A.
Poem to Complement Other Poems, A.
Poet: What Ever Happened to Luther?
Possibilities: Remembering Malcolm X.
Primitive, The.
Re-act for Action.
Self-Hatred of Don L. Lee, The.
Sun House.
Union of Two, The.
We Walk the Way of the New World.

Madigan, Rick (fl. 20th cent.)
Curtis Fuller.
Stereo Time with Booker Little.

Madison, Dolley (1768–1849)
Lafayette.

Madonick, Michael David (b. 1950)
Settled In.

Maeterlinck, Maurice (1862–1949)
Last Words, The.
Song: "Three little maidens they have slain."

Magdeburg, Mechthild von (1210–94)
Desert Has Many Teachings, The.
Effortlessly, / Love flows from God into man.
Fish cannot drown in water, A.
God's Absence.
God Speaks to the Soul.
How God Answers the Soul.
How God Comes to the Soul.
How the Soul Speaks to God.
I cannot dance, O Lord.
Love Flows from God.
Of all that God has shown me.

True love in every moment praises God.

Magee, John Gillespie, Jr. (1922–41)
High Flight.

Magee, Wes (b. 1939)
British Garden, A.
Giant Rocket.
How to Reach the Sun . . . on a Piece of Paper.

Mager, Don (b. 1942)
Beloved, / What does it take to put a house in order?

Magidson, Herb (1906–86)
Continental (You Kiss While You're Dancing), The.
Gone with the Wind.
(I'm Afraid) The Masquerade Is Over.
Music, Maestro, Please!
T'Ain't No Use.

Maginn, William (1793–1842)
Rime of the Auncient Waggonere, The.

Magowan, Robin (b. 1936)
Days of 1956.
Paros.
Susan.
Zeimbekiko.

Magrelli, Valerio (b. 1957)
Before the last curve of the day.
Each photographed face.
Especially in weeping.
Every evening, bent over the bright.
I have a brain populated by women.
I have finally learned.
I have from you this red.
I have often imagined that glances.
I look for a way of writing.
I love uncertain gestures.
I'm what is missing.
I prefer to come from silence to talk.
I sit, in treatment, at the movies, devoted.
If I must dial a number to call you.
If you melt some lead.
In summer, like the theaters, I close up.
In the evening when the light is dim.
Like ground that's been walked over, it echoes.
Pen slides, The.
Side by side after the meal.
Ten poems written in one month.
There are words that coast alongside thought.
There's silence between one page and another.
Things have an admirable life.
This handwriting wears itself away.
Tomorrow morning I will take a shower.
We go through life this way.
Wood of my thoughts is on fire, The.

Maguire, Sarah (b. 1957)
Communion.
Divorce Referendum, The.
Fall, The.
Invisible Mender, The.
Perfect Timing.
Spilt Milk.

Mahadevi (Mahadeviyakka) (fl. 12th cent.)
I do not call it his sign.
It was like a stream.
Like an elephant.
Like / treasure hidden in the ground.
O brothers, why do you talk.
On Her Decision to Stop Wearing Clothes.
Other men are thorn.
People, / male and female.
Riding the blue sapphire mountains.
So long as this breath fills your nostrils.
Vein of sapphires, A.
When I am hungry.
When the body becomes Your mirror.
Would a circling surface vulture.

Mahadeviyakka See **Mahadevi**

Mahapatra, Anuradha (b. 1956)
Spell.

Mahapatra, Jayanta (b. 1928)
Ash.
Main Temple Street, Puri.
Monsoon Day Fable, A.
October Morning, An.
Sanskrit.
Summer Poem, A.

Taste for Tomorrow.
Mahapatra, Sitakant (b. 1937)
　Election, The.
Mahdi, Sami (b. 1940)
　Inheritance, The.
　Mistake, The.
　Morning.
　On Details.
　World of Fancy.
Maher, Mary
　Not like a sock. The one.
Mahfouz, 'Isam (b. 1939)
　Weariness in the Evening of January Thirty-
　　Second.
Mahlmann, Siegfried August (1771–1826)
　Allah.
Mahmoud, Fatima
　What Was Not Conceivable.
Mahon, Derek (b. 1941)
　Achill.
　Afterlives.
　Another Sunday Morning.
　Antarctica.
　As It Should Be.
　Banished Gods, The.
　Consolations of Philosophy.
　Courtyards in Delft.
　Dark Country, A.
　Death and the Sun.
　Dejection.
　Derry Morning.
　Disused Shed in Co. Wexford, A.
　Dog Days.
　Dying Art, A.
　Ecclesiastes.
　Everything Is Going to Be All Right.
　Ford Manor.
　Garage in Co. Cork, A.
　Girls in Their Seasons.
　Glengormley.
　Globe in North Carolina, The.
　Going Home.
　Grandfather.
　Hunt by Night, The.
　I Am Raftery.
　Image from Beckett, An.
　In Carrowdore Churchyard.
　Kinsale.
　Last of the Fire Kings, The.
　Lives.
　Matthew V. 29–30.
　My Wicked Uncle.
　Poem Beginning with a Line by Cavafy.
　Postcard from Berlin, A.
　Rathlin.
　Refusal to Mourn, A.
　Snow Party, The.
　Spring Vacation, The.
　St. Eustace.
　Table Talk.
　Tractatus.
　Unborn Child, An.
　Woods, The.
**Mahony, Francis Sylvester ("Father Prout")
(1805–66)**
　Bells of Shandon, The.
Mahsati (fl. 12th cent.)
　Better to live as a rogue and a bum.
　Gone are the games we played all night.
　Good-looking, I'll never stoop for you.
　I knew like a song your vows weren't strong.
　Unless you can dance through a common bar.
Māhtābcānd, Mahārājādhirāja (1825–79)
　Who is this, all alone? Whose woman is She.
Maiden, Jennifer (b. 1949)
　Air.
　Anorexia.
　Climbing.
　Dew.
　Foundations, The.
　Green Side, The.
　In the Gloaming.
　Language.
　Mother-in-Law of the Marquis de Sade, The.
　New.

Slides.
　Taste.
Mailer, Norman (b. 1923)
　Devils.
Maillard, Claude
　Christmas Mass for a Little Atheist Jesus.
Mainwaring, M. G.
　Gothic columns of petrified motion.
Mair, Charles (1838–1927)
　I love you better than I love my race.
　Song: "Hear me, ye smokeless skies and grass-
　　green earth."
　There was a time on this fair continent.
Maitland, Sir Richard (1496–1586)
　Solace in Age.
Maitland, Sir Thomas
　Sir Thomas Maitland's Satyr upon Sir Niel
　　Laing.
Majaj, Lisa Suhair (fl. 20th cent.)
　Arguments.
　First Light.
　In Season.
　Jerusalem Song.
　Recognized Futures.
Majer, Hugo
　On my winter walk.
　Spring.
Major, Clarence (b. 1936)
　All the Same.
　Apple Core.
　Balance and Beauty.
　Beaulieu.
　Bruce and Nina.
　Funeral.
　Giant Red Woman.
　I Was Looking for the University.
　Inside Diameter.
　Isolate.
　Jefferson Company, The.
　Large Room with Wood Floor.
　Little Girls Posing All Dressed Up.
　Lost in the Desert.
　On Trying to Imagine the Kiwi Pregnant.
　On Watching a Caterpillar Become a Butterfly.
　Round Midnight.
　Self World.
　Swallow the Lake.
　Vietnam.
　Vietnam #4.
Majorino, Giancarlo (b. 1928)
　Doing.
　Hints.
　Kisses.
　Mirrored.
　My Flesh in its Sweat.
　Say—So I'll Say.
　Scene-Script.
Majumdar, Benoy (b. 1934)
　Time Wins.
Majumdār, Harināth (1833–96)
　Jaya / Don't wake up Hara's wife.
Mak, Lev (b. 1939)
　Farewell to Russia.
Makabo, Calvin (d. 1943)
　Desert Conflict.
**Makarov [or Makarov-Krotkov], Aleksandr (b.
1959)**
　Life lasts the course of a kiss.
　Twenty years / I tamed an ant.
Makeda (Queen of Sheba) (fl. 1000 B.C.)
　I fell.
　Wisdom is / sweeter than honey.
Makhfi Zibu'n-Nisa (1639–1703)
　Beauty of the Friend it was that taught me,
　　The.
Makidemewabe, Samuel
　Born Tying Knots.
　Saw the Cloud Lynx.
　Tree Old Woman.
Makin, Bathsua Pell (fl. 17th cent.)
　To Frederick V, by the Grace of God.
　Upon the Much Lamented Death of the Right
　　Honourable, the Lady Elizabeth Langham.
Maksimovic, Desanka (fl. c.1898)
　For All Mary Magdalenes.

For the Barren Woman.
　Matthew 22:15–22; Then the Pharisees went
　　and.
Makuck, Peter
　Prey.
Makusho, Layman
　Loving old priceless things.
Malachi
　Psalm of Silk.
Malallah, Zakiyya (b. 1959)
　Little Tales.
　Women.
Malam, Charles (b. 1906)
　Steam Shovel.
Malancioui, Ileana (b. 1940)
　Bear's Blood.
　My Sister, the Empress.
Malangatana, Valente Goenha (b. 1936)
　To the Anxious Mother.
　Woman.
Malange, Nise (b. 1960)
　This Poem Is Dedicated to Brother Andries
　　Raditsela.
Malczewski, Anton (1793–1826)
　After the Battle.
Malé, Belkis Cuza (b. 1942)
　And Here are the Poets in Their Sad Portraits.
　Creed.
　For the Moment.
　Glance.
　Greek Metamorphosis.
　Poet's Biography.
　Women Don't Die on the Front Lines.
Mallarmé, Stéphane (1842–98)
　Afternoon of a Faun, The.
　Album Leaf.
　Anguish.
　End / conscience.
　Favn in the Afternoon, A.
　Fine suicide fled victoriously, The.
　Gift of the Poem.
　Glazier, The.
　L'Après-Midi d'un Faune.
　Saint.
　Sea Breeze.
　Sea-Wind.
　Sigh.
　This virginal long-living lovely day.
　Toast.
　Tomb.
　Tomb of Charles Baudelaire, The.
　Tomb of Edgar Allan Poe, The.
　Tomb of Edgar Poe, The.
　Virginal, Vibrant, and Beautiful Dawn, The.
　Virginal, Vivid, Beautiful, Will This Be.
　When the shade threatened with the fatal
　　decree.
　With her pure nails offering their onyx high.
Mallet, David (1705–65)
　On an Amorous Old Man.
　Rule, Britannia!
　William and Margaret.
**"Malley, Ern" (James McAuley and Harold
Stewart)**
　Baroque Exterior.
　Boult to Marina.
　Coda.
　Colloquy with John Keats.
　Culture as Exhibit.
　Documentary Film.
　Dürer: Innsbruck, 1495.
　Egyptian Register.
　Night Piece.
　Palinode.
　Perspective Lovesong.
　Petit Testament.
　Sonnets for the Novachord.
　Sweet William.
　Sybilline.
　Young Prince of Tyre.
Malloch, Donald (1877–1938)
　Manly Love.
Malloch, Douglas (1877–1938)
　Up and Doing.
Malloch, William Hurrell (1849–1923)
　Brussels and Oxford.

Christmas Thoughts, by a Modern Thinker.
Marriage Prospect, A.

Malneek, Matt
I'm Through with Love.

Malone, Walter (1866–1915)
Opportunity.

Maloney, Frank R.
Grandmothers in Green and Orange.

Malouf, David (b. 1934)
Asphodel.
Bicycle.
Die Musik, An.
Early Discoveries.
For Two Children.
Guide to the Perplexed.
Judas Touch, The.
Snow.
This Day, under My Hand.
Wolf-Boy.
Year of the Foxes, The.

Malroux, Claire (b. 1935)
Every morning.
Fingers probe.
In October.
Octet Before Winter.

Maltby, Richard, Jr. (b. 1937)
I Don't Remember Christmas.
Little Bit Off, A.
Today Is the First Day of the Rest of My Life.

Maltseva, Nadezhda Elizarovna (b. 1950)
To the Muse.

Malveisin, William (d. 1238)
Fergus attempts to make off with the Sheild of Dunottar.

Mamalatan
What She Said.

Man Giac (1051–1096)
Rebirth.

Manaka, Matsemela (b. 1956)
Chorus: "Babylon, I did not come to you for the sake of coming."
Chorus: "In the name of the people."

Manan (1591–1654)
Unfettered at last, a traveling monk.

Manchán, Saint (d. 665)
Manchán's Prayer.

Mancini, Henry
Moon River.

Mandal, Bhadreśvar
I'm not a child any more, Syama.

Mandel, Eli W. (b. 1922)
Envoi: "My country is not a country."
Four Songs from the Book of Samuel.
From the North Saskatchewan.
Houdini.
Madwomen of the Plaza de Mayo, The.
My father was always out in the garage.
On the 25th Anniversary of the Liberation of Auschwitz.
Song: "When the echo of the last footstep dies."

Mandel, Naum Moiseievich *See* "Korzhavin, Naum"

Mandel, Tom (b. 1942)
Jews in Hell.
Realism.
Say Ja.

Mandela, Zindzi (b. 1959)
I Have Tried Hard.
I Saw as a Child.
I Waited for You Last Night.
Lock the Place in Your Heart.
Saviour.
There's an Unknown River in Soweto.

Mandelbaum, Harriet
Deus "Sex" Machina.

Mandell, Arlene L.
Middle Age.

Mandelstam [*or* Mandelshtam], Osip Emilevich (1892–1938)
And then my country spoke to me.
And you, my sister Moscow, are at ease.
Ariosto.
Batyushkov.

Because I Let Go Your Hands.
Body was given to me—what to do with it, A.
Both Schubert on the waters and Mozart in the din of birds.
Bread is poisoned and the air's drunk dry, The.
By denying me the seas, the right to run and fly.
Charlie Chaplin Poem, The.
Enough of snivelling! Shove our papers in the desk.
Finder of a Horseshoe, The.
Finding a Horseshoe.
For the resounding valor of millennia to come.
I Am Deaf.
I drink to military asters, to all that I'm censured about.
I Drink to the Asters of War.
I Hate the Light.
I'll chase through the gypsy camp of dark streets.
I'll tell you bluntly.
I must read only children's books.
I Was Washing Outside in the Darkness.
In This Cool Transparent Spring.
Insomnia.
Insomnia. Homer. Taut Sails.
Lamarck.
Last night I tell you, I do not lie.
[Last Poems].
Leningrad.
Lightheartedly Take from the Palms of My Hands.
Like Grumbling Roman Plebs.
Mounds of Human Heads.
Mounds of Human Heads Are Wandering into the Distance.
Not yet dead, not yet alone.
Notre Dame.
O how much I would like.
O Lord, Help Me to Live Through This Night.
Ode on Slate, The.
On Stony Pierian Spurs.
Petersburg Strophes.
Petropolis.
Phaedra.
Poem No. 286 (On Stalin)
Shy speechless sound, The.
Silentium.
Skillful mistress of guilty glances.
Stalin Epigram, The.
Still far from patriarch or sage.
Tell me, draftsman of the desert.
Three Octets.
Thy image, wavering, agonizing.
To A. A. A. (Akhmatova)
Tristia.
Valley Bleeds with Roman Rust, The.
What is the name of this street?
When Psyche, Who Is Life, Descends Among the Shades.
Where Can I Hide in January.
Whoever Finds a Horseshoe.
You Took Away All the Oceans and All the Room.
Your image, tormenting and elusive.

Mandeville, Bernard (1670–1733)
On Honour.

Mandiela, Ahdri Zhina
Mih Feel It.
Speshal Rikwes.

"Mang Ke" (Jiang Shi-wei) (b. 1951)
Section II.

Mangan, James Clarence (1803–49)
Christ, as a light.
Karamanian Exile, The.
Lament over the Ruins of the Abbey of Teach Molaga.
Nameless One, The.
O'Hussey's Ode to the Maguire.
Rest Only in the Grave.
Siberia.
To Amine.
To Sultan Murad II.
Twenty Golden Years Ago.
Vision of Connaught in the Thirteenth Century, A.

Manger, Itsik [*or* Itzig] (1901–69)
Adam and Eve.
Autumn.
I Am the Autumn.
Jealous Adam.
Mother Sarah's Lullaby.

Manguso, Sarah (b. 1974)
Rider, The.

Manhire, Bill (b. 1946)
Brazil.
Children.
Contemplation of the Heavens.
Distance between Bodies, The.
Late Victorian Girl, The.
On Originality.
Out West.
Prayer: "What do you take."
Selenologist, The.
Trees, The.
Zoetropes.

Manifold, John Streeter (1915–85)
Assignation with a Somnambulist.
Defensive Position.
Deserter, The.
Fencing School.
Fife Tune.
Garcia Lorca Murdered in Granada.
Griesly Wife, The.
L'Embarquement pour Cythère.
Makhno's Philosophers.
Making Contact.
Night Piece.
Sirens, The.
Tomb of Lt. John Learmonth, A.I.F., The.

Manilius, Marcus (*fl. c.* 1st cent. A.D.)
Why do we in worries waste our lives, and torture.

Manley, Delariviere (1670–1724)
Prologue [Spoken by Mr. Horden]: "First Adventurer for her fame I stand, The."
Song and Musick, Set by Mr. Eccles, and Sung by Mrs. Leveridge.
To the Author of Agnes de Castro.

Manley, Rachel
Bob Marley's Dead.

Mann, Chris (b. 1948)
Comrades Marathon, The.
Poet's Progress, The.

Mann, David
In the Wee Small Hours of the Morning.
No Moon at All.

Manner, Eeva-Liisa (b. 1921)
Lunar Games, The.

Manning, Frederic (1882–1935)
Grotesque.
Leaves.
Trenches, The.

Mannyng [*or* Manning], Robert (1288–1338)
Dancers of Colbek, The.
Praise of Women.

Manrique, Jaime
Barcelona Days.
Baudelaire's Spleen.
My Night with Frederico García Lorca (As Told by Edouard Roditi)
Tarzan.

Mansei *See* Sami Mansei

Mansel, William Lort (1753–1820)
Sun's Perpendicular Rays, The.

Mansfield, Katherine (Kathleen Beauchamp Murry) (1888–1923)
Friendship.
Man with the Wooden Leg, The.
Meeting, The.
Secret Flowers.
To L. H. B.

Mansour, Joyce (b. 1928)
Anti-mnemonic self-vaccination.
Auditory Hallucinations.
Beyond the breakers.
Desire as Light as a Shuttle.
Embrace the Blade.
Empty Black Haunted House.
From an ass to an analyst and back.
Gently stroke a wound.

Going and Coming of Sequins.
I Opened Your Head.
I Saw the Red Electric.
I Saw You through My Closed Eye.
In the Gloom on the Left.
Into the Red Velvet.
Last night I saw your corpse.
Lovely Monster.
Mango, A.
Men's Vices.
Naked / I float among the wreckage with steel
　mustaches.
Night in the Shape of a Bison.
North Express.
Of Sweet Rest.
Regulation equipment.
Seated on her bed legs spread open.
Sun is in Capricorn, The.
Ten to One to No.
They Have Weighed.
Tinfoil.
Vices of Men, The.
Wild Glee from Elsewhere.
Woman Kneeling in the Sorry Jelly, A.
Yesterday evening I saw your corpse.
Your Figure or the War Against Fat.

Mansour, Khairi (b. 1945)
Day.
I see trees breaking off their branches.

Mansour [or Mansur], Monica (b. 1946)
Desert 1.
My Memory.

Mansur, Abul Kasim See **Firdowsi**

Mant, Bishop Richard (1776–1848)
Church Bells, The.
House of God, The.
Social Worship.
True Knowledge.

Manyarrows, Victoria Lena (fl. 20th cent.)
Lakota Sister/Cherokee Mother.
See No Indian, Hear No Indian.
Today We Will Not Be Invisible Nor Silent.

Manzan (1635–1714)
One minute of sitting, one inch of Buddha.

Manzano, Juan Fransico (1797–1854)
My Thirty Years.

Mao Tse-tung [or Mao Zedong] (1893–1976)
Chinese Ballad.
Glitter of a northern kingdom.
I stand alone in the cold autumn.
Midstream.
Return to Shaoshan.
"Spring in Ch'in's Garden."
Tune: "Deva-like Barbarian"—Ta-po-ti.
Tune: "Full River Red"—A Reply to Kuo Mo-
　jo.
Tune: "Remembering the Lady of Ch'in"—
　Loushan Pass.
Tune: "Song of Divination"—On the Plum
　Tree, after a Poem by Lu Yu.
Tune: "Song of Picking Mulberry" Double-
　Ninth Festival.
Tune: "Spring in Ch'in's Garden."
Tune: "The Charm of Nien-nu"—Kunlun
　Mountains.

Mao Wen-hsi (fl. c.930)
Drunk Among the Flowers.
Tune: Drunk among the Flowers.

Mapanje, Jack A.
After Wiriyamu Village Massacre by
　Portuguese.
Another Fools' Day Touches Down: Shush.
At the Metro: Old Irrelevant Images.
Baobab Fruit Picking; or, Development in
　Monkey Bay.
Before Chilembwe Tree.
Cheerful Girls at Smiller's Bar, 1971, The.
Elegy for Mangochi Fishermen, An.
From Florrie Abraham Witness, December
　1972.
Glory Be to Chingwe's Hole.
Making Our Clowns Martyrs.
Messages.
On African Writing.
On Being Asked to Write a Poem for 1979.
On His Royal Blindness Paramount Chief

Kwangala.
Steve Biko Is Dead.
These Too Are Our Elders.
Visiting Zomba Plateau.
We Wondered about the Mellow Peaches.

Mar, Laureen (b. 1953)
My Mother, Who Came from China, Where
　She Never Saw Snow.

Mar, Yekhi'el [or Yehiel] (1921–69)
Handfuls of Wind.

Maraini, Dacia (b. 1936)
Family Stories.
I Am Two.
I Dreamt a Pig.
I Spent the Night.
Lemon, Hot Water and a Blood Clot.
Little Woman with Medusa Eyes, A.
Love If This Is Love.
Man with Long Legs, The.
Your Face Has No Name.

Marais, Eugène (1871–1936)
Deep River.
Here We have No Firm Dwelling-Place.
Radio Cradle-song.

Maran, René (1887–1960)
Human Soul.
Silence.
"Tropicals."

Marbod of Rennes (1035–1123)
Enemy in the Fortress, The.
Epitaph for Bruno of Angers.
Horace composed an ode about a certain boy.
Hymn of the Magdalen.
I Give You No Greeting.
Meditation among Trees.
Now must I mend my manners.
Of the Resurrection of the Body.
Prayer to God the Father.
This vision of a face, radiant and full of
　beauty.

Marcabrun (fl. 12th cent.)
At the Fountain.

**Marcela de Carpio de San Felix, Sister (fl. 16th
cent.)**
Amor Mysticus.

March, Ausiàs (1397?–1459)
As someone on his back for months of illness.
Day's in dread of losing her bright features,
　The.
Know what I'm like? Some captain moors his
　ship.
Let others hail the holidays with laughter.
Much as a man who takes delight in dreaming.
Not so with me as with the little page.
Out scouting for sound counsels? How to
　prosper?

March, Joseph Moncure (1899–1977)
Gang was there when midnight came, The.
Queenie was a blonde, and her age stood still.

Marchant, Frederick
Screen Porch.

Marchenko, Nikolai Nikolaevich See **"Morshen,
Nikolai Nikolaevich"**

Marckant, John (fl. 16th cent.)
Lamentation, The.

Marcus, Ben
Battle at Horizon.
Delaying Relevance.
Justice.
Plagiarism.

Marcus, Morton (b. 1936)
I Think of Those Mornings.
Letter, The.
Picnic on the Bay Bridge.
Poem for Gonzales, California, The.
Whales.

Mardale, W. R. (fl. c.1853)
Pop Goes the Weasel!

Mardhekar, B. S. (1909–56)
Forest of Yellow Bamboo Trees, The.

Marechera, Dambudzo (1954–87)
Cemetery in the Mind, The.
Desert Crossing.
Neither Innocence or Experience.

Old Man Inside Me, The.
When Love's Perished.

Margarido, Maria Manuela (b. 1926)
Landscape.
Roça.
Socope.
You Who Occupy Our Land.

Margul-Sperber, Alfred
Day of the Landscape, The.

Margulies, Stephen (b. 1951)
Relentlessly Lovelorn, the Non-Sleeper
　Whispers and Re-Whispers a Magic Charm
　Against His Wound's Roar.

"Maria, Laura" See **Robinson, Mary**

Mariah, Paul (b. 1937)
Christmas 1962.
Quarry/Rock.

Mariani, Paul (b. 1940)
Betty.

Marianus (fl. c.500–c.600)
In this bath Cypris once was bathed by Love,
　her son.

Marichiko
Every morning.
I cannot forget.
I hold your head tight.
I wish I could be.
Who is there? Me.

Marie de France (c.1155–1189)
Honeysuckle (Chevrefoil)
Lanval.
Lay of the Honeysuckle, The.
Nightingale, The.
Song from "Chartivel."
Two Lovers, The.
Wolf and the Lamb, The.
Wolf and the Sow, The.
Would I Might Go Far over Sea.

Marinetti, Filippo Tommaso (1876–1944)
Correction of proofs + desires in speed.
Futurism Wants to Transform the Variety
　Theater into a Theater of Amazement,
　Record-setting, and Body-madness.
They are Coming.
We had stayed up all night, my friends and I,
　under hanging mosque lamps.
Landscape Heard, A.

**Marino, Giambattista [or Giovanni Battista]
(1569–1625)**
Fading Beauty.
Lips and Eyes.
Out of the Italain.
Steps to the Temple.
Yet on the other side, faine would he start.

Marinoni, Rosa Zagnoni (1888?–1970)
At Sunrise.
For a New Home.
Who Are My People?

Marion, George, Jr. (1909–68)
Ladies Who Sing with a Band, The.
Love Is a Random Thing.
My Future Just Passed.
There's a Man in My Life.

Maris, Hyllus
Season's Finished, The.
Spiritual Song of the Aborigine.

Mark, Diane Mei Lin
Suzie Wong Doesn't Live Here.

Markham, E. A. (b. 1939)
Sea, The.

Markham, Edwin (1852–1940)
After Reading Shakspere.
Avengers, The.
In Death Valley.
Leaf from the Devil's Jest-Book, A.
Lincoln, the Man of the People.
Man with the Hoe, The.
Outwitted.
Preparedness.
Right Kind of People, The.
There Is a High Place.

Markham, Gervase (1568–1637)
Fragment, A: "I walked [or walk'd] along a
　stream for pureness rare."

Markish, Perets [*or* Peretz] (1895–1952)
We Reached Out Far.
Markman, Stephanie
They lived out in a women's house.
Markoe, Merrill
Ballad of Winky.
Lewis Describes His Day.
Markov, Sergey [*or* Sergei] Nikolaevich (1906–79)
Stendhal.
Marks, Gerald
All of Me.
Is It True What They Say About Dixie?
Spanish Jake.
Marks, S. J. (b. 1939)
Losing Myself.
November Woods.
Poem in Three Parts.
Poem With Two Seasons Right Now.
Returning in Wind and Drizzle to My Home.
To Go Through Life Is to Walk Across a Field.
To the Ocean.
Markus, Peter (b. 1966)
Black Light.
Light.
Shooting Crows.
Marlatt, Daphne (b. 1942)
Coming to You.
Femina.
Imagine: A Town.
Marlatt, David (b. 1963)
Bruce and the Bluegills.
Katherine's Hair.
Summer of the New Well.
Working Girl.
Marlatt, Earl Bowman (1892–1976)
Spirit of Life, in This New Dawn.
Through the Dark the Dreamers Came.
Marlowe, Christopher (1564–93)
Dido, Queen of Carthage, *sels*.
Doctor Faustus, *sels*.
Edward the Second, *sels*.
Hero and Leander, *sels*.
Lucan's Pharsalia, *sels*.
Ovid's Elegies, *sels*.
Passionate Shepherd to His Love, The.
Tamburlaine the Great, *sels*.
"Marnia" (1968–92)
Accoutrement.
I Must be Able to Protect You.
I Want to Love You Very Much.
Maro, Publius Vergilius *See* **Virgil [*or* Vergil]**
Maroon, Bahiyyih (b. 1973)
Fire Keeper.
Neighbor.
Nude Woman Spotted in Cappuccino Cup as Advertising Dollar co-opts another life.
Marot, Clément (1495–1544)
Friar Lubin.
Love-Lesson, A.
Madame d'Albert's Laugh.
Posy Ring, The.
Marquis, Don (Donald Robert Perry Marquis) (1878–1937)
Aesop Revised by Archy.
Archy at the Zoo.
Archy Confesses.
Archy Interviews a Pharoah.
Certain Maxims of Archy.
Coming of Archy, The.
Expression is the need of my soul.
I once heard the survivors.
Limerick: "It needn't have ribaldry's taint."
Limerick: "There was a young fellow named Sydney."
Mehitabel S Extensive Past.
Song of Mehitabel, The.
Tom-Cat, The.
When One Loves Tensely.
Marquis, Donald Robert Perry *See* **Marquis, Don**
Marriott, Anne (b. 1913)
As You Come In.
Beaver Pond.
Prairie Graveyard.
Marsden, James (1908–73)
What Is Time?

Marsh, Barbara
Papa.
Marshak, Samuel (1887–1904)
Immortality.
Marshall, Archibald (1866–1934)
Limerick: "There was a young man of Devizes."
Marshall, Edward (b. 1932)
Leave the Word Alone.
Marshall, Jack (b. 1937)
Air Dagger.
Letter to My Father on the Other Side.
Months of Love, The.
Still.
Thirty-Seven.
United Way, The.
Wing and Prayer.
Marshall, Rex (b. 1943)
Buddgelin Bey.
Burrel Bullai.
Little Brown Jacks Nyimbung.
Marshall-Stoneking, Billy (b. 1947)
On the Death of Muriel Rukeyser.
Passage.
Picture Postcard.
Seasons of Fire, The.
Marshall, Tom (b. 1938)
Interior Monologue 666.
Politics.
Summer.
Marsman, Hendrik (1899–1940)
Holland.
Landscape.
Memory of Holland.
Paradise Regained.
Polderland.
Marsman, Henk *See* **Bernstein, Charles**
Marston, John (1575–1634)
Cynic Satire, A.
Humours.
Metamorphosis of Pigmalion's Image, The, *sels*.
Scourge of Villanie, The, *sels*.
To Detraction I Present My Poesie.
To Everlasting Oblivion.
Marston, Philip Bourke (1850–87)
After.
Inseparable.
Love's Music.
Old Churchyard of Bonchurch, The.
Speechless: Upon the Marriage of Two Deaf and Dumb Persons.
Vain Wish, A.
Martelli, Jennifer
Mal'Occhio.
Martí, José (1853–95)
I am an honest man.
I Dream Awake.
I know: from flesh.
I want, in the shade of a wing.
In the shadow of a wing.
Lonely trembling soul can ache, The.
Opposite of Ornate and Rhetorical Poetry, The.
Simple Verses.
Two Countries.
Martial (Marcus Valerius Martialis) (c.40–c.104)
Ad Quintilianum.
After her wedding-night, the nymph.
Agriculture.
Aulus, my girlfriend's in a dreadful plight.
Believe me, sir, I'd like to spend whole days.
Bought Locks.
Breath of balm from foreign branches pressed, The.
Cornelius sighs . . . the lines I write.
Country Pleasures.
Critics.
Cure of my unquietness.
Dasius, chucker-out / at the Turkish Baths.
De Cœnatione Micae.
Did he have eyes and, if so, did he look.
Don't pay any attention.
Either get out of the house or conform to my tastes, woman.
Epigrams, *sels*.

Epitaph for Erotion.
Erotion.
Erotion rests here, in the.
For rank, descent and title famed.
Fronto, Father, Flaccilla, Mother, extend.
Garland of roses, whether you come.
Happy Life, A.
He scanned me closely, Rufus, just as.
Hinted Wish, A.
How to Do It.
I send you a lock of hair.
Irresolute the down upon your cheek.
Just half our three score years and ten.
Laid with papyrus to catch fire.
Lentinus! thou dost nought but fume, and fret.
Let every prudish reader use his feet.
Ligurra's fearful I'll contrive.
Lycoris darling, once I burned for you.
Lydia is as wide and slack.
My carefree Namesake, this the art.
My taste in women, Flaccus? Give me one.
Near Neighbors.
Near the Vipsanian columns where the aqueduct.
Oh If the Gods Would Make Me Rich.
On the Death of a Young and Favorite Slave.
Out of an Epigram of Martial.
Out of the house or be the wife I want.
People have the oddest kinks.
Post-Obits and the Poets.
Pre-eminent among scholars.
Procrastination.
Read of *Thyestes, Oedipus*, dark suns.
Roman Presents.
Roman Thank-You Letter, A.
Rome, I am Scorpus, foremost in the race.
Sextus the Usurer.
Since you, Charmenion, come from Corinth.
Since your marriage you have lost the look.
Slipshod writing, premature publication.
Temperament.
Thais, why do you call me old.
They smell of *Corycian* saffron, of A.
This was the young Camonus; this his face.
To Cloe.
To His Book[e].
To Julius.
To Sextus.
Traveller on the Flaminian Way.
Verses on Blenheim.
Were lives of ease, dear Namesake, ours.
What a host you are, Mancinus.
What Makes a Happy Life.
When you say, 'Quick, I'm going to come.'
Whenever you drink all night you make.
While unquiet, *Juvenal*, you haunt.
Who deem epigrams mere trifles.
Why, Hyllus, do you deny to me today.
Would you, my friend, in little room express.
You are a stool pigeon and.
You are the most beautiful.
You gave Bithynicus thousands yearly; still.
You rocked my cradle, Charidemus, once.
You say, *Postumus*, you'll live tomorrow.
You Serve the Best Wines Always, My Dear Sir.
You've Told Me, Maro.
You want me to call you generous.
You were a swan, you're now a crow.
Martialis, Marcus Valerius *See* **Martial**
Martien, Jerry
In Wild Iris Time.
Late 20th Century: Spring.
Rocks Along the Coast, The.
Martin, C. D. (b. 1943)
His Eye Is on the Sparrow.
Martin, Charles (b. 1942)
E. S. L.
Easter Sunday, 1985.
Metaphor of Grass in California.
Satyr, Cunniliguent: To Herman Melville.
Speech Against Stone.
Victoria's Secret.
"Martin, David" (Ludwig Detsinyi) (b. 1915)
Dreams in German.
Martin, Herbert (b. 1933)
Miss Rosie Mae Watches Elvis Presley on The

Ed Sullivan Show.

Martin, Hugh (b. 1914)
Ev'ry Time.
Have Yourself a Merry Little Christmas.
Here Come the Dreamers.
I Never Felt Better.
Love: "Love can be a moment's madness."
Occasional Man, An.
On Such a Night As This.
That Face.
Trolley Song, The.

Martin, Philip (b. 1931)
Tongues.

Martin, Sarah Catherine (1768–1826)
Comic Adventures of Old Mother Hubbard and
Her Dog, The.

Martin, William
Apple Orchard in the Spring, An.

Martinaitis, Marcelijus
Forbid!
Kukutis Describes His Hut.
Kukutis in the Reich's Guard House.
Kukutis's Consciousness Becomes Alienated.
Kukutis's Fruitless Bread.
Kukutis's Lament under the Heavens.
Kukutis's Sermon to the Pigs.
Kukutis's Sinful Spirit.
Kukutis's Song.
Kukutis's Swallow's Hymn.
Kukutis's Trip on the Samogitian Highway.
Last Farewell to Kukutis.
Pony in Kukutis's Ear, A.
Silly Spring.
Unhappy Kukutis in the Potato Patch.
Zuveliskes's Women Mourn Over Kukutis.

Martínez de Navarrete, José Manuel (1768–1809)
Separation from Clorila, The.

Martinez, Dionisio D.
Altruism.
Carp.
Cole Porter.
Cultivation of Orchids, The.
Death of Isadora Duncan, The.
Discreet Prayer, A.
In a Duplex Near the San Andreas Fault.
Kinescope.
Matisse: Blue Nude, 1952.
Nocturnes: "He closed the deal on the night. A
real."
Pain.
Room itself, The. The women. The absence of
women.
Standard Time: Novena for My Father.

Martínez, Valerie (b. 1961)
Absence, Luminescent.
Camera Obscura.
Children of the Disappeared.
Coastal.
Ever So, Between.
Human Universe, The.
Into the Next One.
It Is Not.
New World, The.
Night of Fathers.
Nocturne: "To the interior, limbs folded."
Reliquaries, The.
Tesoro.
Traveler.

Martins, Maria (1900–1973)
I Am the Tropical Night's High Noon.

Martinson, Harry Edmund (b. 1904)
Cable Ship, The.
Cotton.
Dusk in the Country.
Earthworm, The.
On the Congo.
Peonies.

Martory, Pierre (d. 1998)
Blues.

Marty, Sid (b. 1944)
In the Dome Car of the "Canadian."

Martynov, Leonid Nikolaevich (1905–80)
Be kind / Be iron.
Daedalus.
River Silence, The.

Idlers.
It seems to me I'm resurrected.
Lord of Nature.
Seashore, The.
Sunflower.

Marula (fl. c.1156)
Meeting after Separation.

Marvell, Andrew (1621–78)
After two sittings, now our Lady State.
And now to the ab[b]yss I pass.
At the demolishing, this seat.
Bermudas.
Character of Holland, The.
Charles II.
Clorinda and Damon.
Coronet, The.
Damon the Mower.
Definition of Love, The.
Dialogue between the Resolved Soul and
Created Pleasure, A.
Dialogue between the Soul and [the] Body, A.
Execution of King Charles, The.
Eyes and Tears.
Fair Singer, The.
First Anniversary of the Government under His
Highness the Lord Protector, 1655, The.
Flecknoe, an English Priest at Rome.
For Santacruze the glad fleet takes her way.
From that blest bed the hero came.
Gallery, The.
Garden, The.
Garden of Appleton House, The ("When in the
east the morning ray")
Garden, The ("How vainly men themselves
amaze")
Holland, that scarce deserves the name of land.
Horatian Ode upon Cromwell's Return from
Ireland, An.
'Is this, saith one, the Nation that we read.'
Match, The.
Mower Against Gardens, The.
Mower's Song, The.
Mower to the Glowworms [or Glow-Worms or
Glo-Worms], The.
Nymph and Her Fawn, The.
Nymph Complaining for the Death of Her
Faun [or Fawn], The.
Oh thou, that dear and happy isle.
On a Drop of Dew.
On Mr Milton's "Paradise Lost."
Paint Castlemaine in colours that will hold.
Picture of Little T. C. in a Prospect of Flowers,
The.
To His Coy Mistress.
Upon Appleton House [To My Lord Fairfax].
Upon the Hill and Grove at Bilbrough.
Young Love.

Marx, Pearson
Hugs.

"Mary, Aunt" *See* **Lathbury, Mary Artemisia**

Mary, Queen of Scots *See* **Mary Stuart, Queen of Scots**

Mary Stuart, Queen of Scots (1542–87)
For him also I powrit out mony teiris.
He is, in truth, lacking in civility.
In my sweet and sad song.
My lord and my God, I have hoped in Thee.
Verses in Italian and French, Written by the
Queen of Scots to the Queen of England.

**Maryam bint Abi Ya'qub al-Ansari (fl. early 11th
cent.)**
What can you expect.

Marzán, Julio (b. 1946)
Emergency.
Eve.
In the Backyard.
Sunday Morning in Old San Juan.

Marzials, Théophile Julius Henry
Tragedy, A.

Masahide (1657–1723)
Barn's burnt down.
Now that my storehouse.
When bird passes on.
While I walk on.

Masaoka Shiki (1867–1902)
Aged nightingale / How sweet.

All the hot night.
Among Saga's / Tall weeds.
Autumn come / Cicada husk.
Autumn wind / Gods, Buddha.
Barrelful of phlegm, A.
Dew, clinging / To potato field.
Evening bell / Persimmons pelt.
Fresh From the Void.
Frozen in the ice.
Heath grass / Sandals.
I can see the stones.
Imagine / The monk took off.
Indian summer / Dragonfly shadows seldom.
Loofah blooms and, The.
Loofah water.
Midnight sound / Leap up.
On the eve of death.
Shitting in the winter turnip field.
Spring night.
Stone / On summer plain.
Storm—chestnuts / Race along.
Such silence / Snow tracing wings.
Sudden rain / Rows of horses.
Summer sky / Clear after rain.
Thing long forgotten.
White butterfly / Darting among pinks.
Wicker chair / In pinetree's shade.
Wild geese cry, The.

Maschwitz, Eric (1901–69)
Nightingale Sang in Berkeley Square, A.
Paris Is Not the Same.
These Foolish Things (Remind Me of You)

Mase, Sidney Warren
It's Simply Great.

Masefield, John (1878–1967)
Autumn Ploughing.
C. L. M.
Captain Stratton's Fancy.
Cargoes.
Choice, The.
Consecration, A.
Crowd, The.
Dead Knight, The.
Epilogue: "I have seen flowers come in stony
places."
Fellow Mortal, A.
Fox knew well, that before they tore him, The.
From '41 to '51.
Is there a great green commonwealth of
Thought.
Laugh and Be Merry.
Meet was at "The Cock and Pye," The.
Night on the Downland.
No man takes the farm.
On Growing Old.
Other bright days of action have seemed great.
Partridges.
Passing Strange, The.
Port of Holy Peter.
Port of Many Ships.
Posted.
Roadways.
Rose of the World, The.
Rounding the Horn.
Run to Mourne End Wood, The.
Sea Change.
Sea Fever.
Sonnet: "Here in the self is all that men can
know."
Sonnet: "There, on the darkened deathbed, dies
the brain."
Sorrow of Mydath.
To-morrow.
Trade Winds.
Twilight.
Up on the Downs.
Valediction (Liverpool Docks), A.
Waggon-Maker, The.
Wanderer's Song, A.
West Wind, The.

Masham, Damaris, Lady (1659–1708)
Irreconcilable, The.
On Damons Loveing of Clora.

Masini, Donna
Two Men, Two Grapefruits.

Mason, Francis Claiborne
Sunken Sailor.

Mason, Ronald Allison Kells (1905–71)
Be Swift O Sun.
Body of John.
Ecce Homunculus.
Footnote to John II: 4.
Judas Iscariot.
Latter-day Geography Lesson.
Old Memories of Earth.
On the Swag.
Prelude: "This short straight sword."
Sonnet of Brotherhood.
Spark's Farewell to Its Clay, The.
Young Man Thinks of Sons, The.
Mason, William (1725–97)
Alcander's Flower Garden.
Heroic Epistle to Sir William Chambers, An.
Some Early gardenists.
Thomas Gray's View of Nature.
To a Gravel Walk.
Masri, Maram
Small Sins.
You who.
Massey, Gerald (1828–1907)
All's Right with the World.
And thou hast stolen a jewel, Death.
As proper mode of quenching legal lust.
Desolate.
Diakka, The.
O, Lay Thy Hand in Mine, Dear!
Womankind.
Worker, The.
Massimi, Pacifico (fl. 15th cent.)
Advice to Paulinus.
Love Song for Marcus, A.
On Happiness.
Massinger, Philip (1583–1640)
Men May Talk of Country-Christmasses.
Masson, Thomas Lansing See **Masson, Tom**
Masson, Tom (Thomas Lansing Masson) (1866–1934)
Enough.
He Took Her.
My Poker Girl.
Tragedy, A.
Massoni, Marie-Dominique (b. 1947)
How Old Is the Old Mole?
Two Seconds.
Masters, Edgar Lee (1869–1950)
A. D. Blood.
Amanda Barker.
Anne Rutledge.
Archibald Higbie.
Battle of Gettysburg, The.
Benjamin Pantier.
Business Reverses.
"Butch" Weldy.
Carl Hamblin.
Cassius Hueffer.
Circuit Judge, The.
Cities of the Plain.
Constance Hately.
Daisy Fraser.
Doctor Meyers.
Dora Williams.
Editor Whedon.
Elliott Hawkins.
Elsa Wertman.
Emily Sparks.
English Thornton.
Father Malloy.
Fiddler Jones.
Flossie Cabanis.
Gettysburg.
Hamilton Greene.
Harry Williams.
Herman Altman.
Hill, The.
Indignation Jones.
Jennie McGrew.
Jonathan Houghton.
Jonathan Swift Somers.
Judge Somers.
Justice Arnett.
Knowlt Hoheimer.
Lost Orchard, The.
Lucinda Matlock.

Many Soldiers.
Margaret Fuller Slack.
Marx the Sign Painter.
Minerva Jones.
Mrs. Benjamin Pantier.
Mrs. Meyers.
On the way to the grove you'll pass the Fates.
Oscar Hummel.
Petit, the Poet.
Ralph Rhodes.
Reuben Pantier.
Rutherford McDowell.
Serepta Mason.
Sexsmith the Dentist.
Silence.
Spooniad, The.
Starved Rock.
Supplication.
This is the city of great doges hidden.
Trainor, the Druggist.
Unknown Soldiers.
Veterans of the Wars.
Webster Ford.
Wedding Feast, The.
Week-End by the Sea.
Widows.
Willie Metcalf.
Masters, Marcia Lee (b. 1910)
At My Mother's Bedside.
Masters, Mary (c.1694–1771)
To the Same; Enquiring Why I Wept.
Mastin, Florence Ripley (b. 1896)
From the Telephone.
Mastoraki, Jenny (b. 1949)
Crusaders knew the Holy Places, The.
Death of a Warrior, The.
Prometheus.
Then they paraded Pompey's urn.
Vandals, The.
Wooden Horse then said, The.
Masumi Kato (d. 1725)
I draw the willow.
Masumi Kato (d. 1796)
Path to paradise, The.
Masumi Kato (d. 1825)
Surface, The.
Mataira, Katerina Te Hei Koko (b. 1932)
Restoring the Ancestral House.
Mataka, Laini (b. 1949)
Next Door.
Ornithology.
Matar, Muhammad ʿAfifi (b. 1935)
Recital.
Matchett, William H. (b. 1923)
Water Ouzel.
Mateo, Noel
Jeepneyfying.
There Is No Word for Sex in Taglog.
Matevski, Mateja
This is an hour of calm, a quiet hour.
Mathema, N. C. G. (b. 1949)
Maze of Blood, A.
Mather, Cotton (1663–1728)
Dummer the Shepherd Sacrific'd.
Epitaph: "Dummer the shepherd sacrific'd."
Eternal God, How They're Increased.
Excellent Wigglesworth, Remembered by some Good Tokens, The.
Go then, my dove, but now no longer mine.
I Lift My Eyes Up to the Hills.
My Heart, How Very Hard It's Grown.
O Glorious Christ of God; I live.
Vigilantius, or a Servant of the Lord Found Ready.
When the Seed of Thy Word Is Cast.
Mather, Joseph (1737–1804)
File-Hewer's Lamentation, The.
God Save Great Thomas Paine.
Mather, Tinker
If you're looking for water.
Matherne, Beverly
La Fabrique de Tabac (Tobacco Harvest)
Les Fils (Sons)
Matheson, George (1842–1906)
Christian Freedom.

O Love That Wilt Not Let Me Go.
Mathew, Ray (b. 1929)
Good Thing, A.
Lover's Meeting.
One Day.
Poem in Time of Winter.
Seeing St. James's.
Wynyard Sailor.
Mathews, Aidan Carl (b. 1956)
At the Wailing Wall.
Caedmon.
Death of Irish, The.
Descartes at Daybreak.
Letter Following.
Library, The.
Minding Ruth.
Persons Unknown.
Severances.
Spectrum.
Two Months Married.
Mathews, Cornelius (1817–89)
Journalist, The.
Masses, The.
Sculptor, The.
Mathews, Eliza Kirkham (1772–1802)
Indian, The.
Mathews, Harry (b. 1930)
Aboard a Boat at Night, Drinking with My Wife.
At Night, Hearing Someone Singing in the House Next Door.
Back from Green Dragon, Presented to Hsieh Shih-chih.
Histoire.
Lunar Eclipse.
My Neighbor to the South, the Office Clerk Hsiao, Came in the Evening to Say Good-bye.
Out and Back on the Fifteenth Night of the First Month.
Sad Birds, The.
Mathias, Roland (b. 1915)
Brechfa Chapel.
Cae Iago: May Day.
Craswall.
Departure in Middle Age.
Flooded Valley, The.
God Is.
Grasshoppers.
Laus Deo.
Memling.
Porth Cwyfan.
Sanderlings.
Sir Gelli to R. S
Testament.
Mathis, Cleopatra (b. 1942)
Angels, The.
Blues: Late August.
Getting Out.
Given What Manages.
Mathison, Thomas (d. 1754)
Victory on the Last Green.
"Matilda, Anna" See **Cowley, Hannah**
"Matilda, Rosa" See **Dacre, Charlotte**
Matshoba, Mtutuzeli (b. 1950)
Mantatee Horde, The.
Matson, Clive
Bedside.
Mattawa, Khaled (fl. 20th cent.)
Before.
Bus Driver Poem, The.
Cricket Mountain.
Heartsong.
History of My Face.
Ismailia Eclipse.
Letter to Ibrahim.
White Nile Elegy.
Mattera, Don (b. 1935)
Day They Came for Our House, The.
Giovanni Azania.
Matthews, Harley (b. 1889)
Women Are Not Gentlemen.
Matthews, Marc (b. 1937)
By a Ways.
Language.

Matthews, Tom (b. 1945)
Cowboy Film.
Even the Whales.
Happy Arabia.
Private But Sulphurous.
Robert Sat.

Matthews, William (1942–97)
Buddy Bolden Cylinder, The.
Cheap Seats, the Cincinnati Gardens, Professional Basketball, 1959.
Descriptive Passages.
Elegy for Bob Marley, An.
Foul Shots: A Clinic.
Good Company.
Grandmother, Dead at 99 Years and 10 Months.
In Memory of the Utah Stars.
Mail Order Catalogs.
Mingus at the Showplace.
Mood Indigo.
Names.
Old Folsom Prison.
Onions.
Penalty for Bigamy Is Two Wives, The.
Psychopathology of Everyday Life, The.
Story Often Told in Bars: The *Reader's Digest* Version, A.
This Spud's for You.
Unrelenting Flood.
Vermin.

Maturaikkataiayattar Makan Vennakan
What She Said to Her Girl-Friend.

Matveyev, Ivan Venediktovich *See* **"Elagin, Ivan Venediktovich"**

Matveyeva [or Matvieiva], Novella Nikolaevna (b. 1934)
Dream.
Eggplants Have Pins and Needles, The.
Ginger-Haired Girl, The.
Hymn to the Pepper.
I, he says, am not a warrior.
I'm no fighting man, he says.
Laughter of a Faun, The.
Lighthouse.
Procurers.
Re-Conversion.
Robert Frost.
Wood.

Maule, Thomas (c.1645–1724)
To Cotton Mather, from a Quaker.

Maunick, Edouard J. (b. 1931)
Accept from me not silence.
And I have chosen the sea as no man's land.
Enter in the circle.
For there is an African virtue of the tree.
Further off is the measured force the word of the sea.
I am from everywhere.
I have mentioned it by name.
I have understood nothing.
I love to encounter you in strange cities.
I made the motions of the sacred place.
Letter to Ellen Conroy Kennedy.
Ofatedo / seek it out upon the skin of Africa.
Point no scornful finger at Yoruba Land.
Seven Sides and Seven Syllables.
Speaking of Gethsemane in Yoruba Land.
This is where the warrior from Ibokun came.
This Strange Calculation of Roots.
Trees were forbidden me, The.
Where does this poem come from?

Maura, Sister (b. 1915)
Creation of Light, The.
Each Day.

"Maurice, Furnley" (Frank Wilmot) (1881–1942)
Echoes of Wheels.
Victoria Markets Recollected in Tranquility, The.
Whenever I Have.

Maurice, Thomas (1754–1824)
Chiswick.
How cursed that country, how severe its doom.

Maurus, Hrabanus *See* **Charlemagne**

Maurus, Hrabanus (776–856)
To Grimold, Abbot of St. Gall.

Max, Lin
Equal Temperament.
Pedagogy.

Maxted, Eleanor
Slow train, A. Few travellers. If.

Maxton, Hugh (b. 1947)
At the Protestant Museum.
Cernunnos.
Deutschland.
Elegies.
Ode.
Urgent Letter, An.
Waking.

Maxwell, Glyn (b. 1962)
Mild Citizen.
Poisonfield.
Rumplestiltskin.

Maxwell-Hall, Agnes (b. 1894)
Jamaica Market.

Maxwell, James Clerk (1831–79)
Rigid Body Sings.

Maxwell, Ruth Fortney
Mother's Joy, A.

May, Edward (fl. c.1633)
Five Things White.
On a Young Man and an Old Man.
To a Covetous Churl.
To Barba.
To Her Love.
You tender virgins, fairer than the snow with which you play.

May, Kenneth (fl. 20th cent.)
Valentine's Day.

Mayakovsky [or Maiakovskii], Vladimir Vladimirovich (1893–1930)
At the Top of My Voice.
But Could You?
Can't Stand It.
Cloud in Trousers, A.
Crimea.
For a Violin, Somewhat Nervously.
Good Attitude to Horses, A.
How I Became a Dog.
I know the force of words, I know their clarion call.
In Re Conferences.
It's already past one. You'll have gone to bed.
Last Page of the Civil War.
Last Statement.
Listen.
Maria! Maria! Maria!
Mayakovsky's Suicide Note.
My most respected / comrades of posterity!
No matter how much more waiting I'll have to do.
Now Listen!
Ode on the Revolution.
On Being Kind to Horses.
On Trash.
Our March.
Past One O'Clock.
Prologue: "I'll mock those thoughts of yours."
Screaming My Head Off.
They Don't Understand a Thing.
You!
You think this is some malarial dream?

Maybe, Ellyn (b. 1964)
Umbilical Cord.

Mayer, Bernadette (b. 1945)
Aeschyleans, The.
Birthday Sonnet for Grace.
Boats.
Earthworker's God is Healed, The.
End of Human Reign on Bashan Hill, The.
First Turn to Me.
Garden, The.
Gay Full Story.
Generic Elbows.
House Cap.
Port, The.
Sonnet: "Beauty of songs your absence I should not show."
Sonnet: "Dawn and night of fighting, lovers like actual wars."
Sonnet: "Thousand apples you might put in

your theories."
We've Solved the Problem.

Mayer, Gerda (b. 1927)
Ballad: "Knight went down to the river's rim, A."
Bilberries.
Count Carrots.
Crunch, The.
Dandelions.
Drip Drip or Not Bloody Likely.
Echo and Narcissus.
529 1983.
Make Believe.
Narcissus.
Noah.
Old Mrs. Lazibones.
Poor Mrs. Prior.
Song: "Does the policeman sleep with his boots on."

Mayer, Hansjörg (b. 1943)
Oil.

Mayes, Jane
Descant.
Orchestration.

Mayhall, Jane (b. 1921)
City Sparrow.
For the Market.
Human Animal, The.
Marshes, The.

Mayne, Jasper (1604–72)
Time.

Mayne, John (1759–1836)
Logan Braes.

Mayne, Seymour (b. 1944)
Before Passover.
In Memory of Aaron, Murdered Grandfather.
Roots.
Zalman.

Mayo, Edward Leslie (b. 1904)
Diver, The.

Mayröcker, Friederike (b. 1924)
Ostia Will Receive You.
Patron of Flawless Serpent Beauty.
Spirit of '76, The.

Mazur, Gail (b. 1937)
Acorn, The.
After the Storm, August.
Common, The.
Keep Going.
Then.

'Mbala' (Michael Bailey)
History of Dub Poetry, The.
New Dub, A.

M'Baye d'Erneville, Annette (b. 1927)
Kassacks.
Labane.
Requiem.

Mbuyazi *See* **Fynn, Henry Francis**

McAdams, Janet
Leaving the Old Gods.

McAlmon, Robert (1896–1956)
Frost in the Corn, The.

McAlpine, Rachel (b. 1940)
Bird-Woman.
Te Kaha.

McAuley, James (1917–76)
Art of Poetry, An.
Because.
Blue Horses, The.
Cloak, The.
Convalescence.
Dear John, whoever now takes pen to write.
Dialogue.
Envoi.
Gnostic Prelude.
In a Late Hour.
In the Huon Valley.
In the Twentieth Century.
Jesus.
Keep the Season.
Late Winter.
Legendary.
Liberal, or Innocent by Definition.
Merry-go-round.
New Guinea.

Nocturne.
One Tuesday in Summer.
Pietà.
Released on Parole.
Seventh Day, The.
Song of Shem.
Terra Australis.
Tomb of Heracles, The.
Wet Day.
Winter Drive.
World on Sunday.
McBride, Mekeel (b. 1950)
Knife-Thrower's Wife, The.
McCabe, Victoria (b. 1948)
For Starters.
People at the Pay Telephone, The.
McCaffery, Steve (b. 1947)
Can there be a collision between picture and application?
Homines qouque si taceant, vocem invenient libri.
Little Hans.
McCaig, Norman (b. 1910)
Betweens.
Poem: "There is a wailing baby under every stone and you walk."
McCallum, Shara (b. 1972)
Calypso.
Collage.
Deer, The.
Fugue.
In My Other Life.
In the Beginning.
Jamaica, October 18, 1972.
Perfect Heart, The.
McCarriston, Linda
Billy.
Castle in Lynn, A.
Healing the Mare.
January, Anchorage.
Riding Out at Evening.
To Judge Faolain, Dead Long Enough: A Summons.
McCarthy, Eugene (1916–1970?)
Ending.
Kilroy.
McCarthy, Gerald
Arrival.
Fall of Da Nang, The.
Hooded Legion, The.
Med Building.
Finding the Way Back.
Sound of Guns, The.
McCarthy, Joseph (1885–1943)
Alice Blue Gown.
I'm Always Chasing Rainbows.
You Made Me Love You (I Didn't Want to Do It)
McCarthy, Joseph, Jr. (1922–75)
Cloudy Morning.
I'm Gonna Laugh You Right Out of My Life.
Riviera, The.
Why Try to Change Me Now?
McCarthy, T. L.
Limerick: "Immaculate Sir Walter Raleigh, The."
Limerick: "Mrs. Whitehouse, mixed bathing at Deal."
McCarthy, Thomas (b. 1954)
Claud Cockburn.
Dying Synagogue at South Terrace, The.
Emigration Trains, The.
Feeding Ground.
Mr. Nabokov's Memory.
November in Boston.
Party Shrine.
Persephone, 1978.
Phenomenology of Stones, The.
Poet of the Mountains, The.
Quatrain without Sparrows, Helpful Bells or Hope.
Question Time.
Shopkeepers at the Party Meeting.
Sorrow Garden, The.
Standing Trains, The.

State Funeral.
Toast.
Wisdom of AE, The.
Word "Silk," The.
McClanahan, Rebecca
Bridal Rites.
McClatchy, J. D. (b. 1945)
At a Reading.
Bishop Reading.
Capriccio of Roman Ruins and Sculpture with Figures, A.
1871.
First Steps.
Method, The.
My Mammogram.
1946, 1957.
1971.
Old Song Ended, An.
Spirit sets about its task, but slowly, The.
Tattoos.
McClaurin, Irma (b. 1945)
I, Woman.
Mask, The.
To a Gone Era.
McClellan, George Marion (b. 1860)
September Night, A.
McClennan, Tommy
Brown Skin Girl.
McClintock, Michael
Across the sands.
Bluebird alights, The.
Broken window, A.
Dead cat.
Drizzling rain, A.
First melt, The.
Glimmering morning.
Grasshopper, A.
Hamburger Hill.
Hearing.
Here's a guy.
Hungry / without money—.
I eat alone.
Letting my tongue.
Long summer day.
Look it's clear.
Merry-go-round, The.
Overtaken.
Peering out.
Poppy, A.
Pushing.
Rowing downstream.
Sat down.
She leaves.
Side-canyon, A.
Single tulip!, A.
Small girl, A.
Thought i'd / never grow old.
Tonight . . . wishing.
Twisting inland.
While we wait.
McClure, Michael (b. 1932)
Aelf-Scin, The.
Breech, The.
Canticle.
Clear—the senses bright—sitting in the black chair—Rocker.
Flowers of Politics, I, The.
Flowers of Politics, II, The.
For Artaud.
For Monk.
From the Window of the Beverly Wilshire Hotel.
(Fuck Ode)
Gesture the gesture the gesture the gesture, The.
Hymn to Saint Geryon.
Jazz at the Intergalactic Nightclub.
Mad Sonnet 1.
Mad Sonnet: Fame.
Mad Sonnet: Grace.
May Morn.
Moiré.
Ode for Soft Voice.
Ode to Jackson Pollock.
Peyote Poem.
Pleasure fears me, foot rose, foot breath.

Rant Block.
Reading Frank O'Hara in a Mexican Rainstorm.
Rug, The.
Senate Hearings.
Silence the eyes! becalm the senses!
Small Secret Book, A.
Song: "Platinum fur and brass revolver shine."
Trees are elephants' heads, The.
With Tendrils of Poems.
McCord, David (b. 1897)
Ascot Waistcoat.
Axolotl, The.
Baccalaureate.
Blessed Lord, What It Is to Be Young.
Books Fall Open.
Cocoon.
Crickets.
Crows.
Crows, The.
Epitaph on a Waiter.
Every Time I Climb a Tree.
Five Chants.
Gloss.
Glowworm.
History of Education.
Mantis.
Mr. Bidery's Spidery Garden.
Pickety fence, The.
Singular Indeed.
Song of the Train.
Summer Shower.
This Is My Rock.
To a Certain Most Certainly Certain Critic.
Walnut Tree, The.
When I Was Christened.
McCrae, Hugh Raymond (1876–1958)
Mimshi Maiden, The.
Song of the Rain.
Winds.
McCrae, John (1872–1918)
In Flanders Fields.
McCree, Junie (fl. 1910)
Put Your Arms Around Me, Honey.
McCreery, John Luckey (1835–1906)
There Is No Death.
McCuaig, Ronald (b. 1908)
Au Tombeau de Mon Père.
Betty by the Sea.
Recitative: "Farmer's son is good and mad," The.
McCullagh, James C.
Mermaid's Song.
McDade, Thomas Michael
Potatoes of the Field, The.
McDaniel, Jeffrey
D.
Disasterology.
Following Her to Sleep.
Leonard.
Logic in the House of Sawed-Off Telescopes.
Obvious, The.
Play It Again, Salmonella.
McDaniel, Wilma Elizabeth
Asking Favors.
California Entertainment, 1936.
First Spring in California, 1936.
My Room at Aunt Eura's, 1937.
Realist of 1939–40, A.
Ruby Red's Migrant Camp.
McDonald, Charles (b. 1957)
Asdrubral Jiménez.
At the Gwen John Exhibition.
Cheers.
Fresh Mussels.
Nightfishing.
Oxford Gardens.
McDonald, Dorothy Nell
Birthday Wish, A.
McDonald, Ellie (b. 1937)
Itherness.
McDonald, Nan (1921–73)
Burragorang.
Hatters, The.
McDonald, Peter (b. 1962)
Cash Positive.

Christmas.
Peacetime.
Pleasures of the Imagination.
Sunday in Great Tew.
Totalled.

McDonald, Roger (b. 1941)
1915.
Apis Mellifica.
Bachelor Farmer.
Blizzard, The.
Components.
Flights.
Hollow Thesaurus, The.
Incident in Transylvania.
Two Summers in Moravia.

McDonald, Walter (b. 1934)
After the Noise of Saigon.
Children of Saigon, The.
Christmas Bells, Saigon.
Faraway Places.
For Harper, Killed in Action.
For Kelly, Missing in Action.
Hauling Over Wolf Creek Pass in Winter.
Honky-Tonk Blues.
Interview with a Guy Named Fawkes, U.S. Army.
Last Still Days in a Bunker, The.
Caliban in Blue.
Once You've Been to War.
Retired Pilot to Himself, The.
Rocket Attack.
Songs We Fought For, The.
Veteran.
War Games.
Winter Before the War, The.

McDuffie, Carrington
Finally the Rain.

McElroy, Colleen J. (b. 1935)
Caledonia.
End of Civilization as We Know It, The.
Foul Line—1987.
From Homegrown: An Asian-American Anthology of Writers.
Ghost-Who-Walks, The.
Griots Who Know Brer Fox, The.
Horoscope.
Illusion.
In My Mother's Room.
Ruth.
Learning to Swim at Forty-Five.
Looking for a Country under Its Original Name.
Mae West Chats It Up with Bessie Smith.
Pike Street Bus.
Tapestries.
Under the Oak Table.
Woman's Song, A.

McFadden, David (b. 1940)
Form of Passion, A.
House Plants.
Lennox Island.

McFadden, Roy (b. 1921)
Bigamy.
Contemplations of Mary.
Epithalamium: "So you are married, girl. It makes me sad."
First Letter to an Irish Novelist.
For the Record.
Grand Central Hotel, The.
My Mother's Young Sister.
Stringer's Field.

McFee, Michael (b. 1954)
First Radio.

McFerrin, Bobby
23rd Psalm, The.

McGinley, Phyllis (1905–78)
5:32, The.
About Children.
Adversary, The.
Ballade of Lost Objects.
City Christmas.
Daniel at Breakfast.
Day after Sunday, The.
Demagogue, The.
Evening Musicale.
Garland of Precepts, A.

Giveaway, The.
How to Start a War.
Independent, The.
J's the Jumping Jay-Walker.
Lady Selecting Her Christmas Cards.
Last Year's Discussion: The Nobel Russian.
Midcentury Love Letter.
Muted Screen of Graham Greene, The.
Notes for a Southern Road Map.
Occupation: Housewife.
Ode to the End of Summer.
Office Party.
Old Beauty, The.
On the Farther Wall, Marc Chagall.
Portrait of a Girl with Comic Book.
Public Journal.
Publisher's Party.
Reflections at Dawn.
Robin Hood.
Spring Comes to the Suburbs.
Squeeze Play.
Temptations of Saint Anthony, The.
Theology of Jonathan Edwards, The.
Trial and Error.
Trinity Place.
Triolet Against Sisters.
Twelfth Night.
Velvet Hand, The.
Village Spa.
Women of Jericho, The.

McGlashan, June
Island of Women, The.

McGonagall, William (1825–1902)
Accidents will happen by land and by sea.
Alas! Lord and Lady Dalhousie are dead, and buried at last.
All hail to the Empress of India, Great Britain's Queen.
And my opinion is that God sent the whale in time of need.
As the procession passes the palace the blinds are drawn.
Beautiful new railway bridge of the Silvery Tay.
Beautiful Railway Bridge of the Silv'ry Tay!
By taking the impressions of watch-cases he discovered, one day.
Calamity in London; Family of Ten Burned to Death.
Famous Tay Whale, The.
Hen It Is a Noble Beast, The.
Late Sir John Ogilvy, The.
Railway Bridge of the Silvery Tay, The.
Tay Bridge Disaster, The.
'Twas on the 8th April, on the afternoon of that day.

McGough, Robert
Fight of the Year, The.

McGough, Roger (b. 1937)
Away from you.
Bully Night.
Defying Gravity.
Harum Scarum.
40—Love.
If Life's a Lousy Picture, Why Not Leave before the End.
Italic.
Kleptomaniac, The.
Leader, The.
Let Me Die a Youngman's Death.
My Cat and I.
Noah's Ark.
P. C. Plod versus the Dale St. Dog Strangler.
Poem With a Limp.
Potato Clock.
Prayer to Saint Grobianus.
Snow Poem.
Snowman in a field.
Snowman, The.
Storm.
Survivor.
Though giving pleasure to many.

McGrane, Paul
Jukebox Saturday Night.

McGrath, Beth
Concert Choir.

McGrath, Campbell
At the Freud Hilton.
Capitalist Poem #36.
Delphos, Ohio.
First Trimester, The.
Florida.
Florida Anasazi, The.
Jack Gilbert.
Jeffrey Lee Pierce.
Shrimp Boats, Biloxi.
Spring Comes to Chicago.
Wheatfield Under Clouded Sky.

McGrath, Thomas (1916–90)
Advertisements.
And I hear the pad of feet to the union hall.
And we, of the damned poor, trot our frost-furred horses.
Begun before Easter.
Black Train, The.
Blues for Warren.
Bread of this World; Praises III, The.
Celebration.
Coal Fire in Winter, A.
Death for the Dark Stranger.
End of a Season.
End of the Line, The.
End of the World, The.
Epitaph: "Again, traveller, you have come a long way led by that star."
Evening—another evening—and the lights flare.
Fresco: Departure for an Imperialist War.
From here it is necessary to ship all bodies east.
Go Ask the Dead.
Guiffre's Nightmusic.
Half Measures.
Jig Tune: Not for Love.
Language of the Dead, The.
Letter for Marian, A.
Long Way Outside Yellowstone, A.
Longing.
Night Meeting.
Nocturne Militaire.
Nuclear Winter.
Ode for the American Dead in Korea.
Offering.
On the Head of a Pin.
Ordonnance.
Poem: "My little son, laughing, singing."
Poem: "When I carry my little son in the cold."
Probable Cause.
Reading by Mechanic Light.
Reading the Names of the Vietnam War Dead.
Return, The.
Skull of the Horse.
Song: "Lovers in ladies' magazines."
Song: Miss Penelope Burgess, Balling the Jack.
Visit to the House of the Poet—Nicaragua, 1987—Homage to Rubén Darío on His Birthday, A.
We go out in the stony midnight.
Windless city built on decaying granite, loose ends.
Working in Darkness.

McGraw, Erin
Drunk Dog.

McGregor, Duncan Campbell
Limerick: "There was a young curate called Lloyd."

McGuckian, Medbh (b. 1950)
Aphrodisiac, The.
Coleridge.
Collusion.
Dream-Language of Fergus, The.
Flitting, The.
Flower Master, The.
Folk Museum, The.
Gateposts.
Laurentia.
Little House, Big House.
Lychees.
Mast Year, The.
Mr. McGregor's Garden.

On Ballycastle Beach.
On Not Being Your Lover.
Orchid House, The.
Presence, The.
Sea or Sky?
Seed-Picture, The.
Sitting, The.
Sofa, The.
Speaking Into the Candles.
To a Cuckoo at Coolanlough.
Tulips.
Waterford.

McGuire, Jack
Streets of Forbes, The.

McHugh, Heather (b. 1948)
After You Left.
Coming.
Etymological Dirge.
Ghazal of the Better-Unbegun.
My One.
My Shepherd.
Night in a World, A.
Past All Understanding.
Sizing.
Three To's and an Oi.
20-200 on 737.
What Could Hold Us.

McHugh, Jimmy (1895–1969)
Blue Again.
Don't Blame Me.
I Can't Believe That You're in Love with Me.
I Just Found Out About Love.
I'm in the Mood for Love.
I'm Livin' in a Great Big Way.
It's a Most Unusual Day.
Lovely to Look At.
On the Sunny Side of the Street.
Spreadin' Rhythm Around.
Where Are You?

McHugh, Vincent See **Kwock, C. H.**

McIlroy, Leslie Anne (b. 1965)
Good-Bye, Valentine.
How to Change a Flat.
Siesta.

McIntyre, James (1827–1906)
Ancient poets ne'er did dream, The.
Disaster to Steamer Victoria at London.
Prophecy of a Ten Ton Cheese.
We have scarcely time to tell thee.
When we do trace out nature's laws.
Wooden Leg.

McKay, Claude (1889–1948)
Africa.
America.
Birds of Prey.
Castaways, The.
Dawn in New York.
Enslaved.
Harlem Dancer, The.
Harlem Shadows.
I Know My Soul.
If We Must Die.
Jasmine.
Lynching, The.
My Mother.
My Mother.
Negro's Tragedy, The.
Negro Spiritual.
Outcast.
Pagan Isms, The.
Spring in New Hampshire.
St. Isaac's Church, Petrograd.
Subway Wind.
Tiger.
Tired Worker, The.
To O. E. A.
To the White Fiends.
Tropics in New York, The.
Truth.
White City, The.
White House, The.
Wild Goat, The.

McKay, Don (b. 1942)
Barbed Wire Fence Meditates upon the
    Goldfinch, A.
I Scream You Scream.

March Snow.

McKean, James (fl. 20th cent.)
After Listening to Jack Teagarden.
Good 'D.'

McKendrick, Jamie (b. 1955)
Shortened History in Pictures, A.

McKinney, Irene
Chrysanthemums.
Dance, The.
Deep Mining.
Rapt.
Sunday Morning, 1950.
Twilight in West Virginia: Six O'Clock Mine
    Report.
Visiting My Gravesite: Talbott Churchyard,
    West Virginia.

McKinney, Laurence (b. 1944)
Oboe.

McKinnon, Barry (b. 1944)
Bushed.
North, The.

McKuen, Rod (b. 1933)
Thoughts on Capital Punishment.

McLachlan, Alexander (1818–40)
Arrival, The.
Song: "Old England is eaten by Knaves."
We Live in a Rickety House.

McLain, Paula (b. 1965)
Beauty, That Lying Bitch.
Connor in the Wind and Rain with His Coat
    on.
Fishing.
Residue.
Willing.

McLaughlin, Joe-Anne
Black Irish Blues.

McLeod, Irene (b. 1891)
Lone Dog.

McLoughland, Beverly
Crazy Boys.
Whippoorwill Calls, The.

McMahon, Lynne
All quail to the wallowing.
Elvis for the Ages, An.
Not Falling.
Peace Studies.

McManus, Frank R.
Limerick: "Precede us, O Lord, with Thy
    Grace."

McManus, James (b. 1951)
Commercials exaggerate.

McMaster, Rhyll (b. 1947)
Back Steps Lookout.
Clockface.
Mutton Bird Man.
Profiles of My Father.
Round Song, A.
Tanks.

McMichael, James (b. 1939)
Cat came, A.
My parents had teased that if I ever caught a
    fish I'd take it to bed.
Posited.

McMorris, Mark (b. 1960)
Evening.
Near Speech, The.

McNair, Wesley (b. 1941)
Mina Bell's Cows.
Where I Live.

McNaughton, Anne
Balls.

McNeil, Rodney M. (b. 1966)
Angel in the Temple of Luxor, An.
It Just Doesn't Matter.
Mirrors in the Room.

McNeill, Anthony (fl. c.1941)
Bob Marley New King of the Music.
For the D.
Ode to Brother Joe.
Saint Ras.

McNulty, Tim
Bodhidharma Crossing the Graywolf River on
    a Ry-Krisp.

McOrlan, Pierre (1882–1970)
Accessories shop, The.

Battery woman.
Hairdresser's, The.
Horse butcher, The.
Modern circus, The.
Produce from the colonies.
Weighing-machine, The.
Wood merchant's parlour, The.

McPherson, Heather (b. 1942)
Close-up.
Have You Heard of Artemisia?
Theology and a Patchwork Absolute.

McPherson, Sandra (b. 1943)
1943.
Ability to Make a Face Like a Spider While
    Singing Blues: Junior Wells, The.
Bedrooms.
Bittern, The.
Black Soap.
Children.
Coconut for Katerina, A.
Games.
Genius of Fog at Ecola Creek Mouth.
Gnawing the Breast.
Helen Todd: My Birthname.
His Body.
Microscope in Winter, The.
Museum of the Second Creation, The.
Some Metaphysics of Junior Wells.
Outsider: Minnie Evans.
Peter Rabbit.
Pornography, Nebraska.
Pregnancy.
Quilt of Rights.
Resigning from a Job in a Defense Industry.
Streamers.
Suspension: Junior Wells on a Small Stage in a
    Converted Barn.
Wanting a Mummy.
Wings and Seeds.

McPower, Kate
Limerick: "Teacher of tots at Uttoxeter, A."

McQueen, Cilla (b. 1949)
Studio Poem.
To Ben, at the Lake.

McRay, Paul
Performance.

McVeigh, Jane
Eve Falling.

McWilliam, George
Limerick: "When the census man called upon
    Gail."

Mead, Jane (b. 1958)
Delphi, Coming Around the Corner.
However.
Incomplete Scenario Involving What the Voice
    Said.
La Guardia, the Story.
Point and Counter-Point in All Things.
Sometimes the Mind.

Mead, Philip (b. 1953)
Cinema Point.
From a Republican Grave: Daniel Henry
    Deniehy, 1828–1865.
Man and the Tree, The.
Melbourne or the Bush.
There.

Meador, Betty De Shong
Fields Belong to Woman, The.

Means, Alex (1801–83)
What Wondrous Love Is This.

Mearns, Hughes (1875–1965)
Perfect Reactionary, The.

Mechain, Gwerfyl (c.1460–1500)
Female Genitals, The.
Hostess of the Ferry Inn, The.
In the Snowfall.
Lady of the Ferry Inn.
Snowfall, The.

Mécs, László (1895–1978)
Going Down, Please.
My Dear Little Fellow.
On the Tomb of the Unknown Soldier.
Prayer for the Great Lunatic.
Who Can Understand This?

Meddemmen, J. G.
L. R. D. G.

Medici, Lorenzo de' (1449–92)
Triumph of Bacchus and Ariadne.
Two Lyrics.

Medicine-Tail
He was there / Old Man Coyote.

Medina, Pablo
Exile, The.
Nocturno de Washington.

Medina, Tony (b. 1966)
After the Verdict.
Big House Revisited, The.
Don't Say Goodnight to Etheridge Knight.
Poem for Teacup Mantlepiece Poets Palpitating
Poot Booty Plagiarists Imprisoned in Ivy
League White Supremacist Mental
Biological Warfare Labs.
Rhudine Rhudine.

Medrano, Francisco de (1570–1607)
Sonnet 41.

Meehan, Paula (b. 1955)
Child Burial.
Laburnum.
Pattern, The.

Meeks, Brian (b. 1953)
Is Culcha Weapon?
March 9 1976.
Twin Barrel Bucky: A Kingston 12 Dub, The.

Meenakshi, R. (b. 1944)
If Hot Flowers Come to the Street.

Megnen, Jeanne
Noise Will Start Tomorrow, The.

Mehri (1404–47)
Coming Across.

Mehrotra, Arvind Krishna (b. 1947)
Roys, The.

Mei Ch'eng (d. 140 B.C.)
Seven Stimuli.

Mei Sheng and Fu I
Nineteen Old Poems of the Han.

Mei Yao Ch'en (1002–60)
Aboard a Boat at Night, Drinking with My
Wife.
At Night, Hearing Someone Singing in the
House Next Door.
Back from Green Dragon.
Boat-pullers, The.
Borrowing Rice from Ju-hui.
Chiang Lin-chi Treats Me to Mudfish.
Crescent Moon, The.
Dappled Horse, The.
Dream at Night, A.
Eating Shepherd's-purse.
Elegy for a White Cock.
Excuse for Not Returning the Visit of a Friend,
An.
Fish Peddler.
I Remember the Blue River.
I Remember the River at Wu Sung.
In Broad Daylight I Dream of My Dead Wife.
Lice, The.
Little Village, A.
Lunar Eclipse.
Marrying Again.
Meeting the Herdsmen.
Melon Girl.
Mourning for My Wife.
My Neighbor to the South, the Office Clerk
Hsiao, Came in the Evening to Say Good-
bye.
Necessities.
Next Door.
Offering for the Cat, An.
On Hearing that Holders of the *Chin-shih*
Degree Are Dealing in Tea.
On Seeing a Painting of Plants and Insects by
Chü-ning.
On the Death of a New Born Child.
On the Death of His Wife.
On the Night of the Fifteenth Day of the First
Month I Go Out and Return.
On the Thirteenth Day of the Eleventh Month I
Went to the Granary for the First Time since
My Illness.
Out and Back on the Fifteenth Night of the
First Month.

Poverty on the Bank.
Sad Remembrance.
Second Marriage.
Sharing Lodging with Hsieh Shih-hou.
Shih-hou Pointed Out to Me That from Ancient
Times There Had Never Been a Poem on the
Subject of Lice.
Solitary Falcon above the Buddha Hall of the
Monastery of Universal Purity, A.
Sorrow.
Swarming Mosquitoes.
Year Wu-tzu [1048], The, First Month, Night
of the Twenty-sixth: A Dream.

Meidhre, Brian MacGiolla *See* **Merriman** [*or*
Merryman], **Brian** [*or* **Bryan**]

Meigs, Mildred Plew (Mildred Plew Merryman)
(d. 1944)
Abraham Lincoln.
Pirate Don Durk of Dowdee, The.
Shepherd Left Behind, The.

Meilyr Brydydd (*fl.* **1100–1137**)
Poem on His Death-Bed.

Meinke, Peter
Advice to My Son.
Atomic Pantoum.
Death of the Pilot Whales, The.
Helen.
Poet, Trying to Surprise God, The.
Sonnet on the Death of the Man Who Invented
Plastic Roses.
Supermarket.
This is a poem to my son Peter.
Unnatural Light.

Meïr of Rothenburg (1215–53)
Burning of the Law, The.

Meireles, Cecília (1901–64)
Ballad of the Ten Casino Dancers.
Dead Horse, The.
Portrait.
Sketch.
Song: "I placed my dream in a boat."
Vigil.

Melbourne, Hirini (b. 1949)
Tamaki of a Hundred Lovers.
Why the Wind Comes.

Meleager (*fl.* **1st cent. B.C.**)
All that he is . . . does . . . is attractive.
Asclepias who loves to love.
Epigram: "At 12 o'clock in the afternoon."
Burn not too oft who flutters at thy flame.
Busy with love, the bumble bee.
By Cypris, Cupid!
By Timo's locks.
Cicala stoned with dew.
Counts itself lucky.
Cup takes its sweet joy and tells how it
touches, The.
Cupid at Venus' breast.
Did I not tell you, my soul, "By Cypris, you
will be caught."
Dorcas, be off! & tell her this.
Down through the earth as a last gift.
Epigram: "And now I, Meleager, am among
them."
Epigram: "As honey in wine / wine, honey."
Epigram: "Breath of my life—no less, The."
Epigram: "I was thirsty."
Epigram: "It is true that I held Thero fair."
Eyes / flatterers of Soul.
Flower-feasting bee, why do you touch upon.
Foresworn now the love-vows!
Garland for Heliodora, A.
Goat-foot Pan has quit his flocks.
Heliodora's Brows.
Hot day. Dying of thirst. Slake myself.
I foster a Love fond of playing ball. It throws.
I'll weave in the white violet. I'll weave in.
I'm down. Step on my neck, you savage god,
with your heel.
I say that my sweetly prattling Heliodora will
someday.
I swear by desire.
I was a quick-footed, long-eared hare, just
snatched from my mother's.
If you burn my scorched soul too often, Love,
she'll fly.

In heart's space hath Eros.
In the Spring.
Inconstant Dawn, thou tak'st thy time.
Little Love-God, The.
Lost! Cupid!/ One lost Cupid!
Lost Desire.
Love at the Door.
Love cast!
Love fed Heliodora's fingernail and made.
Love in silence shall.
Love-prone Asclepias with eyes like a
summer's day.
Love's night and a lamp.
More than Apollo's golden lyre.
Mosquito, may you fly, a swift courier for me.
Mosquitoes, shameless and shrill of voice,
sucking the blood.
Mother of gods.
Night Alone, The.
Night and Night's longing.
Now the white violet blooms and narcissus that
loves.
O Gentle Ships.
Of Himself.
Of His Death.
Petals fall from Heliodora's image, The.
Pour and say again and again and yet again.
Pour for Heliodora Persuasion and pour for
Cypris.
Pour this wine.
Regions of Tyre are noted, The.
Sell it, though it sleeps still at its mother's
breast!
She's gone! Call Rape! Call Robbers!
Violence!
Shrilling cicada, drunk on drops of dew, you
sing.
Soul counsels flight.
Spring.
Still in his mother's lap the baby Love played.
Sweetly hath Dorcas of Lycaenis learnt.
Tears beneath the earth, Heliodora, I give.
'Tis Timarion.
To Aristogoras.
To Diodorus, Dorotheus, Callicrates et al.
Tread lightly, Stranger!
Upon a Maid That Died [*or* Dyed] the Day She
Was Married [*or* Married].
Volatile mosquito.
What have you got to crow about.
White violets flower.
Whose the hand unloosed Clearista's zone.
Within my heart Love himself made Heliodora.
Yes, I'd rather hear Heliodora's voice.
You're sleeping, Zenophila, my tender bloom. I
wish.

Meléndez, Jesús Papoleto
Oye Mundo/Sometimes.

Melhem, Diana Helen (b. 1926)
Boy in a Hospital.
Grandfather: Frailty Is Not the Story.
It was warm in Grandma's kitchen. Throughout
this, her second.
Lamentation After Jeremiah to Exorcise High
Rental / High Rise Building Scheduled for
Construction with Public Funds.
Person place thing tree.
Say french.
To an Ethiopian Child.
To write the country.

Melican, Terence
Limerick: "There was a young man of
Newcastle."

Melinescu, Gabriela (b. 1942)
Birth.
Time of Fish Dying.

Melinno (*fl.* **2nd cent. A.D.**)
Hail, Roma, daughter of Ares.

Mell, Max
Homeland.

Melly, George (b. 1926)
Homage to René Magritte.

Melnyczuk, Askold
Usual Immigrant Uncle Poem, The.

Melo, David Abenatar (b. 1550)
Thanksgiving.

Melo, Michael
Red Lipstick on a Straw.
Scrambled Eggs and Garlic Pork.
Unlearning English.

Melo Neto, João Cabral de (b. 1920)
Cemetery in Pernambuco.
Daily Space.
Education by Stone.
Emptiness of Man, The.
End of the World, The.
Knife All Blade, A.
Landscape of the Capibaribe River.
Sea and the Canefield, The.
Two of the Festivals of Death.
Weaving the Morning.

Meltzer, David (b. 1937)
17:II:82.
Eyes, the Blood, The.
Prayerwheel: 2.
Ragas.
Revelations.
Tell Them I'm Struggling to Sing with Angels.
Third Shell, The.
Tishah B'Ov / 1952.
What Do I Know of Journey.
Who's the Jew.

Melville, Elizabeth, Lady Culross (*fl.* c.1603)
Godly Dream, A.
I luikit up unto that Castell fair.
Sonnet sent to Blackness to Mr. John Welsch, by the Lady Culross, A.
Upon one day as I did mourn full sore.

Melville, Herman (1819–91)
Aeolian Harp, The.
After the Pleasure Party.
Afterward.
Ah! / These under-formings in the mind.
America.
Apparition—A Retrospect, The.
Arch, The.
Archipelago, The.
Art.
Attic Landscape, The.
Ball's Bluff.
Battle Summers, The.
Bench of Boors, The.
Berg, The.
Billy in the Darbies.
Blue-Bird, The.
By the Jordan.
Chipmunk, The.
College Colonel, The.
Coming Storm, The.
Commemorative of a Naval Victory.
Concerning Hebrews.
Conflict of Convictions, The.
Cypriote, The.
Dirge for McPherson, A.
Dirge: "Stay, Death. Not mine the Christus-wand."
Easter.
Enthusiast, The.
Enviable Isles, The.
Epilogue: "If Luther's day expand to Darwin's year."
Formerly a Slave.
Fragments of a Lost Gnostic Poem of the Twelfth [*or* 12th] Century.
Fruit and Flower Painter.
Greek Architecture.
Guide and Guard.
Haglets, The.
Herba Santa.
Hostel, The.
House-Top, The.
Immolated.
In a Bye-Canal.
In a Church of Padua.
In a Garret.
In Piranesi's rarer prints.
In the Desert.
In the Pauper's Turnip-Field.
In the Prison Pen.
Inscription: The: "While yet Rolfe's foot in stirrup stood."
Inscription: "To them who crossed the flood."

Iris.
Island, The.
Little Good Fellows, The.
Lover and the Syringa-Bush, The.
Maldive Shark, The.
Malvern Hill.
Man-of-War Hawk, The.
March into Virginia, The.
Martyr, The.
Medallion, The.
Memorial on the Slain at Chickamauga.
Misgivings.
Monody.
My Jacket Old.
New Ancient of Days, The.
Of Mortmain.
Of Rome.
Old Age in His Ailing.
On Mammon.
Parthenon, The.
Pebbles.
Pillow, The.
Pontoosuce.
Portent, The.
Ravaged Villa, The.
Recluse, The.
Requiem[:] for Soldiers Lost in Ocean Transports, A.
Return of the Sire de Nesle *A.D. 16*, The.
Ribs and Terrors, The.
Rolfe and the Palm.
Rosary Beads.
Rose Farmer, The.
Rose Window.
Rusty Man, The.
Shelley's Vision.
Sheridan at Cedar Creek.
Shiloh [A Requiem].
Since as in night's deck-watch ye show.
Song from *Mardi*.
Southern Cross.
Spirit Appeared to Me, A.
Stonewall Jackson.
Swamp Angel, The.
Symphonies.
Temeraire, The.
They felt how far beyond the scope.
Time's Betrayal.
Timoleon.
To.
To Ned.
Tom Deadlight.
Tuft of Kelp, The.
Ungar's Harangue.
Uninscribed Monument on One of the Battlefields of the Wilderness, An.
Utilitarian View of the Monitor's Fight, A.
Venice.
Via Crucis.
We Fish.

Menahem ben Jacob (d. 1203)
Harvesting of the Roses, The.
Martyr's Death, A.

Menahem ben Makhir of Ratisbon (*fl.* 11th cent.)
How Sweet Thy Precious Gift of Rest.

Menai, Huw (1887–1961)
Pieces of Coal.
Rooks: December.
To One Who Died in a Garret in Cardiff.
Where shall the eyes a darkness find.

Menander (342–290 B.C.)
On Epicurus and Themistokles.

Menashe, Samuel (b. 1925)
Annunciation, The.

Mendelssohn, Moses (1728–86)
Self-Portrait.

Mendès, Catulle (1841–1909)
I Go by Road.
Mother, The.

Mendes, Moses (d. 1758)
Chaplet, The.
On the Death of a Lady's Owl.

Mendes Zapata, Santiago
Story of the Eaters, A.

Meng Chiao (751–814)
After Passing the Examination.

Autumn finds me old and poorer.
Ballad of Ching Mountain.
Bones of the lonely-wretched spend no quiet nights.
Despair.
Don't let freezing hands play with these pearls.
Edges of the gorges hack up sun and moon, The.
Expressing My Feelings.
Failing the Examination.
In autumn moonlight the face turns icy.
In vain I gather up these stars from the ground.
It must have been a single thread of tears.
Lament for Lu Yin.
Nipping chill, the frost killed spring.
Old and sick, many strange broodings.
On Failing the Examination.
Owls mimic human speech.
Seeing Off Master Tan.
When I tread the earth, I fear to hurt the ground.
When my son was born, the moon was not bright.

Meng Hao Jan (689–740)
Crossing the Hsiang River at Night.
First of Autumn, The.
Lake of the Ten Thousand Mountains, The.
Night on the Great River.
On the Street of Lo-yang.
Parting from Wang Wei.
Passing Seven-League Rapids.
Passing the Night on a River in Chien-te.
Paying a Visit to Monk Yung's Cloister.
Returning by Night to Lu-Men.
Returning Late to Lu-men Shan.
Seeking Hsin E in the Western Hills.
Seeking out Master Chan on Incense Mountain.
Spending the Night at the Hillside Lodge of Master Yeh and Waiting for My Friend Ting.
Spring Dawn.
Spring Dreams.
Springtime Sleep.
Starting Early from Yü-p'u Deep.
Stayover at Chien-Teh River.
Stopping at a Friend's Farm.
Written for Old Friends in Yang-Jou City While Spending the Night on the Tung-Lu River.

Menicanti, Daria (b. 1914)
Biographical News.
Chameleon.
Epigram for a Worm.
Felines.
I Don't Know.
If.
Love Says.
Seagulls.
To the Readers Who Write to Me.
What's Left of You.

Menken, Adah Isaacs (1839?–1868)
Adelina Patti.
Answer Me.
Aspiration.
Autograph on the Soul, The.
Battle of the Stars.
Dreams of Beauty.
Drifts That Bar My Door.
Dying.
Fragment: "Cold chain of life presseth heavily on me tonight, The."
Genius.
Hear, O Israel!
Hemlock in the Furrows.
In Vain.
Infelix.
Into the Depths.
Judith.
Karazah to Karl.
Memory, A.
Miserimus.
My Heritage.
Myself.
One Year Ago.
Pro Patria.
Release, The.
Resurgam.

Sale of Souls.
Saved.
Ship That Went Down, The.
To&m3rdash;, Sleeping.
Venetia.
Where the Flocks Shall Be Led.
Working and Waiting.

Meogo, Pero (*fl.* **c.1250**)
Cantiga de Amigo.
Cossante.

Mercer, Johnny (1909–76)
Accentuate the Positive.
Arthur Murray Taught Me Dancing in a Hurry.
Blues in the Night.
Come Rain or Come Shine.
Day In—Day Out.
Early Autumn.
Glow-Worm, The.
Hooray for Hollywood.
How Little We Know.
I'm an Old Cowhand.
I'm Old-Fashioned.
I Remember You.
I Thought About You.
I Wonder What Became of Me.
Jeepers Creepers.
Jubilation T. Cornpone.
Laura.
Midnight Sun.
Moon River.
My Shining Hour.
On the Atchison, Topeka and the Santa Fe.
One for My Baby (And One More for the Road)
Out of This World.
P.S. I Love You.
Satin Doll.
Skylark.
Something's Gotta Give.
Tangerine.
That Old Black Magic.
Too Marvelous for Words.
You Must Have Been a Beautiful Baby.
You Were Never Lovelier.

Mercer, Thomas (*fl.* **c.1770**)
Where is the gallant race that rose.

Meredith, Christopher (b. 1954)
Christening Pot Boiler.
Jets.
Plasnewydd Square.

Meredith, George (1828–1909)
Ballad of Past Meridian, A.
Camelus Saltat.
Camelus Saltat: Continued.
Dirge in Woods.
Empty Purse, *sels.*
Flat as to an eagle's eye.
King Harald's Trance.
Love in the Valley.
Lucifer in Starlight.
Modern Love, *sels.*
Phoebus with Admetus.
Square along the couch, and stark.

Meredith, Louisa (1812–95)
Tasmanian Scenes.

"Meredith, Owen" (Edward Robert Bulwer-Lytton, 1st Earl of Lytton) (1831–91)
Going Back Again.
Last Wish, The.
Midges, *sels.*
Tears.
Vampyre, The, *sels.*
We may live without poetry, music and art.

Meredith, William (b. 1919)
American Living-room: A Tract, The.
Bachelor.
Country Stars.
Crossing Over.
Dying Away.
For Guillaume Apollinaire.
His Plans for Old Age.
Iambic Feet Considered as Honorable Scars.
Illiterate, The.
Jain Bird Hospital in Delhi, The.
John and Anne.
June: Dutch Harbor.

Last Things.
My Acts.
Myself, Rousseau, a Few Others.
Of Choice.
Of Love.
On Falling Asleep by Firelight.
Open Sea, The.
Partial Accounts.
Rhode Island.
Thoughts on One's Head.
To the Thoughtful Reader.
Traveling Boy.
Tree Marriage.
Two Masks Unearthed in Bulgaria.
Wholesome.
Winter Verse for His Sister.

Meredith, William Tuckey (b. 1839)
Farragut, Farragut.

Merezhkovsky [*or* **Merezhkovskii**], **Dmitry** [*or* **Dmitrii**] **Sergeievich (1866–1941)**
She Loves Me, She Loves Me Not.

Merini, Alda (b. 1931)
Ah If at Least I Could.
Bird of Fire, The.
Dies Merini.
Genesis.
Hymn: "If in my womb and mind You placed."
I Leave You These Imprints on the Earth.
I Open the Cigarette.
I Was Born on the Twenty-First in Spring.
Overcoat, The.
Song of Reply.

Merkureva, Vera (1876–1943)
Grandmother of Russian Poetry: A Self-Portrait, The.

Merriam, Eve (b. 1916)
Catch a Little Rhyme.
Counting-out Rhyme.
Coward, The.
Esther.
How to Eat a Poem.
Landscape.
Lazy Thought, A.
Lullaby "Purple."
Of Dogs and Ostriches.
One, Two, Three—Gough!
Restricted.
Sing a Song of Subways.
Spell of Weather, A.
Tube Time.
Wall, The.
Weather.
Which Washington?
Windshield Wiper.
Wonderful Whale, The.

Merriam, Lillie Fuller
At the Door.

Merrick, A. of Aylesbury
Hartwell Gardens.

Merrill, Bob (1920–98)
Don't Rain on My Parade.
Music That Makes Me Dance.
People.
Staying Young.

Merrill, Boynton, Jr. (b. 1925)
Fossil, The.
Mite, The.
Mule, The.

Merrill, Christopher
Boy Juggling a Soccer Ball, A.
Diver, The.
Erosion.

Merrill, James (1926–95)
About the Phoenix.
After Greece.
Annie Hill's Grave.
Between Us.
Book of Ephraim, *sels.*
Broken Home, The.
Changing Light at Sandover, The.
Charioteer of Delphi, The.
Charles on Fire.
Childlessness.
Clearing the Title.
Coda, the Higher Keys, *sels.*

Country of a Thousand Years of Peace, The.
David's Night in Veliès.
Days of 1941 and '44.
Days of 1964.
Foliage of Vision.
Furnished Room, The.
Geode, the troll's melon.
Grand Canyon, The.
In the Dark.
Kimono, The.
Kite Poem.
Laboratory Poem.
Last Words.
Losing the Marbles.
Mad Scene, The.
Maisie.
Manos Karastefanís.
Matinees.
Midnight Snack, The.
Mirabell: Books of Number, *sels.*
Mirror.
Octopus, The.
Parrot Fish, The.
Peacock, The.
Pier: Under Pisces, The.
Power Station, The.
Preface to the Memoirs, A.
Renewal, A.
Samos.
Scenes of Childhood.
Swimming By Night.
Syrinx.
Thistledown.
Tomorrows.
Up and Down.
Upward Look, An.
Urban Convalescence, An.
Victor Dog, The.
Voices from the Other World.
Watching the Dance.
Willowware Cup.
World and the Child, The.
Casual Wear.

Merrill, Stuart (1863–1915)
Ballade of the Chinese Lover.
Ballade of the Outcasts.

Merrill, William Pierson (1867–1954)
Not Alone for Mighty Empire.
Rise Up, O Men of God.

Merriman [*or* **Merryman**], **Brian** [*or* **Bryan**] **(1747–1805)**
Country's Crisis, The.
Husband's Lament, The.
Irish Marriage Night, An.
Lament of the Unmarried Girl, The.
Maiden's Plight, The.
Midnight Court, The.
Now God Stand Up for Bastards.
Old Man's Tale, The.
Solution, The.
Walk.

Merritt, Constance (b. 1966)
Lullaby: "Say to me: out there are only streets, and cars."
Mute Swan, The.
Woman of Color.

Merritt, Dixon Lanier (1879–1972)
Limerick: "Wonderful bird is the pelican, A."

Merry, Robert ("Della Crusca") (1755–98)
Adieu and Recall to Love, The.
Genius, or Muse, whate'er thou art! whose thrill.
Madness.
Sir Roland; a Fragment.
To Anna Matilda.

Merryman, Mildred Plew *See* **Meigs, Mildred Plew**

Merryweather, Anne (d. after 1702)
Prince who said an English Senate can, The.

Mersal, Iman
Solitude Exercises.

Mersar
Allace! So Sobir Is the Micht.

Merson, Billy (1881–1947)
Spaniard That Blighted My Life, The.

Merton, Thomas (1915–68)
Cana.
Elegy for the Monastery Barn.
Evening Prayer.
Lent in a Year of War.
Place Names.
Reader, The.
Responsory, 1948, A.
St. Malachy.
St. Paul.
There Has to Be a Jail for Ladies.
Merwin, W. S. (b. 1927)
Animals, The.
Another Year Come.
Approaches, The.
Asians Dying, The.
Avoiding News by the River.
Ballad of John Cable and Three Gentlemen.
Ballade of Sayings.
Bathers, The.
Berryman.
Birds Waking.
Black Jewel, The.
Black Plateau, The.
Bread.
Broken, The.
Burning the Cat.
Burnt Child, The.
Caesar.
Calling, A.
Carol of the Three Kings.
Carol: "On vague hills the prophet bird."
Daybreak.
Dead Hand.
Dictum: For a Masque of Deluge.
Diggers, The.
Distances, The.
Door, A.
Drunk in the Furnace, The.
Dusk in Winter.
Early January.
Elegy: "Who would I show it to."
Encampment at Morning, An.
Evening.
Exercise.
Feast Day.
February.
Fields, The.
Finding a Teacher.
Fly.
Footprints on the Glacier.
For a Coming Extinction.
For the Anniversary of My Death.
Gardens of Zuñi, The.
Glass.
Glassy Sea.
Grandmother Watching at Her Window.
Hearing.
Home for Thanksgiving.
In the Winter of My Thirty-eighth Year.
Initiate, The.
Judgment of Paris, The.
Last One, The.
Letter.
Leviathan.
Looking for Mushrooms at Sunrise.
Losing a Language.
Low Fields and Light.
Marfa Lights, The.
Migrants by Night.
Moths, The.
Mountain, The.
Native, The.
Night of the Shirts, The.
Noah's Raven.
Odysseus.
Old Boast, The.
On the Subject of Poetry.
Piper, The.
Plea for a Captive.
"Prodigal Son," The.
Rain Travel.
River of Bees, The.
Room, The.
Second Psalm: The Signals.
Separation.
Sire.

Small Woman on Swallow Street.
Snowfall.
Some Last Questions.
Song of Man Chipping an Arrowhead.
Song of Three Smiles.
St. Vincent's.
Strawberries.
Surf-casting.
Things.
Thorn Leaves in March.
Tide Line Garden.
To My Brother Hanson.
To the Hand.
Utterance.
Vineyard, The.
Voice.
Way to the River, The.
West Wall.
Wheels of the Trains, The.
When I Came from Colchis.
When the War Is Over.
When You Go Away.
Widow, The.
Witnesses.
Yesterday.
Mesens, E. L. T.
Arid Husband, The.
Mesmer, Sharon
Lonely Tylenol.
My Life in Yonago.
What Becomes Us.
Messerli, Douglas (b. 1947)
Actually Swallowed.
Angry with China.
Annunciation, The.
Closure.
Essay on Concrete, An.
From Hear to Air.
Going to Sea.
Harrowing.
Scared Cows.
Suddenly someone wakes me. Still half-asleep,
    I see standing in front.
This That and Then.
Metastasio, Pietro (1698–1782)
Age of Gold.
On thy grey bark, in witness of my flame.
Metcalf, Richard
These Are Not Lost.
Metcalfe, James J.
Visit the Sick.
Metras, Gary
Anniversary.
Vanishing Point.
Mew, Charlotte (1870–1928)
À Quoi Bon Dire.
Absence.
Again.
At the Convent Gate.
Beside the Bed.
Cenotaph, The.
Fame.
Farmer's Bride, The.
"Find rest in Him!" One knows the parsons'
    tags.
Forest Road, The.
Here Lies a Prisoner.
How old was Mary out of whom you cast.
I Have Been Through the Gates.
I So Liked Spring.
In Nunhead Cemetery.
In the Fields.
June, 1915.
Ken.
Madeleine in Church.
My Heart is Lame.
Ne Me Tangito.
Not for That City.
Old Shepherd's Prayer.
On the Asylum Road.
On the Road to the Sea.
Pedlar, The.
Quiet House, The.
Rambling Sailor, The.
Rooms.
Saturday Market.

Sea Love.
Smile, Death.
Song: "Love, love today, my dear."
To a Child in Death.
Trees Are Down, The.
Mey, Mildred T.
Quiet Days.
Meyer, George W.
Everything Is Peaches Down in Georgia.
For Me and My Gal.
Meyer, Joseph
California, Here I Come.
Crazy Rhythm.
Cup of Coffee, a Sandwich, and You.
If You Knew Susie (Like I Know Susie)
Meyers, Bert (1928–79)
Daybreak.
Pigeons.
Suburban Dusk.
**Meynell, Alice Thompson (Mrs. Wilfrid Meynell)
(1847–1922)**
After a Parting.
At Night.
Beyond Knowledge.
Chimes.
Christ in the Universe.
Cradle-Song at Twilight.
Crucifixion, The.
Easter Night.
Father of Women, A [Ad Sororem E. B.].
Roaring Frost, The.
Fugitive, The.
General Communion, A.
Girl on the Land, The.
"I Am the Way."
In Portugal, 1912.
In Sleep.
Lady Poverty, The.
Launch, The.
Letter from a Girl to Her Own Old Age, A.
Maternity.
Messina, 1908.
Modern Mother, The.
November Blue.
October Redbreast, The.
Parentage.
Parted.
Rainy Summer, The.
Renouncement.
Shepherdess, The.
Singers to Come.
Song of Derivations, A.
Study, A.
Summer in England, 1914.
Sunderland Children, The.
Thoughts in Separation.
Threshing Machine, The.
Thrush before Dawn, A.
To a Daisy.
To Conscripts.
To "A Certain Rich Man."
To Silence.
To the Beloved.
To the Body.
Two Questions, The.
Unto Us a Son Is Given.
Veni Creator.
Watershed, The.
Wind Is Blind, The.
Meynell, Viola (1886–1956)
Sympathy.
Meyrelles, Isabel (b. 1929)
I Will Tell You During the Walk.
Night Words.
Once again.
To forget.
Tyger, Tyger.
Mezey, Robert (b. 1935)
At the Point.
Evening, An.
Evening Wind.
From a thousand Chinese dinners, one cookie.
How Much Longer?
My Mother.
Owl.
Reaching the Horizon.

Silence, The.
To Levine on the Day of Atonement.
Touch It.
Twilight Under Pine Ridge.
Wandering Jew, The.
Mezhirov, Aleksandr Petrovich (b. 1923)
Ballad about the Circus.
Farewell to Arms, A.
From the War.
I can usually feel at home in rooms.
Ice of Ladoga, The.
Lines about a Little Boy.
Loneliness chases me.
Man lives in the wide world, A.
Troop Train.
We are huddled in a crowd before Kolpino.
We would awaken in a twilight gloom.
Mhac an tSaoi, Máire (b. 1922)
Lament.
Mary Hogan's Quatrains.
Mhlongo, Swidi-Nonkamfela (b. 1948)
His Praises.
Mhlophe, Gcina (b. 1958)
Sometimes When It Rains.
Miadesnia
Postscript to Orwell's *Animal Farm*, A.
Mibu no Tadami (*fl.* 10th cent.)
Since I left her.
Yes, I am in love.
Miccolis, Leila (b. 1947)
I wanted to see you, / thighs showing.
Till Death Do Us Part.
Michael of Kildare, Friar (*fl.* 14th cent.)
Swet Jesus.
Michaelis, Hanny (b. 1922)
Brilliantly Philosophising.
I Was About Three Years of Age.
Michaux, Henri (1899–1984)
He who knows how to shave the razor, will
   know how to erase the.
One evening an exceptionally abstract
   communication came over the airwaves.
Michelangelo Buonarroti (1474–1564)
Celestial Love.
Dante.
Doom of Beauty, The.
Flee, lovers, from Love, flee from his fire.
From sweet weeping to a painful smile.
Garland and the Girdle, The.
I live in sin, and dying to myself I live.
I see in your beautiful face, my lord.
It was over here that my love, in his mercy.
Joy May Kill.
Like dry wood in a burning fire.
Love's Entreaty.
Love's Justification.
Love, the Light-Giver [*or* To Tommaso de'
   Cavalieri].
"Night" in the Medici Chapel.
On the Brink of Death.
Prayer for Purification, A.
Soul tries a thousand remedies in vain, The.
Three Poems.
To Vittoria Colonna.
Transfiguration of Beauty, The.
Very dear though it was I have bought you.
Violent burning for prodigious beauty, A.
Why should I still pour out my intense desire.
You know that I know, my lord, that you
   know.
Michelson, Joan
Rings.
Michelson, Max
Bird, The.
Hymn to Night, A.
Michelson, Peter
Enduring Witness, the Mosques of Kattankudi.
Michelson, Richard
Faraway Landscape.
Genuine Jewish Flesh.
Interrogation.
Jews That We Are, The.
Queen Esther Award, The.
Where I Sat.
Michie, James (b. 1927)
Arizona Nature Myth.

Discoverer.
Dooley Is a Traitor.
Nine Times.
To My Daughter.
Michie, Susan
Connecting Light.
Michikaze (d. 1709)
Today I put on summer.
Michitsuna, the Mother of (*fl.* late 10th cent.)
Have you any idea.
Mickiewicz, Adam (1798–1855)
Ackermann Steppe, The.
Storm, The.
Year 1812, The.
Mickle, William Julius (1735–88)
Cumnor Hall.
Sailor's Wife, The.
Middleton, Christopher (b. 1926)
Adelaide's Dream.
Anasphere: Le torse antique.
Edward Lear in February.
In Some Seer's Cloud Car.
In the Secret House.
News from Norwood.
Oystercatchers.
Saloon with Birds.
Middleton, Richard (1882–1911)
Carol of the Poor Children, The.
Middleton, Thomas (1580–1627)
Melancholy.
Song: "In a maiden-time professed."
Midge, Tiffany
Written in Blood.
Miedzyrzecki, Artur (b. 1922)
At the Cave.
At Work.
Can You Imagine.
End of the Game.
Golden Age, The.
Penguins.
29-77-02.
What Does the Political Scientist Know?
Mif
Terezin.
Migliore, Maestro (*fl.* 1250)
Love taking leave, my heart then leaveth me.
Mignon, Auguste
One Heart's Enough for Me.
Mihalic, Slavko (b. 1928)
Atlantis.
Drinking Spree Beneath the Open Sky.
Elegy: "From the old settlements only the
   writings."
Exile's Return, The.
I Cannot Say the Name of the City.
Large Grieving Women.
Morning Roar of the City, The.
On the Carpet, Staring at Myself.
Screams in the Dark.
Second-Class Citizen.
Under the Microscope.
Miidhu
War Dance.
**Mikata Shami [*or* Mikata no Sami] (*fl.* late 7th
cent.)**
Bound up it always.
Mikata, Yamada *See* **Mikata Shami [*or* Mikata
no Sami]**
Mikes, Margit (1897–1976)
Glassworks.
Identity.
Poet in the Kitchen.
To My Daughter.
Mikhail, Dunya (b. 1965)
Chaldean Ruins, The.
Dawn Fairy, The.
Rain.
Milan, Jyotsna (b. 1941)
Woman, 2.
Miles, Dick
Coffee Song (They've Got an Awful Lot of
   Coffee in Brazil), The.
Miles, Josephine (1911–85)
After noon I lie down.

Album.
All Hallow.
As Difference Blends into Identity.
Belief.
Bibliographer.
Bounty.
Bureau 2.
Campaign, The.
Civilian.
Conception.
Concert.
Day the Winds, The.
Dear Frank, Here is a poem.
Doctor Who Sits at the Bedside of a Rat, The.
Doll.
Dolor.
Entrepreneur chicken shed his tail feathers,
   surplus, The.
Family.
Fields of Learning.
Find.
Forecast.
Gypsy.
Housewife.
In the town where every man is king.
Made Shine.
Merchant Marine.
Officers.
None.
Oedipus.
On Inhabiting an Orange.
Parent.
Preliminary to Classroom Lecture.
Reason.
Ride.
Sale.
So Graven.
Summer.
Tally.
Travelers.
Why We Are Late.
Miles, Susan (Ursula Roberts) (b. 1887)
Hares, The.
Microcosmos.
Plumbers.
Miliauskaite, Nijole (b. 1950)
In the Damp Places.
On Winter Nights.
Temporary City.
These are Lilacs.
Miljkovic, Branko (1934–60)
Agon.
Miners.
Sea Without Poets.
Sleepers.
Millar, Joseph
Midlife.
**Millay, Edna St. Vincent (Nancy Boyd) (1892–
1950)**
Afternoon on a Hill.
All I could see from where I stood.
Ancient Gesture, An.
And you as well must die, belovèd dust.
Apostrophe to Man.
Armenonville.
Bean-Stalk, The.
Bluebeard.
Buck in the Snow, The.
Cameo, The.
Childhood Is the Kingdom Where Nobody
   Dies.
Conscientious Objector.
Counting-out Rhyme.
Courage that my mother had, The.
Departure.
Dirge Without Music.
Eel-Grass.
Elegy: "Let them bury your big eyes."
"Euclid Alone Has Looked on Beauty Bare."
Even in the moment of our earliest kiss.
Evening on Lesbos.
Exiled.
First Fig.
Fitting, The.
From a Train Window.
From a Very Little Sphinx.

God's World.
Grow not too high, grow not too far from home.
Grown-up.
Hearing Your Words, and Not a Word Among Them.
Here lies, and none to mourn him but the sea.
I, Being Born a Woman.
I do but ask that you be always fair.
I Dreamed I Moved among the Elysian Fields.
I Forgot for a Moment.
I know I am but summer to your heart.
I shall forget you presently, my dear.
I shall go back.
I think I should have loved you presently.
I too beneath your moon, almighty Sex.
I will put Chaos into fourteen lines.
If I should learn, in some quite casual way.
If in the years to come you should recall.
In the Grave No Flower.
Inland.
It is the fashion now to wave aside.
Justice Denied in Massachusetts.
Love Is Not All.
"Love is not all: it is not meat nor drink."
Love me no more, now let the god depart.
Loving you less than life, a little less.
Make Bright the Arrows.
Menses.
My most distinguished guest and learnèd friend.
Never May the Fruit Be Plucked.
Night is my sister, and how deep in love.
Not in a silver casket cool with pearls.
O Earth, unhappy planet born to die.
O God, I Cried, No Dark Disguise.
O, loveliest throat of all sweet throats.
Oh, Oh, you will be sorry for that word!
"Oh, sleep forever in the Latmian cave."
On Hearing a Symphony of Beethoven.
On the Wide Heath.
Only until this cigarette is ended.
Passer Mortuus Est.
Pear Tree, The.
Pity me not because the light of day.
Poet and His Book, The.
Portrait by a Neighbour.
Ragged Island.
Recuerdo.
Renascence.
Rendezvous.
Return, The.
Scrub.
Second Fig.
See where Capella with her golden kids.
Siege.
Since of no creature living the last breath.
Snow Storm, The.
So she came back into his house again.
Song of a Second April.
Sonnet 17.
Sonnet: "Oh, my belovèd, have you thought of this."
Sonnet to Gath.
Sonnet: "What lips my lips have kissed, and where, and why."
Sonnets from an Ungrafted Tree.
Sorrow.
Spring.
Strawberry Shrub, The.
Think not, nor for a moment let your mind.
Time does not bring relief; you all have lied.
To a Calvinist in Bali.
To a Young Poet.
To Inez Milholland.
To Jesus on His Birthday.
Travel.
True Encounter, The.
What Rider Spurs Him from the Darkening East.
When I too long have looked upon your face.
When we are old and these rejoicing veins.
When you, that at this moment are to me.
Wild Swans.
Winter Night.
Witch-Wife.
Women have loved before as I love now.

Wood Road, The.
You loved me not at all, but let it go.
Miller, Adam David (b. 1922)
Africa Thing, The.
Hungry Black Child, The.
Mulch.
Pruning, The.
Miller, Arthur
Lola's Lament.
Miller, Carolyn
Night in San Francisco.
Miller, Cincinnatus Heine [or Hiner] See Miller, Joaquin
Miller, E. Ethelbert (b. 1950)
Another Love Affair/Another Poem.
Boys of Summer, The.
Jasmine.
Mississippi.
My Father's Girlfriend.
Night Before the First Day of School, The.
Players.
Rebecca.
She is Flat on Her Back.
Tomorrow.
What the Women Told Me.
You Send Me: Bertha Franklin, December 11, 1964.
Miller, E. S. (b. 1904)
To My Lady.
Miller, Jane (b. 1925)
American Odalisque.
Any Two Wheels.
August Zero.
Foundered Star.
Giants.
Impossible, The.
O Pioneers!
Poetry.
Sonnet Against Nuclear Weapons.
Topos.
Which Religion Vouchsafes.
Miller, Jeannette (b. 1944)
Bird dressed as solitude and tears.
Crazed Woman, The.
Four times during the night.
I remember the long corridors.
Rise of the Afternoon is a Wide Glory, The.
These Green Paths.
This sense of space.
Woman I Know, The.
Miller, Joaquin (Cincinnatus Heine [or Hiner] Miller) (1841–1913)
Africa.
At Our Golden Gate.
Bravest battle that ever was fought, The.
Columbus.
For Those Who Fail.
In Père La Chaise.
Sierras.
Miller, Mary Britton (1883–1975)
Cat.
Miller, May (b. 1918)
Closing, A.
Gift from Kenya.
Not That Far.
Miller, Patricia Cleary
Molly O'Rourke Cleary Explains.
Miller, Peter (b. 1920)
Capture of Edwin Alonzo Boyd, The.
Prevention of Stacy Miller, The.
Miller, Philip L.
Peeling Potatoes.
Miller, Russell
Limerick: "If you dream, said the eminent Freud."
Miller, Ruth (b. 1919)
Aspects of Love.
Mantis.
Sterkfontein.
Miller, Thomas (1807–74)
Evening.
Miller, Vassar (b. 1924)
Beat Poem by an Academic Poet.
Bird in the Hand, A.

Bout with Burning.
Christmas Mourning.
Defense Rests.
Dirge in Jazz Time.
How Far?
Judas.
Light Reading.
Quarry, The.
Slump.
Spinster's Lullaby.
Without Ceremony.
Miller, William (1810–72)
Willie Winkie.
Milligan, James (fl. 1800)
In ages past [animals] lived and died.
Milligan, Spike (b. 1918)
Bad Report—Good Manners.
Christmas 1970.
Limerick: "Man who was asked out to dinner, A."
My Sister Laura.
Teeth.
Thousand Hairy Savages, A.
Millikin, Richard Alfred (1764–1815)
Groves of Blarney, The.
Million, Dian
Housing Poem, The.
Millis, Christopher
IRT at Rush Hour, The.
Mills, Billy (b. 1954)
Ballad: Of Motion.
Mills, David S. (b. 1965)
And Now Yu.
Chembank Card.
Mills, Irving
Minnie, the Moocher.
Prelude to a Kiss.
Solitude.
Sophisticated Lady.
Mills, Ralph J., Jr.
Evening Song.
For Lorine Niedecker in Heaven.
Water Lilies.
Mills, William G.
Arise, O Glorious Zion.
Milman, Henry Hart
Crucifixion, The.
For thou didst die for me, O Son of God!
Holy Field, The.
Hymn: "When our heads are bowed with woe."
O help us, Lord! Each hour of need.
Where the Wicked Cease from Troubling, and the Weary Are at Rest.
Milne, Alan Alexander (1882–1956)
Bad Sir Brian Botany.
Disobedience.
Happiness.
Hoppity.
Hush! Hush! Whisper who dares!
King's Breakfast, The.
More It Snows, The.
Milne, Ewart (b. 1903)
Diamond Cut Diamond.
Martyred Earth, The.
Vanessa Vanessa.
Milner-Brown, A. L.
Who Knows?
Milnes, Richard Monckton, 1st Baron Houghton (1809–85)
England and America, 1863.
Lady Moon.
Men of Old, The.
Sir Walter Scott at the Tomb of the Stuarts in St. Peter's.
Youth, That Pursuest.
Milosz, Czeslaw (b. 1911)
Abundant Catch (Luke 5:4–10)
And Yet the Books.
Bypassing Rue Descartes.
Cafe.
Campo dei Fiori.
Child of Europe.
"Christ has risen." Whoever believes that / Should not behave as we do.
Dedication: "You whom I could not save."

Elegy for N. N.
Encounter.
Esse.
Faith.
Felicitous Life, A.
Goddess, A.
House in Krasnogruda.
In Szetejnie.
Incantation.
Luke 5:1–11; While the people pressed upon him.
Mark 5:21–43; And when Jesus had crossed.
Matthew 4:1–11; Then Jesus was led up by the spirit.
Matthew 28:1–6; Now after the sabbath.
My Faithful Mother Tongue.
On Angels.
On Pilgrimage.
On the Other Side.
Poor Christian Looks at the Ghetto, A.
Preparation.
Proof.
Reading the Japanese Poet Issa: (1762–1826)
Readings.
Report.
Song on the End of the World, A.
Sun, The.
Task, A.
Temptation.
Tidings.
To Raja Rao.
Who?
With Her.

Milosz, O. V. de L. (1877–1939)
Bridge, The.
King Don Luis.
La Berline Arrêtée Dans la Nuit.

Milton, John (1608–74)
Comus; a Masque Presented at Ludlow Castle, *sels.*
Il Penseroso.
L'Allegro.
Lament for Damon.
Lycidas, *sels.*
On His Blindness.
On His Deceased Wife.
On Shakespear[e].
On the Detraction Which Followed upon My Writing Certain Treatises.
On the Late Massacre [*or* Massacher] in Piedmont [*or* Piemont].
On the Lord Gen[eral] Fairfax at the Siege of Colchester.
On the Morning of Christ's Nativity, *sels.*
On the New Forcers of Conscience Under the Long Parliament.
On the University Carrier Who Sick'n'd [*or* Sickened] in the Time of His Vacancy [, Being Forbid to go to London, by Reason of the Plague].
On Time.
Paradise Lost, *sels.*
Paradise Regained, *sels.*
Sabrina Fair.
Samson Agonistes, *sels.*
Song: "Nymphs and Shepherds dance no more."
Song: "O're [*or* O'er] the smooth enamel'd [*or* enameled *or* enamelled] green."
Sonnet 9: "Ladie [*or* Lady], that in the prime of earliest youth."
Sonnet: On the Religious Memorie of Mrs. Catherine Thomason My Christian Freind Deceas'd Decem. 1646.
Spring Song.
Spring Time.
To Charles Diodati.
To Cyriack Skinner.
To Mr. Cyriack Skinner upon His Blindness.
To Mr. H. Lawes on His Airs.
To Mr. Lawrence.
To Sir Henry Vane the Younger.
To the Lady Margaret Ley.
To the Lord General Cromwell.
Upon the Circumcision.
When the Assault Was Intended to the City.

Mimnermus (c.650–c.590 B.C.)
Youth and Age.

Min, Neeltje Maria (b. 1944)
Deep in the Pit.
My Mother Has Forgotten My Name.

Minamoto no Morotada (*fl.* 12th cent.)
In the mountain village.

Minamoto no Tōru (d. 949)
Like Michinoku.

Minamoto no Tsunenobu (*fl.* late 11th cent.)
In the evening / The rice leaves in the garden.

Ming, T'ao T'ung *See* T'ao Hung Ching

Minhinnick, Robert (b. 1952)
Aerial, The.
After a Friendship.
Boathouse, The.
Catching My Breath.
Children, The.
Drinking Art, The.
Grandfather in the Garden.
House, The.
Looters, The.
Sap.
She Drove a 'Seventies Plymouth.
Sunday Morning.
Surfers.
Twenty-Five Laments for Iraq.

Minnigerode, Meade (*fl.* 1911)
Whiffenpoof Song.

Minot, George
Down.

Minot, Susan
Devotion.

"Minsky, Nicolai Maksimovich" (Nicolai Maksimovich Vilenkin)
Immortality.

Minteisengan (d. 1844)
Fall, plum petals.

Minuchihri (d. 1041?)
Demon in Paradise.
I Send You My Verses.
Recantation.

Mir, M. Safdar
Elegy: "In the May breeze."

Mirabai [*or* Mira Bai] (1498–1547)
All I Was Doing Was Breathing.
At the Holi festival of color.
Clouds, The.
Dark One, / all I request is a portion of love.
Dark one, / how can I sleep?
Don't block my way, friend.
Friend, don't be angry.
Friend, how can I meet my lord?
Glimpse of your body, A.
Hari helps his people.
Hari, look at me a while.
Having wet me with love.
Heat of Midnight Tears, The.
I can't break with the Dark One.
I don't sleep. All night.
I was going to the river for water.
It's True I Went to the Market.
Let me see you.
Mira is dancing with bells tied on her ankles.
My eyes are thirsty.
My love is in my house.
O friend, understand: the body.
O friends, I am mad.
O friends on this Path.
O King, I know you gave me poison.
O my friends.
Rana, I know you gave me poison.
Rana, why do you treat me as your enemy?
Song of the flute, O sister, is madness, The.
Wake, child with the flute.
Wake up, dear boy that holds the flute!
Why Mira Can't Go Back to Her Old House.
Wild woman of the forests, The.
Yogi, don't go away.

Miri, Angela (b. 1959)
Do Not Stop Me!

Mirikitani, Janice
Doreen.
Fisherman, The.
Shadow in Stone.
Sing with Your Body.
Soul Food.

Suicide Note.

Mirsal, Iman (b. 1966)
Abortion.
Confessions.
I Usually Look Around Me.

Mishler, Richard M.
Ceremony.

Mishol, Agi (b. 1947)
Estate.
Gravity, Death.
Sacred Cow of Hardship, The.
Shopping.

Mishra, Soubhagya Kumar (b. 1941)
Robinson Crusoe.

Miss Queenie *See* Kennedy, Imogene Elizabeth

Mistral, Frédéric (1830–1914)
Leaf-picking, The.
Mares of the Camargue, The.

Mistral, Gabriela (Lucila Godoy Alcayaga) (1889–1957)
Absence.
Autumn.
Ballad: "He was strolling with another woman."
Ballad: "He went by with another."
Bread.
Caribbean Sea.
Close to Me.
Dawn.
Death Sonnet I.
Decalogue of the Artist.
Drops of Gall.
Dusk.
Earthen Jugs.
Empty Walnut, The.
Final Tree.
Flower of Air, The.
House, The.
I Love, Love.
Intimate.
Liana, The.
Like those jars that women put out to catch the dew of night.
Little Box From Olinalá.
Martha and Mary.
Midnight.
Morning.
My Mother.
Night.
One Word.
Pious One, The.
Rocking.
Rose, The.
Serene Words.
Sister.
Song.
Stranger, The.
Those Who Do Not Dance.
To the Children.
Woman, A.

Mitcalfe, Barry (b. 1930)
Lamentation on Ninety-Mile Beach.

Mitcham, Judson
On the Otis Redding Bridge.

Mitchell, Adrian (b. 1937)
Autobahnmotorwayautoroute.
Beggar, The.
Celia Celia.
Dumb Insolence.
Fifteen Million Plastic Bags.
From Rich Uneasy America to My Friend Christopher Logue.
Giving Potatoes.
Goodbye.
Icarus Schmicarus.
Nature Poem.
Not a Very Cheerful Song, I'm Afraid.
Nothingmas Day.
Oxford Hysteria of English Poetry, The.
Private Transport.
Quite Apart from the Holy Ghost.
Remember Suez?
Riddle: "Their tongues are knives, their forks are hands and feet."
Speck Speaks, A.
To Whom It May Concern.

Watch Your Step—I'm Drenched.
Mitchell, Cyprus R.
Soul of Jesus Is Restless, The.
Mitchell, David (b. 1940)
At Pakiri Beach.
My Lai / Remuera / Ponsonby.
Silences.
Van Gogh.
Mitchell, Elma (b. 1919)
I wear bright colours.
Mother, Dear Mother.
Passenger Opposite, The.
Thoughts after Ruskin.
Mitchell, Frank (b. 1912)
13th Horse Song of Frank Mitchell (White), The.
12th Horse Song of Frank Mitchell (Blue), The.
Mitchell, Jonathan (1624–68)
On the Following Work and Its Author.
Mitchell, Karen L. (b. 1955)
Monster, The.
Night Rain.
On the Anniversary Of Your Death.
Tree Stillness.
Mitchell, Larry (b. 1938)
Faggots and their friends now live in Ramrod, The.
Men love papers, The. They love to sign them, file them and.
Men spread disease among the faggots, one of the things they, The.
Sons and Fathers.
Women Wisdom.
Mitchell, Lorna
Hermaphrodite's Song, The.
Mitchell, Lucy Sprague (1878–1967)
House of the Mouse, The.
Mitchell, Matthew (b. 1928)
Printing Jenny.
Mitchell, Mrs. James Herbert *See* **Strobel, Marion**
Mitchell, Roger
It.
North.
Out Here.
Mitchell, Sam
Thunderstorm.
Mitchell, Stephen (b. 1943)
Annunciation, The.
Good Samaritan et Al, The.
Luke 10:25–37; And behold, a lawyer.
Matthew 13:1–9; That same day Jesus.
Parable of the Sower, The.
Vermeer.
Mitchell, Susan (b. 1944)
Golden Bough: The Feather Palm.
Grove at Nemi, The.
Smoke.
Mitchell, Susanna Valentine
Of Earthly Love.
Mitchison, Naomi (b. 1897)
My True Love Hath My Heart.
Mitford, Mary Russell (1787–1855)
Forget-Me-Not, The.
On a Beautiful Woman.
Song: "Fairest things are those which live, The."
Written in a Blank-Paper Book Given to the Author by a Friend.
Mitoku (d. 1669)
Foam on the last water, The.
Mitsuhashi, Takajo (1899–1972)
Hair ornament of the sun, The.
Mitsui, James Masao (b. 1940)
At Bon Odori.
Because of My Father's Job.
Destination: Tule Lake Relocation Center, May 20, 1942.
Katori Maru, October 1920.
Nisei: Second Generation Japanese-American.
Photograph of a Child, Japanese-American Evacuation, Bainbridge Island, Washington, March 30, 1942.

Picture of a Japanese Farmer, Woodland, California, May 20, 1942.
Mitsune (Oshikochi no Mitsune) (*fl.* c.900)
Ceaseless snow.
Mitsune, Oshikochi no *See* **Mitsune**
Mitterer, Erika (b. 1906)
City Park.
To Austria.
Miu Hsi (186–245)
Bearer's Song.
Poem in the Form of a Coffin-Puller's Song.
Miyazawa Kenji (1896–1933)
Daydreaming on the Trail.
Pictures of the Floating World.
Snow on Saddle Mountain, The.
Spring and the Ashura.
Miyoshi Toyoichiro
Shadow 1.
Mkangelwa, Luvuyo (b. 1977)
Observations.
Women Sing, The.
Mnasalces (*fl.* 3rd cent. B.C.)
Aristocrateia, / You've crossed the dark stream.
Broad-acred Ascra bore me.
I, wretched Virtue, sit.
My fighting days are done.
No longer, cricket, sitting.
Promachus hangs here.
Say, stranger, that this is the tomb of the mare Aethyia.
Setting their country free.
Mnookin, Wendy
Signs.
Mnotoza, Zim (b. 1961)
Still There's No Trace.
Mnthali, Felix (b. 1933)
Celebration, The.
My Father.
Neocolonialism.
Sizeline.
Stranglehold of English Lit, The.
To the Writers' Worship in Zomba.
Mó, Alonzo Gonzales
Conversations in Mayan.
How Just One Poor Man Lives.
Things That Happen to You.
Wizards.
Mo Shih-lung (c.1539–1587)
Drinking Wine.
Flower Shadows.
Friend Comes to Visit on a Summer Night, A.
Gathering Lotus with Singing Girls.
I Waited for Chuang Hsüan-yüan but He Never Came.
I Went to Gold Mountain to Visit a Ch'an Master but He Was Not at Home.
Meditation Rock, The.
On a Cold Day I Climbed Tiger Hill With Professor Ho. At the Time, the Local Prefect Had Prohibited Pleasure Excursions and Feasts, but the Mountain Was Quiet and Tranquil, So We Stayed All Day.
Saying Good-bye to a Singing Girl Who Has Decided to Become a Nun.
Saying Good-Bye to Feng the Hermit.
Staying Overnight at Blue Cloud Temple.
To the Monk Wu-hsia on the Occasion of His Editing the Lotus Sutra.
Moan
Clear, clear—clearest!
Moat, John
Twilight by the plantation.
Mocoancoeng, J. G.
Drought.
Modena, Leone da (1571–1648)
Epitaph: "Implacable angel / Has shot his dart, The."
Modisane, Bloke (1923–86)
Black Blues.
Blue Black.
Lonely.
Moerman, Ernst (*fl.* 20th cent.)
Louis Armstrong.
Moffett, Judith (b. 1942)
Now or Never.

Moffi, Larry
Putting an End to the War Stories.
Mohammad, Hala (b. 1959)
At the Door of Anticipation.
Love Burned Out the Light.
Man Who Offers Me His Chest, The.
What Am I Chasing!
Mohodahi (*fl.* between c.700 and c.1050)
On the holy day of your going out to war.
Mohr, Joseph (1792–1848)
Christmas Song.
Silent Night.
Silent Night! Holy Night!
Moir, Lyn (b. 1934)
Handnotes.
Moiro
Beneath Aphrodite's golden portico you now lie.
Great Zeus was reared in Krete and no one.
Hail, forest nymphs, daughters of the river.
Now you lie—a grape-offering.
Tree nymphs, daughters of River, ambrosial.
Moise, Penina (1797–1880) and Edward N. Calisch
God Supreme! To Thee We Pray.
Newspaper, The.
To Persecuted Foreigners.
Mok, Judith (b. 1958)
Winter Mirror.
Winter Mirror II.
Mokudo (d. 1788)
I constantly aspire.
Mokusen (1847–1920)
On Climbing the Mountain Where Buddha Trained.
Mokusetsu (*fl.* 17th cent.)
Long summer rains / Barley's tasteless.
Moldaw, Carol (b. 1956)
Nest, The.
Mole, John
Jack-in-the-Box.
Mine is the ungloved.
Musical Monkey, The.
Song of the Hat-Raising Doll.
Taking the Plunge.
Trick, The.
Mole, Lyndon T.
Limerick: "Texan Rhodes Scholar named Fred, A."
Molière (Jean Baptiste Poquelin) (1622–73)
To Monsieur de la Mothe le Vayer.
Molina, Enrique (b. 1910)
As the Great Days Flow.
To Vahine (Painted by Gaugin)
Way It Must Be, The.
Molina, Paz (b. 1945)
Events Like Palaces.
Scream Is a Kind of Coffin, The.
Things of the Blind.
Your Anger.
Molinari, Ricardo (b. 1898)
Little Ode to Melancholy.
Ode to a Long Sorrow.
Poem of the Girl from Velázquez.
Moll, Billy
Wrap Your Troubles in Dreams.
Moll, Ernest G. (b. 1900)
Beware the Cuckoo.
Bush Speaks, The.
Clearing for the Plough.
Mollineux, Mary (1651–95)
Another Letter to a Friend.
Even what the hungry Wolf in Field would do.
Lord of them that hurt his Saints, doth say, The.
Meditations on Persecution.
Solitude.
Molodovsky [*or* Molodowsky], Kadya (1894–1975)
God of Mercy.
Prayers: I.
Song of the Sabbath.
Molony, Linda (b. 1960)
Cat Washing.

Momaday, N. Scott (b. 1934)
Angle of Geese.
Bear, The.
Burning, The.
But Then and There the Sun Bore Down.
Carriers of the Dream Wheel.
Delight Song of Tsoai-Talee, The.
Eagle-Feather Fan, The.
Earth and I Gave You Turquoise.
Forms of the Earth at Abiquiu.
Four Notions of Love and Marriage.
Gift, The.
Gourd Dancer, The.
Headwaters.
North Dakota, North Light.
Pit Viper.
Plainview: 3.
Rainy Mountain Cemetery.
Simile.
Story of a Well-made Shield, The.
To a Child Running with Outstretched Arms in
    Canyon de Chelly.
Trees and Evening Sky.
Two Figures.
Walk on the Moon.
Wide Empty Landscape with a Death in the
    Foreground.
Winter Holding off the Coast of North
    America.
Mombert, Alfred (b. 1872)
Along the Strand.
Idyl: "And my young sweetheart sat at board
    with me."
Sleeping They Bear Me.
Momen (d. 1788)
Clouds breaking up.
Monaco, James V.
Ain't It a Shame About Mame.
I've Got a Pocketful of Dreams.
Row, Row, Row.
You Made Me Love You (I Didn't Want to Do
    It)
You're Gonna Lose Your Gal.
Monaghan, Patricia
Persephone's Journey.
Venus of Laussel.
Monck, Mary (1678–1715)
Masque of the Virtues against Love.
On a Romantic Lady.
Verses Written on Her Death-bed at Bath to
    Her Husband in London.
Money-Coutts, Francis Burdett (1852–1923)
On a Wife.
Monju-Shindo
Joshu's 'Oak in the courtyard.'
"Monk" See **Lewis, Matthew Gregory**
Monk, Geraldine (b. 1952)
A C.
C S
La Tormenta.
South Bound: Facing North.
Monk, Mary (1677?–1715)
Fire Us with Ice, Burn Us with Snow.
Verses Written on Her Death-Bed at Bath to
    Her Husband in London.
Monk, Thelonius
'Round Midnight.
Monkhouse, Cosmo (1840–1901)
Any Soul to Any Body.
Limerick: "There was a young lady of Riga."
There Was a Young Lady of Niger.
Monks, Arthur W.
Twilight's Last Gleaming.
Monro, Harold (1879–1932)
Bird at Dawn, The.
Bitter Sanctuary.
Carrion.
Cat's Meat.
Children of Love.
City-Storm.
Dog.
Every Thing.
Flower Is Looking, A.
Hearthstone.
Hurrier, The.

If Suddenly a Clod of Earth.
Man Carrying Bale.
Midnight Lamentation.
Milk for the Cat.
Nightingale near the House, The.
Solitude.
Street Fight.
Terrible Door, The.
Thistledown.
Train, The! The twelve o'clock for paradise.
Vixen woman, The.
When you and I go down.
Monroe, Arthur W.
To W. S. M.
Monroe, Bill
In the Pines.
Monroe, Harriet (1861–1936)
Garden, The.
Meeting, The.
Radio.
Rubens.
These Two.
Monsour, Leslie
Dream of Dying, A.
Emily's Words.
Sweeping.
Montagu, Lady Mary Wortley (1689–1762)
Addressed to ——.
Answer to a Love-Letter in Verse, An.
Between Your Sheets.
Epistle from Mrs. Yonge to Her Husband.
Epistle: "How happy you who varied joys
    pursue."
Epitaph: "Here lie John Hughes and Sarah
    Drew."
Farewell to Bath.
Hymn to the Moon.
Ill fates pursue me, may I never find.
Lady's Resolve, The.
Lover, The; a Ballad.
Man in Love, A.
On the Death of Mrs. Bowes.
Reasons That Induced Dr. Swift to Write a
    Poem Called "The Lady's Dressing-Room,"
    The.
Receipt to Cure [or for] the Vapours, A.
Saturday: The Small-Pox.
Summary of Lord Lyttleton's 'Advice to a
    Lady,' A.
To a Lady Making Love.
Town Eclogues.
Verses Addressed to the Imitator of the First
    Satire of the Second Book of Horace: An
    Attack on Pope.
Verses Written in a Garden.
Verses Written in the Chiosk [of the British
    Palace], at Pera, Overlooking [the City of]
    Constantinople.
When God created thee, one would believe.
Montague, John (b. 1929)
Above the Pool.
All Legendary Obstacles.
Answer, The.
At Last.
Bright Day, A.
Cage, The.
Cassandra's Answer.
Cave.
Deer Park.
Dowager.
Drink of Milk, A.
11 rue Daguerre.
Falls Funeral.
Family Conference.
Flowering Absence, A.
Footnote on Monasticism: Dingle Peninsula, A.
Grafted Tongue, A.
Hearth Song.
Herbert Street Revisited.
Hero's Portion.
King & Queen.
Lament for the O'Neills.
Last Journey.
Like Dolmens Round My Childhood, the Old
    People.
Little Flower's Disciple, The.

Locket, The.
Lost Tradition, A.
Mother Cat.
Mount Eagle.
Old Mythologies.
Point, The.
Process.
Same Gesture, The.
She Cries.
Silver Flask, The.
Small Secrets.
That Room.
Tracks.
Trout, The.
Walking Late.
Welcoming Party, A.
Well-beloved, The.
Wild Dog Rose, The.
Wild Sports of the West.
Windharp.
Witness.
Woodtown Manor.
Montale, Eugenio (1896–1981)
Bird-Shooting.
Black and white, The.
Bring me the sunflower, I'll plant it here.
Day and Night.
Don't ask us for the word to frame.
Dora Markus.
Ecologue.
Eel, The.
Elegy of Our Times.
Fan, The.
Far away, still I was with you.
Frost on the windowpanes; the sick.
Haul Your Paper Boats.
Here is the sign: it trembles.
I had almost lost.
I repeat I'm ready, but ready for what?
If the green lizard darts.
In the Greenhouse.
Lemon Trees, The.
Little Testament.
Long goodbyes, the whistles in the dark, The.
Many years, and one of them a little harder.
Murder's not my forte.
My Muse.
Ours is group solitude.
Personae Separatae.
Prisoner's Dream, The.
Soliloquy.
Storm, The.
Story of Every Day, The.
Thrust and Riposte.
You know, I must leave you again and I can't.
You know this: I must lose you again and
    cannot.
Montejo, Eugenio (b. 1938)
Marina.
Montemayor, Carlos (b. 1947)
Cytherea.
Montgomerie, Alexander (1540?–1610?)
Away Vane World.
Description of Tyme, A.
Dreame, Ane.
Night Is Near [or Neir] Gone, The.
Remembers thou in Æsope of a taill.
Royall Palice of the Heichest Hewin, The.
Solsequium, The.
Sonet: "Thocht Polibus, pisander, and with
    them."
To Henry Constable and Henry Keir.
To His Maistres [or Mistress].
To R. Hudson.
Montgomerie, William (b. 1904)
Author Unknown.
Elegy for William Soutar.
Epitaph: "My brother is skull and skeleton
    now."
Glasgow Street.
Is there no vision in a lovely place?
Montgomery, James (1771–1854)
Come to Calvary's holy mountain.
Nativity.
On the Loss of Friends.
Once on the mountain's balmy lap reclined.

Stranger and His Friend, The.

Montgomery, Niall
Eyewash.

Montgomery, Scott
Crying.
Evening lecture.
Her silence at dinner.
Moonrise white cat eating the cardinal.
With the last lamp.

Montrose, James Graham, Marquess of (1612–50)
His Metrical Vow.
My Dear and Only Love.
On Himself, upon Hearing What Was His Sentence.

"Monty Python"
All Things Dull and Ugly.

Moody, Elizabeth (d. 1814)
Dr. Johnson's Ghost.
Housewife's Prayer on the Morning Preceding a Fete, The.
Sappho Burns Her Books and Cultivates the Culinary Arts.
To a Friend, Who Gave the Author a Reading Glass.
To a Gentleman Who Invited Me to Go a-Fishing.
To a Lady, Who Was a Great Talker.

Moody, William Vaughn (1869–1910)
Bracelet of Grass, The.
Departure, The.
Faded Pictures.
Gloucester Moors.
Harmonics.
I Stood within the Heart of God.
Ode in Time of Hesitation, An.
On a Soldier Fallen in the Philippines.

Moolten, David (b. 1961)
Bio 7.
Brandy Station, Virginia.
Madame Butterfly.
Motorcycle Ward.
Voyeur.

Mooney, Martin (b. 1964)
Anna Akhmatova's Funeral.

Moore, Alan (b. 1960)
Girls' School.

Moore, Bertha
Child's Thought, A.

Moore, Clement Clarke (1779–1863)
Lord of Life, All Praise Excelling.
Visit from St Nicholas, A.

Moore, Edward (1712–57)
Nun, The.
Poet and His Patron, The.
Song 3: "As Phyllis the gay, at the break of the day."
To the Right Hon. Henry Pelham.
Why, Celia, is your spreading waist.

Moore, Egbert ("Lord Beginner")
Victory Calypso, Lord's 1950.

Moore, Honor (b. 1945)
Edward.
First Time: 1950.
Girl in a Fur-Trimmed Dress.
Green Place, A.
Memoir.
Poem for the End.
Runaway.
Window at Key West, A.

Moore, James
One Reason I Went to Prison.

Moore, Julia A. (1847–1920)
And now, kind friends, what I have wrote.
Ashtabula Disaster, The.
Enos Page the youngest brother.
Grand Rapids.
Hiram Helsel.
On a moonlight evening, in the month of May.
One morning in April, a short time ago.
She had blue eyes and light flaxen hair.
Sketch of Lord Byron's Life.
Some people are getting so they think a poor girl.
When Mr. Dennis does well play.

Moore, Lenard D. (b. 1958)
Again.
Bluesman's Blues, A.
Eternal Landscape, The.
Farther and farther.
From the Field.
Gifts.
Haiku.
Homeplace, The.
Indian Girl.
Silent deer the sound of a waterfall.
Song Poem, The.
Stars.
Summer noon.
Tanka.
Winter 1967.

Moore, Lilian (b. 1909)
Bedtime Story.
In the Fog.
Listen!
No One.
Pigeons.
Sometimes.
Spectacular.
Until I Saw the Sea.

Moore, Marianne Craig (1887–1972)
At Rest in the Blast.
Baseball and Writing.
Bird-witted.
Black Earth.
Blessed Is the Man.
Bowls.
Carriage from Sweden, A.
Charity Overcoming Envy.
Critics and Connoisseurs.
Egyptian Pulled Glass Bottle in the Shape of a Fish, An.
England.
Enough.
Face, A.
Fish, The.
Four Quartz Crystal Clocks.
Grave, A.
He "Digesteth Harde Yron."
He Wrote the History Book.
Hero, The.
His Shield.
Hometown Piece for Messrs. Alston and Reese.
I May, I Might, I Must.
In Distrust of Merits.
In the Public Garden.
Is Your Town Nineveh?
Jellyfish, A.
Jerboa, The.
Labors of Hercules, The.
Like a Bulrush.
Love in America.
Marriage.
Mind Is an Enchanting Thing, The.
Monkeys, The.
Nevertheless.
New York.
No Swan So Fine.
O to Be a Dragon.
Pangolin, The.
Paper Nautilus, The.
Past Is the Present, The.
Peter.
Poetry: "I, too, dislike it: there are things that are important beyond all this fiddle."
Saint Nicholas.
Sea Unicorns and Land Unicorns.
Silence.
Smooth Gnarled Crape Myrtle.
Sojourn in the Whale.
Spenser's Ireland.
Steeple-Jack, The.
Student, The.
Talisman, A.
That Harp You Play So Well.
To a Chameleon.
To a Snail.
To a Steam Roller.
To an Intra-Mural Rat.
Tom Fool at Jamaica.
W. S. Landor.

What Are Years?
When I Buy Pictures.

Moore, Merrill (1903–57)
Americans in 1933–4–5–6–7–8–, Etc.
And to the Young Men.
Book of How, The.
Cumae.
How She Resolved to Act.
In Magic Words.
It Is Winter, I Know.
Literature: The God, Its Ritual.
Noise That Time Makes, The.
Odor of a Metal Is Not Strong, The.
Old Men and Old Women Going Home on the Street Car.
Pandora and the Moon.
Shot Who? Jim Lane!
Unknown Man in the Morgue.
Village Noon; Mid-Day Bells.
Warning to One.

Moore, Nicholas (b. 1918)
Island and the Cattle, The.
Patient, The.
Song: "Little onion lay by the fireplace, A."

Moore, Richard (b. 1927)
It Took TV to Civilize Our Village.
Though the New Teacher Is a Trifle Odd.
Unable, Father, Still, to Disavow.
Visitors, The.

Moore, Rosalie (b. 1910)
Catalog [or Catalogue].
Dirge for the Living.
Doors.
Height.
Memory of Quiet.
Mind's Disguise, The.
Personal Atlas.
Ripeness Is Rapid.
Shipwreck.
Still Without Life.

Moore, Thomas (1779–1852)
After dreaming some hours of the land of Cockaigne.
And is there then no earthly place.
Announcement of a New Grand Acceleration Company for the Promotion of the Speed of Literature.
Argument, An.
At length, my Lord, I have the bliss.
Believe Me, If All Those Endearing Young Charms.
Canadian Boat Song, A.
Cherries; a Parable, The.
Comforter, The.
Copy of an Intercepted Despatch from His Excellency Don Strepitoso Diabolo.
Dear Harp of My Country.
Did Not.
Duke Is the Lad [to Frighten a Lass], The.
Echo.
Epitaph on Robert Southey.
Epitaph on Tuft-Hunter.
Fancy.
Fly to the desert, fly with me.
From Miss Biddy Fudge to Miss Dorothy———.
Fum and Hum, the Two Birds of Royalty.
Harp That Once through Tara's Halls, The.
How Oft Has the Banshee Cried.
Irish Antiquities.
Journey Onwards, The.
Kiss, The.
Letter 1.
Meeting of the Waters, The.
Minstrel Boy, The.
No—Leave My Heart to Rest.
Nonsense.
Oft in the Stilly Night.
Oh! blame not the bard, if he fly to the bowers.
Oh Dick! You may talk of your writing and reading.
Oh! ever thus from childhood's hour.
Oh! where's the slave so lowly.
Pastoral Ballad by John Bull, A.
Petition of the Orangemen of Ireland, The.
Pro Patria Mori.

Scene from a Play, Acted at Oxford, Called
   "Matriculation."
She Is Far from the Land.
Song of Fionnuala, The.
Song: "When the heart's feeling."
Song: "Where is the nymph, whose azure eye."
Sound the Loud Timbrel.
This World Is All a Fleeting Show.
Time I've Lost in Wooing, The.
'Tis the Last Rose of Summer.
To Ladies' Eyes.
To Miss———.
To Sir Hudson Lowe.
Tory Pledges.
Venetian Air.
Weep, Children of Israel.
What's My Thought Like?
When I loved you, I can't but allow.
Young May Moon, The.

Moore, Thomas Sturge (1870–1944)
Daughter of Admetus, A.
Duet, A.
Dying Swan, The.
Event, The.
Gazelles, The.
Kindness.
On Harting Down.
Response to Rimbaud's Later Manner.
Sent from Egypt with a Fair Robe of Tissue to
   a Sicilian Vinedresser.
Variation on Ronsard.

Moorer, Lizelia Augusta Jenkins
Accompanying a Gift.
Africa.
Benefits of Sorrow.
Bible, The.
Birthday Wishes to a Husband.
Birthday Wishes to a Minister of the Gospel.
Birthday Wishes to a Physician.
Christmas Eve.
Christmas Tree, The.
Circle, The.
Claflin's Alumni.
Crum Appointment, The.
Dedication Day Poem.
Dialogue, A.
Door of Hope, The.
Duty, or Truth at Work.
Easter; or, Spring-Time.
Emancipation Day.
Eutawville Lynching, The.
Hallowe'en.
Immortality.
In Memoriam of E. B. Clark.
Injustice of the Courts.
Jim Crow Cars.
Legal Mouse, A.
Lela's Charms.
Lines to a Graduate.
Loyalty to the Flag.
Lynching.
Misunderstood.
Mountain Tops.
Must Be Freed.
Negro Ballot, The.
Negro Heroines.
Negro Schools, The.
Notable Dinner, A.
Peonage System, The.
Pharaohs of Today, The.
Prejudice.
Presidents, The.
Price of Disrespect, The.
Refining Fire.
Retribution.
Russia's Resentment.
Social Glass, The.
Social Life, The.
Song of the Angels.
Southern Press, The.
Southern Pulpit, The.
Southern Work of Dr. and Mrs. L. M. Dunton.
Sympathy.
Thanksgiving.
Tree of Knowledge, The.
Truth Suppressed, The.
Voice of the Negro, The.

What We Teach at Claflin.
Whisper Words of Love to Me.
Why Is It?
Why Negroes Don't Unite.
Why We Meet.

Moossy, Brenda J.
I Can No Longer Care for the Dying.
Notion of Grace, A.
When Fat Women Fear Famine.

Mopev
Would you care for a smoke or a sherry?

Mor, Amus (fl. 20th cent.)
Coming of John, The.

Mora, Pat (fl. 1986)
Castanet Clicks.
Cortez's Horse.
Depression Days.
Elena.
Gentle Communion.
Immigrants.
La Migra.
One Potato.
Sonrisas.
Tall Walking Woman.

Moraes, Dom (b. 1938)
1668.
Altermann, sipping wine, reads with a look.
Babur.
Gardener.
Kanheri Caves.
Santa Claus.
Snow on a Mountain.

Moraes, Vinícius de (b. 1913)
Song: "Never take her away."

Moraga, Cherríe (b. 1952)
Feed the Mexican Back into Her.
For the Color of My Mother.
For You, Mamá.
Half-Breed.

Morales, Aurora Levins (b. 1954)
1930.
Child's Christmas in Puerto Rico, A.
Ending Poem.
Immigrants.
Kitchens.
Old Countries.
Other Heritage, The.
Puertoricanness.
South.
Sugar Poem.
Tita's Poem.

Morales, Rosario
Africa.
Dinner, The.
Ending Poem.
Getting Out Alive.
I Am the Reasonable One.
I Recognize You.
My Revolution.
Spring Fever.

Moran, Michael ("Zozimus")
Pharao's Daughter.

Moran, Rod (b. 1952)
Cross Country.
Wire.

Morant, Harry (1864–1902)
Last Rhyme and Testament of Tony Lumpkin.

Morcott, Anne (fl. 1692)
Loyal English Man's Wish for the Preservation
   of the King and Queen, The.

Mordaunt, Charles, Earl of Peterborough (1658–1735)
I Said to My Heart.

Mordaunt, Elizabeth, Viscountess (d. 1678)
Sepr. ye 6th 1666 Thursday a Thanks Geving
   for the Stoping of the Fire in London.

Mordaunt, Thomas Osbert (1730–1809)
Sound, Sound the Clarion.

Mordecai ben Isaac (fl. 13th–14th cent.)
Fair Thou Art.
Rock of My Salvation.

Mordecai, Pamela (b. 1942)
Jesus Is Condemned to Death.

More, Dame Gertrude (1604–33)
Dittie to the Same Subject, A.

Short Oblation of This Small Work by the
   Writer Gatherer Thereof to Our Most Sweet
   and Merciful God, A.

More, Hannah (1745–1833)
Cheap Repository: The Story of Sinful Sally.
   Told by Herself.
Cold Ceremony.
Come, neighbour, take a walk with me.
Epilogue: "Child! we must quit these visionary
   scenes."
Florio: A Tale, and The Bas-bleu; or,
   Conversation.
From The Slave Trade.
Hackney Coachman, The; Or, The Way to Get
   a Good Fare.
Inscription in a Beautiful Retreat Called Fairy
   Bower.
Long was Society o'er-run.
Patient Joe; or, The Newcastle Collier.
Perish th' illiberal thought which would
   debase.
Riot; or, Half a Loaf Is Better than No Bread,
   The.
Sacred Dramas.
Sensibility: A Poetical Epistle to the Hon. Mrs
   Boscawen.
Slavery.

More, Henry (1614–87)
Charity and Humility.
Contrition.

More, Saint Thomas See **More, Sir Thomas**

More, Sir Thomas (Saint Thomas More) (1478–1535)
Astrologer, The.
Child's Song.
Consider Well.
De Principe Bono et Malo.
Fortune.
Good Princes and Bad.
Mine high estate, power and auctority.
Prayer, A.
Quis Optimus Reipublicae Status.

Morejón, Nancy (b. 1944)
Angela Dominguez, Ever Present.
Carpet.
Disillusion for Rubén Darío.
Havana Harbor.
I Never Saw Great Lakes.
Love, Attributed City.
Mother.
Poem Fifty.
Reason for Poetry, The.
Requiem for the Left Hand.
Richard Brought His Flute.
Tame and Ferocious Animal, A.
To a Boy.
Tree of Earthly Delights.
Will-o'-Wisp.

Moret, Neil
She's Funny That Way (I Got a Woman, Crazy
   for Me)

Morgan, Angela (1874–1957)
God the Artist.

Morgan-Browne, L. E.
Purple, White and Green, The.

Morgan, Edwin (b. 1920)
Cinquevalli.
Coin, The.
Columba's Song.
Computer's First Christmas Card, The.
Dowser, The.
First Men on Mercury, The.
From the Domain of Arnheim.
Glass, The.
Itinerary.
King Billy.
Loch Ness Monster's Song, The.
Message Clear.
My Greenhouse.
Opening the Cage.
Second Life, The.
Shilpit dog fucks grimly by the close, A.
Siesta of a Hungarian Snake.
Sir James Murray.
Strawberries.
To Hugh MacDiarmid.

Video Box: 25, The.
View of Things, A.
"Morgan, Emanuel" *See* Bynner, Witter
Morgan, Frederick (b. 1922)
February 11, 1977.
I Saw My Darling.
1904.
Morgan, John (1827–1903)
My Welsh Home.
Morgan, Robert (b. 1920)
Blood Donor.
Shadow Valley.
Morgan, Robert (b. 1944)
Bellrope.
Grandma's Bureau.
Honey.
Stretching.
Morgan, Robin (b. 1941)
And blessed be the women who get you
through.
As it was in the beginning.
Battery.
On the Watergate Women.
Morganfield, McKinley *See* Waters, Muddy
Morganwg, Iolo *See* Williams, Edward
Morgenstern, Christian (1871–1914)
Anxiety for the Future.
Blueprint for Disaster.
Delayed Action.
Fish's Nightsong.
Hen, The.
Knee, The.
Midnightmouse, The.
Summons.
Mori, Kyoko
Barbie Says Math is Hard.
Heat in October.
Speaking Through White: For My Mother.
Morikawa Kyoroku (1656–1715)
Even the dumplings / Are smaller.
Summer airing / On one pole.
**Mörike [or Möricke], Eduard Friedrich (1804–
75)**
Beauty Rohtraut.
Forest Murmurs.
Forsaken Girl, The.
Remember It, My Soul.
Moritake (d. 1549)
Those falling blossoms.
Today.
Moritaké *See* Arakida Moritaké
**Moritz [or Morits] Yunna Petrovna [or Iunna
Pinkhusovna] (b. 1937)**
Autumn.
Baltic Summer.
Between Scylla and Charybdis.
Crow.
Fisherman, The.
In Memory of Titian Tabidze.
In that town I was twenty. Snow there lay.
Leader, The.
Memorandum.
My apple-tree, my willow.
Parting the curtains on the other world.
Some Lines on My Mother's Illness.
Morley, Christopher Darlington (1890–1957)
Dial Call.
Elegy Written in a Country Coal-Bin.
Forever Ambrosia.
Gospel of Mr. Pepys, The.
In Honour of Taffy Topaz.
Pennsylvania Deutsch.
Plumpuppets, The.
Public Beach (Long Island Sound)
Morley, David (b. 1964)
Air Street.
Answers on a Postcard.
Enniskillen.
Errand.
Exact Fares.
Jerusalem.
Metal-work.
On Fire.
Politicisation of the North Wind, The.
White, White.

Morley, Hilda (b. 1916)
Curve of the Water.
For Elaine de Kooning.
Lizard, The.
Made Out of Links.
Parents.
Morley, I. D. M.
Limerick: "Far beyond all the girls of Pirelli."
Morley, Thomas
Sing We and Chant It.
You Black Bright Stars.
Mörling, Malena (b. 1965)
For F. M. Who Did Not Get Killed Yesterday
on 57th Street.
For the Woman with the Radio.
In a Motel Room at Dawn.
Three-Card Monte.
Moro, César (1903–56)
Battle at the Edge of the Falls.
Moronelli da Fiorenza, Pier (*fl.*** 13th cent.)**
Canzonetta: A Bitter Song to His Lady.
Moross, Jerome
Lazy Afternoon.
Morozov, Sergey
Poem about the Blue Horse.
Morpurgo, Rachel [*or* Rahel] (1790–1871)
Song: "Ah, vale of woe, of gloom and
darkness moulded."
Sonnet: "My soul surcharged with grief now
loud complains."
Morra, Rawia (b. 1966)
Powerless.
Morriën, Adriaan (b. 1912)
Farewell.
Morris, Betty
Limerick: "Poet from Cheltenham Spa, A."
Morris, Brian (b. 1930)
Dinas Emrys.
Morris, Charles (1745–1838)
Address to Lady———, Who Asked What the
Passion of Love Was?
Country and Town.
Morris, George Pope (1802–64)
Woodman, Spare That Tree.
Morris, Harry (b. 1924)
Because Thou Did'st Give.
Maine Lake at Night.
Where Lie All the Slain.
Morris, Herbert (b. 1928)
Road, The.
This Alice.
Morris, John N. (b. 1931)
Untrimming the Tree.
Morris-Jones, John (1864–1929)
North Star, The.
Old Age.
Wind's Lament, The.
Morris, Joseph
One Step at a Time.
Morris, Lewis (1701–65)
Fishing Lass of Hakin, The.
Miner's Ballad, The.
Poem of the Frost and Snow.
Morris, Sir Lewis (1833–1907)
Here in these fretted caverns whence the sea.
Salt sprays deluge it, wild waves buffet it,
hurricanes rave.
Morris, Mary
Missing: A Dog's Doggerel.
Morris, Mervyn (b. 1937)
For Consciousness.
Rasta Reggae.
Valley Prince.
Morris, Thomas (1732–1806?)
Sapphics: At the Mohawk-Castle, Canada.
Morris, William (1834–96)
Another for the Briar Rose.
Apology, An.
Death Song, A.
Defense of Guenevere, The.
End of May, The.
For the Briar Rose.
French Noel.

Garden by the Sea, A.
Haystack in the Floods, The.
In Prison.
Inscription for an Old Bed.
Judgement of God, The.
Love Is Enough.
Outlanders, The.
Pomona.
Prologue: The Wanderers.
Riding Together.
Shameful Death.
Summer Dawn.
Two Red Roses across the Moon.
Morrison, Blake
Ower t'ills o Bingley.
Morrison, Lillian (b. 1917)
Rural Recreation.
Sidewalk Racer Or, On the Skateboard, The.
Surf.
Morrissey, Sinéad (b. 1972)
After the Hurricane.
Hazel Goodwin Morrissey Brown.
My New Angels.
There was Fire in Vancouver.
Thoughts in a Black Taxi.
To Look Out Once from High Windows.
Morse, Brian
Day on the Planet, A.
Morse, Carl (b. 1934)
Dream of the Artfairy.
Fairy Straighttalk.
Scenes of Childhood.
Morse, Gail
He kneels on the rumpled bed.
**"Morshen, Nikolai Nikolaevich" (Nikolai
Nikolaevich Marchenko) (b. 1917)**
Andreyevsky Church, The.
At the Lighthouse.
He lived so little: only forty years.
In superstitious panic.
Storm, A.
Morstein, Petra von (b. 1941)
Anthology Poem.
For one who says he feels.
In the Case of Lobsters.
Justice.
Nineteen Sixty Eight.
Thing Poem.
Morsztyn, Zbigniew (1620–90)
Emblem 51.
Mortál, Anna
Cork Examiner, December 4, 1846: More
Starvation, The.
**Morton, John Bingham ("Beachcomber") (1893–
1979)**
Another Canto.
Dancing Cabman, The.
Epitaph: "Glassblower lies here at rest, A."
Epitaph: "Tread softly; bid a solemn music
sound."
Hush, Hush.
John Percy.
Let poets praise the softer winds of spring.
On Sir Henry Ferrett, M.P.
Someone Asked the Publisher.
Spring in London.
To Hilda Dancing.
Morton, Thomas (1764–1838)
Carmen Elegiacum.
Epitaph: "Time that brings [*or* bringes] all
things to light."
New Canaans Genius; Epilogus.
New English Canaan; Prologue.
Poem: "I sing th' adventures of mine worthy
wights."
Poem, The: "Rise Oedipus, and if thou canst
unfold."
Poem, The: "What ailes Pigmalion? Is it
lunacy."
Song: "Drinke and be merry, merry, merry
boyes."
Song, The: "Drink and be merry, merry, merry
boys."
Morungen, Heinrich von (d. 1222)
Alas, shall I not see again.

I believe there is no one alive who weeps for
  my sorrow.
I heard on the meadow.
It has gone with me as with a child.
Legacy, The.
Many a man gets bewitched by the elves.
Wound of Love, The.

Morus, Huw (1622–1709)
In Praise of a Girl.

Mosby, George, Jr.
To Josh Gibson (Legendary Slugger of the Old
  Negro Baseball League)

Moschus (fl. 3rd cent. B.C.)
Cupid Turned Plowman.
Europa.
Lament for Bion.
Ocean, The.
Pan, Echo, and the Satyr.

Moser, Leo
Limerick: "Quadratic function, ambitious, A."

Moses, Daniel David (b. 1952)
Corn, The.
Party Favour.
Report on Her Remains.
Some Grand River Blues.

Moses, Gavin
Black Banana House.
Poem for Trish, A.

Moskowitz, Faye
Bird Lives.

Moss, Howard (b. 1922)
Arsenic.
Cats and Dogs.
Einstein's Bathrobe.
Elegy for My Father.
Elegy for My Sister.
Finding Them Lost.
Geography: a Song.
Gift to Be Simple, The.
Great Spaces.
Hand, The.
King Midas.
Long Island Springs.
Ménage à Trois.
Miami Beach.
Morning Glory.
New York Notebooks, The.
Persistence of Song, The.
Pruned Tree, The.
Rules of Sleep.
Shall I Compare Thee to a Summer's Day?
Tourists.
Underwood.
Wars, The.
Water Island.

Moss, Stanley (b. 1935)
Clouds.
Dog, The.
Exchange of Hats, An.
God Poem.
Hangman's Love Song, The.
Sailing from the United States.
Squall.
Two Fishermen.

Moss, Thomas (1740?–1803)
Beggar, The.

Moss, Thylias (b. 1954)
Anointing, An.
Botanical Fanaticism.
Fisher Street.
Landscape with Saxophonist.
Last Chance for the Tarzan Holler.
Lessons from a Mirror.
Lynching, The.
November and Aunt Jemima.
Owl in Daytime, The.
Raising a Humid Flag.
Reconsideration of the Blackbird, A.
Sunrise Comes to Second Avenue.
Tornados.
Undertaker's Daughter Feels Neglect, The.
Wonder, The.

Mother Goose (fl. 17th–18th cent.)
Aristotle's Story.
As I was going along, long, long.

As I was going to St. Ives.
As I was going up Pippen Hill.
As Tommy Snooks and Bessy Brooks.
At the siege of Belle Isle.
Awake, arise, / Pull out your eyes.
Baa, baa, black sheep, have you any wool?
Baby, baby, naughty baby.
Balloon, The.
Bandy Legs.
Barber, barber, shave a pig.
Bat, bat, come under my hat.
Bell horses, bell horses, what time of day?
Bessy Bell and Mary Gray.
Betty Blue.
Betty Pringle's Pig.
Birthdays.
Black Hen, The.
Black I am and much admired.
Bless you, bless you, burnie-bee [or bonnie-
  bee].
Blind man, blind man.
Blow the fire, blacksmith.
Blow, wind, blow! and go, mill, go!
Bob Robin.
Bobby Shaftoe.
Bonny Cravet, The.
Bow-wow, says the dog.
Boy and Girl.
Boy and the Sparrow.
Boys and girls come out to play.
Buttons.
By the Fire.
Bye, baby bunting.
Caesar's Song.
Candle, A.
Carrion crow sat upon [or on] an oak,
  The [or A].
Catch.
Chimney, A.
Christmas comes but once a year.
Clock, The.
Coachman, The.
Cobbler, cobbler, mend my shoe.
Cock-a-doodle-doo! / My dame has lost her
  shoe.
Cock doth crow / To let you know, The.
Come, butter, come.
Come dance a jig.
Come, let's to bed.
Cross Patch / Draw the latch.
Curly Locks [!] Curly Locks [!] wilt thou be
  mine?
Curr dhoo, curr dhoo.
Cushy cow bonny, let down thy milk.
Daffadowndilly.
Dame Trot and her cat.
Dance a baby diddy.
Dance, Little Baby.
Dance, Thumbkin, dance.
Dance to your [or thee] daddy.
Dapple-gray.
Dickery [or dickory], dickery [or dickory],
  dare.
Diddle, diddle, dumpling, my son John.
Diddlety, diddlety, dumpty.
Difficult Rhyme, A.
Ding, dong, bell, / Pussy's in the well.
Dingty diddlety.
Doctor Faustus was a good man.
Doctor Foster went to Gloucester [or Glo'ster].
Dove and the Wren, The.
Ducks and Drakes.
Elizabeth, Elspeth, Betsy, and Bess.
Every lady in this land.
Flying-Man.
For every evil under the sun.
For want of a nail.
Forehead, Eyes, Cheeks, Nose, Mouth, and
  Chin.
Formed long ago, yet made today.
Frog He Would a-Wooing Go, A.
Georgie Porgie, pudding and pie.
Girl in the lane, The.
God made the bees.
Good Advice.
Goosey, goosey, gander, where [or whither]
  shall I wander? shall I wander?

"Hark, Hark, the Dogs Do Bark."
Hart he loves the high wood, The.
Hector Protector was dressed all in green.
Hickety, pickety, my black hen.
Hickory, dickory, dock.
Hie, hie, says Anthony.
High Diddle Diddle.
Higher than a house, / Higher than a tree.
Hot cross buns! Hot-cross buns! / One a penny,
  two a penny.
Hot Pease Man, The.
House That Jack Built, The.
How many days has my baby to play?
How many miles to Babylon?
Humpty Dumpty sat on a wall.
Hush-a-bye, baby, on the tree-top.
I had a little hobby horse, it was well shod.
I have a little sister, they call her Peep-Peep.
I'll tell you a story / About Jack a Nory.
I love sixpence, jolly [or pretty] little sixpence.
I saw a ship a-sailing.
I saw three ships come sailing by.
I would, if I could.
If all the seas were one sea.
If all the world were apple-pie.
If I had [or I'd] as much money as I could
  spend.
If wishes were horses.
In marble walls [or halls] as white as milk.
Intery, mintery, cutery corn.
Is John Smith within?
Jack and Gill.
Jack and His Fiddle.
Jack be nimble.
Jack Sprat could eat no fat.
Jenny Wren.
Jerry Hall, / He is so small.
John Cook had a little grey mare.
Johnny shall have a new bonnet.
King Arthur.
King of France, the king of France / with forty
  thousand men, The.
Ladybird, Ladybird fly away home.
Leg over leg.
Lion and the unicorn, The.
Little Bird, The.
Little Bo-Peep.
Little Boy Blue, come blow [up] your horn[!].
Little Girl.
Little Jack Horner/ Sat in a corner.
Little Jumping Joan.
Little King Pippin.
Little maid, pretty maid, / Whither goest thou?
Little Moppet, The.
Little Polly Flinders.
London Bridge.
Long-tailed pig, A.
Lucy Locket lost her pocket.
Man in the wilderness asked [of] me [or said
  to me], The [or A].
March, march, head erect.
Margery Mutton-pie.
Mary, Mary, quite contrary.
Master and Man.
Merchants of London, The.
Milk Maid, The.
Miss Muffet.
My Father Died.
My Kitten.
My maid Mary, / She minds the dairy.
Niddle Noddle.
North wind doth blow, The.
Nut Tree, A.
Old King Cole was a merry old soul.
Old Mother Goose.
Old Mother Twitchett had [or has] but one eye.
Old Woman of Surrey.
Old Woman, Old Woman.
One misty, moisty morning.
One, two, / Buckle my shoe.
One to Ten.
One, two, three, four, / Mary at the cottage
  door.
Other Little Tune, T'
Pancake Day.
Pat-a-cake, pat-a-cake, baker's man.
Pease porridge [or pudding] hot.

Peter Piper picked a peck of pickled pepper[s].
Peter White will ne'er go right.
Piper and His Cow, The.
Pit, pat, well-a-day.
Plum Pudding, A.
Polly and Sukey.
Poor old Robinson Crusoe!
Pretty John Watts.
Pumpkin-Eater, The.
Pussy-Cat, Pussy-Cat,/ where have you been?
Pussycat.
Quarrle, The.
Rain, rain, go to Spain.
Riddle: "Two legs sat upon three legs."
Riddle me, riddle me ree.
Ride a cock-horse [or a-cock horse] to
  Banbury Cross, / To see a fine lady upon a
  white horse.
Ride away, ride away / Johnny shall ride.
Ring-a-ring o' roses.
Robert Barnes, or [my] fellow fine.
Robert Rowley rolled a round roll round.
Robin-a-bobin.
Robin and Richard.
Robin Hood, Robin Hood, / Is in the mickle
  wood.
Rock-a-bye, baby, thy cradle is green.
Rub a dub dub.
Saturday, Sunday.
See-saw, Margery Daw, / Jack[y] shall have a
  new master.
See-saw, Margery Daw, / The old hen flew
  over the malt house.
See-saw, sacradown [or Sacaradown].
See, see, what shall I see?
Shall We Go A-Shearing?
Shoeing.
Sieve, A.
Simple Simon.
Sing a song of sixpence.
Sing, sing, / What shall I sing?
Six Little Mice.
Smiling girls, rosy boys.
Snail, The.
Solomon Grundy.
Sow came in with the saddle, The.
Speak when you're spoken to, / Come for one
  call.
Strange Old Woman, A.
Sulky Sue.
Sunshine.
Taffy was a Welshman, Taffy was a thief.
Tarts, The.
Teeth and Gums.
Ten O'Clock Scholar, [The].
That's All.
There Was a Crooked Man.
There Was a Little Girl.
There was a little man, / and he wooed a little
  maid.
There was a man and he had nought.
There was an old man in a velvet coat.
Old Woman and the Pedlar, The.
There was an old woman called Nothing-at-all.
There was an old woman lived under a hill.
There was an old woman / Lived under a hill /
  She put a mouse in a bag.
There Was an Old Woman Who Lived in a
  Shoe.
They That Wash on Monday.
Thirty days hath September.
This is the House that Jack Built.
This is the way the ladies ride.
This Little Pig Went to Market.
Three blind mice, see how they run!
Three Children.
Three crooked cripples went through
  Cripplegate.
Three wise men of Gotham.
To make your candles last for aye.
To market, to market / To buy a plum bun.
Tom, Tom, the piper's son.
Tommy Tittlemouse.
Tommy Tucker.
Tongs.
Trip upon trenchers, and dance upon dishes.
Tweedledum and Tweedledee.

Twelve pears hanging high.
Two Comical Folk.
Ungrateful Jenny.
Walnut, A.
Wash the dishes, wipe the dishes.
Well, The.
What Are Folks Made Of.
When I was a bachelor/ I lived by myself.
When I was a little girl, / About seven years
  old.
When the wind is in the east.
Where Is He?
Who Killed Cock Robin?
Willy boy, Willy boy, / Where are you going?
Willy, Willy Wilkin.
Winter.

Mother Maria [or Mat' Mariia] See **Kuzmina-
  Karavayeva, Elizaveta**

Motherwell, William (1797–1935)
  Jeanie Morrison.

Mothibi, Chief
  Speech.

Motion, Andrew (b. 1952)
  Anne Frank Huis.
  Close.
  Letter, The.
  One Life.
  Reading the Elephant.
  These Days.
  Writing.

Motojo
  Drone of the mosquitoes.

Motoyoshi Prince (fl. late 9th cent.)
  I am unhappy. / I do not care what happens.

**Motteux, Peter Anthony (Pierre Antoine) (1660–
  1718)**
  Song, A: "Slaves to London, I'll deceive you."

Mottram, Eric
  Elegy 11: Ford.
  Zuni Dancers.

Moulds, Julie (b. 1962)
  Late Summer Litany.
  Renoir's Bathers.
  When Bad Angels Love Women.

Moulsworth, Martha
  Memorandum of Martha Moulsworth, Widow,
    The.

**Moulton, Louise Chandler (Ellen Louise
  Chandler) (1835–1908)**
  At End.
  Shall I Complain.

Moultrie, John (1799–1874)
  Fairy Maimounè, The.
  Forget Thee?

Mounsey, Messenger (1693–1788)
  Here lie my old bones: my vexation now ends.

Mountain, Marlene
  After your visit.
  At dusk hot water from the hose.
  Beneath / leaf mold.
  C o y O t e.
  Empty mailbox.
  End of the cold spell.
  Faded flowers of the bed sheets autumn night.
  Frog.
  Gosling following its neck to the bug.
  He leans on the gate going staying.
  Hoot.
  In her old voice the mountains.
  In / the / woods.
  K k k k k.
  Krĭk'ĭt.
  My neighbor's rooster hops the stick i throw.
  Old towel folding it again autumn evening.
  On this cold.
  One fly everywhere the heat.
  Pick-up truck.
  Pig and i spring rain.
  Quiet day, A.
  Rain.
  Seed catalog in the mailbox cold drizzle.
  Smoke from a neighbor's chimney loneliness.
  Sn wfl k s.
  Summer night clothes whirling in a dryer.
  Wood pile.

Mountjoy, Cyril
  Limerick: "Gay soccer spectator from Wix, A."
  Limerick: "Psychic researcher's elation, A."
  Limerick: "Slow-footed stockman called
    Beales, A."
  Limerick: "Victoria was bitterly short."
  Limerick: "Young Joseph's new coat was real
    nice."

Mouré, Erin
  Thirteen Years.

Moussa, Amal (b. 1971)
  Autumn Rose.
  Formal Poem, A.
  Love Me.

Moxon, Edward
  Loud midnight-soothing melancholy bird.

Mozeen, Thomas (d. 1768)
  Bedlamite, The.
  Kilruddery Hunt, The.

Mozley, Abigail (b. 1947)
  Summer I Taught English to the French, The.

Mphahlele, Ezekiel (b. 1919)
  Exile in Nigeria.
  Homeward Bound.
  Poem, A: "What is there that we can do or
    say."

Mphande, Lupenga (b. 1947)
  I Was Sent For.
  Pain.
  Walking the Plateau.
  Why the Old Woman Limps.
  Wood-Cutter, The.

Mpina, Edison
  Reborn.
  Summer Fires of Mulanje Mountain.

Mpondo, Simon (b. 1935?)
  Season of the Rains, The.

Mqhayi, S. E. K. (1875–1945)
  Pleiades, The.

Mririda n'Ait Attik
  Azouou.
  Mririda.
  Praise to the Tattoo Mistress.

Msham, Mwana Kupona (c.1810–1860)
  Daughter, take this amulet.

Mtshali, Mbuyiseni Oswald (b. 1940)
  Birth of Shaka, The.
  Boy on a Swing.
  Day We Buried Our Bully, The.
  Farewell to My Scooter.
  Inside My Zulu Hut.
  Removal of Our Village, KwaBhanya, The.
  Ride upon the Death Chariot.

Mudie, Ian (1911–76)
  This Land.

Mudrooroo Narogin (b. 1938)
  Hide and Seek.
  Jacky Demonstrates for Land Rights.
  Jacky Hears the Century Cry.
  Jacky Sings His Songs.
  Peaches and Cream.
  Reincarnation.
  Song Circle of Jacky.
  Song Thirty-Four.
  Streets.
  They give Jacky rights.

Mueller, Lisel (b. 1924)
  Alive Together.
  American Literature.
  Animals Are Entering Our Lives.
  Another Version.
  Commuter.
  Concert, The.
  Curriculum Vitae.
  Deaf Dancing to Rock, The.
  Happy and Unhappy Families 1.
  Happy and Unhappy Families 2.
  Highway Poems.
  Late-Born Daughters, The.
  Lonesome Dream, The.
  Losing My Sight.
  Monet Refuses the Operation.
  Moon Fishing.
  Naming the Animals.
  Nude by Edward Hopper, A.

Palindrome.
Statues.
Triage.
What the Dog Perhaps Hears.
Muffareh, Sa'adyya
Spell of Blazing Trees, The.
Mugo, Micere Githae
I Want You to Know.
Look How Rich We are Together.
Where are those Songs?
Wife of the Husband.
Mugrón, Abbot of Iona (d. 980)
Christ's Cross.
Muhammad ibn Ghalib al-Rusafi (d. 1177)
Blue River.
Muhammadi, Habiba
In the Forests of Sleep.
Mühlenberg, William Augustus (1796–1877)
I Would Not Live Alway.
Like Noah's Weary Dove.
Saviour, Who Thy Flock Art Feeding.
Muir, Edwin (1887–1959)
Abraham.
Absent, The.
Adam's Dream.
Animals, The.
Annunciation, The.
Ballad of Hector in Hades.
Brothers, The.
Child Dying, The.
Childhood.
Combat, The.
Confirmation, The.
Face, The.
Fathers, The.
For Ann Scott-Moncrieff.
Good Man in Hell, The.
Horses.
Horses, The.
In Love for Long.
Incarnate One, The.
Interrogation, The.
Killing, The.
Labyrinth, The.
Late Wasp, The.
Love's Remorse.
Mary Stuart.
Merlin.
Milton.
Myth, The.
Mythical Journey, The.
One Foot in Eden.
Refugees, The.
Robert the Bruce.
Scotland 1941.
Scotland's Winter.
Suburban Dreams.
Then.
Three Mirrors, The.
Transfiguration, The.
Troy.
Wayside Station, The.
Wheel, The.
Muir, Lewis F.
Rag Time Cowboy Joe.
Mukai Kyorai (1651–1704)
After the green storm / True color.
Each year it is but a peck of rice.
Even in my town / Now, I sleep.
Returning from a funeral.
Mukand, Jon
First Payment.
Lullaby.
Mukhopādhyāy, Kalyānkumār
Am I afraid of the tenth day?
Is there any treasure like the Mother's name?
Ma, the mail train is leaving now.
Mukhopādhyāy, Nīlkantha (1841–1912)
Use your mental eye.
Mukhopādhyāy, Rāmrenu
Why should I sit alone, eyes closed.
Mukhopadhyay, Subhash (b. 1919)
Task, The.
Mukhopadhyay, Vijaya (b. 1937)
Monday.

Mukta Bai (fl. 13th cent.)
Although he has no form.
Muktibodh, G. M. (1917–64)
Void, The.
Muldoon, Paul (b. 1951)
Aisling.
Anseo.
Avenue, The.
Bearded Woman, by Ribera, The.
Birth, The.
Briefcase, The.
Brock.
Cauliflowers.
Centaurs, The.
Christo's.
Clonfeacle.
Cuba.
Dancers at the Moy.
Electric Orchard, The.
Field Hospital, The.
Gathering Mushrooms.
Glad Eye, The.
Hard Drive.
Hedgehog.
Ireland.
Lass of Aughrim, The.
Long Finish.
Lunch with Pancho Villa.
Ma.
Making the Move.
Meeting the British.
Milkweed and Monarch.
Mixed Marriage, The.
More a Man Has the More a Man Wants, The.
Mules.
Narrow Road to the Deep North, The.
Our Lady of Ardboe.
Quoof.
Right Arm, The.
Rune.
Sightseers, The.
Soap-Pig, The.
Something Else.
Something of a Departure.
Sushi.
Truce.
Weepies, The.
Why Brownlee Left.
Wind and Tree.
Wishbone, The.
Yggdrasill.
Mulford, Wendy
Nevrazumitelny.
Mulholland, Rosa (Lady Gilbert) (1841–1921)
Stolen Visit, A.
Mulkey, Rick (b. 1963)
Blind-Sided.
Why I Believe in Angels.
Mullen, F.
I took him by the arm and said.
Let Observation, Shuddering the While.
Mullen, Harryette
Dance She Does, The.
Momma Sayings.
Music for Homemade Instruments.
Roadmap.
Saturday Afternoon, When Chores Are Done.
Mullen, Laura (b. 1958)
After I Was Dead.
For the Reader (Blank Book)
House.
Self-Portrait as Somebody Else.
Müller, Wilhelm (1794–1827)
Whither?
Mulock, Dinah Maria
Labor and Rest.
Mulso, Hester (1727–1801)
To Stella.
Mumon-Ekai (1183–1260)
Thunderbolt—eyes wide, A.
Mumon Gensen (1323–1390)
Life: a cloud crossing the peak.
Life is an ever-rolling wheel.
Life is like a cloud of mist.
Munby, Arthur Joseph (1828–1910)
One Way of Looking at It.

Post Mortem.
Serving Maid, The.
'Munda, Constantia' (fl. 1617)
To the Right Worshipful Lady Her Most Dear
Mother, the Lady Prudentia Munda, the True
Pattern of Piety and Virtue, C. M. Wisheth
Increase of Happiness.
Munday, Anthony (1553–1633)
Beauty Bathing.
Dirge: "Weep, weep, ye woodmen, wail."
I Serve a Mistress.
Muneyuki (Minamoto no Muneyuki) (b. 939)
I can feel the loneliness.
Muneyuki, Minamoto no See **Muneyuki**
Mungoshi, Charles (b. 1947)
Dotito is Our Brother.
Letter to a Son, A.
Munib-ur-Rahman (b. 1924)
Tall Buildings.
Muñiz Huberman, Angelina
Ablution.
Cabalists, The.
Cascades of Death.
Circle of the Golem, The.
Eye of Creation, The.
Manuscript.
Obsession.
Prodigal Daughter.
Sanctuary.
Munkittrick, Richard Kendall (1853–1911)
Molasses River.
Old King Cabbage.
Redingote and the Vamoose, The.
Song of the Owl, The.
Muñoz, Alicia
Hunting Accident.
Munro, Hector Hugh See **"Saki"**
Mura, David
Argument: On 1942, An.
Blueness of the Day, The.
Colors of Desire, The.
Gardens We Have Left.
Grandfather and Grandmother in Love.
Grandfather-in-law.
Hibakusha's Letter (1955), The.
Huy Nguyen: Brothers, Drowning Cries.
Letters from Poston Relocation Camp (1942–
45)
Natives, The.
Nisei Picnic: From an Album, A.
To H. N.
Murakami Kijo
Against far off snow mountains.
Murasaki Shikibu (974–1031)
Lady Murasaki says.
Someone passes.
Troubled waters, The/ are frozen fast.
Warblers are today as long ago, The.
Muratori, Fred
Re-Emergence of the Trombone, The.
Mure, Sir William (1594–1657)
O Heavens! O Earth! heer I must pause a
space.
Murford, Nicholas (fl. 1647–52)
Storm and Calm: Sent from Embden to M.
Edw. Ma. and M. Tho. Ly, The.
Murger, Henry (1822–61)
Old Loves.
Spring in the Students' Quarter.
Murillo, Rosario
Angel in the Deluge.
Conversation in Front of a Helicopter.
Murphy, E. G. (1867–1939)
Smiths, The.
Thank you, Mr Rason, for the Apples.
Murphy, Gerry (b. 1952)
Small Fat Boy Walking Backwards, A.
Vision at Knock.
Murphy, Kay
Eighties Meditation.
Girl with the Bad Rep, The.
Murphy, Peter E.
Manifesto.
New Boy, The.

Murphy, Richard (b. 1927)
Archaeology of Love, The.
Beehive Cell.
Casement's Funeral.
Convenience.
Deep red bogs divided.
Elixir.
Epitaph on a Fir-Tree.
Gate Lodge.
Girl at the Seaside.
Green Martyrs.
Gym.
High Island.
Kylemore Castle.
Last Galway Hooker, The.
Little Hunger.
Luttrell.
Morning Call.
Natural Son.
Nest in a Wall, A.
Orange March.
Pat Cloherty's Version of *The Maisie*.
Philosopher and the Birds, The.
Planter.
Poet on the Island, The.
Rapparees.
Reading Lesson, The.
Roof-Tree.
Sailing to an Island.
Seals at High Island.
Slate.
Stormpetrel.
Tony White.
Wolfhound.

Murray, Charles (1864–1941)
Dockens afore his Peers.
Whistle, The.

Murray, G. E. (b. 1920)
American Cheese.
Art of a Cold Sun.
On Being Disabled by Light at Dawn in the
   Wilderness.
Rounds, The.
Shopping for Midnight.

Murray, Joan (1917–1942)
And As I Came Out from the Temples.
Epithalamium, An.
Here We Stand Before the Temporal World.
Lullaby.
Men and Women Have Meaning Only as Man
   and Woman.
There Has Been More Than Beginning and
   End to Face.

Murray, John (1741–1815)
Hark! 'Tis the Saviour of Mankind.

Murray, L. *and* **F. Leigh**
Charlie Piecan.

Murray, Les A. (b. 1938)
Absolutely Ordinary Rainbow, An.
Broad Bean Sermon, The.
Burning Want.
Cotton Flannelette.
Dog Fox Field.
Dream of Wearing Shorts Forever, The.
Drugs of War, The.
Easter 1984.
Equanimity.
Flight from Manhattan, The.
Gods, The.
Greenhouse Vanity, The.
Hearing Impairment.
It Allows a Portrait in Line Scan at Fifteen.
Lament for the Country Soldiers.
Last Hellos, The.
Louvres.
Morse.
Names of the Humble, The.
Noonday Axeman.
Once in a Lifetime, Snow.
People are eating dinner in that country north
   of Legge's Lake, The.
Portrait of the Autist as a New World Driver.
Powerline Incarnation, The.
Quality of Sprawl, The.
Satis Passio.
Smell of Coal Smoke, The.

Sydney and the Bush.
Tall Wood twins, The.
Tin Wash Dish, The.
Transposition of Clermont, The.
Widower in the Country, The.

Murray, Paul (b. 1947)
Canticle of the Void, The.
Introit.
Rain.

Murray, Pauli (b. 1910)
Conquest.
Dark Testament.
Inquietude.
Redemption.
Returning Spring.
Song: "Because I know deep in my own
   heart."

Murray, Robert Fuller (1863–94)
Wasted Day, The.

Murray, Rona (b. 1924)
Lizard, The.

Murry, Ann (b. c.1755, d. after 1816)
Familiar Epistle, A.
Tête à Tête; or, Fashionable Pair: an Eclogue,
   The.

Murry, Kathleen Beauchamp *See* **Mansfield,
Katherine**

Murthy, Janaki Srinivas *See* **"Vaidehi"**

Musgrave, Susan (b. 1951)
Burial of the Dog.
Hidden Meaning.
I Am Not a Conspiracy Everything Is Not
   Paranoid The Drug Enforcement
   Administration Is Not Everywhere.
Judas Goat, The.
Returning to the Town Where We Used to
   Live.
Salad Days.
You Didn't Fit.

Musho Josho (d. 1306)
When it comes—just so!

Muske, Carol (b. 1945)
At the School for the Gifted.
August, Los Angeles, Lullaby.
Blue Kashmir, '74.
Blue Rose.
Coming Over Coldwater.
Epith.
Eulogy, The.
Fault, The.
Field Trip.
Former Love, a Lover of Form, A.
Last Take.
Like This.
Miracles.
Our Kitty.
Pediatrics.
Red Trousseau.
Stage and Screen, 1989.
Intensive Care.
Wish Foundation, The.
Wyndmere, Windemere.

Muslih-Din *See* **Sadi** [*or* **Saadi** *or* **Sa'di**]

Muso Soseki (1275–1351)
Abiding Mountain.
All on my own I'm happy.
All worries and troubles.
Among rocks and valleys.
Ancient Origin.
Another Summit.
Ashikaga Tadayoshi's Palace.
At Gen's Embarkation for Yuan China.
At Iku's Embarkation for Yuan China.
At Kan's Embarkation for Yuan China.
At the Nachi Kannon Hall.
At Whole-World-In-View-Hut.
Bamboo Garden.
Beyond Light.
Beyond the World.
Bridge Where the Moon Crosses, The.
Buddha's Satori.
By the sea.
Cave of the Thousand Pines.
Chick feed is what I eat.
Clear Valley.

Climbing Down the Snowy Mountain.
Cloud Mountain.
Curtain of cloud hangs, A.
Digging Out the Buddha Relic.
Don't ask suspiciously.
Dragon-Gate House.
Dry Tree.
East of the strait.
East Peak.
Flat Mountain.
For a Monk Going West.
For Gen the New Head Priest of Erin-ji.
For Ko Who Has Come Back from China.
For Myo's Departure for Anzen-ji.
For Myo's Departure for Shofuku-ji.
For Sho the New Head Priest of Erin-ji.
For Taihei Osho.
For Tetsu the New Head Priest of Erin-ji.
For the Death of a Monk.
For years I dug in the earth.
Fragrance of the Udumbara, The.
Free Old Man.
From My Hut in Miura.
From the beginning.
Garden at the General's Residence, The.
Gate of Universal Light, The.
Gem Creek.
Gem Forest.
Gem Mountain.
Green mountains.
Hall of the Guardian God.
Heaven Peak.
House of Spring.
Hui-neng's Pond.
Hut in Harmony.
I'm not so deep in it.
I wake from my noon nap.
In these mountain villages and harbor towns.
In this small hut.
Inauguration of Fukusan Dormitory.
Incomparable-Verse Valley.
It.
Jewel Cliff.
Jewel Field.
Joy Mountain.
Lamenting the Civil War.
Laughing Mountain.
Lodging House in Town, A.
Loud thunder.
Lover of Mountains.
Magnificent Peak.
Many times the mountains have turned from
   green to yellow.
Moon Mountain.
Moon Tree Cliff.
Mourning for the Layman Named Cloud Peak.
Mugoku Osho's Snow Poem.
My thatched hut.
No End Point.
No Gain.
No Precedent.
No-Word Hut.
Old Creek.
Old Hut.
Old Man Advancing.
Old Man at Leisure.
Old Man in Retirement.
Old Man of Few Words.
Old Man to-the-Point.
Old Mountain.
On the blue waves.
On the Wall of Cloud-Friend Hut.
One Hut.
Ox Turned Loose.
Patriarch Peaks.
Peak of the Held-Up Flower, The.
People's abuse.
Pine Shade.
Plum Window.
Poem on Dry Mountain (A Zen Garden)
Pure Sound Pavilion of the Riverside Temple,
   The.
Reizan Osho Visits Me.
Reply to a Friend's Poem.
Reply to Bukko Zenji's Poem at Seiken-ji.
Reply to Gen'no Osho's Poem.
Reply to Reizan Osho.

Reply to Suzan Osho's Snow Poem.
Snow.
Snow at Rohatsu Sesshin.
Snow Garden.
Snow Valley.
Spring Cliff.
Strange Peak.
Suzan Osho's Visit.
Suzan Oshos's Visit to My West Mountain
    Hut.
Temple of Eternal Light.
Tengan Osho's Visit to Erin-ji.
Thanks for Daisen Osho's Visit.
Thanks Sent to Taihei Osho.
Three-Step Waterfall.
Thus have I rolled my life throughout.
Tiger Valley.
Time for a walk.
To Kengai Osho of Engaku-ji.
To the Emperor's Messenger.
Toki-no-Ge (Satori Poem)
Truth Hall.
Turtle Head Stupa.
Vainly I dug for a perfect sky.
Very high this mountain.
Visiting My Old Hut in Late Spring.
Wandering.
With compassionate hands.
Withered Zen.

Musset, Alfred de (1810–57)
Juana.
Muse, The.
Poet, The.
Souvenir.

"Mustafa" See Johnson, Don Allen

Mu'tamid, King of Seville (1040–95)
Tears of the World.
Woo Not the World.

Mutanabbi (915–65)
Shame Kept My Tears Away.

Mutén, Burleigh
Demeter's Blessing.
Hesperides, The.
Queen Hera.
Queen Medusa.
Urania.

Mutis, Alvaro
Amen.
East Song.
Sonata.
Word, A.
You Are a Daughter of the Lagides.

Mutran, Khalil (1872–1949)
Boycott.
Evening.

Mutswairo, Solomon (b. 1924)
My Birds.

Muuse, 'Abdillaahi
Elder's Reproof to his Wife, An.

Muyassar, Orkhan (1914–65)
Graves.
Lost.
Race.
Statue, The.
Transformations.
Wall of Tomorrow, The.

Muzaffar, May
Absent, The.
Flash, A.
Friends.
Reticence.
Spinning.
Voice, The.

Muzahim al-Ugaili (fl. 700)
Earth Outside, The.

Mycall, John (d. 1833)
Our States, O Lord.

Myer, Michael
Cool Cat.

Myers, Frederic William Henry (1843–1901)
Hymn: "Hark what a sound, and too divine for
    hearing."
Surrender to Christ.

Myers, Jack (b. 1941)
Experts, The.

Instinct, The.
Mom Did Marilyn, Dad Did Fred.
What's Left.

Myles, Eileen (b. 1949)
American Poem, An.
December 9th.
Eileen's Vision.
Merk.
Milk.
New England Wind.
Maxfield Parrish.
Rotting Symbols.
Sadness of Leaving, The.
School of Fish.
Sleepless.
Taxing.
Woman like Me, A.

Mylonas, Eva (b. 1936)
Holidays.

Myŏng'ok (fl. 16th cent.)
Dreams.

Myoyu (1333–93)
Defying the power of speech, the Law
    Commission on Mount Vulture!

Myrddyn (Merlin)
Yscolan.

Myrinos
"L" may stand for fifty, Lais.
Time topples Statyllios like a doddery oak.

Myrow, Josef
You Make Me Feel So Young.

Mystic, Rabi'a the See Rabi'a al-Adawiyya

N

Na'car, Pancho (1909–63)
Foreigner Who Died in Juchitán, The.

Na Ceapaich, Sileas (c.1660–c.1729)
Alasdair of Glengarry.
Conversation with Death, A.

Na-lan Hsing-te (Nara Singde) (1655–85)
Tune: "Autumn Waters"—Listening to Rain.
Tune: "Big String of Words A"—The Great
    Wall.
Tune: "Butterflies Lingering over Flowers"—
    Leaving the Border.
Tune: "Immortal at the River"—Winter
    Willow.
Tune: "Partridge Sky"—Parting Sorrows.
Tune: "Remembering the Lady of Ch'in—At
    the Mouth of Dragon Pool."
Tune: "Remembering the Prince."
Tune: "Song of Dandy"—Hunting in Autumn.

Nabbes, Thomas (1605?–1641)
Song, The: "Beauty no more the subject be."
Song: "What a dainty life the milkmaid leads!"

Nabhan, Gary Paul
Coming Out on Solid Ground After the Ice
    Age.

Nâbî (c. 1642–1712)
In the Garden of Time and Destiny.

**Nabokov, Vladimir Vladimirovich (Vladimir
    Sirin) (1899–1977)**
Execution, The.
Fame.
Literary Dinner, A.
Lolita.
Ode to a Model.
On Translating 'Eugene Onegin.'
To Russia.
What Is the Evil Deed.

Naden, Constance (1858–1889)
Evolutional Erotics.
Love's Mirror.
Love Versus Learning.
Moonlight and Gas.
Natural Selection.
Pantheist's Song of Immortality, The.
Pessimist's Vision, The.
Poet and Botanist.
Scientific Wooing.
Sister of Mercy, The.
Solomon Redivivus, 1886.

Two Artists, The.

Nadir, Moishe (Yitzhok Reis) (1885–1943)
Adjectives.

Nadja (1902–1940)
Blue Wind, The.

Nadson, Semion Yakovlevich (1862–87)
Brother, The.

Nádvorníková, Alena (b. 1942)
Art History (Sandro Botticelli)
Determination of Time.

Nag Hammadi Library
Look upon me.
Sent from the Power.

Nagai, Mariko
Histories of Bodies.

Naganawa, Arlene
Learning to Swim.

Nagase, Kiyoko (b. 1906)
Mother.
Surf.

Nagy, László (1925–1978)
Bartók.
City's Coat of Arms, The.
Coalmen, The.
Csontváry.
Frosts are Coming.
Grasshoppers on the Bell.
Hymn for All Seasons.
Who'll Ferry Love to the Yonder Shore.
Young Miracle Stag, The.

**Nahman [or Nachman] of Bratzlav, Rabbi (1770–
    1811)**
Annul Wars.
From "The Torah of the Void."
Heart of the World, The.

Nahum (fl. c.1300)
Spring Song.

Naimy, Mikhail (1889–1988)
Autumn Leaves.
Close Your Eyes and See.
Hope is agony.
Hunger.
My Brother.
Rotating Tombs.
Solemn Vow, A.

Nairne, Carolina Oliphant, Baroness (1766–1845)
Caller Herrin'
Heiress, The.
Laird o' Cockpen, The.
Land o' the Leal, The.
Will Ye No Come Back Again?

Naisby, T. H. (1931–89)
Reflections on Hillsborough in Memoriam.

Naito Joso (Joso) (1662–1704)
About the grave / Waves of spring mist.
Autumn cicada, The.
Fields and mountains.
Gruel heaped / In a perfect bowl.
How green— / Flowering slopes.
I've just come up.
No need to cling: "No need to cling."
These branches: "These branches."

Naito Meisetsu (1847–1926)
My only hope against.

Najara, Israel (1555–1628)
God of the World.
Loved of My Soul.

Naji, Ibrahim (1848–1953)
Farewell: "Leave me, my love, it's time to
    part."
Oblivion.

Nakamichi (d. 1893)
At the crossroad.

Nakasuk
Great Farter, The.
Invisible Men, The.
Magic Words to Feel Better.

Nakhla, Amin (1901–76)
Black Song.
To the Beloved Grown Past Youth.

Nalungiaq
Heaven and Hell.

Namagusai Tazukuri (d. 1858)
In fall.

Na'mani, Huda (b. 1930)
Both Earth and Heaven.
Love Poem: "In your quest or request God is remote."
To You.

Nameroff, Rochelle
California Dreaming.
Elvis Presley.

Namjoshi, Suniti (b. 1941)
Caliban's Journal.
From the Travels of Gulliver.
Not loved enough, nor yet quite lost.

Namjoshi, Suniti and Gillian Hanscombe
Well, Then Let Slip the Masks.

Nampijinpa, Jennie Hargraves
Child, leave the tape recorder.

Nampo Jomyo (d. 1308)
This year, the twenty-ninth of the twelfth.
To hell with the wind!

Nan-o-myo
Not falling, not ignoring.

Nandai (d. 1817)
Since time began.

Nandī Majumdār, Rāmkumār
Mind, I'm talking to you.

Nandī, Rāmdulāl (d. 1851)
I understand how, Tara, I understand.
Mind, let's go to an estate that's decent.

Nanei (1363–1438)
Splitting the void in half.

Nannestad, Elizabeth (b. 1943)
Portrait of a Lady.
Queen of the River.

Nantembo (1839–1925)
On New Year's Day.

Naone, Dana (b. 1949)
Girl with the Green Skirt.
I make all the poetic pauses.
Long Distance.
Presence, The.
Sleep.

Napaljarri, Pansy Rose (b. 1966)
Kangaroo, The.
Two women sit in the shade away from the hot sun.

Napanangka, Valerie Patterson
Horse, The.
Rain, The.

Napier, Felicity
Houseplant.
I Do Not Want the Ceiling of the Sistine Chapel.
I Have Taken the Suits and Shoes to Oxfam.

Napurrurla, Irene James (b. 1962)
Water, The.

Napurrurla, Rhonda Samuel (b. 1966)
Two Mothers, The.

Nara See **Narayana Rao, V.**

Nara Singde (1655–85)
Tune: 'As If in a Dream.'
Tune: 'Butterflies Lingering over Flowers.'
Tune: 'Sand of Silk-Washing Brook' In Memoriam.

Narain, Kunwar (b. 1927)
Towards Delhi.

Naranjo, Carmen (b. 1930)
Part One: The Orders Begin.

Naranjo-Morse, Nora
Gia's Song.
Tradition and Change.

Narasimhaswami, K. S. (b. 1915)
Consolation to Empty Pitchers.

Narayana Rao, V. (Nara) (b. 1932)
White Paper.

Narbut, Vladimir Ivanovich (1888–1944)
October.

Narihira (Ariwara no Narihira) (825–80)
Even in the age.
Facing His Own Death.
I have always known / That at last I would.
Is that the same moon.
Regretting the Past.
This is not the moon.

Narihira, Ariwara no See **Narihira (Ariwara no Narihira)**

Narovchatov, Sergey [or Sergei] Sergeievich (1919–81)
In Those Years.
Wolf Cub.

Nartsissov, Boris (b. 1906)
Marated Bastilled age, A.

Nash, Ogden (1902–71)
Adventures of Isabel.
Anatomy of Happiness, The.
Ant, The.
Arthur.
Benjamin.
Canary, The.
Cat, The.
Come On In, the Senility Is Fine.
Cook called McMurray, A.
Cow, The.
Curl Up and Diet.
Dog, The.
Duck, The.
Eel, The.
Emmet, The.
England Expects.
Evening Out, The.
Experiment Degustatory.
Family Court.
First Limick.
Genealogical Reflection.
Germ, The.
Golly, How Truth Will Out.
Grackle, The.
Grandpa Is Ashamed.
Ha! Original Sin!
Here Usually Comes the Bride.
I Can't Have a Martini, Dear, but You Take One, or, Are You Going to Sit There Guzzling All Night?
I'm a Stranger Here Myself.
I pray the Lord my soul to take.
Spring Comes to Murray Hill.
Inter-Office Memorandum.
Introspective Reflection.
Invocation: "Senator Smoot (Republican, Ut.)"
It Figures.
Lama, The.
Limerick: "Careless explorer named Blake, A."
Limerick: "Crusader's wife slipped from the garrison, A."
Limerick: "Cute secretary, none cuter, A."
Limerick: "Elderly bride of Port Jervis, An."
Limerick: "Jolly young fellow from Yuma, A."
Limerick: "Lama of Outer Mongolia, A."
Limerick: "Novelist of the Absurd, A."
Limerick: "Old Danish jester named Yorick, An."
Limerick: "There was a young fellow named Fonda."
Limerick: "There was a young girl of old Natchez."
Limerick: "There was a young lady called Harris."
Limerick: "There was an old gossip called Baird."
Limerick: "There was an old man in a trunk."
Lines to a World-famous Poet Who Failed to Complete a World-famous Poem; or, Come Clean, Mr. Guest!
Lines Written to Console Those Ladies Distressed by the Lines 'Men Never Make Passes, etc.'
Man Can Complain, Can't He?, A.
Mermaid, The.
Seven Spiritual Ages of Mrs. Marmaduke Moore, The.
Mr. Artesian's Conscientiousness.
Necessary Dirge, A.
Octopus, The.
Lion, The.
Old Men.
Panther, The.
Parent, The.
Parsnip, The.
Peekaboo, I Almost See You.
Pig, The.
Portrait of the Artist as a Prematurely Old Man.
Private Dining Room, The.
Purist, The.
Reflection on Babies.
Reflection on Ingenuity.
Reflections on Ice-breaking.
Requiem: "There was a young belle of old Natchez."
Rhinoceros, The.
Round About.
Samson Agonistes.
Sea-Gull and the Ea-Gull, The.
Sea-Gull, The.
Song of the Open Road.
Song to Be Sung by the Father of Infant Female Children.
Speak Low.
Sweet Bye and Bye.
Sweet Dreams.
Taboo to Boot.
Tale of Custard the Dragon, The.
Termite, The.
Terrible People, The.
They Don't Speak English in Paris.
Third Limick.
Turtle, The.
Tweedledee and Tweedledoom.
Up from the Egg; the Confessions of a Nuthatch Avoider.
Very like a Whale.
Wapiti, The.
What Do You Want: A Meaningful Dialogue, or a Satisfactory Talk?
Which the Chicken, Which the Egg?
Winter Morning.
Word to Husbands, A.
Young flirt of Ceylon, A.

Nashe [or Nash], Thomas (1567–1601)
Adieu, Farewell, Earth's Bliss[e].
Autumn.
Choise of valentines, The.
Fair Summer Droops.
Spring, the Sweet Spring.

Nasir, Amjad (b. 1955)
Bent Branches.
Exile.
Loneliness.

Naso, Publius Ovidius See **Ovid**

Nasrin, Taslima (b. 1962)
Another Life.
At the Back of Progress.
Border.
Character.
Eve Oh Eve.

Nasser, Eugene Paul (b. 1935)
Arab woman is wailing in the parlor, The.
Lebanon, land of our birth and hopefully of our dying.

Nathan, Leonard (b. 1924)
At the Well.
Bladder Song.
Body Count.
Breathing Exercises.
Election, The.
Hole.
Letter.
So?
Toast.

Nathan, Robert (1894–1985)
Christian, Be Up.
Mountaineer, The.
Sonnet: "Because my grief seems quiet and apart."
These Are the Chosen People.

Natzler, Caroline
There.

Navajo Oral Tradition
Coyote, Skunk, and the Prairie Dogs.
Creation of the Earth, The.
Ground-Squirrel Song.
There Are No People Song.

Nawaz, Gharib (1143–1236)
Riddle.

Naylor, James Ball (1860–1945)
Authorship.

"Nayo" *See* Watkins, Nayo-Barbara
Nazareno, Clovis L.
  Bohol's Tarsier Population.
  Cortes Swamp, The.
Nazario, Amanda
  Kevin and Nicole.
  Melt me.
Ndebele, Njabulo S. (b. 1948)
  Revolution of the Aged, The.
Ndlovu, Thembinkosi
  Elegy for the Dead of Soweto.
Ndu, Pol N (1940–78)
  Evacuation.
  Udude.
Ne Jame, Adele
  About the Men.
  Somnambulist.
  Song of a Thousand Empty Hands.
  World Is a Wedding, The.
Neal, John (1793–1876)
  Fresher and fresher comes the air. The blue.
  It is that hour when listening ones will weep.
  O save thy children blue Ontario!
  There's a fierce gray Bird, with a bending
    beak.
Neal, Larry (b. 1937)
  Harlem Gallery: From the Inside.
  James Powell on Imagination.
  Lady's Days.
  Malcolm X—an Autobiography.
  Middle Passage and After, The.
Neale, John Mason (1818–66)
  Guide from St. Stephen the Sabaite, The.
  Hymn for Easter Morn.
  Oh, Give Us Back the Days of Old!
Neander, Joachim (*fl.* 1680)
  Praise to the Lord the Almighty.
Nedîm (d. 1730)
  Take Yourself to the Rose-Garden.
Needham, Frederick B.
  One! strikes the clock in the belfry tower.
Neely, Letta
  Eight Ways of Looking at Pussy.
  Multiple Assaults.
  Rhonda, Age 15, Emergency Room.
Neiburg, A. J. (*fl.* 1933)
  It's the Talk of the Town.
Neidjie, Bill (*fl.* 1987)
  This earth.
Neihardt, John Gneisenau (1881–1973)
  In vain against the formless wolves of air.
  Summer turned.
Neilson, John Shaw (1872–1942)
  Crane Is My Neighbor, The.
  Flowers in the Ward.
  In the Street.
  May.
  Orange Tree, The.
  Schoolgirls Hastening.
  Soldier Is Home, The.
  Sundowner, The.
  Take Down the Fiddle, Karl!
  To the Red Lory.
  You Cannot Go Down to the Spring.
Nekipelov, Viktor Aleksandrovich (1928–89)
  Alabushevo.
Nekrasov, Nikolai Alekseyevich (1821–77)
  Capitals Are Rocked, The.
Nekrasov, Vsevolod (b. 1934)
  And I Speak of Cosmic Things.
  I repeat.
  So who of us.
  Somehow I really want to go.
  What kind of Pushkin am I.
Nekrasova, Ksenya [*or* Kseniia] (1912–58)
  Blind Man, The.
  Rublyov XVth Century.
  Street, The.
Nelligan, Emile (1879–1941)
  Watteau, a Dream.
Nelson, David (1793–1844)
  My Days are Gliding Swiftly By.
Nelson, Frank Carleton
  Human Heart, The.

Nelson, Helena
  With my Mother, Missing the Train.
Nelson, Howard
  My Father Went to Funerals.
  Peepers.
Nelson, Jo
  Our Love.
Nelson, John
  For Whom the Bells Toll and Toll and Toll.
  If a Fish Fell in a Forest.
  If You Knew September.
  Just Word Wranglin'
  Never Eat Oranges!
  Teed Off.
Nelson, Lynn *See* Waniek, Marilyn Nelson
Nelson, Maggie (b. 1973)
  Brightness.
  56 Westervelt.
  Molino.
  Motel Story.
  Proposal.
  Shiner.
  Vallejo.
  Wish.
  Wish Fulfillment.
Nelson, Marilyn (b. 1946)
  Balance.
  Ballad of Aunt Geneva, The.
  Chopin.
  Chosen.
  Cover Photograph.
  How I Discovered Poetry.
  Juneteenth.
  Love Song.
  Sacrament of Poverty, The.
Nelson, Willie (b. 1933)
  Heaven and Hell.
Nemerov, Howard (b. 1920)
  Amateurs of Heaven, The.
  At a Country Hotel.
  Author to His Body on Their Fifteenth
    Birthday, 29.ii.80, The.
  Backward Look, The.
  Because You Asked about the Line between
    Prose and Poetry.
  Blue Suburban.
  Blue Swallows, The.
  Bluejay and the Mockingbird, The.
  Boom!
  Boy with Book of Knowledge.
  Brainstorm.
  Brief Journey West, The.
  Cabinet of Seeds Displayed, A.
  Carol: "Now is the world withdrawn all."
  Casting.
  Celestial Emperor, The.
  Creation Myth on a Moebius Band.
  Death of God, The.
  Debate with the Rabbi.
  Dependencies, The.
  Easter.
  Epigrams.
  Eve.
  Extract from Memoirs.
  Fable of the War, A.
  Fall Again, The.
  Fugue.
  Ginkgoes in Fall.
  "Good-bye," said the river, "I'm going
    downstream."
  Goose Fish, The.
  Grace to Be Said at the Supermarket.
  Gyroscope.
  Historical Judas, The.
  History of a Literary Movement.
  I Only Am Escaped Alone to Tell Thee.
  Icehouse in Summer, The.
  IFF.
  In the Beginning.
  Insomnia I.
  Intimations.
  John 3:1–15; Now there was a man.
  Learning by Doing.
  Learning the Trees.
  Life, A.
  Life Cycle of Common Man.

  Low-Level Cross-Country.
  Makers, The.
  Manners.
  Metamorphoses.
  Models.
  Money.
  More Joy in Heaven.
  Mousemeal.
  Murder of William Remington, The.
  Mystery Story.
  Negro Cemetery Next to a White One, A.
  Nicodemus.
  Night Operations, Coastal Command RAF.
  Old Picture, An.
  On Being Asked for a Peace Poem.
  On Certain Wits.
  Ozymandias II.
  Picture, A.
  Playing the Machine.
  Primer of the Daily Round, A.
  Reading Pornography in Old Age.
  Redeployment.
  Reflexions on the Seizure of the Suez, and on a
    Proposal to Line the Banks of That Canal
    with Billboard Advertisements.
  Remorse for Time, The.
  Sacrificed Author, A.
  Salt Garden, The.
  Santa Claus.
  September, the First Day of School.
  Singular Metamorphosis, A.
  Snowflakes.
  Song of Degrees, A.
  Speculation.
  Statues in the Public Gardens, The.
  Storm Windows.
  Style.
  Sweeper of Ways, The.
  Thirtieth Anniversary Report of the Class of
    '41.
  To David, about His Education.
  To My Least Favorite Reviewer.
  To the Rulers.
  Town Dump, The.
  Translation.
  Ultima Ratio Reagan.
  Vacuum, The.
  View from an Attic Window, The.
  War in the Air, The.
  Way of Life, A.
  Western Approaches, The.
  Wolves in the Zoo.
  Writing.
Nemes Nagy, Ágnes (1922–91)
  Between.
  Bird.
  Carbon Dioxide.
  Comparison, A.
  Conciousness.
  Conversation.
  Defend It.
  Four-Light Window, A.
  Garden of Eden, The.
  Geyser, The.
  Ghost, The.
  I Carried Statues.
  Ice.
  Lake Balaton.
  Lazarus.
  Like One Who.
  Pinetree.
  Scene, The.
  Shapelessness, The.
  Simile.
  Sincerity.
  Storm.
  To a Poet.
  To Freedom.
  To Liberty.
  To My Craft.
  Towards Springtime.
  Trees.
  Winter Angel.
  Winter Trees.
  Words to a Song.
Nensho (1409–82)
  Only genuine awakening results in that.

Nepo, Mark
  Oil of Her Hands, The.
Neri, Giampiero (b. 1927)
  Case of the Same Name, A.
  Inn of Angels, The.
  Natural History.
  Seasons.
Neruda, Pablo (Neftalí Ricardo Reyes Basualto) (1904–73)
  Almería.
  America, I Do Not Call Your Name Without Hope.
  Amor America (1400)
  Poetry.
  And what did the rubies say.
  Body of a Woman.
  Burial in the East.
  Come up with me, American love.
  Dead Gallop.
  Dictators, The.
  Different Ship, A.
  Drunk As Drunk.
  Every Day, Matilde.
  Final.
  Flag, The.
  Forgive me if my eyes see.
  From the explosion to the iron split.
  Funeral in the East.
  Gross innocent.
  Hero, The.
  Homecomings.
  How did the grapes come to know.
  I did not touch your night, or your air, or dawn.
  I Explain a Few Things.
  I love the handful of the earth you are.
  I'm Explaining a Few Things.
  If Each Day Falls.
  Introduction: My Themes.
  Leaning into the Afternoons.
  Letter to Miguel Otero Silva, in Caracas.
  Love Song: "I love you, I love you, is my song."
  Melancholy inside Families.
  Men grow with all that grows.
  My love, if I die and you don't.
  Nothing but Death.
  Ode to César Vallejo.
  Ode to Laziness.
  Ode to My Socks.
  Ode to Salt.
  Ode to the Cat.
  Ode to the Lemon.
  Ode to the Watermelon.
  Pardon me, if when I want.
  Past.
  Poem.
  Poem 15.
  Poem 20.
  Poet's Obligation.
  Rise up, brother, be born with me.
  Sexual Water.
  Some Beasts.
  Sonnet 4.
  Still, I am here.
  Stone upon stone, and man, where was he?
  Stone within stone, and man, where was he?
  Tell me, is the rose naked.
  Then up the ladder of the earth I climbed.
  They Receive Instructions Against Chile.
  To the Foot from Its Child.
  Tonight I Can Write the Saddest Lines.
  Too Many Names.
  United Fruit Co.
  Walking Around.
  We Are Many.
  Who works harder on earth.
Nerval, Gérard de (Gérard Labrunie) (1808–55)
  El Desdichado.
  Fantasy.
  Golden Sayings.
  Old Tune, An.
  To J—Y Colonna.
Nervo, Amado (1870–1919)
  Cowardice.
  Ecstasy.

  Gift, The.
  Revenge.
  Sorrow Vanquished.
Nesbit, Edith (Edith Nesbit Bland) (1858–1924)
  Among His Books.
  Appeal.
  At Parting.
  Child's Song in Spring.
  Claim, The.
  Dead to the Living, The.
  Goose-Girl, The.
  Gray Folk, The.
  Great Industrial Centre, A.
  Haunted.
  Husband of To-Day, The.
  Kiss, The.
  Love's Guerdons.
  Song: "Oh, baby, baby, baby dear."
  Things That Matter, The.
  To Vera, Who Asked a Song.
  Vies Manquées.
  Villeggiature.
  Wife of All Ages, The.
Neto, Agostinho (1922–79)
  African Poem.
  Grieved Lands, The.
  Kinaxixi.
  Saturday in the Sand-Slums.
  We Must Return.
Neufeld, Amos
  Children of Night.
  Family Album.
  Pictures and Stories.
Neumark, Georg (fl. 1641)
  If thou but suffer God to guide thee.
Nevill, Frances Manners, Lady Abergavenny (b. after 1527, d. 1576)
  Necessarie Praier in Meeter Against Vices, A.
Nevin, Edwin H. (1814–89)
  Happy, Saviour, Would I Be.
  When Our Earthly Sun Is Setting.
Newbolt, Sir Henry John (1862–1938)
  Clifton Chapel.
  Commemoration.
  Drake's Drum.
  From Generation to Generation.
  Gillespie.
  He Fell among Thieves.
  Master and Man.
  Messmates.
  Moonset.
  Non-Combatant, The.
  Song: "Flowers that in thy garden rise, The."
  Vitaï Lampada.
Newburn, Laura
  Office Geraniums.
Newell, Catherine Parmenter
  Dream House.
Newell, Elizabeth (fl. 1655–68)
  Dialogue, A.
Newell, Robert Henry See "Kerr, Orpheus C."
Newley, Anthony
  Candy Man, The.
  Goldfinger.
  What Kind of Fool Am I?
  Who Can I Turn To (When Nobody Needs Me?)
Newlove, John (b. 1938)
  America.
  Double-headed Snake, The.
  Pride, The.
  Samuel Hearne in Wintertime.
  What Do You Want?
Newman, Edward (fl.1840)
  Earwigs.
Newman, Gail
  Anti-Semitic Demonstration, An.
  Photograph of Survivors.
  Recording History.
Newman, John Henry, Cardinal (1801–90)
  Angel.
  Chorus of Angels.
  Desolation.
  Elements, The.
  Melchizedek.

  Path of the Just, The.
  Pillar of the Cloud, The.
  Sensitiveness.
  Taormini.
Newman, Louis I. (b. 1895)
  Voice of God, The.
Newson, Dyan (b. 1952)
  Crowther—Ours.
  Turnabouts.
Newton, Byron Rufus (1861–1938)
  Owed to New York.
Newton, Charles (b. 1776?)
  Wild Nature.
Newton, John (1725–1807)
  Amazing Grace.
  Glorious Things of Thee Are Spoken.
  "In Evil Long I Took Delight."
  Name of Jesus, The.
Nezahualcoyotl (1402–72)
  Be Indomitable, O My Heart.
  Can It Be True That One Lives on Earth?
  Flowers of Red and Blue.
  Our Lord.
  Where Will I Go?
Nezval, Vitězslau (1900–58)
  City With Towers.
  Lilac by the Museum on St. Wenceslas Square, The.
  Moon over Prague.
  Prague in the Midday Sun.
  Trap Door.
  Walker in Prague.
Ng Shao (fl. 6th cent.)
  New Wife, The.
Ngata, Apirana (1874–1945)
  Cream Song, The.
Ngatho, Stella (b. 1953)
  Footpath.
Ngawai, Tuini (1910–65)
  Great King.
  News, The.
Ngo Chi Lan (fl. 15th cent.)
  Autumn.
  Winter.
Ngunaitponi (David Unaipon) (1873–1967)
  Song of Hungarrda, The.
Nguyen Binh Khiem (1491–1585)
  Hated Rats, The.
  Worried.
Nguyễn Chí Thiện (b. 1933)
  Jungle Night, A.
  Model Children of the Regime, The.
  Party holds you down and you lie still, The.
  This Land's No Joy.
  Travel with Grief—Goodbye to Joy.
Nguyễn Gia Thiều (1741–98)
  You were a fool, Old Man of the Moon.
Nguyễn Khuyễn (1835–1909)
  Man Who Feigns Deafness, The.
  To the Singing Girl Named Luu.
Nguyễn Trãi (1380–1442)
  Bamboo Hut, The.
  Plough and a Spade, A.
Nguyễn Văn Lạc (1842–1915)
  Shrimps.
Ngwenya, Malangatana (b. 1936)
  Woman.
Nhan, Dieu See Ly Ngoc Kieu
Ní Chuilleanáin, Eiléan (b. 1942)
  At alarming bell daybreak, before.
  Dead Fly.
  Deaths and Engines.
  Informant, The.
  Letter to Pearse Hutchinson.
  Old Roads.
  Pygmalion's Image.
  Real Thing, The.
  Rose-Geranium, The.
  Saint Margaret of Cortona.
  Second Voyage, The.
  Street.
  Studying the Language.
  Swineherd.
  Tale of Me, The.

Wash.

Ni Dhomhnaill, Nuala (b. 1952)
Annunciations.
As for the Quince.
Aubade: "It's all the same to morning what it dawns on."
Bond, The.
Broken Doll, The.
Cathleen.
Feeding a Child.
I Cannot Lie Here Anymore.
Labasheedy (The Silken Bed)
Language Issue, The.
Leaba Shíoda.
Marvellous Grass.
Miraculous Grass.
Parthenogenesis.
Poem for Melissa.
Race, The.
Shannon Estuary Welcomes the Fish, The.
Shannon Estuary Welcoming the Fish, The.
Unfaithful Wife, The.
Venio ex Oriente.

Ni Tsan (1301–74)
Following the Rhymes of the Six Poems "Thinking of the Past at Ku-su and Ch'ien-t'ang."
Inscribed on a Painting.
Inscribed on a Painting by Myself.
Inscribed on the Painting, "River in Autumn."
Lamenting Noble Scholar Chu.
Man in Hangchou Spread Word that I Had Died. Chen-chü Heard of This and Was Upset, So I Have Written This to Send Him, A.
On the Fifteenth Day of the Ninth Month of the Year Kuei-mao of the Chih-cheng Period (Oct. 22, 1363), I Painted This to Send to the Summoned Scholar, Sheng-po, and Inscribed This Poem on It.
On the Twentieth Day.
Painting "Solitary Fisherman by a Spring River," The.
To the Retired Scholar Chang.
Two Poems to the Tune "Hsiao-t'iao hung."
Two Poems to the Tune "Jen-yüeh yüan."
Waking from a Nap.
Woodpecker, The.
You ask when I will go back home.

Niatum, Duane (b. 1938)
After the Death of an Elder Klallam.
Apology.
Art of Clay, The.
Ascending Red Cedar Moon.
Chief Leschi of the Nisqually.
Crow's Way.
Drawings of the Song Animals.
Elegy for Chief Sealth.
First Spring.
Homage to Chagall.
In the Labyrinth of Elements.
Indian Rock, Bainbridge Island, Washington.
Lines for Roethke Twenty Years after His Death.
Maggie.
No One Remembers [Abandoning] the Village of White Fir.
Novelty Shop, The.
Old Woman Awaiting the Greyhound Bus.
On Hearing the Marsh Bird's Water Cry.
On Leaving Baltimore.
On Visiting My Son, Port Angeles, Washington.
Pieces.
Reality of Autumn, The.
Rufous Hummingbird.
Salmon, The.
Slow Dancer That No One Hears but You.
Snowy Owl near Ocean Shores.
Stones Speak of an Earthless Sky.
To Your Question.
Traveler, The.

Nibenegenesabe, Jacob
I try to make wishes right.
One time I wanted two moons.
Quiet until the Thaw.

Niblett, Peter
Tiger, The.

Nicaenetus (fl. 3rd cent. B.C.)
Not in the city, Philoterus.
Speaks Bito's tomb to whomsoever reads.

Nicarchos
Sweet Nicarete, who served Athene's shuttle.

Nicarchus of Alexandria (fl. A.D. 1st cent.)
Agelaus was kind to Acestorides.
All great events have harbingers.
Another doctor story. Our G.P., Marcus.
Diodorus the hunchback / Went to Socles the quack.
Have you heard the latest miser story.
I like a woman built on ample lines.
If blocked, a fart can kill a man.
Law should have ear-plugs, not bandaged eyes, The.
Listen! The night-raven's song.
Niconoë has just inched past her prime.
One deaf man went to law with.
Path of glory leads but to the grave, The.
Phido the miser's crying.
Take note who stoop.

Niccolai, Giulia (b. 1934)
Careful that these *Frisbees*.
Clear Form Clashes, The.
Frisbees on Light.
From the Novissimi.
Geographical History, The.
Harry's Bar Ballad.
Only Indirectly.
So Inferred.
Syntactic and Verbal.
' What's that?' the boy asks his mother, pointing to the flag.

Nichol, B. P. (b. 1944)
Ferry Me Across.
Gorg, a Detective Story.
Hill Songs of Saint Orm, The.
Monotones.
Scraptures: 7th Sequence.
Scraptures: 17th Sequence.
Some Nets.
St. Anzas IX.
St. Anzas VI.
Two Words; a Wedding.

Nicholl, Theodore (1902–73)
His Friend's Last Battle.

Nicholls, Horatio
Among My Souvenirs.

Nicholls, Judith
Journey.
Mary Celeste.
Polar Cub.
Season Song.
Storytime.

Nichols, Alberta
Until the Real Thing Comes.
Why Shouldn't It Happen to Us?
You Can't Stop Me from Lovin' You.

Nichols, Carrie May
Boomerang, The.

Nichols, Grace (b. 1950)
Beverley's Saga.
Black.
Come up and see me sometime.
Configurations.
Holding My Beads.
Like a Beacon.
Long-Man.
Praise Song for My Mother.
Wha Me Mudder Do.
White.

Nichols, Kevin
Feast of Stephen, The.

Nichols, Robert Malise Bowyer (1893–1944)
Aurelia.
Don Juan's Address to the Sunset.
Flower of Flame, The, *sels.*
Get-Away, *sels.*
Harlot's Catch.
Moon between High Tranquil Leaves, The.
Sonnets to Aurelia.
Sprig of Lime, The.

Talking of Ezra Pound and long-dead pantos.
To D'Annunzio: Lines from the Sea.

Nicholson, John (1790–1843)
On a Calm Summer's Night.

Nicholson, Norman (1914–87)
Blackberry, The.
Caedmon.
Carol for the Last Christmas Eve.
Carol: "Mary laid her Child among."
Cleator Moor.
Comet Come.
Cowper's Tame Hare.
Epithalamium for a Niece.
Five Minutes.
For Hokey and Henrietta.
From a Boat at Coniston.
Halley's Comet.
Michaelmas.
On the Closing of Millom Ironworks.
Rockferns.
Shepherds' Carol.
Song at Night.
To the River Duddon.
Tune the Old Cow Died Of, The.
Weather Ear.

Nicias (c.470–413 B.C.)
Fountain at the Tomb, The.
I, Hermes, guard Cyllene's wooded slopes.
Spring blossoms, honey-bee, in the colours you parade.

Nickerson, Sheila
At Auke Bay the whales dance.
Seal's cry has lain against my leg, A.

Nicol, Abioseh (b. 1924)
African Easter.
Meaning of Africa, The.

Nicolson, Adela Florence Cory See "Hope, Laurence"

Nicolson, Veronica
Limerick: "I once took my girl to Southend."

Niedecker, Lorine (b. 1903)
As praiseworthy / the power of breathing.
Clothesline post is set, The.
Darwin.
Death of my poor father, The.
Element Mother, The.
Fancy Another Day Gone.
Far reach.
For best work.
Get a load.
Graves, The.
He lived—childhood summers.
I Married.
I rose from marsh mud.
Lake Superior.
Lobster, The.
Men leave the car, The.
My friend tree.
My Life by Water.
My life is hung up.
My mother saw the green tree toad.
News.
Old man who seined.
Paean to Place.
Paul / when the leaves.
Poems at the Porthole.
Remember my little granite pail?
Sewing a Dress.
Smile / to see the lake.
Stone / and that hard.
Subliminal.
There's a better shine.
Thomas Jefferson.
War.
What horror to awake at night.
Who was Mary Shelley?
Will You Write Me a Christmas Poem?
Woman in middle-life.
You are my friend.
Young in Fall I said: the birds.

Nielsen, Kristy
Self Portrait as Nancy Drew, Girl Sleuth.

Niemoller, Pastor (1892–1984)
First They Came for the Jews.

Nienhauser, William H.
Sent to the Taoist of Dragon Mountain, Hsu

Fa-leng.
Nietzsche, Friedrich Wilhelm (1844–1900)
Against the Laws.
Notes.
Solitary, The.
Star Morals.
Undiscouraged.
Niger, Paul (1917–62)
What?/ a rhythm.
Nighean Dhonnchadh (The Daughter of Duncan Campbell of Glenlyon) (*fl.* 1570)
Early on Lammas Morning.
Nighean Uisdein, Mor (*fl.* c.1615)
Ay, Bashful Thou!
Nigot
You surprise me, crow.
Nijhoff, Martinus
At a Grave.
Dancer.
Last Day.
Light.
Light, The.
Musician, The.
New Stars, The.
Soldier Who Crucified Jesus, The.
Nikitin, Ivan Savvich (1824–77)
Night in a Village, A.
Nikolayeva [or Nikolaeva], Olesya [or Olesia] (b. 1955)
Daughter.
Here, everything gets eaten: drippings, marinade.
Party on Women's Day, A.
Seven Beginnings.
Nikolic, Georg (b. 1949)
Key to Dreams.
Under the Ninth Sky.
Niles, John Jacob (1892–1980)
In All the Magic of Christmas-Tide.
Niles, Nathaniel (1741–1828)
Why Should Vain Mortals Tremble.
Nilsson, HeidiLynn (b. 1974)
How Came What Came Alas.
My Least Skirtable Deficiency.
On Inheriting Departure.
We Are Easily Reduced.
Nimatullah [or Ni'matu'llah], Seid [or Sayyid] (d. 1431)
Song of Seyd [or Seid] Nimetollah of Kuhistan.
Nimmo, Dorothy
Exorcism.
My Father's Shadow.
Nims, Bonnie
On a Cold Autumn Day.
Nims, John Frederick (b. 1913)
Agamemnon before Troy.
Christmas.
Contemplation.
Evergreen, The.
Freight.
Knowledge of God.
Love Poem: "My clumsiest dear, whose hands shipwreck vases."
New Year's Eve, 1938.
Tide Turning.
Trainwrecked Soldiers.
Trick or Treat.
Young Ionia, The.
"Nirala" (Suryakant Tripathi) (1896–1961)
Betrayal, The.
Nisbet, Hume (1849–1921?)
Isandula.
Nishiwaki Junzaburo (b. 1894)
January in Kyoto.
Man Who Reads Homer, A.
Nishiyama Soin (1605–82)
Cherry blossoms / dizzying.
Settling, white dew.
Nitschmann, Anna (1715–60)
This Flock So Small.
Niu Hsi-chi (*fl.* c.930)
Where the mist has torn.
Niyazi [or Niazi], Salah (b. 1935)
Hameed.

Um Hakeem.
Nizami Arudi (*fl.* 1110)
Calling the Doctor (1000 A.D.)
No Ch'ŏn-myŏng (1913–57)
Nameless Woman, A.
Noailles, Anna de (1876–1933)
Poem on Azure.
Noble, Ray (1903–78)
Good Night, Sweetheart.
I Hadn't Anyone Till You.
Touch of Your Lips, The.
Very Thought of You, The.
Nobleman, Blythe
Tabloid News.
Noel, Linda
Understanding Each Other.
Noel-Scott, Barbara
Hansel and Gretel.
"Nogar, Rui" (b. 1933)
Poem of the Conscripted Warrior.
Noguchi, Rick (b. 1967)
Breath He Holds, The.
From Rooftops, Kenji Takezo Throws Himself.
His Waves.
I, the Neighbor Mr. Uskovich, Watch Every Morning Kenji Takezo Hold His Breath.
Kenji Takezo Becomes Water.
Not Surfing Some Days.
Really Long Ride, The.
Turn of Privacy, The.
When for Weeks the Sea Is Flat.
Noguere, Suzanne (b. 1947)
Barney Bigard.
Scribes, The.
Secret, The.
Soma.
Whirling Round the Sun.
Noho-mai-te-Rangi (*fl.* c.18th cent.)
Song for Te Hauapu.
Noin (988?–1050)
After the storm / On Mount Mimuro.
As I approach / The mountain village.
Spring in a Mountain Village.
Spring twilight.
Nokan, Charles (b. 1937)
My Head Is Immense.
Nolens, Leonard (b. 1947)
Address.
Origins.
Paranoia.
Place and Date.
Poetic License.
Saint Vitus's Dance in October 10.
Tributary.
Noll, Bink (b. 1927)
Abraham's Madness.
Nolla, Olga (b. 1938)
Erotic Suite.
Greek History.
Manifest, The.
Reencournter with the Goddess.
Thoughts on Innocence.
Troubadour Love.
Nomberg, David
Russian Cradle Song, A.
Nonnus (*fl.* 5th cent.)
But Dionysos had no healing physic for his comrade fallen, of dancing he thought no more.
Dionysus and Ampelos.
Eros came near in the horned shape of a shaggy Silenos.
Where Carpos wandered and died, I will fall headlong.
Nooteboom, Cees (b. 1933)
Basho 1.
Basho 2.
Basho 3.
Basho 4.
Nordbrandt, Henrik
China Observed Through Greek Rain in Turkish Coffee.
No Matter Where We Go.
Our Love Is Like Byzantium.

Sailing.
Streets.
Norman, Peter
I could have been Lord Dacre or a balalaika-maker.
Norman, Pierre
When I Take My Sugar to Tea.
Norman, Rosemary (b. 1946)
Cabbage.
My Son and I.
Norris, Alfred (b. 1914)
Humble Heart, A.
Norris, Anne
Limerick: "Rose gives a tremulous glance, The."
Norris, John (1657–1711)
Meditation, The.
My Estate.
Norris, John W. (b. 1893)
Give Peace, O God, the Nations Cry.
Norris, Kathleen (b. 1947)
Lilith and the Doctor.
Memorandum / The Accountant's Notebook.
Naming the Living God.
Persephone.
Prayer to Eve, A.
Stomach.
Wedding in the Courthouse, The.
Norris, Leslie (b. 1921)
Ballad of Billy Rose, The.
Barn Owl.
Belonging.
Bridges.
Cage Bird and Sky Bird.
Early Frost.
Elegy for David Beynon.
Elegy for Lyn James.
His Father, Singing.
Hudson's Geese.
Hyperion.
Merlin and the Snake's Egg.
Mice in the Hay.
Pit Ponies, The.
Ravenna Bridge.
Shepherd's Dog, The.
Stone and Fern.
Thin Prison, The.
Tiger in the Zoo, A.
Water.
Norse, Harold (b. 1926)
Believing in the Absurd.
Business of Poetry, The.
Colosseum.
I'm Not a Man.
I Would Not Recommend Love.
Picasso Visits Braque.
We Bumped Off Your Friend the Poet.
You Must Have Been a Sensational Baby.
Norte, Marisela (b. 1955)
Angel.
Peeping Tom Tom Girl.
North, Charles (b. 1941)
Air and Angels.
Elizabethan & Nova Scotian Music.
Few Facts about Me, A.
From the French.
Hospital.
Leap Year.
Little Cape Cod Landscape.
Note to Tony Towle (After W S), A.
Philosophical Songs.
Sunrise with Sea Monster.
Year of the Olive Oil, The.
"North, Christopher" *See* **Galt, John**
North, Dudley, 3rd Baron North (1581–1666)
Air: "So full of courtly reverence."
Platonic.
North, Frank Mason (1850–1935)
Where Cross the Crowded Ways of Life.
North, Mick (b. 1958)
Account, An.
Ordnance Survey in the Northern Counties.
Pheasant Plucker's Son, The.
Pinder.
Poems to My Father.

Portrait in a Brass Gong.
Red Desiré.
Shap.

Nortje, Arthur (1942–73)
Asseverations.
At Lansdowne Bridge.
At Rest from the Grim Place.
Autopsy.
Letter from Pretoria Central Prison.
Cosmos in London.
Immigrant.
Native's Letter.
Newcombe at the Croydon Gallery.
Up Late.
Waiting.

Norton, Andrews (1786–1853)
My God, I Thank Thee.

Norton, Caroline Elizabeth (1808–76)
Bingen on the Rhine.
I Do Not Love Thee.
In the cold change, which time hath wrought
on love.
Laura was lightsome, gay, and free from guile.
Like an enfranchised bird, who wildly springs:
"Like an enfranchised bird, who wildly
springs."
Obscurity of Woman's Worth.
Picture of Sappho, The.
To My Books.
Voice from the Factories, A.

Norton, George (*fl.* 1912)
My Melancholy Baby.

Norton, John (1651–1716)
Funeral Elegy upon That Pattern and Patron of
Virtue, A.

Norton, Thomas
O all ye nations of the Lord.

Norwid, Cyprian (1821–83)
But Just to See.
Recipe for a Warsaw Novel.
Those Who Love.

Norworth, Jack (1879–1959)
Take Me Out to the Ball Game.

Nossis (*fl.* c.290 B.C.)
Even from a distance, this picture is known.
It seems that Aphrodite took with joy.
Kallo dedicated her portrait in the house of
golden.
Laugh aloud, then pass by, with a kind.
Let us go into the temple.
Let us go to the temple.
Melinna herself is re-created: notice the face.
Melinna herself! It *is*—see how kindly.
Most honoured Hera, who descends from
heaven.
Nothing is sweeter than love.
Nothing is sweeter than love, all other
blessings.
Nothing is sweeter than love, all other riches.
O Artemis of Delos and lovely Ortygia.
O Honored Hera, who often descending from
heaven.
Shields Bruttians threw from their doomed
shoulders.
Stranger, if you sail to the land of lovely
dances, Mitylene.
This is Thaumareta's picture, and how well it
captures.
This portrait captures Thaumareta's form—it
renders.
When we go to the temple, let's see
Aphrodite's.
When you've laughed out loud and said a
friendly.

Notari, Luciana (b. 1944)
Body and Soul.
Brief Ecstasy.
Distance.
Harsh Metropolitan Season.
If One Always Denies.
Winter Landscape.

Notley, Alice (b. 1945)
Baby Is Born Out of a White Owl's
Forehead—1972, A.
Beginning with a Stain.

California Girlhood, A.
How Spring Comes.
I—Towards a Definition.
Jack Would Speak Through the Imperfect
Medium of Alice.
Mysteries of Small Houses.
Overhead at night, above the planet.
Poem: "You hear that heroic big land music?"
Where Leftover Misery Goes.
White Peacock, The.
White Phosphorus.

Novakovich, Josip (b. 1956)
Shadow.

**"Novalis" (Friedrich von Hardenberg) (1772–
1801)**
Longing for Death.
When geometric diagrams and digits.
Yearning for Death.

Novello, Ivor
And Her Mother Came Too.
We'll Gather Lilacs.

Novikov, Denis Gennad'evich (b. 1967)
On my right hand I'll seat one of my loves.

Novikov, Nikolay (b. 1933)
In our world it's unusual.
White on white's a flatness.

Nowlan, Alden (1933–83)
Beginning.
For Jean Vincent d'Abbadie, Baron St.-Castin.
God Sour the Milk of the Knacking Wench.
Grove beyond the Barley, The.
I, Icarus.
In the Operating Room.
Mother and Son.
Only When My Heart Freezes.
Rites of Manhood, The.
Stoney Ridge Dance Hall.
Suppose This Moment Some Stupendous
Question.
Thief, The.
Wickedness of Peter Shannon, The.

Noyes, Alfred (1880–1958)
Anvil, The.
Art, I.
Art, II.
Barrel-Organ, The.
Butterfly Garden, The.
Double Fortress, The.
Epilogue: "Carol, every violet has."
Highwayman, The.
Night Journey.
Resurrection.
Spring, and the Blind Children.

Noyes, Nicholas (1647–1717)
Consolatory Poem Dedicated unto Mr. Cotton
Mather, A.
Præfatory Poem to the Little Book, Entituled,
Christianus per Ignem, A.
Prefatory Poem, on . . . *Magnalia Christi
Americana*.
Rev. Nicholas Noyes to the Rev. Cotton
Mather, The.
To My Worthy Friend, Mr. James Bayley.

Ntiru, Richard (b. 1946)
Listen—listen.

Nu'aima [or Nuaymah], Mikha'il (b. 1889)
Seek Out Another Heart.
To a Worm.

Nuccoli, Cecco (*fl.* 14th cent.)
Since I abandoned and tied my soul to your
sweet appearance and manners oh Sir, guide
and light of my life, will I ever see you
before I die?
You have the light of my life, in your clear and
pleasing face, and don't see me.
Your promises come to me always together
with your betrayals, which you have more of
than the fox.

Nugent, Robert, Earl Nugent (1709–88)
Epigram: "I loved thee beautiful and kind."
Epigram: "My heart still hovering round about
you."
Epigram: "Since first you knew my am'rous
smart."
To Clarissa.

Nungarrayi, Julie Watson
Sorry.

Nuriddin, Jalauddin Mansur (b. 1944)
Children of the Future.

Nurkse, Dennis
Olmos.

Nurske, D.
Involuntary Music.

Nutter, Mrs. Charles Read *See* **Addison, Medora
C.**

Nuur, Faarah (d. 1930)
Limits of Submission, The.

Nwankwo, Chimalum (b. 1945)
Asphalt.
Poem: "In sand."

Nweke, Chuba
Moon Song.

Nye, Naomi Shihab (b. 1952)
Across the Bay.
Arabic.
Art of Disappearing, The.
At Mother Teresa's.
Blood.
Catalogue Army.
Famous.
For Lost and Found Brothers.
Fuel.
Going for Peaches, Fredericksburg, Texas.
I Still Have Everything You Gave Me.
Lunch in Nablus City Park.
Making a Fist.
Man Who Makes Brooms, The.
Mother of Nothing.
My Father and the Fig Tree.
My Uncle Mohammed at Mecca, 1981.
Negotiations with a Volcano.
New Year.
Ongoing.
Rebellion against the North Side.
Small Vases from Hebron, The.
Steps.
Traveling Onion, The.
Whole Self, The.
Yellow Glove.

Nystrom, Debra (b. 1954)
Insomnia.

O

O Brolchain, Mael Isu (*fl.* c.1086)
I give Thee thanks, my King.
My sins in their completeness.
To an Elderly Virgin.

O Dalaigh, Lochlann Og (*fl.* mid–16th cent.)
In Praise of Three Young Men.

Ó Dálaigh, Muireadhach Albanach (*fl.* 1200–24)
Elegy on Mael Mhedha, his Wife.

O Direain, Mairtin (1910–88)
Axle Song.
Berkeley.
Era's End.
Essence Is Not in the Living, The.
Homage to John Millington Synge.
Memory of Sunday.
Strong Beams.
That Face.

O Domhnaill, Maghnas (d. 1563)
Famished end to my tale this night, A.
Heart made full of thought, A.
Love, I think, is a disease.

O Heigeartaigh, Padraig (1871–1936)
My sorrow, Donncha, my thousand-cherished.

O Riordain, Sean (1917–77)
Claustrophobia.
Death.
Fever.
Frozen Stiff.
Ice Cold.
Moths, The.
Mount Melleray.
My Mother's Burial.
Switch.
Syllabling.

Ó Searcaigh, Cathal (b. 1956)
Clay Pipes, The.
Lament: "I cried on my mother's breast, cried sore."
Runaway Cow, A.

Oakes-Smith, Elizabeth (1806–93)
Annihilation.
Ode to Sappho.
'Tis the summer prime, when the noiseless air.

Oakes, Urian (1631–81)
Away loose-reined careers of poetry!
Elegie upon the Death of the Reverend . . . Mr. Thomas Shepard, An.
To the Reader.

Oakland, Ben
I'll Take Romance.

Oandasan, William (b. 1947)
Acoma.
Grandmothers Land.
Song of Ancient Ways, The.

Oates, Joyce Carol (b. 1938)
Edward Hopper's Nighthawks, 1942.
In Jana's Garden.
Insomnia.
Waiting on Elvis, 1956.

Obejas, Achy
Dancing in Paradise.
Lifes.
Public Place (After Olga Broumas), The.
Sunday.

Oberkofler, Joseph Georg
Heir, The.

Obi, Dorothy S.
Winds of Africa.

Obolduyev [or Obolduev], Georgy [or Georgii] Nikolaevich (1898–1954)
Rod, The.
Tongue, The.

O'Brien, Fitz-James (1828–62)
Ghost, The.

O'Brien, Geoffrey (b. 1948)
Lake, The.

O'Brien, John
Revelation on a Summer Walk.

"O'Brien, John" See **Hartigan, Patrick Joseph**

O'Brien, Lawrence F.
Diabolus in Musica.

O'Brien, Michael
Poem: "Little bones of."

O'Brien, Sean (b. 1952)
Before.
In Residence: A Worst Case View.

O'Bruadair [or Ó Bruadair], David [or Daibhí] [or Daithí] (c.1625–1698)
Adoramus Te, Christe.
Change, The.
Eire.
For the Family of Cuchonnacht O Dalaigh.
New Style, The.
O'Bruadair.
O it's best to be a total boor.
Shrewish, barren, bony, nosy servant, A.

Occom, Samson (1723–92)
Waked [or Wak'd] by the Gospel's Powerful Sound.

O'Connell, Eibhlin Dubh (Eibhlin Dubh Ni Chonaill) (b. 1743)
My steadfast love!
Your Grave Disfigures Me.

O'Connor, Frank (Michael Francis O'Donovan) (1903–66)
Angry Poet, The.

O'Connor, Mark (b. 1945)
Fire.
Sun-Hunters, The.
Turtles Hatching.

O'Connor, Philip (b. 1916)
Fag-End.
Raspberry in the Pudding, The.
Poems (I–XI)
Writing in England Now.

O'Curry, Eugene
Litany to Our Lady.

O'Dalaigh, Gofraidh Fionn (d. 1387)
Child in Prison, A.

Under Sorrow's Sign.

O'Dalaigh, Muireadhach Albanach (Muireadhach Albanach) (c.1180–1220)
Invocation: "Last night my soul departed."
Mighty Mary, hear me.
On the Death of His Wife.
On the Gift of a Knife.
Young man of alien beauty.

O'Daly, Bill
Whale in the Web, The.

O'Donovan, Michael Francis See **O'Connor, Frank**

O'Daly, Murragh (fl. c.1250)
On Killing a Tax Collector.

Odarchenko, Yury [or Iurii] Pavlovich (1903–60)
And you, Vanya.
Bears became cucumbers.
Cap, a sword, flowers, A.
Claudia Petrovna.
On Red Square, on the chopping block.
Only for you my tea roses.
Path I'm following, The.
There are perfect illustrations.
What a sweet little day, what a day!

Oden, Gloria C. (b. 1923)
Bible Study.
Private Letter to Brazil, A.
Review from Staten Island.
Riven Quarry, The.
Testament of Loss.
This Child Is the Mother.

Odio, Eunice (b. 1947)
Creation.
I'm at the point of hurting myself and listening to myself.
It is not true that you are far from 'the light that can find you.'
It is the dawn.
Letter to Carlos Pellicer.
Memory of My Private Childhood.
Prologue to a Time That Is Not Itself.

O'Donnell, Brigid (Bríd Iníon Iarla Chille Dara) (b. c.1590, d. after 1607)
O young man who composes the poem.

O'Donnell, Charles Leo (1884–1934)
Process.
Resolution.
Security.

O'Donnell, Hugh See **MacWard, Owen Roe**

O'Donoghue, Bernard (b. 1945)
Apparition, The.
Nun Takes the Veil, A.
Weakness, The.

O'Donoghue, Gregory (b. 1951)
Web, The.

O'Dowd, Bernard (1866–1953)
Cupid.
To other eyes and ears you are a great.

Odoyevtseva [or Odoevtseva], Irina (Iraida Gustavovna Geinike Ivanova) (1901–90)
Ground Glass.

Ōe no Chisato (fl. 9th cent.)
As I watch the moon.

Oehlenschläger, Adam (1779–1850)
There Is a Charming Land.

Oengus Céile Dé (fl. late 10th cent.)
Time is ripe and I repent, The.

Ofeimun, Odia
Beyond Fear.
Gong, A.
Handle for the Flutist, A.
How Can I Sing.
Judgement Day.
Landing on the Moon.
Let Them Choose Paths.
Naming Day, A.
New Brooms, The.
Poet Lied, The.
Prologue: "I have come down."
Song: "You are the sandstorm beneath my skin."

Og MacWard, Fearghal (fl. early 17th cent.)
All Ireland's now one vessel's company.

Ogarev, Nikolay Platonovich (1813–79)
Road, The.

Ogata Kenzon (1663–1743)
Retrospective.

O'Gillan, Angus (fl. 14th cent.)
Dead at Clonmacnois [or Clonmacnoise], The.

Ogilvy, Eliza (1822–1912)
Grannie's Birthday.
Natal Address to My Child, March 19th 1844, A.
Newly Dead and Newly Born.

O'Gnive [or O'Gnihm], Fearflatha (fl. c.1562)
After the Flight of the Earls.
Downfall of the Gael, The.
Passing of the Poets, The.

O'Grady, Desmond (b. 1935)
Berlin Metro.
Day concludes burning, The.
Dying Gaul, The.
Finn's Wishes.
Great Horse Fair, The.
Here, because of the shock, the sudden.
If I Went Away.
In the valleys of the future we shall walk.
My darling, my love.
Page from a Diary.
Poet in Old Age Fishing at Evening, The.
Professor Kelleher and the Charles River.
Purpose.
Reading the Unpublished Manuscripts of Louis MacNeice at Kinsale Harbour.
This introspective exile here today.
Tipperary.
Twist of cloth on the flat stones, A.

O'Grady, Jennifer (b. 1963)
Anonymous Wedding Photo.
Buster's Last Hand.
Poem for the Womb.

O'Grady, Standish (fl. c.1793–c.1841)
Winter in Lower Canada.

Ogundipe-Leslie, Molara
Nigeria of the Seventies.
On Reading an Archeological Article.
Rain at Noon-time.
Song at the African Middle Class.
Tendril Love of Africa.
Yoruba Love.

O'Hara, Frank (1926–66)
Abortion, An.
Animals.
Answer to Voznesensky and Evtushenko.
Aus Einem April.
Autobiographia Literaria.
Ave Maria.
Blocks.
Captains Courageous.
Chez Jane.
Cornkind.
Easter.
Rhapsody.
For James Dean.
Forest Divers.
Greek Girl at Riis Beach, A.
Having a Coke with You.
Homosexuality.
Hôtel Transylvanie.
Hunter, The.
Ideal Bar, The.
Image of Leda, An.
In Favor of One's Time.
In Hospital.
In Memory of My Feelings.
Interior (With Jane).
Day Lady Died, The.
Lebanon.
Les Luths.
Litany, A.
Madrid.
Mary Desti's Ass.
Meditations in an Emergency.
Military Ball, A.
1951.
Ode: "Idea of justice may be precious, An."
Ode: Salute to the French Negro Poets.
Ode to Joy.
Ode to Michael Goldberg's Birth and Other Births.
On Rachmaninoff's Birthday.

Painter's Son, The.
Personal Poem.
Poem: "At night Chinamen jump."
Poem: "Eager note on my door said Call me, The."
Poem: "Hate is only one of many responses."
Poem: "I don't know as I get what D. H. Lawrence is driving at."
Poem: "Khrushchev is coming on the right day!"
Poem: "Lana Turner has collapsed!"
Poem: "O solo mio, hot diggety, nix I wather think I can."
Poem: "There I could never be a boy."
Poetry.
Rogers in Italy.
Shine, "O world!" don't weary the gulping Pole.
Sleeping on the Wing.
Song: "Did you see me walking by the Buick Repairs?"
Step Away from Them, A.
Steps.
To Hell with It.
To John Ashbery on Szymanowski's Birthday.
To the Film Industry in Crisis.
To the Harbormaster.
Today.
Trout Quintet, The.
True Account of Talking to the Sun at Fire Island, A.
War, The.
Why I Am Not a Painter.
Windows.
You Are Gorgeous and I'm Coming.
You at the Pump.

O'Hara, Geoffrey (fl. 1918)
K-K-K-Katy.

O'Heffernan, Mahon (fl. early 17th cent.)
My Son, Forsake Your Art.
Who Will Buy a Poem?

Ohnishi, Takajiro
Blossoms in the Wind.

O'Huiginn, Tadhg Dall (1550–91)
Difference, The.
Present of Butter, A.
Satire on the O'Haras, A.
Visit to Enniskillen, A.

O'Huiginn, Tadhg Og (d. 1448)
Lament for Fearghal Ruadh.

O'Hussey [or **O'Heughusa**], **Eochadh** [or **Eochy**] (d. 1612)
Change in Style, A.
Mag Uidhir's Winter Campaign.
O'Hussey's Ode to the Maguire.

Ojaide, Tanure
Ward 6.
Consolation.
Daydream of Ants, The.
Emergency Kit.
Fate of Vultures, The.
Launching Our Community Developement Fund.
Verdict of Stone, A.
What They Said.
When Tomorrow Is Too Long.
Where Everybody Is King.
Where the Nightmare Begins.

Ojibwa Oral Tradition
Loon upon the Lake, The.

Okai, Atukwei (b. 1941)
999 Smiles.

Okano Kin'emon Kanehide (d. 1703)
Over the fields of.

Okantah, Mwatabu (fl. 20th cent.)
Afreeka Brass.
Southern Road.

Okara, Gabriel (b. 1921)
Call of the River Nun, The.
Mystic Drum, The.
Once upon a Time.
One Night at Victoria Beach.
Piano and Drums.
Spirit of the Wind.
To Adhiambo.

You Laughed and Laughed and Laughed.

O'Keefe, Eamer
Chords.

O'Keefe [or **O'Keeffe**], **John** (1747–1833)
Air: "Flaxen-headed cow-boy, as simple as may be, A."
I Want a Tenant; a Satire.

O'Keeffe, Adelaide (1776–1855)
Kite, The.

Okigbo, Christopher (1932–67)
Banks of reed.
Bridge.
Come Thunder.
Death lay in ambush.
Elegy for Alto.
Elegy for Slit-Drum.
Elegy of the Wind.
Eyes Watch the Stars.
For he was a shrub among the poplars.
From flesh into phantom.
Hurrah for Thunder.
Image insists, An.
Lament of the Flutes.
Lion-hearted cedar forest, gonads for our thunder.
Lustra.
On the New Year.
Overture.
Passion Flower.
Sacrifice.
Suddenly becoming talkative.
Thunder Can Break.
Water Maid.

Okikaze, Fujiwara No
Who shall I have for friends.

Okita, Dwight
Nice Thing About Counting Stars, The.
Notes for a Poem on Being Asian American.

Okkur Macatti (fl. between 1st and 3rd cent.)
What Her Girlfriends Said to Her.

Oku, Princess (661–701)
How will you cross the autumn mountain alone?

Okudzhava, Bulat Shalvovich (b. 1924)
Ah, Nadya, Nadyenka.
As a child I came upon a grasshopper.
As I Sat in the Armchair of the Tsar.
Departure.
Everything here is curtained in darkness.
François Villon.
How the young flutist smiles.
I don't believe in God and fate.
I have never soared, never soared.
I need to worship someone.
I never soared, and never did I soar.
In the City Park.
Midnight Trolleybus.
Not About Death.
Once there was a soldier boy.
Paper Soldier.
Reflections Near the House Where Titian Tabidze Lived.
Ruispiri—A Comic Ballad.
Save us, the poets, save us, we have but.
Soldier's Ditty, A.
They exterminate poets.
To me, Muscovites are sweethearts out of old stories.

Okura See **Yamanoé** [or **Yamanoué**] **no Okura**

Okyo (d. 1890)
This phantasm.

O'Lahsen, Malika (b. 1930)
Dead Erect, The.
It Took One Hundred Years.

Older, Julia (b. 1941)
Two Worlds.

Oldham, John (1653–83)
Cup, The.
If you're so out of love with happiness.
London.
Of all the creatures, in the world, that be.
On Butler who can think without rage.
One night, as I was pondering of late.
Quiet Soul, A.
Upon a Bookseller.

Oldham, Perry
Noon.
War Stories.

Olds, Peter (b. 1944)
Psycho.
My Mother Spinning.
Thoughts of Jack Kerouac—& Other Things.

Olds, Sharon (b. 1942)
Knowing, The.
April, New Hampshire.
Clasp, The.
Connoisseuse of Slugs, The.
Death of Marilyn Monroe, The.
Ecstasy.
Elder Sister, The.
First.
Glass, The.
Greed and Aggression.
Guild, The.
Her First Week.
Her List.
His Costume.
I Go Back to May 1937.
In the Hospital Near the End.
Indictment of Senior Officers.
Language of the Brag, The.
Last Acts.
Leningrad Cemetery, Winter of 1941.
Lifelong.
Lifting, The.
May 1968.
Moment of My Father's Death, The.
Mother, The.
New Mother.
On the Subway.
One Girl at the Boys Party, The.
Promise, The.
Quake Theory.
Race, The.
Request, The.
Satan Says.
Saturn.
Seventh Birthday of the First Child.
Sex without Love.
Sisters of Sexual Treasure, The.
Station.
True Love.
Unjustly Punished Child.
Victims, The.
Wedding Vow, The.
Wellspring, The.

Oldys, William (1687–1761)
On a Fly Drinking out of [or from] His Cup.
On Himself.

Oles, Carole (b. 1939)
For the Drunk.
To a Daughter at Fourteen Forsaking the Violin.

Oleynikov, Nikolai Makarovich ("Makar Svirepy") (1891–1942)
Beetle, The.

Olinka, Sharon
Bird of Death.

Olitski, Leib (1894–1975)
My Song to the Jewish People.

Oliveira, David
Little Travel Story, A.
Paso Robles, San Luis Obispo, San Luis Obispo.
San Joaquin.
Summer.

Oliver, Douglas (b. 1937)
Little Night, A.
Oracle of the Drowned, The.
'u', 'je', 'r', 'r', 'im', 'a', 'finally.'
Walnut and Lily.

Oliver, Louis (**LittleCoon**) (b. 1904)
Empty Kettle.
Horned Snake, The.
Wagon Full of Thunder.

Oliver, Mary (b. 1935)
At the Shore.
Bats.
Black Walnut Tree, The.
Design.

Diviners, The.
Fox, The.
Goldenrod.
Grandmothers, The.
Hawk.
Hummingbird Pauses at the Trumpet Vine.
In Blackwater Woods.
Kingfisher, The.
Landscape.
Lilies.
Morning.
Picking Blueberries, Austerlitz, New York, 1957.
Poem 12.
Rain in Ohio.
Rice.
Roses, Late Summer.
Singapore.
Snapshots.
Some Questions You Might Ask.
Summer Day, The.
Swans on the River Ayr.
Through Ruddy Orchards.
Waking on a Summer Morning.
White Night.
Wild Geese.
Wings.

Oliver, W. H. (b. 1925)
Augury.
Counter-Revolution.
Parihaka.

Olivers, Thomas (1725–99)
God of Abraham praise, The.

Ologboni, Tejumola ("Rockie D. Taylor") (b. 1945)
Black Henry.
Changed Mind (or the Day I Woke Up)
I Wonta Thank Ya.

Ologoudou, Emile (b. 1935)
Liberty.
Vespers.

O'Loughlin, Michael (b. 1958)
Bunkers, The.
Cuchulainn.
Elegy for the Unknown Soldier.
Glasnevin Cemetery.
Irish Requiem, An.
Posthumous.

Olson, Charles (1910–70)
Across Space and Time.
Added to / making a Republic.
All/ wrong.
Anecdotes of the Late War.
As Cabeza de Vaca was.
As the Dead Prey upon Us.
At Yorktown.
Boats' lights in the dawn going so swiftly the, The.
Celestial Evening, October 1967.
Chain of memory is resurrection   I am a vain man, The.
Cole's Island.
Colored pictures.
Colored pictures/ of all things to eat: dirty.
Death of Europe, The.
Distances, The.
I, Maximus of Gloucester, to You ("By ear, she sd")
I, Maximus of Gloucester, to You ("Off-shore, by islands hidden in the blood")
In Cold Hell, in Thicket.
Kingfishers, The.
La Chute.
La Préface.
Letter 3.
Librarian, The.
Lordly and Isolate Satyrs, The.
Maximus from Dogtown-II.
Maximus, to Gloucester, Letter 2.
Maximus, to Gloucester, Letter 27.
Maximus, to Gloucester, Sunday, July 19.
Maximus, to Himself.
Merce of Egypt.
Moon Is the Number 18, The.
My memory is.
Newly Discovered "Homeric" Hymn, A.

O Quadriga.
Ocean, The.
Peloria the dog's upper lip kept curling.
Perfume / of flowers! A haw, The.
Plan for a Curriculum of the Soul, A.
Poem 143.
Praises, The.
Ring of, The.
Songs of Maximus.
Telesphere, The.
These Days.
Variations Done for Gerald Van De Wiele.

Olson, Elder (1909–92)
Ballad of the Scarecrow Christ.
Childe Roland, etc.
Four Black Bogmen, The.
Presence, The.
Reflections on Mirrors.

Olson, Ernst W. (1870–1958)
God of Peace, in Peace Preserve Us.

Olson, Ted (b. 1899)
Hypothesis.

Olstein, Lisa
We Still Have Basketball, Sara.

O'Malley, Mary (b. 1954)
Shoeing the Currach.

Omar ben Abi Rabi'a (d. 720)
Damsel, The.

Ombres, Rossana (b. 1931)
Afternoon Hours.
Angel Who Separated Us with the Flame, The.
Ballad of Noah's Daughter.
Bella and the Golem.
Embalmer.
Ensnaring Flower of Psalms.
Flower Ensnarer of Psalms.
Meadow Bug.
Morning Hours.
Nursery Rhyme in Eight Strophes.
Rondeau Tempo.
Sentimental Suffering of the Oyster of Smoke.
Strange Adventure.
Talin of the Pasta Factory.
Twelve.
White House, A.

Ome Shushiki (1668–1725)
After dream / How real.
Frost of separation / Father, child.
I wake and find.

Onakatomi Yoshinobu (921–91)
Deer on pine mountain, The.

Ondaatje, Michael (b. 1943)
Biography.
Breaking Green.
Burning Hills.
Cinnamon Peeler, The.
Elizabeth.
For you I have slept.
House Divided, A.
Inner Tube.
King Kong Meets Wallace Stevens.
Letters and Other Worlds.
Light.
Notes for the Legend of Salad Woman.
Rat Jelly.
Strange Case, The.
To a Sad Daughter.
Walking to Bellrock.

Onderdonk, Henry Ustic (1789–1858)
On Zion and on Lebanon.
Spirit in Our Hearts, The.
Though I Should Seek.

O'Neal, John
Shades of Pharoah Sanders Blues for My Baby.

O'Neill, Eugene (1888–1953)
Lament of a Subwayite.
To a Bull Moose.

O'Neill, Henrietta (1758–93)
Ode to the Poppy.
Written on Seeing Her Two Sons at Play.

O'Neill, Mary
My Fingers.
Sound of Water.
What Is Black?

"O'Neill, Moira" (Nesta Higginson Skrine) (1870–1955)
Corrymeela.
Her Sister.

O'Neill, Rose Cecil (1874–1944)
I Made a House of Houselessness.

Oness, C. Mikal
August 1990.
Climbing.
Of All There Is.
Pulling in the Nets.

Onitsura (Uejima Onitsura) (1661–1738)
Autumn wind / Across the fields.
Cherry blossoms, The.
Come! Come! Though I call.
Give my dream back.
Leaping trout sees, The.
Plum blossoms / One's nose.
To finally know.
True obedience.

Onitsura, Uejima *See* **Onitsura**

Ono no Komachi (834–80)
Although my feet.
As certain as color.
Autumn nights, it seems.
Color of the flowers / has faded, The.
Diver does not abandon, A.
Doesn't he realize / that I am not / like the swaying kelp.
Following the roads.
I long for him most.
If it were real / Perhaps I'd understand it.
Imperceptible / It withers in the world.
No moon, no chance to meet.
Since I've felt this pain.
So lonely am I.
Thinking about him.
Though I go to you.
When longing for you.
Yielding to a love.

Ono no Yoshiki (d. 902)
My love / Is like the grasses.

Ono, Yoko (b. 1933)
Mother of the Universe.

Oodgeroo of the tribe Noonuccal (Kath Walker) (1920–93)
Colour Bar.
Dawn Wail for the Dead.
Flea's Hymn.
Gooboora, the Silent Pool.
Last of His Tribe.
Municipal Gum.
No More Boomerang.
Past, The.
Time Is Running Out.
Unhappy Race, The.
We Are Going.

O'odham, Tohono [Owl Woman] [Juana Manwell]
Healing Songs.
Songs for the Four Parts of the Night.

Ōoka Mokoto (b. 1931)
Marilyn.

"Ophelia" (fl. mid–18th cent.)
Snaith Marsh; a Yorkshire Pastoral.

Opie, Amelia Alderson (1769–1853)
Negro Boy's Tale, A.
Ode to Borrowdale in Cumberland.
On the Approach of Autumn.
To a Maniac.
To Mr. Opie, On His Having Painted for Me the Picture of Mrs Twis.
To Winter.

Opitz, Martin (1597–1639)
Ah Dearest, let us haste us.
Concerning the Wolffsbrunnen near Heidelberg.
I'll lay this halfway me, which we the body name.
To This Book.
With snowy light of moon I cannot you compare.
You golden freedom, both my wish and my desire.

Opoku-Agyemang, Kwadwo (b. 1951?)
King Tut in America.

Opoku, Andrew Amankwa (b. 1912)
River Afram.
Oppen, George (b. 1908)
And Their Winter and Night in Disguise.
Animula.
Anniversary Poem.
Book of Job and a Draft of a Poem to Praise
the Paths of the Living, The.
But So As By Fire.
Confession.
Daedalus: The Dirge.
Disasters.
Discrete Series.
Eclogue: "Men talking, The."
Exodus.
Fear.
Forms of Love, The.
From Disaster.
From Virgil.
Gesture, The.
Gold on Oak Leaves.
Gold on Oak Leaves Said Young.
From a Photograph.
Image of the Engine.
Impossible Poem, The.
In Memoriam Charles Reznikoff.
It is difficult now to speak of poetry.
Morality Play: Preface, A.
Moving over the hills, crossing the irrigation.
Myself I Sing.
Myth of the Blaze.
No interval of manner.
O withering seas.
Occurrences, The.
Penobscot.
Product.
Psalm: "In the small beauty of the forest."
Quotations.
Resort.
Route.
Sara in Her Father's Arms.
Silver as / The needle's eye.
Survival: Infantry.
Taste, The.
To the Poets: To Make Much of the World.
Translucent Mechanics, The.
Whirl Wind Must, The.
Oppenheim, James (1882–1932)
Action.
As to Being Alone.
Future, The.
Handful of Dust, A.
Hebrews.
Runner in the Skies, The.
Slave, The.
Oppenheim, Meret (1913–1985)
Finally.
If You Say the Right Word, I Can Sing.
My Friend's Dog.
Round the World with the Rumpus God.
Where Is the Wagon Going?
Without Me Anyway.
Oppenheimer, Joel (b. 1930)
Bath, The.
Blue Funk.
Bus Trip, The.
Father Poem.
Feeding, The.
Innocent Breasts, The.
Leave It to Me Blues.
Love Bit, The.
Mare Nostrum.
Mother Poem.
Poem in Defense of Children.
Undefined Tenderness, An.
Opperman, D. J. (b. 1914)
Christmas Carol: "Three outas from the [High]
bleak Karoo."
Fable: "Under a dung-cake."
Oppezzo, Piera (b. 1934)
Demand.
Iteration.
Now Melanctha Had neither Home, nor
Regular Occupation. Life Was Just
Beginning for Her.
Project.

Ready-Made World.
Oppian (fl. 3rd cent)
Loves of the Tortoise, The.
Then from the teeming Filth, and putrid Heap.
Oquendo de Amat, Carlos (1905–36)
Poem of the Sea and of Her.
**O'Rahilly [or O'Reilly], Egan [or Ó Rathaille,
Aodhagán](1670–1726)**
Brightest of the Bright, The.
Brightness most bright I beheld on the way,
forlorn.
Drenching night drags on: no sleep or snore,
The.
Grey Eye Weeping, A.
Inis Fal.
Lament for Banba.
Lament for Tadhg Cronin's Children, sels.
More Power.
No help I'll call till I'm put in the narrow
coffin.
Time of Change, A.
Valentine Browne.
Vision, The.
O'Reilly, John Boyle (1844–90)
Builder's Lesson, A.
What Is Good?
White Rose, A.
O'Reilly, Michael (d. 1988)
Abused Child.
House Call to a Man with Parkinson's
Disease, A.
Potter.
Small Girl Brings an Injured Bird into the
Surgery, A.
Orerulavanar
What He Said.
"Orestes" (fl. c.1796)
Sonnet to Opium; Celebrating Its Virtues, A.
Orfalea, Gregory (b. 1949)
Age of Cruelty, The.
Bomb That Fell on Abdu's Farm, The.
Gift You Must Lose, A.
Jellyfish Eggs.
My Father Writing Joe Hamrah in a Blackout.
Rose of Brooklyn, The.
Sunken Road, Antietam 1980, The.
Wave.
Orientius (c. 450)
Bulk of these years is already gone out of
mind, The.
"Orinda" See Philips, Katherine
Orlandi, Guido
Friend, well I know thou knowest well to bear.
If thou hadst offered, friend, to blessed Mary.
Now of the hue of ashes are the Whites.
Orléans, Charles, Duc d' (1391–1465)
Alons au bois le may cueillir.
Balade.
Ballade: "I was in blossom when I was a
child."
Dieu Qu'il La Fait.
Go forth myn hert wyth my lady: "Go forth
myn hert wyth my lady."
Honure, joy, helthe, and plesaunce.
Las! Mort Qui T'a Fait Si Hardie.
Lost.
My Ghostly Fader.
Quant Souvenir Me Ramentoit.
Rondel: "Strengthen, my Love, this castle of
my heart."
Roundel: "Take, take this cosse, atonys, atonys,
my hert!"
Smiling Mouth and Laughing Eyen Grey, The.
Spring.
Le Temps a Laissié.
Well, Wanton Eye.
Orlen, Steve [or Stephen] (b. 1942)
Androgyny.
Orlov, Sergey [or Sergei] Sergeievich (1921–77)
They buried him in the terrestrial globe.
Orlovsky, Peter (b. 1933)
Collaboration: Letter to Charlie Chaplin.
Dick Tracy's Yellow Hat.
Dream May 18, 1958.
Lepers Cry.

I Dream of St. Francis.
Second Poem.
Snail Poem.
Some One Liked Me when I Was Twelve.
Poems from Subway to Work.
Ormerod, V. R.
Limerick: "In dealing with time it is found."
Limerick: "Night's bible-black darkness
prevails."
Limerick: "There was a young student called
Fred."
Ormond, John (b. 1923)
Ancient Monuments.
At His Father's Grave.
Cathedral Builders.
Certain Questions for Monsieur Renoir.
Definition of a Waterfall.
Design for a Quilt.
Design for a Tomb.
Gift, The.
In September.
Key, The.
Lament for a Leg.
My Dusty Kinsfolk.
My Grandfather and His Apple-Tree.
To a Nun.
Ormsby, Eric (b. 1941)
My Mother in Old Age.
Origins.
Skunk Cabbage.
Starfish.
Ormsby, Frank (b. 1947)
At the Jaffé Memorial Fountain, Botanic
Gardens.
Day in August, A.
Home.
Interim.
L'Orangerie.
Landscape with Figures.
My Careful Life.
Ornaments.
Padre, The.
Passing the Crematorium.
Soldier Bathing.
Some of us stayed forever, under the lough.
Spot the Ball.
Survivors.
Under the Stairs.
War Photographers, The.
Apples, Normandy, 1944.
Winter Offerings.
Orozco, Olga (b. 1920)
Miss Havisham.
Olga Orozco.
Reality and Desire.
Sphinxes Inclined to Be.
There Are No Doors.
To Make a Talisman.
Twilight (Between Dog and Wolf)
Orpingalik
Alcheringa Definitions.
In a Time of Sickness.
"Songs are Thoughts, Sung Out with the
Breath."
Orr, Bob (b. 1949)
Here.
Parable.
Orr, Gregory (b. 1947)
All Morning.
City of Salt, The.
Elegy for a Child.
In an Empty Field at Night.
Insomnia Song.
Litany, A.
Sweater, The.
Who'd Want to Be a Man?
Orrick, John
Little Things.
Wild Plum.
Orten, Jiri
Last Poem, The.
Whispered.
Ortiz, Simon J. (b. 1941)
At the Salvation Army.
Bend in the River.

Bony.
Creation.
Dry Root in a Wash.
Earth and Rain, the Plants & Sun.
8:50 A.M. Ft. Lyons VAH.
Final Solution: Jobs, Leaving.
Forming Child Poems.
Four Bird Songs.
Look to the Mountain.
My Father's Song.
On late-night television, two U.S. scientists
   talk about why the U.S
Pretty Woman, A.
Returned from California.
San Diego Poem, A.
Serenity in Stones, The.
Speaking.
Spreading Wings on Wind.
Story of How a Wall Stands, A.
Survival This Way.
Telling About Coyote.
To Insure Survival.
Travelling.
Travels in the South.
Upstate.
Vision Shadows.
Waiting for You to Come By.
War Poem.
Watching Salmon Jump.
Watching You.
What I Tell Him.
Wind and Glacier Voices.
Wisconsin Horse, The.

Ortleb, Chuck (b. 1950)
Metaphor as Illness.
Militerotics.
On Finding Out that the One You Slept with
   the Night Before Was Murdered the Next
   Day.
Some Boys.

Orton, Barbara J. (b. 1969)
Bacchanal.
Beekeeper.
Love Poem.
Sea Monkeys, The.

Orwell, George (Eric Blair) (1903–50)
As One Non-Combatant to Another.
Dressed man and a naked man, A.
Italian soldier shook my hand, The.

Osadebay, Dennis C. (b. 1911)
African Trader's Complaint, The.

Osaki, Mark (b. 1952)
Amnesiac.

Osbey, Brenda Marie (b. 1951)
Everything Happens to (Monk and) Me.
Geography.

Osborn, John
Whaling Song, A.

Osborn, Mary I. ("Mary I")
My Playmate.

Osborne, Jennie
Naming of Flowers, The.

Osen (d. 1696)
What a lark!

Osgood, Frances Sargent (1811–50)
Ah! Woman Still.
Ellen Learning to Walk.
Garden of Friendship, The.
He Bade Me Be Happy.

Osgood, Francis P. (b. 1910)
Winter Fairyland in Vermont.

Osgood, Kate Putnam (1841–1910)
Driving Home the Cows.

O'Shaughnessy, Arthur William Edgar (1844–81)
Ode: "We are the music-makers."
Song: "I made another garden, yea."

Osherow, Jacqueline
Ghazal: Comet.
My Cousin Abe, Paul Antschel and Paul
   Celan.
Phantom Haiku/Silent Film.
Song for the Music in the Warsaw Ghetto.
To Eva.
Villanelle for the Middle of the Night.
Villanelle from a Sentence in a Poet's Brief

Biography.
Yiddish Muses, The.

Ōshima Ryōta (1718–87)
No one spoke.
On rainy leaves / Glow.
Pure brush-clover / Basket of flowers.
They look / like newlyweds.

Osofisan, Femi (b. 1946)
Longing.
Paris Latin Quarter.
Release.
She Thinks in Song.

Osorio Benitez, Miguel Angel See **"Barba-Jacob, Porfirio"**

"Ossian" See **Macpherson, James**

Ossip, Kathleen (b. 1959)
Nature of Things, The.

Osterhaus, Joe (b. 1960)
Gambier.
New York Minute.
Pepper.
Shall We Dance.

Ostriker, Alicia (b. 1937)
Boys, the Broom Handle, the Retarded Girl,
   The.
Bride, The.
Bridge, The.
Eighth and the Thirteenth, The.
Healing.
I Brood about Some Concepts, for Example.
If your mother is a Jew, you are a Jew.
In the Twenty-Fifth Year of Marriage, It Goes
   On.
Lamenting the Inevitable.
Meditation in Seven Days, A.
Millennial Polka.
Minor Van Gogh (He Speaks), A.
Opinion of Hagar, The.
Story of Abraham, The.
Story of Joshua.
Studio, The (Homeage to Alice Neel)
Wintering.

O'Sullivan, Maggie (b. 1951)
Dancer, The.
Giant Yellow.
Hill Figures.
Lesson from the Cockerel.
Narrative Charm for Ibbotroyd.
2nd Lesson from the Cockerel.

**O'Sullivan, Owen Roe (Eoghan Rua O
Suilleabhain) (1748–84)**
His Request.
Magic Mist, A.
Seamus, light-hearted and loving friend of my
   breast.
Volatile Kerryman, The.

"O'Sullivan, Seumas" (James Starkey) (1879–1958)
In North Great George's Street.
Lamplighter, The.
Starling Lake, The.

O'Sullivan, Vincent (b. 1937)
Dogknotting in Quezaltenango.
Don't Knock the Rawleigh's Man.
Elegy for a Schoolmate.
Figure who stands on the beach, A.
Home.
Last things/ the turning leaves slip in the wind.
Look Sheila Seeing You've Asked Me.
Medusa.
Still Shines When You Think of It.
To be in a place for spring and not have lived
   its winter.
Waikato-Taniwha-Rau.

Osundare, Niyi (b. 1947)
And the snake says to the toad.
Excursion.
Eyeful Glances.
Frantic as a prentice poet.
Goree.
I Sing of Change.
Ikoyi / The moon here.
Madding moon, A.
Moon is an exile, The.
Our Earth Will Not Die.

Sand Seer, The.
We called the statue.
Who Says That Drought Was Here?
Word is an Egg, The.

Oswald, Alice (b. 1966)
Ballad of a Shadow.
Melon Grower, The.
Mountains.
Pilchard-Curing Song, The.
Sea Sonnet.
Wedding.

Oswald, H. S. (1751–1834)
O let him whose sorrow.

Oto (d. 1935)
At night my sleep.

Otogami
In the blackberry.

Otomo no Sakanoé, Lady (c.728–746)
Do not smile to yourself.
Don't you cut the brush.
It is other people who have separated.
My brother has on / a thin robe.
My heart, thinking / "How beautiful he is."
Sent from the Capital to Her Elder Daughter.
Though in my heart.
Till the rough-gem moon.
Where the plovers cry.

Otomo no Sakanoé, *the elder daughter of* Lady (*fl.* 8th cent.)
Were you a string of beads.
When we could have met.

Otomo no Tabito (Tabito) (665–731)
Better get drunk and cry.
To sit silent.

"Otrada, Nikolai Karpovich" (Nikolai Karpovich Turochkin) (1918–40)
Football.

Otsuchi (d. 1872)
O white chrysanthemum.

Otsuin (d. 1807)
Hidden among the roots.

Otsuji (1881–1920)
Winter midnight.

Otsup, Georgii Avdeievich See **"Rayevsky [*or* Raevskii], Georgy [*or*" Georgii] Avdeievich**

Otsuyu (1674–1739)
Cry of the deer / Where at its depths.

Otten, Willem Jan (b. 1951)
All Soul's Day.
Mud-Flat.
Poet Dives, The.

Otto, Heinrich (*fl.* 18th cent.)
Lord, Dear God! to Thy Attending.

Otway, Thomas (1652–85)
Enchantment, The.

Ou-yang Chiung (896–971)
Offering Congratulations to the Enlightened
   Reign.

Ou-yang Hsiu (1007–72)
Answer to Ting Yuan Ch'en, An.
Calligraphy Practice.
Cicada, The.
Cutting, A.
Deep, Deep in the Shade of the Court.
Distant Mountains.
East Wind.
Faint Thunder Drifts beneath the Willow.
Fisherman.
Green Jade Plum Trees in Spring.
In the Evening I Walk by the River.
Inscribed on the Arbor of the Old Drunkard
   (Tsui-weng-t'ing) at Ch'u-chou.
Old Age.
Old Fisherman.
Pear Leaves Redden, Cicada's Song Is Done,
   The.
Pool Is Full of Autumn Sky, Rippled by Gentle
   Breezes, The.
Reading the Poems of an Absent Friend.
Song of "Hand-in-Hand," A.
Song of Liang Chou.
Song of "Night After Night," A.
Song of Picking Mulberry.
Song of Spring at West Lake, Sent to Circuit

Officer Hsieh, A.
Song of the Radiant Lady, Replying to a Poem
 by Wang Chieh-fu.
Spring Day on West Lake.
Spring Walk to the Pavilion of Good Crops
 and Peace.
Thoughts on the First Day of Autumn, Sent to
 Su Tzu-mei.
Tune: 'Drunk in Fairyland.'
Tune: 'Gathering Mulberry Leaves.'
Tune: "Butterflies Lingering over Flowers."
Tune: "Butterflies Lingering over Flowers."
Tune: "Song of Picking Mulberry"—
 Recollections of West Lake.
Tune: "Treading on Grass."
Tune: 'Magnolia Flower.'
Tune: Treading on Grass.
When the Moon Is in the River of Heaven.
Written for the Pavilion of the Drunken Old
 Man at Ch'u-chou.

Ouologuem, Yambo (b. 1940)
Dear Husband.

Outram, George (1805–51)
Annuity, The.
On Hearing a Lady Praise a Certain Rev.
 Doctor's Eyes.

Ouwens, Kees (b. 1944)
Farmer, The.
New Sweater.
Some Tears.

Overbury, E. J.
Springtime It Brings On the Shearing, The.

Overstreet, Bonaro W. (b. 1902)
Count Ten.

Overton, Ron
Blues in "C."

Ovid (Publius Ovidius Naso) (43 B.C.–A.D. 17)
Amores, sels.
De Ponto.
Death of Orpheus, The.
Elegies, sels.
Heroides, sels.
Invective against Ibis, sels.
Metamorphoses, sels.
Tristia, sels.

Owen, Catherin See **Llwyd, Catherin Owen**

Owen, Ellis (1789–1868)
Epitaph: On the Near-Death Experience.

Owen, Gareth (b. 1922)
Gathering in the Days.
Half Asleep.
Jonah and the Whale.
This and That.
Uncle Alfred's Long Jump.
Waterfall.
Winter Days.

Owen, Goronwy (1723–69)
Elegy for His Daughter Ellen.
Invitation, The.
Prudent Simplicity.

Owen, Guy (1925?–1981)
Epitaph for a Beatnik Poet.
Epitaph for a Meat-Packer.

Owen, Jan
Visitation, The.

Owen, Louise
Chart Showing Rain, Winds, Isothermal Lines
 and Ocean Currents.

Owen, Maureen (b. 1943)
African Sunday.
All That Glitters.
For Emily (Dickinson)
Narcolepsy.

Owen, R. C.
Limerick: "Said philosopher-physicist Jeans."

Owen, Wilfred (1893–1918)
À Terre.
Anthem for Doomed Youth.
Apologia Pro Poemate Meo.
Arms and the Boy.
At a Calvary near the Ancre.
Chances, The.
Conscious.
Disabled.
Dulce et Decorum Est.

End, The.
Exposure.
From My Diary, July 1914.
Futility.
Greater Love.
Hospital Barge at Cérisy.
Insensibility.
Maundy Thursday.
Mental Cases.
Miners.
Music.
Next War, The.
Parable of the Old Men and the Young, The.
Roads Also, The.
Send-Off, The.
Sentry, The.
Shadwell Stair.
Show, The.
Smile, Smile, Smile.
Sonnet, to a Child.
Spring Offensive.
Strange Meeting.
To a Child.
To Eros.
To My Friend (With an Identity Disc)
To ———: "Three rompers run together, hand
 in hand."
Unreturning, The.
We'd found an old Boche dug-out, and he
 knew.
Wild with All Regrets.
Yes, there's the orderly. He'll change the
 sheets.

Owens, Philip (b. 1947)
Croeso i Gymru.

Owens, Rochelle (b. 1936)
Dedication.
I Am the Babe of Joseph Stalin's Daughter.
It is for me poetry.

Owenson, Sydney, Lady Morgan (1783?–1859)
Fragment 3.
Fragment 10. The Boudoir.
Fragment 19. L'Amant Mutin.
Fragment 35. The Irish Jig.
Joy.

Owl Woman See **O'odham (Owl Woman) (Juana
 Manwell), Tohono**

**Oxenham, John (William Arthur Dunkerley)
 (1861–1941)**
All One in Christ.
Art Thou Lonely?
Dies Ire-Dies Pacis.
Everymaid.
Fair Raiment.
Hammer and Anvil.
My Treasure.
Profit and Loss.
Pruner, The.
So Little and So Much.
Vimy Ridge.
Watchman! What of the night?

Oxley, William
Men stare at me more than at women.

Oxlie, Mary, of Morpeth (fl. c.1656)
To William Drummond of Hawthornden.

Oyake
Hidden in the clouds.

Ozick, Cynthia (b. 1928)
In the Synagogue.
Origins, Divergences.
When That with Tragic Rapture Moses Stood.
Wonder-Teacher, The.
Yom Kippur, 5726.

Ozui (d. 1738)
Still tied to the world.

P

Pace, Ser (fl. 1280)
Fresh content of fresh enamouring, A.
Pacernick [or Pacernik], Gary (b. 1941)
Louie the Tailor.
Pacheco, José Emilio (b. 1939)
Boundaries.

Enquiry Concerning the Bat, An.
High Treason.
Job 18, 2.
On the Fragile Labyrinth.
Song to Be Written on a Wave.

Pack, Richardson (1682–1728)
Epistle from a Half-Pay Officer in the Country
 to His Friend in London, An.

Pack, Robert (b. 1929)
Boat, The.
Proton Decay.
Thrasher in the Willow by the Lake, The.

Padel, Ruth
Angel.
On the Line.
On the Venom Farm.
Scotch.
Tell Me About It.
Trial.
Yew Berries.

Padeshah Khatun (fl. 14th cent.)
Sovereign Queen.

Padgaonkar, Mangesh (b. 1929)
Salaam.

Padgett, Ron (b. 1942)
After the Broken Arm.
Strawberries in Mexico.
Big Bluejay Composition.
Early Triangles.
Chocolate Milk.
December.
Detach, Invading.
First Drift.
Louisiana Perch.
Lucky Strikes.
Nothing in That Drawer.
Orange Jews.
Sandwich Man, The.
Something or Other.
Symbols of Transformation.
Tell Us, Josephine.
Three Animals.
Who and Each.
Wonderful Things.

Padilla, Heberto (b. 1932)
Daily Habits.
Discourse on Method, The.
Fountain, a House of Stone, A.
History.
In Trying Times.
Landscapes.
Legacies.
Man on the Edge.
Nuclear Umbrella.
Prayer for the End of the Century, A.
Promise, The.
Question for the Frankfurt School, A.
Self-Portrait of the Other.
Sometimes I plunge into the ocean.
Song of the Juggler.

Page, G. K.
Kaleidoscope.

Page, Geoff (b. 1940)
Country Nun.
Elegist, The.
Grit.
In Dante's Hell.
Inscription at Villers-Bretonneux.
Jerry's Plains, 1848.
Late Night Radio.
Premeditations.
Road Show.
Smalltown Memorials.

Page, Patricia K. (b. 1916)
After Rain.
Arras.
Brazilian Fazenda.
Deaf-Mute in the Pear Tree.
Element.
Evening Dance of the Grey Flies.
Images of Angels.
Man with One Small Hand.
Permanent Tourists, The.
Photos of a Salt Mine.
Puppets.
Schizophrenic.

Snowman, The.
Stenographers, The.
Stories of Snow.
Suffering.
T-Bar.
Typists.
War Lord in the Early Evening.

Pagis, Dan (b. 1930)
Autobiography.
Balloons.
Battle, The.
Conversation.
Draft of a Reparations Agreement.
Ein Leben.
End of the Questionnaire.
Europe, Late.
Evidence.
Footprints.
In the Laboratory.
Instructions for Crossing the Border.
Last Ones, The.
Late Author: Snapshot in the Rain, The.
Lesson in Observation, A.
Mosquito, The.
Picture Postcard from Our Youth.
Ready.
Roll-Call in the Concentration Camp.
Roll Call, The.
Scrawled in Pencil in a Sealed Car.
Snake.
Story, The.
Testimony.
Twelve Faces of the Emerald.
Wall Calendar.
Winter's End.
Written in Pencil in the Sealed Railway-Car.

Pain, D. W.
Limerick: "Modern young curate called
    Hyde, A."

Pain, Philip (d. 1668?)
Meditation 8.
Meditation 10.
Meditation 62.
Meditations for August 1, 1666.
Meditations for July 19, 1666.
Meditations for July 25, 1666.
Meditations for July 26, 1666.
Porch, The.
Whilst in This World I Stay.

Paine, Albert Bigelow (1861–1937)
Cooky-Nut Trees, The.
Dancing Bear, The.

Paino, Frankie
Matter of Division, A.
1965.
Truth, The.

Pak Mokwŏl (1919–78)
Prayer in Four Verses.

Palagyi, Louis (b. 1866)
Aimless.

Palasovszky, Ödön (1899–1980)
Humiliating the Laser-Beam.
Lapiade, Opus 3.
Susannah Bathing.

Palazzeschi, Aldo (1885–1974)
Nuns Go Walking.
Stranger, The.

Palés Matos, Luis (1898–1959)
Calling, The.
Elegy for the Duke of Marmalade.
Pueblo.

Paley, Grace (b. 1922)
Here.
People in My Family.
Sad Children's Song, The.
Some days I am lonesome   I want to talk to
    my mother.
Two Villages.
Warning, A.

Palgrave, Francis Turner (1824–97)
Eutopia.
Linnet in November, The.

Palis, Yolanda
Floor, The.
Waking Up.

Palitz, Morty
While We're Young.

Palladas [or Pallades] (360–430)
Blacksmith's quite a logical man, The.
Born crying, and after crying, die.
Born naked. Buried naked. So why fuss?
Cuckolded husbands have no certain sign.
Death feeds us up, keeps an eye on our weight.
Don't fash yourself, man! Don't complain.
Drink to drown my sorrows and restart, A.
Each new daybreak we are born again.
Fate didn't hustle Gessius to his death.
God rot the guts and the guts' indulgences.
God's philosophical and so can wait.
Grammar commences with a 5-line curse.
Grammarian's daughter, The.
Having Slept with a Man.
Hope! Fortune! Je m'en fous!
I was promised a horse but what I got instead.
Ignorant man does well to shut his trap, The.
Ignorant of all logic and all law.
It's no great step for a poor man to the grave.
Just look at them, the shameless well-to-do.
Let this life of worry.
"I know all," you say; of incompleteness, you
    have enough.
Life's a performance. Either join in.
Life's an ocean crossing where winds howl.
Lifetime's teaching grammar come to this, A.
Loving the rituals that keep men close.
Lyf So Short, The.
Man stole fire, and Zeus created flame.
Maurus.
Meditation.
Mein Breast, mein Corset und mein Legs.
Mere ants and gnats and trivia with stings.
Monks.
Murderer and Sarapis, The.
Poor devil that I am, being so attacked.
Poor little donkey! It's no joke.
Racing, reckoning fingers flick.
Sad and great evil is the expectation of
    death, A.
So, Mister Moneybags, you're loaded? So?
Thanks for the haggis. Could you really spare.
Theft of fire, The. Man's worst bargain yet.
Think of your conception, you'll soon forget.
This is all the life there is.
This is my mule, a poor long-suffering hack.
This Life a Theater.
Totting up the takings, quick Death can /
    reckon much faster than the businessman.
We Greeks have fallen on evil.
When he comes up to the bedroom.
When you send out invitations, don't ask me.
Where's the public good in what you write.
Where the Three Roads Meet.
Whose baggage from land to land is despair.
Why this desperation to move heaven and
    earth.
Women all / cause rue.
Women all shout after me and mock, The.
Zeus isn't such a raving Casanova.

Pallottini, Renata
Message.

Palma, Michael (fl. 20th cent.)
Coming of Age.

Palmer, E. Harriet (1840–82)
Parterre, The.

Palmer, Herbert Edward (b. 1880)
Aunt Zillah Speaks.
Ishmael.
Rock Pilgrim.
Woodworker's Ballad.
Wounded Hawk, The.

Palmer, John F. (b. c.1870)
Band Played On, The.

Palmer, John Williamson (1825–1906)
Stonewall Jackson's Way.

Palmer, Julea (fl. 1671–3)
Fruit of Sin, or a Lamentation for England,
    The.

Palmer, Michael (b. 1943)
Autobiography 2 (hellogoodby)
Construction of the Museum.
Dearest Reader.

Eighth Sky.
Erolog.
Fifth Prose.
H.
Here the image of a child on a hill.
I Do Not.
Letter 5.
Lines through these words, The.
Ninth Symmetrical Poem.
Notes for Echo Lake 3.
Of this cloth doll which.
Or anything resembling it.
Painted Cup, The.
Project of Linear Inquiry, The.
Prose 22.
Prose 31.
Recursus.
Seven Forbidden Words.
Sonnet: "Now I see them sitting me before a
    mirror."
Sun.
Theory of the Flower, The.
Twenty-four Logics in Memory of Lee
    Hickman.
Untitled (April '91)
Untitled (February 2000)
Voice and Address.
Wheel.

Palmer, Opal (b. 1954)
Wasting Time.

Palmer, R. F.
Conchie, The.

Palmer, Ray (1808–87)
Hymn: "Jesus these eyes have never seen."
Jesus, These Eyes Have Never Seen.
Lord, My Weak Thought in Vain Would Climb.
My Faith Looks Up to Thee.

Palmer, T. H. (1782–1861)
Try, Try Again.

Palmer, Vance (1885–1959)
Farmer Remembers the Somme, The.
Snake, The.

Paloff, Benjamin
On Transportation.

Palquera, Shem-Tob ben Joseph (1225–90)
Adapt Thyself.
Mouth and the Ears, The.

Paman, Clement (fl. c.1660)
On Christmas Day to My Heart.

Pambardu
Windmill at Mandanthanunguna.

Pamphilus
To the Swallow.

Pan Chao (A.D. 48–117?)
Needle and Thread.

Pan Chieh-yû (fl.c.48–46 B.C.)
Poem in Rhyme-Prose Form.
Present from the Emperor's New
    Concubine, A.
Song of Regret.

P'an Lang (d. 1009)
Tune: "Song of the Wine Spring."
Written on Lake View Tower.

P'an Yüeh (d. 300)
In Mourning for His Dead Wife.
Lamenting the Dead.
Rhyme-Prose on the Idle Life.
Thinking of My Wife.

Panchenko, Nikolai Vasil'evich (b. 1928)
Ballad of the Shot Heart.

Pande, Mrinal (b. 1946)
Two Women Knitting.

Pandeya, Sudama See "Dhoomil"

Paniker, K. Ayyappa (b. 1930)
Itch, The.

Pankey, Eric (b. 1959)
As We Forgive Those.
Confession of Cleopas, The.
Luke: 24:13–32; That very day two of them.
Reason, The.

**Panmure, Margaret Maule, Countess of (c.1667–
1731)**
Now let us unto some fair Medow goe.

Pannonius, Janus (1434–72)
About a Transdanurban Almond Tree.

About the Shipwrecked Frandus.
Difficult and Weighty Question, A.
Farewell to Várad.
On the Bird Which Still Flew, Though Its Head Was Severed.
One For Pope Paul.
To Mars, a Prayer for Peace.

Pant, Sumitranandan (1900–77)
Almora Spring.

"Pantycelyn" *See* **Williams, William**

Pao Chao (414–66)
Ascend Lu-Shan.
Do you not see the riverside grass.
Do you not see the young men off to war.
Going Out Through the North Gate of Chi.
Have you not seen the grasses on the riverbank?
Imitating the Old Poems.
In Imitation of Ancient-style Poetry.
In Imitation of "The King of Huai-nan."
Magic Cinnabar.
Presented as a Farewell to Secretary Fu.
Rhyme-Prose on the Desolate City.
Ruined City, The.
Scholar Recruit.
Splash water on level ground.
To you, fine wine in gold cup.
Water spilled on level ground.

Pao-chen, Liu *See* **"Tan Ying"**

Pao Ling-hui (*fl.* 5th cent.)
Added to a Letter Sent to a Traveler.

Pao Yu (*fl.* 5th cent.)
Viaticum.

Papago
There was a mountain, over its black roots [the deer].

Papaionnou, Yannis (1913–1972)
Nights without Hope (Rebetiko Song)

Papaleo, Joseph (*fl.* 20th cent.)
American Dream: First Report.

Pape, Gertrude (1907–1988)
Lake, The.

Pape, Greg (b. 1947)
Birds of Detroit.
Dinner on the Miami River.
In Line at the Supermarket.
In the Bluemist Motel.
Indian Ruins Along Rio de Flag.
Minotaur Next Door, The.
Storm Pattern.
Storm Surf.
Street Music.

Papertalk-Green, Charmaine (b. 1963)
Are We the Same.
No One to Guide Us.
Pension Day.
Wanna Be White.

Paquet, Basil T.
Basket Case.
Easter '68.
Graves Registration.
Group Shot.
In a Plantation.
It Is Monsoon at Last.
Morning—A Death.
Mourning the Death, by Hemorrhage, of a Child from Honai.
Night Dust-off.
They Do Not Go Gentle.

Paramore, Edward E., Jr. (1895–1956)
Ballad of Yukon Jake, The.

Pardo, Patrick (b. 1969)
I was on the couch when the Jehova's Witnesses came.

Parini, Jay (b. 1948)
Coal Train.

Parish, Mitchell
Deep Purple.
Sophisticated Lady.
Star Dust.
Stars Fell on Alabama.
Sweet Lorraine.

Park, Roswell (1807–69)
Jesus Spreads His Banner o'er Us.

Park, Song-Jook
On Such A Day.

Parker, Alan Michael
Abandoing All Pretense, the Vandals.
Above the Timberline.
After the Poem Who Knows.
Alchemy.
Another Poem about the Vandals.
Cruelty, the Vandals Say.
Days like Prose.
God of Pepper, The.
Lullaby: "Sleep and rain, two gangsters."
Magpie.
No Fool, the God of Salt.
Vandals, Horses.
Vandals in the Garden.
Vandals, The.

Parker, C. J.
Old soak from Stoke, An.

Parker, Dominique (b. 1964)
Art of the Nickname, The.
Foxfire.
Sand.
When Mark Deloach Ruled the World.

Parker, Dorothy (1893–1967)
Alexandre Dumas and His Son.
Alfred, Lord Tennyson.
Ballade at Thirty-Five.
Bohemia.
Bric-à-Brac.
Certain Lady, A.
Chant for Dark Hours.
Charles Dickens.
Coda: "There's little in taking or giving."
Comment.
D. G. Rossetti.
De Profundis.
Experience.
Flaw in Paganism, The.
General Review of the Sex Situation.
George Gissing.
George Sand.
Godmother.
Harriet Beecher Stowe.
Indian Summer.
Inventory.
Little Old Lady in Lavender Silk, The.
Lives and Times of John Keats, Percy Bysshe Shelley, and George Gordon Noel, Lord Byron, The.
Maid-Servant at the Inn, The.
Men.
News Item.
Observation.
One Perfect Rose.
Oscar Wilde.
Partial Comfort.
Penelope.
Pictures in the Smoke.
Prophetic Soul.
Red Dress, The.
Résumé.
Sanctuary.
Social Note.
Song of One of the Girls.
Symptom Recital.
Thomas Carlyle.
Unfortunate Coincidence.
Walter Savage Landor.

Parker, Edwin Pond (1836–1925)
Master, No Offering.

Parker, Sir Gilbert (1862–1932)
Reunited.

Parker, Martin (c.1600–c.1656)
King Enjoys His Own Again, The.
Maunding Soldier; or, The Fruits of Warre Is Beggery, The.
Thou knowst I lov'd thee well.
Whither away good neighbour.

Parker, Patricia (b. 1944)
For Willyce.
From the Cavities of Bones.
I Followed a Path.
My Brother.
Prologue from "Legacy."
There Is a Woman in This Town.

Where Will You Be?

Parkerson, Michelle (b. 1953)
Statistic.

Parkes, Bessie Rayner (1829–1925)
Dream Fears.
For Adelaide.
Lilian's Second Letter.
To an Author who Loved Truth More than Fame.
To Elizabeth Barrett Browning.

Parkes, Francis Ernest Kobina (b. 1932)
Apocalypse.
Blind Steersmen.
Three Phases of Africa.

"Parley, Peter" *See* **Goodrich, Samuel Griswold**

Parmenion of Macedon
Gutsy bugs grabbed grub from me till disgusted, The.
Protection of a cheap coat suffices, The.
Statue of Nemesis at Rhamnus, The.
Thermopylai.
You poured down like gold, / Olympian Zeus
Zeus paid Danaé in gold:/ thus I pay you.

Parnell, Pat
Apotheosis of Medusa.
Medusa and Perseus III: Lilith.
Sheila the Hat.
Sile Na gCioch.

Parnell, Thomas (1679–1718)
Elegy, to an Old Beauty, An.
From the black beach and broad expanse of sea.
How deep yon azure dyes the sky!
Hymn to Contentment, A.
Night Piece on Death.
On Bishop Burnet's Being Set on Fire in His Closet.
On Riding to See Dean Swift in the Mist of the Morning.
Riddle, A: "Upon a bed of humble clay."
Song: "When thy beauty appears."

Parnok, Sofiya (1885–1933)
Childhood memory: those pears, A.
I shall not lie to find a lurid rhyme.
Through a Window-Light.

Paros, Euenus the Grammarian, Euenus of Askelon, Euenus of *See* **Euenus**

Parr, Joyce
Limerick: "There was an old sage of New Delhi."

Parr, Katherine, Lady Borough (1512–48)
Christ was obedient unto his father.

Parra, Nicanor (b. 1914)
Anti-Lazarus, The.
Discourse of the Good Thief, The.
I Move the Meeting Be Adjourned.
Individual's Soliloquy, The.
Inflation.
Journey Through Hell.
Letters from the Poet Who Sleeps in a Chair.
Letters to an Unknown Woman.
Litany of the Little Bourgeois.
Lord's Prayer.
Man, A.
Modern Times.
Mummies.
Piano Solo.
Pilgrim, The.
Poems of the Pope, The.
Roller Coaster.
Sentences.
Test.
Tunnel, The.
Vices of the Modern World.
Viper, The.
Warnings.
Who are my friends / the sick / the weak / the poor in spirit.

Parra, Violeta (1917–62)
At the Center of Injustice.
Attention Young Bachelors.
Because the Poor Have Nothing.
Here's to Life.
I Curse in the Highest Sky.
I Thank Life for So Many Gifts.

Song for a Seed.
To Be Seventeen Again.
Why Is It This Way, Almighty God?
Parrhasios (*fl.* **5th cent. B.C.**)
Herakles.
I tell you (you needn't believe it)
Parrington, Georgia Bailey (*fl.* **1907**)
Sweet Dog! now cold and stiff in death.
Parrish, Elsie
Essie Parrish in New York.
Parrish, John (*fl.* **c.1793**)
Democratic Barber; or, Country Gentleman's
Surprise, The.
Parrot, Henry (*fl.* **1600–26**)
Fatales Poetae.
On a Poet.
Parrott, E. O.
Limerick: "Bashful young fellow of
Brighton, A."
Limerick: "Brickie who had a fine tool, A."
Limerick: "Carpenter living in Crewe, A."
Limerick: "Couturier from Haverford
West, A."
Limerick: "I spotted these daffs by the lake."
Limerick: "O, I yearn to go back to the Cam!"
Limerick: "Said a girl in green Mansfield
Park."
Limerick: "Shepherd who lived up in
Gwent, A."
Limerick: "There was a young man of
Ostend."
Limerick: "There was a young outlaw named
Hood."
Limerick: "There was an old housewife of
Staines."
More Bagpipe Music.
There's a man at Crewe.
Parry, David Fisher (b. **1908?**)
Miniver Cheevy, Jr.
Parry, Edward Abbott (**1803–1943**)
I Would Like You for a Comrade.
Parry, Joseph (**1841–1903**)
New Friends and Old Friends.
Parry, R. Williams (**1884–1956**)
Branwen's Starling.
Fox, The.
Miraculous Dawn.
Old Boatman of Death's River, The.
On a Soldier Killed in the Great War.
Two Hearts Divided.
Parry-Williams, T. H. (**1887–1975**)
Christmas Carol: "Close to a quarter of a
century since then."
Llyn y Gadair.
These Bones.
Parshchikov, Aleksey [*or* **Aleksei**] **Ivanovich** (b.
1954)
Prelude, Spoken to My Work Tools.
Parson-Nesbitt, Julie
Strange Country.
Parsons, Clere (**1908–31**)
Different.
Introduction: "I bespeak words."
Parsons, William (**1758?–1828**)
To a Friend in Love during the Riots.
Parthasarathy, Rajagopal (b. **1934**)
Speaking of Places.
Parulekar, Rajani (b. **1945**)
Birthmarks.
Parun, Vesna (b. **1922**)
Return to the Tree of Time, A.
Pascal, Paul (b. **1925**)
Tact.
Paschen, Elise
Between the Acts.
Confederacy.
Litany.
Potatoes Coriander.
Sam's Ghazals.
12 East Scott Street.
Two Standards.
Paschi de' Bardi, Lippo (*fl.* **1280**)
Wert thou as prone to yield unto my prayer.
Páskándi, Géza (**1933–95**)
Close your eyes over my sins.

First Resurrection.
I have laboured a virgin by being born.
In the grass of the twilight: the seventh day is
God.
Last Will and Testament.
Mother of God, you tired Mary.
My shirt got torn to rags.
You don't even have any sins!
Pasman, Heinz
Black Hairs, The.
Pasolini, Pier Paolo (**1922–75**)
As in a film by Godard: alone.
Civil Song.
Day of My Death, The.
John 12:24–25; Truly, truly, I say to you.
Lines from the Testament.
Part of a Letter to the Codignola Boy.
Prayer to My Mother.
Presence, The.
Redefining 'Orthodoxy.'
Roman Evening.
Sex, Consolation for Misery.
Southern Dawn.
Pasos, Joaquín (**1914–47**)
This Is Not Her.
Passerat, Jean (**1534–1602**)
Love in May.
Song: "Shephard loveth thow me vell?"
Sonnet Addressed to Henry III on the Death of
Thulène, the King's Fool.
Pastan, Linda (b. **1932**)
Agoraphobia.
Ars Poetica.
Aspects of Eve.
At the Jewish Museum.
Baseball.
David.
Early Afterlife, An.
Egg.
Erosion.
Ethics.
Hat Lady, The.
Imperfect Paradise, The.
Jump Cabling.
Last Train, The.
Love Poem.
Marks.
Name, A.
Old Photograph Album.
Orpheus.
Overture.
Passover.
Returning.
Self-Portrait.
September.
To a Daughter Leaving Home.
At the Train Museum.
Turnabout.
Pasternak, Boris Leonidovich (**1890–1960**)
As with Them.
At dusk you appear, a school-girl still.
Autumn.
Christmas Star.
Christmas Star, The.
Courage.
Definition of the Soul.
Don't Touch.
Evil Days, The.
Feasts, The.
February. Get your ink and weep.
Fresco Come to Life.
Fresh Paint.
From Superstition.
Garden of Gethsemane, The.
Hamlet.
Highest Sickness, The.
Hops.
I too have been in love, and my sleepless.
In the Breeze.
Indian Summer.
Let the Words.
Magdalene (I)
Marburg.
Mark 14:26–42; And when they had sung.
Mary Magdalene (I)
Matthew 21:1–11.

Matthew 26:47–56; While he was still
speaking, Judas came.
May It Be.
Miracle, The.
Mirror, The.
Moochkap.
Night.
O had I known that it ends like this.
On Early Trains.
Piano, trembling, makes the lips grow dry, The.
Poem: "So they begin. With two years gone."
Snow Is Falling.
Storm, an Endless Instant.
Sultry Night, A.
Three Variations.
To a Friend.
To be famous is not in good taste.
To Be Famous Isn't Decent.
To Love.
Waving a Bough.
White Night.
Wind, The.
Winter Night.
Pastorius, Francis Daniel (**1651–1720**)
As often as some where before my feet.
Delight in books from evening.
Epigram: "At ten a clock, when I the fire
rake."
Extract the quint-essence.
Great God, Preserver of All Things.
I have a pretty little flow'r.
If Any Be Pleased to Walk into My Poor
Garden.
If thou wouldest roses scent.
Learn, lads and lasses, of my garden.
Most weeds, whilst young.
On His Garden Book.
Penance, A.
Though My Thoughts.
Thy garden, orchard, fields.
To God alone, the only donour.
When I solidly do ponder.
When one or other rambles.
Patacara (*fl.* **6th cent. B.C.**)
When they plow their fields.
Patchen, Kenneth (**1911–72**)
Animal I wanted, The.
Biography of Southern Rain.
Body Beside the Ties, The.
Character of Love Seen as a Search for the
Lost, The.
Deer and the Snake, The.
Do the Dead Know What Time It Is?
Figure Motioned with Its Mangled Hand
Toward the Wall Behind It, The.
From My High Love.
Horses of Yilderin, The.
I have lighted the candles, Mary.
In Judgment of the Leaf.
In Memory of Kathleen.
Like a Mourningless Child.
'In the footsteps of the walking air.'
Lions of fire, The.
'O Now the Drenched Land Wakes.'
Lonesome Boy Blues.
Magical Mouse, The.
Midnight Special.
Moon, Sun, Sleep, Birds, Live.
Naked Land, The.
O All Down within the Pretty Meadow.
O my love / The pretty towns.
O terrible is the highest thing.
Origin of Baseball, The.
Pastoral: "Dove walks with sticky feet, The."
Religion Is That I Love You.
Saturday Night in the Parthenon.
State of the Nation, The.
Street Corner College.
Temple, A.
23rd Street Runs into Heaven.
Village Tudda, The.
We Go Out Together.
Patel, Essop (b. **1943**)
Haanetjie's Morning Dialogue.
Patel, Gieve (b. **1940**)
Forensic Medicine.

Patel, Ravji (1939–68)
Whirlwind.
Pater, Walter (1839–94)
Mona Lisa.
Paterson, Alistair (b. 1929)
Incantations for Warriors.
Overture for Bubble-Gum and Flute.
They do it with knives.
Paterson, Andrew Barton (1864–1941)
Father Riley's Horse.
Man from Snowy River, The.
Old Australian Ways.
Road to Hogan's Gap, The.
Travelling Post Office, The.
Waltzing Matilda.
Paterson, Don (b. 1963)
Chartres of Gowrie, The.
Private Bottling, A.
Paterson, Evangeline
Griselda.
Pāthak, Ganapti
I'll worship You with tears, Ma.
Patil, Chandrashekhar (b. 1939)
Freak.
Patmore, Coventry Kersey Dighton (1823–96)
Arbor Vitae.
Attainment, The.
Constancy Rewarded.
County Ball, The.
Departure.
Farewell, A.
Flesh-Fly and the Bee, The.
Fool and Wise.
From the small life that loves with tooth and
nail.
Going to Church.
How fair a flower is sown.
King William's Dispatch to Queen Augusta.
Kiss, The.
London Fete, A.
Love at Large.
Love Serviceable.
Lover, The.
Married Lover, The.
Music of Forefended Spheres, The.
Night and Sleep.
Paragon, The.
Parting.
Perspective.
Rainbow, The.
Revelation, The.
Rods and Kisses.
Rosy Bosom'd Hours, The.
Sahara.
Save by the Old Road none attain the new.
Science, the agile ape, may well.
Spirit's Epochs, The.
Storm, The.
To the Body.
Toys, The.
Tribute, The.
'Twas When the Spousal Time of May.
Vesica Piscis.
Warning, A.
Patrick, Bishop (d. 1084)
Invocation: "Almighty God, who fillest the
recesses of the heavens."
Patrick, Saint (fl. c.5th cent.)
St Patrick's Breastplate.
Pattanshetti, Siddhalinga (b. 1939)
Woman.
Patten, Brian (b. 1946)
After Frost.
Bee's Last Journey to the Rose, The.
Complacent Tortoise, The.
Frogologist, The.
How the New Teacher Got Her Nickname.
I Don't Believe in Human-tales.
Lion and the Echo, The.
Ode on Celestial Music.
Party Piece.
Portrait of a Young Girl Raped at a Suburban
Party.
Squeezes.
Terrible Path, The.

Through All Your Abstract Reasoning.
Through frost and snow and sunlight.
What Happened to Miss Frugle.
Patterson, G. E. (b. 1960)
Autobiography of a Black Man.
Lament.
Letter from Home.
Patterson, Lindsay (b. 1942)
When I Woke.
Patterson, Raymond R. (b. 1929)
Black Power.
Hopping Toad Blues.
Schwerner, Chaney, Goodman.
Sundown Blues.
This Age.
Twenty-Six Ways of Looking at a Blackman.
What We Know.
When I Awoke.
"Word to the Wise Is Enough, A."
You Are the Brave.
Pattison, William (1706–27)
Ad Coelum.
Patton, Charlie (1887–1934)
High Water Everywhere.
Patumanār
What She Said.
Pātunī, Nīlmani (d. 1825)
Ma, Hara's Beloved, Tara.
Pau-Llosa, Ricardo
Kendall Gulls.
Paredón.
Pauker, Ted (b. 1917)
Garland for a Propagandist.
Grouchy Good Night to the Academic Year, A.
Limeraiku.
Limerick: "There was a great Marxist called
Lenin."
Trifle for Trafalgar Day, A.
"Paul, John" See Webb, Charles Henry
Paul, Louis (1901–70)
Cynical Portraits.
Paul the Deacon (c.720–800)
Epitaph for His Niece, Sophia.
He Intercedes with Charlemagne for His
Brother in Exile.
Paulding, James Kirke (1779–1860)
Here lay dark Pittsburgh, from whose site there
broke.
In truth it was a landscape wildly gay.
Neglected Muse! of this our western clime.
'Tis true—yet 'tis no pity that 'tis true.
'Twas sunset's hallow'd time—and such an
eve.
Paulin, Tom (b. 1949)
Anastasia McLaughlin.
And Where Do You Stand on the National
Question.
Black Bread.
Cadaver Politic.
Desertmartin.
Impossible Pictures, The.
In the Lost Province.
Lonely Tower, The.
Lyric Afterwards, A.
Manichean Geography I.
Of Difference Does It Make.
Off the Back of a Lorry.
Other Voice, The.
Peacetime.
Personal Column.
Pot Burial.
Presbyterian Study.
Settlers.
Still Century.
Sting, The.
Surveillances.
Ulster Unionist Walks the Streets of London,
An.
Under the Eyes.
Where Art Is a Midwife.
Written Answer, A.
Paulinus of Aquileia (c.726–802)
Lament for Aquileia Destroyed, and Never to
Be Built Again.
Paulinus of Nola (353–431)
To Ausonius.

Paulus [or Paulos] Silentiarius (fl. c.560)
And there lay the lovers, lip-locked.
Choicer than all / flush of youth.
Come, give me kisses, Rhodope.
Don't tell me I'm getting gray.
Epigram: "Kissing Hippomenes, I crave."
Epitaph: Atticus.
Epitaph: Chryseomallus the Mime.
Epitaph: "Here I— / What does."
Eros has changed his quiver.
Even clothed in wrinkles, dear Philinna.
For whom now will you comb your hair in
lover's fashion?
Giving her mother's / zealous eye.
Gold cut the knot of otherwise.
Goodbye: I bite the word back.
I saw them, caught them in the act.
In Peterborough Churchyard.
Man (they say), A.
Mild, of sweet / countenance.
No Matter.
On a Bath-House in which Both Men and
Women Bathe.
On a High House in Byzantium.
Our kisses / Rhodope / let us steal.
Set foot once beyond Nilotic Meroë.
She has not come.
She lay all night beside me.
She plucked one thread.
Slip off that gown.
Soft are Sappho's kisses.
Take off your clothes, my love!
Tantalos.
These wreaths, Lais.
United.
You're right, Lais' smile is sweet.
Pavese, Cesare (1908–50)
August Moon.
Goat God, The.
Grappa in September.
Words from Confinement.
Pavlich, Walter
Black Flower.
Pavlova, Karolina (1807–93)
Crone, The.
Life calls us, and we go, massing our courage.
Pavlovski, Radovan
Climate and Lyre.
Pawar, Daya (b. 1935)
Buddha, The.
Pawlak, Mark
After Burying Her Son, a Mother Speaks.
Payne, John Howard (1791–1852)
Home, Sweet Home!
Paz, Octavio (b. 1914)
All is transformed and is sacred.
Along Galeana Street.
And the banquet, the exile, the first crime.
Better the crime.
Between Going and Staying.
Between What I See and What I Say.
Brotherhood.
Certainty.
Crystal willow, a poplar of water, A.
Exclamation.
Girl.
Grove, The.
Here.
Hymn Among the Ruins.
I Speak of the City.
I travel your body as I would travel the world.
Lake.
Landscape.
Madrid, 1937.
Mystery.
Native Stone.
Pause.
Shrine.
Small Variation.
Solo for Two Voices.
Stanzas for an Imaginary Garden.
Stirring, A.
Touch.
Tree Within, A.
Village.
Was it I making plans.

P'Bitek
Wind and Water and Stone.
P'Bitek, Okot (1931–82)
Woman with Whom I Share My Husband, The.
Peabody, Josephine Preston (1874–1922)
After Music.
Far-Off Rose, A.
House and the Road, The.
Peacock, Molly (b. 1947)
Anger Sweetened.
Breakfast with Cats.
Chriseaster.
Desire.
Dream Come True.
Fare, The.
Good Girl.
Have You Ever Faked an Orgasm?
How I Come to You.
How I Had to Act.
Lullaby: "Big as a down duvet the night."
Matins.
My God, Why Are You Crying?
Purr, The.
Return, The.
Seeing a Basket of Lobelia the Color of a
  Bathrobe.
Spell, The.
Surge, The.
Those Paperweights with Snow Inside.
Wheel, The.
Devolution.
Why I Am Not a Buddhist.
Peacock, Thomas Love (1785–1866)
Andonis, My Daughter.
Chorus: "If I drink water while this doth last."
Earth Song.
Fear.
For the Children.
Ghosts, The.
Grave of Love, The.
In Respect of the Elderly.
In the days of old.
Love and Age.
Magic and mystery, spells Circæan.
Newark Abbey.
Over, Over.
Priest and the Mulberry-Tree, The.
Rich and Poor; or, Saint and Sinner.
Robin Hood and the Grey Friars.
Six Eagles.
War Song of Dinas Vawr, The.
Peacocke, M. R. (b. 1930)
At the Entrance.
Final reductions.
Goddess, The.
In Memoriam.
Railway Allotments.
Remembrance.
Soap.
We're Staying at the Castlemount, Western
  Esplanade.
Peake, Mervyn Laurence (1911–68)
Babe was born in the reign of George, A.
Conceit.
Frivolous Cake, The.
I cannot give the reasons.
It Makes a Change.
My Uncle Paul of Pimlico.
O here it is! And there it is!
Sensitive, Seldom and Sad.
Pearce, Norman V.
Blind.
Pearl, Robert
Mourning Song.
Pearlberg, Gerry Gomez
Dog Star.
Loop-the-Loop in Prospect Park (1905)
Marianne Faithfull's Cigarette.
Sailor.
Think Back.
Pearse, Jimmy
As he stood in their shop, Mr. Boosey.
Willesden Gree.
Pearse, Padraic (1880–1916)
I Am Ireland.
Ideal.

Naked I Saw You.
Renunciation.
Peaux, Augusta (1859–1944)
Cold Landscape.
Old Houses on the Quays.
Spring Landscape.
Peck, John (b. 1941)
Anti-dithyrambics.
Archeus Terrae.
Campagna.
End of July.
From the Viking Museum.
Here Is a Song.
Metal Denser Than, and Liquid, A.
Monologue of the Magdalene.
Mount Bromley Hymn.
Vega over the rim of the Val Verzasca.
What If the Saint Must Die.
Woods Burial.
Peck, Robert Newton
Four of July.
Peck, Samuel Minturn (b. 1854)
Kiss in the Rain, A.
Pecor, Amanda
Product of Evolution, I Invest in a Mutual
  Fund, A.
Pederson, Cynthia S.
Summer Recital.
Pedrick, Jean (b. 1922)
Hats.
Pedro, Joao (b.1948)
Homecoming.
Pedroso, Regino
Opinions of the New Student.
Peele, George (1559–96)
Bethsabe's Song.
Fair and Fair.
His Golden Lock[e]s [Time Hath to Silver
  Turned].
Song: "Whenas [or When as] the Rye [or Rie]
  reach to the chin."
Spread, table, spread.
Three merry men, and three merry men.
Voice [Speaks] from the Well, A.
Write write yow Croniclers of Tyme and Fame.
Peeradina, Saleem (b. 1944)
Sisters.
Pegram, Amelia Blossom
Burials.
Deliverance.
I Will Still Sing.
Mr. White Discoverer.
Towards Abraham's Bosom.
Peirce, Kathleen
Alcoholic's Son at Ten, The.
Farmers.
Near Burning.
Need Increasing Itself by Rounds.
Quilts.
Peire Cardenal (c.1225–1272?)
Clerks pretend to be shepherds, and under,
  The.
Peire Vidal (c.1175–1205)
Song of Breath.
Peiyu, Gong *See* **"Shu Ting"**
Pelham, Sarah
When I was young.
Pelizzon, V. Penelope (b. 1967)
Clever and Poor.
Feast of San Silvestro, The.
Late Apostasy, A.
Wedding Day, The.
Pelletiere, Marcia
Under Her Crib.
Pellicer, Carlos (1899–1977)
Flocks of Doves.
Studies.
To Poetry.
Wishes.
**Pembroke, Mary Sidney Herbert, Countess of
  (1562–1621)**
Dialogue between two shepherds, Thenot and
  Piers, in praise of Astræa.
He placed all rest, and had no resting place.

If Ever Hapless Woman Had a Cause.
To the Thrice-Sacred Queen Elizabeth.
Pembroke, William Herbert, Earl of (1580–1630)
Song: "Soules joy, now I am gone."
Pender, Lydia
Lizard, The.
Penfold, Merimeri (b. 1824)
Land Laws, The.
Tamaki of a Hundred Lovers.
Peniarth Poet, The (fl. after 1484)
Loke that none of you departe.
Penn, Maggie
Calling Up the Spirit of the Lost Child.
Penn, Robert E.
Hand.
Morning Songs.
Penna, Sandro (1906–77)
Always boys in my poems!
Found—my little angel.
Lady on Streetcar.
Life...is remembering waking up.
My poetry will not be.
Pitiless war of love I fought, A.
Shadowless sun on male bodies.
When I don't feel well, I wander among.
Pennecuik, Alexander (d. 1730)
Below fair Peebles, on the river's side.
Penny, Anne (1731–84)
Sung at Table by the Same Choir.
Sung by a Choir of Boys Marching Round the
  Room.
Penrose, Roland (1900–1984)
Road Is Wider Than Long: An Image Diary
  from the Balkans, July–August 1938, The.
Penrose, Thomas (1742–79)
Helmets; a Fragment, The.
Penrose, Valentine
Beautiful or Ugly It Doesn't Matter.
Datura the Serpent, The.
I Dream.
May—1941.
There Is the Fire.
To a Woman to a Path.
Pepler, H. D. C. (1878–1951)
Concerning Dragons.
Percival, James Gates (1795–1856)
Coral Grove, The.
Morning among the Hills.
Percy, William (1575–1648)
Judged by my goddess' doom to endless pain.
Relent, my dear yet unkind Coelia.
Percy, William Alexander (1885–1942)
They Cast Their Nets in Galilee.
Perdomo, Willie
Nigger-Reecan Blues.
Revolutionary.
Unemployed Mami.
Pereira, Francesca Yetunde (b. 1933)
Burden, The.
Mother Dark.
Paradox, The.
Two Strange Worlds.
Pereira, Sam
Entity of Its Word, An.
**"Pereleshin, Valery Frantsevich" (Valerii
  Frantsevich Salatko-Petrishche) (b. 1913)**
In the final hour, dear.
Path, The.
Perelman, Bob (b. 1947)
Broken Mirror, The.
China.
Chronic Meanings.
Cliff Notes.
Let's Say.
Marginalization of Poetry, The.
Seduced by Analogy.
Things.
Money.
Péret, Benjamin (1899–1959)
Hymn of the Patriotic War Veterans.
Joan of Arc.
Listen.
Little Song of the Maimed.
Making Feet and Hands.

Nungesser und Coli Sind Verreckt.
On All Fours.
One good mistress deserves another.
Staircase with a Hundred Steps, The.
My Final Agonies.
Where Are You.

Peretz [or Perets], Isaac Leibush [or Yitskhok Leybush] (1852?–1915)
All through the Stranger's Wood.
Believe Not.
Eternal Sabbath.
Hope and Faith.
In the Silent Night.
Little People.
Three Seamstresses, The.

Peri Rossi, Cristina (b. 1941)
Tired of women.

Perillo, Lucia Maria (b. 1958)
Body Mutinies, The.
Dangerous Life.
For Edward Hopper, from the Floor.
For I Have Taught the Japanese.
Ghost Shirt, The.
Lament in Good Weather.
Needles.
Skin.
Sweaters, The.

Perk, Jacques (1859–1881)
Iris.

Perkins, Emily Swan (1866–1941)
Thou Art, O God, the God of Might.

Perkins, Frank
Stars Fell on Alabama.

Perkins, Silas H.
Common Road, The.

Perkoff, Stuart Z. (1930–74)
Feasts of Death, Feasts of Love.
Flowers for Luis Bunuel.
Recluses, The.

Perreault, John (b. 1937)
Boomerang.
Metaphysical Paintings, The.
Readymade.
Shoe.

Perrine, Laurence (b. 1915)
Janus.

Perronet, Edward (1725–92)
All Hail the Power of Jesus' Name.

Perry, Grace (b. 1927)
Time of Turtles.

Perry, Nora (1831–76)
Coming of Spring, The.
Next Year.
Too Late.

Perry, Stephen
Fugue.
Orpheus.
Toadfish.

"Perse, St.-John" (Alexis Saint-Léger Léger) (1887–1975)
Anabasis.
Bird, The.
Doors open on the sands, doors open on exile.

Perses (fl. 316 B.C.)
Artemis.
Death came before Marriage, Philaenion.
Lucina, Care.
Mnasylla, the daughter you lament.
Time & prayer fitting, I, the god.

Persius (Aulus Persius Flaccus) (A.D. 34–62)
Prologue to the First Satire.
Satire 1.
Satire 5.
Satire 6.

Peruñcattan
What Her Girl-Friend Said.

Peseroff, Joyce
Hardness Scale, The.

Peshkov, Aleksey Maksimovich See **"Gorky [or Gorkii], Maksim"**

Peskett, William (b. 1952)
Bottles in the Zoological Museum.
From Belfast to Suffolk.
Inheritors, The.

Question of Time, The.
Star and Sea.
Window Dressing.

Pessoa, Fernando (1888–1935)
Ah, pirates, pirates, pirates!
Ascent of Vasco da Gama, The.
Autopsychography.
Blighter, The.
I the Roses Love in the Gardens of Adonis.
If, after I Die.
No One in the Wide Wilderness of the Wood.
[Poem 2]: "Inside, the church lights up today's rain."
Portuguese Sea, The.
Rather the Bird Flying By and Leaving No Trace.
Segue O Teu Destino.
"Startling Reality of Things, The."

Pestel [or Pestell], Thomas (1585–1667)
Psalm for Christmas Day.

Petchenik, Kenneth
Limerick: "There was a young faggot called Willy."

Peter, Robert (fl. 1800)
On Time, Death, and Eternity.

Peters, Lenrie (b. 1932)
After They Put Down Their Overalls.
Home Coming.
I am asking about the way ahead.
Isatou Died.
One Long Jump.
Parachute Men.
Song: "Clawed green-eyed."
We Have Come Home.

Peters, Nancy Joyce (b. 1936)
General Strike.
To the Death of Mirrors.

Peters, Robert (b. 1924)
Potatoes.

Petersen, Donald (b. 1928)
Walking along the Hudson.

Peterson, Jim
Stand Still.

Peterson, Mattie J.
I Kissed Pa Twice after His Death.
I sometimes alligators heard.

Peterson, Robert (b. 1924)
Autumn.
Brief History of the City.
Now and Then.
San Quentin 1968.
September 5.

Peterson, Ruth Delong (b. 1606)
Midwest Town.

Petit, Pascale (b. 1953)
Embrace of the Electric Eel.
My Father's Clothes.
My Mother's Clothes.

Petőfi, Sándor (1823–49)
At the End of September.
Autumn Again.
Cart with Four Oxen,The.
Farmer puts his field under the plow, The.
Fate Give Me Space.
Glorious night! / The giant moon, the tiny evening star.
How many drops has the ocean sea?
How will the earth die? . . . will she freeze? will she burn?
Humankind has not declined!
Hungary.
I'll Be a Tree.
I'm Troubled by One Thought.
I often wonder who will find.
If all the hearts that shrivelled in their graves.
Is the spirit the true lover of the flesh?
Like Clouds.
National Song.
Okato-Otaia.
On Hope.
Plans Gone Up in Smoke.
Puszta in Winter, The.
Shepherd Rides on Donkey-Back, The.
Some Old How.
Song of the Dogs, The.

Song of the Wolves,The.
Sorrow? A Great Ocean.
Time of Fear, A.
Tisza, The.
To János Arany.
Upon the shepherd-boy the summer sun.
What happens to laughter.
What's the merriest burial ground?

Petrarca, Francesco See **Petrarch**

Petrarch (Francesco Petrarca) (1304–74)
Apollo, if the sweet desire is still alive that inflamed you beside.
Bicause I have the still kept fro lyes and blame.
Blest be the day, and blest the month and year.
Clear, fresh, sweet waters, where she who alone seems lady.
Complaint of a Lover Rebuked.
Description of the Contrarious Passions in a Lover.
Ever mine [or myn] hap[pe] is slack and slo[w] in coming [or commyng].
Eyes that drew from me such fervent praise, The.
Father in heaven, after each lost day.
First day she passed up and down through the Heavens, The.
For Whatever Animals Dwell On Earth.
Galley, The.
Go, grieving rimes of mine, to that hard stone.
Great is my envy of you, earth, in your greed.
He Understands the Great Cruelty of Death.
Heart on the Hill, The.
How the Lover Perisheth in His Delight, As the Fly in the Fire.
I saw a Phoenix in the Wood Alone.
If constancy in love, if a brave heart.
If It Be Destined.
In the years of her age the most beautiful.
It was the day when the sun's rays turned pale with grief for his.
It was the morning of that blessed day.
Long[e] love that in my thought do[e]th [or I] harbour [or harber or harbar], The.
Loose to the wind her golden tresses streamed.
Love delivers to me its sweetest thoughts.
Love's Fidelity.
My Galley.
My ship laden with forgetfulness passes through a harsh sea, at.
Oh! place me where the burning noon.
She used to let her golden hair fly free.
Signs of Love.
Sonnet: "When she walks by here."
Translation from Petrarch, A.
Visions, The.
When Simon received the high idea which, for my sake, put his.
Woods Are Wild and Were Not Made for Man, The.
Ye vales and woods! fair scenes of happier hours.
You who hear in scattered rhymes the sound of those sighs with.

Petri, György (b. 1913)
By an Unknown Poet from Eastern Europe, 1955.
Christmas 1956.
Electra.
Gratitude.
To Be Said Over and Over Again.
Morning Coffee.
Night Song of the Personal Shadow.
To S. V.

Petrie, Paul (b. 1936)
Dream, The.
Indoor Cat, The.
Not Seeing Is Believing.
Old Pro's Lament, The.
Phases of Darkness, The.

Petröczy [or Petröczi], Kata Szidónia (1662–1708)
Light of Our Souls.
Rapid Floods.
Swift Floods.

Petronius Arbiter (Caius Petronius Arbiter) (d. A.D. 66)
Beauty is not enough; who wishes to be fair.

Coition's brief, a nasty cheat.
Doing, a filthy pleasure is, and short.
Encouragement to Exile.
Fornication is a filthy business.
Good God, What a Night That Was.
I had just gone to bed.
Long may our hearts, Nealce, guard that night.
Malady of Love Is Nerves, The.
Man in the Middle of the Street.
My bed was soft, the early night was bliss.
Satyricon, *sels*.
That night will long delight us, Nealce.
There, sea and sky are at a mortal war.
Waking, my eyes, and in the night.
We Are Such Stuff as Dreams.
Why do you frown on me, you puritans.

Petrosky, Anthony (b. 1948)
V.A. Hospital.

Petrovykh, Maria (b. 1908)
Air Is Motionless with Heat, The.

Pettit, Michael
Self-Portrait Approaching Promontory, Utah.
Vanna White's Bread Pudding.

Petty, Noel
Great Poll-Tax Victory of '88, The.
It was in the Spring of 1825.
There's a Breathless Hush.

Pewhairangi, Kumeroa Ngoingoi (b. 1922)
Do Not Turn Away.
I Sit Here.

Peynetsa, Andrew
Boy and the Deer, The.
Shumeekuli, The.

Pfeiffer, Emily Jane (1827–90)
Among the Hebrides.
Any Husband to Many a Wife.
Aspiration.
Bower among the Beans, The.
Chrysalis, A.
Cruse of Tears, The. A Russian Legend.
Fight at Rorke's Drift, The.
If we be fools of chance, indeed, and tend.
Klytemnestra.
Lost Light, The.
Mid-Ocean.
Nathaniel to Ruth.
O Nature! thou whom I have thought to love.
Peace to the odalisque, the facile slave.
Peace to the odalisque, whose morning glory.
So the river—yes, the river; I have come to
that at last.
Song of Winter, A.
Sonsy Milkmaid, The.
Studies from the Antique.
To a Moth that Drinketh of the Ripe October.
Witch's Last Ride, The.

Phá ch, Lê Cụ' *See* **Du Tũ' Lê**

Phaedrus (*fl.* c. 8 A.D.)
Aesop at Play.
Dog in the River, The.
Man and the Weasel, The.
Purpose of Fable-writing, The.
Widow and the Soldier or: The Measure of a
Woman's Inconstancy and Lust, The.
Wolf and the Lamb, The.

Phalaicus (*fl.* c.300 B.C.)
This gift, her gold-hemmed saffron gown.

Pham Tien Duat (b. 1941)
To Return to the Urges Unconscious of their
Beginnings.

Phanias
By Themis & the wine that made me tipsy.
Here Lysis set an empty tomb.
It's a sign of the times when even barbers.
Stick he used to tap out feet, The.

Phelp, J. A.
Duke Of Buccleuch, The.

Phelps, Sylvanus D. (1816–95)
Saviour, Thy Dying Love.

Philetas (b. c.320 B.C.)
Past fifty and cloyed at last.
This tombstone heavy with grief announces.

Philip, John (b. 1927)
Manly Ferry.

Philip of Thessalonica (*fl.* A.D. 1st cent.)
Bronze warship-beaks, old voyage-avid

weapons.
Epigram: "You were a pretty boy once,
Archestratus, and."
His anchor, seaweed-probing, boat-securing.
I, a ship, built on the profits / from my
master's amorous trade.
I am a plane-tree. I was sound and strong when
the blasts.
Long farewell to all you universe-swivelling
optics, A.
Look at these most wretched remains of a man.
Moment ago the shrill flute whistled in the
bridal chamber, A.
Old Nico brought wreaths to the tomb of
Melite.
Queen of black-earth Egypt, divine Isis.
Sky will extinguish its stars, and the sun, The.
Sosicles the farmer dedicated these sheaves.
Stranger, beware! This terrible tomb.
To Pan the forest-ranger, Gelo the hunter.
Whistling bellows of his furnace, The.
Yellow-coated pomegranate, figs like lizards'
necks, A.
Young Hermes, who placed you at the starter's
mark?

Philip V, King of Macedon (238–179 B.C.)
Traveller, on this ridge a leafless, barkless tree.

Philipott, Thomas (c.1616–1682)
To Sir Henry Newton, upon His Re-edifying
the Church of Charleton in Kent.

Philips, Ambrose (1675–1749)
Happy Swain, The.
Ode: To Miss Margaret Pulteney.
To Miss Charlotte Pulteney in Her Mother's
Arms.
Winter-Piece, A.
Wit and Wisdom.

Philips, Joan *See* **"Ephelia"**

Philips, John (1676–1704)
Apple-Culture.
War Poetry.

Philips, Katherine ("Orinda") (1631–64)
Advice to Virgins.
Against Love.
Answer to Another Persuading a Lady to
Marriage, An.
Cornelia's Defiance.
Country Life, A.
Enquiry, The.
Epitaph on her Son H. P. at St. Syth's Church.
Friendship in Emblem[e], or the Seal[e], to my
dearest Lucasia.
Friendship's Mystery[s], to my dearest Lucasia.
L'Amitie: To Mrs. Mary [*or* M.] Awbrey.
Lucasia, Rosania and Orinda Parting at a
Fountain, July 1663.
Married State, A.
On the 3 of September, 1651.
On the Death of My First and Dearest Child[e],
Hector Philip[p]s.
On the Welsh Language.
Orinda to Lucasia.
Orinda to Lucasia Parting, October, 1661, at
London.
Retired Friendship, To Ardelia, A.
Sea-Voyage from Tenby to Bristol, A.
Song: "'Tis true our life is but a long dis-ease."
To Antenor.
To Mr. Henry Lawes.
To Mrs M. A. at Parting.
To My Excellent Lucasia, On Our Friendship.
To My Lucasia, in Defence of Declared
Friendship.
To Rosania (now Mrs Montague) Being with
Her, 25th September 1652.
To the Queen of Inconstancy, Regina Collier,
in Antwerp.
Upon the Double Murther of King Charles I.
Upon the graving of her Name upon a Tree in
Barnelmes Walks.
Wiston Vault.

Phillimore, John Swinnerton (1873–1926)
In a Meadow.

Phillips, Carl (b. 1959)
Abundance.
Africa Says.

As from a Quiver of Arrows.
Chamber Music.
Clearing, The.
Cotillion.
In the blood, Winnowing.
Kill, The.
Little Dance Outside the Ruins of Unreason.
Luncheon on the Grass.
Reach, The.
Passing.
Recumbent.
Regalia Figure.
Sunday.
Toys.
Undressing for Li Po.
You Are Here.

Phillips, David (1922–88)
Limerick: "Heart of O'Leary, S. J., The."

Phillips, Dennis (b. 1951)
Five.
From Arena.
Hounds are either the work of wind, The.
I Held the Vein, But Death.
If It's Only Rhythm.
On Entries Emptiness.

Phillips, Douglas (b. 1929)
Maridunum.

Phillips, Harriet C. (1806–84)
We Bring No Glittering Treasures.

Phillips, John (1676–1709)
Happy the man, who, void of cares and strife.

Phillips, Louis (b. 1942)
My Son Shows Me a Photograph of Michael
Jordan Performing a Slam Dunk.

Phillips, Pauline
Limerick: "I've combed out my beard and I've
found."

Phillips, Robert (b. 1938)
Arsh Potatoes.
Death of Janis Joplin, The.
Running on Empty.

Phillips, Stephen (1864–1915)
Apparition, The.

Phillpotts, Eden (b. 1862)
Houses, The.
Man's Days.
Miniature.

"Philo-Philippa" (*fl.* c.1667)
To the Excellent Orinda.

Philodemus (c.110–c.30 B.C.)
Antikrates knew the stars.
Cypris who puts the sea to rest.
Death has torn ten years from us.
Demo and Thermion Both Slay Me.
Double-horned, nocturnal Moon.
Hello. Hello. What's your name?
Hello There.
Herakles' rebuttal was too much.
Here it's rose-time again, chick-peas in season.
I fell in love with Demo of Paphos. No big
surprise.
"I know, fair lady, how to love the lover well."
I Loved—Who Hasn't?
I've been in love. Who hasn't? I went out and
got drunk.
I, who used to score five, even nine times.
In the middle of the night.
In the middle of the night I slipped away from
my husband.
Make the Bedlamp Tipsy with Oil.
Naked warmth of you is still, The.
O foot, O leg, O thighs for which I rightly
died.
O two-horned moon, you love the parties that
last all night.
Oh feet, oh legs, oh thighs / that formed the
deathrow.
Once I was in love. Who's been exempted?
Philaenion is small and swart, but her hair
curls more.
Philainis is short and.
Roses are already here.
Seven plus thirty years are gone.
Sixty sun-decked years Charito has gotten to.
Small thing and moreover black is she, A.

Strumming and patter / the meaningful glances, The.
That silent publicizer of unheard-of news.
This *quidam* gives that *quidam* for *one* round.
This stone incorporates three gods:/ the head is unmistakably goat-horned Pan's.
To Piso, on Epicurus' Birthday.
Wax-contoured, in your face a Muse.
White violets again and lyre orchestras.
With Demo I fell in love, of Paphian origins.
With the night half over.
Xanthippe's strumming, her chatter, her speaking eye, her song.
Xanthippe, singing at her lyre.
You cry, carry on in tones of pity.
You Cry, Whine, Peer Strangely at Me.

Philp-Carmichael, Beryl (Yungha-Dhu) (b. 1935)
Dust Storm.
Mother.
My Dad.
Pemulwy—A Visitation.

Philp, Geoffrey
Dance Hall.
Dance Hall: Version.
Heirlooms.
One Song.

Philpot, Tracy (b. 1961)
How to Live in the Elegy.
Louisa's Wedding.
Wildlife.

Philpot, William (1823–89)
Maritae Suae.

Phipson, Thomas (1815–76)
Press, The.

Phylip, Siôn (d. 1620)
Seagull, The.

Phylip, William (d. 1670)
Farewell to Hendre Fechan.

P'i Jih-hsiu (c.833–883)
Impromptu on a Hangover.
Lament for the People of Lung.
Lament of a Woman Acorn-gatherer.
Mosquitoes.
On a Crab.
Reading.
Song of a Farmer.
Thoughts in Early Autumn: Thirty Rhymes Sent to Lu-wang.
Woodcutter's Ax, A.

Piatt, John James (1835–1917)
Farther.
Fires in Illinois.
My Shadow's Stature.
Taking the Night-Train.
To the Statue on the Capitol.

Piatt, Sarah Morgan Bryan (1836–1919)
Answering a Child.
Army of Occupation.
Child's Party, A.
Doubt, A.
Giving Back the Flower.
Her Word of Reproach.
If I Had Made the World.
In A Queen's Domain.
In Her Prison.
Lesson in a Picture, A.
No Help.
Palace-Burner, The.
Pique at Parting, A.
Sad Spring-Song.
Stone for a Statue.
This World.

"Pibwob"
Limerick: "Van Gogh, feeling devil-may-care."

Picabia, Francis (1879–1953)
Aphorisms.
Eunuch Unique.
Spermal Chimney.

Picasso, Pablo (1881–1973)
9.1.59: II.
9.1.59: VI.
Bottle of Suze, A.
Poem: "Hasten on your childhood to the hour when white."

Piccione, Anthony
Watching Ants Play Soccer in Central Park.

Piccolo, Lucio (1903–69)
Veneris Venefica Agrestis.

Pichamurti, N. (1900–78)
National Bird.

Pickard, Tom (b. 1946)
Bush Telegram.
Devil's Destroying Angel Exploded, The.
My Pen.
Rape.
What Maks Makems.

Pickering [or Pikerying], John (b. 1567)
Haltersick's Song.
Song Sung by Egistus and Clytemnestra.
Vice's Song, The.

Picková, Eva (1929–43)
Fear.

Pickthall, Marjorie Lowry Christie (1883–1922)
Bridegroom of Cana, The.
Lost Friend, The.
Père Lalement.
Quiet.
Resurgam.
Two Souls.

Pien Kung (1476–1532)
At the Lake—Remembering My Dead Son, Yü.
First Day of Spring, The.
Inscribed on an Album Leaf Painted by Dr. Lin.
Mooring at K'ou-ch'üeh—Sent to Dr. Lin.
New Year's Day—Following the Rhymes of Inspector Luan-chiang.
On Hearing That San-p'ing's Newly Brewed Chrysanthemum Wine Is Ready to Drink— Investigating with a Poem.
On the Sixteenth Day I Visit the Temple Again.
Paintings.
Paintings of Various Subjects by Fang Jih-sheng: Baby Chicks Following Their Mother.
Song of the Boat-Pullers.
Song of the Transport Workers—Seeing Off Fang Wen-yü on His Way to His Post as Inspector of Transportation.
Song of the Woodcutter of the Sea.
Walking Outside the City Walls on the Day of the Cold Food Festival.

Piercy, Marge (b. 1936)
Apron Strings.
At the New Moon: Rosh Hodesh.
Attack of the Squash People.
Barbie Doll.
Battle of Wills Disguised, A.
Candle in a Glass, A.
Cast Off, The.
Crabs.
Cyclist, The.
Development, The.
Friend, The.
Growing Up Haunted.
Hello Up There.
Implications of One Plus One.
It Arrives Suddenly and Carries Us Off As Usual.
Last Scene in the First Act.
Learning Experience.
Letter to be Disguised as a Gas Bill.
Maggid.
Moon Is Always Female, The.
Morning Athletes.
Morning Love Song.
My Rich Uncle, Whom I Only Met Three Times.
Peaceable Kingdom, The.
Postcard from the Garden.
Quiet Fog, The.
September Afternoon at Four O'Clock.
Song of the Fucked Duck.
Spring Offensive of the Snail, The.
To Be of Use.
To Have without Holding.
Token Woman, The.
We Become New.
What's That Smell in the Kitchen?
When a Friend Dies.

You Don't Understand Me.

Pierman, Carol J.
Apparition, The.

Pierpoint, F. S. (1835–1917)
For the beauty of the earth.

Pierpoint, Katherine (b. 1961)
Combustion Engine.
In the Outhouse.
Steeplejack.
Swim Right Up to Me.
This Dead Relationship.

Pierpont, James S.
Jingle Bells.

Pierpont, John (1785–1866)
Ballot, The.
Fugitive Slave's Apostrophe to the North Star, The.
Here let us pause:—the opening prospect view.
In what rich harmony, what polished lays.
Now, he recalls the lamentable wail.
O Thou, to Whom in Ancient Time.
On Arno's bosom, as he calmly flows.

Piers, Lady Sarah (d. 1720)
To My Much Esteemed Friend on Her Play Call'd Fatal-Friendship.

Piersanti, Umberto (b. 1941)
In Times and Places.
Second Image Sequence.
When Slow October Changes Color.

Pierson, Jennifer M.
Thrift Shop Ladies.

Pietri, Pedro Juan (b. 1940)
First Day of Spring, The.
First Rock and Roll Song of 1970, The.
1st Untitled Poem.
How Do Your Eggs Want You (?)
Intermission from Friday.
Intermission from Monday.
Intermission from Saturday.
Intermission from Sunday.
Intermission from Thursday.
Intermission from Wednesday.
Night Is out of Sight, The.
9th Untitled Poem.
Old Buildings, The.
7th Untitled Poem.
10th Untitled Poem.
3rd Untitled Poem.
Title of This Poem Was Lost, The.
Traffic Misdirector.

Pigott, Jean Sophia
Jesus I am resting, resting.

Pilinszky, János (1921–1981)
Agonia Christiana.
Apocrypha.
Auschwitz.
Crime and Punishment.
Depression.
Desert of Love, The.
Difference.
Extract from a Diary.
Fable: "Once upon a time / there was a lonely wolf."
Fish in the Net.
Frankfurt.
French Prisoner, The.
Hangman's Room, The.
Harbach 1944.
Homage to Issac Newton.
Introitus.
Life Sentence.
Monstrance.
On the Back of a Photograph.
On the Third Day.
On the Wall of a KZ-Lager.
One Fine Day.
Oratorio for a Concentration Camp.
Passion of Ravensbrück.
Relationship.
Rest Is Grace, The.
Scaffold in Winter.
Stone Wall and Celebration.
Stone Wall and Fiesta.
Three-Coloured Banner.
Veil.

Your Death and Mine.
Pilkington, Laetitia (1712?–1750)
Dol and Roger.
Fair and Softly goes far or, The Wary
    Physician.
Memory, a Poem.
Song, A.
Song, A: "Lying is an occupation."
Song, A: "Strephon, your breach of faith and
    trust."
Sorrow.
Wish, By a Young Lady, The.
Pillen [or Pillin], William (1910–85)
Ascensions, The.
Pilling, Christopher (b. 1936)
Adoration of the Magi, The.
Affair With a Chair, An.
Cast Away.
Dear Ez.
Earth, The.
Encounter at the Post Office Counter.
Field, The.
Fran.
Ophelia.
She Lies Silent.
Specimen.
Triptych.
Webern.
You and You, in the Pink.
Pinar, Florencia del (b. c.1460)
Another Song of the Same Woman, to Some
    Partridges, Sent to Her Alive.
Pinchas-Cohen, Chava (b. 1955)
Her, Me, and Yochanan.
Journey of a Doe.
My English Teacher.
Remembering Our Fathers.
Yearning of Karakashian, The.
Pindar (c.518–c.438 B.C.)
For Midas, the Man from Akragas First in the
    Flute Match.
Hyperboreans, The.
Ode on Theoxenos.
Olympia 11—For Agesidamus of the
    Westwind Locrians: Winner in the Boys'
    Boxing Match.
"Pindar, Peter" (John Wolcot) (1738–1819)
Apple Dumplings and a King, The.
Epigram: "Midas, they say, possessed the art of
    old."
George III and the Sailor.
George III Visits Whitbread's Brewery.
Hymn to the Guilotine.
Ode: "That I have often been in love, deep
    love."
Ode to a Country Hoyden.
On a Stone Thrown at a Very Great Man, but
    Which Missed Him.
Royal Tour, and Weymouth Amusements, The.
Royal Tour, The.
Sons of Saint Crispin, 'tis in vain!
Susan, the constant slave to mop and broom.
To a Fly, Taken out of a Bowl of Punch.
Town Eclogue, A.
Piñero, Miguel
La Bodega Sold Dreams.
Lower East Side Poem, A.
On the Day They Buried My Mother.
Running Scared.
This Is Not the Place Where I was Born.
"Ping Hsin" (Hsieh Wang-ying) (b. 1900)
In shaping the snow into blossoms.
O, Lord/ If in life eternal.
Orphan beat of my heart, The.
Stars, The.
Ping, Wang (b. 1957)
No cloud or rain all night long.
Pinkard, Maceo (fl. 1925)
Gimme a Little Kiss (Will Ya, Huh?)
Sweet Georgia Brown.
Pinkerton, Helen
On Dorothea Lange's Photograph "Migrant
    Mother" (1936)
On Vermeer's "Young Woman with a Water
    Jug" (1658) in the Metropolitan Museum.

Pinkney, Edward Coote [or Coate] (1802–28)
Health, A.
Italy.
On Parting.
Serenade: "Look out upon the stars, my love."
To ———: "'Twas eve; the broadly shining
    sun."
Voyager's Song, The.
Pinosová, Katerina
Piece of Bone, The.
Pinsky, Robert (b. 1940)
At Pleasure Bay.
Avenue.
Braveries.
Dionysus as Psychiatrist.
Doctor Frolic.
Dying.
Figured Wheel, The.
First Early Mornings Together.
From the Childhood of Jesus.
Hearts, The.
Invocation: "It's crazy to think one could
    describe them."
Jersey Rain.
Living, The.
Long Branch Song, A.
Mad, The.
Memorial.
Night Game, The.
Ode to Meaning.
Peroration, Concerning Genius.
Physical Comparison with Professors and
    Others.
Poem about People.
Poem with Refrains.
Proposition.
Questions, The.
Ralegh's Prizes.
Serpent Knowledge.
Shirt.
Some Terms.
Song of Reasons.
Street, The.
Their Patients.
Their Philistinism Considered.
Their Seriousness, with Further Comparisons.
Their Speech, Compared with Wisdom and
    Poetry.
Woman, A.
Pinto, Vivian de Sola (1895–1969)
At Piccadilly Circus.
Pinytos (fl. A.D. 1st cent.)
Epitaph: Sappho.
Piombino, Nick (b. 1942)
Frozen Witness, The.
My Lady Carries Stones.
Pyramids, The.
Time Travel.
Piontek, Heinz
In the Woods.
Piper, Edwin Ford (1871–1939)
Big Swimming.
Indian Counsel.
Piper, Linda (b. 1949)
Missionaries in the Jungle.
Sweet Ethel.
Piron, Alexis (1689–1773)
Here lies Piron—a man of no position.
Pise, Constantine (1801–66)
Let the Deep Organ Swell.
Pitcher, Oliver (b. 1923)
Pale Blue Casket, The.
Pitchford, Kenneth (b. 1930)
Surgery.
Pitiroirangi, Nga See Habib, Rowley
Pitman, Hassall
Limerick: "Cynical sage with a kink, A."
Pitt, Christopher (1699–1748)
Fable of the Young Man and His Cat, The.
On the Masquerades.
Pitt-Kethley, Fiona
God made the sex-shop keeper.
Limerick: "Platinum blonde, Goldilocks, A."
Limerick: "There was a young boy, Jack
    Horner."

Limerick: "Two playwrights called Beaumont
    and Fletcher."
Pitter, Ruth (1897–1992)
But for Lust.
Coffin-Worm, The.
Diehards, The.
Dun-Colour [or Dun-Color].
Eternal Image, The.
Hen under Bay-Tree.
If You Came.
Irish Patriarch, The.
Lost Tribe, The.
Military Harpist, The.
Morning Glory.
Old, Childless, Husbandless.
Old Nelly's Birthday.
Old Woman Speaks of the Moon, An.
Other People's Glasshouses.
Sparrow's Skull, The.
Swan Bathing, The.
Task, The.
Time's Fool.
Unicorn, The.
Viper, The.
Yorkshire Wife's Saga.
Pix, Mary (1666–c.1709)
To Mrs. Manley, upon Her Tragedy Call'd The
    Royal Mischief.
To Mrs S. F. on Her Poems.
Pixner, Stef (b. 1945)
Day in the Life, A.
Pizarnik, Alejandra (1936–1972)
Ashes.
Caroline von Günderode.
Exile.
Paths of the Mirror.
Poem for the Father.
Silences.
Piznarnick, Alejandra (1936–1972)
Awakening, The.
Deaf Lantern.
Existing.
Foundation Stone.
Fragments to Overcome Silence.
I gave the surge of myself to the dawn.
Poem for My Father.
Recognition.
Shadow of Days to Come.
Speaking Your Name.
Suspicion.
Pizzarelli, Alan
Bearded lady, The.
Bending back.
Bright awning is cranked, A.
Brim-shadow, The.
BuzzZ.
Driving.
Drop of ocean.
Fat lady, The.
Flinging the frisbee.
Fwap!
Girl / loosens her bra, The.
Just before dawn.
Just before the storm.
Late in the evening.
Meteor.
Moving van zooms, A.
On the merry-go-round.
Opening the mailbox.
Piece of buttered popcorn, A.
Scarecrow.
Shade springs open, The.
Snow falls from trees.
Spark, A.
Stranger passing, A.
Sun brightens.
Tattoo'd man, The.
Tiny fish.
Tonite.
Under the boardwalk.
Waterbug running by the frogulp.
Wiping the chrome.
With no money.
"Placido" (1809–44)
Farewell to My Mother.
Prayer to God.

Plaiwon
Limerick: "I once knew a spinster of Staines."
Planché, James Robinson (1796–1880)
Ching a Ring.
Love, You've Been a Villain.
Self-Evident.
Plantier, Thérèse (b. 1911)
Doors.
Overdue Balance Sheet.
Plarr, Victor Gustave (1863–1929)
Epitaphium Citharistriae.
Of Change of Opinions.
Shadows.
Plath, Sylvia (1932–63)
Among the Narcissi.
Applicant, The.
Ariel.
Arrival of the Bee Box, The.
Balloons.
Barren Woman.
Bee Meeting, The.
Black Pine Tree in an Orange Light.
Black Rook in Rainy Weather.
Blackberrying.
Child.
Colossus, The.
Couriers, The.
Crossing the Water.
Cut.
Daddy.
Death and Co.
Disquieting Muses, The.
Edge.
Elm.
Event.
Fever 103°.
Flute Notes from a Reedy Pond.
Frog Autumn.
Getting There.
Gulliver.
Hanging Man, The.
Incommunicado.
Insomniac.
Kindness.
Lady Lazarus.
Life, A.
Love Letter.
Magi.
Manor Garden, The.
Mary's Song.
Medallion.
Medusa.
Metaphors.
Mirror.
Moon and the Yew Tree, The.
Morning in the Hospital Solarium.
Morning Song.
Most Beds Are Beds.
Mushrooms.
New Year on Dartmoor.
Nick and the Candlestick.
Night Dances, The.
Owl.
Paralytic.
Parliament Hill Fields.
Pheasant.
Point Shirley.
Polly's Tree.
Poppies in July.
Poppies in October.
Rhyme.
Rival, The.
Sheep in Fog.
Sleep in the Mojave Desert.
Soliloquy of the Solipsist.
Spinster.
Stings.
Street Song.
Swarm, The.
Tulips.
Watercolor of Grantchester Meadows.
Winter's Tale, A.
Winter Trees.
Wintering.
Words.
You're.

Platke, Stan
Gut Catcher.
Plato (fl. 492–347 B.C.)
Apple, The.
Aristophanes.
Aster.
Dion.
Farewell: "Far from the deep roar of the
Aegean main."
Kiss, The.
Kissing Helena.
Leaving behind for ever the thundering
Aegean.
Love Sleeping.
Lover to His Lady, The.
On a Seal.
On Alexis.
On Archaeanassa.
Pan Piping.
Pindar.
Sappho.
Sit down under the high crown.
Sokrates to Agathon.
Sokrates to Xanthippé.
To Stella.
We are Eretrians from Euboia.
Plato, Ann (b. 1820)
Advice to Young Ladies.
Natives of America, The.
Reflections, Written on Visiting the Grave of a
Venerated Friend.
To the First of August.
True Friend, The.
Plato the Younger (fl. 1st–2nd cent.)
Life brings everything, time's length can shift.
Satyr by Diodorus, A.
**"Platonov, Andrey" (Andrei Platonovich
Klimentov) (1899–1951)**
Wanderer, The.
Platt, Frederic W.
Coincidentally.
Plazewska, Irene (b. 1949)
Newton's Descent.
Plenty-hawk
If all of me is still there.
**Plisetsky [or Plisetskii], German Borisovich (b.
1931)**
Papers have been sold. In them it's all made
clear, The.
Pipe, The.
Plomer, William (1903–73)
Atheling Grange; or, The Apotheosis of Lotte
Nussbaum.
Azure, or Green, or Purple.
Devil-Dancers, The.
Fall of Rock, A.
French Lisette: A Ballad of Maida Vale.
Headline History.
In the Snake Park.
Levantine, A.
Limerick: "There was an old person of Persia."
Mews Flat Mona.
Namaqualand after Rain.
Playboy of the Demi-World[: 1938], The.
Right-of-Way: 1865, A.
Scorpion, The.
Seven Rainy Months.
To the Moon and Back.
Tugela River.
White Gloves.
Plotnick, Harvey M.
Jewish.
Plowman, Max
Dead Soldiers, The.
Plumly, Stanley (b. 1939)
After Grief.
After Whistler.
Alms.
Cardinals in a Shower at Union Square.
Constable's Clouds for Keats.
Digging Potatoes, 1950.
For Esther.
Giraffe.
Iron Lung, The.
Karate.

Nobody Sleeps.
Out-of-the-Body Travel.
Peppergrass.
Wildflower.
Plumpp, Sterling (b. 1940)
Another Mule.
Billie Holiday.
Poem.
Remembered.
Saturday Night Decades.
Survivors.
Turf Song.
Plumptre, Annabella (1761–1838)
To thee, whose cautious step and specious air.
Plumptre, James (1770–1832)
Where Cumbria's mountains in the north arise.
Plunkett, Joseph Mary (1887–1916)
Spark, The.
Plutzik, Hyam (1912–62)
Airman Who Flew over Shakespeare's
England, The.
And in the 51st Year of That Century, While
My Brother Cried in the Trench, While My
Enemy Glared from the Cave.
As the Great Horse Rots on the Hill.
Cancer and Nova.
Commentary.
Dream about Our Master, William
Shakespeare, The.
For T. S. E. Only.
I Am Disquieted when I See Many Hills.
Jim Desterland.
Of Objects Considered as Fortresses in a
Baleful Place.
Portrait.
Winter, Never Mind Where.
Po Chü-i (772–842)
After Collecting the Autumn Taxes.
After Getting Drunk, Becoming Sober in the
Night.
After Passing the Examination.
After Reading Lao Tzu.
Alarm at First Entering the Yang-tze Gorges.
Arriving at Hsün-yang.
At the End of Spring.
Bamboo by Li Ch'e Yun's Window, The.
Beginning of Summer, The.
Being on Duty All Night in the Palace and
Dreaming of the Hsien-yu Temple.
Being Visited by a Friend during Illness.
Better Come Drink Wine with Me.
Bitter Cold, Living in the Village.
Buying Flowers.
Chancellor's Gravel-Drive, The.
Children.
Chrysanthemums in the Eastern Garden, The.
Chu Ch'ên Village.
Chuang Tzu, The Monist.
Climbing the Ling-ying Terrace and Looking
North.
Climbing the Terrace of Kuan-yin and Looking
at the City of Ch'ang-an.
Cold Night.
Going Alone to Spend a Night at the Hsien-Yu
Temple.
Cranes, The.
Crow Cries at Night, The.
Dream of Mountaineering, A.
Dreaming of Yüan Chên.
Dreaming that I Went with Li and Yü to Visit
Yüan Chên.
Drunk, Facing Crimson Leaves.
Early Levée, An.
Ease.
Eating Bamboo-Shoots.
Escorting Candidates to the Examination Hall.
Evening View at River Pavilion, Inviting
Guest.
Feelings Wakened by a Mirror.
Fifteenth Volume, The.
Fishing in the Wei River.
Five-string, The.
Flower, A.
Flower Market, The.
Getting Up Early on a Spring Morning.
Going to the Mountains with a Little Dancing

Girl, Aged Fifteen.
Golden Bells.
Golden Bells.
Good-bye to the People of Hangchow.
Grand Houses at Lo-yang, The.
Grass on Ancient Plain, a Song of Farewell.
Half in the Family, Half Out.
Half-recluse, The.
Harp, The.
Hat Given to the Poet by Li Chien, The.
Having Climbed to the Topmost Peak of the Incense-Burner Mountain.
Hearing the Early Oriole.
Hermit and Politician.
How can the tide of the river be compared to your love?
Idle Droning.
Illness.
Illness and Idleness.
Immeasurable Pain.
In Early Summer Lodging in a Temple to Enjoy the Moonlight.
Invitation to Hsiao Ch'u-shih.
Iranian Whirling Girls.
Kept Waiting in the Boat at Chiu-K'ou Ten Days by an Adverse Wind.
Lao Tzŭ.
Last Poem.
Lazy Man's Song.
Letter, The.
Light Furs, Fat Horses.
Lodging with the Old Man of the Stream.
Lonely Night in Early Autumn.
Looking in the Lake.
Losing a Slave-Girl.
Lotus-gatherer's Song.
Mad Poem Addressed to My Nephews and Nieces, A.
Madly Singing in the Mountains.
My Servant Wakes Me.
New Thatched Hall, A.
Night Duty in the Palace, Dreaming of a Hsien-yu Temple.
Night Snow.
Old Age.
Old Charcoal Seller, An.
Old Lute, The.
Old Man of Hsin-feng witih the Broken Arm, The.
Old Man with the Broken Arm, The.
On a Box Containing His Own Works.
On a Moonlit Night, Sent to My Brothers and Sisters.
On a Portrait of the Poet.
On an Ancient Tomb East of the Village.
On Being Removed from Hsün-yang and Sent to Chung-chou.
On Being Sixty.
On Board Ship: Reading Yüan Chên's Poems.
On Hearing Someone Sing a Poem by Yüan Chên.
On His Baldness.
On the Way to Hangchow: Anchored on the River at Night.
Painting Bamboo, a Song.
Parrot.
Parting from the Winter Stove.
Passing T'ien-mên Street in Ch'ang-an and Seeing a Distant View of Chung-nan Mountains.
Philosophers: Lao-Tzu, The.
Pine Sounds.
Pine-trees in the Courtyard, The.
Planting Flowers on the Eastern Embankment.
Poem on the Wall, The.
Poems in Depression, at Wei Village.
Pouring out My Feelings after Parting from Yüan Chen.
Prisoner, The.
Pruning Trees.
Question Addressed to Liu Shih-chiu, A.
Quiet House in Ch'ang-lo Ward, A.
Rain.
Reading the Collected Works of Li Po and Tu Fu: A Colophon.
Reading Yuan Chen on a Boat.
Realizing the Futility of Life.

Red Cuckatoo, The.
Red Embroidered Carpet.
Rejoicing at the Arrival of Chi'en Hsiung.
Releasing a Migrant 'Yen' (Wild Goose)
Remembering Golden Bells.
Resignation.
Rising Late, and Playing with A-ts'ui, Aged Two.
River Flute.
Seeing Hsia Chan off by River.
Sentimental Poem.
Separation.
Sick Leave.
Since I Lay Ill.
Sitting at Night.
Sleeping on Horseback.
Song of Everlasting Sorrow.
Song of Lasting Regret, The.
Song of the Lute.
Song of the P'i-P'a.
Song of the Pines.
Song of the Rear Palace.
Starting Early from the Ch'u-ch'êng Inn.
Stopping the Night at Jung-yang.
Taoism and Buddhism.
Temple of Bequeathed Love, The.
Temple, The.
There'll be a day when dust flies at the bottom of the sea.
Thinking of the Past.
To a Portrait Painter Who Desired Him to Sit.
To a Talkative Guest.
To a Young Widow.
To His Brother Hsing-chien.
To His Brother Hsing-chien, Who Was Serving in Tung-ch'uan.
To Li Chien.
To Liu Yü-hsi.
To the Distant One.
To Yuan Chen.
Traveler's Moon, A.
Traveler's Moon, The.
Tune: "Flower unlike Flower."
Tune: 'Memories of the South.'
Village Night.
Visiting the Hermit Cheng.
Visiting the Hsi-lin Temple.
Watching the Reapers.
Watching the Wheat-Reapers.
Winter Night.
Writing Again on the Same Theme.
Written when Governor of Soochow.

Poe, Edgar Allan (1809–49)
Al Aaraaf.
Alone.
Annabel Lee.
Bells, The.
City in the Sea, The.
Coliseum, The.
Conqueror Worm, The.
Dream-Land [or Dreamland].
Dream within a Dream, A.
Dreams.
Eldorado.
Enigma, An.
Fairyland [or Fairy-Land].
For Annie.
Happiest Day, the Happiest Hour, The.
Haunted Palace, The.
Israfel.
Lake: To——, The.
Lenore.
Monody on Doctor Olmsted.
Oh! that my young life were a lasting dream!
Raven, The.
Romance.
Sleeper, The.
Song: "Neath blue-bell or streamer."
Song: "Young flowers were whispering in melody."
Sonnet—Silence.
Sonnet—To Science.
Stanzas.
Stanzas: "How often we forget all time, when lone."
To F——.

To Helen.
To My Mother.
To One in Paradise.
Ulalume [or Ulalume—a Ballad].
Valley of Unrest, The.
Poets of the Tixall Circle (*fl.* 1630s–50s)
Confession, A.
From a Sick Poetesse to Mrs St George on Her Feeding the Swans.
To a Gentleman that Courted Several Ladys.
Pogson, Patricia (b. 1944)
Amaryllis Belladonna.
Apples.
Bee.
Bo Tree.
Deep.
Exits.
Face Mask.
Fifteen.
Going Home.
Hairdressing.
In Dreams.
Resin.
Sleeper.
Pointon, Priscilla (c.1740–1801)
Address to a Bachelor on a Delicate Occasion.
In a post-coach and four, with postillions as fine.
On Her Blindness.
Polak, Jirka (b. 1925)
Storm, The.
Polglaze, Pascoe
There's a cut-price whore.
Politian *See* Poliziano, Angelo [or Andrea]
Polito, Robert
Overheard in the Love Hotel.
Poliziano, Angelo [or Andrea] (Politian) (1454–94)
Love Song for Chrysokomos (Goldenlocks)
On the Love of Two Boys.
Splendor and pride I celebrate.
Three Ballate.
To Giovan Battista Buoninsegni.
What song will ever be so sorrowful.
Polkowski, Jan (b. 1953)
I Don't Know That Man.
Noli Me Tangere.
World Is Only Air, The.
Pollack, Lew
Two Cigarettes in the Dark.
Pollak, Felix (b. 1909)
Dream, The.
Pollard, Adelaide A.
Have thine own way, Lord! Have thine own way!
Pollard, Clare (b. 1978)
Breakfast Poem.
Heavy-Petting Zoo, The.
I enjoy dancing.
On the first of January.
Pollard, Velma (b. 1937)
Heavens Cherubim High Horsed or The Meeting of the Two Sevens (May 1977)
Pollarolo, Giovanna (b. 1955)
At Breakfast.
During Recess.
Foretold Futures.
Good Marriage, A.
Grocer's Dream, The.
In My Days.
Man Went to See the Doltons, A.
S.L.A.M.
Sunny Afternoon Dream, The.
They All Think.
When We Meet Again.
While My Father.
Pollitt, Katha (b. 1949)
Mind-Body Problem.
Of the Scythians.
Onion.
Two Fish.
Pollock, Thomas Benson
We have not known thee as we ought.
Pollok, Robert
Happiness.

Polwhele, Elizabeth (b. before 1648, d. after 1672)
On His Royal Highness His Expedition Against the Dutch.
Song: "If I were tortur'd with greensickness."

Polwhele, Richard (1760–1838)
Alas! in every aspiration bold.
Thou, who with all the poet's genuine rage.
Visit to the Author's Paternal Seat, A.

Pomeroy, George S. (fl. 1911)
Whiffenpoof Song.

Pomeroy, Ralph (b. 1926)
Gay Love and the Movies.
Tardy Epithalamium for E. and N, A.

Pomfret, John (1767–1802)
Choice, The.

Pommy-Vega, Janine (b. 1942)
Ah certainty of love in the hand.
Here before the sunrise blue and in this solitude.

Pompeius (d. 33 A.D.)
Even if I am only more dust.
Lais, who was a lovely flower.

Ponge, Francis (1899–1988)
Delights of the Door, The.
Frog, The.
Oyster, The.
Pleasures of the Door, The.
Prairie, The.
Rhetoric.
Silent World Is Our Only Homeland, The.
Sun as a Spinning Top (I), The.
Water of Tears, The.

Ponika, Kohine Whakarua (b. 1920)
Call Together.
Song of Yearning, A.

Ponsonby, Sarah (1755–1831)
Song: "By vulgar Eros long misled."

Ponsot, Marie (b. 1921)
Analogue.
Communion of Saints: The Poor Bastard under the Bridge.
I've Been Around: It Gets Me Nowhere.
La Une, A.
Matins and Lauds.
Multipara: Gravida 5.
One Is One.
Possession.
Rockefeller the Center.
Story after the Story, The.
Subject.
To the Age's Insanities.
Trois Petits Tours et Puis.
Winter.

Pook, John (b. 1942)
In Chapel.
Weekend at Home.

Poole, Richard (b. 1945)
Dark, The.

Popa, Vasco [or Vasko] (b. 1922)
Adventure of the Quartz Pebble, The.
Battle on the Blackbird's Field, The.
Be Seeing You.
Burning Shewolf.
Dream of the Quartz Pebble, The.
Echo.
Games.
He.
Heart of the Quartz Pebble, The.
Heaven's Ring.
In the Ashtray.
In the Village of My Forefathers.
Journey.
Life of St Sava, The.
Look that is that uninvited.
Love of the Quartz Pebble, The.
Nail, The.
Petrified Echoes.
Quartz Pebble, The.
Secret of the Quartz Pebble, The.
Seed, The.
Song of the Tower of Skulls.
St Sava's Forge.
St Sava's Journey.
Streets of your glances, The.

These are your lips.
Time Swept Up.
Two Quartz Pebbles.
Wise Triangle, A.
Yawn of Yawns, The.

Pope, Alexander (1688–1744)
Alley; an Imitation of Spenser, The.
Another [Epigram].
Dunciad, The, sels.
Eloisa to Abelard, sels.
Epigram Engraved on the Collar of a Dog Given [or Which I Gave] to His Royal Highness.
Epigram from the French: "Sir, I admit your general [or gen'ral] Rule."
Epigram in a Maid of Honour's Prayer-Book.
Epigram on One Who Made Long Epitaphs.
Epigrams Occasioned by Cibber's Verses in Praise of Nash, sels.
Epilogue to the Satires, in Two Dialogues, sels.
Epistle [II,] to a Lady[: Of the Characters of Women].
Epistle to Dr. Arbuthnot, sels.
Epistle [III,] to Allen Lord Bathurst, sels.
Epistle [IV,] to Richard Boyle, Earl of Burlington, sels.
Epistle to Miss [or Miss Teresa] Blount, on Her Leaving the Town after the Coronation.
Epistle to Sir Richard Temple, sels.
Epitaph for One Who Would Not Be Buried in Westminster Abbey.
Epitaph on James Moore Smythe.
Epitaph: "See here, nice Death, to please his palate."
Essay on Criticism, An, sels.
Essay on Man, An, sels.
Farewell to London in the Year 1715, A.
First Epistle of the First Book of Horace Imitated, The, sels.
First Epistle of the Second Book of Horace Imitated, The, sels.
First Satire of the Second Book of Horace [Imitated], The, sels.
For ever cursed be this detested day.
Garden, The.
Happy Life of a Country Parson, The.
Hymn: "What conscience dictates to be done."
Imitation of Chaucer.
Impromptu to Lady Winchelsea.
Inscriptio.
Intended for Sir Isaac Newton.
Lines Written in Windsor Forest.
Lord Coningsby's Epitaph.
Messiah [a Sacred Eclogue, in Imitation of Virgil's Pollio], sels.
Ode on Solitude.
Ode: The Dying Christian to His Soul.
On a Certain Lady at Court.
On a Lady Who P-ssed [or P———st] at the Tragedy of Cato.
On Authors and Booksellers [or Publishers].
On Certain Ladies.
On Dennis.
On Dullness.
On J. M. S. Gent.
On Poets.
On Queen Caroline's Deathbed.
On Riding to See Dean Swift in the Mist of the Morning.
On the Benefactions in the Late Frost.
On the Candidates for the Laurel.
On the Erection of Shakespeare's Statue in Westminster Abbey.
Quoth Cibber to Pope, tho' in verse you foreclose.
Rape of the Lock, The; an Heroi-Comical Poem, sels.
Three Epitaphs on John Hewet and Sarah Drew, sels.
To a Lady.
To Dr. Jonathan Swift.
To Mr. C., St. James's Place, London, October 22nd.
To Mrs. M. B. on Her Birth-Day.
Two or Three; a Recipe [or Receipt] to Make a Cuckold.
Universal Prayer [Deo Opt. Max.], The.

Upon a Girl of Seven Years Old.
Windsor-Forest [⁢ or &xit; Windsor Forest] sels.
You think this cruel? take it for a rule.

Pope, J. R. (1909–91)
Word of Encouragement, A.

Pope, Jessie (Mrs. Babington Lenton) (d. 1941)
Beau Ideal, The.

Pope, Walter (c.1636–1714)
Old Man's Wish, The.

Popham, Hugh (b. 1920)
Usual exquisite boredom of patrols, The.

Poplavsky [or Poplavskii], Boris Iulianovich (1903–35)
Another Planet.

Popov, Aleksandr Iakovlevich See "Yashin [or "Iashin"], Aleksandr Iakovlevich"

Popova, Olga (b. 1960)
Among black trees.
Curve of your lips, The.
Lay your head in my lap.
What's left for me to say? God.

Popovski, Anté
There was nothing left for man.

Poquelin, Jean Baptiste See **Molière**

Pordage, Samuel (1633–c.1691)
To Lucia Playing on Her Lute, Another.

Porete, Marguerite
Beloved, what do you want of me?

Porson, Richard (1759–1808)
Bathos, The.
Mutual Congratulations of the Poets Anna Seward and Hayley, The.
Note on the Latin Gerunds, A.
On a Doctor of Divinity.
Porson on German Scholarship.
Porson's Visit to the Continent.

Porta, Antonio (b. 1935)
Age of unhappiness has arrived, or is it, The.
Dialogue with Herz.
I'm walking out on Rome.
Nearby creatures of the air.
To become a tree.
To Open.
Traveler.
White bars from the window.

Portal, Magda (b. 1901)
Attitude.
Thirst for the Sea.
Watch of Time.
Woman.

Porteous, Katrina (b. 1960)
Calf.
Charlie Douglas.
Decommissioning.
I Envy the Cracked, Black Basalt.
Wrecked Creeves.

Porter, Adrian
Perfect Child, The.

Porter, Anne (b. 1911)
Another Sarah.
Consider the Lillies of the Sea.
Five Wishes.
Oaks and Squirrels.
Winter Twilight.

Porter, Cole (1891–1964)
All of You.
Always True to You in My Fashion.
Anything Goes.
At Long Last Love.
Begin the Beguine.
Brush Up Your Shakespeare.
Down in the Depths.
Ev'ry Time We Say Good-bye.
Friendship.
From This Moment On.
Get Out of Town.
I Concentrate on You.
I Get a Kick out of You.
I'm a Gigolo.
I've Got You under My Skin.
If a custom-tailored vet.
In the Still of the Night.
It's All Right with Me.

It's De-Lovely.
Just One of Those Things.
Katie Went to Haiti.
Laziest Gal in Town, The.
Let's Do It, Let's Fall in Love.
Let's Not Talk About Love.
Love for Sale.
Miss Otis Regrets.
My Heart Belongs to Daddy.
Night and Day.
Old-Fashioned Garden, An.
Red, Hot and Blue.
Ridin' High.
So in Love.
Tale of the Oyster, The.
They Couldn't Compare to You.
Too Darn Hot.
Well, Did You Evah?
What Is This Thing Called Love?
Where Is the Life That Late I Led?
You Don't Know Paree.
You're the Top.

Porter, Dorothy (b. 1954)
Lollies Noir.
P. M. T.

Porter, Hal (b. 1917)
Four Winds.
Hobart Town, Van Diemen's Land (11th June, 1837)
In a Bed-Sitter.

Porter, Peter (b. 1929)
Affair of the Heart.
And No Help Came.
Angel in Blythburgh Church, An.
Annotations of Auschwitz.
Australian Garden, An.
Consumer's Report, A.
Cost of Seriousness, The.
Exequy, An.
Gertrude Stein at Snails Bay.
Happening at Sordid Creek.
In the New World Happiness Is Allowed.
It's there, somewhere in the Platonic cold store.
Japanese Jokes.
King of the Cats Is Dead, The.
Last of England, The.
London is full of chickens, on electric spits.
Managed as they say about such men.
May, 1945.
Metamorphosis.
Mort aux Chats.
Non Piangere, Liù.
Now it's in all the novels, what's pornography to do?
On First Looking into Chapman's Hesiod.
On This Day I Complete My Fortieth Year.
Sex and the Over Forties.
Soliloquy at Potsdam.
St Cecilia's Day Epigram.
Sydney Cove, 1788.
Talking to You Afterwards.
What I Have Written I Have Written.
World of Simon Raven, The.
Your Attention Please.

Portnoy, Michael
Dinogon.
Evolution of Lather, The.
Hints at Distance.
Instant Control.
Of Titmouse.
Roget, Papier, Schism!
Voucher.

Ports, Kim
Desire.

Porumbacu, Veronica (1921–77)
Of Autumn.

Porzecanski, Teresa
Every Month.
What Matters.

Posamentier, Evelyn
Being Modern in Jerusalem.
Bird Named Isidore, The.
Counting Backwards.
Hungarian Medical Student, The: 1928.

Poseidippus (fl. c.270 B.C.)
Doricha.

Doricha, your soft bones are.
Here in this rough trench lies.
If Pythias has a customer.
If someone's with her.
On sea and land alike.
Three-year-old Archianax.
You who visit in turn.

Posey, Alexander L.
Autumn.
July.
Midsummer.
Nightfall.
Song of the Oktahutchee.

Potamkin, Harry Alan (1900–33)
Cargoes of the Radanites.

Potocki, Waclaw (1625–96)
Winter, Before the War.

Potter, Beatrix (1866–1943)
Old Woman, The.

Potts, Paul (b. 1911)
For My Father.
Muse to an Unknown Poet, The.

Poulin, A., Jr. (b. 1938)
Red Clock.

Pound, Ezra (1885–1972)
Ancient Music.
Ancient Wisdom, Rather Cosmic.
And the Days Are Not Full Enough.
And Thus in Nineveh.
Ballad for Gloom.
Ballad of the Goodly Fere.
Ballatetta.
Bathtub [or Bath Tub], The.
Beautiful Toilet, The.
Cantico del Sole.
Cantos, sels.
Cino.
Coda.
Coming of War, The; Actaeon.
Commission.
Curl-grass, curl-grass.
Dance Figure.
De Aegypto.
Doria.
Encounter, The.
Epilogue: "O chansons foregoing."
Fan-Piece, for Her Imperial Lord.
Faun, The.
Fine fish to net.
For an officer / in the old Capital, fox fur.
For deep deer-copse beneath Mount Han.
Full be the year, abundant be the grain.
Garden, The.
Girl, A.
Great Digest of Confucius, The.
Greek Epigram.
Green robe, green robe, lined with yellow.
Gypsy, The.
Heaven conserve thy course in quietness.
"Hid! Hid!" the fish-hawk saith.
Homage to Sextus Propertius, sels.
Hugh Selwyn Mauberley (Life and Contacts), sels.
I dreamt that I was God Himself.
Immorality, A.
In a Station of the Metro.
Ité.
Know then: / Toward summer when the sun is in Hyades.
L'Art, 1910.
Lake Isle, The.
Langue d'oc, sels.
Les Millwin.
Lies a dead deer on younder plain.
Liu Ch'e.
Locusts a-wing, multiply.
Long Wind, the Dawn Wind.
Lustra, sels.
Meditatio.
Monumentum Aere, Etc.
Mr. Housman's Message.
Near Perigord.
Night Litany.
Temperaments, The.
Of Jacopo del Sellaio.
Pact, A.

Papyrus.
Phyllidula.
Pick a fern, pick a fern, ferns are high.
Pisan Canto 124, sels.
Pine boat a-shift.
Planh for the Young English King.
Portrait d'une Femme.
Provincia Deserta.
Quia Pauper Amavi, sels.
Reflection and Advice.
Return, The.
River-Merchant's Wife: A Letter, The.
Salutation.
Salutation the Second.
Sandalphon.
Seafarer, The.
Sestina: Altaforte.
Silet.
Soirée.
Song of the Bowmen of Shu.
Song of the Degrees, A.
South-Folk in Cold Country.
Speech for Psyche in the Golden Book of Apuleius.
Study in Aesthetics, The.
Tame Cat.
Tea Shop, The.
To Whistler, American.
Toujours la Politesse.
Translator to Translated.
Tree, The.
Ts'ai Chi'h.
Villanelle: The Psychological Hour.
Virginal, A.
Vitex in swamp ground.
What thou lovest well remains.
Wide, ho?
Yeux Glauques.

Powell, Anthony (b. 1905)
Caledonia.

Powell, Craig (b. 1941)
Nativity.

Powell, D. A. (b. 1963)
Always Returning: Holidays and Burials. Not Every Week.
Darling can you kill me: with your mickeymouse pillows.
How his body stood against a thicket. rich in hardwood gentry: ponderous and gloomy.
Long line of bohunks and hunyaks, A: we settled in podunk. thirteen consonants.
Minotaur at Supper: Spare the Noritake and the Spode, The.
My Father and Me Making Dresses: Together.
Nicholas the ridiculous: you will always be 27 and impossible. No more expectations.
Ode: "Where have you gone blue middle of a decade? the gates creak. a sigh is so vastly different."
Sleek mechanical dart: the syringe noses into the blue vein marking the target of me.
Sonnet: "Morsels of my lifework: the story of a professional party hostess."
Studs and Rings: Favors of the Piercing Party.
Tall and thin and young and lovely the michael with kaposi's sarcoma goes walking.
Thicknesses of victor decreased: blanket→sheet→floss. Until no material would do, The.
Triptych.
What direction will you take when the universe collapses. you who when you go must go someplace.
Who won't praise green. each minute to caress each minute blade of spring. green slice us open.
You're thin again handsome. in our last.

Powell, James Henry (fl. 1850)
Lines Written for a Friend on the Death of His Brother, Caused by a Railway Train Running over Him Whilst He Was in a State of Inebriation.

Powell, Jim (b. 1951)
It Was Fever That Made the World.

Powell, Kevin (b. 1966)
Don't Feel No Way.

For Aunt Cathy.
Genius Child.
Harlem: Neo-Image.
Love / a Many Splintered Thing.
Mental Terrorism.
Southern Birth.

Powell, Padgett
Full Neurological Work-up.

Powers, Jessica Agnes
Garments of God, The.

Powys, John Cowper (1872–1963)
Aye! What a thing is the passing of Cronos, the
angular-minded.
In a Hotel Writing-Room.

Pozdnyayev [or Pozdniaev], Mikhail (b. 1953)
Remembrance of Five Loaves.

**Pozhenyan [or Pozhenian], Grigory [or Grigorii]
Mikhailovich (b. 1922)**
Cities.
Clear fall afternoon beckons, A.
Poet and Tsar.

Prabhu, Allama
For the Lord of Caves.

Prado, Adelia (b. 1936)
Easter.
Fluency.
Grace.
Heart's Desire.
In Portuguese.
Murmur.
Pelican, The.
Serenade.
Siesta.
Stained Glass Window.
Successive Deaths.
Time.

Praed, Winthrop Mackworth (1802–39)
Arrivals at a Watering-Place.
Beauty and Her Visitors.
Chancery Morals.
Chaunts of the Brazen Head, The.
Goodnight to the Season!
I think the thing you call Renown.
Letter of Advice, A.
Portrait of a Lady in the Exhibition of the
Royal Academy.
Royal Education.
School and Schoolfellows.
Talented Man, The.
To Helen.
Vicar, The.
Belle of the Ball-Room, The.

Prager, Marie-Francoise (b. 1925?)
I'll act out a weird dream.

Prandstetter, Martin Joseph
Song of Thanks.
To Chloe.

Prassinos, Gisèle (b. 1920)
Conversation, A.
Hair Tonic.

Pratt, Claire
Fog has settled, The.

Pratt, Edwin John (1882–1964)
Come Not the Seasons Here.
Final Moments, The.
From Stone to Steel.
Gathering, The.
Martyrdom of Brébeuf and Lalemant, 16
March 1649, The.
Precambrian [or Pre-Cambrian] Shield, The.
Shark, The.
Silences.
There is a language in a naval log.
Thousand years now had his breed, A.
Truant, The.
Where Cape Delgado strikes the sea.

Pratt, John Clark
Words and Thoughts.

Pratt, Marjory Bates
Not a breath of air.

Pratt, Minnie Bruce (b. 1946)
Bury and Dig.
Child Taken from the Mother, The.
Crime Againts Nature.
Eating Clay.

Elbows.
Other Side, The.
Poem for My Sons.
Red String.
Shades.
Waulking Song: Two.
White Star, The.

Pratt, Samuel Jackson (1749–1814)
Cottage Pictures.

Praxilla (fl. c.450 B.C.)
Adonis, Dying.
Fairest thing I leave behind is sunlight, The.
Learning from the tale of Admetos, my friend,
love the brave.
Most beautiful of things I leave is sunlight.
Peeking in through.
Watch for a scorpion, my friend, under every
stone.
Yet they never persuaded your heart.
You gaze at me teasingly through the window.
You who look lovely from the windows.

Prayton, Michael
Paradice on earth is found, A.

Preece, Peter (b. 1936)
Cormorant.

Preil, Gabriel (b. 1910)
Brief Note from Jerusalem, A.
Eternal Present, The.
From a Late Diary.
Lesson in Translation, A.
Little Research in Snow, A.
Night. And I am drinking smoky black tea
from China.
Rain Poem.
Tired Hunter, The.
With Walter and Amati.
Words of Oblivion and Peace.

Prelutsky, Jack (b. 1940)
Bring on the Clowns.
First Thanksgiving, The.
Ghoul, The.
Goblin, The.
Harvey Always Wins.
Homework! Oh, Homework!
It's Halloween.
Mother Goblin's Lullaby.
Pancake Collector, The.
Skeleton Parade.
Visitor, The.

Prentiss, Elizabeth Payson (1818–78)
More Love to Thee, O Christ.

Preradovic, Paula von
Chronicle in Verse, Vienna 1945.
Land of Mountains, Riverland.
Upper-Austrian Landscape.

Prescod, Marsha
Vicious Circle.
Women Are Different.

Prescot, Kenrick (1702–79)
Balsham Bells.

Press, J. E.
Limerick: "Lord, since it's hard to explain."

Press, John (b. 1920)
African Christmas.
Farewell: "Smell of death was in the air, The."
Womanisers.

Pressoir, Charles (b. 1910)
Black Island.
Country Graveyard.

Preston, James (b. 1951)
Sunfish Races.

Preston, Keith (1884–1927)
Complete Cynic, The.
Effervescence and Evanescence.
Lapsus Linguae.
Parental Critic, The.
Probably.

Preston, Margaret Junkin (1820–77)
Erinna's Spinning.
Grave in Hollywood Cemetery, Richmond, A.
Ready.

Preston, Rohan B. (b. 1966)
Champion Chant.
Chicago Blues.
Deep-Sea Bathing (Inna Reggae Dancehall)

Italist Chant.
Mama.
Music.
Ten Seconds.

Prestwich, Edmond (fl. 1651)
How to Choose a Mistress.

Prévert, Jacques (1900–77)
Alicante.
August Bank Holiday.
Barbara.
Discourse on Peace, The.
Dunce, The.
Familial.
I'm the Way I Am.
Inventory.
Last Supper, The.
Message, The.
Quartier Libre.
River, The.
Song in the Blood.
Song of the snails on their way to a funeral.
Whale hunt, The.

Previn, André
Thanks A Lot, but No Thanks.

Previn, Dory Langdon (fl. 1962)
Morning After, The.

Prewett, Frank (1893–1962)
I Shall Take You in Rough Weather.
If I Love You.
Pack, The.
Plea for Peace.
Red-Man, The.

**Preygel [or Preigel'], Sofiya [or Sofiia] Iul'evna
(1904–86)**
Hospital, The.

Price, Caroline
Night Fishing.

Price, Jonathan (1931–85)
Considered Reply to a Child, A.

Price, Laurence (fl. 1625–80?)
Maidens of London's Brave Adventures, or, A
Boon Voyage Intended for the Sea, The.
Win at First and Lose at Last; or, A New
Game at Cards.

Price, W. H. G.
Limerick: "Said a Marxist who stood on the
pier."

Prichard, Thomas Jeffrey Llewelyn (fl. 1824–61)
What can you see in yonder bay.

Pridvorov, Efim Alekseyevich See "Bedny [or
Bednyi], Demyan" [or Dem'ian]

**Prigov, Dmitry [or Dmitrii] Aleksandrovich (b.
1940)**
Dialogue No. 5.
Entry into Jerusalem.
Imagine this: a mighty giant asleep.
In the Desert.
It's better not to live in Moscow.
People are on the one side understandable.
Whenever I live, like simple.

Primrose, Lady Diana (fl. c.1630)
Eighth Pearle, The: Science.
Fourth Pearl, The: Temperance.

Prince, Frank Templeton (b. 1912)
Babiaantje, The.
Epistle to a Patron, An.
False Bay.
For Fugitives.
Question, The.
Soldiers Bathing.
Somewhere in Mauriac a girl.
Token, The.
Wind in the Tree, The.

Prince, Hughie
Boogie Woogie Bugle Boy.

Prince, Thomas (1687–1758)
Give Ear, O God, to My Loud Cry.
O Lord, Bow Down Thine Ear.
With Christ and All His Shining Train.

Pringle, Thomas (1789–1834)
Caffer Commando, The.
Emigrant's Cabin, The.
Ghona Widow's Lullaby, The.

Prior, Edwyna
I am first mouth, then hand.

Prior, Matthew (1664–1721)
Another True Maid.
Answer to Cloe [or Chloe] Jealous.
Chameleon, The.
Chaste Florimel.
Democritus and Heraclitus.
Dutch Proverb, A.
Earning a Dinner.
Enigma.
Epigram: "Thy nags (the leanest things alive)"
Epigram: "To John I ow'd great obligation."
Epigram: "Tom's sickness did his morals mend."
Epigram: "When Bibo thought fit from the world to retreat."
Epigram: "Yes, every poet is a fool."
Epitaph, An: "Interred [or Interr'd] beneath this marble stone."
Epitaph: "Meek Francis lies here, friend, without stop or stay."
Fable, A: "In Æsop's tales an honest wretch we find."
Fatal Love.
For My Own Monument.
Hans Carvel.
Human Life.
In Britain's isles, as Heylyn notes.
In Imitation of Anacreon.
Insatiable Priest, The.
Jinny the Just.
Lady Who Offers Her Looking-Glass to Venus, The.
Les Estreines.
Letter to the Honourable Lady Miss Margaret Cavendish Holles-Harley, A.
Mercury and Cupid.
Nonpareil.
Ode, An: "Merchant, to secure his treasure, The."
Oft have I said, the praise of doing well.
On Exodus 3:14: "I am that I am."
On Himself.
On My Birthday, July 21.
Orange, The.
Paraphrase from the French, A.
Pass we the ills, which each man feels or dreads.
Phillis's Age.
Question to Lisetta, The.
Quid Sit Futurum Cras Fuge Quaerere.
Reasonable Affliction, A.
Remedy Worse than the Disease, The.
Simile, A.
To a Child of Quality [Five Years Old, the Author Supposed Forty].
To a Lady: She Refusing to Continue a Dispute with Me, and Leaving Me in the Argument.
True Maid, The.
Woman's Wish, The.
Written in an Ovid.
Written in the Beginning of Mezeray's History of France.

Prior-Pitt, Pauline
Fitting.

Prismanova, Anna Semionovna (1898–1960)
Brontë Sisters, The.
Lomonosov.
Siren.

Pritam, Amrita (b. 1919)
Annunciation, The.
Creative Process, The.

Pritchard, Angharad (1677–1749)
Conversation between Two Sisters, One Choosing an Aged Man, and the Other Choosing Youth, A.

Pritchard, Norman Henry, II
Burnt Sienna.
Cassandra and Friend.
Cloak, The.
Landscape with Nymphs and Satyrs.
Love Poem.
Narrow Path, The.
Paysagesque.
Signs, The.
Springtime.

Probyn, May
After.

Anniversaries.
As the Flower of the Grass.
Ballade of Lovers.
Barcarolle.
Blossom.
Changes.
China Maniacs.
Before.
End of the Journey, The.
Frustrated.
Is It Nothing to You?
Kyrielle.
Lai.
Love in Mayfair.
Masquerading.
Mésalliance, A.
Model, The.
More than They that Watch for the Morning.
Rondelet: "Say what you please."
Rondelet: "Which way he went?"
Song Out of Season, A.
Tête-à-Tête.

Procter, Adelaide Anne (1825–64)
Address to the Ocean.
Dark Side, The.
Divine Presence, The.
Envy.
Give Me Thy Heart.
Homeless.
Incompleteness.
Judge not; the workings of his brain.
Legend, A.
Legend of Provence, A.
My Journal.
Philip and Mildred.
Pilgrims, The.
Present, The.
Lost Chord, A.
Strive, Wait, and Pray.
Thankfulness.
Three Evenings in a Life.
Unexpressed.
Woman's Answer, A.
Woman's Last Word, A.
Words.

Proctor, Bryan Waller See "Cornwall, Barry"
Proctor, Thomas (fl. c.1578)
Respice Finem.

Prodromos, Theodore (1098–1150)
To the Emperor.

Prokofiev, Aleksandr Andreievich (1900–71)
Betrothed, The.

Propertius (Sextus Propertius) (c.54 B.C.–A.D. c.2)
Ah Woe Is Me.
Ariadne Lay, Theseus' Ship Sailing Away.
Elegies.
Ghost, The.
Hylas.
Night's best of all. Night brings delight.
Revenge to Come.
When Thou Must Home.

Propertius, Sextus See **Propertius**
Propp, Karen
Train Passage.

Prospere, Susan (b. 1946)
Heart of the Matter.

"Prout, Father" See **Mahony, Francis Sylvester**
Prudentius (Prudentius Aurelius Clemens) (348–c.410)
At Cock-crow.
Come from the confines of the sunset world.
Easter Eve.
For the Kindling of the Light on Easter Eve.
Hymn for Morning.
Of the Father's love begotten Ere the worlds began to be.
Ye clouds and darkness, hosts of night.

Prufer, Kevin (b. 1969)
Babysitter's Devotion, The.
For the Dead.
My Father Recounts a Story from His Youth.
On Finding a Swastika Carved on a Tree in the Hills above Heidelberg.

Prunty, Wyatt
Coach.

Elderly Lady Crossing on Green.
Ferris Wheel, The.
Insomnia.
Note of Thanks, A.
Reading Before We Read, Horoscope and Weather.
To be Sung on the Fourth of July.
Vegetable Garden, The.
Winter's Tale, A.

Pryde, Alison
I'll See You Down the Lane.

Prynne, J. H.
Chromatin.
Evening Walk, An.
Landing Area.
Melanin.
Of Movement towards a Natural Place.

Prynne, Martha Dorsett (b. 1577, d. after 1632)
Memorandum of Martha Moulsworth Widdowe, The.

Prys, Edmwnd (1544–1623)
Welsh Ballad, A.

Prys-Jones, A. G. (b. 1888)
Cors-y-Gwaed: Fenland of Blood.
Day Which Endures Not, A.
Henry Morgan's March on Panama.
Limerick: "Artist who lived in St. Ives, An."
Limerick: "There was a young man of Porthcawl."
Ploughman: In Welsh Uplands, The.
St. Govan.
Unfortunate Occurrence at Cwm-Cadno.
Wife of Carcassone, The.

Prys, Thomas (c.1564–1639)
Poem to Show the Trouble That Befell Him When He Was at Sea, A.

Ptolemaeus, Claudius See **Ptolemy**
Ptolemy (Claudius Ptolemaeus) (fl. 121–51 B.C.)
From the Greek.
Star-Gazing.

Public Enemy (fl. 1986)
Don't Believe the Hype.
Party for Your Right to Fight.

Pudjipangu
Aeroplane.

Pudney, John (1909–77)
For Johnny.
Missing.

Pugh, Sheenagh (b. 1950)
Allegiance.
Coming into Their Own.
Do you think we'll ever get to see Earth, sir?
Frozen Field, The.
Guest, The.
Guys.
King Billy on the Walls.
Railway Signals.
Shoni Onions.
Sometimes.
Woodcarver of Stendal, The.

Pugliesi, Giacomino (fl. 13th cent.)
Canzone: Of His Dead Lady.
Canzonetta: Of His Lady in Absence.
To see the green returning.

Pulsford, Doris
Limerick: "Budding young playwright named Coward, A."

Pulter, Hester Lee (1596–1678)
Complaint of Thames 1647 When the Best of Kings Was Imprisoned by the Worst of Rebels at Holmbie, The.
On Those Two Unparalleld Friends, Sr: G: Lisle and Sr: C: Lucas, Who Were Shott to Death at Colechester.
Upon the Death of My Deare and Lovely Daughter J. P. Jane Pulter, Baptized May 1 1625 and Died Oct 8 1646 Aet. 20.
Upon the Imprisonment of His Sacred Majesties that Unparaleld Prince King Charles the First.

Purdy, Alfred Wellington (b. 1919)
Alive or Not.
Cariboo Horses, The.
Blue City, The.
Country North of Belleville, The.

Dead Poet, The.
Dead Seal.
Evergreen Cemetery.
Lament for the Dorsets.
Madwoman on the Train, The.
Night Song for a Woman.
Poem: "You are ill and so I lead you away."
Remains of an Indian Village.
Spinning.
What Do the Birds Think?
Wilderness Gothic.
Winemaker's Beat-étude, The.
Winter Walking.
Purdy, James
Do You Wonder Why I Am Sleepy.
From rivers, and from the earth itself.
Purohit, Swami (1882–1936?)
I Know That I Am a Great Sinner.
Miracle Indeed, A.
Shall I Do This.
Pushkin, Alexander Sergeyevich (1799–1837)
Autumn.
Autumn (A Fragment)
Demons.
I Loved You.
Imitation of the Arabic.
Lines Written at Night during Insomnia.
Message to Siberia.
Ode on the Hills of Georgia.
On the Statue of a Player at Svaika.
Prophet, The.
Tale of St. Petersburg, A.
With Freedom's Seed.
Work.
Püsküllüoğlu, Ali (b. 1935)
Old Pirate in These Waters, An.
Putnam, Howard Phelps (Phelps Putnam) (1874–1948)
Ballad of a Strange Thing.
Bill Gets Burned.
Hasbrouck and the Rose.
Words of an Old Woman.
Putnam, Phelps See Putnam, Howard Phelps
Puttenham, George (1529–90)
Her Majestie resembled to the crowned piller.
Ye must read upward.
O mightye Muse.
Pye, Henry James (1745–1813)
Air Balloon, The.
"Pygge, Edward" See Hamilton, Ian
Pyle, Katharine (1863–1938)
August.
Circus Parade, The.
Clever Peter and the Ogress.
Toys Talk of the World, The.
Waking.
Wonder Clock, The.
Pyrlaeus, Johann C. (1713–85)
Jesu, Come on Board.

Q

"Q" See Quiller-Couch, Sir Arthur Thomas
Qabbani, Nizar (b. 1923)
Actors, The.
Between Us.
Child Scribbles, The.
Cup and Rose.
Day I met you I tore up, The.
Disrobe, my love.
Equation.
Foolishness.
God how is it that we surrender.
I am afraid to.
I Conquer the World with Words.
I knew when I said.
If an audience could be arranged.
Language.
Testament.
There is nothing I can do.
Twenty years on the road of love.
Two African Breasts.
When God gave you to me.
Who are you.

Woman in whose voice.
You ask for the date.
Your eyes are like a night of rain.
Your image is engraved.
Your love threw me down.
Qabula, Alfred Temba (b. 1942)
Migrant's Lament: A Song.
Qaisi, Aziz (b. 1945)
Outside the Furnace.
Qaqatcguk
I keep dreaming I'm dead.
Qasmi, Ahmad Nadeem (b. 1916)
Thought.
Qorratu'l-Ayn (1814–52)
Cupbearer, O victorious Falcon, come!
Quagliano, Tony
Edward Hopper Retrospective, The.
Edward Hopper's 'Lighthouse at Two Lights.'
Quarles, Francis (1592–1644)
Are all such off'rings, as are crusht, and bruis'd.
At length, by flight, I over-went the Pack.
Be Sad, My Heart.
Before a Pack of deep-mouth'd Lusts I flee.
Behold thy darling, which thy lustfull care.
Booke of Common Pray'r excels the rest, The.
Born in Winter.
Can he be fair that withers at a blast.
Christ and Our Selves.
Come then, my soule, approach this royall Burse.
Crucified.
David's Epitaph on Jonathan.
Deuteronomy 30.19.
Eclogue 8.
Epigram: "My soul, sit thou a patient looker-on."
Galatians 6.14.
Hos Ego Versiculos.
How shall my tongue expresse that hallow'd fire.
I saw him dead; I saw his Body fall.
I wish a greater knowledge, then t'attaine.
If lust should chase my soule, made swift by fright.
Isaiah 66.11.
Let Grace conduct thee to the paths of peace.
Like to the Arctic Needle.
Luke 6.25.
Matthew 9.12.
On Zacheus [or Zacchaeus].
Meditatio Septima.
Meditatio Tertia Decima.
Mercy Tempering Justice.
My Beloved Is Mine, and I Am His; He Feedeth among the Lillies.
My soul, what's lighter than a feather? Wind.
My Soule is like a Bird; my Flesh, the Cage.
Nahum 2.10.
Not as the thirsty soyle desires soft showres.
Of Common Devotion.
Of St Stephen.
On a Feast.
On Balaam's Ass.
On Change of Weathers.
On Death.
On Dinah.
On God's Favour.
On God's Law.
On Jacob's Purchase.
On Judas Iscariot.
On Our Saviour's Passion.
On Saul and David.
On the Babel-Builders.
On the Gospel.
On the Holy Scriptures.
On the Life of Man.
On the Ploughman [or Plough-Man].
On the Two Great Floods.
On the World.
On Those That Deserve It.
On Zacchaeus [or Zacheus].
Philippians 1.23.
They Gave Him Vinegar and Gall (Matt. 27) and Wine Mingled with Myrrh (Mark 15)
This furnisht Ark presents the greedy view.

Upon the Day of Our Saviour's Nativity.
What is the World? A great Exchange of ware.
Whene'er the old exchange of profit rings.
Why dost thou shade thy lovely face? O[h] why.
World's a Floore, whose swelling heapes retaine, The.
Worldly wisdome of the foolish man, The.
Yet a Little While Is the Light with You.
Quarles, John (1624–65)
At Home.
Quasimodo, Salvatore (1901–68)
19 January 1944.
And Suddenly It Is Evening.
Anno Domini MCMXLVII.
Auschwitz.
Dead of Winter.
From the Willow Branches.
Insomnia.
Milan, August 1943.
Street in Agrigento.
To the Fifteen of Piazzale Loreto.
Quayle, Lesley
Woman Who Drank Us Up, The.
Queen Latifah
Evil That Men Do, The.
Quennell, Peter (b. 1905)
Divers, The.
Music met Leviathan returning, A.
Procne.
Quevedo y Villegas, Francisco de (1580–1645)
Ah, What of Life! Does No One Answer Me?
Amorous Sonnet Defining Love.
Birds Are in the Air at Ease.
Continues in the Same State of Feeling.
Everything Is Swept Away by the Brief Year.
From the White Day to Take Me.
Happy and Contented in Your Hut.
He Points Out the Brevity of Life, Unthinking and Suffering, Surprised by Death.
I Gaze Upon My Country's Walls.
I'll not be silent, though you put your finger.
Love Beyond Death.
Love Constant Beyond Death.
Mighty Lord Is Money, A.
Now Great and Awesome in My Heart.
On a Chaplain's Nose.
On Lisi's Golden Hair.
Rosebush, Less Presumption.
Sonnet: Death Warnings.
To a Nose.
To Rome Entombed in Her Ruins.
Toothpuller Who Wanted to Turn a Mouth into a Grinding Machine, The.
Quickenden, Beatrice (1902–67)
Hail, Oh Hail to the King.
Quiller-Couch, Sir Arthur Thomas ("Q") (1863–1944)
Doom Ferry.
Harbour of Fowey, The.
Lady Jane.
Planted Heel, The.
Sage Counsel.
Quillet, Claude (1602–61)
Process of Conception, The.
Quillinan, Edward (1791–1851)
Hour Glass, The.
Quinn, Roderic (1867–1949)
Fisher, The.
Quirino, Giovanni (fl. c.1300)
To Dante Alighieri (He Commends the Work of Dante's Life)
Quisenberry, Dan (d. 1998)
Skinning.
Qunta, Christine (b. 1952)
Know, The.

R

Ra-in (d. 1779)
My body in its autumn.
Raab, Esther (b. 1899)
Folk Tune.

Serenade for Two Poplars, A.
Today I am modest like an animal.

Raab, Lawrence (b. 1946)
After Edward Hopper.
Being a Monster.
Katie's Words.
Sudden Appearance of a Monster at a Window.

Rab (Abba Arika) *(fl.* 3rd cent.)
Kingdom of God, The.

Rabbitt, Thomas (b. 1943)
Dancing Sunshine Lounge, The.

Rabe, Olive *See* **Fisher, Aileen**

Rabéarivelo [*or* Rebéarivelo], Jean-Joseph (1901–37)
Black glassmaker, The.
Cactus.
Close by, to the north, there were two oranges.
Here is.
Here She Stands.
Hide of the black cow is stretched, The.
Imaginary tremolo.
May I come in? May I come in?
One day some young poet.
Reading.
Rondo for the Poet's Children.
Slowly / like a crippled cow.
There you are.
Three Dawns.
What Invisible Rat.
Wife is like a blade of grass, A.
You built yourself a tower in the wind.
You delude yourself.
Your Work.

Rabémanganjara, Jacques (b. 1913)
In hermetic enclosure.
Lament: "Blue, so blue that eye of sky."
Song: "Isle! / Island of the syllables of flame!"

Rabi'a al-Adawiyya (Rabi'a the Mystic) (712–801)
I am fully qualified to work as a doorkeeper, and for this reason.
My Lord / if I worship Thee from fear of Hell.
O my Lord.
O my Lord, if I worship you from fear of Hell.
O my Lord, the stars glitter and eyes of men are closed.
Stars are shining / the eyes of men are closed.
Two ways I love Thee, selfishly.

Rabi'a bint Isma'il of Syria (d. 755)
Sufi Quatrain.

Rabi'a of Balkh *(fl.* 10th cent.)
My wish for you / that God should make your love.

Rabinowich, Sholem *See* **"Aleichem, Sholom"**

Rabinowitz, Anna
Of Joy Illimited: Polyphonic Soundings: Shore to Ship.

Raboni, Giovanni (b. 1932)
Alibi of a Dead Man.
For C., Who Died of Childbirth at the Age of One Year and Eleven Months.
Hospital Interiors.
Madrigal.
Moon.

"Rachel" [*or* "Rahel"] (Rahel Blumstein [*or* Blaustein *or* Bluwstein]) (1890–1931)
Aftergrowth.
At the Window.
Barn, The.
Barren.
Dawn.
He too will soon go away.
Here on Earth.
His Wife.
In my great loneliness.
Jonathan.
Kinnereth.
Love was late in coming, and coming.
Messenger came in the night, The.
My Dead.
Only of Myself I Knew How to Tell.
Surrender.
Tiny joys, joys like a lizard's tail.
Wrestling.

Radcliffe, Alexander *(fl.* 1669–96)
As Concerning Man.

Radcliffe, Ann (1764–1823)
Butterfly to His Love, The.
Night.
Scene on the Northern Shore of Sicily.
Sea-View, A.
Song of a Spirit.
Sonnet: "Now the bat circles on the breeze of eve."
Stanzas: "How smooth that lake expands its ample breast!"
Storied Sonnet.
Sun-Rise: A Sonnet.
To the Bat.
To the Visions of Fancy.
To the Winds.

Radford, Dollie (Mrs. Ernest Radford) (b. 1858)
Soliloquy of a Maiden Aunt.

Radford, Mrs. Ernest *See* **Radford, Dollie**

Radiguet, Raymond (1903–23)
Handless Clock.
Map.
Poem: "Horizon line."
Poem: "Red eiderdown at the window, A."

Radnóti, Miklós (1909–44)
Á La Recherche.
Angel of Dread, The.
Clouded Sky.
Eighth Eclogue.
Forced March.
Fourth Eclogue, The.
Fragment: "I lived on this earth in an age."
Il Faut Laisser.
Images.
Just Walk On, Condemned to Die.
Letter to My Spouse.
Letter to My Wife.
Paris.
Peace, Horror.
Picture Postcards.
Portrait.
Postcard (Found on His body after He Was Killed by the Nazis)
Razglednica (1)
Razglednica (2)
Razglednica (3)
Razglednica (4)
Root.
Seventh Eclogue.
Thursday.

Rae, Simon (b. 1952)
Pulling the Chain.
Vile World.

Raen, Michaela
La Sombra of Who I Am.

Raffalovich, Marc André (1864–1934)
Rose Leaves when the Rose Is Dead.
Sonnet 120.
World Well Lost 4, The.
World Well Lost 18, The.

Rafferty, Charles (b. 1965)
Arsonist Tells His Story to the Attorney, The.
Man on the Tower, The.
Story of the Man Whose Tastes Were Too Refined.

Rafferty, Peter
66°7' N/22°17' W.
After Carnival.
Back End.
In the Madonna Dell' Orto.
Off the Beaten Track.
Passage.
Personal.
View from the Bathysphere.
Willowherb.

Raftery [*or* Raifteiri], Anthony [*or* Antoine] (1784–1835)
I Am Raftery [*or* Raferty].
I am Raifteiri, the poet, full of courage and love.
Lass from Bally-na-Lee, The.

Ragan, James
Child Christ at the Top of the Stairs.
Huckster at Noontime.
Standing at Pasternak's Table, Peredelkino.

Rago, Henry (1915–69)
Child's Birthday, A.

Childhood Painting Lesson.
Distances, The.
Green Afternoon, The.
Knowledge of Light, The.
Summer Countries, The.

Rahon, Alice (1904–87)
Appellants, The.
Cave of bronze amplifier of the storms.
Ferns in a Hollow of Absence.
For those parallel destinies.
Glances changed their source.
Hourglass Lying Down.
In the night of the beginning.
Pointed Out Like the Stars.
Sublimated Mercury.

"Raimar, Freimund" *See* **Rückert, Friedrich**

Raimund, Ferdinand
Farewell.
My Brother Dear.
Valentin's Song.

Raine, Craig (b. 1944)
Attempt at Jealousy, An.
City Gent.
Dandelions.
Gardener, The.
In Modern Dress.
Man Who Invented Pain, The.
Martian Sends a Postcard Home, A.
Nature Study.
Onion, Memory, The.
Plain Song.

Raine, Kathleen Jessie (b. 1908)
Air.
Angelus.
Envoi: "Take of me what is not my own."
Envoi: "What has want to give."
From a place I came.
Good Friday.
Heirloom.
Heroes.
Human Form Divine, The.
In Time.
Invocation of Death.
Isis Wanderer.
Kore in Hades.
Love-Poem: "Yours is the face that the earth turns to me."
Tu Non Se' in Terra, Si Come Tu Credi.
Message from Home.
On its way I see.
Prayer.
Pythoness, The.
Question and Answer.
Rose.
Spell of Creation.
Summit, The.
To My Mountain.
What substance had Euridice.
Wilderness, The.
World, The.
Worry about Money.
Written in Exile.

Rainey, Gertrude "Ma" ("Ma" Rainey) (1886–1939)
Prove It on Me Blues.
See, See Rider.

Rainger, Ralph
Easy Living.
Thanks for the Memory.

Rairai (d. 1780)
I take leave.

Raishi (d. 1795)
You've done your duty.

Raizan *See* **Konishi Raizan**

Rajeevan, Savithri (b. 1955)
Pair of Glasses, A.

Rajendra, Cecil
My Message.

Rakan-Keinan
Today Rakan, riding an iron horse.

Rakosi, Carl (b. 1903)
Americana 3.
Amulet.
Avocado Pit, The.
Discoveries, Trade Names, Genitals, and

Ancient Instruments.
Figures in an Ancient Ink.
Florida.
Fluteplayers from Finmarken.
Founding of New Hampshire, The.
Good Morning.
In a Warm Bath.
Instructions to the Player.
Israel.
January of a Gnat, The.
Journey Away, A.
Lord, What Is Man?
Lying in Bed on a Summer Morning.
Menage, The.
Ode on Arrival.
Old Country, The.
Origins.
Paraguay.
Sandalwood Comes to My Mind.
Services.
Song: "There never was."
To an Anti-Semite.
To the Man Inside.
Two Variations on a Theme.
Unswerving Marine.
Woman.
Young Girl.

Raksin, David
Laura.

Ralegh, Sir Walter (1552?–1618)
Authours Epitaph, Made by Himself, The.
On the Card[e]s, and Dice.
Even Such Is Time.
Farewell to False Love, A.
Farewell to the Court.
Fortune Hath Taken Away, *sels*.
Epitaph on the Earl of Leicester [*or* Leceister].
Lie, The.
Likes to a hermit poor in place obscure.
Nature, That Washed [*or* Washt] Her Hands in Milk[e].
Nymph's [*or* Nimphs] Reply to the Shepherd [*or* Sheepheard], The.
Ocean's Love to Cynthia, The, *sels*.
On the Snuff of a Candle.
Passionate Man[']s Pilgrimage, The.
Homage to Diana.
Silent Lover, The.
Sir Walter Ra[u]le[i]gh to His Son[ne].
Sir Walter Ralegh to the Queen.
To His Love When He Had Obtained Her.
Vision upon This Concei[p]t of the Faerie [*or* Faery] Queen[e], A.
What Is Our Life?

Raleigh, Sir Walter Alexander (1861–1922)
Lie, The.
Lines Suggested by an Edition of Blake's Poems.
Wishes of an Elderly Man[, Wished at a Garden Party, June 1914].

"Ramal, Walter" *See* De la Mare, Walter

Ramanujan, A. K. (b. 1929)
At Forty.
Breaded Fish.
Death and the Good Citizen.
Elements of Composition.
Foundlings in the Yukon.
Hindoo: He Doesn't Hurt a Fly or a Spider Either, The.
Hindu to His Body, A.
In the Zoo.
Last of the Princes, The.
Love Poem for a Wife, 2.
Pleasure.
Routine Day Sonnet.
Salamanders.
Self-Portrait.
Small-scale Reflections on a Great House.
Snakes.
Some Indian Uses of History on a Rainy Day.
Some People.

Ramke, Bin (b. 1947)
Astronomer Works Nights: A Parable of Science, The.
Difference Between Night and Day, The.
Paul Verlaine at the Grave of Lucien Létinois.

Revealing Oneself to a Woman.

Ramler, Karl Wilhelm (1725–98)
Yearning for Winter.

Rampolekeng, Leseko (b. 1965)
Welcome to the New Consciousness.
Wet Pain . . . Tread with Care.

Ramsay, Allan (1686–1758)
Carle He Came o'er the Croft, The.
Epigram: "Lasses, like nuts at bottom brown."
Lass of Patie's Mill, The.
Lass with a Lump of Land.
Lucky Spence's Last Advice.
Ode to Mr. F— [*or* Mr. Forbes].
Poet's Wish; an Ode, The.
Polwart on the Green.
Thou Were My Ain Thing, An.
Twa Books, The.
Up in the Air.
Wawking of the Fauld, The.

Ramsay, Andrew Michael (1686–1743)
Friendship in Perfection.

Ramsdell, Heather (b. 1968)
Bright Receding.
Nearly Circle.

Ramsey, Hettye Rayburn
Home and Mother.
Mother.

Ramsey, Jarold (b. 1937)
Comet and Treefrog.
Hand-Shadows.
Ontogeny.
Power Quest, Sooke Park.
Tally Stick, The.

Ramsey, Paul (b. 1924)
Angels, The.
Hours, The.
Images for the Gospel of Christ.
On Words and Concepts and Things.
Poet Defended, A.
Three Epigrams.

Ranaivo, Flavien (b. 1914)
Carry Me.
Choice.
Distress.
Humped Ox, The.
Love Song: "Do not love me, my friend."
Old Merina Theme.
Song of a Common Lover.
Song of a Young Girl.

Ranaldo, Lee
Five Weeks.
Flash me.
HIS:STORY.
Killed.
No Deal.
Refugee, A.
Steel.
Time Presses Me.
Ttest.
Wrong #.

Ranasinghe, Anne
Auschwitz from Colombo.
Holocaust 1944.
Sinhala New Year 1975.

Randall, Belle (b. 1940)
Be He Ezra Pound, Kennedy, or King.
City Hall.
Mabel Woo.
Playing at Cards.

Randall, Deborah (b. 1957)
Ballygrand Widow.
Blue Dome, The.
Haymakers.
His Favourite Seat.
Nightwatchman.

Randall, Dudley (b. 1914)
Abu.
Analysands.
Ancestors.
Bag Woman.
Ballad of Birmingham.
Black Poet, White Critic.
Blackberry Sweet.
Booker T. and W. E. B.
Different Image, A.

George.
Hail, Dionysos.
Idiot, The.
Langston Blues.
Melting Pot, The.
Memorial Wreath.
Old Witherington.
Poet Is Not a Jukebox, A.
Primitives.
Profile on the Pillow, The.
Roses and Revolutions.
Southern Road, The.
Souvenirs.
To the Mercy Killers.
Vacant Lot.

Randall, James A., Jr. (b. 1938)
Don't Ask Me Who I Am.
Execution.
Jew.
When Something Happens.
Who Shall Die.
Why should I be eaten by love.

Randall, James Ryder (1839–1908)
My Maryland.

Randall, Julia (b. 1923)
Miracles.
Rockland.
To William Wordsworth from Virginia.

Randell, Elaine (b. 1951)
And if my light should.
Digging up weeds by the little hedge.
Hard to Place.
Hedge breaks out in bud, The.
It's this familiar black line from the tops.
Jetty, The.
O house, o sloping field, o poplar trees whose tall arms salute.
Our hands crushed.
She had the stance of a snowdrop.
Temperament is related to physique.
Tomorrow I shall.
Waiting.
Walking towards the village.

Rando (d. 1686)
For a moment there.

Randolph, Innes (1837–87)
Rebel, The.

Randolph, Thomas (1605–35)
Answer to Master [*or* Mr.] Ben Jonson's Ode, to Persuade Him Not to Leave the Stage, An.
Come from Thy Palace.
Devout Lover, A.
Elegy, An: "Love, give me leave to serve thee, and be wise."
Elegy upon the Lady Venetia Digby, An.
Epitaph: "Beauty itself lies here, in whom alone."
Gratulatory to Mr. Ben Johnson for His Adopting of Him to Be His Son, A.
He Lives Long Who Lives Well.
In Praise of Women in General.
Mask for Lydia, A.
Milkmaid's Epithalamium, The.
Ode to Master [*or* Mr.] Anthony Stafford to Hasten Him into the Country, An.
On Sir Robert Cotton the Antiquary.
On the Death of a Nightingale.
Pastoral Courtship, A.
Phyllis.
Poet, The.
Second Epode of Horace Translated, The.
Song, A: "Music, thou queen of souls, get up and string."
This definition poetry doth fit.
Upon His Picture.
Upon Love Fondly Refused [*or* Refus'd] for Conscience's Sake.
Upon the Loss[e] of His Little Finger.

Rands, William Brighty ("Matthew Browne") (1823–80)
Cat of Cats, The.
Thought, The.

Rangai (d. 1845)
I wish to die.

Rankei Doryu (d. 1278)
Thirty years and more.

Rankin, Jennifer (1941–79)
Forever the Snake.
Love Affair 36.
Man is following me, A.
Old Circles.
Old Currawong.
Sea and Other Stories, The.
Sea-bundle.
Tale.

Rankin, Jeremiah Eames (1828–1904)
God Be with You till We Meet Again.
Laboring and Heavy Laden.

Rankin, Rush
Tourists, Potatoes, and Genocide.

Rankine, Claudia
Eden.
Elsewhere, Things Tend.
Man. His Bowl. His Raspberries, The.
New Windows.
Quotidian, The.
Short Narrative of Breasts and Wombs in
Service of Plot Entitled, A.
Short Narrative of Hand and Face in Service of
PLOT, Entitled, A.
Testimonial.

Rankins, William (fl. 1588–1601)
By this time long-gowned Lumen walked
abroad.

Ranseki (d. 1782)
Each day the absent grow.
This last night of nights.

Ransetsu (Hattori Ransetsu) (1653–1708)
All by itself.
Deep in the night.
Each morn / From the straw raincoat.
Fields and mountains turn.
Five rice dumplings.
Fly, dare take / The rice grain.
Large slug slides, A.
Melon / How well.
On the old plum tree.
One leaf lets go, and.
One plum blossom blooms.
Single leaf falls, A.
Traveling / old armor.
Without a sound.

Ransetsu, Hattori *See* **Ransetsu**

Ransom, John Crowe (1888–1974)
Agitato Ma Non Troppo.
Amphibious Crocodile.
Antique Harvesters.
Armageddon.
Bells for John Whiteside's Daughter.
Blackberry Winter.
Blue Girls.
Captain Carpenter.
Dead Boy.
Dog.
Emily Hardcastle, Spinster.
Equilibrists, The.
Good Ships.
Her Eyes.
Here Lies a Lady.
Janet Waking.
Judith of Bethulia.
Lady Lost.
Man without Sense of Direction.
Necrological.
Nocturne.
Old Man Pondered.
Old Mansion.
Our Two Worthies.
Painted Head.
Painting: A Head.
Parting, without a Sequel.
Persistent Explorer.
Philomela.
Piazza Piece.
Prelude to an Evening.
Spectral Lovers.
Spiel of [the] Three Mountebanks.
Survey of Literature.
Tall Girl, The.
Two in August.
Vaunting Oak.
Vision by Sweetwater.

Winter Remembered.

Ransom, W. M. (b. 1945)
Catechism, 1958.
Critter.
Grandpa's .45.
Indian Summer: Montana, 1956.
Message from Ohanapecosh Glacier.
On the Morning of the Third Night above
Nisqually.
Pastime Café.
Statement on Our Higher Education.

Ransome-Davies, Basil
Limerick: "Cassandra declining to follow."
Limerick: "Finding God's taboos totalitarian."
Limerick: "Is it really so very unthinkable."
Limerick: "Said Plato: 'The things that we
feel.'"
Limerick: "There was a collection of
schemers."
Limerick: "There was a young person of
Leigh."
Limerick: "Trouble with General Sherman,
The."
Limerick: "Two earnest young fellows named
Wright."
Limerick: "Young Oedipus learned from the
Sphinx."
Raymond Chandler: The Big Sleep.

Rao, B. R. Lakshman
Green Snake.

Rao, Bhanuji (b. 1926)
Fish.

Rapin, Rene (1621–87)
Of Gardens.

Rapp, Elizabeth
I hang from a thin green rope.

Rappoport, Solomon *See* **"Ansky, S."**

Ras, Barbara
In the New Country.
My Train.
Pregnant Poets Swim Lake Tarleton, New
Hampshire.
Sadness of Couples, The.
Sadness of Memory, The.

Rashad, Johari M.
Morning After, The.
Place Setting.

Rashid, N. M.
Izhab-O-Rasai (Expression and Reach)

Rashidi Samarqandi (fl. 1100)
Complaint to a Court Poet.

Raskin, Willie
Wedding Bells Are Breaking Up That Old
Gang of Mine.

Ratcliff, Carter
Big Bad Art Thing, The.

Rathkey, W. A.
Limerick: "G. B. Shaw wrote to Yeats: 'P'raps
it's mad of me.'"

Ratner, Rochelle (b. 1948)
Potato, The.

Rattigan, Terence
Limerick: "'I would doubt,' said the Bishop of
Balham."

Rattray, David
They Don't Have to Have That Look.

Ratushinskaya [or Ratushinskaia], Irina (b. 1954)
But Only Not to Think.
For the cry from the well of 'mama!'
I Will Live and Survive.
Like Mandelstam's Swallow.
Try to Cover Your Shivering Shoulders.
Why is the snow pale blue?

Raut, Paresh Chandra (b. 1936)
Snake.

Rauter, Rose
Peach.

Raven, John (b. 1936)
Assailant.
Inconvenience, An.
Roach, The.

Ravenel, Beatrice Witte (1870–1956)
Alligator, The.

Ravenscroft, Edward (c.1643–1707)
In Derision of a Country Life.

Ravenscroft, Thomas (c.1592–c.1635)
Belmans Song, A.
Hawking for the Partridge.
Madrigal: "My mistress is as fair as fine."
Sing we now merily.

Ravikovitch [or Ravikovich], Dahlia (b. 1936)
Blood Heifer.
Clockwork Doll.
Dress of Fire, A.
Everlasting Forests, The.
Hills of Salt.
On the Road at Night There Stands the Man.
Poem of Explanations.
Real Love Isn't What It Seems.
Sound of Birds at Noon, The.
Surely You Remember.
Trying Again.
Unusual Autumn, An.
You Can't Kill a Baby Twice.

**"Ravitch, Melech" (Zekharye Khone Bergner)
(1893–1976)**
Twelve Lines about the Burning Bush.

Rawling, Tom
Gas Drill.

Rawlins, C. L.
Living in at Least Two Worlds.

Rawlinson, Gloria (b. 1918)
Islands Where I Was Born, The.
Simple Matter, A.

Raworth, Tom (b. 1938)
Bolivia: Another End of Ace.
Collapsible.
Dark Senses.
Empty Pain-Killer Bottles, The.
Future Models May Have Infra-Red Sensors.
Hot Day at the Races.
Jungle Book.
Lion Lion.
My Face Is My Own, I Thought.
Out of a Sudden.
That More Simple Natural Time Tone
Distortion.

Rawson, Grindall (1659–1715)
To the Learned and Reverend Mr. Cotton
Mather, on His Excellent Magnalia.
Upon the Death of His Much Esteemed Friend
Mr. Jno Saffin Junr.

Rawson, Joanna (b. 1964)
Border, The.
Map Burnt Through.
Self-portraits by Frida Kahlo.

Ray, Cyril
Limerick: "At last I've seduced the *au pair*."
Limerick: "I was sitting there, taking my ease."
Limerick: "Not that it always transpired."
Limerick: "Well, if it's a sin to like Guinness."

Rāy, Dāśarathi (1807–57)
It's no one else's fault, Syama Ma.
Wake up, wake up, Mother!
Who is this black.

Ray, David (b. 1932)
At the Washing of My Son.
Automat.
Brides of Elvis, The.
Card-Players, The.
Eskimo Girl, The.
Greens.
In the Third Month.
Midnight Diner by Edward Hopper, A.
On a Fifteenth-Century Flemish Angel.
Sunday Morning.
Ursula.
Widower.

Ray, Henrietta Cordelia (1861?–1916)
After the Storm.
Afterglow, The.
Ambition.
Among the Berkshire Hills.
Anita and Giovanni.
Antigone and Oedipus.
April.
Aspiration.
At Christmas-Tide.
At Nature's Shrine.
At Sunset.

At the Cascade.
August.
Awakening.
Beethoven.
Boat Song.
Broken Heart.
Charity.
Charles Sumner.
Chateaux en Espagne.
Cloud Fantasy.
Cloud Song.
Coming of Spring, The.
Compensation.
Cuckoo Song.
Dante.
Dawn of Love, The.
Dawn's Carol.
December.
Dream of Elfland, A.
Dream within a Song, A.
Easter Carol.
Echo Reverie.
Echo's Complaint.
Emerson.
Enchanted Shell, The.
Evening Prayer.
Fading Skiff, The.
Failure.
Fancy and Imagination.
February.
Fisherman's Story, The.
Fragment, A: "Our fancies are but joys all
    unexprest."
Full Vision.
God's Ways, Not Our Ways.
Greeting.
Group of Musings, A.
Hermit and the Soul, The.
Hidden Essence.
Hour's Glory, The.
Hymn to the Thousand Islands.
Ideal, An.
Idyl.
Idyl of Spring, An.
In Memoriam Frederick Douglass.
In Memoriam Paul Laurence Dunbar.
Incompleteness.
Instability.
Invocation to the Muse.
January.
July.
June.
Life.
Life's Boundary.
Limitations.
Lincoln.
Lines Written on a Farewell View of the
    Franconia Mountains at Twilight.
Listening Nydia.
Little Fay's Thanksgiving.
Longfellow.
Lost Opportunities.
Love's Vista.
Maid of Ehrenthal, The.
March.
May.
May's Invocation after a Tardy Spring.
Messengers, The.
Mignon.
Mildred's Doves.
Milton.
Mist Maiden, The.
Musidora's Vision.
My Easter Dove.
My Spirit's Complement.
Nature's Minor Chords.
Nature's Uplifting.
Niobe.
November.
O Restless Heart, Be Still!
Ocean Musing, An.
October.
Ode on the Twentieth Century.
On a Nook Called Fairyland.
On the Concord River.
On the Picture of a Child.
On the Rapids of the St. Lawrence.

Our Task.
Pastoral: "Annette came through the
    meadows."
Perfect Orchestra, The.
Picture, A.
Poet's Ideal, The.
Poet's Ministrants, The.
Prayer: "O Christ, who in Gethsemane."
Quebec.
Quest of the Ideal, The.
Questioning.
Raphael.
Recompensed?
Repose.
Retrospection.
Reunited.
Reverie.
Rhyme of the Antique Forest.
Robert G. Shaw.
Sculptor's Vision, The.
Sea Cadences.
Self-Mastery.
September.
Shadow and Sunrise.
Shakespeare.
Siren Bird, The.
Sky Picture.
Snow Song.
Song: "O sweet, sad, singing river."
Soul Incense.
Soul's Courts, The.
Star Song.
Sunrise.
Sunset.
Sunset Picture.
Thought at Walden, A.
Thought of Lake Ontario, A.
Tireless Sculptor, The.
To Laura.
To My Father.
To My Mother.
Toussaint L'Ouverture.
Triple Benison, The.
Two Musicians, The.
Venus of Milo, The.
Verses to My Heart's-Sister.
Vision of Eve, The.
Vision of Moonlight, A.
Voices of the Rain.
Wendell Phillips.
William Lloyd Garrison.
Wood Carols.

Rāy, Kumār Śambhucandra (*fl.* early 19th cent.)
    Tara, You are Cintamayi, Full of Thought.
Rāy, Mahārāja Nandakumār (d. 1775)
    You've enchanted the world.
Rāy, Mahārāja Rāmkrsna (d. 1795)
    Give me food.
    Moon flashes in Her blessed face, The.
Ray, Maude Louise
    My Task.
Rāy, Naracandra (*fl.* early 19th cent.)
    Everything is Your wish, Tara.
Rāy, Raghunāth (d. 1836)
    Who is this.
Rāy, Rasikcandra (1820–93)
    Mountain / Whose woman have you brought
        home to our mountain city?
Rāy, Tāpas
    Wait a moment, Death.
Raye, Don (1909–85)
    Boogie Woogie Bugle Boy.
    I'll Remember April.
    Milkman, Keep Those Bottles Quiet!
    Mister Five by Five.
    You Don't Know What Love Is.
"Rayevsky [*or* Raevskii], Georgy [*or* Georgii]
    Avdeievich" (Georgii Avdeievich Otsup)
    (1897–1962)
    O, he who flashed above the moon afar.
    War.
    You think: won't fate tap.
Rayl, Johanna
    Spring Storm.
Raymond, Vicki (b. 1949)
    Extinguish, One by One.

People, No, The.
Reculver Bay.
Raymund, Bernard
    Well, The.
Raz, Hilda
    Before John and Maria's Wedding.
    Fast Car on Nebraska I-80: Visiting Teacher.
    Volunteers.
Razaf, Andy (1895–1973)
    Ain't Misbehavin'
    Guess Who's in Town? (Nobody but That Gal
        of Mine)
    Honeysuckle Rose.
    I'd Give a Dollar for a Dime.
    Joint is Jumpin', The.
    Keepin' Out of Mischief Now.
    Memories of You.
    My Handy Man.
    My Handy Man Ain't Handy No More.
    My Man o' War.
    My Special Friend (Is Back in Town)
    Porter's Love Song to a Chambermaid, A.
    S'posin'
    Stompin' at the Savoy.
    Tan Manhattan.
    (What Did I Do to Be So) Black and Blue?
    You're Lucky to Me.
Rea, Tom
    Lugs Benedict on the Coast, 1934.
Read, Sir Herbert (1893–1968)
    1945.
    Beata l'Alma.
    Cranach.
    End of a War, The.
    Falcon and the Dove, The.
    Garden Party.
    Happy Warrior, The.
    My Company.
    Phoenix, bird of terrible pride.
    Short Poem for Armistice Day, A.
    Sic et Non.
    To a Conscript of 1940.
    White Isle of Leuce, The.
Read, Thomas Buchanan (1822–72)
    Sheridan's Ride.
    Summer Shower, The.
Read, Vail (b. 1909)
    This New Day.
Reader, Willie
    When Paul Bunyan Was Ill.
Reading, Peter (b. 1946)
    Ballad: "I'll tell you a story / concerning John
        and Joan."
    Camping Provencial. Notices: (1)
    Correspondence.
    Soon and silently.
    Who would have thought it Sir, actually
        putting ME in a WRITING!
    Ye haue heard this yarn afore.
Realuyo, Bino A.
    Querida, La.
    Sojourners, The.
Reaney, James (b. 1926)
    Branwell's Sestina.
    Granny Crack.
    Katzenjammer Kids, The.
    Le Tombeau de Pierre Falcon.
    Lost Child, The.
    School Globe, The.
    To the Avon River above Stratford, Canada.
    Upper Canadian, The.
Reavey, George (1907–76)
    Bridge of Heraclitus, The.
    Dismissing Progress and Its Progenitors.
    How many fires.
    Never.
Rebelo, Jorge
    Poem: "Come, brother, and tell me your life."
    Poem for a Militant.
Rebolledo, Efrén (1877–1927)
    Sapho's Kiss.
Receveur, Don
    Eagle in the Land of Oz.
    Doper's Dream.
    Night Fear.

August 17, 1970.

Rector, Liam (b. 1949)
David's Rumor.
Him, His Place.
My Grandfather Always Promised Us.
Showing.

Red Elk, Lois
For Thieves Only.

Redcloud, Prince
Farmer.

Redding, Edward C. (*fl.* **1950)**
End of a Love Affair, The.

Redel, Victoria
Singing to Tony Bennett's Cock.

Redenius, Jeannette
Potato Garden.

Redgrove, Peter (b. 1932)
Christiana.
Corposant.
Curiosity-Shop, The.
Design.
Dog Prospectus.
For No Good Reason.
Idea of Entropy at Maenporth Beach, The.
Intimate Supper.
Light Hotel.
Million, The.
Minerals of Cornwall, Stones of Cornwall.
Negotium Perambulans.
Red Indian Corpse.
Required of You This Night.
Secretary, The.
Serious Readers.
Song: "I chuck my Bible in the parlour fire."
Visible Baby, The.

Redi, Francesco (1626–98)
Bacchus's Opinion of Wine, and Other
Beverages.
Creation of My Lady, The.

Redmond, Eugene B. (b. 1937)
Aerolingual Poet of Prey.
Dance Bodies #1.
Definition of Nature.
Distance.
Gwensways.
Love Necessitates.
Milestone: The Birth of an Ancestor.
My Tongue Paints a Path.
Parapoetics.
Poetic Reflections Enroute to, and During, the
Funeral and Burial of Henry Dumas, Poet.
River of Bones and Flesh and Blood.
Spearo's Blues (or: Ode to a Grecian Yearn)

Redwing, A. K. (b. 1948)
Agent of Love.
Blue Jeaned Rock Queen in Search of
Happiness on a Blind Thursday at 1/3 Speed
and Crying, A.
Chrome Babies Eating Chocolate Snowmen in
the Moonlight.
Cosmic Eye.
Hoofer, The.
Lost Mohican Visits Hell's Kitchen, A.
Sitting Bull's Will versus the Sioux Treaty of
1868 and Monty Hall.
Tornado Soup.
Two Hookers.
World's Last Unnamed Poem, The.
Written in Unbridled Repugnance near Sioux
Falls, Alabama—April 30, 1974.

Reed, Henry (1914–86)
Auction Sale, The.
Chard Whitlow.
Château, The.
Door and the Window, The.
Dull Sonnet.
Judging Distances.
Lessons of the War.
Map of Verona, A.
Naming of Parts.
Philoctetes.
Sailor's Harbor.
Unarmed Combat.

Reed, Ishmael (b. 1938)
.05.

Badman of the Guest Professor.
Beware: Do Not Read This Poem.
Black Cock, The.
Black Power Poem.
Catechism of d Neoamerican Hoodoo Church.
Chattanooga.
Dualism.
El Paso Monologue.
I Am a Cowboy in the Boat of Ra.
I am not the walrus.
Feral Pioneers, The.
Jacket Notes.
Nov 22, 1988.
Oakland Blues.
Paul Laurence Dunbar in The Tenderloin.
Railroad Bill, a Conjure Man.
Reactionary Poet, The.
Turning Pro.
White Hope.
Why I Often Allude to Osiris.

Reed, John (1887–1920)
I have watched the summer day come up from
the top of a pier of the Williamsburgh
Bridge.

Reed, Langford (1889–1954)
Limerick: "Consider the lowering Lynx."
Limerick: "Goddess capricious is Fame, A."
Limerick: "Indolent vicar of Bray, An."
Limerick: "Patriot living at Ewell, A."
Limerick: "Said a fair-headed maiden of
Klondike."
Limerick: "Said a foolish young lady of
Wales."
Limerick: "To his wife said the lynx-eyed
detective."

Reed, Mary Davis
One Year to Live.

Reedy, Carlyle (b. 1938)
Doll Museum, The.

Rees, John Machreth
Merioneth.

Rees-Jones, Deryn (b. 1968)
And Please Do Not Presume.
Great Mutando, The.
I Know Exactly the Sort of Woman I'd Like to
Fall in Love With.
It Will Not Do.
Largo.
Making for Planet Alice.
Service Wash.

Reese, Doc
Ol' Hannah.

Reese, Lizette Woodworth (1856–1935)
April in Town.
At Cockcrow.
Christmas Folk-Song, A.
Crows.
Day before Spring, The.
Death's Guerdon.
Flower of Mullein, A.
Fog.
In Time of Grief.
Indian Summer.
Lavender Woman, The.
Little Song of Life, A.
Love, Weeping, Laid This Song.
Lyric on the Lyric, A.
Mid-March.
Mystery.
Nocturne: "Topple the house down, wind."
Old Belle, An.
One Night.
Ownership.
Prayer of an Unbeliever.
Puritan Lady, A.
Rachel.
Renunciation.
Reserve.
Spicewood.
Spring Ecstasy.
Street Scene, A.
Tears.
Telling the Bees.
To Life.
Trust.
White Fury of the Spring, The.

Wind.

Reeve, Clara (1729–1807)
Character, A.
New Cantata, A.
Sacred Heliconian spring, The.

Reeves, James (1909–78)
Animals' Houses.
Black Pebble, The.
Cows.
Double Autumn, The.
Four Horses, The.
Giant Thunder.
Grasshopper and the Bird, The.
Horn, The.
If Pigs Could Fly.
Little Brother, The.
Mr. Tom Narrow.
Noah.
Old Wife and the Ghost, The.
Others.
Sea, The.
Slowly.
Stone Gentleman, The.
Things to Come.
Waiting.
You in Anger.

Reeves, Trish (b. 1947)
Of Potatoes.

Reeves, W. James
W.

Reeves, William Pember (1857–1932)
Passing of the Forest, The.

Regan, J. M. (b. 1947)
Partial Luetic History of an Individual at Risk.

Rege, P. S. (1910–78)
Pact, The.

Rege, Sadanand (1923–82)
Old Leaves from the Chinese Earth.

Reginald, Francis
À l'Ange Avantgardien.
Cloth of Gold.
Lass in Wonderland, A.
Vision.

Reichard, William (b. 1963)
Cloud Game, The.
Monster's Dream, The.

Reid, Alastair (b. 1926)
Curiosity.
Pigeons.
Scotland.
Spell for Sleeping, A.

Reid, Christopher (b. 1949)
Baldanders.
Firs / born Xmas day.
Gardeners, The.
Howl, Howl.
Perversion, A.
Stones and Bones.

Reid, Dorothy E.
Between Aphorisms.

Reid, John, of Stobo (c.1430–1505)
In Peblis town sum tyme, as I heard tell.

Reilly, Patricia Lynn
Imagine a woman who honors the face of the
Goddess in her own changing face.

Reimer, Nadia Hazboun
Middle East, The.
To an Old Friend.
Workaholic.

Rein, Yevgeny [or Evgenii] Borisovich (b. 1935)
Black Music.
Breakfast on the Balcony.
Calendar of the Air.
Galya, Mother, and My Daughter Anna.
Glimpsed through a Lens.
Monastery.
Moscow Station, The.
Nanny Tanya.
Return, The.
Secret Agent, A.

Reinmar der Alte (*fl.* **1185–1205)**
Messenger, hear what I say.
No one needs to ask.

Reis, Patricia
Ancient Ones, The.

Reis, Yitzhok *See* **Nadir, Moishe**

Reisen, Abraham (1876–1953)
Burn Out Burn Quick.
Healing.
Household of Eight.
Watchman, The.

Reiss, Annaliese *See* **Ress, Lisa**

Reiter, Thomas
Class Bully.
Rights of Way.

Reito
Ox bridle tossed, vows taken.

Reitz, F. W. (1844–1934)
Proclamation, or Paper Bomb, The.

Reizan (d. 1411)
Myriad differences resolved by sitting, all
doors opened, The.

Rekisen (d. 1834)
Let them bloom or.

Relph, Josiah (1712–43)
Hay-Time; or, The Constant Lovers. A
Pastoral.

Remoto, Danton R.
Black Silk Pajamas.
Exile.
Images of John (1967–92)
Rain.

Rendall, Robert (1898–1967)
Angle of Vision.
Planticru, The.
Shore Tullye.

Rendon, Marcie
You See This Body.

Rendra, W. S.
Baby at the Bottom of the River.
Moon's Bed, the Bride's Bed, The.
Tall Weeds.
World's First Face, The.

Renseki (d. 1789)
I cleansed the mirror.

Renton, William
After Nightfall.
Crescent Moon.
Foal, The.
Fork of the Road, The.
Moon and Candle-light.
Shadow of Himself, The.

Repetto, Vittoria
6th Grade—Our Lady of Pompeii.

Replansky, Naomi (b. 1918)
Dangerous World, The.
Good Day's Work, A.
I Met My Solitude.
In the Sea of Tears.

Resnikoff, Alexander
Bad and Good.

Ress, Lisa (Annaliese Reiss) (b. 1939)
Family Album, The.
Household Rules. Farwell Avenue, Chicago,
1946.
Learning the Ropes. Custer Street. Evanston,
1949.
Visit, Auschwitz, 1971, The.
Waving Her Farewell. Train Station, Vienna
XV, 1939.

Retallack, Joan (b. 1941)
Biographia Literaria.
Here's Looking at You Francis Bacon.
Japanese Presentation I and II.
Not a Cage.
Secret Life of Gilbert Bond, The.
Western Civ, 4 and 5.
Woman Dragged by Welsh Corgis.

Reti, Irene
I Never Knew I Was Jewish.

Retsuzan (d. 1826)
Night I understood, The.

Reuental, Neidhart von (*fl.* 13th cent.)
On the Mountain.
Sing, my golden cock, I'll give thee grain!
Summer, now we must live without your sweet
weather.
There is pain in my heart.
Young and old, rejoice.

Reuther, Linda
And the Great Mother said.

Revard, Carter (b. 1931)
Advice from Euterpe.
And Don't Be Deaf to the Singing Beyond.
Another Sunday Morning.
Birch Canoe.
But Still in Israel's Paths They Shine.
Christmas Shopping.
Coming of Age in the County Jail.
Coyote, The.
Discovery of the New World.
Dragon-Watching in St. Louis.
Driving in Oklahoma.
ESP.
In Kansas.
Getting Across.
Home Movies.
January 15 as a National Holiday.
Looking Before and After.
My Right Hand Don't Leave Me No More.
North of Santa Monica.
Not Just Yet.
October, Isle of Skye.
On the Bright Side.
Parading with the Veterans of Foreign Wars.
Support Your Local Police Dog.

Revel, Harry
Head over Heels in Love.
Love Thy Neighbor.
Meet the Beat of My Heart.
There's a Lull in My Life.
You Hit the Spot.

Revell, Donald
1919.
At the Exhibition of Parables.
Fauviste.
World, The.

Reverdy, Pierre (1889–1960)
Adieu.
Air: "Forgetting."
Departure.
Endless Journeys.
For the Moment.
On the Threshold.
Post.
Road.
Secret.
Squares.

Revere, Paul (1735–1818)
Unhappy Boston.

Revett, Eldred (b. c.1635)
Ode: Hastening His Friend into the Country.

Reviczky, Gyula (1855–89)
Death of Pan, The.
I Am the Son of King Gog of Magog.
To János Arany in Answer to His Poem
'Cosmopolitan Poetry.'

Rexroth, Kenneth (1905–82)
Andrée Rexroth.
As I came from the.
As the wheel follows the hoof.
Asagumori.
Bad Old Days, The.
Bestiary, A.
Buddha took some Autumn leaves.
Chilled through, I wake up.
Come to me, as you come.
Dawn in a tree of birds, A.
Did you take me because you loved me?
Every morning, I.
Fact.
Fifty.
Fires / Burn in my heart.
Fish Peddler and Cobbler.
Floating.
For a Masseuse and Prostitute.
For Eli Jacobson.
Fox.
Frost covers the reeds of the marsh.
Further Advantages of Learning.
Half in a dream.
Heart of Herakles, The.
Here is Klito's little shack.
Horse.
How long, long ago.

How many lives ago.
I am sad this morning.
I cannot forget.
I hate this shadow of a ghost.
I have sworn ten thousand times.
I hold your head tight between.
I Lais, once an arrow.
I pass the day tense, day.
I scream as you bite.
I sit at my desk.
I wish I could be.
If I thought I could get away.
In the park a crow awakes.
It Is a German Honeymoon.
It is the time when.
Just us.
Let us sleep together here tonight.
Letter to William Carlos Williams, A.
Long Lifetime, A.
Lute Music.
Lyell's Hypothesis Again.
Lying in the meadow, open to you.
Lysidike dedicates.
Naked out of the dark we came.
Night is too long to the sleepless, The.
Night without end. Loneliness.
Now the fireflies of our youth.
Observations in a Cornish Teashop.
Oh the anguish of these secret meetings.
On Flower Wreath Hill.
On the bridges.
On the Eve of the Plebiscite.
Once I shone afar like A.
Only Years.
Poem: "As the full moon rises."
Proust's Madeleine.
Quietly.
Raccoon.
Vulture.
Scorched with love, the cicada.
Signature of All Things, The.
Some day in six inches of.
Song for a Dancer.
Sottoportico San Zaccaria.
Spring, Coast Range.
Spring is early this year.
Strength through Joy.
This flesh you have loved.
Time Is the Mercy of Eternity.
Two flowers in a letter.
Uguisu sing in the blossoming trees.
Uguisu sleeps in the bamboo grove, The.
Vitamins and Roughage.
Wednesday of Holy Week, 1940.
Wheel Revolves, The.
Who is there? Me.
Without me you can only.
Wolf.
You ask me what I thought about.
You wake me.
Your tongue thrums and moves.

Reyes, Alfonso (1889–1959)
Menace of the Flower, The.
Monterrey Sun.
Scarcely.
Tarahumara Herbs.
To-and-Fro of Saint Theresa.

Reyes, Carlos
Arizona Nocturne.

Reyes, Myrna Peña
San Juan.
Toads Mate and Father Cleans the Pool.

Reynolds, Craig (b. 1952)
Worst of it, The.

Reynolds, Henry (*fl.* 1628)
Black Maid to the Fair Boy, The.

Reynolds, John (*fl.* 17th cent.)
Mysteries Revealed after Death.
Nosegay, A.

Reynolds, John Hamilton (1796–1852)
To Keats: On Reading His Sonnet Written in
Chaucer.
To Spenser.

Reynolds, Lucile Hargrove
To the New Owner.

Reynolds, Oliver (b. 1957)
Bestiary.

Eous.
Hazel.
Spanish Dancer.

Reynolds, Rebecca (b. 1962)
Object of Burial Is Intent, The.
Peridot.
Surplus.

Reynolds, Samuel F. (b. 1967)
Moon/light quarter/back sack.
Open Letter to All Black Poets, An.
Whipping, The.

Reznikoff, Charles (1894–1976)
About an Excavation.
After I had worked all day at what I earn my
living.
Amelia was just fourteen and out of the orphan
asylum.
Among the heaps of brick and plaster lies.
Aphrodite Vrania.
April.
Babylon: 539 B.C.E.
Testimony: The United States (1901–1910)
Recitative / The South.
Children.
David.
Day of Atonement.
Dead gull in the road, A.
Deserter, A.
Dew.
Epidemic.
Epitaph.
Epitaphs.
Exodus.
Free Verse.
Grove of small trees, branches thick with
berries, A.
Hebrew of Your Poets, Zion, The.
Her work was to count linings.
Highway I was walking on, The.
House-wreckers, The.
How difficult for me is Hebrew.
How Shall We Mourn You Who Are Killed
and Wasted.
I.
I Do Not Believe That David Killed Goliath.
I had been bothered by a secret weariness.
I have learnt the Hebrew blessing before eating
bread.
I like this secret walking.
I met in a merchant's place.
I Will Go into the Ghetto.
I Will Write Songs against You.
Idiot, The.
If There Is a Scheme.
In steel clouds.
In the shop, she, her mother, and grandmother.
Israel I.
Israel II.
Joshua at Schechem.
Kaddish.
Lamps Are Burning, The.
Luzzato.
Massacres.
Millinery District: "Clouds, piled in rows like
merchandise, The."
Millinery District: "Many fair hours have been
buried here."
My grandfather, dead long before I was born.
My work done, I lean on the window-sill.
New Year's.
Of course, we must die.
On Brooklyn Bridge I saw a man drop dead.
Out of the hills the trees bulge.
Rainy Season.
She who worked patiently.
Shopgirls leave their work, The.
Showing a torn sleeve, with stiff and shaking
fingers the old man.
Similes.
Te Deum.
Testimony.
These Days the Papers in the Street.
Though our thoughts often, we ourselves.
Two Witches.
What are you doing in our street among the
automobiles, horse?
When the Second World War began.

Rhau, Daisy
Potatoes.

Rhianos
To Theodorus et al.

Rhianus (fl. 3rd cent. B.C.)
Archinos, this retsina bottle contains.

Rhodenbaugh, Suzanne
Civil War, The.

Rhodes, Martha
All the Soups.
Bare Windows.
Behind Me.
Disguised.
How Fast.
Inside Father's Pockets.
It Being Forbidden.
Robe, The.
Through Clouds, Their Whispers.
Why She Hurries Out, Then Home.

Rhys, Ernest (1859–1946)
Ballad of the Homing Man, The.

Rhys, Keidrych (b. 1915)
Interlude.

Ribemont-Dessaignes, Georges (b. 1884)
Artichokes.
Sliding Trombone.

Rice, Nicky
Mother's Room.

Rich, Adrienne (b. 1929)
5:30 A.M.
Abnegation.
After Dark.
After Twenty Years.
Afterwake, The.
Amends.
Architect.
Art of Translation, The.
At a Bach Concert.
At the Jewish New Year.
Attention.
August.
Aunt Jennifer's Tigers.
Autumn Sequence.
Bears.
Blood-Sister.
Burning of Paper instead of Children, The.
Burning Oneself Out.
Camino Real.
Can it be growing colder when I begin.
Catch if you can your country's moment,
begin.
Charleston in the Eighteen-sixties.
Children Playing Checkers at the Edge of the
Forest.
Clock in the Square, A.
Culture and Anarchy.
Dark lintels, the blue and foreign stones, The.
Dark woman, head bent, listening for
something, A.
Delta.
Dialogue.
Diving into the Wreck.
Every peak is a crater. This is the law of
volcanoes.
Face to Face.
Floating Poem, Unnumbered, The.
Focus.
Food Packages: 1947.
For a Friend in Travail.
For an Album.
For the Dead.
For the Record.
From a Survivor.
From an Old House in America.
From the Prison House.
Gabriel.
Ghazal.
Grandmothers.
Harpers Ferry.
Here is a map of our country.
History.
I Am in Danger—Sir.
I come home from you through the early light
of spring.
I Dream I'm the Death of Orpheus.
I know you are reading this poem.

I wake up in your bed. I know I have been
dreaming.
In a Classroom.
In the Wake of Home.
In Those Years.
Insusceptibles, The.
Integrity.
Jerusalem.
Late Ghazal.
Late summers, early autumns, you can see
something that binds.
Letters in the Family.
Letters to a Young Poet.
Like This Together.
Living in Sin.
Living Memory.
Loser, The.
Lucifer in the Train.
Mare's skeleton in the clearing: another sign of
life, The.
Mathilde in Normandy.
Memory lifts her smoky mirror: 1943.
Memory says: Want to do right? Don't count
on me.
Merced.
Middle-Aged, The.
Mirror in Which Two Are Seen as One, The.
Mourning Picture.
My mouth hovers across your breasts.
Necessities of Life.
Newsreel.
Ninth Symphony of Beethoven Understood at
Last as a Sexual Message, The.
No one's fated or doomed to love anyone.
Not Like That.
Of simple choice they are the villagers; their
clothes come.
Old blanket, The. The crumbs of rubbed wool
turning up.
On this earth, in this life, as I read your story,
you're lonely.
One night on Monterey Bay the death-freeze of
the century.
Origins and History of Consciousness.
Orion.
Paula Becker to Clara Westhoff.
Peeling Onions.
Phantasia for Elvira Shatayev.
Phenomenology of Anger, The.
Planetarium.
Power.
Primary Ground, A.
Prospective Immigrants Please Note.
Rain on the West Side Highway.
Re-forming the Crystal.
Readings of History.
Roofwalker, The.
Sleeping, turning in turn like planets.
Snapshots of a Daughter-in-Law.
Soledad. = f.Solitude, loneliness,
homesickness; lonely retreat.
Song: "You're wondering if I'm lonely."
Splittings.
Storm Warnings.
Stranger, The.
Suppose you want to write.
Tattered Kaddish.
That conversation we were always on the edge of.
That "old last act"!
They come to you with their descriptions of
your soul.
To the Days.
Toward the Solstice.
Translations.
Trees, The.
Trying to Talk with a Man.
Twenty-one Love Poems.
Two Songs.
Upper Broadway.
Valediction Forbidding Mourning, A.
Versailles.
Waking in the Dark.
Walking down the Road.
We are driven to odd attempts; once it would
not have occurred to.
What homage will be paid to a beauty built to
last.

What Kind of Times Are These.
Whatever it was: the grains of the glacier caked in the boot-cleats.
Woman wired in memories, A.
Women.
Yom Kippur 1984.
Your small hands, precisely equal to my own.

Rich, Moss
Limerick: "I wonder how King Arthur felt."
Limerick: "It is clear that Napoleon's Queen."
Opera Teacher neemed Enna, An.

Richard I, Coeur de Lion (1157–99)
Ja Nul Homs Pris Ne Ira a Raison.

Richard, Mark
Y'All Are Bird Dogs, Aren't You?

Richardowlands See **Verstegan** [or **Verstegen**], **Richard**

Richards, Edward Hersey (b. 1874)
Wise Old Owl, A.

Richards, Frank
Limerick: "Boastful young fellow of Neath, A."
Limerick: "From the elephant paddock one day."
Limerick: "George Stephenson said: 'These repairs.'"
Limerick: "George Washington said to his dad."
Limerick: "Goliath was known for ferocity."
Limerick: "Great-grandfather at Waterloo."
Limerick: "In Pinter's new play that's now running."
Limerick: "Keeper who worked at the zoo, A."
Limerick: "Come now,' said Bell, 'This is choice.'"
Limerick: "'No more mistresses,' King Edward said."
Limerick: "Monkey exclaimed with great glee, A."
Limerick: "Poor Ophelia sighed: 'I deplore.'"
Limerick: "Ronald Reagan screamed out in dismay."
Limerick: "Rupert Murdoch, with glee, shouted: 'What.'"
Limerick: "Said a boastful young student from Hayes."
Limerick: "Said Freud: 'I've discovered the Id.'"
Limerick: "Said Paisley: 'I've given up hope.'"
Limerick: "Said the vet as he looked at my pet."
Limerick: "Said Wellington: 'What's the location.'"
Limerick: "Said Wilbur Wright, 'Oh, this is grand.'"
Limerick: "Victoria said: 'We've no quarrel.'"
Limerick: "Victorian gent said: 'This dance,' A."

Richards, George (c.1755–1814)
Almighty Spake, and Gabriel Sped, Th'
Long as the Darkening Cloud Abode.

Richards, Ivor Armstrong (1893–1974)
End of a Course.
Nothing at All.
Trinity Brethren Attend.

Richards, Johnny
Young at Heart.

Richards, Laura Elizabeth (1850–1943)
Alibazan.
Antonio.
Eletelephony.
Kindness to Animals.
King of the Hobbledygoblins, The.
Mermaidens, The.
Molly Pitcher.
Mouse, The.
Nicholas Ned.
Old Joe Jones.
Owl and the Eel and the Warming-Pan, The.
Punkydoodle and Jollapin.
Why Does It Snow?

Richards, Michael (b. 1915)
After Christmas.
Christmas Spider, The.

Richards, Tad
Challenge to the Reader, A.

Richardson, Anthony
Song to Hymen: 1942.

Richardson, James
Vectors: Forty-five Aphorisms and Ten-second Essays.

Richardson, Jonathan (1667?–1745)
On My Late Dear Wife.
Self-Consciousness Makes All Changes Happy; Ode.

Richardson, Justin (b. 1889)
O To Scuttle From the Battle.
Retort Perfect, The.

Richardson, Kate C.
Aubade: "Geese flew by as you entered me, The."

Richardson, Lloyd
Poet Sings His Painting, The.

Richardson, Mamie A. (fl. 1920s)
Sonnet: "I still shall smile and go my careless way."

Richie, Eugene
Airports of the World.

Richman, Liliane
Rue de Rosiers: To My Brother Fred.
To Valenton: Impressions circa 1947.

Richter, C. F. (1676–1711)
My Soul before Thee Prostrate Lies.

Richter, Jennifer
Nothing but Bad News.

Rickword, Edgell (1898–1982)
Cascade.
Contemporary Muse, The.
Cosmogony.
Encounter, The.
Handmaid of Religion, The.
Moon-talk.
Moonrise over Battlefield.
Soldier Addresses His Body, The.
Trench Poets.
Winter Warfare.

Riddell, Alan (1927–77)
At the Hammersmith Palais.

Riddell, Elizabeth (b. 1909)
Children March, The.
Letter, The.
News of a Baby.
Soldier in the Park, The.
Suburban Song.
Wakeful in the Township.

Ridge, John Rollin (1827–67)
And shall we view these miracles and more.
Cherokee Love Song, A.
Mount Shasta.
Rainy Season in California, The.
Stolen White Girl, The.

Ridge, Lola (Mrs. David Lawson) (1873–1941)
Because you are four years old.
Cool inaccessible air.
Electrocution.
Fifth-Floor Window, The.
In this dingy café.
Kerensky.
Réveille.
Saint's Bridge.
Salvation Army lass, The.
Song, The: "That day, in the slipping of torsos and straining flanks."
Spring.
Veteran.

Ridl, Jack (b. 1944)
Video Mama.

Ridler, Anne (b. 1912)
At Parting.
Backgrounds to Italian Paintings: Fifteenth Century.
Before Sleep.
Choosing a Name.
Christmas and Common Birth.
Cranmer and the Bread of Heaven.
Edlesborough.
For a Child Expected.
Making Love, Killing Time.
Modern Love.
Nothing Is Lost.
Now Phillipa Is Gone.

Some Time After.

Ridley, George
Cushie Butterfield.

Ridlon, Marci (b. 1942)
Fernando.
That Was Summer.

Riei (d. 1794)
All freezes again.

Riesco, Laura (b. 1939)
Burdens.
So You Would Listen to Me.
When I Passed in the Afternoon.

Rieu, Emile Victor (1887–1972)
Unicorn, The.

Rifat, Oktay
Flute, The.

Rifqa [or **Rifka**], **Fu'ad** [or **Fuad**] **(b. 1930)**
Fortune Teller, The.
Mirrors.
Threshold, The.
Ultimate Distance, The.

Rifu (d. 1762)
I'm happy through and through.

Riggs, Lynn
Santo Domingo Corn Dance.

Rihaku
Exile's Letter.
Lament of the Frontier Guard.
River-Merchant's Wife: A Letter, The.

Riley, Denise (b. 1948)
Disintegrate Me.
Flip, Flop.
I Take Two of These Tablets Tonight and in the Morning Go On Living.
Lure, 1963.
Misremembered Lyric, A.

Riley, James Whitcomb (1849–1916)
As one who cons at evening o'er an album, all alone.
Craqueodoom.
Days Gone By, The.
Diners in the Kitchen, The.
Eternity.
Few of the Bird-Family, A.
Good-by er Howdy-do.
'Heigho!' said a voice of low laughter.
Country Pathway, A.
I come upon it suddenly, alone.
I'm nine years old! An' you can't guess how much I weigh, I bet.
I'm thist a little crippled boy, an' never goin' to grow.
I Strayed, all alone, where the Autumn.
King of Oo-Rinktum-Jing, The.
Leaves on the branches still swinging, The.
Little Orphant Annie.
Nine Little Goblins, The.
Nonsense Rhyme, A.
Old Sweetheart of Mine, An.
Old Swimmin'-Hole, The.
Raggedy Man, The.
Rose in October, A.
Silence.
Smitten Purist, The.
Jack the Giant-Killer.
Us-folks is purty pore—but Ma.
When the Frost Is on the Punkin.

Riley, John
At the Stanley Spencer Exhibition.
Summer Seeming.
Travel Notes.

Riley, Peter
Another damp Sunday morning up and walk over.
E Questa Vita Un Lampo.
Elf Shots.

Rilke, Rainer Maria (1875–1926)
Abishag.
Ah, not to be cut off.
Annunciation.
As once the winged energy of delight.
Autumn.
Autumn Day.
Before Summer Rain.
Birth of the Smile, The.

Buddha in Glory.
Death.
Departure of the Prodigal Son, The.
Dove that ventured outside, flying far from the dovecote.
Duino Elegies, *sels.*
Entrance.
Flamingos, The.
For, Lord, the Crowded Cities Be.
From a Childhood.
Going Blind.
I Find You, Lord, All Things and In All.
I Have Faith.
I live my life in growing orbits.
Imaginary Career.
Initiation.
John 2:1–12; On the third day there was a marriage.
John 11:30–44; Now Jesus had not yet come to the village.
John 20:11–18; But Mary stood weeping outside the tomb.
Joseph's Suspicion.
Just as the Watchman.
Just as the Winged Energy of Delight.
Lament: "Oh, everything is far."
Last Evening.
Leda.
Luke 1:39–56: In those days Mary arose.
Luke 15:11–19; And he said, "There was a man."
Man Watching, The.
Mary at Peace with the Risen Lord.
Mary's Visitation.
Matthew 26:17–29.
Matthew 27:57–61; When it was evening, there came a rich man.
Merry-go-round, The.
Olive Garden, The.
On the Marriage at Cana.
Orpheus, Eurydice, Hermes.
Panther, The.
Pietà.
Prayer of the Maidens to Mary.
Presaging.
Roman Fountain.
Rose, oh pure contradiction, joy.
Silent Hour.
Solemn Hour.
Solitary, The.
Solitude.
Sometimes a Man Stands Up during Supper.
Song of Love, The.
Sonnets to Orpheus, The, *sels.*
Spanish Dancer.
Swan, The.
Three Holy Kings, The.
Tombs of the Hetaerae.
Unicorn, The, *sels.*
Walk, A.
We Must Die because We Have Known Them.
Youth Dreams, The.

Rimbaud, Arthur (1854–91)
After the Flood.
Being Beauteous.
Blackcurrant River.
Cheated Heart.
Les Chercheuses de Poux.
City.
Dawn.
Decidedly we are out of the world. No longer any sound.
Departure.
Drunken Boat.
Evil.
Farewell.
Hearing the thunder of the intransitive weirs.
Hunger.
In Tseghi.
Lice-Seekers.
Lovely Morning Thought.
Morning.
Morning of Drunkenness.
My Bohemia.
Napoleon after Sedan.
Night in Hell.
O Saisons, O Châteaux.

O seasons, o châteaux.
Obscur et froncé.
Our Assholes Are Different.
Poster of Our Dazzling Victory at Saarbrucken, A.
Promontory.
Romance.
Rooks, The.
Runt of a Dream, A.
Sales.
Seascape.
Sensation.
Sleeper in the Valley, The.
Sleeper of the Valley, The.
Song of the Highest Tower.
Thirst.
Vowels.
Voyelles.
To the French of the Second Empire.

Rimington, John
God of the Flies.

Rimos of Majorca, Moses (1406–30)
Elegy (for Himself)

Rinckhart [*or* Rinkhart], Martin (1586–1649)
Now Thank We All Our God.

Riordan, Maurice (b. 1953)
Milk.
Time Out.
Word from the Loki, A.

Ríos, Alberto A. (b. c.1952)
Advice to a First Cousin.
At Kino Viejo, Mexico.
Domingo Limón.
Dream of Husbands, A.
I Held His Name.
Island of the Three Marias.
Language of Great-Aunts, The.
Madre Sofía.
Man She Called Honey, and Married, The.
Man Then Suddenly Stops Moving, A.
Man Who Became Old, The.
Mi Abuelo.
Incident at Imuris.
Nani.
Teodoro Luna's Two Kisses.
Wet Camp.

Rist, Johann (1607–67)
Eternity, thou thunderous word.
She Boasts of Her Constancy.

Ritchie, Elisavietta (b. 1932)
Sorting Laundry.

Ritchie, Elspeth Cameron
Electroconvulsive Therapy.

Ritsos, Yannis (b. 1909)
After the Defeat.
Afternoon.
Audible and Inaudible.
Distant, The.
End of Dodona II, The.
Erotica 12.
His Lamp near Daybreak.
Marpessa's Choice.
Meaning of Simplicity, The.
Miniature.
Missing, The.
Naked Face.
Not Even Mythology.
Our Land.
Requiem on Poros.
Second Series.
Unanswered.
Underneath Oblivion.

Rittenhouse, Jessie Belle (Mrs. Clinton Scollard) (1869–1948)
Debts.
My Wage.

Ritterbusch, Dale
Search and Destroy.

Rivard, David
1966.
Baby Vallejo.
Consolation.
Cures.
Fall River.
Firestone.

How It Will Always Seem.
One Too Many Mornings.
Summons.
Torque.

Rive, Richard (b. 1931)
Where the Rainbow Ends.

Rivera, Diana
Dinner Together.
Under the Apple Tree.

Rivers, Conrad Kent (1933–68)
Death of a Negro Poet, The.
Four Sheets to the Wind and a One-Way Ticket to France.
In Defense of Black Poets.
Mourning Letter from Paris, A.
Underground.

Rivner, Tuvia (b. 1924)
Fire in the Stone, The.
Lullaby: "Nocturnal, my panther, has eyes that spark, The."
Sunflower.
Wicked Clamor, The.

Rizal, José (1861–96)
Water and Fire.

Roach, Eric (1915–74)
At Guaracara Park.

Robbins, Howard Chandler (1876–1952)
And Have the Bright Immensities.
Put Forth, O God, Thy Spirit's Might.
Sabbath Day Was By, The.

Roberson, Ed (b. 1939)
Blue Horses.
Eclipse.
Four Lines of a Black Love Letter Between Teachers.
Poor Houses, The.
Sonnet.
True We Are Two Grown Men.

Roberts, Allan (1905–66)
Put the Blame on Mame.
That Old Devil Called Love.
Tired.

Roberts, Sir Charles G. D. (1860–1943)
Herring Weir, The.
Mowing, The.
Pea-Fields, The.
Potato Harvest, The.
Skater, The.
Tantramar Revisited, The.

Roberts, Daniel C. (1841–1907)
God of Our Fathers, Whose Almighty Hand.

Roberts, David ("Dewi Havhesp") (1831–84)
Beloved, The.

Roberts, Dorothy (b. 1907)
Cold.
Dazzle.

Roberts, Elizabeth Madox (1886–1941)
Christmas Morning.
Cold Fear.
Disconsolate Morning.
Evening Song.
Firefly.
Hens, The.
Milking Time.
Mr. Wells.
Old Love in Song, An.
Orpheus.
People, The.
Rabbit, The.
Sky, The.
Stranger.
Woodpecker, The.

Roberts, G. D. (1860–1943)
Burnt Lands.
Marsyas.
Night Sky, The.

Roberts, Katrina
How Late Desire Looks.
Postcard from the Coast.

Roberts, Kim (b. 1961)
Darkness Was upon the Face of the Deep.
Night Tumbles into Town by Rail.
Plastic Cup, The.
Tilt, The.

Roberts, Len
Acupuncture and Cleansing at 48.

And Where Were You.
Another Spring on Olmstead Street.
Assignment, The.
God's Blessing.
My Father's Whistle.
Sister Ann Zita Shows Us the Foolishness of
    the Forbidden Books.
Roberts, Lucky
Moonlight Cocktail.
Roberts, Lynnette (b. 1909)
Poem from Llanybri.
Roberts, Michael (1902–48)
H. M. S. *Hero.*
Hymn to the Sun.
In the Flowering Season.
Les Planches-en-Montagnes.
Midnight.
St. Gervais.
Roberts, Michele (b. 1949)
Madwoman at Rodmell.
Magnificat.
Out of Chaos out of Order Out.
Sibyl's Song, The.
Your job's to work the surface. Don't.
Roberts, Nigel (b. 1941)
After / the Moratorium Reading.
Gull's Flight, The.
Max Factor Pink.
Mona Lisa Tea Towel, The.
Nigger and Some Poofters, A.
Roberts, Teresa Noelle
Apotheosis of the Kitchen Goddess II.
Roberts, Theodore Goodridge (1877–1953)
Blue Heron, The.
Roberts, Ursula *See* **Miles, Susan**
Roberts, Walter Adolphe (1886–1962)
On a Monument to Martí.
Robertson, Alexander (d. 1916)
Song of the Dove, The.
Robertson, Edith Anne (b. 1883)
Deean Tractorman, Clear, The.
Deean Tractorman, Deleerit, The.
Robertson, Eliza (1771–1805)
O place us, dear Saviour! in some small
    retreat.
Robertson, James Logie (1846–1922)
Discovery of America, The.
Schule Laddie's Lament on the Lateness o' the
    Season, A.
Robertson, Robin (b. 1955)
Aberdeen.
Robertson, T. A. (b. 1909)
Tuslag.
Robey, George (1869–1954)
Limerick: "There was an old person of
    Slough."
Robin, Leo (1895–1984)
Beyond the Blue Horizon.
Diamonds Are a Girl's Best Friend.
Easy Living.
For Every Man There's a Woman.
Hallelujah!
Hooray for Love.
In Love in Vain.
Little Girl from Little Rock.
Louise.
Love Is Just around the Corner.
My Cutey's Due at Two-to-Two Today.
My Ideal.
No Love, No Nothin'
Prisoner of Love.
Thanks for the Memory.
True Blue Lou.
Robins, Gurdon (1813–83)
There Is a Land Mine Eye Hath Seen.
When Thickly Beat the Storms of Life.
**Robinson, Agnes Mary Frances (Mme Duclaux)
(1857–1944)**
Art and Life.
Aubade Triste.
Celia's Home-Coming.
Darwinism.
Dead Friend, The.
Etruscan Tombs.

Idea, The.
Love, Death, and Art.
Neurasthenia.
Oasis, An.
Orchard at Avignon, An.
Pallor.
Personality.
Posies.
Rosa Rosarum.
Scape-Goat, The.
Search for Apollo, A.
Sibyl, The.
Song: "Oh for the wings of a dove."
Stornelli and Strambotti.
To a Dead Friend.
To My Muse.
Tuscan Olives.
Unum est Necessarium.
Valley, The.
Venetian Nocturne.
Wise-Woman, The.
Robinson, Annie Douglas Green *See* **"Douglas,
Marian"**
Robinson, Corinne Roosevelt (1861–1933)
Path that Leads to Nowhere, The.
We Who Have Loved.
Robinson, Edwin Arlington (1869–1935)
Aaron Stark.
Ballade of Broken Flutes.
Ben Jonson Entertains a Man from Stratford.
Bewick Finzer.
Boston.
Calvary.
Calverly's.
Cassandra.
Charles Carville's Eyes.
Children of the Night, The.
Christmas Sonnet, A.
Clavering.
Clerks, The.
Cliff Klingenhagen.
Companion, The.
Credo.
Dark Hills, The.
Eros Turannos.
Eutychides.
Exit.
Field of Glory, The.
Firelight.
Flammonde.
Fleming Helphenstine.
For a Dead Lady.
George Crabbe.
Gift of God, The.
Hillcrest.
House on the Hill, The.
How Annandale Went Out.
Inscription by the Sea, An.
Isaac and Archibald.
James Wetherell.
John Evereldown.
John Gorham.
Karma.
L'Envoi.
Lais to Aphrodite.
Lingard and the Stars.
Luke 15:20–32; And he arose and came.
Luke Havergal.
Man against the Sky, The.
Many Are Called.
Master, The.
Matthew 22:1–14; And again Jesus spoke to
    them.
Mighty Runner, A.
Mill, The.
Miniver Cheevy.
New England.
New Tenants, The.
Mr Flood's Party.
Old Story, An.
Pity of the Leaves, The.
Poem for Max Nordau, A.
Poor Relation, The.
Prodigal Son, The.
Raven, The.
Reuben Bright.
Reunion.

Richard Cory.
Shadrach O'Leary.
Sheaves, The.
Sonnet: "Master and the slave go hand in hand,
    The."
Sonnet: "Oh for a poet—for a beacon bright."
Souvenir.
Supremacy.
Tact.
Tavern, The.
Three Quatrains.
Too Much Coffee.
Torrent, The.
Uncle Ananias.
Unforgiven, The.
Verlaine.
Veteran Sirens.
Vickery's Mountain.
Walt Whitman.
Why He Was There.
Zola.
Robinson, Elizabeth (b. 1961)
For Karen.
Fountain.
Meshes.
Salisbury Plain.
Shatter.
Robinson, Elsie (1883–1956)
Beauty as a Shield.
Help Me Today.
Pain.
Robinson, Frank K.
Brief day ending.
Down rippling, The.
Today too.
Robinson, Kit (b. 1949)
First Thing.
Intent to consider.
Nesting of Layer Protocols.
Nursery Rhyme.
On the Corner.
Pontoon.
Severance.
Robinson, Martha
Stanzas Written between Dover and Calais, in
    July, 1792.
Robinson, Mary ("Laura Maria") (1758–1800)
Bids Farewell to Lesbos.
Birth-Day, The.
Bower of Pleasure, The.
Camp, The.
Canzonet.
Conclusion to Book 1.
Contemns its Power.
Contemns Philosophy.
Describes Her Bark.
Describes Phaon.
Describes the Characteristics of Love.
Describes the Fascinations of Love.
Determines to Follow Phaon.
Dreams of a Rival.
Foresees her Death.
Haunted Beach, The.
Her Address to the Moon.
Her Confirmed Despair.
Her Last Appeal to Phaon.
Her Passion Increases.
Her Reflections on the Leucadian Rock before
    She Perishes.
Invokes Reason.
January, 1795.
Laments Her Early Misfortunes.
Laments the Volatility of Phaon.
Laura to Petrarch.
London's Summer Morning.
Modern Female Fashions.
Modern Male Fashions.
Negro Girl, The.
Ode Inscribed to the Infant Son of S. T.
    Coleridge, Esq.
Phaon Awakes.
Phaon Forsakes Her.
Poet's Garret, The.
Previous to Her Interview with Phaon.
Reaches Sicily.
Rejects the Influence of Reason.

Reproaches Phaon.
Resolves to Take the Leap of Leucata.
Sappho Discovers Her Passion.
Sappho Rejects Hope.
Sappho's Address to the Stars.
Sappho's Conjectures.
Sappho's Prayer to Venus.
Savage of Aveyron, The.
She Endeavors to Fascinate Him.
[Sonnet] Conclusive.
Sonnet Introductory.
Stanzas: "In this vain, busy world, where the good and the gay."
Suspects His Constancy.
Temple of Chastity, The.
To a Sigh.
To Liberty.
To Phaon.
To the Eolian Harp.
To the Muses.
Tyranny of Love, The.
Visions Appear to Her in a Dream.
Walsingham; or, the Pupil of Nature.

Robinson, Robert
Come, thou Fount of ev'ry blessing.

Robinson, Roland (b. 1912)
Cradle, The.
Creek, The.
I am at Deep Well where the spirit-trees.
I reached that waterhole, its mud designed.
Jarrangulli.

Robison, Willard
Cottage for Sale, A.

Robles, Al
Cutting Back the Ifugao Past.
Feasting with Etang a Hundred Times Around.
Manong with a Thousand Tribal Visions, The.
Remembering the Past.

Robson, Jeremy (b. 1939)
Blues for the Lonely.

Robun (d. 1725)
Water bird, asleep, A.

Rocha, Jofre (b. 1941)
Guerilla Fighter.
Poem of Return.

Rochester, Elizabeth Wilmot, Countess of (d. 1681)
Song: "Nothing ades to Loves fond fire."

Rochester, John Wilmot, 2nd Earl of (1647–80)
Against Constancy.
Constancy.
Description of Maidenhead, A.
Disabled Debauchee, The.
Epitaph on Charles II.
Fall, The.
Grecian Kindness.
Imperfect Enjoyment, The.
Impromptu on Charles II.
Letter from Artemisa in the Town, to Chloe [or Cloe], in the Country, A.
Love and Life.
Mistress, The: A Song.
Platonic Lady, The.
Poet, whoe'er thou art, God damn thee.
Ramble in St. James's Park, A.
Restless he rolls about from whore to whore.
Rochester Extempore.
Rodomontade on His Cruel Mistress, A.
Satire on Charles II, A.
Satire [or Satyre or Satyr] against [Reason and] Mankind, A.
Signior Dildo.
Song: "Absent from thee, I languish still."
Song: "By all love's soft, yet mighty powers."
Song: "Give me leave to rail at you."
Song: "Leave this gaudy gilded stage."
Song: "Love a woman? You're [or Y'are] an ass."
Song of a Young Lady to Her Ancient Lover, A.
Song: "Oh gentle Venus, ease a tarse."
Song: "Quoth the Duchess of Cleveland to counselor Knight."
To His Mistress.
To My More Than Meritorious Wife.
Tunbridge Wells.

Upon Drinking in a Bowl.
Upon [His] Leaving His Mistress.
Upon Nothing.
Were I (who to my cost already am)
Written in a Lady's Prayer Book.
You see how far Mans wisedom here extends.

Rochu (d. 1744)
Is it only me?

Rock, Daphne
Changing.
Mother.

Rodas, Ana María (b. 1937)
Poems from the Erotic Left.

Rodd, Sheila Desiré Savory See **Flynn, Desiré**

Rodefer, Stephen (b. 1940)
Codex.
My mind to me mangles iron. An error is mirror to the truth.
Pretext.

Rodenko, Paul (1920–76)
Bombing.
February Sun.

Roderick, David
Curlers at Dusk.

Rodgers, Carolyn M. (b. 1942)
Black Heart as Ever Green, The.
Breakthrough.
For H. W. Fuller.
For Sistuhs Wearin' Straight Hair.
Group Therapy.
It Is Deep.
Jesus Was Crucified or: It Must Be Deep.
Masquerade.
Now Ain't That Love?
One.
Poem for Some Black Women.
Poem No. 1.
Slave Ritual.
Testimony.
U Name This One.
What Color Is Lonely.
Written for Love of an Ascension—Coltrane.
Yuh Lookin Good.

Rodgers, Mary
Very Soft Shoes.

Rodgers, Richard (1902–79)
All er Nothin'
Blue Moon.
Blue Room, The.
Dancing on the Ceiling.
Falling in Love with Love.
Gentleman Is a Dope, The.
Happy Talk.
Have You Met Miss Jones?
He Was Too Good to Me.
Hello, Young Lovers.
I Cain't Say No.
I Didn't Know What Time It Was.
I've Got Five Dollars.
If I Loved You.
It Might As Well Be Spring.
It Never Entered My Mind.
It's Got to Be Love.
June Is Bustin' Out All Over.
Lady Is a Tramp, The.
Manhattan.
Many a New Day.
Mister Snow.
Most Beautiful Girl in the World, The.
Mountain Greenery.
My Favorite Things.
My Funny Valentine.
My Heart Stood Still.
My Romance.
Nobody's Heart.
Oh, What a Beautiful Mornin'!
People Will Say We're in Love.
Shall We Dance?
Ship without a Sail, A.
Soliloquy.
Some Enchanted Evening.
Sound of Music, The.
Spring Is Here.
Surrey with the Fringe on Top, The.
Ten Cents a Dance.
There's a Small Hotel.

This Can't Be Love.
Thou Swell.
To Keep My Love Alive.
Wait Till You See Her.
Where or When.
With a Song in My Heart.
Wonderful Guy, A.
You Are Too Beautiful.
You'll Never Walk Alone.
You Took Advantage of Me.
Younger Than Springtime.
Zip.

Rodgers, William Robert (1909–69)
Beagles.
Carol: "Deep in the fading leaves of night."
Field Day.
Home Thoughts from Abroad.
Irish Lake, An.
It was a lovely night.
Lent.
Life's Circumnavigators.
Lovers, The.
Neither Here nor There.
Net, The.
Paired Lives.
Party, The.
Raider, The.
Scapegoat.
Sing, Brothers, Sing!
Snow.
Stormy Night.
Swan, The.
War-Time.
White Christmas.
Winter's Cold.
Words.

Roditi, Edouard (b. 1910)
Aurora Borealis.
Hand.
Night Prayer of Glückel of Hameln, The.
Seance.

Rodrigues, Julia Park
Half-.

Rodriguez, Judith (b. 1936)
About This Woman.
At the Nature-Strip.
Eskimo Occasion.
Handloom, The.
How Come the Truck-Loads?
In-flight Note.
Lifetime Devoted to Literature, A.
Mahogany Ship, The.
Nasturtium Scanned.
New York Sonnet.
Nu-plastik Fanfare Red.
Rebeca in a Mirror.

Rodriguez, Luis J.
Always Running.
Fire.
Heavy Blue Veins.
Rant, Rave and Ricochet.
Reflection on El Train Glass.
Speaking with Hands.
To the Police Officer Who Refused to Sit in the Same Room as My Son because He's a 'Gang Banger.'
We Never Stopped Crossing Borders.

Rodriguez, Magdalena de
June 10.

Roe, Barbara
Into Concrete Mixer Throw.

Roe, Sir Thomas (1581–1644)
On Gustavus Adolphus, King of Sweden.

Roeske, Paulette (b. 1945)
Preparing the Dead.

Roethke, Theodore (1908–63)
Academic.
All the Earth, All the Air.
Bat, The.
Big Wind.
Bring the Day!
Carnations.
Ceiling, The.
Child on Top of a Greenhouse.
Coming of the Cold, The.
Cow, The.

Cuttings.
Decision, The.
Dinky.
Dolor.
Donkey, The.
Dream, The.
Duet.
Elegy for Jane.
Far Field, The.
Field of Light, A.
First Meditation.
Flight, The.
Follies of Adam, The.
For an Amorous Lady.
Four for Sir John Davies.
Frau Bauman, Frau Schmidt, and Frau
　Schwartze.
Geranium, The.
Heard in a Violent Ward.
Her Longing.
Her Reticence.
Her Time.
Heron, The.
Hippo, The.
I Knew a Woman.
I'm Here.
In a Dark Time.
In Evening Air.
Infirmity.
Journey to the Interior.
Judge Not.
Kitty-Cat Bird, The.
Lady and the Bear, The.
Light Listened.
Lizard, The.
Long Live the Weeds.
Lost Son, The.
Marrow, The.
Matthew 7:1–2; "Judge not, that you be not."
Meadow Mouse, The.
Meditation at Oyster River.
Mid-Country Blow.
Minimal, The.
Mips and ma the mooly moo.
Mistake, The.
Monotony Song, The.
Moss-Gathering.
Night Crow.
Night Journey.
Old Florist.
Open House.
Orchids.
Otto.
Pike, The.
Pipling.
Prayer: "If I must of my Senses lose."
Premonition, The.
Renewal, The.
Right Thing, The.
Root Cellar.
Rose, The.
Rouse for Stevens, A.
Running Lightly over Spongy Ground.
Saginaw Song, The.
Serpent, The.
Shape of the Fire, The.
She.
Sloth, The.
Snake.
Song for the Squeeze-Box.
Swan, The.
Thing, The.
Three Epigrams.
Visitant, The.
Voice, The.
Waking, The.
Walk in Late Summer, A.
Weed Puller.
What Can I Tell My Bones?
Where Knock Is Open Wide.
My Papa's Waltz.
Wish for a Young Wife.
Words for the Wind.
Roffé, Mercedes (b. 1954)
Landscape of return is drawn, A.
Lighthouse of Alexandria, The.
Scene of Return Is Sketched, A.

Wanted.
Rogan (d. 1693)
On the ground.
Rogen (d. 1691)
Times are torn asunder, The.
Rogers, Elymas Payson (1815–61)
In 'Fifty Congress Passed a Bill.
Rogers, George (1805–46)
As Gentle Dews Distill.
Rogers, John (1630–84)
Upon Mrs. Anne Bradstreet, Her Poems, Etc.
Rogers, Pattiann (b. 1940)
Before the Beginning: Maybe God and a Silk
　Flower Concubine Perhaps.
Family Is All There Is, The.
Into the Light.
Kingdom of Heaven, The.
Opus from Space.
Rogers, Samuel (1763–1855)
Boy of Egremond, The.
Epitaph on a Robin Redbreast, An.
Ginevra.
On J. W. Ward.
Sleeping Beauty, The.
To the Fragment of a Statue of Hercules,
　Commonly Called the Torso.
Wish, A.
Written in a Sick Chamber.
Rogetsu, Ishii
Roasting chestnuts.
Roggeman, Willem M. (b. 1935)
African Queen.
Archaeological Find.
Fata Morgana in Flanders.
Rohrer, Jane
Bad Truth.
In the Kitchen before Dinner.
Orchard in the Spring.
Rohrer, Matthew (b. 1970)
After the Wedding Party.
Brooklyn Bridge.
Childhood Stories.
Comet.
Gliding toward the Lamps.
Hotel de L'Étoile.
Hummock in the Malookas, A.
Hunger of the Lemur, The.
Last Look at the Mutineers, A.
Precision German Craftmanship.
Quick Sell the Pig.
Short History of Illumination, A.
Starfish Waving to Me from the Sand.
Rojas, Gonzalo (b. 1917)
And to Be Born Is Here an Unnameable Feast.
Beautiful Ones, The.
Bed with Mirrors.
Chapter and Verse.
What Do We Love when We Love?
Roka (d. 1703)
Evening shadows steal.
Rokeah [or Rokeakh], David (b. 1916)
Beyond Imagination.
Hands Full of Sun.
Jerusalem.
Negev.
Open-Eyed Angel.
Solar Years.
Whirlwind.
Zealots of Yearning.
Rokushi (d. 1881)
I wake up.
Roland Holst, Adriaan (1888–1976)
Autumn Wind.
Beggar Love.
Being.
I Who Was Born.
Night Visit.
Outside in the Open.
Quatrain: "We're snug as a bug in a heated
　house."
Time Now Please.
Time, Please.
Visitation.
Roland-Holst, Henriëtte (1869–1952)
Concerning the Awakening of My Soul.

I Looked for a Sounding-Board.
Small Paths.
Rolfe, Edwin (1909–54)
Casualty.
First Love.
No Man Knows War.
Paris—Christmas 1938.
Song: "Keep the dream alive and growing
　always."
Rolland, John (c.1530–c.1580)
In haist ga hy thee to sum hoill.
Rolle of Hampole, Richard (1300–49)
Cantus Amoris 2.
Ghostly Gladness.
Love Is Life.
Prayer to Jesus 1.
Song of the Passion, A.
Rolle, Sojourner Kincaid
Birds' Refuge, The.
Blue Rock, The.
Hands in the Motion of Prayer.
Keeping Watch.
Rollings, Alane (b. 1950)
Dirty Dreams and God Smiling.
For Dear Life.
In Your Own Sweet Time.
Light Years and the Love Lost in the
　Oleanders.
Rollinson, Neil (b. 1960)
Ecstasy of St Saviour's Avenue, The.
Rolls, Eric (b. 1923)
Bamboo.
Dog Fight.
Rain Forest.
Rolnik, Joseph (1879–1955)
Thank God.
Roma, Luke
I drink your love.
I picture your face.
Romains, Jules (b. 1885)
Another Spirit Advances.
Romanelli, Samuele (1757–1814)
From Battle Clamour.
Love.
Romano, Emily
August heat.
Romano, Jennie
Old Houses.
Romano, Rose (fl. 20th cent.)
Bucket, The.
But My Blood.
So I Lost My Temper.
Romberg, Sigmund
Lover, Come Back to Me!
Rome, Harold (1908–93)
(All of a Sudden) My Heart Sings.
Call Me Mister.
Chain Store Daisy.
Doing the Reactionary.
Don't Wanna Write about the South.
F. D. R. Jones.
Military Life, The.
Money Song, The.
Nobody Makes a Pass at Me.
Ring on the Finger.
South America, Take It Away!
Who Knows?
Wish You Were Here.
Romero, Leo
If Marilyn Monroe.
Marilyn Monroe Indian.
Romero, Nidia Sanabria de (b. 1928)
New Suit, The.
Romo-Carmona, Mariana
Crows.
Daylight.
Fish.
Signs.
Romtvedt, David
Glass Canyons.
Kiev, the Ukraine, Nuclear Accident.
Ronald of Orkney, Saint
Attributes of a Gentleman, The.
Ronan, Richard
Love among Lepers.

Ronsard, Pierre de (1524–85)
And Lightly, like the Flowers.
By looking too long on your perfect face.
Corinna in Vendome.
Deadly Kisses.
Fragment of a Sonnet.
Génèvres Hérissez, et Vous, Houx Espineux.
His Lady's Death.
His Lady's Tomb.
Invective against Denise, a Witch.
Of His Lady's Old Age.
On His Lady's Waking.
Paradox of Time, The.
Revenge, The.
Rose, The.
Roses.
Time to Be Up, Marie, Young Sleepyhead.
To His Young Mistress.
To the Moon.
When you are old, at evening candle-lit.

Root, George Frederick (1820–95)
Battle-Cry of Freedom, The.

Root, William Pitt (b. 1941)
Sonnet 20: Remembering, from a Nazi Prison,
a Teacher Years Before.

Rope, Henry E. G. (1880–1978)
City of the Grail, The.
Wasted years, the wasted years, The.

**"Ropshin, V." (Boris Viktorovich Savinkov)
(1879–1925)**
Guillotine's / Sharp blade?, The.

Roripaugh, Lee Ann (b. 1965)
Pearls.
Peony Lover.

Ros, Amanda (1860–1939)
End of 'Pain,' The.
I Love to See a Lady Nice and Natural at Any
Price.
Little Belgian Orphan, A.
Old Home, The.
On a Girl Who Took Action for Breach of
Promise.
On Visiting Westminster Abbey.
Thoughts.

Roscoe, William (1823–59)
Butterfly's Ball [and the Grasshopper's Feast],
The.

Roscoe, William Stanley
Camellia, The.
On Being Forced to Part with His Library for
the Benefit of His Creditors.
To the Harvest Moon.

Rose, Billy (1899–1966)
Barney Google.
Cup of Coffee, a Sandwich, and You.
Does the Spearmint Lose Its Flavor on the
Bedpost Overnight?
Don't Bring Lulu.
Great Day.
I Found a Million Dollar Baby (In a Five and
Ten Cent Store)
I Wanna Be Loved.
It's Only a Paper Moon.
More Than You Know.
Night Is Young and You're So Beautiful, The.
Without a Song.
Would You Like to Take a Walk?

Rose, Sir George (1782–1873)
Forensic Jocularities.

Rose, Harriet
Mellisandra.
Succubus, The.
Wedding Coat, The.

Rose, Juan Gonzalo (b. 1929)
Marisel.

Rose, Peter (b. 1955)
Anglo-Saxon Comedy.
Terminus.
Wind Debates Asian Immigration, The.

Rose, Rachel (b. 1970)
What the Japanese Perhaps Heard.
What We Heard about the Japanese.

Rose, Wendy (b. 1948)
Alaskan Fragments June 1981—Summer
Solstice.

America.
Celebration for My Mother.
Comparison of Hands One Day Late Summer
El Sobrante.
Day They Cleaned Up the Border El Salvador,
February, 1981, The.
Endangered Roots of a Person.
Epitaph: "Roots of mankind are tangled in my
hair, The."
For My People.
For Steph.
For Walter Lowenfels.
Grunion.
I Expected My Skin and My Blood to Ripen.
If I Am Too Brown or Too White for You.
Leaving Port Authority for the St. Regis Rezz.
Long Division; a Tribal History.
Loo-wit.
Naayawva Taawi.
Naming Power.
Oh Father.
Oh My People I Remember.
Poem to a Redskin.
Poet Haunted, The.
Robert.
Saint Patrick's Day, 1973.
Self Dirge.
Six Nations Museum Onchiota, New York—
January.
Story Keeper.
They Sometimes Call Me.
Throat Song: The Whirling Earth.
To an Imaginary Father.
Truganinny.

Roseliep, Raymond (1917–83)
After Beethoven.
After Tosca.
Banker, The.
Birthcry!
Black hen, The.
Blind man's, The.
Blues are the big thing.
Brushing my sins.
Buttoning his fly.
Campfire Extinguished.
Cat, The.
Child.
Flea.
He removes his glove.
In white tulips.
Morning-Glory, The.
On the apple.
Ordering my tombstone.
Pacing.
Piano practice.
Rain.
Sailor, The.
Seance.
Sistine Chapel.
Sky.
Unable.
Under.
White orchid.

Rosemont, Penelope
Bad Days Will End, The.
Candle.
Passage.
Rising Asleep.

Rosemurgy, Catie (b. 1969)
Angel Finally Admits What She Knows to Lou
Binkler of Bethany, Missouri, An.
Hard Put.
Mostly Mick Jagger.
Why God Invented the Cold.

Rosen (d. 1743)
Sweep away.

Rosen, Kenneth (b. 1940)
Along the Charles.

Rosen, Michael (b. 1940)
Chivvy.
Christmas Dinner.
Eddie and the Birthday.
From the winter wind.
Here Is the News.
One, Two, Three.
Teasing Toads, The.

This Morning.
You need me for sitting.

Rosen, Michael and Susanna Steele
Humpty Dumpty.

Rosen, Michael J. (b. 1954)
Total Eclipse.

Rosenbaum, Benjamin (b. 1897?)
O Pity Our Small Size.

Rosenberg, David (b. 1943)
Isaiah: Chapter 66.

Rosenberg, Isaac (1890–1918)
August 1914.
Beauty.
Break of Day in the Trenches.
Burning of the Temple, The.
Chagrin.
Daughters of War.
Dead Heroes, The.
Dead Man's Dump.
Destruction of Jerusalem by the Babylonian
Hordes, The.
Expression.
Female God, The.
Fine! Fine!
Girl to Soldier on Leave.
God.
I Am the Blood.
Immortals, The.
Jew, The.
Louse Hunting.
Love and Lust.
Marching.
Mirror, The.
On Receiving News of the War.
One Lost, The.
Returning, We Hear the Larks.
Sick. . .Sick. . .I will lie down and die. How.
Slime clung, The.
Soldier: Twentieth Century.
Spiritual Isolation.
Spring.
Through These Pale Cold Days.
Tower of Skulls, The.
Troop Ship, The.
Worm Fed on the Heart of Corinth, A.

Rosenberg, Liz (b. 1955)
Accident, The.
City Baseball.
Edith B—— and her mother on a Sunday
afternoon.
Lesson in Anatomy, A.
Longing for Eternal Life, The.
Married Love.
No Boundaries.
Silence of Women, The.
Story of My Life, The.
Suburban Childhood, A.
Thanksgiving.
They Are Planning to Cancel the School Milk
Program to Fund a Tax Cut for the Middle
Class.
Which One Is the Grown-up? Haiku.

Rosenberg, Sydell
In the laundermat.
Library closing.

Rosenblatt, Joe (b. 1933)
Ant Trap, The.
Cat.
Fish.
Ichthycide.
It's in the Egg.
Metamorpho I.
Of Dandelions & Tourists.
Saphire (Metamorpho's Chick)

Rosenblatt, Sarah (b. 1962)
Leaving Home.
Mom and Dad Getting Older.
Procession, The.
Second Half of Our Lives, The.
Should I Stay or Should I Go?
Visiting New York.

Rosenfeld, Morris Jacob (1862–1923)
Another While.
Cry from the Ghetto, A.
Jewish May, The.
My Camping Ground.

Simchas Torah.
So Long Ago.

Rosenhane, Gustav (1619–84)
Sonnet: "And then I sat me down, and gave the rein."
Sonnet: "Deep in a vale where rocks on every side."

Rosenius, Carl Olof (1816–68)
With God and His Mercy.

Roshu (d. 1899)
Time to go.

Rosidi, Ajip (b. 1938)
Only in Poetry.

Rosner, Elizabeth
Souvenirs.

Rospigliosi, Veronica
Leavetaking.

Ross, Abram Bunn (b. 1866)
Two in Bed.

Ross, Alan (b. 1922)
Cricket at Oxford.
Destroyers in the Arctic.
En Route.
In Bloemfontein.
Mess Deck.
Off Brighton Pier.
Stanley Matthews.

Ross, Alexander (1699–1784)
Wooed and Married and A'

Ross, Charles Henry (c.1842–97)
Jack.
John, Tom, and James.

Ross, Charles Sarsfield
Old Mothers.

Ross, David
Beyond Compare.
Shall We Join the Ladies?

Ross, J. M.
Limerick: "There once was a person of Chiswick."

Ross, Jerry *See* **Adler, Richard**

Ross, Jerry (1926–55)
Heart.
Hernando's Hideaway.
Hey There.
There Once Was a Man.
Whatever Lola Wants (Lola Gets)

Ross, Leo (b. 1934)
Requiescat.

Ross, Linwood M. (b. 1959)
Indecent Exposure (A True Story)
James Brown.

Ross, W. W. Eustace (1894–1966)
Creek, The.
Diver, The.
Fish.
If Ice.
On Angels.
Snake Trying, The.

Ross [or Ros], William [or Villeam] (1762–90)
Another Song.

Rosselli, Amelia (b. 1930)
Actions in my brain: these verbs, whose celerity.
Around This Body of Mine.
Blue That Isn't Even Blue or in Any Case, A.
Dawn Presented Itself Bare-Armed and Immodest.
Dialogue with the Dead.
Feeble Little Voice: All It Takes Is Barely Opening the Shutter, A.
From relief to relief, the white lines, the white paper.
How many fields which like a sponge.
I Dreamt of Visiting Relatives.
If the Soul Loses Its Gift Then It Loses Ground, if Hell.
In the Evening the Sky Roams, a Meager.
In the lethargy which follows the machinations of the.
Infinite We Count the Dead! The Dance Is Almost Finished! Death.
Letter to Her Brother.
Mirrors!, The.

Negro blood flowing on his brown.
Sex violent as an object (whitened quarry of marble)
Tonight with Bold Desire.
Worthless as was her itinerary to fame.
You might as well think one thing or another.

Rossetti, Christina Georgina (1830–94)
Advent.
After Communion.
After Death.
Aloof.
Amen.
Apple Gathering, An.
Ash Wednesday.
At Home.
Autumn.
Autumn Violets.
Bed of Forget-Me-Nots, A.
Before the Beginning.
Before the Paling of the Stars.
Better Resurrection, A.
Birthday, A.
Blessed that flock safe penned in Paradise.
Bride Song.
Bruised Reed Shall He Not Break, A.
By the Sea.
Cardinal Newman.
Caterpillar, The.
Chilly Night, A.
Christ our All in All, *sels.*
Christmas Carol, A: "In the bleak mid-winter."
Christmas Eve.
City Mouse and the Garden Mouse, The.
City plum is not a plum, A.
Cobwebs.
Convent Threshold, The.
Cousin Kate.
Dead before Death.
Dirge, A: "Why were you born when the snow was falling?"
Despised and Rejected, *sels.*
Dream Land.
Dream-Love.
Easter Monday.
Echo.
Endure Hardness.
Enrica, 1865.
Eve.
Ferry Me across the Water.
First Spring Day, The.
Flint.
Fly Away, Fly Away.
Frisky Lamb, A.
Frog's Fate, A.
From Sunset to Star Rise.
From the Antique.
Goblin Market, *sels.*
Gone Before.
Good Friday.
Grown and Flown.
Handy Mole who plied no shovel, A.
Heaviness May Endure for a Night, but Joy Cometh in the Morning.
Hopping frog, hop here and be seen.
Horses of the Sea, The.
Hurt No Living Thing.
I caught a little ladybird.
I dug and dug amongst the snow.
I tell you what I dreamed last night.
If a pig wore a wig.
If Only.
In an Artist's Studio.
In Progress.
Iniquity of the Fathers upon the Children, The.
Introspective.
Is the Moon Tired?
Italia, Io Ti Saluto!
L. E. L.
Last Rites.
Later Life: A Double Sonnet of Sonnets, *sels.*
Laughed every goblin.
Let's Be Merry.
"Good folk," said Lizzie.
"I, if I perish, perish"—Esther spake.
Life's Parallels, A.
Kookoorookoo! kookoorookoo!
"Love me, for I love you"—and answer me.

Long Barren.
Lord, Grant Us Calm.
Lord Jesus, who would think that I am Thine?
Lowest Place, The.
Marvel of Marvels.
Maude Clare.
May.
Mirage.
Mix a Pancake.
Monna Innominata, *sels.*
My Dream.
No, Thank You, John.
Noble Sisters.
None other Lamb, none other Name.
Old-World Thicket, An.
On the Wing.
Pain or Joy.
Passing away, saith the World, passing away.
Pause, A.
Pause of Thought, A.
Promises like Pie-Crust.
Queen of Hearts, The.
Reflection.
Remember [Me].
Rest.
Royal Princess, A.
St. Peter.
Sappho.
Shut Out.
Sketch, A.
Sleeping at Last.
Somewhere or Other.
Song: "Oh roses for the flush of youth."
Song: "She sat and sang alway."
Song: "When I am dead, my dearest."
Soul, A.
Spring Quiet.
St. Michael and All Angels.
Study (A Soul), A.
Summer Is Ended.
Symbols.
They lie at rest, our blessed dead.
Three Enemies, The.
Triad, A.
Twice.
Two Pursuits.
Two Thoughts of Death.
Under Willows.
Uphill.
Venus's Looking-Glass.
Verse II.
Verse III.
Wednesday in Holy Week.
What Are Heavy?
What are these that glow from afar.
What's in a Name?
What Would I Give?
Where Innocent Bright-Eyed Daisies Are.
Who Has Seen the Wind?
Who Shall Deliver Me?
Wind Has Such a Rainy Sound, The.
Winter: My Secret.
World, The.

Rossetti, Dante Gabriel (1828–82)
Antwerp to Ghent.
Aspecta Medusa.
Blessed Damozel, The.
Boulogne to Amiens and Paris.
Constant keeping-past of shaken trees.
Even So.
For a Venetian Pastoral by Giorgone (In the Louvre)
For "An Allegorical Dance of Women" by Andrea Mantegna.
For "Our Lady of the Rocks."
For "The Wine of Circe" by Edward Burne-Jones.
For Spring by Sandro Botticelli.
For the Holy Family by Michelangelo.
Fragment, A: "'I saw the Sibly at Cumæ'"
Half-Way Pause, A.
He and I.
Heart of the Night, The.
House of Life, *sels.*
Insomnia.
Limerick: "There is a creature called God."
Limerick: "There is an old he-wolf named

Gambart."
Limerick: "There once was a painter named Scott."
Limerick: "There's a combative artist named Whistler."
Limerick: "There's a Portuguese person named Howell."
Limerick: "There's a publishing party named Ellis."
Lost Days.
Marriage of St. Katharine, by the same; in the Hospital of St. John at Bruges.
Match with the Moon, A.
Memory.
My Sister's Sleep.
Old Song Ended, An.
On Himself.
On Refusal of Aid between Nations.
On Robert Buchanan, Who Attacked Him under the Pseudonym of "Thomas Maitland."
On the Painter Val Prinsep.
On the Poet, Arthur O'Shaughnessy.
Orchard-Pit, The.
Retro me, Sathana!
Saint Luke the Painter.
Same, The.
Sea-Limits, The *sels*.
Smithereens.
Sonnet, A [*or* 'A Sonnet is a moment's monument'].
Soul's Beauty.
Stratton Water.
Sudden Light.
There is a big artist named Val.
Think thou and act; to-morrow thou shalt die.
Tom Agnew, Bill Agnew.
Virgin and Child, by Hans Memmeling; in the Academy of Bruges, A.
White Ship, The.
Woodspurge, The.
Rossetti, William Michael (1829–1919)
Jesus Wept.
Rossi, Azariah di (1513–78)
Epitaph: "From out the stormy sea unto the shore."
Rossi, Tiziano (b. 1935)
Beach.
Insomnia.
Law.
Leaving.
Possibility.
Pot.
System.
Rossini, Clare (b. 1954)
Valediction.
Rossiter, Charles
Nostalgia.
Your Body Glistens from the Bath.
Rossman, Ed
Double Features.
Rosten, Norman (1914–95)
Black Boy.
I am immortal in Cheyenne!
Out of Our Shame.
This Child.
We came during those years.
Roston, Ruth
Program Notes.
Rostopchina, Evdokiya (1812–58)
Unfinished Sewing, The.
"Rostrevor, George" *See* **Hamilton, George Rostrevor**
Rotella, Alexis
After he leaves.
After the full moon.
Against his coat.
Asparagus I bite off their heads.
At the edge.
Barefoot through clover.
Breakfast alone.
Butterfly lands on Park Place, A.
Clutching a fist of hair.
Discussing divorce.
During our argument.

Everyone talking at once.
From green to grey.
From her neon window.
From the window.
His footsteps in the room.
Holding his gaze.
In his wedding band watching the clouds pass.
In the garbage bin.
In the guest room.
In the Queen Anne's lace a toad.
Late August.
Leading him in.
Left to the wind.
Lying in the wet grass.
Not speaking.
Only I laugh.
Opening his.
Phone call.
Rainbow, A.
Starrynight Ienteryourmirror.
Surrendering to a rain-washed stone.
Swans stir of his breath against my hair.
Trying to forget him.
Undressed.
Vase of peonies.
Waterlilies.
With wine glasses.
Roth, Hal
Argument ended.
Evening star.
Her black negligee.
Her eyes still closed.
Rothenberg, Jerome (b. 1931)
12th Horse-Song of Frank Mitchell (Blue), The.
48 Words for a Woman's Dance Song.
Aleph Poem.
At the Castle.
Beadle's Testimony, The.
Cokboy.
Connoisseur of Jews, The.
Corkby, Part Two.
Crazy Dog Events.
Dibbukim (Dibbiks).
Dos Geshray (The Scream).
Dos Oysleydikn (The Emptying).
Esther K. Comes to America: 1931.
Hunger.
In the Dark Word, Khurbn.
Lorca Variations (XXVIII), The.
Nokh Aushvits (After Auschwitz).
Numerology.
Others Hunters in the North the Cree, The.
Poem in Yellow after Tristan Tzara, A.
Poland / 1931 "The Wedding."
Portrait of a Jew Old Country Style.
Portrait of Myself with Arshile Gorky and Gertrude Stein.
Praises of the Bantu Kings (1–10).
Prologomena to a Poetics.
Realtheater Piece Two.
Seneca Journal 1: "A Poem of Beavers."
Seven Hells of Jigoku Zoshi, The.
Soap (II).
Song of Quavering, A.
Structural Study of Myth, The.
That Dada Strain.
Visions of Jesus.
Water of the Flowery Mill (II), The.
Young Woman's Neo-Aramaic Jewish Persian Blues.
Rothman, David J. (b. 1959)
Let It Snow.
One of the Lords of Life.
Resurrection of a Mouse.
Shape of Water Most Like Love, The.
When the Wind and Dark Waves Come.
Whistling in January.
Youth.
Rottman, Larry
APO 96225.
Roubaud, Jacques (b. 1932)
Section V.
Roughton, Roger
Building Society Blues.
Soluble Noughts and Crosses; or, California,

Here I Come.
Roumain, Jacques (1907–44)
Dirty Niggers.
Guinea.
Negro peddler of revolt.
New Negro Sermon.
When the Tom-Tom Beats.
Roumer, Emile (b. 1903)
Black Girl Goes By, A.
Peasant Declares His Love, The.
Ten Lines.
Rous, Francis (1579–c.1658)
Help, Lord, because the Godly Man.
I to the Hills Will Lift Mine Eyes.
Rouse, Anne (b. 1954)
Birthday, A.
England Nil.
Glass.
Her Retirement.
Lilies of the Field.
Memo to Auden.
Narrows, The.
Queynt.
Sacrificial Wolf.
Spunk Talking.
Sunday Morning.
Timing.
Uni-Gym, The.
Virginian Arcady.
Rouweler, Hannie (b. 1951)
Landscape.
Silent Time.
Rowbotham, David (b. 1934)
Bus-Stop on the Somme, The.
Cliff, The.
Mullabinda.
Nebuchadnezzar's Kingdom-Come.
Prey to Prey.
Rowe, Elizabeth Singer (1674–1737)
Athenians' Answer, The.
Chapter II.
Chapter IV.
Chapter V.
Expostulation, The.
Forgo the charming Muses! No, in spite.
Hymn: "In vain the dusky night retires."
Laplander's Song to His Mistress, A.
Parthenea, an Elegy.
Pindaric, to the Athenian Society, A.
Platonic Love.
Poetical Question concerning the Jacobites, sent to the Athenians, A.
Reflection, The.
Reply to Mr.&m3rdash;, The.
To a Very Young Gentleman at a Dancing-School.
To Celinda.
To Cleone.
To Orestes.
Upon the Death of Her Husband.
Rowe, Henry (1754–1819)
Moon.
Sun.
Rowe, Nicholas (1674–1718)
Epigram: "Whilst maudlin Whigs deplore their Cato's fate."
Rowe, Vernon
MRI of a Poet's Brain.
Time Heals All Wounds—but One.
Youth.
Rowland, J. R. (b. 1925)
Canberra in April.
London.
Seven Days.
Traveller, A.
Rowlands, Samuel (1570?–1630?)
Boreas.
Epigram 29: "Gentlewoman of the dealing trade, A."
Prologue: "Under the shadow of the gloomy night."
Sir Eglamour.
Sir Revel.
Thraso.
Rowlandson, Thomas (1756–1827)
Epitaph on a Willing Girl.

Rowley, William (1585?–1642?)
Art Thou Gone in Haste?
Rowse, Alfred Leslie (b. 1903)
White Cat of Trenarren, The.
Rowswell, Albert K.
Should You Go First.
Roy, Lucinda
Bread Man, The.
Ride, The.
Suffering the Sea Change: All My Pretty Ones.
Triple Overtime.
Roy, Tushar (b. 1938)
Nowadays.
Różewicz, Tadeusz (b. 1921)
Busy with Many Jobs.
Fight with an Angel.
Homework Assignment on the Subject of
Angels.
I See Madmen.
Lament: "I turn to you high priests."
Larva, The.
Memory of a Dream from the Year 1963.
Pigtail.
Posthumous Rehabilitation.
Proofs.
Questions about Poetry since Auschwitz.
Return, The.
She Looked at the Sun.
Survivor, The.
To the Heart.
Transformations.
Voice, A.
Warning.
What Happens.
What Luck.
Who Is a Poet.
**Rozhdestvensky [or Rozhdestvenskii], Robert
Ivanovich (b. 1932)**
In the Night.
Nonflying Weather.
Nostalgia.
They Killed the Lad.
Winter of Thirty-Eight, The.
You Live on a Drifting Road.
Ruark, Gibbons (b. 1941)
Larkin.
Rose Growing into the House, The.
Rubadiri, James David (b. 1930)
African Thunderstorm, An.
Stanley Meets Mutesa.
Rubin, Larry (b. 1930)
Houses of Emily Dickinson, The.
Rubin, Ron
Limerick: "I'm getting deep lines on my
forehead."
Limerick: "'I'm glad pigs can't fly,' said young
Sellers."
Limerick: "There was a trombonist called
Herb."
Limerick: "There was a young Japanese
geisha."
Limerick: "There was an old drunk called
Hieronymus."
Limerick: "There was an old drunkard of
Devon."
Limerick: "There was an old Welshman called
Morgan."
Limerick: "Vain old Professor of Greek, A."
Rubisova, Yelena [or Elena] (b. 1910)
Humility is the eye of the needle.
Rubtsov, Nikolai Mikhailovich (1936–71)
Farewell Song.
Good Filya.
Ruby, Harry (1895–1974)
Give Me the Simple Life.
Nevertheless (I'm in Love with You)
Three Little Words.
What a Perfect Combination.
Who's Sorry Now?
Ruby, Harry *See* **Kalmar, Bert**
**Rückert, Friedrich ("Freimund Raimar") (1788–
1866)**
And Then No More.
Barbarossa.
Ride round the Parapet, The.

Rudaki (870?–c.940)
All the teeth ever I had are worn down and
fallen out.
Came to me.
Prayer.
Quatrain: "With you away—despair!"
Spring.
Young or Old We Die.
Ruddock, Margot
Autumn, Crystal Eye.
Child Compassion, The.
I Take Thee Life.
Love Song: "Though to think / Rejoiceth me."
O Holy Water.
Spirit, Silken Thread.
Take Away.
Ruden, Sarah (b. 1962)
Beggar outside Cape Town Station, A.
Letter.
Stubble Burning, The.
Rudman, Andrew (d. 1708)
When Shall My Pilgrimage, Jesus My Saviour,
Be Ended?
Rudman, Mark (b. 1948)
What about that girl in first grade? The one
who hopped up on her desk.
Rudolf, Anthony (b. 1942)
Edward Hopper.
Ruefle, Mary
Controlling Factors.
Furtherness.
Minor Figure.
School of Denial.
Stopwatch.
Topophilia.
Ruffilli, Paolo (b. 1949)
Malaria.
Ruffin, Paul (b. 1941)
Hotel Fire: New Orleans.
Rufinus (fl. 2nd cent. B.C.?)
Amymone.
Dear God, I didn't know that Cytherea was
bathing.
Did I not say we grow old.
Europa's kiss.
Her eyes are gold.
Her foot sparkled like silver.
Here Rhodoklea.
How could I have known.
I do not enjoy.
I hate an easy woman.
I have armoured my feelings.
If girls were nice.
In Spite.
Kiss from Her, A.
Lamplighter, if you can't set two equally.
Lay neither the scrawny.
Leaving the Boys Behind.
Let us wash each other's body.
Letter from Ephesos.
Lover's Posy, The.
Melissias.
Melissias denies her love, but her body
screams.
Pallas and / golden-shoed Hera.
Prodike.
Rhodoclea, I send you this wreath which I
wove with my own hands.
Rhodope is so stuck up.
Rhodope, Melite and Rhodoklea.
Silver-footed girl was bathing, letting the
water, The.
Silvertoed virgin, A.
Slave Girl, The.
So it's hullo now.
Time has not quenched your beauty. Much of
your bygone prime.
Waterfront Girls, The.
When Pallas and golden-sandaled Hera saw
Maeonis.
Where is Praxiteles where.
You have Hera's eyes Melite.
Rugge, Heinrich von (fl. 12th cent.)
He that Loves a Rosy Cheek.
Ruhani, Ghulam-Rezi
Gaffer Speaks.

Rûhî (1548–1605)
Curse the Thorns of Fate.
Rühm, Gerhard
Few Things, A.
Flower Piece.
Ruiz, Juan, Archpriest of Hita (fl. c.1343)
Charms of Small Women.
Praise of Little Women.
Rukeyser, Muriel (1913–80)
Ajanta.
Akiba.
Alloy.
Along History.
Ballad of Orange and Grape.
Believing in Those Inexorable Laws.
Birth of Venus, The.
Blood Is Justified, The.
Book of the Dead, The.
Boy with His Hair Cut Short.
Boys of These Men Full Speed.
Bubble of Air.
Bunk Johnson Blowing.
Burning the Dreams.
Ceiling Unlimited.
Children, the Sandbar, That Summer.
Columbus.
Darkness Music.
Death and the Dancer.
Don Baty, the Draft Resister.
Easter Eve.
Effort at Speech between Two People.
Even during war, moments of delicate peace.
Eyes of Night-Time.
Fields Where We Slept.
For My Son.
Gates, The.
Gauley Bridge.
George Robinson: Blues.
Gyroscope, The.
He Had a Quality of Growth.
Holy Family.
Homage to Literature.
Hostages, The.
In the Underworld.
Iris.
Käthe Kollwitz.
Leg in a Plaster Cast, A.
Long Enough. Long Enough.
Looking at Each Other.
Madboy's Song.
Meeting, The.
More of a Corpse than a Woman.
Myth.
Nevertheless the Moon.
Night Feeding.
Nuns in the Wind.
Outer Banks, The.
Painters.
Paper Anniversary.
Poem as Mask, The.
Poem: "I lived in the first century of world
wars."
Power of Suicide, The.
Question, The.
Rational Man.
Reading Time: 1 Minute 26 Seconds.
Resurrection of the Right Side.
Rondel: "Now that I am fifty-six."
Sand-Quarry with Moving Figures.
Seventh Avenue.
Soul and Body of John Brown, The.
Speaking Tree, The.
St. Roach.
That is what they say, who were broken off
from love.
Then.
Then I Saw What the Calling Was.
They Came to Me and Said, "There Is a
Child."
This Morning.
This Place in the Ways.
To Be a Jew in the Twentieth Century.
Traditional Tune.
Waiting for Icarus.
Who in One Lifetime.
Woman as Market.
Yes.

Rukeyser, Muriel *and* **Leif Sjoberg**
Believe that we bloom upon this stalk of time.
My night awake.
Speed of Darkness, The.
Rumaker, Michael (b. 1932)
Fairies Are Dancing All over the World, The.
Rumann, Son of Colman
Storm at Sea.
Rumens, Carol (b. 1944)
Before These Wars.
Double Bed.
Easter Garland, An.
From a Conversation during Divorce.
Geography Lesson.
In the Cloud of Unknowing.
Like cancer cells, ivy, arthritis.
Limerick: "Ancient biologist, Heine, An."
Vocation.
Rumi, Jelaluddin [*or* Jalal al-Din] (1207–73)
All day and night, music.
Answers from the Elements.
Beauty That All Night Long, A.
Caring for My Lover.
Come, come, for the rosebower has blossomed;
come, come, for the beloved has arrived.
Core of Masculinity, The.
Daylight, full of small dancing particles.
Do you think I know what I'm doing?
Drunkards, The.
Friend remarks to the Prophet, "Why is it," A.
Has Anyone Seen the Boy?
Human shape is a ghost, The.
I am your mother, your mother's mother.
I died as mineral and became a plant.
I have lived on the lip.
I, you, he, she, we.
If there be any lover in the world, O Moslems,
'tis I.
If you're not going to sleep.
In the shambles of love, they kill only the best.
In this river the heart is like a ruined
waterwheel; in whichever direction it turns,
there is water before it.
Inside water, a waterwheel turns.
Keep walking, though there's no place to get
to.
Let the lover be disgraceful, crazy.
Light You Give Off, The.
Like the rose I am laughing with all my body,
not only with.
Like This.
Little by little, wean yourself.
Lo, for I to myself am unknown, now in God's
name what must I do?
Love you alone have been with us.
Man of God is drunken without wine, The.
Minute I heard my first love story, The.
Morning: a polished knifeblade.
Never too many fish in a swift creek,.
New Rule, The.
Night and Sleep.
Night comes so people can sleep like fish.
Night full of talking that hurts, A.
Out beyond ideas of wrongdoing and
rightdoing.
Outside, the freezing desert night.
Praise to the emptiness that blanks out
existence. Existence.
Quatrain: "I cry: / but you want comforting."
Say Yes Quickly.
Someone Digging in the Ground.
Song of the spheres in their revolutions, The.
Strange Business.
That Journeys Are Good.
That moon which the sky never saw.
Thief in the Night, A.
This night there are no limits to what may be
given.
Tonight with wine being poured.
Totally conscious, and apropos of nothing, he
comes to see me.
Two strong impulses: One.
We can't help being thirsty.
We take long trips.
What I want to see is your face.
When grapes turn.

When I see Your Face, the stones start
spinning!
When it's cold and raining.
When the heart bursts into flame.
Where is a foot worthy to walk a garden.
Who Says Words with My Mouth.
Wise teacher tell me.
You are the notes, and we are the flute.
You're song.
You that love Lovers.
Rummel, Mary Kay
Letter to a Former Mother Superior.
Runcie, John (1864–1939)
Slumber Song of the Gardens, A.
Rungano, Kristina (b. 1963)
After the Rain.
Labour.
Mother.
This Morning.
Woman, The.
Rupp, Joyce
Sophia.
Rushin, Kate (b. 1951)
Black Back-Ups, The.
Bridge Poem, The.
Rushing, Jimmy (1903–72)
Good Morning, Blues.
Sent for You Yesterday.
Rushton, Edward (1756–1814)
Human Debasement; a Fragment.
Ruskhan (*fl.* 1550)
In Praise of Krishna.
Ruskin, Harry (*fl.* 1929)
I May Be Wrong (But I Think You're
Wonderful)
Ruskin, John (1817–1900)
La Madonna dell' Acqua.
Trust Thou Thy Love.
Zodiac Song, The.
**Russell, Bertrand Arthur William Russell, 3rd
Earl (1872–1970)**
Limerick: "There was a young girl of
Shanghai."
Russell, Bob (1915–70)
Ballerina.
Crazy She Calls Me.
Don't Get Around Much Anymore.
I Didn't Know about You.
You Came a Long Way from St. Louis.
Russell, G. J.
It Might Have Been Worse.
Russell, George William *See* **"Æ"**
Russell, Norman H. (b. 1921)
Message of the Rain, The.
Russell, Sanders
Poem: "I keep feeling all space as my image."
Russell, Thomas (1762–88)
Dear Babe, whose meaning by fond looks
expressed.
Sonnet: Suppos'd to Be Written at Lemnos.
Sonnet to Valclusa.
To Boccaccio.
To Oxford.
To the Owl.
To the Spider.
Russell, W. Les (b. 1949)
Developers, The.
God Gave Us Trees to Cut Down.
Ngarnbarndtar.
Nuclear Winter, The.
Red.
Tali Karng: Twilight Snake.
Rutilius (*fl.* c.416)
Roma.
Rutsala, Vern (b. 1934)
Shame.
Silence, The.
Wilderness.
Words.
Rutter, Joseph (*fl.* 1635)
Epithalamium: "Hymen, god of marriage bed."
Rux, Carl Hancock (b. 1967)
Asphalt Musings.
Asylum of Gestures.

Excavation, The.
Pledge of Allegiance.
Shunning an Imperative.
Suite Repose.
Ryan, Abram Joseph (Father Ryan) (1839–86)
Better than Gold.
Lines: "Gather the sacred dust."
Sword of Robert Lee, The.
Thought, A.
Ryan, Father *See* **Ryan, Abram Joseph**
Ryan, Gig (b. 1956)
Cruising.
Elegy for 6 So Far.
If I Had a Gun.
In the Purple Bar.
Ode to My Car.
Orbit.
Too Bad.
Ryan, Kay
Elephant Rocks.
If She Only Had One Minute.
Surfaces.
Why Isn't It All More Marked.
Woman Who Wrote Too Much, The.
Ryan, Michael (b. 1946)
Complete Semen Study.
God Hunger.
Moonlight.
Passion.
Pure Loneliness, The.
Speaking.
Talking about Things.
This Is a Poem for the Dead.
Use of Poetry, The.
Your Own Image.
Ryan, Richard (b. 1949)
At the End.
Deafness.
El Dorado.
Father of Famine.
From My Lai the Thunder Went West.
Ireland.
Lake of the Woods, The.
Wet Night, A.
Winter in Minneapolis.
Ryan, Tracy
Eclipse, Kenwick, 1974.
Enough.
Lunar Eclipse.
Spin.
Trompe l'oeil.
**Ryashentsev [*or* Riashentsev], Yury [*or* Iurii] (b.
1931)**
April in Town.
Rybicki, John
Brother Ben.
Dogman, The.
For Daniel Beels, Third Generation Bricklayer.
In Directions.
This Sun.
Ryden, Ernest Edwin (1886–1981)
Twilight Shadows round Me Fall, The.
Rye, Anthony
Redbreast, The.
Rykard, Richard (b. 1964)
Whole two weeks after The Million Man
March, A; and still, if you'd ask me, this is
all I could say about it.
Rylander, Edith
Dancing on Beethoven's Birthday.
Midnight Rocker, Tiananmen Square, May 27,
1989.
Rylant, Cynthia
Living in Cheston.
Ryman, James (*fl.* late 15th cent.)
Farewell Advent.
Have mynde how I mankynde have take.
Nunc Puer Nobis Natus Est.
Sancta Maria, ora pro nobis.
Song of the Eucharist, A.
Ther is a chielde, a heuenly childe.
Rymer, Thomas (1641–1713)
To ———: "Let those with cost deck their ill-
fashioned clay."
Ryojin Hisho (Hisho) (*fl.* c.1179?)
May the man who gained my trust yet did not

come.

Ryokan (1758–1831)
Done with a long day's begging.
First Days of Spring.
I've forgotten.
In all ten directions of the universe.
In my begging bowl.
Late at night, listening to the winter rain.
Now it reveals its hidden side.
Picking violets.
To lazy to be ambitious.
Without a jot of ambition left.

Ryosa (d. 1807)
Is man A.

Ryoto (d. 1717)
I understand.
Till now.

Ryou (d. 1794)
Plover rises, A.

Ryozan (fl. 10th cent.)
When I am lonely.

Ryuho (d. 1669)
Now I understand how.

Ryuichi, Tamura (b. 1923)
Invisible Tree.
My Imperialism.
October Poem.
Standing Coffin.

Ryusai (d. 1895)
Brittle pampas grass.

Ryushi (d. 1764)
Man is Buddha.

Ryushu Shutaku (1308–88)
For all these years, my certain Zen.
Mind set free in the Dharma-realm.
Why bother with the world?

Ryu'u (d. 1934)
New Year, The.

Ryuzan (1274–1358)
Clear in the blue, the moon!

S

Saar, Ferdinand von
Again!
Age.
Fall.
Landscape in Late Autumn.
Lullaby: "Grown still loud voices of the day."
Second Viennese Elegy.

Saarikoski, Pentti (b. 1937)
No, Quetzalcoatl, don't come back.
Potato Thief.
Winter solstice.

Saavedra, Guadalupe de
If You Hear that a Thousand People Love You.

Saba, Umberto (1883–1957)
Goat, The.
Insomnia on a Summer Night.
Ulysses.
Winter Noon.

Sabgir, Genrikh
Radio Gibberish.

Sabina, María (b. 1894)
13th Horse Song of Frank Mitchell, The.
Ah, Jesu Kri.
Midnight Velada, The.
Shaman.

Sabines, Jaime
Capriccios.
Entresol.
I Do Not Know It for Sure.
If Someone Tells You It's Not for Sure.
Lovers, The.

Sabti, Kamal (b. 1958)
What remains in the hands.

Sacchetti, Franco (1335–1400?)
Ballata: His Talk with Certain Peasant Girls.
Catch: On a Wet Day.
On a Fine Day.

Sachdev, Padma (b. 1940)
Well, The.

Sachs, Hans (1494–1576)
Fair Melody: To Be Sung by Good
Christians, A.

Sachs, Nelly (1891–1969)
Already Embraced by the Arm of Heavenly
Solace.
But Perhaps.
Chorus of the Dead.
Chorus of the Rescued.
Chorus of the Stars.
Dead Child Speaks, A.
How Long Have We Forgotten How to Listen!
If I Only Knew.
If the Prophets Broke In.
In flight in escape.
In the blue distance.
In the Evening Your Vision Widens.
Last one, The.
Line Like.
O Sister.
O the Chimneys.
Rushing at Times like Flames.
Someone.
Someone Will Take the Ball.
What Secret Cravings of the Blood.
White Serpent.
World, Do Not Ask Those Snatched from
Death.
You.
Your Eyes, O My Beloved.

Sackett, Frances (b. 1948)
Another Kind of Skin.

**Sackville, Charles, 6th Earl of Dorset (1688–
1706)**
My Opinion.
On Mr. Edward Howard, upon His British
Princes.
On the Countess of Dorchester.
Song Written at Sea in the First Dutch War
(1665), the Night before an Engagement.

**Sackville, Thomas, 1st Earl of Dorset (1536–
1608)**
Induction, The.

Sackville-West, Victoria Mary (1892–1962)
Bull, The.
Craftsmen.
Garden, The.
Greater Cats, The.
Land, The.
No Obligation.
On the Lake.
Persia.
Sometimes When Night.
Young Stock.

Sadi [or Saadi or Sa'di] (1184–1291)
Alas!
Courage.
Dancer, The.
Friendship.
Gift of Speech, The.
Great Physician, The.
He glanced at me one day—but then his mean.
He Hath No Parallel.
Help.
If you should say to me Don't mention love.
Last night without sight of you my brain was
ablaze.
Love's Last Resource.
Mesnevi.
O I repented, wore my pious cloak.
Ode: "Until thine hands clasp girdlewise the
waist of the Belov'd."
On the Deception of Appearances.
Sooth-Sayer, The.
Take the Crust.
This I write, mix ink with tears.
Until you can correct and heal yourself.
Wealth.
When once the soul is ready to depart, sir.

Sadiq, Mohammed (fl. 20th cent.)
Tuskegee Experiment.

Sadoff, Ira (b. 1945)
Civil Rights.
Depression, The.
February: Pemaquid Point.
Grazing.

Hopper's "Nighthawks" (1942)
Izzy.
Nazis.
Soul, The.
Standard Time.
There's No Rigor like the Old Rigor 2.

Sadoleto, Jacopo (1477–1547)
Poem of Jacobus Sadoletus on the Statue of
Laocoon, The.

Sadongei, Alice (b. 1959)
After Seeing Paintings in a Small Book by T.
C. Cannon (1946–1978)
Don't Forget.
For Carlos Charles Bucillio.
Poems Come to Me in the Night.
Wind Blew like Water.

Saenz, Jaime (1921–86)
Let your permanency under the brilliance of
the stars be long.

Saffarzadeh, Tahereh (b. 1939)
Birthplace.

Saffin, John (1626–1700)
Acrostick on Mrs. Elizabeth Hull, An.
Acrostick on Mrs. Winifret Griffin, An.
Brief Elegie on My Dear Son John, A.
Consideratus Considerandus.
Elegie on the Deploreable Departure of the
Honered and Truely Religious Chieftain
John Hull, An.
Lamentation on My Dear Son Simon, A.
One Presenting a Rare Book to Madame Hull.
Sweetly (my Dearest) I left thee asleep.
To His Excellency Joseph Dudley.

Safford, June Billings
Very Floor of Our Existence, The.

Saffoti, Carol Lee (fl. 20th cent.)
Espresso.

Safie, Doris (b. 1940)
Danger, Men in Trees.
In the Middle of Reading One More Poem
with Brueghel as a Metaphor.
Meditation by the Xerox Machine.

Safiya bint Musafir (fl. early 7th cent.)
At the Badr Trench.

Sagami, Lady (fl. c.1000)
In the gathering dew.

Sage, Kay (1898–1963)
Chinoiserie.
Fragrance.
Observation, An.
Window, The.

"Sagittarius" (Olga Katzin) (b. 1896)
Come into the Army, Maud.
Croaked the Eagle: "Nevermore."
Freedom in Peril.
Limerick: "Rather extreme vegetarian, A."
Nerves.
Passionate Profiteer to His Love, The.
Servant of the House.
Stalin Moy Golubchik.

Sagoff, Maurice
Preface Shrink Lit: Elements of Style.
Robinson Crusoe Daniel Defoe.

Sahay, Raghuvir (1929–90)
Our Hindi.

Sāheb, Anthony
Victory to Yogendra's Wife, Great Illusion!

Saiba (d. 1858)
I shift my pillow.

Said, Amina (b. 1953)
Africa of the Statue, The.
And We Were Born.
Bird Is Meditation, The.
I Present Myself to the World.
My Woman's Transparence.
On the Fringe.
On the Tattered Edges.
One Day I Know the Page.
Vultures Grow Impatient, The.

Sa'id, Hameed (b. 1941)
Daily Delights.
Dying at the Edge of Death.
Emanations.

Saigyo (Saigyo Hoshi) (1118–90)
Although I do not know.

I don't even know.
In a tree standing.
In my boat that goes.
Like those boats which are returning.
Mingling my prayer.
My heart emptied.
Out in the high waves.
Since I am convinced.
Startled / By a single scream.
Those ships which left.
Saikaku (d. 1693)
In this delusive world.
Saikaku (d. 1730)
I borrow moonlight.
Sail, Lawrence (b. 1942)
Christmas Night.
Up and down I go, my stock.
Saimaro (1656–1737)
I'll cross the ridge.
Mirrored by stream.
Saimu (d. 1679)
Dawn breaks.
Saint, Assotto (b. 1957)
Heart and Soul.
Triple Trouble.
Saint-Gelais, Mellin de (1491–1558)
Sonnet of the Mountain, The.
St. John, David (b. 1949)
Black Poppy (At the Temple)
California.
Dolls.
Grandfather's Cap, My.
Guitar.
Homage to Robert Johnson.
Hush.
I will tell you. Maybe.
Iris.
My Friend.
Quote Me Wrong Again and I'll Slit the Throat
   of Your Pet Iguana.
Slow Dance.
Temporary Situation, A.
Twin memory, we all seek it.
Wedding Preparations in the Country.
St. John, Primus (b. 1939)
Biological Light.
Carnival.
Lynching and Burning.
Ocean of the Streams of Story.
Pearle's Poem.
Song.
Sunday.
We Are Going to Be Here Now.
Saiokuken Socho (Socho) (1448–1532)
Moon this evening, The.
Saisho (d. 1506)
On Joshu's Nothingness.
Saitō Mokichi (1882–1953)
From far off I have brought medicines, she
   watches me because I am her son.
Sakanoe No Korenori
In the dawn.
"Saki" (Hector Hugh Munro) (1870–1916)
Carol: "While shepherds watched their flocks
   by night."
Sakyoku (d. 1790)
How sad.
Salaam, Kalamu ya (b. 1947)
5 Minutes, Mr. Salaam.
All Nite Long.
Always Know.
Everywhere You Eat.
French Quarter Intimacies.
Funeraled Fare Well.
Height, Breadth, Depth.
I Just Heard John Buffington Died.
I Live in the Mouth of History.
Makes You Go Oohhh!
Name the Oldest Member of Your Family.
New Orleans Rainbow.
Our Natures Rise.
Our World Is Less Full Now that Mr. Fuller Is
   Gone.
Quarter Moon Rise.
Round Midnight, Place de Congo.

Secondline Send Off.
Spice of Life, The.
Spiritual Geography.
St. Louis Cemetery Crypt.
Sunrise on the River.
Til Death Do Us Part.
Salatko-Petrishche, Valerii Frantsevich *See*
   "Pereleshin, Valery Frantsevich"
Salazar, Dixie (*fl.* 20th cent.)
Cricket at Central California Women's Facility.
E Is in Heaven.
Hotel Fresno.
Meteor Showers—Yosemite.
Moulton Transformations.
Piñon Nuts.
Taking It Back.
Saldaña, Diego de (*fl.* 15th cent.)
Eyes So Tristful.
Saleh, Dennis (b. 1942)
Beach, Later.
Crabs.
December Nap.
Sentry.
Summer.
Salganicoff, Matilde
Being an Immigrant.
Girl Refugee, The.
Nightmare.
Shame.
Salih, Saniyya (1939–89)
Choking.
Exile.
Goodbye, Zenobia.
Salimon, Vladimir (b. 1952)
Food-Factory Kitchen.
Salute, Friends!
Salinas, Luis Omar (b. 1937)
For Larry Levis in Memory.
I Go Dreaming Roads in My Youth.
Middle Age.
My Fifty-Plus Years Celebrate Spring.
Nights in Fresno.
Sea Song.
Sometimes Mysteriously.
Salinas, Raul
Trip through the Mind Jail, A.
Salis-Seewis, Johann Gaudenz von (1763–1834)
Song of the Silent Land.
Salkey, Andrew (b. 1943)
Dry River Bed.
Sall, Amadou Lamine (b. 1951)
Cloak of Dawn.
Letter to a Roving Poet.
Sallah, Tijan M. (b. 1958)
Elders Are Gods, The.
Mr. Agama.
No Argument Tonight.
Television as God.
Salmon, André (1881–1957)
Painting.
Prikaz.
Salom, Philip (b. 1950)
Ghazal on signs of Love and Occupation.
Walking at Night.
Well, The.
Winter.
World of Dreams, The.
Salsbury, Nate (b. 1888)
Apex.
Salter, Mary Jo (b. 1954)
Absolute September.
Chernobyl.
Distance.
England.
Frost at Midnight.
Half a Double Sonnet.
Liam.
Rainbow over the Seine, A.
Rebirth of Venus, The.
Robin's Nest, A.
Summer 1983.
Sunday Skaters.
Welcome to Hiroshima.
What Do Women Want?
Young Girl Peeling Apples.

Saltus, Francis Saltus (1847–89)
Come! show your jolly tricks, and be
   possessed.
Kiss, The.
Mothers.
Posthumous Revenge.
Sad, on Broadway next afternoon.
Two loves found refuge in my happy heart.
Salzman, Eric
Double Dactyls.
Salzman, Eva (b. 1960)
Bargain with the Watchman.
Double Crossing.
English Earthquake, The.
Grandmother.
Homesteading.
Sama, Balakrishna
Song, The.
Samain, Albert (1858–1900)
Pannyra of the Golden Heel.
Samara, Munia (b. 1955)
Door of Roses.
Door of the Cities.
Samaras, Nicholas
After the Children Have Gone to Bed.
Aubade: Macedonia.
Crossing the Strait.
Elegy for a Professor.
Farasa.
Mute Prophets.
Notes in Jerusalem.
Translation.
Sami Mansei (Mansei) (*fl.* 8th cent.)
Our Life in This World.
This world of ours.
Samik
Hunger.
"Samoylov [or Samoilov], David Samuilovich"
   (David Samuilovich Kaufman) (1920–1990)
Ballad about the German Censor, The.
Death of Ivan, The.
Forties, The.
Ivan and the Serf.
Old Derzhavin.
Pestel, the Poet, and Anna.
Poem not flowery but bare, A.
Words.
Sampson, Edgar
Stompin' at the Savoy.
Sampter, Jessie E. (b. 1883–1938)
Kadia the Young Mother Speaks.
Promised Land, The.
Summer Sabbath.
Sampu (Sugiyama Sampu) (1647–1732)
Moving / Deep into mist.
Sampu, Sugiyama *See* **Sampu**
Samwell, David (1751–98)
Negro Boy, The.
Samyn, Mary Ann (b. 1970)
Art of Kissing, The.
Poem with Light on Its Shoulder.
Trompe L'Oeil in Winter.
San Geminiano [or Gimignano], Folgore da (*fl.*
   13th cent.)
And every Wednesday, as the swift days move.
And on the morrow, at first peep o' the day.
April.
August.
Because ye made your backs your shields, it
   came.
December.
Dedication: "Unto the blithe and lordly
   fellowship."
February.
For Thursday be the tournament prepar'd.
I've jolliest merriment for Saturday:—.
January.
July.
June.
Let Friday be your highest hunting-tide,—.
March.
May.
November.
Now with the moon the day-star Lucifer.
October.

On Knighthood.
September.
Sonnet: Of Virtue.
Sonnets of the Months.
Sonnets of the Months: Conclusion.
Sonnets of the Months: September.
There is among my thoughts the joyous plan.
To a new world on Tuesday shifts my song.
Were ye but constant, Guelfs, in war or peace.

San Juan, Jr., E.
End of the Affair, The.
Entelechy on the Libidinal Fringe.
Owl of Minerva Takes Flight in the Evening, The.
Three for the Road.

Sana'i (d. 1131)
Invocation.

Sanchez, Carol Lee (b. 1934)
Corn Children.
Tribal Chant.

Sánchez Peláez, Juan (b. 1922)
Portrait of the Beautiful Unknown Woman.

Sanchez, Sonia (b. 1935)
Answer to Yo / Question.
Anthem, An.
Black Magic.
Blues.
Chant for Young / Brothas and Sistuhs, A.
Depression.
Earth Mother.
Elegy (for MOVE and Philadelphia)
Father and Daughter.
Haiku.
Haiku: "Was it yesterday."
Haiku: "Your voice unwrapping."
Hospital / Poem.
July.
Liberation / Poem.
Listenen to Big Black at S. F. State.
Memorial.
Nigger.
Norma.
On Watching a World Series Game.
Personal Letter No. 3.
Philadelphia: Spring, 1985.
Poem at Thirty.
Poem for Etheridge.
Poem for July 4, 1994.
Poem for My Father, A.
Prelude to Nothing.
Present.
Reflections after the June 12th March for Disarmament.
Right On: White America.
Song No. 2: "I say. all you young girls waiting to live."
Song No. 3: "Cain't nobody tell me any different."
Summary.
Summer Words of [or for] a Sistuh [or Sister] Addict.
This Is Not a Small Voice.
To All Brothers.
To Anita.
To P. J. (2 Yrs Old Who Sed Write a Poem for Me in Portland, Oregon)

Sandall, Harold C.
Song: "Love that is hoarded, moulds at last."

Sandburg, Carl (1878–1967)
A. E. F.
Adelaide Crapsey.
Aprons of Silence.
At a Window.
Auctioneer.
Balloon Faces.
Bar of steel—it is only, A.
Bas-Relief.
Be Ready.
Bilbea.
Blue Island Intersection.
Bones.
Broadway.
Broken-Face Gargoyles.
Buffalo Dusk.
Bundles.
Cahoots.

Chicago.
Child of the Romans.
Choose.
Circles.
Cool Tombs.
Crapshooters.
Early Copper.
Early Lynching.
Elephants Are Different to Different People.
Fish Crier.
Flash Crimson.
Fog.
For You.
Four Preludes on Playthings of the Wind.
Galoots.
Gargoyle.
Gone.
Grass.
Halsted Street Car.
Happiness.
Harbor, The.
Harrison Street Court.
Haze.
Hits and Runs.
I Am the People, the Mob.
Ice Handler.
Illinois Farmer.
Jazz Fantasia.
Languages.
Lawyers Know Too Much, The.
Limited.
Lines Written for Gene Kelly to Dance To.
Little Girl, Be Careful What You Say.
Little girl saw her first troop parade and asked, 'What are those?' , The.
Long Shadow of Lincoln: A Litany, The.
Losers.
Love in Labrador.
Mag.
Mamie.
Man in the street is fed, The.
Manual System.
Moist Moon People.
Murmurings in a Field Hospital.
Nocturne in a Deserted Brickyard.
Old Timers.
On a Flimmering Floom You Shall Ride.
One Modern Poet.
Osawatomie.
People know what the land knows, The.
People, yes, the people, The.
Population Drifts.
Portrait of a Motorcar.
Prairie Waters by Night.
Prayer after World War.
Prayers of Steel.
Precious Moments.
Primer Lesson.
Psalm of Those Who Go Forth before Daylight.
Right to Grief, The.
River Roads.
Sea-Wash.
Shirt.
Shovel Man, The.
Sins of Kalamazoo, The.
Skyscraper.
Smoke of the fields in spring is one.
Soup.
Southern Pacific.
Splinter.
Stars.
Sunset from Omaha Hotel Window.
Sunsets.
Teamster's Farewell, A.
They All Want to Play Hamlet.
They have yarns.
Three Spring Notations on Bipeds.
Threes.
Under a Hat Rim.
Upstream.
Washerwoman.
We Must Be Polite.
What the people learn out of lifting and hauling and waiting and losing.
When I asked for fish in the restaurant facing

the Ohio River.
Who shall speak for the people?
Why did the children.
Why repeat? I heard you the first time.
Wilderness.
Wind Song.
Window.
You can go now yes go now. Go east or west, go north or.

Sandeen, Ernest (b. 1908)
Late Twentieth-Century Prayer, A.
Plaint of Flowers, A.
Poète Manqué.
They Are Wicked.
Way Down, The.

Sanders, Donald T. (b. 1944)
Poem for Shane on Her Brother's Birthday.

Sanders, Edward (b. 1939)
Content of History Will Be Poetry, The.
Cutting Prow, The.
Fugs, The.
Holy Was Demeter Walking th' Corn Furrow.
Leaves of Heaven, The.
Pindar's Revenge.

Sanders, Peter A.
Tripoli.

Sandys, Edwin (1561–1629)
In Pilgrim Life Our Rest.

Sandys, George (c.1577–1644)
Again when all the radiant sons of light.
Bounty of Jehovah Praise, The.
Hymn Written at the Holy Sepulchre in Jerusalem.
Judah in Exile Wanders.
"O Father, I acknowledge, " Job replied.
O Blest Estate, Blest from Above.

Saner, Reg (b. 1931)
Autumn Aspens: Cumbres Pass.
Camping Clean.
Desert Wisdom.
Indian Peaks, Colorado.
Morning Snowfield.
Rain near Heart Lake.
Report to the Stockholders.
Sierra Cup.
This Grizzly.
Waking at the Middle of Nowhere.

Sanesada (Fujiwara no Sanesada) (1139–91)
Cuckoo calls.

Sanesada, Fujiwara no *See* **Sanesada**

Sangster, Charles (1822–93)
Our life is like a forest, where the sun.
Thousand Islands, The.

Sangster, Margaret Elizabeth (b. 1894)
Blind Man, The.
Prayer for Faith, A.

Sangster, Margaret Elizabeth Munson (1838–1912)
At Sunset.
Forgiven.
Oh, face to face with trouble.
Our Own.
Patience with the Living.

Sanguineti, Edoardo (b. 1930)
And now a few questions to end with.
At the offset it was calculated.
I defended Genet on the subject of terror in London.
I tell you it was a hard punch to my brain.
Last Stroll, The: Homage to Pascoli.
Like a disk, a trembling coin spinning on its own diameter.
So it takes very little indeed: a brasserie.
To the mini-skirted customs official who with sibyl-dove eyes.
What you're reading (if you're reading me) are the effects.
Wind shoves my New Year's Day sun in my face, The.

Sanjō Emperor (fl. 11th cent.)
Involuntary, / I may live on.

Sankichi, Tōge (1917–53)
Dying.
Flames.

Sannazarius, Actius Sincerus *See* **Sannazaro,**

Jacopo

Sannazaro, Jacopo (Actius Sincerus Sannazarius) (1458–1530)
Like to these unme[a]surable montains [or mountayns].

Sanpu (1647–1732)
First cherry blossoms.
May rains!

Sansom, Ann
Confinement.
Cross Country.
From the Moment I Picked Up Your Book.
Prince.
Romance.
Voice.
World is everything, The.

Sansom, Clive (1910–81)
Innkeeper's Wife, The.
Me—Pirate.
Snowflakes.

Sansom, Martha (1690–1736)
Invitation from a Country Cottage, The.
It was not that I lost direction.
NoTL.
Song: "Foolish eyes, thy streams give over."
To Cleon's Eyes.
To My Heavenly Charmer.

Sant, Andrew (b. 1950)
Homage to the Canal People.
Soundwaves.

Sant, Indira (b. 1914)
Household Fires.

Santal
Witch, The.

Santalucia, Jason
Sustenance.

Santayana, George (1863–1952)
Before a Statue of Achilles.
Cape Cod.
Echo.
I Would I Might Forget that I Am I.
O world, thou choosest not the better part!
Ode V: "Of thee the Northman by his beachèd galley."
On a Piece of Tapestry.
On an Unfinished Statue.
Sonnet V: "Dreamt I today [or to-day] the dream of yesternight."
Sonnet XLIII: "Candour of the gods is in thy gaze, The."
Sonnet XLVIII: "Of Helen's brothers, one was born to die."
Sonnet XXV: "As in the midst of battle there is room."
To W. P.
When I discover that the substance of the beautiful is a certain rhythm.

Santly, Lester (fl. 1921)
I'm Nobody's Baby.

Santob de Carrion (fl. 14th cent.)
Jewish Poet Counsels a King, A.

Santos Chocano, José (1875–1934)
Dream of the Caiman, The.
Dream of the Condor, The.
Indignation.
Manifesto, A.
Volcanoes, The.
Who Knows?

Santos, Sherod (b. 1949)
Jeffers Country.
Late November.
Married Love.
Midsummer.
Near the Desert Test Sites.
On the Last Day of the World.
Sheltering Ground, The.
Tahoe Nocturne.

Sapgir, Genrik Veniaminovich (b. 1928)
Dionysus.
Fearless One.
From an Album.
Psalm 1.
Psalm 137.

Sapia, Yvonne (b. 1946)
Grandmother, a Caribbean Indian, Described

by My Father.
Valentino's Hair.

"Sapphire"
American Dreams.

Sappho (fl. c.612 B.C.)
About the Cool Water.
All the while, believe me, I prayed.
Alone.
Anaktoria.
And you, Dika, put lovely garlands round your hair.
Andromache's Wedding.
Andromeda / forgot.
Arbor, The.
Atthis, for you the thought of me has become hateful.
Beneath its wings.
Black Dream, you come.
Bride: Virginity, virginity, where have you gone leaving me behind?
But as my friend, take to a younger bed.
But I am not someone of spiteful.
Come, divine lyre, speak to me.
Come, holy tortoise shell.
Come to me from Crete to this holy temple.
Come to me from Krete to this holy.
Delicate Adonis is dying, Kytheria—what should we do?
Do I still desire virginity?
Doorkeeper has feet seven fathoms long, The.
Dust of Timas, The.
Equal to the Gods.
[Eros] came from heaven wearing a purple cloak.
Eros seizes and shakes my very soul.
Evening Star who gathers everything.
Farewell to Anactoria.
For me neither honey nor bee.
For you beautiful ones my mind.
Forever Dead.
Full Moon.
Full moon was rising, The.
Glow and beauty of the stars, The.
Gongyla.
Handsome man is good to look at, A.
Happy bridegroom, the marriage that you prayed for.
He is almost a god, a man beside you.
Herald came, The.
Herdsmen crush under their feet.
Here are fine gifts, children.
Hermes came to me in a dream. I said.
Hesperos, you bring home all the bright dawn disperses.
Honestly I'd as soon be dead!
Honestly I wish I were dead!
Horses in Flowers.
I could not hope / to touch the sky.
I don't expect to touch heaven.
I don't know what I should do—I'm of two minds.
I fell in love with you, Atthis.
I have a beautiful child, her form.
I have no embroidered headband.
I love / love's delicacy.
I loved you Atthis once long ago.
I say someone in another time will remember us.
I simply wish to die.
I think no woman of such skill.
I urge you.
I will now sing this beautifully.
I wish to say something to you, but shame.
If my nipples were to drip milk.
In gold sandals.
In the house of those who serve the Muses, a dirge.
In the young spring evening.
It's no use.
It would be wrong for us. It is not right.
Kypris and Nereids, let that brother.
Kypris, / May she find you very bitter.
Leave Krete and come to this holy temple.
Leaving Crete, come visit again our temple.
Like a mountain whirlwind.
Like a sweet apple reddening on the high.
Like the sweet-apple.

Like the very gods in my sight is he who.
Love.
Love—bittersweet, irrepressible.
Love shook my senses.
Many-colored sandal, A.
Marriage of Hector and Andromache, The.
May I, goldencrowned Aphrodite.
May winds and sorrows.
May you sleep on the breast of a tender companion.
Mika / But I will not allow you.
Moon and the Pleiades have set, The.
Moon has set, The.
Mother darling, I cannot work the loom.
My Atthis, although our dear Anaktoria.
My mother always said.
My mother / In her youth it was a great.
Night / Virgins.
Now in my.
O dream from the blackness.
O Gongyla, my darling rose.
Ode to Anactoria.
Ode to Aphrodite.
Of love.
On a Lady Indifferent to Poetry.
On the throne of many hues, Immortal Aphrodite.
On your dazzling throne, Aphrodite.
On your throne, a marvel of art, immortal.
Once again Love [Eros], the loosener of limbs, shakes me.
Once again that loosener of limbs, Love.
One Girl.
Peer of the gods is that man, who.
Percussion, Salt and Honey.
Pleiades disappear, The.
Prayer to Aphrodite.
Prayer to my lady of Paphos.
Queen Hera, may your [graceful form].
Raise high the roof.
Round about Me.
Sappho, if you do not come out.
Sardis.
Since yes you [were] once a child.
Some prefer a glory of horsemen; warships.
Some say an army of horsemen, others.
Some say cavalry and others claim.
Some there are who say that the fairest thing seen.
Someone, I tell you.
Star of Evening.
Stars around the fair moon, The.
Stars around the luminous moon—how soon they.
Superior, as a singer from Lesbos to those of other lands.
Sweet apple reddens on a high branch, The.
Sweet mother, I cannot weave.
That labor / a face to remember in wonder.
That one seems to me to be like the gods, the man whosoever sits facing you and listens nearby to your sweet speech and desirable laughter.
Their souls became cold.
Then I said to the elegant ladies.
There a bowl of ambrosia.
There is no other girl, bridegroom, like this.
There's a man, I really believe, compares with.
There's a man I really believe's in heaven.
They say that once Leda found.
This is the dust of Timias.
Throned in splendor, deathless, O Aphrodite.
To goldenhaired Phoibos whom Leto bore.
To me he seems like a god.
To me it seems.
Tonight I've watched.
Verses Made by Sappho, Done from the Greek by Boyleau, and from the French by a Lady of Quality.
What country woman bewitches your mind.
When anger spreads in the breast.
When you die you'll lie dead, no memory of you.
With what, dear bridegroom, can I fairly compare you?
You came and did (well); I felt for you.
You came. And you did well to come.

You lay in wait.
You / Put success in the mouth.

Sarangapani (*fl.* c.1720)
Madam to a Young Courtesan, The.

Sargant, Jane Alice (*fl.* 1817–21)
How gladly would I lay my aching head.
'Lo, on her dying couch, the sufferer lies.

Sargent, Epes (1813–80)
Planet Jupiter, The.
Rockall.
Sea-Breeze at Matanzas, The.

Sárközi, György (1899–1945)
Cursed Is a Man.
Fog.
Hope for a Miracle.
Hymn of Love, The.
Like Gulliver.
Raindrops.
Unknown World, The.

Sarmèd the Yahud (*fl.* 17th cent.)
Quatrain: "Sarmèd, whom they intoxicated from the cup of love."
Quatrain: "This existence has, without the azure sphere, no reality."

Sarmiento, Félix Rubén García *See* **"Dario, Rubén"**

"Sarnicol" *See* **Thomas, Thomas Jacob**

Sarson, H. M.
Shell, The.

Sarton, May (1914–95)
After a Train Journey.
After All These Years.
At Lindos.
Eine Kleine Snailmusik.
February Days.
If I can let you go as trees let go.
It is time for the invocation.
Letter from Chicago.
Love: "Fragile as a spider's web."
Moving In.
Muse as Medusa, The.
My Sisters, O My Sisters.
Nursery Rhyme.
On a Winter Night.
Small Joys.
Snow Light, The.
Tortured, The.
When a Woman Feels Alone.

Sarumaru (*fl.* 9th cent.)
Deep in the mountain.

Saruo (d. 1923)
Cherry blossoms fall.

Sassoon, Siegfried (1886–1967)
Aftermath.
Ancient History.
At the Grave of Henry Vaughan.
Attack.
Babylon.
Base Details.
Blighters.
Blues at Lord's, The.
Christ and the Soldier.
Conclusion: "Image dance of change, An."
Counter-Attack.
Death-Bed, The.
Does It Matter?
Dreamers.
Dug-Out, The.
Elected Silence.
Everyman.
Everyone Sang.
Falling Asleep.
General, The.
Glory of Women.
Grandeur of Ghosts.
Hero, The.
In Barracks.
In Heytesbury Wood.
In Me, Past, Present, Future Meet.
Invocation: "Come down from heaven to meet me when my breath."
Lamentations.
Limitations.
Memorial Tablet.
Morning Glory.

On Passing the New Menin Gate.
One Who Watches.
Power and the Glory, The.
Prehistoric Burials.
Presences Perfected.
Rank stench of those bodies haunts me still, The.
Rear-Guard, The.
Repression of War Experience.
Sporting Acquaintances.
Stand-to: Good Friday Morning.
Strangeness of Heart.
Suicide in [the] Trenches.
They.
To His Dead Body.
Two Old Ladies.
Wisdom of the World, The.
Working Party, A.

Satchell, Marlon D. (b. 1977)
Grandfather Grandfather.
Velvet Blanket.

Satchidanandan, K. (b. 1946)
Genesis.

Satyamurti, Carole (b. 1939)
Day Trip.
Erdywurble.
Where Are You?

Satyrus
Echo, tongueless, sings her sweet.

Sa'udi, Mona (b. 1945)
How do I enter the silence of stones.
When the loneliness of the tomb went down into the marketplace.
Why don't I write in the language of air?

Saudi, Mona (b. 1945)
Blind City.
So Drunk Am I with the Night, the Air, and the Trees.

Saunders, Lesley
Mothers of Sons.

Saunders, R. Crombie (b. 1914)
Empty Glen, The.
Ressaif My Saul.

Saunders, Ruby C. (Fareedah Allah)
Cinderella.
Funky Football.
Generation Gap, The.
Hush Honey.
Lawd, Dese Colored Chillum.
You Made It Rain.

Sauser-Hall, Frédéric-Louis *See* **Cendrars, Blaise**

Sauter, Lilly
Full Moon in Salzburg.
Longing.

Savage, Mary (*fl.* 1763–77)
Disaster, The.
Letter to Miss E. B. at Bath.
Letter to Miss E. B. on Marriage.
To a School-Boy at Eton, Yes and No.

Savage, Richard (1698–c.1743)
First, let me view what noxious nonsense reigns.
In gayer hours, when high my fancy ran.
Now in the patron's mansion see the wight.

Savageau, Cheryl
All Night She Dreams.
At the Powwow.
Henri Toussaints.
Like the Trails of Ndakinna.
Looking for Indians.
To Human Skin.
Trees.

Savenko, Eduard Veniaminovich *See* **"Limonov, Eduard Veniaminovich"**

Savinkov, Boris Viktorovich *See* **"Ropshin, V."**

Sawyer, Anna (*fl.* 1794–1801)
Lines, / Written on Seeing My Husband's Picture, Painted when He Was Young: "Those are the features, those the smiles."
Sunday Schools.

Sawyer, Ruth (b. 1880)
Feast o' Saint [*or* St.] Stephen, The.

Saxe, John Godfrey (1816–87)
Blind Men and the Elephant, The.

News, The.
Story of Life, The.

Saxe, Susan (b. 1949)
Questionnaire.

Saxena, Sarveshwar Dayal (1927–84)
Black Panther, The.

Sayers, A. M.
Limerick: "I admire your felicitous phrasing."
Limerick: "There once was a wise politician."
Limerick: "There was an old dame of Toulouse."
Limerick: "Three wonderful people called Wick."
Limerick: "When I sit in the Churchyard at Stoke."

Sayers, Dorothy Leigh (1893–1957)
Choice of the Cross, The.
War Cat.

Sayigh, Mai (b. 1940)
Departure.
Lament: "Those we love die like birds."

Sayigh, Tawfiq [*or* **Taufiq**] (1923–71)
Out of the Depths I Cry unto You, O Death!
Phantom.

Sayles, James M. (b. 1948)
Star of the Evening.

Sayres, Cortlandt W. (b. 1927)
Bankrupt.

Sa'id, 'Ali Ahmad *See* **"Adonis"** [*or* **"Adunis"**]

Scalapino, Leslie (b. 1948)
Considering How Exaggerated Music Is.
Flush / a Play.
Instead of an Animal.
Or a Play.
Picasso and Anarchism.
Playing ball—so it's like paradise, not because it's in the past, we're on A.
Series—3, The.
There's still on the rim of night (having been in it) which is (in night)

Scalise, Gregorio (b. 1939)
Amiti' Amoureuse.
Days pass on that face, The.
Dora Markus and Her Actors.
Man comes last: he's got to.
Passion circles round our body, A.
Testing out the door-posts.
There have never been men crazier than these.

Scamell, Ben (b. 1966)
Actor Speaks, An.
Diaries.
For a Six Year Old.
From the Provinces.
More Rain.
My Lost Brother.
Party, The.
Sin.
Stranger to a Small Child.
Working for British Telecom.

Scammell, Michael *See* **Taufer, Veno**

Scammell, William
Christmas at Bristol.
Eclogue: Clerk of the Weather.
Inventions.
Jean Rhys.
Men rigged my chamfered oak.
Nicola.
One Man.
Poem for a Younger Son.
Retrospective.
Screes, The.
St Bees in Winter.
Trains.
Walk, The.

Scannell, Vernon (b. 1922)
Any Complaints?
Apple-raid, The.
Autumn.
Bayonet Training.
Dead Dog.
Discriminator, The.
Five Domestic Interiors.
Great War, The.
Hide and Seek.
Incendiary.

Jailbird.
Moth, The.
Old Books, The.
Poem on Bread.
Poetry Reading.
Popular Mythologies.
Protest Poem.
Six Reasons for Drinking.
Walking Wounded.
Words and Monsters.

Scarfe, Francis (b. 1911)
Grenade.
Kitchen Poem.
Merry Window, The.
Ode in Honour.

Scarlatti, Filippo (c.1442–c.1487)
Lanza 51.

Scates, Maxine
1956.
Angel.
Angel's Flight.
Going to Mass after Fifteen Years.
Floor Plans.
Working.

Scève, Maurice
Les Dizains.
Every Wide and Long Expanse of Sea.

Schaefer, Sister M. Cherubim (b. 1886)
Rejoice, Let Alleluias Ring.

Schaeffer, Susan Fromberg (b. 1941)
Dog, The.
May Levine.
Yahrzeit.

Schafer, Bob
My Special Friend (Is Back in Town)

Schafer, John C.
Battle Lines.

Schapiro, Jane
Tourist, The.

Schaukal, Richard von
Early Spring.
Images.
To the Lord.

Schechter, Ruth Lisa (1927–89)
What Were You Patching?

Scheffauer, Ethel Talbot
Limerick: "Mr Lear, I'm the Akond of Swat."

Scheffler, Johannes *See* **"Angelus Silesius"**

Schertzinger, Victor
Arthur Murray Taught Me Dancing in a Hurry.
I Remember You.
Sand in My Shoes.
Tangerine.

Schevill, James (b. 1920)
Freud: Dying London, He Recalls the Smoke
of His Cigar Beginning to Sing.
Green Frog at Roadstead, Wisconsin.
Huck Finn at Ninety, Dying in a Chicago
Boarding House Room.
London Pavement Artist.
Screamer Discusses Methods of Screaming, A.

Schick, Eleanor
Last summer.

Schierbeek, Bert (b. 1918)
Animal Has Drawn a Human, The.
Sun, The: Day.

Schiff, Hilda
Discovery.
German Frontier at Basel: 1942 and 1992, The.
When It Happened.

Schifrin, Lalo
Right to Love, The.

Schiller, Johann Christoph Friedrich von (1759–1805)
Maid of Orleans, The.
Thekla's Song.
To My Friends.
Unrealities, The.

Schilpp, Margot (b. 1962)
Devotions in Confidence.
Non Sequitur.
Triage.
Under the Scorpion's Heart.

Schinto, Jeanne
Stalker.

Schippers, K. (Gerard Stigter) (b. 1936)
No, No, Nanette.

Schirmer, David (1623–83)
He Loves.

Schlegel, Katharina von
Be Still, My Soul.

Schluger, Bill
I Love Being Here with You.

Schmitz, Dennis (b. 1937)
Abbott's Lagoon.
Bird-Watching.
Carmel.
Climbing Sears Tower.
Letter to Ron Silliman on the Back of a Map
of the Solar System, A.
Making a Door.
Making Chicago.
Mile Hill.
Monstrous Pictures of Whales.
Picture of Okinawa, A.
Queen of Heaven Mausoleum.
Star & Garter Theater.
String.

Schnack, Anton
Nocturnal Landscape.

Schnackenberg, Gjertrud (b. 1953)
Advent Calendar.
Darwin in 1881.
Nightfishing.
Paperweight, The.
Signs.
Supernatural Love.
Walking Home.
When Clumsy harks the gladsome ting-a-lings.

Schneemann, Carolee
Interior Scroll.

Schneider, Isidor (1896–1977)
History of the Caesars, A.
Insects.
Joy of Knowledge.

Schneider, Myra (b. 1936)
Photograph, The.
Soup and Slavery.

Schneiders, Jay
Weight.

Schneour, Zalman (b. 1887)
Besieged.
Cherries.
Forsaken.
Fruited Month, The.
Last Words of Don Henriquez, The.
Like Water down a Slope.
Middle Ages Draw Near!, The.
Poppies.
Road, The.
Song of the Snow.
War Comes.
Welcome, Queen Sabbath.

Schneurson [or Mishkovsky], Zelda *See* **"Zelda"**

Schnitzler, Arthur
Sayings in Verse.

Schnüffis, Laurentius von
Praise, Oh You Heavens, the Highest on High.

Schoenberger, Nancy (b. 1950)
Epithalamion.

Scholasticus, Agathias *See* **Agathias**

Scholl, J. W.
Gooing babies, helpless pygmies.

Schomberg, Ralph (1714–92)
Judgment of Paris, The.

Schonborg, Virginia (b. 1913)
Rumble, A.

Schoolcraft, Jane Johnston (1800–41)
Otagamiad.

Schreiber, Ron (b. 1934)
Alarming New Development, An.
House Is Old, The.

Schreiner, Olive (1855–1920)
Cry of South Africa, The.

Schubert, David (1913–46)
It Is Sticky in the Subway.
Monterey.
No Title.
Prospect Park.

Successful Summer, A.
Victor Record Catalog.

Schulman, Grace
American Solitude.
Burial of a Fisherman in Hydra.
Crossing the Square.
False Move.
New Netherland, 1654.
Notes from Underground: W. H. Auden on the
Lexington Avenue IRT.
Prayer.
Two Trees.

Schultz, Philip (b. 1945)
Bar Mitzvah, The.
For My Father.
For the Wandering Jews.
I'm Not Complaining.

Schultz, Robert (b.1951)
She Speaks to Her Husband, Asleep.

Schulzová, Eva (1931–43)
Evening in Terezin, An.

Schuyler, James (1923–91)
Along Overgrown Paths.
Buried at Springs.
Crocus Night.
Crystal Lithium, The.
Elizabethans Called It Dying, The.
Father or Son.
February.
Freely Espousing.
Greetings from the Chateau.
Growing Dark.
Head, A.
I Think.
Korean Mums.
Letter to a Friend: Who Is Nancy Daum?
Man in Blue, A.
Master of the Golden Glow, The.
Noon Office.
Our Father.
Red Brick and Brown Stone.
Reserved Sacrament.
Roof Garden.
Royals.
Salute.
Self-Pity Is a Kind of Lying, Too.
Shimmer.
Sleep.
Song: "I'm about to go shopping."
Sunday.
Tom.
View, A.

Schwartz, Arthur
Alone Together.
Blue Grass.
Dancing in the Dark.
Haunted Heart.
I Guess I'll Have to Change My Plan.
I See Your Face before Me.
If There Is Someone Lovelier than You.
It's All Yours.
Make the Man Love Me.
Rhode Island Is Famous for You.
Something to Remember You By.
That's Entertainment.
Then I'll Be Tired of You.
They're Either Too Young or Too Old.
Triplets.
You and the Night and the Music.

Schwartz, Delmore (1913–66)
Abraham.
All Clowns Are Masked.
All of us always turning away for solace.
Ballet of the Fifth Year, The.
Baudelaire.
Beautiful American Word, Sure, The.
Darkling Summer, Ominous Dusk, Rumorous
Rain.
Do the Others Speak of Me Mockingly,
Maliciously?
Dogs Are Shakespearean, Children Are
Strangers.
Far Rockaway.
For the One Who Would Take Man's Life in
His Hands.
Heavy Bear Who Goes with Me, The.

I Am a Book I neither Wrote nor Read.
I Am Cherry Alive.
In the Naked Bed, in Plato's Cave.
In the Slight Ripple, the Mind Perceives the Heart.
Jacob.
Let Us Consider Where the Great Men Are.
Lincoln.
Look, in the Labyrinth of Memory.
Mind Is an Ancient and Famous Capital, The.
O Child, Do Not Fear the Dark and Sleep's Dark Possession.
Passionate Shepherd to His Love, The.
Prothalamion.
Sarah.
Sonnet on Famous and Familiar Sonnets and Experiences.
Starlight like Intuition Pierced the Twelve.
Time's Dedication.
Tired and Unhappy, You Think of Houses.
Today Is Armistice, a Holiday.
Winter Twilight, Glowing Black and Gold, The.
You Are a Jew!

Schwartz, Hillel
Recruiting Poster.

Schwartz, Jean
Rock-a-Bye Your Baby with a Dixie Melody.

Schwartz, Lloyd (b. 1941)
Leaves.

Schwartz, Perla (b. 1955)
Snapshots of the Chameleon Woman.

Schwartz, Ruth L.
AIDS Education, Seventh Grade.
Can Pigeons Be Heroes?
Edgewater Park.
Falling in Love after Forty.
Flamenco Guitar.
Grief.
Late Summer.
Midnight Supper.
Possible.
When They Know.
Why I Forgive My Younger Self Her Transgressions.

Schwarz, Ida
To a Cloud.

Schwarz, Sibylla (1621–38)
Sonnet: "If love is chaste, what bears adultery?"

Schwerner, Armand
He is not quite dead.
Next Two Tablets, The.
Tablet II.
Tablet V.
Tablet X.
Tablet XV.
Work, The.

Schwitters, Kurt (1887–1948)
Anna Blossom Has Wheels.
Anna Blume.
Desire.
Murder Machine 43.
Third movement.

Schwob, Marcel (1867–1905)
Actions.
Moments.
Things Dead.

Scliar-Cabral, Leonor
Deceiving Words.
Fire and Embers.
Sephirot.

Scollard, Clinton (1860–1932)
As I Came Down from Lebanon.
Bit of Marble, A.

Scollard, Mrs. Clinton See **Rittenhouse, Jessie Belle**

Scott, Alexander (1525?–84)
Coronach.
Hence, heart, with her that must depart.
Letter to Robert Fergusson.
My Heart Is High Above.
Of May.
Return thee, heart.
Rondel of Luve [or Love], A.

To luve unluvit it is ane pane.
Up, Helsum Hairt.
Welcum, illustrat Ladye, and oure Quene!

Scott, Alexander (b. 1920)
Calvinist Sang.
Scotch God / Kent His / Faither.

Scott, Bob
Limerick: "Sky's are a pitiful lot, The."
Limerick: "There was a young girl from Uttoxeter."
Limerick: "There was an old Doctor called Coué."

Scott, David (b. 1947)
Church Boiler, The.
Churchyard under Snow.
Flanking Sheep in Mosedale.
For Norman Nicholson.
Hopkins Enters the Roman Catholic Church.
Illness.
Kirkwall Auction Mart.
Letters from Baron Von Hügel to a Niece.
Locking the Church.
Playing for England.
Scattering Ashes.
Skiddaw House.
Surplice, The.
Winston Churchill.

Scott, Dennis (1939–91)
Apocalypse Dub.
Dreadwalk.
More Poem.

Scott, Diana (b. 1947)
Lucy Taking Birth.
Prayer for the Little Daughter between Death and Burial.
Winter Solstice Poem.

Scott, Duncan Campbell (1862–1947)
At Gull Lake; August, 1810.
At the Cedars.
En Route.
Forsaken, The.
On the Way to the Mission.

Scott, Elizabeth (1708–76)
Now Let Our Hearts Their Glory Wake.
See How the Rising Sun.

Scott, Francis Reginald (1899–1985)
Bangkok.
Brébeuf and His Brethren.
Canadian Authors Meet, The.
Lakeshore.
Laurentian Shield.
Night Club.
W. L. M. K.

Scott, Frederick George (1861–1944)
Sting of Death, The.
Unnamed Lake, The.

Scott, Geoffrey (1884–1924)
All Our Joy Is Enough.
Frutta di Mare.
Hector, the captain bronzed, from simple fight.
What Was Solomon's Mind?

Scott-Heron, Gil (b. 1949)
Revolution Will Not Be Televised!, The.
Winter in America.

Scott, John A. (b. 1948)
Changing Room.
Helen Paints a Room (1984)
Plato's Dog.
Typing the Letters.

Scott, Lady John (1810–1900)
Ettrick.

Scott, Margaret (b. 1934)
Portrait of a Married Couple.

Scott, Mary (1752?–93)
On Anna Laetitia Aikin.
On Elizabeth Montagu.
Women of the Future.

Scott, Maurice
I've Got Rings on My Fingers.

Scott of Amwell, John (1730–83)
Ode: "I hate that drum's discordant sound."
Ode: Written after Reading Some Modern Love-Verses.

Scott, Peter Dale (b. 1929)
Argenteuil County.

Loon's Egg, The.

Scott, Robert Balgarnie Young (1899–1987)
O Day of God, Draw Nigh.

Scott, W. N. (b. 1923)
Bundaberg Rum.

Scott, Sir Walter (1771–1832)
Bonny [or Bonnie] Dundee.
Charge at Waterloo.
Chase, The.
Datur Hora Quieti.
Dreary Change, The.
Fire, The.
Fitz-Eustace's Song.
Flowers and Trees.
Hie Away, Hie Away.
Hour with Thee, An.
Hunting Song.
Jock of Hazeldean.
Lady of the Lake, The, sels.
Lay of the Last Minstrel, sels.
Lochinvar.
Love.
Lucy Ashton's Song.
MacGregor's Gathering.
Maid of Neidpath, The.
Marmion, sels.
Melrose Abbey.
Minstrel, The.
Nativity Chant, The.
Nelson, Pitt, Fox.
On Having Piles.
Oyster, The.
Peveril of the Peak, sels.
Pibroch of Donuil Dhu.
Proud Maisie.
Red Harlaw.
Rosabelle.
Serenade, A: "Ah! County Guy, the hour is nigh."
Soldier Rest! [Thy Warfare O'er].
Sound, Sound the Clarion.
To a Lock of Hair.
To-Day I Leave Mrs. Brown's Lodgings.
Youth! Thou Wear'st to Manhood Now.

Scott, William Bell (1812–90)
Continuity of Life.
Death.
Early Aspirations.
Garland for Advancing Years, A.
Music.
My Mother.
Rhyme of the Sun-Dial, A.
Witch's Ballad, The.

Scott, Winfield Townley (1910–68)
Annual Legend.
Crocus Air.
Five for the Grace of Man.
Flowering Quince.
Mr. Whittier.
Mrs. Severin.
O Lyric Love.
U.S. Sailor with the Japanese Skull, The.
Winslow Homer.

Scovel, Myra
Silence, The.

Scovell, Edith Jay (b. 1907)
After Midsummer.
Boy Fishing, The.
Days Drawing In.
Ghosts, The.
Listening to Collared Doves.
Past Time.
River Steamer, The.
Sandy Yard, The.
Shadows of Chrysanthemums.
Stream, The.
Swan's Feet, The.
Tidal River, The.
Well, The.

Scrimgeour, James R.
Lines Started outside Filene's Basement.

Scriven, Joseph
Unfailing Friend, The.

Scudder, Antoinette (b. 1898, d. after 1949)
Tea Making.

Scudder, Eliza (1821–96)
Thou Grace Divine, Encircling All.

Thou Long Disowned, Reviled, Oppressed.

Scully, James (b. 1937)
Glass Blower, The.
Midsummer.

Scully, Maurice (b. 1952)
Variations.

Scully, W. C. (1855–1943)
'Nkongane.

Scupham, Peter (b. 1933)
After Ovid, Tristia.
Although you never asked to come with me.
Beach, The.
Birthday Triptych.
Key, The.
Nondescript, The.
Pompeii: Plaster Casts.
Service.
Twelfth Night.

Scurfield, George
Bitter Mangoes, The.

Scythinus
Calamity and conflagration! Strife!

Se Praj (fl. 17th cent.)
Your breasts will not fall.

Seager, Jane (fl. 1589)
Lybica.
To Queen Elizabeth.

Seagrave, Artis (fl. 18th cent.)
Let All Created Things.

Seale, Jane Epton
Playing the Flute for the TMR Class.

Seaman, E. William (b. 1927)
Double Dactyls.

Seaman, Sir Owen (1861–1936)
Ballad of a Bun, A.
Birthday Ode to Mr. Alfred Austin, A.
England Expects?
England's Alfred Abroad.
Nocturne at Danieli's, A.
Plea for Trigamy, A.
Sitting Bard, The.
To a Boy-Poet of the Decadence.

Sears, Edmund Hamilton (1810–76)
Calm, on the Listening Ear of Night.
It Came upon the Midnight Clear.

Sears, Peter
One Polar Bear, The.
Volcanic Ash.

Sears, Vickie
Pubescence at 39.

Seaton, Maureen
Blonde Ambition.
Cannibal Women in the Avocado Jungle of Death.
Fear of Shoplifting.
Fear of Subways.
Fiddleheads.
Ice.
Malleus Maleficarum 4.
Man Who Killed Himself to Avoid August, The.
Nostradamus Predicts the Destruction of Chicago.
Story of Stonewall, A.
Tagging.
Wings.

Seaver, Edwin (b. 1900)
To My People.

Seay, James (b. 1939)
Audubon Drive, Memphis.
Johnny B. Goode.

'Secundus, Johannes' (Jan Nicolai Everaerts) (1511–36)
Kisses, The.
Not always give a melting kiss.

Sedakova, Olga
Female Figure.
Fifth Stanzas. De Arte Poetica.
Grasshopper and the Cricket, The.

Sedley, Sir Charles (1639–1701)
Child and Maiden.
Marriage and Money.
On a Cock at Rochester.
On Fruition.

On the Happy Corydon and Phyllis.
Out of French.
See! Hymen comes; how his torch blazes!
Song: "Hears not my Phillis how the birds."
Song: "Love still has something of the sea."
Song: "Phillis is my only joy."
Song: "Phillis, let's shun the common fate."
Song to Celia.
To Cloris.
To Nysus.
To Scilla.
To Sergius.

Sedulius Scottus (d. 858 A.D.)
Apologia pro Vita Sua.
Battle is joined on the open plain.
Death of a Ram.
Heavens, ocean, and all earth, rejoice!
Nunc Viridant Segetes.
Request for Meat and Drink.

See, Patti
Shotgun.

Seed, John
During War, the Timeless Air.
'From Escomb, County Durham': July 1990.
Sofia.
This Curious Involvement, a Dominant Species.

Seeger, Alan (1888–1916)
I Have a Rendezvous with Death.

Seeger, Pete
Where Have All the Flowers Gone?

Seferis, George (1900–71)
Argonautica.
Bottle in the Sea.
Day was cloudy, The. No one could come to a decision.
Days of April '43.
Euripides the Athenian.
Interlude of Joy.
Last Day, The.
Last Stop.
Mathios Paskalis among the Roses.
Memory 1.
Memory 2.
Narration.
Old Man on the River Bank, An.
Our Sun.
Poplar Leaf, The.
Stratis the Sailor by the Dead Sea.
Word for Summer, A.

Segal, Jack (b. 1918)
I Keep Going Back to Joe's.
Nothing Ever Changes My Love for You.
When Sunny Gets Blue.
Wind in the Willow.

Segalen, Victor (1878–1919)
Hidden Name.

Segers, Michael
In the eggshell after the chick has hatched.

Seibert, T. Lawrence
Casey Jones.

Seibles, Tim
Manic: A Conversation with Jimi Hendrix.
Who.

Seidel, Frederick (b. 1936)
Fucking.
Scotland.
To Robert Lowell and Osip Mandelstam.

Seidman, Hugh (b. 1946)
Bleecker Street.
Composition.
Dirt to Dirt.
End.
Gail.
Laureate.
Making of Color, The.
Modes of Vallejo Street, San Diego, Los Angeles, The.
Photos.
Poem: "War and greed stop food."
Stroke.
Tale of Genji.

Seiferle, Rebecca
Catch, The.
Mother Tongue.

Welcome to Ithaca.

Seifert, Jaroslav (1901–86)
Candlestick, The.
Never Again.

Seifū (1650–1721)
Faces of dolls, The.

Seigan Soi (d. 1661)
Joy of living.

Seigen-yuiin
How vast karma.

Seiho
Sky's not high, earth not solid.

Seiju (d. 1776)
Not even for a moment.
Water veins.

Seiken-Chiju
Twenty years a pilgrim.

Seiler, Barry (b. 1946)
Digging in the Streets of Gold.

Seira (d. 1791)
Boarding the boat.

Seisa (d. 1722)
My body, useless.

Seisetsu Shucho (d. 1820)
My hour draws near and I am still alive.

Seishu (d. 1817)
Rain clouds clear away.

Sekioku-Seikyo
This body won't pollute.

Sekishitsu-Soei
Fifty-three years.

Sekula, Sonia (1918–63)
Womb.

Selerie, Gavin
23.
47.
52.

Seligman, Ulma (fl. 16th–17th cent.)
Truth Has Perished.

Sellar, W. C. *See* **Yeatman, R. J.**

Sellers, Bettie M. (b. 1926)
In the Counselor's Waiting Room.

Selman, Robyn
21 East 10th, 2BR, WBF, EIK.
Descent.
Exodus.
For the Field.
Work Song.

Seltzer, George R. (1902–74)
Come, All Ye People.

Selvinsky [or Sel'vinskii], Ilya [or Karl] L'vovich (1899–1968)
I Saw It!
Mighty Ocean, The.
Portrait of My Mother.
Reader of Poetry, The.
Sebastopol.

Selyns, Henricus (1636–1701)
Epitaph for Peter Stuyvesant.
O Christmas Night.
Of Scolding Wives and the Third Day Ague.
On Maids and Cats.
On Mercenary and Unjust Bailiffs.
Reasons for and against Marrying Widows.
Upon the Bankruptcy of a Physician.

Semeonoff, B. and C. Semeonoff
Limerick: "There once was a flock of wild geese."

Semeonoff, C. *See* **Semeonoff, B.**

Semonides
God in His Wisdom from the start.

Sempill, Francis (1616–82)
Maggie Lauder.
Pox fa that pultron Povertie.

Sempill, Robert (c.1595–c.1665)
Life and Death of [Habbie Simson] the Piper of Kilbarchan, The.

Sempo (d. 1730)
Deep in the underbrush.

Sen, Rāmprasād (c.1718–75)
At last I have a way to understand.
Black clouds have risen in my sky.
Brother / This world.

Can someone.
Death, get out of here!
Her face.
Hey, it's not wine I drink.
Hey! Who is She, dark as clouds.
How wonderful! Look what.
I came to this world.
I have learned.
I'll die of mental anguish.
It's not Siva.
It's silly to hope for Father's wealth.
Kali, Ma.
Kulakundalini, Goddess Full of Brahman, Tara.
Let me tell You a thing or two, Tara.
Look here.
Love Her, Mind.
Ma, You're inside me.
Managing the house is a big problem.
Meditate on Kali! Why be anxious?
Mind, don't be duped by others' sneers.
Mind, how do you think you'll find Her?
Mind, why this separation from the Mother's feet?
Mind, you're still not rid of your illusions.
Mother, make me Your treasurer.
My Mind.
My Mind, my helmsman.
Oh Kali Full of Brahman!
Oh Mind, you don't know how to farm.
Oh my Mind, worship Kali.
Oh my Mind! You're just spinning.
So, Mind / You've decided to go on pilgrimage?
Supreme Savior of Sinners.
Tara, what more are You planning?
Tell me.
This is a fine mess.
This time I've realized the essence.
This time, Kali.
Tongue, call out.
Wait a minute, Death.
What a joke!
What's the fault of the poor mind?
Who can understand Kali?
Who is that Syama woman.
World-Mother's police chief, The.
World's a shoreless ocean, The.

Sen, Samar (b. 1916)
Love.
Solitary.

Senard, Jacqueline
Polar.

Senchojo (d. 1802)
I cup my ears.

Seneca (4 B.C.–A.D. 65)
After Death Nothing Is.
Britannia, free from foes and foreign kings.
Chorus.
Climb at court for me that will.
Deaths of Orpheus and Hercules, The.
Flee every friendship and live: a greater truth.
Let him that will, ascend the tottering seat.
Let oken club now strike, and poast of might.
Let other mount aloft, let other sore.
Let who so lyst with mighty mace to raygne.
Medea's Frenzy.
O barbarous Corsica, locked in by crags.
O yee, whome lorde of lande and waters wyde.
Stand [or Stond] who so list upon the slipper top[pe].
This said, she twirled the thread on an ugly spool.
Trojan Women.
Upon the slippery tops of human[e] state.
Voracious Time, uprooting all, consumes it.

Senesh, Hannah (1921–44)
Blessed Match, The.
One—Two—Three.

Seng-ts'an (d. 606 A.D.)
Mind of Absolute Trust, The.

Sengai Gibon (1750–1837)
He who comes knows only his coming.
If you say, Come back later.
On Basho's 'Frog.'
Young bride.

Senghor, Léopold Sédar (b. 1906)
After this day's hope—see how the Somme,

the Seine, and the wild Slav.
African Image Is Not An Image by Equation, The.
All Day Long.
Be Not Amazed.
Before Night Comes.
Black Woman.
Blues.
Camp 1940.
Elephant of Moissel, hear my pious prayer.
French Garden.
I Am Alone.
I Know Not When It Was.
I walked you to the village where the granaries are at the threshold of Night.
I Want to Say Your Name.
I Will Pronounce Your Name.
In Memoriam.
Joal.
Kaya-Magan, The.
Long, long between your hands you held the warrior's black face.
Lord God, forgive white Europe!
Lord Jesus, at the end of this book which I offer you.
Luxembourg 1939.
Man and Beast.
Midnight Elegy.
Negro Mask.
Night of Sine.
Nocturne (I Accompanied You)
Nocturne (She Flies She Flies)
On the Appeal from the Race of Sheba: II.
Paris in the Snow.
Pearls.
Porte Dorée.
Prayer to the Masks.
Song of the Initiate.
Songs for a Three-String Guitar.
Speech and Image: An African Tradition of the Surreal.
Suddenly Startled.
Taga for Mbaye Dyôb.
To New York.
Totem.
Visit.
We Delighted, My Friend.
We shall bathe, my love, in an African presence.
You Held the Black Face.
Your face, the beauty of a time long past evokes the perfumed robes in faded hues.

Senior, Olive (b. 1943)
Brief Lives.
Meditation on Yellow.
Together, babe, we could have had the world sewn up.

Senkei (d. 1775)
Somehow or other.

Senryu (d. 1827)
Like dewdrops.

Senryu (d. 1818)
Willow tree in fall, A.

Senryu (d. 1790)
Bitter winds of winter.

Senseki (d. 1742)
At long last I am leaving.

Sentoku (d. 1726)
Like ice in storage.

Sepamla, Sipho (b. 1932)
Civilization Aha.
If.
Law That Says, The.
Measure for Measure.
Odyssey, The.
On Judgement Day.
I Remember Sharpeville.
Silence: 2.
Talk to the Peach Tree.
When I Lost Slum Life.

Sepúlveda-Pulvirenti, Emma (b. 1950)
From Now Until Chile.
September 11, 1973.
To the Child That Never Was.

Serapion of Alexandria (c.200–150 B.C.)
This is the skull of a hard-working man.

Serge, Victor (1890–1947)
Asphyxiated Man, The.
Constellation of Dead Brothers.
Dialectic.
Hands.

Sergeant, Howard (b. 1914)
Inundation, The.
Man Meeting Himself.

Serote, Mongane Wally (b. 1944)
Alexandria.
Another Alexandra.
Breezing Dawn of the New Day, The.
City Johannesburg.
Death Survey.
Growing, The.
Hell, Well, Heaven.
Ofay-Watcher Looks Back.
Poem, A: "Gasp sounded, The."
This Old Woman.

Serraillier, Ian (b. 1912)
After Ever Happily or, The Princess and the Woodcutter.
Anne and the Field-Mouse.
Mouse in the Wainscot, The.
Old Sussex Road, The.
Tickle Rhyme, The.

Servasius, Sulpicius Lupercus (4th cent. A.D.)
Rivers level granite mountains.

Service, Robert W. (1874–1958)
Cremation of Sam McGee, The.
Inspiration.
Pot of Tea, A.
Shooting of Dan McGrew, The.
Woman and the Angel, The.

Seshadri, Vijay
Lifeline.
Scholar, The.

Seth, Vikram (b. 1952)
Doctor's Journal Entry for August 6, 1945, A.
God's Love.
How ugly babies are! How heedless.
Pigeons.
Week ago, when I had finished, A.

Seto, Thelma
Blood Ties.
Jihad.

Setsudo (d. 1776)
Now then.

"Seuss, Dr." (Theodore Seuss Geisel) (b. 1904)
Too Many Daves.

Sevelingen, Meinloh von (fl. c.1170)
My Eyes Have Seen and Chosen.
Woe Then to the Gossips.

"Severyanin [or Severianin], Igor" (Igor' Vasilievich Lotaryov) (1887–1941)
Epilogue: "I, the genius Severyanin."
Lilac Ice Cream.
Minor Elegy, A.
Prologue: "Mirra Lokhvitskaia's ashes are now entombed."
Russian Woman.
Same Old Way, The.
Spring Day.

Sewall, Samuel (1652–1730)
Once More, Our God, Vouchsafe to Shine!
This Morning Tom Child, the Painter, Died.
To Be Engraven on a Dial.
To the Rev'd Mr. Jno. Sparhawk on the Birth of his Son.
Upon the Springs Issuing out from the Foot of Plimouth Beach.

Seward, Anna (1742–1809)
Behold that tree, in Autumn's dim decay.
By Derwent's rapid stream as oft I strayed.
December Morning.
Eyam.
Farewell, false Friend!—our scenes of kindness close!
In every breast affection fires, there dwells.
In scenes paternal, not beheld through years.
Invocation, to the Genius of Slumber Written Oct. 1787.
Lake, The; Or, Modern Improvement in Landscape.
Old Cat's Dying Soliloquy, An.

On a Lock of Miss Sarah Seward's Hair Who
   Died in Her Twentieth Year.
On Catania and Syracuse Swallowed Up by an
   Earthquake, from the Italian of Filicaja.
On the damp margin of the sea-beat shore.
On the fleet streams, the Sun, that late arose.
On the Use of New and Old Words in Poetry.
Scene of superfluous grace, and wasted bloom.
Seek not, my Lesbia, the sequestered dale.
Sonnet 31.
Sonnet: "From a rived tree, that stands beside
   the grave."
Sonnet: Ingratitude.
Sonnet: "Stranger, when o'er yon slant, warm
   field no cloud."
Sonnet Written from an Eastern Apartment in
   the Bishop's Palace at Lichfield, Which
   Commands a View of Stowe Valley.
Speech of the Nymph.
To a Friend, Who Thinks Sensibility a
   Misfortune.
To a Young Lady, Purposing to Marry a Man
   of Immoral Character in the Hope of His
   Reformation.
To Colebrooke Dale.
To Honora Sneyd.
To Mr. Henry Cary, on the Publication of His
   Sonnets.
To the Poppy.
To Time Past.
Verses Inviting Stella to Tea on the Public
   Fast-Day.
When Life's realities the Soul perceives.
While neighbouring cities waste the fleeting
   hours.
While one sere leaf, that parting autumn yields.
Written December 1790.

Sewell, Elizabeth (b. 1919)
   Job.
Sewell, George (1688–1726)
   Dying Man in His Garden, The.
Sewell, Lisa (b. 1960)
   Denied, The.
   Expulsion.
   Release.
Sexton, Anne (1928–74)
   Abortion, The.
   All My Pretty Ones.
   And One for My Dame.
   Author of the Jesus Papers Speaks, The.
   Boat, The.
   Child Bearers, The.
   Cinderella.
   Consorting with Angels.
   Crossing the Atlantic.
   End, Middle, Beginning.
   For My Lover, Returning to His Wife.
   From the Garden.
   Funnel.
   Furies, The.
   Fury of Abandonment, The.
   Fury of Beautiful Bones, The.
   Fury of Cocks, The.
   Fury of Earth, The.
   Fury of Flowers and Worms, The.
   Fury of God's Good-bye, The.
   Fury of Guitars and Sopranos, The.
   Fury of Hating Eyes, The.
   Fury of Jewels and Coal, The.
   Fury of Overshoes, The.
   Fury of Sundays, The.
   Fury of Sunrises, The.
   Fury of Sunsets, The.
   Her Kind.
   Housewife.
   How We Danced.
   I Remember.
   In Celebration of My Uterus.
   In the Deep Museum.
   January 1st.
   Jesus Asleep.
   Jesus Dies.
   Jesus Suckles.
   Jesus Unborn.
   Lament: "Someone is dead."
   Letter Written on a Ferry while Crossing Long
      Island Sound.
   Little Girl, My String Bean, My Lovely
      Woman.
   Lobster.
   Moss of His Skin, The.
   Music Swims Back to Me.
   Noon Walk on the Asylum Lawn.
   Nude Swim, The.
   Red Roses.
   Ringing the Bells.
   Risk, The.
   Room of My Life, The.
   Rowing.
   Self in 1958.
   Sixth Psalm.
   Small Wire.
   Snow White and the Seven Dwarfs.
   Some Foreign Letters.
   Somewhere in Africa.
   Starry Night, The.
   Sylvia's Death.
   That Day.
   Third Psalm.
   To a Friend Whose Work Has Come to
      Triumph.
   Truth the Dead Know, The.
   Unknown Girl in the Maternity Ward.
   Us.
   Wanting to Die.
   Welcome Morning.
   What's That.
   With Mercy for the Greedy.
   You, Doctor Martin.
Sexton, Tom
   Seal Island.
   Skimming the Ice.
Seyburn, Patty (b. 1962)
   Good Water.
   Persuasion.
   You and Them.
**Seymour, Frances, Countess of Hertford (1699–
   1754)**
   Life at Richkings.
   Story of Inkle and Yarico, The.
Seymour, Jane (1541–61)
   This sacred urn holds the ashes of the Queen
      of Navarre.
Seymour-Smith, Martin (b. 1928)
   He Came to Visit Me.
   What Schoolmasters Say.
**Seymour, Sir Thomas (Baron Seymour of
   Sudeley) (1508?–49)**
   Forgetting God.
Shaben, Sekeena
   Fourteenth Ode.
   Tempest.
   Thirteenth Ode.
Shafer, Audrey
   Gurney Tears.
   Monday Morning.
Shagai (d. 1795)
   Reality is flowerlike.
Shahid (Roosevelt Williamson) (b. 1951)
   Letters Come to Prison.
**"Shahryar" (Akhlaq Mohammad Khan) (b.
   1936)**
   Still Life.
Shaka, King of the Zulus (1787–1828)
   Battle Song.
Shakespeare, William See also **Fletcher, John**
Shakespeare, William (1564–1616)
   All's Well That Ends Well, *sels.*
   Antony and Cleopatra, *sels.*
   As You Like It, *sels.*
   Comedy of Errors, The, *sels.*
   Coriolanus, *sels.*
   Cymbeline, *sels.*
   Hamlet, *sels.*
   Julius Caesar, *sels.*
   King Henry IV, Pt. I, *sels.*
   King Henry IV, Pt. II, *sels.*
   King Henry V, *sels.*
   King Henry VI, Pt. I, *sels.*
   King Henry VI, Pt. II, *sels.*
   King Henry VI, Pt. III, *sels.*
   King John, *sels.*
   King Lear, *sels.*
   King Richard II, *sels.*
   King Richard III, *sels.*
   Love's Labour's Lost, *sels.*
   Macbeth, *sels.*
   Measure for Measure, *sels.*
   Merchant of Venice, The, *sels.*
   Midsummer Night's Dream, A, *sels.*
   Much Ado about Nothing, *sels.*
   Othello, *sels.*
   Pericles, *sels.*
   Phoenix and the Turtle, *sels.*
   Rape of Lucrece, *sels.*
   Romeo and Juliet, *sels.*
   Sonnets, *sels.*
   Taming of the Shrew, The, *sels.*
   Tempest, The, *sels.*
   Timon of Athens, *sels.*
   Troilus and Cressida, *sels.*
   Twelfth Night, *sels.*
   Two Gentlemen of Verona, *sels.*
   Venus and Adonis, *sels.*
   Winter's Tale, The, *sels.*
Shakhova, Elizaveta (1821–99)
   Autobiographical Response from a Provincial
      Wasteland (in Reply to a New Year's
      Greeting Sent with a Bouquet)
Shalamov, Varlam Tikhonovich (1907–82)
   Pegasus.
Shalom, Shin (b. 1904)
   At Evening when Flicker.
   Drink Wonder.
   Guard Me, Oh God.
   In the World's Heart Burns a Torch of Fire.
   Stoker, The.
   Suddenly We Will Wake.
   They That Sow at Night.
Shamaqmaq, Abu (fl. 770)
   Hungry Master and Hungry Cat.
Shange, Ntozake (b. 1948)
   About Atlanta.
   Ancestral Messengers / Composition 13.
   At 4:30 A.M. / she rose.
   Bocas: A Daughter's Geography.
   Dark Phrases.
   Different Love Poem / We Need a Change, A.
   Dream of Pairing.
   Elegance in the Extreme.
   I Live in Music.
   It's Not so Good to Be Born a Girl /
      Sometimes.
   No More Love Poems #1.
   Oh, I'm 10 Months Pregnant.
   Nappy Edges.
   Nappy Edges (A Cross Country Sojourn)
   Frank Albert and Viola Benzena Owens.
   Somebody almost walked off wid alla my stuff.
   Tango.
   We Need a God Who Bleeds Now.
   Where the Heart Is.
   Where the Mississippi Meets the Amazon.
   You Are Sucha Fool.
Shanks, Edward Richard Burton (1892–1953)
   Drilling in Russell Square.
   Going In to Dinner.
   High Germany.
   Sleeping Heroes.
Shao Yung (1011–77)
   Arriving in Lo-yang Again.
   Song of Delight.
   Song on Being Too Lazy to Get Up.
   Thoughts on T'ien-chin Bridge.
Shaoxuan, Cui
   Black hair and red cheeks: for how long?
Shapcott, Jo (b. 1953)
   I am always behind.
Shapcott, Thomas William (b. 1935)
   Autumn.
   Bicycle Rider, The.
   Blue Paisley Shirt, The.
   City of Home, The.
   Flying Fox.
   June Fugue.
   Litanies of Julia Pastrana (1832–1860), The.
   Near the School for Handicapped Children.

Piano Pieces.
Post Operative.
Sestina with Refrain.
Shadow of War, 1941.
Turning Fifty.

Shapiro, Alan (b. 1952)
Basement, The.
Christmas Story, A.
Familiar Story.
Mezuzah.

Shapiro, David (b. 1947)
Archaic Torsos.
Book of Glass, A.
Canticle.
Commentary Text Commentary Text
 Commentary Text.
Counter-Example, The.
House (Blown Apart)
In a Blind Garden.
Lord I Sleep and I Sleep.
Old Poems.
Pin's Fee, or Painting with Star, A.
Realistic Bar and Grill, A.
Song of the Eiffel Tower.
Tracing of an Evening.
Traumerei.
Weak Poet, The.

Shapiro, Harvey (b. 1924)
6/20/97.
Bible Lesson.
Death of a Grandmother.
Feast of the Ram's Horn.
For Paul Celan and Primo Levi.
Loyalty.
Mountain, Fire, Thornbush.
National Cold Storage Company.

Shapiro, Karl (1913–2000)
151st Psalm, The.
All Tropic Places Smell of Mold.
Alphabet, The.
Aubade: "What dawn is it?"
Auto Wreck.
Bourgeois poet closes the door of his study and
 lights his pipe, The.
California Winter.
Confirmation, The.
Conscientious Objector, The.
Crossing Lincoln Park.
Cut Flower, A.
Dirty Word, The.
Dome of Sunday, The [or A].
Drug Store.
Each in her well-lighted picture window,
 reading a book or magazine.
Editing *Poetry*.
Elegy for a Dead Soldier.
Elegy for Two Banjos.
Exile.
First Time, The.
Fly, The.
Full Moon: New Guinea.
Funeral of Poetry, The.
Geographers, The.
Girls Working in Banks.
Going to School.
Haircut.
Hollywood.
Homecoming.
Hospital.
I Am an Atheist Who Says His Prayers.
I drove three thousand miles to ask a question.
 No answer, naturally.
Jew at Christmas Eve, The.
Leg, The.
Look of shock on an old friend's face after
 years of not meeting, The.
Love for a Hand.
Lower the Standard: That's My Motto.
Manhole Covers.
Midnight Show.
My Father's Funeral.
My Grandmother.
Nigger.
Nostalgia.
October 1.
Of love and death in the Garrison State I sing.

Oriental, you give and give. No Christian ever
 gave like you.
Piano Tuner's Wife, The.
Poet.
Prophets say to Know Thyself: I say it can't be
 done, The.
Puritan, The.
Quintana lay in the shallow grave of coral.
Recapitulations.
Recognition of Eve, The.
Rice around the lingam stone will be
 distributed in the dying sun, The.
Sickness of Adam, The.
Teachers of culture hate science but the
 teachers of science do not hate culture, The.
Terminal.
To make the child in your own image is a
 capital crime.
Travelogue for Exiles.
Troop Train.
Twins, The.
Two-Year-Old Has Had a Motherless Week,
 The.
University.
V-Letter.
Waiting in Front of the Columnar High School.
World is my dream, says the wise child, ever
 so wise, The.

Shapiro, Myra
To Jerusalem, 1990.

Shapiro, Ted
If I Had You.

Sharah, Jemal (b. 1969)
Package for Another World.
Parting Roundel.

Share, Don
Divorced.

Sharkey, Michael (b. 1946)
Greenwood's.
Hots, The.

Sharma, B. C. Ramachandra
American Tourist.

Sharma, Prageeta
Action-Packed Sonnet.
Performance Test.
Poorly Matched.
Potter's Field.
Principles, When I Felt Them.
Transit.

Sharman, Ruth
By Heart.

Sharp, Saundra (b. 1942)
Good Nights.
In the Tradition of Bobbitt.
Tribal Marks.

Sharpe, R. L.
Bag of Tools, A.

Sharples, Pita (b. 1941)
Haka: The Blossoming.
Space Invaders Machine, The.

Sharpless, Stanley J. (b. 1910)
Chaucer: The Wogan's Tale.
Costa Geriatrica.
Does That Answer Your Question, Mr
 Shakespeare?
Go to the Ant.
Hamlet.
In Praise of Cocoa, Cupid's Nightcap.
Limerick: "Albert Einstein's the man we must
 credit."
Limerick: "April. Bad month. Visit spa."
Limerick: "Archimedes, the early truth-seeker."
Limerick: "In Illyria, the love-sick Orsino."
Limerick: "Let the eugenist reach for his gun!"
Limerick: "'We're not amused,' said Victoria."
Limerick: "Marconi, whose ardour was
 tireless."
Limerick: "Monsieur Gauguin? 'E's gone to
 Tahiti."
Limerick: "Ninety summers—and never a
 platitude."
Limerick: "Said a herring one day to a sole."
Limerick: "Said Orville to Wilbur 'Hold
 tight!'"
Limerick: "Smile on the famed Mona Lisa,

 The."
Limerick: "There was a young girl from
 Uttoxeter / Who sported a tight-fitting
 baroque sweater."
Limerick: "There was a young girl of Uttoxeter
 / Who worked nine to five as a choc-setter."
Limerick: "There was a young lady of Ulva /
 Whose boy-friend said: 'Look, I will
 pulver.'"
Limerick: "There was a young lady. . .tut, tut!"
Limerick: "Widow (conscious that time's on
 the wing)"
Low Church.
Moment of Eschatological Doubt, A.
Paradise Lost as a Haiku.
Pied Beauty.
Sonnet: "How do I hate you? Let me count the
 ways."
There's a Breathless Hush on the Centre Court.

Sharyu (d. mid-19th cent.)
I have gone through.

Shaughnessy, Brenda (b. 1970)
Postfeminism.
Rise.
Your One Good Dress.

Shauqi, Ahmad (1869–1932)
Andalusian Exile, An.
Bois de Boulogne.
Thoughts on Schoolchildren.

Shaw, Angela (b. 1967)
April.
Bird Nests.
Crepuscule.
Pornography.
Rear Window.
Small Pleasures.

Shaw, Arthur
Limerick: "Certain young pate who was
 addle, A."
Limerick: "Chap was so pose that was adi, A."
Limerick: "In gonia once which was Pata."
Limerick: "Nice pot of gold that was mari, A."

Shaw, Charles (b. 1892)
Search, The.

Shaw, Dunstan
Retrospection.

Shaw, Frances
Who Loves the Rain.

Shaw, Luci (b. 1928)
Craftsman.
For They Shall See God.
Getting inside the Miracle.
Groundhog, The.
It is as if infancy were the whole of
 incarnation.
Man Cannot Name Himself.
Need Is Our Name.
Onlookers.
Reluctant Prophet.
Stars in Apple Cores.
To a Christmas Two-Year-Old.

Shaw, Robert B. (b. 1916)
Gargoyle.
Grass Widows.

Shaw, Robert B. (b. 1947)
Shut In.

Shaw, Stanley
Christopher Smart.

Shayo (d. 1776)
Hold on!

**Shchapova, Yelena [or Elena] Sergeievna,
 Countess de Carli (b. 1950)**
Smells.

Shcherbina, Tatiana (b. 1954)
Eros Poesis.
Stepmother, The.
Still-Life.
Whole city seductively lit up, The.

**Shchipachov [or Shchipachiov], Stepan Petrovich
 (1899–1980)**
Blue spaces do not see themselves, The.
Little Birch Tree, The.

**Shchirovsky [or Shchirovskii], Vladimir (1909–
 41)**
Dance of the Soul.

I don't enclose the universe in my grasp.
I really don't want to die now.
Shea, Martin
Bolted space.
Caught shoplifting.
Held it.
Long night, The.
Moving.
Red-flashing lights.
Sparrows sunning.
Terminal.
Those corner winds.
Through the wall.
Walk's end.
Warehouse-theatre's.
Shearing, George
Lullaby of Birdland.
Sheehan, Marc J.
My Father's Singing.
Shefatiah, Amittai ben (*fl.* c.900)
Hymn of Weeping.
Sheffield, John, Duke of Buckingham and Normandy (1648–1721)
On One Who Died Discovering Her Kindness.
Reconcilement, The.
Shefner, Vadim Sergeievich (b. 1915)
Forest Fire.
Lily, The.
Shehabi, Deema K.
Breath.
Cemetery at Petit Saconnex, The.
Glistening, The.
Sheikh, Ghulam Mohammed (b. 1937)
Jaisalmer, 1.
Sheldon, Glenn
Blames, for Rane and Diane.
Shelley, Mary Wollstonecraft (1797–1851)
Stanzas: "Oh, come to me in dreams, my love!"
Shelley, Percy Bysshe (1792–1822)
Adonais; An Elegy on the Death of John Keats, *sels.*
Alastor; or, The Spirit of Solitude, *sels.*
As I Lay Asleep in Italy, *sels.*
Autumn: A Dirge.
Aziola, The.
Charles the First, *sels.*
Cloud, The.
Conclusion.
Dirge, A: "Rough wind, that moanest loud."
England in 1819.
Epipsychidion, *sels.*
Feelings of a Republican on the Fall of Bonaparte.
Fragment: "Wake the serpent not—lest he."
From the Arabic: An Imitation.
Hate-Song, A.
Hymn of Pan.
Hymn to Intellectual Beauty.
Indian Serenade, The.
Julian and Maddalo; A Conversation, *sels.*
Lament, A: "O world! O life! O time!"
Lines to a Reviewer.
Lines: "When the lamp is shattered [*or* shatter'd]."
Lines Written in the Bay of Lerici.
Love's Philosophy.
Mask [*or* Masque] of Anarchy, The.
Mont Blanc.
Mutability.
Ode to the West Wind.
On a Painted Woman.
On the Medusa of Leonardo da Vinci in the Florentine Gallery.
Ozymandias.
Peter Bell the Third, *sels.*
Prometheus Unbound [A Lyrical Drama in Four Acts], *sels.*
Question, The.
Revolt of Islam, *sels.*
Sensitive Plant, The.
Similes for Two Political Characters of 1819.
Song: "Rarely, rarely, comest thou."
Song to the Men of England.
Sonnet: Lift Not the Painted Veil.

Sonnet: Political Greatness.
Stanzas—April, 1814.
Stanzas Written in Dejection, near Naples [*or* —December 1818, near Naples].
Summer and Winter.
To a Skylark.
To ——: "I fear thy kisses, gentle maiden."
To ——: "Music, when soft voices die."
To ——: "One word is too often profaned."
To Jane: The Invitation.
To Jane: The keen stars were twinkling.
To Maria Gisborne in England, from Italy.
To Night.
To the Moon.
To Wordsworth.
Tribute to America.
Triumph of Life, The.
Waning Moon, The.
Widow Bird, A.
With a Guitar, to Jane.
World's Great Age, The.
World's Wanderers, The.
Worlds on Worlds.
You are now / In London, that great sea.
Shelton, Richard (b. 1933)
Job the Father.
Letter to a Dead Father.
Promises.
Eden after Dark.
Shelton, Thomas Russell
Patches.
Shen Chou (1427–1509)
Bamboo Villa, The.
Consoling Wu Te-cheng on the Death of His Son.
Drinking at Night with Yen Kung-mou.
Inscribed on a Painting.
Inscribed on the Fan of a Wealthy Old Man.
Lady Picking Flowers, A.
Moon in a Winecup, The.
On the Fifteenth Day of the Seventh Month I Came Home Late from the City.
Painting of Peach Blossom Spring, A.
Paying a Sick-call to Yao Ts'un-tao in the Rain.
Returning Home at Dusk from Town, on the Fifteenth of the Seventh Month.
Sent in Parting to Yen Kung-su.
South of the Bridge.
Taoist Huang Has Died of Alcoholism, The.
Temple of the Ocean of Awakening.
To the Tune "Bamboo at West Lake."
To the Tune "Nan-hsiang-tzu."
White clouds like a scarf enfold the the mountain's waist.
Wine Cup and Bright Moon.
Written on a Landscape Painting in an Album.
Shen Ch'üan (*fl.* 17th cent.)
Therefore We Preserve Life.
Shen Yüeh (441–513)
Farewell to Fan Yun at An Ch'eng.
Fishing Rod, The.
Four Recollections.
Fragrant Tree, The.
Hand in Hand; a Song.
Harmonizing with a Poem by Left Assistant Yu Kao-chih Requesting Sick Leave.
I Say Goodby to Fan An-ch'eng.
I think of when she comes.
Lament for Hsieh T'iao.
Listening to Gibbons at Rock-Pool Creek.
Out Early One Morning, I Met an Old Acquaintance.
Response to Wang Ssu-yüan's Poem on the Moon, A.
Returning to My Garden Home: In Respectful Response to the Master of Hua-yang.
Seeing the Beloved in a Dream.
Six Poems on Remembering.
Song of Woe.
Spending the Night in the Eastern Park.
Wild Geese on the Lake.
Written for My Neighbor.
Shengeli, Georgy [*or* Georgii] Arkadevich (1894–1956)
27 July 1830.

Derzhavin.
Shenstone, William (1714–63)
Elegy 11: "Ah me, my friend! it will not, will not last!"
Hint from Voiture.
Lines Written on a Window at The Leasowes.
On the Clerk of a Country Parish.
School-Mistress, The.
Solemn Meditation, A.
To the Virtuosos.
Written at [*or* in] an Inn at Henley.
Shepard, Jim
Love Song of Audrey.
Shepard, Karen
Birch.
Glom: Labrador, 110 pounds.
Shepard, Ollie (1897–1984)
It's a Low Down Dirty Shame.
Sheperd, Luke (*fl.* 1548)
Who hath not knowne or herd.
Shepherd, Sir Fleetwood (1634–98)
Epitaph on the Duke of Grafton.
Shepherd, Reginald (b. 1963)
Another Version of an Ocean.
Difficult Music, The.
Eros in His Striped Blue Shirt.
Gods at Three A.M., The.
Hygiene.
Lucky One, The.
Man Named Troy, A.
Maritime.
Motive.
Narcissus Learning the Words to This Song.
Provisional.
That Man.
Three A.M. Eternal.
West Willow.
What Cannot Be Kept.
Where When Was.
White Days.
Who Owns the Night and Lease Stars.
Shepherd, Richard
Tribute to Matthew Arnold in a Moment of Self-Abuse, A.
"Shepherd, The Ettrick" *See* Hogg, James
Shepherd, William (1768–1847)
Ode on Lord Macartney's Embassy to China.
Sheppard, Robert (b. 1955)
Empty Diary 1905.
Empty Diary 1936.
Empty Diary 1944.
Empty Diary 1954.
Empty Diary 1968.
Empty Diary 1987.
Empty Diary 1990.
Sherburne, Sir Edward (1618–1702)
And She Washed His Feet with Her Tear[e]s, and Wiped Them with the Hairs of Her Head.
Dream, The.
Weeping and Kissing.
Sheridan, Helen Selina (1807–67)
Charming Woman, The.
Sheridan, Richard Brinsley (1751–1816)
Air: "I ne'er could any lustre see."
Clio's Protest.
Drinking Song.
Geranium, The.
Lines by a Lady on the Loss of Her Trunk.
Oh, the days when I was young.
On Lady Anne Hamilton.
Song: "Give Isaac the nymph who no beauty can boast."
Sheridan, Thomas (*fl.* 1724)
Tom Punsibi's Letter to Dean Swift.
Sherman, Charlotte Watson (b. 1958)
Roots.
Sherman, Frank Dempster (1860–1916)
Baseball.
Blossoms.
Sherman, Maurina
Blackberries.
San Buenaventura.
This Body.

Towards Sunset at Camino Cielo.
Sherrill, Jan-Mitchell
Woodstock.
Sherrill, Steven (b. 1961)
Katyn Forest.
Sherry, James (b. 1946)
Free Radicals.
Hazardous Waste.
Lepidoptery.
Pay Cash Only.
Radiant.
What should be the title of a king. Too, how
also to include. What happened when.
Shershenevich, Vadim Gabrielevich (1893–1942)
Plot with Bitterness.
Sherwin, Judith Johnson (b. 1936)
Gentle Heart, A: Two.
Goddess.
Just.
Light Woman's Song, The.
Nightpiece.
Rhyme for the Child as a Wet Dog.
To Whom it may concern.
Sherwin, Manning
Nightingale Sang in Berkeley Square, A.
Sherwood, Grace Buchanan (b. 1883)
Love and Life.
Satire against Reason and Mankind, A.
Sherwood, Kate Brownlee (1841–1914)
Albert Sidney Johnston.
Sherwood, Robert E. (1896–1955)
Old Hokum Buncombe, The.
Shevin, David (b. 1951)
What He Hated.
Shi-wei, Jiang See "Mang Ke"
Shiba Sonome (1664–1726)
Skies at dawn.
Shibafune, Onoe No
In the spring ravine.
Shidoken (d. 1765)
Returning as it came.
Shiei (d. 1715)
Of such a time as this.
Shiffert, Edith Marcombe (b. 1916)
Manners.
Monkeys on Mt. Hiei.
Shadow of a Branch, The.
Shiffrin, Nancy
Anna's Dream.
Shigan (d. 1838)
Farewell to 'Blessed be.'
Shigenobu (d. 1832)
Willow branch, A.
Shih Shu
Enlightenment.
Shih-te (Pickup) (fl. c.8th cent.)
Far, faraway, steep mountain paths.
I laugh at my failing strength in old age.
Since apes are still able to learn.
You can see the moon's brightness.
Shikaku (d. 1767)
To grass it comes.
Shiki, Prince (668–716)
Full moon ringed, The.
In the winter river.
Just when the sermon.
O autumn winds.
Skylark school, The.
Thunderstorm breaks up, The.
Shikibu, Izumi See Izumi, Lady
Shikishi, Princess (d. 1201)
Blossoms have fallen, The.
Shiko (d. 1743)
I vanish.
Shiko (d. 1845)
Cricket, crying, A.
Shillaber, B. P.
Picture, A.
Sagamore, The.
Shimon, Louis C.
I Know Something Good about You.
Shimoni, David (1886–1957)
At Times Spirit Surges.

Flower Pot, The.
Gleaning.
Shinder, Jason (b. 1955)
One Secret That Has Carried, The.
Waitress.
Shinga (d. 1843)
Feast of the dead.
Shinseki (d. 1764)
Fickle winter shower.
Shipley, Vivian
At Fifty.
Faithful Daughter Dreams of Spring Break
While Installing a Bird Feeder for Her
Mother by a Window in the Courtyard of
Safe Harbour, The.
Heart with Little or No Bedrock for Anchor, A.
Shipman, Thomas (1632–80)
Kiss, The 1656. To Mrs. C.
Streams are fettered, and with us as rare, The.
Shiraishi, Kazuko (b. 1931)
Man Root, The.
Phallic Root.
Phallus.
Shire, David
I Don't Remember Christmas.
Little Bit Off, A.
Today Is the First Day of the Rest of My Life.
Shirley, Aleda
Hours Musicians Keep, The.
Late Night Radio.
Long Distance.
Shirley, James (1596–1666)
Cupid's Call.
Fie on Love.
Garden, The.
Glories of our blood and state, The.
Good-night.
Love for Enjoying.
Love's Hue and Cry.
Lover that Durst Not Speak to His
M[istress], A.
On the Duke of Buckingham.
Piping Peace.
Song to the Masquers.
To a Lady upon a Looking-Glass Sent.
To His Honored Friend Thomas Stanley
Esquire, upon His Elegant Poems.
To His Mistress.
To Odelia.
To the Excellent Pattern of Beauty and Virtue,
Lady Elizabeth, Countess of Ormonde.
Two Gentlemen That Broke Their Promise of a
Meeting.
Would you know what's soft? I dare.
Shirley, Lady Dorothy (1600–36)
LD Ansure, The.
Shiroa See Kaya Shirao
Shiseki (1676–1759)
My old thighs.
Shishin-Goshin (d. 1339)
Talking: seven steps, eight falls.
Shivarudrappa, G. S. (b. 1926)
This Man.
Shiyo (d. 1703)
And won't there be.
Snow on the pines.
Surely there's a teahouse.
Shizan (d. 1775)
Willingly.
Shkapskaya, Maria Mikhailovna (1891–1952)
My body had no entrance, and the black.
No Dream.
Shklyarevsky [or Shkliarevskii], Igor (b. 1938)
My Younger Brother.
Shlonsky, Avraham (1900–73)
Grape-gathering.
Jezrael.
Morning in My City.
Prayer: "Forgive me, you whom they cast in a
name."
Shepherd.
Tiller of the Soil.
Toil.
Shofu
No dust speck anywhere.

One moon.
Shogetsu (d. 1899)
Autumn ends.
Shogo (d. 1798)
Today the sky above Mount Hiei, too.
Shoha (Kuroyanagi Shoha) (d. 1771)
Shameful / Dead grass.
When the bush warbler.
Shoha, Kuroyanagi See Shoha
Shohaku (d. 1722)
Swollen bottle gourd, A.
Yesterday, it was hibiscus.
Shohi (d. 1750)
O morning glory.
Shoichi (1202–80)
All-meaning circle, The.
Shokaku
High wind, cold moon.
Shokei (d. 1895)
My shame in this world.
Shokushi, Princess
Guide me on my way.
O cord of life!
Shoku'u (d. 1772)
Chilling cold.
Sholl, Betsy
Dawn.
Distinct Call of the Alligator, The.
Girl Named Spring, A.
Hospital State, The.
Midnight Vapor Light Breakdown.
Outside the Depot.
Past, The.
Small Patch of Ice, A.
Something to Say.
Soup Kitchen.
Thinking of You, Hiroshima.
To the Dregs.
Shomer, Enid
Falling for Jesus.
Freestyle, on the First of Tishri.
From the Wailing Wall.
Letter Home from Brooklyn.
Refusing the Call.
Shards.
Women Bathing at Bergen-Belsen.
Shore, Jane (b. 1947)
High Holy Days.
Shoro (d. 1894)
Pampas grass, now dry.
Short, John (b. 1911)
Carol: "There was a boy bedded in bracken."
Leave in Mid-Winter.
Shorter, Dora Sigerson (1866–1918)
Ireland.
Mother, The.
Skeleton in the Cupboard, The.
Wind on the Hills, The.
Shoshun (d. betw. 1660 and 1672)
Flowers bloomed yesterday.
Shove, Fredegond Maitland (1889–1949)
Farmer, The.
New Ghost, The.
Shozan (1717–1800)
Fall of leaves, The.
Guest gone / I stroke the brazier.
No mind, no Buddha.
Shpolyansky, Aminado Petrovich See "Aminado,
Don"
Shrine Priestess of Ise
My mind is dazzled.
**Shteiger, Anatoly [or Anatoli] Sergeievich (1907–
44)**
No one waits down below, as when we were
young.
Shu Hsi (c. 265–306)
Hot Cake.
Shu-jen, Chou See "Lu Hsün"
"Shu Ting" (Gong Peiyu) (b. 1952)
'?.!'
Assembly Line.
Bits of Reminiscence.
Brother, I Am Here.

Fairy Tales.
Gifts.
Maple Leaf.
Mirror, The.
Missing You.
Perhaps.
Returning Home.
Singing Flower, The.
To.
To the Oak.
Unexpected Meeting.
When You Come Past My Window.

Shúa, Ana Maria
Golem and Rabbi 3.
Golem and Rabbi 4.
Golem and Rabbi 5.

Shuckburg, Richard *and* **Edward Bangs**
Yankee Doodle.

Shuho (d. 1767)
Cicada shell.

Shukabo (d. 1775)
Is it me the raven calls.

Shukyo (d. 1826)
Above the fence.

Shulman, Max (b. 1919)
Honest Abe Lincoln.

Shumaker, Peggy (b. 1952)
Ajo Lily.
Bush Navigator: The Last Morning of Hands.
Circle of Totems, The.
First Winter: Joy.
Inupiat Christmas Pageant, The.
Waitress's Kid, The.

Shumpan (d. 1703)
Winter fowl, The.

Shumpo Soki (d. 1496)
My sword leans against the sky.
No single bone in my body is holy.

Shun 'Oku Soen (d. 1611)
Adrift between the earth and sky.

Shune (fl. c.1160–c.1180)
All during a night.

Shunoku (1311–88)
After the spring song, 'Vast emptiness, no holiness.'

Shunzei (Fujiwara no Shunzei; Toshinari) (1114–1204)
Cormorant-boat, The.
Shall I see it again.

"Shunzei's Daughter" (1171?–1252?)
Brought by the breeze.
Burning in Secret.

Shuraikh
Distich.

Shurin, Aaron (b. 1947)
Blue Shade.
City of Men.
Exorcism of the Straight / Man / Demon.
His Promise.
Forward or Back.
Material's Daughter.
Sailed.
Saturated.

Shurtleff, Ernest W. (1862–1917)
Lead On, O King Eternal.

Shuster, Dana
Mellow on Morphine.

Shutei (d. 1858)
Frost on a summer day.

Shuttle, Penelope (b. 1947)
Early Pregnancy.
Expectant Mother.
Gone Is the Sleepgiver.
Locale.
Many creatures don't have one.
Maritimes.
Old Man, The.
Passion.

Shwarts [or Schvarts], Yelena [or Elena] (b. 1948)
Beast Flower.
Dump, The.
Elegies on the Cardinal Points.
Elegy on an X-ray Photo of My Skull.
Imitation of Boileau.

My heart's cloth I shall spread before the Savior's feet.
Parrot at Sea, A.
Remembrance of Strange Hospitality.
Sale of a Historian's Library.
What That Street Is Called.

"Shy, Timothy" *See* **Lewis, Dominic Bevan Wyndham**

Sia, Beau (b. 1976)
Claim to Fame.
Enemy.
Howl.
No Words Empty.
Things to Do in Holland.

Siamanto (1878–1915)
Dance, The.
Grief.

Sica, Gabriella (b. 1950)
I.
I wish I were spring water.
Lightening, The.
Monotomy.
Nudity.
On the Sea.

Sicoli, Dan
All Shook Up.

Siddal, Elizabeth (1834–62)
At Last.
Dead Love.
Lust of the Eyes, The.
Silent Wood, A.

Sidgwick, Henry
Strenuous Life, The.

Sidney, Sir Philip (1554–86)
Arcadia, *or* The Countesse of Pembroke's Arcadia, *sels.*
Astrophil and Stella, *sels.*
Delight of Solitariness, The.
Dirge: "Ring out your bells [*or* belles], let mourning shows [*or* shewes] be spread."
Eighth Song.
Eleventh Song.
Epithalamium: "Let mother Earth."
First Song.
Fortune, Nature, Love.
Fourth Song.
His Being Was in Her Alone.
Leave Me O Love.
Like Those Sick Folks.
Love Me, O Love.
Madrigal.
My muse, what ails this ardour?
My Sheep Are Thoughts.
My true love hath my heart [*or* hart], and I have his.
Nightingale, The.
Ninth Song.
Second Song.
Since wailing is a bud of causeful sorrow.
Sleep, Baby Mine, Desire.
Sonnet 1: "Loving in truth, and fain[e] in verse my love to show."
Sonnet 2: "Not at [the] first sight, nor with a dribbed shot."
Sonnet 3: "Let dainty wits cry on the sisters nine."
Sonnet 5: "It is most true that eyes are formed to serve."
Sonnet 6: "Some lovers speak, when they their Muses entertain."
Sonnet 7: "When Nature made her chief work, Stella's eyes."
Sonnet 9: "Queen Virtue's court, which some call Stella's face."
Sonnet 10: "Reason, in faith thou art well served, that still."
Sonnet 11: "In truth, O Love, with what a boyish kind."
Sonnet 14: "Alas, have I not pain enough, my friend."
Sonnet 15: "You that do search for every purling spring."
Sonnet 16: "In nature apt to like when I did see."
Sonnet 18: "With what sharp checks I in myself am shent."

Sonnet 19: "On Cupid's bow how are my heart-strings bent."
Sonnet 20: "Fly, fly, my friends."
Sonnet 21: "Your words my friend (right healthful caustics) blame."
Sonnet 22: "In highest way of heav'n the sun did ride."
Sonnet 25: "Wisest scholar of the wight most wise, The."
Sonnet 26: "Though dusty wits dare scorn astrology."
Sonnet 27: "Because I oft, in dark abstracted guise."
Sonnet 28: "You that with allegory's curious frame."
Sonnet 30: "Whether the Turkish new moon minded be."
Sonnet 31: "With how sad steps, O Moon[e], thou climb'st the skies."
Sonnet 33: "I might, unhappy word, O me, I might."
Sonnet 37: "My mouth doth water, and my breast doth swell."
Sonnet 39: "Come Sleep! O sleep the certain knot of peace."
Sonnet 40: "As good to write as for to lie and groan."
Sonnet 41: "Having this day my horse, my hand, my lance."
Sonnet 45: "Stella oft sees the very face of woe."
Sonnet 47: "What, have I thus betrayed my liberty?"
Sonnet 48: "Soul's joy, bend not those morning stars from me."
Sonnet 49: "I on my horse, and Love on me doth try."
Sonnet 52: "Strife is grown between Virtue and Love, A."
Sonnet 53: "In martial sports I had my cunning tried."
Sonnet 54: "Because I breathe not love to every one."
Sonnet 56: "Fie, school of Patience, fie; your lesson is."
Sonnet 61: "Oft with true sighs, oft with uncalled tears."
Sonnet 64: "No more, my dear, no more these counsels try."
Sonnet 65: "Love, by sure proof I may call thee unkind."
Sonnet 69: "O joy, too high for my low style to show."
Sonnet 71: "Who will in fairest book of Nature know."
Sonnet 72: "Desire, though thou my old companion art."
Sonnet 74: "I never drank of Aganippe well."
Sonnet 74: "Love still a boy, and oft a wanton is."
Sonnet 75: "Of all the kings that ever here did reign."
Sonnet 81: "O kiss, which dost those ruddy gems impart."
Sonnet 82: "Nymph of the garden where all beauties be."
Sonnet 84: "Highway, since you my chief Parnassus be."
Sonnet 87: "When I was forced from Stella ever dear."
Sonnet 89: "Now that of absence the most irksome night."
Sonnet 90: "Stella, think not that I by verse seek fame."
Sonnet 91: "Stella, while now by honour's cruel might."
Sonnet 92: "Be your words made (good sir) of Indian ware."
Sonnet 98: "Ah bed, the field where joy's peace some do see."
Sonnet 99: "When far-spent night persuades each mortal eye."
Sonnet 100: "O tears, no tears, but rain from beauty's skies."
Sonnet 103: "O happy Thames, that didst my Stella bear."
Sonnet 104: "Envious wits, what hath been

mine offence."
Sonnet 107: "Stella, since thou so right a Princess art."
Sonnet 108: "When sorrow (using mine own fire's might)"
Such maner time there was (what time I n'ot)
Then do I thinke in deed, that better it is to be private.
Thou Blind Man's Mark.
What Length of Verse?
When, to my deadly [or deadlie] pleasure.
White Great Nimble Cat, A.
Ye Goat-herd Gods.

Sidney, Robert (1563–1626)
Ah dearest limbs, my life's best joy and stay.
Alas, why say you I am rich? when I.
Forsaken woods, trees with sharp storms oppressed.
Songe 17: "Sun is set, and masked night, The."
Sonnet 25: "Yow that take pleasure in yowr cruelty."

Siegel, Joan I.
Drought.
How the Tortoise Knew It Was Her Time.
Wild Hyacinth.

Sigman, Carl
Ballerina.
Civilization (Bongo, Bongo, Bongo)
Crazy She Calls Me.

Sigourney, Lydia Huntley (1791–1865)
Advertisement of a Lost Day.
Blessed Comforter Divine.
Death of an Infant.
Erin's Daughter.
God Save the Plough.
Indian Names.
Indian's Welcome to the Pilgrim Fathers, The.
Laborers of Christ! Arise.
Onward, Onward, Men of Heaven.
Poetry.
Request of a Dying Child.
Stars, The.
To the First Slave Ship.
We Praise Thee, If One Rescued Soul.
Western Emigrant, The.

Sík Sándor (1889–1963)
English, The.
Summer and Dawn.

Silabhattarika (fl. before 11th cent.)
He who stole my virginity / is the same man.

Silano, Martha (b. 1961)
In Henry Carlile's *Writing 213.*
Moon, The.
Such a Way to Go.
Sweet Red Peppers, Sun-Drieds, the Hearts of Artichokes.

Silcock, Ruth
Limerick: "Hibiscus is flaming and frillier."
Limerick: "In the rain in a yard in Cessnock."
Limerick: "Land of blue skies, and sunlight, A."
Limerick: "There's an emerald frog down the loo."
Pioneer Village.

Silesky, Barry
Kingdom, The.
Screens.

Silex, Edgar
Acts of Love.
Departure.
Elegy: "What remains of the suicide's voice is the last conversation."
Gift, The.

Silkin, Jon (b. 1930)
Death of a Son.
Lilies of the Valley.
Space in the Air, A.

Silkin, Jon *See* **McDuff, David**

Silko, Leslie Marmon (b. 1948)
Alaskan Mountain Poem #1.
Deer Song.
Four Mountain Wolves.
Hawk and Snake.
Horses at Valley Store.
In Cold Storm Light.

Indian Song: Survival.
Invention of White People, The.
It Was a Long Time Before.
Long Time Ago.
Love Poem: "Rain smell comes with the wind."
Poem for Ben Barney.
Poem for Myself and Mei: Abortion.
Prayer to the Pacific.
Preparations.
Slim Man Canyon.
Sun Children.
Time We Climbed Snake Mountain, The.
Toe'osh; a Laguna Coyote Story.
When Sun Came to Riverwoman.
Where Mountain Lion Lay [or Laid] Down with Deer.

Sill, Edward Rowland (1841–87)
California Winter.
Fool's Prayer, The.
Opportunity.
Truth at Last.

Sillè, Nicasius de (b. 1610)
God Set Us Here.

Silliman, Ron (b. 1946)
Lucky my ears 'pop' at the hilltop.
Not this. / What then?
Revolving door.
Sentence in the evening. Today the boxscores are green. Tonight, A.

Sillitoe, Alan (b. 1928)
Picture of Loot.
Synagogue in Prague.

"Silurist" *See* **Vaughan, Henry**

Silva, Clara (1908–1976)
In the Darkness of the Other.
Magical Devices.
Moon's Cadaver, The.
Tea at the Magdalene.
Who Will Throw the First Stone?

Silva, José Asunción (1865–96)
Nocturne: "One night / One night full of perfumes, music of wings and murmurs."

Silva, Luis Andrade (b. 1943)
Emigrant's Son, The.
Island and Europe, The.

Silveira, Onésima (b. 1936)
Different Poem, A.

Silvers, Louis
April Showers.

Silverstein, Shel [or Shelley] (b. 1932)
Clarence.
Dirtiest Man in the World, The.
Friendship.
Hug o' War.
Jimmy Jet and His TV Set.
Lazy People, The.
Longmobile.
Nobody.
One Inch Tall.
Sarah Cynthia Sylvia Stout Would Not Take the Garbage Out.
Sick.
Slithergadee, The.
Whatif.

Simcox, George Augustus (1841–1905)
Love's Votary.

Simic, Charles (b. 1938)
Against Whatever It Is That's Encroaching.
Ancient Autumn.
Animal Acts.
Austerities.
Ballad: "What's that approaching like dust like poverty."
Begotten of the Spleen.
Bestiary for the Fingers of My Right Hand.
Book Full of Pictures, A.
Breasts.
Brooms.
Butcher Shop.
Charon's Cosmology.
Classic Ballroom Dances.
Clouds Gathering.
Club Midnight.
Cold, The.

Concerning My Neighbors, the Hittites.
Congress of the Insomniacs, The.
Country Fair.
Crepuscule with Nellie.
Dark Farmhouses.
Elementary Cosmogony.
Empire of Dreams.
Errata.
Eyes Fastened with Pins.
Fear.
Fork.
Great Infirmities.
Harsh Climate.
Hearing Steps.
Hunger.
Inner Man, The.
Lesson, The.
Live at Club Mozambique.
Lives of Alchemists, The.
Marvels of the City, The.
Miracle Glass Co.
Mirrors at 4 A.M.
My Shoes.
Night Picnic.
Nothing.
Old Couple.
Pain.
Pastoral: "I came to a field."
Poem: "Every morning I forget how it is."
Poem without a Title.
Popular Mechanics.
Prodigy.
Promises of Leniency and Forgiveness.
Psalm: "Old ones to the side."
Shelley.
Shirt.
Sleep.
Something, The.
Spoon, The.
Stone.
Story, The.
Strictly for Posterity.
Tapestry.
Wall, A.
Watching the Hearse.
Watermelons.
We were so poor I had to take the place of the.
Winter Night.

Simmerman, Jim (b. 1952)
Child's Grave, Hale County, Alabama.

Simmias [or Simias] of Rhodes (fl. c. 300 B.C.)
At the Tomb of Sophokles.
Decoy Partridge, A.

Simmias of Thebes (fl. 5th cent. B.C.)
To Prote.

Simmons, James (b. 1933)
After Eden.
Archæologist, The.
Birthday Poem, A.
Cavalier Lyric.
Claudy.
Didn't He Ramble.
Eden.
End of the Affair, The.
Experience.
Fear Test: Integrity of Heroes.
For Imelda.
For Thomas Moore.
From the Irish.
Goodbye, Sally.
Honeymoon, The.
In the Wilderness.
Influence of Natural Objects, The.
John Donne.
Join Me in Celebrating.
Long Way After Ronsard, A.
Lullaby for Rachael.
October in the Country: [1983].
One of the Boys.
Outward Bound.
Playing with Fire.
Pleasant Joys of Brotherhood, The.
Reformer to His Father, A.
Rogation Day: Portrush.
Stephano Remembers.
West Strand Visions.

Westport House, Portrush.
Written, Directed by and Starring.

Simms, Colin
First English Wildcat, The.
Grey Wagtail on the Tyne.
Lochside silverschistsand disturbed-to-black-
below distributed.
Pallid Harrier.

Simms, William Gilmore (1806–72)
By the Swannanoa.
Glory and Enduring Fame.
Lost Pleiad, The.
New Moon, The.
Triumph, The.
With ruder pomp, in more barbaric taste.

Simon, Leslie
Bernice Got Next to Isis.
Hattie Went to Market.
Kali.
Nellie Gives into Blanche.

Simon, Maurya (b. 1950)
All Soul's Day.
Atomic Psalm.
Blue Movies.
Boy Crazy.
Coward.
Dolphin, The.
Doomsday.
Keeping Track.
Night.
Sea Sprite, Hermosa Beach, The.
Search, The.
Shiva's Prowess.
Standing Between Two Ideas.

Simon, Paul (b. 1942)
Richard Cory.

Simonides (c.556–468 B.C.)
All things come to one hideous Charybdis.
As whenever.
Because of these men's courage, no smoke
rose.
Being human, don't ever say what happens
tomorrow.
Cenotaph at the Isthmos.
Countless birds.
Danae and Perseus.
Distinguishes the fair and the shameful.
Drinker, glutton supreme.
For the Athenian Dead at Plataia.
For the Spartan Dead at Plataia.
Great light was born in Athens when, A.
Greek Dead at Thermopylae, The.
Here lies Anacreon.
Human strength.
I Brotachos of Gortyn lie here. This.
It is hard to become a truly good.
No alien dust covers your tomb.
No leaf-shaking blast of winds.
On a Hound.
On His Friend Megistias, Who Died at
Thermopylai.
On the Spartan Dead at Thermopylae.
On Theodoros.
On Two Brothers.
Stone of Megakles who's dead, The.
Stranger, when you come to / Lakedaimon.
There is a tale.
Thermopylae.
Thermopylai's dead.
They wept for the violet-wreathed [lady's].
When in the skillfully welded chest.
While bringing Apollo the pick of the Etruscan
plunder.
Who, trusting his mind, could praise the man
of Lindos, Kleoboulos.
Without pleasure.

Simonov, Konstantin Mikhailovich (1915–79)
Blind Man, The.
By the Campfire.
Cricket, The.
Death Struck Him.
Lieutenant, The.
Remember, Alyosha, the roads of Smolensk.
Wait for me, and I'll come back.

Simons, Seymour
All of Me.

Breezin' Along with the Breeze.
Simpson, Jane Cross (1811–86)
Oh! if thou lov'st me, love me not so well!
Simpson, Joshua McCarter (1820–76)
Grieve not, my wife—grieve not for me.
Simpson, Louis (b. 1923)
After Midnight.
American Poetry.
Appointment, The.
As Birds Are Fitted to the Boughs.
Ash and the Oak, The.
Battle, The.
Before the Poetry Reading.
Boarder, The.
Boots and Saddles.
Carentan O Carentan.
Chocolates.
Climate of Paradise, The.
Country House, The.
Custom of the World, The.
Doubting.
Dvonya.
Early in the Morning.
Friend of the Family, A.
Heroes, The.
Hot Night on Water Street.
Hubert's Museum.
I Dreamed That in a City Dark as Paris.
In the Suburbs.
Inner Part, The.
Isidor.
Laurel Tree, The.
Letter from Brazil, A.
Listeners, The.
Long Afternoon, The.
Man Who Married Magdalene, The.
Memories of a Lost War.
Middleaged Man, The.
Morning Light, The.
My Father in the Night Commanding No.
New Lines for Cuscuscaraway and Mirza
Murad Ali Beg.
Night in Odessa, A.
On the Lawn at the Villa.
Outward.
Redwoods, The.
Riders Held Back, The.
Runner, The.
Silent Piano, The.
Son of the Romanovs, A.
Squeal.
Story about Chicken Soup, A.
Stumpfoot on 42nd Street.
Summer Storm.
Sway.
Tailor's Wedding, The.
There Is.
Things.
To the Western World.
Tonight the Famous Psychiatrist.
Troika, The.
Variations on a Poem by Reznikoff.
Walt Whitman at Bear Mountain.
White Oxen.
Simpson, Margaret Winefride (1893–1939)
Villanelle: "O winter wind, lat grievin be."
Simpson, Mercer (b. 1926)
Homo Erectus, Cerne Abbas.
Simpson, Ronald Albert (b. 1929)
All Friends Together.
Antarctica.
Diver.
Lake.
Sims, George R. (1847–1922)
Christmas Day in the Workhouse.
Garden Song, A.
He gazed on the face of the high-born maid.
To-night is a midnight meeting, and the Earl is
in the chair.
Undertones.
Sims, Hylda
Left Rites.
Sims, Steve
It's night, an extra quilt.
Sinason, Valerie (b. 1946)
In the Beginning.

Renaming, The.
Will You Come Out Now?
Sinclair, Iain
Serious of Photographs, A.
Snow Lip.
World's Oldest Comedian Is Dead.
Sinclair, Keith (b. 1922)
Bomb Is Made, The.
Memorial to a Missionary.
Sonnet from Below the Age Gap.
Sinda, Martial (b. c.1930)
To the Banquet of the Earth.
You Shall Walk in Peace!
Sing, Dorothy Wong Loi
Baap-Nemesthe Reggae Song.
Singde, Nara *See* **Na-lan Hsing-te**
Singer, Burns (James Burns Singer) (1928–64)
Birdsong.
Corner Boy's Farewell.
Epilogue: "That death might not be casual."
Marcus Antoninus Cui Cognomen Erat
Aurelius.
Nothing.
Peterhead in May.
Still and All.
Your Words, My Answers.
Singer, Elizabeth (1674–1737)
Cant. 5.6 & c.
Singer, James Burns *See* **Singer, Burns**
Singh, Kedarnath (b. 1934)
On Reading a Love Poem.
Singh, Shamsher Bahadur (1911–93)
On the Slope of This Hill.
Sinha, Kabita (b. 1931)
Diamond of Character, The.
Sinka, István (1897–1969)
Bobbin Stops, The.
Dear Stars, Rock Me to Sleep.
Memories of Mudland-Meadow.
My Mother Dances a Ballad.
Only the Sun.
Shepherd's Wife's Farewell to the Old Pasture,
The.
Siôn Cent (fl. 1400–30)
Vanity of the World, The.
Sirin, Vladimir *See* **Nabokov, Vladimir
Vladimirovich**
Sirowitz, Hal
Equality.
Sirr, Peter (b. 1960)
Beginnings.
Collector's Marginalia, The.
Few Helpful Hints, A.
Guide to Holland, A.
'Phoning.
Troubadour.
Understanding Canada.
Sissay, Lemn (b. 1967)
I have a voice in my head that talks
backwards.
Sissle, Noble (1889–1975)
Baltimore Buzz.
I'm Craving for That Kind of Love.
I'm Just Wild about Harry.
Sissman, Louis Edward (b. 1928)
Big Rock-Candy Mountain, The.
Bruisingly cradled in a Harvard chair.
Cockaigne: A Dream.
Deathplace, A.
Disappearance in West Cedar Street, A.
December 27, 1966.
Upon Finding Dying: An Introduction, by L. E.
Sissman, Remaindered at IS.
West Forties: Morning, Noon, and Night, The.
Sissoko, Fily-Dabo (1900–64)
Bombax Tree, The.
Brush Fire.
Dawn in the Valley.
Grandmother.
Like a Flower.
Meeting Bida.
Whirlwinds.
Sisson, Charles Hubert (b. 1914)
Adam and Eve.

A and B.
At First.
Black Rocks.
Carmen Saeculare.
Cato.
Cranmer.
Easter.
Family Fortunes.
Herb-Garden, The.
In Autumn.
In Flood.
Knole.
Letter to John Donne, A.
Marcus Aurelius.
Money.
Nature of Man, The.
Over the Wall: Berlin, May 1975.
Person, The.
Queen of Lydia, The.
Red Admiral, The.
Temple, The.
Tristia.
Un-Red Deer, The.
Usk, The.

Sitwell, Dame Edith (1887–1964)
Ass-Face.
Aubade: "Jane, Jane, / Tall as a crane."
Bat, The.
Bells of Grey Crystal.
Bird's Song, A.
Colonel Fantock.
Country Dance.
Dark Song.
Dirge for the New Sunrise.
Drum; the Narrative of the Demon of
   Tedworth, The.
En Famille.
Gardener Janus Catches a Naiad.
Governante, The.
Green Song.
Hambone and the Heart, The.
Heart and Mind.
Hornpipe.
How Many Heavens.
I Do Like to Be Beside the Seaside.
Innocent Spring, The.
Interlude.
King of China's Daughter, The.
Lament of Edward Blastock, The.
Lullaby: "Though the world has slipped and
   gone."
Madam Mouse Trots.
Madwoman in the Park, The.
Mauve summer rain, The.
Most Lovely Shade.
Neptune—Polka.
One fantee wave.
Panope.
Poet Laments the Coming of Old Age, The.
Princess, The.
Said King Pompey.
Scotch Rhapsody.
Serenade: Any Man to Any Woman.
Shadow of Cain, The.
Sir Beelzebub.
Solo for Ear-Trumpet.
Song: "Now that Fate is dead and gone."
Song: "We are the darkness in the heat of the
   day."
Song: "Where is all the bright company gone."
Spinning Song.
Still Falls the Rain.
Swans, The.
Trams.
Trio for Two Cats and a Trombone.
Waltz.
When we come to that dark house.
Youth with Red-gold Hair, The.

Sitwell, Sir Osbert (1892–1969)
Continually they cackle thus.
Elegy for Mr. Goodbeare.
Fountains.
In the Potting Shed.
In the Winter.
Judas and the Profiteer.
Mrs. Busk.
Next War, The.

On the Coast of Coromandel.

Sitwell, Sacheverell (1897–1988)
Agamemnon's Tomb.
Fountains.
Kingcups.
One by one, as harvesters, all heavy laden.
Psittachus Eois Imitatrix Ales ab Indis.
Red-Gold Rain, The.
River God, The.
Tulip Tree.

Skeen, Anita (b. 1946)
Women Who Cook.

Skeeter, Sharyn Jeanne (b. 1945)
California, 1852.
Midwest, Midcentury.
Western Trail Cook, 1880.

Skelley, Jack (b. 1956)
To Marie Osmond.

Skelton, John (1460?–1529)
And if ye stand in doubt.
Calliope.
Doctors that learned be.
For though my rhyme be ragged.
Garden of the Muses: Iopas' Song, The.
Gup, Scot!
Instead of coin and money.
Lullay, Lullay, Like a Child.
Mannerly Margery Mylk and Ale.
My name is Parrot, a bird of Paradise.
Now, Parrot, my sweet bird, speak our yet once
   again.
Now Sing We, as We Were Wont.
O benign Jesu, my sovereign Lord and King.
O ye wretched Scots.
Over this the foresayd lay.
Parrot's Soliloquy.
Phillip Sparow.
Phyllyp Sparowe.
Pla ce bo! Who is there, who?
Prayer to the Father of [*or* in] Heaven, A.
Rose both white and Rede, The.
Sail is up, Fortune ruleth our helm, The.
So many cloisters closed.
Sparrow's Dirge, The.
Spirituality vs. the Temporality, The.
Stow, birde, stow, stow!
Such a prelate, I trow.
Than, if this noble kyng.
Then Margery [*or* Marjorie] Milkduck.
Though Ye Suppose.
To Mistress Margery Wentworth.
To Mistress [*or* Maystres] Isabell Pennell.
To Mistress [*or* Maystres] Margaret Hussey.
Unto this process briefly compiled.
Upon a Dead Man's Head.
Woefully Arrayed.
Ye remembre the gentylman ryghte nowe.

Skelton, Robin (b. 1925)
Eagle.
Lakeside Incident.

Skinner, Jeffrey
City out of the Boy, The.
Earth Angel.
For Stuart Porter, Who Asked for a Poem That
   Would Not Depress Him Further.
Late Afternoon, Late in the Twentieth Century.
Objects in Mirror Are Closer Than They
   Appear.
Restoration.
Silk Robe.
Starling Migration, The.

Skinner, John (1721–1807)
Tullochgorum.

Skinner, Knute (b. 1929)
Cold Irish Earth, The.

Skinner, Richard
Conjure with me: three letters.

Skipsey, Joseph (*fl.* c.1892)
Get Up!
Hey Robin.
Mother Wept.
Not as Wont.

Skirrow, Desmond (1924–76)
Ode on a Grecian Urn Summarized.

Skirving, Adam (1719–1803)
Johnnie Cope.

Sklarew, Myra (1934–87?)
After Theresienstadt.
At three-thirty in the morning in America.
Holocaust.
How Metaphor Can Save Your Life.
Instructions for Elijah.
Ninth of Av.
On Muranowska Street.
Speech Warts.
Teaching the Children.
Three-Course Meal for the New Year, A.
What Is a Jewish Poem?

Skloot, Floyd (b. 1947)
Closer to Home.
Everly Brothers, The.
Hook.
Music Appreciation.
Twilight Time.
Year the Space Age Was Born, The.

Skovron, Alex (b. 1948)
Election Eve, with Cat.

Skrine, Nesta Higginson *See* "O'Neill, Moira"

Skrzynecki, Peter (b. 1945)
Cattle.
Feliks Skrzynecki.
Hunting Rabbits.

Skythinos (c.90 B.C.–A.D. 50)
Epigram: "Great woe, fire & war come on
   me."

Sladen, Douglas Brook Wheelton (1856–1947)
Summer Christmas in Australia, A.

Slater, Eleanor (b. 1903)
Search.

Slater, Francis Carey (1876–1958)
Songless Land, The.
Stars in Sand.

Slauerhoff, J. (1898–1936)
Columbus.
Within My Life.

Slegman, Ann
Sex and the Single Spud.

Sleigh, Tom
To the Sun.

Slessor, Kenneth (1901–71)
All-night Taxi Stand, The.
Beach Burial.
Bushranger, A.
Choker's Lane.
Country Towns.
Five Bells.
Fixed Ideas.
Full Orchestra.
Last Trams.
Leaning against the golden undertow.
Metempsychosis.
North Country.
Nuremberg.
Polarities.
Sleep.
South Country.
To Myself.
Up in Mabel's Room.
William Street.

Sloman, Joel (b. 1943)
In a Remote Cloister Bordering the Empyrean.
Tree, The.

Slonimski, Antoni (1895–1976)
All.
Elegy: "No more, no more Jewish townships in
   Poland."
He Is My Countryman.
London Spring.
Morning and Evening.
Remembrance.

**Sluchevsky [*or* Sluchevskii], Konstantin
Konstantinovich (1837–1904)**
I told her: the sidewalks are muddy.
Nothing but anniversaries, anniversaries...
Yes, for the multitude of people it's hard to
   avoid.

Slugs, Slocum (*fl.* 1857)
I Saw Her in Cabbage Time.

Slutsky [or Slutskii], Boris Abramovich (1919–86)
Bathhouse, The.
Boss, The.
Burnt.
Clerks.
Coppers.
Filled with the final weariness.
God.
Horses in the Ocean.
Horses in the Sea.
Hospital.
Hospital, The.
How Did They Kill My Grandmother?
How They Killed My Grandmother.
Law, which each citizen knows well.
My Friends.
My old men are dying.
Pit of Cologne, The.
Prosaics.

Small, Adam (b. 1936)
Brown Lullaby.
Second Coming.
There's Somethin'
What abou' de Law?

Small, Robin *See* **"Jerry, Bongo"**

Smallpiece, Anna Maria (fl. 1805)
Veil's removed, the gaudy, flimsy veil, The.
Written in Ill Health.

Smart, Christopher (1722–71)
Ascension of Our Lord Jesus Christ, The.
Author Apologizes to a Lady, for His Being a
　Little Man, The.
Beauty.
Christmas Day.
Crucifixion of Our Blessed Lord.
Elegance.
Epiphany.
Faith.
Conclusion of the Matter, The.
For Saturday.
Fortitude.
Gratitude.
Hope.
Hymn to the Supreme Being, *sels*.
Jubilate Agno, *sels*.
Long-Suffering of God.
Loveliness.
Moderation.
Morning-Piece; or, An Hymn for the Hay-
　Makers, A.
Mutual Subjection.
My Cat Jeoffry, *sels*.
Nativity of Our Lord and Saviour Jesus Christ,
　The.
Nativity of St. John the Baptist, The.
New Year.
Night-Piece; or, Modern Philosophy, A.
On a Bed of Guernsey Lilies.
Pray Remember the Poor.
Psalm 58.
Song to David, A, *sels*.
Song: "Where shall Celia fly for shelter."
St. Philip and St. James.
St. Thomas.
Strength.
Taste.
To the Rev. Mr. Powell.

Smedley, Jonathan (1671–1729)
Fancy.

Smedley, Menella Bute (1820–77)
Cavour.
Contrast, A.
Face from the Past, A.
Irish Fairy, The.
Sorrowful Sea-Gull, The.

Smelcer, John E.
Animal Spirits.
Bonanza Creek.
My Indian Grandmother Speaks to Animals.

Smelyakov, Yaroslav Vasilevich (1912–72)
Blind Man, The.
Dancing, phosphorescent drops.
Earth.
From My Diary.
Judge, The.

Locomotives' Graveyard, The.
Lovely Leda.
Manon Lescaut.
Menshikov.
Monument, The.
Peter and Aleksey.
Portrait.
Should I ever fall ill.

Smiler Narautjarri
Witch Doctor's Magic Flight, The.

Smith, Alexander (1830–67)
Sing, Poet, 'tis a merry world.
Steamer left he black and oozy wharves, The.

Smith, Ali (b. 1962)
Genesis.

Smith, Anna Deavere
Roslyn Malamud the Coup.

Smith, Anne K.
Giving Thanks.
Praise.

Smith, Arthur James Marshall (1902–80)
Ballade un Peu Banale.
Brigadier.
Common Man, The.
Dead, The.
Lonely Land, The.
News of the Phoenix.
Political Intelligence.
Resurrection of Arp.
Watching the Old Man Die.
What the Emanation of Casey Jones Said to
　the Medium.

Smith, Barbara (b. 1946)
Bowl, The.

Smith, Beasley
That Lucky Old Sun.

Smith, Bessie (1895–1937)
Backwater Blues.
Black Mountain Blues.
Empty Bed Blues.
In the House Blues.

Smith, Bruce (b. 1949)
Address.
How Garnett Mims and the Enchanters Came
　into Your Life.
Laundry.
O My Invisible Estate.

Smith, Caroline Sprague (1827–88)
Tarry with Me, O My Saviour.

Smith, Charlie (b. 1947)
Beds.
Santa Monica.

Smith, Charlotte (1749–1806)
Beachy Head.
Blessed is yon shepherd on the turf reclined.
By the Same.
By the Same. To Solitude.
Captive Escaped in the Wilds of America, The.
　Addressed to the Hon. Mrs. O'Neill.
Composed during a Walk on the Downs, in
　November 1787.
Dead Beggar, an Elegy Addressed to a Lady,
　The.
Disillusion with the French Revolution.
Early worshipper at Nature's shrine, An.
Emigrants, The.
Fragment Descriptive of the Miseries of War.
From Beachy Head.
Glow-Worm, The.
I once was happy, when while yet a child.
Nepenthe.
Ode to Death.
On Being Cautioned against Walking on an
　Headland Overlooking the Sea, because It
　Was Frequented by a Lunatic.
On Passing over a Dreary Tract of Country,
　and near the Ruins of a Deserted Chapel,
　during a Tempest.
On the Aphorism "L'Amitié est l'Amour sans
　Ailes."
On the Departure of the Nightingale.
Partial muse has, from my earliest hours, The.
Pressed by the Moon, Mute Arbitress of Tides.
Sea View, The.
Should the lone Wanderer, fainting on his way.

Sighing I see yon little troop at play.
Sonnet Written at the Close of Spring [or
　Elegiac Sonnet].
Stanzas: "Ah! think'st thou, Laura, then, that
　wealth."
Supposed to Be Written by Werter.
Thirty-eight: Addressed to Mrs H—y.
To a Friend.
To a Nightingale.
To a Querulous Acquaintance.
To Dependence.
To Fancy.
To Friendship.
To Hope.
To Melancholy. Written on the Banks of the
　Arun, October 1785.
To Miss C—on Being Desired To Attempt
　Writing a Comedy.
To Mr. Hayley, on Receiving Some Elegant
　Lines from Him.
To Mrs. G.
To Night.
To Sleep.
To Spring.
To the Countess of A—. Written on the
　Anniversary of Her Marriage.
To the Earl of Egremont.
To the Insect of the Gossamer.
To the Moon.
To the Naiad of the Arun.
To the River Arun.
To the Shade of Burns.
To the South Downs.
Unhappy exile, whom his fates confine, The.
Verses Intended to Have Been Prefixed to the
　Novel of Emmeline, but Then Suppressed.
Where the wild woods and pathless forests
　frown.
Written at Bignor Park in Sussex, in August,
　1799.
Written in Farm Wood, South Downs, in May
　1784.
Written in October.
Written on the Sea Shore.—October, 1784.
Written September 1791, during a Remarkable
　Thunder Storm.

Smith, Christopher
Ballin' the Jack.
He's a Cousin of Mine.

Smith, Dave Jeddie (b. 1942)
American Roadside Elegy, An.
August, on the Rented Farm.
Bats.
Between the Moon and the Sun.
Cleaning a Fish.
Cumberland Station.
Desks.
Elegy in an Abandoned Boatyard.
Hawktree.
Hole, Where Once in Passion We Swam.
Roundhouse Voices, The.
Lake Drummond Dream.
Looking for the Melungeon.
Morning Light at Wanship, Utah.
On a Field Trip at Fredericksburg.
Pink Slip at Tool & Dye.
Rain Forest.
Reading the Books Our Children Have Written.
Sea Owl.
Smithfield Ham.
Snapshot of a Crab-Picker among Barrels
　Spilling Over, Apparently at the End of Her
　Shift.
Spring Poem, The.

Smith, Edgar (1857–1938)
Heaven Will Protect the Working-Girl.

Smith, Eunice (fl. late 18th cent.)
Dear Brethren, Are Your Harps in Tune?
Dear Happy Souls.

Smith, Francis J. (b. 1920)
First Prelude.

Smith, Gary
Penitential Cries of Jupiter Hammond, The.

Smith, George (1713–76)
Country Lovers; or, Isaac and Marget Going to
　Town, on a Summer's Morning, The.

Smith, Harry Bache (1860–1936)
My Angeline.

Smith, Horace [or Horatio] (1779–1849)
Ozymandias.
To the Wine Treasurer of the Circuit Mess.

Smith, Horace (1779–1849) and James Smith (1775–1839)
Cui Bono?

Smith, Iain Crichton (b. 1928)
Clearances, The.
Contrasts.
Culloden and After.
Deer looks through you to the other side, A.
Exiles, The.
For Angus MacLeod.
For My Mother.
Gaelic Stories.
Ghost, The.
Herring Girls, The.
John Knox.
Listen.
Nose, The.
Old Woman, The.
Shall Gaelic Die?
Two Girls Singing.
You Are at the Bottom of My Mind.

Smith, Jack
Gimme a Little Kiss (Will Ya, Huh?)

Smith, James (1775–1839)
Playhouse Musings.

Smith, James See **Smith, Horace**

Smith, Jessie Welborn
Sew a Pocket.

Smith, John (1580–1631)
In the Due Honor of the Author Master Robert
Norton.
John Smith of His Friend Master John Taylor.
Sea Marke.

Smith, John (1662–1717)
Solitary Canto to Chloris the Disdainful, A.

Smith, Kay (b. 1911)
Annunciation.
Heaven which art in Heaven Our Father in
Heaven.

Smith, Ken (b. 1938)
Encounter at St. Martin's.
End of All History, The.
Possessions.
Train.
Writing in Prison.

Smith, Langdon (1858–1908)
Evolution.

Smith, Laurence
Christmas Tree.
Skeleton House.

Smith, Lawrence R. See **Hayward, Max**

Smith, Lee
In the Heat of the Night.

Smith, Michael (1954–83)
Asleep in the City.
Chimes.
City.
Fall.
From the Chinese.
In Prison.
Mitching.
Stopping to Take Notes.
Visit to the Village, A.

Smith, Michael S.
Springtime at Twilight.
Watering the New Lawn.

Smith, Patricia (b. 1955)
Annie Pearl Smith Discovers Moonlight.
Biting Back.
Blonde White Women.
Building Nicole's Mama.
Dylan, Two Days.
Finding His Fist.
Meanwhile, in Rwanda.
So Motown taught me all about men. Men
worshipped.
They Say That Black People.
What It's Like to Be a Black Girl (For Those
of You Who Aren't)

Woman Who Died in Line, The.

Smith, Pauline (1882–1959)
Katisje's Patchwork Dress.

Smith, R. T. (b. 1904)
Halcion.
Softball at Julia Tutwiler Prison.

Smith, Ray (b. 1915)
Apple, The.

Smith, Ruth
Bluetits.

Smith, Sam
Rumoured thief.

Smith, Samuel Francis (1808–95)
America.
As Flows the Rapid River.
Down to the Sacred Wave.
Morning Light Is Breaking, The.
My country, 'tis of thee.
Softly Fades the Twilight Ray.

Smith, Samuel J. (1771–1835)
Arise, My Soul! With Rapture Rise!

Smith, Stevie (1902–71)
Admire Cranmer!
After-Thought, The.
Airy Christ, The.
Angel Boley.
Anger's Freeing Power.
Animula, Vagula, Blandula.
Away, Melancholy.
Be Off!
Bereaved Swan, The.
Black March.
Bog-Face.
Celts, The.
Childe Rolandine.
Christmas.
Cock-a-Doo.
Commuted Sentence, The.
Conviction IV.
Correspondence between Mr. Harrison in
Newcastle and Mr. Sholto Peach Harrison in
Hull.
Dear Female Heart.
Death Sentence, The.
Deserter, The.
Dirge: "From a friend's friend I taste
friendship."
Distractions and the Human Crowd.
Donkey, The.
Dream of Comparison, A.
Drugs Made Pauline Vague.
Edmonton, thy cemetery.
Emily Writes Such a Good Letter.
Exeat.
Fairy Story.
Freddy.
Frog Prince, The.
Galloping Cat, The.
God the Eater.
Goodnight.
Grange, The.
Great Unaffected Vampires and the Moon.
He Told His Life Story to Mrs. Courtly.
Heavenly City, The.
Holiday, The.
Hop hop, thump thump.
House of Mercy, A.
How Cruel Is the Story of Eve.
Human Affection.
I Forgive You.
I Remember.
I Rode with My Darling.
In My Dreams.
Infelice.
Is It Wise?
Jungle Husband, The.
Lads of the Village, The.
Lady "Rogue" Singleton.
Lightly Bound.
Little Boy Lost.
Lord Barrenstock.
Love Me!
Magna Est Veritas.
Major Macroo.
Man Is a Spirit.
Mrs Simpkins.

Mother Love.
Murderer, The.
My Hat.
My Muse Sits Forlorn.
New Age, The.
No Categories!
None of the Other Birds.
Not Waving but Drowning.
On the Death of a German Philosopher.
One of Many.
Our Bog Is Dood.
Pad, Pad.
Papa Love Baby.
Persian, The.
Pretty.
Private Means Is Dead.
Quand on n'a pas ce que l'on aime, il faut
aimer ce que l'on a—.
Reversionary.
River God, The.
Satin-Clad.
Scorpion.
Singing Cat, The.
Songe d'Athalie.
Souvenir de Monsieur Poop.
Sunt Leones.
Tenuous and Precarious.
This Englishwoman.
Thoughts about the Person from Porlock.
To Carry the Child.
To School!
To the Tune of The Coventry Carol.
Valuable.
Wanderer, The.
Was He Married?
Was It Not Curious?
Weak Monk, The.
White Thought, The.
Who Is This Who Howls and Mutters?

Smith, Sydney (1771–1845)
On Seeing Francis Jeffrey Riding on a Donkey.

Smith, Sydney Bernard
Deadly Seven, The.
Limerick: "Angst, poetry, urbanized fret."
Limerick: "I haven't a clue where I've been."
Limerick: "Sign your name in the book. It's
just ink."
Limerick: "Very apt question struck me, A."

Smith, Sydney Goodsir (1915–75)
Bishop Blomfield's First Charge to His Clergy.
But ae braithless note.
Cokkils.
Deevil's Waltz, The.
Epistle to John Guthrie.
Grace of God and the Meth-Drinker, The.
Ineffable Dou, The.
Kenless Strand, The.
Leander Stormbound.
Mandrake Hert, The.
Mither's Lament, The.
Salad, A.
Slugabed.
War in Fife, The.
Ye Mongers Aye Need Masks for Cheatrie.

Smith, Thomas (1883–1969)
Why Why Should I the World Be Minding.

Smith, Vivian (b. 1933)
At an Exhibition of Historical Paintings,
Hobart.
Early Arrival: Sydney.
Fishermen, Drowned beyond the West Coast.
Reflections.
Summer Band Concert.
Tasmania.

Smith, Walter Chalmers (1824–1908)
Glenaradale.
Immortal, invisible, God only wise.

Smith, Welton
Malcolm.
Nigga Section, The.

Smith, William (fl. c.1596)
Feed, silly sheep, although your keeper pineth.
To the Most Excellent and Learned Shepherd,
Colin Clout.

Smith, William Jay (b. 1918)
American Primitive.

Around My Room.
Bachelor's-Buttons.
Brooklyn Bridge.
Closing of the Rodeo, The.
Crocodile.
Dachshunds.
Floor and the Ceiling, The.
Independence Day.
Journey to the Interior.
Lovers, The.
Park in Milan, The.
Pavane for the Nursery, A.
Persian Miniature.
Plain Talk.
Polar Bear.
Quail in Autumn.
Random Generation of English Sentences; or,
    The Revenge of the Poets.
Said Dorothy Hughes to Helen Hocking.
Tempest, The.
There Was an Old Lady Named Crockett.
There Was an Old Woman Named Piper.
Toaster, The.

Smither, Elizabeth (b. 1941)
Best Cowboy Movie, The.
Casanova's Ankle.
City Girl in the Country.
Temptations of St. Antony by His
    Housekeeper.
Terrapin, The.

Smithyman, Kendrick (b. 1922)
Circus at the Barber's Shop.
Colville 1964.
Hint for the Incomplete Angler.
Tomarata.

Smolensky [or Smolenskii], Vladimir
Aleksandrovich (1901–61)
No matter how I shout—there's no reply.

Smollett, Tobias (1721–71)
Tears of Scotland, The.
To Leven Water.

Smukler, Linda (b. 1954)
Days Inn.
Home in Three Days. Don't Wash.
Marry.
Shower, The.
Sign.
Trash.

Smyth, Paul (b. 1944)
Spring that I was six I found in the woods,
    The.

Sneak, Hymie
Limerick: "Lad of the brainier kind, A."

Sneeden, Ralph (fl. 20th cent.)
Coltrane and My Father.

Snider, P. M.
Communion.

Snodgrass, C. A.
Poem for Christmas, A.

Snodgrass, William DeWitt ("S. S. Gardons") (b.
1926)
Adolf Hitler———1 April, 1945.
Adolf Hitler———20 April, 1934; 1900 hours.
After Experience Taught Me..
Albert Speer.
April Inventory.
Campus on the Hill, The.
Child of My Winter Born.
Coroner's Inquest.
Easter has come around.
Eva Braun.
He fed them generously who were his flocks.
Hermann Fegelein.
I thumped on you the best I could.
Late April and you are three; today.
Leaving the Motel.
Lobsters in the Window.
Locked House, A.
Lying Awake.
Matisse: "The Red Studio."
Mementos, 1.
Men's Room in the College Chapel, The.
Monet: 'Les Nymphéas.'
Mutability.
No Use.

One. now another. one.
Operation, The.
Powwow.
Song: "Sweet beast, I have gone prowling."
Ten Days Leave.
Vuillard: "The Mother and Sister of the Artist."

Snow, A. H. (b. 1910)
Gardener.

Snow, Eliza R. (1804–87)
Think Not when You Gather to Zion.

Snow, Wilbert (1884–1977)
Advice to a Clam-Digger.

Snyder, Gary (b. 1930)
Above Pate Valley.
After weeks of watching the roof leak.
After Work.
All the Spirit Powers Went to Their Dancing
    Place.
All through the Rains.
As for Poets.
August on Sourdough, a Visit from Dick
    Brewer.
August Was Foggy.
Autumn Morning in Shokoku-ji, An.
Avocado.
Axe Handles.
Bath, The.
Bedrock.
Before the Stuff Comes Down.
Beneath My Hand and Eye the Distant Hills,
    Your Body.
Building.
Burning.
Burning Island.
Burning the Small Dead.
Cartagena.
Changing Diapers.
Circumambulating Arunachala.
It.
Dead by the Side of the Road, The.
Dragonfly.
Earrings Dangling and Miles of Desert.
Eight Sandbars on the Takano River.
Elwha River, The.
Feathered Robe, The.
Fire in the Hole.
First Shaman Song.
For a Far-out Friend.
For a Stone Girl at Sanchi.
For John Chappell.
For Nothing.
For the Children.
Four Poems for Robin.
Front Lines.
Gaia.
Geese Gone Beyond.
Getting in the Wood.
Grand Entry, The.
Hay for the Horses.
Heifer Clambers Up, A.
Hitch Haiku.
Hop, Skip, and Jump.
How Do You Shape an Axe Handle?
How Poetry Comes to Me.
Hump-Backed Flute Player, The.
I Went into the Maverick Bar.
John Muir on Mt. Ritter.
L M F B R.
Late October Camping in the Sawtooths.
Lodgepole Pine: the wonderful reproductive.
Long Hair.
Looking at Pictures to Be Put Away.
Manichaeans, The.
Meeting the Mountains.
Message from Outside.
Mid-August at Sourdough Mountain Lookout.
Milton by Firelight.
Mother Earth: Her Whales.
My home was at Cold Mountain from the start.
Nansen.
Night Herons.
Night Song of the Los Angeles Basin.
No Shoes No Shirt No Service.
Old Dutch Woman, The.
Old Woman Nature.
Out of the soil and rock.

Out West.
Pine Tree Tops.
Piute Creek.
Praise for Sick Women.
Prayer for the Great Family.
Removing the Plate of the Pump on the
    Hydraulic System of the Backhoe.
Right in the Trail.
Riprap.
River Snow.
Second Shaman Song.
Sixth-Month Song in the Foothills.
Some Good Things to Be Said for the Iron
    Age.
Song of the Taste.
Spring Night in Shokoku-ji, A.
Text, The.
They Didn't Hire Him.
Things to Do around a Lookout.
This Poem Is for Bear.
This Poem Is for Deer.
This Tokyo.
What Happened Here Before.
Trail Crew Camp at Bear Valley. 9000 Feet.
Truth Like the Belly of a Woman Turning,
    The.
Two Fawns That Didn't See the Light This
    Spring.
Uses of Light, The.
Vapor Trails.
Walk, A.
Water.
What Do They Say.
What Happened Here Before.
What Have I Learned.
What You Should Know to Be a Poet.
Why Log Truck Drivers Rise Earlier than
    Students of Zen.
Work to Do Toward Town.

Snyder, Jennifer
Roses, The.
Train.

Snyder, Richard (b. 1905)
Mongoloid Child Handling Shells on the
    Beach, A.

Snyder, Ted
Who's Sorry Now?

So Chong-Ju (b. 1915)
Beside a Chrysanthemum.
Elephants of Thailand.
Flower-Patterned Snake.
If I Became a Stone.
Owl.
Peony Afternoon.
Self-Portrait.
Sneeze, A.
Untitled.
Wanderer's Bouquet.
Winter Sky.

Soa (d. 1742)
Whether or not a paradise.

Soan
Sailing on Men River, I heard.

Sobaku (1728–92)
Cherry blossoms.

Sobiloff, Hy (1912–70)
Child's Sight, The.
Wisdom.

Sobin, Gustaf (b. 1935)
Eleven Rock Poems.
Girandole.
Irises.
Out of the Identical.
What the Music Wants.

Socho *See* **Saiokuken Socho**

Södergran, Edith (1892–1923)
Arrival in Hades.
Forest Lake.
Hell.
Homecoming.
Instinct.
My Childhood Trees.
Net, The.
On Foot I Had to Walk through the Solar
    Systems.

Pain.
Question.
There is no one.
Vierge Moderne.
Violet Twilights.
We Women.

Sodo (*fl.* c.1868)
Full autumn moon.
Late spring / Paling rose.
Question clear, the answer deep, The.
Sudden shower / Cooling lava.

Soen (1859–1919)
Calm, activity—each has its use. At times.
Master Joshu and the dog.
On Visiting Shorin Temple, Where
    Bodhidharma Once Lived.

Sofu (d. 1891)
Festival of Souls.

Sogetsuni (d. c.1804)
After the Dance for the Dead.
Divine mystery.

Sogi *See* Iio Sogi

Sohoku (d. 1743)
Empty are.
This winter.

Sokan (Yamazaki Sokan) (1465–1553)
Cold, yes / But don't test.

Sokan, Yamazaki *See* Sokan

Sokin (d. 1818)
Road I take, The.

Soko (d. 1897)
Shadows from a lingering sun.

Soko (d. 1770)
Like full, plump.

Sokolov, Vladimir Nikolaevich (b. 1928)
Artist has to be enslaved, An.
Beginning, The.
Everything as in a good old-fashioned novel.
Garland, The.
Recollections of the Cross.
Snow's white pencil outlining the buildings.

Solari, Rose (b. 1960)
Currents.
December 25, 1991.
Truro.

Soldati, Joseph A.
Surroundings.

Soldofsky, Alan
Chin Music.

Sologub, Fyodor [*or* Fiodor] Kuz'mich (1863–1927)
Amphora, The.
Austere the Music of My Songs.
Devil's Swing, The.

Sologuren, Javier (b. 1922)
Oh, Astonishing Love.

Solomon ibn Gabirol (1021–58)
Almighty! What Is Man?
Before I Was Born.
Defiance.
Degenerate Age, A.
From Thee to Thee.
His Illness.
In Praise of Wisdom.
In the Morning I Look for You.
Invitation.
Meditations.
Morning Song.
My God.
My Heart Thinks as the Sun Comes Up.
Night.
Night-Thoughts.
O Soul, with Storms Beset.
Pen, The.
Royal Crown, The.
Separation from the Torah.
Song of the Wind and the Rain.
Stanzas: "With tears thy grief thou dost
    bemoan."
Water Song.
Wine and Grief.

Solomon, Mark
Comment on My Host, A.

Solomos, Dionysios (1798–1857)
Destruction of Psara, The.

Solon (c.635–c.559 B.C.)
Love of Boys, The.

Solonche, J. R.
Chopin Preludes, Opus 28.

Soloukhin, Vladimir Alekseievich (b. 1924)
Apple, The.
For the Tree to Sing.
How to Drink the Sun.
Lost Songs.
To Make Birds Sing.
Wind, The.
Wolves.

Solovyov [*or* Solov'iov], Vladimir Sergeievich
(1853–1900)
Panmongolism.

Solt, Mary Ellen
Forsythia.
Lilac.
Marriage.
Moonshot Sonnet.
Rain Down.
Wild Crab.

Somali Oral Tradition
Woman's Love Song.

Somaru (d. 1795)
Green gourd, A.

Somervile [*or* Somerville], William (1675–1742)
Hare-hunting.
Hudibras and Milton Reconciled.
Inquisitive Bridegroom, The.
On the Village Green.
See! there she goes.
Where fair Sabrina's wand'ring currents flow.

Sommer, Jason
Mengele Shitting.

Sondheim, Stephen (b. 1930)
All I Need Is the Girl.
America.
Another Hundred People.
Comedy Tonight.
Everybody Says Don't.
Everything's Coming Up Roses.
Gee, Officer Krupke.
I'm Still Here.
I Never Do Anything Twice (Madam's Song)
In Buddy's Eyes.
Ladies Who Lunch, The.
Losing My Mind.
Remember?
Send in the Clowns.
Some People.
Somewhere.
Together Wherever We Go.

Soné
Blessed.

Sone Yoshitada (*fl.* late 10th cent.)
Lower leaves of the trees, The.

Song, Cathy (b. 1955)
Beauty and Sadness.
Easter: Wahiawa, 1959.
Father and Daughter.
Girl Powdering Her Neck.
Heaven.
Ikebana.
Journey.
Leaf.
Leaving.
Lost Sister.
Mehinaku Girl in Seclusion, A.
Out of Our Hands.
Picture Bride.
Small Light, A.
Spaces We Leave Empty.
Vegetable Air, The.
Waterwings.
White Porch, The.
Wind in the Trees, The.
Youngest Daughter, The.

Song Sun (1493–1583)
Ten Years It Took.

Soniat, Katherine
Dog Days.
Harp / Desire.

Sonnenberg, Ben
Stay.

Sonnevi, Göran (b. 1939)
Child Is Not a Knife, A.
Demon Colors, Dark.

Sono-Jo, Lady (1649–1723)
How cool / forehead touched.
Shameful / These clothes.

Sontonga, Enoch (c.1860–1904)
Lord Bless Africa.

Sontrop, Theo (b. 1931)
Acorn Speaks, The.
Park, A.

So'oku (d. 1766)
Walking westward.

Sophocles (c.495–c.406 B.C.)
Antigone.
Chorus: "Fair Salamis, the billow's roar."
Chorus: "What man is he that yearneth."
Colonus' Praise.
Endure what life God gives and ask no longer
    span.
Kupris bears trophies away.
Oedipus the King [*or* Oedipus Rex].
This disease is an evil bound upon the day.
Torn between griefs, which grief shall I lament.

Soprovsky [*or* Soprovskii], Aleksandr (1953–90)
Notes from the house of the dead.

Sora (Kaai Sora) (1649–1710)
Skylark / Soaring—her young.

Sora, Kaai *See* Sora

Sorby, Angela
Gossip.
Land of Lincoln.
Man without a Middle, The.
Synchronized Swimming.

Sorescu, Martin (b. 1936)
Fountains in the Sea.
Fresco.
Map.
Perseverance.
Precautions.
Start.
Tear, The.
With a Green Scarf.

Sorley, Charles Hamilton (1895–1915)
All the Hills and Vales Along.
Expectans Expectavi.
Hundred Thousand Million Mites, A.
Rooks.
Saints have adored the lofty soul of you.
Song of the Ungirt Runners, The.
Sonnet: "When you see millions of the
    mouthless dead."
Such, such is Death: no triumph: no defeat.
To Germany.
Two Sonnets.

Sornberger, Judith
When She Laughs.

Sorrell, Martin (*fl.* 20th cent.)
Time and again we're cut down to size.

Sorrells, Helen (b. 1908)
From a Correct Address in a Suburb of a
    Major City.
Mountain Corral.
To a Child Born in Time of Small War.

Sorrentino, Gilbert (b. 1929)
Classic Case, A.
Good Night!
Land of Cotton.
Magic Composer.
Oranges Returned, The.
Razzmatazz.
Zoo, The.

Soryu (d. 1797)
Autumn winds.

Sosa, Roberto
Most Ancient Names of Fire, The.

Sosei (*fl.* 9th cent.)
She said she would come.

Sosen (d. 1776)
Lotus seeds.

Sosnora, Viktor Aleksandrovich (b. 1936)
Crow.
Do you envy, my comrades-in-arms.
Footsteps of an Owl and His Lament, The.

Letter, A.
Owl and the Mouse, The.
Supreme Hour, The.
There it all was: the gaslamp, drugstore.
Where are our horses.

Sotheby, William (1757–1833)
Netley Abbey; Midnight.

Soto, Gary (b. 1952)
After Tonight.
Behind Grandma's House.
Black Hair.
Blanco.
Braly Street.
Brown Girl, Blonde Okie.
Chiapas.
Dizzy Girls in the Sixties.
Drought, The.
Effects of Abstract Art, The.
Elements of San Joaquin, The.
Field Poem.
Graciela.
Harvest.
Heaven.
History.
Hoeing.
How Things Work.
Making Money: Drought Year in Minkler,
    California.
Jungle Café, The.
Soup, The.
Map, The.
Mexicans Begin Jogging.
Morning They Shot Tony Lopez, Barber and
    Pusher Who Went Too Far, 1958, The.
Not Knowing.
Ode to Señor Leal's Goat.
Oranges.
Rain.
Small Town with One Road.
Street.
Sun.
Tale of Sunlight, The.
Teaching Numbers.
Telephoning God.
Trees that Change Our Lives.
TV in Black and White.
Who Will Know Us?
Wind.

Sour, Robert
Body and Soul.

Sotoba, Layman (1036–1101)
Mountain—Buddha's body, The.

Soudijn, Karel (b. 1944)
Cleaning.
Régime.

Soupault, Philippe (b. 1897)
Comrade.
Condemned.
Epitaph: André Breton.
Epitaph: Tristran Tzara.
Georgia.
Life-Saving Medal.
One o'Clock.
One Two or Three.
Poems from Saint Pelagia Prison.
Route.
Sporting Goods.
Sunday.
To Drink.
Twilight.
You Who Sleep.

Sour, Robert
Body and Soul.

Sousa, John Philip (1854–1932)
Feast of the Monkeys, The.
Have You Seen the Lady?

Sousa, Noémia da (b. 1927)
Appeal.
Call.
Let My People Go.
Our Voice.
Poem of a Distant Childhood.
Poem of João, The.

Souster, Raymond (b. 1921)
Choosing Coffins.
Flight of the Roller Coaster.
Hunter, The.
Ladybug.

Lagoons, Hanlan's Point.
Man Who Finds that His Son Has Become a
    Thief, The.
May 15th.
On the Rouge.
Six-Quart Basket, The.
Ties.
Young Girls.

Soutar, William (1898–1943)
Auld House, The.
Auld Sang.
Makar, The.
Permanence of the Young Men, The.
Philosophic Taed, The.
Riddle, A: "Yon laddie wi' the gowdan pow."
Room, The.
Scotland.
Song: "Whaur yon broken brig hings owre."
Summer Is By.
Supper.
Three Puddocks, The.
Tryst [or Trysting Place], The.
Whigmaleerie, A.

Southard, O. Mabson
Across the still lake.
At the window, sleet.
By mist.
Down to dark leaf-mold.
Gleaming—sunken stones.
Hushed, the lake-shore's pines.
In the garden pool.
In the sea, sunset.
Mirrored by the spring.
Now the leaves are still.
Old rooster crows, The.
On a leaf, a leaf.
On the top fence-rail.
One breaker crashes.
Patter of rain, A.
Perching bolt upright.
Snow-laden bushes.
Steadily it snows.
Still sunlit, one tree.
This morning's rainbow.
Waves now fall short, The.

Southerland, Ellease
Blue Clay.
Night in Nigeria.
Pale Ant.
Recitation.
Two Fishing Villages.

Southern Bushmen Oral Tradition
Day We Die, The.

Southerne, Thomas (1660–1746)
Song: "Pursuing beauty, men descry."

Southey, Caroline Anne Bowles (1786–1854)
Mariner's Hymn.

Southey, Robert (1774–1843)
Battle of Blenheim, The.
Cold! cold! 'tis a chilly clime.
Devil, The.
Did then the bold slave rear at last the sword.
Go, Valentine.
High in the air exposed the slave is hung.
Hold your mad hands! for ever on your plain.
How does the water / Come down at Lodore?
Inchcape Rock, The.
Kehama's Curse.
Ode to a Pig while His Nose Was Being Bored.
Oh he is worn with toil! the big drops run.
Old Man's Comforts and How He Gained
    Them, The.
Remembrance.
Scholar, The.
Ship, The.
Soldier's Wife, The.
'Tis night; the mercenary tyrants sleep.
To a Goose [or Gosse].
Why dost thou beat thy breast and rend thine
    hair.
Widow, The.
Wrinkled, crabbèd man they picture thee, A.

Southgate, Christopher
Man.

Southwell, Lady Anne Harris (1571–1636)
All married men desire to have good wives.

Elegie Written by the Lady A. S. to the
    Countesse of London Derrye Supposyenge
    Hir to be Dead by Hir Long Silence, An.
Epitaph, uppon Cassandra Mac Willms Wife to
    Sr Thomas Ridgway Earle of London Derry
    by ye Lady A. S., An.
To the Kinges Most Excellent Majestye.

Southwell, Robert (1561?–95)
At Home in Heaven.
Before my face the picture hangs.
Burning Babe, The.
Child[e] My Choice [or Choyse], A.
Child My Choice, A.
Christ[e]'s Childhood[e].
Christs Sleeping Friends.
Content and Ri[t]ch[e].
David's Peccavi.
I Dye Alive.
Look[e] Home.
Loss[e] in Delay[e].
Man's Civil[l] War[re].
Marie [or Mary] Magdalens Complaint at
    Christs Death.
Nativity of Christ[e], The.
New Heaven, New War[re].
New Prince, New Pomp[e].
Of the Blessed Sacrament of the Altar [or
    Aulter].
Seek[e] Flowers of Heaven.
Sinnes Heavie Loade.
Times [or Tymes] Go[e] By Turn[e]s.
Upon the Image of Death.
Vale of Tear[e]s, A.

Southwick, Marcia
Earthly Light.

Souza, Eunice De (b. 1940)
De Souza Prabhu.
Women in Dutch Painting.

Sowbel, S. B.
If You're Lost.

Sowle, Jane (fl. 1680)
Short Testimony for Anne Whitehead, A.

Soyfer, Jura
Song of Dachau.

Soyinka, Wole (b. 1934)
Abiku.
After the Deluge.
Apologia (Nkomati)
Bearings III: Amber Wall.
Civilian and Soldier.
Death in the Dawn.
Fado Singer.
Funeral Sermon, Soweto.
Harvest of Hate.
He escape the lynch days. He survives.
Huge with Time, a wombfruit lanced.
Hunchback of Dugbe, The.
I Think It Rains.
Ikeja, Friday, Four O'Clock.
"No!" He Said.
Massacre, October '66.
Night.
Post Mortem.
Prisoner.
Rust and silence fill the thatch.
Season.
Telephone Conversation.
To My First White Hairs.
Ujamaa.
We wish only to bury our dead. Shorn.

Sozan-Kyonin (fl. 9th cent.?)
Rootless tree, A.

Spafford, Horatio G. (1828–1888)
It Is Well with My Soul.

Spahr, Juliana
Story goes like this: the light, The.

Spalding, A. W.
High Adventure.

Spalding, Susan Marr (fl. 19th cent.)
Fate.

Spark, Muriel (b. 1918)
Faith and Works.
Kensington Gardens.

Sparrow, John (1906–92)
Apology and Explanation.

Epitaph: "This stone, with not unpardonable pride."
To an Angel in the House.

Sparshott, Francis (b. 1926)
Entanglement.
Improperia.
Naming of the Beasts, The.
Paysage Choisi.
Reply to the Committed Intellectual.
Three Seasons.

Spatola, Adriano (b. 1941)
Poem Stalin, The.
Risk of Abstraction, The.

Spaziani, Maria Luisa (b. 1924)
Aegean, The.
Comet, The.
Convent in '45, The.
Crossroads, The.
Destiny.
Duomo, The.
Figurehead, The.
Grain of Sand, The.
I shall find in paradise that emaciated rose shoot.
If it were a sea, this immense wind.
It Is Said by Some Sailors, the Old.
Journey in the Orient.
Memory's Usefulness.
Merciful Shore, The.
Present, The.
Prison, The.
Pure Dust.
Role Reversal.
Rome has a thousand fountains, and in May they sing.
Spark of Green.
Sunday in the provinces, a plaintive Norman bell-peal.
Tender heart, hairy muscle.
To the Readers.
To the Victims of Mauthausen.
Traveling with too much baggage is not a good idea.
Ultrasound.
Via Margutta.
White on White.
Your life is a baby not yet born.

Speak, Margaret
Ingredients of Glass.

Speakes, Richard
Heartbreak Hotel Piano-Bar.
Mama Loves Janis Joplin.
Patsy Cline.

Spear, Charles (b. 1910)
At a Danse Macabre.
Disinherited, The.
Environs of Vanholt I.
Memoriter.
Remark.
Vineta.
Watchers, The.

Spear, Roberta (b. 1948)
Good Men.
Nest for Everyone, A.
River Song.

Spee, Friedrich (1591–1635)
Spouse of Jesus Laments Her Heart's Flame, The.

Speed, Samuel
Peace.

Speers, Edith (b. 1949)
Australorp.

Speght, Rachel (b. 1597)
Disswasion hearing her assigne my helpe.
Dream[e], The [*or* A].
My grief, quoth I, is called Ignorance.
When splendent Sol, which riseth in the East.

Spellman, Alfred B. (b. 1934)
Did John's Music Kill Him?
In Orangeburg My Brothers Did.
Twist, The.
When Black People Are.

Spence, Lewis (1874–1955)
Prows O' Reekie, The.

Spence, Michael
Fig Curtain of Atherton, The.

Spencer, Anne (1882–1975)
At the Carnival.
Before the Feast of Shushan.
Dunbar.
Lady, Lady.
Letter to My Sister.
Lines to a Nasturtium.
Substitution.
Wife-Woman, The.

Spencer, Bernard (1909–63)
Blue Arm.
Boat Poem.
Castanets.
Delos.
Egyptian Dancer at Shubra.
Invaders, The.
Night-Time: Starting to Write.
Olive Trees.
Passed On.
Rendezvous, The.
Spring Wind, A.
Thousand Killed, A.
Yachts on the Nile.

Spencer, James Harvey (1870–1950)
For You.

Spencer, Kate Clark
When I Died on My Birthday.

Spender, Stephen *See also* **Leishman, J. B.**

Spender, Stephen (1909–95)
Abrupt and charming mover.
Acts passed beyond the boundary of mere wishing.
After They Have Tired of the Brilliance of Cities.
Air Raid across the Bay at Plymouth.
Auden at Milwaukee.
Auf dem Wasser zu Singen.
Beethoven's Death Mask.
Daybreak.
Elementary School Classroom in a Slum, An.
Epilogue: "Time is a thing."
Epilogue to a Human Drama.
Express, The.
Farewell in a Dream.
Funeral, The.
History and Reality.
"I" Can Never Be a Great Man, An.
I Think Continually of Those Who Were Truly Great.
Ice.
In Railway Halls.
Judas Iscariot.
Landscape near an Aerodrome, The.
Marston.
Mask.
Memento.
Missing My Daughter.
My Parents.
New Year.
Not Palaces.
One More New Botched Beginning.
Polar Exploration.
Port Bou.
Prisoners, The.
Pylons, The.
Rejoice in the Abyss.
Room above the Square, The.
Shapes of Death, The.
Song: "Stranger, you who hide my love."
Sonnet: "You were born; must die; were loved; must love."
Statistics.
Thoughts during an Air Raid.
To T.A.R.H.
Two Armies.
Ultima Ratio Regum.
Unemployed.
What I Expected.
Whim of Time, A.
Winter and Summer.
Winter Landscape.
Without That Once Clear Aim.
Word.
Your Body Is Stars.

Spenser, Edmund (1552?–99)
Amoretti, *sels.*
Astrophel, *sels.*
Elegy, An: "She fell away in her first ages spring."
Epithalamion.
Faerie Queene, The, *sels.*
Fox and the Ape Go to Court, The.
Hymn[e] of Heavenly Beauty [*or* Beautie], An.
Hymn of Heavenly Love, An.
Iambicum Trimetrum.
Merry Cuckoo, The.
Prothalamion.
Ruines of Time, The.
Shepeardes Calender, The, *sels.*
To the Right Worshipfull, My Singular Good Frend, Master Gabriell Harvey, Doctor of the Lawes.
Who lists to see, what ever nature, arte.

"Speranza" *See* **Wilde, Lady Jane Francesca**

Speyer, Leonora (1872–1956)
To a Song of Sappho Discovered in Egypt.
Witch!

Spicer, Jack (b. 1925)
6.
Army Beach with Trumpets.
Book of Galahad, The.
Book of Gawain, The.
Book of Music, A.
Cantata.
Cardplayers, The.
Conspiracy.
Duet for a Chair and a Table.
Five Words for Joe Dunn on His 22nd Birthday.
Four Poems for *The St. Louis Sporting News.*
Ghost Song.
God must have a big eye to see everything.
God's other eye is good and gold. So bright.
Good Friday: For Lack of an Orchestra.
Graphemics.
Imaginary Elegies, I-IV.
Improvisations on a Sentence by Poe.
Jungle Warfare.
Lament for the Makers: "No call upon anyone but the timber drifting in the waves."
Morphemics.
Mummer.
Orfeo.
Phonemics.
Poem without a Single Bird in It, A.
Poetry, almost blind like a camera.
Song of a Prisoner.
Thing Language.
Transformations.
Valentine, A.
Walden Pond / All those noxious gases rising from it.
Yes, be like God. I wonder what I thought.

Spiess, Robert
Asparagus bed.
Becoming dusk.
Blue jays in the pines.
Chain saw stops, The.
Dirt road, A.
Dry, summer day.
Lean-to of tin.
Light river wind, A.
Long wedge of geese, A.
Marsh marigold.
Muttering month.
Ostrich fern on shore.
Patches of snow.
Shooting the rapids!
Tar paper cabin.
Winter moon.
Winter wind.
Wispy autumn clouds.

Spire, André (1886–1968)
Abishag.
Dust.
Hear, O Israel!
It Was Not You.
Lonely.
Now You're Content.
Nudities.
Spring.

Spireng, Matthew J.
Snowy Owl.

Spires, Elizabeth (b. 1952)
0°.
Apology.
Bodies, The.
Comb and the Mirror, The.
Interrogations of the Sparrow.
Robed Heart, The.
Rock, The.
Two Shadows.
Woman on the Dump, The.
Worldling.

Spivack, Kathleen (b. 1938)
Dust.
Judgment, The.
Love U.S.A.

Spofford, Harriet Prescott (1835–1921)
Fossil Raindrops, The.
Magdalen.
Tryst, The.

Spooner, Lawrence
On Giving Up Smoking.

Sprague, Achsa W. (c.1828–62)
'Tis near the time. I'm glad 'tis getting late.

Spratt, Thomas (1635–1713)
On His Mistress Drown'd.

Sprigg, Christopher St. John See **"Caudwell, Christopher"**

Springer, Philip
How Little We Know (How Little It Matters)

Springer, Thomas Grant
Giving and Forgiving.
Harmony.

Squire, Sir John Collings ("Solomon Eagle") (1884–1950)
Ballade of the Poetic Life.
Interior.
It did not last; the Devil howling Ho.
Stockyard, The.
Under.
Vision of Truth, A.
When I Leapt over Tower Bridge.
Winter Nightfall.

Sri Sri (1910–83)
Man walks on the bridge and gives away the change in his, A.

Ssu-k'ung Shu (740–790?)
Exhorting Myself.
In Heaven.
In Illness, Dismissing My Singing Girl.
In the Country.
In the Mountains.
Occasional Poem, An.
Oxhead Temple.

Ssu-ma Hsiang-ju (c.179–118 B.C.)
Cock-Phoenix, Hen-Phoenix.
Sir Fantasy.

St. Germain, Sheryl
Addiction.
Cajun.

Stadler, Ernst
Decampment.

Staff, Leopold (1878–1957)
Duckweed.
Foundations.
Kingdom.
Portrait.
Speech.

Stafford, Kim R.
Inside the Fence: Tule Lake Internment Camp.

Stafford, William (1914–93)
Accountability.
After Arguing against the Contention That Art Must Come from Discontent.
Among Strangers.
Animal That Drank Up Sound, The.
Ask Me.
At Cove on the Crooked River.
At the Bomb Testing Site.
At the Edge of Town.
At the Klamath Berry Festival.
At the Playground.
At the Un-National Monument along the Canadian Border.
August.
Bess.

Bi-Focal.
Bring the North.
British Columbia.
Broken Home.
Ceremony.
Chair in the Meadow, The.
Christianite.
Epitaph Ending in And, The.
Escape, The.
Farm on the Great Plains, The.
For the Barn at Bread Loaf.
For the Grave of Daniel Boone.
Glimpses.
Gulls at Cannon Beach.
Holding the Sky.
Humanities Lecture.
In a Museum in the Capital.
In the Deep Channel.
In Time of Need.
Indian Cave Jerry Ramsey Found, The.
Juncos.
Late at Night.
Moment, The.
Monuments for a Friendly Girl at a Tenth Grade Party.
Near.
Notice What This Poem Is Not Doing.
Now.
Observation Car and Cigar.
One Home.
One of the Years.
Vacation.
People of the South Wind.
Priorities at Friday Ranch.
Religion Back Home.
Report from an Unappointed Committee.
Report to Crazy Horse.
Rescued Year, The.
Returned to Say.
Ritual to Read to Each Other, A.
Run before Dawn.
Scars.
School Days.
Serving with Gideon.
Sound from the Earth, A.
Stared Story, A.
Story, A.
Story That Could Be True, A.
Stranger Not Ourselves, The.
Strangers.
Strokes.
Survey, A.
Textures.
These Days.
These Leaves.
Things That Happen.
Time.
Tourist Country.
Traveling through the Dark.
Visions.
Walking West.
Well Rising, The.
Oregon Message, An.
Whole Story, The.
With Kit, Age Seven, at the Beach.
With My Crowbar Key.

Stagnelius, Erik Johann (1793–1823)
Memory.

Stainer, Pauline (b. 1941)
Bleaklow.
Honeycomb, The.
I am black-browed.
Sarcophagus.
Seals, The.
Sighting the Slave Ship.
Wound-dresser's Dream, The.
Xochiquetzal.

Stallworthy, Jon (b. 1935)
Again.
Almond Tree, The.
Beginning of the End, The.
Letter from Berlin, A.
Letter to a Friend.
Miss Lavender.
Mother Tongue.
Poem about Poems about Vietnam, A.
Question of Form and Content, A.

Sindhi Woman.
Pour Commencer.
Walking against the Wind.
War Story.

Stam, Betty Scott
Ring Sonnet.
Stand Still, and See.
Two Names.

Stamp, Catriona (b. 1950)
Rebirth.

Stampa, Gaspara (c.1523–1554)
At dawn of the day the Creator.
Deeply repentant of my sinful ways.
Holy angels, in envy I cast no sigh.
Hunger.
I am now so weary with waiting.
Often when alone I liken my lord / to the cosmos.
When before those eyes, my life and light.
Women, whoever wishes to know my lord.

Stanard, Christopher (b. 1967)
Baseball.
Rap Is.
Washington Square Park and a Game of Chess.
Wrong Color.

Standing, Sue
Hopper's Women.
Mouvance.

Stanford, Ann (1916–87)
Beating, The.
Brother Symmes conversed with her on the ship.
Night of Souls.
Riders, The.

Stanley, John
Limerick: "Bells from the steeple resound, The."
Limerick: "Fact of the matter is, Jack, The."
Limerick: "Miranda, remember that Inn?"

Stanley, Mary (1919–80)
Put Off Constricting Day.
Sestina: "Body of my love is a familiar country, The."
Wife Speaks, The.

Stanley, Thomas (1625–78)
All Things Drink.
Beauty.
Bracelet, The.
Celia Singing.
Changed, Yet Constant.
Combat, The.
Divorce, The.
Exequies, The.
Expectation.
Glowworm, The.
Grasshopper, The.
La Belle Confidente.
Love Deposed.
Love's Innocence.
Magnet, The.
Ode XV.
Old I Am.
On a Violet in Her Breast.
On Mr. Shirley's Poems.
On S. John the Baptist.
Paraphrase Upon Part of the CXXXIX Psalm, A.
Pythagoric Letter, The.
Relapse, The.
Repulse, The.
Self-Deceaver, The.
Snow-Ball, The.
Song: "Fool, take up thy shaft again."
Song: "I prithee let my heart alone."
Speaking and Kissing.
Swallow, The.
Time Recover'd.
Wish, The.
Would I were air that thou with heat opprest.

Stanley-Wrench, Margaret (1917–1974)
Hinterland.
Storm, The.

Stansbury, Joseph (1740–1809)
To Cordelia.

Stanton, Frank Lebby (1857–1927)
Keep a-Goin'

Stanton, Maura (b. 1946)
Ballad of the Magic Glasses.
Comfort.
Conjurer, The.
Few Picnics in Illinois, A.
In Ignorant Cadence.
Judith Recalls Holofernes.
Little Ode for X.
Ode to Mozart.
Posthuman.
Shoplifters.
Short Story.
Sorrow and Rapture.
Space.
Veiled Lady, The.
Visibility.
Voice for the Sirens, A.

Stanton, Will D. (b. 1918)
Dandelions.

Stapleton, Francellina (fl. 1655)
Upon a Joynted Ring.

Starbird, Kaye (b. 1916)
Hound, The.

Starbuck, George (b. 1931)
Bone Thoughts on a Dry Day: Chicago.
Chip.
Communication to the City Fathers of Boston.
High Renaissance.
Margaret Are You Drug.
Monarch of the Sea.
New Strain.
Of Late.
On First Looking in on Blodgett's Keats's
    "Chapman's Homer."
Prognosis.
Said.
Said / Agatha Christie to.
Sonnet with a Different Letter at the End of
    Every Line.
Technologies.
Translations from the English.

Starhawk
Demeter's Song.

Starkey, David
Scrabble.

Starkey, James See "O'Sullivan, Seumas"

Statius, Publius Papinius (c.61–96 A.D.)
Book 10.
First of December, The.
In Memory of His Father.
Jocular Lines to Plotius Grypus.
Sleep.
Thanksgiving to the Emperor Augustus
    Germanicus Domitianus.
To Sleep.

Staub, Herta Felicia
September.

Staughton, William (1770–1829)
Tell Us, Ye Servants of the Lord.

Stead, Christian Karlson (b. 1932)
Air New Zealand.
All over the plain of the world lovers are being
    hurt.
April Notebook.
Between.
Fucking, I feel at one with the world.
Odysseus under wet snapping sheets.
Rain, and a flurry of wind shaking the pear's
    white blossom.
That the balls of the lover are not larger than
    the balls of the priest.
Walking westward/ you have it all before you.

Stead, W. T. (1849–1912)
Now that war is in the air, e'en the parson in
    his lair.

Stead, William Force (b. 1884)
How Infinite Are Thy Ways.
I Closed My Eyes To-Day and Saw.

Stedman, Edmund Clarence (1833–1908)
Ballad of Lager Bier, The.

Steede, Vejay
Reggae.

Steele, Nancy
Diminutive.

Steele, Peter (b. 1939)
Cana.

Marking Time.

Steele, Sir Richard (1672–1729)
Trim's Song: The Fair Kitchen-Maid.

Steele, Susanna See Rosen, Michael

Steele, Timothy (b. 1948)
At Will Robers Beach.
Aubade, An: "As she is showering, I wake to
    see."
Aurora.
Devotional Sonnet, A.
Epitaph: "Here lies Sir Tact, a diplomatic
    fellow."
Eros.
In the King's Rooms.
Joseph.
Library, The.
One Morning.
Rural Colloquy with a Painter.
Sheets, The.
Timothy.
Waiting for the Storm.
Wartburg, 1521–22, The.

Steendam, Jacob (1616–72)
Oh, Sing to God.
When I Admire the Greatness.

Steere, Richard (1643–1721)
Earth Felicities, Heavens Allowances.
Monumental Memorial of Marine Mercy, A.
On a Sea-Storm nigh the Coast.
Poem upon the Caelestial Embassy, A.

Stefanile, Felix (b. 1920)
How I Changed My Name, Felice.

Stefanovich, Nikolai (1912–79)
For all of us destiny is undivided.

Steiger, Anatoly (1908–43)
Ancient Custom, An.
Dull rattle of shutters being lowered, The.
Friendship.
How do we break the habit of big words.
Nobody waits at the foot of the stairs any
    more.
Not an epilogue, but everything coming to an
    end.
They will not ask us: have you sinned?
Until the sun sinks into a green.
We believe books and music.

Stein, Charles (b. 1944)
Parmenides Machine, A.

Stein, Gertrude (1874–1946)
Bundles for Them.
Cézanne.
Cloth, A.
Colored Hats.
Concluding Aria.
Dog, A.
Frightful Release, A.
From Stanzas in Meditation.
George Hugnet.
How do you like what you have.
I Am Rose.
I think very well of Susan but I do not know
    her name.
Identity a Poem.
In This Way.
It is not a range of a mountain.
Kiss my lips. She did.
Kneeling.
Leave, A.
Let Us Describe.
Lifting belly. Are you. Lifting.
Light in the moon the only light is on
    Sunday, A.
More.
Mounted Umbrella, A.
New Cup and Saucer, A.
On Her Way.
Petticoat, A.
Pigeons on the grass alas.
Purse, A.
Put a sun in Sunday, Sunday.
Red Roses.
Sacred.
Scenes from the Door.
Sound, A.
Stanza 10.
Suppose an Eyes.

Susie Asado.
Teachers taught her, The.
Umbrella, An.
Valentine to Sherwood Anderson, A.
What Do I See.
Which I wish to say is this.
White Hunter, A.
Why Do You Feel Differently.

Stein, Kevin
Because You're American.
First Performance of the Rock 'n Roll Band
    Puce Exit.
In the Kingdom of Perpetual Repair.
It Didn't Begin with Horned Owls Hooting at
    Noon.
Night Shift, after Drinking Dinner, Container
    Corporation of America, 1972.
Past Midnight, My Daughter Awakened by
    Miles Davis' Kind of Blue.
Upon Finding a Black Woman's Door Sprayed
    with Swastikas, I Tell Her This Story of
    Hands.
World Without End.

Stein, Rose M. (d. 1938)
Lines to Mother.

Steinbarg, Eliezer (1880–1932)
Terrible Thought, A.

Steinberg, David
Image Was of Me Flowing through You, The.
Purple Is the Color of Longing.
Slowly, slowly.
With you I begin.

Steinberg, Jakov [or Jacob] (1887–1947)
All of a Summer.
Heart, The.
It has been long since first my fears grew light.
Rain at Night.
Till Evening.
Turn towards the end, be a leaf dying.

Steingesser, Martin
Spring Forward.

Steinmar (fl. late 13th cent.)
Farmhand lay all hidden, A.
Since She Gives So Little Pay.

"Stella" See Johnson, Esther

Stephanou, Lydia (b. 1922)
"Case of Assault, A."

"Stephany"
I have spent my life.
It is again.
Moving deep.
What marked the river's flow.
Who collects the pain.

Stephen, James Kenneth (1859–92)
Drinking Song.
In the Backs.
Last Ride Together (from Her Point of View),
    The.
Malines.
On a Parisian Boulevard.
On a Rhine Steamer.
Remonstrance, A.
She's not a faultless woman; no!
Sincere Flattery of R. B.
Sincere Flattery of W. W. (Americanus)
Sonnet, A: "Two voices are there: one is of the
    deep."
To R. K.

Stephens, Brunton (1835–1902)
Gentle Anarchist, The.

Stephens, James (1880–1950)
Blue Blood.
Cage, The.
Christmas at Freelands.
Crest Jewel, The.
Daisies, The.
Deirdre.
Evening.
Glass of Beer, A.
Goat Paths, The.
Good and Bad.
Hate.
In the Night.
In the Poppy Field.
In Waste Places.

Lake, The.
Little Things.
Main-Deep, The.
Odell.
Outcast, The.
Red-haired Man's Wife, The.
Rivals, The.
Seumas Beg.
Shell, The.
Snare, The.
To the Four Courts, Please.
Twins, The.
Watcher, The.
What Thomas an Buile Said in a Pub.
White Fields.
Wind, The.

Stephens, Meic (b. 1938)
Elegy for Llywelyn Humphries.
Hooters.
Ponies, Twynyrodyn.

Stephens, Michael (b. 1946)
After Asia.

Stephens, Philip (b. 1966)
God Shed His Grace.
Hangman.
Signalmen, The.

Stept, Sam H. (fl. 1928)
That's My Weakness Now.

Steptoe, Lamont B. (b. 1949)
Election Time.
Mississippi Blues.
Notes for a Poem from the Middle Passage of
    Years.
O' Yes.
Such a Boat of Land.
Sweet Brown Rice and Red Bones.
Window Shopping.
Wired In.

Sterling, Andrew B. (1874–1955)
Meet Me in St. Louis, Louis.
Under the Anheuser Bush.
What You Goin' to Do When the Rent Comes
    'Round?

Sterling, George (1869–1926)
Aldebaran at Dusk.
Black Vulture, The.

Stern, Anatol (1899–1968)
Europa.

Stern, Gerald (b. c.1925)
Adler.
Behaving Like a Jew.
Bela.
Blue Skies, White Breasts, Green Trees.
Cow Worship.
Dancing, The.
Dear waves, what will you do for me this
    year?
Diary.
Dog, The.
Expulsion, The.
Faces I Love, The.
For Song.
Fritz.
Hinglish.
Kissing Stieglitz Goodbye.
Lucky Life.
Modern Love.
Morning Harvest.
Night.
On the Far Edge of Kilmer.
Pile of Feathers.
Red Bird.
Romania, Romania.
Royal Manor Road.
Self-Portrait.
Soap.
Sounds, The.
Tashlikh.
There Is Wind, There Are Matches.

Sternberg, Jacob (b. 1890)
Little Birds.

Sternhold, Thomas (c.1500–49)
I Lift My Heart to Thee.
Majesty of God, The.
My Shepherd Is the Living Lord.

Sternlieb, Barry (b. 1947)
Right of Way.
Survivor.

Stesichoros (fl. 6th cent. B.C.)
Across from glorious Erytheia.
Don't pile cruel cares upon those griefs.
Helen suddenly saw a divine omen.
Since Tyndareos.
They flung many quinces toward the chariot.
This story is not true.

Stevens, Cat
Wild World.

Stevens, George Alexander (1710–84)
Bartleme Fair.
Repentance.
Simple Pastoral, A.

Stevens, Michael
Carp, The.

Stevens, Wallace (1879–1955)
American Sublime, The.
Anecdote of the Jar.
Anecdote of the Prince of Peacocks.
Angel Surrounded by Paysans.
Anglais Mort à Florence.
Annual Gaiety.
Arrival at the Waldorf.
Asides on the Oboe.
Auroras of Autumn, The.
Autumn Refrain.
Bantams in Pine-Woods.
Beginning, The.
Bouquet of Belle Scavoir.
Bowl.
Brave Man, The.
Candle a Saint, The.
Comedian as the Letter C, The.
Contrary Theses (I)
Course of a Particular, The.
Dance of the Macabre Mice.
Death of a Soldier, The.
Debris of Life and Mind.
Depression before Spring.
Discovery of Thought, A.
Disillusionment of Ten O'Clock.
Domination of Black.
Dry Loaf.
Earthy Anecdote.
Emperor of Ice-Cream, The.
Evening without Angels.
Farewell to an idea...A cabin stands.
Farewell to an idea...The mother's face.
Farewell to Florida.
Final Soliloquy of the Interior Paramour.
First idea was not our own, The. Adam.
Flyer's Fall.
Gallant Château.
Girl in a Nightgown.
Glass of Water, The.
God Is Good. It Is a Beautiful Night.
Gray Stones and Gray Pigeons.
Gubbinal.
He was at Naples writing letters home.
High-Toned Old Christian Woman, A.
Holiday in Reality.
Homunculus et la Belle Étoile.
House Was Quiet and the World Was Calm,
    The.
I cannot bring a world quite round.
I feel an apparition.
Idea of Order at Key West, The.
Idiom of the Hero.
In the Carolinas.
Infanta Marina.
Irish Cliffs of Moher, The.
Is there an imagination that sits enthroned.
It feels good as it is without the giant.
It is a theatre floating through the clouds.
It Must Be Abstract.
John Smith and His Son, John Smith.
Landscape with Boat.
Large Red Man Reading.
Le Monocle de Mon Oncle.
Less and Less Human, O Savage Spirit.
Life Is Motion.
Lunar Paraphrase.
Major abstraction is the idea of man, The.

Man bent over his guitar, The.
Man on the Dump, The.
Martial Cadenza.
Meditation Celestial and Terrestrial.
Men Made Out of Words.
Metamorphosis.
Metaphor as Degeneration.
Metaphors of a Magnifico.
Motive for Metaphor, The.
Mozart, 1935.
Mrs. Alfred Uruguay.
No Possum, No Sop, No Taters.
Nomad Exquisite.
Not Ideas about the Thing but the Thing Itself.
Notes toward a Supreme Fiction.
O Florida, Venereal Soil.
Of Mere Being.
Of Modern Poetry.
Old Lutheran Bells at Home, The.
On the Adequacy of Landscape.
Ordinary Women, The.
Owl in the Sarcophagus, The.
Paltry Nude Starts on a Spring Voyage, The.
Peter Quince at the Clavier.
Phosphor Reading by His Own Light.
Plain Sense of Things, The.
Planet on the Table, The.
Pleasures of Merely Circulating, The.
Plot against the Giant, The.
Ploughing on Sunday.
Poem That Took the Place of a Mountain, The.
Poems of Our Climate, The.
Poetry Is a Destructive Force.
Postcard from the Volcano, A.
Primitive like an Orb, A.
Puella Parvula.
Quiet Normal Life, A.
Rabbit Is King of the Ghosts, A.
Reader, The.
Reality Is an Activity of the Most August
    Imagination.
River of Rivers in Connecticut, The.
Rock, The.
Room on a Garden, A.
Sad Strains of a Gay Waltz.
Sea Surface Full of Clouds.
Sense of the Sleight-of-Hand Man, The.
Snow Man, The.
So-and-So Reclining on Her Couch.
Soldier's Wound, The.
Soldier, There Is a War between the Mind.
Song of Fixed Accord.
Stars at Tallapoosa.
Study of Two Pears.
Sun, in clownish yellow, but not a clown, The.
Sun This March, The.
Sunday Morning.
Table Talk.
Tea at the Palaz of Hoon.
Thinking of a Relation between the Images of
    Metaphors.
Thirteen Ways of Looking at a Blackbird.
This is where the serpent lives, the bodiless.
This Solitude of Cataracts.
This was the salty taste of glory.
To an Old Philosopher in Rome.
To Henry Church.
To the One of Fictive Music.
To the Roaring Wind.
Two Figures in Dense Violet Night.
Unhappy people in a happy world, An.
Vacancy in the Park.
Valley Candle.
Waving Adieu, Adieu, Adieu.
What shall we say to the lovers of freedom.
World as Meditation, The.
World without Peculiarity.
Worms at Heaven's Gate, The.

Stevenson, Alec Brock (b. 1895)
Death, My Companion.
He Who Loved Beauty.
Hemlock at Sunset, A.
Icarus in November.
Sonnet: "If it be night . . . ."

Stevenson, Anne (b. 1933)
Arioso Dolente.
By the Boat House, Oxford.

Demolition, The.
Epitaph for a Good Mouser.
Fiction-Makers, The.
From an Asylum; Kathy Chattle to Her
    Mother, Ruth Arbeiter.
Gales.
Giving Rabbit to My Cat Bonnie.
Himalayan Balsam.
Larousse Gastronomique.
In the Orchard.
Making Poetry.
Marriage, The.
Price, The.
Ragwort.
Re-reading Jane.
Respectable House.
Sous-Entendu.
Spirit Is Too Blunt an Instrument, The.
Suicide.
Temporarily in Oxford.
Utah.
When the Camel Is Dust it Goes through the
    Needle's Eye.
Willow Song.

Stevenson, Matthew (*fl.* **1654–85**)
Here in this homely cabinet.

Stevenson, Robert Louis (1850–94)
Alcaics; to H. F. B.
Armies in the Fire.
As from the house your mother sees.
As with heaped bees at hiving time.
At the Seaside [*or* Sea-Side].
Auntie's Skirts.
Autumn Fires.
Bed in Summer.
Block City.
Blows the Wind Today.
Brilliant kernel of the night, The.
Browning.
Celestial Surgeon, The.
Christmas at Sea.
Christmas Prayer, A.
Cow, The.
Epitaph: "Angler rose, he took his rod, The."
Escape at Bedtime.
Evensong.
Fair Isle at Sea—thy lovely name.
Fragment, A: "Thou strainest through the
    mountain fern."
From a Railway Carriage.
Gardener, The.
Good and Bad Children.
Good Boy, A.
Good Play, A.
Happy Thought.
He hears with gladdened heart the thunder.
Home no more home to me, whither must I
    wander?
House Beautiful, The.
I Am a Hunchback.
I saw red evening through the rain.
Ille Terrarum.
In autumn when the woods are red.
In the highlands, in the country places.
In the States.
It's an overcome sooth for age an' youth.
Lamplighter, The.
Land of Counterpane, The.
Land of Nod, The.
Land of Story-Books, The.
Last night we had a thunderstorm in style.
Light-Keeper, The.
Limerick: "There was an old man of the
    Cape."
Looking Forward.
Mile an' a Bittock, A.
Moon, The.
Morning drum-call on my eager ear, The.
My Bed Is a Boat.
My house, I say. But hark to the sunny doves.
My Shadow.
Nay, but I fancy somehow, year by year.
Not I.
O dull cold northern sky.
O to Be Up and Doing.
Over the Sea to Skye.
Pirate Ditty.

Pirate Story.
Rain.
Requiem: "Under the wide and starry sky."
Say not of me that weakly I declined.
So live, so love, so use that fragile hour.
Song of a Traveller, The.
Spaewife, The.
Summer Sun.
Swallows travel to and fro.
Swing, The.
System.
Ticonderoga: A Legend of the West Highlands.
To A Gardener.
To Henry James.
To Mrs. Will H. Low.
To S.C.
To the Muse.
Travel.
Tropics vanish, and meseems that I, The.
Vagabond, The.
Where Go the Boats?
Whole Duty of Children.
Windy Nights.
Winter Time [*or* Winter-Time].
Wishes.
Young Night Thought.

Stevenson, William (1530?–75) *and* **John Still**
Back and Side Go Bare, Go Bare.
Jolly Good Ale and Old.

Stevenson, William Frederick (*fl.* **c.1883**)
Life and Impellance.
Planet of Descendance, A.

Stever, Ed
Her Back to Me.

Steward, Joseph (1752–1822)
God from His Throne with Piercing Eye.
My Soul Would Fain Indulge a Hope.

Steward of Baldynneis [*or* Stewart of Baldynnis],
John (1550–1605?)
To His Darrest Freind.

Stewardess of the Empress Kōka (*fl.* **12th cent.**)
For the sake of a night.

Stewart, Bob
August Town.
Words Is Not Enough.

Stewart, Douglas (1913–85)
At the Entrance.
Country Song, A.
Garden of Ships, The.
Leopard Skin.
Oh the corrugated-iron town.
Sigh, wind in the pine.
Silkworms, The.
Terra Australis.
Two Englishmen.

Stewart, Frank
Black Winter.

Stewart, George Craig (1879–1940)
As I Went Down to David's Town.

Stewart, Harold (b. 1916)
Sage in Unison, The.

Stewart, James McAuley *and* **Harold** *See*
"Malley, Ern"

Stewart, Pamela (b. 1943)
Against Silence.
August.
Estes' Backyard, The.
Martin.
Punk Pantoum.
What's It For.

Stewart, Pauline (b. 1962)
Singing down the Breadfruit.

Stewart, Robert
Tonight I Thank the Potato.

Stewart, Susan (b. 1952)
Apple.
Arbor 1937, The.
Slaughter.

Stewart, W. (*fl.* **c.1849**)
Limerick: "Democracy works (*entre nous*)"
There was an old chap who said: "Well."

Stewart, William (1481?–1550?)
Thir Lenterne Dayis Ar Luvely Lang.

Stickney, Trumbull (1874–1904)
Age in Youth.

And, the last day being come, Man stood
    alone.
As a Sad Man, when Evenings Grayer Grow.
At Sainte-Marguerite.
Athenian Garden, An.
Autumn's done; they have the golden corn in,
    The.
Be Still. The Hanging Gardens Were a Dream.
Departure, The.
Dramatic Fragment.
Eride, V.
He Said: "If in His Image I Was Made."
Here in the North I chase an old despair.
I heard a river thro' the valley wander.
In Ampezzo.
In the Past.
Lakeward.
Live Blindly and upon the Hour.
Melancholy Year [Is Dead with Rain], The.
Mnemosyne.
Mount Lykaion.
On Rodin's "L'Illusion, Sœur d'Icare."
On Sandro's Flora.
On Some Shells Found Inland.
On the Concert.
Pandora's Songs.
Pity.
Quiet after the Rain of Morning.
Requiescam.
Sir, say no more.
Six o'Clock.
Sonnets from Greece.
You say, Columbus with his argosies.

Stidger, William Leroy (1886–1949)
Day, A.
Lest Thou Forget.

Stieler, Kaspar (1632–1707)
Hatred Surely Does Not Kiss.
Night's Delights.

Stifter, Adalbert
Autumn Evening.

Stigall, John (d. 1942)
Dying.

Stigter, Gerard *See* **Schippers, K.**

Stiles, Nina
Thank You, God.

Still, John *See* **Stevenson, William**

Stillman, Al (*fl.* **1942**)
Jukebox Saturday Night.

Stillman, Michael (b. 1940)
In Memoriam John Coltrane.
Lullaby for Suzanne.
Song: "Love is a green girl."
Whiskers Meets Polly.

Stilwell, Joseph W. (1883–1946)
Lyric to Spring.

Stirling, Sir William Alexander, Earl of (1567–
1640)
Echo, An.
I Envy Not Endymion.
I Hope, I Fear.
O happy Tithon! if thou know'st thy harp.
Oh, If Thou Knew'st How Thou Thyself Dost
    Harm.
Sonnet: "Cleare moving cristall, pure as the
    Sunne beames."
Sonnet: "I dreamed the nymph that o'er my
    fancy reigns."
Sonnet: "Ile give thee leave my love, in
    beauties field."

Stitch, Wilhelmina
Blessed Are They.
Little Roads to Happiness.

Stites, Edgar P. (b. 1837)
I've Reached the Land of Corn and Wine.

Stockbridge, Patricia
My True Love Hath My Heart and I Have His.

Stockenström, Wilma (b. 1933)
L'Agulhas, A Walk.
On the Suicide of Young Writers.
Rank Harvest of Betrayal, The.

Stocking, Jay Thomas (1870–1936)
O Master-Workman of the Race.

Stockton, John H. (1813–77)
Come, Every Soul.

Stodart, M. A.
One Thing at a Time.

Stoddard, Elizabeth (1823–1902)
Above the Tree.
Before the Mirror.
House by the Sea, The.
Nameless Pain.
One Morn I Left Him in His Bed.
Wife Speaks, The.

Stoddart, Thomas Tod (1810–80)
Beautiful Lunacy! that shapest flight.
He sate like winter o'er the wasted year.
Song: "'Tis light to love thee living, girl, when
hope is full and fair."

Stoessl, Otto
Love.
Moon Fable.

Stoker, Andrew
Limerick: "Student from Pembroke once
said, A."

Stokes, Terry (b. 1943)
Elvis Elevator, The.

Stokesbury, Leon (b. 1945)
Evening's End.

Stone, Alison
Rocket to Russia.
Spofford Hall.

Stone, John A. (b. 1936)
Bass, The.
Confabulation.
Early Sunday Morning.
Gaudeamus Igitur: A Valediction.
Getting to Sleep in New Jersey.
He Makes a House Call.
Rosemary.
Talking to the Family.
Truck, The.

Stone, Ruth (b. 1915)
Burned Bridge, The.
Cocks and Mares.
Codicil.
Dark Conclusions.
Denouement.
Earth Quake.
Hummingbirds.
In an Iridescent Time.
It Follows.
Liberation.
Magnet, The.
My Son.
Nose, The.
On the Mountain.
Periphery.
Reading.
Repetition of Words and Weather.
Resonance.
Room.
Secondhand Coat.
So Be It.
Song of Absinthe Granny, The.
Talking Fish, The.
Up There.
Vernal Equinox.
Whose Scene?
Winter.
Years Later.

Stone, Samuel John (1602–63)
Church's One Foundation, The.

Storace, Patricia
Archaeology of Divorce, The.
King Lear Bewildered.
Wedding Song.

Stordahl, Axel
Day by Day.
I Should Care.

Storer, Thomas (1571–1604)
Rivers.

Storey, Violet Alleyn (b. 1899)
Prayer for Broken Little Families, A.

Storm, Theodor (1817–88)
At the Desk.
Woman's Ritornelle.

Storni, Alfonsina (1892–1938)
Ancestral Burden.
Ancestral Weight.

Camp Fire.
Encounter.
I Am Going to Sleep (Suicide Poem)
I'm Going to Sleep.
Lighthouse in the Night.
Lost Caress, The.
Lyrical Letter to the Other Woman.
Me at the Bottom of the Sea.
My Sister.
Pain.
Siren, The.
Sorrow.
They've Come.
To Eros.
White Claw, The.
Words to My Mother.
World is Bitter, The.

Story, William Wetmore (1819–95)
Cleopatra.
He thanked me for my kindness, disagreed.

Stoutenburg, Adrien (1916–82)
Midnight Saving Time.

Stow, Randolph (b. 1935)
Landfall.
Calenture, The.
Dust.
Enemy, The.
Ghost at Anlaby, The.
My Wish for My Land.
Ruins of the City of Hay.
Singing Bones, The.
Thailand Railway.

Stowe, Harriet Beecher (1811–96)
Abide in Me, O Lord, and I in Thee.
Hymn: "When winds are raging."
Only a Year.
Still, Still, with Thee.

Strabo, Walafrid (809–849)
Dearest, You Come Suddenly and Suddenly
You Depart.
Elegy on Reichenau.

Strachan, W. J.
Limerick: "Said a parson, addressing his
flock."

Strachey, James
Paris Is Not the Same.
These Foolish Things (Remind Me of You)

Stradling, Sir John (1563–1637)
Abraham's Sacrifice of Isaac.

Stramm, August
Battlefield.
Encounter.
Guard-Duty.
Urdeath.

Strand, Mark (b. 1934)
Always.
Breath.
Coming of Light, The.
Coming to This.
Courtship.
Dance, The.
Dead, The.
Door, The.
Dreadful Has Already Happened, The.
Eating Poetry.
Elegy for My Father.
Empty Body, The.
End, The.
Garden, The.
In Celebration.
It is true, as someone has said, that in.
Keeping Things Whole.
Kite, The.
Last Bus, The.
Late Hour, The.
Letter.
Man in Black, The.
Man in the Tree, The.
Marriage, The.
Morning, A.
Morning, Noon and Night.
My Life.
New Year, The.
Night, The Porch, The.
Pot Roast.
Prediction, The.

Shooting Whales.
Story of Our Lives, The.
Tunnel, The.
Where Are the Waters of Childhood?

Strange, Sharan (b. 1959)
Acts of Power.
Barbershop Ritual.
Childhood.
Crazy Girl, The.
Offering.
Still Life.
Streetcorner Church.
Transits.

Strangman, Honor (fl. 1616), and others
Yf there be any man that can tell me quicklye.

**"Strannik" (Prince Ioann Shakhovskoy,
Archbishop of San Francisco) (1902–89)**
Solar Loneliness.

Stratanovsky, Sergey (b. 1944)
Herostratos and Herostratos.
Leningrad stairwell, A.
Terrorist, The.

Stratidakis, Eileen
Need for Armor, A.

Strato [or Straton] (d. 270 B.C.)
A. To start with, grapple your opponent 'round.
Bath-house bench pinched Graphicus' bottom,
The.
'Begin with Zeus,' Aratus said; but, Muse.
Boys' members, Diodorus, come in three.
Despite the ruddy down upon your cheek.
Don't hitch your dear little cunt against that
wall.
Epigram: "Boy's cocks, Diodore."
Epigram: "I am provoked."
Epigram: "I delight in the prime of a boy of
twelve."
Epigram: "Long hair, endless curls trained by
the devoted."
Epigram: "There was this gym-teacher."
Epigram: "Those snooty boys in all their
purple drag!"
Fitness expert. Big gym-man.
Give, and take the cash.
Grey already the hair at my temples.
He's a dragon, see.
Heterosexual Poem.
I loathe a boy who won't be hugged and
kissed.
I swore to you, son of Kronos, never.
If my kisses wrong you, then tit for tat.
In the bed are two, submissive.
In years to come, I ask, be kind.
Let's start from Zeus.
Long hair, and curls woven not by Nature but
by Art.
Meeting a lovely boy face to face.
Numbers in ass, The.
Off with you, boy! Pretended prude!
Once I came across / some beardless doctors.
Pair of brothers love me, A.
Private Poem.
Someone later may hear these playthings,
thinking.
To Kyris.
Twelve-year-old looks fetching in his prime, A.
Two Plus Two.
Vive La Différence.
Who knows when love has had its day.
Yesterday in the bath Diodes' penis.
Your rosy-fingered prick that used to charm.

Straus, Marc J.
Log of Pi, The.
Luck.
Neuroanatomy Summer.
Scarlet Crown.
What I Heard on the Radio Today.

Strauss, Jennifer (b. 1933)
Love Notes.
Tending the Graves.

"Strauss, Yawcob" See **Adams, Charles Follen**

Strayhorn, Billy (1915–67)
Lonely Coed, A.
Lush Life.
Satin Doll.
Something to Live For.

"Streamer, Col. D." *See* Graham, Harry

Strebeck, George (*fl.* late 18th cent.)
Joyful Sound It Is, A.

Street, Douglas
Love Letters of the Dead.

Street, T. (b. 1941?)
Tim tryeth truth convicting all that strive.

Streeter, Sebastian (*fl.* early 19th cent.)
King Shall Reign in Righteousness, A.
Lo, What Enraptured Songs of Praise.

Strehlenau, Nikolaus Franz Niembsch von *See* **Lenau, Nikolaus**

Strejilevich, Nora
When They Robbed Me of My Name.

Strelchenko, Vadim Konstantinovich (1912–42)
My Photograph.

Strickland, Agnes (1796–1874)
Forsaken, The.
Infant, The.
Maniac, The.
Self-Devoted, The.

Strickland, Stephanie
Absent from Dances 1925.
FigTree.
Gustave Thibon, How Simone Weil Appeared to Me/2.
Gustave Thibon, How Simone Weil Appeared to Me/3.
Gustave Thibon, How Simone Weil Appeared to Me/4.
Gustave Thibon, How Simone Weil Appeared to Me/5.
Intact.

Strobel, Marion (Mrs. James Herbert Mitchell) (b. 1895)
Encounter.

Strode, William (1600–43)
Bracelets.
Ear-string, An.
Epitaph on the Monument of Sir William Strode.
Girdle, A.
In Commendation of Music.
Justification.
Kisses.
Nightingale, The.
On a Gentlewoman that Sung and Played upon a Lute.
On a Good Leg and Foot.
On Chloris Walking in the Snow.
On Fairford Windows.
On the Death of Mistress Mary Prideaux.
On Westwall Downes [*or* On Westwell Downs].
Opposite to Melancholy.
Riddle: On a Kiss, A.

Stroffolino, Chris
Lingua Franca.

Strong, George A. (1832–1912)
Modern Hiawatha, The.

Strong, Leonard Alfred George (1896–1958)
Appointment, The.
Brewer's Man, The.
Coroner's Jury.
Door, The.
Evening before Rain.
Knowledgeable Child, The.
Lowery Cot.
Mad Woman of Punnet's Town, The.
March Evening.
Memory, A.
Old Dan'l.
Old Man at the Crossing, The.
Old Woman, Outside the Abbey Theater, An.
Rufus Prays.
Two Generations.
Zeke.

Strong, Nathan (1748–1816)
Almighty Sovereign of the Skies!
Summer Harvest Spreads the Fields, The.
Swell the Anthem, Raise the Song.

Strong, Phillips Burrows
Tongue, The.

Stroud, Joseph (b. 1943)
Grandfather.

Homage: Summer/Winter, Shay Creek.
Manna.
Oh Yes.

Stroud, William
Rustler.

Strouse, Charles
But Alive.
Kids!
Once Upon a Time.
Put on a Happy Face.
Those Were the Days.

"Struther, Jan" (Joyce Anstruther Maxtone Graham) (1901–53)
Freedom.

Strutz, Herbert
Farmer's Son Writes from the City, A.
Grace of the Homeland.
Maidens in Spring.
March Night.

Stryk, Lucien (b. 1924)
After night in.
Awakening.
Black Bean Soup.
Blood.
Charcoal fire.
Cherry blossoms.
Child in the City, A.
Cormorant.
Dawn.
Frog and I.
Into the house.
Morning glory.
My empty face.
My thinning hair.
New Year's Day.
Oeuvre.
Plum in bloom.
Return to DeKalb.
Snail—baring / Shoulders.
Song of skylark.
What a moon.
Winter moon.
Winter Storm.
Wonderful / Under cherry blossoms.
Woodpecker on.

Stryker, Melancthon Woolsey (1851–1929)
Almighty Lord, with One Accord.
God of Our Fathers.

Stuart, Alice V. (1899–1981)
Lintie in a Cage.
Plait of Hair, The.

Stuart, Dabney (b. 1937)
Fishing with Elvis.
Swinging on the First Pitch.
Where the Deer Go.

Stuart, Francis (b. 1902)
Remembering Yeats.

Stuart, Muriel (1889–1967)
In the Orchard.

Stuart, Ruth McEnery (1856–1917)
Endless Song, The.

Stubbs, William (1825–1901)
Hymn on Froude and Kingsley, A.

Studdert-Kennedy, Geoffrey Anketell ("Woodbine Willie") (1883–1929)
Great Wager, The.
Indifference.
Is It a Dream?

Sturm, Frank Pearce (1879–1942)
Still-Heart.

Styne, Jule
Adventure.
All I Need Is the Girl.
All of My Life.
Diamonds Are a Girl's Best Friend.
Don't Rain on My Parade.
Everything's Coming Up Roses.
Guess I'll Hang My Tears Out to Dry.
I Don't Want to Walk without You.
I Fall in Love Too Easily.
I'll Walk Alone.
If You Hadn't—But You Did.
It's Magic.
Just in Time.
Let It Snow! Let It Snow! Let It Snow!

Little Girl from Little Rock.
Music That Makes Me Dance.
Not Mine.
Party's Over, The.
People.
Put 'Em in a Box, Tie 'Em with a Ribbon (And Throw 'Em in the Deep Blue Sea)
Some People.
Things We Did Last Summer, The.
Time after Time.
Together Wherever We Go.
You Mustn't Feel Discouraged.

Su, Adrienne (b. 1967)
Address.
Antidepressant.
Four Sonnets about Food.
I Can't Become a Buddhist.
Wedding Gifts.

Su Man-shu (Hsüan-ying) (1884–1918)
Addressed to a Koto-player.
Chanting These Verses on My Way to Yodoe.
Exile in Japan.
Inscribed on Byron's Poetic Works.
On the bank of Lake Rouge a chestnut steed treads proudly.
Passing by Kamata.
She puts on a silken blouse and comes down from the western chamber.
Shouldn't I pilfer wantonly this famed fragrance of a foreign land?
Written during My Stay at White Clouds Monastery on West Lake.

Su Shih *See* **Su Tung-p'o (Su Shih)**

Su Shun-ch'in (1008–48)
Commandeering the Wind.
Summertime.

Su Tung-p'o (Su Shih) (1036–1101)
Abandoned earthworks nobody tends.
At Gold Hill Monastery.
At the Heng-ts'ui Pavilion of Fa-hui Monastery.
At the Temple of Kuan Yin in the Rain.
At the Washing of My Son.
Autumn.
Bathing the Infant.
Beginning of Autumn: A Poem to Send to Tzu-yu.
Begonias.
Black Clouds—Spilled Ink.
Black Muzzle.
Children.
Climbing Yun-lung Mountain.
Days of Rain; the Rivers Have Overflowed.
Drinking at the Lake, First It's Sunny, Then It Rains.
End of the Year, The.
Epigram.
Fisherman drinks, The.
Fisherman, laughing, The.
Fisherman's drunk, The.
Fisherman wakes, The.
Harvest Sacrifice.
Hibiscus.
I planted rice before Spring Festival.
I Travel Day and Night.
In a Boat, Getting Up at Night.
Lament of the Farm Wife of Wu.
Last Day of the Year, The.
Listening to the River.
Little stream used to cross my land, A.
Long Ago I Lived in the Country.
Looking from the Pavilion over the Lake.
Lyrics to the Tune 'Fairy Grotto.'
Lyrics to the Tune 'The Charms of Niennu': At the Red Cliff I Ponder Over Antiquity.
Mid-Autumn Moon.
Monk of Auspicious Fortune Monastery Asking Me to Name a Pavilion, A.
Moon, Flowers, Man.
New Year's Blizzard, The.
New Year's Eve.
On a Painting by Wang the Clerk of Yen Ling.
On a Snail.
On a Toad.
On the Birth of His Son.
On the Death of His Baby Son.

On the Road to Hsin-ch'eng.
On the Siu Cheng Road.
On the Tower of Gathering Remoteness.
Plum Blossoms.
Presented to Liu Ching-wen.
Purple Peach Tree, The.
Rain during the Cold Food Festival.
Rain in the Aspens.
Reading the Poetry of Meng Chiao: Two
    Poems.
Red Cliff, The.
Remembering Min Ch'e.
Remembering My Wife.
Rhyming with Tzu-yu's "Treading the Green."
Roadside flowers are blooming, butterflies on
    the wing.
Roaring waterfall, the.
Seeking Spring beyond the City.
Sent to Chief Abbot of Tung-lin Monastery.
Shadow of Flowers, The.
Since coming to Huang-chou.
Sitting at Night with My Nephew Who Has
    Just Come from Afar.
Southern Room Over the River, The.
Spring.
Spring Day.
Spring flood is coming up to my door.
Spring Night.
Spring Scene.
Sunflower.
Terrace in the Snow, The.
Thoughts in Exile.
To a Traveler.
Tune: 'A Riverside Town.'
Tune: 'Always Having Fun.'
Tune: "As in a Dream; a Song."
Tune: 'Butterflies Lingering over Flowers.'
Tune: 'Calming Windswept Waves.'
Tune: 'Charming Nien-Nu.'
Tune: 'Fragrance Fills the Courtyard.'
Tune: "Immortal at the River."
Tune: "Immortal by the River."
Tune: "Joy of Eternal Union"—Passing the
    Seven-league Shallows.
Tune: 'Partridge Sky.'
Tune: "Prelude to Water Music."
Tune: 'River Town.'
Tune: "Song of Divination."
Tune: "Water Dragon's Chang" After Chang
    Chi-fu's Lyric on the Willow Catkin.
Tune: "Sand of Silk-washing Stream."
Tune: "Sand of Silk-washing Stream" ("Flutter,
    flutter, on clothes and cap, jujube flowers
    fall")
Tune: "Sand of Silk-washing Stream" ("Layer
    on layer of hemp leaves, jute leaves
    shining")
Tune: "Sand of Silk-washing Stream" ("Soft
    grasses, a plain of sedge fresh with passing
    rain")
Tune: "Sand of Silk-washing Stream" ("Throw
    on rouge and powder, watch the governor
    pass!")
Tune: "Song of River City"
Tune: 'Water Mode Song.'
Turning Year, The.
Under the Heaven of Our Holy Ruler.
Verses: "I am old, sick and lonely."
Weaker the Wine, The.
Wealth and honor in life were dew on the grass
    leaf.
When Yü-k'o painted bamboo.
White Crane Hill.
Who Says a Painting Must Look Like Life?
Wild roadside flowers, blooming in boundless
    numbers.
Su Wu (*fl.* **2nd cent.**)
Drafted.
To His Wife.
Suárez, Clementina (b. 1906)
Another Poem to My Mother.
Like the Magic Glow of Paradise.
Now That I Have Grown Up, Mother.
Poem for Mankind and Its Hope.
Poem, The: "If you start to write a poem."
Worker Dies, A.
Suárez, Virgil (b. 1962)
Cuban-American Gothic.

Donatilia's Unrequited Love Remedy.
Rice Comes to El Volcán.
Song for the Sugar Cane.
Song to the Banyan.
Sub-ok
Spring at Yesan Station.
Subbiah, Shanmuga (b. 1924)
Salutations.
Subido, Trinidad Tarrosa (b. 1912)
Paganly.
Subramanyam, Kaa Naa (b. 1912)
Situation.
Suckling, Sir John (1609–42)
Against Absence.
Against Fruition.
Ballad[e] [upon a Wedding], A.
Barley-Break , A.
Candle, A.
Constant Lover, A [*or* The].
Dream, A.
Farewell to Love.
Love and Debt Alike Troublesome.
Love's Clock.
Love's Offence.
Love's Siege.
Loving and Beloved.
Metamorphosis, The.
Miracle, The.
My dearest rival, lest [*or* least] our love.
Sonnet: "O[h]! for some honest lover's ghost."
On King Richard the Third, Who Lies Buried
    under Leicester Bridge.
Pedlar of Small-Wares, A.
Soldier, A.
Song: "I prithee spare me, gentle boy."
Song: "No, no, fair heretic[k], it needs must
    be."
Song to a Lute, A.
Song: "Why so pale and wan, fond lover?"
Sonnet: "Dost see how unregarded now."
Sonnet: "Of thee, kind boy, I ask no red and
    white."
Summons to Town, A.
To a Lady That Forbade to Love before
    Company.
To B. C.
To Master Davenant for Absence.
Upon My Lady Carlisle's Walking in Hampton
    Court Garden.
Upon My Lord Brohall's Wedding.
Upon Sir John Lawrence's Bringing Water
    over the Hills [to My L. Middlesex His
    House at Witten].
Upon Stephen Stoned.
Wits, The; A Session[s] of the Poets.
Woman's Constancy.
**Suckling, Sir John (1609– 42) *and* Owen
Felltham (c.1602–68)**
Song: "When, dearest, I but think on [*or* of]
    thee."
Sudeley, Baron Seymour of *See* **Seymour, Sir
Thomas**
Suessdorf, Karl (*fl.* **1944**)
Moonlight in Vermont.
Suesse, Dana
Ho Hum.
Moon about Town.
Night Is Young and You're So Beautiful, The.
Sueyoshi, Fujiwara No
Crying plovers, The.
Sugetsu (d. 1830)
Years have piled up, The.
Sugioka, Stephanie
Legacy.
Suhl, Yuri (1908–86)
And the Earth Rebelled.
Permanent Delegate, The.
Sui Ching-ch'en (*fl* **c.1300**)
Tune: "Slow Chant"—Kao-tsu's Homecoming.
Suian
Traceless, no more need to hide.
Suibne Geilt (*fl.* **12th cent.**)
Bellower with the antlers.
I am in great misery tonight.
I am Suibne the wanderer.

My fixed abode is Glen Bolcain.
Rich tuft of ivy, A.
Starry frost descends, The.
Sweet voice of the Garb.
Though my wanderings are many.
Suikoku (d. 1734)
By the fifth month.
Suilleabhain, Eoghan Rua O *See* **O'Sullivan,
Owen Roe**
Suknaski, Andrew (b. 1942)
Chinese Camp, Kamloops (circa 1883)
Snake, The.
Sullam, Sarah Copia (1592–1641)
My Inmost Hope.
Sullivan, Breda
Hair.
Sullivan, Charles (b. 1933)
Nights along the River.
Sullivan, Francis (b. 1929)
Prayer: "You may be right, divinity."
Still Life.
Sullivan, Henry
I May Be Wrong (But I Think You're
    Wonderful)
Sullivan, Jonny Kyoko
Sagimusume: The White Heron Maiden.
Sullivan, Nancy (b. 1929)
Eclipses.
His Necessary Darkness.
Telling It.
To My Body.
**Sully-Prudhomme, René François Armand
(1839–1907)**
Struggle, The.
Sulpicia (*fl.* **c.20 B.C.**)
At last love has come. I would be more
    ashamed.
Darling, I won't be your hot love.
Do you have a sweet thought, Cerinthus.
Have you heard? The troubles.
It's nice that though you are casual about me.
My hated birthday is here, and I must go.
Sumangala, *the mother of* (*fl.* **19th cent.**)
Free woman, A. At last free!
Sumangalamata (*fl.* **6th cent. B.C.**)
At last free.
Summerfield, Geoffrey
Tall Story for Fred Dibnah.
Washday Battles.
Yesterday the House was Full of Flies.
Summers, Hal (b. 1911)
My Old Cat.
Summers, Thomas O. (1812–82)
Morning Bright, with Rosy Light, The.
Sun Ch'o (320?–80 A.D.)
Orchid Pavilion.
Sun Kuang-hsien (898?–968)
Tune: "Eight-beat Barbarian Tune."
Tune: "Paying Homage at the Golden Gate."
Tune: "Song of a Dandy."
Sun Yün-feng (1764–1814)
On the Road through Chang-te.
Trail up Wu Gorge, The.
Sunao (d. 1926)
Spitting blood.
Sund, Robert (b. 1929)
Considering Poverty and Homelessness.
Sundiata, Sekou (*fl.* **c.1990–95**)
Ear Training.
Making Poems; on the road in Minneapolis.
Notes from the Defense of Colin Ferguson.
Open Heart.
Sung Fang-hu (*fl.* **c.1317**)
Traveler's Life, A.
Sung Sammun (1418–56)
White Banners.
Sung Tzu-hou (*fl.* **c.120 A.D.**)
Song: "On the Eastern Way at the city of Lo-
    yang."
Sung Yu (*fl.* **3rd cent. B.C.**)
Wind, The.
Suo, Lady (*fl.* **11th cent.**)
That Spring Night I Spent.

Supervielle, Jules (1884–1960)
Early in the morning.
Earth.
Entangled.
Like an ox.
Missing France.
Rain and the Tyrants.
Return to Paris.
Some day shall I be.
Sphere.
Traveller, traveller.
Voyages.

Surkov, Aleksey [or Aleksei] Aleksandrovich (1899–1983)
Tenderness.

Surrey, Henry Howard, Earl of (1517?–47)
Complaint by Night, A.
Epitaph for [or on] Thomas Clere.
Excellent Epitaffe of Syr Thomas Wyat, An.
Exhortation to Learn of Others' Trouble.
Frailty and Hurtfulness of Beauty, The.
Golden Mean, The.
I, Solomon, David's son, King of Jerusalem.
Laid in My Quiet Bed.
Love, That Doth Reign and Live Within My Thought.
Prison in Windsor Castle.
Prisoned in Windsor, He Recounteth His Pleasure There Passed.
Sardanapalus.
Seafarer, The.
Soote Season, The.
When I bethought me well, under the restless sun.
When Raging Love.
When that repentant tears hath cleansed clear from ill.

Surve, Narayan (b. 1926)
Lifetime.

Trimberg, Süsskind von (c.1250–1300)
Power of Thought, The.
Virtuous Wife, The.
Why Should I Wander Sadly.

Sutcliffe, Alice (fl. c.1633)
God by his Wisdome, and all seeing Pow'r.

Sute-Jo, Lady Den (1633–98)
Are there / Short-cuts in the sky.
Woman.

Sutherland, Robert See **Garioch, Robert**

Sutherland-Smith, James
Something you won't ever bring pressure to bear on.

Sutskever [or Sutzkever], Abraham (b. 1913)
1974.
1980.
Cartload of Shoes, A.
Here I Am.
How?
Like Groping Fingers.
Secret Town, The.

Sutter, Barton (b. 1949)
Hoarfrost and Fog.
Peregrine.
Shoe Shop.

Sutu, S. D. R. (d. 1965)
Night.

Svankmajerová, Eva (b. 1940)
I Don't Know Exactly.
Stunned by Freedom.

Svetlov, Mikhail Arkadyevich [orArkad'evich] (1903–64)
Friends.
Grenada.
Italian, The.
On Reconnaissance.
To a Rabfak Student.
Two.

"Svirepy, Makar" See Oleynikov, Nikolai Makarovich

Svoboda, Terese (b. 1951)
Appomattox.
Cosmo Dog.
Epithalamion.
Goddess Corn Finds Her Dress in Disarray,The.

Swaanswijk, L. J. See **"Lucebert"**

Swain, Charles (fl. c.1870)
Home Is Where There Is One to Love Us.
Take the world as it is!—with its smiles and its sorrow.

Swain, Leonard (1821–69)
My Soul, Weigh Not Thy Life.

Swainson, Eric
Limerick: "I fear, Mr. Lear, you're a clot."

Swan, E. A. (fl. 1931)
When Your Lover Has Gone.

Swan, Guida
I pull opposites together.

Swanger, David (b. 1940)
Knob Pines.
Natural Disaster.
Wayne's College of Beauty, Santa Cruz.

Swann, Brian (b. 1940)
Land at the World's End, The.
Old Song of the Musk Ox People.
Walking at Night.

Swann, Roberta
EFT.

Sward, Robert (b. 1933)
American Heritage.
Concert.
Uncle Dog; the Poet at 9.

Swart, Edward Vincent (1911–62)
Convict.
This Is Not a Poem but a Proem.

Swarth, Hélène (1859–1941)
Candles.
Ecstasy.

Swartwout, Susan
Gypsy Teaches Her Grandchild Wolfen Ways, The.
I Wannabe Your Queen.
Siamese Twins in Love.

Swede, George
After I step.
After the search for meaning bills in the mail.
At dawn remembering her bad grammar.
At my father's.
At the edge of the precipice I become logical.
At the end of myself pencil tip.
August sky, The.
Christmas Eve.
Dawn.
Frozen breaths, The.
In one corner.
In the town dump I find a still-beating heart.
Leaving my loneliness inside her.
Mental hospital my shadow stays outside.
Night begins to gather between her breasts.
On the face.
One button undone.
One by one to the floor all of her shadows.
Panties on the clothesline lingering mist.
Passport check.
Stars crickets.
Summer night.
Swinging on the hanger.
Unhappy wife.
Windless summer day.

Sweeney, Matthew (b. 1952)
Couple Waiting, A.
To the Building Trade.
Tube Ride to Martha's.
Where Fishermen Can't Swim.

Sweet, Bruce
' New World' Interview.

Sweet, Denise
My Mother and I Had a Discussion One Day.

Sweet, Frank Herbert
Before It Is Too Late.

Swenson, Karen (b. 1936)
Landlady in Bangkok, The.

Swenson, May (b. 1919)
Almanac.
Bleeding.
Bronco Busting, Event #1.
Cardinal Ideograms.
Cat and the Weather.
Centaur, The.

Colors without Objects.
Death Invited.
Distance and a Certain Light.
Electronic Sound.
Fire Island.
First Walk on the Moon.
Flying Home from Utah.
Four-Word Lines.
Frontispiece.
Goodbye, Goldeneye.
Green Red Brown and White.
He That None Can Capture.
How Everything Happens.
How to Be Old.
James Bond Movie, The.
Landing on the Moon.
Living Tenderly.
Morning at Point Dume.
Motherhood.
Notes Made in the Piazza San Marco.
On Its Way.
One of the Strangest.
Painting the Gate.
Poet to Tiger.
Question.
Riding the 'A.'
Secret in the Cat, The.
Shape of Death, The.
Shu Swamp, Spring.
Something Goes By.
Southbound on the Freeway.
Staring at the Sea on the Day of the Death of Another.
Staying at Ed's Place.
Stone Gullets.
Strawberrying.
Stripping and Putting On.
Teleology.
Unconscious Came a Beauty.
Waking from a Nap on the Beach.
Watch, The.
Waterbird.
Willets, The.
Women.
Written while Riding the Long Island Rail Road.

Swift, Joan (b. 1926)
Anthuriums, Pahoa.
Spider.
Steelhead in the Whitehorse Rearing Pond.
Wild Salmon: Stillaguamish Tribal Hatchery.

Swift, Jonathan (1667–1745)
All human race would fain be wits.
As I strole the city, oft I.
Baucis and Philemon.
Beautiful Young Nymph Going to Bed, A.
Behold the fatal day arrive!
Character of Sir Robert Walpole, The.
Clever Tom Clinch Going to Be Hanged.
Critics.
Daphne.
Day of Judgement, The.
Day will come, when't shall be said, The.
Description of a City Shower, A.
Description of the Morning, A.
Dick, a Maggot.
Doctors tender of their fame, The.
Epigram on Fasting.
Epigram on Scolding, An.
Fool, to put up four crosses at your door.
Gentle Echo on Woman, A.
Here shift the scene, to represent.
Holyhead. September 25, 1727.
In Sickness.
Lady's Dressing Room, The.
From Life and Character of Dean Swift, The.
Mary the Cook-Maid's Letter to Dr. Sheridan.
My female friends, whose tender hearts.
New Song of Wood's Halfpence, A.
Now Curll his shop from rubbish drains.
On Dreams.
On Poetry: a Rhapsody.
On the Astrologer and Almanac Maker, John Partridge.
On the Collar of Mrs. Dingley's Lap-Dog.
On the Irish Club.
Onyons.

Oysters.
Perhaps I may allow, the Dean.
Phyllis [or Phillis] [or Progress of Love, The].
Place of the Damned [or Damn'd], The.
Power of Time, The.
Progress of Poetry, The.
Satirical Elegy on the Death of a Late Famous General, A.
Stella at Wood-Park.
Stella's Birthday [1721].
Stella's Birthday, 1725.
Stella's Birthday ([March 13,] 1727)
Stella's Birthday; Written in the Year 1718[/9].
Suppose me dead; and then suppose.
Three Epigrams.
Thy curate's place, thy fruitful wife.
Time is not remote when I, The.
To Stella.
To the Earl of Oxford, Late Lord Treasurer.
To Their Excellencies the Lords Justices of Ireland, the Humble Petition of Frances Harris, Who Must Starve, and Die a Maid if It Miscarries.
Twelve Articles.
Verses on the Death of Dr. Swift, D. S. P. D., Occasioned by Reading a Maxim in Rochefoucauld.
Virtue conceal'd within our breast.
Wretched Ierne! with what grief I see.
Swift, Kay
Can't We Be Friends?
Can This Be Love?
Fine and Dandy.
Swigart, Rob See Mather, Richard
Swinburne, Algernon Charles (1837–1909)
After Death.
Aholibah.
Anactoria.
Ave atque Vale.
Ballad of François Villon, A.
Before Parting.
Before the Beginning of Years.
Before the Mirror.
Come into the orchard, Anne.
Dolores, sels.
Duriesdyke.
Étude Réliste, sels.
Forsaken Garden, A.
Free Thought.
Garden of Proserpine, The.
Higher Pantheism in a Nutshell, The.
Hymn to Proserpine.
I Will Go Back to the Great Sweet Mother.
Ilicet.
In the Orchard.
Itylus.
King Mark, Tristram, and Palamede.
Lake of Gaube, The.
Leave-taking, A.
Leper, The.
Limerick: "There was a young girl of Aberystwyth."
Limerick: "There was a young lady of Norway / Who hung by her toes in a doorway."
Limerick: "There was a young man of Cape Horn."
Love and Sleep.
Love at Sea.
Lyke-Wake Song, A.
Match, A.
Nephelidia.
On Arthur Hugh Clough.
On the Russian Persecution of the Jews.
Oscar Wilde.
Sapphics.
Satia Te Sanguine.
Sestina: "I saw my soul at rest upon a day."
Sonnet for a Picture.
Sonnets of English Dramatic Poets.
Sundew, The.
Vision of Spring in Winter, A.
When the Hounds of Spring.
Swiontkowski, Gale
Old Moon with Her Youth In Her Arms.
Swir, Anna
Bitch, A.

My Father's Workshop.
Swirszczynska, Anna (1909–84)
Conversation through the Door, A.
Good Lord Saved Her, The.
Greatest Love, The.
He Is Gone.
He Was Lucky.
I Am Afraid of Fire.
I Starve My Belly for a Sublime Purpose.
I Talk to My Body.
I Wash the Shirt.
Poetry Reading.
Same Inside, The.
Sea and the Man, The.
Second Madrigal, The.
She Does Not Remember.
Terminally Ill.
Thank You, My Fate.
They Lay Dying Side by Side.
Troubles with the Soul at Morning Calisthenics.
Very Sad Conversation at Night, A.
Visit, A.
We Are Going to Shoot at the Heart.
We Survived Them.
White Wedding Slippers.
Sykes, Arthur A.
Splendid Bankrupt, The.
Sykes, Bobbi (b. 1943)
Cycle.
Fallin'
Final Count.
One Day.
Prayer to the Spirit of the New Year.
Rachel.
Requiem.
Sylvain, Patrick (b. 1966)
Collective Search.
Constant Memories.
Panama.
Sylvester, Janet (b. 1950)
Arrowhead Christian Center and No-Smoking Luncheonette.
Sylvester, János Edrosi
To the Hungarian People.
Sylvester, Joshua (1561–1618)
Acrostiteliostichon.
Aestas.
But, fair Iëmpsar (wife of Potiphar)
Cunning Painter, that with curious care, The.
Father, The.
Fuimus Fumus.
Garden, The.
I hate these phrases: Of power absolute.
If patience true could termine passions warr.
Job's Epitaph.
Mundus Qualis.
Of a Husbandman.
Omnia Somnia.
Rare type of gentrie, and true Vertues Starr.
Rome, Conqueror, Conquered.
Sweet Mouth, That Send'st a Musky-Rosed Breath.
Variable.
War is the mistress of enormity.
Were I as Base as Is the Lowly Plain.
When wine runs low, it is not worth the sparing.
Sylvester, June
Palms.
Sylvester, Stephen
Limerick: "'How much,' sighed the gentle Narcissus."
Symeon (949–1022)
We awaken in Christ's body.
Symes, Marty (fl. 1933)
It's the Talk of the Town.
Symonds, John Addington (1840–93)
Camera Obscura, The.
In years of old.
Love and Death: A Symphony.
Lux Est Umbra Dei.
Midnight at Baiae.
Rebuke Me Not.
Sonnet (III), The.

Thou dost establish—and our hearts receive.
To Night, the Mother of Sleep and Death.
What Cannot Be.
Symons, Arthur (1865–1945)
Absinthe-Drinker, The.
And yet, there was a hunger in your eyes.
At Seventeen.
At the Cavour.
Barrel-Organ, The.
Bianca.
During Music.
Episode of a Night of May.
Faint Love.
Grey and Green.
Grey Wolf, The.
In Kensington Gardens.
Isolation.
La Mélinite: Moulin-Rouge.
Laus Virginitatis.
Maquillage.
Nerves.
Palm Sunday: Naples.
Paris.
Pastel: Masks and Faces.
Tune, A.
Venice.
White Heliotrope.
Symons, Julian (b. 1912)
Central Park.
Harvard.
Syms, Barbara (fl. 1663)
Song: "Goe turne away those Cruell Eyes."
Synge, John Millington (1871–1909)
Beg-Innish.
Curse, The.
Danny.
Dread.
Epitaph after Reading Ronsard's Lines from Rabelais.
I curse my bearing, childhood, youth.
I read about the Blaskets and Dunquin.
I've Thirty Months.
In Glencullen.
In Kerry.
In May.
Is It a Month.
'Mergency Man, The.
On a Birthday.
On an Anniversary.
On an Island.
Passing of the Shee, The.
Patch-Shaneen.
Prelude: "Still south I went and west and south again."
Queens.
Question, A.
Rendez-vous Manqué dans la Rue Racine.
To the Oaks of Glencree.
Winter.
Wish, A.
Synková, Alena (b. 1926)
I'd Like to Go Alone.
I've met enough people.
Tears.
To Olga.
Syrkin, Marie (1899–1989)
My Uncle in Treblinka.
Szabédi, László (1907–59)
Creative Poverty.
Irrationale.
Marriage of Death, The.
Szabó, Dávid Baróti (1739–1819)
To a Fallen Walnut Tree.
To Hungarian Youth.
To The Moon.
Szabó, Lőrinc (1900–57)
All for Nothing.
Babits.
Dream of Tsuang Tsi, The.
Dreams of the One, The.
English Poetry.
Hay Wagon.
Lóci Becomes a Giant.
Materialism.
Moment, The.
Night on the Boulevard.

On a Raft.
Prisons.
Private Truce.
Quarter-Hour between God and the Office.
Shame.
They Say She Is Lovely.
To Forget?
Tranquil Miracle, The.
With Flute, with Violin.

Sze, Arthur (b. 1950)
Black Java Pepper.
Day can become a Zen garden of raked sand, The.
Every Where and Every When.
Great White Shark, The.
In Your Honor.
June Ghazal.
Leaves of a Dream Are the Leaves of an Onion, The.
Network, The.
Parallax.

Szécsi, Margit (1928–90)
Genius.
July.
Letter.
Love's Fool.
Noah.
Old Trees with Hands Sawing the Air.
Only with Radiance.
Twilight.

Székely, János (1929–92)
Analogy.
Galileo.
Nothing-Never.

Szirtes, George
Even now I cannot help thinking of them.

Szporluk, Larissa (b. 1967)
Axiom of Maria.
Duressor.
Grass and the Sin, The.
Holy Ghost.
Libido.
Meteor.
Occupant of the Hose.
Triage.

Szumigalski, Anne (b. 1926)
Angels.
In the Heat of the Morning.
Midwife's Story; Two, A.
Visitor's Parking.
Want of þ Want of ð.

Szymborska, Wislawa (b. 1923)
Born of Woman.
Clothes.
Contribution on Pornography, A.
End and the Beginning, The.
Experiment.
Four in the Morning.
Homecoming.
I Am Too Near.
In Praise of My Sister.
In Praise of Self-Deprecation.
Innocence.
Laughter.
Memory at Last.
Miracle Mart.
Monologue for Cassandra.
Museum, The.
Notes from a Nonexistent Himalayan Expedition.
Once we knew the world well.
Onion.
π.
Pietà.
Reality Demands.
Seen from Above.
Starvation Camp near Jaslo.
Still.
Terrorist, He Watches, The.
Terrorist Is Watching, A.
Theater Impressions.
Two Apes of Brueghel, The.
Under a Certain Little Star.
Unexpected Meeting.
View with a Grain of Sand.
Voices.

Women of Rubens, The.
Words.
Writing a Curriculum Vitae.

T

"T., B. L." *See* **Taylor, Bert Leston**

"T., J." *(fl. late 19th cent.)*
Sea-Chaplain's Petition to the Lieutenants in the Ward-Room, for the Use of the Quarter-Gallery, A.

Ta' Abbata Sharra *(fl. 7th cent.)*
Ever Watchful.

Tabb, John Banister (1845–1909)
Bicycles! Tricycles!
Bridge, The.
Christ and the Pagan.
Close Quarters.
Echo.
Echoes.
Evolution.
Foot Soldiers.
Mid-Day Moon, The.
Milton.
Rub, A.
Shadow, The.
Sisters, The.
Tenebræ.
Tryst, The.
Whisper.
Winter Twilight, A.

"Tabitha"
Sweet it is to be a child.

Tabito *See* **Otomo no Tabito**

Tablada, José Juan (1871–1945)
I Built My Hut.

Tachibana Akemi (1812–68)
Happiness is when.

Tada, Chimako (b. 1930)
Mirror.
Odyssey or "On Absence," The.
Poetry Calendar, A.
Universe of the Rose.
Wind Invites Wind.

Tadamichi (Fujiwara no Tadamichi) (1097–1164)
As I row over the plain.

Tadamichi, Fujiwara no *See* **Tadamichi**

Tadatomo (d. 1676)
This frosty month.

Tadic, Novica (b. 1949)
Antipsalm.
Dogs Gambol.
Jesus.
Laocoon / Serpent.
Man from the Death Institute.
Nobody.

Tadjo, Veronique (b. 1955)
He is my shadow.
Life is made.
Over there, people.

Tafolla, Carmen
Allí por la Calle San Luis.

Tagami, Jeff (b. 1954)
Mussel Rock / Lowtide—Santa Cruz, California 1959.
Song of Pajaro.
Tobera.

Tagami Kikusha-Ni (1752–1826)
Only the moon.

Taggard, Genevieve (Mrs. Kenneth Durant) (1894–1948)
All around the Town.
American Farm, 1934.
Bounding Line.
Demeter.
Dilemma of the Elm.
Doomsday Morning.
Enamel Girl, The.
Everyday Alchemy.
Fructus.
Geraniums, The.
Hymn to Yellow.
In the Tail of the Scorpion.

Little Girl with Bands on Her Teeth, The.
Millions of Strawberries.
Solar Myth.
Song for Unbound Hair.
Squirrel near Library.
Thirst.
To Mr. Maunder Maunder, Professional Poet.
To One Loved Wholly within Wisdom.
To the Natural World: at 37.
To the Powers of Desolation.
Train: Abstraction.
Try Tropic.
Weed, The.
With Child.

Taggart, John
Body and Soul: Poem for Two Readers.
Monk.
Never Too Late.
Pen Vine and Scroll.
Sainte-Chapelle.
Slow Song for Mark Rothko.

Tagliabue, John (b. 1923)
Maine Vastly Covered with Much Snow.

Tagore, Rabindranath (1861–1941)
Day after Day.
Flute-music.
Gardener, The.
Gift.
I Have Got My Leave.
If It Is Not My Portion.
On the Slope of the Desolate River.
Song That I Came to Sing, The.
Thou Art the Sky.
You Did Not Find Me.

Taha, Ahmed (b. 1948)
Abode of Arrival.
Arabesque.
December 31.
State of Butterfly.
Wall of Dreams (2)

Taha, 'Ali Mahmud (1902–49)
Blind Musician, The.
Egyptian Serenade.

Tahureau, Jacques (1527–55)
Moonlight.
Shadows of His Lady.

Tai Piao-yüan (1244–1310)
As My Way Passed through T'ung-ch'uan, I Wished to Visit the Policy Critic of the Right, Mei, but Did Not Know Where to Find Him.
Cheng-tao Temple.
In the Year Chi-hai (1299), while Returning by Way of Purple Fungus Mountain at Springmouth, I Lamented for Lecture Master Chin.
Painting, *"Mist and Rain on the Spring River,"* by Hsiao Chao, The.
Painting of One Hundred Wild Geese, A.
Returning to Yin-ch'eng Early in the Year *Ting-ch'ou* (1277)
South of the house, north of the house.
Supervisor, Han Chün-mei, Has Shown Me Five Poems He Has Written Called, The Trees Flourish in Early Summer. I Have Therefore Written Down My Own Ignoble Feelings and Sent Them Via Inspector Juan. At This Time, Chün-mei Is Lecturing to the.

T'ai-shang *(fl. 10th? cent.)*
In Reply to Questions.

Tai Shu-lun (732–89 A.D.)
Accidental Meeting with an Old Friend while Traveling at Night, An.
Living in the Mountains.
Wang Chao-chün.

Taigen Sofu (d. 1555)
I raise the mirror of my life.

Taikyo (d. 1770)
Deutzia has bloomed, The.

Tairyu (d. 1747)
Flowers bloom a score of days.

Tait, William J. (b. 1918)
Gallow Hill.

Takahashi Mutsuo (b. 1937)
Monkey-eaters.

Myself in the Disguise of an Ancient Queen.
Myself with a Glory Hole.

Takahashi, Shinkichi (1901–87)
Absence.
Afterimages.
Afternoon.
Beach.
Braggart Duck.
Burning Oneself to Death.
Camel.
Canna.
Clay Image.
Cloud.
Destruction.
Downy Hair.
Drizzle.
Eternity.
Explosion.
Fish.
Flight of the Sparrow.
Four Divine Animals.
Gods.
Hand.
Lap Dog.
Let's Live Cheerfully.
Little Sunlight, A.
Moon.
Moon and Hare.
Mother and I.
Mushroom.
Near Shinobazu Pond.
Peach Blossom and Pigeon (painting by Kiso)
Peach, The.
Pipe, The.
Position of the Sparrow.
Quails.
Railroad Station.
Rain.
Raw Fish and Vegetables.
Rocks.
Sea of Oblivion.
Sheep.
Shell.
Sky.
Snowy Sky.
Sparrow and Bird-Net Building.
Sparrow in Withered Field.
Spinning Dharma Wheel.
Spring.
Stitches.
Stone Wall.
Sweet Potato.
Thistles.
Toad.
Urn.
Vimalakirti.
What Is Moving.
Wood in Sound, A.

Takai Kito (1741–89)
Barley-reaping song / Smith's hammer.
Contending / Temple bell.
Nightingale / Rarely seen.
Seaweed / Between rocks.

Takako Uchino Lento (b. 1941)
Glass.

Takamura Kotaro (1883–1956)
Whale Spouting.

Takao (d. 1660)
Brittle autumn leaves.

Takarai [or Enomoto] Kikaku (1661–1707)
Blind child / Guided by his mother, A.

Takomaq (fl. late 19th cent.)
Improvised Song of Joy.

Takuan (1573–1645)
Though night after night.

Takuchi (d. 1846)
When summoned.

Takuro (d. 1866)
Soon I shall hear.

Takushitsu (1290–1367)
Breeze strokes the water of the spring, A.

Talbot, Charles Remington See **"Brownjohn, John"**

Talbot, Kirkham
Limerick: "King Henry the Eighth was a Tudor."

Talbot, Norman (b. 1936)
Ballad of Old Women & of How They Are Constrained to Simulate Youth In Order to Avoid Shocking the Young.

Talfourd, Sir Thomas N.
Friend, A.
'Tis a Little Thing.

"Talhaiarn" See **Jones, John**

Taliesin (fl. c.550)
Battle of Argoed Llwyfain, The.
Death Song for Owain ab Urien.
Song to the Wind, A.

Talvikki, Ansel
Afterwards: Caliban.
Flemish Beauty.
For Want.
My Shining Archipelago.
Origin Charm against Uncertain Injuries.
You Don't Know What Happened When You Froze.

Tallet, José Zacarías (b. 1983)
Rumba.

"Tallis"
Limerick: "Conclusion I reach at the Tate, The."

Tallmountain, Mary
Good Grease.
Hands of Mary Joe, The.
Indian Blood.
Last Wolf, The.
Matmiya.
Peeling Pippins.
There Is No Word for Goodbye.

Talpalar, Morris
True Happiness.

Tam'si, Tchicaya U See **U'Tamsi, Felix Tchicaya [or TchiKaya]**

Tamanari
Cool.

Tamashichi (d. 1910)
Lone monk, A.

Tammaro, Thom
'Mericn Fst Fd.

Tan Taigi (1709–71)
Barley's season / Dust mutes.
Beyond serenity / Gray kites.
' Don't touch!' my host cried.
Fallen leaves / Raking.
In the boat / Crescent moon's light.
In the melon-patch / Thief, fox.
Swellfish eaten / He chants nembutsu.
Temple in / Deep winter grove.
Thunder / Voices of drowned.
Winter withering.
Zazen / Fat mosquitoes.

"Tan Ying" (Liu Pao-chen) (b. 1943)
Drinking the Wind.

T'an Yüan-ch'un (1586–1631)
Heard on a Boat.

Tana, Patti
I Have Touched.
Marvelous Beast.
No.
River, The.
You Bring Me Back.

"Tanaquil, Paul" (J. G. Clemenceau Le Clerq) (b. 1893)
Very Young Man Speaks, A.

Tanehiko (d. 1842)
Such is the world's way.

Tanfield, Lady Elizabeth (fl. 1565–1628)
Epitaph for Sir Lawrence Tanfield.

T'ang Hsien-tsu (1550–1616)
Autumn River.
Cave of Gold Essence—in Ning-tu, The.
Descending the Ridge of Flying Clouds.
Evening View from the Bell Tower at P'ing-ch'ang.
Hsiu-chou.
Inspector Hsü Claims He Has Found the Secret of Youth.
My son, you loved telling the story of Prince Nata.
On the Day of Washing the Buddha in the Year.
Paintings on My Wall Have Been Damaged by the Weather, The.
Spending the Night on the River.

T'ang Wan (fl. 12th cent.)
To the Tune "The Phoenix Hairpin."

T'ang Yen-ch'ien (fl. c.880)
Walk in the Country, A.

T'ang Yin (1470–1523)
Fog of night envelops the flowering trees, The.
Galloping around, north and south.
Inscribed on a Painting: At the country inn, thousands of peach trees.
Inscribed on a Painting: Light mist girdles the mountain.
Inscribed on a Painting: On the mountain, old trees, still green in autumn.
Inscribed on a Painting: Places I go, leaning on my bramble cane, The.
Inscribed on a Painting: Thatched hut among the pines, door open near a cliff.
Inscribed on a Painting of a Cock.
Inscribed on a Painting of a Fisherman.
Inscribed on a Painting of Bamboo.
Inscription for a Portrait.
On a Painting of a Woman Shown Half-Length.
On the Butterflies.
Poems Inscribed on Paintings.
Scene at Heaven Gate, The.
Song of Peach Blossom Retreat.
Ten days of wind and rain, depressing darkness!

Tanikawa, Shuntaro (b. 1931)
Concerning a Girl.
Cycle of Months (Menstruation)
Dusk.
Family Portrait.
Growth.
I know how worthless this poem will be.
Landscape with Yellow Birds.
Nero.
Picnic to the Earth.
Porno-Bach.
Rain Please Fall.
Request.
River.
Sadness.
Stone and Light.
Twenty Billion Light Years of Loneliness.
Two Tokyos.
Zoo.

Tanko (d. 1735)
First snow, The.

Tanko (d. 1735)
Life-cutting axe.
Moon leaks out, The.
Today too.

Tanko (d. 1884)
For eight and fifty years.

Tannahill, Robert (1774–1810)
Eild.
O! Are Ye Sleepin [or Sleeping], Maggie?
Tap-Room, The.

Tantan (1674–1761)
Morning frost / Mount Fuji.
On the rock / Waves can't reach.
With my cane.

Tanzan (1819–92)
Madness, the way they gallop off to foreign shores!

Tao-chi (1642–1707)
Bend after bend, the long embankment.
Flower-Rain Terrace, The.
Inscribed on a Painting: Little boat floats by the dock, The.
Inscribed on a Painting of a Wu-t'ung Tree by Myself.
Inscribed on "Drunk in the Autumn Woods."
Inscribed on My Ink Landscape Painting.
Inscribed on My Large Landscape Hanging Scroll "Listening to a Waterfall."
Inscribed on My Little Painting of Plum Blossom and Bamboo.

Inscribed on the Wall at the Temple of the Auspicious Talisman.
Mood comes on—I want to cross Hsi-ling, The.
Riding a Boat on Wu-ling Stream.
Searching for Herb Brazier and Cinnabar Well, I Also Saw the Waterfall of Singing Strings.
Alongside Was the Cliff of the Lord of the Mountain.
Trip to Hua-yang Mountain, A.
Trip to the Village of the River of White Sand, A.

T'ao Ch'ien [or T'ao Yuan-ming] (365–427)
Autumn chrysanthemums have beautiful color.
Bank to bank, the stream is wide.
Bearers' Song.
Begging for Food.
Blaming Sons.
Bright blossoms seldom last long.
Bright sun lights out over the western bank.
By and by, the seasons come and go.
Drinking Alone in the Rainy Season.
Drinking Wine.
Fire, Sixth Month, 408.
Green pine grows in eastern garden, A.
I built my hut in a place where people live.
I plant beans at the foot of the southern hill.
I Return to the Place I Was Born.
In Praise of Poor Scholars.
In the morning and at night.
In the Year with the Cyclical Sign *Mou-shen.*
Lament: "Ways of heaven are mysterious, The."
Long time ago, A.
Man has no roots, A.
Motionless Clouds.
Noble ambition spans the four seas, A.
Old friends know what I like.
Once More Fields and Gardens.
Passing Ch'ien-hsi as Military Adviser in the Third Month of the Year Yi-ssu.
Passing through Ch'ien-hsi, Third Month, 405.
Peering into the depths of the stream.
Poem on Returning to Dwell in the Country.
Prosperity and decline have no fixed dwelling.
Reading *The Classic of Hills and Seas.*
Reply to Prefect Liu.
Return, The.
Returning to My Fields and Gardens.
Shady, Shady.
Stopping Wine.
Substance, Shadow, and Spirit.
Thinking of Impoverished Ancients.
To My Cousin, Ching-yuan, Twelfth Month, 403.
Unsettled, a bird lost from the flock.
Untitled.
Way's been lost for a thousand years, The.
When I was young and in my prime.
When I was young, I did not fit into the common mold.
Years ago, when I heard the words of my elders.

T'ao Hung Ching (T'ao T'ung Ming) (452–536)
Freezing Night.
Poem Written in Answer to His Majesty's Question: 'What Is There in the Mountains?'

Tapahonso, Luci (b. 1954)
All I Want.
I Am Singing Now.
Pay Up or Else.
They Were Alone in the Winter.
What Danger We Court.

Tappan, William Bingham (1794–1849)
He stood, the last—the last of all.
Obey Your Parents.
Onward! though ever in our march.
Ransomed Spirit to Her Home, The.

Tappenden, Sandra
I'm ugly but I don't know why.

Tarkovsky [or Tarkovskii], Arseny [or Arsenii] Aleksandrovich (1907–89)
First Meetings.
Poet, The.
Sight grows dim—my power.

Tarn, Nathaniel (b. 1928)
Journal of the Laguna de San Ignacio.

Section: America (2): Seen as a Bird.

Tarpley, Natasha (b. 1971)
Feel Free.

Tassis y Peralta, Juan de (1582–1622)
Love Is Not Will but Destiny.
To a Lady Combing Her Hair.

Tasso, Torquato (1544–95)
All wilie sleights, that subtile women know.
Drearie trumpet blew a dreadfull blast, The.
Erminia's steed this while his mistress bore.
Golden Age, The.
Golden Age, The. A Paraphrase on a Translation out of French.
Joyous birds, hid under greenewood shade, The.
Love: Love, the great master of true eloquence.
Palace great is builded rich and round.
Sweet Armida tooke this charge on hand, The.
To His Mistress in Absence.
Who first of Christian warriors now did chance.

Tatarunis, Paula (b. 1952)
Before the Brain Surgery.
Chest X-Ray.
I Have Two Sons and the One I Love Best Is Robert.

Tate, Allen (1899–1979)
Aeneas at Washington.
Ah, Christ, I love you rings to the wild sky.
Battle of Murfreesboro.
Cross, The.
Emblems.
Horatian Epode to the Duchess of Malfi.
Idiot.
Ivory Tower, The.
Last Days of Alice.
Mediterranean, The.
Mother and Son.
Mr. Pope.
Non Omnis Moriar.
Oath, The.
Ode to the Confederate Dead.
Paradigm, The.
Seasons of the Soul.
Shadow and Shade.
Sonnet: To a Portrait of Hart Crane.
Sonnets at Christmas.
Subway, The.
Swimmers, The.
This is the day His hour of life draws near.
To the Lacedemonians.
Twelve, The.
Winter Mask.
Wolves, The.

Tate, Garth (1952–92)
Last Instructions.

Tate, Greg S. (b. 1957)
Tonguing.

Tate, James (b. 1943)
Blue Booby, The.
Book of Lies, The.
Breathing.
Cages, The.
Chaste Stranger, The.
Coming Down Cleveland Avenue.
Conjuring Roethke.
Deaf Girl Playing.
Dear Reader.
Death on Columbus Day.
Descent, The.
Diagnosis, The.
Dream On.
Dreamy Cars Graze on the Dewy Boulevard.
Figure in the Carpet, The.
Goodtime Jesus.
Head of a White Woman Winking.
I Am a Finn.
I Am Still a Finn.
In a Motel on Lake Erie.
Inspiration.
Intimidations of an Autobiography.
Land of Little Sticks, 1945.
Lost Pilot, The.
Lousy in Center Field.
Love Making.
Manna.

Miss Cho Composes in the Cafeteria.
Motorcyclists, The.
My Great Great Etc. Uncle Patrick Henry.
Neighbors.
Never Again the Same.
Nirvana.
Non-Stop.
Pet Deer, The.
Poem to Some of My Recent Poems.
President Slumming, The.
Rescue.
Rooster.
Shadowboxing.
Stray Animals.
Vagabond, A.
Wedding, A.
Wheelchair Butterfly, The.

Tate, Nahum *See also* **Dryden, John**

Tate, Nahum (1652–1715)
Choice, The.
While Shepherds Watched [Their Flocks by Night].

Tate, Nahum (1652–1715) and Nicholas Brady
Lord, Who's the Happy Man.

Tatersal, Robert (*fl.* c.1734)
Bricklayer's Labours, The.

Tatham, John (*fl.* 1632–64)
Ostella forth of Town: To My Heart.

Tati-Loutard, Jean-Baptiste (b. 1939)
Death and Rebirth.
Early.
News of My Mother.
Noonday in Immaturity.
Pilgrimage to Loango Strand.
Submarine Tombs.
Voices, The.

Taub, Debra (b. 1954)
Exquisite Alchemy.
Secret Melodies.

Taufer, Veno and Michael Scammell
Mother loves me loves me not.

Tayankannanar
Overspread with Salty Soil.

Taylor, Andrew (b. 1940)
Beast with Two Backs, The.
Clearing Away.
Developing a Wife.
Fitzroy.
Goethe and Brentano.
Invention of Fire, The.

Taylor, Ann (1782–1866)
Air.
Earth.
Fire.
Maniac's Song, The.
Water.

Taylor, Apirana (b. 1955)
Sad Joke on a Marae.
Taiaha Haka Poem.
Womb, The.

Taylor, Bayard (1825–78)
Ballad of Hiram Hover, The.
Bedouin Song.
Camerados.
Gettysburg Ode.
Goblet, The.
Hylas.
Love Returned.
Nauvoo.
Night the Eighth: Camerados.
Night the Second: All or Nothing.
Night the Sixth: Hadramaut.
On the Headland.
On the Sea.
Paean to the Dawn, A.
Palabras Grandiosas.
Proposal.
To a Persian Boy in the Bazaar at Smyrna.

Taylor, Bert Leston ("B. L. T.") (1866–1921)
Aprilly.
Canopus.
Doxology.
Passionate Professor, The.
Those Flapjacks of Brown's.
Upon Julia's Arctics.

Taylor, Caleb J. (1763–1817)
O Jesus, My Savior, I Know Thou Art Mine.
Taylor, Cheryl Boyce
Forever Arima.
Plenty Time Pass Fast, Fas Dey So.
Round Irving High School.
Taylor, Edward (1645–1729)
Address to the Soul Occasioned by a Rain, An.
All Dull, my Lord, my Spirits flat, and dead.
Angels Sung a Carol, The.
Another Meditation at the same Time.
Christ's Reply.
Deity of Love Incorporate, A.
Dull. Dull indeed! What shall it e'er be thus?
Ebb and Flow, The.
Fiery Darts of Satan stob my heart, The.
Fig for Thee, Oh! Death, A.
Frowardness of the Elect in the Work of
Conversion, The.
Here is a Mudwall tent, whose Matters are.
Huswifery.
Joy of Church Fellowship Rightly Attended,
The.
Like to the marigold, I blushing close.
Lord with thine Altars Fire, mine Inward man.
Meditation 8 (First Series)
Meditation 16 (First Series)
Meditation 22 (First Series)
Meditation 26.
Meditation 38.
Meditation 42 (First Series)
Meditation 150 (Second Series)
Meditation. Can. 1.3. Thy Good Ointment.
Meditation. Heb. 13.10. Wee have an Altar.
Meditation. Joh. 15.5. Without me yee can do
nothing.
Meditation. Numb. 28.4.9. One Lamb shalt
thou offer in the Morning, and the other at
Even. And on the Sabbath day two Lambs
etc.
Meditation. Rom. 9.5. God blessed forever.
Methinks I spy Almighty holding in.
My gracious Lord, I would thee glory doe.
My Metaphors are but dull Tacklings tag'd.
My shattred phancy stole away from mee.
My sin! my sin, my God, these cursed dregs.
O! what a thing is Love? who can define.
Oh! Golden Rose! Oh. Glittering Lilly White.
Oh! Good, good, good, my Lord. What more
love yet.
Oh leaden heeld. Lord, give, forgive I pray.
Oh that I was the Bird of Paradise!
Pit indeed of Sin: No water's here, A.
Preface, The: "Infinity, when all things it
beheld."
Prologue: "Lord, can a crumb of dust the earth
outweigh."
Reflexion, The.
Should I with Silver Tooles Delve through the
Hill.
Soul's Groan to Christ for Succo[u]r, The.
State, a state, oh! dungeon state indeed, A.
Stupendous love! all saints astonishment.
Thou Art the Tree of Life.
Thy grace, dear Lord's my golden wrack I find.
Thy human frame, my glorious Lord, I spy.
Upon a Spider Catching a Fly.
Upon a Wasp Chilled [or Child] with Cold.
Upon Wedlock and Death of Children.
View, all ye eyes above, this sight which flings.
Was Ever Heart Like Mine?
What love is this of thine, that cannot be.
What shall I say, my Lord? With what begin?
Why should my bells, which chime thy praise,
when thou.
Ye angells bright, pluck from your wings a
quill.
Taylor, Eleanor Ross (b. 1920)
Few Days in the South in February, A.
In the Churchyard.
This Year's Drive to Appomattox.
Welcome Eumenides.
Taylor, Elizabeth (fl. c.1680)
Off the Dutchesse.
To Mertill Who Desired Her to Speak to
Clorinda of His Love.

Taylor, Ellen (fl. c.1792)
Written by the Barrow Side, Where She Was
Sent to Wash Linen.
Taylor, Geoffrey (1900–1957)
Admonition to the Muse.
Cruel, Clever Cat.
English Liberal.
Epitaph: "Nor practising virtue nor committing
crime."
Gentlemen.
Taylor, George Lansing (1835–1903)
Dare to Do Right.
Taylor, Hannah
Virtue alone can never die. but lives to.
Taylor, Henry (1711–85)
Country Curate, The.
Taylor, Sir Henry (1800–86)
Elena's Song.
Taylor, Henry (b. 1942)
At the Swings.
Riding a One-eyed Horse.
Riding Lesson.
Speech.
View from a Cab, The.
Taylor, James Bayard (1825–78)
To G. H. B.
Taylor, Jane (1783–1824)
Fairies' Song, The.
My Mother.
Squire's Pew, The.
Star, The.
Violet, The.
Recreation.
Taylor, Jeremy (1613–67)
Hymn for Advent.
Prayer, A: "My soul doth pant towards thee."
Prayer, A: "O beauteous God! uncircumscribed
treasure."
Prayer for Charity, A.
Taylor, John (1580–1653)
As Gold is better that's in fire tride.
Epigram, A Supposed Construction.
Epigram: "Fair Beatrice tucks her coat up
somewhat high."
Epigram: "Look how yon lecher's legs are
worn away."
Epigram: "Lusty wench as nimble as an
eel, A."
Epigram: "There chanced to meet together in
an inn."
Gods Houses, almost like Troyes Ilion,.
It was in June the eight and thirtieth day.
Libra, September.
Me thinks I heare some Cavillers object.
10 Commandments, are the Law Divine.
Trumpet of Liberty, The.
Virgo, August.
Taylor, Rachel Annand (1876–1960)
Princess of Scotland, The.
Taylor, Richard
Limerick: "Sexy young student once toyed, A."
"Taylor, Rockie D." See Ologboni, Tejumola
Taylor, Rod (b. 1947)
Dakota: October, 1822, Hunkpapa Warrior.
Taylor, Susan
I am true in the land of ancient sounds.
Taylor, William (1765–1836)
Ellenore.
Vision, The.
Tayo-jo (1772–1865)
People, more people.
Tayson, Richard
Chase, The.
First Sex.
Nightsweats.
Phone Sex.
**Tchernichowsky [or Tchernichovsky], Saul [or
Shaul] (1875–1943)**
Before the Statue of Apollo.
Bells, The.
Dance of Saul with the Prophets, The.
Death of Tammuz, The.
Grave in Ukraine, A.
I Believe.

I have been to my God like the iris and the
anemone.
Images of a faded world possessed me, I
cannot flee!
Levivot.
Or the image-kingdom's idol of the past
generation.
They Say There Is a Country.
This Be Our Revenge.
To Ashtaroth and Bel.
Te Aomuhurangi te Maaka (b. 1927)
Go Down, O Sun, Out from the Motu River.
Haka: Hinemotu.
Te Heuheu Tukino
Lament for Te Heuheu Herea.
Te Kooti Rikirangi (c.1830–93)
Song of Instruction, A.
Te Puea Herangi (1884–1952)
Remain, Rata.
Te Whetu (fl. c.1880)
Sound of My Sneezing Nose, The.
Teasdale, Sara (1884–1933)
After Love.
Appraisal.
At Night.
August Night.
Barter.
Broken Field, The.
Crystal Gazer, The.
Enough.
Falling Star, The.
February Twilight.
Flight, The.
Full Moon; Santa Barbara.
Gift, The.
I Am Not Yours.
I Shall Live to Be Old.
I Shall Not Care.
I Would Live in Your Love.
Jewels.
Lines.
Little While, A.
Long Hill, The.
Look, The.
Moods.
Moon's Ending.
Moonlight.
Mystery, The.
Night.
Night Song at Amalfi.
On the Dunes.
On the South Downs.
Open Windows.
Over the Roofs.
Philosopher, The.
Sanctuary, The.
Shrine, The.
Solitary, The.
Song: "Let it be forgotten, as a flower is
forgotten."
Song: "You bound strong sandals on my feet."
Spring Night.
Summer Night, Riverside.
There Will Come Soft Rains.
Those Who Love.
Unchanging, The.
Water-Lilies.
What Do I Care.
Wisdom.
Wood Song.
Teddy
At Terezin.
**"Teffi" (Nadezhda Aleksandrovna Lokhvitskaia)
(1872–1952)**
Before the Map of Russia.
Teft, Elizabeth (fl. 1741–47)
On a Friend's Taking a Journey.
On Learning.
On Snuff-Taking.
On Viewing Herself in a Glass.
To a Gentleman Who Disordered a Lady's
Handkerchief, and Immediately Cut His
Thumb.
Tegnér, Esaias (1782–1846)
Frithiof's Saga.
Teiga (1744–1826)
In the poor man's house.

Teika, Fujiwara no *See* **Fujiwara no Teika**
Teikitsu (d. 1760)
  Open the shutters.
Teillier, Jorge (b. 1935)
  Bridge in the South.
  In the Secret House of Night.
  No Sign of Life.
  Portrait of My Father, Militant Communist.
Teisa (d. 1747)
  Plover wades through, A.
Teishi (d. 1700)
  Morning glory, A.
Teishitsu *See* **Yasuharau Teishitsu**
"Tekahionwake" *See* **Johnson, Emily Pauline**
Tekeyan, Vahan
  Country of Dust, The.
  Dream.
  Forgetting.
  Prayer on the Threshold of Tomorrow.
  Sacred Wrath.
Tekkan
  No mind, no Buddha, no being.
Telemaque, Harold Milton (b. 1911)
  Adina.
Telesilla (*fl.* 5th cent.)
  But Artemis, my girls.
  O Artemis and your virgin girls.
Tellegen, Toon (b. 1941)
  If Just For Once.
  Visit, The.
Tembo (d. 1823)
  I wish this body.
Templeton, Fiona (b. 1951)
  Act II—Crossing at the Tracks.
ten Berge, H. C. (b. 1938)
  Dança Mortal.
  Duel.
  Fortunes in knee breeches.
Tendo-Nyojo (1163–1228)
  Sixty-six years.
Teng Yu-pin (*fl.* late 13th cent.)
  Taoist Song: "Empty bag of skin filling with
    desire."
  Taoist Song: "Heaven and hell are men's
    unhappy inventions."
  Taoist Song: "In white clouds, in green
    mountains."
  Tune: "Wild Geese Have Come Down; Song of
    Victory"—Idle Leisure.
Tengour, Habib (b. 1947)
  Traces/Renown/Shades/Urns/Life(s)/Epoch/
    Zenith.
Tenji, Emperor (626–71 A.D.)
  Because.
Tennant, Edward Wyndham (1895–1916)
  A Bas la Gloire!
  Mad Soldier, The.
Tennant, William (1784–1848)
  My pulse beats fire—my pericranium glows.
  Sang First.
  Upon a little dappled nag, whose mane.
Tennyson, Alfred Tennyson, 1st Baron (1809–92)
  Ancient Pistol, peacock Payne.
  Ancient Sage, The.
  As through [*or* thro'] the Land [at Eve We
    Went].
  As when with downcast eyes we muse and
    brood.
  Ask Me No More.
  Audley Court.
  Babylon.
  Boädicea, *sels.*
  Break, Break, Break.
  Brook; An Idyl, The.
  Buonaparte.
  Charge of the Light Brigade, The.
  Check every outflash, every ruder sally.
  City Child, The.
  Come Down, O Maid [from Yonder Mountain
    Height].
  Crossing the Bar.
  Daisy, The.
  Dawn, The.
  Dedication, A: "Dear, near and true—no truer

    Time himself."
  Dying Swan, The.
  Eagle, The.
  Epic, The [Morte d'Arthur].
  Fatima.
  Flower in the Crannied Wall.
  Forgiving.
  Frater Ave Atque Vale.
  From Sorrow Sorrow Yet Is Born.
  Gardener's Daughter, The.
  Go By.
  Guess well, and that is well. Our age can find.
  Hendecasyllabics.
  Higher Pantheism, The.
  How thought you that this thing could
    captivate?
  Human Cry, The.
  Idylls of the King, *sels.*
  I ran upon life unknowing, without or science
    or art.
  I Stood on a Tower in the Wet.
  If I were loved, as I desire to be.
  In Memoriam A. H. H., *sels.*
  In my youth the growls.
  In the Garden at Swainston.
  In the Valley of Cauteretz.
  June Bracken and Heather.
  Kraken, The.
  Lady of Shalott, The.
  Late, late, so late! and dark the night and chill!
  Letter, The.
  Lines: "Here often, when a child, I lay
    reclined."
  Lines on Cambridge of 1830.
  Locksley Hall.
  Lotus-Eaters, The.
  Mariana.
  Maud [A Monodrama], *sels.*
  May Queen, The.
  Merlin and the Gleam.
  Merman, The.
  Miller's Daughter, The.
  Milton [Alcaics].
  Mine be the strength of spirit fierce and free.
  Minnie and Winnie.
  Morte d'Arthur, *sels.*
  Northern Cobbler, The.
  Northern Farmer: New Style.
  Not only with no sense of shame.
  Now Sleeps the Crimson Petal.
  O Swallow, Swallow.
  On the Jubilee of Queen Victoria.
  Owl, The.
  Palace of Art, The, *sels.*
  Passing of Arthur, The.
  Pelleas and Ettarre.
  Poet's Song, The.
  Popular.
  Prayer: "Pray for my soul. More things are
    wrought by prayer."
  Princess, The, *sels.*
  Recollections of the Arabian Nights.
  Revenge, The, *sels.*
  Ring Out, Wild Bells.
  Rizpah.
  Sadness.
  Sailor Boy, The.
  Sisters, The.
  Somebody.
  Song: "Who can say."
  Sonnet: "She took the dappled partridge
    fleckt [*or* fleckt] with blood."
  Spinster's Sweet-Arts, The, *sels.*
  Splendour Falls, The.
  St. Agnes' Eve.
  St. Simeon Stylites.
  Sweet and Low.
  Tears, Idle Tears.
  Tithonus.
  To Christopher North.
  To E. Fitzgerald.
  To the Rev. F. D. Maurice.
  To Virgil [*or* Vergil].
  To —. With the Following Poem.
  Ulysses.
  Woman's Cause Is Man's, The.
Tennyson, Frederick (1807–98)
  Holy Tide, The.

  Incident, An.
  Iona.
  Old Age.
  Poetical Happiness.
**Terapiano, Yury [*or* Iurii] Konstantinovich
  (1892–1980)**
  Lights shining above the Neva.
  Ships that sail forth.
**Teresa de Cepeda Y Ahumada (Teresa of Avila)
  (1515–82)**
  (Lines Written on a Bookmark Found in Her
    Breviary)
Terranova, Elaine
  Self-Examination.
Terrazas, Francisco de (1525?–1600?)
  To a Lady.
  To a Pair of Legs.
Terris, Virginia R.
  Roots: To My Daughter.
Terry, Lucy (1730–1821)
  Bar[']s Fight, [August 28, 1746].
Teschke, Holger (b. 1958)
  Minutes of Hasiba, The.
Tesshi (d. 1707)
  Among the barley stalks.
Tessho
  Finally out of reach.
Tesshu (*fl.* 14th cent.)
  How heal the phantom body of its phantom ill.
  On Visiting Sokei, Where the Sixth Patriarch
    Lived.
  When I leave.
Tessimond, Arthur Seymour John (1902–62)
  Jamaican Bus Ride.
  Postscript to a Pettiness.
Tester, William
  Complacencies of the Fenced Yard.
Teton Sioux Oral Tradition
  I Sing for the Animals.
Tetsugen Doko (d. 1682)
  Full of great changes.
Tetto Giko (d. 1369)
  I look now at the very moment.
Tewa Oral Tradition
  Song of the Sky Loom.
Thacker, Labhshankar (b. 1935)
  Poem: "Word is fast asleep, The."
Thackeray, William Makepeace (1811–63)
  At the Zoo.
  Ballad of Bouillabaisse, The.
  Damages, Two Hundred Pounds.
  Dear Jack.
  Due of the Dead, The.
  Georges, The.
  King of Brentford's Testament *abr,* The.
  Little Billee.
  Mahogany Tree, The.
  Mr. Molony's Account of the Crystal Palace.
  Napoleon.
  Sorrows of Werther, The.
  Speculators, The.
  Wearied arm, and broken sword.
Thallus (*fl.* A.D. 1st cent.)
  Now the green plane-tree hides the lovers,
    hides the lovers'/ rites.
Thamnaret
  Nightsong.
Thatcher, Charles Robert (1831–82)
  Dick Briggs from Australia.
  Moggy's Wedding.
  Taking the Census.
Thatcher, Thomas (1620–78)
  Love Letter to Elizabeth Thatcher, A.
Thaxter, Celia Laighton (1835–94)
  Alone.
  Chanticleer.
  Cruise of the *Mystery*, The.
  Favorite Flower, The.
  Imprisoned.
  Jack Frost.
  Sandpiper, The.
  Schumann's Sonata in a Minor.
Thayer, Ernest Lawrence (1863–1940)
  Casey at the Bat.

Thayer, Louis E. (1870–1966)
Little Child's Faith, The.

Thế Lũ' (Nguyễn Thú' Lễ) (b. 1907)
Green Nostalgia.

Theaitetus (fl. 6th cent.)
Already the field, fair with leaves, in her fruitful bringing to birth.
Krantor.

Thelwall, John (1764–1834)
Anacreontic.
Cell, The.
Day of my double birth, if such the year.
On the Rapid Extension of the Suburbs.
To Ancestry.
To Tyranny.
Vanity of National Grandeur, The.

Theocritus (c.310–c.250 B.C.)
Along that footpath, shepherd, past the oaks.
Cyclops ("For love there is no other drug")
Damoetas and Daphnis.
Daphnis the fair-skinned, who plays country songs.
Death of Adonis, The.
Death of Daphnis, The.
Enchantment, The.
Epitaph: Justice.
Epitaph of Cleonicus.
Epitaph of Hipponax.
Fishermen, The.
Gorgo and Praxinoa.
Harvest-Home.
Herdsmen, The.
Hylas.
Idyll 1.
Idyll.
Idyll 29.
Incantations, The.
Little Heracles.
Look on this statue, traveller; look well.
Neteheard.
O NICIAS, there is no other remedy for love.
Ortho's Epitaph.
Take, friend, Orthon of Syracuse' advice.
This bank makes welcome citizen and foreigner.
This is the grave of Eusthenes the wise.
Those dew-moist roses and that bushy thyme.
What do you gain, poor Thyrsis, by these tears?
Words are Doric, Doric too the man, The.
You left behind, Eurymedon, an infant child.
You sleep here, Daphnis, on the leafy ground.

Theodoridas (fl. 3rd cent. B.C.)
I am the tomb of a shipwrecked man. Sail on.
Roused by November seas, wrecked on Italian rocks.
To the triple goddess of Amarynthus.

Theodulf of Orleans (c.750–821)
Wherefore the Scars of Christ's Passion Remained in the Body of His Resurrection.

Theognis (fl. c.545 B.C.)
Boy and horse, a similar brain: The horse doesn't cry when its rider lies in the dust.
Captive.
Enjoyment.
Hope.
It's a thrill to love a boy: Even Kronos' son, king of immortals, once longed for Ganymede.
Man who doesn't love boys and single-foot horses and dogs, his heart will never know pleasure, The.
Poverty.

Theon (fl. 5th cent.)
For the Cenotaph of a Lost Soldier.

Theophanes (fl. 6th cent.)
I wish I could be.

Theresa [or Teresa], Saint, of Avila (1515–82)
En las Internas Entrañas.
I Die because I Do Not Die.
I gave myself to Love Divine.
If, Lord, Thy Love for Me Is Strong.
Let Mine Eyes See Thee.
Lines Written in Her Breviary.
Poem: "Nothing move thee."
Shepherd, Shepherd, Hark.

Soul, thou must seek thyself in Me.
To-Day a Shepherd.

Thésée, Lucie
Beautiful As.
Buckets in My Head, The.

Thesen, Sharon (b. 1946)
Kirk Lonegren's Home Movie Taking Place Just North of Prince George, with Sound.
Loose Woman Poem.
Mean Drunk Poem.

Thibaudeau, Colleen (b. 1925)
Brown Family, The.
Green Family, The.
Poem: "I do not want only."

Thicknesse, Lily (fl early 20th cent.)
Siena.

Thiele, Colin (b. 1920)
Radiation Victim.
Tom Farley.

Thimelby, Gertrude Aston (c.1615–c.1670)
Mrs Thimelby, on the Death of Her Only Child.
To Her Husband, on New Year's Day 1651.
Upon a Command to Write on My Father.

Thom, William (1799?–1848)
Blind Boy's Pranks, The.

Thomas, Abigail
Doggerel.

Thomas, Ann (fl. 1784–95)
To Laura, on the French Fleet Parading before Plymouth.

Thomas Aquinas, Saint (c.1225–74)
Thee we adore, O hidden Saviour, thee.
With my heart I worship.
Word went forth, The.

Thomas, Claire Richcreek
Flesh will heal and pain will fade.
Heart Wounds.
Treasures.

Thomas, D. M.
Puberty Tree, The.

Thomas, Delaina (b. 1955)
Turning of the Year, The.

Thomas, Dylan (1914–53)
After the Funeral.
Altarwise by owl-light in the half-way house.
Among Those Killed in the Dawn Raid Was a Man Aged a Hundred.
And Death Shall Have No Dominion.
Author's Prologue.
Because the Pleasure-Bird Whistles.
Before I Knocked.
Ceremony after a Fire Raid.
Conversation of Prayer, The.
Countryman's Return, The.
Death is all metaphors, shape in one history.
Do Not Go Gentle into That Good Night.
Ears in the Turrets Hear.
Especially When the October Wind.
Fern Hill.
Force That through the Green Fuse Drives the Flower, The.
Ghost Story.
Hand That Signed the Paper, The.
Hunchback in the Park, The.
I Have Longed to Move Away.
I, in My Intricate Image.
I shall never forget his blue eye.
In My Craft or Sullen Art.
In The Beginning.
It is the sinners' dust-tongued bell claps me to churches.
Johnnie Crack and Flossie Snail.
Let the tale's sailor from a Christian voyage.
Light Breaks Where No Sun Shines.
Limerick: "Last time I slept with the Queen, The."
Marriage of a Virgin, The.
Now stamp the Lord's Prayer on a grain of rice.
On No Work of Words.
On the Marriage of a Virgin.
Over Sir John's Hill.
Poem in October.
Refusal to Mourn the Death, by Fire, of a

Child in London, A.
Should Lanterns Shine.
Song of the Mischievous Dog, The.
There Was a Saviour.
This Bread I Break.
Tombstone told when she died, The.
Twenty-four Years.
Walking in Gardens.
What is the metre of the dictionary?
When All My Five and Country Senses See.

Thomas, Edith Matilda (1854–1925)
Cricket Kept the House, The.
Cries of the Newsboy.
Deep-Sea Pearl, The.
Frost To-night.
Mrs. Kriss Kringle.
Shooting Star, A.

Thomas, Edward ("Edward Eastaway") (1878–1917)
Adlestrop.
And You, Helen.
As the Team's Head-Brass.
Aspens.
Barn and the Down, The.
Birds' Nests.
Bob's Lane.
By the Ford.
Celandine.
Cherry Trees, The.
Clouds That Are So Light, The.
Cock-Crow.
Combe, The.
Digging.
February Afternoon.
Fifty Faggots.
Gallows, The.
Glory, The.
Gone, Gone Again.
Green Roads, The.
Gypsy, The.
Haymaking.
Here once flint walls.
Hollow Wood, The.
I never saw that land before.
If I Should Ever by Chance.
In Memoriam (Easter, 1915)
It Rains.
Lights Out.
Like the Touch of Rain.
Man and Dog.
Mill-Pond, The.
New House, The.
No One So Much As You.
October.
Old Man.
Out in the Dark.
Owl, The.
Penny Whistle, The.
Private, A.
Rain.
Roads.
Snow.
Some Eyes Condemn.
Sun Used to Shine, The.
Swedes.
Tale, A.
Tall Nettles.
Tears.
Thaw.
This Is No Case of Petty Right or Wrong.
Trumpet, The.
Two Houses.
Unknown Bird, The.
What Shall I Give?
When First.
When I First Came Here.

Thomas, Elizabeth (1675–1731)
Dream, The; An Epistle to Mr. Dryden.
Epistle to Clemena, Occasioned by an Argument She Had Maintained against the Author.
Execration, The.
Forsaken Wife, The.
Midnight Thought, A [on the Death of Mrs. E. H. and Her Little Daughter].
New Litany, Occasioned by an Invitation to a Wedding, A.

Nine times the sun his yearly course had run.
On Sir J—— S—— Saying in a Sarcastic
  Manner, My Books Would Make Me Mad;
  An Ode.
Remedia Amoris.
To Almystrea, on her Divine Works.
To Clemena.
To Colindra.
Triumvirate, The.
True Effigies of a Certain Squire: Inscribed to
  Clemena, The.
Thomas, Evan (c.1710–c.70)
  To the Gentlewoman of Llanarth Hall.
Thomas, Evan J. (1903–30)
  Return, The.
  Spectator, The.
Thomas, Graham (b. 1944)
  At Ynysddu.
  Lessons.
Thomas, Gwyn (b. 1936)
  Horses.
  Little Death.
  Microscope.
Thomas, Harry
  Limerick: "Strip," Leofric said, "and you'll
    find."
Thomas, John L. (Ieuan Ddu) (1795–1871)
  His father did intend that Harry should.
Thomas, Lorenzo (b. 1944)
  Cameo in Sudden Light.
  Clear Channel.
  Electricity of Blossoms.
  Excitation.
  Historiography.
  Inauguration.
  Instructions for Your New Osiris.
  Marvelous Land of Indefinitions, The.
  Onion Bucket.
  Subway Witnesses, The.
Thomas of Celano (1200?–55?)
  Dies Irae.
Thomas of Erceldoune (c.1225–c.1300)
  Tristrem and the Hunters.
Thomas, Peter (b. 1939)
  Lascars, The.
Thomas, Ronald Stuart (b. 1913)
  After Jericho.
  Ancients of the World, The.
  Ann Griffith.
  Aside.
  At It.
  Blackbird Singing, A.
  Bright Field, The.
  Calling, The.
  Centuries.
  Coleridge.
  Country Clergy, The.
  Cynddylan on a Tractor.
  Echoes.
  Empty Church, The.
  Evans.
  Evening.
  Expatriates.
  Geriatric.
  Gifts.
  Hand, The.
  Here.
  Hill Farmer Speaks, The.
  In a Country Church.
  Ire.
  Island, The.
  Judgment Day.
  Line from St. David's, A.
  Llanrhaeadr Ym Mochnant.
  Lonely Farmer, The.
  Lore.
  Madrigal: "Your love is dead, lady, your love
    is dead."
  Marriage, A.
  Moor, The.
  Navigation.
  Nocturne by Ben Shahn.
  On the Farm.
  One Furrow, The.
  Other.

Pavane.
Peasant, A.
Period.
Person from Porlock, A.
Petition.
Pietà.
Pisces.
Poetry for Supper.
Porch, The.
Postscript.
Raptor.
Reservoirs.
Rhodri.
Selah.
Sir Gelli Meurig.
Song for Gwydion.
Still.
Survivor, The.
Taliesin 1952.
They.
Via Negativa.
View from the Window, The.
Village, The.
Welsh Hill Country, The.
Welsh History.
Welsh Landscape.
Welsh Testament, A.
Welshman at St. James' Park, A.
Welshman to Any Tourist, A.
White Tiger, The.
Woman, The.
Thomas, Thomas Jacob ("Sarnicol") (1873–1945)
  Dic Siôn Dayfydd.
Thompson, Alexander R. (1812–95)
  Wayfarers in the Wilderness.
Thompson, Benjamin (1642–1714)
  Seaconk Plain Engagement.
Thompson, Clara Ann (b. 1887?)
  After-Glow of Pain, The.
  Angel's Message, The.
  Autumn Day, An.
  Autumn Leaves.
  Christmas Rush, The.
  Church Bells.
  Doubt.
  Drift-Wood.
  Dying Year, The.
  Easter Bonnet, The.
  Easter Light, The.
  Empty Tomb, The.
  His Answer.
  Hope.
  Hope Deferred.
  I'll Follow Thee.
  If Thou Shouldst Return.
  Johnny's Pet Superstition.
  Lullaby: "Hush ye, hush ye! honey, darlin'"
  Memorial Day.
  Mrs. Johnson Objects.
  Not Dead, but Sleeping.
  Oh List to My Song!
  Old and the New, The.
  Opening Service, An.
  Out of the Deep.
  Parted.
  She Sent Him Away.
  Skeptic, The.
  Storm-Beaten.
  Submission.
  To My Dead Brother.
  Uncle Rube on the Race Problem.
  Uncle Rube's Defense.
  Uncle Rube to the Young People.
  Watcher, The.
Thompson, Donald
  On the Relative Merit of Friend and Foe,
    Being Dead.
Thompson, Dorothy Brown (b. 1896)
  Good Will to Men—Christmas Greetings in
    Six Languages.
Thompson, Dorothy Perry (b. 1944)
  Blues at 1.
  Dancing in Menopause.
  Intelligence Quotients.
  Laurel Street, 1950.
  Sister Lakin and Lally.

Thompson, Douglas
  Days of Yore, The.
Thompson, Earle (b. 1950)
  Juniper Moon Pulls at My Bones, The.
  Love Song: "She is a reed swaying in blue."
  Mythology.
  No Deposit.
  Song: "Woman sits on her porch."
Thompson, Edward (1739?–86)
  I've served my country nine and twenty years.
  Indian Maid, The; Demararie, Oct. 27, 1781.
  To Emma, Extempore; Hyaena, off Gambia,
    June 4, 1779.
Thompson, Eloise Bibb *See* Bibb, Eloise
Thompson, Francis (1859–1907)
  Ad Amicam.
  All's Vast.
  Any Saint.
  Arab Love-Song, An.
  At Lord's.
  But lo! at length the day is lingered out.
  Counsel of Moderation, A.
  Daisy.
  End of It, The.
  Envoy: "Go, songs, for ended is our brief,
    sweet play."
  Epilogue: "Heaven, which man's generations
    draws."
  Fallen Yew, A.
  Heart you hold too small and local thing, The.
  Heaven and Hell.
  Hound of Heaven, The.
  I fled Him, down the nights and down the
    days.
  Kingdom of God, The.
  Love's Varlets.
  Non Pax—Expectatio.
  Now of that vision I, bereaven.
  Past Thinking of Solomon.
  Poppy, The.
  Sun, The.
  To a Snowflake.
  To Olivia.
  To the Dead Cardinal of Westminster.
Thompson, J. W.
  Work.
Thompson, James W. (b. 1936)
  Constant Labor, A.
  Greek Room, The.
  Plight, The.
  Spawn of Slums, The.
Thompson, John (1907–68)
  Bread Hot from the Oven, The.
  Now You Have Burned.
  Onion, The.
Thompson, John Randolph (b. 1838)
  Lee to the Rear.
  Obsequies of Stuart.
Thompson, John Reuben (1823–73)
  Burial of Latané, The.
  Music in Camp.
Thompson, Maurice (1844–1901)
  Address by an Ex-Confederate Soldier to the
    Grand Army of the Republic, An.
  Lincoln's Grave.
  To the South.
Thompson, Priscilla Jane (b. 1882)
  Address to Ethiopia.
  Adieu, Adieu, Forever.
  Adown the Heights of Ages.
  After the Quarrel.
  Afternoon Gossip, An.
  Alberta.
  Athelstane.
  Autumn.
  Christmas Ghost, A.
  Common Occurrence, A.
  Consumptive, The.
  David and Goliath.
  Death and Resurrection.
  Domestic Storm, A.
  Emancipation.
  Evelyn.
  Examination, The.
  Favorite Slave's Story, The.

Freedom at McNealy's.
Fugitive, The.
Glimpses of Infancy.
Happy Pair, A.
Home Greeting, A.
Husband's Return, The.
Hymn: "Lord, within thy fold I be."
In the Valley.
Inner Realm, The.
Insulted.
Interrupted Reproof, The.
Just How It Happened.
Kindly Deed, A.
King's Favorites, The.
Knight of My Maiden Love.
Lines on a Dead Girl.
Lines to an Old School-House.
Lines to Emma.
Little Wren, A.
Muse's Favor, The.
My Father's Story.
Oh, Whence Comes the Gladness?
Old Freedman, The.
Old Saint's Prayer, The.
Old Year, The.
Prayer, A: "Oh, Lord! I lift my heart."
Precious Pearl, The.
Raphael.
Snail's Lesson, The.
Snow-Flakes, The.
Soft Black Eyes.
Song of the Moon.
Song, The: "Oh, foully slighted Ethiope maid!"
Southern Scene, A.
They Are the Same.
Thwarted.
To a Deceased Friend.
To a Little Colored Boy.
To the New Year.
Tribute to the Bride and Groom, A.
Turncoat, The.
Uncle Ike's Holiday.
Uncle Jimmie's Yarn.
Unromantic Awakening, An.
Valentine, A.
Vineyard of My Beloved, The.
While the Choir Sang.
Winter Night, A.

Thompson, Samuel (1766–1816)
April.
To a Hedgehog.

Thompson, Ted
Limerick: "Having rid Hamelin town of its vermin."

Thompson, Will Henry (1848–1918)
High Tide at Gettysburg, The.

Thompson, William (1712?–66?)
Happy Life, The.
Next, in a low-browed cave, a little hell.

Thomson, Derick (b. 1921)
Herring Girls, The.

Thomson, Edward William (1849–1924)
Aspiration.

Thomson, James (1700–48)
All–intellectual eye, our solar round.
And what, my thoughtless sons, should fire you more.
Behold yon breathing prospect bids the Muse.
Evening and Night.
Flushed by the spirit of the genial year.
For, see! where Winter comes, himself, confest.
Forenoon. Summer Insects Described.
How sweet and innocent are country sports.
Hymn on Solitude.
Hymn on the Seasons, A.
Keener tempests come, The.
Land of Indolence, The.
Leper-House and the Impenitents, The.
Night. Summer Meteors. A Comet.
Now, when the cheerless empire of the sky.
On the Death of a Particular Friend.
Paraphrase of the Latter part of the Sixth Chapter of St. Matthew, A.
Rule, Britannia!
See, Winter comes, to rule the varied year.

Songs in the Desert! songs of husky breath.
Spring Flowers.
These, as they change, Almighty Father! these.
This happy place with all delights abounds.
Thy Church has long been becoming the Fossil of a Faith.
'Tis done! Dread Winter spreads his latest glooms.
'Tis raging noon; and vertical, the sun.
To Fortune.
To the God of Fond Desire.
What art thou, frost? and whence are thy keen stores.
When from the pallid sky the sun descends.
Winter Night, A.
Winter Tragedy, A.

Thomson, James (1834–82)
Although lamps burn along the silent streets.
Because he seemed to walk with an intent.
City is of Night, The; perchance of Death.
City's Queen, The.
Gifts.
He stood alone within the spacious square.
How the moon triumphs through the endless nights!
I wandered in a suburb of the north.
In a Christian Churchyard.
In the Room.
Large glooms were gathered in the mighty fane.
Mighty river flowing dark and deep, The.
Mr. MacCall at Cleveland Hall.
Once in a Saintly Passion.
Proem: "Lo, thus, as prostrate, In the dust I write."
Singing is sweet; but be sure of this.
What men are they who haunt these fatal glooms.
Wine of Love, The.

Thomson, Mary A. (1834–1923)
O King of Saints, We Give Thee Praise and Glory.
O Sion, Haste, Thy Mission High Fulfilling.

T'Hooft, Jotie (1956–77)
Death, Dark Agent.
Death, Dark Doer.
Worn-Out Pop Song, A.

Thoreau, Henry David (1817–62)
All Things Are Current Found.
Any Fool Can Make a Rule.
Brother Where Dost Thou Dwell.
Dong, Sounds the Brass in the East.
Each More Melodious Note I Hear.
Fog.
For Though the Eaves [or Caves] Were Rabbeted [or Rabbited].
Great God, I Ask Thee for No Meaner Pelf.
Guido's Aurora.
I Am a Parcel of Vain Strivings Tied.
I Am Bound, I Am Bound.
Indeed Indeed, I Cannot Tell.
Inspiration.
Light-Winged Smoke, Icarian Bird.
Love Equals Swift and Slow.
Low-Anchored Cloud.
Men Say They Know Many Things.
Music.
My Life Has Been the Poem I Would Have Writ.
Nature.
O nature I do not aspire.
On Fields oer Which the Reaper's Hand Has Passed.
On Ponkawtasset, Since, We Took Our Way.
On the Sun Coming Out in the Afternoon.
Poet's Delay, The.
Pray to What Earth Does This Sweet Cold Belong.
River Swelleth More and More, The.
Rumors from an Aeolian Harp.
Salmon Brook.
Sympathy.
They Made Me Erect and Lone.
They Who Prepare My Evening Meal below.
Though All the Fates Should Prove Unkind.
To the Maiden in the East.

What's the Railroad to Me?
Winter and Spring Scene, A.
Winter Memories.
Woof of the Sun, Ethereal Gauze.

Thorley, Wilfrid (b. 1878)
Chant for Reapers.

Thornbury, George Walter (1828–76)
Court Historian, The.
Smith of Maudlin.

Thorne, Ellin (fl. c.1576)
Ellin Thorne Songe.

Thorne, Tim (b. 1944)
High Country.
Whatever Happened to Conway Twitty?

Thorneley, Thomas
Limerick: "Candid Professor confesses, A."
Limerick: "Cynic says: Now that we know, A."
Limerick: "Fascist, erect and irate, A."
Limerick: "Figure is not anatomical, The."
Limerick: "Life-Force, afflicted with doubt, The."
Limerick: "Man who had lately declared, A."
Limerick: "Millionaire, filled with elation, A."
Limerick: "Mordant and decadent Youth, A."
Limerick: "Novelist, flushed with success, A."
Limerick: "Painter, encumbered with cash, A."
Limerick: "Said a Tripper: 'O joy, to have found.'"
Limerick: "Said the Stoic, tormented by gout."
Limerick: "There was a great German Grammarian."

Thornton, R. K. R.
Limerick: "'Political women,' thought Yeats."
Limerick: "There once was a writer called James."

Thorold Rogers, J. E. (1823–90)
Here X. lies dead, but God's forgiving.
On a Distinguished Politician.
On the Historians Freeman and Stubbs.
Suggestion Made by the Posters of the Globe, A.
Upon the man who's buried here.
Vulgar Error, A.

Thorpe, Rose Hartwick (1850–1939)
Curfew Must Not Ring Tonight [or To-Night].

Thorson, Marie
Closed Doors.

Thrale [later Mrs. Piozzi], Hester Lynch Salusbury (1741–1821)
Ode to Society, An.
Winter in Wales, A.

Three Marias, The (Maria Isabella Barreno, Maria Teresa Horta (b. 1937) and Maria Velho da Costa)
Saddle and Cell.

Thribb, E. J. (b. 1960?)
Erratum.
In Memoriam Krishna Menon.
In Memoriam Larry Parnes ("Mr Parnes Shillings and Pence.")
In Memoriam Salvador Dali.
In Memoriam the Master—Noel Coward (1900–1973)
Lines on the Award "Pipe Man of the Year" to Magnus Magnusson.
Lines on the Hundredth Anniversary of the Birth of W. Somerset Maugham.
Lines on the Return to Britain of Billy Graham.

Thrilling, Isobel
Mother.

Thucydides (b. c.460 B.C.)
Euripides.

Thurayya, Malhas
False...False.
Orphan, An.

Thurman, Judith (b. 1946)
Clockface.
Oil Slick.
Zebra.

Thurtle, Ida
Limerick: "Certain young man of Hilgay, A."
Limerick: "Flighty young lady from Loddon, A."
Limerick: "Retired Civil Servant from

Gateley, A."
Limerick: "Said a wife to her husband near Scole."
Limerick: "Said the boy driving home towards Clere."
Limerick: "Young man who lived at Holme Hale, A."

Thwaite, Anthony (b. 1930)
Ali Ben Shufti.
At Evening.
Dream Time.
Freedom.
Girdle round the Earth, A.
Great Foreign Writer Visits Age-Old Temple, Greeted by Venerable Abbess, 1955.
Mr. Cooper.
On Consulting "Contemporary Poets of the English Language."
Simple Poem.
Sunday Afternoons.

Thwaites, Michael (b. 1917)
On either side the *Jervis Bay* the convoy was dipping.

Thyillos
Already swallows build their homes of mud.

Thymocles (Timocles) (fl. 3rd cent. B.C.)
Remember, do you remember those solemn words.
Remember now? Do you.

Tibble, Anne (b. 1912)
Trials of a Tourist.

Tibi, Lina (b. 1963)
Failure.
If Only.
Striding, shuddering.
Suicide.
Voice, A.

Tibullus (Albius Tibullus) (c.59–c.19 B.C.)
Cross the Aegean Without Me, Then, Messalla.
Fill up my glass again! The anodyne.
Pastoral Elegy, A.
Priapus, may this shady roof forever.

Tichborne [or Tichbourne], Chidiock (1558?–86)
Tichborne's Elegy.

Tickell, Thomas (1686–1740)
Ah! curst Ambition, to thy lures we owe.
Such be the dog, I charge, thou mean'st to train.
To the Earl of Warwick, on the Death of Mr. Addison.

Ticknor, Francis Orrery [or Orray] (1822–74)
Little Giffen.

Tico, Tom
After gazing at stars.
Tinkle of chimes, The.
Wisp of spring cloud, A.

Tidjani-Cissé, Ahmed (b. 1947)
Home News.
Of Colours and Shadows.

Tieck, Johann Ludwig (1773–1853)
Autumn Song.

Tiempo, César (Israel Zierlin) (b. 1906)
I Tell of Another Young Death.
Harangue on the Death of Hayyim Nahman Bialik.

T'ien Hung (fl. 3rd cent. B.C.)
Dew on the Young Garlic Leaves.

Tierney, Harry
Alice Blue Gown.

Tiger, Madeline J.
Lovepoem Writing Me.

Tighe, Mary (1772–1810)
1802.
As one who late hath lost a friend adored.
Can I look back, and view with tranquil eye.
From Psyche.
Illumined bright now shines the splendid dome.
'Mid the thick covert of that woodland shade.
On Receiving a Branch of Mezereon Which Flowered at Woodstock, December 1809.
Poor, fond deluded heart! wilt thou again.
Psyche.
Sonnet Addressed to My Mother.

To Death.
When glowing Phoebus quits the weeping earth.
Wine, I Say! I'll Drink to Madness!
Written at Killarney. July 29, 1800.
Written at Rossana. November 18, 1799.
Written at Scarborough. August, 1799.
Written at the Eagle's Nest, Killarney. July 26, 1800.
Written in Autumn.

Tikhonov, Nikolai Semionovich (1896–1979)
Ballad of the Blue Envelope, The.
Ballad of the Nails, The.
Fire and Rope, Bullet and Axe.
Gulliver Plays Cards.
We have forgotten how to offer alms.

Tilden, Stephen (1690–1766)
O Heaven Indulge.

Tillam, Thomas (fl. 17th cent.)
Uppon the First Sight of New England, June 29, 1638.

Tillema, Mieke (b. 1944)
Considering Tulips.
So Soon.
Tulips.

Tiller, Terence (b. 1916)
Reading a Medal.
Street Performers, 1851.

Tilley, H. H.
Democracy, my grannie's foot!

Timocles *See* **Thymocles**

Timrod, Henry (1828–67)
Carolina.
Charleston.
Christmas.
Cotton Boll, The.
Dreams.
Ethnogenesis.
Faint Falls the Gentle Voice.
I know not why, but all this weary day.
La Belle Juive.
Ode: "Sleep sweetly in your humble graves."
Retirement.

Tindal, Henrietta (1818–79)
Birth Wail, The.
Cry of the Oppressed, The.

Tindley, Charles A. (1859–1933)
Stand by Me.

Tinódi, Sebestyén (1505 [or] 1510–56)
Fall of Zolnok, The.
I've heard it sung—it may be true or no.
You, who are lieutenants in the army.

Tinturin, Peter
Foolin' Myself.

Tió, Elsa (b. 1950)
I am furious with myself.

"Tipcuca" *See* **Wilson, T. P. Cameron**

Tipper, Elizabeth (fl. 1698–1704)
Some Experimental Passages of My Life, with Reflections upon Jacob's Words, Few and Evil Have the Days of the Years of My Life Been.
To a Young Lady That Desired a Verse of My Being Servant One Day and Mistress Another.

Tipping, Richard (b. 1949)
Casino.
Just after Michael's Death, the Game of Pool.
Mangoes.
Men at Work.
Poet at Work.
When You're Feeling Kind of Bonkers.

Tipton, James
All day.
I Want to Speak With the Blood that Lies Down.
I Wanted You in the Kitchen of My Heart.
There Are Rivers of Oranges.

Tirolien, Guy (b. 1917)
Ghetto.
Little Black Boy's Prayer, A.
Marie Galante.
Soul of the Black Land, The.

Tirumalesh, K. V. (b. 1940)
Face to Face.

Tiruvalluvar (fl. c.500)
Gift of Children, The.
Kindness and Generosity.
Learning.

Titherage, Dion (1889–1934)
And Her Mother Came Too.

Tjanara-Williams, Pam
Torn Apart.

Tjinapirrgarri
Emu Shot.

Tkachenko, Aleksandr Petrovich (b. 1945)
Battle.
Dynamo Stadium, 1980.
Engraving, An.
Like Thousands of Others.
Requiem for Eduard Streltsov.

Tlingit Oral Tradition
Carrying My Mind Around.

Tobin, Daniel
At the Egyptian Exhibit.
Deep Shit.
Floor Scrapers.
Hunt-Cup, The.
Pigeons.

Tobrise, Mabel (b. 1965)
Dyeing.

Todd, Mark
Game Trail, The.
Grandmother's Farm.
Mud Season.
Post Scriptum.
Rigby.
Son et Lumière.
To Kill Stray Dogs.
Wire Song.

Todd, Ruthven (b. 1914)
Joan Miró.
Of Moulds and Mushrooms.
Paul Klee.
Poem: "I walk at dawn across the hollow hills."

Todros ben Judah Abulafia
From Prison.

Tofte, Robert (d. 1620)
Unto Thy Favor.
When She Was Born.

Togyu (d. 1749)
When autumn winds blow.

Tohe, Laura
She Was Telling It This Way.

Toho (d. 1730)
Food is steaming.

Tojaku (d. 1799)
I go back.

Tojun (d. 1695)
Even dew distilled.

Toko (d. 1795)
Death poems.

Tokugen (d. 1647)
My life was.

Tokuo (1649–1709)
Town's aflame with summer heat, The.

Tolkien, John Ronald Reuel (1892–1973)
Man in the Moon Stayed up Too Late, The.

Toller, Ernst (1893–1939)
Book I Held Grew Cold, The.
Corpses in the Wood.
O Heavy Step of Slow Monotony.
O Master Masons.
O My Swallows!
One Who Struggles, The.
To the Mothers.

Tollerud, Jim
Bird of Power.
Buzz.
Earth.
Elementary.
Eye of God.
Rainier.
Sunrise.
Thirsty Island.
Week-Seek.

Tollet, Elizabeth (1694–1754)
On a Death's Head.

On Loving Once and Loving Often.
On the Prospect from Westminster Bridge.
Rose, The.
To My Brother at St. John's College in
    Cambridge.
What cruel laws depress the female kind.
Winter Song.

Tolson, Melvin B. (1898–1966)
African China.
Alpha.
Ex-Judge at the Bar, An.
Birth of John Henry, The.
Dark Symphony.
Festus Conrad.
Legend of Versailles, A.
Lena Lovelace.
Mu.
Note, The.
Old Houses.
Old Pettigrew.
On the Founding of Liberia.
Satchmo.
Ti.
Victor Garibaldi.

Tomioka, Taeko (b. 1935)
Just the Two of Us.
Life Story.
Please Say Something.

Tomlinson, Charles (b. 1927)
After a Death.
Against Extremity.
Ararat.
At Barstow.
Chances of Rhyme, The.
Charlotte Corday.
Chestnut Avenue: At Alton House, The.
Civilities of Lamplight.
Crane, The.
Death of Will, The.
Descartes and the Stove.
Door, The.
Dream, A.
Farewell to Van Gogh.
Fiascherino.
For Danton.
Icos.
In Arden.
In Defence of Metaphysics.
In the Borghese Gardens.
Jam Trap, The.
John Maydew or The Allotment.
Juliet's Garden.
Las Trampas U. S. A.
Macduff.
More Foreign Cities.
Mr. Brodsky.
On a Pig's Head.
On the Hall at Stowey.
Oxen: Ploughing at Fiesole.
Paring the Apple.
Picture of J. T. in a Prospect of Stone, The.
Prometheus.
Radial wheels of the season spiked with
    knives, The.
Rhymes.
Saving the Appearances.
Shaft, The.
Snow Signs.
Stone Speech.
Swimming Chenango Lake.
Tramontana at Lerici.
Two Views of Two Ghost Towns.
Ute Mountain.
Weather Report.
Word in Edgeways, A.

Tomoana, Paraire Henare (1868–1946)
Full Tide.
Waters of Waiapu, The.

Tomoemon
Sound of a melody.

Tompa, Mihály (1817–68)
Autumn.
Bird, to Its Young, The.
Haven of Rest.
Last Poem.
To the Stork.

Tompson, Benjamin (1642–1714)
Chelmsfords Fate.
Edmund Davie 1682; Annagram.
Marlburyes Fate.
New-England's Crisis.
On a Fortification at Boston Begun by Women.
Seaconk or Rehoboths Fate.
Supplement, a.
To My Honoured Patron Humphery Davie.
Town Called Providence, Its Fate, The.

**"Tomson, Graham R." See Watson, Rosamund
Marriott**

Tong, Raymond
Then suddenly his brain became the sound.

Tonkin, S.
Limerick: "Since my overdraft threatens to
    be."

Tonks, Rosemary
Badly-Chosen Lover.
Farewell to Kurdistan.
Hydromaniac.
Story of a Hotel Room.

Toomer, Jean (1894–1967)
Beehive.
Cotton Song.
Delivered at the Knighting of Lord Durgling
    by Great Bruce-Jean.
Evening Song.
Georgia Dusk.
Gods Are Here, The.
Gum.
Harvest Song.
Her Lips Are Copper Wire.
I Sit in My Room.
It is Everywhere.
Merl.
November Cotton Flower.
Nullo.
People.
Portrait in Georgia.
Prayer.
Reapers.
Seventh Street.
Song of the Son.
Storm Ending.

Toplady, Augustus Montague (1740–78)
Hymn: "Inspirer and hearer of prayer."
Rock of Ages.

Torberg, Friedrich (b. 1908)
Prater's Tree-Lined Boulevard.
View from the Kobenzl.

Torlino
Therefore I Must Tell the Truth.

Tormé, Mel
Christmas Song, The.

Torneol, Nuño Fernández (fl. c.1225)
Lady's Farewell, The.

Torrance, Chris (b. 1941)
Acrospirical Meanderings in a Tongue of the
    Time.
It Is Difficult to Exaggerate the Importance of
    Mushrooms as Food.
Maen Madoc.

Torregian, Sotère (b. 1941)
Newark Public Library Reading Room, The.
Poem for the Birthday of Huey P. Newton.
Travois of the Nameless.

Torrence, Frederic Ridgely (1875–1950)
Son, The.

Torres, Anabel (b. 1948)
Eskimo's Woman, The.
Kettle Rooted to the Void.
Small Miracle, A.
Smash Your Fist.
These Are the Sweet Girls.
Warmness.

Torres Bodet, Jaime (1902–74)
Exodus.
Labyrinth.
Living.
My Country.
Summary.

Torres, Edwin
Bio-Rodent-Oriole.
Breezy Delicious Day.

Drowning in the Last Days of Luxury.
Elbow in Dumberland, An.
Elder Dubb.
Gigabyte Me—How Much RAM in Your
    Summer of Love?
How Long Does the Curator Dance For?
Lipsticktion.
Of My Nipple Ring Halos.
Poetry Detective.
Summertime Late Show.
Vase of the Universe, The.

Toshinari, Fujiwara No
I remember a grass hut.
Twilight.

Toshinari, Fujiwara no Shunzei; See Shunzei

Toshiyuki (Fujiwara no Toshiyuki)
Autumn has come invisibly.
In the Bay of Sumi.

Tosui Unkei (d. 1683)
Content with chipped bowl and tattered robe.
Seventy years and more.
Though my dwelling be small.
Today is the end of religion's work.

Tóth, Árpád (1886–1928)
Berzsenyi.
Elegy on a Broom Bush.
Evening Halo of Light, An.
From Soul to Soul.
Non Piu Leggevano.
Pendulum, The.
Retreat.
Serenade at Dawn.
Soul Woven of Shadows.
Until New Spring or Death.

Tóth, Judit (b. 1936)
Dead Embryos.
To the Newborn.

Touma, Khalil (b. 1945)
Song of Job, A.

Toure, Askia M. (b. 1958)
Azuri.
Frontier of Rage, The.
Imani in Sunburst Summer: A Chant.

Touré, Askia Muhammad (b. 1938)
JuJu.
O Lord of Light! A Mystic Sage Returns to
    Realms of Eternity!

Tourneur, Cyril (1575?–1626)
Art thou beguild now? tut, a Lady can.
Duke: royall letcher; goe, gray hayrde adultery.

Toussaint L'Ouverture, Isaac (1782–1854)
Farewell: "Shores of my native land."

Towanbucket
Limerick: "There once was a doctor who said."
Limerick: "There was a French bard who said:
    'Hell!'"

Towers, Tarin
Mission Poem.
Three Observations on Belief.

Towle, Tony (b. 1939)
North.
Painting the Eaves.
Postmodern Maturity.
Random (Re-arrangeable) Study for *Views*.

Towne, Charles Hanson (1877–1949)
Around the Corner.
Roof-Tops.

Townley, Roderick
Potato, The.

Townley, Wyatt
Swimming Lesson.

Townsend, Ann (fl. 20th cent.)
After the End.
Bicycle Racers, The.
Butane, Kerosene, Gasoline.
Comings and Goings.
Eighteenth-Century Medical Illustration: The
    Infant in its Little Room.
First Death.
First Quilt.
Institutional Blue.
Mardi Gras Premortem.
Night Watch in the Laboratory.
Outdoor Chums in the Forest.

Purple Loosestrife.
Rouge.
Shirt Collar, The.

Townsend, Charles (1789–1870)
On the Lake Poets.

Townsend, F. H. (b. 1893)
To the Cuckoo.

Townsend, George Alfred (1841–1914)
Fire Guest, The.

Townshend [or Townsend], Aurelian (c.1583–c.1651)
Dialogue betwixt Time and a Pilgrim[e], A.
Let not thy beauty make thee proud.
Song: "Though regions farr divided."
Song: "What mak's me so unnimbly ryse."
To the Lady May.
Upon Kind[e] and True Love.

Toxaoci
I don't know why you tell me I'm drunk.

Toya, Debra Haaland
Hunter's Dance in Early Fall.

Toyama, Jean Yamasaki
Red.

Toyo Eicho (d. 1504)
All four pillars of enlightenment.

Toyokuni (d. 1825)
Is it like.

Tozan-Gyoso
Way's not for the blind.

Traherne, Thomas (1636–74)
All music, sauces, feasts, delights and pleasures.
Amendment.
Anticipation, The.
Apostacy, The.
Bible, The.
Childhood.
Contentment.
Corn was Orient and Immortal Wheat, which never should, The.
Demonstration, The.
Eden.
Hosanna.
Hymn upon St. Bartholomew's Day, An.
In Salem Dwelt a Glorious King.
Innocence.
Insatiableness.
Instruction, The.
Life of sabbaths here beneath, A!
Love.
My Spirit.
News.
On Leaping over the Moon.
On the Bible.
Poverty.
Preparative, The.
Rapture, The.
Recovery, The.
Return, The.
Salutation [or Salutations], The.
Shadows in the Water.
Sin! / O only fatal Woe.
Thanksgivings for the Beauty of His Providence.
That childish thoughts such joys inspire.
Third Day.
Wonder.

Trainin, Avner (b. 1928)
Cat in the Dovecote.
Sunbeams.

Trajan (A.D. 53–117)
Point your nose to the sun.

Trakl, Georg (1887–1914)
Autumn of the Lonely.
De Profundis.
Decline.
Dejection.
Downfall.
Effulgent Autumn.
Elis.
Evening, The.
Grodek.
In the East.
Lament: "Sleep and death, the dusky eagles."
Night.

Revelation and Decline.
Romance to Night, A.
To the Child Elis.
Trumpets.
Winter Evening, A.

Tran, Barbara
From Rosary.

Tran Nhan-tong
Spring View.

Trần Tế Xu'o'ng (1870–1907)
New Year's Season and Its Poetasters, The.
Women.

Trần Thái-Tông, King
To the Monk Dúc Son at Thanh-phong Monastery.

Tranströmer, Tomas (b. 1931)
After a Death.
Allegro.
Alone.
Below Freezing.
Black Postcards.
Breathing Space July.
Elegy.
Gallery, The.
Homewards.
It's been a hard winter, but summer is here and the fields.
Man Awakened by a Song above His Roof, The.
Open and Closed Space.
Outskirts.
Scattered Congregation, The.
Sketch in October.
Solitude.
Syros.
To Friends behind a Frontier.
Track.

Tranter, John (b. 1943)
Alphabet Murders, The.
Backyard.
Chicago "Manuel of Style" is really neat, The.
Death Circus, The.
Debbie and Co.
Enzensberger at 'Exiles.'
Glow-boys.
Giving up women is worse than animal laxatives.
Great Artist Reconsiders the Homeric Simile, The.
Having Completed My Fortieth Year.
It's bad luck with a coughing baby.
Lufthansa.
Mark.
Moment of Waking, The.
Moonshine Sonata.
Spy bears his bald intent like a maniac, The.
Sweat is a style of the body.
They burn the radio and listen to the blues.
Un-American Women, The.

Trapnell, Anna (c.1622–c.60)
Having Prayed for, and Made Much Mention of the Merchants, She Sings the Following Hymn to Them.
O he is a rest that requires.
Therefore John read how that thou wouldst.

Trapnell, N. J.
Lament of a Desert Rat.

Trask, Haunani-Kay
Sisters.

Traubel, Horace Logo (1858–1919)
How Are You, Dear World, This Morning?
What Can I Do?

Travis, Nancy (b. 1967)
At My Father's House.
Church Ladies.
Sunbathing.

Treasone, Grace
Life.

Tree-Leaf Woman
Who speaks the sound of an echo?

Treece, Henry (1912–66)
Conquerors.
Horror.
Magic Wood, The.
Three Pleas.

Y Ddraig Goch.

Trefusis, Elizabeth (fl early 19th cent.)
Valentine, A.

Tregear, Edward (1846–1931)
Te Whetu Plains.

Tregian, Francis (1548–1608)
Imprisoned Recusant Writes to His Wife, An.

Trejo, Ernesto
Cloud Unfolding, The.

Tremayne, Sydney (b. 1920)
Moses.

Tremblay, Bill
Home Front.
Mayday.

Tremblay, Gail (b. 1945)
Indian Singing in 20th Century America.
It Is Important.
Medicine Bearer.
Night Gives Old Woman the Word.
Not Sense.
Reflections on a Visit to the Burke Museum, University of Washington, Seattle.
To Grandmother on Her Going.

Trench, Herbert (1865–1923)
Charge, A.
Jean Richepin's Song.
She Comes Not When Noon Is on the Roses.

Trench, M.
Limerick: "Dear Sir, You're quite wrong about me."

Trench, Richard Chenevix (1807–86)
Lord, Many Times.
What is Man?

Trenet, Charles
I Wish You Love (Que Reste-t-il de Nos Amours?)

Trethewey, Natasha (b. 1966)
Bellocq's Ophelia.
Cameo.
Collection Day.
Domestic Work, 1937.
Drapery Factory, Gulfport, Mississippi, 1956.
Flounder.
Hot Comb.
Naola Beauty Academy, New Orleans, Louisiana, 1943.
Photograph of a Bawd Drinking Raleigh Rye.
Secular.
White Lies.
Zebra.

Triem, Eve (b. 1902)
For Paul.

Trinidad, David (b. 1953)
Answer Song.
As one young guy screwed another young guy.
Doll Not Included.
Double Trouble.
For Joe Brainard.
He said his name was Nick; later I learned.
Meet the Supremes.
Monday, Monday.
Moonstones.
More than anything, I wanted Charlie.
Movin' with Nancy.
Of Mere Plastic.
Shower Scene in Psycho, The.
Things to Do in Valley of the Dolls (The Movie)
Tom used spit for lubricant and fucked me.

Tripathi, Suryakant See "Nirala"

Tripathy, Sunanda (b. 1964)
Tryst.

Triplett, Pimone (b. 1965)
Fractal Audition.
Manora.
Spectral Dues.
Spider of Doubt.
Studies in Desire.
Winter Swim.

Tripp, John (b. 1927)
Armistice Day '77, Honiton.
Capital.
Caroline Street, Cardiff.
Connection in Bridgend.

Diesel to Yesterday.
Eglwys Newydd.
Father.
Headmaster.
In Memory of Idris Davies.
Last at Lucy's, The.
On My Fortieth Birthday.
Ploughman.
Twilight in the Library.
Welcome to Wales.

Trocchi, Alexander (1925–84)
For John Donne: Master Metaphysical.

Trommer, Rosemerry Wahtola
Climbing the Ridge.
If You Listen.
March.
Sonnet for July.

Tropp, Stephen (b. 1930)
My Wife Is My Shirt.

Troup, Bobby (1910–99)
Baby, Baby All the Time.
Daddy.
(Get Your Kicks On) Route 66!
You're in Love.
You're Lookin' at Me.

Troupe, Quincy (b. 1943)
And Syllables Grow Wings There.
Avalanche.
Boomerang: A Blatantly Political Poem.
Conjuring against Alien Spirits.
Conversation Overheard.
Day in the Life of a Poet, A.
Forty-one Seconds on a Sunday in June, in Salt
   Lake City, Utah.
Impressions / of Chicago; For Howlin' Wolf.
In Jimmy's Garden.
One for Charlie Mingus.
Poem for "Magic", A.
Poem for My Father; for Quincy Troupe, Sr.
Reflections on Growing Older.
River Town Packin House Blues.
Sense of Coolness, A.
Syntax of the Mind Grips, The.
View from Skates in Berkeley, The.
You Come to Me.

Trowbridge, John Townsend (1827–1916)
Circumstance.
Darius Green and His Flying-Machine.
Farmer John.
Filling an Order.
Idyl of Harvest Time, An.
Old Lobsterman, The.
Recollections of "Lalla Rookh."

Trowbridge, William (b. 1941)
Bad Birds.
Kong Breaks a Leg at the William Morris
   Agency.
Viet Kong.

Trubin, Aleksandr (b. 1961)
And we kill blood.

Trubridge, B. A. See **"Vrepont, Brian"**

Trudell, Dennis
Jump Shooter, The.

Truitt, Sam (b. 1960)
Kerf, The.
Old World Monkeys.

Trumbull, John (1750–1831)
Town-Meeting, A.M., The.

Trussell, Donna
Choice.

Truth, Sojourner (1797–1883)
Ain't I a Woman?

**Tryapkin [or Triapkin], Nikolai Ivanovich (b.
1918)**
How much there was of everything:
   kettledrums and horns and bells!
We banished the tyrant-tsars.
We've inherited something from our ancestors,
   the serfs.

Tryphon
Terpander.

Ts'an, Ts'en See **Ts'en Shen**

Ts'ai Yen (162?–239?)
I have no desire to live, but I am afraid of

death.
I never believed that in my broken life.
I was born in a time of peace.
Lamentation, The.
Seventeenth stanza, The. My heart aches, my
   tears fall.
Sun sets, The. The wind moans.
Tatar chief forced me to become his wife, A.

Tsakak
I'm gonna die & won't see you all any more.

Tsaloumas, Dimitris (b. 1921)
Autumn Supper.
Consolation.
Falcon Drinking.
Grudge, The.
Note.
Old Friend.
Progressive Man's Indignation, A.
Return of an Ikon.
They brought him one morning.

Tsang, K'o Chia (b. 1905)
Street Angel, The.

Ts'ao Chih (192–232)
Ballad of the Orioles in the Fields.
Cock-fight, The.
Forsaken Wife, The.
Presented to Piao, the Prince of Pai-ma.
Roaming Immortal.
Ruins of Lo-yang, The.
Seven Poems of Lament.
Song of Heavenly Ascent.
Song of Lament, A.
Vision, A.
Woe Indeed!
Written on Parting from Mr. Ying.

Ts'ao Ching-chao (fl. 1620)
Palace Poem.

Ts'ao P'i (187–226)
Deep and boundless, the long autumn night.
In the northwest there is a drifting cloud.
Lotus Lake.
Lotus Pond, The.
Song of Yen.

Ts'ao Sung (fl. c.870–c.920)
Protest in the Sixth Year of Ch'ien Fu, A.

Ts'ao Ts'ao (155–220)
Bitter Cold: A Song.
Drinking Song.
Song on Enduring the Cold.
Variant on the Songs of the East and West
   Gates.
View of the Blue Sea.

Ts'en Shen (Ts'en Ts'an) (715–70)
Autumn Thoughts.
Composed at Sunset at the Dunes of Ho-yen.
Fisherman.
On Climbing the Pagoda of the Temple of
   Gracious Benevolence with Kao Shih and
   Hsüeh Chü.
Replying to "On the Occasion of Morning
   Audience after Snow" Poem by Assistant
   Secretary Wang of the Board of Sacrifices.
Song of the Bay Steed of Governor Wei, A.
Song of the Running Horse River, A: Presented
   on Saying Farewell to the Army Going on
   Campaign to the West.
Song of the Running Horse River, A: Presented
   on Seeing General Feng Off on a Campaign
   to the West.
Song of the White Snow: Saying Farewell to
   Supervisor Wu Returning to the Capital.

Tseng Jui (fl. c.1300)
Cock's cunning means profit, The.
Great success need not be proud.

Tso Ssu (fl. 3rd cent.)
Day Dreams.
Scholar in the Narrow Street, The.

Tso Yen-nien (fl. 3rd cent.)
Call to Arms.

Tsogyel, Yeshe (757?–817?)
Listen.

Tsugen Jakurei (1322–91)
From the day of my coming hither.
Not a mote in the light above.

Ts'ui Hao (704–54)
By the City Gate.

Songs of Ch'ang-kan.

Tsui, Kitty
Chinese Banquet, A.
Suzy Wong's Been Dead a Long Time.

Tsung Ch'en (1525–60)
Drinking at the Cave Mouth.
Miscellaneous Words on the Lake.
On Hearing That the Sea-Barbarians Are about
   to Attack Hu-chou—Expressing My
   Feelings to Tzu-yü.
On the spring river, you depart.
Rebels' cavalry are everywhere, The.
Side by side, we ride out of the city.
Snowstorm: At a Gathering at Chang Chu-fu's
   House, with Tzu-yeh Attending, We All
   Wrote Poems on This Subject—I Got the
   Ryhme-Word, "Hu."
Snowy Mountains.
Song of Meeting.
Song of Selling Flowers.
When you enter Chin-hua Mountain.

Tsurayuki (Ki no Tsurayuki) (c.868–c.946)
I went out in the Spring.
When.

**Tsvetayeva [or Tsvetaeva], Marina Ivanovna
(1892–1941)**
Ancient Song, An.
And, Not Crying in Vain.
Ars.
Attempt at Jealousy, An.
Bethlehem.
Beware.
Cupolas flame, in Moscow where I live.
Daughter of Jairus, The.
Den—for the beast, A.
Fatal Volume, The.
Garden.
Gentle ghost.
God (3)
Gold that was my hair has turned, The.
Here's another window.
Homesickness.
Horn of Roland, The.
I am happy to live correctly and simply.
I Bless the Daily Labor.
I'd like to live with you.
I didn't want this, not.
I know the truth—give up all other truths!
If the Soul was Born with Pinions.
In my enormous city it is—night.
In my melodious city cupolas burn.
Last bridge I won't.
Like a thick horse's mane.
Magdalene.
Not quite remembering, not quite.
O what tears in eyes now.
Poem: "When I look at the falling leaves."
Praise to the Rich.
Readers of Newspapers.
Single post, a point of rusting, A.
Staircase.
They thought: Human!
They took quickly, they took hugely.
To Kiss a Forehead Is to Erase Worry.
Tonight—I am alone in the night.
We shall not escape Hell, my passionate.
White Low Sun . . . , A.
Who sleeps at night? No one is sleeping.
Yesterday he could still look in my eyes, yet.
You're going by, west of the sun.
You, Walking Past Me.
Your name—a bird on my hand.

Tsvetkov, Aleksey [or Aleksei] Petrovich (b. 1947)
I had a dream. I walked in a field of feather
   grass.
Like a ruddy child you fall asleep in
   september.
Pupil of fever chills and bewilderment, A.
To be mistaken in old age and not to be afraid.
To the apostles of history.
What remained of our meetings?
Yes, it's me. I appear thus to myself.

Tsybin, Vladimir Dmitrievich (b. 1932)
Eyes.

Tu Fu (712–76)
Adviser to the Court.

After Rain.
After Solstice.
After the Harvest.
All day, all night, I worry.
Another Spring.
At Horizon's End, Thinking of Li Po.
At the Thatched Hall of the Ts'ui Family.
Autumn Night.
Ballad of the Army Carts.
Banishment.
Banquet at the Tso Family Manor.
Becoming a Farmer.
Blown by winds, the thistledown.
Brimming Water.
Broken Boat, A.
By the Winding River I.
By the Winding River II.
By Yangtze and Han.
Ch'iang Village.
Chaos of mountains upon mountains, A.
Chengtu.
Chüeh-chü.
City of White Emperor, The.
Clear after Rain.
Clear Evening after Rain.
Climbing on the Double Ninth Day.
Climbing the Heights.
Coming Home Late at Night.
Country Cottage.
Cricket, The.
Crooked River Meditation.
Dawn Over the Mountains.
Daytime Dream.
Déjeuner sur l'herbe.
Departing from Ch'in-chou.
Descending through Dragon Gate.
Draft Board at Shih-hao, The.
Dragon Gate Gorge.
Dragon sleeps three winter months, A.
Drawing a bow you must draw a strong one.
Dreaming of Li Po.
Drifting clouds pass by all day long.
Drinking at Crooked River.
Drinking with Elder Cheng the Eighth at
   Crooked River.
Early Rising.
Elegant Women, The.
Emperor, The.
Empty Purse.
Evening after Rain.
Evening near Serpent River.
Excursion, The.
Facing the Snow.
Far up the River.
Farewell of an Old Man.
Farewell Once More to My Friend Yen at Feng
   Chi Station.
Farewell Rhyme.
Firefly.
Flocks of chicken clucking from every corner.
For Li Po.
From the jagged edges of purple clouds to the
   west.
Full Moon.
Going to the Palace with a Friend at Dawn.
Grieved, I idle and doze.
Guest, A.
Guest Arrives, A.
Hawk in a Painting, A.
Heading South.
Hearing of Imperial Forces Retaking Ho-Nan
   and Ho-Pei.
Heavenly River.
Homage to the Painter General Ts'ao.
Homecoming—Late at Night.
Homestead.
Hundred Worries, A.
I have a sister, little sister, living in Chung-li.
I have brothers, younger brothers in a place far
   away.
I have heard the affairs in Ch'ang-an are like a
   game of chess.
I Pass the Night at General Headquarters.
I Spend the Night in a Room by the River.
I Stand Alone.
If you draw a bow, draw the strongest.
Impromptu.

In a Village by the River.
In Praise of Rain.
In Seclusion.
Jade dews deeply wilt and wound the maple
   woods.
Jade Flower Palace.
Journey North.
Lament for Ch'en T'ao.
Leaving Ch'in-chou.
Leaving Government Offices.
Light rain doesn't slick the road.
Listless.
Lo Yu Park.
Lone Wild Goose.
Loneliness.
Long hoe, long hoe, handle of white wood.
Looking at Mount T'ai.
Looking at Mount T'ai-Shan.
Lovely Lady.
Madman, The.
Man with No Family to Take Leave of, The.
Masses of flowers and plants envelop the
   riverbanks.
Meandering River Poems, The.
Moon Festival.
Moon on the Cold Flood Festival.
Moon, Rain, Riverbank.
Moonlight Night.
Moonlit Night.
New Moon.
New Year's Eve at the Home of Tu Wei.
Night.
Night feast at the Tsos.
Night in a Room by the River.
Night in the House by the River.
Night in the Villa by the River.
Night Thoughts aboard a Boat.
Night Thoughts While Traveling.
Night Up in the Tower.
No Word.
On a Portrait of a Falcon.
On Climbing the Heights on the Ninth Day of
   the Ninth Moon.
On the Border, First Series.
On the River.
On the Spur of the Moment.
Overlooking the Desert.
P'eng-ya Road.
Parted by death, we swallow remorse.
Passing Chao-ling Again.
Passing Mr. Sung's Old House.
Passing the Night.
Peach and plum I planted were my own, The.
Poem for Mr. Li in Early Spring.
Poem for My Brother Returning to My Farm.
Prelude: "This fugitive between the Earth and
   Sky."
Presented to Wei Pa, Gentleman in Retirement.
Quatrain: "Before you praise Spring's advent
   note."
Quatrain: "Beyond the gate the cormorant had
   gone and not returned."
Quatrain: "Birds the more white, against green
   stream."
Quatrain: "I lounge on the jetty in the
   fragrance of catalpa."
Quatrain: "Late sun, the stream and the hills;
   the beauty."
Random Pleasures.
Recruiting Officer of Shih-hao.
Restless Night.
Restless Night in Camp, A.
Return, The.
Returning from court day after day, I pawn my
   spring clothes.
Rising Spring Waters.
River Pavilion.
River swallows know my shack is humble.
Running from Trouble.
Sad, sad they leave their old village.
Sent to the Magistrate of P'eng-chou.
Servant Boy Delivers, The.
Seven Songs Written During the Ch'ien-yüan
   Era.
Seven Songs Written while Living at T'ung-ku
   in 759.
Sharpen the sword in the Sobbing Waters.

Sick Horse.
Singing Girls (Written in Jest)
Single petal swirling diminishes the spring, A.
Six Choruses.
Sleepless Nights.
Snow Storm.
Song for a Young General.
Song of P'eng-ya.
Song of T'ung-ku.
Song of the Beautiful Ladies.
Song of the Vermeil Phoenix.
Song of the War-Chariots (Yueh-Fu)
Song of the War Wagons.
South Wind.
Spring.
Spring Day: Thinking of Li Po.
Spring Homecoming.
Spring Night, A—Rejoicing in Rain.
Spring Prospect.
Spring Rain.
Spring Scene.
Spring View.
Spring Vigil in the Imperial Chancellery.
Summer Night.
Summit, A.
Sunset.
T'ao Ch'ien withdrew from all the world.
Taking Leave of Two Officials.
Testament.
Thatched Hut, The.
They Say You're Staying in a Mountain
   Temple.
Thinking of Li Po.
Thinking of My Brothers on a Moonlit Night.
Thinking of My Little Boy.
This southern rain nourishes the mossy stones.
Thoughts on Historical Sites: Wang Chao-
   chün.
Thwarted.
Tired Night, A.
'Tis not I pity the flowers are about to die.
To a Guest.
To Abbot Min the Compassionate.
To Li Po.
To Li Po on a Spring Day.
To Li Po on a Winter Day.
To My Younger Brother.
To Pi Ssu Yao.
To the south there is a dragon living in a
   mountain pool.
To Wei Pa, a Retired Scholar.
Traveler, a traveler, Tzu-mei his name, A.
Traveler at Night Writes His Thoughts, A.
Traveler's Pavilion.
Traveling at Night.
Travelling Northward.
Two Poems on Night.
Unemployed and lazy, I wander around the
   village.
Upon Seeing the Fireflies.
Visit in Winter to the Temple of His Mystical
   Majesty, A.
Visiting the Monastery at Lung-men.
Visiting Tsan, Abbot of Ta-Yun.
Visitors.
Waiting for Audience on a Spring Night.
Watching the Distances.
Waters of K'un-ming Pool recalled the
   achievements of Han times, The.
We recruits have our commanders to send us
   off.
West of my hut, I grow mulberry.
Willow, The.
Winter Dawn.
Word from My Brothers.
Written on the Thirtieth Day, Ninth Month,
   Second Year of the Ta-li Reign [767].
Written on the Wall at Chang's Hermitage.
Wu-Chueh.
Wu-Chuen.
Yen-chou City Wall Tower.

Tu Hsün-ho (846–907)
   Climbing to a Mountain Monastery.
   Traveler's Thoughts.
Tu Mo (1900–76)
   Mandarins Got Their Raise, The.
Tu Mu (803–53)
   Climbing Up to the Lo-yu Plain.

Crane, The.
Departing in Early Morning.
Early Geese.
Egrets.
Mooring at River Ch'in-Huai.
Pond in a Basin.
Red Embankment.
Returning Home.
Sent in Parting.
Sighing over Flowers.
View from the Cliffs.
We Drink Farewell.

Tu Shan-fu (*fl.* 1230)
Tune: 'Shua Hai-erh' Country Cousin at the
    Theater.

Tu Shen-yen (648–708)
Harmonizing a Spring Poem by Premier Lu of
    Chin-Ling.

Tuck, Lily
Sniff.

Tucker, F. Bland (b. 1895)
All Praise to Thee.
Our Father, by Whose Name.

Tucker, Mary E. (b. 1838?)
Adieu.
All Alone.
Apple Dumplings.
Arria to Poetus.
Autumn Thoughts.
Beautiful Sea, The.
Beautiful, The.
Blight of Love, The.
Burial of a Fairy Queen.
Charley du Bignon.
Child Life.
Christmas Eve, South, 1865.
Christmas, South, 1866.
Crazed.
Crushed Flower, The.
"Did You Call Me, Father?"
Disappointment.
Drink On.
Drunkard's Wife, The.
Evanishings.
Family Portraits.
Father's Love, The.
First Grey Hair, The.
Found—Who Lost?
Gone.
Heart's Ease.
Hope.
Hugging the Shore.
Humming-Bird, The.
I Am Fashion's Toy.
I Am Weary, Mother.
I Smile, but Oh! My Heart Is Breaking.
"I Was a Stranger and Ye Took Me In."
Kindness.
Kiss, A.
Knitting.
Life.
Life for a Life.
Lift Me Higher.
Light in Darkness.
Lines on the Death of the Rev. S. K. Talmage.
Lines to an Old Dress.
Little Bell.
Love-letter, A.
Mail Has Come, The.
Mine.
Mistletoe.
Mother's Lament, The.
Mrs. Myrick's Lecture.
My Mother's Voice.
Mysteries of Life.
No Letter.
Old Crib, The.
Only a Blush.
Opium-Eater, The.
Revenge.
Signal Gun, The.
Silvery Fountain.
Soldier Boy's Dream, The.
Speak to Her Tenderly.
Spring.

That Glove.
To Annie.
To Don Juan Baz.
To Fannie.
To Father.
To Mary.
To One Who Sleepeth.
Tryst, The.
Upon Receipt of a Pound of Coffee in 1863.
Wail of the Divorced.
We Met.
Weariness.

Tucker, St. George (1752–1827)
Cynic, The.
Discontented Student, The.
Judge with the Sore Rump, The.
Once at a merry wedding feast.

Tuckerman, Frederick Goddard (1821–73)
And change[,] with hurried hand, has swept
    these scenes.
And two I knew, an old man and a boy.
As Sometimes in a Grove.
As when, down some broad River dropping,
    we.
But war his overturning trumpet blew.
But we are set to strive to make our mark.
Coralie.
Cricket, The.
Dark fens of cedar; hemlock-branches gray.
Gertrude and Gulielma, sister-twins.
Hast thou seen reversed the prophet's miracle.
Here, where the red man swept the leaves
    away.
His heart was in his garden; but his brain.
How Oft in Schoolboy Days.
How well do I recall that walk in state.
Infatuation.
"Last night I dreamed we parted once again."
Let me give something!—as the years unfold.
Let me give something!—though my spring be
    done.
Morning comes; not slow, with reddening gold,
    The.
No! Cover not the fault. The wise revere.
Nor strange it is, to us who walk in bonds.
Not sometimes, but to him that heeds the
    whole.
November.
Question, The.
Refrigerium.
Rhotruda.
Roll on, sad world! Not Mercury or Mars.
Some truths may pierce the spirit's deeper
    gloom.
Sometimes I walk where the deep water dips.
Sonnet: "And so, as this great sphere (now
    turning slow)"
Sonnets: First Series.
Sonnets: "Starry flower, the flower-like stars
    that fade, The."
Still pressing through these weeping solitudes.
Tall stately plants with spikes and forks of
    gold.
Thin little leaves of wood fern, ribbed and
    toothed.
Under the Locust Blossoms.
Under the mountain, as when first I knew.
Upper chamber in a darkened house, An.
Yes: though the brine may from the desert
    deep.
Yet, even 'mid merry boyhood's tricks and
    scapes.

Tudur Aled (*fl.* c.1480–c.1525)
Stallion, The.

Tuéni, Nadia (1935–83)
Baalbeck.
Beirut.
Cedars.
In the Lebanese Mountains.
Nothing but a man.
Tripoli.
Would you come back if I said the earth.

Tufts, Carol
We Take the New Young Couple Out to
    Dinner.

Tugend, Alina
Every Few Months.

Tuglik (*fl.* 19th cent.)
Tuglik's Song.

Tuite, Eliza Cobbe, Lady (1764–1850)
To a Friend, Fearful of Being Forgotten in
    Absence.

Tukaram (1598–1649)
In My View.

Tung-shan (807–69)
If you look for the truth outside yourself.

Tuqan [or Tuquan], Fadwa (b. 1917)
After Twenty Years.
Behind Bars, Sel.
Elegy of a Knight.
Face Lost in the Wilderness.
From the Diary of.
I Found It.
I Won't Sell His Love.
In the Aging City.
In the Flux.
Prayer to the New Year, A.
Song of Becoming.

Tuqan, Ibrahim (1905–41)
Martyr, The.
Perplexity.

Turberville, George (c.1540–c.1610)
Epitaph of Maister Win Drowned in the
    Sea, An.
Of Drunkenness.
Of One That Had a Great Nose.
Poor Ploughman to a Gentleman for Whom He
    Had Taken a Little Pains, A.
To an Old Gentlewoman That Painted Her
    Face.
To His Friend P. of Courting, Traveling,
    Dicing, and Tennis.
To Spencer.

Turell, Jane Colman (1708–35)
Though my small incomes never can afford.
You Beauteous Dames.

Turk, Roy (1892–1934)
Ain't That the Way It Goes?
Are You Lonesome Tonight?
Gimme a Little Kiss (Will Ya, Huh?)
I Don't Know Why (I Just Do)
I'll Get By (As Long As I Have You)
Mean to Me.
Walkin' My Baby Back Home.

Turki, Fawaz (b. 1940)
Being a Good *Americani*.
I leave the child to grow up by itself as a
    beggar from the killing.
In Search of Yacove Eved.
Moments of Ridicule and Love.

Turnbull, Gael (b. 1928)
Residues: Thronging the Heart.
Takings.
There Are Words.

Turner, Alberta (b. 1921)
Drift.
Fourth Wish.
In Love with Wholes.
Making Old Bones.
On the Nature of Food.
Three Easters.
Water Eased of Its Cliffs by Falling.

Turner, Ann
Clean.
Red-Dress Girl.
Red Flower.

Turner, Brian (b. 1944)
Coming Home.
Nichita Stanescu.
Responses to Montale.

Turner, Charles Tennyson (1808–79)
Bliss of Heaven, Maria, shall be thine, The.
Brilliant Day, A.
Buoy-Bell, The.
Calvus to a Fly.
Country Dance, A.
Dream, A.
Drowned Spaniel, The.
East or West?
From Harvest to January.
Gout and Wings.
Great Britain through the Ice: Or, Premature

Patriotism.
Hence with your jeerings, petulant and low.
His was a chamber in the topmost tower.
Julius Caesar and the Honey-Bee.
Letty's Globe.
Lion's Skeleton, The.
No trace is left upon the vulgar mind.
O'erladen with sad musings, till the tear.
Old Ruralities: A Regret.
Old Stephen.
On a Vase of Gold-Fish.
On Seeing a Little Child Spin a Coin of
    Alexander the Great.
On Shooting a Swallow in Early Youth.
Orion.
Seaside: In and Out of the Season, The.
When lovers' lips from kissing disunite.
White Horse of Westbury, The.
Wind on the Corn.
Turner, Frederick (b. 1943)
April Wind.
On the Pains of Translating Miklós Radnóti.
Spring Evening.
Turner, Godfrey (*fl. c.*1878)
Journal of Society, The.
Synchoresis.
Tattle.
Turner, Jack (b. 1947)
Plan, The.
Turner, James
In cities I'm as rare as I'm unwelcome.
Turner, Nancy Byrd (b. 1880)
First Thanksgiving of All.
Let Us Have Peace.
When Young Melissa Sweeps.
Turner, S. C.
Limerick: "Youth and a maiden from
    Costessey, A."
Turner, Steve (b. 1951)
Christmas Is Really for the Children.
Turner, Walter James (1889–1946)
Dancer, The.
Epithalamium: "Can the lover share his soul."
Hymn to Her Unknown.
In Time like Glass.
India.
Life and Death.
Lion, The.
Love-song: "Beautiful, delicate bright gazelle,
    The."
Magic.
Marriage.
Men Fade Like Rocks.
Music of a Tree, The.
Navigators, The.
Reflection.
Robber, The.
Romance.
Seven Days of the Sun, The.
Silence.
Song: "Lovely hill-torrents are."
Sun, The.
Talking with Soldiers.
Tragic Love.
Word Made Flesh, The.
Turner, William Price (b. 1927)
Alien.
Coronary Thrombosis.
University Curriculum.
Turochkin, Nikolai Karpovich *See* "Otrada",
Tusser, Thomas (c.1524–1580)
Advice of Housewives.
December's Husbandry.
Tutchin, John (1661?–1707)
Foreigners, The.
Tuwhare, Hone (b. 1922)
Friend.
Heemi.
Monologue.
No Ordinary Sun.
Ron Mason.
Song in Praise of a Favourite
    Humming-Top, A.
Talk with My Cousin Alone, A.
Tuwim, Julian [or Juljan] (Juljan) (1894–1953)
Prayer, A: "I pray Thee O Lord."

Pursuit.
There Is No Country.
**Tvardovsky [or Tvardovskii], Aleksandr
    Trifonovich (1910–71)**
Crossing, The.
From a crumpled wartime diary.
No, I have not been cheated by life.
Poem: "Blue snow is turning black, The."
**"Twain, Mark" (Samuel Langhorne Clemens)
    (1835–1910)**
Aged Pilot Man, The.
Emmeline Grangerford's "Ode to Stephen
    Dowling Bots, Dec'd."
He Done His Level Best.
Imitation of Julia A. Moore.
Limerick: "Man hired by John Smith
    and Co., A."
Tweedy, Henry Hallam (1868–1953)
Eternal God, Whose Power Upholds.
O Gracious Father of Mankind.
Twichell, Chase (b. 1950)
Aisle of Dogs.
City Animals.
Condom Tree, The.
Horse.
Kerosene.
My Taste for Trash.
Private Airplane.
Tea Mind.
Twiss, Horace (1786 [or] 1787–1849)
Our Parodies are Ended.
Patriot's Progress, The.
Tyfield, Thelma (1906–68)
Gifts.
Tyler, Royall (1757–1826)
Anacreontic to Flip.
Father and I went to camp.
Gambling.
Hail to the Joyous Day.
Love Song: "By the fierce flames of love I'm
    in a sad taking."
Marblehead's a rocky place.
Original Epitaph on a Drunkard.
Prologue: "Exult each patriot heart!—this night
    is shewn."
Song: "Sun sets in night, and the stars shun the
    day, The."
Widower, The.
Tymnes (*fl. 2nd cent. B.C.)*
Dear little bird, the Graces' favourite.
Don't let it matter much, Philaenis.
Eumelos had a Maltese dog.
Maltese Dog, A.
Stone says that it covers here the white dog,
    The.
**Tynan, Katharine (Katharine Tynan Hinkson)
    (1861–1931)**
Doves, The.
I would choose to be a doorkeeper.
Lux in Tenebris.
Of an Orchard.
Prayer, A.
Sheep and Lambs.
Witch, The.
Tyrwhit, Lady Elizabeth (*fl. c.*1548–82)
Hymne of the Daie of Judgment, The.
Hymne of the State of all Adams
    Posteritie, An.
Tyson, Ian *See* **John, Richard Johnny**
**Tyutchev, Fyodor [or Feodor] Ivanovich (1803–
    73)**
As Ocean's Stream.
At Vshchizh.
Last Love.
Past, The.
Silentium.
To His Wife.
Tzara, Tristan (1896–1963)
Chanson Dada.
Dada Manifesto on Feeble and Bitter Love.
Dance of the Greased Women, The.
For Robert Desnos.
Great Lament of My Obscurity Three, The.
Maison Aragon.
Metal Coughdrops.

[Part One].
Proclamation without Pretention.
Waking.
Zurich Chronicle February 1916.
Tzara, Tristan *See also* **Huelsenbeck, Richard**
Tzu Yeh (*fl. 3rd–4th cent.*)
Admonition.
All Night.
Bare branches tremble, The.
Bitter Harvest.
Busy in the Spring.
End to Spring, An.
I had not fastened my sash over my gown.
Illusions.
It is night again.
Late Spring.
Lotus Lover, The.
Smile, A.
So soon. Today, love, we.
Song: "Longing, I watch out the open
    window."
Song: "Winter skies are cold and low."
When I started wanting.

U

U Tam'si Tchicaya (b. 1929)
Bad Blood.
Brush-Fire.
Communion II.
Dance to the Amulets.
Epitaph.
Headline to Summarize a Passion.
Here is the stream again under the rainbow.
I am no longer master of my tears.
I tear at my belly.
I was naked for the first kiss of my mother.
'Congo is myself' (Lumumba), The.
Mat to Weave, A.
Promenade, The.
Scorner, The.
Sea Nocturne.
Treasure, The.
Viaticum.
What do I want with a thousand stars in broad
    daylight.
Uceda, Julia (b. 1925)
2976.
Time Reminded Me.
Uda Emperor (*fl. 9th cent.*)
Like a wave crest.
Udall, L. G.
Limerick: "Each Lon was a notable man."
Limerick: "Pulmonary tuberculosis."
'Udwan, Mamdouh (b. 1941)
Casbah, The.
Elegy for a Man Who Died and Died.
Uflyand [or Ufliand], Vladimir (b. 1937)
It has for ages been observed.
Now, at last, even Nikifor's a suitor.
Peasant, The.
Working week comes to an end, The.
**Uhland, Ludwig (Johann Ludwig Uhland) (1787–
    1862)**
Castle by the Sea, The.
Durand of Blonden.
Hostess' Daughter, The.
Ichabod! The Glory has Departed.
In a Lovely Garden Walking.
Leaf, A.
Luck of Edenhall, The.
Spirits Everywhere.
Ujejski, Kornel (1823–97)
Polish Eagle, The.
Ukihashi (*fl. late 17th cent.*)
Whether I sit or lie.
Uko (d. 1820)
Voice of the nightingale.
Uko (d. 1743)
Cuckoo.
Ukon, Lady (*fl. 10th cent.*)
Me.
Ulacia, Manuel (b. 1953)
Stone at the Bottom, The.

Ulku, Alpay (b. 1964)
History.
Lullaby: "You are safe / You are lying in a
    hammock."
Spring Forward, Fall Back.

Ullman, Leslie (b. 1947)
1945.
Dreams by No One's Daughter.
Living near the Plaza of Thieves.
Memo.
Rain.
Resolve.
Rose Quartz.
Running.
Why There Are Children.

Ulrich, Anton (1633–1714)
Dying Song.

Umpierre, Luz Maria (b. 1947)
No Hatchet Job.
Only the Hand That Stirs Knows What's in the
    Pot.
Statue, The.

Unaipon, David See **Ngunaitponi**

Unamuno, Miguel de (1864–1936)
Throw Yourself Like Seed.

Uncho
Forty-nine years / —What a din!

U'ng Bình (1877–1961)
At the Exiled King's River Pavilion.

Ungaretti, Giuseppe (1888–1970)
Agony.
Babel.
Brothers.
I Am a Creature.
Italy.
Morning.
No More Crying Out.
Rivers.
San Martino del Carso.
Soldiers.
Vigil.
Wake.
Watch.
Where the Light.
You Were Broken.

Unger, Barbara
Observance.
Photo Taken in Winter, 1944.

Ungo Kiyo (1583–1659)
I came into the world after Buddha.
Whirled by the three passions, one's eyes go
    blind.

Ungria, Ricardo M. de
Carillonneur.
Commerce and the Man.
Culture Nervous.
Sui Veneris / The Poet of No Return.

Unik, Pierre
Manless Society, The.

Unknown
A, a, a, a, / Yet I love whereso I go.
A B C D.
A, B, C, D, E, F, G, Little Robin Redbreast.
A, dere God, what I am fayn.
A! Mercy, Fortune; have pitee on me.
A! Sone, tak hede to me whos sone thou wast.
A was an archer, who [*or* and] shot at a frog.
ABC, An.
Abenamar, Abenamar.
Abide, gud men, and hald your pays.
Aborigine Sound Poem.
About the bush, Willie.
Abram Brown.
Absent Lover.
Abu Nowas for the Barmacides.
Achaian Invasion of Sparta, The.
Aching nostalgia.
Acorn Song, The.
Acrostic on Wharton, An.
Adam Bell, Clim of the Clough, and William
    of Cloudesly.
Adam Lay Ybounden [*or* I-bounden].
Adieu, the years are a broken song.
Adonis.
Adoration of the Disk by King Akhnaten and

Princess Nefer Neferiu Aten.
Adore we the Lord.
Advent Lyrics.
Advertising Agency Song, The.
Advice from Poor Robin's Almanack.
Advice to a Young Man.
Adze-Head.
After spring has come.
After the Inscription on a Greek Stele of a
    Woman Holding Her Grandchild on Her
    Knees.
After the rushing waters had subsided the
    Lenape of the turtle were close together, in
    hollow houses, living together there.
After the Seizer there were ten chiefs, and
    there was much warfare south and east.
Against a Wen.
Age of War, The.
Agincourt Carol, The.
Aging.
Ah blackbird, giving thanks.
Ah, ra, chickera.
Ah, silly pug, wert thou so sore afraid?
Aiken Drum.
Al worldly welthe passed me fro.
Ala, mala, mink, monk.
Alas! alas! the while.
Alas, departing is ground of wo!
Alas! How should I sing?
Alas, that ever that speche was spoken.
Alba Innominata.
Alba, With a Refrain from the Provençal.
Alexander's Song.
Algy.
Alison.
Alison and Willie.
Alison [*or* Allison] Gross.
All, All a-Lonely.
All alone in my little cell.
All day I hoe weeds.
All Is Phantom.
All-Knowing God, 'Tis Thine to Know.
All Night by the Rose.
All night I could not sleep.
All other love is like the mone.
All Other Love Is Like the Moon.
All Seasons in One.
All Ten Commandments I Have Broken.
All the Pretty Little Horses.
All the World.
All Through the Night.
All Too Late.
All too soon, I fear.
All work and no play makes Jack a dull boy.
Second Epitaph, A.
All Year Long.
Allansford Pursuit, The.
Alleluia, alleluia, / Alleluia, now sing we.
Almanac Verse.
Alone, I live alone.
Alone retired in my native cell.
Alone up here on the mountain.
Alphabet.
Alphabet Calendar of Amergin, The.
Alphabetical Song on the Corn Law Bill.
Although I Conquer All the Earth.
Am I to go on.
American Indian, The.
American jump, American jump.
Among the dead we come.
Among the yeomen's sons on my estate.
Anagram, An.
Ancient Song of a Woman of Fez, An.
Andalusian merchant, that returns, The.
And here's the child's Dad.
And in the mountains of Kiev, Sviatoslav.
And now one prayer.
And when thus the night availed.
And Yet the Earth Remains Unchanged.
Angel of Death, The.
Angelica the Doorkeeper.
Angels Came a-Mustering, The.
Angels in the House, The.
Angling.
Anglo-American Chainpoem.
Angry Bride, The.
Animal Fair.

Ankotarinya.
Anna Elise.
Annette Myers.
Annie of Tharaw.
Another Little Boy.
Another Man Done Gone.
Another Song about That Same Dead Person
    or Mole—Whichever it Was.
Another year it may betide.
Aoibhinn, A Leabhráin, Do Thriall.
Apple-pie, apple-pie.
Approaching Dance, The.
Arab and His Donkey, An.
Aranda Song.
Archaic Song of Dr. Tom the Shaman.
Archie o [*or* of] Cawfield.
Archpoet's Confession, The.
Arise, Ye Saints of Latter Days.
Arithmetic.
Arjuna, his war flag a rampant monkey.
Arjuna sat dejected.
Army Dance, The.
Army, Navy.
Around the Green Gravel.
Around the rick, around the rick.
Arran.
Arrow Song.
Art.
Art Thou That She.
Artist, The.
As black as ink and isn't ink.
As I Came in by Fiddich-Side.
As I me rod this endre day.
As I Sat on a Sunny Bank.
As I Walked [*or* Walk'd] by Myself.
As I wandrede her by weste.
As I was a-walking on Westminster Bridge.
As I was going o'er Tipple Tine.
As I was going to Banbury.
As I Was Standing in the Street.
As I was walking in a field of wheat.
As I went over the water.
As I Went to Bonner.
As I went up the Brandy hill.
As in thee resteth my joye and confort.
As Life What Is So Sweet?
As night follows night.
As night succeeds night.
As round as an apple, as deep as a pail.
As the thread of my breath.
At Brill on the hill.
At Fifteen I Went Off to the Army.
At Fifteen I Went to War.
At first in that place, at all times, above the
    earth.
At Great Torrington, Devon.
At last these two stout erles did meet.
At Mass.
At sixty I, Dionysios of Tarsos, lie here.
At sunset I come out of the door.
At the beginning of winter a cold spirit comes.
At the northe ende of Selver White.
At the Tavern.
At the time when blossoms.
At Upton-on-Severn.
Aubade.
Auld Matrons.
Auld Seceder Cat, The.
Author of this is Ossian, The.
Auto-erotic.
Autumn.
Autumn 1710.
Ave Maris Stella.
Awake all night till the.
Away down East, away down West.
Away from Home.
Ay, 'Tis Thus.
B C D Goldfish, A.
Babes in the Wood, The.
Baby and I.
Baby Dolly.
Baby Verse, A.
Babylon; or, The Bonnie Banks o' Fordie.
Baffled Knight, The.
Bailiff's Daughter of Islington, The.
Bailiff, why your useless plaints about.
Baith Gud[e] and Fair and Womanlie [*or*

Womanly].
Bakchos the wine-god / dissolver of limbs.
Bald Mountain Zaum-Poems.
Balgu Song.
Ballad of Mulan, The.
Ballad of the Cool Fountain.
Ballad of the Mulberry Road.
Ballad of the Western Island in the North Country.
Ballad of William Bloat, The.
Ballade de Marguerite.
Ballata: Of True and False Singing.
Ballata: One Speaks of the Beginning of His Love.
Ballet [or Ballit] of de Boll Weevil, De.
Bamboos Grow Well Under Good Rule, The.
Banks of the Condamine, The.
Bar, The.
Barbara Allen.
Barber shaved the mason, The.
Barney Bodkin broke his nose.
Baron o [or of] Leys, The.
Baron of Brackley, The.
Baron of Braikley, The.
Bastard from the Bush, The.
Battle of Bothwell Bridge, The.
Battle of Brunanburh.
Battle of Finnsburg, The.
Battle of Flodden, The.
Battle of Harlaw, The.
Battle of Inverlochy, The.
Battle of Maldon, The.
Battle of Otterburn [or Oterborne], The.
Battle of Philiphaugh, The.
Battles of Joshua.
Be always in time.
Be Careful.
Be glad, of all maidens floure.
Be Merry.
Be punctual then to know.
Bear's Song, The.
Because of this love.
Because We're Here.
Bedtime.
Bee-Keeper, The.
Been in the Storm So Long.
Before jade pavilions the new moon dims.
Before light became time.
Before my back was bent I was eloquent.
Before Sleeping.
Before your hair was ever cut.
Beggar-Laddie, The.
Beguines who hear these words.
Behold.
Being helpless.
Belfast Lough.
Bellman's Song, The.
Bells of hell go ting-a-ling-a-ling, The.
Bells, The.
Beneath this smooth stone by the bone of his bone.
Benedicite, What Dreamed I This Night?
Bent Sae Brown, The.
Bents and Broom, The.
Beoleopard; or, The Witan's Whail.
Beowulf.
Beowulf and Wiglaf Slay the Dragon.
Beowulf's Death.
Bequests.
Bessy [or Bessie] Bell and Mary Gray.
Betsy Baker.
Betty Botter bought some butter.
Between a Contractor and His Wife.
Between an Unemployed Artist and His Wife.
Between his hands.
Beulah Railway, The.
Bewick and Graham.
Bewteis of the Fute-Ball, The.
Bewwitching the blossoms of the spring grove.
Beyond.
Beyond the East Gate.
Beyond the Profit of Today.
Big box / Little box.
Big Chariot, The.
Big house / Little house.
Big Rabbit goes to see his baby.
Big rats! Big rats!

Big Rock Candy Mountains, The.
Big Ship Sails, The.
Billy, Billy.
Bingo.
Binnorie; The Two Sisters.
Bird Catcher, The.
Bird is calling from the willow, A.
Bird on Briar.
Bird saw the young Burara girls, twisting their strings, making string figures, The.
Bird Scarer, The.
Bird Starver's Cry.
Birds.
Birds of a Feather.
Birth of Robin Hood, The.
Bitter Cold.
Bitter Withy, The.
Black Hair.
Blackbird calls in grief, The.
Blackbird of Derrycairn, The.
Blackbird, The.
Blacksmiths, The.
Blancheflour and Jellyflorice.
Bleeding Nun, The.
Bless Him.
Blessed Art Thou, O Lord.
Blessed be thou, levedy.
Blessed Is Everyone.
Blessed Mary.
Blessing without Company.
Blind Musicians, The.
Blind musicians, the blind musicians, The.
Blow, Boys, Blow [or Blow, Bullies, Blow].
Blow, Northern Wind.
Blow the Winds, I-Ho.
Blow Your Trumpet, Gabriel.
Blowflies Buzz, The.
Blue Bell Boy.
Blue Blue Your Collar.
Bo-peep / Little Bo-peep.
Bo peeper.
Boar's Head Carol, The.
Bobby Snooks.
Bold Pedlar and Robin Hood, The.
Bon jour, bon jour a vous!
Boney.
Bonnie Annie.
Bonnie Annie Livieston.
Bonnie House o' Airlie, The.
Bonnie James Campbell.
Bonnie Laddie's Lang a-Grouwin', The.
Bonnie [or Bonny] George [or James] Campbell.
Bonny Baby Livingston.
Bonny Barbara Allan ("In Scarlet Town where I was born)."
Bonny Bee Hom.
Bonny Birdy, The.
Bonny Bunch of Roses O, The.
Bonny Earl of Murray, The.
Bonny Hind, The.
Bonny John Seton.
Bonny Lass of Anglesey, The.
Bonny Lizie Baillie.
Boots / Shoes.
Borrow to your heart's content.
Boss Rat.
Boss's Wife, The.
Boston in Distress.
Bounce, buckram, velvet's dear.
Boy and the Mantle, The.
Boy in the Barn, The.
Boyne Water, The.
Boys Make Men.
Boys of Mullabaun [or Mullaghbawn], The.
Braes of Yarrow, The.
Brainsick race that wanton youth ensues, The.
Bran at the Island of Women.
Brave news is come to town.
Breach in the Wall, The.
Brian O'Linn.
Bridegroom, beloved of my heart.
Bridge engineer, Mister Crumpett, A.
Bridge instead of a Wall, A.
Bridge of Death, The.
Brief Autumnal.
BRIGHT moon illumines the night-prospect.

Bright moon, oh how white it shines, The.
Bright moon white and silver, The.
Bring Daddy home.
Bring Us In Good Ale.
British Grenadiers, The.
Broom, Green Broom.
Broom of Cowdenknows, The.
Broom Squire's Song, The.
Broomfield Hill, The.
Brotherless Sisters.
Broughty Wa's.
Brow, brow, brenty.
Brown Adam.
Brown Girl, The.
Brown Robin.
Brown Robyn's [or Robin's] Confession.
Brunanburg.
Buffalo are coming. We will feed and feast. We wish to be fortunate and we expect it, The.
Buffalo Gals.
Buffalo Skinners, The.
Bugs.
Building of a New Church, The.
Bull's eyes and targets.
Bunch of Blue Ribbons, The.
Burd Ellen and Young Tamlane.
Burd Isabel and Earl Patrick.
Burial Songs.
Burma-Shave Roadside Signs.
Burmese Figures.
Burnie bee, burnie bee.
Busy yellow bee, after his mighty quest, A.
But the lady's longing would not allow her to sleep.
Butcher of Abbeville, The.
Butter Charm.
Butterfly Song.
Button to chin.
Buzz Buzz, the Blue Flies.
By a forest as I gan fare.
By Heaven!
By Heraclides.
By west, under a wilde wode-side.
Bye, bye, baby bunting / Daddy's gone a-hunting.
Ca' the Yowes to the Knowes.
Cackle, cackle, Mother Goose.
Cala-Achí! Ha! Aha! Yeha! Ahau! Wow! Achí!
Call of the Soul, The.
Call, The.
Calvary.
Camel-Rider, The.
Cameleon Lover, The.
Cameleon's Defence, The.
Can't You Line It?
Can Ye Sew Cushions?
Can you keep a secret?
Can you make me a cambric [or cambriek] shirt.
Candy Man, The.
Cannibal Hymn, The.
Captain Car; or, Edom o Gordon.
Captain Ward and the *Rainbow*.
Captain Wedderburn's Courtship.
Captive's Song.
Care Away.
Care away, away, away / Care away for evermore!
Care away, away, away, / Murninge away!
Careless Love.
Carmen Possum.
Carnal and the Crane, The.
Carnation Milk.
Carol, for Candlemas Day.
Carpenter's Wife, The.
Case to the Civilians, A.
Casey Jones.
Cat May Look at a King, A.
Cat sat asleep by the side of the fire, The.
Catch him, crow! Carry him, kite!
Cathleen.
Cats of Kilkenny, The.
Cauld Lad of Hilton, The [or] The Wandering Spectre.
Cautionary Limerick.
Cautiously bubbles that spring water.

Caw Caw the Crows Caw Caw.
Ch'i-yü-ko.
Ch'in Chia's Wife's Reply.
Ch'ing-yang Ford.
Chairs to Mend.
Chalcan Female Song.
Chance led me once, when idling through the street.
Changeful Beauty.
Chant from the Iroquois Book of Rites.
Chant to the Fire-Fly.
Chanting Buddha's name.
Chants to the Deity.
Chapmen.
Character of a Roundhead, The.
Charade.
Charles II.
Charles the King, our Emperor, the great.
Charley Barley, butter and eggs.
Charley, Charley.
Charley Warlie had a cow.
Charlie MacPherson.
Charm.
Charm for Lighting the Fire, A.
Charm for Love and Lasting Affection, A.
Charm of the Nine Healing Herbs.
Charm Rhyme, A.
Charms for a Sudden Stitch.
Charms for Unfruitful Land.
Chaste Maiden, shining scarlet, The.
Cheetie-Poussie-Cattie, O.
Chen and Wei are brimming, The.
Cherished Daughter, The.
Cherry, A.
Cherry-Tree Carol, The.
Cherry year, A.
Chevy Chase.
Chick! my naggie.
Chicken blessed and caressed.
Child Maurice.
Child Owlet.
Child's Christmas Day, A.
Child's Grace, A.
Child this Day is Born, A.
Child Waters.
Childe Maurice.
Children's Ball-Bouncing Song.
Children's Rhymes and Parodies.
Chilling breath of midwinter arrives, The.
Chinese Figures 1.
Chinese Figures 2.
Chinese Figures 3.
Chinook Songs.
Chippewa Love Song.
Chirp Chirp the Katydids.
Chook, chook, chook, chook, chook.
Chou and the South.
Christ.
Christ 1.
Christ's Kirk on the Grene.
Christ's Love-Song.
Christ's Prayer in Gethsemane.
Christ the Apple-Tree.
Christ Triumphant.
Christ was the Word that spake it.
Christian Epigram.
Christmas is coming [or a-coming], / And the geese are getting fat.
Christmas Rhyme: North Tyrone.
Christopher White.
Chuck Will's Widow Song.
Chung Tzu.
Church Bell in the Night, The.
Church / Chapel.
Cicada cries out, The.
Cicada sings, The.
Cid Calls His Vassals Together, The. They'll Go into Exile with Him.
Cid Enters Burgos, The.
Cill Chais.
City Called Heaven.
Clap Handies.
Clap hands, clap hands / Hie, Tommy Randy.
Clap hands, clap hands / Till father comes home.
Clap hands, Daddy comes / With his pocket full of plums.

Clap hands, Daddy's coming / Up the waggon way.
Clapping Chant, A.
Claude Allen.
Clear full moon.
Clear moon brightly shining in the night.
Clementine.
Cleric Courts His Lady, A.
Clerihew: "Spinoza / Collected curiosa."
Clerk Colvill.
Clerk's Twa Sons o Owsenford, The.
Clerk Saunders.
Clever Hen, The.
Cloe to Artimesa.
Clonakilty.
Clonmel Jail.
Close by the shore, the shore.
Clothed in yellow, red and green.
Cloudy morning.
Clyde's Water.
Cnut's Song.
Coach / Carriage.
Coble o Cargill, The.
Cocaine Lil [and Morphine Sue].
Cock-A-Doodle-Do.
Cock and Bull Story, A.
Cock and the Hen, The.
Cock-Crow.
Cock-crow Song.
Cock Robin got up early.
Cock's on the wood pile, The.
Coffee and Tea.
Coilyear, gudlie in feir, tuke him be the hand, The.
Cold! Cold! / Wide Lurg Plain is cold tonight.
Cold Fountain, Cold Fountain.
Cold Is the North Wind.
Cold is the winter. The wind is risen.
Colleen Rue.
Colon Bay.
Columbia, Trust the Lord.
Combat of Ferdia and Cúchulainn.
Come All You Tonguers.
Come all you young ladies and make no delay.
Come at dawn, good friend.
Come, come, my companion.
Come, Happy Children.
Come Harken unto Me.
Come in, Tom longtail, come short hose and round.
Come, Landlord, Fill the Flowing Bowl.
Come, Let's to Bed.
Come Not Near My Songs.
Come, Precious Soul.
Come up, my horse, to Budleigh Fair.
Come with clean hands.
Coming of Enkidu, The.
Coming of Grendel, The.
Common people are very weary, The.
Company in Loneliness.
Comparatives.
Concert, The.
Confederate Memorial Day.
Confide In a Friend.
Constant Penelope sends to thee, careless Ulysses.
Constantinople (New Rome).
Conversation between the Chevalier de Chamilly and Mariana Alcoforado in the Manner of a Song of Regret.
Convicts' Rum Song.
Cool breezes—I sleep by the open window.
Cormac Mac Airt Presiding at Tara.
Corn-grinding Song.
Corn Song.
Corpse-Keeper, The.
Corpus Christi Carol, The.
Corpus Inscriptionum Latinarum 14.3565.
Corydon's Farewell, on Sailing in the Late Expedition Fleet.
Cosmogony.
Cosmology.
Could I but become a crimson rose.
Counsels of Sigrdrifa.
Counterlove, A.
Counting-Out Rhyme, A.
Country Lassie, The.

Country School, The.
Courage shall grow keener, clearer the will.
Cow and a calf, A.
Cowboy's Lament, The.
Cowboy Sayings.
Coyote and the Locust, The.
Cradle Song: "Sleep, my child, my little daughter."
Crafty Farmer, The.
Crafty Miss of London; or, The Fryar Well Fitted, The.
Crane Calls.
Crateas the doctor and Damon the sexton.
Creation Hymn.
Creide's Lament for Cael.
Créide's Lament for Dínertech.
Cries of London, The.
Cripple Creek.
Cripple Dick upon a stick.
Croppy Boy, The.
Cross-Patch.
Crossing the river I pluck the lotus flowers;.
Crow and Pie.
Crow caws in the moonlight, A.
Crown of all travailing.
Crown of Days.
Crowned with flowers, I saw fair Amarillis.
Crows on City Walls.
Crucifixion.
Cruel Brother, The.
Cruel Mother, The.
Cruel Sister, The.
CRUEL, you pull away too soon your lips whenas you kiss me.
Cry, Baby.
Cu Chuimne in youth.
Cuckoo Calls from the Bamboo Grove, The.
Cuckoo, cherry tree.
Cuckoo comes in April, The.
Cuckoo, cuckoo, cherry tree.
Cuckoo, cuckoo / What do you do?
Cuckoo Song, The.
Cuckoo, The.
Cumberland Gap.
Cunning Clerk, The.
Curse, A.
Curtain rung down on his wise old age, The.
Cut them on Monday, you cut them for health.
Cut thistles in May.
Cutty Wren, The.
Cypress Boat.
D . . . dronken.
Dahn the Plug'ole.
Dame, get up and bake your pies.
DAMON and Phyllis squared.
Dance of the Rain Gods.
Dance Song.
Dance the Boatman.
Dances and Songs of the Winter Ceremonial.
Darby and Joan were dressed in black.
Dark House, The.
Darky Sunday School.
Darling, you only, there is no duplicate.
Darwinism in the Kitchen.
Dates.
David Lowston.
Davy Crockett.
Davy Davy Dumpling.
Dawn.
Dawn Has Arisen, Our Welfare Is Assured.
Dawning Fair, Morning Wonderful.
Day began with dismal dougt, The.
Days of Our Youth, The.
De Ramis Cadunt Folia (Love in Winter)
Dead are gone and with them we cannot converse, The.
Dead Man Ariseth and Singeth a Hymn to the Sun, The.
Dead Man Asks for a Song, The.
Dead on the War Path.
Deadly Dance, The.
Dear Black Head.
Dear earth, take old Amyntichus to your heart.
Dear Son, Leave Thy Weeping.
Death.
Death and Burial of Cock Robbin, The.
Death Is before Me Today.

Death ("Once he will miss, twice he will miss.")
Death of Alexander, The.
Death of Don Pedro, The.
Death of Enkidu, The.
Death of King Edward VII, The.
Death of Lord Warriston, The.
Death of Moses, The.
Death of My Aunt.
Death of Nelson, The.
Death of Parcy Reed, The.
Death of Yesugei, The.
Death Rites II.
Death Song.
Death Songs.
Decision.
Declair, ye bankis of Helicon.
Deep in the Forest.
Deep River.
Deep Spring.
Deirdre's [or Deidre's] Lament for the Sons of Usnach.
Delia Very Angry.
Demon Lover, The.
Dentist, A.
Deor.
Deor's Lament.
Derby Ram, The.
Dere's No Hidin' Place Down Dere.
Description of Spring in London, A.
Dese Bones Gwine to Rise Again.
Deserted Mountain, The.
Deserter, The.
Desolate City, The.
Desolation.
Devil and the Princess.
Devil in Texas, The.
Dew on the Leek.
Dialogue between Death and Youth, A.
Dick o' the Cow.
Did you eever, iver, over?
Did you see my wife, did you see, did you see.
Didn't My Lord Deliver Daniel?
DIE not before thy day, poor man condemned.
Die, pussy, die.
Died from fatigue, three laundresses together all.
Died, Sir Charles Wetherell's laundress, honest Sue.
Diggers' Song, The.
Digging Sing, A.
Diggins-Oh, The.
Dilly Dilly.
Ding dang, bell rang.
Dingle dingle doosey.
Dink's Song.
Dinky Di.
Dinogad's Petticoat.
Dion of Tarsus.
Dirge for the Ninth of Ab.
Dirge for Three Trumpets.
Dirge: "I make this dirge for you Miss Mary Binning I miss you."
Dish for a Poet, A.
Dispraise of Absalom, The.
Dispute between Women, A.
Dispute over Suicide, A.
Distant and faint the Herd-Boy Star.
Distant as the Duchess of Savoy.
Distressed: single cane, I return.
Ditties Lamentation for the cruelty of this age.
Dives and Laz'us.
Dives and Lazarus.
Divorce Song.
Do not look at me.
Do not torment me, lady.
Do you carrot all for me?
Do You Remember That Night.
Doctor Foster went to Gloucester.
Doddledy, doodledy, doodledy, dan.
Doggies went to the mill, The.
Dole of the King's Daughter, The.
Domestic Philosopher, The.
Don't care didn't care.
Don't cry / over the happy dead.
Don't Walk beside the Big Carriage.
Don't You Be like the Foolish Virgin.

Donal[l] Oge [or Og]: Grief of a Girl's Heart.
Donal Og.
Donkey, donkey, do not bray.
Donkey, donkey, old and gray.
Double Vision of Manannan, The.
Dowie Dens of Yarrow, The.
Dowie Houms o' Yarrow, The.
Down by the river.
Down in the Lonesome Garden.
Down to the Mire.
Down with the lambs.
Dr. Foster.
Dragon Speaks, The.
Draw a bucket of water.
Draw a pail of water.
Dream.
Dream of the Cross, The.
Dream of the Rood, The.
Dream Song.
Dream, The.
Dreams.
Dress me in green.
Drill's the Thing.
Drinking Song.
Drinking Wine.
Drive a Tractor.
Driving in the Park.
Drop a Stone.
Drunk Man, The.
Drunkard and the Pig, The.
Dry Leaves, Dry Leaves.
Dry River.
Duel with Verses over a Great Man.
Dugall Quin.
Duke o' Athole's Nurse, The.
Duke of Gordon's Daughter, The.
Dum Diana Vitrea.
Dunce, The.
Dunt Dunt Dunt Pittie Pattie.
Durham.
Durham Field.
Dusty Miller, The.
Dyer, The.
Dying Airman, The.
Dynastic Hymn.
E-ri-e, The.
Eadwacer.
Eagle above Us, The.
Eagle of Pengwern.
Eagle of the tomb, whose tomb is this? Why.
Eaper Weaper, chimney sweeper.
Earl Bothwell.
Earl Brand.
Earl Crawford.
Earl of Aboyne, The.
Earl of Errol, The.
Earl of Westmoreland, The.
Earl Rothes.
Early morning glows.
East Gate, The.
Easter Song, An.
Eastern Gate, The.
Eastern Wall stands high and long, The.
Eccho, An.
Ecstasy.
Edom o' Gordon.
Edward.
Eenie, meenie, mackeracka.
Eenie, meenie, minie, mo / Catch a thief by the toe.
Eenity, feenity, fickety, feg.
Eeny, weeny, winey, wo.
Egan O Rahilly.
Eh-Ros-ka, the Warrior's Dance.
Ejaculating into their vaginas—young girls of the western tribes.
Elected Knight, The.
Election Time.
Elegy upon the Death of Mrs. A. Behn, the Incomparable Astrea, An.
Elephant [I], The.
Elephant [II], The.
Elfer Hill.
Elfin Knight, The.
Elsie Marley is grown so fine.
Emulation, The: A Pindarick Ode.
En un Vergier Soiz Folha D'Albespi.

Encountering Sorrow.
End of Clonmacnois, The.
England.
English Girl.
Enlisted Today.
Epigram: "Broad and ample he warms himself."
Epigram: "Gold priests, wooden chalices."
Epigram: "Heat goes deep as cold."
Epigram: "Loss of our learning brought darkness, weakness and woe."
Epigram: On Sir Roger Phillimore.
Epigram: "Says a Reverend Priest to a less Rev'rend friend."
Epigram: "While Adam slept, from him his Eve arose."
Epigram: "Why all the racket, you chattering birds?"
Epigram: "World laid low, and the wind blew like a dust, The."
Epitaph.
Epitaph, An: "Here lieth under this marble ston."
Epitaph for Cú Chuimne.
Epitaph for Mael Mhuru.
Epitaph for Mr. Moses Levy.
Epitaph for One Killed at Roncesvalles.
Epitaph for Sir Henry Lee.
Epitaph for Thomas Johnson, Huntsman. Charlton, Sussex.
Epitaph: "Fortune's darling, king's content."
Epitaph from a Tomb in Asia Minor.
Epitaph from Athens.
Epitaph from Piraeus.
Epitaph in St. Olave's, Southwark, on Mr. Munday.
Epitaph in the Borghese Gardens.
Epitaph: "It was for you that the mountains shook at Sinai."
Epitaph: "Man who in his life trusts in this world, A."
Epitaph: "My friend, judge not me."
Epitaph of a Dog.
Epitaph of a Girl.
Epitaph of a Nicene Actor.
Epitaph of Dionysia.
Epitaph of Sardanapalos, The.
Epitaph of Sir Griffith ap Rhys, The.
Epitaph on a Child Killed by Procured Abortion.
Epitaph on a Tomb near Rome.
Epitaph on Achilles.
Epitaph on an Irish Priest.
Epitaph on John Knott.
Epitaph on the Duke of Buckingham.
Epitaph on William Jones.
Epitaph on William Whitehead.
Epitaph: "Stone cries from the wall, The."
Epithalamium: "Lo! Hymen passes through th' admiring crowds."
Eppie Morrie.
Equal, An.
Erasers.
Erlinton.
Erthe tok of erthe erthe with woh.
Essay on Man.
Eulogy for Hasdai ibn Shaprut.
Eve.
Eve am I, great Adam's wife.
Even He Was Abashed.
Even though my hands / are rough from much rice-pounding.
Evening darkens until.
Evening Prayer.
Evening red and morning gray.
Evermore, wher-so-evere I be.
Every Bullet Has Its Billet.
Every Christian Born of God.
Every [or Ev'ry] Time I Feel the [or de] Spirit.
Everyman.
Evyn as mery as I make myght.
Examination Question.
Execution of Alice Holt.
Exile of Erin, The.
Exile of Rákóczi, The.
Exile of the Sons of Uisliu.
Extensive the lands flanking that southern

mountain.
Eye winker.
Eyes of men running, falling, screaming.
Ezekiel Saw de [or the] Wheel.
Fa, Mi, Fa, Re, La, Mi.
Factory Girl's Come-All-Ye, The.
Factory Workers' Song.
Fading Beauty.
Fair and Scornful.
Fair Annie.
Fair Cassidy.
Fair Flower of Northumberland, The.
Fair Hills of Ireland, The.
Fair Isabell of Rochroyall.
Fair Janet.
Fair Maid of Amsterdam, The.
Fair Margaret and Sweet William.
Fair Mary of Wallington.
Fair rosa.
Faire, fresshest erthly creature.
Fairweill.
Faith.
Faking Boy, The.
Fals fox came unto our croft, The.
False Knight upon [or on] the Road, The.
False Lover Won Back, The.
Famous Flower of Serving-Men; or, The Lady Turn'd Serving-Man, The.
Far Away.
Far far away, the Herdboy Star.
Far inland / go my sad thoughts.
Far off brough, A.
Farewel ye guilded follies, pleasing troubles.
Farewel, dear love! Since thou wilt needs be gone.
Farewell Poem.
Farewell, that was my lef so dere.
Farewell, this world! I take my leve for ever.
Farewell to Kingsbridge.
Farewell, Unkind! Farewell! to me, no more a father!
Farmer's Curst Wife, The.
Farmer's Pride, The.
Farthing, A.
Fates of Men (Exeter Book)
Father, have pity on me.
Father's gone a-flailing.
Father says so—E'yayo!, The.
Father Short came down the lane.
Fause Foodrage.
Fears and Tears.
Fee, fi, fo, fum.
Feed still thy self, thou fondling, with belief.
Feltons Epitaph.
Female Transport, The.
Female Wits, The: A Song by a Lady of Quality.
Festal Song.
Fiddler and his wife, The.
Field, A.
Fighting South of the Castle.
Fighting South of the Ramparts.
Fine Knacks for Ladies.
Finnegan's Wake.
Finnesburh Fragment, The.
Fire.
Fire-Dragon and the Treasure, The.
Fire! Fire! said [or says] the town crier.
Fire of Frendraught, The.
Firm Belief.
First dawn comes, The.
First Daylight Song.
First in a carriage.
First Invasion of Ireland, The.
First Lawcase, The.
First Lay of Gudrun, The.
First Merseburg Spell.
First month of winter: cold air comes.
First Nowell, The.
First of May, The.
First of summer, lovely sight.
First Song of the Exploding Stick.
First Song of the Thunder.
First Stone of the New Castle, The.
First time I saw you, The.
First William the Norman.
Fish at Mass, The.

Fish Weeps, The.
Fisherman's Rhyme.
Fishermen's Song.
Fishes swim in water clear.
Five Arabic Verses in Praise of Wine.
Five Flower World Variations.
Flavia's a name a deal too free.
Flodden Field.
Flood Water.
Flowering War, The.
Flowers in the Valley.
Flowers will do us no good on our tombstones.
Foggy, Foggy Dew, The.
Follow my Bangalorey Man.
Foolish Child.
Foot Race Song.
For a Swarm of Bees.
For Baby.
For no love borne by me.
For Sale or Rent.
For that noble princess pressed him so hard.
For the Children or the Grown-ups?
For the God of Peyote.
For the nightemare.
For the Sin.
For the Theft of Cattle.
For Those Who Always Fear the Worst.
For Thy Sake Let the World Call Me Fool.
For We Are Thy People.
For wele or wo I wyl not flee.
Force.
Forest Trees of the Sea.
Forever Martial.
Fort of Ard Ruide, The.
Fort of Rathangan, The.
Fortune.
Fortune's Legacy.
Fortunes of Men, The.
Fortunes of War, I Tell You Plain, The.
Found dead a rat—no case could sure be harder.
Four Glosses.
Four May Poems, II.
Four May Poems: "Be glaid, al ye that luvaris bene."
Four on a Sidewalk.
Four stiff-standers.
Four Tz'u from Tun-huang.
Fourth Month, The.
Fowls [or Foweles or Fowles] in the Frith.
Fox and the Goose, The.
Fox, The.
Foxes move in pairs.
Fragment of a Song on the Beautiful Wife of Dr. John Overall.
Fragrance comes from the scent I wear, The.
Fragrance is due to perfumes.
Frail, frail, lone-growing bamboo.
Frankie and Albert.
Frankie and Johnny [or Johnnie or Albert].
Franks come down the hill with a random course, The.
Fray of Suport, The.
Free Parliament Litany, A.
Freedom a Come Oh!
Freedom in the Air.
French, 1870–1871, The.
Fressh lusty beautee joyned wyth gentilesse.
Friar in the Well.
Friar of Orders Gray, The.
Friend, A.
Friendship.
Frog, The.
From a Lavatory Wall.
From a London Bookshop.
From here to there / To Washington Square.
From the South.
From the South: 2.
From Tomorrow On.
From Wibbleton to Wobbleton is fifteen miles.
Frozen Logger, The.
Fruit Plummets from the Plum Tree.
Full and True Account of a Dreaded Fire, that Lately Broke out in the Pope's Breeches, A.
Funeral Lament (Kommos) from Epiros.
Funeral Oration.
Funeral Pyre, The.

Fuzzy Wuzzy was a bear.
Gaberlunzie Man, The.
Galway Races.
Gardener, The.
Gasbags.
Gawain and the Lady of the Castle.
Gawain Journeys North.
Gay Old Hag, The.
Gaze North-east.
Gee up, Neddy, to the fair.
General wonder in our land.
Generals Ride in Cars.
Gentle River, Gentle River.
Gentle Word, A.
Gentlemen, for this day's work our chance has not been ill.
Gentlewoman yt Married a Yonge Gent Who after Forsooke Whereupon She Tooke Hir Needle in Which She Was Excelent and Worked upon Hir Sampler Thus, A.
Gentlewomans Answer to One, that Sayd He Should Dye, if Shee Refuse His Desires, A.
Gently, gently prithee, time.
Geordie [An Old Ballad].
George Aloe and the *Sweepstake,* The.
George Copway's Dream Song.
Gereint ab Erbin.
Gereint Son of Erbin.
Gest of Robyn Hode.
Get ready your money and come to me.
Get Up and Bar the Door.
Get Up, Get Up.
Get up, Mountain, get up!
Getting Berries.
Getting Firewood.
Getting to Rome.
Ghost & Shaman.
Gift, A.
Gift for the Queen.
Gil Brenton.
Gil Morrice.
Gilbertus Glanvil, whose heart was a hard as an anvil.
Gilly Silly Jarter.
Gipsy Laddie, The.
Girl.
Girl by Green River, The.
Girl's Song.
Girl threw an apple to a cloud, A.
Girl with the Dark Hair.
Girls and Boys Come out to Play.
Give Me Jesus.
Give me my knife.
Give me sweet nectar in a kiss.
Giving.
Glance, A.
Glasgerion.
Glasgow Peggie.
Glenlogie; or, Jean o Bethelnie.
Gloomy Night of Sadness, The.
Gloria mundi est.
Glorious Strike of the Builders, The.
Glyn Cynon Wood.
Go bet, penny, go bet, go!
Go Down, Moses.
Go Down, Old Hannah.
Go hert, hurt with adversité.
Go, litel bille, and do me recomaunde.
Go, litel ryng, to that ilke swete.
Go on, / Muses, / and sing the Moon with her big wings.
Go Right along the Seashore.
Go tell the king—the carven hall is felled.
Go to Bed.
Go to bed late.
Go to bed, Tom.
Goanna.
God and Man Set as One.
God and Yet a Man, A?
God be here, God be there.
God Be with You.
God bless our meat.
God bless this house from thatch to floor.
God Bless You.
God of Abraham, of Isaac, and of Jacob.
God of his goodnes, praysed that he be.
God of Might, God of Right.

God Rest Ye Merry, Gentlemen.
God's A-Gonna Trouble the Water.
God send euerie Preist ane wyfe.
God, that all this mightes may.
Goddess Chiao, The.
Goddesse bade the nymphs remove, The.
Godlie Instructione for Old and Young, Ane.
Goes through the mud.
Goin' to Chicago Blues.
Going on always on and on.
Gold, / Silver.
Golden God, the Self, the immortal Swan, The.
Golden Island, The; or, the Darian Song.
Golden Palace, The.
Golden Vanity, The.
Goll Mac Morna Parts from His Wife.
Good and Better.
Good Christian men, rejoice.
Good Counsel.
Good King Wenceslas.
Good Lord in That Heaven.
Good medicin for sor eyen.
Good Medicine.
Good morning, Father Francis.
Good morning, Mistress and Master.
Good morrow to you, Valentine.
Good night, God bless you.
Good night, sweet repose.
Good Scholars Make Bad Husbands.
Good Wish.
Goose and the Gander, The.
Gospel Train, The.
Got a Home in That Rock.
Grace after Meals.
Graces, if the beautiful Dionysios.
Gracius and gay.
Grandfa' Grig / Had a pig.
Grania's Song to Diarmuid.
Grapes.
Grass on the Mountain, The.
Grasshopper Wings.
Grave, The.
Graves the rain makes wet and sleek, The.
Gravestone at Corinth, A.
Gray [or Grey] Goose and Gander.
Gray She-Wolf, The.
Great land and a wide land was the east
    land, A.
Great Silkie of Sule Skerry, The.
Great Spirit.
Great Spirit, whose dry lands thirst, help us to
    find.
Great Summons, The.
Great tempest on the Plain of Ler, A.
Great War Dance, The.
Greed.
Greedy Man, The.
Greedy Tom.
Green beyond green, the grass along the river.
Green cheese, yellow laces.
Green Grass.
Green Gravel.
Green, green.
Green green, river bank grasses.
Green, green riverside grass.
Green green the cypress on the ridge.
Green is the grass on riverbanks.
Green Willow, The.
Greensleeves.
Greetings! you seven students of Professor
    Aristides.
Gregory Griggs, Gregory Griggs.
Grenadier, The.
Grey Cock, or, Saw You My Father, The?
Grey goose and gander.
Grey Selchie of Sule Skerry, The.
Grey Time moves silently, and creeping on.
Grief.
Grief of Love, The.
Grizzel Grimme.
Ground-Thumping Song.
Grumble Family, The.
Gud Ber.
Gude Wallace.
Gudrun Laments over Sigurd.
Guest, The.
Gunpowder Plot Day.

Gwan! Gwan! Cry the Fish Hawks.
Gypsies in the Wood.
Gypsy Laddie, The.
Ha-Kon-E-Crase, the Eagle Dance.
Had Gadyaa Kid, a Kid.
Hag of Béara, The.
Hag of Beare, The.
Haida Cradle-Song.
Haif hairt in hairt ye hairt of hairtis haill.
Hail, Queen of Heaven.
Hail South Australia!
Hail, thou once despised Jesus.
Hail to the Queen.
Hairy Toe, The.
Half Sigh.
Hammer-Song.
Hand by Hand We Shall Us Take.
Hand-clapping Rhyme.
Handy dandy.
Hang up the Baby's Stocking!
Hannah Bantry.
Happy Day Will Soon Appear, The.
Hard Road Blues.
Hares on the Mountain.
Hark, All Ye Lovely Saints.
Hark, and Hear My Trumpet Sounding.
Harmony.
Haroun Al-Rachid for Heart's-Life.
Haroun's Favorite Song.
Harper's Song for Inherkhawy, The.
Harpkin.
Harriet Tubman.
Harrowing, The.
Harry Parry.
Harry Pollit Was a Bolshie.
Hart Loves the High Wood, The.
Harvest Song.
Have good day, now, Mergerete.
Have oon god in worshipe.
Have You Been at Carrick?
Having left behind its cutting.
Hawk Chant of the Saginaws.
Hawthorn, The.
Hay, ay, hay, ay.
Hay is for horses.
He Approacheth the Hall of Judgment.
He Asked Them What Did They Know &
    They Told Him.
He Asketh Absolution of God.
He bare him [or hym] up, he bare him [or
    hym] down.
He Biddeth Osiris to Arise from the Dead.
He Cometh Forth into the Day.
He Commandeth a Fair Wind.
He Defendeth His Heart against the Destroyer.
He dwelt there all that day, and at dawn on the
    morrow.
He Embarketh in the Boat of Ra.
He Entereth the House of the Goddess Hathor.
He Establisheth His Triumph.
He followed his own mind.
He Holdeth Fast to the Memory of His
    Identity.
He is coming, Adzed-Head.
He Is Declared True of Word.
He Is Far.
He Is like the Lotus.
He Is like the Serpent Saka.
He is my love / my sweet nutgrove.
He Kindleth a Fire.
He Knoweth the Souls of the East.
He Knoweth the Souls of the West.
He loves me.
He Maketh Himself One with Osiris.
He Maketh Himself One with the God Ra.
He Maketh Himself One with the Only God,
    Whose Limbs Are the Many Gods.
He Measured Out His Spirit Tower.
He Never Said a Mumblin' Word.
He Overcometh the Serpent of Evil in the
    Name of Ra.
He Paid Me Seven.
He Praises the Trees.
He Prayeth for Ink and Palette That He May
    Write.
He Raise a Poor Lazarus.
He's Jus' de Same Today.

He Singeth a Hymn to Osiris, the Lord of
    Eternity.
He Singeth in the Underworld.
He That Hath No Mistress.
He that in youthe no vertu will yowes.
He that spendes muche and getes nothing.
He that would thrive must rise at five.
He Walketh by Day.
He was the Word that Spake it.
He! When I met him approaching.
He who would acclaim Cleanness in becoming
    style.
He Whose Hand and Eye Are Gentle.
Head bumper.
Healing Song.
Hear father yet thou Long-Armed Lord! these
    latest words I say.
Hear me / helper of mankind.
Hearse Song, The.
Hearts, like doors, will ope with ease.
Heavenly Aeroplane, The.
Heavens Do Declare, The.
Heavily Flapping Are the Bustards' Plumes.
Heavyweight champ of Seattle, The.
Hebe and Ganymede.
Hedge before me, one behind, A.
Heigh ho! my heart is low.
Heir of Linne, The.
Helen of Kirconnell.
Hell and Heaven.
Helpe, crosse, fairest of timbres three.
Hems gathered up, sash not yet tied.
Henpecked Husband, A.
Henry Martyn.
Hēr Æoelstān cyning, eorla drihten.
Her bracelets tinkle.
Her Elegy.
Her Rival for Aziza.
Her saffron gown.
Herdsman's Song.
Here are my lady's knives and forks.
Here Comes a Lusty Wooer.
Here comes my lady with her little baby.
Here Goes My Lord.
Here I am with my rabbits.
Here I ame and fourthe I mouse.
Here I was and here I drank.
Here in my garden.
Here is the church, and here is the steeple.
Here let the Muse perform the painter's art.
Here lies I, no wonder I'm dead.
Here lies my dear wife, a sad slattern and a
    shrew.
Here lies my poor wife, much lamented.
Here lies my poor wife, without bed or
    blanket.
Here lies Sir John Plumpudding of the Grange.
Here lies the body of Daniel Saul.
Here lies the body of Sir John Guise.
Here lies the corpse of Doctor Chard.
Here lies the great. False marble, where?
Here's a ball for baby.
Here's a jolly couple! Oh the jolly jolly cuple!
Here's a poor widow from Babylon.
Here's Dog Diogenes, you ferryman.
Here's Finiky Hawkes.
Here's to thee, old apple tree.
Here's two or three jolly boys.
Here stand I, for whores as great.
Here We Come A-wassailing.
Here we go round ring by ring.
Heriger and the False Prophet.
Herkeneth, lordinges, grete and smale.
Hermit Marbán, The.
Hermit's Song, A.
Hestia, / you who have received the highest
    honor.
Heven, it es a riche ture.
Hey, Boys! Up Go We!
Hey diddle diddle.
Hey diddle dout, / My candle's out.
Hey ding a ding.
Hey, dorolot, dorolot!
Hey, ey, hey, ey / Make we myrie as we may.
Hey, hey, hey, hey!
Hey Nonny No!
Hey noyney! I will love our Sir John and I love

eny.
Heye Louerd, thou here my bone.
Hic, Hoc, the Carrion Crow.
Hic jacet Tom Shorthose.
Hickety pickety i sillickety [*or* i-silicity].
Hidden-in-winter.
Hidden People and the Star People, The.
Hie to the market, Jenny come trot.
Hierusalem.
High Priest, The.
High Resolve.
High Skip, The.
Highest Divinity.
Highwayman, The.
Him I'm thinking of.
Hind Etin.
Hind Horn.
Hinx! minx! / The old witch winks!
Hiraeth.
His Confession.
His Son's / A Jew.
Hitty Pitty within the wall.
Hoatchunk' Narwoanar, or Winnebago War
  Song.
Hob, shoe, hob; hob, shoe, hob.
Hob upon a Holiday.
Hobie [*or* Hobbie] Noble.
Hoddley, poddley, puddle and fogs.
Hoddy doddy.
Hogyn.
Hokey, pokey, whisky, thum.
Hold my Rooster.
Hold up your head.
Holly and Ivy.
Holly and the Ivy, The.
Holy Goddess Tellus.
Holy is the moon and our own Selene.
Holy Nunnery, The.
Holy Priestess of Heaven, The.
Holy Well, The.
Homage to Tara Our Mother.
Home.
Home on the Range, A.
Home to Farm.
Home Truths from Abroad.
Honey, Take a Whiff on Me.
Hope.
Horny-Goloch, The.
Horse Cursed by the Sun, The.
Horse Sense.
Hospital Duties.
Hot Boiled Beans.
Hot Codlins.
Hot cross buns, hot cross buns / One a penny
  poker.
Hot Day in Sydney, A.
Hours of Sleep.
Hours of the Passion, The.
House full, a hole full, A.
House Song to the East.
House That Jack Built, The.
How, butler, how! bevis a tout!
How come alle ye that ben i-broght.
How Death Came.
How do you cut an ax-handle?
How far from enough.
How Goes the Night?
How Her Teeth Were Pulled.
How! hey! it is non les.
How I wish I had known / beforehand of this
  journey.
How Is the Night?
How lovely it is today!
"How Quick You Are!"
How terrible it is to trust no one.
How the First Hielandman of God Was Made.
How to Choose a Mistress.
How to Get Grizzly Spirit.
How to Obtain Her.
How was I born? Where from? Why did I
  come.
Hrothgar Answered.
Hugh Spencer's Feats in France.
Hughie [the] Gra[e]me.
Humble Petition of the British Jacobins to their
  Brethren of France, The.
Hunger.

Hungering Hearts.
Hunter Poems of the Yoruba.
Hunter's Song.
Hunting of the Gods, The.
Hunting-Song.
Hunting the Wren.
Hurly, hurly, roon the table.
Hurry On, My Weary Soul.
Husband's Message, The.
Hush-a-ba birdie [*or* burdie], croon, croon.
Hush-a-baa, baby / Dinna mak' a din.
Hush-a-Bye.
Hush-a-bye a baa lamb.
Hush-a-bye, baby / The beggar shan't have 'ee.
Hush-a-bye, baby, they're gone to milk.
Hush, little baby, don't say a word.
Hush, my baby, do not cry.
Hush thee, my babby.
Hushie ba, burdie beeton.
Hwæt, wē gār-dena in gēardagum.
Hyder Iddle.
Hye Nonny Nonny Noe.
Hyena.
Hyena Addressing Her Young Ones, The.
Hymn for Seedtime and a Safe Harvest (Arval
  Hymn)
Hymn for St. John's Eve.
Hymn: "O God of Hosts, thine Ear incline."
Hymn of Unity.
Hymn to Aphrodite.
Hymn to Athena.
Hymn to Castor and Pollux.
Hymn to Earth the Mother of All.
Hymn to Night.
Hymn to Nut.
Hymn to Selene.
Hymn to the Earth, The.
Hymn to the Fallen.
Hymn to the Orange.
Hymn to the Sun.
Hymn to the Virgin.
I am a pretty wench.
I am a young girl, gay.
I am as light as any roe.
I am climbing.
I am constantly wounded.
I am I, but also the other.
I am making / a wind come here.
I am olde whan age doth apele.
I Am Taliesin. I Sing Perfect Metre.
I Am Your Wife.
I ame not she by proweff of syt.
I ask all blessings.
I ask you to witness, Priapus.
I asked my mother for fifty cents.
I Been Working on the Railroad.
I beg you, beg you, mother.
I Believe.
I bring you news.
I Came from under the Earth.
I Can No Longer Untangle My Hair.
I can sing a true song about myself.
I can sing of myself a true song.
I cannot go to you.
I Climb That Barren Ridge.
I conjour hem in the name of the Fader, and
  Sone.
I cross the river to pluck hibiscus.
I crossed the deep sea.
I do not care if.
I don't care.
I don't care if you're married, I'll still get you.
I don't want to be a nun.
I Don't Want to Be a Soldier.
I drive my carriage from the Upper East Gate.
I fell in love. I kissed her.
I find my love fishing.
I found in Munster, unfettered of any.
I Found My Love by the Secret Canal.
I Go before, my darling.
I Got a Home in Dat Rock.
I Got the Blues.
I grew from the earth.
I Had a Black Man.
I had a cat and the cat pleased me.
I had a dog / Whose name was Buff.
I had a little cow.

I had a little dog and his name was Blue Bell.
I had a little hobby-horse.
I had a little horse, his name was Dappled
  Grey.
I had a little husband.
I had a little nag.
I Had But Fifty Cents.
I had my good and my.
I Have a Gentle Cock [*or* Gentil Cok].
I Have a New Garden.
I have a whim to speak in verse.
I Have a Young Sister.
I Have Been a Foster.
I have heard that far from here.
I Have Lived and I Have Loved.
I have no pain, dear mother, now.
I Have Some Friends before Me Gone.
I have thee, thou hast me.
I have twelve oxen that be faire and brown.
I have two sicknesses, Love.
I heard a cow low, a bonnie cow low.
I heard my love was going to Yang-chou.
I Know de Moonlight.
I know him / He'll give no horse for a poem.
I know I am poor.
I Know Moon-Rise [*or* Moonrise].
I like sleeping with somebody.
I like to crawl around the house after my
  brother's wife.
I'll buy you a tartan bonnet.
I'll shoot a little bird for little brother.
I'll sing you a song / Nine verses long.
I'll sing you a song / The days are long.
I'll tell my own daddy.
I'll Wear Me a Cotton Dress.
I loathe the twin seas.
I lost my mare in Lincoln Lane.
I love little pussy, her coat is so warm.
I Love the Lord.
I love thee, Betty.
I love thee for thy fickleness.
I loved / secretly.
I'm a little butterfly.
I'm a-Rollin'
I'm Agoing to Lay Down My Sword.
I'm ashamed of my thoughts.
I'm called by the name of a man.
I'm gonna marry my brother's wife.
I'm on My Way to Canaan.
I may wel sike for grevous is my peyne.
I ne have joy, pleasauns, nor comfort.
I need not your needles.
I passed thurgh a gardyn grene.
I peeped through the window.
I pray you, be mery and synge with me.
I Pressed Her Rebel Lips.
I Saw a Fish-Pond All on Fire.
I Saw a Peacock [with a Fiery Tail].
I saw Esau sawing wood.
I Saw My Lady Weep.
I Saw Three Ships Come Sailing In.
I See the Moon.
I sent a letter to my love.
I Shall Not Pass This Way Again.
I Sing of a Maiden.
I Sit with My Dolls.
I sleep alone.
I Sometimes Think.
I Stood in the Maytime Meadows.
I Thank God I'm Free at Las.'
I thank the, Lord so dere, that wold vowchsayf.
I think of him / Who lives south of the big sea.
I Think over Again My Small Adventures.
I think this is something you should get clear.
I thought that Love had been a boy.
I to the Lord from My Distress.
I trained me a falcon, for more than a year.
I turn the carriage, yoke and set off.
I've Had the Wagon Hauled Out.
I've lost my rifle and bayonet.
I Vision God.
I Wait My Lord.
I waited for my.
I walk in loneliness through the greenwood.
I want the robes, the skins of the game
  animals, the meat of the game animals.
  Bring them to me. Let us enjoy ourselves.

I want to be in a garden with my love.
I want to be with my love in a garden.
I Was Born Almost Ten Thousand Years Ago.
I was sent forth from the power.
I Was Surprised to Find Myself Out Here & Acting like a Crow.
I watch the sanitary state.
I wende to deeth, knight stith in stour.
I went down to my garden patch.
I Went Downtown.
I went to Noke.
I went to the toad that lies under the wall.
I Will Bow and Be Simple.
I will carry my coat and not put on my belt.
I Will Give My Love an Apple [Without E'er a Core].
I will make love.
I will not die for you.
I, Willie Wastle.
I Wish I Were.
I wish I were the wind, and you.
I wish to paint my eyes.
I wot a tree XII bowes betake.
I Would Be Clad in Christ's Skin.
I Would but I Can't.
I'yehe! my children.
Icarus.
Ichot a burde in a bour ase beryl so bright.
Ickle ockle, blue bockle.
If All the World Were Paper.
If bees stay at home.
If I Could Shut the Gate against My Thoughts.
If I don't take anything to the party I'll feel bad.
If I had a donkey that wouldn't go.
If I had a little wife.
If I Might Be an Ox.
If I might offer.
If I singe, ye will me lakke.
If I were but a bird.
If it is but sleep.
If "ifs" and "ans" [or If ifs and ands were pots and pans.].
If only Life-and-Death.
If Sanct Paules day be fair and cleir.
If the clouds come good, our tobacco will grow. We will be happy.
If the oak is out before the ash.
If there be a rainbow in the eve.
If to the Pump Room in the morn we go.
If true that notion, which but few contest.
If you'd died I would've cut off my hair.
If you don't like my apples.
If you go away / why should I adorn myself?
If you really care for me.
If you really love me honey, hey- yah.
If You Think Kindly of Me.
Ignotum per Ignotius, or a Furious Hodge-Podge of Nonsense; A Pindaric.
I'm Callicratia / who bore / 29 children.
Imperious bath-maid, O why.
Imploration for Clear Weather.
Impossible to Trust Women.
In al this world nis a murier lyf.
In Bath a wanton wife did dwell.
In Beauty May I Walk.
In 8 is alle my love.
In her boudoir, the young lady—unacquainted with grief.
In Honour of St. David's Day.
In May it muryeth when it dawes.
In Memory of Captain Underwood Who Was Drowned.
In Merche, after the first C.
In Praise of Ivy.
In Praise of Tenby.
In Praise of Wine.
In Slumber Late.
In Spring I look gay.
In Spring We Gather Mulberry Leaves.
In the casket of the Hours.
In the Chung Mode, to the Tune of 'P'u T'ien Lo.'
In the courtyard is a marvelous tree.
In the Days of Old Rameses.
In the early hours of the next morning dawning.

In the evening / The mists trail.
In the Garden.
In the garden a strange tree grows.
In the greenhouse lives a wren.
In the hottest time, when all is still and windless.
In the Meadow There's a Dead Deer.
In the Night.
In the north-west there is a high house.
In the open sea.
In the Seventh Month.
In the seventh month, declining is the Fire Star.
In the Shadows of the Wu-t'ung Tree.
In the Town.
In the vale of resteles mynde.
In the wilds, a dead doe.
In the Wilds There Is a Dead Doe.
In what estate so ever I be.
In wrath and grief away the Paynims fly.
Inanna spoke.
Incantation Songs of the Klamath Lake People.
Incantations of Modoc Conjurers.
Independence Bell—July 4, 1776.
Independence Day.
Indian Bagman's Toast.
Indra, the Supreme God.
Infir Taris.
Inky gloss of your mane, The.
Innsbruck, now I must depart.
Inordinate Love.
Inscribed in Melrose Abbey.
Inscribed on a Statue of Hermes.
Inscription at Mount Vernon.
Inscription for a Statue of Pan.
Inscription in Osmington Church, Dorset.
Inscriptions at the City of Brass.
Insult, An.
Inter, mitzy, titzy, tool.
International Chainpoem.
(Invocation for Storing Corn)
Invocation To Dsilyi N'Eyani.
Invocation to the U' wannami.
Ipsey Wipsey spider.
Is it not sure a deadly pain.
Is There No Balm in Christian Lands?
It Can Be Done.
It Don't Mean a Thing (If It Ain't Got That Swing)
It is far from just between us.
It is the day of all the year.
It Is the Third Watch.
It is well for small birds that can rise up on high.
It's once I courted as pretty a lass.
It's raining, it's pouring.
It's Spring Returning, It's Spring and Love.
It's the Enobarbus Complex.
It's you puts the green sprig in my hatband.
It takes a very stupid dolt.
Ivied Tree-Top, An.
Jack and Dinah Want Freedom.
Jack and Gye.
Jack and Jill went up the hill.
Jack in the Pulpit.
Jack Jelf.
Jack Jingle.
Jack Sprat's Cat.
Jack the Piper.
James Grant.
James Harris (The Daemon Lover)
James Hatley.
Jamie Douglas.
Jamie Telfer of [or in] the Fair Dodhead.
Japanese Figures 1.
Japanese Figures 2.
Jellon Grame.
Jenny Nettles.
Jeremiah, blow the fire.
Jeremiah Obadiah.
Jerusalem, My Happy Home.
Jesse James.
Jesu Christ, my Leman Swete.
Jesu Crist, heovene king.
Jesu, for thy muchele might.
Jesu that is most of might.

Jesus Bids Man Remember.
Jesus, Master, O Discover.
Jesus Reproaches His People.
Jesus, the very thought of thee with sweetness fills my breast.
Jesus to Those Who Pass By.
Jewels wherever we look.
Jewish Arabic Liturgies.
Jim Jones.
Jimmy's Enlisted; or, The Recruited Collier.
Jingle bells! jingle, bells!
Jinny.
Jo Jo, My Child.
Jock o' the Side.
Jock the Leg and the Merry Merchant.
John Bun.
John Dory.
John Gilbert Was a Bushranger.
John Hardy.
John Henry.
John of Hazelgreen.
John of Tours.
John Rogers' Exhortation to His Children.
John Smith, fellow fine.
John Thomson and the Turk.
Johnie Armstrang.
Johnie Cock.
Johnie Scot.
Johnnie Norrie.
Johnny Armstrong killed a calf.
Johnny come down de hollow.
Johnny Dow [or Doo].
Johnny, I Hardly Knew Ye.
Johnny's the Lad I Love.
Johny Faa.
Jolly Jugger, The.
Jolly Pinder of Wakefield, The.
Jolly Shepherd, The.
Jonah and the Whale.
Joshua Fit de Battle of Jericho [or ob Jerico].
Joy and Temperance.
Juce of lekes with gotes galle.
Judas.
Judas Sells His Lord.
Judge, judge, tell the judge.
Judged by the Company One Keeps.
Juggy's Christening.
Julius Caesar.
Jump-Rope Rhyme.
Just because of you.
Just Like Me.
Justice to Scotland.
Kalapuya Prophecy, A.
Katharine Jaffray.
Keep away from asps and toads.
Keep It Dark.
Keep Ye Holy Sabbath Rest.
Keep your kiss to yourself.
Kemp Owyne.
Kentucky Moonshiner.
Ki-u-nad'-dis-si's Song.
Kilaben Bay Song.
Kilcash.
Kill That Crowing Cock.
Kindely is now my coming.
Kindness to Animals.
King Arthur and King Cornwall.
King Berdok.
King Charles the First.
King Charles the First walked and talked.
King Edward the Fourth and a Tanner of Tamworth.
King Estmere.
King Henry.
King Henry Fifth's Conquest of France.
King James and Brown.
King John and the Bishop.
King of the Castle.
King Orfeo.
King's Disguise, and Friendship with Robin Hood, The.
King's Dochter Lady Jean, The.
King's Last Farewell to the World, The.
Kinges baneres beth forth ilad, The.
Kinmont Willie.
Kiss in the Ring.
Kiss me and hug me.

Kiss me then, my merry May.
Kitchie-Boy, The.
Knight and Shepherd's Daughter, The.
Knight of Liddesdale, The.
Knight's Ghost, The.
Knight's Prayer, The.
Knock at the doorie.
Know er thou knitte; prove er thou preise it.
Koel (Rainbird) and Effigy.
Koocoo, The.
Korean Figures.
Kū′ siut Song.
Kuan-kuan call the ospreys.
Kuan-kuan, the ospreys.
Kudzu Spreads Till It Darkens the Brier, The.
Kyrie, So Kyrie.
Labours of the Months.
Ladies, you see time flieth.
Lads of Wamphray, The.
Lady Alice.
Lady / baby.
Lady Diamond.
Lady Elspat.
Lady in the Wood, The.
Lady Isabel.
Lady Isabel and the Elf-Knight.
Lady Laments for Her Lost Lover, by Similitude of a Falcon, A.
Lady Lowbodice.
Lady Maisry.
Lady of Arngosk, The.
Lady of High Degree, A.
Lady of shrouding hair.
Lady of the Morning, The.
Lady Queen Anne she sits in the sun.
Lady T-rc----l's Ring.
Lady, those cherries plenty.
Lady Who Ascends into the Heavens, The.
Lady, you think you spite me.
Ladybird.
Laily Worm and the Machrel of the Sea, The.
Laird, a lord, A.
Laird o Drum, The.
Laird o' Logie, The.
Laird o' Ochiltree Wa's, The.
Laird of Wariston, The.
Lais' Mirror.
Lament: "Cheek by cheek on our pillow[s]."
Lament for a Husband.
Lament for Hathimoda, Abbess of Gandesheim.
Lament for Prince Chagoo.
Lament for Tawhiao.
Lament for Te Iwi—ika.
Lament for the Death of Guillén Peraza.
Lament for Urien, The.
Lament of a Man for His Son.
Lament of Gilgamesh for Enkidu, The.
Lament of Hsi-Chün.
Lament of Maev Leith-Dherg, The.
Lament of Mary, The.
Lament of the Border Widow, The.
Lament over the Ruins of the Abbey of Teach Molaga.
Lament: "Spell, treasure-bearing spell, prop up the sky standing above."
Lamentation for Celin, The.
Lamentations of the Fallen Angels.
Lamkin.
Land Is Gone, The.
Land of Cokaygne, The.
Lang Johnny More.
Lanigan's Ball.
Lao Figures.
Large-headed beauty, head so alluring, The.
Lark, The.
Lass A-Laundering.
Lass in the Female Factory, The.
Lass of Roch Royal, The.
Last Battle and Death of Chingis Khan, The.
Last Daybreak Song.
Last Drink, A.
Last Judgment, The.
Last night with hair unbrushed.
Last Oracle from Delphi.
Last Song of the Exploding Stick.

Last Survivor's Speech, The.
Last Utterance of the Delphic Oracle, The.
Last Words of the Prophet.
Laudanum.
Law of God be to thee thy rest, The.
Lawyers.
Lay of Finn, The.
Lay of King Saint Ladislas, The.
Lay of the Lash, The.
Lay [or Short Lay] of Sigurd, The.
Lazy deuks that sit i' the coal-neuks.
Lazy Man, The.
Le Père Sévère.
Learn from me, Son of Kunti! also this.
Learn now, dear Prince! how, if thy soul be set.
Learn to Count.
Learn to Wait.
Learned Mistress, A.
Leesome Brand.
Leezie Lindsay.
Leith police dismisseth us, The.
Lengthening Days.
Lenten Is [or Ys] Come [with Love to Toune].
Lesson from a Sundial [Sun-Dial].
Let all mortal flesh keep silence, and with fear and trembling stand.
Let Christian Hearts Rejoice Today.
Let dirty streets be paved with flow'ry green.
Let Him with Kisses of His Mouth.
Let Me Gallop, Let Me Go.
Let My People Go.
Let's go to the wood, says this pig.
Let the first syllable of PEnelope be followed by the first of DIdo, the first of CAnus by that of REmus.
Let Thy Kingdom.
Let Us Break Bread Together.
Let Us Cheer the Weary Traveler.
Lettre Sende by on Yonge Woman to A-noder, Whiche Aforetyme Were Felowes To-geder, A.
Levedy Fortune is bothe frend and fo, The.
Levis Exsurgit Zephirus.
Liadain.
Líadan and Cuirithir.
Líadan Laments Cuirithir.
Life.
Life Is Long.
Life of this world, woe betide thee!
Life Owes Me Nothing.
Light and Rejoicing to Israel.
Like the tides' flood.
Like to a ring without a finger.
Lilies are white.
Lily Events.
Limejuice Tub, The.
Limerick.
Limerick: "According to old Sigmund Freud."
Limerick: "After lunch the old Duchess of Teck."
Limerick: "Amoeba named Sam, and his brother, An."
Limerick: "Amorous maiden antique, An."
Limerick: "Argentine gaucho named Bruno, An."
Limerick: "As dull as the life of the cloister."
Limerick: "As he filled up his order book pp."
Limerick: "As Mozart composed a sonata."
Limerick: "As the elevator car left our floor."
Limerick: "Astute Melanesians on Munda."
Limerick: "At Harvard a randy old Dean."
Limerick: "At the orgy I humped twenty-two."
Limerick: "Authoress, armed with a skewer, An."
Limerick: "Bather whose clothing was strewed, A."
Limerick: "Big cities are reeking with grief."
Limerick: "Binary mathematician, A."
Limerick: "Book and a jug and a dame, A."
Limerick: "Bottle of perfume that Willie sent, The [or A]."
Limerick: "Breasts of a barmaid of Crale, The."
Limerick: "Business-like harlot named Draper, A."
Limerick: "Careless old cook of Salt Ash, A."
Limerick: "Certain young chap named Bill

Beebee, A."
Limerick: "Certain young sheik I'm not namin', A."
Limerick: "Come and see our French goods— you can try 'em."
Limerick: "Come to Noah's for wine and strong waters."
Limerick: "Comely young widow named Ransom, A."
Limerick: "Complacent old Don of Divinity, A."
Limerick: "Concerning the bees and the flowers."
Limerick: "Concert conductor in Rio, A."
Limerick: "Connoisseurs of coition aver."
Limerick: "Consider the Emperor Nero."
Limerick: "Creature of charm is the gerbil, A."
Limerick: "Daring young lady of Guam, A."
Limerick: "Desperate spinster of Clare, A."
Limerick: "Divine by the name of McWhinners, A."
Limerick: "Enjoyment of sex, although great, The."
Limerick: "Epicure, Dining at Crewe, An."
Limerick: "Ethnologists up with the Sioux."
Limerick: "Exquisite bartender at Sweeney's, The."
Limerick: "Fabulous Wizard of Oz, The."
Limerick: "Famous theatrical actress, A."
Limerick: "Fellow who fucked but as few can, A."
Limerick: "Fencing instructor named Fisk, A."
Limerick: "'For the tenth time, dull Daphnis,' said Chloe."
Limerick: "For Widower—wanted, house-keeper."
Limerick: "French are a race among races, The."
Limerick: "French poodle espied in the hall, A."
Limerick: "From the crypt of the church of St. Giles."
Limerick: "From the west to the fabulous east."
Limerick: "Girl who was touring Zambesi, A."
Limerick: "Given faith," sighed the vicar of Deneham."
Limerick: "God's plan made a hopeful beginning."
Limerick: "Handsome young monk in a wood, A."
Limerick: "Herder who hailed from Terre Haute, A."
Limerick: "Highly bored damsel called Brown, A."
Limerick: "Honourable Winifred Wemyss, The."
Limerick: "Husband who lived in Tiberias, A."
Limerick: "I, Caesar, when I learned of the fame."
Limerick: "'I must leave here,' said Lady De Vere."
Limerick: "I sat next to the Duchess at tea."
Limerick: "I wouldn't be bothered with drawers."
Limerick: "If intercourse gives you thrombosis."
Limerick: "If you find for your verse there's no call."
Limerick: "In considering things gastronomic."
Limerick: "In history's mysteries vast."
Limerick: "In the days of mild Jerry Ford."
Limerick: "In the Garden of Eden lay Adam."
Limerick: "Innocent bride from the Mission, An."
Limerick: "Innocent maiden of Gloucester, An."
Limerick: "It occurred when she crossed the Atlantic."
Limerick: "It seems I impregnated Marge."
Limerick: "It's my custom," said dear Lady Norris."
Limerick: "Ivy Compton-Burnett's irritations."
Limerick: "King Louis gave lessons in Class."
Limerick: "Kings of Peru were the Incas, The."
Limerick: "Lady of features cherubic, A."
Limerick: "Lady on climbing Mount

Shasta, A."
Limerick: "Lady there was in Antigua, A."
Limerick: "Lesbian girl of Khartoum, A."
Limerick: "Let's enter the literary scene."
Limerick: "Limerick lacks the precision, The."
Limerick: "Limerick packs laughs anatomical, The."
Limerick: "Limerick realm now prepares, The."
Limerick: "Limerick's birth is unclear, The."
Limerick: "Limerick's callous and crude, The."
Limerick: "Lisping young lady called Beth, A."
Limerick: "Lissom psychotic named Jane, A."
Limerick: "Lonely old maid named Loretta, A."
Limerick: "Lonely young fellow of Eton, A."
Limerick: "Mechanical marvel was Bill, A."
Limerick: "Menagerie came to Cape Race, A."
Limerick: "Minister up in Vermont, A."
Limerick: "Mosquito was heard to complain, A."
Limerick: "Much-worried mother once said, A."
Limerick: "Near-sighted fellow named Walter, A."
Limerick: "New cinematic emporium, The."
Limerick: "None could better our sex limousine."
Limerick: "Of a sudden, the great prima donna."
Limerick: "Of my husband I do not ask much."
Limerick: "Old archaeologist, Throstle, An."
Limerick: "On a date with a charming young bird."
Limerick: "On an outing with seventeen Czechs."
Limerick: "On May Day, the girls of Penzance."
Limerick: "On Saturn the sexes are three."
Limerick: "On the chest of a barmaid in Sale."
Limerick: "Orgy was held on the lawn, The."
Limerick: "Pansy who lived in Khartoum, A."
Limerick: "Plumber from Lowater Creek, A."
Limerick: "Policeman from Nottingham Junction, A."
Limerick: "Professor of Ethical Culture, A."
Limerick: "Prudish old lady called Muir, A."
Limerick: "Publisher went off to France, A."
Limerick: "Rapist, who reeked of cheap booze, A."
Limerick: "Rascal far gone in treachery, A."
Limerick: "Remarkable race are the Persians, A."
Limerick: "Revelations—we've come to the lewd."
Limerick: "Reverend Mr. Uprightly, The."
Limerick: "Riverrun where can you guess?"
Limerick: "Round-bottomed babe from Mobile, A."
Limerick: "Said a diffident lady named Drood."
Limerick: "Said a luscious young lady called Wade."
Limerick: "Said an ape as he swung by his tail."
Limerick: "Said an eminent, erudite ermine."
Limerick: "Said Miss Farrow, on one of her larks."
Limerick: "Said Queen Isabella of Spain."
Limerick: "Said the Duchess of Alba to Goya."
Limerick: "Said the mythical King of Algiers."
Limerick: "Said the newly-weds staying near Kitely."
Limerick: "Salvation lassie named Claire, A."
Limerick: "Sculptor remarked: "I'm afraid," A."
Limerick: "Señorita who strolled on the Corso, A."
Limerick: "Sensitive girl called O'Neill, A."
Limerick: "Sermon our Pastor, Rt. Rev., The."
Limerick: "Shed a tear for the WREN named McGinnis."
Limerick: "Shiftless young fellow of Kent, A."
Limerick: "Some lives are so odd—you agree?"
Limerick: "Sometimes there are airs grave and

gentle."
Limerick: "Southern hill-billy named Hollis, A."
Limerick: "Staid schizophrenic named Struther, A."
Limerick: "There isn't a shadow of doubt."
Limerick: "There once was a couple named Mound."
Limerick: "There once was a Fellow of Trinity."
Limerick: "There once was a Fellow of Wadham / Who approved of the doings of Sodom."
Limerick: "There once was a girl from St. Paul."
Limerick: "There once was a judge of Assize."
Limerick: "There once was a lady called Lily."
Limerick: "There once was a monarch of Spain."
Limerick: "There once was a plesiosaurus."
Limerick: "There once was a sculptor named Phidias."
Limerick: "There once was a vicar of Ryhill."
Limerick: "There once was an eccentric old boffin."
Limerick: "There's a notable family named Stein."
Limerick: "There's a sensitive type in Tom's River."
Limerick: "There's a very prim girl called McDrood."
Limerick: "There's a wonderful family called Stein."
Limerick: "There was a crusader of Parma."
Limerick: "There was a faith-healer of Deal."
Limerick: "There was a fat lady of Clyde."
Limerick: "There was a rash fellow called Weir."
Limerick: "There was a sick man of Tobago."
Limerick: "There was a young artist called Saint."
Limerick: "There was a young bride named McWing."
Limerick: "There was a young curate of Kew."
Limerick: "There was a young curate of Salisbury."
Limerick: "There was a young fellow called Baker."
Limerick: "There was a young fellow called Bliss."
Limerick: "There was a young fellow called Cager."
Limerick: "There was a young fellow called Chubb."
Limerick: "There was a young fellow called Clyde."
Limerick: "There was a young fellow called Hall."
Limerick: "There was a young fellow called Lancelot."
Limerick: "There was a young fellow called Price."
Limerick: "There was a young fellow called Wyatt."
Limerick: "There was a young fellow from Tyne."
Limerick: "There was a young fellow named Fisher."
Limerick: "There was a young fellow named Menzies."
Limerick: "There was a young Fellow of Caius."
Limerick: "There was a young fellow of Ceuta."
Limerick: "There was a young Fellow of King's."
Limerick: "There was a young fellow of Lyme."
Limerick: "There was a young fellow of Perth."
Limerick: "There was a young fellow of Trinity."
Limerick: "There was a young Fellow of Wadham."
Limerick: "There was a young Fellow of Wadham / Who asked for a ticket to Sodom."

Limerick: "There was a young girl called Bianca."
Limerick: "There was a young girl of Australia."
Limerick: "There was a young girl of Cape Cod."
Limerick: "There was a young girl of Darjeeling."
Limerick: "There was a young girl of La Plata."
Limerick: "There was a young girl of Penzance."
Limerick: "There was a young girl of Siam."
Limerick: "There was a young girl of St. Cyr."
Limerick: "There was a young girl of Tralee."
Limerick: "There was a young girl whose frigidity."
Limerick: "There was a young Jap on a syndicate."
Limerick: "There was a young lady called Alice."
Limerick: "There was a young lady called Etta."
Limerick: "There was a young lady called Flynn."
Limerick: "There was a young lady called Gloria."
Limerick: "There was a young lady called Hilda."
Limerick: "There was a young lady called Kate."
Limerick: "There was a young lady called Maud."
Limerick: "There was a young lady called Muffet."
Limerick: "There was a young lady called Smith."
Limerick: "There was a young lady called Starky."
Limerick: "There was a young lady from Pecking."
Limerick: "There was a young lady named Kent."
Limerick: "There was a young lady of Aenos."
Limerick: "There was a young lady of Brabant."
Limerick: "There was a young lady of Chichester."
Limerick: "There was a young lady of Chiswick."
Limerick: "There was a young lady of Ealing."
Limerick: "There was a young lady of fashion."
Limerick: "There was a young lady of Florence."
Limerick: "There was a young lady of Joppa."
Limerick: "There was a young lady of Kew."
Limerick: "There was a young lady of Ryde / Who ate some green apples and died."
Limerick: "There was a young lady of Ryde / Who was carried too far by the tide."
Limerick: "There was a young lady of Rye."
Limerick: "There was a young lady of Slough."
Limerick: "There was a young lady of Spain."
Limerick: "There was a young lady of Tottenham."
Limerick: "There was a young lady of Trent."
Limerick: "There was a young lady of Wantage."
Limerick: "There was a young lady of Where?"
Limerick: "There was a young lass of Pitlochry."
Limerick: "There was a young lawyer called Rex."
Limerick: "There was a young maid who said, "Why."
Limerick: "There was a young maiden from Multerry."
Limerick: "There was a young maiden of Devon."
Limerick: "There was a young man from Darjeeling."
Limerick: "There was a young man named Racine."
Limerick: "There was a young man of

Australia."
Limerick: "There was a young man of Calcutta."
Limerick: "There was a young man of Cape Race."
Limerick: "There was a young man of Dumfries."
Limerick: "There was a young man of Ghent."
Limerick: "There was a young man of Japan."
Limerick: "There was a young man of Madras."
Limerick: "There was a young man of Nepal."
Limerick: "There was a young man of St John's."
Limerick: "There was a young man of Wood's Hole."
Limerick: "There was a young man who said: 'Ayer."
Limerick: "There was a young monarch called Ed."
Limerick: "There was a young monk from Siberia."
Limerick: "There was a young peasant named Gorse."
Limerick: "There was a young plumber of Leigh."
Limerick: "There was a young poet of Kew."
Limerick: "There was a young poet of Thusis."
Limerick: "There was a young priest of Dun Laoghaire."
Limerick: "There was a young student called Jones."
Limerick: "There was a young student of John's."
Limerick: "There was a young woman called Myrtle."
Limerick: "There was a young woman of Dee."
Limerick: "There was an archdeacon who said."
Limerick: "There was an old Bey of Calcutta."
Limerick: "There was an old fellow named Hewing."
Limerick: "There was an old fellow of Fife."
Limerick: "There was an old madam called Rainey."
Limerick: "There was an old maid of Duluth."
Limerick: "There was an old man of Boulogne."
Limerick: "There was an old man of Dundee."
Limerick: "There was an old man of [or from] Peru / Who dreamt [or dreamed] he was eating his shoe."
Limerick: "There was an old man who averred."
Limerick: "There was an old miser at [or of] Reading."
Limerick: "There was an old person of Fratton."
Limerick: "There was an old Scot called McTavish."
Limerick: "There was an Old Woman of Gloster."
Limerick: "There was an Old Woman of Lynn."
Limerick: "They say that I was in my youth."
Limerick: "Though clerical errors are fun."
Limerick: "Though his plan, when he gave her a buzz."
Limerick: "Though the limerick can not be deaded."
Limerick: "Throughout the whole world, experts say."
Limerick: "Thus spake an old Chinese mandarin."
Limerick: "To her gardener, a lady named Liliom."
Limerick: "To his bride said a numbskull named Clarence."
Limerick: "Tone-deaf old person of Tring, A."
Limerick: "Traveller to Timbuktu, A."
Limerick: "Truth about truth is elusive, The."
Limerick: "Try our Rubber Girl-Friend (air-inflatable)"
Limerick: "Two middle-aged ladies from Fordham."
Limerick: "Two she-camels spied on a goat."

Limerick: "Unfortunate lad from Madrid, An."
Limerick: "Unpopular man of Cologne, An."
Limerick: "Up the street sex is sold by the piece."
Limerick: "Vice most obscene and unsavoury, A."
Limerick: "Wanton young lady of Wimley, A."
Limerick: "We all place a great deal of reliance."
Limerick: "We've got a new maid called Chrysanthemum."
Limerick: "We've socially-conscious biography."
Limerick: "Well-buggered boy named Delpasse, A."
Limerick: "Well, I took your advice, Doc," said Knopp."
Limerick: "Well, it's partly the shape of the thing."
Limerick: "'What have I done?' said Christine."
Limerick: "When he raped a young maid in a train."
Limerick: "When I thought of this Duchess affair."
Limerick: "When Lazarus came back from the dead."
Limerick: "When the judge with his wife having sport."
Limerick: "Whenever he got in a fury, A."
Limerick: "While Titian was grinding rose madder."
Limerick: "Whilst Titian was mixing rose madder."
Limerick: "Winter is here with his grouch."
Limerick: "Yogi from far-off Beirut, A."
Limerick: "Young bride and groom of Australia, A."
Limerick: "Young girl of English nativity, A."
Limerick: "Young girl who was no good at tennis, A."
Limerick: "Young Irish servant in Drogheda, A."
Limerick: "Young man by a girl was desired, A."
Limerick: "Young man with passions quite gingery, A."
Limerick: "Young men who frequent picture palaces."
Limericks and Puns.
Lincolnshire Poacher, The.
Linen Weaver, The.
Lines are cast and the nets are set and waiting, The.
Lines from Love Letters.
Lines in the Corner of a Manuscript.
Linstead Market.
Lion over the Tomb of Leonidas, The.
Litany to Our Lady.
Little Billy Breek.
Little bird of paradise.
Little Bird, The.
Little Birds, The.
Little black dog ran round the house, The.
Little Black Rose.
Little Black Train Is A-Comin'
Little Blue Ben.
Little Blue Betty.
Little Britain.
Little by Little.
Little Chap Who Follows Me, The.
Little Dicky Dilver.
Little fishes in a brook.
Little Fred.
Little Friend.
Little General Monk.
Little Hundred.
Little Jack Dandy-prat.
Little Jack Sprat / Once had a pig.
Little Jenny Wren.
Little Jock Elliot.
Little John a Begging.
Little John Jiggy Jag.
Little John Nobody.
Little King Boggen.
Little lad, little lad.
Little lady lairdie, The.

Little Lady of Ch'ing-ch'i, The.
Little Lamb, A.
Little More Cider, A.
Little Mouse, The.
Little Musgrave and Lady Barnard.
Little old man of Derby, A.
Little Pig.
Little Poll Parrot.
Little pretty Nancy girl.
Little Random Creatures, The.
Little Rose.
Little Tee-wee.
Little Things.
Little Tom Tittlemouse / Lived in a bell-house.
Little Tommy Tacket.
Little Word, The.
Little work, a little play, A.
Lizie Lindsay.
Lo! As the Potter Mouldeth.
Lo, How a Rose E'er Blooming.
Lo, how a rose is growing.
Lo, I Am Stricken Dumb.
Lo! I have learned of the loveliest of lands.
Lo, where with flowery head and hair all brightsome.
Lo, Who Could Stand.
Lo! ye children of men and the Mother.
Lochmaben Harper, The.
Lock and Key.
Lock the dairy door.
Locust, The.
Lofty trees of the south, The.
London Bells.
London Lickpenny.
Lone Buck.
Lonesome Valley.
Long ago there was a mighty snake, and beings evil to men.
Long night: unable to sleep.
Long Time Back, A.
Look out there.
Looking-Glass for Men and Maids, A.
Loom of Time, The.
Loon I Thought It Was, A.
Loosed from Winter's prison.
Lord among the Clouds, The.
Lord Delamere.
Lord Derwentwater.
Lord, I Want to Be a Christian.
Lord Ingram and Chiel Wyet.
Lord into His Garden Comes, The.
Lord Is King, The.
Lord Jesus Christ, in whose hand is the breath.
Lord Livingston.
Lord Lovel.
Lord Maxwell's Last Goodnight.
Lord of Lorn and the False [or Fals] Steward, The.
Lord of the River.
Lord of the World.
Lord Randal.
Lord, Remember Me!
Lord Saltoun and Auchanachie.
Lord Thomas and Fair Annet.
Lord Thomas and Lady Margaret.
Lord Thomas Stuart.
Lord, thou clepedest me.
Lord William; or, Lord Lundy.
Lost for a Rose's Sake.
Lost Shoe, The.
Loudon Hill; or, Drumclog.
Louerd, thu clepedest me.
Love.
Love Charm, The.
Love-goddess, saviour / Of the sea-wrecked.
Love he to morrow, who lov'd never.
Love Is a Secret Feeding Fire.
Love Is Weal, Love Is Wo.
Love ("Love was before the light began")
Love Me Not [for Comely Grace].
Love of women leaves me cold; desire, The.
Love's Ending.
Love Secret, The.
Love Song.
Love Song: "Beautiful is she, this woman."
Love Song: "Early I rose."
Love Song: "I passed by the house of the

young man who loves me."
Love Song: "I will walk into some one's
dwelling."
Love Song: "Like pain of fire runs down my
body my love to you, my dear!"
Love Song: "Little sycamore, The."
Love-Song: "Little wild birds have come
flying, The."
Love Song: "My boat sails downstream."
Love Song: "My love is a lotus blossom."
Love Song: "My loved one is unique, without
a peer."
Love Song: "On the hill tops I visit the
snares."
Love Song: "Your handkerchief should be
blue."
Love Undeclared.
Love, Why Don't You Come.
Love Will Find Out the Way.
Lovely Étan, The.
Lovely Is the Modest Girl.
Lovely Rose Is Sprung, A.
Lovely Young Moor, A.
Lover Compareth Himself to the Painful
Falconer, The.
Lover's Arithmetic, The.
Lover's Lament [or] The Willows by the Water
Side, A.
Loving Mad Tom.
Lowlands.
Lowlands o' [or of] Holland, The.
Lowlands of Holland, The.
Lubin.
Lullabies, 2:174.
Lullaby: "O! hush thee, my darling, sleep
soundly my son."
Lullaby of Donald Gorm, by his Nurse.
Lullaby: "Puva, puva, puva."
Lullaby: "Sleep, baby, sleep."
Lullaby: "Someone would like to have you for
her child."
Lullay, lullay, litel child, child reste thee a
throwe.
Lullay, lullay, litel child, why wepest thu so
sore?
Luminous winds flicker in the moonrise.
Lusty May.
Lutel wot it any mon.
Lydia Pinkham.
Lying Down.
Lyke-Wake Dirge, The [or A].
Lyric by Nine.
Lythe and listin, gentilmen.
Mackerel sky.
Madrigal: "If that a sinner's sighs be angels'
food."
Madrigal: "My Love in her attire doth show
her wit."
Mæg ic be me sylfum so?ogied wrecan.
Maggot Song.
Magic Formula.
Magic Song.
Magic Words.
Magic Words for Hunting Caribou.
Magic Words for Hunting Seal.
Magpie, magpie, flutter and flee.
Magpies.
Maid and the Palmer, The.
Maid Freed from the Gallows, The.
Maid Mars Me, A.
Maid of Kent, A.
Maid's Complaint for Want of a Dil Doul, The.
Maiden in the Moor [or Mor], A.
Maiden moder milde.
Maiden There Lived, A.
Make Me Loathe Earthly Likings.
Make quiet, so quiet, your awesome bearing.
Make three fourths of a cross, and a circle
complete.
Make we mery bothe more and lasse.
Make Ye a Joyful Sounding Noise.
Malay Figures.
Malediction.
Malvern Waters.
Man Be Merie as Bryd on Berie.
Man, bewar of thine wowing.
Man in Our Town.

Man in the Moon.
Man in the mune, The / Is making shune.
Man meye longe him lives wene.
Man of Bombay, The.
Man of Words, A.
Man on the Flying Trapeze, The.
Man once married who hunts wife once
more, A.
Man's Song, about His Daughter, A.
Man's years fall short of a hundred.
Man United.
Man went a-hunting at Reigate, A.
Manners in the dining-room.
Marban, a Hermit Speaks.
March winds and April showers.
Maria to Henric.
Marie moder, wel thee be!
Marriage of Sir Gawain, The.
Marriage of the Frog and the Mouse, The.
Marrying Maiden, The.
Marsh's Bewilder, The.
Marsilion sees his people's martyrdom.
Mary had a little lamb.
Mary [or Marie] Hamilton.
Mary's Canary.
Mary's Dream.
Mary Suffers with Her Son.
Mary Weeps for Her Child.
Matthew, Mark, Luke and John.
Maud Fitzgerald.
Maunder's Praise of His Strowling Mort, The.
Maxim Revised, A.
Maxims (Cotton MS.)
Maxims (Exeter Book)
May Colven [or May Colvin].
"May Grace be with you all" said the bishop.
May I for my own self song's truth reckon.
May in the Green-Wood.
May Isis heal me.
May no man slepe in youre halle.
Mayden in the moor lay.
Maytime.
Mbuyazi (Henry Francis Fynn)
McNaughtan.
Me and My Captain.
Me thinks I see our mighty monarch stand.
Meaning of a Letter, The.
Meda Songs.
Medicina pro morbo caduco et le fevre.
Medicine Song of an Indian Lover.
Medicine Songs.
Medieval Norman Song.
Medieval Poem of the Nativity, A.
Meet-on-the-Road.
Meeting in the Road.
Memory Song, A.
Men's loving is a false affection.
Mena, deena, deina, duss.
Mer-Man, and Marstig's Daughter, The.
Merchant and the Fidler's Wife, The.
Mercy.
Mercy abid and loke all day.
Mermaid, The.
Merry, Merry Is My Lord.
Mervell nothyng, Joseph, that Mary be with
chyld.
Mery it is in May morning.
Message of King Sakis and the Legend of the
Twelve Dreams He Had in One Night, The.
Messe of Nonsense, A.
Metre Colombian, The.
Michael Row the Boat Ashore.
Mid-West, The.
Middelerd for mon wes mad.
Midnight Special.
Midwife's Invocation, A.
Militaris Cantio.
Milk White Doe, The.
Milla.
Millery, millery, dustipole.
Millets in full rows.
Minutes of Gold.
Mirabile Misterium.
MIRACULOUS love's wounding!
Mischievous Raven, The.
Miserere, My Maker.

Miss Buss and Miss Beale.
Miss Foggerty's Cake.
Miss One, Two, and Three.
Miss You.
Mission Work-Boat.
Mist, The.
Mocking-Bird's Song, The.
Mode of France, The.
Moder Phoebe.
Modern Love Songs.
Moll-in-the-wad and I fell out.
Money and the Mare.
Money Is What Matters.
Money, Money.
Monk, step further off.
Montague Michael.
Months Go By, The.
Months, The.
Mony klyf he overclambe in contrayes
straunge.
Moon Eclipse Exorcism.
Moon is full, The.
Moon Is Rising, The.
Moon-like Is All Other Love.
Moon, moon / Mak' me a pair o'shoon.
Moon shines bright, The.
Moon shines on valley.
Moon Sings, The.
Moon, The.
Morant Bay.
More Love.
More than the color.
Moreton Bay.
Morning.
Morning Glory, The.
Morning Prayer.
Morning's sun.
Morning Star, O Cheering Sight!
Morrigan, The.
Moses.
Most I riden by Ribbesdale.
Moth ate words; a marvellous event, A.
Mother.
Mother Dear, O! Pray for Me.
Mother, I want to go.
Mother, May I Go Out to Swim?
Mother's Choice, The.
Mother's Malison; or, Clyde's Water, The.
Mother's Song.
Mother's Song to a Baby.
Mother with the life-giving power now comes.
Motto for a Sundial.
Mountain Spirit, The.
Mouse in Her Room, A.
Mr. and Mrs. Vite's Journey.
Mr. Ibister.
Mr Nobody.
Mrs. Mason's Basin.
Mu-Lan.
Much Ado about Nothing in the City.
Much Distressed.
Mulberry Bush, The.
Mulberry by the Path.
Mulberry up the Lane.
Muse of Amergin, The.
Music and Poetry of the Indians.
Muspilli.
Musselburgh Field.
Muu's Way; or Pictures from the Uterine
World.
My Aunt Jane.
My Boy Willie.
My cares comen ever anew.
My children, when at first I liked the whites.
My Cousin German came from France.
(My Daily Creed)
My dame hath a lame tame crane.
My Dancing Day.
My Dark Night Has Come Round Again.
My Darlings' Shoes.
My Fair Lady.
My Father's Close.
My father was a Frenchman.
My grandmother sent me a new-fashioned
three-cornered cambric country-cut
handkerchief.
My grief on the ocean.

My Hairt Is Heich Aboif.
My hands are withered.
My Heart Is in Merioneth.
My heart was split, and a flower.
My Hope Is in God.
My Hope, My Love.
My Husband, Before Leaving.
My Lady Carenza of the lovely body.
My Lady Is a Pretty One.
My Last Tooth.
My Lief Is Faren in Londe.
My Little Maid.
My Little Pretty Mopsy.
My little ship, three-masted.
My Lord Is Full of Delight.
My Lord's Gone to Service.
My Love.
My Love For You.
My love forever!
My Love I Gave for Hate.
My love is falle upon a may.
My love sent me a chicken without e'er a bone.
My Lover Will Soon Be Here.
My mill grinds pepper and spice.
My Mistress.
My mistress in a hive of bees.
My mother and your mother.
My Mother's Hands.
My Neighbor's Reply.
My own dark head (my own, my own)
My passion is like turbulence at the head of waters.
My perfume?
My purpose is to tell my own true tale.
My Purse.
My Sodger Laddie.
My Soul in the Bundle of Life.
My spouse, Chunaychunay.
My Thought Was on a Maid So Bright.
Myrie a tyme I telle in May.
Myself.
Names of the Hare, The.
Nancy Dawson.
Nature's Travail.
Nauty Pauty Jack-a-Dandy.
Nay, but of such an one.
Ne hath my soule but fyr and yse.
Near the East Gate.
Needles of the lofty pine, The.
Negro Soldier's Civil War Chant.
Net of Moon, The.
Nettle.
Never Say Fail.
Never Tell.
New Moon, The.
New-slain Knight, The.
New Year Carol, A.
Newly Wed Girl, The.
Next Morning.
Nievie nievie nick nack.
Night after night, I do not.
Night and Morning.
Night before Larry Was Stretched, The.
Night Chant, The.
Night passes on, and the bright day appears.
Night so.
Night Was Growing Cold, The.
Night Without End.
Nightfall.
Nile the Hermit.
Nine Lyric Poets, The.
Nine Times a Night.
Niobe.
No Balls at All.
No Cold Approach.
No lake is so still but that it has its wave.
No money yet, why then let's terrify with swords.
No More Auction Block.
No More beneath the Oppressive Hand.
No More Booze.
No more ne will I wicked be.
No One Will Put the Cid up. Only a Small Girl Addresses Him and That to Tell Him to Go Away. The Cid Finds He Has to Make Camp Outside of Town, on the Sand of the

Riverbank.
No ring, no Wedding.
No sickness worse than secret love.
No weather is ill.
Noble Fisherman; or, Robin Hood's Preferment, The.
Noble sighed ceaselessly in restless slumber, The.
Nobody Knows de Trouble I've Seen.
Nobody Knows the Trouble I've Had.
Noise of the Village, The.
Nonsense.
North-East.
Northern har, A.
Northumberland Betray[e]d by Douglas [or Dowglas].
Northwest the tall tower stands.
Not Much Talking.
Not of Itself but Thee.
Not to Us, Not unto Us, Lord.
Nottamun Town.
Now.
Now! The Red Tobacco has come to strike your soul.
Now bernes, buirdes, bolde and blithe.
Now every man at my request.
Now Fade the Rose and Lily-Flower.
Now for that slawnders sake.
Now Goeth [or goth or goothe] Sun [or Sonne or Sunne] under Wood.
Now goth sonne under wode.
Now Help Us, Lord.
Now I Lay Me down to Take My Sleep.
Now Is the Month of Maying.
Now Roland feels that he is at death's door.
Now skrinketh rose and lilie-flour.
Now springes the spray.
Now that the fragrance.
Now thise foweles syngen and maken her blisse.
Now we flourish / as others have / before.
Now we have heard stories of high valor.
Now what do you think.
Now will I open unto thee—whose heart.
Nowel, el, el, el, el!
Nowell Sing We.
Noye, to me thou arte full able.
Nu thu, unsely body, upon bere list.
Nut-brown Maid, The.
Nut Tree, A.
Nuts an' May.
O Christ, our hope, our heart's desire, Redeption's only spring!
O Come, All Ye Faithful.
O come, O come, Emmanuel.
"O Cormac, grandson of Conn," said Carbery.
O Earnest Be.
O excellent sovereigne, most semely to see.
O flowers of Mekhmekh, give us peace!
O Fortune.
O[h], Dear! What Can the Matter Be?
O happy hour.
O Heavens!
O I hae tint my rosy cheek.
O I'm a jolly old cowboy.
O King of the Friday.
O Lamb Give Me My Salt.
O Lord, Almighty God.
O Lord, How Lovely Is the Place.
O Lord, Save We Beseech Thee.
O Lord, Thou Hast Been to the Land.
O Magnificent and Many.
O, Magyar.
'O, My Heart Is Woe.'
"O my Joseph, Jacob's son."
O, No, John [or The One Answer].
O restless, caressing eyes.
O Ride On, Jesus.
O sea-gulls that are crying.
O the little rusty dusty miller.
O thow archbishop and metropolitan.
O You Jolly Augustine.
Oak and the Ash, The.
Oath of Friendship.
Ode on Gas, An.
Ode to a Ditch.
Ode to a Jacobin.

Ode to the German Drama.
Of a little take a little.
Of a mon Matheu thoghte.
Of a Rose, a Lovely Rose.
Of all the sayings in this world.
Of all the seas that's coming.
Of alle the enemies that I can fynde.
Of Jesu Christ I Sing.
Of Sir Frauncis Walsingham Sir Phillipp Sydney, and Sir Christopher Hatton, Lord Chancelor.
Of this day's glorious feast and revel.
Of Three Friendly Warnings This Is the Second.
Of Three Friendly Warnings This Is the Third.
Of Tyndarus, That Frumped a Gentlewoman.
Off Womanheid Ane Flour Delice.
Oft in the hall I have heard my people.
Oh Cruel Was the Press-Gang.
Oh, Dear!
Oh! Fucking Halkirk.
Oh! the time that is past.
Oh! What is the matter?
Oh moon, oh moon!
Oh My Own Little Daughter, Four Years Old.
Oh send to me an apple that hasn't any kernel.
Oh that I were / Where I would be.
Oh Trial.
Ojibwa War Songs.
Ol' Clothes.
Old and New.
Old Boniface he loved good cheer.
Old *Chüeh-chü.*
Old Doctor Foster.
Old Farmer Giles.
Old Father Greybeard.
Old Folks' Room, The.
Old Forty-five Per Cent.
Old Joe.
Old Joe Clark.
Old Lady of Harrow, An.
Old maid, an old maid, An.
Old Man from Darjeeling.
Old Man Know-All.
Old Man of Nantucket, The.
Old Man's Complaint, The.
Old Man's Song, about His Wife, The.
Old Marse John.
Old Mother Niddity Nod.
Old Mother Shuttle.
Old Mother, The.
Old [or Ould] Orange Flute, The.
Old Poem.
Old Robin of Portingale.
Old Roger.
Old-Saxon Fragment.
Old Section Boss, The.
Old Sir Simon the king.
Old Song.
Old Song of Rejoicing, An.
Old-Time Religion.
Old Woman from France, The.
Old woman must stand, The.
Old Woman of Beare Regrets Lost Youth, The.
Old Woman of Beare, The.
Old Woman of Gloucester, The.
Old Woman of Harrow.
Old Woman of Leeds, The.
Old woman was sweeping her house, and she found, An.
Old woman went to market and bought a pig, An.
Ole Sheep Dey Know de Road, De.
Oliver's climbed upon a hilly crest.
Omagh Post Office Rhyme.
Omens.
Omens on the Road to Burgos.
Omnes Gentes Plaudite!
On a Clergyman's Horse Biting Him.
On a Female Rope-Dancer.
On a Gentleman's Complaining to a Lady That He Could Not Eat Meat.
On a New Duke.
On a Nomination to the Legion of Honour.
On a Small Bath.
On a Statue of Pan.
On a Worthless Politician.

On an Old Woman Who Sold Pots.
On and on, always on and on.
On Asuka River.
On Board Starship *Enterprise*.
On Bond the Usurer.
On Button the Grave-Maker.
On Buying a Horse.
On Christians, Mercy Will Fall.
On Christmas Eve I turned the spit.
On Dr. Evans Cutting Down a Row of Trees.
On Dr. Lettsom.
On Eleanor Freeman, Who Died 1650, Aged 21.
On Elizabeth Ireland.
On Epiktetos the Stoic.
On hire is al my lyf ylong.
On His Mistress Going from Home [Song].
On How the Cobler.
On Jocky Bell.
On John So.
On Komochi Mountain.
On Late-acquired Wealth *or* Riches.
On May-day, when the lark began to rise.
On Meeting a Gentlewoman in the Dark.
On Meeting——, Esq., in St. James's Park.
On Melancholy.
On Mike O'Day.
On Mr. Pricke.
On Plato's Grave.
On Prince Frederick.
On Queen Caroline.
On Rÿneveld, an Unpopular Dutch Judge.
On Sir John Calf.
On the Athenians Who Died at the Hellespont, 440–39 B.C.
On the Bible.
On The Death of King Matthias.
On the Death of Mr. Persall's Little Daughter, in the Beginning of the Spring, at Amsterdam.
On the Death of Mr. Pope.
On the Death of Old Bennet the News-Crier.
On the Death of the Great Chef Alexis Soyer.
On the Death of the Lord Treasurer.
On the Earl of Leicester.
On the Meetings of the Scotch Covenanters.
On the offering mound, a dead roe.
On the Reverend Jonathan Doe.
On the Slope of Hua Mountain.
On the Statue of Epaminondas in Thebes.
On the Welch.
On Tom Holland and Nell Cotton.
On Tom-o-Combe.
On Tomato Ketchup.
On William Wilson, Tailor.
Once Did My Thoughts.
Once in our lives, / Let us drink to our wives.
Once, twice, thrice / I give thee warning.
One-erum, two-erum.
One-ery, two-ery, [*or* ore-ery], ickery, Ann.
One-ery, two-ery, tickery, seven.
One for Coyote.
One for money.
One for sorrow, two for joy.
One, he loves; two, he loves.
One Horse Chay, The.
One I love, two I love.
One Little Boy.
One misty moisty morning.
One More River.
One of the Awl Songs.
One son of God, The.
One thing at a time.
One, Two, Three, Four, Five!
One to Ten.
One, two, three, / I love coffee.
One, two, whatever you do.
One who first gave birth to our people, The.
'One with this world.'
One Writing against His Prick.
Only Jealousy of Emer, The.
Only One Life.
Only rule is enjoy yourself, The.
Only Way to Have a Friend, The.
Open the Gates.
Orange Lily, The.
Oranges and lemons, say the bells of St.

Clement's.
Orchid Door, The.
Origin-Legend of the Chou Tribe.
Origin of the Snake, The.
Oriki Erinle.
Orphan, The.
Oshun, the River Goddess.
Other Side of the Valley, The.
Other World, The.
Our Father, Our King.
Our Flag.
Our Goodman.
Our Lady's Song.
Our Little Sister is Worried.
Our love is infinite.
Out the southern gate at sundown.
Outgoing Sabbath.
Outlaw Murray, The.
Outlaw of Loch Lene, The.
Over the Hills and Far Away.
Over the reeds the.
Over the water and over the lea [*or* sea].
Overlander, The.
Owl / whose home was in the hemlock, The.
Owl Woman's Death Song.
Oxaitoq's Song.
Paddling Song.
Pan in Battle.
Panchatantra, The.
Pangur Ban.
Panther, The.
Papa's Letter.
Parcy Reed.
Parting Is Hard.
Parting of the Red Sea, The.
Pass Office Song.
Pastoral, A: "There went out in the dawning light."
Path of Independence, The.
Patience is a virtue.
Pawnee War-Song.
Peace.
Peace Be Still.
Peace is made with a warlike man.
Peace Maketh Plenty.
Peach Tree Young and Fresh.
Peacock Southeast Flew, A.
Pear-Tree, The.
Peas.
Penal Servitude for Mrs. Maybrick.
Penny.
Penny and penny.
Penny lost in the lak, The.
Perle, plesaunte to prynces paye.
Pessimist, The.
Petelia Tablet, The.
Petition to Father and Son and Holy Ghost, A.
Pettitoes are little feet, The.
Phebus fonde first the craft of medecine.
Philippine Figures.
Phillida Flouts Me [*or* The Disdainful Shepherdess].
Pick ferns, pick ferns.
Picking Rushes.
Pieces of Snot.
Pig, The.
Piggish young person from Leeds, A.
Pilgrimage Song.
Pilgrims in Mexico.
Pilot's Psalm, The.
Pindarick To Mrs. Behn on her Poem on the Coronation, A.
Pinionjay shits pebbles.
Piper o' Dundee, The.
Pitman's Lovesong, A.
Place of the Fian is bare tonight, The.
Plain Dealing's Downfall.
Plain of Adoration, The.
Plaint of the Wife, The.
Planting Initiation Song.
Playing the Game.
Pleasant Songs of the Sweetheart Who Meets You in the Fields.
Pleasant the House.
Please, Chung Tzu.
Please, Sir Second-born.
Pluck Wins.

Plucking The Rushes.
Plum flowers all fallen and gone.
Plum Tree Drops Its Fruit, The.
Po, po, po, po.
Poem about a Wolf Maybe Two Wolves, A.
Poem for Jacqueline Hill.
Poem of Medicine Puns.
Poem to Answer the Question: How Old Are Fleas?
Poem to Be Recited Every 8 Years While Eating Unleavened Tamales.
Poem to Ease Birth.
Poem to the Mother of the Gods, A.
Poem Written in Time of Trouble by an Irish Priest Who Had Taken Orders in France, A.
Poems for the Game of Silence.
Poet Dreamt of Heaven, The.
Poet's Prayer, The.
Poet's Request, The.
Poetess's Bouts-Rimés, The.
Pointless Pride of Man, The.
Polly Perkins.
Polly Wolly Doodle.
Pomegranate speaks, The.
Pomelo, The.
Poor Adam and Eve were from Eden turned out.
Poor Girl's Meditation, The.
Poor Lazarus.
Poor Old Lady.
Poor Paddy Works on the Railway.
Poor Wayfaring Stranger.
Popol Vuh, The.
Popular Songs of Tuscany.
Portrait of a Stupid Teacher of Rhetoric.
Postscript to Verses on the History of France, A.
Potter, The.
Poussie, poussie, baudrons.
Poverty Knock.
Pox on't, says Time to Thomas Hearne.
Praise of God.
Praise Song for the Oba of Benin.
Praises of the Canna, The.
Prayer for Every Day.
Prayer for Redemption.
Prayer for the Journey.
Prayer for the Speedy End of Three Great Misfortunes.
Prayer of a Woman in Charge of Berry Picking in Knights Inlet.
Prayer to the God Thot.
Prayer to the Gods of the Night.
Prayer to the Sockeye Salmon.
Prayer upon Cutting down the Sacred Tree.
Prayer yo Hymen.
Prelude to Akwasidae.
Present to a Lady, A.
Preston.
Priapus Poems, The.
Pride is his pity, artifice his praise.
Priest of Felton.
Prince Eugene.
Prince Heathen.
Prince Robert.
Prognostication on Will Laud, Late Archbishop of Canterbury, A.
Promises of Freedom.
Proper Song, Entitled: Fain Would I Have a Pretty Thing to Give unto My Lady, A.
Prophetic Powers.
Proud in Thy Love.
Proud Lady Margaret.
Proud Margret.
Proud Queen of the Earth Gods, Supreme among the Heaven Gods.
Proverb.
Proverbial Advice on Marriage.
Psalm 58.
Psalm 137.
Psalm of Battle.
Puberty Rite Dance Song (Traditional)
Purity of the moonlight, The.
Purple, yellow, red and green.
Pushan, God of Pasture.
Puss came dancing out of a barn.
Pussicat, wussicat, with a white foot.

Pussy-Cat Mew.
Pussy Cat Mole.
Put your finger in Foxy's hole.
Putting on Nightgown.
Quaco Sam.
Quaker's wife got up to bake, The.
Queen Eleanor's Confession.
Queen Nefertiti.
Queen of Elfan's [or Elfland's] Nourice [or Nourrice], The.
Queen of Scotland, The.
Queen, Queen Caroline.
Queen's Dream, The.
Queen's Marie, The.
Queen wept but thought: It is not appropriate to show such grief, The.
Question, A.
Quhy Sowld Nocht Allane Honorit Be?
Quia Amore Langueo.
Quiet Mind, The.
Qwhen Alexander our kynge was dede.
Raid of the Reidswire, The.
Railroad Blues, The.
Railroad Cars Are Coming, The.
Railroad Man for Me, A.
Railroad Section Leader's Song.
Rain before [or Raan afoor] seven.
Rain, rain, go away.
Rain Song of the Quer'ränna Chai'än, A.
Rain Song of the Shu'-wi Chai'än (Snake Society), A.
Rain, The.
Rainbow i'th'morning.
Raise a "Rucus" To-Night.
Rakes of Mallow, The.
Rapier of Treason, A.
Rare sight, a woman lost in the trance.
Rare Willie Drowned in Yarrow; or, The Water o Gamrie.
Rat, The.
Ratcatcher's Daughter, The.
Rath in front of the oak wood, The.
Rebuke to Robert Southey, A.
Receipt to Cure a Love Fit, A.
Red Cloud's Song.
Red sky at night [is the shepherd's delight], A.
Red stockings, blue stockings.
Redesdale and Wise William.
Reid in the Loch Sayis, The.
Rejoice, O Bridegroom!
Remeidis of Luve.
Remember, Sinful Youth.
Remember that night.
Removal, The.
Reply, A.
Resplendent studs of heaven's frame.
Rest.
Restored Terrace is new and fresh, The.
Return from Battle.
Revolutionaries, The.
Rhyme from Lincolnshire, A.
Rich Is the Year with Much Millet and Rice.
Richard Dick upon a stick.
Richie Story.
Richmond Gardens: A Poem.
Riddle: "As I went down that yella bank."
Riddle: "As I went through a guttery gap / I met a wee man with a red cap."
Riddle: "As I went through yon guttery gap / I met my Uncle Davy."
Riddle: "Black'm saut'm rough'm glower'm saw."
Riddle: "Chip chip cherry."
Riddle: "Cuckoo and the gowk, The."
Riddle: "He went to the wood and caught it."
Riddle: "Hickamore hackamore."
Riddle: "High as the sky it flies."
Riddle: "Highty, tighty, paradighty, clothed [all] in green."
Riddle: "Hopper o'ditches, A."
Riddle: "House full, [a] yard full, [A]."
Riddle: "It has a head like a cat, feet like a cat."
Riddle: "Land was white, The."
Riddle: "Little trotty hetty coat."
Riddle: "Lives in winter."
Riddle: "Long slick black feller."

Riddle: "Riddle a riddle as I suppose, A."
Riddle: "Riddlum riddlum ranty pole."
Riddle: "Round the house and round the house / and there lies a black glove in the window."
Riddle: "Round the house and round the house / and there lies a white glove in the window."
Riddle: "Shoemaker makes shoes without leather, A."
Riddle: "White bird featherless."
Riddle: "White sheep, white sheep, on a blue hill."
Riddle: "Wooden belly iron back."
Riddles.
Riddles Wisely Expounded.
Riddling Knight, The.
Ride a cock-horse to Banbury Cross / To buy little Johnny a galloping horse.
Ride a cock-horse to Banbury Cross / To see what Tommy can buy.
Rigadoon, rigadoon, now let him fly.
Right best beloved and most in assurance.
Ring That Controlled Erections, The.
Ripe Plums.
Rise and Progress of the Present Taste in Planning Parks, Pleasure Grounds, Gardens, etc, The.
Rising in the North, The.
River, The.
Rob Roy.
Robin-a-Bobbin.
Robin and a robin's son, A.
Robin Goodfellow.
Robin Hood.
Robin Hood and Allen [or Allin] -a-Dale.
Robin Hood and Guy of Gisborne.
Robin Hood and Little John.
Robin Hood and Maid Marian.
Robin Hood and Queen Katherine.
Robin Hood and the Beggar, I.
Robin Hood and the Beggar, II.
Robin Hood and the Bishop.
Robin Hood and the Bishop of Hereford.
Robin Hood and the Butcher.
Robin Hood and the Curtal Friar.
Robin Hood and the Golden Arrow.
Robin Hood and the Monk.
Robin Hood and the Pedlars.
Robin Hood and the Potter.
Robin Hood and the Prince of Aragon.
Robin Hood and the Ranger.
Robin Hood and the Scotchman.
Robin Hood and the Shepherd.
Robin Hood and the Tanner.
Robin Hood and the Tinker.
Robin Hood and the Valiant Knight.
Robin Hood's Progress to Nottingham.
Robin Hood Newly Revived.
Robin Hood Rescuing Three Squires.
Robin Hood Rescuing Will Stutly.
Robin Hood's Birth, Breeding, Valor, and Marriage.
Robin Hood's Chase.
Robin Hood's Death.
Robin Hood's Delight.
Robin Hood's Golden Prize.
Robinets and Jenny Wrens.
Robyn and Gandeleyn.
Rock, Ball, Fiddle.
Rock O' My Soul.
Roman Earl, The.
Roman Numerals.
Romance of Love.
Romans, I appeal to you.
Roncevalles.
Rookhope Ryde.
Rooks, The.
Room for a Jovial Tinker: Old Brass to Mend.
Rose and grape, pear and bean.
Rose is red, the grass is green, The.
Rose is red, the rose is white, The.
Rose is red, the violet's blue, The.
Rose of England, The.
Rose That Bore Jesu, The.
Rose the Red and White Lil[l]y.
Roses are red.

Round about, round about, / Catch a wee mouse.
Round about, round about, here sits the hare.
Round about, round about, / maggotty pie.
Round about the rosebush.
Round about there / Sat a little hare.
Round and round the cornfield.
Round and round the garden.
Round and round the rugged rock.
Roy Bean.
Royal health to the Rising Sun, The.
"Rufinianus" was once just Rufus.
Ruin, The.
Rumpty-iddity, row, row, row.
Run, Nigger, Run!
Rural Dance about the Maypole, The.
Rye Whiskey.
Sacrament of the Altar, The.
Sacred Formula to Destroy Life.
Sad, lost in thought, and mute I go.
Sad Song.
Sad Story of a Little boy That Cried, The.
Sadness in Spring.
Saga of Gisli, The.
Sailor, ask not whose this tomb.
Sailor Boy's Song.
Sailors, I wish you safety on sea and land.
St. Dunstan, as the story goes.
Saint Patrick's Breastplate.
St. Thomas's Day is past and gone.
Sally go round the sun.
Sally, Sally Waters.
Salve Regina.
Sam [or Samuel] Hall.
Sam, Sam, the butcher man.
Sandy he belongs to the mill.
Sandy Kildandy.
Sang of the Outlaw Murray, The.
Satire.
Satire: "This way of writing I observed by some."
Sâvitrî; or, Love and Death.
Saxons of Flint, The.
Say, Dwarf, for it seems to me.
Say well and do well.
Scarborough Fair.
Scaring Crows.
Scholar and the Cat, The.
Scholar's Life, The.
Schoolboy's Lot, A.
Scissors and string, scissors and string.
Scones.
Scottsboro.
Seafarer.
Season Song.
Second Honeymoon.
Second Merseburg Spell.
Second Shepherd's Play, The.
SECRET murder hath been done of late.
See a pin and pick it up.
See columns rang'd in proud Palladian style!
See! Here, My Heart.
See-saw, down in my lap.
See-saw, Margery Daw.
See-saw, Margery Daw, / Sold her bed and lay upon straw.
See the great vultures.
See the Rat—at Least It's Got a Hide.
See there, that tree is a digging stick.
Seize the moment!
Seized with a sudden fancy for fresh meat.
Self-Examination, The.
Send Him Back Hard by Your Lady's Small Window.
Senful man, bethink and see.
Serenade: "Come now, and let us wake them: time."
Serenader, The.
Servant-Girl's Holiday, A.
Seven, The.
Seven Sins, The.
Seven Songs and Song Pictures.
Seven Virgins, The.
Seven Wonders of North Wales, The.
Shades of the Newly Buried Complain to the Gods, The.
Shady Grove.

Shaka, King of the Zulus.
Shall we stay in the.
Shalom Aleichem.
Shan Van Vocht, The.
Shango.
Shari Wag El Burka.
She Hugged Me and Kissed Me.
She Lay All Naked.
She likes it, the conjugal act.
She said she don't love me anymore because I drink whiskey.
She Says, Cocks Are Crowing!
She Sells Sea-shells.
She Smiled like a Holiday.
She stood in her scarlet gown.
She talks not, plays not, visits not, in bed.
She Was Poor but She Was Honest.
She Who First Bore Our People.
She Will Gather Roses.
Shearing, The.
Sheath and Knife.
Sheepheards Description of Love, The.
Shema Yisrael.
Shickered As He Could Be.
Shine and the *Titanic*.
Ship's Nail, A.
Ship That Sails, The.
Shirt of a Lad, The.
Shoe a little horse.
Shoe the little horse.
Shoemakker, The.
Shon a Morgan.
Shooting of His Dear.
Shootingway Ceremony Prayer.
Short and Sweet Sonnet Made by One of the Maids of Honour, upon the Death of Queen Elizabeth, which She Sewed upon a Sampler, in Red Silke, A.
Should I believe you, e'en my oaths are witty.
Shu Has Gone Hunting.
Shu is away in the hunting-fields.
Siesta, The.
Signifying Monkey, The.
Silk / Satin.
Silly Boy.
Silver Swan, The.
Simon and Susan.
Simple Ploughboy, The.
Simple Rustic You Seemed, A.
Since Bonny-Boots Was Dead.
Since First I Saw Your Face.
Since I'm a girl.
Since the night is dark.
Sing Ivy.
Sing, My Soul.
Sioux Metamorphoses.
Sir Aldingar.
Sir Andrew Bart[t]on.
Sir Cawline.
Sir Colin.
Sir Dilberry Diddle, Captain of Militia.
Sir Gawain and the Green Knight.
Sir Hugh; or, The Jew's Daughter.
Sir Isaac Newton.
Sir James the Rose.
Sir John Butler.
Sir Lionel.
Sir Patrick Spens [*or* Spence].
Sir, so suspicious.
Sir Walter Raleigh Sailing in the Lowlands.
Sister, Awake!
Sith al that in this world hath ben in rerum natura.
Six to Six.
Sixth Song of the Holy Young Men.
Sixty-Six Poems for a Blackfoot Bundle.
Skin the Goat's Curse on Carey.
Sky Clears, The.
Sky is a dark bowl, the stars die and fall, The.
Sky is strewn with stars, The.
Sky, The.
Slaughter of the Laird of Mellerstain, The.
Slave Girl's Song.
Slave Marriage Ceremony Supplement.
Sleep, baby, sleep.
Sleep, baby, sleep / Our cottage vale is deep.
Sleeper, The.

Slender Lad, The.
Sluggy and slowe, in spetinge muiche.
Small bird, forgive me.
Smile, A.
Smoke-Blackened Smiths.
Snail, snail, put out your horns.
Sneezing.
Snoring Bedmate, The.
Snow, snow faster.
Snowman, The.
Snowy Day, A.
So faire, so fressh, so goodly on-to see.
So Hrothgar's men lived happy in his hall.
So it is because.
So plentiful, the babes-in-a-pot.
So small are the flowers of Seamu.
So soon. Today, love, we.
So well is me begone.
Sodeynly affrayed, half wakyng, half slepyng.
Soldier brave, sailor true.
Soldier's Song.
Soldier's Tale, The.
Soldier stood at the pearly gate.
Soldier That Has Seen Service, The.
Soldier, Won't You Marry Me?
Soldiers.
Soldiers' Chorus from Faust.
Some folks in looks take so much pride.
Some say the deil's deid.
Somebody.
Somebody's Mother.
Somer is comen and winter gon.
Somer is comen with love to toune.
Sometimes I feel like a motherless child.
Sometimes I Go about Pitying Myself.
Sometimes I sauntered from my lone abode.
Son David.
Song, A: "My head on moss reclining."
Song, A: "While a thousand fine projects are planned ev'ry day."
Song about a Dead Person—or Was It a Mole, A?
Song and Poetry.
Song: "At the center of the earth."
Song Bewailing the Time of Christmas, So Much Decayed in England, A.
Song Cycle of the Moon-Bone.
Song for a Fallen Warrior.
Song for a Girl on Her First Menstruation.
Song for a Scalp Dance.
Song for a Young Girl's Puberty Ceremony.
Song for Fine Weather.
Song for Joseph.
Song for the Dead, III.
Song for the Newborn.
Song for the Sun That Disappeared behind the Rainclouds.
Song: "Hang sorrow, cast away care."
Song: "I keep running around."
Song: "I'm living in a cave."
Song I sing of my sea adventure, A.
Song: "In the middle of the sea."
Song: "Know what I'll promise you?"
Song: "Might have known it."
Song: "Mother Mother shave me."
Song: "Now and then there will arise."
Song Inscribed on an Earthenware Vessel.
Song of a Marriageable Girl.
Song of a Woman Abandoned by the Tribe.
Song of an Old Gray Wolf.
Song of Bekotsidi, The.
Song of Blodeuwedd, The.
Song of Crede, The.
Song of Lewes, The.
Song of Lo-fu, The.
Song of My Song, in Three Parts, A.
Song of Parable, A.
Song of Parents Who Want to Wake up Their Son.
Song of Sixpence.
Song of Sorrow.
Song of Starvation.
Song of Summer.
Song of the Bald Eagle.
Song of the Bear.
Song of the Black Bear, The.
Song of the Boatswain of Yüeh.

Song of the Breaking of the Willow.
Song of the Crab Medicine-Bag.
Song of the Dew.
Song of the Elk.
Song of the English Bowmen.
Song of the Fallen Deer.
Song of the Fire-Charm.
Song of the Flood.
Song of the Galley, The.
Song of the Graves, The.
Song of the Gun.
Song of the Horse.
Song of the Ill-Married.
Song of the Lenape Warriors Going against the Enemy, The.
Song of the Lioness for Her Cub.
Song of the Little Miss by the Green Rill.
Song of the Man Who Succeeded.
Song of the Narcissus, The.
Song of the Old Woman.
Song of the Open Road, A.
Song of the Owl.
Song of the Pheasant.
Song of the Pleiades.
Song of the Poor Man.
Song of the Promise of the Buffalo.
Song of the Prophet.
Song of the Rain Chant.
Song of the Red & Green Buffalo, A.
Song of the Rising Sun Dance.
Song of the Seeress.
Song of the Snow-white Heads.
Song of the Stars, The.
Song of the Thunders.
Song of the Transportationist, The.
Song of the Trees.
Song of the Viet Boatman.
Song of the Weasel.
Song of the White Man.
Song of Tzu-yeh.
Song: "Red young men under the ground, The."
Song Set by John Farmer.
Song: "Sound is fading out."
Song: "Sure thing / I'm a spirit!"
Song: The Railway Train.
Song to a Child.
Song to a Lover.
Song to Bring Fair Weather.
Song to Promote Growth.
Song to the Mountains.
Song to the Runaway Slave.
Song to the Trees and Streams.
Song: "Water's flowing."
Song: "We raise de wheat."
Song: "When I show up."
Song: "When the water's calm."
Song: "Yellow dust drifts down the road to Ch'ang-an."
Songe bewailing the tyme of Christmas, So much decayed in Englande, A.
Songs and Chants.
Songs from the Great Feast to the Dead.
Songs of Courtship.
Songs of Spirits.
Songs of the Arapaho.
Songs of the Kiowa.
Songs of the Paiute.
Songs of the Sacred Mysteries.
Songs of the Sioux.
Songs to Welcome the Society of the Mystic Animals.
Sons d'un Cornet, Li.
Soon I Will Be Done.
Sophocles.
Sorrow.
Sorrow of Kodio, The.
Soul's Desire, The.
Sound Advice.
Soup Kitchen Song.
South Mount Soaring High.
South of the Great Sea.
South of the Yangtze.
Southeast the Peacock Flies.
Southern Blues.
Southern Paiute Poetry.
Sovereign soul, The / Of him who lives self-

governed and at peace.
Spanish Ladies.
Sparrow-Hawk, A.
Specimens of Indian Songs.
Speeding carriage climbs through eastern
gate, A.
Spell, A.
Spell against Predatory Animals.
Spell against Twisting an Ankle.
Spell for Making the First Man.
Spin, Dame, spin.
Spirit of Plato.
Spirit Song.
Spoils of Annwn, The.
Spoken by Venus on Seeing Her Statue Done
by Praxiteles.
Spoken Extempore on the Death of Mr. Pope.
Spring.
Spring breeze stirs a springtime heart.
Spring Fiord.
Spring from the earth, food for our children.
Give us good health. Let us grow up, and
become ripe.
Spring garlands the earth with leaves.
Spring in the Bronx.
Spring Song.
Spring Song from 'Tzu-Yeh' Songs of the Four
Seasons.
Spring under a Thorn, The.
Springfield Mountain.
Spyglass Conversations.
Squire and Milkmaid; or, Blackberry Fold.
Squirrel, The.
St. Andrew's Voyage to Mermedonia.
St Jerome and His Lion.
St. Paul's Steeple.
St. Stephen and King Herod.
St. Swithin's Day, if thou dost rain.
Stackalee.
Stagolee.
Stand out, maids, and look on the land of
Cynddylan.
Standing beside you, fiddler.
Stanza: "What, my Lord, shall I do with."
Stars Begin to Fall.
Stars Stand Up in the Air, The.
Start, The.
Starving to Death on a Government Claim.
State of Arkansas, The.
Statesmen, in your exalted station know.
Steadfast a lamp burns sheltered from the
wind.
Steal Away to Jesus.
Stealing of Apollo's Cattle, The.
Sthenelais.
Stiff winds blow.
Stond well, moder, under Rode.
Stone Castle Music.
Stop! Don't touch me.
Stormalong!
Strange Visitor, The.
Streams of Bunclody, The.
Streams of Lovely Nancy, The.
Strength for To-Day.
Stringybark Cockatoo, The.
Strip Me Naked, or Royal Gin for Ever; A
Picture.
Student, The.
Substituted Poem of Laureate Quynh, The.
Success.
Such Is the Grief of the Grey-Haired Man.
Suffolk Miracle, The.
Sukey [or Suky], you shall be my wife.
Sumer Is Icumen [or Ycomen] In.
Summe men sayen that I am blac.
Summer.
Summer Is Gone.
Summer Niight.
Summer Song.
Summer Sunday.
Sun and Moon So High and Bright, The.
Song of Lo-fu, The.
Sun sinks low, The.
Sunrise Sequence.
Sunshine and Music.
Sunshiny shower, A.
Sure, a little bit of shrapnel fell from out the

sky one day.
Sure Test, A.
Surprise, Surprise.
Susannah and the Elders.
Suspiria.
Swallow flies away, The.
Swallow sings "Dawn," The.
Swampland Mulberries Are Lovely.
Swan Sequence, The.
Swan, The.
Swarm of Bees, A.
Sweat-House Ritual No. 1.
Sweet Betsey from Pike.
Sweet, Let Me Go!
Sweet nymph, come to thy lover.
Sweet Polly Oliver.
Sweet Suffolk Owl.
Sweet Was the Song.
Sweet William's Ghost or Sweet William and
May Margaret.
Sweet Willie.
Sweetest Thing, The.
Sweetness.
Swete Jesu, king of blisse.
Swete sone, reu on me.
Swift Is That Falcon.
Swing Low, Sweet Chariot.
Swinging.
Synge we alle and seye we thus.
Tae titly.
Taffy was born.
Tailor of Bicester.
Táin, The.
Taisigh Agat Fein Do Phog.
Tak' Your Auld Cloak about Ye.
Take a Whiff on Me.
Take My Hand, Precious Lord.
Take my song of love to heart.
Tale I frame shall be found to tally.
Tale of Lord Lovell, The.
Tale of Sigemund, The.
Talk not of strength, till your heart has known.
Talmud, The.
Tam Lin.
Tam o' the linn cam up the gait.
Tammy Messer.
Tamping Ties.
Tantric Praise of the Goddess.
Tarpauling Jacket.
Tatar Songs.
Tatton Parachute Training School.
Tayis Bank.
Tchirek Song (Northern Yueh-Fu)
Te Deum, The.
Teddy Bear, Teddy Bear.
Tehkarihhoken! / Continue to listen!
Tell Her So.
Tell Him, O Night.
Tell me.
Tell Me, Wight in the Broom.
Temper.
Temujin Becomes Chingis Khan.
Ten Commandments, Seven Deadly Sins, and
Five Wits.
Ten little nigger boys went out to dine.
Tepehua Thought-Songs.
Terence McDiddler.
Thai passit in thare pilgramage.
Thair is nocht ane Winche.
Thank God!
Thank You: A Poem in Seventeen Parts.
Thanks and a Plea to Mary.
Thanksgivings, The.
That Broad and Spreading Sweet Pear.
That Cypress Boat Is Drifting.
That Hypocrite.
That mayden mylde hir childe dide kepe.
That Mountain Far Away.
That peachtree so frail.
That's a rich man coming.
That the earth be made safer for men, and
more stable.
Thatcher of Thatchwood went to Thatchet a-
thatching, A.
Theh Thet Hi Can Wittes Fule-Wis.
Thei I singe and murthes make.
Then the drawbridge came down, and the thick

gates.
Thenk, man, of min harde stundes.
Theophilus Thistledown.
Ther bloweth a cold wynd to-day, to-day.
There are flowers of Zait in the garden.
There are four Graces, two Aphrodites, ten
Muses.
There are three who await my death.
There in the flower garden.
There Is a Balm in Gilead.
There is a greater charm to me.
There Is a Lady Sweet and Kind.
There Is a Mystery in Human Hearts.
There is a soldier on the battlefield.
There is smoke above the hawks in the hall of
the king.
There is so much of loneliness.
There Once Was a Spinster of Ealing.
There once was a time.
There's No Lust like to Poetry.
There's Someone I Think Of.
There was a girl in our town.
There Was a King.
There was a king met a king.
There Was a Lady Loved a Swine.
There was a little boy went into a barn.
There was a little maid, and she was afraid.
There was a little man.
There was a little one-eyed gunner.
There Was a Man and He Was Mad.
There was a man, and his name was Dob.
There was a man, he went mad.
There was a man of double deed.
There was a man rode through our town.
There was a man who had no eyes.
There Was a Monkey.
There was a rat, for want of stairs.
There was a stange student from Yale.
There was a thing a full month old.
There was a wee bit wifie.
There was a young lady called Dawes.
There was a young lady of Riga.
There was a young man of Bengal.
There was an old crow.
There was an old man / And he had a calf.
There was an old man of Tobago.
There Was an Old Woman.
There was an old woman / And nothing she
had.
There was an old woman had three cows.
There was an old woman, her name was Peg.
There was an old woman / Lived under a hill /
And if she's not gone.
There was an old woman / Sold puddings and
pies.
There was an old woman / Who lived in
Dundee.
There was an owl lived in an oak.
There were three cooks of Colebrook.
There were three sisters in a hall.
There were two royal children.
There were two wrens upon a tree.
Therefore, who doeth work rightful to do.
"There's not a husband whom storms don't
benight."
Theris, whose hands were cunning.
These Women Plunder My Husband.
They arm themselves with Saracen hauberks.
They Fought South of the Wall.
They have crucified their Lord afresh.
They saw the young girls twisting their strings,
Goulburn Island.
They say there is.
They seize the young girls of the western
tribes, with their swaying.
They toke togyder theyr counsell.
They wear.
They Went to the Moon Mother.
Things Forbidden.
Things That Go Bump in the Night.
Thinking of Lady Yang at Midnight.
This cattle shed is Heaven now.
This Feast of the Law.
This, for my soul's peace, have I heard from
Thee.
This is a sailor's grave, while opposite.
This is no lif, alas, that I do lede.

This Is the Key.
This is the way the farmers ride.
This is the way the gentlemen ride.
This is Willy Walker, and that's Tam Sim.
This kyng lay at Camylot upon Krystmasse.
This little pig had a rub-a-dub.
This little stone, dear Sabinos.
This Morning Our Boat Left.
This Newly Created World.
This pig got in the barn.
This sad world we inhabit.
This Stone.
This Sun Is Hot.
This Train.
This world of ours.
This year / Next year.
This Yonder Night I Sawe a Sighte.
Thomas Cromwell.
Thomas Dudley, Ah! Old Must Dye.
Thomas o Yonderdale.
Thomas the Rhymer [or Rimer].
Thorn, A.
Thorn Vine on the Wall.
Those gone are day by day remote.
Those Who Died for Their Country.
"Those who realize true wisdom."
Those Women.
Those words, said the lady, are the worst there
    could be.
Thou Beautiful Sabbath.
Thou ermined judge, pull off that sable cap!
Thou Great God.
Thou shalt die.
Thou Who Createdst Everything.
Though Amaryllis Dance in Green.
Though I am dark.
Though I've a Clever Head.
Though Mine Eye Sleep Not.
Though riders be thrown in black disgrace.
Though the purity.
Thought on Human Life, A.
Thousand doves, A.
Thread the Needle.
Three Butchers, The.
Three Captains, The.
Three Friends.
Three Ghostesses.
Three grey geese in a green field grazing.
Three Hunchbacks, The.
Three Ravens, The.
Three rounded flanks I loved.
Three Songs of Mad Coyote.
Three Sons, The.
Three Straws.
Three Things Come Without Seeking.
Three Ways to Screw up on Your Way to The
    Doings Three Ways.
Three Young Rats.
Through Nurseryland.
Through storm and wind.
Through the front gate.
Throw me a quince.
Thumb bold.
Thumb he.
Thumbikin, Thumbikin, broke the barn.
Thumbkin says, I'll dance.
Thus Bonny-Boots the Birthday Celebrated.
Thus feverish fancies floated in my brain.
Thus I complain my grevous hevynesse.
Thy eyes and eyebrows I could spare.
Thy Heart.
Thyrsis, Sleep'st Thou?
Thys Endris Nyght.
Ti-ch'ü Song Words.
Tickly, tickly, on your knee.
Tiddle liddle lightum.
Tidinges I bring you, for to tell.
Tig.
Till Christ ("Till Christ, quhome I am haldin
    for to lufe.")
Till the good morning star.
Time stands still, with gazing on her face!
Timothy Titus took two ties.
Tinker / Tailor.
Tired as I Can Be.
'Tis a Little Journey.
'Tis Midnight.

'Tis the Gift to Be Simple.
Titanic, The.
Titty cum tawtay.
To a Gentleman, Who Desired Proper
    Materials for a Monody.
To a Living Author.
To a New Daughter-in-Law.
To a Schoolboy.
To a Traitor.
To an Ancient Tune.
To Astarte.
To be long silent was my thought.
To Buonaparte.
To Caelia.
To Colman Returning.
To G.
To His Love.
To Keep the Cold Wind Away.
To learn how to die.
To Lighten My Darkness.
To market, to market, to buy a fat pig.
To me nothing seems as splendid nor as
    praiseworthy.
To-morrow shall be my dancing day.
To Mr. Punchinello.
To Mrs B. from a Lady Who Had a Desire to
    See Her, and Who Complains on the
    Ingratitude of Her Fugitive Lover.
To My Niece, A.M., with a New Pair of Shoes.
To my trew love and able.
To Priapos.
To Purity and Truth.
To Show How Humble.
To sleep easy all night.
To the Archbishop of Tuam.
To the Holy Goste my goodes I bequeth.
To the Holy Trinity.
To the Marquis of Graham on His Marriage.
To the Poets.
To the Tune: Beautiful Barbarian.
To the Tune 'The Drunken Young Lord.'
To you, dere herte, variant and mutable.
To your question: why are my private parts.
Tobacco is a filthy weed.
Toe tipe.
Toe, trip and go.
Toishan Song, A.
Toltecs were wise, The.
Tom Brown's two little Indian boys.
Tom, He Was a Piper's Son.
Tom o' Bedlam.
Tom o' Bedlam's Song.
Tom Potts.
Tom Thumbkin.
Tomb of Diogenes, The.
Tomb of Ibykos, The.
Tommy kept a chandler's shop.
Tommy O'Linn was a Scotsman born.
Tommy Tibule.
Tommy Trot, a man of law.
Tone of Voice, The.
Too Late for a Husband.
Toss not my soul, O Love, 'twixt hope and
    fear.
Tournament of Tottenham, The.
Toward Winter.
Towering is that southern mountain.
Town of Passage, The.
Traditional Funeral Songs.
Traditional Women's Song of Algeria.
Train is A-Comin'
Train, The.
Translation of "Pax Bello Potior."
Tree Toad.
Tree-topped Hill.
Tree we plant will, when its boughs are grown,
    The.
Trees of the Forest, The.
Trees So High, The.
Triads ("Three excellent qualities in narration")
Trial of Renard, The.
Tribute on the Passing of a Very Real Person.
Trit trot to market to buy a penny doll.
Trot, and a canter, a gallop, and over, A.
Trousers of Wind.
True Heroism.
True Love.

True storyteller is a, The.
True Tale of Robin Hood, A.
Truly now.
Trumpet of Liberty, The.
Trumpeter of Fyvie, The.
Trust in Me.
Try Smiling.
Tryst, The.
Trystan and Esyllt.
Tumadir al-Khansa for Her Brother.
Tumult in the street, A!
Tune: Eternal Longing.
Tune: "Celebration in the Eastern Plain"—
    Replying to a Lyric Song by the Senior Poet
    Ma Chih-yüan.
Tune: "Deva-like Barbarian."
Tune: "Eternal Longing."
Tune: "Full Moon in the Human World"—
    Spring Evening: Replying to a Song.
Tune: "Joy in Spring's Coming"—Seven
    Songs.
Tune: Magpie on the Branch.
Tune: "Red Embroidered Slippers"—Spring
    Night.
Tune: 'San-fan Yü-lou Jen.'
Tune: "Sheep on Mountain Slope"—Boudoir
    Thoughts.
Tune: "Tartar Tune of Eighteen Beats."
Tune: "Wild Geese Have Come Down; Song of
    Victory."
Tune: "Willow Branches."
Tune: 'Wu Yeh-erh' Twitting the Teller of Tall
    Tales.
Turbulent Water, The.
Turkey in the Straw.
Turkey is dancing near the rocks, A.
Turkish Love Songs.
Turning my chariot I yoke my horses and go.
Turtle-Dove, The.
Turtle's Song, The.
Tutivillus, the Devil.
Twa Brothers, The.
Twa Corbies, The.
Twa Knights, The.
Twa Magicians, The.
Twa Sisters, The.
'Twas Rollog, and the Minim Potes.
Twats in the Ops Room.
Tweed and Till.
Twelfth Song of the Holy Young Men.
Twelfth Song of the Thunder.
Twelve Days of Christmas, The.
Twist about, turn about.
Two Appeals to John Harralson, Agent.
Two birds, one of them mortal, the other
    immortal.
Two bodies have I.
Two brothers we are.
Two Bulls, The.
Two Cherokee Songs of Friendship.
Two-Faced Too.
Two Gifts.
Two Gray Kits.
Two Laments.
Two little dicky birds.
Two little dogs / Sat by the fire.
Two Little Kittens.
Two Magicians, The.
Two More about a Crow, in the Manner of
    Zukofsky.
Two Pigeons.
Two Seabirds.
Two Soldier's Songs.
Two Songs about Flowers & Where I Was
    Walking.
Two Spring Charms.
Two sweeter babes you nare did see.
Two Tongue-Pointing (Satirical) Songs.
Ubi Sunt Qui Ante Nos Fuerunt?
Ugly your uproar at my side.
Uguisu on the flowering plum, The.
Under a hill.
Under the Bram Bush.
Under the Drooping Willow Tree.
Under the Linden Tree.
Under the oak tree, oak tree.
Under the Pondweed.

Under this plaque I lie, the famous woman.
Understanding.
Undo!
Undo thy dore, my spuse dere!
Undo Your Heart.
Unexpected Pleasure, An.
Unfair to Men.
Unfair to Women.
Unfaithful Shepherdess, The.
Unfortunate Miller; or, The Country Lasses
    Witty Invention, The.
Unhappy pedophiles, cease your inane.
Unquiet Grave, The.
Until life goes out.
Up hill and down dale.
Up in the North.
Up street and down street.
Up the wooden hill.
Upon a cock-horse to market I'll trot.
Upon a lady my love is lente.
Upon a Notorious Shrew.
Upon a Rich Country Gentleman.
Upon Arch-bishop Laud, Prisoner in the
    Tower. 1641.
Upon Sir Francis Drake's Return from His
    Voyage about the World, and the Queen's
    Meeting Him.
Upon the Duke of Buckingham.
Urumbula Song, The.
Utitia' q's Song.
Van Dieman's Land.
Verbum caro factum est.
Verses Made by a Catholic in Praise of
    Campion That Was Executed at Tyburn for
    Treason, as Is Made Known by the
    Proclamation.
Verses of a True Hungarian Patriot, The.
Verses on Daniel Good.
Very handsome gentleman, A.
Vicar of Bray, The.
Vigil of Venus, The.
Vikings, The.
Village Choir, The.
Villancico.
Virgin Mary, The.
Virgin's Song, The.
Visit, The.
Visitor.
Voice, A.
Voice of the Swallow, Flittering, Calls to Me,
    The.
Voice That Beautifies the Land, The.
Volunteer, The.
Voluspo.
Vote for Lunn.
Wa-Sissica, the War Song.
Wag a leg, wag a leg.
Wag ballock wag.
Wait!
Wait a Little!
Wake at the Well, The.
Waldere 1.
Waldere 2.
Walk down the path.
Walk on again walk on.
Walk Softly.
Walk Together Children.
Walking in a Meadowe Greene.
Walking the Wide Road.
Wall of woodland overlooks me, A.
Walter Lesly.
Waly, Waly [Love Be Bonny].
Wanderer, The.
Wandering Gentleman, The.
War (?) in the Desert, A.
War Dance.
War God's Horse Song, The.
War Lament: "Autumn flowers."
War Lament: "Every plant is burnt yellow."
War Song of the Basotho, A.
War Songs.
War the Source of Riches.
Warm hands, warm.
Warning, A.
Warsong of the Kwakiutl.
Wash me in the water.
Wassailing Song.

Water and nblod for thee I swete.
Water Bug and the Shadows, The.
Water pouring from clouds.
Water the Horses at a Breach in the Great
    Wall.
Watering Horses at a Long Wall Hole.
Waverly Pen, The.
Waves.
Wayle whit as whalles bon, A.
Wazir Dandan for Prince Sharkan, The.
We are all in the dumps.
We are Fred Karno's army.
We Are on Our Journey Home.
We are, you and me.
We cannot tell now.
We four lads from Liverpool are.
We Got Everything We Needed Here and Aint
    It Something.
We Have Chosen a Timely Day.
We have forgotten who we are.
We hold a splendid feast today.
We join with the earth and with each other.
We love the daylight.
We made a mistake in this song.
We mean to thrash these Prussian Pups.
We Pick Ferns, We Pick Ferns.
We Read of a People.
We Shall Know.
We shall live again.
We Shall Overcome.
We Sit Solitary.
We Three Kings.
We've all been invited up to Killisnoo.
We will go to the wood, says Robin to Bobbin.
Wearing of [or Wearin' o'] the Green, The.
Weather.
Weddings.
Wee Cooper of Fife, The.
Wee Falorie Man, The.
Wee Jenny Wren, The.
Wee Tammy Tyrie.
Wee Wee Man, The.
Weep [or Weepe] You No More [Sad
    Fountains].
Weingarten Travel Blessing, The.
Wel, who shal thise hornes blowe.
Welcome be ye when ye go.
Wele, thu art a waried thing.
Well I never, did you ever.
Well of Vertew and Flour of Womanheid, The.
Well, the war is done.
Weping haveth min wonges wet.
Wer ther outher in this toun.
Were I to send word.
Were You There.
Were You There When They Crucified My
    Lord?
West-Country Damosel's Complaint, The.
Western Wind.
Westphalian Song.
Whale, The.
Whaler's Rhyme.
Whan I thenke on the rode.
Whan I thenke thynges three.
Whan the nyghtengale syngeth the wodes
    waxen grene.
Whanne mine eyhnen misten.
What are you doing, my lady, my lady.
What Became of Them?
What business, this? What reason should we
    give.
What care I how black I be?
What Care I Though the World Reprove.
What Do We Geese Wear for Clothes?
What does a bird in Cross's air.
What God never sees.
What grass not yellowed?
What Happened to a Young man in a Place
    Where He Turned to Water.
What Hiawatha Probably Did.
What Is the Matter With Me?
What Makes a Home?
What mean these loud aerial cracks I hear?
What meanest thou, my fortune.
What profit to Darius of his reign?
What Really Goes on in the College of
    Cardinals.

What's in the Cupboard?
What's in there?
What's that in which good housewives take
    delight.
What Shall We Do for the Striking Seamen?
What the Informant Said to Franz Boas in
    1920.
What, why didest thou wink whan thou a wyf
    toke?
What Women Are Not.
What Yo' Gwine to [or t'] Do When Yo' [or
    de] Lamp Burn Down?
Whatever the cost.
When Adam dalf and Eve span.
When Aphrodite saw the *Aphrodite* of Knidos.
When as I do record.
When clouds appear like rocks and towers.
When he saw her.
When He Says so We Dance in All
    Directions—Wow!
When I Am Dead.
When I am dead and thou wouldst try.
When I Have Time.
When I look at her.
When I pick up my koto.
When I see blosmes springe.
When I See on Rood.
When I start my fast driving.
When I started wanting.
When I Think about Why.
When I was a bachelor, I lived by myself.
When I was a good and quick little girl.
When I was a lad and so was my dad.
When I Was a Little Boy.
When I was a little boy / I had but little wit.
When I was a little boy / I lived by myself.
When I was a little boy / My mammy kept me
    in.
When I was young I little thought.
When I went with you.
When ice on the pond is three feet thick.
When in My Pilgrimage.
When Jenny Wren Was Young.
When land is gone and money spent.
When, lo, by break of morning.
When morning gilds the skies.
When Shall We All Meet Again?
When shall we be married.
When the birds sang.
When the clouds are upon the hills.
When the dew is on the grass.
When the last greyness dwells throughout the
    air.
When the Lord climbed.
When the nightegale singes.
When the Rain Raineth.
When the Saints Go Marchin' [or Marching]
    In.
When the Snow is on the Ground.
When the wind blows.
When the wind is asleep and the weather set
    fair.
When we in kind embracements had agre'd
    [agreed].
When you look on my grave.
Whenceness of the Which.
Whenneso will wit oversteeth.
Where Are You Going, My Pretty Maid.
Where hae ye been a' the day.
Where have you been all the day, Billy boy,
    Billy boy?
Where Now Are the Hebrew Children?
Where the Song Went Where She Went &
    What Happened When They Met.
Whether I see you now.
Which is worse.
While I asked myself.
While thou hast gode and getest gode.
Whirlpool, The.
Whistle, Daughter, Whistle.
White Fisher, The.
WHITHER away so fast.
Who hath that conning by wisdam or
    prudence.
Who is that BRAHMA? What that Soul of Souls.
Who redes this boke of imagerie.
Who's that ringing at my door bell?

Who Says the River is Wide?
Who Would List.
Whole world is coming, The.
Whoops!
Whore that rides in us abides, The.
Whose Hand.
Whose little pigs are these, these, these?
Whoso saw on rode.
Whummil Bore, The.
Why do these prudes fear Prakrit poetry.
Why Have You No Ruth?
Wicked Who Would Do Me Harm, The.
Wide Walls.
Widow's Curse, The.
Widow's Lament.
Widsith, the Minstrel.
Wife of Usher's Well, The.
Wife's Complaint, The.
Wife's Lament.
Wife Wrapt [or Wrapped] in Wether's Skin,
    The.
Wild Dreams, The.
Wild Man Comes to the Monastery, The.
Wild Negro Bill.
Wildcat was walking.
Wilful waste brings woeful want.
Will He No Come Back Again?
Will Stewart and John?
Will to be tickled wants; has got the itch.
Will Ye Na Can Ye Na Let Me Be.
Will you lend me your mare to ride but a mile?
Will You Love Me When I'm Old?
William and Mary / George and Anne.
William the Conqueror, ten sixty-six.
Willie and Earl Richard's Daughter.
Willie and Lady Margerie [or Maisry].
Willie Macintosh.
Willie o Douglas Dale.
Willie o [or of] Winsbury.
Willie's Fatal Visit.
Willie's Lyke-Wake.
Willie the Poisoner.
Willie the Weeper.
Willie's Lady.
Willow by the Eastern Gate.
Willy Drowned in Yarrow.
Wind Blows High, The.
Wind is thin.
Wind is wild tonight, The.
Wind Last Night Blew Down.
Wind piercing, hill bare, hard to find shelter.
Wind, The.
Winds, The.
Wine and cakes for gentlemen.
Wine & bath-house sensualities.
Wings.
Winifreda.
Winter [or Wynter] Wakeneth All [or Al] My
    Care.
Winter's thunder.
Winter Wise.
Wise Rejoice with Ganymede, The.
Wishing Poem.
Witches, The.
With candour I confess my love.
With every note / of the mountain temple.
With huntis vp, with huntis vp.
With right all my herte now I you grete.
With Tears A-Flowing.
With the first light of the early morning
    dawning.
With your beautiful hair and seemly.
Wizard's Chant, The.
Wolde God that hyt were so.
Wolves for Company.
Woman.
Woman is by aptitude.
Woman-love can't touch my heart.
Woman of Exeter, The.
Woman of Three Cows, The.
Woman's Hard Fate.
Woman's Love.
Woman's Song, about Men, A.
Woman Who Married a Caterpillar, The.
Women as women, me had never charmed.
Women's Rondo.
Women's Songs.

Women Transport Corps.
Women, women, love of women.
Wonders.
Wonders of Nature.
Wood-chuck.
Woodcutter on His Way Home, A.
Wooing of Etain, The.
Wooyeo Ball, The.
Words 'I love you,' The.
Words of the All-Wise, The.
Working on the Railway.
World is Turned Upside Down, The.
World Needs, the.
World, the Devil, and Tom Paine, The.
Worldes bliss ne last no throwe.
Worldes blisse, have good day!
Worries.
Worry.
Would you be a man in fashion?
Wounds, as Wells of Life, The.
Wrecche mon, why artou proud.
Written on a Leaf.
Written on a Looking-Glass.
Wulf and Eadwacer.
Wulf and Eadwacer: A Woman's Lament.
Wynter wakeneth al my care.
Yankee Doodle.
Yankee Man-of-War, The.
Ye Scattered Nations.
Years of a lifetime do not reach a hundred,
    The.
Yellow Bittern, The.
Yellow dusk: messenger fails to appear.
Yellow Rose of Texas, The.
Yes, by Golly.
Yet hard / The travail is for such as bend their
    minds.
Yit is God a curteis lord.
Yong wyf and an harvest-gos, A.
York Play of the Crucifixion, The.
Yoshino River.
You all by yourself fulfilled.
You and I.
You and I will go to Finegall.
You are desolate, fort of kings.
You govern the locks, You open life.
You intend, it seems.
You know that I love you, sweatheart, but
    every time I come around.
You Love Her.
You May Go But This Will Bring You Back.
You might easy know a doffer.
You're the Top.
You sweet soft murderess.
You Tell on Yourself.
You that are jealous and have a wife.
You That Have Been Often Invited.
You too, Clenorides, homesickness drove.
You Will Die.
You Will See Your Lord a-Coming.
You Worthless.
Young Allan.
Young Bearwell.
Young Beichan.
Young Benjie.
Young Earl of Essex's Victory over the
    Emperor of Germany, The.
Young Hunting.
Young Johnstone.
Young [or Younge] Andrew.
Young Peggy.
Young Ronald.
Young swallows trill their new tune.
Young Waters.
Young Woman from Aenos, The.
Your Beauty and My Reason.
Your Thwarts in Pieces, Your Mooring Rope
    Cut.
Your way / is turning bad.
Yourself and Myself.
Z, Y, X, and W, V.
Zealous Puritan, The.
Zebra, The.
Zeus as an eagle came to Ganymede.
Zion me wan go home.
Zuni Derivations.

Unknown, after Etienne Pasquier
    My Three Wives.

Unknown, after the Greek of Plato
    Lais now old, that erst attempting lass.
Unknown, after the Latin of George Buchanan
    Cure for Poetry, A.
Unknown, after the Latin of Joachim du Bellay
    At thieves I bark; at lovers wag my tail.
Unknown, formerly at. to Homer
    Among the springs which flow from Ida's
        head.
    But when the golden-thron'd Aurora made.
Unknown, fr. Egyptian hieroglyphics
    He is the love-wolf.
    Is there anything sweeter than this hour?
    Little sycamore she planted, The.
    My lover is a lotus blossom.
Unknown, fr. Terezin Concentration Camp
    Birdsong.
    Birdsong 2.
    Closed Town, The.
    Concert in the Old School Garret.
    Dusk.
    Forgotten.
    Homesick.
    Letter to Daddy, A.
    Night in the Ghetto.
    On a Sunny Evening.
    Pain Strikes Sparks on Me, the Pain of Terezin.
    Theresienstadt's Hospital.
Unknown, sometimes at. to Sir Walter Ralegh
    As You Came from the Holy Land [of
        Walsingham].
Unrei (d. 1717)
    Second of the second month, The.
Untermeyer, Jean Starr (1886–1970)
    Autumn.
    Country of No Lack.
    Dew on a Dusty Heart.
    False Enchantment.
    High Tide.
    Lake Song.
    Passionate Sword, The.
    Sinfonia Domestica.
Untermeyer, Louis (1885–1977)
    Archibald MacLeish Suspends the Five Little
        Pigs.
    Caliban in the Coal Mines.
    Dark Chamber, The.
    Edna St. Vincent Millay Exhorts Little Boy
        Blue.
    Feuerzauber.
    Food and Drink.
    Glad Day.
    Goliath and David.
    Infidelity.
    Irony.
    John Masefield Relates the Story of Tom, Tom,
        the Piper's Son.
    Koheleth.
    Last Words before Winter.
    Long Feud.
    Portrait of a Machine.
    Prayer for This House.
    Prayer: "God, though [or although] this life is
        but a wraith."
    Repentance.
    Song Tournament: New Style.
    To a Vine-clad Telegraph Pole.
    Walter de la Mare Tells the Listener about Jack
        and Jill.
Unwin, Richard
    Limerick: "My beard's overcrowded. Now
        that."
Updike, John (b. 1932)
    Amish, The.
    August.
    Dea ex Machina.
    Ex-Basketball Player.
    I Missed His Book, but I Read His Name.
    In Extremis.
    Insomnia the Gem of the Ocean.
    Love Sonnet.
    May.
    Meditation on a News Item.
    Movie House.
    Newlyweds, The.

On the Inclusion of Miniature Dinosaurs in
   Breakfast Cereal Boxes.
Player Piano.
Recital.
Richmond.
Seagulls.
September.
Seven Stanzas at Easter.
Snapshots.
Some Frenchmen.
Two Hoppers.
Upon Learning That a Bird Exists Called the
   Turnstone.
Upon Shaving Off One's Beard.
V. B. Nimble, V. B. Quick.
Vow.
Winter Ocean.

Upham, Thomas Cogswell (1799–1872)
Fear Not, Poor Weary One.

Upton, Charles
When I was very young.

Urbiciani, Bonaggiunta (fl. 1250)
Lady, my wedded thought.
Never was joy or good that did not soothe.
Such wisdom as a little child displays.
Whoso abandons peace for war-seeking.

Urchard, T. (1611–60)
Truly Rich, The.

Urdang, Constance (b. 1922)
All Around Us.
At Frank 'n' Helen's.
Back Far Enough, down Deep Enough.
Children, The.
Muse Is Always the Other Woman, The.
My Father's Death.
Old Wives' Tales.
Portrait.
Returning to the Port of Authority, A
   Picaresque.
This Poem.

Urin, Viktor Arkad'evich (b. 1924)
Oh, Maika in a maika, there's the smell of
   summer.

Urmy, Clarence Thomas (1858–1923)
Old Year, The.

Urusova, Ekaterina (1747–1816?)
O Muses! I beseech you, fire my heart with
   song.

Usborne, Richard (b. 1910)
Epitaph on a Party Girl.

Usei (d. 1764)
Six and sixty.

Usha, S. (b. 1954)
To Mother.

Ushakov, Nikolai Nikolaevich (1899–1973)
Craftsmanship.
Lady Macbeth.
Wine.

Usher, Leila (1859–1955)
I Am the Cat.

Ushida, May
Deep in the rippling spring.

Utemorrah, Daisy (b. 1922)
Mary's Plea.

Utkin, Iosif Pavlovich (1903–44)
Komsomol Song.
Letter.
Tale of Red-Haired Motl, Mister Inspector,
   Rabbi Isaiah, and Commissar Blokh, The.

Utsu (d. 1863)
Owner of the cherry blossoms, The.

Utting, Susan
Spoon Maker's Daughter, The.

Uvavnuk (fl. 19th–20th cent.)
Great sea has set me in motion, The.
Shaman Song.

Uyematsu, Amy
30 Miles from J-Town.
December 7 Always Brings Christmas Early.
Fortune Cookie Blues.
Near Roscoe and Coldwater.
Same Month They Bombed Cambodia, The.
Ten Million Flames of Los Angeles, The.
To All Us Sansei Who Wanted to Be Westside.

V

**Vaginov, Konstantin Konstantinovich (1899–
1934)**
Song of Words.

Vagura
Love Poem, A.

"Vaidehi" (Janaki Srinivas Murthy) (b. 1945)
Girl in the Kitchen.

Vajda, János (1827–97)
Comet, The.
In the Forest of Vaal.
Lusitanian Song.
On The Reedy Lake.
Thirty Years After.
Times Gone By.
Twenty Years After.

Vakaló, Eléni (b. 1921)
But there was / once / a time.
My Father's Eye.

Valachová, Lenka (b. 1973)
Sterile Dish, The.

Valduga, Patrizia (b. 1953)
And This is a Beautiful Night That in the
   Heart.
I Despair Because I Don't Have Words.
Other Simulation, The.
Why Are Those Who Are Loved So Dull and
   Leaden?
Word Knows How to Seduce the Flesh, The.

Valentine, Jean (b. 1934)
After Elegies.
American River Sky Alcohol Father.
Anaesthesia.
April.
Bride's Hours, A.
Death Asphodel.
December 21st.
Dream Barker.
Field, The.
First Station, The.
Forgiveness Dream.
Free Abandonment Blues, The.
He Said.
Lines in Dejection.
Living Together.
Messenger, The.
One You Wanted to Be Is the One You Are,
   The.
Orpheus and Eurydice.
Pen, The.
Pilgrims.
Sasha and the Poet.
Second Dream, The.
Sex.
Silences; A Dream of Governments.
Sleep Drops Its Nets.
Sunset at Wellfleet.
To My Soul.
Truth.
Under Voice, The.
Waiting.
X.
Yield Everything, Force Nothing.

Valerie, Jean (b. 1953)
Lesson on Braces.
On Apologies.

Valéry, Paul (1871–1945)
Crusoe.
Girl with Mind Wandering.
Graves by the Sea, The.
Graveyard by the Sea, The.
Helen.
Helen, the Sad Queen.
Narcissus.

Valiente, Doreen
Charge of the Goddess, The.

Vallejo, César (1892–1938)
Agape.
'And don't bother telling me anything.'
And What If after So Many Words.
Anger.
Anger that Breaks the Man into Chidren, The.
Black Cup, The.
Black Messengers, The.

Black Riders, The.
Black Stone Lying on a White Stone.
Black Stone on a White Stone.
Dead Idyll.
Distant Footsteps, The.
Down to the Dregs.
Eternal Dice, The.
Finished the stranger, with whom, late.
Good Sense.
Have You Anything to Say in Your Defense?
Hungry Man's Wheel, The.
I Am Going to Speak of Hope.
I Am Going to Talk About Hope.
'I have a terrible fear of being an animal.'
I'm thinking of your sex.
In That Corner Where We Slept Together.
Intensity and Height.
It was Sunday in the fair ears of my burro.
Man Walks by with a Loaf of Bread on His
   Shoulder, A.
Mass.
Masses.
Our Daily Bread.
Poem to Be Read and Sung.
Right Meaning, The.
Rollcall of Bones, The.
Short Prayer for a Loyalist Hero.
Spain, Take This Cup from Me.
Spider, The.
Telluric and Magnetic.
To My Brother Miguel.
Today I like life much less.
Trilce.

Valli, Maria
Crows, The.

Van Alstyne, Egbert
Pretty Baby.

Van de Woestijne, Karel (1878–1929)
Fever Tune.
I Am the Hazel-Nut.
Oars Heavy with Seaweed, The.

Van den Bergh, Herman (1896–1967)
Nocturn: "Moon rows burning, The."

Van den Heuvel, Cor
After the shower.
Autumn twilight.
Branch, A.
From behind me.
Geese have gone, The.
Hot night.
In the parking lot.
Late autumn.
My mind takes a leap.
November evening.
Raining at every window.
Shading his eyes.
Shadow in the folded napkin, The.
Starting to rise.
Stick goes over the falls at sunset, A.
Summer breeze.
Sun goes down, The.
Through the small holes.
Tidepool, A.
Twilight.

Van Doesburg, Theo (1883–1991)
Remembrance of the Founts of Night.
Still Life: The Table.

Van Doren, Mark (1894–1973)
Ancient Couple on Lu Mountain, The.
And Did the Animals?
Axle Song.
Distant Runners, The.
Dream of Trains, A.
Escape, The.
Family Prime.
First Poem, The.
Former Barn Lot.
Good Appetite.
Immortal.
Midland.
Near House, The.
Praise Him Who Makes Us Happy.
Proper Clay.
Pulse, The.
Runaways, The.
So Simple.

This Amber Sunstream.
Where I Saw the Snake.
Whisperer, The.
Why, Lord.

Van Duyn, Mona (b. 1921)
Christmas Card, After the Assassinations, A.
Condemned Site.
Falling in Love at Sixty-Five.
Gardener to His God, The.
Homework.
Into Mexico.
Late Flight of the Love God.
Letters from a Father.
Mockingbird Month.
Moose in the Morning, Northern Maine.
One Strategy for Loving the World.
Poets in Late Winter.
Sonnet for Minimalists.
Stream, The.
This seems, in a world where love must take
    its chances.
Twins, The.
View, A.
Vision Test, The.
What the Motorcycle Said.

Van Dyke, Cheryl
Birth, 1975.

Van Dyke, Henry (1852–1933)
America for Me.
America's Welcome Home.
Foundation.
Four Things.
Gospel of Labor, The.
Jesus, Thou Divine Companion.
Lost Word of Jesus, A.
Peace Hymn of the Republic.
Reliance.
Victoria.
Work.

Van Eeden, Frederick (1860–1932)
North Wind, The.

Van Hanh (d. 1018)
Body of Man, The.

Van Haren, Elma (b. 1954)
Stepping Out With Edvard Munch.

Van hee, Miriam (b. 1952)
December.

Van Heusen, Jimmy
All the Way.
But Beautiful.
Call Me Irresponsible.
Come Fly with Me.
Darn That Dream.
Good Time Charlie.
Here's That Rainy Day.
I Thought about You.
It Could Happen to You.
Like Someone in Love.
Love and Marriage.
(Love Is) The Tender Trap.
Moonlight Becomes You.
My Heart Is a Hobo.
Personality.
Polka Dots and Moonbeams.
Road to Morocco, The.
Second Time around, The.
Shake down the Stars.
Sleigh Ride in July.
Swinging on a Star.
Welcome to My Dream.
You May Not Love Me.

van Hirtum, Marianne (1935–88)
And I Shall Be the Mouth of Copper.
In Those Rooms.
Naked Truth, The.
Vampiro Nox.
While We Spend Our Lives Ironing.

Van Jordan, A.
Dance Lesson, A.
If I Write a Poem.
My Father's Retirement.

Van Ostaijen, Paul (1896–1928)
Landscape.
Murderers, The.
Ode to Singer.

Song of the Alpine Hunter.
Souvenir.

Van Peenen, H. J.
Insulin Receptor.
Will Campbell Displays His Craniotribe.

Van Riessen, René (b. 1954)
Old in Overijssel.

Van Rooten, Luis d'Antin (1906–73)
Jacques s'apprête.
Lit-elle messe, moffette.
Polis poutre catalane.
Pousse y gâte, pousse y gâte.

Van Sertima, Ivan (b. 1935)
Volcano.

Van Toorn, Peter (b. 1944)
Shake'nbake Ballad.
Mountain Study.

Van Vliet, Eddy (b. 1942)
City, The.
Coastline, The.
Courtyard, The.
Old Champagne Glass.
Party.
Valediction—To My Father.

Van Vriesland, Victor (b. 1891)
Ars Poetica.
Evening.

Van Walleghen, Michael (b. 1938)
Crabapples.
Elephant in Winter, The.
In the Chariot Drawn by Dragons.
More Trouble with the Obvious.
Walking the Baby to the Liquor Store.

Van Wyk, Chris (b. 1957)
Ballot and the Bullet, The.
Reason, The.

Vance-Watkins, Lequita
Passacaglia.

Vancrevel, Laurens (b. 1941)
About Time.

Vandas, Drahomira (b. 1919)
Egg Hatches Out a Flame, An.
Light Throws Shadows.
Rain Man.

Vando, Gloria
Blanca's Red Lips.
Commonwealth, Common Poverty.
Father's Day.
In the Crevices of Night.
In the Dark Backward.
Knife.
Lydia's Phantasmagoria.
My Mother Cunning, Yet Innocent.
Ode to Your Back.
On Hearing that a Potato Costs $70 in
    Sarajevo.
Swallows of Salangan.

Vanhomrigh, Esther (fl early 18th cent.)
Hail, Blushing Goddess, Beauteous Spring!

Vanshenkin, Konstantin Iakovlevich (b. 1925)
Forest in winter, The! From edge to edge.
Girl dreams of her lover at night, The.
Path, The.
Rain.
Sunset fades, and from the little hill, The.
Urchin, The.
We came back late from visiting.

Varchi, Benedetto (1503–1565)
What part of my holiest and most beautiful
    feelings.

Varela, Blanca (b. 1926)
Before the Pacific.
Captain, The.
Nobody will open the door for you.
Things I Say Are True, The.

Varma, Archana (b. 1946)
Man.

Várnai, Zseni (1890–1981)
To My Soldier Son.

Vas, István (1910–91)
Armageddon.
Beethoven's Old Age.
Coventry Cathedral.
Deaf Mute Girl, The.

From the Admonitions of St. Theresa of Avila.
In the Roman Forum.
Invisible Element, The.
Lion, The.
Rhapsody: Keeping Faith.
Romanus Sum.
Santa Maria Antiqua.
Through the Smoke.
Through Time's Segments.
Understanding.
Upon a Drawing.
Xenophon's Song.

Vasalis, M. (b. 1909)
Idiot in the Bath, The.
Sotto Voce.

Vásárhelyi, András (d. 1526)
Song to the Virgin Mary.

Vashon, George Boyer (1824–78)
Vincent Ogé.

**Vasilyev [or Vasil'ev], Pavel Nikolaevich
(1910–37)**
Lines in Honor of Natalya.
Prince Foma.
Wedding, The.

**Vasilyev [or Vasil'ev], Sergey Aleksandrovich
(1911–75)**
Pigeon of My Childhood.

Vasquez, Robert
At the Rainbow.
Early Morning Test Light over Nevada, 1955.
For Jose Mercado Vasquez and Frances Roman
    Vasquez.
Pismo, 1959.

**Vatsyayan, Sachidananda Hirananda See
"Agyeya"**

Vaughan, Henry ("Silurist") (1622?–95)
Abel's Blood.
Admission.
And do they so?
Anguish.
As Time One Day by Me Did Pass.
Ascension-Day.
Ascension Hymn.
Begging.
Bird, The.
Book, The.
British [or Brittish] Church, The.
Burial.
Charnel-house, The.
Childhood.
Christ's Nativity.
Cock-crowing.
Come, come, what doe I here?
Corruption.
Dawning, The.
Day of Judgement.
Death.
Dedication, The: "My God, thou that didst dye
    for me."
Disorder and Frailty.
Distraction.
Dressing.
Dwelling-Place, The.
Easter-Day.
Easter Hymn.
Eclipse, The.
Epitaph Upon the Lady Elizabeth, Second
    Daughter to His Late Majesty, An.
Evening-Watch, The.
H. Scriptures.
Here, take again thy sackcloth! and thank
    heaven.
Holy Communion, The.
I Walked [or Walkt] the Other Day to Spend
    My Hour.
Idle Verse.
Incarnation and Passion, The.
Isaac's Marriage.
Jacob's Pillow, and Pillar.
Joy of My Life! While Left Me Here.
Kingdom of Heaven Compared to a Grain of
    Mustard-Seed, The.
Knot, The.
Lamp[e], The.
Leave, leave, thy gadding thoughts.
Leaves Come Again, The.

Love and Discipline.
Man.
Mans Fall, and Recovery.
Match, The.
Midnight.
Morning-Watch, The.
Mount of Olives.
Nativity, The.
Night, The.
Palm-tree, The.
Passion, The.
Peace.
Pilgrimage, The.
Praise.
Pursuit[e], The.
Quickness.
Rainbow, The.
Regeneration.
Relapse, The.
Religion.
Resolve, The.
Resurrection and Immortality.
Retirement.
Retreat[e], The.
Revival, The.
Rhapsody, A.
Rules and Lessons.
Sap, The.
Search, The.
Seed Growing Secretly, The.
Shepherds [or Shepheards], The.
Should we go now a wandering [or a-
 wand'ring], we should meet.
Shower [or Showre], The.
Silence and Stealth of Day[e]s!
Since last we met, thou and thy horse, my
 dear.
Son-Days [dayes].
Song to Amoret, A.
Starre, The.
Stone, The.
Sure, there's a tie of bodies! and as they.
Tempest, The.
They Are All Gone into the World of Light!
Timber, The.
To Amoret.
To Amoret Gone from Him.
To Amoret, of the Difference 'twixt Him and
 Other Lovers, and What True Love Is.
To Amoret, Walking in a Starry Evening.
To His Books.
To My Ingenuous Friend, R. W.
To the Best, and Most Accomplished Couple.
To the Most Excellently Accomplished Mrs.
 Katherine Philips.
To the Pious Memory of C. W. Esquire.
Town believes thee lost, and didst thou see,
 The.
Twenty-first Day of the Seventh Month.
Unprofitablenes.
Upon a Cloak [or Cloke] Lent Him by Mr. J.
 Ridsley.
Upon the Priory Grove, His Usual Retirement.
Vanity of Spirit.
Waterfall [or Water-Fall], The.
World, The (1)

Vaughan, Jane (*fl.* mid-17th cent.)
Debate between Jane Vaughan of Caergai and
 Cadwaladr the Poet.
O my merciful Lord God, you, who are one in
 three.

Vaughan, Thomas (1622?–66)
Stone, The.
When he did read how did we flock to hear.

Vaughan-Thomas, Wynford (b. 1908)
Farewell to New Zealand.
Hiraeth in N.W.3.
To His Not-so-coy Mistress.

**Vaux, Thomas, 2nd Baron Vaux of Harrowden
 (1510–66)**
Aged Lover Renounceth Love, The.

Vazakas, Byron
Epitaph for the Old Howard.
Pavilion on the Pier, The.

Vazirani, Reetika (b. 1962)
Daughter-Mother-Maya-Seeta.

Dream of the Evil Servant.
E-Mail.
Maya to Herself and Then to Her Gardener.
Mrs. Biswas Breaks Her Connection with
 Another Relative.
Mrs. Biswas Goes through a Photo Album.
Mrs. Biswas of Maryland on the Phone.

Veale, Peter (b. 1919)
Bold Troubleshooters.
I put my hat upon my head.

Veenendaal, Cornelia
On My Fourteenth Wedding Anniversary I
 Ride on Trains.

Vega (b. 1954)
Brothers Loving Brothers.

Vegin, Pyotr (b. 1939)
Explanation of a Sign.
' Moscow' Pool.

Veiga, Amélia (b. 1931)
Angola.
Wind of Liberty.

Veinberg, Jon
Next to Tut.
Owl's Landscape, An.
To an Exeter City Cocktail Waitress.

Veldeke, Heinrich von (1140?–1210?)
In April when the flowers spring.
Tristan had no choice.
Whoever hurts my favor with my lady.

Vélez, Elizabeth Ash
Elvis P. and Emma B.

Velichansky, A.
Flame's speech is confused, The. The
 muttering of the water is hollow.
In the evil time.
Infant is white, like down, The. And the youth
 dark-complexioned, like shingle.
Kalmyk poppies, horde of pan-Mongol tulips.
Memory of the past grows paler with each day.
Policeman does not blow his whistle, The.
Trunks of birches, like scrolls.

Venantius Fortunatus (*fl.* 14th cent.)
Holy Cross.

Venantius Fortunatus, Saint (c.530–c.610)
Standards of the King go forth, The.

Venclova, Tomas
Canto Eleven.

Venugopalan, T. S. (b. 1929)
Family Pride.

Vere, Mary Ainge De *See* **"Bridges, Madeline"**

Verhaeren, Emile (1855–1916)
Poor, The.

Verlaine, Paul (1844–96)
A la Promenade.
Art of Poetry, The.
Art Poétique.
Asleep in the Valley.
Autumn Song.
Balanide 2.
Beams.
Beauty of women, their weakness, those pale
 hands.
Brussels: Simple Frescos 1.
Brussels: Simple Frescos 2.
Chansons d'Automne.
Clair de Lune.
Clymène, A.
Cold wind hurls itself at, A.
Colombine.
Cortège.
Cythère.
Dans l'Allée.
En Bateau.
Endless sameness.
Exchange of Feelings.
Falling tears in my heart.
Fantoches.
Femme et Chatte.
Green.
He's an awkward bedfellow and I love to keep.
Hope like a wisp of straw shines in the stable.
Humble life of dull and easy work, The.
Il Pleut Doucement sur la Ville.
It's languor and ecstasy.
Malines.

Mandoline.
Mille e tre.
Moonlight.
Muted Tones.
On the Grass.
Pantomime.
Parsifal.
Peaceful eyes my only wealth.
Piano kissed by a slender hand, The.
Sadness, the languor of the human body, The.
Sky above the roof's, The.
Sky is up above the roof, The.
Slumber dark and deep.
Sonnet to the Asshole.
Spleen.
Streets 1.
Streets 2.
Tears Fall in My Heart.
Uneven rows of hedges.
Voice of Pride: shout of blaring trumpets.
Weird as Puppets.
White Moonglow, The.
Without Guile.
Woman and Cat.
Wooden Horses.
You see, we have to be forgiven things.
You Would Have Understood Me.
Young Fools, The.

Verma, Shrikant (1931–86)
Pleasure Dome, The.

**Verstegan [or Verstegen], Richard
 (Richardowlands) (1565–1620)**
Lullaby: "Upon my lap my sovereign sits."
Times Go by Turns.

Vertinsky, Aleksandr (1889–1957)
I remember the night.
In the Moldavian Steppe.

Vertreace, Martha (b. 1945)
Black Tulips.
Caged Stone.

Verwey, Albert (1865–1937)
Beautiful World, The.
North-Sea, The.
Soul and Love, The.

Very, Jones (1831–80)
Autumn Flowers.
Autumn Leaves.
Beauty.
Birds of Passage, The.
Clouded Morning, The.
Columbine, The.
Cottage, The.
Created, The.
Cross, The.
Cup, The.
Day of Denial, The.
Dead, The.
Eagles, The.
Earth, The.
Enoch.
Eye and Ear, The.
Fair Morning, The.
Faith.
Fear Not: For They That Be With Us.
First Atlantic Telegraph, The.
Forevermore.
Fugitive Slaves, The.
Garden, The.
God Not Afar Off.
Grave-Yard, The.
Hand and Foot, The [or Hand and the Foot,
 The].
Harvest, The.
Hath the Rain a Father?
He Was Acquainted with Grief.
I Was Sick and in Prison.
In Him We Live [and Move and Have Our
 Being].
Indian's Retort, The.
Jacob Wrestling with the Angel.
John.
Laborers, The.
Lament of the Flowers, The.
Latter Rain, The.
Lost, The.
Morning Watch, The.

Moses in Infancy.
Mountain, The.
My Meat and Drink.
My People Are Destroyed for Lack of
    Knowledge.
Nature.
New Birth, The.
New Man, The.
New World, The.
Night.
On Finding the Truth.
On the Completion of the Pacific Telegraph.
On Visiting the Graves of Hawthorne and
    Thoreau.
One Generation Passeth Away.
Origin of Man, I, The.
Origin of Man, The.
Poor, The.
Prayer of Jabez, The.
Prayer, The.
Presence, The.
Promise, The.
Robe, The.
Robin, The.
Rock, The.
Serpent, The.
Settler, The.
Silent, The.
Slave, The.
Slavery.
Slowness of Belief in a Spiritual World, The.
Son, The.
Song, The: "When I would sing of crooked
    streams and fields."
Sower, The.
Spirit Land, The.
Spirit, The.
Strangers, The.
Sumach Leaves, The.
Take Ye Heed, Watch and Pray.
Thy Better Self.
Thy Brother's Blood.
Today.
Trees of Life, The.
Wild Rose of Plymouth, The.
Winter Rain, The.
Word, The.
Yourself.
"Vesey, Paul" *See* Allen, Samuel
Vetus, Gaius Antistius *See* Antistius Vetus
Vice, Lisa (b. 1951)
    Pants.
Vicente, Gil (c.1465–1536)
    Song: "If thou art sleeping, maiden."
Vicinelli, Patrizia (b. 1943)
    Crossing the River.
    I Met the Thieving Miss Magpie.
    When time--irreversible--begins to doze.
Vicioso, Chiqui (b. 1948)
    Fazal.
    Haiti.
    Perspectives.
    Survival 1.
    Survival 2.
    Wo/men.
Victor, Geraldo Bessa (b. 1917)
    Note on a Shop in the Muceque.
    That Old Mulemba.
Vicuña, Cecilia (b. 1948)
    Five Notebooks for Exit Art.
    I saw a word in the air.
Vidya (Vijjika) (fl. c.659)
    And What of Those Arbors of Vines.
    Fate Is a Cruel and Proficient Potter.
    Friends, / you are lucky you can talk.
    Hiding in the.
    I praise the disk of the rising sun.
    Love Poem, A.
    On Makeshift Bedding.
    Please keep an eye on my house for a few
        moments.
    You are fortunate, dear friends, that you can
        tell.
Vidyapati (fl. 15th cent.)
    First Love.
Viereck, Peter (b. 1916)
    1912–1952, Full Cycle.

Blindman's Buff.
Homecoming.
Insulted and the Injured, The.
Kilroy.
Love Song to Eohippus.
Poet.
To Helen of Troy (N.Y.).
Vale from Carthage.
Viertel, Berthold
    Emigrants.
    February.
    German Language, The.
Vietnamese Oral Tradition
    Across the Field of the Old Corporal.
    Arranged Marriage, The.
    Autumn.
    Bare Rocks and Stars.
    Body Is Pain, The.
    Carp, The.
    Cat, The.
    Clear Skies, Still Sea.
    Coins of Van-Lich.
    Colonial Troops Transport, The.
    Complaining about the Second Wife.
    Concubine, The.
    Difficulties at Love.
    Egret's Death and Funeral Preparations.
    Evening.
    From *So* Mountain.
    Girl with the Binh Tien Hairdo, The.
    Harmony in the Kingdom.
    Homesick Bride, The.
    Husband and Wife.
    Impossible Tasks.
    Ke-Mo Village Girl.
    King Star, The.
    Leaving the Village.
    Linked Verses.
    Looking Out in All Directions.
    Love Lament.
    Lullaby.
    Mandarin Who Couldn't Do Anything, The.
    Mother Egret.
    Outpost Soldier, The.
    Painting, The.
    Phoenixes and Sparrows.
    Pole at the Village Pagoda, The.
    Red Cloth, The.
    Replies.
    Saigon River, The.
    Ship of Redemption.
    Singer with a Bad Voice, The.
    Talking about Birds.
    Tao.
    Testing the Confucian Ideal.
    Tiny Bird, A.
    Venturing Out.
    Whisky Lovers.
    Wicked Women.
    Woman's Heart, A.
Vigil, Anthony R. (b. 1968)
    As the Beer Trucks Eclipse the Light of
        Morning.
    At the Stop Light, the Braided Blond Man.
    El Hogarcito de La Madrugada.
    That's the Way, Uh Huh, Uh Huh, I Liked It.
Vigny, Alfred de (1797–1863)
    Nature.
    Sound of the Horn, The.
Viidikas, Vicki (b. 1948)
    Future.
Vijjika *See* **Vidya**
Vilakazi, B. W. (1906–47)
    In the Gold Mines.
    Now I Do Believe.
    Now I Will Only Believe.
Vilariño, Idea (b. 1920)
    Each Afternoon.
    How Awful.
    How disgusting.
    How to shrug off.
    If I Died Tonight.
    Lifelong farewell.
    Like a dog howling endlessly.
    Like a Floating Jasmine.
    Like that man who kicks off his shoes.

Maybe Then.
No.
No More.
There is no hope.
Visitor, A.
What Was Life.
Vildrac, Charles (b. 1882)
    After Midnight.
    Relief.
Vilenkin, Nicolai Maksimovich *See* **"Minsky,
    Nicolai Maksimovich"**
Villa, Dario (1953–96)
    Blades and slime, the limits, The.
    In the end.
    It is.
    Remember the goose that.
    Sometimes, Doctor, I awake.
    Then if I think about it.
    What counts in any action.
Villa, Emilio (b. 1914)
    It is world of the back hune wone it is.
    Lend me a battle of unavoidable suggestions.
    Natus de Muliere, Brevi Vivens.
    Trees were moving.
    Ugly season of putrifying buzzards, An.
Villa, José Garcia (b. 1914)
    I Was Speaking of Oranges to a Lady.
    Inviting a Tiger for the Weekend.
    Now I Prize Yellow Strawberries.
    To Become an Archer.
Villalongo, José Angel Sr. (*fl.* 20th cent.)
    In the Good Old U. S. A.
Villana [*or* **Vallane**] (*fl.* betw. 8th and 12th cent.)
    After he stripped off my clothes.
Villanueva, Alma (b. 1944)
    Even the Eagles Must Gather.
    From the Healing Dark.
    Mother, May I?
    Peace #3.
    Planet Earth Speaks, The.
    Power.
    Song of the Self: The Grandmother.
    They Didn't Get Me.
Villanueva, Tino (b. 1941)
    Haciendo Apenas la Recolección.
    Scene from the Movie *Giant*.
Villaurrutia, Xavier (1903–50)
    Los Angeles Nocturne.
    Nocturnal Sea.
    Nocturne.
    Nocturne of the Statue.
    Nocturne: The Eternal.
    Our Love.
    Poetry.
    They and I.
**Villiers, George, 2nd Duke of Buckingham
    (1628–87)**
    Cabin-Boy, The.
    Epitaph upon Thomas, Lord Fairfax, An.
Villon, François (1431–65)
    Arbor Amoris.
    Ballad against the Enemies of France.
    Ballad[e] of Dead Ladies.
    Ballad of the Gibbet.
    Ballad of the Lords of Old Time.
    Ballad of the Women of Paris.
    Ballad of Villon and Fat Madge, The.
    Ballad Written for a Bridegroom.
    Ballade of the Ladies of Time Past.
    Ballade of the Men Who Were Hanged.
    Ballade: "Tell me where, in what country,
        where."
    Ballade to End With, A.
    Ballade to His Mistress.
    Ballat o the Hingit.
    Ballat o the Leddies o Langsyne.
    Complaint of the Fair Armoress [*or*
        Armouress], The.
    Dispute of the Heart and Body of François
        Villon, The.
    Double Ballad of Good Counsel, A.
    Epistle in Form of a Ballad to His Friends.
    Epitaph in Form of a Ballad, The.
    Fragment on Death, A.
    Gone Ladies.

His Mother's Service to Our Lady.
I Die of Thirst While at the Fountain Side.
I love and serve my lady with a will.
No, I Am Not as Others Are.
Now I think I hear the laments.
Old Lady's Lament for Her Youth, The.
Old Woman's Lamentations, An.
Prayer of the Old Woman.
Quatrain: "France's I am; my lookout's glum."
Remember, Imbeciles and Wits.
Rondel: "Good-by, the tears are in my eyes."
To Death, of His Lady.

Vinal, Harold (1891–1967)
To Persephone.

Vinkenoog, Simon
(Hollanditis)

Vinokurov, Yevgeny [or Evgenii] Mikhailovich (b. 1925)
Adam.
All Grows Old.
And when my legs had already grown numb.
Every store keeps a book for complaints.
Eyes.
Forget-Me-Nots.
Hamlet.
Has the time come to draw up the accounts?
I ate and drank with you, fellow men.
I do not like the circus.
I don't remember him.
I feel the reasonableness of existence.
In the Dresden Gallery.
Mother of Judas, The.
My beloved was laundering.
Objects.
On the hall stand hangs a fur coat.
Poetry Editor.
Prophet, The.
Rhythm.
She.
Shows.
When the Parachute Does Not Open.

Vinz, Mark (b. 1942)
Blues, The.

Violi, Paul (b. 1944)
Harold and Imogene.
Hazards of Imagery, The.
Index.
Rifacimento.
When to Slap a Woman.

Viorst, Judith (b. 1931)
Honeymoon is Over, The.
Mother Doesn't Want a Dog.
Night Fun.

Virág, Benedek (1754–1830)
Invocation: "O holy Justice! Hiding your puissance."
Spartan Mother, The.

Viray, Manuel A. (b. 1917)
Patio.
Saturday Morning, A.
Two Strangers, The.

Virgil [or Vergil] (Publius Vergilius Maro) (70–19 B.C.)
Aeneid, The, *sels.*
Death Plucks My Ear.
Eclogues, *sels.*
Georgics, *sels.*

Virgil, Anita
Another year!
Awakening.
Behind sunglasses.
Bitterness.
Black spaces, The.
Claiming.
Coal train, The.
Dark, The.
Darkening.
Emerging hot and rosy.
First hot night, The.
Grass Path Lasts.
Holding you.
Hot afternoon.
Knifing deep.
Laughing softly.
Low tide.
Morning bath.

Mullein.
Not seeing.
Over and over.
Phoebe's cry, A.
Quiet afternoon.
Rainy day, A.
Red flipped out.
She turns the child.
Spring breeze.
Swan's head, The.
Trickling.
Twilight.
Walking the snow-crust.

Virgilio, Nicholas
Adding father's name.
After father's wake.
Alone on the road.
Another autumn.
At the open grave.
Autumn twilight.
Autumn wind, The.
Beyond empty pews.
Cathedral bell, The.
Crow in the snowy pine, A.
Deep in rank grass.
Distant balloon, A.
Empty highway, The.
Flag-covered coffin.
Heat before the storm.
Hinge of the year, The.
In the empty church.
Into the blinding sun.
Junkyard dog, The.
Lily.
Lone red-winged blackbird.
My dead brother.
My gold star mother.
Now the swing is still.
Pressing my forehead.
Sack of kittens, The.
Town barberpole.
Town clock's face, The.
Viet Nam Monument.
Winter evening.

Viscusi, Robert (fl. 20th cent.)
Autobiography.

Visick, Mary
Wordsworth on Lloyd George.

Vita-Finzi, C.
Limerick: "Her husband was *hors de combat*."
Limerick: "Lecherous young Lilliputian, A."
Limerick: "Some people may think I'm a bit la-di."
Limerick: "Three scribblers whose names end in Bert."
Limerick: "Unperson from West Oceania, An."
Limerick: "When an amorous youth from Atlantis."

Vitale, Marianne
Become Your Face.
I Read That It Was All a Chain.
Joy Island.
Loop, Fleck, Sound *and So On*.
Patois.
Three Written Poems, Unconnected.
Truth Put It.
Who trusteth in hilarity.
You Oh Even.

Vitéz, Mihály Csokonai (1773–1805)
Constantinople.
Evening.
Happiness.
Love Song to the Foal-Hide Flask.
On My Pneumonia.
Once More to Lilla.
Shy Request.
Susie's Lament for Johnny.
To Hope.
To Solitude.
To the Echo of Tihany.

Vitiello, Justin (fl. 20th cent.)
Letter to a Cretan Flute-Maker.

Vittorelli, Jacopo (1749–1803)
On a Nun.

Vivar, Alicia Galaz
Delivery.

Femmemasochism.
Love Is Round.
Order and the Days, The.

Vizenor, Gerald (b. 1934)
Anishinabe Grandmothers.
Family Photograph.
February Park.
Haiku: "August heat."
Indians at the Guthrie.
North to Milwaukee.
Raising the Flag.
Seasons in Santa Fe.
Seven Woodland Crows.
Shaman Breaks.
Surrendered Names.
Thumbing Old Magazines.
Tropisms on John Berryman.
Tyranny of Moths.
Unhappy Diary Days.
White Earth.

Voce, Lello (b. 1957)
Your eyes stolen.

Voeten, Bert (1918–92)
Sun On My Hand, The.

Vogel, David (1891–1943)
How Can I See You, Love.
I Saw My Father Drowning.
On autumn nights.
Silently you stand before me.
Single and last carriage is ready for the journey, A.
There Is a Last, Solitary Coach.
Waiting-rooms.
With gentle fingers.

Vogelweide, Walther [or Walter] von der (1170?–1230?)
Alas, all my years, where have they disappeared?
Alas, that wisdom, and youth.
Alas! Where Have They Vanished, All Those Years of Mine!
Awake!
Dancing Girl.
Dearly beloved gentle girl.
I sat down on a rock.
I Sat Upon a Stone.
"Lady, take this garland."
Now My Life Has Gained Some Meaning.
There Is a Lady.
Translation from Walter von der Vogelweide, A.
Under the Lindens [or Lime Tree].
Under the Lindentree.
Will anyone tell me what Minne is?
With a Rod No Man Alive.
You excellent women, you valiant men.
You should bid me welcome.

Voigt, Ellen Bryant (b. 1943)
All ears, nose, tongue and gut.
At the Movie: Virginia, 1956.
Blue Ridge.
Exile.
Farm Wife.
Farmer, The.
For My Mother.
Nocturne.
Spire, The.
Why She Says No.
Woman Who Weeps.
Year's End.

Voiture, Vincent (1597–1648)
Rondeau: "Lord, I'm done for: now Margot."
You Know Where You Did Despise.

Volach, Yona (1944–85)
Bird.
Hebrew.
I Have a Stage in My Head.
Life You Have, The.
Tefillin.
When You Come Sleep with Me.

Volkman, Karen (b. 1967)
Create Desire.
Daffodils.
Evening.
Infernal.
Pregnant Lady Playing Tennis, The.

Seasonal.
Shipwreck Poem.
Theft.
Untitled.
Untitled: "If it be event, I go towards and not
back. I go tower, not floor."
Untitled: "Shrewd star, who crudes our
naming: you should be flame."
Untitled: "There comes a time to rusticate the
numbers. The way the birds, jug."
Volkow, Veronica
Washerwoman, The.
Vollmer, Judith
Nursing the Sunburn.
Wildsisters Bar.
Vollmoeller, Karl Gustav (b. 1878)
Nocturne in G Minor.
**Voloshin, Maksimilian Aleksandrovich
(Maksimilian Kirilenko-Voloshin) (1877–
1932)**
Bourgeoisie.
Civil War.
Holy Russia.
In the Bottomless Pit.
Peter the Great, first Bolshevik.
Red Guard.
Voltaire (François Marie Arouet) (1694–1778)
Mountain Mountainous in Parturition, A.
Woeful mankind, born to a woeful earth!
Von Freytag-Loringhoven, Else (1874–1927)
Affectionate.
Café du Dôme.
Dozen Cocktails—Please, A.
Klink—Hratzvenga (Deathwail)
Holy Skirts.
X-Ray.
Von Tilzer, Albert
My Cutey's Due at Two-to-Two Today.
Put Your Arms around Me, Honey.
von Zweck, Dina
One Man's Potato Chip.
Vories, William M. (b. 1880)
Let There Be Light.
Vörös, Mátyás Nyéki (1575–1654)
Of what avail are palaces in hell.
Vörösmarty, Mihály (1800–55)
Ancient Gypsy, The.
Another for Miss Pardo's Album.
Appeal.
Bitter Cup, A.
Fair Ilonka.
Flight of Zalán, The.
For Laura.
Gutenberg Inscription.
On Mankind.
One For Miss Pardo's Travel Diary.
Prologue: "I wrote this when the sky was still
serene."
Soliloquy of the Night, The.
Thoughts in the Library.
To Ferencz Liszt.
To the Day-Dreamer.
Young Pete.
Voznesensky, Andrey [or Andrei] Andreievich
Anguish.
Arrow in the Wall.
Autumn.
Autumn in Sigulda.
Autumn Prelude.
Beatnik's Monologue, The.
Boat on the Shore.
Call of the Lake, The.
Cashier, The.
Chagall's Cornflowers.
Chorus of Nymphs, A.
Darkmotherscream.
Dead Still.
December Pastures.
Dogalypse.
Edge, The.
Elegy for My Mother.
Epitaph for Vysotsky.
First Ice, The.
For a Portrait of Annette Vallon.
Forgive Me!

From the Window of a Plane.
Genealogy of Crosses, The.
Give Me Peace.
Hunting a Hare.
I Am Goya.
In the Mountains.
Ironical Elegy, Composed in Those Terribly
Sad Moments When I Cannot Write.
Look Back into the Future.
Mayakovsky in Paris.
Monologue with Commentary.
New Year's Letter in Warsaw, A.
New York Airport at Night.
Old Song.
On the Metamorphoses Brought about by
Emotion: The Rebellion of the Eyes.
Poem: "From us, like appendicitis."
Portrait of Plisetskaya.
Public Beach No. 2.
Recommendation.
Saga.
Someone Is Beating a Woman.
Striptease.
Big Fire at the Architectural College, The.
Two Poems.
War.
War Ballad.
Why.
"Vrepont, Brian" (B. A. Trubridge) (1882–1955)
Bomber, The.
Vroman, Leo (b. 1915)
Flowers.
Regeneration.
Thin Wire.
Wrinkling Together.
Vroomkoning, Victor (b. 1938)
Returning.
Rubbish Bags.
Together Again.
**Vvedensky [or Vvedenskii], Aleksandr Ivanovich
(1904–41)**
I wish I were a wild beast.
Maybe There's a God Around.
Where.
Vyazemsky, Prince P. A. (1792–1878)
Russian God, The.
**Vysotsky [or Vysotskii], Vladimir Semionovich
(1938–80)**
And ice below, and above—I toil somewhere
in between.
I never believed in mirages.
Unruly Horses.

W

"W., A." (fl. c.1586)
Hopeless Desire Soon Withers and Dies.
In Praise of the Sun.
Upon Visiting His Lady by Moonlight.
Where His Lady Keeps His Heart.
"W., C. A."
To have it out or not? that is the question.
"W——, Miss" (fl. 18th cent.)
Gentleman's Study, in Answer to The Lady's
Dressing-Room, The.
Waddell, Helen (1889–1965)
But we, whose sands run low.
December nights are frosts and stars.
Dim grey wastes of the silent hills.
Earth Said to Death.
Hitler Speaks.
I Shall Not Go to Heaven When I Die.
I stood within the empty House of Youth.
New York City.
Waddell, P. Hately (1817–91)
David and Goliath.
Wadding [or Waddinge], Luke (1588–1657)
Christmas Day [Is Come].
For Innocents' Day.
On the Circumcision: New Year's Day.
Waddington, Miriam (b. 1917)
Advice to the Young.
Catalpa Tree.
Icons.

My Lessons in the Jail.
Old Women of Toronto.
Season's Lovers, The.
Ten Years and More.
Ulysses Embroidered.
Women's Jail, The.
Waddleton, Joan
Fatherhood.
Wade, Barrie
Goldfish.
Truth.
Wade-Gayles, Gloria B. (1940)
Inquisition.
Loving Again.
Wade, Sidney (b. 1951)
Dog Sonnet.
Gas.
Wadsworth, Connemara
Desire.
Wadsworth, William
Need for Attention, The.
Wagenlander, Lydia
Mother's Birthday.
Wagin (d. 1758)
New Year's dawn.
Wagner, Charles L. H.
Let's Forget.
Wagner, Maryfrances Cusumano (fl. 20th cent.)
Miss Clement's Second Grade.
Wagner, Richard (1813–83)
Smile his lips, A.
Wagoner, David (b. 1926)
Advice to the Orchestra.
Author of American Ornithology Sketches a
Bird, Now Extinct, The.
Best Slow Dancer, The.
Chorus: "That rain-strewn night in the woods,
the chorus, chorus."
Diary.
Elegy for a Forest Clear-Cut by the
Weyerhaeuser Company.
Excursion of the Speech and Hearing Class,
The.
Five Dawn Skies in November.
In the Badlands.
Leaving Something Behind.
Looking for Mountain Beavers.
Loons Mating.
Making Camp.
Making up for a Soul.
Man of the House, The.
Meeting a Bear.
My Father's Garden.
Naval Trainees Learn How to Jump Overboard,
The.
Nuthatch.
On Motel Walls.
Peacock Display.
Poem about Breath.
Poets Agree to Be Quiet by the Swamp, The.
Shooting of John Dillinger outside the
Biograph Theater July 22, 1934, The.
Singing Lesson, The.
Source, The.
Staying Alive.
To a Farmer Who Hung Five Hawks on His
Barbed Wire.
Victorian Idyll, A.
Walking in a Swamp.
Young Girl with a Pitcher Full of Water, A.
Wah, Fred (b. 1939)
Breathe Dust.
Wain, John (b. 1925)
Anniversary.
Apology for Understatement.
Arrival.
Au Jardin des Plantes.
Brooklyn Heights.
Song about Major Eatherly, A.
Wainwright, Jeffrey (b. 1944)
1815.
Apparent Colonnades, The.
Fierce Dream, The.
Illumination.
Thomas Müntzer.

Waits, Tom (b. 1949)
Swordfishtrombone.
Wake, W. Bernard
Limerick: "Student of nuclear fission, A."
Wakefield, Samuel (1799–1895)
Music of His Steps, The.
Wakolele, Nguno
Southern Africa.
Wakoski, Diane (b. 1937)
Apology, An.
Belly Dancer.
Blue Monday.
Blue Suede Shoes.
Canoer, The.
Father of My Country, The.
For Craig Who Leapt off a Cliff in to
    Hummingbird Light.
George Washington and the Loss of His Teeth.
Hitchhikers, The.
Hummingbird Light.
Ice Eagle, The.
Imagining Point Dume.
Inside Out.
Light.
Mirror of a Day Chiming Marigold, The.
My Trouble.
Night a Sailor Came to Me in a Dream, The.
Night Blooming Jasmine.
Patriotic Poem.
Photos, The.
Placing a $2 Bet for a Man Who Will Never
    Go to the Horse Races Any More.
Poet Recognizing the Echo of the Voice, A.
Reading *Bonjour, Tristesse* at the Florence
    Crittenden Home for Unwed Mothers.
Remembering the Pacific.
Ring of Irony, The.
Ringless.
Singer, The.
Summer.
Valentine for Ben Franklin Who Drives a
    Truck in California, A.
Walking Past Paul Blackburn's Apt. on 7th St.
Wakuan-Shitai (1108–69)
Iron tree blooms.
Wakyu (d. 1692)
My four and forty years.
Wakyu (d. 1759)
In the end.
Walafrid Strabo (809–49)
To His Friend in Absence.
With His Book, of Gardening.
Walcott, Derek (b. 1930)
Adios, Carenage.
Ajax, / lion-coloured stallion from Sealey's
    stable.
Arkansas Testament, The.
Camps hold [*or* held] their distance—[of]
    brown chestnuts and grey smoke, The.
Chicago's avenues, as white as Poland.
Cloud, The.
Codicil.
Country Club Romance, A.
Crusoe's Island.
Eulogy to W.H. Auden.
Far Cry from Africa, A.
Fist, The.
Force.
Fortunate Traveller, The.
Frederiksted, Dusk.
Gauguin.
Glory Trumpeter, The.
Gulf, The.
He yawned and watched the lilac horns of his
    island.
Hotel Normandie Pool, The.
In the middle of the harbour.
Italian Eclogues.
Le Loupgarou.
Letter from Brooklyn, A.
Man o' War Bird.
Man Who Loved Islands, The.
Midsummer.
Midsummer, Tobago.
Missing the Sea.
Nearing La Guaira.

New World.
Nights in the Gardens of Port of Spain.
Oak inns creak in their joints as light declines,
    The.
Polish Rider, The.
Pomme arac.
Port of Spain.
Rest, Christ! from tireless war. See, it's
    midsummer.
Ruins of a Great House.
Saddhu of Couva, The.
Schooner Flight, The.
Sea Canes.
Sea-Chantey, A.
Sea Grapes.
Season of Phantasmal° Peace, The.
Tales of the Islands.
Tomorrow, Tomorrow.
Upstate.
Villa Restaurant, The.
Village Life, A.
Virgins, The.
Voice out of the Sabbaths, A.
Volcano.
Whale, His Bulwark, The.
Winding Up.
Young Wife, The.
Walden, Gale Renée
Misguided Angels.
Walders, Davi
Anniversary.
Waldinger, Ernst
Beethoven Sonata.
Even the Beating Heart Is Already Indicated.
False Prophet, The.
Forgive, But Do Not Forget.
I Am a Son of the German Language.
Lidice.
Memorials, The.
Mozart, Piano Concerto No. 20 in D Minor,
    K.466.
Music for This Time.
On Love of the Homeland.
Pope John XXIII.
Report from Germany, 1944.
They Killed Our Longing for Our Homeland.
Waldman, Anne (b. 1945)
& Now the book is closed.
Baby's Pantoum.
Berthe Morisot.
Fait Accompli.
Iovis XIX: Why That's a Blade Can Float.
Lady Tactics.
Nerves.
Pressure.
Skin / Meat / BONES
Under My Breath.
Waldrop, Keith (b. 1932)
Balancing. Austere. Life.
Proposition II.
Wandering Curves.
Will to Will.
Waldrop, Rosmarie (b. 1935)
Chapter XXIII: Of Marriage.
Chapter XXIV: Concerning Their Coyne.
Feverish Propositions.
Lawn of Excluded Middle.
Relaxed Abalone, The.
To explore the nature of rain I opened the door
    because inside the workings of language
    clear vision is impossible.
Waley, Arthur (1889–1966)
Censorship.
Walker, Alice (b. 1944)
Early Losses: A Requiem.
Even as I Hold You.
Good Night, Willie Lee, I'll See You in the
    Morning.
Kiss, The.
Medicine.
On Stripping Bark from Myself.
Once.
Remember?
Revolutionary Petunias.
Women.
Walker, Frank X. (b. 1961)
Crooked Afro.

Sweet Bread.
Wishbone.
Walker, J. (1881–1946)
Love Song of J. Alfred Prufrock, The.
Walker, James (b. 1940)
Safe.
Walker, Jeanne Murray (b. 1944)
Studying Physics with My Daughter.
Walker, Kath *See* **Oodgeroo of the tribe**
    Noonuccal (Kath Walker)
Walker, Margaret Abigail (1915–98)
Ballad of the Hoppy-Toad.
Childhood.
Dark Blood.
Delta.
For Andy Goodman—Michael Schwerner—
    and James Chaney.
For Malcolm X.
Girl Held without Bail.
Kissie Lee.
Lineage.
Molly Means.
Poppa Chicken.
Prophets for a New Day.
Since 1619.
Street Demonstration.
Whores.
Walker, Robert (1958–84)
Life Is Life.
Okay, Let's Be Honest.
Solitary Confinement.
Unreceived Messages.
Walker, Ted (b. 1934)
Owl.
Walker, William (1623–84)
High o'er the Hills.
Walker, William Sidney (1795–1846)
Too solemn for day, too sweet for night.
Wallace-Crabbe, Chris (b. 1934)
Abhorring a Vacuum.
And the World was Calm.
Binary.
Citizen.
Collective Invention, The.
Dirigible, The.
Double Dactyl.
Nub.
Life of Ideas, The.
Mental Traveller's Landfall, The.
Opener.
Rebel General, The.
Secular, The.
Shape-Changer, The.
Sonnet IV.
Sporting the Plaid.
Tribunal, The.
Windows, The.
Wallace, Edgar (1875–1932)
Song of the Bounder, The.
War.
Wallace, Robert (1858–1938)
Dog's Song.
Problem in History, A.
Under the September Peach.
Wallace, Ronald (b. 1945)
Basketball.
Building an Outhouse.
Facts of Life, The.
Makings of Happiness, The.
Nightline: An Interview with the General.
Sestina for the House.
Smoking.
Sound Systems.
State Poetry Day.
Thirteen.
Wallace, William Ross (1819–81)
Hand That Rocks the Cradle Is the Hand That
    Rules the World, The.
Wallāda (*fl.* 11th cent.)
To Ibn Zaidun.
Wait till the darkness is deep.
Wallbank, Susan (b. 1943)
Why So Many of Them Die.
Wallenstein, Barry (*fl.* 20th cent.)
Blues 1.

Blues 2.

Waller, Edmund (1606–87)
Aid me Bellona, while the dreadful fight.
At Penshurst [Another].
Budd, The.
Fall, The.
Love's Farewell.
Of English Verse.
Of Loving at First Sight.
Of My Lady Isabella Playing on the Lute.
Of the Last Verses in the Book.
Of the Marriage of the Dwarfs.
On a Girdle.
On St. James's Park, as Lately Improved by His Majesty.
Seas are quiet when the winds give o'er, The.
Song: "Go[e], lovely rose."
Song: "Stay Phoebus, stay."
Story of Phoebus and Daphne Applied, [etc.], The.
To a Fair Lady Playing with a Snake.
To a Lady in a Garden.
To a Very Young Lady.
To Chloris, upon a Favour Received.
To Mr. Henry Lawes, Who Had Then Newly Set a Song of Mine in the Year 1635.
To One Married to an Old Man.
To Phyllis.
To the King, on His Navy.
To the Mutable Fair.
Under a Lady's Picture.
Upon Ben Johnson [or Jonson].
Upon His Majesty's [or Majesties] Repairing of Paul's.
While I Listen to Thy Voice.
Waller, Sir John
Limerick: "Artist who lived near Montmartre, An."
Waller, Marey (fl. 1674)
To; Oxon.
Waller, Thomas ("Fats")
Ain't Misbehavin'
Honeysuckle Rose.
Joint is Jumpin', The.
Keepin' Out of Mischief Now.
Ladies Who Sing with a Band, The.
There's a Man in My Life.
(What Did I Do to Be So) Black and Blue?
Walley, Dean
Limerick: "Inept young person, Miss Muffet, The."
Wallis, Hannah (fl. 1787)
Female's Lamentations, The; or, The Village in Mourning.
To a Sick Friend.
To Mrs.———, on the Death of Her Husband.
Wallis, John (1616–1703)
Twister Twisting Twine.
Wallis, Severn Teackle (1816–94)
Prayer for Peace, A.
Walls, Doyle Wesley
Summer the Beatles Went over Seven Minutes on a Single, The.
Walpole, Horace, 4th Earl of Orford (1717–97)
All praise your face, your verses none abuse.
Epitaphs [or Epitaph] on Two Piping-Bullfinches of Lady Ossory's, Buried under a Rose-Bush in Her Garden.
Estate and an earldom at seventy-four, An!
On the Translation of Anacreon.
To Lady Anne Fitzpatrick, When about Five Years Old, with a Present of Shells, 1772.
To the Gardener at Nuneham.
Walsh, Catherine (b. 1964)
Matter / of fact.
Nearly Nowhere.
Walsh, Chad (b. 1914)
Psalm of Christ, The.
Quintina of Crosses, A.
Walsh, Christina (b. 1964)
Prayer to Isis.
Woman to Her Lover, A.
Walsh, John (1911–1972)
I've Got an Apple Ready.
Walsh, Marnie
Thomas Iron-Eyes.

Walsh, Octavia (1677–1706)
At length my soul the fatal union finds.
Walsh, William (1663–1708)
Despairing Lover, The.
Love and Jealousy.
Lyce.
Phillis's Resolution.
Rivals.
Walsh, William (1663–1708) and Sir George Etherege (1653–91)
Imperfect Enjoyment, The.
Rivals.
Song: "If she be not as kind as fair."
Walter, Nehemiah (1663–1750)
Elegiack Verse on Mr. Elijah Corlet, An.
Walters, Anna (b. 1946)
Hartico.
I Am of the Earth.
I Have Bowed before the Sun.
My Brothers.
Simplicity Aims Circularly.
Teacher Taught Me, A.
Walters, Dorothy (b. 1924)
Flannery O'Connor.
Walters, Elizabeth
Elizabeth Walters is my name.
Walters, Muru (b. 1935)
Haka: The Feathered Albatross.
Walton, Alfred Grant
First Impressions.
Recipe for Living.
Sincere Man, The.
World We Make, The.
Walton, Anthony
Dissidence.
Third Shift.
Walton, Eda Lou (b. 1896)
In Recompense.
Walton, John
God, the Port of Peace.
Walwicz, Ania (b. 1951)
Abattoir, The.
Big Tease.
Daredevil.
Little Red Riding Hood.
Tattoo, The.
Wonderful.
Walworth, Clarence A. (1820–1900)
Holy God, We Praise Thy Name.
Wanek, Connie
Duluth, Minnesota.
Wang An-shih (1021–86)
At Home.
At the Chiang-ning River Mouth.
Autumn Sun over the *t'ung* Tree.
Bald Mountain.
By a Stream on Mount T'ien-t'ung.
By the River.
Composed on Horseback, Returning from Lakeview Pavilion at Hangchow, Presented to Yü-ju and Lo-tao.
Confiscating Salt.
Fresh Flowers.
Had I been an ox or horse.
Hastily Composed on the Mo-ling Road.
Hui-chu Temple, Mount K'un.
Impromptu; Late Spring at Pan-shan.
In the Mountains.
Night Watch.
Old Pine, An.
On Chung Mountain.
On the Yangtze.
Once I was a cow, a horse.
Plum Blossoms on Solitary Hill.
Sketch of Mount Chung, A.
Song of the Radiant Lady.
Spring Evening on Pan Mountain.
Tune: "Mountain Hawthorns."
Tune: "Sand of Silk-washing Stream."
Walking in the Countryside.
Wind blew, a tile fell from the roof, The.
Working for the Government.
Written at Hsiang-kuo Temple on the Occasion of Watching Actors in the Hsing-hsiang Garden of the T'ung-t'ien-chieh Tao-ch'ang.

Written for My Own Amusement.
Written on the Wall of Halfway Mountain Temple.
Written on the Wall of Pan-shan Temple.
Wang Ch'ang-ling (698–757)
At Jad Gate Pass mountain ridges several thousand-fold.
Castleside Song.
Complaint from a Lady's Chamber.
In the citadel of Jade Gate Pass, elm leaves early scatter yellow.
Listening to a Wanderer's "Water Melody."
P'i-p'a begins the dance, midst changing new sounds, The.
Silent at Her Window.
Sorrow in the Harem, A.
Wang Chi (fl. c.700)
In Praise of Carnations.
Sent to Recluse Ch'eng.
Tell Me Now.
Viewing Mr. Yü's Landscape Painting on the Wall.
Wang Chien (768?–833?)
At home I loved to wear old clothes.
Boatman's Song, A.
Early autumn, white rabbits.
Hearing That His Friend Was Coming Back from the War.
Her silken gown rustles.
Long the flimsy skirts.
Pair of green-painted eyebrows, A.
Palace girls up early.
Palace Song.
Red lantern calls the spring clouds from my sleep, A.
South, The.
Spring breeze blows the rain, A.
Wanting to welcome the emperor.
Weaving at the Window.
Wang Chih-huan (688?–742)
Ascend the Heron Tower.
Climbing the Stork Pavilion.
View from Heron Tower.
Wang Ch'ing-hui (fl. 13th cent.)
Now the lotuses in the imperial lake.
Wang Chiu-ssu (1468–1551)
After Reading the Poems of Master Han Shan.
Ballad of Selling a Child.
Ballad of the Fatherless Boy.
Chanting Poems.
Floating, floating, the river waters.
For Several Days I Have Not Visited the Garden Pavilion—A Poem Sent to My Pet Crane.
I love the serenity of living in the woods.
Quiet Sitting.
Recording My Happiness.
Rising from Sleep.
Song of the Painting of the Long-Life Star.
This crazy man has escaped the world.
Thunder.
Today I am a farmer in the fields.
Total failure—Master Han Shan, A.
You think I am happy.
Wang Fan-chih (590?ND/660?)
Drinking Alone.
Grass hovel filled with wind and dust.
Having power is nothing to be concerned about.
I, Fan-chih, wear my socks inside out.
I have a couple acres of land.
I saw another man die.
No one lives past a hundred.
On the outskirts, dumplings of mud.
Poem: "When the rich pass proudly by."
Reclusive.
Requiem: "Houses in country and city."
That fellow rides a big horse.
Yellow gold's not precious.
Wang Ho-ch'ing
Tune: 'Po Pu-tuan' Fat Couple.
Tune: 'Po Pu-tuan' Long-Haired Little Dog.
Tune: 'Tsui-chung T'ien' To the Giant Butterfly.
Wang Hsi-chih (321–79)
Orchid Pavilion.

Wang I (*fl.* c.120)
Lychee, The.
Lychee-tree, The.

Wang , Jiaosheng
Tune: 'Magnolia Flowers.'
Tune: 'The Charm of a Maiden Singer;' Spring Thoughts.

Wang K'ang-chü (*fl.* 4th cent.)
Refuting the "Invitation to Hiding."

Wang Kuo-wei (1877–1927)
To Try to Find.
Tune: "Butterflies Lingering over Flowers."
Tune: "Echoing Heaven's Everlastingness."
Tune: "Immortal at the River."
Tune: 'Rouged Lips.'
Tune: 'Sand of Silk-Washing Brook.'
Tune: "Sand of Silk-washing Stream."
Tune: "Song of Picking Mulberry."

Wang Pin-chih (*fl.* 400)
Orchard Pavilion.

Wang Po (c.650–76)
In the Mountains.

Wang Po-ch'eng (*fl.* c.1279)
Song of Parting.

Wang Seng-ju (465–522)
Describing a Dream for Someone.

Wang Seng-ta (423–58)
I think of when she sits.
I think of when she sleeps.
Out Early One Morning, I Met an Old Acquaintance.
To Match the Prince of Lang-yeh's Poem in the Old Style.
Written for My Neighbor.

Wang Shih-chieng (1634–1711)
After Rain, Visiting the Temple of Heavenly Peace.
After Snow, Longing for Elder Brother Hsi-ch'iao.
Arriving after Rain at the Temple of Heavenly Peace.
At Ch'en Ch'u.
Bamboo Branch Song of Han-chia.
Ch'ai-kuan Mountain Pass.
Composed at the West Wall of Tsou-p'ing Three Days after the Festival of Pure Brightness.
Crossing the Yangtze in a Strong Wind.
Dawn at Chiao Mountain, Seeing off K'un-lun on His Way Back to Ching-k'ou.
Echoing Old Man Mu's Poem, "Inscribed on Shen Lang-ch'ien's Little Landscape, Autumn Willows at Stone Cliff."
Lamenting for My Wife.
Lieh Mountain.
Medicine.
Moonlit Night at Fragrant Mountain Temple.
Mooring at Night at Kao-yu.
Mooring at Night at the River Mouth, I Heard a Flute—Sent to My Elder Brother Hsi-ch'iao.
Occasionial Poem: Upon Seeing Lotuses Bloom in a Vase.
On the Way to Huang-ch'ang River.
Pure Sound Pavilion.
Quatrain at Chen-chou.
Sailing along the Tai Stream from Stone Bridge to the Foot of Mo-ho Peak.
Seeing off Editor Wang Chou-tz'u and Secretary Lin Shih-lai on Their Mission as Envoys to the Ryūkyū Islands.
Song of the Ch'in-Dynasty Mirror—Written for Yüan Sung-li.
Things Seen.
Thinking of the Past on an Autumn Night at Tz'u-jen Temple.
What Strikes My Eye.
Written beneath Hui Mountain, When Tsou Liu-yi Comes by for a Visit.

Wang T'ing-hsiang (1474–1544)
At Arrow Rapids, the water splashes foam.
Climbing to the Top of the City Walls at Kan-yü.
Don't ask about the Six Dynasties of the Sui Palace.
Flowering Tree, The.

Miscellaneous Poems on Spirit-Valley Temple.
Miscellaneous Poems Written in the Snow.
On New Year's Day of the Year Kuei-ssu (1533), Releasing Live Creatures.
Song of the Wanderer.
Songs of Chiang-nan.
Written in the Office Precincts.

Wang Ts'an (177–217)
Joining the Army: A Song.
Land of the Ching tribes is not my home, The.
Occasional Verse.
Seven Sorrows.
This frontier post brings me sorrow.
Tribes of Ching—that's not my home.
Western Capital is in turmoil, The.

Wang Wan (693–751?)
Stayover at Pei-Ku-Shan.

Wang Wei
After Long Rain.
After Source of the Peach Blossom Stream.
Answer to Vice-Prefect Chang.
Army Ballad.
Arriving at Ba Gorge in the Morning.
At a House in the Bamboo Grove.
At Lake Yi.
At Li's Mountain Hermitage.
At My Country Home in Chung-nan.
At the Hermitage of Master Fu.
Autumn.
Autumn Dusk at a Mountain Lodge.
Autumn Twilight in the Mountains.
Bamboo Grove.
Bird and Waterfall Music.
Bird-Singing Stream.
Birdsong Brook.
Birdsong Valley.
Chi River Gardens and Fields.
Climbing Pien-chueh Temple.
Cold Mountain, The.
Crossing the Yellow River.
Deep in the Mountain Wilderness.
Deer Enclosure.
Deer Park.
Departure.
Duckweed Pond.
Enjoying Coolness.
Farms at Wei River, The.
Floating on the River Han.
Four Examples from the Poems of River Wang Deer Enclosure.
Hermitage at Chung-nan Mountain.
Hsin-I Village.
In the Hills.
In the Mountain.
Lush, lush, fragrant grasses in autumn green.
Meal for the Monks, A.
Morning.
Mount Chung-Nan.
Mourning for Yin Yao.
On Returning to Sung Mountain.
Passing the Temple of Teeming Fragrance.
Red Peonies.
Reply to a Magistrate.
Return to Wang River.
Rill of the House of the Luans.
Sailing Down the Han.
Second Song for the Worship of the Goddess at Yu Mountain: 'Bidding the Goddess Farewell.'
Seeing Someone Off.
Seeking a Mooring.
Sitting Alone on an Autumn Night.
Song for Wei City, A.
Song of Peach Tree Spring.
Spring Night at Bamboo Pavillion, Presenting a Poem to Subprefect Qian about His Staying for Good in Blue Field Mountains.
Suffering from Heat.
Thinking of My Brother in Shantung on the Ninth Day of the Ninth Moon.
To See a Friend Off.
To Subprefect Chang.
Twenty Views of Wang-ch'uan.
Twilight Comes.
Verses: "You who come from the old village."
Villa at the Foot of Mount Chungnan.
Visiting Hsiang-Chi Monastery.

Visiting the Mountain Hermitage of a Monk at Gan-hua Monastery.
Visiting the Temple of Accumulated Fragrance.
Walking at Leisure.
Way to the Temple, The.
Weather Newly Cleared.
Weeping for Ying Yao.

Wang Ya (c.764–835)
Palace Poem.
Song of Autumn Night.
Song of Spring Journeying.

Wang Yang-ming (1472–1529)
Magic City Monastery.
Taoist Song.

Wang Yen-Shou (*fl.* 2nd cent. A.D.)
Nightmare, The.
Wangsun, The.

Wang-ying, Hsieh *See* "Ping Hsin"

Wang Yü-ch'eng (954–1001)
Journey to a Village.
Journeying to the Village.
Random Thoughts Written in Spring.
Song of the Crow Pecking at My Scarred Donkey.

Wang Yung (468–85)
River Song, The.

Waniek, Marilyn Nelson (Lynn Nelson) (b. 1946)
Alderman.
Balance.
Bali Hai Calls Mama.
Ballad of Aunt Geneva, The.
Canticle for Abba Jacob, A.
Chosen.
Daughters, 1900.
Diverne's Waltz.
Emily Dickinson's Defunct.
Freeman Field.
House on Moscow Street, The.
Letter to a Benedictine Monk.
Lonely Eagles.
My Grandfather Walks in the Woods.
Porter.
Sacrament of Poverty, The.
Sleepless Nights.
Star-Fix.
Three Men in a Tent.
Tuskegee Airfield.
Women's Locker Room.

Wanley, Nathaniel (1634–80)
Resurrection, The.
Royal[l] Presents.

Warburton, N. J.
Snake on D. H. Lawrence, The.

Warburton, R. E. Egerton (1804–91)
Past and Present.

Ward, David Scott (b. 1961)
Hunting in Twilight.
My Brothers Make a Lantern.

Ward, Diane (b. 1956)
Absolution.
Approximately.
Crossing.
Glass House.
Immediate Content Recognition.
Limit.
Lovely Stuff.
Re-Verse.
Shakeout.
Tables in Pictures.

Ward, Edward (1667–1731)
Ballad on the Taxes, A.
Dialogue between a Squeamish Cotting Mechanic and His Sluttish Wife, in the Kitchen.
Extravagant Drunkard's Wish, The.
Parish Poor-Officers, The.
South Sea Ballad, A.

Ward, J. P. (b. 1937)
To Get Clear.
Unusual View of the Town.

Ward, Jerry W., Jr. (b. 1943)
Comfort-Maker.

Ward, John Powell (b. 1937)
Here, Home.
London Welsh v. Bridgend.

Marathon.
Wye below Bredwardine, The.
Ward, Nathaniel (1578–1652)
Mercury shew'd Apollo, Bartas Book.
Mr. Ward of Anagrams Thus.
Poetry's a gift wherein but few excell.
World's a well strung fidle, man's tongue the quill, The.
Ward, Thom (b. 1963)
Dark Underfoot.
In the Interest of Possibility.
On Being Kicked Out of the Harold Washington Library Center for Napping on the Floor.
Stray Dogs, Foaming.
Tacit.
Wardman, Gordon
I have horns, but am not beast.
Ware, Henry, Jr. (1794–1843)
Great God, the Followers of Thy Son.
Lift Your Glad Voices in Triumph on High.
Warfield, Catherine Anne (1816–77)
Forests and Caverns.
Sun-Struck Eagle, The.
Waring, Anna L. (1823–1950)
My Times Are in Thy Hand.
Waring, Belle
Baby Random.
Baltazar Beats His Tutor at Scrabble.
Breeze in Translation.
Look.
Nothing Happened.
Our Lady of the Laundromat.
Refuge at the One Step Down.
Reprieve on the Stoop.
So Get over It, Honey.
Tip, The.
When a Beautiful Woman Gets on the Jutiapa Bus.
Warn, Emily
After Reading the Book of Splendor.
Dwelling.
Warner, Anna Bartlett ("Amy Lothrop") (1827–1915)
Jesus Loves Me, This I Know.
One More Day's Work for Jesus.
We Would See Jesus.
Warner, Eva
Irony of God.
Warner, Rex (b. 1905)
Chough.
Egyptian Kites.
Warner, Sylvia Townsend (1893–1978)
Absence, The.
After He Had Gone.
Alarum, The.
Become as little children.
Benicasim.
Building in Stone.
Clock Plods on, The.
Country Thought.
Elizabeth.
Epitaph: "Her grieving parents cradled here."
Epitaph: "I, an unwedded wandering dame."
Epitaph: "I, Richard Kent, beneath these stones."
Epitaph: "John Bird, a laborer, lies here."
Eyes of [or the] body, being blindfold by night, The.
Gloriana Dying.
Green Valley, The.
Modo and Alciphron.
Killing No Murder.
King Duffus.
Nelly Trim.
Rival, The.
Sad Green.
Sailor, The.
Since the first toss of gale that blew.
Song from the Bride of Smithfield.
Song: "She has left me, my pretty."
To no believable blue I turn my eyes.
Triumph of Sensibility.
Warner, William (1558?–1609)
Tale of the Beginning of Friars and

Cloisterers, A.
Warr, Bertram J. (1917–43)
Working Class.
Warr, Michael (fl. 20th cent.)
Brain on Ice.
Malcolm Is 'Bout More Than Wearing a Cap.
Warren, Harry
Chattanooga Choo-Choo.
Dames.
Forty-second Street.
Gold Digger's Song (We're in the Money), The.
Great Big Bunch of You, A.
I Found a Million Dollar Baby (In a Five and Ten Cent Store)
I'll String along with You.
I Only Have Eyes for You.
I've Got a Gal in Kalamazoo.
I, Yi, Yi, Yi, Yi (I Like You Very Much)
Jeepers Creepers.
Lullaby of Broadway.
Lulu's Back in Town.
Nagasaki.
No Love, No Nothin'
On the Atchison, Topeka and the Santa Fe.
Remember Me?
September in the Rain.
Serenade in Blue.
She's a Latin from Manhattan.
Shuffle off to Buffalo.
Spring Isn't Everything.
There Will Never Be Another You.
This Heart of Mine.
Would You Like to Take a Walk?
You're Getting to Be a Habit with Me.
Young and Healthy.
Warren-Moore, Jackie (b. 1950)
All-Night Issue, The.
Dannemora Contraband.
For Etheridge Knight.
For Paula Cooper.
Pink Poem.
Warren, Mrs. Mercy (1728–1814)
Limerick: "Maiden at college called Breeze, A."
Warren, Robert Penn (1905–89)
Acquaintance with Time in Early Autumn.
After Night Flight Son Reaches Bedside of Already Unconscious Father, Whose Right Hand Lifts in a Spasmodic Gesture, as Though Trying to Make Contact: 1955.
After the Dinner Party.
Afterward.
All is nothing, nothing all.
Amazing Grace in the Back Country.
Apology for Domitian.
Arizona Midnight.
Aubade for Hope.
Audubon: A Vision.
Ballad of Billie Potts, The.
Bearded Oaks.
Birth of Love.
Confederate Veteran Tries to Explain the Event, A.
Covered Bridge.
Crime.
Dawn.
Dead Horse in Field.
Death of Time.
Debate: Question, Quarry, Dream.
Evening Hawk.
Fall Comes in Back-Country Vermont.
Flaubert in Egypt.
Gold Glade.
Heart of Autumn.
History among the Rocks.
History during Nocturnal Snowfall.
I Can't Even Remember the Name.
Blow, West Wind.
If.
Last Meeting.
Lessons in History.
Letter from a Coward to a Hero.
Letter of a Mother.
Letter to a Friend.
Little Girl Wakes Early.

Love and Knowledge.
Man in the Street.
Mango on the Mango Tree, The.
Masts at Dawn.
Muted Music.
Myth on Mediterranean Beach: Aphrodite as Logos.
Nameless Thing.
Natural History.
Night Walking.
Old-Time Childhood in Kentucky.
Only Poem, The.
Original Sin.
Owl, The.
Patriotic Tour and Postulate of Joy.
Picnic Remembered.
Pondy Woods.
Pro Sua Vita.
Pursuit.
Rattlesnake Country.
Return: An Elegy, The.
Revelation.
Riddle in the Garden.
Sila.
Tale of Time.
Tell Me a Story.
There once, on that goat island, I.
There's a Grandfather's Clock in the Hall.
To a Face in a Crowd.
Two Studies in Idealism: Short Survey of American and Human History.
Vermont Ballad: Change of Season.
Vermont Thaw.
Vision.
Was Not the Lost Dauphin.
Way to Love God, A.
Wet Hair: If Now His Mother Should Come.
What Voice at Moth-Hour.
When the Century Dragged.
Where the Slow Fig's Purple Sloth.
Whole Question, The.
You Sort Old Letters.
Warren, Rosanna (b. 1954)
Daylights.
Funerary Portraits.
Hagar.
His Long Home.
History as Decoration.
In Creve Coeur, Missouri.
Interior at Petworth: From Turner.
Man, That Is Born of a Woman.
Max Jacob at Saint Benoît.
Renoir.
Song: "Yellow coverlet, A."
To Max Jacob.
Warren, William F. (1833–1929)
I Worship Thee, O Holy Ghost.
Warrior, Emma Lee (b. 1941)
Enemy's Eyes, The.
How I Came to Have a Man's Name.
New Indian Medicine.
Reginald Pugh, The Man Who Came from the Army.
Warsh, Lewis (b. 1944)
Downward Mobility.
Elegy: "Leaves have a sense of, The."
Enmeshment.
Good Omen.
Gout.
Man Escaped, A.
Mistaken Identity.
Static, The.
Suicide Rates, The.
Travelogue.
White Nights.
Warshawski, Morrie
Sonia at 32.
Warton, Joseph (1722–1800)
Dying Indian, The.
Enthusiast: or, The Lover of Nature, The.
O warm, enthusiastic maid.
Ode to Evening.
Revenge of America, The.
Verses Written at Montauban in France, 1750.
Ye green-robed Dryads, oft at dusky eve.
Warton, Thomas, the Elder (fl. late 17th cent.)
Fashioned after the Manner of Master Geoffrey

Chaucer in His Assembly of Fowls.
Ode on the Passion.
On the Spirit Adulterated by the Flesh.
Stanzas Imitated From Psalm CXIX.
Stanzas on the Psalms.

Warton, Thomas, the Younger (1728–90)
Beneath yon ruin'd abbey's moss-grown piles.
Come, gentle sleep, death's image though thou art.
On Bathing.
On King Arthur's Round Table, at Winchester.
On Leander's Swimming over the Hellespont to Hero.
Prologue on the Old Winchester Playhouse over the Old Butchers' Shambles.
Sonnet: To the River Lodon.
Tapered choir, at the late hour of prayer, The.
To Mr. Gray.
Verses on Sir Joshua Reynolds's Painted Window at New College, Oxford.
While summer-suns o'er the gay prospect played.
Written at Stonehenge.

Washbourne, Thomas (1606–87)
Casting All Your Care upon God, for He Careth for You.
Circulation, The.
God's Two Dwellings.
Upon a Great Shower of Snow That Fell on May-Day, 1654.

Washburn, Henry Stevenson (1813–1903)
Almighty God, Thy Constant Care.

Washington, Ned
Give Me a Heart to Sing To.
Hundred Years from Today, A.
Love Is the Thing.
My Foolish Heart.
Nearness of You, The.
Woman's Intuition, A.

Washington, Raymond
Freedom Hair.
Moon Bound.
Vision from the Ghetto.

Wastell, Simon (d. 1632)
Man's Mortality.

Wat, Aleksander (1900–67)
By a great, swift water.
Facing Bonnard.
From "Songs of a Wanderer."
Imagerie d'Epinal.
Japanese Archery.
Joke, A.

Waterbury, Jared Bell (1799–1876)
I Have Fought the Good Fight.
Sinner, Is Thy Heart at Rest?

Waterman, Nixon (1857–89)
Cheer for the Consumer.
If We Didn't Have to Eat.
Rose to the living is more than, A.

Waters, Michael (b. 1949)
American Bandstand.
Burden Lifters, The.
Christ at the Apollo, 1962.
Horse.
'Night in the Tropics' (1858–59?).

Waters, Muddy (McKinley Morganfield) (1915–83)
Hoochie Coochie.

Watkins, Nayo-Barbara ("Nayo" Barbara Malcolm)
Bedtime Story.
Black Woman Throws a Tantrum.
Easy way out.
First time I was sweet sixteen.
I watched little black boys.

Watkins, Vernon (1906–67)
Collier, The.
Feather, The.
Foal.
For a Wine Festival.
Healing of the Leper, The.
Heron, The.
Indolence.
Lady with the Unicorn, The.
Mare, The.

Music of Colours: The Blossom Scattered.
Music of Colours—White Blossom.
Ode to Swansea.
Old Triton Time.
Ophelia.
Peace in the Welsh Hills.
Replica, The.
Returning to Goleufryn.
Swedenborg's Skull.
Taliesin and the Mockers.
Two Decisions.

Watkyns, Rowland (fl. 1635–64)
Anabaptist, The.
Antipathy.
Bad company is a disease.
Blackamoors, The.
Common People, The.
Gardener, The.
Golden Grove, Carmarthen.
Holy Sepulchre, The.
New Illiterate Lay-Teachers, The.
Peace and War.
Periwig, The.
Saul did much care and diligence express.
Shrew, The.
Strange Monsters.
To the Reader.
Upon Christ's Nativity or Christmas.
Upon the mournful death of our late Soveraign Lord Charles the First, King of England, etc.
Worldly Wealth.

Watson, Clyde (b. 1947)
Dilly Dilly Piccalilli.
Do the Baby Cake-Walk.
Knickerbocker Knockabout.
Phoebe in a Rosebush.
Rock, Rock, Sleep, My Baby.

Watson, Ellen
Battered Toddler, Page B6.

Watson, Frank
Limerick: "Said a practical thinker: "One should."

Watson, Maureen
Black Child.
Female of the Species.
Memo to J. C.
Stepping Out.

Watson, Rosamund Marriott (1863–1911)
Aubade: "Lights are out in the street, and a cool wind swings, The."
Ave atque Vale.
Ballad of the Bird-Bride.
Ballad of the Were-Wolf, A.
Betty Barnes, the Book-Burner.
Cage, The.
Children of the Mist.
Die Zauberflöte.
Enchanted Princess, An.
Hic Jacet.
Midnight Harvest, A.
Moor Girl's Well, The.
Nirvana.
Of the Earth, Earthy.
Ruined Altar, A.
Serenade: "Who is it sings the gypsies' song to-night."
Vespertilia.
White Bird, The.
White Lady, The.

Watson, Roy W. (b. 1926)
View on Death, A.
Who a Mother Is.

Watson, Thomas (c.1557–92)
Go Idle Lines.
I Saw the Object.
My Love Is Past.

Watson, W. F. N.
Limerick: "Couple there was in Blefuscu, A."
Limerick: "Dear Albert, of Saxe-Coburg-Gotha."
Limerick: "Fellow from far Erewhon, A."
Limerick: "Feminine mouth in Utopia, The."
Limerick: "Few things to desire can so prod us."
Limerick: "Lady from Vanity Fair, A."
Limerick: "There was a young lady of Lundy."

Limerick: "Young couple who lived at "The Laurels", A."

Watson, Wilfred (b. 1911)
Canticle of Darkness.
Emily Carr.
Invocation: "Appear, O Mother, was the perpetual cry."
Lines: I Praise God's Mankind in an Old Woman.
O My Poor Darling.
White Bird, The.

Watson, Sir William (1858–1935)
Epitaph, An: "His friends he loved. His direst earthly foes."
Ode in May.
Song: "April, April / Laugh thy girlish laughter."

Watta, Oumarou (b. 1951)
Cloud Rains.
Stone at the Tip of the Tongue, A.

Watteau, Otto
Limerick: "Oh, halt!" cried Virginia, "Enough!"

Watten, Barrett (b. 1948)
Complete Thought I - XXV.
Isolate and.
Radio.
Relax, / stand at attention, and.
Statistics.

Watterman, Catharine H. (1812–97)
Come unto Me, When Shadows Darkly Gather.

Watts, Alaric Alexander (1797–1864)
Austrian Army, An.
Ten Years Ago.

Watts-Dunton, Theodore (1832–1914)
Coleridge.
Sonnet's Voice, The.

Watts, Isaac (1674–1748)
Adventurous Muse, The.
Broad Is the Road.
Christ hath a garden walled around.
Church the Garden of Christ, The.
Cradle Hymn, A.
Day of Judg[e]ment, The; An Ode.
Felicity.
Few Happy Matches.
Flying Fowl, and Creeping Things, Praise Ye the Lord.
Heaven.
Hosanna to Christ.
How Doth the Little Busy Bee.
How sweet and awful is the place.
Hurry of the Spirits, in a Fever and Nervous Disorders, The.
Hymn: "When I survey the wondrous cross."
Incomprehensible, The.
Innocent Play.
Jesus shall reign where'er the sun.
Joy to the World.
Launching Into Eternity.
Law Given at Sinai, The.
Look on Him Whom They Pierced, and Mourn.
Man Frail, and God Eternal.
Miracles at the Birth of Christ.
Passion and Exaltation of Christ, The.
Praise for Mercies Spiritual and Temporal.
Psalm 58.
Shortness and Misery of Life, The.
Sluggard, The.
Spare Us, O Lord, Aloud We Pray.
Submission to Afflictive Providences.
Sweet Muse, Descend.
Where-e'er My Flatt'ring Passions Rove.
Where Nothing Dwelt but Beasts of Prey.
Why Do We Mourn Departing Friends?

Watts, May Thielgaard (fl 1920s)
Vision.

Waugh, Evelyn (1903–66)
They told me, Francis Hinsley, they told me you were hung.

Wayman, Tom (b. 1945)
Another Poem about the Madness of Women.
Chilean Elegies: 5, The. The Interior.
Despair.

Hating Jews.
Picketing Supermarkets.
Teething.
Wayman in Love.

Wayne, Jane O. (b. 1938)
By Accident.
Cleaning Indian Dahl.
Eavesdropper, The.
In Praise of Zigzags.

Wayne, Mabel
Dreamer's Holiday, A.

Wearne, Alan (b. 1948)
Elise.
Go on, tell me the season is over.
Terri.
Division of O'Dowd, The.

Weatherly, Tom (b. 1942)
Autobiography.
Blues for Franks Wooten.
Mud Water Shango.
Your Eyes Are Mirth.

Weaver, Michael S.
Appaloosa, The.
Beginnings.
Black and White Galaxie, The.
Black Man's Sonata, A.
Blind Solo.
Borders.
Brooklyn.
Dogs, The.
Easy Living.
Imitation of Life.
Improvisation for Piano.
Left Bank Jazz Society, The.
Luxembourg Garden.
Message on Cape Cod, The.
Missing Patriarch, The.
My Father's First Baseball Game.
My Father's Geography.
Picnic, an Homage to Civil Rights, The.
Providence Journal V: Israel of Puerto Rico.
Sub Shop Girl.
Water Song.
Weekend Equestrian, The.

Webb, Charles
Potato Bug.
Rumpelstiltskin Convention.

Webb, Charles Harper
Arson.
At Summer's End.
Invaders from South of the Border Imperil
    Native Population.
You Missed the Earthquake, Bill.

Webb, Charles Henry ("John Paul") (b. 1834)
At the Ball!
Autumn Leaves.

Webb, Chick
Stompin' at the Savoy.

Webb, Francis (1925–73)
Airliner.
Art.
Clouds.
Death at Winson Green, A.
End of the Picnic.
Gunner, The.
Hospital Night.
Laid Off.
Port Phillip Night.
Sea, The.
This Runner.
Tip for Saturday, A.
Towards the Land of the Composer.
Ward Two.
Wild Honey.

Webb, Harri (b. 1920)
Abbey Cwmhir.
Cywydd o Fawl.
Epil y Filiast.
Nightingales, The.
Ode to the Severn Bridge.
Stone Face, The.
Synopsis of the Great Welsh Novel.
Thanks in Winter.
Vive Le Sport.

Webb, Mary (1881–1927)
Why?

Webb, Phyllis (b. 1927)
Days of the Unicorns, The.
Imperfect Sestina.
Poetics against the Angel of Death.
Propositions.
Spots of Blood.
Syllables disintegrate ingrate alphabets.
Time of Man, The.
To Friends Who Have Also Considered
    Suicide.

Webbe, Charles (fl. c.1678)
Against Indifference.

Weber, Ilse
Road to Terezin, The.

Weber, Richard (b. 1932)
Elizabeth in Italy.
Envying the Pelican.
Poet's Day, The.
Primer for Schoolchildren, A.
Visit to Bridge House, A.

Weber, Ron
Concise History of the Vietnam War: 1965–
    1968, A.

**Webster, Augusta Davies ("Cecil Home")
(1837–94)**
By the Looking-Glass.
Circe.
Dead is he? Yes, our stranger guest said dead.
Enigma No. 6.
Faded.
Flood of Is in Brittany, The.
Her father lessons me I at times am hard.
Little child she, half defiant came, A.
Love's Mourner.
Oh smooth adder / who with fanged kisses
    changedst my natural blood.
Passing Away.
Poor little diary, with its simple thoughts.
She will not have it that my day wanes low.
Since first my little one lay on my breast.
Sometimes, as young things will, she vexes
    me.
That she is beautiful is not delight.
That some day death who has us all for jest.
There's one I miss. A little questioning maid.
Well, well, I know the wise ones talk and talk.
Where Home Was.

Webster, John (1580?–1625?)
Art Thou Gone in Haste?
Burial, The.
Call for the Robin-Redbreast and the Wren.
Do'st thou thinke we shall know one an other.
Duchess of Malfi, The.
Hark, Now Everything Is Still.
Thou wretched thing of blood.
What death?

Webster, Paul Francis
Baltimore Oriole.
Black Coffee.
Doctor, Lawyer, Indian Chief.
I Got It Bad and That Ain't Good.
Jump for Joy.
Love Is a Many-Splendored Thing.
Secret Love.
Two Cigarettes in the Dark.
What's Your Story, Morning Glory.

Wechsler, Elina
Child is Born, A.
Lilith, Adam's First Companion.
Once Again, Anne Frank.

Weckherlin, Georg Rudolph (1584–1653)
Concerning the King of Sweden.
Love Is Life and Death.
She Is the Greatest Wealth.
To Breisach, Taken by That Supremely
    Celebrated Hero, Bernhard, Duke of Saxony.
To Germany.

Wedde, Ian (b. 1946)
And this is where.
Beggar at the Gate, The.
By day and also by night and you are.
Diesel trucks past the Scrovegni chapel.
Hardon ("Get One Today.")
"If thy wife is small bend down to her and."
King Solomon Vistas.
Power Transformer.

Those Others.

Wedderburn, Robert *See* **James, John**

Wedgefarth, W. Dayton
Mother in gladness, Mother in sorrow.
Mother's Hands.

Weeks, Dora
When I was ten.

Weeks, James Eyre (b. 1719?)
On the Great Fog in London, December 1762.

Weelkes, Thomas (fl. c.1600)
Fara Diddle Dyno.
Madrigal: "Ay me, alas, heigh ho, heigh ho!"

Weems, Mary (b. 1954)
B.B. Blues.
Dime after Dime.
Funk.
Return to Temptation.
Yesterday.

Weever, John (1576–1632)
De Se.

Wei Chuang (836–910)
Against Conscription.
Lament of the Lady of Ch'in, The.
Late Rising on Spring Days.
Spoken to Pines and Bamboos.
To the Tune: Beautiful Barbarian.
Tune: Deva-like Barbarian.
Tune: Lotus-leaf Cup.
Tune: "Sand of Silk-washing Stream."
Tune: 'The Bodhisattva Foreigner.'
Tune: The Taoist Priestess.
Tune: 'Thinking of the Imperial Capital.'

Wei Wên-Ti (d. 220)
On the Death of His Father.

Wei Ying-wu (b. 736)
Autumn Night: A Letter Sent to Ch'iu.
Crossing the Lang-yeh Mountain with a
    Friend.
In Imitation of T'ao P'eng-tse.
Longing in My Heart.
On Dewdrop.
On Sound.
Sent to the Taoist Holy Man of Ch'üan-chiao.
To Send to Li Tan and Yüan Hsi.
Tune: Flirtatious Laughter.
Tune: "Song of Flirtatious Laughter."
West Creek at Ch'u-chou.

Weigl, Bruce (b. 1949)
Ambassador, The.
Amnesia.
Anna Grasa.
Burning Shit at An Khe.
Girl at the Chu Lai Laundry.
Her Life Runs Like a Red Silk Flag.
Him, on the Bicycle.
Homage to Elvis, Homage to the Fathers.
Impossible, The.
Last Lie, The.
Mercy.
Mines.
Monkey.
Our 17th Street Years.
Red Squirrel.
Regret for the Mourning Doves Who Failed to
    Mate.
Sailing to Bien Hoa.
Sharing, The.
Snowy Egret.
Song for the Lost Private.
Song of Napalm.
Surrounding Blues on the Way Down.
Temple Near Quang Tri, Not on the Map.
Way of Tet, The.
Why We Are Forgiven.

Weill, Kurt
I'm a Stranger Here Myself.
It Never Was You.
Lost in the Stars.
My Ship.
One Life to Live.
Saga of Jenny, The.
September Song.
Speak Low.
Tchaikowsky (And Other Russians)

Weiman, Andrew (b. 1956)
Andy-Diana DNA Letter.

Wein, Jules Alan
Genesis.
Weinberger, Florence
He Wears Old Socks.
Survivor.
Weinblatt, Jennifer
Marriage Song for Many Voices.
Weiner, Hannah (b. 1928)
From *Spoke / Aug 19.*
How can I describe anything when all these
interruptions keep *arriving* and then.
Little Books / 137 / Silence Mar 22 79.
Mar 7 SIGNAL.
Remembered Sequel.
Sand.
Seen Words.
Weiners, John (b. 1934)
Act #2.
Acts of Youth, The.
Children of the Working Class.
My Mother.
Poem for museum goers, A.
Poem for Painters, A.
Poem for Trapped Things, A.
Poem for the Insane, A.
Poem for vipers, A.
With Meaning.
Weinheber, Josef
In the Grass.
Liebhartstal.
Old Ottakring.
Weinstein, Norman
Drummond's Lover Sings the Blues.
Ethiopian Apocalypse of Don, The.
Garvey's Head as Value.
Migration of Drummond's Organs (After
Death), The.
Weise, Christian (1642–1708)
Upon the Birth of a Young and Highly Desired
Son.
Weiser, Conrad (1696–1760)
Jehovah, Lord and Majesty.
Weismiller, Edward (b. 1915)
Crystal Moment.
Hemlocks in Autumn.
Skull.
Vermont: Spring Rains.
Weiss, George David (b. 1921)
Lullaby of Birdland.
Oh! What It Seemed to Be.
Too Close for Comfort.
Weiss, Renée
Conference, A.
For Gil and Other Incurables.
Lost Wood, The.
Weiss, Theodore (b. 1916)
Another and Another and.
As You Like It.
Barracks Apt. 14.
Clothes Maketh the Man.
Conference, A.
Dab of Color, A.
Egyptian Passage, An.
Fire at Alexandria, The.
Flypaper.
For Gil and Other Incurables.
Grey and dankish thing, A.
Last Day and the First, The.
Letter from the Pygmies, A.
Lost Wood, The.
"Yes, But . . . ."
Off to Patagonia.
Pair of Shoes, A.
Preface: "Sonja Henie, the young girl."
Shorthand.
Ten Little Rembrandts.
To Forget Me.
Ultimate Antientropy, The.
Web, The.
Weissbort, Daniel (b. 1935)
Mourning.
Weisz, Olga Klein
Jerusalem, I am a pilgrim.
Sefarad.
Welburn, Ron (b. 1944)
And universals / are not that world.

Ben Webster: "Did You Call Her Today?"
Black is beautiful.
Bones and Drums.
Condition Blue/ Dress.
Gonsalves.
It is overdue time.
Lyrics shimmy like.
Put u red-eye in.
Tu / cson's of blackmens.
Whichway.
Welch, James (b. 1940)
Across to the Peloponnese.
Arizona Highways.
Blue like Death.
Christmas Comes to Moccasin Flat.
D-Y Bar.
Day after Chasing Porcupines.
Directions to the Nomad.
Going to Remake This World.
Grandma's Man.
Harlem, Montana.
In My First Hard Springtime.
In My Lifetime.
Magic Fox.
Man from Washington, The.
Never Give a Bum an Even Break.
Please Forward.
Renegade Wants Words, The.
Snow Country Weavers.
Surviving.
Thanksgiving at Snake Butte.
Verifying the Dead.
Why I Didn't Go to Delphi.
Welch, Lew (b. 1920)
After Anacreon.
Empress Herself Served Tea to Su Tung-Po,
The.
He Thanks His Woodpile.
Chicago Poem.
In Answer to a Question from P. W.
Sausalito Trash Prayer.
Song of the Turkey Buzzard.
This Book Is for Magda.
Whenever I Make a New Poem.
Wobbly Rock.
Welch, Myra Brooks
Touch of the Master's Hand, The.
Weldon, Charles
Poem of the Universe, The.
Welish, Marjorie (b. 1944)
Blood or Color.
Casting Sequences.
Crossing Disappearing behind Them.
If I Blindfold You.
Kiss Tomorrow Goodbye.
Respected, Feared, and Somehow Loved.
Scalpel in Hand.
Skin.
Veil.
Wild Sleeve.
Within This Book, Called Marguerite.
Wellburn, Ron
Pitching Coups.
Weller, Archie (b. 1957)
And now we watch you crawl, you crawl.
Children play like Yukana, The.
From the bottomless waterhole.
Ho! Brother.
I am waetch.
Kinigar.
Midgiegooroo.
New earth mother.
Ngungalari.
Oh, Domjum!
Once, when walking down the wet grey streets.
Pinjarra warrior, where were you that day.
Rain comes over the hills, The.
Spilt blood and tears like rivers flow.
Story of Frankie . . . My Man, The.
These coloured lights.
To the Moore River Settlement we now go.
Willy-willy man.
Wurarbuti.
Yesterday old Nundah's eldest daughter's son.
**Wellesley, Dorothy, Duchess of Wellington
(1891–1956)**
As Lambs into the Pen.

Asian Desert.
Epilogue: "He is not dead nor liveth."
Fire.
Fishing.
Horses.
Lighthouses.
Lost Lane.
Maiden Castle.
Morning after, The.
So I came down the steps to Lenin.
Spiritual, the carnal, are one, The.
Walled Garden.
Wellman, Mac (b. 1945)
All the way clear to Aliquippa.
Blue sky in a human face.
Endowed fiction of a mouse ear.
Evil Raven, have paper pity upon those.
Having Led a Charmed Life, He Had to Be
Hanged Twice.
Lost from an airy.
Mad Wolf in Lunar Web, Mad Crow on the
Beach.
Most simple things repel.
Moth house is taking over, Sir Footfall.
Needle growing in ancient basalt.
No point mortgages wilt in daynights.
No tongue but bumbles, has.
Of Power, Money, Cheese, Real Estate,
Conboberation, Hoohah.
Silvery tells no sphere to go and.
So perfectly done and yet.
Two hollow eyes follow a cat's crie.
United bolt and screw.
Who lowers the unseen hat from on high.
Wells, Amos Russel (1862–1935)
Ambitious Ant, The.
Considerate Crocodile, The.
Inn That Missed Its Chance, The.
Length of Life, The.
Wells, Anna Maria (1795–1868)
Cow-Boy's Song, The.
Little Maid, The.
Wells, Carolyn (1862–1942)
Alone.
Baker's Dozen of Wild Beasts, A.
Diversions of the Re-Echo Club.
Fate.
How To Tell the Wild Animals.
Limerick: "Canner, Exceedingly Canny, A."
Limerick: "There was a young person called
Tate."
Limerick: "Tutor who tooted a flute, A."
Marvel, A.
Of Modern Books.
Original Summer Girl, The.
Pastoral in Posters, A.
Poster Girl's Defence, The.
Problem, A.
Puzzled.
Universal Favorite, The.
Wells, H. G.
Limerick: "Mr. Wells of the big cerebellum."
Limerick: "Our novels get longa and longa."
Wells, Laury (b. 1938)
Distress upon the Farm.
Nomads, The.
Prelude: "Track is my companion, The."
Sorcerer, The.
Wells, Marcus Morris (1815–95)
Holy Spirit, Faithful Guide.
Wells, Nigel (b. 1944)
Owl Wives.
Up.
Wells, Robert (fl. 1947)
Christmas Song, The.
Wells, Will
Beatings.
Welshimer, Helen
Dusk.
Welsted, Leonard (1688–1747)
Invitation, The.
Welt, Bernard (b. 1952)
I stopped writing poetry.
Wen Cheng-ming (1470–1559)
All of you are seeing me off, east of the

Emperor's city.
Around the temple, pines and cedars.
As flowers fall at the river city, memories
come to me.
At the lacquered table—my recent calligraphy.
Beneath the Shrine of the Three Loyal Ones.
Day drags on, as long as a year, The!
Evening Bell from a Misty Temple.
Fine breeze blows through the temple halls, A.
Floating clouds and worldly affairs.
Floating threads of spider webs hang.
For three years I sadly listened.
Hearing a Flute on the River Chi.
I remove my court gown and part from the
Emperor's precincts.
I sit on horseback at Twin Bridges.
In the past when I saw friends off.
In the sixth month, outside the gate.
Mooring My Boat on the Ssu River and
Watching the Moon.
New Year's Eve.
On First Returning from Taking the
Examinations: Feelings at Cloud-Stop
Pavilion.
Painting a Picture, The Tranquil Boat—Sent to
Ko Ju-ching.
Quiet courtyard fills with greenery, The.
Recording My Happiness upon Returning
Home.
Smiling, we set the testing tray before the hall.
Staying Overnight at Spirit-Source Temple.
Tea bowls, incense burning—a good feeling
here!
There was no reason to expect sadness.
These long verandahs seem to be washed
clean.
This little courtyard—the wind is pure.
This man of leisure for twenty years.
Volumes of books, tea and incense.
Walking to the Temple of Precious Light.
Where among the blue clouds.
While It Was Raining.
Wine of parting flowed and flowed, The.
Wishing to try retirement, I requested release
from duty.
Written While Sick.
Year *Chi-wei* (Fifteen Fifty Nine), New Year's
Day, The.
Year Hsin-hai (Fifteen Fifty One), New Year's
Eve: Keeping Watch, The.
Year I-mao (Fifteen Fifty Five), New Year's
Eve, The.

Wen-Ti Chien (6th cent.)
Lo-yang.

Wen T'ien-hsiang (1236–82)
Chin-ling Post Station.

Wen T'ing-yün (812–72)
Crossing South of Li-chou, A.
Deva-like Barbarian.
Early Autumn in the Mountains.
Early Walk on Shang Mountain, An.
Fishing Trapping Song, A.
I remember that year, under the blossoms.
In the Mountains as Autumn Begins.
Last night at midnight.
Passing a Ruined Palace.
People all say the southland's better.
Song Of Chang Ching-Yüan Picking Lotus
Flowers, A.
Song of Distant Waters, A.
Song of Wildfire, A.
Spring Day in the Countryside, A.
To the Tune: Southern Song.
To the Tune: The Water Clock.
Tune: 'Beautiful Barbarians.'
Tune: Deva-like Barbarian.
Tune: Dreaming of the South.
Tune: "Lotus-leaf Cup."
Tune: "Pacifying the Western Barbarians."
Tune: "River Messages."
Tune: "Southern Song, A."
Tune: "Telling of Innermost Feelings."

Wen Yi-tuo *or* Wen I-to (1898–1946)
Dead Water.
Miracle.

Wenberi
Wenberi's Song.

Wendel, Ngudia (b. 1940)
We Shall Return, Luanda.

Wenderoth, Joe (b. 1966)
Aesthetics of the Bases Loaded Walk.
All That Really Happens.
As Hour and Year Collapsed.
Billy's Famous Lounge.
Death.
Detailed History of the Western World.
Disfortune.
Each Sentence Is Into the Fast.
First Impression.
Moon River.
Museum.
My Life.
Only Fortunate Thing, The.
Outside the Hospital.
Promise.
Send New Beasts.
We Were a Whole Army Underground.
Writer.

Wentworth, Anne (*fl.* 1676–79)
Revelation 5, October 8.
Revelation 8, March 31.

Weöres, Sándor (1913–89)
Another World.
Ars Poetica.
Brambleberry, The.
Clouds.
Coolie.
Dissolving Presence, A.
Dragon-Steed, The.
Eternal Moment.
Eternity.
Four Elements, The.
In Memoriam Gyula Juhász.
Insect.
Monkeyland.
Moon and Farmstead.
Never Again Another Garden.
On Death.
Plain, The.
Rain.
Rayflower.
Saturn Declining.
Seventh Symphony, The.
Sheep School.
Song: Boundless Space.
Storm from the Far Heights.
Time's Come up Pearls.
To Die.
Twentieth Century Fresco.
Valse Triste.
Where metalled road invades light thinning air.
Whisper in the Dark.
Wingless.

Werfel, Franz (1890–1945)
Exaltation.
For I Have Done a Good and Kindly Deed.
Litany of the Rooms of the Dead.
Loneliness.
Song of Life, A.
Strangers Are We All Upon the Earth.
Teach Us to Mark This, God.
To a Lark in War-Time.
Ye Sorrowers.

Wergeland, Henrik Arnold Thaulov (1808–45)
Wall-Flower, The.

Werner, Martina (b. 1929)
Monogram 4.
Monogram 23.
Monogram 29.

Wertheimer, Paul (1874–1948)
Souls.

Wesley, Charles (1707–88)
Ah! Lovely Appearance of Death!
Arise, my soul, arise, Shake off thy guilty
fears.
Catholic Love.
Come on, my partners in distress.
Come, Thou Almighty King.
During His Courtship.
For His Wife, on Her Birthday.
For the Anniversary Day of One's Conversion.
Free Grace.
Hark, how all the welkin rings! Glory to the

King of Kings.
Hark! the herald angels sing, Glory to the
newborn King.
He Shook off the Beast.
Incarnation, The.
Let earth and heaven combine.
Love Divine, All Loves Excelling.
Morning Hymn.
N T.
None is like Jeshuron's God.
O Thou Eternal Victim Slain.
On Sympathisers with the American
Revolution.
On the Death of His Son.
On Worldly Prelates.
Rejoice! The Lord is King.
Sinners, abhor the Fiend.
Still, O Lord, for Thee I Tarry.
True Use of Music, The.
Whole Armour of God, The.
Wrestling Jacob.

Wesley, John (1703–91)
Hymn: "Thou hidden love of God, whose
height."

Wesley, Samuel (1691–1739)
Anacreontic, on Parting with a Little Child.
Epitaph, An: "Here lie I, once a witty fair."
Freeborn Pindaric never does refuse.
Full doelful Tales have oft been told.
Monument, The.
On the Setting Up of Mr. Butler's Monument
in Westminster Abbey.
Pindaric on the Grunting of a Hog, A.

Weslowski, Dieter
Dry World.
Heart.
Pablo.
Zoe and the Ghosts.

West, Arthur Graeme
Night Patrol, The.

West, Errol (b. 1947)
I feel the texture of her complexion with both
hand and heart.
Misty mountains tell me the secrets you hold,
of men.
Please mista do'n take me chilen, please mista
do'n.
Sitting, wondering, do I have a place here?
There is no one to teach me the songs that
bring the Moon Bird, the fish or any other
thing that makes me what I am.
White man's vision.

West, Gilbert (1703–56)
Lives there on Earth to whom I am unknown.
Stowe, the Gardens of the Rt. Hon. Richard
Lord Viscount Cobham.

West, Jane (1758–1852)
Married, poor soul! your empire's over.
To May.
To the Hon. Mrs. C——e.

West, Jean
I paid a spring-time visit to your country.

West, Kathleene
By Water Divined.
On Track.
To My Twin Sister Who Died at Birth.

West, Robert A. (1809–65)
Come, Let Us Tune Our Loftiest Song.

**Westmorland, Mildmay Fane, 2nd Earl of
(1602–65)**
Dedication of My First Son, A.
Happy Life, A.
How to Ride Out a Storm.
In Obitum Ben. Jons.
In Praise of Fidelia.
Man Leavens the Batch.
My Carol.
My Close-Committee.
My Country Audit.
My Observation at Sea.
Occasioned by Seeing a Walk of Bay Trees.
Reveille Matin, or Good Morrow to a Friend.
Shamed by the Creature.
To Kiss God's Rod; Occasioned upon a Child's
Sickness.

To Retiredness.
To Sir John Wentworth, Upon His Curiosities
  and Courteous Entertainment at Summerly
  in Lovingland.
Upon the Times.
Weston, Mildred (b. 1900)
Departure.
Primitive Place.
Weston, Paul
Day by Day.
I Should Care.
Weston, R. P. (1878–1936)
Epitaph: "Beneath this stone lies William
  Burke."
I've Got Rings on My Fingers.
Westphalen, Emilio Adolfo (b. 1911)
You Came to Rest.
Westwood, Thomas (1814–88)
Motionless sat the shadow at the helm.
Wetzsteon, Rachel (B. 1967)
Coming Back to the Cave.
Dinner at Le Caprice.
Drinks in the Town Square.
Late Show, The.
Learning from the Movies.
Poem for a New Year.
Rival, A.
Surgical Moves.
Thoughts While Walking.
Three Songs.
Urban Gallery.
Witness.
Wever, Robert (fl. c.1550)
In Youth Is Pleasure.
Wevill, David (b. 1935)
Birth of a Shark, The.
Body of a Rook.
In Love.
Snow.
Spiders.
Wexionius, Olof (1656–90?)
On the Death of a Pious Lady.
Wexler, Evelyn
Governess, The.
Whalen, Philip (b. 1923)
2 Variations: All about Love.
10:X:57, 45 Years Since the Fall of the Ch'ing
  Dynasty.
25:I:68.
Chanson d'Outre Tombe.
Complaint: To the Muse.
Denunciation; or, Unfrock'd Again.
For C.
Further Notice.
Hymnus Ad Patrem Sinensis.
International Date Line, Monday/Monday
  27:XI:67.
Life in the City: In Memoriam Edward
  Gibbon.
Martyrdom of Two Pagans.
"Never Apologize; Never Explain."
Regalia in Immediate Demand!
Same Old Jazz, The.
For Kai Snyder.
Slop Barrel, The.
Sourdough Mountain Lookout.
Take I, 4:11:58.
Technicalities for Jack Spicer.
To the Muse.
Walking beside the Kamogawa, Remembering
  Nansen and Fudo and Gary's Poem.
Where or When.
Whalley, George (b. 1915)
Affair of Honour.
Wharton, Anne (1659–85)
Elegy on the Earl of Rochester.
My Fate.
Wharton, Edith (1862–1937)
Autumn Sunset, An.
Chartres.
Experience.
Last Giustiniani, The.
Life.
Mona Lisa.
Mortal Lease, The.

Terminus.
Tomb of Ilaria Giunigi, The.
Two Backgrounds.
**Wharton, Thomas Wharton, 1st Marquess of
(1648–1715)**
Lilli Burlero [A New Song.]
Whateley, Mary (1738–1825)
Ode to Truth.
On the Author's Husband Desiring Her to
  Write Some Verses.
Power of Destiny, The.
Vanity of External Accomplishments, The.
Whately, Richard, Archbishop (1787–1863)
There Is a Place in Distant Seas.
Wheatley, John (d. 1830)
Cape of Storms, The.
Wheatley, Phillis (c.1753–84)
America.
As reason's pow'rs by day our God disclose.
Farewell to America, A. To Mrs. S. W.
Hymn to the Evening, An.
Hymn to the Morning, An.
Liberty and Peace, a Poem.
Lo! Freedom comes. Th' prescient Muse
  foretold.
No more, America, in mournful strain.
On Being Brought from Africa to America.
On Imagination.
On the Death of a Young Gentleman.
On the Death of the Rev. Mr. George
  Whitefield, 1770.
On Virtue.
Should You, My Lord.
Thoughts on the Works of Providence.
To a Gentleman and Lady on the Death of the
  Lady's Brother and Sister, and a Child of the
  Name Avis, Aged One Year.
To a Lady on the Death of Her Husband.
To His Excellency General Washington.
To Mæcenas.
To S.M., a Young African Painter, on Seeing
  His Works.
To the King's Most Excellent Majesty.
To the Rev. Dr. Thomas Amory on Reading
  His Sermons on Daily Devotion, in Which
  that Duty Is Recommended and Assisted.
To the Right Honourable William, Earl of
  Dartmouth, His Majesty's Principal
  Secretary of State for North America.
To the University of Cambridge, in New-
  England.
Wheeler, Ruth Winant
Prayer for Shut-Ins.
Wheeler, Susan (b. 1955)
He or She That's Got the Limb, That Holds
  Me Out on It.
Produce, Produce.
Song for the Spirit of Natalie Going.
That Been to Me My Lives Light and Saviour.
Wheelock, C. Webster (b. 1939)
Divorcee.
Wheelock, John Hall (1886–1978)
Afternoon: Amagansett Beach.
Earth.
Earth, Take Me Back.
Fish-Hawk, The.
House in the Green Well, The.
Love and Liberation.
Nirvana.
Sunday Evening in the Common.
This Quiet Dust.
Triumph of Love.
Wheelwright, John (1897–1940)
Abel.
Anathema. Maranatha!
Bread-Word Giver.
Come over and Help Us; A Rhapsody.
Cross Questions.
Esprit d'Escalier.
Father.
Fish Food.
In the Bathtub, to Mnemosyne.
Live, Evil Veil.
Second Ascension of Christ, The.
Slow Curtain.
Train Ride.

Why Must You Know?
Would You Think?
Whipple, Laura
My Dad.
Whisenand, Emma Bridge
Open Your Eyes.
Whistler, Laurence (b. 1912)
Form of Epitaph, A.
Portrait in the Guards, A.
White-arm
Child listen / I am singing.
White, Bukka (1909–77)
Fixin' to Die.
White, Dorothy (1630–1685)
Epistle of Love and of Consolation unto
  Israel, An.
White, Elwyn Brooks (1899–1985)
Chairs in Snow.
Commuter.
Critic.
I Paint What I See.
Listener's Guide to the Birds, A.
Marble-Top.
Red Cow Is Dead, The.
Window Ledge in the Atom Age.
White, Gail
Dead Armadillos.
Leopard in Eden, The.
White, Gilbert (1720–93)
Naturalist's Summer-Evening Walk, The.
On the Dark, Still, Dry, Warm Weather
  Occasionally Happening in the Winter
  Months.
White, Henry Kirke (1785–1806)
Give me a cottage on some Cambrian wild.
Winter Traveler, The.
White, J. P. (b. 1940)
In Ecclesiastes I Read.
White, James L. (1936–81)
Making Love to Myself.
Oshi.
White, Joseph Blanco (1775–1841)
To Night.
White, Michael
Recurrence.
White, Viola C.
Child of Adam.
Whitehead, Charles (1804–62)
Lamp, The.
Whitehead, Christiania (b. 1969)
Brutus' Last Song.
Daybreak.
Girls Sitting Together Like Dolls.
Grass Crust, The.
Marian Hymn.
Morning Thesis.
Whitehead, Paul (1710–74)
As when two monarchs of the brindled breed.
Boxers, The.
Hunting Song.
Whitehead, William (1715–85)
If nature prompts you, or if friends persuade.
Life of writing, unless wondrous short, A.
New Night Thoughts on Death; a Parody.
On the Late Improvements at Nuneham, the
  Seat of the Earl of Harcourt.
Song for Ranelagh.
Sweepers, The.
Venus Attiring the Graces.
Whitely, Opal (d. 1991)
Today the Grandpa Dug Potatoes.
Whiteman, Roberta Hill (Roberta Hill) (b. 1947)
Beginning the Year at Rosebud, S. D.
Blue Mountain.
Climbing Gannett.
Depot in Rapid City.
Direction.
Dream of Rebirth.
E Uni Que A The Hi A Tho, Father.
Falling Moon.
For Heather, Entering Kindergarten.
From the Sun Itself.
Horses in Snow.
In the Longhouse, Oneida Museum.

In the Madison Zoo.
Leap in the Dark.
Lines for Marking Time.
Midnight on Front Street.
Nation Wrapped in Stone, A.
Night along the Mackinac Bridge.
One More Sign.
Patterns.
Reaching Yellow River.
Seal at Stinson Beach.
Sleeping with Foxes.
Song for Healing.
Star Quilt.
Steps.
Swamp.
Variations for Two Voices.
Waiting for Robinson.
Whispers.
White Land, The.
Winter Burn.
Woman Seed Player.

Whiteside, Mary Brent (d. 1962)
Carpenter, The.

Whitfield, James M. (1823–78)
America.
America, it is to thee.
From America.
From Year to Year the Contest Grew.
Self-Reliance.
To A. H.
Yes! Strike Again That Sounding String.

Whiting, George (fl. 1925)
My Blue Heaven.

Whiting, Richard A.
Ain't We Got Fun.
Beyond the Blue Horizon.
Breezin' Along with the Breeze.
Guilty.
Hooray for Hollywood.
Louise.
My Future Just Passed.
My Ideal.
On the Good Ship Lollipop.
She's Funny That Way (I Got a Woman, Crazy for Me)
Sleepy Time Gal.
Too Marvelous for Words.
True Blue Lou.
You're an Old Smoothie.

Whiting, William (1825–78)
Eternal Father, Strong to Save.

Whitlow, Carolyn Beard
Book of Routh.
Poem for the Children.
Rockin' A Man, Stone Blind.

Whitman, Albery Allson (1851–1901)
Have I not seen the hills of Candahar.
I had a dream: Columbia the Great.
Is manhood less because man's face is black?
Lute of Afric's Tribe, The.

Whitman, Ruth (b. 1922)
Bubba Esther, 1888.
Castoff Skin.
Cutting the Jewish Bride's Hair.
Laughing Gas.
Listening to Grownups Quarreling.
My Greatgreatuncle the Archbishop.
Touro Synagogue.
Uncle Harry at the La Brea Tar Pits.

Whitman, Sarah Helen (1803–78)
Morning-Glory, The.
November Landscape, A.
Past, The.
To &m3rdash;: "Vainly my heart had with thy sorceries striven."

Whitman, Teresa
Hunger and Imagination.
Scissortails.

Whitman, Walt (1819–92)
Aboard at a Ship's Helm.
Afoot and light-hearted I take to the open road.
After the Sea-Ship.
After the Supper and Talk.
Ah Poverties, Wincings, and Sulky Retreats.
All the Past We Leave Behind.

All truths wait in all things.
Alone far in the wilds and mountains I hunt.
America.
Among the Multitude.
And as to you Death, and you bitter hug of mortality, it is idle to try to alarm me.
And I saw askant the armies.
Are You the New Person Drawn toward Me?
Army Corps on the March, An.
Artilleryman's Vision, The.
As Adam Early in the Morning.
As I Ebb'd with the Ocean of Life.
As I Lay with My Head in Your Lap Camerado.
As I Sit Writing Here.
As If a Phantom Caress'd Me.
As Toilsome I Wander'd Virginia's Woods.
Ashes of Soldiers.
Base of All Metaphysics, The.
Bearing the bandages, water and sponge.
Beat! Beat! Drums!
Beauty.
Beginning My Studies.
Behold This Swarthy Face.
Big doors of the country stand open and ready, The.
Bivouac on a Mountain Side.
Blind loving wrestling touch! Sheathed hooded sharptoothed touch!
Boston Ballad [1854], A.
Broad-Ax, The.
Broadway.
By Blue Ontario's Shore.
By That Long Scan of Waves.
By the Bivouac's Fitful Flame.
Call in the midst of the crowd, A.
Carol of Death, The.
Cavalry Crossing a Ford.
Centenarian's Story, The.
Chanting the Square Deific.
Child said What is the grass? fetching it to me with full hands, A.
City of Orgies.
Clear Midnight, A.
Come, Said My Soul.
Come up from the Fields Father.
Commonplace, The.
Crossing Brooklyn Ferry.
Dalliance of the Eagles, The.
Dazzling and tremendous how quick the sunrise would kill me.
Death's Valley.
Dirge for Two Veterans.
Dismantled Ship, The.
Earth expanding right hand and left hand, The.
Earth, My Likeness.
Efflux of the soul is happiness, here is happiness, The.
Eidolons.
Epigraph to "Drum-Taps."
Europe, the 72nd and 73rd Year of These States.
Evening Lull, An.
Facing West from California's Shores.
Farm Picture, A.
Fast-Anchor'd Eternal O Love!
Flood-tide below me! I see you face to face!
For You O Democracy.
From Pent-up Aching Rivers.
Full of Life Now.
Give Me the Splendid Silent Sun.
Glimpse, A.
Good-Bye, My Fancy!
Had I the Choice.
Halcyon Days.
Hand-Mirror, A.
Has any one supposed it lucky to be born?
Hast Never Come to Thee an Hour.
Here the Frailest Leaves of Me.
Houses and rooms are full of perfumes, the shelves are crowded with perfumes.
Hush'd Be the Camps To-Day.
I Am He That Aches with Love.
I am of old and young, of the foolish as much as the wise.
I Am the Poet.
I am the poet of the Body and I am the poet of

the Soul.
I am the teacher of athletes.
I believe a leaf of grass is no less than the journey-work of the stars.
I believe in you my soul, the other I am must not abase itself to you.
I celebrate myself, and sing myself.
I Dream'd in a Dream.
I have heard what the talkers were talking, the talk of the beginning and the end.
I have perceiv'd that to be with those I like is enough.
I have said that the soul is not more than the body.
I Hear America Singing.
I Hear It Was Charged against Me.
I Heard You Solemn-Sweet Pipes of the Organ.
I knew a man, a common farmer, the father of five sons.
I know I have the best of time and space, and was never measured and will never be measured.
I Saw in Louisiana a Live-Oak Growing.
I Sing the Body Electric.
I Sit and Look Out.
I think I could turn and live with animals, they are so placid and self-contained.
I understand the large hearts of heroes.
I wander all night in my vision.
In Paths Untrodden.
Is this then a touch? . . . quivering me to a new identity.
Italian Music in Dakota.
Joy, Shipmate, Joy!
Last Invocation, The.
Leaf for Hand in Hand, A.
Little one sleeps in its cradle, The.
Live Oak, with Moss.
Long I Thought That Knowledge Alone Would Suffice.
Male is not less the soul nor more, he too is in his place, The.
Man's body at auction, A.
Mannahatta.
March in the Ranks Hard-Prest, and the Road Unknown, A.
Me Imperturbe.
Miracles.
Muse in the New World, The.
My Picture-Gallery.
Native Moments.
No Labor-Saving Machine.
Noiseless Patient Spider, A.
Not Heat Flames up and Consumes.
Not Heaving from My Ribb'd Breast Only.
Now I will do nothing but listen.
Now Precedent Songs, Farewell.
Now what my mother told me one day as we sat at dinner / together.
O Captain! My Captain!
O Living Always, Always Dying.
O Tan-Faced Prairie-Boy.
O the engineer's joys! to go with a locomotive!
O You Whom I Often and Silently Come.
Of the Terrible Doubt of Appearances.
Old Man's Thought of School, An.
Old War-Dreams.
On the Beach at Night.
On the Beach at Night Alone.
On the Same Picture.
Once I Pass'd through a Populous City.
One's-Self I Sing.
Orange Buds by Mail from Florida.
Osceola.
Out of the Cradle Endlessly Rocking.
Ox-Tamer, The.
Passage to India.
Past and present wilt—I have filled them, emptied them, The.
Patrolling Barnegat.
Pensive on Her Dead Gazing.
Poet, The.
Prairie-Grass Dividing, The.
Prairie Sunset, A.
Promise to California, A.
Proud Music of the Storm.
Pure contralto sings in the organloft, The.

Reconciliation.
Recorders Ages Hence.
Respondez!
Roots and Leaves Themselves Alone.
Rounded Catalogue Divine Complete, The.
Runaway slave came to my house and stopt outside, The.
Runner, The.
Scented Herbage of My Breast.
Ship Starting, The.
Shut Not Your Doors.
Sight in Camp in the Daybreak Gray and Dim, A.
Sleepers, The.
Sometimes with One I Love.
Song for All Seas, All Ships.
Song of Myself.
Song of the Open Road.
Sparkles from the Wheel.
Spirit Whose Work Is Done.
Spontaneous Me.
Spotted hawk swoops by and accuses me, he complains of my gab and my loitering, The.
Stretch'd and still lies the midnight.
Swiftly arose and spread around me the peace and knowledge that pass all the argument of the earth.
Tears.
Thanks in Old Age.
That Shadow My Likeness.
There is that in me—I do not know what it is—but I know it is in me.
There Was a Child Went Forth.
There was a child went forth every day.
These I Singing in Spring.
This Compost.
This is the female form.
This is the meal pleasantly set . . . this is the meat and drink for natural hunger.
This Moment Yearning and Thoughtful.
Thought.
To a Certain Cantatrice.
To a Certain Civilian.
To a Common Prostitute.
To a Locomotive in Winter.
To a President.
To a Stranger.
To a Western Boy.
To be in any form, what is that?
To Old Age.
To the East and to the West.
To the Garden the World.
To the Man-of-War Bird.
To the Pending Year.
To the States.
To the States, To Identify the 16th, 17th, or 18th Presidentiad.
Torch, The.
Trickle Drops.
Trippers and askers surround me.
Twenty-eight young men bathe by the shore.
Untold Want, The.
Vigil Strange I Kept on the Field One Night.
Walt Whitman, a kosmos, of Manhattan the son.
We Two Boys Together Clinging.
What Am I After All.
What Think You I Take My Pen in Hand?
When I Heard At The Close of The Day.
When I Heard the Learn'd Astronomer.
When I Peruse the Conquer'd Fame.
When I Read the Book.
When Lilacs Last in the Dooryard Bloom'd.
Who goes there? hankering, gross, mystical, nude.
Whoever You Are Holding Me Now in Hand.
Wild gander leads his flock through the cool night, The.
Will you seek afar off? you surely come back at last.
Woman Waits for Me, A.
World below the Brine, The.
Would you hear of an old-time [or old-fashioned] sea fight?
Wound-Dresser, The.
Year That Trembled and Reel'd beneath Me.
Years of the Modern.

Yonnondio.
You sea! I resign myself to you also—I guess what you mean.

Whitmore, Susan M. (b. 1962)
Bird, The.
Gamelia.
Lenaia.
Outside.

Whitney, Helen Hay
To a Woman.

Whitney, Isabella (b. c.1540, d. after 1580)
And now let mee dispose such things.
And (though I am perswade) that I.
Aucthour Maketh Her Wyll and Testament, The.
For Women shall you Taylors have.
I.W. to her unconstant Lover.
I whole in body and in minde.
Manner of Her Will and What She Left to London and to All Those in It, at Her Departing, The.
Now for the people in thee left.
Now London have I (for thy sake)
Now when thy folke are fed and clad.
Rejoice in God that I am gon.
Sweet Nosegay, A, or Pleasant Posy.
Ye virgins that from Cupid's tents.
Yf they that keepe what I you leave.

Whitney, Joan
Candy.

Whitson, Beth Slater (fl. 1910)
Let Me Call You Sweetheart.

Whittemore, Elizabeth
My Friends Are Little Lamps to Me.

Whittemore, Reed (b. 1919)
Clamming.
Crow and the Fox, The.
Day with the Foreign Legion, A.
Departure, The.
Mother's Past.
On the Suicide of a Friend.
Party, The.
Projection, A.
Smiling Through.
Still Life.
Tarantula, The.
Thinking of Tents.
Walk Home, The.

Whittier, John Greenleaf (1807–92)
Abraham Davenport.
All's Well.
Astræa.
Barbara Frietchie.
Barefoot Boy, The.
Battle Autumn of 1862, The.
Brown of Ossawatomie.
Burning Drift-Wood.
Call of the Christian, The.
Changeling, The.
Christian Slave, The.
Cities of the Plain, The.
Clerical Oppressors.
Dear Lord and Father of mankind.
Dedication: "I would the gift I offer here."
Ezekiel.
Farewell, The: "Gone, gone,—sold and gone."
Firelight.
First-Day Thoughts.
Forgiveness.
Fruit-Gift, The.
Garden.
Godspeed.
Haschish, The.
Help.
Henchman, The.
I know not what the future hath.
Ichabod[!].
Immortal Love, Forever Full.
In School-Days.
Laus Deo!
Lost Occasion, The.
Maud Muller.
My Playmate.
My Triumph.
O Thou! Whose Presence Went Before.
Official Piety.

Oh for boyhood's painless play.
Over-Heart, The.
Overruled.
Palm-Tree, The.
Pardon, Lord, the lips that dare.
Pipes at Lucknow, The.
Prelude: "Along the roadside, like the flowers of gold."
Proem: "I love the old melodious lays."
River Path, The.
Robin, The.
Sisters, The.
Skipper Ireson's Ride.
Slave-Ships, The.
Snow-Bound [or Snow-Bound; a Winter Idyl.].
Song of Slaves in the Desert.
Sun that brief December day, The.
Telling the Bees.
Tent on the Beach: [The Dreamer.].
To a Cape Ann Schooner.
To My Old Schoolmaster.
Vesta.
What the Birds Said.
Word for the Hour, A.
Worship.

Whittingham, William (1524–79)
Now Israel May Say, and That Truly.

Whitworth, John
Big sleep, the high window, The.

Whur, Cornelius (1782–1853)
Alas! Alas! the father said.
In a dark and trying hour.

Whyte-Melville, George John
Coyotes.

Wickham, Anna (Mrs. Patrick Hepburn) (1884–1947)
Affinity, The.
After Annunciation.
Cherry-Blossom Wand, The.
Creatrix.
Dedication of the Cook.
Divorce.
Domestic Economy.
Envoi: "God, thou great symmetry."
Fired Pot, The.
Friend Cato.
Gift to a Jade.
Last Round, The.
Letter to a Boy at School.
Marriage, The.
Meditation at Kew.
Nervous Prostration.
Nursery Song.
Paradox.
Sehnsucht.
Self-Analysis.
Singer, The.
Slighted Lady, The.
Song: "I was so chill, and overworn, and sad."
Song-Maker, The.
Soul's Liberty.
Sung in a Graveyard.
Tired Woman, The.
To a Crucifix.
To Men.
Vanity.
Weapons.

Wicks, Susan (b. 1947)
Buying Fish.
Clever Daughter, The.
Joy.
Knot.
Moderato.
On Re-recording Mozart.
Protected Species.
Rain Dance.
Stilt-walker.
Voice.

Widdows, P. F.
Minutiae 3.

Widerberg, Siv (b. 1931)
At Annika's Place.
Best?
Once.

Wied, Martina
Saint Stephen's.

Wieder, Laurance (b. 1946)
Tower of Babel, The.

Wieners, John (b. 1934)
Acceptance.
Anniversary of Death, An.
Doll.
Glimpse, A.
King Solomon's Magnetic Quiz.
Le Chariot.
Loneliness, The.
Long Nook.
Moon Poems.
My Mother.
Poem for Cocksuckers, A.
Poem for Museum Goers, A.
Poem for Painters, A.
Poem for the Old Man, A.
Poem for Trapped Things, A.
Suck, The.
To H.
Two Years Later.
Waning of the Harvest Moon, The.
What Happened?

Wiese, Brooke
Everyone Who Wants to Work Can.
Going Home Madly.

Wiesel, Elie
Behold, God of Abraham, God of mercy.
Never Shall I Forget.

Wiesinger, Steve
Snow Climbers.

Wiethüchter, Blanca (b. 1942)
At This Juncture.
Movement.
Song: "Among the clamor the single shout."
Without Histories.

Wiggin, Larry
Crickets.
Dreaming.
Fly.
Scouring pans.
Wind.

Wigglesworth, Michael (1631–1705)
Adulterers and whoremongers / were there, with all unchaste.
All filthy facts, and secret acts.
All silence keep, both goats and sheep.
Apostates and run-aways.
Blasphemers lewd, and swearers shrewd.
But all too late, grief's out of date.
Can God delight in such a sight.
Christ's Flock of Lambs there also stands.
Come, blessed ones, and sit on thrones.
Day of Doom, The.
Farewell to the World, A.
For at midnight brake forth a Light.
For Just Men Light Is Sown.
Glorious Judge will priviledge, The.
God's Controversy with New-England.
Had your intent been to repent.
Others argue, and not a few.
Prayer unto Christ the Judge of the World, A.
Song of Emptiness to Fill up the Empty Pages Following, A.
Still was the night, Serene and Bright.
Then to the bar, all they drew near.
There also stand a num'rous band.
These words appall and daunt them all.
They rush from Beds with giddy heads.
They wring their hands, their caitiff-hands.
Thus all men's pleas the Judge with ease.
Thus every one before the Throne.
Thus he doth find of all mankind.
Thus shall they lie, and wail, and cry.
Unto the saints with sad complaints.
Wallowing in all kind of sin.
Welcome, Sweet Rest.
With cords of love often strove.
Wond'rous crowd then 'gan aloud, A.

Wigmore, Paul
Limerick: "Man called Andronicus (Titus), A."

Wigson, John (b. c.1711)
On the Death of Squire Christopher.

Wilberforce, Ernest R.
Just for To-Day.

Wilberforce, Samuel (1805–73)
Impromptu.

Wilbur, Richard (b. 1921)
Advice to a Prophet.
After the Last Bulletins.
All These Birds.
April 5, 1974.
Ballade for the Duke of Orléans.
Baroque Wall-Fountain in the Villa Sciarra, A.
Beasts.
Beautiful Changes, The.
Bell Speech.
Black November Turkey, A.
Boy at the Window.
Caserta Garden.
Catch, The.
Ceremony.
Christmas Hymn, A.
Cicadas.
Cottage Street, 1953.
Death of a Toad, The.
Digging for China.
Epistemology.
Exeunt.
Fire-Truck, A.
First Snow in Alsace.
For the Student Strikers.
Grasse: The Olive Trees.
Grasshopper, A.
Hamlen Brook.
Hole in the Floor, A.
In a Churchyard.
In the Elegy Season.
In the Field.
In the Smoking-Car.
John Chapman.
Juggler.
Junk.
Late Aubade, A.
Leaving.
Looking into History.
Love Calls Us to the Things of This World.
Loves of the Puppets.
Lying.
Marché aux Oiseaux.
Matthew 8:28–34; And when he came to the other side.
Mind.
Mind-Reader, The.
Museum Piece.
My Father Paints the Summer.
On the Marginal Way.
Pangloss's Song: A Comic-Opera Lyric.
Parable.
Pardon, The.
Piazza di Spagna, Early Morning.
Place Pigalle.
Playboy.
Potato.
Praise in Summer.
Prisoner of Zenda, The.
Proof, The.
Rillons, Rillettes.
Running.
Shame.
She.
Simile for Her Smile, A.
Sleepless at Crown Point.
Some Opposites.
Someone Talking to Himself.
Sonnet: "Winter deepening, the hay all in, The."
Star System, The.
Still, Citizen Sparrow.
Stop.
Summer Morning, A.
Teresa.
Thyme Flowering among Rocks.
To an American Poet Just Dead.
To the Etruscan Poets.
Transit.
Tywater.
Undead, The.
Voice from under the Table, A.
Walking to Sleep.
What is the opposite of nuts?
What's Good for the Soul is Good for Sales.
What should I tell them?
"World Without Objects Is a Sensible Emptiness, A."
Writer, The.
Year's End.

Wilcox, Carlos (1794–1827)
Sultry noon, not in the summer's prime, A.

Wilcox, Ella Wheeler (1850–1919)
Accept My Full Heart's Thanks.
And he held me fast, and he said, at last.
Answered Prayers.
Attraction.
Beautiful Land of Nod, The.
Belief.
Burdened.
Come Back Clean.
Communism.
Dawn.
Engine, The.
Faith.
Fault of the Age, The.
Friendship.
Friendship after Love.
In the Night.
Inspiration, An.
Law, The.
Life.
Life's Journey.
Love much. Earth has enough of bitter in it.
Mistakes.
Morning Prayer, A.
My Grave.
No Classes!
Nothing New.
One of Us Two.
Optimism.
Peace and Love.
Peace at the Goal.
Room beneath the Rafters, The.
Secret Thoughts.
Solitude.
Sonnet, The.
There Comes a Time.
Those We Love the Best.
Was, Is, and Yet-To-Be.
Way of It, The.
What Love Is.
Whatever Is—Is Best.
Will.
Winds of Fate, The.
Woman.
World, The.
Worthwhile.
You Never Can Tell.

Wilczek, Frank (b. 1951)
Virtual Particles.

Wild, Robert (1609–79)
Epitaph for a Godly Man's Tomb, An.
Epitaph on Some Bottles of Sack and Claret Laid in Sand.
In a melancholly studdy.

Wilde, J. (fl. c.1779)
Verses to Miss———.

Wilde, Lady Jane Francesca ("Speranza") (1820–96)
Corinne's Last Love-Song.
Désillusion.
Poet's Destiny, The.
Who Will Show Us Any Good?

Wilde, Oscar Fingall O'Flahertie Wills (1854–1900)
Ave Imperatrix!
Ave Maria, Gratia Plena.
Ballad of Reading Gaol, The.
By the Arno.
E Tenebris.
Easter Day.
Fin-de-Siècle Cat.
For oak and elm have pleasant leaves.
Harlot's House, The.
He did not wear his scarlet coat.
He does not sit with silent men.
Hélas!
How subtle-secret is your smile! Did you love none then? Nay, I know.
Impression Du Matin.
In Debtor's Yard the stones are hard.
Les Ballons.

Les Silhouettes.
Magdalen Walks.
My Voice.
Preface: "Artist is the creator of beautiful
  things, The."
Requiescat.
Santa Decca.
Symphony in Yellow.
Theocritus.
There is no chapel on the day.
Vita Nuova.
Wasted Days.
Yet each man kills the thing he loves.

Wilde, Richard Henry (1789–1847)
Across the Prairie's silent waste I stray.
Beyond Vermont's green hills, against the
  skies.
Change blots out change—their very memory
  dies.
Father of Rivers! standing by thy side.
If the romantic land whose soil I tread.
Lament of the Captive, The.
Mount Auburn! loveliest city of the dead.
Saint Augustine, thy praise was sung by one.
To the Mocking-Bird.
Where dost thou lie, great Nimrod of the West!

Wilder, Alec (1907–80)
Crazy in the Heart.
Did You Ever Cross Over to Sneden's.
I'll Be Around.
It's So Peaceful in the Country.
Photographs.
Trouble Is a Man.
While We're Young.
Who Can I Turn To?

Wilder, Amos Niven (1895–1993)
Those sultry nights we used to pass outdoors.

Wildgans, Anton
Austrian Song.
Chord.
Final Knowledge.
I Am a City Child.

Wildman, Eugene
Cure, The.

Wilkes, John (1727–97)
Awake my Fanny! leave all meaner things.
He who the hoop's immensity can pierce.
Pleased to the last, she likes the luscious food.
Then, in the scale of Pricks, 'tis plain.
Then, say not Man's imperfect, Heaven in
  fault.

Wilkes, Kennette
Dolce.

Wilkie, William (1721–72)
True Knowledge.

Wilkins Freeman, Mary E.
Ostrich Is a Silly Bird, The.

Wilkinson, Anne (1910–61)
Adam and God.
Daily the Drum.
Falconry.
In June and Gentle Oven.
Leda in Stratford, Ont.
Lens.
Nature Be Damned.
Red and the Green, The.
Variations on a Theme.

Wilkinson, Iris Gulver See "Hyde, Robin"

Willard, Emma Hart (1787–1870)
Rocked in the Cradle of the Deep.

Willard, Nancy (b. 1936)
Angels in Winter.
Ballad of Biddy Early, The.
Blake Leads a Walk on the Milky Way.
Cat's Second Song, The.
Feast of St. Tortoise, The.
How the Hen Sold Her Eggs to the Stingy
  Priest.
Insects, The.
King of Cats Sends a Postcard to His Wife,
  The.
Night Light.
Original Strawberry.
Questions My Son Asked Me, Answers I
  Never Gave Him.

Saint Pumpkin.
Sand Shark.
Sleep of the Painted Ladies, The.
Speckled Hen's Morning Song to Biddy Early,
  The.

Willemer, Marianne von
To the West Wind.

William of Aquitaine (1071–1127)
From the Provençal of William of Poitiers.
Since now I have a mind to sing.
Spring Song.

William of Shoreham (*fl.* early 14th cent.)
Song to Mary, A.

Williams, Ann (*fl.* 1660s)
Greifes Farwell, to an Inherritor of Joy.

Williams, Anna (1706–83)
Nunnery, The.
Verses to Mr. Richardson on his History of Sir
  Charles Grandison.

Williams, Bertye Young (d. 1951)
Friend Who Just Stands by, The.

Williams, Beryle
Night Flute, The.

Williams, Charles (1886–1945)
At the "Ye That Do Truly."
Dream, A.
Kings Came Riding.
Mount Badon.
Night Song for a Child.
Taliessin's Song of the Unicorn.

Williams, Sir Charles Hanbury (1709–57)
Monkey, lap-dog, parrot, and her Grace, The.
Song upon Miss Harriet Hanbury, Addressed to
  the Revd Mr Birt.
Verses: "Poor fellow, what is it to you."

Williams, Charles Kenneth (b. 1936)
Alzheimer's: The Wife.
Bone.
Critic, The.
Day for Anne Frank, A.
Dog, The.
Gas Station, The.
It Is This Way with Men.
Loss.
My Fly.
My Mother's Lips.
Poem: "I think I came close to being insane a
  few months ago."
Racists.
Repression.
Sanctity, The.
Shock.
Spit.
Tar.
Vessel, The.

Williams, Clarence (1893–1965)
Gulf Coast Blues.

Williams, Cootie
'Round Midnight.

Williams, Crystal (b. 1970)
For the White Lady Holding Me.
In Search of Aunt Jemima.

Williams, David
In Praise of the Potato.

Williams, Edward (Iolo Morganwg) (1747–1826)
I live on my farm in a beautiful vale.
Poet's Arbour in the Birchwood, The.
Why, Cambria did I quit thy shore.

Williams, Edward W. (1863–91)
At Harper's Ferry Just before the Attack.

Williams, Eliseus (1867–1926)
Heather Flowers.

Williams, Emmett (b. 1925)
He said it two days ago.
Like Attracts Like.
Rose is a Rose is a Rose is a Rose.
Rose is a Violin is a Codpiece.
What.

Williams, George See Awoonor, Kofi

Williams, Gwyn (b. 1904)
After Reading *Poems to Einhir*.
City Under Snow.
Jet Planes.
Saint Ursula of Llangwyryfon.

Today has it all, sunshine.
Wild Night at Treweithan.

Williams, Helen Maria (1762–1827)
Bastille, a Vision, The.
Blest Poesy! Oh sent to calm.
Elegy on a Young Thrush Which Escaped from
  the Writer's Hand.
Farewell, for Two Years, to England, A. A
  Poem.
On the Death of the Rev. Dr. Kippis.
Part of an Irregular Fragment, Found in a Dark
  Passage of the Tower.
Poem on the Bill Lately Passed for Regulating
  the Slave-Trade, A.
Song, A: "No riches from his scanty store."
Sonnet 6. To the Torrid Zone.
Sonnet on Reading the Poem upon the
  Mountain Daisy, by Mr. Burns.
Sonnet to Twilight.
To Dr. Moore, in Anser to a Poetical Epistle
  Written by Him in Wales.
To Hope.
To Mrs. K————, On Her Sending Me an
  English Christmas Plum-Cake at Paris.
To the Curlew.
To the Moon.
To the Strawberry.
To the White Bird of the Tropic.

Williams, Herbert (b. 1932)
Like Father.
Old Tongue, The.

Williams, Hugo (b. 1942)
Butcher, The.
Last Poem.
Prayer.
Some Kisses from *The Kama Sutra*.
When I Grow Up.

Williams, John (1664–1729)
Some Contemplations of the Poor, and
  Desolate State of the Church at Deerfield.

Williams, John (1761–1818)
Matrimony.
On Reading Aloud My Early Poems.

Williams, John Hartley (b. 1942)
Script Conference.

Williams, John Stuart (b. 1920)
Early Days.
In Duffryn Woods.
Pastoral: "You see that forest on the height?"
Rhyfel y Sais Bach.
River Walk.

Williams, Jonathan (b. 1929)
Adhesive Autopsy of Walt Whitman, The.
Anthropophagites See a Sign on NC Highway
  177 That Looks like Heaven, The.
Bitch-Kitty, The.
Distances to the Friend, The.
Fast Ball.
Hermit Cackleberry Brown, on Human Vanity,
  The.
Honey Lamb, The.
Little Tumescence, A.
Mrs. Sadie Grindstaff, Weaver and Factotum.
Ovid, Meet a Metamorphodite.
Switch Blade; or, John's Other Wife, The.
Symphony No. 3, in D Minor.
Those Troublesome Disguises.
Three Sayings from Highlands, North Carolina.
Uncle Iv Surveys His Domain from His
  Rocker.
Vulnerary, The.

Williams, Joy (b. 1942)
Memories of Christmas.
Rachel.
Shadows.
Sometimes I look at the needle.
Thousand years ago I loved you, A.

Williams, Lisa (b. 1966)
Crater.
Interruption of Flight.

Williams, Lucy (b. 1893)
Origin of the Skagit Indians, The.

Williams, M. L.
152 Into 5, *El Centro Palabra de Fe*.
Astronomy.

South.

Williams, Mary Lou
What's Your Story, Morning Glory.

Williams, Max
Empty House, The.

Williams, Merryn
Heading for the Heights.

Williams, Miller (b. 1930)
Death of Chet Baker, The.
On the Symbolic Consideration of Hands and
the Significance of Death.
Poem for Emily, A.
Shrinking Lonesome Sestina, The.
Thinking about Bill, Dead of AIDS

Williams, Oscar (b. 1900)
Picture Postcard of a Zoo.
Spritely Dead, The.
With Me.

Williams, Palorine
Libation.

Williams, Patrick (b. 1950)
Baby in the House, A.
In the Dark.
Lost Seed.
Passing Through.
Rhapsody on Main Street.
Trails.

Williams, Peter (b. 1937)
When She Was Here, Li Bo.

Williams, Rhydwen (b. 1916)
Baboon, The.

Williams, Robert (1830–77)
On a Woman.

Williams, Roger (c.1603–1683)
Adulteries, murthers, robberies, thefts.
Boast not proud English, of thy birth and
blood.
Courteous Indian, The.
God gives them sleep on ground, on straw.
God makes a path, provides a guide.
How busie are the sonnes of men?
I have heard ingenuous Indians say.
If Birds That neither Sow nor Reap.
Indians count of men as dogs, The.
Indians prize not English gold, The.
Mans restlesse soule hath restlesse eyes and
ears.
Observation Generall from Their Eating, Etc.,
The.
One step twix't me and death, (twas Davids
speech)
Our English gamesters scorne to stake.
Pagans wild confesse the bonds, The.
They see Gods wonders that are call'd.
Truth is a native, naked beauty; but.
What Habacuck once spake, mine eyes.
When Sun Doth Rise.

Williams, Sarah (1837–68)
Youth and Maidenhood.

Williams, Sherley Anne (b. 1944)
Buildings of the, The.
California Light.
Driving Wheel.
Empress Brand Trim: Ruby Reminisces, The.
Green Eyed Monsters of the Valley Dusk, The.
House of Desire, The.
I Want Aretha to Set This to Music.
Letters from a New England Negro.
Peacock Poems: 1, The.
Say Hello to John.
She Had Known Brothers.
Straight Talk from Plain Women.
Summer mornings we.
Town less, A.
Wishon Line, The.
You Were Never Miss Brown to Me.

Williams, Shirley
If He Let Us Go Now.
Killing of the Birds, The.
You Know It's Really Cold.

Williams, Simon
Inscrutable question, The.

Williams, Spencer
My Man o' War.

Williams, Taliesin (1787–1847)
Tourist, as he views the place, The.

**Williams, Tennessee (Thomas Lanier Williams)
(1914–83)**
Beanstalk Country, The.
Carrousel Tune.
Gold Tooth Blues.
Kitchen Door Blues.
Life Story.
Sugar in the Cane.
You and I.

Williams, Theodore Chickering (1855–1915)
Hast Thou Heard It, O My Brother.
My Country, to Thy Shore.
When Thy Heart with Joy O'erflowing.

Williams, Thomas Lanier *See* **Williams,
Tennessee**

Williams, Waldo (1904–72)
Daffodil.
In Two Fields.
Summer Cloud, A.

Williams, William ("Pantycelyn") (1717–91)
Christian Pilgrim's Hymn.
Guide Me, O Thou Great Jehovah.
Hymn: "Now the shadows flee and vanish."
Hymn: "What is the world, and what is life."
I Gaze across the Distant Hills.
Marriage in Eden, The.

Williams, William Carlos (1883–1963)
Act, The.
Adoration of the Kings, The.
Apology.
Approach to a City.
Approaching death.
Après le Bain.
At Kenneth Burke's Place.
At the Ball Game.
At the Faucet of June.
Ballad of Faith.
Between Walls.
Bird Song.
Black Winds, The.
Breakfast.
Brilliant Sad Sun.
Bull, The.
Burning the Christmas Greens.
Catholic Bells, The.
Chicory and Daisies.
Children, The.
Classic Scene.
Clouds, The.
Coda.
Complaint.
Complete Destruction.
Coronal, A.
Daisy.
Dance, The.
Danse Russe.
Dawn.
Dead Baby, The.
Death.
Delineaments of the Giants, The.
Descent, The.
Desert Music, The.
Desolate Field, The.
Drink.
Edward / Paterson has grown older.
El Hombre.
Episode 17.
Exercise No. 2.
First Praise.
Flight to the City.
Flowers by the Sea.
For Eleanor and Bill Monahan.
Fragment: "As for him who."
Gift, The.
Good Night.
Goodnight, A.
Great Figure, The.
Grotesque.
Gulls.
Hard Listener, The.
Haymaking.
Hemmed-in Males.
High Bridge above the Tagus River at Toledo,
The.
History of Love, A.
Horse Show, The.

House, The.
Hunters in the Snow, The.
Illegitimate Things.
Intelligent Sheepman and the New Cars, The.
Iris.
It Is a Small Plant.
It is dangerous to leave written that which is
badly written.
It is far to Assisi.
Italian Garden, The.
Ivy Crown, The.
January.
January Morning.
Lament: "What face, in the water."
Landscape with the Fall of Icarus.
Last Words of My English Grandmother, The.
Late Singer, The.
Lear.
Locust Tree in Flower, The.
Lonely Street, The.
Love Song: "Sweep the house clean."
Luke 6:39.
Metric Figure.
Mezzo Forte.
Artist, The.
Mists Over the River.
Moon, the dried weeds, The.
Mujer.
Nantucket.
Negro Woman, A.
New Clouds, The.
Ol' Bunk's Band.
On Gay Wallpaper.
Orchestra, The.
Overture to a Dance of Locomotives.
Parable of the Blind, The.
Pastoral: "Little sparrows, The."
Pastoral: "When I was younger."
Paterson, Book 5: The River of Heaven.
Paterson: The Falls.
Paterson—The Strike.
Pathology literally speaking is a flower garden.
Perpetuum Mobile: The City.
Philomena Andronico.
Pink Locust, The.
Poem: "As the cat."
Poem: "On getting a card."
Poem: "Rose fades, The."
Poor, The.
Portrait of a Lady.
Pot of Flowers, The.
Predicter of Famine, The.
Preface: "Rigor of beauty is the quest. But how
will you find beauty when it is locked."
Preface: "To make a start."
Prelude to Winter.
Proletarian Portrait.
Queen-Anne's-Lace.
Question and Answer.
Raleigh Was Right.
Rapid Transit.
Red Wheelbarrow, The.
Revelation, The.
Rigamarole.
Right of Way, The.
Romance Moderne.
Rose, The.
Russia.
Sadness of the Sea, The.
Sea-Elephant, The.
Self-Portrait.
Semblables, The.
Shoot It Jimmy!
Short Poem.
Silence.
Smell.
Some fools once were listening to a poet
reading his poem.
Sort of a Song, A.
Sparrow, The.
Spring and All.
Spring Strains.
Sunday in the Park.
Sympathetic Portrait of a Child.
There are no perfect waves.
There is a woman in our town.
There is neither beginning nor end to the

imagination.
There's force to this cold sun, makes beard
  stubble stand shinily.
These.
These Purists.
This Is Just to Say.
This is the time of year.
Thursday.
To.
To a Dog Injured in the Street.
To a Friend Concerning Several Ladies.
To a Man Dying on His Feet.
To a Poor Old Woman.
To a Solitary Disciple.
To a Sparrow.
To an Old Jaundiced Woman.
To Be Recited to Flossie on Her Birthday.
To Close.
To Daphne and Virginia.
To Elsie.
To Flossie.
To Ford Madox Ford in Heaven.
To freight cars in the air.
To Greet a Letter-Carrier.
To Mark Anthony in Heaven.
To the Shade of Po Chü-I.
To Waken an Old Lady.
Tract.
Tulip Bed, The.
Turtle, The.
Unison, A.
Waiting.
Why go further? One might conceivably rectify
  the rhythm.
Widow's Lament in Springtime, The.
Willow Poem.
Wind Increases, The.
Woman Walking.
World Contracted to a Recognizable Image,
  The.
Yachts, The.
Yellow Flower, The.
Yellow Season, The.
Young Housewife, The.
Young Laundryman, The.
Young Love.
Young Sycamore.
Young Woman at a Window.

Williamson, Alan (b. 1944)
Light's Reading, The.

Williamson, Greg (b. 1964)
Annual Returns.
Appalachian Trees Encircled by Police Tape.
Belvedere Marittimo.
Bodies of Water.
Counterfeiter, The.
Dark Days, The.
Drawing Hands.
Kites at the Washington Monument.
Neighboring Storms.
On His Birthday.
Origami.
Up in the Air.
Walter Parmer.
Waterfall.

Williamson, Roosevelt *See* **Shahid**

"Willie, Woodbine" *See* **Studdert-Kennedy,**
Geoffrey Anketell

Willis, Humphrey *(fl. 1647)*
Time's Whirligig, Or, The Blue-New-Made-
  Gentleman Mounted.

Willis, Love Maria (1824–1908)
Father, Hear the Prayer We Offer.

Willis, Nathaniel Parker (1806–67)
Ambition.
Calm and lovely paradise, A.
City Lyrics.
Confessional, The.
Declaration, The.
January 1, 1829.
Lady in the White Dress, Whom I Helped into
  the Omnibus, The.
Lady Jane, The.
New Year, The.
Psyche, before the Tribunal of Venus.
To Charles Roux, of Switzerland.

To Helen in a Huff.
To the Lady in the Chemisette with Black
  Buttons.

Willmot, Rod
Away from eyes.
Breathing.
Cheeses, pâté.
Her breasts lift with her arms.
Her hand on the doorknob.
Humiliated again.
I find her huddled on the bed.
If I go alone.
Listening.
Mail on the counter.
May rain.
Musty shed.
Novel's end.
Now the spade.
Page of Shelley, A.
Quiet rustle, A.
Shadows in the grass.
Small noise, A.
Weak sun.

Wills, John
Another bend.
Below the dam.
Beyond the porch.
Bittern booms, A.
Bluegill rises, A.
Bluejay sails, A.
Boulders.
Box of nails, A.
Coolness.
Day wears on, The.
Den of the bear.
Dusk from rock to rock a waterthrush.
Evening sun, The.
Forest stands, The.
Goats on the roof.
Hills, The.
I catch.
In an upstairs room.
Larger.
Laurel in bloom.
Looking deeper.
Moon at dawn, The.
Mourning cloak, A.
My hand moves out.
November evening.
Old cow lags, The.
Pebble falls, A.
Rain in gusts.
River, The.
Stagnant pond, A.
Summer drizzle.
Sun lights up a distant ridge another, The.
Water lilies.
Water pools.
White horse.
Winter again.

Willson, Dixie
Tip-Toe Tail.

Willson, Forceythe (1837–67)
Estray, The.
In State.
To Hersa.

Willson, Meredith
Seventy Six Trombones.
Till There Was You.
Ya Got Trouble.

Wilmer, Sydney
Mess Boy, The.

Wilmot, Frank *See* **"Maurice, Furnley"**

Wilner, Eleanor (b. 1931)
Abstraction.
All the Wide Grin of Him.
Conversation with a Japanese Student.
Epitaph: "Young then, / we were bored
  already."
Her Body Is Private.
High Noon at Los Alamos.
Judgment.
Meditation on the Wen Fu.
Miriam's Song.
Muse, The.
Reading the Bible Backwards.

Sarah's Choice.
Secret Garden, The.
When Asked to Lie Down on the Altar.
You, Failed Pronoun.

Wilson, Anne *(fl. 1778)*
In Praise of Drainage.

Wilson, Anthony
Everything opauqe about us, perhaps.

Wilson, Edmund (1895–1972)
Disloyal Lines to an Alumnus.
Drafts for a Quatrain.
Enemies of Promise.
Epitaphs.
Lakeside.
Miniature Dialogue.
Nursery Vignette.
Scène de Boudoir.
Something for My Russian Friends.

Wilson, Edwin H. (b. 1898)
Where Is Our Holy Church?

Wilson, Frances
Bathing My Mother.

Wilson, John (1591–1667)
Confess We All, before the Lord.
For Lo! My Jonah How He Slumped.
Whoso Would See This Song of Heavenly
  Choice.

Wilson, John (1627?–96)
Claudius Gilbert.
Copy of Verses, A.

Wilson, Keith (b. 1927)
Dusk in My Backyard.

Wilson, Mary
Diary.
I went out of the conf'rence to get a pint of
  beer.

Wilson, Ramona (b. 1945)
Bags Packed and We Expected This.
Dry Rivers—Arizona.
Eveningsong.
Eveningsong 2.
Keeping Hair.
Late in Fall.
Meeting, The.
Overnight Guest.
Reading Indian Poetry.
Spring at Fort Okanogan.
Spring in Virginia.
Summer.

Wilson, Robert (d. 1600?)
Simplicity's Song.

Wilson, Robert Noble Denison (1899–1953)
Elegy in a Presbyterian Burying-Ground.

Wilson, Robley, Jr. (b. 1936)
Envoi: "Sun in the mouth of the day."
I Wish in the City of Your Heart.
Mechanical Cow, The.
Military-Industrial Complex, The.
Potato Escape, A.
Rejoicing That Attend the Murder of Famous
  Men, The.
Say Girls in Shoe Ads: "I Go for a Man Who's
  Tall!"
Sparrow Hills.

Wilson, Sandy (b. 1924)
Boy Friend, The.
It's Never Too Late to Fall in Love.
Room in Bloomsbury, A.

Wilson, Steve (b. 1960)
Contemporary Poet, A.
Experiments in the Impersonal.
Picture on the Purple Wall, the.
Recreational Mathematics.

Wilson, T. P. Cameron (1889–1918)
Magpies in Picardy.

Wilson, Thomas Zvi
Alice Potato.

Wilson, Woodrow (1856–1924)
Limerick: "I went with the Duchess to tea."

Wiman, Christian (b. 1966)
Hearing Loss.
In Lakeview Cemetery.
Sweet Dreams.

Winant, Fran (b. 1943)
Sacred Grove, A.

To Begin.

Winch, Terence (b. 1945)
Shadow Grammar.

Winchcombe, Mrs. (fl. 1614)
I lovd thee living and lament thee dead.

Winchester, Caleb T. (1847–1920)
Lord Our God Alone Is Strong, The.

Winchester, Elhanan (1751–97)
Behold with Joy.

Winchilsea, Anne Finch, Countess of (1661–1720)
Adam Posed.
Answer, The.
Ballad to Mrs. Catherine Fleming in London from Malshanger Farm in Hampshire, A.
Bolder Youth, grown of capable arms, A.
Caesar and Brutus.
Circuit of Apollo, The.
Enquiry after Peace. A Fragment.
Epistle from Alexander to Hephaestion in His Sickness, An.
Friendship between Ephelia and Ardelia.
Give me, O indulgent fate!
Glass.
Hog, the Sheep and Goat, Carrying to a Fair, The.
Hymn, The: "To the Almighty on his radiant throne."
Introduction, The: "Did I, my lines intend for public[k] view."
Letter to Daphnis, A.
Life's Progress.
Nocturnal Reverie, A.
On Myself.
Pastoral Dialogue between Two Shepherdesses, A.
Petition for an Absolute Retreat, The.
Power of Spleen, The.
Reformation.
Sigh, A.
Some Reflections.
Song, A: "Nymph in vain bestows her pains, The."
Song of the Cannibals, A.
Song on the South Sea, A.
Spleen, The.
Tale of the Miser and the Poet, A.
To Death.
To Melancholy.
To the Nightingale.
Trail All Your Pikes.
Unequal Fetters, The.
Upon My Lord Winchilsea's Converting the Mount in His Garden to a Terrace.
White Mouses Petition to Lamira the Right Honble the Lady Anne Tufton now Countess of Salisbury, The.

Winder, Barbara
Lesson.
On Fourteen Maple Street.
Unaccompanied Suite.

Wine, Maria (b. 1912)
Woman, you are afraid of the forest.

Wingfield, Sheila (1906–73)
Winter.

Winkfield, Trevor
Nature Study.

Winkler Prins, Jacob (1849–1904)
Shower.

Winnebago Oral Tradition
Felix White Sr.'s Introduction to Wakjankaga.

Winner, Joseph E. (1837–1918)
Little Brown Jug.

Winner, Robert (b. 1930)
Segregated Railway Diner—1946.

Winner, Septimus (1827–1902)
Coolie Chinee, The.
Lilliputian's Beer Song.
Listen to the Mocking Bird.
Ten Little Injuns.

Winslow, Pete
I blink and half my life is over.
O god of spring forgive me.

Winstanley, Gerrard (1609?–76)
Digger's Song, The.

Winstanley, John (1678–1750)
Epigram on Florio.

Epigram on the First of April.
Fanny's Removal in 1714.
Inventory of the Furniture of a Collegian's Chamber, An.
Last Will and Testament, A.
Miss Betty's Singing-Bird.
On a Certain Effeminate Peer.
On a Stingy Beau.
To the Revd. Mr. ——— on His Drinking Sea-Water.
Upon a Friend's Pet Cat, Being Sick.

Wintchevsky, Morris (1856–1934)
Child-King, The.
If I Felt Less.

Winter, Max (b. 1970)
Dux Bellorum.
Elegy: "There is a question."
Long Distance.
Space Parable.

Winter, Miriam Therese
In the Beginning.

Winter, William (1836–1917)
Heart's Anchor, The.

Winters, Yvor (1900–68)
Alas, that I should be.
Apollo and Daphne.
At the San Francisco Airport.
Barnyard, The.
Cold, The.
Elegy: "Noon is beautiful, The."
Elegy on a Young Airedale Bitch Lost Two Years Since in the Salt-Marsh.
Fable, The.
Fall of Leaves, The.
For My Father's Grave.
For the Opening of the William Dinsmore Briggs Room.
Fragment: "I cannot find my way to Nazareth."
In Praise of California Wines.
Inscription for a Graveyard.
John Sutter.
Magpie's Shadow, The.
Manzanita, The.
Nocturne: "Moonlight on stubbleshining."
October.
On a View of Pasadena from the Hills.
On Teaching the Young.
Orpheus.
Precision, The.
Realization, The.
Rows of Cold Trees, The.
Sir Gawaine and the Green Knight.
Slow Pacific Swell, The.
Solitude of Glass, The.
Song in Passing, A.
Summer Noon: 1941.
Theseus: A Trilogy.
Time and the Garden.
To a Military Rifle, 1942.
To a Young Writer.
To Emily Dickinson.
To My Infant Daughter.
To the Holy Spirit.
To the Moon.
Two Songs of Advent.
Vacant Lot.
Wild Sunflower.

Wisdome, Robert (d. 1568)
Religious Use of [Taking] Tobacco, A.

Wise, Isaac M. (1819–1900)
In Mercy, Lord, Incline Thine Ear.

Wise, Joseph (b. 1940)
Glory.

Wise, Suzanne (b. 1965)
50 Years in the Career of an Aspiring Thug.
Closure Opening Its Trap.
I Was Very Prolific.

Wise, William (b. 1923)
When I Grow Up.

Wishik, Heather (b. 1950)
Visitation Rights.

Wiswall, Ichabod (1637–1700)
Judicious Observation of That Dreadful Comet, A.

With, Elizabeth (fl. 1659)
How Elizabeth Foole and Her Husband Parted

by Means of Her Sister in Law.

Witheford, Hubert (b. 1921)
At the Discharge of Cannon Rise the Drowned.
Barbarossa.
Mid Winter.
What Is Happening Now?

Wither, George (1588–1667)
Choice, The.
Conversion of S. Paul, The.
Epigram: "Women, as some men say, unconstant be."
First Song of Moses, The.
First think, my soul, if I have foes.
For a Poet.
Husbandman, The.
I Loved a Lass.
If by mischance the people in the street.
Lord, Many Times Thou Pleased Art.
Marigold, The.
Ninth Canticle, The.
Planting.
Prayer for His Wife and Children, Written in Newgate.
Prayer of Hezekiah, The.
Prayer of Nehemiah, The.
Shall I, Wasting in Despair.
Sonnet: "I that erstwhile the world's sweet air did draw."
Sonnet: "I wandered out a while agone."
Spade and the Wreath, The.
Spade, The.
Sun hath run his course through all the Signes, The.
When We Cannot Sleep.
Widow's Hymn, A.

Witherspoon, Naomi Long *See* **Madgett, Naomi Long**

Withington, Leonard (1789–1885)
O Saviour of a World Undone.

Witt, Sir Robert
Limerick: "Arnolfinis both sat to Van Eyck."

Witt, Sam (b. 1970)
Americana.
Everlasting Quail.
Michael Masse.
Waterfowl Descending.

Witting, Amy (b. 1918)
Beauty Is the Straw.
Blinkered Mind, The.
Curse on Herod, A.

Woddis, Roger (b. 1917)
All Clear.
Believers' Best Buy.
Do Not Go Sober.
Doctor, The.
Eat Your Heart Out, Edward Lear!
Ethics for Everyman.
Final Curtain.
I Shall Vote Centre.
Limerick: "Said a God-fearing lady called Whitehouse."
Limerick: "Said Powell: "Don't call me insane""
Limerick: "There once were two Babes in the Wood."
Limerick: "There was an Old Man with a Beard / Who said: "I demand to be feared."
Moral Tale, A.
Nothing Sacred.
Rewards and Fairies.
Rolling Chinese Wall, The.

Wodehouse, Pelham Grenville (1881–1975)
Bill.
Bill (Original Version)
Bungalow in Quogue.
Cleopatterer.
Gourmet's Love-Song, The.
It's a Hard, Hard World for a Man.
Land Where the Good Songs Go, The.
Napoleon.
Outcast, The.
Printer's Error.
That Was before I Met You.
Till the Clouds Roll By.
To William (Whom We Have Missed)
Tulip Time in Sing Sing.

You Can't Make Love by Wireless.
You Never Knew about Me.
Woessner, Warren
Jungle Music.
Wohlfeld, Valerie (b. 1956)
Sea.
That Which Is Fugitive, That Which Is
Medicinally Sweet or Alterable to Gold,
That Which Is Substantiated by Unscientific
Means.
Wojahn, David (b. 1953)
Allegory: Attic and Fever.
Assassination of John Lennon as Depicted by
the Madame Tussaud Wax Museum, Niagara
Falls, Ontario, 1987, The.
Assassination of Robert Goulet as Performed
by Elvis Presley: Memphis, 1968, The.
At Graceland with a Six Year Old, 1985.
Buddy Holly.
Buddy Holly Watching *Rebel Without a Cause*,
Lubbock, Texas, 1956.
Colorizing: Turner Broadcasting Enterprises,
Computer Graphics Division, Burbank,
California, 1987.
Custom Job: Hank Williams, Jr., and the Death
Car, 1958.
Distance.
Elvis Moving a Small Cloud: The Desert Near
Las Vegas, 1976.
Fab Four Tour Deutschland: Hamburg, 1961.
Francis Ford Coppola and Anthropologist
Interpreter Teaching Gartewienna Tribesmen
to Sing 'Light My Fire,' Philippine Jungle,
1978.
Homage: Light from the Hall.
Inside, The.
'It's Only Rock and Roll but I Like It': The
Fall of Saigon, 1975.
John Berryman Listening to Robert Johnson's
"King of the Delta Blues," January 1972.
"Mystery Train": Janis Joplin Leaves Port
Arthur for Points West, 1964.
Matins: James Brown and His Famous Flames
Tour the South, 1958.
My Father's Pornography.
Necromancy: The Last Days of Brian Jones,
1968.
Nixon Names Elvis Honorary Federal
Narcotics Agent at Oval Office Ceremony,
1973.
Pharaoh's Palace.
Photo of My Father in a Snowbound Train.
Rajah in Babylon.
Riding the Empire Builder, 1948.
Satin Doll.
Song of the Burning.
Tattoo, Corazon: Ritchie Valens, 1959.
Trashmen Shaking Hands with Hubert
Humphrey at the Opening of Apache Plaza
Shopping Center, Suburban Minneapolis,
August 1963, The.
W.C.W. Watching Presley's Second
Appearance on The Ed Sullivan Show:
Mercy Hospital, Newark, 1956.
Woody Guthrie Visited by Bob Dylan:
Brooklyn State Hospital, New York, 1961.
Workmen Photographed inside the Reactor.
Wolcot, John *See* "Pindar, Peter"
Wojtyla, Karol (b. 1920)
Marble Floor.
Song of the Brightness of Water.
Wolcott, Roger (1679–1767)
Heart Is Deep, The.
Matthew X. 28.
Wolcott, Samuel (1813–86)
Christ for the World! We Sing.
Father! I Own Thy Voice.
Wolf, Tommy
Ballad of the Sad Young Men, The.
Say 'Cheese!'
Spring Can Really Hang You up the Most.
Wolfe, Aaron R. (1821–1902)
Complete in Thee, No Work of Mine.
Parting Hymn We Sing, A.
Wolfe, Charles (1791–1823)
Burial of Sir John Moore [after [*or* at]

Corunna], The.
Song: "Oh say not that my heart is cold."
To Mary.
Wolfe, Ffrida
Choosing Shoes.
Wolfe, Humbert (1885–1940)
A. E. Housman and a Few Friends.
Blackbird, The.
British Journalist, The.
D. H. Lawrence and James Joyce.
Dead Fiddle, The.
Dean Inge.
G. K. Chesterton.
Gray Squirrel, The.
Green Candles.
Hilaire Belloc.
Iliad.
Journey's End.
Love Is a Keeper of Swans.
Man.
Things Lovelier.
This Is Not Death.
Tulip.
Wardour Street.
Waters of Life, The.
Wolfe, Marianne
Thaw, The.
Wolfe, Thomas Clayton (1900–1938)
For, Brother, What Are We?
Wolff, David
While We Slept.
Wolfli, Adolf (1864–1930)
And now: And now: here begins Our Voyage,
hunters and naturalists of indefatigable
enthusiasm.
Nostalgic Song for My Beloved.
Wolfram von Eschenbach (1170?–1220?)
His Own True Wife.
"Its claws have struck through the clouds."
You always sang at break of day.
Wolfskehl, Karl (1869–1948)
And Yet We Are Here!
Shekhinah.
To Be Said at the Seder.
We Go.
Wolkenstein, Oswald von (1377–1445)
O Margie, Marge, Dear Margaret.
Wolley, Hannah (c.1621–74)
Ladies, I do here present you.
Wölmyŏng, Master (c.742–765)
Requiem.
Wolstenholme-Elmy, Elizabeth (1834–1918)
Marriage, which might have been a mateship
sweet.
Wolverton, Terry
Black Slip.
Dead Stepfather, The.
In China.
Tubes.
Wong, Janet S. (b. 1962)
Good Luck Gold.
One to Ten.
Wong, Nellie (b. 1934)
Dreams in Harrison Railroad Park.
For an Asian Woman Who Says My Poetry
Gives Her a Stomachache.
Grandmothers' Song.
How a Girl Got Her Chinese Name.
Ironing.
Ma, my heart must be made of rice straw.
Mama, Come Back.
On Plaza Garibaldi.
On Thinking of Photographing My Fantasies.
Picnic.
When I Was Growing Up.
Can't Tell.
Where Is My Country?
Wonodi, Okogbule (b. 1936)
Planting.
Salute to Icheke.
Woo, David (b. 1959)
Eden.
Expatriates.
Grandfather's Rockery.
Great Helmsman, The.

Habit.
Woo, Merle
Untitled: "In the deepest night and a full
moon."
Whenever You're Cornered, the Only Way Out
Is to Fight.
Wood, Charles Erskine Scott
I have entered into the Desert, the place of
desolation.
Wood, Dilys
Christmas Fare.
Wood, Eve (b. 1967)
Recognition.
Wood, Robert Williams (1868–1955)
Elk, The Whelk, The.
Pecan, The Toucan, The.
Pen-guin. The Sword-fish, The.
Wood, Susan (b. 1946)
Eggs.
Wood, Victoria (b. 1953)
Saturday Night.
Wood, William (1606–c.37)
Kinds of Shel-fish.
Kingly lyon, and the strong arm'd beare, The.
Princely eagle, and the soaring hawke, The.
Sea's Abundant Progeny, The.
Trees both in hills and plaines, in plenty be.
Woodard, Deborah
Tower.
Woodbridge, Benjamin (1622–84)
Upon the Author. By a Known Friend.
Upon the Tomb of the Most Reverend Mr.
John Cotton.
Woodcock, George (1912–95)
Imagine the South.
Island, The.
Pacifists.
Paper Anarchist Addresses the Shade of Nancy
Ling Perry.
Poem for Garcia Lorca.
Woodhouse, James (1735–1820)
Life and Lucubrations of Crispinus Scriblerus,
The.
Woodhouse, Peter
I see a Soldiers service is forgot.
Woods, Donald (1957–92)
Prescription.
Waiting.
Woods, Harry
Over My Shoulder.
Paddlin' Madelin' Home.
River, Stay 'Way from My Door.
Side by Side.
Try a Little Tenderness.
We Just Couldn't Say Good-bye.
When the Red, Red Robin Comes Bob, Bob,
Bobbin' Along.
Woods, John (b. 1926)
Looking Both Ways before Crossing.
What Do You Do When It's Spring?
Woods, Margaret Louisa (b. 1856)
Genius Loci.
Woods, Stuart
Limerick: "Couple from old Aberystwyth, A."
Woodsford, David
Limerick: "Hoover, in grim silence, sat, The."
Woodward, Charles (fl. c.1731)
Midnight Ramble, The.
Woodward, Gerard (b. 1961)
Lighthouse.
Woodworth, Samuel (1784–1842)
Old Oaken Bucket, The.
Woody, Elizabeth
Girlfriends, The.
She-Who-Watches . . . The Names are Prayer.
Woolagoodjah, Sam
Lalai (Dreamtime).
Woolsey, Sarah Chauncey *See* "Coolidge, Susan"
Woolson, Constance Fenimore (1840–94)
Detroit River.
Florida Beach, The.
Kentucky Belle.
Love Unexpressed.

One.
Other, The.
"Worcester"
Pastoral; in the Modern Style, A.
Wordsworth, Christopher (1807–85)
All Saints' Day, Nov. 1.
O Day of Rest and Gladness.
See the Conqueror mounts in triumph.
Wordsworth, Dorothy (1771–1855)
Address to a Child during a Boisterous Winter Evening.
Cottager to Her Infant, (By My Sister), The.
Floating Island at Hawkshead.
Irregular Verses.
Lake was covered all over, The.
Loving and Liking [Irregular Verses Addressed to A Child].
Peaceful Our Valley, Fair and Green.
Thoughts on my sick-bed.
Wordsworth, Elizabeth (1840–1932)
Good and Clever.
Wordsworth, William (1770–1850)
1801.
Admonition to a Traveller.
Affliction of Margaret—The.
Alice Fell; or, Poverty.
Animal Tranquillity and Decay.
Complaint, A.
Composed after a Journey across the Hamilton Hills, Yorkshire.
Composed at Neidpath Castle, the Property of Lord Queensberry,1803.
Composed by the Sea-Side, near Calais, August, 1802.
Composed in One of the Valleys of Westmoreland, on Easter Sunday.
Composed upon Westminster Bridge, September 3, 1802.
Decay of Piety.
Domestic carnage now filled the whole year.
Ecclesiastical Sonnets, sels.
Elegiac Stanzas Suggested by a Picture of Peele Castle, in a Storm, Painted by Sir George Beaumont.
England, 1802, III.
England, 1802, V.
Ere I had told / Ten birthdays when among the mountain-slopes.
Even as a river,—partly (it might seem)
Excursion, The, sels.
Expostulation and Reply.
Extempore Effusion upon the Death of James Hogg.
Farewell, A: "Farewell thou little Nook of mountain-ground."
Farmer of Tilsbury Vale, The.
Fountain, The.
Gravestone upon the Floor in the Cloisters of Worcester Cathedral, A.
Green Linnet, The.
Here, calling up to mind what then I saw.
How sweet it is, when mother Fancy rocks.
Hymn: "Blest are the moments, doubly blest."
I Wandered Lonely As a Cloud.
I watch, and long have watched, with calm regret.
Idiot Boy, The.
If thou indeed derive thy light from Heaven.
Inscription for the Moss-Hut at Dove Cottage.
It is a beauteous evening.
Kitten and [the] Falling Leaves, The, sels.
Lesson, A.
Lines Composed a Few Miles above Tintern Abbey on Revisiting the Banks of the Wye during a Tour, July 13, 1798.
Lines Written in Early Spring.
London 1802.
London, MDCCCII.
Lucy, sels.
Lucy Gray; or, Solitude.
Man is dear to man: the poorest poor.
Memorials of a Tour of the Continent; 1820, sels.
Methought I saw the footsteps of a throne.
Michael [A Pastoral Poem].
London, 1802.

Most Alluring Clouds That Mount the Sky, The.
Most Sweet It Is with Unuplifted Eyes.
My Heart Leaps Up.
Newton's Statue.
November, 1806.
Nutting.
October, 1803.
Ode: Intimations of Immortality [from Recollections of Early Childhood], sels.
Ode to Duty.
Old Man by the Brook, The.
Old Man Travelling [Animal Tranquillity and Decay, a Sketch].
On the Departure of Sir Walter Scott from Abbotsford, for Naples.
On the Extinction of the Venetian Republic.
On the Projected Kendal and Windermere Railway.
Perfect Woman.
Personal Talk.
Poems Composed or Suggested during a Tour, in the Summer of 1833, sels.
Prelude, The; Growth of a Poet's Mind [1850 vers.], sels.
Primrose of the Rock, The.
Recluse; Home at Grasmere, The, sels.
Resolution and Independence, sels.
Reverie of Poor Susan, The.
River Duddon [A Series of Sonnets], The, sels.
Ruined Cottage, The.
Ruth [or, The Influences of Nature].
Scorn not the Sonnet; Critic, you have frowned.
September 1, 1802.
She dwelt among the untrodden ways.
Simon Lee [the Old Huntsman].
Solitary Reaper, The.
Sonnet: "England! the time is come when thou shouldst wean."
Sonnet: "Nuns fret not at their convent's narrow room."
Sonnet on Catherine Wordsworth.
Sonnet: Where Lies the Land.
Sonnets upon the Punishment of Death, sels.
Stepping Westward.
Tables Turned, The.
These words were uttered in a pensive mood.
This Prayer I Make.
Thorn, The, sels.
Thought[s] of a Briton on the Subjugation of Switzerland.
To a Child [Written in Her Album].
To a Sky-Lark, sels.
To My Sister.
To Sleep.
To the Cuckoo.
To the Daisy.
To the Highland Girl of Inversneyde.
To the Men of Kent (October, 1803)
To Toussaint L'Ouverture.
Tradition of Oker Hill in Darley Dale, Derbyshire, A.
Trosachs, The.
Two April Mornings, The.
We Are Seven, sels.
What aspect bore the Man who roved or fled.
Where Lies the Truth? Has Man in Wisdom's Creed.
With how sad steps, O Moon, thou climb'st the sky.
With Ships the Sea Was Sprinkled Far and Nigh.
World Is Too Much With Us, The.
Written in London, September, 1802.
Written in March [While Resting on the Bridge at the Foot of Brother's Water].
Yarrow Unvisited [1803].
Yarrow Visited [September, 1814].
Yew-Trees.
Work, Henry Clay (1932–84)
Come home, Father[!].
Grandfather's Clock.
Marching through Georgia.
Worley, Demetrice A. (b. 1960)
Dancing in the Dark.
Las Flores para una Niña Negra.

Sandra.
Tongues in My Mouth.
Wormser, Baron (b. 1948)
By-Products.
Fans.
It's a Party (1959)
Pigeons.
Shoplifting.
Soul Music.
Worth, Valerie (b. 1933)
Chairs.
Clock.
Dinosaurs.
Door.
Duck.
Fireworks.
Goldfish in the Garden Pond.
Magnet.
McDonald's, New Hartford, NY.
Sun.
Zinnias.
Wortman, Denis (1835–1922)
God of the Prophets! Bless the Prophets' Sons.
Today beneath Benignant Skies.
Wotton, Sir Henry (1568–1639)
Character of a Happy Life, The.
De Morte.
Dialogue betwixt God and the Soul, A.
Hymn to My God in a Night of My Late Sickness[e], A.
On a Bank [or Banck] as I Sat[e] [a-]Fishing; a Description of the Spring.
On His Mistress [or Mistris], the Queen of Bohemia.
Poem Written by Sir Henry Wotton, in His Youth, A.
To John Donne.
Upon the Death of Sir Albert Morton's Wife.
Upon the Sudden Restraint of the Earl[e] of Somerset, Then Falling from Favor [or Favour].
Woty, William (1731–91)
I now solicit not the Muses nine.
Lines Written in the Dog-Days.
White Conduit House.
Wray, Ruby Marion (b. 1888)
You'll Never Know.
Wren, Andrea M. (b. 1969)
Day at School, A.
Harmony.
Surrogate Mothers.
Wrigglesworth, Anne (fl. 1584)
Yf I had as faire a face as John Williams.
Wright, C.
May God Go with You, Son.
Wright, C. D. (1932–78)
Complete Birth if the Cool, The.
Further Adventures With You.
Legend of Hell, The.
Meanwhile the cars continued in a persistent flow down.
Obedience of the Corpse.
On the Eve of Our Mutually Assured Destruction.
Provinces.
Spread Rhythm.
Woman Looking through a Viewmaster.
Wright, Celeste Turner (b. 1906)
State of Preservation.
Yugoslav Cemetery.
Wright, Charles (b. 1935)
Appalachian Book of the Dead III, The.
April.
Autumn.
California Spring.
California Twilight.
Cicada Blue.
Clear Night.
Daughters of Blum, The.
Dead are a cadmium blue, The.
Dead Color.
Delta Traveller.
Disjecta Membra.
Dog Creek Mainline.
Dog Day Vespers.

Edvard Munch.
Hawaii Dantesca.
Homage to Paul Cézanne.
Laguna Blues.
Looking West from Laguna Beach at Night.
March Journal.
New Poem, The.
Northhanger Ridge.
Other Side of the River, The.
Saturday 6 A.M.
Self-Portrait.
Sitting at Night on the Front Porch.
Skins.
Snow.
Spider Crystal Ascension.
Stone Canyon Nocturne.
Tattoos.
Two Stories.
Virgo Descending.

Wright, David (b. 1920)
Caleb Barnes.
Cockermouth.
Funeral Oration, A.
Juxtapositions.
Lakes, The.
Musician, The.
On Himself.
This was as far as I had got.
Those Walks We Took.
To the Gods the Shades Flavinus of the
    Cavalry Regiment.
Winter at Gurnard's Head.

Wright, David McKee (b. 1867 or 1869, d. 1928)
While the Billy Boils.

Wright, Ernest Vincent (1872–1939)
When Father Carves the Duck.

Wright, Franz (b. 1953)
Alcohol.
Blood.
Depiction of Childhood.
Drinking Back.
I Did Not Notice.
Joseph Come Back as the Dusk.
Mosquitoes.
Journey, The.
Old, The.
Untitled.

Wright, Hetty (1697–1751)
Wedlock; a Satire.

Wright, Ivan Leonard
Want of You, The.

Wright, James (1643–1713)
Out of Horace.

Wright, James (1927–80)
American Twilights, 1957.
And Yet I Know.
Angel, The.
Arrangements with Earth for Three Dead
    Friends.
Art of the Fugue, The: A Prayer.
At the Executed Murderer's Grave.
At the Slackening of the Tide.
At Thomas Hardy's Birthplace, 1953.
Autumn Begins in Martins Ferry, Ohio.
Before the [or a] Cashier's Window in a
    Department Store.
Beginning.
Blessing, A.
Breath of Air, A.
Complaint.
Confession to J. Edgar Hoover.
Depressed by a Book of Bad Poetry, I Walk
    toward an Unused Pasture and Invite the
    Insects to Join Me.
Evening.
Four Dead Sons.
Gesture by a Lady with an Assumed Name, A.
Handsome Is as Handsome Does.
Having Lost My Sons, I Confront the
    Wreckage of the Moon: Christmas, 1960.
Horse, The.
I slouch in bed.
I Try to Waken and Greet the World Once
    Again.
In Ohio.
In Response to a Rumor that the Oldest

Whorehouse in Wheeling, West Virginia,
    Has Been Condemned.
Inscription for the Tank.
Jewel, The.
Journey, The.
Late November in a Field.
Life, The.
Lifting Illegal Nets by Flashlight.
Living by the Red River.
Love in a Warm Room in Winter.
Lying in a Hammock at William Duffy's Farm
    in Pine Island, Minnesota.
Mad Fight Song for William S. Carpenter,
    1966, A.
Magnificence.
Mantova.
Milkweed.
Miners.
Minneapolis Poem, The.
Mutterings over the Crib of a Deaf Child.
My Grandmother's Ghost.
Names in Monterchi: To Rachel.
Nocturne, Aubade, and Vesper: "To call it a
    wet dream would be too barren."
Northern Pike.
Note Left in Jimmy Leonard's Shack, A.
Ohio Valley Swains.
Ohioan Pastoral.
Old Age Compensation.
Old Dog in the Ruins of the Graves at Arles,
    The.
On a Phrase from Southern Ohio.
Outside Fargo, North Dakota.
Poem about Breasts, A.
Poem Written under an Archway in a
    Discontinued Railroad Station, Fargo, North
    Dakota, A.
Prayer to the Lord Ramakrishna, A.
Presentation of Two Birds to My Son, A.
Redwings.
Revelation, The.
Romeo, Grown Old.
Saint Judas.
Sappho.
Saying Dante Aloud.
Secret Gratitude, A.
Silent Angel, The.
Simon and the Tarantula.
Sirmione.
Small Frogs Killed on the Highway.
Snowfall; a Poem about Spring.
Song for the Middle of the Night, A.
Sparrows in a Hillside Drift.
Speak.
Stages on a Journey Westward.
Three Sentences for a Dead Swan.
To a Beautiful Pear Tree.
To a Troubled Friend.
To Flood Stage Again.
To the Evening Star: Central Minnesota.
To the Muse.
To the Poets in New York.
Trying to Pray.
Twilights.
Two Hangovers.
Two Poems about President Harding.
Two Postures beside a Fire.
Verona.
Way to Make a Living, A.
Willy Lyons.
Winter Daybreak above Vence, A.
Written in a Copy of Swift's Poems, for Wayne
    Burns.
You and I Saw Hawks Exchanging the Prey.
Young Don't Want to Be Born.

Wright, Jay (b. 1935)
Albuquerque Graveyard, The.
Benjamin Banneker Sends His *Almanac* to
    Thomas Jefferson.
Compassion's Bird.
Death as History.
Desire's Persistence.
Don José Gorostiza Encounters El Cordobés.
End of an Ethnic Dream, The.
Homecoming Singer, The.
Invention of a Garden, The.
Invitation to Madison County, An.

Jalapeña Gypsies.
Journey to the Place of Ghosts.
Lake in Central Park, The.
Love in the Weather's Bells.
Madrid.
Meta-A and the A of Absolutes.
Neighborhood House, The.
Sketch for an Aesthetic Project.
Wednesday Night Prayer Meeting.
What is Beautiful.
White Deer, The.

Wright, John (fl. 1708–27)
Poor Man's Province, The.
Portugal Laurel, The.
Therapy.
Transfiguration.
Walking the Dog.

Wright, Judith (b. 1915)
And Mr. Ferritt.
At Cooloolah.
Australia 1970.
Beanstalk, Meditated Later, The.
Birds.
Black Cockatoos.
Bora Ring.
Brevity.
Brother and Sisters.
Bullocky.
Camphor Laurel.
Child, The.
Country Dance.
Cup, The.
"Dove-Love."
Drought Year.
Dust.
Eli, Eli.
Eve to Her Daughters.
Finale.
Flood Year.
Gum-trees Stripping.
Habitat.
Half-Caste Girl.
Hawthorn Hedge, The.
I to my Brothers.
Ishtar.
Killer, The.
Lament for Passenger Pigeons.
Legend.
Metho Drinker.
Naked Girl and Mirror.
Nigger's Leap, New England.
Night After Bushfire.
Old Prison, The.
Oppositions.
Patterns.
Pelicans.
Portrait.
Precipice, The.
Rainforest.
Remittance Man.
Request to a Year.
River Bend.
Rockpool.
Rosina Alcona to Julius Brenzaida.
Sanctuary.
Sisters, The.
Skins.
Sonnet for Christmas.
South of My Days.
Storm.
Summer.
Surfer, The.
Tableau.
To a Child.
To Another Housewife.
Train Journey.
Two Fires, The.
Wings.
Winter.
Woman's Song.
Woman to Child.
Woman to Man.

Wright, Kit (b. 1944)
Dad and the Cat and the Tree.
Doll's House, A.
Fortunes of War.
Greedyguts.

Heads or Tails?
How I See It.
How the Wild South East Was Lost.
I go through the wood in silence.
Limerick: "Her limp lover Maud couldn't pardon."
New World Symphony, A.
Our Hamster's Life.
Red Boots On.
Sergeant Brown's Parrot.
Underneath the Archers *or* What's All This about Walter's Willy?
Unlikely Obbligato of Andersonstown.
Victorian Family Photograph.

Wright, Mehetabel (1697–1750)
Address to Her Husband.
Epitaph on Herself, An.
To an Infant Expiring the Second Day of Its Birth.
Wedlock, a Satire.

Wright, Richard (1808–60)
Between the World and Me.
Bloody knife blade, A.
Bulging yellow clouds.
Bursting ripe plum, A.
Chill autumn dusk, The.
Consumptive man, The.
FB Eye Blues, The.
For you, O gulls.
From under the house.
From a red tile roof.
From the woods at night.
Haiku: "Coming from the woods."
Haiku: "Green cockleburs, The."
Haiku: "Just enough of rain."
I am nobody.
I Have Seen Black Hands.
In the falling snow.
O finicky cat.
On winter mornings.
Rustling dry paper.
Sound of the rain, The.
Spring lingers on, The.
Stars are dredging, The.
Twisting tendril, A.
Wild winter wind, A.

Wright, Robert (b. 1914)
And This Is My Beloved.
Baubles, Bangles, and Beads.
It's a Blue World.
Strange Music.
Stranger in Paradise.

Wright, Stephen Caldwell (b. 1946)
Out of the Wailing.

Wrigley, Ammon
Owdham Footbo'.

Wrigley, Robert
For the Last Summer.
Milkflowers.
Prophecy, The.
Sinking of Clay City, The.

Wroth [*or* Wroath], Mary Sidney, Countess of Montgomery (1587?–1651?)
Did I boast of liberty?
Here all alone in silence might I mourne.
Railing Rimes Returned upon the Author by Mistress Mary Wrothe.
Song 2: "All night I weep[e], all day I cry, Ay me[e]."
Song 4: "Sweetest love return[e] again[e]."
Song: "Dearest [*or* Deerest] if I by my deserving."
Song: "Love a child is ever crying [*or* criing]."
Song: "Love what art thou? A vain thought."
Song: "O[h] me[e], the time is [*or* has] come to part."
Sonnet 1: "In this strang[e] labyrinth [*or* labourinth] how shall I turn[e]?"
Sonnet 1: "When night's black mantle could most darknes[s] prove."
Sonnet 2: "Is to leave all, and take the thread of love."
Sonnet 2: "Late in the Forest I did Cupid See."
Sonnet 2: "Love like a jugler, comes to play his prize [*or* prise]."
Sonnet 3: "His flames ar[e] joy[e]s, his bands

true lovers' might."
Sonnet 3: "Juno still jealous[e] of her husband Jove."
Sonnet 5: "And burn[e], yet[t] burning you will love the smart."
Sonnet 6: "My pain[e], still smothered [*or* smother'd] in my grieved bre[a]st."
Sonnet 6: "Ô[h] strive not[t] still to heap[e] disdain[e] on me[e]."
Sonnet 7: "How blest be[e] they then, who his favo[u]rs prove."
Sonnet 7: "Love leave to urge, thou know'st thou hast the hand."
Sonnet 8: "Led by the pow'r [*or* powre] of grief[e], to wailings [*or* waylings] brought."
Sonnet 9: "Be[e] you all pleased [*or* pleas'd]? your pleasures grieve not[t] me[e]."
Sonnet 9: "My muse now hap[p]y, lay thy self to rest."
Sonnet 11: "Unprofitably pleasing, and unsound."
Sonnet 13: "Free from all fogs but[t] shining fair[e], and clear [*or* cleere]."
Sonnet 14: "Am I thus conquered [*or* conquer'd]? have I lost the powers."
Sonnet 14: "Except my hart which you beestow'd before."
Sonnet 19: "Come darkest night, be[e]coming sorrow best."
Sonnet 21: "When last I saw thee, I did not[t] thee see."
Sonnet 22: "Like to the Indians, scorched with the sun[ne]."
Sonnet 23: "When every one to pleasing pastime hies."
Sonnet 26: "Deare cherish this, and with it[t] my soules will."
Sonnet 27: "Fie [*or* Fy] tedious Hope, why do[e] you still rebel[l]?"
Sonnet 32: "How fast thou fliest, O Time, on loves swift wings."
Sonnet 34: "Take heed mine eyes, how you your look[e]s do[e] cast."
Sonnet 35: "False [*or* Faulce] hope which feeds but[t] to destroy, and spill."
Sonnet 37: "Night, welcome art thou to my mind destrest."
Sonnet 38: "What pleasure can a bannish'd creature have."
Sonnet 42: "If ever love had force in huma[i]ne bre[a]st?"
Sonnet 48: "How like a fire doth love increase in me[e]."

Wruber, Allie
Gone with the Wind.
(I'm Afraid) The Masquerade Is Over.
Lady in Red, The.
Music, Maestro, Please!

Wu Chen (1280–1354)
Fantastic Rock, The.
Inscribed on a Painting of Bamboo.
Level forest stretching far and wide, A.
Moonlight Bay.
Ni Tsan Poem Following Rhyme-Words of Wu Chen.
Paintings of Fishermen.
Poems Inscribed on Paintings of Bamboo.
To the Tune "Chiu-ch'üan tzu."

Wu Chia-chi (1618–84)
East of the salt village, low and narrow.
Grain-Barge Wife, The.
In the morning they build embankments against floods.
My Hut.
Old saltman, hair turned white, The.
To Ch'eng Fei-t'ao.
Woman Née Wu, The.
Woman Tung.

Wu Chün (469–520)
Song of Spring.

Wu Li (1632–1718)
Singing of the Source of Holy Church.
Tune: 'Happily Flitting Oriole.'

Wu-Men (1183–1260)
Great Way has no gate, The.
Moon and clouds are the same.

One instant is eternity.
Ten Thousand Flowers in Spring, the Moon in Autumn.

Wu of Han [*or* Wu Ti *or* Ou-ty *or* Liu Ch'e *or* Liu Ch'u] Emperor
Autumn Wind, The.
From the Most Distant Time.
Li Fu-Jên.
People Hide Their Love.
Skein, The.
Song of the Autumn Wind.
Summer Song.

Wu of Liang, Emperor (464–519)
Morning Sun Shines, The.
Water Lilies Bloom.

Wu Tsao (*fl.* c.1800)
For the Courtesan Ch'ing Lin.
In the Home of the Scholar Wu Su-chiang.
To the Tune "The Joy of Peace and Brightness."

Wu Wei-yeh (1609–72)
Ancient Feeling.
At the Mountain of the Mysterious Tomb Visiting Master P'ou.
At the River Tower Parting from My Younger Brother, Fu-ling.
At Yuen Yang Lake.
Autumn Night—Sleepless.
Ballad of Yüan-yüan.
Broken Lampstand, The.
Climbing P'iao-miao Peak.
Country Scene.
Distant Roads.
Feelings Come As I Pass through Wu-chiang.
Garden Living.
Impromptu.
Lamenting for My Late Daughter.
On the Twenty-fourth of the Third Month, in the Year Ting-wei Sailed across Lake T'ai from Behind the Mountain.
Passing by Huai-yin I Have Feelings.
Poem of the Western Fields.
Reading the Annals of Emperor Wu of the Han Dynasty.
Sailing at Dusk from T'u-sung.
Seeing Off Sun Ling-hsiu on His Journey to Chen-ting.
Seeing Off Wang Yüan-chao—Reprise.
Setting Out at Dawn.
Song to the Tune "Perching Crows."
Tune: "Sand of Silk-washing Stream."
Tune: "Song of River City"—On a Kite.
View of the Countryside.
Visiting the Garden at Monk Wen Ko's Home.

Wu Wen-ying (c.1200–c.1260)
Tune: 'Rouged Lips' Rain Just over on the Night of the Lantern Preview.
Tune: 'Sand of Silk-Washing Brook' a Reminiscence.

Wu Yun (469–520)
Apotheosis.
From the mountain's end, sight of coming smoke.

Wunderlich, Mark
Anchorage, The.
Aubade.
Bruise of This, The.
Chapel of the Miraculous Medal.
Continent's Edge.
Difficult Body.
East Seventh Street.
From a Vacant House.
Given in Person Only.
On Opening.
One Explanation of Beauty.
Simplify Your Combination Therapy.
Suture.
Take Good Care of Yourself.
Thirst.
Trick, The.

Wyat, Hester
What makes me write my dearest Freind you aske.

Wyatt, Sir Thomas (1503?–42)
Alas, madam[e], for stealing [*or* stelying] of a kiss [*or* kysse].

Argument, The.
Blame Not My Lute.
Courtier's Life, The.
Divers[e] [or Dyvers] doth[e] use, as I have heard and kno[w].
Enemy [or en'my] of life, decayer of all kind, The [or Th'].
Face that should content me wonders [or wondrous] well, A.
Farewell, love, and all thy law[e]s forever [or for ever].
Farewell: "What should I say."
Fortune doth frown.
Furious Gun, The.
He is not de[a]d that sometime [or somtyme] hath a fall.
His Reward.
Honesty.
I abide and abide and better abide.
I am as I am and so will I be.
I must go walk the woods so wild.
If waker care, if sudden [or sodayne] pale colo[u]r.
In aeternum I was once determed.
In Eternum.
In mourning wise since daily I increase.
In Spayn.
Introductory Poem to the Penitential Psalms.
Long love that in my thought doth harbo[u]r, The.
Lover's Appeal, The.
Lux, My Faire Falcon.
Madam, Withouten Many Words.
Madame, withouten Many Wordes.
Marvel No More.
"My galley charged with forgetfulness."
My Lute, Awake!
My mother's maids [or maydes] when they did sew [or sowe] and spin [or spynne].
My Pen.
Of the Courtier's Life.
Penitential Psalms, sels.
Pillar [or Piller] perished [or pearisht] is whe[a]rto I le[a]nt, The.
Prologue: "Love, to give law unto his subject hearts."
Promise, A.
Quondam was I in my lady's grace.
Satires, sels.
Sighs are my food, drink are my tears.
So unwarely was never no man caught [or cawght].
Sometime I fled the fire that me brent.
Sonnet: 'My galley charged.'
Stand Whoso List.
Steadfastness.
Thenmy of liff decayer of all kynde.
Lover Showeth How He Is Forsaken of Such as He Sometime Enjoyed, The.
Thou sleepest fast and I with woeful heart.
To cause accord or to ag[g]re[e].
To Sir Francis Brian.
Unstable dream[e] [or dreme], according [or accordyng] to the place.
Varium et Mutabile.
What nedeth these thretning wordes and wasted wynde?
What rage is this? What furo[u]r of what kind [or kynd]?
What should I say.
Who list his wealth and ease retain.
Whoso List to Hunt.
Wycherley, Lynne
Cat's Cradle.
Earth Man.
Wylie, Elinor (1885–1928)
Address to My Soul.
Atavism.
August.
Beauty.
Birthday Sonnet.
Castilian.
Cold-blooded Creatures.
Confession of Faith.
Crowded Trolley Car, A.
"Desolation Is a Delicate Thing."
Doomsday.

Eagle and the Mole, The.
Ejaculation.
Epitaph: "For this she starred her eyes with salt."
Escape.
Full Moon.
Golden Bough.
Green Hair.
Hughie at the Inn.
Hymn to Earth.
In our content, before the autumn came.
Incantation.
Innocent Landscape.
King Honour's Eldest Son.
Knight Fallen on Evil Days, The.
Let No Charitable Hope.
Little Beauty That I Was Allowed, The.
Madman's Song.
Malediction Upon Myself.
Nebuchadnezzar.
Now That Your Eyes Are Shut.
O Virtuous Light.
Parting Gift.
Pastiche.
Pebble, The.
Pegasus Lost.
Peter and John.
Portrait in Black Paint, with a Very Sparing Use of Whitewash.
Preference.
Pretty Words.
Prophecy.
Puritan Sonnet, IV.
Sanctuary.
Self-Portrait.
Simon Gerty.
Sonnet: "How many faults you might accuse me of."
Sonnet: "I hereby swear that to uphold your house."
Sonnet: "Let us leave talking of angelic hosts."
Sonnet: "You are the faintest freckles on the hide."
Spring Pastoral.
This Corruptible.
To a Lady's Countenance.
Twelfth Night.
Velvet Shoes.
Village Mystery.
Wild Peaches.
Wyrebek, M. (b. 1960)
Example, An.
Healing Logic, A.
Recovery.
Trendelenburg Position.

X

Xenophanes
War Memories.
Xu, Haixin See **Barnstone, Tony**
Xuanjing, Zhou (fl. 12th cent.)
Meditating at midnight.

Y

Yaba (d. 1740)
Voice calls me, A.
Yaitsu (d. 1807)
I pass beneath.
Paradise.
Yakamochi (Otomo no Yakamochi) (718–85)
Better never to have met you.
Cry of the stag, The.
Frost lies white, The.
I lie long abed.
I send you a box.
I will come to you.
Late evening finally comes.
Mist floats on the Spring meadow.
Now to meet only in dreams.
[These] meetings in dreams.
We were together.

When I see the first.
When my wife left home.
Wind rustles the bamboos, The.
Yakuo Tokuken (d. 1320)
My six and seventy years are through.
Yakusai, Layman
Deafening peal, A.
Yalden, Thomas (1670–1736)
Advice to a Lover.
Miner thus through perils digs his way, The.
Yamada, Mitsuye (b. 1923)
American Son.
Camp Notes.
Cincinnati.
Club, The.
Yamanoé [or Yamanoué] no Okura (Okura) (660?–733?)
Lament for the Evanescence of Life, A.
Longing for His Son, Furuhi.
Yamato-himé, Empress (fl. c.671)
Others may forget you, but not I.
Yambo, Ouologuem (b. 1940)
When Negro Teeth Speak.
Yamei (18th cent.)
Spring plain / Gulped.
Yang Chi (c.1334–c.1383)
After my illness, so hard to be a traveler.
Describing My Feelings While Living in Retirement by the Riverside: Seven Poems to the Tune "Ch'ing-p'ing-yüeh."
Describing My Feelings While Living in the Spring Quarters at Chiang-ning: Four Poems to the Tune "Ching-p'ing-yëh."
Eastern neighbor, western neighbor.
Five-Color.
Living in a Riverside Village—Miscellaneous Impressions.
Living in Master Fang's Garden.
Living in the Country at Kou-ch'ü in Autumn—Miscellaneous Impressions.
Meeting My Fellow Countryman, Yü Wu-chung.
Nesting among Clouds.
Noble Scholar Playing the Lute, A.
On Seeing a Firefly in My Room.
Painting of Bamboo by Ni Yün-lin, A.
Pitch-Ball.
Poem Making Fun of Chi-ti for His Eye Illness, A.
Poem on Passing by Hsin-k'ai Lake at Kao-yu in Light Rain, A.
Reviewing the Troops at Kuei-lin with Military Inspectors Chiang And Chang.
Selling My Official Robe.
Spring Dreams.
Springtime Embroidery.
Studio for Listening to the Snow, The.
Submitting a Memorial Requesting Permission to Return Home and Care for My Parents.
Thousands of flowers, thousands of petals.
Up at the prow, I wash my mouth, dripping water on my robe.
Walking in the Country outside T'ai-yüan on a Spring Day.
Wu Shan-yang.
Yang Fang (fl. 4th cent.)
Joy of Union, The.
Yang Hsiung (52 B.C.–18 A.D.)
Poverty.
Yang Hsün-chi (1456–1544)
Inscribed on the Doors of My Bookshelves.
Yang Lian (b. 1955)
Crocodile 1–15.
Yang Na
Tune: 'Hung Hsiu-hsieh' to a Flea.
Yang of Sui, Emperor (fl. 6th–7th cent.)
Spring River Flowers Moon Night.
Yang Shen (1488–1559)
Four Poems from the Sequence "Singing of the Moon."
To the Tune, "Ch'ing-p'ing Yüeh."
To the Tune "Chao-chün's Sorrow."
To the Tune "Chiang ch'eng tzu."
To the Tune "Child at Play."
To the Tune "Flowers in the Rain."

To the Tune "Heavenly Immortal."
To the Tune "Moon Over West River."
To the Tune "New Moon."
To the Tune "Partridge Sky."
To the Tune "Song of the Plum Blossom at the River Town."
To the Tune "Spring in Tien Is Fine."
To the Tune "Stopping My Horse to Listen."
To the Tune "The Southerner."
To the Tune "Yellow Oriole."

Yang Shih-ch'i (1365–1444)
After the rain, the vegetables from your garden.
Beyond the temple, a hidden cliff.
Crossing the River.
Dawn: Clear Skies.
Dragon-Tiger Terrace.
Enclosed with a Letter to My Family—For Shu.
Eulogy on My Own Portrait, A.
Even ordinarily, parting is difficult.
Evening of My Birthday, The.
Following the Rhymes of Shao-pao Huang's Poem on Being Moved while Visiting the Farmers.
Forty *li* through Chü-yang Pass.
Herdboy returns, none too early, The.
I've drawn a salary in the capital for forty years now.
I Was Received in an Early Audience at Heaven-Gate and Then at Noon I Was Summoned to the Yu-shun Gate. In the Evening I Withdrew, and Improvised This Poem.
Inscribed on the Painting, Stabbing a Tiger, by Chao Tzu-ang, in the Collection of Scholar Yang.
Night Rain: A Wall Collapses—Sent to My Neighbors.
Night Rain beneath the City Walls of P'i-chou.
Not sobered up from my muddy Kao-yang drunk.
On the Hall of Precious Virtue.
Recording a Dream.
Red Heart Station.
Rhymed Words Sent to My Eldest Son.
Searching for the Ruins of the Pavilion of the Drunken Old Man.
Sha-ch'eng, "Sand City."
Song of the Merchant's Wife.
Ten Scenes at the Hsiao Family Stone Ridge.
Three Poems on Ch'ang-sha.
White Stone Slope.

Yang-Ti, Emperor of Sui Dynasty (*fl.* 7th cent.)
Flowers and Moonlight on the Spring River.

Yang Wan-li (1127–1206)
Bubbles on the Water.
Cold Fly.
Cold Lantern, The.
Crossing Ts'en River.
Don't Read Books!
Drying Clothes.
Early Summer Waking from a Nap.
Fallen Blossoms.
I don't feel like reading another book.
I finish chanting my new poems.
Master Liu Painted a Portrait of Me in My Old Age and Asked Me to Write a Poem about the Picture.
Moored for the Night at the Lan-chi Riverside Courier Station.
Passing by Waterwheel Bay.
Replying to a Poem by Li T'ien-lin.
Sailing through the Gorges.
Sitting at Night on the Moon-viewing Terrace.
Sitting at Night on the Moonlit Terrace.
Stanza Written in Jest.
Staying Overnight at the Temple of the Holy Vulture.
Trip to Stone Man Peak, A.
Watching a Village Festival.
Written on a Cold Evening.

Yang Wei-chen (1296–1370)
Bamboo Branch Song of the Seacoast.
Bamboo Branch Song of West Lake.
Horse-Watering Hole, The.

Horseman at the Roadside, The.
Impromptu Inspirations.
Mating.
Painting Her Nails.
Residence of the Emperors of Ch'en, The.
Song of a Dream Journey over the Vast Sea.
Song of the Merchant's Wife.
Song of the Waterfall at Mount Lu.
Songs of Lake Tung-t'ing.
Taking the Ferry at Ta-kao at Dawn.
Tu-lu Poem.

Yang Wen-li (*fl.* 16th cent.)
New Year's Eve.
Thinking of My Family on an Autumn Day.

Yang Yi (974–1020)
Blue mist rises from fragrant herbs in the bronze plate.
Lang Mountain Monastery.
Prisons Are Full of Convicts, The.

Yannai (*fl.* 7th cent.)
And It Came to Pass at Midnight.

Yao Chen (1448–1478)
Ballad on the Investigation of a Disaster.

Yao K'uan
To an Ancient Tune.

Yao Sui (1239–1314)
Tune: 'Full Court of Fragrance.'

Yaohiko (d. 1777)
Clouds of flowers.

Ya'oz-kest, Itamar (1732–1815)
Smoke Rose.

Yarrow, Ruth
Baby's pee, The.
Low winter moon.
Sunrise path.
Warm rain before dawn.

Yashashchandra, Sitanshu (b. 1941)
Drought.

"Yashin [*or* "Iashin"]**, Aleksandr Iakovlevich" (Aleksandr Iakovlevich Popov) (1913–68)**
Eagle, The.
I am fated to perform a heroic deed.

Yasuda, Kenneth
Crimson dragonfly, A.
On the bench I wait.
Shadow of the trees, The.

Yasuharau Teishitsu (Teishitsu) (1610–73)
New year.

Yates, J. Michael (b. 1938)
I persist in a little fabric between me and the world.

Yates, John H.
Model Church, The.

Yau, John (b. 1950)
Angel Atrapado 7.
Avila.
Cenotaph.
Chinese Landscape Above Caracas.
Chinese Villanelle.
Corpse and Mirror III.
Engines of Gloom and Affection.
Painter Asks, The.
Picadilly or Paradise.
Postcard from Trakl.
Radiant Silhouette I.
Radiant Silhouette II.
Radiant Silhouette III.
Radiant Silhouette IV.
Radiant Silhouette V.

Yayu (1701–83)
My sickness lingers; I part from this world.
One sneeze / Skylark's.
Short night, A.
Transplanting rice / He pisses.
Yesterday? Today?

Ye, Zi
All night I could not sleep.

Yearley, Reg
Limerick: "Naïve young lady of Cork, A."

Yearsley, Ann (1752–1806)
Addressed to Sensibility.
Familiar Poem from Nisa to Fulvia of the Vale.
Mira, as they dear Edward's senses grow.
On Mrs. Montagu.

Reflections on the Death of Louis XVI.
Rural Lyre, The.
Soliloquy: "What folly to complain."
These feeble sounds.
To ———: "Lo! dreary Winter, howling o'er the waste."
To Mr. ———, an Unlettered Poet, on Genius Unimproved.
To the Right Hon. and Right Revd. Fredrick, Earl of Bristol, Bishop of Derry, Etc., Etc.

Yeatman, R. J. (1898–1968)
How I Brought the Good News from Aix to Ghent (or Vice Versa)

Yeats, William Butler (1865–1939)
Acre of Grass, An.
Adam's Curse.
After Long Silence.
All Souls' Night.
All Things Can Tempt Me.
Among School Children.
Ancestral Houses.
Apparitions, The.
At Galway Races.
At the Abbey Theatre.
At the Grey Round of the Hill.
Ballad of Father Gilligan, The.
Before the World Was Made.
Beggar to Beggar Cried.
Brown Penny.
Byzantium.
Cap and Bells, The.
Cast a cold eye.
Cat and the Moon, The.
"Calvary."
Choice, The.
Chosen.
Circus Animals' Desertion, The.
Coat, A.
Cold Heaven, The.
Collarbone [*or* Collar-Bone] of a Hare, The.
Coming of Wisdom with Time, The.
Consolation.
Coole Park, 1929.
Coole Park and Ballylee, 1931.
Cradle Song, A: "Angels are stooping, The."
Cradle Song: "Angels are bending, The."
Crazed Girl, A.
Crazy Jane Grown Old Looks at the Dancers.
Crazy Jane on God.
Crazy Jane Talks with the Bishop.
Cuchulain Comforted.
Curse of Cromwell, The.
Death.
Deep-sworn Vow, A.
Dialogue of Self and Soul, A.
Dolls, The.
Down by the Salley Gardens.
Drinking Song, A.
Easter 1916.
Everlasting Voices, The.
Fascination of What's Difficult, The.
Fiddler of Dooney, The.
Fisherman, The.
Folly of Being Comforted, The.
For Anne Gregory.
Four Ages of Man, The.
Fragments: "Locke sank into a swoon."
Friends.
Gratitude to the Unknown Instructors.
Great Day, The.
Gyres, The.
He Hears the Cry of the Sedge.
He Remembers Forgotten Beauty.
He Thinks of Those Who Have Spoken Evil of His Beloved.
He Wishes for the Cloths of Heaven.
Her Anxiety.
High Talk.
Hosting of the Sidhe, The.
I am Judas.
Lake-Isle of Innisfree, The.
In Memory of Eva Gore-Booth and Con Markievicz.
In Memory of Major Robert Gregory.
In the Seven Woods.
Indian upon God, The [*or* An].
Irish Airman Foresees His Death, An.

Irish poets, learn your trade.
John Kinsella's Lament for Mrs. Mary Moore.
Lady's Third Song, The.
Lamentation of the Old Pensioner, The.
Lapis Lazuli.
Last Confession, A.
Leaders of the Crowd, The.
Leda and the Swan.
Living man is blind and drinks his drop, A.
Lonely the Sea-Bird Lies at Her Rest.
Long-Legged Fly.
Lover Mourns for the Loss of Love, The.
Lullaby: "Beloved, may your sleep be sound."
Mad as the Mist and Snow.
Madness of King Goll, The.
Magi, The.
Man Who Dreamed of Faeryland, The.
Many ingenious lovely things are gone.
Matthew 24:15–31.
Matthew 28:16–20; Now the eleven disciples went to Galilee.
Memory.
Men Improve with the Years.
Meru.
Michael Robartes Bids His Beloved Be at Peace.
Mohini Chatterjee.
Moods, The.
Mother of God, The.
Municipal Gallery Revisited, The.
Must we part, Von Hügel, though much alike.
My fiftieth year had come and gone.
Never Give All the Heart.
New Faces, The.
News for the Delphic Oracle.
Nineteenth Century and After, The.
No Second Troy.
Old Man Stirs the Fire to a Blaze, An.
Old Men Admiring Themselves in the Water, The.
On a Political Prisoner.
On Being Asked for a War Poem.
On Hearing That the Students of Our New University Have Joined the Agitation against Immoral Literature.
On Those That Hated "The Playboy of the Western World" 1907.
On Woman.
Parting.
Paudeen.
Pilgrim, The.
Pity of Love, The.
Politics.
Prayer for My Daughter, A.
Prayer for My Son, A.
Red Hanrahan's Song about Ireland.
Renowned Generations, The.
Reprisals.
Ribh Considers Christian Love Insufficient.
Road at My Door, The.
Rose of the World, The.
Rose Tree, The.
Running to Paradise.
Sailing To Byzantium.
Scholars, The.
Second Coming, The.
Secret Rose, The.
September 1913.
Seven Sages, The.
Sixteen Dead Men.
Solomon and the Witch.
Some moralist or mythological poet.
Song of the Happy Shepherd, The.
Song of the Old Mother, The.
Song Of Wandering Aengus, The.
Sorrow of Love, The.
Spilt Milk.
Spur, The.
Stare's Nest by My Window, The.
Statesman's Holiday, The.
Statues, The.
Stick of Incense, A.
Stolen Child, The.
Swift's Epitaph.
Symbols.
Thought from Propertius, A.
Three Bushes, The.

Three Movements.
Three Things.
To a Friend Whose Work Has Come to Nothing.
To a Poet, Who Would Have Me Praise Certain Bad Poets, Imitators of His and Mine.
To a Shade.
To a Squirrel at Kyle-Na-No.
To a Young Girl.
To an Isle in the Water.
To Be Carved on a Stone at Thoor Ballylee.
To Ireland in the Coming Times.
To the Rose upon the Rood of Time.
Tower, The.
Travail of Passion, The.
Two Songs from a Play.
Two Songs of a Fool.
Under bare Ben Bulben's head.
Under Ben Bulben.
Upon a Dying Lady.
Vacillation.
Wheel, The.
When You Are Old.
Whence Had They Come?
Where My Books Go.
Who Goes with Fergus?
Wild Old Wicked Man, The.
Wild Swans at Coole, The.
Wind Blows out of the Gates of the Day, The.
Wisdom.
Youth and Age.

Yee, Marian
Handbook of Sex of the Plain Girl, The.
Wintermelons.

Yehoash (1870–1926)
At the Tomb of Rachel.
Harp of David, The.
Hunting.
Jephthah's Daughter.
Mystery.
Old Song, An.
Prayer, A: "Eternal God, our life is but."
Prophet, The.
Psalm: "Happy is the man whom Thou hast set apart."
Shadows.
Song, A: "Song of grass, A, / A song of earth."
Song as Yet Unsung, A.
Strongest, The.
Terror.
Thanksgiving.
That Is All I Heard.
Tool of Fate, The.
Wanderer, The.
Withered Rose, A.
Yang-Se-Fu.

Yellen, Jack (1892–1991)
Ain't She Sweet?
Are You Havin' Any Fun?
Glad Rag Doll.
Happy Days Are Here Again.
Hard-Hearted Hannah (The Vamp of Savannah)
Louisville Lou (The Vampin' Lady)
Mamma Goes Where Papa Goes.

Yellen, Samuel (b. 1906)
Nighthawks.

Yen Chen (fl. c.1960)
On the Willow Bank.

Yen Chi-tao (1030?–1106?)
Drunk with wine, I slap my spring robe.
Tune: "Butterflies Lingering over Flowers."
Tune: "Mountain Hawthorns."

Yen Shu (991–1055)
Song: "Old song with new words, An."
Tune: "Spring in Jade Pavilion."
Tune: "Treading on Grass."
Tune: 'Sand of Silk-Washing Brook.'
Tune: 'Spring in the Jade House.'
Tune: 'Treading on Fragrant Grass.'

Yen Yü (fl. c.1200)
My Boat Moored on a River.

Yenser, Stephen (b. 1941)
Another Lo-Cal Elegy.

Yeryomenko [or Eremenko], Aleksandr (b. 1950)
Addition to the Opposition.

I look at you from such deep graves.

Yeryomin, Mikhail (b. 1937)
Drake pays court to the duck, The.
Faceted grains of wisdom.
Helioptér of a skyscraper hotel.
House over the garden is a bouquet of evening windows, The.
Polyhedral kernels of wisdom.
Seamstress stitches on a sewing machine, The.
Street lamp. Something missing. Drugstore.

Yesenin [or Essenin], Sergey [or Sergei] (1895–1925)
All Too Soon.
Bitch, The.
Black Man, The.
Blue Mist.
Do You Not Love Me.
Esenin's Suicide Note.
Field Upon Field Upon Field.
Flowers say goodbye to me, The.
For My Sister Shura.
From the start, each living thing's.
Golden Birch Grove's, The.
Golden Grove, The.
Goodbye, my friend, goodbye.
Horn of doom is blaring, The!
I do not regret, complain, or weep.
I Regret Nothing.
Letter to My Mother.
My leafless maple tree, your icy coating.
Mysterious, Ancient World of Mine.
Now piece by piece we slip away.
Only one final trick remains—.
Rowan Tree Fire, The.
Sleigh, The.
To Kachalov's Dog.
Today I asked the money changer.
Winds, Winds, Winds.
Years of my youth, years of dissipation.
Yesterday's rain.
You feel no love or pity for me.

Yevtushenko [or Evtushenko], Yevgeny Aleksandrovich (b. 1933)
At Forty.
Babii Yar.
Cemetery of the Whales, The.
City of Yes and the City of No, The.
Disbelief in Yourself Is Indispensable.
Dwarf Birches.
Fear (Extracts)
From a Talk.
Half-Measures.
Hand-Rolled Cigarettes.
Heirs of Stalin, The.
Hundred miles from the capital city of hope, A.
I am.
I am a purse.
John Reed's Monologue.
Loss.
Metamorphoses.
Monologue of a Blue Fox.
My love will come.
New York Elegy.
Saints of Jazz.
Siberian Wooing.
Sleep, My Beloved.
Streetcar Named Poetry, A.
When your face dawned.

Yi Chöngbo (c. 1690–1760)
Memory, A.

Yi Inbok (fl. 1350)
Drumbeats.

Yi Jang'hi (Jang-hi Lee) (1902–28)
Spring is a Cat, The.

Yi Jung (fl. 16th cent.)
River Darkens on an Autumn Night, The.

Yi Kyubo
Evening on the Mountain: Song to the Moon in the Well.

Yi, Mu See Seaton, Jerome P.

Yi, Sang (1910–38)
Paper Memorial Stone.
Poem No. II.
Poem No. III.
Poem No. V.

Poem No. VII.
Poem No. X.
Poem No. XV.
Precipice.
Soyŏng Problems.
Yi Talch'ung
Neglected Wife, The.
Yin Shih (fl. early 7th cent.)
Parting from the Courtier Sung.
Yip Wai-lim (b. 1937)
In and Out of Check Points.
Yitzhak, Avraham ben- (1883–1950)
Blessed Are They That Sow.
Yo Inlŏ (c.1050–1100)
Meditating on the Start of a New Era.
Yo, Shên
Dreaming of a Dead Lady.
Yoketsu
Nothing longed for.
Yoldugu
It would be very pleasant to die with a wolf
  woman.
Yolen, Jane (b. 1939)
Caterpillar's Lullaby.
Dragon Night.
First Robin.
Graffiti.
Shepherd's Night Count.
Sky Scrape / City Scape.
Troll to her Children, The.
Yondo, Elolongue Epanya (b. 1930)
Love.
Lullaby.
My Country.
To You.
Woman.
"Yorick"
Limerick: "Emperor Marcus Aurelius, The."
Limerick: "Old gourmet who's grown
  somewhat stout, An."
York, Sarah E. (1819–51)
I Am Weary of Straying.
Yorke, Philip
Our Gardener here, James Phillips see.
Yosano, Akiko (1878–1942)
Amidst the notes.
As I am unhappy.
At the beginning.
Bird comes, A / delicately as a little girl.
Channel Boat, The.
Come at last to this point.
Hair unbound, in this.
He tempted me to.
I can give myself to her.
Left on the beach.
Like tiny golden.
Once, far over the breakers.
Over the old honeymoon cottage.
Spring is short.
Swifter than hail.
That evening when.
This autumn will end.
Thousand lines, A.
Uguisu has not come, The.
Wave of coldness, A.
What shall I wear to sleep in alone?
You never touch.
Yosef, Hamutal Bar
Angel on the Beach, An.
In the Library.
Jaffa, July 1948.
Reflections on a Dove.
Yoshifusa, Fujiwara No
Years have touched me, The.
Yoshihara, Sachiko (b. 1932)
Air Raid.
Madness.
Yoshioka Minoru (1919–1990)
Pilgrimage.
Yoso Soi (d. 1458)
Katsu!
Yost, Chryss
California Poem.
Descano, California.

Escaping from Autopia.
From San Diego.
Youmans, Vincent
Flying down to Rio.
Great Day.
Hallelujah!
I Know That You Know.
I Want to Be Happy.
More Than You Know.
Sometimes I'm Happy.
Tea for Two.
Time on My Hands.
Too Many Rings around Rosie.
Without a Song.
Young, Al (b. 1939)
Blue Monday.
Blues Don't Change, The.
Conjugal Visits.
Dance For Ma Rainey, A.
Dance for Militant Dilettantes, A.
Dance of the Infidels.
Detroit 1958.
Fifty-Fifty.
From Bowling Green.
How Stars Start.
How the Rainbow Works.
California Peninsula: El Camino Real.
Jazz as Was.
Leaving Syracuse.
Lester Leaps In.
Little More Traveling Music, A.
Mountains of California: Part 1, The.
Mountains of California: Part 2, The.
One Snapshot I Couldn't Take in France, The.
One West Coast.
Poem for Players, A.
Prestidigitator 1, The.
Prestidigitator 2, The.
Ravel: Bolero.
Studio up over In Your Ear.
Written in Bracing, Gray L.A. Rainlight.
Young, Andrew (1885–1971)
Ba Cottage.
Black Rock of Kiltearn.
Christmas Day.
Culbin Sands.
Dead Crab, The.
Dead Mole, A.
Fairy Ring, The.
Falls of Glomach, The.
Field-Glasses.
In Teesdale.
Last Snow.
Man and Cows.
March Hares.
Nest, The.
Scarecrow, The.
Shepherd's Hut, The.
Stay, Spring.
Stockdoves, The.
Suilven.
Wet Day, A.
Wiltshire Downs.
Young, Augustus (b. 1943)
Advice of an Efficiency Expert, The.
After Five Years.
Ballad of Fat Margot.
Elegy for a School-Friend.
Heritage.
Last Refuge, The.
Woman, Don't Be Troublesome.
Young Bear, Ray A. (b. 1950)
Another Face.
Before the Actual Cold.
Black Dog.
Celebration.
Coming Back Home.
Cook, The.
Crow-Children Walk My Circles in the Snow,
  The.
Drive to Lone Ranger, A.
Emily Dickinson, Bismarck and the
  Roadrunner's Inquiry.
First Dimension of Skunk, The.
From the Spotted Night.
I am walking and I.

In Dream: The Privacy of Sequence.
In Missing.
King Cobra as Political Assassin, The.
Language of Weather, The.
My reflection.
Nothing Could Take Away the Bear-King's
  Image.
Personification of a Name, The.
Place of O, The.
Place of V, The.
Poem for Diane Wakoski, A.
Race of the Kingfishers.
Remembrance of a Color inside a Forest, A.
Rushing.
Significance of a Water Animal, The.
Song Taught to Joseph, The.
Star Blanket.
These Horses Came.
This House.
This little house swallows.
Through the cracks.
Trains Made of Stone.
Wadasa Nakamoon, Vietnam Memorial.
Waiting to Be Fed.
War Walking Near.
Way the Bird Sat, The.
What We Can.
Young, David
Project for Freight Trains, A.
Young, Dean
Frottage.
Pleasure.
Rothko's Yellow.
Sources of the Delaware.
White Crane.
Young, Douglas (1913–73)
Caller rain frae abune.
Deid sall ye ligg, and ne'er a memorie.
For a Wife in Jizzen.
Last Lauch.
Minnie, I canna caa my wheel.
Steekit, consecrat, fou o fire but fuel.
Winter Homily on the Calton Hill.
Young, Edward (1683–1765)
Bell strikes *one*: We take no note of time.
Consolation, The.
Infidel Reclaimed, The.
Languid lady next appears in state, The.
Love of Fame, the Universal Passion.
Night Thoughts.
On Women ("Britannia's daughters.")
On Women ("Lavinia is polite.")
One to destroy, is murder by the law.
Satires.
These labouring wits, like paviours, mend our
  ways.
What am I? and from whence?—I nothing
  know.
Young, Francis Brett (1884–1954)
Seascape.
Young, Gary (b. 1951)
Eating Wild Mushrooms.
Fog descends over the tidal surge and the
  shallow lagoons.
I don't know where the owls go when they
  leave this place.
It's Sunday, October ninth, and the earth here
  is barren after harvest.
Our Life in California.
Owl drifts slowly through the canyon where
  three flickers worry a pitted oak for
  grubs, An.
Young, George
Damien.
Letter to William Carlos Williams, A.
Miracle, The.
Night Call.
Young, George W. (1846–1919)
Lips That Touch Liquor.
Young, Irene
Mermaid Knows, A.
Visit to the Palace of Venus.
Young, Joe (1889–1939)
Dinah.
Five Foot Two, Eyes of Blue (Has Anybody
  Seen My Girl?)

Young (cont.)
How 'Ya Gonna Keep 'Em down on the Farm? (After They've Seen Paree).
I'm Gonna Sit Right down and Write Myself a Letter.
I'm Sitting on Top of the World.
I Wonder Why She Kept on Saying 'Si-Si-Si-Si-Senor.'
Life Is a Song, Let's Sing It Together.
Rock-a-Bye Your Baby with a Dixie Melody.
Was That the Human Thing to Do?
You're Gonna Lose Your Gal.

Young, Joseph
Hundred Years from Today, A.

Young, Kevin (b. 1970)
Almanac, 1939, An.
Campbell's Black Bean Soup.
Casting.
Central Standard Time.
Clyde Peeling's Reptiland in Allenwood, Pennsylvania.
Degrees.
Eddie Priest's Barbershop and Notary.
Escape Artist, The.
Field Trip.
Langston Hughes.
Letters from the North Star.
No Offense.
Preserving, The.
Quivira City Limits.
Reward.
Southern University, 1962.

Young, Marguerite (b. 1909)
Angels, The.
Noah's Ark.
Whales, The.
Winter Scene.

Young, Mary Julia (fl. 1789–1809)
Anxiety.
Friendship.
On an Early Spring.
To Dreams.
To My Pen.
To Time.

Young-Prottengeier, Merra
Lithuanian Grandmother.

Young, Sally
I love your plumpness.

Young, Stanley
Epitaph for a Concord Boy.

Young, Victor
Give Me a Heart to Sing To.
Hundred Years from Today, A.
Love Is the Thing.
My Foolish Heart.
Street of Dreams.
When I Fall in Love.
Woman's Intuition, A.

Young, Virginia Brady (b. 1911)
At twilight.
Fallen birch leaf.
In a circle of thaw.
On the first day of spring.
Persimmons.
Sight of a lark's, The.
Silence, The.
Violets.

Yount, Alan
Sharing.

Yoyotte, Simone (c.1910–1933)
Half-Season.
Pale Blue Line in a Forced Episode, I Cut a Hole in the Flag of the Republic.

Yozei Emperor (fl. 9th cent.)
Falling from the ridge.

Yu Ch'an (c.286–339)
Third Day of the Third Month at the Meandering River, The.

Yü Chi (1272–1348)
After Snow—Impromptu.
Following the Rhymes of Autumn Night Song by Meng Tzu-chou, Signatory Official of the Board of Rites.
Following the Rhymes of Bamboo Branch Songs in Response to Yüan Po-chang.
Getting on Horseback.

Going to the Ministry with Chao Tzu-ch'i.
Hearing Loom and Shuttle.
Inscribed on a Painting.
Inscribed on the Painting, Solitary Crane, in the Collection of Jao Shih-ying.
Late in the Year K'uei-yu (1333), Staying at the Temple of the Upper Regions.
Little Landscape by Chao Ch'ien-li, A.
Little Landscape by Yen Wen-kuei, A.
Sent To Be Inscribed on the Temple of P'u-jun (Universal Fructification) at Lou-fu Mountain.
Sitting Alone in the Courtyard.
Traveling Early through a Snowy Valley.
What Family?
When I Was Young, I Stopped by a Wine Shop in Chi-men and Wrote This Poem, Inscribed It and Signed It, "Written by Lien the Eighteenth." The People of That District Have Since Taken It To Be a Poem of [the God] Lü Tung-pin! I Have Re.

Yü Ch'ien (1394–1457)
Poem on Coal, A.

Yu Chien-wu (487–550)
Spring Day.

Yü Ch'ing-tsêng (fl. 19th cent.)
To the Tune "Intoxicated with Shadows of Flowers."

Yü, Hsiang See Hsiang Chi

Yu Hsin (513–81)
Bidding Farewell to Secretary Chou.

Yü Hsüan-chi (c.843–868)
Answering Li Ying Who Showed Me His Poems about Summer Fishing.
At the End of Spring.
Boudoir Lament.
Composed on the Theme "Willows by the Riverside."
Elegy for the Wife of a Friend.
For Hidden Mist Pavilion.
For Kuo Hsiang.
Letting My Feelings Out.
Living in the Summer Mountains.
On a Visit to Ch'ung Chen Taoist Temple.
On the River.
Poem to the Tune "Riverbank Willows."
Regretful Thoughts.
Replying to a Poem by a New Graduate Lamenting the Loss of His Wife.
Rhyming a Friend's Poem.
Rhyming with a Friend.
Selling Ruined Peonies.
Sent to Wen T'ing-yün on a Winter Night.
Spring Thoughts Sent to Tzu-an.
Staying in the Mountains in Summer.
Telling My Feelings.
To the Minister Liu.
To Tzu-an.

Yü Hu (b. 745)
Thoughts South of the Yangtze.

Yü Wu-ling (fl. 9th cent.)
Offered to a Man Who Sells Pines.
Offering Wine.

Yu Xuanji
At Home in the Summer Mountains.

Yüan Chên (779–831)
Airing Painful Memories.
Apricot Garden.
Bamboo Mat.
Dreaming of My Wife.
Drunk Too Soon.
Elegy: "O loveliest daughter of Hsieh."
Empty House.
Iranian Whirling Girls.
Late Spring.
Letter Smuggled in a Fish.
Mourning My Son.
On Lien-ch'ang Palace.
Oriole.
Peach Blossoms.
Pitcher, The.
Remembering.
Retirement.
Sent to Lo-t'ien for Thinking of Me after the Rainfall.
Sobering Up.

Song of the Weaving Woman.
Three Dreams at Chiang-ling.
To the Waters of the Chia-ling.
When We Are Apart.
White Dress.

Yuan Chi (210–163)
Deep Night.
Regret.

Yüan Chieh (719–72)
Palace of Rocks, THe.
Stone Fish Lake.
Civilization.

Yüan Chiu-ts'ai (fl. early 18th cent.)
Warm Invitation, A.

Yüan Chüeh (1266–1327)
Shipboard Song.

Yüan Hao-wen (1190–1257)
Autumn Sentiments.
Clustered trees filled with the sounds of autumn.
Croaking frog in a well sees the sky from end to end, A.
Crossing the Yellow River: June 12.
Fade the kingfisher blue, trim the red, blend the colors.
Poet's heart is wrenched and wrenched again until his head turns white, A.
Quatrain: "Above the creek dallies a bright moon."
Song of the Maidens.
Winding creek and scattered maple groves, A.

Yüan Hung-tao (1568–1610)
Climbing Mount Yang.
Eastern mountains/ and western mountains.
On Board a Boat at Chi-ning.
On Receiving My Letter of Termination.
Pei-mang Cemetery.
Record of My Trip to Mount She, A.
Slowly, Slowly Poem, The.
Woman's Room in Autumn, A.

Yüan Mei (1716–98)
Arriving at Hangchou.
Ballad of Peach Blossom Spring.
Busy.
Finding Serenity.
Five Poems on Returning to Hangchou.
Flying Bells.
Fog at Liang-hsiang.
Growing Old (1)
Growing Old (2)
Happy about Being Old.
I Know Nothing.
In Late Spring of the Year Keng-hsü (1790), I Stayed at the Sun Family's Gemstone Mountain Villa at West Lake. Before Leaving, I Wrote These Poems as Mementos.
Last Poem: Goodbye to My Garden.
Ma-wei.
Miscellaneous Feelings in the Sui Garden.
Miscellaneous Poems on Growing Old.
Moments of Fullfillment—Writing Down Miscellaneous.
Motto.
Next Day the Fog Was Even Worse, The.
Night of the Fifteenth, Second Month.
Old and Traveling.
On the Road to T'ien-t'ai.
On the Twenty-First Day of the Fifth Month, I Reached Home.
On the Way to Pa-ling.
Rains Pass.
Returning Home.
Rough Ridge.
Summer Day.
Things Seen.
Things Seen on Spring Days.
Winter Night.
Words from the Goblet of Wisdom.
Writing My Feelings.
Writing What I've Seen.

Yüan-ti
Ejected Wife, The.

Yud, Nachum (b. 1888)
Like the Eyes of Wolves.

Yuhara, Prince (fl. 8th cent.)
Let us bribe the Moon God.

Yuishun (d. 1544)
Why, it's but the motion of eyes and brows!
Yun'er
Yun'er's Bell.
Yün-k'an Tzu (*fl.* first half of 14th cent.)
Out of chaos.
Tune: "Greeting the Immortal Guest."
Yün Shou-p'ing (1633–90)
As old age approaches.
As we say farewell to autumn.
Autumn Plants, Flowers, Bamboo, Rocks.
Brush in rocks, draw a stream.
Early Summer in the Year Jen-tzu (1672)—
Playfully Painted in the Manner of Ts'ao
Yün-hsi.
Essence of ink, The.
Facing evil, on the wall, across from your bed.
For a hundred miles the west wind carries the
fragrance of millet.
Green Banana Leaves.
Hearing a Flute at Broken Bridge.
In a hidden spot on the northern mountain.
Inscribed on a Painting.
Inscribed on a Painting of Sailboats on the
River—Seeing Off Yen-chi on His Journey
to Ch'ang-an.
Inscribed on a Snowscape.
Lament for the Willows outside the City
Walls, A.
On a Landscape by Myself.
On a Painting "Ancient Trees and Flowing
Stream."
On a Painting of Mushrooms.
On the Painting, Mist Over Ten Thousand
Mountains by Shih-ku.
Painting in the Style of Secretary Kao, A.
Painting of Chrysanthemums in the Boneless
Style of Hsü Ch'ung-ssu, A.
Painting of Yams, A.
Sadness in the Autumn Chambers.
Scorpion's tails, silver hooks.
Through the windy valley.
War ships, cold tides.
Waterside Village.
Written on the Night of the Twenty-ninth of
the First Month.
Yun Sŏndo (1587–1671)
Is it a cuckoo that cries?
Sun's fair rays are shining, The.
Yusef, Imam
Love Your Enemy.
Yuson, Alfred A. (b. 1944)
Andy Warhol Speaks to His Two Filipino
Maids.
Dead Center.
Love Before Dinner.
World Poetry Circuit.
Yusuf, Sa'di (b. 1943)
Departure of '82.
Hamra Night.
Hot Evening, A.
Sentiment.
State of Fever, A.
Three Dispositions Regarding One Woman.
Woman, A.
Woods, The.
Yuwaku
I think about you & it's like having spirits
come down on me.

Z

"Z., Z."
Here lies a poet—where's the great surprise!
**Zabolotsky [*or* Zabolotskii], Nikolai Alekseievich
(1903–58)**
All That My Soul Possessed.
At the Fishmonger's.
Circus, The.
Face of a Horse, The.
Ivanovs, The.
Last Love.
Loop Canal, The.
Metamorphoses.

Movement.
Nocturnal Garden.
Peoples House.
Poem about Rain.
Popryshchin.
Signs of the Zodiac are fading, The.
Snakes.
Soccer.
Somewhere in a field near Magadan.
Strolling Musicians.
Thistle.
Ugly Girl, The.
Walk, A.
Warning.
Wedding.
Yesterday Reflecting Upon Death.
Zach, Natan (b. 1930)
Against Parting.
Be Attentive.
Be Careful.
Failure.
Greater Courage.
King Solomon's Camel.
Seven.
Zagajewski, Adam (b. 1945)
At Daybreak.
Auto Mirror.
Betrayal.
Electric Elegy.
Moths.
To Go to Lvov.
Watching Shoah in a Hotel Room in America.
When Death Came.
Zaid, Gabriel
Circe.
Cloister.
Furious Clarity, A.
Mortal Practice.
Song of Pursuit.
Sundial.
Zaishiki (d. 1719)
Frost on grass.
Zamora, Daisy (b. 1959)
Celebration of the Body.
Downpour.
Hand Mirror.
Lineage.
Loyal Housewife.
Mother's Day.
Precisely.
Report on the Protest in Front of the United
States Embassy by the Pino Grande
Movement, A.
Vision of Your Body.
Zamora-Linmark, R.
Day 1: Portrait of the Artisit, Small-kid Time.
Election Day.
Zandvakili, Katayoon (b. 1967)
County.
Love Letter.
No Trespassing (Private Beach)
Zangwill, Israel (1864–1926)
At the Zoo.
Death's Transfiguration.
Despair and Hope.
Dreams.
Evolution.
In the Morgue.
Inexhaustible.
Israel.
"Might Is Right."
Moses and Jesus.
Seder-Night.
Sundered.
Tabernacle Thought, A.
Theodor Herzl.
To a Pretty Girl.
Vanitas Vanitatum.
Vision.
Why Do We Live?
Yom Kippur.
Zanker, Arthur
Grandparents' House.
Wedding Sonnet.
Zant, Johan van der *See* **Andreus, Hans**
Zanzotto, Andrea (b. 1921)
Behold the Thin Green.

Campèa.
Distance.
Eclogue 4: "Shell-bursting births, comas, and
the mute."
Epiphany.
Eva, forma futuri.
Existing Psychically.
How Long.
If It Were Not.
Subnarcosis.
Zaragoza Clubs (*fl.* 1860)
My heart tells me.
When the French, to their shame.
Zarco, Cyn (b. 1950)
Manila Paper.
My Worst Fear.
Once upon a Seesaw with Charlie Chan.
Zarin, Cynthia (b. 1959)
Ant Hill, The.
Song: "My heart, my dove, my snail, my sail,
my."
Zarou-Zouzounis, Lorene (b. 1958)
Embroidered Memory.
Her Heart Is a Rose Petal and Her Skin Is
Granite.
Zarzyski, Paul
How Near Vietnam Came to Us.
Hurley High.
**Zaturenska, Marya Alexandrovna (Mrs. Horace
Gregory) (1902–82)**
Daisy, The.
Descent of the Vulture, The.
Head of Medusa, The.
Lovers, The.
Tempest, The.
White Dress, The.
Woman at the Piano.
**Zavalnyuk [*or* Zaval'niuk], Leonid Andreievich
(b. 1931)**
Earlobe.
I Love My Enemies.
Zawgee (1907–1990)
Way of the Water-Hyacinth.
Zawinski, Andrena
You Touch Me.
Zayyad, Tawfiq (b. 1932)
Before Their Tanks.
Here We Will Stay.
Pagan Fires.
Passing Remark.
Salman.
They Know.
Zeb-un-Nissa, Princess (1638–1702)
Though I am Laila of the Persian romance.
Zeiger, David
Mostly Mozart at Planting Fields Arboretum.
Zekkai Chushin (1336–1405)
Void has collapsed upon the earth, The.
**"Zelda" (Zelda Schneurson [*or* Mishkovsky]) (b.
1914)**
Crippled beggar who lives, The.
Wicked Neighbor, The.
Zeldis, Chayyim (b. 1927)
Holy Ones, the Young Ones, The.
Zenodotus (b. c.325 B.C.)
Statue Of Eros, A.
Zepeda, Ofelia
Bury Me with a Band.
Zephaniah, Benjamin
According to my Mood.
Speak.
Sun, The.
Zeppa, Mary
Aleatory.
Zerbe, Evelyn Arcad
In Memory of My Arab Grandmother.
Zesen, Philipp von (1619–89)
Evening Song.
To the Superhuman Adelmund, When She
Would Undo the Kiss Already Done.
Zhao, Pan (48–117?)
Needle and Thread.
Zhdanov, Ivan (b. 1948)
Home.

I'm not the branch, only the prebranchness.

Zhenkai, Zhao ("Bei Dao") (b. 1949)
Accomplices.
Answer, The.
August Sleepwalker, The.
Collection, The.
Discovery.
End or a Beginning, An.
Evening Scene, An.
He Opens Wide a Third Eye.
Résumé.
Stretch out your hands to me.

Zhigulin, Anatoly [or Anatolii] (b. 1930)
Campfireburners.

Zibu'n-Nisa See **Makhfi**

Zide, Norman H. See **Naim, C. M.**

Ziedonis, Imants
At Maruža's.

Zierlin, Israel See **Tiempo, César**

Zieroth, Dale (b. 1946)
Baptism.
Beautiful Woman.
Hunters of the Deer, The.

Zimmer, Paul (b. 1934)
Apple Blight.
But Bird.
Day Zimmer Lost Religion, The.
Duke Ellington Dream, The.
Eisenhower Years, The.
Example, The.
Lord Fluting Dreams of America on the Eve of
    His Departure from Liverpool.
Phineas Within and Without.
Romance.
Sitting with Lester Young.
Zimmer Drunk and Alone, Dreaming of Old
    Football Games.
Zimmer Imagines Heaven.
Zimmer in Fall.
Zimmer in Grade School.
Zimmer's Head Thudding against the
    Blackboard.

Zimmerman, Robert See **"Dylan, Bob"**

Zimunya, Musaemura Bonus
After the Massacre.
Arrivants.
Kisimiso.
Let It Be.
Mr. Bezuidenthout's Dogs.
White Poetess.

Zinnemann-Hope, Pam
Taking Tea with My Father and Mother.

**Zinzendorf, Nikolaus [or Nicolaus] Ludwig, Graf
von (1700–1760)**
For Us No Night Can Be Happier.
Jesu, to Thee My Heart I Bow.
Jesus, thy blood and righteousness.
On Earth There Is a Lamb So Small.
Slain Lamb of God.

Zipper, Arizona
Farmer drives by, A.
Football, The.
I stop to listen.
Right in the middle.

Wedding over, The.

Zisquit, Linda (b. 1947)
After Years of Feasting and No Sacrifice.
Because passion is the absence we speak.
Because passion is the silence we share.
There is always a sound.
Word before the Last about Loss, A.

Znamenskaya [or Znamenskaia], Irina (b. 1952)
Estonia. A private dacha.

Zolotow, Charlotte (b. 1915)
Bridge, The.
Enemies.
Riddle, A: "Once when I was very scared."

Zolynas, Al (b. 1945)
Love in the Classroom.
Zen of Housework, The.

Zonas (fl. 90 B.C.)
Pass me the sweet earthenware jug.

**Zorgenfrey [or Zorgenfrei], Wilgelm
Aleksandrovich (1882–1938)**
Over the Neva.

Zoroaster [or Zarathustra] (fl. 7th cent. B.C.)
Sacred Book, The.

Zosan Junku (d. 1308)
You must play.

Zoso Royo (d. 1276)
I pondered Buddha's teaching.

"Zozimus" See **Moran, Michael**

Zrínyi, Miklós (1620–64)
Early in the spring-time a huntsman full of
    sorrow.
Elegy: "Outworn year has altered his apparel,
    The."
Epilogue.
Invocation: "I, who in times before, with
    youthful mind."
Sortie, The.

Zu-Bolton, Ahmos, II (b. 1935)
Struggle-Road Dance.

Zubick, Kalleen
Evolution of Appetite.

Zucker, Rachel (b. 1971)
In Your Version of Heaven I am Younger.

Zuckermann, Hugo
Cavalry Song.

Zuckmayer, Carl (b. 1896)
My Death.

Zuian
Sky-piercing sword, gleaming cold.

Zukofsky, Louis (1904–78)
'A' 4.
'A' 11.
As to How Much.
Blue light is the night harbor-slip.
Can a mote of sunlight defeat its purpose.
Cars Once Steel and Green, Now Old.
Cocktails / and signs of.
Ferry.
Fifth Movement: Autobiography.
For you I have emptied the meaning.
Green leaf that will outlast the winter.
He has become as / talkative as Bottom a
    weaver and says for.
Hinny / by / stallion, An.

I Sent Thee Late.
I Walk in the Old Street.
In Arizona.
In peace.
In that this happening.
It's hard to see but think of a sea.
Like Grandpa Paul / The water is all of my
    mind.
Lines of this new song are nothing, The.
Non Ti Fidar.
Not much more than being.
Poem Beginning 'The.'
Red horse, A.
(Ryokan's scroll)
Shang Cup.
Song for the Year's End, A.
To my wash-stand.
Two Dedications: Tibor Serly.
Unearthing / my valentine, An.
Ways, The.
Weeping: the food he eats.
When the crickets.
When they use elbow or arm boards to.
William / Carlos / Williams / alive!
Xenophanes.

Zulu, Phumzile
You are Mad: and I Mean It!

Zuma, Nongejeni (1870–1942)
Praises of Field-marshal J. C. Smuts, The.

Zuni Oral Tradition
Dismissal of the Koyemshi.
Following their road of exit, they stooped over
    and came out.
House Blessing.
Indeed, the enemy.
Perhaps if we are lucky.

Zurita, Raúl (b. 1951)
6.
Even Forsaken They'd Flower.
March of the Cordilleras, The.
Sparkling Beaches, The.
Splendor in the Wind.

Zweig, Paul (1935–84)
Aunt Lil.
Eternity's Woods.
Father.
Life Story.

Zweig, Stefan (1881–1942)
Jeremiah.

Zwein, Sabah Al-Kharrat (b. 1954)
Abysmal circle is in the sky, An. At the
    moment we are an infinite line,.
I have already lost the style and maze of
    language.

Zweter, Reinmar von (fl. 13th cent.)
I Came a-Riding.

Zwicky, Fay (b. 1933)
Jack Frost.
Reckoning.
Stone Dolphin, The.
Summer Pogrom.

Zych, Adam
Auschwitz, 1987.

SUBJECT INDEX

*Poems under each subject are listed alphabetically by author. Subjects range from specific (for example, persons) to general (for example, **Faith**).*

*Some subjects headings show cross-references to related subjects. Some subjects, such as **Love,** are so broad that they appear here only to refer the user to related subjects and to anthologies. In other cases as well, anthologies are listed that in whole or in part focus on the subject in question. Anthologies that are mainly translations into English are listed under their appropriate countries or languages.*

There may be cross-references to related subjects.

A

Aaron (Bible)
Carey, T. Zohar.
Herbert, G. Aaron.
Abandonment
Arrillaga. Mariana II.
  Rosa/Filí.
Atwood. Beauharnois (1).
  Beauharnois (3).
  Beauharnois, Glengarry (2).
  Dufferin, Simcoe, Grey (4).
  Four Small Elegies.
Ben-Lev, D. Broken Helix.
Berlin. Supper Time.
Berssenbrugge. Chronicle.
Blake, W. Love's Secret.
Clark, T. "Like Musical Instruments."
Daley, V. Mother Doorstep.
Davis, C. Belongings.
  Nod.
Dove, R. Adolescence—III.
Frost, R. Hill Wife, The.
  House Fear.
  Impulse, The.
  Loneliness.
  Oft-Repeated Dream, The.
González, R. Death of the Farm Workers' Cat.
Hammerstein. Don't Ever Leave Me.
Hughes, L. Mama and Daughter.
Hugo, R. Death of the Kapowsin Tavern.
  Degrees of Gray in Philipsburg.
  River Now, The.
Kern, J. Don't Ever Leave Me.
Kimbrell, J. My Father at the North Street Boarding House.
Kingsley, C. Airly Beacon.
Kooser. Abandoned Farmhouse.
Landor, W. What News.
Madhubuti. After Her Man Had Left Her for the Sixth Time That Year (An Uncommon Occurrence).
Meynell, A. Study, A.
Mickle. Cumnor Hall.
Moore, L. Winter 1967.
Nowlan. Only When My Heart Freezes.
Owen, W. To Eros.
Papertalk-Green, C. Wanna Be White.
Randell. Hard to Place.
Ransom, J. Lady Lost.
Realuyo. La Querida.
Rich, A. In the Wake of Home.
Rilke. Olive Garden, The.
Scarfe. Merry Window, The.
Smith, R. Bluetits.
Sorrentino. Land of Cotton.
Spender, S. Song: "Stranger, you who hide my love."
Stickney, T. Departure, The.

Szporluk. Meteor.
Tomlinson, C. Two Views of Two Ghost Towns.
Vando. My Mother Cunning, Yet Innocent.
Weissbort. Mourning.
Wenderoth, J. Disfortune.
Wither. I Loved a Lass.
Wyatt, S. Lover Showeth How He Is Forsaken of Such as He Sometime Enjoyed, The.
  Lover's Appeal, The.
Yeats. John Kinsella's Lament for Mrs. Mary Moore.
Abbey Theatre, Dublin
Strong, L. Old Woman, Outside the Abbey Theater, An.
Yeats. At the Abbey Theatre.
Abelard and Heloise
Pope, A. Eloisa to Abelard.
Read, S. Sic et Non.
Abolitionists
Dunbar, P. Douglass.
Forten. To W. L. G. on Reading His "Chosen Queen."
Harper, F. Bible Defence of Slavery.
  Bury Me in a Free Land.
Hayden, R. Runagate Runagate.
Rukeyser, M. Soul and Body of John Brown, The.
Whittier. Brown of Ossawatomie.
Williams, E. At Harper's Ferry Just before the Attack.
Aborigines
Barney, S. Black People Cry.
Bostock, G. Night Marauders.
Brady, G. Voice from the Bush—Through Me.
Clayton, I. Black Rat, The.
  Kidnappers.
  Last Link, The.
  River Bidgee.
Clayton, S. Redfern at Night.
Davis, J. Aboriginal Australia.
  Aboriginal Reserve.
  Desolation.
  First-born, The.
  My Brother, My Sister.
  One Hundred and Fifty Years.
  Slum Dwelling.
  Urban Aboriginal.
  Warru.
Doolan, F. Last Fullblood, The.
  Whiteman Is the Judge, The.
  Who Owns Darling Street?
Durack. Lament for the Drowned Country.
Duroux, M. Dirge for a Hidden Art.
  Lament for a Dialect.
Everett, J. Ode to Salted Mutton Birds.
  Old Co'es.
  Rest Our Spiritual Dead.
  White Man Problem, The.
Fogarty, L. Ecology.

No Grudge.
  Remember Something Like This.
  Shields Strong, Nulla Nullas Alive.
  Worker Who, the Human Who, the Abo Who, The.
Gilbert, K. Gularwundul's Wish.
  Kiacatoo.
  Same Old Problem.
Grandfather Koori. Never Blood So Red.
  Song in the Symbol, The.
Hughes, S. Got No Shame.
  Home on Palm.
Johnson, E. Letter to My Mother, A.
  Right to Be.
  Weevily Porridge.
Maris, H. Spiritual Song of the Aborigine.
Marshall, R. Buddgelin Bey.
  Burrel Bullai.
  Little Brown Jacks Nyimbung.
Marshall-Stoneking. Passage.
Momaday. Carriers of the Dream Wheel.
Mudrooroo Narogin. Jacky Demonstrates for Land Rights.
  Peaches and Cream.
  Reincarnation.
  Streets.
Napurrurla, R. Two Mothers, The.
Newson, D. Crowther—Ours.
  Turnabouts.
Nungarrayi, J. Sorry.
Oodgeroo of the tribe Noonuccal. Colour Bar.
  Gooboora, the Silent Pool.
  Last of His Tribe.
  No More Boomerang.
  Time Is Running Out.
  Unhappy Race, The.
  We Are Going.
Papertalk-Green, C. No One to Guide Us.
  Wanna Be White.
Philp-Carmichael. Pemulwy—A Visitation.
Russell, W. Developers, The.
  God Gave Us Trees to Cut Down.
  Ngarnbarndtar.
  Red.
  Tali Karng: Twilight Snake.
Sykes, B. Fallin'
  One Day.
  Requiem.
Watson, M. Black Child.
  Stepping Out.
Weller. Midgiegooroo.
  Story of Frankie. . . My Man, The.
  Wurarbuti.
Wells, L. Nomads, The.
  Sorcerer, The.
Wright, J. Bora Ring.
Abortion
Ai. Abortion.
  Country Midwife: A Day, The.
Alkalay-Gut. Life Goes On.

Abraham

Anderson, A. Suicide Year, The.
Atkins. Lakefront, Cleveland.
Baumel. Snow-Day.
Carroll, K. Truth About Karen, The.
Clifton, L. Lost Baby Poem, The.
Hewett, D. This Version of Love.
Hope, A. Massacre of the Innocents.
Jonson, B. To Fine Lady Would-Be.
Peacock, M. ChrisEaster.
Sexton. Abortion, The.
Unknown. Epitaph on a Child Killed by
  Procured Abortion.
Woddis. Moral Tale, A.

Abraham

Lasker-Schüler. Abraham and Isaac.
Muir, E. Abraham.
Nemerov. Nicodemus.
Nichols, R. Harlot's Catch.
Noll. Abraham's Madness.
Ostriker. Story of Abraham, The.
Owen, W. Parable of the Old Men and the
  Young, The.
Schwartz, D. Abraham.
Stradling. Abraham's Sacrifice of Isaac.
Wilner, E. Sarah's Choice.
Zisquit. After Years of Feasting and No
  Sacrifice.

Absalom

Rosenberg, I. Chagrin.

Absence

Allingham. Across the Sea.
Baxter, E. In Your Absence.
Blunden. Late Light.
Brent, E. Angel Eyes.
Brion, R. Good Friday.
Browning, R. Never the Time and the Place.
Byron, G. To Thyrza.
Cahn, S. I'll Walk Alone.
Carew, T. To Her in Absence; a Ship.
  Upon Some Alterations in My Mistress, after
  My Departure into France.
Cervantes. Isla Mujeres.
Chambers, G. If Only for One Night.
Crane, H. Carrier Letter.
Crase. Astropastoral.
Creeley. Song: "Those rivers run from that
  land."
  Turn, The.
De la Mare. Alone.
Dennis, M. Angel Eyes.
Dickinson, E. My Life Closed Twice.
Dooley, M. No, Go On.
Drummond, W. Sonnet: "Slide soft, fair forth,
  and make a crystal plain."
Duncan, R. Passage Over Water.
Georgiou, E. Space Between, The.
Grierson. To Miss Laetitia Van Lewen.
Habington. To Castara, Being to Take a
  Journey.
  Upon Castara's Departure.
Harburg. When I'm Not Near the Girl I Love.
Hardy, T. Voice, The.
Hashimoto, S. Mirror of Matsuyama, The.
Hass, R. Song: "Afternoon cooking in the fall
  sun."
Hazo. Silence Spoken Here.
Herd. Missing.
Hoskyns [or Hoskins]. Absence.
Hove. Lost Bird.
Hughes, L. So Long.
Inada. Filling the Gap.
Jago. Absence.
Knott. Goodbye.
Lane, B. When I'm Not Near the Girl I Love.
Lawrence, D. Quite Forsaken.
Lewis, A. Song (On Seeing Dead Bodies
  Floating Off the Cape).
Liu, T. Sunday.
Lovelace, R. Elinda's [or Ellinda's] Glove.
Lowell, R. Home After Three Months Away.
MacDiarmid, H. Empty Vessel.
Martínez, V. Absence, Luminescent.
Mathews, A. Letter Following.
Mercer, J. I Thought About You.
Merwin, W. S. Separation.
Mew. Absence.

Millay, E. Oh, Oh, you will be sorry for that
  word!
Monro. Solitude.
Montgomerie, A. Dreame, Ane.
Muldoon, P. Why Brownlee Left.
Nairne. Will Ye No Come Back Again?
Nortje. Waiting.
Novello, I. We'll Gather Lilacs.
Olson, E. Presence, The.
Raine, K. Angelus.
  Wilderness, The.
Ransom, J. Winter Remembered.
Rich, A. Splittings.
Rochester, J. Song: "Absent from thee, I
  languish still."
Rome, H. Wish You Were Here.
Romo-Carmona, M. Daylight.
  Fish.
Seed. Sofia.
Silex, E. Gift, The.
Smukler. Home in Three Days. Don't Wash.
St. John, D. Hush.
Stevens, W. Gallant Château.
Styne, J. I'll Walk Alone.
Suckling, S. Against Absence.
  To Master Davenant for Absence.
Surrey. Seafarer, The.
Tatham. Ostella forth of Town: To My Heart.
Teasdale. At Night.
Tennyson, A. Daisy, The.
Unknown. I Believe.
  Western Wind.
Van Heusen, J. I Thought About You.
Vaughan, H. To Amoret Gone from Him.
Warner, S. Absence, The.
Wilbur. "World Without Objects Is a Sensible
  Emptiness, A."
Wright, F. Joseph Come Back as the Dusk.

See also **Isolation; Loneliness; Separation**

Abundance

Pankey. Reason, The.

Acacia

Brion, R. If Fortune Smiles.
"Field." Leaves.

Academia

Berryman. Professor's Song, A.
Cunningham, J. To a Friend, on Her
  Examination for the Doctorate in English.
DiPalma. Each Moment is Surrounded.
Glaser, E. Confluences at San Francisco.
Kleinzahler. Autumnal Sketch, An.
Larkin, P. Posterity.
Perelman. Marginalization of Poetry, The.
Roethke. Academic.
Whitman, W. When I Heard the Learn'd
  Astronomer.
Worley, D. Dancing in the Dark.

Acadia and Acadians

Longfellow, H. Tale of Acadie, A.

Accent

Hare, M. Alfred de Musset.
Joseph, A. On Being Told I Don't Speak Like a
  Black Person.
Lees, J. Jone o' Grinfilt.

Acceptance

Bradstreet, A. Here Follows Some Verses upon
  the Burning of Our House [July 10th, 1666.
  Copied Out of a Loose Paper].
Derricotte. Promise, The.
Emerson, R. Terminus.
France, L. North and South.
Frost, R. Acceptance.
Herrick. To Vulcan.
Johnson, J. To America.
Joseph, J. Dog Body and Cat Mind.
MacNeice. Selva Oscura.
McDaniel, J. Obvious, The.
Olson, C. Kingfishers, The.
Rich, A. Loser, The.
Shelley, P. To————: "One word is too often
  profaned."
Whitman, W. Me Imperturbe.
  To a Common Prostitute.

Accidents

Aytoun [or Ayton], R. Upon Mr Thomas

Murrays Fall.
Belieu. How the Elderly Drive.
Carruth, H. Wreck of the Circus Train, The.
Cooper, D. 10 Dead Friends.
Dickey, J. Falling.
Esteves. Lil' Pito.
Frost, R. "Out, Out—."
  Objection to Being Stepped On, The.
Gibson, W. White Dust, The.
Godden, J. Lost.
Greenlaw. Earliest Known Representation of a
  Storm in Western Art, The.
Heaney, S. Summer of Lost Rachel, The.
Herd. Coronach.
Herrick. Casualties.
Hume, C. Helicopter Wrecked on a Hill.
Knight, E. Poem of Attrition, A.
Larkin, P. Whatever Happened?
Lawrence, D. Collier's Wife, The.
Livingstone, D. One Time.
McElroy, C. Ruth.
McGonagall. Tay Bridge Disaster, The.
McIntyre. Disaster to Steamer Victoria at
  London.
Merrill, C. Diver, The.
Mother Goose. Jack and Jill.
Murray, L. Cotton Flannelette.
Plath. Cut.
Rawling. Gas Drill.
Roethke. Elegy for Jane.
Seshadri. Lifeline.
Shumaker. Circle of Totems, The.
Townsend, A. Bicycle Racers, The.
Unknown. Mischievous Raven, The.
Warren, R. I Can't Even Remember the Name.
Wayne, J. By Accident.
Weber, R. Concise History of the Vietnam War:
  1965–1968, A.

See also **Airplane Crashes; Automobile
  Accidents; Disasters; Nuclear Accidents;
  Railroad Wrecks; Shipwrecks**

Accordions

Hall, D. Wedding Party.

Achilles

Auden. Shield of Achilles, The.
Duncan, R. Achilles' Song.
Ewart. Personal Footnote, A.
Santayana. Before a Statue of Achilles.
Whittemore, R. Thinking of Tents.

Acorns

Nicholls, J. Journey.

Acquiescence

Hammerstein. I Cain't Say No.
Herrick. To Fortune.
Kunitz, S. Knot, The.
Rodgers, R. I Cain't Say No.

Acrobatics and Acrobats

Lefevre, A. Halftime.
Redmond. Dance Bodies #1.
Swenson, M. He That None Can Capture.

See also **Circus; Gymnastics and Gymnasts;
  Tightropes and Tightrope Walkers; Trapezes
  and Trapeze Artists**

Acrostic (form)

Hall, R. Crickhowel.
  Pontypool.

Actaeon

Bewe. I Would I Were Actaeon.
Heppenstall. Actaeon.

Acting and Actors

Allston. On Kean's Hamlet.
Baraka. Poem for Willie Best, A.
Bernstein, C. Caught.
Chrystos. Soap Bubbles.
Conway, J. Marlo Thomas in Seven Parts and
  Epilogue.
Cook, E. To Charlotte Cushman.
Coward. Boy Actor, The.
Garrigue. Movie Actors Scribbling Letters Very
  Fast in Crucial Scenes.
Ginsberg, A. Blue Angel, The.
Harrison, T. Continuous.
Hassall. Santa Claus.
Henley, W. Ballade of Dead Actors.
Holman, B. Performance Poem.

Jonson, B.   To Edward Alleyn.
Klipschutz.   Funicello at 50.
Lindsay, N.   To Mary Pickford—Moving Picture
   Actress.
McKinney, I.   Rapt.
Melville, H.   Coming Storm, The.
Muske, C.   Last Take.
O'Hara, F.   To the Film Industry in Crisis.
Parker, D.   Certain Lady, A.
Pasternak, B.   Hamlet.
Reid, C.   Howl, Howl.
Sandburg, C.   They All Want to Play Hamlet.
Scamell, B.   Actor Speaks, An.
Speakes.   Patsy Cline.
Stern, G.   Adler.
Stevens, W.   Of Modern Poetry.
Szymborska.   Theater Impressions.
Trinidad.   Things to Do in Valley of the Dolls
   (The Movie).
Wheelwright.   Slow Curtain.
Wilbur.   Prisoner of Zenda, The.
See also Show Business

Adam and Eve
Andrews, N.   Notes for a Sermon on the Mount.
Blake, W.   Ghost of Abel, The.
Booth, P.   Original Sequence.
Bowers, E.   Adam's Song to Heaven.
Chaucer.   Chaucer's Wordes unto Adam, his
   Owne Scriveyn.
Clive.   Mother, The.
Copus, J.   Making of Eve, The.
   Masaccio's Expulsion from Paradise.
Crane, H.   Garden Abstract.
Dharker.   Namesake.
Dickey, J.   Poisoned Man, The.
Donnelly, S.   Eve Names the Animals.
Duncan, R.   Strains of Sight.
Graves, R.   Apple Island.
   Quiet Glades of Eden, The.
Hardy, J.   Computer Aided Design: Creation.
Hecht, A.   Naming the Animals.
Hirsch, E.   Husband and Wife.
Hollander, J.   Adam's Task.
Hood, T.   Reflection, A.
Hope, A.   Imperial Adam.
   Paradise Saved.
Hough, G.   Age of Innocence.
Hughes, T.   Childish Prank, A.
   Theology.
Jensen, L.   To a Stranger (At the End of a
   Caboose).
Lanier, S.   Whate'er Has Been.
Macpherson, J.   Fisherman, The.
Muir, E.   Adam's Dream.
Roethke.   Follies of Adam, The.
Sassoon.   Ancient History.
Sewell, L.   Expulsion.
Shapiro, K.   Exile.
   Recognition of Eve, The.
   Sickness of Adam, The.
Sisson.   Adam and Eve.
Snyder, G.   Milton by Firelight.
Sparshott.   Naming of the Beasts, The.
Thomas, D.   Ceremony after a Fire Raid.
Tomlinson, C.   In Arden.
Unknown.   Adam Lay Ybounden [or I-
   bounden].
Epigram: "While Adam slept, from him his Eve
   arose."
Very.   Serpent, The.
Walcott.   Cloud, The.
   New World.
White, G.   Leopard in Eden, The.
Whitman, W.   As Adam Early in the Morning.
   To the Garden the World.
Winchilsea.   Adam Posed.
Wright, J.   Eve to Her Daughters.
Yeats.   Adam's Curse.
See also Eve

Adams, John
Monks.   Twilight's Last Gleaming.

Adams, John Quincy
Benét, R. et al.   John Quincy Adams.

Addison, Joseph
Tickell.   To the Earl of Warwick, on the Death

of Mr. Addison.

Adelaide, Empress Consort
Middleton, C.   Adelaide's Dream.

Admiration
Aldrich, T.   Fannie.
Bacon, C.   Outlook.
Behn, A.   To My Lady Morland at Tunbridge.
Bell, M.   Mystery of Emily Dickinson, The.
Burns, R.   Of A' the Airts [the Wind Can Blaw].
Byron, G.   She Walks In Beauty.
Carew, T.   Comparison, The.
   To A. L.; Persuasions [or Perswasions] to Love.
   To My Worthy Friend Master George Sands [or
      Sandys], on His Translation of the Psalms.
Cavalieri.   First, The.
Ezekiel.   Goodbye Party for Miss Pushpa T. S.
Ferlinghetti, L.   Pound at Spoleto.
Fisher, R.   Paraphrases.
Garrigue.   Primer of Plato.
Gay, J.   Molly Mog [or, The Fair Maid of the
   Inn].
Gilyard, K.   Letter.
Guiney.   Salutation, A.
Herrick.   Upon the Nipples of Julia's Breast.
Hood, T.   Parental Ode to My Son, Aged Three
   Years and Five Months, A.
Johnston, E.   Lines: To a Young Gentleman of
   Surpassing Beauty.
Keats.   Addressed to Haydon.
   Great Spirits Now on Earth.
Kinnell.   Hen Flower, The.
Koch, K.   To Marina.
Levy, A.   To Lallie.
Lindsay, N.   To a Golden-Haired Girl in a
   Louisiana Town.
Lowell, R.   Alfred Corning Clark.
Melville, H.   College Colonel, The.
   Sheridan at Cedar Creek.
Meredith, G.   When I Would Image.
Nesbit, E.   Love's Guerdons.
Ponsot.   A La Une.
Praed.   Talented Man, The.
Silex, E.   Gift, The.
Sondheim.   In Buddy's Eyes.
Song.   Father and Daughter.
Waller, E.   Song: "Go[e], lovely rose."
Warren, R.   Birth of Love.
Whitfield.   To A. H.
Wilbur.   Piazza di Spagna, Early Morning.
   Praise in Summer.
Williams, S.   Song upon Miss Harriet Hanbury,
   Addressed to the Revd Mr Birt.
Wood, E.   Recognition.
Wright, K.   Unlikely Obbligato of
   Andersonstown.
Young, A.   Mountains of California: Part 1, The.

Adolescence
Alexander, E.   Nineteen.
   Zodiac.
Arnold, C.   Why I Skip My High School
   Reunions.
Auden.   Adolescence.
Ayres, R.   Corporeal.
Bandele, A.   1980–1990: A Poet's Personal
   Review.
Barresi.   Vacation, 1969.
Brainard, J.   I Remember.
Burris.   Very True Confessions.
Clinton, M.   I Wanna Be Black.
DeFoe, M.   Dream Lover.
Delgado, J.   Two Timer.
Dickey, J.   Sheep Child, The.
Dove, R.   Adolescence—I.
   Adolescence—II.
   Hully Gully.
Duhamel.   Bicentennial Barbie.
Dybek.   My Neighborhood.
Ellis, K. N.   Girl.
Forché.   As Children Together.
Goetsch, D.   Beach, The.
Goldbarth.   Counterfeit Earth!, The.
Graham, D.   Father of the Man.
Hernández Cruz.   Three Days/out of Franklin.
Howe, M.   Sixth Grade.
Jackson, M. L.   Blunts.
Jennings, E.   Young Ones, The.

Joseph, A.   Adolescence.
Kessler, S.   Marty's Mother.
Kirstein.   Double Date.
La Loca.   Why I Choose Black Men for My
   Lovers.
LaFemina.   Her Rose Tattoo.
Long, R.   What's So Funny 'bout Peace, Love
   and Understanding.
Lorde.   Hanging Fire.
Lux.   Little Tooth, A.
Machan.   In 1969.
Manrique, J.   Tarzan.
Mariani.   Betty.
Matthews, W.   Mood Indigo.
McClatchy.   1871.
   1946, 1957.
   1971.
   First Steps.
McGinley.   Portrait of a Girl with Comic Book.
McPherson, S.   1943.
Meinke.   Helen.
Merrill, J.   Matinees.
Murray, L.   Burning Want.
Neely, L.   Rhonda, Age 15, Emergency Room.
Oles.   To a Daughter at Fourteen Forsaking the
   Violin.
Ondaatje.   Burning Hills.
Pape.   Street Music.
Rukeyser, M.   Question, The.
Samyn, M.   Art of Kissing, The.
Sanchez, S.   Norma.
   Prelude to Nothing.
Seidman.   Gail.
Sexton.   Little Girl, My String Bean, My Lovely
   Woman.
Shapiro, K.   Confirmation, The.
   Drug Store.
   Waiting in Front of the Columnar High School.
Simon, M.   Boy Crazy.
Smith, P.   What It's Like to Be a Black Girl (For
   Those of You Who Aren't).
Soto.   Heaven.
Souster.   Young Girls.
Stein, K.   First Performance of the Rock 'n Roll
   Band Puce Exit.
Trinidad.   Double Trouble.
   Meet the Supremes.
   Movin' with Nancy.
Turner, W.   Romance.
Uyematsu.   To All Us Sansei Who Wanted to Be
   Westside.
Valerie, J.   Lesson on Braces.
Vasquez, R.   At the Rainbow.
Wallace, R.   Smoking.
   Thirteen.
Walls, D.   Summer the Beatles Went Over
   Seven Minutes on a Single, The.
Warren-Moore.   For Paula Cooper.
Wilson, R.   Say Girls in Shoe Ads: "I Go for a
   Man Who's Tall!"
Wilson, S.   Boy Friend, The.
Zarzyski.   Hurley High.

Adonis
Ayres.   Death of Adonis, The.
Bion.   Lament for Adonis.
Doolittle, H.   Adonis.

Adoption and the Adopted
Barben, D.   To Look Yet Not Find.
Ben-Lev, D.   Broken Helix.
Johnson, E.   Letter to My Mother, A.
Kay, J.   Waiting Lists, The.
Keller, D.   Man Who Knew the Words to
   'Louie, Louie', The.
Lavieri, J.   Autobiography of John Doe, The.
Tjanara-Williams, P.   Torn Apart.
Wren, A.   Surrogate Mothers.

Adultery and Adulterers
Amis, K.   Nothing to Fear.
Berssenbrugge.   Jealousy.
Boyd, E.   Guess Who I Saw Today.
Carew, T.   Secrecy [or Secresie] Protested.
Cope, W.   Reading Scheme.
Creeley.   Anger.
Curtis, T.   Gambit.
Dickey, J.   Adultery.
Ewart.   Old Husband Suspects Adultery, An.

Advent

Goetsch, D. Beach, The.
Grand, M. Guess Who I Saw Today.
Heaney, S. Punishment.
Herrick. Upon Scobble [Epigram].
Hope, A. Gloss to Matthew V 27–28.
Hope, M. Only Days.
Hughes, L. Sister.
Kasischke. My Heart.
Kazantzis. In Memory, 1978.
Lochhead, L. Hickie, The.
Lomax, M. Other Woman, The.
Maguire, S. Spilt Milk.
Papertalk-Green, C. Wanna Be White.
Quarles. On Dinah.
Sexton. For My Lover, Returning to His Wife.
Shepard, O. It's a Low Down Dirty Shame.
Simmons, J. End of the Affair, The.
St. John, D. California.
Unknown. Frankie and Johnny [*or* Johnnie *or* Albert].
  Queen Eleanor's Confession.

Advent

Auden. After Christmas.
Hartigan, A. Advent.
Rossetti, C. Advent.

Adventure and Adventurers

Brontë, C. Young Man Naughty's Adventure.
Brown, S. Odyssey of Big Boy.
Comden, B. Adventure.
Dehn, P. Alternative Endings to an Unwritten Ballad.
Green, A. Adventure.
Nash, O. Adventures of Isabel.
Owen, M. For Emily (Dickinson).
Stafford, W. Run before Dawn.
Stevenson, R. Mile an' a Bittock, A.
Styne, J. Adventure.
Tennyson, A. Sailor Boy, The.
Unknown. I Think Over Again My Small Adventures.
  Ship That Sails, The.

Advertising

Adams, F. Double Standard, The.
Benét, S. Hymn in Columbus Circle.
Cummings, E. Poem, or Beauty Hurts Mr. Vinal.
Dawe, B. Copy-writer's Dream, The.
Francia, L. Video Victim.
Fuhrman, J. Personal Ad.
Hughes, L. Neon Signs.
Nash, O. Song of the Open Road.
Padilla. Landscapes.
Portnoy, M. Voucher.
Rouse. Lilies of the Field.
Silverstein, S. Clarence.
Unknown. Advertising Agency Song, The.
  Burma-Shave Roadside Signs.
  Carnation Milk.

See also **Billboards**

Advice

Alexander of Pleuron. Epitaph for Cleonicus.
Berrigan, A. Advice to a Young Philosopher.
Bland, P. Notes for the Park Keeper.
Brown, L. Button Up Your Overcoat.
Burns, R. Epistle to a Young Friend.
Carroll, L. Rules and Regulations.
Cook, E. Building upon the Sand.
Creeley. Way, The.
Davidson, D. Sanctuary.
Delmore, E. Such Sweet Sorrow.
DeSylva, B. G. Button Up Your Overcoat.
Dodge, M. Early to Bed.
Dufferin. Charming Woman, The.
Emerson, R. To Rhea.
Farjeon, E. Advice to a Child.
Fearing. Any Man's Advice to His Son.
Floyd. Lance Corporal Purdue Grace, U. S. M. C.
Grimké, A. At April.
Henderson, R. Button Up Your Overcoat.
Herbert, G. Perirrhanterium.
Holm, B. Advice.
Housman, A. Carpenter's Son, The.
  When I Was One-and-Twenty.
Hughes, L. Mother to Son.

Warning: Augmented.
Johnson, B. Advice to a Reckless Youth.
Jonson, B. Martial. Epigram XLVII, Book X.
Kasdorf. Eve's Striptease.
Keyes, S. Advice for a Journey.
Kipling, R. If—.
Lewis, E. Advice to a Young Lady Lately Married.
Lovelace, R. Advice to My Best Brother, Colonel Francis Lovelace.
Meinke. Advice to My Son.
Montagu, L. Summary of Lord Lyttleton's 'Advice to a Lady', A.
Ralegh, S. Sir Walter Ra[u]le[i]gh to His Son[ne].
Rios, A. Advice to a First Cousin.
Simmons, J. Lullaby for Rachael.
Unknown. Penny.
Vaughan, H. Rules and Lessons.
Whitehead, W. Song for Ranelagh.
Wotton, S. To John Donne.

Aegean Sea

Flecker. Santorin.

Aeneas

Tate, A. Aeneas at Washington.

Aeneid, The (Virgil)

Lowell, R. Falling Asleep over the Aeneid.

Aengus

Yeats. Song Of Wandering Aengus, The.

Aesop

Crane, H. Black Tambourine.
Hecht, A. Improvisations on Aesop.
Marquis. Aesop Revised by Archy.

Affection

Adamson. My Tenth Birthday.
Ahlert, F. I'll Get By (As Long As I Have You).
'Andrews, C.' Morn's Recompense.
Armantrout. Sense.
  Winter.
Armitage, S. Poem: "And if it snowed and snow covered the drive."
Baldwin, J. Guilt, Desire and Love.
Barbauld. Rights of Woman, The.
Bawer. On Leaving the Artists' Colony.
Bell, M. To Dorothy.
Bennett, G. Sonnet—2: "Some things are very dear to me—."
Bernstein, C. Poem: "Here. Forget."
Berryman. He Resigns.
Bishop, E. Casabianca.
Blaga. I Will Not Crush the World's Corolla of Wonders.
Blake, W. How Sweet I Roamed [*or* Roam'd] from Field to Field.
Bobis, M. Driving to Katoomba.
Bognini. Earth and Sky.
Boland, E. Ready for Flight.
  That the Science of Cartography Is Limited.
Boyd, M. Fra Bank to Bank, Fra Wood to Wood I Rin.
Bradstreet, A. Another.
  Before the Birth of One of Her Children.
  Letter to Her Husband, Absent upon Public[k] Employment, A.
  To Her Father, with Some Verses.
Breton, A. Free Union.
Brooke, R. Hill, The.
  Sonnet: "Oh! Death will find me, long before I tire."
Broumas, O. Privacy.
Brown, L. Button Up Your Overcoat.
Browning, E. L. E. L.'s Last Question.
Browning, R. Lost Mistress, The.
  Meeting At Night.
  Porphyria's Lover.
  Two in the Campagna.
Burns, R. Highland Mary.
  O [*or* Oh] Wert Thou in the Cauld Blast.
  Song: "O my love's [*or* luve's *or* love is *or* luve is] like a red, red rose."
Byron, G. She Walks In Beauty.
  To Thyrza.
Campion, T. Follow Thy Fair Sun[ne] [Unhappy Shadow].

When to Her Lute Corinna [*or* Corrina] Sings.
Carew, T. Fly That Flew into My Mistress'[s] Eye, A.
  In Praise of His Mistress.
  Song, [A]: "Ask[e] me no more where Jove bestow[e]s."
  To my Friend G. N. from Wrest.
  To My Rival.
Castillo, S. At the Havana Hilton.
Cherry, K. Late Afternoon at the Arboretum.
Cisneros, S. You Bring Out the Mexican in Me.
Clare, J. To Mary: 'It Is the Evening Hour'
Cleveland, J. Antiplatonic[k], The.
Cook, E. Building upon the Sand.
Cope, W. Flowers.
  Valentine.
Cory, W. Preparation.
Crabbe. Marriage Ring, The.
Creeley. Act of Love, The.
Cummings, E. Somewhere i have never travelled, gladly beyond.
Cunningham, J. To My Wife.
Curbelo. Dreaming Horse.
  Tonight I Can Almost Hear the Singing.
Davenant [*or* D'Avenant]. Countess of Anglesey lead Captive by the Rebels, at the Disforresting of Pewsam, The.
De la Mare. Ghost, The.
Delmore, A. Girl by the River, The.
DeSylva, B. G. Button Up Your Overcoat.
Disch. Clouds, The.
Dixon, M. Great Big Bunch of You, A.
Donne. Canonization, The.
  Ecstasy, The.
  Funeral[l], The.
  Good-Morrow, The.
  Nocturnal[l] upon Saint Lucy's [*or* S. Lucy's *or* S. Lucies] Day, Being the Shortest Day, A.
  Relic, The.
  Song: "Sweetest love, I do not go[e]."
  Valediction: Forbidding Mourning, A.
  Valediction: of Weeping, A.
Dowson. Non Sum Qualis Eram Bonae sub Regno Cynarae.
Duhig, I. From the Irish.
Duke, V. I Can't Get Started.
  I Like the Likes of You.
Dunbar, P. Negro Love Song, A.
Dyer, S. Lowest Trees Have Tops, The.
Elizabeth I. When I Was Fair and Young.
Elizabeth, M. Manon Reassures Her Lover.
Elledge. 14 Reasons Why I Mention Mario Lanza to the Man I Love Every Chance I Get Tonight.
Elmslie, K. One Night Stand.
"Ephelia." In the Person of a Lady, to Bajazet, Her Unconstant Gallant.
Feirstein. Mark Stern Wakes Up.
  Rune-Maker, The.
Fenton, J. In Paris with You.
Ferguson, G. Silent as Roses.
  Winter Sunflowers.
Flanner. True Western Summer.
Garcia, R. Los Amantes.
Gardner, I. Cock-a-Hoop.
  In the Museum.
Gascoigne. For That He Looked Not upon Her.
  Lullaby [*or* Lullabie] of a Lover, The.
Gershwin. I Can't Get Started.
  They All Laughed.
Ginsberg, A. To Aunt Rose.
Giovanni. Winter Poem.
Glück, L. Garden, The.
  Hawk's Shadow.
Gorges. Her Face, Her Tongue, Her Wit.
Graves, R. In Perspective.
  Lost Love.
  Pure Death.
  She Tells Her Love While Half Asleep.
Green, D. R. Names and sorrows.
Greenwald, T. And, Hinges.
  I Hear a Step.
Gross, W. Tenderly.
Guevara, M. Buddy Holly Poem, The.
Gunn, T. Tamer and Hawk.
Hall, D. Love-Letter-Burning.

Hampton. Yugoslav Story.
Harbach, O. Love Nest, The.
Harburg. I Like the Likes of You.
Hardy, T. After a Journey.
 Church Romance, A.
 Going, The.
 She Hears the Storm.
Henderson, R. Button Up Your Overcoat.
Herbert, G. Affliction (1).
 Bitter-Sweet.
Hikmet. Things I Didn't Know I Loved.
Hirsch, L. Love Nest, The.
Holiday. Fine and Mellow.
Holmes, O. Tartarus.
"Hope." I Shall Forget.
Hope, A. Return of Persephone, The.
Horton, G. Early Affection.
 Lover's Farewell, The.
Housman, A. Because I liked you better.
Hughes, L. Gal's Cry for a Dying Lover.
 Gypsy Man.
 Night Funeral in Harlem.
Jefferson, B. Long Distance Moan.
Johnson, G. I Want to Die While You Love Me.
Jonson, B. Elegy, An: "Though beauty be the
 mark of praise."
 My Picture Left in Scotland.
 Song: To Celia.
 Sonnet to the Noble Lady, the Lady Mary
 Wroth, A.
Keats. La Belle Dame sans Merci [A Ballad].
 To———: "Had I a man's fair form, then might
 my sighs."
Keithley. Thunder Storm.
Kemble. Noonday Vision, A.
 Sonnet: "If there were any power in human
 love."
Kenney. Aubade: "Cold snap. Five o'clock."
King, H. Exequy, The.
Koch, K. Permanently.
Landon. Bonds of Affection.
Lanier, S. Song for "The Jacquerie."
Lau, C. Zhoukoudian Bride's Harvest.
Lawrence, J. Tenderly.
Leithauser. Ghost of a Ghost, The.
Levertov. Love Poem.
 Woman Meets an Old Lover, A.
Lewis, A. Goodbye.
 Post-Script: for Gweno.
Loesser. Luck, Be a Lady.
Lomax, M. Amor Diving.
Longfellow, H. Children's Hour, The.
Lovelace, R. Gratiana Dancing [or Daucing]
 and Singing.
 On Sanazar's being honoured with six hundred
 Duckets by the Clarissimi of Venice, for
 composing an Elegiack Hexastick of The
 City. A Satyre.
 To Althea, from Prison.
Lowell, A. Aubade.
Lowell, J. Contrast, A.
Lowell, R. Grandparents.
Malloch, D. Manly Love.
Marston, P. Speechless: Upon the Marriage of
 Two Deaf and Dumb Persons.
Martinez, D. Cole Porter.
 In a Duplex Near the San Andreas Fault.
 Matisse: Blue Nude, 1952.
Marvell. Definition of Love, The.
 Fair Singer, The.
 Gallery, The.
 Mower to the Glowworms [or Glow-Worms or
 Glo-Worms], The.
Mayer, B. Sonnet: Kamikaze.
McAuley, J. Because.
McCree, J. Put Your Arms Around Me, Honey.
Melhem, D. Grandfather: Frailty Is Not the
 Story.
Mercer, J. Midnight Sun.
Mignon, A. One Heart's Enough for Me.
Millay, E. I shall go back.
Mitchison. My True Love Hath My Heart.
Montagu, L. Lover, The; a Ballad.
Montague, J. All Legendary Obstacles.
Montgomerie, A. Remembers thou in Æsope of
 a taill.

Moore, T. Did Not.
 Echo.
 Oft In the Stilly Night.
Muir, E. In Love For Long.
Musgrave. You Didn't Fit.
Nathan, L. Toast.
Nims, J. Love Poem: "My clumsiest dear,
 whose hands shipwreck vases."
Olds, S. Knowing, The.
Parker, D. One Perfect Rose.
Pasolini. Prayer to My Mother.
Pfeiffer, E. Nathaniel to Ruth.
Phillips, S. Apparition, The.
Piatt, S. Lesson in a Picture, A.
 Pique at Parting, A.
 This World.
Poe. To One in Paradise.
Pope, A. Hampton Court.
 Rape of the Lock, The; an Heroi-Comical Poem.
 Toilet, The.
 Voyage on the Thames, The.
Porter, C. I Concentrate on You.
Rainger, R. Easy Living.
Ramsey, J. Tally Stick, The.
Reavey. Dismissing Progress and Its
 Progenitors.
Roberts, M. Magnificat.
Robin, L. Easy Living.
Rochester, J. Love And Life.
Roethke. For An Amorous Lady.
 I Knew A Woman.
Rossetti, C. L. E. L.
 Somewhere Or Other.
Rushing. Sent for You Yesterday.
Ryan, G. Orbit.
Salom. Ghazal on signs of Love and
 Occupation.
Salter. Summer 1983.
Schnackenberg. Supernatural Love.
Seidman. Gail.
Shapiro, K. Twins, The.
Shelley, P. To———: "Music, when soft voices
 die."
 To Jane: The keen stars were twinkling.
Sherwood, G. Love and Life.
Sidney, R. Sonnet 25: "Yow that take pleasure
 in yowr cruelty."
Sidney, S. Dirge: "Ring out your bells [or
 belles], let mourning shows [or shewes] be
 spread."
 Nightingale, The.
Silverstein, S. Hug o' War.
Simic. Old Couple.
Simpson, L. As Birds Are Fitted to the Boughs.
Skelton, J. Mannerly Margery Mylk and Ale.
Smith, S. Freddy.
 Human Affection.
Snodgrass, W. Mementos, 1.
Sparrow, J. To an Angel in the House.
Spencer, A. Wife-Woman, The.
Spenser. Epithalamion: "Ye learned sisters
 which have oftentimes."
Strand. Coming to This.
Strauss, J. Love Notes.
Surrey. Love, That Doth Reign and Live Within
 My Thought.
Swenson, M. Staying at Ed's Place.
Swift, J. Stella's Birthday ([March 13,] 1727).
Swirszczynska. Greatest Love, The.
 Same Inside, The.
Synge. In May.
Taggart, J. Body and Soul: Poem for Two
 Readers.
Taylor, B. Love Returned.
 Proposal.
Teasdale. "I Am Not Yours."
Thomas, E. No One So Much As You.
Thomas, L. Cameo in Sudden Light.
 Clear Channel.
Tipton. I Wanted You in the Kitchen of My
 Heart.
Tonks. Story of a Hotel Room.
Traherne. Salutation [or Salutations], The.
Tranter. Moonshine Sonata.
Tsaloumas. Return of an Ikon.
Tuckerman, F. Coralie.

Rhotruda.
Turk, R. I'll Get By (As Long As I Have You).
Unknown. Country Lassie, The.
 I Have a Young Sister.
 I Saw My Lady Weep.
 Lowest Trees Have Tops, The.
 Rare Willie Drowned in Yarrow; or, The Water
 o Gamrie.
 Sweet Polly Oliver.
 There Is a Lady Sweet and Kind.
 To His Love.
 Waly, Waly [Love Be Bonny].
 Will You Love Me When I'm Old?
Unknown, sometimes at. to Sir Walter Ralegh.
 As You Came from the Holy Land [of
 Walsingham].
Vando. Ode to Your Back.
Von Tilzer, A. Put Your Arms Around Me,
 Honey.
Waldrop, R. Lawn of Excluded Middle.
Waller, E. Love's Farewell.
Warren, H. Great Big Bunch of You, A.
Warsh. Enmeshment.
Wayne, J. By Accident.
Wheelwright. Slow Curtain.
Whitman, W. Base of All Metaphysics, The.
 Live Oak, with Moss.
 Sometimes with One I Love.
 When I Heard at the Close of the Day.
 Woman Waits for Me, A.
Whitney, I. I. W. To her unconstant Lover.
Wieners. Doll.
Wilcox, E. Friendship After Love.
Williams, C. Dog, The.
Williams, M. Poem for Emily, A.
Williams, W. Love Song: "Sweep the house
 clean."
Wilson, R. I Wish in the City of Your Heart.
Winchilsea. Friendship Between Ephelia and
 Ardelia.
 Letter to Daphnis, A.
Wyatt, S. Long love that in my thought doth
 harbo[u]r, The.
 Lover Showeth How He Is Forsaken of Such as
 He Sometime Enjoyed, The.
 My Lute, Awake!
Yeats. Down by the Salley Gardens.
 Drinking Song, A.
 Folly of Being Comforted, The.
 Lullaby: "Beloved, may your sleep be sound."
 When You Are Old.
Yount, A. Sharing.
Yuson. Love Before Dinner.
Zawinski, A. You Touch Me.
Zolynas. Love in the Classroom.

Affliction
Herbert, G. Affliction (1).
Wright, C. Appalachian Book of the Dead III,
 The.

Afghanistan
Allingham. In Snow.

Africa
Abena, B. Exiles.
 Mawu of the Waters.
Acam-Oturu. Agony . . . A Resurrection, An.
Acholonu. Harvest of War.
Acquah. They're Tearing Up the Old
 Graveyard.
Adisa. Count Ossie.
Aiyejina. When the Monuments.
Amadiume. Nok Lady in Terracotta.
 Oya Now.
Angelou. Africa.
Angira. Newscast.
 Obbligato from a Public Gallery.
 Old Wharf Canto.
 Symphony from the Balcony.
Anyidoho. Elegy for the Revolution.
 Tsitsa.
Baker, H. Toward Guinea: For Larry Neal,
 1937–1981.
Baraka. Ka 'Ba.
 Kenyatta Listening to Mozart.
Barlow, G. 4½ Months: Halfway Song.
Bennett, G. Heritage.
Bolamba. Portrait.

Bontemps.   Nocturne at Bethesda.
Nocturne of the Wharves.
Brathwaite, E.   Mmenson.
Brew.   Plea for Mercy, A.
Brooks, G.   To the Diaspora.
Browning, R.   Home-Thoughts, from the Sea.
Through the Metidja to Abd-el-Kadr.
Césaire, A.   Macumba Word.
Miraculous Weapons, The.
Cheney-Coker.   Analysis.
Childhood.
Peasants.
Poet Among Those Who Are Also Poets.
Chipasula.   Everything to Declare.
Singing Drum, The.
Clark Bekedermo.   Epilogue to Casualties.
New from Ethiopia and the Sudan, The.
Crouch, S.   Riding Across John Lee's Finger.
Cullen, C.   Heritage.
Cumbo.   Ceremony.
De Kok.   Our Sharpeville.
Dei-Anang.   My Africa.
Dempster, R.   Africa's Plea.
Is This Africa.
Diop, D.   Africa.
Dipoko.   Poem of Villeneuve St Georges, A.
Dumas, H.   Root Song.
Dunbar, P.   Ode to Ethiopia.
Ezenwa-Ohaeto.   I Wan Bi President.
Fawcett, B.   Hand, The.
Fuller, R.   In Africa.
Gashe.   Village, The.
Gibbon, P.   Answer, An.
Giovanni.   They Clapped.
Guillén, N.   Sensemayá.
Hardy, T.   Drummer Hodge.
Harper, F.   Ethiopia.
Horne, N.   Messages.
Note to My Liberal Feminist Sister, A.
Hughes, L.   Cubes.
Danse Africaine.
Ismaili.   Bajji.
Lagos.
Solange.
Jacinto, A.   Monangamba.
Jackson, B.   Another Impostor.
Jackson, M.   Return from Luluabourg.
Jordan, J.   Mid-Year Report: For Haruko.
Karade, B.   Yemoja.
Kaufman, B.   African Dream.
Kizer, C.   Race Relations.
Knight, E.   Idea of Ancestry, The.
Koch, K.   Geography.
Kombem.   Another Moment.
Kunene.   Echoes, The.
Elegy.
La Grone.   Suncoming.
Laing, K.   Africa Sky.
Steps.
Lane, P.   Girl at the Window.
Lindsay, N.   Congo, The.
Lumumba.   Dawn in the Heart of Africa.
Mabuza.   Love Song, A.
Tired Lizi Tired.
Macgoye.   Letter to a Friend.
Macha, F.   Artist and a Wailing Mother, An.
Corruption.
Madhubuti.   Change Is Not Always Progress.
Knocking Donkey Fleas off a Poet from the
Southside of Chi.
Mandela.   I Have Tried Hard.
Mapanje.   After Wiriyamu Village Massacre by
Portuguese.
Messages.
On Being Asked to Write a Poem for 1979.
These Too Are Our Elders.
Visiting Zomba Plateau.
Marchera, D.   Desert Crossing.
McKay, C.   Africa.
Miller, A.   Africa Thing, The.
Miller, J.   Africa.
Milner-Brown.   Who Knows?
Mnthali.   Celebration, The.
My Father.
Stranglehold of English Lit, The.
Moore, M.   Jerboa, The.

Moorer.   Africa.
Morales.   Africa.
Morales, A.   Other Heritage, The.
Mphande.   I Was Sent For.
Pain.
Walking the Plateau.
Mpina.   Reborn.
Summer Fires of Mulanje Mountain.
Mpondo.   Season of the Rains, The.
Neely, L.   Multiple Assaults.
Nicol.   Meaning of Africa, The.
Nortje.   Waiting.
Ofeimun.   New Brooms, The.
Ogundipe-Leslie.   Tendril Love of Africa.
Ojaide.   Fate of Vultures, The.
Verdict of Stone, A.
Where Everybody is King.
O'Lahsen, M.   Dead Erect, The.
Opoku-Agyemang.   King Tut in America.
Osofisan.   She Thinks in Song.
Parkes, F.   Three Phases of Africa.
Pegram, A.   Deliverance.
I Will Still Sing.
Mr. White Discoverer.
Penn, R.E.   Morning Songs.
Phillips, C.   Africa Says.
Rampolekeng.   Welcome to the New
Consciousness.
Rich, A.   Letters in the Family.
Rothenberg, J.   Praises of the Bantu Kings (1–
10).
Sall, A.   Cloak of Dawn.
Sallah, T.   Elders Are Gods, The.
Senghor.   "African Image Is Not An Image by
Equation . . . , The."
Kaya-Magan, The.
Man and Beast.
Taga for Mbaye Dyôb.
Serote.   This Old Woman.
Shange.   Bocas: A Daughter's Geography.
Sousa, N.   Appeal.
Southerland.   Pale Ant.
Steptoe.   Mississippi Blues.
Tati-Loutard.   Pilgrimage to Loango Strand.
Tidjani-Cissé.   Home News.
Tobrise.   Dyeing.
Tolson, M.   On the Founding of Liberia.
Ti.
Wakolele.   Southern Africa.
Walcott.   Far Cry from Africa, A.
Weaver, M.   My Father's Geography.
Wonodi.   Planting.
Zimunya.   Let It Be.
Mr. Bezuidenthout's Dogs.
African Americans
Ai.   Endangered Species.
Riot Act, April 29, 1992.
Self Defense.
Akiwumi, V.   Different Ones #6—Future
Possibilities (An Aids Soliloquy).
Alexander, E.   Affirmative Action Blues (1993).
Boston Year.
Deadwood Dick.
Feminist Poem Number One.
Kevin of the N.E. Crew.
Ladders.
Ode.
Today's News.
Algarin.   Broadway Opening.
Allen, S.   Moment Please, A.
View from the Corner.
Anderson-Thompkins.   Brken Promises.
Epitaph for Willie or Little Black Poet with No
Future.
Angelou.   Sepia Fashion Show.
Still I Rise.
As-Sabah.   I'll Never Know No Sunday in This
Weekday Room.
Jubilee.
Asim, J.   Dumas.
Askhari.   Colorstruck.
Isalutu.
REcreation.
Aubert, A.   Opposite of Green, The.
Bandele, A.   1980–1990: A Poet's Personal
Review.

Prayer for the Living, A.
Baraka.   Beautiful Black Women.
Black Art.
Black Dada Nihilismus.
Clay.
Each Morning.
Funk Lore.
Hymn for Lanie Poo.
I don't love you.
Ka 'Ba.
Leadbelly Gives an Autograph.
Leroy.
Nation Is Like Ouselves, The.
Pause of Joe, The.
Poem for Black Hearts, A.
Poem Some People Will Have to Understand, A.
Short Speech to My Friends.
SOS.
Three Movements and a Coda.
W. W.
Baraka, R.   Five-0.
For the Brothers Who Aint Here.
I Remember Malcolm.
In the Tradition Too.
Barlow, G.   Painting Drunken Twilight.
Place Where He Arose, The.
Barras, J.   Peace.
Barrax.   For a Black Poet.
Beatty, P.   Gription.
I Know You Are, But What Am I?
Independent Study.
New York Newsday: Truth, Justice and Vomit.
That's Not in My Job Description.
Why That Abbott and Costello Vaudeville Mess
Never Worked with Black People.
Bennett, G.   Heritage.
Song: "I am weaving a song of waters."
Sonnet—2: "Some things are very dear to
me—."
To a Dark Girl.
To Usward.
Benson, L.   P Word Poem, The.
Asante.
Bernie, B.   Sweet Georgia Brown.
Bishop, E.   Cootchie.
Songs for a Colored Singer.
Black, I.   Racist Psychotherapy.
Bontemps.   God Give to Men.
Brathwaite, E.   Journeys, The.
Braxton, C.   Arts Are Black, The.
Breedlove, N.   Black and Divided or Chittlins
and Caviar.
New Miz Praise de Lawd, The.
Brooks, G.   Ballad of Rudolph Reed, The.
Gay Chaps at the Bar.
My Dreams, My Works, Must Wait Till After
Hell.
Primer for Blacks.
Still Do I Keep My Look, My Identity.
Third Sermon on the Warpland, The.
To the Diaspora.
We Real Cool.
Young Heroes.
Brooks, S.   Darktown Strutter's Ball, The.
Grandma Talk.
Brown, J. et al.   Say It Loud—I'm Black and
I'm Proud.
Brown, M.   Survival Motion: Notice.
Brown, S.   Odyssey of Big Boy.
Old Woman Remembers, An.
Scotty Has His Say.
Slim in Atlanta.
Southern Cop.
Sporting Beasley.
Strong Men.
To Sallie, Walking.
Browning, E.   Runaway Slave at Pilgrim's Point,
The.
Buddy.   Callin Buddy / Bolden.
Burroughs, M.   Black Pride.
Only in This Way.
To Soulfolk.
Casey, K.   Sweet Georgia Brown.
Cassells.   Soul Make a Path Through Shouting.
Chambers, G.   Meditations on Stevie.
Waxing Poetic on Marvin.

Clarke, T. For Babies Unborn.
Clemmons. Freedom Song for the Black
  Woman, A.
Cliff. Within the Veil.
Clifton, L. 4/30/92 for rodney king.
  For de Lawd.
  Good Times.
  In Salem.
  In White America.
  Listen Children.
  Thirty-Eighth Year, The.
  Way It Was, The.
Clinton, M. Black Rape.
  I Wanna Be Black.
  Warning to Young Bright Sisters / White AM.
    Culture 101A.
Coleman, H. Black Soldier Remembers, A.
  OK Corral East Brothers in the Nam.
Coleman, W. African Sleeping Sickness.
  American Sonnet (10).
  Coffee.
  Emmett Till.
  Essay on Language.
  Where I Live.
Collins, K. I Am Africa.
  Sisters.
Conyus. Confession to Malcolm.
Corpus. Blkfern-jungal.
Corrothers. At the Closed Gate of Justice.
  Indignation Dinner, An.
Cortez, J. How Long Has Trane Been Gone.
Craighead, L. Whole Truth So Help Me God—
    Also Known as the Gettin' Rid of Nigguz
    Business.
  Wo/man's Voice Must Be Heard, A.
Crane, H. Black Tambourine.
Crawley, W. Bud.
  Poetry for the Goddess.
Cullen, C. Black Majesty.
  Brown Girl Dead, A.
  From the Dark Tower.
  Heritage.
  Litany of the Dark People, The.
  Shroud of Color, The.
  Yet Do I Marvel.
Cumbo. Black Sister.
Cuney. No Images.
Cyril. Children's Games.
  Jump Black Honey Jump Black.
  Just Because I Am.
Dabney, F. That's Why They Call Me 'Shine'
Damas. Just Like the Legend.
  S.O.S.
Danner. At Home in Dakar.
  Grandson Is a Hoticeberg, A.
Dent. For Cool Papa Bell.
Derricotte. Blackbottom.
  For Black Women Who Are Afraid.
  In an Urban School.
  St. Peter Claver.
  Struggle, The.
Dove, R. Wingfoot Lake.
DuBois, W. Song of the Smoke, The.
Dumas, H. Zebra Goes Wild Where the
    Sidewalk Ends, The.
Dunbar, P. Colored Soldiers, The.
  Negro Love Song, A.
  Unsung Heroes, The.
  We Wear the Mask.
  When Dey 'Listed Colored Soldiers.
Eady. Why Do So Few Blacks Study Creative
    Writing?
Ellis, T. Hush Yo Mouf.
Emanuel, J. Whitey, Baby.
Encarnacion. Bulosan Listens to a Recording of
    Robert Johnson.
Evans, M. How Will You Call Me, Brother.
  I Am a Black Woman.
  Status Symbol.
  Vive Noir!
Fauset. Touché.
Ferdinand. Food for Thought.
Finney, N. Uncles.
Fisher, S. Assumption about the Harlem Brown
    Baby.
Fleming, R. For All Unwed Mothers.

Ford, C. Plaint.
Forman, R. Green Boots n Lil Honeys.
Foster, S. Old Folks at Home[, The].
Gilbert, C. Time with Stevie Wonder in It.
Gilmore, B. To be or not to be.
Giovanni. Beautiful Black Men.
  Ego Tripping [(There May Be a Reason Why)].
  Genie in the Jar, The.
  Nikki-Rosa.
  Poem for Flora.
  Woman Poem.
Giscombe. (1962 At the Edge of Town).
  (1980).
Grandmaster Flash and the Furious Five.
  Message, The.
Gray-Kontar, D. Cuz' mama played jazz.
  Not no socialism/communism classical, but
    some power to the people jazz.
Handy, W. Beale Street Blues.
Harland-Watts, J. For a Woman's Rights.
  Let It Be Known.
  Resist Confinement.
Harper, F. She's Free!
Harper, M. Archives.
  Grandfather.
  High Modes: Vision as Ritual: Confirmation.
  Homage to the Brown Bomber.
  Song: I Want a Witness.
Harris, W. Daddy Poem, A.
  Rib Sandwich.
Hayden, R. Aunt Jemima of the Ocean Waves.
  Beginnings.
  Frederick Douglass.
  O Daedalus, Fly Away Home.
Hemphill. Cordon Negro.
  Family Jewels.
  To Some Supposed Brothers.
Henderson-Holmes. Failure of an Invention.
Holman, M. Mr. Z.
Holmes, D. Time for Guns, A.
Hope, M. Sacrifice.
Hopkins, L. Nat Love: Black Cowboy.
Hughes, L. Be-Bop Boys.
  Cross.
  Dinner Guest: Me.
  Dream Boogie.
  Dream Variation[s].
  Gal's Cry for a Dying Lover.
  High to Low.
  I, Too.
  Low to High.
  Merry-Go-Round.
  Negro Servant.
  Negro Speaks of Rivers, The.
  Neighbor.
  Nightmare Boogie.
  Red Silk Stockings.
  Shame on You.
  Stars.
  Theme for English B.
  Trumpet Player.
  Uncle Tom.
  Visitors to the Black Belt.
  Weary Blues, The.
  When She Wears Red.
Hummer, T. Ideal, The.
Irvine, W. To be Young, Gifted, and Black.
Iverem, E. Daddy's Friends.
  Journalist's Convention 1987.
Jackson, A. Make/n My Music.
  Miz Rosa Rides the Bus.
  Spinster Song: African-American Woman Guild.
Jackson, B. Another Impostor.
  In Exchange for Forty Acres.
Jackson, G. Fugitive Slaves.
  Some of Betty's Story Round 1850.
Jackson, R. After the Dance.
  Albert James.
  Jamal's Lamentation.
Jacobs, H. On Growing Up the Darker Berry.
Jeffers, L. My Blackness Is the Beauty of This
  Land.
  Nina Simone.
  When I Know the Power of my Black Hand.
Johnson, F. Tired.
Johnson, H. Bottled [New York].

  Sonnet to a Negro in Harlem.
Johnson, J. Brothers.
  Creation, The.
  Lift Every [or Ev'ry] Voice and Sing.
  O Black and Unknown Bards.
Johnson, T. Until He Comes.
Jonas, R. Ballade des Belles Milatraisses.
  Brother Baptis' on Woman Suffrage.
Jones, G. Tripart.
Jones, I. Echoes of the Murder of Emmett Till.
Jones, L. et al. Poem for Black Hearts, A.
Jordan, J. If You Saw a Negro Lady.
  Poem about Intelligence for My Brothers and
    Sisters, A.
  Something Like a Sonnet for Phillis Miracle
    Wheatley.
Jordan, N. Be You.
Joseph, A. My Father's Heroes.
  Numbers.
  On Being Told I Don't Speak Like a Black
    Person.
  Reading Room.
  Soul Train.
Kaufman, B. Oregon.
  Untitled.
Kendrick, D. Solo: The Good Blues.
  We are the Writing on the Wall.
Kgositsile. Song for Ilva Mackay and Mongane.
Kinnell. Avenue Bearing the Initial of Christ
    into the New World, The.
Knight, E. Another Poem for Me (after
    Recovering from an O.D.).
  Black Poet Leaps to His Death, A.
  Bones of My Father, The.
  For Black Poets Who Think of Suicide.
  Hard Rock Returns to Prison from the Hospital
    for the Criminal Insane.
  Idea of Ancestry, The.
  My Life, the Quality of Which.
  Once on a Night in the Delta: A Report From
    Hell.
  Warden Said to Me the Other Day, The.
Komunyakaa. Gift Horse.
  "Kush." Message for Langston, A.
Lee, K. On South Africa.
Lindsay, N. Congo, The.
  John Brown.
  Simon Legree—A Negro Sermon.
Loftin. Weeksville Women.
Loftis, N. Big John.
Long, D. Black Love Black Hope.
Lorde. Between Ourselves.
  Coal.
  For the Record.
  Harriet.
  Naturally.
Lowell, R. For the Union Dead.
  Mad Negro Soldier Confined at Munich, A.
Mack, C. That's Why They Call Me 'Shine.'
Madgett. Black Woman.
  Images.
  Midway.
Madhubuti. B Network, The.
  Big Momma.
  Gwendolyn Brooks.
  Malcolm Spoke / Who Listened?
  My Brothers.
  Poem to Complement Other Poems, A.
  Poet: What Ever Happened to Luther?
  Possibiliites: Remembering Malcolm X.
McClaurin. I, Woman.
  Mask, The.
  To a Gone Era.
McElroy, C. Ghost-Who-Walks, The.
  Griots Who Know Brer Fox, The.
  Illusion.
  Tapestries.
  Under the Oak Table.
  Woman's Song, A.
McKay, C. Harlem Dancer, The.
  If We Must Die.
  Negro Spiritual.
  Negro's Tragedy, The.
  Outcast.
  To the White Fiends.
  White House, The.

McNeil, R.   Angel in the Temple of Luxor, An.
Medina, T.   Big House Revisited, The.
  Don't Say Goodnight to Etheridge Knight.
  Poem for Teacup Mantlepiece Poets Palpitating
    Poot Booty Plagiarists Imprisoned in Ivy
    League White Supremacist Mental Biological
    Warfare Labs.
Melville, H.   Formerly a Slave.
  Swamp Angel, The.
Moses, G.   Poem for Trish, A.
Moss, T.   Raising a Humid Flag.
Neal, L.   Harlem Gallery: From the Inside.
Neely, L.   Eight Ways of Looking at Pussy.
  Multiple Assaults.
  Rhonda, Age 15, Emergency Room.
Nelson, M.   Balance.
  Ballad of Aunt Geneva, The.
  Chopin.
Nemerov.   Negro Cemetery Next to a White
  One, A.
Ofeimun.   Gong, A.
Parker, D.   Sand.
Patterson, G.   Autobiography of a Black Man.
Patterson, R.   Black Power.
  Twenty-Six Ways of Looking at a Blackman.
  What We Know.
Perdomo, W.   Nigger-Reecan Blues.
Phillips, C.   Passing.
Piatt, S.   Child's Party, A.
Pinkard, M.   Sweet Georgia Brown.
Pomeroy, R.   Gay Love and the Movies.
Powell, K.   Don't Feel No Way.
  For Aunt Cathy.
  Genius Child.
  Mental Terrorism.
  Southern Birth.
Public Enemy.   Don't Believe the Hype.
  Party for your Right to Fight.
Queen Latifah.   Evil That Men Do, The.
Randall, D.   Abu.
  Blackberry Sweet.
  Booker T. and W. E. B.
  Different Image, A.
  Melting Pot, The.
  Roses and Revolutions.
Razaf, A.   (What Did I Do to Be So) Black and
  Blue?
Reed, I.   Railroad Bill, A Conjure Man.
Reynolds, H.   Black Maid to the Fair Boy, The.
Rivers, C.   In Defense of Black Poets.
  Underground.
Roach.   At Guaracara Park.
Roberts, N.   Nigger and Some Poofters, A.
Rodgers, C.   For Sistuhs Wearin' Straight Hair.
  It Is Deep.
  Jesus Was Crucified or: It Must Be Deep.
  Poem for Some Black Women.
Ross, L.   Indecent Exposure (A True Story).
  James Brown.
Rosten.   Black Boy.
Rukeyser, M.   George Robinson: Blues.
Rushin.   Black Back-Ups, The.
Rykard, R.   Whole two weeks after The Million
  Man March; and still, if you'd ask me, this is
  all I could say about it, A.
Sadiq, M.   Tuskegee Experiment.
Saint.   Heart and Soul.
Sanchez, S.   Blues.
  Memorial.
  Poem at Thirty.
  Present.
  Reflections After the June 12th March for
    Disarmament.
  Song No. 2: "I say. all you young girls waiting
    to live."
  Song No. 3: "Cain't nobody tell me any
    different."
  To Anita.
Saunders, R.   Generation Gap, The.
  Hush Honey.
  Lawd, Dese Colored Chillum.
Senghor.   To New York.
  You Held the Black Face.
Sepamla.   Civilization Aha.
  On Judgement Day.
Shange.   About Atlanta.

Nappy Edges.
Nappy Edges (A Cross Country Sojourn).
Shapiro, K.   Nigger.
Sharp, S.   Tribal Marks.
Shepherd, R.   Difficult Music, The.
Sherman, C.   Roots.
Simon, L.   Nellie Gives into Blanche.
Smith, P.   Blonde White Women.
  Building Nicole's Mama.
  They Say That Black People . . . .
  What It's Like to Be a Black Girl (For Those of
    You Who Aren't).
Smith, W.   Malcolm.
Soyinka.   Telephone Conversation.
Spellman.   Did John's Music Kill Him?
  When Black People Are.
Stafford, W.   Monuments for a Friendly Girl at a
  Tenth Grade Party.
Stanard, C.   Baseball.
Steptoe.   Window Shopping.
Sykes, B.   One Day.
Sylvain, P.   Collective Search.
Thomas, L.   Excitation.
Thompson, C.   Mrs. Johnson Objects.
Tolson, M.   Dark Symphony.
  Ex-Judge at the Bar, An.
Touré, A.   JuJu.
  Frontier of Rage, The.
  Imani in Sunburst Summer: A Chant.
Travis, N.   Sunbathing.
Troupe.   Poem for My Father; for Quincy.
  River Town Packin House Blues.
Unknown.   Me and My Captain.
  Shine and the Titanic.
  Song: "We raise de wheat."
Van Jordan, A.   If I Write a Poem.
Vega.   Brothers Loving Brothers.
Voigt.   At the Movie: Virginia, 1956.
Wade-Gayles.   Inquisition.
Walker, M.   Poppa Chicken.
Waller, T.   (What Did I Do to Be So) Black and
  Blue?
Waniek.   Balance.
  Ballad of Aunt Geneva, The.
  Diverne's Waltz.
  Three Men in a Tent.
  Tuskegee Airfield.
Washington.   Freedom Hair.
Watkins, N.   Bedtime Story.
Watkyns.   Blackamoors, The.
Weaver, M.   Black and White Galaxie, The.
  Black Man's Sonata, A.
  Easy Living.
  Imitation of Life.
  Left Bank Jazz Society, The.
  Luxembourg Garden.
  Picnic, an Homage to Civil Rights, The.
Weiss, T.   Dab of Color, A.
Welburn.   Bones and Drums.
Wheatley, P.   On Being Brought from Africa to
  America.
Whitlow.   Poem for the Children.
Williams, C.   For the White Lady Holding Me.
  In Search of Aunt Jemima.
Williams, S.   I Want Aretha to Set This to
  Music.
  Letters from a New England Negro.
  Peacock Poems: 1, The.
  Straight Talk from Plain Women.
  Wishon Line, The.
  You Were Never Miss Brown to Me.
Wordsworth, W.   September 1, 1802.
Worley, D.   Dancing in the Dark.
Wormser.   It's a Party (1959).
Wren, A.   Harmony.
Wright, J.   Albuquerque Graveyard, The.
  Confession to J. Edgar Hoover.
  End of an Ethnic Dream, The.
Wright, R.   Between the World and Me.
  Haiku: "Green cockleburs, The."
  I Have Seen Black Hands.
Young, A.   Dance for Militant Dilettantes, A.
  Poem for Players, A.

African-American Power
Baraka.   Ka 'Ba.
  Last Word, The.

Sacred Chant for the Return of Black Spirit and
  Power.
State/meant.
DuBois, W.   Song of the Smoke, The.
Evans, M.   Vive Noir!
Ferdinand.   2 B BLK.
Giovanni.   My Poem.
Harper, M.   High Modes: Vision as Ritual:
  Confirmation.
  Song: I Want a Witness.
Hoagland, E.   Anti-Semanticist, The.
Hughes, L.   I, Too.
Jackson, R.   Big Chill Variations.
Jeffers, L.   I Do Not Know the Power of My
  Hand.
Knight, E.   Dark Prophecy: I Sing of Shine.
Madhubuti.   Poem to Complement Other
  Poems, A.
Ologboni.   Black Henry.
Reed, I.   Badman of the Guest Professor.
Sanchez, S.   Liberation / Poem.
Tolson, M.   Dark Symphony.

Afterlife
Crane, H.   Circumstance, The.
Deanovich.   American Avalon.
Dickinson, E.   Of nearness to her sundered
  Things.
Faber, F.   After-State.
Fenton, J.   Kingfisher's Boxing Gloves, The.
Herrick.   Plaudite, or End of Life, The.
Hine.   Man's Country.
MacNeice.   This Is the Life.
Merrill, J.   Voices from the Other World.
Oliver, M.   Roses, Late Summer.
Smith, S.   Mrs Simpkins.
Wright, J.   Willy Lyons.

Afternoon
Bevington, L.   Afternoon.
Cofer, J.   Hour of the Siesta, The.
Creeley.   Place, The.
Guggenberger.   Afternoon.
Hinsey, E.   Roman Arbor, The.
Howell, C.   Reminder to the Current
  President, A.
Latouche, J.   Lazy Afternoon.
Levertov.   Sunday Afternoon.
Longfellow, H.   Afternoon in February.
Lowell, A.   September, 1918.
McAuley, J.   One Tuesday in Summer.
Millay, E.   Afternoon on a Hill.
Moross, J.   Lazy Afternoon.
Senghor.   Visit.
Stickney, T.   Quiet after the Rain of Morning.

Afton River, Scotland
Burns, R.   Flow Gently, Sweet Afton.

Aggression
Clare, J.   Turkeys.
Gilbert, S.   Thought from Ruddigore, A.
Griffiths, S.   Just a Product of a Certain
  Situation.
Guiducci.   Perhaps One Day There Will Be
  Ways.
Nash, O.   Tweedledee and Tweedledoom.
Young, A.   Dance for Militant Dilettantes, A.

Agincourt, Battle of (1415)
Unknown.   Agincourt Carol, The.
  Song of the English Bowmen.
Drayton.   Battle of Agincourt, The.

Aging
Anderson, M.   September Song.
Arnold, M.   Growing Old.
Auden.   Doggerel by a Senior Citizen.
Awad, J.   Autumnal.
  First Snow.
Baillie, J.   Song: "What voice is this, thou
  evening gale!"
Barker, J.   To My Young Lover.
Bartlett, E.   Contre Jour.
Beckett, S.   Saint-Lô.
Beer, P.   Jane Austen at the Window.
  Middle Age.
Berry, W.   Ripening.
Betjeman.   Senex.
Blood, B.   Late.
Bly, R.   Dream of Retarded Children, A.

For My Son Noah, Ten Years Old.
Boland, E.   Anna Liffey.
Braithwaite.   Turn Me to My Yellow Leaves.
Brasch.   Ambulando.
Brontë, E.   Love and Friendship.
  Why do I hate that lone green dell?
Brooks, G.   Marie Lucille.
  Sunset of the City, A.
Brown, S.   Feminine Intuition.
Browning, R.   By the Fire-Side.
  Rabbi Ben Ezra.
  Youth and Art.
Burns, R.   John Anderson, My Jo.
Byron, G.   On This Day I Complete My Thirty-sixth Year.
  Stanzas for Music.
Campion, T.   First Love.
Carew, T.   Disdain Returned.
  True Beauty, The.
Carlson, R.   Max Who Caught a Car.
Carruth, H.   Capper Kaplinski at the North Side Cue Club.
  Testament.
  Twilight Comes.
Causley.   Nursery Rhyme of Innocence and Experience.
Cavendish, M.   Woman drest by Age, A.
Christopher.   Palm Reader, The.
Chrystos.   Portrait of Assimilation.
Clarke, A.   Martha Blake at Fifty-one.
Clifton, L.   Climbing.
  Thirty-Eighth Year, The.
Cole, T.   Dial, The.
Coleridge, H.   Long Time a Child.
Coleridge, S.   Old Man's Sigh, The. A Sonnet.
  This Lime-Tree Bower My Prison.
Cooley.   Brother Body.
Corn.   To Hermes.
Cornford, F.   All Souls' Night.
  Childhood.
Cowley, H.   Departed Youth.
Cowper, W.   To Mary.
  To William Hayley, Esq.: In Reply to His Solicitation to Write with Him in a Literary Work.
Cranch.   My Old Palette.
Creeley.   Age.
  Body.
Cunningham, J.   To My Wife.
Davie.   Heigh-ho on a Winter Afternoon.
Davis, O.   Thirty Years Rising.
Disch.   Entropic Villanelle.
d'Oettingen.   To Il y a.
Donne.   Canonization, The.
Donovan, K.   Grooming.
Dransfield.   Portrait of the Artist as an Old Man.
Dudley, E.   Pathologist.
Earle, J.   May Tree, The.
Eberhart, R.   Hardy Perennial.
Elmusa.   Two Angels, The.
Emerson, R.   Awed I Behold Once More.
  Terminus.
"Ephelia."   Maidenhead.
Erdrich, H.   Hopi Prophet Chooses a Pop.
Feinstein, E.   Bathroom.
  Getting Older.
Feinstein, S.   Blues for Zoot.
Field, E.   Little Boy Blue.
Fisher, J.   Gooseflesh.
Flynn, D.   Collector, The.
Forché.   As Children Together.
Frost, R.   To Earthward.
Fusselman, A.   Puffy Jacket.
Gahagan.   Colour of the Old Man's Eyes, The.
Galvin, J.   Two Horses and a Dog.
Galvin, P.   Plaisir d'Amour.
Gay, J.   Toilette, The.
Ginsberg, A.   Charnel Ground, The.
Giovanni.   Life I Led, The.
Glück, L.   For My Mother.
Goodman, M.   Upkeep.
Graves, R.   Change.
Gray, S.   On a Cat Aging.
Greenberg, S.   To Dear Daniel.
Guevara, M.   Hands of the Old Métis, The.
Guthrie, W.   Turkey in the Corn.

Hall, D.   Dusting.
  My Son, My Executioner.
Hardy, T.   Church Romance, A.
  Circus-Rider to Ringmaster.
  Colonel's Soliloquy, The.
  Voice of Things, The.
Hemingway.   Age Demanded, The.
Herbert, G.   Answer, The.
  Mortification.
Herrick.   His Age, Dedicated to His Peculiar Friend, Master John Wickes, under the Name of Posthumus.
  To a Bed of Tulips.
  To a Gentlewoman Objecting to Him His Grey Hairs.
  To His Friend, on the Untunable Times.
  To His Mistress[es].
Hicok.   Alzheimer's.
Hilton, D.   I Try to Turn in My Jock.
Hinsey, E.   Body in Youth, The.
Hollander, J.   Carmen Ancillae.
Housman, A.   Loveliest of Trees, the Cherry Now.
Howe, J.   My Last Dance.
Hughes, L.   Young Gal's Blues.
Hugo, R.   From Altitude, the Diamonds.
  In Your Young Dream.
  Letter to Blessing from Missoula.
  Letter to Libbey from St. Regis.
  Places and Ways to Live.
Ingram-Roberts, A.   Poem 2 (for Duckie Simpson of Black Uhuru).
Jarrell.   Island, The.
  Next Day.
  Player Piano, The.
Jeffers, R.   Age in Prospect.
  But I Am Growing Old and Indolent.
  For Una.
Johnson, J.   Girl of Fifteen.
Jones, L. et al.   Look for You Yesterday, Here You Come Today.
Jones, P.   Modris.
Jones, R.   Song of the Old Man.
Jonson, B.   My Picture Left in Scotland.
  To the World [A Farewell for a Gentlewoman, Virtuous and Noble].
Joseph, J.   Warning.
Joyce, J.   Bahnhofstrasse.
Justice, D.   Men at Forty.
Kantaris.   Stocking Up.
Kaufman, S.   Next Year, in Jerusalem.
Keats.   In Drear-nighted December.
Kennedy, X.   In a Prominent Bar in Secaucus [One Day].
Kenyon, J.   Finding a Long Gray Hair.
Kinsella, T.   Oldest Place, The.
Knoepfle.   Dark Spaces: Thoughts on All Souls Day.
Kowit.   Cosmetics Do No Good.
Lamb, C.   Gipsy's Malison, The.
  Old Familiar Faces, The.
Larkin, J.   My Body.
Larkin, P.   Age.
  Dockery and Son.
  Love Songs in Age.
  Nothing to Be Said.
  Old Fools, The.
Lem.   Temple City Blvd. and Ellis Ln.
Levertov.   What Wild Dawns There Were.
  Woman Alone, A.
Levine, P.   28.
  Red Dust.
Lieberman, M.   Regret.
Linton.   Epicurean.
Lisick, B.   Empress of Sighs.
Lockhart.   Lines: "When youthful faith hath fled."
Loftin.   Weeksville Women.
Longley, M.   Ash Keys.
Lowell, A.   New Heavens for Old.
Lowell, R.   For Sheridan.
Loy.   Jules Pascin.
Lum.   Riding the North Point Ferry.
Lux.   Little Tooth, A.
Lyman Jr., D. B.   Eternal Controversy, The.
MacLeish.   Old Men in the Leaf Smoke, The.

Madonick, M.   Settled In.
Mallet.   On an Amorous Old Man.
Mandell, A.   Middle Age.
Marshall, J.   Still.
Marvell.   To His Coy Mistress.
Marzán.   Emergency.
Mayakovsky [or Maiakovskii].   Mayakovsky's Suicide Note.
McClatchy.   My Mammogram.
Meredith, W.   His Plans for Old Age.
Merrill, J.   Kimono, The.
  Mirror.
Merwin, W. S.   Another Year Come.
Meynell, A.   Letter from a Girl to Her Own Old Age, A.
Miles, J.   Album.
Millar, J.   Midlife.
Millay, E.   Grown-up.
  Sonnet: "What lips my lips have kissed, and where, and why."
Moody, E.   To a Friend, Who Gave the Author a Reading Glass.
Moore, H.   Girl in a Fur-Trimmed Dress.
Morgan, E.   Second Life, The.
Mueller, L.   Curriculum Vitae.
Muir, E.   Late Wasp, The.
  Myth, The.
Murray, J.   And As I Came Out from the Temples.
Ndebele.   Revolution of the Aged, The.
Nemerov.   Boy with Book of Knowledge.
  Thirtieth Anniversary Report of the Class of '41.
Noguchi, R.   His Waves.
O'Grady, D.   Purpose.
O'Grady, J.   Buster's Last Hand.
Oliveira, D.   Paso Robles, San Luis Obispo, San Luis Obispo.
Ormsby, E.   My Mother in Old Age.
Owen, W.   Sonnet, to a Child.
Paley, G.   Sad Children's Song, The.
Parker, D.   Ballade at Thirty-Five.
Patchen.   Street Corner College.
Peters, L.   One Long Jump.
Petrie.   Old Pro's Lament, The.
Phillips, C.   In the blood, Winnowing.
Plath.   Mirror.
Poe.   Eldorado.
  Happiest Day, the Happiest Hour, The.
Pope, A.   To Mrs. M. B. on Her Birth-Day.
Porter, P.   On This Day I Complete My Fortieth Year.
  What I Have Written I Have Written.
Pound, E.   Beautiful Toilet, The.
  Return, The.
  Tea Shop, The.
Preston, R.   Mama.
Ralegh, S.   Nymph's [or Nimphs] Reply to the Shepherd [or Sheepheard], The.
Randall, D.   Haymakers.
Randall, J.   Rockland.
Rankin, J.   Sea-bundle.
Ransom, J.   Blue Girls.
Reed, H.   Chard Whitlow.
Reed, I.   Turning Pro.
Reid, C.   Howl, Howl.
Rexroth, K.   Fifty.
  Only Years.
Reynolds, R.   Peridot.
Rich, A.   Middle-Aged, The.
  Necessities of Life.
  Upper Broadway.
Roberson.   True We Are Two Grown Men.
Robinson, E.   Isaac and Archibald.
  Veteran Sirens.
Rochester, J.   Disabled Debauchee, The.
Romo-Carmona, M.   Signs.
Rosenblatt, S.   Mom and Dad Getting Older.
  Second Half of Our Lives, The.
Rowse.   White Cat of Trenarren, The.
Salinas, L.   Middle Age.
  My Fifty-Plus Years Celebrate Spring.
Sanchez, S.   July.
  Personal Letter No. 3.
Sanders, E.   Cutting Prow, The.
Saxe, J.   Story of Life, The.

Schilpp, M. Non Sequitur.
Schoenberger. Epithalamion.
Schwartz, R. L. Falling in Love after Forty.
  Midnight Supper.
Scott, W. Garland for Advancing Years, A.
Scovell. Ghosts, The.
  Listening to Collared Doves.
Shapcott, T. Blue Paisley Shirt, The.
  Turning Fifty.
Shenstone. Elegy 11: "Ah me, my friend! it will
  not, will not last!"
Sisson. In Autumn.
  Tristia.
Smith, C. Thirty-eight: Addressed to Mrs H—y.
Smith, K. Writing in Prison.
Smith, M. City.
Smith, S. Pad, Pad.
Southey, R. Old Man's Comforts and How He
  Gained Them, The.
  Remembrance.
Soyinka. To My First White Hairs.
Speakes. Mama Loves Janis Joplin.
Spender, S. What I Expected.
St. John, D. My Friend.
Stephens, P. Hangman.
Stevenson, A. Willow Song.
Stevenson, R. Over the Sea to Skye.
Strickland, A. Forsaken, The.
Sullivan, B. Hair.
Swenson, M. How to Be Old.
Swift, J. Stella's Birthday, 1725.
  Stella's Birthday; Written in the Year 1718[/9].
  Stella's Birthday [1721].
Tallmountain. Hands of Mary Joe, The.
Tate, A. Last Days of Alice.
Taylor, B. Love Returned.
Tennyson, A. June Bracken and Heather.
Thomas, E. Gone, Gone Again.
Thomas, R. Geriatric.
  Pavane.
Tomlinson, C. On the Hall at Stowey.
Toomer. Delivered at the Knighting of Lord
  Durgling by Great Bruce-Jean.
Trinidad. Answer Song.
Tripp. On My Fortieth Birthday.
Troupe. Reflections on Growing Older.
Unknown. Will You Love Me When I'm Old?
Van Duyn. Stream, The.
Very. Autumn Flowers.
Volkman. Theft.
Walcott. Codicil.
Waniek. Sleepless Nights.
Warren, R. Acquaintance with Time in Early
  Autumn.
  Vermont Ballad: Change of Season.
Warton, T. Sonnet: To the River Lodon.
Weill, K. September Song.
Whitman, R. Laughing Gas.
Whittemore, R. Walk Home, The.
Whittier. To My Old Schoolmaster.
Wilcox, E. Friendship After Love.
  Life.
Williams, C. Alzheimer's: The Wife.
Williams, W. Descent, The.
  To a Man Dying on His Feet.
Wiman, C. Hearing Loss.
Wright, C. Hawaii Dantesca.
Wright, J. Brother and Sisters.
  Old Age Compensation.
  Sonnet for Christmas.
Yeats. Coming of Wisdom with Time, The.
  Crazy Jane Grown Old Looks at the Dancers.
  Crazy Jane Talks with the Bishop.
  Folly of Being Comforted, The.
  Lamentation of the Old Pensioner, The.
  Men Improve with the Years.
  New Faces, The.
  Wild Swans at Coole, The.
  Youth and Age.
See also **Middle Age; Old Age**

Agnosticism and Agnostics
Burris. On Living with a Fat Woman in
  Heaven.
Ginsberg, L. Biography of an Agnostic.
Hardy, T. Impercipient, The.
Joseph, L. It's Not Me Shouting at No One.

See also **Doubt**

Agoraphobia
Wayman. Another Poem about the Madness of
  Women.

Agriculture
Roscoe, W. To the Harvest Moon.
See also **Farming and Farmers**

AIDS
Addonizio. Conversation in Woodside.
Akiwumi, V. Different Ones #6—Future
  Possibilities (An Aids Soliloquy).
Alarcon, F. Blues del SIDA / AIDS Blues.
Ameen. Monologue of a Dying Beast.
  Sonnet No. 21.
Campo. Allegory.
  Her Final Show.
  Towards Curing AIDS.
Chin, J. Undetectable.
Conway, J. Marlo Thomas in Seven Parts and
  Epilogue.
  Weight Belt.
Corn. Long-Distance Call to Gregg, Who Lived
  with AIDS as Long as He Could.
Dixon, M. Heartbeats.
Doty, M. Tiara.
Drake, N. Very Rich Hours, The.
Gates, B. Cathy.
  Homeless.
  Ron.
  Triptych.
Gunn, T. In the Post Office.
  J Car, The.
  Lament: "Your dying was a difficult enterprise."
  Man With Night Sweats, The.
  Missing, The.
  Reassurance, The.
  Terminal.
Hacker, M. Dusk: July.
Hamer. Different Strokes Bar, San Francisco,
  The.
Healy, E. Louganis.
Hemphill. Better Days.
Holland, W. Journal of the Plague Years, A.
Larkin, J. Inventory.
Lassell. How to Watch Your Brother Die.
  Kissing Ramén.
  Sunset Stripping: Visiting L.A.
  Three Poems.
Liu, T. Thoreau.
Moore, H. Edward.
  Memoir.
Neely, L. Multiple Assaults.
Reynolds, C. Worst of it, The.
Schreiber, R. Alarming New Development, An.
Schwartz, R. L. AIDS Education, Seventh
  Grade.
  Grief.
Stein, K. It Didn't Begin with Horned Owls
  Hooting at Noon.
Vando. Blanca's Red Lips.
Waniek. Sacrament of Poverty, The.
Wiese, B. Everyone Who Wants to Work Can.
Williams, M. Thinking about Bill, Dead of
  AIDS.
Woods, D. Prescription.
Wunderlich, M. Given in Person Only.

Air
Ashbery. Melodic Trains.
Atwood. Variation on the Word *Sleep*.
Benedikt. Some Feelings.
Duncan, R. Eyesight II.
Ekelof. If You Ask Me.
"Field." Nightfall.
Gardelle, C. Air.
  Rain.
Guest, B. Roses.
Hardy, T. Garden Seat, The.
Hays, H. January.
  Manhattan.
Hopkins, G. Blessed Virgin Compared to the
  Air We Breathe, The.
Jackson, H. Distance.
Kgositsile. Air I Hear, The.
Kleinzahler. Poetics.
Kuroda. Afternoon 3.
Levin, P. Citizens and Sky.

Maiden. Air.
Mörling, M. For F. M. Who Did Not Get Killed
  Yesterday on 57th Street.
Peters, L. Parachute Men.
Raine, K. Air.
Robinson, E. For Karen.
Sanchez, S. Haiku: "Was it yesterday."
Strand. Marriage, The.
Taylor, A. Air.
Wright, J. Breath of Air, A.

Air Plants
Crane, H. Air Plant, The.

Air Travel
Alexopoulos. Night Flight.
Birney. Twenty-third Flight.
Cahn, S. Come Fly with Me.
Cardiff. It has something to do with final words.
Davis, J. Day Flight.
Dove, R. Vacation.
Grant, J. Planes Landing.
Harjo, J. White Bear.
Kooser. Flying at Night.
Larkin, P. Naturally the Foundation Will Bear
  Your Expenses.
McHugh, H. 20-200 on 737.
Swenson, M. Flying Home from Utah.
Van Heusen, J. Come Fly with Me.
Winters, Y. At the San Francisco Airport.
See also **Airports**

Air Warfare
Bayliss. Reported Missing.
Bowers, E. Stoic: for Laura von Courten, The.
Brinnin. Ascension: 1925, The.
Dickey, J. Firebombing, The.
Eberhart, R. Dam Neck, Virginia.
  Fury of Aerial Bombardment, The.
Everson, W. Raid, The.
Ewart. When a Beau Goes In.
Field, E. World War II.
Fuller, R. During a Bombardment by
  V-Weapons.
Hall, D. Airstrip in Essex, 1960, An.
Jarrell. Dead Wingman, The.
  Death of the Ball Turret Gunner, The.
  Eighth Air Force.
  Front, A.
  Gunner.
  Losses.
  Pilot from the Carrier, A.
  Pilots, Man Your Planes.
  Range in the Desert, The.
  Second Air Force.
Lawrence, D. Bombardment.
Lowell, R. Dead in Europe, The.
MacGreevy [or McGreevy]. De Civitate
  Hominum.
MacNeice. Brother Fire.
Nemerov. IFF.
  Models.
  Night Operations, Coastal Command RAF.
  War in the Air, The.
Rodgers, W. Raider, The.
Sitwell, D. Still Falls the Rain.
Spender, S. Air Raid Across the Bay at
  Plymouth.
  Thoughts During an Air Raid.
Stephens, M. Hooters.
Tate, J. Lost Pilot, The.
Thomas, D. Ceremony after a Fire Raid.
  Refusal to Mourn the Death, by Fire, of a Child
  in London, A.
Unknown. Little Friend.
  Pilot's Psalm, The.
Webb, F. Gunner.
Yeats. Irish Airman Foresees His Death, An.
  Reprisals.

Airline Stewardesses
Dickey, J. Falling.

Airplane Crashes
Bang, M. Crossed-Over, Fiend-Snitched, X-ed
  Out.
Ewart. When a Beau Goes In.
Herd. Survivors, The.
Jarrell. Front, A.
  Pilot from the Carrier, A.

Long, J.   Bermuda Triangle.
Music's Wife.
Rukeyser, M.   Ceiling Unlimited.
Schwartz, R. L.   When They Know.
Stainer.   Bleaklow.

Airplanes
Bawer.   View from an Airplane at Night, over California, The.
Chamberlain, K.   Airlift.
Clarke, G.   No Hands.
Dauer.   Falling.
Deanovich.   Zombie Jet.
Duran, J.   Mere Pleasure of Flying, The.
Graham, J.   What the End Is For.
Hall, D.   Old Pilot, The.
Hamod, S.   Libyan/Egyptian Acrobats/Israeli Air Circus.
Hazo.   Toys, The.
Heyen.   For Hermann Heyen.
McDonald, W.   Retired Pilot to Himself, The.
Meredith, C.   Jets.
O'Donoghue, B.   Apparition, The.
Rankine.   New Windows.
Rawson, J.   Border, The.
Revard.   Dragon-Watching in St. Louis.
Reverdy.   Adieu.
Sandburg, C.   Bas-Relief.
Thomas, R.   Navigation.
Tranter.   Lufthansa.
Unknown.   Heavenly Aeroplane, The.
Pilot's Psalm, The.
Twats in the Ops Room.
Waniek.   Porter.
Weigl.   Sailing to Bien Hoa.
Williams, C.   Jet Planes.
Williamson, G.   Up in the Air.
Young, K.   Central Standard Time.
See also **Aviation and Aviators**

Airports
Hobson, G.   Buffalo Poem #1.
Ignatow, D.   Night at an Airport.
Mead, J.   La Guardia, the Story.
Richie, E.   Airports of the World.
Winters, Y.   At the San Francisco Airport.
See also **Air Travel**

Ajanta, India
Rukeyser, M.   Ajanta.

Akhmatova, Anna
Balaban.   Anna Akhmatova Spends the Night on Miami Beach.
Cheney-Coker.   Letter to a Tormented Playwright.
Chimombo.   Messengers, The.
Mooney, M.   Anna Akhmatova's Funeral.
Nortje.   Asseverations.

Alabama (state)
Berlin.   When the Midnight Choo-Choo Leaves for Alabam'
Brecht, B.   Alabama Song.
Parish.   Stars Fell on Alabama.

Alaska
Corn.   Walrus Tusk from Alaska, A.
Fordham.   Alaska.
Haines, J.   Train Stops at Healy Fork, The.
Harjo, J.   Anchorage.
Rose.   Alaskan Fragments June 1981—Summer Solstice.

Albatrosses
Coleridge, S.   Rime of the Ancient Mariner, The.
Ewart.   Lines: "Other day I was loving a sweet little fruitpie-and-cream, The."
Masefield.   Sea Change.

Albinos
Belieu.   Legend of the Albino Farm.

Alchemy and Alchemists
Bogan, L.   Alchemist, The.
Browning, R.   Song: "Heap cassia, sandal-buds and stripes."
Thus the Mayne Glideth.
Wanderers, The.
Chubb, T.   Merlin.
Donne.   Love's Alchemy [*or* Alchemie].
Jonson, B.   To Alchemists.
Simic.   Lives of Alchemists, The.

Poem without a Title.
Alcoholism and Alcoholics
Anderson, D.   Itinerary.
Anstett.   Shift.
Berryman.   4th Weekend.
5th Tuesday.
Alcoholic in the 3rd Week of the 3rd Treatment, The.
Dry Eleven Months.
Group.
Phase Four.
Bradford, E.   His Mother Drinks.
Cavin.   Christmas with the Holy Family.
Coulehan, J.   I'm Gonna Slap Those Doctors.
Cunningham, J.   Interview with Doctor Drink.
Cuthand, B.   She Ties Her Bandanna.
Ewart.   Sonnet: The Last Things.
Hass, R.   Bookbuying in the Tenderloin.
Haug.   Tennessee Waltz, The.
Heaney, S.   Casualty.
Hirsch, E.   Two Suffering Men.
Hollander, F.   Boys in the Backroom, The.
Hugo, R.   Letter to Logan from Milltown.
Larkin, J.   Clifton.
Good-Bye.
Loesser.   Boys in the Backroom, The.
Louis, A.   Something About Being an Indian.
MacIntyre, T.   Yellow Bittern, The.
McGraw, E.   Drunk Dog.
Nash, O.   Reflections on Ice-breaking.
Which the Chicken, Which the Egg?
Notley.   Jack Would Speak Through the Imperfect Medium of Alice.
Olinka, S.   Bird of Death.
Papertalk-Green, C.   Pension Day.
Parker, A.   Another Poem about the Vandals.
Peirce.   Alcoholic's Son at Ten, The.
Near Burning.
Roberts, L.   Assignment, The.
Roethke.   My Papa's Waltz.
Stone, J.   Confabulation.
Townsend, A.   Mardi Gras Premortem.
Trethewey, N.   Photograph of a Bawd Drinking Raleigh Rye.
Troupe.   River Town Packin House Blues.
Walker, F. X.   Crooked Afro.
Wetzsteon.   Drinks in the Town Square.
Wright, J.   Metho Drinker.
See also **Drunkards**

Ale
Unknown.   Bring Us In Good Ale.

Aleichem, Sholom
Lieberman, E.   Sholom Aleichem.

Alexander the Great, King of Macedon
Dryden, J.   Alexander's Feast; or, The Power of Music [*or* Musique].
Dugan, A.   How We Heard the Name.
Flecker.   Santorin.
Killigrew, A.   Alexandreis.
Moore, R.   Ripeness Is Rapid.
Rukeyser, M.   Speaking Tree, The.

Alexander, Sir William
James I, King of England.   Sonnet on Sir William Alexander's Harsh Verses after the English Fashion, A.

Alfonso X, King of Castile and León
Emerson, R.   Alphonso of Castile.

Ali, Muhammad
Alexander, E.   Narrative: Ali.

Alice in Wonderland
Tate, A.   Last Days of Alice.

Alienation
Allen, P.   Kopis'taya.
Anderson, L.   Dog Show.
Arnold, M.   Buried Life, The.
Baraka.   Invention of Comics, The.
Barben, D.   Eight Beds, Eight Lockers.
Berryman.   Traveller, The.
Bly, R.   Snowbanks North of the House.
Bruner.   On City Streets.
Christopher.   Far from Home.
Clare, J.   I Am.
Clarke, G.   Baby-Sitting.
Creeley.   Form of Women, A.
Moon, The.

Croft, J.   D-Zug.
Diop, D.   Renegade, The.
Duncan, R.   Passage Over Water.
Eliot, T.   Gerontion.
Journey of the Magi.
Love Song of J. Alfred Prufrock, The.
Portrait of a Lady.
Ellis, T.   T.A.P.O.A.F.O.M.
Emerson, R.   Blight.
Intellect.
Fearing.   Dirge: "1-2-3 was the number he played but today the number came 3-2-1."
Forbes, C.   Blue Monday.
Frost, R.   In Neglect.
Glück, R.   Invaders from Mars.
Hall, D.   Exile.
Harry, J.   Honesty-Stones.
Hayden, R.   Soledad.
Heaney, S.   Guttural Muse, The.
Hernton.   Poem.
Hongo.   Legend, The.
Housman, A.   Laws of God, the Laws of Man, The.
Howell, C.   Liberty and Ten Years of Return.
Livingston, M.   Poor.
Lovecraft.   Alienation.
Lowell, J.   Street, The.
Madhubuti.   Back Again, Home.
Empty Warriors.
"Marnia."   I Must be Able to Protect You.
McDonald, R.   Incident in Transylvania.
McKay, C.   Outcast.
Merwin, W. S.   Fields, The.
Nelson, M.   Wish Fulfillment.
Oppen.   Resort.
Paulin.   Ulster Unionist Walks the Streets of London, An.
Piñero.   This Is Not the Place Where I was Born.
Pinsky.   Poem about People.
Pound, E.   In a Station of the Metro.
Raffalovich, M. A.   Sonnet 120.
World Well Lost 4, The.
Reed, I.   Dualism.
Rich, A.   After Dark.
Stranger, The.
Robinson, E.   Mr Flood's Party.
Rodgers, W.   Winter's Cold.
Rodriguez, L.   We Never Stopped Crossing Borders.
Rukeyser, M.   Effort at Speech between Two People.
Samaras, N.   Farasa.
Schnackenberg.   Paperweight, The.
Seferis.   Word for Summer, A.
Senghor.   To New York.
Shapiro, K.   My Grandmother.
Travelogue for Exiles.
Sharp, S.   Tribal Marks.
Solomon, M.   Comment on My Host, A.
Stanton, M.   Space.
Tomlinson, C.   Mr. Brodsky.
Tranter.   Great Artist Reconsiders the Homeric Simile, The.
Warren, R.   To a Face in a Crowd.
Warsh.   Enmeshment.
Wordsworth, W.   World Is Too Much With Us, The.
Wright, C.   Stone Canyon Nocturne.

Aliens
Conoley.   World, The.
Kinsella, J.   Visitant Eclogue.
Morgan, E.   First Men on Mercury, The.
Nuriddin, J. M.   Children of the Future.
Pugh.   'Do you think we'll ever get to see Earth, sir?'
Raine, C.   Martian Sends a Postcard Home, A.
Violi.   Harold and Imogene.

All Souls' Day
Atkins.   Lisbon.
Bidgood.   All Souls'
Knoepfle.   Dark Spaces: Thoughts on All Souls Day.

All Souls' Night
Cornford, F.   All Souls' Night.
Glück, L.   All Hallows.

Allen, Richard
  Heard, J. Rt. Rev. Richard Allen.
Alligators
  Bly, R. Day We Visited New Orleans, The.
  Hall, D. Alligator Bride, The.
  Nash, O. Purist, The.
  Ravenel. Alligator, The.
See also **Crocodiles**
Almanacs
  Bishop, E. Sestina: "September rain falls on the house."
  Wright, J. Benjamin Banneker Sends His *Almanac* to Thomas Jefferson.
Almond Trees and Almonds
  Herrick. Upon Sibilla.
  Lawrence, D. Bare Almond-Trees.
Alphabet
  Caesar. Animal Crackers in My Soup.
  Dodge, M. Letters at School, The.
  Peacock, M. Spell, The.
  Shapiro, K. Alphabet, The.
Alphabet Poems
  Disch. Abecedary.
    Zewhyexary.
  Humphries, B. Edna's Alphabet.
  Lear, E. Twenty-Six Nonsense Rhymes.
  Nemerov. Primer of the Daily Round, A.
  Watts. Austrian Army, An.
Alphonsus Rodriguez, Saint
  Hopkins, G. In Honour of St. Alphonsus Rodriguez.
Alps
  Bunting. On the Fly-Leaf of Pound's Cantos.
  Byron, G. Manfred.
  Coleridge, S. Hymn before Sunrise, in the Vale of Chamouni.
  MacGreevy [*or* McGreevy]. Nocturne of the Self-evident Presence.
  Meynell, A. Watershed, The.
  Radcliffe, A. Storied Sonnet.
Alsace, France
  Wilbur. First Snow in Alsace.
Altars
  Chin. Altar.
  Herbert, G. Altar, The.
  Taylor, B. Goblet, The.
Altgeld, John Peter
  Lindsay, N. Bryan, Bryan, Bryan, Bryan.
    Eagle That Is Forgotten, The.
Alumni
  Eberhart, R. I Went to See Irving Babbitt.
  Nemerov. Thirtieth Anniversary Report of the Class of '41.
  Wilson, E. Disloyal Lines to an Alumnus.
Amaryllis (mythology)
  Campion, T. I Care Not for These Ladies.
Amazons
  Coleridge, M. White Women, The.
  Killigrew, A. Alexandreis.
Ambition
  Berger, B. Ambition.
  Bottrall. Icarus.
  Brydges. To Miss M———, Written by Moonlight, July 18, 1782.
  Cary, A. West Country, The.
  Clampitt. Cormorant in His Element, The.
  Clifton, L. Climbing.
  Cornish, S. Generations 2.
  Davies, W. Ambition.
  Gladding. Fisherman's Wife, The.
  Herrick. Ambition.
  Horton, G. George Moses Horton, Myself.
  Johnson, M. Ambition.
  Johnson, S. Scholar's Life, The.
    Vanity of Human Wishes, The; The Tenth Satire of Juvenal Imitated.
  Longfellow, H. Mezzo Cammin.
  Mitchell, K. Monster, The.
  Pietri. Title of This Poem Was Lost, The.
  Ray, H. Ambition.
  Waniek. Sleepless Nights.
Ambulances
  Fanthorpe. Resuscitation Team.
  Larkin, P. Ambulances.

Moore, L. Tanka.
America
  Ai. More.
  Alexie. Vision (2).
  Allen, P. Zen Americana.
  Appleman, P. Peace with Honor.
  Ashbery. One Thing That Can Save America, The.
    Pyrography.
  Awoonor. America.
    American Memory of Africa, An.
    On Having Been an Experimental Sacred Cow for Four Years, and a Token African on Faculty.
  Baca. How We Carry Ourselves.
  Balaban. After Our War.
    Dead for Two Years, Erhart Arranges to Meet Me in a Dream.
    In Celebration of Spring.
  Baraka. Each Morning.
    Hymn for Lanie Poo.
    Nation Is Like Ouselves, The.
    Three Modes of History and Culture.
  Bates, K. America the Beautiful.
  Benét, S. American Names.
    Ballad of William Sycamore, The.
    Daniel Boone.
  Berrigan, D. My Name.
  Blake, W. Desire and Jealousy.
    Visions of the Daughters of Albion.
  Bly, R. After the Industrial Revolution, All Things Happen at Once.
  Brathwaite, E. Colombe.
  Brock, V. Sphinx.
  Bromige. Eastward Ho! A Succession.
  Brown, M. Survival Motion: Notice.
  Bryant, W. Not Yet.
  Bursk. Lies.
  Campo. Battle Hymn of the Republic, The.
  Cary, A. West Country, The.
  Cheney-Coker. Analysis.
  Chin. How I Got That Name.
    We Are Americans Now, We Live in the Tundra.
  Clark, T. Going to School in France or America.
  Clover, J. Ceriserie.
  Cohan. You're a Grand Old Flag.
  Cook, E. Sot-Weed Factor, The.
  Costanzo. Everything You Own.
    Jeane Dixon's America.
  Creeley. America.
  Cross, F. When Chicken Man Came Home to Roost.
  Cummings, E. I Sing of Olaf Glad and Big.
    Next to of Course God America I.
  Davidson, M. Sensation Type and His Friends, The.
  Davis, L. Mown Lawn, A.
  Djanikian. In the Elementary School Choir.
    When I First Saw Snow.
  Dorn, E. Home on the Range, February 1962.
  Drake, J. To a Friend.
  Dumas, H. America.
    Zebra Goes Wild Where the Sidewalk Ends, The.
  Ehrhart. Invasion of Grenada, The.
    Relative Thing, A.
  Ferlinghetti, L. Starting from San Francisco.
  Finnell. Over *Voice of America*.
  Floyd. Corporal Kevin Spina, U. S. M. C.
  Follen, E. For the Fourth of July.
  Freneau. On the Emigration to America [and Peopling the Western Country].
  Frost, R. America Is Hard to See.
    Gift Outright, The.
  Gibbons, R. American Trains.
  Gilmore, B. Bow to Allah.
  Ginsberg, A. America.
    Bayonne Turnpike to Tuscarora.
    Crossing Nation.
  Grenier. Wrath to Sadness.
  Hagedorn, J. Filipino Boogie.
  Harms. Tomorrow, We'll Dance in America.
  Harper, M. American History.
  Hasford. Bedtime Story.

Hayden, R. [American Journal].
Hazo. Some Words for President Wilson.
Healy, E. From Los Angeles Looking South.
Hernández Cruz. Areyto.
  It's Miller Time.
Herrera. Cherry Bowl with Blue Revolver: Neo-American Landscape.
  Poetry of America, The.
  When He Believed Himself to Be a Young Girl Lifting the Skin of the Water.
Hirsch, E. Edward Hopper and the House by the Railroad.
Howe, J. Battle Hymn [*or* Battle-Hymn] of the Republic, The.
Howe, S. Thorow.
Howell, C. Liberty and Ten Years of Return.
Hughes, L. I, Too.
  Let America Be America Again.
Hugo, R. What Thou Lovest Well Remains American.
Huidobro. Cow Boy.
Jeffers, L. My Blackness Is the Beauty of This Land.
Jeffers, R. Shine, Perishing Republic.
Johnson, E. Joe.
Johnson, J. To America.
Kaufman, B. Heavy Water Blues.
Key. Star-Spangled Banner, The.
Kizer, C. Ashes, The.
Kumin, M. Height of the Season, The.
Larkin, P. Faith Healing.
Laughlin, J. Kind-, The.
Lauterbach. Novelist Speaks, The.
Lawrence, D. Evening Land, The.
Lazarus, E. 1492.
  How Long?
Levertov. Fragrance of Life, Odor of Death.
  In Thai Binh (Peace) Province.
  Weeping Woman.
Lim, S. Learning to Love America.
Lincoln, A. Gettysburg Address, The.
Lindsay, N. Bryan, Bryan, Bryan, Bryan.
Long, R. Conspiracy, The.
Lum. Chinese Hot Pot.
Mabuza. Tired Lizi Tired.
MacLeish. Empire Builders.
McClure, M. Reading Frank O'Hara in a Mexican Rainstorm.
McKay, C. America.
Meinke. Supermarket.
Melville, H. America.
Miller, J. American Odalisque.
  Sierras.
Mitchell, A. From Rich Uneasy America to My Friend Christopher Logue.
Moise *et al.* To Persecuted Foreigners.
Moore, M. Love in America.
Morales, A. Immigrants.
Mueller, L. American Literature.
  Highway Poems.
Myles, E. American Poem, An.
Nemerov. Boy with Book of Knowledge.
O'Grady, D. Great Horse Fair, The.
O'Hara, F. Ave Maria.
  You at the Pump.
Ologboni. Changed Mind (or the Day I Woke Up).
Olson, C. Across Space and Time.
Opoku-Agyemang. King Tut in America.
Orfalea, G. Age of Cruelty, The.
Ortiz. Travels in the South.
  War Poem.
Padgett, R. Early Triangles.
Parkerson. Statistic.
Piatt, J. Farther.
  To the Statue on the Capitol.
Piercy. Peaceable Kingdom, The.
Pierman. Apparition, The.
Pietri. Intermission from Wednesday.
Prunty. To be Sung on the Fourth of July.
Randall, D. Melting Pot, The.
Ras. In the New Country.
Roethke. Night Journey.
Romano, R. But My Blood.
Rukeyser, M. Blood is Justified, The.
  Book of the Dead, The.

Saint. Triple Trouble.
Sallah, T. Television as God.
Sanchez, S. Poem for July 4, 1994.
  Right On: White America.
Sandburg, C. Threes.
Schulman. American Solitude.
Scott-Heron. Winter in America.
Seay. Johnny B. Goode.
Sexton. Sixth Psalm.
Shapiro, H. National Cold Storage Company.
Shapiro, K. Manhole Covers.
Shelley, P. Tribute to America.
Simpson, L. To the Western World.
  Walt Whitman at Bear Mountain.
Smith, S. America.
Snyder, G. I Went Into the Maverick Bar.
  What Happened Here Before.
Spicer, J. Book of Galahad, The.
St. John, P. We Are Going to Be Here Now.
Stein, K. Because You're American.
Steptoe. Such a Boat of Land.
Sternlieb. Right of Way.
Stevenson, R. Ticonderoga: A Legend of the
  West Highlands.
Su, A. Address.
Thorne, T. Whatever Happened to Conway
  Twitty?
Tomlinson, C. Word in Edgeways, A.
Toomer. It is Everywhere.
Turki, F. Being a Good *Americani*.
Very. Slavery.
Walcott. Glory Trumpeter, The.
  Gulf, The.
  Upstate.
Wayman. Despair.
Weaver, M. My Father's Geography.
Weiners. Poem for Painters, A.
Welburn. Bones and Drums.
Wheatley, P. America.
Whitman, W. By Blue Ontario's Shore.
  For You O Democracy.
  Full of Life Now.
  Heroes.
  Hub of the Universe, The.
  I Hear America Singing.
  Orange Buds by Mail from Florida.
  Poet, The.
  Prairie-Grass Dividing, The.
  Respondez!
  Song of Myself.
  Swiftly Arose.
  To the East and to the West.
  Would You Hear of an Old-Time [*or* Old-
  Fashioned] Sea fight?
  Wound-Dresser, The.
  Years of the Modern.
  Yonnondio.
Williams, W. To Elsie.
Willis, N. To Charles Roux, of Switzerland.
Woolson. Detroit River.
Wright, J. American Twilights, 1957.
  Stages on a Journey Westward.
Yuson. Dead Center.
Zimmer. Eisenhower Years, The.
See also **United States**

American Indians
Alexie. November 22, 1983.
Chrystos. Soap Bubbles.
Grieves, C. Indian Car.
Romero, L. Marilyn Monroe Indian.
Smelcer. My Indian Grandmother Speaks to
  Animals.
See also **Native Americans**

American Revolution
Bly, R. Poem Against the British.
Davidson, M. Landing of Rochambeau, The.
Emerson, R. Concord Hymn.
Freneau. To the Memory of the Brave
  Americans.
Hassett. Christmas.
Hopkinson, F. Battle of the Kegs, The.
Hunt, L. Iterating Sonnet.
Kandel. Spring 61.
Richards, L. Molly Pitcher.
Seward. Verses Inviting Stella to Tea on the
  Public Fast-Day.

Shuckburg *et al.* Yankee Doodle.
Sigourney. God Save the Plough.
Unknown. Boston in Distress.
  Farewell to Kingsbridge.
  Little Britain.
Wesley, C. On Sympathisers with the American
  Revolution.
Whitman, W. Centenarian's Story, The.
Young, S. Epitaph for a Concord Boy.

Americans
Allston. America to Great Britain.
Auden. On the Circuit.
Charara, H. Thinking American.
Chesterton, G. Ballad of Abbreviations, A.
Chin. Composed Near the Bay Bridge (after a
  wild party).
Chrystos. Okeydoekey Tribe, The.
Ferlinghetti, L. Baseball Canto.
Frost, R. Gift Outright, The.
Hughes, L. Madam's Calling Cards.
Hugo, R. What Thou Lovest Well Remains
  American.
Jeffers, R. Ave Caesar.
Knight, E. Idea of Ancestry, The.
Koch, K. You Were Wearing.
Lawrence, D. English Are So Nice!, The.
Pound, E. Soirée.
Rose, R. What the Japanese Perhaps Heard.
  What We Heard About the Japanese.
Simic. Crepuscule with Nellie.
Simpson, L. Inner Part, The.
  Runner, The.
Smith, W. American Primitive.
Very. Indian's Retort, The.
Whitman, W. For You O Democracy.
  I Hear America Singing.
  Prairie-Grass Dividing, The.
Williams, W. Question and Answer.

Amish, The
Becker, R. Why We Fear the Amish.
Dubie. Peace of Lodi, The.
Kasdorf. Dying with Amish Uncles.
  Green Market, New York.
  Grossdaadi's Funeral.
Owen, J. Visitation, The.
Updike. Amish, The.

Amnesia
Sansom, A. World is everything, The.
Weigl. Amnesia.

Amon Ra
Reed, I. I Am a Cowboy in the Boat of Ra.

Amputees
Coleman, H. Black Soldier Remembers, A.
Coulehan, J. D-Day, 1994.
Crawford, R. Downtown Sunday.
Hood, T. Faithless Nelly Gray.
MacDiarmid, H. In the Children's Hospital.
Ormond. Lament for a Leg.
Owen, W. Disabled.
Sassoon. Does It Matter?
Shapiro, K. Leg, The.
Williams, L. Interruption of Flight.

Amsterdam, Netherlands
Garlick, R. Capitals.
Garrigue. Amsterdam Letter.

Amusement Parks
Allbery. Carnies.
Berlin, E. Sea World.
Brouwer, J. Steve's Commando Paintball, San
  Adriano, California.
Cooley, N. Diane Arbus, New York.
Foerster. Playland.

Anarchism and Anarchists
Pietri. 10th Untitled Poem.
Shelley, P. Mask [*or* Masque] of Anarchy, The.
Woodcock. Paper Anarchist Addresses the
  Shade of Nancy Ling Perry.

Ancestry and Ancestors
Acholonu. Going Home.
Baker, H. Toward Guinea: For Larry Neal,
  1937–1981.
Balaban. Riding Westward.
Bennett, G. Heritage.
Blaeser. Certificate of Live Birth.
Blunden. Forefathers.

Boland, E. Oral Tradition, The.
Brew. Ancestral Faces.
Brooks, G. Sundays of Satin-Legs Smith, The.
Cabico, R. Mango Poem.
Campo. Belonging.
Cariaga. Family Tree, The.
Cervantes. Archeology.
Chin. Barbarian Suite.
  Floral Apron, The.
Clayton, I. Last Link, The.
Clinton, M. History as Trash.
Cohan. Nothing New Beneath the Sun.
Conran. Death of a Species.
Cortez, J. I See Chano Pozo.
Creeley. And.
Cullen, C. Heritage.
de Aerenlund, C. Cuando el tecolote canta, el
  Indio muere.
DeCormier-Shekejian. Grandmother.
Delmore, E. Willow.
Diop, B. Viaticum.
Dixon, M. Tour Guide: La Maison des
  Esclaves.
Doolan, F. Last Fullblood, The.
E'der, E. Once We Were Farmers.
Emerson, R. Forerunners.
Everett, J. Old Co'es.
Finnell. Belladonna.
Forman, R. Kin.
France de Bravo, B. Unrepentant.
Frost, R. Pride of Ancestry.
Garlick, R. Ancestors.
Gilbert, C. Sorrow Since Sitting Bull, A.
  This Bridge Across.
Guiterman. Heredity.
Hacker, M. Squares and Courtyards.
Hayden, R. Beginnings.
Hewitt, J. Search, The.
Howe, S. Thorow.
Hugo, V. Boaz Asleep.
Humphreys, E. Ancestor Worship.
Kennelly. My Dark Fathers.
Kinsella, T. Ancestor.
  His Father's Hands.
Klein, A. Heirloom.
Knight, E. Bones of My Father, The.
  Idea of Ancestry, The.
Komunyakaa. Salt.
Kunene. Elegy.
Levertov. Illustrious Ancestors.
Limburg, J. Seder Night with My Ancestors.
Manyarrows. Lakota Sister/Cherokee Mother.
Mattawa. History of My Face.
Mora. Sonrisas.
Morales. Africa.
Morales, A. 1930.
Muir, E. Absent, The.
  Scotland 1941.
Nungarrayi, J. Sorry.
Oandasan. Song of Ancient Ways, The.
Oodgeroo of the tribe Noonuccal. Past, The.
Quiller-Couch. Planted Heel, The.
Ramanujan. Elements of Composition.
Randall, D. Ancestors.
Redmond. Milestone: The Birth of an Ancestor.
Reid, C. Stones and Bones.
Robles. Cutting Back the Ifugao Past.
Rose. Story Keeper.
Rukeyser, M. Bubble of Air.
  Bunk Johnson Blowing.
  For My Son.
Salaam. Name the Oldest Member of Your
  Family.
Sanchez, S. Present.
Senghor. In Memoriam.
Shapiro, K. Nigger.
Smith, M. Stopping to Take Notes.
  Visit to the Village, A.
Song. Heaven.
Tate, J. My Great Great Etc. Uncle Patrick
  Henry.
Taylor, J. Squire's Pew, The.
Thelwall. To Ancestry.
Troupe. Sense of Coolness, A.
Utemorrah, D. Mary's Plea.
Valentine, J. Forgiveness Dream.

Walker, A. Women.
Walker, M. Lineage.
Welburn. Bones and Drums.
Winchilsea. Upon My Lord Winchilsea's Converting the Mount in His Garden to a Terrace.
Worley, D. Tongues in My Mouth.
Young Bear. Wadasa Nakamoon, Vietnam Memorial.

Anchorage, Alaska
Harjo, J. Anchorage.

Anchors
Blight. Anchor, The.
Herrick. End of His Work, The.
His Hope or Sheet-Anchor.
Williamson, G. Up in the Air.

Andrea Doria (ship)
Hollander, J. Last Words.

Andromache
Iremonger. Hector.

Andromeda
Fay, J. Mother of Andromeda, The.
Hopkins, G. Andromeda.

Anemones
Copus, J. Sea-Polyp, The.
Harwood, G. Sea Anemones, The.

Anesthesia
Centolella. Woman of Three Minds, The.

Angels
Andrews, N. That Cold Summer.
Bontemps. Nocturne at Bethesda.
Browning, R. Guardian-Angel, The.
Butts, A. Skin.
Carroll. Ode to the Angels Who Move Perpetually toward the Dayspring of Their Youth.
Carson, C. Slate Street School.
Causley. Angel's Song.
Christie. In My Dream.
Cole, H. 40 Days and 40 Nights.
Crashaw. Flaming Heart, The.
Upon the Book and Picture of the Seraphical Saint Teresa.
Dana, R. Chanting Cherubs, The [A Group by Greenough].
David, M. Sinner Kissed an Angel, A.
Dickinson, E. God's Residence.
Donne. Air[e] and Angels.
Doyle, S. Hell To Pay.
Dubin, A. I'll String Along with You.
Dunn, S. Guardian Angel, The.
"Dylan." Three Angels.
Elmusa. Two Angels, The.
Field, R. Angel's Visit, The.
Gilbert, J. It Is Clear Why the Angels Come No More.
Goldbarth. Talk Show, The.
Gonzalez, R. Angels of Juárez, Mexico, The.
Graves, R. Gardener.
Hass, R. Privilege of Being.
Hawker. Are They Not All Ministering Spirits?
Hemans. Vigil of Rizpah, The.
Howard, R. Vocational Guidance, with Special Reference to the Annunciation of Simone Martini.
Howitt, M. Dying Child, The.
Hunt, L. Abou Ben Adhem.
Jennings, E. Annunciation, The.
Johnson, L. Dark Angel, The.
Jones, A. Communal Living.
Joseph, R. Sinner Kissed an Angel, A.
Kandel. First They Slaughtered the Angels.
Kelly, B. Imagining Their Own Hymns.
Kelly, R. In June.
Killeen, G. My Father's Angels.
Kimball, H. Angel of the Rain.
Kimbrell, J. True Descenders.
Levertov. Jacob's Ladder, The.
Where Is the Angel?
Levi, P. Annunciation.
Lewis, C. Sonnet: "Bible says Sennacherib's campaign was spoiled, The."
Liu, T. Vox Angelica.
Longfellow, H. Sandalphon.
Mackey, N. Song of the Andoumboulou.

Song of the Andoumboulou: 6.
Song of the Andoumboulou: 7.
Winged Abyss.
McIlroy, L. Good-Bye, Valentine.
Melville, H. Swamp Angel, The.
Menashe. Annunciation, The.
Mew. Trees Are Down, The.
Meynell, A. Thoughts in Separation.
Milosz, C. On Angels.
Mitchell, S. Annunciation, The.
Morrissey, S. My New Angels.
Moulds, J. When Bad Angels Love Women.
Mulkey, R. Why I Believe in Angels.
North, C. Air and Angels.
O'Hara, F. In Favor of One's Time.
Padel. Angel.
Page, P. Images of Angels.
Poe. Israfel.
Porter, A. Another Sarah.
Porter, P. Angel in Blythburgh Church, An.
Radnóti. Angel of Dread, The.
Ramsey, P. Angels, The.
Ray, D. On a Fifteenth-Century Flemish Angel.
Rich, A. Gabriel.
Rilke. Olive Garden, The.
Rosemurgy, C. Angel Finally Admits What She Knows to Lou Binkler of Bethany, Missouri, An.
Ross, W. On Angels.
Rózewicz. Homework Assignment on the Subject of Angels.
Schuyler, J. Head, A.
Schwartz, D. Sarah.
Sears, E. It Came upon the Midnight Clear.
Seaton, M. Wings.
Sewell, L. Expulsion.
Sexton. Consorting with Angels.
Smith, S. Galloping Cat, The.
I Rode With My Darling.
No Categories!
Southwell. New Heaven, New War[re].
Stevens, W. Angel Surrounded by Paysans.
Szumigalski. Angels.
Taggart, J. Body and Soul: Poem for Two Readers.
Torres, E. Of My Nipple Ring Halos.
Triplett, P. Fractal Audition.
Unknown. Angels in the House, The.
Warren, H. I'll String Along with You.
Wesley, C. Wrestling Jacob.
Willard, N. Angels in Winter.
Wordsworth, W. Perfect Woman.
Wright, J. Angel, The.
Secret Gratitude, A.
Young, M. Angels, The.

Anger
Allen, S. Moment Please, A.
Awoonor. To the Eminent Scholar and Meddler.
Baugh, E. Carpenter's Complaint, The.
Baxter, C. Purest Rage, The.
Bloch, M. While Bouncing the Shema Back and Forth in Shul.
Bolamba. Fistful of News, A.
Bruner. Angry Word, An.
Clifton, L. Fury.
Creeley. Anger.
Daryush. Anger Lay by Me All Night Long.
Derricotte. Promise, The.
Estep, M. I Have to Go Now.
"Field." Wheat-miners.
Ford, C. There's No Place to Sleep in This Bed, Tanguy.
Glück, L. Labor Day.
Goodman, M. Open Poem.
Griffiths, B. For P—Celtic: found text from Machen.
Griffiths, S. Mines in Sepia Tint, The.
Hacker, M. Fifteen to Eighteen.
Hejinian. Mask of Anger, A.
Hernandez, D. Martin and My Father.
Herrick. Gods Anger without Affection.
Hodgson, R. Gipsy Girl, The.
Hongo. Yellow Light.
Iverem, E. Daddy's Friends.
Jemie. Toward a Poetics.
Kahaney, P. Germany, 1981.

Kaufman, S. Mothers, Daughters.
Komunyakaa. Seven Deadly Sins.
Konie, G. In the Fist of Your Hatred.
Koroneu. Funeral Eva.
Kunitz, S. Portrait, The.
Laing, K. Many Worlds Are Walked Once.
Lamb. Anger.
Leonard, T. Fathers and Sons.
Levine, P. Fox, The.
Horse, The.
Louis, A. Dust World.
Matherne, B. Les Fils (Sons).
Mayer, B. Sonnet: "Thousand apples you might put in your theories."
McClure, M. Rant Block.
McKay, C. White City, The.
Myles, E. Maxfield Parrish.
Neruda. Walking Around.
Neufeld, A. Children of Night.
Olds, S. Clasp, The.
Overstreet. Count Ten.
Pastorius. Penance, A.
Peacock, M. Anger Sweetened.
Pietri. 9th Untitled Poem.
Rankin, J. Love Affair 36.
Rich, A. Phenomenology of Anger, The.
Rodgers, W. Lovers, The.
Rosenberg, L. Silence of Women, The.
Samaras, N. Elegy for a Professor.
Sandburg, C. Choose.
Smith, S. Anger's Freeing Power.
Soto. Behind Grandma's House.
Spender, S. Prisoners, The.
Stead, C. Between.
Tayson, R. Chase, The.
Thomas, D. Do Not Go Gentle into That Good Night.
Thomas, E. Execration, The.
Torres, E. Vase of the Universe, The.
Troupe. Boomerang: A Blatantly Political Poem.
Unknown. Temper.
Warsh. Enmeshment.
Watta. Stone at the Tip of the Tongue, A.
Wetzsteon. Urban Gallery.
Wicks, S. Voice.
Wong, N. For an Asian Woman Who Says My Poetry Gives Her a Stomachache.
Wright, J. Revelation, The.
See also **Quarrels**

Angkor Wat, Cambodia
Devlin, D. Ank'hor Vat.

Animal Migration
Bryant, W. To a Waterfowl.
Field, R. Something Told the Wild Geese.

Animals
Albrecht, A. Passing Piedras Blancas.
Amherst. Verses Designed to Be Sent to Mr. Adams.
Amirthanayagam. Elephants Are in the Yard, The.
Angira. Look in the Past, A.
Atwood. Animals in That Country, The.
Auden. Our Hunting Fathers.
Barnes, W. Sam'el Down vrom Lon'on.
Benson, G. Cat and the Pig, The.
Berger, B. Photo Safari.
Bishop, E. Armadillo, The.
Blaser. Ruler, The.
Blevins, S. New York.
Blight. Into the Ark.
Bly, R. Extra Joyful Chorus for Those Who Have Read This Far, An.
Bobrowski. Latvian Songs.
Brooke, L. Johnny Crow's Garden.
Brooks, F. Barnyard Melodies.
Bruchac. Prayer: "Let my words."
Burke, J. Swinging on a Star.
Burnham, D. Maintaining the Species.
Caesar. Animal Crackers in My Soup.
Campbell, J. Ad Limina.
Carruth, H. Little Citizen, Little Survivor.
Causley. On Being Asked to Write a School Hymn.
Cavendish, M. Discourse of Beasts, A.
Sea Similized to Meadows and Pastures: the

Mariners, to Shepherds: the Mast, to a May-Pole: the Fish, to Beasts, The.
Centolella. Small Acts.
Ceravolo. Ho Ho Ho Caribou.
  Spring of Work Dream.
Chang, E. After the Storm.
Clairmont. Answers, The.
Clare, J. Hares at Play.
Clark, P. Zoo.
Clifton, L. Earth is a living thing, The.
Cooley. Sleep of Beasts, The.
Corso. Mad Yak, The.
Cortez, J. Heavy Headed Dance, The.
Couzyn. Spell to Protect Our Love.
Dauer. Mammals.
Davies, W. Dumb World, The.
Davis, H. Proud Riders.
DeFrees. Census of Animal Bodies: Driving Home.
Deutsch. Creatures in the Zoo.
Dewdney. Grid Erectile.
Dickey, J. Heaven of Animals, The.
  Hedge Life.
Dugan, A. Letter to Eve.
Estes, A. Nocturne.
Evans, A. Under Cover.
Faigao, B. Kundiman.
Ferril. Something Starting Over.
Flint, F. Eau-Forte.
Galvin, B. Bullfrog.
Garcia, R. Death in Larkspur Canyon, A.
Garrigue. Song in Sligo.
Godfrey. Radiant Dog.
Gonzalez, R. San Jacinto Plaza.
Goodrich. Higglety, Pigglety, Pop!
Graves, R. Allie.
Gray, J. Mishka.
Hale, S. Mary's Lamb [or Mary and Her Lamb].
Haley, M. Tropicalia.
Hall, D. Sudden Things.
Hejinian. Nights.
Holcroft. Fool's Song.
Hollander, J. Adam's Task.
Howitt, M. Cry of the Animals, The.
Hughes, T. I See a Bear.
Jeffers, R. Animals.
  Hurt Hawks.
Jenkins, N. Castration.
Johnson, J. Brer Rabbit, You's de Cutes' of 'Em All.
Kearney, M. Nature Poetry.
Kinnell. Cells Breathe in the Emptiness.
  When One Has Lived a Long Time Alone.
Kipling, R. Eddi's Service.
Knott. Poem: "After your death."
Lawrence, D. Glory.
  Self-Pity.
Lear, E. Calico Pie.
  Quangle Wangle's Hat, The.
Levertov. Come into Animal Presence.
  Else a great Prince in prison lies.
Levine, P. Animals Are Passing from Our Lives.
Long, H. Cobweb.
Lovelace, R. Her Muffe.
Lowry, M. Xochitepec.
MacCaig. Feeding Ducks.
  Summer Farm.
MacDiarmid, H. Parley of Beasts.
Maiden. Taste.
Matthews, W. Names.
Meredith, W. On Falling Asleep by Firelight.
Milton. On the Detraction Which Followed upon My Writing Certain Treatises.
"Monty Python." All Things dull and Ugly.
Moore, M. Jerboa, The.
  Like a Bulrush.
  Monkeys, The.
  Pangolin, The.
Moss, S. Dog, The.
Mueller, L. Naming the Animals.
Muir, E. Animals, The.
Nichol. Scraptures: 7th Sequence.
North, M. Shap.
Quiller-Couch. Sage Counsel.

Ransom, J. Spiel of [the] Three Mountebanks.
Reese, L. Christmas Folk-Song, A.
Reeves, J. Animals' Houses.
Rexroth, K. Bestiary, A.
  Fox.
  Horse.
  Raccoon.
  Vulture.
  Wolf.
Roethke. For An Amorous Lady.
  Running Lightly over Spongy Ground.
Roripaugh, L. Peony Lover.
Roscoe, W. Butterfly's Ball [and the Grasshopper's Feast], The.
Rossetti, C. Hurt No Living Thing.
Sackville-West. Young Stock.
Scammell, W. Screes, The.
Sharma, P. Performance Test.
Simic. Animal Acts.
Simms, C. First English Wildcat, The.
Smelcer. Animal Spirits.
  My Indian Grandmother Speaks to Animals.
Squire. Stockyard, The.
Stein, G. What Do I See.
Stephens, J. Cage, The.
  Little Things.
Stern, G. Behaving Like a Jew.
Stevens, W. Poetry Is a Destructive Force.
Stevenson, A. Giving Rabbit to My Cat Bonnie.
Swirszczynska. I Talk to My Body.
Szymborska. In Praise of Self-Deprecation.
  Unexpected Meeting.
Tate, J. Descent, The.
Thackeray. At the Zoo.
Twichell. City Animals.
Unknown. Animal Fair.
  Birds of a Feather.
  Kindness to Animals.
  Little Lamb, A.
Van Doren. And Did the Animals?
Wells, C. How To Tell the Wild Animals.
Wenderoth, J. My Life.
Whitman, W. Ox-Tamer, The.
  World below the Brine, The.
Wilbur. Beasts.
Winchilsea. Hog, the Sheep and Goat, Carrying to a Fair, The.
Wright, J. Pelicans.
  To the Evening Star: Central Minnesota.
Young Bear. Significance of a Water Animal, The.
See also **Death of Animals; Cruelty to Animals**

Animism
Gardner, I. That "Craning of the Neck."
Rich, A. Trees, The.

Anniversaries
Bruner. Wedding Anniversary.
Cofer, J. Anniversary.
Donne. Anniversary [or Anniversarie], The.
Ellis, T. T.A.P.O.A.F.O.M.
Hewett, D. Anniversary.
Lovelace, R. Anniversary on the Hymeneals of My Noble Kinsman, Thomas Stanley, Esquire, An.
Merwin, W. S. For the Anniversary of My Death.
Probyn. Anniversaries.
Smith, C. To the Countess of A—. Written on the Anniversary of Her Marriage.

Annunciation of the Virgin
Gunn, T. Jesus and His Mother.
Levi, P. Annunciation.
Menashe. Annunciation, The.
Messerli. Annunciation, The.
Mitchell, S. Annunciation, The.
Muir, E. Annunciation, The.
Smith, K. Annunciation.

Antarctica
Mahon. Antarctica.

Anteaters
Moore, M. Pangolin, The.

Anthony, Saint
McGinley. Temptations of Saint Anthony, The.

Anthropology and Anthropologists
Arnett. Powwow.

Daruwalla. Of Mohenjo Daro at Oxford.
Kinsella, J. Visitant Eclogue.
Wojahn. Francis Ford Coppola and Anthropologist Interpreter Teaching Gartewienna Tribesmen to Sing 'Light My Fire,' Philippine Jungle, 1978.

Anti-Semitism
Becker, R. Crypto-Jews, The.
Bell, M. Book of the Dead Man (#58), The.
Feinstein, E. Annus Mirabilis 1989.
Freed, F. Private School for Girls, May 14, 1948, New York City, A.
Kahaney, P. Pogrom.
Kumin, M. Riddle of Noah, The.
Lifshin. After the Anti-Semitic Calls on a Local Talk Station.
  Crystal Night.
Newman, G. Anti-Semitic Demonstration, An.
Plotnick, H. M. Jewish.
Rakosi. To an Anti-Semite.
Rodriguez, J. How Come the Truck-Loads?
Sadoff. Nazis.
Wayman. Hating Jews.

Anticipation
Ashbery. At North Farm.
  One Thing That Can Save America, The.
Beresford. Courtship, The.
Bock, J. Tonight at Eight.
Coleman, C. Best Is Yet to Come, The.
Doolittle, H. At Ithaca.
Everwine. From the Meadow.
Gay, N. Leaning on a Lamppost.
Gilbert, J. To See if Something Comes Next.
Grennan. Pause.
Harnick. Tonight at Eight.
Hayden, R. Night-Blooming Cereus, The.
Hinsey, E. Approach of War, The.
Larkin, P. Next, Please.
Lawrence, D. Suspense.
Levy, A. Twilight.
Maltby, R. Today Is the First Day of the Rest of My Life.
Novello, I. We'll Gather Lilacs.
Palmer, O. Wasting Time.
Thompson, F. Non Pax—Expectatio.

Antigone
Nathan, L. Letter.
Ray, H. Antigone and Oedipus.

Antiques
Zukofsky, L. Shang Cup.

Antony (Marc Antony)
Hemans. Last Banquet of Antony and Cleopatra, The.
Pascal. Tact.
Simpson, L. Early in the Morning.
Williams, W. To Mark Anthony in Heaven.

Ants
Benson, A. Ant-Heap, The.
Campbell, D. Anguish of Ants, The.
Clare, J. Ants, The.
"Douglas." Ant-Hills.
Empson. Ants, The.
Frost, R. Departmental.
Johnson, S. *ad. fr.* the Bible, Proverbs, 6, 6.
Knott. Ant Dodger.
Kreymborg. Ants.
Lovelace, R. Ant, The.
Matthews, W. Vermin.
McGrath, T. Skull of the Horse.
Moore, M. Critics and Connoisseurs.
Nash, O. Ant, The.
  Emmet, The.
Piccione. Watching Ants Play Soccer in Central Park.
Rosenblatt. Ant Trap, The.
Sharpless. "Go to the Ant."
Wallace, R. Dog's Song.
Zarin. Ant Hill, The.

Anxiety
Ashbery. Problem of Anxiety, The.
Atwood. Up.
Baillie, J. Song: Woo'd and married and a'
Berry, W. Peace of Wild Things, The.
Bukowski. I Am Dead But I Know the Dead Are Not Like This.

Apartheid
Creeley. Waiting.
Di Prima. Abyss.
Dobyns. Allegorical Matters.
Frost, R. Armful, The.
Garrigue. Forest.
Gilyard, K. Daughter, That Picture of You.
Hamod, S. Letter.
Hayden, R. Ice Storm.
Hazo. Drenching, The.
Herbert, G. Conscience.
Hopkins, G. She Schools the Flighty Pupils of
  Her Eyes.
Hugo, R. In Your Racing Dream.
Kumin, M. Excrement Poem, The.
Lagier. Second Class Citizen.
Lifshin. After the Anti-Semitic Calls on a Local
  Talk Station.
Liu, T. Mama.
  Size of It, The.
MacNeice. Prognosis.
McGrath, T. Letter for Marian, A.
Mora. Elena.
  Immigrants.
Naimy, M. Solemn Vow, A.
Pietri. Intermission from Thursday.
Powell, D. A. Minotaur at Supper: Spare the
  Noritake and the Spode, The.
Ramanujan. Snakes.
Robinson, M. Dreams of a Rival.
Shepherd, R. Eros in His Striped Blue Shirt.
Simic. Clouds Gathering.
Smith, C. To a Friend.
Sweeney, M. Couple Waiting, A.
Weaver, M. Improvisation for Piano.
Wright, C. Laguna Blues.
Young, M. J. Anxiety.

Apartheid
Brooks, G. Near-Johannesburg Boy, The.
Johnson, L. Mi Revalueshanary Fren.
Rive. Where the Rainbow Ends.
Ross, A. In Bloemfontein.
Sepamla. Measure for Measure.
Vilakazi. In the Gold Mines.
Zulu, P. You are Mad: and I Mean It!

Apartments
As-Sabah. I'll Never Know No Sunday in This
  Weekday Room.
Bodenheim. Rear Porches of an Apartment
  Building.
Cooper, J. Rent.
Davis, J. Time Bum.
Dunn, D. Modern Love.
Greenlaw. Five O'Clock Opera.
Hogan, L. New Apartment.
Hughes, L. Madam and the Rent Man.
Osterhaus, J. New York Minute.
Rich, A. Living in Sin.

Apathy
Atwood. Notes towards a Poem That Can
  Never Be Written.
Auden. Musée des Beaux Arts.
De la Mare. Pooh!
Eliot, T. Love Song of J. Alfred Prufrock, The.
Hughes, T. View of a Pig.
Ignatow, D. First on TV, A.
Lindsay, N. Leaden-eyed, The.
Shapiro, K. Hospital.
Stafford, W. Ritual to Read to Each Other, A.
Stevenson, R. Celestial Surgeon, The.
Studdert-Kennedy. Indifference.

Apes
Edson, R. Ape.
Hayes, T. Goliath Poem.
Huxley, A. First Philosopher's Song.
Robinson, A. Darwinism.
Sassoon. Sporting Acquaintances.

Aphrodisiacs
McGuckian. Aphrodisiac, The.
Sharpless. In Praise of Cocoa, Cupid's
  Nightcap.

Aphrodite
"Field." To the Winter Aphrodite.
Ghiselin. Bath of Aphrodite.
Lawrence, D. Man of Tyre, The.
Olson, C. Ring of, The.

Warren, R. Myth on Mediterranean Beach:
  Aphrodite as Logos.
See also **Venus (goddess)**

Apocalypse
Baraka, R. After-Word.
Bayliss. Apocalypse and Resurrection.
Braxton, C. Apocalypse.
Hirsch, E. American Apocalypse.
Holmes, O. Latter-Day Warnings.
Ingalls, J. Vision of St. Michael and St. John,
  The.
Lowell, R. Harriet.
McAuley, J. One Tuesday in Summer.
McGrath, T. End of the World, The.
Melo Neto. End of the World, The.
Muir, E. Horses.
Sherry, J. Hazardous Waste.
Unknown. Steal Away to Jesus.
Wilbur. Advice to a Prophet.
Wylie. Doomsday.
See also **End of the World; Judgment Day**

Apollinaire, Guillaume
Ginsberg, A. At Apollinaire's Grave.
Grier. I Am Almost Asleep.
Kaufman, B. Unhistorical Events.

Apollo
Davidman. Lament for Evolution.
Doolittle, H. Evadne.
Douglas, L. Rejected.
Drayton. Sacrifice to Apollo, The.
Drummond, W. Invocation: "Pheobus, arise! /
  And paint the sable skies."
Herrick. Canticle to Apollo, A.
Kunitz, S. Flight of Apollo, The.
Melville, H. Ravaged Villa, The.
Meredith, G. Phoebus with Admetus.
Robinson, A. Search for Apollo, A.
Robinson, E. Many Are Called.
Shepherd, R. Man Named Troy, A.
Waller, E. Story of Phoebus and Daphne
  Applied, [etc.], The.
Winchilsea. Circuit of Apollo, The.
Winters, Y. Apollo and Daphne.

Apostles
Herrick. Salutation.
Pound, E. Ballad of the Goodly Fere.
Schwartz, D. Starlight like Intuition Pierced the
  Twelve.
Southwell. Christs Sleeping Friends.
Tate, A. Twelve, The.

Apple Blossoms
Farrar, J. Comparison, A.

Apple Trees and Apples
Barker, G. How many apples grow on the tree?
Bogan, L. Crossed Apple, The.
Booth, P. Original Sequence.
Causley. Apple-Tree Man, The.
Coiffait, C. Last Apple, The.
Crane, H. Sunday Morning Apples.
Dauenhauer. Tlingit Concrete Poem.
De la Mare. Miss T.
Drinkwater. Moonlit Apples.
Dufault. Burden.
Freneau. On Observing a Large Red-Streak
  Apple.
Frost, F. Deserted Orchard.
Frost, R. After Apple-Picking.
  Unharvested.
  Wood-Pile, The.
Guernsey, B. Apple, The.
Hall, D. Apples.
Heyen. Windfall.
Humphreys, E. Apple Tree and a Pig, An.
Larkin, P. As Bad as a Mile.
Lawrence, D. Medlars and Sorb-Apples.
  Mystic.
Livesay, D. Eve.
Major, C. Apple Core.
Martin, W. Apple Orchard in the Spring, An.
Merriam, E. Counting-out Rhyme.
Morris, W. Pomona.
Murphy, E. Thank you, Mr Rason, for the
  Apples.
Nemerov. Primer of the Daily Round, A.
Ormond. My Grandfather and His Apple-Tree.

Pogson, P. Apples.
Porter, A. Another Sarah.
Rivera, D. Under the Apple Tree.
Rossetti, C. Apple Gathering, An.
Rossetti, D. Orchard-Pit, The.
Salter. Young Girl Peeling Apples.
Scannell. Apple-raid, The.
Stewart, S. Apple.
Tomlinson, C. Paring the Apple.
Unknown. Harry Parry.
  I Will Give My Love an Apple [Without E'er a
    Core].
  St. Paul's Steeple.
Updike. September.
Wilbur. John Chapman.
Yeats. Song of Wandering Aengus, The.

Apprentices
Muldoon, P. Sushi.

Approval
Hamill, G. Limerick: "'If you're aristocratic,'
  said Nietzsche."

Apricot Trees and Apricots
Isanos. Apricot Tree.

April
Benét, S. For City Spring.
Bridges, R. April, 1885.
Browning, R. Home-Thoughts, From Abroad.
Carman, B. *et al.* Earth's Lyric.
Clare, J. Last of April, The.
De Paul, G. I'll Remember April.
DeSylva, B. G. April Showers.
Duke, V. April in Paris.
Dunbar-Nelson. April Is on the Way.
Eberhart, R. This Fevers Me.
Grimké, A. At April.
Grosholz. Remembering the Ardèche.
Gurney, I. April Gale.
Jeffers, R. Gale in April.
Kenney. In April.
Keyes, S. Elegy: "April again, and it is a year
  again."
Klein, A. Break-up, The.
Levine, P. Sleepless Night, A.
Loveman. April Rain.
Lowell, A. April.
Masefield. West Wind, The.
Millay, E. Song of a Second April.
  Spring.
Nesbit, E. Dead to the Living, The.
Raye, H. April.
Sandburg, C. Three Spring Notations on
  Bipeds.
Shaw, A. April.
Snodgrass, W. April Inventory.
Taylor, B. Aprilly.
Turner, F. April Wind.
Watson, S. Song: "April, April, / Laugh thy
  girlish laughter."
Winstanley, J. Epigram on the First of April.

Aquariums
Bush, D. Aquarium du Trocadéro.
Hammial. Petit Guignol.
Lowell, R. For the Union Dead.

Arab-Israeli Wars
Alkalay-Gut. Public Outcry.
Back, R. Gaza, Undated.

Arabia
Falkner. Arabia.
Tennyson, A. Recollections of The Arabian
  Nights.

Arabs
Awad, J. Autumnal.
Bennani, B. Camel's Bite.
Blind. Fantasy, A.
Browning, R. Through the Metidja to Abd-el-
  Kadr.
Charara, H. Holy Water.
Elmusa. Expatriates.
  Father Lullabies the Unborn.
Hamod, S. Dying with the Wrong Name.
  Libyan/Egyptian Acrobats/Israeli Air Circus.
Hazo. Silence Spoken Here.
  To My Mother.
Joseph, L. Curriculum Vitae.
  It's Not Me Shouting at No One.

That's All.
Minhinnick. Twenty-Five Laments for Iraq.
Nye, N. Blood.
  For Lost and Found Brothers.
  Mother of Nothing.
  My Father and the Fig Tree.
  Small Vases from Hebron, The.
Orfalea, G. Bomb That Fell on Abdu's Farm,
  The.
  Gift You Must Lose, A.
  Jellyfish Eggs.
  Rose of Brooklyn, The.
Samaras, N. Notes in Jerusalem.
Taylor, B. Bedouin Song.
Thompson, F. Arab Love-Song, An.
Turki, F. In Search of Yacove Eved.
Zolotow. Enemies.

Arachne
Kazantzis. Arachne.

Arbor Day
Morris, G. Woodman, Spare That Tree.

Arcadia
Taylor, B. Paean to the Dawn, A.

Archaeology and Archaeologists
Betjeman. Archaeological Picnic, The.
Cervantes. Archeology.
Daruwalla. Of Mohenjo Daro at Oxford.
Murphy, R. Archaeology of Love, The.
Phillips, D. Maridunum.
Prufer, K. My Father Recounts a Story from
  His Youth.
Storace. Archaeology of Divorce, The.

Archery
Gascoigne. Gascoigne's Woodmanship.
Longfellow, H. Arrow and the Song, The.
Unknown. Song of the English Bowmen.
Villa. To Become an Archer.

Architecture and Architects
Blake, E. J. Within and Without.
Cabico, R. Art in Architecture.
Denney. Building the Dam.
Emerson, R. Problem, The.
Evans, A. On Sir John Vanbrugh [Architect].
Garrigue. Grand Canyon, The.
Gier, J. Going Baroque.
"Malley." Baroque Exterior.
Melville, H. Greek Architecture.
Rich, A. Architect.

Arctic
Booth, P. Stefansson Island.
Gunn, T. From the Highest Camp.
Nicholls, J. Polar Cub.
Spender, S. Polar Exploration.

Argentina
Coward. Nina.
Mandel, E. Madwomen of the Plaza de Mayo,
  The.

Arguments
Gershwin. Let's Call the Whole Thing Off.
Gonzalez, N. How the Heart Aches.
Rivard. Cures.
Sallah, T. No Argument Tonight.
See also **Quarrels**

Aristocracy
Coward. Stately Homes of England, The.
Graves, R. Cloak, The.
Thomas, R. Sir Gelli Meurig.
Unknown. Vicar of Bray, The.

Aristotle
Stafford, W. Humanities Lecture.

Arithmetic
Adcock, F. Halfway Street, Sidcup.
Carroll, L. Sum, A.

Arizona (state)
Carruth, H. Rimrock, Where It Is.
Johnson, D. Incognito Lounge, The.
Pape. In the Bluemist Motel.
Reyes, C. Arizona Nocturne.
Santos, S. Near the Desert Test Sites.
Warren, R. Arizona Midnight.

Ark, The
Blight. Into the Ark.
Kendall, M. Vision of Noah, The.
Levertov. Ache of Marriage, The.

Nemerov. Fall Again, The.
Thomas, D. Author's Prologue.
Tomlinson, C. Ararat.
Wallace, R. Problem in History, A.
Warren, R. Gold Glade.
Wright, J. Pelicans.
See also **Noah**

Arkansas (state)
Angelou. My Arkansas.
Ortiz. Bend in the River.
Robin, L. Little Girl from Little Rock.
Unknown. State of Arkansas, The.
Walcott. Arkansas Testament, The.

Armadillos
Cumpian. Armadillo Charm.
White, G. Dead Armadillos.

Armenia and Armenians
Hill, G. Song from Armenia, A.
Hovanessian, D. Two Voices.

Armistice
Hillyer. Eternal Return, The.
Sassoon. Everyone Sang.
Schwartz, D. Today Is Armistice, a Holiday.
Van Dyke. America's Welcome Home.
See also **Peace**

Armstrong, Johnie (Scot, *fl.* **1530)**
Unknown. Johnie Armstrong.

Armstrong, Louis
Allen, S. I Say, Mr. A.
Brock-Broido. Radiating Naïveté.
Fabio. For Louis Armstrong, A Ju-Ju.
Moerman. Louis Armstrong.
Tolson, M. Satchmo.

Armstrong, William (Scot, *fl.* **1596)**
Unknown. Kinmont Willie.

Army Life
Berlin. Oh! How I Hate to Get Up in the
  Morning.
  This Is the Army, Mr. Jones.
Brookes, J. Officers and Gentlemen Down
  Under.
Brownjohn. Class Incident from Graves.
Campo. Battle Hymn of the Republic, The.
Carmichael, H. Don't Forget to Say No, Baby.
Clare, J. Soldier, The.
Corfield, J. Morse Lesson.
Dawe, B. Weapons Training.
Day, J. North Sea.
Ewart. Officers' Mess.
  Personal Footnote, A.
Fuller, R. Spring 1942.
Gurney, I. Bohemians, The.
Housman, A. Grenadier.
  New Mistress, The.
Jackson, F. Elvis Goes to the Army.
Jarmain. Embarkation, 1942.
Jarrell. Second Air Force.
Kipling, R. 'Eathen, The.
  Boots.
  Cholera Camp.
  Danny Deever.
  Gentlemen-Rankers.
  Gunga Din.
  Mandalay.
Kirstein. Rank.
Lewis, A. All Day It Has Rained.
  Infantry.
Long, H. For Tony, Embarking in Spring.
Prince, H. Boogie Woogie Bugle Boy.
Razaf, A. My Man o' War.
Rosenberg, I. Troop ship, The.
Sassoon. Stand-to: Good Friday Morning.
Scannell. Bayonet Training.
Service. Pot of Tea, A.
Shanks. Going In to Dinner.
Shapiro, K. Troop Train.
Smith, A. Political Intelligence.
Stevenson, R. Armies in the Fire.
Unknown. Army Dance, The.
  Deserter, The.
Waniek. Freeman Field.
  Three Men in a Tent.
West, A. Night Patrol, The.
Whitman, W. Bivouac on a Mountain Side.
  By the Bivouac's Fitful Flame.

  Cavalry Crossing a Ford.
Williams, S. My Man o' War.
See also **Soldiers**

Arnold, Matthew
Hecht, A. Dover Bitch, The.

Arrows
Longfellow, H. Arrow and the Song, The.
Unknown. Arrow Song.
Wilner, E. Meditation on the Wen Fu.

Art and Artists
Agee. To Walker Evans.
Ai. Back in the World.
Albert-Birot. In the Paul Guillaume Gallery.
Allston. Art.
  On Rembrant; Occasioned by His Picture of
    Jacob's Dream.
  On Seeing the Picture of Æolus by Pelegrino
    Tibalbi, in the Institute at Bologna.
  On the Group of the Three Angels Before the
    Tent of Abraham, by Raffaelle, in the Vatican.
  On the Statue of an Angel, by Bienaimé, in the
    Possession of J. S. Copley Greene, Esq.
  To My Venerable Friend, the President of the
    Royal Academy.
Baraka. Black Art.
  State/meant.
Bawer. On Leaving the Artists' Colony.
Bishop, E. Monument, The.
  One Art.
Blake, W. Orator Prigg.
Bogan, L. To an Artist, to Take Heart.
Braxton, C. Arts Are Black, The.
Browning, E. Hiram Powers' "Greek Slave."
Browning, R. Fra Lippo Lippi.
  How It Strikes a Contemporary.
  Youth and Art.
Carruth, H. This Decoration.
Cendrars. Head, The.
  My Dance.
Cheng Hsieh. For Contemporary Artist Pien
  Wei-Ch'I.
Cherry, K. Bride of Quietness, The.
Clark, T. Suicide with Squirtgun.
Clarke, A. Japanese Print.
Cole, T. Painter, A.
Coleridge, M. On a Bas-relief of Pelops and
  Hippodameia.
Coleridge, S. Apologia pro Vita Sua.
Connolly, C. On Geoffrey Grigson.
Copus, J. Art of Interpretation, The.
Creeley. Figures, The.
Cummings, E. If I Have Made, My Lady.
Davie. Hill Field, The.
  With the Grain.
DeFrees. Beetle Light.
Delaunay, S. Greetings, Blaise Cendrars.
Drake, N. Foley Artist, The.
Duchamp. Speculations.
Eberhart, R. Cancer Cells, The.
Edson, R. Performance at Hog Theater, A.
Ellis, T. T.A.P.O.A.F.O.M.
Emanuel, L. Sleeping, The.
Emerson, R. Art.
Fawcett, B. Hand, The.
Fearing. Art Review.
Ferlinghetti, L. Monet's Lilies Shuddering.
"Field." L'indifférent.
  La Gioconda; Leonardo Da Vinci, The Louvre.
Forbes, J. Four Heads & How to Do Them.
Fox, S. Peaches.
Galbreath. Limerick: "There once was an artist
  called Pat."
Goldbarth. Counterfeit Earth!, The.
Graves, R. Epitaph on an Unfortunate Artist.
Griffin, S. To the Far Corners of Fractured
  Worlds.
Guest, B. Roses.
  Wild Gardens Overlooked by Night Lights.
Gunn, T. Expression.
Hacker, M. Ballad of Ladies Lost and Found.
Hannan, M. Life Model.
Hass, R. Image, The.
  Pornographer, The.
Hecht, A. Death the Painter.
Hernández Cruz. Art of Hurricanes, The.
Herrera. Resurrection of the Flesh, The.

Herrick. Art above Nature, to Julia.
Hewitt, J. From a Museum Man's Album.
Hill, G. Pre-Raphaelite Notebook, A.
  Vergine bella.
Hirschman, J. Painting, The.
Holloway, G. Bash on Basho: Six of the Best.
Hovey. Accident in Art.
Howard, R. Nikolaus Mardruz to his Master
  Ferdinand, Count of Tyrol, 1565.
  Venetian Interior, 1889.
Jeffers, R. Artist, An.
Jennings, E. Works of Art.
Johnson, J. Before a Painting.
Justice, D. Anonymous Drawing.
Kates. No Altarpiece.
Kaufman, B. To My Son Parker, Asleep in the
  Next Room.
Keats. On Seeing the Elgin Marbles.
Kinsella, J. Warhol at Wetlands.
Kinsella, J. Portrait of the Artist, A.
Kipling, R. Conundrum of the Workshops, The.
  Evarra and His Gods.
  L'Envoi.
Lanier, S. To Bayard Taylor.
Lee-Hamilton. Luca Signorelli to His Son.
Lefroy. Palaestral Study, A.
Liu, T. Vox Angelica.
Livesay, D. Three Emily's, The.
Loftis, N. Delirium.
Macha, F. Artist and a Wailing Mother, An.
MacLeish. Corporate Entity.
Maiden. New.
Martinez, D. Matisse: Blue Nude, 1952.
McDonald, C. At the Gwen John Exhibition.
Melville, H. Art.
  Attic Landscape, The.
Michelson, R. Faraway Landscape.
Milosz, C. Sun, The.
Monroe, H. Rubens.
Moore, M. When I Buy Pictures.
Morse, C. Dream of the Artfairy.
Muldoon, P. Christo's.
Mullen, H. Music for Homemade Instruments.
Murray, G. Art of a Cold Sun.
Naden. Two Artists, The.
Napier, F. I Do Not Want the Ceiling of the
  Sistine Chapel.
Nemerov. Intimations.
Norse. Business of Poetry, The.
  Picasso Visits Braque.
Nortje. Newcombe at the Croydon Gallery.
O'Hara, F. Why I Am Not a Painter.
O'Shaughnessy, A. Ode: "We are the music-
  makers."
Opie. To Mr. Opie, On His Having Painted for
  Me the Picture of Mrs Twis.
Peacocke. Remembrance.
Phillips, C. Luncheon on the Grass.
Pilling. Ophelia.
Pinkerton, H. On Vermeer's "Young Woman
  with a Water Jug" (1658) in the Metropolitan
  Museum.
Porter, P. And No Help Came.
Pound, E. L'Art, 1910.
  Of Jacopo del Sellaio.
Randall, D. Primitives.
Ransom, J. Painted Head.
Ratcliff, C. Big Bad Art Thing, The.
Reed, I. Catechism of d Neoamerican Hoodoo
  Church.
Rich, A. Architect.
  At a Bach Concert.
  Aunt Jennifer's Tigers.
  Burning Oneself Out.
Richardson, L. Poet Sings His Painting, The.
Robinson, A. Art and Life.
Rossetti, C. In an Artist's Studio.
Rossetti, D. For "Our Lady of the Rocks."
  For a Venetian Pastoral by Giorgone (In the
  Louvre).
Rouse. Memo to Auden.
Rukeyser, M. Homage to Literature.
  Käthe Kollwitz.
  Painters.
Ryan, T. Trompe l'oeil.
Salmon, A. Painting.

Salter. Rebirth of Venus, The.
Sanders, E. Cutting Prow, The.
Scalapino. Picasso and Anarchism.
Scammell, W. Eclogue: Clerk of the Weather.
  Retrospective.
Schevill. London Pavement Artist.
Schuyler, J. Red Brick and Brown Stone.
Serote. Hell, Well, Heaven.
Shapiro, K. Poet.
Slessor. Nuremberg.
Smith, S. New Age, The.
Smith, V. At an Exhibition of Historical
  Paintings, Hobart.
Snodgrass, W. Matisse: "The Red Studio."
Song. Girl Powdering Her Neck.
Soto. Effects of Abstract Art, The.
Stevens, W. Anecdote of the Jar.
  So-and-So Reclining on Her Couch.
Stevenson, R. To the Muse.
Stickney, T. On the Concert.
  Requiescam.
Tate, A. Sonnet: To a Portrait of Hart Crane.
Taylor, B. Paean to the Dawn, A.
Tennyson, A. Palace of Art, The.
Thomas, D. In My Craft or Sullen Art.
Tomlinson, C. Chances of Rhyme, The.
Tranter. Great Artist Reconsiders the Homeric
  Simile, The.
  Having Completed My Fortieth Year.
Troupe. View from Skates in Berkeley, The.
Tzara. Chanson Dada.
Unknown. Art.
  Limerick: "There was a young artist called
  Saint."
Updike. Two Hoppers.
Van Duyn. Homework.
Violi. Hazards of Imagery, The.
Wagoner, D. Author of American Ornithology
  Sketches a Bird, Now Extinct, The.
Weiners. Poem for Painters, A.
Weiss, T. Dab of Color, A.
Whitman, W. Eidolons.
Whittemore, R. Departure, The.
Wilbur. Museum Piece.
Williams, W. Artist, The.
Wilner, E. Conversation with a Japanese
  Student.
  Meditation on the Wen Fu.
Wilson, T. Magpies in Picardy.
Winters, Y. To My Infant Daughter.
Wright, J. Request to a Year.
Yeats. Curse of Cromwell, The.
  Lapis Lazuli.
Young, K. Campbell's Black Bean Soup.
Yuson. Andy Warhol Speaks to His Two
  Filipino Maids.
Zukofsky, L. Shang Cup.
See also **Artists' Colonies**
Arthurian Legend
Hill, G. Merlin.
Keyes, S. Grail, The.
Morris, W. Defense of Guenevere, The.
Spicer, J. Book of Galahad, The.
Tennyson, A. Epic, The [Morte d'Arthur].
  Lady of Shalott, The.
  Morte d'Arthur.
Unknown. Marriage of Sir Gawain, The.
Warton, T. On King Arthur's Round Table, at
  Winchester.
Winters, Y. Sir Gawaine and the Green Knight.
Artifacts
Hughes, T. Relic.
Kroetsch. Stone Hammer Poem.
Martínez, V. Reliquaries, The.
Nungarrayi, J. Sorry.
Pound, E. Papyrus.
Rich, A. Power.
Artists' Colonies
Robinson, E. Hillcrest.
Ascension Day
Vaughan, H. Ascension-Day.
  They Are All Gone into the World of Light!
Ashbery, John
Koch, K. Circus, The.

Ashes
Bibbins, M. Mud.
"Field." Your Rose is Dead.
Kizer, C. Ashes, The.
Mahapatra, J. Ash.
Sears, P. Volcanic Ash.
Asia
Kaufman, S. Poem in November.
Merrill, J. Willoware Cup.
Purdy, A. Blue City, The.
Asian-Americans
Cerenio. Family Photos: Black and White:
  1960.
Chang, D. Foreign Ways.
Chin. Floral Apron, The.
  We Are Americans Now, We Live in the
  Tundra.
Divakaruni. Indian Movie, New Jersey.
Fletcher, L. After Delivering Your Lunch.
Hawkins, R. Issei Men: The First Generation.
  Nisei Daughter: The Second Generation.
  Sansei: The Third Generation.
Inada. Making It Stick.
  Projected Scenario of a Performance to Be
  Given Before the UN.
Kim, A. Sewing Woman.
Kim, M. Into Such Assembly.
Lau, C. Zhoukoudian Bride's Harvest.
Lee, L. Cleaving, The.
  Persimmons.
Lem. So Now You're Chicana.
Lim, S. Lost Name Woman.
  Modern Secrets.
  Riding into California.
Mark, D. Suzie Wong Doesn't Live Here.
Okita. Notes for a Poem on Being Asian
  American.
Robles. Remembering the Past.
Su, A. Address.
Uyematsu. 30 Miles from J-Town.
  To All Us Sansei Who Wanted to Be Westside.
Vazirani, R. Mrs. Biswas Goes Through a Photo
  Album.
  Mrs. Biswas of Maryland on the Phone.
Wong, N. When I Was Growing Up.
Yee, M. Wintermelons.
Asians
Alvi, M. Presents from My Aunts in Pakistan.
Divakaruni. Founding of Yuba City, The.
  Leaving Yuba City.
Sharma, P. Action-Packed Sonnet.
See also **Chinese, The; Filipinos; Japanese, The**
Aspen Trees
Hopkins, G. Binsey Poplars (Felled 1879).
Thomas, E. Aspens.
See also **Poplar Trees**
Asphodels
Williams, W. Paterson, Book 5: The River of
  Heaven.
Aspirations
Chin. Elegy for Chloe Nguyen.
Hughes, L. Deferred.
Kennedy, X. Keep a Hand on Your Dream.
Larkin, J. Inventory.
Porter, C. Tale of the Oyster, The.
Procter, A. Incompleteness.
Rolfe, E. Song: "Keep the dream alive and
  growing always."
Salaam. I Live in the Mouth of History.
Scott, W. Early Aspirations.
Trethewey, N. Domestic Work, 1937.
Assassinations and Assassins
Barrax. King: April 4, 1968.
Emanuel, J. Panther Man.
Felltham [or Feltham]. On the Duke of
  Buckingham, Slain by Felton, the 23rd August,
  1628.
Gunn, T. Claus von Stauffenberg.
Herd. Pink Rose Rings, The.
Ismaili. Bajji.
Justice, D. Assassination, The.
Kazantzis. In Memory, 1978.
Knight, E. It Was a Funky Deal.
Livingston, M. Arthur Thinks on Kennedy.
Madhubuti. Assassination.

Melville, H. Martyr, The.
Randall, B. Be He Ezra Pound, Kennedy, or King.
Reed, I. Nov 22, 1988.
Tomlinson, C. Charlotte Corday.
Whitehead, C. Brutus' Last Song.

Assurance
Crosby, F. Blessed Assurance.

Assyrians
Byron, G. Destruction of Sennacherib, The.
Moore, M. Is Your Town Nineveh?

Asteroids
Cumpian. Estrellitas.

Astrology and Astrologers
Beatty, P. Independent Study.
Crashaw. Love's Horoscope.
Kipling, R. Astrologer's Song, An.
Longfellow, H. Poet's Calendar, The.
McElroy, C. Horoscope.
Ramke. Difference Between Night and Day, The.

Astronauts
Alexander, E. Apollo.
Hayden, R. Astronauts.
Morgan, E. From the Domain of Arnheim.
Whittemore, R. Projection, A.

Astronomy and Astronomers
Adcock, F. Blue Glass.
Ex-Queen Among the Astronomers, The.
Donne. Good Friday [or Goodfriday], 1613.
Riding Westward.
Goldbarth. Talk Show, The.
Griffin, J. Night Sky Hiss.
Keyes, S. Greenwich Observatory.
Ramke. Astronomer Works Nights: A Parable of Science, The.
Rich, A. Planetarium.
Very. Slowness of Belief in a Spiritual World, The.
Volkman. Untitled: "Shrewd star, who crudes our naming: you should be flame."
Whitman, W. When I Heard the Learn'd Astronomer.
Williams, M. Astronomy.
Young, K. Letters from the North Star.

Astrophysics and Astrophysicists
Hoover, P. Letter to Einstein Beginning Dear Albert.
Lumsden, R. Beginning of the End, The.
Salazar. Moulton Transformations.

Atalanta
Swinburne. Before the Beginning of Years.
When the Hounds of Spring.

Atheism
Chesterton, G. On Reading "God."
Dobell, S. Liberty to M. le Diplomate.
Flynn, N. Emptying Town.
Hardy, T. Impercipient, The.
Lowell, R. For George Santayana.
Shapiro, K. I Am an Atheist Who Says His Prayers.

Athens, Greece
Byron, G. Maid of Athens, Ere We Part.
Gibran. Two Poems, The.
Lefroy. Idler Listening to Socrates Discussing Philosophy with His Boy-Friends, An.
Muldoon, P. Dancers at the Moy.
Spencer, B. Spring Wind, A.

Athletics and Athletes
Allen, S. To Satch.
Barresi. Called Up: Tinker to Evers to Chance.
Dean, D. K. Back to Back.
Evans, D. Song of Racquetball.
Higgins, F. Tennis in the City.
Hope, A. Massacre of the Innocents.
Housman, A. To an Athlete Dying Young.
Lacavaro, A. Advantages of Being a World Class Athlete, The.
Matthews, W. Foul Shots: A Clinic.
In Memory of the Utah Stars.
Piercy. Morning Athletes.
Updike. Ex-Basketball Player.
Wellburn, R. Pitching Coups.
Whitman, W. Runner, The.

Atlanta, Georgia
DuBois, W. Litany of [or at] Atlanta, A.
Fordham. Atlanta Exposition Ode.
Shange. About Atlanta.
Touré, A. Imani in Sunburst Summer: A Chant.

Atlantic Ocean
Aiken, C. Hatteras Calling.
Cowper, W. Castaway, The.
Ford, C. Somebody's Gone.
Hayley. To Mrs. Hayley, On Her Voyage to America. 1784.
Longfellow, H. Seaweed.
Osundare. Goree.
Sargent, E. Rockall.
Sexton. Crossing the Atlantic.

Atlantis
Fuhrman, J. Atlantis.

Atomic Bomb
Ai. Chance.
Armour. Hiding Place.
Braun, H. To Fat Boy, the Bomb.
Curnow. Pacific 1945-1995.
Dugan, A. Actual Vision of Morning's Extrusion.
Enright, D. Monuments of Hiroshima, The.
Frost, R. U. S. 1946 King's X.
Ginsberg, A. America.
Herd. Bombshell.
Mura. Hibakusha's Letter (1955), The.
Santos, S. Near the Desert Test Sites.
Seth. Doctor's Journal Entry for August 6, 1945, A.
Sherry, J. Free Radicals.
Hazardous Waste.
Stafford, W. At the Bomb Testing Site.
Wheelock, J. Earth.
Wilner, E. High Noon at Los Alamos.
See also **Hiroshima, Japan; Nuclear War**

Atoms
Cavendish, M. Of Many Worlds in This World.
Dickinson, E. Choice.
Pack, R. Proton Decay.

Atonement
Guiney. Atoning Yesterday, The.
Smart, C. Hymn to the Supreme Being.

Atterbury, Francis, Bishop of Rochester
Prior. Epitaph: "Meek Francis lies here, friend, without stop or stay."

Attics
Coulette. Attic, The.
Goetsch, D. Walls, The.
Nemerov. View from an Attic Window, The.
Peacocke. We're Staying at the Castlemount, Western Esplanade.

Attucks, Crispus
Hayden, R. Crispus Attucks.

Auctions
Brouwer, J. Space Memorabilia Auction, Superior Stamp and Coin, Beverly Hills, California.
Bynner. Highest Bidder, The.
Byrom. To Henry Wright of Mobberley, Esq. on Buying the Picture of Father Malebranche.
DeLeeuw. Auction Sale—Household Furnishings.
Hardy, T. Bags of Meat.
Reed, H. Auction Sale, The.
Sandburg, C. Auctioneer.
Scott, D. Kirkwall Auction Mart.

Auden, Wystan Hugh
Empson. Just a Smack at Auden.
Loftis, N. In Memorium: Robert Hayden.
Rouse. Memo to Auden.
Spender, S. Auden at Milwaukee.
Walcott. Eulogy to W. H. Auden.

Aughrim, Battle of (1691)
Lawless, E. After Aughrim.

August
Bly, R. August Rain.
Canton. Day-Dreams.
Eberhart, R. Loon Call, A.
Garland, H. In August.
Hardy, T. August Midnight, An.
Jacobik, G. Turkeys in August.

Kennedy, X. One Winter Night in August.
Kenyon, J. August Rain, after Haying.
Ray, H. August.
Rich, A. August.
Sexton. I Remember.
Snyder, G. Mid-August at Sourdough Mountain Lookout.
Wylie. August.
Zhenkai. August Sleepwalker, The.

Augustine, Saint
Grosholz. Back Trouble.

Aunt Jemima
Hayden, R. Aunt Jemima of the Ocean Waves.
Williams, C. In Search of Aunt Jemima.

Aunts
Alvi, M. Presents from My Aunts in Pakistan.
Boss. Candy Lady, The.
Campo. Aunt Toni's Heart.
Dacey, P. Thumb.
Dittberner-Jax. Blues for Aunt Ruth.
Dybek. Cherry.
Eliot, T. Aunt Helen.
Ginsberg, A. To Aunt Rose.
Graham, H. Waste.
Gylys, B. Family Reunion—Aunt Vern's Two Cents.
Harrison, T. Study.
Holmes, O. My Aunt.
Lee, W. Aunt Martha.
Michelson, R. Where I Sat.
Powell, K. For Aunt Cathy.
Rich, A. Aunt Jennifer's Tigers.
Ríos, A. Language of Great-Aunts, The.
Seto, T. Blood Ties.
Sexton. Some Foreign Letters.
Stevenson, R. Auntie's Skirts.
Tolson, M. Old Houses.
Trethewey, N. Flounder.
Unknown. My Aunt Jane.
Wojahn. Satin Doll.

Auschwitz, Poland
Bond, E. If.
Brock, V. Remembering Dresden.
Fainlight, R. Archive Film Material.
Gershon. Experiments with God.
Mandel, E. On the 25th Anniversary of the Liberation of Auschwitz.
Porter, P. Annotations of Auschwitz.
Your Attention Please.
Schiff, H. Discovery.

Australia
Adamson. Elm Tree in Paddington, An.
Bobis, M. Driving to Katoomba.
Word Gifts for an Australian Critic.
Brookes, J. Officers and Gentlemen Down Under.
Brown, F. Last of England, The.
Buckmaster. Wilpena Pound.
Catalano. Australia.
Cataldi. 13 November 1983.
Darwin. Visit of Hope to Sydney Cove, near Botany-Bay.
Davidson, R. Gravy Train, The.
Davis, J. Aboriginal Australia.
Desolation.
First-born, The.
One Hundred and Fifty Years.
Dransfield. Minstrel.
That Which We Call a Rose.
Ewart. Short Time.
Freeth. Botany Bay.
Gilbert, K. Celebrators '88.
New True Anthem, The.
Gray, R. Journey: the North Coast.
Harris, R. Sydney.
Hart-Smith. Nullarbor.
Hope, A. Australia.
Humphries, B. Edna's Hymn.
Jones, T. Rhiannon.
"Malley." Dürer: Innsbruck, 1495.
Sweet William.
Marshall-Stoneking. Picture Postcard.
McAuley, J. Envoi.
Terra Australis.
Mead, P. Melbourne or the Bush.

Murphy, E.   Thank you, Mr Rason, for the
  Apples.
Napurrurla, I.   Water, The.
Oodgeroo of the tribe Noonuccal.   No More
  Boomerang.
  We are Going.
Page, G.   Jerry's Plains, 1848.
Porter, P.   Australian Garden, An.
  Last of England, The.
  Sydney Cove, 1788.
  Talking to You Afterwards.
Rankin, J.   Old Currawong.
Rodriguez, J.   Mahogany Ship, The.
Sladen.   Summer Christmas in Australia, A.
Slessor.   Five Bells.
  South Country.
Smith, V.   Early Arrival: Sydney.
Stewart, D.   Terra Australis.
Thorne, T.   High Country.
Tranter.   Enzensberger at 'Exiles'
Unknown.   Hail South Australia!
  Hot Day In Sydney, A.
Wallace-Crabbe.   Collective Invention, The.
  Mental Traveller's Landfall, The.
Webb, F.   Towards the Land of the Composer.
Wright, J.   At Cooloolah.
  Australia 1970.

Authorship and Authors
Belloc.   On His Books.
Bradstreet, A.   Author to Her Book, The.
Campbell, R.   On the Same.
Drummond, W.   Sonnet: "I know that all
  beneath the moon decays."
Fitzgerald, F.   Obit on Parnassus.
Freneau.   To an Author.
Herrick.   Argument of His Book, The.
  Poetry Perpetuates the Poet.
Holmes, O.   Cacoëthes Scribendi.
Kennedy, B.   On ["Who Wrote Icon Basilike"
  by Dr.] Christopher Wordsworth, Master of
  Trinity.
Killigrew, A.   Upon the Saying That My Verses
  Were Made by Another.
Macpherson, J.   Boatman, The.
Ondaatje.   Burning Hills.
Pound, E.   Lake Isle, The.
Robinson, E.   George Crabbe.
  Verlaine.
Scott, F.   Canadian Authors Meet, The.
Updike.   I Missed His Book, but I Read His
  Name.

Autism
Silkin.   Death of a Son.

Automation
Moore, M.   Four Quartz Crystal Clocks.

Automobile Accidents
Abbey, L.   Broken Silence.
Corob, T.   Either Way.
Delgado, J.   I-5 Incident.
Fearing.   Obituary.
Geiger.   Disproportionate.
Glück, L.   Racer's Widow, The.
McCarthy, T.   Persephone, 1978.
Oness, C.   August 1990.
Shapiro, K.   Auto Wreck.
Williams, W.   Romance Moderne.

Automobile Racing
Dubie.   Death of the Race Car Driver, The.
Glück, L.   Racer's Widow, The.

Automobiles
Atkins.   New Storefront.
Baranczak, S.   Three Magi, The.
Barrax.   Adagio.
Betjeman.   Meditation on the A30.
Bishop, E.   Filling Station.
Bishop, M.   Gas and Hot Air.
Blanco, R.   El Malibú.
Bly, R.   Driving toward the Lac Qui Parle River.
Bolt, T.   Meditation in Loudoun County.
Burns, J.   Revisionism.
Chavez, L.   After the Prom.
Connor, T.   Last of the Poet's Car.
Davis, C.   Nod.
Dawe, B.   Abandonment of Autos.
Dickey, J.   Cherrylog Road.

Duggan, L.   Three xlvii.
Eady.   Song.
Edson, R.   Automobile, The.
Finkel.   Gesture.
Flanders, J.   Big Cars.
Forman, R.   Green Boots n Lil Honeys.
Gilbert, C.   Now.
Gilmore, B.   Gas Station Attendant.
Guest, B.   Way of Being, A.
Haines, J.   Flight, The.
Hammial.   Automobiles of the Asylum.
Hope, A.   Brides, The.
Jackson, M. L.   Some Kind of Crazy.
Jacob, M.   Invitation to a Voyage.
Jarman, M.   Black Riviera, The.
Johnson, J.   Eclipse.
Kharms.   Event on the Street, An.
Larsen, L.   Lips.
Liu, T.   Highway 6.
Livingston, M.   Car Wash.
Markus, P.   Light.
Mateo.   Jeepneyfying.
McIlroy, L.   How to Change a Flat.
McKuen.   Thoughts on Capital Punishment.
Merriam, E.   Landscape.
Meyers, B.   Suburban Dusk.
Miles, J.   Reason.
Mitchell, A.   Autobahnmotorwayautoroute.
Monroe, H.   Meeting, The.
Morrison, L.   Sidewalk Racer, or, On the
  Skateboard, The.
Moss, T.   Wonder, The.
Murray, L.   Portrait of the Autist as a New
  World Driver.
Nemerov.   Fugue.
Parker, D.   One Perfect Rose.
Pastan.   Jump Cabling.
Prunty.   Elderly Lady Crossing on Green.
Ryan, G.   Ode to My Car.
Sandburg, C.   Portrait of a Motorcar.
Seyburn, P.   Persuasion.
Shepherd, R.   Who Owns the Night and Lease
  Stars.
Silverstein, S.   Longmobile.
Stafford, W.   Traveling Through the Dark.
Swenson, M.   Southbound on the Freeway.
Tayson, R.   Chase, The.
Unknown.   Generals Ride in Cars.
Vigil, A.   At the Stop Light, the Braided Blond
  Man.
Weaver, M.   Black and White Galaxie, The.
Williams, W.   Ballad of Faith.
  Intelligent Sheepman and the New Cars, The.
Young, K.   Quivira City Limits.

See also **Driving and Drivers; Cars**
Autumn
Alexander, M.   October Journey.
Awad, J.   Autumnal.
Barker, G.   Gardens of Ravished Psyche, The.
Blake, W.   To Autumn.
Bobrowski.   Latvian Autumn, The.
Bogan, L.   Simple Autumnal.
Braithwaite.   Turn Me to My Yellow Leaves.
Bridges, R.   Garden in September, The.
Brock-Broido.   Of the Finished World.
Bronk.   Where It Ends.
Brontë, E.   Song.
Brooks, G.   Sunset of the City, A.
Browning, R.   By the Fire-Side.
Bryant, W.   Autumn Woods.
  Death of the Flowers, The.
  November.
  October.
  To the Fringed Gentian.
Burns, R.   Early Autumn.
Campbell, R.   Autumn.
Campbell, W.   How One Winter Came in the
  Lake Region.
Carman, B.   Vagabond Song, A.
Carruth, H.   Emergency Haying.
Cary, A.   Autumn.
Ceravolo.   Invisible Autumn.
Chesterton, G.   Gold Leaves.
Chin.   Autumn Leaves.
Clare, J.   Autumn.
Clover, J.   Archive of Confessions, a Genealogy

  of Confessions, An.
Cole, T.   Written in Autumn.
Corbett, W.   Vermont Apollinaire.
Cranch.   Autumn Rain, The.
Crane, H.   Sunday Morning Apples.
Crapsey.   November Night.
Cristall.   Song: "Through springtime walks, with
  flowers perfumed."
Curry.   Anne Hathaway Composes Her 18th
  Sonnet.
Cushing, J.   Autumn Leaves.
Davison, P.   From the Outland.
Day Lewis.   Maple and Sumach.
  Stand-To, The.
Dickinson, E.   Morns are meeker than they
  were, The.
  Name—of it—is "Autumn," The.
Dixon, R.   Song: "Feathers of the willow, The."
  Winter Will Follow.
Dowson.   Autumnal.
Duke, V.   Autumn in New York.
Dunbar, P.   Signs of the Times.
Eberhart, R.   Loon Call, A.
  Spider, The.
Ekelof.   Absentia Animi.
Encarnacion.   Seattle, Autumn, 1933.
Farjeon, E.   Down! Down!
Field, R.   Something Told the Wild Geese.
Finch, B.   Written in a Shrubbery Towards the
  Decline of Autumn.
Francis, R.   Fall.
Freneau.   On Observing a Large Red-Streak
  Apple.
Frost, R.   Clear and Colder.
  My November Guest.
Fuller, M.   Lines Written in Boston on a
  Beautiful Autumnal Day.
Garland, H.   Plowing: A Memory.
Glück, L.   All Hallows.
Gray, D.   Sonnet: "October's gold is dim—the
  forests rot."
Gunn, T.   Autumn Chapter in a Novel.
Hayne, P.   October.
Henson, L.   Scattered Leaves.
Herman, W.   Early Autumn.
Hiestand, E.   Witch-Hazel Wood, The.
Hood, T.   Autumn.
  No!
Hopkins, G.   Hurrahing in Harvest.
  Spring and Fall.
Housman, A.   Tell Me Not Here [It Needs Not
  Saying].
  They Say My Verse Is Sad: No Wonder.
Howells, W.   November.
Hulme, T.   Autumn.
Irwin, M.   Autumnal.
Jackson, H.   September [Days Are Here].
James, J.   Sister Midnight.
Jeffers, R.   Autumn Evening.
Jennings, E.   Song at the Beginning of Autumn.
Keats.   To Autumn.
Kennedy, X.   Landscapes with Set-Screws.
Kenney.   Apples on Champlain.
Kinsella, T.   Another September.
Kunitz, S.   End of Summer.
  Hornworm: Autumn Lamentation.
Larkin, P.   Afternoons.
Lawrence, D.   Butterfly.
  Ship of Death, The.
Levine, P.   Zaydee.
Lewis, A.   Autumn, 1939.
Li Po.   Verses: "Clean is the autumn wind."
Linden, M.   Fall Is Here, The.
Lodge, G.   Fall.
Longfellow, H.   Aftermath.
  Autumn.
  Harvest Moon, The.
Lorde.   What My Child Learns of the Sea.
Lowell, A.   Hoar-Frost.
  Wind and Silver.
MacLeish.   Autumn.
  Immortal Autumn.
  Old Men in the Leaf Smoke, The.
  Tourist Death.
Maiden.   Green Side, The.
Mathews, H.   Sad Birds, The.

McGrath, T.   Black Train, The.
Melville, H.   Pontoosuce.
Mercer, J.   Early Autumn.
Millay, E.   God's World.
Milosz, O.   Bridge, The.
Muir, E.   Late Wasp, The.
Nelson, J.   If You Knew September.
O'Hara, F.   Poem: "Eager note on my door said 'Call me', The."
Ologoudou.   Vespers.
Opie.   On the Approach of Autumn.
Parker, D.   Indian Summer.
Peterson, R.   Autumn.
Po Chü-i.   Lonely Night in Early Autumn.
Porumbacu.   Of Autumn.
Posey, A.   Autumn.
Riley, J.   When the Frost Is on the Punkin.
Rilke.   Autumn Day.
Robinson, A.   Art and Life.
Rossetti, C.   Autumn.
Scannell.   Autumn.
Schuyler, J.   Master of the Golden Glow, The.
Shelley, P.   Autumn: A Dirge.
Ode to the West Wind.
Simic.   Ancient Autumn.
Smith, C.   To Melancholy. Written on the Banks of the Arun, October 1785.
Written in October.
Stevens, W.   Autumn Refrain.
Lunar Paraphrase.
Stevenson, R.   Autumn Fires.
Stickney, T.   Mnemosyne.
Tate, A.   Seasons of the Soul.
Tennyson, A.   Dedication, A: "Dear, near and true—no truer Time himself."
Thomas, D.   Poem in October.
Thomas, E.   Digging.
October.
Thomas, R.   Still.
Thompson, C.   Autumn Day, An.
Autumn Leaves.
Thompson, P.   Autumn.
Tighe.   Written in Autumn.
Tucker, M.   Autumn Thoughts.
Ungaretti.   Soldiers.
Unknown.   Autumn.
Untermeyer, J.   Autumn.
Updike.   September.
Very.   Autumn Flowers.
Autumn Leaves.
Sumach Leaves, The.
Waller, E.   Fall, The.
Wang Wei.   In the Hills.
Warren, R.   Acquaintance with Time in Early Autumn.
Heart of Autumn.
Weismiller.   Hemlocks in Autumn.
Welburn.   Gonsalves.
Whittier.   Battle Autumn of 1862, The.
Fruit-Gift, The.
Wieners.   Waning of the Harvest Moon, The.
Williams, W.   Prelude to Winter.
Yellow Season, The.
Wilson, R.   Late in Fall.
Wright, C.   Autumn.
Wright, J.   Autumn Begins in Martins Ferry, Ohio.
Zimmer.   Zimmer in Fall.

Avalanches
Simon, M.   Keeping Track.

Aviation and Aviators
Ewart.   When a Beau Goes In.
Hall, D.   Airstrip in Essex, 1960, An.
Old Pilot, The.
Iremonger.   Icarus.
Jarrell.   Dead Wingman, The.
Death of the Ball Turret Gunner, The.
Losses.
Kazantzis.   Frightened Flier Goes North, The.
Plutzik.   Airman Who Flew over Shakespeare's England, The.
Snyder, G.   Vapor Trails.
Spender, S.   Landscape near an Aerodrome, The.
Tate, J.   Lost Pilot, The.
Trowbridge, J.   Darius Green and His Flying-

Machine.
See also **Air Travel; Air Warfare; Airports**

Avignon, France
Robinson, A.   Orchard at Avignon, An.

Avoca, Ireland
Moore, T.   Meeting of the Waters, The.

Avocados
Rakosi.   Avocado Pit, The.

Avon River, Canada
Reaney.   To the Avon River above Stratford, Canada.

Axes
Adamson.   Private, The.
Evans, M.   Boss Communication.
Frost, R.   Axe-Helve, The.
Morris, G.   Woodman, Spare That Tree.
Plath.   Words.
Snyder, G.   Axe Handles.

Ayr, Scotland
Burns, R.   Flow Gently, Sweet Afton.

B

Baal-Shem-Tov
Klein, A.   Baal Shem Tov.

Babel, Tower of
Quarles.   On the Babel-Builders.
Wieder.   Tower of Babel, The.

Babies
Adisa.   Rainbow, The.
Aldis, D.   Little.
Armitage, J.   To Our Daughter.
Auden.   Mundus et Infans.
Baillie, J.   Mother to Her Waking Infant, A.
Barbauld.   To a Little Invisible Being Who Is Expected Soon to Become Visible.
Barker, G.   Verses for a First Birthday.
Barlow, G.   4½ Months: Halfway Song.
Barnes, J.   Clinic Day.
Barnstone, A.   To a Friend's Child.
Beers, E.   Weighing the Baby.
Bennett, G.   Secret.
Blake, W.   Cradle Song, A: "Sleep, sleep, beauty bright."
Bowering, G.   In the Forest.
Breton, N.   Cradle Song: "Come, little babe."
Brooks, F.   New Baby, The.
Bruce, D.   Two Couples.
Byrd.   My Sweet Little Baby.
Campbell, R.   Zulu Girl, The.
Causley.   Infant Song.
Cave.   Written a Few Hours before the Birth of a Child.
Cerenio.   13 June 1994.
20 July 1994.
Chernoff.   How Lies Grow.
Clifton, L.   I Am Accused of Tending to the Past.
Coleridge, H.   First Birthday, The.
Coleridge, S.   Frost at Midnight.
Sonnet to a Friend Who Asked How I Felt When the Nurse First Presented My Infant to Me.
Cornford, F.   New-Born Baby's Song, The.
Cowper, M.   On Viewing Her Sleeping Infant.
Dalton, A.   Dad-Baby, The.
Davie.   Christening, A.
Day Lewis.   Carol, A.
Dickey, J.   Magus, The.
Dougherty.   Double Helix.
Dove, R.   Pastoral: "Like an otter, but warm."
Dunbar, P.   Little Brown Baby.
Duncan, R.   Coming out of.
Duran, J.   Stillborn.
Elmusa.   Father Lullabies the Unborn.
Feinstein, E.   Mother Love.
Ferguson, G.   Inhaling His Hair.
Scan.
Galvin, J.   Station (1).
García Lorca.   Comet.
Garrett, E.   Airborne.
Graves, R.   Call It a Good Marriage.
Maternal Despotism; or, The Rights of Infants.

Griffin, S.   Song My.
Guthrie, W.   Turkey in the Corn.
Hannan, M.   Tom Passey's Child.
Hardy, T.   New Toy, The.
Hashimoto, S.   Standing in the Doorway, I Watch the Young Child Sleep.
Hazo.   Child of Our Bodies.
Heaney, S.   Peacock's Feather, A.
Herrick.   Upon a child.
Houghton, L.   Caustic Soda.
Ingelow.   Little babe, while burns the west.
Jacobsen, J.   Primer, The.
Jarrell.   Bats.
Johnson, S.   Ballad: "Tender infant, meek and mild, The."
Kelly, I.   To an Unborn Infant.
King, H.   Dream Maiden, A.
Kinnell.   Under the Maud Moon.
Kinzie.   Sound Waves.
Kirchwey.   He Considers the Birds of the Air.
Kirkup.   Baby's Drinking Song.
Koch, K.   Girl and Baby Florist Sidewalk Pram Nineteen Seventy Something.
Lamb, C.   First Tooth, The.
Gipsy's Malison, The.
Lamb, M.   First Tooth, The.
Leigh, H.   Natural Child, The.
Lipsitz.   Feeding, The.
Locker-Lampson.   Terrible Infant, A.
Lorde.   Now That I Am Forever with Child.
Luther.   Away in a Manger.
Madan.   To Lysander.
Mahon.   Unborn Child, An.
McAdams, J.   Leaving the Old Gods.
McCaig.   Poem: "There is a wailing baby under every stone and you walk."
Mercer, J.   You Must Have Been a Beautiful Baby.
Moffett.   Now or Never.
Mother Goose.   Rock-a-bye, baby, thy cradle is green.
Murray, L.   Cotton Flannelette.
Nash, O.   Come On In, the Senility Is Fine.
Reflection on Babies.
Song to Be Sung by the Father of Infant Female Children.
Nesbit, E.   Song: "Oh, baby, baby, baby dear."
Ogilvy.   Natal Address to My Child, March 19th 1844, A.
Newly Dead and Newly Born.
Oppen.   Sara in Her Father's Arms.
Osgood, F.   Ellen Learning to Walk.
Owen, M.   All That Glitters.
Philips, A.   To Miss Charlotte Pulteney in Her Mother's Arms.
Plath.   Death and Co.
Event.
Gulliver.
Magi.
Morning Song.
New Year on Dartmoor.
Nick and the Candlestick.
Night Dances, The.
You're.
Probyn.   End of the Journey, The.
Raworth.   My Face Is My Own, I Thought.
Ray, D.   At the Washing of My Son.
Riley, J.   King of Oo-Rinktum-Jing, The.
Rolfe, E.   Song: "Keep the dream alive and growing always."
Rukeyser, M.   Night Feeding.
Salter.   Summer 1983.
Sampter.   Kadia the Young Mother Speaks.
Sanchez, S.   To P. J. (2 Yrs Old Who Sed Write a Poem for Me in Portland, Oregon).
Sexton.   Unknown Girl in the Maternity Ward.
Smith, P.   Dylan, Two Days.
Smith, S.   Valuable.
Snyder, G.   Changing Diapers.
Stevenson, A.   Spirit Is Too Blunt an Instrument, The.
Thomas, E.   Triumvirate, The.
Unknown.   Baby Dolly.
Clap Handies.
Cry, Baby.
For Baby.

Hush-a-Bye.
Mother's Song to a Baby.
Van Walleghen. Walking the Baby to the Liquor Store.
Very. Moses in Infancy.
Waldman, A. Baby's Pantoum.
Waring, B. Baby Random.
Whitman, W. From Pent-up Aching Rivers.
Williams, M. Poem for Emily, A.
Wordsworth, D. Cottager to Her Infant, (By My Sister), The.
Wright, J. Song for the Middle of the Night, A.
Yeats. Dolls, The.
Young, K. Almanac, 1939, An.
See also **Infants**

Baboons
Belloc. Big Baboon, The.

Baby-Sitting and Baby-Sitters
Clarke, G. Baby-Sitting.
Gomez, M. Making It.
Hashimoto, S. Eleven A.M. on My Day Off,
My Sister Phones Desperate for a Babysitter.
Prufer, K. Babysitter's Devotion, The.

Babylon
Aiken, C. And in the Hanging Gardens.
Bishop, E. Burglar of Babylon, The.
Mother Goose. How many miles to Babylon?
Reznikoff. Babylon: 539 B.C.E.
Sandburg, C. Bilbea.
Sassoon. Babylon.
Soutar. Song: "Whaur yon broken brig hings owre."
Stickney, T. Be Still. The Hanging Gardens Were a Dream.
Tennyson, A. Babylon.

Bacchus
Emerson, R. Bacchus.
Ransom, J. Nocturne.
Whitmore, S. Lenaia.

Bach, Johann Sebastian
Bly, R. Six Winter Privacy Poems.
Dacey, P. Musician, The.
Gurney, I. Bach and the Sentry.
Holm, B. Playing the Goldberg Variations on Sunday Morning.
Max, L. Equal Temperament.

Bachelors
Eberhart, R. New England Bachelor, A.
Garrett, E. Bachelors, The.
Herrick. Upon the Loss[e] of His Mistresses.
Porter, C. I'm a Gigolo.
Unknown. Starving to Death on a Government Claim.

Backs
Grosholz. Back Trouble.
Portnoy, M. Voucher.

Badgers
Clare, J. Badger.
Clarke, C. Tortoise and Badger.
Ghiselin. Catch, The.
Heaney, S. Badgers, The.
Muldoon, P. Brock.
Thomas, E. Combe, The.

Bagels
Ignatow, D. Bagel, The.

Bagpipes
MacNeice. Bagpipe Music.
Scarfe. Kitchen Poem.
Sempill, F. Maggie Lauder.
Tomlinson, C. Mr. Brodsky.
Whittier. Pipes at Lucknow, The.

Baker, Chet
Ai. Archangel.
Doty, M. Almost Blue.
Hull, L. Lost Fugue for Chet.
Komunyakaa. Speed Ball.
Williams, M. Death of Chet Baker, The.

Baker, Josephine
Cortez, J. So Many Feathers.

Balaam
Causley. Balaam.

Baldness
Donne. Licentious Person, A.
Henderson-Holmes. 'C' ing in Colors: Red.

Baldwin, James
Troupe. In Jimmy's Garden.

Ballet
Merrill, J. Watching the Dance.
Russell, B. Ballerina.
Wright, S. Out of the Wailing.

Balloons
Bishop, E. Armadillo, The.
Freneau. To Mr. Blanchard, the Celebrated Aeronaut in America.
Gylys, B. Balloon Heart.
Kelly, B. Visitation, The.
Knight, E. Green Grass and Yellow Balloons.
Plath. Balloons.
Morning Song.
Sandburg, C. Balloon Faces.
Wilde, O. Les Ballons.

Ballrooms
Dickson, J. Aragon Ballroom, The.

Balls
Berryman. Ball Poem, The.
Brooks, S. Darktown Strutter's Ball, The.
Clark, T. Superballs.
Farjeon, E. Over the Garden Wall.
Fitzgerald, E. 70.
Weber, R. Concise History of the Vietnam War: 1965–1968, A.
Wilbur. Juggler.

Ballylee, Ireland
Yeats. Coole Park and Ballylee, 1931.
To Be Carved on a Stone at Thoor Ballylee.

Baltimore, Maryland
Blake, E. Baltimore Buzz.
Carmichael, H. Baltimore Oriole.
Cullen, C. Incident.
Romtvedt. Glass Canyons.
Sissle, N. Baltimore Buzz.
Weaver, M. Imitation of Life.
Weekend Equestrian, The.
Webster, P. Baltimore Oriole.

Bamboo
Rolls. Bamboo.

Bananas
Edwards [*or* Edwardes], R. When I Was Three.
Hernández Cruz. Tale of Bananas, A.

Bands
Berger, B. Salad Days.
Berlin. Alexander's Ragtime Band.
Knight, S. Double Writing.
Palmer, J. Band Played On, The.
Stein, K. First Performance of the Rock 'n Roll Band *Puce Exit.*

Bangkok, Thailand
Clifton, H. Monsoon Girl.
Scott, F. Bangkok.
Swenson, K. Landlady in Bangkok, The.
Townsend, A. Comings and Goings.

Bangladesh
Duran, J. Time Zones.

Banjos
Foster, S. Oh! Susanna.
Kipling, R. Song of the Banjo, The.

Banking and Bankers
Kooser. At the Office Early.
Mills, D. Chembank Card.
Shapiro, K. Girls Working in Banks.
Unknown. War the Source of Riches.
See also **Financiers**

Baptism
Coleridge, S. My Baptismal Birthday [*or* Birth-Day].
Crashaw. On the Water of Our Lord's Baptism[e].
Heaney, S. Peacock's Feather, A.
Herbert, G. Love.
Unknown. Jesus, Master, O Discover.
See also **Christenings**

Bar Kokba, Simon
Lazarus, E. Bar Kochba.
Vollmer. Wildsisters Bar.

Barbecues
Barresi. How It Comes.
Rivera, D. Dinner Together.
See also **Picnics and Barbecues**

Barbers and Barbershops
Awad, J. Stopping at the Mayflower.
Beardsley. Ballad of a Barber, The.
Fuller, J. Alex at the Barber's.
Gray, J. Barber, The.
Kooser. Self-Portrait at Thirty-Nine.
Levine, P. To a Child Trapped in a Barber Shop.
Paquet. Night Dust-off.
Strange. Barbershop Ritual.

Barcelona, Spain
Lewis, S. I Wonder Why She Kept on Saying 'Si-Si-Si-Si-Senor.'

Bards
Benson, G. Limerick: "There once was a bard of Hong Kong."
Gray, T. Bard, The [A Pindaric Ode].
Progress of Poesy, The.
Johnson, J. O Black and Unknown Bards.
Keats. How Many Bards Gild the Lapses of Time!
Kipling, R. In the Neolithic Age.
O'Heffernan. Who Will Buy a Poem?
Webb, H. Cywydd o Fawl.
Whitman, W. By Blue Ontario's Shore.
Poet, The.

Barley
Burns, R. John Barleycorn [a Ballad].

Barmaids
Lumsden, R. Tricks for the Barmaid.
Stephens, J. Glass of Beer, A.

Barns
Blunden. Barn, The.
Carter, A. B. Cobb's Barns.
Heaney, S. Barn, The.
Lux. Barn Fire.
Merton. Elegy for the Monastery Barn.
Pritchard, N. Paysagesque.

Barons' War (1263-1267)
Unknown. Song of Lewes, The.

Baroque
Bogan, L. Baroque Comment.
Fenton, J. Lollipops of the Pomeranian Baroque.
Gier, J. Going Baroque.

Bars and Bartenders
Auden. September 1, 1939.
Bukowski. Crucifix in a Deathhand.
Corn. Billie's Blues.
Coxon, W. Flash Colonial Barman, The.
Croft, J. Greenhalgh's Pub.
Daniels, J. Ted's Bar and Grill.
Davis, J. You Turn Around.
Dugan, A. Swing Shift Blues.
Elmslie, K. Big Bar.
Espada. Dándole la mano a Mongo.
Shaking Hands with Mongo.
Gallagher, T. Instructions to the Double.
Galloway, T. Whiffenpoof Song.
Harms. From Now On.
Hecht, A. Third Avenue in Sunlight.
Herrera. Iowa Blues Bar Spiritual.
Hollander, F. Boys in the Backroom, The.
Hughes, L. Bar.
Hugo, R. Letter to Reed from Lolo.
Letter to Welch from Browning.
Milltown Union Bar, The.
Jenkins, A. Murphy's Law.
Kennedy, X. In a Prominent Bar in Secaucus [One Day].
LaFemina. Her Rose Tattoo.
Levine, P. Poem Circling Hamtramck, Michigan, All Night in Search of You, The.
Lim, S. Starlight Haven.
Loesser. Boys in the Backroom, The.
Lowry, M. Delirium in Vera Cruz.
McRay. Performance.
Middleton, C. Saloon with Birds.
Minhinnick. Drinking Art, The.
Patchen. State of the Nation, The.
Peterson, R. September 5.
Reynolds, R. Surplus.
Roberts, K. Plastic Cup, The.
Rouse. Glass.
Shepherd, R. Gods at Three A.M., The.

Snyder, G.   I Went into the Maverick Bar.
Speakes.   Heartbreak Hotel Piano-Bar.
Stephens, J.   Glass of Beer, A.
Tannahill.   Tap-Room, The.
Tolson, M.   Ex-Judge at the Bar, An.
Unknown.   Bar, The.
Welch, J.   D-Y Bar.
Wenderoth, J.   Billy's Famous Lounge.
Whitman, W.   Glimpse, A.
See also **Barmaids**

Barters
Blake, M.   Barter.
Moore, M.   New York.

Barth, Karl
Clemo.   On the Death of Karl Barth.

Baseball
Allen, S.   To Satch.
Barresi.   Called Up: Tinker to Evers to Chance.
Carlson, D.   Russ Joy Little League.
Clark, T.   Baseball and Classicism.
Corso.   Dream of a Baseball Star.
Dent.   For Cool Papa Bell.
Djanikian.   How I Learned English.
Espada.   Pitching the Potatoes.
Fairchild.   Body and Soul.
Feinstein, S.   Blues for Zoot.
Ferlinghetti, L.   Baseball Canto.
Fincke.   Class A, Salem, the Rookie League.
Fitzgerald, R.   Cobb Would Have Caught It.
Francis, R.   Base Stealer, The.
  Catch.
  Pitcher, The.
Galvin, B.   Knot Hole Gang, The.
Gilbert, C.   Theory of Curve.
Gildner.   4th Base.
Gregerson.   Line Drive Caught by the Grace of
  God.
Hall, D.   Eighth Inning, The.
  Fifth Inning, The.
Hamer.   Allegiance.
Harper, M.   Archives.
Heyen.   Mantle.
Holden, J.   How to Play Night Baseball.
  Poem for Ed "Whitey" Ford, A.
Hoover, P.   Baseball.
Hugo, R.   From Altitude, the Diamonds.
  Letter to Mantsch from Havre.
Kizer, C.   One to Nothing.
Lopez, L.   NEHI Strawberry Down-and-Away.
Miller, E.   Boys of Summer, The.
  Players.
Monroe, H.   Radio.
Moore, M.   Baseball and Writing.
  Hometown Piece for Messrs. Alston and Reese.
Morrison, L.   Rural Recreation.
Mosby.   To Josh Gibson (Legendary Slugger of
  the Old Negro Baseball League).
Norworth.   Take Me Out to the Ball Game.
Pastan.   Baseball.
Patchen.   Origin of Baseball, The.
Richter, J.   Nothing but Bad News.
Rosenberg, L.   City Baseball.
Sandburg, C.   Hits and Runs.
Sherman, F.   Baseball.
Smith, D.   Roundhouse Voices, The.
Soldofsky, A.   Chin Music.
Soto.   Black Hair.
Stanard, C.   Baseball.
Stuart, D.   Swinging on the First Pitch.
Tate, J.   Lousy in Center Field.
Thayer, E.   Casey at the Bat.
Troupe.   Poem for My Father; for Quincy
  Trouppe, Sr.
Weaver, M.   My Father's First Baseball Game.
Wellburn, R.   Pitching Coups.
Wenderoth, J.   Aesthetics of the Bases Loaded
  Walk.
Williams, W.   At the Ball Game.

Basketball
Alexie.   Defending Walt Whitman.
  Father and Farther.
  Penance.
  Why We Play Basketball.
Bowen, K.   Playing Basketball with the Viet
  Cong.

Bowman, C.   My Knicks Are Going to Beat
  Your Spurs—NBA Souvenir Bracelet 1999 for
  My Long Distance Love.
De Los Santos, M.   Women Watching
  Basketball.
Ellis, T.   Being There.
Fairchild.   Old Men Playing Basketball.
Giovanni.   Basketball.
Harper, M.   Makin' Jump Shots.
Hilton, D.   I Try to Turn in My Jock.
Hirsch, E.   Fast Break.
Hugo, R.   In Your Young Dream.
Jenkins, L.   Basketball.
Kleinzahler.   Winter Ball.
Komunyakaa.   Slam, Dunk, and Hook.
Kraushaar, M.   Free Throw.
Matthews, W.   Cheap Seats, the Cincinnati
  Gardens, Professional Basketball, 1959.
  Foul Shots: A Clinic.
  In Memory of the Utah Stars.
McKean.   Good 'D.'
Olstein, L.   We Still Have Basketball, Sara.
Phillips, L.   My Son Shows Me a Photograph of
  Michael Jordan Performing a Slam Dunk.
Ridlon.   Fernando.
Troupe.   Poem for "Magic," A.
Trudell.   Jump Shooter, The.
Updike.   Ex-Basketball Player.

Bastogne, Battle of (1944-1945)
Simpson, L.   Battle, The.

Bathrooms
Machan.   Hazel Tells LaVerne.

Baths and Bathing
Adamson.   Rimbaud Having a Bath.
Africa-Bolasco.   Sauna 2.
Ammons, A. R.   Foot-Washing, The.
Becker, R.   Bath, The.
Cabalquinto.   Value Added in Smashing a
  German Roach on the Bathroom Door, The.
Campo.   El Curandero.
Carver, R.   Woman Bathing.
Clarke, C.   What Goes Around Comes Around,
  or The Proof is in the Pudding.
Cole, H.   Roman Baths at Nîmes, The.
Davis, T.   Susannah.
Ewart.   Miss Twye.
Feinstein, E.   Bathroom.
Fisher, A.   After a Bath.
Giovanni.   Trips.
Godfrey.   Bath.
Graves, R.   I Wonder What It Feels Like to Be
  Drowned?
Hollo.   That Old Sauna High.
Kipling, R.   Naaman's Song.
Lawrence, D.   Gloire de Dijon.
Mackey, N.   Dream Thief.
Miller, E.   Another Love Affair/Another Poem.
Nash, O.   Samson Agonistes.
Patchen.   Saturday Night in the Parthenon.
Peacocke.   Soap.
Phillips, C.   In the blood, Winnowing.
Pilling.   Ophelia.
Portnoy, M.   Evolution of Lather, The.
Pound, E.   Bathtub [or Bath Tub], The.
Rakosi.   In a Warm Bath.
Rossiter.   Your Body Glistens From the Bath.
Smukler.   Home in Three Days. Don't Wash.
Snyder, G.   Bath, The.
Steele, T.   Aubade, An: "As she is showering, I
  wake to see."
Trinidad.   Shower Scene in *Psycho*, The.
Warton, T.   On Bathing.
Wheelwright.   In the Bathtub, to Mnemosyne.
Wilson, F.   Bathing My Mother.

Bats
Bennett, R.   Witch of Willowby Wood, The.
Dickinson, E.   Bat, The.
Jarrell.   Bats.
Kizer, C.   Intruder, The.
Lawrence, D.   Bat.
  Man and Bat.
Llewellyn-Williams.   Feeding the Bat.
Oliver, M.   Bats.
Radcliffe, A.   Sonnet: "Now the bat circles on
  the breeze of eve."
  To the Bat.

Roethke.   Bat, The.
Safie, D.   In the Middle of Reading One More
  Poem with Brueghel as a Metaphor.
Smith, D.   Bats.
Wicks, S.   Protected Species.
Wilbur.   Mind.

Battlefields
Aldington.   Battlefield.
Campbell, T.   Hohenlinden.
Collins, W.   How Sleep the Brave.
Douglas, K.   Vergissmeinicht.
Emerson, R.   Concord Hymn.
Fenton, J.   Wind.
Heóghusa.   Winter Campaign, A.
Hill, G.   Distant Fury of Battle, The.
  Pastoral, A: "Mobile, immaculate and austere."
Jarmain.   El Alamein.
Johnstone, P.   High Wood.
Kennedy, B.   Bad Luck to This Marching.
McCrae, J.   In Flanders Fields.
Melville, H.   Battle Summers, The.
  Inscription: "To them who crossed the flood."
  Shiloh [A Requiem].
Muir, E.   Combat, The.
Murray, P.   Redemption.
Sandburg, C.   Grass.
Smith, D.   On a Field Trip at Fredericksburg.
Southey, R.   Battle of Blenheim, The.
Stevenson, R.   Ticonderoga: A Legend of the
  West Highlands.
Tennyson, A.   Epic, The [Morte d'Arthur].
  Morte d'Arthur.
Whitman, W.   Vigil Strange I Kept on the Field
  One Night.
Wilson, T.   Magpies in Picardy.

Baucis and Philemon
Swift, J.   Baucis and Philemon.

Baudelaire, Charles
Cronin, A.   Baudelaire in Brussels.
Duncan, R.   After a Passage in Baudelaire.
Fanning, R.   Baudelaire's Ablutions.
Hochman.   Sphinxes.
Manrique, J.   Baudelaire's Spleen.
Schwartz, D.   Baudelaire.
Swinburne.   Ave atque Vale.

Bayous
St. Germain, S.   Cajun.

Beaches
Agran, R.   Door Thrown Open to Daisies.
Ammons, A. R.   Constant, The.
Arnold, M.   Dover Beach.
Beer, P.   Jane Austen.
Beevers.   Atameros.
Berryman.   Traveller, The.
Betjeman.   East Anglian Bathe.
Bridges, R.   Snow Lies Sprinkled on the Beach,
  The.
Brown, G.   Beachcomber.
Brutus.   Sand Wet and Cool, The.
Ceravolo.   Wind Is Blowing West, The.
Clampitt.   Baroque Sunburst, A.
  Beach Glass.
Clark, T.   On the Beach.
Coccimiglio.   Night Beach.
Corben.   On the Beach.
Cornford, F.   Summer Beach.
Cummings, E.   Maggie and Milly and Molly
  and May.
Davie.   Across the Bay.
Dickinson, E.   By the Sea.
Dugan, A.   Memorial Service for the Invasion
  Beach Where the Vacation in the Flesh Is
  Over.
Dunn, S.   Because You Mentioned the Spiritual
  Life.
Goetsch, D.   Beach, The.
Graves, D.   Beach, The.
Hannon.   Homeless.
Heaney, S.   Strand at Lough Beg, The.
Kees.   Beach in August, The.
Kennedy, X.   Emily Dickinson in Southern
  California.
Koch, C.   Shelly Beach.
Lee, S.   Letter from Turtle Beach.
Lipsitz.   Prospect Beach.

Martínez, V. Coastal.
McGuckian. On Ballycastle Beach.
Meredith, W. Rhode Island.
Millay, E. Eel-Grass.
Mitchell, K. Tree Stillness.
Nemerov. Salt Garden, The.
Orlen. Androgyny.
Plath. Point Shirley.
Richman, L. To Valenton: Impressions circa 1947.
Robinson, M. Haunted Beach, The.
Rukeyser, M. Children, the Sandbar, That Summer.
Saleh. Beach, Later.
Santos, S. Midsummer.
  On the Last Day of the World.
Satyamurti. Day Trip.
Schwartz, R. L. Edgewater Park.
Scupham. Beach, The.
Solari, R. December 25, 1991.
  Truro.
Stafford, W. Gulls at Cannon Beach.
  With Kit, Age Seven, at the Beach.
Stevenson, R. At the Seaside [or Sea-Side].
Stickney, T. At Sainte-Marguerite.
Swenson, M. Waking from a Nap on the Beach.
Szporluk. Duressor.
Teasdale. Unchanging, The.
Thaxter. Sandpiper, The.
Tomlinson, C. Stone Speech.
Toomer. Merl.
Vasquez, R. Pismo, 1959.
Wakoski. Imagining Point Dume.
Warren, R. Myth on Mediterranean Beach: Aphrodite as Logos.
Wheelock, J. Afternoon: Amagansett Beach.
Whitman, W. As If a Phantom Caress'd Me.
  On the Beach at Night.
  On the Beach at Night Alone.
Wilbur. On the Marginal Way.
Winch. Shadow Grammar.
Woolson. Florida Beach, The.
Wright, C. Looking West from Laguna Beach at Night.
Wright, J. At the Slackening of the Tide.
Wunderlich, M. Continent's Edge.
Zandvakili, K. No Trespassing (Private Beach).
See also **Shores**

Beagles
Rodgers, W. Beagles.

Bean, Judge Roy
Unknown. Roy Bean.

Beans
Herbert, W. Coco-de-Mer.
Murray, L. Broad Bean Sermon, The.
Unknown. Hot Boiled Beans.

Beards
Bachner. Yes, That's the Way Things Are.
Blanco, R. Shaving.
Dove, R. This Life.
Löwy, H.
Lear, E. There Was an Old Man With a Beard.
Ríos, A. Domingo Limón.
Updike. Upon Shaving Off One's Beard.

Bears
Barnett, R. Taxidermist at the Zoo, The.
Birney. Bear on the Delhi Road, The.
Blue Cloud. Bear: A Totem Dance As Seen by Raven.
Bottoms. Sierra Bear.
Césaire, A. Three for Bear.
Dubie. Elizabeth's War with the Christmas Bear.
Dunbar, P. Cabin Tale, A.
Fanning, R. Parable of the Boy and the Polar Bear.
Field, R. Dancing Bear, The.
Frost, R. Bear, The.
García Lorca. Ursa Major.
Harjo, J. White Bear.
Housman, A. Infant Innocence.
Hughes, T. Bear, The.
  I See a Bear.
Kelen. Rabbit Shoeshine.
Kinnell. Bear, The.

Lastness.
Kyger. Destruction.
Levertov. To the Reader.
Merwin, W. S. Feast Day.
Momaday. Bear, The.
Nemerov. Goose Fish, The.
Nicholls, J. Polar Cub.
Rich, A. Bears.
Roberson. Sonnet.
Roethke. Lady and the Bear, The.
Saner. This Grizzly.
Sears, P. One Polar Bear, The.
Smith, W. Polar Bear.
Snyder, G. Right in the Trail.
Unknown. Algy.
  Song of the Black Bear, The.
Wagoner, D. Meeting a Bear.
Willard, N. Cat's Second Song, The.

Beatings
Algarin. Trampling.
Knight, E. Hard Rock Returns to Prison from the Hospital for the Criminal Insane.
Larkin, J. Beatings.
Morrissey, S. Thoughts in a Black Taxi.
Ross, C. Jack.
Unknown. No More Auction Block.

Beatniks
Baraka. All is One for Monk.
Ginsberg, A. 'Back on Times Square, Dreaming of Times Square.'
  Bop Lyrics.
  Dream Record: June 8 1955.
  Howl.

Beaufort, South Carolina
Heard, J. National Cemetery, Beaufort, South Carolina, The.

Beaumont, Francis
Jonson, B. To Francis Beaumont.

Beauty
Abu Sa'id. I Asked My Love.
"Æ." Great Breath, The.
Ager, M. Ain't She Sweet?
  Everything Is Peaches Down in Georgia.
Alexander, C. All Things Bright and Beautiful.
Allerton. Beautiful Things.
Amirthanayagam. So Beautiful.
Arnold. Growing Old.
Ashbery. Le Livre Est sur la Table.
Baillie, L. Werena My Heart Licht I Wad Dee.
Baraka. Cold Term.
  Return of the Native.
Barnes, B. To the Most Beautiful Lady, the Lady Bridget Manners.
Barnfield [or Barnefield]. Affectionate Shepherd, The.
Barras, J. Peace.
Bates, K. America the Beautiful.
Behn, A. To My Lady Morland at Tunbridge.
Berlin. Pretty Girl Is Like a Melody, A.
Bernie, B. Sweet Georgia Brown.
Berryman. Canto Amor.
Binyon. Beauty.
Bishop, J. Metamorphoses of M.
Blane, R. That Face.
Blind. Beautiful Beeshareen Boy, The.
Blunden. One among the Roses.
Blunt, W. On Her Vanity.
Bogan, L. Juan's Song.
Borodin, A. And This Is My Beloved.
Braithwaite. Sic Vita.
Bridges, R. I Love All Beauteous Things.
Brown, L. Maybe This Is Love.
Brown, N. You Stepped Out of a Dream.
Browning, E. Best Thing in the World, The.
  Hiram Powers' "Greek Slave."
Browning, R. Guardian-Angel, The.
  Women and Roses.
Burke, J. Little Bit Independent, A.
  Moonlight Becomes You.
Burns, R. Bonnie Lesley.
Burrington. Beautiful, The.
Bynner. Lightning.
Byron, G. She Walks In Beauty.
  Sonnet, to the Same.
  Stanzas for Music.

Campbell, J. Old Woman, The.
Carew, T. Beautiful Mistress, A.
  Comparison, The.
  Disdain Returned.
  Divine Mistress, A.
  Fancy, A.
  Ingrateful[l] Beauty Threatened.
  On Sight of a Gentlewoman's Face in the Water.
  On the Marriage of T. K. and C. C.: The Morning Stormy.
  Song, [A]: "Ask[e] me no more where Jove bestow[e]s."
  Tinder, The.
  To a Lady That Desired I Would Love Her.
  To A. L.; Persuasions [or Perswasions] to Love.
  To my Friend G. N. from Wrest.
  True Beauty, The.
Casey, K. Sweet Georgia Brown.
Cassells. Beautiful Signor.
Cawein. Beauty.
  Unimaginative, The.
Chaucer. Mercile[s]s Beaute [or Beautée or Beauty].
  Merciless Beauty.
  To Rosamounde.
Chin, J. Cocksucker's Blues.
Chippewa Oral Tradition. Love-Charm Song.
Chivers. To Isa Sleeping.
Chudleigh. Song: "Why Damon, why, why, why so pressing?"
Clare, J. First Love.
Clarke, A. Planter's Daughter, The.
Clifton, L. Song at midnight.
Coatsworth. Swift Things Are Beautiful.
Coffman. Cheerleaders.
Cohan. When a Fellow's on the Level with a Girl That's on the Square.
Coleridge, M. On a Bas-relief of Pelops and Hippodameia.
  Wasted.
Conquest. Rokeby Venus, The.
Cowley, H. Departed Youth.
Cranch. Evening Primrose, The.
Cristall. Elegy on a Young Lady.
Cummings, E. Poem, or Beauty Hurts Mr. Vinal.
Cuney. No Images.
Darley. It Is Not Beauty I Demand.
Davenant [or D'Avenant]. Lover and Philosopher.
De la Mare. Epitaph, An: "Here lies a most beautiful lady."
  Three Cherry Trees, The.
Derricotte. Minks, The.
DeSylva, B. G. Maybe This Is Love.
Dietz, H. If There Is Someone Lovelier Than You.
Dixon, M. Lady in Red, The.
Donne. Undertaking, The.
Doolittle, H. Song: "You are as gold."
D'Orleans. Smiling Mouth, The.
Dowson. Villanelle of His Lady's Treasures.
Drake, N. Very Rich Hours, The.
Drayton. Roundelay Between Two Shepherds, A.
Drummond, W. Madrigal: "Like the Idalian Queen[e]."
  Stolen Pleasure.
Dubin, A. Dames.
Dugan, A. American Variation on How Rilke Loved a Princess and Got to Stay in Her Castle.
Duhamel. Bicentennial Barbie.
Duncan, R. Poetry, a Natural Thing.
Edwards, M. World Is Full of Beauty, The.
Ehrmann. If You Made Gentler the Churlish World.
Elizabeth I. When I Was Fair and Young.
Emerson, R. Each and All.
  Harp, The.
  Rhodora, The [On Being Asked Whence Is the Flower].
Empson. Villanelle: "It is the pain, it is the pain, endures."
"Ephelia." To a Proud Beauty.
Evelyn, M. Mundus Muliebris.

"Field." Elsewhere.
 Girl, A.
 Portrait, A.
 So jealous of your beauty.
Fields, D. Lovely to Look At.
 Way You Look Tonight, The.
 You Couldn't Be Cuter.
Fitzgerald, M. Rendezvous.
Fletcher, J. Take, Oh, Take Those Lips Away.
Forché. Kalaloch.
Forman, R. You So Woman.
Forrest, G. And This Is My Beloved.
Freed, R. You Leave Me Breathless.
Garrett, E. Vista.
Garrigue. Primer of Plato.
Giovanni. Beautiful Black Men.
 Poem for Flora.
Godolphin. Song: "Noe more unto my thoughts appeare."
Gorges. Her Face, Her Tongue, Her Wit.
Graves, R. Down, Wanton, Down!
Gray, J. Les Demoiselles de Sauve.
Grimké, A. Mona Lisa, A.
Hamlish, M. One.
Harford, L. Beauty and Terror.
Harjo, J. Eagle Poem.
 Woman Who Fell from the Sky, The.
Harris, W. Daddy Poem, A.
Hart, L. Most Beautiful Girl in the World, The.
 Wait Till You See Her.
 You Are Too Beautiful.
Hemphill. Soft Targets.
Henderson, R. Maybe This Is Love.
Herbert, E. La Gialletta Gallante, or the Sunburned Exotic Beauty.
 Sonnet of Black Beauty.
 To One Black, and Not Very Handsome, Who Expected Commendation.
Herbert, G. Sonnet: "Sure Lord, there is enough in thee to dry."
Hernández Cruz. Problems With Hurricanes.
Herrick. Apron of Flowers, The.
 Art above Nature, to Julia.
 Definition of Beauty, The.
 Delight in Disorder.
 Epitaph upon a Virgin, An.
 Request to the Graces, A.
 To Anthea Lying in Bed.
 Upon Her Feet.
 Upon Julia's Clothes.
 Upon the Nipples of Julia's Breast.
Hewett, D. This Version of Love.
Hill, A. Garden Window, The.
Hoagland, E. Anti-Semanticist, The.
Hodgson, R. Gipsy Girl, The.
Hoffman, D. At Provincetown.
Hollander, F. You Leave Me Breathless.
Hood, T. Ruth.
Hookes. To Amanda Walking in the Garden.
Hopkins, G. Pied Beauty.
Hughes, L. Harlem Sweeties.
 I, Too.
 My People.
 When Sue Wears Red.
Hull, A. Another Rhythm.
Ismaili. Solange.
Jackson, H. Her Eyes.
Jackson, L. Divestment of Beauty.
 Helen's Burning.
 Mask, The.
Jacobs, H. On Growing Up the Darker Berry.
Jakiela. Personal History of Hands, A.
Jamie. Queen of Sheba, The.
Jeffers, L. My Blackness Is the Beauty of This Land.
Jeffers, R. Beauty of Things, The.
 Birds and Fishes.
 Divinely Superfluous Beauty.
 Rearmament.
Jennings, E. Ugly Child, The.
Johnson, J. White Witch, The.
Johnston, E. Lines: To a Young Gentleman of Surpassing Beauty.
Jones, M. After the Small Pox.
Jones, P. If I Were Rita Hayworth.
Jonson, B. Elegy, An: "Though beauty be the

mark of praise."
 To Mary, Lady Wroth.
Joyce, J. My Dove, My Beautiful One.
Kahal, I. Night Is Young and You're So Beautiful, The.
Kahn, G. You Stepped Out of a Dream.
Kasischke. Pall.
Katz, J. Imperfect Is Our Paradise, The.
Keats. Ode on a Grecian Urn.
Kemble. Sonnet: "What is my lady like? thou fain would'st know."
Kenney. Plume.
Kenny, M. Still-Life.
Kern, J. Cleopatterer.
 You Were Never Lovelier.
Kinnell. Saint Francis and the Sow.
Kinsella, T. Portrait of the Artist, A.
 Soft, To Your Places.
Kizer, C. Hera, Hung from the Sky.
Kleban, E. One.
Knott. Sonnet: "Way the world is not, The."
Koch, K. Energy in Sweden.
Košek, M. It All Depends on How You Look at It.
Kynaston. To Cynthia.
 To Cynthia, on Concealment of Her Beauty.
Lake, P. Introduction to Poetry.
Lamb, C. Timid grace sits trembling in her eye, A.
Landon. Banquet, The.
Landor, W. Rose Aylmer.
Le Gallienne. Beauty Accurst.
Leapor. Strephon to Celia.
Lefroy. Palaestral Study, A.
Legaré. To a Lily.
Leigh, R. On a Fair Lady, Looking in the Glass.
Leslie, E. Little Bit Independent, A.
Li Ch'ing-chao. Tune: 'Magnolia Flowers.'
Lochhead, L. Grim Sisters, The.
Lorde. Naturally.
Lovelace, R. Fair Beggar, The.
 Gratiana Dancing [or Dauncing] and Singing.
 To Amaranta, That She Would Dishevel[l] Her Hair[e].
Lowell, J. In a Copy of Omar Khayyám.
Lyttelton. Soliloquy of a Beauty in the Country.
MacLean, S. Turmoil, The.
MacLeish. Not Marble nor the Gilded Monuments.
MacNeice. Circe.
Madgett. Black Woman.
Martin, H. That Face.
Masefield. On Growing Old.
McCarthy. Alice Blue Gown.
McKay, C. To O.E.A.
McLain, P. Beauty, That Lying Bitch.
Meinke. Sonnet on the Death of the Man Who Invented Plastic Roses.
Mercer, J. Jeepers Creepers.
 Tangerine.
 You Must Have Been a Beautiful Baby.
Meredith, G. When I Would Image.
Merrill, J. Peacock, The.
Michelson, R. Queen Esther Award, The.
Millay, E. "Euclid Alone Has Looked on Beauty Bare."
 Spring.
Mitford. On a Beautiful Woman.
 Song: "Fairest things are those which live, The."
Montagu, L. Between Your Sheets.
Moore, T. Believe Me, If All Those Endearing Young Charms.
Morley, H. Parents.
Myers, J. Mom Did Marilyn, Dad Did Fred.
Nabbes. Song, The: "Beauty no more the subject be."
Nairne. Heiress, The.
O'Hara, F. Having a Coke with You.
 Poem: "O solo mio, hot diggety, nix 'I wather think I can'."
Olson, C. Kingfishers, The.
 La Chute.
Parker, A. God of Pepper, The.
 No Fool, the God of Salt.
Parnell, T. Elegy, to an Old Beauty, An.
Percival. Morning among the Hills.

Phillips, C. Toys.
Piatt, S. Lesson in a Picture, A.
Piercy. Barbie Doll.
Pinkard, M. Sweet Georgia Brown.
Poe. Al Aaraaf.
 Israfel.
 Lake: To———, The.
 Sleeper, The.
 Song: "Young flowers were whispering in melody."
 Stanzas: "How often we forget all time, when lone."
 To Helen.
 Valley of Unrest, The.
Pogson, P. Exits.
 Face Mask.
 Hairdressing.
Porter, C. All of You.
 It's All Right with Me.
Pound, E. Dance Figure.
 Study in Aesthetics, The.
Praed. Beauty and Her Visitors.
Prestwich. How to Choose a Mistress.
Prince, F. Token, The.
Prior. Nonpareil.
 To a Lady: She Refusing to Continue a Dispute with Me, and Leaving Me in the Argument.
Probyn. Frustrated.
Procter, A. Lost Chord, A.
Rafferty, C. Arsonist Tells His Story to the Attorney, The.
Ransom, J. Judith of Bethulia.
Roberson. Eclipse.
Robin, L. Louise.
Robinson, E. Beauty as a Shield.
Roethke. I Knew A Woman.
Rohrer, M. Quick Sell the Pig.
Romero, L. If Marilyn Monroe.
Rosenberg, I. Beauty.
Rossetti, C. Cousin Kate.
Sanchez, S. Song No. 3: "Cain't nobody tell me any different."
Sandburg, C. Flash Crimson.
 Murmurings in a Field Hospital.
Sansom, M. To Cleon's Eyes.
Santayana. On a Piece of Tapestry.
Sepamla. Odyssey, The.
Sexton. Snow White and the Seven Dwarfs.
Shakespeare, W. Phoenix and the Turtle, The.
Shapiro, K. Cut Flower, A.
Shaughnessy, B. Your One Good Dress.
Shelley, P. Hymn to Intellectual Beauty.
Sherwin, J. Nightpiece.
Shirley, J. Love's Hue and Cry.
Siddal. Lust of the Eyes, The.
Simms, C. Grey Wagtail on the Tyne.
Singer, E. Cant. 5.6 & c.
Slessor. William Street.
Smith, P. Blonde White Women.
Smith, S. Pretty.
Smith, W. Independence Day.
St. John, P. Pearle's Poem.
Stanley, T. Celia Singing.
 Glowworm, The.
Stein, G. Bundles for Them.
 Suppose an Eyes.
Stevens, W. Peter Quince at the Clavier.
 Sunday Morning.
Stevenson, A. He Who Loved Beauty.
Stevenson, R. To Henry James.
Strode. On a Good Leg and Foot.
 On Fairford Windows.
Suckling, S. Sonnet: "Dost see how unregarded now."
 To B. C.
Suckling, S. et al. Song: "When, dearest, I but think on [or of] thee."
Surrey. Frailty and Hurtfulness of Beauty, The.
Swanger. Wayne's College of Beauty, Santa Cruz.
Swift, J. Lady's Dressing Room, The.
 Stella's Birthday; Written in the Year 1718[/9].
 Stella's Birthday [1721].
Swinburne. Aholibah.
 Sapphics.
Symons, A. Faint Love.

Taylor, B.   Paean to the Dawn, A.
Teasdale.   Moonlight.
Tennyson, A.   To—. With the Following Poem.
Thaxter.   Alone.
Thomas, E.   Glory, The.
Thompson, D. P.   Sister Lakin and Lally.
Tierney, H.   Alice Blue Gown.
Traherne.   Salutation [or Salutations], The.
Trethewey, N.   Hot Comb.
Tuckerman, F.   Question, The.
Unknown.   Art Thou That She.
  First of May, The.
  I Saw My Lady Weep.
  Madrigal: "My Love in her attire doth show her
    wit."
  Question, A.
  There Is a Lady Sweet and Kind.
Unknown, sometimes at. to Sir Walter Ralegh.
  As You Came from the Holy Land [of
    Walsingham].
Unknown, fr. Terezin Concentration Camp.
  Birdsong 2.
Wakoski.   Poet Recognizing the Echo of the
    Voice, A.
Waller, E.   Song: "Go[e], lovely rose."
Wang, J.   Tune: 'Magnolia Flowers.'
Waring, B.   When a Beautiful Woman Gets on
    the Jutiapa Bus.
Warren, H.   Dames.
  Jeepers Creepers.
Warren, R.   Arizona Midnight.
Wat.   From "Songs of a Wanderer."
Webster, A.   Faded.
Wells, C.   Poster Girl's Defence, The.
Wenderoth, J.   Aesthetics of the Bases Loaded
    Walk.
  Disfortune.
Whiting, R.   Louise.
Whitman, W.   Beauty.
Wiese, B.   Going Home Madly.
Wilbur.   Beautiful Changes, The.
  Caserta Garden.
  Piazza di Spagna, Early Morning.
  Potato.
  Still, Citizen Sparrow.
  Thyme Flowering among Rocks.
  Transit.
Wilde, L.   Poet's Destiny, The.
Williams, S.   Song upon Miss Harriet Hanbury,
    Addressed to the Revd Mr Birt.
  Straight Talk from Plain Women.
Willson, F.   Estray, The.
  To Hersa.
Wither.   Ninth Canticle, The.
Witting.   Beauty Is the Straw.
Wodehouse, P.   Cleopatterer.
Wordsworth, W.   Composed upon Westminster
    Bridge, September 3, 1802.
  I Wandered Lonely as a Cloud.
  To the Highland Girl of Inversneyde.
Wright, J.   What Is Beautiful.
Wright, K.   Unlikely Obbligato of
    Andersonstown.
Wright, R.   And This Is My Beloved.
Wruber, A.   Lady in Red, The.
Wunderlich, M.   One Explanation of Beauty.
Wylie.   Beauty.
  Preference.
Yeats.   Before the World Was Made.
  Crazed Girl, A.
  Crazy Jane Talks with the Bishop.
  Folly of Being Comforted, The.
  He Remembers Forgotten Beauty.
  Memory.
  No Second Troy.
  Old Men Admiring Themselves in the Water,
    The.
  Secret Rose, The.
  Symbols.
  Thought from Propertius, A.
Yee, M.   Handbook of Sex of the Plain Girl,
    The.
Yellen, J.   Ain't She Sweet?
Young, A.   Dance For Ma Rainey, A.
Young, D.   Rothko's Yellow.

Beauty and the Beast
Brown, E.   Beauty and the Prince Formerly
    Known as Beast.
Beauty Parlors
Dauer.   Lois at the Hair Salon.
Beavers
Rothenberg, J.   Seneca Journal 1: "A Poem of
    Beavers."
See also **Mountain Beavers**
Bedouins
Taylor, B.   Bedouin Song.
Bedrooms
Berger, D.   Lincoln Bedroom, The.
Cornford, F.   Country Bedroom, The.
Jacob, M.   Little Poem.
Komunyakaa.   Between Days.
Smith, S.   Goodnight.
Beds
Alvi, M.   Bed, The.
Arnold, M.   Last Word, The.
Benét, S.   For City Spring.
Blagg, T.   In Bed This Morning.
Coleman, W.   Bedtime Story.
Davison, P.   Bed Time.
"Field."   Love rises up some days.
Herrick.   Her Bed.
Hope, A.   Bed, The.
Janeczko.   Blanket Hog.
Jewsbury.   Verses: "I am monarch of troubles a
    host."
Larkin, P.   Sad Steps.
  Talking In Bed.
Lovelace, R.   To Lucasta: The Rose.
Lowell, R.   Man and Wife.
Madhubuti.   Loneliness, A.
Matson, C.   Bedside.
Montagu, L.   Between Your Sheets.
Morley, C.   Plumppuppets, The.
Ni Dhomhnaill.   Leaba Shíoda.
Ramsay, A.   Polwart on the Green.
Ross, A.   Two in Bed.
Schilpp, M.   Non Sequitur.
Shapiro, D.   House (Blown Apart).
Smith, C.   Beds.
Stevenson, R.   Bed in Summer.
  Land of Counterpane, The.
  My Bed Is a Boat.
Stillman, M.   Lullaby for Suzanne.
Surrey.   Laid in My Quiet Bed.
Swinburne.   Love and Sleep.
Unknown.   Get Up, Get Up.
  Lord Randal[l].
Updike.   Insomnia the Gem of the Ocean.
Warren-Moore.   All-Night Issue, The.
Beech Trees and Beechnuts
Frost, R.   Boundless Moment, A.
Beef
Unknown.   Little More Cider, A.
Beer
Alexie.   Reservation Love Song.
Allen, F.   Fall, The.
Arnold, G.   Beer.
Brown, G.   Old Women, The.
Bukowski.   Crucifix in a Deathhand.
Chavez, L.   After the Prom.
Gay, J.   Birth of the Squire; an Eclogue, The.
Housman, A.   Terence, This Is Stupid Stuff.
Leland, C.   Hans Breitmann's Party [or Barty].
Leonard, T.   Jist Ti Let Yi No.
Roberts, K.   Plastic Cup, The.
Stedman, E.   Ballad of Lager Bier, The.
Stephens, J.   Glass of Beer, A.
Sterling, A.   Under the Anheuser Bush.
Thackeray.   Dear Jack.
Unknown.   Gud Ber.
Webster, A.   Enigma No. 6.
Winner, S.   Lilliputian's Beer Song.
Bees and Beekeeping
Baxter, J.   Wild Bees.
Blunden.   Forefathers.
Booth, P.   Bee.
Bukowski.   b.
Carew, T.   Upon a Mole in Celia's Bosom.
Clare, J.   To an Angry Bee.
Dickinson, E.   Bee, The.

Bees.
  Letter to Bee.
Emerson, R.   Humble-Bee, The.
"Field."   Penetration.
Frost, R.   White-Tailed Hornet, The.
Gerstler.   BZZZZZZZ.
Graham, H.   Opportunity.
Herrick.   Captived Bee; or, The Little Filcher,
    The.
Lear, E.   Limerick: "There was an Old Man in a
    tree."
Levin, P.   Lost Bee, The.
  Planting Roses.
Lovelace, R.   Black Patch on Lucasta's Face, A.
Morgan, R.   Honey.
Mtshali.   Inside My Zulu Hut.
Orton, B.   Beekeeper.
Patten, B.   Bee's Last Journey to the Rose, The.
Peck, J.   Mount Bromley Hymn.
Plath.   Arrival of the Bee Box, The.
  Stings.
  Swarm, The.
  Wintering.
Pogson, P.   Bee.
  Resin.
Reese, L.   Telling the Bees.
Stainer.   Honeycomb, The.
Toomer.   Beehive.
Turner, C.   Julius Caesar and the Honey-Bee.
Unknown.   Bee-Keeper, The.
  Swarm of Bees, A.
Watts, I.   How Doth the Little Busy Bee.
Winkfield, T.   Nature Study.
Beethoven, Ludwig van
Berger, B.   To Answer Your Question.
Clampitt.   Beethoven, Opus 111.
Lanier, S.   To Beethoven.
Levy, A.   Sinfonia Eroica.
Millay, E.   On Hearing a Symphony of
    Beethoven.
Ray, H.   Beethoven.
Rich, A.   Ninth Symphony of Beethoven
    Understood at Last as a Sexual Message, The.
Rylander, E.   Dancing on Beethoven's Birthday.
Seaman, E.   Double Dactyls.
Spender, S.   Beethoven's Death Mask.
Beetles
Blind.   Scarabæus Sisyphus.
Fisher, A.   Upside Down.
Kaufman, S.   Beetle on the Shasta Daylight.
Sorrentino.   Zoo, The.
Szymborska.   Seen from Above.
Beets
Nash, O.   Parsnip, The.
Begging and Beggars
Aleshire.   Double, The.
Arnold, M.   West London.
Ayres.   On a Fair Beggar.
Berry, W.   Music, A.
Bishop, E.   Pink Dog.
Browning, R.   Twins, The.
Bruner.   Beggar, The.
Coleman, H.   Black Soldier Remembers, A.
Coleridge, M.   Insincere Wish Addressed to a
    Beggar, An.
Dana, R.   Mark, The.
Dickinson, E.   I Never Lost as Much.
Douglas, K.   Egypt.
González, R.   Marías, Old Indian Mothers.
Herrick.   Beggar to Mab, the Fairy [or Fairie]
    Queen, The.
Hippolyte.   So Jah Sey.
Hughes, F.   Foxes.
Jackson, H.   Grab-Bag.
King, W.   Beggar Woman, The.
Kleinzahler.   Ebenezer Californicus.
Moss, T.   Beggar, The.
Mother Goose.   "Hark, Hark, the Dogs Do
    Bark."
Parker, M.   Maunding Soldier; or, The Fruits of
    Warre Is Beggery, The.
Plath.   Applicant, The.
Ruden, S.   Beggar Outside Cape Town
    Station, A.
Stephens, J.   Glass of Beer, A.
Swirszczynska.   Same Inside, The.

Thomas, D.   Hunchback in the Park, The.
Unknown.   Gaberlunzie Man, The.
   Oh Cruel Was the Press-Gang.
Yeats.   Beggar to Beggar Cried.
See also **Homeless, The; Vagabonds**

Behn, Aphra
Unknown.   Elegy upon the Death of Mrs. A.
   Behn, the Incomparable Astrea, An.

Beirut, Lebanon
Adnan.   Beirut-Hell Express, The.
"Adonis" [*or* "Adunis"].   Diary of Beirut Under
   Siege, 1982, The.
Hammad, S.   Broken and Beirut.
Tuéni.   Beirut.

Belfast, Northern Ireland
Brodsky, J.   Belfast Tune.
Carson, C.   Belfast Confetti.
   Campaign.
   Slate Street School.
Causley.   HMS *Glory.*
Craig, M.   Ballad to a Traditional Refrain.
Heaney, S.   Summer nineteen sixty nine.
MacNeice.   Belfast.
Mahon.   Afterlives.
Montague, J.   Falls Funeral.
Morrissey, S.   Thoughts in a Black Taxi.
Muldoon, P.   Aisling.
Paulin.   Under the Eyes.

Belgium
Auden.   Brussels in Winter.
Craig, M.   Ballad to a Traditional Refrain.
Sassoon.   On Passing the New Menin Gate.

Belief
Apotheker, A.   Burning Bush.
Cary, P.   Hymn: "How dare I in thy courts
   appear."
Chasin.   In Communication with a UFO.
Duncan, R.   Song of the Borderguard, The.
Empson.   Invitation To Juno.
Everson, W.   Narrows of Birth, The.
Forché.   Ancapagari.
Gaskill, C.   I Can't Believe That You're in Love
   with Me.
Greene, R.   Ideals.
Howard, B.   Would You Believe It?
Killigrew, A.   Upon the Saying That My Verses
   Were Made by Another.
Kiser.   My Creed.
Landor, W.   You Smiled, You Spoke, and I
   Believed.
Levine, P.   Belief.
Loesser.   I Believe in You.
Morton, J.   On Sir Henry Ferrett, M.P.
Nichol.   St. Anzas IX.
Pack, R.   Proton Decay.
Rukeyser, M.   This Place in the Ways.
Smith, S.   God the Eater.
Thayer, L.   Little Child's Faith, The.
Towers, T.   Three Observations on Belief.
Unknown.   Firm Belief.
See also **Faith**

Belisarius
Longfellow, H.   Belisarius.

Bellbirds
Kendall, H.   Bell-Birds.

Belloc, Hilaire
Beerbohm, M.   After Hilaire Belloc.
Wolfe, H.   Hilaire Belloc.

Bells
Adams, L.   Bell Tower.
Becker, C.   Door-Bell, The.
Bungay.   Creeds of the Bells.
Crane, H.   Broken Tower, The.
Cummings, E.   Anyone Lived in a Pretty How
   Town.
Curtis, T.   To My Father.
Ekelof.   Greece.
Fordham.   Bells of St. Michael.
Guiney.   Sunday Chimes in the City.
Heard, J.   Sabbath Bells.
Herrick.   Bellman, The.
Housman, A.   Bredon Hill.
Ingelow.   High Tide on the Coast of
   Lincolnshire, 1571, The.
Jackson, L.   Ding-Donging.

Linden, M.   Church Bells, The.
Loesser.   If I Were a Bell.
Longfellow, H.   Bells of San Blas, The.
   Christmas Bells.
Mant, R.   Church Bells, The.
McDonald, W.   Christmas Bells, Saigon.
Meynell, A.   Chimes.
Owen, W.   Anthem for Doomed Youth.
Poe.   Bells, The.
Prescot.   Balsham Bells.
Probyn.   Changes.
Reverdy.   Secret.
Sexton.   Ringing the Bells.
Sidney, S.   Dirge: "Ring out your bells [*or*
   belles], let mourning shows [*or* shewes] be
   spread."
Slessor.   Five Bells.
Smith, M.   Chimes.
Thompson, C.   Church Bells.
Thoreau.   Dong, Sounds the Brass in the East.
Turner, C.   Buoy-Bell, The.
Unknown.   Bells, The.
   London Bells.
   Upon Arch-bishop Laud, Prisoner in the Tower.
   1641.
Warsh.   Suicide Rates, The.
Whittier.   Skipper Ireson's Ride.
Wilbur.   Bell Speech.
Williams, W.   Catholic Bells, The.

Belshazzar
Bibb.   Belshazzer's Feast.

Ben Bulben, Ireland
Yeats.   Under Ben Bulben.

Bennett, Susan Eugenia
Fordham.   In Memoriam. Susan Eugenia
   Bennett.

Beowulf
Amis, K.   Beowulf.
De Los Santos, M.   Wiglaf.
Heaney, S.   Beowulf.
Unknown.   Beowulf.

Bergman, Ingmar
Duncan, R.   Ingmar Bergman's "Seventh Seal."

Berkeley, George
Davie.   Fountain, The.

Berkshire Hills, Massachusetts
Ray, H.   Among the Berkshire Hills.

Berlin, Germany
Mahon.   Postcard from Berlin, A.
Sisson.   Over the Wall: Berlin, May 1975.
Villanueva, A.   Even the Eagles Must Gather.

Bermuda
Long, J.   Bermuda Triangle.
Marvell.   Bermudas.

Berrigan, Daniel
Rich, A.   Burning of Paper instead of Children,
   The.

Berryman, John
Harper, M.   Tongue-tied in Black and White.
Meredith, W.   John and Anne.
Merwin, W. S.   Berryman.
Vizenor.   Tropisms on John Berryman.

Bertrand de Born
Pound, E.   Near Perigord.
   Sestina: Altaforte.

Bestiality
Dickey, J.   Sheep Child, The.
Donovan, K.   Entering the Mare.

Bethlehem
Brooks, P.   O Little Town of Bethlehem.
Longfellow, H.   Three Kings, The.
Parker, D.   Maid-Servant at the Inn, The.
Roberts, E.   Christmas Morning.
Yeats.   Second Coming, The.

Betjeman, Sir John
Causley.   Betjeman, 1984.

Betrayal
Bibbins, M.   Mud.
Breton, N.   Cradle Song: "Come, little babe."
Brown, L.   (Here Am I) Broken Hearted.
Burns, R.   Hughie Graham.
Cabico, R.   Gameboy.
Cheney-Coker.   Poem for a Guerrilla Leader.
Creeley.   Anger.

Davidman.   And Pilate Said.
Davidson, J.   Ballad of Hell, A.
De Tabley.   Song of Faith Forsworn, A.
Galvin, J.   Station (4).
Goodman, M.   Open Poem.
Graves, R.   Lost Jewel, A.
   Not at Home.
   Wreath, The.
Greenwell, D.   Fidelity Rewarded.
Harbach, O.   Poor Pierrot.
Hardy, T.   Broken Appointment, A.
Housman, A.   Is my team plowing?
Ismaili.   Bajji.
   Queue.
Kern, J.   Poor Pierrot.
Kossman.   Judas' Reproach.
Medina, T.   Big House Revisited, The.
Millay, E.   Bluebeard.
Myles, E.   Maxfield Parrish.
Newson, D.   Turnabouts.
Ralegh, S.   Farewell to False Love, A.
Ransom, J.   Winter Remembered.
Seto, T.   Blood Ties.
Sitwell, S.   Judas and the Profiteer.
Tayson, R.   Phone Sex.
Unknown.   Frankie and Johnny [*or* Johnnie *or*
   Albert].
   Lamkin.
Whittier.   Ichabod[!].
Wyatt, S.   Lover Showeth How He Is Forsaken
   of Such as He Sometime Enjoyed, The.

Biafra
Achebe.   Christmas in Biafra (1969).
See also **Civil War, Nigeria**

Bible
Abse.   Inscription on the Flyleaf of a Bible.
Bishop, E.   Over 2000 Illustrations and a
   Complete Concordance.
Blanchard, F.   Word of God, Across the Ages.
Branch, A.   In the Beginning Was the Word.
Cowper, W.   To Mary Unwin.
Dickinson, P.   Moses and the Princess.
Eliscu, E.   Great Day.
Equi.   Things to Do in the Bible.
"Field."   Will You Crucify Your King?
Gershwin.   It Ain't Necessarily So.
Giovanni.   Poem for Flora.
Hardy, T.   Respectable Burgher, The.
Harte, B.   Colenso Rhymes for Orthodox
   Children.
Heaney, S.   Other Side, The.
Hemans.   Vigil of Rizpah, The.
Herbert, G.   Thanksgiving, The.
Johnson, J.   Creation, The.
Longfellow, H.   Sand of the Desert in an Hour-
   Glass.
Mahon.   Ecclesiastes.
McAuley, J.   Art of Poetry, An.
Merritt, C.   Woman of Color.
Merwin, W. S.   Calling, A.
Moore, M.   Is Your Town Nineveh?
Moorer.   Bible, The.
   Mountain Tops.
Oden.   Bible Study.
Ostriker.   Story of Abraham, The.
Plutzik.   And in the 51st Year of That Century,
   While My Brother Cried in the Trench, While
   My Enemy Glared from the Cave.
Quarles.   On the Gospel.
   On the Holy Scriptures.
Reznikoff.   Isreal I.
Rose, B.   Great Day.
Simic.   Begotten of the Spleen.
   Concerning My Neighbors, the Hittites.
Smart, C.   My Cat Jeoffry.
   Song to David, A.
   Strength.
Traherne.   On the Bible.
Ullman.   Rain.
Unknown.   From a London Bookshop.
   On the Bible.
Vaughan, H.   Book, The.
   H. Scriptures.
Warton, T.   Stanzas on the Psalms.
Wesley, C.   N T.
White, V. C.   Child of Adam.

Wilner, E.   Reading the Bible Backwards.
Youmans, V.   Great Day.
Young, K.   Central Standard Time.

Bicycles and Bicycling
Alpaugh, D.   Herbie.
Beeching, H.   Going Down Hill on a Bicycle.
Jarry.   Passion of Jesus Considered as an Uphill Race, The.
Laing, K.   Race on Gathering Bites.
Malouf.   Bicycle.
Noguchi, R.   When for Weeks the Sea is Flat.
Piercy.   Cyclist, The.
Rhys, K.   Interlude.
Shapcott, T.   Bicycle Rider, The.
Townsend, A.   Bicycle Racers, The.
Tzara.   Chanson Dada.
Weigl.   Him, on the Bicycle.

Billboards
Larkin, P.   Sunny Prestatyn.
Nash, O.   Song of the Open Road.

Billiards
Willson, M.   Ya Got Trouble.

Bingen, Germany
Norton, C.   Bingen on the Rhine.

Biography
Buchanan, G.   Lyle Donaghy, Poet, 1902-1949.
Burkard.   2 Poems on the Same Theme.
Cooper, D.   In New York.
   In School.
Greacen.   Captain Fox.
Larkin, P.   Posterity.
McFadden, R.   Contemplations of Mary.
Violi.   Index.
Whitman, W.   When I Read the Book.

Birch Trees
Coleridge, M.   Lady of Trees, The.
Frost, R.   Birches.
   Young Birch, A.
Levy, A.   Birch-Tree at Loschwitz, The.

Bird-watching
Endrezze.   Birdwatching at Fan Lake.
Kinnell.   Gray Heron, The.
Nash, O.   Up from the Egg; the Confessions of a Nuthatch Avoider.
Van Duyn.   Letters from a Father.

Birds
Addonizio.   Bird.
Albrecht, A.   Below White Cliffs.
   Elkhorn Slough.
Alvarez, J.   Redwing Sonnets.
Ammons, A. R.   City Limits, The.
Asquith.   Birds on a Powerline.
Auden.   Bird-Language.
   Decoys, The.
   Their Lonely Betters.
Awoonor.   Weaver Bird, The.
Axelrod, D.   Guide to Urban Birds, A.
Baker, D.   Envoi: Waking After Snow.
Balaban.   Along the Mekong.
Bampfylde.   To the Redbreast.
Barham.   Jackdaw of Rheims, The.
Barnes, D.   Portrait of a Lady Walking.
Barnes, W.   Lullaby.
Belieu.   Radio Nebraska.
Berger, B.   Plagiarist, The.
   Silver-Paced.
   Transmigration.
Berry, W.   Wild, The.
Bidgood.   Safaddan.
Bishop, E.   Some Dreams They Forgot.
Blake, W.   How Sweet I Roamed [or Roam'd] from Field to Field.
Blight.   Oyster-Eaters, The.
Blind.   Entangled.
Blodgett.   Fossil.
Bogan, L.   Statue and Birds.
Boruch.   Camouflage.
Bosley.   Bird Sips Water.
Bottomley.   Dawn.
Brautigan.   Surprise.
Bridgeman, P.   Cockatoo.
Brontë, A.   Captive Dove, The.
Bryant, W.   Robert of Lincoln.
   To a Waterfowl.
Budy.   On High Street.

Campbell, D.   Hear the Bird of Day.
Carbone, L.   Flight from the Marriage Bed.
Carroll, L.   Little Birds Are Playing.
Carter, E.   Ode to Wisdom.
Castro, M.   New York City.
Ceravolo.   Sunset.
Christie.   Hollywood Finch, The.
Clampitt.   Syrinx.
Clare, J.   Birds' Nest.
   Birds' Nests.
   Little Trotty Wagtail.
   Nightingale's Nest, The.
   Wren, The.
   Wryneck's Nest, The.
   Yellowhammer, The.
Clarke, A.   Japanese Print.
Coatsworth.   No Shop Does the Bird Use.
   Swallows, The.
Cohen, M.   Evensong.
Cokinos.   Earth Movers, The.
Coleridge, S.   Answer to a Child's Question.
Coles, G.   Heron in the Alyn.
Collier, M.   Brave Sparrow.
Conyus.   Day in the Life of . . . , A.
Cook, E.   On Seeing a Bird-Catcher.
   Song of the Imprisoned Bird.
Cording.   Peregrine Falcon, New York City.
Corey, S.   Complicated Shadows.
Costanzo.   In the Aviary.
Cranch.   Bird Language.
Crane, H.   Carrier Letter.
Crane, S.   Little Birds of the Night.
Cullinan.   M. François le Vaillant Recalls His Travels to the Interior Parts of Africa.
Curry.   Mute Swans.
   Swallows and Tortoises.
Davies, W.   Truth, The.
Davis, O.   Panic of Birds, The.
De la Mare.   Owl, The.
   Spotted Flycatcher, The.
   Thomas Hardy.
Dean, D. K.   Arrival.
DeFoe, M.   Aviary.
Dickinson, E.   "Hope" is the thing with feathers.
   Cat.
Dipoko.   Our Life.
Dissanayake.   Freedom.
Dogen.   On Non-dependence of Mind.
Doolittle, H.   Birds in Snow.
Dove, R.   In the Old Neighborhood.
Dransfield.   Strange Bird, A.
Dunbar, P.   Sympathy.
Eigner.   Live /, Bird Which.
Elmslie, K.   Feathered Dances.
Erdrich.   I Was Sleeping Where the Black Oaks Move.
Everson, W.   Canticle to the Waterbirds, A.
Fagan.   Weather They Were Written In, The.
Faigao, B.   Kundiman.
Faust, H.   After the Storm.
"Field."   Goad, The.
Finch, P.   Scaring Hens.
Follain.   Taxidermist, A.
Francis, R.   Waxwings.
Frost, R.   Hill Wife, The.
   House Fear.
   Impulse, The.
   Last Word of a Bluebird, The.
   Loneliness.
   Minor Bird, A.
   Never Again Would Birds' Song Be the Same.
   Oft-Repeated Dream, The.
   On a Bird Singing in its Sleep.
   Oven Bird, The.
Gallagher, T.   Little Invitation in a Hushed Voice.
   Unsteady Yellow.
Galvin, B.   Running.
Ghigna.   Lesson of Night, A.
Ghiselin.   Food of Birds, The.
Gilbert, C.   African Sculpture.
Goldbarth.   Seriema Song.
Golding, L.   O Bird, So Lovely.
Graham, J.   Thinking.
Greger.   Penguin Jane Austen, The.
Grosholz.   Last of the Courtyard, The.

Guest, B.   Geese Blood.
Guevara, M.   Once When I Was in the Eighth Grade.
Guillén, N.   Usurers, The.
Gunn, T.   On the Move.
Hall, D.   Short Circuit.
Hall, H.   Listening Macaws, The.
Hanzlicek, C.   Feeding Frenzies.
Hardy, T.   Weathers [or Weather].
Harrison, J.   Birds That Woke Us: An Urban Pastoral, The.
   Swifts at Evening.
Harryman.   Allegory.
Hart-Smith.   Boomerang.
Hartnett.   I Have Exhausted the Delighted Range.
Heath-Stubbs.   Jays, The.
Hemans.   Written on the Sea-Shore.
Henry, P.   Love Birds.
Hernandez, D.   Pigeons.
Heyen.   Crane in Reeds.
   Derailment.
Higginson, W.   Interstices.
Hirshfield, J.   Story, A.
Hope, A.   Death of the Bird, The.
Hopkins, G.   As Kingfishers Catch Fire.
   Windhover, The.
Hove.   Lost Bird.
   Migratory Bird.
Hughes, F.   Bird.
   Birds.
   Kookaburra.
Hughes, T.   Crow and the Birds.
   October Robin, An.
   Rooks love excitement.
   Swifts.
Hugo, V.   Be Like the Bird.
Hull, L.   Ornithology.
Inez.   Monologue of the Falconer's Wife.
Jarrell.   Country Life, A.
   Mockingbird, The.
Jeffers, R.   Birds.
   Birds and Fishes.
Jenkins, M.   Diver-Bird.
   Martins.
Johnson, G.   Heart of a Woman, The.
Jones, G.   Esyllt.
Keats.   How Many Bards Gild the Lapses of Time!
Kenyon, J.   Insomnia at the Solstice.
Kimbrell, J.   Rooftop.
Kinnell.   Gray Heron, The.
   Last Songs.
Kinsella, J.   Sick Woman.
Kirchwey.   He Considers the Birds of the Air.
Kirkup.   Scarecrows.
Knowles, S.   Tails and Heads.
Lake, P.   Blue Jay.
Lampert, D.   Poem for Sophie.
Lawrence, D.   Blue Jay, The.
Lear, E.   Limerick: "There was an old man of Whitehaven."
Lennon, J.   Fat Budgie, The.
Levertov.   Claritas.
   Wren, A.
Levine, P.   Red Dust.
Lewis, J.   Footprint on the Air, A.
Linden, M.   Bird Song, The.
Lindley, D.   Nearness.
Liu, T.   Highway 6.
Livingstone, D.   Bateleur.
   Lake Morning in Autumn.
Lloyd, J.   Thoughts of Boyhood.
Logan, W.   Moorhen.
Longenbach.   What You Find in the Woods.
Lovelace, R.   Falcon, The.
MacBeth [or Macbeth].   Owl.
MacCaig.   Blue Tit on a String of Peanuts.
   Ringed Plover by a Water's Edge.
MacDiarmid, H.   Caledonian Antisyzygy, The.
   Ex Vermibus.
   Perfect.
   Storm-Cock's Song, The.
   Whip-the-World.
Mackey, N.   Winged Abyss.
Madge.   Birds of Tin, The.

Magowan. Days of 1956.
Major, C. Apple Core.
  On Trying to Imagine the Kiwi Pregnant.
Makuck. Prey.
Marshall, J. Air Dagger.
Masefield. Sea Change.
Mathias, R. Sanderlings.
Mattawa. Letter to Ibrahim.
Mayes, J. Descant.
McAuley, J. Nocturne.
McCarthy, G. Sound of Guns, The.
McKay, C. Birds of Prey.
Melly. Homage to René Magritte.
Melville, H. Man-of-War Hawk, The.
Meyers, B. Daybreak.
Meynell, A. October Redbreast, The.
  Roaring Frost, The.
Michelson, M. Bird, The.
Middleton, C. Oystercatchers.
Miller, V. Beat Poem by an Academic Poet.
Monro. Bird at Dawn, The.
Moore, L. Spectacular.
Moore, M. Bird-witted.
  Smooth Gnarled Crape Myrtle.
Moore, N. Island and the Cattle, The.
Morley, D. Politicisation of the North Wind,
  The.
Mother Goose. Aristotle's Story.
  Who Killed Cock Robin.
Murray, L. Equanimity.
Nash, O. Grackle, The.
  Up from the Egg; the Confessions of a Nuthatch
  Avoider.
Nemerov. More Joy in Heaven.
Nesbit, E. Vies Manquées.
Norris, L. Cage Bird and Sky Bird.
O'Hara, F. Easter.
Okara. Spirit of the Wind.
Oliver, M. Kingfisher, The.
Olson, C. Variations Done for Gerald Van De
  Wiele.
Oness, C. Climbing.
O'Reilly, M. Small Girl Brings an Injured Bird
  into the Surgery, A.
O'Sullivan, M. Giant Yellow.
  Hill Figures.
Pack, R. Thrasher in the Willow by the Lake,
  The.
Page, P. Deaf-Mute in the Pear Tree.
Palgrave. Linnet in November, The.
Pfeiffer, E. Aspiration.
Plumly. Cardinals in a Shower at Union Square.
Plumpp. Survivors.
Poe. Romance.
Pogson, P. Deep.
Posamentier, E. Bird Named Isidore, The.
Probyn. Tête-à-Tête.
Pryde, A. I'll See You Down the Lane.
Radiguet. Poem: "Red eiderdown at the
  window, A."
Raine, K. Good Friday.
Rakosi. Good Morning.
  Paraguay.
Ramanujan. In the Zoo.
Rankin, J. Old Currawong.
Ransom, J. Lady Lost.
Ravikovitch [or Ravikovich]. Sound of Birds at
  Noon, The.
Reeves, J. Grasshopper and the Bird, The.
Riley, J. Few of the Bird-Family, A.
Roberts, N. Gull's Flight, The.
Roethke. Kitty-Cat Bird, The.
  Rose, The.
Rolle, S. Birds' Refuge, The.
Rossetti, C. Birthday, A.
  Fly Away, Fly Away.
Russell, S. Poem: "I keep feeling all space as
  my image."
Russell, T. To the Owl.
Sandburg, C. River Roads.
  Three Spring Notations on Bipeds.
Seed. During War, the Timeless Air.
Shakespeare, W. Phoenix and the Turtle, The.
Shapcott, T. Shadow of War, 1941.
Shearing, G. Lullaby of Birdland.
Shepherd, R. Provisional.

Simic. Fork.
Simpson, L. As Birds Are Fitted to the Boughs.
Smith, S. None of the Other Birds.
Sorby. Man without a Middle, The.
Spenser. Sonnet 73: 'Being my self captived
  here.'
Stafford, W. Juncos.
Stephens, J. Rivals, The.
Stern, G. Pile of Feathers.
  Red Bird.
Stevens, W. Of Mere Being.
Sutter. Peregrine.
Swenson, M. Waterbird.
Sylvester, J. Palms.
Synge. In Glencullen.
Taggard. Thirst.
Tate, J. Blue Booby, The.
Teasdale. Moods.
Thomas, D. Because the Pleasure-Bird
  Whistles.
  Over Sir John's Hill.
Thomas, E. Snow.
  Unknown Bird, The.
Tobin, D. Pigeons.
Todd, R. Joan Miró.
Townsend, A. Butane, Kerosene, Gasoline.
Trowbridge, W. Bad Birds.
Tsaloumas. Falcon Drinking.
Unknown. Bird Scarer, The.
  Bird Starver's Cry.
  Cuckoo Song, The.
  Cutty Wren, The.
  Death and Burial of Cock Robbin, The.
  Examination Question.
  Fowls [or Foweles or Fowles] in the Frith.
  Riddle: "Cuckoo and the gowk, The."
  Rooks, The.
  Two Pigeons.
  Warning, A.
  When Jenny Wren Was Young.
Unknown, fr. Terezin Concentration Camp.
  Birdsong.
Updike. Upon Learning That a Bird Exists
  Called the Turnstone.
Van Duyn. Letters from a Father.
  Mockingbird Month.
Vaughan, H. Bird, The.
Veinberg, J. Owl's Landscape, An.
Very. Birds of Passage, The.
Virgil. Grass Path Lasts.
Wagoner, D. Author of American Ornithology
  Sketches a Bird, Now Extinct, The.
  Loons Mating.
  Nuthatch.
Walcott. Season of Phantasmal Peace, The.
Warner, R. Chough.
  Egyptian Kites.
Warren, R. Death of Time.
  Heart of Autumn.
  Patriotic Tour and Postulate of Joy.
Warsh. Gout.
Warton, T. Fashioned After the Manner of
  Master Geoffrey Chaucer in His Assembly of
  Fowls.
Watson, R. Ballad of the Bird-Bride.
  Cage, The.
  Die Zauberflöte.
  White Bird, The.
Weiss, G. Lullaby of Birdland.
Whalen. "Never Apologize; Never Explain."
White, E. Listener's Guide to the Birds, A.
Whitman, W. Out of the Cradle Endlessly
  Rocking.
  To the Man-of-War Bird.
Whitmore, S. Bird, The.
Wilberforce, S. Impromptu.
Wilbur. All These Birds.
  Marché aux Oiseaux.
  Still, Citizen Sparrow.
Williams, C. Shock.
Williams, H. To the Curlew.
  To the White Bird of the Tropic.
Williams, W. Breakfast.
  To Waken an Old Lady.
Wise, S. Closure Opening Its Trap.
Witt, S. Waterfowl Descending.

Wordsworth, W. Reverie of Poor Susan, The.
Wright, D. Juxtapositions.
  Those Walks We Took.
Wright, J. Birds.
  Black Cockatoos.
  Invention of a Garden, The.
  Presentation of Two Birds to My Son, A.
Yeats. Lonely the Sea-Bird Lies at Her Rest.
Yenser, S. Another Lo-Cal Elegy.
Young Bear. Song Taught to Joseph, The.
Young, A. Stockdoves, The.
See also **Waterfowl**

Birds of Paradise
Coleridge, M. In London Town.
Lovelace, R. Lucasta's Fan[ne], with a
  Looking-Glass[e] in It.

Birds' Nests
Blind. On a Forsaken Lark's Nest.
Clare, J. Green Woodpecker's Nest, The.
  Hen's Nest.
  Nightingale's Nest, The.
  Pewits Nest.
  Sky Lark, The.
Larcom. Brown Thrush, The.
Thomas, E. Birds' Nests.
Unknown. Warning, A.
Young, A. Nest, The.

Birmingham, Alabama
Giscombe. (1962 at the Edge of Town).
  (Recent Past, The).
Randall, D. Ballad of Birmingham.

Birmingham, England
MacNeice. Birmingham.

Birth
Acholonu. Nigeria in the Year 1999.
Ai. Country Midwife: A Day, The.
Barber, D. Small Hours.
Berg, S. May 1970.
Berger, J. Between Worlds.
Bernstein, C. Dysraphism.
Blaser. Ruler, The.
Bradstreet, A. Before the Birth of One of Her
  Children.
Brecht, B. Mary.
Brooks, G. Birth in a Narrow Room, The.
Broumas, O. Pealing, The.
Buckley, V. Origins.
Cave. Written a Few Hours before the Birth of
  a Child.
Charach, R. Labour and Delivery.
Chesterton, G. Donkey, The.
Copus, J. Sea-Polyp, The.
Couzyn. Creation.
  Pain, The.
  Spell for Birth.
  Transformation.
Creeley. River Wandering Down.
De Kok. Small Passing.
De la Mare. Birthnight: To F, The.
Durcan. Birth of a Coachman.
Erdrich. Birth.
Esteves. Celebration of Home Birth: November
  15th, 1981, A.
Fanthorpe. Nativities.
Feinstein, E. Calliope in the Labour Ward.
Fenton, J. Born Too Soon.
Garrett, E. Airborne.
Gay, J. Birth of the Squire; an Eclogue, The.
Gilbert, C. Midwives, The.
Glück, L. Garden, The.
Goodison. Birth Stone.
Goodtimes. Learning to Smile.
Hardy, T. To an Unborn Pauper Child.
Harjo, J. For Alva Benson, and for Those Who
  Have Learned to Speak.
  White Bear.
Harper, M. Deathwatch.
Hejduk. Sleep of Adam, The.
Herrick. Epitaph upon a Sober Matron, An.
  Upon Batt.
Hope, A. Imperial Adam.
Hughes, T. February 17th.
  Yesterday He Was Nowhere to Be Found.
Joyce, J. Ecce Puer.
Kay, J. What Jenny Knows.

Kazantzis. Midwife.
Kennelly. Bread.
Lee, D. There Was a Man.
Leigh, H. Natural Child, The.
Levertov. Map of the Western Part of the County of Essex in England, A.
Lorde. Now That I Am Forever with Child.
Macgoye. August the First; Court Martial. The Mother Speaks.
Madhubuti. Men and Birth: the Unexplainable.
Mattera. Giovanni Azania.
McCallum, S. Jamaica, October 18, 1972.
Meynell, A. Maternity.
Miles, J. Conception.
Miller, E. Jasmine.
Minhinnick. Catching My Breath.
Muldoon, P. Mules.
Murphy, R. Beehive Cell.
O'Donoghue, B. Weakness, The.
Ogilvy. Newly Dead and Newly Born.
Olds, S. Language of the Brag, The.
Olson, C. Ring of, The.
Oppen. Eclogue: "Men talking, The."
Ortiz. To Insure Survival.
Parker, D. Maid-Servant at the Inn, The.
Plath. Morning Song.
Ponsot. Multipara: Gravida 5.
Porteous. Calf.
Pratt, M. Poem for My Sons.
Prunty. Winter's Tale, A.
Quarles. Born in Winter.
Ramanujan. Foundlings in the Yukon.
Ridler. Christmas and Common Birth.
Rogers, P. Opus from Space.
Rome, H. F. D. R. Jones.
Rossetti, C. Before the Paling of the Stars.
Rungano. Labour.
Sanchez, S. Present.
Savageau. Henri Toussaints.
Shange. Oh, I'm 10 Months Pregnant.
Simmons, J. Join Me in Celebrating.
Slessor. Sleep.
Spires. Robed Heart, The.
Stallworthy, J. Almond Tree, The.
Stevens, W. Discovery of Thought, A.
To the One of Fictive Music.
Stewart, S. Apple.
Sykes, B. Cycle.
Szymborska. Born of Woman.
Taylor, J. Epigram: "Fair Beatrice tucks her coat up somewhat high."
Tindal. Birth Wail, The.
Townsend, A. Eighteenth-Century Medical Illustration: The Infant in its Little Room.
Van Dyke, C. Birth, 1975.
Van Peenen, H. Will Campbell Displays His Craniotribe.
Waniek. Chosen.
Whitman, W. Out of the Cradle Endlessly Rocking.
Woman Waits for Me, A.
Wilde, O. Ave Maria, Gratia Plena.
Williams, O. With Me.
Williams, S. Say Hello to John.
Wohlfeld. That Which Is Fugitive, That Which Is Medicinally Sweet or Alterable to Gold, That Which Is Substantiated by Unscientific Means.
Woods, J. What Do You Do When It's Spring?
Wright, J. Lake in Central Park, The.
Yeats. Consolation.
Stick of Incense, A.
Young, D. For a Wife in Jizzen.

Birth Control
Jonson, B. To Fine Lady Would-Be.
Miller, E. She Is Flat on Her Back.
See also **Abortion; Contraception**

Birth Defects
Charach, R. Labour and Delivery.
Gorey. Limerick: "To his club-footed child said Lord Stipple."
Stallworthy, J. Almond Tree, The.
Van Peenen, H. Will Campbell Displays His Craniotribe.

Birthdays
Adamson. My Tenth Birthday.

Byron, G. On My Thirty-third Birthday.
On This Day I Complete My Thirty-sixth Year.
Coleridge, H. First Birthday, The.
Geier. On Your Twenty-First Birthday.
Geiger. Soundtracks.
Goodman, P. Birthday Cake.
Hahn, K. Hula Skirt, 1959, The.
Heard, J. My Husband's Birthday.
Johnson, S. Short Song of Congratulation [*or* To a Young Heir], A.
To Mrs Thrale [on Her Thirty-fifth Birthday].
Jonson, B. Ode. To Sir William Sydney, on His Birthday.
Jordan, J. If You Saw a Negro Lady.
Komunyakaa. Gift Horse.
Kunitz, S. Passing Through.
Kusano Shimpei. Birthday Party.
Kuskin. Rose on My Cake, The.
Lee, D. Jan's Birthday.
Lowell, J. Sixty-Eighth Birthday.
Madigan. Curtis Fuller.
Moorer. Birthday Wishes to a Husband.
Birthday Wishes to a Minister of the Gospel.
Birthday Wishes to a Physician.
Mother Goose. Birthdays.
Myles, E. December 9th.
Ogilvy. Grannie's Birthday.
Paschen. Potatoes Coriander.
Pope, A. To Mrs. M. B. on Her Birth-Day.
Porter, P. On This Day I Complete My Fortieth Year.
Rago. Child's Birthday, A.
Robinson, M. Birth-Day, The.
Rosen, M. Eddie and the Birthday.
Rossetti, C. Birthday, A.
Rouse. Birthday, A.
Rukeyser, M. Rondel: "Now that I am fifty-six."
Scupham. Birthday Triptych.
Sholl. Thinking of You, Hiroshima.
Simmons, J. Birthday Poem, A.
Steele, T. Epitaph: "Here lies Sir Tact, a diplomatic fellow."
Swift, J. Stella's Birthday ([March 13,] 1727).
Stella's Birthday, 1725.
Stella's Birthday; Written in the Year 1718[/9].
Stella's Birthday [1721].
Thomas, D. Poem in October.
Thribb. Lines on the Hundredth Anniversary of the Birth of W. Somerset Maugham.
Torregian. Poem for the Birthday of Huey P. Newton.
Tranter. Having Completed My Fortieth Year.
Tripp. On My Fortieth Birthday.
Wagenlander. Mother's Birthday.
Wenderoth, J. Disfortune.
Wesley, C. For His Wife, on Her Birthday.
Williamson, G. On His Birthday.

Birthmarks
Carew, T. Upon a Mole in Celia's Bosom.

Birthplaces
Alvi, M. Presents from My Aunts in Pakistan.
Corso. Birthplace Revisited.
Hardy, T. Domicilium.
Heaney, S. Birthplace, The.
Jonson, B. To Penshurst.

Bishop, Elizabeth
McClatchy. Bishop Reading.

Bitterness
Amadiume. Bitter.
Amichai [*or* Amikhai]. Quick and Bitter.
Aytoun [*or* Ayton], R. To His Forsaken Mistress.
Baugh, E. Nigger Sweat.
Brown, S. Bitter Fruit of the Tree.
Carew, T. To Celia, upon Love's Ubiquity.
To My Inconstant Mistress [*or* Mistris].
Eliot, T. Lines for an Old Man.
Ellis, C. Adder's Epigrams.
Ford, C. There's No Place to Sleep in This Bed, Tanguy.
Graves, R. Laureate, The.
Hartnett. Small Farm, A.
Hughes, T. Her Husband.
Jones, T. Cwmchwefri.
Jong. Colder.

Kooser. Widow, A.
Kunitz, S. Thief, The.
Landon. Castle of Chillon, The.
Lorde. New York City 1970.
Major, C. Isolate.
Millay, E. Scrub.
Mura. Blueness of the Day, The.
Piercy. Letter to Be Disguised as a Gas Bill.
Smith, S. Lightly Bound.
Teasdale. After Love.
Thomas, R. Island, The.

Black (color)
Crosby, H. Photoheliograph (For Lady A.).
Herbert, E. Sonnet of Black Beauty.
Knott. Goodbye.
Levertov. Wings, The.
Nichols, G. Black.
Sanchez, S. Haiku: "Was it yesterday."
Strand. Man in Black, The.
Vertreace, M. Black Tulips.

Black Power
Baraka. State/meant.
Clinton, M. I Wanna Be Black.
Gilmore, B. Revolution.
"Jerry." Mabrak.
See also **African-American Power**

Blackberries
Heaney, S. Blackberry-Picking.
Kinnell. Blackberry Eating.
Nicholson, N. Blackberry, The.
Plath. Blackberrying.
Sherman, M. Blackberries.
Turner, J. Plan, The.
Van den Bergh. Nocturn: "Moon rows burning, The."

Blackbirds
Cohen, L. All There Is to Know about Adolph Eichmann.
Dixon, M. Bye Bye Blackbird.
Forbes, C. Killer Blues.
Ledwidge. Lament for the Poets: 1916.
Moss, T. Reconsideration of the Blackbird, A.
Satyamurti. Where Are You?
Stevens, W. Thirteen Ways of Looking at a Blackbird.
Stevenson, A. In the Orchard.
Thomas, R. Blackbird Singing, A.
Unknown, fr. Terezin Concentration Camp. Birdsong.
Wolfe, H. Blackbird, The.

Blackouts
Orfalea, G. My Father Writing Joe Hamrah in a Blackout.

Blacks
Adisa. No, Women Don't Cry.
Ai. Riot Act, April 29, 1992.
Alexander, E. Venus Hottentot, The.
Allen, L. Rub a Dub Style inna Regent Park.
Baraka. Ka 'Ba.
Bontemps. God Give to Men.
Brooks, G. To Black Women.
To the Diaspora.
Brown, S. Let Them Call It Jazz.
Strong Men.
Carroll, K. Domino Theory (or Snoop Dogg rules the world), The.
Something easy for Ultra Black nationalists.
Upper Marlboro.
Clinton, M. History as Trash.
Traditional Post-Modern Neo-HooDoo Afra-Centric Sister in a Purple Head Rag Mourning Death and Cooking.
Coleman, W. Where I Live.
Corpus. Blkfern-jungal.
Cullen, C. From the Dark Tower.
D'Aguiar. Dreadtalk.
Damas. Just Like the Legend.
S.O.S.
Davis, F. Christ is a Dixie Nigger.
Derricotte. Black Boys Play the Classics.
Family Secrets.
Passing.
Doyle, R. E. Ma Ramon.
DuBois, W. Song of the Smoke, The.
Ellis, T. T.A.P.O.A.F.O.M.

Farr, R.   At general Electric, where they eat their/young.
Giovanni.   Ego Tripping [(There May Be a Reason Why)].
Nikki-Rosa.
Hamer.   Line Up.
Hayden, R.   Beginnings.
Henderson-Holmes.   'C' ing in Colors: Red.
Holman, M.   Mr. Z.
Hopkins, L.   Nat Love: Black Cowboy.
Hughes, L.   Cross.
Cubes.
Dream Variation[s].
Negro Speaks of Rivers, The.
Neighbor.
Visitors to the Black Belt.
Irvine, W.   To Be Young, Gifted, and Black.
Jeffers, L.   My Blackness Is the Beauty of This Land.
Johnson, L.   Reggae Sounds.
Jordan, J.   Something Like a Sonnet for Phillis Miracle Wheatley.
Joseph, A.   On Being Told I Don't Speak Like a Black Person.
Traitor.
Kaufman, B.   Untitled.
King, J.   Intercity Dub.
Loftin.   Weeksville Women.
Lorde.   Between Ourselves.
Harriet.
Naturally.
Lowell, R.   For the Union Dead.
Madhubuti.   B Network, The.
Magnificent Tomorrows.
Mandiela, A.   Speshal Rikwes.
McKay, C.   If We Must Die.
Nichols, G.   Beverley's Saga.
Pomeroy, R.   Gay Love and the Movies.
Reynolds, S. F.   Open Letter to All Black Poets, An.
Roberts, N.   Nigger and Some Poofters, A.
Salaam.   I Live in the Mouth of History.
Sanchez, S.   This is Not a Small Voice.
Smith, P.   What It's Like to Be a Black Girl (For Those of You Who Aren't).
Sundiata.   Notes from the Defense of Colin Ferguson.
Sykes, B.   One Day.
Toure, A.   Azuri.
Travis, N.   Sunbathing.
Valerie, L.   On Apologies.
Walker, A.   Remember?
Weems, M.   Funk.
Wheatley, P.   On Being Brought from Africa to America.
See also **African Americans**

Blacksmiths
Dibdin, C.   Anchorsmiths, The.
Hopkins, G.   Felix Randal.
Longfellow, H.   Village Blacksmith, The.
Unknown.   Blacksmiths, The.
Smoke-Blackened Smiths.

Blake, William
Kinzie.   Engraving of Blake, An.
Rukeyser, M.   Homage to Literature.

Blasphemy
Benét, S.   For All Blasphemers.
"Field."   Trinity.

Blenheim, Battle of (1704)
Southey, R.   Battle of Blenheim, The.

Blessings
Clare, J.   God Looks on Nature With a Glorious Eye.
Dawe, B.   Beatitudes.
Everson, W.   High Embrace, The.
Frost, R.   Answer, An.
Herrick.   Crutches.
Good-Night, or Blessing, The.
Grace for a Child.
To Dianeme.
Wassaile, The.
Herzog, A.   God Bless the Child.
Jarrell.   Blind Sheep, The.
Landon.   Bonds of Affection.
Luterman, A.   Justice of the Peace, The.

Tremblay, G.   It Is Important.
Tsvetayeva [*or* Tsvetaeva].   I Bless the Daily Labor.
Unknown.   God Bless You.
I See the Moon.
My Darlings' Shoes.
Vaughan, H.   To the Best, and Most Accomplished Couple.
Whittier.   Barefoot Boy, The.
Godspeed.
Wright, C.   May God Go with You, Son.

Blindness
Berry, W.   Music, A.
Butts, A.   Nature of Braille, The.
Campbell, J.   Blind Man at the Fair, The.
Cary, P.   True Love.
Cibber.   Blind Boy, The.
Crashaw.   Samson to His De [*or* a] lilah.
Cristall.   Blind Man, The.
De la Mare.   All but Blind.
Dubin, A.   I Only Have Eyes for You.
Dunn, D.   War Blinded.
Echeruo.   Melting Pot.
Gibson, W.   Sight.
Holmes, O.   Prelude to a Volume Printed in Raised Letters for the Blind.
Jarrell.   Blind Sheep, The.
Keller, H.   In the Garden of the Lord.
Kohler, S.   Shepherd.
Levertov.   Uncertain Oneiromancy.
Loy.   Der Blinde Junge.
Mapanje.   On His Royal Blindness Paramount Chief Kwangala.
Milton.   On His Blindness.
On His Deceased Wife.
To Mr. Cyriack Skinner upon His Blindness.
Norris, L.   Ballad of Billy Rose, The.
Noyes, A.   Spring, and the Blind Children.
Pearce, N.   Blind.
Piper, E.   Indian Counsel.
Rossetti, C.   Sketch, A.
Sangster, M.   Blind Man, The.
Sassoon.   Does It Matter?
Saxe, J.   Blind Men and the Elephant, The.
Tabb.   Milton.
Williams, W.   Parable of the Blind, The.
Young, G.   Miracle, The.

Blizzards
"Antler."   Thoughts Breathing in a Blizzard.
Dougherty.   Cocoons.
See also **Storms**

Blocks (toys)
Stevenson, R.   Block City.

Blood
Ai.   Country Midwife: A Day, The.
Amadiume.   Bloody Masculinity.
Benn.   Bunch of Drifter Sons Hollered, A.
Berrigan, T.   Orange Jews.
Blunden.   1916 Seen from 1921.
Midnight Skaters, The.
Brontë, C.   Lonely Lady, The.
Campbell, T.   Hohenlinden.
Cassian.   Blood, The.
Celan.   Tenebrae.
Chin, D.   Sterling Williams' Nosebleed.
Dickey, J.   Poisoned Man, The.
Dickinson, E.   Name—of it—is "Autumn," The.
Dipoko.   Pain.
Donne.   Flea, The.
Donovan, K.   Underneath Our Skirts.
Duncan, R.   My Mother Would Be a Falconress.
Everson, W.   Passion Week.
"Field."   Flaw, A.
Grandfather Koori.   Never Blood So Red.
Gunn, T.   Faustus Triumphant.
Hachenburg, H.   Terezin.
Hall, D.   Poet at Twenty, A.
Harper, M.   Breaded Meat, Breaded Hands.
Herrick.   Upon a Child That Died [*or* Dyed].
Hughes, L.   Negro Speaks of Rivers, The.
Iverem, E.   Keeper.
Jackson, R.   For Thurman Thomas.
Jarrell.   Islands, The.
Kees.   Conversation in the Drawing Room, The.
Larsen, L.   Red.

Lawrence, D.   Mosquito Knows, The.
Levin, D.   Red Water.
MacDiarmid, H.   One of the Principal Causes of War.
Mayer, G.   Drip Drip or Not Bloody Likely.
Moore, M.   Odor of a Metal Is Not Strong, The.
Naden.   Poet and Botanist.
O'Hara, F.   Poem: "Eager note on my door said 'Call me', The."
Padgett, R.   Orange Jews.
Polak, J.   Storm, The.
Raworth.   Hot Day at the Races.
Rodriguez, L.   Heavy Blue Veins.
Rouse.   Sunday Morning.
Sherry, J.   Lepidoptery.
Simic.   Butcher Shop.
Stafford, W.   Ceremony.
Sternlieb.   Right of Way.
Strange.   Transits.
Thomas, L.   Subway Witnesses, The.
Thomas, R.   Welsh Landscape.
Ungaretti.   Babel.
Unknown, fr. Terezin Concentration Camp.   Pain Strikes Sparks on Me, the Pain of Terezin.
Vaughan, H.   Abel's Blood.
Washbourne.   Circulation, The.
Wheelwright.   Esprit d'Escalier.
Whitman, W.   Trickle Drops.
Wright, F.   Blood.
Wright, J.   Living by the Red River.

Blue (color)
Berlin.   Blue Skies.
Cherry, K.   Reading, Dreaming, Hiding.
DeCarteret, M.   Coloring.
Divakaruni.   Indigo.
Edwards [*or* Edwardes], R.   Blue Room, The.
Evans, A.   Fringed Gentians.
Forrest, G.   It's a Blue World.
Francis, R.   Blue Winter.
Exclusive Blue.
Gahagan.   Colour of the Old Man's Eyes, The.
Hart, L.   Blue Room, The.
Jacobs, H.   Goree.
Keats.   Blue! 'Tis the Life of Heaven, the Domain.
Kelly, R.   Coming.
Larsen, W.   Bluebird in Cutleaf Beech.
Lowry, M.   About Ice.
McCarthy, J.   Alice Blue Gown.
Ormond.   Certain Questions for Monsieur Renoir.
Rodgers, R.   Blue Room, The.
Shapcott, T.   Blue Paisley Shirt, The.
Silano, M.   Such a Way to Go.
Stanard, C.   Wrong Color.
Stein, K.   Past Midnight, My Daughter Awakened by Miles Davis' *Kind of Blue.*
Tate, J.   Blue Booby, The.
Tierney, H.   Alice Blue Gown.
Toure, A.   Azuri.
Volkman.   Untitled.
Wakoski.   Blue Monday.
Wright, C.   Cicada Blue.
Wright, R.   It's a Blue World.

Blue Jays
Carryl, G.   Patrician Peacocks and the Overweening Jay, The.
Francis, R.   Blue Jay [*or* Bluejay].

Blueberries
Layton.   Berry Picking.
Moore, L.   Indian Girl.

Bluebirds
Frost, R.   Last Word of a Bluebird, The.
Melville, H.   Blue-Bird, The.
Padgett, R.   Big Bluejay Composition.

Blues (mood)
Akst, H.   Am I Blue?
Arlen, H.   I Gotta Right to Sing the Blues.
Baraka.   Funk Lore.
Beeks.   Parker's Mood.
Berlin.   Blue Skies.
Brown, L.   Sunny Side Up.
Caldwell, A.   Left All Alone Again Blues.
Davis, T.   Rogue and Jar: 4/27/77.
Derricotte.   Blackbottom.

Blues (music)

DeSylva, B. G.   Sunny Side Up.
Ellington, D.   I Ain't Got Nothin' But the Blues.
Encarnacion.   Bulosan Listens to a Recording of Robert Johson.
Fields, D.   Blue Again.
Fisher, M.   When Sunny Gets Blue.
Forrest, G.   It's a Blue World.
Gardinier.   Blues.
Hart, L.   Blue Moon.
Henderson, R.   Sunny Side Up.
Hernton.   Long Blues, The.
Hughes, L.   Blues, The.
  Hard Daddy.
  Homesick Blues.
  Miss Blues'es Child.
  Weary Blues, The.
Jefferson, B.   Easy Rider Blues.
Jones, P.   Song: "I have so little sorrow."
Jordan, M.   When a Woman Gets Blue.
Kern, J.   In Love in Vain.
Knight, E.   Poem for Myself (Or Blues for a Mississippi Black Boy), A.
McHugh, J.   Blue Again.
Medina, T.   Rhudine Rhudine.
Perdomo, W.   Nigger-Reecan Blues.
Porter, C.   I Concentrate on You.
Randall, D.   Langston Blues.
Razaf, A.   (What Did I Do to Be So) Black and Blue?
Rodgers, R.   Blue Moon.
Segal, J.   When Sunny Gets Blue.
Smith, B.   Empty Bed Blues.
St. John, D.   Homage to Robert Johnson.
Unknown.   Railroad Blues, The.
  Southern Blues.
Williams, T.   Kitchen Door Blues.
Wright, R.   It's a Blue World.
Young, A.   Blue Monday.
  Blues Don't Change, The.

See also **Melancholy**

Blues (music)

Arlen, H.   I Gotta Right to Sing the Blues.
Aubert, A.   Bessie Smith's Funeral.
Baker, H.   Tobacco Warehouse Blues.
Ball, A.   Jazz.
Baraka.   Legacy.
Bauer, G.   So You Want to Hear the Blues.
Bottoms.   Homage to Lester Flatt.
Brathwaite, E.   Blues.
Brooks, G.   Queen of the Blues.
Brown, L.   Birth of the Blues, The.
Caldwell, A.   Left All Alone Again Blues.
Carr, L.   How Long Blues.
Cortez, J.   How Long Has Trane Been Gone.
Dent.   For Walter Washington.
DeSylva, B. G.   Birth of the Blues, The.
Dittberner-Jax.   Blues for Aunt Ruth.
Dumas, H.   Concentration Camp Blues.
Eady.   Muddy Waters and the Chicago Blues.
Encarnacion.   Bulosan Listens to a Recording of Robert Johnson.
Ferdinand.   Blues (in Two Parts), The.
France, L.   Blues for Bird.
Gibb.   Paul Butterfield, Dead at 44.
Gilbert, C.   Enclosure.
Harper, M.   For Bud.
  Narrative of the Life and Times of John Coltrane: Played by Himself, A.
Hayden, R.   Homage to the Empress of the Blues.
Henderson, R.   Birth of the Blues, The.
Hopkins, L.   Death Bells.
Hughes, L.   Brass Spittoons.
  Note on Commercial Theatre.
  Weary Blues, The.
Hunter, A.   Down-Hearted Blues.
Jackson, A.   Choosing the Blues.
Johnson, R.   Hellhound on My Trail.
Jones, R.   Trouble in Mind.
Lea, S.   One White Face in the Place, The.
Lowe, J.   With Thanks to Eddie Shaw.
McClaurin.   Mask, The.
McDonald, W.   Honky-Tonk Blues.
McLaughlin, J.   Black Irish Blues.
Moore, L.   Bluesman's Blues, A.
  Haiku.

Overton, R.   Blues in "C."
Patterson, R.   Hopping Toad Blues.
  Sundown Blues.
Plumpp.   Remembered.
Powell, J.   It Was Fever That Made the World.
Robson, J.   Blues for the Lonely.
Rushing.   Good Morning, Blues.
Sanchez, S.   Liberation / Poem.
Senghor.   Blues.
Smith, B.   Backwater Blues.
  Black Mountain Blues.
  In the House Blues.
Unknown.   Railroad Blues, The.
Vinz.   Blues, The.
Wallenstein.   Blues 1.
  Blues 2.
Weatherly, T.   Blues for Franks Wooten.
Weinstein, N.   Drummond's Lover Sings the Blues.
Williams, C.   Gulf Coast Blues.
Wojahn.   John Berryman Listening to Robert Johnson's "King of the Delta Blues," January 1972.
Young, A.   Blues Don't Change, The.
Zu-Bolton.   Struggle-Road Dance.

Boarding Houses

Acorn.   On Saint-Urbain Street.
Kipling, R.   Ballad of Fisher's Boardinghouse, The.
Larkin, P.   Mr Bleaney.
Van Duyn.   Condemned Site.

Boasting

Forman, R.   This Poem.
Griffiths, S.   Just a Product of a Certain Situation.
Hardy, T.   Epitaph for George Moore.
McDaniel, J.   Logic in the House of Sawed-Off Telescopes.
Sandburg, C.   Primer Lesson.

Boats and Boating

Asekoff, L.   North Star.
Ashbery.   Archipelago, The.
Bishop, E.   Arrival at Santos.
  Fish, The.
Blind.   Russian Student's Tale, The.
Campbell, R.   Fishing Boats in Martigues.
Chute, M.   My Plan.
Clark, T.   Time.
Davis, J.   Boat, A.
Davison, P.   Equinox 1980.
Deutsch.   Barges on the Hudson.
Dickey, J.   Lifeguard, The.
Duncan, R.   New Poem, A.
Eberhart, R.   Chart Indent.
  Immortal Picture, The.
Emmett.   Boatman's Dance.
"Field."   As two fair vessels side by side.
Finlay, I.   Boat's Blueprint, The.
Garrigue.   Song in Sligo.
Guiney.   Down Stream.
Hall, D.   Long River, The.
Hirsch, E.   Tristan Tzara.
Holmes, O.   Old Ironsides.
"Ingoldsby."   Lines Left at Mr Theodore Hook's House in June, 1834.
Jackson, H.   My Lighthouses.
Jeffers, R.   Boats in a Fog.
Komunyakaa.   Boat People.
Lake, P.   In Rough Weather.
Lear, E.   Limerick: "There was an Old Man in a boat."
Lim-Wilson.   Raising the Dead.
Loesser.   Sit Down, You're Rockin' the Boat.
MacCaig.   So Many Summers.
Marvell.   Bermudas.
Mayer, B.   Boats.
Merrill, J.   Parrot Fish, The.
Moore, J.   One Reason I Went to Prison.
Morley, D.   Enniskillen.
Mura.   Huy Nguyen: Brothers, Drowning Cries.
Murphy, R.   Last Galway Hooker, The.
Nicholson, N.   From a Boat at Coniston.
Oppen.   Product.
Ou-yang Hsiu.   Old Fisherman.
Pape.   Dinner on the Miami River.
Pilling.   You and You, In the Pink.

Plath.   Crossing the Water.
Porteous.   Decommissioning.
Rafferty, P.   Passage.
Ríos, A.   Domingo Limón.
Robinson, M.   Describes her Bark.
Rollings.   For Dear Life.
Samaras, N.   Crossing the Strait.
Share, D.   Divorced.
Spencer, B.   Boat Poem.
Stevenson, R.   Travel.
  Where Go the Boats?
Synková, A.   To Olga.
Wang Wei.   Seeking a Mooring.
Zukofsky, L.   Ways, The.

See also **Ferry Boats; Freighters; Ships and Shipbuilding; Tugboats; Yachts**

Bobolinks

Bryant, W.   Robert of Lincoln.

Bodies

Abse.   Lunch and Afterwards.
  Pathology of Colours.
Armantrout.   Disown.
  Winter.
Ayres, R.   Corporeal.
Ball, J.   And This Is So.
Barnett, R.   Anorexic, The.
Baudelaire.   Snake That Dances, The.
Benedikt.   Thoughts.
Berlin.   Heat Wave.
Bethel, M.   Reggae Prophecy.
Bidart.   Ellen West.
Blagg, T.   In Bed This Morning.
Bogan, L.   Cartography.
Braun, Henry.   To Fat Boy, the Bomb.
Breton, A.   Free Union.
Bringhurst.   Parśvanatha.
Broumas, O.   Masseuse, The.
Bui-Burton.   Look at Me.
  My Love Is Like a Lily.
Butts, A.   Skin.
Cabico, R.   Antonio Banderas in His Underwear.
  Art in Architecture.
Caldwell, E.   Love Poem: "Olfactory paradise."
Campo.   What the Body Told.
Carter, E.   Dialogue, A.
Cavendish, M.   Dialogue betwixt the Body and the Mind, A.
  Of the Animal Spirits.
  Soul and Body.
  Soul's Garment, The.
Cendrars.   Great Fetishes, The.
Charach, R.   Question of Vitamins, A.
Child, A.   Squeeze.
Chubb, R.   Song of My Soul.
  Transfiguration.
Clarke, A.   Martha Blake at Fifty-one.
Clarke, C.   Rondeau: "They are bodies left unburied."
Clifton, L.   11/10 Again.
  Homage to My Hips.
  Lost Baby Poem, The.
Clover, J.   There Is the Body Lying in State.
Colby, T.   Dear, I Love.
Cooley.   Brother Body.
Cooper, J.   Waiting.
Couani.   Map of the World, The.
Coulehan, J.   Anatomy Lesson.
Coultas, B.   Human Museum, The.
Couzyn.   Creation.
  Mystery, The.
Creeley.   Body.
Crowley, A.   Rondels.
Cuddihy.   This Body.
Dawes, K.   Some Tentative Definitions 4.
Derricotte.   Invisible Dreams.
Donald.   Eye for an Eye, An.
  I Expect You Think This Huge Dark Coat.
Donne.   Ecstasy, The.
  Resurrection, Imperfect.
Dooley, M.   Does It Go Like this?
D'Orleans.   Smiling Mouth, The.
Douskey.   Wet Bodies.
Drieu la Rochelle.   Roundness.
Dudley, E.   Pathologist.
Duncan, R.   I Am a Most Fleshly Man.
  Torso / Passages 18, The.

Dyer, E.   Painting the Nude.
Ehret, T.   Lost Body.
Eliot, T.   Dedication to My Wife, A.
Elizabeth I.   Written in Her French Psalter.
Elizabeth, M.   She Teaches Him to Reach Out.
Emanuel, L.   She.
Equi.   Autobiographical Poem.
Erdrich.   Lady in the Pink Mustang, The.
Erdrich, H.   Fat in America.
Eyton, F.   Body and Soul.
Fatchen.   Hullo, Inside.
  Tailpiece.
Feinfeld, D.   Wound Man, The.
Felltham [or Feltham].   To Phryne.
"Field."   Sweet-Briar in Rose.
Fisk, M.   Late Afternoon.
Follain.   Mirror, A.
  Taxidermist, A.
Fox, S.   Miss Pimberton Of.
Foy, J.   Autopsy.
France, L.   Body Language.
Gallagher, T.   Each Bird Walking.
  Sea Inside the Sea.
Garcia, R.   Brief Entanglements.
Ginsberg, A.   After Lalon.
Graham-Pole, J.   Venipuncture.
Graves, R.   Thieves, The.
Green, J.   Body and Soul.
Gunn, T.   Man with Night Sweats, The.
Hacker, M.   Year's End.
Hadas, R.   Winged Words.
Hagiwara Sakutaro.   Lover of Love.
Halpern, D.   Her Body.
Harper, M.   Studs.
Hecht, A.   Feast of Stephen, The.
Herrera.   Resurrection of the Flesh, The.
Herrick.   Body, The.
  Life Is the Body's [or Bodies] Light.
Heyman, E.   Body and Soul.
Hilberry.   Body and Mind.
Hill, M.   Sleep.
Holst-Warhaft.   In the End Is the Body.
Holt, R.   Pleasure of Feeling Inside Your Body,
  The.
Holub.   Vanishing Lung Syndrome.
Hughes, L.   Red Silk Stockings.
Hume, C.   Birthday.
Hunter, T.   Wanting You.
Jackson, L.   Starved.
Jenyns.   Temple of Venus, The.
Jones, A.   Anorexia.
  Tap.
Josefowitz, N.   Music.
Joseph, A.   Learning to Laugh.
  Pleasure.
Kennedy, L.   Moonburn.
Klinger, A.   Transformation.
Klugman, S.   God's Body.
Komunyakaa.   Jeanne Duval's Confession.
  Slam, Dunk, and Hook.
Kowit.   In the Morning.
  What Chord Did She Pluck.
Lacavaro, A.   Advantages of Being a World
  Class Athlete, The.
LaFemina.   White Dwarf.
Larkin, J.   Legacy.
  My Body.
Larkin, P.   Mr Bleaney.
Laux.   China.
Lawrence, D.   Body of God, The.
  Eloi, Eloi, Lama Sabachthani?
Lee, L.   Interrogation, The.
  This Room and Everything in It.
Lee, W.   Lovers' Duet.
Levertov.   Our Bodies.
Levin, D.   Red Water.
Levis.   Morning After My Death, The.
Liu, T.   Size of It, The.
Livesay, D.   Other.
Loy.   Three Moments in Paris.
Lux.   Commercial Leech Farming Today.
MacDiarmid, H.   Scunner.
Maiden.   In the Gloaming.
"Malley."   Egyptian Register.
Manhire.   Distance between Bodies, The.
Marcus, B.   Justice.

Marks, G.   All of Me.
Martínez, V.   It Is Not.
  Night of Fathers.
Martinez, D.   Pain.
Marvell.   Dialogue between the Soul and [the]
  Body, A.
Marzán.   Emergency.
Matthews, W.   Descriptive Passages.
McClatchy.   My Mammogram.
McPherson, S.   His Body.
Metras, G.   Vanishing Point.
Morley, H.   Made out of Links.
Moulds, J.   Renoir's Bathers.
Muldoon, P.   Hard Drive.
Mulkey, R.   Why I Believe in Angels.
Muske, C.   Our Kitty.
Nagai, M.   Histories of Bodies.
Nelson, D.   Vallejo.
Niedecker.   News.
Noguere.   Soma.
Olds, S.   Language of the Brag, The.
Oppenheimer, J.   Innocent Breasts, The.
Palmer, M.   Eighth Sky.
  Erolog.
Perelman.   Cliff Notes.
Perillo.   Body Mutinies, The.
Phillips, C.   As From a Quiver of Arrows.
  Recumbent.
  Toys.
Piercy.   Friend, The.
Pollitt.   Mind-Body Problem.
Porter, C.   All of You.
Ports, K.   Desire.
Pratt, M.   Elbows.
Raine, K.   Love-Poem: "Yours is the face that
  the earth turns to me."
Ralegh, S.   Lie, The.
Ramanujan.   Elements of Composition.
  Hindu to His Body, A.
Ranaldo, L.   Five Weeks.
Rankin, J.   Tale.
Rayl, J.   Spring Storm.
Receveur.   Night Fear.
Reichard, W.   Monster's Dream, The.
Reverdy.   Squares.
Reynolds, R.   Peridot.
Rich, A.   Splittings.
Rilke.   Tombs of the Hetaerae.
Roberts, N.   Max Factor Pink.
Rollings.   Dirty Dreams and God Smiling.
Rosenberg, L.   Lesson in Anatomy, A.
Ryan, G.   Cruising.
Schneiders, J.   Weight.
Schwartz, R. L.   Late Summer.
  Possible.
Seibles.   Who.
Sexton.   In Celebration of My Uterus.
Sherman, M.   This Body.
Smart, C.   Author Apologizes to a Lady, for His
  Being a Little Man, The.
Smith, A.   Praise.
Smith, S.   Man Is a Spirit.
  This Englishwoman.
Snyder, G.   Bath, The.
Södergran.   Instinct.
Solomon, M.   Comment on My Host, A.
Sour, R.   Body and Soul.
Spender, S.   Abrupt and charming mover.
Spires.   Bodies, The.
Steinberg, D.   Image Was of Me Flowing
  Through You, The.
Stevenson, A.   Spirit Is Too Blunt an Instrument,
  The.
Stever, E.   Her Back to Me.
Strode.   On a Good Leg and Foot.
Sullivan, N.   To My Body.
Swenson, M.   Question.
Swirszczynska.   I Starve My Belly for a
  Sublime Purpose.
  I Talk to My Body.
Tana, P.   I Have Touched.
  Marvelous Beast.
  You Bring Me Back.
Triplett, P.   Spectral Dues.
  Studies in Desire.
Unknown.   I Have a Gentle Cock [or Gentil

  Cok].
  I Know Moon-Rise [or Moonrise].
  Joy and Temperance.
Unknown, fr. Terezin Concentration Camp.   Pain
  Strikes Sparks on Me, the Pain of Terezin.
Updike.   In Extremis.
Van Peenen, H.   Insulin Receptor.
Vaughan, H.   Resurrection and Immortality.
Volkman.   Untitled.
Waldman, A.   Skin / Meat / BONES.
Waller, E.   Of the Last Verses in the Book.
  On a Girdle.
Wanley.   Resurrection, The.
Ward, D.   Absolution.
  Limit.
Wat.   Facing Bonnard.
Weinstein, N.   Migration of Drummond's
  Organs (After Death), The.
Wenderoth, J.   First Impression.
Wheelwright.   Esprit d'Escalier.
Whitman, W.   Come, Said My Soul.
  I Sing the Body Electric.
Wiesinger, S.   Snow Climbers.
Wilner, E.   Muse, The.
Woods, D.   Prescription.
Wright, J.   Jewel, The.
  What Is Beautiful.
Wylie.   Preference.
Yeats.   Crazy Jane Talks with the Bishop.
  Lady's Third Song, The.
Yi, S.   Poem No. V.
See also **Nudity and Nudists**
Bodybuilding
  Katz, J.   Women Must Put Off Their Rich
    Apparel.
  Nilsson, H.   My Least Skirtable Deficiency.
Boer War
  Davidson, J.   Battle.
  Hardy, T.   Christmas Ghost-Story, A.
  Colonel's Soliloquy, The.
  Departure.
  Drummer Hodge.
  Embarcation.
  Wife in London, A.
  Kipling, R.   Absent-Minded Beggar, The.
  Bridge-Guard in the Karroo.
  Return, The.
  Morant, H.   Last Rhyme and Testament of Tony
    Lumpkin.
Boethius, Anicius Manlius Severinus
  Macoubrie.   Boethius at Cavalzero.
Bogs
  Heaney, S.   Bog Queen.
  Bogland.
  Tollund Man, The.
  Smith, S.   Our Bog is Dood.
Bohemian Life
  Gurney, I.   Bohemians, The.
  Herbert, S.   Lines for a Worthy Person Who Has
    Drifted by Accident into a Chelsea Revel.
  Parker, D.   Bohemia.
Boleyn, Anne
  Bibb.   Anne Boleyn.
  Wyatt, S.   Whoso List to Hunt.
Bolsheviks
  Unknown.   Harry Pollit Was a Bolshie.
Bombay, India
  Dharker.   Living Space.
Bombs and Bombing
  Back, R.   Untitled.
  Brock, V.   Remembering Dresden.
  Fiacc.   Intimate Letter 1973.
  Fisher, R.   Entertainment of War, The.
  Floyd.   Corporal Charles Chungtu, U. S. M. C.
  Garioch.   Phooie!
  Wire, The.
  Hitchcock.   Scattering Flowers.
  Holden, J.   Why We Bombed Haiphong.
  Ignatow, D.   All Quiet.
  Jarrell.   Truth, The.
  Layne, M.   Intersection in the Sky.
  Levertov.   Fragrance of Life, Odor of Death.
  Lipsitz.   Feeding, The.
  McDonald, W.   For Kelly, Missing in Action.
  Retired Pilot to Himself, The.

War Games.
Michelson, P. Enduring Witness, the Mosques of Kattankudi.
Miller, V. Light Reading.
O'Keefe, E. Chords.
Randall, D. Ballad of Birmingham.
Receveur. Eagle in the Land of Oz.
Reed, H. Chard Whitlow.
Rolfe, E. Casualty.
Paris—Christmas 1938.
Spender, S. Epilogue to a Human Drama.
Rejoice in the Abyss.
Stafford, W. At the Bomb Testing Site.
Szymborska. Terrorist, He Watches, The.
Todd, R. Joan Miró.
Weigl. Her Life Runs Like a Red Silk Flag.
See also **Air Warfare**

Bonaparte, Josephine
Hollander, J. Appearance and Reality.

Bones
Abse. Origin of Music, The.
Bly, R. Counting Small-Boned Bodies.
Coultas, B. Capitalist Projections.
Lecture #1.
Craveirinha. Seed Is in Me, The.
Donaldson, W. T'ain't No Sin to Dance Around in Your Bones.
Donne. Relic, The.
Evans, C. Lucy's Bones.
Garcia, R. Los Amantes.
Gehrke, S. Near the Mississippi.
Geiger. Dry Spell of Faith, A.
Hannan, M. Bone Die, The.
Harries, E. Bone Prison, The.
Harwood, G. Bone Scan.
Herd. Hyperion's Bones.
Hollander, J. Lady's-Maid's Song, The.
Hope, A. Meditation on a Bone.
Hughes, T. Relic.
Loden. Conversations with Dr. M.
Milton. On Shakespear[e].
Ramke. Paul Verlaine at the Grave of Lucien Létinois.
Roy, L. Suffering the Sea Change: All My Pretty Ones.
Stevens, W. Postcard from the Volcano, A.
Stow. Singing Bones, The.
Unknown. Epitaph on William Jones.
Williams, C. Bone.
Wylie. Full Moon.
See also **Skeletons**

Bonn, Germany
Garlick, R. Capitals.

Bonneau, Jennette
Fordham. Death of a Grandparent. Mrs. Jennette Bonneau.

Boobies
Tate, J. Blue Booby, The.

Books
Adams, F. To a Thesaurus.
Amis, K. Bookshop Idyll, A.
Balaban. Opening Le Ba Khon's Dictionary.
Beer, P. Footbinding.
Belloc. On His Books.
Bogan, L. Man Alone.
Bradstreet, A. Author to Her Book, The.
Brown, S. Marginalia.
Brownell, H. Suspiria Noctis.
Burns, J. How.
Reading.
Burns, R. Book-Worms, The.
Carew, T. Fancy, A.
Cavendish, M. Common Fate of Books, The.
Cerenio. 13 June 1994.
Collins, B. Tomes.
Coolidge, C. This Garden Being: The Hanging of Books.
Corso. I Held a Shelley Manuscript.
Dana, R. Pleasure Boat, The [*or* Pleasure-Boat, The].
Davidson, M. Dream Dream, The.
Disch. Bookmark, A.
Dove, R. First Book, The.
Drummond, W. Book, The.
Earle, J. Saturday in the '20s, A.

Elmusa. Bookishness.
Fearing. Literary.
Garcia, R. Book of Dreams, The.
Glaser, M. Changing Address Books.
Guiney. In the Reading-Room of the Brtish Museum.
Hadas, R. Moments of Summer.
Harmon, B. E. Chanson Delice.
Harwood, L. "Utopia," The.
Hass, R. Bookbuying in the Tenderloin.
Herrick. Argument of His Book, The.
To God.
To His Book[e].
To My Ill Reader.
To the Most Illustrious and Most Hopeful[l] Prince, Charles, Prince of Wales.
Holmes, O. Iris, Her Book.
Ignatow, D. Against the Evidence.
Jackson, L. Troubles of a Book, The.
Jarrell. Author to the Reader, The.
Joseph, A. In the Bookstore.
Reading Room.
Searching for *Melinda's Magic Moment.*
Keats. Keen, Fitful Gusts Are Whispering Here and There.
Keyes, S. War Poet.
Kirby, D. To a French Structuralist.
Larkin, P. Fiction and the Reading Public.
Study of Reading Habits, A.
Lawrence, A. Robert Penn Warren's Book.
Le Gallienne. Library in a Garden, A.
McCord, D. Books Fall Open.
Milosz, C. And Yet the Books.
Milton. On the Detraction Which Followed upon My Writing Certain Treatises.
Moore, M. He Wrote the History Book.
Muldoon, P. Making the Move.
Nesbit, E. Among His Books.
Norton, C. To My Books.
Palis, Y. Waking Up.
Pilling. Fran.
Reese, L. Love, Weeping, Laid This Song.
Rich, A. Burning of Paper instead of Children, The.
Shapiro, D. Book of Glass, A.
Sissman. Upon Finding Dying: An Introduction, by L. E. Sissman, Remaindered at 1s.
Southey, R. Scholar, The.
Stevens, W. House Was Quiet and the World Was Calm, The.
Poem That Took the Place of a Mountain, The.
Stevenson, R. Armies in the Fire.
Land of Story-Books, The.
Strand. Eating Poetry.
Swirszczynska. He Was Lucky.
Thomas, E. On Sir J——S——Saying in a Sarcastic Manner, My Books Would Make Me Mad; an Ode.
Thornbury. Court Historian, The.
Tipping. Poet at Work.
Tranter. Enzensberger at 'Exiles.'
Trowbridge, J. Recollections of "Lalla Rookh."
Unknown. Domestic Philosopher, The.
Vaughan, H. Book, The.
To His Books.
Veenendaal. On My Fourteenth Wedding Anniversary I Ride on Trains.
Wakoski. Light.
Walcott. Volcano.
Waller, E. Of the Last Verses in the Book.
Watson, R. Betty Barnes, the Book-Burner.
Weiss, T. Fire at Alexandria, The.
Wells, C. Of Modern Books.
Whitman, W. Shut Not Your Doors.
Whoever You Are Holding Me Now in Hand.
Williams, C. Critic, The.
Williams, W. Coronal, A.
Wordsworth, W. Expostulation and Reply.
Tables Turned, The.
Yeats. When You Are Old.

Books of Hours
Ramsey, P. Hours, The.

Bookworms
Burns, R. Book-Worms, The.

Boone, Daniel
Benét, S. Daniel Boone.

Stafford, W. For the Grave of Daniel Boone.

Booth, Edwin
Melville, H. Coming Storm, The.

Booth, William
Lindsay, N. General William Booth Enters into Heaven.

Boots
Wright, K. Red Boots On.

Borden, Lizzie
Gallagher, T. Instructions to the Double.

Boredom
Belieu. Radio Nebraska.
Belloc. Ballade of Hell and of Mrs. Roebeck.
Brownstein. War.
Clampitt. Meridian.
'Dermée.' Poem.
Elliott, A. Stay Behind, The.
Fanning, R. Baudelaire's Ablutions.
Hope, A. Observation Car.
Hummell, A. I Never Saw a Goddess Go.
Larkin, P. Vers de Société.
Lawrence, D. Last Lesson of the Afternoon.
Leonard, T. Song: "Yi surta."
McDaniel, J. Leonard.
Moss, H. Ménage à Trois.
Nash, O. Spring Comes to Murray Hill.
Robinson, E. Help Me Today.
Simic. Book Full of Pictures, A.
Sondheim. I Never Do Anything Twice (Madam's Song).
Some People.
Wickham. Nervous Prostration.

Bores
Betjeman. Reproof Deserved; or After the Lecture.
De la Mare. Pooh!

Borgia, Lucretia
Landor, W. On Seeing a Hair of Lucretia Borgia.

Bosch, Hieronymus
MacGreevy [*or* McGreevy]. Homage to Hieronymus Bosch.

Boston Tea Party
Seward. Verses Inviting Stella to Tea on the Public Fast-Day.

Boston, Massachusetts
Aiken, C. South End.
Bossidy. Boston.
Doty, M. Days of 1981.
Espada. Bully.
Hall, D. Woolworth's.
Harnick. Boston Beguine, The.
Houghton, F. Mr. Frost Goes South to Boston.
Lowell, R. At the Indian Killer's Grave.
Death from Cancer.
For the Union Dead.
Public Garden, The.
Where the Rainbow Ends.
McCarthy, T. November in Boston.
Moore, M. In the Public Garden.
Plath. Winter's Tale, A.
Revere. Unhappy Boston.
Robinson, E. Boston.
Starbuck, G. Communication to the City Fathers of Boston.
Whitman, W. Boston Ballad [1854], A.

Boswell, James
Moody, E. Dr. Johnson's Ghost.

Bottles
Bishop, M. Song of the Pop-Bottlers.
Noguchi, R. His Waves.
Stevens, W. Anecdote of the Jar.

Bouillabaisse
Thackeray. Ballad of Bouillabaisse, The.

Boundaries
Alarcon, F. Frontera / Border.
Back, R. Untitled.
Dharker. Minority.
France, L. North and South.
Gonzalez, R. Angels of Juárez, Mexico, The.
Lomax, M. Kith.
Mtshali. Boy on a Swing.
Rose. Long Division; a Tribal History.
Yip Wai-lim. In and Out of Check Points.

Bourgeoisie
Abinader, E. Gentry, The.
Angelou. Sepia Fashion Show.
Auden. Unknown Citizen, The.
Corso. Marriage.
Cummings, E. Cambridge ladies who live in furnished souls, The.
Feirstein. Mark Stern.
Larkin, P. Toads.
Lawrence, D. How Beastly the Bourgeois Is. Worm Either Way.
Levertov. Tenebrae.
Myles, E. Merk.
Nemerov. Life Cycle of Common Man.
Wickham. Fired Pot, The.
See also **Proletariat**

Bowling and Bowlers
Costanzo. Old Neighborhood, The.
Kooser. Genuine Poem, Found on a Blackboard in a Bowling Alley in Story City, Iowa.
Moore, M. Bowls.
Skloot. Hook.

Boxing and Boxers
Acorn. Fights, The.
Addonizio. Event.
Late Round.
Alexander, E. Narrative: Ali.
Today's News.
Barlow, G. Dream of the Ring: The Great Jack Johnson, A.
Cuney. My Lord, What a Morning.
Davis, O. Moorer Denies Holyfield in Twelve.
Dugan, A. On Hurricane Jackson.
Dybek. My Father's Fights.
Espada. Man Who Beat Hemingway, The.
Harper, M. Homage to the Brown Bomber.
Hayden, R. Free Fantasia: Tiger Flowers.
Ignatow, D. Boxing Match, The.
Komunyakaa. Boxing Day.
Levine, P. Right Cross, The.
Reed, I. White Hope.
Tate, J. Shadowboxing.

Boyne (river), Ireland
Higgins, F. Father and Son.

Boyne, Battle of the (1690)
Unknown. Boyne Water, The.

Boys
Adams, S. Rough Boys.
Aldis, D. Hiding.
Ammons, A. R. Widespread Implications.
Baker, H. Advice to a Man Who Lost a Dog.
Beeching, H. Going Down Hill on a Bicycle.
Betjeman. False Security.
Bishop, E. Casabianca.
Blind. Beautiful Beeshareen Boy, The.
Brecht, B. Three Fragments.
Burroughs, W. My Legs Señor.
Ciardi. All about Boys and Girls.
Cornish, S. Generations 1.
de Gillies, G. De Puerorum osculis.
De la Mare. Tired Tim.
Eberhart, R. Horse Chestnut Tree, The.
Fanning, R. In the Barn.
Field, E. Little Boy Blue.
Gunn, T. Allegory of the Wolf Boy, The.
Hamer. Allegiance.
Higgins, F. Tennis in the City.
Hogg, J. Boy's Song, A.
Holmes, J. Four and a Half.
Howes, B. Portrait of the Boy as Artist.
Hughes, L. Tag.
Jewett, S. Country Boy in Winter, A.
Kinnell. First Song.
Kipling, R. If—.
Lamb, M. Two Boys, The.
Larcom. Little Cavalier, A.
Lauterbach. Boy Sleeping.
Longfellow, H. My Lost Youth.
Martinez, D. Cultivation of Orchids, The.
McDonald, C. Nightfishing.
Olds, S. One Girl at the Boys Party, The.
Patchen. Street Corner College.
Praed. School and Schoolfellows.
Reznikoff. Testimony: The United States (1901–1910) Recitative/The South.

Riley, J. Jack the Giant-Killer.
Rivard. 1966.
Robinson, E. Meshes.
Savage, M. To a School-Boy at Eton, Yes and No.
Schuyler, J. Head, A.
Solari, R. December 25, 1991.
Truro.
Taylor, C. B. Round Irving High School.
Unknown. One Little Boy.
Sad Story of a Little Boy That Cried, The.
Walwicz. Tattoo, The.
Whitman, W. We Two Boys Together Clinging.
Wilmer, S. Mess Boy, The.
Wise, W. When I Grow Up.
Wright, R. Haiku: "Green cockleburs, The.".
See also **Childhood and Children; Youth**

Bradstreet, Anne
Norton, J. Funeral Elegy Upon that Pattern and Patron of Virtue, A.
Rogers, J. Upon Mrs. Anne Bradstreet, Her Poems, An.
Unknown. Anagram, An.
Woodbridge. Upon the Author. By a Known Friend.

Brahma
Emerson, R. Brahma.
Jones, S. Hymn to Na'ra'yena, A.

Brahms, Johannes
Berger, B. Stout Brahms.
Derricotte. Black Boys Play the Classics.
Stevens, W. Anglais Mort à Florence.

Brains
Abse. In the Theatre.
Arlen, H. If I Only Had a Brain (If I Only Had a Heart) (If I Only Had the Nerve).
Auden. Ode to the Diencephalon.
Ferguson, G. In Hospital-land.
Lowell, J. Darkened Mind, The.
Rowe, V. MRI of a Poet's Brain.
Straus, M. Neuroanatomy Summer.

Brancusi, Constantin
Loy. Brancusi's Golden Bird.

Brandy
Fallon, P. Flask of Brandy, A.

Braque, Georges
Norse. Picasso Visits Braque.

Brazil
Eliscu, E. Flying Down to Rio.
Gordon, M. I, Yi, Yi, Yi, Yi (I Like You Very Much).
Hilliard, B. Coffee Song (They've Got an Awful Lot of Coffee in Brazil), The.
Loden. Conversations with Dr. M.
Manhire. Brazil.
Oden. Private Letter to Brazil, A.

Bread
Brontë, C. Like wolf—and black bull or goblin hound.
Brooks, G. My Dreams, My Works Must Wait Till after Hell.
Burnshaw. Bread.
Crashaw. On the Miracle of Multiplied [or Multiplyed] Loaves.
Dickinson, E. Indian Summer.
Dunbar, P. Dinah Kneading Dough.
Fulton, A. Wonder Bread.
Hartnett. Domestic Scene.
Levy, A. Epitaph: "This is the end of him, here he lies."
Lux. One Meat Ball.
McGrath, T. Bread of this World; Praises III, The.
Merwin, W. S. Bread.
Moss, T. Wonder, The.
Roy, L. Bread Man, The.
Simic. Austerities.
Tapahonso. All I Want.
Thomas, D. This Bread I Break.
Tsvetayeva [or Tsvetaeva]. I Bless the Daily Labor.

Breakfast
Graham, H. Breakfast.
Griffin, S. Song My.
Kinnell. Oatmeal.

Lowry, M. Eye-Opener.
Peacock, M. Breakfast with Cats.
Rankine. Man. His Bowl. His Raspberries, The.
Rosenblatt. It's in the Egg.
Unknown. Morning.

Breasts
Adcock, F. Soho Hospital for Women, The.
Bernstein, C. Caught.
Brion, R. Love Song.
Carew, T. Upon a Mole in Celia's Bosom.
Chernoff. Breasts.
Coleman, W. Breast Examination.
Hacker, M. Cancer Winter.
Hass, R. Story about the Body, A.
Herman, G. Clinic, The.
Herrick. Fresh Cheese and Cream.
How Roses Came Red.
Upon Julia's Breasts.
Upon the Nipples of Julia's Breast.
Jenyns. To a Nosegay in Pancharilla's Breast.
Kasischke. My Heart.
Martinez, D. In a Duplex Near the San Andreas Fault.
McClatchy. My Mammogram.
Miller, E. Rebecca.
Oppenheimer, J. Innocent Breasts, The.
Pratt, M. Poem for My Sons.
Rankine. Short Narrative of Breasts and Wombs in Service of Plot Entitled, A.
Schwartz, R. L. Possible.
Simic. Breasts.
Smith, S. This Englishwoman.
Terranova. Self-Examination.
Unknown. Lady Lowbodice.
Wright, J. Poem about Breasts, A.
Wrigley, R. Milkflowers.

Breath
Biespiel, D. Heat Sours, The.
Burkard. Foolish Thing.
Dickey, J. Basics.
Freed, R. You Leave Me Breathless.
Garnett, R. Dealing Scraps.
Gehrke, S. Mouth to Mouth.
Gerner, K. House of Breath.
Harjo, J. Call It Fear.
Herrick. To Julia.
Hollander, F. You Leave Me Breathless.
Holub. Vanishing Lung Syndrome.
Kinsella, J. Chess Piece Cornered.
Nathan, L. Breathing Exercises.
Noguchi, R. Breath He Holds, The.
Raworth. Collapsible.
Reichard, W. Monster's Dream, The.
Strand. Breath.
Tate, J. Breathing.
Wagoner, D. Poem about Breath.

Brebeuf, Jean de
Pratt, E. Martyrdom of Brébeuf and Lalemant, 16 March 1649, The.

Brecht, Bertolt
Mueller, L. Triage.

Bricks and Bricklayers
Bruce, W. Holland Brick, A.
Rybicki, J. For Daniel Beels, Third Generation Bricklayer.
This Sun.
Tatersal. Bricklayer's Labours, The.

Brides
Akhmadulina. Bride, The.
Bang, M. Constant Bride, The.
Bayly. We Met.
Cary, A. Bridal Veil, The.
Dubrava. Miraculous Marriage of Zarife Dominquez.
Groarke, V. Trousseau.
Hall, D. Alligator Bride, The.
Hemans. Bride of the Greek Isle, The.
Bride's Farewell, The.
Herrick. Tithe [or Tythe]: To the Bride, The.
Hope, A. Brides, The.
Levine, M. Wedding Day.
Lovelace, R. Anniversary on the Hymeneals of My Noble Kinsman, Thomas Stanley, Esquire, An.
McClanahan, R. Bridal Rites.

Smedley, M. Contrast, A.
Smith, S. I Remember.
Somervile [or Somerville]. Inquisitive Bridegroom, The.
Song. Picture Bride.
Spenser. Epithalamion: "Ye learned sisters which have oftentimes."
Unknown. Slave Marriage Ceremony Supplement.
Valentine, J. Bride's Hours, A.
Veenendaal. On My Fourteenth Wedding Anniversary I Ride on Trains.
See also **Weddings**

Bridges
Alegría. From the Bridge.
Carpenter, W. Ghosts.
Dromgoole. Building the Bridge.
Gregerson. Waterborne.
Hammond, M. GWB in the Rain, The.
Hardy, T. On Sturminster Foot-Bridge.
Kinnell. Under the Williamsburg Bridge.
Longfellow, H. Bridge, The.
Marcus, M. Picnic on the Bay Bridge.
McGonagall. Tay Bridge Disaster, The.
McPherson, S. Suspension: Junior Wells on a Small Stage in a Converted Barn.
Minhinnick. Catching My Breath.
Mitcham. On the Otis Redding Bridge.
Mother Goose. London Bridge.
Norris, L. Bridges.
Ravenna Bridge.
Nortje. At Lansdowne Bridge.
Plumpp. Poem.
Smith, W. Brooklyn Bridge.
Stone, R. Burned Bridge, The.
Tabb. Bridge, The.
Unknown. Bridge instead of a Wall, A.
Warren, R. Covered Bridge.
Webb, H. Ode to the Severn Bridge.
Wilbur. Simile for Her Smile, A.
Wordsworth, W. Composed upon Westminster Bridge, September 3, 1802.
Zolotow. Bridge, The.

Bridges, Robert
Hopkins, G. To R. B.

Brighton, England
Collins, M. Winter in Brighton.

Bristol, England
Lloyd, C. Written at the Hotwells, near Bristol.

British Columbia, Canada
Lowry, M. Christ Walks in This Infernal District Too.
Marty. In the Dome Car of the "Canadian."
Stafford, W. British Columbia.
Wah. Breathe Dust.

British Empire
Aytoun, W. Royal Banquet, The.
Kipling, R. Arithmetic on the Frontier.
Ballad of East and West, The.
Boots.
Cholera Camp.
Christmas in India.
Ford o' Kabul River.
Gunga Din.
Mandalay.
New Knighthood, The.
Recessional.
Screw-Guns.
Song of the Banjo, The.
Widow at Windsor, The.
Logue, C. Song of the Dead Soldier, The.
Magee, W. British Garden, A.
Muldoon, P. Meeting the British.
Murphy, E. Thank you, Mr Rason, for the Apples.
Shepherd, W. Ode on Lord Macartney's Embassy to China.

British Museum, London
Empson. Homage to the British Museum.
Guiney. In the Reading-Room of the Brtish Museum.
Levy, A. To Lallie.
MacNeice. British Museum Reading Room, The.

Brittany, France
James, J. Idyl: "Tiny fish."
Webster, A. Flood of Is in Brittany, The.

Broadway, New York City
Algarin. Broadway Opening.
Brown, N. Broadway Melody.
Cohan. Down by the Erie Canal.
Forty-five Minutes from Broadway.
Give My Regards to Broadway.
Dubin, A. Lullaby of Broadway.
Freed, R. Babes on Broadway.
Gardinier. To Peace.
Hughes, L. Note on Commercial Theatre.
Jackson, B. Another Impostor.
Rich, A. Upper Broadway.
Sandburg, C. Broadway.
Whitman, W. Broadway.

Brontë, Anne
Brontë, C. On the Death of Anne Brontë.

Brontë, Charlotte
"Coolidge." Charlotte Brontë.
Hayne, P. Charlotte Brontë.
Howard, F. Sampler from Haworth.

Brontë, Emily
Brontë, C. On the Death of Emily Jane Brontë.
Day Lewis. Emily Brontë.
Wright, J. Rosina Alcona to Julius Brenzaida.

Bronx, The, New York City
Di Prima. April Fool Birthday Poem for Grandpa.
Drake, J. Bronx.
Esteves. For South Bronx.
South Bronx Testimonial.
Figueroa, J. Boricua.
Foerster. Bronx Park.
Henderson-Holmes. My First Riot: Bronx, NYC.
Ignatow, D. East Bronx.
Morales. Getting Out Alive.

Brooklyn Bridge
Al-Rihani. It Was All for Him.
Crane, H. Bridge, The.
Denby. New York Face, A.
Hernández Cruz. Side 4.
Rohrer, M. Brooklyn Bridge.
Shapiro, H. National Cold Storage Company.
Smith, W. Brooklyn Bridge.

Brooklyn, New York City
Blackburn, P. Brooklyn Narcissus.
Di Prima. Backyard.
Espada. Moon Shatters on Alabama Avenue, The.
Owl and the Lightning, The.
Liu, T. Brooklyn Botanic Garden, The.
Montague, J. Cage, The.
Orfalea, G. Rose of Brooklyn, The.
Pearlberg, G.G. Loop-the-Loop in Prospect Park (1905).
Shapiro, H. National Cold Storage Company.
Shomer. Letter Home from Brooklyn.
Wain. Brooklyn Heights.
Waters, M. Horse.
Weaver, M. Brooklyn.
Whitman, W. Centenarian's Story, The.
Crossing Brooklyn Ferry.

Brooks and Streams
Bastard. Ad Henricum Wottonem.
Burns, R. Birks of Aberfeldy, The [Composed on the Spot].
Frost, R. Brook in the City, A.
Hyla Brook.
West-Running Brook.
Hopkins, G. Inversnaid.
Winter with the Gulf Stream.
Janzen, J. At Summer's End.
Kendall, H. Orara.
Lee, L. Interrogation, The.
Roethke. Lady and the Bear, The.
Ross, W. Creek, The.
Seward. Sonnet: "Stranger, when o'er yon slant, warm field no cloud."
Smollett. To Leven Water.
Snyder, G. Water.
Spratt. On His Mistress Drown'd.
Unknown. River, The.

Wagoner, D. Source, The.
Wilbur. Hamlen Brook.
Wordsworth, W. Old Man by the Brook, The.
See also **Rivers**

Brooks, Gwendolyn
Madhubuti. Gwendolyn Brooks.

Brooms
Lear, E. Limericks, I (ii).
Ledwidge. June.
Simic. Brooms.

Brotherhood
Baraka. Return of the Native.
Burns, R. For A' That and A' That ['Is there, for honest poverty'].
Ceravolo. Wild Provoke of the Endurance Sky.
Clifton, L. Listen Children.
Cronin, J. Motho Ke Motho Ka Batho Babang (A Person Is a Person Because of Other People).
Dame. Seder, The.
Encarnacion. Bulosan Listens to a Recording of Robert Johson.
Frost, R. Tuft of Flowers, The.
Ginsberg, A. Who Be Kind To.
Hayden, R. In the Mourning Time.
Heine, H. To Edom.
Hogan, L. New Apartment.
Hopkins, G. Epithalamion: "Hark, hearer, hear what I do; lend a thought now, make believe."
Hughes, L. Projection.
Hunt, L. Abou Ben Adhem.
Johnson, G. Interracial.
Kinsella, T. Brotherhood.
Kipling, R. Ballad of East and West, The.
Lum. Chinese Hot Pot.
MacLeish. Speech to Those Who Say Comrade.
Mason, R. Sonnet of Brotherhood.
Miles, J. Family.
Moore, M. In Distrust of Merits.
Muir, E. Brothers, The.
Ransom, J. Armageddon.
Rive. Where the Rainbow Ends.
Rolfe, E. First Love.
Rosten. Out of Our Shame.
Rukeyser, M. Hostages, The.
Saint. Heart and Soul.
Sandburg, C. Long Shadow of Lincoln: A Litany, The.
Symonds. Love and Death: A Symphony.
Untermeyer, L. Goliath and David.
Whitman, W. Full of Life Now.
I Dream'd in a Dream.
I Hear It Was Charged against Me.
To the East and to the West.
Wylie. Pebble, The.

Brothers
Aldis, D. Little.
Amadiume. Be Brothers.
Anderson, A. Licking Wounds.
Bly, R. Things My Brother and I Could Do.
Bryan, M. To My Brother.
Burkard. Weather.
Carroll, L. Brother and Sister.
Chipasula. My Blood Brother.
Creeley. World, The.
Forbes, C. Hand Me Down Blues.
Geiger. Soundtracks.
Harper, M. Drowning of the Facts of a Life, The.
Hemans. To My Eldest Brother, With the British Army in Portugal.
Herrick. To His Dying Brother, Master William Herrick.
Hicok. Heroin.
Keats. To My Brothers.
Lake, P. In Rough Weather.
Lamb, C. To John Lamb, Esq.: Of the South-Sea House.
Lassell. How to Watch Your Brother Die.
Leigh, H. Twins, The.
Leithauser. Old Bachelor Brother.
Levine, P. You Can Have It.
Lovelace, R. Advice to My Best Brother, Colonel Francis Lovelace.
Mapanje. Making Our Clowns Martyrs.

Mattawa. Letter to Ibrahim.
Melville, H. Timoleon.
Muir, E. Brothers, The.
Nye, N. For Lost and Found Brothers.
Robinson, A. Scape-Goat, The.
Robinson, E. Prodigal Son, The.
Ross, A. Two in Bed.
Rybicki, J. Brother Ben.
Samaras, N. After the Children Have Gone to Bed.
Sanchez, S. To P. J. (2 Yrs Old Who Sed Write a Poem for Me in Portland, Oregon).
Scamell, B. My Lost Brother.
Shapiro, K. Two-Year-Old Has Had a Motherless Week, The.
Skloot. Everly Brothers, The.
Year the Space Age Was Born, The.
Soldati. Surroundings.
Soto. Not Knowing.
Thompson, C. To My Dead Brother.
Thoreau. Brother Where Dost Thou Dwell.
Turner, F. On the Pains of Translating Miklós Radnóti.
Unknown. Twa Brothers, The.
Van Duyn. Twins, The.
Vaughan, H. Silence and Stealth of Day[e]s!
Walker, F. X. Crooked Afro.
Wallis, H. Female's Lamentations, The; or, The Village in Mourning.
Wang Shih-chieng. After Snow, Longing for Elder Brother Hsi-ch'iao.
Ward, D. My Brothers Make a Lantern.
Wordsworth, W. Tradition of Oker Hill in Darley Dale, Derbyshire, A.

Brown (color)
Grimké, A. At April.

Brown, Andrew
Heard, J. Rev. Andrew Brown, over the Hill to Rest.

Brown, John
Atkins. Narrative.
Brownell, H. John Brown's Body.
Melville, H. Portent, The.
Rukeyser, M. Soul and Body of John Brown, The.
Sandburg, C. Osawatomie.
Whittier. Brown of Ossawatomie.

Brown, Mrs. E. Cohrs
Fordham. Mrs. E. Cohrs Brown.

Brown, Sterling A.
Harper, M. Br'er Sterling and the Rocker.

Brown, Thomas
Chappell, F. Truth at Last, The.

Browning, Elizabeth Barrett
Blagden. To George Sand on Her Interview with Elizabeth Barrett Browning.
Browning, R. Lost Mistress, The.
Greenwell, D. To Elizabeth Barrett Browning, in 1851.
To Elizabeth Barrett Browning, in 1861.
Lowell, A. Sisters, The.
Parkes, B. To Elizabeth Barrett Browning.

Browning, Robert
Chesterton, G. From a Spanish Cloister.
Landor, W. To Robert Browning.
Stevenson, R. Browning.

Bruce, Robert
Barbour, J. Before Bannockburn.
Freedom [*or* Fredome].
Burns, R. Scots Wha Hae.

Brueghel, Pieter
Auden. Musée des Beaux Arts.
Berryman. Winter Landscape.
Dubie. February; the Boy Breughel.
Safie, D. In the Middle of Reading One More Poem with Brueghel as a Metaphor.
Williams, W. Dance, The.
Haymaking.
Hunters in the Snow, The.
Landscape with the Fall of Icarus.
Parable of the Blind, The.
Self-Portrait.

Brummell, "Beau" (George Bryan Brummell)
Glassco. Brummell at Calais.

Brussels, Belgium
Auden. Brussels in Winter.

Brutus (Marcus Junius Brutus)
Cowley, A. Brutus.
Whitehead, C. Brutus' Last Song.

Brutus, Dennis
Awoonor. To Dennis Brutus.

Bryan, William Jennings
Lindsay, N. Bryan, Bryan, Bryan, Bryan.

Bubbles
Bacon, F. Life of Man, The.
Drummond, W. Madrigal: "This life, which seems so fair."
Greenberg, S. Glass Bubbles, The.
Herrick. Bubble; a Song, The.

Buber, Martin
Harris, M. Martin Buber in the Pub.

Buccaneers
Prys-Jones. Henry Morgan's March on Panama.

Buckingham, George Villiers, 2d Duke of
Felltham [*or* Feltham]. On the Duke of Buckingham, Slain by Felton, the 23rd August, 1628.
Shirley, J. On the Duke of Buckingham.
Unknown. Epitaph: "Fortune's darling, king's content."
Epitaph on the Duke of Buckingham.
Upon the Duke of Buckingham.

Budapest, Hungary
Jamie. Flower-sellers, Budapest.

Buddha and Buddhism
Adams, H. Buddha and Brahma.
Barry, J. Nun in Ninh Hoa, A.
Casey, M. On What the Army Does with Heads.
Di Prima. Death Sunyata Chant: A Rite for Passing Over.
Gerstler. Max's Lecture on Canine Buddhism.
Ginsberg, A. Reflections at Lake Louise.
Guest, B. Walking Buddha.
Guevara, M. Buddy Holly Poem, The.
Izumi. In the Autumn, on Retreat at a Mountain Temple.
Kaufman, B. Unanimity Has Been Achieved, Not a Dot Less for Its Accidentalness.
Kaufman, S. Buddha of Sökkuram, The.
Lanier, S. Nirvâna.
Lieberman, L. God's Measurements.
McNulty, T. Bodhidharma Crossing the Graywolf River on a Ry-Krisp.
Rexroth, K. Further Advantages of Learning.
Sansom, A. Cross Country.
Snyder, G. Avocado.
Circumambulating Arunachala.
Su, A. I Can't Become a Buddhist.
Whalen. Walking beside the Kamogawa, Remembering Nansen and Fudo and Gary's Poem.
White, J. Oshi.
Wright, C. Disjecta Membra.
See also **Zen Buddhism**

"Buffalo Bill" (William Frederick Cody)
Cummings, E. Portrait.

Buffaloes
Barnes, J. Bone Yard.
Belloc. Bison, The.
Dobyns. Nouns of Assemblage.
Hobson, G. Buffalo Poem #1.
Hume, C. Dirty Money.
Lindsay, N. Flower-fed Buffaloes, The.
Ghosts of the Buffaloes, The.
Lindsay, V. Flower-Fed Buffaloes, The.
Sandburg, C. Buffalo Dusk.
Unknown. Buffalo Skinners, The.

Bugles and Buglers
Day, J. Picket before Bull Run, The.
Fallon, P. Bit of Brass, A.
LeFlore, S. B. Rayboy Blk & Bluz.
Merwin, W. S. Second Psalm: The Signals.
Prince, H. Boogie Woogie Bugle Boy.
Whitman, W. Beat! Beat! Drums!

Buildings and Builders
Awad, J. Variations on a Theme.
Browning, R. Apparent Failure.

Creeley. Invitation, The.
Damacion, K. Canciones.
Dugan, A. Love Song: I and Thou.
Esteves. Ahora.
Graves, R. Fallen Tower of Siloam, The.
Hacker, M. Squares and Courtyards.
Harbach, O. Love Nest, The.
Hartnett. Visit to Castletown House, A.
Heaney, S. Scaffolding.
Hernández Cruz. Man Who Came to the Last Floor, The.
Hirsch, L. Love Nest, The.
Hulme, T. Image.
Jonson, B. To Penshurst.
Kelly, R. Bittersweet Growing Up the Red Wall.
Komunyakaa. Instructions for Building Straw Huts.
Larkin, J. Housework.
Lear, E. There Was an Old Man With a Beard.
Macdonald, G. Song.
MacLeish. Burying Ground by the Ties.
Marvell. Garden of Appleton House, The ("When in the east the morning ray").
Garden, A.
Upon Appleton House [To My Lord Fairfax].
Melhem, D. Lamentation After Jeremiah to Exorcise High Rental / High Rise Building Scheduled for Construction with Public Funds.
Moore, H. Window at Key West, A.
Mother Goose. House That Jack Built, The.
Oden. Review from Staten Island.
Ormond. Cathedral Builders.
O'Shaughnessy, A. Ode: "We are the music-makers."
Pietri. 7th Untitled Poem.
Rafferty, C. Man on the Tower, The.
Reznikoff. About an Excavation.
Sandburg, C. Shovel Man, The.
Skeeter. Midwest, Midcentury.
Snyder, G. Building.
Stein, K. It Didn't Begin with Horned Owls Hooting at Noon.
Stevenson, R. Block City.
Stryk, L. Oeuvre.
Sweeney, M. To the Building Trade.
Tomlinson, C. Crane, The.
Watts, I. How Doth the Little Busy Bee.
Williams, C. Sanctity, The.

Bulgaria
Meredith, W. Two Masks Unearthed in Bulgaria.

Bull Run, Battles of (1861, 1862)
Day, J. Picket before Bull Run, The.
Lowell, R. March 1, The.
Melville, H. March into Virginia, The.

Bullets
Dove, R. Teach Us to Number Our Days.
Harte, B. What the Bullet Sang.

Bullfights and Bullfighters
Beckman, J. Lament for the Death of a Bullfighter.
Frost, C. Custom.
Herrera. Hallucinogenic Bullfighter.
Jacobsen, J. Matadors, The.
Swenson, M. Death Invited.

Bullfinches
Cowper, W. On the Lamented Death of Mrs. Throckmorton's Bullfinch.

Bulls
Dinka Oral Tradition. Magnificent Bull, The.
Heaney, S. Outlaw, The.
Hodgson, R. Bull, The.
Layton. Bull Calf, The.
Phelp. Duke Of Buccleuch, The.
Sackville-West. Bull, The.
Williams, W. Bull, The.
Wright, R. Haiku: "Coming from the woods."

Bullying and Bullies
Parker, D. When Mark Deloach Ruled the World.
Reiter, T. Class Bully.
Spender, S. My Parents.
Walsh, J. I've Got an Apple Ready.

Bunker Hill, Battle of (1775)
Freeth.   Bunker's Hill, or the Soldier's
Lamentation.
Bunyan, John
James, J.   Of John Bunyan's Life.
Bureaucracy and Bureaucrats
Ashbery.   On the Empress's Mind.
Auden.   Unknown Citizen, The.
Burke, K.   Frigate Jones, the Pussyfooter.
Devlin, D.   Anteroom: Geneva.
Frost, R.   Departmental.
Hughes, L.   Un-American Investigators.
Miles, J.   Bureau 2.
Burial
Abena, B.   Exiles.
Beckett, S.   Malacoda.
Berryman.   Poet's Final Instructions, The.
Carson, J.   I Am Asking You to Come Back
Home.
Clarke, C.   Rondeau: "They are bodies left
unburied."
Currey.   Burial Flags.
Davies, D.   At Branwen's Grave.
Dickey, J.   Sled Burial, Dream Ceremony.
Everett, J.   Rest Our Spiritual Dead.
France de Bravo, B.   Unrepentant.
Freneau.   Indian Burying Ground, The.
Frost, R.   Home Burial.
Giovanni.   Women Gather, The.
Goodison.   For Don Drummond.
Guevara, M.   Magic Carpet, The.
Hardy, T.   I Found Her Out There.
Harper, F.   Bury Me in a Free Land.
Herbert, E.   Epitaph on Sir Philip Sidney Lying
in St Paul's without a Monument, to be
Fastned upon the Church Door.
Herrick.   Upon a Child That Died [or Dyed].
Upon Himselfe Being Buried.
Upon Prue [or Prew], His Maid.
Hudgins.   Burial Detail.
Jeffers, R.   Shane O'Neill's Cairn.
Mackenzie, K.   Earth Buried.
McKinney, I.   Visiting My Gravesite: Talbott
Churchyard, West Virginia.
Mitchell, K.   On the Anniversary Of Your
Death.
Nash, O.   Tweedledee and Tweedledoom.
Newson, D.   Crowther—Ours.
Pegram, A.   Burials.
Piñero.   On the Day They Buried My Mother.
Powell, D. A.   Always Returning: Holidays and
Burials. Not Every Week.
Ramanujan.   Death and the Good Citizen.
Robinson, A.   Etruscan Tombs.
Southerland.   Blue Clay.
Stevenson, A.   Temporarily in Oxford.
Unknown.   Hearse Song, The.
Rhyme from Lincolnshire, A.
Vaughan, H.   Burial.
Whitman, W.   Vigil Strange I Kept on the Field
One Night.
Wright, D.   Caleb Barnes.
To the Gods the Shades Flavinus of the Cavalry
Regiment.
See also **Cemeteries; Funerals; Graves;
Mausoleums; Tombs**
Burke, Edmund
Wilbur.   Marché aux Oiseaux.
Burma
Kipling, R.   Mandalay.
Burne-Jones, Edward
Rossetti, D.   For "The Wine of Circe" by
Edward Burne-Jones.
Burns, Robert
Landor, W.   Had We Two Met.
Smith, C.   To the Shade of Burns.
Stevenson, R.   Fragment, A: "Thou strainest
through the mountain fern."
Williams, H.   Sonnet on Reading the Poem upon
the Mountain Daisy, by Mr. Burns.
Burroughs, William
Glück, R.   Burroughs.
Bus Terminals
Johnson, J.   Unmarked Stop in Front of
Westmond General Store, Westmond, Idaho.

Buses
Atkins.   Late Bus (After a Series of Hold-Ups).
Bishop, E.   Moose, The.
Clarke, C.   Passing.
Cohen, L.   Bus, The.
Cope, W.   Bloody Men.
Hirschman, J.   Tremor, The.
Jackson, A.   Miz Rosa Rides the Bus.
Kalamaras, G.   Mud.
Mattawa.   Bus Driver Poem, The.
McElroy, C.   Pike Street Bus.
Morley, D.   Exact Fares.
Williams, S.   Wishon Line, The.
Willis, N.   Lady in the White Dress, Whom I
Helped into the Omnibus, The.
Business and Businessmen
Baca.   So Mexicans Are Taking Jobs from
Americans.
Berlin.   There's No Business Like Show
Business.
Betjeman.   Business Girls.
Executive.
Brown, G.   Trout Fisher.
Codrescu.   Poetry Paper.
Farr, R.   At general Electric, where they eat
their/young.
Fearing.   Dirge: "1-2-3 was the number he
played but today the number came 3-2-1."
Florsheim.   Business in Germany.
Ginsberg, A.   Who Runs America?
Hughes, L.   Madam's Past History.
Leonard, T.   Opting for Early Retirement.
MacLeish.   Corporate Entity.
Unknown.   Between a Contractor and His Wife.
See also **Accounting and Accountants;
Advertising; Banking and Bankers;
Capitalism; Financiers; Commerce; Insurance**
Butchering and Butchers
Hampton.   Crafty Butcher, The.
Hardy, T.   Bags of Meat.
Hood, T.   Butcher, A.
Lee, L.   Cleaving, The.
Levine, P.   Animals Are Passing from Our
Lives.
Robinson, E.   Reuben Bright.
Simic.   Butcher Shop.
Squire.   Stockyard, The.
Tipping.   Casino.
Tomlinson, C.   On a Pig's Head.
Walwicz.   Abattoir, The.
Williams, C.   Racists.
Butler, Samuel (1612-1680)
Taylor, G.   English Liberal.
Butter
Calverley.   Ballad: "Auld wife sat at her ivied
door, The."
Heaney, S.   Churning Day.
Nash, O.   Arthur.
Thorold Rogers.   On the Historians Freeman and
Stubbs.
Unknown.   Butter Charm.
Butterflies
Becker, R.   Monarchs of Parque Tranquilidad.
Bensko.   Butterfly Net, The.
Boruch.   Camouflage.
Cole, H.   Cabbage Butterfly, The.
Coleridge, M.   September.
Davies, W.   Example, The.
Dickinson, E.   Caterpillar.
Duncan, R.   Roots and Branches.
Friedmann.   Butterfly, The.
Frost, R.   Tuft of Flowers, The.
Fuller, J.   Butterfly, The.
Gould, H.   Butterfly's Dream, The.
Graves, R.   Flying Crooked.
Grimké, A.   Butterflies.
Hagiwara Sakutaro.   So Terrifyingly
Melancholy.
Hawker.   Butterfly, The.
Humes.   Butterfly Effect, The.
Lawrence, D.   Butterfly.
Layton.   Butterfly on Rock.
Lee, K.   Haiku #3.
Levertov.   Dead Butterfly, The.
Lim, S.   Monarchs Steering.

Lindsay, N.   King of Yellow Butterflies, The.
Major, C.   On Watching a Caterpillar Become a
Butterfly.
Milosz, C.   Abundant Catch (Luke 5:4–10).
Moore, M.   To a Steam Roller.
Muldoon, P.   Milkweed and Monarch.
Noyes, A.   Butterfly Garden, The.
Redwing.   Hoofer, The.
Sherry, J.   Lepidoptery.
Swenson, M.   Unconscious Came a Beauty.
Wieners.   Poem for Trapped Things, A.
Wilde, O.   Symphony in Yellow.
Willard, N.   ›Sleep of the Painted Ladies, The.
Wright, J.   Wings.
Yi, S.   Poem No. X.
Buzzards
Curtis, T.   Pembrokeshire Buzzards.
Rossetti, C.   Sketch, A.
Warren, R.   Pondy Woods.
Welch, L.   Song of the Turkey Buzzard.
See also **Vultures**
Byrd, Mary Furman Weston
Fordham.   Mrs. Mary Furman Weston Byrd.
Byron, George Gordon Noel Byron, 6th Baron
Arnold, M.   Memorial Verses.
Chesterton, G.   Sea Replies to Byron, The.
Coogler.   Byron.
Moore, J.   Sketch of Lord Byron's Life.
Nash, O.   Very like a Whale.
Porter, P.   On This Day I Complete My Fortieth
Year.
Praed.   Chancery Morals.
Byzantium
Notley.   Where Leftover Misery Goes.
Yeats.   Byzantium.
Sailing To Byzantium.

C

Cézanne, Paul
Brutus.   Under House Arrest.
Salmon, A.   Painting.
Strange.   Still Life.
Cabbages
Kinnell.   Cells Breathe in the Emptiness.
Norman, R.   Cabbage.
Ormsby, E.   Skunk Cabbage.
Slugs, S.   I Saw Her in Cabbage Time.
Unknown.   Mid-West, The.
Cadavers
Abse.   Carnal Knowledge.
Coulehan, J.   Anatomy Lesson.
Dudley, E.   Pathologist.
Foy, J.   Autopsy.
See also **Corpses**
Cads
Bowen, C.   Rain It Raineth, The.
Caedmon
Levertov.   Caedmon.
Nicholson, N.   Caedmon.
Caesar, Julius
Auden.   Fall of Rome, The.
Bukowski.   b.
Fitzgerald, E.   19.
Jonson, B.   To Clement Edmonds, on His
Caesar's Commentaries Observed, and
Translated.
Murray, J.   Here We Stand Before the Temporal
World.
Turner, C.   Julius Caesar and the Honey-Bee.
Unknown.   Julius Caesar.
Whitehead, C.   Brutus' Last Song.
Cafés
Dobson, R.   In a Café.
Eliot, T.   Sweeney Among the Nightingales.
Gotera.   Manong Chito Tells Manong Ben about
His Dream over Breakfast at the Manilatown
Cafe.
Gray, S.   Apollo Café.
Johnson, J.   View Café, The.
Tripp.   Connection in Bridgend.
Von Freytag-Loringhoven.   Café du Dôme.
Wetzsteon.   Drinks in the Town Square.

Cain and Abel
Back, R.   After Eden.
Blake, W.   Ghost of Abel, The.
Capetanakis.   Abel.
Hope, A.   Imperial Adam.
Pagis.   Autobiography.
Vaughan, H.   Abel's Blood.
Wheelwright.   Abel.

Cakes
Agran, R.   Cakes Continue to Rise.
Cook, E.   Mouse and the Cake, The.
Hume, C.   Birthday.
Prior-Pitt.   Fitting.
St. John, D.   Wedding Preparations in the
    Country.
Williams, H.   To Mrs. K———, On Her
    Sending Me an English Christmas Plum-Cake
    at Paris.

Calcutta, India
Nye, N.   At Mother Teresa's.

Caliban
Brathwaite, E.   Caliban.
Browning, R.   Caliban upon Setebos; or, Natural
    Theology in the Island.
McDonald, W.   Caliban in Blue.
Namjoshi, S.   Caliban's Journal.
Talvikki, A.   Afterwards: Caliban.

California (state)
Alarcon, F.   Viernes Santo / Good Friday.
Berlin.   White Christmas.
Castillo, A.   Napa, California.
Cervantes.   Como lo Siento.
    Freeway 280.
    Poema para los Californios Muertos.
Davie.   Across the Bay.
    In California.
Davis, G.   August Fires.
DeSylva, B. G.   California, Here I Come.
Fagan.   California, *She Replied.*
    In California.
Gier, J.   California Coast.
Gioia.   California Hills in August.
    In Chandler Country.
Gould, J.   Easter Sunday.
Harms.   Dogtown.
    When You Wish Upon a Star That Turns into a
    Plane.
Hass, R.   Concerning the Afterlife, the Indians
    of Central California Had Only the Dimmest
    Notions.
    Late Spring.
    Palo Alto: the Marshes.
    Spring Rain.
    Tahoe in August.
Hillman.   Geology, A.
Hongo.   Mendocino Rose.
    Off from Swing Shift.
Hoover, P.   California.
Inada.   Fresno Truth, The.
Jarrell.   In Montecito.
Jeffers, R.   Carmel Point.
    Clouds of Evening.
    Return.
Kramer, L.   Strong Winds Below the Canyons.
Kyger.   And with March a Decade in Bolinas.
Lem.   California Dreaming.
Lim, S.   In California with Neruda.
Luschei, G.   Here.
    Water Song, The.
Martin, C.   Metaphor of Grass in California.
McClure, M.   May Morn.
Montague, J.   All Legendary Obstacles.
Nameroff, R.   California Dreaming.
Oliveira, D.   San Joaquin.
Plath.   Sleep in the Mojave Desert.
Reed, I.   Oakland Blues.
Rich, A.   Walking Down the Road.
Ridge, J.   Mount Shasta.
Salazar.   Hotel Fresno.
Salinas, L.   Nights in Fresno.
Sherman, M.   Towards Sunset at Camino Cielo.
Sill.   California Winter.
Snyder, G.   Before the Stuff Comes Down.
    Burning the Small Dead.
    Hay for the Horses.
Song.   Beauty and Sadness.

Soto.   Elements of San Joaquin, The.
    Rain.
    Wind.
St. John, D.   California.
Stroud, J.   Grandfather.
Troupe.   View from Skates in Berkeley, The.
Voigt.   Blue Ridge.
Wakoski.   Imagining Point Dume.
    Night Blooming Jasmine.
Whitman, W.   Facing West from California's
    Shores.
    Promise to California, A.
Winters, Y.   John Sutter.
Yost, C.   California Poem.
    Descano, California.
Young, A.   California Peninsula: El Camino
    Real.
    One West Coast.

Callas, Maria
Field, E.   Callas.

Calligraphy
Zukofsky, L.   (Ryokan's scroll).

Calliope (muse)
Skelton, J.   Calliope.

Calm
Baxter, J.   Morning and Evening Calm.
Brainard, J.   I Saw Two Clouds at Morning.
Donne.   Calm[e], The.
Hayden, R.   Islands, The.
Hazo.   Drenching, The.
Herrick.   To Music, to Becalm a Sweet-sick
    Youth.
Hughes, L.   Sea Calm.
Hughes, T.   Horses, The.
Morgan, R.   Honey.
Rossetti, C.   In Progress.
Warren, R.   Masts at Dawn.
Wordsworth, W.   It is a beauteous evening.
Wunderlich, M.   One Explanation of Beauty.

Calvary
Awoonor.   Easter Dawn.
Robinson, E.   Calvary.
See also **Crucifixion, The**

Calves
Parry, E.   I Would Like You for a Comrade.
Porteous.   Calf.
Tomlinson, C.   Macduff.

Calvinism
Clough.   Latest Decalogue, The.
Kipling, R.   McAndrew's Hymn.
Lowell, R.   Mr. Edwards and the Spider.
Millay, E.   To a Calvinist in Bali.

Calypso (mythology)
McCallum, S.   Calypso.
Morley, C.   Forever Ambrosia.

Calypso Music
Brathwaite, E.   Calypso.
Brode.   Calypsomania.
McCallum, S.   Calypso.

Camaraderie
Djanikian.   How I Learned English.
Jarmain.   Embarkation, 1942.
Owen, W.   Apologia Pro Poemate Meo.
Stone, J.   Confabulation.
See also **Friendship**

Cambodia and Cambodians
Bowman, C.   Jackie in Cambodia.
Fenton, J.   Cambodia.
    Dead Soldiers.
Long, R.   Conspiracy, The.
Receveur.   Eagle in the Land of Oz.

Cambridge University
Cornford, F.   Autumn Morning at Cambridge.
Davie.   On Bertrand Russell's "Portraits from
    Memory."
Ewart.   Semantic Limerick According to Dr.
    Johnson's Dictionary (Edition of 1765), The.
    Semantic Limerick According to the Shorter
    Oxford English Dictionary (1933), The.
Levy, A.   Cambridge in the Long.
Tennyson, A.   Lines on Cambridge of 1830.

Cambridge, England
Calverley.   Hic Vir, Hic Est.
Cornford, F.   Autumn Morning at Cambridge.

    In the Backs.
Cambridge, Massachusetts
Alexander, E.   Boston Year.
O'Grady, D.   Professor Kelleher and the Charles
    River.
See also **Harvard University**
Cambridgeshire, England
Brooke, R.   Old Vicarage, Grantchester, The.
Camden, William
Jonson, B.   To William Camden.
Camellias
Roscoe, W.   Camellia, The.
Camelot
Chubb, T.   Merlin.
Lerner, A.   Camelot.
Tennyson, A.   Epic, The [Morte d'Arthur].
    Lady of Shalott, The.
    Morte d'Arthur.
Camels
Lewis, J.   How to Tell a Camel.
Cameras
Ciardi.   On a Photo of Sgt. Ciardi a Year Later.
Herd.   Marilyn Climbs Out of the Pool.
"Malley."   Documentary Film.
McDonald, W.   For Harper, Killed in Action.
Paquet.   Group Shot.
Vando.   Lydia's Phantasmagoria.
See also **Photography and Photographers**
Campaigns, Political
Lindsay, N.   Bryan, Bryan, Bryan, Bryan.
See also **Voting and Voters**
Camões, Luis de
Campbell, R.   Luis de Camões.
Camping
Empson.   Camping Out.
Fisher, J.   Camp.
Kinnell.   Night in the Forest.
Kumin, M.   Despair.
Rexroth, K.   Fish Peddler and Cobbler.
    Floating.
Roseliep.   Campfire Extinguished.
Saner.   Camping Clean.
Snyder, G.   August on Sourdough, a Visit from
    Dick Brewer.
    Late October Camping in the Sawtooths.
Wagoner, D.   Making Camp.
    Staying Alive.
Wright, C.   Other Side of the River, The.
Canada
Birney.   Can. Lit.
Cohen, L.   Only Tourist in Havana Turns His
    Thoughts Homeward, The.
Layton.   From Colony to Nation.
Moore, T.   Canadian Boat Song, A.
Sirr.   Understanding Canada.
Smith, I.   Exiles, The.
Canals
Freneau.   On the Great Western Canal of the
    State of New York.
Lowell, A.   Spring Longing.
Melville, H.   In a Bye-Canal.
"Twain."   Aged Pilot Man, The.
Wainwright, J.   1815.
Canaries
Amherst.   Verses Designed to Be Sent to Mr.
    Adams.
Heard, J.   My Canary.
Jewett, S.   Caged Bird, A.
Nash, O.   Canary, The.
Unknown.   Mary's Canary.
Canberra, Australia
Rowland.   Canberra in April.
Cancer (disease)
Adcock, F.   Soho Hospital for Women, The.
Agard, J.   For Bob Marley.
Agran, R.   Swimming with Seiger.
Ammons, A. R.   Improvisation for the Stately
    Dwelling, An.
Auden.   Miss Gee.
Benn.   Man and Woman Go Through the Cancer
    Ward.
Blaser.   Ruler, The.
Campo.   Her Final Show.
Charara, H.   Holy Water.

Coulehan, J. D-Day, 1994.
Curbelo. Tourist Weather.
Dickey, J. For the Death of Vince Lombardi.
Dubie. Funeral, The.
Dunn, D. Sundial, The.
Eberhart, R. Cancer Cells, The.
Espada. Spanish of Our Out-Loud Dreams, The.
Geiger. Dry Spell of Faith, A.
Glatt. Amanda.
　What We Did After My Mother's Mastectomy.
Graham-Pole, J. Candor.
Hacker, M. Cancer Winter.
　Invocation: "This is for Elsa, also known as
　　Liz."
　Year's End.
Haldane, J. Cancer's a Funny Thing.
Henderson-Holmes. 'C' ing in Colors: Blue.
　'C' ing in Colors: Red.
Herman, G. Clinic, The.
Hodgins. Death Who.
Kenyon, J. Pharaoh.
Kessler, S. Jack's Last Words.
Kimbrell, J. My Father at the North Street
　Boarding House.
Kizer, C. American Beauty, An.
Martinez, D. In a Duplex Near the San Andreas
　Fault.
McClatchy. My Mammogram.
Miller, E. Rebecca.
Olds, S. Glass, The.
　In the Hospital Near the End.
Paino. Matter of Division, A.
Perillo. Needles.
Pinsky. Memorial.
Shaw, A. Bird Nests.
Stafford, W. Bess.
Terranova. Self-Examination.
Van Walleghen. Crabapples.
Wunderlich, M. On Opening.
Wyrebek, M. Healing Logic, A.

Candlemas
Clampitt. Procession at Candlemas, A.
Herrick. Ceremonies for Candlemas[se] Eve.
　Ceremony upon Candlemas Eve.
Madeleva. Candlemas Day.

Candles
Adams, F. If.
Creeley. Warning, The.
Drake, E. Just for Today.
Empson. Legal Fiction.
Leithauser. Haunted, The.
Light, K. Idea of Love Between Us, The.
Lowell, A. Bungler, The.
Millay, E. First Fig.
　Second Fig.
Mother Goose. Candle, A.
　To make your candles last for aye.
Stevens, W. Valley Candle.
Suckling, S. Candle, A.
Unknown. Riddle: "Little trotty hetty coat."
Warsh. Static, The.
Willard, N. Cat's Second Song, The.
Wilson, K. Dusk in My Backyard.

Candy
Bang, M. Crossed-Over, Fiend-Snitched, X-ed
　Out.
Bidart. Ellen West.
Bricusse, L. Candy Man, The.
Clare, S. On the Good Ship Lollipop.
David, M. Candy.
Ford, C. There's No Place to Sleep in This Bed,
　Tanguy.
González, R. Day of the Dead.
Kramer, A. Candy.
Nash, O. Reflections on Ice-breaking.
Newley, A. Candy Man, The.
Simpson, L. Chocolates.
Whitney, J. Candy.

Cannibalism and Cannibals
Brion, R. One Morning Beside a Pond.
Chase, K. Venison.
Gilbert, S. Yarn of the *Nancy Bell*, The.
Goodison. Jamaica 1980.
Irwin, W. Constant Cannibal Maiden, The.
Reid, C. Perversion, A.
Wright, J. "Dove-Love."

Yambo. When Negro Teeth Speak.

Canning
Van Duyn. Homework.
Young, K. Preserving, The.

Canoes and Canoeing
Johnson, E. Wave-Won.
Mapanje. Elegy for Mangochi Fishermen, An.
Revard. Birch Canoe.
Rexroth, K. Floating.
Woods, H. Paddlin' Madelin' Home.

Canonical Hours
Davie. Horae Canonicae.

Cape Cod, Massachusetts
Dudek. Provincetown.
Santayana. Cape Cod.
Weaver, M. Message on Cape Cod, The.

Capital Punishment
Cendrars. Head, The.
MacDiarmid, H. Facing the Chair.
McKuen. Thoughts on Capital Punishment.
Montrose. On Himself, upon Hearing What
　Was His Sentence.
Peterson, R. San Quentin 1968.
Warren-Moore. For Paula Cooper.
See also **Executions and Executioners**

Capitalism
Chrystos. Okeydoekey Tribe, The.
Codrescu. Circle Jerk.
Cumpian. No Deposit Returns.
Drake, N. Man in the White Suit, The.
Harland-Watts, J. Resist Confinement.
Joseph, L. That's All.
Kandel. First They Slaughtered the Angels.
Knight, S. Eyeball Works, The.
Larkin, P. Homage to a Government.
Lawrence, D. Mosquito Knows, The.
Lopez, T. No Transport.
MacLeish. Empire Builders.
McNeill, A. Saint Ras.
Merrill, J. Clearing the Title.
Mills, D. Chembank Card.
Reed, I. El Paso Monologue.
Rich, A. In Those Years.
San Juan. Owl of Minerva Takes Flight in the
　Evening, The.
Shapiro, A. Drug Store.
Spender, S. After They Have Tired of the
　Brilliance of Cities.
Thomas, R. Other.
Umpierre, L. Statue, The.
See also **Banking and Bankers; Business and
　Businessmen; Financiers**

Captivity
Barben, D. Four White Walls.
Belieu. Sleeping Man Must Be Awakened to Be
　Killed, A.
Bryant, W. African Chief, The.
Chippewa Oral Tradition. Song of the Captive
　Sioux Woman.
Coleman, W. Prisoner of Los Angeles (2).
Davenant [or D'Avenant]. Countess of
　Anglesey lead Captive by the Rebels, at the
　Disforresting of Pewsam, The.
Dunbar, P. Sympathy.
Jewett, S. Caged Bird, A.
Karp. Harm.
Kipling, R. Half-Ballad of Waterval.
Knight, S. Mermaid Tank, The.
Komunyakaa. Chastity Belt.
Landon. Castle of Chillon, The.
Levy, A. Captivity.
Lovelace, R. Lady A. L., My Asylum [in a
　Great Extremity], The.
Lowell, A. Captured Goddess, The.
Noguchi, R. His Waves.
Rohrer, M. Last Look at the Mutineers, A.
Rowe, E. Expostulation, The.
Sisson. Money.
Steptoe. Wired In.
"Struther." Freedom.
Szporluk. Occupant of the Hose.
Thwaite. Freedom.
Trethewey, N. Bellocq's Ophelia.
Very. I Was Sick and in Prison.
Wilde, R. Lament of the Captive, The.

Caravaggio, Michelangelo Merisi da
Gunn, T. In Santa Maria del Popolo.
Levis. Caravaggio: Swirl and Vortex.

Card Games
Cataldi. Advice.
Davis, T. Playing Solitaire.
Hitchcock. Solitaire.
Larkin, P. Card-Players, The.
O'Grady, J. Buster's Last Hand.
Rossetti, C. Queen of Hearts, The.
Spicer, J. Cardplayers, The.
Webster, A. Enigma No. 6.

Cardiff, Wales
Abse. Return to Cardiff.
Garlick, R. Capitals.
Tripp. Capital.

Cardinals (ornithology)
Plumly. Cardinals in a Shower at Union Square.
Stern, G. Red Bird.

Cargoes
Masefield. Cargoes.
See also **Freighters**

Caribbean Islands
Brathwaite, E. Calypso.
Esteves. From Fanon.
　It Is Raining Today.
Hernández Cruz. Islandis.
　It's Miller Time.
See also **West Indies**

Caribbean Sea
Barrax. Scuba Diver Recovers the Body of a
　Drowned Child, The.
See also **West Indies**

Caring
Ackerman, J. First Night.
Bart, L. As Long As He Needs Me.
Cooper, J. Rent.
Foster, A. Starting School.
Klein, M. Guardian Life.
Loesser. Somebody, Somewhere.
Prufer, K. Babysitter's Devotion, The.
Wright, J. Arrangements with Earth for Three
　Dead Friends.
　Mutterings Over the Crib of a Deaf Child.

Carmel, California
Jeffers, R. Carmel Point.
　Tor House.
Santos, S. Jeffers Country.
Schmitz. Carmel.

Carnivals
Bishop, E. Pink Dog.
Brautigan. Boat, A.
Brown, G. Hamnavoe Market.
Kasischke. Fatima.
Keplinger, D. Distance Between Zero and One,
　The.
Rafferty, P. After Carnival.
Spencer, A. At the Carnival.
St. John, P. Carnival.

Caroline of Ansbach
Pope, A. On Queen Caroline's Deathbed.

Carp
Martinez, D. Carp.
Wright, J. Lifting Illegal Nets by Flashlight.

Carpe Diem
Angelou. Come, and Be My Baby.
Braley, B. Start Where You Stand.
Browning, R. Youth and Art.
Carew, T. To A. L.; Persuasions [or
　Perswasions] to Love.
Carson, J. I Am Asking You to Come Back
　Home.
Catina. Philosophy.
Cohan. I'm Mighty Glad I'm Living and That's
　All.
　If I'm Going to Die I'm Going to Have Some
　　Fun.
Coslow, S. (Up on Top of a Rainbow) Sweepin'
　the Clouds Away.
Cowley, A. Age.
Cummings, E. My Father Moved Through
　Dooms of Love.
　What If a Much of a Which of a Wind.
De Vries, P. Bacchanal.

Dowson. Villanelle of the Poet's Road.
Dubin, A. Young and Healthy.
Finch, A. There's No To-Morrow.
Foley, H. Touch Wood.
Gershwin. One Life to Live.
Harte, B. California Madrigal.
Herman, J. Before the Parade Passes By.
Herrick. Anacreontic.
Corinna's Going a-Maying.
To the Virgins, to Make Much of Time.
Jacob, H. Alarm, The.
Jordan, T. Careless Gallant, The.
Kaufman, H. This Is Your Hour.
Keats. Fancy.
Ode on a Grecian Urn.
Lovelace, R. To Amarantha, That She Would
Dishevel[l] Her Hair[e].
MacLeish. Speech to a Crowd.
Marlowe. Passionate Shepherd To His Love,
The.
Marvell. To His Coy Mistress.
Young Love.
Masefield. Laugh and Be Merry.
Meinke. Advice to My Son.
Melville, H. Rosary Beads.
Moore, T. Young May Moon, The.
Morley, T. Sing We and Chant It.
Perry, N. Next Year.
Plato. Apple, The.
Prior. Quid Sit Futurum Cras Fuge Quaerere.
Ralegh, S. Nymph's [or Nimphs] Reply to the
Shepherd [or Sheepheard], The.
Ransom, J. Blue Girls.
Southwell. Loss[e] in Delay[e].
Stickney, T. Live Blindly and upon the Hour.
Unknown. Sister, Awake!
Waller, E. Song: "Go[e], lovely rose."
Warren, H. Young and Healthy.
Washington, N. Hundred Years from Today, A.
Weill, K. One Life to Live.
Wilcox, E. Was, Is, and Yet-To-Be.

Carpentry and Carpenters
Baugh, E. Carpenter's Complaint, The.
Carter, M. Bitter Wood.
Davie. With the Grain.
Dove, R. Genie's Prayer Under the Kitchen
Sink.
Shaw, L. Craftsman.
Stein, K. In the Kingdom of Perpetual Repair.
Wilbur. Hole in the Floor, A.

Carriages
Hammerstein. Surrey with the Fringe on Top,
The.
Moore, M. Carriage from Sweden, A.

Cars
Berger, B. Silver-Paced.
Bottoms. In the Black Camaro.
Carlson, R. Max Who Caught a Car.
Erdrich. Lady in the Pink Mustang, The.
Espada. Jeep Driver, The.
Grieves, C. Indian Car.
Healy, E. Changing the Oil.
Jacobik, G. Turkeys in August.
Minhinnick. She Drove a 'Seventies Plymouth.
Moore, H. Edward.
Parnell, P. Sile Na gCioch.
Pau-Llosa. Kendall Gulls.
Pearlberg, G. G. Dog Star.
Rhodes, M. How Fast.
Savageau. Trees.
Snyder, G. Night Song of the Los Angeles
Basin.
Stein, K. Because You're American.
Williams, C. Shock.
See also **Automobiles**

Cartoons
Flynn, N. Cartoon Physics, Part 1.
Cartoon Physics, Part 2.

Cary, Sir Lucius
Jonson, B. To the Immortal[l] Memory [or
Memorie] and Friendship of That Noble
Pair[e], Sir Lucius Cary and Sir H. [or Henry]
Morison.

Casabianca, Louis
Hemans. Casabianca.

Cassandra
Bogan, L. Cassandra.
Dickey, W. Cassandra.
Jeffers, R. Cassandra.
Robinson, E. Cassandra.

Castlereagh, Robert Stewart, 2d Viscount
Shelley, P. Similes for Two Political Characters
of 1819.

Castles
Beevers. Atameros.
Bowles, W. Written at Bamborough Castle.
Burn. Welsh Love Letter.
Carr, M. Castle in the Fire, The.
Corben. Harlech Castle.
Holloway, G. Ford Castle: The Borders.
Hugo, R. Ferniehirst Castle.
Landon. Castle of Chillon, The.
Lang, A. Romance.
Levertov. Psalm Concerning the Castle.
Leyeles. Castles.
O'Huiginn, T. Visit to Enniskillen, A.
Pau-Llosa. Paredón.
Poe. Haunted Palace, The.
Reed, H. Château, The.
Rothenberg, J. At the Castle.
Sitwell, D. Trams.
Spires. Robed Heart, The.
Stevenson, R. Song of a Traveller, The.
Wordsworth, W. Elegiac Stanzas Suggested by
a Picture of Peele Castle, in a Storm, Painted
by Sir George Beaumont.

Castration
Jenkins, N. Castration.
Morris, M. Missing: A Dog's Doggerel.
Sharp, S. In the Tradition of Bobbitt.

Castro, Fidel
Espada. Fidel in Ohio.
Esteves. For Fidel Castro.
Ferlinghetti, L. One Thousand Fearful Words
for Fidel Castro.
Updike. Meditation on a News Item.

Catalpa Trees
Waddington, M. Catalpa Tree.

Caterpillars
Dickinson, E. Caterpillar.
Fisher, A. Caterpillars.
Foster, A. Caterpillar.
McCord, D. Cocoon.
Rossetti, C. Caterpillar, The.
Serraillier. Tickle Rhyme, The.
Yolen. Caterpillar's Lullaby.

Catfish
Engels, J. Bullhead.

Cathedrals
Chester, T. Candle at Canterbury, A.
Fields, J. Citizen.
Hardy, T. In a Cathedral City.
Johnson, J. Before a Painting.
Milosz, C. Abundant Catch (Luke 5:4–10).
Ormond. Cathedral Builders.
Wharton, E. Chartres.

Catholicism and Catholics
Ayres. Invites Poets and Historians to Write in
Cynthia's Praise.
Coles, R. Christmas, Belfast.
Crashaw. To the Noblest and Best of Ladies,
the Countess of Denbigh.
Derricotte. St. Peter Claver.
Devlin, D. Lough Derg.
Dryden, J. Churches of Rome and of England,
The.
Presbyterians, The.
Eliot, T. Hippopotamus, The.
Gildner. They Have Turned the Church Where I
Ate God.
Kennedy, X. First Confession.
Kinnell. Avenue Bearing the Initial of Christ
into the New World, The.
LaFemina. Her Rose Tattoo.
Lehmann, G. Pope Alexander VI.
Lim-Wilson. Explaining the Origin of My
Name.
Longley, M. Letter to Derek Mahon.
Lowell, R. Beyond the Alps.
For George Santayana.

Myles, E. Eileen's Vision.
Scates. Going to Mass after Fifteen Years.
Williams, W. Catholic Bells, The.

Cats
Alegría. Savoir Faire.
Algarin. Tiger Lady.
Amherst. Verses Designed to Be Sent to Mr.
Adams.
Arnold, M. Atossa.
Bates, C. Gray Thrums.
Benson, G. Cat and the Pig, The.
Bodecker. Cats and Dogs.
Brautigan. Surprise.
Brown, L. Sonnet Around Stephanie.
Bukowski. Mockingbird, The.
Startled into Life Like Fire.
Charles, D. Concrete Cat.
Coatsworth. Bad Kittens, The.
On a Night of Snow.
Open Door, The.
Cox, P. Lazy Pussy, The.
Cranch. Old Cat's Confessions, An.
Crane, H. Chaplinesque.
Dickinson, E. Cat.
Eliot, T. Bustopher Jones: The Cat About Town.
Cat Morgan Introduces Himself.
Growltiger's Last Stand.
Gus: The Theatre Cat.
Macavity: The Mystery Cat.
Mr Mistoffelees.
Naming of Cats, The.
Rum Tum Tugger, The.
Skimbleshanks: The Railway Cat.
Song of the Jellicles, The.
Ewart. 14-Year-Old Convalescent Cat in the
Winter, A.
Jubilate Matteo.
Lifelines.
Who Likes the Idea of Guide Cats?
Fanning, R. In the Barn.
Farjeon, E. Cats.
Field, E. Duel, The.
Fisher, A. Cat in the Snow.
Listening.
Flatman. Appeal to Cats in the Business of
Love, An.
Fuhrman, J. Watching Trains.
Fuller, R. Family Cat, The.
Fyleman. Cat, The.
Gallico, P. Application.
Confession.
Garrigue. Epitaph for My Cat.
Georges. Alley Cat.
Gibbons, R. Hoppy.
Gilbert, S. Gilbertian Cats.
González, R. Death of the Farm Workers' Cat.
Graves, R. Cat Goddesses.
Gray, S. On a Cat Aging.
Gray, T. Ode on the Death of a Favourite [or
Favorite] Cat, Drowned in a Tub [or Bowl] of
Gold Fishes.
Grimes, A. Alice's Cat, New Year's Eve 1990.
Hall, D. Alligator Bride, The.
Halpern, D. Dance, The.
Hare, M. Alfred de Musset.
Harris, W. Samantha Is My Negro Cat.
Hass, R. Elegy Residence on Earth.
Hemingway. Earnest Liberal's Lament, The.
Hirsch, E. Wild Gratitude.
Hood, T. Choosing Their Names.
Hope, A. House of God, The.
Hudgins. Two Ember Days in Alabama.
Hughes, T. Esther's Tomcat.
Jarrell. Lonely Man, The.
Johnston, E. Nelly's Lament for the Pirnhouse
Cat.
Keats. To a Cat.
Kinnell. Supper after the Last, The.
Kumin, M. Plans.
Larsen, L. Lips.
Lear, E. Children of the Owl and the Pussy-Cat,
The.
Owl and the Pussy-Cat, The.
Leax. Her Seventeenth Winter.
Levertov. Cat as Cat, The.
Innocent, The.

Scenes from the Life of the Peppertrees.
Lindsay, N. Mysterious Cat, The.
Loncar, M. As My Cat Eats the Head of a Field Mouse He Has Caught.
Marquis. Mehitabel S Extensive Past.
  Song of Mehitabel, The.
  Tom-Cat, The.
McGough, R. My Cat and I.
Merrill, J. Maisie.
Merwin, W. S. Burning the Cat.
Miller, M. Cat.
Milne, E. Diamond Cut Diamond.
Molony. Cat Washing.
Monro. Cat's Meat.
  Milk for the Cat.
Montague, J. Mother Cat.
Moore, M. Peter.
Morley, C. In Honour of Taffy Topaz.
Mother Goose. Pancake Day.
  Six Little Mice.
Myer, M. Cool Cat.
Nash, O. Cat, The.
Oliver, M. Morning.
Owen, G. This and That.
Peacock, M. Breakfast with Cats.
Petrie. Indoor Cat, The.
Pitt. Fable of the Young Man and His Cat, The.
Rands. Cat of Cats, The.
Reid, A. Curiosity.
Robinson, E. New England.
Rosenblatt. Cat.
Rowse. White Cat of Trenarren, The.
Sackville-West. Greater Cats, The.
Sayers, D. War Cat.
Seward. Old Cat's Dying Soliloquy, An.
Shamaqmaq, A. Hungry Master and Hungry Cat.
Sidney, S. White Great Nimble Cat, A.
Smart, C. My Cat Jeoffry (Jubilate Agno).
Smith, S. Galloping Cat, The.
  Singing Cat, The.
Stevenson, A. Epitaph for a Good Mouser.
Straus, M. Neuroanatomy Summer.
Summers, H. My Old Cat.
Swenson, M. Cat and the Weather.
  Secret in the Cat, The.
Taylor, G. Cruel, Clever Cat.
Unknown. Cats of Kilkenny, The.
  Pangur Bán.
  Pussy-Cat Mew.
  Two Gray Kits.
Usher, L. I Am the Cat.
Verlaine. Femme et Chatte.
Ward, J. To Get Clear.
Wenderoth, J. Detailed History of the Western World.
Whalen. Walking beside the Kamogawa, Remembering Nansen and Fudo and Gary's Poem.
Willard, N. King of Cats Sends a Postcard to His Wife, The.
Williams, W. Complete Destruction.
  Mujer.
  Poem: "As the cat."
Winstanley, J. Upon a Friend's Pet Cat, Being Sick.
Wright, K. Dad and the Cat and the Tree.
Yeats. Cat and the Moon, The.
  Two Songs of a Fool.
See also **Kittens**
Cattle
Ba. Familiar Oxen.
  Ox-Soldier, The.
Colum, P. Drover, A.
Currey. Jersey Cattle.
Davis, H. Proud Riders.
García Lorca. Prelude.
Gibson, W. Drove-Road, The.
Hardy, T. Bags of Meat.
Moore, N. Island and the Cattle, The.
Murray, L. Names of the Humble, The.
Skrzynecki. Cattle.
See also **Bulls; Cowboys; Cows; Meat**
Catullus
Huxley, A. Second Philosopher's Song.
Landor, W. On Catullus.

MacLeish. You Also, Gaius Valerius Catullus.
Millay, E. Passer Mortuus Est.
Tennyson, A. Frater Ave Atque Vale.
Caution
Brodsky, J. Belfast Tune.
Brown, L. Button Up Your Overcoat.
Creeley. I Know a Man.
Gascoigne. For That He Looked Not upon Her.
Hewitt, J. Search, The.
Lewis, A. To a Comrade in Arms.
Montagu, L. Lover, The; a Ballad.
Moore, T. Duke Is the Lad [to Frighten a Lass], The.
Roethke. Monotony Song, The.
Slessor. Up in Mabel's Room.
Washington, N. My Foolish Heart.
Weigl. Mines.
Yeats. Never Give All the Heart.
Cavafy, Constantine P.
Jarman, M. Cavafy in Redondo.
Cavalcanti, Guido
Dante Alighieri. Sonnet: To Guido Cavalcanti.
Cavaliers
Herrick. His Cavalier.
Larcom. Little Cavalier, A.
Cavalry
Davidson, D. Sequel of Appomattox.
Housman, A. Lancer.
Newbolt. Gillespie.
Tennyson, A. Charge of the Light Brigade, The.
Whitman, W. Cavalry Crossing a Ford.
Cavemen
Eshleman, C. Placements I.
Kipling, R. King, The.
Mahon. Hunt by Night, The.
Pratt, E. From Stone to Steel.
Rukeyser, M. Painters.
See also **Man, Primitive**
Caves
Cary, A. Sea-Side Cave, The.
Cawein. Caverns.
Crashaw. Come See the Place Where the Lord Lay.
Dodd, E. Like Memory, Caverns.
Eshleman, C. Notes on a Visit to Le Tuc d'Audoubert.
Fairburn. Cave, The.
"Field." Maidenhair.
Hedin, R. At Betharram.
Knott. Sleep.
Lee, E. Forests and Caverns.
Merrill, J. Power Station, The.
Merwin, W. S. Bread.
Moraes, D. Kanheri Caves.
Nungarrayi, J. Sorry.
Rukeyser, M. Ajanta.
Stafford, W. Indian Cave Jerry Ramsey Found, The.
Warfield. Forests and Caverns.
Wetzsteon. Coming Back to the Cave.
Cecilia, Saint
Auden. Song for St. Cecilia's Day.
Dryden, J. Alexander's Feast; or, The Power of Music [or Musique].
  Song for St Cecilia's Day, 1687, A.
Celan, Paul
Halperin. Two Lines from Paul Celan.
Hirsch, E. In Memoriam Paul Celan.
Celandine
Thomas, E. Celandine.
Wordsworth, W. Lesson, A.
Celibacy
Clarke, A. Celibacy.
Hubbell, L. W. Birth-Hour.
See also **Bachelors; Virginity and Virgins**
Cellars
De la Mare. John Mouldy.
Hope, M. Bare Floors.
Kumin, M. In the Root Cellar.
Roethke. Root Cellar.
Cellos
Winder. Unaccompanied Suite.
Celts
Smith, S. Celts, The.

Cemeteries
Aldington. Battlefield.
Barton, J. Mistress, The.
Behar, R. Jewish Cemetery in Guanabacoa, The.
Bowers, E. Mountain Cemetery, The.
Causley. At the British War Cemetery, Bayeux.
  By St. Thomas Water.
Cervantes. Meeting Mescalito at Oak Hill Cemetery.
Clarke, M. In the Graveyard.
Clifton, L. At the Cemetery, Walnut Grove Plantation, South Carolina, 1989.
Creeley. Stairway to Heaven.
Dickinson, E. Cemetery, A.
Dorn, E. Air of June Sings, The.
Fairfax, J. Forest of the Dead, The.
Flecker. Town without a Market, The.
Fordham. Magnolia.
Freneau. Indian Burying Ground, The.
Frost, R. Home Burial.
Gray, T. Elegy Written in a Country Churchyard.
  Epitaph: "Here rests his head upon the lap of earth."
Haines, J. Flight, The.
Hardy, T. Friends Beyond.
  Levelled Churchyard, The.
  Voices from Things Growing in a Churchyard.
Heard, J. National Cemetery, Beaufort, South Carolina, The.
Hill, G. Distant Fury of Battle, The.
Howe, F. Seeking Out His Face in a Cup.
Hugo, R. Graves at Elkhorn.
Kaufman, S. Mount of Olives, The.
Lawrence, D. Giorno dei Morti.
Longfellow, H. In the Churchyard at Cambridge.
  Jewish Cemetery at Newport, The.
Lowell, R. Quaker Graveyard in Nantucket, The.
Marriott. Prairie Graveyard.
Marston, P. Old Churchyard of Bonchurch, The.
McCarthy, T. Sorrow Garden, The.
McCrae, J. In Flanders Fields.
Mew. In Nunhead Cemetery.
Miller, J. In Père La Chaise.
Moore, L. Again.
Nemerov. Negro Cemetery Next to a White One, A.
Olds, S. Leningrad Cemetery, Winter of 1941.
Pelletiere, M. Under Her Crib.
Ryan, A. Lines: "Gather the sacred dust."
Sandburg, C. Cool Tombs.
Smith, C. Pressed by the Moon, Mute Arbitress of Tides.
Smith, S. Great Unaffected Vampires and the Moon.
Stevenson, R. Blows the Wind Today.
Tate, A. Ode to the Confederate Dead.
Thomson, J. In a Christian Churchyard.
Timrod. Ode: "Sleep sweetly in your humble graves."
Tomlinson, C. After a Death.
Unknown. Of Sir Frauncis Walsingham Sir Phillipp Sydney, and Sir Christopher Hatton, Lord Chancelor.
Wilbur. In a Churchyard.
Williams, W. Children, The.
Wilson, R. Elegy in a Presbyterian Burying-Ground.
Wiman, C. In Lakeview Cemetery.
Winters, Y. To the Holy Spirit.
Wright, C. Yugoslav Cemetery.
Wright, J. Albuquerque Graveyard, The.
  Way to Make a Living, A.
See also **Burial; Graves; Mausoleums; Tombs**
Censorship
Clarke, A. Penal Law.
Donne. Raderus.
Duchamp. SURcenSURE.
Hirschman, J. Painting, The.
Kramer, L. Night Bird, The.
Lawrence, D. Innocent England.
Nash, O. Invocation: "Senator Smoot (Republican, Ut.)."

Paulin. Where Art Is a Midwife.
Waley. Censorship.

Centaurs
Bowers, E. Centaur Overheard, The.
Swenson, M. Centaur, The.

Centipedes
Dove, R. Centipede.
Kendall, M. Education's Martyr.

Central America
Rose. Day They Cleaned up the Border El
Salvador, February, 1981, The.
See also **Latin America and Latin Americans**

Central Park, New York City
Brouwer, J. Conservatory Pond, Central Park,
New York, New York.
Cooley, N. Diane Arbus, New York.
Hughes, N. Dive.
Symons, J. Central Park.
Wright, J. Lake in Central Park, The.

Cereus, Night-blooming
Hayden, R. Night-Blooming Cereus, The.

Certainty
Jeffers, R. Nova.

Chagall, Marc
Cohen, L. Out of the Land of Heaven.
Ferlinghetti, L. Don't Let That Horse.
Niatum. Homage to Chagall.

Chairs
Borson. After a Death.
Cambridge, R. On Seeing a Tapestry Chair-
Bottom Beautifully Worked by His Daughter
for Mrs Holroyd.
Campbell, S. Chairmaker, The.
Cook, E. Old Arm-Chair, The.
Hagiwara Sakutaro. Chair.
Hardy, T. Garden Seat, The.
Klein, A. Rocking Chair, The.
Pietri. 3rd Untitled Poem.
Pilling. Affair With a Chair, An.
Townsend, A. Rouge.
White, E. Chairs in Snow.
Worth, V. Chairs.

Chameleons
Kinnell. Gray Heron, The.
Moore, M. To a Chameleon.
Unknown. Cameleon Lover, The.

Chamois
Hemans. Chamois Hunter's Love, The.

Champions
Preston, R. Champion Chant.

Chance
Aiken, C. Chance Meetings.
Bawer. On Leaving the Artists' Colony.
Bond, E. If.
Burke, J. It Could Happen to You.
Cataldi. We Could Have Met.
Charara, H. On the Murder of an Ice Cream
Man.
Creeley. Song: "Those rivers run from that
land."
Duhamel. Art.
Duke, V. Taking a Chance on Love.
Ehrhart. Letter.
Elizabeth I. Ah silly pugg wert thou so sore
afraid.
Gioia. Summer Storm.
Gylys, B. Fat Chance.
Herrick. Casualties.
Kalmar. Nevertheless (I'm in Love with You).
Kinnell. Little Sleep's-Head Sprouting Hair in
the Moonlight.
Knott. At the Crossroads.
Madge. On One Condition.
Melville, H. Guide and Guard.
Mulkey, R. Blind-Sided.
Simic. Elementary Cosmogony.
Szymborska. Terrorist, He Watches, The.
Van Heusen, J. It Could Happen to You.
Wotton, S. Upon the Sudden Restraint of the
Earl[e] of Somerset, Then Falling from Favor
[*or* Favour].
Wyatt. Varium et Mutabile.
See also **Fate; Fortune**

Chancellorsville, Battle of (1863)
Hudgins. At Chancellorsville.

Change
Ammons, A. R. Corsons Inlet.

Ashbery. My Philosophy of Life.
Atwood. Eventual Proteus.
Auden. As I Walked Out One Evening.
Backus. Then Laugh.
Blamire. When Home We Return.
Boss. My Ringless Fingers on the Steering
Wheel Tell the Story.
Bowman, C. Demographics.
Bradley, G. E Pur Si Muove.
Brontë, A. Fragment, A.
Bryant, W. Mutation.
Rivulet, The.
Carew, T. Persuasions to Enjoy.
Upon Some Alterations in My Mistress, after
My Departure into France.
Cartwright, W. On the Great Frost (1634).
Chavez, L. Woman Who Raised Dogs, The.
Chipasula. Friend, Ah You Have Changed!
Ciardi. On Learning to Adjust to Things.
Clinton, M. Traditional Post-Modern Neo-
HooDoo Afra-Centric Sister in a Purple Head
Rag Mourning Death and Cooking.
Coleman, C. Why Try to Change Me Now?
Coleridge, M. Marriage.
Moment, A.
Coleridge, S. Constancy to an Ideal Object.
Duty Surviving Self-Love.
Garden Year, The.
Congreve. False Though She Be.
Cook, E. Song of the Modern Time.
Corso. Whole Mess . . . Almost, The.
Cowper, W. Yardley Oak.
Cranch. Spirit of the Age, The.
Creeley. For Love.
Crunk, T. Visiting the Site of One of the First
Churches My Grandfather Pastored.
Davies, M. Vow for New Year's, A.
Dawe, G. Lundys Letter, The.
Day Lewis. Poem for an Anniversary.
Dickinson, E. Presentiment.
Dove, R. Ö.
Sunday Greens.
Wingfoot Lake.
Eberhart, R. Immortal Picture, The.
Elizabeth I. When I Was Fair and Young.
Ellington, D. Maybe I Should Change My
Ways.
English, T. Ben Bolt.
Espada. Bully.
Fisher, M. Nothing Ever Changes My Love for
You.
Forbes, J. Age of Plastic, The.
Forman, R. Someone.
We Are the Young Magicians.
Frost, R. Directive.
Nothing Gold Can Stay.
Ginsberg, A. Change: *Kyoto-Tokyo Express*,
The.
Glück, L. Cottonmouth Country.
Goldsmith, O. Deserted Village, The.
Village, The.
Graves, R. Change.
Hall, D. Hermit with Landscape.
Porcelain Couple, The.
Wedding Party.
Hardy, T. Ancient to Ancients, An.
Going and Staying.
His Visitor.
Places.
Voice of Things, The.
Harjo, J. Anchorage.
For Alva Benson, and for Those Who Have
Learned to Speak.
Hayden, J. Full Moon.
Healy, E. Changing What We Mean.
Herbert, C. Everything Changes.
Hernandez, D. Martin and My Father.
Herrick. Fair[e] Days; or, Dawn[e]s
Deceitful[l].
Impossibilities to His Friend.
Hewitt, J. Postscript, 1984.
Hinsey, E. Art of Measuring Light, The.
Body in Youth, The.
Hirschman, J. Headlands.
Hogan, L. Crossings.
Holland, J. Sleep.

Hollander, J. Old-Fashioned Song, An.
Holloway, G. Things.
Housman, A. Oh, When I Was In Love.
Hugo, R. Letter to Gale from Ovando.
Jarrell. In Montecito.
Jeffers, R. Beaks of Eagles, The.
Summer Holiday.
Jefferys [*or* Jeffries]. We Have Lived and
Loved Together.
Jonson, B. Epistle. To Katharine, Lady
Aubigny.
Jordan, J. Roman Poem Number Nine.
Keats. After Dark Vapours Have Oppressed Our
Plains.
Bright Star.
Keplinger, D. Another Century.
Kiser. Bargain Sale, A.
Komunyakaa. Way the Cards Fall, The.
Kooser. Country School.
Landor, W. What News.
Lear, E. Calico Pie.
Levine, P. Later Still.
Levis. Picking Grapes in an Abandoned
Vineyard.
Lovelace, R. Apostasy of One and But One
Lady, The.
Grasshopper, The.
Lucasta's World.
Lucy. Missing Link.
MacCaig. Return to Scalpay.
MacNeice. Figure of Eight.
Precursors.
Snow.
Madhubuti. Poem to Complement Other
Poems, A.
Magidson, H. (I'm Afraid) the Masquerade Is
Over.
Manyarrows. Today We Will Not Be Invisible
Nor Silent.
Mapanje. At the Metro: Old Irrelevant Images.
McCarthy, J. Why Try to Change Me Now?
Merwin, W. S. Dictum: For a Masque of
Deluge.
Grandmother Watching at Her Window.
Miller, A. Pruning, The.
Minhinnick. Boathouse, The.
Mitchell, R. Out Here.
Montague, J. Mount Eagle.
Moody, W. Departure, The.
Moulds, J. Late Summer Litany.
Nelson, J. Teed Off.
Nemerov. Dependencies, The.
Western Approaches, The.
Nye, N. New Year.
O'Connor, P. Poems (I- XI).
Olson, C. In Cold Hell, in Thicket.
Kingfishers, The.
Palazzeschi. Stranger, The.
Pope, A. C[h]loe.
Epistle [II,] to a Lady[: Of the Characters of
Women].
To a Lady.
Powell, D. A. Always Returning: Holidays and
Burials. Not Every Week.
Reynolds, R. Object of Burial Is Intent, The.
Rich, A. Necessities of Life.
Phenomenology of Anger, The.
Prospective Immigrants Please Note.
Riley, J. Old Swimmin'-Hole, The.
Robinson, E. Ballade of Broken Flutes.
Rossetti, C. In Progress.
Rossini, C. Valediction.
Sanchez, S. Norma.
Sandburg, C. Languages.
Sarton. On a Winter Night.
Schwartz, L. Leaves.
Schwartz, R. L. Falling in Love after Forty.
Midnight Supper.
Scott, J. Changing Room.
Shapiro, D. Archaic Torsos.
Shelley, P. Lament, A: "O world! O life! O
time!"
Lines: "When the lamp is shattered [*or*
shatter'd]."
Mutability.
Simic. Poem without a Title.
Smith, S. Grange, The.

Snodgrass, W. Mutability.
St. John, P. Carnival.
Stevenson, R. In the States.
Thomas, R. View from the Window, The.
Unknown. Deor.
  Force.
  Will You Love Me When I'm Old?
  World is Turned Upside Down, The.
Van Duyn. Condemned Site.
Viidikas. Future.
Walker, J. Studying Physics with My Daughter.
Wallace-Crabbe. Shape-Changer, The.
Warren, R. Blow, West Wind.
Webb, C. At Summer's End.
Whittier. My Playmate.
Wilbur. Beautiful Changes, The.
Worth, V. Door.
Wright, D. Cockermouth.
Wright, J. On a Phrase from Southern Ohio.
Wunderlich, M. On Opening.
Yeats. Lamentation of the Old Pensioner, The.
  Old Men Admiring Themselves in the Water,
  The.
Young, A. California Peninsula: El Camino
  Real.
See also **Transience**

Changelings
Cofer, J. Changeling, The.
Unknown. Tam Lin.

Channing, William Henry
Emerson, R. Ode, Inscribed to W. H. Channing.

Chaos
Aiken, C. Room, The.
Artaud. Spurt of Blood, The.
Ashbery. Hotel Lautréamont.
Bernstein, C. Gradation.
Berrigan, A. Looking Up My Balance.
Breton, A. Mystery Corset, The.
Brownstein. Glass Enclosure, The.
Byron, G. Darkness.
Daumal. Short Revelation Concerning Death
  and Chaos.
Desnos. Language Event Two.
Drieu la Rochelle. Roundness.
Ekelof. Absentia Animi.
Fisher, R. Rules and Ranges for Ian Tyson.
Ginsberg, A. Friday the Thirteenth.
Glatshteyn. To a Friend Who Wouldn't Bother
  to Strain His Noodleboard Because Even So It
  Is Hard to Go Hunting When Your Rifle Is
  Blunt and Love Is Soft as an Old Blanket.
Kelly, R. Looking.
Kowit. Notice.
Kunitz, S. Reflection by a Mailbox.
Lowell, R. For the Union Dead.
Mac Low. Mani-Mani Gatha.
Messerli. Essay on Concrete, An.
Millay, E. I will put Chaos into fourteen lines.
Ribemont-Dessaignes. Artichokes.
Riley, J. Silence.
Robinson, K. First Thing.
  Severance.
Rothenberg, J. That Dada Strain.
Rukeyser, M. Nuns in the Wind.
Sorley. Hundred Thousand Million Mites, A.
St. John, P. Carnival.
Stein, G. Scenes from the Door.
Stevens, W. Idiom of the Hero.
Szymborska. Seen from Above.
Van Doesburg. Remembrance of the Founts of
  Night.
  Still Life: The Table.
Yeats. Second Coming, The.

Chaplin, Charlie
Crane, H. Chaplinesque.
Mandelstam [*or* Mandelshtam]. Charlie Chaplin
  Poem, The.
Orlovsky. Collaboration: Letter to Charlie
  Chaplin.

Chapman, George (1559?-1634)
Keats. On First Looking into Chapman's
  Homer.

Chapman, John ("Johnny Appleseed")
Lindsay, N. Apple-Barrel of Johnny Appleseed,
  The.

Wilbur. John Chapman.

Charity
Bhatt. Go To Ahmedabad.
Browning, R. Twins, The.
Chatterton. Excelente Balade of Charitie, An.
Chesterton, G. From a Spanish Cloister.
Crashaw. C[h]aritas Nimia; or, The Dear[e]
  Bargain.
Dobson, A. Virtuoso, A.
Foss, S. Husband and Heathen.
Graves, R. Certain Mercies.
Guiterman. Offer, An.
Herrick. Upon Sibilla.
Kelly, B. Imagining Their Own Hymns.
Klappert. To Whom.
Moore, M. Charity Overcoming Envy.
Mukand, J. First Payment.
Pritchard, N. Cloak, The.
Ray, H. Charity.
  Triple Benison, The.
Robinson, E. Karma.
Unknown. I Shall Not Pass This Way Again.
See also **Philanthropy and Philanthropists**

Charlemagne
Tuckerman, F. Rhotruda.

Charles I, King of England
Cartwright, W. New Year's Gift, A.
Herrick. Bad Season Makes the Poet Sad, The.
  To the King.
  To the King and Queen[e], upon Their Unhappy
  Distances.
  To the King, upon His Com[m]ing with His
  Army into the West.
  To the King, Upon His Welcome to Hampton
  Court.
Johnson, L. By the Statue of King Charles [*or*
  Charles I] at Charing Cross.
Jonson, B. Epigram. To the Household. 1630,
  An.
Lovelace, R. To My Worthy Friend Mr. Peter
  Lely [*or* Lilly].
Philips, K. Upon the Double Murther of King
  Charles I.
Shelley, P. Widow Bird, A.

Charles II, King of England
Dryden, J. Absalom and Achitophel.
  Achitophel: The Earl of Shaftsbury.
  Shaftsbury.
  Zimri: "In the first rank of These did Zimri
  stand."
  Zimri: The Duke of Buckingham.
Herrick. To the Most Illustrious and Most
  Hopeful[l] Prince, Charles, Prince of Wales.
Lovelace, R. Mock Song, A.
Marvell. Charles II.
Rochester, J. Epitaph on Charles II.
  Impromptu on Charles II.
  Satire on Charles II, A.

Charles VI, King of France
Boland, E. Glass King, The.

Charles River, Massachusetts
Hyde, L. Goldfish in the Charles River.
O'Grady, D. Professor Kelleher and the Charles
  River.
Rosen, K. Along the Charles.
Share, D. Divorced.

Charles, Ray
Cecil. Richard's Blues.
Dent. Ray Charles at Mississippi State.

Charleston, South Carolina
Derricotte. 1994 Inventory.
Heard, J. New Organ, The.
Johnson, J. Charleston.
Rich, A. Charleston in the Eighteen-Sixties.
Timrod. Charleston.
  Ode: "Sleep sweetly in your humble graves."

Charm
Burke, J. Personality.
Herrick. Charme, or an Allay for Love, A.
Hutchinson, P. Bright after Dark.
Plomer. French Lisette: A Ballad of Maida
  Vale.
Ransom, J. Vision by Sweetwater.
Van Heusen, J. Personality.
Yeats. Memory.

Charms (genre)
Campion, T. Thrice Toss[e] These Oaken Ashes
  in the Air [*or* Ayre].
Herrick. Another.
  Another Charme for Stables.
  Another to Bring in the Witch.
  Charmes.
  Spell, The.
Talvikki, A. Origin Charm Against Uncertain
  Injuries.
Unknown. Butter Charm.
  Charm Rhyme, A.

Charon
Belloc. To Dives.
MacNeice. Charon.
Prior. Epigram: "When Bibo thought fit from
  the world to retreat."
Simic. Charon's Cosmology.

Chartism
Jenkins, M. Chartist Meeting.

Chartres, France
Wharton, E. Chartres.

Chastity
"Field." Tragic Mary Queen of Scots, The.
Komunyakaa. Chastity Belt.
Montagu, L. Lover, The; a Ballad.
Philips, K. Answer to Another Persuading a
  Lady to Marriage, An.
Thomas, E. Remedia Amoris.
Yeats. Three Bushes, The.

Chattahoochee River, Georgia
Lanier, S. Song of the Chattahoochee.

Chatterton, Thomas
Keats. To Chatterton.

Chaucer, Geoffrey
Longfellow, H. Chaucer.
Waller, E. Of English Verse.

Cheerfulness
Creeley. Be of Good Cheer.
Wordsworth, W. I Wandered Lonely As a
  Cloud.

Cheese
Cole, W. What a Friend We Have in Cheeses!
Hall, D. O Cheese.
Herrick. Fresh Cheese and Cream.
Hughes, T. Cheese for the Archdeacon, A.
Landesman. Say 'Cheese!'
McGrath, C. Capitalist Poem #36.
McIntyre. Prophecy of a Ten Ton Cheese.
Murray, G. American Cheese.
Unknown. Sukey [*or* Suky], you shall be my
  wife.

Chekhov, Anton
Berg, S. Prayer: "Nobody understands so let the
  Rabbi."
Bolton, J. Fin de Siècle.
Hirshfield, J. In Praise of Coldness.
Simpson, L. Chocolates.

Chemical Warfare
Kipling, R. Gethsemane.
Owen, W. Dulce et Decorum Est.

Chemistry and Chemists
Lehrer. Elements, The.
Masters, E. Trainor, the Druggist.

Chernobyl
Salter. Chernobyl.
Stainer. Xochiquetzal.
Wojahn. Workmen Photographed inside the
  Reactor.
See also **Nuclear Accidents**

Cherry Trees and Cherries
Brown, L. Life Is Just a Bowl of Cherries.
Burrows, S. Time of Cherries, A.
Gunn, T. Cherry Tree, The.
Herrick. Cherry-ripe [*or* Cherrie-ripe].
  Upon Mistresse Susanna Southwell, Her
  Cheeks.
Housman, A. Loveliest of Trees, the Cherry
  Now.
Jenkins, N. Wild Cherry.
Lawrence, D. Cherry Robbers.
Lowry, M. Wild Cherry, The.
Rossetti, C. Let's Be Merry.
Thomas, E. Cherry Trees, The.

Unknown. Cherry, A.
Ward, T. In the Interest of Possibility.

Chesapeake Bay
Orfalea, G. Jellyfish Eggs.
Wylie. Puritan Sonnet, IV.
Wild Peaches.

Chess
Harwood, G. Game of Chess, A.
Lovelace, R. To Dr. F. B. on His Book of Chess[e].
Rossetti, D. On the Poet, Arthur O'Shaughnessy—.
Simic. Prodigy.
Stanard, C. Washington Square Park and a Game of Chess.

Chesterton, Gilbert Keith
Belloc. Lines to a Don.
Wolfe, H. G. K. Chesterton.

Chestnut Trees and Chestnuts
Aldrich, T. Song: "Chestnuts shine through the cloven rind, The."
Eberhart, R. Horse Chestnut Tree, The.
Longfellow, H. Village Blacksmith, The.
Tomlinson, C. Chestnut Avenue: at Alton House, The.
Unknown, fr. Terezin Concentration Camp. On a Sunny Evening.

Chicago, Illinois
Alexander, M. Chicago.
Anderson, S. Evening Song.
Brooks, F. Foreigners at the Fair.
Dobyns. Freight Cars.
Fordham. Chicago Exposition Ode.
Harris, D. Landscapes.
Harte, B. Chicago.
Hernandez, D. Rooftop Piper.
Hirsch, E. American Apocalypse.
Loftis, N. Big John.
McGrath, C. Spring Comes to Chicago.
Piatt, J. Fires in Illinois.
Rexroth, K. Bad Old Days, The.
Rodgers, C. U Name This One.
Rodriguez, L. Fire.
Sandburg, C. Chicago.
Mamie.
Schmitz. Climbing Sears Tower.
Making Chicago.
Seaton, M. Nostradamus Predicts the Destruction of Chicago.
Tagging.
Shepherd, R. Maritime.
Squire. Stockyard, The.
Troupe. Impressions / of Chicago; For Howlin' Wolf.
Unknown. Goin' to Chicago Blues.
Welch, L. Chicago Poem.

Chicanos and Chicanas
Anzaldúa. Horse.
Encarnacion. Bulosan Listens to a Recording of Robert Johson.
Lem. Office Hour.
Mora. Depression Days.
La Migra.
Salinas, R. Trip Through the Mind Jail, A.
Soto. Black Hair.
Mexicans Begin Jogging.

Chickens
Bly, R. As a Child.
Brown, G. Hawk, The.
Burdette. Orphan Born.
Finch, P. Scaring Hens.
Garcia, R. Nobody Here But Us.
Hernández Cruz. If Chickens Could Talk.
Kinnell. Supper after the Last, The.
Nash, O. Experiment Degustatory.
Orton, B. Bacchanal.
Patchen. In the footsteps of the walking air.
Rankine. Eden.
Roberts, E. Hens, The.
Shange. Ancestral Messengers/Composition 13.
Williams, W. Red Wheelbarrow, The.
Wright, J. Presentation of Two Birds to My Son, A.

Child Abuse
Addonizio. Broken Sonnets.
Ai. Child Beater.
Anderson, A. Suicide Year, The.
Budbill. What I Heard at the Discount Department Store.
Cary, P. Granny's House.
Chin, J. Why a Boy.
Clifton, L. Sorrow Song.
Hayden, R. Whipping, The.
Holloway, G. Non-Accidental Injury Slides.
Larkin, J. Origins.
Lawrence, D. Discord in Childhood.
Lorde. Chain.
McCarriston. Billy.
Castle in Lynn, A.
Mouré. Thirteen Years.
O'Reilly, M. Abused Child.
Smith, S. Lord Barrenstock.
Papa Love Baby.
Watson, E. Battered Toddler, Page B6.

Child Labor
Cleghorn. Golf Links, The.
Cook, E. Our Father.

Childhood and Children
Abad, G. Toys.
Abinader, E. Making It New.
Adams, F. Those Two Boys.
Adams, L. Kids!
Adcock, F. Halfway Street, Sidcup.
Addonizio. Broken Sonnets.
Adkins, G. Children in Armour.
"Æ." Frolic.
Germinal.
Aguilar-Cariño. Familiar.
Ai. Good Shepherd: Atlanta, 1981, The.
Aldis, D. Hiding.
Alexander, E. Aspirin.
Minnesota Fats Describes His Youth.
Algarin. Meeting Gaylen's 5th Grade Class.
Allbery. Offering.
Alley, R. Growing Days, The.
Anderson, A. Licking Wounds.
Angela, F. Old Stone Age.
Angus. Blue Jacket, The.
Ashbery. Young Son, The.
Ashe. Vision of Children, A.
Asquith. Sunday Afternoons.
Awad, J. First Snow.
Widower, The.
Bachhuber, D. Mozart in a Classroom of Children.
Baillie, J. Child to His Sick Grandfather, A.
Barber, D. Spirit Level, The.
Barber, M. Written for My Son, and Spoken by Him at His First Putting on Breeches.
Barlow, G. Painting Drunken Twilight.
Barrax. Scuba Diver Recovers the Body of a Drowned Child, The.
Strangers Like Us: Pittsburgh, Raleigh, 1945–1985.
Visit.
Bass, F. Garden, The.
Beeching, H. Going Down Hill on a Bicycle.
Belieu. Radio Nebraska.
Bell, J. Indian Children Speak.
Belloc. Jim Who Ran Away from His Nurse, and Was Eaten by a Lion.
Rebecca, Who Slammed Doors for Fun and Perished Miserably.
Benson, S. Beaten Track, The.
Berger, B. Without.
Berrigan, T. Kirsten.
Berryman. Ball Poem, The.
Berssenbrugge. Chronicle.
Betjeman. False Security.
NW5 and N6.
Beveridge. Catching Webs.
Bevington, L. One More Bruised Heart!
Binyon. Little Dancers, The.
Bishop, E. In the Waiting Room.
Bishop, M. Sales Talk for Annie.
Bly, R. As a Child.
Things My Brother and I Could Do.
Bogan, L. Kept.
Borthwick, P. Out of Bounds.
Bostock, G. Childhood Revisited.
Boyd, M. Why?

Bradstreet, A. Author to Her Book, The.
In Reference to Her Children, 23 June, 1659.
To My Dear Children.
Braithwaite. City Garden, A.
Brontë, C. Orphan Child, The.
Brooks, G. "Do Not Be Afraid of No."
"Pygmies Are Pygmies Still, Though Percht on Alps."
Beverly Hills, Chicago.
Bronzeville Woman in a Red Hat.
Children of the Poor, The.
First Fight. Then Fiddle.
Notes from the Childhood and the Girlhood.
Old Relative.
Parents: People Like Our Marriage Maxie and Andrew, The.
Rites for Cousin Vit, The.
Sunday Chicken.
Throwing Out the Flowers.
Broumas, O. Sometimes, as a Child.
Brown, M. Survival Motion: Notice.
Brown, S. Children's Children.
Chillen Get Shoes.
Conjured.
Browning, E. Cry of the Children, The.
Bruck. Childhood.
Bryan, S. Lunch with Girl Scouts.
Burns, J. Marble surfaces.
Burroughs, W. Cold Lost Marbles.
Butts, A. Nature of Braille, The.
Cabalquinto. Depths of Fields.
Caesar. Animal Crackers in My Soup.
Caldwell, A. Raggedy Ann.
Campo. Lost Plaza Is Everywhere, The.
My Childhood in Another Part of the World.
Carbó, N. Civilizing the Filipino.
In Tagalog Ibon Means Bird.
When the Grain Is Golden and the Wind Is Chilly, Then It Is the Time to Harvest.
Carroll. In the Shakespeare Garden at Northwestern University.
Casey, M. On What the Army Does with Heads.
Cassells. From the Theater of Wine.
Castillo, S. Letter to Yeni on Peering into Her Life.
Cave. Poem for Children, A; or, On Cruelty to the Irrational Creation.
Cerenio. 13 June 1994.
20 July 1994.
Chamberlain, K. Airlift.
Cheney-Coker. Childhood.
Chippewa Oral Tradition. Sioux Woman Defends Her Children, The.
Ciardi. Sometimes Even Parents Win.
Clark, T. Daily News.
Superballs.
Clarke, A. Three Poems about Children.
Clarke, G. Baby-Sitting.
Cleghorn. Golf Links, The.
Clements, S. Matinee.
Reservation, The.
Susans.
Clifton, L. C. C. Rider.
Listen Children.
Sorrow Song.
Cofer, J. How to Get a Baby.
Coleman, W. Coffee.
Coleridge, H. Long Time a Child.
Coleridge, M. In London Town.
Coleridge, S. Youth and Age.
Coles, R. Goddam Street, The.
Cook, E. Our Father.
Song of the Rushlight.
Cooley, N. Diane Arbus, New York.
Coolidge, C. Album—A Runthru.
Cooper, D. After School, Street Football, Eighth Grade.
Cooper, J. My Young Mother.
Cope, J. Solstice for John.
Copus, J. Back Seat of My Mother's Car, The.
Cornford, F. Childhood.
"Cornwall." To My Child.
Cotton, N. To a Child [of] Five Years Old.
Coultas, B. Human Museum, The.
Creeley. Company, The.

Cruickshank, H.   Shy Geordie.
Cullen, C.   Incident.
  Saturday's Child.
Cummings, E.   In Just.
Dalton, A.   How to Disappear.
Davis, D.   Childhood of a Spy.
Davis, G.   Children in the Arbor.
De Kok.   Al Wat Kind Is.
De la Mare.   Reserved.
Dean, D. K.   In the Way Back.
Denning.   Night on the Kho Bha Dinh.
Derricotte.   Fears of the Eighth Grade.
Deutsch.   'To an Amiable Child.'
Dharker.   Namesake.
Dickey, R.   Father.
  Mulatto Lullaby.
Dickey, W.   Memoranda.
Dietz, H.   Triplets.
Divakaruni.   Childhood.
  Yuba City School.
Djanikian.   How I Learned English.
  In the Elementary School Choir.
  When I First Saw Snow.
Dodd, W.   Of His Life.
Doyle, S.   This Shade.
Dubie.   Poem: "Mule kicked out in the trees, A.
  An Early."
Duhig, I.   First Second, The.
Dunbar, P.   Little Brown Baby.
Duncan, R.   Ark for Lawrence Durrell, An.
  Childhood's Retreat.
Durcan.   Weeping Headstones of the Isaac
  Becketts, The.
Earle, J.   Saturday in the '20s, A.
E'der, E.   La Puente.
Edmond, L.   Jardin des Colombières.
Edwards [or Edwardes], R.   When I Was Three.
Eliot, T.   Animula.
Elliot, A.   Latitudes of Home, The.
Ellis, T.   Star Child.
Elmusa.   She Fans the Word.
Emerson, R.   Motto to "The Poet."
Erdrich.   Windigo.
Esteves.   Take the Hearts of Children.
Evans, B.   Waltz for Debby.
Farjeon, E.   Over the Garden Wall.
Field, E.   Jest 'fore Christmas.
  Little Boy Blue.
  Sugar-Plum Tree, The.
Fitzgerald, R.   Figlio Maggiore.
Floyd.   Sergeant Brandon Just, U. S. M. C.
Flynn, N.   Cartoon Physics, Part 1.
Follen, E.   Children in Slavery.
Forbes, C.   Picture of a Man.
Forché.   As Children Together.
Foster, A.   Gap, The.
Frame.   Yet Another Poem about a Dying Child.
Francis, R.   Farm Boy after Summer.
Frost, R.   Birches.
  Home Burial.
Gallup.   Backing into the Future.
Galvin, B.   Knot Hole Gang, The.
Galvin, J.   Station (1).
  Station (2).
García Lorca.   Little Mute Boy, The.
Garrett, E.   Vista.
Geiger.   Soundtracks.
Gilbert, C.   Pushing.
Gilmore, B.   Revolution.
Giovanni.   Nikki-Rosa.
Glück, L.   Apple Trees, The.
  Descending Figure.
  Drowned Children, The.
  Firstborn.
  Gift, The.
  Illuminations.
  School Children, The.
  Time.
Gloria.   Assimilation.
Goodison.   Songs of the Fruits and Sweets of
  Childhood.
Goodman, M.   Cobwebs.
Gordon, J.   Love.
Graham, H.   L'Enfant Glacé.
Graham, W.   Loch Thom.
Graham-Pole, J.   Candor.

Graves, R.   I'd Love to Be a Fairy's Child.
  Warning to Children.
  Wm. Brazier.
Gray, T.   Ode on a Distant Prospect of Eton
  College.
Greacen.   Carnival at the River.
Gregory, H.   Cage of Voices, The.
Grennan.   Pause.
Grey, C.   Hallelujah!
Grosholz.   Eden.
Guevara, M.   Once When I Was in the Eighth
  Grade.
Gunn, T.   Courage, a Tale.
Gwynn, R.   Drive-In, The.
Hachenburg, H.   Terezin.
Hadas, R.   Moments of Summer.
  Red Hat, The.
Hagedorn, J.   Souvenirs.
Hagiwara Sakutaro.   Chair.
Hale, J.   Aaron Nicholas, Almost Ten.
Hale, S.   Mary's Lamb [or Mary and Her
  Lamb].
Hall, D.   Sleeping Giant, The.
  Sudden Things.
Hardy, T.   Oxen, The.
Harms.   Sky.
Harper, F.   Thank God for Little Children.
Harris, D.   What we have lost.
Harrison, G.   Playground, The.
Harte, B.   Miss Edith's Modest Request.
Harwood, G.   Father and Child.
Hashimoto, S.   Standing in the Doorway, I
  Watch the Young Child Sleep.
Hass, R.   Late Spring.
Hayden, R.   Those Winter Sundays.
  Whipping, The.
Hayes, T.   At Pegasus.
Hays, H.   Sacred Children, The.
Hazo.   Child of Our Bodies.
Heaney, S.   Follower.
  Railway Children, The.
  Terminus.
Hecht, A.   "It Out-Herods Herod. Pray You,
  Avoid It."
  Book of Yolek, The.
  Sarabande on Attaining the Age of Seventy-
  Seven.
Hemans.   Bride's Farewell, The.
  Return, The.
Henderson-Holmes.   Friendly Town #1.
  Friendly Town #3.
  To Hell and Back, with Cake.
Herbert, G.   Holy Baptism (2).
Herbert, W.   Praise of Italian Chip-Shops.
Herd.   Bathing Girls, The.
  Survivors, The.
Herrick.   Grace for a Child.
Heyen.   Blue.
Hoagland, E.   Big Zeb Johnson.
Hogg, J.   Boy's Song, A.
Holland, J.   Spin-Cycle.
Holloway, G.   Non-Accidental Injury Slides.
Holt, J.   To Mr. Wren, My Valentine Six Year
  Old.
Hongo.   Winnings.
Hood, T.   I Remember, I Remember.
  Parental Ode to My Son, Aged Three Years and
  Five Months, A.
Hopkins, G.   Handsome Heart, The.
  Spring and Fall.
Horne, F.   Mamma!
Housman, A.   African Lion, The.
  Fragment of an English Opera.
  Infant Innocence.
  Purple William or The Liar's Doom.
Hove.   Child's Parliment.
Howe, M.   Sixth Grade.
Howitt, M.   Dying Child, The.
Hudgins.   Childhood of the Ancients.
  Tree.
Hughes, L.   Children's Rhymes.
  Genius Child.
Hugo, R.   White Center.
Ignatow, D.   Ritual Three.
Ilio, D.   Children of the Atomic Age.
Ingelow.   Echo and the Ferry.

Jacinto, J.   Heaven Is Just Another Country.
Jackson, M.   Red Flag, The.
Jacob, M.   Little Poem.
Jacobsen, J.   Only Alice.
Jarrell.   Cinderella.
  Elementary Scene, The.
  Lost Children, The.
  Sick Child, A.
  Thinking of the Lost World.
  Truth, The.
Jennings, E.   Child's Story, The.
  Ugly Child, The.
Jensen, L.   Age, An.
  Ajax Samples, The.
Jones, P.   In the Formal Garden.
Jordan, J.   Test of Atlanta 1979, The.
Joseph, A.   On Sidewalks, on Streetcorners, as
  Girls.
  Searching for *Melinda's Magic Moment*.
Joyce, J.   Ecce Puer.
  On the Beach at Fontana.
Jurmann, W.   All God's Chillun Got Rhythm.
Justice, D.   Childhood.
  Children Walking Home from School through
  Good Neighborhood.
  Poet at Seven, The.
  Sonatina in Yellow.
Kaneko.   Bailey Gatzert: The First Grade, 1945.
Kasdorf.   First TV in a Mennonite Family.
  Grossdaadi's Funeral.
  Leftover Blessings.
Kaufman, S.   Accuser, The.
Kavanagh, P.   Long Garden, The.
Keeshig-Tobias.   I Grew Up.
  Mother with Child.
Kelly, B.   To the Lost Child.
Kendall, M.   In the Toy Shop.
Kennedy, X.   Help!
  Last Child.
  Poets.
Kenny, N.   Patty-Poem.
Kern, J.   Raggedy Ann.
Kinnell.   First Song.
  Freedom, New Hampshire.
  Lackawanna.
  Little Sleep's-Head Sprouting Hair in the
  Moonlight.
Kinsella, J.   Fall, The.
Kinzie.   Boy.
Klein, A.   Baal Shem Tov.
Kleinzahler.   Lunatic of Lindley Meadow, The.
Knight, E.   Green Grass and Yellow Balloons.
  Poem of Attrition, The.
Knight, S.   In Case of Monsters.
Knott.   Two Vietnam Poems: (1966).
Koch, K.   You Were Wearing.
Koethe.   From the Porch.
Komey.   Change, The.
Kumin, M.   Height of the Season, The.
  Nuns of Childhood: Two Views, The.
Kunitz, S.   Testing-Tree, The.
Kuskin.   I Woke Up This Morning.
  Question, The.
  Rose on My Cake, The.
Lamb, C.   Childhood Fled.
Lamb, M.   Parental Recollections.
Langford.   Speak Gently.
Larcom.   What the Train Ran Over.
Larkin, P.   I Remember, I Remember.
  This Be the Verse.
Larsen, L.   Red.
Lauterbach.   Boy Sleeping.
Laux.   Children's Train, The.
Lawrence, D.   Piano.
  Piano, The.
  White Horse, The.
Lea, S.   Clouded Evening, Late September.
Lee, L.   Gift, The.
  Milkmaid.
Levertov.   Earliest Spring.
Levin, P.   Dark Horse.
Levine, P.   Belle Isle, 1949.
  Milkweed.
  Old Testament, The.
  To a Child Trapped in a Barber Shop.
Lewis, J.   For the Father of Sandro Gulotta.

Lewis, N. Footprint on the Air, A.
Lifshin. Bergen-Belsen 1945.
Lim, G. Children are Colorblind.
Lim-Wilson. Alphabet Soup.
Lincoln, A. My Childhood-Home I See Again.
Liu, T. Echoes.
Livesay, D. Waking in the Dark.
Livingston, M. Coming from Kansas.
  Lemonade Stand.
Llewellyn-Williams. Making Babies.
Loftis, N. Ruth.
Logan, J. Picnic, The.
Longfellow, H. Children's Hour, The.
  My Lost Youth.
Lorde. Song for a Thin Sister.
  What My Child Learns of the Sea.
  Woman Thing, The.
Love, M. Initiation.
Lowell, R. Child's Song.
  My Last Afternoon with Uncle Devereux
  Winslow.
Lumsden, R. Show and Tell.
Lux. There Were Some Summers.
MacCaig. Intruder in a Set Scene.
MacDiarmid, H. Of John Davidson.
Macgoye. August the First: The Shadow. Patel
  Speaks.
Mackenzie, K. Children Go, The.
Mackey, N. Phantom Light of All Our Day,
  The.
MacLeish. Eleven.
MacNeice. Soap Suds.
Madgett. Offspring.
Mahapatra, J. Main Temple Street, Puri.
Manhire. Children.
Mapanje. On Being Asked to Write a Poem for
  1979.
Markus, P. Black Light.
  Light.
Marlatt, D. Summer of the New Well.
Marshall, J. Still.
  Thirty-Seven.
Martínez, V. Children of the Disappeared.
Marvell. Picture of Little T. C. in a Prospect of
  Flowers, The.
McCallum, S. In My Other Life.
  Perfect Heart, The.
McCarriston. Billy.
McClatchy. 1871.
  1946, 1957.
  1971.
  First Steps.
McDaniel, J. Leonard.
McDonald, W. Children of Saigon, The.
McFadden, R. Stringer's Field.
McGinley. About Children.
McGrath, C. Delphos, Ohio.
McLain, P. Connor in the Wind and Rain with
  His Coat on.
McPherson, S. Children.
Mehrotra. Roys, The.
Melhem, D. To an Ethiopian Child.
Merrill, J. Broken Home, The.
  Days of 1941 and '44.
  Scenes of Childhood.
  Up and Down.
  World and the Child, The.
Mew. Ne Me Tangito.
Meynell, A. Cradle-Song at Twilight.
  Parentage.
Mhlophe. Sometimes When It Rains.
Miles, J. Doll.
Millay, E. Childhood Is the Kingdom Where
  Nobody Dies.
  From a Very Little Sphinx.
Milligan, S. Bad Report—Good Manners.
Minhinnick. Children, The.
Mitchell, A. Dumb Insolence.
Mitsui. Photograph of a Child, Japanese-
  American Evacuation, Bainbridge Island,
  Washington, March 30, 1942.
Momaday. To a Child Running with
  Outstretched Arms in Canyon de Chelly.
Moore, B. Child's Thought, A.
Moore, H. First Time: 1950.
Moore, T. Oft In the Stilly Night.

Morales, A. Child's Christmas in Puerto
  Rico, A.
Morris, G. Woodman, Spare That Tree.
Morse, B. Day on the Planet, A.
Muir, E. Childhood.
  Myth, The.
Muldoon, P. Right Arm, The.
Muske, C. Field Trip.
Ní Chuilleanáin. Tale of Me, The.
Naganawa, A. Learning to Swim.
Nash, O. Come On In, the Senility Is Fine.
  Grandpa Is Ashamed.
  Parent, The.
Nemerov. Icehouse in Summer, The.
  Remorse for Time, The.
Nesbit, E. Dead to the Living, The.
  Haunted.
Noguchi, R. Not Surfing Some Days.
Norris, L. Ravenna Bridge.
Notley. California Girlhood, A.
Nye, N. Mother of Nothing.
  Yellow Glove.
Ogilvy. Natal Address to My Child, March 19th
  1844, A.
O'Hara, F. Autobiographia Literaria.
  Blocks.
  Cornkind.
  Poem: "There I could never be a boy."
Olds, S. Seventh Birthday of the First Child.
O'Neill, H. Written on Seeing Her Two Sons at
  Play.
Oppen. From a Photograph.
Oppenheimer, J. Poem in Defense of Children.
O'Reilly, M. Small Girl Brings an Injured Bird
  into the Surgery, A.
Owen, W. To————: "Three rompers run
  together, hand in hand."
  To a Child.
Paino. 1965.
  Matter of Division, A.
Paley, G. Sad Children's Song, The.
Palgrave. Eutopia.
Pankey. As We Forgive Those.
Paquet. Mourning the Death, by Hemorrhage,
  of a Child from Honai.
Parker, D. When Mark Deloach Ruled the
  World.
Parry, E. I Would Like You for a Comrade.
Paulin. Peacetime.
Peters, L. Isatou Died.
Philips, A. Ode: To Miss Margaret Pulteney.
Piatt, S. Answering A Child.
  Child's Party, A.
  Lesson in a Picture, A.
  Palace-Burner, The.
Pinsky. Woman, A.
Plath. Child.
  Getting There.
Poe. "Alone."
Porter, A. Perfect Child, The.
Posamentier, E. Counting Backwards.
Pound, E. Girl, A.
  River-Merchant's Wife: A Letter, The.
Praed. School and Schoolfellows.
Preston, R. Mama.
Prior. To a Child of Quality [Five Years Old,
  the Author Supposed Forty].
Prunty. Winter's Tale, A.
Ramsey, J. Ontogeny.
Randell. Hard to Place.
Ravikovitch [or Ravikovich]. You Can't Kill a
  Baby Twice.
Ray, H. On the Picture of a Child.
Reaney. Lost Child, The.
  School Globe, The.
Reeves, J. Little Brother, The.
  Others.
Rich, A. Afterwake, The.
  Bears.
  Children Playing Checkers at the Edge of the
  Forest.
  In the Wake of Home.
  Not Like That.
Richman, L. Rue de Rosiers: To My Brother
  Fred.
Riddell, E. Children March, The.

Ridler. For a Child Expected.
Riley, J. Days Gone By, The.
  Little Orphant Annie.
Rilke. From a Childhood.
Ríos, A. Language of Great-Aunts, The.
Robin, L. Hallelujah!
Robinson, E. For Karen.
  Meshes.
Roethke. Child on Top of a Greenhouse.
  My Papa's Waltz.
  Where Knock Is Open Wide.
Rohrer, M. Childhood Stories.
Roripaugh, L. Pearls.
Rosenberg, L. No Boundaries.
  Suburban Childhood, A.
  Which One Is the Grown-up? Haiku.
Rossetti, C. Frisky Lamb, A.
Roy, L. Suffering the Sea Change: All My
  Pretty Ones.
Rukeyser, M. Boy with His Hair Cut Short.
  Children, the Sandbar, That Summer.
Russell, N. Message of the Rain, The.
Salter. Half a Double Sonnet.
Sanchez, S. Poem at Thirty.
  Song No. 3: "Cain't nobody tell me any
  different."
Sandburg, C. Three Spring Notations on
  Bipeds.
Sanders, E. Leaves of Heaven, The.
Sawyer, A. Sunday Schools.
Scalapino. Or a Play.
Scamell, B. For a Six Year Old.
Scammell, W. Nicola.
Scannell. Hide and Seek.
Schiff, H. When It Happened.
Schwartz, A. Triplets.
Schwartz, D. I Am Cherry Alive.
Scott, D. Dreadwalk.
Seale, J. Playing the Flute for the TMR Class.
Sergeant. Man Meeting Himself.
Serraillier. Anne and the Field-Mouse.
Sexton. Fury of Overshoes.
  January 1st.
  Red Roses.
Shapiro, D. Book of Glass, A.
Sherman, M. San Buenaventura.
Sholl. Dawn.
Silverstein, S. Nobody.
  One Inch Tall.
  Sick.
Simic. Austerities.
  Book Full of Pictures, A.
  Prodigy.
Simon, M. Sea Sprite, Hermosa Beach, The.
Simpson, L. My Father in the Night
  Commanding No.
Smith, C. Glow-Worm, The.
Smith, D. Roundhouse Voices, The.
Smith, P. Biting Back.
Smith, S. Bog-Face.
  One of Many.
  Our Bog is Dood.
  To Carry the Child.
Snyder, G. Dragonfly.
Sobiloff. Child's Sight, The.
Södergran. Homecoming.
Song. Wind in the Trees, The.
Sorrentino. Classic Case, A.
Soto. Behind Grandma's House.
  Black Hair.
Spender, S. Elementary School Classroom in a
  Slum, An.
  My Parents.
Stefanile. How I Changed My Name, Felice.
Stevens, W. In the Carolinas.
Stevenson, R. Auntie's Skirts.
  Bed in Summer.
  Cow, The.
  Escape at Bedtime.
  Good and Bad Children.
  Good Boy, A.
  Good Play, A.
  Lamplighter, The.
  Land of Counterpane, The.
  Land of Nod, The.
  Land of Story-Books, The.

Looking Forward.
My Bed Is a Boat.
My Shadow.
Pirate Story.
Swing, The.
System.
Where Go the Boats?
Whole Duty of Children.
Winter Time [or Winter-Time].
Young Night Thought.
Strand. Where Are the Waters of Childhood?
Strange. Acts of Power.
  Childhood.
Strickland, A. Infant, The.
Strouse, C. Kids!
Stryk, L. Child in the City, A.
Suárez, V. Rice Comes to El Volcán.
Sullivan, B. Hair.
Surrey. Prison in Windsor Castle.
Sward. Uncle Dog; the Poet at 9.
Swenson, M. Centaur, The.
Taggard. Little Girl with Bands on Her Teeth,
  The.
Taylor, C. B. Plenty Time Pass Fast, Fas Dey
  So.
Tayson, R. First Sex.
Tennyson, A. City Child, The.
  Lines: "Here often, when a child, I lay
    reclined."
  Minnie and Winnie.
Thaxter. Favorite Flower, The.
Thayer, L. Little Child's Faith, The.
Thomas, D. Conversation of Prayer, The.
  Fern Hill.
Thomas, R. Song for Gwydion.
Thompson, J. Mrs. Johnson Objects.
Tomlinson, C. Picture of J. T. in a Prospect of
  Stone, The.
Troupe. Boomerang: A Blatantly Political
  Poem.
Tucker, M. Old Crib, The.
  We Met.
Turner, C. Letty's Globe.
Ullman. Why There Are Children.
Unknown. Bitter Withy, The.
  Blue Bell Boy.
  Girls and Boys Come out to Play.
  Little Rose.
  Mulberry Bush, The.
  Oh My Own Little Daughter, Four Years Old.
  Old Folks' Room, The.
  On the Death of Mr. Persall's Little Daughter, in
    the Beginning of the Spring, at Amsterdam.
  To My Niece, A. M., with a New Pair of Shoes.
  Walk Together Children.
Valentine, J. After Elegies.
Valerie, J. On Apologies.
Van Dyke, C. Birth, 1975.
Van Jordan, A. If I Write a Poem.
Vaughan, H. Childhood.
  Retreat[e], The.
Villanueva, A. They Didn't Get Me.
Wagner, M. Miss Clement's Second Grade.
Walker, A. Childhood.
Wallace, R. Facts of Life, The.
Walsh, J. I've Got an Apple Ready.
Waniek. Sacrament of Poverty, The.
Warren, R. Little Girl Wakes Early.
  Old-Time Childhood in Kentucky.
  What Voice at Moth-Hour.
Watson, E. Battered Toddler, Page B6.
Watson, M. Black Child.
Watson, R. Children of the Mist.
  White Lady, The.
Weaver, M. Improvisation for Piano.
Weems, M. Yesterday.
Weigl. Last Lie, The.
Whitehead, C. Girls Sitting Together Like
  Dolls.
Whitman, W. There Was a Child Went Forth.
Whittemore, R. Party, The.
Whittier. Barefoot Boy, The.
  In School-Days.
  My Playmate.
Wilbur. Boy at the Window.
  Digging for China.

Pardon, The.
Williams, C. For the White Lady Holding Me.
  My Mother's Lips.
Williams, J. Memories of Christmas.
  Rachel.
Williams, P. Baby in the House, A.
Williams, S. Peacock Poems: 1, The.
Williams, W. Sympathetic Portrait of a Child.
  To.
  Waiting.
Williamson, G. Drawing Hands.
  Origami.
Wordsworth, W. My Heart Leaps Up.
  Ode: Intimations of Immortality [from
    Recollections of Early Childhood].
  Ruth [or, The Influences of Nature].
  To a Child [Written in Her Album].
  We Are Seven.
Work. Come Home, Father[!].
Wright, K. Untitled.
Wright, J. Evening.
  Mutterings Over the Crib of a Deaf Child.
  Note Left in Jimmy Leonard's Shack, A.
  Sappho.
  Song for the Middle of the Night, A.
  To a Child.
  Twilights.
Wright, K. How the Wild South East Was Lost.
Wyrebek, M. Healing Logic, A.
Yeats. Among School Children.
  Cradle Song, A: "Angels are stooping, The."
  Prayer for My Daughter, A.
Yost, C. From San Diego.
Youmans, V. Hallelujah!
Young, D. Sources of the Delaware.
Young, K. No Offense.
Zamora-Linmark. Day 1: Portrait of the Artist,
  Small-kid Time.
Zarco. Manila Paper.
  Once upon a Seesaw with Charlie Chan.
Zarin. Ant Hill, The.
Zimmer. Zimmer's Head Thudding against the
  Blackboard.

See also **Adolescence; Boys; Death in Childhood;
Girls; Youth**

Chile
Ali, A. I See Chile in My Rearview Mirror.
Larsen, L. Peach.
Neruda. They Receive Instructions Against
  Chile.

Chilembwe, John
Mapanje. Before Chilembwe Tree.

Chimney Sweepers
Alcock. Chimney-Sweeper's Complaint, The.
Graves, R. Wm. Brazier.

Chimneys
Bennett, R. Windy Nights.
Bidgood. Chimneys.
Graves, R. Under the Pot.
Summerfield. Tall Story for Fred Dibnah.

Chimpanzees
Sassoon. Sporting Acquaintances.

China
Auden. Spain 1937.
Beer, P. Footbinding.
Benét, W. Merchants from Cathay.
Berssenbrugge. Chronicle.
Bynner. Tiles.
Chin. Barbarian Suite.
  Prelude.
Clifton, H. Monsoon Girl.
Digby, J. Sooner or Later.
Hovey. Sea Gypsy, The.
Kaufman, S. Emperor of China, The.
Kizer, C. Ashes, The.
Lim, S. Visting Malacca.
Lindsay, N. Chinese Nightingale, The.
Merrill, S. Ballade of the Chinese Lover.
Messerli. Angry with China.
O'Hara, F. Poem: "At night Chinamen jump."
Roberts, N. Mona Lisa Tea Towel, The.
Rylander, E. Midnight Rocker, Tiananmen
  Square, May 27, 1989.
Silko. Prayer to the Pacific.
Song. Heaven.

  Lost Sister.
Whalen. Hymnus Ad Patrem Sinensis.
Wilbur. Digging for China.
Wolverton, T. In China.

Chinaware
Gay, J. To a Lady on Her Passion for Old
  China.
Merrill, J. Willowware Cup.
Moore, M. No Swan So Fine.
Probyn. China Maniacs.

Chinese, The
Addonizio. China Camp, California.
Carruth, H. Of Distress Being Humiliated by
  the Classical Chinese Poets.
Chin. Composed Near the Bay Bridge (after a
  wild party).
  How I Got That Name.
Chinn. Not Translation, Not Poetry.
Harte, B. Plain Language from Truthful James.
Kerouac. Thrashing Doves, The.
Lau, A. Upside Down Basket, The.
Liu. My Father's Martial Art.
Mar, L. My Mother, Who Came from China,
  Where She Never Saw Snow.
Song. Heaven.
  Lost Sister.
Su, A. Address.
Suárez, V. Rice Comes to El Volcán.
Tate, J. Miss Cho Composes in the Cafeteria.
Wong, N. How a Girl Got Her Chinese Name.
  When I Was Growing Up.

Chipmunks
Jarrell. Chipmunk's Day, The.
Melville, H. Chipmunk, The.

Chivalry
Black, S. Hoopla.
Melville, H. Rusty Man, The.

Chocolates
Gomez, M. Chocolate Confessions.
Rosner. Souvenirs.
Simpson, L. Chocolates.

Choices
Baraka. Kenyatta Listening to Mozart.
Cassells. Marathon.
Di Prima. Abyss.
Elizabeth, M. She Teaches Him to Reach Out.
Elmusa. Two Angels, The.
Emanuel, L. Like God.
Frost, R. Lovely Shall Be Choosers, The.
Garrett, E. Tyranny of Choice.
Graves, R. Down, Wanton, Down!
  Sharp Ridge, The.
Gregg. Edge of Something, The.
Grennan. Pause.
Healy, E. Changing What We Mean.
Jonson, B. Epode: "Not to know vice at all, and
  keep[e] true state."
Joseph, L. When One Is Feeling One's Way.
Kenyon, J. Otherwise.
Larkin, P. Dockery and Son.
Meredith, W. Myself, Rousseau, a Few Others.
Olson, C. In Cold Hell, in Thicket.
Rich, A. Roofwalker, The.
Sandburg, C. Choose.
Sund. Considering Poverty and Homelessness.
Turner, C. East or West?
Williams, H. Prayer.
Yeats. Choice, The.

Choking
Char. Man flees suffocation.

Cholera
Kipling, R. Cholera Camp.
MacKay, C. Mowers: An Anticipation of the
  Cholera, 1848, The.

Chopin, Frédéric François
Solonche. Chopin Preludes, Opus 28.

Christchurch, New Zealand
Curnow. Skeleton of the Great Moa in the
  Canterbury Museum, Christchurch, The.

Christianity and Christians
Abad, G. Holy Order.
"Ada." Appeal to Women, An.
  Scroll is open, The.
Adams, S. Nearer, My God, to Thee.
Alarcon, F. Viernes Santo / Good Friday.

Awoonor. Easter Dawn.
Baxter, J. Morning and Evening Calm.
Bishop, E. Brazil, January 1, 1502.
Blunden. Report on Experience.
Breedlove, N. New Miz Praise de Lawd, The.
Caballero-Robb, M. Dear Rosario.
Clarke, A. Martha Blake at Fifty-one.
Cleyre, V. Love's Compensation.
Cofer, J. Campesino's Lament, The.
  Magdalenas, Las.
Cooke, R. Schemhammphorasch.
"Coolidge." My Rights.
Corbet [or Corbett]. Proper New Ballad Entitled
  [or Intituled] The Fairies' [or Faeryes]
  Farewell, or God-a-Mercy Will, A.
Crashaw. Howres for the Hours of Matines,
  The.
Crosby, F. Blessed Assurance.
  I Am Thine, O Lord.
  Thoughts in Midnight Hours.
Delgado, J. Mexican Fire Breather, A.
Doty, M. Homo Will Not Inherit.
Duhig, I. Fundamentals.
Dwight. I Love Thy Kingdom, Lord.
Erdrich. Immaculate Conception.
Ferlinghetti, L. Sometime During Eternity.
"Field." Lovers.
Fuller, M. Meditations.
  One in All, The.
Galvin, J. Station (4).
Gilman, C. Christian Virtues.
Glaser, M. Magnificat!
Gomez, M. Lost Daughter.
  Troubled Awakening.
Harper, F. Bible Defence of Slavery.
Harwood, G. Bone Scan.
Heaney, S. Westering.
Heath-Stubbs. For the Nativity.
Herbert, G. British Church, The.
  Cross[e], The.
  Priesthood, The.
Herrick. Crosses.
  On Himself[e].
Heynen. Clean People, The.
Hope, M. INRI.
Hugo, R. Letter to Hill from St. Ignatius.
Hyneman, R. Woman's Rights.
Jackson, H. Distance.
  Opportunity.
Jennings, E. Annuciation, The.
Jones, D. A, a, a, Domine Deus.
Jones, R. Blasphemy, A.
Jonson, B. Carol.
Kelly, B. Imagining Their Own Hymns.
Kinnell. Avenue Bearing the Initial of Christ
  into the New World, The.
Lawrence, D. Retort to Jesus.
Levin, P. Third Day, The.
Lim-Wilson. Raising the Dead.
MacNeice. Belfast.
McVeigh, J. Eve Falling.
Milosz, C. Poor Christian Looks at the
  Ghetto, A.
Milton. On His Blindness.
Montrose. On Himself, upon Hearing What
  Was His Sentence.
Muldoon, P. Our Lady of Ardboe.
Obejas, A. Sunday.
O'Curry, E. Litany to Our Lady.
Owen, W. Maundy Thursday.
Pavlich. Black Flower.
Plath. Medusa.
Plato. True Friend, The.
Plotnick, H. M. Jewish.
Ragan, J. Child Christ at the Top of the Stairs.
Reese, L. Trust.
Robinson, E. Christmas Sonnet, A.
Sandburg, C. Washerwoman.
Shomer. Falling for Jesus.
Skelton, J. Now Sing We, as We Were Wont.
Smart, C. Ascension of Our Lord Jesus Christ,
  The.
  Beauty.
  Christmas Day.
  Conclusion of the Matter, The.
  Crucifixion of Our Blessed Lord.

Elegance.
Epiphany.
Faith.
For Saturday.
Fortitude.
Gratitude.
Hope.
Long-Suffering of God.
Loveliness.
Moderation.
Mutual Subjection.
My Cat Jeoffry.
Nativity of Our Lord and Saviour Jesus Christ,
  The.
Nativity of St. John the Baptist, The.
New Year.
Pray Remember the Poor.
Song to David, A.
St. Philip and St. James.
St. Thomas.
Strength.
Taste.
Stein, K. In the Kingdom of Perpetual Repair.
Stevens, W. High-Toned Old Christian
  Woman, A.
Sunday Morning.
Swinburne. On the Russian Persecution of the
  Jews.
Thomas, D. Before I Knocked.
Thomas, R. Navigation.
Unknown. Gospel Train, The.
  Hand by Hand We Shall Us Take.
  I Will Bow and Be Simple.
  Let Us Cheer the Weary Traveler.
  Litany to Our Lady.
  Saint Patrick's Breastplate.
Vaughan, H. British [or Brittish] Church, The.
  Nativity, The.
  Retirement.
Very. Enoch.
  John.
Viray, M. Saturday Morning, A.
Watson, M. Memo to J. C.
Wheatley, P. On Being Brought from Africa to
  America.
Whittier. Call of the Christian, The.
Williams, W. Hymn: "What is the world, and
  what is life."
Wordsworth, W. Decay of Piety.
Yeats. Ribh Considers Christian Love
  Insufficient.

Christmas
Achebe. Christmas in Biafra (1969).
Anderson, D. Executive Geochrone.
Arrowsmith, P. Christmas Story (1980).
Bampfylde. On Christmas.
Belloc. Noël.
Berlin. White Christmas.
Betjeman. Christmas.
Bishop, M. Dark Christmas on Wildwood Road,
  The.
Blane, R. Have Yourself a Merry Little
  Christmas.
Bridges, R. Noel; Christmas Eve, 1913.
Brooks, P. Christmas Everywhere.
Calil, A. Blouse of Felt.
Carruth, H. Essay on Death.
Causley. Ballad of the Bread Man.
  Sailor's Carol.
Chesterton, G. House of Christmas, The.
Chute, M. Day before Christmas.
Clare, J. December.
Coatsworth. Barn, The.
Coleridge, M. I Saw a Stable.
Coleridge, S. Christmas Carol, A: "Shepherds
  went their hasty way, The."
Cooper, R. To See the Cross at Christmas.
Coots, J. Santa Claus Is Comin' to Town.
Corn. Navidad, St. Nicholas Ave.
Corrothers. Indignation Dinner, An.
Cortes, F. Fish 2.
Crashaw. In the Holy Nativity of Our Lord
  God.
  Shepherds' Hymn, The.
Crowell, G. Eternal Values.
Cullen, C. Christus Natus Est.

Dafydd [or David] Bach ap Madog Wladaidd.
  Christmas Revel, A.
Dickinson, P. Advent; a Carol.
Djanikian. When I First Saw Snow.
Dunn, G. Journey Back to Christmas.
Falkner. Christmas Day; the Family Sitting.
Fanthorpe. BC:AD.
  What the Donkey Saw.
Farber. Bow Down, Mountain.
Farjeon, E. Advice to a Child.
Ferlinghetti, L. Christ Climbed Down.
Field, E. Jest 'fore Christmas.
Finch, R. Crib, The.
Fordham. Nativity, The.
Freeman, C. Christmas Morning I.
Frost, F. Christmas in the Wood.
Gilmore, B. Bow to Allah.
Glück, L. Nativity Poem.
Godolphin. Hymn: "Lord, when the wise men
  came from far[r]."
Graves, R. Carol of Patience.
  Christmas Robin, The.
Gregory. Christmas Lullaby for a New-Born
  Child.
Hardy, T. House of Hospitalities, The.
  Oxen, The.
  Reminder, The.
Heaney, S. Turkeys Observed.
Heard, J. Birth of Jesus, The.
Heber. Brightest and Best of the Sons of the
  Morning.
Hecht, A. Christmas Is Coming.
Herbert, G. Christmas.
Herrick. Ceremonies for Christmas[se].
  Ode on the Birth of Our Saviour, An.
Holland, J. Christmas Carol, A: "There's a song
  in the air!"
Hopkins, J. We Three Kings of Orient Are.
Horne, F. Kid Stuff.
Image. Meditation for Christmas, A.
Jennings, E. Afterthought.
Johnson, G. Christmas Rhyme, A.
Johnson, M. Christmas Times.
  Krismas Dinnah.
Jonson, B. Hymn[e] on the Nativity [or
  Nativitie] of My Saviour, A.
  Masque of Christmas, The.
Kinnell. To Christ Our Lord.
Kipling, R. Christmas in India.
  Eddi's Service.
Kirkup. Shepherd's Tale, The.
Kleinzahler. Ebenezer Californicus.
Knott. Christmas at the Orphanage.
Levertov. Advent 1966.
  Christmas 1944.
Lewis, C. Nativity, The.
Longfellow, H. Christmas Bells.
  Three Kings, The.
Lowell, R. Christmas Eve under Hooker's
  Statue.
MacIntyre, S. Christmas Present for My
  Mother.
McClatchy. Old Song Ended, An.
McDonald, W. Christmas Bells, Saigon.
McGinley. City Christmas.
McGrath, T. Bread of this World; Praises III,
  The.
Middleton, R. Carol of the Poor Children, The.
Millay, E. To Jesus on His Birthday.
Miller, V. Christmas Mourning.
Milton. Hymn on the Morning of Christ's
  Nativity.
  On the Morning of Christ's Nativity.
Mitchell, A. Nothingmas Day.
Montgomery, J. Nativity.
Moore, C. Visit from St Nicholas, A.
Moore, L. Gifts.
Moorer. Christmas Eve.
Morales, A. Child's Christmas in Puerto
  Rico, A.
Morgan, E. Computer's First Christmas Card,
  The.
Morris, W. French Noel.
Nemerov. Eve.
  Santa Claus.
Nicholson, N. Shepherds' Carol.

Niedecker. Will You Write Me a Christmas Poem?
Nims, J. Christmas.
Norris, L. Mice in the Hay.
Shepherd's Dog, The.
Paman. On Christmas Day to My Heart.
Pasternak, B. Christmas Star.
Plath. Winter's Tale, A.
Ray, H. At Christmas-Tide.
Reese, L. Christmas Folk-Song, A.
Revard. Christmas Shopping.
Roberts, E. Christmas Morning.
Robinson, E. Karma.
Rodgers, W. White Christmas.
Rossetti, C. Before the Paling of the Stars.
Christmas Carol, A: "In the bleak mid-winter."
Christmas Eve.
Sansom, C. Innkeeper's Wife, The.
Scammell, W. Christmas at Bristol.
Schnackenberg. Advent Calendar.
Sears, E. It Came upon the Midnight Clear.
Shapiro, A. Christmas Story, A.
Shapiro, K. Jew at Christmas Eve, The.
Shaw, L. Groundhog, The.
Stars in Apple Cores.
Shorter. Skeleton in the Cupboard, The.
Snodgrass, C. Poem for Christmas, A.
Southwell. Burning Babe, The.
Child[e] My Choice [or Choyse], A.
Nativity of Christ[e], The.
New Prince, New Pomp[e].
Stephens, J. Christmas at Freelands.
Stevenson, R. Christmas at Sea.
Christmas Prayer, A.
Stewart, G. As I Went Down to David's Town.
Tate, A. Sonnets at Christmas.
Tate, N. While Shepherds Watched [Their Flocks by Night].
Thackeray. Mahogany Tree, The.
Thompson, C. Christmas Rush, The.
Timrod. Christmas.
Tormé, M. Christmas Song, The.
Tucker, M. Christmas, South, 1866.
Turner, S. Christmas Is Really for the Children.
Unknown. As I Sat on a Sunny Bank.
Carnal and the Crane, The.
Carol, for Candlemas Day.
First Nowell, The.
God Rest Ye Merry, Gentlemen.
Here We Come A-wassailing.
Holly and the Ivy, The.
I Sing of a Maiden.
Jolly Shepherd, The.
Medieval Poem of the Nativity, A.
Song Bewailing the Time of Christmas, So Much Decayed in England, A.
Thys Endris Nyght.
Twelve Days of Christmas, The.
Van Duyn. Christmas Card, After the Assassinations, A.
Vaughan, H. Christ's Nativity.
Shepherds [or Shepheards], The.
Wadding [or Waddinge]. Christmas Day [Is Come].
Waldman, A. Baby's Pantoum.
Watkyns. Upon Christ's Nativity or Christmas.
Watts, I. Cradle Hymn, A.
Miracles at the Birth of Christ.
Wells, A. Inn That Missed Its Chance, The.
Wells, R. Christmas Song, The.
Wesley, C. Incarnation, The.
Wilbur. Christmas Hymn, A.
Williams, J. Memories of Christmas.
Williams, W. Burning the Christmas Greens.
Wolfe, H. Dean Inge.
Wood, D. Christmas Fare.
Young, A. Christmas Day.
Zinzendorf. For Us No Night Can Be Happier.

Christmas Cards
McGinley. Lady Selecting Her Christmas Cards.
Morgan, E. Computer's First Christmas Card, The.

Christmas Carols
Brooks, P. O Little Town of Bethlehem.
Clare, J. December.

Luther. Away in a Manger.
Pierpont, J. Jingle Bells.
Sears, E. It Came upon the Midnight Clear.
Tate, N. While Shepherds Watched [Their Flocks by Night].
Unknown. First Nowell, The.
Here We Come A-wassailing.
I Saw Three Ships Come Sailing In.
Nowell Sing We.
Twelve Days of Christmas, The.
Watts, I. Joy to the World.
Wolfe, H. Dean Inge.

Christmas Eve
Algarin. Christmas Eve: Nuyorican Café.
Anderson, D. Executive Geochrone.
Bly, R. Christmas Eve Service at Midnight at St. Michael's.
Davie. Devil on Ice.
De la Mare. Christmas Eve.
Farjeon, E. Advice to a Child.
Feinstein, S. Christmas Eve.
Hall, D. Christmas Eve in Whitneyville, 1955.
Hardy, T. Oxen, The.
Moore, C. Visit from St Nicholas, A.
Thompson, P. Christmas Ghost, A.
Tucker, M. Christmas Eve, South, 1865.

Christmas Trees
Berry, W. Our Christmas Tree.
Burford, W. Christmas Tree, A.
Cook, S. Christmas Tree.
Day Lewis. Christmas Tree, The.
Moorer. Christmas Tree, The.
Morris, J. Untrimming the Tree.
Smith, L. Christmas Tree.
Tate, J. Miss Cho Composes in the Cafeteria.
Williams, W. Burning the Christmas Greens.

Christmas, the Virgin
Unknown. Cherry-Tree Carol, The.
Sweet Was the Song.

Chrysanthemums
Lee, L. Between Seasons.
McKinney, I. Chrysanthemums.
Scovell. Shadows of Chrysanthemums.

Chungking, China
Stilwell. Lyric to Spring.

Church of England
Herbert, G. British Church, The.
Herrick. Persecutions Purifie.
Smart, C. Ascension of Our Lord Jesus Christ, The.
Christmas Day.
Crucifixion of Our Blessed Lord.
Epiphany.
Nativity of Our Lord and Saviour Jesus Christ, The.
Nativity of St. John the Baptist, The.
New Year.
St. Philip and St. James.
St. Thomas.
Unknown. Vicar of Bray, The.
Vaughan, H. British [or Brittish] Church, The.
Wordsworth, W. Mutability.
Obligations of Civil to Religious Liberty.
Persuasion.
Point at Issue, The.
Trepidation of the Druids.

Churches
Arnold, M. Rugby Chapel.
Beer, M. Church in the Heart, The.
Belieu. At St. Sulpice.
Berkeley, S. Mass is Over, The.
Betjeman. Diary of a Church Mouse.
St. Saviour's, Aberdeen Park, Highbury, London, N.
Sunday Afternoon Service in St. Enodoc Church, Cornwall.
Sunday Morning, King's Cambridge.
Undenominational.
Booth, P. Within.
Buckley, V. Good Friday and the Present Crucifixion.
Burns, R. Kirk's Alarm, The.
Tam o' Shanter; A Tale.
To a Louse [On Seeing One on a Lady's Bonnet at Church].

Clemmons. Greater Friendship Baptist Church, The.
Clifton, L. In White America.
Corbet [or Corbett]. Upon Fairford Windows.
Crane, H. Broken Tower, The.
Doolittle, H. Trance.
Durcan. Divorce Referendum, Ireland, 1986, The.
Ekelof. Greece.
Emerson, R. We Love the Venerable House.
Fuller, J. St. Sophia.
Graham, D. Jesus Never Sleeps.
Haines, J. Snowbound City, The.
Hardy, T. Afternoon Service at Mellstock.
Church Romance, A.
Hawker. Poor Man and His Parish Church, The.
Hayden, R. Those Winter Sundays.
Herbert, G. Perirrhanterium.
Prayer (1): "Prayer the Church's banquet, Angels' age."
Herrick. Fairy Temple; or, Oberon's Chapel, The.
Temple, The.
Horne, F. On Seeing Two Brown Boys in a Catholic Church.
Jewett, S. At Home from Church.
Kantaris. Airing the Chapel.
Keats. On Oxford.
Kendall, M. Church Echoes.
Kennedy, X. Hangover Mass.
Larkin, P. Church Going.
Lawrence, D. Tabernacle.
Lee, D. Benediction.
Leithauser. Old Bachelor Brother.
Lieberman, L. Organist's Black Carnation, The.
Lowell, A. Meeting-House Hill.
Mahapatra, J. Taste for Tomorrow.
Mathias, R. Brechfa Chapel.
Matthews, W. Old Folsom Prison.
McCarthy, T. Dying Synagogue at South Terrace, The.
McKay, C. St. Isaac's Church, Petrograd.
McKinney, I. Sunday Morning, 1950.
Melville, H. In a Church of Padua.
Moore, L. Tanka.
Morgan, R. Bellrope.
Mullen, H. Dance She Does, The.
Olds, S. Wedding Vow, The.
Orlovsky. Dream May 18, 1958.
Paino. 1965.
Palazzeschi. Nuns Go Walking.
Philipott. To Sir Henry Newton, upon His Re-edifying the Church of Charleton in Kent.
Pook. In Chapel.
Porter, P. Angel in Blythburgh Church, An.
Roberts, E. Mr. Wells.
Scott, D. Church Boiler, The.
Locking the Church.
Scupham. Service.
Seward. Eyam.
Shiffert. Manners.
Simic. Winter Night.
Sisson. Knole.
Spires. Comb and the Mirror, The.
Stevens, W. Gray Stones and Gray Pigeons.
Synge. Dread.
Tate, A. Sonnets at Christmas.
Taylor, J. Squire's Pew, The.
Thomas, R. In a Country Church.
Thompson, C. Opening Service, An.
Tolson, M. Lena Lovelace.
Tomlinson, C. Las Trampas U. S. A.
Travis, N. Church Ladies.
Unknown. Building of a New Church, The.
Little More Cider, A.
Preston.
Waller, E. Upon His Majesty's [or Majesties] Repairing of Paul's.
Warner, S. Building in Stone.
Country Thought.
Watts, I. Church the Garden of Christ, The.
Weigl. Temple Near Quang Tri, Not on the Map.
Whitman, W. March in the Ranks Hard-Prest, and the Road Unknown, A.
Wright, J. Wednesday Night Prayer Meeting.

Wrigley, R. Prophecy, The.
Zagajewski. Auto Mirror.

Churchill, Winston Leonard Spencer
Scott, D. Winston Churchill.

Churchyards
Collins, W. Ode on the Poetical Character.
"Fane, V." In an Irish Churchyard.
Gray, T. Elegy Written in a Country Churchyard.
Epitaph: "Here rests his head upon the lap of earth."
Gutteridge. Man into a Churchyard.
Mahon. In Carrowdore Churchyard.
McKinney, I. Visiting My Gravesite: Talbott Churchyard, West Virginia.
Pierpoint, K. Steeplejack.
Scott, D. Churchyard under Snow.

Cicadas
Eady. Dance, The.
Wilbur. Cicadas.

Cigarettes
Campo. Lost in the Hospital.
Ehrhart. One That Died, The.
Gibbons, R. "Luckies."
Iozia, J. Last Night at the Flamingo.
Loncar, M. Picasso Shag.
Mitchell, S. Smoke.
Pearlberg, G. G. Marianne Faithfull's Cigarette.
Pollack, L. Two Cigarettes in the Dark.
Rodgers, C. Group Therapy.
Shaw, A. Crepuscule.
Yevtushenko [or Evtushenko]. Hand-Rolled Cigarettes.
See also **Smoking and Smokers**

Cigars
Low, S. To a Segar.

Cinderella
Jarrell. Cinderella.
Sexton. Cinderella.

Circe
De Tabley. Circe.
Doolittle, H. Circe.
Gunn, T. Moly.
MacNeice. Circe.

Circumcision
Herrick. To His Savior [or Saviour]. The New Years [or yeers] Gift.
Lowell, R. New Year's Day.
Milton. Upon the Circumcision.
Okigbo. Elegy of the Wind.
Ostriker. Story of Abraham, The.
Wadding [or Waddinge]. On the Circumsision: New Year's Day.

Circus
Alexander, E. Venus Hottentot, The.
Bursky, R. Decisions, The.
Cable, G. Song of Cayetano's Circus, The.
Carruth, H. Wreck of the Circus Train, The.
Cendrars. Medrano Academy.
Fallon, P. Flask of Brandy, A.
Ferlinghetti, L. Constantly Risking Absurdity.
Goldbarth. Book of Human Anomalies, The.
Jordan, J. What Happens.
Larkin, P. For Sidney Bechet.
Lim-Wilson. Ringmaster's Wife.
Padgett, R. First Drift.
Pyle. Circus Parade, The.
Shapcott, T. Litanies of Julia Pastrana (1832-1860), The.
Williams, W. Artist, The.

Cities
Aguilar, M. Pall Hanging over Manila.
Al-Rihani. Lilatu Laili.
Ammons, A. R. City Limits, The.
Apollinaire. Voyager, The.
Windows.
Asekoff, L. Invisible Hand.
Ashbery. Rain.
Rivers and Mountains.
These Lacustrine Cities.
Auden. Paysage Moralisé.
Axelrod, D. Guide to Urban Birds, A.
Barot, R. Portishead Suite.
Riffing.
Bateman, E. Cockney's Garden, The.

Bell, M. Street Fair: The Quartet.
Bernard, A. Praise Psalm of the City-Dweller.
Bernstein, C. Matters of Policy.
Betjeman. Business Girls.
Bierce. Passing Show, The.
Bishop, E. One Art.
Blackburn, P. Assistance, The.
Blind. Manchester by Night.
Braithwaite. City Garden, A.
Brannon, J. Evolution on 38th Street.
Broumas, O. Next to the *Café* Chaos.
Browning, R. Up at a Villa—Down in the City.
Bruner. On City Streets.
There Is a Loneliness.
Brutus. Nightsong: City.
Buscani. Barefoot in the City.
Cabalquinto. Ordinance, The.
Campana. Genoa.
Cawein. Dead Cities.
Cendrars. Hammock.
Clarke, C. 14th Street Was Gutted in 1968.
Clifton, H. Eccles Street, Bloomsday, 1982.
Euclid Avenue.
Clifton, L. In the Inner City.
Clough. Sic Itur.
Clover, J. Archive of Confessions, a Genealogy of Confessions, An.
Coe, C. Possibility.
Coleridge, M. Day-dream, A.
Corn. Water: City Wildlife and Greenery.
Cortes, F. Poem Composed During a Brownout.
Costanzo. Jeane Dixon's America.
Washington Park.
Craighead, L. Dancin' Our Lives Away.
Crawford, R. Love Song of Tommo Frogley.
Creeley. City, The.
Crow, C. City Park.
Cumbo. Nocturnal Sounds.
Davies, A. Thirty East Forty-Second Street.
DeFoe, M. Aviary.
Dharwadker. New Delhi, 1974.
Di Prima. Montezuma.
Donne. To Sir Henry Wotton.
Doty, M. Homo Will Not Inherit.
Dougherty. Puerto Rican Girls of French Hill, The.
Douglas, L. Impression de Nuit; London.
Dransfield. Day at a Time.
Drummond de Andrade. Motionless Faces.
Drummond, W. Content and Resolute.
Dumdum. Li Pos of the Polis.
Dunn, D. On Roofs of Terry Street.
Ehrmann. Away.
"Eliot." In a London Drawingroom.
Eliot, T. *Boston Evening Transcript*, The.
Morning at the Window.
Preludes.
Rhapsody on a Windy Night.
Ellis, T. Break of Dawn, The.
Esteves. Ahora.
For South Bronx.
Evans, R. Buttons and Bows.
Fenton, J. German Requiem, A.
Fields, J. Citizen.
Fleckenstein, M. Getting Even.
Forman, R. We Are the Young Magicians.
Fructuoso, E. Astig.
Gamalinda, E. Denials.
Garlick, R. Capitals.
Georgiou, E. Week in the Life of the Ethnically Indeterminate, A.
Ginsberg, A. My Sad Self.
Godfrey. What It Takes.
What Say.
Goetsch, D. Urban Poem.
Gonzalez, R. San Jacinto Plaza.
Greenberg, A. City Life.
Gregerman, D. Silent Globe.
Guest, B. Bleat.
Gunn, T. Map of the City, A.
Haines, J. Nocturnal.
Harwood, G. Nightfall.
Hausman. September City.
Hearne, B. Commuters.
Hecht, A. Third Avenue in Sunlight.
Hemans. Illuminated City, The.

Hernández Cruz. Energy.
Entering Detroit.
Man Who Came to the Last Floor, The.
Mountain Building.
Side 18.
Side 4.
Slick.
Swans' Book, The.
Urban Dream.
Heyen. Numinous, The.
Hogan, L. Heartland.
Hollander, J. Lion Named Passion, A.
Hubbell, P. Streetcleaner's Lament, The.
Huidobro. Express.
Ilio, D. Children of the Atomic Age.
Prokosch in Tehran, 1978.
Inada. Fresno Truth, The.
Inez. Courtyard Noises from the North, Twenty-fourth Precinct.
Irby. January 1965, Looking on.
Ismaili. Lagos.
Iverem, E. Earth Screaming.
Jackson, L. City Seems, A.
Jordan, J. Speculations on the Present through the Prism of the Past.
Jussawalla. Sea Breeze, Bombay.
Kaplinski, J. My Wife and Children.
Kaufman, B. Battle Report.
Kearney, M. Nature Poetry.
Kefala. Industrial City.
Kimbrell, J. Rooftop.
Kooser. City Limits.
Interchange.
Korican, L. City Goddess.
Kramer, L. Strong Winds Below the Canyons.
Krohn. Can Tho.
Lane, P. Wind Thoughts.
Lang, A. Tired of Towns.
Lawson, H. Faces in the Street.
Lee, L. City in Which I Love You, The.
Lehman. Towards the Vanishing Point.
Lenski, L. Sing a Song of People.
Levertov. World Outside, The.
Levin, P. Citizens and Sky.
Levy, A. London Plane-Tree, A.
Liu, T. Brooklyn Botanic Garden, The.
Livingston, J. Buttons and Bows.
Lodge, G. Lower New York.
Logan, J. Trip to Four or Five Towns, A.
Logan, M. Verses on Hearing That an Airy and Pleasant Situation, near a Populous and Commercial Town, Was Surrounded with New Buildings.
Lowell, J. Street, The.
Lowry, M. Christ Walks in This Infernal District Too.
MacNeice. Birmingham.
Morning Sun.
Masters, E. Cities of the Plain.
Mattawa. Bus Driver Poem, The.
McKay, C. White City, The.
Meléndez. Oye Mundo/Sometimes.
Melhem, D. Lamentation After Jeremiah to Exorcise High Rental / High Rise Building Scheduled for Construction with Public Funds.
Mew. I Have Been Through the Gates.
Not for That City.
Milosz, C. Temptation.
Mueller, L. Commuter.
Noguere. Whirling Round the Sun.
Noyes, A. Barrel-Organ, The.
O'Loughlin. Posthumous.
Oodgeroo of the tribe Noonuccal. Municipal Gum.
O'Shaughnessy, A. Ode: "We are the music-makers."
Paloff, B. On Transportation.
Patchen. 23rd Street Runs into Heaven.
Penn, R.E. Morning Songs.
Piercy. Learning Experience.
Pietri. Intermission from Monday.
Piñero. La Bodega Sold Dreams.
Running Scared.
Plumpp. Another Mule.
Survivors.
Poe. City in the Sea, The.

Pope, A.   Epistle to Miss [or Miss Teresa] Blount, on Her Leaving the Town after the Coronation.
Purdy, A.   Blue City, The.
Radiguet.   Map.
Redmond.   Definition of Nature.
Reverdy.   Post.
Rivard.   Consolation.
Robles.   Remembering the Past.
Roditi.   Hand.
Rosenberg, L.   City Baseball.
Rux, C. H.   Asphalt Musings.
   Asylum of Gestures.
Salazar.   Hotel Fresno.
Sandburg, C.   Blue Island Intersection.
   Cahoots.
   Chicago.
   Osawatomie.
   Prayers of Steel.
   Skyscraper.
Scalapino.   Considering How Exaggerated Music Is.
Seferis.   Word for Summer, A.
Shapcott, T.   City of Home, The.
Shepherd, R.   Provisional.
Sherwin, J.   Nightpiece.
Simic.   Marvels of the City, The.
Simpson, L.   There Is.
Sitwell, D.   Trams.
Skinner, J.   City Out of the Boy, The.
Smith, M.   Asleep in the City.
   Visit to the Village, A.
Snyder, G.   Cartagena.
Sondheim.   Another Hundred People.
Stevenson, R.   Block City.
Stewart, P.   Estes' Backyard, The.
Stryk, L.   Child in the City, A.
Sutter.   Peregrine.
Swift, J.   Description of a City Shower, A.
   Description of the Morning, A.
Taggard.   All Around the Town.
Taylor, A.   Fitzroy.
Tennyson, A.   City Child, The.
Thomas, D.   Countryman's Return, The.
Thomas, E.   Cries of the Newsboy.
Thomas, R.   Rhodri.
Thurman.   Zebra.
Tomlinson, C.   More Foreign Cities.
Toomer.   Gum.
Trowbridge, W.   Bad Birds.
Turner, A.   Clean.
   Red Flower.
Twichell.   City Animals.
Ungria, R.   Carillonneur.
Voigt.   Nocturne.
Wakoski.   Night Blooming Jasmine.
   Walking Past Paul Blackburn's Apt. on 7th St.
Walcott.   Tomorrow, Tomorrow.
Wanek.   Duluth, Minnesota.
Weiners.   With Meaning.
Weston, M.   Primitive Place.
Wetzsteon.   Urban Gallery.
Wharton, E.   Two Backgrounds.
Whitman, W.   Once I Pass'd through a Populous City.
   Sparkles from the Wheel.
Whittemore, R.   Departure, The.
Wilbur.   After the Last Bulletins.
   Shame.
Williams, G.   City under Snow.
Williams, W.   Approach to a City.
   Grotesque.
   Perpetuum Mobile: The City.
   Predicter of Famine, The.
Wordsworth, W.   Composed upon Westminster Bridge, September 3, 1802.
Wormser.   Pigeons.
Wunderlich, M.   Chapel of the Miraculous Medal.
Yeats.   Coole Park, 1929.
Yolen.   Sky Scrape / City Scape.

See also **Towns; Villages**

Citizenship
Ashbery.   One Thing That Can Save America, The.
Cabalquinto.   Ordinance, The.

Civil Defense
Burke, K.   Civil Defense.
Civil Rights Movement
Carroll, K.   Theory on Extinction or what happened to the dinosaurs?
See also **Protest, Social**
Civil War, Spain
Auden.   Spain 1937.
Campbell, R.   Toledo.
Cornford, J.   Full Moon at Tierz; before the Storming of Huesca.
   Letter from Aragon, A.
Hughes, L.   Madrid—1937.
Livesay, D.   Spain.
MacDiarmid, H.   Spanish War, The.
Spender, S.   Port Bou.
   Two Armies.
See also **Spain**
Civil War, United States
Aldrich, T.   By the Potomac.
Ball, C.   Jacket of Gray, The.
Beers, E.   All Quiet along the Potomac Tonight.
Bierce.   Confederate Flags, The.
   Death of Grant, The.
   Hesitating Veteran, The.
   To E. S. Salomon.
Bishop, E.   From Trollope's Journal.
Breckenridge.   General John Cabell Breckinridge.
Bristol.   Crime of the Ages, The.
Bryant, W.   Death of Slavery, The.
   Not Yet.
Davidson, D.   Lee in the Mountains.
   Sequel of Appomattox.
Dickey, J.   Hunting Civil War Relics at Nimblewill Creek.
Dugan, A.   Fabrication of Ancestors.
Dunbar, P.   Colored Soldiers, The.
   Robert Gould Shaw.
   Unsung Heroes, The.
   When Dey 'Listed Colored Soldiers.
Emerson, R.   Boston Hymn.
   Voluntaries.
Emmett.   Dixie [or Dixie's Land].
Finch, R.   Blue and the Gray, The.
Foss, S.   House by the Side of the Road, The.
Frost, R.   Black Cottage, The.
Gilmore, P.   When Johnny Comes Marching Home.
Harte, B.   John Burns of Gettysburg.
   Second Review of the Grand Army, A.
Hayden, R.   Dream, The.
Horgan.   Tintype of a Private in the Fifteenth Georgia Infantry.
Horton, G.   General Grant—the Hero of the War.
Howe, J.   Battle Hymn [or Battle-Hymn] of the Republic, The.
   Robert E. Lee.
Hudgins.   After the Wilderness.
   Around the Campfire.
   Burial Detail.
   Serenades in Virginia.
   Soldier on the Marsh, A.
Irving, M.   Marching Still.
Jarrell.   Description of Some Confederate Soldiers, A.
Jordan, J.   Grand Army Plaza.
Kenyon, J.   Gettysburg, July 1, 1863.
Lanier, S.   Dying Words of Stonewall Jackson, The.
Larcom.   Volunteer's Thanksgiving, The.
Lazarus, E.   South, The.
Lincoln, A.   Gettysburg Address, The.
Longfellow, H.   Building of the Ship, The.
   Cumberland, The.
   Killed at the Ford.
Lowell, J.   Memoriae Positum R. G. Shaw.
   Ode Recited at the Harvard Commemoration (July 21, 1865).
Lowell, R.   For the Union Dead.
Masters, E.   Battle of Gettysburg, The.
   Veterans of the Wars.
Melville, H.   Apparition, The—A Retrospect.
   Ball's Bluff.

Battle Summers, The.
   College Colonel, The.
   Dirge for McPherson, A.
   House-Top, The.
   Malvern Hill.
   March into Virginia, The.
   Memorial on the Slain at Chickamauga.
   Portent, The.
   Requiem[:] for Soldiers Lost in Ocean Transports, A.
   Sheridan at Cedar Creek.
   Shiloh [A Requiem].
   Stonewall Jackson.
   Swamp Angel, The.
   Uninscribed Monument on One of the Battlefields of the Wilderness, An.
   Utilitarian View of the Monitor's Fight, A.
Meredith, W.   Farragut, Farragut.
Milnes.   England and America, 1863.
Moody, W.   Ode in Time of Hesitation, An.
Moolten, D.   Brandy Station, Virginia.
Olson, C.   Anecdotes of the Late War.
Orfalea, G.   Sunken Road, Antietam 1980, The.
Osgood, K.   Driving Home the Cows.
Palmer, J.   Stonewall Jackson's Way.
Randall, D.   Memorial Wreath.
Randall, J.   My Maryland.
Randolph, I.   Rebel, The.
Ray, H.   Robert G. Shaw.
Read, T.   Sheridan's Ride.
Reed, I.   Chattanooga.
Reese, L.   Old Belle, An.
Rhodenbaugh.   Civil War, The.
Rich, A.   Charleston in the Eighteen-Sixties.
Root, G.   Battle-Cry of Freedom, The.
Ryan, A.   Lines: "Gather the sacred dust."
   Sword of Robert Lee, The.
Sherwood, K.   Albert Sidney Johnston.
Tate, A.   Battle of Murfreesboro.
   Ode to the Confederate Dead.
Taylor, B.   Gettysburg Ode.
Taylor, E.   Few Days in the South in February, A.
   This Year's Drive to Appomattox.
Thompson, J.   Burial of Latané, The.
   Lee to the Rear.
   Music in Camp.
   Obsequies of Stuart.
Thompson, M.   Address by an Ex-Confederate Soldier to the Grand Army of the Republic, An.
   Lincoln's Grave.
   To the South.
Ticknor.   Little Giffen.
Timrod.   Carolina.
   Charleston.
   Christmas.
   Cotton Boll, The.
   Ethnogenesis.
   Ode: "Sleep sweetly in your humble graves."
Unknown.   Confederate Memorial Day.
   Enlisted Today.
   Hospital Duties.
   Negro Soldier's Civil War Chant.
Updike.   Richmond.
Wallis, S.   Prayer for Peace, A.
Whitman, W.   Army Corps on the March, An.
   Artilleryman's Vision, The.
   As I Lay with My Head in Your Lap Camerado.
   As Toilsome I Wander'd Virginia's Woods.
   Beat! Beat! Drums!
   Bivouac on a Mountain Side.
   By the Bivouac's Fitful Flame.
   Cavalry Crossing a Ford.
   Come Up from the Fields Father.
   Dirge for Two Veterans.
   Epigraph to "Drum-Taps."
   Give Me the Splendid Silent Sun.
   March in the Ranks Hard-Prest, and the Road Unknown, A.
   Reconciliation.
   Sight in Camp [in the Daybreak Gray and Dim], A.
   Spirit Whose Work Is Done.
   To a Certain Civilian.
   Vigil Strange I Kept on the Field One Night.

Wound-Dresser, The.
Year That Trembled and Reel'd beneath Me.
Whittier. Barbara Frietchie.
  Battle Autumn of 1862, The.
  Laus Deo!
  Lost Occasion, The.
  What the Birds Said.
  Word for the Hour, A.
Williams, E. At Harper's Ferry Just before the
  Attack.
Woolson. Kentucky Belle.
Work. Marching through Georgia.

Civil Wars, England
Cowley, A. Powers of Darkness.
Herrick. Bad Season Makes the Poet Sad, The.
  Upon the Troublesome Times.
Milton. On the Lord Gen[eral] Fairfax at the
  Siege of Colchester.
  On the New Forcers of Conscience Under the
  Long Parliament.
  To the Lord General Cromwell.
  When the Assault Was Intended to the City.
Parker, M. King Enjoys His Own Again, The.
Unknown. Eccho, An.

Civilization
Bible, Apocrypha. Steel Usurps the Forests;
  Silence Dethrones Dialogue.
Bowman, C. Demographics.
Campbell, D. Anguish of Ants, The.
Cavafy. Waiting for the Barbarians.
Dickey, W. For Easter Island or Another Island.
Dransfield. Day at a Time.
  That Which We Call a Rose.
Durcan. Wife Who Smashed Television Gets
  Jail.
Eliot, T. Waste Land, The.
Emerson, R. Water.
  World-Soul, The.
Ford, C. There's No Place to Sleep in This Bed,
  Tanguy.
Freneau. On the Civilization of the Western
  Aboriginal Country.
Hall, D. New Hampshire.
Hall, R. Text for These Distracted Times, A.
Harris, W. We Live in a Cage.
Hilliard, B. Civilization (Bongo, Bongo,
  Bongo).
Hope, A. Australia.
  Under Sedation.
Hughes, L. Letter to the Academy.
Iverem, E. Earth Screaming.
Jeffers, R. New Mexican Mountain.
Johnson, F. Tired.
Johnstone, R. Eden Says No.
Mahon. Image from Beckett, An.
"Malley." Dürer: Innsbruck, 1495.
Miller, E. Tomorrow.
Moore, R. Personal Atlas.
Neruda. Walking Around.
Oodgeroo of the tribe Noonuccal. No More
  Boomerang.
Ormond. Ancient Monuments.
Perillo. Skin.
Raine, K. Martian Sends a Postcard Home, A.
Rakosi. Journey Away, A.
Roughton. Building Society Blues.
Sepamla. Civilization Aha.
Shange. Ancestral Messengers/Composition 13.
Simpson, L. Riders Held Back, The.
Stafford, W. At Cove on the Crooked River.
Stern, G. Morning Harvest.
  There Is Wind, There Are Matches.
Stevens, W. Anecdote of the Jar.
Thomas, R. Period.
Unknown. Money, Money.
Wright, J. Horse, The.
Yeats. Long-Legged Fly.
  Meru.

Clams and Clamming
Snow, W. Advice to a Clam-Digger.
Tennyson, A. Minnie and Winnie.
Whittemore, R. Clamming.
See also **Oysters; Shells**

Clarke, Austin
Weber, R. Visit to Bridge House, A.

Class
Breedlove, N. Black and Divided or Chittlins
  and Caviar.
Ebb, F. Class.
Kander, J. Class.
Kinsella, J. Bright Cigar-Shaped Object Hovers
  Over Mount Pleasant, A.
Kizer, C. To an Unknown Poet.
Komunyakaa. Salt.
Medina, T. Poem for Teacup Mantlepiece Poets
  Palpitating Poot Booty Plagiarists Imprisoned
  in Ivy League White Supremacist Mental
  Biological Warfare Labs.
See also **Social Class**

Classicism
Derricotte. Black Boys Play the Classics.
Hardy, T. Liddell and Scott.
Jonson, B. Fit of Rhyme [*or* Rime] against
  Rhyme [*or* Rime], A.
Pinkney, E. Italy.
Poe. To Helen.
Sandburg, C. Child of the Romans.
  Southern Pacific.
Tate, A. Aeneas at Washington.
  Mediterranean, The.
Walcott. Sea Grapes.

Cleanliness
Alvarez, J. How I Learned to Sweep.
Brown, E. Jezebel to the Eunuchs.
Burgess, F. Table Manners.
Dove, R. Great Palaces of Versailles, The.
Giles, B. Mrs. Lorris, Who Died of Being
  Clean.
Graves, R. It Was All Very Tidy.
Henderson-Holmes. Goodhousekeeping #17.
Heynen. Clean People, The.
Housman, A. Oh, When I Was In Love.
Hubbell, P. Streetcleaner's Lament, The.
Locke, A. So Foul Is Sin and Loathsome in Thy
  Sight.
Monsour. Sweeping.
Silano, M. Such a Way to Go.
Silverstein, S. Dirtiest Man in the World, The.
Tolson, M. Old Houses.
Trethewey, N. Domestic Work, 1937.
Turner, A. Clean.

Cleopatra
Hemans. Last Banquet of Antony and
  Cleopatra, The.
Hughes, T. Cleopatra to the Asp.
Kern, J. Cleopatterer.
Pascal. Tact.
Rossetti, C. Study (A Soul), A.
Simpson, L. Early in the Morning.
Story, W. Cleopatra.

Clergy
Arnold, M. In Harmony with Nature.
Barham. Jackdaw of Rheims, The.
Bowering, G. Grandfather.
Browning, R. Bishop Orders His Tomb at Saint
  Praxed's Church, The.
  Soliloquy of the Spanish Cloister.
Burns, R. Kirk's Alarm, The.
Burroughs, W. My Legs Señor.
Clarke, A. Irish-American Dignitary.
Cook, E. Idiot-Born, The.
Corbet [*or* Corbett]. On Mr. Rice the Maniple
  of Christ Church in Oxford.
Crashaw. Upon Bishop Andrewes's [*or*
  Andrewes His] Picture before His Sermons.
Didsbury. Priest in the Sabbath Dawn
  Addresses His Somnolent Mistress, A.
Doane, W. Preacher's Mistake, The.
Donne. To Mr. Tilman after He Had Taken
  Orders.
Dryden, J. Character of a Good Parson, The.
Elliott, E. Poet vs. Parson.
Gilbert, S. Rival Curates, The.
Graham, H. Breakfast.
Herbert, G. Aaron.
  Collar, The.
  Priesthood, The.
  Windows, The.
Hopkins, G. Habit of Perfection, The.
Hughes, L. Madam and the Minister.
Hughes, T. Cheese for the Archdeacon, A.

Ken. Priest of Christ, The.
Kipling, R. Eddi's Service.
Lloyd, E. Portrait of a Bishop.
Marvell. Flecknoe, an English Priest at Rome.
Milton. Lycidas.
Moorer. Birthday Wishes to a Minister of the
  Gospel.
Norse. Believing in the Absurd.
Outram. On Hearing a Lady Praise a Certain
  Rev. Doctor's Eyes.
Quarles. On Those That Deserve It.
Scott, D. Hopkins Enters the Roman Catholic
  Church.
  Locking the Church.
  Surplice, The.
Stevens, W. Gray Stones and Gray Pigeons.
"T., J." Sea-Chaplain's Petition to the
  Lieutenants in the Ward-Room, for the Use of
  the Quarter-Gallery, A.
Taylor, H. Country Curate, The.
Tennyson, A. To the Rev. F. D. Maurice.
Thomas, R. Country Clergy, The.
Unknown. Kyrie, So Kyrie.
  On a Clergyman's Horse Biting Him.
  Vicar of Bray, The.
Whittier. Clerical Oppressors.
  Official Piety.
Yeats. Ballad of Father Gilligan, The.
See also **Rabbis**

Clerks
Davidson, J. Thirty Bob a Week.
DeCarteret, M. Town Clerk, The.
Hamill, G. Song of the GPO, A.
Robinson, E. Clerks, The.
Roethke. Dolor.
Weaver, M. Sub Shop Girl.
See also **Office Workers**

Cleveland, Ohio
Atkins. Lakefront, Cleveland.

Clichés
Grigson. On a Lover of Books.
Guiterman. Everything in Its Place.
Silveira. Different Poem, A.

Cliffs
Coleridge, S. Blest is the tarn which towering
  cliffs o'ershade.
Curry. St Kilda.
Hardy, T. Beeny Cliff.
Millay, E. Ragged Island.
Robinson, E. Salisbury Plain.

Climbing
Benjamin, P. Press On.
Herd. Coronach.
MacCaig. Climbing Suilven.
Oness, C. Climbing.
Pierpoint, K. Steeplejack.
Rafferty, C. Man on the Tower, The.
Schmitz. Climbing Sears Tower.
Trommer, R. Climbing the Ridge.

Clive, Robert
Warner, S. Alarum, The.

Clocks
Barnes, W. Wold Clock, The.
Ginsberg, L. Clocks.
Graves, R. Counting the Beats.
Greenlaw. Five O'Clock Opera.
Hall, D. Alligator Bride, The.
Longfellow, H. Old Clock on the Stairs, The.
Lowell, R. Fall 1961.
Mansfield, K. Meeting, The.
McMaster, R. Clockface.
Moore, M. Four Quartz Crystal Clocks.
Mother Goose. Clock, The.
Pietri. 3rd Untitled Poem.
Poulin. Red Clock.
Radiguet. Handless Clock.
Rich, A. Clock in the Square, A.
Thurman. Clockface.
Warren, R. There's a Grandfather's Clock in the
  Hall.
Wilbur. Bell Speech.
Work. Grandfather's Clock.
Worth, V. Clock.
See also **Watches**

Clonmacnoise, Ireland
Clarke, A.   Pilgrimage.

Clothing
Adair, T.   Violets for Your Furs.
Alvarez, J.   Naming the Fabrics.
Alvi, M.   Presents from My Aunts in Pakistan.
Arnold, C.   Party She Outdid Herself, The.
Ball, C.   Jacket of Gray, The.
Bang, M.   It Says, I Did So.
Barber, M.   Written for My Son, and Spoken by
  Him at His First Putting on Breeches.
Brown, S.   Sporting Beasley.
Burrell.   Picture of a Fine Gentleman, The.
Butler, W.   Nothing to Wear.
Cerenio.   My Mother.
Chester, T.   Running Hares.
Clarke, G.   Second Hand Rose.
Cliff.   History of Costume, A.
Codrescu.   Grammar, A.
Cofer, J.   Spring.
Conway, J.   Clothes Make the Man.
Copus, J.   Clothes, The.
Crozier, A.   Driftwood and Seacoal.
Dennis, M.   Violets for Your Furs.
Dixon, S.   Verses Left on a Lady's Toilet.
Dubin, A.   Lulu's Back in Town.
Dybek.   Windy City.
Espada.   My Native Costume.
Feaver.   Coat.
Feldman, I.   Se Aprovechan.
Fergusson.   Braid Claith.
Ferlinghetti, L.   Underwear.
Fishman, L.   Diagnosis: My Mother's Breast.
Flynn, F.   Clothes on the Washing Line.
Gallagher, T.   Black Silk.
Goodman, M.   Lullabye for a Butch.
Hadas, R.   House Beside the Sea, The.
Hagedorn, J.   Vulva Operetta.
Hahn, K.   Hula Skirt, 1959, The.
Hanley, J.   Second Hand Rose.
Hardy, T.   Pink Frock, The.
  Thunderstorm in Town, A.
Herrick.   Art above Nature, to Julia.
  Clothes Do But Cheat and Cozen [or Cousen]
    Us.
  Delight in Disorder.
  Julia's Petticoat.
  Upon Electra.
  Upon Julia's Ribband.
  Upon Julia's Clothes.
Hoberman.   Let's Dress Up.
Hudgins.   At Chancellorsville.
Hughes, L.   When Sue Wears Red.
Jackson, L.   One Self.
  Only Daughter, The.
Jenkins, N.   Shirts.
Johnson, M.   Wintah Styles, De.
Katz, J.   Women Must Put Off Their Rich
  Apparel.
Kendrick, D.   Alone for a Week.
Kowit.   Notice.
Koyama.   Downtown Seattle in the Fog.
Lear, E.   New Vestments, The.
Lee, D.   Coat, The.
Lifshin.   Bergen-Belsen 1945.
Lochhead, L.   Neckties.
Lovelace, R.   To a Lady with Child that Asked
  [or Ask'd] an Old Shirt.
Lovibond.   To Miss Kitty Phillips.
Lowell, A.   Bright Sunlight.
McAuley, J.   Cloak, The.
Merritt, C.   Woman of Color.
Morales.   My Revolution.
Moss, H.   Persistence of Song, The.
Mother Goose.   Daffadowndilly.
Nash, O.   Requiem: "There was a young belle of
  old Natchez."
Padgett, R.   Tell Us, Josephine.
Peacock, M.   How I Had to Act.
Peacocke.   Final reductions.
Petit, P.   My Father's Clothes.
  My Mother's Clothes.
Phillips, C.   Cotillion.
Pierson, J.   Thrift Shop Ladies.
Pinsky.   Shirt.
Portnoy, M.   Dinogon.

Powell, D. A.   My Father and Me Making
  Dresses: Together.
Probyn.   After.
  Before.
Ravikovitch [or Ravikovich].   Dress of Fire, A.
Redmond.   Poetic Reflections Enroute To, and
  During, The Funeral and Burial of Henry
  Dumas, Poet.
Remoto.   Black Silk Pajamas.
Robinson, M.   Modern Female Fashions.
  Modern Male Fashions.
Romo-Carmona, M.   Signs.
Rosenblatt, S.   Should I Stay or Should I Go?
Ryan, G.   Cruising.
Sansom, A.   Cross Country.
Shaughnessy, B.   Your One Good Dress.
Smith, W.   Said Dorothy Hughes to Helen
  Hocking.
Snyder, G.   No Shoes No Shirt No Service.
Steptoe.   Window Shopping.
Stevenson, R.   Auntie's Skirts.
Stillman, M.   Whiskers Meets Polly.
Strand.   Man in the Tree, The.
Swenson, M.   Question.
Tobrise.   Dyeing.
Townsend, A.   Shirt Collar, The.
Trinidad.   Doll Not Included.
Tucker, M.   Lines to an Old Dress.
Unknown.   Brian O'Linn.
  Madrigal: "My Love in her attire doth show her
    wit."
Waller, E.   On a Girdle.
Warren, H.   Lulu's Back in Town.
Weinberger, F.   He Wears Old Socks.
Weiss, T.   Clothes Maketh the Man.
Wilbur.   Catch, The.
  Love Calls Us to the Things of This World.
Wolverton, T.   Black Slip.
Wunderlich, M.   Take Good Care of Yourself.
Young, A.   Wet Day, A.

See also **Jewelry**

Clouds
Atkins.   Dark Area.
Bogan, L.   Train Tune.
Bolton, G.   Till the Clouds Roll By.
Brooke, R.   Clouds.
Coleridge, M.   Moment, A.
Coleridge, S.   Fancy in Nubibus.
Crane, H.   To the Cloud Juggler.
Davies, W.   Black Cloud, The.
  Moon and a Cloud, The.
DeSylva, B. G.   Look for the Silver Lining.
Digby, J.   Sooner or Later.
Disch.   Clouds, The.
Edgar, C.   Cloud of Unknowing, The.
Evance, S.   To the Clouds.
Figueroa, J.   Confessions from the Last Cloud.
Finlay, I.   Cloud's Anchor, The.
Fisher, M.   Cloudy Morning.
Frost, R.   Lost in Heaven.
Fuller, M.   Meditations.
Galassi.   Argument.
Harwood, L.   "Utopia" The.
  Final Painting, The.
  Words, The.
Herrick.   Her Bed.
Jensen, L.   Cloud Parade, The.
Kern, J.   Look for the Silver Lining.
  Till the Clouds Roll By.
Levertov.   Clouds.
Levin, P.   Citizens and Sky.
Levine, P.   Clouds.
Littlebird.   For the Girls 'cause They Know.
Livingstone, D.   On Clouds.
Lowell, A.   Night Clouds.
McCarthy, J.   Cloudy Morning.
Monk, G.   AC.
  CS.
Morgan, E.   King Billy.
Moss, S.   Clouds.
Pastan.   Last Train, The.
Ray, H.   Cloud Song.
Reichard, W.   Cloud Game, The.
Romo-Carmona, M.   Fish.
Rubadiri.   African Thunderstorm, An.
Shelley, P.   Cloud, The.

Sitwell, D.   Song: "We are the darkness in the
  heat of the day."
Stevens, W.   Sea Surface Full of Clouds.
Strand.   Marriage, The.
Sundiata.   Making Poems; on the road in
  Minneapolis.
Thomas, E.   Clouds That Are So Light, The.
Very.   Clouded Morning, The.
Watta.   Cloud Rains.
Williams, W.   Clouds, The.
Williamson, G.   Up in the Air.
Wodehouse, P.   Till the Clouds Roll By.
Wordsworth, W.   I Wandered Lonely As a
  Cloud.
  Most Alluring Clouds That Mount the Sky, The.

Clough, Arthur Hugh
Arnold, M.   Thyrsis.
Swinburne.   On Arthur Hugh Clough.

Clover
Bell, M.   White Clover.
Higginson, E.   Four-Leaf Clover.

Clowns
Beer, P.   Ninny's Tomb.
Bruner.   Clown, The.
Cendrars.   Medrano Academy.
Prelutsky.   Bring on the Clowns.
Sondheim.   Send in the Clowns.

See also **Circus**

Clumsiness
Lowell, A.   Bungler, The.
Nims, J.   Love Poem: "My clumsiest dear,
  whose hands shipwreck vases."

Coal Mining and Coal Miners
Armstrong, F.   Collier Lass, The.
Ballowe, J.   Coal Miners, The.
Bryant, W.   Meditation on Rhode Island
  Coal, A.
Bush, D.   Pneumoconiosis.
Collier, M.   North Corridor.
Davies, I.   High Summer on the Mountains.
Dorn, E.   Los Mineros.
Lawrence, D.   Collier's Wife, The.
Lopez, L.   To a Coal Miner in Madrid, New
  Mexico.
Lorde.   Coal.
MacBeth [or Macbeth].   Miner's Helmet, The.
Morgan, R.   Blood Donor.
Morris, L.   Miner's Ballad, The.
Nicholson, N.   Cleator Moor.
Owen, W.   Miners.
Parini.   Coal Train.
Pettit.   Self-Portrait Approaching Promontory,
  Utah.
Untermeyer, L.   Caliban in the Coal Mines.
Watkins, V.   Collier, The.

Cobblers
Gibran.   Cobbler in Jerusalem, A.
See also **Shoes and Shoemakers**

Coca Cola
Cumpian.   No Deposit Returns.
Erdrich, H.   Hopi Prophet Chooses a Pop.
Espada.   Coca-Cola and Coco Frío.
Fusselman, A.   Mother Nature.
Hiestand, E.   Moon Winx Motel.
Hollander, R.   You Too? Me Too—Why Not?
  Soda Pop.
McGrane, P.   Jukebox Saturday Night.
O'Hara, F.   Having a Coke with You.
Stillman, A.   Jukebox Saturday Night.

Cocaine
Ai.   Self Defense.
Clifton, L.   White Lady.
Espada.   Prisoners of Saint Lawrence, The.
Harper, M.   Elvin's Blues.
Unknown.   Cocaine Lil [and Morphine Sue].

Cockaigne, Land of
Sissman.   Cockaigne: A Dream.
Unknown.   Land of Cokaygne, The.

Cockfighting
Garrett, E.   Grandfather's Mint.
Hernández Cruz.   Side 26.
See also **Roosters**

Cockroaches
Espada.   Cockroaches of Liberation.

My Cockroach Lover.
Greenlaw. Love from a Foreign City.
Raven. Roach, The.
Rukeyser, M. St. Roach.
Stone, R. Whose Scene?

Cocks
Henryson. Cock and the Fox, The.
Jacobik, G. Turkeys in August.
Raine, K. Good Friday.
See also **Roosters**

Cocoa
Sharpless. In Praise of Cocoa, Cupid's
Nightcap.

Coconuts
Espada. Coca-Cola and Coco Frío.

Coercion
Flanders, M. Have Some Madeira, M'dear?

Coffee
Alegría. Documentary.
Berlin. Let's Have Another Cup of Coffee.
Bernstein, C. Cup of Coffee, The.
Brown, L. You're the Cream in My Coffee.
Burke, S. Black Coffee.
Coleman, W. Coffee.
DeSylva, B. G. You're the Cream in My
Coffee.
Hall, D. Je Suis une Table.
Henderson, R. You're the Cream in My Coffee.
Hilliard, B. Coffee Song (They've Got an
Awful Lot of Coffee in Brazil), The.
Iozia, J. Last Night at the Flamingo.
Loncar, M. Picasso Shag.
McClure, M. May Morn.
Miles, D. Coffee Song (They've Got an Awful
Lot of Coffee in Brazil), The.
Peacock, M. Breakfast with Cats.
Saffoti. Espresso.
Tucker, M. Upon Receipt of a Pound of Coffee
in 1863.
Unknown. Little More Cider, A.
Walcott. Gulf, The.
Webster, P. Black Coffee.

Coffins
Baugh, E. Carpenter's Complaint, The.
Hernández, M. War.
Monsour. Emily's Words.
Ruefle. Furtherness.

Coins
Hughes, L. Fact.
Tomorrow.
Hume, C. Dirty Money.
Kramer, L. Strong Winds Below the Canyons.
Nemerov. Money.
Weems, M. Dime after Dime.
Weinstein, N. Garvey's Head as Value.

Cold
Abse. Hunt the Thimble.
Ager, M. Hard-Hearted Hannah (The Vamp of
Savannah).
Atwood. You Are Happy.
Bacon, C. Outlook.
Berlin. I've Got My Love to Keep Me Warm.
Brown, L. Turn On the Heat.
Brutus. Cold.
Bryant, W. November.
Burns, R. O [*or* Oh] Wert Thou in the Cauld
Blast.
Bynner. Wintry Mind, The.
Ceravolo. Stolen Away.
Corfield, J. Morse Lesson.
Ford, R. Twenty Below.
Francis, R. Cold.
Galvin, J. Two Horses and a Dog.
Gbadamosi. Death of the Polar Explorers.
Guest, B. Nebraska.
Haines, J. Into the Glacier.
Heath, R. On the Unusual Cold and Rainy [*or*
Rainie] Weather in the Summer, 1648.
Henderson, R. Turn On the Heat.
Hughes, T. November.
Hulme, T. Embankment, The (The fantasia of a
fallen gentleman on a cold, bitter night).
Keithley. First Morning.
Kenney. Aubade: "Cold snap. Five o'clock."
Loesser. Baby, It's Cold Outside.

Mahon. Antarctica.
McCarriston. January, Anchorage.
Merrill, J. David's Night in Veliès.
Moore, L. Winter 1967.
Nash, O. Samson Agonistes.
Po Chü-i. Bitter Cold, Living in the Village.
Roberts, D. Cold.
Rosemurgy, C. Why God Invented the Cold.
Sansom, A. Confinement.
Scupham. After Ovid, Tristia.
Service. Cremation of Sam McGee, The.
Simic. Winter Night.
Snyder, G. Late October Camping in the
Sawtooths.
Thomas, E. Frost To-night.
Thoreau. Pray to What Earth Does This Sweet
Cold Belong.
Tomlinson, C. Tramontana at Lerici.
Ward, D. Hunting in Twilight.
Warner, S. After He Had Gone.
Williams, C. You Know It's Really Cold.
Winters, Y. Cold, The.

Colds (illness)
Adams, C. To Bary Jade.
Roethke. Ceiling, The.

Cole, Thomas
Bryant, W. To Cole, the Painter, Departing for
Europe.

Coleridge, Samuel Taylor
Barbauld. To Mr. S. T. Coleridge.
Coleridge, H. Dedicatory Sonnet to S. T.
Coleridge.
Written on the Anniversary of Our Father's
Death.
Coleridge, S. Father! no amaranths e'er shall
wreathe my brow.
De la Mare. Bards, The.
Ewart. Lines: "Other day I was loving a sweet
little fruitpie-and-cream, The."
Fanthorpe. Person's Tale, The.
Frost, R. Most of It, The.
Smith, S. Thoughts about the Person from
Porlock.
Thomas, R. Coleridge.
Person from Porlock, A.
Watts-Dunton. Coleridge.

Colleges and Universities
Brown, L. Varsity Drag, The.
DeSylva, B. G.
Frost, R. Lucretius versus the Lake Poets.
Heaney, S. Mid-Term Break.
Henderson, R. Varsity Drag, The.
Herrick. To His Kinsman, Master Thomas
Herrick, Who Desired to Be in His Book.
Holmes, J. Old Professor, The.
Jarrell. Soldier Walks under the Trees of the
University, The.
Kern, J. Tulip Time in Sing Sing.
Kirby, D. Dear Derrida.
Moore, M. Student, The.
Moorer. Claflin's Alumni.
Dedication Day Poem.
What We Teach at Claflin.
Nazario, A. Kevin and Nicole.
Olds, S. I Go Back to May 1937.
Samaras, N. Elegy for a Professor.
Shapiro, K. University.
Spender, S. One More New Botched Beginning.
Strayhorn, B. Lonely Coed, A.
Symons, J. Harvard.
Travis, N. At My Father's House.
Turner, W. University Curriculum.
Unknown. Miss Buss and Miss Beale.
Waniek. Letter to a Benedictine Monk.
Wheatley, P. To the University of Cambridge, in
New-England.
Wilson, E. Disloyal Lines to an Alumnus.
See also **Students**

Collies
MacCaig. Praise of a Collie.

Cologne, Germany
Coleridge, S. Cologne.
Gier, J. Examining the I.

Colonialism
Abad, G. Light in One's Blood, The.

Mahon. Antarctica.

Adisa. No, Women Don't Cry.
Aguilar, M. Pall Hanging over Manila.
Allingham. In Snow.
Bain, A. Address.
Baxter, J. New Zealand.
Bradstreet, A. Dialogue between Old England
and New, A.
Chrystos. I Bring You Greetings: How.
Okeydoekey Tribe, The.
Creeley. America.
D'Aguiar. Mama Dot.
Davis, J. Aboriginal Australia.
Urban Aboriginal.
Doolan, F. Who Owns Darling Street?
Duhig, I. Fundamentals.
Esteves. From Fanon.
Gardiner, A. Natal Hunters, The.
Gier, J. California Coast.
Going Baroque.
Gilbert, K. Celebrators '88.
Kiacatoo.
New True Anthem, The.
Same Old Problem.
Gloria. Touch.
Hagedorn, J. Souvenirs.
Hemans. England's Dead.
Hernández Cruz. New/Aguas Buenas/Jersey.
Johnson, E. Letter to My Mother, A.
Kearns, L. Environment.
Foreign Aid.
Landor, W. To Arthur de Noé Walker.
Lazarus, E. 1492.
How Long?
Lim-Wilson. Alphabet Soup.
Livingstone, D. Sleep of My Lions, The.
Lopez, T. Path Marked with Breadcrumbs, A.
Mapanje. Baobab Fruit Picking; or,
Development in Monkey Bay.
Mateo. There Is No Word for Sex in Taglog.
Mnthali. Neocolonialism.
Mudrooroo Narogin. They give Jacky rights.
Nichols, G. Beverley's Saga.
O'Connor, P. Poems (I- XI).
Oodgeroo of the tribe Noonuccal. Unhappy
Race, The.
Pietri. Intermission from Wednesday.
Plomer. Fall of Rock, A.
Pringle. Caffer Commando, The.
Putnam. Words of an Old Woman.
Robles. Feasting with Etang a Hundred Times
Around.
San Juan. Owl of Minerva Takes Flight in the
Evening, The.
Schoolcraft. Otagamiad.
Schulman. New Netherland, 1654.
Senior. Meditation on Yellow.
Sykes, B. Fallin'
Requiem.
Sylvain, P. Constant Memories.
Unknown. Mbuyazi (Henry Francis Fynn).
Vando. Commonwealth, Common Poverty.
Walcott. Far Cry from Africa, A.
Weller. Midgiegooroo.
Wurarbuti.
Zimunya. White Poetess.
See also **British Empire; Imperialism**

Colorado (state)
Saner. Indian Peaks, Colorado.
Stafford, W. Holding the Sky.

Colors
Abse. Pathology of Colours.
Albert-Birot. Balalaïka.
Alexander, E. Stravinsky in L.A.
Brown, G. Shroud.
Bynner. Tiles.
DeCarteret, M. Coloring.
Depero. Colors.
Dickinson, E. Yellow Man, Purple Man.
Diop, B. Ball.
Ebb, F. My Coloring Book.
Esteves. Weaver.
Gray-Kontar, D. Not no socialism/communism
classical, but some power to the people jazz.
Guest, B. River Road Studio.
Hughes, L. Little Song.
Kander, J. My Coloring Book.

Koyama.   Downtown Seattle in the Fog.
Madhubuti.   Poem Looking for a Reader, A.
Mathews, A.   Spectrum.
McPherson, S.   Quilt of Rights.
Merritt, C.   Woman of Color.
Milosz, C.   Sun, The.
Morley, H.   Curve of the Water.
  For Elaine de Kooning.
Nichols, G.   Black.
  White.
Oppenheimer, J.   Love Bit, The.
Pilling.   You and You, In the Pink.
Pitter.   Dun-Colour [or Dun-Color].
Pound, E.   Song of the Degrees, A.
Riley, D.   Lure, 1963.
Seidman.   Making of Color, The.
Snyder, G.   Gaia.
Stanard, C.   Wrong Color.
Steinberg, D.   Purple is the Color of Longing.
Steptoe.   Sweet Brown Rice and Red Bones.
Stevens, W.   Domination of Black.
Tidjani-Cissé.   Of Colours and Shadows.
Toomer.   People.
Watkins, V.   Music of Colours—White Blossom.
  Music of Colours: The Blossom Scattered.
Wolverton, T.   Tubes.
Wylie.   Green Hair.
Young, D.   Project for Freight Trains, A.

Colosseum, Rome
Browne, M.   Survey of the Amphitheatre, A.
Norse.   Colosseum.
Poe.   Coliseum, The.

Coltrane, John
Baraka.   Am/Trak.
Brathwaite, E.   Naima.
Early, G.   Country or Western Music.
Etter.   Monk's Dream.
Gordon, G.   Gas.
Graham, M.   After the War; When Coltrane
  Only Wanted to Play Dance Tunes.
Greenlee.   Memorial for Trane.
Harjo, J.   Healing Animal.
Harper, M.   Dear John, Dear Coltrane.
  Here Where Coltrane Is.
  Narrative of the Life and Times of John
    Coltrane: Played by Himself, A.
Hayes, T.   Boxcar.
Henderson, D.   Elvin Jones Gretsch Freak.
Jordan, N.   Silent Prophet, The.
Kgositsile.   Acknowledgement.
Levine, P.   Soloing.
Madhubuti.   Don't Cry, Scream.
Mor.   Coming of John, The.
Okantah.   Afreeka Brass.
Rodgers, C.   Written for Love of an
  Ascension—Coltrane.
Sneeden.   Coltrane and My Father.
Spellman.   Did John's Music Kill Him?
Stillman, M.   In Memoriam John Coltrane.
Touré, A.   JuJu.

Colts
Frost, R.   Runaway, The.
See also **Horses**

Columba, Saint
Morgan, E.   Columba's Song.
See also **Columcille, Saint**

Columbia University
Hughes, L.   Theme for English B.

Columbus, Christopher
Brathwaite, E.   Colombe.
Durham.   Columbus Day.
Freneau.   Columbus to Ferdinand.
Frost, R.   America Is Hard to See.
Gardinier.   Admirals (Columbus).
Gustafson, R.   Columbus Reaches Juana, 1492.
Lazarus, E.   1492.
Miller, J.   Columbus.
Robertson, J.   Discovery of America, The.
Rukeyser, M.   Columbus.
Sylvain, P.   Constant Memories.
Whitman, W.   Passage to India.

Columcille, Saint
Dallán Forgaill.   Poem in Praise of Colum
  Cille, A.

Comas
Khalvati.   Coma.
Meredith, G.   King Harald's Trance.

Combs
Cardiff.   Combing.
Trethewey, N.   Hot Comb.

Comedians
Bernstein, C.   Of Time and the Line.
Hathaway, W.   Why That's Bob Hope.

Comets
Johnson, S.   Comets and Princes.
Marvell.   Mower to the Glowworms [or Glow-
  Worms or Glo-Worms], The.
Nicholson, N.   Comet Come.
  Halley's Comet.
Noguere.   Soma.
Ramsey, J.   Comet and Treefrog.

Comfort
Angus.   Blue Jacket, The.
Baraka.   Political Poem.
Bauer, G.   She Calms the Savage Beast with Her
  Aubade.
Berry, W.   Wild Geese, The.
Bock, J.   Too Close for Comfort.
Browning, E.   Comfort.
  Thought for a Lonely Death-Bed, A.
Clark, T.   Touch of Human Hands, The.
Crowell, G.   Courage to Live.
Foster, A.   Starting School.
Hammerstein.   My Favorite Things.
Harbach, O.   Love Nest, The.
Haskins, L.   To Play Pianissimo.
Herrick.   Comfort to a Youth That Had Lost His
  Love.
Hirsch, L.   Love Nest, The.
Hopkins, G.   No Worst, There Is None. Pitched
  Past Pitch of Grief.
Johnson, H.   Fringe-Area Reception.
Keats.   Why Did I Laugh Tonight?
Lerner, A.   I've Grown Accustomed to Her
  Face.
Liu, T.   Ikon.
Melville, H.   Herba Santa.
Murphy, P.   Manifesto.
Sandburg, C.   At a Window.
Talfourd.   'Tis a Little Thing.
Thayer, L.   Little Child's Faith, The.
Walders, D.   Anniversary.

Comic Strips
Ashbery.   Farm Implements and Rutabagas in a
  Landscape.
Reaney.   Katzenjammer Kids, The.
Sorrentino.   Zoo, The.
Wallace-Crabbe.   Collective Invention, The.

Commencement Day
Carrier, C.   Commencement.

Commerce
Brown, L.   Best Things in Life Are Free, The.
Elliott, E.   Fatal Birth, The.
Ginsberg, A.   Studying the Signs.
Griffith, L.   Office Window.
Gwynn, R.   Classroom at the Mall, The.
Hacker, M.   Elysian Fields.
Hall, D.   Hermit with Landscape.
Knight, E.   Eyeball Works, The.
Koch, K.   You Were Wearing.
Martin, C.   Victoria's Secret.
Spender, S.   Ultima Ratio Regum.
Zukofsky, L.   Song for the Year's End, A.
See also **Barters; Business and Businessmen**

Communes
Jones, A.   Communal Living.
Piatt, S.   Palace-Burner, The.

Communication
Aiken, C.   Annihilation.
Ashbery.   Train Rising Out of the Sea.
Atwood.   Against Still Life.
Behn, A.   Love's Witness.
Bowers, M.   Answer.
Bowes-Lyon.   Feather, The.
Bronk.   Mayan Glyphs Unread, The.
Carruth, H.   Sonnet: "Well, she told me I had an
  aura. 'What?' I said."
Creeley.   Act of Love, The.
Cummings, E.   May I Feel Said He.

Davidson, D.   Utterance.
Dooley, M.   No, Go On.
Dow, R.   How Should I Say This?
Eliot, T.   Conversation Galante.
Gardner, I.   That "Craning of the Neck."
Gaspar.   Part of What I Mean.
Ginsberg, A.   Stroke.
Harwood, G.   In The Park.
Herrick.   Upon Love, by Way of Question and
  Answer.
Hoffman, D.   Signatures.
Jackson, L.   Summary for Alastor.
  World and I, The.
Joseph, J.   Lost Continent, The.
Kipling, R.   Fabulists, The.
Lloyd, M.   Simplest and the Hardest, The.
Lum.   Going Home.
Maguire, S.   Communion.
Mansfield, K.   Meeting, The.
Matthews, T.   Even the Whales.
McGrath, T.   Letter for Marian, A.
Millay, E.   Hearing Your Words, and Not a
  Word Among Them.
Morgan, E.   First Men on Mercury, The.
Piercy.   You Don't Understand Me.
Ransom, J.   Two in August.
Rich, A.   Valediction Forbidding Mourning, A.
Robinson, E.   Tact.
Rukeyser, M.   Effort at Speech between Two
  People.
Sexton.   From the Garden.
Singer, B.   Your Words, My Answers.
Stafford, W.   Ritual to Read to Each Other, A.
Voznesensky [or Voznesenskii].   Dogalypse.
Walker, R.   Unreceived Messages.
Watta.   Stone at the Tip of the Tongue, A.
Woolson.   Love Unexpressed.

Communism
Cornford, J.   Full Moon at Tierz; before the
  Storming of Huesca.
Crosby, H.   Firebrand.
Duff, V.   Letters from an Exile.
Eastman, M.   To John Reed.
Elliott, E.   Epigram: "What is a communist?
  One who hath yearnings."
Ginsberg, A.   Kral Majales.
Hikmet.   Angina Pectoris.
Jones, R.   End of Communism, The.
Kay, J.   Waiting Lists, The.
Mandelstam [or Mandelshtam].   Poem No. 286
  (On Stalin).
Niemoller.   First They Came for the Jews.
Pauker.   Garland for a Propagandist.
Ridge, L.   Réveille.
"Sagittarius."   Stalin Moy Golubchik.
Sims, H.   Left Rites.
Tomlinson, C.   Prometheus.
Wilcox, E.   Communism.
Worley, D.   Las Flores para una Niña Negra.

Commuting and Commuters
As-Sabah.   Transition #2.
Clarke, C.   Passing.
Elledge.   Duckling, Swan.
Hearne, B.   Commuters.
Hopkins, L.   Subways Are People.
Manrique, J.   Baudelaire's Spleen.
Rodriguez, L.   Reflection on El Train Glass.
Ross, L.   Indecent Exposure (A True Story).
Rouse.   Her Retirement.
White, E.   Commuter.
See also **Suburbs and Suburban Life**

Companionship and Companions
Adamson.   Action Would Kill It / A Gamble.
Ager, M.   Mamma Goes Where Papa Goes.
Alford, H.   You and I.
Amadiume.   Union, The.
Anderson, J.   Waking Up Twice.
Arlen, H.   For Every Man There's a Woman.
Ashbery.   Love Poem, A.
Atwood.   Circle Game, The.
  Eventual Proteus.
Auden.   Lullaby: "Lay your sleeping head, my
  love."
Belieu.   Part of the Effect of the Public Scene Is
  to Importune the Passing Viewer.
Bendall, M.   Matinée Idylls.

Berrigan, A. Various Multitudes Contained by the Loves of My Love, The.
Blaser. Ah.
Bloom, R. Good for Nothin' Joe.
Bock, J. Matchmaker.
Broughton, J. Twin Flames.
Buchanan, G. I Suddenly.
Burns, R. O [or Oh] Wert Thou in the Cauld Blast.
Song: "O my love's [or luve's or love is or luve is] like a red, red rose."
Carruth, H. Little Citizen, Little Survivor.
Carter, J. Adagio at Twilight.
Cataldi. We Could Have Met.
Chester, T. Buttons.
Colby, T. Boy and the Girl, The.
Think Eight.
Cooper, J. Rent.
Coslow, S. Cocktails for Two.
Couzyn. Heartsong.
Creeley. For Love.
Curbelo. Among Strangers.
Dietz, H. Alone Together.
Donne. Canonization, The.
Dooley, M. Does It Go Like this?
Up on the Roof.
Duncan, R. And If He Had Been Wrong for Me.
Erdman, E. No, No, Nora.
Toot, Toot, Tootsie! (Good-bye).
Etherege. To a Lady Asking Him How Long He Would Love Her.
Evans, R. Never Let Me Go.
Everson, W. Stone Face Falls.
Fletcher, L. Way April Leads to Autumn, The.
Ford, C. There's No Place to Sleep in This Bed, Tanguy.
Freeman, S. Other Half of Me, The.
Frost, R. Pasture, The.
Garshman, B. Keys.
Giovanni. World Is Not a Pleasant Place to Be, The.
Goodman, M. Open Poem.
Graves, R. Narrow Sea, The.
Green, J. You're Mine, You!
Gunn, T. Touch.
Harnick. Matchmaker.
Hart, L. There's a Small Hotel.
Herd. On the Glittering Beaches.
Herrick. Not To Love.
To Phyllis to Love and Live with Him.
Heyman, E. You're Mine, You!
Hirshfield, J. Music Like Water, The.
Hollander, J. Some Walks With You.
Hovanessian, D. On Commonwealth Avenue and Brattle Street.
Hugo, R. Letter to Libbey from St. Regis.
Jennings, K. Just the Two of Us.
Johnston, A. Cocktails for Two.
Josefowitz, N. Foreplay.
Kefala. Sunday Visit.
Kern, J. You Never Knew About Me.
King, H. Exequy, The.
Kizer, C. For Jan as the End Draws Near.
Klein, M. Guardian Life.
Koehler, T. Good for Nothin' Joe.
Koyama. Currents.
Kunitz, S. After the Last Dynasty.
Route Six.
Lanier, S. To Bayard Taylor.
Lawrence, J. Other Half of Me, The.
Lees, G. Right to Love, The.
Lerner, A. Heather on the Hill, The.
Levertov. Bedtime.
Losing Track.
Light, K. Idea of Love Between Us, The.
Livingston, J. Never Let Me Go.
Loewe, F. Heather on the Hill, The.
Marion, G. There's a Man in My Life.
Mathews, A. Spectrum.
Matson, C. Bedside.
McGrath, T. Celebration.
McKay, C. Wild Goat, The.
Merrill, B. People.
Moore, T. 'Tis the Last Rose of Summer.
Mueller, L. Alive Together.

Naimy, M. Solemn Vow, A.
Nash, O. Which the Chicken, Which the Egg?
Nelson, J. Our Love.
Nelson, J. 56 Westervelt.
Nemerov. Blue Suburban.
Owen, W. Apologia Pro Poemate Meo.
Parker, A. Magpie.
Penn, R.E. Hand.
Perreault, J. Metaphysical Paintings, The.
Piercy. Implications of One Plus One.
To Have without Holding.
Porter, C. From This Moment On.
Ramsey, J. Tally Stick, The.
Rashad, J. Place Setting.
Rees-Jones. I Know Exactly the Sort of Woman I'd Like to Fall in Love With.
It Will Not Do.
Rich, A. After Twenty Years.
Blood-Sister.
Living in Sin.
Paula Becker to Clara Westhoff.
Ritchie. Sorting Laundry.
Robin, L. For Every Man There's a Woman.
Robinson, E. Companion, The.
Firelight.
Rodgers, R. There's a Small Hotel.
Safford, J. Very Floor of Our Existence, The.
Scamell, B. Working for British Telecom.
Schifrin, L. Right to Love, The.
Schwartz, A. Alone Together.
Shelley, P. From the Arabic: An Imitation.
To Maria Gisborne in England, from Italy.
Sondheim. Together Wherever We Go.
Styne, J. People.
Together Wherever We Go.
Swift, J. Stella's Birthday, 1725.
To Stella.
Twelve Articles.
Sykes, B. One Day.
Taggard. Everyday Alchemy.
Thompson, D. P. Sister Lakin and Lally.
Walcott. Village Life, A.
Waller, T. et al. There's a Man in My Life.
Warren, R. After the Dinner Party.
Wodehouse, P. You Never Knew About Me.
Woods, H. Side by Side.
Wright, F. Alcohol.
Wright, J. Transfiguration.
Yellen, J. Mamma Goes Where Papa Goes.
See also **Friendship**
Compassion
Brecht, B. World's One Hope, The.
Brontë, A. Song.
Brown, L. Never Swat a Fly.
Bursk. Lies.
Crane, H. Chaplinesque.
Creeley. Token, A.
World, The.
DeSylva, B. G. Never Swat a Fly.
Dickinson, E. This Is My Letter to the World.
Fletcher, L. After Delivering Your Lunch.
Ginsberg, A. Is About.
Line Drive.
Hamburger, M. Between the Lines.
Henderson, R. Never Swat a Fly.
Knott. Two Vietnam Poems: (1966).
Levine, P. Coming Home, Detroit, 1968.
Mukand, J. Lullaby.
North, C. Few Facts about Me, A.
O'Reilly, M. Small Girl Brings an Injured Bird into the Surgery, A.
Peck, J. Metal Denser Than, and Liquid, A.
Spender, S. History and Reality.
Unknown. Homage to Tara Our Mother.
Williams, C. Day for Anne Frank, A.
Witt, S. Americana.
Wright, J. Compassion's Bird.
Saint Judas.
Wunderlich, M. From a Vacant House.
Zukofsky, L. Song for the Year's End, A.
Competition
Emerson, R. Fable: "Mountain and the squirrel, The."
Holden, J. Saturday Afternoon, October.
Holland, J. Baize Queens.
Jarry. Passion of Jesus Considered as an Uphill

Race, The.
Johnson, J. Brer Rabbit, You's de Cutes' of 'Em All.
O'Hara, F. Hôtel Transylvanie.
Suckling, S. Wits, The; A Session[s] of the Poets.
Winchilsea. Circuit of Apollo, The.
See also **Rivalry**
Complacency
Bradley, G. E Pur Si Muove.
Browning, E. Loved Once.
Creeley. Warning, The.
Ingalls, J. Apprehension.
Ulku, A. Lullaby: "You are safe / You are lying in a hammock."
Computers
Clayton, S. Boom Time.
Hardy, J. Computer Aided Design: Creation.
Morgan, E. Computer's First Christmas Card, The.
von Zweck, D. One Man's Potato Chip.
Comraderie
Clifton, L. Lost Women, The.
Gottlieb, L. Greeting Shekinah.
Williams, C. Sanctity, The.
Concentration
Meredith, W. Traveling Boy.
Noguchi, R. Not Surfing Some Days.
Concentration Camps
Alkalay-Gut. Kitzbuhl Church.
Bachner. Yes, That's the Way Things Are.
Berg, S. Desnos Reading the Palms of Men on Their Way to the Gas Chambers.
Bienek. Our Ashes.
Vorkuta.
Carruth, H. Camps, The.
Cohen, L. Heirloom.
Dambroff. Resistance.
Durcan. Death by Heroin of Sid Vicious, The.
Fenton, J. German Requiem, A.
Florsheim. Real Chocolate.
Weekend in Palm Springs.
Fogel, E. Shipment to Maidanek.
Forché. Elegy.
Hachenburg, H. Terezin.
Hecht, A. 'More Light! More Light!'
Book of Yolek, The.
Henderson, D. Alvin Cash/Keep on Dancin'
Heyen. Blue.
Hyett. Assembling the Dead at Dachau.
Inada. Concentration Constellation.
Jarrell. Camp in the Prussian Forest, A.
In the Camp There Was One Alive.
Protocols.
Košek, M. It All Depends on How You Look at It.
Yes, That's the Way Things Are.
Lifshin. Bergen-Belsen 1945.
Hearing of Reagan's Trip to Bitburg.
Seeing the Documentary by the British Liberating Bergen-Belsen.
Lindtvoj, A. Campfire.
Mandel, E. On the 25th Anniversary of the Liberation of Auschwitz.
Michelson, R. Faraway Landscape.
Queen Esther Award, The.
Mif. Terezin.
Nepo. Oil of Her Hands, The.
Pilinszky, J. On the Wall of a KZ-Lager.
Posamentier, E. Counting Backwards.
Radnóti. Seventh Eclogue.
Ress. Visit, Auschwitz, 1971, The.
Reti, I. I Never Knew I Was Jewish.
Schapiro, J. Tourist, The.
Schulzová, E. Evening in Terezin, An.
Simic. Begotten of the Spleen.
Spender, S. Memento.
Syrkin. My Uncle in Treblinka.
Szymborska. Starvation Camp near Jaslo.
Teddy. At Terezin.
Unger, B. Photo Taken in Winter, 1944.
Unknown, fr. Terezin Concentration Camp.
Closed Town, The.
On a Sunny Evening.
Pain Strikes Sparks on Me, the Pain of Terezin.

Theresienstadt's Hospital.
Williams, C.   Day for Anne Frank, A.
See also **Auschwitz, Poland; Internment**
Conception
Erdrich.   Immaculate Conception.
Herrick.   Tithe [*or* Tythe]: To the Bride, The.
Kasdorf.   Streak, The.
Reyes, M.   Toads Mate and Father Cleans the
Pool.
Rouse.   Birthday, A.
Concerts
Blunden.   Concert Party: Busseboom.
North, C.   Hospital.
Smith, V.   Summer Band Concert.
Concord, Massachusetts
Emerson, R.   Concord Hymn.
Musketaquid.
Young, S.   Epitaph for a Concord Boy.
Concrete Poetry
Cabico, R.   Art in Architecture.
O'Sullivan, M.   Narrative Charm for Ibbotroyd.
See also **Shaped Poetry**
Confederacy
Ball, C.   Jacket of Gray, The.
Bierce.   Confederate Flags, The.
Davidson, D.   Lee in the Mountains.
Sequel of Appomattox.
Emmett.   Dixie [*or* Dixie's Land].
Preston, M.   Grave in Hollywood Cemetery,
Richmond, A.
Randall, J.   My Maryland.
Tate, A.   Battle of Murfreesboro.
Ode to the Confederate Dead.
Thompson, M.   To the South.
Timrod.   Charleston.
Ode: "Sleep sweetly in your humble graves."
Unknown.   Confederate Memorial Day.
Walcott.   Arkansas Testament, The.
See also **Civil War, United States**
Confessions
Berg, S.   On This Side of the River.
Blunt, W.   To One Who Would Make a
Confession.
Clarke, A.   Ancient Lights.
Clover, J.   Archive of Confessions, a Genealogy
of Confessions, An.
Creeley.   Hill, The.
Dauer.   Lois at the Hair Salon.
Derricotte.   Weakness, The.
Dunn, S.   What They Wanted.
Faber, F.   Confessional, The.
Figueroa, J.   Confessions from the Last Cloud.
Gomez, M.   Chocolate Confessions.
Hahn, S.   Confession.
Herbert, G.   Trinity Sunday.
Hudgins.   Praying Drunk.
Hughes, L.   Third Degree.
Kennedy, X.   First Confession.
Kern, J.   That Was Before I Met You.
Komunyakaa.   Jeanne Duval's Confession.
Lee-Hamilton.   Ipsissimus.
Leonard, T.   Jist Ti Let Yi No.
Lowell, R.   At the Altar.
Melville, H.   In a Church of Padua.
Muldoon, P.   Cuba.
Pankey.   Confession of Cleopas, The.
Tobin, D.   Deep Shit.
Whitman, W.   As I Lay with My Head in Your
Lap Camerado.
Trickle Drops.
Whitney, I.   Aucthour Maketh Her Wyll and
Testament, The.
Manner of Her Will and What She Left to
London and to All Those in It, at Her
Departing, The.
Wilbur.   Mind-Reader, The.
Wodehouse, P.   That Was Before I Met You.
Wright, J.   Confession to J. Edgar Hoover.
Confidence
Fields, D.   Pick Yourself Up.
Townshend [*or* Townsend].   Upon Kind[e] and
True Love.
Troup, B.   You're Lookin' at Me.
Conflict
Berg, S.   On This Side of the River.

Berryman.   Recognition, The.
Bursk.   Lies.
Cleary, B.   Slouch.
Creeley.   Fancy.
Whip, The.
Wife, The.
Derricotte.   Invisible Dreams.
Foster, A.   No Dice.
Hardy, J.   Difference, The.
Huddle.   Music.
Johnson, M. F.   Widow's Remarriage, The.
Keithley.   Thunder Storm.
Mapanje.   On Being Asked to Write a Poem for
1979.
Melville, H.   After the Pleasure Party.
America.
O'Brien, L.   Diabolus in Musica.
Pollitt.   Mind-Body Problem.
Seaton, M.   Fiddleheads.
Southwell.   Man's Civil[l] War[re].
Turner, G.   Synchoresis.
Wilder, A.   Trouble Is a Man.
Conformity
Auden.   Unknown Citizen, The.
Bly, R.   Executive's Death, The.
Boland, E.   Self-Portrait on a Summer Evening.
Crozier, A.   Driftwood and Seacoal.
Egerton, S.   Emulation, The.
Liberty, The.
Graves, R.   It Was All Very Tidy.
Harland-Watts, J.   Resist Confinement.
Joseph, J.   Warning.
Laing, K.   Huge Car with the Sad Voice, The.
Lindsay, N.   Congo, The.
McGrath, T.   Ode for the American Dead in
Korea.
Melville, H.   Enthusiast, The.
Musgrave.   You Didn't Fit.
Ofeimun.   Let Them Choose Paths.
Shapiro, K.   University.
Stevens, W.   Disillusionment of Ten O'Clock.
Wilson, S.   Contemporary Poet, A.
Confusion
Adams, L.   But Alive.
Ashbery.   Chapter 2, Book 35.
Barbour, D.   I Don't Know Enough About You.
Beckett, S.   Saint-Lô.
Carew, T.   Lover, upon an Accident
Necessitating His Departure, Consults with
Reason, A.
Creeley.   Fancy.
Davis, J.   Fire Barns.
Delmore, E.   Such Sweet Sorrow.
Forhan, C.   Big Jigsaw.
Frost, R.   Cabin in the Clearing, A.
Gascoyne.   Cubical Domes, The.
End Is Near the Beginning, The.
Graves, R.   In Broken Images.
Hadas, R.   Lair, The.
Hollander, J.   Carmen Ancillae.
Koch, K.   To World War Two.
Larkin, J.   Rape.
Lee, P.   I Don't Know Enough About You.
Levin, P.   Lost Bee, The.
Piercy.   Song of the Fucked Duck.
Pietri.   Intermission from Friday.
Intermission from Saturday.
Portnoy, M.   Hints at Distance.
Instant Control.
Of of Titmouse.
Shepherd, R.   Another Version of an Ocean.
Smedley, M.   Irish Fairy, The.
Strouse, C.   But Alive.
Szporluk.   Holy Ghost.
Occupant of the Hose.
Toomer.   I Sit in My Room.
Torres, E.   Breezy Delicious Day.
Poetry Detective.
Vitale, M.   You Oh Even.
Volkman.   Untitled.
Von Freytag-Loringhoven.   Café du Dôme.
Dozen Cocktails—Please, A.
Waniek.   Bali Hai Calls Mama.
Wetzsteon.   Three Songs.
Urban Gallery.
Winchilsea.   Adam Posed.

Congo River
Bethune, L.   For Singing In Good Mood.
Kgositsile.   Gods Wrote, The.
Sanchez, S.   Haiku: "Your voice unwrapping."
Congreve, William
Dryden, J.   To My Dear Friend Mr Congreve
[on His Comedy Called "The Double-Dealer"].
Connaught, Ireland
Mangan, J.   Vision of Connaught in the
Thirteenth Century, A.
Connecticut (state)
Branch, A.   Connecticut Road Song.
Hall, D.   Sleeping Giant, The.
Stevens, W.   River of Rivers in Connecticut,
The.
Connecticut River
Stevens, W.   River of Rivers in Connecticut,
The.
Conquistadors
Brathwaite, E.   Colombe.
Crane, H.   Imperator Victus.
MacLeish.   Prologue: "And the way goes on in
the worn earth."
Ryan, R.   El Dorado.
Conrad, Joseph
Walcott.   Volcano.
Conscience
Byron, G.   Answer to——'s Professions of
Affection.
Heaney, S.   From the Republic of Conscience.
Herrick.   Sabbaths.
To His Conscience.
To Oenone.
Hopkins, G.   Candle Indoors, The.
Nash, O.   Inter-Office Memorandum.
Ramsdell, H.   Nearly Circle.
Simic.   Inner Man, The.
Stevens, W.   High-Toned Old Christian
Woman, A.
Szymborska.   In Praise of Self-Deprecation.
Ungria, R.   Culture Nervous.
Unknown.   Little Chap Who Follows Me, The.
Wilbur.   Mind-Reader, The.
Conscientious Objectors
Gardinier.   Supremer Sacrifice, The.
Lowell, R.   After the Surprising Conversions.
Memories of West Street and Lepke.
Shapiro, K.   Conscientious Objector, The.
See also **Pacifism and Pacifists**
Consciousness
Baraka.   Minute of Consciousness, The.
Collins, B.   Going Out for Cigarettes.
Deming, A.   Tilden Park.
Edwards, K.   Unconsciously.
Frost, R.   Silken Tent, The.
Glück, L.   Wild Iris, The.
Hardy, T.   New Year's Eve.
Simic.   Inner Man, The.
Sisson.   Person, The.
Stafford, W.   Ritual to Read to Each Other, A.
Conscription, Military
Ewer.   Only Way, The.
Loesser.   They're Either Too Young or Too Old.
Logue, C.   Song of the Dead Soldier, The.
Murray, C.   Dockens afore his Peers.
Schwartz, A.   They're Either Too Young or Too
Old.
Consolation
Berg, S.   Prayer: "Nobody understands so let the
Rabbi."
Brontë, E.   To Imagination.
Buscani.   Miss Mary Mack.
Cook, E.   To My Lyre.
Davis, C.   Belongings.
Fishman, L.   Promiscuity.
Giovanni.   Women Gather, The.
Hooks.   Woman's Mourning Song, The.
Kocot, N.   Consolations Before an Affair, Upper
West Side.
Longfellow, H.   Rainy Day, The.
Mahon.   Consolations of Philosophy.
Porter, C.   I Concentrate on You.
It's All Right with Me.
Rivard.   Consolation.

Tsaloumas. Consolation.
White, D. Epistle of Love and of Consolation unto Israel, An.

Conspiracy
Komunyakaa. Fragging.
Nuriddin, J. M. Children of the Future.
Wise, S. I Was Very Prolific.

Constantinople, Turkey
Al-Rihani. Constantinople.
Montagu, L. Verses Written in the Chiosk [of the British Palace], at Pera, Overlooking [the City of] Constantinople.

Constellations
Barnard, M. Pleiades, The.
Berssenbrugge. Constellation Quilt, The.
Bryant, W. Constellations, The.
De la Mare. Ride-by-Nights, The.
Eliot, T. Sweeney Among the Nightingales.
Frost, R. Canis Major.
Graves, R. Star-Talk.
Grennan. Conjunctions.
Healy, R. Size of This Universe, The.
Hollander, J. Great Bear, The.
Lion Named Passion, A.
Mahon. Globe in North Carolina, The.
Rich, A. Orion.
Planetarium.
Sigourney. Stars, The.
Stevenson, A. Sonnet: "If it be night . . . ."
Storace. Wedding Song.
Tuckerman, F. Sonnets: "Starry flower, the flower-like stars that fade, The."
Turner, C. Orion.
Wilbur. In the Field.
See also **Sky; Stars**

Constitution (ship)
Holmes, O. Old Ironsides.

Construction Workers
Delgado, J. Con Los Pájaros.
See also **Buildings and Builders**

Consumerism
Chrystos. Real Indian Leans Against, The.
Cummings, E. Poem, or Beauty Hurts Mr. Vinal.
Francia, L. Video Victim.
Lazard. In Answer to Your Query.
Moore, T. Announcement of a New Grand Acceleration Company for the Promotion of the Speed of Literature.
Nemerov. Life Cycle of Common Man.
Thomas, R. Period.
Unknown. Lydia Pinkham.
Warr, M. Malcolm Is 'Bout More Than Wearing a Cap.
Waterman, N. Cheer for the Consumer.

Contempt
Levertov. Grace-Note, The.
Millay, E. Oh, Oh, you will be sorry for that word!
Rochester, J. Ramble in St. James's Park, A.
Rossetti, C. Frog's Fate, A.
Sia, B. Things to Do in Holland.

Contentment
Ahlert, F. I'll Get By (As Long As I Have You).
Anderson, S. American Spring Song.
Baraka. Song Form.
Berlin. I Got the Sun in the Morning.
Little Things in Life, The.
Blane, R. I Never Felt Better.
Bontemps. God Give to Men.
Brown, L. Life Is Just a Bowl of Cherries.
Brown, S. Odyssey of Big Boy.
Burns, R. Birks of Aberfeldy, The [Composed on the Spot].
Byrom. Careless Content.
Calverley. Peace.
Carruth, H. Twilight Comes.
Chudleigh. Resolve, The.
Clare, J. Sabbath Bells.
Creeley. Innocence, The.
Rain, The.
David, M. I'm Just a Lucky So-and-So.
Davie. Heigh-ho on a Winter Afternoon.
Davies, W. Truly Great.

De Vere, E. Poem: "Were I a king, I could command content."
Dekker, T. Art thou poore yet hast thou golden Slumbers.
Dixon, M. Great Big Bunch of You, A.
Donaldson, W. My Blue Heaven.
Dubin, A. Cup of Coffee, a Sandwich, and You.
Duke, V. Not a Care in the World.
Dyer, J. Grongar Hill.
Dyer, S. My Mind to Me a Kingdom Is.
Ehrhart. Time on Target.
Ellington, D. I'm Just a Lucky So-and-So.
Emerson, R. Day's Ration, The.
Garrigue. Song for "Buvez les Vins du Postillion"—Advt.
Gershwin. I Got Plenty o' Nuthin'
I Got Rhythm.
Nice Work If You Can Get It.
Greenwell, D. Content.
Haines, J. To Turn Back.
Henderson, R. I'm Sitting on Top of the World.
Life Is Just a Bowl of Cherries.
Herbert, G. Family [*or* Familie], The.
Jesu.
Herrick. His Content in the Country.
His Grange, or Private Wealth.
Hikmet. Letters from a Man in Solitary.
Hilliard, B. Civilization (Bongo, Bongo, Bongo).
Jackson, M. L. Some Kind of Crazy.
Kyger. And with March a Decade in Bolinas.
Lampman. In November: "Hills and leafless forests slowly yield, The."
Landor, W. Ireland Never Was Contented.
Lanier, S. Nirvâna.
Latouche, J. Not a Care in the World.
Longfellow, H. Day Is Done, The.
Lowell, A. Decade, [A].
Martin, H. I Never Felt Better.
Marvell. Garden, The.
Meyer, J. Cup of Coffee, a Sandwich, and You.
Parnell, T. Hymn to Contentment, A.
Pomfret, J. Choice, The.
Rivera, D. Under the Apple Tree.
Robinson, E. Firelight.
Sexton. I Remember.
Sill. California Winter.
Smith, C. To Spring.
To the Moon.
Written September 1791, During a Remarkable Thunder Storm, in which the Moon Was Perfectly Clear, While the Tempest Gathered in Various Directions Near the Earth.
Stern, G. Red Bird.
Swenson, M. Staying at Ed's Place.
Turk, R. I'll Get By (As Long As I Have You).
Unknown. Another Little Boy.
Quiet Mind, The.
Warren, H. Great Big Bunch of You, A.
Washington, N. Love Is the Thing.
Whiting, G. My Blue Heaven.
Whitman, W. Glimpse, A.
Wilbur. Ballade for the Duke of Orléans.
Wilson, S. Room in Bloomsbury, A.
Wordsworth, D. Peaceful Our Valley, Fair and Green.
Wordsworth, W. Farmer of Tilsbury Vale, The.
Sonnet: "Nuns fret not at their convent's narrow room."
Wotton, S. Character of a Happy Life, The.
Wylie. Puritan Sonnet, IV.
Wild Peaches.
Yeats. Lake-Isle of Innisfree, The.
Young, J. I'm Sitting on Top of the World.
Young, V. Love Is the Thing.
See also **Happiness**

Continuity
Ammons, A. R. Eternal City, The.
Anderson, J. Re-member Us.
Atwood. Circle Game, The.
Bell, M. Drawn by Stones, by Earth, by Things That Have Been in the Fire.
Bethell. Warning of Winter.
Clampitt. Procession at Candlemas, A.
Creeley. Again.
Hardy, T. Heredity.

Harper, M. High Modes: Vision as Ritual: Confirmation.
Hopkins, E. Life in Death.
Kumin, M. Excrement Poem, The.
Kunitz, S. Layers, The.
Levine, P. Milkweed.
Marshall-Stoneking. Passage.
Meynell, A. Song of Derivations, A.
Nemerov. Dependencies, The.
O'Grady, D. Berlin Metro.
Oliver, M. In Blackwater Woods.
Rich, A. Readings of History.
Snodgrass, W. Leaving the Motel.
Vitale, M. I Read That It Was All a Chain.
Young, A. How Stars Start.

Contraception
Twichell. Condom Tree, The.

Contrariness
Melville, H. Parthenon, The.
Salmon, A. Prikaz.

Contrition
Smith, C. Santa Monica.

Convalescence
Chester, T. Running Hares.
Emerson, R. Give All to Love.
McCarriston. Healing the Mare.
Plath. Among the Narcissi.

Conventionality
Ransom, J. Nocturne.
Thomas, L. Electricity of Blossoms.

Convents
Brownjohn. In a Convent Garden.
Mew. At the Convent Gate.
Williams, A. Nunnery, The.
See also **Nuns**

Conversation
Adamson. Action Would Kill It / A Gamble.
Albert-Birot. In the Paul Guillaume Gallery.
Ashbery. Life As a Book That Has Been Put Down.
Berg, S. On This Side of the River.
Bottke, A. How to Approach Your Lover's Wife.
Coleman, W. Be Quiet, Go Away.
Crane, H. Praise for an Urn.
Dixon, M. Would You Like to Take a Walk?
Fearing. How Do I Feel?
Frost, R. Meeting and Passing.
Hodgins. Death Who.
Jackson, M. L. Blunts.
Kasdorf. Green Market, New York.
Larkin, P. Talking In Bed.
Longfellow, H. Fire of Drift-Wood, The.
Menashe. Annunciation, The.
Merrill, J. Charles on Fire.
Millay, E. I, Being Born a Woman.
Morley, H. For Elaine de Kooning.
Oden. Bible Study.
Oppen. Eclogue: "Men talking, The."
Prior. To a Lady: She Refusing to Continue a Dispute with Me, and Leaving Me in the Argument.
Rich, A. Dialogue.
Richardson, J. Retort Perfect, The.
Rose, B. Would You Like to Take a Walk?
Schuyler, J. Master of the Golden Glow, The.
Scott, D. Dreadwalk.
Shurin. Sailed.
Simpson, L. Chocolates.
Sitwell, D. Said King Pompey.
Stevens, W. Table Talk.
Stevenson, A. Sous-Entendu.
Taylor, J. Recreation.
Thomas, D. Conversation of Prayer, The.
Thomas, E. Sun Used to Shine, The.
Tomlinson, C. Word in Edgeways, A.
Troupe. Conversation Overheard.
Turner, G. Synchoresis.
Warren, H. Would You Like to Take a Walk?
Webb, F. Tip for Saturday, A.
Welish. Blood or Color.

Conversion
Crashaw. To the Noblest and Best of Ladies, the Countess of Denbigh.

Merton. St. Paul.
Ransom, J. Persistent Explorer.
Unknown. Vicar of Bray, The.
Wheatley, P. On Being Brought from Africa to America.
Whittier. Call of the Christian, The.
Williamson, G. Dark Days, The.
Wither. Conversion of S. Paul, The.

Conviction
Creeley. Way, The.

Cooking and Cooks
Aguilar-Cariño. Dinakdakan.
Aiken, J. Palace Cook's Tale.
Bernstein, L. I Can Cook, Too.
Cavendish, M. Nature's Cook.
Clifton, L. Cutting Greens.
Daniels, J. Short-Order Cook.
Delmore, E. Marmalade.
Ellis, C. On a Gentleman Marrying His Cook.
Everett, J. Ode to Salted Mutton Birds.
Forbes, C. Potlicker Blues.
Forché. Skin Canoes.
Gilbert, S. Ferdinando and Elvira; or, The Gentle Pieman.
Graves, R. Under the Pot.
Green, A. I Can Cook, Too.
Hamod, S. Leaves.
Harper, M. Breaded Meat, Breaded Hands.
Jong. Woman Who Loved to Cook, The.
Keplinger, D. Another Century.
Kleinschmidt. Cooking to Music.
Lorde. From the House of Yemanjá.
Marlatt, D. Bruce and the Bluegills.
Massinger. Men May Talk of Country-Christmasses.
McDonald, C. Fresh Mussels.
McGrath, T. Bread of this World; Praises III, The.
Moody, E. Sappho Burns Her Books and Cultivates the Culinary Arts.
Moore, L. Tanka.
Morales. Dinner, The.
Morales, A. Kitchens.
Muldoon, P. Sushi.
Piercy. What's That Smell in the Kitchen?
Rossetti, C. Mix a Pancake.
Saffoti. Espresso.
Simic. Lives of Alchemists, The.
Skeeter. Western Trail Cook, 1880.
Smith, B. Bowl, The.
Strange. Offering.
Tafolla. Allí por la Calle San Luis.
Tapahonso. All I Want.
Taylor, C.B. Forever Arima.
Umpierre, L. Only the Hand That Stirs Knows What's in the Pot.

Coole, Ireland
Yeats. Coole Park and Ballylee, 1931.
Coole Park, 1929.
In the Seven Woods.
Wild Swans at Coole, The.

Copernicus, Nicholas
Leapor. Epistle to a Lady, An.

Coral
Lieberman, L. Coral Reef, The.
Percival. Coral Grove, The.

Cormac Mac Art
Ferguson, S. Burial of King Cormac, The.

Cormorants
Blight. Cormorants.
Clampitt. Cormorant in His Element, The.
Clifton, L. To the Unborn and Waiting Children.
Isherwood. Common Cormorant [*or* Shag], The.
Kinsella, J. Cormorants.
Preece. Cormorant.
Stryk, L.

Corn
Apache Oral Tradition. Corn Ceremony.
Bly, R. Snowfall in the Afternoon.
Equi. Lesbian Corn.
Lanier, S. Waving of the Corn, The.
McAlmon. Frost in the Corn, The.
Riggs, L. Santo Domingo Corn Dance.

Sandburg, C. Early Copper.
Willard, N. Speckled Hen's Morning Song to Biddy Early, The.

Cornwall, England
Gray, J. On the South Coast of Cornwall.
Redgrove, P. Minerals of Cornwall, Stones of Cornwall.
Strong, L. March Evening.

Corpses
Alegría. From the Bridge.
Bly, R. Counting Small-Boned Bodies.
Dobson, A. Before Sedan.
Guevara, M. Postmortem.
Heaney, S. Grauballe Man, The.
Hemans. Image in Lava, The.
Herd. Exhibits, The.
Hughes, F. Kookaburra.
Kasischke. Pall.
Kinnell. Quick and the Dead, The.
MacDiarmid, H. Dead Liebknecht, The.
Meyers, B. Suburban Dusk.
Phillips, C. As From a Quiver of Arrows.
Radnóti. Picture Postcards.
Roeske, P. Preparing the Dead.
Rosenberg, I. Dead Man's Dump.
Southerland. Blue Clay.
Soyinka. Post Mortem.
Swinburne. After Death.
Unknown. Hearse Song, The.
Young, G. Damien.
See also **Necrophilia**

Correggio (Antonio Allegri)
De Vere, A. Correggio's Cupolas at Parma.

Corruption
Baraka. Three Modes of History and Culture.
Bly, R. Executive's Death, The.
Bock, J. Little Tin Box.
Byron, G. Answer to——'s Professions of Affection.
Drake, N. Man in the White Suit, The.
Graves, R. Wigs and Beards.
Harnick. Little Tin Box.
Hemphill. Family Jewels.
Holmes, O. Latter-Day Warnings.
Hughes, L. Un-American Investigators.
Jeffers, R. Stars Go Over the Lonely Ocean, The.
Johnson, F. Minister, The.
Jonson, B. On English Monsieur.
Lamb, C. Gipsy's Malison, The.
Lindsay, N. What the Moon Saw.
McClure, M. Senate Hearings.
Melhem, D. Lamentation After Jeremiah to Exorcise High Rental / High Rise Building Scheduled for Construction with Public Funds.
Milton. Lycidas.
Rios, A. Advice to a First Cousin.
Spenser. Address to Venus.
Arthur's Fight with Orgoglio and Duessa.
Belphoebe and Timias.
Book 1.
Bower of Bliss, The.
Britomart at Isis' Church.
Britomart chaseth Ollyphant.
Britomart in the House of the Enchanter Busyrane.
Cave of Despair, The.
Fight of the Red Cross Knight and the Heathen Sansjoy, The.
Garden of Adonis, The.
Guardian Angels.
Guyon's Voyage to the Bower of Bliss.
Hill of the Graces, The.
House of Busyrane, The.
In the Bower of Bliss.
Legend of Britomartis, or of Chastitie, The.
Legend of the Knight of the Red Crosse, or of Holinesse, The.
Maske of Cupid, The.
Mutability Claims to Rule the World.
Nature's Reply to Mutability.
Scudamor in the Temple of Venus.
Song of Bliss.
Vision of the Graces, The.
Visit to Merlin, The.

Unknown. Epitaph on the Duke of Buckingham.

Coruña, La, Spain
Wolfe, C. Burial of Sir John Moore [after [*or* at] Corunna], The.

Cosmetics
Borthwick, P. Out of Bounds.
Clarke, C. Make-Up.
Donne. Phryne.
Fanning, R. In the Barn.
Herrick. Upon Sibilla.
Kowit. Cosmetics Do No Good.
Naden. Two Artists, The.
Prior. Phillis's Age.
Symons, A. Maquillage.
Wolverton, T. Tubes.

Cosmology
Buckley, C. Presocratic, Surfing, Breathing Cosmology Blues, The.
Clairmont. Answers, The.
Fox, S. Almagest, Last Letter to Zakarias.
Healy, R. Size of This Universe, The.

Cosmos
Fabian, C. On reading the new physics—Creation and Cosmology.
Gottlieb, A. Meditation on the Feminine Nature of Shekinah, A.
Hildebrandt, Z. In Hecate's Garden.
Hillman. Black Series.
Hixon, L. My blissful Mother exists fully through every creature!
Mutén, B. Queen Hera.
Urania.
Sornberger. When She Laughs.
Tuckerman, F. Sonnet: "And so, as this great sphere (now turning slow)."
Villanueva, A. Planet Earth Speaks, The.
See also **Creation**

Cotswold Hills, England
Gurney, I. High Hills, The.
Thomas, E. Adlestrop.

Cotton
Bontemps. Southern Mansion.
Timrod. Cotton Boll, The.
Toomer. Cotton Song.
November Cotton Flower.
Whittier. Haschish, The.

Counterfeiting and Counterfeiters
Goldbarth. Counterfeit Earth!, The.
Williamson, G. Counterfeiter, The.

Counting
Justice, D. Counting the Mad.
Kendrick, D. Sophie, Climbing the Stairs.
Lehrer. Wernher von Braun.
Mora. Castanet Clicks.
Mother Goose. One to Ten.
Robinson, E. Fountain.
Rosen, M. One, Two, Three.
Soto. Teaching Numbers.
Unknown. Counting-out Rhyme, A.
One to Ten.
One, Two, Three, Four, Five!
Wong, J. One to Ten.
Yolen. Shepherd's Night Count.

Country Life
Adams, L. Country Summer.
Ammons, A. R. Hardweed Path Going.
Anderson, M. Country Wisdoms.
Ashe. City Clerk, The.
Baillie, J. Disappointment, A.
Blunt, W. Old Squire, The.
Bogan, L. Old Countryside.
Brereton, C. To Miss A[——]a M[——]a Tra[——]s; an Epistle from Scotland.
Brown, S. Virginia Portrait.
Burns, R. Cotter's Saturday Night [Inscribed to Robert Aiken [*or* R. A****], Esq.], The.
Byron, H. Rural Simplicity.
Centlivre. From the Country, to Mr. Rowe in Town.
Clare, J. Noon.
Cohan. Forty-five Minutes from Broadway.
Cornford, F. Country Bedroom, The.
Cowper, W. Against Slavery.
Arrival of the Mail.
Crazy Kate.

Effeminate Englishmen.
Frosty Morning, A.
Landscape Described, A.
Reading the Newspaper.
Stricken Deer, The.
Winter Evening, The: A Brown Study.
Winter Walk at Noon, The.
Creeley. City, The.
Cunningham, J. Montana Pastoral.
Davies, O. Urban.
DeFoe, M. Aviary.
Denham. Cooper's Hill.
Donne. To Sir Henry Wotton.
Dunn, D. In the Grounds.
Evans, A. Old Yellow Shop, The.
Evans, R. Buttons and Bows.
Francis, R. Silent Poem.
Frost, R. Directive.
  Need of Being Versed in Country Things, The.
Gale, N. Country Faith, The.
Garland, H. Goin' Back T'morrer.
Garrigue. After Reading "The Country of the
  Pointed Firs."
Gashe. Village, The.
Gogarty. Farrell O'Reilly.
Goldsmith, O. Deserted Village, The.
  Village, The.
Graves, R. On Dwelling.
Greenaway. Three Little Girls.
Gregg. Adult.
Grierson. To Miss Laetitia Van Lewen.
Hall, D. Names of Horses.
  Ox Cart Man.
Hardy, T. In Time of "The Breaking of
  Nations."
Hart, L. Mountain Greenery.
Henley, S. Verses Addressed to a Friend, Just
  Leaving a Favourite Retirement.
Herrick. Country Life, to the Honored Mr.
  Endymion Porter[, Groome of the Bed-
  Chamber to His Maj.], The.
  Country Life: To His Brother, M. Tho: Herrick.
  His Content in the Country.
  His Grange, or Private Wealth.
  To Phyllis to Love and Live with Him.
Hogg, J. Boy's Song, A.
Jarrell. Country Life, A.
Jewett, S. Country Boy in Winter, A.
Johnson, J. Unmarked Stop in Front of
  Westmond General Store, Westmond, Idaho.
Jonson, B. To Penshurst.
Kavanagh, P. Epic: "I have lived in important
  places, times."
  Spraying the Potatoes.
Keats. Dawlish Fair.
  To One Who Has Been Long in City Pent.
  Where Be You [or Ye] Going, You [or Ye]
  Devon Maid?
Keller, D. After Supper.
Kern, J. Bungalow in Quogue.
Kinnell. When One Has Lived a Long Time
  Alone.
Lanyer. Description of Cooke-ham [or
  Cookham], The.
Lawrence, D. Love On the Farm.
  Whether or Not.
Layton. Aubade, An.
Livingston, J. Buttons and Bows.
Lloyd, R. Cit's Country Box, The.
Longfellow, H. Fire of Drift-Wood, The.
Longley, M. Gorse Fires.
  West, The.
Lux. There Were Some Summers.
Mahon. Woods, The.
Marlatt, D. Summer of the New Well.
Marvell. Garden, The.
McGuckian. Gateposts.
McMorris, M. Evening.
Melville, H. Immolated.
Millay, E. Return, The.
Miller, J. Which Religion Vouchsafes.
Mother Goose. This is the House that Jack
  Built.
Murray, C. Dockens afore his Peers.
Murray, L. Noonday Axeman.
Nemerov. At a Country Hotel.

O'Donoghue, B. Nun Takes the Veil, A.
Pope, A. Epistle to Miss [or Miss Teresa]
  Blount, on Her Leaving the Town after the
  Coronation.
  Happy Life of a Country Parson, The.
Purdy, A. Country North of Belleville, The.
Ravenscroft, E. In Derision of a Country Life.
Rawlins, C. Living in at Least Two Worlds.
Reaney. Upper Canadian, The.
Riley, J. Country Pathway, A.
  When the Frost Is on the Punkin.
Rodgers, R. Mountain Greenery.
Rogers, S. Wish, A.
Sackville-West. Bull, The.
Sansom, M. Invitation from a Country Cottage,
  The.
Schuyler, J. Korean Mums.
Seymour, F. Life at Richkings.
Simic. Ballad: "What's that approaching like
  dust like poverty."
Slessor. Country Towns.
Smart, C. Morning-Piece; or, An Hymn for the
  Hay-Makers, A.
Snyder, G. After Work.
Sylvester, J. Of a Husbandman.
Tate, J. Land of Little Sticks, 1945.
Tennyson, A. City Child, The.
Thomas, E. Haymaking.
Thomas, R. Village, The.
Unknown. Country Lassie, The.
Untermeyer, J. Country of No Lack.
Vaughan, H. Retirement.
Walcott. Upstate.
Walker, M. Childhood.
Waller, E. At Penshurst [Another].
Warren, R. Renoir.
Weöres. Plain, The.
Westmorland. My Country Audit.
  To Retiredness.
Whitman, W. Farm Picture, A.
Wilder, A. It's So Peaceful in the Country.
Williams, W. Raleigh Was Right.
  Woman Walking.
Winchilsea. Ballad to Mrs. Catherine Fleming
  in London from Malshanger Farm in
  Hampshire, A.
Wodehouse, P. Bungalow in Quogue.
Wordsworth, W. Inscription for the Moss-Hut at
  Dove Cottage.
Wright, C. Two Stories.
Wright, K. How the Wild South East Was Lost.
Yeats. Lake-Isle of Innisfree, The.

County Antrim, Northern Ireland
MacNeice. Carrickfergus.
Mahon. Rathlin.

County Cork, Ireland
Mahon. Garage in Co. Cork, A.
  Kinsale.
Millikin. Groves of Blarney, The.

County Galway, Ireland
Murphy, R. High Island.
  Sailing to an Island.

County Kerry, Ireland
Synge. In Kerry.

County Meath, Ireland
Higgins, F. Father and Son.

County Monaghan, Ireland
Kavanagh, P. Shancoduff.
  Stony Grey Soil.

County Sligo, Ireland
Yeats. Lake-Isle of Innisfree, The.

Courage
Amis, K. Autobiographical Fragment.
Ammons, A. R. Coward.
Anstett. Man Saves Own Life.
Arlen, H. If I Only Had a Brain (If I Only Had
  a Heart) (If I Only Had the Nerve).
Atwood. Notes towards a Poem That Can
  Never Be Written.
Babcock, M. Be Strong.
Brontë, E. No Coward Soul is Mine.
Brooke, R. Hill, The.
Butler, C. E. Other Places, The.
Cameron, N. Thespians at Thermopylae, The.
Cary, P. Leak in the Dike, The.

Clough. Say Not the Struggle Nought Availeth.
Coffman. Courage, or One of Gene Horner's
  Fiddles.
Colesworthy. Be Never Discouraged.
Cook, E. "No!"
Cooke, E. How Did You Die?
Crowell, G. Courage to Live.
  I Think That God is Proud.
Dambroff. Resistance.
Delgado, J. Dandelion.
Douglas, K. Gallantry.
Fishman, C. Not Only in the Six-Day War.
Freed, F. Private School for Girls, May 14,
  1948, New York City, A.
Gilbert, J. Abnormal Is Not Courage, The.
Gordon, A. Question Not.
Jonson, B. On Playwright.
Karr. Hubris.
Kay, J. Twelve Bar Bessie.
Kennelly. Dream of a Black Fox.
Konie, G. In the Fist of Your Hatred.
Legaré. Tallulah.
McKay, C. If We Must Die.
Moore, J. One Reason I Went to Prison.
Owen, W. Spring Offensive.
Palmer, R. F. Conchie, The.
Parker, D. Penelope.
Patterson, R. You Are the Brave.
Ralegh, S. On the Snuff of a Candle.
Rich, A. Trying to Talk with a Man.
Salter. Frost at Midnight.
Sassoon. Hero, The.
Scannell. Any Complaints?
Schwartz, R. L. Can Pigeons Be Heroes?
Skirving. Johnnie Cope.
Taylor, G. Dare to Do Right.
Tennyson, A. Charge of the Light Brigade, The.
Thomas, R. Lore.
Unknown. (My Daily Creed).
  It Can Be Done.
Very. Fear Not: For They That Be With Us.
Wagner, C. Let's Forget.
Walwicz. Daredevil.
Whittier. Barbara Frietchie.
Wright, J. Legend.
  Mad Fight Song for William S. Carpenter,
  1966, A.

Coureurs de Bois
Le Pan. Coureurs de Bois.

Courtesy
Robinson, E. Flammonde.
Sansom, A. From the Moment I Picked Up
  Your Book.

Courtiers
Donne. To Sir Henry Wotton.
Ransom, J. Vaunting Oak.
Steele, T. Epitaph: "Here lies Sir Tact, a
  diplomatic fellow."
Unknown. Mode of France, The.

Courtship
Alexie. Reservation Love Song.
Anderson, M. September Song.
Anderson-Thompkins. Broken Promises.
Angira. Request.
Angus. Doors of Sleep, The.
Anthony, M. Ugly Heart, The.
Auden. As I Walked Out One Evening.
Aytoun [or Ayton], R. Answer, The.
  Rejection, The.
  Song: "What means this strangeness now of
  late."
  To His Coy Mistress.
  Upon His Unconstant Mistress.
Baillie, J. Song: Woo'd and married and a'.
Barnes, W. Bit o' Sly Coorten, A.
  White an' Blue.
Behn, A. To Lysander.
Betjeman. Subaltern's Love-Song, A.
Blake, W. How Sweet I Roamed [or Roam'd]
  from Field to Field.
  Love's Secret.
Blamire. Auld Robin Forbes.
Brooks, G. Lovely Love, A.
Brooks, S. Some of These Days.
Brown, S. Scotty Has His Say.
Browning, E. Lord Walter's Wife.

Man's Requirements, A.
Year's Spinning, A.
Burns, R.   Comin[g] thro' [or through] the Rye.
  Duncan Gray.
  Halloween.
  Mary Morison.
  Whistle, and I'll Come to You, My Lad.
Caesar.   Too Many Rings Around Rosie.
Calverley.   In the Gloaming.
Campbell, T.   Freedom and Love.
Campion, T.   I Care Not for These Ladies.
  Now Winter Nights Enlarge.
  Shall I Come, Sweet Love.
  Think'st thou to seduce me then.
  Thus I Resolve.
  What Fair[e] Pomp[e].
Carew, T.   Boldness[e] in Love.
  To a Lady That Desired I Would Love Her.
  To A. L.; Persuasions [or Perswasions] to Love.
Carey, H.   Roger and Dolly.
Carmichael, H.   Don't Forget to Say No, Baby.
Carmichael, R.   Young Lass's Soliloquy, A.
Chaucer.   Catalogue of the Birds.
  Complaint of Troilus, The.
  Love Unfeigned.
  Now Welcom[e], Somer [or Summer].
  Rondel: "And whan this werk al brought was to
    an ende."
  Song of Troylus, The.
  To Rosamounde.
Chippewa Oral Tradition.   Love-Charm Song.
Chudleigh.   Song: "Why Damon, why, why,
  why so pressing?"
Cohan.   Twentieth-Century Love.
Cook, E.   Song of the Ugly Maiden.
Corso.   Love Poem for Three for Kaye & Me.
  Marriage.
Coward.   Irish Song [Rosie O'Grady].
Craighead, L.   Whole Truth So Help Me God—
  Also Known as the Gettin' Rid of Nigguz
  Business.
Crawley, W.   Poetry for the Goddess.
Dante Alighieri.   New Love and the Gentle
  Heart.
Davies, S.   Faith (wench) I cannot court thy
  sprightly eyes.
De la Mare.   Some One.
Delmore, A.   Girl by the River, The.
DeSylva, B. G.   I'll Say She Does.
Dodsley.   Progress of Love, The.
Donne.   Prohibition, The.
Dove, R.   Adolescence—III.
  Courtship.
Drummond, W.   All Changeth.
Du Bois.   Song: "Scholar first my Love
  implor'd, A."
Duffy, M.   Semi-Skilled Lover.
Edwards, G.   By the Light of the Silvery Moon.
Elmusa.   Bookishness.
"Ephelia."   On a Bashful Shepherd.
Fields, D.   Have Feet, Will Dance.
Garrigue.   Cracked Looking Glass.
  Grenoble Café.
  To Speak of My Influences.
Gay, J.   To a Young Lady, with Some Lampreys.
Gershwin.   Embraceable You.
Gershwin, G.
Gilbert, S.   Ferdinando and Elvira; or, The
  Gentle Pieman.
Godfrey.   Our Lady.
Greger.   Penguin Jane Austen, The.
Grimké, A.   Caprichosa.
Hall, J.   Call, The.
Hammerstein.   Surrey with the Fringe on Top,
  The.
Hands, E.   Favourite Swain, The.
  Lob's Courtship.
  Perplexity: A Poem.
  Widower's Courtship, The.
Harbach, O.   Let's Begin.
  Poor Pierrot.
Hardy, T.   Epitaph on a Pessimist.
Harland-Watts, J.   Let It Be Known.
Heard, J.   To Clements' Ferry.
Hecht, A.   Ghost in the Martini, The.
  Samuel Sewall.

Hein, S.   He's a Cousin of Mine.
Herrick.   Chop-Cherry.
  Corinna's Going a-Maying.
  To the Virgins, to Make Much of Time.
  Up Tail[e]s All.
Holmes, O.   Ballad of the Oysterman, The.
Hookes.   To Amanda Walking in the Garden.
Hughes, L.   Up-Beat.
Hupfeld, H.   Are You Makin' Any Money?
Jerome, W.   Row, Row, Row.
Jolson, A.   I'll Say She Does.
Jonson, B.   Song: To Celia.
Kahn, G.   I'll Say She Does.
Keats.   To———: "Had I a man's fair form,
  then might my sighs."
  Where Be You [or Ye] Going, You [or Ye]
    Devon Maid?
Kern, J.   Let's Begin.
  Poor Pierrot.
Komunyakaa.   Thorn Merchant's Mistress, The.
Lane, B.   Have Feet, Will Dance.
Larcom.   Little Cavalier, A.
Lawrence, D.   Cherry Robbers.
Leapor.   Strephon to Celia.
Lear, E.   Courtship of the Yonghy-Bonghy-Bo,
  The.
Livingstone, D.   One Time.
Loesser.   Luck, Be a Lady.
  Murder, He Says.
MacCaig.   Wild Oats.
Mack, C.   He's a Cousin of Mine.
Madden, E.   By the Light of the Silvery Moon.
Madhubuti.   My Brothers.
"Malley."   Boult to Marina.
  Perspective Lovesong.
Marlowe.   Passionate Shepherd To His Love,
  The.
Marvell.   To His Coy Mistress.
McDaniel, W.   Realist of 1939–40, A.
Meredith, G.   Love in the Valley.
Merrill, S.   Ballade of the Chinese Lover.
Miller, E.   Another Love Affair/Another Poem.
Monaco, J.   Row, Row, Row.
  You're Gonna Lose Your Gal.
Monck.   On a Romantic Lady.
Montagu, L.   'Between your sheets.'
  Answer to a Love-Letter in Verse, An.
  Lady's Resolve, The.
  To a Lady Making Love.
Moore, T.   Time I've Lost in Wooing, The.
Mother Goose.   Frog He Would A-Wooing
  Go, A.
Naden.   Love Versus Learning.
Nairne.   Heiress, The.
  Laird o' Cockpen, The.
North, D.   Platonic.
Novello, I.   And Her Mother Came Too.
O'Hara, G.   K-K-K-Katy.
Palmer, O.   Wasting Time.
Parker, D.   One Perfect Rose.
  Unfortunate Coincidence.
Patchen.   Figure Motioned with Its Mangled
  Hand Toward the Wall Behind It, The.
  We Go Out Together.
Pearlberg, G. G.   Sailor.
Philips, K.   Answer to Another Persuading a
  Lady to Marriage, An.
Porter, C.   Brush Up Your Shakespeare.
  Red, Hot and Blue.
Posamentier, E.   Hungarian Medical Student,
  The: 1928.
Pound, E.   River-Merchant's Wife: A Letter,
  The.
Prior.   Les Estreines.
  Ode, An: "Merchant, to secure his treasure,
  The."
Ralegh, S.   Nymph's [or Nimphs] Reply to the
  Shepherd [or Sheepheard], The.
  Sir Walter Ralegh to the Queen.
Ramsay, A.   Polwart on the Green.
Rankin, J.   Man Is Following Me, A.
Ransom, J.   Piazza Piece.
Richards, L.   Antonio.
Roethke.   For an Amorous Lady.
Rossetti, C.   Bride Song.
  Cousin Kate.

No, Thank You, John.
Noble Sisters.
Triad, A.
Rowe, E.   To Orestes.
Safie, D.   Danger, Men in Trees.
Salter.   Young Girl Peeling Apples.
Scott, A.   Return Thee, Heart.
Sedley.   Song: "Love still has something of the
  sea."
Smith, C.   He's a Cousin of Mine.
  On the Aphorism "L'Amitié est l'Amour sans
  Ailes."
  Stanzas: "Ah! think'st thou, Laura, then, that
  wealth."
Soto.   Oranges.
  Trees that Change Our Lives.
Stevenson, R.   Song of a Traveller, The.
Stirling, S.   Echo, An.
Strand.   Courtship.
Suckling, S.   Barley-Break , A.
  Love's Siege.
  Loving and Beloved.
  Song: "I prithee spare me, gentle boy."
  Sonnet: "Of thee, kind boy, I ask no red and
  white."
Sullivan, J.   Sagimusume: The White Heron
  Maiden.
Surrey.   "Love, That Doth Reign and Live
  Within My Thought."
Titherage.   And Her Mother Came Too.
Toure, A.   Frontier of Rage, The.
Unknown.   Bailiff's Daughter of Islington, The.
  Bonny Barbara Allan ("In Scarlet Town where I
  was born").
  Do you carrot all for me?
  Dowie Dens of Yarrow, The.
  Four on a Sidewalk.
  Lord Thomas and Fair Annet.
  Polly Perkins.
  Visit, The.
Wade-Gayles.   Inquisition.
Weill, K.   September Song.
Whalen.   Slop Barrel, The.
Whitman, W.   Dalliance of the Eagles, The.
Williams, W.   First Praise.
Willis, N.   City Lyrics.
Wroth [or Wroath].   Song: "Love what art thou?
  A vain thought."
Wyatt, S.   Long love that in my thought doth
  harbo[u]r, The.
  Madam, Withouten Many Words.
Yeats.   Cap and Bells, The.
Youmans, V.   Too Many Rings Around Rosie.
Young, J.   You're Gonna Lose Your Gal.
Zarzyski.   How Near Vietnam Came to Us.

Cousins
Browning, E.   Aurora Leigh.
  First Book: Young Aurora's Fostermother.
  Sweetness of England, The.
Clanchy, K.   For a Wedding.
Eliot, T.   Cousin Nancy.
Hein, S.   He's a Cousin of Mine.
Jordan, J.   Through These Halls.
Mack, C.   He's a Cousin of Mine.
Paino.   Matter of Division, A.
Smith, C.   He's a Cousin of Mine.
Winder.   On Fourteen Maple Street.

Coventry, England
Larkin, P.   I Remember, I Remember.

Cowardice and Cowards
Ammons, A. R.   Coward.
Benjamin, P.   Press On.
Bhatt.   Go To Ahmedabad.
Crosland.   White Feather Legion, The.
Dalton, A.   Kitchen Beast.
Eliot, T.   Gerontion.
  Love Song of J. Alfred Prufrock, The.
France, L.   Body Language.
Ingalls, J.   Apprehension.
Lawrence, D.   Willy Wet-Leg.
Levine, P.   Heaven.

Cowboys
Abrahams, M.   Rag Time Cowboy Joe.
Alexander, E.   Deadwood Dick.

Campbell, D.   Song for the Cattle.
Causley.   Cowboy Song.
Clarke, G.   Rag Time Cowboy Joe.
Dorn, E.   Vaquero.
Fletcher, C.   High-loping Cowboy, The.
Hopkins, L.   Nat Love: Black Cowboy.
Huidobro.   Cow Boy.
Major, C.   I Was Looking for the University.
McDonald, W.   Honky-Tonk Blues.
  Songs We Fought For, The.
McElroy, C.   Mae West Chats It Up with Bessie
  Smith.
Mercer, J.   I'm an Old Cowhand.
Michie.   Arizona Nature Myth.
Muir, L.   Rag Time Cowboy Joe.
Reed, I.   I Am a Cowboy in the Boat of Ra.
Smith, W.   Closing of the Rodeo, The.
Swenson, M.   Bronco Busting, Event #1.
Tomlinson, C.   At Barstow.
Unknown.   Buffalo Skinners, The.
  Cowboy Sayings.
  Cowboy's Lament, The.
Warren, R.   Rattlesnake Country.

Cowper, William
Browning, E.   Cowper's Grave.

Cows
Burgess, F.   Cinq Ans Après.
  Purple Cow, The.
Carruth, H.   Cows at Night, The.
Clarke, A.   Lost Heifer, The.
Clifton, L.   My Dream About the Cows.
Crozier, A.   Heifer, The.
Frost, R.   Cow in Apple Time, The.
Graves, R.   Dead Cow Farm.
Hands, E.   Written, Originally Extempore, on
  Seeing a Mad Heifer Run through the Village.
Herrick.   Supreme Fortune Falls Soonest.
Hillyer.   Moo!
Johnson, J.   Music for the Cows.
Kinnell.   Freedom, New Hampshire.
Kocan.   Cows.
MacCaig.   Fetching Cows.
McNair.   Mina Bell's Cows.
Moore, T.   Response to Rimbaud's Later
  Manner.
Musgrave.   I Am Not a Conspiracy Everything
  Is Not Paranoid the Drug Enforcement
  Administration Is Not Everywhere.
Nash, O.   Cow, The.
Nicholson, N.   Tune the Old Cow Died of, The.
O'Donoghue, B.   Weakness, The.
Porteous.   Calf.
Rector.   My Grandfather Always Promised Us.
Reeves, J.   Cows.
Roberson.   Blue Horses.
Roberts, E.   Milking Time.
Roethke.   Cow, The.
Scully, J.   Midsummer.
Stern, G.   Cow Worship.
Stevenson, R.   Cow, The.
Tomlinson, C.   Macduff.
Unknown.   Sukey [or Suky], you shall be my
  wife.
Wells, A.   Cow-Boy's Song, The.
White, E.   Red Cow Is Dead, The.
Young, A.   Man and Cows.

Coyote (mythology)
Blue Cloud.   Sweat Song.
Ortiz.   Telling About Coyote.
Silko.   Toe'osh; a Laguna Coyote Story.

Coyotes
Blue Cloud.   Sweat Song.
Goodtimes.   Roadkill Coyote.
Hannon.   Beneath Cold Mountain.
Navajo Oral Tradition.   Coyote, Skunk, and the
  Prairie Dogs.
Silko.   Toe'osh; a Laguna Coyote Story.
Warren, R.   Arizona Midnight.
Whyte-Melville.   Coyotes.

Crab Apple Trees and Crab Apples
Van Walleghen.   Crabapples.

Crabbe, George
Robinson, E.   George Crabbe.

Crabs and Crabbing
Atwood.   Landcrab I.

Landcrab II.
Dove, A.   Crab.
Fuller, R.   Crustaceans.
Gotera.   Pacific Crossing.
Magowan.   Paros.
Saleh.   Crabs.
Szporluk.   Duressor.
Young, A.   Dead Crab, The.
See also **Hermit Crabs; Horseshoe Crabs**

Craftsmanship
Garrett, E.   Unguentarium.
Guevara, M.   Miniaturist, The.
Kirkup.   Correct Compassion, A.
Nye, N.   Man Who Makes Brooms, The.
Sackville-West.   Craftsmen.
Snyder, G.   Axe Handles.
Tohe.   She Was Telling It This Way.

Crane, Hart
Doty, M.   Almost Blue.
Wheelwright.   Fish Food.

Cranes (ornithology)
Faust, H.   Six Cranes at Dusk.
Heyen.   Crane in Reeds.
Young, D.   White Crane.

Cranmer, Thomas
Sisson.   Cranmer.
Smith, S.   Admire Cranmer!

Crashaw, Richard
Cowley, A.   On the Death of Mr. Crashaw.

Crazy Horse (Oglala Sioux Chief)
Blue Cloud.   Crazy Horse Monument.
Clifton, L.   Death of Crazy Horse, The.
Stafford, W.   Report to Crazy Horse.
  Sound from the Earth, A.

Creation
Addison, J.   Ode: "Spacious firmament on high,
  The."
Alexander, C.   All Things Bright and Beautiful.
Amadiume.   Creation.
Apuleius, L.   I who am Nature, mother of all.
Ballou, S.   Almighty God in Being Was.
Berman, C.   Poem for the Shechina.
Blood, B.   Late.
Brewster, M.   Stately Structure of This Earth,
  The.
Browning, R.   Johannes Agricola in Meditation.
Bryant, W.   Song of the Stars.
Caedmon.   Caedmon's Hymn.
Ceravolo.   Data.
Chesterton, G.   Donkey, The.
Clare, J.   I Feel I Am.
Clifton, L.   Earth is a living thing, The.
Copus, J.   Making of Eve, The.
Couzyn.   Creation.
  Mystery, The.
De la Mare.   Scribe, The.
Di Prima.   Loba au bout.
Doyle, S.   To an Undiscerning Critic.
Drake, N.   Foley Artist, The.
Eclipse.   Cicada.
Emerson, R.   Rhodora, The [On Being Asked
  Whence Is the Flower].
Essbaum, J.   In the Beginning.
Everson, W.   South Coast, The.
Fabian, C.   On reading the new physics—
  Creation and Cosmology.
Fordham.   Creation.
Fuller, J.   Whole New Scene, A.
Gidlow.   Creed for Free Women, A.
Glück, L.   Lamentations.
Goodtimes.   Sartor Resartus.
Gottlieb, A.   Meditation on the Feminine Nature
  of Shekinah, A.
Gould, J.   Coyotismo.
Grahn.   Grand Grand Mother is returning.
Grainger, J.   Solitude: An Ode.
Graves, R.   Dead Cow Farm.
Griffin, S.   Our Mother.
Gurr.   Creation.
Hamburger, M.   Treblinka.
Hardy, J.   Computer Aided Design: Creation.
Harjo, J.   Perhaps the World Ends Here.
Harvey, A.   Prayer to the Divine Mother, A.
Herbert, G.   Man.
  Pulley, The.

Herrick.   Eye, The.
Hildebrandt, Z.   In Hecate's Garden.
  Kali.
Hill, G.   Genesis.
Hillman.   Formation of Soils, The.
Hollander, J.   What the Lovers in the Old Songs
  Thought.
Hollander, V.   Rosh Chodesh Tisheri.
Hoogerhuis.   Search, The.
Howe, J.   Kosmos.
Hughes, T.   Crow's First Lesson.
Hummell, A.   Sculpture Garden.
Ironbiter, S.   Song to the Mother of the World.
Jackson, A.   Transformable Prophecy.
Jennings, E.   In Praise of Creation.
Johnson, J.   Creation, The.
Karade, B.   Yemoja.
Kayo.   War.
Kilmer, J.   Trees.
Klugman, S.   God's Body.
Kreymborg.   Ants.
Lawrence, D.   Let There Be Light!
Levine, P.   Rain Downriver.
Logghe.   Madonna of the Peaches.
Longfellow, H.   Kéramos.
Macpherson, J.   Fisherman, The.
McVeigh, J.   Eve Falling.
Meador, B.   Fields Belong to Woman, The.
Melville, H.   Venice.
Miller, A.   Mulch.
Monaghan.   Persephone's Journey.
Moore, M.   Book of How, The.
Navajo Oral Tradition.   Creation of the Earth,
  The.
Ndu.   Udude.
Nemerov.   Creation Myth on a Moebius Band.
O'Shaughnessy, A.   Ode: "We are the music-
  makers."
Olson, T.   Hypothesis.
Ormsby, E.   Origins.
Ortiz.   Creation.
Pastan.   Imperfect Paradise, The.
Piatt, S.   If I Had Made the World.
Reis, P.   Ancient Ones, The.
Rossetti, D.   On the Painter Val Prinsep.
Rukeyser, M.   Gyroscope, The.
  He Had a Quality of Growth.
Seidman.   Making of Color, The.
Shange.   We Need a God Who Bleeds Now.
Simic.   Austerities.
Southwell.   Vale of Tear[e]s, A.
Starhawk.   Demeter's Song.
Stevens, W.   Bowl.
Stevenson, A.   Spirit Is Too Blunt an Instrument,
  The.
Swinburne.   Aholibah.
Thomas, R.   Echoes.
Tuckerman, F.   Sonnets: "Starry flower, the
  flower-like stars that fade, The."
Unknown.   Holy Goddess Tellus.
Valéry.   Crusoe.
Very.   Origin of Man, I, The.
Villanueva, A.   Planet Earth Speaks, The.
Warren, R.   Where the Slow Fig's Purple Sloth.
Wilbur.   On the Marginal Way.
  Praise in Summer.
Winter, M.   In the Beginning.
Woody.   Girlfriends, The.
Yeats.   Before the World Was Made.
  Rose of the World, The.
See also **Cosmology**

Creativity
Allston.   Art.
Berssenbrugge.   Duration of Water.
Bidart.   For the Twentieth Century.
Brown, L.   Birth of the Blues, The.
Creeley.   Figures, The.
Ginsberg, A.   Mescaline.
Hovey.   Accident in Art.
Levertov.   For Those Whom the Gods Love
  Less.
  To the Muse.
Snodgrass, W.   Matisse: "The Red Studio."

Creatures
Alexander, C.   All Things Bright and Beautiful.
Brown, M.   Little Black Bug.

Morgan, E.   First Men on Mercury, The.
Shenstone.   To the Virtuosos.
Stephens, J.   Little Things.
Yeats.   High Talk.
See also **Animals**

Cremation
Bibbins, M.   Mud.
Fletcher, L.   Higashiyama Crematorium, November 6, 1983.
Fogel, E.   Shipment to Maidanek.
Hesketh.   Dilemma.
Jeffers, R.   Cremation.
Ormsby, F.   Passing the Crematorium.
Ramanujan.   Death and the Good Citizen.
Service.   Cremation of Sam McGee, The.
Williams, W.   Complete Destruction.

Crete
Constantine, D.   Lasithi.
Corso.   Paranoia in Crete.
Duran, J.   Time Zones.
Vitiello.   Letter to a Cretan Flute-Maker.

Cricket (game)
Lang, A.   Brahma.
Moore, E.   Victory Calypso, Lord's 1950.
Petty.   There's a Breathless Hush.
Ross, A.   Cricket at Oxford.
Sassoon.   Blues at Lord's, The.
Thompson, F.   At Lord's.
Wodehouse, P.   Outcast, The.

Crickets
Bly, R.   Listening to a Cricket in the Wainscoting.
Etter.   Roma Higgins.
Heath-Stubbs.   Winter Cricket.
Hunt, L.   To the Grasshopper and the Cricket.
Izumi.   In the Autumn, on Retreat at a Mountain Temple.
Keats.   On the Grasshopper and [the] Cricket.
Klein, A.   Rocking Chair, The.
Lear, E.   Incidents in the Life of My Uncle Arly.
Lovelace, R.   Ant, The.
McCord, D.   Crickets.
Merwin, W. S.   Black Jewel, The.
Salazar.   Cricket at Central California Women's Facility.
Sandburg, C.   Splinter.
Thomas, E.   Cricket Kept the House, The.
Tuckerman, F.   Cricket, The.

Crime and Criminals
Atkins.   Late Bus (After a Series of Hold-Ups).
Atwood.   Marrying the Hangman.
Bart, L.   Fings Ain't Wot They Used t'Be.
Reviewing the Situation.
Bernstein, L.   Gee, Officer Krupke.
Bishop, E.   Burglar of Babylon, The.
Butts, A.   Poe Story, A.
Caesar.   Spanish Jake.
Calloway, C.   Minnie, the Moocher.
Eliot, T.   Macavity: The Mystery Cat.
Enright, D.   Since Then.
Fisher, J.   Life, A.
Gaskill, C.   Minnie, the Moocher.
Gay, J.   Newgate's Garland.
Ginsberg, A.   Mugging.
Hamer.   Line Up.
Hardy, T.   In the Servants' Quarters.
Harington [or Harrington].   Of honest Theft. To my good friend Master Samuel Daniel.
Hattersley, G.   Remembering Dennis's Eyes.
Henley, W.   Villon's Straight Tip to All Cross Coves.
Kingston, M.   Absorption of Rock.
Lerner, S.   Spanish Jake.
Matthews, W.   Old Folsom Prison.
McGuire.   Streets of Forbes, The.
Miller, P.   Capture of Edwin Alonzo Boyd, The.
Mills, I.   Minnie, the Moocher.
Mother Goose.   Tarts, The.
Tom, Tom, the Piper's Son.
Muldoon, P.   More a Man Has the More a Man Wants, The.
Newbolt.   He Fell among Thieves.

Noyes, A.   Highwayman, The.
Pope, A.   Hampton Court.
Rape of the Lock, The; an Heroi-Comical Poem.
Toilet, The.
Voyage on the Thames, The.
Ransome-Davies.   Raymond Chandler: The Big Sleep.
Raworth.   Collapsible.
Future Models May Have Infra-Red Sensors.
Sandburg, C.   Cahoots.
Service.   Shooting of Dan McGrew, The.
Sondheim.   Gee, Officer Krupke.
Stephens, M.   Elegy for Llywelyn Humphries.
Tennyson, A.   Rizpah.
Unknown.   Claude Allen.
Crafty Farmer, The.
Geordie [An Old Ballad].
Highwayman, The.
Jesse James.
John Gilbert Was a Bushranger.
Johnie Armstrong.
Wagoner, D.   Shooting of John Dillinger outside the Biograph Theater July 22, 1934, The.
Walsh, C.   Nearly Nowhere.
Warren, R.   Crime.
Whittier.   Slave-Ships, The.
See also **Prisons and Prisoners**

Crimean War
Forster, W.   Sonnet on the Crimean War.
Landor, W.   Crimean Heroes, The.
Tennyson, A.   Charge of the Light Brigade, The.
Thackeray.   Due of the Dead, The.

Criticism and Critics
Barnett, A.   Critique.
Belloc.   Lines to a Don.
Browning, R.   Dialogue between Father and Daughter.
Bukowski.   Black Poets, The.
Burrell.   School for Satire, The.
Ciardi.   To a Reviewer Who Admired My Book.
Coleridge, S.   Modern Critics.
Cope, W.   Emily Dickinson.
Serious Concerns.
Cullen, C.   To Certain Critics.
Davie.   Rejoinder to a Critic.
Doyle, S.   To An Undiscerning Critic.
Drayton.   His Defence Against the Idle Critic.
Dunbar, P.   To a Captious Critic.
Durem.   I Know I'm Not Sufficiently Obscure.
Elliott, E.   Criticism.
Enright, D.   Evil Days, The.
Ewart.   Black Box, The.
Falconar, M.   Prefatory Epistle, A.
Fields, J.   Owl-Critic, The.
Greenwell, D.   Saturday Review, The.
Hartnett.   Man Who Wrote Yeats, the Man Who Wrote Mozart, The.
Hemingway.   Valentine.
Herrick.   To Critic[k]s.
To the Detracter.
Upon the Same.
Hewitt, J.   Because I Paced My Thought.
Hood, T.   Poet's Fate, The.
Johnson, S.   Prologue to Hugh Kelly's *A Word to the Wise*.
Jonson, B.   Ode to Himself[e].
To Censorious Courtling.
To Fool or Knave.
To John Donne.
To My Mere English Censurer.
Kirby, D.   Dear Derrida.
Kunitz, S.   Choice of Weapons, A.
Landor, W.   Critic, A.
Lehman.   One Size Fits All: a Critical Essay.
Maule.   To Cotton Mather, from a Quaker.
Meredith, G.   Camelus Saltat.
Camelus Saltat: Continued.
Nemerov.   On Certain Wits.
To My Least Favorite Reviewer.
O'Hara, F.   Answer to Voznesensky and Evtushenko.
Osterhaus, J.   Gambier.

Piercy.   Letter to be Disguised as a Gas Bill.
Pope, A.   Art of Poetry, The.
Bookful Blockhead, The.
Essay on Criticism.
On Dennis.
Plain Fools.
Servile Herd, The.
Porter, P.   St Cecilia's Day Epigram.
Randall, D.   Black Poet, White Critic.
Rochester, J.   Song: "Give me leave to rail at you."
Shelley, P.   Lines to a Reviewer.
Starbuck, G.   On First Looking in on Blodgett's Keats's "Chapman's Homer."
Swift, J.   Epigram on Scolding, An.
Tennyson, A.   Hendecasyllabics.
Popular.
To Christopher North.
Whalen.   Chanson d'Outre Tombe.
Williams, C.   Critic, The.
Yeats.   On Those That Hated "The Playboy of the Western World" 1907.
To a Poet, Who Would Have Me Praise Certain Bad Poets, Imitators of His and Mine.

Crockett, Davy (David Crockett) (1786-1836)
Unknown.   Davy Crockett.

Crocodiles
Nash, O.   Purist, The.
Rossetti, C.   My Dream.
Speyer.   To a Song of Sappho Discovered in Egypt.
Wells, A.   Considerate Crocodile, The.
See also **Alligators**

Crocuses
Harper, F.   Crocuses, The.

Cromwell, Oliver
Brome.   On Sir G. B. his defeat.
Lovelace, R.   Mock Song, A.
Marvell.   First Anniversary of the Government under His Highness the Lord Protector, 1655, The.
Horatian Ode upon Cromwell's Return from Ireland, An.
Milton.   To the Lord General Cromwell.
Wright, C.   State of Preservation.
Yeats.   Curse of Cromwell, The.

Croquet
MacNeice.   Soap Suds.

Cross, The
Cooper, R.   To See the Cross at Christmas.
Everson, W.   Making of the Cross, The.
Garrett, E.   Lost Property.
Herrick.   Crosses.
MacCaig.   Celtic Cross.
Sanchez, S.   Father and Daughter.
Sexton.   With Mercy for the Greedy.
Tate, A.   Cross, The.
See also **Crucifixion, The**

Crowds
Alvi, M.   Houdini.
Berlin.   Manhattan Madness.
Brontë, C.   Obscure and little seen my way.
Hoffman, D.   Center of Attention, The.
Hughes, L.   Subway Rush Hour.
Lowell, J.   Street, The.
Mew.   Fame.
Millis, C.   IRT at Rush Hour, The.
Perkins, S.   Common Road, The.
Pound, E.   In a Station of the Metro.
Romtvedt.   Glass Canyons.
Sandburg, C.   I Am the People, the Mob.
Sondheim.   Another Hundred People.
Williams, W.   At the Ball Game.

Crowns
Coleridge, M.   Moment, A.
Mortal Combat.
Marvell.   Coronet, The.

Crows
Berger, B.   Transmigration.
Chippewa Oral Tradition.   Song of the Crows.
Clarke, P.   In Air.
Digby, J.   Sooner or Later.

Eady. Crows in a Strong Wind.
Frost, R. Dust of Snow.
Glück, R. Pasolini.
Graham, J. Thinking.
Grenier. Crow.
Hughes, T. Crow's Theology.
Lindsay, N. Two Old Crows.
MacCaig. Solitary crow.
Markus, P. Shooting Crows.
McCord, D. Crows.
Menai. Rooks: December.
Ortiz. Telling About Coyote.
Reese, L. Crows.
Roethke. Night Crow.
Romo-Carmona, M. Crows.
Shapiro, K. Crossing Lincoln Park.
Silko. Preparations.
Sorley. Rooks.
Unknown. Twa Corbies, The.
Volkman. Seasonal.

Crucifixion, The
Alabaster. Of the Reed That the Jews Set in
Our Saviour's Hand.
Upon the Ensigns of Christ's Crucifying.
Auden. Shield of Achilles, The.
Barnes, D. Chuang Tzu and Hui Tzu*.
Beaumont, J. Garden, The.
Bevington, L. Dreamers?
Borges. John 1:14 (1964).
Carmichael, A. Yet Listen Now.
Carruth, H. Crucifixion.
Emergency Haying.
Causley. I Am the Great Sun.
Colman, H. On the Inscription Over the Head
of Christ on the Cross.
On the Strange Apparitions at Christ's Death.
Cowley, A. Christ's Passion.
Crashaw. To Our Blessed Lord upon the Choice
of His Sepulchre.
Cullen, C. Simon the Cyrenian Speaks.
Donne. Good Friday [*or* Goodfriday], 1613.
Riding Westward.
Everson, W. Zone of Death.
Fletcher, P. Ocean of Light.
Fordham. Crucifixion, The.
Uranne.
Gascoyne. Tenebrae.
Herbert, G. Sacrifice, The.
Herrick. Cross-tree, The.
His Saviour[']s Words, Going to the Cross[e].
Observation.
Hill, G. Canticle for Good Friday.
Hughes, T. God, A.
Kates. No Altarpiece.
Keble. Fill High the Bowl.
Lanier, S. Ballad of Trees and the Master, A.
Leax. That Day.
Levertov. Ikon: The Harrowing of Hell.
Milman. Crucifixion, The.
Muir, E. Killing, The.
Patchen. Pastoral: "Dove walks with sticky feet,
The."
Prince, F. Soldiers Bathing.
Quarles. Crucified.
They Gave Him Vinegar and Gall (Matt. 27)
and Wine Mingled with Myrrh (Mark 15).
Robinson, E. Calvary.
Rossetti, C. Good Friday.
Rukeyser, M. Gates, The.
Sandburg, C. Early Lynching.
Sexton. In the Deep Museum.
Sisson. Easter.
Sitwell, D. Still Falls the Rain.
Studdert-Kennedy. Indifference.
Thompson, P. Death and Resurrection.
Unknown. 'O, My Heart Is Woe.'
He Never Said a Mumblin' Word.
Hours of the Passion, The.
Now Goeth [*or* goth *or* goothe] Sun [*or* Sonne
or Sunne] under Wood.
Seven Virgins, The.
Were You There When They Crucified My
Lord?
York Play of the Crucifixion, The.
Very. Cross, The.
Warton, T. Ode on the Passion.

Watts, I. Hymn: "When I survey the wondrous
cross."
Look on Him Whom They Pierced, and Mourn.
Yeats. "Calvary."
See also **Cross, The; Calvary**

Cruelty
Ager, M. Hard-Hearted Hannah (The Vamp of
Savannah).
Louisville Lou (The Vampin' Lady).
Ahlert, F. Mean to Me.
Allen, S. Moment Please, A.
Bigelow, B.
Bloom, R. Good for Nothin' Joe.
Borawski. Cheers, Cheers for Old Cha Cha Ass.
Carew, T. Looking-Glass, A.
Ciardi. Faces.
Cleary, B. Slouch.
Collier, M. Robert Wilson.
Creeley. Hill, The.
Delgado, J. Lame Boy Returns, The.
Dickey, W. Memoranda.
Dixon, S. Request of Alexis, The.
Fain, S. Was That the Human Thing to Do?
Herrick. Cruelties.
Holden, J. Liberace.
Jackson, G. Some of Betty's Story Round 1850.
Jarrell. Snow-Leopard, The.
Johnston, E. Address to Nature on its Cruelty,
An.
Koehler, T. Good for Nothin' Joe.
Lane, P. On Being Head of the English
Department.
Lawrence, D. Cherry Robbers.
Levertov. Innocent, The.
Lovelace, R. La Bourbon, A.
Lumsden, R. Show and Tell.
Michelson, R. Interrogation.
Morris, W. Haystack in the Floods, The.
Orfalea, G. Age of Cruelty, The.
Parker, A. Cruelty, the Vandals Say.
Piercy. Friend, The.
Reynolds, S. F. Whipping, The.
Shange. It's Not so Good to be Born a Girl/
Sometimes.
Smith, S. How Cruel Is the Story of Eve.
Swinburne. Satia Te Sanguine.
Tsvetayeva [*or* Tsvetaeva]. I know the truth—
give up all other truths!
Turk, R. Mean to Me.
Ulku, A. History.
Wetzsteon. Three Songs.

Cruelty to Animals
Addonizio. Bird.
Cave. Poem for Children, A; or, On Cruelty to
the Irrational Creation.
Clare, J. Badger.
Derricotte. From a Letter: About Snow.
Espada. Do Not Put Dead Monkeys in the
Freezer.
Hodgson, R. Bells of Heaven, The.
Kinnell. Bear, The.
Porcupine, The.
Livingstone, D. Bad Run at King's Rest.
McKuen. Thoughts on Capital Punishment.
Merwin, W. S. Fly.
Prior. Epigram: "Thy nags (the leanest things
alive)."
Stephens, J. Snare, The.
Straus, M. Neuroanatomy Summer.
Thomas, E. Gallows, The.

Crum, William
Moorer. Crum Appointment, The.

Crusades
Chesterton, G. Lepanto.

Crystals
Bishop, E. Vague Poem.
MacDiarmid, H. Crystals like Blood.

Cuba
Baraka. Cuba Libre.
Behar, R. Jewish Cemetery in Guanabacoa,
The.
Campo. Belonging.
My Voice.
Castillo, S. Cuba.
En el Sol de Mi Barrio.

Monday Night at Pedro's.
Rincón.
Esteves. 1st Poem for Cuba.
For Fidel Castro.
Hupfeld, H. When Yuba Plays the Rumba on
the Tuba.
Lowell, R. Fall 1961.
Padilla. Landscapes.
Roberts, W. On a Monument to Martí.
Rollings. For Dear Life.
Suárez, V. Cuban-American Gothic.
Rice Comes to El Volcán.
Song for the Sugar Cane.
Song to the Banyan.

Cuchulain (Irish legendary hero)
Yeats. Cuchulain Comforted.

Cuckoldry and Cuckolds
Bishop, M. My Friend the Cuckold.
Montagu, L. Epitaph: "Here lies John Hughes
and Sarah Drew."
Unknown. Unfortunate Miller; or, The Country
Lasses Witty Invention, The.
See also **Adultery and Adulterers**

Cuckoos
Alcuin. Lament for the Cuckoo.
Campbell, D. Pallid Cuckoo.
Davies, W. Great Time, A.
Desnos. Cuckoo.
Heywood, J. Of Use.
Hopkins, G. Cuckoo, The.
McAuley, J. Late Winter.
Ray, H. Cuckoo Song.
Spenser. Merry Cuckoo, The.
Townsend, F. To the Cuckoo.
Unknown. Cuckoo Song, The.
Cuckoo, The.
Koocoo, The.
Sumer Is Icumen [*or* Ycomen] In.
Wee Jenny Wren, The.
Wordsworth, W. To the Cuckoo.

Cucumbers
Hikmet. Cucumber, The.
Unknown. Cautionary Limerick.

Culture
Abad, G. Jeepney.
Anzaldúa. Cultures.
Bell, M. Footnote to Enright's "Apocalypse."
Blanco, R. Letter to El Flaco on His Birthday.
Burns, J. Revisionism.
Cabico, R. Check One.
Gameboy.
Campo. Belonging.
Collins, K. I Am Africa.
Corn. Contemporary Culture and the Letter
"K."
Davie. Meeting of Cultures, A.
de Aerenlund, C. Cuando el tecolote canta, el
Indio muere.
DeCormier-Shekejian. Snow.
Divakaruni. Indian Movie, New Jersey.
Evasco, M. Heron-Woman.
Fenton, J. Lollipops of the Pomeranian
Baroque.
This Octopus Exploits Women.
Georgiou, E. Week in the Life of the Ethnically
Indeterminate, A.
Ginsberg, A. Studying the Signs.
Gonzales, R. Praise the Tortilla, Praise the
Menudo, Praise the Chorizo.
Gotera. Pacific Crossing.
Hewitt, J. Once Alien Here.
Hovanessian, D. Mixed Marriage.
Hufana, A. Contemporary.
Ilio, D. Marikudo in Kalibo, 1979.
Joseph, L. Curriculum Vitae.
Kessler, S. Names the Dead Speak.
Kim, M. Rose of Sharon, A.
Koch, K. You Were Wearing.
Lee, L. Cleaving, The.
Levi, S. Abbienti.
MacEwen, G. Breakfast for Barbarians, A.
"Malley." Culture as Exhibit.
Maris, H. Spiritual Song of the Aborigine.
Mayne, S. Zalman.
Meléndez. Oye Mundo/Sometimes.

Melo, M.   Red Lipstick on a Straw.
Mueller, L.   Highway Poems.
Nazareno, C.   Bohol's Tarsier Population.
Okita.   Notes for a Poem on Being Asian American.
Older.   Two Worlds.
Olson, C.   Kingfishers, The.
Opoku-Agyemang.   King Tut in America.
Posamentier, E.   Being Modern in Jerusalem.
Retallack, J.   Western CIV, 4 and 5.
Reyes, M.   San Juan.
Robles.   Manong with a Thousand Tribal Visions, The.
Rome, H.   Who Knows?
Salazar.   Taking It Back.
Shapiro, K.   Drug Store.
Smith, I.   Shall Gaelic Die?
Snyder, G.   Axe Handles.
St. Germain, S.   Cajun.
Ungria, R.   Culture Nervous.
Weaver, M.   Brooklyn.
Weems, M.   Funk.
Young-Prottengeier.   Lithuanian Grandmother.
Yuson.   Dead Center.
Zamora-Linmark.   Day 1: Portrait of the Artisit, Small-kid Time.

Cumberland, England
Nicholson, N.   To the River Duddon.

Cumberland, Virginia
Smith, D.   Cumberland Station.
Unknown.   Cumberland Gap.

Cunningham, James Vincent
Kennedy, X.   Terse Elegy for J.V. Cunningham.

Cunningham, Merce
Olson, C.   Merce of Egypt.

Cupboards
De la Mare.   Cupboard, The.

Cupid
Baillie, J.   To Cupid.
Behn, A.   On Her Loving Two Equally.
  Song: Love Armed [or Arm'd].
Bridges, R.   Eros.
Carew, T.   Song: The Willing Prisoner to His Mistress.
Drayton.   Cupid, I Hate Thee.
Elizabeth I.   When I Was Fair and Young.
Emerson, R.   Dæmonic and the Celestial Love, The.
Gay, J.   Damon and Cupid.
Greene, R.   Night Visitor, A.
Herrick.   Cheat of Cupid; or, The Ungentle Guest, The.
  How Lillies Came White.
  How Roses Came Red.
  Hymne to Love, An.
  To Oenone.
  Upon Love.
  Wounded Cupid, The.
Jonson, B.   Why I Write Not of Love.
Knox, E.   To the God of Love.
Lovelace, R.   Cupid Far Gone.
North, D.   Platonic.
Sedley.   To Cloris.
Stanley, T.   Song: "Fool, take up thy shaft again."
Suckling, S.   Metamorphosis, The.
  To B.C.

Cups
Harwood, G.   Cups.
Roberts, K.   Plastic Cup, The.
Schuyler, J.   Shimmer.
Zukofsky, L.   Shang Cup.

Curfew
Clayton, S.   Redfern at Night.
Espada.   Toque de queda: Curfew in Lawrence.
Thorpe, R.   Curfew Must Not Ring Tonight [or To-Night].

Curie, Marie
Brock-Broido.   Radiating Naïveté.
Rich, A.   Power.

Curiosity
DeSylva, B. G.   Somebody Loves Me.
Gershwin, G.   Somebody Loves Me.
Kinnell.   For Robert Frost.
MacDonald, B.   Somebody Loves Me.

Olds, S.   Connoisseuse of Slugs, The.
Reid, A.   Curiosity.
Robinson, M.   Sappho's Conjectures.

Curses
Browning, E.   Curse for a Nation, A.
Burns, R.   Epitaph on Mr. Burton.
Coleridge, S.   Rime of the Ancient Mariner, The.
Graves, R.   Travel[l]er's Curse after Misdirection[, The].
Herrick.   Curse. A Song, The.
  To the Sour[e] Reader.
Maitland, T.   Sir Thomas Maitland's Satyr upon Sir Niel Laing.
Quarles.   On Judas Iscariot.
Sedley.   On a Cock at Rochester.
Smith, S.   Thoughts about the Person from Porlock.
Stephens, J.   Glass of Beer, A.
  Odell.
Swinburne.   After Death.
Synge.   Curse, The.
Thomas, E.   Execration, The.
Unknown.   Bonny Barbara Allan ("In Scarlet Town where I was born").
  Skin the Goat's Curse on Carey.
Wright, J.   Song for the Middle of the Night, A.

Custer, George Armstrong
Alexie.   Crazy Horse Speaks.
Kelen.   Rabbit Shoeshine.

Custom
Curry.   St Kilda.
France de Bravo, B.   Unrepentant.

Cyclamen
"Field."   Cyclamens.
Lawrence, D.   Sicilian Cyclamens.

Cymon
Dryden, J.   Cymon and Iphigenia.
  Militia.

Cynicism and Cynics
Adnan.   Beirut-Hell Express, The.
Berrigan, A.   Four Minute History of Getting It Together in Order to Be Fabulous, Briefly, A.
Bukowski.   Secret, The.
Doyle, S.   To an Undiscerning Critic.
Frost, R.   Demiurge's Laugh, The.
Hardy, T.   Christmas: 1924.
  He Never Expected Much.
Hughes, J.   Knowingness.
Lowell, R.   As a Plane Tree by the Water.
McDonald, P.   Totalled.
Ojaide.   Launching Our Community Developement Fund.
Parker, D.   Certain Lady, A.
  Symptom Recital.
  Unfortunate Coincidence.
Raleigh.   Lines Suggested by an Edition of Blake's Poems.
Southey, R.   Battle of Blenheim, The.

Cypress Trees
Francis, R.   Cypresses.
Jeffers, R.   Granite and Cypress.
Kelly, R.   Life of Intimate Fleeing, A.
Lawrence, D.   Cypresses.

Czechoslovakia
Goldberg, B.   Our Father.
Harwood, L.   Czech Dream.
Hirsch, E.   Milena Jesenká.
Milosz, C.   My Faithful Mother Tongue.
Rumens.   Geography Lesson.
Walker, A.   Kiss, The.

D

Déjà Vu
Hart, L.   Where or When.
Ransom, J.   Vision by Sweetwater.

Dürer, Albrecht
Hill, N.   Dürer's 'Young Hare'
Jarrell.   Knight, Death, and the Devil, The.
"Malley."   Dürer; Innsbruck, 1495.

Dachshunds
Arnold, M.   Geist's Grave.

Daedalus
Oppen.   Daedalus: The Dirge.

Daffodils
Davies, I.   In Gardens in the Rhondda.
Herrick.   Divination by a Daffadill [or Daffodil].
  To Daffodils [or Daffadills].
Loveman.   April Rain.
Majer.   Spring.
McGrath, T.   Black Train, The.
Mother Goose.   Daffadowndilly.
Wordsworth, W.   I Wandered Lonely As a Cloud.

Daisies
Gray, J.   Poem: "Geranium, houseleek, laid in oblong beds."
Herrick.   To Daisies, Not to Shut So Soon[e].
Meynell, A.   To a Daisy.
Probyn.   Blossom.
Rossetti, C.   Where Innocent Bright-Eyed Daisies Are.
Tennyson, A.   Daisy, The.
Williams, H.   Sonnet on Reading the Poem upon the Mountain Daisy, by Mr. Burns.
Williams, W.   Chicory and Daisies.
  Daisy.
Wordsworth, W.   To a Child [Written in Her Album].
  To the Daisy.
Zaturenska.   Daisy, The.

Dali, Salvador
Gascoyne.   Salvador Dali.
Thribb.   In Memoriam Salvador Dali.

Damascus, Syria
Orfalea, G.   Bomb That Fell on Abdu's Farm, The.

Damnation and the Damned
Bliss, P.   Almost Persuaded.
Empson.   This Last Pain.
Graves, R.   Song: Lift-Boy.
Hill, G.   Ovid in the Third Reich.
Hunter, W.   "Go Bring Me," Said the Dying Fair.
Raffalovich, M. A.   World Well Lost 18, The.
Swift, J.   Place of the Damned [or Damn'd], The.
Unknown.   Ubi Sunt Qui Ante Nos Fuerunt?

Dams
Guiney.   Reason for Silence, A.
Hall, D.   Town of Hill, The.
Woody.   She-Who-Watches . . . The Names are Prayer.

Dancing and Dancers
Adams, A.   Her Dancing Days.
Adamson, H.   Make with the Feet.
Ai.   More.
Alden, J.   Sleepy Time Gal.
Alexander, E.   Ode.
Algarin.   Dante Park.
  El Jibarito Moderno.
Allen, L.   Rub a Dub Style inna Regent Park.
Altizer.   Sonnet 5: "No, I'll not, carrion, comfort you. Comfort."
Amherst.   Welford Wedding, The.
Awad, J.   Man Who Loved Flamenco, The.
Ayres.   On Lydia Distracted.
Barlow, G.   Nook.
Belloc.   Tarantella.
Bendall, M.   Conversation with Isadora Duncan.
Berke.   Fifties Rock Party, 1985.
Berlin.   Change Partners.
  Cheek to Cheek.
  Heat Wave.
  Let's Face the Music and Dance.
Bernstein, J.   Tango'd Love.
Bernstein, L.   Conga.
Berryman.   King David Dances.
Binyon.   Little Dancers, The.
Birney.   Bear on the Delhi Road, The.
Blake, E.   Baltimore Buzz.
Bloom, R.   Truckin'
Bond, S.   Tuesday Night Affair.
Bontemps.   Dark Girl.
Brooks, S.   Darktown Strutter's Ball, The.
  Walkin' the Dog.
Brown, L.   Turn On the Heat.

Varsity Drag, The.
Brownjohn. Of Dancing.
Buchanan, G. Theatrical Venus.
Burbank, E. I Danced to the Rumble of the
  Drum.
Burris, J. Ballin' the Jack.
Caddel. Against Numerology.
Caldwell, A. Raggedy Ann.
Camp, J. Female Dancer.
Campbell, J. Dancer, The.
Clampitt. Dancers Exercising.
Clayton, S. Soul Music.
Coffman. Cheerleaders.
Comden, B. Conga.
Conrad, C. Continental (You Kiss While You're
  Dancing), The.
Cooper, A. Stepping to da Muse/Sic.
Cortez, J. Heavy Headed Dance, The.
  So Many Feathers.
Coward. Nina.
Craighead, L. Dancin' Our Lives Away.
Creeley. Quick-Step.
Cristall. Song: "Come, let us dance and sing."
Crouch, S. Riding Across John Lee's Finger.
Cumming, P. Midsummer.
Cuthand, B. Dancing with Rex.
Cyril. Jump Black Honey Jump Black.
Davies, S. Orchestra; or, A Poem[e] of
  Da[u]ncing.
  Praise of Dancing, The.
  Speach of Love persuading men to learn
  Dancing, The.
Davis, T. Boppin' is Safer than Grindin'
  Trickster 4 (for Sister Patra).
Dawes, K. Some Tentative Definitions 4.
DeSylva, B. G. Turn On the Heat.
  Varsity Drag, The.
Di Prima. I Ching.
Dietz, H. Dancing in the Dark.
Donaldson, W. T'ain't No Sin to Dance Around
  in Your Bones.
Dubin, A. Forty-second Street.
  She's a Latin from Manhattan.
Duke, V. Make with the Feet.
Duncan, R. Presence of the Dance / The
  Resolution of the Music, The.
Dunn, S. Dancing with God.
Eady. Jazz Dancer.
  Johnny Laces Up His Red Shoes.
  My Mother, If She Had Won Free Dance
  Lessons.
Egan, R. Sleepy Time Gal.
Ellington, D. Satin Doll.
Evasco, M. Dancing a Spell.
Eyen, J. New Dream, A (Wuski A-Baw-Tan).
Ferlinghetti, L. Retired Ballerinas, Central Park
  West.
Field, R. Dancing Bear, The.
Fields, D. Bojangles of Harlem.
  Have Feet, Will Dance.
  I Won't Dance.
  Never Gonna Dance.
Fusselman, A. Puffy Jacket.
García, D. Turns at the Dance.
Gilbert, C. Directions, The.
Giovanni. Three/Quarters Time.
Goodman, B. Stompin' at the Savoy.
Green, A. Conga.
Gregg. Dark Thing Inside the Day, A.
Grenfell, J. Stately as a Galleon.
Hagedorn, J. Latin Music in New York.
Hahn, S. Nijinsky's Dog.
Halpern, D. Dance, The.
Hammerstein. Shall We Dance?
Hart, L. Dancing on the Ceiling.
  Ten Cents a Dance.
Hayes, T. At Pegasus.
Healy, E. What It Was Like the Night Cary
  Grant Died.
Heath, R. Seeing Her Dancing.
Henderson, D. Alvin Cash/Keep on Dancin'
Henderson, R. Turn On the Heat.
  Varsity Drag, The.
Herman, J. Tap Your Troubles Away.
Hernández Cruz. Ironing Goatskin.
  Latin and Soul for Joe Bataan.

Loíza Aldea.
  Poem: "Think with your body."
  Side 12.
Hippolyte. Antonette's Boogie.
Holst-Warhaft. Old Men of Athens, The.
Housman, A. Fancy's Knell.
Hughes, L. College Formal: Renaissance
  Casino.
  Dream Boogie.
  Dream Variation[s].
  Sunday by the Combination.
Hummell, A. Saraband.
Ilio, D. Marikudo in Kalibo, 1979.
Iverem, E. Journalist's Convention 1987.
Jacobsen, J. Limbo Dancer, The.
Jeffers, R. New Mexican Mountain.
Johnson, A. Joint is Jumpin', The.
Johnson, H. Bottled [New York].
Johnson, J. Charleston.
  Joint is Jumpin', The.
Jonson, B. Masque of Christmas, The.
Joseph, A. Junior High Dance.
  Soul Train.
  Wedding Party.
Justice, D. Dancer's Life, A.
Kayo. Song of the Initiate.
Kendrick, D. Jenny in Love.
Kern, J. Bojangles of Harlem.
  I Won't Dance.
  Never Gonna Dance.
  Raggedy Ann.
Koehler, T. Truckin'
Landon. Dancing Girl, The.
Lane, B. Have Feet, Will Dance.
Laurencin, M. Zebra, The.
Lear, E. Limerick: "There was an old man of
  Whitehaven."
  Owl and the Pussy-Cat, The.
Lerner, A. I Could Have Danced All Night.
Leslie, E. T'ain't No Sin to Dance Around in
  Your Bones.
Lewis, S. I Wonder Why She Kept on Saying
  'Si-Si-Si-Si-Senor.'
Li Po. For the Dancer of the King of Wu.
Loewe, F. I Could Have Danced All Night.
Lorenzo, A. Sleepy Time Gal.
Lovelace, R. Gratiana Dancing [or Dauncing]
  and [or &] Singing.
  Loose Saraband, A.
Mack, C. Charleston.
MacKenzie, R. Square.
Magidson, H. Continental (You Kiss While
  You're Dancing), The.
Major, C. Large Room with Wood Floor.
Martinez, D. Death of Isadora Duncan, The.
McDonald, W. Songs We Fought For, The.
McKay, C. Harlem Dancer, The.
McKinney, I. Dance, The.
McRay. Performance.
Mercer, J. Arthur Murray Taught Me Dancing
  in a Hurry.
  Satin Doll.
Merrill, B. Music That Makes Me Dance.
Merrill, J. Watching the Dance.
Morton, J. To Hilda Dancing.
Moss, T. Tornados.
Mottram. Zuni Dancers.
Mueller, L. Deaf Dancing to Rock, The.
Mullen, H. Dance She Does, The.
Mutén, B. Urania.
Nye, N. Whole Self, The.
Obejas, A. Dancing in Paradise.
Ogundipe-Leslie. Rain at Noon-time.
Olson, C. Merce of Egypt.
Osterhaus, J. New York Minute.
Page, G. Road Show.
Palmer, J. Band Played On, The.
Philp, G. Dance Hall.
Pound, E. Dance Figure.
Pratt, M. Other Side, The.
Preston, R. Deep-Sea Bathing (Inna Reggae
  Dancehall).
Ragan, J. Child Christ at the Top of the Stairs.
Razaf, A. Joint is Jumpin', The.
  Stompin' at the Savoy.
Redmond. Dance Bodies #1.

Reed, I. Black Cock, The.
Reynolds, O. Spanish Dancer.
Riggs, L. Santo Domingo Corn Dance.
Rodgers, R. Dancing on the Ceiling.
  Shall We Dance?
  Ten Cents a Dance.
Rome, H. Doing the Reactionary.
Rossiter. Your Body Glistens From the Bath.
Rumaker. Fairies Are Dancing All Over the
  World, The.
Russell, B. Ballerina.
Rylander, E. Dancing on Beethoven's Birthday.
Sampson, E. Stompin' at the Savoy.
Sandburg, C. Lines Written for Gene Kelly to
  Dance To.
Schertzinger, V. Arthur Murray Taught Me
  Dancing in a Hurry.
Schwartz, A. Dancing in the Dark.
Seibles. Who.
Sempill, F. Maggie Lauder.
Shange. Dream of Pairing.
Shepherd, R. Gods at Three A.M., The.
  Narcissus Learning the Words to This Song.
Sigman, C. Ballerina.
Simpson, L. Riders Held Back, The.
Sissle, N. Baltimore Buzz.
Skinner, J. Tullochgorum.
Smith, C. Ballin' the Jack.
Smith, P. They Say That Black People . . . .
Spellman. Twist, The.
Spencer, B. Castanets.
  Egyptian Dancer at Shubra.
St. John, D. Slow Dance.
Stafford, W. At the Klamath Berry Festival.
Stein, G. Susie Asado.
Stevens, W. Dance of the Macabre Mice.
Strayhorn, B. Satin Doll.
Stuart, M. In The Orchard.
Styne, J. Music That Makes Me Dance.
Symons, A. La Mélinite: Moulin-Rouge.
Synge. On an Island.
Tarpley. Feel Free.
Thompson, D. P. Dancing in Menopause.
Tu Fu. Coming Home Late at Night.
Unknown. Harry Parry.
  Mode of France, The.
  Old Woman from France, The.
  On a Female Rope-Dancer.
  Rural Dance about the Maypole, The.
  Wooyeo Ball, The.
U Tam'si Tchicaya. Dance to the Amulets.
Van Jordan, A. Dance Lesson, A.
Vasquez, R. At the Rainbow.
Vigil, A. That's the Way, Uh Huh, Uh Huh, I
  Liked It.
Wagoner, D. Best Slow Dancer, The.
Wakoski. Belly Dancer.
Wallenstein. Blues 2.
Waller, T. et al. Joint is Jumpin', The.
Waniek. Diverne's Waltz.
Warren, H. Forty-second Street.
  She's a Latin from Manhattan.
Waters, M. American Bandstand.
Webb, C. Stompin' at the Savoy.
Whiting, R. Sleepy Time Gal.
Wicks, S. Joy.
  Rain Dance.
Williams, W. Artist, The.
  Dance, The.
  Danse Russe.
  Overture to a Dance of Locomotives.
  Philomena Andronico.
Wordsworth, W. I Wandered Lonely As a
  Cloud.
Wright, S. Out of the Wailing.
Wunderlich, M. Take Good Care of Yourself.
Yeats. Fiddler of Dooney, The.
Young, A. Ravel: Bolero.

See also **Ballet; Waltzes and Waltzing**

Dandelions
Curry. Dandelion.
Friedmann. Butterfly, The.
Holloway, G. Virtue of Slovenliness, The.
Mayer, G. Dandelions.
Rosenblatt. Of Dandelions & Tourists.

Stanton, W.   Dandelions.

Danger
Auden.   Legend.
Benjamin, P.   Press On.
Lomax, M.   Gulf.
Noguchi, R.   From Rooftops, Kenji Takezo
   Throws Himself.
O'Lahsen, M.   Dead Erect, The.
Rollings.   For Dear Life.
Volkman.   Infernal.

Daniel
Glück, L.   Gretel in Darkness.
Keats.   Nebuchadnezzar's Dream.
Rowbotham.   Nebuchadnezzar's Kingdom-
   Come.
Unknown.   Didn't My Lord Deliver Daniel?

Dante Alighieri
Bryant, W.   Dante.
Emerson, R.   Solution.
Goetsch, D.   Nobody's Hell.
Longfellow, H.   Dante.
Ray, H.   Dante.
Wright, J.   Saying Dante Aloud.

Daphne
Glück, L.   Mythic Fragment.
   Undertaking, The.
Pound, E.   Tree, The.
Waller, E.   Story of Phoebus and Daphne
   Applied, [etc.], The.
Winters, Y.   Apollo and Daphne.

Dare, Virginia
Benét, R. *et al.*   Peregrine White and Virginia
   Dare.

Darkness
Aiken, J.   Rhyme for Night.
Aldis, D.   No One Heard Him Call.
Armstrong, F.   Out of the Darkness.
Asekoff, L.   Crowdoll.
Barber, D.   Small Hours.
Bly, R.   Snowfall in the Afternoon.
Bobrowski.   Latvian Songs.
Brontë, E.   Spellbound.
Bush, D.   Sunday the Power Went Off, The.
Butler, C. E.   Darkness, The.
   Other Places, The.
Byron, G.   Darkness.
Carew, T.   Beautiful Mistress, A.
Cleyre, V.   Out of the Darkness.
Cortes, F.   Poem Composed During a Brownout.
Creeley.   Anger.
   I Know a Man.
   Somewhere.
Curzon, D.   Instructions to a Seed.
Dunbar, P.   Slow Through the Dark.
Ellis, T.   Shooting Back.
Evans, R.   No Moon at All.
Everwine.   Perhaps It's as You Say.
"Field."   They Shall Look on Him.
Fisher, R.   Rules and Ranges for Ian Tyson.
Francis, R.   Three Darks Come Down Together.
Garrigue.   Forest.
Gioia.   Insomnia.
Gore-Booth.   Vision of Niamh, The.
Greenlaw.   Five O'Clock Opera.
Gunn, T.   Feel of Hands, The.
Harjo, J.   White Bear.
Hecht, A.   Christmas Is Coming.
Hemphill.   Where Seed Falls.
Herd.   Survivors, The.
Herrick.   In the Dark None Dainty.
Hewitt, J.   Calling on Peadar O'Donnell at
   Dungloe.
Hickey, E.   For Richer, For Poorer.
Hippolyte.   Reggae Cat (for Boston Jack).
Jarrell.   90 North.
Justice, D.   Insomnia of Tremayne, The.
Kirkup.   Who's That?
Knott.   Funny Poem.
Kooser.   Late Lights in Minnesota.
Lane, P.   Lake Murry.
Lawrence, D.   Young Wife, A.
Levertov.   Closed World, The.
Lindtová, A.   Campfire.
Long, H.   In the Dark World.
Longfellow, H.   Children's Hour, The.

Lowell, J.   Darkened Mind, The.
MacCaig.   Likenesses.
Magowan.   Zeimbekiko.
Mann, D.   No Moon at All.
Meinke.   Unnatural Light.
Milton.   Il Penseroso.
Novakovich.   Shadow.
Peck, J.   Metal Denser Than, and Liquid, A.
Peterson, J.   Stand Still.
Petrie.   Phases of Darkness, The.
Poole, R.   Dark, The.
Probyn.   More than They that Watch for the
   Morning.
Roethke.   In a Dark Time.
Rossetti, C.   Remember [Me].
Satchell.   Velvet Blanket.
Simic.   Night Picnic.
Smith, K.   Train.
Snyder, G.   How Poetry Comes to Me.
Spender, S.   Abrupt and charming mover.
Stafford, W.   Traveling Through the Dark.
Stevens, W.   Sun This March, The.
Stoutenburg.   Midnight Saving Time.
Sullivan, N.   His Necessary Darkness.
Swinburne.   Lake of Gaube, The.
Symons, A.   Pastel: Masks and Faces.
Szymborska.   Four in the Morning.
Thomas, E.   Out in the Dark.
Thomas, R.   Still.
Tomlinson, C.   Civilities of Lamplight.
Torres, E.   Elbow in Dumberland, An.
Unknown, fr. Terezin Concentration Camp.
   Night in the Ghetto.
Welch, L.   Empress Herself Served Tea to Su
   Tung-Po, The.
White, J.   To Night.
Whitman, S.   Past, The.
Wright, J.   Beginning.
   Revelation, The.
Wunderlich, M.   On Opening.
Wylie.   Incantation.

Darwin, Charles
Edson, R.   Darwin Descending.
Niedecker.   Darwin.
Robinson, A.   Darwinism.
Schnackenberg.   Darwin in 1881.
See also **Evolution**

Dating
Aytoun [*or* Ayton], R.   Rejection, The.
   Song: "What means this strangeness now of
      late."
   Upon His Unconstant Mistress.
Behn, A.   On Her Loving Two Equally.
Bock, J.   Tonight at Eight.
Brown, E.   Bitcherel.
Brown, L.   Don't Bring Lulu.
Campbell, T.   Freedom and Love.
Chrystos.   I Bought a New Red.
Cooper, D.   David Cassidy Then.
Cope, W.   Exchange of Letters.
DeFoe, M.   Dream Lover.
Dunbar, P.   Negro Love Song, A.
Foerster.   Playland.
Goodman, M.   Lullaby for a Butch.
Gylys, B.   Family Reunion—Aunt Vern's Two
   Cents.
Harnick.   Tonight at Eight.
Henderson, R.   Don't Bring Lulu.
Mariani.   Betty.
McGrane, P.   Jukebox Saturday Night.
North, D.   Platonic.
Reading.   Ballad: "I'll tell you a story /
   concerning John and Joan."
   Correspondence.
Robin, L.   My Cutey's Due at Two-to-Two
   Today.
Rose, B.   Don't Bring Lulu.
Stillman, A.   Jukebox Saturday Night.
Wallace, R.   Sound Systems.
Wilson, S.   Boy Friend, The.

Daughters
Acholonu.   Dissidents, The.
Armitage, J.   To Our Daughter.
Arrillaga.   Mariana II.
Baraka.   Preface to a Twenty Volume Suicide
   Note.

Ben-Lev, D.   Broken Helix.
Betjeman.   Old Land Dog, The.
Boland, E.   Pomegranate, The.
Bolger.   Dublin Girl, Mountjoy, 1984.
BonniLee.   White Candles.
Booth, P.   First Lesson.
Brooks, G.   Jessie Mitchell's Mother.
   Maxie Allen.
Burns, R.   Poet's Welcome to His Love-
   Begotten Daughter [the First Instance that
   Entitled Him to the Venerable Appellation of
   Father], A.
Byron, G.   Jephtha's Daughter.
Campbell, D.   Mothers and Daughters.
Campbell, S.   Constant Welcome, The.
Carruth, W.   Essay on Death.
Clarke, A.   Planter's Daughter, The.
Clifton, L.   Admonitions.
Cofer, J.   Unspoken.
Coleman, H.   Black Soldier Remembers, A.
   Poem for a "Divorced" Daughter.
Coleman, W.   Cousin Mary.
Creeley.   Fire, The.
Curtis, T.   Games with My Daughter.
Darr.   Gift, The.
Dove, R.   After Reading *Mickey in the Night
   Kitchen* for the Third Time Before Bed.
Dufferin.   Mother's Lament, The.
Eliot, T.   Marina.
Elmusa.   She Fans the Word.
Fay, J.   Santorini Daughter.
Finkel.   Father, The.
Friedman, S.   Answering Machine Message.
Galvin, B.   For a Daughter Gone Away.
García, D.   Green Corn Season.
Garcia, R.   Note Folded Thirteen Ways.
Gardinier.   Ghost of Santo Domingo, The.
Gilyard, K.   Daughter, That Picture of You.
Gioia.   Counting the Children.
Goldberg, B.   Our Father.
Gomez, M.   Lost Daughter.
Goodison.   I Am Becoming My Mother.
Graves, R.   Frosty Night, A.
Hai-Jew, S.   Father's Belt.
Harper, M.   Eve (Rachel).
Hashimoto, S.   Standing in the Doorway, I
   Watch the Young Child Sleep.
Herd.   Exhibits, The.
Hughes, L.   Mama and Daughter.
Jackson, G.   Only Daughter, The.
Jarrell.   Lost Children, The.
Johnson, E.   Letter to My Mother, A.
Jonson, B.   On My First Daughter.
   To Elizabeth, Countess of Rutland.
Joseph, A.   Numbers.
Joyce, J.   Flower Given to My Daughter, A.
Kaufman, S.   Mothers, Daughters.
Kay, E.   Phoenix.
Kees.   For My Daughter.
Kgositsile.   To My Daughter.
Khalvati.   Blue Moon.
Kinnell.   Little Sleep's-Head Sprouting Hair in
   the Moonlight.
Kizer, C.   Thrall.
Krysl.   Persephone, to Demeter.
Kumin, M.   Envelope, The.
   Making the Jam without You.
Landor, W.   Mother, I Cannot Mind My Wheel.
Larkin, J.   Cold River.
   Legacy.
Laux.   Finding What's Lost.
Livingston, M.   Working with Mother.
Lomax, M.   July.
Longfellow, H.   Wreck of the *Hesperus*, The.
Lowell, R.   Home After Three Months Away.
Lux.   Little Tooth, A.
MacCaig.   Intruder in a Set Scene.
MacKay, C.   Louise on the Door-Step.
Macpherson, J.   Beauty of Job's Daughters, The.
Madgett.   Offspring.
Mayer, G.   Make Believe.
McDonald, W.   Faraway Places.
McElroy, C.   In My Mother's Room.
Meynell, A.   Girl on the Land, The.
Michie, S.   Connecting Light.
Moss, T.   Undertaker's Daughter Feels

Neglect, The.
Mullen, H. Saturday Afternoon, When Chores Are Done.
Mutén, B. Queen Hera.
Napurrurla, R. Two Mothers, The.
Norris, K. Persephone.
Nye, N. Making a Fist.
Olds, S. Her List.
  Quake Theory.
Oppen. Exodus.
Pastan. To a Daughter Leaving Home.
Paterson, E. Griselda.
Pelizzon, V. Wedding Day, The.
Posamentier, E. Counting Backwards.
Ransom, J. Bells for John Whiteside's Daughter.
Rodgers, C. It Is Deep.
Seaton, M. Blonde Ambition.
  Fear of Shoplifting.
Sexton. Little Girl, My String Bean, My Lovely Woman.
Shumaker. Waitress's Kid, The.
Shurin. Material's Daughter.
Siddal. At Last.
Smith, S. Human Affection.
Song. Lost Sister.
  Youngest Daughter, The.
Spender, S. Missing My Daughter.
Stead, C. Between.
Thomas, E. If I Should Ever by Chance.
Unknown. Execution of Alice Holt.
Utting, S. Spoon Maker's Daughter, The.
Van Dyke, C. Birth, 1975.
Vazirani, R. Daughter-Mother-Maya-Seeta.
Vertreace, M. Caged Stone.
Waniek. Daughters, 1900.
Weems, M. Dime after Dime.
Whittier. Farewell, The: "Gone, gone,—sold and gone."
Wilbur. Writer, The.
Williams, J. Rachel.
Williams, M. Poem for Emily, A.
Wilson, K. Dusk in My Backyard.
Winters, Y. To My Infant Daughter.
Wright, C. Daughters of Blum, The.
Wright, J. Eve to Her Daughters.
Yeats. Prayer for My Daughter, A.
Yee, M. Wintermelons.
Young, I. Mermaid Knows, A.

David (Bible)
Abelard. David's Lament for Jonathan.
Amis, K. After Goliath.
Benét, S. King David.
Berryman. King David Dances.
Byron, G. Harp the Monarch Minstrel Swept, The.
Graves, R. Goliath and David.
Lamb, C. David in the Cave of Adullam.
Lindsay, N. In Which Roosevelt Is Compared to Saul.
Moore, M. That Harp You Play So Well.
Naylor. Authorship.
Quarles. On Saul and David.
Reznikoff. David.
  I Do Not Believe That David Killed Goliath.
Smart, C. Song to David, A.
  Strength.
Steele, T. In the King's Rooms.
Thompson, P. David and Goliath.
Traherne. In Salem Dwelt a Glorious King.
Untermeyer, L. Goliath and David.
Waddell, P. David and Goliath.

Davies, Dr. John
Howell, J. Upon Dr. Davies's British Grammar.

Davies, Sir John
Roethke. Four for Sir John Davies.

Davis, Angela
Cobb, A. Angela Davis.

Davis, Miles
Brathwaite, E. Blues.
Ford, W. Of Miles Davis.
Gordon, G. Tercios del Muerte.
Harper, M. Alone.
Hayes, T. Boxcar.
Hoagland, E. Kinda Blue Miles Davis Died

Today.
Jauss. Black Orchid.
Kelly, R. Ode to Language.
Komunyakaa. Boxing Day.
Redmond. Milestone: The Birth of an Ancestor.
Rux, C. H. Shunning an Imperative.
Sundiata. Open Heart.
Whitlow. Poem for the Children.

Davis, Thomas Osborne
Ferguson, S. Lament for the Death of Thomas Davis.

Dawn
Angeles, C. Light Invested.
Beckett, S. Alba.
Belloc. Early Morning, The.
Campbell, R. Mass at Dawn.
  Sisters, The.
Carmichael, H. Two Sleepy People.
Dana, R. Daybreak.
Davenant [*or* D'Avenant]. Lark Now Leaves His Watery [*or* Wat'ry] Nest.
Davison, P. Equinox 1980.
De la Mare. Stranger, The.
De Tabley. Nuptial Song.
Dixon, R. Dawning.
Drummond, W. Invocation: "Pheobus, arise! / And paint the sable skies."
Ellis, T. Break of Dawn, The.
Ginsberg, A. Fourth Floor, Dawn, Up All Night Writing Letters.
Grimké, A. Dawn.
Guiney. When on the Marge of Evening.
Hearn, M. At Dawn.
Herrick. To Anthea Lying in Bed.
Higginson, E. Dawn.
  Dawn on the Willamette.
Housman, A. Fairies Break Their Dances, The.
  Reveille.
Hudgins. Two Ember Days in Alabama.
Hughes, T. Roe-Deer.
Irwin, T. With the Dawn.
Jaccottet. Dawn.
Jones, G. Morning.
Kinsella, T. First Light.
Lane, P. Spring.
Lawrence, D. Quite Forsaken.
Levertov. What Wild Dawns There Were.
Lewis, A. Dawn on the East Coast.
Lodge, G. Lower New York.
Loesser. Two Sleepy People.
Longfellow, H. Children's Hour, The.
  Daybreak.
Mahapatra, J. October Morning, An.
McKay, C. Dawn in New York.
Millay, E. Recuerdo.
Montgomerie, A. Night Is Near [*or* Neir] Gone, The.
Morris, W. Summer Dawn.
North, C. Sunrise with Sea Monster.
O'Rahilly [*or* O'Reilly] [*or* Ó Rathaille]. Vision, The.
Percival. Morning among the Hills.
Philips, A. Happy Swain, The.
Ray, H. Dawn's Carol.
Skloot. Closer to Home.
Stevens, W. Brave Man, The.
Stryk, L. Dawn.
Taylor, B. Paean to the Dawn, A.
Tennyson, A. Dawn, The.
  Owl, The.
Thomas, D. Light Breaks Where No Sun Shines.
Thomas, E. Cock-Crow.
  Trumpet, The.
Thoreau. Guido's Aurora.
Unknown. Dawn, The.
  I Think Over Again My Small Adventures.
Unknown, fr. Terezin Concentration Camp. Night in the Ghetto.
Vaughan, H. Cock-crowing.
Very. Fair Morning, The.
Wagoner, D. Five Dawn Skies in November.
Warren, R. Dawn.
  Masts at Dawn.
Watson, R. Aubade: "Lights are out in the street, and a cool wind swings, The."

Westmorland. Reveille Matin, or Good Morrow to a Friend.
Whitehead, C. Daybreak.
  Morning Thesis.
Wilcox, E. Dawn.
Williams, W. Dawn.
Wright, C. Saturday 6 a.m.
See also **Morning; Sunrise**

Dawson, F. W.
Fordham. Tribute to Capt. F. W. Dawson.

Day
Adamson, H. It's a Most Unusual Day.
Barbauld. Tomorrow.
Barbour, D. It's a Good Day.
Belloc. Early Morning, The.
Bourdillon. Night Has a Thousand Eyes, The.
Cahn, S. Day by Day.
Codrescu. Work.
Coleridge, M. Shadow.
Collins, B. Snow Day.
Cummings, E. Impression.
Doolittle, H. Mid-day.
Emerson, R. Days.
Hernández Cruz. Thursday.
Herrick. Dream[e]s.
Hesketh. Love's Advocate.
Kalidasa. Salutation to the Dawn.
Kimball, H. In Reverie.
Lanier, S. Song for "The Jacquerie."
Larkin, P. Days.
McCrae, J. In Flanders Fields.
Motherwell. Jeanie Morrison.
Owen, G. Gathering in the Days.
Prynne. Of Movement towards a Natural Place.
Romo-Carmona, M. Daylight.
Roseliep. Morning-Glory, The.
Rossetti, C. Is the Moon Tired?
Sigourney. Advertisement of a Lost Day.
Stevens, W. Brave Man, The.
Stevenson, R. Bed in Summer.
  Moon, The.
Stidger. Day, A.
Thoreau. Guido's Aurora.
Wilbur. Death of a Toad, The.

Daydreams
Ashbery. Instruction Manual, The.
  Mixed Feelings.
Brontë, E. Little while, a little while, A.
Coleridge, M. Day-dream, A.
Eskimo Oral Tradition. Song of Kuk-ook, the Bad Boy, The.
Foster, S. Jeanie with the Light Brown Hair.
Harrison, G. Playground, The.
Hecht, A. Hill, A.
Jones, J. Watching the Wheat.
Nash, O. Spring Comes to Murray Hill.
Robinson, E. Miniver Cheevy.
Safie, D. Meditation by the Xerox Machine.
See also **Dreams and Dreaming**

De Hooch, Pieter
Tomlinson, C. Paring the Apple.

De Soto, Hernando
Harjo, J. New Orleans.
Van Doren. Distant Runners, The.

Deafness
Clayton, S. Soul Music.
Davies, E. Portrait of Auntie Blodwen.
Marston, P. Speechless: Upon the Marriage of Two Deaf and Dumb Persons.
Mueller, L. Deaf Dancing to Rock, The.
Murray, L. Hearing Impairment.
Page, P. Deaf-Mute in the Pear Tree.
Ryan, R. Deafness.
Tate, J. Deaf Girl Playing.
Wiman, C. Hearing Loss.
Wright, D. On Himself.
Wright, J. Mutterings over the Crib of a Deaf Child.

Dean, James
Jones, R. James Dean.
Like, J. James Dean and the Pig.
O'Hara, F. For James Dean.

Death and the Dead
Abbey, L. Broken Silence.
Abena, B. Exiles.

Abse. Carnal Knowledge.
Lunch and Afterwards.
Millie's Date.
Pathology of Colours.
Peachstone.
Winter Visit, A.
Acholonu. Going Home.
"Ada." Oh, when this earthly tenement.
Adams, L. Death and the Lady.
Adamson. My House.
Adcock, F. Poem Ended by a Death.
"Æ." Immortality.
Agard, J. For Bob Marley.
Ai. Deserter, The.
Aiken, C. Tetélestai.
Akhmatova, A. Dedication.
Everything Is Plundered.
Alarcon, F. Blues del SIDA / AIDS Blues.
Aldrich, T. Lycidas.
Memory.
Alegría. Desire.
From the Bridge.
Alexander, M. Her Garden.
Alexie. Theology.
Allingham. Dream, A [or The].
Allott. Statue, The.
Alvarez, J. How I Learned to Sweep.
Amiel. Death Is a Matter of Mathematics.
Amis, K. Last War, The.
Anderson, J. Re-member Us.
Anderson-Thompkins. To Love a Stranger.
Andrews, M. Elegy on the Death of Mr Sterne.
Angira. Country of the Dead, The.
Arnold, M. Memorial Verses.
Requiescat.
Thyrsis.
Youth and Calm.
Arp. Kaspar Is Dead.
Asalache. Death of a Chief.
Asekoff, L. Will.
Ashbery. Fear of Death.
How Much Longer Will I Be Able to Inhabit the
Divine Sepulcher.
Ashe. Corpse-bearing.
"Asphodel." Winter Solstice—for Frank.
Aston, A. Everything in the Garden is Lovely.
Atkins. Narrative.
Atwood. Beauharnois (1).
Beauharnois (3).
Beauharnois, Glengarry (2).
Dufferin, Simcoe, Grey (4).
Four Small Elegies.
Settlers, The.
This Is a Photograph of Me.
Auchterlonie. Waiting for the Post.
Auden. As I Walked Out One Evening.
Cultural Presupposition, The.
In Memory of W. B. Yeats.
Limerick: "As the poets have mournfully sung."
O What Is That Sound [Which So Thrills the
Ear].
Auslander, J. Elegy: "Fled is the swiftness of all
the white-footed ones."
Awad, J. Autumnal.
Widower, The.
Awoonor. Song of War.
Songs of Sorrow.
Aytoun [or Ayton], R. On the Prince's Death, to
the King.
Balaban. Graveyard at Bald Eagle Ridge.
News Update.
Bang, M. Crossed-Over, Fiend-Snitched, X-ed
Out.
Baraka. Clay.
Crow Jane.
Incident.
Invention of Comics, The.
Baraka, R. For the Brothers Who Aint Here.
Barker, G. In Memory of a Friend.
Barlow, G. Mingus Speaks: Found Poems.
Barnes, W. Mater Dolorosa.
Sonnet: "In every dream thy lovely features
rise."
Wife A-Lost, The.
Barrax. Scuba Diver Recovers the Body of a
Drowned Child, The.

Barry, J. Green Hell, Green Death.
Harvest Moon.
Baugh, E. Carpenter's Complaint, The.
Baxter, J. East Coast Journey.
Becker, R. Crypto-Jews, The.
Beckett, S. Alba.
Beckman, J. Lament for the Death of a
Bullfighter.
Beddoes. Death Sweet.
Bedient, C. When the Gods Put on Meter.
Beer, P. Grave Doubts.
Lemmings.
Beerbohm, M. On the Imprint of the First
English Edition of "The Works of Max
Beerbohm."
Behn, A. Epitaph on the Tombstone of a Child,
the Last of Seven That Died Before.
On the Death of the Late Earl of Rochester.
Belieu. Nocturne: My Sister Life.
Sleeping Man Must Be Awakened to Be
Killed, A.
Bell, C. Lying in Small Pieces.
Bell, M. Book of the Dead Man #43, The.
Book of the Dead Man #87, The.
Someone Is Probably Dead.
Bellerby. With Music.
Belloc. Obiter Dicta.
Statue, The.
Bendall, M. Conversation with Isadora Duncan.
Bensko. Bones of Lazarus.
Last Look in the Sambre Canal, A.
Bently, S. River Dove: a Lyric Pastoral, The.
Berg, S. Nostalgia.
Berger, J. Between Worlds.
Bernstein, C. Cup of Coffee, The.
Profaning the Dead.
Berry, W. Ripening.
Slip, The.
Berryman. Poet's Final Instructions, The.
To My Father.
Bethune, L. For Singing in Good Mood.
Harlem Freeze Frame.
Betjeman. Before the Anæsthetic; or, A Real
Fright.
City.
Death in Leamington.
House of Rest.
Inevitable.
Remorse.
Bevington, L. Twilight.
Bibbins, M. Mud.
Bidart. Sacrifice, The.
To the Dead.
Bidgood. Burial Path.
Bienek. Exodus.
Our Ashes.
Vorkuta.
Bierce. General B. F. Butler.
Bion. Lament for Adonis.
Bishop, E. Cootchie.
First Death in Nova Scotia.
Man-Moth, The.
Bishop, J. Hours, The.
Sleep Brought Me Vision.
Blagden. To George Sand on her Interview with
Elizabeth Barrett Browning.
Blake, W. Another [Epitaph]: "Here lies John
Trot, the Friend of all mankind."
Epitaph, An: "I was buried near this dyke [or
Dike]."
Blamire. Auld Robin Forbes.
Blaser. Ruler, The.
Blaustein, N. Water and Light.
Blight. Death of a Whale.
Bly, R. Christmas Eve Service at Midnight at
St. Michael's.
Looking at New-Fallen Snow from a Train.
Things My Brother and I Could Do.
Bodenheim. Death.
Bogan, L. My Voice Not Being Proud.
Boland, E. Anna Liffey.
Boleyn, G. O Death, Rock Me Asleep.
Bolton, J. In Memory of the Boys of Dexter,
Kentucky.
Booth, P. Sixty-Six.
Borson. After a Death.

Boss. Candy Lady, The.
Bowers, E. Centaur Overheard, The.
Bowles, W. On the Death of William Linley,
esq.
Boyle, K. Complaint for M and M, A.
Bradstreet, A. Before the Birth of One of Her
Children.
In Memory of My Dear Grandchild Anne
Bradstreet Who Deceased June 20, 1669,
Being Three Years and Seven Months Old.
To My Dear and Loving Husband.
To the Memory of My Dear and Ever Honored
Father Thomas Dudley Esq. Who Deceased
July 31, 1653, and of His Age 77.
Brant, B. Stillborn Night.
Brass. There Isn't Any Death.
Brecht, B. To Those Born Later.
Breidenbach, T. Confessional.
Brewer, G. Teen Drowns in Rehabilitation
Camp Days Before 17th Birthday, Questions
Persist.
Breytenbach. Out There.
Bridges, R. When Death to Either Shall Come.
Bringhurst. For the Bones of Josef Mengele,
Disinterred June 1985.
Brodrick. Epitaph on a Diamond Digger.
On a Government Surveyor.
Brodsky, J. Belfast Tune.
Brontë, A. Night.
Brontë, E. Diving.
Is this my tomb, this humble stone.
On the Death of Anne Brontë.
On the Death of Emily Jane Brontë.
Reason.
Young Man Naughty's Adventure.
Brontë, E. Aye there it is! It wakes tonight.
Death.
Death Scene, A.
Long Neglect Has Worn Away.
Night Wind, The.
No Coward Soul is Mine.
Philosopher, The.
Remembrance.
Song: "Linnet in the rocky dells, The."
Stanzas: "I'll not weep that thou art going to
leave me."
Stanzas to———.
Brooke, R. Great Lover, The.
Hill, The.
Sonnet: "Oh! Death will find me, long before I
tire."
Brooks, G. Boy Died in My Alley, The.
Last Quatrain of the Ballad of Emmett Till, The.
Medgar Evers.
Mentors.
We Real Cool.
White Troops Had Their Orders but the Negroes
Looked Like Men.
Broumas, O. On Earth.
Brown, A. Assassination of Charlie Parker, The.
Brown, D. Still Later There Are War Stories.
Brown, E. Jezebel to the Eunuchs.
Brown, G. Kirkyard.
Old Fisherman with Guitar.
Brown, M. Created Clay.
Brown, S. Conjured.
Sister Lou.
Browne, E. When I Am Dead.
Browne, W. On the Countess Dowager of
Pembroke.
Browning, E. Died..
Grief.
L.E.L.'s Last Question.
Mother and Poet.
Sleep, The.
Thought for a Lonely Death-Bed, A.
Browning, R. Bishop Orders His Tomb at Saint
Praxed's Church, The.
Evelyn Hope.
Lost Leader, The.
May and Death.
Prospice.
Bruchac. Elegy for Jack Bowman.
Brutus. At a Funeral.
Endurance.
Bryan, M. To———: "O timeless guest!—so

soon returned art thou."
Bryant, W.   Death of Lincoln, The.
Death of the Flowers, The.
Thanatopsis.
To the Fringed Gentian.
Buchanan, G.   Jill's Death.
Buckmaster.   Seed.
Bukowski.   I Am Dead But I Know the Dead
Are Not Like This.
Bunting.   To Violet [with Prewar Poems].
Burns, R.   Death and Doctor Hornbook [A True
Story].
Epitaph: "Lo worms enjoy the seat of bliss."
Epitaph for William Nicol.
Epitaph on a Schoolmaster.
Epitaph on Mr. Burton.
Fishing in Winter.
Highland Mary.
Man Was Made to Mourn, a Dirge.
On a Noisy Polemic.
On W. R———, Esq.
Prayer, in the Prospect of Death, A.
Burt, D.   On the Death of Lisa Lyman.
Butler, G.   In Memoriam, J.A.R., Drowned, East
London.
Bynner.   Donald Evans.
Byron, G.   Aristomenes.
Destruction of Sennacherib, The.
If Sometimes in the Haunts of Men.
Last Words on Greece.
Love and Death.
Manfred.
One Struggle More, and I Am Free.
To Thyrza.
Césaire, A.   In Memory of a Black Union
Leader.
Caballero-Robb, M.   Memoranda for Rosario.
Caddel.   Against Numerology.
Cameron, N.   She and I.
Campbell, J.   Dancer, The.
Campbell, T.   Hohenlinden.
Last Man, The.
Campo.   El Día de los Muertos.
Her Final Show.
Carbó, N.   Verso Libre.
Carew, T.   Another [On the Duke of
Buckingham].
Elegy upon the Death of the Dean of [St.]
Paul's, Dr. John Donne, An.
For a Picture Where a Queen Laments over the
Tomb of a Slain Knight.
Maria Wentworth.
On the Death of Donne.
Carroll, J.   Maybe I'm Amazed.
Carruth, H.   Crucifixion.
Essay on Death.
Paragraph 36.
Quality of Wine.
Carter, E.   On the Death of Mrs. Rowe.
Casey, M.   LZ Gator Body Collector, The.
Cassells.   Courtesy, A Trenchant Grace, A.
Caston, A.   Burden, The.
Causley.   By St. Thomas Water.
Death of a Poet.
Song of the Dying Gunner A.A.1.
Cavendish, M.   Common Fate of Books, The.
Nature's Cook.
Soul and Body.
Woman drest by Age, A.
Cawein.   Uncalled.
Celan.   Death Fugue, A.
Chamberlain, B.   Dead Ponies.
Islandman.
Chandler, M.   My Own Epitaph.
Chang, E.   Bamboo Elegy: Two.
Chapman, G.   Homer and the Brazen Head of
Rumour.
Cheney-Coker.   Letter to a Tormented
Playwright.
Chester, T.   Candle at Canterbury, A.
Chesterfield.   On Lord Ila's Improvements, near
Hounslow Heath.
Chimombo.   Four Ways of Dying.
Chin.   Autumn Leaves.
Elegy for Chloe Nguyen.
Chingono.   Epitaph, An: "Here lies Stephen

Pwanya."
Chisholm, A.   Contact.
Chivers.   Avalon.
Chock.   Poem for George Helm: Aloha Week
1980.
Clampitt.   What the Light Was Like.
Clanchy, K.   Deadman's Shoes.
Clare, J.   Death.
I Am.
To the Memory of John Keats.
Clark Bekedermo.   Death of a Lady.
Family Procession, A.
Order of the Dead, The.
Clark, P.   Kleptomaniac.
Clifton, H.   Death of Thomas Merton.
Clifton, L.   At Jonestown.
Sam.
Clough.   Epi-strauss-ium.
Clover, J.   There Is the Body Lying in State.
Codrescu.   Grammar, A.
Cofer, J.   Lesson of the Teeth, The.
My Grandfather's Hat.
Coleman, E.   Liberator, The.
Coleman, M.   Remembrance of Things Past.
Coleman, W.   Today I Am a Homicide in the
North of the City.
Coleridge, H.   Think upon Death.
Written on the Anniversary of Our Father's
Death.
Coleridge, M.   'But in that Sleep of Death What
Dreams may Come?'
'I envy not the dead that rest'
Death.
Marriage.
Witch, The.
Coleridge, S.   Epitaph: "Stop, Christian passer-
by!—Stop, child of God."
Father! no amaranths e'er shall wreathe my
brow.
W. H. Eheu!
Collier, M.   Robert Wilson.
Collins, B.   Memento Mori.
Tomes.
Collins, W.   Fidele, A.
How Sleep the Brave.
Conway, J.   Weight Belt.
Cook, E.   Song of the Rushlight.
Written at the Couch of a Dying Parent.
Cook-Lynn.   My Grandmother's Burial Ground.
Cooke, E.   How Did You Die?
Cooke, P.   Florence Vane.
Cooper, D.   10 Dead Friends.
Dreamt Up.
Drugs.
Cope, J.   Solstice for John.
Copus, J.   Clothes, The.
Corbet [or Corbett].   Elegy upon the Death of
His Own Father, An.
On the Lady Arabella.
Corcoran.   When Suzy Was.
Corman.   Deceased.
Cornford, F.   Recollection, A.
Watch, The.
Corso.   Mad Yak, The.
Cotton, C.   Epitaph on M. H., An.
Coulehan, J.   Azalea Poem, The.
Cowley, A.   On the Death of Mr. Crashaw.
On the Death of Mr. William Hervey [or
Harvey].
Cowper, W.   Epitaph on a Hare.
Crane, H.   Broken Tower, The.
Circumstance, The.
Praise for an Urn.
Crane, S.   Man Adrift on a Slim Spar, A.
There Is a Grey Thing That Lives in the Tree-
Tops.
Crapsey.   Lonely Death, The.
Moon-Shadows.
Crase.   There Is No Real Peace in the World.
Crashaw.   Epitaph Upon Husband and Wife
Who Died and Were Buried Together, An.
Crawford, R.   Downtown Sunday.
Creeley.   After Lorca.
And.
Death of Venus, The.
For My Mother: Genevieve Jules Creeley.

Heroes.
Road, The.
World, The.
Cristall.   Elegy: "Wander, my troubled soul, sigh
mid the night thy pain."
Song: "Both gloomy and dark was the shadowy
night."
Cross, F.   Fifty Gunner, The.
Rice Will Grow Again.
Cross, Jr.   Gliding Baskets.
Csoori.   Thin, Black Band, A.
Cullen, C.   Brown Girl Dead, A.
For Hazel Hall, American Poet.
Only the Polished Skeleton.
Cummings, E.   One X.
Portrait.
Since feeling is first.
Sonnet IV.
When God Lets My Body Be.
Cuney.   Death Bed, The.
Cunningham, J.   Epigram: "Life flows to death
as rivers to the sea."
Curry.   St Kilda.
Cust.   Non Nobis.
d'Oettingen.   Kilimanjaro.
D'Orleans.   Oft in My Thought.
Dalton, A.   Dad-Baby, The.
Dana, R.   At the Vietnam War Memorial,
Washington, D. C.
Dying Raven, The.
Husband's and Wife's Grave, The.
Daniels, K.   Ethiopia.
Darley.   Pass of Death, The.
Darr.   At Sixteen.
Daumal.   Short Revelation Concerning Death
and Chaos.
Davey, V.   Shadow of Life, The.
Davidson, D.   Lines for a Tomb.
Redivivus.
Davidson, J.   Price, The.
Davidson, L.   Charnel Ship, The.
Davie.   G. M. B.
Davies, D.   At Branwen's Grave.
Davies, J.   Remembrance of My Friend Mr.
Thomas Morley, A.
Davies, W.   Bed-Sitting Room, The.
Dawe, B.   Family Man, The.
Going.
On the Death of Ronald Ryan.
Day Lewis.   Reconciliation.
Day, J.   Man's Natural Infirmity.
De Kok.   Al Wat Kind Is.
Our Sharpeville.
Small Passing.
De la Mare.   Autumn.
Epitaph, An: "Here lies a most beautiful lady."
Fare Well.
Motley.
Peace.
Shubble, The.
Silver Penny, The.
Slim Cunning Hands.
De Vere, E.   Poem: "Were I a king, I could
command content."
Deane, S.   Burial, A.
DeFrees.   Census of Animal Bodies: Driving
Home.
Delanty.   Tie.
Delgado, J.   Winter Fruit.
Denham.   Song, A: "Morpheus, the humble god,
that dwells."
Denning.   Fire Support Burk.
Kim-San.
Movie, The.
Night on the Kho Bha Dinh.
This Time.
Dennis, C.   St. Francis and the Nun.
Desnos.   Epitaph: "I lived in those times. For a
thousand years."
Di Prima.   Death Poems in September.
Death Sunyata Chant: A Rite for Passing Over.
For the Dead Lecturer.
Diaz-Duque.   Why Don't I?
Dibdin, C.   Poor Tom.
Dickey, J.   Hospital Window, The.
Sled Burial, Dream Ceremony.

Dickey, W.   Cassandra.
Death of John Berryman,The.
Plot, The.
Dickinson, E.   Choice.
Flags Vex a Dying Face.
He fumbles at Your Spirit.
Heart Asks Pleasure—First, The.
I Felt a Funeral in My Brain.
I Never Lost as Much.
Last Night that She Lived, The.
My Life Closed Twice.
Of nearness to her sundered Things.
That after horror that was us.
Word is dead, A.
Divakaruni.   At Muktinath.
Dixon, M.   Grandmother: Crossing Jordan.
Dixon, R.   Wizard's Funeral, The.
Dobell, S.   Tommy's Dead.
Dobson, R.   Being Called For.
Dobyns.   Allegorical Matters.
Dodd, E.   Like Memory, Caverns.
Dodd, W.   Of His Life.
Dodge, M.   Two Mysteries, The.
Donne.   Blossom [or Blossome], The.
Computation, The.
Expiration, The.
Funeral[l], The.
Hero and Leander.
Hymn to the Saints, and to Marquis Hamilton[,
An].
Hymn[e] to God My God, In My
Sickness[e], A.
Paradox, The.
Song: "Sweetest love, I do not go[e]."
Valediction: Forbidding Mourning, A.
Valediction: of Weeping, A.
Donnelly, C.   Tolerance of Crows, The.
Dooley, M.   Heart.
Doolittle, H.   Epitaph: "So I may say."
Helen.
Wine Bowl.
Doty, M.   Tiara.
Douglas, K.   How to Kill.
Offensive, The.
Prisoner, The.
Simplify Me When I'm Dead.
Dove, R.   Event, The.
Oriental Ballerina, The.
Political.
Teach Us to Number Our Days.
Tou Wan Speaks to Her Husband Liu Sheng.
Dowson.   Dregs.
Extreme Unction.
Last Word, A.
Dressel.   You, Benjamin Jones.
Drummond de Andrade.   Motionless Faces.
Drummond, W.   Madrigal: "This world a
hunting is."
Dryden, J.   To the Memory of Mr Oldham.
To the Pious Memory of the Accomplished [or
Accomplisht] Young Lady, Mrs. Anne
Killigrew, [Excellent in the Two Sister-Arts of
Poesie and Painting].
Du Maurier.   Music.
Dubie.   Death of the Race Car Driver, The.
Sanctuary.
Dudek.   Dead, The.
Dudley, E.   Pathologist.
Dufault.   First Night, A.
Dugan, A.   Memorial Service for the Invasion
Beach Where the Vacation in the Flesh Is
Over.
Duhamel.   How Much Is This Poem Going to
Cost Me?
Duhig, I.   Fred.
Dunbar, P.   Compensation.
Frederick Douglass.
Paradox, The.
When All Is Done.
Dunbar, W.   Lament for the Makaris.
Translation by Mark Willhardt.
Duncan, R.   After a Long Illness.
Dunn, D.   Kaleidoscope, The.
Supreme Death.
Durcan.   Ireland 1972.
Tullynoe: Tête-à-Tête in the Parish Priest's

Parlour.
Earle, J.   Tea Party, The.
Eastman, M.   To John Reed.
Eberhart, R.   Flux.
Hardy Perennial.
Horse Chestnut Tree, The.
I Walked over the Grave of Henry James.
Edson, R.   Bringing a Dead Man Back into Life.
Edwards, M.   Time to Die, The.
We Are Passing Away.
Egan, T.   Drover's Boy, The.
Ehrhart.   Letter.
One That Died, The.
Eigner.   Letter for Duncan.
Eliot, T.   Aunt Helen.
Hollow Men, The.
Marina.
Song for Simeon, A.
"Eliza."   To My Husband.
Ellis, T.   Star Child.
"Elmo."   Our Ernest.
Emerson, R.   Dirge: "I reached the middle of the
mount."
Good-bye.
Terminus.
Visit, The.
Emmett.   Blue Tail Fly or Jimmy Cracked Corn,
The.
Empson.   Ignorance of Death.
Missing Dates.
Teasers, The.
Engels, J.   Bullhead.
Engle, P.   Hart Crane.
Erdrich, H.   Future Debris.
Quiet Earth, The.
Eshleman, C.   Lich Gate, The.
Espada.   Latin Night at the Pawnshop.
Espinet, R.   Merchant of Death.
Etter.   Drink and Agriculture.
Roma Higgins.
Evance, S.   Written at Netley Abbey.
Written in Ill Health at the Close of Spring.
Evans, G.   Horse on a Fence.
Evans, M.   Rebel, The.
Everson, W.   Poet Is Dead, The.
Ewart.   Sonnet: The Last Things.
Faber, F.   After-State.
"Fane, V."   In an Irish Churchyard.
Fanthorpe.   At the Ferry.
Fanfare.
Fauset.   Oblivion.
Fearing.   Dirge: "1-2-3 was the number he
played but today the number came 3-2-1."
Evening Song.
Obituary.
Feinfeld, D.   Carmelita.
Feldman, A.   Contemporary American Poetry.
Fenton, J.   Cambodia.
Dead Soldiers.
God, A Poem.
Ferguson, G.   Swimming Pool Ghost, The.
Ferlinghetti, L.   Sometime During Eternity.
Fernandez, R.   Legacy of a Brother.
Ferry.   Cythera.
Fiacc.   Saint Coleman's Song for Flight/ An Ite
Missa Est.
Fiawoo.   Soliloquy on Death.
"Field."   Almoner, An.
Dying Viper, A.
Picture, A.
Portrait, A.
Your Rose is Dead.
Field, E.   Little Boy Blue.
Little Peach, The.
Finch, A.   Reply From His Coy Mistress, A.
Fisher, R.   As He Came near Death.
Occasional Poem 7.1.72.
Fishman, C.   Death March.
Fitzgerald, F.   Obit on Parnassus.
Flatman.   Thought of Death, A.
Fletcher, J.   Blue Symphony.
Lincoln.
Fletcher, L.   Higashiyama Crematorium,
November 6, 1983.
Fletcher, P.   Dying Husband's Farewell, The.
Floyd.   Captain James Leson, U. S. M. C.

Corporal Kevin Spina, U. S. M. C.
Sergeant Brandon Just, U. S. M. C.
Flynn, E.   After Grave Deliberation.
Foerster.   Mozart's Death.
Forbes, J.   Death, an Ode.
Fordham.   Dying Girl, The.
Magnolia.
On Parting with a Friend.
To My Mother.
Twilight Musings.
Foster, A.   Ashes.
Nest of Hats, A.
Fox, G.   It Is Her Cousin's Death.
Francia, L.   Is there There in dying.
Francis, R.   That Dark Other Mountain.
While I Slept.
Freneau.   Indian Burying Ground, The.
Frost, R.   "Out, Out—."
Away!
Death of the Hired Man, The.
Departmental.
Fire and Ice.
Hill Wife, The.
Home Burial.
House Fear.
Impulse, The.
Loneliness.
Oft-Repeated Dream, The.
Stopping by Woods on a Snowy Evening.
Fuller, M.   Let Me Gather from the Earth.
Fuller, R.   Death.
Memorial Poem.
Galvin, J.   Shadow-Casting.
Garcia, R.   Dangerous Hats.
Death in Larkspur Canyon, A.
Gardinier.   Ghost of Santo Domingo, The.
Two Girls.
Gardner, I.   Cock-a-Hoop.
Garioch.   Elegy: "They are lang deid, folk that I
used to ken."
Gascoyne.   De Profundis.
Tenebrae.
Gay, J.   My Own Epitaph.
Gbadamosi.   Death of the Polar Explorers.
Gehrke, S.   Mouth to Mouth.
George, D.   Wreck of the Old 97.
Gibb, B.   Vigil.
Gibbons, O.   Silver Swan, The.
Gibson, W.   All Being Well.
Gilbert-Lecomte.   Son of the Bone Speaks, The.
Gilmore, M.   Tenancy, The.
Ginsberg, A.   After Lalon.
At Apollinaire's Grave.
Death News.
Dream Record: June 8 1955.
Line Drive.
Memory Gardens.
On Neal's Ashes.
Ginsberg, L.   Soon at Last My Sighs and
Moans.
Giorno.   Scum & Slime.
Gioseffi.   American Sonnets for My Father.
Giovanni.   Women Gather, The.
Glück, L.   Apple Trees, The.
Descending Figure.
Drowned Children, The.
Firstborn.
Garden, The.
Hyacinth.
Racer's Widow, The.
Glaser, E.   Coroner.
Glaser, M.   Changing Address Books.
Glatt.   Amanda.
Godfrey.   Air.
Goethe.   Erl-King, The.
Gogarty.   Per Iter Tenebricosum.
To Death.
Goldbarth.   Complete with Starry Night and
Bourbon Shots.
González, R.   Day of the Dead.
Gonzalez, R.   At the Rio Grande Near the End
of the Century.
Without Villages.
Goodison.   For Don Drummond.
Goodman, M.   Coming and Going.
Goodman, P.   Sonnet 21: "I start awake at night

afraid of death."
Goodtimes. Roadkill Coyote.
Googe. Epitaph of the Death of Nicholas
 Grimald, An.
Gordon, G. Tercios del Muerte.
Gorges. Written upon the death of the most
 Noble Prince Henrie.
Graham, H. Opportunity.
Waste.
Graham-Pole, J. Candor.
Grahn. Funeral Plainsong from a Younger
 Woman to an Older Woman, A.
Graves, R. It Was All Very Tidy.
Narrow Sea, The.
Pure Death.
Sharp Ridge, The.
Gray, D. Sonnet: "October's gold is dim—the
 forests rot."
Gray, T. Descent of Odin, The.
Elegy Written in a Country Churchyard.
Epitaph: "Here rests his head upon the lap of
 earth."
Ode on the Death of a Favourite [or Favorite]
 Cat, Drowned in a Tub [or Bowl] of Gold
 Fishes.
Sonnet [on the Death of Mr. Richard West].
Greacen. Summer Day, A.
Greening, M. Missing—Believed Drowned.
Greenlee. Memorial for Trane.
Greenwell, D. Christina.
To Christina Rossetti.
Gregg. Past Perfect.
Singers Change, The Music Goes On, The.
Grimké, A. Epitaph on a Living Woman.
Grossman, A. Enough Rain for Agnes Walquist.
Guevara, M. Abuelo, Answers and Questions.
Magic Carpet, The.
Postmortem.
Tuesday Shaman.
Guiney. Open, Time.
Gunn, T. In the Post Office.
J Car, The.
Lament: "Your dying was a difficult enterprise."
My Sad Captains.
Reassurance, The.
Victim, The.
Gurney, I. First Time In.
Gwynn, R. Approaching a Significant Birthday,
 He Peruses The Norton Anthology of Poetry.
Habington. Solum Mihi Superest Sepulchrum.
To the Moment Last Past.
Hachenburg, H. Terezin.
Hacker, M. Ballad of Ladies Lost and Found.
Dusk: July.
Year's End.
Hadas, R. In the Grove.
Hahn, S. Perennial.
Haines, J. Flight, The.
Halfe, L. Pāhkahkos.
Hall, D. Christmas Eve in Whitneyville, 1955.
Dusting.
My Son, My Executioner.
Raisin, The.
Small Fig Tree, A.
White Apples.
Hall, H. Woman Death.
Halleck, F. On the Death of Joseph Rodman
 Drake.
Halswell. Upon Mr. Hopton's Death.
Hamburger, M. Treblinka.
Hammial. Petit Guignol.
Hamod, S. After the Funeral of Assam
 Hamady.
Dying with the Wrong Name.
Hanson, M. Occasioned by Reading Mrs. M.
 Robinson's Poems.
Hanzlicek, C. Sierra Noon.
Harchik. Requiem: "Your names ring clearly."
Hardy, T. Afterwards.
At Castle Boterel.
Beeny Cliff.
Channel Firing.
Choirmaster's Burial, The.
Drummer Hodge.
During Wind and Rain.
Epitaph: "I never cared for Life: Life cared for

me."
Fallow Deer at the Lonely House, The.
Friends Beyond.
Going, The.
I Found Her Out There.
Lodging-House Fuchsias, The.
Nettles, The.
Neutral Tones.
She Hears the Storm.
Subalterns, The.
Thoughts of Phena.
Transformations.
Voice, The.
Where the Picnic Was.
Wife in London, A.
Harington, L. Elegy: "Death be not proud, thy
 hand gave not this blow."
Harjo, P. Death.
Harms. Soon.
Harper, F. Night of Death, The.
Harper, M. Mother Speaks: The Algiers Motel
 Incident, Detroit, A.
Nightmare Begins Responsibility.
Reuben, Reuben.
We Assume: On the Death of Our Son, Reuben
 Masai Harper.
Harries, E. Bone Prison, The.
Harrison, T. Heartless Art, The.
Study.
Harry, J. Honesty-Stones.
Harter. Sister Death.
Turtle Blessing.
Hartnett. All the Death-Room Needs.
Death of an Irishwoman.
Last Vision of Eoghan Rua Ó Súilleabháin, The.
Harwood, G. Death Has No Features of His
 Own.
Hassett. Patriot's Day.
Havergal. Just When Thou Wilt.
Hawkesworth, P. Two Statues.
Hay, G. Bizerta.
Hayden, R. Broken Dark, The.
Mourning Poem for the Queen of Sunday.
Paul Laurence Dunbar.
Hays, H. For One Who Died Young.
Healy, E. What It Was Like the Night Cary
 Grant Died.
Heaney, S. Badgers, The.
Casualty.
Funeral Rites.
Grauballe Man, The.
In Memoriam Francis Ledwidge.
Mid-Term Break.
Ship of Death, A.
Summer of Lost Rachel, The.
Heard, J. Message to a Loved One Dead, A.
Resting.
Hecht, A. 'More Light! More Light!'
Death the Painter.
Hedin, R. Wreck of the Great Northern, The.
Heithaus. What a Little Moonlight Can Do.
Hemans. Bring Flowers.
Effigies, The.
England's Dead.
Grave of a Poetess, The.
Graves of a Household, The.
Hour of Death, The.
Image in Lava, The.
Imelda.
Indian Woman's Death-Song, The.
Juana.
Magic Glass, The.
Properzia Rossi.
Statue of the Dying Gladiator, The.
To a Departed Spirit.
Hemingway. Champs d'Honneur.
Henderson, H. End of a Campaign.
We Show You That Death as a Dancer.
Henley, W. Madam Life's A Piece in Bloom.
Herbert, E. Elegy over a Tomb.
Herbert, G. Death.
Doomsday.
Life.
Mortification.
Redemption.
Virtue [or Vertue].

Herbert, J. Dossers at the Imperial War
 Museum.
Herbert, Z. Our Fear.
Herd. Coronach.
Exhibits, The.
Gia.
Hyperion's Bones.
Missing.
Herrera. Atavistic: Traces after the Rain.
Yellow Room, The.
Herrick. Comfort to a Youth That Had Lost His
 Love.
Dirge of Jephthah's Daughter, The.
Funeral[I] Rites of the Rose, The.
Gods Keyes.
Grace for a Child.
His Winding-Sheet.
Ode to Master Endymion Porter, upon His
 Brother's Death, An.
On Himself.
On Himselfe.
To Death.
To His Lovely Mistresses.
To Julia.
To Perilla.
To the Reverend Shade of His Religious Father.
Transfiguration, The.
Upon a child.
Upon Ben Jo[h]nson.
Upon Prue [or Prew], His Maid.
Widow's Tears [or Widdowes Teares]: or, Dirge
 of Dorcas, The.
Hesketh. Death of a Gardener.
Dilemma.
Hewitt, J. Father's Death, A.
Scar, The.
Heyen. Crane in Reeds.
Derailment.
Hill, G. Guardians, The.
In Memory of Jane Fraser [or Frazer].
Merlin.
White Ship, The.
Hillyer. Dead Man's Corner.
Hirsch, E. Fast Break.
Hirschhorn, N. Number Our Days.
Hirshfield, J. Story, A.
Hodgins. Death Who.
Hoffmann, H. Story of Augustus Who Would
 Not Have Any Soup, The.
Holden, M. Seaman, 1941.
Hollander, F. Boys in the Backroom, The.
Holst-Warhaft. In the End Is the Body.
Hongo. Legend, The.
Honig, E. Now, My Usefullness Over.
Hood, T. Bridge of Sighs, The.
Death in the Kitchen.
Death-Bed, The.
Jack Hall.
Hooks. Body Inside the Soul, The.
Hope, A. Death of the Bird, The.
Inscription for a War.
Hopkins, E. Life in Death.
Hopkins, G. Felix Randal.
No Worst, There Is None. Pitched Past Pitch of
 Grief.
Horan. Soft Swimmer, Winter Swan.
Houghton, L. Caustic Soda.
Housman, A. Because I liked you better.
Bredon Hill.
Crossing Alone the Nighted Ferry.
Epitaph.
Is my team plowing?
Isle of Portland, The.
Night Is Freezing Fast, The.
To an Athlete Dying Young.
When I Watch the Living Meet.
With Rue My Heart Is Laden.
Howard, R. 1915: A Pre-Raphaelite Ending,
 London.
Howe, F. Doubt.
Seeking Out His Face in a Cup.
Howe, W. Funeral Hymn.
Howell, J. Elegy upon His Tomb in Herndon-
 Hill Church, Erected by His Wife, Who
 Speaks, An.
Howes, B. Death of a Vermont Farm Woman.

Howitt, M.   Dying Child, The.
Hudgins.   After the Wilderness.
  Burial Detail.
  Dead Christ.
  Elegy for My Father, Who Is Not Dead.
  Hereafter, The.
Hufana, A.   Floating Epitaphs, Their Possible
  Explanations in Poro Point.
Hughes, F.   In the Shadow of Fire.
  Kookaburra.
Hughes, L.   Cross.
  Drum.
  Gal's Cry for a Dying Lover.
  Peace.
  Song for a Dark Girl.
  Stony Lonesome.
  Sylvester's Dying Bed.
  Wake.
  World War II.
  Young Gal's Blues.
Hughes, T.   Day He Died, The.
  Examination at the Womb-Door.
  Heptonstall.
  Leaves.
Hugo, R.   Elegy: "I expected him to look dead
  in the casket."
Huidobro.   Midnight.
Hummer, T.   Train Wreck, 1890: My
  Grandmother Lies Down with the Dead.
Humphreys, E.   From Father to Son.
Hunt, L.   On the Death of His Son Vincent.
Hunt, S.   My Father Today.
Hunter, A.   North American Death Song.
Hunter, W.   Monologue in a Rand Hospital.
Hyett.   Assembling the Dead at Dachau.
Ingelow.   High Tide on the Coast of
  Lincolnshire, 1571, The.
Ives, G.   With Whom, then, should I Sleep?
Jacinto, J.   Absence.
Jackson, F.   Death of Gladys Presley, The.
Jackson, G.   Some of Betty's Story Round 1850.
Jackson, L.   Elegy in a Spider's Web.
Jacobsen, J.   Limbo Dancer, The.
James, A.   Honor (1969).
James, T.   Lines on His Companions Who Died
  in the Northern Seas.
Jarman, M.   Ground Swell.
Jarrell.   Black Swan, The.
  Death of the Ball Turret Gunner, The.
  In the Camp There Was One Alive.
  Islands, The.
  Knight, Death, and the Devil, The.
  Losses.
  Say Good-bye to Big Daddy.
  Seele im Raum.
  Truth, The.
Jeffers, R.   Antrim.
  Bed by the Window, The.
  Cremation.
  Deer Lay Down Their Bones, The.
  May-June, 1940.
  Original Sin.
  Purse-Seine, The.
  Vulture.
  Where I?
Jewsbury.   Summer Eve's Vision, A.
Johnson, F.   My God in Heaven Said to Me.
  Song of the Whirlwind.
Johnson, G.   I Want to Die While You Love Me.
Johnson, J.   Color Sergeant, The.
  Go Down Death.
Johnson, L.   Collins.
  Dark Angel, The.
  Death of the Bosun's Mate.
Johnson, S.   On the Death of Dr [or Mr] Robert
  Levet [a Practiser in Physic].
Johnston, E.   Mother's Love, A.
  Nelly's Lament for the Pirnhouse Cat.
Johnston, M.   In Memoriam.
Johnstone, R.   Robot Camera.
  Undertakers.
Jones, E.   Development of Idiotcy, A.
Jones, G.   Merthyr.
Jones, M.   Stella's Epitaph.
Jones, S.   Community.
Jones, T.   My Grandmother Died in the Early

Hours of the Morning.
Jonson, B.   Epitaph on Elizabeth, L. H.
  Epitaph on Master Philip Gray, An.
  Epitaph on Master Vincent Corbet[t], An.
  Little Shrub Growing By, A.
  Ode To Himself, An.
  Of Life and Death.
  To the World [A Farewell for a Gentlewoman,
  Virtuous and Noble].
Justice, D.   Incident in a Rose Garden.
  On the Death of Friends in Childhood.
  Psalm and Lament.
  White Notes.
Kasdorf.   Dying with Amish Uncles.
  Grossdaadi's Funeral.
Kavanagh, P.   In Memory of My Mother.
Keats.   Bright Star.
  To Chatterton.
  When I Have Fears [That I May Cease to Be].
Kees.   For My Daughter.
  If this Room is Our World.
Kelen.   Gods Ash Their Cigarettes, The.
Kendrick, D.   Inpatient.
Kennedy, X.   Epitaph for a Postal Clerk.
Kenyon, J.   Travel: After a Death.
Kessler, S.   Jack's Last Words.
Keyes, S.   Death and the Plowman.
  Elegy: "April again, and it is a year again."
Kgositsile.   Acknowledgement.
  Air I Hear, The.
Killigrew, A.   On Death.
King, H.   Exequy, The.
Kingsley, C.   Three Fishers [Went Sailing], The.
Kinnell.   Cells Breathe in the Emptiness.
  Freedom, New Hampshire.
  Quick and the Dead, The.
Kinsella, T.   Cover Her Face.
  Death Bed.
Kinzie.   Lunar Frost.
Kirsch, D.   Dvora.
Kizer, C.   On a Line from Valéry.
Klappert.   In Memory of H. F.
Klein, M.   Guardian Life.
  Scenes for an Elegy.
Knevet.   Navigation.
Knight, E.   Poem of Attrition, A.
Knott.   At the Crossroads.
  Death.
  Funny Poem.
  Poem: "After your death."
  Two Vietnam Poems: (1966).
Košek, M.   It All Depends on How You Look at
  It.
Komey.   Oblivion.
Komunyakaa.   April Fools' Day.
  Between Days.
  Seven Deadly Sins.
Kumin, M.   How It Is.
  Retrieval System, The.
Kunene.   Elegy for My Friend E. Galo.
Kunitz, S.   Dragonfly, The.
Lacavaro, A.   Advantages of Being a World
  Class Athlete, The.
Laing, K.   I Am the Freshly Dead Husband.
Lake, P.   Blue Jay.
Lamb, C.   Hester.
  Old Familiar Faces, The.
Landon.   Child Screening a Dove from a
  Hawk, A.
  Marriage Vow, The.
Landor, W.   Age.
  Alas! 'Tis Very Sad to Hear.
  Death of the Day.
  Death Stands above Me.
  Rose Aylmer.
  To Arthur de Noé Walker.
Lane, P.   Rain Ditch.
Lanier, S.   Nirvâna.
Larkin, J.   Inventory.
Larkin, P.   Ambulances.
  Aubade: "I work all day, and get half-drunk at
  night."
  Church Going.
  Dublinesque.
  Next, Please.
Lassell.   Brady Street, San Francisco.

How to Watch Your Brother Die.
  Sunset Stripping: Visiting L.A.
  Three Poems.
Lattimore.   Witness to Death.
Laurencin, M.   Horse, The.
Lawrence, D.   Bride, The.
  Cherry Robbers.
  Fatality.
  Giorno dei Morti.
  Hymn to Priapus.
  Shadows.
  Ship of Death, The.
Layne, M.   On Hats and Things.
Layton.   Cold Green Element, The.
  Street Funeral.
Le Guin.   Child on the Shore, The.
Le Pan.   Incident, An.
Lea, S.   At the Flyfisher's Shack.
  Feud, Dust.
  Wrong Way Will Haunt You, The.
Leaf, E.   Her Son.
Leapor.   Epistle to a Lady, An.
  Mira's Will.
Lee, L.   Between Seasons.
  Eating Together.
  Visions and Interpetations.
Leigh, H.   Twins, The.
Leithauser.   Haunted, The.
Levertov.   Change, The.
  Clouds.
  Dead Butterfly, The.
  Death in Mexico.
  Note to Olga (1966), A.
  Olga Poems.
  What Were They Like?
Levin, P.   Shadow Returns, The.
Levine, P.   1933.
  And the Trains Go On.
  Baby Villon.
  Belief.
  Death of Saul, The.
  Horse, The.
  On a Drawing by Flavio.
  Red Dust.
  To My God in His Sickness.
  Uncle.
  Water's Chant, The.
Levis.   Morning After My Death, The.
Levy, A.   Cross-Road Epitaph, A.
  Epitaph: "This is the end of him, here he lies."
  Felo de Se.
  In the Mile End Road.
  London Poets.
  Magdalen.
  Old House, The.
  On the Threshold.
  Reminiscence, A.
  Sequel to 'A Reminiscence,' The.
  Straw in the Street.
  Twilight.
Lewis, A.   All Day It Has Rained.
  Autumn, 1939.
  Easter at Christmas.
  Song (On Seeing Dead Bodies Floating Off the
  Cape).
  Unknown Soldier, The.
Lewis, C.   Ballade of Dead Gentlemen.
  Epitaph, An: "Erected by her sorrowing
  brothers."
  Evensong.
Lewis, G.   Flyover Elegies.
Lewis, M.   Alonzo the Brave and the Fair
  Imogine.
Lieberman, L.   Compass of the Dying.
Lieberman, M.   Los Olivos.
  On the Anniversary of My Father's Death.
Lifshin.   Yahrtzeit Light, The.
Lightfoot.   Wreck of the Edmund Fitzgerald,
  The.
Limburg, J.   Return, The.
Lincoln, A.   My Childhood-Home I See Again.
Liu, T.   Vox Angelica.
  Wellfleet.
Lockhart.   Lines: "When youthful faith hath
  fled."
Loden.   Conversations with Dr. M.

Loesser. Boys in the Backroom, The.
Loftis, N. In Memorium: Robert Hayden.
Lomax, M. Amor Diving.
July.
Longenbach. What You Find in the Woods.
Longfellow, H. Cross of Snow, The.
Dante.
Excelsior.
Jewish Cemetery at Newport, The.
Nature.
Longley, M. In Memoriam.
In Memory of Gerard Dillon.
Kindertotenlieder.
Third Light, The.
Wounds.
Lorde. Day They Eulogized Mahalia, The.
Father Son and Holy Ghost.
Hanging Fire.
Lourie. For All My Brothers and Sisters.
Lovecraft. Well, The.
Lovelace, R. Black Patch on Lucasta's Face, A.
La Bourbon, A.
Lowell, J. First Snowfall [or Snow-Fall], The.
Memoriae Positum R. G. Shaw.
Sixty-Eighth Birthday.
Lowell, R. Alfred Corning Clark.
Death and the Bridge.
Falling Asleep over the Aeneid.
For Sale.
Harriet.
History.
Mr. Edwards and the Spider.
Quaker Graveyard in Nantucket, The.
Sailing Home from Rapallo.
Where the Rainbow Ends.
Lowry, M. Epitaph: "Malcolm Lowry."
For *Under the Volcano*.
Strange Type.
Volcano is Dark, The.
Lucie-Smith. Lesson, The.
Lumsden, R. Mercy.
Lux. Plague Victims Catapulted over Walls into Besieged City.
Lyte. Abide With Me.
Mörling, M. In a Motel Room at Dawn.
Mabuza. Death to the Gold Mine!
MacCaig. So Many Summers.
MacDiarmid, H. At My Father's Grave.
Dead Liebknecht, The.
Empty Vessel.
Of John Davidson.
Under the Greenwood Tree.
Watergaw, The.
Macgoye. Freedom Song, A.
MacKay, C. Louise on the Door-Step.
Mackenzie, K. Door swung open, The.
Sick Men Sleeping.
MacLean, S. Ebb.
Heroes.
MacLeish. Burying Ground by the Ties.
Epistle to Be Left in the Earth.
Mother Goose's Garland.
MacNeice. Charon.
Sunlight on the Garden, The.
This Is the Life.
Maguire, S. Invisible Mender, The.
Mahapatra, J. Ash.
Mahon. Image from Beckett, An.
In Carrowdore Churchyard.
Maiden. Air.
Climbing.
Major, C. Swallow the Lake.
Malange. This Poem Is Dedicated to Brother Andries Raditsela.
"Malley." Egyptian Register.
Mandelstam [or Mandelshtam]. I Was Washing Outside in the Darkness.
Mounds of Human Heads Are Wandering into the Distance.
Petropolis.
Mangan, J. O'Hussey's Ode to the Maguire.
Rest Only in the Grave.
Manguso, S. Rider, The.
Manley, R. Bob Marley's Dead.
Mansfield, K. To L. H. B.
Mapanje. Steve Biko is Dead.

Markham, E. In Death Valley.
Lincoln, the Man of the People.
Marlatt, D. Summer of the New Well.
Marshall-Stoneking. On the Death of Muriel Rukeyser.
Marston, P. Inseparable.
Martínez, V. Absence, Luminescent.
Tesoro.
Martin, C. Easter Sunday, 1985.
Martin, P. Tongues.
Martinez, D. Altruism.
Death of Isadora Duncan, The.
Discreet Prayer, A.
Standard Time: Novena for My Father.
Marvell. Damon the Mower.
To His Coy Mistress.
Marzials. Tragedy, A.
Masefield. Dead Knight, The.
Sonnet: "There, on the darkened deathbed, dies the brain."
To-morrow.
Mason, R. Spark's Farewell to Its Clay, The.
Matherne, B. Les Fils (Sons).
Mathews, A. At the Wailing Wall.
Mathias, R. Departure in Middle Age.
Maxton. Elegies.
McAuley, J. Cloak, The.
Pietá.
Pietà.
McCarthy, T. Sorrow Garden, The.
McClatchy. Tattoos.
McCrae, J. In Flanders Fields.
McCreery. There Is No Death.
McDonald, W. For Harper, Killed in Action.
For Kelly, Missing in Action.
McGonagall. Calamity in London; Family of Ten Burned to Death.
Late Sir John Ogilvy, The.
McGough, R. Let Me Die a Youngman's Death.
Survivor.
McGrath, C. First Trimester, The.
Jeffrey Lee Pierce.
McGrath, T. Blues for Warren.
Death for the Dark Stranger.
Epitaph: "Again, traveller, you have come a long way led by that star."
Go Ask the Dead.
McKay, C. If We Must Die.
My Mother.
McLaughlin, J. Black Irish Blues.
Mei Yao Ch'en. I Remember the River at Wu Sung.
Meltzer, D. 17: II:82.
Melville, H. Ball's Bluff.
Haglets, The.
Monody.
Time's Betrayal.
Menai. To One Who Died in a Garret in Cardiff.
Menken. Dying.
Resurgam.
Meredith, G. Ballad of Past Meridian, A.
Dirge in Woods.
Meredith, W. Dying Away.
To the Thoughtful Reader.
Merrill, C. Diver, The.
Merrill, J. Annie Hill's Grave.
Broken Home, The.
Country of a Thousand Years of Peace, The.
Merton. Responsory, 1948, A.
Merwin, W. S. Asians Dying, The.
Ballad of John Cable and Three Gentlemen.
For the Anniversary of My Death.
Strawberries.
Mew. À Quoi Bon Dire.
At the Convent Gate.
Beside the Bed.
In Nunhead Cemetery.
Smile, Death.
Meynell, A. Maternity.
Parentage.
Mezey. Touch It.
Michelson, P. Enduring Witness, the Mosques of Kattankudi.
Miles, J. Conception.
Millay, E. Buck in the Snow, The.

Childhood Is the Kingdom Where Nobody Dies.
Conscientious Objector.
I Dreamed I Moved among the Elysian Fields.
Passer Mortuus Est.
Miller, E. Players.
Miller, M. Closing, A.
Mills, R. For Lorine Niedecker in Heaven.
Milosz, C. Dedication: "You whom I could not save."
With Her*.
Milosz, O. Bridge, The.
Milton. Lycidas.
On His Blindness.
On His Deceased Wife.
On Shakespear[e].
On the University Carrier Who Sick'n'd [or Sickened] in the Time of His Vacancy [, Being Forbid to go to London, by Reason of the Plague].
On Time.
Sonnet: On the Religious Memorie of Mrs. Catherine Thomason My Christian Freind Deceas'd Decem. 1646.
Mirikitani. Fisherman, The.
Shadow in Stone.
Mitchell, A. Not a Very Cheerful Song, I'm Afraid.
Mitchell, K. On the Anniversary Of Your Death.
Mitchell, S. Parable of the Sower, The.
Momaday. Rainy Mountain Cemetery.
Two Figures.
Monck. Verses Written on Her Death-bed at Bath to Her Husband in London.
Monk, M. Verses Written on Her Death-Bed at Bath to Her Husband in London.
Monsour. Emily's Words.
Montagu, L. Epitaph: "Here lies John Hughes and Sarah Drew."
On the Death of Mrs. Bowes.
Montague, J. Mother Cat.
Montgomerie, W. Epitaph: "My brother is skull and skeleton now."
Moolten, D. Brandy Station, Virginia.
Moore, M. Grave, A.
What Are Years?
Moore, R. Dirge for the Living.
Shipwreck.
Still Without Life.
Moore, T. 'Tis the Last Rose of Summer.
Echo.
Moorer. In Memoriam of E. B. Clark.
More, S. Minstrel Boy, The.
Morgan, R. Blood Donor.
Mori. Heat in October.
Speaking Through White: For My Mother.
Morris, W. Death Song, A.
Morrissey, S. To Look Out Once from High Windows.
Moss, H. Elegy for My Sister.
Water Island.
Moss, T. Fisher Street.
Mother Goose. Six Little Mice.
Who Killed Cock Robin.
Mtshali. Ride upon the Death Chariot.
Muir, E. Child Dying, The.
For Ann Scott-Moncrieff.
Muldoon, P. Soap-Pig, The.
Munby. Post Mortem.
Mura. Grandfather-in-law.
Murray, G. Rounds, The.
Murray, L. Lament for the Country Soldiers.
Muske, C. Eulogy, The.
Myles, E. December 9th.
Naganawa, A. Learning to Swim.
Nairne. Land o' the Leal, The.
Napier, F. I Have Taken the Suits and Shoes to Oxfam.
Nash, O. Old Men.
Tweedledee and Tweedledoom.
Nashe [or Nash]. Adieu, Farewell, Earth's Bliss[e].
Autumn.
Fair Summer Droops.
Spring, the Sweet Spring.
Nelson, H. My Father Went to Funerals.

Nemerov. Easter.
  Grace to Be Said at the Supermarket.
  Speculation.
Nesbit, E. Dead to the Living, The.
Neufeld, A. Pictures and Stories.
Newbolt. Messmates.
Nezval. Trap Door.
Nichol. Ferry Me Across.
Nicholson, N. Five Minutes.
Nims, J. Trainwrecked Soldiers.
Noguchi, R. I, the Neighbor Mr. Uskovich,
  Watch Every Morning Kenji Takezo Hold His
  Breath.
Norris, J. Meditation, The.
Norris, L. Elegy for Lyn James.
Nortje. Autopsy.
Norton, C. Obscurity of Woman's Worth.
Notley. Beginning with a Stain.
  Poem: "You hear that heroic big land music?"
Nowlan. Suppose This Moment Some
  Stupendous Question.
Noyes, A. Highwayman, The.
O'Connor, P. Fag-End.
O'Grady, D. Dying Gaul, The.
  Reading the Unpublished Manuscripts of Louis
    MacNeice at Kinsale Harbour.
O'Hara, F. Day Lady Died, The.
  Hôtel Transylvanie.
  Ode to Joy.
  Poem: "Eager note on my door said "Call me",
    The."
O'Lahsen, M. Dead Erect, The.
O'Loughlin. Irish Requiem, An.
  Posthumous.
O'Reilly, M. Abused Child.
  Small Girl Brings an Injured Bird into the
    Surgery, A.
Ogilvy. Newly Dead and Newly Born.
Olds, S. Leningrad Cemetery, Winter of 1941.
  Lifting, The.
  Moment of My Father's Death, The.
  Race, The.
Oliver, D. Little Night, A.
Oliver, M. Wings.
Ologoudou. Liberty.
Olson, C. As the Dead Prey upon Us.
  At Yorktown.
  Death of Europe, The.
  La Chute.
  La Préface.
  Newly Discovered "Homeric" Hymn, A.
  Variations Done for Gerald Van De Wiele.
Oodgeroo of the tribe Noonuccal. Dawn Wail
  for the Dead.
Ormond. At His Father's Grave.
  My Dusty Kinsfolk.
Ormsby, F. Day in August, A.
Ortleb. On Finding Out that the One You Slept
  with the Night Before Was Murdered the Next
  Day.
Owen, W. End, The.
  Futility.
  Miners.
  Next War, The.
  Strange Meeting.
  To My Friend (With an Identity Disc).
  Unreturning, The.
Padgett, R. Something or Other.
Page, G. Elegist, The.
  Inscription at Villers-Bretonneux.
Pagis. Autobiography.
Paino. Matter of Division, A.
  Truth, The.
Paquet. Easter '68.
  In a Plantation.
  It Is Monsoon at Last.
  Morning—A Death.
  Mourning the Death, by Hemorrhage, of a Child
    from Honai.
  They Do Not Go Gentle.
Parker, D. Foxfire.
Parkerson. Statistic.
Parnell, T. Night Piece on Death.
Pasolini. Day of My Death, The.
Pastan. Hat Lady, The.
  Turnabout.

Patchen. Body Beside the Ties, The.
  Do the Dead Know What Time It Is?
  From My High Love.
  In Memory of Kathleen.
  O All Down within the Pretty Meadow.
  Religion Is That I Love You.
Patel, G. Forensic Medicine.
Peacock, M. Dream Come True.
Peacocke. In Memoriam.
Pegram, A. Burials.
  Towards Abraham's Bosom.
Perry, N. Too Late.
Peters, L. Isatou Died.
  One Long Jump.
Peterson, M. I Kissed Pa Twice after His Death.
Philips, K. Epitaph on her Son H. P. at St.
  Syth's Church.
Piatt, S. Army of Occupation.
  Giving Back the Flower.
  Her Word of Reproach.
Picasso. Bottle of Suze, A.
Picková, E. Fear.
Pickthall, M. Resurgam.
Piercy. Barbie Doll.
Pietri. Night Is out of Sight, The.
Pilling. Ophelia.
Pinsky. Dying.
  Memorial.
Pitcher. Pale Blue Casket, The.
Plath. Bee Meeting, The.
  Daddy.
  Death and Co.
  Edge.
  Getting There.
  Lady Lazarus.
  Point Shirley.
  Stings.
Plato. Reflections, Written on Visiting the
  Grave of a Venerated Friend.
Plumly. After Grief.
Poe. Annabel Lee.
  City in the Sea, The.
  Conqueror Worm, The.
  For Annie.
  Lenore.
  Monody on Doctor Olmsted.
  Raven, The.
  Sleeper, The.
  To My Mother.
  To One in Paradise.
  Ulalume [or Ulalume—a Ballad].
Pogson, P. Bee.
Pope, A. Epitaph for One Who Would Not Be
  Buried in Westminster Abbey.
  Ode: The Dying Christian to His Soul.
Porter, D. Lollies Noir.
Porter, P. Exequy, An.
  Talking to You Afterwards.
Pound, E. Coda.
  Planh for the Young English King.
  Sandalphon.
Powell, J. Lines Written for a Friend on the
  Death of His Brother, Caused by a Railway
  Train Running Over Him Whilst He Was in a
  State of Inebriation.
Pratt, M. Red String.
Preston, M. Ready.
Prior. Epigram: "When Bibo thought fit from
  the world to retreat."
  Reasonable Affliction, A.
Probyn. Kyrielle.
  Rondelet: "Which way he went?"
Procter, A. Envy.
  Philip and Mildred.
  Three Evenings in a Life.
Prufer, K. For the Dead.
Prys-Jones. Unfortunate Occurrence at Cwm-
  Cadno.
Pudney. Missing.
Purdy, A. Winter Walking.
Quarles. David's Epitaph on Jonathan.
Quiller-Couch. Doom Ferry.
Ríos, A. Mi Abuelo.
Radcliffe, A. Storied Sonnet.
Radnóti. Forced March.
  Picture Postcards.

Ragan, J. Huckster at Noontime.
Raine, K. Invocation of Death.
Ralegh, S. Authours Epitaph, Made by Himself,
  The.
  Even Such Is Time.
  On the Snuff of a Candle.
  Passionate Man[']s Pilgrimage, The.
  Sir Walter Ra[u]le[i]gh to His Son[ne].
Ramanujan. Breaded Fish.
  Death and the Good Citizen.
  Hindu to His Body, A.
  Some People.
Randall, D. Blue Dome, The.
  Old Witherington.
Randolph, T. On Sir Robert Cotton the
  Antiquary.
Rankin, J. Forever the Snake.
Ransom, J. Piazza Piece.
Ravikovitch [or Ravikovich]. You Can't Kill a
  Baby Twice.
Ray, D. Eskimo Girl, The.
Rector. Showing.
Redmond. Milestone: The Birth of an Ancestor.
  Poetic Reflections Enroute To, and During, The
    Funeral and Burial of Henry Dumas, Poet.
Reed, I. I am not the walrus.
  Oakland Blues.
Reese, L. Telling the Bees.
Reid, A. Curiosity.
Rexroth, K. Andrée Rexroth.
  Andree Rexroth.
  For Eli Jacobson.
Reynolds, C. Worst of it, The.
Reznikoff. Epitaph.
  Epitaphs.
  Testimony: The United States (1901–1910)
    Recitative/The South.
Rich, A. For the Dead.
  From a Survivor.
  I Dream I'm the Death of Orpheus.
  Mourning Picture.
  Paula Becker to Clara Westhoff.
  Phantasia for Elvira Shatayev.
  Readings of History.
  Tattered Kaddish.
Richards, I. End of a Course.
Rickword. Moonrise Over Battlefield.
Ridge, L. Fifth-Floor Window, The.
Rilke. Death.
Robinson, A. Dead Friend, The.
  Pallor.
  To a Dead Friend.
  Venetian Nocturne.
Robinson, E. Exit.
  For a Dead Lady.
  Luke Havergal.
  Many Are Called.
  Old Story, An.
  Walt Whitman.
Robinson, M. Foresees her Death.
  Her Reflections on the Leucadian Rock Before
    She Perishes.
  Resolves to Take the Leap of Leucata.
  To the Muses.
Rochester, J. Song: "Absent from thee, I
  languish still."
Rock, D. Mother.
Rodgers, C. Written for Love of an
  Ascension—Coltrane.
Roditi. Seance.
Roeske, P. Preparing the Dead.
Roethke. Elegy for Jane.
  Judge Not.
Rogers, S. Boy of Egremond, The.
Rolfe, E. Paris—Christmas 1938.
Root, W. Sonnet 20: Remembering, from a Nazi
  Prison, a Teacher Years Before.
Rose. Truganinny.
Rose, P. Terminus.
Rosenberg, I. Dead Man's Dump.
Rossetti, C. After Death.
  Amen.
  At Home.
  Before the Beginning.
  Bride Song.
  Cardinal Newman.

Chilly Night, A.
Convent Threshold, The.
Dead before Death.
Dirge, A: "Why were you born when the snow was falling?"
Dream Land.
Easter Monday.
Eve.
From the Antique.
Gone Before.
Heaviness May Endure for a Night, But Joy Cometh in the Morning.
Iniquity of the Fathers upon the Children, The.
Pause, A.
Remember [Me].
Rest.
Sappho.
Sleeping at Last.
Song: "Oh roses for the flush of youth."
Triad, A.
Two Thoughts of Death.
Under Willows.
Uphill.
Wednesday in Holy Week.
Rossetti, D. My Sister's Sleep.
Orchard-Pit, The.
Sudden Light.
Rothenberg, J. Water of the Flowery Mill (II), The.
Rowbotham. Bus-Stop on the Somme, The.
Rowe, E. Upon the Death of Her Husband.
Rowswell. Should You Go First.
Ruefle. Furtherness.
Rukeyser, M. Book of the Dead, The.
Death and the Dancer.
Iris.
Madboy's Song.
Outer Banks, The.
Power of Suicide, The.
Then.
Rungano. Mother.
Rutsala. Silence, The.
Ryan, G. Elegy for 6 So Far.
Ryan, M. Talking about Things.
Ryan, R. At the End.
Ryan, T. Eclipse, Kenwick, 1974.
Trompe l'oeil.
Sachs, N. Chorus of the Dead.
Salaam. I Just Heard John Buffington Died.
Our World Is Less Full Now That Mr. Fuller Is Gone.
Salazar. E is in Heaven.
Piñon Nuts.
Salinas, L. For Larry Levis in Memory.
Sanchez, S. Blues.
Philadelphia: Spring, 1985.
Sandburg, C. Bones.
Cool Tombs.
Grass.
Haze.
Illinois Farmer.
Losers.
Murmurings in a Field Hospital.
Right to Grief, The.
Southern Pacific.
Sarson, H. Shell, The.
Sarton. Letter from Chicago.
Sassoon. Counter-Attack.
Death-Bed, The.
General, The.
In Heytesbury Wood.
One Who Watches.
Rear-Guard, The.
To His Dead Body.
Working Party, A.
Scammell, W. Inventions.
Schechter. What Were You Patching?
Schnackenberg. Nightfishing.
Schreiner, O. Cry of South Africa, The.
Schwartz, R. L. Grief.
When They Know.
Scott, D. Forsaken, The.
Prayer for the Little Daughter between Death and Burial.
Scott, W. Death.
My Mother.

U.S. Sailor with the Japanese Skull, The.
Seeger, A. I Have a Rendezvous with Death.
Seeger, P. Where Have All the Flowers Gone?
Seferis. Our Sun.
Sempill, R. Life and Death of [Habbie Simson] the Piper of Kilbarchan, The.
Seth. Doctor's Journal Entry for August 6, 1945, A.
Seward. On a Lock of Miss Sarah Seward's Hair Who Died in her Twentieth Year.
Sonnet 31.
Sewell, G. Dying Man in His Garden, The.
Sexton. All My Pretty Ones.
Jesus Dies.
Lament: "Someone is dead."
Moss of His Skin, The.
Somewhere in Africa.
Starry Night, The.
Truth the Dead Know, The.
Wanting to Die.
Seymour-Smith. He Came to Visit Me.
Shapiro, K. Auto Wreck.
Cut Flower, A.
Hospital.
My Grandmother.
Shelley, P. Adonais; An Elegy on the Death of John Keats.
Lament, A: "O world! O life! O time!"
Mask [or Masque] of Anarchy, The.
To Night.
Sherrill, S. Katyn Forest.
Sia, B. Howl.
Siddal. At Last.
Dead Love.
Sidney, S. Dirge: "Ring out your bells [or belles], let mourning shows [or shewes] be spread."
Leave Me O Love.
Sigourney. Death of an Infant.
Silesky. Kingdom, The.
Silkin. Space in the Air, A.
Simic. Charon's Cosmology.
Eyes Fastened with Pins.
Simmons, J. From the Irish.
Simpson, L. Riders Held Back, The.
Singer, B. Epilogue: "That death might not be casual."
Sirr. Beginnings.
Sissman. Deathplace, A.
Upon Finding Dying: An Introduction, by L. E. Sissman, Remaindered atts.
Skeeter. Western Trail Cook, 1880.
Skelton, J. Upon a Dead Man's Head.
Smedley, M. Cavour.
Face from the Past, A.
Smith, A. Dead, The.
Smith, C. By the Same.
Dead Beggar, an Elegy Addressed to a Lady, The.
Ode to Death.
Pressed by the Moon, Mute Arbitress of Tides.
To the Shade of Burns.
To the South Downs.
Smith, D. Roundhouse Voices, The.
Smith, J. Sew a Pocket.
Smith, K. Train.
Smith, P. Building Nicole's Mama.
Woman Who Died in Line, The.
Smith, S. Angel Boley.
Black March.
Death Sentence, The.
Exeat.
Mrs Simpkins.
Not Waving But Drowning.
Private Means Is Dead.
Quand on n'a pas ce que l'on aime, il faut aimer ce que l'on a—.
Reversionary.
Snodgrass, W. Monet: 'Les Nymphéas'
Snyder, G. Dragonfly.
For John Chappell.
Sorby. Land of Lincoln.
Sorley. All the Hills and Vales Along.
Sorrentino. Zoo, The.
Sousa, N. Appeal.
Soutar. Song: "Whaur yon broken brig hings

owre."
Southey, R. Scholar, The.
Southwell. I Dye Alive.
Upon the Image of Death.
Sowle, J. Short Testimony for Anne Whitehead, A.
Soyinka. Civilian and Soldier.
Funeral Sermon, Soweto.
Massacre, October '66.
Post Mortem.
Sparrow, J. Epitaph: "This stone, with not unpardonable pride."
Spellman. Did John's Music Kill Him?
Spender, S. Beethoven's Death Mask.
Funeral, The.
Stafford, W. Bess.
Traveling Through the Dark.
Stainer. Bleaklow.
Sarcophagus.
Xochiquetzal.
Stanley, T. On S. John the Baptist.
Stanton, M. Few Picnics in Illinois, A.
Starbuck, G. Prognosis.
Stephens, P. Signalmen, The.
Steptoe. Notes for a Poem from the Middle Passage of Years.
Stern, G. Behaving Like a Jew.
Pile of Feathers.
Stevens, W. Death of a Soldier, The.
Emperor of Ice-Cream, The.
Flyer's Fall.
Owl in the Sarcophagus, The.
Postcard from the Volcano, A.
Sunday Morning.
Table Talk.
Worms at Heaven's Gate, The.
Stevenson, A. Death, My Companion*.
Epitaph for a Good Mouser.
Stevenson, R. Celestial Surgeon, The.
Epitaph: "Angler rose, he took his rod, The."
Requiem: "Under the wide and starry sky."
Ticonderoga: A Legend of the West Highlands.
To Mrs. Will H. Low.
Stewart, S. Apple.
Stone, J. Truck, The.
Stowe. Only a Year.
Strand. Dead, The.
End, The.
Prediction, The.
Strauss, J. Tending the Graves.
Strickland, A. Forsaken, The.
Strode. Epitaph on the Monument of Sir William Strode.
Suckling, S. Song: "I prithee spare me, gentle boy."
Summers, H. My Old Cat.
Surrey. Epitaph for [or on] Thomas Clere.
Excellent Epitaffe of Syr Thomas Wyat, An.
Swenson, M. Question.
Shape of Death, The.
Swift, J. In Sickness.
Satirical Elegy on the Death of a Late Famous General, A.
To the Earl of Oxford, Late Lord Treasurer.
Verses on the Death of Dr. Swift, D.S.P.D., Occasioned by Reading a Maxim in Rochefoucauld.
Swinburne. After Death.
Forsaken Garden, A.
Garden of Proserpine, The.
Lyke-Wake Song, A.
Swirszczynska. I Wash the Shirt.
They Lay Dying Side by Side.
Synge. Question, A.
Synková, A. I'd Like to Go Alone.
Szymborska. Seen from Above.
Tabb. Echoes.
Taggard. To the Powers of Desolation.
Tallmountain. Hands of Mary Joe, The.
Tate, A. Cross, The.
Non Omnis Moriar.
Oath, The.
Tate, G. Last Instructions.
Tate, J. Death on Columbus Day.
Diagnosis, The.
Tati-Loutard. Death and Rebirth.

Submarine Tombs.
Voices, The.
Taylor, E. Fig for Thee, Oh! Death, A.
Upon a Spider Catching a Fly.
Taylor, W. Ellenore.
Teasdale. I Shall Live To Be Old.
On the Dunes.
Tennyson, A. Crossing the Bar.
Dying Swan, The.
Epic, The [Morte d'Arthur].
Go By.
In the Garden at Swainston.
In the Valley of Cauteretz.
Lady of Shalott, The.
Morte d'Arthur.
Sailor Boy, The.
Sonnet: "She took the dappled partridge flecked [or fleckt] with blood."
St. Simeon Stylites.
Tithonus.
Thackeray. Dear Jack.
Sorrows of Werther, The.
Thomas, D. After the Funeral.
Among Those Killed in the Dawn Raid Was a Man Aged a Hundred.
And Death Shall Have No Dominion.
Conversation of Prayer, The.
Do Not Go Gentle into That Good Night.
Force That Through the Green Fuse Drives the Flower, The.
Hand That Signed the Paper, The.
Thomas, E. Gallows, The.
Lights Out.
Rain.
Snow.
Spectator, The.
Thomas, R. Madrigal: "Your love is dead, lady, your love is dead."
Pisces.
Still.
Thompson, C. Not Dead, but Sleeping.
To My Dead Brother.
Thompson, P. Afternoon Gossip, An.
Consumptive, The.
Lines on a Dead Girl.
Song, The: "Oh, foully slighted Ethiope maid!"
To a Deceased Friend.
Thornbury. Smith of Maudlin.
Tichborne [or Tichbourne]. Tichborne's Elegy.
Tighe. 1802.
To Death.
Timrod. Ode: "Sleep sweetly in your humble graves."
Tipping. Just after Michael's Death, the Game of Pool.
Todd, R. Joan Miró.
Tollet. On a Death's Head.
Tolson, M. Festus Conrad.
Old Pettigrew.
Townsend, A. First Death.
Trakl. In the East.
Tranter. Death Circus, The.
Triem. For Paul.
Tripp. Armistice Day '77, Honiton.
In Memory of Idris Davies.
Troupe. Conjuring Against Alien Spirits.
Day in the Life of a Poet, A.
Tsvetayeva [or Tsvetaeva]. I know the truth— give up all other truths!
Tucker, M. "Did You Call Me, Father?"
Gone.
Lift Me Higher.
Tuckerman, F. Coralie.
Turner, C. Julius Caesar and the Honey-Bee.
Turner, W. Life and Death.
Tuwhare. Ron Mason.
Twichell. Aisle of Dogs.
Tzara. For Robert Desnos.
Waking.
Unger, B. Photo Taken in Winter, 1944.
Unknown. Beyond.
Bonny Earl of Murray, The.
Cauld Lad of Hilton, The *or* The Wandering Spectre.
Cowboy's Lament, The.
Créide's Lament for Dínertech.

Death.
Dying Airman, The.
Elegy upon the Death of Mrs. A. Behn, the Incomparable Astrea, An.
Epitaph.
Epitaph on the Duke of Buckingham.
Feltons Epitaph.
Finnegan's Wake.
Grave, The.
Hearse Song, The.
I Know Moon-Rise [or Moonrise].
I Thank God I'm Free at Las'
Limerick.
Lonesome Valley.
Lord, Remember Me!
Lyke-Wake Dirge, The [or A].
Man of Words, A.
My Boy Willie.
No More Auction Block.
On an Old Woman Who Sold Pots.
On Bond the Usurer.
On Prince Frederick.
On the Death of Mr. Persall's Little Daughter, in the Beginning of the Spring, at Amsterdam.
Rare Willie Drowned in Yarrow; or, The Water o Gamrie.
Silver Swan, The.
Since Bonny-Boots Was Dead.
Soon I Will Be Done.
Springfield Mountain.
Steal Away to Jesus.
Stormalong!
Swing Low, Sweet Chariot.
Thank God!
Three Ravens, The.
Twa Brothers, The.
Twa Corbies, The.
Ubi Sunt Qui Ante Nos Fuerunt?
Unquiet Grave, The.
We Shall Know.
Wife of Usher's Well, The.
Unknown, fr. Terezin Concentration Camp.
Birdsong I.
Closed Town, The.
Concert in the Old School Garret.
Homesick.
On a Sunny Evening.
Theresienstadt's Hospital.
Untermeyer, L. Irony.
To a Vine-clad Telegraph Pole.
Urdang. My Father's Death.
Usborne. Epitaph on a Party Girl.
Van Duyn. Stream, The.
Van Walleghen. More Trouble with the Obvious.
Vando. In the Crevices of Night.
Vaughan, H. As Time One Day by Me Did Pass.
Death.
Easter Hymn.
Pursuit[e], The.
They Are All Gone into the World of Light!
To the Pious Memory of C. W. Esquire.
Waterfall [or Water-Fall], The.
Veinberg, J. Next to Tut.
Owl's Landscape, An.
Very. Autumn Leaves.
Cup, The.
Dead, The.
Son, The.
Yourself.
Vilakazi. Now I Will Only Believe.
Villiers. Epitaph upon Thomas, Lord Fairfax, An.
Vinal. To Persephone.
Vizenor. Unhappy Diary Days.
Voigt. For My Mother.
Volkman. Infernal.
Voznesensky [or Voznesenskii]. Call of the Lake, The.
Waddell, H. Earth Said to Death.
I Shall Not Go to Heaven When I Die.
Wagoner, D. Author of American Ornithology Sketches a Bird, Now Extinct, The.
Wainwright, J. 1815.
Walcott. Letter from Brooklyn, A.

Sea Canes.
Village Life, A.
Young Wife, The.
Walker, A. Good Night, Willie Lee, I'll See You in the Morning.
Wallis, H. Female's Lamentations, The; or, The Village in Mourning.
To Mrs.———, on the Death of Her Husband.
Walsh, M. Thomas Iron-Eyes.
Wanley. Resurrection, The.
Warren, R. After the Dinner Party.
Confederate Veteran Tries to Explain the Event, A.
Fall Comes in Back-Country Vermont.
In Creve Coeur, Missouri.
Max Jacob at Saint Benoît.
There's a Grandfather's Clock in the Hall.
Way to Love God, A.
Warsh. Gout.
Watson, E. Battered Toddler, Page B6.
Watson, R. View on Death, A.
Watson, W. O My Poor Darling.
Watts, I. Heaven.
Weaver, M. Water Song.
Webb, C. You Missed the Earthquake, Bill.
Webb, F. Death at Winson Green, A.
Webster, A. Passing Away.
Weems, M. Return to Temptation.
Weigl. Temple Near Quang Tri, Not on the Map.
Weinstein, N. Migration of Drummond's Organs (After Death), The.
Weismiller. Skull.
Welish. Kiss Tomorrow Goodbye.
Wesley, C. Ah! Lovely Appearance of Death!
Weston, R. Epitaph: "Beneath this stone lies William Burke."
Whalen. Walking beside the Kamogawa, Remembering Nansen and Fudo and Gary's Poem.
Wheatley, P. On the Death of a Young Gentleman.
On the Death of the Rev. Mr. George Whitefield, 1770.
Thoughts on the Works of Providence.
To a Gentleman and Lady on the Death of the Lady's Brother and Sister, and a Child of the Name Avis, Aged One Year.
Wheelock, J. Earth, Take Me Back.
Whistler. Form of Epitaph, A.
White, B. Fixin' to Die.
White, D. Epistle of Love and of Consolation unto Israel, An.
White, G. Dead Armadillos.
Whitehead, W. New Night Thoughts on Death; a Parody.
Whitlow. Rockin' a Man, Stone Blind.
Whitman, W. As If a Phantom Caress'd Me.
As Toilsome I Wander'd Virginia's Woods.
Ashes of Soldiers.
Come Up from the Fields Father.
Death's Valley.
Joy, Shipmate, Joy!
Last Invocation, The.
O Living Always, Always Dying.
On the Same Picture.
Osceola.
Out of the Cradle Endlessly Rocking.
Sight in Camp [in the Daybreak Gray and Dim], A.
This Compost.
Vigil Strange I Kept on the Field One Night.
Whitmore, S. Outside.
Whittier. Telling the Bees.
Wicks, S. On Re-recording Mozart.
Wigglesworth. Farewell to the World, A.
Welcome, Sweet Rest.
Wilbur. Bell Speech.
In a Churchyard.
Pardon, The.
To an American Poet Just Dead.
Tywater.
Voice from under the Table, A.
Year's End.
Wild, R. Epitaph on Some Bottles of Sack and Claret Laid in Sand.

Wilde, O. Requiescat.
Willard, N. King of Cats Sends a Postcard to His Wife, The.
Williams, H. On the Death of the Rev. Dr. Kippis.
Williams, M. Death of Chet Baker, The.
On the Symbolic Consideration of Hands and the Significance of Death.
Williams, O. With Me.
Williams, W. Complete Destruction.
Death.
Last Words of My English Grandmother, The.
Rapid Transit.
To a Dog Injured in the Street.
Widow's Lament in Springtime, The.
Winchilsea. To Death.
Trail All Your Pikes.
Winner, S. Listen to the Mocking Bird.
Winters, Y. For My Father's Grave.
Inscription for a Graveyard.
Realization, The.
Song in Passing, A.
Time and the Garden.
To the Holy Spirit.
Wojahn. Buddy Holly.
John Berryman Listening to Robert Johnson's "King of the Delta Blues," January 1972.
Riding the Empire Builder, 1948.
Wolfe, C. To Mary.
Wolfe, H. Journey's End.
Wolverton, T. Dead Stepfather, The.
Wong, N. Mama, Come Back.
Woods, D. Waiting.
Woody. She-Who-Watches . . . The Names are Prayer.
Wordsworth, W. Perfect Woman.
Sonnet on Catherine Wordsworth.
Two April Mornings, The.
Wotton, S. De Morte.
Wright, C. Appalachian Book of the Dead III, The.
Delta Traveller.
Hawaii Dantesca.
Homage to Paul Cézanne.
Obedience of the Corpse.
Sitting at Night on the Front Porch.
Wright, J. Angel, The.
Arrangements with Earth for Three Dead Friends.
At the Executed Murderer's Grave.
At the Slackening of the Tide.
At Thomas Hardy's Birthplace, 1953.
Don José Gorostiza Encounters El Cordobés.
Eli, Eli.
Gesture by a Lady with an Assumed Name, A.
Inscription for the Tank.
Journey to the Place of Ghosts.
Life, The.
Metho Drinker.
Minneapolis Poem, The.
Northern Pike.
Note Left in Jimmy Leonard's Shack, A.
Old Age Compensation.
Saint Judas.
Small Frogs Killed on the Highway.
Speak.
Three Sentences for a Dead Swan.
To the Muse.
Two Poems about President Harding.
Way to Make a Living, A.
Willy Lyons.
Wright, M. Epitaph on Herself, An.
Wunderlich, M. East Seventh Street.
Wyatt, S. Stand Whoso List.
Wylie. Prophecy.
Yeats. Byzantium.
Circus Animals' Desertion, The.
Cold Heaven, The.
Death.
Irish Airman Foresees His Death, An.
Last Confession, A.
Man Who Dreamed of Faeryland, The.
Sailing To Byzantium.
Three Bushes, The.
Three Things.
To a Shade.

Upon a Dying Lady.
Vacillation.
Young, A. Elegy for a School-Friend.
Young, D. White Crane.
Young, G. Damien.
Young, K. Clyde Peeling's Reptiland in Allenwood, Pennsylvania.
Escape Artist, The.
Young, S. Epitaph for a Concord Boy.
Zangwill. Death's Transfiguration.
Zepeda, O. Bury Me with a Band.

Death in Childhood
Ai. Good Shepherd: Atlanta, 1981, The.
Atwood. Death of a Young Son by Drowning.
Austen, K. Dec. 5th 1644 Upon Robin Austins Recovery of the Smal Pox and General Popams Son John Diing of Them.
Beaumont, S. Of My Dear Son [or Deare Sonne], Gervase Beaumont.
Behn, A. Epitaph on the Tombstone of a Child, the Last of Seven That Died Before.
Bigelow, M. Two Smothered Children.
Bishop, E. First Death in Nova Scotia.
Bourdillon. Night Has a Thousand Eyes, The.
Bradstreet, A. In Memory of My Dear Grandchild Anne Bradstreet Who Deceased June 20, 1669, Being Three Years and Seven Months Old.
In Memory of My Dear Grandchild Elizabeth Bradstreet Who Deceased August, 1665, Being a Year and Half Old.
On My Dear Grandchild Simon Bradstreet, [Who Died on 16TH November, 1669, Being But A Month And One Day Old].
Bridges, R. On a Dead Child.
Carew, T. Another [Epitaph on the Lady Mary Villiers].
Epitaph on the Lady Mary Villiers.
Carey, M. Wretten by Me at the Death of My 4th Sonne and 5th Child Perigrene Payler.
Coleridge, S. On an Infant Which Died before Baptism.
Collier, M. Robert Wilson.
Dawe, B. Elegy for Drowned Children.
Dubie. Annual of the Dark Physics, An.
Duran, J. Stillborn.
Egerton, E. On My Boy Henry.
Emerson, R. Threnody: "South-wind brings, The."
Esteves. Lil' Pito.
Field, E. Little Boy Blue.
Fordham. In Memoriam. Alphonse Campbell Fordham.
Queenie.
To an Infant.
Frame. Yet Another Poem about a Dying Child.
Frost, R. "Out, Out—."
Home Burial.
Gilman, C. Dead Sister, The.
Glück, L. Mount Ararat.
Goethe. Erl-King, The.
Gould, H. Dying Child's Request, The.
Harper, M. Nightmare Begins Responsibility.
Reuben, Reuben.
Heaney, S. Limbo.
Mid-Term Break.
Heard, J. Solace.
Hecht, A. Book of Yolek, The.
Hemans. Wreck, The.
Herrick. Epitaph upon a Child, An.
Upon a Child That Died [or Dyed].
Holmes, O. Iris, Her Book.
Howitt, M. Dying Child, The.
Jarrell. Come to the Stone.
Lost Children, The.
Protocols.
Jones, R. Portrait of My Father and His Grandson.
Jonson, B. Epitaph on S. P. [Salomon or Salathiel Pavy], a Child of Q[ueen] El[izabeth's] Chapel.
On My First Daughter.
On My First Son[ne].
Why I Write Not of Love.
Jordan, J. Test of Atlanta 1979, The.
Justice, D. On the Death of Friends in

Childhood.
Kennedy, X. Little Elegy.
Landon. Dying Child, The.
Liu, T. Kindertotenlieder.
Martinez, D. Discreet Prayer, A.
Meehan, P. Child Burial.
Mew. To a Child in Death.
Meynell, A. Maternity.
Montague, J. Falls Funeral.
Moore, J. Hiram Helsel.
Moorer. Russia's Resentment.
Morgan, F. February 11, 1977.
Muir, E. Child Dying, The.
Muske, C. Wish Foundation, The.
Norris, L. Elegy for David Beynon.
O'Reilly, M. Abused Child.
Ondaatje. Strange Case, The.
Peters, L. Isatou Died.
Randall, D. Ballad of Birmingham.
Ransom, J. Bells for John Whiteside's Daughter.
Dead Boy.
Reznikoff. Children.
Sachs, N. Dead Child Speaks, A.
Schuyler, J. Head, A.
Shorter. Mother, The.
Sigourney. Request of a Dying Child.
Silkin. Death of a Son.
Simmerman. Child's Grave, Hale County, Alabama.
Smith, P. Meanwhile, in Rwanda.
Soyinka. Abiku.
Strode. On the Death of Mistress Mary Prideaux.
Sykes, B. Final Count.
Taylor, E. Upon Wedlock and Death of Children.
Thimelby, G. Mrs Thimelby, on the Death of Her Only Child.
Thomas, D. Refusal to Mourn the Death, by Fire, of a Child in London, A.
Thompson, D. P. Laurel Street, 1950.
Unknown. Babes in the Wood, The.
Papa's Letter.
Voigt. Year's End.
Watson, S. Epitaph, An: "His friends he loved. His direst earthly foes."
Wesley, C. On the Death of His Son.
Whittier. Vesta.
Wilde, O. Requiescat.
Wordsworth, W. Lucy Gray; or, Solitude.
Sonnet on Catherine Wordsworth.
We Are Seven.
Wright, J. Flood Year.

Death in War
Allen, H. Dragon's Breath.
Allingham. In Snow.
Bendall, F. Outposts.
Bishop, J. Young Men Dead.
Brodsky, J. Bosnia Tune.
Buck, H. Mort, Le.
George, P. Battle Won Is Lost.
Graham, W. Conscript Goes, The.
Graves, R. When I'm Killed.
Kipling, R. Nativity, A.
Levis. Caravaggio: Swirl and Vortex.
Logue, C. Song of the Dead Soldier, The.
Meddemmen, J. G. L.R.D.G.
Monroe, H. These Two.
Nisbet, H. Isandula.
Raine, K. Heroes.
Rawling. Gas Drill.
Rimington, J. God of the Flies.
Southey, R. Soldier's Wife, The.
Spencer, B. Passed On.
Thousand Killed, A.
Thompson, D. On the Relative Merit of Friend and Foe, Being Dead.
Unknown. Battle of Inverlochy, The.
See also **War Dead**

Death of Animals
Albee, E. Samantha.
Algarin. Tiger Lady.
Ammons, A. R. Widespread Implications.
Bly, R. Dead Seal [near McClure's Beach], The.
Hollow Tree, A.

Braun, R.   Goose.
  Lilies, The.
Brown, L.   Never Swat a Fly.
Brown, S.   Marriage.
Chamberlain, B.   Dead Ponies.
Coccimiglio.   St. Francis Speaks to Me at a
  Young Age.
Coleman, W.   Dog Suicide.
Cowper, W.   Epitaph on a Hare.
Cummings, E.   Me Up at Does.
Davis, C.   Murderer, The.
Dickey, J.   Heaven of Animals, The.
Dunn, S.   Buster's Visitation.
Eberhart, R.   For a Lamb.
Espada.   Cada Puerco Tiene Su Sábado.
Faust, H.   After the Storm.
Ferrell, A.   Out.
Frost, R.   Draft Horse, The.
Garrigue.   Epitaph for My Cat.
  Mouse, The.
González, R.   Death of the Farm Workers' Cat.
Gray, T.   Ode on the Death of a Favourite [or
  Favorite] Cat, Drowned in a Tub [or Bowl] of
  Gold Fishes.
Hartley, M.   As the Buck Lay Dead.
Hayden, R.   Plague of Starlings, A.
Herrick.   Upon His Spaniel[l] Tracie [or Tracy].
Hughes, F.   Different Voice, The.
  Kookaburra.
Hughes, T.   Old Age Gets Up.
  View of a Pig.
Irving, J.   Untitled.
Jeffers, R.   Hurt Hawks.
Kinnell.   Hen Flower, The.
Kumin, M.   Gus Speaks.
Kunitz, S.   Wellfleet Whale, The.
Larsen, L.   Lips.
Lawrence, A.   Cro-Kill.
Lindsay, N.   Eagle That Is Forgotten, The.
Lish, G.   Rusty.
Lovelace, R.   Fly Caught in a Cobweb, A.
Lowry, M.   Salmon Drowns Eagle.
MacCaig.   Interruption to a Journey.
Marlatt, D.   Bruce and the Bluegills.
Marvell.   Nymph and Her Fawn, The.
  Nymph Complaining for the Death of Her Faun
  [or Fawn], The.
Mattawa.   Letter to Ibrahim.
Millay, E.   Buck in the Snow, The.
Minot, S.   Devotion.
Moran, R.   Cross Country.
Mother Goose.   Who Killed Cock Robin.
Muñoz, A.   Hunting Accident.
Musgrave.   Burial of the Dog.
Nicholson, N.   Tune the Old Cow Died of, The.
Prunty.   Coach.
Randolph, T.   On the Death of a Nightingale.
Ransom, J.   Janet Waking.
Rossetti, C.   Last Rites.
Sharah.   Package for Another World.
Simon, M.   Dolphin, The.
Snodgrass, W.   Coroner's Inquest.
Snyder, G.   Dead by the Side of the Road, The.
Sonnenberg, B.   Stay.
Spencer, K. C.   When I Died on My Birthday.
Stafford, W.   Traveling Through the Dark.
Stern, G.   Dog, The.
Thomas, E.   Gallows, The.
Townsend, A.   After the End.
Turner, C.   Drowned Spaniel, The.
Unknown.   Madrigal: "Ay me, alas, heigh ho,
  heigh ho!"
  Two Gray Kits.
Van Walleghen.   More Trouble with the
  Obvious.
Weelkes.   Madrigal: "Ay me, alas, heigh ho,
  heigh ho!"
White, G.   Dead Armadillos.
Wilbur.   Death of a Toad, The.
  Pardon, The.
Williams, H.   Elegy on a Young Thrush Which
  Escaped from the Writer's Hand.
Wright, J.   Small Frogs Killed on the Highway.
  Sparrows in a Hillside Drift.
Death Poetry
Basho.   On a journey, ill.
Daido Ichi'i.   Tune of non-being.
Dairin Soto.   My whole life long I've sharpened
  my sword.

Dokyo Etan.   Here in the shadow of death.
Doyu.   In all my six and fifty years.
Gessu Soko.   Inhale, exhale.
Kogaku Soko.   My final words are these.
Muso Soseki.   Thus have I rolled my life
  throughout.
Ruefle.   Furtherness.
Debauchery
Awoonor.   To the Eminent Scholar and Meddler.
Giorno.   Pornographic Poem.
Graves, R.   Blue-Fly, The.
Johnson, S.   Short Song of Congratulation [or
  To a Young Heir], A.
Jonson, B.   On Gut.
Rochester, J.   Disabled Debauchee, The.
  Ramble in St. James's Park, A.
Thomas, E.   Epistle to Clemena, Occasioned by
  an Argument She Had Maintained Against the
  Author.
"W——, Miss."   Gentleman's Study, in Answer
  to The Lady's Dressing-Room, The.
Whitman, W.   Hand-Mirror, A.
Wyatt, S.   Courtier's Life, The.
Debt
Bayly.   Out, John.
Coward.   Stately Homes of England, The.
De Vries, P.   To His Importunate Mistress.
Dunbar, P.   Debt, The.
Herrick.   Bell-Man, The.
  Upon Bunce: Epigram.
Horton, G.   Creditor to His Proud Debtor, The.
Hughes, L.   Little Lyric (of Great Importance).
Mather, J.   File-Hewer's Lamentation, The.
Suckling, S.   Love and Debt Alike Troublesome.
Westmorland.   My Country Audit.
Decadence
El-Hadi, S.   Drama, The.
Eliot, T.   Burial of the Dead, The.
  Death by Water.
  Fire Sermon, The.
  Game of Chess, A.
  Sweeney among the Nightingales.
  Sweeney Erect.
  Waste Land, The.
Ewart.   One for the Anthologies.
Jenyns.   Modern Fine Lady, The.
MacNeice.   Belfast.
  Goodbye to London.
  Individualist Speaks, The.
Seaman, S.   To a Boy-Poet of the Decadence.
Sitwell, D.   Waltz.
Warren, R.   Bearded Oaks.
Wyatt, S.   Lux, My Faire Falcon.
Decay
Auden.   Paysage Moralisé.
Awoonor.   Songs of Sorrow.
Bolt, T.   Meditation in Loudoun County.
Brutus.   This Sun on this Rubble.
Davies, H.   Poem: "In the stump of the old tree,
  where the heart has rotted out."
Disch.   Entropic Villanelle.
Dooley, M.   Does It Go Like This?
Dransfield.   War of the Roses, The.
Drummond, W.   Sonnet: "I know that all
  beneath the moon decays."
Eberhart, R.   Groundhog, The.
Eliot, T.   Burial of the Dead, The.
  Death by Water.
  Fire Sermon, The.
  Game of Chess, A.
  Gerontion.
  Hollow Men, The.
  Portrait of a Lady.
  Rhapsody on a Windy Night.
  Sweeney Erect.
  Waste Land, The.
Frost, R.   Range-finding.
  Wood-Pile, The.
Ginsberg, A.   Sunflower Sutra.
Graham, J.   Opulence.
Gwynn, R.   Approaching a Significant Birthday,
  He Peruses The Norton Anthology of Poetry.
Hall, D.   Old Pilot, The.
Heath-Stubbs.   Footnote to Belloc's "Tarantella."
Herbert, G.   Decay.
Herrick.   All Things Decay and Die.
Hugo, R.   Death of the Kapowsin Tavern.
Jeffers, R.   For Una.
  Prescription of Painful Ends.

Kefala.   Freedom Fighter.
Kelly, R.   Recessional.
Lawrence, A.   Robert Penn Warren's Book.
Li Po.   On Climbing the Phoenix Tower at
  Chinling.
Long, H.   Our Spring Needs Shoveling.
Lowell, R.   As a Plane Tree by the Water.
McAuley, J.   Wet Day.
McCarthy, J.   Alice Blue Gown.
Merwin, W. S.   Losing a Language.
Olson, C.   Kingfishers, The.
Pack, R.   Proton Decay.
Pierpoint, K.   In the Outhouse.
Portnoy, M.   Evolution of Lather, The.
Ramanujan.   Elements of Composition.
Rich, A.   Diving into the Wreck.
Robinson, E.   Ballade of Broken Flutes.
  House on the Hill, The.
Rodefer.   Pretext.
Scott, D.   Skiddaw House.
Seed.   'From Escomb, County Durham': July
  1990.
Shelley, P.   Ozymandias.
Simpson, L.   Inner Part, The.
Slessor.   Choker's Lane.
Stevens, W.   Worms at Heaven's Gate, The.
Trakl.   Revelation and Decline.
Turner, C.   Lion's Skeleton, The.
Unknown.   Song Bewailing the Time of
  Christmas, So Much Decayed in England, A.
Vaughan, H.   They Are All Gone into the World
  of Light!
Wanley.   Resurrection, The.
Ward, T.   Stray Dogs, Foaming.
Wilbur.   Junk.
Williams, H.   Sonnet 6. To the Torrid Zone.
Williams, W.   Raleigh Was Right.
December
Cane.   Tree in December.
Clare, J.   December.
Clark, L.   Singing in the Streets.
Cranch.   December.
Fergusson.   Daft Days, The.
Francis, R.   December.
Giovanni.   December of My Springs, The.
Heaney, S.   Exposure.
Heard, J.   December.
Herford.   I Heard a Bird Sing.
Keats.   In a Drear-nighted December.
Kenny, M.   December.
Lovelace, R.   Grasshopper, The.
Ray, H.   December.
Whittier.   Firelight.
  Snow-Bound [or Snow-Bound; a Winter Idyl].
Deception
Barbauld.   Tomorrow.
Bayly.   Out, John.
Boruch.   Camouflage.
Brecht, B.   From a German War Primer.
Brown, D.   First Person—1981.
Brownjohn.   Negotiation.
Campion, T.   Blame Not My Cheekes.
Carew, T.   Deposition from Love, A.
  Looking-Glass, A.
Carryl, G.   Sycophantic Fox and the Gullible
  Raven, The.
Chesterton, G.   Aristocrat, The.
Clark, T.   Society.
Coulehan, J.   Dynamizer and the Oscilloclast,
  The.
Creeley.   If You.
Davis, T.   Playing Solitaire.
Derricotte.   Passing.
Dickey, W.   Plot, The.
Dunbar, P.   Made to Order Smile, The.
  We Wear the Mask.
Dunbar, W.   Translation by Mark Willhardt.
Dunn, S.   What They Wanted.
Elizabeth I.   On Monsieur's Departure.
Emerson, R.   Maia.
"Ephelia."   In the Person of a Lady, to Bajazet,
  Her Unconstant Gallant.
Floyd.   Captain James Leson, U. S. M. C.
Frost, R.   Revelation.
Graves, R.   Beauty in Trouble.
  Full Moon.
  Sick Love.
  Theseus and Ariadne.

Hare, P.   Deceit in the Park.
Heffernan, M.   Message, The.
Herrick.   Chop-Cherry.
   Fair[e] Days; or, Dawn[e]s Deceitful[l].
Horan.   Soft Swimmer, Winter Swan.
Hughes, T.   Childish Prank, A.
Johnson, J.   White Witch, The.
Jones, M.   Lass of the Hill, The.
Landor, W.   You Smiled, You Spoke, and I
   Believed.
Loftis, N.   Brief Encounter.
McElroy, C.   Horoscope.
Navajo Oral Tradition.   Coyote, Skunk, and the
   Prairie Dogs.
Ojaide.   When Tomorrow Is Too Long.
Ostriker.   Lamenting the Inevitable.
Peacock, M.   Have You Ever Faked an Orgasm?
Phillips, C.   Clearing, The.
Plomer.   French Lisette: A Ballad of Maida
   Vale.
Pope, J.   Word of Encouragement, A.
Prescod.   Vicious Circle.
Prior.   Ode, An: "Merchant, to secure his
   treasure, The."
   Phillis's Age.
Silverstein, S.   Sick.
Spender, S.   Song: "Stranger, you who hide my
   love."
Stanton, M.   Shoplifters.
Stephens, J.   Blue Blood.
Thomas, L.   Instructions for Your New Osiris.
Unknown.   Me and My Captain.
   Signifying Monkey, The.
Warren, R.   Picnic Remembered.
Welch, J.   Man from Washington, The.
Whitehead, C.   Brutus' Last Song.
Whitlow.   Book of Routh.
Yeats.   Three Bushes, The.

Decisions
Carew, T.   Mediocrity in Love Rejected.
"Field."   Second Thoughts.
Frost, R.   Road Not Taken, The.
Herrick.   Neutrality Loathsome.
Marcus, M.   Poem for Gonzales, California,
   The.
Roethke.   Decision, The.

See also **Free Will**

Declaration of Independence
Hopkins, L.   John Hancock.

Decorum
Glück, L.   My Neighbor in the Mirror.
Kinnell.   To William Carlos Williams.
Meynell, A.   Shepherdress, The.

Deer
Addonizio.   Alone in Your House.
Benét, S.   Daniel Boone.
Benét, W.   Fawn in the Snow, The.
Biespiel, D.   There Were No Deer in the
   Thicket.
Booth, P.   Deer Isle.
Conyus.   Upon Leaving the Parole Board
   Hearing.
Davidson, J.   Runnable Stag, A.
Dickinson, E.   Wounded Deer Leaps Highest, A.
Erdrich.   Strange People, The.
Flanner.   Fern Song.
   Moment.
Frost, C.   To Kill a Deer.
Frost, R.   Two Look at Two.
Glück, L.   Messengers.
Hardy, T.   Fallow Deer at the Lonely House,
   The.
Hartley, M.   As the Buck Lay Dead.
Hass, R.   Image, The.
Hughes, T.   Roe-Deer.
Jeffers, R.   Deer Lay Down Their Bones, The.
   Fawn's Foster-Mother.
Levien.   In the Falling Deer's Mouth.
Lewis, J.   Grandmother Remembers, A.
Lovelace, R.   La Bella Bona-Roba.
Marvell.   Nymph and Her Fawn, The.
   Nymph Complaining for the Death of Her Faun
   [*or* Fawn], The.
McCallum, S.   Deer, The.
Millay, E.   Buck in the Snow, The.
More, S.   Child's Song.

Morley, D.   Air Street.
Oliver, M.   Picking Blueberries, Austerlitz, New
   York, 1957.
Oppen.   Psalm: "In the small beauty of the
   forest."
Patchen.   Deer and the Snake, The.
Silko.   Deer Song.
Sisson.   Knole.
Snyder, G.   Long Hair.
   Two Fawns That Didn't See the Light This
   Spring.
Stafford, W.   Traveling through the Dark.
Stuart, D.   Where the Deer Go.
Tate, J.   Pet Deer, The.
U Tam'si Tchicaya.   Dance to the Amulets.
Warren, R.   Sila.
Weismiller.   Crystal Moment.
Wright, J.   White Deer, The.
Wyatt, S.   Whoso List to Hunt.

See also **Hunting and Hunters**

Defeat
Arnold, M.   Last Word, The.
Awad, J.   I Think Continually of Those Who
   Were Truly Failures.
Fitzgerald, E.   19.
Foley, M.   On the Waterfront.
Gibran.   Defeat.
Herrick.   To Virgins.
Hugo, R.   Degrees of Gray in Philipsburg.
Keyes, S.   Dunbar, 1650.
Komunyakaa.   After the Fall of Saigon.
Kunitz, S.   Dragonfly, The.
Padilla.   Discourse on Method, The.
Ramanujan.   At Forty.
Robinson, E.   Mighty Runner, A.
Spencer, B.   Invaders, The.
Thayer, E.   Casey at the Bat.
Wright, J.   Speak.

Deformities
Elizabeth I.   Written in Her French Psalter.
Mother Goose.   Tongs.

Degas, Edgar
Wilbur.   Museum Piece.

Dehumanization
Amadiume.   Nok Lady in Terracotta.
Mitsui.   Destination: Tule Lake Relocation
   Center, May 20, 1942.
Owen, W.   Anthem for Doomed Youth.
Plath.   Applicant, The.
Simic.   Cold, The.

See also **Bureaucracy and Bureaucrats**

Deirdre
Stephens, J.   Deirdre.

Deism
Addison, J.   Ode: "Spacious firmament on high,
   The."

Dejection
Carroll, L.   Rules and Regulations.
Coleridge, S.   Dejection: An Ode.
Mahon.   Dejection.
Shelley, P.   Stanzas Written in Dejection, near
   Naples [*or*—December 1818, near Naples].
Valentine, J.   Lines in Dejection.

See also **Melancholy**

Delaware (state)
Kinnell.   Memory of Wilmington.

Delft, Holland
Mahon.   Courtyards in Delft.

Delight
Dunbar, W.   Translation by Mark Willhardt.
Eliot, T.   Dedication to My Wife, A.
Freed, A.   Fit As a Fiddle.
Oliver, M.   Summer Day, The.
Porter, C.   It's De-Lovely.
Shelley, P.   Song: "Rarely, rarely, comest thou."
Stevens, W.   Poems of Our Climate, The.
Swinburne.   Sestina: "I saw my soul at rest upon
   a day."

Deliverance
Jarrell.   Jews at Haifa.
Jeffers, R.   Home.
Unknown.   Didn't My Lord Deliver Daniel?
   I to the Lord from My Distress.

Delphi, Oracle of
Lindsay, C.   Love or Fame.

Merrill, J.   Charioteer of Delphi, The.
Yeats.   News for the Delphic Oracle.

Delvaux, Paul
Guthrie, R.   Homage to Paul Delvaux.

Demeter
Doolittle, H.   Mysteries, The.
Dove, R.   Demeter, Waiting.
   Persephone Underground.
   Political.
Greenwell, D.   Demeter and Cora.
Krysl.   Persephone, to Demeter.
Mutén, B.   Demeter's Blessing.
Starhawk.   Demeter's Song.
Taggard.   Demeter.

Democracy
"Ada."   Scroll is open, The.
Belloc.   On a General Election.
Freneau.   On Mr. Paine's Rights of Man.
Hughes, L.   Democracy.
Kizer, C.   Election Day, 1984.
Scott-Heron.   Winter in America.
Skovron.   Election Eve, with Cat.
Unknown.   Equal, An.
Van Wyk.   Ballot and the Bullet, The.
Whitman, W.   Commonplace, The.
   For You O Democracy.
   One's-Self I Sing.

See also **Campaigns, Political; Voting and Voters**

Demons
Brown, K.   Good Devil, The.
Burns, R.   De'il's [*or* Deil's] Awa wi' th' [*or*
   the] Exciseman, The.
Kimbrell, J.   True Descenders.
Wright, J.   Killer, The.

See also **Monsters**

Dempsey, William Harrison ("Jack")
Ignatow, D.   Boxing Match, The.

Denial
Clifton, L.   At the Cemetery, Walnut Grove
   Plantation, South Carolina, 1989.
Dove, R.   Poem in Which I Refuse
   Contemplation.
Gamalinda, E.   Denials.
Glazer.   Drinking with the Nazis.
Graves, R.   Cool Web, The.
   Nobody.
   She Is No Liar.
Hardy, T.   In the Servants' Quarters.
Heyen.   Numinous, The.
Ismaili.   Solange.
Kahaney, P.   Germany, 1981.
Larkin, J.   Origins.
MacNeice.   Mixer, The.
Meynell, A.   Renouncement.
Posamentier, E.   Counting Backwards.
Ransom, J.   Good Ships.
   Nocturne.
Reti, I.   I Never Knew I Was Jewish.

Dentistry and Dentists
Kay, J.   Crown and Country.
Marzán.   Emergency.
Valerie, J.   Lesson on Braces.

Denver, Colorado
Ferril.   Waltz against the Mountains.

Department Stores
Alexander, E.   Ladders.
Derricotte.   Weakness, The.
Farber.   For a Quick Exit.

Deportation
Lavieri, J.   Autobiography of John Doe, The.
Unknown.   On Queen Caroline.

Depression (economic)
Justice, D.   Pantoum of the Great Depression.
Walker, M.   Delta.

See also **Great Depression**

Depression (psychological)
Alley, R.   Dissecting Uncle Sorrow.
Butler, C. E.   Darkness, The.
Cleyre, V.   Out of the Darkness.
Gerstler.   Fan Letter, A.
Hayden, R.   Ice Storm.
Holmes, J.   Depressive Episode.
Howe, F.   Doubt.
Hughes, L.   Neighbor.

Hugo, R.　Letter to Bell from Missoula.
Kenyon, J.　From the Nursery.
　Having It Out With Melancholy.
　In and Out.
　Often.
　Once There Was Light.
　Pardon.
　Suggestion from a Friend.
Lake, P.　Crime and Punishment.
McGough, R.　Survivor.
Randall, D.　His Favourite Seat.
Sadoff.　Depression, The.
Sanchez, S.　Depression.
Sears, P.　One Polar Bear, The.
Smith, C.　To Night.
Stevens, W.　Anglais Mort à Florence.
Stoddard, E.　Nameless Pain.
Su, A.　Antidepressant.
Szymborska.　Four in the Morning.
Thomas, R.　Evans.
Trinidad.　Things to Do in Valley of the Dolls
　(The Movie).
Wordsworth, W.　I Wandered Lonely As a
　Cloud.
See also **Melancholy; Mental Illness**

Dereliction
Wordsworth, W.　Decay of Piety.

Descartes, René
Tomlinson, C.　Descartes and the Stove.

Deserts
Ali, A.　Desert Landscape.
Benton, S.　Lilith.
Carruth, H.　Rimrock, Where It Is.
Currey.　Burial Flags.
Forbes, C.　Dark Mirror.
Garioch.　Property.
Gilbert, K.　Peace and the Desert.
Greenberg, S.　African Desert.
Hope, A.　Australia.
Illyés, G.　Logbook of a Lost Caravan.
Jarrell.　Range in the Desert, The.
Kunitz, S.　Old Cracked Tune, An.
Longfellow, H.　Sand of the Desert in an Hour-
　Glass.
Major, C.　Lost in the Desert.
Marchera, D.　Desert Crossing.
Markham, E.　In Death Valley.
Martínez, V.　It Is Not.
McAuley, J.　Envoi.
Melville, H.　In the Desert.
Merrill, C.　Erosion.
Mora.　La Migra.
Morgan, E.　Dowser, The.
Plath.　Sleep in the Mojave Desert.
Ramke.　Difference Between Night and Day,
　The.
Rawson, J.　Border, The.
Robinson, A.　Oasis, An.
Saner.　Desert Wisdom.
Santos, S.　Near the Desert Test Sites.
Shelley, P.　Ozymandias.
Trapnell, N.　Lament of a Desert Rat.
Weslowski.　Dry World.
Whittemore, R.　Day with the Foreign
　Legion, A.
Whittier.　Song of Slaves in the Desert.
Woo, D.　Eden.

Desire
Adamson.　Action Would Kill It / A Gamble.
Adler, R.　Whatever Lola Wants (Lola Gets).
"Æ."　Desire.
Ager, M.　Ain't She Sweet?
　Hard-Hearted Hannah (The Vamp of Savannah).
　Louisville Lou (The Vampin' Lady).
Ahlert, F.　Ain't That the Way It Goes?
　I Don't Know Why (I Just Do).
　Mean to Me.
Akst, H.　Dinah.
　Guilty.
　What a Perfect Combination.
Al-Rihani.　Lilatu Laili.
Alegría.　Savoir Faire.
Alford, H.　You and I.
Amadiume.　Union, The.
Amichai [*or* Amikhai].　Quick and Bitter.
Ammons, A. R.　Spit.

Anderson, M.　It Never Was You.
Angelou.　On Diverse Deviations.
Angus.　Invitation.
Arlen, H.　As Long As I Live.
　Let's Fall in Love.
　Sing, My Heart.
Armantrout.　Attention.
Arnheim, G.　I Cried for You.
Ashbery.　Blessing in Disguise, A.
Atwood.　Against Still Life.
　There Is Only One of Everything.
　Variation on the Word *Sleep*.
　Woman Who Could Not Live With Her Faulty
　　Heart, The.
Ayer, N.　If You Were the Only Girl in the
　World.
Ayres, R.　Corporeal.
Baker, H.　Love.
　Rapture, The.
Baldwin, J.　Guilt, Desire and Love.
Baratier, D.　She Wants.
Barker, J.　To My Young Lover.
Barnett, A.　Music of the Spheres.
Becker, R.　Story I Like to Tell, The.
Beckett, S.　Cascando.
Behn, A.　In Imitation of Horace.
　Thousand Martyrs I Have Made, A.
　To the Fair Clarinda [*or* Clorinda], Who Made
　　Love to Me, Imagined [*or* Imagin'd] More
　　Than Woman.
Bell, M.　Book of the Dead Man #43, The.
Bensley.　Desires.
Bergman, D.　Blueberry Man.
Berlin.　Change Partners.
　Fools Fall in Love.
　Heat Wave.
　How Deep Is the Ocean? (How High Is the
　　Sky?).
　I Got Lost in His Arms.
　I've Got My Love to Keep Me Warm.
　Isn't This a Lovely Day (To Be Caught in the
　　Rain?).
　It's a Lovely Day Today.
　Let's Face the Music and Dance.
　Remember.
　They Say It's Wonderful.
　What'll I Do?
　You'd Be Surprised.
　You're Laughing at Me.
Berrigan, A.　Various Multitudes Contained by
　the Loves of My Love, The.
Beveridge.　Dining Out.
Bibbins, M.　Bluebeard.
　Whitman on the Beach.
Blagg, T.　In Bed this Morning.
Blake, E.　I'm Craving for That Kind of Love.
　I'm Just Wild About Harry.
Blind.　Once We Played.
Bly, R.　French Generals, The.
Bogan, L.　Dream, The.
Boland, E.　In Her Own Image.
Braley, B.　Success.
Breton, A.　Assurance, An.
Brion, R.　Love Song.
Broumas, O.　She Loves.
Brown, E.　Beauty and the Prince Formerly
　Known as Beast.
Brown, L.　(Here Am I) Broken Hearted.
　If I Had a Talking Picture of You.
　It All Depends on You.
　Magnolia.
　Maybe This Is Love.
　Never Swat a Fly.
　That Old Feeling.
　You're the Cream in My Coffee.
Brown, N.　All I Do Is Dream of You.
　I've Got a Feelin' You're Foolin'
　You Stepped Out of a Dream.
　You Were Meant for Me.
Browning, E.　Man's Requirements, A.
Browning, R.　Song: "Moth's kiss, first, The!"
Bryan, M.　To————: "O thou unknown
　disturber of my rest."
Burke, J.　Little Bit Independent, A.
Burns, R.　Green Sleeves [and Tartan Ties].
　Mary Morison.

O Were My Love Yon Lilac[k] Fair.
　Tam Glen.
Butts, A.　Nature of Braille, The.
Cady.　Starting 1973: What to Do Now that
　Peace Has Been Announced.
Caldwell, A.　I Know That You Know.
Cambridge, A.　Desire.
Camlan.　Lady Charlotte Guest.
Campion, T.　Fain Would I Wed.
　First Love.
　Sleep, Angry Beauty.
Campo.　For J. W.
Carew, T.　Mediocrity in Love Rejected.
　Second Rapture, The.
　To My Worthy Friend Master George Sands [*or*
　　Sandys], on His Translation of the Psalms.
Carmichael, H.　Nearness of You, The.
Cervantes.　A un Desconocido.
Chase, N.　My Ideal.
Cheney-Coker.　On Being a Poet in Sierra
　Leone.
Chesterton, G.　Joseph.
Chudleigh.　Song: "Why Damon, why, why,
　why so pressing?"
Cisneros, S.　You Called Me Corazón.
Clare, J.　First Love.
Clark, T.　Doors.
Coffman.　Girl/Spit.
Cohan.　When a Fellow's on the Level with a
　Girl That's on the Square.
Columbo, R.　Prisoner of Love.
Comden, B.　Not Mine.
　Party's Over, The.
Cooley, N.　Undine.
Cooper, D.　My Past.
Coots, J.　For All We Know.
　You Go to My Head.
Corey, S.　Complicated Shadows.
Corn.　Older Men.
Crane, H.　Legend.
Creamer, H.　If I Could Be with You.
Creeley.　Ballad of the Despairing Husband.
　For W.C.W.
Crowley, A.　Rondels.
Cullen, C.　Timid Lover.
Cummings, E.　First of All My Dreams, The.
　It Is At Moments After I Have Dreamed.
　Item.
　Somewhere i have never travelled, gladly
　　beyond.
Cutts.　To a Lady, Who Desired Me Not To Be
　in Love with Her.
Dacre, C.　Power of Love, The.
　Sappho; or, The Resolve.
Darr.　At Sixteen.
Davidson, M.　Century of Hands.
Davies, H.　Love Song: "There is a strong wall
　about me to protect me."
Davis, C.　Little Crisis Framed in My Window.
Davis, J.　You Turn Around.
Davis, T.　Desire 1.
de Gillies, G.　De Puerorum osculis.
Delgado, J.　Dandelion.
'Dermée.'　Silver Clasps.
Dipoko.　Poem of Villeneuve St Georges, A.
Dixon, M.　I Found a Million Dollar Baby (In a
　Five and Ten Cent Store).
Dixon, S.　Request of Alexis, The.
Donaldson, W.　Kansas City Kitty.
　Little White Lies.
　Love Me or Leave Me.
　My Baby Just Cares for Me.
　Okay, Toots.
　One I Love (Belongs to Someone Else), The.
　Yes, Sir! That's My Baby.
　You're Driving Me Crazy (What Did I Do?).
Donne.　Canonization, The.
　Lovers' Infiniteness[e].
Doolittle, H.　Helmsman, The.
Douskey.　Dog Days and Delta Nights.
　Wet Bodies.
Dove, R.　Secret Garden, The.
　Sunday Greens.
Dowson.　Non Sum Qualis Eram Bonae sub
　Regno Cynarae.
Dransfield.　Epiderm.

Memoirs of a Velvet Urinal.
Dubin, A. Cup of Coffee, a Sandwich, and You.
I Only Have Eyes for You.
I'll String Along with You.
Lulu's Back in Town.
You're Getting to Be a Habit with Me.
Young and Healthy.
Duffy, C. Words, Wide Night.
Duffy, M. I Am Beset with a Dream of Fair Woman.
Semi-Skilled Lover.
Duhamel. Kinky.
Duke, V. I Can't Get Started.
Duncan, R. Eyesight II.
Dunn, S. Tenderness.
Eliot, T. Dedication to My Wife, A.
Elizabeth I. When I Was Fair and Young.
Elizabeth, M. She Teaches Him to Reach Out.
Ellington, D. It Shouldn't Happen to a Dream.
Emerson, R. To Rhea.
"Ephelia." To J.G. on the News of His Marriage.
Estes, A. You Stand There Fishing.
Etter. Andy Hasselgard.
Evans, D. Dinner at the Hotel de la Tigresse Verte.
Ewart. Office Friendships.
Faber, F. Dream of Blue Eyes, A.
Fabian, C. Qadesha (Sacred Whore).
Fagan. Desire.
"Field." Ebbtide at Sundown.
Fields, D. I'm in the Mood for Love.
Make the Man Love Me.
Fishman, L. V's Farmhouse.
Fletcher, J. Blue Symphony.
Take, Oh, Take Those Lips Away.
Flynn, N. Cartoon Physics, Part 2.
Forman, R. Someone.
Fournier, R. Encounter.
Freed, A. Fit As a Fiddle.
This Heart of Mine.
Frost, R. Fire and Ice.
Garrigue. From Venice Was That Afternoon.
Grenoble Café.
To Speak of My Influences.
Gascoigne. For That He Looked Not upon Her.
Lullaby [or Lullabie] of a Lover, The.
Gaskill, C. I Can't Believe That You're in Love with Me.
Gensler, L. Love Is Just Around the Corner.
George, D. It Shouldn't Happen to a Dream.
Gershwin. I Can't Get Started.
Gibbons, S. Truce, The.
Ginsberg, A. Green Automobile, The.
Kaddish.
Shrouded Stranger, The.
Why Is God Love, Jack?
Giorno. Life Is a Killer.
Scum & Slime.
Glück, L. Aubade: "World was very large, The. Then."
Elms.
Gladding. Fisherman's Wife, The.
Glatt. Amanda.
Gleason, K. After Fighting for Hours.
Godfrey. One or More Together.
Wings.
Goese, M. Love Ghost.
Gonzalez, R. Beyond Having.
Goodman, P. Long Lines: Youth and Age.
Graves, R. Quiet Glades of Eden, The.
Symptoms Of Love.
Green, A. Not Mine.
Party's Over, The.
Gregg. What Is Kept.
Grey, C. If You Were the Only Girl in the World.
Guillén, N. Don't Know No English.
Guiney. Borderlands.
Gunn, T. In the Post Office.
Hadas, R. Mars and Venus.
Three Silences.
Hagiwara Sakutaro. Lover of Love.
Hall, D. "Reclining Figure."
Mangosteens.
Hammerstein. Bill.

Harbach, O. Let's Begin.
She Didn't Say 'Yes.'
Harford, L. I Count the Days Until I See You, Dear.
Harms. Tomorrow, We'll Dance in America.
Harryman. Matter.
Hass, R. Story about the Body, A.
Hattersley, G. Frank O'Hara Five, Geoffrey Chaucer Nil.
Henderson, R. Five Foot Two, Eyes of Blue (Has Anybody Seen My girl?).
Henry, B. Skin.
Herd. Bathing Girls, The.
Marilyn Climbs Out of the Pool.
Herrick. Charme, or an Allay for Love, A.
Frozen Zone; or, Julia Disdainful, The.
Hymne to Love, An.
Julia's Petticoat.
Night-Piece, to Julia, The.
To Electra.
To His Mistress[es].
Upon Julia's Clothes.
Upon Julia['s] Washing Herself in the River.
Upon Love, by Way of Question and Answer.
What Kind of Mistress[e] He Would Have.
Hewett, D. You Gave Me Hyacinths First a Year Ago.
Hill, M. Bad Karma.
Hirshfield, J. Of Gravity and Angels.
To Drink.
Hodges, J. It Shouldn't Happen to a Dream.
Hovey. Song by the Shore, A.
Hughes, L. Advice.
Hugo, R. Letter to Welch from Browning.
Hunter, T. Wanting You.
Jackson, H. Tides.
Jackson, T. Pretty Baby.
Jacob, V. Tam i' the Kirk.
James, J. Shakin All Over.
Jeffers, R. Divinely Superfluous Beauty.
Jennings, E. First Love.
Thinking of Love.
Johnson, J. My Special Friend (Is Back in Town).
Jones, I. I'll See You in My Dreams.
It Had to Be You.
Josefowitz, N. Foreplay.
Joseph, A. Pure Pop.
Kalmar et al. Nevertheless (I'm in Love with You).
Kantaris. Body Language.
Katz, J. Concerning the Islands Newly Discovered.
Kenyon, J. August Rain, after Haying.
Kern, J. Bill (Original Version).
That Was Before I Met You.
Koehler, T. Stop! You're Breakin' My Heart.
Komunyakaa. Thorn Merchant's Mistress, The.
Kowit. What Chord Did She Pluck.
LaFemina. White Dwarf.
Larkin, P. Wants.
Lasker-Schüler. To the Barbarian.
Laughlin, J. O Best of All Nights, Return and Return Again.
Laux. Fast Gas.
Lawrence, D. Desire Is Dead.
Grasshopper Is a Burden.
In Trouble and Shame.
Leapor. Strephon to Celia.
Lee, L. Irises.
Lefroy. Idler Listening to Socrates Discussing Philosophy with His Boy-Friends, An.
Levertov. Quest, The.
Sea's Wash in the Hollow of the Heart, The.
Levine, P. Poem Circling Hamtramck, Michigan, All Night in Search of You, The.
Lewis, S. I Wonder Why She Kept on Saying 'Si-Si-Si- Si-Senor.'
Lomax, M. Gruoch.
Long, H. Daphnis and Chloe.
Lovelace, R. Love Made in the First Age[: To Chloris].
To a Lady That Desired Me I Would Bear My Part with Her in a Song.
Lowell, A. Opal.
Lum. Urban Love Songs.

Lyons, S. Loving Along Western Rivers.
Mackenzie, K. Fool, The.
Maguire, S. Divorce Referendum, The.
"Malley." Night Piece.
Mandel, T. Say Ja.
Mansfield, K. Secret Flowers.
Marlatt, D. Working Girl.
Martínez, V. Into the Next One.
New World, The.
Traveler.
Marvell. Match, The.
Mower's Song, The.
Masini. Two Men, Two Grapefruits.
Mattawa. Heartsong.
Mayakovsky [or Maiakovskii]. Mayakovsky's Suicide Note.
McAuley, J. Legendary.
McCarthy, J. You Made Me Love You (I Didn't Want to Do It).
McDaniel, J. D.
McLain, P. Beauty, That Lying Bitch.
Willing.
Melville, H. After the Pleasure Party.
In a Bye-Canal.
Mercer, J. Laura.
Something's Gotta Give.
Merrill, J. Kimono, A.
Octopus, The.
Merritt, C. Mute Swan, The.
Merry. Adieu and Recall to Love, The.
Mesens. Arid Husband, The.
Monk, M. Fire Us with Ice, Burn Us with Snow.
Montagu, L. Man in Love, A.
Receipt to Cure [or for] the Vapours, A.
To a Lady Making Love.
Montgomerie, A. Dreame, Ane.
Moore, T. Did Not.
Moraes, D. Snow on a Mountain.
Muldoon, P. Something of a Departure.
Muske. C. Red Trousseau.
Nazario, A. Kevin and Nicole.
Nelson, M. Proposal.
Noble, R. Touch of Your Lips, The.
Norse. You Must Have Been a Sensational Baby.
North, C. From the French.
O'Hara, F. Poem: "O solo mio, hot diggety, nix 'I wather think I can' ."
O'Reilly, J. White Rose, A.
Obejas, A. Public Place (After Olga Broumas), The.
Ofeimun. Gong, A.
Ojaide. What They Said.
Oppen. Forms of Love, The.
Orton, B. Love Poem.
Owen, W. Music.
Paley, G. Here.
Parra, N. Pilgrim, The.
Peacock, M. Desire.
Wheel, The.
Phillips, C. Cotillion.
Pinkard, M. Gimme a Little Kiss (Will Ya, Huh?).
Poe. Dream within a Dream, A.
To F——.
Pope, J. Beau Ideal, The.
Porter, C. All of You.
At Long Last Love.
Get Out of Town.
I've Got You Under My Skin.
In the Still of the Night.
It's All Right with Me.
It's De-Lovely.
Laziest Gal in Town, The.
Let's Do It, Let's Fall in Love.
Porter, D. Lollies Noir.
P. M. T.
Ports, K. Desire.
Pratt, M. Elbows.
Rabinowitz. Of Joy Illimited: Polyphonic Soundings: Shore to Ship.
Randall, D. Haymakers.
Nightwatchman.
Randolph, T. Milkmaid's Epithalamium, The.
Rankin, J. Love Affair 36.

Ravikovitch [or Ravikovich]. Surely You Remember.
  Trying Again.
Rich, A.   Re-forming the Crystal.
  Two Songs.
Ridge, J.   Cherokee Love Song, A.
  Stolen White Girl, The.
Roberts, K.   How Late Desire Looks.
Robin, L.   Louise.
Robinson, C.   We Who Have Loved.
Robinson, E.   John Evereldown.
  Tavern, The.
Robinson, K.   On the Corner.
Robinson, M.   Describes Phaon.
  Laments the Volatility of Phaon.
  Phaon Awakes.
  Rejects the Influence of Reason.
  She Endeavors to Fascinate Him.
Rochester, E.   Song: "Nothing ades to Loves fond fire."
Roethke.   Four for Sir John Davies.
  Her Longing.
  I Knew A Woman.
  Marrow, The.
  Renewal, The.
  She.
  Swan, The.
  Voice, The.
Rome, H.   Nobody Makes a Pass at Me.
Roripaugh, L.   Peony Lover.
Rosenberg, L.   Lesson in Anatomy, A.
Rossetti, C.   What Would I Give?
Roughton.   Soluble Noughts and Crosses; or, California, Here I Come.
Rowe, E.   To Orestes.
Rukeyser, M.   Eyes of Night-Time.
  Looking at Each Other.
  Meeting, The.
Rux, C. H.   Shunning an Imperative.
Södergran.   Instinct.
Sackville-West.   No Obligation.
Samyn, M.   Art of Kissing, The.
Sandburg, C.   Adelaide Crapsey.
  At a Window.
  Gone.
Sansom, M.   To My Heavenly Charmer.
Santos, S.   Midsummer.
Schuyler, J.   Tom.
Schwartz, R. L.   Falling in Love after Forty.
  Possible.
Schwitters.   Anna Blossom Has Wheels.
  Desire.
Sexton.   Jesus Asleep.
Seyburn, P.   Persuasion.
Shapiro, K.   Haircut.
Shaughnessy, B.   Rise.
Shaw, A.   Rear Window.
  Small Pleasures.
Shelley, M.   Stanzas: "Oh, come to me in dreams, my love!"
Shirley, J.   Lover that Durst Not Speak to His M[istress], A.
Shurin.   Forward or Back.
Sidney, S.   Thou Blind Man's Mark.
Sitwell, D.   Heart and Mind.
  King of China's Daughter, The.
Skelton, J.   Mannerly Margery Mylk and Ale.
Smith, B.   Empty Bed Blues.
Smith, S.   Love Me!
Snyder, G.   Autumn Morning in Shokoku-ji, An.
  Beneath My Hand and Eye the Distant Hills, Your Body.
  For a Far-out Friend.
  Four Poems for Robin.
  Manichaeans, The.
  Spring Night in Shokoku-ji, A.
Song.   White Porch, The.
Soniat.   Harp/Desire.
Spencer, B.   Egyptian Dancer at Shubra.
Spender, S.   Abrupt and charming mover.
Spenser.   Sonnet 73: 'Being my self captived here'
Stanton, M.   Voice for the Sirens, A.
Steele, T.   Aubade, An: "As she is showering, I wake to see."
  Eros.

Stevens, W.   Bouquet of Belle Scavoir.
  Peter Quince at the Clavier.
Stewart, S.   Apple.
Stone, J.   Rosemary.
Stramm.   Encounter.
Strand.   Courtship.
Strauss, J.   Love Notes.
Styne, J.   Not Mine.
  Party's Over, The.
Suárez, V.   Donatilia's Unrequited Love Remedy.
Suckling, S.   Against Absence.
  Miracle, The.
  Sonnet: "Dost see how unregarded now."
Surrey.   Complaint by Night, A.
Swinburne.   Love And Sleep.
  Sapphics.
Swiontkowski, G.   Old Moon With Her Youth in Her Arms.
Symonds.   What Cannot Be.
Sze.   Great White Shark, The.
Szporluk.   Axiom of Maria.
  Grass and the Sin, The.
  Libido.
Taylor, B.   Goblet, The.
Tennyson, A.   O Swallow, Swallow.
Thomas, E.   Remedia Amoris.
  To Colindra.
Thomson, J.   To Fortune.
  To the God of Fond Desire.
Timrod.   La Belle Juive.
Tollet.   On Loving Once and Loving Often.
Tomlinson, C.   Death of Will, The.
Traherne.   Insatiableness.
Trethewey, N.   Photograph of a Bawd Drinking Raleigh Rye.
Trinidad.   Of Mere Plastic.
Triplett, P.   Studies in Desire.
Tuckerman, F.   Question, The.
Tufts, C.   We Take the New Young Couple Out to Dinner.
Turell, J.   You Beauteous Dames.
Unknown.   Art Thou That She.
  Hares on the Mountain.
  There Is a Lady Sweet and Kind.
  To His Love.
  Wonders.
Vallejo.   Poem to Be Read and Sung.
Vanhomrigh.   Hail, Blushing Goddess, Beauteous Spring!
Vaughan, H.   To Amoret, of the Difference 'twixt Him and Other Lovers, and What True Love Is.
Villanueva, A.   Peace #3.
Volkman.   Create Desire.
  Untitled.
Wadsworth, C.   Desire.
Waller, E.   On a Girdle.
Walls, D.   Summer the Beatles Went Over Seven Minutes on a Single, The.
Walton, E.   In Recompense.
Walwicz.   Tattoo, The.
Warren, R.   Birth of Love.
Weill, K.   It Never Was You.
Welish.   Veil.
Wetzsteon.   Dinner at Le Caprice.
  Three Songs.
Whitman, W.   As Adam Early in the Morning.
  Fast-Anchor'd Eternal O Love!
  From Pent-up Aching Rivers.
  I Heard You Solemn-Sweet Pipes of the Organ.
  Not Heat Flames Up and Consumes.
  O You Whom I Often and Silently Come.
  To the Garden the World.
  When I Heard at The Close Of The Day.
Whitson, B.   Let Me Call You Sweetheart.
Whittier.   Henchman, The.
Widdows.   Minutiae 3.
Wilbur.   Playboy.
  She.
  Voice from under the Table, A.
Wilcox, E.   Attraction.
Williams, W.   Woman Walking.
Willis, N.   Lady in the White Dress, Whom I Helped into the Omnibus, The.
Witt, S.   Everlasting Quail.

  Michael Masse.
  Wohlfeld.   Sea.
Wright, C.   On the Eve of Our Mutually Assured Destruction.
Wright, J.   Angel, The.
  Desire's Persistence.
  Metho Drinker.
  Poem about Breasts, A.
  Sappho.
  To a Child.
Wunderlich, M.   From a Vacant House.
Wyatt, S.   Long love that in my thought doth harbo[u]r, The.
  Lover Showeth How He Is Forsaken of Such as He Sometime Enjoyed, The.
Yeats.   Politics.
Youmans, V.   I Know That You Know.
Zandvakili, K.   County.
See also **Erotic Love; Lust**

Desks
Mahon.   Table Talk.
Smith, D.   Desks.

Desolation
Belloc.   Ha'nacker Mill.
Bontemps.   Blight.
Brontë, E.   Remembrance.
Byron, G.   Darkness.
Creeley.   Marriage, A.
Delmore, E.   Marmalade.
Finch, R.   Last Visit.
Ginsberg, A.   In Back of the Real.
Henri, A.   Adrian Henri's Talking after Christmas Blues.
Hugo, R.   Letter to Scanlon from Whitehall.
Jeffers, R.   Place for No Story, The.
Jordan, N.   When a Woman Gets Blue.
Joseph, L.   Do What You Can.
Knight, E.   Feeling Fucked/Up Up.
Muir, E.   Milton.
Ransom, J.   Emily Hardcastle, Spinster.
Roberts, G.   Burnt Lands.
Stanton, M.   Shoplifters.
Thomas, D.   Hand That Signed the Paper, The.
Thomas, R.   Reservoirs.
Very.   Lament of the Flowers, The.
Yeats.   Meru.
Zimmer.   Eisenhower Years, The.

Despair
Ai.   Man with the Saxophone, The.
Akhmatova, A.   Everything Is Plundered.
Alexie.   Exaggeration of Despair, The.
Baraka.   Poem Some People Will Have to Understand, A.
Barber, M.   On Seeing an Officer's Widow Distracted.
Beckett, S.   Cascando.
Berg, S.   Nostalgia.
Blake, W.   Song: "My silks and fine array."
Blamire.   Written on a Gloomy Day, in Sickness.
Bly, R.   Snowbanks North of the House.
  When the Dumb Speak.
Borson.   Save Us From.
Brody.   Cry of the Peoples, The.
Bronk.   World, The.
Brontë, E.   F. de Samara to A. G. A.
Browning, E.   Loved Once.
  Mask, The.
Brutus.   Endurance.
Byron, G.   Lines Written beneath a Picture.
  One Struggle More, and I Am Free.
Campbell, S.   Big John's Tears Fall to the River.
Cary, A.   In Bonds.
Castro, R.   Black Mood.
Cervantes.   Poet Is Served Her Papers, The.
Chin.   We Are Americans Now, We Live in the Tundra.
  Year Passes in My Morning Teacup, The.
Chitre.   My Father Travels.
Colby, T.   Captain's Log.
Coleridge, H.   Other Side of a Mirror, The.
Coleridge, S.   Work without Hope.
Cowper, W.   Castaway, The.
  Lines Written During a Period of Insanity.
Creeley.   Ballad of the Despairing Husband.
  For Love.

Crunk, T. Leaving.
Dalton, A. How to Disappear.
Davis, J. Aboriginal Reserve.
Deane, S. Roots.
Disch. Zewhyexary.
Dowson. Last Word, A.
Drummond, W. Madrigal: "My thoughts hold mortal[l] strife."
Dunbar, P. Ships That Pass in the Night.
Worn Out.
Empson. This Last Pain.
"Field." Maidenhair.
Giorno. Life Is a Killer.
Godfrey. Where the Weather Suits My Clothes.
Gomez, M. Desert Cry, A.
Gonzalez, N. Deepest Well in Madras, The.
Grandmaster Flash and the Furious Five. Message, The.
Gu Cheng. Ark.
Hardy, T. Darkling Thrush, The.
Hayes, A. Epistle to the Gentiles.
Hemans. Indian Woman's Death-Song, The.
Herbert, G. Affliction (4).
Collar, The.
Decay.
Denial[l].
Longing.
Hewitt, J. Postscript, 1984.
Hope, A. Return of Persephone, The.
Hopkins, G. Carrion Comfort.
I Wake and Feel the Fell of Dark, Not Day.
Leaden Echo and the Golden Echo, The.
No Worst, There Is None. Pitched Past Pitch of Grief.
Thou Art Indeed Just, Lord.
Hove. Red Hills of Home.
Hugo, R. Letter to Levertov from Butte.
My Buddy.
Jenkins, L. In a Tavern.
Johnson, J. To America.
Kaplan, M. Knife, The.
Kaufman, S. Security.
Kavanagh, P. Memory of Brother Michael.
Kayo. Song of the Initiate.
Keats. Day Is Gone and All Its Sweets Are Gone, The.
La Belle Dame sans Merci [A Ballad].
Kinnell. Another Night in the Ruins.
Kumin, M. Despair.
Kunitz, S. Night Letter.
Laing, K. Senior Lady Sells Garden Eggs.
Lane, B. T'Ain't No Use.
Lansdown. Golgotha.
Lear, E. Limericks, II (v).
Levis. Rhododendrons.
Levy, A. To Vernon Lee.
Lewis, A. Karanje Village.
Mountain over Aberdare, The.
Locke, A. Sin and Despair Have So Possess'd My Heart.
Lodge, G. Lower New York.
Lorde. Generation.
Macaulay, T. Jacobite's Epitaph, A.
Macdonald, G. Shall the Dead Praise Thee?
MacKay, I. Meeting, The.
Magidson, H. T'Ain't No Use.
Mangan, J. Twenty Golden Years Ago.
McCarthy, J. Quatrain without Sparrows, Helpful Bells or Hope.
McCord, D. Five Chants.
McGrath, T. End of the Line, The.
Nuclear Winter.
Melville, H. Island, The.
Mew. Quiet House, The.
Mezey. How Much Longer?
Montagu, L. Addressed to.
Nathan, R. Mountaineer, The.
Nemerov. Redeployment.
Niedecker. I Married.
Notley. Poem: "You hear that heroic big land music?"
O'Hara, F. Meditations in an Emergency.
Oppen. Survival: Infantry.
Parker, D. Coda: "There's little in taking or giving."
Piñero. Running Scared.

Plath. Event.
Moon and the Yew Tree, The.
Street Song.
Raab, L. Being a Monster.
Ralegh, S. Fortune Hath Taken Away.
Rankine. Short Narrative of Breasts and Wombs in Service of Plot Entitled, A.
Robinson, M. Her Address to the Moon.
Her Confirmed Despair.
Sappho Discovers her Passion.
Sappho Rejects Hope.
Stanzas: "In this vain, busy world, where the good and the gay."
Roethke. In a Dark Time.
Rosenfeld, C. Another While.
Rossetti, C. Better Resurrection, A.
If Only.
L.E.L.
Old-World Thicket, An.
What Would I Give?
Sassoon. Lamentations.
Sepamla. Silence: 2.
Sexton. Her Kind.
Shelley, P. England in 1819.
Lament, A: "O world! O life! O time!"
Stanzas Written in Dejection, near Naples [or—December 1818, near Naples].
Shelton, R. Eden After Dark.
Smith, C. Composed During a Walk on the Downs, in November 1787.
Nepenthe.
Ode to Death.
To Fancy.
To Spring.
Written at Bignor Park in Sussex, in August, 1799.
Smith, M. City.
Smith, S. Bereaved Swan, The.
Bog-Face.
I Rode With My Darling.
Spender, S. Memento.
Spicer, J. Transformations.
Stickney, F. At Sainte-Marguerite.
Swift, J. Phyllis [or Phillis] [or Progress of Love, The].
Swinburne. Satia Te Sanguine.
Tennyson, A. Mariana.
Thomson, J. In the Room.
Thoreau. Poet's Delay, The.
Unknown. Love Is a Secret Feeding Fire.
Miserere, My Maker.
Untermeyer, L. Koheleth.
Vaughan, H. Anguish.
Very. Forevermore.
Walsh, W. Despairing Lover, The.
Weissbort. Mourning.
Weller. Story of Frankie . . . My Man, The.
Whalen. Complaint: To the Muse.
Wieners. Waning of the Harvest Moon, The.
Wilde, O. Vita Nuova.
Williams, C. Loss.
Williams, W. These.
Woods, D. Prescription.
Wordsworth, W. Reverie of Poor Susan, The.
Written in London, September, 1802.
Wright, J. Lying in a Hammock at William Duffy's Farm in Pine Island, Minnesota.
Wunderlich, M. Bruise of This, The.
Wyatt, S. "My galley charged with forgetfulness."
Sonnet: 'My galley charged'
Wylie. Let No Charitable Hope.
Yamada. Cincinnati.
Zangwill. Moses and Jesus.

Destiny
Frost, R. Gift Outright, The.
Harjo, J. Woman Who Fell from the Sky, The.
Hecht, A. Jason.
Simon, M. Standing between Two Ideas.
Turner, F. Julius Caesar and the Honey-Bee.
Unknown. She Will Gather Roses.
See also **Fate**

Destruction
Aiken, C. Summer.
Anderson, D. Domi Solus.
Atwood. Beauharnois (1).

Beauharnois (3).
Beauharnois, Glengarry (2).
Dufferin, Simcoe, Grey (4).
Four Small Elegies.
It Is Dangerous to Read Newspapers.
Awoonor. Sea Eats the Land at Home, The.
Back, R. Gaza, Undated.
Baratier, D. Fall of Because, The.
Borawski. Power of One.
Brooks, G. Boy Breaking Glass.
Brown, S. Schadenfreude.
Di Prima. Brief Wyoming Meditation.
Donne. Broken Heart, The.
Duncan, R. Passage Over Water.
Elliott, E. War.
Emerson, R. Water.
Fenton, J. Wind.
Gallagher, T. Unsteady Yellow.
Gould, A. Demolisher.
Graves, R. Twins.
Griffin, J. Emperor, The.
Gwangwa'a. Leaking Roof.
Hawoldar. Destruction.
Hill, L. Let Him Return.
Jeffers, R. Summer Holiday.
Jonson, B. Execration upon Vulcan, An.
Kinnell. Ruins under the Stars.
Kinsella, J. Pig Melons.
Kocbek. Dialectics.
Kooser. Shooting a Farmhouse.
Kowit. Notice.
Kunitz, S. Last Picnic, The.
Kyger. Destruction.
Kyle, C. J. Fire in Early Morning.
LeFlore, S. B. Dream/Eaters.
Lewis, A. Raiders' Dawn.
Lifshin. Crystal Night.
Lux. Barn Fire.
Manyarrows. See No Indian, Hear No Indian.
Mapanje. Glory Be to Chingwe's Hole.
Mattera. Day They Came for Our House, The.
McLain, P. Beauty, That Lying Bitch.
Melville, H. Iris.
Ravaged Villa, The.
Merrill, J. Urban Convalescence, An.
Momaday. Burning, The.
Moulds, J. When Bad Angels Love Women.
Nichol. Some Nets.
Oppen. Survival: Infantry.
Owen, W. To Eros.
Poe. Sonnet—To Science.
Porter, P. May, 1945.
Prior. Dutch Proverb, A.
Pugh. 'Do you think we'll ever get to see Earth, sir?'
Rich, A. For the Record.
Rukeyser, M. Sand-Quarry with Moving Figures.
Sandburg, C. Prayers of Steel.
Seferis. Last Stop.
Seyburn, P. Good Water.
Tate, J. Death on Columbus Day.
Tennyson, A. Babylon.
Thelwall. On the Rapid Extension of the Suburbs.
Vaughan, H. Charnel-house, The.
Waldrop, K. Wandering Curves.
Watts, I. Day of Judg[e]ment, The; an Ode.
Williams, C. Shock.
Williamson, G. Walter Parmer.
Winter, M. Elegy: "There is a question."
Winters, Y. Summer Noon: 1941.
Wordsworth, W. Composed at Neidpath Castle, the Property of Lord Queensberry,1803.
Wylie. Doomsday.

Detectives
Hughes, L. Café: 3 A.M.
Nielsen, K. Self Portrait as Nancy Drew, Girl Sleuth.
Orlovsky. Dick Tracy's Yellow Hat.
Ransome-Davies. Raymond Chandler: The Big Sleep.

Determination
Angelou. Still I Rise.
Creeley. En Famille.
Kunitz, S. Knot, The.

Lefevre, A.   Halftime.
Moore, M.   I May, I Might, I Must.
Rich, A.   Power.
Williams, W.   To an Old Jaundiced Woman.

Detroit, Michigan
Bly, R.   Andrew Jackson's Speech.
Butts, A.   Belle Isle Men, The.
Charara, H.   Thinking American.
Daniels, J.   Time, Temperature.
Davis, O.   Thirty Years Rising.
Hernández Cruz.   Entering Detroit.
Joseph, L.   Then.
Levine, P.   Belle Isle, 1949.
  Coming Home, *Detroit*, 1968.
  Snow.
  You Can Have It.
Pape.   Birds of Detroit.

Developing Countries
Enright, D.   Underdeveloped Country, An.
Hove.   Country Life.
Ojaide.   Ward 6.

Devil
Brown, K.   Good Devil, The.
Fisher, D.   That Old Devil Called Love.
See also **Satan**

Devonshire, England
Herrick.   Discontents in Devon.

Dew
Bell, M.   Dew at the Edge of a Leaf.
Bryant, W.   To a Waterfowl.
Clare, J.   Clock-A-Clay.
Marvell.   On a Drop of Dew.
Miles, J.   Fields of Learning.
Unknown.   I Sing of a Maiden.

Diabetes
Hacker, M.   Fifteen to Eighteen.
Hoagland, E.   Big Zeb Johnson.

Dialects
Herbert, W.   Cabaret McGonagall.
  To a Mousse.
Porteous.   Charlie Douglas.
Torres, E.   Elder Dubb.

Diana (mythology)
Gallagher, T.   Instructions to the Double.
Killigrew, A.   On a Picture Painted by Herself
  [*or* Her self], Representing Two Nymphs [*or*
  Nimphs] of Diana's, One in a Posture to Hunt,
  the Other Bath[e]ing.
Ralegh, S.   Homage to Diana.
Simms, W.   New Moon, The.

Diaries
Abse.   New Diary, A.
Allingham.   Writing.
Bishop, E.   From Trollope's Journal.
Brewer, G.   Journals, The.
Colby, T.   Captain's Log.
Dibdin, C.   Lady's Diary, The.
Dugan, A.   On a Seven-Day Diary.
Fusselman, A.   Ticker.
Larkin, P.   Forget What Did.
Procter, A.   My Journal.
Scamell, B.   Diaries.
Wilson, M.   Diary.

Diaspora
Becker, R.   Crypto-Jews, The.
Behar, R.   Survivals.
Brathwaite, E.   Journeys, The.
Brooks, G.   To the Diaspora.
Carruth, H.   Little Citizen, Little Survivor.
Nye, N.   For Lost and Found Brothers.

Dickinson, Emily
Bell, M.   Mystery of Emily Dickinson, The.
Bly, R.   Visiting Emily Dickinson's Grave with
  Robert Francis.
Cope, W.   Emily Dickinson.
Crane, H.   To Emily Dickinson.
Finch, A.   Dickinson.
Finnell.   Over *Voice of America*.
Fulton, A.   Wonder Bread.
Kennedy, X.   Emily Dickinson in Southern
  California.
Longley, M.   Emily Dickinson.
Lowell, A.   Sisters, The.
Peacock, M.   Desire.
Rich, A.   I Am in Danger—Sir.

Rubin, L.   Houses of Emily Dickinson, The.
Ruefle.   Furtherness.
Waniek.   Emily Dickinson's Defunct.
Winters, Y.   To Emily Dickinson.
Young Bear.   Emily Dickinson, Bismarck and
  the Roadrunner's Inquiry.

Dictionaries
Alvi, M.   Throwing Out My Father's Dictionary.
Hardy, T.   Liddell and Scott.

Dieting
Burge.   Diet, The.
King, S.   Breakfast Song in Time of Diet.
Nash, O.   I Can't Have a Martini, Dear, but You
  Take One, or, Are You Going to Sit There
  Guzzling All Night?
Prys-Jones.   Wife of Carcassone, The.
Unknown.   On a Gentleman's Complaining to a
  Lady That He Could Not Eat Meat.

Digby, Lady Venetia
Jonson, B.   Picture of the Body, The.

Digging and Diggers
Gildner.   Digging for Indians.
Gruffydd, P.   Digging Soil.
Merwin, W. S.   Diggers, The.
Parker, A.   Alchemy.
Rux, C. H.   Excavation, The.
Stephens, P.   Signalmen, The.
Stevenson, R.   At the Seaside [*or* Sea-Side].
Unknown.   Digging Sing, A.
Wilbur.   Digging for China.

Dikes
Cary, P.   Leak in the Dike, The.
Kipling, R.   Dykes, The.

Dillinger, John
Wagoner, D.   Shooting of John Dillinger outside
  the Biograph Theater July 22, 1934, The.

Diners
Atwood.   They Eat Out.
Johnson, M.   All-Night Diner, The.
Liu, T.   Ikon.
Waring, B.   Tip, The.

Dinosaurs
Armour.   Pachycephalosaurus.
Couto.   Living in the La Brea Tar Pits.
Updike.   On the Inclusion of Miniature
  Dinosaurs in Breakfast Cereal Boxes.
Worth, V.   Dinosaurs.

Dionysus
Randall, D.   Hail, Dionysos.

Diplomacy and Diplomats
Barrington, P.   I Had a Duck-Billed Platypus.
Weigl.   Ambassador, The.

Disabilities
Lim, S.   Pantoun for Chinese Women.
Owen, W.   Disabled.

Disappointment
Arlen, H.   Man That Got Away, The.
Baillie, J.   Werena My Heart Licht I Wad Dee.
Behn, A.   Disappointment, The.
Carroll, H.   I'm Always Chasing Rainbows.
Clifton, L.   Thirty-Eighth Year, The.
Comden, B.   Party's Over, The.
Davis, O.   Small Number, A.
Dietz, H.   I Guess I'll Have to Change My Plan.
Duke, V.   Love Turned the Light Out.
  Round About.
Gershwin.   But Not for Me.
  Man That Got Away, The.
Gershwin, G.   But Not for Me.
Glatt.   One Night With a Stranger at 30.
Hardy, T.   Broken Appointment, A.
Herrick.   Invitation, The.
Heyman, E.   Blame It on My Youth.
Howe, F.   Doubt.
Joseph, A.   Wedding Party.
Kyle, C. J.   Argument, The.
Lazard.   Ordinance on Arrival.
Levine, P.   Blasting from Heaven.
McCarthy, J.   I'm Always Chasing Rainbows.
McDaniel, J.   Play It Again, Salmonella.
Meynell, A.   Modern Mother, The.
Parker, D.   One Perfect Rose.
Rafferty, C.   Story of the Man Whose Tastes
  Were Too Refined.

Ralegh, S.   Farewell to False Love, A.
Rich, A.   Snapshots of a Daughter-in-Law.
Rosenberg, I.   Chagrin.
Schwartz, A.   I Guess I'll Have to Change My
  Plan.
Smith, C.   To Mrs. G.
Tate, J.   My Great Great Etc. Uncle Patrick
  Henry.
Thayer, E.   Casey at the Bat.
Troup, B.   You're Lookin' at Me.
Whitehead, C.   Morning Thesis.
Wordsworth, W.   Yarrow Visited [September,
  1814].

Disarmament
Lehmann, J.   This Excellent Machine.
See also **Militarism; Pacifism and Pacifists**

Disasters
Ammons, A. R.   Eternal City, The.
Balaban.   Hurricane.
Graves, R.   Fallen Tower of Siloam, The.
Kasischke.   Grace.
Kramer, L.   Images of the San Francisco
  Disaster.
Larkin, P.   Explosion, The.
Longfellow, H.   Disasters.
McGonagall.   Tay Bridge Disaster, The.
Moore, J.   Ashtabula Disaster, The.
Swanger.   Natural Disaster.
Urdang.   All Around Us.

Discipline
Berlin.   This Is the Army, Mr. Jones.
Blount, R.   Country Dog in the City (On a
  Leash, Which Is Bizarre Enough) Comes Upon
  an Obedience Class, A.
Ellis, T.   Sticks.
Gilmore, B.   Revolution.
Herbert, G.   Discipline.
Matthews, W.   Foul Shots: A Clinic.
Ross, C.   Jack.
Stevenson, R.   Good and Bad Children.

Discontent
Abrahams, L.   Whiteman Blues, The.
Betjeman.   Meditation on the A30.
Brathwaite, E.   Naima.
Coleman, W.   African Sleeping Sickness.
Creeley.   Gift, The.
  Something for Easter.
Dobyns.   How to Like It.
Fagan.   Desire.
Fanthorpe.   Not My Best Side.
Fields, D.   Fine Romance, A.
Glancy.   Kemo Sabe.
Graves, R.   Lovers in Winter.
Gunn, T.   Autumn Chapter in a Novel.
Gurney, I.   Not-Returning, The.
Herbert, G.   Affliction (1).
Herrick.   Discontents in Devon.
  Not To Love.
Jennings, E.   Afterthought.
Kern, J.   Fine Romance, A.
Kunitz, S.   Night Letter.
Lear, E.   O dear! How disgusting is life!
MacNeice.   Nature Morte.
  Wolves.
Mathew.   Poem in Time of Winter.
McCord, D.   Five Chants.
McGough, R.   Prayer to Saint Grobianus.
Millay, E.   Hearing Your Words, and Not a
  Word among Them.
  Rendezvous.
Murray, P.   Inquietude.
O'Brien, S.   In Residence: A Worst Case View.
Plath.   Spinster.
Porter, P.   Consumer's Report, A.
Sewell, L.   Release.
Smith, C.   Pressed by the Moon, Mute Arbitress
  of Tides.
Thomas, D.   I Have Longed to Move Away.
Toomer.   I Sit in My Room.
Trapnell, N.   Lament of a Desert Rat.
Unknown.   Grumble Family, The.
Wickham.   Nervous Prostration.
Williams, W.   Raleigh Was Right.
Yeats.   He Hears the Cry of the Sedge.

Discothèques
Ginsberg, A.　Chances "R."
Lowe, J.　Club House.
Merrill, J.　Watching the Dance.

Discovery
Adamson, H.　I Just Found Out About Love.
Auden.　Legend.
Carew, T.　Ingrateful[l] Beauty Threatened.
Gershwin.　How Long Has This Been Going On?
Gunn, T.　Discovery of the Pacific, The.
Hass, R.　After I Seized the Pentagon.
Heffernan, M.　Message, The.
Henry, B.　Discovery.
Hernández Cruz.　Discovery.
Hewitt, J.　Tryst.
Katz, J.　Concerning the Islands Newly Discovered.
Levertov.　Overland to the Islands.
MacLeish.　Voyage West.
MacNeice.　Truisms, The.
McHugh, J.　I Just Found Out About Love.
Millay, E.　"Euclid Alone Has Looked on Beauty Bare."
Owen, W.　Music.
Shapiro, K.　Leg, The.
Stern, G.　For Song.

Disdain
Cahn, S.　Put 'Em in a Box, Tie 'Em with a Ribbon (And Throw 'Em in the Deep Blue Sea).
Campion, T.　Follow Thy Fair Sun[ne] [Unhappy Shadow].
Chesterton, G.　World State, The.
Creeley.　Gift, The.
Memory, The.
Florian.　Send My Spinach.
Glück, L.　My Neighbor in the Mirror.
Godolphin.　Chloris, It Is Not Thy Disdain.
Hewitt, J.　Turf-Carrier [or Turf Carrier] on Aranmore.
Plath.　Daddy.
Rafferty, C.　Story of the Man Whose Tastes Were Too Refined.
Unknown.　Mode of France, The.
Wyatt, S.　My Lute, Awake!

Disease
Abse.　X-Ray.
Ai.　Chance.
Becker, R.　Medical Science.
Beckett, S.　Ooftish.
Bruce, D.　Prognosis.
Chimombo.　Derailment: A Delirium.
Coulehan, J.　Azalea Poem, The.
Lovesickness: A Medieval Text.
Crosby, F.　Mandan Chief, The.
Dickson, J.　Poemectomy.
Elliott, A.　Angel.
García, D.　Tísica.
Hicok.　Alzheimer's.
Kees.　For My Daughter.
Lux.　Plague Victims Catapulted over Walls into Besieged City.
MacBeth [or Macbeth].　Worst Fear, The.
MacKay, C.　Mowers: An Anticipation of the Cholera, 1848, The.
Martínez, V.　Tesoro.
Mukand, J.　First Payment.
Muldoon, P.　Aisling.
O'Reilly, M.　House Call to a Man with Parkinson's Disease, A.
Potter.
Perillo.　Body Mutinies, The.
Picková, E.　Fear.
Piercy.　Crabs.
Pitchford.　Surgery.
Scott, D.　Apocalypse Dub.
Stone, J.　Gaudeamus Igitur: A Valediction.
Straus, M.　Luck.
Teddy.　At Terezin.
Wilbur.　Pangloss's Song: A Comic-Opera Lyric.
Williams, C.　Alzheimer's: The Wife.
Williams, M.　Thinking about Bill, Dead of AIDS.
Woods, D.　Waiting.

Disgrace
Thackeray.　Napoleon.

Dishonesty
Cary, P.　When Lovely Woman.
Nesbit, E.　Appeal.
Piercy.　Song of the Fucked Duck.

Dishonor
Jonson, B.　To Captain Hungry.
Melville, H.　Stonewall Jackson.
Surrey.　Sardanapalus.
Unknown.　She Was Poor but She Was Honest.

Disillusion
Adair, T.　Will You Still Be Mine?
Arlen, H.　I Wonder What Became of Me.
Bishop, J.　Return, The.
Blunden.　Report on Experience.
Browning, R.　Patriot, The [An Old Story].
Carew, T.　Ingrateful[l] Beauty Threatened.
Ceravolo.　Caught in the Swamp.
Comden, B.　If You Hadn't—But You Did.
Conley, L.　Cottage for Sale, A.
Ellington, D.　Sophisticated Lady.
Fuller, R.　Spring 1942.
Ginsberg, A.　America.
My Alba.
Hall, D.　Hardy's 'Shelley's Skylark.'
Hart, L.　Falling in Love with Love.
Hass, R.　Story about the Body, A.
Koch, K.　Thanksgiving.
Macaulay, T.　Jacobite's Epitaph, A.
Mew.　Rooms.
Montague, J.　Well-Beloved, The.
Owen, W.　Dulce et Decorum Est.
Sonnet, to a Child.
To———: "Three rompers run together, hand in hand."
Parker, D.　Symptom Recital.
Ransom, J.　Blackberry Winter.
Ras.　Sadness of Couples, The.
Reese, L.　Lyric on the Lyric, A.
Shelley, P.　Alastor; or, The Spirit of Solitude.
Invocation: "Earth, ocean, air, belovèd brotherhood!"
Swan, E.　When Your Lover Has Gone.
Tomlinson, C.　Jam Trap, The.
Wilbur.　Someone Talking to Himself.
Wright, C.　May God Go with You, Son.

Disorder
Bishop, E.　Filling Station.
Gunn, T.　Wheel of Fortune, The.
Herrick.　Delight in Disorder.
Wang Ts'an.　Seven Sorrows.
Welish.　Blood or Color.
Wild Sleeve.
Whitman, W.　Beat! Beat! Drums!

Displacement
Dean, D. K.　Stitches.
Dharker.　Postcards from God (1).
Griffiths, J.　Migration.

Disraeli, Benjamin
Brooks, S.　To Disraeli.

Distrust
Amis, K.　Last War, The.
Dunn, S.　Man Who Closed Shop, The.
Herrick.　Distrust.
Morgan, E.　Cinquevalli.
Padilla.　Prayer for the End of the Century, A.
Ransom, J.　Her Eyes.
Rich, A.　Like This Together.

Diversity
Blake, E.　Tan Manhattan.
Dunbar, P.　Accountability.
Hewitt, J.　Frontier, The.
Hughes, L.　Mystery.
Longfellow, H.　Kéramos.

Diving and Divers
Biespiel, D.　Tower.
Brontë, C.　Diving.
Garcia, R.　Diver for the NYPD Talks to His Girlfriend, A.
Garrett, E.　Reprieve, The.
Goese, M.　Dive, The.
Hayden, R.　Diver, The.
Healy, E.　Louganis.
Hemans.　Diver, The.

Knight, E.　Poem of Attrition, A.
Livesay, D.　Fantasia.
Livingstone, D.　One Time.
Merrill, C.　Diver, The.
Mole, J.　Taking the Plunge.
Quennell.　Divers, The.
Rich, A.　Diving into the Wreck.
Ross, W.　Diver, The.
Simpson, R.　Diver.
Smith, I.　You Are at the Bottom of My Mind.

Divining and Diviners
Herrick.　Divination by a Daffadill [or Daffodil].

Divorce
Boss.　My Ringless Fingers on the Steering Wheel Tell the Story.
Byron, G.　To Penelope, January 2, 1821.
Coleman, H.　Poem for a "Divorced" Daughter.
Copus, J.　Back Seat of My Mother's Car, The.
Dibdin, C.　Popular Functionary, A.
Durcan.　Divorce Referendum, Ireland, 1986, The.
Pietà 's Over, The.
Elliott, A.　X-Ray, The.
Ferlinghetti, L.　People Getting Divorced.
Gewanter, D.　Divorce and Mr. Circe.
Gylys, B.　Family Reunion—Aunt Vern's Two Cents.
"H., C. G."　Power of Innocence, The.
Hollander, J.　For Both of You, the Divorce Being Final.
Koehn.　Divorce.
Kunitz, S.　River Road.
Levertov.　Wedding-Ring.
Lowell, R.　Katherine's Dream.
Maguire, S.　Divorce Referendum, The.
Mathis.　Getting Out.
McCabe, V.　For Starters.
McCarriston.　To Judge Faolain, Dead Long Enough: A Summons.
Merrill, J.　Broken Home, The.
Mew.　Madeleine in Church.
Moulds, J.　Late Summer Litany.
Nowlan.　Beginning.
Olds, S.　Victims, The.
Realuyo.　Sojourners, The.
Snodgrass, W.　Mementos, 1.
Storace.　Archaeology of Divorce, The.
Tucker, M.　Wail of the Divorced.
Unknown.　Jamie Douglas.
Wickham.　Divorce.

Doctors
Abse.　Carnal Knowledge.
Case History.
Doctor, The.
Lunch and Afterwards.
Origin of Music, The.
Stethoscope, The.
X-Ray.
Campo.　El Curandero.
Lost in the Hospital.
S. W.
Coles, R.　On Dutch's Death.
Coulehan, J.　Dynamizer and the Oscilloclast, The.
I'm Gonna Slap Those Doctors.
Donze, R.　Vermont Has a High Suicide Rate.
Dyer, E.　'Round Killar.
Painting the Nude.
Ginsberg, A.　Chief of Medicine, The.
Line Drive.
Graham-Pole, J.　Venipuncture.
Guevara, M.　Postmortem.
Hirsch, E.　Two Suffering Men.
Hirschhorn, N.　Number Our Days.
Loden.　Conversations with Dr. M.
Mukand, J.　Lullaby.
Norris, K.　Lilith and the Doctor.
O'Reilly, M.　Small Girl Brings an Injured Bird into the Surgery, A.
Palmer, R. F.　Conchie, The.
Platt, F.　Coincidentally.
Rowe, V.　Time Heals All Wounds—But One.
Shafer, A.　Gurney Tears.
Monday Morning.
Stainer.　Wound-dresser's Dream, The.
Stone, J.　Gaudeamus Igitur: A Valediction.

Dogs

Getting to Sleep in New Jersey.
Talking to the Family.
Straus, M.   Log of Pi, The.
Sykes, B.   Rachel.
Unknown, fr. Terezin Concentration Camp.   Pain Strikes Sparks on Me, the Pain of Terezin.
Van Peenen, H.   Insulin Receptor.
Will Campbell Displays His Craniotribe.
Wright, J.   Portugal Laurel, The.
Young, G.   Letter to William Carlos Williams, A.
Miracle, The.
Night Call.

See also **Physicians**

Dogs

Albee, E.   Samantha.
Allen, J.   War Poem, A.
Amherst.   Verses Designed to Be Sent to Mr. Adams.
Anderson, D.   Domi Solus.
Anderson, J.   Ye Bruthers Dogg.
Anderson, L.   Dog Show.
Armitage, S.   Before You Cut Loose.
Arnold, M.   Geist's Grave.
Baker, H.   Advice to a Man Who Lost a Dog.
Bangs, J.   My Dog.
Barry, L.   I love my master I love my master.
Bass, R.   Odyssey, The.
Baxter, C.   Dog Kibble: A Villanelle.
Beddoes.   Sonnet: To Tartar, a Terrier Beauty.
Beerbohm, M.   Brave Rover.
Benson, R.   Lab Lines.
Bertolino.   Baying, The.
Bishop, E.   Pink Dog.
Blount, R.   Country Dog in the City (On a Leash, Which Is Bizarre Enough) Comes Upon an Obedience Class, A.
Bodecker.   Cats and Dogs.
Brent.   I Think I Know No Finer Things than Dogs.
Browning, E.   Flush or Faunus.
Bruner.   Beyond the Grave.
Dog's Vigil, A.
Lonely Dog, The.
Burkard.   Dogs on the Cliffs, The.
Burns, R.   On a Dog of Lord Eglinton's.
Carlson, R.   Max Who Caught a Car.
Chavez, L.   Woman Who Raised Dogs, The.
Chute, M.   My Dog.
Ciardi, J.   Suburban.
Ciment, J.   Mommy.
Coleman, W.   Dog Suicide.
Cooper, B.   Pet Names.
Toast to the Cook, A.
Cornford, F.   Child's Dream, A.
Cowper, W.   Beau's Reply.
On a Spaniel Called Beau Killing a Young Bird.
Creeley.   Messengers, The.
Davies, W.   D is for Dog.
Dawe, B.   Dogs in the Morning Light.
Drifters.
Day Lewis.   Sheepdog Trials in Hyde Park.
Stand-To, The.
Delmore, E.   Difference, The.
Derricotte.   From a Letter: About Snow.
Doty, M.   Beau: Golden Retrievals.
Dugan, A.   Memorial Service for the Invasion Beach Where the Vacation in the Flesh Is Over.
Dunn, S.   Buster's Visitation.
Fanthorpe.   Our Dog Chasing Swifts.
Ferrell, A.   Out.
Field, E.   Duel, The.
Frost, R.   Canis Major.
One More Brevity.
Galvin, J.   Little Dantesque.
Gerstler.   Max's Lecture on Canine Buddhism.
Gilbert, C.   Glimpses.
Giscombe.   (1978, Remembering 1962).
Graham, M.   Greta's Song.
Greenwell, D.   Fidelity Rewarded.
Grue.   Dogs of New York, The.
Guiterman.   Little Lost Pup.
Gunn, T.   Yoko.
Hahn, S.   Nijinksy's Dog.
Hamilton, D. O.   Ajax.

Hansen, R.   Do Not Let Skeezix Go in There: Winslow's Villanelle.
Hardy, T.   Ah, Are You Digging on My Grave?
Harper, M.   Sandra: At the Beaver Trap.
Haxton.   Nietzsche Possessed.
Heimel, C.   Sally.
Hempel, A.   Rain.
Hodgins.   Shooting the Dogs.
Hoffman, D.   In the Days of Rin-Tin-Tin.
Holland, N.   Alice.
Hudgins.   Buddy.
Rosie.
Two Ember Days in Alabama.
Hughes, L.   Warning: Augmented.
Hughes, T.   Roger the Dog.
Iremonger.   Dog, The.
Irving, J.   Untitled.
Jensen, L.   Red Dog, The.
Johnson, D.   Harold's Bowl and Food.
Johnson, J.   Midnight Run.
Johnson, M.   Old Dog.
Johnson, S.   Translation of Du Bellay's *Epigram on a Dog*.
Johnston, G.   Noctambule.
Jones, R. S.   Shelter.
Kinnell.   Supper after the Last, The.
Kirn, W.   Envoy: "I left. I'd finished raising you. I walked."
Klee.   Wolf Speaks, The.
Kohler, S.   Shepherd.
Kumin, M.   Gus Speaks.
Kusz, N.   Retired Greyhound, I.
Retired Greyhound, II.
Lamott, A.   Spoon River Sadie Louise.
Lea, S.   Wrong Way Will Haunt You, The.
Levertov.   Overland to the Islands.
Lewis, E.   My Dog.
Lewis, J.   Stories.
Lish, G.   Rusty.
Lombreglia, R.   Daisy, Five, Speaks to Sophia, Two.
MacCaig.   Praise of a Collie.
Markoe, M.   Ballad of Winky.
Lewis Describes His Day.
Martin, S.   Comic Adventures of Old Mother Hubbard and Her Dog, The.
Marx, P.   Hugs.
McGraw, E.   Drunk Dog.
McHugh, H.   My Shepherd.
McLeod.   Lone Dog.
Merrill, J.   Victor Dog, The.
Miller, A.   Lola's Lament.
Minot, G.   Down.
Minot, S.   Devotion.
Mnookin.   Signs.
Momaday.   Two Figures.
Monro.   Dog.
Montgomerie, A.   Remembers thou in Æsope of a taill.
Moore, H.   Runaway.
Moore, N.   Island and the Cattle, The.
More, S.   De Principe Bono et Malo.
Morris, M.   Missing: A Dog's Doggerel.
Muñoz, A.   Hunting Accident.
Mueller, L.   What the Dog Perhaps Hears.
Musgrave.   Burial of the Dog.
Nash, O.   Dog, The.
Norris, L.   Shepherd's Dog, The.
Ondaatje.   Biography.
Oodgeroo of the tribe Noonuccal.   Flea's Hymn.
Ortiz.   Bony.
Paschen.   Sam's Ghazals.
Perry, S.   Fugue.
Pope, A.   Epigram Engraved on the Collar of a Dog Given [*or* Which I Gave] to His Royal Highness.
Powell, P.   Full Neurological Work-up.
Procter, A.   Homeless.
Prunty.   Coach.
Raab, L.   Katie's Words.
Retallack, J.   Woman Dragged by Welsh Corgis.
Richard, M.   Y'All Are Bird Dogs, Aren't You?
Riley, J.   Diners in the Kitchen, The.
Rybicki, J.   Dogman, The.
Salom.   Winter.
Schaeffer.   Dog, The.

Schinto, J.   Stalker.
Schwartz, D.   Dogs Are Shakespearean, Children Are Strangers.
Shepard, J.   Love Song of Audrey.
Shepard, K.   Birch.
Glom: Labrador, 110 pounds.
Smith, L.   In the Heat of the Night.
Smith, S.   Goodnight.
Soniat.   Dog Days.
Sonnenberg, B.   Stay.
Spencer, K. C.   When I Died on My Birthday.
Starbird.   Hound, The.
Stein, G.   Identity A Poem.
Stern, G.   Dog, The.
Svoboda.   Cosmo Dog.
Sward.   Uncle Dog; the Poet at 9.
Swift, J.   On the Collar of Mrs. Dingley's Lap-Dog.
Tester, W.   Complacencies of the Fenced Yard.
Thomas, A.   Doggerel.
Thomas, D.   Song of the Mischievous Dog, The.
Thompson, P.   Unromantic Awakening, An.
Todd, M.   To Kill Stray Dogs.
Tuck, L.   Sniff.
Unknown.   Bingo.
Viorst.   Mother Doesn't Want a Dog.
Wade, S.   Dog Sonnet.
Wallace, R.   Dog's Song.
Ward, T.   Stray Dogs, Foaming.
Warren, R.   Sila.
Wilbur.   Pardon, The.
Williams, C.   Dog, The.
Williams, W.   To a Dog Injured in the Street.
Winters, Y.   Elegy on a Young Airedale Bitch Lost Two Years Since in the Salt-Marsh.
Wright, J.   Old Dog in the Ruins of the Graves at Arles, The.
Simon and the Tarantula.
Walking the Dog.
Wright, K.   Heads or Tails?
Zimunya.   Mr. Bezuidenthout's Dogs.

See also **Puppies**

Dollhouses

Schmitz.   Making a Door.

Dolls

Black, J.   Paper Doll.
Boland, E.   Dolls Museum in Dublin, The.
Caldwell, A.   Raggedy Ann.
Dubie.   Poem: "Mule kicked out in the trees, A. An Early."
Duhamel.   Barbie's Molester.
Bicentennial Barbie.
Kinky.
Evans, B.   Waltz for Debby.
Freeman, C.   Christmas Morning I.
Gioia.   Counting the Children.
González, R.   Perla at the Mexican Border Assembly Line of Dolls.
Hemphill.   Soft Targets.
Kern, J.   Raggedy Ann.
Lees, G.   Waltz for Debby.
Levertov.   Partial Resemblance.
Livingston, M.   Doll.
Miles, J.   Doll.
Mori.   Barbie Says Math is Hard.
Palmer, M.   Of this cloth doll which.
Paterson, E.   Griselda.
Reedy, C.   Doll Museum, The.
St. John, D.   Dolls.
Hush.
Trinidad.   Of Mere Plastic.
Yeats.   Dolls, The.

Dolphins

Constantine, D.   Watching for Dolphins.
Griffiths, B.   Dolphins.
Simon, M.   Dolphin, The.

Dominican Republic

Dove, R.   Parsley.

Don Juan

Byron, G.   Canto I.
Canto the Eleventh.
Canto the First.
Dedication: "Bob Southey! You're a poet—poet-laureate."
Evening.

Fragment: "I would to heaven that I were so much clay."
Growing Old.
Juan and Haiidée.
Juan in England.
Juan's Puberty.
On Wellington.
Poetical Commandments.
Shipwreck, The.

Don Quixote
Melville, H. Rusty Man, The.
Reavey. Bridge of Heraclitus, The.
Wilbur. Parable.

Donaghy, Lyle (1902-49)
Buchanan, G. Lyle Donaghy, Poet, 1902-1949.

Donkeys
Al-Rihani. I Dreamt I Was a Donkey Boy Again.
Causley. Balaam.
Chesterton, G. Donkey, The.
Fanthorpe. What the Donkey Saw.
Gibson, W. Advice to Travelers.
Gonzalez, R. Calling the White Donkey.
Hecht, A. Pig.
Hewitt, J. Turf-Carrier [or Turf Carrier] on Aranmore.
Montgomerie, A. Remembers thou in Æsope of a taill.
Roethke. Donkey, The.
Monotony Song, The.
Smith, S. Donkey, The.
Thomas, D. After the Funeral.
Unknown. Lock and Key.

Donne, John
Carew, T. Elegy upon the Death of the Dean of [St.] Paul's, Dr. John Donne, An.
On the Death of Donne.
Coleridge, S. On Donne's Poetry.
Corbet [or Corbett]. Epitaph on Dr. Donne, Dean of Paul's, An.
Godolphin. Elegy on D. D.
Jonson, B. To John Donne.
Kenyon, J. Travel: After a Death.
King, H. Upon the Death of My Ever Desired Friend Doctor [or Dr] Donne Dean of Paul's.
Maxton. Elegies.
Rukeyser, M. Homage to Literature.
Simmons, J. John Donne.
Sisson. Letter to John Donne, A.
Trocchi, A. For John Donne: Master Metaphysical.
Wotton, S. To John Donne.

Doors
Barrington, J. Villanelle VI.
Bayliss. Seven Dreams.
Bennett, R. Windy Nights.
Bible, *O.T.* Song: "I was asleep but my heart stayed awake."
Budenz. Poeta Fui.
Clark, T. Doors.
Coleridge, M. Broken Friendship.
Gone.
Witch, The.
Creeley. Door, The.
Davis, W. In a Room.
Frost, R. Lockless Door, The.
Garrison, T. Closed Door, The.
Herrick. No Lock against Lechery.
Hill, M. Sleep.
Imbs. Sleep.
Kafka. Before the Law.
Larkin, P. Mr Bleaney.
Levy, A. Minor Poet, A.
Mackenzie, K. Door swung open, The.
Mackey, N. Dream Thief.
Maiden. In the Gloaming.
McKay, C. White House, The.
Merwin, W. S. Door, A.
To the Hand.
Miller, M. Closing, A.
Monro. Terrible Door, The.
Moore, R. Doors.
Reed, H. Door and the Window, The.
Reed, I. Why I Often Allude to Osiris.
Reznikoff. House-Wreckers, The.

Shorter. Skeleton in the Cupboard, The.
Sorby. Gossip.
Thomas, E. Like the Touch of Rain.
Tomlinson, C. Door, The.

Dorset, England
Bastard. Ad Henricum Wottonem.
Hardy, T. Domicilium.
Roman Road, The.

Doubt
Arnold, M. Dover Beach.
Bontemps. Miracles.
Brontë, A. Doubter's Prayer, The.
Brownjohn. Looking at Her.
Creeley. Token, A.
Davies, W. Inquest, The.
Dickinson, E. This World Is Not Conclusion.
Dunn, S. Guardian Angel, The.
Green, D. R. Names and sorrows.
Herbert, G. Affliction (1).
Hewitt, J. Substance and Shadow.
Howe, F. Doubt.
Hudgins. Elegy for My Father, Who Is Not Dead.
Johnson, S. Lines Contributed to Hawkesworth's 'The Rival.'
Nesbit, E. Love's Guerdons.
O'Hara, F. Ode: "Idea of justice may be precious, An."
To the Harbormaster.
Ostriker. Story of Abraham, The.
Pankey. Confession of Cleopas, The.
Piatt, S. Doubt, A.
Public Enemy. Don't Believe the Hype.
Reese, L. Prayer of an Unbeliever.
Robinson, A. Sibyl, The.
Robinson, E. Christmas Sonnet, A.
Rossetti, C. After Communion.
Shapiro, D. House (Blown Apart).
Stevens, W. Landscape with Boat.
Thompson, C. Doubt.
Skeptic, The.
Tuckerman, F. As Sometimes in a Grove.
Unknown. Essay on Man.
See also **Agnosticism and Agnostics**

Douglass, Frederick
Bibb. In Memoriam Frederick Douglass.
Dunbar, P. Douglass.
Frederick Douglass.
Hayden, R. Frederick Douglass.
Heard, J. Welcome to Hon. Frederick Douglass.
Hughes, L. Frederick Douglass: 1817-1895.
Ray, H. In Memoriam Frederick Douglass.

Dover, England
Arnold, M. Dover Beach.

Doves
Brontë, A. Captive Dove, The.
De la Mare. Dove, The.
"Field." I sing thee with the stock-dove's throat. Trinity.
Hall, D. Short Circuit.
Kerouac. Thrashing Doves, The.
Miller, E. What the Women Told Me.
Moldaw. Nest, The.
Montagu, L. Verses Written in a Garden.
Mother Goose. Dove and the Wren, The.
Probyn. Lai.
Ray, H. My Easter Dove.
Robertson, A. Song of the Dove, The.
Robinson, A. Song: "Oh for the wings of a dove."
Scovell. Listening to Collared Doves.
Stainer. Sarcophagus.
Stevens, W. Song of Fixed Accord.
Weigl. Regret for the Mourning Doves Who Failed to Mate.
Wright, J. "Dove-Love."
Young, A. Stockdoves, The.
See also **Turtle Doves**

Down's Syndrome
Alpaugh, D. Herbie.
Snyder, R. Mongoloid Child Handling Shells on the Beach, A.
Stallworthy, J. Almond Tree, The.
See also **Mental Retardation**

Dowries
Ramsay, A. Lass with a Lump of Land.

Dowsing and Dowsers
Morgan, E. Dowser, The.

Drag
Campo. Her Final Show.
Olds, S. His Costume.
White, J. Oshi.
Wieners. Poem for Cocksuckers, A.

Dragonflies
Bogan, L. Dragonfly, The.
Kunitz, S. Dragonfly, The.
Paloff, B. On Transportation.
Snyder, G. Dragonfly.

Dragons
Allen, P. Tattoo #47, 'Happy Dragon.'
Bottoms. Chinese Dragons.
Dove, O. Dragon.
Fanthorpe. Not My Best Side.
Moore, M. O To Be A Dragon.
Nash, O. Tale of Custard the Dragon, The.
Nicholls, J. Storytime.
Pepler. Concerning Dragons.
Revard. Dragon-Watching in St. Louis.
Smith, W. Toaster, The.
Stevens, M. Carp, The.
Treece. Magic Wood, The.

Drake, Joseph Rodman
Halleck, F. On the Death of Joseph Rodman Drake.

Drake, Sir Francis
Beedome. To the Noble Sir Francis Drake.
Newbolt. Drake's Drum.
Unknown. Upon Sir Francis Drake's Return from His Voyage about the World, and the Queen's Meeting Him.

Drawing
Behn, H. Circles.
Cowper, W. To George Romney, Esq.
Forbes, C. Picture of a Man.
Levine, P. On a Drawing by Flavio.
Rago. Childhood Painting Lesson.
Rector. David's Rumor.

Dreams and Dreaming
Adams, J. Dream, or the Type of the Rising Sun, A.
Adcock, F. Dreaming.
Addison, M. Names.
Al-Rihani. I Dreamt I Was a Donkey Boy Again.
Alexander, E. Feminist Poem Number One.
Overture: Watermelon City.
Alexander, P. Scherzo.
Ali, A. Dream of Glass Bangles, A.
I See Chile in My Rearview Mirror.
Allingham. Dream, A [or The].
Alvi, M. Bed, The.
Fish.
Amis, K. Against Romanticism.
Dream of Fair Women, A.
Anderson, L. Dog Show.
Angira. If.
Anyidoho. Hero and Thief.
Arnold, M. Longing.
Ashbery. Improvement, The.
Atwood. Variation on the Word *Sleep*.
Baca. Voz de la Gente.
Work We Hate and Dreams We Love.
Baillie, J. Reverie, A.
Balaban. Dead for Two Years, Erhart Arranges to Meet Me in a Dream.
Bampfylde. On a Frightful Dream.
Bang, M. Like a Fire in a Fire.
Baraka. New World, The.
Barer, M. Here Come the Dreamers.
Barnes, W. Sonnet: "In every dream thy lovely features rise."
Barney, S. Vision.
Barris, H. Wrap Your Troubles in Dreams.
Becker, R. Dreaming at the Rexall Drug.
Beddoes. Dream-Pedlary.
Belieu. Sleeping Man Must Be Awakened to Be Killed, A.
Berg, S. May 1970.
Bevington, L. Dreamers?

Bishop, E.   Summer's Dream, A.
Blockcolski.   My Dream.
Bly, R.   Dream of Retarded Children, A.
Bogan, L.   Dream, The.
  Meeting, The.
Bolger.   Dublin Girl, Mountjoy, 1984.
Bona.   Dream Poem.
Bowers, E.   Le Rêve.
Brecht, B.   I, the Survivor.
Breckenridge.   General John Cabell
  Breckinridge.
Brock, V.   Mary's Dream.
Brontë, C.   'Again I find myself alone'
  'What does she dream of'
  Pilate's Wife's Dream.
Brontë, E.   Day Dream, A.
  Stars.
Brooke, R.   Sonnet: "Oh! Death will find me,
  long before I tire."
Brooks, G.   My Dreams, My Works Must Wait
  Till after Hell.
Brown, D.   Illumination.
Brown, N.   All I Do Is Dream of You.
  You Stepped Out of a Dream.
Browning, E.   True Dream, A.
Browning, R.   Women and Roses.
Brydges.   On Dreams, October 15, 1782.
Buckley, C.   Sycamore Canyon Nocturne.
Burke, J.   I've Got a Pocketful of Dreams.
  Polka Dots and Moonbeams.
  Welcome to My Dream.
Busch, T.   Heartland.
Bynner.   Wistaria.
Byron, G.   Darkness.
Campbell, T.   Soldier's Dream, The.
Campo.   Allegory.
Carter, R.   Vietnam Dream.
Cartwright, W.   Dream Broke, A.
Cavalieri.   Grandmother.
Cherry, K.   Reading, Dreaming, Hiding.
Chin, D.   Sleeping Father.
Chin, J.   Night.
Christie.   In My Dream.
  Overture.
Clark, T.   "Before Dawn."
Clifton, L.   Death of Crazy Horse, The.
  Mary's Dream.
  Night Vision.
  Powell (officer charged with the beating of
    Rodney King).
  Women you are accustomed to, The.
Codrescu.   Work.
Coleridge, M.   'But in that Sleep of Death What
  Dreams May Come?'
Coleridge, S.   Blest is the tarn which towering
  cliffs o'ershade.
  Kubla Khan: or, A Vision in a Dream.
Conkling, G.   I Will Not Give Thee All My
  Heart.
Conoley.   Beckon.
Cornford, F.   Child's Dream, A.
Corrothers.   Snapping of the Bow, The.
Corso.   30th Year Dream.
  Dream of a Baseball Star.
Cortes, F.   Poem Composed During a Brownout.
Couzyn.   Morning.
Creeley.   Death of Venus, The.
  For No Clear Reason.
  Place, The.
  Talking.
  Three Ladies, The.
Cullen, C.   For a Poet.
Cumbo.   I'm a Dreamer.
Cummings, E.   First of All My Dreams, The.
  It Is at Moments After I Have Dreamed.
Curbelo.   Bedtime Stories.
  Lake Has Swallowed the Whole Sky, The.
Daley, V.   Vision of Sunday in Heaven, A.
Davis, T.   C. T. at the Five Spot.
Dawe, B.   Copy-writer's Dream, The.
De la Mare.   Miss Loo.
  Voices.
De Vries, R.   On Alabama Ave., Paterson, NJ,
  1954.
DeLange, E.   Darn That Dream.
Delgado, J.   I-5 Incident.

Dickey, J.   Sled Burial, Dream Ceremony.
Digges.   Rough Music.
Dodge, M.   Poor Crow!
Donne.   Dream[e], The.
Doolittle, H.   At Baia.
Douglas, L.   Dead Poet, The.
  Two Loves.
Dove, R.   Oriental Ballerina, The.
  This Life.
Dransfield.   That Which We Call a Rose.
Driscoll, L.   Hold Fast Your Dreams.
Dubie.   Sanctuary.
Duhamel.   Sex with a Famous Poet.
Dunbar, P.   Ere Sleep Comes Down to Soothe
  the Weary Eyes.
Duncan, R.   Often I Am Permitted to Return to
  a Meadow.
  Sentinels, The.
Eady.   Success.
Early, G.   Innocency or Not Song X.
Elledge.   Their Hats Is Always White.
Ellington, D.   It Shouldn't Happen to a Dream.
Equi.   In a Monotonous Dream.
Erdrich.   Strange People, The.
Espada.   My Cockroach Lover.
Etter.   Monk's Dream.
Everson, W.   Narrows of Birth, The.
Faigao, B.   Balitaw.
Ferguson, G.   In Hospital-land.
"Field."   Elsewhere.
Field, E.   Little Boy Blue.
  Sugar-Plum Tree, The.
  Wynken, Blynken, and Nod.
Figueroa, J.   Pablo Neruda.
Frost, R.   After Apple-Picking.
  Hill Wife, The.
  House Fear.
  Impulse, The.
  Loneliness.
  Oft-Repeated Dream, The.
Fuller, C.   My Father's Dreams.
Gannon, K.   Dreamer's Holiday, A.
Garcia, R.   Book of Dreams, The.
Gardner, I.   Nightmare.
Garrett, E.   Moules à la Marinière.
Gascoyne.   And the Seventh Dream Is the
  Dream of Isis.
George, D.   Asenath.
Gershwin.   Long Ago (And Far Away).
  Man I Love, The.
Gilbert, C.   Kite-Flying.
Giscombe.   (1980).
  (The Recent Past).
Glück, L.   Condo.
Glancy.   Kemo Sabe.
Goodtimes.   Sartor Resartus.
Gotera.   Manong Chito Tells Manong Ben about
  His Dream over Breakfast at the Manilatown
  Cafe.
Graves, R.   Hag-Ridden.
  In Procession.
  Pinch of Salt, A.
  Theseus and Ariadne.
  Window Sill, The.
Gray, J.   Barber, The.
Greenlaw.   Shape of Things, The.
Guevara, M.   Reader of This Page.
Gunn, T.   Wheel of Fortune, The.
Hachenburg, H.   Terezin.
Hacker, M.   Wagers.
Hadas, R.   Journey Out.
Hall, D.   Town of Hill, The.
  White Apples.
  Woolworth's.
Hamill, S.   Abstract.
Hammerstein.   Happy Talk.
Hardy, T.   Self-Unseeing, The.
Harms.   Los Angeles, The Angels.
  My Own Little Piece of Hollywood.
Hart, L.   Blue Room, The.
Harte, B.   Second Review of the Grand
  Army, A.
Hass, R.   Palo Alto: the Marshes.
  Pornographer, The.
Hayden, R.   Bone-Flower Elegy.
Hemans.   Dreaming Child, The.

Henry, J.   Out of the Frying Pan into the Fire.
Herrick.   Dream[e]s.
  Vine, The.
  Vision, The.
Higginson, E.   Dream of Sappho, A.
Hill, M.   Sleep.
Hollo.   Le Jazz Hot.
Hope, A.   Gateway, The.
Howes, B.   Chimera.
Hughes, L.   Dream Boogie.
  Dream Variation[s].
  Morning After.
  Water-Front Streets.
Hugo, R.   In Your Bad Dream.
  In Your Dream after Falling in Love.
  In Your Racing Dream.
  In Your Young Dream.
Hugo, V.   Boaz Asleep.
Hunt, L.   Nile, The.
Ignatow, D.   Dream, The.
Imbs.   Sleep.
Jackson, H.   Dreams.
Jarrell.   Dead Wingman, The.
  Girl in a Library, A.
  House in the Wood, The.
Jenkins, P.   Six Small Fires.
Jewsbury.   Summer Eve's Vision, A.
Johnson, G.   My Little Dreams.
Johnson, M.   Dream, A.
Johnston, M.   Directions for Dreamfishing.
Jones, E.   Dream, A.
Jones, I.   I'll See You in My Dreams.
Jonson, B.   Dream[e], The.
Kane, P.   Disciples Asleep at Gethsemane.
Kaufman, B.   African Dream.
Keats.   Fall of Hyperion; A Dream, The.
  Nebuchadnezzar's Dream.
Kendall, M.   Pure Hypothesis, A.
King, H.   Dream Maiden, A.
Kinsella, T.   Nuchal, a Fragment.
  Wormwood.
Kipling, R.   If—.
Koehler, T.   Wrap Your Troubles in Dreams.
Komey.   Change, The.
Kossman.   Pilate's Wife.
Kumin, M.   Making the Jam without You.
Kyle, C. J.   Fire in Early Morning.
Lane, P.   Girl at the Window.
Levertov.   Don't You Hear that Whistle Blowin'
Levine, P.   Soloing.
Levy, A.   Cambridge in the Long.
  Old House, The.
  On the Threshold.
Lewis, S.   Street of Dreams.
Lim, S.   Modern Secrets.
Litsey.   Dreams Ahead, The.
Loesser.   Sit Down, You're Rockin' the Boat.
Longfellow, H.   Golden Mile-Stone, The.
Lopez, L.   To a Coal Miner in Madrid, New
  Mexico.
Lowell, J.   Aladdin.
Lowell, R.   Katherine's Dream.
Lum.   Chinese Hot Pot.
Mabuza.   Dream Cloud.
Mackenzie, K.   Sick Men Sleeping.
Mackey, N.   Winged Abyss.
MacNeice.   Bad Dream.
Major, C.   Round Midnight.
Martin, H.   Here Come the Dreamers.
McAuley, J.   Dialogue.
Melville, H.   Rose Window.
  To.
Merrill, J.   Mad Scene, The.
Merton.   Lent in a Year of War.
Merwin, W. S.   Carol: "On vague hills the
  prophet bird."
  To the Hand.
Mew.   Ne Me Tangito.
  Not for That City.
Milton.   On His Deceased Wife.
Mitchell, K.   Monster, The.
Miyazawa Kenji.   Daydreaming on the Trail.
Moll, B.   Wrap Your Troubles in Dreams.
Momaday.   Carriers of the Dream Wheel.
Monaco, J.   I've Got a Pocketful of Dreams.
Montgomerie, A.   Dreame, Ane.

Moore, H. Window at Key West, A.
Moore, N. Patient, The.
Muir, E. Adam's Dream.
Brothers, The.
Labyrinth, The.
Murray, P. Rain.
Nash, O. It Figures.
Nelson, M. Motel Story.
Niedecker. Subliminal.
Nikolic, G. Key to Dreams.
Notley. Where Leftover Misery Goes.
O'Hara, F. Sleeping on the Wing.
O'Rahilly [or O'Reilly] [or Ó Rathaille].
Vision, The.
O'Shaughnessy, A. Ode: "We are the music-
makers."
Orlovsky. Dream May 18, 1958.
I Dream of St. Francis.
Orpingalik. Alcheringa Definitions.
Owen, W. Strange Meeting.
Palmer, M. Erolog.
Parker, A. Vandals, Horses.
Parkes, B. Dream Fears.
Pastan. September.
Phillips, D. On Entries Emptiness.
Pietri. Intermission from Saturday.
Night Is out of Sight, The.
Plutzik. Dream about Our Master, William
Shakespeare, The.
Poe. Dream within a Dream, A.
Dream-Land [or Dreamland].
Dreams.
Fairyland [or Fairy-Land].
To One in Paradise.
Pogson, P. In Dreams.
Pollak, F. Dream, The.
Pyle. Waking.
Rózewicz. Memory of a Dream From the Year
1963.
Rafferty, P. Personal.
Rakosi. Journey Away, A.
Ramke. Difference Between Night and Day,
The.
Rees-Jones. Making for Planet Alice.
Rexroth, K. Fish Peddler and Cobbler.
Poem: "As the full moon rises."
Rich, A. Jerusalem.
Richardson, J. On My Late Dear Wife.
Robinson, A. Pallor.
Robinson, E. Miniver Cheevy.
Robinson, M. Dreams of a Rival.
Visions Appear to her in a Dream.
Rodgers, W. Scapegoat.
Roethke. Dream, The.
Rolfe, E. Song: "Keep the dream alive and
growing always."
Rossetti, C. Echo.
Mirage.
My Dream.
Old-World Thicket, An.
On the Wing.
Reflection.
Rossetti, D. Orchard-Pit, The.
Rukeyser, M. Burning the Dreams.
Nevertheless the Moon.
Salom. World of Dreams, The.
Sanchez, S. Blues.
Sandburg, C. Gone.
Mamie.
Murmurings in a Field Hospital.
Portrait of a Motorcar.
Prayers of Steel.
Sarton. Nursery Rhyme.
Sayres. Bankrupt.
Schwartz, D. O Child, Do Not Fear the Dark
and Sleep's Dark Possession.
Seward. Invocation, To the Genius of Slumber
Written Oct. 1787.
Sexton. Author of the Jesus Papers Speaks,
The.
Shange. Dream of Pairing.
Shapiro, K. Love for a Hand.
Sharma, P. Action-Packed Sonnet.
Shelley, Mary. Stanzas: "Oh, come to me in
dreams, my love!"
Shelley, P. Indian Serenade, The.

Sherburne. Dream, The.
Simic. Empire of Dreams.
Simon, L. Kali.
Simpson, L. I Dreamed That in a City Dark as
Paris.
Smith, C. To Sleep.
Smith, S. Be Off!
In My Dreams.
My Hat.
Songe d'Athalie.
Snyder, G. For a Stone Girl at Sanchi.
Spender, S. Daybreak.
Stern, G. Lucky Life.
Stevens, W. Disillusionment of Ten O'Clock.
Stevenson, R. Escape at Bedtime.
Land of Nod, The.
Young Night Thought.
Suckling, S. Dream, A.
Swift, J. On Dreams.
Swinburne. Love And Sleep.
Synková, A. To Olga.
Taggard. Demeter.
Talvikki, A. You Don't Know What Happened
When You Froze.
Thwaite. Dream Time.
Timrod. Dreams.
Todd, M. To Kill Stray Dogs.
Tomlinson, C. Dream, A.
Toomer. Evening Song.
Turner, C. Dream, A.
Turner, W. Romance.
Unknown. Dreams.
Limerick: "There was an old man of [or from]
Peru / Who dreamt [or dreamed] he was
eating his shoe."
Poet Dreamt of Heaven, The.
She Lay All Naked.
Valentine, J. Dream Barker.
Sleep Drops Its Nets.
Van Doren. Dream of Trains, A.
Van Heusen, J. Darn That Dream.
Polka Dots and Moonbeams.
Welcome to My Dream.
Van Walleghen. In the Chariot Drawn by
Dragons.
Wainwright, J. Fierce Dream, The.
Wakoski. Night a Sailor Came to Me in a
Dream, The.
Watson, R. Nirvana.
Wayne, M. Dreamer's Holiday, A.
Weaver, M. Blind Solo.
Whitman, W. Old War-Dreams.
Whitmore, S. Bird, The.
Wieners. King Solomon's Magnetic Quiz.
Wilbur. Beasts.
In the Smoking-Car.
Walking to Sleep.
Wilde, L. Corinne's Last Love-Song.
Williams, W. Revelation, The.
Thursday.
Williamson, G. Annual Returns.
Wiman, C. Sweet Dreams.
Winner, S. Listen to the Mocking Bird.
Winter, M. Elegy: "There is a question."
Wojahn. Allegory: Attic and Fever.
Woodard. Tower.
Wordsworth, W. Expostulation and Reply.
Wright, C. Further Adventures With You.
Wright, J. American Twilights, 1957.
Compassion's Bird.
End of an Ethnic Dream, The.
Poem about Breasts, A.
Wyatt, S. Lover Showeth How He Is Forsaken
of Such as He Sometime Enjoyed, The.
Yeats. He Wishes for the Cloths of Heaven.
Rose of the World, The.
To the Rose upon the Rood of Time.
Young, M. J. To Dreams.
Young, V. Street of Dreams.

Dress
Chrystos. I Bought a New Red.
Dixon, M. Lady in Red, The.
Duran, J. For the Woman Who Dressed Up to
Listen to Gigli on the Radio.
McCarthy, J. Alice Blue Gown.
Muske, C. Epith.

Parker, D. Red Dress, The.
Pearlberg, G.G. Loop-the-Loop in Prospect
Park (1905).
Sondheim. All I Need Is the Girl.
See also **Clothing**
Driftwood
Bynner. Driftwood.
Drinking Water
Bishop, E. Under the Window: Ouro Prêto.
Goldbarth. Complete with Starry Night and
Bourbon Shots.
Drinks and Drinking
Ade. R-E-M-O-R-S-E.
Ai. I Can't Get Started.
Aldrich, H. Catch, A.
Allen, P. Tattoo #47, 'Happy Dragon.'
Allison, D. When I Drink I Become the Joy of
Faggots.
Arlen, H. One for My Baby (And One More for
the Road).
Arnold, G. Beer.
Banus. Eighteen.
Barnes, B. Something Cool.
Belloc. West Sussex Drinking Song.
Bishop, M. Song of the Pop-Bottlers.
Bitar. Happy Hour.
Boyd, M. Beer Drops.
Brecht, B. Three Fragments.
Brooks, G. We Real Cool.
Bukowski. Crucifix in a Deathhand.
Not Much Singing.
Burns, R. Auld Lang Syne.
Scotch Drink.
Tam o' Shanter; A Tale.
Willie Brew'd [or Brewed] a Peck o' Maut.
Bynner. Drinking Alone with the Moon.
Ceravolo. Geological Hymn.
Chavez, L. After the Prom.
Claman, E. Show Biz Parties.
Cleary, B. Boys' Own.
Coolidge, C. Some Glow on the Sill.
Coots, J. You Go to My Head.
Cope, W. Usquebaugh.
Cornish, S. His Fingers Seem to Sing.
Coslow, S. Cocktails for Two.
Cowley, A. Epicure, The.
Crane, H. Wine Menagerie, The.
Cunningham, J. Interview with Doctor Drink.
Curbelo. Drinking Song.
Last Call.
Davis, J. Desolation.
De Vries, P. Bacchanal.
Dickinson, E. I Taste a Liquor Never Brewed.
Dow, P. Drunk Last Night with Friends, I Go to
Work Anyway.
Doyle, S. Hell To Pay.
Dressel. Dai, Live.
Dugan, A. Drunken Memories of Anne Sexton.
Dumas, H. Knees of a Natural Man.
Etter. Drink and Agriculture.
Fergusson. Daft Days, The.
Fincke. Class A, Salem, the Rookie League.
Flanders, M. Have Some Madeira, M'dear?
Forbes, C. Potter's Wheel, The.
Gannon, K. Moonlight Cocktail.
Garrigue. Song for "Buvez les Vins du
Postillion"—Advt.
Glaser, E. Blues for the Nightowl.
Glazer. Drinking with the Nazis.
Gorey. Limerick: "From the bathing machine
came a din."
Greenwell, D. To Christina Rossetti.
Gregerman, D. High Speed.
Guest, B. Green Revolutions.
Guillén, N. Wake for Papa Montero.
Gunn, T. Donahue's Sister.
Halleck, F. Song: "There's a barrel of porter at
Tammany Hall."
Hardy, T. Great Things.
Harms. From Now On.
Haug. Tennessee Waltz, The.
Heaney, S. Sloe Gin.
Hecht, A. Ghost in the Martini, The.
Hernández Cruz. Perlas.
Herrick. Anacreontic[k] Verse.
Frolic[k], A.

To Live Merrily, and To Trust to Good Verses.
Wassaile, The.
Welcome to Sack, The.
Holmes, O.　Ode for a Social Meeting.
Housman, A.　Terence, This Is Stupid Stuff.
Hudgins.　Praying Drunk.
Hughes, L.　Neighbor.
Iozia, J.　Last Night at the Flamingo.
Jacobsen, J.　Bush.
Johnston, A.　Cocktails for Two.
Johnston, M.　Sea-Cucumber, The.
Jonson, B.　Song: To Celia.
Kasischke.　Grace.
Kennedy, X.　Hangover Mass.
　In a Prominent Bar in Secaucus [One Day].
Komunyakaa.　White Port and Lemon Juice.
Landor, W.　Had We Two Met.
Larkin, J.　Good-Bye.
Larkin, P.　Aubade: "I work all day, and get
　half-drunk at night."
Lewis, G.　Hedge, The.
Li Po.　Awakening from Drunkenness on a
　Spring Day.
Drinking Alone in Moonlight.
Drinking Alone in the Moonlight.
Drinking Alone under Moonlight.
For the Dancer of the King of Wu.
Livingston, M.　Lemonade Stand.
Lopez, L.　NEHI Strawberry Down-and-Away.
Lovelace, R.　Vintage to the Dungeon, The.
Lowry, M.　Delirium in Vera Cruz.
Eye-Opener.
Mac Giolla Ghunna.　Yellow Bittern, The.
MacDiarmid, H.　Old Wife in High Spirits.
Madgett.　Sally: Twelfth Street.
Masefield.　Captain Stratton's Fancy.
Mathias, R.　Testament.
McIlroy, L.　Siesta.
Merriam, E.　Counting-out Rhyme.
Messerli.　Actually Swallowed.
Moorer.　Circle, The.
Social Glass, The.
Morton, T.　Song, The: "Drink and be merry,
　merry, merry boys."
Mother Goose.　Strange Old Woman, A.
Nash, O.　Reflections on Ice-breaking.
Padel.　Scotch.
Paschen.　Confederacy.
Prior.　Epigram: "When Bibo thought fit from
　the world to retreat."
Rafferty, C.　Man on the Tower, The.
Ramsay, A.　Up in the Air.
Randall, D.　Old Witherington.
Roberts, L.　Moonlight Cocktail.
Robinson, A.　Oasis, An.
Robinson, E.　Miniver Cheevy.
Mr Flood's Party.
Rochester, J.　Ramble in St. James's Park, A.
Upon Drinking in a Bowl.
Roethke.　My Papa's Waltz.
Rossetti, C.　Better Resurrection, A.
Rouse.　England Nil.
Glass.
San Juan.　Entelechy on the Libidinal Fringe.
Three for the Road.
Sanders P.　Tripoli.
Scott, J.　Plato's Dog.
Smith, S.　Grace of God and the Meth-Drinker,
The.
Snyder, G.　I Went into the Maverick Bar.
Stephen, J.　Drinking Song.
Stephens, J.　Glass of Beer, A.
What Thomas an Buile Said in a Pub.
Strayhorn, B.　Lush Life.
Suárez, V.　Donatilia's Unrequited Love
Remedy.
Turberville.　Of Drunkenness.
Tyler, R.　Anacreontic to Flip.
Unknown.　At the Tavern.
Drinking Song.
Finnegan's Wake.
Judged by the Company One Keeps.
Last Drink, A.
Little More Cider, A.
Love.
Omnes Gentes Plaudite!

Riddle: "As I went through yon guttery gap / I
　met my Uncle Davy."
Rye Whisky.
Strip Me Naked, or Royal Gin for Ever; a
　Picture.
Tale of Lord Lovell, The.
Ward, E.　Extravagant Drunkard's Wish, The.
Wilbur.　Voice from under the Table, A.
Willard, N.　Ballad of Biddy Early, The.
Williams, W.　Drink.
Winch.　Shadow Grammar.
Winner, S.　Lilliputian's Beer Song.
Wright, J.　Journey to the Place of Ghosts.
Yeats.　Drinking Song, A.
Young, G.　Lips That Touch Liquor.

See also **Alcoholism and Alcoholics; Drunkards**

Driving and Drivers
Allen, P.　Pickup.
Anania.　Interstate 80.
Belieu.　How the Elderly Drive.
Betjeman.　Meditation on the A30.
Blackburn, P.　El Camino Verde.
Bly, R.　Driving toward the Lac Qui Parle River.
　Three Kinds of Pleasures.
Brock, V.　Sphinx.
Brown, E.　You Got You Got to Be Told.
Cherry, K.　Late Afternoon at the Arboretum.
Cofer, J.　Seizing the Day.
Creeley.　I Know a Man.
Dauenhauer, R.　Driving in a Snowstorm, King
　Salmon to Naknek.
Davis, G.　August Fires.
Erdrich.　Lady in the Pink Mustang, The.
Espada.　Fidel in Ohio.
Jeep Driver, The.
Ginsberg, A.　Bayonne Turnpike to Tuscarora.
Gioia.　Cruising with the Beach Boys.
Gloria.　Touch.
Heaney, S.　From the Frontier of Writing.
Peninsula, The.
Keller, D.　After Supper.
Lea, S.　Tempted by the Classical on Returning
　from the Store at Twenty Below Zero.
Lehman.　First Offense.
Levine, P.　I Caught a Glimpse.
Livingston, M.　4-Way Stop.
Mateo.　Jeepneyfying.
Miles, J.　Reason.
Muldoon, P.　Hard Drive.
Muske, C.　Coming Over Coldwater.
Revard.　Driving in Oklahoma.
Rukeyser, M.　Sand-Quarry with Moving
　Figures.
Smukler.　Home in Three Days. Don't Wash.
Stevens, W.　Reality Is an Activity of the Most
　August Imagination.
Van Duyn.　Vision Test, The.
Wallace, R.　Smoking.
Williams, M.　152 Into 5, *El Centro Palabra de
Fe.*
South.
Williams, W.　Right of Way, The.
Yost, C.　Escaping from Autopia.

See also **Automobiles**

Drought
Dressel.　Drouth, The.
Hannon.　Subterranean.
Hummell, A.　Salt Longing.
Lewis, A.　Mahratta Ghats, The.
Osundare.　Who Says That Drought Was Here?
Siegel, J.　Drought.
Wright, J.　Drought Year.

Drowning
Atwood.　Death of a Young Son by Drowning.
　This Is a Photograph of Me.
Barrax.　Scuba Diver Recovers the Body of a
　Drowned Child, The.
Benn.　Little Aster.
Brewer, G.　Teen Drowns in Rehabilitation
　Camp Days Before 17th Birthday, Questions
　Persist.
Brewster, E.　Death by Drowning.
Cofer, J.　Drowned Sailor, The.
Cowper, W.　Castaway, The.
Dawe, B.　Elegy for Drowned Children.

Delgado, J.　La Llorona.
Dobson, R.　Three Fates, The.
Donne.　Burnt Ship, A.
Hero and Leander.
Glück, L.　Drowned Children, The.
Gonzalez, R.　Angels of Juárez, Mexico, The.
Gray, T.　Ode on the Death of a Favourite [*or*
　Favorite] Cat, Drowned in a Tub [*or* Bowl] of
　Gold Fishes.
Greening, M.　Missing—Believed Drowned.
Heaney, S.　Limbo.
Hill, G.　White Ship, The.
Holden, M.　Seaman, 1941.
Holmes, O.　Ballad of the Oysterman, The.
Hopkins, G.　Wreck of the Deutschland, The.
Hugo, R.　Lady in Kicking Horse Reservoir,
　The.
Janzen, J.　At Summer's End.
Johnson, J.　Midnight Run.
Jones, D.　These Trees Are No Forest of
　Mourners.
Jones, R.　Portrait of My Father and His
　Grandson.
Lear, E.　Limerick: "There was an Old Man in a
　boat."
Lowry, M.　Salmon Drowns Eagle.
Miles, J.　Family.
Milton.　Lycidas.
Moss, H.　Water Island.
Oliver, D.　Oracle of the Drowned, The.
Salom.　Winter.
Smith, S.　Not Waving But Drowning.
Sweeney, M.　Where Fishermen Can't Swim.
Synge.　'Mergency Man, The.
Thomas, E.　Midnight Thought, A [on the Death
　of Mrs. *E. H.* and Her Little Daughter].
Unknown.　*Golden Vanity*, The.
Golden Vanity, The.
Lowlands o' [*or* of] Holland, The.
May Colven [*or* May Colvin].
Sir Patrick Spens [*or* Spence].
Tweed and Till.
Wheelwright.　Fish Food.
Witheford.　At the Discharge of Cannon Rise the
　Drowned.
Wright, J.　Eli, Eli.
In Response to a Rumor that the Oldest
　Whorehouse in Wheeling, West Virginia, Has
　Been Condemned.
Note Left in Jimmy Leonard's Shack, A.
To the Muse.

Drug Addiction
Adamson.　Passing through Experiences.
Ai.　Archangel.
Self Defense.
Anderson, D.　Itinerary.
Baraka.　Babylon Revisited.
Barresi.　Venice Beach: Brief Song.
Barth, R.　Insert, The.
Beatty, P.　Doggin the Rockman.
Brooks, G.　Coora Flower, The.
Brown, P.　I Remember Dexedrine. 1970.
Carroll, J.　Paregoric Babies.
Withdrawal Letter.
Clark, T.　Going to School in France or
　America.
Clifton, L.　White Lady.
Cuthand, B.　She Ties Her Bandanna.
Dransfield.　Fix.
Dubin, A.　You're Getting to Be a Habit with
　Me.
Fanthorpe.　Person's Tale, The.
Forbes, J.　Speed, a Pastoral.
Gould, J.　I Learn a Lesson About Our Society.
Gunn, T.　Street Song.
Harrison, W.　In Praise of Laudanum.
Hicok.　Heroin.
Hirsch, E.　Art Pepper.
Hope, A.　Under Sedation.
Hughes, L.　Junior Addict.
Jarrell.　Say Good-bye to Big Daddy.
Jauss.　Black Orchid.
Jones, J.　Drugs.
Knight, E.　Another Poem for Me (after
　Recovering from an O.D.).
Idea of Ancestry, The.

Welcome Back, Mr. Knight: Love of My Life.
Komunyakaa. Speed Ball.
Mackey, N. Falso Brilhante.
McLaughlin, J. Black Irish Blues.
Medina, T. Rhudine Rhudine.
Murray, L. Drugs of War, The.
Sanchez, S. Summer Words of [or for] a Sistuh
    [or Sister] Addict.
Smith, S. Drugs Made Pauline Vague.
St. Germain, S. Addiction.
Stone, A. Spofford Hall.
Thomas, L. Historiography.
Tucker, M. Opium-Eater, The.
Unknown. Cocaine Lil [and Morphine Sue].
    Laudanum.
    Willie the Weeper.
Waring, B. Refuge at the One Step Down.
Warren, H. You're Getting to Be a Habit with
    Me.
Warsh. White Nights.
Worley, D. Sandra.

Drugs
Anderson, D. Itinerary.
Barry, L. I love my master I love my master.
Carroll, J. Maybe I'm Amazed.
Cooper, D. Drugs.
Espinet, R. Merchant of Death.
Fisher, J. Life, A.
Ford, C. Bad Habit, The.
Galvin, J. Station (4).
Ginsberg, A. Mescaline.
Goodtimes. Learning to Smile.
Gunn, T. Painkillers.
    Victim, The.
Herrera. Future Martyr of Supersonic Waves.
Hollo. Discovery of LSD a True Story, The.
Iozia, J. Last Night at the Flamingo.
Jackson, R. Tee.
Jarman, M. Black Riviera, The.
Jones, J. Drugs.
Katz, J. Falling.
Knight, E. Feeling Fucked/Up Up.
    Idea of Ancestry, The.
Kolodny, S. Tsuneko—Psychiatric Medications
    Clinic.
Lopez, T. Path Marked with Breadcrumbs, A.
Muldoon, P. Gathering Mushrooms.
Pietri. How Do Your Eggs Want You (?).
Selman, R. Exodus.
Unknown. Cocaine Lil [and Morphine Sue].
Weiners. Act #2.
    Poem for vipers, A.
White, J. Oshi.
Wojahn. Necromancy: The Last Days of Brian
    Jones, 1968.

Drugstores
Anstett. Pharmacy.

Druids
Nichols, G. Long-Man.

Drums
Adisa. Count Ossie.
Andrews, L. Time Signature.
Baca. Voz de la Gente.
Barlow, G. 4½ Months: Halfway Song.
Bethune, L. For Singing in Good Mood.
Bontemps. Dark Girl.
Brathwaite, E. Making of the Drum, The.
Chipasula. Singing Drum, The.
Dacey, P. Drummer, The.
DiPasquale. Rain.
Etter. Stuffy Turkey.
Gould, R. Amateur Drummer.
Hardy, T. Drummer Hodge.
Hernández Cruz. Ironing Goatskin.
Hernton. Distant Drum, The.
Hughes, L. Danse Africaine.
    Drum.
Komunyakaa. Back Then.
Kyei. Talking Drums, The.
MacLeish. End of the World, The.
Momaday. Eagle-Feather Fan, The.
Okara. Piano and Drums.
Okigbo. Sacrifice.
Olson, C. La Chute.
Pegram, A. I Will Still Sing.
Scott of Amwell. Ode: "I hate that drum's

discordant sound."
Smith, P. They Say That Black People.
Whitman, W. Beat! Beat! Drums!
Young, K. Escape Artist, The.

Drunkards
Baillie, J. Hooly and Fairly.
Barnes, J. Lying in a Yuma Saloon.
Berryman. Alcoholic.
Burns, R. Johnie Blunt.
Cary, A. Telling Fortunes.
Chesterton, G. Rolling English Road, The.
Cunningham, J. Interview with Doctor Drink.
Dickinson, E. I Taste a Liquor Never Brewed.
Dove, R. Genie's Prayer Under the Kitchen
    Sink.
Endrezze. Eclipse.
    Song-Maker.
Evans, G. Renaissance Drunk, A.
Fenton, J. Skip, The.
Graves, R. Point of No Return.
Hattersley, G. New Mr Barnsley Something,
    The.
Hernández Cruz. Scarlet Skirt.
Herrick. Vision, The.
Housman, A. Terence, This Is Stupid Stuff.
Hugo, R. Neighbor.
Kipling, R. Cells.
Knight, S. Resentments Composed because of
    the Clamor of Town Topers Outside My
    Apartment.
Leland, C. Wein Geist.
Levine, P. Sweet Will.
Lowry, M. Delirium in Vera Cruz.
McGrath, T. On the Head of a Pin.
Merwin, W. S. Drunk in the Furnace, The.
Notley. Jack Would Speak through the
    Imperfect Medium of Alice.
Oles. For the Drunk.
Paul, L. Cynical Portraits.
Powell, J. Lines Written for a Friend on the
    Death of His Brother, Caused by a Railway
    Train Running over Him Whilst He Was in a
    State of Inebriation.
Prior. Epigram: "When Bibo thought fit from
    the world to retreat."
Randall, D. Old Witherington.
Robinson, E. Miniver Cheevy.
    Mr Flood's Party.
Södergran. Question.
Smith, S. Grace of God and the Meth-Drinker,
    The.
Symons, A. Absinthe-Drinker, The.
Thatcher, C. Moggy's Wedding.
Tucker, M. Drunkard's Wife, The.
Turberville. Of Drunkenness.
Tyler, R. Original Epitaph on a Drunkard.
Unknown. Drunk Man, The.
    Limerick.
    Pig, The.
    Shickered As He Could Be.
    Tarpauling Jacket.
Ward, E. Extravagant Drunkard's Wish, The.
Wilbur. Voice from under the Table, A.
Willard, N. Ballad of Biddy Early, The.
Woodward, C. Midnight Ramble, The.
Work. Come Home, Father[!].
Wright, J. Inscription for the Tank.
    Note Left in Jimmy Leonard's Shack, A.
Zimmer. Zimmer Drunk and Alone, Dreaming
    of Old Football Games.
See also **Alcoholism and Alcoholics**

Dryads
Doolittle, H. Acon.

Dryden, John
Behn, A. On Mr. Dryden, Renegade.
Thomas, E. Dream, The; An Epistle to Mr.
    Dryden.

Du Bois, William Edward Burghardt
Randall, D. Booker T. and W. E. B.

Dublin, Ireland
Durcan. Bewley's Oriental Café, Westmoreland
    Street.
Ford, R. Back to Dublin.
Garlick, R. Capitals.
Kavanagh, P. Canal Bank Walk.

Elegy for Jim Larkin.
Lines Written on a Seat on the Grand Canal,
    Dublin.
Larkin, P. Dublinesque.
MacDonagh, D. Dublin Made Me.
Montague, J. Herbert Street Revisited.
Ormsby, F. At the Jaffé Memorial Fountain,
    Botanic Gardens.

Duchamp, Marcel
Kennedy, X. Nude Descending a Staircase.

Ducks
Allingham. Four Ducks on a Pond.
Barnard, M. Solitary, The.
Davison, P. From the Outland.
Donaghy, J. Duck.
Dupree, E. At Present I Am Working as a
    Security Guard.
Heaney, S. Widgeon.
Kinnell. Duck-chasing.
McDonald, W. Faraway Places.
Nash, O. Duck, The.
Oles. For the Drunk.
Swenson, M. Goodbye, Goldeneye.
Worth, V. Duck.

Duels
Field, E. Duel, The.
Unknown. Dowie Houms o' Yarrow, The.

Dullness
Dryden, J. Crown Prince of Dullness, The.
    Mac Flecknoe [or, A Satire upon the True-Blue
    Protestant Poet T. S.].
Mother Goose. Simple Simon.
Pound, E. Les Millwin.

Dumbness
Hall, D. Je Suis une Table.
Hirsch, E. Song: "This is a song for the
    speechless."
Lear, E. Limericks, I (v).
Marston, P. Speechless: Upon the Marriage of
    Two Deaf and Dumb Persons.
Reznikoff. Idiot, The.
Samaras, N. Mute Prophets.

Dumont, Margaret
Hollander, J. To the Lady Portrayed by
    Margaret Dumont.

Dumps
Nemerov. Town Dump, The.
Spires. Woman on the Dump, The.
Stevens, W. Man on the Dump, The.

Dunbar, Paul Laurence
Hayden, R. Paul Laurence Dunbar.
Linden, M. Paul Laurence Dunbar.
Ray, H. In Memoriam Paul Laurence Dunbar.
Reed, I. Paul Laurence Dunbar in The
    Tenderloin.
Spencer, A. Dunbar.

Dunes
Ammons, A. R. So I Said I Am Ezra.
Frost, R. Sand Dunes.
Teasdale. On the Dunes.

Duns Scotus
Hopkins, G. Duns Scotus's Oxford.

Dusk
Abinader, E. Dar a Luz.
Dunn, D. Land Love.
Everwine. Distance.
Faust, H. Six Cranes at Dusk.
Gray, R. Dusk, The.
Lang, A. Twilight on Tweed.
Longfellow, H. Afternoon in February.
McMorris, M. Evening.
Rohrer, M. Quick Sell the Pig.
Unknown, fr. Terezin Concentration Camp.
    Dusk.
Voigt. Nocturne.
Volkman. Evening.
Ward, D. Hunting in Twilight.
    My Brothers Make a Lantern.
Warren, R. What Voice at Moth-Hour.
See also **Twilight**

Dust
Borges. John 1:14 (1964).
Chesterton, G. Praise of Dust, The.
Chin. Altar.

Davies, J.   Remembrance of My Friend Mr. Thomas Morley, A.

"Field."   Mummy Invokes His Soul, The.

Finch, A.   Sapphics for Patience.

Frost, R.   Meeting and Passing.

Gascoyne.   Yves Tanguy.

Hall, D.   Dusting.

Janzen, J.   Claiming the Dust.

Johnson, G.   Common Dust.

Philp-Carmichael.   Dust Storm.

Rukeyser, M.   George Robinson: Blues.

Wheelock, J.   This Quiet Dust.

Dutch Wars

Marvell.   Character of Holland, The.
   Charles II.

Sackville, C.   Song Written at Sea in the First Dutch War (1665), the Night before an Engagement.

Duty

Clough.   Duty.

Emerson, R.   Voluntaries.

Frost, R.   Stopping by Woods on a Snowy Evening.

Hay, J.   Jim Bludso of the Prairie Belle.

Herrick.   Duty to Tyrants.

Kingsley, C.   Three Fishers [Went Sailing], The.

Kipling, R.   Eddi's Service.

McCrae, J.   In Flanders Fields.

Milton.   On His Blindness.

Monk, M.   Verses Written on Her Death-Bed at Bath to Her Husband in London.

Moorer.   Duty, or Truth at Work.

Ralegh, S.   Sir Walter Ralegh to the Queen.

Stafford, W.   Traveling through the Dark.

Stevenson, A.   In the Orchard.

Tennyson, A.   Charge of the Light Brigade, The.

Van Jordan, A.   My Father's Retirement.

Watts, I.   How Doth the Little Busy Bee.

Whittier.   Abraham Davenport.

Wordsworth, W.   Ode to Duty.

Dwarfs

Ewart.   Lines: "Other day I was loving a sweet little fruitpie-and-cream, The."

Karr.   Hubris.

Smart, C.   Author Apologizes to a Lady, for His Being a Little Man, The.

Wallace-Crabbe.   Windows, The.

Waller, E.   Of the Marriage of the Dwarfs.

E

Eagles

Altamirano, S.   Eagle above Us, The.

Arlen, H.   Eagle and Me, The.

Asim, J.   Dumas.

Darley.   Free-booter, The.

Dickey, J.   Eagles.

Dodge, M.   Taking Time to Grow.

Duncan, R.   Letting the Beat Go.

Fordham.   To the Eagle.

Hale, S.   Mole and the Eagle, The.

Harjo, J.   Eagle Poem.

Hughes, L.   Fact.

Jeffers, R.   Beaks of Eagles, The.
   Fire on the Hills.

Kavanagh, P.   Goldie Sapiens.

Lee, E.   Sun-Struck Eagle, The.

Lindsay, N.   Eagle That Is Forgotten, The.

Lowry, M.   Salmon Drowns Eagle.

Momaday.   Eagle-Feather Fan, The.
   Story of a Well-made Shield, The.

Ortiz.   Vision Shadows.

Pfeiffer, E.   Aspiration.

Skelton, R.   Eagle.

Sylvain, P.   Panama.

Tennyson, A.   Eagle, The.

Todd, R.   Poem: "I walk at dawn across the hollow hills."

Very.   Eagles, The.

Villanueva, A.   Even the Eagles Must Gather.

Wakoski.   Ice Eagle, The.

Warfield.   Sun-Struck Eagle, The.

Whitman, W.   Dalliance of the Eagles, The.

Wylie.   Eagle and the Mole, The.

Ears

Forché.   Colonel, The.

Haines, J.   Awakening.

Hannan, M.   Tap.

Lovelace, R.   To a Lady That Desired Me I Would Bear My Part with Her in a Song.

Powell, D. A.   Studs and Rings: Favors of the Piercing Party.

Sirowitz, H.   Equality.

Smith, P.   Finding His Fist.

Thoreau.   Each More Melodious Note I Hear.

Earth

Allen, S.   Moment Please, A.

Atwood.   You Begin.

Begay.   Mother's Lace.

Bingen, Hildegard von.   Earth is at the same time mother, The.

Bly, R.   Extra Joyful Chorus for Those Who Have Read This Far, An.

Bognini.   Earth and Sky.

Bronk.   Aspects of the World like Coral Reefs.

Bryant, W.   Thanatopsis.

Buckley, C.   Concerning Paradise.

Césaire, A.   Bucolic.

Cavendish, M.   Of the Animal Spirits.

Channing.   Hymn of the Earth.

Clairmont.   Answers, The.

Clare, J.   Loves Lives Beyond the Tomb.

Clifton, L.   Earth Is a Living Thing, The.

Coleridge, M.   O Earth, My Mother! Not Upon Thy Breast.

Couzyn.   Spell for Birth.

Creeley.   Here.

Cummings, E.   O Sweet Spontaneous.

De la Mare.   Snow.

Deloney.   Weavers Song, The.

DiPrima, C.   Her Eyes a Thousand Times Over.

Donne.   To Mr. Tilman after He Had Taken Orders.
   Valediction: of Weeping, A.

Dransfield.   Strange Bird, A.

Eberhart, R.   Hard Structure of the World, The.

Echeruo.   Melting Pot.

Edwards, M.   World Is Full of Beauty, The.

Emerson, R.   Hamatreya.

Empson.   To an Old Lady.

Faber, F.   World, The.

Fitzgerald, E.   73.

Götter-Abendroth.   Thou Gaia Art I.

Gilbert, S.   To the Terrestrial Globe.

Griffin, J.   One's Country.

Griffin, S.   Our Mother.

Haines, J.   Cloud Factory, The.
   Tundra, The.

Heaney, S.   Bog Queen.

Herrick.   White Island.

Hewitt, J.   Because I Paced My Thought.

Hill, G.   Genesis.
   In Piam Memoriam.

Hillman.   Formation of Soils, The.

Hollo.   Read the Fear.

Hoogerhuis.   Search, The.

Hopkins, G.   God's Grandeur.

Howe, J.   Kosmos.

Hughes, T.   River.

Hummell, A.   Salt Longing.

Ingelow.   Divided.

Iverem, E.   Earth Screaming.

Jarrell.   Blind Sheep, The.

Jeffers, R.   Autumn Evening.
   Eye, The.
   Shine, Perishing Republic.

Jemie.   Iroko.

Johnston, G.   O Earth, Turn!

Kelber, M.   Pledge of Allegiance to the Family of Earth, A.

Kinnell.   Quick and the Dead, The.

Kipling, R.   Sestina of the Tramp-Royal.

Koch, K.   Geography.

Kusano Shimpei.   Skylarks and Fuji.

Levertov.   O Taste and See.

Levine, P.   Clouds.
   How Much Earth.
   On a Drawing by Flavio.
   Rain Downriver.
   Snow.

They Feed They Lion.
   To My God in His Sickness.

Lovelace, R.   To My Noble Kinsman, Thomas Stanley, Esquire, on His Lyric Poems Composed by Master John Gamble.

MacDiarmid, H.   Bonnie Broukit Bairn, The.
   Little White Rose, The.

MacLeish.   Speech to a Crowd.

Mahon.   Tractatus.

Meador, B.   Fields Belong to Woman, The.

Merriam, E.   Landscape.

Merrill, J.   Childlessness.

Miles, J.   Merchant Marine.
   On Inhabiting an Orange.

Millay, E.   God's World.

Muir, E.   One Foot in Eden.

Murray, P.   Conquest.

Mutén, B.   Queen Hera.

Neidjie.   This Earth.

Noguere.   Whirling Round the Sun.

Ortiz.   Earth and Rain, the Plants & Sun.

Osundare.   Eyeful Glances.
   Goree.
   I Sing of Change.
   Our Earth Will Not Die.
   Who Says That Drought Was Here?

Padilla.   Fountain, a House of Stone, A.

Patchen.   Temple, A.

Perelman.   China.

Peters, L.   Parachute Men.

Pilling.   Earth, The.

Raine, K.   World, The.

Rexroth, K.   Lute Music.
   Lyell's Hypothesis Again.

Reynolds, S. F.   Moon/light Quarter/back Sack.

Roberts, E.   People, The.

Robinson, A.   Sibyl, The.
   Unum est Necessarium.

Robinson, K.   Nursery Rhyme.

Rossetti, C.   Advent.
   Horses of the Sea, The.

Rukeyser, M.   He Had a Quality of Growth.

Sandburg, C.   Be Ready.
   Early Copper.

Simic.   Poem: "Every morning I forget how it is."

Snyder, G.   For Nothing.
   Gaia.

Sornberger.   When She Laughs.

Southwell.   Vale of Tear[e]s, A.

Southwick.   Earthly Light.

St. John, P.   Lynching and Burning.

Stevens, W.   Bowl.
   Gubbinal.
   Planet on the Table, The.

Sylvester, J.   "Were I as Base as Is the Lowly Plain."

Sze.   Every Where and Every When.
   Network, The.

Taylor, A.   Earth.

Thomas, D.   This Bread I Break.

Tomlinson, C.   Ararat.

Tuckerman, F.   Sonnet: "And so, as this great sphere (now turning slow)."

Unknown.   This Newly Created World.

Vaughan, H.   World, The (1).

Vigil, A.   Hogarcito de La Madrugada, El.

Villanueva, A.   From the Healing Dark.
   Planet Earth Speaks, The.

Ward, T.   Dark Underfoot.

Watson, R.   Of the Earth, Earthy.

Weston, M.   Departure.

Wheelock, J.   Earth.

White, J.   In Ecclesiastes I Read.

Whitman, S.   November Landscape, A.

Whitman, W.   Earth, My Likeness.
   This Compost.

Whitmore, S.   Gamelia.

Wilbur.   Caserta Garden.

Williams, W.   At Kenneth Burke's Place.

Wordsworth, W.   Composed upon Westminster Bridge, September 3, 1802.

Wright, J.   Arrangements with Earth for Three Dead Friends.
   At Thomas Hardy's Birthplace, 1953.
   Horse, The.

Wylie. Hymn to Earth.
Yeats. Before the World Was Made.

Earthquakes
Ford, R. Earthquake.
Gould, J. Earthquake Weather.
Guevara, M. After the Colombian Earthquake.
Heard, J. Earthquake of 1886, The.
Kramer, L. Images of the San Francisco Disaster.
Olds, S. Quake Theory.
Salzman, E. English Earthquake, The.
Seward. On Catania and Syracuse Swallowed Up by an Earthquake, from the Italian of Filicaja.
Sharp, S. Good Nights.
Webb, C. You Missed the Earthquake, Bill.

Easter
Ammons, A. R. Easter Morning.
Awoonor. Easter Dawn.
Berlin. Easter Parade.
Carr, S. Easter Outing.
Hadas, R. Easter Afternoon.
Heard, J. Easter Morn.
Herbert, G. Easter.
  Easter Wings.
Hope, A. Easter Hymn.
Hopkins, G. That Nature Is a Heraclitean Fire and of the Comfort of the Resurrection.
Hopkins, J. Alleluia! Christ Is Risen Today.
Housman, A. Easter Hymn.
  Loveliest of Trees, the Cherry Now.
Mörling, M. Three-Card Monte.
Meynell, A. Easter Night.
Moorer. Easter; or, Spring-Time.
Nemerov. Easter.
Nicol. African Easter.
Paquet. Easter '68.
Peacock, M. Chriseaster.
Ray, H. Easter Carol.
Rossetti, C. Easter Monday.
Schaefer, S. Rejoice, Let Alleluias Ring.
Sisson. Easter.
Thompson, C. Easter Light, The.
Turner, A. Three Easters.
Turner, S. Christmas Is Really for the Children.
Updike. Seven Stanzas at Easter.
Vaughan, H. Easter Hymn.
  Easter-Day.
Wilde, O. Easter Day.
Wordsworth, W. Composed in One of the Valleys of Westmoreland, on Easter Sunday.
Yeats. Easter 1916.

Easter Island
Dickey, W. For Easter Island or Another Island.

Easter Rebellion (1916)
Ledwidge. Lament for the Poets: 1916.
  Lament for Thomas MacDonagh.
MacDonagh, D. Veterans, The.
Yeats. Easter 1916.
  Rose Tree, The.
  Sixteen Dead Men.

Eatherly, Claude R.
Crashaw. Luke 11: Blessed Be the Paps Which Thou Hast Sucked.
Wain. Song about Major Eatherly, A.

Eating
Alexander, E. Nineteen.
Barrax. In the Restaurant.
Belloc. Vulture, The.
Beveridge. Dining Out.
Brooks, G. Bean Eaters, The.
Burgess, F. Table Manners.
Chase, K. Venison.
De la Mare. Miss T.
Dickey, J. Bread.
Edson, R. Ape.
Evasco, M. Baked Oysters Rockefeller.
France, L. Eater of Wives, The.
Gonzalez, R. Brown Pot.
Gunn, T. J Car, The.
Hanzlicek, C. Feeding Frenzies.
Harjo, J. Perhaps the World Ends Here.
Harper, M. Fireplace, The.
Herbert, G. Love (3).
Herrick. Panegyric to Sir Lewis Pemberton, A.

Upon Jack and Jill: Epigram.
Upon Showbread [or Shewbread]: Epigram.
Highfill, M. Rebis.
Hoffmann, H. Story of Augustus Who Would Not Have Any Soup, The.
Hughes, F. Foxes.
Jaques, F. There Once Was a Puffin.
Jonson, B. Inviting a Friend to Supper.
  On Gut.
Keller, D. After Supper.
Kinnell. Supper after the Last, The.
Kossman. Judas' Reproach.
Larsen, L. Peach.
  Red.
Lee, L. Eating Together.
Lipsitz. Feeding, The.
MacCaig. Fetching Cows.
Madge. Birds of Tin, The.
Maguire, S. Communion.
Merriam, E. How to Eat a Poem.
Mirikitani. Soul Food.
Mother Goose. Strange Old Woman, A.
Myles, E. Merk.
Nash, O. Experiment Degustatory.
  Termite, The.
O'Hara, F. Blocks.
Oliver, M. Kingfisher, The.
Peacock, M. Anger Sweetened.
  Devolution.
Rakosi. Good Morning.
Ramanujan. Pleasure.
Rukeyser, M. Night Feeding.
Shaughnessy, B. Rise.
Stevenson, R. Cow, The.
Strand. Eating Poetry.
Tallmountain. Good Grease.
Torres, E. Bio-Rodent-Oriole.
Unknown. Limerick: "There was an old man of [or from] Peru / Who dreamt [or dreamed] he was eating his shoe."
Weinberger, F. He Wears Old Socks.
Williams, W. This Is Just to Say.
  To a Poor Old Woman.
Wright, E. When Father Carves the Duck.
See also **Food; Gluttony and Gluttons**

Eating Disorders
Barnett, R. Anorexic, The.
Bidart. Ellen West.
Hoffmann, H. Story of Augustus Who Would Not Have Any Soup, The.
Jones, A. Anorexia.
Maiden. Anorexia.
Nash, O. Curl Up and Diet.

Echo (mythology)
Jones, A. M. To Echo.
Ray, H. Echo's Complaint.
Rossetti, C. Echo.
Spenser. Epithalamion: "Ye learned sisters which have oftentimes."
See also **Narcissus (mythology)**

Echo Lake, New Hampshire
Ray, H. Echo Reverie.

Echoes
Barnes, W. Echo, The.
Cawein. Echo.
Cofer, J. Life of an Echo, The.
De la Mare. Echo.
Lazarus, E. Echoes.
Lorde. Echoes.
Madgett. Echoes.
Swift, J. Gentle Echo on Woman, A.
Tabb. Echo.

Eclipses
Bly, R. Seeing the Eclipse in Maine.
Hummell, A. Sculpture Garden.
Roberson. Eclipse.
Rosen, M. Total Eclipse.
Ryan, T. Eclipse, Kenwick, 1974.
  Lunar Eclipse.

Ecology and Ecologists
Buckmaster. End to Myth, An.
Cole, T. Lament of the Forest, The.
Cowper. Poplar Field, The.
Dutton, G. Stranded Whales, The.
Ellis, C. Bungaloid Growth.

Fogarty, L. Ecology.
Hodgson, R. Hymn to Moloch.
Hopkins, G. Binsey Poplars (Felled 1879).
  Inversnaid.
Kunitz, S. War against the Trees, The.
Lindsay, N. Flower-fed Buffaloes, The.
Marshall, J. Wing and Prayer.
Milne, E. Martyred Earth, The.
Morris, G. Woodman, Spare That Tree.
Purdy, A. Dead Seal.
Ransom, W. Statement on Our Higher Education.
Roethke. Moss-Gathering.
Snyder, G. Front Lines.
  Mother Earth: Her Whales.
Spender, S. I Think Continually of Those Who Were Truly Great.
Stephens, J. Little Things.
See also **Conservation; Pollution**

Economics and Economists
Ai. Riot Act, April 29, 1992.
McGrath, C. Capitalist Poem #36.
Nash, O. What Do You Want: A Meaningful Dialogue, or a Satisfactory Talk?

Ecstasy
Browning, R. Now.
Donne. Ecstasy, The.
Fullerton. Poetry.

Eden
Aisenberg, N. Leaving Eden.
Armantrout. Plan, The.
Auchterlonie. Tree, The.
Ayer, N. If You Were the Only Girl in the World.
Back, R. After Eden.
Beaumont, J. Garden, The.
Chin. Disorder, The.
Coolbrith. Longing.
Cotton, N. On Lord Cobham's Garden.
Crane, H. Garden Abstract.
Dickey, J. Poisoned Man, The.
Dickinson, E. Eden is that Old-Fashioned House.
Donnelly, S. Eve Names the Animals.
Fitzgerald, E. 13.
Goodison. Jamaica 1980.
Grosholz. Eden.
Hartigan, A. Brazen Image.
Higginson, E. Eve.
Hopkins, G. Spring.
Howitt, M. Cry of the Animals, The.
Hughes, T. Theology.
Kavanagh, P. Long Garden, The.
Kendrick, D. Gethsemane A. D.
Kipling, R. L'Envoi.
Larkin, P. High Windows.
Lawrence, D. Paradise Re-entered.
Leapor. Man the Monarch.
MacNeice. Apple Blossom.
Merton. Lent in a Year of War.
Muir, E. Adam's Dream.
  One Foot in Eden.
Probyn. Ballade of Lovers.
Robinson, A. Unum est Necessarium.
Rochester, J. Fall, The.
Smith, R. Apple, The.
Sparshott. Naming of the Beasts, The.
Tomlinson, C. In Arden.
  John Maydew or The Allotment.
Unknown. Adam Lay Ybounden [or I-bounden].
Vaughan, H. Corruption.
Very. Garden, The.
Walcott. Crusoe's Island.
  New World.
Wallace-Crabbe. And the World was Calm.
White, G. Leopard in Eden, The.
Whitman, W. To the Garden the World.
Whittier. Garden.
See also **Adam and Eve**

Edinburgh, Scotland
Dunbar, W. To the Merchantis of Edinburgh.
Fergusson. Daft Days, The.
Garioch. Embro to the Ploy.

Editors
Betjeman. Ballad of George R. Sims, The.
Byron, G. To Mr. Murray.
Cummings, E. Mr U.
Shapiro, K. Editing *Poetry*.

Education
Awoonor. On Having Been an Experimental Sacred Cow for Four Years, and a Token African on Faculty.
Belloc. Lines to a Don.
Bentley, E. On Education, December 1789.
Berkeley, G. On the Prospect of Planting Arts and Learning in America.
Camlan. Education in Wales.
Clark, T. Going to School in France or America.
Dodge, M. Shepherd John.
Dove, R. Flash Cards.
Enright, D. University Examinations in Egypt.
Finney, N. Fishing Among the Learned.
Forbes, J. Speed, a Pastoral.
Forten. Poem: "In the earnest path of duty."
Freed, F. Private School for Girls, May 14, 1948, New York City, A.
Ginsberg, A. Sather Gate Illumination.
Gregory, H. Cage of Voices, The.
Gwynn, R. Classroom at the Mall, The.
Heard, J. Advance of Education, The.
Heath-Stubbs. One.
Hecht, A. Mysteries of Caesar, The.
Holmes, J. Old Professor, The.
Lilley. Sewing Lesson, The.
Lorde. Learning to Write.
Lucy. Supervising Examinations.
Martin, C. E. S. L.
McCord, D. History of Education.
Milton. To Cyriack Skinner.
Naden. Love Versus Learning.
Nemerov. Sweeper of Ways, The. To David, about His Education.
Palmer, T. Try, Try Again.
Praed. Talented Man, The.
Prelutsky. Homework! Oh, Homework!
Samaras, N. Elegy for a Professor.
Schwartz, R. L. AIDS Education, Seventh Grade.
Snodgrass, W. Campus on the Hill, The.
Spender, S. Elementary School Classroom in a Slum, A.
Teft. On Learning.
Thomas, E. On Sir J——S—— Saying in a Sarcastic Manner, My Books Would Make Me Mad; an Ode.
Travis, N. At My Father's House.
Unknown. Arithmetic. Dr. Foster.
Villalongo. In the Good Old U. S. A.
Whitman, W. When I Heard the Learn'd Astronomer.
See also **Colleges and Universities; Scholarship and Scholars; Students; Teaching and Teachers**

Edward IV, King of England
Unknown. King Edward the Fourth and a Tanner of Tamworth.

Edward VII, King of England
Unknown. Death of King Edward VII, The.
Beerbohm, M. Addition to Kipling's "The Dead King (Edward VII), 1910.".
Harkness, J. New Song on the Birth of the Prince of Wales, A.
Murphy, E. Thank you, Mr Rason, for the Apples.

Edwards, Jonathan
Lowell, R. After the Surprising Conversions. Mr. Edwards and the Spider.
McGinley. Theology of Jonathan Edwards, The.

Eels
Guiterman. Song of Hate for Eels.
Montale. Eel, The.
Muldoon, P. Briefcase, The.
Nash, O. Eel, The.
Petit, P. Embrace of the Electric Eel.
Unknown. Lord Randal[l].
See also **Lampreys**

Eggs
Blanco, R. Tía Olivia Serves Wallace Stevens a Cuban Egg.
Blind. On a Forsaken Lark's Nest.
Cabico, R. Afternoon in Pangasinan with No Electricity, An.
Caston, A. Blowing Eggs.
Cook, S. Boiling an Egg.
Day, C. Egg, The.
Garrett, E. History Goes to Work.
Gogarty. Leda and the Swan.
Grass. In the Egg.
Herrick. Her Legs.
Hoban. Egg Thoughts.
Hughes, L. Bar.
Lamport. Eggomania.
Moore, N. Song: "Little onion lay by the fireplace, A."
Okita. Notes for a Poem on Being Asian American.
Pastan. Egg.
Pietri. How Do Your Eggs Want You (?).
Rosenblatt. It's in the Egg.
Unknown. Dirge for Three Trumpets. Warning, A.
Willard, N. How the Hen Sold Her Eggs to the Stingy Priest.

Egotism and Egotists
Berlin. Couple of Swells, A.
Carew, T. Ingrateful[l] Beauty Threatened.
Creeley. Immoral Proposition, The.
Davie. In the Stopping Train.
Ewart. It's Hard to Dislike Ewart.
Giovanni. Ego Tripping [(There May Be a Reason Why)].
Komrij. Poet, The.
Landon. Gifts Misused.
Meredith, G. Lucifer in Starlight.
Sia, B. Claim to Fame.
Torres, E. Drowning in the Last Days of Luxury.
Waters, M. Hoochie Coochie.
See also **Individualism and Individualists**

Egrets
Tu Mu. Egrets.
Weigl. Snowy Egret.

Egypt
Blodgett. Snails.
Bringhurst. Song of Ptahhotep, The.
Doolittle, H. Egypt.
Douglas, K. On a Return from Egypt.
Dufault. Mud Dauber Wasp, The.
Ford, R. Sakhara.
Fyleman. Cat, The.
Giovanni. Ego Tripping [(There May Be a Reason Why)].
Hunt, L. Nile, The.
Kern, J. Cleopatterer.
Kipling, R. Naaman's Song.
"Malley." Egyptian Register.
McKay, C. Africa.
McNeil, R. Angel in the Temple of Luxor, An.
Reed, I. I Am a Cowboy in the Boat of Ra. Why I Often Allude to Osiris.
Shelley, P. Ozymandias.
Tobin, D. At the Egyptian Exhibit.
Unknown. Go Down, Moses. Shari Wag Iel Burka.
Warner, R. Egyptian Kites.
Warren, R. Flaubert in Egypt.
Wodehouse, P. Cleopatterer.

Eichmann, Adolf
Levertov. Crystal Night.
Peachtree, The. When We Look Up.

Eiffel Tower
Huidobro. Eiffel Tower.

Einstein, Albert
Feinstein, E. Annus Mirabilis 1989.
Hoover, P. Letter to Einstein Beginning Dear Albert.
Jordan, J. Poem about Intelligence for My Brothers and Sisters, A.
Kizer, C. Twelve O'Clock.
Moss, H. Einstein's Bathrobe.

Gift to Be Simple, The.

Eisenhower, Dwight David
Lowell, R. Inauguration Day: January 1953.

El Dorado
Poe. Eldorado.

El Salvador
Alegría. Documentary.
Forché. Colonel, The.
Healy, E. From Los Angeles Looking South.
Rose. Day They Cleaned Up the Border El Salvador, February, 1981, The.

Elands
Jarrell. Seele im Raum.

Eleanor of Aquitaine
Masefield. Rose of the World, The.
Unknown. Queen Eleanor's Confession.

Electricity
Carver, R. Window, The.
Cranch. Spirit of the Age, The.
Dickey, J. Power and Light.
Duchamp. Electricity Breadthwise.
Lawrence, D. Storm in the Black Forest.
Merrill, J. Power Station, The.
Ritchie, E. Electroconvulsive Therapy.
Smith, W. There Was an Old Lady Named Crockett.
Spender, S. Pylons, The.
Thomas, L. Electricity of Blossoms.

Elephants
Amirthanayagam. Elephants Are in the Yard, The.
Brooks, G. Pete at the Zoo.
Housman, A. Elephant, or the Force of Habit, The.
Lawrence, D. Two Performing Elephants.
Link, L. Holding Hands.
Moore, M. Black Earth.
Richards, L. Eletelephony.
Sandburg, C. Elephants Are Different to Different People.
Saxe, J. Blind Men and the Elephant, The.
Unknown. Signifying Monkey, The.
Van Walleghen. Elephant in Winter, The.

Elgin Marbles
Keats. On Seeing the Elgin Marbles.

Elijah (Bible)
Hayes, A. Angel, The.

Eliot, Thomas Stearns
Auden. T. S. Eliot.
Cope, W. Waste Land Limericks.
Crawford, R. Love Song of Tommo Frogley.
Ferlinghetti, L. Sea and Ourselves at Cape Ann, The.
Hecht, A. Vice.
Levi, P. New Year's Eve Poem 1965.
Lowell, R. T. S. Eliot.
Shepard, J. Love Song of Audrey.
Wallace-Crabbe. Double Dactyl.
Webb, H. Thanks in Winter.

Elizabeth I, Queen of England
Bradstreet, A. In Honour of that High and Mighty Princess Queen Elizabeth of Happy Memory.
Dubie. Elizabeth's War with the Christmas Bear.
Elizabeth I. Doubt of Future Foes. Written with a Diamond On Her Window at Woodstock.
Kipling, R. Looking Glass, The.
Ondaatje. Elizabeth.
Pembroke, M. Dialogue between two shepherds, Thenot and Piers, in praise of ASTRÆA. To the Thrice-Sacred Queen Elizabeth.
Puttenham. Her Majestie resembled to the crowned piller. Ye must read upward.
Seager, J. To Queen Elizabeth.
Unknown. Short and Sweet Sonnet Made by One of the Maids of Honour, upon the Death of Queen Elizabeth, which She Sewed upon a Sampler, in Red Silke, A.

Elizabeth, Queen of Bohemia
Wotton, S. On His Mistress [*or* Mistris], the Queen of Bohemia.

Elk
Ceravolo. Ho Ho Ho Caribou.
Dugan, A. On the Elk, Unwitnessed.
Nash, O. Wapiti, The.

Ellington, Edward Kennedy (Duke)
Baraka. Duke's World.
Dana, R. Elegy for the Duke.
Jackson, R. For duke ellington.
Komunyakaa. Twilight Seduction.

Elm Trees
Ayres, R. Neighbor's Elm, The.
Clare, J. Fallen Elm, The.
Elliott, E. Drone v. Worker.
"Field." Leaves.
Gibbons, R. Affect of Elms, The.
Kessler, R. Elm Tree on Lafayette Street, The.
Melville, H. Malvern Hill.
Mueller, L. Triage.
Plath. Elm.
Taggard. Dilemma of the Elm.
Thomas, E. October.

Elopement
Campbell, T. Lord Ullin's Daughter.
Derricotte. Family Secrets.
Keats. Eve of St Agnes, The.
Longfellow, H. Skeleton in Armor [or Armour], The.
Scott, S. Jock of Hazeldean.
Unknown. Bleeding Nun, The.
To His Love.

Elves
Bangs, J. Little Elf, The.
Bishop, M. How to Treat Elves.
Keats. La Belle Dame sans Merci [A Ballad].
Ray, H. Dream of Elfland, A.
Unknown. Tam Lin.
See also **Fairies**

Emancipation (1863-1865)
Heard, J. General Robert Smalls.
Howe, J. Battle Hymn [or Battle-Hymn] of the Republic, The.
Moorer. Emancipation Day.
Thompson, P. Emancipation.
Freedom at McNealy's.
Hymn: "Lord, within thy fold I be."
Unknown. No More Auction Block.
Whittier. Laus Deo!

Embryos
Traherne. Preparative, The.
Return, The.
Wright, J. Woman to Man.

Emerson, Ralph Waldo
Lee, L. Cleaving, The.
Ray, H. Emerson.

Emigration and Emigrants
Bennett, L. Colonization in Reverse.
Boyle, K. New Emigration, The.
Bunting. Complaint of the Morpethshire Farmer, The.
Gin the Goodwife Stint.
Dunn, D. Landscape with One Figure.
Griffiths, J. Emigrants.
Hall, D. Sister on the Tracks, A.
Hemans. Song of Emigration.
Hernández Cruz. New/Aguas Buenas/Jersey.
Jackson, H. Emigravit.
McCarthy, T. Emigration Trains, The.
Sigourney. Western Emigrant, The.

Emmet, Robert
Moore, T. She Is Far from the Land.

Empire State Building, New York City
Berrigan, T. Bean Spasms.

Emptiness
Berry, W. Wild, The.
Clark, T. "Like Musical Instruments.."
Cooper, J. Waiting.
Creeley. Language, The.
Davies, H. Music in an Empty House.
Eliot, T. Burial of the Dead, The.
Conversation Galante.
Death by Water.
Fire Sermon, The.
Game of Chess, A.
Gerontion.

Hollow Men, The.
Waste Land, The.
Graves, R. Not at Home.
Hardy, T. Exeunt Omnes.
Harms. After Yes.
Herbert, G. Dotage.
Johnson, D. Incognito Lounge, The.
Kees. Heat in the Room, The.
Kipling, R. Derelict, The.
Knight, E. Cell Song.
Kyle, C. J. Argument, The.
Lindsay, N. Leaden-eyed, The.
Mahon. Achill.
Mew. I Have Been Through the Gates.
Millay, E. Bluebeard.
Orr, G. Who'd Want to Be a Man?
Quarles. Nahum 2.10.
Simic. Mirrors at 4 A.M.
Towers, T. Mission Poem.
Williams, W. These.
Wright, C. Disjecta Membra.

Emus
Philp-Carmichael. Dust Storm.

Enchantment
Brontë, E. Spellbound.
Carew, T. In Praise of His Mistress.
Tinder, The.
Disch. Rapist's Villanelle, The.
Hardy, T. First Sight of Her and After.
Herrick. To Music: A Song.
Keats. La Belle Dame sans Merci [A Ballad].
Landon. Enchanted Island, The.
Yeats. Sorrow of Love, The.

End of the World
Bottomley. End of the World, The.
Browning, R. Childe Roland to the Dark Tower Came.
Byron, G. Darkness.
Cummings, E. What If a Much of a Which of a Wind.
Derricotte. Fears of the Eighth Grade.
Eady. Dance, The.
Figueroa, J. Confessions from the Last Cloud.
Frost, R. Fire and Ice.
Once by the Pacific.
Gascoyne. And the Seventh Dream Is the Dream of Isis.
End Is Near the Beginning, The.
Graves, R. Warning to Children.
Jackson, A. Transformable Prophecy.
Jauss. After the End of the World.
Lieberman, M. Prediction.
MacLeish. End of the World, The.
Macpherson, J. Ordinary People in the Last Days.
McGrath, T. End of the World, The.
Nuriddin, J. M. Children of the Future.
Pack, R. Proton Decay.
Patterson, R. When I Awoke.
Rowland. Seven Days.
Snyder, G. L M F B R.
Stafford, W. Epitaph Ending in And, The.
Very. First Atlantic Telegraph, The.
Wade-Gayles. Loving Again.
Wilbur. Advice to a Prophet.
Winters, Y. Summer Noon: 1941.
Wylie. Doomsday.
See also **Apocalypse; Judgment Day**

Endangered Species
Atwood. Elegy for the Giant Tortoises.
Hope, A. Moschus Moschiferus.
Wojahn. Rajah in Babylon.

Endurance
Baca. Cloudy Day.
Bowles, W. Time and Grief.
Brutus. Endurance.
Cameron, N. Unfinished Race, The.
Cervantes. Archeology.
Coleridge, S. Forbearance.
Delgado, J. I-5 Incident.
Di Prima. For H.D.
Emerson, R. Character.
Humphrey, D. Hope.
Jeffers, R. Granite and Cypress.
Justice, D. Pantoum of the Great Depression.

Kipling, R. Old Men, The.
Kunitz, S. Welcome the Wrath.
Lawrence, D. Race and Battle.
MacLeish. Snowflake Which Is Now and Hence Forever, The.
Merrill, J. After Greece.
Porteous. I Envy the Cracked, Black Basalt.
Strange. Still Life.
Voznesensky [or Voznesenskii]. Autumn.
Warren, R. To a Face in a Crowd.
Yeats. Travail of Passion, The.
See also **Fortitude**

Endymion
Keats. Song of the Indian Maid.
Millay, E. "Oh, sleep forever in the Latmian cave."

Enemies
Barrax. In the Restaurant.
Coleridge, M. Gifts.
De la Mare. Hare, A.
Elizabeth I. Written on a Wall at Woodstock.
Hannah, S. My Enemies.
Hardy, T. Man He Killed, The.
Henderson, H. Ninth Elegy: Fort Capuzzo.
Iman. Love Your Enemy.
Lovelace, R. Fly Caught in a Cobweb, A.
Marcus, B. Battle at Horizon.
Millay, E. First Fig.
Robinson, E. New Tenants, The.
Sia, B. Enemy.
Thompson, D. On the Relative Merit of Friend and Foe, Being Dead.
Whitman, W. Reconciliation.
Zarco. My Worst Fear.
Zolotow. Enemies.

Energy
Georgiou, E. Intimate Mixture.
Gunn, T. My Sad Captains.
Hernández Cruz. Energy.
Kendall, M. Ether Insatiable.
Koch, K. Energy in Sweden.
Lawrence, D. We Are Transmitters.
MacCaig. Blue Tit on a String of Peanuts.
Sorrentino. Razzmatazz.

Energy Crisis
Morley, C. Elegy Written in a Country Coal-Bin.

Engineers
Bolt, T. Glimpse of Terrain.
Cope, W. Engineers' Corner.
Kipling, R. McAndrew's Hymn.
Unknown. Casey Jones.

England
Agard, J. Palm Tree King.
Allingham. In Snow.
Alvi, M. Laughing Moon, The.
Auden. On This Island.
Barker, G. Channel Crossing.
Beer, P. Millennium.
Belloc. Ha'nacker Mill.
Imitation.
South Country, The.
Betjeman. Christmas.
In Westminster Abbey.
Bond, E. If.
Bradstreet, A. Dialogue between Old England and New, A.
Brome. On Sir G. B. his defeat.
Brooke, R. Old Vicarage, Grantchester, The.
Browning, R. Home-Thoughts, From Abroad.
Home-Thoughts, from the Sea.
Burns, R. Such a Parcel of Rogues in a Nation.
Causley. Armistice Day.
At the British War Cemetery, Bayeux.
Chesterton, G. Elegy in a Country Churchyard.
Rolling English Road, The.
Collins, W. How Sleep the Brave.
Coward. Stately Homes of England, The.
D'Aguiar. English Sampler, An.
Davidson, J. Crystal Palace, The.
Day Lewis. You That Love England.
Dryden, J. Crown Prince of Dullness, The.
Mac Flecknoe [or, A Satire upon the True-Blue Protestant Poet T. S.].
Duffy, C. In Your Mind.

Dunbar, W.   Lament for the Makaris.
Furber, D.   Lambeth Walk.
Gay, N.
Gorges.   Written upon the death of the most
  Noble Prince Henrie.
Hardy, T.   On an Invitation to the United States.
  Earthen Lot, The.
Harry, J.   Shot of War, A.
Heath-Stubbs.   One.
Hemans.   England's Dead.
  Homes of England, The.
Henley, W.   England, My England.
Herbert, G.   British Church, The.
Hewitt, J.   Once Alien Here.
Housman, A.   1887.
  New Mistress, The.
  On Wenlock Edge.
Hunt, L.   Iterating Sonnet.
Hutchinson, P.   Fleadh Cheoil.
Jonson, B.   To Penshurst.
Keats.   Happy Is England! I Could Be Content.
Kingsley, C.   Last Buccaneer, The.
Kipling, R.   Absent-Minded Beggar, The.
  Broken Men, The.
  Brown Bess.
  Dane-Geld.
  Glory of the Garden, The.
  Land, The.
  Return, The.
Lanyer.   Description of Cooke-ham [or
  Cookham], The.
Larkin, P.   MCMXIV.
  Naturally the Foundation Will Bear Your
  Expenses.
Lawrence, D.   English Are So Nice!, The.
  Innocent England.
Lopez, T.   No Transport.
Lovelace, R.   Mock Song, A.
"Malley."   Sweet William.
Mapanje.   At the Metro: Old Irrelevant Images.
Marvell.   Charles II.
  First Anniversary of the Government under His
  Highness the Lord Protector, 1655, The.
  Garden of Appleton House, The ("When in the
  east the morning ray").
  Garden, A.
  Upon Appleton House [To My Lord Fairfax].
Meynell, A.   Summer in England, 1914.
Miller, J.   At Our Golden Gate.
More, H.   Riot; or, Half a Loaf Is Better than No
  Bread, The.
Nichols, G.   Long-Man.
O'Connor, P.   Writing in England Now.
"O'Neill."   Corrymeela.
Pembroke, M.   To the Thrice-Sacred Queen
  Elizabeth.
Philips, K.   On the 3 of September, 1651.
"Pindar."   Hymn to the Guilotine.
Plutzik.   Airman Who Flew over Shakespeare's
  England, The.
Pope, A.   Hunting and Fishing.
  Progress.
Porter, P.   Last of England, The.
Prior.   Fable, A: "In Æsop's tales an honest
  wretch we find."
Retallack, J.   Secret Life of Gilbert Bond, The.
Rosenberg, I.   Worm Fed on the Heart of
  Corinth, A.
Salter.   England.
Salzman, E.   English Earthquake, The.
Scott, D.   Playing for England.
Shelley, P.   England in 1819.
  Song to the Men of England.
Smith, C.   Beachy Head.
  From Beachy Head.
Spenser.   Ruines of Time, The.
Swinburne.   Forsaken Garden, A.
Thackeray.   Mr. Molony's Account of the
  Crystal Palace.
Thelwall.   To Ancestry.
Thomas, E.   Adlestrop.
Tighe.   Written at Scarborough. August, 1799.
Tomlinson, C.   John Maydew or The Allotment.
Unknown.   Agincourt Carol, The.
  Diggers' Song, The.

England.
  Free Parliament Litany, A.
  I Don't Want to Be a Soldier.
  Of Sir Frauncis Walsingham Sir Phillipp
  Sydney, and Sir Christopher Hatton, Lord
  Chancelor.
  Song Bewailing the Time of Christmas, So
  Much Decayed in England, A.
Vaughan, H.   British [or Brittish] Church, The.
  Charnel-house, The.
Walcott.   Far Cry from Africa, A.
Wheatley, P.   Farewell to America. To Mrs. S.
  W. A.
Wilde, O.   Ave Imperatrix!
Williams, H.   Farewell, for Two Years, to
  England, A. A Poem.
Wordsworth, W.   Composed by the Sea-Side,
  near Calais, August, 1802.
  England, 1802, V.
  London 1802.
  Sonnet: "England! the time is come when thou
  shouldst wean."
Yeats.   On a Political Prisoner.
See also **Civil Wars, England**

English Channel
Barker, G.   Channel Crossing.
Smith, C.   Beachy Head.
  From Beachy Head.

English, The
Allston.   America to Great Britain.
Campbell, T.   Ye Mariners of England.
Chesterton, G.   Secret People, The.
Cleveland, J.   Rebel Scot, The.
Coleridge, S.   Fears in Solitude.
Coward.   Mad Dogs and Englishmen.
Cowley, A.   London Subverted by the Furies.
D'Aguiar.   Dreadtalk.
Finch, P.   Why Do You Want to Be English?
Kay, J.   English Cousin Comes to Scotland.
"Kerr."   Neutral British Gentleman, The.
Kipling, R.   Absent-Minded Beggar, The.
  Fuzzy-Wuzzy.
  Gentlemen-Rankers.
  Ladies, The.
Lawrence, D.   English Are So Nice!, The.
  How Beastly the Bourgeois Is.
Lees, J.   Jone o' Grinfilt.
Limburg, J.   Barton in the Beans.
Longfellow, H.   Rhyme of Sir Christopher, The.
Macaulay.   Jacobite's Epitaph, A.
Milligan, S.   Teeth.
Milton.   To the Lord General Cromwell.
Morgan, E.   Sir James Murray.
Nash, O.   England Expects.
Nichols, G.   Beverley's Saga.
Nisbet, H.   Isandula.
Pembroke, M.   To the Thrice-Sacred Queen
  Elizabeth.
Pfeiffer, E.   Fight at Rorke's Drift, The.
Rexroth, K.   Observations in a Cornish Teashop.
Rouse.   England Nil.
Sackville, C.   My Opinion.
Shelley, P.   Song to the Men of England.
Simpson, L.   Runner, The.
Smith, S.   Celts, The.
  This Englishwoman.
Stewart, D.   Two Englishmen.
Unknown.   Song of the English Bowmen.
  To Buonaparte.
Wolfe, H.   British Journalist, The.
Wordsworth, W.   Decay of Piety.

Engraving and Engravers
Kinzie.   Engraving of Blake, An.

Envy
Burrell.   School for Satire, The.
Coleridge, M.   'I envy not the dead that rest.'
Cook, E.   Lines / Suggested by the Song of a
  Nightingale.
Donne.   Song: "Go and catch a falling star."
Fenton, J.   Skip, The.
"Field."   So jealous of your beauty.
Kipling, R.   My Rival.
Komunyakaa.   Seven Deadly Sins.
Lochhead, L.   My Rival's House.
Moore, M.   Charity Overcoming Envy.

Porteous.   I Envy the Cracked, Black Basalt.
Procter, A.   Envy.
Ramanujan.   Love Poem for a Wife, 2.
Synge.   Dread.
Wilbur.   All These Birds.
See also **Jealousy**

Epic Poetry
Kavanagh, P.   Epic: "I have lived in important
  places, times."
Tennyson, A.   Epic, The [Morte d'Arthur].
  Morte d'Arthur.

Epictetus
Arnold, M.   To a Friend.

Epicureanism
Cowley, A.   Epicure, The.

Epigrams
Coleridge, S.   What Is an Epigram?
Ellis, C.   Adder's Epigrams.
Jonson, B.   To My Book.
  To My Mere English Censurer.
Mahon.   As It Should Be.
  Dying Art, A.

Epiphany
Beaumont, J.   Of the Epiphany.
Fitzgerald, R.   Epiphany.
Garrett, E.   Reprieve, The.
Kyle, C. J.   Season of Locking-In, The.
See also **Twelfth Night**

Epitaphs
Behn, A.   Epitaph on the Tombstone of a Child,
  the Last of Seven That Died Before.
Bliss, D.   Epitaph of John Jack.
Cunningham, J.   Epigram: "Within this mindless
  vault."
Davidson, D.   Lines for a Tomb.
Freneau.   Epitaph for Jonathan Robbins.
Gay, J.   My Own Epitaph.
Gray, T.   Elegy Written in a Country
  Churchyard.
  Epitaph: "Here rests his head upon the lap of
  earth."
Hardy, T.
Herbert, E.   Epitaph on Sir Philip Sidney Lying
  in St Paul's without a Monument, to be
  Fastned upon the Church Door.
Jackson, L.   Dimensions.
Levy, A.   Epitaph: "This is the end of him, here
  he lies."
Masters, E.   Trainor, the Druggist.
Ralegh, S.   Authours Epitaph, Made by Himself,
  The.
  Epitaph on the Earl of Leicester [or Leceister].
Rochester, J.   Epitaph on Charles II.
Shirley, J.   Garden, The.
Whitman, W.   As Toilsome I Wander'd
  Virginia's Woods.
Wordsworth, W.   Gravestone upon the Floor in
  the Cloisters of Worcester Cathedral, A.

Equality
Adisa.   Women at the Crossroad / (May Elegba
  Forever Guard the Right Doors).
Barbauld.   Rights of Woman, The.
Burns, R.   For A' That and A' That ['Is there,
  for honest poverty'].
Carew, T.   Rapture, A.
Cowper, W.   Negro's Complaint, The.
Dickey, J.   Basics.
Dugan, A.   On the Elk, Unwitnessed.
Eady.   Why Do So Few Blacks Study Creative
  Writing?
Hughes, L.   Democracy.
Jordan, J.   What Would I Do White?
Kelber, M.   Pledge of Allegiance to the Family
  of Earth, A.
Konie, G.   We Are Equals.
Lincoln, A.   Gettysburg Address, The.
Public Enemy.   Party for your Right to Fight.
Sanchez, S.   Poem for July 4, 1994.
Sirowitz, H.   Equality.
Spender, S.   Not Palaces.
Symonds.   Love and Death: A Symphony.
Walsh, C.   Woman to Her Lover, A.
Whitman, W.   America.
Yeats.   Paudeen.
See also **Social Class**

Erie Canal
Allen, W.   Erie Canal, The.
Cohan.   Down by the Erie Canal.
Unknown.   E-ri-e, The.

Erie, Lake
Weems, M.   Dime after Dime.

Erne (river), Ireland
Muldoon, P.   Yggdrasill.

Eros
Shepherd, R.   Eros in His Striped Blue Shirt.
See also **Cupid**

Erosion
Wilbur.   On the Marginal Way.

Erotic Love
Abbott, D.   All Day at Work.
Ackerman, D.   Sweep Me through Your Many-Chambered Heart.
Adair, T.   Night We Called It a Day, The.
Will You Still Be Mine?
Adams, F.   If.
Adamson, H.   Everything I Have Is Yours.
I Just Found Out About Love.
Time on My Hands.
Adler, R.   Hey There.
There Once Was a Man.
Ai.   Twenty-Year Marriage.
Altman, A.   All or Nothing at All.
Amichai [*or* Amikhai].   Quick And Bitter.
'Andrews, C.'   Morn's Recompense.
Angira.   Request.
Angus.   Invitation.
Arlen, H.   Come Rain or Come Shine.
Down with Love.
Fun to be Fooled.
Happiness Is Just a Thing Called Joe.
Hooray for Love.
Last Night When We Were Young.
Morning After, The.
That Old Black Magic.
Armantrout.   Plan, The.
Arnold, C.   My Love Is Sick.
Ashbery.   My Erotic Double.
Auden.   As I Walked Out One Evening.
Legend.
Uncle Henry.
Ball, J.   And This Is So.
Bangs, C.   Touching Each Other's Surfaces.
Barer, M.   Beyond Compare.
On Such a Night As This.
Barnfield [*or* Barnefield].   Affectionate Shepherd, The.
Daphnis to Ganymede.
Barot, R.   Three Amoretti.
Baudelaire.   Snake that Dances, The.
Becker, R.   Sonnet to the Imagination.
Behn, A.   Song: "I led my Silvia to a grove."
To the Fair Clarinda [*or* Clorinda], Who Made Love to Me, Imagined [*or* Imagin'd] More Than Woman.
Benjamin, B.   Oh! What It Seemed to Be.
Bergman, A.   Summer Me, Winter Me.
Berlin.   Always.
Say It Isn't So.
You're Just in Love.
Bernstein, J.   Tango'd Love.
Bernstein, L.   Little Bit in Love, A.
Berrigan, A.   Various Multitudes Contained by the Loves of My Love, The.
Betjeman.   Invasion Exercise on the Poultry Farm.
Licorice Fields at Pontefract, The.
Potpourri from a Surrey Garden.
Bizet, G.   Dat's Love (Habanera).
Black, S.   Hoopla.
Blake, E.   You're Lucky to Me.
Blake, W.   Desire and Jealousy.
Visions of the Daughters of Albion.
Blane, R.   Love: "Love can be a moment's madness."
Blind.   Many Will Love You.
Bloom, R.   Day In—Day Out.
Bly, R.   Listening to the Köln Concert.
Bock, J.   She Loves Me.
Too Close for Comfort.
Bogan, L.   Frightened Man, The.

Juan's Song.
Borodin, A.   And This Is My Beloved.
Boyse.   On Platonic Love.
Breton, A.   On the Road to San Romano.
Bricusse, L.   What Kind of Fool Am I?
Bridges, R.   Eros.
Broughton, J.   Twin Flames.
Wondrous the Merge.
Broumas, O.   After *The Little Mariner*.
Privacy.
Brown, L.   Best Things in Life Are Free, The.
Browning, E.   Romance of the Swan's Nest, The.
Browning, R.   Confessions.
Last Ride Together, The.
Meeting at Night.
Bui-Burton.   My Love is Like a Lily.
Poem for R.
Burke, J.   But Beautiful.
Like Someone in Love.
Misty.
You May Not Love Me.
Burns, R.   Patriarch, The.
Song: "O my love's [*or* luve's *or* love is *or* luve is] like a red, red rose."
Burwell, C.   Sweet Lorraine.
Bynner.   Lovers.
Byron, G.   Cornelian, The.
Last Words on Greece.
Love and Death.
On This Day I Complete My Thirty-sixth Year.
One Struggle More, and I Am Free.
So We'll Go No More A-Roving.
To Thyrza.
Caesar.   Sometimes I'm Happy.
Cahn, S.   (Love Is) The Tender Trap.
All the Way.
Day by Day.
I Fall in Love Too Easily.
Put 'Em in a Box, Tie 'Em with a Ribbon (And Throw 'Em in the Deep Blue Sea).
Second Time Around, The.
Time After Time.
Until the Real Thing Comes.
Caldwell, E.   Love Poem: "Olfactory paradise."
Campbell, J.   Good Night, Sweetheart.
If I Had You.
Campion, T.   I Care Not for These Ladies.
It Fell on a Summer's [*or* Sommers] Day [*or* Daie].
Carew, T.   On the Marriage of T. K. and C. C.: The Morning Stormy.
Rapture, A.
Second Rapture, The.
Song, [A]: "Ask[e] me no more where Jove bestow[e]s."
Carle, F.   Oh! What It Seemed to Be.
Carmichael, H.   Doctor, Lawyer, Indian Chief.
How Little We Know.
Two Sleepy People.
Carroll, K.   Short Poem.
Cartwright, W.   No Platonic [*or* Platonique] Love.
Song of Dalliance, A.
Carver, R.   Woman Bathing.
Cassian.   Lady Gulliver.
Chaplin, S.   Until the Real Thing Comes.
Chase, K.   Venison.
Cheney-Coker.   Poem for a Lost Lover.
Chubb, R.   Song of My Soul.
Clare, J.   First Love.
Clark, C.   Border Affair, A.
Clarke, A.   Envy of Poor Lovers, The.
Penal Law.
Clarke, C.   Rondeau: "They are bodies left unburied."
Cleage.   Confession.
Clifton, H.   Monsoon Girl.
Clough.   Natura Naturans.
Clover, J.   Map Room, The.
Coates, E.   Sleepy Lagoon.
Coleman, C.   I've Got Your Number.
It Amazes Me!
Rules of the Road, The.
Comden, B.   Adventure.
Just in Time.

Little Bit in Love, A.
Connelly, R.   Good Night, Sweetheart.
If I Had You.
Cook, E.   'Tis Well to Wake the Theme of Love.
Cortez, J.   Pray for the Lovers.
Cory, W.   Desiderato.
Deteriora.
Parting.
Coslow, S.   (I'm In Love With) The Honorable Mr. So and So.
It's Love Again.
My Old Flame.
Couzyn.   Spell to Protect Our Love.
Coward.   Let's Do It.
Crowley, A.   Ballad of Passive Paederasty, A.
Dedicace.
Go into the Highways and Hedges, And Compel Them to Come In.
Rondels.
Cullen, C.   Wind Bloweth Where It Listeth, The.
Cummings, E.   May I Feel Said He.
Cushing, J.   Lover Man.
Dacre, C.   Kiss, The.
Darley.   It Is Not Beauty I Demand.
Song: "Sweet in her green dell the flower of beauty slumbers."
David, M.   Candy.
Davie.   Rejoinder to a Critic.
Time Passing, Beloved.
de Gillies, G.   De Puerorum osculis.
De Paul, G.   You Don't Know What Love Is.
De Veaux.   Sisters, The.
DeLange, E.   Shake Down the Stars.
Denniker, P.   S'posin'
Dennis, M.   Night We Called It a Day, The.
Will You Still Be Mine?
'Dermée.'   Silver Clasps.
DeSylva, B. G.   Best Things in Life Are Free, The.
Somebody Loves Me.
Dickey, J.   Cherrylog Road.
Dietz, H.   Dancing in the Dark.
Haunted Heart.
You and the Night and the Music.
Dodsley.   Stolen Kiss, The.
Donaldson, W.   Because My Baby Don't Mean Maybe Now.
Dongala.   Fantasy under the Moon.
Donne.   Air[e] and Angels.
Anniversary [*or* Anniversarie], The.
Bait[e], The.
Canonization, The.
Confined Love.
Dream[e], The.
Ecstasy, The.
Farewell to Love.
Flea, The.
Good-Morrow, The.
Indifferent, The.
Love's Deity [*or* Deitie].
Love's Growth.
Love's Alchemy [*or* Alchemie].
Sun Rising, The.
To Mr. C.B.
Donovan, K.   These Last Days.
Dorcey.   Night.
Douglas, L.   Two Loves.
Dove, R.   Persephone Underground.
Dransfield.   Memoirs of a Velvet Urinal.
Drieu la Rochelle.   Tennis.
Dryden, J.   Song: "SYLVIA the fair, in the bloom of fifteen."
Duhamel.   Sex with a Famous Poet.
Duke, V.   Honey in the Honeycomb.
Love Turned the Light Out.
Taking a Chance on Love.
What Is There to Say?
Dunbar, P.   Negro Love Song, A.
Eliscu, E.   More Than You Know.
Elizabeth I.   On Monsieur's Departure.
Elledge.   Triptych.
Ellington, D.   I Didn't Know About You.
I'm Beginning to See the Light.
Maybe I Should Change My Ways.
Something to Live For.
Emanuel, L.   Sleeping, The.

Emerson, R. Eros.
Give All to Love.
"Ephelia." On a Bashful Shepherd.
Evans, D. Dinner at the Hotel de la Tigresse
Verte.
Evans, R. To Each His Own.
Fain, S. Love Is a Many-Splendored Thing.
Love Is a Random Thing.
Secret Love.
Springtime Cometh, The.
When I Take My Sugar to Tea.
Fenton, E. Olivia.
Fetter, T. Taking a Chance on Love.
"Field." Ah, Eros Doth Not Always Smite.
As Two Fair Vessels Side by Side.
Constancy.
Lovers.
Palimpsest, A.
Unbosoming.
Fields, D. Don't Blame Me.
I Can't Give You Anything but Love.
Remind Me.
There Must Be Somethin' Better Than Love.
Fisher, D. That Old Devil Called Love.
Fisher, M. Nothing Ever Changes My Love for
You.
Flatman. Appeal to Cats in the Business of
Love, An.
Floyd. Private First Class Brooks Morgenstern,
U. S. M. C.
Follain. Taxidermist, A.
Forrest, G. And This Is My Beloved.
Strange Music.
Fowler, W. Ship-broken Men Whom Stormy
Seas Sore Toss.
Francis, R. Swimmer.
Furber, D. Me and My Girl.
Gannon, K. Reciprocity.
Garner, E. Misty.
Gay, N. Leaning on a Lamppost.
Me and My Girl.
George, D. I'm Beginning to See the Light.
Gershwin. 'S Wonderful.
But Not for Me.
Do, Do, Do.
Fun to be Fooled.
I Got Rhythm.
Isn't It a Pity?
Long Ago (And Far Away).
Love Is Here to Stay.
Love Is Sweeping the Country.
Man I Love, The.
Nice Work If You Can Get It.
Of Thee I Sing.
Someone to Watch over Me.
Who Cares?
Gershwin, G. 'S Wonderful.
But Not for Me.
Do, Do, Do.
I Got Rhythm.
Isn't It a Pity?
Long Ago (And Far Away).
Love Is Here to Stay.
Love Is Sweeping the Country.
Man I Love, The.
Nice Work If You Can Get It.
Of Thee I Sing.
Somebody Loves Me.
Someone to Watch over Me.
Who Cares?
Gilyard, K. Portraits of a Moment.
Glück, L. Garden, The.
Happiness.
Goetz, E. For Me and My Gal.
Gonzalez, R. Beyond Having.
Gordon, I. Be Anything (But Be Mine).
Unforgettable.
Gordon, M. Head Over Heels in Love.
Mam'selle.
There Will Never Be Another You.
There's a Lull in My Life.
Time on My Hands.
You Hit the Spot.
Gould, M. There Must Be Somethin' Better
Than Love.
Goulding, E. Mam'selle.

Graves, R. Down, Wanton, Down!
Not at Home.
She Tells Her Love While Half Asleep.
Gray, J. Barber, The.
Green, A. Adventure.
Just in Time.
Little Bit in Love, A.
Green, B. That's My Weakness Now.
Green, J. Easy Come, Easy Go.
I Wanna Be Loved.
You're Mine, You!
Grieg, E. Strange Music.
Grossmith, G. You Can't Make Love by
Wireless.
Grunke, A. Learning to Live with the Piano.
Gunn, T. Hug, The.
Hacker, M. Ballad of Ladies Lost and Found.
Eight Days in April.
Rondeau after a Transatlantic Telephone Call.
Villanelle: "Every day our bodies separate."
Hamilton, N. How High the Moon.
Hammerstein. All er Nothin'
All the Things You Are.
Can't Help Lovin' Dat Man.
Dat's Love (Habanera).
Don't Ever Leave Me.
Hello, Young Lovers.
I'll Take Romance.
I've Told Ev'ry Little Star.
If I Loved You.
Make Believe.
Many a New Day.
Mister Snow.
People Will Say We're in Love.
Some Enchanted Evening.
Song Is You, The.
Who?
Wonderful Guy, A.
Younger Than Springtime.
Harbach, O. Who?
Harburg. Down with Love.
Fun to be Fooled.
Happiness Is Just a Thing Called Joe.
If This Isn't Love.
Last Night When We Were Young.
Old Devil Moon.
Springtime Cometh, The.
Then I'll Be Tired of You.
What Is There to Say?
When I'm Not Near the Girl I Love.
Hardy, T. Beeny Cliff.
Neutral Tones.
Harnick. She Loves Me.
Hart, L. Bewitched, Bothered and Bewildered.
Blue Moon.
Falling in Love with Love.
Have You Met Miss Jones?
I Didn't Know What Time It Was.
I've Got Five Dollars.
It's Got to Be Love.
Most Beautiful Girl in the World, The.
My Funny Valentine.
My Heart Stood Still.
My Romance.
Ship Without a Sail, A.
This Can't Be Love.
To Keep My Love Alive.
Where or When.
You Took Advantage of Me.
Heath, R. Seeing Her Dancing.
Hecht, A. Gardens of the Villa D'Este, The.
Hemans. Chamois Hunter's Love, The.
Properzia Rossi.
To a Wandering Female Singer.
Henderson, R. Best Things in Life Are Free,
The.
Herbert, G. Love (3).
Herrick. Her Bed.
Her Legs.
No Loathsomnesse in Love.
To Anthea, Who May Command Him Anything.
To Dianeme.
To Electra.
Upon Julia's Breasts.
Upon Julia's Clothes.
Vine, The.

Hesketh. Love's Advocate.
Heyman, E. Blame It on My Youth.
Easy Come, Easy Go.
Ho Hum.
I Wanna Be Loved.
When I Fall in Love.
You're Mine, You!
Hill, A. On a Lady, Preached into the Colic, by
One of Her Lovers.
Hill, B. Glory of Love, The.
Hirsch, E. Lectures on Love, The.
Hirshfield, J. Painting.
Hodges, J. I'm Beginning to See the Light.
Hogg, J. When Maggy Gangs Away.
Holiner, M. Until the Real Thing Comes.
Why Shouldn't It Happen to Us?
You Can't Stop Me from Lovin' You.
Holofcener, L. Too Close for Comfort.
Hope, A. Blason, A.
Housman, A. Because I Liked You Better.
When I Was One-and-Twenty.
Howard, B. Fly Me to the Moon (In Other
Words).
Who Besides You.
Would You Believe It?
Year After Year.
Huang O [or Huang Ho]. To the Tune "Red
Embroidered Shoes."
Huddle. Music.
Hupfeld, H. As Time Goes By.
Huxley, A. Armour.
James, H. I'm Beginning to See the Light.
James, J. Sister Midnight.
James, P. Can This Be Love?
Fine and Dandy.
Jeffers, R. For Una.
Jenkins, G. P.S. I Love You.
Johnson, G. I Want to Die While You Love Me.
Johnson, J. Guess Who's in Town? (Nobody
but That Gal of Mine).
Porter's Love Song to a Chambermaid, A.
Johnston, A. My Old Flame.
Jones, S. Force of Love, The.
Jordan, J. Grand Army Plaza.
Kahal, I. When I Take My Sugar to Tea.
Kahn, G. I'm Through with Love.
Kalmar et al. Three Little Words.
Kasdorf. Eve's Striptease.
Keats. Bright Star.
Dawlish Fair.
Eve of St Agnes, The.
Kennelly. Bread.
Kent, W. Reciprocity.
Kern, J. All the Things You Are.
Can't Help Lovin' Dat Man.
Don't Ever Leave Me.
I've Told Ev'ry Little Star.
In Love In Vain.
Make Believe.
Remind Me.
Song Is You, The.
Who?
You Can't Make Love by Wireless.
Koch, K. Sleeping with Women.
Kramer, A. Candy.
Kumin, M. After Love.
Lamantia. Winter Day, A.
Landon. Girl at Her Devotions, A.
Landor, W. Mother, I Cannot Mind My Wheel.
Rose Aylmer.
Lane, B. Everything I Have Is Yours.
If This Isn't Love.
Lady's in Love with You, The.
Old Devil Moon.
When I'm Not Near the Girl I Love.
Latouche, J. Honey in the Honeycomb.
Love Turned the Light Out.
Maybe I Should Change My Ways.
Taking a Chance on Love.
Laughlin, J. Rhyme.
Laurencin, M. Present, The.
Lawrence, D. Gloire de Dijon.
New Year's Eve.
Young Wife, A.
Lawrence, J. All or Nothing at All.
Foolin' Myself.

Sleepy Lagoon.
What's Your Story, Morning Glory.
Lee, P.   I Love Being Here with You.
Lee, W.   Lovers' Duet.
Lees, G.   Right to Love, The.
Legrand, M.   Summer Me, Winter Me.
Leigh, C.   How Little We Know (How Little It Matters).
  I've Got Your Number.
  It Amazes Me!
  Rules of the Road, The.
Lerner, A.   Almost Like Being in Love.
Leslie, E.   For Me and My Gal.
Levant, O.   Blame It on My Youth.
Levertov.   Eros at Temple Stream.
  Hymn to Eros.
  Love Poem.
Levy, A.   Sinfonia Eroica.
Lewis, M.   How High the Moon.
Livingston, J.   I'm Through with Love.
  To Each His Own.
Livingstone, D.   One Time.
Loesser.   Guys and Dolls.
  I Wish I Didn't Love You So.
  Lady's in Love with You, The.
  Once in Love with Amy.
  Two Sleepy People.
Loewe, F.   Almost Like Being in Love.
Lorde.   Love Poem.
  On a Night of the Full Moon.
  Recreation.
Lovelace, R.   Love Made in the First Age[: To Chloris].
  To Lucasta, [on] Going to the War[re]s.
Lowe, J.   With Thanks to Eddie Shaw.
Lowell, A.   April.
  Aubade.
Lowell, R.   Man And Wife.
Lowry, M.   Volcano is Dark, The.
Mabuza.   Love Song, A.
MacDonald, B.   Somebody Loves Me.
Madan.   Abelard to Eloisa.
Magidson, H.   (I'm Afraid) The Masquerade Is Over.
Maguire, S.   Perfect Timing.
"Malley."   Perspective Lovesong.
Malneek, M.   I'm Through with Love.
Maltby, R.   Little Bit Off, A.
Marion, G.   Love Is a Random Thing.
  My Future Just Passed.
  There's a Man in My Life.
Marks, G.   All of Me.
Marlowe.   Passionate Shepherd To His Love, The.
Martin, H.   Love: "Love can be a moment's madness."
  On Such a Night As This.
Marvell.   To His Coy Mistress.
Maschwitz, E.   Nightingale Sang in Berkeley Square, A.
McDaniel, J.   D.
McHugh, J.   Don't Blame Me.
  I Just Found Out About Love.
Mercer, J.   Come Rain or Come Shine.
  Day In—Day Out.
  How Little We Know.
  I Remember You.
  P.S. I Love You.
  That Old Black Magic.
Metras, G.   Vanishing Point.
Mew.   À Quoi Bon Dire.
Meyer, G.   For Me and My Gal.
Middleton, C.   Adelaide's Dream.
Montagu, L.   'Between your sheets.'
Moore, E.   Nun, The.
  Song 3: "As Phyllis the gay, at the break of the day."
Moore, H.   Green Place, A.
Moraes, D.   Snow on a Mountain.
Moret, N.   She's Funny That Way (I Got a Woman, Crazy for Me).
Namjoshi, S.   From the Travels of Gulliver.
Nash, O.   I'm a Stranger Here Myself.
  Speak Low.
Nashe [or Nash].   Choise of valentines, The.
Nelson, J.   Our Love.

Nesbit, E.   Vies Manquées.
Newley, A.   What Kind of Fool Am I?
Nichols, A.   Until the Real Thing Comes.
  Why Shouldn't It Happen to Us?
  You Can't Stop Me from Lovin' You.
Nichols, G.   Configurations.
Noble, R.   Good Night, Sweetheart.
  I Hadn't Anyone Till You.
  Very Thought of You, The.
Norman, P.   When I Take My Sugar to Tea.
Noyes, A.   Highwayman, The.
Oakland, B.   I'll Take Romance.
Olds, S.   Wellspring, The.
Orton, B.   Love Poem.
Owen, W.   Music.
  To Eros.
Parish.   Stars Fell on Alabama.
  Sweet Lorraine.
Parker, D.   Unfortunate Coincidence.
Patchen.   Character of Love Seen as a Search for the Lost, The.
  In Judgment of the Leaf.
  In Memory of Kathleen.
  Religion Is That I Love You.
Patten, B.   Party Piece.
Perkins, F.   Stars Fell on Alabama.
Philips, K.   L'Amitie: To Mrs. Mary [or M.] Awbrey.
Pickard, T.   Bush Telegram.
Pilkington, L.   Dol and Roger.
  Fair and Softly goes far or, The Wary Physician.
Pollack, L.   Two Cigarettes in the Dark.
Porter, C.   Let's Not Talk About Love.
  Love for Sale.
  Ridin' High.
  So in Love.
  What Is This Thing Called Love?
Porter, P.   Affair of the Heart.
Previn, D.   Morning After, The.
Prior.   Les Estreines.
Probyn.   After.
  Barcarolle.
  Before.
  Blossom.
  China Maniacs.
  Lai.
  Love in Mayfair.
Procter, A.   Philip and Mildred.
  Woman's Answer, A.
  Woman's Last Word, A.
Raffalovich, M. A.   Rose Leaves When the Rose Is Dead.
  World Well Lost 18, The.
Raine, K.   Love-Poem: "Yours is the face that the earth turns to me."
Ralegh, S.   Nymph's [or Nimphs] Reply to the Shepherd [or Sheepheard], The.
Randall, D.   Blackberry Sweet.
Rankine.   Testimonial.
Ransom, J.   Equilibrists, The.
Rashad, J.   Morning After, The.
Raye, D.   You Don't Know What Love Is.
Razaf, A.   Guess Who's in Town? (Nobody but That Gal of Mine).
  Keepin' Out of Mischief Now.
  Porter's Love Song to a Chambermaid, A.
  S'posin'
  You're Lucky to Me.
Revel, H.   Head Over Heels in Love.
  There's a Lull in My Life.
  You Hit the Spot.
Riley, P.   E Questa Vita Un Lampo.
Roberts, A.   That Old Devil Called Love.
Roberts, E.   Old Love in Song, An.
Robin, L.   Hooray for Love.
  In Love In Vain.
Robinson, A.   Posies.
  Tuscan Olives.
Rochester, J.   Imperfect Enjoyment, The.
Rodgers, C.   Now Ain't That Love?
Rodgers, R.   Blue Moon.
  Falling in Love with Love.
  Have You Met Miss Jones?
  I Didn't Know What Time It Was.
  I've Got Five Dollars.
  It's Got to Be Love.

Most Beautiful Girl in the World, The.
My Funny Valentine.
My Heart Stood Still.
My Romance.
Ship Without a Sail, A.
This Can't Be Love.
To Keep My Love Alive.
Where or When.
You Took Advantage of Me.
Rodgers, W.   Net, The.
Roethke.   I Knew A Woman.
Rohrer, M.   Gliding Toward the Lamps.
Rollings.   Dirty Dreams and God Smiling.
Rome, H.   Who Knows?
Rose, B.   I Wanna Be Loved.
  More Than You Know.
Ross, D.   Beyond Compare.
Ross, J.   Hey There.
  There Once Was a Man.
Rossetti, C.   Bed of Forget-Me-Nots, A.
  Birthday, A.
Rossetti, D.   Sudden Light.
Ruby, H.   Three Little Words.
Rukeyser, M.   Nevertheless the Moon.
Rungano.   This Morning.
Russell, B.   Crazy She Calls Me.
  I Didn't Know About You.
Schertzinger, V.   I Remember You.
Schifrin, L.   Right to Love, The.
Schluger, B.   I Love Being Here with You.
Schwartz, A.   Dancing in the Dark.
  Haunted Heart.
  Then I'll Be Tired of You.
  You and the Night and the Music.
Schwartz, R. L.   Falling in Love after Forty.
Scott, A.   Rondel of Luve [or Love], A.
Sedley.   On the Happy Corydon and Phyllis.
  Song: "Phillis, let's shun the common fate."
  To Cloris.
Segal, J.   Nothing Ever Changes My Love for You.
Sexton.   That Day.
  Us.
Shakespeare, W.   Phoenix and the Turtle, The.
Shange.   Where the Mississippi meets the Amazon.
Shapiro, T.   If I Had You.
Sharkey.   Hots, The.
Shaw, A.   April.
Shearing, G.   Lullaby of Birdland.
Shelley, P.   Indian Serenade, The.
Sheridan, R.   Geranium, The.
Sherwin, M.   Nightingale Sang in Berkeley Square, A.
Shire, D.   Little Bit Off, A.
Sidney, S.   When, to my deadly [or deadlie] pleasure.
Sigman, C.   Crazy She Calls Me.
Simic.   Breasts.
Simmons, J.   Goodbye, Sally.
Simons, S.   All of Me.
Smith, C.   On the Aphorism "L'Amitié est l'Amour sans Ailes."
Smith, W.   Pavane for the Nursery, A.
Snyder, G.   After Work.
Song.   White Porch, The.
Soutar.   Tryst [or Trysting Place], The.
Spender, S.   Abrupt and charming mover.
  Daybreak.
  To T.A.R.H.
Spenser.   Epithalamion: "Ye learned sisters which have oftentimes."
Springer, P.   How Little We Know (How Little It Matters).
St. John, D.   My Friend.
Stainer.   Honeycomb, The.
Stept, S.   That's My Weakness Now.
Steptoe.   Sweet Brown Rice and Red Bones.
Stordahl, A.   Day by Day.
Strayhorn, B.   Something to Live For.
Styne, J.   Adventure.
  I Fall in Love Too Easily.
  Just in Time.
  Put 'Em in a Box, Tie 'Em with a Ribbon (And Throw 'Em in the Deep Blue Sea).
  Time After Time.

Suckling, S.   Against Fruition.
  Farewell to Love.
  Love's Clock.
  Love's Siege.
  Miracle, The.
  Sonnet: "O[h]! for some honest lover's ghost."
  To a Lady That Forbade to Love before
    Company.
  Upon My Lady Carlisle's Walking in Hampton
    Court Garden.
Suesse, D.   Ho Hum.
Swift, K.   Can This Be Love?
  Fine and Dandy.
Swinburne.   In The Orchard.
  Love And Sleep.
Swirszczynska.   Second Madrigal, The.
  Thank You, My Fate.
Symonds.   Love and Death: A Symphony.
Symons, A.   Faint Love.
  Nerves.
  White Heliotrope.
Synge.   In May.
Tana, P.   River, The.
Teasdale.   Enough.
  Summer Night, Riverside.
  Unchanging, The.
Thomas, D.   In My Craft or Sullen Art.
  Tiger. Lovepoem Writing Me.
Tinturin, P.   Foolin' Myself.
Tremblay, G.   Not Sense.
Trocchi, A.   For John Donne: Master
  Metaphysical.
Troup, B.   You're in Love.
Troupe.   You Come to Me.
Unknown.   Black Hair.
  Cripple Creek.
  Hark, All Ye Lovely Saints.
  I Have a Gentle Cock [*or* Gentil Cok].
  Love Me Not [for Comely Grace].
  Now Is the Month of Maying.
  Pitman's Lovesong, A.
  She Lay All Naked.
  There Was a Lady Loved a Swine.
  Unquiet Grave, The.
Van Duyn.   Falling in Love at Sixty-Five.
Van Heusen, J.   (Love Is) The Tender Trap.
  All the Way.
  But Beautiful.
  Like Someone in Love.
  Second Time Around, The.
  Shake Down the Stars.
  You May Not Love Me.
Villon.   Ballad of Villon and Fat Madge, The.
Wade-Gayles.   Loving Again.
Wakoski.   Inside Out.
Walker, F. X.   Sweet Bread.
Waller, E.   Budd, The.
Waller, T. *et al.*   Keepin' Out of Mischief Now.
  There's a Man in My Life.
Waniek.   Ballad of Aunt Geneva, The.
Warren, H.   There Will Never Be Another You.
Warren-Moore.   Pink Poem.
Washington, N.   Hundred Years from Today, A.
  Love Is the Thing.
  Woman's Intuition, A.
Webster, A.   By the Looking-Glass.
Webster, P.   Doctor, Lawyer, Indian Chief.
  Love Is a Many-Splendored Thing.
  Secret Love.
  Two Cigarettes in the Dark.
  What's Your Story, Morning Glory.
Weill, K.   I'm a Stranger Here Myself.
  Speak Low.
Weiss, G.   Lullaby of Birdland.
  Oh! What It Seemed to Be.
  Too Close for Comfort.
Weston, P.   Day by Day.
Wharton, E.   Mortal Lease, The.
Whiting, R.   My Future Just Passed.
  She's Funny That Way (I Got a Woman, Crazy
    for Me).
Whitman, W.   Among the Multitude.
  As Adam Early in the Morning.
  From Pent-up Aching Rivers.
  Live Oak, with Moss.
  Spontaneous Me.

  When I Heard at the Close of the Day.
  Whoever You Are Holding Me Now in Hand.
Whitney, J.   Candy.
Wilbur.   Late Aubade, A.
  Loves of the Puppets.
  Pangloss's Song: A Comic-Opera Lyric.
  Someone Talking to Himself.
Wilde, L.   Corinne's Last Love-Song.
Wilde, O.   Ballad of Reading Gaol, The.
  Vita Nuova.
Williams, M.   What's Your Story, Morning
  Glory.
Williams, W.   Queen-Anne's-Lace.
Willson, M.   Till There Was You.
Wilson, S.   It's Never Too Late to Fall in Love.
Wodehouse, P.   You Can't Make Love by
  Wireless.
Woods, H.   Over My Shoulder.
  Paddlin' Madelin' Home.
  We Just Couldn't Say Good-bye.
Wright, J.   Gesture by a Lady with an Assumed
  Name, A.
  Sappho.
Wright, R.   And This Is My Beloved.
  Strange Music.
Wruber, A.   (I'm Afraid) The Masquerade Is
  Over.
Wyatt, S.   His Reward.
  Lover Showeth How He Is Forsaken of Such as
    He Sometime Enjoyed, The.
  Varium et Mutabile.
Wylie.   Confession of Faith.
Yalden.   Advice to a Lover.
Yeats.   Brown Penny.
  Last Confession, A.
  Lullaby: "Beloved, may your sleep be sound."
Youmans, V.   More Than You Know.
  Sometimes I'm Happy.
  Time on My Hands.
Young, J.   Hundred Years from Today, A.
Young, V.   Love Is the Thing.
  When I Fall in Love.
  Woman's Intuition, A.

See also **Sex**
Error
Peacock, M.   How I Had to Act.
Preston, K.   Lapsus Linguae.
Probyn.   Masquerading.
Ransom, J.   Parting, without a Sequel.
Ruskin, H.   I May Be Wrong (But I Think
  You're Wonderful).
Simic.   Errata.
Sullivan, H.   I May Be Wrong (But I Think
  You're Wonderful).
Unknown.   Erasers.
Escapes
Ai.   Kid, The.
Alexander, E.   Passage.
Alvi, M.   Houdini.
Balaban.   Heading Out West.
Bayly.   Out, John.
Bennett, R.   Gingerbread Man, The.
Brathwaite [*or* Brathwait], R.   Vandunk's Four
  Humours, in Quality and Quantity.
Causley.   What Has Happened to Lulu?
Ciardi.   Sometimes Even Parents Win.
Cleary, B.   Sealink.
Corn.   Kimchee in Worcester (Mass.).
Durcan.   Death by Heroin of Sid Vicious, The.
Erdrich.   Indian Boarding School: The
  Runaways.
Ewart.   Wanting Out.
Farber.   For a Quick Exit.
Glaser, M.   Magnificat!
Gonzalez, R.   There.
Harper, F.   Eliza Harris.
  Slave Mother, The.
Hayden, R.   O Daedalus, Fly Away Home.
  Runagate Runagate.
Hernández Cruz.   Swans' Book, The.
Holzer, R.   Current 'Now, Voyager' Fantasy.
Jackson, G.   Fugitive Slaves.
Kendrick, D.   Sadie Snuffs a Candle.
Lazard.   Ordinance on Arrival.
"Leadbelly."   Take this Hammer.
Lear, E.   Limerick: "There was an old person of

  Basing."
Levine, P.   And the Trains Go On.
Longfellow, H.   Slave in the Dismal Swamp,
  The.
MacEwen, G.   Manzini; Escape Artist.
Mandel, E.   Houdini.
McLain, P.   Residue.
Morales.   Getting Out Alive.
Probyn.   Anniversaries.
Ress.   Waving Her Farewell. Train Station,
  Vienna XV, 1939.
Robinson, A.   To My Muse.
Rodriguez, L.   Always Running.
Salzman, E.   Double Crossing.
Seward.   Eyam.
Stevenson, R.   Escape at Bedtime.
Villanueva, A.   They Didn't Get Me.
Wong, N.   Can't Tell.
Wylie.   Escape.
Yamada.   Club, The.
Yost, C.   Escaping from Autopia.
Young, K.   Escape Artist, The.
Eskimos
Berg, S.   Orpingalik's My Breath: Eskimo Song.
Brown, L.   Turn On the Heat.
"Dylan."   Quinn the Eskimo.
Koch, K.   Geography.
Purdy, A.   Lament for the Dorsets.
Ray, D.   Eskimo Girl, The.
Tallmountain.   Indian Blood.
Warren, R.   Sila.
Watson, R.   Ballad of the Bird-Bride.
Essex, England
Levertov.   Map of the Western Part of the
  County of Essex in England, A.
Essex, Robert Devereux, 2d Earl of
Unknown.   Young Earl of Essex's Victory over
  the Emperor of Germany, The.
Esther, Book of (Bible)
Harper, F.   Vashti.
Spencer, A.   Before the Feast of Shushan.
Estrangement
Bendall, M.   After Estrangement.
Byron, G.   Lines on Hearing That Lady Byron
  Was Ill.
Cope, W.   At 3 A.M.
Crane, H.   Stark Major.
Crozier, L.   So This Is Love.
Godfrey.   Where the Weather Suits My Clothes.
Hogan, L.   Heritage.
Jeffers, R.   Birth-Dues.
Jong.   Colder.
Kantaris.   Body Language.
Light, K.   My Worst Nightmare.
Lowell, R.   Man and Wife.
  To Speak of Woe That Is in Marriage.
MacNeice.   Selva Oscura.
Major, C.   Isolate.
Mansfield, K.   Meeting, The.
'Marnia.   Accoutrement.
Merrill, J.   Renewal, A.
Olson, C.   Distances, The.
Ransom, J.   Two in August.
Rich, A.   After Dark.
  Like This Together.
Rumens.   Double Bed.
Scott, L.   Ettrick.
Stanley-Wrench.   Storm, The.
Unknown.   Since First I Saw Your Face.
Viorst.   Honeymoon is Over, The.
Walker, F. X.   Wishbone.
Whitehead, C.   Grass Crust, The.
Young, A.   Dance of the Infidels.
Eternity
Ammons, A. R.   Eternal City, The.
Beaumont, S.   Description of Love, A.
Berlin.   Always.
Betjeman.   NW5 and N6.
Brontë, E.   No Coward Soul is Mine.
Browning, R.   Last Ride Together, The.
Bursk.   Tearing Up the Tracks.
Clare, J.   Vision, A.
Coleridge, M.   Some in a Child Would Live,
  Some in a Book.
"Cornwall."   Address to the Ocean.

Cowley, A.   Muse, The.
Donne.   Anniversary [or Anniversarie], The.
Emerson, R.   Days.
  Spiritual Laws.
Ferlinghetti, L.   Cro-Magnons.
  River Still To Be Found, A.
Fitzgerald, R.   Face of the Waters, The.
Gershwin.   Love Is Here to Stay.
Glück, L.   White Lilies, The.
Habington.   To the Moment Last Past.
Hannon.   Beyond Freedom.
Heard, J.   Eternity.
Herrick.   Love What It Is.
  Sabbaths.
  White Island.
Heyman, E.   When I Fall in Love.
Housman, A.   Immortal Part, The.
Hughes, T.   Pibroch.
Kaufman, B.   Private Sadness.
Keats.   Bright Star.
Kinnell.   Quick and the Dead, The.
MacLeish.   Pole Star for This Year.
Meynell, A.   To a Daisy.
Moore, T.   Response to Rimbaud's Later
  Manner.
Procter, A.   Address to the Ocean.
Rands.   Cat of Cats, The.
Riley, J.   Eternity.
Roberts, G.   Night Sky, The.
Rochester, J.   Song: "Absent from thee, I
  languish still."
Roethke.   I Knew a Woman.
Rossetti, C.   Bed of Forget-Me-Nots, A.
  From the Antique.
  Life's Parallels, A.
  Rest.
Sandburg, C.   Sea-Wash.
Simic.   Mirrors at 4 A.M.
Smith, W.   Pavane for the Nursery, A.
Spender, S.   To T.A.R.H.
Sylvester, J.   Father, The.
Vaughan, H.   World, The (1).
Yeats.   Whence Had They Come?
Young, A.   Blues Don't Change, The.
Young, V.   When I Fall in Love.
See also **Immortality**

Ethiopia
Adisa.   Ethiopia Unda a Jamaican Mango Tree.
Clark Bekederemo.   New from Ethiopia and the
  Sudan, The.
Dunbar, P.   Ode to Ethiopia.
Melhem, D.   To an Ethiopian Child.

Etiquette
Alcock.   Modern Manners.
Betjeman.   How to Get On in Society.
Bishop, E.   Manners.
Browning, R.   Respectability.
Bruner.   On City Streets.
Burgess, F.   Table Manners.
Creeley.   Way, The.
Gilbert, S.   Etiquette.
Guiterman.   Of Courtesy.
Herrick.   Panegyric to Sir Lewis Pemberton, A.
  Upon Showbread [or Shewbread]: Epigram.
Macklin.   House Style, The.
Probyn.   Mésalliance, A.
Sandburg, C.   We Must Be Polite.
Stevenson, R.   Good and Bad Children.
  Good Boy, A.
  Whole Duty of Children.
Waniek.   Daughters, 1900.

Eton College
Connolly, C.   On Himself.
Gray, T.   Ode on a Distant Prospect of Eton
  College.

Etruscan Civilization
Lawrence, D.   Cypresses.
Wilbur.   To the Etruscan Poets.

Eucharist
Clarke, A.   Martha Blake.
Conder.   Bread of Heaven, on Thee We Feed.
Constable, H.   To the Blessed Sacrament.
Herbert, G.   Agony [or Agonie], The.
  Banquet, The.
  H[oly] Communion, The.

  Love (3).
  Superliminare.
Hopkins, G.   Bugler's First Communion, The.
L'Engle.   At Communion.
Lyon, G.   Foot-Washing, The.
Meynell, A.   General Communion, A.
  In Portugal, 1912.
Ryman.   Song of the Eucharist, A.
Snider.   Communion.
Southwell.   Of the Blessed Sacrament of the
  Altar [or Aulter].
Thomas, D.   This Bread I Break.
Unknown.   Let Us Break Bread Together.
  Sacrament of the Altar, The.
Vaughan, H.   Holy Communion, The.
See also **Last Supper**

Euclid
Lovelace, R.   Snail [or Snayl], The.
Millay, E.   "Euclid Alone Has Looked on
  Beauty Bare."

Eunuchs
Cannell.   King, The.

Europe
Apollinaire.   Zone.
Barker, G.   Channel Crossing.
Bryant, W.   To Cole, the Painter, Departing for
  Europe.
Douglas, K.   On a Return from Egypt.
Gascoyne.   Snow in Europe.
Gustafson, R.   In the Yukon.
Hollander, J.   Late August on the Lido.
Ignatow, D.   Europe and America.
Jenkins, J. *et al.*   In Ferrara.
Lassell.   Going to Europe.
Lewis, C.   Pentecost.
Lowell, R.   Beyond the Alps.
Oliver, D.   Walnut and Lily.
Scarfe.   Kitchen Poem.
Sergeant.   Inundation, The.
Sirr.   Guide to Holland, A.
Whitman, W.   Europe, the 72d and 73d Year of
  These States.
Wordsworth, W.   Column Intended by
  Buonaparte for a Triumphal Edifice in Milan,
  Now Lying by the Way-Side in the Simplon
  Pass, The.
  Hymn for the Boatmen, as They Approach the
  Rapids under the Castle of Heidelberg.

Eurydice
Glück, L.   Eurydice.
Hill, G.   Orpheus and Eurydice.
Lovelace, R.   Orpheus to Beasts.
Valentine, J.   Orpheus and Eurydice.

Eutaw Springs, South Carolina, Battle of (1781)
Freneau.   To the Memory of the Brave
  Americans.

Euthanasia
Berger, J.   Between Worlds.
Jeffers, R.   Hurt Hawks.
Lumsden, R.   Mercy.
Randall, D.   To the Mercy Killers.

Evangelism and Evangelists
Hayden, R.   Witch Doctor.
Oden.   This Child Is the Mother.
Strange.   Streetcorner Church.
Warren, R.   Amazing Grace in the Back
  Country.

Evanston, Illinois
Ress.   Learnng the Ropes. Custer Street.
  Evanston, 1949.

Eve
Berryman.   Gislebertus' Eve.
Bull.   Eve.
Copus, J.   Masaccio's *Expulsion from Paradise.*
Frost, R.   Never Again Would Birds' Song Be
  The Same.
Gascoyne.   Eve.
Harper, M.   Eve (Rachel).
Hartigan, A.   Brazen Image.
Hejduk.   Sleep of Adam, The.
Higginson, E.   Eve.
Hildebrandt.   O Eve.
Hodgson, R.   Eve.
Hood, T.   Reflection, A.
Hope, A.   Imperial Adam.

Hough, G.   Age of Innocence.
Hughes, T.   Theology.
Marzán.   Eve.
McVeigh, J.   Eve Falling.
Nasrin.   Eve Oh Eve.
Norris, K.   Prayer to Eve, A.
Pastan.   Aspects of Eve.
Probyn.   Ballade of Lovers.
Ray, H.   Vision of Eve, The.
Rossetti, C.   Eve.
Sharpless.   *Paradise Lost* as a Haiku.
Sinason.   In the Beginning.
Sisson.   Adam and Eve.
Smith, S.   Dream of Comparison, A.
  How Cruel Is the Story of Eve.
Triplett, P.   Fractal Audition.
Wells, C.   Original Summer Girl, The.
Wilbur.   She.
Wright, J.   Eve to Her Daughters.
Yeats.   Adam's Curse.

Evening
Abinader, E.   Dar a Luz.
Adams, L.   Home-coming.
Aldington.   Evening.
Allingham.   Evening, An.
Auden.   As I Walked Out One Evening.
Balingit, J.   Quiet Evening, Home Away.
Barnes, W.   Evenen in the Village.
Blake, W.   To the Evening Star.
Bly, R.   Surprised by Evening.
Bowles, W.   Sonnet 5: "Evening, as slow thy
  placid shades descend."
Bridges, R.   Winter Nightfall.
Clare, J.   Evening.
  Gypsy's Evening Blaze, The.
  Mist in the Meadows.
  To Mary: 'It Is the Evening Hour.'
Collins, W.   Ode to Evening.
Creeley.   Buffalo Evening.
Cristall.   Evening, Gertrude.
De la Mare.   Summer Evening.
  Thomas Hardy.
Doolittle, H.   Evening.
Fearing.   Evening Song.
Frost, R.   Stopping by Woods on a Snowy
  Evening.
Gascoigne.   Gascoigne's [or Gascoygnes] Good-
  Night.
Gray, T.   Elegy Written in a Country
  Churchyard.
  Epitaph: "Here rests his head upon the lap of
  earth."
Guest, B.   Otranto.
Guiney.   When on the Marge of Evening.
Haines, J.   Evening Change.
Hammerstein.   Some Enchanted Evening.
Harrison, J.   Swifts at Evening.
Herrick.   Evensong.
Hodgson, R.   Late, Last Rook, The.
Hughes, T.   Full Moon and Little Frieda.
Jeffers, R.   Autumn Evening.
Johnson, M. F.   Second Evening.
Jurmann, W.   Tomorrow Is Another Day.
Kenyon, J.   Let Evening Come.
Kimbrell, J.   Rooftop.
Lampman.   Winter Evening.
Larkin, P.   Coming.
  Going.
Lewis, C.   Evensong.
Longfellow, H.   Curfew.
  Fire of Drift-Wood, The.
Longfellow, S.   Again as Evening's Shadow
  Falls.
Lovelace, R.   Another.
Merriam, E.   Lullaby "Purple."
Merwin, W. S.   Witnesses.
Meynell, A.   November Blue.
Mezey.   Evening, An.
Miller, T.   Evening.
Miller, W.   Willie Winkie.
Mills, R.   Evening Song.
Moss, H.   Persistence of Song, The.
Radnóti.   Seventh Eclogue.
Rodgers, R.   Some Enchanted Evening.
Roethke.   In Evening Air.
Scarfe.   Ode in Honour.

Senghor. Man and Beast.
Shapiro, D. Tracing of an Evening.
Shaw, A. Crepuscule.
Snyder, G. Work to Do Toward Town.
Stephens, J. Evening.
Stevens, W. Evening without Angels.
Stevenson, R. Evensong.
Teasdale. February Twilight.
Toomer. Georgia Dusk.
Turner, F. Spring Evening.
Unknown, fr. Terezin Concentration Camp. On a Sunny Evening.
Warren, R. Evening Hawk.
White, G. Naturalist's Summer-Evening Walk, The.
Wordsworth, W. It Is a Beauteous Evening.
Wright, C. Complete Birth if the Cool, The.
See also **Twilight**

Evening Star
Blake, W. To the Evening Star.
Bogan, L. Evening-Star.
Clare, J. Hesperus.
Jeffers, R. Evening Ebb.
Longfellow, H. Evening Star, The.
Stevens, W. Homunculus et la Belle Étoile.
Martial Cadenza.
See also **Venus (planet)**

Evers, Medgar
Brooks, G. Medgar Evers.
Ignatow, D. For Medgar Evers.

Evictions
Clinton, M. Eviction.
Espada. Imagine the Angels of Bread.
See also **Inclosure Movement**

Evil
Blake, W. Marriage of Heaven and Hell, The.
Memorable Fancy, A.
Pride of the Peacock, The.
Song of Liberty, A.
Brecht, B. To Those Born Later.
Byrom. On the Origin of Evil.
Coleridge, S. Christabel.
In the Touch of This Bosom There Worketh a Spell.
El-Hadi, S. Drama, The.
"Field." Dying Viper, A.
Frost, R. Bearer of Evil Tidings, The.
Design.
Gray, T. Tophet.
Gurney, I. To God.
Hecht, A. "It Out-Herods Herod. Pray You, Avoid It."
Herrick. Neutrality Loathsome.
Spell, The.
Hope, A. Möbius Strip-Tease.
Hughes, L. Bad Man.
Jackson, M. L. Don Pullen at the Zanzibar Blue Jazz Cafe, 1994.
Jarrell. Blind Sheep, The.
Kaufman, S. Emperor of China, The.
Kendall, M. Legend of the Crossing-Sweeper.
Lawrence, D. Root of Our Evil, The.
Snake.
Longfellow, H. Rhyme of Sir Christopher, The.
McGrath, T. Death for the Dark Stranger.
Picková, E. Fear.
Poe. Sonnet—Silence.
Raine, K. Pythoness, The.
Shapiro, K. Puritan, The.
Smith, S. Angel Boley.
Lord Barrenstock.
To the Tune of the Coventry Carol.
Soto. Who Will Know Us?
Vaughan, H. Kingdom of Heaven Compared to a Grain of Mustard-Seed, The.
Wesley, C. He Shook off the Beast.
Wheelwright. Live, Evil Veil.
Whitman, W. I Sit and Look Out.

Evolution
Allen, G. Ballade of Evolution, A.
Bevington, L. Midnight.
Morning.
Blight. Evolution.
Ciardi. On Evolution.
Davidman. Lament for Evolution.

Edson, R. Darwin Descending.
Emerson, R. Nature [1836].
Hahn, S. Incontinence.
Hiestand, E. Day Lily and the Fox, The.
Howe, J. Kosmos.
Kendall, M. Lay of the Trilobite.
Lower Life, The.
Lawrence, D. Self-Protection.
Lewis, C. Evolutionary Hymn.
Peskett. Inheritors, The.
Question of Time, The.
Sandburg, C. Wilderness.
Schnackenberg. Darwin in 1881.
Smith, L. Evolution.
Stoutenburg. Midnight Saving Time.
Very. Origin of Man, I, The.
Viereck, P. Love Song to Eohippus.
See also **Darwin, Charles; Extinction; Genetics and Geneticists**

Ex-lovers
Adamson, H. It's Been So Long.
Anania. Judy Travaillo Variations, The.
Arlen, H. Tess's Torch Song (I Had a Man).
Bang, M. It Says, I Did So.
Barber, W. Gay Poet, The.
Barker, G. To Whom Else.
Bloom, R. Don't Worry 'Bout Me.
Bolton, J. Parthenon at Nashville, The.
Brown, L. That Old Feeling.
Carnevali. Serenade.
Chin, J. Ex-Boyfriends Named Michael.
Clark, P. Walk in the Rain.
Corn. Billie's Blues.
Donaldson, W. It's Been So Long.
Engvick, W. Who Can I Turn To?
Estep, M. I Have to Go Now.
Fain, S. That Old Feeling.
Fairburn. Farewell, A: "What is there left to be said?"
Fisher, M. I Keep Going Back to Joe's.
Groarke, V. Riverbed, The.
Hart, L. He Was Too Good to Me.
James, P. Can't We Be Friends?
Killeen, G. Rewind.
Klenner, J. Just Friends.
Koehler, T. Don't Worry 'Bout Me.
Tess's Torch Song (I Had a Man).
Lau, C. Zhoukoudian Bride's Harvest.
Lewis, S. Just Friends.
Lumsden, R. Yeah Yeah Yeah.
Martínez, V. Absence, Luminescent.
Porter, C. Just One of Those Things.
Rainger, R. Thanks for the Memory.
Ramke. Paul Verlaine at the Grave of Lucien Létinois.
Rees-Jones. And Please Do Not Presume.
Robin, L. Thanks for the Memory.
Rodgers, R. He Was Too Good to Me.
Rouse. Timing.
Segal, J. I Keep Going Back to Joe's.
Swift, K. Can't We Be Friends?
Teasdale. After Love.
Jewels.
Unknown. Scarborough Fair.
Warren, R. You Sort Old Letters.
Wilder, A. Who Can I Turn To?
Wilson, S. Recreational Mathematics.

Excavations
Phillips, D. Maridunum.
Rux, C. H. Excavation, The.
Unknown. Clementine.
Weston, M. Primitive Place.

Excrement
Bhatt. Muliebrity.
Brecht, B. Three Fragments.
Ciardi. Suburban.
Kumin, M. Excrement Poem, The.
Nathan, L. Bladder Song.
Ward, T. In the Interest of Possibility.
Weigl. Burning Shit at An Khe.

Executions and Executioners
Bruchac. Let the Midnight Special.
Burns, R. Hughie Graham.
Cable, G. Dirge of St. Malo, The.
Fairfax of Cameron. On the Fatal Day January

30, 1648.
Shortness of Life.
Frankau. Deserter, The.
Garlick, R. Anthem for Doomed Youth.
Greene, A. Four Roads, The.
Gunn, T. No Speech from the Scaffold.
Gwynn, R. Among Philistines.
Harington [*or* Harrington]. Tragicall Epigram, A.
Hecht, A. 'More Light! More Light!'
Housman, A. Carpenter's Son, The.
Eight O'Clock.
Kipling, R. Danny Deever.
Marinoni. At Sunrise.
Martínez, V. Children of the Disappeared.
McKendrick, J. Shortened History in Pictures, A.
Newbolt. He Fell among Thieves.
Patmore, C. London Fete, A.
Pau-Llosa. Paredón.
Peterson, R. San Quentin 1968.
Ralegh, S. Sir Walter Ra[u]le[i]gh to His Son[ne].
Ridge, L. Electrocution.
Smith, S. Death Sentence, The.
One of Many.
Swift, J. Clever Tom Clinch Going to Be Hanged.
Tekeyan. Sacred Wrath.
Tennyson, A. Rizpah.
Thorpe, R. Curfew Must Not Ring Tonight [*or* To-Night].
Tichborne [*or* Tichbourne]. Tichborne's Elegy.
Unknown. Croppy Boy, The.
Frankie and Johnny [*or* Johnnie *or* Albert].
John Hardy.
Mary [*or* Marie] Hamilton.
Mary Hamilton.
Night before Larry Was Stretched, The.
Queen's Marie, The.
Wat. Imagerie d'Epinal.
Weller. Midgiegooroo.
See also **Capital Punishment; Hanging**

Exercise
Rouse. Uni-Gym, The.
Swirszczynska. Troubles with the Soul at Morning Calisthenics.

Exhilaration
Browning, R. Now.

Exile
Abena, B. Exiles.
Aisenberg, N. Leaving Eden.
Alcott, L. Lay of a Golden Goose, The.
Auden. Exiles, The.
Back, R. Notes: From the Wait.
Bernard [*or* Bernart] de Ventadour [*or* Ventadorn]. Lark, The.
Bienek. Exodus.
Bly, R. Dream of Retarded Children, A.
Breeze. Riddym Ravings (The Mad Woman's Poem).
Brontë, E. Visionary, The.
Brooke, R. Old Vicarage, Grantchester, The.
Burns, R. Highland Harry Back Again.
My Heart's in the Highlands.
Castillo, S. Letter to Yeni on Peering into Her Life.
Primos.
Cheney-Coker. Road to Exile Thinking of Vallejo, The.
Cleary, B. Sealink.
Slouch.
Clover, J. El periférico, or Sleep.
Curnow. House and Land.
Dharker. Minority.
Diop, D. Renegade, The.
Dipoko. Exile.
Poem of Villeneuve St Georges, A.
Dowson. Exile.
Driver. Letter to Breyten Breytenbach from Hong Kong.
Duff, V. Letters from an Exile.
Duffy, C. Foreign.
Elmusa. Expatriates.
Fordham. Exile's Reverie, The.
Gilfillan, R. Exile's Song, The.

Griffith, L.   Exile: Welsh Service from Daventry.
Griffiths, J.   Emigrants.
  Migration.
Hamilton, S.   Farewell to France.
Healy, E.   From Los Angeles Looking South.
Hecht, A.   Alceste in the Wilderness.
Hemans.   Ancient Greek Song of Exile.
Hovanessian, D.   Exiles.
Hove.   Red Hills of Home.
Ingalls, J.   For the Intellectuals.
Jones, T.   Welshman in Exile Speaks, The.
Kipling, R.   Broken Men, The.
  St. Helena Lullaby, A.
Lazard.   Ordinance on Arrival.
Levertov.   Contraband.
Lovelace, R.   Another.
Martinez, D.   Altruism.
Mattawa.   Before.
McDonald, C.   Asdrubral Jiménez.
Medina, P.   Exile, The.
Millay, E.   Exiled.
Milosz, C.   My Faithful Mother Tongue.
Mphahlele.   Exile in Nigeria.
Nurkse.   Olmos.
Raine, K.   Written in Exile.
Ralegh, S.   Farewell to the Court.
Remoto.   Exile.
Robinson, E.   Aaron Stark.
Schiff, H.   German Frontier at Basel: 1942 and
  1992, The.
Shapiro, K.   Travelogue for Exiles.
Smith, I.   Exiles, The.
Solomon, M.   Comment on My Host, A.
Soyinka.   Massacre, October '66.
Stansbury, J.   To Cordelia.
Stewart, F.   Black Winter.
Suárez, V.   Song to the Banyan.
Tidjani-Cissé.   Home News.
Unknown.   Edward [or Edward, Edward].
  Exile of Erin, The.
  Songe bewailinge the tyme of Christmas, So
    much decayed in Englande, A.
Voigt.   Exile.
Walcott.   Hotel Normandie Pool, The.
Wat.   From "Songs of a Wanderer."
Watkins, V.   Returning to Goleufryn.
Woodcock.   Pacifists.

Existentialism and Existentialists
Hillman.   Black Series.
  Dark Existence.
Katz, J.   Imperfect Is Our Paradise, The.
Mattawa.   Before.
  Heartsong.
McNeil, R.   It Just Doesn't Matter.
Pietri.   7th Untitled Poem.
Roethke.   Duet.
Schwartz, R. L.   Why I Forgive My Younger
  Self Her Transgressions.
Talvikki, A.   My Shining Archipelago.
Thoreau.   All Things Are Current Found.
Tomlinson, C.   Juliet's Garden.
Williams, C.   Gas Station, The.

Exodus
Dunbar, P.   Ante-Bellum Sermon, An.
Moore, T.   Sound the Loud Timbrel.
Oppen.   Exodus.
Reznikoff.   Exodus.
Unknown.   Go Down, Moses.
  Let My People Go.

Experience
Anania.   On the Conditions of Place.
Blunden.   Report on Experience.
Brontë, E.   Why do I hate that lone green dell?
Bruce, D.   Plunder.
Chubb, R.   Song of My Soul.
Cohan.   I'm Mighty Glad I'm Living and That's
  All.
Coleridge, S.   Christabel.
  In the Touch of This Bosom There Worketh a
    Spell.
Crane, S.   Little Birds of the Night.
Cummings, E.   Since feeling is first.
Dunn, S.   Tenderness.
Ellington, D.   Sophisticated Lady.
Emerson, R.   Experience.
Empson.   Let It Go.

García, D.   Serpentine Voices.
Ginsberg, A.   II.
  Howl.
Hirshfield, J.   Lives of the Heart,The.
Hope, A.   Observation Car.
Hughes, L.   Esthete in Harlem.
Kerouac.   Poem.
Kipling, R.   Bonfires, The.
  Sestina of the Tramp-Royal.
Levertov.   In Mind.
Levine, P.   28.
MacLeish.   L'An Trentiesme de Mon Eage.
McHugh, H.   Night in a World, A.
Mills, I.   Sophisticated Lady.
Prescod.   Vicious Circle.
Ransom, J.   Blue Girls.
Rich, A.   Diving into the Wreck.
Richardson, J.   Vectors: Forty-five Aphorisms
  and Ten-second Essays.
Robinson, E.   Isaac and Archibald.
Rolle, S.   Keeping Watch.
Rosemurgy, C.   Angel Finally Admits What She
  Knows to Lou Binkler of Bethany, Missouri,
  An.
Seidman.   Gail.
Sitwell, D.   Green Song.
Sondheim.   I Never Do Anything Twice
  (Madam's Song).
  I'm Still Here.
Stern, G.   Royal Manor Road.
Van Duyn.   Moose in the Morning, Northern
  Maine.
Walcott.   Tomorrow, Tomorrow.
Wharton, E.   Experience.
Whitman, W.   When I Heard the Learn'd
  Astronomer.
Winner, R.   Segregated Railway Diner—1946.
Wordsworth, W.   World Is Too Much With Us,
  The.
Young, A.   Prestidigitator 1, The.

Exploring and Explorers
Atwood.   Explorers, The.
Bishop, J.   O Pioneers!
Booth, P.   Stefansson Island.
Curry.   Galapagos.
Donne.   Calm[e], The.
  Storm at Sea, A.
  Storm[e], The.
Drayton.   To the Virginian Voyage.
Falkner.   Arabia.
Fetherling.   Explorers as Seen by the Natives.
Frost, R.   America Is Hard to See.
Hinsey, E.   Planisféria, Map of the World,
  Lisbon, 1554.
Hoffman, D.   Exploration.
MacLeish.   Voyage West.
Marvell.   Bermudas.
Melville, H.   To Ned.
Merwin, W. S.   Gardens of Zuñi, The.
Miller, J.   Columbus.
Newlove.   Samuel Hearne in Wintertime.
Simpson, L.   To the Western World.
Stafford, W.   For the Grave of Daniel Boone.
Unknown.   Wonders.
Waniek.   Star-Fix.
Whitman, W.   Passage to India.

Explosions
Komunyakaa.   Fragging.
Larkin, P.   Explosion, The.
Pelizzon, V.   Feast of San Silvestro, The.

Exterminating and Exterminators
Browning, R.   Pied Piper of Hamelin, The.
Matthews, W.   Vermin.

Extinction
Blight.   Death of a Whale.
Buckmaster.   End to Myth, An.
Burnham, D.   Maintaining the Species.
Carroll, K.   Theory on Extinction or what
  happened to the dinosaurs?
Clayton, I.   Last Link, The.
Davis, J.   Aboriginal Australia.
  First-born, The.
Doolan, F.   Last Fullblood, The.
Dransfield.   Endsight.
Dunn, D.   St Kilda's Parliament: 1879–1979.
Hope, A.   Moschus Moschiferus.

Kendall, M.   Ballad of the Ichthyosaurus.
MacBeth [or Macbeth].   Bedtime Story.
Matthews, W.   Names.
Merwin, W. S.   For a Coming Extinction.
Oodgeroo of the tribe Noonuccal.   Gooboora,
  the Silent Pool.
  Last of His Tribe.
  We Are Going.
Porteous.   Charlie Douglas.
  Decommissioning.
Sandburg, C.   Buffalo Dusk.
Wells, L.   Sorcerer, The.

Extrasensory Perception
Wilbur.   Mind-Reader, The.

Extreme Unction
Dowson.   Extreme Unction.

Eyeglasses
Clark, T.   Eyeglasses.
Evans, D.   En Monocle.
Fanthorpe.   Relief of Myopia, The.

Eyes
Atwood.   You Fit into Me.
Benedikt.   Eye, The.
Birney.   Slug in Woods.
Bogan, L.   Medusa.
Bourdillon.   Night Has a Thousand Eyes, The.
Brontë, E.   God of Visions.
Clanchy, K.   Recognition.
Coulehan, J.   Man with a Hole in His Face, The.
Crashaw.   Weeper, The.
Curtis, L.   Only One Eye.
Donne.   Message, The.
Dowson.   Extreme Unction.
Dubin, A.   I Only Have Eyes for You.
Duncan, R.   Coming out of.
  Eyesight II.
Eliot, T.   Eyes That Last I Saw in Tears.
"Field."   Already to mine eyelids' shore.
  Dying Viper, A.
  La Gioconda; Leonardo Da Vinci, The Louvre.
Field, E.   Wynken, Blynken, and Nod.
Field, R.   Dancing Bear, The.
Gahagan.   Colour of the Old Man's Eyes, The.
Gilbert-Lecomte.   Wink.
González, R.   Perla at the Mexican Border
  Assembly Line of Dolls.
Greenlaw.   Millefiori.
Grenier.   Wrath to Sadness.
Haines, J.   Awakening.
Halpern, D.   Her Body.
Harburg.   Old Devil Moon.
Harwood, L.   Soft White.
Herrick.   Eye, The.
  Upon Her Eyes.
Holland, J.   Pulse.
Hopkins, G.   She Schools the Flighty Pupils of
  Her Eyes.
Hovanessian, D.   Inside Green Eyes, Black
  Eyes.
Hummell, A.   I Never Saw a Goddess Go.
Jackson, H.   Her Eyes.
Jonson, B.   Song: To Celia.
Joseph, A.   Chalazion.
Kandinsky [or Kandinskii].   Sounds.
Kaufman, B.   Would You Wear My Eyes?
Kendrick, D.   Note to the Ophthalmologist.
Kizer, C.   Through a Glass Eye, Lightly.
Knight, E.   He Sees Through Stone.
Knight, S.   Eyeball Works, The.
Knott.   Goodbye.
Lane, B.   Old Devil Moon.
Lowell, R.   Eye and Tooth.
MacCaig.   Instrument and Agent.
Magowan.   Susan.
Marvell.   Eyes and Tears.
Mercer, J.   Jeepers Creepers.
Merwin, W. S.   Diggers, The.
  Glass.
Meynell, A.   Cradle-Song at Twilight.
Montgomery, N.   Eyewash.
Nelson, M.   Shiner.
Olds, S.   Knowing, The.
Pack, R.   Thrasher in the Willow by the Lake,
  The.
Pfeiffer, E.   Any Husband to Many a Wife.
Porter, P.   Non Piangere, Liù.

Ransom, J.   Her Eyes.
Rosenblatt, S.   Visiting New York.
Rukeyser, M.   Eyes of Night-Time.
Salter.   Half a Double Sonnet.
Sandburg, C.   Under a Hat Rim.
Sansom, M.   To Cleon's Eyes.
Schafer.   Battle Lines.
Sedley.   To Cloris.
Siddal.   Lust of the Eyes, The.
Sondheim.   In Buddy's Eyes.
Stein, G.   I Am Rose.
  Suppose an Eyes.
Thomas, E.   Some Eyes Condemn.
Thompson, P.   Soft Black Eyes.
Tsaloumas.   Return of an Ikon.
Unknown.   Alexander's Song.
Ward, D.   Approximately.
Warren, H.   I Only Have Eyes for You.
  Jeepers Creepers.
Wordsworth, D.   Lake was covered all over,
  The.
Wylie.   Now That Your Eyes Are Shut.
Yeats.   Cat and the Moon, The.
  Drinking Song, A.

Ezra
Ammons, A. R.   So I Said I Am Ezra.

F

Faces
Blane, R.   That Face.
Bogan, L.   Song for the Last Act.
Bridges, R.   Eros.
Bringhurst.   Parśvanatha.
Brontë, A.   Fragment, A.
Campbell, J.   Old Woman, The.
Chin.   Altar.
Clare, J.   First Love.
Coulehan, J.   Man with a Hole in His Face, The.
Creeley.   Just Friends.
Dietz, H.   I See Your Face Before Me.
Dunn, S.   Criminal.
Eigner.   In Imitation.
"Field."   Elsewhere.
Fyleman.   (Mice).
Gallagher, T.   Not There.
Graves, R.   Face in the Mirror, The.
Hall, D.   Raisin, The.
Herrick.   Upon Mistresse Susanna Southwell,
  Her Cheeks.
Hughes, L.   125th Street.
  Chord.
Kay, J.   Pride.
Komunyakaa.   Facing It.
Kooser.   Self-Portrait at Thirty-Nine.
Lerner, A.   I've Grown Accustomed to Her
  Face.
Lewis, A.   Unknown Soldier, The.
Lindsay, C.   To My Own Face.
Liu, T.   Ikon.
Lorde.   From the House of Yemanjá.
Lovelace, R.   Another.
  Black Patch on Lucasta's Face, A.
  Scrutiny [*or* Scrutinie], The.
Marcus, B.   Plagiarism.
Martin, H.   That Face.
Mattawa.   History of My Face.
McPherson, S.   Ability to Make a Face Like a
  Spider While Singing Blues: Junior Wells, The.
Moore, M.   Face, A.
Patterson, R.   Sundown Blues.
Pinkerton, H.   On Dorothea Lange's Photograph
  "Migrant Mother" (1936).
Pound, E.   In a Station of the Metro.
Probyn.   Model, The.
Rodgers, C.   Poem No. 1.
Sandburg, C.   Halsted Street Car.
  Under a Hat Rim.
Schwartz, A.   I See Your Face Before Me.
Simon, L.   Nellie Gives into Blanche.
Smedley, M.   Face from the Past, A.
Sylvester, J.   Sweet Mouth, That Send'st a
  Musky-Rosed Breath.
Symons, A.   Maquillage.

Valentine, J.   After Elegies.
Vitale, M.   Become Your Face.
Webster, A.   By the Looking-Glass.
  Faded.
Wylie.   To a Lady's Countenance.
Yi, S.   Soyŏng Problems.
Zandvakili, K.   Love Letter.

Factories
Alexander, M.   Chicago.
Johnston, E.   Lines to Ellen, the Factory Girl.
Kelly, R.   Bittersweet Growing Up the Red
  Wall.
Knight, S.   Eyeball Works, The.
Lindsay, N.   Factory Windows Are Always
  Broken.
Longfellow, H.   Ropewalk, The.
Nicholson, N.   On the Closing of Millom
  Ironworks.
Shepherd, R.   What Cannot Be Kept.
Stein, K.   Night Shift, after Drinking Dinner,
  Container Corporation of America, 1972.
Unknown.   Factory Workers' Song.
Williams, W.   Classic Scene.

Failure
Altizer.   Sonnet 5: "No, I'll not, carrion, comfort
  you. Comfort."
Awad, J.   I Think Continually of Those Who
  Were Truly Failures.
Backus.   Then Laugh.
Bly, R.   August Rain.
Coleridge, H.   He Lived amidst th' Untrodden
  Ways.
Eady.   Hank Mobley's.
Finlay, I.   Great Frog Race.
Gilder, R.   Failure and Success.
Ginsberg, A.   Last Night in Calcutta.
Gioia.   Failure.
  Guide to the Other Gallery.
Giovanni.   Stars.
Glück, L.   Legend.
Gleason, K.   After Fighting for Hours.
Goode.   Failure.
Guillén, N.   Don't Know No English.
Gwynn, R.   Anacreontic.
Gylys, B.   Fat Chance.
Henry, B.   Discovery.
Hughes, T.   Crow's First Lesson.
Hunt, L.   Rondeau: "Jenny kissed [*or* kiss'd] me
  when we met."
James, C.   Book of My Enemy Has Been
  Remaindered, The.
Jonson, B.   Ode To Himself, An.
  Ode to Himself[e].
Kendall, M.   Failures.
Kooser.   Abandoned Farmhouse.
Lake, P.   Crime and Punishment.
Lowell, A.   Epitaph on a Young Poet Who Died
  before Having Achieved Success.
Masefield.   Consecration, A.
Miller, J.   For Those Who Fail.
Rafferty, P.   Back End.
Ray, H.   Failure.
Robinson, E.   Bewick Finzer.
  Clavering.
  Shadrach O'Leary.
Rossetti, C.   Symbols.
Rukeyser, M.   Paper Anniversary.
Sassoon.   Counter-Attack.
Silano, M.   In Henry Carlile's *Writing 213.*
Trowbridge, J.   Farmer John.
Unknown.   Never Say Fail.
Updike.   Player Piano.
Wilbur.   In the Smoking-Car.
Yeats.   To a Friend Whose Work Has Come to
  Nothing.
Zimmer.   Zimmer in Grade School.

Fairies
Allingham.   Fairies, The.
Bangs, J.   Little Elf, The.
Bishop, M.   How to Treat Elves.
Burgess, F.   Trapping Fairies.
Cary, A.   To Mother Fairie.
Cavendish, M.   Pastime of the Queen of Fairies,
  The.
Corbet [*or* Corbett].   Proper New Ballad Entitled
  [*or* Intituled] The Fairies' [*or* Faeryes]

Farewell, or God-a-Mercy Will, A.
Cox, P.   Brownies' Celebration, The.
Fyleman.   Goblin, The.
Graves, R.   I'd Love to Be a Fairy's Child.
  Lollocks.
Hardy, T.   On a Midsummer Eve.
Herrick.   Beggar to Mab, the Fairy [*or* Fairie]
  Queen, The.
  Fairy Temple; or, Oberon's Chapel, The.
  Oberon's Feast.
  Oberon's Palace.
  Temple, The.
Housman, A.   Fairies Break Their Dances, The.
Keats.   La Belle Dame sans Merci [A Ballad].
Lowell, J.   Hob Gobbling's Song.
More, H.   Inscription in a Beautiful Retreat
  Called Fairy Bower.
Morley, C.   Plumppuppets, The.
Morse, C.   Dream of the Artfairy.
Moultrie.   Fairy Maimounè, The.
Peake.   O here it is! And there it is!
Poe.   Fairyland [*or* Fairy-Land].
Ray, H.   On a Nook Called Fairyland.
Riley, J.   Little Orphant Annie.
Rumaker.   Fairies Are Dancing All Over the
  World, The.
Shakespeare, W.   Asleep, My Love?
  Bottom's Song.
  Fairies' Lullaby, The.
  Flower of This Purple Dye.
  Now the Hungry Lion.
  Through the Forest Have I Gone.
  Through the House.
  Up and Down.
  Yet but Three?
Smedley, M.   Irish Fairy, The.
Taylor, J.   Fairies' Song, The.
Unknown.   Thomas the Rhymer.
  Wee Wee Man, The.
Wright, J.   Evening.
Yeats.   Stolen Child, The.
See also **Elves; Goblins**

Fairs
Clarke, A.   Fair at Windgap, The.
Gardinier.   Agricultural Show, Flemington,
  Victoria, The.
Gay, J.   Two Monkeys, The.
Hardy, T.   After the Fair.
  Ballad-Singer, The.
  Former Beauties.
MacDiarmid, H.   Cattle Show.
Stevens, G.   Bartleme Fair.
Thackeray.   Mr. Molony's Account of the
  Crystal Palace.
Williams, P.   Rhapsody on Main Street.
Williams, W.   Dance, The.
Winchilsea.   Hog, the Sheep and Goat, Carrying
  to a Fair, The.

Fairy Tales
Aguilar-Cariño.   Gabi.
Ashbery.   Märchenbilder.
Bennett, B.   True Story of Snow White, The.
Cooley, N.   Family History, The.
Dacey, P.   Jack, Afterwards.
Galvin, J.   Independence Day, 1956: A Fairy
  Tale.
Glück, L.   Gretel in Darkness.
Graves, R.   To Juan at the Winter Solstice.
Jarrell.   House in the Wood, The.
  Märchen, The.
Machan.   Hazel Tells LaVerne.
Marshall, R.   Little Brown Jacks Nyimbung.
Nesbit, E.   Goose-Girl, The.
Posamentier, E.   Bird Named Isidore, The.
Smith, S.   Fairy Story.
  Frog Prince, The.
Unknown, fr. Terezin Concentration Camp.
  Forgotten.

Fairyland
Alexander, C.   Dreams.
More, H.   Inscription in a Beautiful Retreat
  Called Fairy Bower.

Faith
Aaronson.   Homeward Journey, The.
Arnold, M.   Dover Beach.

Rugby Chapel.
Askew, A.　Ballad Which Anne Askew Made and Sang When She Was in Newgate, The.
Bangs, J.　Blind.
Ben-Lev, D.　Sensualist Speaks on Faith, A.
Berman, C.　Mother Lakshmi's Poem.
Bible, Apocrypha.　Jeremie .17.
Blake, W.　Mock On, Mock On, Voltaire, Rousseau.
Bonar.　Thy Way, Not Mine.
Brontë, A.　Doubter's Prayer, The.
Brontë, E.　No Coward Soul is Mine.
Visionary, The.
Brooke, R.　Heaven.
Bryant, W.　To a Waterfowl.
Byrom.　My Spirit Longeth for Thee.
Cane.　Tree in December.
Cary, A.　My Creed.
Chesterton, G.　Convert, The.
Clark, T.　Faith for Tomorrow.
Coleridge, S.　Hexameters[; Paraphrase of Psalm XLVI].
Coverdale.　Song of the Virgin Mary, The.
Cowper, W.　Contentment.
Ephraim Repenting.
Exhortation to Prayer.
Future Peace and Glory of the Church, The.
House of Prayer, The.
Hymn: "Jesus, where'er thy people meet."
Jehovah Our Righteousness.
Joy and Peace in Believing.
Light Shining out of Darkness.
Lord Will Happiness Divine, The.
Love Constraining to Obedience.
Lovest Thou Me?
My Soul Thirsteth for God.
Old-Testament Gospel.
Praise for the Fountain Opened.
Retirement.
Sardis.
Self-Acquaintance.
Sower, The.
Walking with God.
Wisdom.
Crane, H.　Recitative.
Creeley.　En Famille.
Crowell, G.　Courage to Live.
I Think That God is Proud.
Crunk, T.　Visiting the Site of One of the First Churches My Grandfather Pastored.
Cummings, E.　I Thank You God.
Dharker.　Living Space.
Dickinson, E.　I Never Lost as Much.
This World Is Not Conclusion.
Dobell, S.　Liberty to M. le Diplomate.
Donne.　To Mr. Roland Woodward.
Dowland.　Dear, If You Change.
Drayton.　Other Song of the Faithful, for the Mercies of God, An.
Song of the Faithful, A.
Dunbar, P.　Resignation.
Slow Through the Dark.
Dunn, S.　Guardian Angel, The.
Emerson, R.　Character.
Problem, The.
Worship.
Fenton, J.　God, A Poem.
Fields, J.　Ballad of the Tempest.
Floyd.　Corporal Kevin Spina, U. S. M. C.
Flynn, N.　Emptying Town.
Frost, R.　Sitting by a Bush in Broad Daylight.
Gale, N.　Country Faith, The.
Gilbert, C.　Directions, The.
Glück, L.　Celestial Music.
Greenlaw.　Earliest Known Representation of a Storm in Western Art, The.
Guiney.　Wild Ride, The.
Hall, J.　Praise of Faith, The.
Hardy, T.　Impercipient, The.
Harris, R.　Isaiah by Kerosene Lantern Light.
Hartnett.　There Will Be a Talking.
Herbert, G.　Affliction: "Kill me not every [or ev'ry] day."
Affliction (1).
Artillery [or Artillerie].
Bag, The.

Banquet, The.
Bitter-Sweet.
Church-Floor[e], The.
Collar, The.
Complaining.
Discipline.
Divinity.
Elixir [or Elixer], The.
Employment (1).
Flower, The.
Forerunners, The.
Glance, The.
Grace.
Holy Baptism (2).
Love.
Love (1).
Peace.
Pearl, The. Matth. 13:45.
Pilgrimage, The.
Quidditie [or Quiddity], The.
Search, The.
Sepulchre.
Sin (1).
Sonnet: "My God, where is that ancient heat towards Thee."
Superliminare.
Temper (1), The.
Temper (2), The.
Thanksgiving, The.
Windows, The.
Herrick.　His Creed.
His Litany to the Holy Spirit.
Hirsch, E.　For the Sleepwalkers.
Holmes, O.　Our Limitations.
Hopkins, G.　Carrion Comfort.
God's Grandeur.
Howard, R.　Vocational Guidance, with Special Reference to the Annunciation of Simone Martini.
Howe, S.　Silence Wager Stories.
Hunt, L.　Abou Ben Adhem.
Faith, Hope, and Charity Are the Prospects of Manhood.
Jeffers, R.　Credo.
Johnson, F.　Song of the Whirlwind.
Keats.　O Thou Whose Face Hath Felt the Winter's Wind.
Keble.　See Lucifer Like Lightning Fall.
Kemble.　Faith.
Kipling, R.　Recessional.
Knevet.　Harp, The.
Komunyakaa.　Instructions for Building Straw Huts.
Kumin, M.　Getting the Message.
Landon.　Bonds of Affection.
Lawrence, D.　Hills, The.
Levine, P.　28.
Lim-Wilson.　Raising the Dead.
Locke, A.　Sin and Despair Have So Possess'd My Heart.
Longfellow, H.　Bells of San Blas, The.
Lowell, J.　After the Burial.
In a Copy of Omar Khayyám.
Lowell, R.　As a Plane Tree by the Water.
Malone, W.　Opportunity.
McAuley, J.　In the Twentieth Century.
McKay, C.　Pagan Isms, The.
Melville, H.　Conflict of Convictions, The.
Swamp Angel, The.
Milton.　On His Blindness.
On Time.
More, H.　Patient Joe; or, The Newcastle Collier.
More, S.　Prayer, A.
Murray, A.　There Has Been More Than Beginning and End to Face.
Murray, P.　Canticle of the Void, The.
Newman, J.　Pillar of the Cloud, The.
Newton, J.　Amazing Grace.
Noll.　Abraham's Madness.
Palmer, R.　My Faith Looks Up to Thee.
Parker, A.　Above the Timberline.
Pfeiffer, E.　Any Husband to Many a Wife.
Powers, J.　Garments of God, The.
Procter, A.　Incompleteness.
Strive, Wait, and Pray.
Ralegh, S.　Even Such Is Time.

Ray, H.　Triple Benison, The.
Reichard, W.　Cloud Game, The.
Robinson, E.　Children of the Night, The.
Christmas Sonnet, A.
Credo.
Rossetti, C.　Somewhere or Other.
Rossetti, D.　"Retro Me, Sathana."
Rowbotham.　Nebuchadnezzar's Kingdom-Come.
Rowe, E.　Hymn: "In vain the dusky night retires."
Ryan, T.　Spin.
Sangster, M.　Prayer for Faith, A.
Sexton.　Small Wire.
"Shu Ting."　Fairy Tales.
Sigourney.　Poetry.
Smith, P.　Annie Pearl Smith Discovers Moonlight.
Smith, S.　Dream of Comparison, A.
God the Eater.
Stevenson, R.　Evensong.
Stradling.　Abraham's Sacrifice of Isaac.
Tabb.　Sisters, The.
Tenebræ.
"Tanaquil."　Very Young Man Speaks, A.
Taylor, E.　Meditation Eight.
Thomas, L.　Electricity of Blossoms.
Thomas, R.　In a Country Church.
Island, The.
Thompson, F.　Hound of Heaven, The.
Traherne.　Innocence.
Tuckerman, F.　As Sometimes in a Grove.
Sonnets: First Series.
Unknown.　Angels in the House, The.
Faith.
God and Yet a Man, A?
I Believe.
Lonesome Valley.
Shema Yisrael.
Van Dyke.　Four Things.
Vaughan, H.　Retreat[e], The.
Very.　Nature.
Night.
Rock, The.
Slavery.
Slowness of Belief in a Spiritual World, The.
Vitale, M.　Three Written Poems, Unconnected.
Wallace-Crabbe.　Secular, The.
Warton, T.　On the Spirit Adulterated by the Flesh.
Watts, I.　Incomprehensible, The.
Wesley, C.　Come on, my partners in distress.
Wesley, J.　Hymn: "Thou hidden love of God, whose height."
Whitehead, C.　Daybreak.
Wilcox, E.　Faith.
Nothing New.
Willard, E.　Rocked in the Cradle of the Deep.
Winters, Y.　Precision, The.
Wyatt, S.　Farewell: "What should I say."
Steadfastness.

Faith Healers
García, D.　Curandera, La.
Larkin, P.　Faith Healing.

Falcons
Cording.　Peregrine Falcon, New York City.
Duncan, A.　My Mother Would Be a Falconress.
Hopkins, G.　Windhover, The.
Inez.　Monologue of the Falconer's Wife.
Lovelace, R.　Lady with a Falcon on Her Fist, A.
Read, S.　Falcon and the Dove, The.
Rossetti, C.　Noble Sisters.
Sutter.　Peregrine.
Unknown.　Lover Compareth Himself to the Painful Falconer, The.
Villon.　Ballad Written for a Bridegroom.
Wyatt, S.　Lux, My Faire Falcon.
Yenser, S.　Another Lo-Cal Elegy.

Falkland, Lucius Cary, Viscount
Conway, H.　Falkland at Newbury, 1643.

Fall
Ammons, A. R.　Improvisation for the Stately Dwelling, An.
Crapsey.　November Night.
See also **Autumn**

Falling
Anania. Fall, The.
Berlin. I Got Lost in His Arms.
Cherry, K. Pines Without Peer, The.
Curbelo. Bedtime Stories.
Davis, T. Boppin' is Safer than Grindin'
Dickinson, E. It Dropped So Low in My
   Regard.
Grigson. Before a Fall.
Hayes, T. Goliath Poem.
Hooks. Body Inside the Soul, The.
Jacobsen, J. Primer, The.
Kimbrell, J. True Descenders.
Kinsella, J. Fall, The.
Martinez, D. Discreet Prayer, A.
O'Malley, M. Shoeing the Currach.
Palmer, M. Theory of the Flower, The.
Rózewicz. Homework Assignment on the
   Subject of Angels.
Sewell, L. Denied, The.
Sharma, P. Transit.
Unknown. Haida Cradle-Song.

Fame
Berlin. There's No Business Like Show
   Business.
Bradstreet, A. In Honour of that High and
   Mighty Princess Queen Elizabeth of Happy
   Memory.
Brontë, E. Stanzas to———.
Byron, G. Stanzas Written on the Road between
   Florence and Pisa.
Chudleigh. Resolve, The.
Coleridge, S. Epitaph: "Stop, Christian passer-
   by!—Stop, child of God."
Cooper, D. In New York.
   In School.
Coward. Mad About the Boy.
Cowley, A. Motto, The.
Davies, I. Consider Famous Men, Dai Bach.
De Tabley. Sonnet: "Record is nothing, and the
   hero great."
Dickinson, E. Aurora.
Dietz, H. Rhode Island Is Famous for You.
Finnell. Over *Voice of America.*
Fisher, R. Paraphrases.
Fitzgerald, E. 13.
Frost, R. Provide, Provide.
Greenhalgh, C. Night I Met Marilyn, The.
Heard, J. Fame.
Hemans. Woman and Fame.
Herrick. Fame.
   Fame Makes Us Forward.
   Pillar of Fame, The.
   To His Book[e].
Jewsbury. Summer Eve's Vision, A.
Jones, M. Epistle to Lady Bowyer, An.
Jonson, B. To Sir Henry Cary.
Keats. Addressed to Haydon.
   Great Spirits Now on Earth.
   To Kosciusko.
   When I Have Fears [That I May Cease to Be].
Kemble. Sonnet: "Thou poisonous laurel leaf,
   that in the soil."
   Wish, A.
Killigrew, A. Upon the Saying That My Verses
   Were Made by Another.
Kinsella, J. Warhol at Wetlands.
Kizer, C. Ashes, The.
Lazarus, E. Success.
Lihn. Favorite Little Shrine, A.
Lindsay, C. Love or Fame.
Lowell, J. In an Album.
   Sonnet.
Lowry, M. After Publication of Under the
   Volcano.
Macgillivray. Return, The.
McClure, M. Mad Sonnet: Fame.
Mew. Fame.
Milton. On Shakespear[e].
Nathan, L. So?
Norton, C. Picture of Sappho, The.
Nye, N. Art of Disappearing, The.
   Famous.
Owen, W. To My Friend (With an Identity
   Disc).
Parkes, B. To an Author who Loved Truth

More than Fame.
Pettit. Vanna White's Bread Pudding.
Pietri. Intermission from Sunday.
Rich, A. Focus.
Robinson, E. Three Quatrains.
Robinson, M. [Sonnet] Conclusive.
   Sonnet Introductory.
Sandburg, C. Soup.
Schwartz, A. Rhode Island Is Famous for You.
Shelley, P. Ozymandias.
Simms, W. Glory and Enduring Fame.
Troupe. Poem for "Magic," A.
Updike. Newlyweds, The.
Waller, E. At Penshurst [Another].
Whalen. International Date Line, Monday/
   Monday 27: XI:67.
Whitman, W. When I Heard at the Close of the
   Day.
Wyatt, S. Stand Whoso List.
See also **Greatness**

Family
Abinader, E. Making It New.
Ai. Blue Suede Shoes.
Alexander, E. Who I Think You Are.
Ali, A. Cracked Portraits.
   Return to Harmony 3.
Anderson, A. Suicide Year, The.
Arrillaga. Dream.
   Like Raquel.
Barresi. How It Comes.
   Vacation, 1969.
Becker, R. Dreaming at the Rexall Drug.
Bensko. Bones of Lazarus.
   Last Look in the Sambre Canal, A.
Bernstein, C. Memories.
Berryman. Henry's Fate.
Bishop, E. Poem: "About the size of an old-
   style dollar bill."
Blaeser. Rituals, Yours—and Mine.
Bobrowski. Latvian Songs.
Brant, B. Stillborn Night.
Broumas, O. Landscape with Next of Kin.
Brown, E. Out.
Buckley, V. Origins.
Burkard. Breathless Storm.
   Weather.
Burns, R. Memory.
Bursk. Lies.
Campo. S. W.
Carbó, N. Verso Libre.
Carson, C. Dresden.
Castillo, S. Monday Night at Pedro's.
   Primos.
Caston, A. Blowing Eggs.
Cerenio. Family Photos: Black and White:
   1960.
Chin. How I Got That Name.
Chrystos. Old Indian Granny, The.
Clark Bekederemo. Abiku.
   Death of a Lady.
   Family Procession, A.
   Order of the Dead, The.
Clover, J. Family Romance.
Cofer, J. They Never Grew Old.
Cook, E. Written at the Couch of a Dying
   Parent.
Cooley, N. Family History, The.
Cooper, D. In New York.
   In School.
Copus, J. Back Seat of My Mother's Car, The.
"Cornwall." To My Child.
Couzyn. Transformation.
Creeley. En Famille.
   Won't It Be Fine?
Crunk, T. Leaving.
   Visiting the Site of One of the First Churches
   My Grandfather Pastored.
Cuthand, B. Dancing with Rex.
Dacey, P. Drummer, The.
Dalton, A. Dad-Baby, The.
Davidson, D. Sanctuary.
Davies, I. Visitor's Book, 9, The.
De Vries, R. On Alabama Ave., Paterson, NJ,
   1954.
Dean, D. K. In the Way Back.
Deane, S. Fording the River.

DeCormier-Shekejian. Snow.
Delgado, J. Flora's Plea to Mary.
Dobbie. Forty Three Years After Hitler My
   Parents Visit Eugene.
Dooley, M. Dancing at Oakmead Road.
Dove, R. Fifth Grade Autobiography.
Drummond de Andrade. Motionless Faces.
Dugan, A. Nomenclature.
Durcan. Wife Who Smashed Television Gets
   Jail.
E'der, E. La Puente.
El-Hadi, S. Drama, The.
Ennis. Drink of Spring, A.
Essbaum, J. When the Kingdom Comes.
Eversley. Just to Be Needed.
Fay, J. Flowers.
Ferré. Message.
Firer. 1956, The Year My Sister, Using Her Ill
   Health Once Again, Blackmailed My Parents
   into an Accordion.
Fish, C. Work and Worry.
Fitzpatrick, K. Highland, 1955.
Florsheim. Weekend in Palm Springs.
Forhan, C. Taste of Wild Cherry, The.
Forman, R. Abraham Got All the Stars N the
   Sand.
Gewanter, D. Xenia: Stranger/Guest.
Gillilan, P. Mistress, The.
Gomez, M. Lost Daughter.
Gonzalez, N. How the Heart Aches.
Goodman, M. Upkeep.
Gotera. Pacific Crossing.
Groarke, V. Family Photograph, The.
   History of My Father's House, The.
Gylys, B. Family Reunion—Aunt Vern's Two
   Cents.
Hagedorn, J. Smokey's Getting Old.
Hahn, K. Hula Skirt, 1959, The.
Hai-Jew, S. Three Gypsies.
Hall, D. X.
Hannan, M. Coming Down from Derry Hill.
Harchik. Requiem: "Your names ring clearly."
Hardy, T. During Wind and Rain.
Harms. Sky.
Hart, J. Only Applebaum Can Make a Tree.
Hawkesworth, P. Two Statues.
Hawkins, R. Issei Men: The First Generation.
   Nisei Daughter: The Second Generation.
   Sansei: The Third Generation.
Hawoldar. You.
Hayden, R. Beginnings.
Heaney, S. Funeral Rites.
Herrera. Portrait of Woman in Long Black
   Dress / Aurelia.
Hewitt, J. From a Museum Man's Album.
Hippolyte. So Jah Sey.
Hogan, L. Heritage.
Hongo. Hilo: First Night Back.
Hopkins, G. Epithalamion: "Hark, hearer, hear
   what I do; lend a thought now, make believe."
Hovanessian, D. Two Voices.
Huddle. Cousin.
Hudgins. Telling, The.
Johnson, M. F. Idiot Girl, The.
Jones, S. New World.
Jones, T. Llanafan Unrevisited.
Jordan, J. Female and the Silence of a Man,
   The.
   Through These Halls.
Joseph, A. My Father's Heroes.
   Numbers.
Kaplinski, J. My Wife and Children.
Kasdorf. Grossdaadi's Funeral.
Kay, J. English Cousin Comes to Scotland.
Kayo. Song of the Initiate.
Kenyon, J. From Room to Room.
Kessler, S. Family Secrets.
   Names the Dead Speak.
Kim, A. Sewing Woman.
Kinzie. Boy.
Knight, E. My Uncle Is My Honor and a Guest
   in My House.
Koch, K. You Were Wearing.
Kollar. Late Arrivals.
Kumin, M. For My Great-Grandfather: A
   Message Long Overdue.

Retrieval System, The.
Kunitz, S. Quinnapoxet.
Kushner, D. Grandma in the Shower.
Larkin, P. Ambulances.
Lee, L. Eating Together.
  Persimmons.
Lee, S. Letter from Turtle Beach.
Levi, S. Abbienti.
Levin, D. Wind.
Lilley. Sewing Lesson, The.
Lim, S. Visting Malacca.
Lim-Wilson. Wave, The.
Lisella. Song of the Third Generation.
Liu, T. Kindertotenlieder.
Livingston, M. Coming from Kansas.
  Invitation.
Lomax, M. Amor Diving.
Lopez, L. Tomás.
Ludvigson. Inventing My Parents.
Lum. Picture of my Mother's Family, A.
Maroon, B. Neighbor.
Matherne, B. La Fabrique de Tabac (Tobacco
  Harvest).
  Les Fils (Sons).
Mathews, A. Letter Following.
Mayne, S. Zalman.
McGinley. Giveaway, The.
McGrath, C. Delphos, Ohio.
  First Trimester, The.
McGuckian. Lychees.
Melville, H. Fragments of a Lost Gnostic Poem
  of the Twelfth [or 12th] Century.
Merwin, W. S. Ballad of John Cable and Three
  Gentlemen.
Michelson, R. Jews That We Are, The.
Miles, J. Belief.
Miller, E. My Father's Girlfriend.
Million, D. Housing Poem, The.
Mills, B. Ballad: Of Motion.
Montague, J. At Last.
Moolten, D. Bio 7.
Moore, L. Haiku.
Morgan, J. My Welsh Home.
Muir, E. Scotland 1941.
Murray, L. Cotton Flannelette.
Myles, E. American Poem, An.
Nepo. Oil of Her Hands, The.
Neufeld, A. Family Album.
  Pictures and Stories.
Nicholson, N. Epithalamium for a Niece.
Niedecker. Paean to Place.
Noguchi, R. Breath He Holds, The.
  I, the Neighbor Mr. Uskovich, Watch Every
    Morning Kenji Takezo Hold His Breath.
Nye, N. For Lost and Found Brothers.
O'Brien, L. Diabolus in Musica.
O'Loughlin. Glasnevin Cemetery.
Olds, S. Clasp, The.
Ondaatje. Light.
Orfalea, G. Gift You Must Lose, A.
Orton, B. Beekeeper.
Parker, P. Prologue from "Legacy."
Paschen. Two Standards.
Peck, J. Woods Burial.
Penn, M. Calling Up the Spirit of the Lost
  Child.
Philp, G. Heirlooms.
Piercy. My Rich Uncle, Whom I Only Met
  Three Times.
Pilling. Specimen.
Porter, A. Five Wishes.
Posamentier, E. Being Modern in Jerusalem.
Powell, K. For Aunt Cathy.
Propp, K. Train Passage.
Ramanujan. In the Zoo.
Reti, I. I Never Knew I Was Jewish.
Rich, A. Letters in the Family.
Richman, L. To Valenton: Impressions circa
  1947.
Ridl. Video Mama.
Roberts, L. My Father's Whistle.
Rodrigues J. P. Half-.
Rogers, P. Family Is All There Is, The.
Rosenblatt, S. Leaving Home.
Rossetti, C. Gone Before.
Rungano. Labour.

Rybicki, J. This Sun.
Saffoti. Espresso.
Savageau. At the Powwow.
  Like the Trails of Ndakinna.
  Looking for Indians.
  Trees.
Scamell, B. My Lost Brother.
Scammell, W. Poem for a Younger Son.
Scott, D. Illness.
Seto, T. Blood Ties.
Seward. On a Lock of Miss Sarah Seward's
  Hair Who Died in her Twentieth Year.
Sexton. All My Pretty Ones.
Shapcott, T. Turning Fifty.
Sheehan, M. My Father's Singing.
Shepherd, R. Difficult Music, The.
Smith, S. Tenuous and Precarious.
Song. Spaces We Leave Empty.
Soto. Braly Street.
Speak, M. Ingredients of Glass.
Stafford, W. One Home.
Stead, C. Between.
Stevenson, A. Arioso Dolente.
Stone, J. Talking to the Family.
Strickland, A. Infant, The.
Suárez, V. Cuban-American Gothic.
  Song for the Sugar Cane.
Sugioka. Legacy.
Tapahonso. I Am Singing Now.
Tate, J. Land of Little Sticks, 1945.
  My Great Great Etc. Uncle Patrick Henry.
Tidjani-Cissé. Home News.
Townsend, A. First Death.
Tran, B. From Rosary.
Tremblay, B. Home Front.
Tucker, M. We Met.
Ullman. Why There Are Children.
Unknown. On Prince Frederick.
Vazirani, R. Daughter-Mother-Maya-Seeta.
  Mrs. Biswas Breaks Her Connection with
    Another Relative.
Vertreace, M. Black Tulips.
Walcott. Glory Trumpeter, The.
Waniek, M. Porter.
Warren, R. Ballad of Billie Potts, The.
Watkins, V. Returning to Goleufryn.
Wayman. Teething.
Weller. Ngungalari.
  Story of Frankie . . . My Man, The.
Wickham. Letter to a Boy at School.
Winder. On Fourteen Maple Street.
Wong, N. Picnic.
Wright, J. Willy Lyons.
Yamada. American Son.
Zarco. Manila Paper.

Family Life
Barrax. Domestic Tranquility.
Berlin. Supper Time.
Brissenden. Verandahs.
Cervantes. Beneath the Shadow of the Freeway.
Clifton, L. Good Times.
Courtney. Be Kind.
Creeley. Gift of Great Value, A.
Di Prima. Poem in Praise of My Husband
  (Taos).
Dove, R. Daystar.
Eshleman, C. Deeds Done and Suffered by
  Light.
Foley, M. Provincial Adolescence, A.
Forman, R. Abraham Got All the Stars N the
  Sand.
Gildner. House on Buder Street, The.
  Nails.
Giovanni. Nikki-Rosa.
Hands, E. On an Unsociable Family.
Hartnett. Small Farm, A.
Harwood, G. In The Park.
Hass, R. Concerning the Afterlife, the Indians
  of Central California Had Only the Dimmest
  Notions.
Song: "Afternoon cooking in the fall sun."
Hayden, R. Those Winter Sundays.
Hogan, L. Heritage.
Hughes, L. Piggy-back.
Jenkins, C. Sunday Morning.
Joseph, L. Sand Nigger.

Kaufman, S. Mothers, Daughters.
Knight, E. Idea of Ancestry, The.
Kunitz, S. Three Floors.
Lopez, T. No Transport.
Lowell, R. My Last Afternoon with Uncle
  Devereux Winslow.
McCarriston. To Judge Faolain, Dead Long
  Enough: A Summons.
McElroy, C. Looking for a Country under Its
  Original Name.
Meltzer, D. Eyes, the Blood, The.
Moss, H. Long Island Springs.
Muldoon, P. Mixed Marriage, The.
Mura. Nisei Picnic: From an Album, A.
Nash, O. Family Court.
O'Hara, F. Ave Maria.
Pastan. Passover.
Peacock, M. Those Paperweights with Snow
  Inside.
Peeradina, S. Sisters.
Rich, A. In the Wake of Home.
Riley, J. King of Oo-Rinktum-Jing, The.
Rilke. From a Childhood.
Roberts, L. Assignment, The.
Roethke. My Papa's Waltz.
Salter. Frost at Midnight.
Sandburg, C. Population Drifts.
Sexton. Funnel.
Simpson, L. My Father in the Night
  Commanding No.
Smith, S. Emily Writes Such a Good Letter.
Stafford, W. Rescued Year, The.
Storey. Prayer for Broken Little Families, A.
Thibaudeau. Brown Family, The.
  Green Family, The.
Tsui. Chinese Banquet, A.
Weaver, M. Picnic, an Homage to Civil Rights,
  The.
Williams, C. Sanctity, The.
Wright, E. When Father Carves the Duck.
Wright, K. Victorian Family Photograph.

Famine
Achebe. Christmas in Biafra (1969).
Binyon. Hunger.
Citino. Famine.
Clark Bekedermo. New from Ethiopia and the
  Sudan, The.
Knoepfle. Skibbereen the Famine Pit.
Longley, J. Famine's End.
Melhem, D. To an Ethiopian Child.
Mortál, A. Cork Examiner, December 4, 1846:
  More Starvation, The.
Rankin, R. Tourists, Potatoes, and Genocide.
Ryan, R. Father of Famine.
Wickham. Nursery Song.

Fancy
Burns, R. Mary Morison.
Smith, C. To Fancy.
See also **Imagination**

Fans
Boland, E. Black Lace Fan My Mother Gave
  Me, The.
Brandling. To a Lady, with a Present of a Fan.
Gerstler. Fan Letter, A.
Lovelace, R. Lucasta's Fan[ne], with a
  Looking-Glass[e] in It.
Momaday. Eagle-Feather Fan, The.
Pound, E. Fan-Piece, for Her Imperial Lord.
Probyn. Tête-à-Tête.

Fantasies
Arnold, M. Longing.
Barlow, G. Dream of the Ring: The Great Jack
  Johnson, A.
Boyd, M. Fra Bank to Bank, Fra Wood to
  Wood I Rin.
Browning, E. Romance of the Swan's Nest,
  The.
Chase, N. My Ideal.
Coleridge, S. Frost at Midnight.
Cooper, D. David Cassidy Then.
Doolittle, H. At Baia.
Dove, R. Adolescence—III.
Duhamel. I'm Dealing with My Pain.
Elledge. Duckling, Swan.
"Field." And on My Eyes Dark Sleep by Night.
Harms. Los Angeles, The Angels.

Hart, L. Dancing on the Ceiling.
Henry, B. Skin.
Jacob, M. Spanish Generosity.
Jarrell. Seele im Raum.
Kunene. Thought on June 26.
Mitchell, A. Celia Celia.
Naden. Love's Mirror.
Padgett, R. Symbols of Transformation.
Pound, E. Dance Figure.
Prescod. Women Are Different.
Ragan, J. Child Christ at the Top of the Stairs.
Robin, L. My Ideal.
Rodgers, R. Dancing on the Ceiling.
Rossetti, C. Echo.
In An Artist's Studio.
Rukeyser, M. Along History.
Sarton. Nursery Rhyme.
Spivack, K. Love U.S.A.
Steptoe. Window Shopping.
Stevenson, A. Sous-Entendu.
Suckling, S. Upon My Lady Carlisle's Walking in Hampton Court Garden.
Unknown. Pitman's Lovesong, A.
She Lay All Naked.
Weems, M. B.B. Blues.
Whiting, R. My Ideal.
Wilbur. Baroque Wall-Fountain in the Villa Sciarra, A.
Williams, W. Good Night.
Winter, M. Space Parable.
Wong, N. On Thinking of Photographing My Fantasies.
Woo, M. Untitled: "In the deepest night and a full moon."
Wylie. Puritan Sonnet, IV.
Wild Peaches.

Farewell
Alexander, E. Farewell to You.
Beaver. Folk Song: "O I'm off to Hullaboola where the climate's never cooler."
Clare, J. Farewell: "Farewell to the bushy clump close to the river."
Cohan. So Long, Mary.
Cushing, J. Every Time We Say Goodbye.
Donne. Expiration, The.
Dryden, J. To the Memory of Mr Oldham.
Elizabeth I. On Monsieur's Departure.
"Ephelia." First Farewell to J.G G.
Etter. Riding the Rock Island Through Kansas.
Ezekiel. Goodbye Party for Miss Pushpa T. S.
Fairburn. Farewell, A: "What is there left to be said?"
Gay, J. Sweet William's Farewell to Black-Eyed [or Black-Ey'd] Susan.
Gonzalez, N. Wanderer in the Night of the World, A.
Harling, W. Beyond the Blue Horizon.
Hemans. Parting Song, A.
Herrick. His Tears to Thamesis [or Thamasis].
To Dianeme.
To His Peculiar Friend Master Thomas Shapcott, Lawyer.
Hesketh. Love's Advocate.
Hogg, J. When Maggy Gangs Away.
Holmes, J. Good Night! Good Night!
Jewsbury. Farewell to the Muse, A.
Kemble. Farewell to Italy.
To Mrs. Norton.
Kipling, R. King, The.
Knight, E. Cell Song.
Landon. Farewell, The.
Song.
Lili'u-o-ka-lani. Aloha'oe.
Moore, H. Poem for the End.
Naden. Sister of Mercy, The.
Osgood, F. He Bade Me Be Happy.
Paschen. Litany.
Pope, A. Farewell to London in the Year 1715, A.
Porter, C. Get Out of Town.
Just One of Those Things.
Praed. Goodnight to the Season!
Procter, A. Woman's Last Word, A.
Ralegh, S. Farewell to False Love, A.
Farewell to the Court.
Robin, L. Beyond the Blue Horizon.

Sidney, S. Leave Me O Love.
Singer, B. Corner Boy's Farewell.
Stevens, W. Farewell to Florida.
Waving Adieu, Adieu, Adieu.
Suckling, S. Farewell to Love.
Swenson, M. Goodbye, Goldeneye.
Walcott. Adios, Carenage.
Schooner Flight, The.
Walker, A. Good Night, Willie Lee, I'll See You in the Morning.
Waller, E. Love's Farewell.
Wheatley, P. Farewell to America. To Mrs. S. W. A.
Whiting, R. Beyond the Blue Horizon.
Wordsworth, W. Farewell, A: "Farewell thou little Nook of mountain-ground."

Fargo, North Dakota
Wright, J. Outside Fargo, North Dakota.

Farming and Farmers
Adams, L. Country Summer.
Alexander, M. Iowa Farmer.
Ammons, A. R. Hardweed Path Going.
Silver.
Arnold, B. No Tool or Rope or Pail.
Baillie, J. Hay Making.
Balaban. Riding Westward.
Bampfylde. Written at a Farm.
Beaver. Silo Treading.
Belieu. Legend of the Albino Farm.
Bishop, E. Prodigal, The.
Blind. Reapers.
Sower, The.
Bly, R. Snowfall in the Afternoon.
Bontemps. Black Man Talks of Reaping, A.
Boston, B. By All Lights: 1959.
Brown, G. Taxman.
Brown, K. Good Devil, The.
Brown, S. After Winter.
Bunting. Complaint of the Morpethshire Farmer, The.
Gin the Goodwife Stint.
Burns, R. Cotter's Saturday Night [Inscribed to Robert Aiken [or R. A****], Esq.], The.
Busch, T. Heartland.
Calverley. Ballad: "Auld wife sat at her ivied door, The."
Campion, T. Jack and Joan.
Carlyle, T. Sower's Song, The.
Carruth, H. Emergency Haying.
Cary, P. Harvest Gathering.
Clampitt. Beethoven, Opus 111.
Clayton, S. Good Old Days, The.
Cofer, J. Campesino's Lament, The.
Coleridge, S. On a Ruined House in a Romantic Country.
Coles, G. Dornier, The.
Colum, P. Drover, A.
Conn. Todd.
Coultas, B. Third Farming Poem.
Creeley. Counterpoint, A.
Divakaruni. Founding of Yuba City, The.
Donaldson, W. How 'Ya Gonna Keep 'Em Down on the Farm? (After They've Seen Paree).
Dorn, E. On the Debt My Mother Owed to Sears Roebuck.
Dove, R. Small Town.
E'der, E. Once We Were Farmers.
Emerson, R. Musketaquid.
Ennis. Coyne's.
Etter. Drink and Agriculture.
Evans, C. Callers.
Fallon, P. Meadow, The.
Finch, A. For Grizzel McNaught (1709–1792).
Francis, R. Curse, The.
Frost, R. Code, The.
Death of the Hired Man, The.
Mowing.
Pasture, The.
Putting in the Seed.
Range-finding.
Strong Are Saying Nothing, The.
Garland, H. Plowing: A Memory.
Gilbert, C. Glimpses.
Glassco. Entailed Farm, The.
Guthrie, W. Turkey in the Corn.

Hall, D. Ox Cart Man.
Hartnett. Retreat of Ita Cagney, The.
Small Farm, A.
Heaney, S. At a Potato Digging.
Follower.
Harvest Bow, The.
Wife's Tale, The.
Hedin, R. At the Olive Grove of the Resistance.
Herrick. His Grange, or Private Wealth.
Hiebert. Farmer and the Farmer's Wife, The.
Hochman. Cannon Hill.
Holmes, O. Ploughman, The.
Howes, B. Death of a Vermont Farm Woman.
Hughes, T. February 17th.
Jarrell. Field and Forest.
Johnson, J. Music for the Cows.
Johnson, M. F. Village Maid, The.
Jones, R. Nell.
Kavanagh, P. Spraying the Potatoes.
Kern, J. Bungalow in Quogue.
Kinsella, J. Visitant Eclogue.
Wild Radishes.
Komunyakaa. Banking Potatoes.
Kooser. Abandoned Farmhouse.
Lanier, S. Waving of the Corn, The.
Lawrence, D. Love On the Farm.
Lee, D. For Jan, with Love.
Hired Hand.
Jan's Birthday.
Lehmann, G. Saving the Harvest.
Lovecraft. Well, The.
Lux. Commercial Leech Farming Today.
MacCaig. Summer Farm.
MacLeish. Eleven.
Markham, E. Man with the Hoe, The.
Matherne, B. La Fabrique de Tabac (Tobacco Harvest).
McAlmon. Frost in the Corn, The.
Meredith, G. Phoebus with Admetus.
Messerli. Harrowing.
Mew. Farmer's Bride, The.
Millay, E. From a Train Window.
Mitsui. Picture of a Japanese Farmer, Woodland, California, May 20, 1942.
Muldoon, P. Why Brownlee Left.
Orfalea, G. Bomb That Fell on Abdu's Farm, The.
Peirce. Farmers.
Prys-Jones. Ploughman: In Welsh Uplands, The.
Rawson, J. Map Burnt Through.
Redcloud. Farmer.
Reed, I. White Hope.
Riley, J. Raggedy Man, The.
Roberts, S. Mowing, The.
Sandburg, C. Illinois Farmer.
Onion Days.
Simmons, J. Rogation Day: Portrush.
Skeeter. Midwest, Midcentury.
Snyder, G. Hay for the Horses.
Soto. Field Poem.
Hoeing.
Sylvester, J. Aestas.
Tennyson, A. Northern Farmer: New Style.
Thomas, E. As the Team's Head-Brass.
Haymaking.
Thomas, R. Cynddylan on a Tractor.
Hill Farmer Speaks, The.
Lonely Farmer, The.
On the Farm.
Peasant, A.
Todd, M. Grandmother's Farm.
Tomlinson, C. Oxen: Ploughing at Fiesole.
Toomer. Reapers.
Torrence. Son, The.
Tripp. Ploughman.
Trowbridge, J. Idyl of Harvest Time, An.
Turberville. Poor Ploughman to a Gentleman for Whom He Had Taken a Little Pains, A.
Voigt. Farmer, The.
Wallace, R. Makings of Happiness, The.
Warner, S. Rival, The.
Whitman, W. Farm Picture, A.
Wilbur. Sonnet: "Winter deepening, the hay all in, The."
Williams, C. Loss.
Williams, J. Pastoral: "You see that forest on

the height?"
Wodehouse, P. Bungalow in Quogue.
Wordsworth, W. Farmer of Tilsbury Vale, The.
  Solitary Reaper, The.
Wright, J. Milkweed.

Farmworkers
Castillo, A. Napa, California.
Espada. Water, White Cotton, and the Rich Man.
García, D. Orchard of Figs in the Fall, An.
Hausman. Appaloosa Hail Storm.
Kinsella, J. Wild Radishes.
Lee, D. Hired Hand.
Marcus, M. I Think of Those Mornings.
See also **Migrant Workers**

Farragut, David Glasgow
Meredith, W. Farragut, Farragut.

Fascism and Fascists
Hill, G. Christmas Trees.
Reed, I. Why I Often Allude to Osiris.

Fashion
Ager, M. Glad Rag Doll.
Barlow, G. Place Where He Arose, The.
Berlin. Puttin' on the Ritz (Original Version).
  Puttin' on the Ritz (Revised Version).
  Top Hat, White Tie, and Tails.
Cavendish, M. Woman drest by Age, A.
Dickinson, E. Morns are meeker than they were, The.
Dorough, B. I'm Hip.
Dougherty, D. Glad Rag Doll.
Herd. Bathing Girls, The.
Jonson, B. On English Monsieur.
Kelly, R. Rainmakers, The.
Nemerov. History of a Literary Movement.
Pope, A. C[h]loe.
  Epistle [II,] to a Lady[: Of the Characters of Women].
  To a Lady.
Robinson, M. Modern Female Fashions.
  Modern Male Fashions.
Rossetti, C. If a Pig Wore a Wig.
Whitehead, W. Venus Attiring the Graces.
Wunderlich, M. Take Good Care of Yourself.
Yellen, J. Glad Rag Doll.
See also **Clothing**

Fate
Adams, F. Those Two Boys.
Arlen, H. For Every Man There's a Woman.
Arnold, S. Destiny.
Ashbery. Brute Image.
Barker, J. Necessity of Fate, The.
Bedient, C. When the Gods Put on Meter.
Benjamin, P. Press On.
Bevington, L. 'Egoisme à Deux.'
  Measurements.
Bibb. Destiny.
Blake, E. I'm Just Wild About Harry.
Blaser. Finder, The.
Bogan, L. Cartography.
  Didactic Piece.
Bradstreet, A. Here Follows Some Verses upon the Burning of Our House [July 10th, 1666. Copied Out of a Loose Paper].
Braithwaite. House of Falling Leaves, The.
Brown, N. You Were Meant for Me.
Brown, S. Schadenfreude.
Burns, R. Tam Glen.
Butler, S. Love.
Carew, T. For a Picture Where a Queen Laments over the Tomb of a Slain Knight.
  To Celia, upon Love's Ubiquity.
Char. Unbending Prayer.
Clifton, L. Kali.
Cooke, R. Arachne.
Creeley. Kore.
  Oh No.
  Window, The.
Dickinson, E. He fumbles at Your Spirit.
  It Dropped So Low in My Regard.
Dunbar, P. Robert Gould Shaw.
Duncan, R. Poem Beginning with a Line by Pindar, A.
Eberhart, R. Flux.
Elizabeth I. Written on a Wall at Woodstock.

Emerson, R. Day's Ration, The.
  Guy.
  Nemesis.
"Ephelia." To One That Asked Me Why I Loved J.G G.
Ferry. Cythera.
  Embarkation for Cythera, The.
Fitzgerald, E. 73.
  74.
Forbes, C. Hand Me Down Blues.
Freed, A. You Were Meant for Me.
Frost, R. Design.
  Draft Horse, The.
  Gift Outright, The.
Glück, L. Mount Ararat.
Grossman, A. Enough Rain for Agnes Walquist.
Gurney, I. Ballad of the Three Spectres.
Hardy, T. Hap.
Hecht, A. Jason.
Herrick. Man's Dying-Place Uncertain.
  Parcæ, The; or, Three Dainty Destinies: The Armilet.
Hood, T. Poet's Fate, The.
Hope, A. Beyond Phigalia.
  Fafnir.
Hughes, L. Bad Luck Card.
Jackson, H. Crossed Threads.
Johnson, S. Scholar's Life, The.
  Vanity of Human Wishes, The; The Tenth Satire of Juvenal Imitated.
Jones, I. It Had to Be You.
Juana Inés de la Cruz. Green Enravishment of Human Life.
Kahn, G. It Had to Be You.
Keats. Song of the Indian Maid.
Kenyon, J. Otherwise.
Khlebnikov, V. Zangezi: R, K, L, G—.
King, H. Sonnet: "Tell me[e] no more how fair[e] she[e] is."
Landon. Stern Truth.
Lieberman, M. Los Olivos.
Lovelace, R. Advice to My Best Brother, Colonel Francis Lovelace.
MacCarthy, C. To the Same.
Marvell. Definition of Love, The.
McAuley, J. Blue Horses, The.
Melville, H. Haglets, The.
  Immolated.
Millay, E. Buck in the Snow, The.
Nash, O. Necessary Dirge, A.
Okigbo. On the New Year.
Peacock, M. Wheel, The.
Perreault, J. Boomerang.
Rattray, D. They Don't Have to Have That Look.
Robin, L. For Every Man There's a Woman.
Robinson, E. Eros Turannos.
  Karma.
Roethke. Waking, The.
Sandburg, C. Mamie.
Seeger, A. I Have a Rendezvous with Death.
Shapiro, K. Auto Wreck.
Shirley, J. Love's Hue and Cry.
"Shu Ting." Assembly Line.
Simon, M. Standing Between Two Ideas.
Sissle, N. I'm Just Wild About Harry.
Sparrow, J. Apology and Explanation.
Stevens, W. Flyer's Fall.
Stevenson, R. Ticonderoga: A Legend of the West Highlands.
Swirszczynska. Thank You, My Fate.
Tannahill. Tap-Room, The.
Thrale [*later* Mrs. Piozzi]. Winter in Wales, A.
Tomlinson, C. Ararat.
Trowbridge, J. Circumstance.
Unknown. Dragon Speaks, The.
Vaughan, H. To Amoret, Walking in a Starry Evening.
Ward, D. Crossing.
Wells, C. Fate.
Whateley. Power of Destiny, The.
Wilcox, E. Way of It, The.
  Winds of Fate, The.
Yeats. Leda and the Swan.
See also **Fortune; Chance**

Fathers
Abinader, E. Letters from Home.
Acholonu. Dissidents, The.
Alexander, E. Who I Think You Are.
Alexie. Father and Farther.
  Penance.
Allen, G. Poem For My Father.
Alvi, M. Throwing Out My Father's Dictionary.
Armitage, S. Poem: "And if it snowed and snow covered the drive."
Arrillaga. Rosa/Filí.
Ashbery. Boy, A.
Atwood. Flowers.
Awad, J. Stopping at the Mayflower.
  Widower, The.
Bailey, R. Father's Things.
Balaban. Words for My Daughter.
Barer, M. Very Soft Shoes.
Barrax. Visit.
Barry, J. Lessons.
Bartlett, E. Smile for Daddy.
Beer, P. John Milton and My Father.
Berry, J. Girls Can We Educate We Dads?
Berryman. Scholars at the Orchid Pavilion.
  To My Father.
Biespiel, D. Lilacs.
Blanco, R. Malibú, El.
  Shaving.
Bly, R. My Father's Wedding.
  My Father's Neck.
Borthwick, P. Forest.
Boss. At the Nuclear Rally.
Bottoms. Desk, The.
Boyd, E. On the Death of an Infant of Five Days Old.
Boyd, M. Sunflowers and Saturdays.
Bradstreet, A. To Her Father, with Some Verses.
  To the Memory of My Dear and Ever Honored Father Thomas Dudley Esq. Who Deceased July 31, 1653, and of His Age 77.
Brown, L. Thank You Father.
Buckley, C. Father, 1952.
Bukowski. My Old Man.
Burns, R. Fishing in Winter.
Campbell, A. Shabby Old Dad.
Carlson, D. Russ Joy Little League.
Cashdan. Laughing All the Way.
Castillo, A. Toltec, The.
Chambers, J. Why Are Daddies So Mean?
Charara, H. My Father Breaks the Neighbor's Nose.
Chin, D. Sleeping Father.
Chisholm, A. Contact.
Chitre. My Father Travels.
Chrystos. Portrait of Assimilation.
Clayton, S. Good Old Days, The.
Clifton, L. Sam.
Clover, J. Family Romance.
Coleman, H. Poem for a "Divorced" Daughter.
Coleman, W. Cousin Mary.
Coleridge, H. Full Well I Know.
  Written on the Anniversary of Our Father's Death.
Coleridge, S. Father! no amaranths e'er shall wreathe my brow.
  Sonnet Composed on a Journey Homeward; the Author Having Received Intelligence of the Birth of a Son, 20 September 1796.
Coles, G. Ithaca-Liverpool.
Cook-Lynn. Grandfather at the Indian Health Clinic.
Cooley, N. Family History, The.
Copus, J. Pulling the Ivy.
Corbet [*or* Corbett]. Elegy upon the Death of His Own Father, An.
Creeley. Fathers.
Cummings, E. My father moved through dooms of love.
Curtis, T. To My Father.
Dalton, A. Dad-Baby, The.
Davis, O. Moorer Denies Holyfield in Twelve.
Deane, S. Fording the River.
Delgado, J. Con Los Pájaros.
  Visiting Father.
DeSylva, B. G. Thank You Father.
Dickey, J. Bee, The.

Hospital Window, The.
Dickey, R.　Father.
Dodd, W.　Of His Life.
Dooley, M.　Dancing at Oakmead Road.
　Heart.
　Mansize.
Dove, A.　Crab.
Dugan, A.　Elegy: "I know but will not tell."
Duhig, I.　First Second, The.
Dumas, H.　Zebra Goes Wild Where the
　Sidewalk Ends, The.
Dunbar, P.　Little Brown Baby.
Dybek.　My Father's Fights.
Earle, J.　At the South Pole.
Ellis, T.　Sticks.
Elmusa.　Father Lullabies the Unborn.
Ennis.　Road to Patmos, The.
Erdrich.　Birth.
Fanthorpe.　Father in the Railway Buffet.
Fearing.　Any Man's Advice to His Son.
Feinstein, E.　Dad.
Ferguson, G.　In Hospital-land.
Finkel.　Father, The.
Fleming, K.　For All Unwed Mothers.
Foley, K.　My Father, Counting Sheep.
Frost, K.　Winners.
Fuller, C.　My Father's Dreams.
Fyfe, A.　Upturn.
Galvin, J.　Shadow-Casting.
Garcia, R.　Note Folded Thirteen Ways.
Gilbert, K.　Won't You Dad?
Gillan.　Arturo.
Gillilan, P.　Looking North.
Gillilan, S.　"Are You There?"
Gilmore, B.　Revolution.
Gilyard, K.　Daughter, That Picture of You.
Gioseffi.　American Sonnets for My Father.
Glück, L.　Departure.
　Mythic Fragment.
Goethe.　Erl-King, The.
Goldberg, B.　Our Father.
Golding, N.　My Father Makes a Lightbox for
　Vivienne Westwood.
Gotera.　Dance of the Letters.
Graham, D.　Father of the Man.
Graham, W.　To My Father.
Gregg.　Not Saying Much.
Grennan.　Pause.
Groarke, V.　History of My Father's House, The.
Grosholz.　Legacies.
　Life of a Salesman.
Hai-Jew, S.　Father's Belt.
Hall, D.　White Apples.
Hamilton, L.　My Father's Words.
Hamlett, J.　Therapist's Comment, The.
Hamod, S.　Lines to My Father.
Hannan, M.　Coming Down from Derry Hill.
Harris, D.　For My Father.
　What we have lost.
Harris, W.　Daddy Poem, A.
Harwood, G.　Father and Child.
Hayden, R.　Those Winter Sundays.
Hazo.　Maps for a Son Are Drawn as You Go.
Heaney, S.　Digging.
　Follower.
Henderson, R.　Thank You Father.
Hernández Cruz.　Ruskie's Boy.
Herrera.　Atavistic: Traces after the Rain.
Herrick.　To the Reverend Shade of His
　Religious Father.
Hewitt, J.　Father's Death, A.
Higgins, F.　Father and Son.
Hill, N.　Dürer's "Young Hare"
Hippolyte.　So Jah Sey.
Hirsch, E.　My Father's Back.
Hollo.　Le Jazz Hot.
Hongo.　Hilo: First Night Back.
　O-Bon: Dance for the Dead.
Houghton, L.　Caustic Soda.
　Saturday with Dad.
Huddle.　My Daddy, Whenever He Went Some
　Place.
Hudgins.　Childhood of the Ancients.
　Elegy for My Father, Who Is Not Dead.
　Tree.
Humphreys, E.　From Father to Son.

Hunt, S.　My Father Scything.
　My Father Today.
Ignatow, D.　Europe and America.
Ilio, D.　Site of My Grandfather's House, The.
Jacinto, J.　Absence.
　Heaven Is Just Another Country.
Jackowska.　Woman Who Mistook Her Father
　for an Irishman, The.
Jagger, B.　Anyway.
Jastrzebska.　Cracking Walnuts.
Jones, R.　Portrait of My Father and His
　Grandson.
Jonson, B.　On My First Son[ne].
Jordan, J.　Clock on Hancock Street.
Joseph, A.　My Father's Heroes.
Joseph, L.　Not Yet.
　Then.
Justice, D.　Men at Forty.
Kasdorf.　Streak, The.
　Vesta's Father.
Kavanagh, P.　Memory of My Father.
Kay, E.　Phoenix.
Kazantzis.　My Dada.
Kessler, M.　Secret Love.
Kessler, S.　Jack's Last Words.
Kgositsile.　To My Daughter.
Kimbrell, J.　My Father at the North Street
　Boarding House.
Kinsella, T.　His Father's Hands.
Kizer, C.　Thrall.
Klein, A.　Heirloom.
Klein, M.　Range of It, The.
Komunyakaa.　Banking Potatoes.
Kramer, L.　Non-Emigrant, The.
Kunitz, S.　Catch, The.
　Portrait, The.
Kyger.　My Father Died This Spring.
Lassell.　Going to Europe.
Lee, L.　Eating Together.
　Gift, The.
　Mnemonic.
　Story, A.
　Weight of Sweetness, The.
Lehman.　Difference Between Pepsi and Coke,
　The.
Leonard, T.　Fathers and Sons.
Levin, P.　Planting Roses.
Levine, P.　1933.
Levis.　Winter Stars.
Lieberman, M.　On the Anniversary of My
　Father's Death.
Lim, S.　Black and White.
　Father from Asia.
Limburg, J.　Return, The.
Liu.　My Father's Martial Art.
Liu, T.　Thoreau.
Livingston, M.　Father.
Longley, M.　In Memoriam.
　Wounds.
Lopez, L.　Images of San Luis.
Lorde.　Father Son and Holy Ghost.
　Love Poem.
Lowell, R.　Commander Lowell.
　Home After Three Months Away.
　Middle Age.
MacDiarmid, H.　At My Father's Grave.
MacNeice.　Truisms, The.
Maiden.　Air.
Marcus, B.　Delaying Relevance.
Markus, P.　Black Light.
　Light.
　Shooting Crows.
Marsh, B.　Papa.
Marshall, J.　Letter to My Father on the Other
　Side.
Martínez, V.　Night of Fathers.
Martinez, D.　Standard Time: Novena for My
　Father.
Mathews, A.　Letter Following.
Maxton.　Waking.
Mayer, G.　Make Believe.
McAuley, J.　Because.
McCarthy, T.　Party Shrine.
　Sorrow Garden, The.
McCuaig.　Au Tombeau de Mon Père.
McGrath, T.　Offering.

McLaughlin, J.　Black Irish Blues.
Meinke.　Advice to My Son.
Merrill, J.　Scenes of Childhood.
Merwin, W. S.　Calling, A.
　Strawberries.
Meynell, A.　Father of Women, A [Ad Sororem
　E. B.].
Michie, S.　Connecting Light.
Millar, J.　Midlife.
Miller, E.　Jasmine.
　My Father's Girlfriend.
　Night Before the First Day of School, The.
Mitsui.　At Bon Odori.
　Because of My Father's Job.
Montague, J.　At Last.
　Cage, The.
　Last Journey.
Moore, L.　Gifts.
　Winter 1967.
Moore, M.　Silence.
Morley, D.　Errand.
Moss, H.　Elegy for My Father.
Moss, T.　Lynching, The.
Muldoon, P.　Wishbone, The.
Murray, G.　Rounds, The.
Musgrave.　You Didn't Fit.
Napier, F.　I Have Taken the Suits and Shoes to
　Oxfam.
Nelson, H.　My Father Went to Funerals.
Nesbit, E.　Song: "Oh, baby, baby, baby dear."
Nicholson, N.　Halley's Comet.
Nimmo, D.　My Father's Shadow.
Norris, L.　His Father, Singing.
North, M.　Pheasant Plucker's Son, The.
　Poems to My Father.
Nowlan.　Only When My Heart Freezes.
Nye, N.　My Father and the Fig Tree.
Olds, S.　Guild, The.
　Last Acts.
　Lifting, The.
　Moment of My Father's Death, The.
　Race, The.
　Saturn.
　Victims, The.
Ondaatje.　Letters and Other Worlds.
Oppen.　Occurrences, The.
Orfalea, G.　My Father Writing Joe Hamrah in a
　Blackout.
Ortiz.　My Father's Song.
　What I Tell Him.
Orton, B.　Beekeeper.
Pankey.　As We Forgive Those.
Peacock, M.　Dream Come True.
Perillo.　Skin.
Petit, P.　Embrace of the Electric Eel.
　My Father's Clothes.
Philp-Carmichael.　My Dad.
Pietri.　Night Is Out of Sight, The.
Plath.　Colossus, The.
　Daddy.
Plumly.　After Grief.
　Out-of-the-Body Travel.
Pogson, P.　Bo Tree.
Powell, D. A.　My Father and Me Making
　Dresses: Together.
Prufer.　My Father Recounts a Story from
　His Youth.
Prunty.　Reading Before We Read, Horoscope
　and Weather.
Rafferty, P.　Passage.
Ray, D.　In the Third Month.
Ray, H.　To My Father.
Rexroth, K.　Andree Rexroth.
Reznikoff.　Idiot, The.
Rhodes, M.　It Being Forbidden.
Rich, A.　After Dark.
Rivard.　Fall River.
　Firestone.
Roberts, L.　My Father's Whistle.
Rodgers, M.　Very Soft Shoes.
Roethke.　Elegy for Jane.
　My Papa's Waltz.
　Premonition, The.
Rosen, M.　This Morning.
Rosner.　Souvenirs.
Rospigliosi.　Leavetaking.

Ryan, M.   This Is a Poem for the Dead.
Ryan, R.   Father of Famine.
Rybicki, J.   In Directions.
Sanchez, S.   Father and Daughter.
  Poem for My Father, A.
Satyamurti.   Erdywurble.
Savageau.   Looking for Indians.
  To Human Skin.
Schnackenberg.   Supernatural Love.
Schneider, M.   Soup and Slavery.
Seward.   Eyam.
Sexton.   All My Pretty Ones.
  And One for My Dame.
  Moss of His Skin, The.
Sharman, R.   By Heart.
Sheehan, M.   My Father's Singing.
Shelton, R.   Letter to a Dead Father.
Silex, E.   Acts of Love.
  Departure.
Simmons, J.   Reformer to His Father, A.
Simpson, L.   My Father in the Night
  Commanding No.
Skloot.   Hook.
Smith, R.   Bluetits.
Smith, S.   Correspondence Between Mr.
  Harrison in Newcastle and Mr. Sholto Peach
  Harrison in Hull.
Smith, W.   American Primitive.
Soto.   Blanco.
Souster.   Man Who Finds That His Son Has
  Become a Thief, The.
Stafford, W.   Rescued Year, The.
Stevens, W.   Irish Cliffs of Moher, The.
Stewart, P.   Singing Down the Breadfruit.
Stone, J.   Bass, The.
Storace.   King Lear Bewildered.
Strand.   "Dreadful Has Already Happened,
  The."
Swirszczynska.   I Wash the Shirt.
Tate, J.   Lost Pilot, The.
Taylor, E.   Few Days in the South in
  February, A.
Tayson, R.   Chase, The.
Thomas, D.   Do Not Go Gentle into That Good
  Night.
Tipping.   Just after Michael's Death, the Game
  of Pool.
Travis, N.   At My Father's House.
Tripp.   Father.
Troupe.   Poem for My Father; for Quincy
  Trouppe, Sr.
Tucker, M.   To Father.
Unknown.   Edward [*or* Edward, Edward].
  Good and Better.
Unknown, fr. Terezin Concentration Camp.
  Letter to Daddy, A.
Urdang.   My Father's Death.
Utting, S.   Spoon Maker's Daughter, The.
Van Duyn.   Letters from a Father.
Van Jordan, A.   My Father's Retirement.
Van Walleghen.   Walking the Baby to the Liquor
  Store.
Vando.   Father's Day.
Vizenor.   Family Photograph.
Waddleton, J.   Fatherhood.
Wakoski.   Father of My Country, The.
  Placing a $2 Bet for a Man Who Will Never Go
  to the Horse Races Any More.
Walcott.   Letter from Brooklyn, A.
Walker, A.   Good Night, Willie Lee, I'll See
  You in the Morning.
Waniek.   Daughters, 1900.
Warren, R.   Night Walking.
Weaver, M.   My Father's First Baseball Game.
  My Father's Geography.
Weems, M.   Dime after Dime.
Whipple, L.   My Dad.
Whitman, W.   Dirge for Two Veterans.
Wicks, S.   Clever Daughter, The.
  Stilt-walker.
Wishik.   Visitation Rights.
Wojahn.   My Father's Pornography.
  Photo of My Father in a Snowbound Train.
  Riding the Empire Builder, 1948.
Wong, N.   Ironing.
Work.   Come Home, Father[!].

Wright, E.   When Father Carves the Duck.
Wright, J.   Evening.
  Having Lost My Sons, I Confront the Wreckage
  of the Moon: Christmas, 1960.
  Revelation, The.
  Two Postures beside a Fire.
Wycherley, L.   Earth Man.
Young, D.   White Crane.
Young, G.   Miracle, The.
Young, K.   Field Trip.
Zweig, P.   Father.

Faults
Brown, E.   Sonnet 43.
Herrick.   In the Dark None Dainty.
  To the Generous Reader.
Larkin, P.   This Be The Verse.
Wakoski.   My Trouble.

Fauns
Pound, E.   Faun, The.

Faust
Ashbery.   Faust.
Crane, H.   For the Marriage of Faustus and
  Helen.
Enright, D.   Royalties.
Gunn, T.   Faustus Triumphant.
Mother Goose.   Doctor Faustus was a good
  man.

Fear
Agosin.   Fear.
  Fear 2.
Amis, K.   Autobiographical Fragment.
Angel.   Breaking the Rock Down.
Angelou.   Life Doesn't Frighten Me.
Antin.   List of the Delusions of the Insane /
  What They Are Afraid Of, A.
Arnold, C.   My Love Is Sick.
Ashbery.   Young Son, The.
Atkins.   Late Bus (After a Series of Hold-Ups).
Auden.   Leap Before You Look.
Baca.   Like an Animal.
Baugh, E.   Nigger Sweat.
Belieu.   Nocturne: My Sister Life.
Bogan, L.   Frightened Man, The.
Brass.   Only Silly Faggots Know.
Brett, L.   La Pathétique.
Brontë, C.   Again I find myself alone.
Brooks, G.   Michael Is Afraid of the Storm.
Brown, D.   When I Am 19 I Was a Medic.
Browning, R.   Prospice.
Bryan, M.   To———: "O timeless guest!—so
  soon returned art thou."
Burns, R.   Prayer, in the Prospect of Death, A.
  To a Mouse; On Turning Her up in Her Nest,
  with the Plough, November, 1785.
Byron, G.   Love and Death.
Carson, A.   Longing, a Documentary.
Chimombo.   Four Ways of Dying.
Clifton, L.   Night Vision.
  Powell (officer charged with the beating of
  rodney king).
Cofer, J.   What We Feared.
Coleman, H.   Night Flare Drop, Tan Son Nhut.
Coleridge, M.   Master and Guest.
Collins, W.   Ode to Fear.
Crapsey.   Warning, The.
Creeley.   Form of Women, A.
Dalton, A.   Kitchen Beast.
Davidson, L.   Fear of Madness, The.
Derricotte.   Fears of the Eighth Grade.
  From a Letter: About Snow.
Dharker.   Postcards from God (1).
Dickey, J.   Sheep Child, The.
Dickinson, E.   Snake, The.
Dixon, M.   Getting Your Rocks Off.
Douglas, K.   On a Return from Egypt.
Dove, R.   Motherhood.
Eberhart, R.   New England Bachelor, A.
Elizabeth I.   Ah silly pugg wert thou so sore
  afraid.
  Doubt of Future Foes.
Ferguson, G.   Fear of the Future.
Forché.   Return.
Foster, A.   Wythop Mill.
Frost, R.   Storm Fear.
Galvin, B.   Cougar.
García, D.   Matter of Control, A.

Glück, L.   Garden, The.
  Gretel in Darkness.
Goethe.   Erl-King, The.
Gould, H.   Apprehension.
Graves, R.   Straw, The.
Gunn, T.   Man With Night Sweats, The.
Gwangwa'a.   Leaking Roof.
Hammerstein.   I've Told Ev'ry Little Star.
Hardy, T.   To an Unborn Pauper Child.
Harjo, J.   Call It Fear.
  I Give You Back.
Harms.   Tomorrow, We'll Dance in America.
Hayden, R.   Soledad.
Hecht, A.   Hill, A.
Henderson-Holmes.   My First Riot: Bronx,
  NYC.
Herbert, Z.   Our Fear.
Herrick.   On Himselfe.
Hogan, L.   Return: Buffalo.
Hudgins.   Hereafter, The.
Hughes, F.   Different Voice, The.
Hughes, L.   Situation.
  Sweet Words on Race.
Jarrell.   Bird of Night, The.
Johnston, M.   Gorey at the Biennale.
Jonson, B.   To Fine Lady Would-Be.
Kazantzis.   Frightened Flier Goes North, The.
Keats.   When I Have Fears [That I May Cease
  to Be].
Kennelly.   Dream of a Black Fox.
Kern, J.   I've Told Ev'ry Little Star.
Killigrew, A.   On Death.
Knight, S.   In Case of Monsters.
Komunyakaa.   After the Fall of Saigon.
Kooser.   Child Frightened by a Thunderstorm.
Kumin, M.   Getting the Message.
Kusz, N.   Retired Greyhound, II.
Laing, K.   Many Worlds Are Walked Once.
Landor, W.   Death Stands above Me.
Lawrence, D.   Snake.
  Song of a Man Who Has Come Through, The.
Levertov.   Clouds.
Loftis, N.   Fights After School.
Lorde.   Litany for Survival, A.
MacBeth [*or* Macbeth].   Worst Fear, The.
McGinley.   Women of Jericho, The.
Melville, H.   To.
Merrill, J.   Days of 1941 and '44.
Mew.   Farmer's Bride, The.
Miller, A.   Lola's Lament.
Millis, C.   IRT at Rush Hour, The.
Moore, R.   Doors.
Mouré.   Thirteen Years.
Myles, E.   Sadness of Leaving, The.
Newman, G.   Anti-Semitic Demonstration, An.
Nilsson, H.   How Came What Came Alas.
Noguchi, R.   I, the Neighbor Mr. Uskovich,
  Watch Every Morning Kenji Takezo Hold His
  Breath.
Nowlan.   Thief, The.
Ologoudou.   Vespers.
Orfalea, G.   My Father Writing Joe Hamrah in a
  Blackout.
Owen, W.   Next War, The.
Palis, Y.   Waking Up.
Parker, D.   When Mark Deloach Ruled the
  World.
Peacock, T.   Fear.
Piñero.   Running Scared.
Picková, E.   Fear.
Pinsky.   Woman, A.
Poole, R.   Dark, The.
Pope, A.   Apologia pro Vita Sua.
  Atticus ("Peace to all such! but were there one
  whose fires").
  Bufo.
  Epistle to Dr. Arbuthnot.
  Sporus.
Pratt, M.   Waulking Song: Two.
Purdy, J.   Do You Wonder Why I Am Sleepy.
Radnóti.   Angel of Dread, The.
Ralegh, S.   On the Snuff of a Candle.
Ramanujan.   Snakes.
Receveur.   Doper's Dream.
  Night Fear.
Reed, H.   Château, The.

Reeves, J. Others.
Robinson, E. Eros Turannos.
  Poem for Max Nordau, A.
Rolfe, E. Casualty.
Seaton, M. Fear of Subways.
Senghor. Visit.
Shange. Where the Heart Is.
Shelley, P. To————: "I fear thy kisses, gentle maiden."
Shinder. One Secret That Has Carried, The.
Shorter. Mother, The.
Silverstein, S. Whatif.
Simic. Empire of Dreams.
  Fear.
  Old Couple.
Simmons, J. Fear Test: Integrity of Heroes.
Smith, C. Captive Escaped in the Wilds of America, The. Addressed to the Hon. Mrs. O'Neill.
Spicer, J. Cantata.
Stanley, T. Expectation.
Stanton, M. Little Ode for X.
Steele, T. Eros.
Stephens, J. In Waste Places.
Surrey. "Love, That Doth Reign and Live Within My Thought."
Swinburne. Lake of Gaube, The.
Szporluk. Holy Ghost.
  Occupant of the Hose.
Talvikki, A. You Don't Know What Happened When You Froze.
Tatarunis, P. Before the Brain Surgery.
Tayson, R. Nightsweats.
Teasdale. Sanctuary, The.
Thomas, P. Lascars, The.
Unknown. Boy in the Barn, The.
  Fears and Tears.
  Firm Belief.
Vando. Father's Day.
Warr, M. Brain on Ice.
Weigl. Mines.
Weslowski. Zoe and the Ghosts.
Wetzsteon. Drinks in the Town Square.
  Poem for a New Year.
Whitman, R. Listening to Grownups Quarreling.
Whittier. Song of Slaves in the Desert.
Williams, G. Wild Night at Trewethan.
Winchilsea. To Death.
Wojahn. Inside, The.
Wright, J. Brother and Sisters.
  Woman to Man.
Wyatt, S. Long love that in my thought doth harbo[u]r, The.
Wylie. Confession of Faith.
Yeats. Who Goes with Fergus?
Zarco. My Worst Fear.

Feasts and Feasting
Aytoun, W. Royal Banquet, The.
Carew, T. Upon a Mole in Celia's Bosom.
Coleridge, M. Unwelcome.
Fisher, A. Thanksgiving Dinner.
Hall, D. Eating the Pig.
Herrick. Ceremonies for Christmas[se].
  Invitation, The.
Lamb, C. To Dora W[ordsworth].
Landon. Banquet, The.
MacNeice. This Is the Life.
Nash, O. Private Dining Room, The.
Pelletiere, M. Under Her Crib.
Robinson, A. Celia's Home-Coming.
"Sagittarius." Passionate Profiteer to His Love, The.
Zisquit. After Years of Feasting and No Sacrifice.

February
Bodecker. When Skies are Low and Days are Dark.
Fisher, J. It's February But.
Given. Song for February, A.
Heath-Stubbs. February.
Kenyon, J. February: Thinking of Flowers.
Kinsella, T. Mirror in February.
Longfellow, H. Afternoon in February.
Ray, H. February.
Schuyler, J. February.

Teasdale. February Twilight.

Federal Bureau of Investigation
Di Prima. Fragmented Address to the FBI.
Durem. Award.

Feebleness
Herrick. Crutches.

Feet
Adamson, H. Make with the Feet.
Buscani. Barefoot in the City.
Dugan, A. Barefoot Homiletics, After Wittgenstein and Boswell.
Duke, V. Make with the Feet.
Gardinier. Democracy.
Herrick. To Dianeme.
  Upon Her Feet.
Hughes, L. Feet O' Jesus.
Jacobsen, J. Limbo Dancer, The.
Lyon, G. Foot-Washing, The.
Major, C. Large Room with Wood Floor.
Neruda. Walking Around.
O'Malley, M. Shoeing the Currach.
Probyn. After.
  Before.
Rilke. Pietà.
Unknown. My Darlings' Shoes.
Whittier. Barefoot Boy, The.
Williams, W. Overture to a Dance of Locomotives.
  Poem: "As the cat."
See also **Toes**

Feminism and Feminists
Allen, P. He Na Tye Woman.
Amadiume. Oya Now.
Armstrong, F. Women of My Land.
Arrillaga. Dream.
"Astra." Daughters.
Barbauld. Rights of Woman, The.
Canan. Radioactive.
Chudleigh. To the Ladies.
Cisneros, S. Loose Women.
Dodge, M. Note.
Egerton, S. Emulation, The.
Esteves. One Woman.
Fell, A. Significant Fevers.
Grahn. I Have Come to Claim Marilyn Monroe's Body.
Hacker, M. Ballad of Ladies Lost and Found.
  Invocation: "This is for Elsa, also known as Liz."
Hamilton, C. March of the Women, The.
Harland-Watts, J. For a Woman's Rights.
Healy, E. Changing the Oil.
Horne, N. Note to My Liberal Feminist Sister, A.
Hugo, R. To Women.
Korican, L. Her Story.
Levertov. Hypocrite Women.
Macaulay, F. Women's Marseillaise, The.
Millay, E. To Inez Milholland.
Morgan-Browne. Purple, White and Green, The.
"O'Neill." Her Sister.
Parker, P. There Is a Woman in This Town.
Rich, A. Ninth Symphony of Beethoven Understood at Last as a Sexual Message, The.
  Snapshots of a Daughter-in-Law.
  Translations.
Rukeyser, M. Myth.
Scott, M. Women of the Future.
Shange. We Need a God Who Bleeds Now.
Shaughnessy, B. Postfeminism.
Stone, R. Liberation.
Tompson. On a Fortification at Boston Begun by Women.
Trinidad. Answer Song.
Truth. Ain't I A Woman?
Unknown. Cloe to Artimesa.
Vollmer. Wildsisters Bar.
Wells, C. Poster Girl's Defence, The.
Yamada. Club, The.

Fences
Blue Cloud. Old Man's Lazy, The.
Dickey, J. Fence Wire.
Frost, R. Mending Wall.
McCord, D. Pickety Fence, The.
McKay, D. Barbed Wire Fence Meditates upon

the Goldfinch, A.
Stow. Singing Bones, The.
See also **Walls**

Fencing and Fencers
Manifold. Fencing School.

Ferns
Seaton, M. Fiddleheads.

Ferry Boats
Dibdin, C. Jolly Young Waterman, The.
Grosholz. On the Ferry, Toward Patras.
Housman, A. Crossing Alone the Nighted Ferry.
Jackson, G. Alice.
Kinnell. Memory of Wilmington.
Millay, E. Recuerdo.
Parnell, P. Sile Na gCioch.
Rossetti, C. Ferry Me across the Water.
Sexton. Letter Written on a Ferry While Crossing Long Island Sound.
Whitman, W. Crossing Brooklyn Ferry.

Fertilizer
Ramanujan. Death and the Good Citizen.

Festivals
Garioch. Embro to the Ploy.
Maiden. Taste.
Ofeimun. Naming Day, A.
Pelizzon, V. Feast of San Silvestro, The.

Feuds
Lea, S. Feud, The.
Prys-Jones. Cors-y-Gwaed: Fenland of Blood.
Unknown. Lads of Wamphray, The.
  Lord Maxwell's Last Goodnight.

Fever
Alexander, E. Aspirin.
Dobson, R. Fever, The.
Pilkington, L. Fair and Softly Goes Far or, The Wary Physician.
Plath. Fever 103°.
Wojahn. Allegory: Attic and Fever.

Fiddles and Fiddlers
Burns, R. Green Sleeves [and Tartan Ties].
Coffman. Courage, or One of Gene Horner's Fiddles.
Evans, S. Seven Fiddlers, The.
Freed, A. Fit As a Fiddle.
Goodhart, A. Fit As a Fiddle.
Hardy, T. Country Wedding, The.
Hoffman, A. Fit As a Fiddle.
Kinnell. First Song.
Neilson, J. Take Down the Fiddle, Karl!
Yeats. Fiddler of Dooney, The.
See also **Violins**

Fidelity
Auden. Legend.
  Lullaby: "Lay your sleeping head, my love."
Barresi. How It Comes.
Beer, P. Faithful Wife, The.
Black, J. Paper Doll.
Blamire. Siller Croun, The.
Brontë, E. Visionary, The.
Browning, E. Man's Requirements, A.
Burns, R. Open the Door to Me, Oh!
  Song: "O my love's [or luve's or love is or luve is] like a red, red rose."
Carmichael, H. Don't Forget to Say No, Baby.
Cary, P. Samuel Brown.
Chaucer. Complaint unto Pity, The.
Coleman, C. When in Rome (I Do As the Romans Do).
Curtis, T. Gambit.
Delgado, J. Two Timer.
Donne. Anniversary [or Anniversarie], The.
  Indifferent, The.
  Lovers' Infiniteness[e].
  Relic, The.
Dowson. Non Sum Qualis Eram Bonae sub Regno Cynarae.
Duhamel. Sex with a Famous Poet.
"Field." Constancy.
Ford, T. There Is a Lady Sweet and Kind.
Greenwell, D. Fidelity Rewarded.
Hammerstein. All er Nothin'
  Don't Ever Leave Me.
Harms. Soon.
Harwood, G. Wine Is Drunk, The.

Hemans. Gertrude, or Fidelity Till Death.
Herrick. Bracelet to Julia, The.
 Love Me Little, Love Me Long.
 To Anthea, Who May Command Him Anything.
Homer. Butchers, The.
 Phemios and Medon.
Housman, A. Shades of Night, The.
Jonson, B. Epistle. To Katharine, Lady Aubigny.
Kern, J. Don't Ever Leave Me.
Leigh, C. When in Rome (I Do As the Romans Do).
Lewis, A. Post-Script: for Gweno.
"Malley." Perspective Lovesong.
McAuley, J. In a Late Hour.
Montagu, L. Verses Written in a Garden.
Mullen, H. Roadmap.
Nesbit, E. Wife of All Ages, The.
O'Neal. Shades of Pharoah Sanders Blues for My Baby.
Poe. Annabel Lee.
Ponsot. La Une, A.
 Matins and Lauds.
Prassinos. Hair Tonic.
Procter, A. Woman's Answer, A.
Ralegh, S. Fortune Hath Taken Away.
Razaf, A. Keepin' Out of Mischief Now.
Robin, L. My Cutey's Due at Two-to-Two Today.
 No Love, No Nothin'
Robinson, E. Luke Havergal.
Robinson, M. Suspects his Constancy.
Rochester, J. Love And Life.
Rodgers, R. All er Nothin'
Sackville-West. Greater Cats, The.
Sherwood, G. Love and Life.
Spenser. Address to Venus.
 Arthur's Fight with Orgoglio and Duessa.
 Belphoebe and Timias.
 Book 1.
 Bower of Bliss, The.
 Britomart at Isis' Church.
 Britomart chaseth Ollyphant.
 Britomart in the House of the Enchanter Busyrane.
 Cave of Despair, The.
 Fight of the Red Cross Knight and the Heathen Sansjoy, The.
 Garden of Adonis, The.
 Guardian Angels.
 Guyon's Voyage to the Bower of Bliss.
 Hill of the Graces, The.
 House of Busyrane, The.
 In the Bower of Bliss.
 Legend of Britomartis, or of Chastitie, The.
 Legend of the Knight of the Red Crosse, or of Holinesse, The.
 Maske of Cupid, The.
 Mutability Claims to Rule the World.
 Nature's Reply to Mutability.
 Scudamor in the Temple of Venus.
 Song of Bliss.
 Vision of the Graces, The.
 Visit to Merlin, The.
Stanley, T. Changed, Yet Constant.
Surrey. "Love, That Doth Reign and Live Within My Thought."
"Tanaquil." Very Young Man Speaks, A.
Taylor, B. Bedouin Song.
Unknown. Lament of the Border Widow, The.
 Love Me Not [for Comely Grace].
 There Is a Lady Sweet and Kind.
 Young Beichan.
Vaughan, H. Song to Amoret, A.
 To Amoret, of the Difference 'twixt Him and Other Lovers, and What True Love Is.
Von Tilzer, A. My Cutey's Due at Two-to-Two Today.
Waller, T. et al. Keepin' Out of Mischief Now.
Warren, H. No Love, No Nothin'
Wickham. Paradox.
 Slighted Lady, The.
Winchilsea. Letter to Daphnis, A.
Wyatt, S. Long love that in my thought doth harbo[u]r, The.
 Steadfastness.

Yeats. Folly of Being Comforted, The.
Young, A. Woman, Don't Be Troublesome.
Young, M. J. To My Pen.
Field-Glasses
Young, A. Field-Glasses.
Fields and Pastures
Alley, R. Cleaning.
Ashbery. Grand Abacus.
Betjeman. Licorice Fields at Pontefract, The.
Browning, R. Meeting At Night.
 Two in the Campagna.
Busch, T. Heartland.
Cabalquinto. Depths of Fields.
Cavendish, M. Sea Similized to Meadows and Pastures: the Mariners, to Shepherds: the Mast, to a May-Pole: the Fish, to Beasts, The.
Clare, J. Hares at Play.
Conyus. Day in the Life of . . . , A.
Cowper, W. Poplar Field, The.
Davie. Hill Field, The.
Duncan, R. Often I Am Permitted to Return to a Meadow.
Everson, W. Muscat Pruning.
Foster, A. Field.
Francis, R. Onion Fields.
Frost, R. Cow in Apple Time, The.
 Pasture, The.
Gehrke, S. Walking Fields at Night South of Hampton, Iowa.
Gunn, T. For Signs.
Herrick. To Meadows [or Meddowes].
Hugo, R. Open Country.
Jarrell. Field and Forest.
Levin, D. Field.
Lovelace, R. Ant, The.
Marlowe. Passionate Shepherd To His Love, The.
Marvell. Mower's Song, The.
Merwin, W. S. Low Fields and Light.
Miles, J. Fields of Learning.
Millay, E. I Dreamed I Moved among the Elysian Fields.
Milton. Lycidas.
Paterson, D. Chartres of Gowrie, The.
Pilling. Field, The.
Pritchard, N. Paysagesque.
Pugh. Frozen Field, The.
Ray, H. Pastoral: "Annette came through the meadows."
Roethke. All the Earth, All the Air.
 Meadow Mouse, The.
Sharma, P. Potter's Field.
Stephens, J. White Fields.
Tarpley. Feel Free.
Tate, J. Love Making.
Teasdale. Broken Field, The.
Thomas, D. I, in My Intricate Image.
Thoreau. On Fields oer Which the Reaper's Hand Has Passed.
Van Doren. Immortal.
Weöres. Plain, The.
Wilbur. Exeunt.
 Grasshopper, A.
Wilcox, E. Attraction.
Williams, W. Desolate Field, The.
Wordsworth, W. Solitary Reaper, The.
Wright, J. Late November in a Field.
 To the Evening Star: Central Minnesota.
Young, A. Field-Glasses.
Fig Trees and Figs
Causley. Figgie Hobbin.
Dove, R. This Life.
García, D. Orchard of Figs in the Fall, An.
Hall, D. Small Fig Tree, A.
Lawrence, D. Bare Fig-trees.
 Figs.
Nye, N. My Father and the Fig Tree.
Pilling. Encounter at the Post Office Counter.
Warren, R. Where the Slow Fig's Purple Sloth.
Fights
Algarin. Always Throw the First Punch.
Belieu. Part of the Effect of the Public Scene Is to Importune the Passing Viewer.
Browning, R. Woman's Last Word, A.
Cameron, N. Fight with a Water-Spirit.
Carroll, L. Brother and Sister.

Coleridge, M. Mortal Combat.
Lawrence, D. What Would You Fight For?
Loftis, N. Fights After School.
Mattawa. Bus Driver Poem, The.
McKay, C. If We Must Die.
Millay, E. Hearing Your Words, and Not a Word Among Them.
Mulkey, R. Blind-Sided.
Ransom, J. Captain Carpenter.
Valerie, J. On Apologies.
Whitman, R. Listening to Grownups Quarreling.
Williamson, G. Neighboring Storms.
Figureheads (ship)
Adams, L. Figurehead, The.
Filipinos
Abad, G. Holy Order.
 Jeepney.
 Light in One's Blood, The.
 Toys.
Africa-Bolasco. Sauna 2.
Aguilar, M. Pall Hanging over Manila.
 Poem from Sierra Madre.
Aguilar-Cariño. Dinakdakan.
 Familiar.
 Gabi.
Balce, N. Pizza and Pretense.
Balingit, J. Quiet Evening, Home Away.
Bobis, M. Driving to Katoomba.
 Word Gifts for an Australian Critic.
Brion, R. Good Friday.
 If Fortune Smiles.
 Love Song.
Caballero-Robb, M. Dear Rosario.
 Memoranda for Rosario.
Cabalquinto. Depths of Fields.
Cabico, R. Afternoon in Pangasinan with No Electricity, An.
 Check One.
 Mango Poem.
Carbó, N. Civilizing the Filipino.
 I Found Orpheus Levitating.
 Little Brown Brother.
Cariaga. Family Tree, The.
Cerenio. 13 June 1994.
 20 July 1994.
 23 October 1992.
 My Mother.
Cortes, F. Dolce Far Niente.
 Fish 2.
 Palace of Fine Arts in San Francisco, The.
 Poem Composed During a Brownout.
Duhamel. Yes.
Dumdum. Li Pos of the Polis.
 Some Die of Light.
 To My Mother.
E'der, E. La Puente.
 Once We Were Farmers.
Escandor, V. Summer Nostalgia.
Evasco, M. Baked Oysters Rockefeller.
 Dancing a Spell.
 Elemental.
 Heron-Woman.
Faigao, B. Balitaw.
 Kundiman.
Francia, L. In Gurgle Veritas.
 Secret in the Roar, The.
Fructuoso, E. Astig.
Gamalinda, E. Denials.
 La Naval De Manila: Selim Sot as a Modern Political Observer.
 Lament Beginning w/a Line after Cavafy.
Garrett, E. Bachelors, The.
 Grandfather's Mint.
Gier, J. California Coast.
 Examining the I.
 First View of the Islands, A.
 Going Baroque.
Gloria. Aleng Maria.
 Assimilation.
 Rizal's Ghost.
 Touch.
Gonzalez, N. Deepest Well in Madras, The.
 How the Heart Aches.
 I Made Myself a Path.
 Wanderer in the Night of the World, A.

Finches

Gotera. First Mango.
Madarika.
Manong Chito Tells Manong Ben about His
     Dream over Breakfast at the Manilatown
     Cafe.
Pacific Crossing.
Hagedorn, J. Souvenirs.
Hufana, A. Contemporary.
Floating Epitaphs, Their Possible Explanations
     in Poro Point.
From the Raw.
Insides of Alfred Hitchcock, The.
Humphrey, D. April in Houston.
Ilio, D. Children of the Atomic Age.
Marikudo in Kalibo, 1979.
Prokosch in Tehran, 1978.
Site of My Grandfather's House, The.
Jacinto, J. Absence.
Heaven Is Just Another Country.
Visitation.
Lim-Wilson. Alphabet Soup.
Raising the Dead.
Mateo. Jeepneyfying.
There Is No Word for Sex in Taglog.
Melo, M. Red Lipstick on a Straw.
Scrambled Eggs and Garlic Pork.
Unlearning English.
Nazareno, C. Bohol's Tarsier Population.
Cortes Swamp, The.
Palis, Y. Floor, The.
Waking Up.
Remoto. Black Silk Pajamas.
Exile.
Images of John (1967–92).
Robles. Cutting Back the Ifugao Past.
Feasting with Etang a Hundred Times Around.
Manong with a Thousand Tribal Visions, The.
Remembering the Past.
San Juan. Owl of Minerva Takes Flight in the
     Evening, The.
Ungria, R. Carillonneur.
Commerce and the Man.
Culture Nervous.
Viray, M. Patio.
Yuson. Andy Warhol Speaks to His Two
     Filipino Maids.
World Poetry Circuit.
Zamora-Linmark. Day 1: Portrait of the Artisit,
     Small-kid Time.
Election Day.
Zarco. Manila Paper.
Once upon a Seesaw with Charlie Chan.
See also **Philippines**

Finches
Christie. Hollywood Finch, The.
Knight, H. Bullfinch in Town, The.
Singer, B. Birdsong.
Wordsworth, W. Green Linnet, The.

Fingers
Buzzi. Finger-nails.
Dacey, P. Thumb.
Davies, H. Poem: "It doesn't look like a finger
     it looks like a feather of broken glass."
Fitzgerald, E. 71.
Halpern, D. Her Body.
Hartnett. I Think Sometimes.
Hope, A. Gateway, The.
Kuroda. Afternoon 3.
Nezval. City With Towers.
O'Neill, M. My Fingers.
Randolph, T. Upon the Loss[e] of His Little
     Finger.
Simic. Bestiary for the Fingers of My Right
     Hand.

Finland
Hacker, M. Rune of the Finland Woman.
Jacobsen, J. Reindeer and Engine.

Fir Trees
Jay, T. Fir.
Murphy, R. Epitaph on a Fir-Tree.

Fire and Fires
Ai. New Crops for a Free Man.
Alexander, E. Overture: Watermelon City.
Anderson, P. Houses Burning; Quebec.
Balaban. Thoughts Before Dawn.

Baxter, J. Firemen, The.
Wild Bees.
Bishop, E. Armadillo, The.
Casabianca.
Bobrowski. Latvian Autumn, The.
Place of Fire.
Bradstreet, A. Here Follows Some Verses upon
     the Burning of Our House [July 10th, 1666.
     Copied Out of a Loose Paper].
Brew. Search, The.
Bromige. Log.
Point, The.
Brown, S. Schadenfreude.
Brydges. To Miss M——, Written by
     Moonlight, July 18, 1782.
Buckley, V. Man, a Woman, A.
Byron, G. Darkness.
Campbell, D. Man in the Honeysuckle, The.
Cardiff. Where Fire Burns.
Carr, M. Castle in the Fire, The.
Clare, J. Gypsy's Evening Blaze, The.
Clifton, L. Fury.
Move.
Coleman, H. Remembrance of Things Past.
Conoley. World, The.
Couzyn. Way Out, The.
Davis, C. Years, The.
Davis, C. August Fires.
Dodge, M. Fire in the Window.
Doolittle, H. Sea Violet.
Fisher, R. Burning Graves at Netherton, The.
Flynn, N. Bag of Mice.
Frost, R. Fire and Ice.
Garland, H. Fighting Fire.
Prairie Fires.
Geiger. Soundtracks.
Graves, R. Under the Pot.
Grimké, A. Epitaph on a Living Woman.
Gunn, T. Faustus Triumphant.
Hall, D. Love-Letter-Burning.
Hamburger, M. Treblinka.
Harper, M. Fireplace, The.
Harte, B. Chicago.
Hassett. Mother's Day.
Hemphill. Soft Targets.
Henderson-Holmes. My First Riot: Bronx,
     NYC.
Herrick. Scar[e]-Fire, The.
Herschberger. Lumberyard, The.
Hirsch, E. American Apocalypse.
Man on a Fire Escape.
Hitchcock. Scattering Flowers.
Hughes, F. In the Shadow of Fire.
Jacobsen, J. Limbo Dancer, The.
Jeffers, R. Fire on the Hills.
Jonson, B. Execration upon Vulcan, An.
Kennedy, X. Lighting a Fire.
King, H. Sonnet: "Tell me[e] no more how
     fair[e] she[e] is."
Kinnell. Another Night in the Ruins.
Under the Maud Moon.
Komunyakaa. How I See Things.
Kyle, C. J. Fire in Early Morning.
Levine, P. Coming Home, *Detroit*, 1968.
Lindley, D. By Fire or Flood.
Lindtová, A. Campfire.
Longfellow, H. Golden Mile-Stone, The.
Lorde. Day They Eulogized Mahalia, The.
Summer Oracle.
Lovelace, R. Fly about a Glass[e] of Burnt
     Claret, A.
Loving. Black Horse Rider, The.
Lowell, J. Darkened Mind, The.
Lux. Barn Fire.
MacNeice. Brother Fire.
McClatchy. Method, The.
McDaniel, J. Leonard.
McDonald, W. Once You've Been to War.
McGrath, T. Coal Fire in Winter, A.
Merrill, J. Charles on Fire.
Merton. Elegy for the Monastery Barn.
Merwin, W. S. Burnt Child, The.
Monk, M. Fire Us with Ice, Burn Us with
     Snow.
Moore, M. To a Chameleon.
Morley, D. On Fire.

Morrissey, S. There was Fire in Vancouver.
Moss, T. Lynching, The.
North, C. Leap Year.
O'Connor, M. Fire.
Patchen. Naked Land, The.
Paulin. Peacetime.
Piatt, J. Fires in Illinois.
Piatt, S. Palace-Burner, The.
Piper, E. Indian Counsel.
Porter, P. Non Piangere, Liù.
Rabinowitz. Of Joy Illimited: Polyphonic
     Soundings: Shore to Ship.
Rafferty, C. Arsonist Tells His Story to the
     Attorney, The.
Ramsdell, H. Bright Receding.
Ravikovitch [*or* Ravikovich]. Dress of Fire, A.
Rawson, J. Map Burnt Through.
Reavey. How many fires.
Redmond. Distance.
My Tongue Paints a Path.
Rhodes, M. How Fast.
Rich, A. Burning Oneself Out.
Rivard. Firestone.
Rodriguez, L. Fire.
Rohrer, M. Short History of Illumination, A.
Roseliep. Campfire Extinguished.
Rossetti, C. Flint.
Roy, L. Ride, The.
Ruffin. Hotel Fire: New Orleans.
Rukeyser, M. Burning the Dreams.
Rybicki, J. This Sun.
Sanchez, S. Elegy (for MOVE and
     Philadelphia).
Philadelphia: Spring, 1985.
Scannell. Incendiary.
Seyburn, P. Good Water.
Smith, S. Persian, The.
Snyder, G. Burning the Small Dead.
Sorrentino. Land of Cotton.
Southwell. Burning Babe, The.
Speyer. Witch!
Stevenson, R. Armies in the Fire.
Autumn Fires.
Taylor, A. Fire.
Todd, M. Grandmother's Farm.
Townsend, A. Butane, Kerosene, Gasoline.
Uyematsu. Ten Million Flames of Los Angeles,
     The.
Vigil, A. Hogarcito de La Madrugada, El.
Volkman. Create Desire.
Warren, R. In Creve Coeur, Missouri.
Watson, R. Ballad of the Were-Wolf, A.
Betty Barnes, the Book-Burner.
Webb, C. Arson.
Weigl. Burning Shit at An Khe.
Weiss, T. Fire at Alexandria, The.
Whitman, W. By the Bivouac's Fitful Flame.
Whittier. Burning Drift-Wood.
Williamson, G. Walter Parmer.
Wright, C. State of Preservation.
Wright, J. Night After Bushfire.
To a Child.
Two Fires, The.
Wright, R. Between the World and Me.
Zu-Bolton. Struggle-Road Dance.

Fire Engines
Baxter, J. Firemen, The.
Wilbur. Fire-Truck, A.
Williams, W. Great Figure, The.

Fire Island
O'Hara, F. True Account of Talking to the Sun
     at Fire Island, A.

Fire-eaters
Delgado, J. Mexican Fire Breather, A.

Firecats
Stevens, W. Earthy Anecdote.

Firefighters
Baxter, J. Firemen, The.
Hampton. Fire Station's Delight, The.
Harris, R. Ambition, The.
Holland, J. Three Tests for Darwin Duke.

Fireflies
Channing. Chant to the Fire-fly.
Fleischman. Fireflies.
Frost, R. Fireflies in the Garden.

Kinzie. Canicula.
Marvell. Mower to the Glowworms [or Glow-Worms or Glo-Worms], The.
Mercer, J. Glow-Worm, The.
Roberts, E. Firefly.
Smith, C. Glow-Worm, The.
Strange. Childhood.
Ward, D. My Brothers Make a Lantern.
See also **Glowworms**

Fireworks
Peck, R. Four of July.
Worth, V. Fireworks.

Firpo, Luis
Ignatow, D. Boxing Match, The.

Fish
Aaronson. Pesci Misti.
Adams, S. Gwbert: Mackerel Fishing.
Adamson. Gutting the Salmon.
Albrecht, A. Below White Cliffs.
Alvi, M. Fish.
Barker, G. How many apples grow on the tree?
Sonnet of Fishes.
Bishop, E. Fish, The.
Blight. Evolution.
Garfish.
Brooke, R. Heaven.
Carroll. Ode on a Bicycle on Halsted Street in a Sudden Summer Thunderstorm.
Cortes, F. Fish 2.
Couzyn. Spell to Protect Our Love.
De la Mare. Alas, Alack!
Dickey, J. Movement of Fish, The.
Donne. Bait[e], The.
Dove, R. Fish in the Stone, The.
Dumas, H. Knees of a Natural Man.
Eigner. Letter for Duncan.
Gray, T. Ode on the Death of a Favourite [or Favorite] Cat, Drowned in a Tub [or Bowl] of Gold Fishes.
Guest, B. Twilight Polka Dots.
Hannan, M. Lamper, The.
Hartley, M. Fishmonger.
Harwood, G. Mid-Channel.
Hitchcock. One Whose Reproach I Cannot Evade, The.
Hughes, T. Pike.
Jaques, F. There Once Was a Puffin.
Jeffers, R. Birds and Fishes.
Purse-Seine, The.
Kelly, B. Leaving, The.
Lawrence, D. Little Fish.
Lowell, R. Fishnet.
MacCaig. Kingfisher.
Major, C. Beaulieu.
Marlatt, D. Bruce and the Bluegills.
McAuley, J. Legendary.
McCaffery. Little Hans.
Melville, H. Maldive Shark, The.
Song from *Mardi*.
We Fish.
Milosz, C. Abundant Catch (Luke 5:4–10).
Montague, J. Trout, The.
Moore, M. Egyptian Pulled Glass Bottle in the Shape of a Fish, An.
Fish, The.
Myles, E. School of Fish.
Nemerov. Goose Fish, The.
Niatum. Salmon, The.
Noguere. Soma.
Pollitt. Two Fish.
Rafferty, P. View from the Bathysphere.
Ramke. Difference Between Night and Day, The.
Romo-Carmona, M. Fish.
Rosen, K. Along the Charles.
Rosenblatt. Fish.
Ichthycide.
Ross, W. Fish.
Sandburg, C. Fish Crier.
Satyamurti. Erdywurble.
Sitwell, S. Mrs. Busk.
Smedley, M. Sorrowful Sea-Gull, The.
Stevens, M. Carp, The.
Swift, J. Steelhead in the Whitehorse Rearing Pond.
Sze. In Your Honor.

Tate, J. Blue Booby, The.
Thomas, R. Pisces.
Song for Gwydion.
Thoreau. Salmon Brook.
Unknown. Fisherman's Rhyme.
Fowls [or Foweles or Fowles] in the Frith.
One, Two, Three, Four, Five!
Wicks, S. Buying Fish.
Wood, W. Sea's Abundant Progeny, The.
Wright, D. Juxtapositions.
Wright, J. Northern Pike.
Yeats. Three Movements.

Fishing and Fishermen
Adams, S. Gwbert: Mackerel Fishing.
Addonizio. China Camp, California.
Balaban. Dragonfish, The.
Barrax. Visit.
Bishop, E. At the Fishhouses.
Fish, The.
Brown, G. Haddock Fishermen.
Old Fisherman with Guitar.
Trout Fisher.
Burns, R. Fishing in Winter.
Carver, R. Catch, The.
Chamberlain, B. Islandman.
Chang Chi. Coming at Night to a Fisherman's Hut.
Chock. Bait, The.
Cooley, N. Undine.
Curnow. Canst Thou Draw Out Leviathan with an Hook.
D'Urfey [or Durfey]. Fisherman's Song, The.
Delp. Fishing the Dream.
Donne. Bait[e], The.
Dunbar, P. Boy's Summer, A.
Eigner. Letter for Duncan.
Ellington, D. I'm Gonna Go Fishin'.
Engels, J. Bullhead.
Estes, A. You Stand There Fishing.
Field, E. Wynken, Blynken, and Nod.
Finney, M. Fishing Among the Learned.
Galvin, J. Shadow-Casting.
Gomez, M. Looking Deep.
Greenlaw. World Where News Travelled Slowly, A.
Grosholz. Old Fisherman, The.
Hamilton, G. Don's Holiday.
Harwood, G. Mid-Channel.
Hass, R. San Pedro Road.
Heaney, S. Hazel Stick for Catherine Ann, A.
Holmes, O. Ballad of the Oysterman, The.
Howes, B. Out Fishing.
Hughes, L. Catch.
Hugo, R. Letter to Wagoner from Port Townsend.
Jeffers, R. Purse-Seine, The.
Salmon Fishing.
Kingsley, C. Three Fishers [Went Sailing], The.
Kinnell. Angling, a Day.
Kunitz, S. Catch, The.
Quinnapoxet.
Lang, A. Last Chance, The.
Lea, S. At the Flyfisher's Shack.
Lee, P. I'm Gonna Go Fishin'.
Leslie, K. Halibut Cove Harvest.
Lieberman, L. Lobsters in the Brain Coral.
Liu Tsung-yüan. River Snow.
Lorde. Fishing the White Water.
Lowell, R. Drunken Fisherman, The.
MacDiarmid, H. With the Herring Fishers.
Mapanje. Elegy for Mangochi Fishermen, An.
McDonald, C. Nightfishing.
McLain, P. Fishing.
Merrill, J. Parrot Fish, The.
Pier: Under Pisces, The.
Merwin, W. S. Finding a Teacher.
Mirikitani. Fisherman, The.
Montague, J. Trout, The.
Moody, E. To a Gentleman Who Invited Me to Go A-Fishing.
Morris, L. Fishing Lass of Hakin, The.
Nairne. Caller Herrin'.
Nemerov. Casting.
Newbolt. Master and Man.
O'Hara, F. Captains Courageous.

Oswald, A. Pilchard-Curing Song, The.
Ou-yang Hsiu. Old Fisherman.
Plutzik. Jim Desterland.
Porteous. Charlie Douglas.
Decommissioning.
Wrecked Creeves.
Price, C. Night Fishing.
Ray, H. Fisherman's Story, The.
Rodgers, R. Mister Snow.
Roethke. Lady and the Bear, The.
Pike, The.
Schnackenberg. Nightfishing.
Scovell. Boy Fishing, The.
Shumaker. Circle of Totems, The.
Smithyman. Hint for the Incomplete Angler.
Snyder, G. River Snow.
St. John, P. Song.
Stafford, W. In the Deep Channel.
Stevens, W. Thinking of a Relation between the Images of Metaphors.
Stevenson, R. Epitaph: "Angler rose, he took his rod, The."
Stone, J. Bass, The.
Stuart, D. Fishing with Elvis.
Su Tung-p'o. Epigram.
Sze. In Your Honor.
Thoreau. Salmon Brook.
Trethewey, N. Flounder.
Trowbridge, J. Old Lobsterman, The.
Voznesensky [or Voznesenskii]. Call of the Lake, The.
Whitman, W. Torch, The.
Whittier. Skipper Ireson's Ride.
Wright, J. Lifting Illegal Nets by Flashlight.
Yeats. Fisherman, The.
Yevtushenko [or Evtushenko]. Hand-Rolled Cigarettes.
Young, K. Casting.
See also **Clams and Clamming; Crabs and Crabbing**

Fitzgerald, Edward
Browning, R. To Edward FitzGerald.
Tennyson, A. To E. Fitzgerald.

Fitzgerald, F. Scott
Davie. Garden Party, The.
Preston, K. Effervescence and Evanescence.

Fixation
Mew. My Heart is Lame.

Flags
Bell, M. Primer about the Flag, A.
Berry, W. Let Us Pledge.
Bidgood. Dragon.
Bierce. Confederate Flags, The.
Cohan. You're a Grand Old Flag.
Key. Star-Spangled Banner, The.
Morgan, E. Itinerary.
Saint. Heart and Soul.
Smith, K. Train.
Thomas, L. Subway Witnesses, The.

Flags, United States
Bennett, H. Flag Goes By, The.
Cohan. You're a Grand Old Flag.
Drake, J. American Flag, The.
Fordham. Stars and Stripes.
Key. Star-Spangled Banner, The.
Unknown. Our Flag.
Whittier. Barbara Frietchie.

Flamingos
Goldbarth. Seriema Song.

Flanders, Belgium
Ford, F. Old Houses of Flanders, The.
Grenfell, J. Into Battle.
McCrae, J. In Flanders Fields.

Flattery
Anderson, W. I'm Naebody Noo.
Carryl, G. Sycophantic Fox and the Gullible Raven, The.
Ewart. It's Hard to Dislike Ewart.
Herrick. To His Kinswoman, Mrs. Penelope Wheeler.
Howitt, M. Spider and the Fly, The.
Jackson, T. Pretty Baby.
Jordan, T. Double Acrostich on Mrs Svsanna Blvnt, A.
Kahn, G. Pretty Baby.

Porter, C. You're the Top.
Van Alstyne, E. Pretty Baby.

Fleas
Bachner. Little Mouse, The.
Donne. Flea, The.
Lindsay, N. Little Turtle, The.
Nichols, R. Harlot's Catch.
Unknown. Poem to Answer the Question: How Old Are Fleas?

Flies
Carew, T. Fly That Flew into My Mistress'[s] Eye, A.
Carey [*or* Cary]. Nulla Fides.
Chang, D. On The Fly.
Clare, J. Clock-A-Clay.
De la Mare. Fly, The.
Dobson, A. In Town.
Emmett. Blue Tail Fly or Jimmy Cracked Corn, The.
Graves, R. Blue-Fly, The.
Herrick. Amber Bead, The.
Hoffman, D. Ephemeridae.
Howitt, M. Spider and the Fly, The.
Kay, J. Virus².
Larkin, R. Housework.
Lear, E. Limerick: "There was an old person of Skye."
Levis. Morning After My Death, The.
Lovelace, R. Fly about a Glass[e] of Burnt Claret, A.
Lowell, R. Harriet.
MacNeice. Mayfly.
Ní Chuilleanáin. Dead Fly.
Oldys. On a Fly Drinking Out of [*or* From] His Cup.
Page, P. Evening Dance of the Grey Flies.
Patmore, C. Flesh-Fly and the Bee, The.
Perreault, J. Readymade.
"Pindar." To a Fly, Taken out of a Bowl of Punch.
Rimington, J. God of the Flies.
Summerfield. Yesterday the House was Full of Flies.
Taylor, E. Upon a Spider Catching a Fly.
Teddy. At Terezin.
Tomlinson, C. Jam Trap, The.
Turner, C. Calvus to a Fly.
Williams, C. My Fly.
Yeats. Long-Legged Fly.

Flight
Alcott, L. Lay of a Golden Goose, The.
Allingham. Swing Song, A.
Bishop, E. Invitation to Miss Marianne Moore.
Boland, E. Ready for Flight.
Branch, A. Ere the Golden Bowl Is Broken.
Brownstein. Stepping Out.
Brutus. Prayer: "O let me soar on steadfast wing."
Coatsworth. And Stands There Sighing.
De la Mare. Ride-by-Nights, The.
Dickey, J. Eagles.
Dickinson, E. Bees.
Dransfield. Flying.
Duncan, R. Letting the Beat Go.
Gunn, T. Tamer and Hawk.
Hall, D. Old Pilot, The.
Hogg, J. Witch o' Fife, The.
Howes, B. Wild Geese Flying.
Hughes, T. Swifts.
Hugo, V. Be Like the Bird.
Imbs. Wind Was There, The.
Lindley, D. Nearness.
Lovelace, R. Falcon, The.
MacCaig. Solitary Crow.
Magee, J. High Flight.
Mataka. Ornithology.
McLoughland. Crazy Boys.
Melville, H. Man-of-War Hawk, The.
Meredith, W. June: Dutch Harbor.
Merwin, W. S. Fly.
Meyers, B. Pigeons.
Mother Goose. Flying-Man.
Old Woman, Old Woman.
Noguere. Barney Bigard.
Pietri. How Do Your Eggs Want You (?).

Probyn. As the Flower of the Grass.
Reverdy. Adieu.
Roberts, N. Gull's Flight, The.
Rossetti, C. Fly Away, Fly Away.
Sexton. To a Friend Whose Work Has Come to Triumph.
Smith, S. No Categories!
Stevenson, R. Swing, The.
Tranter. Lufthansa.
Very. Birds of Passage, The.
Warren, R. Evening Hawk.
Wilbur. All These Birds.
Woo, M. Untitled: "In the deepest night and a full moon."
Wright, J. Presentation of Two Birds to My Son, A.

Flirtation
Ager, M. Louisville Lou (The Vampin' Lady).
Arlen, H. Between the Devil and the Deep Blue Sea.
Aytoun [*or* Ayton], R. Song, A: On His Mistress.
Brooks, H. Ain't Misbehavin'
Browning, E. Lady's "Yes," The.
Burge. Disillusion.
Campbell, D. Small-town Gladys.
Cockburn, C. Caution, The.
Congreve. Doris.
Cullen, C. Timid Lover.
Davies, W. Flirt, The.
Dougherty. Long Coats with Deep Pockets.
Gascoigne. For That He Looked Not upon Her.
Godfrey. Our Lady.
Grimké, A. Caprichosa.
Harbach, O. She Didn't Say "Yes."
Herrick. Lips Tongueless[e].
Sho[o]e Tying, The.
Silken Snake, The.
Koehler, T. Between the Devil and the Deep Blue Sea.
Lumsden, R. Tricks for the Barmaid.
Montagu, L. To a Lady Making Love.
Pinkard, M. Gimme a Little Kiss (Will Ya, Huh?).
Porter, C. My Heart Belongs to Daddy.
Prior. Ode, An: "Merchant, to secure his treasure, The."
Rome, H. Nobody Makes a Pass at Me.
Stanley, T. Divorce, The.
Stevenson, A. Sous-Entendu.
Stuart, M. In The Orchard.
Surrey. "Love, That Doth Reign and Live Within My Thought."
Symons, A. At the Cavour.
Walwicz. Big Tease.
Wetzsteon. Urban Gallery.
Wyatt, S. Long love that in my thought doth harbo[u]r, The.
Lover Showeth How He Is Forsaken of Such as He Sometime Enjoyed, The.
Yellen, J. Louisville Lou (The Vampin' Lady).

Flodden Field, Battle of (1513)
Elliot, J. Flowers of the Forest, The.

Flood, The
Beer, P. Flood, The.
Halsall. Return to Ararat.
Kendall, M. Vision of Noah, The.
Lewis, C. Late Passenger, The.
Merwin, W. S. Noah's Raven.
Reid, C. Stones and Bones.
Synge. 'Mergency Man, The.
Szporluk. Grass and the Sin, The.
Ullman. Rain.

Floods
Burnside. Swimming in the Flood.
Clare, J. Flood, The.
Dixon, M. River, Stay 'Way from My Door.
Erdrich. I Was Sleeping Where the Black Oaks Move.
Foulcher. After the Flood.
Guevara, M. After the Flood.
Knight, E. Poem to Galway Kinnell, A.
Lim-Wilson. Wave, The.
Marvell. Eyes and Tears.

Merwin, W. S. Dictum: For a Masque of Deluge.
Murray, L. Transposition of Clermont, The.
Patton, C. High Water Everywhere.
Quarles. On the Two Great Floods.
Rios, A. Wet Camp.
Solari, R. Currents.
Swanger. Natural Disaster.
Turner, C. Dream, A.
Woods, H. River, Stay 'Way from My Door.
Wright, J. Beanstalk, Meditated Later, The.
Flood Year.
To Flood Stage Again.

Florence, Italy
Agoos, J. Portinaio.
Hamby, B. St. Clare's Underwear.
Hoffman, D. È, the Feasting Florentines.
Lawrence, D. Bat.
Levy, A. Reminiscence, A.

Florida
Becker, R. In Pompano Beach, Florida.
Bishop, E. Florida.
Blanco, R. Silver Sands, The.
Florsheim. Weekend in Palm Springs.
Hughes, L. Florida Road Workers.
Lewis, G. Pentecost.
McElroy, C. End of Civilization as We Know It, The.
McGrath, C. Florida.
Florida Anasazi, The.
Moss, H. Miami Beach.
Rakosi. Florida.
Sholl. Distinct Call of the Alligator, The.
Stevens, W. Farewell to Florida.
Nomad Exquisite.
O Florida, Venereal Soil.
Vollmer. Nursing the Sunburn.
Woolson. Florida Beach, The.

Florists
Koch, K. Girl and Baby Florist Sidewalk Pram Nineteen Seventy Something.
Roethke. Old Florist.

Flowers
Apollinaire. Fete.
Ashbery. Archipelago, The.
Picture of Little J. A. in a Prospect of Flowers, The.
Atwood. Flowers.
Baker, D. Someone's Been Sending Me Flowers.
Belieu. My Field Guide.
Nocturne: My Sister Life.
Benn. Little Aster.
Betham-Edwards. To a Llangollen Rose, the Day After It Had Been Given by Miss Ponsonby.
Bethell. Discipline.
Betjeman. Licorice Fields at Pontefract, The.
Bevan, M. Confrontation with a Bouquet.
Binyon. Harebell and Pansy.
Blunden. Vlamertinghe.
Bodecker. Garden Calendar.
Brooke, R. Old Vicarage, Grantchester, The.
Brooks, G. Coora Flower, The.
Bryant, W. Death of the Flowers, The.
Painted Cup, The.
Bui-Burton. My Love is Like a Lily.
Burns, R. O Were My Love Yon Lilac[k] Fair.
Calil, A. Blouse of Felt.
Carruth, H. Of Distress Being Humiliated by the Classical Chinese Poets.
This Decoration.
Clare, J. First Love.
Primrose, The.
Cobbold, E. On Some Violets Planted in My Garden by a Friend.
Coleridge, M. Poison Flower, The.
September.
Coolbrith. My Cloth of Gold.
Cope, W. Flowers.
Crane, H. To Emily Dickinson.
Crapsey. Guarded Wound, The.
Creeley. Flower, The.
Crouch, S. Chops Are Flyin.
Curry. Poppy Heads.
Curtis, T. Queen's Tears.

Davies, W. Hill-Side Park, The.
Day Lewis. Two Songs.
De la Mare. Two Gardens.
De Tabley. Study of a Spider, The.
Delgado, J. Chuparosa.
DeSylva, B. G. April Showers.
Doolittle, H. At Baia.
  Evening.
  Garden.
  Sea Rose.
  Sea Violet.
  White World.
Dorn, E. Song, A.
Doty, M. Lilacs in NYC.
Douglas, K. Desert Flowers.
Douglas, L. Two Loves.
Dove, R. In the Old Neighborhood.
Duncan, R. Glimpse, A.
Emerson, R. Humble-Bee, The.
  Rhodora, The [On Being Asked Whence Is the
    Flower].
Enright, D. Flowers.
Evance, S. To a Violet.
Fainlight, R. Archive Film Material.
Fay, J. Flowers.
Ferguson, G. Fear of the Future.
  Scan.
"Field." Irises.
  Penetration.
  Sullenness.
  Tiger-Lilies.
  Unbosoming.
Fishman, L. Promiscuity.
Foley, K. Matching Flowers.
Foster, A. Field.
Francis, R. Bouquets.
  Exclusive Blue.
Freneau. Wild Honey Suckle, The.
Frost, R. Leaves Compared with Flowers.
  Subverted Flower, The.
  Tuft of Flowers, The.
Ginsberg, A. In Back of the Real.
Glück, L. Mock Orange.
Goodison. Kenscoff.
Graham, J. Opulence.
Graves, R. Gardener.
  Troll's Nosegay, The.
Gray, J. Poem: "Geranium, houseleek, laid in
  oblong beds."
Greenberg, A. Wintering Over at the End of the
  Century.
Guest, B. Heavy Violets.
Gunn, T. Moly.
Hahn, S. Perennial.
Hamburger, M. Weeding.
Hamilton, S. Poppy, The.
Hardy, T. Lodging-House Fuchsias, The.
Harnick. Someone's Been Sending Me Flowers.
Harter. Tulip.
Harwood, G. Sea Anemones, The.
Hayden, R. Night-Blooming Cereus, The.
Hazo. Only the New Branches Bloom.
Healy, R. Primula Veris.
Heath, R. On Clarastella Walking in Her
  Garden.
Hecht, A. Illumination.
Hemans. Bring Flowers.
  Night-Blooming Flowers.
Herbert, G. Flower, The.
  Life.
Herrick. Meditation for His Mistress[e], A.
  To Blossoms.
  To Daffodils [or Daffadills].
  To Marygolds.
  To Violets.
  Why Flowers Change Color.
Hildebrandt, Z. Persephone.
Hitchcock. Scattering Flowers.
Hope, A. Flower Poem.
Humphrey, D. April in Houston.
  No Immunity.
Jackson, R. Lady's Way.
Jamie. Flower-sellers, Budapest.
Jarmain. El Alamein.
Jenyns. To a Nosegay in Pancharilla's Breast.
Jones, P. In the Formal Garden.

In the Park.
Kenyon, J. Peonies at Dusk.
King, H. Contemplation upon Flowers, A.
Kinnell. Flower Herding on Mount Monadnock.
Kunitz, S. Round, The.
Landon. Death in the Flower.
Lawrence, D. Andraitx—Pomegranate Flowers.
  Bavarian Gentians.
  Flowers and Men.
Le Gallienne. Library in a Garden, A.
Lee, L. Irises.
Levertov. Earliest Spring.
Li Ch'ing-chao. Tune: 'Magnolia Flowers.'
Lili'u-o-ka-lani. Ku'u Pua I Paoakalani.
  Sanoe.
Liu, T. Brooklyn Botanic Garden, The.
Long, H. Day and Night.
Lovelace, R. To Lucasta: The Rose.
Lowell, A. Grotesque.
  Weather-Cock Points South, The.
Luschei, G. Arrangement.
Mackenzie, K. Ginger-flowers.
Madgett. Woman with Flower.
Mansfield, K. Secret Flowers.
Martínez, V. Into the Next One.
Marvell. Picture of Little T. C. in a Prospect of
  Flowers, The.
McGuckian. Collusion.
  Flower Master, The.
  Orchid House, The.
Mitford. Forget-Me-Not, The.
Mori. Heat in October.
Muske, C. Fault, The.
Myles, E. Maxfield Parrish.
Naden. Poet and Botanist.
Neilson, J. Flowers in the Ward.
Newburn, L. Office Geraniums.
Notley. White Peacock, The.
Ohnishi, T. Blossoms in the Wind.
Oliver, D. Walnut and Lily.
Osborne, J. Naming of Flowers, The.
Plath. Among the Narcissi.
Po Chü-i. Buying Flowers.
  Flower, A.
Pogson, P. Amaryllis Belladonna.
  In Dreams.
Pope, A. Garden, The.
Pound, E. Ts'ai Chi'h.
Prince, F. Babiaantje, The.
Radiguet. Poem: "Red eiderdown at the
  window, A."
Rakosi. Menage, The.
Riley, J. At the Stanley Spencer Exhibition.
Robinson, A. Posies.
  Unum est Necessarium.
Rodriguez, J. Nasturtium Scanned.
Roethke. Carnations.
  Geranium, The.
  Shape of the Fire, The.
Roscoe, W. Camellia, The.
Roseliep. Morning-Glory, The.
Russell, S. Poem: "I keep feeling all space as
  my image."
Schilpp, M. Triage.
Schuyler, J. Korean Mums.
  Roof Garden.
Seward. To the Poppy.
Shapiro, K. Cut Flower, A.
  Editing *Poetry*.
Shepherd, R. White Days.
Shumaker. Ajo Lily.
Siegel, J. Wild Hyacinth.
Silvers, L. April Showers.
Sitwell, D. Swans, The.
Sitwell, S. Kingcups.
Slater, E. Search.
Smith, C. Sonnet Written at the Close of Spring
  [or Elegiac Sonnet].
Smith, W. Bachelor's-Buttons.
Stevenson, A. Himalayan Balsam.
Stevenson, R. To A Gardener.
Swinburne. Sundew, The.
Sylvester, J. Garden, The.
Taggard. Weed, The.
Taylor, J. Violet, The.
Teasdale. Summer Night, Riverside.

Tennyson, A. City Child, The.
  Flower in the Crannied Wall.
Tighe. Written at Rossana. November 18, 1799.
Townsend, A. Purple Loosestrife.
Tuckerman, F. Coralie.
Unknown. Lyric by Nine.
Vaughan, H. I Walked [or Walkt] the Other Day
  to Spend My Hour.
Very. Autumn Flowers.
  Columbine, The.
  Lament of the Flowers, The.
Wang, J. Tune: 'Magnolia Flowers.'
Wat. Joke, A.
Watkins, V. Music of Colours—White Blossom.
  Music of Colours: The Blossom Scattered.
Wellesley. Walled Garden.
Whitman, S. Morning-Glory, The.
Whitman, W. Orange Buds by Mail from
  Florida.
  These I Singing in Spring.
Wilbur. In a Churchyard.
  In the Field.
Williams, W. Chicory and Daisies.
  Flowers by the Sea.
  Iris.
  It Is a Small Plant.
  Ivy Crown, The.
  Locust Tree in Flower, The.
  Paterson, Book 5: The River of Heaven.
  Pink Locust, The.
  Pot of Flowers, The.
  Yellow Flower, The.
Wordsworth, W. Primrose of the Rock, The.
Wright, J. Therapy.

Flutes
Browning, E. Musical Instrument, A.
Dryden, J. Song for St Cecilia's Day, 1687, A.
Krohn. My Flute.
Muldoon, P. Lass of Aughrim, The.
Okigbo. Lament of the Flutes.
Sama, B. Song, The.
Seale, J. Playing the Flute for the TMR Class.
Unknown. Old [or Ould] Orange Flute, The.
Watson, R. Die Zauberflöte.
Williams, B. Night Flute, The.

Flying Saucers
Kinsella, J. Bright Cigar-Shaped Object Hovers
  Over Mount Pleasant, A.

Foals
Hughes, T. Yesterday He Was Nowhere to Be
  Found.
Watkins, V. Foal.
See also **Horses**

Fog
Booth, P. Fog-Talk.
Clampitt. Fog.
Clarke, G. Foghorns.
Dickinson, E. Sun and Fog Contested, The.
Eberhart, R. Flux.
Gershwin. Foggy Day (in London Town), A.
Greenwald, T. And, Hinges.
Guiney. Fog.
Jarrell. Front, A.
Jeffers, R. Boats in a Fog.
Merriam, E. Windshield Wiper.
Moore, L. In the Fog.
Oppen. Forms of Love, The.
Piercy. Quiet Fog, The.
Raworth. Hot Day at the Races.
Sandburg, C. Fog.
Sutter. Hoarfrost and Fog.
Thoreau. Fog.
Weeks, J. On the Great Fog in London,
  December 1762.

Folly
Mapanje. On His Royal Blindness Paramount
  Chief Kwangala.
More, H. Riot; or, Half a Loaf Is Better than No
  Bread, The.
Prior. Fable, A: "In Æsop's tales an honest
  wretch we find."
Suckling, S. Barley-Break, A.
Thomas, E. Some Eyes Condemn.
Unknown. Rakes of Mallow, The.
Winnebago Oral Tradition. Felix White Sr.'s

Introduction to Wakjankaga.
Yeats. Down by the Salley Gardens.

Food
Aaronson. Pesci Misti.
Agran, R. Cakes Continue to Rise.
Aguilar-Cariño. Dinakdakan.
Alexander, E. Minnesota Fats Describes His Youth.
Who I Think You Are.
Baratier, D. She Wants.
Barkan. Two Grandmas.
Barker, G. How many apples grow on the tree?
Baxter, C. Dog Kibble: A Villanelle.
Belloc. On Jam.
Berrigan, A. Looking Up My Balance.
Bond, S. Tuesday Night Affair.
Brown, S. After Winter.
Brownstein. Jet Set Melodrama.
Budy. On High Street.
Burns, R. To a Haggis.
Cabico, R. Afternoon in Pangasinan with No Electricity, An.
Cavendish, M. Dissert, A.
Nature's Cook.
Cisneros, S. Good Hot Dogs.
Cleary, B. Chicken & Sex.
Colby, T. Labor Day Picnic Poem.
Cooper, B. Toast to the Cook, A.
Coward. Any Part of Piggy.
Dauenhauer. How To Make Good Baked Salmon from the River.
Davidson, M. Framing.
De la Mare. Miss T.
Delgado, J. Two Timer.
Erdrich. Windigo.
Evans, M. When in Rome.
Evasco, M. Baked Oysters Rockefeller.
Fergusson. To the Principal and Professors of the University of St Andrews, on their Superb Treat to Dr Samuel Johnson.
Fletcher, L. After Delivering Your Lunch.
Gloria. Assimilation.
Milkfish.
Gonzales, R. Praise the Tortilla, Praise the Menudo, Praise the Chorizo.
Grieves, C. Connuche.
Guest, E. Lemon Pie.
Sausage.
Hansen, R. Do Not Let Skeezix Go in There: Winslow's Villanelle.
Herbert, W. To a Mousse.
Herrick. To His Book[e].
Upon Jack and Jill: Epigram.
Hirschman, J. Tremor, The.
Hoffman, D. Lobsterpot Labyrinths.
Hood, T. Epicurean Reminiscences of a Sentimentalist.
Irving, J. Untitled.
Jackson, B. Riot at Winchell's.
Johns. Salon de Vers.
Johnson, D. Harold's Bowl and Food.
Johnson, E. Weevilly Porridge.
Jonson, B. Inviting a Friend to Supper.
Kasdorf. When Our Women Go Crazy.
Kenyon, J. Potato.
King, B. Pessimist, The.
Kleinschmidt. Cooking to Music.
Kollar. Sunday Matinee.
Lawrence, D. Food of the North.
Lee, L. Eating Alone.
Leonard, T. Song: "Yi surta."
Levine, P. Simple Truth, The.
Liu, T. Sunday.
Llewellyn-Williams. Feeding the Bat.
Major, C. Beaulieu.
Markoe, M. Ballad of Winky.
McDonald, C. Fresh Mussels.
McDonald, W. Children of Saigon, The.
McKay, C. Tropics in New York, The.
Mitchell, A. Giving Potatoes.
Moody, E. Sappho Burns Her Books and Cultivates the Culinary Arts.
Moore, M. To a Chameleon.
Mother Goose. King Arthur.
Nash, O. I Can't Have a Martini, Dear, But You Take One, or, Are You Going to Sit There

Guzzling All Night?
Parsnip, The.
Private Dining Room, The.
Nelson, M. Brightness.
Nemerov. Grace to Be Said at the Supermarket.
Nichols, G. Like a Beacon.
Norris, K. Stomach.
North, M. Red Desire.
Nye, N. Lunch in Nablus City Park.
Orton, B. Bacchanal.
Padgett, R. Lucky Strikes.
Parker, A. God of Pepper, The.
Peacock, M. Devolution.
Phillips, C. Sunday.
Piercy. Attack of the Squash People.
Pierpoint, N. In the Outhouse.
Pogson, P. Fifteen.
Powell, D. A. Minotaur at Supper: Spare the Noritake and the Spode, The.
Ransom, J. Survey of Literature.
Rexroth, K. Observations in a Cornish Teashop.
Robles. Feasting with Etang a Hundred Times Around.
Rosen, M. Christmas Dinner.
"Sagittarius." Passionate Profiteer to His Love, The.
Sallah, T. No Argument Tonight.
Schwartz, R. L. Midnight Supper.
Scott, S. Fire, The.
Shepard, K. Birch.
Silano, M. Sweet Red Peppers, Sun-Drieds, the Hearts of Artichokes.
Smith, S. Salad, A.
Snyder, G. Song of the Taste.
Soto. Soup, The.
St. John, P. Biological Light.
Steele, T. Joseph.
Stevenson, A. Larousse Gastronomique.
Strand. Pot Roast.
Su, A. Four Sonnets About Food.
Swift, J. Epigram on Fasting.
Tallmountain. Good Grease.
Tammaro. 'Mericn Fst Fd.
Taylor, B. Those Flapjacks of Brown's.
Taylor, C.B. Forever Arima.
Tripp. Caroline Street, Cardiff.
Turner, A. On the Nature of Food.
Tyler, R. Love Song: "By the fierce flames of love I'm in a sad taking."
Unknown. Dish for a Poet, A.
Fox, The.
I Had But Fifty Cents.
Little King Boggen.
Miss Foggerty's Cake.
On a Gentleman's Complaining to a Lady That He Could Not Eat Meat.
On Tomato Ketchup.
Scones.
Untermeyer, L. Food and Drink.
Updike. On the Inclusion of Miniature Dinosaurs in Breakfast Cereal Boxes.
Very. My Meat and Drink.
Weigl. Last Lie, The.
Wells, C. Universal Favorite, The.
Wilbur. Rillons, Rillettes.
Wodehouse, P. Gourmet's Love-Song, The.
Young-Prottengeier. Lithuanian Grandmother.
Yuson. Love Before Dinner.
See also **Cooking and Cooks; Eating; Gluttony and Gluttons**

Fools
Adler, R. Hey There.
Arlen, H. Fun to be Fooled.
Barnes, W. Sam'el Down vrom Lon'on.
Berlin. Fools Fall in Love.
Blake, W. Lacedemonian Instruction.
Bricusse, L. What Kind of Fool Am I?
Browne, W. Love Who Will, for I'll Love None.
Burns, R. Holy Fair, The.
On W. R———, Esq.
Cameron, N. Compassionate Fool, The.
Creeley. Counterpoint, A.
Dobell, S. Liberty to M. le Diplomate.
Donne. Triple Fool, The.
Egerton, S. Liberty, The.

"Ephelia." To a Proud Beauty.
Farquhar. Song, A.
Gershwin. Fun to Be Fooled.
Hammerstein. Gentleman Is a Dope, The.
Harburg. Fun to Be Fooled.
Hart, L. You Are Too Beautiful.
Hewitt, J. Ireland.
Hoskyns [*or* Hoskins]. Upon a Fool.
Jonson, B. On Don Surly.
On the Famous Voyage.
To Fool or Knave.
Landor, W. Plays.
Mackenzie, K. Fool, The.
Meredith, G. Camelus Saltat: Continued.
Newley, A. What Kind of Fool Am I?
Pope, A. Another [Epigram].
Epigram from the French: "Sir, I admit your general [*or* gen'ral] Rule."
Prior. Epigram: "Yes, every poet is a fool."
Ralegh, S. Sir Walter Ra[u]le[i]gh to His Son[ne].
Rodgers, R. Gentleman Is a Dope, The.
You Are Too Beautiful.
Ross, J. Hey There.
Sill. Fool's Prayer, The.
Thoreau. Any Fool Can Make a Rule.
Unknown. Silly Boy.
Washington, N. My Foolish Heart.
Yeats. Symbols.
Young, V. My Foolish Heart.
See also **Jesters**

Football
Beatty, P. Independent Study.
Cooper, D. After School, Street Football, Eighth Grade.
Dickey, J. Bee, The.
For the Death of Vince Lombardi.
Dyson, E. Friendly Game of Football, A.
Jackson, R. For Thurman Thomas.
Jarrell. Say Good-bye to Big Daddy.
Jenkins, L. Football.
Komunyakaa. White Port and Lemon Juice.
Saunders, R. Funky Football.
Updike. September.
Wright, J. Autumn Begins in Martins Ferry, Ohio.
Wrigley, A. Owdham Footbo'.
See also **Soccer**

Forbidden Fruit
Carew, T. Secrecy [*or* Secresie] Protested.
Garrett, E. Moules à la Marinière.
Hewitt, J. Tryst.
Sharpless. *Paradise Lost* as a Haiku.

Ford, Ed ("Whitey")
Holden, J. Poem for Ed "Whitey" Ford, A.

Ford, Ford Madox
Lowell, R. Ford Madox Ford.
Williams, W. To Ford Madox Ford in Heaven.

Fordham, Alphonse Campbell
Fordham. In Memoriam. Alphonse Campbell Fordham.

Fordham, Edward
Fordham. Mr. Edward Fordham.

Forest Fires
Melville, H. Uninscribed Monument on One of the Battlefields of the Wilderness, An.
Rios, A. Wet Camp.

Foresters
Unknown. I Have Been a Foster.

Forests
Allen, H. In the Forest.
Bentley, N. Iron Man of the Hoh.
Birney. Slug in Woods.
Blind. Entangled.
Bly, R. Solitude Late at Night in the Woods.
Brautigan. Boat, A.
Bryant, W. Forest Hymn.
Forest Hymn, A.
Inscription for the Entrance to a Wood.
Chipasula. Double Song.
Cole, T. Lament of the Forest, The.
Coleridge, M. Witches' Wood, The.
Davenant [*or* D'Avenant]. Countess of Anglesey Lead Captive by the Rebels, at the Disforresting of Pewsam, The.

Davie. Tunstall Forest.
Doolittle, H. Pursuit.
Emerson, R. Waldeinsamkeit.
Frost, F. Christmas in the Wood.
Frost, R. Come In.
Stopping by Woods on a Snowy Evening.
Garrigue. Forest.
Gascoyne. Cage, The.
Graham, W. Imagine a Forest.
Hagiwara Sakutaro. So Terrifyingly Melancholy.
Hall, D. Poet at Twenty, A.
Hardy, T. In a Wood.
Hemans. American Forest Girl, The.
Henderson, D. Song of Devotion to the Forest.
Herbert, E. Sonnet Made upon the Groves near Merlou [or Merlow] Castle.
Hill, M. Abomination.
Hughes, T. Modest Proposal, A.
Jarrell. House in the Wood, The.
Kenyon, J. Depression in Winter.
Kipling, R. Way Through the Woods, The.
Lampman. In November: "With loitering step and quiet eye."
Lanier, S. Ballad of Trees and the Master, A.
Lee, E. Forests and Caverns.
Lee-Hamilton. Among the Firs.
Longenbach. What You Find in the Woods.
MacLean, S. Hallaig.
Mandelstam [or Mandelshtam]. Whoever Finds a Horseshoe.
Merwin, W. S. Asians Dying, The.
Mezey. At the Point.
Minhinnick. Sap.
Murray, L. Noonday Axeman.
Nelson, J. If a Fish Fell in a Forest.
Preston, R. Chicago Blues.
Pritchard, N. Cassandra and Friend.
Landscape with Nymphs and Satyrs.
Narrow Path, The.
Ray, H. Wood Carols.
Reeves, W. Passing of the Forest, The.
Roberts, G. Burnt Lands.
Rolls. Rain Forest.
Rukeyser, M. Then I Saw What the Calling Was.
Siddal. Silent Wood, A.
Simic. Ballad: "What's that approaching like dust like poverty."
Smith, S. I Rode With My Darling.
Sousa, N. Appeal.
Thomas, E. Combe, The.
Green Roads, The.
Tomlinson, C. In Arden.
Treece. Horror.
Magic Wood, The.
Very. Indian's Retort, The.
Wagoner, D. Staying Alive.
Warfield. Forests and Caverns.
Watson, R. Enchanted Princess, An.
Whittemore, R. Departure, The.
Wright, J. Rainforest.
Wright, R. Haiku: "Coming from the woods."

Forges
Heaney, S. Casualty.
Forge, The.

Forgetfulness
Ashbery. Forgotten Song.
Bensley. One's Correspondence.
Benson, S. Now I Have Nothing.
Berlin. Remember.
Bromige. Log.
Browning, R. Memorabilia.
Coleman, C. I'm Gonna Laugh You Right Out of My Life.
Crane, H. Forgetfulness.
Davidson, M. Sensation Type and His Friends, The.
Dooley, M. Does It Go Like this?
Fields, D. Remind Me.
Garrigue. Song for "Buvez les Vins du Postillion"—Advt.
Hall, D. Exile.
Hardy, T. Tess's Lament.
"Hope." I Shall Forget.
Jackson, H. Two Truths.

Kennedy, X. To Someone Who Insisted I Look Up Someone.
Kern, J. Remind Me.
Levertov. Woman Meets an Old Lover, A.
Maltby, R. I Don't Remember Christmas.
McCarthy, J. I'm Gonna Laugh You Right Out of My Life.
Merwin, W. S. Losing a Language.
Michie, S. Connecting Light.
Millay, E. I Forgot for a Moment.
Sonnet: "What lips my lips have kissed, and where, and why."
Mura. Natives, The.
O'Neill, R. I Made a House of Houselessness.
Pietri. Intermission from Friday.
Intermission from Saturday.
Shire, D. I Don't Remember Christmas.
Smith, C. Nepenthe.
Stephens, P. Hangman.
Stickney, T. Pity.
Strand. Always.
Swirszczynska. She Does Not Remember.
Teasdale. Water-Lilies.
Wakoski. Remembering the Pacific.
Williams, C. Alzheimer's: The Wife.
Wyatt, S. Steadfastness.

Forgiveness
Alexie. Penance.
Angel. Evolving Similarities.
Benét, W. Brazen Tongue.
Bidart. Confessional.
Chesterton, G. Ballade D'une Grande Dame.
Coleridge, S. Epitaph: "Stop, Christian passer-by!—Stop, child of God."
Craveirinha. Seed is in Me, The.
Donne. Hymn[e] to God the Father, A.
Fain, S. Was That the Human Thing to Do?
Hardy, T. Burghers, The.
Peace-Offering, The.
Herbert, G. Love (3).
Herrick. His Prayer for Absolution.
Hope, A. Easter Hymn.
Jackson, H. Two Truths.
Keech. True to the Best.
Komunyakaa. Seven Deadly Sins.
Markham, E. Outwitted.
Meynell, A. Beyond Knowledge.
Pankey. As We Forgive Those.
Pollok. Happiness.
Pratt, J. Words and Thoughts.
Preston, R. Ten Seconds.
Reznikoff. Day of Atonement.
Robinson, E. Unforgiven, The.
Rossetti, C. Ash Wednesday.
Sangster, M. Forgiven.
Smart, C. Hymn to the Supreme Being.
Smith, S. I Forgive You.
Springer, T. Giving and Forgiving.
Stein, K. Upon Finding a Black Woman's Door Sprayed with Swastikas, I Tell Her This Story of Hands.
Tennyson, A. Forgiving.
Unknown. Whirlpool, The.
Waddington, M. Ten Years and More.
Warren, R. Revelation.
Whittier. Forgiveness.
Williams, W. This Is Just to Say.
Young, J. Was That the Human Thing to Do?

Forks
Simic. Fork.
Unknown. Lyric by Nine.

Fort McHenry, Maryland
Key. Star-Spangled Banner, The.

Fort Sumter, South Carolina
Timrod. Charleston.

Fortitude
Allen, E. Endurance.
Kipling, R. If—.
Moore, M. Nevertheless.
Porteous. I Envy the Cracked, Black Basalt.
Wilcox, E. Solitude.
Worthwhile.
See also **Endurance**

Fortune
Benjamin, P. Press On.

Bethell. Fortune.
Blamire. I've Gotten a Rock, I've Gotten a Reel.
Brion, R. If Fortune Smiles.
Chudleigh. Wish, The.
Cockburn, A. Flowers of the Forest, The.
Cunningham, J. Epigram: "Good Fortune, when I hailed her recently."
Donaldson, W. When My Ship Comes In.
Emerson, R. Guy.
Forman, R. We Are the Young Magicians.
Fynn, H. Adieu, to Fortune.
Gunn, T. Wheel of Fortune, The.
Hardy, T. Hap.
Harington [or Harrington]. Author, of His Own Fortune, The.
Henry, B. Discovery.
Herrick. Supreme Fortune Falls Soonest.
To Fortune.
Housman, A. Lads in Their Hundreds, The.
Kahn, G. When My Ship Comes In.
Koch, K. Locks.
Spalding, S. Fate.
Unknown. Sneezing.
Wyatt, S. Marvel No More.
Promise, A.
Wylie. Hughie at the Inn.
See also **Fate; Luck; Chance**

Fortunetelling and Fortunetellers
Carruth, H. Sonnet: "Well, she told me I had an aura. 'What?' I said."
Cary, A. Telling Fortunes.
Christopher. Palm Reader, The.
Ríos, A. Madre Sofía.
Stevenson, R. Spaewife, The.
Williamson, G. On His Birthday.

Fossils
Blodgett. Fossil.
Dove, R. Fish in the Stone, The.
Ferlinghetti, L. Cro-Magnons.
Kendall, M. Fossil, A.
Lewis, J. Fossil, 1975.
Merrill, B. Fossil, The.
Ranaldo, L. HIS:STORY.

Fountains
Bogan, L. Roman Fountain.
Davie. Fountain of Cyanë, The.
Fountain, The.
Duncan, R. Drinking Fountain, The.
Eberhart, R. Garden God, The.
Fisher, R. Memorial Fountain, The.
Herrick. To the Water Nymphs, Drinking at the Fountain.
Jennings, E. Fountain.
Lowell, A. Bright Sunlight.
Lowell, J. Fountain, The.
Pound, E. Ts'ai Chi'h.
Robinson, E. Fountain.
Sitwell. Fountains.
Wilbur. Ballade for the Duke of Orléans.
Baroque Wall-Fountain in the Villa Sciarra, A.
Wordsworth, W. Fountain, The.

Fourth of July
Cox, P. Brownies' Celebration, The.
Follen, E. For the Fourth of July.
McGrath, T. End of the Line, The.
Peck, R. Four of July.
Sanchez, S. Poem for July 4, 1994.
Sharp, S. Good Nights.
Unknown. Independence Bell—July 4, 1776.
Independence Day.

Foxes
Carryl, G. Sycophantic Fox and the Gullible Raven, The.
Clare, J. Vixen, The.
Dickey, J. Dog Sleeping on My Feet, A.
Dyment. Fox.
Gibran. Fox, The.
Grennan. Conjunctions.
Henryson. Cock and the Fox, The.
Hughes, F. Different Voice, The.
Foxes.
Hughes, T. Thought-Fox, The.
Kennelly. Dream of a Black Fox.
Knowles, S. Fox Dancing.

Levine, P. Fox, The.
Masefield. Fellow Mortal, A.
Mozeen. Kilruddery Hunt, The.
Murray, L. Gods, The.
Oliver, M. Fox, The.
  Wings.
Padel. Scotch.
Rich, A. Abnegation.
Unknown. Fox and the Goose, The.
  Fox, The.
Ward, J. Here, Home.
Williams, J. In Duffryn Woods.
Wylie. Escape.

France
Ba. Nobility.
Barbauld. On the Expected General Rising of the French Nation.
  Sonnet to France On Her Present Exertions.
Beckett, S. Dieppe.
Cannan. Rouen.
Clark, T. Going to School in France or America.
Coleman, C. Riviera, The.
Dehn, P. St. Aubin d'Aubigne.
Dove, R. Great Palaces of Versailles, The.
Fisher, J. Pearls.
Flecker. Rioupéroux.
Gardelle, C. Air.
  Rain.
Grosholz. Remembering the Ardèche.
Hacker, M. Squares and Courtyards.
Hamilton, S. Farewell to France.
Hemans. Joan of Arc in Rheims.
Hopkins, G. Duns Scotus's Oxford.
Jacob, M. Rooster and the Pearl, The.
Jonson, B. On English Monsieur.
McCarthy, J. Riviera, The.
Merwin, W. S. Tide Line Garden.
Pound, E. Provincia Deserta.
Prévert. Barbara.
Rivers, L. Four Sheets to the Wind and a One-Way Ticket to France.
Shepherd, R. Lucky One, The.
Unknown. Humble Petition of the British Jacobins to their Brethren of France, The.
  Mode of France, The.
Updike. Some Frenchmen.
Warton, J. Verses Written at Montauban in France, 1750.
Weaver, M. Luxembourg Garden.
  My Father's Geography.
Wordsworth, W. England, 1802, III.
Wright, J. Winter Daybreak above Vence, A.

Francis of Assisi, Saint
Dennis, C. St. Francis and the Nun.
Hecht, A. At the Frick.
Hirsch, E. Simone Weil: In Assisi.
Kinnell. Saint Francis and the Sow.
Orlovsky. I Dream of St. Francis.

Franconia Mountains
Ray, H. Lines Written on a Farewell View of the Franconia Mountains at Twilight.

Frank, Anne
Motion. Anne Frank Huis.
Williams, C. Day for Anne Frank, A.

Frankenstein
Barlow, G. Painting Drunken Twilight.
Deanovich. Frankenstein.
Field, E. Bride of Frankenstein, The.

Franklin, Aretha
Giovanni. Poem for Aretha.

Fratricide
Very. Thy Brother's Blood.

Free Will
Atwood. Torture.
Crosby, E. Military Creed, The.
Frost, R. Road Not Taken, The.
Herrick. Predestination.
Jonson, B. Epode: "Not to know vice at all, and keep[e] true state."
Whittier. Overruled.

Freedom
"Ada." Lines.
Ai. Twenty-Year Marriage.
Al-Rihani. Constantinople.

Alegría. From the Bridge.
Angelou. Caged Bird.
Arlen, H. Eagle and Me, The.
Auden. Watch Any Day.
Barbauld. Eighteen Hundred and Eleven.
  On the Expected General Rising of the French Nation.
Bishop, E. Sonnet: "Caught—the bubble."
Blake, W. How Sweet I Roamed [*or* Roam'd] from Field to Field.
Branch, A. Ere the Golden Bowl Is Broken.
Brathwaite, E. Citadel.
Brontë, E. To Imagination.
Browning, E. Hiram Powers' "Greek Slave." Part II.
  Runaway Slave at Pilgrim's Point, The.
Browning, R. Why I Am a Liberal.
Brutus. Prayer: "O let me soar on steadfast wing."
Bryant, W. Conjunction of Jupiter and Venus, The.
  Damsel of Peru, The.
Burns, R. De'il's [*or* Deil's] Awa wi' th' [*or* the] Exciseman, The.
  For A' That and A' That ['Is there, for honest poverty'].
  Scots Wha Hae.
Butler, C. E. Other Places, The.
Byron, G. Stanzas: "When a man hath no freedom to fight for at home."
Campo. Superman Is Dead.
Carew, T. Song: The Willing Prisoner to His Mistress.
Cavendish, M. Claspe, The.
Char. Argument.
Chin. Composed Near the Bay Bridge (after a wild party).
Chubb, R. Transfiguration.
Clare, J. I Feel I Am.
Cohan. You're a Grand Old Flag.
Coleman, E. Liberator, The.
Collins, W. How Sleep the Brave.
Couzyn. Way Out, The.
Cowper, W. Negro's Complaint, The.
Creeley. Ballad of the Despairing Husband.
Crouch, S. Like a Blessing.
Cullen, C. Wind Bloweth Where It Listeth, The.
Diop, D. Africa.
Donne. Canonization, The.
Doolittle, H. Helmsman, The.
Dove, R. Geometry.
  Lady Freedom Among Us.
Dumas, H. Root Song.
Dunbar, P. Ante-Bellum Sermon, An.
  Sympathy.
Egerton, S. Liberty, The.
Emerson, R. Freedom.
  Give All to Love.
Feaver. Coat.
France, L. Blues for Bird.
Garrett, E. Miser.
  Tyranny of Choice.
Gibran. Madman (Prologue), The.
Gillespie, H. Breezin' Along with the Breeze.
Glück, L. Legend.
  Undertaking, The.
Guevara, M. Buddy Holly Poem, The.
Gunn, T. Tamer and Hawk.
Harburg. Eagle and Me, The.
Harper, F. Slave Mother, The.
Hawoldar. I Have Gone into My Prison Cell.
Hayden, R. Frederick Douglass.
  Runagate Runagate.
Hemans. Corinne at the Capitol.
Hernández Cruz. Puerta Rica.
Howe, J. Battle Hymn [*or* Battle-Hymn] of the Republic, The.
Hucks, J. To Freedom.
Hughes, L. Democracy.
  Dream Boogie.
  Dream Variation[s].
  Let America Be America Again.
Jarrell. Woman at the Washington Zoo, The.
Jeffers, L. How High the Moon.
  When I Know the Power of my Black Hand.
Johnson, J. Lift Every [*or* Ev'ry] Voice and

  Sing.
Jordan, J. I Must Become a Menace to My Enemies.
Joseph, J. Warning.
Kefala. Freedom Fighter.
Kendrick, D. Sidney, Looking for Her Mother.
Key. Star-Spangled Banner, The.
Kgositsile. Song for Ilva Mackay and Mongane.
Lazarus, E. In Exile.
Levy, A. Magdalen.
Lewis, J. Time and Music.
Lincoln, A. Gettysburg Address, The.
Lovelace, R. To Althea, from Prison.
  To Lucasta, from Prison.
  Vintage to the Dungeon, The.
MacLeish. Brave New World.
MacNeice. Sunlight on the Garden, The.
Madgett. Midway.
Mandela. Saviour.
Mandelstam [*or* Mandelshtam]. [Last Poems].
Meinke. Supermarket.
Milosz, C. Incantation.
Milton. On the Detraction Which Followed upon My Writing Certain Treatises.
Mkangelwa. Women Sing, The.
Mnthali. Celebration, The.
Moore, T. Harp That Once through Tara's Halls, The.
  Sound the Loud Timbrel.
More, S. Minstrel Boy, The.
Nasrin. Border.
  Character.
Norris, L. Pit Ponies, The.
Nortje. At Rest from the Grim Place.
Ofeimun. Handle for the Flutist, A.
Ologoudou. Liberty.
Oppenheimer, J. Poem in Defense of Children.
Orfalea, G. Sunken Road, Antietam 1980, The.
Patterson, R. Black Power.
Pegram, A. Deliverance.
Perreault, J. Shoe.
Philips, K. Answer to Another Persuading a Lady to Marriage, An.
Pilkington, L. Song, A.
Ransom, J. Dog.
Ray, H. To My Father.
Reed, I. Railroad Bill, A Conjure Man.
Roethke. I Knew A Woman.
Rossetti, C. Promises like Pie-Crust.
Sall, A. Cloak of Dawn.
Sandburg, C. Harbor, The.
  Limited.
Simons, S. Breezin' Along with the Breeze.
Skeeter. California, 1852.
  Midwest, Midcentury.
Smith, P. Meanwhile, in Rwanda.
  Woman Who Died in Line, The.
Smith, S. Anger's Freeing Power.
Stewart, D. Silkworms, The.
"Struther." Freedom.
Swinburne. Free Thought.
Sykes, B. Cycle.
Taylor, J. Trumpet of Liberty, The.
Thelwall. To Ancestry.
Thompson, P. Emancipation.
  Fugitive, The.
  Prayer, A: "Oh, Lord! I lift my heart."
Tolson, M. Festus Conrad.
Unknown. Freedom a Come Oh!
  Freedom in the Air.
  Go Down, Moses.
  I Thank God I'm Free at Las'.
  Let My People Go.
  No More Auction Block.
  No More Beneath the Oppressive Hand.
  Promises of Freedom.
  Swing Low, Sweet Chariot.
Vashon. Vincent Ogé.
Villanueva, A. Even the Eagles Must Gather.
Washington. Freedom Hair.
Watson, R. White Bird, The.
Weller. Ngungalari.
Wendel. We Shall Return, Luanda.
Wheatley, P. To the Right Honourable William, Earl of Dartmouth, His Majesty's Principal Secretary of State for North America.

Whiting, R.   Breezin' Along with the Breeze.
Whitman, W.   Commonplace, The.
To the States.
Years of the Modern.
Whittier.   Laus Deo!
Lost Occasion, The.
Proem: "I love the old melodious lays."
Wilbur.   Still, Citizen Sparrow.
Willis, N.   To Charles Roux, of Switzerland.
Wordsworth, W.   Thought[s] of a Briton on the Subjugation of Switzerland.
Wright, J.   Wednesday Night Prayer Meeting.
Zangwill.   At the Zoo.
Zu-Bolton.   Struggle-Road Dance.

Freezers
Armour.   Hiding Place.

Freighters
Greenberg, A.   Freight Train, Freight Train.
Levertov.   Don't You Hear that Whistle Blowin'
See also **Cargoes**

French Revolution
Barbauld.   On the Expected General Rising of the French Nation.
Coleridge, S.   Fears in Solitude.
"Pindar."   Hymn to the Guilotine.
Tomlinson, C.   Charlotte Corday.
For Danton.
Williams, H.   To Dr. Moore, in Anser to a Poetical Epistle Written by Him in Wales.

French, The
Gay, J.   French Fops.
Hughes, L.   Cubes.
O'Hara, F.   Ode: Salute to the French Negro Poets.
Osofisan.   Paris Latin Quarter.
Savageau.   Like the Trails of Ndakinna.
Unknown.   Epigram: "Says a Reverend Priest to a less Rev'rend friend."

Freud, Sigmund
Auden.   In Memory of Sigmund Freud.
Bang, M.   Crossed-Over, Fiend-Snitched, X-ed Out.
Dugan, A.   Nomenclature.
Field, E.   Whatever Became Of: Freud?
Hannan, M.   Life Model.
Heseltine, P.   Limerick: "Young things who frequent picture-palaces, The."
Howe, F.   Doubt.
Nemerov.   In the Beginning.
Unknown.   Limerick: "Young men who frequent picture palaces."
Wayman.   Wayman in Love.

Friars
Ransom, J.   Necrological.

Friends, Society of
Green, M.   On Barclay's Apology for the Quakers.
Whittier.   First-Day Thoughts.

Friendship
Ackerly.   Prayer of an Unemployed Man.
Aldrich, H.   Catch, A.
Amirthanayagam.   There Are Many Things I Want to Tell You.
Angel.   Breaking the Rock Down.
Annand.   I Winna Let On.
Arlen, H.   Tess's Torch Song (I Had a Man).
Ashbery.   Friends.
Operators Are Standing By.
Some Trees.
Train Rising Out of the Sea.
Awoonor.   First Circle, The.
Aytoun [*or* Ayton], R.   Upon Platonic Love: To Mistress Cicely Crofts, Maid of Honour.
Beatty, P.   Doggin the Rockman.
Berryman.   Winter-Piece to a Friend Away, A.
Bevington, L.   Am I to Lose You?
Bishop, E.   Letter to N.Y.
Manuelzinho.
Shampoo, The.
Blake, W.   On Hayley.
Bowles, W.   To a Friend.
Boyle, D. M.   Curtain, The.
Boyle, K.   Ode to a Maintenance Man and His Family.
Brett, L.   My Mother's Friend.

Brontë, E.   Love and Friendship.
Brown, D.   Still Later There Are War Stories.
Brown, E.   Bitcherel.
Browning, E.   L.E.L.'s Last Question.
Sleep, The.
Browning, R.   Waring.
Brutus.   They Hanged Him, I Said Dismissively.
Burns, R.   Auld Lang Syne.
Second Epistle to Davie.
Caddel.   For Tom.
Campbell, A.   There Is Always a Place for You.
To My Friend.
Cheney-Coker.   Letter to a Tormented Playwright.
Chipasula.   Friend, Ah You Have Changed!
Ciardi.   What Johnny Told Me.
Clark Bekedermo.   Abiku.
Clark, T.   Friends.
Cleary, B.   Boys' Own.
Clough.   Highland Glen near Loch Ericht, A.
Cobbold, E.   On Some Violets Planted in My Garden by a Friend.
Coleridge, H.   To a Friend.
Coleridge, M.   Contents of an Ink-bottle, The.
Friends—With a Difference.
Gifts.
Gone.
Mortal Combat.
Coleridge, S.   Duty Surviving Self-Love.
To William Wordsworth.
Collins, K.   Sisters.
Converse.   Friendship.
Cook, E.   To the Late William Jerdan.
Cooper, D.   Dreamt Up.
Corrothers.   Me 'n' Dunbar.
Cory, W.   Deteriora.
Cowley, A.   On the Death of Mr. William Hervey [*or* Harvey].
Cox, M.   Barbells of the Gods, The.
Craik.   Friendship.
Creeley.   Damon & Pythias.
For Friendship.
Won't It Be Fine?
Cullen, C.   Tableau.
Dante Alighieri.   Sonnet: To Guido Cavalcanti.
Davies, J.   Remembrance of My Friend Mr. Thomas Morley, A.
Davis, J.   Warru.
Delaunay, S.   Greetings, Blaise Cendrars.
Derricotte.   Friendship, The.
Donne.   To Mr. C.B.
Dooley, M.   Letters from Yorkshire.
Drake, E.   Friendliest Thing (Two People Can Do), The.
Duncan, R.   Among My Friends.
Dunn, S.   Men Talk.
E'der, R.   La Puente.
Edwards [*or* Edwardes], R.   When I Was Three.
Emerson, R.   Friendship.
English, T.   Ben Bolt.
Faugeres, M.   Friendship.
"Field."   Ah, Eros doth not always smite.
Field, R.   Some People.
Foss, S.   House by the Side of the Road, The.
Fulton, A.   What I Like.
Garcia, R.   Dangerous Hats.
Gates, B.   Cathy.
Homeless.
Ron.
Triptych.
Gershwin.   Babbitt and the Bromide, The.
Gibb.   Letter to Russel Barron.
Ginsberg, A.   Green Automobile, The.
Googe.   Of Money.
Graham, W.   Lines on Roger Hilton's Watch.
Grahn.   Funeral Plainsong from a Younger Woman on an Older Woman, A.
Graves, R.   At First Sight.
Gunn, T.   J Car, The.
Reassurance, The.
Terminal.
Hacker, M.   Eight Days in April.
Harwood, G.   In The Park.
Hass, R.   Letter to a Poet.
Haynes, C.   Any Wife or Husband.
Herbert, G.   Unkindness.

Herrick.   His Age, Dedicated to His Peculiar Friend, Master John Wickes, under the Name of Posthumus.
To His Honoured and Most Ingenious Friend Mr. Charles Cotton.
Hughes, L.   Poem: "I loved my friend."
Hughes, T.   Six Young Men.
Jackson, H.   Friends.
James, P.   Can't We Be Friends?
Jonson, B.   Epistle Answering to One that Asked to Be Sealed of the Tribe of Ben, An.
Epistle to Master John Selden, An.
To the Immortal[l] Memory [*or* Memorie] and Friendship of That Noble Pair[e], Sir Lucius Cary and Sir H. [*or* Henry] Morison.
Jordan, J.   Grand Army Plaza.
Keats.   Bright Star.
To a Friend Who Sent Me Some Roses.
Kemble.   To Mrs. Norton.
Kessler, S.   Cigarette Case.
King, H.   Change, The.
Exequy, The.
Kinsella, T.   Talent and Friendship.
Kizer, C.   American Beauty, An.
Klee.   Friend, A.
Klenner, J.   Just Friends.
Koch, K.   Circus, The.
Koehler, T.   Tess's Torch Song (I Had a Man).
Lamb, C.   Old Familiar Faces, The.
Langhorne.   Studley Park.
Lansana, Q.   Woolworth's Poem, The.
Lee, K.   Haiku #3.
Levin, P.   Meeting of Friends, A.
Levy, A.   To Vernon Lee.
Lewis, N.   Footprint on the Air, A.
Lewis, R.   If You Had a Friend.
Lewis, S.   Just Friends.
Lloyd, C.   Written at the Hotwells, near Bristol.
Longfellow, H.   Arrow and the Song, The.
Lovelace, R.   Grasshopper, The.
MacCaig.   Chauvinist.
MacDiarmid, H.   To a Friend and Fellow Poet.
MacGill.   Matey.
Macgoye.   Omera.
Malouf.   Judas Touch, The.
Marinoni.   Who Are My People?
Marshall, J.   United Way, The.
Mayer, B.   Birthday Sonnet for Grace.
Menai.   To One Who Died in a Garret in Cardiff.
Merrill, J.   Clearing the Title.
Manos Karastefanís.
Miles, S.   Hares, The.
Milton.   Lycidas.
Minhinnick.   After a Friendship.
Montagu, L.   Lover, The; a Ballad.
Moody, E.   To a Friend, Who Gave the Author a Reading Glass.
To a Lady, Who Was a Great Talker.
Moore, T.   Meeting of the Waters, The.
Morales, A.   Tita's Poem.
Morley, H.   For Elaine de Kooning.
Moss, S.   Exchange of Hats, An.
Muldoon, P.   Soap-Pig, The.
Nelson, F.   Human Heart, The.
Nemerov.   Blue Suburban.
Nesbit, E.   Among His Books.
O'Hara, F.   Aus Einem April.
Olson, C.   Death of Europe, The.
Osgood, F.   Garden of Friendship, The.
Parry, J.   New Friends and Old Friends.
Patchen.   State of the Nation, The.
Pearlberg, G.G.   Think Back.
Pereira.   Burden, The.
Philips, K.   Friendship in Emblem[e], or the Seal[e], to my dearest Lucasia.
Friendship's Mystery[s], to my dearest Lucasia.
L'Amitie: To Mrs. Mary [*or* M.] Awbrey.
To Mrs M. A. at Parting.
To My Excellent Lucasia, On Our Friendship.
To the Queen of Inconstancy, Regina Collier, in Antwerp.
Piercy.   Friend, The.
Morning Athletes.
Planché.   Self-Evident.
Plato.   True Friend, The.

Porter, C.   Friendship.
Ramsay, A.   Friendship in Perfection.
Reverdy.   On the Threshold.
Rich, A.   For a Friend in Travail.
  Ghazal.
Robinson, A.   To a Dead Friend.
Robinson, C.   We Who Have Loved.
Robinson, E.   How Annandale Went Out.
  Old Story, An.
Rochester, J.   Platonic Lady, The.
Rosenblatt, S.   Second Half of Our Lives, The.
Rossetti, C.   After Communion.
  From Sunset to Star Rise.
  Promises like Pie-Crust.
Ruden, S.   Stubble Burning, The.
Sanchez, S.   Song No. 3: "Cain't nobody tell me
  any different."
Schafer.   Battle Lines.
Seward.   Invocation, To the Genius of Slumber
  Written Oct. 1787.
  To a Friend, Who Thinks Sensibility a
  Misfortune.
Silverstein, S.   Friendship.
  Hug o' War.
  Nobody.
Smith, C.   Captive Escaped in the Wilds of
  America, The. Addressed to the Hon. Mrs.
  O'Neill.
  On the Aphorism "L'Amitié est l'Amour sans
  Ailes."
  To Friendship.
Smith, S.   Dirge: "From a friend's friend I taste
  friendship."
  Freddy.
St. John, D.   My Friend.
Stanley, T.   La Belle Confidente.
Stephens, J.   Seumas Beg.
Stevenson, R.   Mile an' a Bittock, A.
  My Shadow.
Stone, J.   He Makes a House Call.
Swift, J.   In Sickness.
  Twelve Articles.
  Verses on the Death of Dr. Swift, D.S.P.D.,
  Occasioned by Reading a Maxim in
  Rochefoucauld.
Swift, K.   Can't We Be Friends?
Talfourd.   'Tis a Little Thing.
  Friend, A.
Teft.   On a Friend's Taking a Journey.
Tennyson, A.   In the Garden at Swainston.
  To E. Fitzgerald.
Towne, C.   Around the Corner.
Troupe.   View from Skates in Berkeley, The.
Tsaloumas.   Old Friend.
Unknown.   And Yet the Earth Remains
  Unchanged.
  Confide In a Friend.
  Epitaph: "My friend, judge not me."
  Friend, A.
  Friendship.
  Only Way to Have a Friend, The.
Vaughan, H.   To My Ingenuous Friend, R. W.
Walcott.   Sea Canes.
  Village Life, A.
Weaver, M.   Left Bank Jazz Society, The.
Whitman, W.   As Toilsome I Wander'd
  Virginia's Woods.
  I Dream'd in a Dream.
  I Saw in Louisiana a Live-Oak Growing.
  In Paths Untrodden.
  Live Oak, with Moss.
  Not Heat Flames Up and Consumes.
  Recorders Ages Hence.
Whittemore, E.   My Friends Are Little Lamps to
  Me.
Whittemore, R.   On the Suicide of a Friend.
Wilcox, E.   Accept My Full Heart's Thanks.
  Friendship.
  Friendship After Love.
Williams, B.   Friend Who Just Stands By, The.
Williams, M.   Thinking about Bill, Dead of
  AIDS.
Winchilsea.   Friendship Between Ephelia and
  Ardelia.
Wordsworth, W.   Tables Turned, The.
  To a Child [Written in Her Album].

Wyatt, S.   Lux, My Faire Falcon.
Yearsley.   To———: "Lo! dreary Winter,
  howling o'er the waste."
Yeats.   Friends.
Young, M. J.   Friendship.
Frietchie, Barbara
Whittier.   Barbara Frietchie.
Frog Prince, The
Smith, S.   Frog Prince, The.
Frogs
Belloc.   Frog, The.
Brion, R.   One Morning Beside a Pond.
Bruchac.   Birdfoot's Grampa.
Dodge, M.   Moon Came Late, The.
Finlay, I.   Great Frog Race.
Flanner.   Frog Song.
Greger.   Frog in the Swimming Pool, The.
Grunberger, A.   Swimming Upstream.
Heaney, S.   Death of a Naturalist.
Hoban.   Tin Frog, The.
Kinnell.   First Song.
  Vapor Trail Reflected in the Frog Pond.
Machan.   Hazel Tells LaVerne.
Mother Goose.   Frog He Would A-Wooing
  Go, A.
Rossetti, C.   Frog's Fate, A.
  Hopping frog, hop here and be seen.
Rothenberg, J.   Song of Quavering, A.
Schevill.   Green Frog at Roadstead, Wisconsin.
Smith, S.   Frog Prince, The.
Unknown.   Frog, The.
Wallace-Crabbe.   Nub.
Wright, J.   Small Frogs Killed on the Highway.
Young Bear.   Wadasa Nakamoon, Vietnam
  Memorial.
Frontiers
Arnold, C.   Extravagance of Zoos, The.
Heaney, S.   From the Frontier of Writing.
Frontiersmen
Ferril.   Jupiter at Beer Springs.
Frost
Barnes, D.   Portrait of a Lady Walking.
Begay.   Mother's Lace.
Coleridge, M.   September.
Coleridge, S.   Frost at Midnight.
Davis, C.   Years, The.
Fisher, C.   Frozen Tarn.
Goetsch, D.   Nobody's Hell.
Herrick.   Farewell Frost; or, Welcome the
  Spring.
Lovelace, R.   Grasshopper, The.
Mangan, J.   O'Hussey's Ode to the Maguire.
McCarriston.   January, Anchorage.
Norris, L.   Early Frost.
Pugh.   Frozen Field, The.
Sandburg, C.   Splinter.
Thaxter.   Jack Frost.
Zwicky.   Jack Frost.
Frost, Robert
Brooks, G.   Of Robert Frost.
Hillyer.   Letter to Robert Frost, A.
Houghton, F.   Mr. Frost Goes South to Boston.
Kinnell.   For Robert Frost.
Salter.   Frost at Midnight.
Fruit Trees and Fruit
Adisa.   Discover Me.
Belitt.   Orange Tree, The.
Cavendish, M.   Of the Theme of Love.
D'Aguiar.   Airy Hall Icongraphy.
Dooley, M.   At Les Deux Magots.
Elmslie, K.   Fruit.
Evasco, M.   Elemental.
"Field."   She is Singing to Thee, Domine!
Fuller, J.   Wild Raspberries.
Garrett, E.   Ribes Rubrum.
Garrigue.   Catch What You Can.
Gonzalez, R.   Beyond Having.
Goodison.   Songs of the Fruits and Sweets of
  Childhood.
Gorham.   Empress Receives the Head of a
  Taiping Rebel, The.
Hall, D.   Mangosteens.
Harpur, C.   Basket of Summer Fruit, A.
Harrison, T.   Kumquat for John Keats, A.
Huelsenbeck, R.   "We Hardly."

Keats.   To Autumn.
Kelly, B.   Leaving, The.
Kinsella, J.   Plumburst.
Kyger.   Caption for a Miniature.
Levertov.   O Taste and See.
Logghe.   Madonna of the Peaches.
MacLeish.   Ars Poetica.
Maguire, S.   Fall, The.
Masini.   Two Men, Two Grapefruits.
Mayer, G.   Bilberries.
McKay, C.   Tropics in New York, The.
Millay, E.   Never May the Fruit Be Plucked.
Moore, M.   Nevertheless.
Naimy, M.   Hunger.
Nelson, J.   Never Eat Oranges!
Nelson, M.   Brightness.
Padel.   Yew Berries.
Piercy.   September Afternoon at Four O'Clock.
Rankine.   Man. His Bowl. His Raspberries, The.
Rossetti, C.   Goblin Market.
Strange.   Still Life.
Taggard.   Fructus.
Tipping.   Mangoes.
Whitman, T.   Hunger and Imagination.
Whittier.   Fruit-Gift, The.
Williams, W.   This Is Just to Say.
Frustration
Bolton, J.   Lights at Newport Beach, The.
Cabico, R.   Gameboy.
Hope, M.   Sacrifice.
Lassell.   Kissing Ramén.
Powell, K.   Don't Feel No Way.
Rosemurgy, C.   Why God Invented the Cold.
Shepherd, R.   That Man.
Stryk, L.   Cormorant.
Wilde, O.   Wasted Days.
Wren, A.   Harmony.
Fuchsia
Hardy, T.   Lodging-House Fuchsias, The.
Fujiyama
Kusano Shimpei.   Skylarks and Fuji.
Fulfillment
Bontemps.   God Give to Men.
Browning, R.   Now.
Cullen, C.   From the Dark Tower.
Donne.   Good-Morrow, The.
Espada.   Tony Went to the Bodega But He
  Didn't Buy Anything.
Owen, W.   Music.
Robinson, E.   Three Quatrains.
Fuller, Margaret
Hacker, M.   Ballad of Ladies Lost and Found.
Masters, E.   Margaret Fuller Slack.
Fun
"Æ."   Frolic.
Berlin.   Pack Up Your Sins and Go to the Devil.
Brown, L.   I Want to Be Bad.
Burke, J.   Good Time Charlie.
Cohan.   If I'm Going to Die I'm Going to Have
  Some Fun.
Coward.   Bar on the Piccola Marina, A.
Ebb, F.   Nowadays.
Egan, R.   Ain't We Got Fun.
Ellington, D.   I Didn't Know About You.
Fain, S.   Are You Havin' Any Fun?
Herrick.   Anacreontic.
  Frolic[k], A.
Hughes, L.   Advice.
Kander, J.   Nowadays.
Keech.   Discovery.
Russell, B.   I Didn't Know About You.
Sondheim.   Some People.
Van Heusen, J.   Good Time Charlie.
Viorst.   Night Fun.
See also Play; Pleasure
Funerals
Asalache.   Death of a Chief.
Ashe.   Corpse-bearing.
Barlow, G.   Salt.
Beaumont, S.   Upon a Funeral.
Bernstein, C.   Profaning the Dead.
Bidgood.   Burial Path.
Booth, P.   Sixty-Six.
Bowering, G.   Está Muy Caliente.
Broumas, O.   On Earth.

Clover, J. There Is the Body Lying in State.
Cullen, C. Brown Girl Dead, A.
Dawe, B. At Shagger's Funeral.
Going.
De Roche. Aunt Laura Moves toward the Open Grave of Her Father.
Dickinson, E. I Felt a Funeral in My Brain.
Donne. Funeral[l], The.
Dove, R. Tou Wan Speaks to Her Husband Liu Sheng.
Dubie. Funeral, The.
Ganges, The.
Erdrich, H. Future Debris.
Evans, M. Rebel, The.
Fisher, J. It's February But.
Graves, R. 1805.
Greacen. St. Andrew's Day.
Summer Day, A.
Gwala. From the Outside.
Hall, D. Funeral, The.
Hamod, S. After the Funeral of Assam Hamady.
Hardy, T. Choirmaster's Burial, The.
Heaney, S. Funeral Rites.
Herrick. Funeral[l] Rites of the Rose, The.
Housman, A. Bredon Hill.
Hughes, L. Ballad of the Man Who's Gone.
Dead in There.
Night Funeral in Harlem.
Kasischke. Pall.
King, H. Exequy, The.
Komunyakaa. April Fools' Day.
Layton. Street Funeral.
Lewis, J. Country Burial.
Longley, M. Detour.
Lowell, R. Death of the Sheriff, The.
McKinney, I. Chrysanthemums.
Melville, H. Dirge for McPherson, A.
Merrill, J. Annie Hill's Grave.
Millay, E. Dirge Without Music.
Mitchell, K. On the Anniversary Of Your Death.
Montague, J. Falls Funeral.
Mooney, M. Anna Akhmatova's Funeral.
Mother Goose. Who Killed Cock Robin.
Murphy, K. Girl with the Bad Rep, The.
Muske. Eulogy, The.
Orfalea, G. Rose of Brooklyn, The.
Plath. Bee Meeting, The.
Poe. Lenore.
Porteous. Decommissioning.
Probyn. Changes.
Ransom, J. Bells for John Whiteside's Daughter.
Emily Hardcastle, Spinster.
Redmond. Poetic Reflections Enroute To, and During, The Funeral and Burial of Henry Dumas, Poet.
Rouse. Sacrificial Wolf.
Ruefle. Furtherness.
Salaam. Our World Is Less Full Now That Mr. Fuller Is Gone.
Schulman. Burial of a Fisherman in Hydra.
Sexton. Truth the Dead Know, The.
Shapiro, K. My Father's Funeral.
Soyinka. Funeral Sermon, Soweto.
Spender, S. Funeral, The.
Stanley, T. Exequies, The.
Stevens, W. Emperor of Ice-Cream, The.
Synge. Question, A.
Tati-Loutard. Submarine Tombs.
Thomas, D. After the Funeral.
Thomas, E. Spectator, The.
Unknown. Cowboy's Lament, The.
Finnegan's Wake.
Williams, M. On the Symbolic Consideration of Hands and the Significance of Death.
Williams, W. Tract.
Wolfe, C. Burial of Sir John Moore [after [or at] Corunna], The.

Furnaces
Merwin, W. S. Drunk in the Furnace, The.

Furniture
Ashbery. Melodic Trains.
Davidson, M. Feeling Type and His Friends, The.

DiPalma. Table, The.
Maiden. In the Gloaming.
McGuckian. Presence, The.
McHugh, H. What Could Hold Us.
Nemerov. Singular Metamorphosis, A.
Pietri. 7th Untitled Poem.
Intermission from Thursday.
Prospere. Heart of the Matter.
Thomson, J. In the Room.
Tsaloumas. Autumn Supper.
Winstanley, J. Inventory of the Furniture of a Collegian's Chamber, An.

Fuseli, Henry
Blake, W. To Hunt.

Future
Adams, F. Those Two Boys.
Ashbery. Brute Image.
Crossroads in the Past.
Atwood. Up.
Auden. Gare du Midi.
Benson, S. Blue Book 18 Pages 1–4.
Braley, B. Start Where You Stand.
Brecht, B. To Those Born Later.
Clark, T. Daily News.
Coleridge, M. Unwelcome.
Davidson, D. Randall, My Son.
de Carvalho. I Come from a South.
Desnos. Trance Event.
Dipoko. Our Life.
Ehrhart. To Those Who Have Gone Home Tired.
Evans, R. Whatever Will Be, Will Be (Que Sera, Sera).
Everwine. From the Meadow.
Fanning, R. Space Needle, The.
Fenton, J. Born Too Soon.
Finch, A. There's No To-Morrow.
Fuller, J. Born Too Soon.
Gallup. Backing into the Future.
Gilbert, C. Sorrow Since Sitting Bull, A.
Gray, R. Flames and Dangling Wire.
Harms. My Androgynous Years.
Hartnett. There Will Be a Talking.
Hawthorne, N. Oh Could I Raise the Darken'd Veil.
Heath-Stubbs. To a Poet a Thousand Years Hence.
Herbert, C. Everything Changes.
Housman, A. Lads in Their Hundreds, The.
Jarrell. On the Railway Platform.
Jeffers, R. Granite and Cypress.
Watch the Lights Fade.
Jurmann, W. Tomorrow Is Another Day.
Kelly, R. Recessional.
Kenyon, J. Otherwise.
King, H. Exequy, The.
Kipling, R. Storm Cone, The.
Larkin, P. Arundel Tomb, An.
Next, Please.
Livingston, J. Whatever Will Be, Will Be (Que Sera, Sera).
Loesser. Make a Miracle.
Lumsden, R. ITMA.
Madhubuti. Union of Two, The.
Marion, G. My Future Just Passed.
Meyers, B. Suburban Dusk.
Milosz, C. Incantation.
Ofeimun. Let Them Choose Paths.
Osundare. I Sing of Change.
Pasolini. Day of My Death, The.
Polak, J. Storm, The.
Porter, C. From This Moment On.
Ríos, A. Mi Abuelo.
Rich, A. Prospective Immigrants Please Note.
Richardson, K. Aubade: "Geese flew by as you entered me, The."
Rossetti, C. Cobwebs.
Salaam. I Live in the Mouth of History.
Sandburg, C. Broken-Face Gargoyles.
Haze.
Stevens, W. Postcard from the Volcano, A.
Strand. Prediction, The.
Toomer. It is Everywhere.
Wallace-Crabbe. Nub.
Washington, N. Hundred Years from Today, A.
Whiting, R. My Future Just Passed.

Whitman, W. Full of Life Now.
Recorders Ages Hence.
To the Pending Year.
Years of the Modern.
Wilcox, E. Was, Is, and Yet-To-Be.
Winter, M. Space Parable.
Wunderlich, M. Suture.
Young, J. Hundred Years from Today, A.
Zukofsky, L. I Sent Thee Late.

G

Gabriel
Jennings, E. Annuciation, The.
Rich, A. Gabriel.
Richards, G. Almighty Spake, and Gabriel Sped, Th'

Galatea
Graves, R. Galatea and Pygmalion.

Galilee, Israel
Barnes, D. Chuang Tzu and Hui Tzu.

Galley Slaves
Kipling, R. Song of the Galley-Slaves.

Gallipoli Campaign (1915)
Stallworthy, J. War Story.

Galoshes
Bacmeister. Galoshes.
Taylor, N. Upon Julia's Arctics.

Galuppi, Baldassaro
Browning, R. Toccata of Galuppi's, A.

Galveston, Texas
Howes, B. On Galveston Beach.

Gambling and Gamblers
Cavafy. Days of 1908.
Clairmont. Hero in the Land of Dough, A.
Gotera. Gambling.
Hacker, M. Wagers.
Hongo. Off from Swing Shift.
Winnings.
Hughes, L. Situation.
Long, D. One Time Henry Dreamed the Number.
Ortiz. Telling About Coyote.
Rochester, J. Ramble in St. James's Park, A.
Sandburg, C. Cahoots.
Crapshooters.
Studdert-Kennedy. Great Wager, The.
Tyler, R. Gambling.
Wakoski. Placing a $2 Bet for a Man Who Will Never Go to the Horse Races Any More.
Young, A. Studio Up Over In Your Ear.
Zeppa, M. Aleatory.

Games
Anderson, L. Red Hot.
Arlen, H. Between the Devil and the Deep Blue Sea.
Atwood. Game after Supper.
Blind. Once We Played.
Brouwer, J. Steve's Commando Paintball, San Adriano, California.
Burns, R. Johnie Blunt.
Caesar. Too Many Rings Around Rosie.
Clare, J. Shepherd Boy, The.
Cleghorn. Golf Links, The.
Cummings, E. May I Feel Said He.
Curtis, T. Games with My Daughter.
Dehn, P. Game of Consequences, A.
Dent. For Cool Papa Bell.
"Dermée." Poem.
Dunn, S. Competition.
Fatchen. It's a Bit Rich.
Fitzgerald, E. 69.
70.
Gilbert, C. This Bridge Across.
Graves, R. Hide and Seek.
Hammerstein. Make Believe.
Hannan, M. Bone Die, The.
Harper, M. Makin' Jump Shots.
Holland, J. Baize Queens.
Jackson, R. For Thurman Thomas.
Kern, J. Make Believe.
Koehler, T. Between the Devil and the Deep Blue Sea.

Laughlin, J. Step on His Head.
McDonald, W. War Games.
Mosby. To Josh Gibson (Legendary Slugger of the Old Negro Baseball League).
Patterson, G. Letter from Home.
Perreault, J. Boomerang.
Roderick, D. Curlers at Dusk.
Roy, L. Triple Overtime.
Sia, B. No Words Empty.
Starkey, D. Scrabble.
Stevenson, R. Good Play, A.
Pirate Story.
Tate, G. Tonguing.
Todd, R. Paul Klee.
Troupe. Poem for "Magic," A.
Unknown. Children's Ball-Bouncing Song.
Youmans, V. Too Many Rings Around Rosie.
See also **Card Games; Sports**
Ganges River, India
Dubie. Ganges, The.
Shange. Where the Mississippi Meets the Amazon.
Gangs and Gangsters
Fructuoso, E. Astig.
Gilbert, S. Mafioso.
Gunn, T. Black Jackets.
Muldoon, P. Sightseers, The.
Weepies, The.
Muske, C. Field Trip.
Rodriguez, L. To the Police Officer Who Refused to Sit in the Same Room as My Son Because He's a 'Gang Banger.'
Soto. Morning They Shot Tony Lopez, Barber and Pusher Who Went Too Far, 1958, The.
Garages
Bethell. Detail.
Mahon. Garage in Co. Cork, A.
Garbage and Garbage Men
Alley, R. Cleaning.
Axelrod, D. Guide to Urban Birds, A.
Berry, W. Wild, The.
Coe, C. Possibility.
Grennan. Wing Road.
Howell, C. Memories of Mess Duty and the War.
Nemerov. Town Dump, The.
North, C. Little Cape Cod Landscape.
Orfalea, G. Age of Cruelty, The.
Silverstein, S. Sarah Cynthia Sylvia Stout Would Not Take the Garbage Out.
Tranter. Glow-boys.
Wilbur. After the Last Bulletins.
Junk.
Wormser. Pigeons.
See also **Sanitary Engineering and Sanitary Engineers**
García Lorca, Federico
Dudek. García Lorca.
Duncan, R. Drinking Fountain, The.
Hazo. World that Lightning Makes, The.
Jackson, R. Eight Ball.
Manifold. Garcia Lorca Murdered in Granada.
Manrique, J. My Night with Federico García Lorca (As Told by Edouard Roditi).
Woodcock. Poem for Garcia Lorca.
Garda, Lake, Italy
Tennyson, A. Frater Ave Atque Vale.
Gardens and Gardening
Aiken, C. And in the Hanging Gardens.
Akenside. Inscription for a Grotto.
Alexander, M. Her Garden.
Anzaldúa. Cultures.
Arkell. What is a Garden?
Aston, A. Everything in the Garden is Lovely.
Auden. Their Lonely Betters.
Barker, G. Gardens of Ravished Psyche, The.
Bass, F. Garden, The.
Bateman, E. Cockney's Garden, The.
Beaver. Déjeuner Sur l'Herbe.
Bethell. Erica.
Time.
Warning of Winter.
Bishop, E. Manuelzinho.
Black, S. Hoopla.
Bodecker. Garden Calendar.

Bridges, R. Garden in September, The.
To Francis Jammes.
Brooke, L. Johnny Crow's Garden.
Brown, T. My Garden.
Brownjohn. In a Convent Garden.
Bullock, M. Garden.
Carroll. In the Shakespeare Garden at Northwestern University.
Chang, E. After the Storm.
Chesterfield. On Lord Ila's Improvements, near Hounslow Heath.
Ciardi. Suburban.
Coleridge, M. Poison Flower, The.
Coleridge, S. Garden Year, The.
Combs. Just after Noon with Fierce Shears.
Cooke, R. Che Sara Sara.
Coolbrith. Ownership.
Cooley, N. Family History, The.
Cotton, N. On Lord Cobham's Garden.
Cowper, W. Shrubbery, The.
Crane, H. Garden Abstract.
Creeley. Door, The.
Cummings, E. Sonnet IV.
Curry. Gardens.
Davie. Gardens No Emblems.
Davies, W. No Man's Wood.
Dawe, B. Homo Suburbiensis.
Day Lewis. Snowfall on a College Garden.
De la Mare. Two Gardens.
De Tabley. Philoctetes.
Dean, D. K. Taproot.
Deanovich. My Favorite Monk Is.
Delgado, J. Dandelion.
Deming, A. Tilden Park.
Denby. Villa d'Este.
Dobson, A. Garden Song, A.
Doddridge, P. Meditations on the Sepulchre in the Garden.
Dodge, M. Someone in the Garden.
Donne. Twicknam [*or* Twickenham] Garden.
Doolittle, H. Garden.
Douglas, L. Two Loves.
Downie. Her Garden.
Druce. Apropos of Garden Statuary: A Disquisition upon a Minor Genre.
Dunn, D. Gardeners.
In the Grounds.
Durrell. In the Garden: Villa Cleobolus.
Edmond, L. Jardin des Colombières.
Emerson, R. Days.
Enright, D. Kyoto Garden, A.
Evasco, M. Elemental.
Ewart. Wanting Out.
Farjeon, E. Over the Garden Wall.
Finney, N. Uncles.
Foster, A. Caterpillar.
Glück, L. Garden, The.
White Lilies, The.
Graves, R. Gardener.
Gregory, H. Chinese Garden, The.
Grigson. Landscape Gardeners, The.
Guest, B. Wild Gardens Overlooked by Night Lights.
Guiney. Garden Chidings.
Gunn, T. Last Days at Teddington.
Pope's Carnations Knew Him.
Habergham. Seeds of Love, The.
Hall, D. Her Garden.
Hamburger, M. Garden, Wilderness.
Weeding.
Hardy, T. Garden Seat, The.
Hawes, S. Epitaph of Graunde [*or* La Graunde] Amoure, The.
Pastime of Pleasure, The.
True Knight [*or* True Knighthood], The.
Healy, R. Primula veris.
Hecht, A. Gardens of the Villa D'Este, The.
Herbert, G. Paradise.
Herrick. To a Bed of Tulips.
Hesketh. Death of a Gardener.
Hildebrandt, Z. In Hecate's Garden.
Hill, A. Garden Window, The.
Hines, P. My Garden.
Hitchcock. One Whose Reproach I Cannot Evade, The.
Hochman. Cannon Hill.

Howard, R. Mrs. Eden in Town for the Day.
Howells, W. November.
Hugo, R. Way a Ghost Dissolves, The.
Ingraham. She Would Have Roses.
Jacinto, J. Visitation.
Jarrell. In a Hospital Garden.
Jennings, E. In a Garden.
Jones, R. Times Like This.
Kaufman, S. Emperor of China, The.
Kavanagh, P. Long Garden, The.
Kendrick, D. Gethsemane A. D.
Kinzie. Sun and Moon.
Kipling, R. Glory of the Garden, The.
Kirkup. Scarecrows.
Kunitz, S. Snakes of September, The.
Lawrence, D. Trees in the Garden.
Layton. Cold Green Element, The.
Layzer. Lawn Roller, The.
Le Gallienne. Library in a Garden, A.
Leithauser. In a Japanese Moss Garden.
Levertov. Death in Mexico.
Levin, P. Planting Roses.
Lewis, J. Garden Note II, March.
Winter Garden.
Lindon. My Garden.
Liu, T. Brooklyn Botanic Garden, The.
Lowell, R. Public Garden, The.
Lucas, T. Town Garden, A.
MacNeice. Sunlight on the Garden, The.
Magee, W. British Garden, A.
Marvell. Garden, The.
Mower Against Gardens, The.
Marzán. In the Backyard.
Mason, W. To a Gravel Walk.
Mayer, B. Garden, The.
McCord, D. Mr. Bidery's Spidery Garden.
McDonald, C. Oxford Gardens.
McMaster, R. Back Steps Lookout.
Melville, H. Ravaged Villa, The.
Merrick, A. Hartwell Gardens.
Merwin, W. S. Tide Line Garden.
Miller, A. Mulch.
Pruning, The.
Millikin. Groves of Blarney, The.
Minhinnick. Grandfather in the Garden.
Mole, J. Trick, The.
Monroe, H. Garden, The.
Montague, J. 11 rue Daguerre.
Moraes, D. Gardener.
More, S. Child's Song.
Nemerov. Salt Garden, The.
Nesbit, E. At Parting.
Noyes, A. Butterfly Garden, The.
Paley, G. Here.
Paz. Stanzas for an Imaginary Garden.
Peacocke. Railway Allotments.
Pitter. Diehards, The.
Other People's Glasshouses.
Plath. Manor Garden, The.
Pope, A. Garden, The.
Porter, C. Old-Fashioned Garden, An.
Porter, P. Australian Garden, An.
Pound, E. Garden, The.
Prunty. Vegetable Garden, The.
Radiguet. Poem: "Red eiderdown at the window, A."
Raine, C. Gardener, The.
Redgrove, P. Negotium Perambulans.
Reid, C. Gardeners, The.
Riley, J. At the Stanley Spencer Exhibition.
Roberts, L. Another Spring on Olmstead Street.
Roethke. Cuttings.
Otto.
Weed Puller.
Rossetti, C. Shut Out.
Sackville-West. Garden, The.
Sassoon. In Heytesbury Wood.
Schuyler, J. Roof Garden.
Sewell, G. Dying Man in His Garden, The.
Shirley, J. Garden, The.
Simmons, J. October in the Country: [1983].
Playing with Fire.
Sims. Garden Song, A.
Sisson. Herb-Garden, The.
Red Admiral, The.
Sitwell, D. Gardener Janus Catches a Naiad.

Sitwell, S.   In the Potting Shed.
  In the Winter.
Smith, K.   Writing in Prison.
Smith, R.   Bluetits.
Snow, A.   Gardener.
Southerland.   Night in Nigeria.
Spark.   Kensington Gardens.
Stanley-Wrench.   Hinterland.
Steele, T.   Wartburg, 1521–22, The.
Stein, G.   In This Way.
Stevens, W.   Room on a Garden, A.
Stevenson, R.   Autumn Fires.
  Gardener, The.
  To A Gardener.
Stewart, P.   Estes' Backyard, The.
Stickney, T.   Athenian Garden, An.
Strand.   Garden, The.
Straus, M.   Scarlet Crown.
Suckling, S.   Upon My Lady Carlisle's Walking
  in Hampton Court Garden.
Swinburne.   Forsaken Garden, A.
  Garden of Proserpine, The.
Sylvester, J.   Garden, The.
Tennyson, A.   Recollections of The Arabian
  Nights.
Thomas, D.   Walking in Gardens.
Thomas, E.   Digging.
  Frost To-night.
Thomas, G.   Lessons.
Tomlinson, C.   In the Borghese Gardens.
  Juliet's Garden.
Unknown.   I Have a New Garden.
  International Chainpoem.
  Man of Words, A.
Van Duyn.   Gardener to His God, The.
Vazirani, R.   Maya to Herself and Then to Her
  Gardener.
Waller, E.   At Penshurst [Another].
  On St. James's Park, as Lately Improved by His
  Majesty.
  To a Lady in a Garden.
Wellesley.   Walled Garden.
Whitehead, W.   On the Late Improvements at
  Nuneham, the Seat of the Earl of Harcourt.
Whittier.   Garden.
Wilbur.   Caserta Garden.
Williams, P.   Lost Seed.
Williams, W.   Italian Garden, The.
  Tulip Bed, The.
  Widow's Lament in Springtime, The.
Wilner, E.   Secret Garden, The.
Winchilsea.   Upon My Lord Winchilsea's
  Converting the Mount in His Garden to a
  Terrace.
Winters, Y.   Time and the Garden.
Wright, J.   Invention of a Garden, The.
Yeats.   Down by the Salley Gardens.
Yee, M.   Wintermelons.

Gargoyles
Hernández Cruz.   La Milagrosa.
Sandburg, C.   Broken-Face Gargoyles.
  Gargoyle.
Shaw, R.

Garland, Judy
Seaton, M.   Story of Stonewall, A.

Garrick, David
Johnson, S.   Prologue Spoken by Mr[.] Garrick
  at the Opening of the Theatre in Drury Lane,
  1747.

Garrison, William Lloyd
Ray, H.   William Lloyd Garrison.

Gasoline Stations
Bishop, E.   Filling Station.
Gilmore, B.   Gas Station Attendant.
Laux.   Fast Gas.
Tapahonso.   Pay Up or Else.
Wade, S.   Gas.

Gates
Barnes, W.   Turnstile, The.
Gorham.   Princess Parade.
Jackson, H.   Opportunity.
Mew.   At the Convent Gate.
Probyn.   Blossom.

Gauguin, Paul
Hearne, V.   Gauguin's White Horse.

Gawaine, Sir
Winters, Y.   Sir Gawaine and the Green Knight.
Gay and Lesbian Poetry
Gomez.   My Chakabuku Mama: A Comic Tale.
Gazelles
Lawrence, D.   Gazelle Calf, The.
Moore, T.   Gazelles, The.
Geese
Alcott, L.   Lay of a Golden Goose, The.
Berry, W.   Wild Geese, The.
Braun, R.   Goose.
  Lilies, The.
Carroll, J.   Withdrawal Letter.
Chamberlain, K.   Stepping in the Same River.
Cheng Hsieh.   For Contemporary Artist Pien
  Wei-Ch'i.
Coatsworth.   And Stands There Sighing.
Davis, J.   He Is Lightning.
Field, R.   Something Told the Wild Geese.
Glück, L.   Messengers.
Howes, B.   Wild Geese Flying.
Imbs.   Wind Was There, The.
Nesbit, E.   Goose-Girl, The.
Norris, L.   Hudson's Geese.
Oliver, M.   Wild Geese.
Piercy.   Last Scene in the First Act.
  Postcard from the Garden.
Plath.   Rhyme.
Richardson, K.   Aubade: "Geese flew by as you
  entered me, The."
Sandburg, C.   Bas-Relief.
Southey, R.   To a Goose [*or* Gosse].
Stafford, W.   Late at Night.
Stallworthy, J.   Poem about Poems about
  Vietnam, A.
Tu Mu.   Early Geese.
Unknown.   Fox and the Goose, The.
  When the Rain Raineth.
Waniek.   Bali Hai Calls Mama.
Warren, R.   Heart of Autumn.
Gems
Byron, G.   Cornelian, The.
Douglas, L.   Impression de Nuit; London.
Herrick.   Amber Bead, The.
  To Julia.
  To the Right Honourable Mildmay, Earl of
  Westmorland.
Lowther.   Stone Diary, A.
McGuckian.   Laurentia.
Rossetti, C.   Flint.
Slater, F.   Stars in Sand.
Taylor, J.   Star, The.
Generals
Betjeman.   Old Land Dog, The.
Bierce.   General B. F. Butler.
Graves, R.   General Elliott, The.
Landor, W.   Crimean Heroes, The.
Marvell.   Garden of Appleton House, The
  ("When in the east the morning ray").
  Garden, A.
  Upon Appleton House [To My Lord Fairfax].
  Upon the Hill and Grove at Bilbrough.
Sassoon.   General, The.
Sherwood, R.   Albert Sidney Johnston.
Wallace, R.   Nightline: An Interview with the
  General.
Generosity
Adamson, H.   Everything I Have Is Yours.
Akst, H.   Straw Hat in the Rain.
Davies, O.   Urban.
Hart, L.   I've Got Five Dollars.
Hughes, L.   Preference.
Lane, B.   Everything I Have Is Yours.
McGinley.   Giveaway, The.
Rodgers, R.   I've Got Five Dollars.
Sanchez, S.   This is Not a Small Voice.
Unknown.   (My Daily Creed).
Genetics and Geneticists
MacKenzie, R.   Category Mistakes in
  Biochemistry.
Moolten, D.   Bio 7.
See also **Evolution**
Genitalia
Andrews, N.   Notes for a Sermon on the Mount.
Burns, R.   Wat ye what my Minnie did.

Crowley, A.   Ballad of Passive Paederasty, A.
Field, E.   Street Instructions at the Crotch.
Giorno.   Pornographic Poem.
Hagedorn, J.   Vulva Operetta.
Liu, T.   Size of It, The.
Neely, L.   Eight Ways of Looking at Pussy.
Purdy, J.   From rivers, and from the earth itself.
Rankine.   Short Narrative of Breasts and Wombs
  in Service of Plot Entitled, A.
Redel, V.   Singing to Tony Bennett's Cock.
Rouse.   Queynt.
Smukler.   Trash.
Unknown.   No Balls at All.
Genius
Blake, W.   All Religions Are One.
Browning, E.   To George Sand: A Recognition.
Graeme.   Mortified Genius, A.
Hughes, L.   Genius Child.
Kizer, C.   Twelve O'Clock.
Menken.   Genius.
Robinson, E.   Ben Jonson Entertains a Man
  from Stratford.
Gentians
Bryant, W.   To the Fringed Gentian.
Evans, A.   Fringed Gentians.
Lawrence, D.   Bavarian Gentians.
Geodes
Dodd, E.   Like Memory, Caverns.
Geography and Geographers
Donne.   Hymn[e] to God My God, In My
  Sickness[e], A.
Goldbarth.   Letter to Friends East and West.
Koch, K.   Geography.
Lomax, M.   Kith.
Osbey.   Geography.
Sharp, S.   Good Nights.
Whitman, W.   Passage to India.
Geology and Geologists
Ciardi.   Goodnight.
Copus, J.   Widower.
Hillman.   Geology, A.
Mulford.   Nevrazumitelny.
Redgrove, P.   Minerals of Cornwall, Stones of
  Cornwall.
Rexroth, K.   Lyell's Hypothesis Again.
Snyder, G.   What Happened Here Before.
Geometry
Bibbins, M.   Geometry Class.
Dove, R.   Geometry.
Harnick.   Ballad of the Shape of Things, The.
Wayne, J.   In Praise of Zigzags.
See also **Euclid**
George I, King of England
Browne, W.   Epigram: "King to Oxford sent a
  troop of horse, The."
George II, King of England
Carey, H.   Lilliputian Ode on Their Majesties'
  Accession, A.
George III, King of England
Freneau.   George the Third's Soliloquy.
Koch, K.   You Were Wearing.
George V, King of England
Betjeman.   Death of King George V.
Hayward, C.   King George V.
Georgia (state)
Ager, M.   Everything Is Peaches Down in
  Georgia.
Bernie, B.   Sweet Georgia Brown.
Bottoms.   In a U-Haul North of Damascus.
Broonzy.   Southern Blues, The.
Brown, S.   Slim in Atlanta.
Burris, J.   Ballin' the Jack.
Carmichael, H.   Georgia on My Mind.
Casey, K.   Sweet Georgia Brown.
Clarke, G.   Everything Is Peaches Down in
  Georgia.
Davis, F.   Robert Whitmore.
Dickey, J.   In the Marble Quarry.
Evans, M.   Daufuskie.
Gorrell, S.   Georgia on My Mind.
Lanier, S.   Song of the Chattahoochee.
Meyer, G.   Everything Is Peaches Down in
  Georgia.
Pinkard, M.   Sweet Georgia Brown.

Smith, C. Ballin' the Jack.
Toomer. Georgia Dusk.
  Portrait in Georgia.
Work. Marching through Georgia.

Geraniums
Dorn, E. Geranium.
Lawrence, D. Red Geranium and Godly
  Mignonette.
Newburn, L. Office Geraniums.
Roethke. Geranium, The.

German (language)
Buckley, V. Teaching German Literature.
Graham, V. Ein Complaint.

Germans, The
Coward. Don't Let's Be Beastly to the
  Germans.
Dobbie. Forty Three Years After Hitler My
  Parents Visit Eugene.
Fenton, J. German Requiem, A.
Heyen. Riddle: "From Belsen a crate of gold
  teeth."
Leland, C. Breitmann in Paris.
  Wein Geist.
Rohrer, M. Precision German Craftmanship.
Smith, S. On the Death of a German
  Philosopher.

Germany
Alkalay-Gut. Kitzbuhl Church.
Bowers, E. Prince, The.
Brecht, B. From a German War Primer.
  War Has Been Given a Bad Name.
Brock, V. Remembering Dresden.
Celan. Death Fugue, A.
Enright, D. No Offence.
Florsheim. Business in Germany.
Gershon. Race.
Heyen. Numinous, The.
Huelsenbeck, R. "We Hardly."
Kahaney, P. Germany, 1981.
Lowell, R. Exile's Return, The.
"Martin." Dreams in German.
Maxton. Deutschland.
Mayne, S. In Memory of Aaron, Murdered
  Grandfather.
Norton, C. Bingen on the Rhine.
Porter, P. May, 1945.
Prufer, K. On Finding a Swastika Carved on a
  Tree in the Hills above Heidelberg.
Schiff, H. German Frontier at Basel: 1942 and
  1992, The.
Shanks. High Germany.
Sisson. Over the Wall: Berlin, May 1975.
Sorley. To Germany.
Sternlieb. Survivor.
Tranter. Enzensberger at 'Exiles.'
  Lufthansa.
Tugend, A. Every Few Months.

Germs
Nash, O. Germ, The.

Gethsemane
Hemans. Agony in the Garden, The.
Kane, P. Disciples Asleep at Gethsemane.
Kipling, R. Gethsemane.
Pasternak, B. Hamlet.
Pratt, E. From Stone to Steel.
Southwell. Christs Sleeping Friends.
  Sinnes Heavie Loade.
Unknown. Christ's Prayer in Gethsemane.

Gettysburg, Battle of (1863)
Harte, B. John Burns of Gettysburg.
Kenyon, J. Gettysburg, July 1, 1863.
Masters, E. Battle of Gettysburg, The.
  Gettysburg.
Taylor, B. Gettysburg Ode.
Thompson, W. High Tide at Gettysburg, The.

Ghana
Ama Ata Aidoo. Cornfields in Accra.
Laing, K. Same Corpse, The.

Ghettos
Algarin. Taos Pueblo Indians: 700 strong
  according to Bobby's last census.
Brody. Ghetto Twilight.
Davis, J. Aboriginal Reserve.
Dumas, H. Concentration Camp Blues.

Friedmann. Butterfly, The.
Jenkins, P. Six Small Fires.
Klein, A. Autobiographical.
Košek, M. It All Depends on How You Look at
  It.
Lorde. New York City 1970.
Meléndez. Oye Mundo/Sometimes.
Milosz, C. Poor Christian Looks at the
  Ghetto, A.
Picková, E. Fear.
Robles. Remembering the Past.
Rodgers, C. U Name This One.
Schulzová, E. Evening in Terezin, An.
Steptoe. Wired In.
Unknown, fr. Terezin Concentration Camp.
  Homesick.
  Night in the Ghetto.
Voznesensky [or Voznesenskii]. Call of the
  Lake, The.

Ghosts
Alcott, L. Our Little Ghost.
Anthony, G. Autumn Evening.
Baillie, J. Ghost of Fadon, The.
Baker, H. Toward Guinea: For Larry Neal,
  1937–1981.
Balaban. After Our War.
Barry, C. Finding.
Beddoes. Phantom-Wooer, The.
Berger, B. Haunts of the Mirage.
Bontemps. Southern Mansion.
Brooks, G. Mentors.
Brown, S. After the Vietnam War.
Cameron, N. Fight with a Water-Spirit.
Causley. By St. Thomas Water.
  Colonel Fazackerley.
Clanchy, K. Deadman's Shoes.
Clare, J. To Mary: 'It Is the Evening Hour.'
Cofer, J. Drowned Sailor, The.
Coleridge, S. On a Ruined House in a Romantic
  Country.
Colvin, I. Flying Dutchman, The.
Cornford, F. All Souls' Night.
De la Mare. Ghost, The.
  Listeners, The.
Dietz, H. Haunted Heart.
Digges. Rough Music.
Donne. Apparition, The.
Edwards [or Edwardes], R. Recollections of an
  Old Spook.
Eyen, J. New Dream, A (Wuski A-Baw-Tan).
Fanthorpe. Father in the Railway Buffet.
Ferguson, G. Swimming Pool Ghost, The.
Gilbert, C. This Bridge Across.
Gloria. Rizal's Ghost.
Graham, J. Underneath (2).
Graves, R. Corporal Stare.
  Welsh Incident.
Gregg. Adult.
Hall, D. Mount Kearsarge.
Hardy, T. Garden Seat, The.
  Haunter, The.
  My Spirit Will Not Haunt the Mound.
  Phantom Horsewoman, The.
Harper, M. Ghost of Soul-making, The.
Heath-Stubbs. Simcox.
Hecht, A. Ghost in the Martini, The.
  Still Life.
Hernández Cruz. Discovery.
  Spirits.
Housman, A. When I Watch the Living Meet.
Hugo, R. Way a Ghost Dissolves, The.
Johnson, M. F. Invocation to the Spirit Said to
  Haunt Wroxall Down.
Justice, D. Beyond the Hunting Woods.
Keesing. Queer Thing, A.
Kipling, R. Looking Glass, The.
Komunyakaa. Dead at Quang Tri, The.
Leithauser. Ghost of a Ghost, The.
Levin, D. Red Water.
Levy, A. Old House, The.
Lindsay, L. Auld Robin Gray.
Livesay, D. Uninvited, The.
Long, J. Bermuda Triangle.
Longfellow, H. Cross of Snow, The.
  Haunted Houses.
Macdonald, G. Song.

MacLean, S. Hallaig.
Maiden. Air.
  Foundations, The.
Mallet. William and Margaret.
"Malley." Coda.
Moody, E. Dr. Johnson's Ghost.
Murphy, P. New Boy, The.
Nesbit, E. Gray Folk, The.
  Haunted.
  Villeggiature.
Noyes, A. Highwayman, The.
Olson, C. As the Dead Prey upon Us.
  At Yorktown.
Owen, W. Shadwell Stair.
Peacock, T. Ghosts, The.
Perillo. Ghost Shirt, The.
Phillips, S. Apparition, The.
Piatt, S. Army of Occupation.
Poe. Conqueror Worm, The.
  Haunted Palace, The.
Ramanujan. Some People.
Ransom, J. Spectral Lovers.
Reese, L. Day Before Spring, The.
Robinson, A. Dead Friend, The.
Robinson, E. Lingard and the Stars.
  Why He Was There.
Robinson, M. Haunted Beach, The.
Rose. Poet Haunted, The.
Rossetti, C. Chilly Night, A.
Schwartz, A. Haunted Heart.
Scovell. Ghosts, The.
Senghor. Visit.
Smith, I. Ghost, The.
Smith, S. Wanderer, The.
Soyinka. Abiku.
  Civilian and Soldier.
Stanton, M. Few Picnics in Illinois, A.
Stevens, W. Rabbit Is King of the Ghosts, A.
Stoddard, E. House by the Sea, The.
Sugioka. Legacy.
Thomas, D. Ghost Story.
Trench, H. She Comes Not When Noon Is on
  the Roses.
Unknown. Cauld Lad of Hilton, The *or* The
  Wandering Spectre.
  Dark House, The.
  Three Ghostesses.
  Wife of Usher's Well, The.
Waniek. House on Moscow Street, The.
Weaver, M. Appaloosa, The.
Whitman, W. As If a Phantom Caress'd Me.
Whittier. Sisters, The.
Wordsworth, W. Lucy Gray; or, Solitude.
  Perfect Woman.
Wright, J. My Grandmother's Ghost.
Wylie. Village Mystery.
Yeats. Apparitions, The.
  To a Shade.
Young Bear. Emily Dickinson, Bismarck and
  the Roadrunner's Inquiry.
Young, A. Shepherd's Hut, The.

Giants
Campbell, S. Big John's Tears Fall to the River.
Hall, D. Sleeping Giant, The.
Major, C. Giant Red Woman.
Mayer, G. Count Carrots.
Millay, E. Bean-Stalk, The.
Namjoshi, S. From the Travels of Gulliver.
Reader. When Paul Bunyan Was Ill.
Riley, J. Jack the Giant-Killer.

Gibbon, Edward
Hardy, T. Lausanne: In Gibbon's Old Garden:
  11–12 p.m.
Landor, W. Distribution of Honours for
  Literature.

Gibraltar
Blunt, W. Gibraltar.

Gifts and Giving
Alford, J. Thanks Be to God.
Anderson, D. Executive Geochrone.
Antiphilus [or Antiphilos]. Gifts to a Lady.
Betjeman. Christmas.
Bishop, M. Dark Christmas on Wildwood Road,
  The.
Bruner. Beggar, The.
  Greater Gift, The.

Byron, G. Cornelian, The.
Causley. Nursery Rhyme of Innocence and Experience.
Clark, P. Kleptomaniac.
Coleridge, M. Broken Friendship.
Comden, B. Thanks a Lot, but No Thanks.
Creeley. Gift, The.
Davenant [or D'Avenant]. For the Lady Olivia Porter; a Present upon a New Year's Day.
Davies, M. Let Me Be a Giver.
Doolittle, H. Acon.
Wine Bowl.
Emerson, R. Give All to Love.
Ewing, J. Gifts.
Farjeon, E. Advice to a Child.
Fisher, A. Fair Exchange.
Fiskin. Magi, The.
Freeman, C. Christmas Morning I.
Frishberg, D. Peel Me a Grape.
Frost, R. Gift Outright, The.
Gay, J. To a Young Lady, with Some Lampreys.
Green, A. Thanks a Lot, but No Thanks.
Gruber, A. My Neighbor's Roses.
Herrick. New-Year's [or New-Yeares] Gift Sent to Sir Simeon Steward, A.
Primrose, The.
Ring Presented to Julia, A.
Ternarie of Littles, upon a Pipkin of Jellie [or Jelly] Sent to a Lady, A.
To His Saviour, a Child; a Present, by a Child.
Holthaus, G. Unexpected Manna.
Huddle. My Daddy, Whenever He Went Some Place.
Irvine, W. To be Young, Gifted, and Black.
Keats. To a Friend Who Sent Me Some Roses.
Knott. Christmas at the Orphanage.
Komunyakaa. Gift Horse.
Lamantia. Time Traveler's Potlatch.
Landon. Gifts Misused.
Lee, D. Jan's Birthday.
Loesser. Take Back Your Mink.
MacIntyre, S. Christmas Present for My Mother.
Milton. On His Blindness.
Momaday. Gift, The.
Moore, L. Gifts.
Moorer. Accompanying a Gift.
Orfalea, G. Gift You Must Lose, A.
Ormond. Gift, The.
Previn, A. Thanks a Lot, but No Thanks.
Prince, F. Token, The.
Raine, K. Heirloom.
Reader. When Paul Bunyan Was Ill.
Roethke. Her Reticence.
Sandall. Song: "Love that is hoarded, moulds at last."
Shange. You are Sucha Fool.
Shelley, P. To————: "One word is too often profaned."
"Shu Ting." Gifts.
Sorrentino. Oranges Returned, The.
Springer, T. Giving and Forgiving.
Teasdale. Gift, The.
Tomlinson, C. Picture of J. T. in a Prospect of Stone, The.
Troup, B. Daddy.
Unknown. Beyond the Profit of Today.
For Baby.
Giving.
I Went Downtown.
My Neighbor's Reply.
Twelve Days of Christmas, The.
Understanding.
Wilcox, E. Morning Prayer, A.
Williams, W. Gift, The.
Wright, J. Request to a Year.
Wunderlich, M. Given in Person Only.
Wylie. Parting Gift.
Yeats. Never Give All the Heart.

Ginkgo Trees
Bell, M. These Green-Going-to-Yellow.
Nemerov. Ginkgoes in Fall.

Ginsberg, Allen
Derricotte. Allen Ginsberg.
Ferlinghetti, L. He.
Ginsberg, A. After Lalon.

My Alba.
This Form of Life Needs Sex.
Why Is God Love, Jack?
Sia, B. Howl.

Giraffes
Beveridge. Domesticity of Giraffes, The.
Hood, T. On the Death of the Giraffe.
Plumly. Giraffe.
Villa. I Was Speaking of Oranges to a Lady.

Girdles
Waller, E. On a Girdle.

Girl Scouts
Bryan, S. Lunch with Girl Scouts.
Perillo. Dangerous Life.

Girls
Agosin. Obedient Girl, The.
Ashbery. Thoughts of a Young Girl.
Bell, M. Mystery of Emily Dickinson, The.
Bontemps. Dark Girl.
Bourne, W. Heart's Fine Gold, The.
Brooks, A. Narcissa.
Brown, L. Don't Bring Lulu.
Brownstein. Jet Set Melodrama.
Campbell, D. Small-town Gladys.
Cassells. Soul Make a Path Through Shouting.
Ciardi. All about Boys and Girls.
Clark, P. My Life with Horses.
Clifton, L. Night Vision.
Cocteau. Fairy Scene.
Cofer, J. Changeling, The.
Coffman. Cheerleaders.
Girl/Spit.
Likely.
Coleman, C. Real Live Girl.
Davis, J. You Turn Around.
Dougherty. Puerto Rican Girls of French Hill, The.
Eliot, T. La Figlia Che Piange.
Ellis, K. N. Girl.
Ewart. Lifelines.
"Field." Girl, A.
Furber, D. Me and My Girl.
Greenaway. Three Little Girls.
Harris, D. What we have lost.
Hart, L. Little Girl Blue.
Heaney, S. New Song, A.
Hemans. Evening Prayer, at a Girls' School.
Henderson, R. Don't Bring Lulu.
Herd. Bathing Girls, The.
Hogg, J. When Maggy Gangs Away.
Hull, A. Another Rhythm.
Jacobs, J. Two Varieties of the Bitter Orange.
Johnson, J. Girl of Fifteen.
Joseph, A. On Sidewalks, on Streetcorners, as Girls.
Landon. Dancing Girl, The.
Leigh, C. Real Live Girl.
Li Po. Girl of Yueh, The.
Longfellow, H. There Was a Little Girl.
Maiden. New.
Marlatt, D. Working Girl.
Martínez, V. Coastal.
McGinley. Portrait of a Girl with Comic Book.
McGough, R. My Cat and I.
McLain, P. Fishing.
Mercer, J. Tangerine.
Miles, J. Travelers.
Moore, H. Girl in a Fur-Trimmed Dress.
Morales, A. Tita's Poem.
Mori. Barbie Says Math is Hard.
Nash, O. Adventures of Isabel.
Olds, S. One Girl at the Boys Party, The.
Padgett, R. Strawberries in Mexico.
Peacock, M. Good Girl.
Penn, M. Calling Up the Spirit of the Lost Child.
"Pindar." Ode to a Country Hoyden.
Pogson, P. Going Home.
Pound, E. Girl, A.
Rafferty, J. Arsonist Tells His Story to the Attorney, The.
Randall, D. Blackberry Sweet.
Rose, D. Don't Bring Lulu.
Roughton. Soluble Noughts and Crosses; or, California, Here I Come.
Sanchez, S. Song No. 2: "I say. all you young girls waiting to live."
Schertzinger, V. Tangerine.
Shurin. Blue Shade.
Simic. Ballad: "What's that approaching like dust like poverty."
Smith, P. What It's Like to Be a Black Girl (For Those of You Who Aren't).
Sondheim. All I Need Is the Girl.
Soto. Dizzy Girls in the Sixties.
Spires. Bodies, The.
Stevens, W. Plot Against the Giant, The.
Styne, J. All I Need Is the Girl.
Tuckerman, F. Coralie.
Unknown. She Will Gather Roses.
Van Jordan, A. Dance Lesson, A.
Volkman. Daffodils.
Walwicz. Little Red Riding Hood.
Whitehead, C. Girls Sitting Together Like Dolls.
Williams, W. Lonely Street, The.
Wordsworth, W. Solitary Reaper, The.
Yeats. Politics.
Zandvakili, K. Love Letter.
See also **Adolescence; Childhood and Children; Youth**

Giving
Berman, C. Mother Lakshmi's Poem.
Kerouac. And What Do I Owe You, God.
See also **Gifts and Giving**

Glaciers
Haines, J. Into the Glacier.
McClure, M. Moiré.
Ransom, W. Message from Ohanapecosh Glacier.

Glasgow, Scotland
Leonard, T. Evidence, The.
Morgan, E. King Billy.

Glass and Glassblowers
Brownstein. Glass Enclosure, The.
Davies, H. Poem: "It doesn't look like a finger it looks like a feather of broken glass."
Draycott. Prince Rupert's Drop, The.
France, L. Blues for Bird.
Garrett, E. Unguentarium.
Merrill, J. Octopus, The.
Moore, M. Egyptian Pulled Glass Bottle in the Shape of a Fish, An.
Morgan, E. Glass, The.
Morton, J. Epitaph: "Glassblower lies here at rest, A."
Scully, J. Glass Blower, The.
Shapiro, D. Book of Glass, A.
Ward, D. Glass House.
Winters, Y. Solitude of Glass, The.

Globes
Donne. Valediction: of Weeping, A.
Reaney. School Globe, The.
Turner, C. Letty's Globe.

Glory
Byron, G. Last Words on Greece.
De Tabley. Sonnet: "Record is nothing, and the hero great."
"Field." Beloved, My Glory in Thee is Not Ceased.
Fellowship.
Garrick. Heart of Oak.
Garrigue. Mouse, The.
Hawthorne, N. I Left My Low amd Humble Home.
Hemans. Bring Flowers.
Lindley, D. Cryptogram, The.
Owen, W. To My Friend (With an Identity Disc).
Rossetti, C. Heaviness May Endure for a Night, But Joy Cometh in the Morning.
St. Michael and All Angels.
Tennant, E. A Bas la Gloire!

Glossolalia
Hamill, S. Gift of Tongues, The.

Gloucester, Massachusetts
Dorn, E. From Gloucester Out.
Olson, C. Librarian, The.

Gloves
Cleage. Confession.
Cornford, F. To a Fat Lady Seen from the Train.

Lovelace, R.   Elinda's [or Ellinda's] Glove.
Nye, N.   Yellow Glove.
Tucker, M.   That Glove.
See also **Mittens**
Glowworms
Marvell.   Mower to the Glowworms [or Glow-Worms *or* Glo-Worms], The.
McCord, D.   Glowworm.
Stanley, T.   Glowworm, The.
See also **Fireflies**
Gluttony and Gluttons
Belloc.   Vulture, The.
Cook, E.   Mouse and the Cake, The.
Jonson, B.   On Gut.
Kizer, C.   Food of Love.
Komunyakaa.   Seven Deadly Sins.
Wright, K.   Greedyguts.
Gnats
Beaumont, J.   Gnat, The.
Eberhart, R.   Gnat on My Paper.
Graves, R.   One Hard Look.
Gnomes
Druce.   Apropos of Garden Statuary: A Disquisition upon a Minor Genre.
Goats
Herford.   Smile of the Goat, The.
Magowan.   Zeimbekiko.
Shange.   Ancestral Messengers/Composition 13.
Soto.   Ode to Señor Leal's Goat.
Stephens, J.   Goat Paths, The.
Winters, Y.   Vacant Lot.
Goblins
Fyleman.   Goblin, The.
Herrick.   Ceremony upon Candlemas Eve.
Prelutsky.   Mother Goblin's Lullaby.
Riley, J.   Little Orphant Annie.
Nine Little Goblins, The.
See also **Elves; Fairies; Ghosts**
God
"Ada."   Lines.
Addonizio.   Broken Sonnets.
Agee.   Permit Me Voyage.
Ai.   Good Shepherd: Atlanta, 1981, The.
Al-Mala'ika.   Lilies for the Prophet.
Alexander, C.   All Things Bright and Beautiful.
Alford, H.   Harvest Home.
Allen, P.   Taku Skanskan.
Ammons, A. R.   Hymn: "I know if I find you I will have to leave the earth."
Anderson, M.   Lost in the Stars.
Andrews, N.   Notes for a Sermon on the Mount.
Apollinaire.   Zone.
Appleman, P.   Waiting for the Fire.
Armantrout.   Plan, The.
Arvey, V.   All That I Am.
Askew, A.   Ballad Which Anne Askew Made and Sang When She Was in Newgate, The.
Auden.   Petition.
Babcock, M.   Be Strong.
This Is My Father's World.
Ballou, S.   Almighty God in Being Was.
Bangs, J.   Blind.
Barbauld.   To the Poor.
Baudelaire.   Fuses I and II.
Berrigan, D.   But God is Silent / Psalm 114.
Berryman.   Certainty Before Lunch.
Eleven Addresses to the Lord.
Lauds.
Betjeman.   In Westminster Abbey.
Bible, *O.T.*   Psalm 1.
Psalm 2.
Psalm 8.
Psalm 14.
Psalm 19.
Psalm 23.
Psalm 29.
Psalm 42.
Psalm 46.
Psalm 50.
Psalm 55.
Psalm 77.
Psalm 90.
Psalm 91.
Psalm 95.
Psalm 103.

Psalm 104.
Psalm 118.
Psalm 121.
Psalm 130.
Psalm 133.
Psalm 136.
Psalm 137.
Blake, W.   Book of Urizen [or First Book of Urizen], The.
There Is No Natural Religion.
Blaser.   Even on Sunday.
Bly, R.   Waking from Sleep.
Bonar.   Hymn: "O Love of God, how strong and true."
Bontemps.   Miracles.
Nocturne at Bethesda.
Booth, P.   Original Sequence.
Bradstreet, A.   Here Follows Some Verses upon the Burning of Our House [July 10th, 1666. Copied Out of a Loose Paper].
Braithwaite.   Rye Bread.
Branch, A.   Monk in the Kitchen, The.
Brontë, C.   Orphan Child, The.
Brontë, E.   No Coward Soul is Mine.
Brooks, G.   Maxie Allen.
Brown, S.   Sister Lou.
Brown, T.   Between Our Folding Lips.
Browning, E.   Child's Thought of God, A.
Only a Curl.
Sleep, The.
Browning, R.   Epilogue: "On the first of the Feast of Feasts."
Johannes Agricola in Meditation.
Porphyria's Lover.
Prospice.
Bruner.   God's Ways Are Strange.
Bryant, W.   Song of the Stars.
To a Waterfowl.
Burns, R.   *First Six Verses* of the Ninetieth Psalm, The.
Holy Willie's Prayer.
Byron, G.   Prayer of Nature, The.
Campbell, R.   St John of the Cross: Song of the Soul That Is Glad to Know God by Faith.
St John of the Cross: Songs of the Soul in Rapture.
Campion, T.   Heart's Music.
O Come Quickly!
Seek the Lord.
To Music Bent Is My Retired Mind.
Caston, A.   Gathering at the River.
Causley.   Bible Story.
Cawein.   Three Elements, The.
Celan.   Tenebrae.
Ceravolo.   Data.
Fill and Illumined.
Chesterton, G.   Holy of Holies, The.
Chubb, T.   Merlin.
Clampitt.   Sun Underfoot Among the Sundews, The.
Clare, J.   First Love.
God Looks on Nature With a Glorious Eye.
Hymn to the Creator.
Clifton, L.   Prayer.
Clough.   With Whom Is No Variableness, Neither Shadow of Turning.
Cole, H.   40 Days and 40 Nights.
Coleridge, S.   To Nature.
Collins, A.   Song: "My straying thoughts, reduced stay."
Collymore.   Ballad of an Old Woman.
Coogler.   God Correctly Understood.
Cook, E.   Song for the Workers, A.
Coolbrith.   Longing.
Copus, J.   Making of Eve, The.
Masaccio's *Expulsion from Paradise*.
Cornish.   Pleasure It Is.
Cowper, W.   Contentment.
Ephraim Repenting.
Exhortation to Prayer.
Future Peace and Glory of the Church, The.
House of Prayer, The.
Hymn: "Jesus, where'er thy people meet."
Jehovah Our Righteousness.
Joy and Peace in Believing.
Light Shining out of Darkness.

Lines Written During a Period of Insanity.
Lord Will Happiness Divine, The.
Love Constraining to Obedience.
Lovest Thou Me?
My Soul Thirsteth for God.
Old-Testament Gospel.
Praise for the Fountain Opened.
Retirement.
Sardis.
Self-Acquaintance.
Sower, The.
Walking with God.
Wisdom.
Cranch.   Correspondences.
Crane, H.   Broken Tower, The.
Crashaw.   Song: "Lord, when the sense of Thy sweet grace."
Creeley.   Awakening, The.
Cullen, C.   For a Mouthy Woman.
Shroud of Color, The.
Yet Do I Marvel.
Cummings, E.   I Thank You God.
Cust.   Non Nobis.
Davie.   Ordinary God.
Their Rectitude Their Beauty.
Davies, J.   Acclamation, An.
Davies, S.   One Thing Needful Generally Neglected, The.
Day, J.   Man's Natural Infirmity.
de Gillies, G.   De Puerorum osculis.
De la Mare.   Last Chapter, The.
De Vere, S.   Reality.
Dickinson, E.   God is indeed a jealous God.
He fumbles at Your Spirit.
Dodson, O.   Black Mother Praying.
Donne.   Good Friday [or Goodfriday], 1613. Riding Westward.
Hymn[e] to Christ, at the Author's Last Going into Germany, A.
Hymn[e] to God My God, In My Sickness[e], A.
Doolittle, H.   Helen.
Dorsey, T.   Take My Hand, Precious Lord.
Drayton.   Song of the Faithful, A.
Drummond, W.   Book, The.
Dunbar, P.   Compensation.
Hymn: "When storms arise."
Hymn, A: "Lead gently, Lord, and slow."
Night.
Not They Who Soar!
Resignation.
Spiritual, A.
Duncan, R.   This Place Rumord to Have Been Sodom.
Torso / Passages 18, The.
Dunn, D.   Gardeners.
Dunn, S.   Dancing with God.
Eady.   My Mother is a God Fearing Woman.
Eberhart, R.   Fury of Aerial Bombardment, The.
On a Squirrel Crossing the Road in Autumn, in New England.
Echeruo.   Man and God Distinguished.
Elizabeth, Queen of Bohemia.   Verses by the Princess Elizabeth, Given to Lord Harington, of Exton, Her Preceptor.
Elliott, E.   Plaint.
Emanuel, L.   Like God.
Emerson, R.   Dear Brother, Would You Know the Life.
History.
Threnody: "South-wind brings, The."
Essbaum, J.   In the Beginning.
Post-Communion Striptease.
When the Kingdom Comes.
Everson, W.   Canticle to the Waterbirds, A.
South Coast, The.
Ewer.   Chosen People, The.
Faber, F.   Eternity of God, The.
Fairfax of Cameron.   On the Fatal Day January 30, 1648.
Fallon, P.   Holy Well.
Fenton, J.   God, A Poem.
Ferguson, G.   Slugs.
"Field."   Beloved, Now I Love God First.
Fields, J.   Jolly Fat Widows, The.
Fishman, L.   Diagnosis: My Mother's Breast.

Fitzgerald, E. 73.
Flynn, N. God Forgotten.
Foster, A. God and the Holy Stones.
Francis of Assisi. Prayer of St. Francis of Assisi for Peace.
Frost, R. Bereft.
Sitting by a Bush in Broad Daylight.
Fuller, J. Whole New Scene, A.
Fuller, M. Sistrum.
Fullerton. Poetry.
Gascoigne. Gascoigne's Good-Morrow.
Gascoigne's Woodmanship.
Gascoyne. Rex Mundi.
Gaspar. Tree, The.
Gershon. Experiments with God.
Gilbert, J. White Heart of God, The.
Gilbert-Lecomte. Preface or The Drama of Absence in an Eternal Heart.
Gillilan, S. "Are You There?"
Gilmore, J. He Leadeth Me.
Ginsberg, A. Why Is God Love, Jack?
Gioia. Prayer.
Giovanni. Poem for Flora.
Glück, L. Gift, The.
Lamentations.
Grahn. They Say She Is Veiled.
Greenberg, S. God.
Greenwell, D. Christina.
Gregg. Fishing in the Keep of Silence.
Grimke, C. Parting Hymn, A.
Grosholz. Eden.
Gunn, T. Pope's Carnations Knew Him.
Gurney, I. To God.
Hölderlin. In the Days of Socrates.
Hall, D. Small Fig Tree, A.
Hall, J. Anthem for the Cathedral of Exeter.
Praise of Godly Love Out of 1 John. 4, The.
Proverb, XXX.
Hardy, J. Computer Aided Design: Creation.
Hardy, T. Agnosto Theo [To an Unknown God].
Bedridden Peasant, The.
God-Forgotten.
New Year's Eve.
Harper, F. Ethiopia.
Heard, J. Hope Thou in God.
I Will Look Up.
Heber. Holy, Holy, Holy.
Hedge. Mighty Fortress Is Our God, A.
Herbert, G. Affliction (1).
Altar, The.
Artillery [or Artillerie].
Bitter-Sweet.
Church-Floor[e], The.
Church-Lock and Key.
Collar, The.
Decay.
Denial [l].
Discipline.
Easter Wings.
Elixir [or Elixer], The.
Employment (1).
Evensong [or Even-Song].
Family [or Familie], The.
Forerunners, The.
Frailty.
Grace.
Hope.
Invitation, The.
Jordan (1).
Jordan (2).
Judgement.
L'Envoy.
Man.
Obedience.
Paradise.
Pearl, The. Matth. 13:45.
Posy [or Posie], The.
Praise (2).
Prayer (1): "Prayer the Church's banquet, Angels' age."
Providence.
Pulley, The.
Redemption.
Search, The.
Sepulchre.
Sion.

Sonnet: "Sure Lord, there is enough in thee to dry."
Thanksgiving, The.
True Hymn, A.
Unkindness.
Vanity [or Vanitie] (1).
Whitsunday.
Windows, The.
World, The.
Herrick. Calling, and Correcting.
Evensong.
God's Mercy.
Gods Anger without Affection.
Gods Keyes.
Gods Presence.
Neutrality Loathsome.
No Coming to God without Christ.
Right Hand, The.
To Find[e] God.
To God.
To His Ever-Loving God.
To His Saviour.
To Marygolds.
Upon Time.
What God Is.
Hirsch, E. American Apocalypse.
Hodgson, R. Mystery, The.
Holan. Resurrection.
Holmes, O. Our Limitations.
Tartarus.
Hope, A. House of God, The.
Hopkins, G. As Kingfishers Catch Fire.
Carrion Comfort.
God's Grandeur.
In the Valley of the Elwy.
Pied Beauty.
Spring and Fall.
Thou Art Indeed Just, Lord.
Housman, A. Mark 16:19–20; So then the Lord Jesus, after.
Howe, S. Silence Wager Stories.
Hudgins. Southern Crescent Was On Time, The.
Hughes, L. High to Low.
Personal.
Hume, A. Of Gods Omnipotencie.
Hunt, L. Abou Ben Adhem.
To Percy Shelley.
To the Same.
Ignatow, D. He Puts Me to Rest.
Ingelow. Divided.
Jackson, M. L. Blunts.
Jacob, M. 1914.
Jeffers, R. Birds and Fishes.
Birth-Dues.
Noon.
Shine, Perishing Republic.
Jemie. Toward a Poetics.
Jerrold, S. John in Prison.
Johnson, F. My God in Heaven Said to Me.
Singing Hallelujia.
Song of the Whirlwind.
Johnson, J. Creation, The.
Go Down Death.
Lift Every [or Ev'ry] Voice and Sing.
Johnson, S. Scholar's Life, The.
Vanity of Human Wishes, The; The Tenth Satire of Juvenal Imitated.
Jones, S. Hymn to Na'ra'yena, A.
Jonson, B. Hymn[e] to God the Father, A.
To Heaven.
Kavanagh, P. Canal Bank Walk.
Kayo. War.
Kelly, R. Rainmakers, The.
Kenyon, J. Bat, The.
Briefly It Enters, and Briefly Speaks.
Kerouac. And What Do I Owe You, God.
Flies.
Kipling, R. Evarra and His Gods.
Rabbi's Song, The.
Recessional.
Klein, A. For the Sisters of the Hôtel Dieu.
Kowit. Cosmetics Do No Good.
Kumin, M. Getting the Message.
Lanier, S. To Beethoven.
Lawrence, D. Body of God, The.
Eloi, Eloi, Lama Sabachthani?

Hands of God, The.
Living Quetzalcoatl, The.
Lord's Prayer.
Man of Tyre, The.
Pax.
When Wilt Thou Teach the People?
Levertov. Task, The.
Levin, P. Night Coach.
Levine, P. On a Drawing by Flavio.
To My God in His Sickness.
Levy, A. Ballad of Religion and Marriage, A.
Lewis, R. If You Had a Friend.
Lima, J. Enormous Hand, The.
Linden, M. God's Electric Power.
Llwyd, M. Come Wisdome Sweet.
Locke, A. So Foul Is Sin and Loathsome in Thy Sight.
Longfellow, H. Galaxy, The.
Lowell, R. Death and the Bridge.
Mr. Edwards and the Spider.
Watchmaker God.
Luther. Mighty Fortress Is Our God, A.
Lydgate. Thank God for All.
MacDiarmid, H. Prayer for a Second Flood.
With the Herring Fishers.
Macdonald, G. At Aberdeen.
Magee, J. High Flight.
Mahon. Ecclesiastes.
Mandela. Saviour.
Mant, R. House of God, The.
Social Worship.
Marckant. Lamentation, The.
Martin, C. His Eye Is On the Sparrow.
Marvell. Bermudas.
Mathias, R. God Is.
Maura. Creation of Light, The.
Mayakovsky [or Maiakovskii]. Listen.
McGinley. Day after Sunday, The.
Meinke. Poet, Trying to Surprise God, The.
Melville, H. Conflict of Convictions, The.
In the Desert.
Merton. Reader, The.
Merwin, W. S. Leviathan.
Meynell, A. To a Daisy.
Mezey. Silence, The.
Miller, T. Evening.
Milton. On His Blindness.
To Cyriack Skinner.
Mitchell, A. Quite Apart from the Holy Ghost.
"Monty Python." All Things Dull and Ugly.
Moore, M. Book of How, The.
Moore, T. Sound the Loud Timbrel.
More, S. Prayer, A.
Morgan, A. God the Artist.
Morrissey, S. After the Hurricane.
Moss, S. God Poem.
Muir, E. Incarnate One, The.
Murray, J. Lullaby.
Murray, P. Canticle of the Void, The.
Nelson, M. Cover Photograph.
Nemerov. Primer of the Daily Round, A.
Newman, J. Sensitiveness.
Nichol. Ferry Me Across.
Nims, J. Knowledge of God.
Norris, K. Naming the Living God.
Olson, T. Hypothesis.
Ormond. Cathedral Builders.
To a Nun.
Ostriker. Story of Abraham, The.
Padgett, R. Lucky Strikes.
Parker, A. Above the Timberline.
Pastan. Imperfect Paradise, The.
Patchen. Deer and the Snake, The.
Origin of Baseball, The.
Temple, A.
Peacock, M. Good Girl.
Pereira. Paradox, The.
Pfeiffer, E. Cruse of Tears, The. A Russian Legend.
Phillips, C. Sunday.
Piatt, S. Answering A Child.
If I Had Made the World.
No Help.
Pique at Parting, A.
Sad Spring-Song.
Pierpont, J. O Thou, to Whom in Ancient Time.

Plutzik. And in the 51st Year of That Century, While My Brother Cried in the Trench, While My Enemy Glared from the Cave.

Pope, A. Messiah: A Sacred Eclogue in Imitation of Virgil's Pollio.

Rise, Crowned with Light Imperial Salem Rise.

Universal Prayer [Deo Opt. Max.], The.

Pound, E. Ballad for Gloom.

Night Litany.

Powers, J. Garments of God, The.

Prabhu. For the Lord of Caves.

Pratt, E. Truant, The.

Prince, F. Question, The.

Probyn. More Than They That Watch for the Morning.

Procter, A. Divine Presence, The.

Three Evenings in a Life.

Words.

Purdy, A. Wilderness Gothic.

Quarles. On God's Law.

On the Life of Man.

Rab. Kingdom of God, The.

Raine, K. Written in Exile.

Ralegh, S. Authours Epitaph, Made by Himself, The.

Ray, H. God's Ways, Not Our Ways.

Reese, L. Christmas Folk-Song, A.

Reznikoff. Luzzato.

Richards, G. Almighty Spake, and Gabriel Sped, Th'

Robbins, H. And Have the Bright Immensities.

Robinson, A. Idea, The.

Valley, The.

Rodgers, C. It Is Deep.

Testimony.

Rodgers, W. Lent.

Scapegoat.

Roethke. Decision, The.

Marrow, The.

Rogers, P. Before the Beginning: Maybe God and a Silk Flower Concubine Perhaps.

Rossetti, C. After Communion.

Before the Beginning.

Christmas Carol, A: "In the bleak mid-winter."

Long Barren.

Lowest Place, The.

St. Michael and All Angels.

Twice.

Two Pursuits.

Rossetti, D. Blessed Damozel, The.

On the Painter Val Prinsep.

Rothenberg, J. Realtheater Piece Two.

Rowe, E. Expostulation, The.

Rukeyser, M. Akiba.

Nuns in the Wind.

Rumi. Say Yes Quickly.

Södergran. Question.

Sargent, E. Planet Jupiter, The.

Schiff, H. Discovery.

Schulzová, E. Evening in Terezin, An.

Scott, W. Mrs. Severin.

Sexton. Author of the Jesus Papers Speaks, The.

Small Wire.

Welcome Morning.

Shapiro, K. 151st Psalm, The.

Simic. Night Picnic.

Simmons, J. Eden.

Singer, E. Cant. 5.6 & c.

Smart, C. Hymn to the Supreme Being.

My Cat Jeoffry.

Psalm 58.

Smith, G. Penitential Cries of Jupiter Hammond, The.

Smith, S. America.

Away, Melancholy.

Distractions and the Human Crowd.

God the Eater.

No Categories!

Snider. Communion.

Southerland. Pale Ant.

Southey, R. Old Man's Comforts and How He Gained Them, The.

Ship, The.

Southwell. At Home in Heaven.

Sowle, J. Short Testimony for Anne

Whitehead, A.

Spellman. Twist, The.

Stafford, W. With My Crowbar Key.

Stephens, J. What Thomas an Buile Said in a Pub.

Stevenson, R. Epitaph: "Angler rose, he took his rod, The."

House Beautiful, The.

Stickney, T. He Said: "If in His Image I Was Made."

Stowe. Abide in Me, O Lord, and I in Thee.

Only a Year.

Still, Still, with Thee.

Strange. Offering.

Strong, N. Almighty Sovereign of the Skies!

Stryker. Almighty Lord, with One Accord.

Subido, T. Paganly.

Sullivan, N. His Necessary Darkness.

Swinburne. Leper, The.

Sylvester, J. Father, The.

Symonds. Lux Est Umbra Dei[1].

Tate, G. Last Instructions.

Taylor, E. Christ's Reply.

Frowardness of the Elect in the Work of Conversion, The.

Joy of Church Fellowship Rightly Attended, The.

Preface, The: "Infinity, when all things it beheld."

Soul's Groan to Christ for Succo[u]r, The.

Upon a Spider Catching a Fly.

Taylor, J. Hymn for Advent.

My Mother.

Prayer, A: "O beauteous God! uncircumscribed treasure."

Tennyson, A. Flower in the Crannied Wall.

Higher Pantheism, The.

Thomas, J. In The Beginning.

Thomas, R. Ann Griffith.

Echoes.

Island, The.

Pisces.

Via Negativa.

Thompson, F. Heaven and Hell.

Hound of Heaven, The.

Thompson, P. In the Valley.

Thoreau. Inspiration.

Tindley, C. Stand by Me.

Toomer. Gods Are Here, The.

Toplady. Hymn: "Inspirer and hearer of prayer."

Traherne. Bible, The.

Salutation [or Salutations], The.

Wonder.

Tranter. Backyard.

Tucker, F. All Praise to Thee.

Tucker, M. Mysteries of Life.

Tuckerman, F. As Sometimes in a Grove.

Sonnets: "Starry flower, the flower-like stars that fade, The."

Sonnets: First Series.

Unknown. All Is Phantom.

All-Knowing God, 'Tis Thine to Know.

Been in the Storm So Long.

Beulah Railway, The.

Didn't My Lord Deliver Daniel?

Freedom in the Air.

God and Man Set as One.

God Be with You.

God of Might, God of Right.

God's A-Gonna Trouble the Water.

Good and Better.

Good Lord in That Heaven.

He Was the Word that Spake it.

He's Jus' de Same Today.

Hospital Duties.

I Believe.

I See the Moon.

I Sing of a Maiden.

I Vision God.

I'm a-Rollin'.

Little Black Train Is A-Comin'.

Loom of Time, The.

Madrigal: "If that a sinner's sighs be angels' food."

Make Me Loathe Earthly Likings.

My Hope Is in God.

Nobody Knows the Trouble I've Had.

Peace Be Still.

Petition to Father and Son and Holy Ghost, A.

Psalm 58.

Sing, My Soul.

Slave Marriage Ceremony Supplement.

Soon I Will Be Done.

Steal Away to Jesus.

Take My Hand, Precious Lord.

U'Tamsi. Scorner, The.

Valéry. Crusoe.

Van Doren. Near House, The.

Van Duyn. Gardener to His God, The.

Van Dyke. Four Things.

Vaughan, H. Anguish.

Book, The.

Cock-crowing.

Knot, The.

Love and Discipline.

Midnight.

Night, The.

Regeneration.

Retirement.

Vanity of Spirit.

Very. Created, The.

Cup, The.

Earth, The.

Eye and Ear, The.

First Atlantic Telegraph, The.

Forevermore.

Hand and Foot, The [or Hand and the Foot, The].

In Him We Live [and Move and Have Our Being].

Lost, The.

Mountain, The.

My Meat and Drink.

Night.

Prayer, The.

Presence, The.

Promise, The.

Rock, The.

Silent, The.

Slavery.

Spirit, The.

Winter Rain, The.

Word, The.

Yourself.

Vitale, M. I Read That It Was All a Chain.

Walworth. Holy God, We Praise Thy Name.

Waniek. Canticle for Abba Jacob, A.

Warren, R. Way to Love God, A.

Warton, T. Stanzas on the Psalms.

Washbourne. God's Two Dwellings.

Washburn, H. Almighty God, Thy Constant Care.

Watts, I. Day of Judg[e]ment, The; an Ode.

Man Frail, and God Eternal.

Psalm 58.

Weill, K. Lost in the Stars.

Wesley, C. Come on, my partners in distress.

None is like Jeshuron's God.

Westmorland. Man Leavens the Batch.

To Kiss God's Rod; Occasioned Upon a Child's Sickness.

Wheatley, P. On Being Brought from Africa to America.

Thoughts on the Works of Providence.

Whitfield. Self-Reliance.

Whitman, W. Chanting the Square Deific.

Whittier. All's Well.

Garden.

Over-Heart, The.

Overruled.

Palm-Tree, The.

River Path, The.

Wickham. To Men.

Wiesel. Never Shall I Forget.

Wilbur. Proof, The.

Tywater.

Williams, C. Loss.

Spit.

Williams, P. In the Dark.

Williams, R. God makes a path, provides a guide.

Williams, W. Guide Me, O Thou Great

Jehovah.
Wilson, E.   Disloyal Lines to an Alumnus.
Winters, Y.   Precision, The.
Wither.   Prayer of Hezekiah, The.
When We Cannot Sleep.
Wolfli.   Nostalgic Song for My Beloved.
Wordsworth, W.   It is a beauteous evening.
Wotton, S.   Hymn to My God in a night of my
late Sicknesse, A.
Wright, C.   Clear Night.
Disjecta Membra.
Wright, J.   Meta-A and the A of Absolutes.
Speak.
Wyatt, S.   Argument, The.
Yeats.   Crazy Jane on God.
Indian upon God, The [or An].
Paudeen.
Rose of the World, The.
Young, M.   Noah's Ark.

God's Protection
Buchanan, R.   Wanderers, The.
Colman, H.   On the Three Children in the Fiery
Furnace.
Emerson, R.   Worship.
Herbert, G.   Affliction (4).
Evensong [or Even-Song].
Invitation, The.
L'Envoy.
Providence.
Kipling, R.   Hymn before Action.
Kunitz, S.   Benediction.
MacNeice.   Prayer Before Birth.
Rous.   I to the Hills Will Lift Mine Eyes.
Unknown.   All Other Love Is Like the Moon.
Got a Home in That Rock.

Gods and Goddesses
Acholonu.   Dissidents, The.
Water Woman.
Apuleius, L.   I who am Nature, mother of all.
Ashur-Nasir-Pal.   Hymn to Ishtar.
Awoonor.   Easter Dawn.
Baring, A.   Song, The: "Beehive source."
Bedient, C.   When the Gods Put on Meter.
Benton, S.   Lilith.
Second Coming, The.
Berezan, J.   Hail Mother full of grace power is
with thee.
Berman, C.   Mother Lakshmi's Poem.
Poem for the Shechina.
Bingen, Hildegard von.   Earth Is at the Same
Time Mother, The.
Bukowski.   Not Much Singing.
Césaire, A.   In Order to Speak.
Canan.   Goddesses, The.
Inanna's Chant.
Mother Dawning.
Oh Kali.
Carew, T.   To the King, at His Entrance into
Saxham: By Master John Crofts.
Chimombo.   Obituary.
Clifton, L.   Calming Kali.
Kali.
Coleridge, S.   Visit of the Gods, The.
Corn.   To Hermes.
Cott, J.   Isis (Lady of Petals).
Couzyn.   Spell for Birth.
Craveirinha.   Three Dimensions.
Dharker.   Postcards from God (1).
Di Prima.   Loba as Eve.
DiPrima, C.   Her Eyes a Thousand Times Over.
Disch.   Ballade of the New God.
Dobson, R.   Three Fates, The.
Donovan, K.   Entering the Mare.
Doolittle, H.   Evadne.
Dove, R.   Demeter, Waiting.
Duhig, I.   Fundamentals.
Duncan, R.   Chords Passages 14.
Structure of Rime XVIII.
Eclipse.   Cicada.
Elledge.   Household Gods.
Enheduanna.   From the Hymn to Inanna.
Fabian, C.   Prayer of Dedication.
Qadesha (Sacred Whore).
Fanthorpe.   Nativities.
Fuhrman, J.   Atlantis.
Gidlow.   Creed for Free Women, A.

Glover, S.   Power of the Soul.
Goode, S.   Lady of Pazardzik.
Gottlieb, A.   Meditation on the Feminine Nature
of Shekinah, A.
Gottlieb, L.   Greeting Shekinah.
Grahn.   Grand Grand Mother is Returning.
Graves, R.   In Her Praise.
Weather of Olympus, The.
White Goddess, The.
Hannon.   Real Estate.
Harvey, A.   Prayer to the Divine Mother, A.
Hildebrandt, Z.   In Hecate's Garden.
Kali.
Hinckley, P.   New Our Father, The.
Hirshfield, J.   Osiris.
Painting.
Hixon, L.   My blissful Mother exists fully
through every creature!
Who can keep a blazing fire tied in a cotton
cloth?
Hogan, L.   Chambered Nautilus.
Return: Buffalo.
Hope, A.   Fafnir.
Ironbiter, S.   Song to the Mother of the World.
Jones, S.   Hymn to Indra, A.
Karade, B.   Yemoja.
Kipling, R.   Gods of the Copybook Headings,
The.
Sacrifice of Er-Heb, The.
Kizer, C.   Muse of Water, A.
Klee.   Wolf Speaks, The.
Klugman, E.   She Who Listens.
Klugman, S.   God's Body.
Kolatkar.   Low Temple, A.
Korican, L.   City Goddess.
Koroneu.   Funeral Eva.
Laing, K.   Godhorse.
Lawrence, D.   Man of Tyre, The.
Maximus.
Lee, D.   Gods, The.
Levertov.   Death in Mexico.
To the Reader.
Logghe.   Madonna of the Peaches.
Lowell, A.   Captured Goddess, The.
Marvell.   Mower Against Gardens, The.
McAdams, J.   Leaving the Old Gods.
McFerrin, B.   23rd Psalm, The.
Merrill, J.   After Greece.
Milton.   Hymn on the Morning of Christ's
Nativity.
On the Morning of Christ's Nativity.
Monaghan.   Venus of Laussel.
Murray, L.   Gods, The.
Muske, C.   Epith.
Mutén, B.   Hesperides, The.
Queen Hera.
Queen Medusa.
Urania.
Namjoshi, S.   Caliban's Journal.
Norris, K.   Prayer to Eve, A.
O'Curry, E.   Litany to Our Lady.
Okara.   Spirit of the Wind.
Okigbo.   Water Maid.
Olson, C.   Distances, The.
In Cold Hell, in Thicket.
Ono.   Mother of the Universe.
Parnell, P.   Apotheosis of Medusa.
Medusa and Perseus III: Lilith.
Sheila the Hat.
Sile Na gCioch.
Peacocke.   Goddess, The.
Rakosi.   Origins.
Ralegh, S.   Homage to Diana.
Reed, I.   I Am a Cowboy in the Boat of Ra.
Reis, P.   Ancient Ones, The.
Rupp.   Sophia.
Shange.   We Need a God Who Bleeds Now.
Shepherd, R.   Gods at Three A.M., The.
Slessor.   Fixed Ideas.
Smith, S.   River God, The.
Snyder, G.   Gaia.
Stainer.   Xochiquetzal.
Stevens, W.   Less and Less Human, O Savage
Spirit.
Swinburne.   Garden of Proserpine, The.
Taggard.   Demeter.

Thoreau.   All Things Are Current Found.
Unknown.   Holy Goddess Tellus.
Homage to Tara Our Mother.
Hymn to Nut.
Litany to Our Lady.
May Isis heal me.
Villanueva, A.   From the Healing Dark.
Wade-Gayles.   Loving Again.
Welish.   Respected, Feared, and Somehow
Loved.
Wilde, O.   Santa Decca.
Winter, M.   In the Beginning.
Wright, D.   To the Gods the Shades Flavinus of
the Cavalry Regiment.
Young, I.   Mermaid Knows, A.
Visit to the Palace of Venus.

Goethe, Johann Wolfgang von
Arnold, M.   Memorial Verses.
Emerson, R.   Solution.
Thackeray.   Sorrows of Werther, The.

Gogol, Nikolai Vasilyevich
Burkard.   Personal Histories, The.

Gold
Bricusse, L.   Goldfinger.
Crabbe.   Marriage Ring, The.
Doolittle, H.   Song: "You are as gold."
Frost, R.   Nothing Gold Can Stay.
Gray, T.   Ode on the Death of a Favourite [or
Favorite] Cat, Drowned in a Tub [or Bowl] of
Gold Fishes.
Greenwell, D.   Broken Chain, The.
Hopkins, G.   My Own Heart Let Me More Have
Pity On.
Lee-Hamilton.   Sunken Gold.
Newley, A.   Goldfinger.
Oppen.   Gold on Oak Leaves.
Wong, J.   Good Luck Gold.

Gold Mining and Gold Miners
Brodrick.   Joe's Luck.
Service.   Cremation of Sam McGee, The.
Skeeter.   California, 1852.
Winters, Y.   John Sutter.
Yost, C.   California Poem.

Golden Age
Whittier.   My Triumph.

Golden Rule, The
Edwards, M.   Do As You Would Be Done By.
Gannon, K.   Reciprocity.

Goldenrod
Oliver, M.   Goldenrod.

Goldfinches
Ammons, A. R.   Mechanism.
Hardy, T.   Caged Goldfinch, The.
Thomas, E.   Hollow Wood, The.

Goldfish
Duhig, I.   Fred.
Hyde, L.   Goldfish in the Charles River.
Turner, C.   On a Vase of Gold-Fish.
Worth, V.   Goldfish in the Garden Pond.

Golem
Colombo.   How They Made the Golem.

Golf
Cleghorn.   Golf Links, The.
Harrison, J.   Hitting Golfballs off the Bluff.
Lowell, R.   Ford Madox Ford.

Goliath
Dressel.   Let's Hear It for Goliath.
Graves, R.   Goliath and David.
Thompson, P.   David and Goliath.
Untermeyer, L.   Goliath and David.

Good
Blake, W.   Marriage of Heaven and Hell, The.
Memorable Fancy, A.
Pride of the Peacock, The.
Song of Liberty, A.
Hardy, T.   Unkept Good Fridays.
Heaney, S.   Disappearing Island, The.
O'Reilly, J.   What Is Good?
Unknown.   Comparatives.
Wright, J.   Meta-A and the A of Absolutes.
Trying to Pray.

Good Friday
Brion, R.   Good Friday.
Clarke, A.   Tenebrae.

Gore-Booth, Eva

D'Aguiar. Mama Dot Warns Against an Easter Rising.
Donne. Good Friday [or Goodfriday], 1613. Riding Westward.
Hardy, T. Unkept Good Fridays.
Herbert, G. Good Friday.
Herrick. Good Friday: Rex Tragicus, or, Christ Going to His Cross[e].
Hill, G. Canticle for Good Friday.
Longley, M. Letter to Derek Mahon.
Rossetti, C. Good Friday.
Thomas, R. Pisces.

Gore-Booth, Eva

Yeats. In Memory of Eva Gore-Booth and Con Markievicz.

Gorillas

Wain. Au Jardin des Plantes.

Gospel Music

Evans, M. And the Old Women Gathered.
Grey, C. Hallelujah!
Waters, M. Burden Lifters, The.
Youmans, V. Hallelujah!

Gossip and Gossips

Auden. Love Feast, The.
Berlin. Say It Isn't So.
Bruner. Monk and the Peasant, The.
Burke, C. Motor Oil Queen.
Fraser, G. Lean Street.
Hammerstein. People Will Say We're in Love.
Leapor. Headache, The.
Linden, M. Gossip.
Livingston, J. It's the Talk of the Town.
O'Hara, F. Personal Poem.
Patterson, G. Lament.
Rodgers, R. People Will Say We're in Love.
Sorby. Gossip.
Symes, M. It's the Talk of the Town.
Taylor, J. Recreation.
Turner, G. Journal of Society, The. Tattle.
Wordsworth, W. Personal Talk.
Wright, K. Underneath the Archers or What's All This about Walter's Willy?

See also **Rumor; Reputation**

Govan, Saint

Prys-Jones. St. Govan.

Government

Bly, R. Johnson's Cabinet Watched by Ants.
Cabico, R. Check One.
Chrystos. I Have Not Signed a Treaty with the United States Government.
Clayton, I. Kidnappers.
Doolan, F. Whiteman Is the Judge, The.
Emerson, R. Ode, Inscribed to W.H. Channing.
Ennis. Coyne's.
Espada. Cockroaches of Liberation.
Ezenwa-Ohaeto. I Wan Bi President.
Freneau. On Mr. Paine's Rights of Man.
Gilbert, K. Celebrators '88. Gularwundul's Wish.
Haines, J. Poem Like a Grenade, A.
Hernández Cruz. It's Miller Time.
Herrick. Ill Government. Power in the People, The. Shame, No Statist.
Hughes, L. Un-American Investigators.
Kipling, R. Death-Bed, A.
Marvell. Charles II. First Anniversary of the Government under His Highness the Lord Protector, 1655, The.
More, S. Quis Optimus Reipublicae Status.
Mphande. I Was Sent For.
Pound, E. Great Digest of Confucius, The.
Sall, A. Cloak of Dawn.
Schneider, I. History of the Caesars, A.
Shelley, P. England in 1819.
Steptoe. Election Time.
Wheelwright. Anathema. Maranatha!
Wordsworth, W. 1801.
Zimunya. Mr. Bezuidenthout's Dogs.

Goya y Lucientes, Francisco José de

Duncan, R. Poem Beginning with a Line by Pindar, A.
Voznesensky [or Voznesenskii]. I Am Goya.

Grace

Ammons, A. R. Grace Abounding.
Askew, A. Ballad Which Anne Askew Made and Sang When She Was in Newgate, The.
Bontemps. God Give to Men.
Brown, S. To Sallie, Walking.
Campion, T. View Mee, Lord.
Creeley. Fire, The.
Cullen, C. Atlantic City Waiter.
Emerson, R. Grace.
Glück, L. Gift, The.
Herbert, G. Conscience. Grace. Love (3). Temper (2), The.
Hopkins, G. Handsome Heart, The. Windhover, The.
Jewsbury. Verses: "I am monarch of troubles a host."
Kasischke. Grace.
Kendrick, D. Gethsemane A. D.
Landor, W. Rose Aylmer.
Lanier [or Lanyer]. To the Lady Arabella.
Levertov. Grace-Note, The.
Ralegh, S. Passionate Man[']s Pilgrimage, The.
Starkey, D. Scrabble.
Taylor, E. Christ's Reply. Frowardness of the Elect in the Work of Conversion, The. Joy of Church Fellowship Rightly Attended, The. Preface, The: "Infinity, when all things it beheld." Soul's Groan to Christ for Succo[u]r, The.
Thompson, F. Hound of Heaven, The.
Unknown. Love Me Not [for Comely Grace]. On a Female Rope-Dancer.
Very. Promise, The.
Warren, R. Amazing Grace in the Back Country.

Grackles

Nash, O. Grackle, The.

Graffiti

Alexander, E. Kevin of the N.E. Crew.
Espada. Courthouse Graffiti for Two Voices.
Goldbarth. Counterfeit Earth!, The.
Hamer. Charlene-N-Booker 4Ever.
Healy, E. Moroni on the Mormon Temple / Angel on the Wall.
Larkin, P. Sunny Prestatyn.
Martin, C. Speech Against Stone.
Meinke. Helen.
Murphy, M. Eighties Meditation.
Philips, K. Upon the Graving of Her Name upon a Tree in Barnelmes Walks.
Seaton, M. Tagging.
Snodgrass, W. Men's Room in the College Chapel, The.
Viereck, P. Kilroy.
Yolen. Graffiti.

Graham, Billy (William Franklin Graham)

Thribb. Lines on the Return to Britain of Billy Graham.

Grammar

Berger, B. Misconstrued, The.
Carryl, G. How a Girl Was Too Reckless of Grammar [by Far].
Cope, J. Dementia.
Cope, W. Uncertainty of the Poet, The.
Disch. Agreement of Predicate Pronouns, The.
Koch, K. Permanently.
Macklin. House Style, The.

Grand Canyon

Garrigue. Grand Canyon, The.

Grand Pré, Nova Scotia

Carman, B. Low Tide on Grand Pré.

Grand Rapids, Michigan

Moore, J. Grand Rapids.

Grandchildren

Bensko. Butterfly Net, The.
Bradstreet, A. On My Dear Grandchild Simon Bradstreet, [Who Died on 16th November, 1669, Being But a Month and One Day Old].
Jones, R. Portrait of My Father and His Grandson.

Grandchildren

Khalvati. Stone of Patience.
Paley, G. Here.
Sanchez, S. Father and Daughter.

Granddaughters

Boss. When You Are Grown, Amanda Rose.
Bradstreet, A. In Memory of My Dear Grandchild Elizabeth Bradstreet Who Deceased August, 1665, Being a Year and Half Old.

Grandfathers

Alexander, E. Who I Think You Are.
Allbery. Offering.
Bachner. Yes, That's the Way Things Are.
Baillie, J. Child to His Sick Grandfather, A.
Berssenbrugge. Chronicle.
Bishop, E. Manners.
Bowering, G. Grandfather.
Bruchac. Birdfoot's Grampa.
Child, L. Thanksgiving Day.
Clarke, G. Taid's Grave.
Clements, A. Elegy.
Coccimiglio. Night Beach.
Cofer, J. My Grandfather's Hat.
Delgado, J. Phone Booth at the Corner, The.
Di Prima. April Fool Birthday Poem for Grandpa.
Dove, R. Musician Talks About 'Process,' The.
Downie. Great-Grandfather.
Fox, S. Grandmother.
Garrett, E. Grandfather's Mint.
Glück, L. Legend.
Gloria. Whisper, The.
Gotlieb. Late Gothic.
Graham, H. Grandpapa.
Guevara, M. Abuelo, Answers and Questions.
Harper, M. Grandfather.
Hirsch, E. My Grandfather's Poems.
Inada. Father of My Father.
Jacinto, J. Visitation.
Khalvati. Baba Mostafa.
Košek, M. Yes, That's the Way Things Are.
Kumin, M. For My Great-Grandfather: A Message Long Overdue.
Levine, P. Zaydee.
Loftis, N. Big John.
Mahon. Grandfather.
Mayne, S. In Memory of Aaron, Murdered Grandfather.
Melhem, D. Grandfather: Frailty Is Not the Story.
Minhinnick. Grandfather in the Garden.
Mosby. To Josh Gibson (Legendary Slugger of the Old Negro Baseball League).
Mura. Grandfather-in-law.
Ormond. My Grandfather and His Apple-Tree.
Paley, G. Here.
Ríos, A. Mi Abuelo.
Rector. My Grandfather Always Promised Us.
Satchell. Grandfather Grandfather.
Schaeffer. Yahrzeit.
Sexton. Funnel.
Song. Easter: Wahiawa, 1959.
St. John, D. Grandfather's Cap, My.
Waniek. My Grandfather Walks in the Woods.
Woo, D. Grandfather's Rockery.
Work. Grandfather's Clock.

Grandmothers

Abinader, E. Letters from Home.
Alexander, M. Her Garden.
Allbery. Offering.
Baca. Green Chile.
Bahe. Grandmother Sleeps.
Barkan. Two Grandmas.
Barnes, W. Grammer's Shoes.
Bernstein, C. Caught. When My Grandmother Said "Pussy."
Berssenbrugge. Chronicle.
Bishop, E. Sestina: "September rain falls on the house."
Bona. Dream Poem.
Brooks, S. Grandma Talk.
Butler, G. Great-great-grandmother.
Caballero-Robb, M. Dear Rosario. Memoranda for Rosario.
Caston, A. Blowing Eggs.
Cavalieri. Grandmother.
Cervantes. Beneath the Shadow of the Freeway.

Refugee Ship.
Crane, H.   My Grandmother's Love Letters.
Davis, T.   It's All the Same.
De la Mare.   Cupboard, The.
DeCormier-Shekejian.   Grandmother.
Derricotte.   Weakness, The.
Dixon, M.   Grandmother: Crossing Jordan.
Downie.   Her Garden.
Field, E.   Both My Grandmothers.
Figueroa, J.   Felipa, La Filosofa de Rincon que Nació a los 98 Años.
Finney, N.   Fishing Among the Learned.
Fish, C.   Work and Worry.
Forché.   Morning Baking, The.
Fox, S.   Grandmother.
Gonzalez, R.   Cabato.
Gotlieb.   Late Gothic.
Grahn.   Grand Grand Mother is Returning.
Hartnett.   For My Grandmother, Bridget Halpin.
Herd.   Big Girls.
Hugo, V.   Grandmother, The.
Hummer, T.   Train Wreck, 1890: My Grandmother Lies Down with the Dead.
Iverem, E.   Murmur.
Jackson, D.   Grandmother Jackson.
Jennings, E.   My Grandmother.
Jones, T.   My Grandmother Died in the Early Hours of the Morning.
Jordan, J.   Sunflower Sonnet Number One.
Kageyama, C.   Mama.
Kaufman, S.   Nechama.
Khalvati.   Rubaiyat.
Stone of Patience.
Kushner, D.   Grandma in the Shower.
Lau, A.   Upside Down Basket, The.
Livesay, D.   Green Rain.
Mabuza.   Tired Lizi Tired.
Maloney, F.   Grandmothers in Green and Orange.
Marlatt, D.   Katherine's Hair.
Matthews, W.   Grandmother, Dead at 99 Years and 10 Months.
Michelson, R.   Where I Sat.
Moore, L.   Tanka.
Morales, A.   1930.
O'Loughlin.   Glasnevin Cemetery.
Ogilvy.   Grannie's Birthday.
Oliver, M.   Grandmothers, The.
Paley, G.   Here.
Plath.   Point Shirley.
Redmond.   Love Necessitates.
Reis, P.   Ancient Ones, The.
Rich, A.   Grandmothers.
Rios, A.   Advice to a First Cousin.
Rossman, E.   Double Features.
Salzman, E.   Grandmother.
Sapia.   Grandmother, a Caribbean Indian, Described by My Father.
Schaeffer.   May Levine.
Sewell, L.   Denied, The.
Shapiro, K.   My Grandmother.
Silko.   In Cold Storm Light.
It Was a Long Time Before.
Long Time Ago.
Snyder, G.   Old Dutch Woman, The.
Soto.   Behind Grandma's House.
Southerland.   Pale Ant.
St. John, D.   Iris.
Tallmountain.   Matmiya.
Thaxter.   Favorite Flower, The.
Todd, M.   Grandmother's Farm.
Trethewey, N.   Drapery Factory, Gulfport, Mississippi, 1956.
Unger, B.   Observance.
Vizenor.   Anishinabe Grandmothers.
Walker, A.   Medicine.
Walker, M.   Lineage.
Weigl.   Anna Grasa.
Williams, W.   Last Words of My English Grandmother, The.
Wilson, R.   Keeping Hair.
Wong, N.   Grandmothers' Song.
Woo, M.   Whenever You're Cornered, the Only Way Out Is to Fight.
Wright, J.   My Grandmother's Ghost.
Request to a Year.

Young-Prottengeier.   Lithuanian Grandmother.
Zerbe.   In Memory of My Arab Grandmother.

Grandparents
Carroll, L.   Poeta Fit, Non Nascitur.
Ellis, K. N.   Tougaloo Blues.
Emanuel, L.   Outside Room Six.
Forché.   Morning Baking, The.
Gioseffi.   Bicentennial Anti-Poem for Italian-American Women.
González, R.   Day of the Dead.
Jones, R.   End of Communism, The.
Lowell, R.   Grandparents.
Lux.   Night above the Town.
Madonick, M.   Settled In.
Moss, H.   Long Island Springs.
Nash, O.   Come On In, the Senility Is Fine.
Neufeld, A.   Pictures and Stories.
Salazar.   Piñon Nuts.

Granicus, Battle of (334 B.C.)
Dugan, A.   How We Heard the Name.

Grant, Ulysses Simpson
Bierce.   Death of Grant, The.
Horton, G.   General Grant—the Hero of the War.
Sandburg, C.   Cool Tombs.

Grapes
Adams, L.   Grapes Making.
Levis.   Picking Grapes in an Abandoned Vineyard.

Grass
Beveridge.   In the Park.
Bly, R.   Poem Against the British.
Snowfall in the Afternoon.
Bowering, G.   Grass, The.
Dickinson, E.   Presentiment.
Snake, The.
Dietz, H.   Blue Grass.
Gosse.   Lying in the Grass.
Grimké, A.   Grass Fingers.
Haines, J.   To Turn Back.
Hall, D.   Granite and Grass.
Kremer.   Epiphany.
Larkin, P.   Cut Grass.
Lovelace, R.   Grasshopper, The.
Lowell, A.   Shore Grass.
MacCaig.   Fetching Cows.
Madhubuti.   Loneliness, A.
Magowan.   Zeimbekiko.
Martin, C.   Metaphor of Grass in California.
Ni Dhomhnaill.   Leaba Shíoda.
Obejas, A.   Public Place (After Olga Broumas), The.
Reese, L.   Trust.
Sandburg, C.   Grass.
Schwartz, A.   Blue Grass.
Swenson, M.   Cardinal Ideograms.
Szporluk.   Grass and the Sin, The.
Unknown.   On a Clergyman's Horse Biting Him.
Untermeyer, L.   Long Feud.
Van Doren.   Former Barn Lot.
Virgil.   Grass Path Lasts.
Warner, S.   Sad Green.

Grasshoppers
Clare, J.   Grasshoppers.
Cowley, A.   Grasshopper, The.
Cummings, E.   R-P-O-P-H-E-S-S-A-G-R.
Hunt, L.   To the Grasshopper and the Cricket.
Keats.   On the Grasshopper and [the] Cricket.
Lovelace, R.   Grasshopper, The.
Mathias, R.   Grasshoppers.
Reeves, J.   Grasshopper and the Bird, The.
Stanley, T.   Grasshopper, The.
Wilbur.   Grasshopper, A.

Gratitude
Abse.   Thankyou Note.
Balaban.   For Miss Tin in Hue.
Brown, L.   Thank You Father.
Comden, B.   Thanks a Lot, but No Thanks.
Congreve.   False Though She Be.
DeSylva, B. G.   Thank You Father.
Everson, W.   Canticle to the Waterbirds, A.
Glück, L.   Gratitude.
Green, A.   Thanks a Lot, but No Thanks.
Henderson, R.   Thank You Father.
Herrick.   To the Most Virtuous Mistress Pot,

Who Many Times Entertained Him.
Koch, K.   Thank You.
Lawrence, D.   Wild Common, The.
Previn, A.   Thanks a Lot, but No Thanks.
Prunty.   Note of Thanks, A.
Scully, M.   Variations.
Smith, A.   Giving Thanks.
Snyder, G.   Prayer for the Great Family.
Thomas, E.   No One So Much As You.
See also **Thankfulness**

Graves
Bachner.   Man Proposes, God Disposes.
Beer, P.   Ballad of the Underpass.
Grave Doubts.
Behn, A.   Epitaph on the Tombstone of a Child, the Last of Seven That Died Before.
Belloc.   Statue, The.
Betjeman.   Lord Cozens Hardy.
Blodgett.   Snails.
Brontë, A.   Night.
Brown, L.   Sonnet Around Stephanie.
Browning, R.   Bishop Orders His Tomb at Saint Praxed's Church, The.
Childe Roland to the Dark Tower Came.
Bynner.   Idols.
Carver, R.   Walk, A.
Chesterton, G.   Elegy in a Country Churchyard.
English Graves, The.
Clarke, G.   Taid's Grave.
Coleridge, S.   Knight's Tomb, The.
Cotton, C.   Epitaph on M. H., An.
Crashaw.   Epitaph Upon Husband and Wife Who Died and Were Buried Together, An.
Creeley.   Fathers.
Crosby, F.   Let Me Die on the Prairie.
Davidson, D.   Lines for a Tomb.
Doddridge, P.   Meditations on the Sepulchre in the Garden.
Donne.   Relic, The.
Durcan.   Weeping Headstones of the Isaac Becketts, The.
Eberhart, R.   I Walked over the Grave of Henry James.
Elledge.   Strangers: An Essay.
Ellis, K. N.   Tougaloo Blues.
"Field."   After Soufrière.
Sometimes I do despatch my heart.
Glück, L.   Mount Ararat.
Goodman, P.   Gravestone, August 8, 1968, A.
Gray, T.   Elegy Written in a Country Churchyard.
Epitaph: "Here rests his head upon the lap of earth."
Gutteridge.   Man into a Churchyard.
Hall, D.   Sister on the Tracks, A.
Hardy, T.   Ah, Are You Digging on My Grave?
Nettles, The.
Poet, A.
Rain on a Grave.
Harper, F.   Bury Me in a Free Land.
Harper, M.   Alice.
Harrison, T.   Earthen Lot, The.
Hayden, R.   Paul Laurence Dunbar.
Herrick.   To Laurels.
Upon Ben Jo[h]nson.
Housman, A.   Because I liked you better.
With Rue My Heart Is Laden.
Hudgins.   Burial Detail.
Jarrell.   Come to the Stone.
Johnson, H.   Invocation: "Let me be buried in the rain."
King, H.   Exequy, The.
Košek, M.   Man Proposes, God Disposes.
Kramer, L.   Red Cross Telegram, The.
Löwy, H.   Man Proposes, God Disposes.
Landon.   Song.
Lawrence, D.   Giorno dei Morti.
Leithauser.   Buried Graves, The.
Levertov.   Despair.
Levy, A.   Sequel to 'A Reminiscence," The.
Lieberman, L.   Compass of the Dying.
Longfellow, H.   Jewish Cemetery at Newport, The.
Lorde.   Father Son and Holy Ghost.
Lowell, R.   At the Indian Killer's Grave.
Sailing Home from Rapallo.

Macdonald, G. At Aberdeen.
MacNeice. Introduction, The.
Mangan, J. Rest Only in the Grave.
Martinez, D. Death of Isadora Duncan, The.
McKinney, I. Visiting My Gravesite: Talbott Churchyard, West Virginia.
Millay, E. In the Grave No Flower.
Milnes. Sir Walter Scott at the Tomb of the Stuarts in St. Peter's.
Moore, M. Grave, A.
Morgan, E. King Billy.
Muldoon, P. Milkweed and Monarch.
Ndu. Udude.
Niedecker. Graves, The.
Orlovsky. Snail Poem.
Ormond. Lament for a Leg.
Paquet. Graves Registration.
Philips, K. On the Death of My First and Dearest Child[e], Hector Philip[p]s.
Pitter. Coffin-Worm, The.
Po Chü-i. On an Ancient Tomb East of the Village.
Preston, M. Grave in Hollywood Cemetery, Richmond, A.
Ramke. Paul Verlaine at the Grave of Lucien Létinois.
Receveur. August 17, 1970.
Rossetti, C. Song: "When I am dead, my dearest."
Two Thoughts of Death.
Under Willows.
Sandburg, C. Cool Tombs.
Sassoon. Prehistoric Burials.
Simmerman. Child's Grave, Hale County, Alabama.
Slessor. Beach Burial.
Smith, C. By the Same.
Soto. Blanco.
Stevenson, A. Temporarily in Oxford.
Stevenson, R. Requiem: "Under the wide and starry sky."
Stowe. Only a Year.
Thompson, M. Lincoln's Grave.
Trethewey, N. Collection Day.
Unknown. Epitaph for Thomas Johnson, Huntsman. Charlton, Sussex.
Unquiet Grave, The.
Warner, S. Elizabeth.
Whistler. Form of Epitaph, A.
Whitman, W. As Toilsome I Wander'd Virginia's Woods.
Dirge for Two Veterans.
Wilcox, E. My Grave.
Wilde, O. Requiescat.
Winters, Y. For My Father's Grave.
Wordsworth, W. Gravestone upon the Floor in the Cloisters of Worcester Cathedral, A.
Wright, C. Yugoslav Cemetery.
Wright, J. Albuquerque Graveyard, The.
Way to Make a Living, A.
Zukofsky, L. I Sent Thee Late.
See also **Burial; Cemeteries; Mausoleums; Tombs**

Graves, Robert
Ewart. Robert Graves.
Graves, R. Face in the Mirror, The.
My Name and I.

Graveyards
Acquah. They're Tearing Up the Old Graveyard.
Randall, D. Blue Dome, The.
See also **Cemeteries**

Gravity
Garrett, E. Miser.
Gustafson, R. In the Yukon.
Porteous. Calf.
Wilbur. Juggler.

Gray, Thomas
Smith, C. To the South Downs.
Warton, T. To Mr. Gray.
Wilbur. In a Churchyard.

Great Britain
Davies, I. Do You Remember 1926?
Dibdin, T. Origins of Naval Artillery.
Gillilan, P. Looking North.
Pickard, T. Devil's Destroying Angel Exploded,

The.
Turner, C. Great Britain Through the Ice: Or, Premature Patriotism.
Zephaniah. Sun, The.
See also **England; Northern Ireland; Scotland; Wales**

Great Depression
Etter. Elwood Collins: Summer of 1932.
Glaser, I. Depression.
Hughes, L. Madam's Past History.
Jones, R. End of Communism, The.
McDaniel, W. First Spring in California, 1936.
Moore, M. Americans in 1933–4–5–6–7–8–, Etc.

Great Lakes
Shepherd, R. Maritime.

Great Wall, China
Blunden. At the Great Wall of China.
Williams, W. World Contracted to a Recognizable Image, The.

Greatness
Guest, E. Equipment.
Guiterman. On the Vanity of Earthly Greatness.
Holloway, G. Hand for Some Others, A.
Howard, R. Nadar.
Jonson, B. To the Memory of My Beloved, the Author Mr [*or* Master] William Shakespeare [And What He Hath Left Us].
Seaton, M. Fiddleheads.
Spender, S. I Think Continually of Those Who Were Truly Great.
Taggard. To the Natural World: at 37.
Thackeray. Napoleon.
Unknown. Beyond the Profit of Today.
Whitman, W. By Blue Ontario's Shore.
Poet, The.
Wordsworth, W. England, 1802, III.
See also **Fame**

Greco, El
Birney. El Greco: Espolio.
Starbuck, G. High Renaissance.

Greece
Abinader, E. Pigeon Rock: Lebanon.
Baker, H. Sappho's Leap.
Broumas, O. Sometimes, as a Child.
Bryant, W. Conjunction of Jupiter and Venus, The.
Byron, G. On This Day I Complete My Thirty-sixth Year.
Written After Swimming from Sestos to Abydos.
Capetanakis. Isles of Greece, The.
Davidson, D. On a Replica of the Parthenon.
Doolittle, H. Islands, The.
Lais.
Duncan, R. Chords Passages 14.
Durrell. Delos.
Nemea.
Ekelof. Greece.
Elytis. Aegean Melancholy.
England, A. Art of the Snake Story, The.
Glück, L. Roman Study.
Grosholz. On the Ferry, Toward Patras.
Hemans. Bride of the Greek Isle, The.
Lawrence, D. Argonauts, The.
Melville, H. Attic Landscape, The.
Merrill, J. After Greece.
Charioteer of Delphi, The.
Rakosi. Origins.
Sarton. At Lindos.
Seferis. Last Stop.
Spicer, J. Transformations.
Stickney, T. Mount Lykaion.
Sonnets from Greece.
Taggart, J. Never Too Late.
Taylor, B. Paean to the Dawn, A.

Greed
Adams, J. Wants of Man, The.
Bierce. Statesmen, The.
Bricusse, L. Goldfinger.
Burns, R. Such a Parcel of Rogues in a Nation.
Coleman, W. Aunt Jessie.
Emerson, R. Hamatreya.
Wealth.
Everett, J. White Man Problem, The.

"Field." Wheat-miners.
Guest, E. What's In It for Me?
Herbert, G. Size, The.
Lucilius. Miser and the Mouse, The.
May, E. To a Covetous Churl.
Melville, H. Time's Betrayal.
Newley, A. Goldfinger.
Pope, A. Duke of Buckingham, The.
Sir Balaam.
Timon's Villa.
Quarles. Philippians 1.23.
Robinson, E. Aaron Stark.
Samwell. Negro Boy, The.
Sexton. With Mercy for the Greedy.
Tennyson, A. Northern Farmer: New Style.
Torres, E. How Long Does the Curator Dance For?
Traherne. Insatiableness.
Unknown. Greedy Man, The.
Money, Money.
War the Source of Riches.
Whittier. Haschish, The.
Williams, W. Question and Answer.
Wordsworth, W. Written in London, September, 1802.

Greek Poetry, Classical
Bogardus. Narcissus to Echo.

Green (color)
Barry, J. Green Hell, Green Death.
Clare, J. Maple Tree, The.
Espada. Green and Red, Verde y Rojo.
Graves, R. Variables of Green.
Lawrence, D. Green.
Mother Goose. Walnut, A.
Rodgers, C. Black Heart as Ever Green, The.
Schuyler, J. I Think.
Stevens, W. Candle a Saint, The.
Phosphor Reading by His Own Light.

Greene, Graham
McGinley. Muted Screen of Graham Greene, The.

Greene, Nathanael
Freneau. To the Memory of the Brave Americans.

Greenhouses
Hardy, T. Frozen Greenhouse, The.
Morgan, E. My Greenhouse.
Pitter. Other People's Glasshouses.
Roethke. Big Wind.
Child on Top of a Greenhouse.

Gregory, Lady Augusta
Yeats. Municipal Gallery Revisited, The.

Gregory, Robert
Yeats. In Memory of Major Robert Gregory.

Grief
Abelard. David's Lament for Jonathan.
Akhmatova, A. Dedication.
Auden. Stop All the Clocks, Cut Off the Telephone.
Barker, G. Summer Song I.
Barnes, W. Wind at the Door, The.
Blind. Mourning Women.
Bogan, L. Juan's Song.
BonniLee. White Candles.
Bowles, W. On the Death of William Linley, esq.
Time and Grief.
Bridges, R. Elegy on a Lady, Whom Grief for the Death of Her Betrothed Killed.
Brody. Lamentations.
Brontë, E. Day Dream, A.
If grief for grief can touch thee.
Stanzas: "Often rebuked, yet always back returning."
Browning, E. Bereavement.
Grief.
Bryant, W. Death of the Flowers, The.
Burns, R. Song: "O my love's [*or* luve's *or* love is *or* luve is] like a red, red rose."
Chivers. Avalon.
Clark, P. Kleptomaniac.
Clifton, L. For de Lawd.
Cofer, J. Campesino's Lament, The.
Coleridge, M. "My True Love Hath My Heart and I Have His."

D'Orleans. Oft in My Thought.
De Kok. Small Passing.
'Dermée.' Poem: "I play tennis with the shells."
De Vere, A. Sorrow.
Dickinson, E. I Can Wade Grief.
Donne. Triple Fool, The.
  Valediction: Forbidding Mourning, A.
Dove, R. "Blown Apart By Loss . . . ."
  Demeter, Waiting.
Dryden, J. To the Memory of Mr Oldham.
Duncan, R. Structure of Rime XXIII.
Dunn, D. Kaleidoscope, The.
Elizabeth I. On Monsieur's Departure.
Evans, M. Where Have You Gone?
"Field." After Soufrière.
  Beloved, My Glory in Thee is Not Ceased.
Ford, C. Somebody's Gone.
Frost, R. Hill Wife, The.
  House Fear.
  Impulse, The.
  Loneliness.
  Oft-Repeated Dream, The.
Gascoigne. For That He Looked Not upon Her.
Gerstler. Sinking Feeling, A.
Gibb, B. Vigil.
Gibbons, R. We Say.
Ginsberg, A. To Aunt Rose.
Gray, T. Death of Hoel, The.
  Sonnet [on the Death of Mr. Richard West].
Gregg. Night Music.
Hardy, T. Bereft.
Hawkesworth, P. Two Statues.
Hawoldar. Destruction.
Heaney, S. Wedding Day.
Heard, J. Bereft.
Hemphill. Homocide.
Herbert, G. Affliction (1).
  Affliction (3).
  Confession.
Herrick. Observation.
Hill, A. Alone in an Inn at Southampton, April the 25th, 1737.
Hine. Apart from You.
Holmes, J. Four and a Half.
Hopkins, G. Felix Randal.
  No Worst, There Is None. Pitched Past Pitch of Grief.
  Spring and Fall.
Housman, A. Bredon Hill.
Howard, A. Good Shepherd's Sorrow for the Death of His Beloved Son, The.
Ismaili. Bajji.
Jones, R. Apology to Andrew.
Jonson, B. On My First Son[ne].
Kaufman, S. Job's Wife.
Kavanagh, P. In Memory of My Mother.
Keble. Rainbow, The.
King, H. Exequy, The.
Knight, E. As You Leave Me.
Lawrence, D. Brooding Grief.
  Hymn to Priapus.
  Sorrow.
Leiser, J. Kol Nidra.
Li Po. Moon over the Mountain Pass, The.
Lindsay, C. To My Own Face.
Lish, G. Rusty.
Littledale. When My Dog Died.
Liu, T. Poem.
Lomax, M. July.
Longfellow, H. Cross of Snow, The.
Lovelace, R. In Allusion to the French Song.
  Vintage to the Dungeon, The.
Lowell, J. After the Burial.
Lucie-Smith. Lesson, The.
MacDiarmid, H. At My Father's Grave.
Marks, S. November Woods.
Martinez, D. Cole Porter.
Matherne, B. Les Fils (Sons).
Mayakovsky [or Maiakovskii]. Mayakovsky's Suicide Note.
Melville, H. Martyr, The.
  Monody.
Millay, E. Song of a Second April.
  Wood Road, The.
Milton. On His Deceased Wife.
Monro. Solitude.

Montagu, L. Receipt to Cure [or for] the Vapours, A.
Moore, J. One Reason I Went to Prison.
Morley, H. Lizard, The.
Mueller, L. Another Version.
Naganawa, A. Learning to Swim.
Nathan, R. Sonnet: "Because my grief seems quiet and apart."
Neufeld, A. Children of Night.
O'Dalaigh, M. Invocation: "Last night my soul departed."
Orr, G. Who'd Want to Be a Man?
Owen, W. Hospital Barge at Cérisy.
Patchen. O Now the Drenched Land Wakes.
Pegram, A. Burials.
Pembroke, M. If Ever Hapless Woman Had a Cause.
Philips, K. Epitaph on her Son H. P. at St. Syth's Church.
  On the Death of My First and Dearest Child[e], Hector Philip[p]s.
Piatt, S. Her Word of Reproach.
  No Help.
Pilkington, L. Sorrow.
Po Chü-i. To the Distant One.
Poe. Annabel Lee.
  For Annie.
Porter, P. Exequy, An.
  What I Have Written I Have Written.
Ralegh, S. Farewell to the Court.
Reese, L. In Time of Grief.
Rexroth, K. Andrée Rexroth.
Richardson, J. On My Late Dear Wife.
Richardson, M. Sonnet: "I still shall smile and go my careless way."
Robinson, E. Reuben Bright.
Rodriguez, J. In-flight Note.
Rose. Long Division; a Tribal History.
Rose, R. What the Japanese Perhaps Heard.
Rosenberg, I. Spiritual Isolation.
Rossetti, C. Gone Before.
  Remember [Me].
  Song: "When I am dead, my dearest."
Sandburg, C. Right to Grief, The.
Sandeen. Plaint of Flowers, A.
Schwartz, R. L. Grief.
Shafer, A. Gurney Tears.
Shelley, P. Dirge, A: "Rough wind, that moanest loud."
Sherburne. Weeping and Kissing.
Sidney, S. Nightingale, The.
Smith, C. Verses Intended to Have Been Prefixed to the Novel of Emmeline, but Then Suppressed.
Surrey. Complaint by Night, A.
Synková, A. Tears.
Tennyson, A. Break, Break, Break.
Thomas, D. In My Craft or Sullen Art.
Unknown. Moon Is Rising, The.
  Unquiet Grave, The.
Vando. In the Dark Backward.
Voznesensky [or Voznesenskii]. I Am Goya.
Wallis, H. Female's Lamentations, The; or, The Village in Mourning.
Wharton, A. Elegy on the Earl of Rochester.
Whitman, W. Come Up from the Fields Father.
Whitney, I. I.W. To her Unconstant Lover.
Whittier. Telling the Bees.
  Vesta.
Wilde, O. Requiescat.
Williams, W. Widow's Lament in Springtime, The.
Wright, J. Complaint.
  Poem Written under an Archway in a Discontinued Railroad Station, Fargo, North Dakota, A.
Wyatt, S. Blame Not My Lute.
  Lover's Appeal, The.
Yearsley. Soliloquy: "What folly to complain."
  To———: "Lo! dreary Winter, howling o'er the waste."
Yeats. Down by the Salley Gardens.

See also **Sorrow; Mourning and Mourners**

Grocers
Chesterton, G. Song against Grocers, The.
Davies, I. Angry Summer, The.

Espada. Tony Went to the Bodega But He Didn't Buy Anything.
Rosenblatt, S. Procession, The.
Stanton, M. Shoplifters.
Suárez, V. Song for the Sugar Cane.
Williams, C. Racists.

Groundhogs
Eberhart, R. Groundhog, The.
Frost, R. Drumlin Woodchuck, A.
Kumin, M. Woodchucks.
Plath. Incommunicado.
Shaw, L. Groundhog, The.

Grouse
Baillie, J. Blackcock, The [or The Black Cock].

Growth
Ashbery. Boy, A.
  Spring Day.
  Young Son, The.
Bangs, J. Little Elf, The.
Brooke, R. Sonnet: In Time of Revolt.
Clare, J. Maple Tree, The.
Cocteau. Cape of Good Hope, The.
Curzon, D. Instructions to a Seed.
Dodge, M. Taking Time to Grow.
Field, R. General Store.
Hadas, R. Red Hat, The.
Herbert, G. Paradise.
Kipling, R. 'Eathen, The.
Limburg, J. Queen of Swords, The.
MacDiarmid, H. To a Friend and Fellow Poet.
Major, C. Giant Red Woman.
Merwin, W. S. Last One, The.
Namjoshi, S. From the Travels of Gulliver.
O'Hara, F. Cornkind.
  Poem: "There I could never be a boy."
Palma. Coming of Age.
Plath. Mushrooms.
Raine, K. Rose.
Roethke. Cuttings.
Serote. Growing, The.
Smith, M. Watering the New Lawn.
Song. Mehinaku Girl in Seclusion, A.
Southwell. Times [or Tymes] Go[e] By Turn[e]s.
Stevenson, R. Looking Forward.
  My Shadow.
Wells, N. Up.
Wise, W. When I Grow Up.
Wordsworth, W. My Heart Leaps Up.

Guadalajara, Mexico
Ashbery. Instruction Manual, The.

Guards
Dupree, E. At Present I Am Working as a Security Guard.
Salzman, E. Bargain with the Watchman.

Guatemala
Espada. Green and Red, Verde y Rojo.
Jordan, J. Poem for Guatemala.
Stevens, W. Arrival at the Waldorf.

Guerrillas
Heaney, S. Requiem for the Croppies.
Kipling, R. Arithmetic on the Frontier.

Guest, Edgar A
Nash, O. Lines to a World-famous Poet Who Failed to Complete a World-famous Poem; or, Come Clean, Mr. Guest!

Guests
Barbauld. Washing-Day.
Bishop, E. House Guest.
Bruce, D. Two Couples.
Child, L. Thanksgiving Day.
Coleridge, M. Master and Guest.
De la Mare. Feckless Dinner-Party, The.
Hall, D. Wedding Party.
Haynes, C. Any Wife or Husband.
Hitchcock. One Whose Reproach I Cannot Evade, The.
Jonson, B. Inviting a Friend to Supper.
O'Hara, F. Poem: "Eager note on my door said 'Call me, The."
Pugh. Guest, The.
Unknown. Guest, The.
Villa. Inviting a Tiger for the Weekend.
Watson, R. White Bird, The.
Yeats. Secret Rose, The.

See also **Hospitality; Visiting and Visitors**
Guggenheim, John Simon
  Hollander, J.   No Foundation.
Guilt
  Akst, H.   Guilty.
  Balaban.   After Our War.
  Baldwin, J.   Guilt, Desire and Love.
  Berrigan, D.   My Name.
  Bidart.   Sacrifice, The.
  Brecht, B.   To Those Born Later.
  Brodsky, J.   Bosnia Tune.
  Brontë, C.   Again I find myself alone.
  Bruner.   Atonement.
  Byron, G.   Prayer of Nature, The.
  Cary, A.   Sea-Side Cave, The.
  Clampitt.   Cormorant in His Element, The.
  Cross, F.   When Chicken Man Came Home to
    Roost.
  Dauer.   Philip the Store Policeman.
  Dunbar, P.   Debt, The.
  Elizabeth I.   Written on a Wall at Woodstock.
  "Field."   Flaw, A.
  Fields, D.   Don't Blame Me.
  Fisher, D.   Put the Blame on Mame.
  Frost, R.   Home Burial.
  Glazer.   Drinking with the Nazis.
  Herbert, G.   Conscience.
  Heyen.   To the Onlookers.
  Hughes, L.   Dinner Guest: Me.
  Jarrell.   Eighth Air Force.
  Jennings, E.   My Grandmother.
  Kahaney, P.   Germany, 1981.
  Kahn, G.   Guilty.
  Kaufman, S.   Accuser, The.
  Kees.   After the Trial.
  Liu, T.   Mama.
  McHugh, J.   Don't Blame Me.
  Merrill, J.   Renewal, A.
  Miles, J.   Belief.
  Nash, O.   Inter-Office Memorandum.
  Oness, C.   August 1990.
  Roberts, A.   Put the Blame on Mame.
  Sarton.   Tortured, The.
  Shevin.   What He Hated.
  Thomas, R.   Here.
  Very.   Slavery.
    Thy Brother's Blood.
  Wain.   Song about Major Eatherly, A.
  Warren, R.   Amazing Grace in the Back
    Country.
    Crime.
    Pursuit.
    Revelation.
  Weigl.   Her Life Runs Like a Red Silk Flag.
  Whiting, R.   Guilty.
  Wright, C.   California Spring.
Guitars
  Cornford, F.   Guitarist Tunes Up, The.
  Hernández Cruz.   Two Guitars.
  St. John, D.   Guitar.
Gulls
  Adams, L.   Gull Goes Up, A.
  Axelrod, D.   Guide to Urban Birds, A.
  De la Mare.   Storm, The.
  Graham, J.   Gulls.
  Hoffman, D.   At Provincetown.
  Hooker, J.   Gull on a Post.
  Nash, O.   Sea-Gull, The.
  Pau-Llosa.   Kendall Gulls.
  Roberts, N.   Gull's Flight, The.
  Sandburg, C.   Harbor, The.
  Schwartz, D.   Ballet of the Fifth Year, The.
  Smedley, M.   Sorrowful Sea-Gull, The.
  Stafford, W.   Gulls at Cannon Beach.
  Updike.   Seagulls.
  Williams, W.   Gulls.
Gum Trees
  Oodgeroo of the tribe Noonuccal.   Municipal
    Gum.
Guns
  Ai.   Kid, The.
  Berger, J.   Gun, The.
  Berlin.   You Can't Get a Man with a Gun.
  Blunden.   Vlamertinghe.
  Brouwer, J.   Steve's Commando Paintball, San

  Adriano, California.
  Brown, G.   Hawk, The.
  Carson, C.   Bloody Hand.
  Coleridge, M.   In London Town.
  Day, J.   Picket before Bull Run, The.
  Feinstein, S.   Blues Villanelle for Sonny Criss.
  Flynn, N.   Fragment (Found Inside My Mother).
  Galvin, J.   Independence Day, 1956: A Fairy
    Tale.
  Gurney, I.   First Time In.
  Haines, J.   Flight, The.
  Hardy, T.   Channel Firing.
  Heaney, S.   From the Frontier of Writing.
  Hemans.   Wreck, The.
  Holmes, D.   Time for Guns, A.
  Howell, C.   Reminder to the Current
    President, A.
  Joans.   .38, The.
  Kipling, R.   Screw-Guns.
  Kunitz, S.   Careless Love.
  Mörling, M.   For F. M. Who Did Not Get Killed
    Yesterday on 57th Street.
  Manifold.   Defensive Position.
  Meeks, B.   Twin Barrel Bucky: A Kingston 12
    Dub, The.
  Melville, H.   Swamp Angel, The.
  Owen, W.   Anthem for Doomed Youth.
    Arms and the Boy.
  Ransom, W.   Grandpa's .45.
  Robinson, E.   Richard Cory.
  Rolfe, E.   Casualty.
  Sandburg, C.   A. E. F.
  Sassoon.   General, The.
  Sharma, P.   Action-Packed Sonnet.
  Spender, S.   Ultima Ratio Regum.
  Unknown.   Epigram: "Says a Reverend Priest to
    a less Rev'rend friend."
    Gunpowder Plot Day.
    Riddle: "Long slick black feller."
  Wadsworth, W.   Need for Attention, The.
  Whitman, W.   Artilleryman's Vision, The.
  Wilson, R.   Military-Industrial Complex, The.
  Yeats.   To a Squirrel at Kyle-Na-No.
  Young, K.   Casting.
**Gustavus II (Gustavus Adolphus), King of
  Sweden**
  Carew, T.   In Answer of an Elegiacal[l] Letter,
    Upon the Death of the King of Sweden [from
    Aurelian Townsend, Inviting Me to Write on
    That Subject].
Gypsies
  Clare, J.   Gipsies: "Gipsies seek wide sheltering
    woods again, The."
    Gypsy's Evening Blaze, The.
  Cofer, J.   What the Gypsy Said to Her Children.
  Hodgson, R.   Gipsy Girl, The.
  Hovey.   Sea Gypsy.
  Hughes, R.   Gipsy-Night.
  Keats.   Meg Merrilies [or Merrilees].
  Kipling, R.   Gipsy Trail, The.
  Levertov.   Gypsy's Window, The.
  Monsour.   Emily's Words.
  Pound, E.   Gypsy, The.
  Swartwout.   Gypsy Teaches Her Grandchild
    Wolfen Ways, The.
  Thomas, E.   Gypsy, The.
  Unknown.   Gypsy Laddie, The.
  Watson, R.   Serenade: "Who is it sings the
    gypsies' song to-night."
  Wright, J.   Jalapeña Gypsies.

H

Habits
  Ai.   I Can't Get Started.
  Barney, N.   Habit.
  Centolella.   Small Acts.
  Coleman, C.   Why Try to Change Me Now?
  Dooley, M.   Mansize.
  Dubin, A.   You're Getting to Be a Habit with
    Me.
  McCarthy, J.   Why Try to Change Me Now?
  O'Reilly, J.   Builder's Lesson, A.
  Peacock, M.   Breakfast with Cats.

  Plath.   Love Letter.
Hades
  Hope, A.   Return of Persephone, The.
  Patterson, G.   Lament.
  Rukeyser, M.   In the Underworld.
  Swinburne.   Garden of Proserpine, The.
Hafiz
  Taylor, B.   To a Persian Boy in the Bazaar at
    Smyrna.
Hagar
  Bibb.   Expulsion of Hagar, The.
Haggard, Sir Henry Rider
  Stephen, J.   To R. K.
Haggis
  Burns, R.   To a Haggis.
Haiku (form)
  Corn.   Long-Distance Call to Gregg, Who Lived
    with AIDS as Long as He Could.
  Holloway, G.   Bash on Basho: Six of the Best.
  Roseliep.   Campfire Extinguished.
  Wilbur.   Sleepless at Crown Point.
Hail
  Hopkins, G.   Hailstorm in May.
Hair
  Agard, J.   For Bob Marley.
  Beardsley.   Ballad of a Barber, The.
  Betjeman.   Licorice Fields at Pontefract, The.
  Bishop, E.   Shampoo, The.
  Bogan, L.   Medusa.
  Borgmann, K.   Rodeo Tangent.
  Cardiff.   Combing.
  D'Aguiar.   Dread.
  Damas.   Just Like the Legend.
  Dauer.   Lois at the Hair Salon.
  Donovan, K.   Grooming.
  Dove, R.   "Blown Apart By Loss . . . ."
  Erdrich.   Butcher's Wife, The.
  Ferguson, G.   Inhaling His Hair.
  "Field."   Embalmment.
  Flanner.   Dumb.
  Georgiou, E.   From Where I Stand.
  Getsi.   Washing Your Hair.
  Gunn, T.   Skateboard.
  Henderson-Holmes.   'C' ing in Colors: Red.
  Herrick.   Art above Nature, to Julia.
  Heyen.   Trains, The.
  Hochman.   Hairbrush, The.
  Jackson, A.   Choosing the Blues.
  Keeshig-Tobias.   Mother with Child.
  Knott.   Hair Poem.
  Landor, W.   On Seeing a Hair of Lucretia
    Borgia.
  Lee, L.   Early in the Morning.
  Love, M.   Initiation.
  Lovelace, R.   To Amarantha, That She Would
    Dishevel[l] Her Hair[e].
  Marlatt, D.   Katherine's Hair.
  Moss, T.   Raising a Humid Flag.
    Tornados.
  Mullen, H.   Saturday Afternoon, When Chores
    Are Done.
  Piercy.   Hello Up There.
  Pogson, P.   Hairdressing.
  Pope, A.   Hampton Court.
    Rape of the Lock, The; an Heroi-Comical Poem.
    Toilet, The.
    Voyage on the Thames, The.
  Pound, E.   River-Merchant's Wife: A Letter,
    The.
  Probyn.   As the Flower of the Grass.
  Rózewicz.   Pigtail.
  Rukeyser, M.   Boy with His Hair Cut Short.
  Sherman, C.   Roots.
  Song.   White Porch, The.
  Sullivan, B.   Hair.
  Toomer.   Portrait in Georgia.
  Trethewey, N.   Naola Beauty Academy, New
    Orleans, Louisiana, 1943.
  Tucker, M.   First Grey Hair, The.
  Unknown.   Black Hair.
    Dirge for Three Trumpets.
  Washington.   Freedom Hair.
  Watkyns.   Periwig, A.
  Wilson, R.   Keeping Hair.
  Wright, R.   Haiku: "Green cockleburs, The."

Wylie.   Green Hair.
Yeats.   For Anne Gregory.
Young, K.   Eddie Priest's Barbershop and
 Notary.
Hairdressers
Dauer.   Lois at the Hair Salon.
Jackson, A.   Choosing the Blues.
Limburg, J.   Queen of Swords, The.
Love, M.   Initiation.
Strange.   Barbershop Ritual.
Swanger.   Wayne's College of Beauty, Santa
 Cruz.
Trethewey, N.   Naola Beauty Academy, New
 Orleans, Louisiana, 1943.
Young, K.   Eddie Priest's Barbershop and
 Notary.
Haiti
Cullen, C.   Black Majesty.
Lane, B.   I Left My Hat in Haiti.
Porter, C.   Katie Went to Haiti.
Halloween
Barry, J.   Harvest Moon.
Burns, R.   Halloween.
Glück, L.   All Hallows.
Guevara, M.   Rhyme for Halloween, A.
Livingston, M.   Lazy Witch.
Moorer.   Hallowe'en.
Nims, J.   Trick or Treat.
Prelutsky.   It's Halloween.
 Skeleton Parade.
Stephens, P.   Hangman.
Ham
Hood, T.   Sonnet to Vauxhall.
McGinley.   Notes for a Southern Road Map.
Smith, D.   Smithfield Ham.
Unknown.   Riddle: "Riddlum riddlum ranty
 pole."
Hamer, Fannie Lou
Davis, T.   Remembering Fannie Lou Hamer.
Harris, D.   On the uptown lexington avenue
 express: Martin Luther King Day 1995.
Hamlet
Allston.   On Kean's Hamlet.
Gilmore, B.   To be or not to be.
Sandburg, C.   They All Want to Play Hamlet.
Sharpless.   Hamlet.
Hammers and Hammering
Bogan, L.   Roman Fountain.
Brown, S.   Southern Road.
Gustafson, R.   Of Green Steps and Laundry.
Hooks.   Body Inside the Soul, The.
"Leadbelly."   Take this Hammer.
Unknown.   Smoke-Blackened Smiths.
Hammocks
Alexander, P.   Scherzo.
Monsour.   Dream of Dying, A.
Pilling.   Earth, The.
Hampstead Heath, London
Hunt, L.   To Hampstead.
Hamsters
Wright, K.   Our Hamster's Life.
Handball
Dunn, S.   Day and Night Handball.
Feldman, I.   Handball Players at Brighton
 Beach, The.
Handicaps and the Handicapped
Cook, E.   Idiot-Born, The.
Delgado, J.   Lame Boy Returns, The.
Gerstler.   True Bride, The.
Ginsberg, A.   Stroke.
Hugo, R.   Freaks at Spurgin Road Field, The.
McIntyre.   Wooden Leg.
Mungoshi.   Dotito is Our Brother.
Owen, W.   Disabled.
Sassoon.   Does It Matter?
Shapcott, T.   Near the School for Handicapped
 Children.
Simic.   Great Infirmities.
Simpson, L.   Stumpfoot on 42nd Street.
Stanton, M.   Space.
Thomas, D.   Hunchback in the Park, The.
Wordsworth, W.   Idiot Boy, The.
See also **Amputees; Birth Defects; Blindness;
 Cripples; Deafness; Mental Retardation**
Hands
Alley, R.   Canary Man and You, The.

Atwood.   You Begin.
Beatty, P.   Gription.
Behn, A.   Oh, How the Hand the Lover Ought
 to Prize.
Bly, R.   Taking the Hands of Someone You
 Love.
Bogan, L.   Heard by a Girl.
Born, A.   End of the Row.
Brooks, G.   Medgar Evers.
Brown, S.   Conjured.
Chisholm, A.   Contact.
Clark, T.   Touch of Human Hands, The.
Couzyn.   My Father's Hands.
Crane, H.   Episode of Hands.
Crapsey.   Amaze.
Creeley.   Figures, The.
 For Friendship.
 People, The.
Cross, F.   Accident, An.
Dacey, P.   Thumb.
Dickinson, E.   Caterpillar.
Dorsey, T.   Take My Hand, Precious Lord.
Feinstein, S.   Sonnets for Stan Gage (1945–
 1992).
Finch, A.   Sapphics for Patience.
Finkel.   Hands.
González, R.   Perla at the Mexican Border
 Assembly Line of Dolls.
Gregerman, D.   Strictly Speaking.
Guevara, M.   Hands of the Old Métis, The.
Gunn, T.   Feel of Hands, The.
 Man With Night Sweats, The.
Harrison, T.   Hands, The.
Herrick.   Right Hand, The.
Jackson, L.   Take Hands.
Jakiela.   Personal History of Hands, A.
Jeffers, L.   I Do Not Know the Power of My
 Hand.
Johnson, S.   Ballad: "I put my hat upon my
 head."
Keats.   This Living Hand, Now Warm and
 Capable.
Knott.   Death.
Kooser.   Hands in the Wind.
Lima, F.   Hand, The.
Loftis, N.   In Memorium: Robert Hayden.
Lovelace, R.   Her Muffe.
Magowan.   Susan.
Merwin, W. S.   Gardens of Zuñi, The.
Moss, H.   Hand, The.
Penn, R.E.   Hand.
Phillips, C.   As From a Quiver of Arrows.
Piercy.   Friend, The.
Randolph, T.   Upon the Loss[e] of His Little
 Finger.
Rolle, S.   Hands in the Motion of Prayer.
Rossetti, C.   Twice.
Shapiro, K.   Love for a Hand.
Shepherd, R.   West Willow.
Snyder, G.   After Work.
St. John, P.   Ocean of the Streams of Story.
Stein, G.   Leave, A.
Tallmountain.   Hands of Mary Joe, The.
Tate, J.   Love Making.
Thomas, D.   Hand That Signed the Paper, The.
Thomas, R.   Hand, The.
 Here.
Tsaloumas.   Return of an Ikon.
Unknown.   My Mother's Hands.
Vallejo.   Poem to Be Read and Sung.
Ward, D.   Glass House.
Wright, R.   I Have Seen Black Hands.
Handwriting
Barbauld.   On a Lady's Writing.
Hume, C.   Various Readings of an Illegible
 Postcard.
Nemerov.   Writing.
Hanging
Atwood.   Marrying the Hangman.
Brutus.   They Hanged Him, I Said Dismissively.
Getsi.   Woman Hanging from Lightpole, Illinois
 Route 136.
Housman, A.   Carpenter's Son, The.
 Eight O'Clock.
Kipling, R.   Danny Deever.
Lowell, J.   Boss, The.

Melville, H.   Portent, The.
Patmore, C.   London Fete, A.
Plath.   Hanging Man, The.
Stephens, P.   Hangman.
Swift, J.   Clever Tom Clinch Going to Be
 Hanged.
Unknown.   Geordie [An Old Ballad].
 Night before Larry Was Stretched, The.
 Receipt to Cure a Love Fit, A.
Young, A.   Wet Day, A.
See also **Executions and Executioners; Lynching**
Hangovers
Conway, J.   Hangover.
Pollard, C.   Breakfast Poem.
Sanders P.   Tripoli.
Wright, J.   I Try to Waken and Greet the World
 Once Again.
Hansel and Gretel
Glück, L.   Gretel in Darkness.
Noel-Scott.   Hansel and Gretel.
Hanukkah
Chaikin.   Light Another Candle.
Lazarus, E.   Kindle the Taper.
Happiness
Adamson, H.   It's a Most Unusual Day.
Ager, M.   Happy Days Are Here Again.
Alarcon, F.   Laughing Tomatoes.
Arlen, H.   Happiness Is Just a Thing Called Joe.
 Happy As the Day Is Long.
 I've Got the World on a String.
Atwood.   You Are Happy.
Barris, H.   Wrap Your Troubles in Dreams.
Berger, B.   Ballad of the Bright Angel.
Berlin.   Cheek to Cheek.
 Let Me Sing and I'm Happy.
 Song Is Ended (But the Melody Lingers On),
 The.
Blane, R.   Have Yourself a Merry Little
 Christmas.
Brecht, S.   Thanksgiving (1974).
Brown, L.   Sunny Side Up.
Brown, N.   Singin' in the Rain.
Brown, S.   Schadenfreude.
Butler, S.   Love.
Caesar.   I Want to Be Happy.
 Sometimes I'm Happy.
Carew, T.   Second Rapture, The.
Chasin.   Joy Sonnet in a Random Universe.
Clifton, L.   Good Times.
Comden, B.   Make Someone Happy.
Coslow, S.   (Up on Top of a Rainbow) Sweepin'
 the Clouds Away.
Creeley.   Air: "The Love of a Woman."
 En Famille.
Cummings, E.   You Shall Above All Things Be
 Glad and Young.
Curzon, D.   Proverbs 6:6.
Davies, W.   Example, The.
Delmore, E.   Is It Not Strange?
DeSylva, B. G.   Sunny Side Up.
Doolittle, H.   White World.
Doty, M.   Embrace, The.
Dove, R.   Bistro Styx, The.
 Wiederkehr.
Ebb, F.   Happy Time, The.
 Quiet Thing, A.
Egan, R.   Ain't We Got Fun.
Ellis, V.   Spread a Little Happiness.
Erdrich, H.   Fat in America.
Evans, R.   Haven't Got a Worry.
Farley, W.   Thinking Happiness.
Feinstein, E.   Getting Older.
Ferlinghetti, L.   21.
Fernández.   If You Happy Would Be.
Freed, A.   Singin' in the Rain.
Frost, R.   Happiness Makes Up in Height for
 What It Lacks in Length.
Gershwin.   Long Ago (And Far Away).
 Things Are Looking Up.
Glück, L.   Happiness.
Gordon, M.   You Make Me Feel So Young.
Green, A.   Make Someone Happy.
Grey, C.   Spread a Little Happiness.
Hammerstein.   Happy Talk.
 It Might As Well Be Spring.
Harjo, P.   Wishes.

Hattersley, G.   Singing.
Hayden, R.   Islands, The.
Hazo.   Only the New Branches Bloom.
Heard, J.   Happy Heart, A.
Henderson, R.   Sunny Side Up.
Herrick.   Four[e] Things Make Us Happy Here.
Holmes, O.   Illustration of a Picture.
Hughes, L.   Dream Boogie.
  World War II.
James, P.   Fine and Dandy.
Justice, D.   But That Is Another Story.
Kander, J.   Happy Time, The.
  Quiet Thing, A.
Keble.   Happiness.
Kinnell.   Crying.
Kizer, C.   Afternoon Happiness.
Klee.   Happy One, The.
Koehler, T.   Happy As the Day Is Long.
  I've Got the World on a String.
  Wrap Your Troubles in Dreams.
Landon.   Mask of Gaiety, The.
Larkin, P.   High Windows.
Lawrence, D.   Bat.
Layton.   Birth of Tragedy, The.
Leonard, P.   Happiness.
Levine, M.   Everybody.
Levy, A.   First Extra, The.
Lisick, B.   Pantoumstone for a Dying Breed.
Livingston, J.   Haven't Got a Worry.
Loesser.   If I Were a Bell.
Lovelace, R.   Grasshopper, The.
Marlowe.   Passionate Shepherd To His Love,
  The.
McHugh, J.   It's a Most Unusual Day.
Mhlophe.   Sometimes When It Rains.
Milne, A.   Happiness.
Milton.   L'Allegro.
Moll, B.   Wrap Your Troubles in Dreams.
Montague, J.   Hearth Song.
Nash, O.   Anatomy of Happiness, The.
Oliver, M.   Hummingbird Pauses at the Trumpet
  Vine.
Paman.   On Christmas Day to My Heart.
Poe.   Dreams.
Pollok.   Happiness.
Pomfret, J.   Choice, The.
Pope, A.   Ode on Solitude.
Porter, C.   Ridin' High.
Porter, P.   In the New World Happiness is
  Allowed.
Pound, E.   Salutation.
Ravenscroft, T.   Sing we now merily.
Robinson, E.   Cliff Klingenhagen.
Rodriguez, J.   Eskimo Occasion.
Roethke.   Waking, The.
Rogers, S.   Wish, A.
Rome, H.   Call Me Mister.
Rosenberg, L.   No Boundaries.
Rouse.   Narrows, The.
Sandburg, C.   Happiness.
Shelley, P.   Song: "Rarely, rarely, comest thou."
Shepherd, R.   West Willow.
Shurin.   Saturated.
Silveira.   Different Poem, A.
Smith, C.   Sonnet Written at the Close of Spring
  [or Elegiac Sonnet].
  To the Countess of A—. Written on the
  Anniversary of Her Marriage.
Smith, S.   Conviction IV.
Stevenson, R.   Happy Thought.
Stickney, T.   Athenian Garden, An.
Stitch.   Little Roads to Happiness.
Stroud, J.   Manna.
Swift, K.   Fine and Dandy.
Talpalar.   True Happiness.
Teasdale.   On the South Downs.
Tennyson, F.   Poetical Happiness.
Thomas, E.   Glory, The.
Toyama.   Red.
Unknown.   Minutes of Gold.
West, K.   On Track.
Westmorland.   Happy Life, A.
Whiting, R.   Ain't We Got Fun.
Whitman, W.   Halcyon Days.
  Live Oak, with Moss.
  When I Heard at the Close of the Day.

Woolson.   Florida Beach, The.
Wotton, S.   Character of a Happy Life, The.
  To John Donne.
Wright, J.   Blessing, A.
  Northern Pike.
  Out of Horace.
  Way to Make a Living, A.
Yellen, J.   Happy Days Are Here Again.
Youmans, V.   I Want to Be Happy.
  Sometimes I'm Happy.
See also **Contentment**

Harbors and Ports
Bethell.   Long Harbour, The.
Channing.   Harbor, The.
Chester, T.   Candle at Canterbury, A.
Green, J.   I Cover the Waterfront.
Hardy, T.   Harbour Bridge, The.
O'Hara, F.   Blocks.
Pau-Llosa.   Paredón.
Quiller-Couch.   Harbour of Fowey, The.
Sandburg, C.   Harbor, The.

Harding, Warren Gamaliel
Wright, J.   Two Poems about President Harding.

Hardy, Thomas
Beerbohm, M.   Luncheon, A.
De la Mare.   Scholars.
  Thomas Hardy.
Hall, D.   Hardy's 'Shelley's Skylark.'
Wright, J.   At Thomas Hardy's Birthplace, 1953.

Hares
Clare, J.   Hares at Play.
Clarke, G.   Hare, The.
Cowper, W.   Epitaph on a Hare.
De la Mare.   Hare, A.
Earle, J.   Jugged Hare.
Lear, E.   Limericks, II (v).
MacCaig.   Interruption to a Journey.
Miles, S.   Hares, The.
Nicholson, N.   Cowper's Tame Hare.
Smart, C.   To the Rev. Mr. Powell.
Unknown.   Riddle: "Hopper o'ditches, A."
Yeats.   Two Songs of a Fool.
Young, A.   March Hares.
See also **Rabbits**

Harlem, New York City
Asim, J.   Harlem Haiku: A Scrapbook.
Baraka.   Return of the Native.
Beatty, P.   Independent Study.
Berlin.   Puttin' on the Ritz (Original Version).
Bethune, L.   Harlem Freeze Frame.
Bloom, R.   Truckin'
Cortez, J.   Under the Edge of February.
Dana, R.   Elegy for the Duke.
Davis, T.   Zoom (The Commodores).
Espada.   Dándole la mano a Mongo.
  Shaking Hands with Mongo.
Fields, D.   Bojangles of Harlem.
Goodman, B.   Stompin' at the Savoy.
Hughes, L.   College Formal: Renaissance
  Casino.
  Dive.
  Esthete in Harlem.
  Harlem Sweeties.
  Jazzonia.
  Juke Box Love Song.
  Neighbor.
  Night Funeral in Harlem.
  Passing.
  Projection.
  Subway Face.
  Theme for English B.
  Visitors to the Black Belt.
  Weary Blues, The.
Johnson, H.   Sonnet to a Negro in Harlem.
Kern, J.   Bojangles of Harlem.
Koehler, T.   Truckin'
McKay, C.   Harlem Dancer, The.
  Harlem Shadows.
Morales, A.   Other Heritage, The.
Neal, L.   Harlem Gallery: From the Inside.
Powell, K.   Harlem: Neo-Image.
Razaf, A.   Stompin' at the Savoy.
Rukeyser, M.   Ballad of Orange and Grape.
Sampson, E.   Stompin' at the Savoy.
Senghor.   To New York.

Tolson, M.   African China.
Webb, C.   Stompin' at the Savoy.

Harper's Ferry, West Virginia
Atkins.   Narrative.
Williams, E.   At Harper's Ferry Just Before the
  Attack.

Harps and Harpists
Cook, E.   'Tis Well to Wake the Theme of Love.
"Fane, V."   Siren, The.
Melville, H.   Aeolian Harp, The.
Moore, T.   Dear Harp of My Country.
  Harp That Once through Tara's Halls, The.
  Minstrel Boy, The.
Pitter.   Military Harpist, The.
Po Chü-i.   Harp, The.
Soniat.   Harp/Desire.

Harrison, Benjamin
Hollander, J.   Historical Reflections.

Harvard University
Eberhart, R.   I Went to See Irving Babbitt.
Symons, J.   Harvard.
Wheatley, P.   To the University of Cambridge, in
  New-England.

Harvest
Akers, E.   Bringing Our Sheaves with Us.
Alford, H.   Harvest Home.
Anyidoho.   Hero and Thief.
Atwood.   November.
Auden.   As I Walked Out One Evening.
Beaver.   Silo Treading.
Blind.   Reapers.
Brock-Broido.   Of the Finished World.
Carlyle, T.   Sower's Song, The.
Carruth, H.   Emergency Haying.
Cary, P.   Harvest Gathering.
De la Mare.   Scarecrow, The.
Fallon, P.   Meadow, The.
Fitzgerald, E.   73.
Glück, L.   All Hallows.
Herrick.   Hock-Cart, or Harvest Home, The.
Hood, T.   Ruth.
Hope, A.   Hay Fever.
Hopkins, G.   Hurrahing in Harvest.
Lawrence, D.   Youth Mowing, A.
Longfellow, H.   Aftermath.
Matherne, B.   La Fabrique de Tabac (Tobacco
  Harvest).
Meynell, A.   Threshing Machine, The.
Prunty.   Vegetable Garden, The.
Read, T.   Summer Shower, The.
Roberts, S.   Potato Harvest, The.
Roscoe, W.   To the Harvest Moon.
Rossetti, C.   Amen.
Schwartz, R. L.   Late Summer.
Soyinka.   Harvest of Hate.
Toomer.   Harvest Song.
  Reapers.
Trowbridge, J.   Idyl of Harvest Time, An.
Unknown.   Harvest Song.
Wilde, O.   Vita Nuova.
Wordsworth, W.   Solitary Reaper, The.

Hashish
Whittier.   Haschish, The.

Hate
Amichai [or Amikhai].   Quick And Bitter.
Baraka.   Agony, An. As Now.
  Poem Some People Will Have to Understand, A.
Bennett, G.   Hatred.
Browning, R.   Soliloquy of the Spanish Cloister.
Bruner.   Retaliation.
Campbell, S.   Constant Welcome, The.
Chesterton, G.   World State, The.
Creeley.   Self-Portrait.
Dickey, W.   Cassandra.
Domina, L.   Pharoah's Army Got Drowned.
Ehrmann.   Hate and the Love of the World, The.
"Ephelia."   To One That Asked Me Why I
  Loved J.G G.
"Field."   As two fair vessels side by side.
Frost, R.   Beyond Words.
  Fire and Ice.
Glaser, I.   Last Good War—and Afterward, The.
Griffiths, B.   For P—Celtic: found text from
  Machen.
Hachenburg, H.   Terezin.

Harjo, J.   Transformations.
Herbert, E.   Ditty: "Why dost thou hate return instead of love."
Hope, A.   Fafnir.
Housman, A.   When I Watch the Living Meet.
Jonson, B.   Little Shrub Growing By, A.
Kaufman, S.   Mothers, Daughters.
Kees.   For My Daughter.
Kombem.   Another Moment.
Konie, G.   In the Fist of Your Hatred.
Lawrence, D.   Eloi, Eloi, Lama Sabachthani? History.
Lowry, M.   Wild Cherry, The.
MacNeice.   Belfast.
McElroy, C.   Illusion.
McKay, C.   Enslaved. White House, The.
O'Hara, F.   Poem: "Hate is only one of many responses."
Ostriker.   Lamenting the Inevitable.
Piatt, S.   Pique at Parting, A.
Piercy.   Letter to be Disguised as a Gas Bill.
Plath.   Daddy.
Plotnick, H. M.   Jewish.
Prelutsky.   Homework! Oh, Homework!
Ryan, G.   If I Had a Gun.
Schafer.   Battle Lines.
Sepamla.   Odyssey, The.
Shelley, P.   Hate-Song, A.
Shore.   High Holy Days.
Soyinka.   Harvest of Hate.
Stephens, J.   Hate.
Suckling, S.   Barley-Break , A.
Unknown.   'Tis a Little Journey. Edward [or Edward, Edward].
Wickham.   Paradox.
Wildman, E.   Cure, The.
Wyatt, S.   Varium et Mutabile.
Wylie.   Full Moon.

Hats
Adams, C.   My Infundibuliform Hat.
Akst, H.   Straw Hat in the Rain.
Berlin.   Easter Parade.
Bishop, E.   Exchanging Hats. Manuelzinho.
Brown, L.   Straw Hat in the Rain.
Burns, R.   To a Louse [On Seeing One on a Lady's Bonnet at Church].
Cleage.   Confession.
Cofer, J.   My Grandfather's Hat.
Cook, E.   My Old Straw Hat.
Durcan.   Hat Factory, The.
Foster, A.   Nest of Hats, A.
Garcia, R.   Dangerous Hats.
Harper, M.   Bandstand.
Johnson, S.   Ballad: "I put my hat upon my head."
Kyger.   Philip Whalen's Hat.
Lane, B.   I Left My Hat in Haiti.
Layne, M.   On Hats and Things.
Lear, E.   Limerick: "There was an Old Man who supposed." Quangle Wangle's Hat, The.
Lerner, A.   I Left My Hat in Haiti.
Little, L.   My Yellow Straw Hat.
Moss, S.   Exchange of Hats, An.
Parnell, P.   Sheila the Hat.
Pastan.   Hat Lady, The.
Pedrick.   Hats.
Probyn.   Frustrated.
Smith, S.   Magna Est Veritas. My Hat.
Stafford, W.   One of the Years.
Thompson, C.   Easter Bonnet, The.
Travis, N.   Church Ladies.

Haunted Houses
Bontemps.   Southern Mansion.
Causley.   Colonel Fazackerley.
De la Mare.   Feckless Dinner-Party, The.
Donne.   Apparition, The.
Edwards [or Edwardes], R.   Recollections of an Old Spook.
Longfellow, H.   Haunted Houses.
Nesbit, E.   Haunted.

Havana, Cuba
Blanco, R.   Last Night in Havana.

Castillo, S.   En el Sol de Mi Barrio.
Komunyakaa.   Boxing Day.
Pau-Llosa.   Paredón.

Hawaii
Birney.   Twenty-third Flight.
Blanding.   Aloha Oe.
Dean, D. K.   In the Way Back.
Hahn, K.   Hula Skirt, 1959, The.
Hernández Cruz.   Borinkins in Hawaii.
Lili'u-o-ka-lani.   Aloha'oe.

Hawks
Axelrod, D.   Guide to Urban Birds, A.
Blackburn, P.   Net of Place, The.
Blue Cloud.   Hawk Nailed to a Barn Door.
Brouwer, J.   Conservatory Pond, Central Park, New York, New York.
Brown, G.   Hawk, The.
Corey, S.   Complicated Shadows.
Flanner.   Hawk Is a Woman.
Gerner, K.   Prey.
Gunn, T.   Tamer and Hawk.
Hopkins, G.   Windhover, The.
Hughes, T.   Hawk Roosting.
Jeffers, R.   Hurt Hawks. Rock and Hawk.
Jonson, B.   To Sir Henry Goodyere.
"Malley."   Sonnets for the Novachord.
Melville, H.   Man-of-War Hawk, The.
Oliver, M.   Hawk.
Ortiz.   Earth and Rain, the Plants & Sun.
Palmer, H.   Wounded Hawk, The.
Thomas, D.   Over Sir John's Hill.
Townsend, A.   After the End.
Unknown.   Sparrow-Hawk, A.
Warren, R.   Evening Hawk.
Wheelock, J.   Fish-Hawk, The.

Hawthorn (botany)
Bidgood.   Hawthorn at Digiff.
Brown, T.   I Bended unto Me.
Heaney, S.   Haw Lantern, The.
Unknown.   Hawthorn, The.
Wright, J.   Hawthorn Hedge, The.

Hawthorne, Nathaniel
Fogle.   Hawthorne Garland, A.
Melville, H.   Monody.
Noguere.   Secret, The.
Very.   On Visiting the Graves of Hawthorne and Thoreau.

Hay and Haymaking
Clampitt.   Stacking the Straw.
Clarke, G.   Hay-Making.
Hodgins.   Making Hay.
Steele, T.   Timothy.

Haydn, Franz Joseph
Ghigna.   Lesson of Night, A.
Holcroft.   To Haydn.

Haydon, Benjamin Robert
Browning, E.   On a Portrait of Wordsworth by B. R. Haydon.
Keats.   Great Spirits Now on Earth. To B.R. Haydon, with a Sonnet Written on Seeing the Elgin Marbles.

Hayworth, Rita
Herd.   Bombshell.

Haze
Henley, W.   At Queensferry.
See also Fog

Hazlitt, William
Coleridge, S.   W. H. Eheu!
Guiney.   W. H.

Heads
Bradstreet, A.   Letter to Her Husband, Absent upon Public[k] Employment, A.
Carnevali.   Queer Things.
Carter, E.   Dialogue, A.
Conquest.   Agents, The.
Davidson, M.   Troth.
Di Cicco.   Head Is a Paltry Matter, The.
Forbes, J.   Four Heads & How to Do Them.
Gorey.   Limerick.
Jackson, H.   Ding-Donging.
Johnson, S.   Ballad: "I put my hat upon my head."
Knoepfle.   Harpe's Head.
Major, C.   Balance and Beauty.

Mandelstam [or Mandelshtam].   Mounds of Human Heads Are Wandering into the Distance.
Meredith, W.   Thoughts on One's Head.
Nokan.   My Head is Immense.
Pope, A.   Another [Epigram].
Schuyler, J.   Head, A.
Skelton, J.   Upon a Dead Man's Head.
Sparrow, J.   To an Angel in the House.
Webb, H.   Stone Face, The.
Wieners.   Glimpse, A.

Healing
Back, R.   Abu Salim, Healer.
Broumas, O.   Etymolgy.
Chester, T.   Buttons.
Goodison.   Heartease 3. Jah Music.
Larkin, J.   Good-Bye.
Mead, J.   However.
Stone, A.   Spofford Hall.
Unknown.   May Isis Heal Me.
Walker, A.   Remember?

Health Clubs
Hillman.   Y, The.
Rouse.   Uni-Gym, The.

Heaney, Seamus
Williamson, G.   Bodies of Water.

Hearne, Samuel
Newlove.   Samuel Hearne in Wintertime.

Hearst, William Randolph
Taylor, B.   Doxology.

Hearts
Alvarez, J.   Woman's Work.
Arlen, H.   If I Only Had a Brain (If I Only Had a Heart) (If I Only Had the Nerve).
Atwood.   Woman Who Could Not Live With Her Faulty Heart, The.
Bang, M.   Louise in Love.
Binyon.   Harebell and Pansy.
Blanvillain, J.   (All of a Sudden) My Heart Sings.
Bogan, L.   Song for the Last Act.
Bourdillon.   Night Has a Thousand Eyes, The.
Breton, A.   Poem-Object.
Browning, E.   My Heart and I. To George Sand: A Recognition.
Browning, R.   Meeting At Night.
Burke, J.   My Heart Is a Hobo.
Burns, R.   My Heart's in the Highlands.
Bynner.   Wintry Mind, The.
Campo.   Aunt Toni's Heart.
Carbó, N.   Robo.
Cisneros, S.   Heart, My Lovely Hobo.
Clare, J.   First Love.
Clark, T.   Superballs.
Clough.   In Stratis Viarum IV.
Coleridge, M.   Broken Friendship. Only a little shall we speak of thee.
Cope, W.   Valentine.
Couzyn.   Heartsong.
Crashaw.   Flaming Heart, The. To the Noblest and Best of Ladies, the Countess of Denbigh. Upon the Book and Picture of the Seraphical Saint Teresa.
Cunningham, J.   To My Wife.
Davis, T.   Playing Solitaire.
Dickinson, E.   Heart asks Pleasure—First, The.
Dietz, H.   Haunted Heart.
Digby, J.   One Night Away from Day.
Donne.   Blossom [or Blossome], The. Broken Heart, The. Message, The.
Dooley, M.   Heart.
Drayton.   Crier, The. Heart, The.
Engvick, W.   Crazy in the Heart.
"Field."   Love rises up some days. Sometimes I Do Despatch My Heart. Unbosoming.
Freed, A.   This Heart of Mine.
Frost, R.   Dust of Snow.
Garrett, E.   Mimesis.
Gilbert, J.   Getting Ready.
Gordon, M.   Meet the Beat of My Heart.

Gylys, B.   Balloon Heart.
Fat Chance.
Hanley, J.   Zing! Went the Strings of My Heart.
Hannah, S.   Where is Talcott Parsons Now?
Hardy, T.   In a Cathedral City.
Hart, L.   My Heart Stood Still.
Nobody's Heart.
With a Song in My Heart.
Hemans.   Stranger's Heart, The.
Herbert, G.   Altar, The.
Herrick.   To Oenone.
Hikmet.   Angina Pectoris.
Hope, A.   Gateway, The.
Wandering Islands, The.
Hopkins, G.   My Own Heart Let Me More Have Pity On.
Jewsbury.   My heart's in the kitchen, my heart is not here.
To My Own Heart.
Johnson, G.   Heart of a Woman, The.
Kasischke.   My Heart.
Kaufman, S.   Emperor of China, The.
King, H.   Sonnet: "Tell me[e] no more how fair[e] she[e] is."
Kunitz, S.   Touch Me.
Lee, W.   Sex Has a Way.
Leigh, C.   Young at Heart.
Lovelace, R.   To Lucasta.
Lowell, R.   Colloquy in Black Rock.
Mayes, J.   Descant.
McCallum, S.   Perfect Heart, The.
Mew.   I Have Been Through the Gates.
Mignon, A.   One Heart's Enough for Me.
Nelson, J.   Our Love.
Ossip, K.   Nature of Things, The.
Paschen.   Confederacy.
Pelizzon, V.   Late Apostasy, A.
Philips, K.   Friendship in Emblem[e], or the Seal[e], to my Dearest Lucasia.
Friendship's Mystery[s], to My Dearest Lucasia.
Poulin.   Red Clock.
Prior.   Les Estreines.
Receveur.   Eagle in the Land of Oz.
Revel, H.   Meet the Beat of My Heart.
Richards, J.   Young at Heart.
Richardson, K.   Aubade: "Geese flew by as you entered me, The."
Roberts, K.   Postcard from the Coast.
Rodgers, C.   Black Heart as Ever Green, The.
Rodgers, R.   My Heart Stood Still.
Nobody's Heart.
With a Song in My Heart.
Rome, H.   (All of a Sudden) My Heart Sings.
Rossetti, C.   Birthday, A.
Twice.
Schwartz, A.   Haunted Heart.
Shelley, P.   From the Arabic: An Imitation.
Lines: "When the lamp is shattered [or shatter'd]."
Sitwell, D.   Heart and Mind.
Sorby.   Man without a Middle, The.
Spires.   Robed Heart, The.
Sundiata.   Open Heart.
Sylvester, J.   "Were I as Base as Is the Lowly Plain."
Teasdale.   Shrine, The.
Thomas, D.   When All My Five and Country Senses See.
Thomas, R.   Lonely Farmer, The.
Tipton.   I Wanted You in the Kitchen of My Heart.
Unknown.   See! Here, My Heart.
Thy Heart.
Woman's Love.
Unknown, fr. Terezin Concentration Camp.
Birdsong.
Van Heusen, J.   My Heart Is a Hobo.
Warren, J.   This Heart of Mine.
Warren, R.   Debate: Question, Quarry, Dream.
Washington, N.   Give Me a Heart to Sing To.
My Foolish Heart.
Watson, R.   Cage, The.
Wilder, A.   Crazy in the Heart.
Williams, S.   Youth and Maidenhood.
Wright, J.   At Thomas Hardy's Birthplace, 1953.
Jewel, The.

Yeats.   Never Give All the Heart.
Young, V.   Give Me a Heart to Sing To.
My Foolish Heart.

Heat
Barnes, B.   Something Cool.
Berlin.   Heat Wave.
I've Got My Love to Keep Me Warm.
Bernard, A.   Praise Psalm of the City-Dweller.
Biespiel, D.   Heat Sours, The.
Brown, L.   Turn On the Heat.
Bryant, W.   Midsummer.
DeSylva, B. G.   Turn On the Heat.
Dickey, J.   Basics.
Dooley, M.   Heat.
Eigner.   It Sounded.
Graves, R.   Cool Web, The.
Hampton.   In Andrea's Garden.
Hass, R.   Late Spring.
Henderson, R.   Turn On the Heat.
Jacobsen, J.   Shade-Seller, The.
Johnson, D.   Heat.
Kusano Shimpei.   4 or 5 Tadpoles.
Lampman.   Heat.
Loftin.   Weeksville Women.
Luschei, G.   Arrangement.
Mackenzie, K.   Heat.
Markus, P.   Black Light.
McDonald, W.   Last Still Days in a Bunker, The.
McIlroy, L.   Siesta.
Myles, E.   Milk.
Oden.   Riven Quarry, The.
Porter, C.   Too Darn Hot.
Powell, J.   It Was Fever That Made the World.
Rabinowitz.   Of Joy Illimited: Polyphonic Soundings: Shore to Ship.
Scott, D.   Church Boiler, The.
Shurin.   Saturated.
Tomlinson, C.   Las Trampas U. S. A.
Unknown.   Hot Day In Sydney, A.
Vando.   Ode to Your Back.
Walcott.   Midsummer, Tobago.
Warren, R.   Rattlesnake Country.

Heather
Bethell.   Erica.
Lerner, A.   Heather on the Hill, The.

Heaven
Abelard.   Hymn for the Close of the Week.
Agee.   Description of Elysium.
Bailey, P.   What Is Heaven?
Baraka.   Dope.
Berlin.   Cheek to Cheek.
Binney.   Eternal Light!
Bishop, E.   Seascape.
Blake, W.   Marriage of Heaven and Hell, The.
Memorable Fancy, A.
Pride of the Peacock, The.
Song of Liberty, A.
Bowers, E.   Adam's Song to Heaven.
Bradstreet, A.   As Weary Pilgrim, Now at Rest.
Brontë, E.   No Coward Soul is Mine.
Stanzas: "Often rebuked, yet always back returning."
Brooke, R.   Heaven.
Brown, S.   Sister Lou.
Burris.   On Living with a Fat Woman in Heaven.
Campion, T.   O Come Quickly!
Cary, P.   Nearer Home.
Cavendish, W.   Love's Sun.
Clare, J.   Vision, A.
Coleridge, M.   Friends—With a Difference.
Impromptu.
Coleridge, S.   Kubla Khan: or, A Vision in a Dream.
Cranch.   Spirit of the Age, The.
Crashaw.   I Am the Door [*or* Doore].
To the Infant Martyrs.
Upon the Infant Martyrs.
Crosby, F.   We Are Going.
Davie.   Jacob's Ladder.
DeSylva, B. G.   Stairway to Paradise.
Dickey, J.   Heaven of Animals, The.
Dickinson, E.   God's Residence.
My Life Closed Twice.

Disch.   Garage Sale as a Spiritual Exercise, The.
Doddridge, P.   Hymn: "Ye golden lamps of heaven, farewell."
Meditations on the Sepulchre in the Garden.
Dolben.   He Would Have His Lady Sing.
Donaldson, W.   My Blue Heaven.
Donne.   Hymn to the Saints, and to Marquis Hamilton[, An].
To Mr. Tilman after He Had Taken Orders.
Dryden, J.   Song for St Cecilia's Day, 1687, A.
Dunbar, P.   Theology.
Dunbar, W.   Amendis to the Telyouris and Sowtaris for the Turnament Maid on Thame, The.
Emerson, R.   Spiritual Laws.
Francis, A.   Stairway to Paradise.
Goethe.   Mignon Aspiring to Heaven.
Hall, D.   Sister on the Tracks, A.
Hartnett.   Wounded Otter, The.
Herbert, G.   Church Lock-and-Key.
Heaven.
Obedience.
Star[re], The.
Herrick.   Comfort to a Youth That Had Lost His Love.
His Creed.
To Heaven.
To His Ever-Loving God.
White Island.
Hopkins, G.   Handsome Heart, The.
Heaven-Haven.
Housman, A.   Easter Hymn.
Mark 16:19–20; So then the Lord Jesus, after.
Howard, R.   Giovanni da Fiesole on the Sublime.
Hudgins.   Elegy for My Father, Who Is Not Dead.
Hughes, L.   Heaven, Heaven, Heaven Is the Place.
Hughes, T.   River.
Ingelow.   Divided.
Jewsbury.   To My Own Heart.
Johnson, F.   My God in Heaven Said to Me.
Singing Hallelujia.
Johnson, S.   Scholar's Life, The.
Vanity of Human Wishes, The; The Tenth Satire of Juvenal Imitated.
Jonson, B.   Pleasures of Heaven, The.
To Heaven.
Kaufman, B.   Untitled.
Kavanagh, P.   Sanctity.
Keats.   Ode: "Bards of passion and of mirth."
Kendall, M.   Legend of the Crossing-Sweeper.
Kennedy, X.   Nothing in Heaven Functions as It Ought.
Knott.   Hair Poem.
Lang, A.   Tired of Towns.
Lasker-Schüler.   Chronica.
Levine, P.   Heaven.
Lindsay, N.   General William Booth Enters into Heaven.
Loesser.   Sit Down, You're Rockin' the Boat.
Lovelace, R.   Falcon, The.
To My Noble Kinsman, Thomas Stanley, Esquire, on His Lyric Poems Composed by Master John Gamble.
Lowry, R.   Beautiful River.
MacDiarmid, H.   Prayer for a Second Flood.
Masefield.   Port of Many Ships.
Melville, H.   Spirit Appeared to Me, A.
Milton.   Adam and Eve.
Adam and Eve Led Out of Paradise.
Adam Describes His Own Creation and That of Eve; Having Repeated His Warning, the Angel Departs.
Adam Fallen.
Adam Unfallen.
Ascent of Species.
Creation.
Eden.
Eve to Adam.
Evening in Paradise.
Expulsion from Eden, The.
Flood, The.

Hail, Holy Light[!].
Immortal Hate.
Invocation to Urania.
March of the Rebel Angels.
Mulciber.
Occupations of Hell.
Paradise.
Paradise Lost.
Prospect of Eden, The.
Raphael's Descent.
Retreat from Paradise, The.
Satan's Journey.
Serpent Finds Eve Alone, The.
Sin and Death.
Temptation of Eve, The.
Tempter Disarmed, The.
Uncloistered Virtue.
What Words Have Passed.
Montgomerie, A. Royall Palice of the Heichest Hewin, The.
Moore, T. This World Is All a Fleeting Show.
Morley, D. Enniskillen.
Nairne. Land o' the Leal, The.
Nemerov. Backward Look, The.
Newton, J. Glorious Things of Thee Are Spoken.
Oliver, M. Roses, Late Summer.
Patchen. Naked Land, The.
Phillips, C. Sunday.
Plath. Sheep in Fog.
Polak, J. Storm, The.
Pope, A. Universal Prayer [Deo Opt. Max.], The.
Procter, A. Lost Chord, A.
Philip and Mildred.
Quarles. On a Feast.
Raffalovich, M. A. World Well Lost 18, The.
Ralegh, S. Passionate Man[']s Pilgrimage, The.
Roberts, G. Night Sky, The.
Robinson, E. Credo.
Supremacy.
Rohrer, M. Hummock in the Malookas, A.
Rossetti, C. Convent Threshold, The.
Gone Before.
Heaviness May Endure for a Night, But Joy Cometh in the Morning.
Marvel of Marvels.
Pause, A.
Two Thoughts of Death.
Uphill.
Rossetti, D. Blessed Damozel, The.
Sanders, E. Leaves of Heaven, The.
Serote. Hell, Well, Heaven.
Shelley, P. To———: "One word is too often profaned."
Sigourney. Stars, The.
Smith, P. Annie Pearl Smith Discovers Moonlight.
Smith, S. Heavenly City, The.
Smith, W. Pavane for the Nursery, A.
Snodgrass, W. Monet: 'Les Nymphéas.'
Song. Heaven.
Southey, C. Mariner's Hymn.
Southwell. At Home in Heaven.
New Heaven, New War[re].
Seek[e] Flowers of Heaven.
Southwick. Earthly Light.
Spofford. Tryst, The.
Stevens, W. Waving Adieu, Adieu, Adieu.
Sylvester, J. "Were I as Base as Is the Lowly Plain."
Traherne. Bible, The.
Innocence.
Unknown. Beulah Railway, The.
City Called Heaven.
Elegy upon the Death of Mrs. A. Behn, the Incomparable Astrea, An.
Good Lord in That Heaven.
I Got a Home in Dat Rock.
Jerusalem, My Happy Home.
Poet Dreamt of Heaven, The.
Swing Low, Sweet Chariot.
Walk Together Children.
Unknown, fr. Terezin Concentration Camp. On a Sunny Evening.

Van Dyke. Four Things.
Vaughan, H. Peace.
Pilgrimage, The.
Resolve, The.
Sap, The.
They Are All Gone into the World of Light!
Very. Birds of Passage, The.
Forevermore.
Waller, E. Of the Last Verses in the Book.
Washburn, H. Almighty God, Thy Constant Care.
Watts, I. Heaven.
Psalm 58.
Yeats. He Wishes for the Cloths of Heaven.
Young, A. Written in Bracing, Gray L.A.
Rainlight.
Zimmer. Zimmer Imagines Heaven.
Zucker, R. In Your Version of Heaven I Am Younger.

Hebrew
Moore, M. Past Is the Present, The.
Reznikoff. Hebrew of Your Poets, Zion, The.

Hebrides
Longley, M. Hebrides, The.
Pfeiffer, E. Among the Hebrides.

Hector
Iremonger. Hector.
Muir, E. Ballad of Hector in Hades.

Hedgehogs
Muldoon, P. Hedgehog.
Thompson, S. To a Hedgehog.

Hedonism
Cummings, E. Since feeling is first.
Melville, H. After the Pleasure Party.
San Juan. Entelechy on the Libidinal Fringe.
Three for the Road.
Weaver, M. Providence Journal V: Israel of Puerto Rico.

Heine, Heinrich
Lazarus, E. Venus of the Louvre.
Lewisohn, L. Heinrich Heine.
Pound, E. Translator to Translated.

Helen of Troy
Crane, H. For the Marriage of Faustus and Helen.
Doolittle, H. Helen.
Jackson, L. Helen's Burning.
Lewis, J. Helen Grown Old.
Poe. To Helen.
Read, S. White Isle of Leuce, The.
Waller, E. Under a Lady's Picture.
Wilbur. Voice from under the Table, A.
Yeats. Leda and the Swan.

Helicopters
Hume, C. Helicopter Wrecked on a Hill.
Mishler. Ceremony.

Heliogabalus
Hollander, J. Heliogabalus.

Hell
Baraka. I don't love you.
Barry, J. Green Hell, Green Death.
Bayliss. Apocalypse and Resurrection.
Belloc. Ballade of Hell and of Mrs. Roebeck.
To Dives.
Berlin. Pack Up Your Sins and Go to the Devil.
Blake, W. Marriage of Heaven and Hell, The.
Memorable Fancy, A.
Pride of the Peacock, The.
Song of Liberty, A.
Boland, E. Pomegranate, The.
Brontë, E. Stanzas: "Often rebuked, yet always back returning."
Burns, R. Kellyburnbraes.
Coleridge, M. Wilderspin.
Cowley, H. Invocation. To Horror.
Crashaw. But Men loved Darkness[e] Rather Than [or Then] Light.
Dickinson, E. My Life Closed Twice.
Dove, R. Political.
Doyle, S. Hell To Pay.
Dunbar, P. Theology.
Elizabeth, Queen of Bohemia. Verses by the Princess Elizabeth, Given to Lord Harington, of Exton, Her Preceptor.

Ford, F. That Exploit of Yours.
Glück, L. Day Without Night.
Graves, R. Sharp Ridge, The.
Gray, T. Descent of Odin, The.
Greenwell, D. Demeter and Cora.
Greer, J. Rodin's "Gates of Hell."
Herrick. Barley-Break; or, Last in Hell.
Hell.
Hill, G. Ovid in the Third Reich.
Housman, A. Hell Gate.
Howard, R. Giovanni da Fiesole on the Sublime.
Kelen. First Circle, The.
Kennedy, X. Nothing in Heaven Functions as It Ought.
Kimbrell, J. True Descenders.
Lister, R. Lament of an Idle Demon.
Mandel, T. Jews in Hell.
Marquis. Tom-Cat, The.
Milton. Adam and Eve.
Adam and Eve Led Out of Paradise.
Adam Describes His Own Creation and That of Eve; Having Repeated His Warning, the Angel Departs.
Adam Fallen.
Adam Unfallen.
Ascent of Species.
Creation.
Eden.
Eve to Adam.
Evening in Paradise.
Expulsion from Eden, The.
Flood, The.
Hail, Holy Light[!].
Immortal Hate.
Invocation to Urania.
March of the Rebel Angels.
Mulciber.
Occupations of Hell.
Paradise.
Paradise Lost.
Prospect of Eden, The.
Raphael's Descent.
Retreat from Paradise, The.
Satan's Journey.
Serpent Finds Eve Alone, The.
Sin and Death.
Temptation of Eve, The.
Tempter Disarmed, The.
Uncloistered Virtue.
What Words Have Passed.
Muir, E. Good Man in Hell, The.
Naden. Pessimist's Vision, The.
Nesbit, E. Great Industrial Centre, A.
Olson, C. In Cold Hell, in Thicket.
Orr, G. Insomnia Song.
Owen, W. Strange Meeting.
Putnam. Bill Gets Burned.
Rich, A. Lucifer in the Train.
Robinson, E. Supremacy.
Södergran. Hell.
Serote. Hell, Well, Heaven.
Simic. Fork.
Tate, A. Cross, The.
Thompson, F. To the Dead Cardinal of Westminster.
Unknown. Dere's No Hidin' Place Down Dere.
Stackolee.
Williams, W. Paterson, Book 5: The River of Heaven.
Winters, Y. Summer Noon: 1941.

Hell's Angels
Gunn, T. Black Jackets.

Help
Dickinson, E. These Strangers, In a Foreign World.
Dorsey, T. Take My Hand, Precious Lord.
Fitzgerald, E. 72.
Gallagher, T. Little Invitation in a Hushed Voice.
Graves, R. Grotesques.
Grosholz. Eden.
Turner, C. Julius Caesar and the Honey-Bee.

Hemingway, Ernest
  Espada. Man Who Beat Hemingway, The.
  Updike. Meditation on a News Item.
Hemlocks
  Ammons, A. R. Bonus.
    Improvisatin for Jerald Bullis, An.
  Stevenson, A. Hemlock at Sunset, A.
  Weismiller. Hemlocks in Autumn.
Henry I, King of England
  Lee-Hamilton. Henry I to the Sea.
  Rossetti, D. White Ship, The.
Henry II, King of England
  Unknown. Queen Eleanor's Confession.
Henry V, King of England
  Unknown. King Henry Fifth's Conquest of
    France.
Henry VIII, King of England
  Harington [*or* Harrington]. Groome of the
    Chambers religion in King Henry the eights
    time, A.
Hens
  Caston, A. Blowing Eggs.
  Clare, J. Hen's Nest.
  Gehrke, S. Walking Fields at Night South of
    Hampton, Iowa.
  Jacobik, G. Turkeys in August.
  Kinnell. Hen Flower, The.
  Magowan. Zeimbekiko.
  McGonagall. Hen It Is a Noble Beast, The.
  Mother Goose. Black Hen, The.
    Hickety, Pickety, My Black Hen.
  Pitter. Hen under Bay-Tree.
  Ransom, J. Janet Waking.
  Roberts, E. Hens, The.
  Unknown. Clever Hen, The.
  Wilbur. Black November Turkey, A.
  Willard, N. Speckled Hen's Morning Song to
    Biddy Early, The.
See also **Chickens**
Heraclitus
  Cory, W. Heraclitus.
  Fore. They Told Me, Heraclitus.
  Hopkins, G. That Nature Is a Heraclitean Fire
    and of the Comfort of the Resurrection.
  MacNeice. Variation on Heraclitus.
Herbs
  Duncan, R. Glimpse, A.
  Emerson, R. Blight.
  Goodison. From the Garden of the Women
    Once Fallen.
  Hufana, A. From the Raw.
  Jacobs, J. Snakeroot.
  Lindley, D. Fennel.
  Rafferty, P. Willowherb.
  Rohrer, M. Short History of Illumination, A.
  Sisson. Herb-Garden, The.
  Thomas, E. Old Man.
Hercules
  Rogers, S. To the Fragment of a Statue of
    Hercules, Commonly Called the Torso.
Herding
  Joyce, J. Tilly.
See also **Shepherds and Shepherdesses**
Heresy and Heretics
  Kendall, M. Fossil, A.
Heritage and Heredity
  Alvi, M. Backgrounds.
  Behar, R. Survivals.
  Cariaga. Family Tree, The.
  Cisneros, S. You Bring Out the Mexican in Me.
  Cooper, A. Stepping to da Muse/Sic.
  Fisher, L. Child of the Sun.
  Kay, J. Pride.
  Larkin, J. Legacy.
  Limburg, J. Seder Night with My Ancestors.
  Morales. Ending Poem.
  Morales, A. Other Heritage, The.
  Penn, M. Calling Up the Spirit of the Lost
    Child.
  Piñero. This Is Not the Place Where I Was
    Born.
  Preston, R. Italist Chant.
  Savageau. Like the Trails of Ndakinna.
    To Human Skin.

  Schwartz, R. L. Flamenco Guitar.
  Song. Spaces We Leave Empty.
  St. Germain, S. Cajun.
  Thomas, R. Gifts.
Hermits
  Bibb. Hermit, The.
  Birney. Bushed.
  Davies, W. Hermit, The.
  Kinnell. When One Has Lived a Long Time
    Alone.
  Lowell, R. Skunk Hour.
  Matthews, T. Private But Sulphurous.
  Ní Chuilleanáin. Studying the Language.
  Ray, H. Hermit and the Soul, The.
  Stevenson, A. He Who Loved Beauty.
  Unknown. Hermit Marbán, The.
  Walcott. Winding Up.
  Whalen. Further Notice.
Hero and Leander
  Byron, G. Written After Swimming from Sestos
    to Abydos.
  Donne. Hero and Leander.
  Warton, T. On Leander's Swimming over the
    Hellespont to Hero.
Herod the Great
  Causley. Innocent's Song.
  Longfellow, H. Three Kings, The.
  Witting. Curse on Herod, A.
  Wylie. Twelfth Night.
Heroes and Heroines
  Adkins, G. Arthur.
  Anstett. Man Saves Own Life.
  Arnold, M. To the Hungarian Nation.
  Auden. O What Is That Sound [Which So
    Thrills the Ear].
  Benjamin, P. Press On.
  Bentley, N. Iron Man of the Hoh.
  Bishop, M. Who'd Be a Hero (Fictional)?
  Campbell, T. Hohenlinden.
  Campo. Superman Is Dead.
  Clifton, L. Note, Passed to Superman.
  Collins, W. How Sleep the Brave.
  Comfort, A. Song for the Heroes.
  Creeley. Heroes.
  Cummings, E. My Father Moved Through
    Dooms of Love.
  De la Mare. Peace.
  De Tabley. Sonnet: "Record is nothing, and the
    hero great."
  "Dylan." Quinn the Eskimo.
  Emerson, R. Forerunners.
  Encarnacion. Threading the Miles.
  Fishman, C. Not Only in the Six-Day War.
  Gunn, T. Byrnies, The.
  Heóghusa. Winter Campaign, A.
  Heaney, S. Beowulf.
  Hemans. Casabianca.
  Joseph, A. My Father's Heroes.
  Keats. To Kosciusko.
  Kefala. Party, The.
  Layne, M. Beautiful Ladies.
  Longfellow, H. Skeleton in Armor [*or* Armour],
    The.
  Lowell, R. For the Union Dead.
  Machan. No, Superman Was Not the Only One.
  MacLean, S. Heroes.
  Mangan, J. O'Hussey's Ode to the Maguire.
  Markham, E. Lincoln, the Man of the People.
  Melville, H. Commemorative of a Naval
    Victory.
  Montague, J. Old Mythologies.
  Nichols, G. Wha Me Mudder Do.
  Olds, S. Language of the Brag, The.
  Raine, K. Heroes.
  Rich, A. Letters in the Family.
  Richards, L. Molly Pitcher.
  Sassoon. Glory of Women.
  Seferis. Last Stop.
  Simpson, L. Heroes, The.
  Spender, S. I Think Continually of Those Who
    Were Truly Great.
  Szymborska. Pietà.
  Thayer, E. Casey at the Bat.
  Unknown. Beowulf.
  Wadsworth, W. Need for Attention, The.
  Wallace-Crabbe. Collective Invention, The.

Heroin
  Durcan. Death by Heroin of Sid Vicious, The.
  Gould, J. I Learn a Lesson About Our Society.
  Groves. Heroine.
  Herd. Gia.
  Hicok. Heroin.
  St. Germain, S. Addiction.
  Warsh. White Nights.
See also **Drug Addiction**
Herons
  Annand. Heron.
  Brannon, J. Evolution on 38th Street.
  Coles, G. Heron in the Alyn.
  Evasco, M. Heron-Woman.
  Gardner, I. That "Craning of the Neck."
  Kizer, C. Great Blue Heron, The.
  Lowell, A. Hoar-Frost.
  Roberts, T. Blue Heron, The.
  Roethke. Heron, The.
  Wright, J. Old Age Compensation.
Herrick, Robert
  Herrick. On Himselfe.
    Upon Himself.
    Upon the Loss[e] of His Mistresses.
Herring
  MacDiarmid, H. With the Herring Fishers.
  Nairne. Caller Herrin'
  Smith, I. Herring Girls, The.
Herzl, Theodor
  Zangwill. Theodor Herzl.
Hiawatha
  Carroll, L. Hiawatha's Photographing.
  Longfellow, H. Famine, The.
    Hiawatha's Wooing.
    Hiawatha: The White Man's Foot.
    Introduction: "Should you ask me, whence these
      stories?"
    Picture-Writing.
Hicks, Edward
  Helwig. For Edward Hicks.
Highwaymen
  Noyes, A. Highwayman, The.
Highways
  Anania. Fall, The.
    Interstate 80.
  Balaban. Heading Out West.
  Beer, P. Ballad of the Underpass.
  Davis, G. August Fires.
  Fraser, S. Looking Out to Sea Again on the
    Uptown Express.
  Getsi. Woman Hanging from Lightpole, Illinois
    Route 136.
  Healy, E. Artemis in Echo Park.
  Keller, D. Melancholy.
  Kooser. Interchange.
  Lewis, G. Flyover Elegies.
  McDaniel, W. California Entertainment, 1936.
  Mueller, L. Highway Poems.
  Paloff, B. On Transportation.
  Troup, B. (Get Your Kicks On) Route 66!
See also **Roads**
Hiking and Hikers
  Betjeman. Hike on the Downs, A.
  Kenyon, J. Depression in Winter.
  McPherson, S. Wings and Seeds.
  Revard. October, Isle of Skye.
Hills and Mountains
  Ammons, A. R. Mountain Talk.
  Bogan, L. Last Hill in a Vista.
  Brontë, E. Stanzas: "Often rebuked, yet always
    back returning."
  Coleridge, M. Lady of Trees, The.
  Coleridge, S. Blest is the tarn which towering
    cliffs o'ershade.
  Creeley. Hill, The.
  De la Mare. Crazed.
  Di Prima. I Ching.
  Douglas, L. Two Loves.
  Dyer, J. Grongar Hill.
  Emerson, R. Fable: "Mountain and the squirrel,
    The."
  "Field." Eros.
  Francis, R. That Dark Other Mountain.
  Frost, R. Meeting and Passing.
  Garner. Summer Solstice.

Hall, D. Sleeping Giant, The.
Hammerstein. Folks Who Live on the Hill, The.
Sound of Music, The.
Hannon. Temporary Heart.
Hanzlicek, C. Sierra Noon.
Harwood, L. "Utopia," The.
Hecht, A. Hill, A.
Helton. Lonesome Water.
Hove. Red Hills of Home.
Hughes, T. Bear, The.
Huntington, W. Lowlands.
Jackson, H. Cheyenne Mountain.
Kavanagh, P. Shancoduff.
Kern, J. Folks Who Live on the Hill, The.
Kipling, R. Sea and the Hills, The.
Komunyakaa. Boat People.
Kooser. City Limits.
Lanier, S. From the Flats.
Luschei, G. Water Song, The.
MacGreevy [or McGreevy]. Nocturne of the
Self-evident Presence.
MacLean, S. Kinloch Ainort.
Meynell, A. Watershed, The.
Milton. On the Late Massacre [or Massacher]
in Piedmont [or Piemont].
Muir, E. Childhood.
Pettit. Self-Portrait Approaching Promontory,
Utah.
Raine, K. To My Mountain.
Robinson, E. Dark Hills, The.
Rodgers, R. Sound of Music, The.
Rohrer, M. Hummock in the Malookas, A.
Rossetti, C. Uphill.
Rukeyser, M. Alloy.
Silko. Alaskan Mountain Poem #1.
Sissman. Big Rock-Candy Mountain, The.
Smith, C. To the South Downs.
Snyder, G. Mid-August at Sourdough Mountain
Lookout.
Stafford, W. Holding the Sky.
Survey, A.
Stevens, W. Thirteen Ways of Looking at a
Blackbird.
Thomas, R. Lonely Farmer, The.
Pietà.
Tomlinson, C. Ute Mountain.
Vaughan, H. Mount of Olives.
Wordsworth, W. Trosachs, The.
See also **Mountain Climbing**

Hilo, Hawaii
Hongo. Hongo Store 29 Miles Volcano Hilo,
Hawaii, The.

Hinduism and Hindus
Bringhurst. Parśvanatha.
Dharker. Purdah, 1.
Hannon. Real Estate.
Hass, R. To Phil Dow, in Oregon.
Hemans. Indian City, The.
Hirshfield, J. Painting.
Kolatkar. Low Temple, A.
Lyall. Badminton.
Parthasarathy. Speaking of Places.
Sama, B. Song, The.
Sharma, P. Action-Packed Sonnet.
Snyder, G. No Shoes No Shirt No Service.
Yeats. Indian upon God, The [or An].

Hip Hop
Asim, J. Hip Hop Bop.
Lynch, C. Ancestral Echoes/Rap Music.
Stanard, C. Rap Is.

Hippies
Lothamer. Allen.
Umpierre, L. Statue, The.

Hippopotamuses
Barrington, P. I Had a Hippopotamus.
Belloc. Hippopotamus, The.
Cole, J. Hippopotamus.
Eliot, T. Hippopotamus, The.
Guiterman. Habits of the Hippopotamus.
Leithauser. Trauma.
Roethke. Hippo, The.

Hips
Clifton, L. Homage to My Hips.
Jacobs, H. About Our Hips.
Magowan. Days of 1956.

Hiroshima, Japan
Enright, D. Monuments of Hiroshima, The.
Levine, P. Horse, The.
Mirikitani. Shadow in Stone.
Salter. Welcome to Hiroshima.
Seth. Doctor's Journal Entry for August 6,
1945, A.
Sitwell, D. Shadow of Cain, The.

Hispanics
Blanco, R. Malibú, El.
Boss. When You Are Grown, Amanda Rose.
Castillo, A. Me and Baby.
Clark, C. Border Affair, A.
Delgado, J. Awakened in a Field.
Campesinos.
Chuparosa.
Dandelion.
I-5 Incident.
Dougherty. Puerto Rican Girls of French Hill,
The.
Dubin, A. She's a Latin from Manhattan.
Espada. Beloved Spic.
González, R. Death of the Farm Workers' Cat.
Perla at the Mexican Border Assembly Line of
Dolls.
Guevara, M. Doña Josefina Counsels Doña
Concepción Before Entering Sears.
Healy, E. Moroni on the Mormon Temple /
Angel on the Wall.
Two Centuries in One Day.
Herández-Ávila. Presente.
Norte, M. Peeping Tom Tom Girl.
Riggs, L. Santo Domingo Corn Dance.
Suárez, V. Donatilia's Unrequited Love
Remedy.
Vigil, A. As the Beer Trucks Eclipse the Light
of Morning.
At the Stop Light, the Braided Blond Man.
Hogarcito de La Madrugada, El.
That's the Way, Uh Huh, Uh Huh, I Liked It.
See also **Chicanos and Chicanas**

History and Historians
Acam-Oturu. Agony . . . A Resurrection, An.
Aiyejina. When the Monuments.
Alexander, E. West Indian Primer.
Ali, A. Dacca Gauzes, The.
Alvi, M. Backgrounds.
Ama Ata Aidoo. Gynae One.
Anzaldúa. Cultures.
Atwood. Marrying the Hangman.
Auden. Fall of Rome, The.
Awad, J. Variations on a Theme.
Baca. Mi Tío Baca el Poeta de Socorro.
Ballowe, J. Starved Rock.
Baraka. Three Modes of History and Culture.
Baraka, R. In the Tradition Too.
Barclay, E. Human Greatness.
Barry, J. In the Footsteps of Genghis Khan.
Beer, P. Millennium.
Berry, W. Let Us Pledge.
Berryman. Boston Common.
Bloch, T. While Bouncing the Shema Back and
Forth in Shul.
Bly, R. After the Industrial Revolution, All
Things Happen at Once.
Boland, E. That the Science of Cartography Is
Limited.
Bond, E. If.
Brathwaite, E. Citadel.
Mmenson.
Brown, S. Let Them Call It Jazz.
Campbell, J. Antiquary, The.
Canan. Mother Dawning.
Casey, M. Learning.
Cherry, K. History.
Chin. Floral Apron, The.
Prelude.
Chinn. Not Translation, Not Poetry.
Cleveland, J. Epitaph on the Earl of Strafford.
Cliff. History of Costume, A.
Clifton, L. I am Accused of Tending to the Past.
Clinton, M. Traditional Post-Modern Neo-
HooDoo Afra-Centric Sister in a Purple Head
Rag Mourning Death and Cooking.
Coke, A. Change, The.
Collins, B. Tomes.

Colman, G. On Sir Nathaniel Wraxall the
Historian.
Conyus. I Rode with Geronimo.
Cooley, N. John Winthrop, 'Reasons to be
Considered for...the Intended Plantation in New
England,' 1629.
Mary Warren's Sampler.
Mother: Dorcas Good, The.
Publick Fast on Account of the Afflicted: March
31, 1692.
Cronin, A. Responsibilities.
Davidson, D. On a Replica of the Parthenon.
Davidson, M. Landing of Rochambeau, The.
Thinking the Alps.
Davis, J. One Hundred and Fifty Years.
De Tabley. Sonnet: "Record is nothing, and the
hero great."
Deane, S. History Lessons.
Deloney. Weavers Song, The.
Dennis, C. History.
Duggan, L. Town on the Ten Dollar Note, The.
Durham. Columbus Day.
Durrell. Sarajevo.
Emerson, R. History.
Solution.
Evans, M. Status Symbol.
Fearing. 1933.
Ferlinghetti, L. Cro-Magnons.
Fife, C. Dear Webster.
Frost, R. Peaceful Shepherd, The.
Galvin, J. Two Horses and a Dog.
Gardinier. Admirals (Columbus).
Ginsberg, A. Café in Warsaw.
Giovanni. Ego Tripping [(There May Be a
Reason Why)].
Gould, J. Easter Sunday.
Graham, J. History.
Graves, R. End of Play.
Gregor, A. History.
Grenier. Has Faded in Part But Magnificent
Also Late for RC / Mirrors.
Guiterman. Ancient History.
Gunn, T. Claus von Stauffenberg.
Gustafson, R. In the Yukon.
Hardy, T. One We Knew.
Rome: Building a New Street in the Ancient
Quarter.
Harper, M. American History.
Goin' to the Territory.
Zocalo.
Harry, J. Poem Films Itself, The.
Hass, R. Palo Alto: the Marshes.
Healy, E. City Beneath the City, The.
Herd. Bombshell.
Hernández Cruz. New/Aguas Buenas/Jersey.
Herrera. Mexican World Mural / 5 x 25.
Poetry of America, The.
Resurrection of the Flesh, The.
Hirsch, E. Simone Weil: In Assisi.
Howard, R. Again for Hephaistos, the Last
Time.
Hughes, J. Dog Day Lesson.
Hugo, R. Ferniehirst Castle.
Joe, R. Expect Nothing Else from Me.
Johnson, L. Reggae Sounds.
Jonson, B. To Sir Henry [or Henrie] Savile
[upon His Translation of Tacitus].
Kahaney, P. Germany, 1981.
Katz, J. Taxonomy.
Kaufman, B. Geneology.
Kennelly. Running Battle, A.
Kenney. Battle of Valcour Island, The.
Kipling, R. Land, The.
Kirsch, D. Dvora.
Koch, C. Shelly Beach.
Koordada, M. You Can't Escape Your Life
Record.
Kusano Shimpei. Skylarks and Fuji.
Landon. History of the Lyre, A.
Larkin, P. Arundel Tomb, An.
Lauterbach. Novelist Speaks, The.
Lear, E. Limericks, II (i).
Lee, E. Forests and Caverns.
Lindley, D. Cromwell: The Last Portrait.
Lowell, R. History.
Lumsden, R. ITMA.

Hitchhiking and Hitchhikers (continued)

Lux.   Bodo.
MacCaig.   Chauvinist.
  Crossing the Border.
Madhubuti.   Possibilites: Remembering
  Malcolm X.
Marvell.   Garden of Appleton House, The
  ("When in the east the morning ray").
Garden, A.
  Upon Appleton House [To My Lord Fairfax].
Matthews, M.   By a Ways.
Mayne, S.   In Memory of Aaron, Murdered
  Grandfather.
Mazur.   Common, The.
McCarthy, T.   Dying Synagogue at South
  Terrace, The.
McGlashan, J.   Island of Women, The.
Midge, T.   Written in Blood.
Moolten, D.   Brandy Station, Virginia.
Morris, B.   Dinas Emrys.
Nemerov.   Historical Judas, The.
  Ultima Ratio Reagan.
Newman, G.   Recording History.
O'Grady, D.   Berlin Metro.
O'Hara, F.   In Memory of My Feelings.
Olson, C.   At Yorktown.
  Kingfishers, The.
  Praises, The.
Oodgeroo of the tribe Noonuccal.   Past, The.
Opoku-Agyemang.   King Tut in America.
Osaki.   Amnesiac.
Osofisan.   She Thinks in Song.
Padilla.   Prayer for the End of the Century, A.
Perelman.   Cliff Notes.
Perillo.   Ghost Shirt, The.
Pickard, T.   Devil's Destroying Angel Exploded,
  The.
Plumpp.   Turf Song.
Pope, A.   Hunting and Fishing.
  Progress.
Porter, C.   They Couldn't Compare to You.
Porter, P.   And No Help Came.
Preston, R.   Music.
Prior.   Written in the Beginning of Mezeray's
  History of France.
Ramanujan.   Some Indian Uses of History on a
  Rainy Day.
Ramsey, J.   Tally Stick, The.
Ranaldo, L.   Time Presses Me.
Redmond.   River of Bones and Flesh and Blood.
Reed, I.   Dualism.
Rendon.   You See This Body.
Reznikoff.   Luzzato.
Rich, A.   Culture and Anarchy.
  In Those Years.
  Letters in the Family.
  Living Memory.
  Mathilde in Normandy.
  Readings of History.
Rodefer.   Pretext.
Rodriguez, J.   Mahogany Ship, The.
Rukeyser, M.   Book of the Dead, The.
Rux, C. H.   Asphalt Musings.
  Asylum of Gestures.
Rylander, E.   Midnight Rocker, Tiananmen
  Square, May 27, 1989.
Salaam.   I Live in the Mouth of History.
Sandburg, C.   Bilbea.
  I Am the People, the Mob.
  Old Timers.
Schwartz, D.   Lincoln.
Seidman.   Making of Color, The.
Simpson, L.   Story About Chicken Soup, A.
Slessor.   Five Bells.
Smith, C.   Beachy Head.
  From Beachy Head.
Smith, K.   End of All History, The.
Smith, S.   How Cruel Is the Story of Eve.
Snyder, G.   Building.
  What Happened Here Before.
Stafford, W.   Indian Cave Jerry Ramsey Found,
  The.
Sze.   Every Where and Every When.
Tate, A.   Mediterranean, The.
Taylor, E.   This Year's Drive to Appomattox.
Thomas, R.   Centuries.
Thornbury.   Court Historian, The.

Thorold Rogers.   On the Historians Freeman and
  Stubbs.
Turner, C.   Julius Caesar and the Honey-Bee.
Vando.   Commonwealth, Common Poverty.
Vaughan, H.   Charnel-house, The.
Warfield.   Forests and Caverns.
Warren, R.   Lessons in History.
Weller.   Wurarbuti.
Whitman, W.   On the Same Picture.
Whittemore, R.   Walk Home, The.
Wilbur.   Looking into History.
Wordsworth, W.   Mutability.
  Obligations of Civil to Religious Liberty.
  Persuasion.
  Point at Issue, The.
  Trepidation of the Druids.
Wright, D.   Cockermouth.
Wright, J.   At Cooloolah.
Yeats.   Lapis Lazuli.
Yevtushenko [or Evtushenko].   Hand-Rolled
  Cigarettes.
Young, K.   Quivira City Limits.

Hitchhiking and Hitchhikers

Allen, P.   Pickup.
Balaban.   Heading Out West.
Ciardi.   Faces.
Corso.   Poets Hitchhiking on the Highway.
Harms.   When You Wish Upon a Star That
  Turns into a Plane.
Kinnell.   Memory of Wilmington.
Wakoski.   Hitchhikers, The.

Hitler, Adolf

Dobbie.   Forty Three Years After Hitler My
  Parents Visit Eugene.
Gunn, T.   Claus von Stauffenberg.
Rukeyser, M.   Traditional Tune.
Waddell, H.   Hitler Speaks.

Ho Chi Minh

Weber, R.   Concise History of the Vietnam War:
  1965–1968, A.

Hobbes, Thomas

Cowley, A.   To Mr. Hobbes [or Hobs].
Hass, R.   Concerning the Afterlife, the Indians
  of Central California Had Only the Dimmest
  Notions.

Hogarth, William

Johnson, S.   Epitaph on William Hogarth, An.

Hogg, James

Wordsworth, W.   Extempore Effusion upon the
  Death of James Hogg.

Holbein, Hans

MacKellar, D.   Fancy Dress.

Holiday, Billie

Corn.   Billie's Blues.
Dove, R.   Canary.
Heithaus.   What a Little Moonlight Can Do.
Jackson, A.   Billie in Silk.
Levis.   1974: My Story in a Late Style of Fire.
May, K.   Valentine's Day.
Neal, L.   Lady's Days.
O'Hara, F.   Day Lady Died, The.
Plumpp.   Billie Holiday.

Holidays

Buchanan, G.   May Morning.
Chesterton, G.   Certain Evening, A.
Dame.   Seder, The.
Davidson, J.   Holiday at Hampton Court.
Durham.   Columbus Day.
Glaser, M.   Preparations for Seder.
González, R.   Day of the Dead.
Harper, M.   Studs.
Herrick.   Ceremonies for Candlemas[se] Eve.
Maltby, R.   I Don't Remember Christmas.
Smith, S.   Holiday, The.

Holland

Sia, B.   Things to Do in Holland.

See also **Netherlands**

Holly

Davies, G.   Holly Gone.
Unknown.   Holly and Ivy.
  Holly and the Ivy, The.
  Riddle: "Highty, tighty, paradighty, clothed [all]
  in green."

Hollywood, California

Coleman, W.   April in Hollywood.
Harms.   My Own Little Piece of Hollywood.
Jarrell.   Thinking of the Lost World.
Klipschutz.   Funicello at 50.
Mercer, J.   Hooray for Hollywood.
Shapiro, K.   Hollywood.

Holocaust

Alkalay-Gut.   Kitzbuhl Church.
  Life Goes On.
Bell, M.   Book of the Dead Man (#58), The.
  Extermination of the Jews, The.
Berg, S.   Desnos Reading the Palms of Men on
  Their Way to the Gas Chambers.
Bloch, T.   While Bouncing the Shema Back and
  Forth in Shul.
Bobrowski.   Kaunas 1941.
Bond, E.   How We See.
Brett, L.   I Keep Forgetting.
  La Pathétique.
  Leaving You.
  My Mother's Friend.
Brock, V.   Remembering Dresden.
Bruck.   Childhood.
Carruth, H.   Camps, The.
Celan.   Death Fugue, A.
  Tenebrae.
Dambroff.   Resistance.
Dorsett, T.   Survivor, The.
Fainlight, R.   Archive Film Material.
Feldman, I.   Pripet Marshes, The.
Fenton, J.   German Requiem, A.
Fishman, C.   Not Only in the Six-Day War.
Florsheim.   Business in Germany.
  Jewish Singles Event, The.
  Real Chocolate.
Fogel, E.   Shipment to Maidanek.
Forché.   Ourselves or Nothing.
Friedman, S.   Skin.
Gardinier.   Two Girls.
Gershon.   I Was Not There.
  Race.
Glaser, M.   English-Speaking Persons Will Find
  Translations.
Goldberg, B.   Our Father.
  Survivor.
Gouri.   Heritage.
Graham, J.   History.
Hamburger, M.   Treblinka.
Harchik.   Earrings.
Harris, R.   Riding Over Belmore Park.
Hecht, A.   "It Out-Herods Herod. Pray You,
  Avoid It."
  'More Light! More Light!'
  Book of Yolek, The.
Heyen.   Blue.
  Numinous, The.
  Passover: the Injections.
  Riddle: "From Belsen a crate of gold teeth."
  To the Onlookers.
  Trains, The.
Hill, G.   Ovid in the Third Reich.
  September Song.
Hirsch, E.   Paul Celan: A Grave and Mysterious
  Sentence.
Hirschhorn, N.   Number Our Days.
Hyett.   Assembling the Dead at Dachau.
Jarrell.   Camp in the Prussian Forest, A.
  In the Camp There Was One Alive.
  Protocols.
Jenkins, P.   Six Small Fires.
Kahaney, P.   Germany, 1981.
Kirsch, D.   Dvora.
Klepfisz.   Perspectives on the Second World
  War.
Kramer, L.   Non-Emigrant, The.
  Red Cross Telegram, The.
Lampert, D.   Poem for Sophie.
Levertov.   Crystal Night.
  Peachtree, The.
  When We Look Up.
Lifshin.   Hearing of Reagan's Trip to Bitburg.
  I Remember Haifa Being Lovely But.
  Seeing the Documentary by the British
  Liberating Bergen-Belsen.
Loden.   Conversations with Dr. M.

MacLean, S. Death Valley.
Mahon. Disused Shed in Co. Wexford, A.
"Martin." Dreams in German.
Mayne, S. In Memory of Aaron, Murdered Grandfather.
Meltzer, D. What Do I Know of Journey.
Michelson, R. Genuine Jewish Flesh.
Interrogation.
Jews That We Are, The.
Where I Sat.
Millis, C. IRT at Rush Hour, The.
Milosz, C. Campo dei Fiori.
Poor Christian Looks at the Ghetto, A.
Murray, L. Dog Fox Field.
Nepo. Oil of Her Hands, The.
Neufeld, A. Children of Night.
Family Album.
Newman, G. Anti-Semitic Demonstration, An.
Photograph of Survivors.
Recording History.
Olson, C. La Préface.
Pacernick [or Pacernik]. Louie the Tailor.
Pagis. Autobiography.
Pilinszky, J. Frankfurt.
On the Wall of a KZ-Lager.
Pillen [or Pillin]. Ascensions, The.
Plath. Daddy.
Mary's Song.
Plotnick, H. M. Jewish.
Porter, P. Annotations of Auschwitz.
Posamentier, E. Bird Named Isidore, The.
Propp, K. Train Passage.
Rózewicz. Pigtail.
Ranasinghe. Auschwitz from Colombo.
Holocaust 1944.
Ress. Learning the Ropes. Custer Street. Evanston, 1949.
Visit, Auschwitz, 1971, The.
Waving Her Farewell. Train Station, Vienna XV, 1939.
Reznikoff. Children.
Massacres.
Rich, A. Letters in the Family.
Rosner. Souvenirs.
Sachs, N. Chorus of the Dead.
Dead Child Speaks, A.
Schapiro, J. Tourist, The.
Schiff, H. German Frontier at Basel: 1942 and 1992, The.
When It Happened.
Shevin. What He Hated.
Shiffrin, N. Anna's Dream.
Shomer. Women Bathing at Bergen-Belsen.
Sillitoe. Synagogue in Prague.
Simpson, L. Story About Chicken Soup, A.
Sklarew. After Theresienstadt.
Holocaust.
Teaching the Children.
Spender, S. History and Reality.
Memento.
Stallworthy, J. Letter from Berlin, A.
Stern, G. Adler.
Soap.
Sternlieb. Survivor.
Sutskever [or Sutzkever]. How?
Voznesensky [or Voznesenskii]. Call of the Lake, The.
Warren, R. Max Jacob at Saint Benoît.
Warshawski. Sonia at 32.
Weinberger, F. He Wears Old Socks.
Survivor.
Wells, W. Beatings.
Wexler, E. Governess, The.
Wiesel. Never Shall I Forget.
Williams, C. Spit.
Young-Prottengeier. Lithuanian Grandmother.
Zach. Against Parting.
Zukofsky, L. Song for the Year's End, A.

Holy Family
Rukeyser, M. Holy Family.
Unknown. Cherry-Tree Carol, The.

Holy Ghost
Audelay [or Awdelay]. Seven Gifts of the Holy Ghost, The.
Herbert, G. Whitsunday.
Herrick. His Litany to the Holy Spirit.

Sassoon. Christ and the Soldier.
Unknown. Petition to Father and Son and Holy Ghost, A.

Holy Innocents
Wadding [or Waddinge]. For Innocents' Day.

Holy Spirit
Constable, H. To God the Holy Ghost.
"Field." Sweet-Briar in Rose.
Langton, S. Hymn to the Holy Spirit.
Very. Lost, The.
Silent, The.

Home
Adamson. Home, the Spare Room, The.
Aldis, D. No One Heard Him Call.
Alexander, E. Who I Think You Are.
Ali, A. Postcard from Kashmir.
Alvi, M. Bed, The.
Ashbery. Rain Moving In.
Awoonor. Sea Eats the Land at Home, The.
Back, R. Gaza, Undated.
Notes: From the Wait.
Bass, F. Home.
Berger, B. Trophy Homes.
Berssenbrugge. Tan Tien.
Blamire. When Home We Return.
Brontë, A. Home.
Brooks, C. Our Island Home.
Brooks, G. Ballad of Rudolph Reed, The.
Brown, D. Coming Home.
Brown, E. Out.
Bunner, H. Home Sweet Home with Variations.
Burns, R. My Heart's in the Highlands.
Byron, C. Minding You.
Channing. Harbor, The.
Clare, J. After Reading in a Letter Proposals for Building a Cottage.
Cleary, B. Sealink.
Clifton, H. Distaff Side, The.
Clifton, L. In the Inner City.
Clinton, M. Eviction.
Clough. Come Home, Come Home!
Clover, J. Alas, That Is the Name of Our Town; I Have Been Concealing It All This Time.
Colum, P. Old Woman of the Roads, The.
"Coolidge." Home, A.
Cowley, M. Long Voyage, The.
Winter Tenement.
Creeley. En Famille.
Cunningham, A. Hame, Hame, Hame.
Das, K. Hot Noon in Malabar.
Davies, A. Thirty East Forty-Second Street.
Dharker. Name of God, The.
Di Prima. Backyard.
Notes on the Art of Memory.
Donne. To Sir Henry Wotton.
Dove, R. Dusting.
Doyle, S. This Shade.
Edwards [or Edwardes], R. Recollections of an Old Spook.
Edwards, M. Home.
Elliot, A. Latitudes of Home, The.
Fong, H. Asylum.
Forbes, C. Home.
Foster, S. My Old Kentucky Home[, Good Night!].
Old Folks at Home[, The].
Frost, R. Death of the Hired Man, The.
Gilman, C. Homes.
Gioia. In Cheever Country.
Gregg. Night Music.
Griffiths, J. Emigrants.
Migration.
Guest, E. Home.
Harbach, O. Love Nest, The.
Harms. Sky.
Harris, J. Home.
Harris, W. Rib Sandwich.
Healy, E. Moroni on the Mormon Temple / Angel on the Wall.
Heard, J. Welcome Home.
Helwig. Considerations.
Herrick. Thanksgiving to God for His House, A.
Hewitt, J. Substance and Shadow.
Hicky. When a Man Turns Homeward.
Hines, N. Home.

Hirsch, L. Love Nest, The.
Hochman. Cannon Hill.
Holan. Resurrection.
Hove. Red Hills of Home.
Hunt, L. To Hampstead.
Jackson, R. Sunday Brunch.
Janzen, J. Claiming the Dust.
Johnson, L. Mystic and Cavalier.
Jones, T. Llanafan Unrevisited.
Kay, J. In my country.
Keeshig-Tobias. I Grew Up.
Kilmer, J. House with Nobody in It, The.
King, S. Hearth and Home.
Kyle, C. J. Fire in Early Morning.
Lanyer. Description of Cooke-ham [or Cookham], The.
Larkin, P. Home Is So Sad.
Lawrence, D. End of Another Home Holiday.
Lim, S. Visting Malacca.
Lisick, B. Empress of Sighs.
Longfellow, H. Golden Mile-Stone, The.
Longley, M. Remembering Carrigskeewaun.
West, The.
Lovelace, R. Another.
Luschei, G. Here.
Lydston. Family, The.
MacCaig. Kingfisher.
Macdonald, G. Baby-Sermon, A.
Shortest and Sweetest of Songs, The.
Mahon. Ford Manor.
Marinoni. For a New Home.
Marshall, R. Burrel Bullai.
Masefield. West Wind, The.
Mathews, A. Two Months Married.
McCrae, H. Song of the Rain.
Merwin, W. S. Odysseus.
Millay, E. On the Wide Heath.
Million, D. Housing Poem, The.
Morgan, J. My Welsh Home.
Mphahlele. Homeward Bound.
Murphy, P. Manifesto.
Nichols, G. Beverley's Saga.
Like a Beacon.
Nilsson, H. On Inheriting Departure.
We Are Easily Reduced.
Oliveira, D. San Joaquin.
Orfalea, G. Rose of Brooklyn, The.
Paschen. 12 East Scott Street.
Confederacy.
Patterson, G. Letter from Home.
Peters, L. We Have Come Home.
Piercy. Spring Offensive of the Snail, The.
Pietri. 7th Untitled Poem.
Pinsky. Street, The.
Pogson, P. Going Home.
Pook. Weekend at Home.
Radnóti. Seventh Eclogue.
Raine, K. Message from Home.
Rhys, E. Ballad of the Homing Man, The.
Riley, J. Travel Notes.
Robinson, E. House on the Hill, The.
Rodgers, C. For Sistuhs Wearin' Straight Hair.
Rosenblatt, S. Leaving Home.
Mom and Dad Getting Older.
Rukeyser, M. Book of the Dead, The.
Rybicki, J. In Directions.
Södergran. Homecoming.
Shapcott, T. City of Home, The.
Shapiro, M. To Jerusalem, 1990.
Sigourney. Western Emigrant, The.
Simmons, J. Westport House, Portrush.
Snodgrass, W. Mutability.
Stafford, W. One Home.
Stevenson, R. Blows the Wind Today.
Ille Terrarum.
Stickney, T. Quiet after the Rain of Morning.
Swain, C. Home Is Where There Is One to Love Us.
Swenson, M. Staying at Ed's Place.
Talvikki, A. For Want.
Thompson, D. Days of Yore, The.
Thorne, T. High Country.
Tremblay, B. Home Front.
Troupe. Conjuring Against Alien Spirits.
Unknown. Deep River.
For Sale or Rent.

Good Lord in That Heaven.
Steal Away to Jesus.
What Makes a Home?
Unknown, fr. Terezin Concentration Camp.
  Homesick.
Untermeyer, J. Autumn.
Untermeyer, L. Prayer for This House.
Van Doren. Family Prime.
Waniek. House on Moscow Street, The.
Ward, J. Here, Home.
  To Get Clear.
Watkins, V. Returning to Goleufryn.
Watson, R. Ruined Altar, A.
Wayman. Teething.
Webster, A. Where Home Was.
Welshimer. Dusk.
Whittemore, R. Still Life.
Williams, G. Wild Night at Treweithan.
Williams, M. Shrinking Lonesome Sestina, The.
Wilson, K. Dusk in My Backyard.
Wordsworth, D. Peaceful Our Valley, Fair and
  Green.
Wordsworth, W. Farewell, A: "Farewell thou
  little Nook of mountain-ground."
  Ruined Cottage, The.
Wright, C. Virgo Descending.
Zolynas. Zen of Housework, The.

Homecoming
Arnold, M. Poet, The.
  Resignation.
Berlin. When the Midnight Choo-Choo Leaves
  for Alabam'
Bishop, J. Return, The.
Brown, L. Sentimental Journey.
Butterfield, F. G. For Services Rendered.
Carew, T. Upon Master Walter Montagu's
  Return from Travel.
Clare, J. Returned Soldier, The.
Davie. Rodez.
DeSylva, B. G. California, Here I Come.
Dobyns. Freight Cars.
Donaldson, W. How 'Ya Gonna Keep 'Em
  Down on the Farm? (After They've Seen
  Paree).
Dubin, A. Lulu's Back in Town.
Ellis, K. N. Tougaloo Blues.
Fisher, S. Hometown.
Graham, W. What's the News?
Green, B. Sentimental Journey.
Hardy, T. His Visitor.
Herman, J. Hello, Dolly!
Hogg, J. Charlie is my Darling.
Homer. Butchers, The.
  Phemios and Medon.
Homer, B. Sentimental Journey.
Howell, C. Liberty and Ten Years of Return.
Jeffers, R. Return.
Jolson, A. California, Here I Come.
Kavanagh, P. In Memory of My Mother.
Kipling, R. Return, The.
Knight, E. Poem for Myself (Or Blues for a
  Mississippi Black Boy), A.
  Welcome Back, Mr. Knight: Love of My Life.
Levine, P. Water's Chant, The.
Louis, A. At the House of Ghosts.
MacCaig. Return to Scalpay.
Mapanje. Making Our Clowns Martyrs.
Melville, H. Return of the Sire de Nesle *A.D.*
  16, The.
Oness, C. Of All There Is.
Owen, W. Send-Off, The.
Peterson, R. Now and Then.
Robin, L. My Cutey's Due at Two-to-Two
  Today.
Robinson, A. Celia's Home-Coming.
Robinson, E. Prodigal Son, The.
Rosenblatt, S. Mom and Dad Getting Older.
Ross, A. En Route.
Rossetti, C. Italia, Io Ti Saluto!
Salkey. Dry River Bed.
Samaras, N. Farasa.
Schuyler, J. Elizabethans Called It Dying, The.
Smith, P. Dylan, Two Days.
Stryk, L. Return to DeKalb.
Tripp. Diesel to Yesterday.
Von Tilzer, A. My Cutey's Due at Two-to-Two

Today.
Wetzsteon. Coming Back to the Cave.
Zimunya. Arrivants.
  Kisimiso.

Homeless, The
Aleshire. Double, The.
Ashbery. Street Musicians.
Baraka. Legacy.
Berryman. Boston Common.
Bibbins, M. Pathology of Proximity, The.
Brooks, G. To An Old Black Woman, Homeless
  and Indistinct.
Cardiff. Grey Woman.
Clifton, L. Miss Rosie.
Colum, P. Old Woman of the Roads, The.
"Coolidge." Home, A.
Dana, R. Mark, The.
Dobyns. Frenchie.
Dressel. Dai, Live.
Gates, B. Cathy.
  Homeless.
  Ron.
  Triptych.
Ginsberg, A. Homeless Compleynt.
Hannon. Homeless.
Haug. Tennessee Waltz, The.
Hecht, A. Christmas Is Coming.
Hirschman, J. X L E B.
Hopkins, L. En-vi-RON-ment.
Hughes, L. Vagabonds.
Hughes, T. November.
McKay, C. Castaways, The.
Medina, T. Rhudine Rhudine.
Mueller, L. Triage.
Myles, E. School of Fish.
Procter, A. Homeless.
Randall, D. Bag Woman.
Rodriguez, L. Rant, Rave and Ricochet.
Serote. This Old Woman.
Spires. Woman on the Dump, The.
Stevenson, R. Ille Terrarum.
Thomas, D. Hunchback in the Park, The.
Unknown. Soup Kitchen Song.
Williams, W. To a Poor Old Woman.

Homer
Bass, R. Odyssey, The.
Cunningham, J. Epigram: "Homer was poor.
  His scholars live at ease."
Eberhart, R. Garden God, The.
Emerson, R. Solution.
Garlick, R. Note on the Iliad.
Kavanagh, P. Epic: "I have lived in important
  places, times."
  On Looking into E. V. Rieu's Homer.
Keats. On First Looking into Chapman's
  Homer.
  To Homer.
Lang, A. Odyssey, The.
Reese, L. Love, Weeping, Laid This Song.
Stephens, P. God Shed His Grace.
Tennyson, A. Lotus-Eaters, The.
Unknown, after the Latin of George Buchanan.
  Cure for Poetry, A.

Homesickness
Al-Rihani. I Dreamt I Was a Donkey Boy
  Again.
Alexander, E. Letter: Blues.
Ashe. City Clerk, The.
Berry, J. Lucy's Letter.
Blind. Fantasy, A.
Blunden. At the Great Wall of China.
Brooke, R. Old Vicarage, Grantchester, The.
Browning, R. Home-Thoughts, From Abroad.
Byron, G. Lachin y Gair.
Carmichael, H. Georgia on My Mind.
  Hong Kong Blues.
Clare, J. Flitting, The.
  Soldier, The.
Cunningham, A. Hame, Hame, Hame.
Glück, L. Legend.
Gorrell, S. Georgia on My Mind.
Homer. Butchers, The.
  Phemios and Medon.
Hughes, L. Homesick Blues.
Jarrell. Island, The.
Kefala. Sunday Visit.

Kipling, R. Broken Men, The.
Lewis, A. In Hospital: Poona (1).
MacLeish. American Letter.
MacNeice. Nostalgia.
Masefield. West Wind, The.
McKay, C. Outcast.
  Tropics in New York, The.
Porter, P. 'In the New World Happiness is
  Allowed.'
Ransom, J. Amphibious Crocodile.
Ryan, R. Winter in Minneapolis.
Tu Fu. Chengtu.
Unknown. Away from Home.
Wang Wei. Thinking of My Brother in
  Shantung on the Ninth Day of the Ninth Moon.
Wright, J. Outside Fargo, North Dakota.

Homesteaders
Salzman, E. Homesteading.

Homophobia
Anzaldúa. Interface.
Avicolli. Rape Poem, The.
Bergman, D. Blueberry Man.
Bibbins, M. Geometry Class.
Borawski. Cheers, Cheers for Old Cha Cha Ass.
  Invisible History.
  Some of Us Wear Pink Triangles.
Brass. Only Silly Faggots Know.
Crew, L. Gay Psalm from Fort Valley, A.
De la Tierra. De Ambiente.
Domina, L. Pharoah's Army Got Drowned.
Doty, M. Homo Will Not Inherit.
Everhard. Curing Homosexuality.
Gates, B. Deadly Weapon.
Hughes, L. Café: 3 A.M.
Liu, T. Strange Fruit.
Morse, C. Fairy Straighttalk.
Norse. We Bumped Off Your Friend the Poet.
Parker, P. My Brother.
  Prologue from "Legacy."
  Where Will You Be?
Pitchford. Surgery.
Pratt, M. Crime Againts Nature.
Raffalovich, M. A. Sonnet 120.
  World Well Lost 18, The.
  World Well Lost 4, The.
Reynolds, C. Worst of it, The.
Van Jordan, A. Dance Lesson, A.
Wilmer, S. Mess Boy, The.

Homosexuality and Homosexuals
Adamson. Action Would Kill It / A Gamble.
Allison, D. When I Drink I Become the Joy of
  Faggots.
Auden. Legend.
Ayres, R. Corporeal.
Barber, W. Explanation.
  Gay Poet, The.
Barnfield [*or* Barnefield]. Daphnis to
  Ganymede.
Becker, R. History of Sexual Preference, A.
  Sad Sestina.
Behn, A. To the Fair Clarinda [*or* Clorinda],
  Who Made Love to Me, Imagined [*or*
  Imagin'd] More Than Woman.
Bibbins, M. Bluebeard.
  Whitman on the Beach.
Blaser. Even on Sunday.
Borawski. Power of One.
  Some of Us Wear Pink Triangles.
  Talking to Jim.
Brainard, J. I Remember.
Brass. I Have This Vision of Madness.
  Only Silly Faggots Know.
Broumas, O. Rapunzel.
Byron, G. Cornelian, The.
  One Struggle More, and I Am Free.
  To Thyrza.
Cabico, R. Antonio Banderas in His Underwear.
  Art in Architecture.
  Gameboy.
Cady. After Hearing Heterosexual Poets in
  October 1974: What It Seems Like To Write a
  Male Homosexual Love Poem Now.
Campo. Asylum.
  Aunt Toni's Heart.
  Battle Hymn of the Republic, The.
  El Día de los Muertos.

Cassells. Beautiful Signor.
Marathon.
New Song of Solomon.
Cataldi. 13 November 1983.
We Could Have Met.
Chin, J. Cocksucker's Blues.
Ex-Boyfriends Named Michael.
Undetectable.
Why a Boy.
Why He Had to Go.
Chubb, R. Song of My Soul.
Transfiguration.
Clarke, C. Of Althea and Flaxie.
Conway, J. Hangover.
Marlo Thomas in Seven Parts and Epilogue.
Modern English.
Weight Belt.
Cooper, D. After School, Street Football, Eighth
Grade.
No God.
Teen Idols.
Corn. Billie's Blues.
Long-Distance Call to Gregg, Who Lived with
AIDS as Long as He Could.
Marriage in the Nineties, A.
To Hermes.
Cox, M. Barbells of the Gods, The.
Crane, H. Modern Craft.
Creeley. All That Is Lovely in Men.
Crowley, A. Ballad of Passive Paederasty, A.
Rondels.
de Gillies, G. De Puerorum osculis.
De Veaux. Sisters, The.
Domina, L. Pharoah's Army Got Drowned.
Doty, M. Days of 1981.
Lilacs in NYC.
Douglas, L. Two Loves.
Duffy, C. Oppenheim's Cup and Saucer.
Fanning, R. In the Barn.
Fisher, S. Hometown.
Gates, B. Cathy.
Homeless.
Ron.
Triptych.
Ginsberg, A. Chances "R."
This Form of Life Needs Sex.
Giorno. Pornographic Poem.
Hacker, M. Ballad of Ladies Lost and Found.
Dusk: July.
Eight Days in April.
Harms. My Androgynous Years.
Hayes, T. At Pegasus.
Healy, E. Louganis.
What It Was Like the Night Cary Grant Died.
Hecht, A. Feast of Stephen, The.
Hemphill. Homicide.
Where Seed Falls.
Holden, J. Why We Bombed Haiphong.
Holland, W. Christopher Street 1979.
Hughes, L. Café: 3 A.M.
Iozia, J. Fag Art.
Last Night at the Flamingo.
Kirstein. Double Date.
Klein, M. Letters from the Front.
Tides, The.
Knight, E. For Freckle-Faced Gerald.
Koestenbaum, W. 1977.
1980.
1992.
Tea Dance.
Lassell. Brady Street, San Francisco.
Going to Europe.
Kissing Ramén.
Sunset Stripping: Visiting L.A.
Three Poems.
Lefroy. Idler Listening to Socrates Discussing
Philosophy with His Boy-Friends, An.
Liu, T. Highway 6.
Reading Whitman in a Toilet Stall.
Thoreau.
Malloch, D. Manly Love.
Manrique, J. My Night with Frederico García
Lorca (As Told by Edouard Roditi).
Tarzan.
McClatchy. 1871.
1946, 1957.

1971.
First Steps.
Meredith, W. Wholesome.
Mew. On the Road to the Sea.
Moore, H. Edward.
Morse, C. Dream of the Artfairy.
Norse. I Would Not Recommend Love.
O'Hara, F. Homosexuality.
Parker, P. For Willyce.
Where Will You Be?
Pearlberg, G.G. Dog Star.
Loop-the-Loop in Prospect Park (1905).
Sailor.
Philips, K. L'Amitie: To Mrs. Mary [or M.]
Awbrey.
Phillips, C. Cotillion.
Kill, The.
Undressing for Li Po.
Pitchford. Surgery.
Pomeroy, R. Gay Love and the Movies.
Pratt, M. Other Side, The.
Raffalovich, M. A. Rose Leaves When the Rose
Is Dead.
Sonnet 120.
World Well Lost 18, The.
World Well Lost 4, The.
Rainey. Prove It on Me Blues.
Roberts, M. Magnificat.
Roberts, N. Nigger and Some Poofters, A.
Rochester, J. Song: "Love a woman? You're [or
Y'are] an ass."
Saint. Heart and Soul.
Scannell. Protest Poem.
Schuyler, J. Tom.
Seaton, M. Story of Stonewall, A.
Shepherd, R. Eros in His Striped Blue Shirt.
Gods at Three A.M., The.
Narcissus Learning the Words to This Song.
That Man.
Three A.M. Eternal.
Shurin. City of Men.
His Promise.
Simon, L. Bernice Got Next to Isis.
Smith, S. Lord Barrenstock.
Symonds. Love and Death: A Symphony.
What Cannot Be.
Taylor, B. Paean to the Dawn, A.
Tayson, R. First Sex.
Nightsweats.
Phone Sex.
Trinidad. Doll Not Included.
For Joe Brainard.
Monday, Monday.
Tsui. Chinese Banquet, A.
Unknown. Limerick: "There was a young
Fellow of King's."
Weiners. Act #2.
Whitman, W. In Paths Untrodden.
Live Oak, with Moss.
Not Heat Flames Up and Consumes.
Recorders Ages Hence.
When I Heard at the Close of the Day.
Whoever You Are Holding Me Now in Hand.
Wieners. Acceptance.
Doll.
King Solomon's Magnetic Quiz.
Loneliness, The.
Poem for Cocksuckers, A.
To H.
Williams, S. She Had Known Brothers.
Wilmer, S. Mess Boy, The.
Wright, J. Sappho.
Wunderlich, M. Continent's Edge.
East Seventh Street.
Given in Person Only.
Take Good Care of Yourself.
Trick, The.

Honesty
Brown, E. Bitcherel.
Campion, T. Heart's Music.
Cleage. Confession.
Creeley. Somebody Died.
Donne. Song: "Go and catch a falling star."
Duhamel. Yes.
Larkin, P. Talking In Bed.
Nesbit, E. Appeal.

Rukeyser, M. Poem as Mask, The.
Vitale, M. Three Written Poems, Unconnected.
Walker, R. Okay, Let's Be Honest.
Walton, A. Sincere Man, The.
Wyatt, S. Honesty.
Wylie. Let No Charitable Hope.
Honey
Brooks, G. My Dreams, My Works Must Wait
Till after Hell.
Doolittle, H. Fragment 113: "Not honey, / not
the plunder of the bee."
Duke, V. Honey in the Honeycomb.
Kelly, R. In June.
Lima, J. Distribution of Poetry.
Morgan, R. Honey.
Rauter. Peach.
Toomer. Beehive.
Unknown. Peas.
Watts, I. How Doth the Little Busy Bee.
Honeymoons
Cahn, S. Come Fly with Me.
Corso. Marriage.
Donaldson, W. Okay, Toots.
Dubin, A. Shuffle Off to Buffalo.
Durcan. Honeymoon Postcard.
Friman. Honeymoon.
Herrick. Epithalamy to Sir Thomas Southwell
and His Lady, An.
Kahn, G. Okay, Toots.
Updike. Newlyweds, The.
Van Heusen, J. Come Fly with Me.
Warren, H. Shuffle Off to Buffalo.
Honeysuckle
Belieu. Nocturne: My Sister Life.
Freneau. Wild Honey Suckle, The.
Razaf, A. Honeysuckle Rose.
Waller, T. et al.
Hong Kong
Carmichael, H. Hong Kong Blues.
Fain, S. Love Is a Many-Splendored Thing.
Honor
Bass, F. I am a Jew.
Berryman. Scholars at the Orchid Pavilion.
Cameron, N. Thespians at Thermopylae, The.
Chaucer. Lak of Stedfastnesse.
Collins, W. How Sleep the Brave.
Daniel, S. Ulysses and the Siren [or Syren].
Dunbar, W. In Prais of Wemen.
In Praise of Women.
Greenlee. Memorial for Trane.
Hughes, L. Shame on You.
Jonson, B. Ode. To Sir William Sydney, on His
Birthday.
Song: To Celia.
To Sir Henry Cary.
Keith, J. Definitions.
Kiser. My Creed.
Legaré. Tallulah.
Lovelace, R. Mock Charon, A.
To Lucasta, [on] Going to the War[re]s.
MacNeice. Elegy for Minor Poets.
Mandeville. On Honour.
McKay, C. If We Must Die.
Melville, H. College Colonel, The.
Stonewall Jackson.
Murray, L. Lament for the Country Soldiers.
Philips, K. On the Welsh Language.
Scarfe. Ode in Honour.
Smith, A. Praise.
Stanley, T. Pythagoric Letter, The.
Suckling, S. Loving and Beloved.
Sze. In Your Honor.
Unknown. Down to the Mire.
Elegy upon the Death of Mrs. A. Behn, the
Incomparable Astrea, an.
She Was Poor but She Was Honest.
Vega. Brothers Loving Brothers.
Villiers. Epitaph upon Thomas, Lord Fairfax,
An.
Weinblatt, J. Marriage Song for Many Voices.
Whitman, W. To a Certain Cantatrice.
Wilde, L. Désillusion.
Hooch, Pieter de
Mahon. Courtyards in Delft.

Hope
Akhmatova, A. Dedication.
Ali, A. Desert Landscape.
Baca. Oppression.
Beer, P. Flood, The.
Bell, C. Where Hope Lives.
Bly, R. Poem in Three Parts.
Brass. I Have This Vision of Madness.
Brecht, B. World's One Hope, The.
Brontë, E. Hope.
Byron, G. Stanzas for Music.
Carrier, C. Pro Patria.
Carstairs. Addressed to a Beech Tree.
Ceravolo. Wild Provoke of the Endurance Sky.
Chimombo. Death Song, A.
Clark, T. Faith for Tomorrow.
Coleman, C. I Walk a Little Faster.
Coleridge, S. Work without Hope.
Collins, A. Song.
Coulehan, J. Azalea Poem, The.
Cullen, C. From the Dark Tower.
Dame. Seder, The.
Di Prima. Revolutionary Letter #1.
Dickinson, E. "Hope" is the Thing with
  Feathers.
Dipoko. From My Parisian Diary.
Divakaruni. Restroom.
Gillilan, S. Be Hopeful.
Ginsberg, A. In Back of the Real.
  Sunflower Sutra.
Giovanni. Poem For My Nephew.
Graves, R. Love Without Hope.
  Lovers in Winter.
Hammerstein. You'll Never Walk Alone.
Hardy, T. Darkling Thrush, The.
  To an Unborn Pauper Child.
Heard, J. Hope.
Hemans. Despondency and Aspiration.
Herbert, G. Hope.
  Size, The.
Herd. Bathing Girls, The.
Hernández Cruz. Today Is a Day of Great Joy.
Herrick. His Hope or Sheet-Anchor.
  Impossibilities to His Friend.
Hood, T. Time, Hope, and Memory.
Hopkins, G. Leaden Echo and the Golden Echo,
  The.
Horton, G. On Liberty and Slavery.
Hudgins. Hereafter, The.
Hughes, L. Hope.
Humphrey, D. Hope.
Jarrell. Jews at Haifa.
Jeffers, L. I Do Not Know the Power of My
  Hand.
Johnson, S. Scholar's Life, The.
  Vanity of Human Wishes, The; The Tenth Satire
  of Juvenal Imitated.
Kenyon, J. Let Evening Come.
King, J. Intercity Dub.
Kiser. Unsubdued.
Knight, E. Green Grass and Yellow Balloons.
Landon. Farewell, The.
Leigh, C. I Walk a Little Faster.
Lodge, G. Fall.
MacLeish. Pole Star for This Year.
Mahon. Everything Is Going to Be All Right.
Melville, H. Immolated.
  Shelley's Vision.
Menken. Aspiration.
Momaday. Gift, The.
Moorer. Door of Hope, The.
Mora. Immigrants.
Muir, E. Good Man in Hell, The.
  Horses, The.
Nicholson, N. From a Boat at Coniston.
Okigbo. On the New Year.
Olson, C. Distances, The.
Oppen. From Disaster.
Pitter. But for Lust.
Poe. Dreams.
Pugh. Sometimes.
Rafferty, P. Back End.
Ransom, J. Blackberry Winter.
Ratushinskaya [or Ratushinskaia]. Try to Cover
  Your Shivering Shoulders.
Ray, H. Aspiration.

Quest of the Ideal, The.
  Triple Benison, The.
Rodgers, R. You'll Never Walk Alone.
Rossetti, C. If Only.
  Pause of Thought, A.
  Song: "She sat and sang alway."
Rukeyser, M. Who in One Lifetime.
Ryan, R. Lake of the Woods, The.
Sall, A. Cloak of Dawn.
Sanchez, S. Anthem, An.
Sassoon. Everyone Sang.
Scott, W. Continuity of Life.
Shelley, P. England in 1819.
"Shu Ting." Fairy Tales.
Simmons, J. For Thomas Moore.
Smith, C. To Hope.
Sondheim. Somewhere.
Stanley, T. Expectation.
Thomas, E. To Colindra.
  When I First Came Here.
Thompson, C. Hope.
  Hope Deferred.
Tucker, M. Hope.
Unknown. Elegy upon the Death of Mrs. A.
  Behn, the Incomparable Astrea, An.
  High Resolve.
  We Shall Overcome.
  Very. Forevermore.
Wagner, C. Let's Forget.
Walker, A. Remember?
Warren, R. Aubade for Hope.
Whitehead, C. Daybreak.
Williams, H. To Hope.
Wright, C. Hawaii Dantesca.
Wright, J. Arrangements with Earth for Three
  Dead Friends.
Wright, K. How I See It.
Wylie. Let No Charitable Hope.
See also **Optimism**

Hope, Bob
Hathaway, W. Why That's Bob Hope.

Hopi, The
Rose. Naayawva Taawi.
  Story Keeper.

Hopper, Edward
Bonds, D. Life of the Body, The.
Boruch. Light.
Carpenter, W. Evening Wind.
  Night Shadows.
Carter, A. B. Cobb's Barns.
Dunn, S. Impediment.
Elton, W. Hopper: In the Cafe.
Greger. Man on the Bed, The.
Hirsch, E. Edward Hopper and the House by
  the Railroad.
Hollander, J. Edward Hopper's Seven A.M.
  Sunday A.M. Not in Manhattan.
Levis. Edward Hopper, 'Hotel Room,' 1931.
Ludvigson. Inventing My Parents.
Mezey. Evening Wind.
Mueller, L. American Literature.
  Nude by Edward Hopper, A.
Quagliano. Edward Hopper Retrospective, The.
  Edward Hopper's 'Lighthouse at Two Lights.'
Raab, L. After Edward Hopper.
Ray, D. Automat.
  Midnight Diner by Edward Hopper, A.
Rudolf. Edward Hopper.
Sadoff. Hopper's "Nighthawks" (1942).
Schulman. American Solitude.
Standing. Hopper's Women.
Stone, J. Early Sunday Morning.
Wade, S. Gas.
Williamson, A. Light's Reading, The.
Yellen. Nighthawks.

Horace
Durrell. On First Looking into Loeb's Horace.
Godley, A. After Horace.
Montagu, L. Verses Addressed to the Imitator
  of the First Satire of the Second Book of
  Horace: An Attack on Pope.

Horse Racing
Foster, S. Camptown Races.
Gordon, A. How We Beat the Favourite.
Hart, K. Flemington Racecourse.

Hayward, D. To the Man Saying 'Come on
  Seis' at Hollywood Park.
Herd. Hyperion's Bones.
  Pat Taffe and Arkle.
Larkin, P. At Grass.
Loesser. Fugue for Tinhorns.
Moore, M. Tom Fool at Jamaica.
Paterson, A. Father Riley's Horse.
Philpot, T. Louisa's Wedding.
Unknown. Galway Races.
Wakoski. Placing a $2 Bet for a Man Who Will
  Never Go to the Horse Races Any More.
Yeats. At Galway Races.

Horseback Riding
Baillie, J. Horse and His Rider, The.
Betjeman. Hunter Trials.
Browning, R. How They Brought the Good
  News from Ghent to Aix.
  Last Ride Together, The.
Campbell, R. Sisters, The.
Cummings, E. All in green went my love
  riding.
Francis, R. Boy Riding Forward Backward.
Guiney. Wild Ride, The.
Hardy, T. Circus-Rider to Ringmaster.
King, H. Moonlight Ride, A.
Kizer, C. Horseback.
Manguso, S. Rider, The.
Morris, W. Haystack in the Floods, The.
Roethke. Elegy for Jane.
Stevenson, R. Windy Nights.
Swenson, M. Bronco Busting, Event #1.
Taylor, H. Riding Lesson.
Unknown. Here Goes My Lord.
Weaver, M. Weekend Equestrian, The.

Horses
Ai. Before You Leave.
Alexie. I Would Steal Horses.
Ammons, A. R. Silver.
Apollinaire. Horse Calligram.
Ayres. Cynthia on Horseback.
Baca. Mantanza to Welcome Spring.
Baillie, J. Horse and His Rider, The.
Barnes, J. Paiute Ponies.
Blaser. Suddenly.
Blind. Fantasy, A.
Boland, E. War Horse, The.
Bowering, G. Dobbin.
Browning, R. How They Brought the Good
  News from Ghent to Aix.
Burns, R. Tam o' Shanter; A Tale.
Bynner. Horses.
Campbell, R. Horses on the Camargue.
  Sisters, The.
Chamberlain, B. Dead Ponies.
Clark, P. My Life with Horses.
Clifton, L. C. C. Rider.
Coatsworth. Circus-Postered Barn, The.
  Daniel Webster's Horses.
  Old Mare, The.
Conn. Todd.
Creeley. Gift of Great Value, A.
  Rescue, The.
Cummings, E. All in green went my love
  riding.
Davis, H. Proud Riders.
Dickey, J. Dusk of Horses, The.
Dietz, H. Blue Grass.
Dodge, M. Wooden Horse, The.
Donovan, K. Entering the Mare.
Dove, R. Horse and Tree.
Espaillat. Metrics.
Fawkes. Elegy on the Death of Dobbin, the
  Butterwoman's Horse, An.
Field, E. Johnny's Team.
Ford, C. 'January wraps up the wound of his
  arm.'
Frankau. Gun Teams.
Frost, R. Draft Horse, The.
  Runaway, The.
Garland, H. Horses Chawin' Hay.
Getsi. Washing Your Hair.
Glück, L. Horse.
Goodge. How We Drove the Trotter.
Gould, H. Apprehension.
Guiney. Wild Ride, The.

Hall, D.   Names of Horses.
Harjo, J.   She Had Some Horses.
Hausman.   Appaloosa Hail Storm.
Heaney, S.   Terminus.
Hearne, V.   Gauguin's White Horse.
Herd.   Hyperion's Bones.
   Pat Taffe and Arkle.
Hogan, L.   Celebration: Birth of a Colt.
Hopkins, G.   Felix Randal.
Hughes, T.   Bones.
   Horses, The.
   Yesterday He Was Nowhere to Be Found.
Jones, R.   Nell.
Kennelly.   Horse's Head, The.
Larkin, P.   At Grass.
Laurencin, M.   Horse, The.
Lawrence, D.   White Horse, The.
Levin, P.   Dark Horse.
Levine, P.   Horse, The.
Levis.   Anastasia and Sandman.
Loving.   Black Horse Rider, The.
Manguso, S.   Rider, The.
McAuley, J.   Blue Horses, The.
McCarriston.   Healing the Mare.
   Riding Out at Evening.
McGrath, T.   End of the Line, The.
Merrill, J.   Charioteer of Delphi, The.
Moore, L.   Eternal Landscape, The.
Moore, M.   Tom Fool at Jamaica.
Muir, E.   Horses.
   Horses, The.
Muldoon, P.   Dancers at the Moy.
Napanangka, V.   Horse, The.
Nelson, J.   For Whom the Bells Toll and Toll
   and Toll.
Norris, L.   Pit Ponies, The.
O'Grady, D.   Great Horse Fair, The.
Parker, A.   Vandals, Horses.
Patchen.   Horses of Yilderin, The.
Peacocke.   Remembrance.
Purdy, A.   Cariboo Horses, The.
Reeves, J.   Four Horses, The.
Renton.   Foal, The.
   Shadow of Himself, The.
Roberson.   Blue Horses.
Romtvedt.   Glass Canyons.
Rossetti, C.   Horses of the Sea, The.
Rothenberg, J.   12th Horse-Song of Frank
   Mitchell (Blue), The.
Roy, L.   Ride, The.
Sabina.   13th Horse Song of Frank Mitchell,
   The.
Schwartz, A.   Blue Grass.
Snyder, G.   All through the Rains.
Stephens, J.   To the Four Courts, Please.
Stephens, M.   Ponies, Twynyrodyn.
Stevens, W.   Room on a Garden, A.
Swenson, M.   Bronco Busting, Event #1.
   Centaur, The.
Taylor, H.   Riding a One-eyed Horse.
Thomas, D.   Because the Pleasure-Bird
   Whistles.
Tomlinson, C.   Saving the Appearances.
Turner, C.   White Horse of Westbury, The.
Unknown.   On a Clergyman's Horse Biting Him.
   On Buying a Horse.
Van Doren.   Distant Runners, The.
Viereck, P.   Love Song to Eohippus.
Walcott.   Polish Rider, The.
Waters, M.   Horse.
Watkins, V.   Foal.
   Mare, The.
Weaver, M.   Appaloosa, The.
Weigl.   Sharing, The.
Wellesley.   Horses.
Woo, M.   Untitled: "In the deepest night and a
   full moon."
Woolson.   Kentucky Belle.
Wright, J.   Blessing, A.
   Horse, The.
   Outside Fargo, North Dakota.
Wunderlich, M.   One Explanation of Beauty.
Yeats.   Michael Robartes Bids His Beloved Be
   at Peace.
See also **Colts; Foals; Horse Racing; Horse
   Shows; Horseback Riding**

Horseshoes
Hopkins, G.   Felix Randal.
Philpot, T.   Louisa's Wedding.
Worth, V.   Magnet.

Hospitality
Belloc.   On a Dead Hostess.
Gurney, I.   La Gorgue.
Hardy, T.   At an Inn.
Herrick.   To the Most Virtuous Mistress Pot,
   Who Many Times Entertained Him.
   Upon Showbread [*or* Shewbread]: Epigram.
Hugo, R.   Places and Ways to Live.
Jonson, B.   Inviting a Friend to Supper.
Kipling, R.   Ballad of East and West, The.
Michelson, P.   Enduring Witness, the Mosques
   of Kattankudi.
Robinson, E.   Cliff Klingenhagen.
See also **Guests**

Hospitals
Adcock, F.   Soho Hospital for Women, The.
Atwood.   Flowers.
Bibbins, M.   Counting.
Campo.   Lost in the Hospital.
Charach, R.   Labour and Delivery.
   MRI.
Conoley.   Masters, The.
Cooke, R.   Hospital Soliloquy, A.
Daniels, K.   Not Singing.
Dickey, J.   Hospital Window, The.
Dransfield.   Visiting Hour (Repatriation
   Hospital).
Flecker.   In Hospital.
Funk, W.   Hospital.
Fusselman, A.   Mother Nature.
Godley, E.   Ninety-Nine.
Graves, R.   Surgical Ward: Men.
Hamilton, I.   Visit, The.
Harwood, G.   Hospital Evening.
Hayden, R.   Broken Dark, The.
Holloway, G.   Monitors.
Howard, R.   Far Cry after a Close Call, A.
Ignatow, D.   Sunday at the State Hospital.
Jarrell.   In a Hospital Garden.
Kavanagh, P.   Hospital, The.
Kinsella, T.   Lady of Quality, A.
Levertov.   Malice of Innocence, The.
Lewis, A.   In Hospital: Poona (1).
MacDiarmid, H.   In the Children's Hospital.
Mackenzie, K.   Hospital—Retrospections, The.
Merwin, W. S.   St. Vincent's.
Muldoon, P.   Field Hospital, The.
Muske, C.   Pediatrics.
North, C.   Hospital.
Owen, W.   Conscious.
   Disabled.
   Hospital Barge at Cérisy.
   Mental Cases.
Parker, D.   Foxfire.
Peacock, M.   Chriseaster.
Petrosky.   V.A. Hospital.
Pilling.   Triptych.
Plath.   Morning in the Hospital Solarium.
   Tulips.
Porter, P.   Happening at Sordid Creek.
Randall, D.   George.
Roeske, P.   Preparing the Dead.
Sassoon.   Death-Bed, The.
Schuyler, J.   Sleep.
Sexton.   Unknown Girl in the Maternity Ward.
   You, Doctor Martin.
Shafer, A.   Monday Morning.
Sholl.   Hospital State, The.
Sissman.   Deathplace, A.
Snodgrass, W.   Operation, The.
Thwaite.   Freedom.
Unknown, fr. Terezin Concentration Camp.
   Theresienstadt's Hospital.
Waring, B.   Baby Random.
Warner, S.   Benicasim.
Webb, F.   Hospital Night.
   Ward Two.
Whitman, W.   Sight in Camp [in the Daybreak
   Gray and Dim], A.
Williams, W.   Between Walls.
   Spring and All.
Wojahn.   W.C.W. Watching Presley's Second

Appearance on The Ed Sullivan Show: Mercy
   Hospital, Newark, 1956.
Wyrebek, M.   Example, An.
   Trendelenburg Position.
Yi, S.   Paper Memorial Stone.

Hotels
Bell, M.   True Story, A.
Betjeman.   Arrest of Oscar Wilde at the
   Cadogan Hotel, The.
Campbell, D.   Hotel Marine.
Christopher.   Far from Home.
Emanuel, J.   Black Man, 13th Floor.
Emanuel, L.   Outside Room Six.
Espada.   Transient Hotel Sky at the Hour of
   Sleep.
Hart, L.   There's a Small Hotel.
Jones, R.   Key, The.
Klein, A.   For the Sisters of the Hôtel Dieu.
Kumin, M.   At the End of the Affair.
Liddy.   Strand Hotel, Rosslare, The.
Lindsay, N.   Jazz of This Hotel, The.
Mueller, L.   Highway Poems.
Polito.   Overheard in the Love Hotel.
Rodgers, R.   There's a Small Hotel.
Rohrer, M.   Hotel de L'Etoile.
Rosemurgy, C.   Hard Put.
Rossetti, C.   Uphill.
Ryan, G.   In the Purple Bar.
Salazar.   Hotel Fresno.
Shenstone.   Written at [*or* in] an Inn at Henley.
Simon, M.   Sea Sprite, Hermosa Beach, The.
Smukler.   Days Inn.
St. John, D.   California.
Tonks.   Story of a Hotel Room.
See also **Motels**

Houdini, Harry
Alvi, M.   Houdini.
Mandel, E.   Houdini.

Hourglasses
Carruth, H.   Testament.
Clare, J.   To an Hour-Glass.
Herrick.   Hour-Glass, The.
Jonson, B.   Hour-Glass [*or* Houre-Glasse], The.

Housekeeping
Alvarez, J.   How I Learned to Sweep.
Campbell, R.   On the Same.
Cerenio.   My Mother.
Curry.   Anne Hathaway Composes Her 18th
   Sonnet.
Dove, R.   Dusting.
Fordham.   Coming Woman, The.
Gilman, C.   Mother's Charge, The.
Henderson-Holmes.   Goodhousekeeping #17.
Johnson, J.   Porter's Love Song to a
   Chambermaid, A.
Kenyon, J.   Finding a Long Gray Hair.
Larkin, J.   Housework.
McGrath, T.   Probable Cause.
North, M.   Portrait in a Brass Gong.
Razaf, A.   My Handy Man.
   Porter's Love Song to a Chambermaid, A.
Rock, D.   Mother.
Schuyler, J.   Song: "I'm about to go shopping."
Silverstein, S.   Sarah Cynthia Sylvia Stout
   Would Not Take the Garbage Out.
Taylor, E.   Huswifery.
Turner, N.   When Young Melissa Sweeps.
Unknown.   Wee Cooper of Fife, The.
Waldman, A.   Baby's Pantoum.
Wayne, J.   In Praise of Zigzags.
Wong, N.   Ironing.
Yuson.   Andy Warhol Speaks to His Two
   Filipino Maids.
See also **Housewives**

Houses
Adamson.   My House.
Armitage, S.   Zoom!
Ashbery.   Old Complex, The.
Ayres.   Invites His Nymph to His Cottage.
Blumenthal, M.   Marriage, A.
Bowering, G.   House, The.
Bradstreet, A.   Here Follows Some Verses upon
   the Burning of Our House [July 10th, 1666.
   Copied Out of a Loose Paper].
Bronk.   Strong Room of the House, The.

Browning, R.   House.
Love in a Life.
Carew, T.   To Saxham.
Carter, E.   Dialogue, A.
Carver, R.   Cobweb, The.
Cary, A.   Window Just Over the Street, The.
Cawein.   Deserted.
Chang Chi.   Coming at Night to a Fisherman's Hut.
Clare, J.   After Reading in a Letter Proposals for Building a Cottage.
Clark, T.   Eyeglasses.
Coleridge, S.   On a Ruined House in a Romantic Country.
Colum, P.   Old Woman of the Roads, The.
Conley, L.   Cottage for Sale, A.
Coward.   Stately Homes of England, The.
Creeley.   House, The.
This House.
D'Lettuso.   Old Houses.
Davie.   Priory of St Saviour, Glendalough, The.
Davies, H.   Music in an Empty House.
Davies, W.   No Man's Wood.
Dawson, W.   House of Pride, The.
De la Mare.   Old Summerhouse, The.
Sleeper, The.
Delgado, J.   Con Los Pájaros.
Dickinson, E.   Eden is that Old-Fashioned House.
God's Residence.
Dodd, W.   Of Rain and Air.
Dodge, M.   Fire in the window.
Dooley, M.   Dancing at Oakmead Road.
Dransfield.   Portrait of the Artist as an Old Man.
Dugan, A.   Love Song: I and Thou.
Dumdum.   Some Die of Light.
Duncan, R.   Coming out of.
Dunn, D.   Modern Love.
On Roofs of Terry Street.
Fisher, A.   Houses.
Forbes, C.   My Father's House.
Ford, F.   Old Houses of Flanders, The.
Frost, R.   Black Cottage, The.
Directive.
Fyleman.   (Mice).
Garrigue.   Country Villa.
Gerner, K.   House of Breath.
Glassco.   Quebec Farmhouse.
Goetsch, D.   Walls, The.
Gould, A.   Demolisher.
Graham, J.   San Sepolcro.
Grass.   Saturn.
Graves, R.   Not at Home.
Gray, T.   On Lord Holland's Seat near Margate, Kent.
Grennan.   Woman at Lit Window.
Groarke, V.   History of My Father's House, The.
Grosholz.   Legacies.
Guest, B.   Defensive Rapture.
Prairie Houses.
Gunn, T.   Last Days at Teddington.
Gwangwa'a.   Leaking Roof.
Hadas, R.   House Beside the Sea, The.
Hagiwara Sakutaro.   Chair.
Hall, D.   Alligator Bride, The.
Hammerstein.   Folks Who Live on the Hill, The.
Hardy, T.   Domicilium.
Fallow Deer at the Lonely House, The.
Hart, L.   Blue Room, The.
Hartnett.   Visit to Castletown House, A.
Harwood, G.   Andante.
Hass, R.   House.
Heaney, S.   Summer Home.
Herbert, G.   Redemption.
World, The.
Herrick.   Thanksgiving to God for His House, A.
Hopkins, G.   In the Valley of the Elwy.
Howe, J.   House of Rest, The.
Howells, W.   Empty House, The.
Huddle.   Gregory's House.
Hughes, L.   Curious.
Hulme, T.   Image.
Hume, C.   Dialogue of Thunder.
Ilio, D.   Site of My Grandfather's House, The.
Iverem, E.   Murmur.

Jackson, H.   My House Not Made with Hands.
Jones, D.   On a Picture of Your House.
Jonson, B.   To Penshurst.
Justice, D.   Beyond the Hunting Woods.
Men at Forty.
Kapos, M.   Pulse, The.
Kenyon, J.   From Room to Room.
Kern, J.   Folks Who Live on the Hill, The.
Khalvati.   Blue Moon.
Kilmer, J.   House with Nobody in It, The.
Koch, K.   Variations on a Theme by William Carlos Williams.
Kooser.   Shooting a Farmhouse.
Kunitz, S.   Three Floors.
Larkin, P.   Home Is So Sad.
Leithauser.   In Minako Wada's House.
Levy, A.   Old House, The.
Lochhead, L.   My Rival's House.
Louis, A.   At the House of Ghosts.
Lowell, R.   For Sale.
Macdonald, G.   Song.
MacNeice.   Château Jackson.
House on a Cliff.
Selva Oscura.
Maiden.   Foundations, The.
Malouf.   For Two Children.
Mayer, B.   House Cap.
Mead, P.   There.
Meredith, W.   American Living-room: A Tract, The.
Merwin, W. S.   Door, A.
Tide Line Garden.
Mew.   Quiet House, The.
Millay, E.   Second Fig.
Miller, A.   Closing, A.
Minhinnick.   House, The.
Moss, H.   Water Island.
Mother Goose.   House That Jack Built, The.
This is the House that Jack Built.
Mtshali.   Inside My Zulu Hut.
Nash, O.   Turtle, The.
Nesbit, E.   Gray Folk, The.
Newell, C.   Dream House.
Padilla.   Fountain, a House of Stone, A.
Paley, G.   Sad Children's Song, The.
Palis, Y.   Floor, The.
Plath.   Point Shirley.
Plumly.   For Esther.
Rago.   Distances, The.
Rakosi.   Founding of New Hampshire, The.
Randall, J.   Rockland.
Ransom, J.   Old Mansion.
Reynolds, L.   To the New Owner.
Reznikoff.   House-wreckers, The.
Roberson.   Poor Houses, The.
Robinson, E.   House on the Hill, The.
Robison, W.   Cottage for Sale, A.
Rodgers, R.   Blue Room, The.
Romano, J.   Old Houses.
Rubin, L.   Houses of Emily Dickinson, The.
Rudolf.   Edward Hopper.
Schuyler, J.   Along Overgrown Paths.
Scott, D.   Skiddaw House.
Selman, R.   21 East 10th, 2BR, WBF, EIK.
Shange.   Where the Heart Is.
Sheridan, T.   Tom Punsibi's Letter to Dean Swift.
Smith, S.   Grange, The.
Smith, W.   Floor and the Ceiling, The.
Soutar.   Room, The.
Stanley-Wrench.   Hinterland.
Stevens, W.   Gallant Château.
House Was Quiet and the World Was Calm, The.
Stevenson, R.   House Beautiful, The.
Stoddard, E.   House by the Sea, The.
Stryk, L.   Oeuvre.
Swenson, M.   Question.
Taylor, A.   Fitzroy.
Thomas, E.   New House, The.
Thoreau.   For Though the Eaves [or Caves] Were Rabbeted [or Rabbited].
Tomlinson, C.   On the Hall at Stowey.
Unknown.   I Will Give My Love an Apple [Without E'er a Core].
Wide Walls.

Untermeyer, L.   Prayer for This House.
Van Doren.   Near House, The.
Vasquez, R.   For Jose Mercado Vasquez and Frances Roman Vasquez.
Vaughan, H.   They Are All Gone into the World of Light!
Walcott.   Ruins of a Great House.
Wallace, R.   Sestina for the House.
Warn.   After Reading the Book of Splendor.
Dwelling.
Weaver, M.   Beginnings.
Water Song.
Whitlow.   Book of Routh.
Wilde, O.   Harlot's House, The.
Williams, M.   Empty House, The.
Williams, W.   House, The.
Wordsworth, W.   Inscription for the Moss-Hut at Dove Cottage.
Ruined Cottage, The.
Wright, C.   Virgo Descending.
Wylie.   Prophecy.
Wyrebek, M.   Example, An.
See also **Home**
Housewives
Bodecker.   Hurry, Hurry, Mary Dear!
Boland, E.   Woman in Kitchen.
Dove, R.   Daystar.
Gilbert, S.   Ladies' Home Journal, The.
Harwood, G.   Long After Heine.
Jarrell.   Next Day.
Mew.   Farmer's Bride, The.
Pastan.   Marks.
Scarfe.   Kitchen Poem.
Sexton.   Housewife.
Risk, The.
Shuttle.   Gone Is the Sleepgiver.
Unknown.   Epitaph.
My Love.
Williams, W.   Young Housewife, The.
Young, A.   California Peninsula: El Camino Real.
See also **Housekeeping**
Housman, Alfred Edward
Auden.   A. E. Housman.
Pound, E.   Mr. Housman's Message.
Hudson River, New York
Corn.   Water: City Wildlife and Greenery.
Goodman, P.   Lordly Hudson, The.
Lowell, R.   Mouth of the Hudson, The.
Teasdale.   Summer Night, Riverside.
Weiss, T.   Egyptian Passage, An.
Hughes, Langston
Blockcolski.   Langston Hughes.
Brooks, G.   Langston Hughes.
D'Aguiar.   Langston.
Danner.   Rhetoric of Langston Hughes, The.
Forbes, C.   Reading Walt Whitman.
Knight, E.   For Langston Hughes.
Madgett.   Simple.
Plumpp.   Saturday Night Decades.
Powell, K.   Genius Child.
Randall, D.   Langston Blues.
Young, K.   Langston Hughes.
Hughes, Ted
Cope, W.   Policeman's Lot, A.
Larkin, P.   Limerick: "There was an old fellow of Kaber."
Huguenots
Bridges, R.   Psalm: "While Northward the hot sun was sinking o'er the trees."
Coleridge, M.   Huguenot, A.
Human Folly
Bensley.   Bloomsbury Snapshot.
Bradstreet, A.   Contemplations.
De Vries, P.   Sacred and Profane Love, or, There's Nothing New under the Moon Either.
Ferlinghetti, L.   25.
Hall, D.   Grace, A.
Hart, L.   I Wish I Were in Love Again.
Herbert, G.   Dotage.
Jeffers, R.   Advice to Pilgrims.
Eagle Valor, Chicken Mind.
Original Sin.
Kerouac.   Poem.
Kessler, R.   Elm Tree on Lafayette Street, The.

McGough, R.   Prayer to Saint Grobianus.
Murray, L.   Quality of Sprawl, The.
Owen, W.   Arms and the Boy.
Patchen.   Origin of Baseball, The.
Pitter.   But for Lust.
Shapiro, K.   Fly, The.
Swift, J.   Verses on the Death of Dr. Swift, D.S.P.D., Occasioned by Reading a Maxim in Rochefoucauld.
Unknown.   Cameleon's Defence, The.
Warren, R.   Man in the Street.

Human Race
Canan.   Mother Dawning.
Cortes, F.   Fish 2.
Forhan, C.   Without Presumptions.
Glück, L.   Matins.
Glover, S.   Power of the Soul.
Griffin, S.   Our Mother.
Kingston, M.   Restaurant.
Klein, M.   Guardian Life.
Laux.   If This Is Paradise.
Lazarus, E.   Success.
Lifshin.   Bergen-Belsen 1945.
Mandela.   Saviour.
McNeil, R.   It Just Doesn't Matter.
Merrill, B.   People.
Mkangelwa.   Observations.
Murray, J.   There Has Been More Than Beginning and End to Face.
Rampolekeng.   Welcome to the New Consciousness.
Spofford.   Tryst, The.
Styne, J.   People.
Tate, J.   Cages, The.
Villanueva, A.   Planet Earth Speaks, The.
Williamson, G.   Bodies of Water.
See also **Mankind**

Humility
Astell.   In Emulation of Mr Cowleys Poem Call'd The Motto.
Bensley.   Charity.
Carew, T.   On the Marriage of T. K. and C. C.: The Morning Stormy.
Chudleigh.   Resolve, The.
Coleridge, S.   Forbearance.
Curzon, D.   Proverbs 6:6.
Di Piero.   Near Damascus.
Durcan.   Kilfenora Teaboy, The.
Emerson, R.   Experience.
Foss, S.   House by the Side of the Road, The.
Frost, R.   Demiurge's Laugh, The.
Herbert, G.   Church-Lock and Key.
   Humility.
   Posy [*or* Posie], The.
Johnson, S.   *Ad. fr.* the Bible, Proverbs, 6, 6.
Kerouac.   And What Do I Owe You, God.
Kipling, R.   If—.
   Recessional.
Knevet.   Contrition.
Mitchell, A.   Icarus Schmicarus.
Norris, A.   Humble Heart, A.
Porter, A.   Oaks and Squirrels.
Ransom, J.   Amphibious Crocodile.
Robinson, E.   Cliff Klingenhagen.
Rochester, J.   Rochester Extempore.
Rossetti, C.   Lowest Place, The.
Stanley, T.   Paraphrase Upon Part of the CXXXIX Psalm, A.
Taylor, J.   Violet, The.
Unknown.   I Will Bow and Be Simple.
Wright, J.   Out of Horace.

Hummingbirds
Corbett, W.   Vermont Apollinaire.
Corman.   Container, The.
Delgado, J.   Chuparosa.
Dickinson, E.   Hummingbird, A.
Dubie.   Hummingbirds.
Hall, D.   Her Garden.
Kennedy, X.   Hummingbird.
Lawrence, D.   Humming-Bird.
Littlebird.   Hummingbird.
Oliver, M.   Hummingbird Pauses at the Trumpet Vine.
Tucker, M.   Humming-Bird, The.

Humorous and Nonsense Verse
Alexie.   Theology.

Beatty, P.   That's Not in My Job Description.
Healy, R.   Mutability Checkers.
Holmes, O.   After-Dinner Poem (Terpsichore), An.
McDaniel, J.   Disasterology.
Myer, M.   Cool Cat.
Noguchi, R.   Turn of Privacy, The.
Poe.   Monody on Doctor Olmsted.
Prys-Jones.   Unfortunate Occurrence at Cwm-Cadno.
Unknown.   Polly Wolly Doodle.
Von Freytag-Loringhoven.   Klink—Hratzvenga (Deathwail).
Williamson, G.   Appalachian Trees Encircled by Police Tape.
   Belvedere Marittimo.
Young, K.   Clyde Peeling's Reptiland in Allenwood, Pennsylvania.

Hunchbacks
Soyinka.   Hunchback of Dugbe, The.
Thomas, D.   Hunchback in the Park, The.

Hundred Years War
Unknown.   King Henry Fifth's Conquest of France.

Hungary
Arnold, M.   To the Hungarian Nation.
Feinstein, E.   Annus Mirabilis 1989.

Hunger
Angira.   Manna.
Asquith.   Banking Potatoes.
Atwood.   More and More.
Auden.   Healthy Spot, A.
Barnett, R.   Anorexic, The.
Bass, F.   I am a Jew.
Bhatt.   Go To Ahmedabad.
Binyon.   Hunger.
Bourne, W.   Heart's Fine Gold, The.
Cambridge, A.   Desire.
Ceravolo.   Ho Ho Ho Caribou.
Chin.   Disorder, The.
Clampitt.   Beethoven, Opus 111.
D'Aguiar.   Sound Bite.
Dodge, M.   Poor Crow!
"Field."   Eros.
Fisher, J.   Camp.
Fyleman.   Punch and Judy.
Gibran.   Fox, The.
Grass.   Saturn.
Hix, H. L.   Man in Novosibirsk.
Hughes, F.   Foxes.
Jones, A.   Anorexia.
Kinsella, J.   Archetypal Chillies.
Levertov.   O Taste and See.
Levine, P.   They Feed They Lion.
Livingston, M.   Poor.
Lorde.   Litany for Survival, A.
   Woman Thing, The.
Merwin, W. S.   Bread.
Mif.   Terezin.
Miller, A.   Hungry Black Child, The.
Naimy, M.   Hunger.
Pegram, A.   Towards Abraham's Bosom.
Pilinszky, J.   Frankfurt.
Pilling.   Cast Away.
Reed, H.   Château, The.
Rothenberg, J.   Hunger.
Sandburg, C.   Galoots.
Shamaqmaq, A.   Hungry Master and Hungry Cat.
Short, J.   Leave in Mid-Winter.
Swirszczynska.   I Starve My Belly for a Sublime Purpose.
Szymborska.   Starvation Camp near Jaslo.
Thomas, E.   Owl, The.
Toomer.   Harvest Song.
Tsaloumas.   Autumn Supper.
Unknown, fr. Terezin Concentration Camp.   Theresienstadt's Hospital.
Vallejo.   Hungry Man's Wheel, The.
Wheeler, S.   Produce, Produce.
Wilbur.   Potato.

Hunt, Leigh
Keats.   To Leigh Hunt, Esq.
   Written on the Day That Mr. Leigh Hunt Left Prison.

Hunting and Hunters
Amirthanayagam.   Elephants Are in the Yard, The.
Atwood.   Dream 2: Brian the Still-Hunter.
Auden.   Decoys, The.
Baker, H.   Advice to a Man Who Lost a Dog.
Barnes, J.   Tracking Rabbits: Night.
Beer, P.   Lion Hunts.
Berg, S.   Orpingalik's My Breath: Eskimo Song.
Berlin.   You Can't Get a Man with a Gun.
Bernstein, M.   Manly Sports.
Berryman.   Winter Landscape.
Blunden.   Winter: East Anglia.
Blunt, W.   Old Squire, The.
Bowman, C.   Dove at Sundown.
Brontë, A.   Song.
Brontë, C.   Young Man Naughty's Adventure.
Carroll, L.   Baker's Tale, The.
   Fit the Second: The Bellman's Speech.
   Fit the Sixth: The Barrister's Dream.
   Hunting of the Snark, The.
   Vanishing, The.
Causley.   I Saw a Jolly Hunter.
Cavendish, M.   Hunting of the Hare, The.
Chase, K.   Venison.
Clare, J.   Badger.
Clarke, C.   Tortoise and Badger.
Cowley, M.   Ernest.
Cummings, E.   All in green went my love riding.
Daniel, G.   After a Storm, Going a Hawking.
Davidson, J.   Runnable Stag, A.
Davies, S.   Scene after Hunting at Swallowfield in Berkshire, A.
Davis, C.   Little Crisis Framed in My Window.
Davis, J.   Warru.
De la Mare.   Hi!
Dickinson, E.   Cat.
Donaghy, M.   Duck.
Driver.   Ballad of Hunters, A.
Drummond, W.   Madrigal: "This world a hunting is."
Ehrhart.   Hunting.
Erdrich.   Jacklight.
   Strange People, The.
Follain.   Black Meat.
Ford, R.   Revenge of the Hunted.
Francis, R.   December.
Frost, C.   To Kill a Deer.
Gascoigne.   Gascoigne's Woodmanship.
Gascoyne.   Rex Mundi.
Graves, J.   John Peel.
Harris, R.   Literary Excellence.
Hartley, M.   As the Buck Lay Dead.
Hartnett.   Possibility That Has Been Overlooked Is the Future, The.
Hemans.   Chamois Hunter's Love, The.
Herbert, G.   Affliction (4).
Hogan, L.   Skin.
Hopkinson, F.   O'er the Hills.
Hughes, T.   Modest Proposal, A.
Jarrell.   Bird of Night, The.
Jonson, B.   To Sir Henry Goodyere.
Killigrew, A.   On a Picture Painted by Herself [*or* Her self], Representing Two Nymphs [*or* Nimphs] of Diana's, One in a Posture to Hunt, the other Bath[e]ing.
Kinnell.   Bear, The.
   To Christ Our Lord.
Kumin, M.   Woodchucks.
Lanier, S.   Revenge of Hamish, The.
Lawrence, D.   Mountain Lion.
Layton.   Black Huntsmen, The.
Lorde.   Woman Thing, The.
Lovelace, R.   La Bella Bona-Roba.
   Love Enthroned.
Lowbury.   Huntsman, The.
Lowry, M.   Salmon Drowns Eagle.
Mahon.   Hunt by Night, The.
   St. Eustace.
Markus, P.   Shooting Crows.
Marvell.   Nymph and Her Fawn, The.
   Nymph Complaining for the Death of Her Faun [*or* Fawn], The.
McDonald, W.   After the Noise of Saigon.
Mozeen.   Kilruddery Hunt, The.

Muñoz, A. Hunting Accident.
Napurrurla, I. Water, The.
O'Hara, F. Hunter, The.
Page, P. Stories of Snow.
Philp-Carmichael. Dust Storm.
Pound, E. Return, The.
Richard, M. Y'All Are Bird Dogs, Aren't You?
Rodgers, W. Beagles.
Scott, S. Hunting Song.
Sisson. Un-Red Deer, The.
Skrzynecki. Hunting Rabbits.
Souster. Hunter, The.
Starbird. Hound, The.
Stein, G. Valentine to Sherwood Anderson, A.
  White Hunter, A.
Tallmountain. Good Grease.
Talvikki, A. You Don't Know What Happened
  When You Froze.
Thesen. Kirk Lonegren's Home Movie Taking
  Place Just North of Prince George, with Sound.
Tobin, D. Hunt-Cup, The.
Tu Mu. Egrets.
Unknown. Buffalo Skinners, The.
  Carmen Possum.
  Epitaph for Thomas Johnson, Huntsman.
    Charlton, Sussex.
  Fox, The.
  Weismiller. Skull.
Wordsworth, W. Simon Lee [the Old
  Huntsman].
Wright, J. White Deer, The.
Wyatt, S. Whoso List to Hunt.
Zieroth. Hunters of the Deer, The.

Hurdy-Gurdies
Calverley. Lines on Hearing the Organ.
Noyes, A. Barrel-Organ, The.
Symons, A. Barrel-Organ, The.

Huron, Lake
Herschberger. Huron, The.

Hurricanes
Balaban. Hurricane.
Crane, H. Hurricane, The.
Freneau. Hurricane, The.
Glatt. Amanda.
Hernández Cruz. Art of Hurricanes, The.
  Problems With Hurricanes.
Morrissey, S. After the Hurricane.
Philp, G. Heirlooms.
See also **Storms**

Husbands
Alvi, M. Backgrounds.
  Carrying My Wife.
  Man Impregnated.
Bang, M. Crossed-Over, Fiend-Snitched, X-ed
  Out.
Bly, R. French Generals, The.
Bradstreet, A. Letter to Her Husband, Absent
  upon Public[k] Employment, A.
  To My Dear and Loving Husband.
Browning, R. Any Wife to Any Husband.
Carey, H. Maid's Husband, The.
Cerenio. 23 October 1992.
Christie. Possible Man, The.
Egerton, S. Emulation, The.
"Eliza." To My Husband.
Ferch Gruffyd, A. Verses Written by Alis
  Daughter of Gryffydd Son of Iefan When Her
  Father Asked Her What Sort of Husband She
  Would Like.
Graves, R. Slice of Wedding Cake, A.
Haynes, C. Any Wife or Husband.
Heard, J. My Husband's Birthday.
Hirsch, E. Husband and Wife.
Jonson, B. So White, So Soft, So Sweet.
Kendrick, D. Sadie Snuffs a Candle.
King, H. Dream Maiden, A.
Lee, L. Gift, The.
Lewis, C. Ballade of Dead Gentlemen.
Lowell, R. To Speak of Woe That Is in
  Marriage.
Madan. To Lysander.
Masini. Two Men, Two Grapefruits.
McBride, M. Knife-Thrower's Wife, The.
Mesens. Arid Husband, The.
Mugo, M. G. Wife of the Husband.

Nash, O. Word to Husbands, A.
Nesbit, E. Husband of To-Day, The.
Pape. Minotaur Next Door, The.
Remoto. Images of John (1967–92).
Rowe, E. Upon the Death of Her Husband.
Rungano. Woman, The.
Sawyer, A. Lines, / Written on Seeing My
  Husband's Picture, painted when he was
  young: "Those are the features, those the
  smiles."
Sexton. And One for My Dame.
Shaw, A. Crepuscule.
Stoddard, E. Wife Speaks, The.
Thomas, E. New Litany, Occasioned by an
  Invitation to a Wedding, A.
Thompson, P. Husband's Return, The.
Unknown. Henpecked Husband, A.
  Tell Me, Wight in the Broom.
Villon. Ballad Written for a Bridegroom.
Wallis, H. To Mrs.———, on the Death of Her
  Husband.
Winchilsea. Letter to Daphnis, A.
Wright, M. Address to Her Husband.

Hyacinths
Eliot, T. Song for Simeon, A.
Glück, L. Hyacinth.
Prince, F. Babiaantje, The.
Siegel, J. Wild Hyacinth.

Hyde, Douglas
Clarke, A. Burial of an Irish President.

Hyenas
Kipling, R. Hyænas [*or* Hyenas], The.

Hymns
Glaser, M. Magnificat!
Unknown. Limerick.

Hypocrisy and Hypocrites
Barben, D. Do You Know What You're Saying.
Blake, W. On Hayley.
Bly, R. Johnson's Cabinet Watched by Ants.
Browning, E. Man's Requirements, A.
Browning, R. Soliloquy of the Spanish Cloister.
Burns, R. Address to the Unco Guid, or the
  Rigidly Righteous.
  Holy Willie's Prayer.
Clough. Latest Decalogue, The.
Congreve. Hue and Cry after Fair Amoret, A.
Connolly, C. To Osbert Sitwell.
Creeley. Wait for Me.
Cummings, E. Next to of Course God America
  I.
Graves, R. Sick Love.
Harington [*or* Harrington]. Groome of the
  Chambers Religion in King Henry the Eights
  Time, A.
Harper, F. Double Standard, A.
Hughes, L. American Heartbreak.
Hutchinson, P. Look, No Hands.
Jonson, B. On Don Surly.
  On the Town's Honest Man.
Kipling, R. Tommy.
Knight, E. On Watching Politicians Perform at
  Martin Luther King's Funeral.
Lawrence, D. Retort to Jesus.
Levertov. Hypocrite Women.
Lindsay, N. At Mass.
  Why I Voted the Socialist Ticket.
Mapanje. Cheerful Girls at Smiller's Bar, 1971,
  The.
Montagu, L. Epistle from Mrs. Yonge to Her
  Husband.
Mudrooroo Narogin. Peaches and Cream.
Piercy. Peaceable Kingdom, The.
Pope, A. Epigram in a Maid of Honour's
  Prayer-Book.
Praed. Chancery Morals.
Robinson, M. Stanzas: "In this vain, busy
  world, where the good and the gay."
Shapiro, K. Drug Store.
Whittier. Christian Slave, The.
  Clerical Oppressors.
Woddis. Ethics for Everyman.
Yeats. On Hearing That the Students of Our
  New University Have Joined the Agitation
  against Immoral Literature.

I

Ibo, The
Kay, J. Pride.
Ibsen, Henrik
Dubie. Fox Who Watched for the Midnight
  Sun, The.
Ibycus
Lazarus, E. Cranes of Ibycus, The.
Icarus
Abse. Brueghel in Naples.
Auden. Musée des Beaux Arts.
Benét, S. Winged Man.
Bottrall. Icarus.
Iremonger. Icarus.
Mitchell, A. Icarus Schmicarus.
Nowlan. I, Icarus.
Rukeyser, M. Waiting for Icarus.
Sexton. To a Friend Whose Work Has Come to
  Triumph.
Stevenson, A. Icarus in November.
Stickney, T. On Rodin's "L'Illusion, Sœur
  d'Icare."
Ice
De la Mare. Ice.
"Field." To the Winter Aphrodite.
Fletcher, J. Skaters, The.
Frost, R. Fire and Ice.
Hayden, R. Ice Storm.
Johnson, J. Midnight Run.
Kenney. Sailing.
Klein, A. Break-up, The.
Livesay, D. Uninvited, The.
Longley, M. Freeze-Up.
Lowry, M. About Ice.
MacCaig. Sleet.
McCarriston. January, Anchorage.
Monk, M. Fire Us with Ice, Burn Us with
  Snow.
Nabhan, G. Coming Out on Solid Ground After
  the Ice Age.
Nemerov. Icehouse in Summer, The.
Rafferty, P. 66°7' N/22°17' W.
Ransom, W. Message from Ohanapecosh
  Glacier.
Rector. My Grandfather Always Promised Us.
Roditi. Aurora Borealis.
Rothman, D. Whistling in January.
Sexton, T. Skimming the Ice.
Siegel, J. Wild Hyacinth.
Wakoski. Ice Eagle, The.
Wilbur. Stop.
Wyrebek, M. Trendelenburg Position.
Ice Cream
Charara, H. On the Murder of an Ice Cream
  Man.
Hempel, A. Rain.
Kaplinski, J. My Wife and Children.
Laing, A. Grace for Ice-Cream, A.
Stanard, C. Washington Square Park and a
  Game of Chess.
Stevens, W. Emperor of Ice-Cream, The.
Ice Skating and Ice Skaters
Dunn, S. Criminal.
Kuzma. Ice Skating.
Salter. Sunday Skaters.
See also **Skating and Skaters**
Icebergs
Bishop, E. Imaginary Iceberg, The.
Hardy, T. Convergence of the Twain, The.
Melville, H. Berg, The.
Iceland
Rafferty, P. 66°7' N/22°17' W.
Icicles
Frost, R. Beyond Words.
Roberson. Poor Houses, The.
Idaho (state)
Crase. There Is No Real Peace in the World.
Johnson, J. Unmarked Stop in Front of
  Westmond General Store, Westmond, Idaho.
Idealism and Idealists
Chase, N. My Ideal.
Collins, M. If.
Herrick. No Loathsomnesse in Love.

Ray, H.   Quest of the Ideal, The.
Robin, L.   My Ideal.
Sanchez, S.   Poem for July 4, 1994.
Unknown.   I Will Give My Love an Apple [Without E'er a Core].
Whiting, R.   My Ideal.

Identity
Anderson, S.   American Spring Song.
Arrillaga.   Dream.
  Like Raquel.
  Rosa/Filí.
Bernstein, L.   Lucky to Be Me.
Berrigan, A.   Bloodletting.
  Ode to Election Day.
Borawski.   Some of Us Wear Pink Triangles.
Brooks, G.   To the Diaspora.
Brown, E.   Out.
Brown, L.   I Want to Be Bad.
Budy.   Ellis Island, September 1907.
Buscani.   Downtime.
Cameron, N.   Meeting My Former Self.
Chin.   We Are Americans Now, We Live in the Tundra.
Cofer, J.   Changeling, The.
Comden, B.   Lucky to Be Me.
Coultas, B.   Human Museum, The.
de Aerenlund, C.   Cuando el tecolote canta, el Indio muere.
DeSylva, B. G.   I Want to Be Bad.
Dietz, H.   Triplets.
Espada.   My Native Costume.
Esteves.   Here.
Fuhrman, J.   Personal Ad.
Goese, M.   You Are.
Gomez, M.   To the Latin Lover I Left at the Candy Store.
Gonzalez, N.   I Made Myself a Path.
Gordon, I.   Be Anything (But Be Mine).
Green, A.   Lucky to Be Me.
Hamer.   Origins.
Hawoldar.   To Be a Woman.
Henderson, R.   I Want to Be Bad.
Henry, B.   Garage Sale.
Highfill, M.   Marginalization of Poetry, The.
Hovanessian, D.   Inside Green Eyes, Black Eyes.
  Mixed Marriage.
  Two Voices.
Jackson, B.   In Exchange for Forty Acres.
Jackson, L.   One Self.
  Reasons of Each, The.
Joseph, A.   Adolescence.
Joseph, L.   That's All.
Kay, J.   In My Country.
  Pride.
  Somebody Else.
Lavieri, J.   Autobiography of John Doe, The.
Lem.   So Now You're Chicana.
Lorde.   Outlines.
Morales.   Ending Poem.
Morales, A.   Puertoricanness.
Mtshali.   Boy on a Swing.
Mudrooroo Narogin.   Jacky Sings His Songs.
Plotnick, H. M.   Jewish.
Raffalovich, M. A.   Sonnet 120.
  World Well Lost 4, The.
Rodrigues J. P.   Half-.
Savageau.   At the Powwow.
  Like the Trails of Ndakinna.
  Looking for Indians.
  To Human Skin.
Schwartz, A.   Triplets.
Sharma, P.   Poorly Matched.
  Principles, When I Felt Them.
Sia, B.   Claim to Fame.
Singer, B.   Still and All.
Sisson.   Person, The.
Song.   Lost Sister.
St. Germain, S.   Cajun.
Su, A.   Address.
Trethewey, N.   Flounder.
  White Lies.
Uyematsu.   To All Us Sansei Who Wanted to Be Westside.
Van Doren.   Midland.
Viray, M.   Patio.

  Two Strangers, The.
Williams, C.   In Search of Aunt Jemima.

Identity Crisis
Baraka.   Agony, An. As Now.
Bona.   Amazone.
Bronk.   I Thought It Was Harry.
Dame.   On the Road to Damascus, Maryland.
de Aerenlund, C.   Cuando el tecolote canta, el Indio muere.
Derricotte.   Struggle, The.
Gier, J.   Examining the I.
Hagedorn, J.   Filipino Boogie.
Hayden, R.   Names.
Healy, E.   Changing What We Mean.
Hewitt, J.   Colony, The.
Hogan, L.   Truth Is, The.
Honig, E.   Being Somebody.
Hughes, L.   Theme for English B.
Hughes, T.   Wodwo.
Jarrell.   Woman at the Washington Zoo, The.
Kumin, M.   After Love.
Madgett.   Exits and Entrances.
Mirikitani.   Doreen.
Nye, N.   Blood.
Olson, C.   In Cold Hell, in Thicket.
Peacock, M.   Spell, The.
Rodgers, C.   Group Therapy.
Rose.   Endangered Roots of a Person.
Shomer.   Falling for Jesus.
Spires.   Interrogations of the Sparrow.
St. John, P.   We Are Going to Be Here Now.
Stephens, J.   Twins, The.
Stone, R.   My Son.
Utemorrah, D.   Mary's Plea.
Wong, N.   When I Was Growing Up.
  Where Is My Country?

Idleness
Keats.   Ode on Indolence.
Silverstein, S.   Jimmy Jet and His TV Set.
Simic.   Against Whatever It Is That's Encroaching.
Spender, S.   Unemployed.
Watts, I.   Sluggard, The.
Welch, L.   This Book is for Magda.
Whalen.   Chanson d'Outre Tombe.
See also **Sloth**

Idolatry
Cooper, D.   Teen Idols.
Hollo.   Italics.
Kipling, R.   Evarra and His Gods.
Lindsay, N.   To a Golden-Haired Girl in a Louisiana Town.
MacNeice.   Leaving Barra.

Ignorance
Aiken, C.   Annihilation.
Beckett, S.   Gnome.
Bunting.   To Violet [with Prewar Poems].
Cary, A.   In Bonds.
Chinn.   Skin Color from the Sun.
Cornford, F.   To a Fat Lady Seen from the Train.
Cowper, W.   Lines Written upon a Window-Shutter at Weston.
Derricotte.   Blackbottom.
Dobell, S.   Liberty to M. le Diplomate.
Heffernan, M.   Message, The.
Hewitt, J.   From the Tibetan.
Hitchcock.   Song of Expectancy.
Hope, M.   Bare Floors.
  Sixth Grade.
Hughes, F.   Different Voice, The.
Hughes, T.   Childish Prank, A.
Ingalls, J.   Apprehension.
Joseph, J.   Back to Base.
Komunyakaa.   Salt.
Leigh, C.   How Little We Know (How Little It Matters).
Lux.   Bodo.
Madgett.   Images.
Mezey.   Reaching the Horizon.
Prys-Jones.   Unfortunate Occurrence at Cwm-Cadno.
Ransom, J.   Man without Sense of Direction.
Rossetti, C.   Sketch, A.
Springer, P.   How Little We Know (How Little It Matters).

Stevens, W.   Sense of the Sleight-of-Hand Man, The.
Wetzsteon.   Coming Back to the Cave.

Illegitimacy
Breton, N.   Cradle Song: "Come, little babe."
Burns, R.   Poet's Welcome to His Love-Begotten Daughter [the First Instance that Entitled Him to the Venerable Appellation of Father], A.
  Rantin Laddie, The.
Hughes, L.   Mulatto.
Leigh, H.   Natural Child, The.
Sexton.   Unknown Girl in the Maternity Ward.
Smith, S.   Valuable.
Unknown.   Limerick.

Illinois (state)
Bly, R.   Three Kinds of Pleasures.
Bradbury, R.   Byzantium I Come Not From.
Brooks, G.   Lovers of the Poor, The.
Getsi.   Woman Hanging from Lightpole, Illinois Route 136.
Goldbarth.   Letter to Friends East and West.
Kinnell.   First Song.
Knoepfle.   Confluence.
  Late Winter in Menard County.
Loncar, M.   Peoria.
Mueller, L.   Another Version.
Sandburg, C.   Illinois Farmer.
Schmitz.   Making Chicago.
Sorby.   Land of Lincoln.
Stanton, M.   Few Picnics in Illinois, A.
  Sorrow and Rapture.

Illiteracy
Meredith, W.   Illiterate, The.
Murphy, R.   Reading Lesson, The.

Illness
Abse.   Doctor, The.
Baillie, J.   Child to His Sick Grandfather, A.
Bartlett, E.   999 Call.
Bass, F.   Illness.
Bell, M.   Book of the Dead Man #1, The.
  Someone Is Probably Dead.
Belloc.   Henry King, Who Chewed Bits of String, and Was Early Cut Off in Dreadful Agonies.
Berg, S.   Orpingalik's My Breath: Eskimo Song.
Berryman.   Recognition, The.
Betjeman.   Devonshire Street W.1.
Bibbins, M.   Counting.
Borawski.   Talking to Jim.
Bradstreet, A.   Deliverance from a Fit of Fainting.
  For Deliverance from a Fever.
Broumas, O.   Touched.
Browning, R.   Confessions.
Burns, R.   Duncan Gray.
Bush, D.   Pneumoconiosis.
Byron, G.   Lines on Hearing That Lady Byron Was Ill.
Campo.   Lost in the Hospital.
Carroll, J.   Paregoric Babies.
Carver, R.   What the Doctor Said.
Chimombo.   Derailment: A Delirium.
Cofer, J.   Counting.
Cohan.   If I'm Going to Die I'm Going to Have Some Fun.
Colby, T.   Dear, I Love.
Coleman, W.   Aunt Jessie.
Conoley.   Masters, The.
Cornford, F.   Watch, The.
Coulehan, J.   Lovesickness: A Medieval Text.
  Rule of Thirds, The.
Cowper, M.   World Not Our Rest, The.
Cowper, W.   To Mary.
D'Aguiar.   Obeah Mama Dot.
Davidson, L.   Fear of Madness, The.
Day, J.   Man's Natural Infirmity.
Disch.   Convalescing in London.
Dixon, M.   Heartbeats.
Donne.   Canonization, The.
  Hymn[e] to God My God, In My Sickness[e], A.
Doty, M.   Embrace, The.
  Tiara.
Duncan, R.   After a Long Illness.
Evance, S.   Written in Ill Health at the Close of

Spring.
Feilding, F.   One the Morening the King was Taken Ill my Dreame of Him.
"Field."   Almoner, An.
  Picture, A.
Fitzgerald, R.   Entreaty.
Frost, K.   Remission.
Gerstler.   Fan Letter, A.
Glück, L.   Descending Figure.
Godley, E.   Ninety-Nine.
Goodman, P.   Sentences After *Defence of Poetry*.
Graham-Pole, J.   Leaving Mother, 1954.
Graves, R.   Symptoms Of Love.
Gunn, T.   Man With Night Sweats, The.
  Missing, The.
Hanson, M.   To Fancy.
Hardy, T.   Sleep-Worker, The.
Hart, L.   It's Got to Be Love.
Harteis.   Star Trek III.
Hayden, R.   Broken Dark, The.
Hayley.   To Mr. William Long, On His Recovery from a Dangerous Illness, 1785.
Herford.   Limerick.
Hernández Cruz.   Spirits.
Herrera.   Weaning of Furniture-Nutrition.
Herrick.   To Music, to Becalm a Sweet-sick Youth.
  To Music, to Becalm His Fever.
  Upon Prudence Baldwin Her Sickness[e].
Hewitt, J.   Scar, The.
Hikmet.   Angina Pectoris.
Holloway, G.   Hypochondriac.
  Monitors.
Holtby, M.   Answer to a Kind Enquiry.
Hopkins, G.   Felix Randal.
Hove.   Other Syllabus, The.
Howard, R.   1915: A Pre-Raphaelite Ending, London.
  Far Cry after a Close Call, A.
Hughes, L.   Madam and the Wrong Visitor.
Jarrell.   Sick Child, A.
Jewsbury.   Verses: "I am monarch of troubles a host."
Jones, P.   If I Were Rita Hayworth.
  Modris.
Jonson, B.   To Sickness.
Kavanagh, P.   Hospital, The.
Kendrick, D.   Inpatient.
Kinsella, J.   Sick Woman.
Kinsella, T.   Tear.
Kizer, C.   For Jan as the End Draws Near.
Larkin, J.   Inventory.
Lawrence, D.   Healing.
Lewis, G.   Flyover Elegies.
Loesser.   Adelaide's Lament.
Lowell, R.   My Last Afternoon with Uncle Devereux Winslow.
MacBeth [or Macbeth].   Worst Fear, The.
MacDiarmid, H.   Two Parents, The.
Mackenzie, K.   Sick Men Sleeping.
Marvell.   Dialogue between the Soul and [the] Body, A.
Maura.   Each Day.
McAuley, J.   Convalescence.
McCarriston.   Healing the Mare.
McClure, M.   Rant Block.
Merrill, J.   Country of a Thousand Years of Peace, The.
Metcalfe.   Visit the Sick.
Miller, V.   Bout with Burning.
Mukand, J.   Lullaby.
Nye, N.   Making a Fist.
Olson, C.   Librarian, The.
Ormsby, F.   Day in August, A.
Paulin.   Anastasia McLaughlin.
Plath.   Among the Narcissi.
  Fever 103°.
Platt, F.   Coincidentally.
Praed.   To Helen.
Purdy, A.   Poem: "You are ill and so I lead you away."
Reader.   When Paul Bunyan Was Ill.
Reed, I.   I Am Not the Walrus.
Rodgers, R.   It's Got to Be Love.
Roethke.   Infirmity.

Rogers, S.   Written in a Sick Chamber.
Rukeyser, M.   George Robinson: Blues.
Schwartz, R. L.   AIDS Education, Seventh Grade.
  Midnight Supper.
Scott, D.   Apocalypse Dub.
  Illness.
Shapcott, T.   Post Operative.
Shaw, A.   Bird Nests.
Smart, C.   Hymn to the Supreme Being.
Spivack, K.   Judgment, The.
Stevenson, R.   Land of Counterpane, The.
Stow.   Calenture, The.
Strickland, A.   Self-Devoted, The.
Swift, J.   In Sickness.
  To Stella.
Swirszczynska.   Terminally Ill.
  Visit, A.
Symons, A.   Nerves.
Szporluk.   Triage.
Taggard.   Try Tropic.
Tate, A.   Mother and Son.
Teasdale.   Open Windows.
Thomas, R.   Evans.
Van Duyn.   Letters from a Father.
Voigt.   Year's End.
Volkman.   Theft.
Walker, A.   Medicine.
Wallis, H.   To a Sick Friend.
Ward, T.   Stray Dogs, Foaming.
Whitman, W.   Evening Lull, An.
Whitmore, S.   Outside.
Winchilsea.   Spleen, The.
Winder.   Unaccompanied Suite.
Winstanley, J.   Upon a Friend's Pet Cat, Being Sick.
Wolverton, T.   In China.
Woods, D.   Prescription.
Wordsworth, D.   Thoughts on my sick-bed.
Wordsworth, W.   Idiot Boy, The.
Wotton, S.   Hymn to My God in a Night of My Late Sickness[e], A.
Wright, J.   Tableau.
Wunderlich, M.   Bruise of This, The.
Wyrebek, M.   Healing Logic, A.

Illusion
Ashbery.   Forties Flick.
  Illustration.
Carew, T.   To T. H., a Lady Resembling My Mistress.
Cullen, C.   Only the Polished Skeleton.
Dickinson, E.   I met a King this afternoon!
Dunbar, P.   We Wear the Mask.
Emerson, R.   Maia.
Fisher, R.   Rules and Ranges for Ian Tyson.
Gier, J.   First View of the Islands, A.
Guest, B.   Emphasis Falls on Reality, An.
Jarman, M.   Black Riviera, The.
Johnson, G.   Lost Illusions.
Kunitz, S.   Illumination, The.
Laughlin, J.   Inn at Kirchstetten, The.
Levine, P.   Old Testament, The.
Raffalovich, M. A.   World Well Lost 4, The.
Slessor.   Choker's Lane.
Stafford, W.   Bi-Focal.
Troup, B.   You're Lookin' at Me.
Volkman.   Untitled: "If it be event, I go towards and not back. I go tower, not floor."
Whitman, W.   Are You the New Person Drawn toward Me?
  Eidolons.
  Of the Terrible Doubt of Appearances.

Imagination
Adkins, G.   Children in Armour.
Ai.   Man with the Saxophone, The.
Ammons, A. R.   Corsons Inlet.
  He Held Radical Light.
  Laser.
  Triphammer Bridge.
Becker, R.   Sonnet to the Imagination.
Bishop, E.   Little Exercise.
  Sleeping on the Ceiling.
Brontë, E.   Aye there it is! It wakes tonight.
  God of Visions.
  Little while, a little while, A.
  To Imagination.

Brooks, G.   Anniad, The.
  Lovers of the Poor, The.
Browning, R.   By the Fire-Side.
Brownstein.   Paris Visitation.
  War.
Bryan, M.   To————: "O timeless guest!—so soon returned art thou."
Burke, J.   Imagination.
Calverley.   In the Gloaming.
Carr, M.   Castle in the Fire, The.
Cavendish, M.   Discourse of Melancholy, A.
  Imagination.
Coleridge, S.   Fancy in Nubibus.
Coulette.   Attic, The.
Creeley.   Again.
  Wicker Basket, A.
  Wife, The.
d'Oettingen.   Outcries.
Dacre, C.   Power of Love, The.
Dalton, A.   Dad-Baby, The.
Davies, W.   Mind's Liberty, The.
Davis, J.   Boat, A.
  Kids on Television Imagine Me, The.
Day, J.   Moving Object.
Donne.   Song: "Go and catch a falling star."
Dove, R.   Banneker.
  Geometry.
Duncan, R.   Often I Am Permitted to Return to a Meadow.
Durcan.   Backside to the Wind.
Eliot, T.   La Figlia Che Piange.
Evance, S.   To the Clouds.
  Written at Netley Abbey.
Giovanni.   Poem For My Nephew.
Goese, M.   Love Ghost.
Graham, W.   Imagine a Forest.
Graves, R.   Warning to Children.
Guest, B.   Wild Gardens Overlooked by Night Lights.
Hanson, M.   To Fancy.
Harjo, J.   Postcolonial Tale, A.
Hass, R.   Heroic Simile.
  Interrupted Meditation.
Hernández Cruz.   Poem: "Think with your body."
Herrick.   Upon Julia's Clothes.
Hewitt, J.   Substance and Shadow.
Hill, G.   Imaginative Life, The.
Holub.   Vanishing Lung Syndrome.
Hutchinson, P.   Amhrán na mBréag.
Jarrell.   Cinderella.
  Girl in a Library, A.
  Sick Child, A.
Johnson, M. F.   Thunder Storm.
Johnstone, R.   Robot Camera.
Keats.   Ode on a Grecian Urn.
Kinnell.   When One Has Lived a Long Time Alone.
Komunyakaa.   Smokehouse, The.
Kunitz, S.   Testing-Tree, The.
Lasker-Schüler.   George Grosz.
Lazarus, E.   City Visions.
Lee, D.   Billy Batter.
Levertov.   In Mind.
Longfellow, H.   Children's Hour, The.
Lopez, L.   Tomás.
Lorde.   Summer Oracle.
Lovecraft.   Alienation.
Lowell, R.   Epilogue: "Those blessed structures, plot and rhyme."
Lux.   Solo Native.
Markham, E.   After Reading Shakspere.
McDonald, P.   Christmas.
  Pleasures of the Imagination.
Mehrotra.   Roys, The.
Melhem, D.   Grandfather: Frailty Is Not the Story.
Mercer, J.   Laura.
Merriam, E.   Wonderful Whale, The.
Merwin, W. S.   On the Subject of Poetry.
Millay, E.   From a Very Little Sphinx.
Mitsui.   Photograph of a Child, Japanese-American Evacuation, Bainbridge Island, Washington, March 30, 1942.
Moore, T.   Fancy.
Morse, B.   Day on the Planet, A.

Moss, H. Underwood.
Muir, E. Childhood.
Nims, B. On a Cold Autumn Day.
Orlovsky. Dick Tracy's Yellow Hat.
Orr, G. Insomnia Song.
Pape. In the Bluemist Motel.
Paz. Stanzas for an Imaginary Garden.
Perelman. Let's Say.
Porter, P. Annotations of Auschwitz.
Radcliffe, A. To the Visions of Fancy.
Radiguet. Poem: "Horizon line."
Rakosi. Unswerving Marine.
Raksin, D. Laura.
Ray, H. Fancy and Imagination.
Rees-Jones. Making for Planet Alice.
Rich, A. Architect.
Robinson, E. Miniver Cheevy.
Romo-Carmona, M. Fish.
Rossetti, C. Somewhere or Other.
Schuyler, J. Greetings from the Chateau.
Seaton, M. Fiddleheads.
Silverstein, S. One Inch Tall.
Simpson, L. My Father in the Night
  Commanding No.
Smith, S. Fairy Story.
  My Hat.
  Our Bog is Dood.
Sorrentino. Classic Case, A.
Stevens, W. Final Soliloquy of the Interior
  Paramour.
  Mrs. Alfred Uruguay.
  Plain Sense of Things, The.
  Puella Parvula.
  Snow Man, The.
  To the One of Fictive Music.
Stevenson, R. Armies in the Fire.
  Block City.
  Good Play, A.
  Land of Counterpane, The.
  Land of Nod, The.
  Land of Story-Books, The.
  My Bed Is a Boat.
  Pirate Story.
Stone, R. Secondhand Coat.
Suckling, S. Upon My Lady Carlisle's Walking
  in Hampton Court Garden.
Swenson, M. Centaur, The.
Szymborska. View with a Grain of Sand.
Thomas, D. Turning of the Year, The.
Thoreau. On Fields o'er Which the Reaper's
  Hand Has Passed.
  They Who Prepare My Evening Meal Below.
Turner, W. Romance.
  Talking with Soldiers.
Unknown. If All the World Were Paper.
  Mr Nobody.
Viray, M. Patio.
Warsh. Downward Mobility.
Wheatley, P. On Imagination.
Whitman, W. Glimpse, A.
Whittemore, R. Party, The.
Wieners. Glimpse, A.
Wilbur. In the Elegy Season.
  Walking to Sleep.
Wise, W. When I Grow Up.
Wood, E. Recognition.
Wordsworth, W. Yarrow Visited [September,
  1814].
Wright, D. Lakes, The.
Yau. Radiant Silhouette IV.
Young, K. Degrees.
Young, M. J. To Dreams.

Immigration and Immigrants
Abinader, E. Letters from Home.
Adcock, F. Immigrant.
Al-Rihani. I Dreamt I Was a Donkey Boy
  Again.
Alarcon, F. Viernes Santo / Good Friday.
Atwood. Disembarking at Quebec.
Baca. Immigrants in Our Own Land.
Blanco, R. Malibú, El.
Brion, R. Good Friday.
Budy. Ellis Island, September 1907.
Burnshaw. House in St. Petersburg.
Capone. In Answer to Their Questions.
Cariaga. Family Tree, The.

Cerenio. 13 June 1994.
  My Mother.
Chin. We Are Americans Now, We Live in the
  Tundra.
Clements, A. Elegy.
Cofer, J. Idea of Islands, The.
Cortes, F. Dolce Far Niente.
Dean, D. K. Immigrants.
Delgado, J. Chuparosa.
Divakaruni. Founding of Yuba City, The.
  Yuba City School.
Djanikian. How I Learned English.
  In the Elementary School Choir.
Elmusa. Expatriates.
Espada. David Leaves the Saints for Paterson.
  Green and Red, Verde y Rojo.
  La tormenta.
  Toque de queda: Curfew in Lawrence.
Field, E. Both My Grandmothers.
Freneau. On the Emigration to America [and
  Peopling the Western Country].
Frost, R. Immigrants.
Geddes, G. Inheritors, The.
Gilbert, S. Mafioso.
Gioseffi. Bicentennial Anti-Poem for Italian-
  American Women.
Glück, L. Legend.
Gonzalez, N. I Made Myself a Path.
Gonzalez, R. Angels of Juárez, Mexico, The.
  At the Rio Grande Near the End of the Century.
Gotera. Madarika.
  Manong Chito Tells Manong Ben about His
    Dream over Breakfast at the Manilatown
    Cafe.
  Pacific Crossing.
Hamod, S. Dying with the Wrong Name.
Hawkins, R. Issei Men: The First Generation.
  Nisei Daughter: The Second Generation.
  Sansei: The Third Generation.
Hazo. Silence Spoken Here.
  To My Mother.
Healy, E. From Los Angeles Looking South.
Hernández Cruz. Ruskie's Boy.
  Snaps of Immigration.
Hernandez, D. Welcome.
Hewitt, J. Once Alien Here.
Ignatow, D. Europe and America.
Ilio, D. Site of My Grandfather's House, The.
Jacinto, J. Heaven Is Just Another Country.
Joseph, L. Curriculum Vitae.
Kageyama, C. Mama.
Kaufman, S. Nechama.
Lavieri, J. Autobiography of John Doe, The.
Lazarus, E. In Exile.
  New Colossus, The.
Lee, L. Cleaving, The.
Lim, S. Riding into California.
Lochhead, L. Something I'm Not.
Long, R. Conspiracy, The.
Luschei, G. Arrangement.
MacLeish. Burying Ground by the Ties.
Mar, L. My Mother, Who Came from China,
  Where She Never Saw Snow.
Mathews, E. K. Indian, The.
McCarthy, T. November in Boston.
Melnyczuk. Usual Immigrant Uncle Poem, The.
Melo, M. Scrambled Eggs and Garlic Pork.
  Unlearning English.
Merwin, W. S. Fields, The.
Mitsui. Katori Maru, October 1920.
  Nisei: Second Generation Japanese-American.
Mora. Immigrants.
  La Migra.
Morales. I Am the Reasonable One.
  I Recognize You.
Morales, A. Immigrants.
  Old Countries.
Papaleo. American Dream: First Report.
Porter, P. Last of England, The.
Prunty. To be Sung on the Fourth of July.
Ras. In the New Country.
Rich, A. Prospective Immigrants Please Note.
Robles. Feasting with Etang a Hundred Times
  Around.
Rollings. For Dear Life.
Rose, P. Wind Debates Asian Immigration, The.

Seiler. Digging in the Streets of Gold.
Shapiro, K. My Grandmother.
Sigourney. Erin's Daughter.
Song. Lost Sister.
Soto. Mexicans Begin Jogging.
Suárez, V. Cuban-American Gothic.
Suknaski. Chinese Camp, Kamloops (circa
  1883).
Turki, F. Being a Good *Americani*.
Unknown. Mid-West, The.
Uyematsu. Near Roscoe and Coldwater.
  Same Month They Bombed Cambodia, The.
Vazirani, R. Mrs. Biswas Breaks Her
  Connection with Another Relative.
Viray, M. Two Strangers, The.

Immortality
"Ada." Oh, when this earthly tenement.
"Æ." Immortality.
Arnold, M. Shakespeare.
Ashbery. How Much Longer Will I Be Able to
  Inhabit the Divine Sepulcher.
Atwood. They Eat Out.
Bly, R. Poem in Three Parts.
Browning, R. Love.
Campo. Superman Is Dead.
Clare, J. Invite to Eternity, An.
Cowley, A. Muse, The.
Dickinson, E. My Life Closed Twice.
  Thirst.
Dobell, S. Liberty to M. le Diplomate.
Donne. Good-Morrow, The.
Duggan, L. Ten ii.
Elder. Carried Away.
Eliot, T. Whispers of Immortality.
Emerson, R. Eros.
Gallagher, T. Instructions to the Double.
Ginsberg, A. Poem Rocket.
Graves, R. To Bring the Dead to Life.
Hall, D. My Son, My Executioner.
Hannon. Real Estate.
Hardy, T. Shelley's Skylark.
Hemans. Woman and Fame.
Herbert, G. Death.
  Virtue [*or* Vertue].
Herrick. His Creed.
  To His Peculiar Friend Master Thomas Shapcott,
    Lawyer.
Hopkins, E. Life in Death.
Howard, R. After 65.
Jackson, L. Poet's Corner, The.
Jeffers, R. Post Mortem.
Jones, A. Communal Living.
Keats. Ode: "Bards of passion and of mirth."
McCreery. There Is No Death.
Meynell, A. Song of Derivations, A.
Milton. On Shakespear[e].
Moorer. Immortality.
Naden. Pantheist's Song of Immortality, The.
Pembroke, W. Song: "Soules joy, now I am
  gone."
Pinkney, E. Voyager's Song, The.
Reese, L. Love, Weeping, Laid This Song.
Robinson, E. Man against the Sky, The.
  Walt Whitman.
Rodriguez, J. Lifetime Devoted to Literature, A.
Teasdale. Little While, A.
Tennyson, A. Tithonus.
Unknown. Inscription at Mount Vernon.
Vaughan, H. Easter Hymn.
  Resurrection and Immortality.
  Waterfall [*or* Water-Fall], The.
Very. Cross, The.
  New Birth, The.
Waller, E. Of English Verse.
Wheatley, P. To a Gentleman and Lady on the
  Death of the Lady's Brother and Sister, and a
  Child of the Name Avis, Aged One Year.
Whitman, W. Joy, Shipmate, Joy!
  On the Beach at Night.
  Woman Waits for Me, A.
Wolfe, H. Iliad.
Yeats. Sailing To Byzantium.

Imperfections
Creeley. Immoral Proposition, The.
Hammerstein. Can't Help Lovin' Dat Man.
Herrick. No Loathsomnesse in Love.

To the Generous Reader.
Kern, J.   Can't Help Lovin' Dat Man.
Reynolds, R.   Object of Burial Is Intent, The.
Stevens, W.   Poems of Our Climate, The.

Imperialism
Appleman, P.   Peace with Honor.
Blok.   Scythians, The.
Brathwaite, E.   Citadel.
Conyus.   Day in the Life of . . . , A.
Daley, V.   When London Calls.
Di Prima.   Goodbye Nkrumah.
Fawcett, B.   Hand, The.
French, W.   Queen's After-Dinner Speech, The.
Gardinier.   Admirals (Columbus).
Kipling, R.   Recessional.
McGrath, T.   Fresco: Departure for an
   Imperialist War.
Mitchell, A.   Remember Suez?
Montague, J.   Wild Sports of the West.
Muir, E.   Combat, The.
Sylvain, P.   Panama.
Wilde, O.   Ave Imperatrix!

Impermanence
Martínez, V.   Tesoro.
See also **Transience**

Impotence
Adcock, F.   Happy Ending.
Automedon.   Impotent Lover, The.
Behn, A.   Disappointment, The.
Everson, W.   Kingfisher Flat.
Harington [*or* Harrington].   Against an Old
   Lecher.
Herrick.   To His Mistress[es].
Hope, A.   Paradise Saved.
Huang O [*or* Huang Ho].   To the Tune "Red
   Embroidered Shoes."
Levy, A.   On the Threshold.
Montagu, L.   Reasons That Induced Dr. Swift to
   Write a Poem Called "The Lady's Dressing-
   Room," The.
Porter, C.   Too Darn Hot.
Rochester, J.   Against Constancy.
   Disabled Debauchee, The.
   Imperfect Enjoyment, The.
   Song of a Young Lady to Her Ancient Lover, A.
Unknown.   One Writing against His Prick.

Impressionism and Impressionists
Mueller, L.   Monet Refuses the Operation.
Waldman, A.   Berthe Morisot.

Impulse
Clark, T.   Time.

Incense
Garrett, E.   Lost Property.
Ginsberg, A.   After Yeats.

Incest
Borawski.   English Was Only a Second
   Language.
Cavin.   Christmas with the Holy Family.
Couzyn.   World War II.
Fallon, P.   Airs and Graces.
Garcia, R.   Note Folded Thirteen Ways.
Lorde.   Chain.
Mitchell, L.   Sons and Fathers.
Smukler.   Shower, The.
Winkfield, T.   Nature Study.

Inclosure Movement
Freeth.   Cottager's Complaint, on the Intended
   Bill for Enclosing Sutton-Coldfield, The.

Incomprehensibility
Coleman, C.   It Amazes Me!
Ford, C.   Bad Habit, The.
Moret, N.   She's Funny That Way (I Got a
   Woman, Crazy for Me).
Whiting, R.

Inconstancy
Behn, A.   To Alexis in Answer to His Poem
   Against Fruition.
Brown, T.   Oaths.
Burns, R.   Bonie Doon.
   Ye Banks and Braes.
Hood, T.   Faithless Nelly Gray.
Jonson, B.   Another. In Defense of Their
   Inconstancy [*or* Inconstancie]. A Song.
Maguire, S.   Fall, The.
Montagu, L.   Answer to a Love-Letter in Verse,

An.
Pilkington, L.   Song, A: "Strephon, your breach
   of faith and trust."
Stevenson, R.   To Henry James.
Tabb.   Shadow, The.
Thomas, E.   Forsaken Wife, The.
Tollet.   On Loving Once and Loving Often.

Indecision
Arlen, H.   Between the Devil and the Deep Blue
   Sea.
Behn, A.   On Her Loving Two Equally.
Gershwin.   Saga of Jenny, The.
Maltby, R.   Little Bit Off, A.
Porter, C.   At Long Last Love.
Weill, K.   Saga of Jenny, The.
See also **Decisions**

Independence
Bennett, L.   Independance.
Burke, J.   Little Bit Independent, A.
Chrystos.   You Know I Like to Be.
Cofer, J.   Learning to Walk Alone.
Eliot, T.   Cousin Nancy.
Frost, R.   Silken Tent, The.
Galvin, J.   Independence Day, 1956: A Fairy
   Tale.
Leslie, E.   Little Bit Independent, A.
Mora.   Cortez's Horse.
Ogilvy.   Grannie's Birthday.
Preston, M.   Erinna's Spinning.
Scott, A.   Return Thee, Heart.
Smith, C.   To Dependence.
Unknown.   Path of Independence, The.
Wordsworth, W.   Resolution and Independence.
Yee, M.   Wintermelons.
Young, A.   Dance for Ma Rainey, A.

India
Jussawalla.   Sea Breeze, Bombay.
Ali, A.   Dacca Gauzes, The.
Birney.   Bear on the Delhi Road, The.
Bringhurst.   Parśvanatha.
Brooks, C.   Lines: Composed at the Old
   Temples of Maralipoor.
Coward.   I Wonder What Happened to Him.
Das, K.   Hot Noon in Malabar.
   Introduction: "I don't know politics but I know
   the names."
Dharwadker.   New Delhi, 1974.
Divakaruni.   Indian Movie, New Jersey.
Greenberg, A.   Man in the Moon, The.
Hemans.   Indian City, The.
Kalamaras, G.   Mud.
Kipling, R.   Cholera Camp.
   Christmas in India.
   Gunga Din.
   Mandalay.
Lewis, A.   Karanje Village.
   Mahratta Ghats, The.
Mahapatra, J.   Main Temple Street, Puri.
   Monsoon Day Fable, A.
   Sanskrit.
   Summer Poem, A.
   Taste for Tomorrow.
Meredith, W.   Jain Bird Hospital in Delhi, The.
Moraes, D.   Babur.
Orlovsky.   Lepers Cry.
Parthasarathy.   Speaking of Places.
Ramanujan.   At Forty.
   Death and the Good Citizen.
   Elements of Composition.
   Last of the Princes, The.
   Pleasure.
   Some Indian Uses of History on a Rainy Day.
Rukeyser, M.   Ajanta.
Vazirani, R.   Mrs. Biswas Goes Through a Photo
   Album.
   Mrs. Biswas of Maryland on the Phone.
Whitman, W.   Passage to India.

Indian Summer
Campbell, W.   Indian Summer.
Chamberlain, K.   Indian Summer.
Dickinson, E.   Indian Summer.
Garland, H.   Indian Summer.
Lindsay, N.   Indian Summer Day on the Prairie,
   An.
Reese, L.   Indian Summer.

Indiana (state)
Fitzgerald, R.   July in Indiana.

Indians, American
Corso.   Spontaneous Requiem for the American
   Indian.
de Aerenlund, C.   Cuando el tecolote canta, el
   Indio muere.
Freneau.   Indian Burying Ground, The.
Lewis, J.   Indians in the Woods, The.
Livingston, M.   First Thanksgiving.
Sigourney.   Indian Names.
Stafford, W.   Indian Cave Jerry Ramsey Found,
   The.
See also **Native Americans**

Indifference
Baraka.   Preface to a Twenty Volume Suicide
   Note.
Byrom.   Careless Content.
Cisneros, S.   I Am So in Love I Grow a New
   Hymen.
Cummings, E.   Anyone Lived in a Pretty How
   Town.
Dowson.   Flos Lunae.
Gershwin.   Who Cares?
Greville, F.   Prayer for Indifference, A.
Hands, E.   On an Unsociable Family.
Levine, P.   Coming Home, *Detroit*, 1968.
Melo Neto.   End of the World, The.
Melville, H.   Pebbles.
Montagu, L.   Lover, The; a Ballad.
Steele, T.   In the King's Rooms.
Thackeray.   Sorrows of Werther, The.
Wenderoth, J.   Death.

Individualism and Individualists
Berry, J.   One.
Brownjohn.   Of Dancing.
Coleridge, S.   Phantom.
Crane, S.   "Think as I think," said a man.
Emerson, R.   Ode, Inscribed to W.H. Channing.
Frost, R.   Road Not Taken, The.
Ginsberg, A.   Is About.
Harper, F.   Mission of the Flowers, The.
Housman, A.   Laws of God, the Laws of Man,
   The.
Huxley, A.   Fifth Philosopher's Song.
Jordan, N.   Be You.
Kreymborg.   Culture.
Lawrence, D.   Don'ts.
Lear, E.   Jumblies, The.
MacNeice.   Individualist Speaks, The.
Madgett.   Offspring.
Parsons, C.   Different.
Walker, A.   On Stripping Bark from Myself.
Whitman, W.   By Blue Ontario's Shore.
   One's-Self I Sing.
   Poet, The.
   Torch, The.
Yeats.   Coat, A.
Zukofsky, L.   Song for the Year's End, A.
See also **Egotism and Egotists**

Indonesia and Indonesians
Brissenden.   Walking down Jalan Thamrin.
Fenton, J.   Dead Soldiers.
See also **Borneo**

Indulgences
Douglas, K.   Cairo Jag.
Sheridan, R.   On Lady Anne Hamilton.

Industrial Revolution
Unknown.   Factory Girl's Come-All-Ye, The.

Industrial Workers of the World (IWW)
Hill, J.   There Is Power in a Union.

Industrialization
Aguilar, M.   Pall Hanging over Manila.
Ama Ata Aidoo.   Cornfields in Accra.
Blind.   Red Sunsets, 1883, The.
Brown, E.   Spiritual Land.
Cranch.   Spirit of the Age, The.
Davies, I.   In Gardens in the Rhondda.
Dransfield.   Endsight.
Eberhart, R.   Hard Structure of the World, The.
Hopkins, G.   God's Grandeur.
Howard, B.   Break.
Johnson, E.   Remember?
Joseph, L.   Here.
Kumin, M.   Chain, The.

Larkin, P. Going, Going.
Lawrence, D. Evening Land, The.
Levine, P. They Feed They Lion.
Morales, A. South.
Nesbit, E. Great Industrial Centre, A.
Russell, W. Developers, The.
  God Gave Us Trees to Cut Down.
Spender, S. Landscape near an Aerodrome, The.
Thomas, R. Cynddylan on a Tractor.
Welch, L. Chicago Poem.

Ineptitude
Burns, R. On Elphinston's Translation of Martial.
Curbelo. Listening to a White Man Play the Blues.
Gibran. Heavy-Laden Is My Soul.

Infant Death
Bawer. Grand Central Station, 20 December 1987.
Boyd, E. On the Death of an Infant of Five Days Old.
Crashaw. To the Infant Martyrs.
  Upon the Infant Martyrs.
Davies, W. Inquest, The.
Geier. On Your Twenty-First Birthday.
Harper, M. We Assume: On the Death of Our Son, Reuben Masai Harper.
Hewett, D. Anniversary.
Jonson, B. On My First Daughter.
Lamb, C. On an Infant Dying as Soon as Born.
Marvell. Picture of Little T. C. in a Prospect of Flowers, The.
McAuley, J. Pietá.
Melville, H. Chipmunk, The.
Muir, E. Child Dying, The.
Muske, C. Intensive Care.
Philips, K. Epitaph on her Son H. P. at St. Syth's Church.
  On the Death of My First and Dearest Child[e], Hector Philip[p]s.
Piatt, S. No Help.
Sigourney. Death of an Infant.
Stoddard, E. One Morn I Left Him in His Bed.
Unknown. Cruel Mother, The.
West, K. To My Twin Sister Who Died at Birth.
Williams, W. Dead Baby, The.
Wright, M. To an Infant Expiring the Second Day of Its Birth.
See also **Death in Childhood**

Infanticide
Boake. At Devlin's Siding.
Browning, E. Runaway Slave at Pilgrim's Point, The.
Davies, W. Inquest, The.
Delgado, J. La Llorona.
France de Bravo, B. Unrepentant.
Unknown. Mary [*or* Marie] Hamilton.
  Mary Hamilton.
  Queen's Marie, The.
Van Walleghen. In the Chariot Drawn by Dragons.

Infants
Figueroa, J. Taino.
Jackson, T. Pretty Baby.
Ortiz. Speaking.
See also **Babies**

Infatuation
Arlen, H. Let's Fall in Love.
  Out of This World.
Behn, A. To the Fair Clarinda [*or* Clorinda], Who Made Love to Me, Imagined [*or* Imagin'd] More Than Woman.
Berlin. Pretty Girl Is Like a Melody, A.
  They Say It's Wonderful.
Blane, R. Trolley Song, The.
Blanvillain, J. (All of a Sudden) My Heart Sings.
Brown, N. You're an Old Smoothie.
Burke, J. Imagination.
Cahn, S. Call Me Irresponsible.
Clark, P. Excitement.
Coleman, C. Real Live Girl.
  You Fascinate Me So.
Coots, J. You Go to My Head.

Cope, W. Two Cures for Love.
Coward. Mad About the Boy.
DeSylva, B. G. I'll Say She Does.
  If You Knew Susie (Like I Know Susie).
  You're an Old Smoothie.
Dietz, H. I Guess I'll Have to Change My Plan.
Donaldson, W. My Baby Just Cares for Me.
Dorsey, J. I'm Glad There Is You (In This World of Ordinary People).
Ellington, D. I Got It Bad and That Ain't Good.
  Satin Doll.
Engvick, W. Crazy in the Heart.
Freed, R. How About You.
Gillespie, H. You Go to My Head.
Gordon, M. Meet the Beat of My Heart.
  You Make Me Feel So Young.
Hamlish, M. One.
Hanley, J. Zing! Went the Strings of My Heart.
Hart, L. Thou Swell.
Herpin, H. (All of a Sudden) My Heart Sings.
Herrick. Epitaph upon a Virgin, An.
  To Oenone.
  Upon a Black Twist, Rounding the Arm of the Countess of Carlisle.
  Upon Love.
Housman, A. Oh, When I Was In Love.
Jolson, A. I'll Say She Does.
Kahn, G. My Baby Just Cares for Me.
Kern, J. You Were Never Lovelier.
Kleban, E. One.
Koch, K. To Marina.
Koehler, T. Let's Fall in Love.
Lane, B. How About You.
Lawrence, J. Linda.
Leigh, C. Real Live Girl.
  You Fascinate Me So.
Lerner, A. On the Street Where You Live.
Locker-Lampson, M. Mr. Placid's Flirtation.
Madeira, P. I'm Glad There Is You (In This World of Ordinary People).
Martin, H. Trolley Song, The.
Mercer, J. Out of This World.
  Satin Doll.
  You Were Never Lovelier.
Meyer, J. If You Knew Susie (Like I Know Susie).
Myrow, J. You Make Me Feel So Young.
Porter, C. At Long Last Love.
  I Get a Kick Out of You.
Revel, H. Meet the Beat of My Heart.
Rodgers, R. Thou Swell.
Rome, H. (All of a Sudden) My Heart Sings.
Ruskin, H. I May Be Wrong (But I Think You're Wonderful).
Schwartz, A. I Guess I'll Have to Change My Plan.
Shirley, J. Love's Hue and Cry.
Sondheim. Losing My Mind.
Strayhorn, B. Satin Doll.
Suckling, S. Upon My Lady Carlisle's Walking in Hampton Court Garden.
Tuckerman, F. Infatuation.
Van Heusen, J. Call Me Irresponsible.
Weaver, M. Sub Shop Girl.
Webster, P. I Got It Bad and That Ain't Good.
Whiting, R. You're an Old Smoothie.
Wilder, A. Crazy in the Heart.

Infertility
Martínez, V. Children of the Disappeared.

Infidelity
Alexander, E. Nineteen.
Angelou. Pickin Em Up and Layin Em Down.
Auden. Lullaby: "Lay your sleeping head, my love."
Berssenbrugge. Jealousy.
Bottke, A. How to Approach Your Lover's Wife.
Browning, E. Bertha in the Lane.
  Bianca Among the Nightingales.
Browning, R. Any Wife to Any Husband.
Byron, G. When We Two Parted.
Campbell, T. Jilted Nymph, The.
Carew, T. Deposition from Love, A.
Chaucer. Complaint of Troilus, The.
  Love Unfeigned.
  Song of Troylus, The.

Cleveland, J. Antiplatonic[k], The.
Dancer. Variety, The.
De Vries, P. To His Importunate Mistress.
Dickey, J. Adultery.
Donne. Indifferent, The.
  Message, The.
  Song: "Go and catch a falling star."
  Woman's Constancy.
Dowson. Non Sum Qualis Eram Bonae sub Regno Cynarae.
Egerton, S. To One Who Said I Must Not Love.
Elizabeth I. Doubt of Future Foes.
"Ephelia." In the Person of a Lady, to Bajazet, Her Unconstant Gallant.
Feirstein. Mark Stern Wakes Up.
  Rune-Maker, The.
France, L. In Kind.
Godolphin. Song: " 'Tis affection but dissembled."
Graves, R. Lament for Pasiphaë.
  Never Such Love.
  Straw, The.
Grosholz. Legacies.
Handy, W. Yellow Dog Blues.
Hardy, T. Burghers, The.
  Newcomer's Wife, The.
Harington [*or* Harrington]. Of an Heroical Answer of a Great Roman Lady to Her Husband.
Harrington, J. Inconstancy.
Hecht, A. Dover Bitch, The.
Heffernan, M. Message, The.
Herrick. Chop-Cherry.
  Upon Scobble [Epigram].
Hughes, L. Gypsy Man.
Hughes, T. Kreutzer Sonata.
Hunter, A. *et al.* Down-Hearted Blues.
Jong. Parable of the Four-Poster.
King, H. Exequy, The.
Koch, K. To Marina.
Kollar. Late Arrivals.
Lindsay, N. At Mass.
Lomax, M. Other Woman, The.
Lovelace, R. Scrutiny [*or* Scrutinie], The.
  To Lucasta, [on] Going to the War[re]s.
Lowell, R. At the Altar.
Masini. Two Men, Two Grapefruits.
Mataka. Next Door.
McDonald, W. Honky-Tonk Blues.
McElroy, C. Caledonia.
  Horoscope.
Montagu, L. Epistle from Mrs. Yonge to Her Husband.
Nesbit, E. Husband of To-Day, The.
Parker, D. Certain Lady, A.
Pilkington, L. Song, A.
Polito. Overheard in the Love Hotel.
Pope, A. Two or Three; a Recipe [*or* Receipt] to Make a Cuckold.
Porter, C. Always True to You in My Fashion.
Pound, E. Temperaments, The.
Rainey. See, See Rider.
Ralegh, S. Farewell to False Love, A.
Realuyo. Querida, La.
Rochester, J. Against Constancy.
Sedley. Song: "Phillis is my only joy."
Taylor, A. Beast with Two Backs, The.
Thomas, R. Madrigal: "Your love is dead, lady, your love is dead."
Unknown. Demon Lover, The.
  Frankie and Albert.
  Frankie and Johnny [*or* Johnnie *or* Albert].
  Queen Eleanor's Confession.
  Shickered As He Could Be.
  Unfortunate Miller; or, The Country Lasses Witty Invention, The.
Waring, B. Our Lady of the Laundromat.
Wickham. Slighted Lady, The.
Williams, C. Gulf Coast Blues.
Wither. I Loved a Lass.
Wyatt, S. Farewell: "What should I say."
  Lover Showeth How He Is Forsaken of Such as He Sometime Enjoyed, The.
  Whoso List to Hunt.
See also **Adultery and Adulterers**

Infinity
Dowden, E.   Two Infinities.
Lane, B.   On a Clear Day You Can See Forever.

Ingratitude
Hayden, R.   Those Winter Sundays.
Herbert, G.   Unkindness.
Seward.   Sonnet: Ingratitude.
Smith, C.   To a Querulous Acquaintance.

Ingres, Jean Auguste Dominique
Rossetti, D.   Same, The.

Inheritance
Gerrard.   Remonstrance, A.
Herrick.   Lyric[k] for Legacies.
Hewitt, J.   From a Museum Man's Album.
Hogan, L.   Truth Is, The.
Jacob, H.   To Geron.
Johnson, S.   Short Song of Congratulation [or
    To a Young Heir], A.
Nairne.   Heiress, The.
Olds, S.   Guild, The.
Sugioka.   Legacy.
Wolfe, T.   For, Brother, What Are We?
Wordsworth, W.   Michael [A Pastoral Poem].

Injuries
Ammons, A. R.   Silver.
Campo.   S. W.
Coulehan, J.   Man with a Hole in His Face, The.
Crane, H.   Episode of Hands.
Creeley.   Man, The.
Cross, F.   Accident, An.
Denning.   Man.
Espada.   Who Burns for the Perfection of Paper.
Feinfeld, D.   Wound Man, The.
Floyd.   Private Ian Godwin, U. S. M. C.
Frost, R.   Not to Keep.
Galvin, J.   Station (2).
Gibson, W.   In the Ambulance.
Grosholz.   Back Trouble.
Gunn, T.   Wound, The.
Highfill, M.   Rebis.
Kooser.   Very Old, The.
Larkin, J.   My Body.
Mackenzie, K.   Hospital—Retrospections, The.
Mansfield, K.   Man with the Wooden Leg, The.
McDonald, W.   Veteran.
Moolten, D.   Motorcycle Ward.
Muldoon, P.   Hard Drive.
Nelson, M.   Shiner.
Paquet.   Basket Case.
    Easter '68.
    Night Dust-off.
    They Do Not Go Gentle.
Petrosky.   V.A. Hospital.
Platke, S.   Gut Catcher.
Rossetti, C.   Hurt No Living Thing.
Shuster, D.   Mellow on Morphine.
Stein, K.   Night Shift, after Drinking Dinner,
    Container Corporation of America, 1972.
Talvikki, A.   Origin Charm Against Uncertain
    Injuries.
Zarco.   Once upon a Seesaw with Charlie Chan.

Injustice
Alexander, E.   Affirmative Action Blues (1993).
Amadiume.   We Have Even Lost our Tongues!
Bierce.   Hesitating Veteran, The.
Bontemps.   Black Man Talks of Reaping, A.
Brecht, B.   World's One Hope, The.
Carroll, L.   Long Tale, A.
Chrystos.   I Walk in the History of My People.
Clifton, L.   1. at nagasaki.
    4/30/92 for rodney king.
Conyus.   I Rode with Geronimo.
Doolan, F.   Whiteman Is the Judge, The.
Dunbar, P.   Haunted Oak, The.
Ezenwa-Ohaeto.   I Wan Bi President.
Grandfather Koori.   Never Blood So Red.
Hagedon, J.   Song of Bullets, The.
Hall, D.   Small Fig Tree, A.
Hardy, J.   Objection Overruled.
Harper, F.   Slave Auction, The.
Horne, N.   Note to My Liberal Feminist
    Sister, A.
Ismaili.   Yet Still.
Lim, G.   Children are Colorblind.
Lindsay, N.   Abraham Lincoln Walks at
    Midnight.
Mabuza.   Death to the Gold Mine!
Macgoye.   Muffled Cry, A.
Millay, E.   Justice Denied in Massachusetts.
Mkangelwa.   Observations.
Moorer.   Injustice of the Courts.
Mudrooroo Narogin.   They give Jacky rights.
Owen, W.   Parable of the Old Men and the
    Young, The.
Papertalk-Green, C.   No One to Guide Us.
Powell, K.   Don't Feel No Way.
Raffalovich, M. A.   Sonnet 120.
Robinson, M.   January, 1795.
    Stanzas: "In this vain, busy world, where the
    good and the gay."
Rodriguez, L.   Speaking with Hands.
Rungano.   Woman, The.
Stanley, T.   Ode XV.
Steptoe.   Notes for a Poem from the Middle
    Passage of Years.
Stevens, W.   Idiom of the Hero.
Unknown.   Lay of the Lash, The.
    Song: "We raise de wheat."
Winchilsea.   Unequal Fetters, The.
Wong, N.   For an Asian Woman Who Says My
    Poetry Gives Her a Stomachache.
Zulu, P.   You are Mad: and I Mean It!
See also **Protest, Social**

Inkwells
Coleridge, M.   Contents of an Ink-bottle, The.

Innisfree, Ireland
Yeats.   Lake-Isle of Innisfree, The.

Innocence
Aldrich, T.   Fannie.
Atkins.   New Storefront.
Aytoun [or Ayton], R.   On the Prince's Death, to
    the King.
Barker, J.   To Her Lover's Complaint.
Bass, F.   Garden, The.
Brock-Broido.   Radiating Naïveté.
Browning, R.   Pippa's Song.
Bryant, W.   Oh [or O] Fairest of the Rural
    Maids.
Campbell, D.   Small-town Gladys.
Carruth, H.   Cows at Night, The.
Chubb, R.   Transfiguration.
Coleridge, H.   Long Time a Child.
Coleridge, S.   Christabel.
    In the Touch of This Bosom There Worketh a
    Spell.
Curbelo.   Listening to a White Man Play the
    Blues.
Drake, N.   Man in the White Suit, The.
Eliot, T.   Hippopotamus, The.
Elizabeth I.   Written on a Wall at Woodstock.
Garcia, R.   Note Folded Thirteen Ways.
Garrett, E.   Womanhood, The.
Gunn, T.   Innocence.
Hart, L.   I Didn't Know What Time It Was.
Hazo.   Child of Our Bodies.
Herbert, G.   Holy Baptism (2).
Holmes, O.   Iris, Her Book.
Jackson, L.   Only Daughter, The.
    Summary for Alastor.
Jarman, M.   Supremes, The.
Kavanagh, P.   Innocence.
Lamb, C.   "Timid grace sits trembling in her
    eye, A."
Lea, S.   Clouded Evening, Late September.
Levertov.   In Mind.
    Innocent, The.
    Overland to the Islands.
Lewis, A.   Sentry, The.
Loftis, N.   Ruth.
MacNeice.   Apple Blossom.
    Autobiography.
Nemerov.   Remorse for Time, The.
Ni Dhomhnaill.   Poem for Melissa.
Ofeimun.   Naming Day, A.
Olds, S.   I Go Back to May 1937.
Oppen.   Quotations.
Padel.   Trial.
Palgrave.   Eutopia.
Philips, K.   To My Excellent Lucasia, On Our
    Friendship.
Pollard, C.   Heavy-Petting Zoo, The.
Ransom, J.   Janet Waking.
    Necrological.
    Vaunting Oak.
Rich, A.   Children Playing Checkers at the Edge
    of the Forest.
Robin, L.   Little Girl from Little Rock.
Robinson, E.   Souvenir.
Rodgers, R.   I Didn't Know What Time It Was.
Salmon, A.   Prikaz.
Scamell, D.   For a Six Year Old.
Smith, C.   Glow-Worm, The.
    To Fancy.
    To Mrs. G.
    Written in Farm Wood, South Downs, in May
    1784.
Sorrentino.   Razzmatazz.
Stanley, T.   Love's Innocence.
Styne, J.   Little Girl from Little Rock.
Thomas, D.   Fern Hill.
    Refusal to Mourn the Death, by Fire, of a Child
    in London, A.
Thoreau.   Rumors from an Aeolian Harp.
Traherne.   Innocence.
Van Jordan, A.   If I Write a Poem.
Vando.   My Mother Cunning, Yet Innocent.
Wallace-Crabbe.   Windows, The.
Waller, E.   To a Fair Lady Playing with a Snake.
Warren, R.   Picnic Remembered.
Whitehead, C.   Girls Sitting Together Like
    Dolls.
Whittier.   Changeling, The.
    In School-Days.
Wilde, O.   Wasted Days.
Williams, C.   Gas Station, The.
Wordsworth, W.   To the Highland Girl of
    Inversneyde.

Inns
Fairfax of Cameron.   Upon the New Building at
    Appleton.
Hardy, T.   At an Inn.
Heath-Stubbs.   Footnote to Belloc's "Tarantella."
Knight, S.   Double Writing.
Laughlin, J.   Inn at Kirchstetten, The.
Rossetti, C.   Uphill.
Warren, R.   Ballad of Billie Potts, The.
Wharton, E.   Terminus.
See also **Hotels; Motels**

Insanity
Bennani, B.   Camel's Bite.
Burkard.   Foolish Thing.
Calloway, C.   Minnie, the Moocher.
Early, G.   Innocency or Not Song X.
Gibran.   Madman (Prologue), The.
Gibson, W.   In the Ambulance.
Liu, T.   Mama.
Pietri.   How Do Your Eggs Want You (?).
    Intermission from Friday.
Rodriguez, L.   Rant, Rave and Ricochet.
See also **Madness**

Insects
Avison.   Nameless One, A.
Barnes, D.   Transfiguration.
Bly, R.   Exhausted Bug, The.
Brooks, G.   Birth in a Narrow Room, The.
Brown, M.   Little Black Bug.
Cabalquinto.   Value Added in Smashing a
    German Roach on the Bathroom Door, The.
Clare, J.   Clock-A-Clay.
DeFrees.   Beetle Light.
Dufault.   Mud Dauber Wasp, The.
Haley, M.   Tropicalia.
Hardy, T.   August Midnight, An.
Hughes, T.   To Paint a Water Lily.
Laing, K.   Race on Gathering Bites.
Matthews, W.   Vermin.
Ortiz.   Speaking.
Perreault, J.   Readymade.
Pfeiffer, E.   Chrysalis, A.
Plath.   Frog Autumn.
Roethke.   Minimal, The.
Shapiro, K.   Fly, The.
Taylor, E.   Upon a Spider Catching a Fly.
Webb, C.   Potato Bug.
Willard, N.   Insects, The.
Wright, J.   Depressed by a Book of Bad Poetry,
    I Walk toward an Unused Pasture and Invite

the Insects to Join Me.
Invention of a Garden, The.

Insomnia and Insomniacs
Alley, R.   Dissecting Uncle Sorrow.
Berryman.   Henry by Night.
Borson.   Save Us From.
Bukowski.   I Am Dead But I Know the Dead Are Not Like This.
Curbelo.   Last Call.
Cushman, S.   Make the Bed.
Davis, W.   Sleep of the Insomniac, The.
Devi.   This Night.
Gioia.   Insomnia.
Glatt.   What We Did After My Mother's Mastectomy.
Hardy, T.   Lying Awake.
Hayden, R.   Broken Dark, The.
Ice Storm.
Hilliard, B.   In the Wee Small Hours of the Morning.
Jarman, M.   Psalm: The New Day.
Justice, D.   Insomnia of Tremayne, The.
Kenyon, J.   Insomnia at the Solstice.
Kirsch, M.   Sleep's Underside.
Knight, H.   Written to a Near Neighbour in a Tempestuous Night.
Lea, S.   Insomnia: The Distances.
Lindsay, N.   Abraham Lincoln Walks at Midnight.
Logghe.   Insomnia Litany.
Loncar, M.   Insomniac.
Mann, D.   In the Wee Small Hours of the Morning.
Margulies, S.   Relentlessly Lovelorn, the Non-Sleeper Whispers and Re-Whispers a Magic Charm Against His Wound's Roar.
Montagu, L.   Between Your Sheets.
Myles, E.   Sleepless.
Nemerov.   Insomnia I.
Nystrom.   Insomnia.
Oates.   Insomnia.
Orr, G.   Insomnia Song.
Plath.   Insomniac.
Prunty.   Insomnia.
Randell.   Songs for the Sleepless.
Rich, A.   Afterwake, The.
Seyburn, P.   You and Them.
Simic.   Congress of the Insomniacs, The.
Smith, R.   Halcion.
Updike.   Insomnia the Gem of the Ocean.
Wilbur.   Walking to Sleep.
Wojahn.   Distance.

Inspiration
Alegría.   Summing Up.
Baraka, R.   In the Tradition Too.
Berryman.   Henry's Fate.
Bryant, W.   I Cannot Forget with What Fervid Devotion.
Creeley.   Door, The.
Delaunay, S.   Greetings, Blaise Cendrars.
Drayton.   Ode Written in the Peak[e], An.
Dufault.   Mud Dauber Wasp, The.
Duhamel.   How Much Is This Poem Going to Cost Me?
Ellington, D.   Something to Live For.
Elliott, E.   Criticism.
Emerson, R.   Art.
Fanthorpe.   Person's Tale, The.
Hannah, S.   Symptoms.
Hanson, M.   To Mrs. Charlotte Smith.
Herrick.   Departure of the Good Daemon, The.
Not Every Day Fit for Verse.
To the Most Illustrious and Most Hopeful[l] Prince, Charles, Prince of Wales.
Jonson, B.   And Must I Sing? What Subject Shall I Choose?
Keats.   'How Many Bards Gild the Lapses of Time!'
On Sitting Down to Read "King Lear" Once Again.
To B.R. Haydon, with a Sonnet Written on Seeing the Elgin Marbles.
Lazarus, E.   Echoes.
Lee, E.   Sun-Struck Eagle, The.
Longfellow, H.   Broken Oar, The.
Melville, H.   Art.

Monroe, A.   To W. S. M.
Norton, C.   To My Books.
Parker, A.   Another Poem about the Vandals.
Vandals, The.
Pound, E.   Virginal, A.
Powell, D. A.   Sonnet: "Morsels of my lifework: the story of a professional party hostess."
Rankine.   Testimonial.
Robinson, E.   Sonnet: "Oh for a poet—for a beacon bright."
Service.   Inspiration.
Sia, B.   Howl.
Stevenson, R.   Happy Thought.
Strayhorn, B.   Something to Live For.
Szporluk.   Holy Ghost.
Thoreau.   Inspiration.
Tomlinson, C.   Death of Will, The.
Warfield.   Sun-Struck Eagle, The.
Watts-Dunton.   Coleridge.
Wheatley, P.   To S.M., a Young African Painter, on Seeing His Works.
Wilbur.   Love Calls Us to the Things of This World.
Winder.   Lesson.
Young, A.   Prestidigitator 2, The.
Young, K.   Langston Hughes.

Installment Buying
Trethewey, N.   Collection Day.

Instinct
Cowper, W.   Beau's Reply.
Hemphill.   Better Days.
Stevens, W.   Poetry Is a Destructive Force.
Thomas, D.   Before I Knocked.

Institutionalization
Bogan, L.   Evening in the Sanitarium.
Delgado, J.   Recommitted.
Visiting Father.
Dowson.   To One in Bedlam.
Gardinier.   Supremer Sacrifice, The.
Kocan.   Sleepers, The.
Lowell, R.   In the Ward.
Waking in the Blue.
Rector.   David's Rumor.
Sexton.   Music Swims Back to Me.
Ringing the Bells.
Szumigalski.   Visitor's Parking.

Insults
Beatty, P.   Stall Me Out.
Belloc.   Frog, The.
Bunting.   What the Chairman Told Tom.
Crawley, W.   Poetry for the Goddess.
Maitland, T.   Sir Thomas Maitland's Satyr upon Sir Niel Laing.
Unknown.   Bonny Barbara Allan ("In Scarlet Town where I was born").

Integrity
Ashbery.   Le Livre Est sur la Table.
Heaney, S.   From the Canton of Expectation.
Rich, A.   Integrity.

Intellect and Intellectuals
Carter, E.   Dialogue, A.
Chin.   Elegy for Chloe Nguyen.
Coleridge, M.   Clever Woman, A.
Cummings, E.   Since feeling is first.
Drummond, W.   Content and Resolute.
Dyer, S.   My Mind to Me a Kingdom Is.
Emerson, R.   Intellect.
Farawell, M.   Everything I Need to Know I Learned in Kindergarten.
Graham, J.   Mind.
Hart, L.   Zip.
Herrick.   His Desire.
Ingalls, J.   For the Intellectuals.
Jones, D.   Perishing Bird, The.
Jordan, J.   Poem about Intelligence for My Brothers and Sisters, A.
Kendall, M.   Woman's Future.
Kirby, D.   Dear Derrida.
Lear, E.   Limerick: "There was an old person of Basing."
Moore, M.   Mind Is an Enchanting Thing, The.
Nemerov.   Blue Swallows, The.
Brainstorm.
Porter, C.   Let's Not Talk About Love.
Rodgers, R.   Zip.

Shelley, P.   Hymn to Intellectual Beauty.
Simic.   Harsh Climate.
Sparshott.   Reply to the Committed Intellectual.
Traherne.   Preparative, The.
Wheelock, J.   Earth.
Wilbur.   Mind.
Wright, J.   End of an Ethnic Dream, The.
See also **Mind; Rationalism and Rationalists; Reason**

Internationalism
Cocteau.   Fairy Scene.
See also **United Nations**

Internment
Hongo.   Redness: Thinking it Through.
Inada.   Concentration Constellation.
Mura.   Argument: on 1942, An.
Blueness of the Day, The.
Letters from Poston Relocation Camp (1942–45).
Okita.   Nice Thing About Counting Stars, The.
Uyematsu.   December 7 Always Brings Christmas Early.
Wong, N.   Can't Tell.

Interracial Love and Marriage
Clark, C.   Border Affair, A.
Clinton, M.   Warning to Young Bright Sisters / White AM. Culture 101A.
Durand, O.   Black Man's Son, The.
Eady.   Sherbet.
Hughes, L.   Cross.
Lorde.   Outlines.
Mattawa.   History of My Face.
Middleton, C.   Adelaide's Dream.
Papertalk-Green, C.   Wanna Be White.
Ridge, J.   Stolen White Girl, The.
Sholl.   Midnight Vapor Light Breakdown.
Tolson, M.   African China.
Williams, C.   Dog, The.
For the White Lady Holding Me.

Intimacy
Agran, R.   Door Thrown Open to Daisies.
Ahlert, F.   Walkin' My Baby Back Home.
Alvi, M.   Fish.
Anderson, J.   Waking Up Twice.
Berger, J.   Getting to Know Her.
Berrigan, A.   Bloodletting.
Biespiel, D.   There Were No Deer in the Thicket.
Blake, E.   I'm Craving for That Kind of Love.
Byron, G.   To Thyrza.
Caesar.   Tea for Two.
Clark, P.   Kleptomaniac.
Colby, T.   Boy and the Girl, The.
Davis, C.   Any Nest I Can't Sleep in Should Be Burned.
Dougherty.   Double Helix.
Elizabeth, M.   Manon Reassures Her Lover.
Fisk, M.   Late Afternoon.
Red River.
Flynn, N.   God Forgotten.
Glatt.   One Night With a Stranger at 30.
Gregerman, D.   Strictly Speaking.
Joseph, A.   Pleasure.
Klinger, A.   Transformation.
Light, K.   Because.
Loesser.   My Darling, My Darling.
Lyons, S.   Remembering.
Marcus, B.   Battle at Horizon.
Justice.
Mayes, J.   Orchestration.
McLain, P.   Fishing.
Nelson, M.   Proposal.
Porter, C.   From This Moment On.
Raffalovich, M. A.   World Well Lost 18, The.
Rossiter.   Nostalgia.
Your Body Glistens From the Bath.
Safford, J.   Very Floor of Our Existence, The.
Samyn, M.   Art of Kissing, The.
Poem with Light on Its Shoulder.
Schilpp, M.   Devotions in Confidence.
Sissle, N.   I'm Craving for That Kind of Love.
Smith, M.   Springtime at Twilight.
Swiontkowski, G.   Old Moon With Her Youth In Her Arms.
Torres, E.   Summertime Late Show.

Turk, R. Walkin' My Baby Back Home.
Wetzsteon. Late Show, The.
Whitehead, C. Grass Crust, The.
Whitney, H. To a Woman.
Wiesinger, S. Snow Climbers.
Youmans, V. Tea for Two.
Yount, A. Sharing.

Intolerance
Ginsberg, A. Uptown.

Introspection
Cavendish, M. Dialogue between Melancholy
   and Mirth, A.
Creeley. Rain, The.
Dunbar, P. Ere Sleep Comes Down to Soothe
   the Weary Eyes.
Dunn, S. Impediment.
Harjo, J. Call It Fear.
Kerouac. Buddha.
Lodge, G. Pastoral: "Slopes of the sun and vine,
   and thou dark stream."
Milton. Il Penseroso.
Moody, W. Harmonics.
Nemerov. Salt Garden, The.
Rexroth, K. Signature of All Things, The.
Rich, A. Necessities of Life.
   Storm Warnings.
Smith, S. After-Thought, The.
Unknown. Self-Examination, The.
Very. Lost, The.
Walcott. Hotel Normandie Pool, The.
Wilbur. Hole in the Floor, A.

Invective
Jeffers, R. Advice to Pilgrims.

Inventions and Inventors
Blumenthal, M. Inventors.
Fenton, J. Born Too Soon.
McLoughland. Crazy Boys.
Meinke. Sonnet on the Death of the Man Who
   Invented Plastic Roses.
Nemerov. Extract from Memoirs.

Invocation
Hacker, M. Invocation: "This is for Elsa, also
   known as Liz."
Herrick. His Prayer to Ben Jonson.

Iona, Scotland
Tennyson, F. Iona.

Iowa (state)
Alexander, M. Iowa Farmer.
Hollo. Amazing Grace.
Kooser. Genuine Poem, Found on a Blackboard
   in a Bowling Alley in Story City, Iowa.
Schmitz. Mile Hill.

Iphigenia
Dryden, J. Cymon and Iphigenia.
   Militia, The.

Ireland
Alcock. Written in Ireland.
Betjeman. Ireland with Emily.
Bigg. Irish Picture, An.
Boland, E. Famine Road, The.
   That the Science of Cartography Is Limited.
Clifton, H. Distaff Side, The.
Colum, P. Poor Scholar of the 'Forties, A.
Davis, T. Nation Once Again, A.
Dawe, G. Names.
Deane, A. Cult of the Celtic, The.
Deane, S. Return.
Donatus. Land Called Scotia, The.
Durcan. Backside to the Wind.
   Birth of a Coachman.
   Going Home to Mayo, Winter, 1949.
   Irish Hierarchy Bans Colour Photography.
Ennis. Alice of Daphne, 1799.
   Coyne's.
Fallon, P. Yeats at Athenry Perhaps.
"Fane, V." In an Irish Churchyard.
Ford, R. Back to Dublin.
Fordham. Song to Erin.
French, W. Queen's After-Dinner Speech, The.
Graves, R. Broken Girth, The.
Harburg. How Are Things in Glocca Morra?
Heóghusa. On Maguire's Winter Campaign.
Heaney, S. Bogland.
   In Memoriam Francis Ledwidge.
   Requiem for the Croppies.

Traditions.
Hewitt, J. Colony, The.
   Irishman in Coventry, An.
   Postscript, 1984.
   Ulster Names.
Howard-Jones. Hibernia.
Hutchinson, P. Fleadh Cheoil.
   Frost is All Over, The.
   Gaeltacht.
   True Story Ending in False Hope, A.
Kavanagh, P. Long Garden, The.
   Memory of Brother Michael.
Kennelly. Limerick Train, The.
Kinsella, T. His Father's Hands.
Landor, W. Ireland Never Was Contented.
Lane, B. How Are Things in Glocca Morra?
Lindley, D. Potato Blight.
Longley, M. Wounds.
Lucy. Missing Link.
MacDonagh, D. Dublin Made Me.
MacNeice. Belfast.
Marvell. Horatian Ode upon Cromwell's Return
   from Ireland, An.
Maxton. Ode.
   Urgent Letter, An.
McCarthy, T. Toast.
McFadden, R. First Letter to an Irish Novelist.
McGuckian. To a Cuckoo at Coolanlough.
Montague, J. Like Dolmens Round My
   Childhood, the Old People.
   Windharp.
Moore, M. Spenser's Ireland.
Moore, T. Dear Harp of My Country.
   Harp That Once through Tara's Halls, The.
   Minstrel Boy, The.
   Pastoral Ballad by John Bull, A.
   Petition of the Orangemen of Ireland, The.
Muldoon, P. Christo's.
   Ireland.
   Ma.
   Sightseers, The.
Murphy, R. Gate Lodge.
O'Loughlin. Glasnevin Cemetery.
   Irish Requiem, An.
O'Rahilly [or O'Reilly] [or Ó Rathaille].
   Vision, The.
Ormsby, F. Home.
Paulin. Desertmartin.
   Impossible Pictures, The.
Skinner, K. Cold Irish Earth, The.
Smedley, M. Irish Fairy, The.
Stevens, W. Irish Cliffs of Moher, The.
Swift, J. On the Irish Club.
Synge. Prelude: "Still south I went and west
   and south again."
Thomas, D. Fern Hill.
Tighe. Written at Killarney. July 29, 1800.
   Written at the Eagle's Nest, Killarney. July 26,
   1800.
Unknown. Croppy Boy, The.
   Orange Lily, The.
   Shan Van Vocht, The.
   Wearin' o' the Green, The.
   Wearing of [or Wearin' o'] the Green, The.
Wilde, L. Who Will Show Us Any Good?
Wright, J. Remittance Man.
Yeats. Easter 1916.
   Hosting of the Sidhe, The.
   Lake-Isle of Innisfree, The.
   Municipal Gallery Revisited, The.
   On a Political Prisoner.
   Prayer for My Daughter, A.
   Red Hanrahan's Song about Ireland.
   Rose Tree, The.
   September 1913.
   To Ireland in the Coming Times.
See also **Northern Ireland**

Ireland, Northern
Coles, R. Christmas, Belfast.
See also **Northern Ireland**

Iris (flower)
Doolittle, H. Sea Iris.
"Field." Irises.
Glück, L. Wild Iris, The.
Grossman, A. Enough Rain for Agnes Walquist.
Martien, J. In Wild Iris Time.

Rukeyser, M. Iris.
Sobin, G. Irises.
St. John, D. Iris.
Williams, W. Iris.

Irish, The
Barnes, F. I've Got Rings on My Fingers.
Boland, E. Emigrant Irish, The.
Carson, C. Insular Celts, The.
Cleary, B. Slouch.
Deane, A. Cult of the Celtic, The.
Donovan, K. Entering the Mare.
Hartnett. Death of an Irishwoman.
   Pity the Man Who English Lacks.
Heaney, S. Docker.
Hewitt, J. Ireland.
   Irishman in Coventry, An.
   Once Alien Here.
   Scar, The.
Hovey. Barney McGee.
Howard-Jones. Hibernia.
Hutchinson, P. Gaeltacht.
Maloney, F. Grandmothers in Green and
   Orange.
McCarthy, T. Emigration Trains, The.
Moore, T. Irish Antiquities.
Muldoon, P. Anseo.
   Cuba.
   More a Man Has the More a Man Wants, The.
   Quoof.
O Direain. That Face.
Scott, M. I've Got Rings on My Fingers.
Unknown. Battle of Inverlochy, The.
   Finnegan's Wake.
   Poor Paddy Works on the Railway.
Williams, C. For the White Lady Holding Me.

Iron
Lawrence, D. Things Made by Iron.
Moore, M. Odor of a Metal Is Not Strong, The.
Snyder, G. Some Good Things to Be Said for
   the Iron Age.

Iron Lungs
Greenlaw. Iron Lung.
Plumly. Iron Lung, The.

Irony
Creeley. Gift of Great Value, A.
Hardy, T. Country Wedding, The.
Hattersley, G. Frank O'Hara Five, Geoffrey
   Chaucer Nil.
Hemingway. Age Demanded, The.
Mahon. As It Should Be.
Matthews, T. Robert Sat.
Mew. My Heart is Lame.
Ryan, M. Your Own Image.
Smith, S. I Forgive You.
Southwick. Earthly Light.
Stevenson, R. System.
Whitney, I. Manner of Her Will and What She
   Left to London and to All Those in It, at Her
   Departing, The.
Wilbur. Parable.

Isaac
Clough. Genesis XXIV.
Cole, P. Isaac: a Poise.
Gouri. Heritage.
Owen, W. Parable of the Old Men and the
   Young, The.
Stradling. Abraham's Sacrifice of Isaac.
Vaughan, H. Isaac's Marriage.
Wilner, E. Sarah's Choice.

Ishmael
Palmer, H. Ishmael.

Ishtar
Ashur-Nasir-Pal. Hymn to Ishtar.
Levertov. Song for Ishtar.

Isis
Gascoyne. And the Seventh Dream Is the
   Dream of Isis.
Simon, L. Bernice Got Next to Isis.
Walsh, C. Prayer to Isis.

Islam
Dharker. Purdah, 1.
Hamod, S. After the Funeral of Assam
   Hamady.
   Lines to My Father.
Jordan, J. Intifada.

Nye, N.   My Uncle Mohammed at Mecca, 1981.
Penn, R.E.   Morning Songs.
See also **Muslims and Islam**

Islands
Albrecht, A.   Anacapa.
Auden.   On This Island.
Barnes, F.   I've Got Rings on My Fingers.
Bishop, E.   Crusoe in England.
Blane, R.   Occasional Man, An.
Bogan, L.   Night.
Brathwaite, E.   Citadel.
Brinnin.   Letter from an Island.
Brooks, C.   Our Island Home.
Brown, G.   Kirkyard.
Césaire, A.   Lagoonal Calendar.
  On the Islands of All Winds.
Campbell, R.   Tristan da Cunha.
Cervantes.   Isla Mujeres.
Coates, E.   Sleepy Lagoon.
Cofer, J.   Idea of Islands, The.
Curry.   Galapagos.
Dumas, H.   Island within Island.
Dunn, D.   St Kilda's Parliament: 1879–1979.
Elmslie, K.   Island Celebration.
Gier, J.   First View of the Islands, A.
Harms.   Elegy as Evening, as Exodus.
Hartley, M.   This Crusty Fragment.
Highfill, M.   Sea Breeze.
Hope, A.   Wandering Islands, The.
Kennelly.   In the Sea.
Koehler, T.   Spreadin' Rhythm Around.
Landon.   Enchanted Island, The.
Lawrence, J.   Sleepy Lagoon.
Lowry, M.   About Ice.
Mahon.   Rathlin.
Martin, H.   Occasional Man, An.
McHugh, J.   Spreadin' Rhythm Around.
McNeill, A.   Saint Ras.
Melville, H.   Archipelago, The.
  Enviable Isles, The.
  Island, The.
  Rolfe and the Palm.
Millay, E.   Ragged Island.
Ojaide.   Verdict of Stone, A.
Oswald, A.   Sea Sonnet.
Phillips, C.   You Are Here.
Pilling.   Cast Away.
Rankin, J.   Sea-bundle.
Rose.   Alaskan Fragments June 1981—Summer
  Solstice.
Russell, T.   Sonnet: Suppos'd to Be Written at
  Lemnos.
Sargent, E.   Rockall.
Scott, M.   I've Got Rings on My Fingers.
Sexton, T.   Seal Island.
Stevenson, R.   To S.C.
Talvikki, A.   My Shining Archipelago.
Walcott.   Crusoe's Island.
Weaver, M.   Easy Living.
Weston, R.   I've Got Rings on My Fingers.
Wordsworth, D.   Floating Island at Hawkshead.
Yeats.   Lake-Isle of Innisfree, The.
  Sorrow of Love, The.

Isolation
Costanzo.   Old Neighborhood, The.
Kaufman, B.   Heavy Water Blues.
Kinsella, J.   Fall, The.
Koertge.   Lazarus.
Rich, A.   I Am in Danger—Sir.
Stanton, M.   Space.
Zarco.   My Worst Fear.
See also **Absence; Absence; Separation**

Israel
Alkalay-Gut.   Public Outcry.
Byron, G.   Oh! Weep for Those.
Curzon, D.   Tour of Ein Kerem, A.
Fishman, C.   Not Only in the Six-Day War.
Ginsberg, A.   Galilee Shore.
Hamod, S.   Libyan/Egyptian Acrobats/Israeli Air
  Circus.
Jarrell.   Jews at Haifa.
Jordan, J.   Intifada.
Kaufman, S.   Déjà Vu.
  Security.
Kirsch, D.   Dvora.
Lazarus, E.   Banner of the Jew, The.

Nye, N.   Small Vases from Hebron, The.
Ravikovitch [*or* Ravikovich].   You Can't Kill a
  Baby Twice.
Rawson, J.   Border, The.
Samaras, N.   Notes in Jerusalem.
Shapiro, M.   To Jerusalem, 1990.
Sillitoe.   Synagogue in Prague.
Turki, F.   In Search of Yacove Eved.
Unknown, fr. Terezin Concentration Camp.
  Dusk.
White, D.   Epistle of Love and of Consolation
  unto Israel, An.

Italians, The
Barolini.   Having the Wrong Name for Mr.
  Wright.
Bona.   Amazone.
Browning, R.   Italian in England, The.
Capone.   In Answer to Their Questions.
Clements, A.   Why I Don't Speak Italian.
Downie.   Italians Are Excited, The.
Elledge.   14 Reasons Why I Mention Mario
  Lanza to the Man I Love Every Chance I Get
  Tonight.
Gillan.   Arturo.
  Growing Up Italian.
  Public School No. 18: Paterson, New Jersey.
Gioseffi.   Bicentennial Anti-Poem for Italian-
  American Women.
Leto.   For Talking.
  Mary Morelle Show, The.
Palma.   Coming of Age.
Repetto.   6th Grade—Our Lady of Pompeii.
Romano, R.   Bucket, The.
  But My Blood.
  So I Lost My Temper.
Rossetti, C.   Enrica, 1865.
Saffoti.   Espresso.
Stefanile.   How I Changed My Name, Felice.
Viscusi.   Autobiography.
Wagner, M.   Miss Clement's Second Grade.

Italy
Auden.   Good-Bye to the Mezzogiorno.
Bona.   Dream Poem.
Brinnin.   Hotel Paradiso e Commerciale.
Browning, E.   Part II.
Browning, R.   Fra Lippo Lippi.
  Love among the Ruins.
  Pippa's Song.
  Up at a Villa—Down in the City.
Campana.   Genoa.
Clements, A.   Why I Don't Speak Italian.
Clough.   Amours de Voyage.
  Claude to Eustace: "Yes, we are fighting at last,
    it appears. This morning, as usual."
  Claude to Eustace—*from Bellagio.*
  Georgina Trevellyn to Luisa: "Dearest Louisa,
    Enquire if you please about Mr. Claude."
  Mary Trevellyn to Miss Roper.
  Rome.
  Spirit from Perfecter Ages.
Coward.   Bar on the Piccola Marina, A.
Cranch.   In the Palais Royal Garden.
Denby.   Villa d'Este.
Divakaruni.   Outside Pisa.
Fitzgerald, R.   Figlio Maggiore.
Flanagan, D. B.   Three Years from Sorrento.
Garrigue.   Country Villa.
Gilbert, S.   Mafioso.
Gregor, A.   Poem: "So many pigeons at
  Columbus."
Guest, B.   Otranto.
Hayes, A.   City of Beggars, The.
Hecht, A.   Hill, A.
Hugo, R.   Letter to Libbey from St. Regis.
  Map of Montana in Italy, A.
  View from Cortona, A.
Kemble.   Farewell to Italy.
Lawrence, D.   Cypresses.
Levi, S.   Abbienti.
Milton.   On the Late Massacre [*or* Massacher]
  in Piedmont [*or* Piemont].
O'Hara, F.   Rogers in Italy.
Older.   Two Worlds.
Pasolini.   Day of My Death, The.
Pelizzon, V.   Late Apostasy, A.
Pinkney, E.   Italy.

Robinson, A.   To My Muse.
Rossetti, C.   Italia, Io Ti Saluto!
Scammell, W.   One Man.
Simpson, L.   On the Lawn at the Villa.
Stickney, T.   In Ampezzo.
Tennyson, A.   Daisy, The.
  Frater Ave Atque Vale.
Walcott.   Italian Eclogues.
Wright, J.   Journey, The.

Itching
Nash, O.   Requiem: "There was a young belle of
  old Natchez."
  Taboo to Boot.
Unknown.   As I Was A-walking by Yon Green
  Garden.

Ivy
Brontë, A.   Home.
Copus, J.   Pulling the Ivy.
Unknown.   Holly and Ivy.
  Holly and the Ivy, The.
  In Praise of Ivy.

J

Jack and the Beanstalk
Dacey, P.   Jack, Afterwards.
Jack the Ripper
Miller, V.   Light Reading.
Jackdaws
Earle, J.   Visiting Light.
Jackson, "Hurricane"
Dugan, A.   On Hurricane Jackson.
Jackson, Andrew
Bly, R.   Andrew Jackson's Speech.
  Three Presidents.
Davidson, D.   Twilight on Union Street.
Jackson, Mahalia
Lorde.   Day They Eulogized Mahalia, The.
Jackson, Michael
Komunyakaa.   Never Land.
Jackson, Thomas Jonathan ("Stonewall")
Lanier, S.   Dying Words of Stonewall Jackson,
  The.
Melville, H.   Stonewall Jackson.
Palmer, J.   Stonewall Jackson's Way.
Stevens, W.   American Sublime, The.
Jacob (Bible)
Burns, R.   Patriarch, The.
Davie.   Jacob's Ladder.
Levertov.   Jacob's Ladder, The.
Quarles.   On Jacob's Purchase.
Schwartz, D.   Jacob.
Vaughan, H.   Jacob's Pillow, and Pillar.
Very.   Jacob Wrestling with the Angel.
Wesley, C.   Wrestling Jacob.
Jacob, Max
Warren, R.   Max Jacob at Saint Benoît.
  To Max Jacob.
Jaguars
Hughes, T.   Second Glance at a Jaguar.
Jails
Hannan, M.   Inmates.
Unknown.   Deserter, The.
  Midnight Special.
See also **Prisons and Prisoners**
Jam- and Jelly-making
Belloc.   On Jam.
Kumin, M.   Making the Jam without You.
Jamaica, West Indies
Baugh, E.   Nigger Sweat.
Bennett, L.   Independance.
Goodison.   Jamaica 1980.
Maxwell-Hall.   Jamaica Market.
McCallum, S.   Calypso.
  In My Other Life.
  Jamaica, October 18, 1972.
James, Henry
Ransom, J.   Old Mansion.
James, Jesse
Benét, W.   Jesse James.
Unknown.   Jesse James.

Jamestown, Virginia
Moore, M.   Enough.
Tati-Loutard.   Pilgrimage to Loango Strand.
January
Bishop, E.   Brazil, January 1, 1502.
Ford, C.   'January wraps up the wound of his arm'
Gibson, D.   January.
Hays, H.   January.
Heath-Stubbs.   January.
McCarriston.   January, Anchorage.
Nishiwaki Junzaburo.   January in Kyoto.
Rakosi.   January of a Gnat, The.
Ray, H.   January.
Robinson, M.   January, 1795.
Rothman, D.   Whistling in January.
Williams, W.   January.
Janus
Carew, T.   To the New Year [For the Countess of Carlisle].
Japan
Burn.   In Japan.
DiPalma.   Annotations Tropes and Lacunae of the Itoku Master.
Ginsberg, A.   Change: *Kyoto-Tokyo Express*, The.
Inada.   Father of My Father.
Leithauser.   In a Japanese Moss Garden.
In Minako Wada's House.
Mahon.   Snow Party, The.
Miyazawa Kenji.   Pictures of the Floating World.
Nishiwaki Junzaburo.   January in Kyoto.
Retallack, J.   Japanese Presentation I and II.
Snyder, G.   Feathered Robe, The.
Song.   Girl Powdering Her Neck.
Thwaite.   Great Foreign Writer Visits Age-Old Temple, Greeted by Venerable Abbess, 1955.
Japanese, The
Calil, A.   Blouse of Felt.
Dickey, J.   Performance, The.
Elmslie, K.   Japanese City.
Hawkins, R.   Issei Men: The First Generation.
Nisei Daughter: The Second Generation.
Sansei: The Third Generation.
Kageyama, C.   Mama.
Kaneko.   Bailey Gatzert: The First Grade, 1945.
Mitsui.   Nisei: Second Generation Japanese-American.
Mura.   Argument: on 1942, An.
Argument: On 1942, An.
Blueness of the Day, The.
Rose, R.   What the Japanese Perhaps Heard.
What We Heard About the Japanese.
Song.   Ikebana.
Sugioka.   Legacy.
Uyematsu.   30 Miles from J-Town.
Fortune Cookie Blues.
Wilner, E.   Conversation with a Japanese Student.
Yamada.   American Son.
Cincinnati.
Club, The.
See also **Blue Jays**
Jasmine
Lorde.   Night-Blooming Jasmine, The.
McKay, C.   Jasmine.
Wakoski.   Night Blooming Jasmine.
Jason
Glover, D.   Old Jason, the Argonaut, The.
Jays
"Field."   Flaw, A.
Hall, D.   Short Circuit.
Lawrence, D.   Blue Jay, The.
Stroud, J.   Homage: Summer/Winter, Shay Creek.
See also **Blue Jays**
Jazz
Ai.   Archangel.
Allen, S.   I Say, Mr. A.
Andrews, L.   Time Signature.
Ashanti.   Just Another Gig.
Asim, J.   Hip Hop Bop.
Aubert, A.   Bessie.
Bessie Smith's Funeral.
Baker, H.   Of Walter White's Father in the Rain.

Tobacco Warehouse Blues.
Ball, A.   Jazz.
Baraka.   All is One for Monk.
Am/Trak.
Barlow, G.   In My Father's House.
Mingus Speaks: Found Poems.
Barrax.   Singer, The.
Barresi.   Venice Beach: Brief Song.
Bauer, G.   So You Want to Hear the Blues.
Brooks, G.   Third Sermon on the Warpland, The.
We Real Cool.
Brooks, S.   (That's the Way) Dixieland Started Jazz.
Brown, A.   Assassination of Charlie Parker, The.
Brown, S.   Cabaret.
Ma Rainey.
Buckley, C.   Nostalgia.
Playing for Time.
Buddy.   Callin Buddy / Bolden.
Castro, M.   Blew It.
Cecil.   Richard's Blues.
Chase, K.   What You Can't See.
Collins, K.   Trio.
Cooper, J.   Wanda's Blues.
Corrie.   How Long Has Trane Been Gone.
Cortez, J.   Jazz Fan Looks Back.
Crouch, S.   Revelation, The.
Up on the Spoon.
Cushing, J.   Autumn Leaves.
Every Time We Say Goodbye.
Lover Man.
Dana, R.   Elegy for the Duke.
Davis, F.   Jazz Band.
Davis, T.   C. T. at the Five Spot.
Rogue and Jar: 4/27/77.
Deanovich.   Requirements for Suggesting Fats Waller.
Diop, B.   Ball.
Doty, M.   Almost Blue.
Dove, R.   Canary.
Listen to the Sound of My Horn.
Eady.   Hank Mobley's.
Jazz Dancer.
William Carlos Williams.
Ebb, F.   And All That Jazz.
Nowadays.
Espada.   Majeski Plays the Saxophone.
Etter.   Monk's Dream.
Stuffy Turkey.
Evans, M.   Boss Communication.
Fabio.   For Louis Armstrong, A Ju-Ju.
Feinstein, S.   Blues Villanelle for Sonny Criss.
Christmas Eve.
Sonnets for Stan Gage (1945–1992).
Summerhouse Piano.
Ford, W.   Of Miles Davis.
Gilbert, C.   Resonance.
Gilyard, K.   On Top of It All.
Giovanni.   Genie in the Jar, The.
Gordon, G.   Gas.
Tercios del Muerte.
Graham, M.   After the War; When Coltrane Only Wanted to Play Dance Tunes.
Harjo, J.   Healing Animal.
Harper, M.   Alone.
Bandstand.
Dear John, Dear Coltrane.
For Bud.
Narrative of the Life and Times of John Coltrane: Played by Himself, A.
Reuben, Reuben.
Harvey, S.   Mighty Tropicale Orchestra, The.
Hayden, R.   Soledad.
Hayes, T.   Boxcar.
Henderson, D.   Elvin Jones Gretsch Freak.
Lee Morgan.
Heyward, D.   Jasbo Brown.
Highfill, M.   Sea Breeze.
Hirsch, E.   Art Pepper.
Hollo.   Le Jazz Hot.
Holm, B.   Scott Joplin.
Hughes, L.   Be-Bop Boys.
Jazz Band in a Parisian Cabaret.
Jazzonia.
Hull, L.   Lost Fugue for Chet.

Ornithology.
Hummer, T.   Poem in the Shape of a Saxophone.
Jackson, A.   Make/n My Music.
Ohnedaruth.
Jackson, M. L.   Don Pullen at the Zanzibar Blue Jazz Cafe, 1994.
Jackson, R.   63rd and Broadway.
Shadows.
Thelonious.
Jacobs, H.   Imagination in flight: an improvisational duet.
Jauss.   After the End of the World.
Black Orchid.
Last Solo: Charlie Parker, Hotel Stanhope, March 12, 1955.
Jeffers, L.   How High the Moon.
Joseph, A.   My Father's Heroes.
Kander, J.   And All That Jazz.
Nowadays.
Kaufman, B.   Battle Report.
Walking Parker Home.
Kelly, R.   Ode to Language.
Kessler, R.   Elm Tree on Lafayette Street, The.
Kgositsile.   Acknowledgement.
For Art Blakey and the Jazz Messengers.
Komunyakaa.   Elegy for Thelonious.
February in Sydney.
Speed Ball.
Twilight Seduction.
Lagrone.   I Heard the Byrd.
Larkin, P.   For Sidney Bechet.
Lindsay, N.   Jazz of This Hotel, The.
Long, D.   Black Love Black Hope.
Longley, M.   Words for Jazz Perhaps.
Lux.   Night above the Town.
Madgett.   Echoes.
Plea for My Heart's Sake.
Madhubuti.   Don't Cry, Scream.
Knocking Donkey Fleas off a Poet from the Southside of Chi.
Madigan.   Curtis Fuller.
Stereo Time with Booker Little.
Matthews, W.   Buddy Bolden Cylinder, The.
Mingus at the Showplace.
May, K.   Valentine's Day.
McClure, M.   For Monk.
Jazz at the Intergalactic Nightclub.
McGrath, T.   Guiffre's Nightmusic.
McPherson, S.   Some Metaphysics of Junior Wells.
Suspension: Junior Wells on a Small Stage in a Converted Barn.
Meltzer, D.   17: II:82.
Miller, V.   Dirge in Jazz Time.
Mitchell, A.   From Rich Uneasy America to My Friend Christopher Logue.
Moerman.   Louis Armstrong.
Mor.   Coming of John, The.
Moskowitz, F.   Bird Lives.
O'Hara, F.   Day Lady Died, The.
Okantah.   Afreeka Brass.
Southern Road.
Redmond.   Distance.
Rivard.   Baby Vallejo.
Rivers, C.   Underground.
Rodgers, C.   Written for Love of an Ascension—Coltrane.
Rukeyser, M.   Bunk Johnson Blowing.
Homage to Literature.
Rux, C. H.   Suite Repose.
Sadiq, M.   Tuskegee Experiment.
Salaam.   I Just Heard John Buffington Died.
Sandburg, C.   Jazz Fantasia.
Seyburn, P.   You and Them.
Shirley, A.   Hours Musicians Keep, The.
Simic.   Crepuscule with Nellie.
Simmons, J.   Didn't He Ramble.
Sneeden.   Coltrane and My Father.
Spellman.   Did John's Music Kill Him?
Stein, K.   Past Midnight, My Daughter Awakened by Miles Davis' *Kind of Blue*.
Thomas, L.   Historiography.
Tolson, M.   Satchmo.
Troupe.   One for Charlie Mingus.
Poem for My Father; for Quincy Trouppe, Sr.
Unknown.   It Don't Mean a Thing (If It Ain't

Got That Swing).
Walton, A.   Dissidence.
Weaver, M.   Left Bank Jazz Society, The.
Welburn.   Ben Webster: "Did You Call Her Today?"
Williams, M.   Death of Chet Baker, The.
Williams, W.   Shoot It Jimmy!
Wojahn.   Satin Doll.
Yevtushenko [or Evtushenko].   Saints of Jazz.
Young, A.   Jazz as Was.
  Lester Leaps In.
Zimmer.   But Bird.
  Duke Ellington Dream, The.
  Romance.
  Sitting with Lester Young.

Jealousy
Baillie, L.   Werena My Heart Licht I Wad Dee.
Berssenbrugge.   Jealousy.
Brown, E.   Bitcherel.
Brown, S.   Chillen Get Shoes.
Browning, R.   My Last Duchess.
Carmichael, R.   Young Lass's Soliloquy, A.
Coleridge, M.   Jealousy.
  Other Side of a Mirror, The.
Comden, B.   Not Mine.
Couzyn.   Spell for Jealousy.
Creeley.   Memory, The.
Davies, W.   J is for Jealousy.
  No Man's Wood.
Dickinson, E.   God is indeed a jealous God.
Doolittle, H.   At Ithaca.
"Ephelia."   To J.G. on the News of His Marriage.
  To My Rival.
Erdman, E.   No, No, Nora.
Fain, S.   When I Take My Sugar to Tea.
Fox, G.   She Lay Wrapped.
Glück, L.   Horse.
Green, A.   Not Mine.
Heaney, S.   Dream of Jealousy, A.
Herrick.   How Marigolds Came Yellow.
Howard, B.   Who Besides You.
Johnson, E.   Jealousy.
Kahal, I.   When I Take My Sugar to Tea.
Kemble.   Petition, A.
Koch, K.   Down at the Docks.
Lamb, C.   First Tooth, The.
Larkin, P.   Love Again.
Lovelace, R.   Cupid Far Gone.
Mayer, B.   Sonnet: "Beauty of songs your absence I should not show."
Norman, P.   When I Take My Sugar to Tea.
Nugent, R.   To Clarissa.
O'Hara, F.   Hôtel Transylvanie.
Poe.   Annabel Lee.
Porter, C.   Always True to You in My Fashion.
Ranaivo.   Song of a Young Girl.
Ransom, J.   Vaunting Oak.
Service.   Shooting of Dan McGrew, The.
Styne, J.   Not Mine.
Tsaloumas.   Grudge, The.
Unknown.   Fair Margaret and Sweet William.
  Frankie and Johnny [or Johnnie or Albert].
Waniek.   Women's Locker Room.
Whitman, W.   Sometimes with One I Love.

See also **Envy**

Jeffers, Robinson
Everson, W.   Man-Fate, The.
  Poet Is Dead, The.
Hass, R.   Return of Robinson Jeffers, The.
Santos, S.   Jeffers Country.
Schmitz.   Carmel.

Jefferson, Thomas
Katz, J.   Taxonomy.
MacLeish.   Brave New World.
Monks.   Twilight's Last Gleaming.
Niedecker.   Thomas Jefferson.

Jellyfish
Kendall, M.   Philanthropist and the Jelly-fish, The.
Moore, M.   Jellyfish, A.
Orfalea, G.   Jellyfish Eggs.

Jericho
McGinley.   Women of Jericho, The.

Jerusalem
Amichai [or Amikhai].   Letter.
Bible, O.T.   Song: "I was asleep but my heart stayed awake."
Blake, W.   Epigraph.
  Fields from Islington to Marybone, The.
  Prelude: "England! awake! awake! awake!"
Gibran.   Cobbler in Jerusalem, A.
Hazo.   For Fawzi in Jerusalem.
Kaufman, S.   Mount of Olives, The.
  Next Year, in Jerusalem.
  Stones.
Litvinoff.   If I Forget Thee.
Mathews, A.   At the Wailing Wall.
Morley, D.   Jerusalem.
Paley, G.   Warning, A.
Posamentier, E.   Being Modern in Jerusalem.
Rich, A.   Jerusalem.
Rukeyser, M.   Traditional Tune.
Samaras, N.   Notes in Jerusalem.
Shapiro, M.   To Jerusalem, 1990.
Unknown.   Hierusalem.
  Jerusalem, My Happy Home.
  Prayer for Redemption.

See also **Zion**

Jesters
Beer, P.   Ninny's Tomb.
Sill.   Fool's Prayer, The.
Storace.   King Lear Bewildered.
Yeats.   Cap and Bells, The.

See also **Fools**

Jesuits
Scott, F.   Brébeuf and His Brethren.

Jesus Christ
Adams, F.   To the Christians.
Alabaster.   Divine Sonnet, A.
  Of the Reed That the Jews Set in Our Saviour's Hand.
  To Christ.
  Upon the Ensigns of Christ's Crucifying.
Amis, K.   New Approach Needed.
Appleman, P.   Mary.
Arnold, M.   Progress.
Askew, A.   Ballad Which Anne Askew Made and Sang When She Was in Newgate, The.
Austin, J.   Love of Christ, The.
Avison.   Dumbfounding, The.
Bacon, L.   Wake the Song of Jubilee.
Baldwin, W.   Christ, My Beloved.
Baraka.   When We'll Worship Jesus.
Barnes, D.   Chuang Tzu and Hui Tzu*.
Bates, K.   Despised and Rejected.
Baxter, C.   Diptych: Jesus and the Stone.
Baxter, R.   Good Shepherd, The.
Berkeley, S.   Mass is Over, The.
Berrigan, D.   Prayer.
Berryman.   Carpenter's Son, The.
Bevington, L.   Dreamers?
Birney.   El Greco: Espolio.
Blake, W.   How Sweet I Roamed [or Roam'd] from Field to Field.
Bly, R.   French Generals, The.
Bolton, S.   His Monument.
Braxton, C.   Apocalypse.
Brecht, B.   Mary.
Brontë, C.   Pilate's Wife's Dream.
Brooks, P.   Christmas Everywhere.
  O Little Town of Bethlehem.
Brooks, W.   Pilate Remembers.
Browning, E.   Thought for a Lonely Death-Bed, A.
Browning, R.   Epistle Containing the Strange Medical Experience of Karshish, the Arab Physician, An.
Byrd.   Lulla, My Sweet Little Baby.
Byrom.   Hymn: "Christians, awake, salute the happy morn."
Carmichael, A.   Do We Not Hear Thy Footfall?
Cary, P.   Hymn: "How dare I in thy courts appear."
Causley.   Ballad of the Bread Man.
  I Am the Great Sun.
Chesterton, G.   Donkey, The.
Cleghorn.   Comrade Jesus.
Clemo.   Christ in the Clay-Pit.

Clifton, L.   How Is He Coming Then.
Clough.   Across the Sea, Along the Shore.
Coleridge, M.   He Came Unto His Own, and His Own Received Him Not.
  I Saw a Stable.
Coleridge, S.   My Baptismal Birthday [or Birth-Day].
Collier, M.   Robert Wilson.
Columba.   Boyhood of Christ, The.
Crabbe.   Resurrection.
Crashaw.   Christ's Victory.
  Come See the Place Where the Lord Lay.
  In the Holy Nativity of Our Lord God.
  Luke 11: Blessed Be the Paps Which Thou Hast Sucked.
  Neither Durst Any Man From That Day Ask Him Any More Questions.
  On the Water of Our Lord's Baptism[e].
  On the Wounds of Our Crucified Lord.
  Shepherds' Hymn, The.
  To Our Blessed Lord upon the Choice of His Sepulchre.
  To the Noblest and Best of Ladies, the Countess of Denbigh.
  Upon the Asse That Bore Our Saviour.
Cullen, C.   Christus Natus Est.
Davis, D.   .Christmas Poem, A.
Davis, F.   Christ is a Dixie Nigger.
Dickey, J.   Magus, The.
Donne.   Resurrection, Imperfect.
Donovan, K.   Underneath Our Skirts.
Drummond, W.   Miserable Estate of the World Before the Incarnation of God.
Dunbar, W.   In Praise of Women.
Elliott, E.   Three Marys at Castle Howard, in 1812 and 1837, The.
Etheridge, K.   Annunciation.
Fanthorpe.   Nativities.
Ferlinghetti, L.   Christ Climbed Down.
  Sometime During Eternity.
"Field."   Constancy.
  They Shall Look on Him.
Fletcher, G.   Crucify Him!
Fletcher, P.   Hymn, An: "Wake, O my soul; awake, and raise."
  Ocean of Light.
Flynn, N.   Emptying Town.
Fordham.   Christ Child, The.
  Nativity, The.
Frear.   Young Workman, The.
Galvin, J.   Station (4).
Gascoigne.   Gloze Upon This Text, Dominus iis opus habet, A.
Gerhardt.   Commit thy way unto the Lord.
Gibran.   Cobbler in Jerusalem, A.
  Mannus the Pompeiian to a Greek.
Glück, L.   Nativity Poem.
Graves, R.   In the Wilderness.
Gunn, T.   Jesus and His Mother.
Hall, D.   Carol, A.
  Small Fig Tree, A.
Hall, J.   For Christmas Day.
Hardy, T.   Unkept Good Fridays.
Harper, F.   He "Had Not Where to Lay His Head."
Harris, R.   Call, The.
Havergal.   Just When Thou Wilt.
  Trusting Jesus.
Hayden, R.   Full Moon.
Heaney, S.   Westering.
Heard, J.   Birth of Jesus, The.
Heath-Stubbs.   For the Nativity.
Hecht, A.   Pig.
Hemans.   Mary at the Feet of Christ.
  Olive Tree, The.
Herbert, G.   Aaron.
  Affliction: "Kill me not every [or ev'ry] day."
  Affliction (3).
  Agony [or Agonie], The.
  Bag, The.
  Bunch of Grapes, The.
  Dawning, The.
  Dialogue, A.
  Dulness[e].
  Easter Wings.
  Good Friday.

Grieve Not the Holy Spirit, etc.
Holy Baptism (1).
Iesu.
Jesu.
Longing.
Love.
Love (3).
Mary [or Marie] Magdalene.
Paradise.
Redemption.
Reprisal[l], The.
Sacrifice, The.
Son[ne], The.
Sunday.
Thanksgiving, The.
Herebert. My Folk, What Have I Done Thee?
Who is This that Cometh from Edom?
Herrick. Good Friday: Rex Tragicus, or, Christ
Going to His Cross[e].
His Offering, with the Rest, at the Sepulcher.
His Saviour['ered]s Words, Going to the Cross[e].
No Coming to God without Christ.
Hillman. Little Furnace.
Holst-Warhaft. In the End Is the Body.
Hope, A. Easter Hymn.
Gloss to Matthew V 27–28.
Hope, M. INRI.
Hopkins, G. As Kingfishers Catch Fire.
Lantern Out of Doors, The.
Soldier, The.
Spring.
Starlight Night, The.
Windhover, The.
Hopkins, J. Alleluia! Christ Is Risen Today.
Hopper, E. Jesus Saviour, Pilot Me.
Housman, A. Easter Hymn.
Mark 16:19–20; So then the Lord Jesus, after.
Hudgins. Dead Christ.
Hughes, L. Feet O' Jesus.
Shepherd's Song at Christmas.
Hughes, T. God, A.
Jarry. Passion of Jesus Considered as an Uphill
Race, The.
Jennings, E. Annuciation, The.
Christ Seen by Flemish Painters.
Johnson, J. Go Down Death.
Johnson, L. Church of a Dream, The.
Jonson, B. Carol.
Hymn[e] on the Nativity [or Nativitie] of My
Saviour, A.
"K." How Firm a Foundation.
Kane, P. Disciples Asleep at Gethsemane.
Kelly, T. Head That Once Was Crowned with
Thorns, The.
Second Advent, The.
Kipling, R. Nativity, A.
Sons of Martha, The.
Kossman. Pilate's Wife.
Kunitz, S. He.
Lanier, S. Ballad of Trees and the Master, A.
Laux. Prayer.
Lawrence, D. My Name Is Jesus.
Quetzalcoatl Looks Down on Mexico.
Retort to Jesus.
Leax. Incarnation Poem.
Levertov. Ikon: The Harrowing of Hell.
Lewis, J. Lullaby: "Lullee, lullay."
Lindsay, N. I Heard Immanuel Singing.
Lowell, R. Drunken Fisherman, The.
Lowry, R. Up from the Grave He Arose.
Luther. Away in a Manger.
From Heaven Above to Earth I Come.
MacDiarmid, H. Innumerable Christ, The.
Martin, C. Easter Sunday, 1985.
Marvell. Clorinda and Damon.
Coronet, The.
Mason, R. Ecce Homunculus.
On the Swag.
McAuley, J. In the Twentieth Century.
Jesus.
Melville, H. Arch, The.
Merton. Cana.
Mew. Madeleine in Church.
Meynell, A. Christ in the Universe.
Fugitive, The.
Unto Us a Son Is Given.

Michael of Kildare. Swet Jesus.
Milman. Crucifixion, The.
Hymn: "When our heads are bowed with woe."
Milosz, C. Temptation.
With Her*.
Milton. Hymn on the Morning of Christ's
Nativity.
Mitchell, C. Soul of Jesus Is Restless, The.
Moorer. Benefits of Sorrow.
Sympathy.
Mordecai. Jesus Is Condemned to Death.
Mtshali. Ride upon the Death Chariot.
Muir, E. Incarnate One, The.
Killing, The.
Muske, C. Coming Over Coldwater.
Nemerov. Carol: "Now is the world withdrawn
all."
Nicodemus.
Santa Claus.
Newman, J. Desolation.
Newton, J. "In Evil Long I Took Delight."
Noyes, A. Resurrection.
Okigbo. On the New Year.
Olson, E. Ballad of the Scarecrow Christ.
Owen, W. At a Calvary near the Ancre.
Palmer, R. Hymn: "Jesus these eyes have never
seen."
Parker, D. Maid-Servant at the Inn, The.
Pasternak, B. Christmas Star.
Peacock, M. Devolution.
Perronet. All Hail the Power of Jesus' Name.
Pestel [or Pestell]. Psalm for Christmas Day.
Pfeiffer, E. Cruse of Tears, The. A Russian
Legend.
Pickthall, M. Bridegroom of Cana, The.
Pierman. Apparition, The.
Pound, E. Ballad of the Goodly Fere.
Powell, C. Nativity.
Quarles. Christ and Our Selves.
Upon the Day of Our Saviour's Nativity.
Quarles, J. At Home.
Ralegh, S. On the Card[e]s, and Dice.
Ransom, J. Armageddon.
Our Two Worthies.
Ray, H. Prayer: "O Christ, who in
Gethsemane."
Rilke. Mary at Peace with the Risen Lord.
Olive Garden, The.
On the Marriage at Cana.
Pietà.
Robinson, E. Calvary.
Christmas Sonnet, A.
Rolle of Hampole. Cantus Amoris 2.
Prayer to Jesus 1.
Song of the Passion, A.
Rossetti, C. Before the Paling of the Stars.
Better Resurrection, A.
Bruised Reed Shall He Not Break, A.
Christmas Eve.
Easter Monday.
If Only.
Long Barren.
Lord, Grant Us Calm.
Lowest Place, The.
Three Enemies, The.
Wednesday in Holy Week.
Rossetti, D. Virgin and Child, by Hans
Memmeling; in the Academy of Bruges, A.
Rossetti, W. M. Jesus Wept.
Rothenberg, J. Visions of Jesus.
Rukeyser, M. Holy Family.
Traditional Tune.
Ryman. Nunc Puer Nobis Natus Est.
Sandburg, C. Early Lynching.
Sandys, G. Hymn Written at the Holy
Sepulchre in Jerusalem.
Sassoon. Christ and the Soldier.
Sexton. Jesus Asleep.
Jesus Dies.
Jesus Unborn.
Shaw, L. It is as if infancy were the whole of
incarnation.
Onlookers.
Shomer. Falling for Jesus.
Sisson. Adam and Eve.
Easter.

Smith, S. Airy Christ, The.
Christmas.
Was He Married?
Southwell. Burning Babe, The.
Child My Choice, A.
Child[e] My Choice [or Choyse], A.
Christ[e]'s Childhood[e].
Christs Sleeping Friends.
New Heaven, New War[re].
New Prince, New Pomp[e].
Sinnes Heavie Loade.
Steele, P. Cana.
Stewart, G. As I Went Down to David's Town.
Stocking. O Master-Workman of the Race.
Stone, S. Church's One Foundation, The.
Tabb. Christ and the Pagan.
Tate, J. Goodtime Jesus.
Tate, N. While Shepherds Watched [Their
Flocks by Night].
Thomas, D. This Bread I Break.
Thomas, R. Pietà.
Thompson, C. Empty Tomb, The.
Thompson, F. Hound of Heaven, The.
Thompson, P. Death and Resurrection.
Toomer. Gum.
Traherne. Hymn upon St. Bartholomew's Day,
An.
Wonder.
Turner, C. Dream, A.
Tynan. Sheep and Lambs.
Unknown. Bitter Withy, The.
Child this Day is Born, A.
Christ the Apple-Tree.
Deep Spring.
Down to the Mire.
Easter Song, An.
For Thy Sake Let the World Call Me Fool.
Give Me Jesus.
Guest, The.
Hand by Hand We Shall Us Take.
I Sing of a Maiden.
In Slumber Late.
Jesu Christ, my Leman Swete.
Jesus Bids Man Remember.
Jesus Reproaches His People.
Jesus to Those Who Pass By.
Lo, How a Rose E'er Blooming.
Man Be Merie as Bryd on Berie.
My Dancing Day.
Now Goeth [or goth or goothe] Sun [or Sonne
or Sunne] under Wood.
Nowell Sing We.
Petition to Father and Son and Holy Ghost, A.
Rock O' My Soul.
Rose That Bore Jesu, The.
See! Here, My Heart.
Steal Away to Jesus.
There Is a Balm in Gilead.
Thys Endris Nyght.
Were You There When They Crucified My
Lord?
When I See on Rood.
Wounds, as Wells of Life, The.
U'Tamsi. Scorner, The.
Van Dyke. Lost Word of Jesus, A.
Vaughan, H. And do they so?
British [or Brittish] Church, The.
Burial.
Christ's Nativity.
H. Scriptures.
Incarnation and Passion, The.
Lamp[e], The.
Match, The.
Midnight.
Mount of Olives.
Passion, The.
Peace.
Rainbow, The.
Search, The.
Shepherds [or Shepheards], The.
Very. Cross, The.
Garden, The.
Morning Watch, The.
New Birth, The.
Serpent, The.
Son, The.

Wadding [or Waddinge]. On the Circumsision: New Year's Day.
Walsh, C. Quintina of Crosses, A.
Warner, E. Irony of God.
Waters, M. Christ at the Apollo, 1962.
Watkyns. Gardener, The.
    Upon Christ's Nativity or Christmas.
Watson, M. Memo to J. C.
Watts, I. Passion and Exaltation of Christ, The.
Wesley, C. Catholic Love.
White, D. Epistle of Love and of Consolation unto Israel, An.
Whiteside. Carpenter, The.
Whittier. Dedication: "I would the gift I offer here."
    Over-Heart, The.
Wickham. To a Crucifix.
Wilde, O. Ave Maria, Gratia Plena.
    E Tenebris.
    Santa Decca.
Williams, W. Gift, The.
Wolfe, H. Dean Inge.
Wordsworth, W. Hymn: "Blest are the moments, doubly blest."
Wright, J. Eli, Eli.
    Saint Judas.
Yeats. "Calvary."
    Stick of Incense, A.
Zangwill. Moses and Jesus.

Jewelry
Alvi, M. Presents from My Aunts in Pakistan.
Bamber, J. Broken Necklace.
Borodin, A. Baubles, Bangles, and Beads.
Herrick. To Julia.
Robin, L. Diamonds Are a Girl's Best Friend.
Stanley, T. Bracelet, The.
Teasdale. Jewels.
Trinidad. Moonstones.
See also **Rings**

Jewish, Hebrew, and Yiddish Poetry
Bass, F. I Am a Jew.

Jezebel
Brown, E. Jezebel to the Eunuchs.
Higgins, F. Song for the Clatter-Bones.

Joan of Arc
Hemans. Joan of Arc in Rheims.
Lowell, M. Rouen, Place de la Pucelle.
Péret. Joan of Arc.
Zubick, K. Evolution of Appetite.

Job (Bible)
Ashbery. Cæsura.
Kaufman, S. Job's Wife.
Macpherson, J. Beauty of Job's Daughters, The.
Sewell, E. Job.
Shelton, R. Job the Father.
Sylvester, J. Job's Epitaph.

Jockeys
Hayward, D. To the Man Saying 'Come on Seis' at Hollywood Park.
Higgins, F. Old Jockey, The.
See also **Horse Racing**

Jogging and Joggers
Ali, A. Jogger on Riverside Drive, 5:00 A.M., The.
See also **Running and Runners**

Johannesburg, South Africa
Serote. City Johannesburg.
Smith, P. Meanwhile, in Rwanda.

John of Austria
Chesterton, G. Lepanto.

John the Baptist, Saint
Constable, H. To St John Baptist.
Drummond, W. For the Baptiste.

John, Saint
Wheelwright. Bread-Word Giver.
Wylie. Peter and John.

Johnson, Lionel
Yeats. In Memory of Major Robert Gregory.

Johnson, Lyndon Baines
Weber, R. Concise History of the Vietnam War: 1965–1968, A.

Johnson, Samuel
Jenyns. Doctor Johnson.
    Epitaph on Dr Samuel Johnson.
    Moody, E. Dr. Johnson's Ghost.
Synge. To the Oaks of Glencree.

Johnston, James Hugo
Johnson, M. James Hugo Johnston.

Jokes
Dumdum. To My Mother.

Jonah (Bible)
Drayton. Song of Jonah in the Whale's Belly, The.
Jarrell. Jonah.
Merriam, E. Wonderful Whale, The.
Owen, G. Jonah and the Whale.
Shapiro, D. In a Blind Garden.
Speyer. To a Song of Sappho Discovered in Egypt.
Unknown. I to the Lord from My Distress.

Jones, Ebenezer
Betjeman. Incident in the Early Life of Ebenezer Jones, Poet, 1828, An.

Jones, John Paul
Unknown. Yankee Man-of-War, The.

Jonson, Ben
Beaumont, F. Letter to Ben Jonson, A.
Carew, T. To Ben Jonson.
Cleveland, J. Elegy on Ben Jonson, An.
Godolphin. On Ben Jonson.
Herrick. His Prayer to Ben Jonson.
    My Ben.
    Ode for Him [or Ben Jonson], An.
    Upon Ben Jo[h]nson.
    Upon M. Ben Jo[h]nson: Epigram.
Howell, J. Upon the Poet of His Time, Ben Jonson: His Honoured Friend and Father.
Randolph, T. Answer to Master [or Mr.] Ben Jonson's Ode, to Persuade Him Not to Leave the Stage, An.
    Gratulatory to Mr. Ben Johnson for His Adopting of Him to Be His Son, A.
Waller, E. Upon Ben Johnson [or Jonson].
Westmorland. In Obitum Ben. Jons.

Joplin, Janis
Matthews, W. Penalty for Bigamy Is Two Wives, The.
Phillips, R. Death of Janis Joplin, The.
Speakes. Mama Loves Janis Joplin.

Jordan, Michael
Troupe. Forty-one Seconds on a Sunday in June, in Salt Lake City, Utah.

Joseph (Bible, O.T.)
George, D. Asenath.
Herbert, G. Joseph's Coat.
Nemerov. September, the First Day of School.
Reznikoff. Israel II.

Joseph, Saint
Rilke. Joseph's Suspicion.

Joshua (Bible)
Kennedy, X. Joshua.
Ostriker. Story of Joshua.
Unknown. Battles of Joshua.
    Joshua Fit de Battle of Jericho [or ob Jerico].

Journalism and Journalists
Black, S. To a War Correspondent.
Forché. Memory of Elena, The.
McFadden, R. For the Record.
Moorer. Southern Press, The.
Ofeimun. Beyond Fear.
Smith, P. Meanwhile, in Rwanda.
Wolfe, H. British Journalist, The.
See also **Magazines; Newspapers**

Joy
Arlen, H. Hooray for Love.
Bangs, J. Today.
Braithwaite. Sic Vita.
Brome. Epithalamy.
Brown, G. Old Women, The.
Browning, R. Now.
Burwell, C. Sweet Lorraine.
Butler, S. Love.
Carter, E. Ode to Wisdom.
Centolella. Joy.
Ceravolo. White Fish in Reeds.
Chalkhill. Coridon's Song.
Chasin. Joy Sonnet in a Random Universe.
Coleridge, M. Solo.
Cullen, C. From Life to Love.
Cummings, E. You Shall Above All Things Be Glad and Young.
Dacre, C. Kiss, The.
Dawe, B. Going.
Dawe, G. Solstice.
Dickey, J. In the Marble Quarry.
Dickinson, E. I Can Wade Grief.
Donne. Ecstasy, The.
Dunbar, P. Little Brown Baby.
Ellington, D. Jump for Joy.
Emerson, R. Water.
Etter. Great Northern.
"Field." To Christina Rossetti.
Gay, J. Cotillion.
Glück, L. Nativity Poem.
Goedicke. After the Second Operation.
Harms. Joy Addict, The.
Hemans. Revellers, The.
Henderson, R. I'm Sitting on Top of the World.
Hopkins, G. Hurrahing in Harvest.
Howe, F. First Chance Twice.
Hulme, T. Embankment, The (The fantasia of a fallen gentleman on a cold, bitter night).
Jonson, B. To Sir Henry Cary.
Joseph, A. Learning to Laugh.
Keats. Fancy.
Keble. Rainbow, The.
Killigrew, A. Farewell to Worldly Joys, A.
Kuller, S. Jump for Joy.
Levertov. Ache of Marriage, The.
    Matins.
    Triple Feature.
Lewis, S. I'm Sitting on Top of the World.
MacKay, I. Meeting, The.
McCord, D. Blessed Lord, What It Is to Be Young.
Miles, S. Plumbers.
Milton. L'Allegro.
    To the Lord General Cromwell.
Nabbes. Song: "What a dainty life the milkmaid leads!"
Nasrin. Eve Oh Eve.
Owenson. Joy.
Parish. Sweet Lorraine.
Phillips, C. Reach, The.
Porter, C. At Long Last Love.
    I Get a Kick Out of You.
Ray, H. Shadow and Sunrise.
Reverdy. On the Threshold.
Robin, L. Hooray for Love.
Roethke. All the Earth, All the Air.
Rossetti, C. Birthday, A.
Rukeyser, M. Reading Time : 1 Minute 26 Seconds.
Rumi. Say Yes Quickly.
Salzman, E. Grandmother.
Sarton. Small Joys.
Sexton. Welcome Morning.
Sherburne. Weeping and Kissing.
Spenser. Epithalamion: "Ye learned sisters which have oftentimes."
    Prothalamion.
Steele, T. Eros.
Stone, J. Gaudeamus Igitur: A Valediction.
Strode. Opposite to Melancholy.
Swift, J. Satirical Elegy on the Death of a Late Famous General, A.
Swirszczynska. Thank You, My Fate.
Thoreau. Winter Memories.
Tolson, M. Victor Garibaldi.
Tzara. Waking.
Watson, R. Of the Earth, Earthy.
Watts, M. Vision.
Webster, J. Jump for Joy.
Whitman, W. I Saw in Louisiana a Live-Oak Growing.
Wicks, S. Joy.
Wilbur. Hamlen Brook.
Wilde, L. Corinne's Last Love-Song.
Wordsworth, W. I Wandered Lonely As a Cloud.
Wright, J. Blessing, A.
Young, J. I'm Sitting on Top of the World.

Joyce, James
McDonald, W. For Kelly, Missing in Action.

Judaism and Jews (continued)

Walcott. Volcano.
Wolfe, H. D. H. Lawrence and James Joyce.

Judaism and Jews

Abse. Footnote Extended, A.
Antin. Real Estate.
Baumel. Let Me In.
Samuel.
To the Parents of a Childhood Friend, a Suicide.
Becker, R. Crypto-Jews, The.
Grief.
On the Eve of the Warsaw Uprising.
Spiritual Morning.
Yom Kippur, Taos, New Mexico.
Behar, R. Jewish Cemetery in Guanabacoa, The.
Survivals.
Bell, M. Book of the Dead Man (#58), The.
Extermination of the Jews, The.
Getting Lost in Nazi Germany.
Israeli Navy, The.
Bibb. Wandering Jew, The.
Bloch, T. While Bouncing the Shema Back and Forth in Shul.
Bobrowski. Elderblossom.
Boss. At the Nuclear Rally.
Budy. Ellis Island, September 1907.
Celan. Death Fugue, A.
Chess, R. Growing Up in a Jewish Neighborhood.
No Music.
Two and One.
Yiddish Poets in America.
Cohen, L. Genius, The.
Durcan. Jewish Bride, The.
Ewer. Chosen People, The.
Falk. Home for Winter.
Sabbath Morning.
Shulamit in Her Dreams.
Fishman, C. Not Only in the Six-Day War.
Florsheim. Jewish Singles Event, The.
Garlick, R. Heiress, The.
Gershon. Experiments with God.
Race.
Gibran. Mannus the Pompeiian to a Greek.
Ginsberg, A. Visiting Father and Friends.
Yiddishe Kopf.
Glaser, M. Magnificat!
Preparations for Seder.
Goetsch, D. Nobody's Hell.
Goldbarth. Gallery.
Shoyn Fergéssin: 'I've Forgotten' in Yiddish.
Steerage.
World Above Suffering, A.
Gouri. Heritage.
Gray, A. Why Your Grandfather Stopped Playing the Viola.
Greenberg, A. Man in the Moon, The.
Hacker, M. Boy, The.
Hamburger, M. Treblinka.
Harchik. Requiem: "Your names ring clearly."
Harris, R. Riding Over Belmore Park.
Hecht, A. 'More Light! More Light!'
Hirsch, E. Ancient Signs.
My Grandfather's Poems.
Hollander, J. At the New Year.
Letter to Jorge Luis Borges: Apropos of the Golem.
Song at the End of a Meal.
Jarrell. Jews at Haifa.
Kamenetz. History of the Invisible.
Missing Jew, The.
This Is the Map.
Why Ten Men?
Kessler, S. Names the Dead Speak.
Kinnell. Avenue Bearing the Initial of Christ into the New World, The.
Kirsch, D. Dvora.
Klein, A. Autobiographical.
Heirloom.
Klepfisz. Fradel Schtok.
My Mother's Sabbath Days.
Klugman, E. She Who Listens.
Klugman, S. God's Body.
Kramer, L. Shoemaker's Wife, The.
Kumin, M. Chain, The.
Living Alone with Jesus.

Lazarus, E. Crowing of the Red Cock, The.
In Exile.
Levi, S. Abbienti.
Levine, P. Old Testament, The.
Lifshin. Being Jewish in a Small Town.
Yahrtzeit Light, The.
Limburg, J. Seder Night with My Ancestors.
Logghe. Insomnia Litany.
Longfellow, H. Jewish Cemetery at Newport, The.
Mayne, S. Before Passover.
Zalman.
Meltzer, D. Tell Them I'm Struggling to Sing with Angels.
Tishah B'Ov / 1952.
Who's the Jew.
Mezey. To Levine on the Day of Atonement.
Wandering Jew, The.
Michelson, R. Genuine Jewish Flesh.
Jews That We Are, The.
Moore, T. Weep, Children of Israel.
Nemerov. Debate with the Rabbi.
Niemoller. First They Came for the Jews.
Osherow. Song for the Music in the Warsaw Ghetto.
To Eva.
Yiddish Muses, The.
Ostriker. Bride, The.
Eighth and the Thirteenth, The.
Meditation in Seven Days, A.
Opinion of Hagar, The.
Ozick. Origins, Divergences.
When That with Tragic Rapture Moses Stood.
Wonder-Teacher, The.
Yom Kippur, 5726.
Paley, G. Warning, A.
Pastan. At the Jewish Museum.
Name, A.
Old Photograph Album.
Passover.
Pelletiere, M. Under Her Crib.
Piercy. At the New Moon: Rosh Hodesh.
Candle in a Glass, A.
Growing Up Haunted.
Maggid.
Pinsky. Avenue.
Night Game, The.
Poem with Refrains.
Plath. Daddy.
Plotnick, H. M. Jewish.
Posamentier, E. Being Modern in Jerusalem.
Hungarian Medical Student, The: 1928.
Quarles. Meditatio Septima.
Rakosi. Israel.
Services.
Ranasinghe. Holocaust 1944.
Reti, I. I Never Knew I Was Jewish.
Reznikoff. Hebrew of Your Poets, Zion, The.
Joshua at Schechem.
Rich, A. At the Jewish New Year.
Food Packages: 1947.
Yom Kippur 1984.
Richman, L. Rue de Rosiers: To My Brother Fred.
Rosenberg, I. Jew, The.
Rothenberg, J. At the Castle.
Cokboy.
Connoisseur of Jews, The.
In the Dark Word, Khurbn.
Nokh Aushvits (After Auschwitz).
Poland / 1931 "The Wedding."
Portrait of a Jew Old Country Style.
Structural Study of Myth, The.
Rukeyser, M. Akiba.
Sachs, N. Chorus of the Dead.
Sadoff. Nazis.
Schaeffer. May Levine.
Yahrzeit.
Schultz, P. Bar Mitzvah, The.
For My Father.
For the Wandering Jews.
Schulzová, E. Evening in Terezin, An.
Seiler. Digging in the Streets of Gold.
Selman, R. Descent.
For the Field.
Work Song.

Shapiro, A. Basement, The.
Christmas Story, A.
Mezuzah.
Shapiro, K. 151st Psalm, The.
Alphabet, The.
Shapiro, M. To Jerusalem, 1990.
Shomer. Falling for Jesus.
Freestyle, on the First of Tishri.
From the Wailing Wall.
Refusing the Call.
Shards.
Shore. High Holy Days.
Simpson, L. Story About Chicken Soup, A.
Sklarew. After Theresienstadt.
On Muranowska Street.
Three-Course Meal for the New Year, A.
What Is a Jewish Poem?
Smith, S. Songe d'Athalie.
Solomon, M. Comment on My Host, A.
Sommer, J. Mengele Shitting.
Spender, S. History and Reality.
Stern, G. Behaving Like a Jew.
Dancing, The.
Self-Portrait.
Swinburne. On the Russian Persecution of the Jews.
Timrod. La Belle Juive.
Unknown. Sir Hugh; or, The Jew's Daughter.
Warren, R. Max Jacob at Saint Benoît.
Wexler, E. Governess, The.
Williams, C. Spit.
Vessel, The.
Wilner, E. Miriam's Song.
When Asked to Lie Down on the Altar.
Young-Prottengeier. Lithuanian Grandmother.
Zolotow. Enemies.
Zukofsky, L. Song for the Year's End, A.

Judas Iscariot

De la Mare. Ballad of Christmas, A.
Kossman. Judas' Reproach.
Malouf. Judas Touch, The.
Mason, R. Judas Iscariot.
Miller, V. Judas.
Nemerov. Historical Judas, The.
Sitwell, S. Judas and the Profiteer.
Spender, S. Judas Iscariot.
Unknown. Judas.
Judas Sells His Lord.
Wright, J. Saint Judas.

Judges

Cooley, N. Mary Warren's Sampler.
Espada. Tires Stacked in the Hallways of Civilization.
Gilyard, K. Letter.
Hölderlin. In the Days of Socrates.
Kees. After the Trial.
Kipling, R. Gallio's Song.
McCarriston. To Judge Faolain, Dead Long Enough: A Summons.
Smart, C. Psalm 58.
Unknown. On Rÿneveld, an Unpopular Dutch Judge.
Roy Bean.
Watts, I. Psalm 58.

Judgment

Adams, J. Wants of Man, The.
Carew, T. To the Reader of Master William Davenant's Play [The Wits].
Cowper, W. Lines Written During a Period of Insanity.
Davis, O. Small Number, A.
Di Prima. Death Sunyata Chant: A Rite for Passing Over.
Dickinson, E. This Is My Letter to the World.
Emerson, R. Prudence.
Galvin, J. Station (4).
Housman, A. Laws of God, the Laws of Man, The.
Jarrell. Variations.
Lear, E. Limerick: "There was an old man of Whitehaven."
Peck, J. Metal Denser Than, and Liquid, A.
Ransom, J. Armageddon.
Simic. Cold, The.
Tate, J. My Great Great Etc. Uncle Patrick Henry.

Unknown. Little Black Train Is A-Comin'
Warren-Moore. For Etheridge Knight.
Wright, J. At the Executed Murderer's Grave.
Judgment Day
Byron, G. Vision of Judgment, The.
Cowley, A. Resurrection, The.
Evans, S. Fifteen Days of Judgment, The.
Farewell. Quaerè.
Fletcher, P. Against a Rich Man Despising Poverty.
Hart, K. Last Day, The.
Herbert, G. Death.
  Doomsday.
  Judgement.
Herrick. Gods Providence.
  Upon Himselfe Being Buried.
Hill, G. Requiem for the Plantagenet Kings.
Johnson, J. Judgment Day, The.
Kipling, R. Last Chantey, The.
Kunitz, S. For the Word Is Flesh.
Macaulay, T. Dies Iræ.
MacDiarmid, H. Crowdieknowe.
Nicholson, N. Carol for the Last Christmas Eve.
Stickney, T. And, the last day being come, Man stood alone.
Swift, J. Day of Judgement, The.
Unknown. Heavenly Aeroplane, The.
  I Know Moon-Rise [*or* Moonrise].
  Pointless Pride of Man, The.
Vaughan, H. Day of Judgement.
Very. New World, The.
Watts, I. How Doth the Little Busy Bee.
Whittier. Abraham Davenport.
Yeats. Second Coming, The.
See also **Apocalypse; End of the World**
Judith (Apocrypha)
Bibb. Judith.
Menken. Judith.
Ransom, J. Judith of Bethulia.
Stanton, M. Judith Recalls Holofernes.
Juggling and Jugglers
Morgan, E. Cinquevalli.
Unknown. Jolly Jugger, The.
Wilbur. Juggler.
July
Bogan, L. July Dawn.
Burke, J. Sleigh Ride in July.
Cole, W. Back Yard, July Night.
Fitzgerald, R. July in Indiana.
Gray-Kontar, D. July.
Posey, A. July.
Ray, H. July.
Sanchez, S. July.
Trommer, R. Sonnet for July.
Van Heusen, J. Sleigh Ride in July.
Wilbur. My Father Paints the Summer.
Jumping
Fisher, R. Supposed Dancer, The.
Peters, L. Parachute Men.
June
Burns, R. Song: "O my love's [*or* luve's *or* love is *or* luve is] like a red, red rose."
Davies, W. All in June.
Feinstein, E. June.
Fordham. June.
Hammerstein. June Is Bustin' Out All Over.
Kelly, R. In June.
Larkin, P. Cut Grass.
Lawrence, D. Andraitx—Pomegranate Flowers.
Ledwidge. June.
Mew. June, 1915.
Nash, O. Here Usually Comes the Bride.
Ray, H. June.
Roberts, S. Mowing, The.
Rodgers, R. June Is Bustin' Out All Over.
Schuyler, J. I Think.
Sze. June Ghazal.
Tennyson, A. June Bracken and Heather.
Wilkinson, A. In June and Gentle Oven.
Jungles
Barry, J. Green Hell, Green Death.
Brown, D. Eating the Forest.
  First Person—1981.
  Returning Fire.
  When I Am 19 I Was a Medic.

Hilliard, B. Civilization (Bongo, Bongo, Bongo).
"K." Jungle Night.
Lane, P. At the Edge of the Jungle.
Lewis, A. Jungle, The.
McDonald, W. Once You've Been to War.
Murray, L. Louvres.
Nazareno, C. Bohol's Tarsier Population.
Scurfield, G. Bitter Mangoes, The.
Smith, S. Jungle Husband, The.
Weigl. Amnesia.
  Sharing, The.
  Surrounding Blues on the Way Down.
Wright, J. Rainforest.
Juniper Trees
Behn, A. On a Juniper Tree, Cut Down to Make Busks.
Evans, A. Juniper.
Francis, R. Juniper.
Junk and Junkyards
Dickey, J. Cherrylog Road.
Disch. Garage Sale as a Spiritual Exercise, The.
Kessler, R. Elm Tree on Lafayette Street, The.
Merwin, W. S. Drunk in the Furnace, The.
Unknown. Ol' Clothes.
Wilbur. Junk.
Jupiter (god)
Fields, J. Jupiter and Ten.
Jupiter (planet)
Sargent, E. Planet Jupiter, The.
Justice
Austin, A. Jameson's Ride.
Ba. Justice is Done.
  Nobility.
Barney, S. Black People Cry.
Bowen, C. Rain It Raineth, The.
Brown, J. *et al.* Say It Loud—I'm Black and I'm Proud.
Browning, R. Instans Tyrannus.
Burns, R. Holy Willie's Prayer.
Carew, T. Upon My Lord Chief Justice's Election of My Lady Anne Wentworth [*or* A.W.] for His Mistress.
Carson, C. Judgement.
Coleridge, S. Good Great Man, The.
Davies, W. Inquest, The.
Elizabeth I. Written on a Wall at Woodstock.
Emerson, R. Astræa.
Fearing. Escape.
Hall, D. Small Fig Tree, A.
"Hope." Youth.
Hughes, L. Justice.
  Who But the Lord?
Jonson, B. On Lieutenant Shift.
Kelber, M. Pledge of Allegiance to the Family of Earth, A.
Kinsella, T. Another September.
Kinzie. Sun and Moon.
Kipling, R. Gallio's Song.
Košek, M. It All Depends on How You Look at It.
Lawrence, D. When Wilt Thou Teach the People?
Linden, E. All We Ask Is Justice.
Mayne, S. In Memory of Aaron, Murdered Grandfather.
O'Hara, F. Ode: "Idea of justice may be precious, An."
Ofeimun. Judgement Day.
Ogundipe-Leslie. On Reading an Archeological Article.
Quarles. Luke 6.25.
Reznikoff. Day of Atonement.
Sepamla. If.
Unknown. Fortune's Legacy.
  Psalm 58.
Vando. Knife.
Wallace-Crabbe. Tribunal, The.
Whittier. Cities of the Plain, The.
  Slave-Ships, The.
Wong, N. For an Asian Woman Who Says My Poetry Gives Her a Stomachache.
See also **Injustice**
Justification
Emerson, R. Compensation.

Page, G. Jerry's Plains, 1848.
Rich, A. Women.
Juvenile Delinquency
Addonizio. Broken Sonnets.
Brooks, G. We Real Cool.
Hamer. Charlene-N-Booker 4Ever.
Neely, L. Rhonda, Age 15, Emergency Room.

K

Kabul, Afghanistan
Kipling, R. Ford o' Kabul River.
Kafka, Franz (1883-1924)
Hirsch, E. Milena Jesenká.
Holub. Jewish Cemetery at Olsany, Kafka's Grave, April, Sunny Weather, The.
Kahlo, Frida
Alexander, E. Painting / (Frida Kahlo).
Guevara, M. Make-Up.
Rawson, J. Self-portraits by Frida Kahlo.
Kalamazoo, Michigan
Gordon, M. I've Got a Gal in Kalamazoo.
Sandburg, C. Sins of Kalamazoo, The.
Warren, H. I've Got a Gal in Kalamazoo.
Kangaroos
Field, B. Kangaroo, The.
Gray, R. Dusk, The.
Hull, C. Flying Kangaroos.
Lawrence, D. Kangaroo.
Napaljarri, P. Kangaroo, The.
Kansas (state)
Bynner. Haskell.
David, M. Sunflower.
Dunn, J. Kansas.
  Ode to Governor Capper, An.
Etter. Riding the Rock Island Through Kansas.
Justice, D. Crossing Kansas by Train.
Levis. Edward Hopper, 'Hotel Room,' 1931.
Stafford, W. Ceremony.
  Rescued Year, The.
Kansas City, Kansas and Missouri
Beeks. Parker's Mood.
Karate
Plumly. Karate.
Katharine of Aragón, Queen of England
Bibb. Catharine of Arragon.
Causley. Ballad for Katharine of Aragon, A.
Katmandu, Nepal
Justice, D. Here in Katmandu.
Katsushika Hokumei
Enright, D. Laughing Hyena, after [*or* by] Hokusai, The.
Katydids
Freneau. To a Caty-did.
Lowell, A. Katydids.
Katzenjammer Kids
Reaney. Katzenjammer Kids, The.
Kayaks
Villanueva, A. Peace #3.
Keaton, Buster
O'Grady, J. Buster's Last Hand.
Keats, John
Baker, T. Armillaria Mellea.
Brown, L. Green Arbor, A.
Clare, J. To the Memory of John Keats.
Harrison, T. Kumquat for John Keats, A.
Hood, T. False Poets and True.
Hunt, L. To John Keats.
Keats. There Was a Naughty Boy.
Kublanovsky [*or* Kublanovskii]. In Memory of John Keats.
Longfellow, H. Keats.
Lowell, A. To John Keats.
Lowell, J. To the Spirit of Keats.
"Malley." Colloquy with John Keats.
Muske, C. Our Kitty.
Owen, W. To My Friend (With an Identity Disc).
Reynolds, J. To Keats: On Reading His Sonnet Written in Chaucer.
Rukeyser, M. Homage to Literature.
Shelley, P. Adonais; An Elegy on the Death of

John Keats.
Skirrow. Ode on a Grecian Urn Summarized.
Stainer. Wound-dresser's Dream, The.
Kells, Book of
Colum, P. Book of Kells, The.
Kennedy, John Fitzgerald
Alexie. November 22, 1983.
Bly, R. Three Presidents.
Cooper, D. In New York.
In School.
Herd. Pink Rose Rings, The.
Livingston, M. Arthur Thinks on Kennedy.
Myles, E. American Poem, An.
Reed, I. Nov 22, 1988.
Kennedy, Robert Francis
Justice, D. Assassination, The.
Kensington Gardens, London
Spark. Kensington Gardens.
Symons, A. In Kensington Gardens.
Kent, England
"Asphodel." On the Pilgrim's Way in Kent, as
It Leads to the Coldrum Stones.
Davidson, J. In Romney Marsh.
Gray, T. On Lord Holland's Seat near Margate,
Kent.
Rochester, J. Tunbridge Wells.
Waller, E. At Penshurst.
Wright, K. How the Wild South East Was Lost.
See also **Cinque Ports, England**
Kentucky
Ager, M. Louisville Lou (The Vampin' Lady).
Bolton, J. American Tragedy.
In Memory of the Boys of Dexter, Kentucky.
Dietz, H. Blue Grass.
Foster, S. My Old Kentucky Home[, Good
Night!].
Loncar, M. Kentucky.
Schwartz, A. Blue Grass.
Tate, A. Swimmers, The.
Warren, R. History among the Rocks.
Williams, W. To Elsie.
Yellen, J. Louisville Lou (The Vampin' Lady).
Kerouac, Jack
Ginsberg, A. Malest Cornifici Tuo Catullo.
Memory Gardens.
Sunflower Sutra.
Sweet Levinsky.
Herrera. Future Martyr of Supersonic Waves.
Kerouac. Hymn.
Kesey, Ken
Ginsberg, A. First Party at Ken Kesey's with
Hell's Angels.
Kew Gardens, London
Noyes, A. Barrel-Organ, The.
Key West, Florida
Moore, H. Window at Key West, A.
Stevens, W. Idea of Order at Key West, The.
Two Figures in Dense Violet Night.
Keys
Bishop, E. One Art.
Clarke, C. Vicki and Daphne.
Coleman, E. Liberator, The.
Forbes, C. Home.
Garcia, R. Story of Keys, The.
Jones, R. Key, The.
Merwin, W. S. To the Hand.
Ormond. Key, The.
Scupham. Key, The.
Stafford, W. With My Crowbar Key.
Kidnapping and Kidnappers
Clayton, I. Kidnappers.
Kinsella, J. Bright Cigar-Shaped Object Hovers
Over Mount Pleasant, A.
Reed, I. Beware: Do Not Read This Poem.
Killing and Killers
Ai. Deserter, The.
Baraka. Incident.
Bendall, F. Outposts.
Brown, S. Sam Smiley.
Causley. On Being Asked to Write a School
Hymn.
Coleman, W. Emmett Till.
Cowper, W. On a Spaniel Called Beau Killing a
Young Bird.

Douglas, K. How to Kill.
Forbes, C. Killer Blues.
Frost, C. To Kill a Deer.
Guest, B. Geese Blood.
Hammial. Sadie.
Hodgins. Shooting the Dogs.
Hughes, T. Esther's Tomcat.
Hawk Roosting.
Kreutzer Sonata.
Kandel. First They Slaughtered the Angels.
Kinnell. Dead Shall Be Raised Incorruptible,
The.
Koch, K. To World War Two.
Komunyakaa. Tiger Lady.
Kooser. Shooting a Farmhouse.
Livingston, M. Arthur Thinks on Kennedy.
Lumsden, R. Mercy.
Owen, W. Strange Meeting.
Todd, M. To Kill Stray Dogs.
Unknown. Edward [*or* Edward, Edward].
Poor Lazarus.
Weigl. Surrounding Blues on the Way Down.
Whalen. Regalia in Immediate Demand!
Kimonos
Merrill, J. Kimono, The.
Kindness
Alford, J. Thanks Be to God.
Bangs, J. On File.
Belloc. Frog, The.
Buchanan, G. Lewis Mumford.
Carey, H. Maid's Husband, The.
Chaucer. Gentilesse.
Courtney. Be Kind.
Fain, S. Was That the Human Thing to Do?
Foley, J. Drop a Pebble in the Water.
Gershwin. Oh, Lady, Be Good!
Ginsberg, A. Who Be Kind To.
Glück, L. Gratitude.
Gordon, A. Question Not.
Gordon, M. Love Thy Neighbor.
Hale, S. Mary's Lamb [*or* Mary and Her
Lamb].
Hemans. Stranger's Heart, The.
Keech. Love Is Kind.
True to the Best.
Kramer, L. Shoemaker's Wife, The.
Langford. Speak Gently.
Laughlin, J. Kind-, The.
Lawrence, D. English Are So Nice!, The.
Martínez, V. Human Universe, The.
Metcalf, R. These Are Not Lost.
Nelson, F. Human Heart, The.
Nichols, C. Boomerang, The.
O'Reilly, J. What Is Good?
Plath. Kindness.
Reed, M. One Year to Live.
Revel, H. Love Thy Neighbor.
Sandall. Song: "Love that is hoarded, moulds at
last."
Sangster, M. Our Own.
Shimon. I Know Something Good about You.
Springer, T. Giving and Forgiving.
Stanard, C. Baseball.
Thompson, P. Kindly Deed, A.
Tucker, M. Kindness.
Unknown. (My Daily Creed).
Gentle Word, A.
Somebody's Mother.
Wayne, J. By Accident.
Wilcox, E. Morning Prayer, A.
Wright, J. Sappho.
Young, J. Was That the Human Thing to Do?
King Kong
Ondaatje. King Kong Meets Wallace Stevens.
Trowbridge, W. Kong Breaks a Leg at the
William Morris Agency.
King Lear
Howe, S. White Foolscap/Book of Cordelia.
Keats. On Sitting Down to Read "King Lear"
Once Again.
Storace. King Lear Bewildered.
Williams, W. Lear.
King, B. B.
Weems, M. B.B. Blues.

King, Martin Luther, Jr
Barrax. King: April 4, 1968.
Fisher, A. *et al.* Martin Luther King.
Fort, C. For Martin Luther King.
Giovanni. Funeral of Martin Luther King, Jr,
The.
Harper, M. Martin's Blues.
Studs.
Hernandez, D. Martin and My Father.
Holmes, D. Time for Guns, A.
Jordan, J. In Memoriam: Martin Luther King,
Jr.
Madhubuti. Assassination.
Troupe. Day in the Life of a Poet, A.
King, William Lyon Mackenzie
Scott, F. W. L. M. K.
Kingfishers
Clampitt. Kingfisher, The.
Davies, W. Kingfisher, The.
Fenton, J. Kingfisher's Boxing Gloves, The.
Heath-Stubbs. Kingfisher, The.
Hopkins, G. As Kingfishers Catch Fire.
Lloyd, J. Kingfisher, The.
Olson, C. Kingfishers, The.
Kings
Aiyejina. Dialogue, The.
Allingham. Swing Song, A.
Belloc. Henry King, Who Chewed Bits of
String, and Was Early Cut Off in Dreadful
Agonies.
Bishop, E. Twelfth Morning; or What You Will.
Browning, R. Solomon and Balkis.
Byron, G. Harp the Monarch Minstrel Swept,
The.
To Belshazzar.
Cannell. King, The.
Causley. Figgie Hobbin.
Cullen, C. Black Majesty.
De Vere, E. Poem: "Were I a king, I could
command content."
Denham. Cooper's Hill.
Dickinson, E. I Met a King This Afternoon!
Donne. Anniversary [*or* Anniversarie], The.
DuBois, W. Song of the Smoke, The.
Fairfax of Cameron. On the Fatal Day January
30, 1648.
Feilding, F. One the Morening the King was
Taken Ill my Dreame of Him.
"Field." Fifty Quatrains.
Will You Crucify Your King?
Fiskin. Magi, The.
Herbert, Z. Return of the Proconsul, The.
Herrick. Difference Betwixt King and Subjects,
The.
Ill Government.
King and No King, A.
Power in the People, The.
Hill, G. Requiem for the Plantagenet Kings.
Landor, W. Georges, The.
Lawrence, D. Snake.
Leapor. Man the Monarch.
Lovelace, R. To Lucasta, from Prison.
Milne, A. King's Breakfast, The.
Montague, J. Deer Park.
More, S. De Principe Bono et Malo.
Quis Optimus Reipublicae Status.
Ojaide. Where Everybody is King.
Philips, K. On the 3 of September, 1651.
Pope, A. Epigram Engraved on the Collar of a
Dog Given [*or* Which I Gave] to His Royal
Highness.
Quarles. On Saul and David.
Rochester, J. Satire on Charles II, A.
Rossetti, C. After Communion.
Shelley, P. England in 1819.
Ozymandias.
Stafford, W. Story That Could Be True, A.
Stevens, W. Emperor of Ice-Cream, The.
Stevenson, R. Happy Thought.
Suckling, S. On King Richard the Third, Who
Lies Buried under Leicester Bridge.
Unknown. Guest, The.
Sir Patrick Spens [*or* Spence].
Veinberg, J. Next to Tut.
Kingston, Jamaica
Espinet, R. Merchant of Death.

Kipling, Rudyard
Carryl, G.   Ballad: "As I was walkin' the jungle round, a-killin' of tigers an' time."
O'Hara, F.   Captains Courageous.
Stephen, J.   To R. K.
Tuck, L.   Sniff.

Kirk, Henry
Unknown.   To the Poets.

Kisses
Alexander, E.   Zodiac.
Angus.   Mary's Song.
Bell, M.   What They Do to You in Distant Places.
Beveridge.   Dining Out.
Browning, E.   Romance of the Swan's Nest, The.
To George Sand: A Desire.
Budenz.   Poeta Fui.
Burns, R.   Ae Fond Kiss.
Carnevali.   Kiss.
Conrad, C.   Continental (You Kiss While You're Dancing), The.
Dacre, C.   Kiss, The.
David, M.   Sinner Kissed an Angel, A.
Davies, I.   Angry Summer 28, The.
Delmore, E.   Marmalade.
DeSylva, B. G.   Do It Again.
Donne.   Expiration, The.
Dove, R.   Adolescence—I.
Drummond, W.   Kisses Desired.
Dunbar, P.   Her Thought and His.
Negro Love Song, A.
Ellington, D.   Prelude to a Kiss.
"Field."   Already to Mine Eyelids' Shore.
Fletcher, J.   Take, Oh, Take Those Lips Away.
Fletcher, L.   Way April Leads to Autumn, The.
Gannon, K.   Reciprocity.
Gay, J.   Sweet William's Farewell to Black-Eyed [*or* Black-Ey'd] Susan.
Gershwin.   How Long Has This Been Going On?
Gershwin, G.   Do It Again.
Gibbons, S.   Truce, The.
Gordon, I.   Prelude to a Kiss.
Grier.   Kissing Natalia.
Hamer.   Berkeley, Late Spring.
Hammerstein.   I Cain't Say No.
Hardy, T.   Thunderstorm in Town, A.
Two Lips.
Herrick.   Barley-Break; or, Last in Hell.
Chop-Cherry.
Kiss[e], A.
Kisses Loathesome.
Kissing and Bussing.
Tithe [*or* Tythe]: To the Bride, The.
To Dianeme.
To Electra.
Upon Jack and Jill: Epigram.
Hughes, L.   Suicide's Note.
Hunt, L.   Rondeau: "Jenny kissed [*or* kiss'd] me when we met."
Jackson, L.   Take Hands.
Joseph, R.   Sinner Kissed an Angel, A.
Kent, W.   Reciprocity.
Lassell.   Kissing Ramén.
Lawrence, D.   Kisses in the Train.
Lightning.
Le Gallienne.   Beauty Accurst.
Lenier.   Finale.
Loesser.   My Darling, My Darling.
Macdonald, G.   Sweet Peril.
Magidson, H.   Continental (You Kiss While You're Dancing), The.
Melo, M.   Red Lipstick on a Straw.
Millay, E.   Sonnet: "What lips my lips have kissed, and where, and why."
Mills, I.   Prelude to a Kiss.
Moore, T.   Did Not.
Kiss, The.
Muske, C.   Former Love, a Lover of Form, A.
Nathan, L.   Bladder Song.
Nesbit, E.   Kiss, The.
O'Hara, F.   Lebanon.
Orléans, C.   Roundel: "Take, take this cosse, atonys, atonys, my hert!"
Paley, G.   Here.

Pinkard, M.   Gimme a Little Kiss (Will Ya, Huh?).
Porter, C.   Old-Fashioned Garden, An.
Powell, D. A.   Triptych.
Ríos, A.   Teodoro Luna's Two Kisses.
Rodgers, R.   I Cain't Say No.
Rossiter.   Nostalgia.
Rux, C. H.   Shunning an Imperative.
Samyn, M.   Art of Kissing, The.
Shelley, P.   Love's Philosophy.
Smith, J.   Gimme a Little Kiss (Will Ya, Huh?).
Stanley, T.   Speaking and Kissing.
Strode.   Kisses.
Riddle: On a Kiss, A.
Tate, J.   Love Making.
Teasdale.   Look, The.
Thomas, L.   Excitation.
Toomer.   Her Lips Are Copper Wire.
Tucker, M.   Kiss, A.
Turk, R.   Gimme a Little Kiss (Will Ya, Huh?).
Unknown.   Bee-Keeper, The.
Black Hair.
Did you eever, iver, over?
My Little Pretty Mopsy.
Walker, A.   Kiss, The.
Waniek.   Canticle for Abba Jacob, A.
Warner, S.   After He Had Gone.
Watts, M.   Vision.
Wharton, E.   Mortal Lease, The.
Whitman, W.   Behold This Swarthy Face.
Wyatt, S.   Lover Showeth How He Is Forsaken of Such as He Sometime Enjoyed, The.

Kitchens
Branch, A.   Monk in the Kitchen, The.
Brooks, G.   Mrs. Small.
Causley.   Old Mrs. Thing-um-e-bob.
Cook, W.   Still-Life with Woodstove.
Davis, T.   Boppin' is Safer than Grindin'.
Dove, R.   Sunday Greens.
Harjo, J.   Perhaps the World Ends Here.
Hartnett.   Domestic Scene.
Jewsbury.   My heart's in the kitchen, my heart is not here.
Morales, A.   Kitchens.
Rutsala.   Silence, The.
Scarfe.   Kitchen Poem.
Silano, M.   Such a Way to Go.
Smith, B.   Bowl, The.
Talvikki, A.   For Want.
Wright, C.   State of Preservation.

Kites (ornithology)
Lloyd, J.   Thoughts of Boyhood.

Kites (toys)
Cohen, L.   Kite Is a Victim, A.
Gilbert, C.   Kite-Flying.
O'Keeffe.   Kite, The.
Strand.
Swenson, M.   Goodbye, Goldeneye.
Thompson, D. P.   Laurel Street, 1950.
Williamson, G.   Kites at the Washington Monument.

Kittens
Follen, E.   Three Little Kittens, The.
Hood, T.   Choosing Their Names.
Lopez, L.   Tomás.
Twichell.   Aisle of Dogs.
Unknown.   Two Little Kittens.
Williams, W.   Mujer.
Wordsworth, W.   Kitten at Play, The.

Klee, Paul
Gould, R.   Amateur Drummer.
Todd, R.   Paul Klee.

Knees
Burns, R.   Memory.

Knife-Grinding and Knife-Grinders
Canning, G. *et al.*   Friend of Humanity and the Knife Grinder, The.
Whitman, W.   Sparkles from the Wheel.

Knight, Etheridge
Medina, T.   Don't Say Goodnight to Etheridge Knight.
Sanchez, S.   Hospital/Poem.

Knighthood and Knights
Askew, A.   Ballad Which Anne Askew Made and Sang When She Was in Newgate, The.

Browning, R.   Childe Roland to the Dark Tower Came.
Chatterton.   Bristowe Tragedie: or, The Dethe of Syr Charles Bawdin.
De Tabley.   Knight in the Wood, The.
Guiney.   Wild Ride, The.
Herebert.   Who is This that Cometh from Edom?
Hogg, J.   Charlie is my Darling.
Ingelow.   Winding-up Time.
Keats.   La Belle Dame sans Merci [A Ballad].
Masefield.   Dead Knight, The.
Mayer, G.   Ballad: "Knight went down to the river's rim, A."
Merry.   Sir Roland; a Fragment.
Morris, W.   Haystack in the Floods, The.
Poe.   Eldorado.
Procter, A.   Legend of Provence, A.
Taylor, J.   Squire's Pew, The.
Unknown.   Three Ravens, The.
Winters, Y.   Sir Gawaine and the Green Knight.

Knights of Pythias
Kipling, R.   New Knighthood, The.
Linden, M.   For the Good of the Pythian Order.

Knitting and Knitters
Gardinier.   On a Grey-haired Old Lady Knitting at an Orchestral Concert.
Tucker, M.   Knitting.

Knives
Adamson.   Gutting the Salmon.
Dumdum.   To My Mother.
Hampton.   Women who Speak with Steak Knives.
Hume, C.   Birthday.
McBride, M.   Knife-Thrower's Wife, The.
O'Dalaigh, M.   On the Gift of a Knife.
Radnóti.   Angel of Dread, The.
Sharp, S.   In the Tradition of Bobbitt.
Symons, A.   Nerves.
Thomas, D.   Because the Pleasure-Bird Whistles.
Unknown.   Dirge for Three Trumpets.
Walwicz.   Big Tease.
Little Red Riding Hood.
Tattoo, The.

Knowledge
Adamson.   Dreaming Up Mother.
Atwood.   Procedures for Underground.
Baraka.   New World, The.
Barbour, D.   I Don't Know Enough About You.
Bhatt.   What Is Worth Knowing?
Bishop, E.   At the Fishhouses.
Blake, W.   All Religions Are One.
Bogan, L.   Knowledge.
Bowers, E.   Adam's Song to Heaven.
Brett, L.   Leaving You.
Bringhurst.   Parśvanatha.
Browning, R.   Song: "Heap cassia, sandal-buds and stripes."
Thus the Mayne Glideth.
Wanderers, The.
Caldwell, A.   I Know That You Know.
Carmichael, H.   How Little We Know.
Cavendish, M.   Of Many Worlds in This World.
Clare, J.   I Feel I Am.
Clough.   Questioning Spirit, The.
Cope, W.   Two Cures for Love.
Couani.   Obvious, The.
Cowley, A.   Tree of Knowledge, The.
Creeley.   Somebody Died.
Crompton.   Epigram LXVII: Time, the Interpreter.
Cummings, E.   You Shall Above All Things Be Glad and Young.
Davison, P.   Star Watcher, The.
Emerson, R.   Limits.
Flynn, N.   Cartoon Physics, Part 1.
Frost, R.   For Once, Then, Something.
From Plane to Plane.
Revelation.
Gamalinda, E.   Light Falls Obliquely.
Garrigue.   Catch What You Can.
Ginsberg, A.   Psalm III: "To God: to illuminate all men. Beginning with Skid Road."
Guiney.   In the Reading-Room of the Brtish Museum.

Herbert, G.   Pearl, The. Matth. 13:45.
Hernández Cruz.   Perlas.
Hughes, T.   Man Seeking Experience Enquires His Way of a Drop of Water, The.
Jackson, L.   Nothing So Far.
Jamie.   Queen of Sheba, The.
Jeffers, R.   Science.
Kavanagh, P.   To Hell with Commonsense.
Kennedy, X.   Hummingbird.
Killeen, G.   At the Black Edge.
Lee, P.   I Don't Know Enough About You.
Levertov.   Contraband.
Loden.   Conversations with Dr. M.
Maybe, E.   Umbilical Cord.
Mercer, J.   How Little We Know.
Montgomerie, A.   Royall Palice of the Heichest Hewin, The.
Moore, M.   To a Snail.
Moore, R.   Mind's Disguise, The.
  Still Without Life.
Murray, J.   Here We Stand Before the Temporal World.
  There Has Been More Than Beginning and End to Face.
Nathan, L.   Hole.
Nemerov.   Boy with Book of Knowledge.
  To David, about His Education.
Nims, J.   Knowledge of God.
Parker, A.   No Fool, the God of Salt.
Parker, D.   Ballade at Thirty-Five.
Parsons, C.   Different.
Poe.   Al Aaraaf.
  Song: "Young flowers were whispering in melody."
Pound, E.   Great Digest of Confucius, The.
  Tree, The.
Raine, K.   Message from Home.
Ramke.   Astronomer Works Nights: A Parable of Science, The.
Rhodes, M.   How Fast.
Roethke.   Marrow, The.
Romo-Carmona, M.   Crows.
Rosemurgy, C.   Angel Finally Admits What She Knows to Lou Binkler of Bethany, Missouri, An.
Rux, C. H.   Pledge of Allegiance.
Salaam.   Always Know.
Shelley, P.   Sonnet: Lift Not the Painted Veil: "Lift not the painted veil which those who live."
Stein, G.   On Her Way.
Straus, M.   Log of Pi, The.
Tennyson, A.   To—. With the Following Poem.
Thomas, E.   On Sir J——S——Saying in a Sarcastic Manner, My Books Would Make Me Mad; an Ode.
  Some Eyes Condemn.
Thomas, R.   Here.
Unknown.   I Was Born Almost Ten Thousand Years Ago.
Very.   Eye and Ear, The.
Viray, M.   Two Strangers, The.
Ward, D.   Approximately.
Washington, N.   Woman's Intuition, A.
Youmans, V.   I Know That You Know.
Young, V.   Woman's Intuition, A.

Knox, George L.
Bibb.   Lines to the Hon. George L. Knox.
Muir, E.   Scotland 1941.

Knoxville, Tennessee
Giovanni.   Knoxville, Tennessee.

Kollwitz, Käthe
Rukeyser, M.   Käthe Kollwitz.

Korean War
Biespiel, D.   Lilacs.
McGrath, T.   Ode for the American Dead in Korea.

Koreans
Corn.   Kimchee in Worchester (Mass.).

Kosciusko, Thaddeus
Keats.   To Kosciusko.

Krafft-Ebing, Richard Von
Gogarty.   On First Looking into Krafft-Ebing's *Psychopathosexualis* [or Psychopathia Sexualis].

Kreisler, Fritz
Stern, M.   Fritz.

Ku Klux Klan
Hayden, R.   Night, Death, Mississippi.
Hughes, L.   Ku Klux.
Kay, J.   Twelve Bar Bessie.
Spellman.   When Black People Are.
St. John, P.   Lynching and Burning.

Kubla Khan
Coleridge, S.   Kubla Khan: or, A Vision in a Dream.
Smith, S.   Thoughts about the Person from Porlock.

Kyoto, Japan
Enright, D.   Kyoto Garden, A.

L

La Plata, Missouri
Barnes, J.   Last Look at La Plata, Missouri.

Labor and Laborers
Aiken, C.   Road, The.
Alegría.   Documentary.
Allbery.   Assembler.
Alvarez, J.   Woman's Work.
Angira.   Manna.
Anstett.   Shift.
Arnold, B.   No Tool or Rope or Pail.
Babcock, M.   Be Strong.
Baca.   So Mexicans Are Taking Jobs from Americans.
  Work We Hate and Dreams We Love.
Baillie, J.   Hay making.
Baraka.   Poem Some People Will Have to Understand, A.
Beatty, P.   That's Not in My Job Description.
Bersohn.   Dignity of Labor, The.
Bevington, L.   Morning.
Brown, G.   Taxman.
Brown, S.   Call Boy.
  Southern Road.
Bunting.   What the Chairman Told Tom.
Bush, D.   Drainlayer.
Césaire, A.   In Memory of a Black Union Leader.
Campbell, R.   Serf, The.
Campbell, S.   Chairmaker, The.
Cary, A.   To Solitude.
Chamberlain, B.   Islandman.
Chipasula.   Those Rainy Mornings.
Chock.   Working Construction.
Ciardi.   All about Boys and Girls.
Clover, J.   El periférico, or Sleep.
Coleridge, S.   Work without Hope.
Collier, M.   Womans Labour, an epistle, The.
Conyus.   Six Ten Sixty-Nine.
Cook, E.   Song for the Workers, A.
Crowell, G.   Common Tasks, The.
Crozier, A.   Driftwood and Seacoal.
Day, L.   Reject Jell-o.
DuBois, W.   Song of the Smoke, The.
Dunbar, P.   Not They Who Soar!
Elliott, E.   Child, Is Thy Father Dead?
Ellis, T.   Atomic Bride.
Flecknoe.   Ant, The.
Frear.   Young Workman, The.
Frost, R.   "Out, Out—."
  Mowing.
  Tuft of Flowers, The.
  Wood-Pile, The.
García.   I Ain't Going to Hurry No More.
García, D.   Orchard of Figs in the Fall, An.
Glück, L.   School Children, The.
Gladding.   Fisherman's Wife, The.
Goodison.   Birth Stone.
Gordon, A.   Question Not.
Gotlieb.   Three-handed Fugue.
Gould, A.   Demolisher.
Hall, D.   X.
Hayden, R.   Those Winter Sundays.
Hayes, A.   Joe Hill.
Herrick.   End of His Work, The.
Hill, G.   Ovid in the Third Reich.
Hill, J.   Preacher and the Slave, The.

Hood, T.   Song of the Shirt, The.
Hopkins, G.   God's Grandeur.
Hove.   Country Life.
  You Will Forget.
Hughes, L.   Florida Road Workers.
Hutchinson, L.   Verses Written by Mrs. Hutchinson.
Ingelow.   Little babe, while burns the west.
Jacinto, A.   Monangamba.
Johnson, M.   What's de Use ob Wukin in de Summer Time at All.
Johnson, S.   ad. fr. the Bible, Proverbs, 6, 6.
Johnston, E.   Lines to Ellen, the Factory Girl.
  Working Man, The.
Jones, E.   Song of the Low, The.
Jordan, J.   If You Saw a Negro Lady.
Kelly, B.   Leaving, The.
Kendall, M.   Underground.
Kennelly.   Thatcher, The.
King, B.   Pessimist, The.
Kinsella, J.   Wild Radishes.
Larkin, P.   Aubade: "I work all day, and get half-drunk at night."
  Toads.
  Toads Revisited.
Lawrence, D.   Morning Work.
Leapor.   Sacrifice: An Epistle to Celia, The.
Levine, P.   You Can Have It.
Littlefield, M.   O Son of Man, Thou Madest Known.
Longfellow, H.   Psalm of Life, A.
  Tell Me Not in Mournful Numbers.
  Village Blacksmith, The.
MacLean, S.   Highland Woman, A.
MacLeish.   Burying Ground by the Ties.
Mar, L.   My Mother, Who Came from China, Where She Never Saw Snow.
Markham, E.   Man with the Hoe, The.
Masefield.   Consecration, A.
Massey.   Worker, The.
McCarthy, T.   Feeding Ground.
  Word "Silk", The.
McKay, C.   Tired Worker, The.
Merriam, E.   Lazy Thought, A.
Meynell, A.   Girl on the Land, The.
Milnes.   England and America, 1863.
Mnthali.   My Father.
Monro.   Man Carrying Bale.
Moore, L.   From the Field.
Moraga.   Half-Breed.
Morris, M.   For Consciousness.
Mphande.   Why the Old Woman Limps.
Niemoller.   First They Came for the Jews.
Orton, B.   Beekeeper.
Pickard, T.   What Maks Makems.
Piercy.   To Be of Use.
Pinsky.   Shirt.
Randall, D.   George.
Reese, L.   Street Scene, A.
Reznikoff.   Millinery District: "Clouds, piled in rows like merchandise, The."
Ridge, L.   Réveille.
Riley, J.   Raggedy Man, The.
Rivard.   Torque.
Rodgers, C.   It Is Deep.
Roscoe, W.   To the Harvest Moon.
Rukeyser, M.   Alloy.
  George Robinson: Blues.
Sadoff.   February: Pemaquid Point.
Samaras, N.   Translation.
Sandburg, C.   Chicago.
  Child of the Romans.
  Ice Handler.
  Onion Days.
  Psalm of Those Who Go Forth before Daylight.
Scott, S.   Hour with Thee, An.
Shange.   Tango.
Shapiro, D.   House (Blown Apart).
Shelley, P.   Song to the Men of England.
Shurin.   Material's Daughter.
Skipsey.   Get Up!
Smith, C.   To Dependence.
Snyder, G.   Hay for the Horses.
Soto.   Elements of San Joaquin, The.
  Rain.
  Wind.

Steele, T. Timothy.
Stephens, P. Signalmen, The.
Steptoe. O' Yes.
Stevenson, R. To a Gardener.
Stickney, T. Requiescam.
  Six o'Clock.
Swift, J. Description of the Morning, A.
Synge. On an Island.
Tagami. Song of Pajaro.
Thomas, R. Sir Gelli Meurig.
Tindal. Cry of the Oppressed, The.
Toomer. Reapers.
Trethewey, N. Drapery Factory, Gulfport,
  Mississippi, 1956.
Troupe. River Town Packin House Blues.
Tsvetayeva [or Tsvetaeva]. I Bless the Daily
  Labor.
Unknown. Another Little Boy.
  Can't You Line It?
  Factory Girl's Come-All-Ye, The.
  Go Down, Old Hannah.
  John Henry.
  Poor Paddy Works on the Railway.
  Tamping Ties.
  This Sun Is Hot.
Van Dyke. Work.
Voznesensky [or Voznesenskii]. Autumn.
Waniek. Balance.
Warner, S. Epitaph: "John Bird, a laborer, lies
  here."
Warr, B. Working Class.
Watts, I. How Doth the Little Busy Bee.
Whipple, L. My Dad.
Whitehead, W. Sweepers, The.
Whiteside. Carpenter, The.
Whitman, W. I Hear America Singing.
Wise, W. When I Grow Up.
Yeats. Adam's Curse.
Zolynas. Zen of Housework, The.

Labor Day
Glück, L. Labor Day.

Labor Unions
Cleghorn. Comrade Jesus.
Hayes, A. Joe Hill.
Hill, J. Preacher and the Slave, The.
  There Is Power in a Union.
Sandburg, C. Ice Handler.
  Teamster's Farewell, A.
See also **Strikes and Strikers**

Labrador, Canada
Crane, H. North Labrador.
Sandburg, C. Love in Labrador.

Labyrinths
Gioia. Maze Without a Minotaur.
Muir, E. Labyrinth, The.

Lade, Sir John
Johnson, S. Short Song of Congratulation [or
  To a Young Heir], A.

Ladybirds
Clare, J. Clock-A-Clay.
Unknown. Ladybird.

Lafayette, Marie Joseph, Marquis de
Madison. Lafayette.

Lakes and Ponds
Ashbery. On Autumn Lake.
Bayliss. Seven Dreams.
Beddoes. Lake, A.
Bendall, M. Fete on the Lake.
Blunden. Midnight Skaters, The.
Byron, G. Sonnet to Lake Leman.
Campbell, W. Winter Lakes, The.
Coleridge, M. Lady of Trees, The.
Creeley. Way, The.
Durrell. Vega.
Eberhart, R. Loon Call, A.
Eimers. Night Without Stars, A.
Endrezze. Birdwatching at Fan Lake.
Frost, R. Spring Pools.
Garrigue. Shore.
Gioia. Country Wife, The.
Glück, L. Pond, The.
Graham, W. Loch Thom.
Guest, B. Twilight Polka Dots.
Henry, B. Moraine Lake.
Hughes, T. Lake, The.

Kelly, B. Leaving, The.
Lane, P. Lake Murry.
Levertov. Quest, The.
Lickbarrow, I. On Esthwaite Water.
MacCaig. Small Lochs.
Major, C. Swallow the Lake.
Marriott. Beaver Pond.
McQueen. To Ben, at the Lake.
Millay, E. Armenonville.
O'Brien, G. Lake, The.
Plath. Crossing the Water.
Poe. Lake: To————, The.
Pound, E. Canto 49.
Pritchard, N. Paysagesque.
Saner. Rain Near Heart Lake.
Scammell, W. Inventions.
Scott, F. Lakeshore.
  Unnamed Lake, The.
Seward. Lake, The; or, Modern Improvement in
  Landscape.
Simpson, R. Lake.
Stickney, T. In the Past.
  Lakeward.
Voznesensky [or Voznesenskii]. Call of the
  Lake, The.
West, K. By Water Divined.
Wordsworth, D. Lake was covered all over,
  The.
Wright, D. Lakes, The.
Wright, J. Lake in Central Park, The.

Lalemant, Gabriel
Scott, F. Brébeuf and His Brethren.

Lamb, Charles
Coleridge, S. This Lime-Tree Bower My Prison.

Lambs
Brock-Broido. Carrowmore.
Campbell, D. Pallid Cuckoo.
Davies, W. Child's Pet, A.
Eberhart, R. For a Lamb.
Hale, S. Mary's Lamb [or Mary and Her
  Lamb].
Hughes, T. February 17th.
Larkin, P. First Sight.
MacCaig. Gone are the Days.
Marquis. Aesop Revised by Archy.
Mew. Fame.
Roberson. Blue Horses.
Rossetti, C. Frisky Lamb, A.
Tekeyan. Sacred Wrath.
Unknown. Little Lamb, A.

Lament (form)
Awad, J. Lament for Philip Larkin, A.
Bobrowski. Pruzzian Elegy.
Carew, T. Elegy upon the Death of the Dean of
  [St.] Paul's, Dr. John Donne, An.
  On the Death of Donne.
De la Mare. Sunk Lyonesse.
Denney. Song: "No use to aim that sextant
  now."
Drayton. To His Coy Love, A Canzonet.
King, H. Exequy, The.
Oodgeroo of the tribe Noonuccal. Dawn Wail
  for the Dead.
Rowe, E. Expostulation, The.
Surrey. Epitaph for [or on] Thomas Clere.

Lamplighting and Lamplighters
"O'Sullivan." Lamplighter, The.
Stevenson, R.
Tomlinson, C. Civilities of Lamplight.

Lampreys
Gay, J. To a Young Lady, with Some Lampreys.
See also **Eels**

Lancashire, England
Carew, T. To Saxham.
Connor, T. Lancashire Winter.

Lancelot du Lac
Henley, W. At Queensferry.

Landlords and Landladies
Atwood. Landlady, The.
Bunner, H. Behold the Deeds!
Espada. Imagine the Angels of Bread.
Farewell. Adieu to My Landlady, An.
Herbert, G. Redemption.
Hughes, L. Ballad of the Landlord.
  Madam and the Rent Man.

Montague, J. Wild Sports of the West.
Soyinka. Telephone Conversation.
Swenson, K. Landlady in Bangkok, The.
Wells, A. Inn That Missed Its Chance, The.

Landor, Walter Savage
Landor, W. For an Epitaph at Fiesole.
Moore, M. W. S. Landor.

Landscape
Barker, G. Morning in Norfolk.
Bawer. View from an Airplane at Night, over
  California, The.
Boston, B. Savage, Our Fathers, The.
Clare, J. Mist in the Meadows.
Denney. Mathematician's Dream, The.
Di Prima. Tassajara, 1969.
Divakaruni. Indigo.
Drake, J. Bronx.
Dunn, D. Land Love.
  Landscape with One Figure.
Elmusa. Snapshots.
Elytis. Origin of Landscape or the End of
  Mercy, The.
Evans, A. Martian Landscape.
Garioch. Wire, The.
Gascoyne. Snow in Europe.
Getsi. Woman Hanging from Lightpole, Illinois
  Route 136.
Ginsberg, A. Wales Visitation.
Gould, J. Easter Sunday.
Gruffydd, P. Slate Quay: Felinheli.
Hewitt, J. Ram's Horn, The.
Higginson, E. Dawn.
  Dawn on the Willamette.
  Opal Sea, The.
Johnson, E. Joe.
Jonson, B. To Sir Robert Wroth.
Kavanagh, P. Come Dance with Kitty Stobling.
Kinnell. Supper after the Last, The.
Lanier, S. From the Flats.
MacLean, S. Kinloch Ainort.
Marvell. Garden of Appleton House, The
  ("When in the east the morning ray").
  Garden, A.
  Upon Appleton House [To My Lord Fairfax].
  Upon the Hill and Grove at Bilbrough.
Mathias, R. Brechfa Chapel.
  Porth Cwyfan.
McNulty, T. Bodhidharma Crossing the
  Graywolf River on a Ry-Krisp.
Mead, P. Cinema Point.
Melville, H. Attic Landscape, The.
  Enviable Isles, The.
Nazareno, A. Cortes Swamp, The.
O'Daly, B. Whale in the Web, The.
Padilla. Fountain, a House of Stone, A.
  Landscapes.
Rukeyser, M. Homage to Literature.
Samyn, M. Trompe L'Oeil in Winter.
Sandburg, C. Nocturne in a Deserted Brickyard.
Seward. Lake, The; Or, Modern Improvement
  in Landscape.
Simms, C. Grey Wagtail on the Tyne.
Spender, S. Mask.
Stow. Singing Bones, The.
Van Duyn. View, A.
Wells, C. Pastoral in Posters, A.
Williamson, G. Up in the Air.
Wilson, S. Picture on the Purple Wall, the.
Wright, J. In Ohio.

Landscapes
Albrecht, A. Elkhorn Slough.
Auden. In Praise of Limestone.
Cary, A. Katrina on the Porch.
Dyer, J. Grongar Hill.
Graves, R. Lost Acres.
Hanzlicek, C. Sierra Noon.
Hilberry. Body and Mind.
Lowell, A. St. Louis.
Madge. Poem: "Character of a landscape stands
  always in a mysterious relation, The."
Melville, H. Enviable Isles, The.
  Pontoosuce.
Moulds, J. Renoir's Bathers.
Muske, C. Coming Over Coldwater.
Oliveira, D. San Joaquin.
Ostriker. Minor Van Gogh (He Speaks), A.

Patchen. Saturday Night in the Parthenon.
Ridler. Backgrounds to Italian Paintings: Fifteenth Century.
Scammell, W. Inventions.
Sherman, M. Towards Sunset at Camino Cielo.
Smith, C. To the South Downs.
Stickney, T. Requiescam.
Strode. On Westwall Downes [*or* On Westwell Downs].
Thomas, R. Welsh Landscape.
Tomlinson, C. Saving the Appearances.
Wordsworth, W. Lines Composed a Few Miles above Tintern Abbey on Revisiting the Banks of the Wye During a Tour, July 13, 1798.
Wright, C. Northhanger Ridge.
Wright, J. Night After Bushfire.
Yost, C. Descano, California.

Landslides
Ammons, A. R. Clarity.

Language
Abad, G. Light in One's Blood, The.
Adams, F. To a Thesaurus.
Agard, J. Listen Mr Oxford Don.
Albert-Birot. Balalaïka.
Allen, P. Zen Americana.
Alvarez, J. Bilingual Sestina.
Andrews, B. DDD.
  Gestalt Me Out!
  Impatient Heart, The.
  Methodology.
  West West.
  While.
Antin. Real Estate.
Apollinaire. Monday rue Christine.
  To Linda.
Arensberg. Arithmetical Progression of the Verb 'To Be.'
  Ing.
Armantrout. Language of Love.
Ashbery. Life As a Book That Has Been Put Down.
  Limited Liability.
  Pantoum.
  Paradoxes and Oxymorons.
  Soonest Mended.
Aubert, A. Opposite of Green, The.
Auden. Their Lonely Betters.
Ball, H. Complete Sound-Poems of Hugo Ball, The.
Barnett, A. Turbulence and Tongue.
Barot, R. Riffing.
Belieu. My Field Guide.
Bell, M. These Green-Going-to-Yellow.
Benson, S. Beethoven's Sixth Symphony.
Berger, D. Language Pile, The.
Berkson, B. Rebecca Cutlet.
Bernstein, C. Age of Correggio and the Carracci, The.
  Wait.
Bienek. Resistance.
Bishop, M. Naughty Preposition, The.
Boland, E. Anna Liffey.
Breeze. Dubbed Out.
Broumas, O. Artemis.
  If I Yes.
Burn. For the Common Market.
Cage. Lecture on Nothing.
Campion, T. Think'st thou to seduce me then.
Carruth, H. Of Distress Being Humiliated by the Classical Chinese Poets.
Carryl, G. How a Girl Was Too Reckless of Grammar [by Far].
Casey, M. Learning.
Castro, M. Blew It.
Causley. Old Mrs. Thing-um-e-bob.
Cheek. Rollercoaster.
Clare, J. Fragment: "Language has not the power to speak what love indites."
Clark, C. Border Affair, A.
Clifton, L. I am Accused of Tending to the Past.
Cobbing. Bird Bee.
  Hymn to the Sacred Mushroom.
Cocteau. Cape of Good Hope, The.
Codrescu. Poetry Paper.
Coffey. Prayers, The.
Coleman, W. Essay on Language.

ISM, The.
Conoley. Beckon.
Coolidge, C. On Induction of the Hand.
Cope, W. Uncertainty of the Poet, The.
Corcoran. In the Red Book.
Corn. Contemporary Culture and the Letter "K."
Cortez, J. Phraseology.
Creeley. Language, The.
Crouch, S. Blackie Thinks of His Brothers.
Crozier, A. Loopy Dupes.
Curbelo. Between Language and Desire.
Curtis, T. We Can Say That.
Darragh. "Legion" to "Lent" for "R."
  "Luteous" to "Lymph" for "F."
  Footnote at "Figure of Speech."
  Lattice at "Split."
  Lattice at/of (Com)pare (Dis)pair.
  Sis Boom Ba.
  Throwing Out at / of (Com)pare (Dis)pair, A.
  Volcanic Tuff.
Davidson, M. Century of Hands.
  Et in Leucadia Ego.
Davie. Hearing Russian Spoken.
  With the Grain.
Davies, A. New Sentience, The.
  Thirty East Forty-Second Street.
Day, J. From Momentary Work, A Wrench.
  Moving Object.
DiPalma. Annotations Tropes and Lacunae of the Itoku Master.
  Bed, The.
  Motion of the Cypher.
  We Forego Mimicry.
Djanikian. How I Learned English.
Dove, R. Poem in Which I Refuse Contemplation.
Drysdale, A. Language Difficulty.
Duhig, I. From the Irish.
Duroux, M. Lament for a Dialect.
Eady. Sherbet.
Eberhart, R. I Went to See Irving Babbitt.
Edwards, K. Good Science.
  Unconsciously.
Eigner. Temporary Language, A.
Ellis, T. Hush Yo Mouf.
  Sir Nose D'VoidofFunk.
Elmslie, K. Stage Duo.
Equi. In a Monotonous Dream.
Ferguson, G. Silent as Roses.
Finch, P. How Callum Innes Paints.
  Marks the English Left on the Map.
  Reds in the Bed.
  Scaring Hens.
Finlay, I. Garden Poem.
Fisher, A. African Boog.
  Birdland.
Fordham. Saxon Legend of Language, The.
Forrest-Thomson. Lemon and Rosemary.
France, L. Body Language.
  North and South.
Francis, R. Hogwash.
Freer, U. TM.
Galvin, J. Post-Modernism.
Gershwin. Let's Call the Whole Thing Off.
Gilbert, J. It Is Clear Why the Angels Come No More.
  Malvolio in San Francisco.
  Perspective He Would Mutter Going to Bed.
Gillan. Public School No. 18: Paterson, New Jersey.
Giovanni. Poem (for Langston Hughes), A.
Glück, L. Illuminations.
Glancy. First Reader Santee Training School, 1873, The.
Glatshteyn. To a Friend Who Wouldn't Bother to Strain His Noodleboard Because Even So It Is Hard to Go Hunting When Your Rifle Is Blunt and Love Is Soft as an Old Blanket.
Goldsworthy. After Babel.
Graham, J. Breakdancing.
  For One Must Want / To Shut the Other's Gaze.
  Underneath (1).
  Underneath (3).
Graves, R. Cool Web, The.
  In Broken Images.

Tilth.
Griffiths, J. Errata.
  Lost and Found.
Guest, B. Advance of the Grizzly, The.
  Red Dye.
  Words.
  You Can Discover.
Guevara, M. Doña Josefina Counsels Doña Concepción Before Entering Sears.
Guillén, N. Don't Know No English.
  Sensemayá.
Hacker, M. Squares and Courtyards.
Hadas, R. Three Silences.
Hale, J. Desmet, Idaho, March 1969.
Hall, D. Je Suis une Table.
  Peaches.
Hamill, S. Gift of Tongues, The.
Hamod, S. Leaves.
Hannan, M. Drive.
Hardy, T. Liddell and Scott.
Harrison, T. Them and [uz].
Harryman. Allegory.
  That Can Not Be Taken Away From It.
Hartnett. Pity the Man Who English Lacks.
Harwood, L. Words, The.
Hass, R. Interrupted Meditation.
  Meditation at Lagunitas.
Heaney, S. Alphabets.
  Traditions.
Helle, A. Poem for Natalia Ginzburg.
Hemensley. Sulking in the Seventies.
Herbert, G. Son[ne], The.
Herrera. Hallucinogenic Bullfighter.
Higgins, B. Genesis.
Hillman. Geology, A.
Holthaus, G. Unexpected Manna.
Hoover, P. Desire.
Hovanessian, D. Two Voices.
Huelsenbeck, R. *et al.* L'amiral cherche une maison à louer.
Hutchinson, P. Frost is All Over, The.
Inman, P. Centered.
  Colloam.
  Subtracted Words.
  XX.
Jackson, L. All Things.
  World and I, The.
"Jerry." Mabrak.
Jonson, B. Fit of Rhyme [*or* Rime] against Rhyme [*or* Rime], A.
Joseph, A. On Being Told I Don't Speak Like a Black Person.
  Traitor.
Kaneko. Bailey Gatzert: The First Grade, 1945.
Kelly, R. Ode to Language.
Kessler, S. Names the Dead Speak.
Khlebnikov, V. Zangezi: R, K, L, G—.
Kim, M. Into Such Assembly.
Kinsella, J. Visitant Eclogue.
Kirchwey. Oracular Degeneration.
Kizer, C. Translation.
Koch, K. Permanently.
Kruchyonykh [*or* Kruchionykh *or* Kruchenykh]. Declaration of the Word as Such.
Landor, W. Death Stands above Me.
Lange, A. Perugia.
Larsen, W. Learning the War.
Laurencin, M. Tiger, The.
Lauterbach. Novelist Speaks, The.
Lee, L. Persimmons.
Lehrer. Wernher von Braun.
Lerner, A. Rain in Spain, The.
Levertov. Caedmon.
  O Taste and See.
Lim-Wilson. Alphabet Soup.
  Upon Overhearing Tagalog.
Loesser. Murder, He Says.
Loewe, F. Rain in Spain, The.
Lorde. Coal.
Loy. Gertrude Stein.
Lum. Going Home.
Lux. Solo Native.
Mac Low. 7th Light Poem: For John Cage—17 June 1962.
  Almost Casanova Electricity.
  Lack of Balance but Not Fatal, A.

MacCaig. No Consolation.
MacDiarmid, H. Caledonian Antisyzygy, The.
Weapon, The.
MacKenzie, R. Like Pornography.
Square.
Mackey, N. Alphabet of Ahtt.
Macneacail. Gaelic is alive.
MacSweeney. Far Cliff Babylon.
Flame Ode.
Ode: "Urals post-master, this is your."
Ode Long Kesh.
Mahapatra, J. Sanskrit.
Maiden. Language.
Mandel, T. Realism.
Martin, C. E. S. L.
Speech Against Stone.
Mateo. There Is No Word for Sex in Taglog.
McCaffery. Little Hans.
McCallum, S. Calypso.
In My Other Life.
McGrath, T. Language of the Dead, The.
McLain, P. Connor in the Wind and Rain with
His Coat on.
McMorris, M. Near Speech, The.
Mead, J. Sometimes the Mind.
Melo, M. Scrambled Eggs and Garlic Pork.
Unlearning English.
Meredith, W. Rhode Island.
Merriam, E. Catch a Little Rhyme.
Merwin, W. S. Encampment at Morning, An.
Home for Thanksgiving.
Last One, The.
Losing a Language.
Midge, T. Written in Blood.
Mills, B. Ballad: Of Motion.
Milosz, C. My Faithful Mother Tongue.
Monk, G. AC.
CS.
La Tormenta.
Montague, J. Grafted Tongue, A.
Mora. Elena.
Morales. I Am the Reasonable One.
I Recognize You.
Morgan, E. Sir James Murray.
Morley, D. Jerusalem.
Nabokov. On Translating 'Eugene Onegin.'
Nash, O. Very like a Whale.
Nemerov. Makers, The.
Translation.
Nichol. Scraptures: 7th Sequence.
St. Anzas IX.
St. Anzas VI.
Noguere. Scribes, The.
O'Sullivan, M. 2nd Lesson from the Cockerel.
Giant Yellow.
Hill Figures.
Lesson from the Cockerel.
Narrative Charm for Ibbotroyd.
Oliver, D. 'u', 'je', 'r', 'r', 'im', 'a', 'finally.'
Olson, C. Moon Is the Number 18, The.
These Days.
Palmer, M. Eighth Sky.
Project of Linear Inquiry, The.
Recursus.
Sun.
Parker, D. One Perfect Rose.
Patchen. Moon, Sun, Sleep, Birds, Live.
Pembroke, M. To the Thrice-Sacred Queen
Elizabeth.
Perelman. Broken Mirror, The.
Chronic Meanings.
Let's Say.
Seduced by Analogy.
Things.
Philips, K. On the Welsh Language.
Phillips, D. I Held the Vein, But Death.
On Entries Emptiness.
Pinsky. Ode to Meaning.
Plath. Incommunicado.
Magi.
Plumpp. Turf Song.
Portnoy, M. Of of Titmouse.
Ríos, A. Language of Great-Aunts, The.
Nani.
Raab, L. Katie's Words.
Radiguet. Poem: "Horizon line."

Ragan, J. Standing at Pasternak's Table,
Peredelkino.
Rankine. Testimonial.
Raworth. Dark Senses.
That More Simple Natural Time Tone
Distortion.
Reedy, C. Doll Museum, The.
Retallack, J. Here's Looking at You Francis
Bacon.
Not a Cage.
Western CIV, 4 and 5.
Riley, D. Lure, 1963.
Rothenberg, J. Aleph Poem.
Rouse. Spunk Talking.
Russell, N. Message of the Rain, The.
Sabina. 13th Horse Song of Frank Mitchell,
The.
Salazar. Piñon Nuts.
Salter. Summer 1983.
Samaras, N. Translation.
Sanchez, S. Nigger.
Sandburg, C. Languages.
Little Girl, Be Careful What You Say.
Precious Moments.
Primer Lesson.
Scully, M. Variations.
Shapiro, K. Dirty Word, The.
Sherry, J. Lepidoptery.
Simic. Errata.
Sisson. Usk, The.
Smelcer. My Indian Grandmother Speaks to
Animals.
Smith, I. Shall Gaelic Die?
Spender, S. Word.
Spicer, J. Duet for a Chair and a Table.
Sze. Black Java Pepper.
Parallax.
Szporluk. Holy Ghost.
Taggart, J. Body and Soul: Poem for Two
Readers.
Monk.
Tester, W. Complacencies of the Fenced Yard.
Thomas, D. Before I Knocked.
Thomas, L. Electricity of Blossoms.
Tipton. I Want to Speak With the Blood that
Lies Down.
Turnbull. Residues: Thronging the Heart.
There Are Words.
Tzara. Great Lament of my Obscurity Three,
The.
Maison Aragon.
Ullman. Living Near the Plaza of Thieves.
Unknown. Aborigine Sound Poem.
Bald Mountain Zaum-Poems.
Valentine, J. Waiting.
Vando. Commonwealth, Common Poverty.
Very. Promise, The.
Von Freytag-Loringhoven. Klink—Hratzvenga
(Deathwail).
Voznesensky [or Voznesenskii]. Dogalypse.
Walcott. Codicil.
Wallace-Crabbe. Life of Ideas, The.
Warren-Moore. For Etheridge Knight.
Watten. Statistics.
Weaver, M. Luxembourg Garden.
Weiss, R. Conference, A.
Welish. Scalpel in Hand.
Williams, H. Old Tongue, The.
Williamson, G. Dark Days, The.
Waterfall.
Wilson, E. Miniature Dialogue.
Winter, M. Dux Bellorum.
Wohlfeld. That Which Is Fugitive, That Which
Is Medicinally Sweet or Alterable to Gold,
That Which Is Substantiated by Unscientific
Means.
Wolfli. Nostalgic Song for My Beloved.
Wong, J. One to Ten.
Wordsworth, D. Loving and Liking [Irregular
Verses Addressed to A Child].
Worley, D. Las Flores para una Niña Negra.
Tongues in My Mouth.
Wylie. Pretty Words.
Zephaniah. Speak.

Lanterns
Brown, S. Long Track Blues.

Coleridge, M. Street Lanterns.
Frost, R. Draft Horse, The.
Ward, D. My Brothers Make a Lantern.
Lanyon, Peter
Graham, W. Thermal Stair, The.
Laos and Laotians
McDonald, W. For Harper, Killed in Action.
Lapwings
Blake, W. O Lapwing!
Larkin, James
Clarke, A. Inscription for a Headstone.
Larkin, Philip
Awad, J. Lament for Philip Larkin, A.
Ruark. Larkin.
Larks
Blind. On a Forsaken Lark's Nest.
Burns, R. Address to the Woodlark.
Earley, T. Lark.
Graves, R. Love Without Hope.
Hardy, T. Shelley's Skylark.
Hopkins, G. Caged Skylark, The.
Sea and the Skylark, The.
Woodlark, The.
Kavanagh, P. Praying.
Leighton, R. Bunch of Larks, The.
Rosenberg, I. Returning, We Hear the Larks.
Shelley, P. To a Skylark.
Unknown. Lark, The.
Warren, R. Death of Time.
See also **Meadowlarks; Skylarks**
Las Vegas, Nevada
Hays, H. Case, The.
Last Judgment
Howard, R. Giovanni da Fiesole on the
Sublime.
Shelley, P. England in 1819.
Last Supper
Southwell. Of the Blessed Sacrament of the
Altar [or Aulter].
Latin
Cummings, E. Noster, The.
Hecht, A. Mysteries of Caesar, The.
Latin America and Latin Americans
Alexander, E. Ode.
Cofer, J. What the Gypsy Said to Her Children.
Espada. La tormenta.
Moon Shatters on Alabama Avenue, The.
Prisoners of Saint Lawrence, The.
Tires Stacked in the Hallways of Civilization.
Toque de queda: Curfew in Lawrence.
Water, White Cotton, and the Rich Man.
Hagedorn, J. Latin Music in New York.
Hernández Cruz. Side 12.
Hernandez, D. Armitage Street.
Morales. Africa.
Morales, A. South.
Rodriguez, L. Fire.
Spear, R. Good Men.
Lauder, William
Edwards, T. To the Editor of Mr. Pope's Works.
Laughter
Alvi, M. Laughing Moon, The.
Berlin. You're Laughing at Me.
Browning, R. Memorabilia.
Charara, H. Holy Water.
Coleman, C. I'm Gonna Laugh You Right Out
of My Life.
Corso. Zizi's Lament.
Creeley. Wicker Basket, A.
Davies, W. Her Merriment.
Day Lewis. Two Songs.
Dipoko. From My Parisian Diary.
Dunbar, P. We Wear the Mask.
Eliot, T. Hysteria.
Foix. When I Sleep, Then I See Clearly.
Foster, A. Nest of Hats, A.
Gershwin. They All Laughed.
Gilbert-Lecomte. Son of the Bone Speaks, The.
Gladding. Locust Shell.
Graham, J. Soul Says.
Hughes, L. Homesick Blues.
Johnson, G. I Want to Die While You Love Me.
Joseph, A. Learning to Laugh.
Keats. Why Did I Laugh Tonight?

Kinnell.   Crying.
Prunty.   Reading Before We Read, Horoscope and Weather.
Ríos, A.   Teodoro Luna's Two Kisses.
Sanchez, S.   Haiku.
Sandburg, C.   Bundles.
Schwartz, D.   Sarah.
Smith, S.   Persian, The.
Sondheim.   Comedy Tonight.
Sornberger.   When She Laughs.
Swirszczynska.   Sea and the Man, The.
Thomas, E.   Some Eyes Condemn.
Unknown.   Me and My Captain.
   Sunshine and Music.
Wagoner, D.   Loons Mating.
See also **Mirth**

Laundry and Laundering
Barbauld.   Washing-Day.
Barrax.   Domestic Tranquility.
Chavez, L.   Clean Sheets.
Davis, J.   Time Bum.
Elmslie, K.   Duo-Tang.
Fordham.   Washerwoman, The.
Fusselman, A.   Journal.
Gustafson, R.   Of Green Steps and Laundry.
Hochman.   Goldfish Wife, The.
Kendrick, D.   Alone for a Week.
Kinsella, T.   Laundress, The.
Merrill, J.   Mad Scene, The.
Moss, T.   Fisher Street.
North, C.   Hospital.
Rankine.   Eden.
Rees-Jones.   Service Wash.
Ritchie.   Sorting Laundry.
Rohrer, M.   Precision German Craftsmanship.
Sandburg, C.   Washerwoman.
Smith, B.   Laundry.
Steele, T.   Sheets, The.
Stone, R.   In an Iridescent Time.
Summerfield.   Washday Battles.
Swirszczynska.   I Wash the Shirt.
Weigl.   Girl at the Chu Lai Laundry.
Wilbur.   Love Calls Us to the Things of This World.
Williams, W.   Young Laundryman, The.
Young, A.   Shepherd's Hut, The.

Laurels
Bogan, L.   Several Voices Out of a Cloud.
Herrick.   Mount of the Muses, The.
   To Laurels.
   To Mistress Katherine Bradshaw, the Lovely, That Crowned Him with Laurel.
Kemble.   Sonnet: "Thou poisonous laurel leaf, that in the soil."
Milton.   Lycidas.
Suckling, S.   Wits, The; A Session[s] of the Poets.
Westmorland.   Occasioned by Seeing a Walk of Bay Trees.
Winchilsea.   Circuit of Apollo, The.
Wright, J.   Portugal Laurel, The.

Laurentian Mountains, Canada
Scott, F.   Laurentian Shield.

Law and Lawyers
Blamire.   Wey, Ned, Man!
Clarke, A.   Penal Law.
Davis, L.   Mown Lawn, A.
Empson.   Legal Fiction.
Greenlaw.   Love from a Foreign City.
Hardy, J.   Objection Overruled.
Housman, A.   Laws of God, the Laws of Man, The.
Kelly, R.   Life of Intimate Fleeing, A.
Landor, W.   Case at Sessions, A.
Macha, F.   Corruption.
Medina, T.   After the Verdict.
Moorer.   Injustice of the Courts.
   Legal Mouse, A.
O'Grady, J.   Anonymous Wedding Photo.
Quarles.   On God's Law.
Russell, W.   Ngarnbarndtar.
Sandburg, C.   Lawyers Know Too Much, The.
Sundiata.   Notes from the Defense of Colin Ferguson.
Thackeray.   Damages, Two Hundred Pounds.

Tolson, M.   Ex-Judge at the Bar, An.
Unknown.   Case to the Civilians, A.
   Lawyers.
Lawes, Henry
Milton.   To Mr. H. Lawes On His Airs.
Philips, K.   To Mr. Henry Lawes.
Waller, E.   To Mr. Henry Lawes, Who Had Then Newly Set a Song of Mine in the Year 1635.
Lawns
Davis, L.   Mown Lawn, A.
Empson.   Rolling the Lawn.
Ramsay, A.   Polwart on the Green.
Smith, M.   Watering the New Lawn.
Lawrence, David Herbert
O'Hara, F.   Poem: "I don't know as I get what D.H. Lawrence is driving at."
Warburton, N.   Snake on D. H. Lawrence, The.
Wolfe, H.   D. H. Lawrence and James Joyce.
Lawrence, Edward
Milton.   To Mr. Lawrence.
Lazarus (Bible)
Baxter, J.   Lazarus.
Bensko.   Bones of Lazarus.
Browning, R.   Epistle Containing the Strange Medical Experience of Karshish, the Arab Physician, An.
Chesterton, G.   Convert, The.
Colman, H.   On Lazarus Raised From Death.
Crashaw.   Upon Lazarus His Teares.
Feinstein, E.   Lazarus' Sister.
Koertge.   Lazarus.
Procter, A.   Homeless.
Yeats.   "Calvary."
Laziness
Arodin, S.   Lazy River.
Barbour, D.   Mañana (Is Soon Enough for Me).
Blake, W.   My Handy Man Ain't Handy No More.
Dunbar, P.   In the Morning.
Herrick.   Ass[e], The.
   Long and Lazy [*or* Lazie].
Hoskyns [*or* Hoskins].   Epitaph, An: On a Man for Doing Nothing.
Latouche, J.   Lazy Afternoon.
Mayer, G.   Old Mrs. Lazibones.
Murray, R.   Wasted Day, The.
Nash, O.   Introspective Reflection.
Porter, C.   Laziest Gal in Town, The.
Prior.   Epitaph, An: "Interred [*or* Interr'd] beneath this marble stone."
Roethke.   Sloth, The.
Sidgwick, H.   Strenuous Life, The.
Thomson, J.   Land of Indolence, The.
   Leper-House and the Impenitents, The.
Unknown.   Get Up, Get Up.
   Nancy Dawson.
Watts, I.   Sluggard, The.
Wilde, O.   Hélas!
Leadership
Brookes, J.   Officers and Gentlemen Down Under.
Crosby, E.   Military Creed, The.
Eliot, T.   Triumphal March.
Jonson, B.   To Sir Horace Vere.
Kavanagh, P.   Elegy for Jim Larkin.
Kipling, R.   Servant When He Reigneth, A.
Lindsay, N.   Abraham Lincoln Walks at Midnight.
MacKay, C.   Clear the Way.
Markham, E.   Lincoln, the Man of the People.
Moses, G.   Poem for Trish, A.
Robinson, E.   Master, The.
Tennant, E.   A Bas la Gloire!
Whitman, W.   Thought.
Leap Year
Johnson, M.   Leap Yeah Party, De.
Palmer, M.   Untitled (February 2000).
Lear, Edward
Auden.   Edward Lear.
Lear, E.   How Pleasant to Know Mr. Lear.
Learning
Ashbery.   Forgotten Song.
Atwood.   You Begin.
Beckett, S.   Gnome.
Berkeley, G.   On the Prospect of Planting Arts

   and Learning in America.
Centolella.   Joy.
Divakaruni.   Yuba City School.
Glück, L.   Illuminations.
Graves, R.   Plea to Boys and Girls, A.
Hazo.   Only the New Branches Bloom.
Kendrick, D.   Sophie, Climbing the Stairs.
Lisella.   Song of the Third Generation.
Pilling.   Specimen.
Pound, E.   Great Digest of Confucius, The.
Shelley, P.   To a Skylark.
Simic.   Lesson, The.
Smith, B.   Bowl, The.
Snyder, G.   Axe Handles.
Sorrentino.   Razzmatazz.
Leaves
Aiken, C.   Room, The.
Ammons, A. R.   Above the Fray Is Only Thin Air.
Bell, M.   Dew at the Edge of a Leaf.
Brontë, A.   Lines Composed in a Wood on a Windy Day.
Cardiff.   Leaves like Fish.
Chin.   Autumn Leaves.
Crapsey.   November Night.
Cullen, C.   Leaves.
Cummings, E.   L(a.
Davies, W.   Leaves.
Feldman, A.   Contemporary American Poetry.
"Field."   Leaves.
Frost, R.   Gathering Leaves.
   In Hardwood Groves.
   Leaf-Treader, A.
   Leaves Compared with Flowers.
Garnett, R.   Fading-Leaf and Fallen-Leaf.
Hiestand, E.   Witch-Hazel Wood, The.
Hirshfield, J.   Ars Poetica.
Hughes, T.   Leaves.
Ignatow, D.   Simultaneously.
Irwin, M.   Autumnal.
Johnson, L.   Church of a Dream, The.
Larkin, P.   Trees, The.
Lindtová, A.   Campfire.
MacLeish.   Old Men in the Leaf Smoke, The.
McDonald, W.   Winter Before the War, The.
Orfalea, G.   Wave.
Pound, E.   Liu Ch'e.
Pritchard, N.   Landscape with Nymphs and Satyrs.
Robinson, E.   Pity of the Leaves, The.
Rossetti, C.   Who Has Seen the Wind?
Seferis.   Poplar Leaf, The.
Sergeant.   Man Meeting Himself.
Shelley, P.   Ode to the West Wind.
"Shu Ting."   Maple Leaf.
Stephens, J.   Wind, The.
Stevens, W.   Course of a Particular, The.
Thompson, C.   Autumn Leaves.
Unknown.   Anglo-American Chainpoem.
Very.   Sumach Leaves, The.
Wang Wei.   Seeking a Mooring.
Webb, C.   Autumn Leaves.
Winters, Y.   Fall of Leaves, The.
Wordsworth, W.   Kitten at Play, The.
See also **Autumn**
Lebanon and Lebanese
Abinader, E.   Letters from Home.
   Pigeon Rock: Lebanon.
Al-Rihani.   I Dreamt I Was a Donkey Boy Again.
Awad, J.   For Jude's Lebanon.
Bennani, B.   Letters to Lebanon.
Charara, H.   Holy Water.
Joseph, L.   Sand Nigger.
Melville, H.   Guide and Guard.
Scollard.   As I Came Down from Lebanon.
Leda
Doolittle, H.   Leda.
Gogarty.   Leda and the Swan.
Meinke.   Helen.
Millay, E.   I Dreamed I Moved among the Elysian Fields.
Watkins, V.   Music of Colours: The Blossom Scattered.
Yeats.   Leda and the Swan.

Ledwidge, Francis
Heaney, S. In Memoriam Francis Ledwidge.
Lee, Robert Edward
Davidson, D. Lee in the Mountains.
Howe, J. Robert E. Lee.
Ryan, A. Sword of Robert Lee, The.
Thompson, J. Lee to the Rear.
Leeds, England
Unknown. Poem for Jacqueline Hill.
Legs
Burroughs, W. My Legs Señor.
Carnevali. Queer Things.
Eady. April.
Graves, R. Legs, The.
Herrera. Weaning of Furniture-Nutrition.
Herrick. Her Legs.
To Dianeme.
Mother Goose. Riddle: "Two legs sat upon
three legs."
Nash, O. Octopus, The.
Ormond. Lament for a Leg.
Receveur. Eagle in the Land of Oz.
Scarfe. Merry Window, The.
Seibles. Who.
Taylor, J. Epigram: "Fair Beatrice tucks her
coat up somewhat high."
Whitman, W. Runner, The.
Williams, W. Portrait of a Lady.
Leicester, Robert Dudley, Earl of
Ralegh, S. Epitaph on the Earl of Leicester [*or*
Leceister*].
Leisure
Adcock, F. Three-Toed Sloth, The.
Blanco, R. Letter to El Flaco on His Birthday.
Ch'ien T'ao. On Reading the Seas and
Mountains Classic.
Clare, J. Nutting.
Woodland Seat, A.
Coleman, C. Riviera, The.
Coward. Poor Little Rich Girl.
Davidson, J. Crystal Palace, The.
Davies, W. Leisure.
Drieu la Rochelle. Tennis.
Frishberg, D. Peel Me a Grape.
Hanson, M. To Fancy.
Hightower, J. R. On Reading the Seas and
Mountains Classic.
Hood, T. Written in the Workhouse.
Jewett, S. At Home from Church.
McCarthy, J. Riviera, The.
McGinley. Evening Musicale.
Village Spa.
Moore, T. Fancy.
Nabbes. Song: "What a dainty life the milkmaid
leads!"
Quiller-Couch. Harbour of Fowey, The.
Radcliffe, A. Sun-Rise: Sonnet, A.
Revett. Ode: Hastening His Friend into the
Country.
Richman, L. To Valenton: Impressions circa
1947.
Rossetti, C. Reflection.
Snyder, G. Walk, A.
Sondheim. Ladies Who Lunch, The.
Stevens, W. Ordinary Women, The.
Stickney, T. In Ampezzo.
Stroud, J. Homage: Summer/Winter, Shay
Creek.
Thompson, W. Happy Life, The.
Unknown. Hob upon a Holiday.
Westmorland. To Retiredness.
Wright, J. Lying in a Hammock at William
Duffy's Farm in Pine Island, Minnesota.
Lemmings
Beer, P. Lemmings.
Lemons
Hadas, R. Lair, The.
Lenin, Vladimir Ilyich
MacDiarmid, H. Skeleton of the Future, The.
Orlovsky. Dream May 18, 1958.
Paulin. Impossible Pictures, The.
Leningrad, Russia
Akhmatova, A. Introduction.
Mandelstam [*or* Mandelshtam]. Leningrad.
See also **Saint Petersburg [*formerly* Leningrad],**

Russia
Lennon, John
Allen, P. Teaching Poetry at Votech High, Santa
Fe, the Week John Lennon Was Shot.
Lent
Herrick. To Keep a True Lent.
Lent Magdalene
Rodgers, W. Lent.
Lentils
Wayne, J. Cleaning Indian Dahl.
Leonardo da Vinci
Bly, R. Leonardo's Secret.
Dowden, E. Leonardo's "Mona Lisa."
Eberhart, R. Cancer Cells, The.
"Field." La Gioconda; Leonardo Da Vinci, The
Louvre.
Rossetti, D. For "Our Lady of the Rocks."
Shelley, P. On the Medusa of Leonardo da
Vinci in the Florentine Gallery.
Leopards
Jarrell. Snow-Leopard, The.
Kariara. Leopard Lives in a Muu Tree, A.
White, G. Leopard in Eden, The.
Leopold III, King of the Belgians
Berryman. Moon and the Night and the Men,
The.
Lepanto, Battle of (1571)
Chesterton, G. Lepanto.
Leprosy and Lepers
Pau-Llosa. Paredón.
Swinburne. Leper, The.
Young, G. Damien.
Lesbians
Begley, T. Sappho's Gymnasium.
Broumas, O. Artemis.
Beauty and the Beast.
Sometimes, as a Child.
Burke, C. Lizzie.
Chrystos. I Bought a New Red.
I Suck.
You Know I Like to Be.
Clarke, C. Passing.
Poet's Death, A.
Vicki and Daphne.
Cyril. Just Because I Am.
Equi. Lesbian Corn.
Forché. Kalaloch.
Gates, B. Cathy.
Homeless.
Ron.
Triptych.
Goodman, M. February Ice Years.
Lullabye for a Butch.
New Comers.
Open Poem.
Hacker, M. Boy, The.
Healy, E. Changing the Oil.
Changing What We Mean.
Hope, M. Sacrifice.
Liu, T. Strange Fruit.
Lorde. On a Night of the Full Moon.
Outlines.
Myles, E. American Poem, An.
Sleepless.
Obejas, A. Dancing in Paradise.
Public Place (After Olga Broumas), The.
Pratt, M. Crime Against Nature.
Schwartz, R. L. Possible.
Selman, R. 21 East 10th, 2BR, WBF, EIK.
Exodus.
Smukler. Days Inn.
Home in Three Days. Don't Wash.
Marry.
Sign.
Trash.
Wolverton, T. Black Slip.
In China.
See also **Homosexuality and Homosexuals**
Lesbos, Greece
Millay, E. Evening on Lesbos.
Lethargy
Gershwin. Bidin' My Time.
Justice, D. Lethargy.
Ransom, W. Pastime Café.

Letters
Ahlert, F. I'm Gonna Sit Right Down and Write
Myself a Letter.
Aiken, J. Do It Yourself.
Amichai [*or* Amikhai]. Letter.
Ashbery. Rain.
Thoughts of a Young Girl.
Atwood. Postcard.
Auden. Letter, The.
Barber, M. Conclusion of a Letter to the Rev.
Mr. C——, The.
Barresi. Late Summer News.
Beer, P. Letter, The.
Bell, M. How I Got the Word.
Bennani, B. Letters to Lebanon.
Bensley. One's Correspondence.
Berry, J. Lucy's Letter.
Berryman. Winter-Piece to a Friend Away, A.
Bethell. Response.
Bishop, E. Letter to N.Y.
Blight. Letter, The.
Bradstreet, A. Another.
Chavez, L. Clean Sheets.
Clare, J. Soldier, The.
Clover, J. Institute for Social Change, The.
Cofer, J. Correspondence.
Comfort, A. Letter to an American Visitor.
Copus, J. Miss Havisham's Letter.
Corman. Deceased.
Crane, H. My Grandmother's Love Letters.
Creeley. Invoice, The.
Daryush. Still-Life.
Deutsch. Destruction of Letters.
Dixon, S. Lines Occasioned by the Burning of
Some Letters.
Dooley, M. Letters from Yorkshire.
Dove, R. Poem in Which I Refuse
Contemplation.
Dransfield. Self-analysis.
Emerson, R. Letters.
Fainlight, R. Handbag.
Gallagher, T. Unanswered Letter.
Under Stars.
Gibb. Letter to Russel Barron.
Gilyard, K. Letter.
Graham, H. Waste.
Graves, R. Not at Home.
Greenlaw. Five O'Clock Opera.
Gregory, H. Postman's Bell Is Answered
Everywhere, The.
Hadas, R. Lair, The.
Hall, D. Love-Letter-Burning.
Hands, E. Lob's Courtship.
Hardy, T. Wife in London, A.
Heard, J. Love Letters.
Hubbard, S. Letter.
Hughes, L. Little Old Letter.
Personal.
Hume, C. Various Readings of an Illegible
Postcard.
Jarrell. Burning the Letters.
Jenkins, G. P.S. I Love You.
Kinnell. Correspondence School Instructor Says
Goodbye to His Poetry Students, The.
Kinsella, T. Artists' Letters.
Klein, M. Letters from the Front.
Koch, K. To Marina.
Koyama. Downtown Seattle in the Fog.
Kramer, L. Love Letters.
Kunitz, S. Night Letter.
Landon. Lines Written Under a Picture of a Girl
Burning a Love-Letter.
Leapor. Epistle of Deborah Dough, The.
Leong, R. Aerogrammes.
Livesay, D. Children's Letters, The.
Lorde. Learning to Write.
Lowell, A. Letter, The.
MacIntyre, S. Letters from the Concertina File
1939–1940.
Madhubuti. Poem Looking for a Reader, A.
Maiden. New.
Marcus, M. Letter, The.
Marshall-Stoneking. Picture Postcard.
Mathews, A. Letter Following.
Mathias, R. Sir Gelli to R. S.
Mattawa. Letter to Ibrahim.

McClure, M. From the Window of the Beverly Wilshire Hotel.
Meredith, W. Illiterate, The.
Meynell, A. Letter from a Girl to Her Own Old Age, A.
Moore, M. Bowls.
Mura. Letters from Poston Relocation Camp (1942–45).
Oliver, D. 'u,' 'je,' 'r,' 'r,' 'im,' 'a,' 'finally.'
Orfalea, G. My Father Writing Joe Hamrah in a Blackout.
Patterson, G. Letter from Home.
Piercy. Letter to Be Disguised as a Gas Bill.
Praed. Talented Man, The.
Radnóti. Letter to My Wife.
    Picture Postcards.
Ransom, J. Parting, without a Sequel.
Raworth. Empty Pain-Killer Bottles, The.
Rich, A. Letters in the Family.
Riddell, E. Letter, The.
Rottman. APO 96225.
Sandburg, C. Bilbea.
Scott, D. Letters from Baron Von Hügel to a Niece.
Scott, J. Typing the Letters.
Sexton. Letter Written on a Ferry While Crossing Long Island Sound.
    Some Foreign Letters.
Smith, S. Emily Writes Such a Good Letter.
    Jungle Husband, The.
Soldati. Surroundings.
Sorrentino. Oranges Returned, The.
Spencer, B. Passed On.
Street, D. Love Letters of the Dead.
Tennyson, A. Letter, The.
Tidjani-Cissé. Home News.
Tsaloumas. Note.
Tucker, M. Love-letter, A.
Unknown. Meaning of a Letter, The.
Unknown, fr. Terezin Concentration Camp. Letter to Daddy, A.
Van Duyn. Letters from a Father.
Vitiello. Letter to a Cretan Flute-Maker.
Walcott. Letter from Brooklyn, A.
Whitman, W. Come Up from the Fields Father.
Wickham. Letter to a Boy at School.
Wicks, S. Protected Species.
Williams, S. Letters from a New England Negro.
Williamson, G. Belvedere Marittimo.
Young Bear. Emily Dickinson, Bismarck and the Roadrunner's Inquiry.
Young, J. I'm Gonna Sit Right Down and Write Myself a Letter.

See also **Mail and Mailmen**

Leukemia
Graham-Pole, J. Venipuncture.

Levet, Robert
Johnson, S. On the Death of Dr [*or* Mr] Robert Levet [a Practiser in Physic].

Leviathan
Levertov. Ache of Marriage, The.
Merwin, W. S. Leviathan.

Levita, Elijah
Unknown. Epitaph: "Stone cries from the wall, The."

Li Po
Dumdum. Li Pos of the Polis.
Grier. On the Subject of Waves.
Phillips, C. Undressing for Li Po.
Tu Fu. To Li Po.
    To Li Po on a Spring Day.

Liberace
Drake, N. Man in the White Suit, The.
Holden, J. Liberace.

Liberalism and Liberals
Browning, R. Lost Leader, The.
    Why I Am a Liberal.
Hummer, T. Ideal, The.
Jackson, R. Lonely Affair, A.

Liberia
Tolson, M. On the Founding of Liberia.
    Ti.

Liberty
Haraway. Midnight Vigil.

Moise *et al.* To Persecuted Foreigners.
Robinson, M. To Liberty.
Thelwall. To Tyranny.
Watson, M. Stepping Out.

See also **Freedom**

Liberty Bell
Bible, *O.T.* Inscription on the Liberty Bell.
Unknown. Independence Bell—July 4, 1776.

Liberty, Statue of
Bierce. To the Bartholdi Statue.
Dove, R. Lady Freedom Among Us.
Haraway. Midnight Vigil.
Lazarus, E. New Colossus, The.

Libraries and Librarians
Brown, S. Chapter One.
    Marginalia.
Collins, B. Tomes.
Deane, S. Scholar II.
Earle, J. Saturday in the '20s, A.
Ellis, T. View of the Library of Congress from Paul Laurence Dunbar High School.
Jarrell. Girl in a Library, A.
Jonson, B. Execration upon Vulcan, An.
Le Gallienne. Library in a Garden, A.
MacNeice. British Museum Reading Room, The.
Roscoe, W. On Being Forced to Part with His Library for the Benefit of His Creditors.
Steele, T. Library, The.
Tripp. Twilight in the Library.
Unknown. Domestic Philosopher, The.
Ward, T. On Being Kicked Out of the Harold Washington Library Center for Napping on the Floor.
Weiss, T. Fire at Alexandria, The.
Williams, C. Critic, The.

Libya
Mattawa. History of My Face.

Lice
Burns, R. To a Louse [On Seeing One on a Lady's Bonnet at Church].
Rosenberg, I. Immortals, The.
    Louse Hunting.
Villa. To Become an Archer.

Lies and Lying
Auden. Their Lonely Betters.
Belloc. Matilda.
Brown, N. I've Got a Feelin' You're Foolin'
Brown, S. I Was a Phony Baloney!
    Schadenfreude.
Carbó, N. Civilizing the Filipino.
Chernoff. How Lies Grow.
Clarke, C. What Goes Around Comes Around, or The Proof Is in the Pudding.
Coleridge, M. Insincere Wish Addressed to a Beggar, An.
    True to myself am I, and false to all.
Collins, M. Lies.
Donaldson, W. Little White Lies.
Dunbar, P. We Wear the Mask.
"Ephelia." To J. G.
Equi. Autobiographical Poem.
Evans, D. In the Vices.
Freed, A. I've Got a Feelin' You're Foolin'
Fuhrman, J. Here, I Say.
Gilbert, S. Ladies' Home Journal, The.
Glatt. One Night with a Stranger at 30.
Goldberg, B. Once a Shoot of Heaven.
Hardy, T. Her Dilemma.
Hein, S. He's a Cousin of Mine.
Highfill, M. Rebis.
Housman, A. Purple William or The Liar's Doom.
Jones, P. If I Were Rita Hayworth.
Kay, J. Stincher, The.
Laing, K. I Am the Freshly Dead Husband.
Lawrence, D. I Am in a Novel.
Mack, C. He's a Cousin of Mine.
Maxwell. Rumplestiltskin.
Nash, O. Golly, How Truth Will Out.
Nesbit, E. Appeal.
Ofeimun. Beyond Fear.
    Poet Lied, The.
Parker, D. Unfortunate Coincidence.
Pilkington, L. Song, A: "Lying is an

    occupation."
Pope, J. Word of Encouragement, A.
Ralegh, S. Lie, The.
Robinson, E. How Annandale Went Out.
    Uncle Ananias.
Rux, C. H. Pledge of Allegiance.
Silverstein, S. Sick.
Tate, J. Book of Lies, The.
Taylor, J. Epigram: "There chanced to meet together in an inn."
Trethewey, N. White Lies.
Weigl. Song of Napalm.
Wilbur. Lying.

Life
Adams, L. But Alive.
Addonizio. Conversation in Woodside.
Ahlert, F. Life Is a Song, Let's Sing It Together.
Aiken, C. Things, The.
Aldrich, T. Lycidas.
Alegría. Documentary.
    Savoir Faire.
    Summing Up.
Ammons, A. R. Cut the Grass.
    Easter Morning.
Anania. Fall, The.
Angelou. Life Doesn't Frighten Me.
Arlen, H. As Long As I Live.
    I've Got the World on a String.
Arnold, M. Written in Butler's Sermons.
Ashbery. Improvement, The.
    Young Prince and the Young Princess, The.
Auden. Precious Five.
Austin, A. Is Life Worth Living?
Bacon, F. Life of Man, The.
Baraka. Minute of Consciousness, The.
Barbauld. Life.
Barker, D. Make Your Mark.
Beaumont, J. Cheat, The.
Beaver. Angels' Weather.
Becker, R. Life Forms.
Beedome. Question and Answer, The.
Belloc. World's a Stage, The.
Berkson, B. Melting Milk.
Berryman. Sympathy, a Welcome, A.
Bevington, L. Afternoon.
Blackburn, P. Park Poem.
Blind. Sower, The.
Blunden. Report on Experience.
Borson. Rain.
Braithwaite. Sic Vita.
    Turn Me to My Yellow Leaves.
Brass. There Isn't Any Death.
Bronk. Life Supports.
    Metonymy as an Approach to a Real World.
Brown, L. Life Is Just a Bowl of Cherries.
Brown, S. Odyssey of Big Boy.
Browning, R. Pisgah-Sights I.
    Pisgah-Sights II.
    Rabbi Ben Ezra.
Buchanan, G. Jill's Death.
Buckley, C. Concerning Paradise.
Bukowski. Crucifix in a Deathhand.
Burkard. Breathless Storm.
Burns, R. Epistle to a Young Friend.
Campbell, D. Here, under Pear-trees.
Campbell, J. Mors et Vita.
Campbell, T. River of Life, The.
Carroll, J. Heroin.
Carruth, H. Wreck of the Circus Train, The.
Cavafy. As Much As You Can.
Ceravolo. New Realism.
Chimombo. Death Song, A.
Clark, T. Take Time to Live.
Clifton, L. Cutting Greens.
    December.
Cohan. I'm Mighty Glad I'm Living and That's All.
    If I'm Going to Die I'm going to Have Some Fun.
    Life's a Funny Proposition after All.
Coleridge, M. 'I envy not the dead that rest'
Coleridge, S. Epitaph: "Stop, Christian passer-by!—Stop, child of God."
Cooper, J. Praise.
Corpus. Blkfern-jungal.
Couani. Never-Dead, The.

Cronin, A. Elegy for the Nightbound.
Cullen, C. For One Who Gayly Sowed His Oats.
From Life to Love.
Cummings, E. Anyone Lived in a Pretty How Town.
My Father Moved Through Dooms Of Love.
Cunningham, J. Epigram: "Life flows to death as rivers to the sea."
Miller, The.
On a Certain Alderman.
Davies, W. Leisure.
De la Mare. Last Chapter, The.
Di Prima. Short Note on the Sparseness of the Language.
Dickinson, E. This Is My Letter to the World.
Word is dead, A.
DiPalma. When Torrid Rhymes with Forehead.
Doolittle, H. White World.
Dove, R. Fish in the Stone, The.
This Life.
Dowson. Vitae Summa Brevis Spem Nos Vetat Incohare Longam.
Drake, N. Foley Artist, The.
Drummond de Andrade. Dead in Frock Coats, The.
Motionless Faces.
Drummond, W. Madrigal: "This life, which seems so fair."
Dugan, A. Last Statement for a Last Oracle.
Duke, V. Round About.
Dunbar, P. Common Things.
Duncan, R. After a Long Illness.
Ebb, F. Cabaret.
Eberhart, R. Hard Structure of the World, The.
Hardy Perennial.
New Hampshire, February.
Ehrmann. I Ponder on Life.
Eigner. Live /, Bird Which.
Temporary Language, A.
Ekelof. If You Ask Me.
Emerson, R. Blight.
Day's Ration, The.
Nominalist and Realist.
Fenton, J. Skip, The.
Ferlinghetti, L. 25.
River Still to Be Found, A.
"Field." Life Plastic.
Field, E. Lower East Side: The George Bernstein Story.
Fisher, J. Gooseflesh.
Life, A.
Fisher, R. Toyland.
Francis, R. Hound, The.
Frost, R. On the Heart's Beginning to Cloud the Mind.
Road Not Taken, The.
Stopping by Woods on a Snowy Evening.
Gambold. Mystery of Life, The.
Gay, J. My Own Epitaph.
Gershwin. One Life to Live.
Gilbert, S. To the Terrestrial Globe.
Gioia. Maze without a Minotaur.
Giorno. Life Is a Killer.
Giovanni. Life I Led, The.
Glück, L. New Life, The.
Godfrey. In Front of a Large Number of People.
Gonzalez, R. Without Villages.
Grahn. Grand Grand Mother is returning.
Graves, R. To Evoke Posterity.
Gurney, I. To God.
Habington. Cogitabo Pro Peccato Meo.
Hadas, R. Sentimental Education.
Hagedorn, J. Smokey's Getting Old.
Something about You.
Hall, D. Raisin, The.
Hammond, W. On the Same [Death of My Dear Brother, Mr. H.S., Drowned]: The Boat.
Hannon. Beneath Cold Mountain.
Hardy, T. Epitaph: "I never cared for Life: Life cared for me."
Necessitarian's Epitaph, A.
Placid Man's Epitaph, A.
Harford, L. Experience.
Harjo, J. Remember.
Harry, J. Poem Films Itself, The.

Harryman. My Story.
Havergal. Just When Thou Wilt.
Hayden, R. Whipping, The.
Heaney, S. Casting and Gathering.
From the Canton of Expectation.
Henderson, R. Life Is Just a Bowl of Cherries.
Henley, W. Madam Life's A Piece in Bloom.
To Robert Louis Stevenson.
Herbert, G. Life.
Herrick. Four[e] Things Make Us Happy Here.
Life Is the Body's [or Bodies] Light.
Hikmet. Since I Was Thrown Inside.
Hillman. Every Life.
Hillyer. As One Who Bears beneath His Neighbor's Roof.
Hirshfield, J. Story, A.
Hoffman, D. Special Train, A.
Hogan, L. Return: Buffalo.
Holland, J. Sleep.
Three Tests for Darwin Duke.
Hongo. Pier, The.
Hoover, P. Family Romance.
Hopkins, G. Thou Art Indeed Just, Lord.
Hoskyns [or Hoskins]. Epitaph, An: On a Man for Doing Nothing.
Housman, A. From Far, from Eve and Morning.
Immortal Part, The.
Is my team plowing?
Terence, This Is Stupid Stuff.
Hughes, L. Advice.
Esthete in Harlem.
Life Is Fine.
Mother to Son.
Still Here.
Hughes, T. Moon-Hops.
Hutchinson, L. Verses Written by Mrs. Hutchinson.
Hutchinson, P. Be Born a Saint.
Ignatow, D. Rescue the Dead.
Ingelow. Little babe, while burns the west.
Story, A.
Jarrell. Country Life, A.
Well Water.
Jeffers, R. Animals.
Ante Mortem.
Purse-Seine, The.
Jones, R. Beginning, A.
Jonson, B. To William Roe.
Kander, J. Cabaret.
Kaufman, B. Grandfather Was Queer, Too.
Heavy Water Blues.
Kaufman, S. Emperor of China, The.
Kavanagh, P. To Hell with Commonsense.
Keats. Human Seasons, The.
Ode to a Nightingale.
Kees. Beach in August, The.
Kennelly. Island, The.
Killigrew, A. On Death.
King, B. Sum of Life, The.
King, H. Sic Vita.
Kinsella, T. All Is Emptiness, and I Must Spin.
Oldest Place, The.
Route of the Táin, The.
Kipling, R. Envoi: "There's a whisper down the field where the year has shot her yield."
Klein, M. Guardian Life.
Knight, E. My Life, the Quality of Which.
Koehler, T. As Long As I Live.
I've Got the World on a String.
Koethe. Songs of the Valley.
Koordada, M. You Can't Escape Your Life Record.
Kunitz, S. Layers, The.
Round, The.
Laing, K. Godhorse.
Huge Car with the Sad Voice, The.
Lake, P. Crime and Punishment.
Lamantia. Romantic Movement, The.
Landon. Lines of Life.
Small Miseries.
Stern Truth.
Lanier, S. Nirvâna.
Larkin, P. Afternoons.
Days.
Nothing to Be Said.
Seventy Feet Down.

Lawrence, D. We Are Transmitters.
Layton. Street Funeral.
Lea, S. Insomnia: The Distances.
Lear, E. O dear! How disgusting is life!
Lefevre, A. Halftime.
Levertov. Living.
O Taste and See.
Levine, P. 28.
Blasting from Heaven.
Clouds.
Genius.
How Much Earth.
I Caught a Glimpse.
Rain Downriver.
Salami.
Sweet Will.
Levy, A. Epitaph: "This is the end of him, here he lies."
Longfellow, H. Nature.
Psalm of Life, A.
Rainy Day, The.
Tell Me Not in Mournful Numbers.
Village Blacksmith, The.
Lovelace, R. La Bourbon, A.
Lowell, R. Book of Wisdom, The.
Lowry, M. Wild Cherry, The.
Lum. Riding the North Point Ferry.
MacNeice. Prayer Before Birth.
"Malley." Palinode.
Petit Testament.
Sybilline.
Young Prince of Tyre.
Marks, S. To the Ocean.
Mase. It's Simply Great.
Masters, E. Jennie McGrew.
Mathews, A. Caedmon.
McAuley, J. Gnostic Prelude.
Released on Parole.
McClure, M. Mad Sonnet: Grace.
McPherson, S. Wings and Seeds.
Melville, H. To.
Menken. Infelix.
Meredith, G. Ballad of Past Meridian, A.
Merrill, J. Last Words.
Mezey. Reaching the Horizon.
Momaday. Delight Song of Tsoai-Talee, The.
Montagu, L. Addressed to———.
Mother Goose. Solomon Grundy.
Mueller, L. Curriculum Vitae.
Ní Chuilleanáin. Pygmalion's Image.
Nash, O. Round About.
Nathan, L. Bladder Song.
Nemerov. Intimations.
Life Cycle of Common Man.
Life, A.
Neruda. Sexual Water.
Walking Around.
Nichol. St. Anzas VI.
North, C. Elizabethan & Nova Scotian Music.
Few Facts about Me, A.
Leap Year.
Nortje. Newcombe at the Croydon Gallery.
O'Grady, D. Purpose.
O'Hara, F. In Favor of One's Time.
In Memory of My Feelings.
Steps.
O'Loughlin. Posthumous.
Ofeimun. Poet Lied, The.
Ohnishi, T. Blossoms in the Wind.
Okigbo. Hurrah for Thunder.
Oldham, P. Noon.
Oliver, M. In Blackwater Woods.
Singapore.
Summer Day, The.
Olson, C. Distances, The.
Ondaatje. Light.
Oness, C. Of All There Is.
Ormsby, F. Landscape with Figures.
Osgood, K. Driving Home the Cows.
Padgett, R. Sandwich Man, The.
Padilla. Man on the Edge.
Palmer, M. Painted Cup, The.
Parker, D. Coda: "There's little in taking or giving."
Pastan. Baseball.
Pasternak, B. Hamlet.

Snow Is Falling.
Patel, G. Forensic Medicine.
Perillo. Dangerous Life.
Perreault, J. Boomerang.
Peters, L. One Long Jump.
Piatt, S. In Her Prison.
Pinsky. Jersey Rain.
Pitcher. Pale Blue Casket, The.
Plath. Life, A.
Poe. Dreams.
Pomfret, J. Choice, The.
Porter, P. Consumer's Report, A.
Pound, E. And the Days Are Not Full Enough.
Prior. Human Life.
Procter, A. Three Evenings in a Life.
Raine, K. Good Friday.
Rainger, R. Easy Living.
Ralegh, S. What Is Our Life?
Ramanujan. Foundlings in the Yukon.
Ray, H. Life.
  Life's Boundary.
Reese, L. Little Song of Life, A.
  Tears.
  To Life.
Rexroth, K. Long Lifetime, A.
Rich, A. Burning Oneself Out.
  Living Memory.
  Tattered Kaddish.
Richardson, J. Vectors: Forty-five Aphorisms and Ten-second Essays.
Robin, L. Easy Living.
Robinson, A. Art and Life.
Robinson, E. Man against the Sky, The.
Rodriguez, J. About this Woman.
Roethke. Decision, The.
  Judge Not.
  Walk in Late Summer, A.
Rolle, S. Keeping Watch.
Rossetti, C. Birthday, A.
  Cobwebs.
  From the Antique.
  Heaviness May Endure for a Night, But Joy Cometh in the Morning.
  Life's Parallels, A.
  Pause of Thought, A.
  Sappho.
  Uphill.
  Wednesday in Holy Week.
  World, The.
Rossetti, D. Choice, The.
Rouse. Birthday, A.
Rowe, E. Expostulation, The.
Ryan, T. Lunar Eclipse.
Sandburg, C. Aprons of Silence.
  Blue Island Intersection.
  Broken-Face Gargoyles.
  Chicago.
  Early Copper.
  Gone.
  Happiness.
  Mag.
  Onion Days.
  Right to Grief, The.
  Shovel Man, The.
  Sins of Kalamazoo, The.
  Southern Pacific.
  Teamster's Farewell, A.
Saxe, J. Story of Life, The.
Sayres. Bankrupt.
Scalapino. Flush / a Play.
Schnackenberg. Darwin in 1881.
Schultz, P. I'm Not Complaining.
Schwartz, D. Passionate Shepherd to His Love, The.
Seferis. Old Man on the River Bank, An.
Sexton. Rowing.
Shange. I Live in Music.
Shapiro, D. Archaic Torsos.
Shelley, P. Sonnet: Lift Not the Painted Veil: "Lift not the painted veil which those who live."
Sherwood, G. Love and Life.
"Shu Ting." Assembly Line.
Simic. Great Infirmities.
  Lesson, The.
  Poem: "Every morning I forget how it is."

Sirr. Collector's Marginalia, The.
Skovron. Election Eve, with Cat.
Slessor. Fixed Ideas.
  Last Trams.
Smith, C. Pressed by the Moon, Mute Arbitress of Tides.
Smith, M. Stopping to Take Notes.
Smith, S. Dream of Comparison, A.
Snodgrass, W. After Experience Taught Me.
  April Inventory.
Spender, S. Sonnet: "You were born; must die; were loved; must love."
St. John, P. Carnival.
Stafford, W. Ask Me.
Stanley, T. Pythagoric Letter, The.
  Quickness.
Stern, G. Lucky Life.
  Royal Manor Road.
Stevens, W. Men Made Out of Words.
  Rock, The.
  Sunday Morning.
  Table Talk.
Stowe. Only a Year.
Strand. Story of Our Lives, The.
Strouse, C. But Alive.
Stryk, L. Oeuvre.
Suckling, S. Song: "I prithee spare me, gentle boy."
Swenson, M. Secret in the Cat, The.
Swinburne. Match, A.
Swirszczynska. Poetry Reading.
Synková, A. Tears.
Sze. Network, The.
Taylor, A. Fitzroy.
Taylor, B. Goblet, The.
Thomas, D. Force That Through the Green Fuse Drives the Flower, The.
  This Bread I Break.
  Twenty-four Years.
Thomas, R. Bright Field, The.
  Lore.
Thoreau. I Am a Parcel of Vain Strivings Tied.
  My Life Has Been The Poem I Would Have Writ.
Toomer. Gods Are Here, The.
  It is Everywhere.
Torres, E. Lipsticktion.
Tranter. Enzensberger at 'Exiles.'
Treasone. Life.
Troupe. Conversation Overheard.
Tsaloumas. Falcon Drinking.
Tucker, M. Life.
  Mysteries of Life.
Tuckerman, F. Sonnets: First Series.
Unknown. 'Tis a Little Journey.
  Be Merry.
  Hell and Heaven.
  I'm a-Rollin'
  Inscription in Osmington Church, Dorset.
  Life Owes Me Nothing.
  Little Things.
  Loom of Time, The.
  Nobody Knows the Trouble I've Had.
  Only One Life.
  Playing the Game.
  Prayer of a Woman in Charge of Berry Picking in Knights Inlet.
  Thank God!
  What Care I Though the World Reprove.
  Wide Walls.
Van Doren. Good Appetite.
Van Duyn. Sonnet for Minimalists.
Van Peenen, H. Insulin Receptor.
Vaughan, H. Pursuit[e], The.
  Quickness.
Vice. Pants.
Viidikas. Future.
Wallace-Crabbe. And the World was Calm.
Walton, A. Recipe for Living.
  World We Make, The.
Watson, R. Of the Earth, Earthy.
Webb, F. Clouds.
Weill, K. One Life to Live.
Wellman, M. Having Led a Charmed Life, He Had to be Hanged Twice.
Wells, A. Length of Life, The.

Wenderoth, J. My Life.
Wharton, E. Life.
Whistler. Form of Epitaph, A.
White, D. Epistle of Love and of Consolation unto Israel, An.
Whitman, W. Beat! Beat! Drums!
  Miracles.
  O Living Always, Always Dying.
  When I Read the Book.
Wilbur. "World Without Objects Is a Sensible Emptiness, A."
  Leaving.
Wilcox, E. Life.
  Life's Journey.
Williams, W. Horse Show, The.
  Love Song: "Sweep the house clean."
  Pastoral: "Little sparrows, The."
Winchilsea. Life's Progress.
Winter, M. Long Distance.
Wordsworth, D. Thoughts on my sick-bed.
Wordsworth, W. World Is Too Much With Us, The.
Wotton, S. De Morte.
Wright, C. Laguna Blues.
Wright, D. Funeral Oration, A.
Wright, J. American Twilights, 1957.
  Angel, The.
  Horse, The.
  Inscription for the Tank.
  Life, The.
  Mutterings over the Crib of a Deaf Child.
  Northern Pike.
  Secret Gratitude, A.
  Trying to Pray.
Wylie. Hughie at the Inn.
  Puritan Sonnet, IV.
  Wild Peaches.
Yeats. Four Ages of Man, The.
  Gyres, The.
  Meru.
  New Faces, The.
  Scholars, The.
  Wild Old Wicked Man, The.
Young, A. Detroit 1958.
  From Bowling Green.
  How Stars Start.
  How the Rainbow Works.
  Little More Traveling Music, A.
Young, G. Our Life in California.
Young, J. Life Is a Song, Let's Sing It Together.
Zach. Be Careful.
Zangwill. Dreams.
Zhenkai. Accomplices.
Zucker, R. In Your Version of Heaven I am Younger.

Lifeguards
Dickey, J. Lifeguard, The.
Klein, M. Tides, The.

Light
Adams, L. Light at Equinox.
Ammons, A. R. City Limits, The.
Angeles, C. Light Invested.
Armantrout. Getting Warm.
Ash, J. Poor Boy: Portrait of a Painting.
Bangs, J. Philosophy.
Barber, D. Small Hours.
Bawer. View from an Airplane at Night, over California, The.
Bernard, A. See It Does Rise.
Biespiel, D. There Were No Deer in the Thicket.
Blake, W. To Morning.
Bogan, L. Evening-Star.
Boland, E. Self-Portrait on a Summer Evening.
Bolton, J. Lights at Newport Beach, The.
Boruch. Light.
Bourdillon. Night Has a Thousand Eyes, The.
Bronk. Where It Ends.
Brown, D. Illumination.
Browning, E. Best Thing in the World, The.
Byron, G. Darkness.
Carew, T. Beautiful Mistress, A.
Ceravolo. New Realism.
Clover, J. El periférico, or Sleep.
Coleridge, M. In Dispraise of the Moon.
Cook, E. Song of the Rushlight.

Cortes, F. Poem Composed During a Brownout.
Cowley, A. Hymn: To Light.
Creeley. World, The.
Crouch, S. Like a Blessing.
DeFrees. Beetle Light.
Delaunay, S. Zenith.
Dickey, J. Power and Light.
Donne. Nocturnal[l] upon Saint Lucy's [or S. Lucy's or S. Lucies] Day, Being the Shortest Day, A.
Dumdum. Some Die of Light.
Earle, J. Visiting Light.
Ellington, D. I'm Beginning to See the Light.
Ferguson, G. Winter Sunflowers.
"Field." They Shall Look on Him.
Fletcher, P. Ocean of Light.
Ford, C. Overturned Lake, The.
Gamalinda, E. Light Falls Obliquely.
Garrett, E. Airborne.
George, D. I'm Beginning to See the Light.
Goodison. Always Homing Now Soul Toward Light.
Gore-Booth. Vision of Niamh, The.
Graham, J. San Sepolcro.
Graves, R. Lament for Pasiphaë.
Guest, B. Wild Gardens Overlooked by Night Lights.
Gunn, T. Map of the City, A.
Harjo, J. White Bear.
Hays, H. Manhattan.
Hecht, A. Illumination.
Hemans. Illuminated City, The.
Herrick. Life Is the Body's [or Bodies] Light.
Hickey, E. For Richer, for Poorer.
Hinsey, E. Art of Measuring Light, The.
Hodges, J. I'm Beginning to See the Light.
Hope, A. Gateway, The.
James, H. I'm Beginning to See the Light.
Knott. (Poem) (Chicago) (The Were-Age).
Kooser. Late Lights in Minnesota.
Kunitz, S. Round, The.
  When the Light Falls.
LaFemina. White Dwarf.
Lawrence, D. Let There Be Light!
Lea, S. Telescope.
Levine, P. Belief.
Love, B. Bryan Ferry.
Mac Low. 59th Light Poem: for La Monte Young and Marian Zazeela—6 November 1982.
MacCaig. Likenesses.
MacNeice. Star-Gazer.
Martinez, D. Nocturnes: "He closed the deal on the night. A real."
Marvell. Mower to the Glowworms [or Glow-Worms or Glo-Worms], The.
Maura. Creation of Light, The.
McGrath, T. Reading by Mechanic Light.
Meinke. Unnatural Light.
Melville, H. In the Desert.
Millay, E. First Fig.
Milton. On His Blindness.
Moore, L. Homeplace, The.
Morley, D. Air Street.
Myles, E. School of Fish.
Nelson, M. Brightness.
Nichol. St. Anzas VI.
Novakovich. Shadow.
Peterson, J. Stand Still.
Phillips, C. Clearing, The.
Prabhu. For the Lord of Caves.
Probyn. More than They that Watch for the Morning.
Ramsdell, H. Bright Receding.
Rankine. Quotidian, The.
Rich, A. Focus.
  Insusceptibles, The.
  Integrity.
Roberts, D. Dazzle.
Roberts, K. Plastic Cup, The.
Roethke. Light Listened.
Romo-Carmona, M. Daylight.
Roseliep. Morning-Glory, The.
Samyn, M. Poem with Light on Its Shoulder.
Schuyler, J. Shimmer.
Simms, C. Pallid Harrier.

Sitwell, D. Aubade: "Jane, Jane, / Tall as a crane."
Snyder, G. How Poetry Comes to Me.
  Uses of Light, The.
St. John, P. Biological Light.
Stanley, T. Glowworm, The.
Stevens, W. Homunculus et la Belle Étoile.
  Sun This March, The.
Stoutenburg. Midnight Saving Time.
Symonds. Lux Est Umbra Dei[1].
Symons, A. Pastel: Masks and Faces.
Tabb. Tenebræ.
Thomas, D. Light Breaks Where No Sun Shines.
Thomas, L. Electricity of Blossoms.
Touré, A. O Lord of Light! A Mystic Sage Returns to Realms of Eternity!
Towle. Painting the Eaves.
Wat. Facing Bonnard.
Webb, F. Port Phillip Night.
White, J. To Night.
Williamson, A. Light's Reading, The.
Wright, C. Appalachian Book of the Dead III, The.
Wright, J. Beginning.
  To the Evening Star: Central Minnesota.
Wylie. Incantation.
  O Virtuous Light.
Young, A. Written in Bracing, Gray L.A. Rainlight.

Lighthouses
Albrecht, A. Passing Piedras Blancas.
Bishop, E. Seascape.
Clampitt. Baroque Sunburst, A.
Gibson, W. Flannan Isle.
Groarke, V. Shale.
Jackson, H. My Lighthouses.
Quagliano. Edward Hopper's 'Lighthouse at Two Lights.'
Sadoff. February: Pemaquid Point.
Wellesley. Lighthouses.

Lightning
Bynner. Lightning.
Chernoff. Man Struck Twenty Times by Lightning, The.
Davis, J. He Is Lightning.
Espada. Owl and the Lightning, The.
Hazo. Drenching, The.
  World that Lightning Makes, The.
Hester. Lightning Rod Salesman, The.
Lawrence, D. Lightning.
  Storm in the Black Forest.
Long, H. Lightning.
Macdonald, G. Baby-Sermon, A.
Montagu, L. Epitaph: "Here lie John Hughes and Sarah Drew."
Unknown. At Great Torrington, Devon.
Lightning Bugs
Unknown. Bugs.
See also **Fireflies**
Lilacs
Biespiel, D. Lilacs.
Lowell, A. Lilacs.
Wright, R. Haiku: "Coming from the woods."
Lilies
Bui-Burton. My Love Is Like a Lily.
Glück, L. White Lilies, The.
Gregory, H. Chinese Garden, The.
Guest, B. Red Lilies.
Herrick. How Lilies Came White.
Keats. La Belle Dame sans Merci [A Ballad].
Kreymborg. Tiger Lily.
Legaré. To a Lily.
Oliver, M. Lilies.
Robinson, A. Pallor.
Sexton. From the Garden.
Smart, C. On a Bed of Guernsey Lilies.
Unknown. Lily Events.
Lilies of the Valley
Silkin. Lilies of the Valley.
Lilith
Benton, S. Lilith.
Fabian, C. Liturgy for Lilith.
Gregg. Lilith.
Norris, K. Lilith and the Doctor.

Parnell, P. Medusa and Perseus III: Lilith.
Limbo
Jacobsen, J. Limbo Dancer, The.
Levy, A. Ballad of Religion and Marriage, A.
Poe. Al Aaraaf.
  Song: "Young flowers were whispering in melody."
Limestone
Auden. In Praise of Limestone.
Lincoln, Abraham
Berger, D. Lincoln Bedroom, The.
Bryant, W. Death of Lincoln, The.
Fletcher, J. Lincoln.
Hughes, L. Lincoln Monument: Washington.
Kennedy, X. Loneliness of Lincoln, The.
Knoepfle. Bath.
Lindsay, N. Abraham Lincoln Walks at Midnight.
Markham, E. Lincoln, the Man of the People.
Meigs, M. Abraham Lincoln.
Melville, H. Martyr, The.
Ray, H. Lincoln.
Robinson, E. Master, The.
Sandburg, C. Cool Tombs.
  Long Shadow of Lincoln: A Litany, The.
Schwartz, D. Lincoln.
Shulman, M. Honest Abe Lincoln.
Sorby. Land of Lincoln.
Tate, J. Diagnosis, The.
Thompson, M. Lincoln's Grave.
Whitman, W. Carol of Death, The.
  Hush'd Be the Camps To-Day.
  O Captain! My Captain!
  When Lilacs Last in the Dooryard Bloom'd.
Lincolnshire, England
Ingelow. High Tide on the Coast of Lincolnshire, 1571, The.
Tennyson, A. Lines: "Here often, when a child, I lay reclined."
Lindbergh, Charles Augustus
Hazo. Maps for a Son Are Drawn as You Go.
Lindsay, Vachel
Ginsberg, A. To Lindsay.
Linen
Longley, M. Linen Industry, The.
Linnets
Bridges, R. I Heard a Linnet Courting.
Brontë, E. Song: "Linnet in the rocky dells, The."
Wordsworth, W. Green Linnet, The.
Lions
Beer, P. Lion Hunts.
Belloc. Jim Who Ran Away from His Nurse, and Was Eaten by a Lion.
  Lion, The.
Carruth, H. Wreck of the Circus Train, The.
Duncan, R. Song of the Borderguard, The.
Edgar, M. Lion and Albert, The.
Ginsberg, A. Lion for Real, The.
Herrick. Upon Umber: Epigram.
Housman, A. African Lion, The.
Jacobsen, J. Bush.
Levy, A. Captivity.
MacLeish. End of the World, The.
Nash, O. Lion, The.
Sackville-West. Greater Cats, The.
Smith, S. Reversionary.
  Sunt Leones.
Turner, C. Lion's Skeleton, The.
Unknown. Signifying Monkey, The.
Watson, W. O My Poor Darling.
Lips
Benedikt. Divine Love.
Coffman. Girl/Spit.
Conquest. Agents, The.
de Gillies, G. De Puerorum osculis.
Dowson. Non Sum Qualis Eram Bonae sub Regno Cynarae.
Herrick. Captived Bee; or, The Little Filcher, The.
  Cherry-ripe [or Cherrie-ripe].
Knott. (Poem) (Chicago) (The Were-Age).
Larsen, L. Lips.
Noble, R. Touch of Your Lips, The.
O'Hara, F. Lebanon.

Simon, L.   Bernice Got Next to Isis.
Toomer.   Evening Song.
  Her Lips Are Copper Wire.
Wolverton, T.   Tubes.
Lipscomb, Eugene
Jarrell.   Say Good-bye to Big Daddy.
Lisbon, Portugal
Atkins.   Lisbon.
Listening and Listeners
Angeles, C.   Words.
Barresi.   Back-Up Singer, The.
Bringhurst.   Song of Ptahhotep, The.
De la Mare.   Dove, The.
Gilbert, J.   Prospero Listens to the Night.
Herrick.   Canticle to Apollo, A.
Hughes, L.   Lady's Boogie.
Mudrooroo Narogin.   Song Circle of Jacky.
Rohrer, M.   Last Look at the Mutineers, A.
Synková, A.   To Olga.
Tomlinson, C.   Word in Edgeways, A.
Trommer, R.   If You Listen.
Wayne, J.   Eavesdropper, The.
Wilcox, E.   In the Night.
Literature
Berryman.   Professor's Song, A.
Birney.   Can. Lit.
Camlan.   Literature and Action.
Ch'ien T'ao.   On Reading the Seas and
  Mountains Classic.
Derricotte.   Passing.
Donne.   To Mr. R. W.
Donnell.   Canadian Prairie's View of Literature,
  The.
Hattersley, G.   *On the Buses* with Dostoyevsky.
Hightower, J. R.   On Reading the Seas and
  Mountains Classic.
Hirshfield, J.   In Praise of Coldness.
Leonard, T.   100 Differences between Poetry
  and Prose.
Lopez, T.   Path Marked with Breadcrumbs, A.
Mnthali.   Stranglehold of English Lit, The.
Mueller, L.   American Literature.
  Another Version.
Nemerov.   History of a Literary Movement.
Ransom, J.   Survey of Literature.
Reed, I.   Badman of the Guest Professor.
Rukeyser, M.   Homage to Literature.
Smith, S.   Souvenir de Monsieur Poop.
Stevens, W.   Poem That Took the Place of a
  Mountain, The.
Waller, E.   Of English Verse.
Williams, W.   Question and Answer.
See also **Authorship and Authors; Criticism and
Critics**
Lithuania
Milosz, C.   With Her.
Pelletiere, M.   Under Her Crib.
Zwicky.   Summer Pogrom.
Little Red Riding Hood
Bolton, G.   Little Red Riding Hood and the
  Wolf.
Lizards
Bethune, L.   Today Tutu Is Beating the Same
  Burru as Me.
Grennan.   Lizards in Sardinia.
Kinnell.   Gray Heron, The.
Lawrence, D.   Lizard.
Magowan.   Zeimbekiko.
Morley, H.   Lizard, The.
Murray, R.   Lizard, The.
Pender.   Lizard, The.
Robinson, R.   Jarrangulli.
Roethke.   Lizard, The.
  Wish for a Young Wife.
Stafford, W.   At the Bomb Testing Site.
Llamas
Arnold, D.   Song to the Alpaca.
Belloc.   Llama, The.
Nash, O.   Lama, The.
Lobsters
Grennan.   Incident.
Hoffman, D.   Lobstepot Labyrinths.
Lieberman, L.   Lobsters in the Brain Coral.
Lowell, R.   Water.
Niedecker.   Lobster, The.

Sexton.   Lobster.
Snodgrass, W.   Lobsters in the Window.
Locker Rooms
Arnold, C.   Locker Room Etiquette.
Locomotives
MacLeish.   Grazing Locomotives.
Wilcox, E.   Engine, The.
See also **Trains; Railroads**
Locusts
Kinzie.   Canicula.
Unknown.   Coyote and the Locust, The.
Lombardi, Vince
Dickey, J.   For the Death of Vince Lombardi.
London, England
Adcock, F.   Immigrant.
Arnold, M.   West London.
Bancks.   Description of London, A.
Barot, R.   Three Amoretti.
Bateman, E.   Cockney's Garden, The.
Belloc.   Ballade of Hell and of Mrs. Roebeck.
Bridges, R.   London Snow.
Chesterton, G.   Old Song, The.
Coward.   London Pride.
Cronin, A.   Responsibilities.
Davidson, J.   London.
Disch.   Convalescing in London.
Douglas, L.   Impression de Nuit; London.
Dower.   New River Head, a Fragment, The.
Dressel.   Intercity, Swansea-London.
Dunbar, W.   To the City of London [*or* In
  Honour of the City of London].
"Eliot."   In a London Drawingroom.
Ewart.   Dell, The.
Fisher, A.   Birdland.
Flecker.   Ballad of the Londoner.
Forster, W.   Poor of London, The.
French, W.   Mountains of Mourne, The.
Gay, J.   Pickpockets.
  Thieves and Whores.
  Winter Sports.
Gershwin.   Foggy Day (in London Town), A.
Ginsberg, A.   Studying the Signs.
Guiney.   Lights of London, The.
  Sunday Chimes in the City.
  W. H.
Herrick.   His Return to London.
Holloway, J.   London, Greater London (After
  Satire III).
Housman, A.   Eight O'Clock.
Howell, C.   Liberty and Ten Years of Return.
Hunt, L.   To Hampstead.
Keats.   Lines on the Mermaid Tavern.
King, J.   Intercity Dub.
Landon.   Scenes in London: Piccadilly.
Levy, A.   London Plane-Tree, A.
  London Poets.
  Straw in the Street.
MacNeice.   Goodbye to London.
  London Rain.
  Streets of Laredo, The.
  Whit Monday.
Maschwitz, E.   Nightingale Sang in Berkeley
  Square, A.
Mason, R.   Latter-day Geography Lesson.
Matthews, W.   By a Ways.
Meynell, A.   November Blue.
Monk, G.   South Bound: Facing North.
Morris, C.   Country and Town.
Morton, J.   Spring in London.
Mother Goose.   London Bridge.
Motteux.   Song, A: "Slaves to London, I'll
  deceive you."
Nortje.   Cosmos in London.
Noyes, A.   Barrel-Organ, The.
Owen, W.   Shadwell Stair.
Pope, A.   Farewell to London in the Year
  1715, A.
Pound, E.   Portrait d'une Femme.
Robinson, M.   London's Summer Morning.
Rowland.   London.
Sherwin, M.   Nightingale Sang in Berkeley
  Square, A.
Spender, S.   Rejoice in the Abyss.
Suckling, S.   Ballad[e] [upon a Wedding], A.
Swift, J.   Description of a City Shower, A.

Thomas, D.   Countryman's Return, The.
  Refusal to Mourn the Death, by Fire, of a Child
  in London, A.
Thomas, R.   Welshman at St. James' Park, A.
Tollet.   On the Prospect from Westminster
  Bridge.
Tonks.   Farewell to Kurdistan.
Unknown.   Annette Myers.
  Cries of London, The.
  London Bells.
  London Lickpenny.
  St. Paul's Steeple.
Vaughan, H.   Rhapsody, A.
Ward, E.   South Sea Ballad, A.
Whitney, I.   Aucthour Maketh Her Wyll and
  Testament, The.
  Manner of Her Will and What She Left to
  London and to All Those in It, at Her
  Departing, The.
Wilde, O.   Impression Du Matin.
  Symphony in Yellow.
Wilson, S.   Room in Bloomsbury, A.
Wordsworth, W.   Composed upon Westminster
  Bridge, September 3, 1802.
  London 1802.
Londonderry, Northern Ireland
Mahon.   Derry Morning.
Loneliness
Abrahams, P.   Lonely Road.
Ackerly.   Prayer of an Unemployed Man.
Ager, M.   Glad Rag Doll.
Aiken, J.   John's Song.
Akst, H.   Am I Blue?
Allingham.   Across the Sea.
"Amorous Lady."   Letter to My Love—All
  Alone, Past 12, in the Dumps, A.
Angel.   Nothing That Is, The.
Arlen, H.   Stormy Weather (Keeps Rainin' All
  the Time).
  When the Sun Comes Out.
Arrowsmith, P.   Political Activist Living Alone.
Ashby.   Stranger in This Land, A.
Aytoun [*or* Ayton], R.   Valediction.
Barnes, W.   Wife A-Lost, The.
Becker, R.   Near Sheridan.
Beckett, S.   Roundelay: "On all that strand."
Berlin.   What'll I Do?
  You Can't Get a Man with a Gun.
Bernstein, L.   Lonely Town.
Berryman.   He Resigns.
Betjeman.   House of Rest.
Bibbins, M.   Mud.
Blaga.   Psalm.
Bly, R.   Snowbanks North of the House.
Borson.   After a Death.
Brontë, A.   Captive Dove, The.
Brontë, C.   'Again I find myself alone.'
  Lonely Lady, The.
Brontë, E.   If grief for grief can touch thee.
  Sun Has Set, The.
Brooks, G.   Sunset of the City, A.
Brown, E.   Tragic Hero.
Bruner.   There Is a Loneliness.
Burke, J.   Good Time Charlie.
Burke, S.   Black Coffee.
Cahn, S.   I'll Walk Alone.
Chin.   Composed Near the Bay Bridge (after a
  wild party).
Clare, J.   Shepherd Boy, The.
  Song: "I peeled bits of straw and I got switches
  too."
Clarke, G.   Am I Blue?
Coleridge, H.   She Was a Queen.
Coleridge, S.   Old Man's Sigh, The. A Sonnet.
Comden, B.   Lonely Town.
Cope, W.   Lonely Hearts.
Cortez, J.   Lonely Woman.
Crapsey.   Lonely Death, The.
Creamer, H.   If I Could Be with You.
Creeley.   Door, The.
  Moon, The.
  Whip, The.
Csoori.   Thin, Black Band, A.
Cummings, E.   L(a.
Dauer.   Mammals.
Davis, B.   I'm Nobody's Baby.

De la Mare. Alone.
 Old Men, The.
Delmore, E. Difference, The.
Deutsch. Solitude.
Dixon, M. Would You Like to Take a Walk?
Donaldson, W. Love Me or Leave Me.
Dougherty, D. Glad Rag Doll.
Ellington, D. Don't Get Around Much
 Anymore.
 It's Kind of Lonesome Out Tonight.
Emerson, R. Good-bye.
 Thine Eyes Still Shined.
Engvick, W. Who Can I Turn To?
Evance, S. To Melancholy.
Evans, M. And the Hotel Room Held Only
 Him.
"Field." Life Plastic.
Field, E. Unwanted.
Field, R. Skyscrapers.
Fields, D. Blue Again.
Forman, R. Someone.
Frost, R. Acquainted with the Night.
 Bereft.
 Desert Places.
 Most of It, The.
Garland, H. Plowing: A Memory.
George, D. It's Kind of Lonesome Out Tonight.
Gershwin. But Not for Me.
Gershwin, G.
Gibbons, R. We Say.
Gizzi. Lonely Tylenol.
Green, A. Lonely Town.
Greenwell, D. Scherzo, A.
Hammerstein. Why Was I Born?
Handman, L. Are You Lonesome Tonight?
Hardy, T. Bereft.
 Fallow Deer at the Lonely House, The.
Harms. After Yes.
 My Own Little Piece of Hollywood.
Hart, L. Dancing on the Ceiling.
 It Never Entered My Mind.
 Nobody's Heart.
 Ship Without a Sail, A.
Hartnett. Death of an Irishwoman.
Hope, M. INRI.
Horovitz, F. Women.
Hovey. At Sea.
Hughes, L. 50—50.
 Hope.
 Miss Blues'es Child.
 Poem: "I loved my friend."
 Stony Lonesome.
Hunter, A. Pastoral Song, A.
Jackson, L. Take Hands.
Jarrell. Game at Salzburg, A.
 Island, The.
 Lonely Man, The.
Jennings, K. Couples.
Jewett, S. Widows' House, The.
Johnson, J. If I Could Be with You.
Jordan, N. When a Woman Gets Blue.
Joseph, L. It's Not Me Shouting at No One.
Kahn, G. Love Me or Leave Me.
Kantaris. Not-loving.
Kennedy, X. B Negative.
Kern, J. Why Was I Born?
Kerouac. Mexican Loneliness.
Knight, E. Poem to Galway Kinnell, A.
Koehler, T. Stormy Weather (Keeps Rainin' All
 the Time).
 When the Sun Comes Out.
Komunyakaa. Never Land.
 When Loneliness Is a Man.
Landesman. Spring Can Really Hang You Up
 the Most.
Landor, W. What News.
Levine, P. At the Fillmore.
 Poem Circling Hamtramck, Michigan, All Night
 in Search of You, The.
Li Po. Verses: "Clean is the autumn wind."
Linden, M. Lonely World.
Loesser. I Don't Want to Walk Without You.
 Spring Will Be a Little Late This Year.
Lowell, A. Letter, The.
 Madonna of the Evening Flowers.
MacNeice. Autobiography.

Nostalgia.
Madgett. Plea for My Heart's Sake.
Mahon. Achill.
Martelli, J. Mal'Occhio.
Masters, E. Lost Orchard, The.
Matthews, W. Cheap Seats, the Cincinnati
 Gardens, Professional Basketball, 1959.
 Good Company.
McElroy, C. In My Mother's Room.
McHugh, J. Blue Again.
McIlroy, L. Good-Bye, Valentine.
Merwin, W. S. Second Psalm: The Signals.
Metcalfe. Visit the Sick.
Millay, E. On the Wide Heath.
Miller, J. American Odalisque.
Modisane. Lonely.
Monro. Solitude.
Oliver, M. Lilies.
Oxenham. Art Thou Lonely?
Park, S. On Such a Day.
Patchen. Lonesome Boy Blues.
Pilinszky, J. Fable: "Once upon a time / there
 was a lonely wolf."
Porter, C. Down in the Depths.
Prince, F. False Bay.
Raab, L. Being a Monster.
Randall, D. Nightwatchman.
 Old Witherington.
Redding, E. End of a Love Affair, The.
Rich, A. Song: "You're wondering if I'm
 lonely."
Robin, L. No Love, No Nothin'
Robinson, E. Mr Flood's Party.
Robson, J. Blues for the Lonely.
Rodgers, C. One.
 Poem for Some Black Women.
 What Color Is Lonely.
Rodgers, R. Dancing on the Ceiling.
 It Never Entered My Mind.
 Nobody's Heart.
 Ship Without a Sail, A.
Rose, B. Would You Like to Take a Walk?
Rossetti, C. At Home.
 Chilly Night, A.
Sappho.
Russell, B. Don't Get Around Much Anymore.
Ryan, G. Elegy for 6 So Far.
Sadoff. February: Pemaquid Point.
Salaam. '5 Minutes, Mr. Salaam.'
Salinas, L. Sometimes Mysteriously.
Sanchez, S. Summary.
Sansom, A. Prince.
Santly, L. I'm Nobody's Baby.
Seshadri. Lifeline.
Shelley, P. Sonnet: Political Greatness.
Shepherd, R. Who Owns the Night and Lease
 Stars.
Stanton, M. Voice for the Sirens, A.
Stickney, T. Mnemosyne.
Strayhorn, B. Lonely Coed, A.
 Lush Life.
Styne, J. I Don't Want to Walk Without You.
 I'll Walk Alone.
Su Tung-p'o. Verses: "I am old, sick and
 lonely."
Surrey. Complaint by Night, A.
Swan, E. When Your Lover Has Gone.
Swirszczynska. Very Sad Conversation at
 Night, A.
Taylor, B. On the Headland.
Tayson, R. Phone Sex.
Teasdale. Spring Night.
Tennyson, A. Mariana.
Tobin, D. Deep Shit.
Turk, R. Are You Lonesome Tonight?
Unknown. Company in Loneliness.
 There Is a Mystery in Human Hearts.
Van Heusen, J. Good Time Charlie.
Vando. In the Dark Backward.
Wang Shih-chieng. After Snow, Longing for
 Elder Brother Hsi-ch'iao.
Warren, H. No Love, No Nothin'
 Would You Like to Take a Walk?
Webster, P. Black Coffee.
Wells, C. Alone.
Whalen. Complaint: To the Muse.

Wheelock, C. Divorcee.
Whitman, W. As If a Phantom Caress'd Me.
 I Saw in Louisiana a Live-Oak Growing.
 Live Oak, with Moss.
 This Moment Yearning and Thoughtful.
 When I Peruse the Conquer'd Fame.
Wilder, A. Who Can I Turn To?
Wolf, T. Spring Can Really Hang You Up the
 Most.
Wordsworth, W. I Wandered Lonely As a
 Cloud.
Wright, F. Journey, The.
Wright, J. Half-Caste Girl.
 Having Lost My Sons, I Confront the Wreckage
 of the Moon: Christmas, 1960.
 Inscription for the Tank.
 Lake in Central Park, The.
 Northern Pike.
 Poem about Breasts, A.
 Revelation, The.
 Speak.
Wunderlich, M. East Seventh Street.
Wylie. Let No Charitable Hope.
Yellen, J. Glad Rag Doll.
See also **Isolation; Absence; Separation**

Long Island, New York
Kern, J. Bungalow in Quogue.
Lazarus, E. Long Island Sound.
Moss, H. Long Island Springs.
Swenson, M. Fire Island.
 Written While Riding the Long Island Rail
 Road.
Wheelock, J. Afternoon: Amagansett Beach.
Whitman, W. As I Ebb'd with the Ocean of
 Life.
 Centenarian's Story, The.
Wodehouse, P. Bungalow in Quogue.

Longfellow, Henry Wadsworth
Adams, F. If.
Betjeman. Longfellow's Visit to Venice.
Carroll, L. Hiawatha's Photographing.
Ray, H. Longfellow.

Longing
Adamson, H. Where Are You?
Ahlert, F. I'm Gonna Sit Right Down and Write
 Myself a Letter.
Albrecht, A. Anacapa.
Alford, H. You and I.
Allingham. Across the Sea.
Anawrok. Each Time.
Anderson, M. It Never Was You.
Arlen, H. It's Only a Paper Moon.
 Man That Got Away, The.
 My Shining Hour.
 Stormy Weather (Keeps Rainin' All the Time).
 Tess's Torch Song (I Had a Man).
Arnold, M. Longing.
Ashbery. Business Personals.
 Walkways, The.
Awad, J. Variations on a Theme.
Barnes, W. Wind at the Door, The.
Barot, R. Three Amoretti.
Barry, C. Finding.
Berkeley, S. Parting, The.
Berlin. Remember.
 Supper Time.
 What'll I Do?
Blake, E. Memories of You.
Blind. Haunted Streets.
Boland, E. In Her Own Image.
Bowles, W. Languid, and sad, and slow.
Brathwaite, E. Naima.
Brent, E. Angel Eyes.
Brontë, E. F. de Samara to A. G. A.
 Shall Earth no more inspire thee.
Brooks, G. To Be in Love.
Brooks, S. Some of These Days.
Brown, L. That Old Feeling.
Browning, R. Never the Time and the Place.
Bryan, M. To———: "O thou unknown
 disturber of my rest."
Burke, S. Black Coffee.
Burns, R. Highland Harry Back Again.
 Mary Morison.
 My Heart's in the Highlands.
Bynner. Sigh, A.

Byron, G.   To Thyrza.
Cahn, S.   Guess I'll Hang My Tears Out to Dry.
Campo.   My Voice.
Carew, T.   Divine Mistress, A.
  To Her in Absence; a Ship.
  To My Mistress[e] in My Absence.
Carmichael, H.   I Get Along Without You Very
  Well.
  Star Dust.
Carter, J.   Adagio at Twilight.
Castillo, S.   At the Havana Hilton.
Cervantes.   A un Desconocido.
  Isla Mujeres.
Chambers, G.   If Only for One Night.
Chin, J.   Bergamot.
Chivers.   Lily Adair.
Clare, J.   I Am.
  Secret Love.
Clarke, C.   Vicki and Daphne.
Clifton, L.   Climbing.
Coleridge, H.   Night.
Coleridge, S.   Love.
Coolbrith.   Longing.
Cortes, F.   Dolce Far Niente.
Cory, W.   Desiderato.
Craik.   Douglas, Douglas, Tender and True.
Crane, H.   Carrier Letter.
Creamer, H.   If I Could Be with You.
Creeley.   In a Boat Shed.
  Messengers, The.
  Song: "Those rivers run from that land."
Curbelo.   Drinking Song.
DeLange, E.   Darn That Dream.
  Solitude.
Dennis, M.   Angel Eyes.
Dooley, M.   Mansize.
Drummond, W.   Sonnet: "How many times
  Nights silent Queene her Face."
Dunbar, P.   Longing.
Elizabeth I.   On Monsieur's Departure.
Ellington, D.   Don't Get Around Much
  Anymore.
  Solitude.
Emerson, R.   To Rhea.
Erdman, E.   Toot, Toot, Tootsie! (Good-bye).
Eyton, F.   Body and Soul.
Faber, F.   Dream of Blue Eyes, A.
Fain, S.   That Old Feeling.
"Field."   Unbosoming.
Fiorito, T.   Toot, Toot, Tootsie! (Good-bye).
Fisher, M.   I Keep Going Back to Joe's.
  Wind in the Willow.
Flynn, N.   Emptying Town.
Forché.   Morning Baking, The.
Ford, C.   Somebody's Gone.
Foster, S.   Jeanie with the Light Brown Hair.
Gallagher, T.   Under Stars.
Gardinier.   To Peace.
Garrigue.   Catch What You Can.
  Stranger, The.
Georgiou, E.   Space Between, The.
Gershon.   Uphold Me.
Gershwin.   Man That Got Away, The.
  Someone to Watch over Me.
Gershwin, G.
Ginsberg, A.   Further Proposal, A.
  Lion for Real, The.
Gordon, M.   There's a Lull in My Life.
Gould, J.   Earthquake Weather.
Green, J.   Body and Soul.
  I Cover the Waterfront.
Gundy, J.   Rain.
Gunn, T.   Autobiography.
Hammerstein.   Lover, Come Back to Me!
  Why Was I Born?
Harbach, O.   Smoke Gets in Your Eyes.
Harburg.   It's Only a Paper Moon.
Hardy, T.   Voice, The.
Hart, L.   He Was Too Good to Me.
  It Never Entered My Mind.
Hass, R.   Pact, A.
Hayden, R.   Ballad of Sue Ellen Westerfield,
  The.
Herbert, G.   Longing.
Herman, J.   If He Walked into My Life.
Hewitt, D.   In Moncur Street.

Hewitt, J.   Ireland.
Heyman, E.   Body and Soul.
  I Cover the Waterfront.
Hill, M.   Abomination.
Hilliard, B.   In the Wee Small Hours of the
  Morning.
Hirshfield, J.   Of Gravity and Angels.
Hogan, L.   Crossings.
Hope, M.   INRI.
Housman, A.   Because I liked you better.
Hovanessian, D.   Exiles.
Howells, W.   Forlorn.
Johnson, J.   If I Could Be with You.
Jones, I.   I'll See You in My Dreams.
Jones, R.   Blasphemy, A.
Jong.   Parable of the Four-Poster.
Joseph, A.   Pure Pop.
Kahn, G.   I'll See You in My Dreams.
  I'm Through with Love.
  Toot, Toot, Tootsie! (Good-bye).
Keats.   Day Is Gone and All Its Sweets Are
  Gone, The.
  I Cry Your Mercy, Pity, Love—Ay, Love!
  Song of the Indian Maid.
Kern, J.   Smoke Gets in Your Eyes.
  Why Was I Born?
Koehler, T.   Stormy Weather (Keeps Rainin' All
  the Time).
  Tess's Torch Song (I Had a Man).
Kynaston.   To Cynthia.
Landor, W.   Rose Aylmer.
Lane, B.   Come Back to Me.
Lang, A.   Romance.
Lassell.   Kissing Ramén.
Lawrence, J.   Linda.
Lerner, A.   Come Back to Me.
Lewis, A.   Dawn on the East Coast.
  In Hospital: Poona (1).
  Song (On Seeing Dead Bodies Floating Off the
  Cape).
Lilley.   You Have to Strike Back.
Liu, T.   Ariel Singing.
Livingston, J.   I'm Through with Love.
Lodge, T.   Shepherd's Sorrow, Being Disdained
  in Love, The.
Loesser.   I Don't Want to Walk Without You.
  Sand in My Shoes.
Loncar, M.   Picasso Shag.
Lovelace, R.   In Allusion to the French Song.
Lowell, A.   Spring Longing.
  Vernal Equinox.
MacDiarmid, H.   Wheesht, Wheesht.
MacKay, I.   Meeting, The.
Mackenzie, K.   Shall Then Another.
Madan.   Abelard to Eloisa.
Maguire, S.   Divorce Referendum, The.
Mahon.   Achill.
Malneek, M.   I'm Through with Love.
Mandela.   I Waited for You Last Night.
Mann, D.   In the Wee Small Hours of the
  Morning.
Matthews, W.   Mood Indigo.
McGrath, T.   Epitaph: "Again, traveller, you
  have come a long way led by that star."
McHugh, J.   Where Are You?
Mercer, J.   I Thought About You.
  My Shining Hour.
Meredith, G.   Love in the Valley.
Mesmer, S.   Lonely Tylenol.
Mew.   Farmer's Bride, The.
Mills, I.   Solitude.
Mitchell, S.   Of Earthly Love.
Moraes, D.   Snow on a Mountain.
Mother Goose.   Bobby Shaftoe.
Nairne.   Will Ye No Come Back Again?
Olson, C.   As the Dead Prey upon Us.
Padel.   Tell Me About It.
Parish.   Star Dust.
Paulin.   Lyric Afterwards, A.
Pfeiffer, E.   Nathaniel to Ruth.
Phillips, C.   Undressing for Li Po.
Piatt, S.   In Her Prison.
Poe.   To One in Paradise.
Pommy-Vega.   [Ah certainty of love in the
  hand].
[Here before the sunrise blue and in this

  solitude].
Porter, C.   In the Still of the Night.
  Night and Day.
  What Is This Thing Called Love?
  Where Is the Life That Late I Led?
Pound, E.   Papyrus.
  River-Merchant's Wife: A Letter, The.
Rabinowitz.   Of Joy Illimited: Polyphonic
  Soundings: Shore to Ship.
Razaf, A.   Memories of You.
Rees-Jones.   Service Wash.
Revel, H.   There's a Lull in My Life.
Rich, A.   Loser, The.
  Paula Becker to Clara Westhoff.
Riddell, E.   Letter, The.
Robin, L.   No Love, No Nothin'
Robinson, E.   Luke Havergal.
Robinson, M.   Laments the Volatility of Phaon.
  Previous to her Interview with Phaon.
Rodgers, R.   He Was Too Good to Me.
  It Never Entered My Mind.
Rohrer, M.   Gliding Toward the Lamps.
Rolfe, E.   First Love.
Rollings.   Light Years and the Love Lost in the
  Oleanders.
Romberg, S.   Lover, Come Back to Me!
Rome, H.   Wish You Were Here.
Romo-Carmona, M.   Daylight.
Roripaugh, L.   Peony Lover.
Rose, B.   It's Only a Paper Moon.
Rukeyser, M.   Believing in Those Inexorable
  Laws.
Russell, B.   Don't Get Around Much Anymore.
Scamell, B.   Diaries.
Schertzinger, V.   Sand in My Shoes.
Schuyler, J.   Sunday.
Scott, S.   Hour with Thee, An.
Segal, J.   I Keep Going Back to Joe's.
  Wind in the Willow.
Shaughnessy, B.   Rise.
Smith, C.   Stanzas: "Ah! think'st thou, Laura,
  then, that wealth."
Snyder, G.   Autumn Morning in Shokoku-ji, An.
  Four Poems for Robin.
  Spring Night in Shokoku-ji, A.
Sour, R.   Body and Soul.
Stanton, M.   Sorrow and Rapture.
  Voice for the Sirens, A.
Steinberg, D.   Purple Is the Color of Longing.
Stevenson, R.   To Mrs. Will H. Low.
Stickney, T.   As a Sad Man, When Evenings
  Grayer Grow.
Strand.   Late Hour, The.
Styne, J.   Guess I'll Hang My Tears Out to Dry.
  I Don't Want to Walk Without You.
Surrey.   Seafarer, The.
Swift, J.   To Stella.
Tagore.   Song That I Came to Sing, The.
Teasdale.   At Night.
  Flight, The.
Thaxter.   Alone.
Thicknesse.   Siena.
Thomas, L.   Cameo in Sudden Light.
Troup, B.   Baby, Baby All the Time.
Tuckerman, F.   "Last night I dreamed we parted
  once again."
Turell, J.   You Beauteous Dames.
Ullman.   Memo.
Unknown.   Jinny.
  Love Undeclared.
  Western Wind.
Unknown, fr. Terezin Concentration Camp.
  Dusk.
  Homesick.
Van Heusen, J.   Darn That Dream.
  I Thought About You.
Volkman.   Untitled: "Shrewd star, who crudes
  our naming: you should be flame."
Wakoski.   Imagining Point Dume.
  Reading *Bonjour, Tristesse* at the Florence
  Crittenden Home for Unwed Mothers.
Walton, E.   In Recompense.
Warren, H.   No Love, No Nothin'.
Webster, P.   Black Coffee.
Weill, K.   It Never Was You.
Whitman, W.   I Heard You Solemn-Sweet Pipes

of the Organ.
O You Whom I Often and Silently Come.
Out of the Cradle Endlessly Rocking.
Whitmore, S.   Gamelia.
Wickham.   Divorce.
Wilbur.   Ballade for the Duke of Orléans.
Wilde, O.   Wasted Days.
Williams, C.   Gas Station, The.
Williams, W.   Paterson, Book 5: The River of
   Heaven.
Willis, N.   Confessional, The.
Witt, S.   Michael Masse.
Wordsworth, W.   With Ships the Sea Was
   Sprinkled Far and Nigh.
Wright, F.   Journey, The.
Wright, J.   Complaint.
To the Muse.
Wunderlich, M.   From a Vacant House.
Wyatt, S.   Promise, A.
Young, J.   I'm Gonna Sit Right Down and Write
   Myself a Letter.

Longshoremen
Heaney, S.   Docker.

Lookout Mountain, Battle of (1863)
Hayden, R.   On Lookout Mountain.

Loons
Eberhart, R.   Loon Call, A.
Harper, M.   Loon, The.

Lorelei
Heine, H.   Lorelei.

Los Angeles, California
Ai.   Riot Act, April 29, 1992.
Alexander, E.   Stravinsky in L.A.
Beatty, P.   Stall Me Out.
Coleman, W.   Prisoner of Los Angeles (2).
Where I Live.
Gioia.   Los Angeles after the Rain.
Harms.   Los Angeles.
Los Angeles, The Angels.
Healy, E.   Artemis in Echo Park.
Two Centuries in One Day.
Hongo.   Yellow Light.
Jarrell.   Thinking of the Lost World.
Lassell.   Sunset Stripping: Visiting L.A.
Lem.   Office Hour.
Levis.   Oldest Living Thing in L.A., The.
Norte, M.   Angel.
Rodriguez, L.   Always Running.
We Never Stopped Crossing Borders.
Snyder, G.   Night Song of the Los Angeles
   Basin.
Uyematsu.   Ten Million Flames of Los Angeles,
   The.
To All Us Sansei Who Wanted to Be Westside.
See also **Hollywood, California**

Loss
Alkalay-Gut.   Transportation.
Allen, D.   Lost Love.
Anderson, W.   I'm Naebody Noo.
Anstett.   Worry.
Antin.   Definitions for Mendy.
Apollinaire.   Fete.
Arnold, M.   Forsaken Merman, The.
Asekoff, L.   Invisible Hand.
Ashbery.   Lost and Found and Lost Again.
Aytoun [or Ayton], R.   Sonnet: on Loss.
Barnett, A.   Music of the Spheres.
Baumel.   Snow-Day.
Bell, M.   To Dorothy.
Benson, S.   Now I Have Nothing.
Berryman.   Ball Poem, The.
Bevington, L.   Am I to Lose You?
Biespiel, D.   Tower.
Bishop, E.   One Art.
Blind.   Haunted Streets.
Boland, E.   What We Lost.
Browning, E.   Year's Spinning, A.
Browning, R.   Any Wife to Any Husband.
Lost Leader, The.
Lost Mistress, The.
Waring.
Youth and Art.
Burns, R.   Ae Fond Kiss.
Man Was Made to Mourn, a Dirge.
Byron, G.   One Struggle More, and I Am Free.

Caddel.   For Tom.
Canning, J.   Indian Gone!, The.
Carew, T.   Deposition from Love, A.
Chernoff.   Lost and Found.
Chin, J.   Ex-Boyfriends Named Michael.
Ciardi.   On Learning to Adjust to Things.
Clifton, L.   To Ms. Ann.
Cofer, J.   Fever.
Coleridge, H.   She Was a Queen.
Copus, J.   Sea-Polyp, The.
Crane, H.   Stark Major.
Voyages.
Creeley.   Parade.
Cronin, J.   Group Photo from Pretoria Local on
   the Occasion of a Fourth Anniversary (Never
   Taken).
Crunk, T.   Leaving.
Cullen, C.   Wind Bloweth Where It Listeth, The.
Cummings, E.   Noster, The.
Curbelo.   Drinking Song.
Darley.   Song: "Sweet in her green dell the
   flower of beauty slumbers."
To Helene.
De la Mare.   Fare Well.
Reserved.
Deane, S.   Fording the River.
Delanty.   Gift, The.
Denney.   Mathematician's Dream, The.
Song: "No use to aim that sextant now."
'Dermée.'   Poem: "I play tennis with the shells."
Dickey, J.   Leap, The.
Donne.   Broken Heart, The.
Computation, The.
Dorcey.   Night.
Dove, R.   "Blown Apart By Loss . . . ."
Drummond, W.   To His Lute.
Dufferin.   Countess of Dufferin, The.
Dugan, A.   American Variation on How Rilke
   Loved a Princess and Got to Stay in Her
   Castle.
Eliot, T.   Eyes That Last I Saw in Tears.
Hollow Men, The.
Journey of the Magi.
Emerson, R.   Give All to Love.
Threnody: "South-wind brings, The."
"Ephelia."   First Farewell to J.G G.
Fagan.   Desire.
Farrar, J.   Song for a Forgotten Shrine to Pan.
Fenton, J.   Skip, The.
Wind.
Forché.   Skin Canoes.
Fuller, R.   Translation.
Gamalinda, E.   Lament Beginning w/a Line after
   Cavafy.
Garrett, E.   Anatomy of Departure.
Garrigue.   After Reading "The Country of the
   Pointed Firs."
Ginsberg, A.   Café in Warsaw.
Godfrey.   Where the Weather Suits My Clothes.
Gotera.   Manong Chito Tells Manong Ben about
   His Dream over Breakfast at the Manilatown
   Cafe.
Graham, J.   What the End Is For.
Graves, R.   Lost Love.
Groarke, V.   Riverbed, The.
Guiterman.   Little Lost Pup.
Gunn, T.   Autobiography.
Halperin.   Two Lines from Paul Celan.
Hamer.   Berkeley, Late Spring.
Harbach, O.   Smoke Gets in Your Eyes.
Harms.   From Now On.
Harper, M.   Drowning of the Facts of a Life,
   The.
Hass, R.   Bookbuying in the Tenderloin.
Meditation at Lagunitas.
Hayden, R.   Road in Kentucky, A.
Hemans.   Lost Pleiad, The.
Henderson, S.   Five Foot Two, Eyes of Blue
   (Has Anybody Seen My Girl?).
Herrick.   Upon the Loss[e] of His Mistresses.
Vine, The.
Hochman.   Manhattan Pastures.
Sphinxes.
Hongo.   Hilo: First Night Back.
Housman, A.   Yon Far Country.
Howe, J.   My Last Dance.

Hughes, L.   Homecoming.
Young Gal's Blues.
Jackson, L.   Summary for Alastor.
Jarrell.   Second Air Force.
Truth, The.
Jonson, B.   Execration upon Vulcan, An.
To the World [A Farewell for a Gentlewoman,
   Virtuous and Noble].
Why I Write Not of Love.
Justice, D.   In Bertram's Garden.
Katz, J.   Falling.
Keats.   In Drear-nighted December.
Kern, J.   Smoke Gets in Your Eyes.
King, H.   Change, The.
Forfeiture, The.
Summer Lost.
Kipling, R.   For to Admire.
Mesopotamia.
Kizer, C.   For Sappho/After Sappho.
Klappert.   In Memory of H. F.
Knight, E.   Feeling Fucked/Up Up.
Knott.   Christmas at the Orphanage.
Koch, K.   To Marina.
Kramer, L.   Strong Winds Below the Canyons.
Kumin, M.   How It Is.
Lamb, C.   Hester.
Old Familiar Faces, The.
Landor, W.   Alas! 'Tis Very Sad to Hear.
Rose Aylmer.
Larcom.   They Said.
Larkin, P.   No Road.
So through that unripe day you bore your head.
Lear, E.   Calico Pie.
Lee, L.   Eating Alone.
Levy, A.   On the Threshold.
Lewis, A.   Song (On Seeing Dead Bodies
   Floating Off the Cape).
Liu, T.   Ariel Singing.
Poem: "Late butterflies gliding through the air."
Lomax, M.   July.
Longfellow, H.   Cross of Snow, The.
Lowell, A.   Patterns.
Lum.   Urban Love Songs.
Macaulay, T.   Jacobite's Epitaph, A.
Mataka.   Next Door.
Mattawa.   Before.
McCarthy, T.   Dying Synagogue at South
   Terrace, The.
McGrath, T.   End of the Line, The.
Meynell, A.   Maternity.
Millay, E.   Sonnet: "What lips my lips have
   kissed, and where, and why."
Moffi.   Putting an End to the War Stories.
Monaco, J.   You're Gonna Lose Your Gal.
Moore, T.   Journey Onwards, The.
Oft in the Stilly Night.
Moulton.   Shall I Complain.
Mura.   To H.N.
Naganawa, A.   Learning to Swim.
Nesbit, E.   Among His Books.
Nilsson, H.   On Inheriting Departure.
Oden.   Testament of Loss.
Oliver, M.   In Blackwater Woods.
Oppen.   From Disaster.
Peacocke.   At the Entrance.
Philips, K.   To the Queen of Inconstancy,
   Regina Collier, in Antwerp.
Pickthall, M.   Lost Friend, The.
Poe.   Dream within a Dream, A.
Happiest Day, the Happiest Hour, The.
Sleeper, The.
To One in Paradise.
Valley of Unrest, The.
Prince, F.   For Fugitives.
Prys-Jones.   Wife of Carcassone, The.
Ransom, J.   Dead Boy.
Reese, L.   Rachel.
Renunciation.
Reid, C.   Stones and Bones.
Rich, A.   Loser, The.
Roberts, E.   Old Love in Song, An.
Robinson, M.   Phaon Forsakes Her.
Roethke.   Visitant, The.
Roscoe, W.   On Being Forced to Part with his
   Library for the Benefit of his Creditors.
Rossetti, C.   Cousin Kate.

Echo.
Grown and Flown.
Ruden, S.   Stubble Burning, The.
Rukeyser, M.   Waiting for Icarus.
Ryan, G.   Too Bad.
Ryan, M.   Talking About Things.
Salaam.   Our World Is Less Full Now That Mr.
Fuller Is Gone.
Samaras, N.   Aubade: Macedonia.
Sanchez, S.   Father and Daughter.
Sassoon.   Lamentations.
Seed.   Sofia.
Seidman.   Tale of Genji.
Seward.   Invocation, To the Genius of Slumber
Written Oct. 1787.
Shapiro, K.   Haircut.
Leg, The.
Sheridan, R.   Lines by a Lady on the Loss of
Her Trunk.
Sigourney.   Advertisement of a Lost Day.
Simmons, J.   Long Way After Ronsard, A.
Simms, W.   Lost Pleiad, The.
Smith, I.   Clearances, The.
Smith, P.   Building Nicole's Mama.
Soldati.   Surroundings.
Sorrentino.   Good Night!
Stafford, W.   Farm on the Great Plains, The.
Stanley, T.   Love Deposed.
Stern, G.   Expulsion, The.
Kissing Stieglitz Goodbye.
Storey.   Prayer for Broken Little Families, A.
Strickland, A.   Forsaken, The.
Sundiata.   Open Heart.
Swirszczynska.   He Is Gone.
Thomas, E.   Return, The.
Thomas, L.   Instructions for Your New Osiris.
Thoreau.   Brother Where Dost Thou Dwell.
Trinidad.   Moonstones.
Unknown.   My Little Maid.
On Prince Frederick.
Volkman.   Evening.
Wakoski.   Ring of Irony, The.
Wang Ts'an.   Seven Sorrows.
Warren, R.   Song: "Yellow coverlet, A."
Whitman, W.   Out of the Cradle Endlessly
Rocking.
Yonnondio.
Whittier.   Farewell, The: "Gone, gone,—sold
and gone."
Wilcox, E.   Friendship After Love.
One of Us Two.
Wilde, O.   Requiescat.
Williams, B.   Night Flute, The.
Williams, C.   Loss.
Williams, P.   Passing Through.
Williams, W.   These.
Wordsworth, W.   Complaint, A.
Sonnet on Catherine Wordsworth.
Written in London, September, 1802.
Wright, F.   Alcohol.
Joseph Come Back as the Dusk.
Wright, J.   Having Lost My Sons, I Confront the
Wreckage of the Moon: Christmas, 1960.
Wycherley, L.   Cat's Cradle.
Yearsley.   To————: "Lo! dreary Winter,
howling o'er the waste."
Yeats.   Lover Mourns for the Loss of Love, The.
Never Give All the Heart.
Young, K.   Letters from the North Star.
Zarco.   My Worst Fear.
Zisquit.   Word before the Last about Loss, A.

Lot (Bible)
Helwig.   Lot.
Hope, A.   Lot and His Daughters II.
Lot and His Daughters I.
Kaufman, S.   His Wife.

Louisiana
As-Sabah.   Jubilee.
Hemans.   Stranger in Louisiana, The.
Kyei.   African in Louisiana.
Whitman, W.   I Saw in Louisiana a Live-Oak
Growing.

Love
Abu Sa'id.   I Asked My Love.
Agee.   Permit Me Voyage.
Allen, A.   This River.

Amadiume.   Union, The.
Ball, A.   Jazz.
Bell, M.   Being in Love.
Betjeman.   Myfanwy.
Bogardus.   Narcissus to Echo.
Breton, A.   Free Union.
Brodsky, J.   Love Song.
Butler, S.   Love.
Campbell, R.   Sisters, The.
Clanchy, K.   Recognition.
Coulehan, J.   Lovesickness: A Medieval Text.
Croly.   Domestic Love.
Dickey, W.   Plot, The.
Dillon, G.   Hours of the Day, The.
Dugan, A.   Letter to Eve.
Duncan, R.   Eyesight II.
Ford, C.   There's No Place to Sleep in This Bed,
Tanguy.
France, L.   Mess With It.
Gander.   Deflection Toward the Relative Minor.
Garrett, E.   Love's Parallel.
Gladding.   Worsted Heather.
Gomez.   My Chakabuku Mama: A Comic Tale.
Greenlaw.   Earliest Known Representation of a
Storm in Western Art, The.
Love from a Foreign City.
Guiducci.   Perhaps One Day There Will Be
Ways.
Hahn, S.   Incontinence.
Hannah, S.   End of Love, The.
Where is Talcott Parsons Now?
Henry, P.   Love Birds.
Hiestand, E.   Day Lily and the Fox, The.
Hochman.   Manhattan Pastures.
Hollander, J.   Carmen Ancillae.
Hoover, P.   Theoretical People.
Howe, F.   Doubt.
Jackson, R.   Poem That Was Once Called
'Desperate' But Is Now Striving to Become the
Perfect Love Poem.
Jonson, B.   Song: To Celia.
Karp.   Harm.
Kaufman, S.   Emperor of China, The.
King, H.   Exequy, The.
Landon.   Bonds of Affection.
Lee, L.   Milkmaid.
Lehman.   Prophet's Lantern, The.
Luschei, G.   Pozo Basket, The.
Luterman, A.   Justice of the Peace, The.
MacDonogh.   She Walked Unaware.
Meredith, W.   Traveling Boy.
Mesens.   Arid Husband, The.
Motherwell.   Jeanie Morrison.
Murray, G.   On Being Disabled by Light at
Dawn in the Wilderness.
Nims, J.   Young Ionia, The.
O'Reilly, M.   House Call to a Man with
Parkinson's Disease, A.
Potter.
Oswald, A.   Ballad of a Shadow.
Peacock, M.   My God, Why Are You Crying?
Perreault, J.   Metaphysical Paintings, The.
Piercy.   Morning Love Song.
Pollok.   Happiness.
Porter, C.   Let's Do It, Let's Fall in Love.
Randolph, T.   Milkmaid's Epithalamium, The.
Reavey.   Dismissing Progress and Its
Progenitors.
Reid, D.   Between Aphorisms.
Rothman, D.   Shape of Water Most Like Love,
The.
Roughton.   Soluble Noughts and Crosses; or,
California, Here I Come.
Samaras, N.   Aubade: Macedonia.
Shapiro, K.   V-Letter.
Shillaber, B.   Picture, A.
Shinder.   One Secret That Has Carried, The.
Stowe.   Only a Year.
"Tanaquil."   Very Young Man Speaks, A.
Taylor, J.   My Mother.
Unknown, fr. Terezin Concentration Camp.
Forgotten.
Letter to Daddy, A.
Vallejo.   Poem to Be Read and Sung.
Walders, D.   Anniversary.
White, D.   Epistle of Love and of Consolation

unto Israel, An.
Wiese, B.   Going Home Madly.
Winters, Y.   To My Infant Daughter.
Wojahn.   Inside, The.
Yeats.   Brown Penny.
Young, D.   Sources of the Delaware.
See also **Affection; Companionship and
Companions; Courtship; Dating; Desire;
Erotic Love; Lust; Sex; Sexuality**

Love Poetry
Jackson, R.   Poem That Was Once Called
'Desperate' But Is Now Striving to Become the
Perfect Love Poem.

Lovebirds
Hippolyte.   Revo Lyric.
Tomlinson, C.   In the Borghese Gardens.

Lowell, Robert
Bishop, E.   North Haven.
"Pygge."   Robert Lowell's Notebook.

Lowry, Malcolm
Lowry, M.   Epitaph: "Malcolm Lowry."

Loyalty
Ager, M.   Mamma Goes Where Papa Goes.
Berlin.   Always.
Boland, E.   Ready for Flight.
Burns, R.   O [or Oh] Wert Thou in the Cauld
Blast.
Song: "O my love's [or luve's or love is or luve
is] like a red, red rose."
Caldwell, A.   I Know That You Know.
Cassells.   Beautiful Signor.
Columbo, R.   Prisoner of Love.
Comden, B.   Thanks a Lot, but No Thanks.
Creeley.   She Went to Stay.
Crosby, F.   I Am Thine, O Lord.
Erdman, E.   No, No, Nora.
Green, A.   Thanks a Lot, but No Thanks.
Hardy, T.   Broken Appointment, A.
Holiner, M.   You Can't Stop Me from Lovin'
You.
Kern, J.   You Never Knew About Me.
Kipling, R.   Gunga Din.
Lovelace, R.   To Lucasta, from Prison.
Malloch, D.   Manly Love.
Melville, H.   Enthusiast, The.
Montgomerie, A.   Sonet: "Thocht Polibus,
pisander, and with them."
Nairne.   Will Ye No Come Back Again?
Nichols, A.   You Can't Stop Me from Lovin'
You.
Porter, C.   Always True to You in My Fashion.
My Heart Belongs to Daddy.
Previn, A.   Thanks a Lot, but No Thanks.
Smith, C.   Stanzas: "Ah! think'st thou, Laura,
then, that wealth."
Song.   Youngest Daughter, The.
Wilder, A.   I'll Be Around.
Wodehouse, P.   You Never Knew About Me.
Yellen, J.   Mamma Goes Where Papa Goes.
Youmans, V.   I Know That You Know.

Luanda, Angola
Wendel.   We Shall Return, Luanda.

Luck
Adair, T.   Everything Happens to Me.
Ahlert, F.   Ain't That the Way It Goes?
Bernstein, L.   Lucky to Be Me.
Blake, E.   You're Lucky to Me.
Blane, R.   Ev'ry Time.
Broumas, O.   If I Yes.
David, M.   I'm Just a Lucky So-and-So.
Dennis, M.   Everything Happens to Me.
Fitzgerald, R.   Favour.
Gaskill, C.   I Can't Believe That You're in Love
with Me.
Googe.   Of Money.
Hay, J.   Good Luck and Bad.
Heath-Stubbs.   Unpredicted, The.
Herrick.   Coming of Good Luck, The.
Hewitt, J.   Local Poet, A.
Hughes, L.   Bad Luck Card.
Luck.
Loesser.   Luck, Be a Lady.
McDonald, C.   Nightfishing.
Meddemmen, J. G.   L. R. D. G.
Merrill, B.   People.

Rossetti, C.   Queen of Hearts, The.
Shepherd, R.   Motive.
Stern, G.   Lucky Life.
Straus, M.   Luck.
Styne, J.   People.
Turk, R.   Ain't That the Way It Goes?
Wong, J.   Good Luck Gold.
See also Chance; Fate; Fortune; Chance

Lucknow, India
Whittier.   Pipes at Lucknow, The.

Lullabies
Auden.   Lullaby: "Lay your sleeping head, my love."
Barber, D.   Nocturne.
Bennett, G.   Secret.
Causley.   Mary's Song.
Cox, P.   Mouse's Lullaby, The.
Dubin, A.   Lullaby of Broadway.
Field, E.   Wynken, Blynken, and Nod.
Fordham.   Serenade: "Sleep, love sleep."
Gascoigne.   Lullaby [or Lullabie] of a Lover, The.
Herrick.   Upon a child.
Jacobsen, J.   Primer, The.
Mother Goose.   Rock-a-bye, baby, thy cradle is green.
Peacock, M.   Lullaby: "Big as a down duvet the night."
Prelutsky.   Mother Goblin's Lullaby.
Shearing, G.   Lullaby of Birdland.
Sidney, S.   Sleep, Baby Mine, Desire.
Tennyson, A.   Minnie and Winnie.
Unknown.   All the Pretty Little Horses.
   Lullaby of Donald Gorm, by his Nurse.
Wordsworth, D.   Cottager to Her Infant, (By My Sister), The.

Lumbering and Lumbermen
Drummond, W.   Log Jam, The.
Kinnell.   Man Splitting Wood in the Daybreak, The.
Morris, G.   Woodman, Spare That Tree.
Rosen, M.   This Morning.
Scott, D.   At the Cedars.
Snyder, G.   Getting in the Wood.
Wagoner, D.   Elegy for a Forest Clear-Cut by the Weyerhaeuser Company.
   To a Farmer Who Hung Five Hawks on His Barbed Wire.
Whitman, W.   Broad-Ax, The.

Lunch
Bachner.   Little Mouse, The.
Burris.   On Living with a Fat Woman in Heaven.
Charach, R.   Question of Vitamins, A.
Nye, N.   Lunch in Nablus City Park.
O'Hara, F.   Step Away from Them, A.
Sondheim.   Ladies Who Lunch, The.

Lungs
Bush, D.   Pneumoconiosis.

Lungworms
Fuller, R.   Autobiography of a Lungworm.

Lust
Auden.   Love Feast, The.
Baraka.   New World, The.
Barot, R.   Portishead Suite.
Betjeman.   Senex.
Blackburn, P.   Once-over, The.
   Slogan, The.
Blake, W.   Desire and Jealousy.
   Visions of the Daughters of Albion.
Brownjohn.   Looking at Her.
Cope, J.   Copula.
Crowley, A.   Ballad of Passive Paederasty, A.
   Dedicace.
   Go into the Highways and Hedges, And Compel Them to Come In.
DeSylva, B. G.   Do It Again.
Drayton.   To His Coy Love, A Canzonet.
Drummond, W.   For a Lady's Summons of Non-Entry.
Dryden, J.   Song: "SYLVIA the fair, in the bloom of fifteen."
Emanuel, L.   Outside Room Six.
France, L.   In Kind.
   New York Spring.

Garnett, R.   Dealing Scraps.
Georgiou, E.   Intimate Mixture.
   Talkin' Trash.
Gershwin, G.   Do It Again.
Gibran.   Love.
Goodman, M.   New Comers.
Graham, W.   Letter VI.
Graves, R.   Blue-Fly, The.
   Down, Wanton, Down!
   Galatea and Pygmalion.
Griffin, P.   To His Importunate Mistress.
Hatton, R.   Epithalamium: "Hymen hath together tied."
Herrick.   Julia's Petticoat.
   Poet Loves a Mistress, but Not to Marry, The.
   Vine, The.
   Vision, The.
Housman, A.   When I Watch the Living Meet.
Jennings, E.   Thinking of Love.
Johnson, L.   Dark Angel, The.
Jonson, B.   On Groin.
Jordan, J.   Sunflower Sonnet Number One.
Kaufman, S.   Emperor of China, The.
Komunyakaa.   Seven Deadly Sins.
Kunitz, S.   She Wept, She Railed.
MacNeice.   Libertine, The.
Manrique, J.   Tarzan.
May, E.   To Barba.
Melville, H.   After the Pleasure Party.
Miles, S.   Hares, The.
Miller, V.   Dirge in Jazz Time.
Myles, E.   Sleepless.
Nelson, M.   Balance.
Norse.   I Would Not Recommend Love.
O'Hara, F.   Poem: "I don't know as I get what D.H. Lawrence is driving at."
Olds, S.   Greed and Aggression.
   Sex without Love.
Orton, B.   Love Poem.
Pearlberg, G. G.   Dog Star.
   Sailor.
Pitter.   But for Lust.
Read, S.   Sic et Non.
Rich, A.   Two Songs.
Robinson, E.   John Evereldown.
Rochester, J.   Ramble in St. James's Park, A.
Rosenberg, L.   Married Love.
San Juan.   End of the Affair, The.
Sanchez, S.   Poem for My Father, A.
Shepherd, R.   Eros in His Striped Blue Shirt.
   That Man.
Simpson, L.   Summer Storm.
Southerne.   Song: "Pursuing beauty, men descry."
Stevenson, A.   Sous-Entendu.
Suckling, S.   Upon My Lady Carlisle's Walking in Hampton Court Garden.
Swinburne.   Aholibah.
Sylvester, J.   Arrowhead Christian Center and No-Smoking Luncheonette.
Taylor, J.   Epigram: "Lusty wench as nimble as an eel, A."
Unknown.   Hares on the Mountain.
   Nine Times a Night.
Villiers.   Cabin-Boy, The.
Walsh, W. et al.   Imperfect Enjoyment, The.
   Song: "If she be not as kind as fair."
Waniek.   Balance.
Whitman, W.   I Am He That Aches with Love.
   Native Moments.
   Spontaneous Me.
Wilbur.   Loves of the Puppets.
Wither.   Epigram: "Women, as some men say, unconstant be."
See also Erotic Love; Sex

Lutes
Campion, T.   When to Her Lute Corinna [or Corrina] Sings.
Drummond, W.   To His Lute.
Suckling, S.   Song to a Lute, A.
Waller, E.   Of My Lady Isabella Playing on the Lute.
Wilde, O.   Hélas!
Wyatt, S.   Blame Not My Lute.
   My Lute, Awake!

Luther, Martin
Auden.   Luther.
Steele, T.   Wartburg, 1521–22, The.

Lying
Clarke, C.   What Goes Around Comes Around, or The Proof Is in the Pudding.
Forché.   Taking Off My Clothes.
Parker, D.   Unfortunate Coincidence.
Stone, J.   Confabulation.
See also Lies and Lying

Lynching
Allan, L.   Strange Fruit.
Brown, S.   Sam Smiley.
Derricotte.   Note on My Son's Face, A.
Dunbar, P.   Haunted Oak, The.
Dunbar-Nelson.   April Is on the Way.
Durem.   I Know I'm Not Sufficiently Obscure.
Emanuel, J.   Emmett Till.
Evans, M.   I Am a Black Woman.
Ford, C.   Plaint.
Gilmore, M.   Fourteen Men.
Harjo, J.   Strange Fruit.
Hayden, R.   Night, Death, Mississippi.
Hughes, L.   Silhouette.
   Song for a Dark Girl.
Lorde.   Afterimages.
McKay, C.   Lynching, The.
Moorer.   Eutawville Lynching, The.
   Lynching.
   Retribution.
Moss, T.   Lynching, The.
Pratt, M.   Red String.
Rosten.   Black Boy.
Skeeter.   Western Trail Cook, 1880.
St. John, P.   Lynching and Burning.
Tate, A.   Swimmers, The.
Toomer.   Portrait in Georgia.
Toure, A.   Frontier of Rage, The.
Wright, R.   Between the World and Me.

Lynx
Eaton, C.   Lynx, The.

Lyonnesse, Cornwall
De la Mare.   Sunk Lyonesse.
Hardy, T.   When I Set Out for Lyonnesse.

Lysergic Acid (LSD)
Ginsberg, A.   Wales Visitation.
Hollo.   Discovery of LSD a True Story, The.

M

"MacDiarmid, Hugh" (Christopher Murray Grieve)
Morgan, E.   To Hugh MacDiarmid.

Mac Liammóir, Micheál
Durcan.   Micheál Mac Liammóir.

Macbeth
Lomax, M.   Gruoch.

Machiavelli, Niccolò
Sansom, A.   Prince.

Machines
Ammons, A. R.   Needs.
Benét, S.   Nightmare Number Three.
Frost, R.   Egg and the Machine, The.
Kenney.   Sawmill.
Kipling, R.   McAndrew's Hymn.
Moore, M.   To a Steam Roller.
Snyder, G.   Removing the Plate of the Pump on the Hydraulic System of the Backhoe.
Tomlinson, C.   Crane, The.
Unknown.   John Henry.
Untermeyer, L.   Portrait of a Machine.
Wilcox, E.   Engine, The.
Wordsworth, W.   Steamboats, Viaducts, and Railways.

Machismo
Norse.   I'm Not a Man.

MacLeish, Archibald
Sandburg, C.   On a Flimmering Floom You Shall Ride.

MacNeice, Louis
Auden.   Cave of Making, The.
MacNeice.   Autobiography.
Mahon.   In Carrowdore Churchyard.

Mad Song (genre)
De la Mare. Song of the Mad Prince, The.
Herrick. Mad Maid's Song, The.
Holcroft. Fool's Song.
Unknown. Tom o' Bedlam's Song.

Madness
Allison, D. To the Bone.
Antin. List of the Delusions of the Insane / What They Are Afraid Of, A.
Baraka. Preface to a Twenty Volume Suicide Note.
Bayliss. Apocalypse and Resurrection.
Bishop, E. Visits to St. Elizabeths.
Blake, W. Mad Song.
To Flaxman.
Boland, E. Glass King, The.
Brass. I Have This Vision of Madness.
Breeze. Riddym Ravings (The Mad Woman's Poem).
Buddy. Callin Buddy / Bolden.
Bukowski. Drooling Madness at St. Liz.
Butler, C. E. Letter to the Survivors.
Carkesse. His Rule of Behaviour: If You Are Civil, I Am Sober.
On the Doctors' Telling Him that till He Left off Making Verses He Was Not Fit to be Discharged.
Carson, C. Asylum.
Chasin. Getting the News.
Clare, J. I Am.
De la Mare. Motley.
DiPalma. Pink Maniac, A.
Donaldson, W. You're Driving Me Crazy (What Did I Do?).
Dowson. To One in Bedlam.
Eady. My Mother, If She Had Won Free Dance Lessons.
Engvick, W. Crazy in the Heart.
Fitzgerald, E. 74.
Floyd. Private Ian Godwin, U. S. M. C.
Galvin, P. Madwoman of Cork, The.
Ginsberg, A. II.
Howl.
Guest, B. Sassafras.
Henderson, R. Five Foot Two, Eyes of Blue (Has Anybody Seen My girl?).
Herrick. Mad Maid's Song, The.
Howard, R. Nikolaus Mardruz to his Master Ferdinand, Count of Tyrol, 1565.
Hugo, R. What Thou Lovest Well Remains American.
Irving, M. Marching Still.
Jarrell. Seele im Raum.
Jeffers, R. Cassandra.
Johnson, L. Five Nights of Bleeding.
Johnson, T. Until He Comes.
Jones, P. Song: "I have so little sorrow."
Justice, D. Counting the Mad.
On a Painting by Patient B of the Independence State Hospital for the Insane.
Kaufman, B. Would You Wear My Eyes?
Kavanagh, P. Come Dance with Kitty Stobling.
Kenyon, J. Travel: After a Death.
Levertov. Mad Song.
Levine, P. On the Edge.
Lillard. Bushed.
Livingston, M. Why?
Lovelace, R. Cupid Far Gone.
Mahon. As It Should Be.
McClure, M. May Morn.
McDonald, N. Hatters, The.
Melville, H. Berg, The.
Merry. Madness.
Mew. Farmer's Bride, The.
Ken.
Millay, E. Siege.
Mozeen. Bedlamite, The.
Nichol. Monotones.
O'Lahsen, M. Dead Erect, The.
Okara. To Adhiambo.
Opie. To a Maniac.
Owen, W. Mental Cases.
Padgett, R. First Drift.
Parra, N. Pilgrim, The.
Plath. Life, A.
Poe. Conqueror Worm, The.

Pogson, P. In Dreams.
Roberts, M. Madwoman at Rodmell.
Roethke. Heard in a Violent Ward.
In a Dark Time.
Rukeyser, M. Rational Man.
Russell, B. Crazy She Calls Me.
Sexton. Noon Walk on the Asylum Lawn.
Ringing the Bells.
Shange. Elegance in the Extreme.
Sitwell, D. Madwoman in the Park, The.
Smith, C. On Being Cautioned against Walking on an Headland Overlooking the Sea, Because It Was Frequented by a Lunatic.
Supposed to Be Written by Werter.
Smith, S. Deserter, The.
St. John, D. Dolls.
Iris.
Stein, G. White Hunter, A.
Stevenson, A. From an Asylum; Kathy Chattle to Her Mother, Ruth Arbeiter.
Stickney, T. Age in Youth.
Pity.
Strong, L. Mad Woman of Punnet's Town, The.
Symons, A. Nerves.
Szumigalski. Visitor's Parking.
Taylor, A. Maniac's Song, The.
Tennant, E. Mad Soldier, The.
Tighe. Wine, I Say! I'll Drink to Madness!
Tucker, M. Crazed.
Unknown. Fowls [or Foweles or Fowles] in the Frith.
Loving Mad Tom.
There Was a Man and He Was Mad.
Tom o' Bedlam's Song.
Watts, I. Hurry of the Spirits, in a Fever and Nervous Disorders, The.
Wayman. Another Poem about the Madness of Women.
Weaver, M. Appaloosa, The.
Weiner, H. Little Books / 137 / Silence Mar 22 79.
Weiners. Poem for the Insane, A.
Wilbur. What is the opposite of nuts?
Wilder, A. Crazy in the Heart.
Williams, W. To Elsie.
Wylie. Nebuchadnezzar.
Yeats. Crazed Girl, A.
Crazy Jane Talks with the Bishop.
See also **Mental Illness**

Madonnas
Muldoon, P. Bearded Woman, by Ribera, The.
Rafferty, P. In the Madonna Dell' Orto.
Rossetti, D. For "Our Lady of the Rocks."

Madrid, Spain
Garlick, R. Capitals.
Hughes, L. Madrid—1937.
O'Hara, F. Madrid.

Magazines
Aiken, J. Do It Yourself.
Codrescu. Paper on Humor.
Gilbert, S. Ladies' Home Journal, The.
Gioia. My Confessional Sestina.
Herd. Gia.
Wilbur. Playboy.
See also **Journalism and Journalists; Newspapers**

Magdalene, Mary
Gibran. Mary Magdalen.
Peck, J. Monologue of the Magdalene.
Spofford. Magdalen.
See also **Mary Magdalene**

Magi
Baranczak, S. Three Magi, The.
Davis, D. Christmas Poem, A.
Dickey, J. Magus, The.
Eliot, T. Journey of the Magi.
Erskine, J. Kings and Stars.
Fiskin. Magi, The.
Glück, L. Magi, The.
Godolphin. Hymn: "Lord, when the wise men came from far[r]."
Guthrie, R. Magi, The.
Hawker. Mystic Magi, The.
Hopkins, J. We Three Kings of Orient Are.
Kunitz, S. He.
Longfellow, H. Three Kings, The.

Merwin, W. S. Carol of the Three Kings.
Pilling. Adoration of the Magi, The.
Plath. Magi.
Ralegh, S. On the Card[e]s, and Dice.
Wanley. Royal[l] Presents.
Williams, C. Kings Came Riding.
Williams, W. Adoration of the Kings, The.
Gift, The.
Yeats. Magi, The.

Magic
Arlen, H. That Old Black Magic.
We're Off to See the Wizard (The Wonderful Wizard of Oz).
Baraka. Ka 'Ba.
Cahn, S. It's Magic.
Cooley, N. Mary Warren's Sampler.
Mother: Dorcas Good, The.
Evasco, M. Dancing a Spell.
Forman, R. We Are the Young Magicians.
Henderson-Holmes. Goodhousekeeping #17.
Hutchinson, P. Bright after Dark.
Jacobs, H. It is not Just.
Jenkins, L. Walking through a Wall.
Keats. La Belle Dame sans Merci [A Ballad].
Kunitz, S. Testing-Tree, The.
Lorde. Summer Oracle.
MacEwen, G. Manzini; Escape Artist.
Mandel, E. Houdini.
Mercer, J. That Old Black Magic.
Muir, E. Merlin.
Nelson, M. 56 Westervelt.
Patchen. Magical Mouse, The.
Reed, I. Black Cock, The.
Stanton, M. Conjurer, The.
Styne, J. It's Magic.
Unknown. Another Man Done Gone.
First Nowell, The.
Magic Formula.
Two Magicians, The.
You May Go But This Will Bring You Back.
Wohlfeld. That Which Is Fugitive, That Which Is Medicinally Sweet or Alterable to Gold, That Which Is Substantiated by Unscientific Means.

Magnolias
Brown, L. Magnolia.
Coffman. Likely.
Hovanessian, D. On Commonwealth Avenue and Brattle Street.
Humphrey, D. April in Houston.
Wicks, S. Moderato.

Magpies
Glover, D. Magpies, The.
Hanzlicek, C. On the Road Home.
Parker, A. Magpie.
Unknown. Magpies.
Wilson, T. Magpies in Picardy.

Magritte, René
Melly. Homage to René Magritte.
Sorby. Man without a Middle, The.

Mahon, Derek
Longley, M. Letter to Derek Mahon.

Mail and Mailmen
Auden. Night Mail, The.
Barresi. Late Summer News.
Cholmondeley-Pennell. Night Mail North, The.
Gibson, W. Advice to Travelers.
Hamill, G. Song of the GPO, A.
Janeczko. Mail King.
Jarrell. Hope.
Jenkins, L. Appointed Rounds.
Kennedy, X. Epitaph for a Postal Clerk.
Kinnell. Getting the Mail.
Kunitz, S. Reflection by a Mailbox.
Matthews, W. Mail Order Catalogs.
Pilling. Encounter at the Post Office Counter.
Tucker, M. Mail Has Come, The.
Unknown. Meaning of a Letter, The.
Omagh Post Office Rhyme.
Whitman, W. Orange Buds by Mail from Florida.
Williams, W. To Greet a Letter-Carrier.
See also **Letters**

Maine (state)
Clampitt. Baroque Sunburst, A.

Eberhart, R.   Chart Indent.
Lowell, R.   Skunk Hour.
   Water.
Millay, E.   Exiled.
Morris, H.   Maine Lake at Night.
Nowlan.   For Jean Vincent d'Abbadie, Baron
   St.-Castin.
Oppen.   Penobscot.
Quagliano.   Edward Hopper's 'Lighthouse at
   Two Lights.'
Toomer.   Merl.
Van Duyn.   Moose in the Morning, Northern
   Maine.

Malachy, Saint
Merton.   St. Malachy.

Malaga, Spain
Hutchinson, P.   Málaga.

Malawi
Chipasula.   Love Poem for My Country, A.
Mapanje.   On His Royal Blindness Paramount
   Chief Kwangala.

Malcolm X (Malcolm Little)
Baraka.   Poem for Black Hearts, A.
Baraka, R.   I Remember Malcolm.
Brooks, G.   Malcolm X.
Clifton, L.   Malcolm.
Conyus.   Confession to Malcolm.
Hayden, R.   El-Hajj Malik El-Shabazz.
Jones, L. *et al.*   Poem for Black Hearts, A.
Knight, E.   It Was a Funky Deal.
Madhubuti.   Malcolm Spoke / Who Listened?
   Possibilities: Remembering Malcolm X.
Neal, L.   Malcolm X—an Autobiography.
Smith, W.   Malcolm.
Walker, M.   For Malcolm X.
Warr, M.   Malcolm Is 'Bout More Than Wearing
   a Cap.
Whitlow.   Poem for the Children.

Maldon, Battle of (991)
Unknown.   Battle of Maldon, The.

Mallards
Barnard, M.   Solitary, The.
Dupree, E.   At Present I Am Working as a
   Security Guard.

Malls
Scrimgeour, J.   Lines Started Outside Filene's
   Basement.
See also **Shopping Malls**

Malta
Forbes, J.   Malta.

Man in the Moon
Hewett, D.   Moon-Man.

Man, Primitive
Heaney, S.   Tollund Man, The.
See also **Cavemen**

Man-of-War Birds
Whitman, W.   To the Man-of-War Bird.

Mandalay, Burma
Kipling, R.   Mandalay.

Mandela, Nelson
Smith, P.   Finding His Fist.
Soyinka.   "No!" He Said.

Mangan, James Clarence
Kinsella, T.   Clarence Mangan.

Mangoes
Adisa.   Cultural Trip, A.
   Ethiopia Unda a Jamaican Mango Tree.
Bethune, L.   Today Tutu Is Beating the Same
   Burru As Me.
Cabico, R.   Mango Poem.
Gotera.   First Mango.
Hernández Cruz.   Problems With Hurricanes.
Waniek.   Canticle for Abba Jacob, A.

Manhattan
Berlin.   Manhattan Madness.
Blake, E.   Tan Manhattan.
Dubin, A.   She's a Latin from Manhattan.
Harburg.   Moon About Town.
Hochman.   Manhattan Pastures.
Porter, C.   Down in the Depths.
Schulman.   New Netherland, 1654.
See also **New York City**

Manitoba, Canada
Purdy, A.   Wilderness Gothic.

Mankind
Aiken, C.   Tetélestai.
Allston.   Word: Man, A.
Arnold, M.   In Harmony with Nature.
Arp.   People.
Ashbery.   Hotel Lautréamont.
Baraka.   Balboa, the Entertainer.
Berry, W.   Slip, The.
Berryman.   Gislebertus' Eve.
   Traveller, The.
Bishop, E.   In the Waiting Room.
Browning, R.   Parting at Morning.
Bryant, W.   Crowded Street, The.
Burns, R.   Epistle to a Young Friend.
   For A' That and A' That ['Is there, for honest
   poverty'].
Campbell, T.   Last Man, The.
Cavendish, M.   Dialogue betwixt Man, and
   Nature, A.
Char.   Man flees suffocation.
Conquest.   Horror Comic.
Couani.   Obvious, The.
Cowley, M.   Ernest.
Cummings, E.   Pity This Busy
   Monster,Manunkind.
Davie.   Christening, A.
   In the Stopping Train.
De la Mare.   All That's Past.
Donne.   To the Countess of Salisbury.
Drummond, W.   Madrigal: "This world a
   hunting is."
Dunbar, P.   Slow Through the Dark.
Ehrhart.   Making the Children Behave.
Finch, R.   Collective Portrait, The.
Flecknoe.   Ant, The.
Frost, R.   Vantage Point, The.
Gray, T.   Ode on a Distant Prospect of Eton
   College.
Guiterman.   Brief Essay on Man.
Gunn, T.   Last Man, The.
Hardy, T.   Heredity.
Henry, B.   Garage Sale.
Herbert, G.   Man.
   Pulley, The.
Hewitt, J.   Ram's Horn, The.
Hopkins, G.   Epithalamion: "Hark, hearer, hear
   what I do; lend a thought now, make believe."
   Lantern Out of Doors, The.
   Sea and the Skylark, The.
   To His Watch.
Howe, F.   What We Learned.
Ignatow, D.   Ritual Three.
Jarrell.   Islands, The.
Jeffers, R.   Inquisitors, The.
   Science.
Jemie.   Iroko.
Johnson, G.   Common Dust.
Johnson, S.   Scholar's Life, The.
   Vanity of Human Wishes, The; The Tenth Satire
   of Juvenal Imitated.
Jurmann, W.   All God's Chillun Got Rhythm.
Kaufman, B.   Geneology.
   To My Son Parker, Asleep in the Next Room.
Kayo.   War.
Keats.   Human Seasons, The.
King, H.   Sic Vita.
Kipling, R.   If—.
Knevet.   Habitation, The.
Krohn.   Farmer's Song at Can Tho.
Lawrence, D.   Elemental.
   When Wilt Thou Teach the People?
Levertov.   Crystal Night.
   Peachtree, The.
   When We Look Up.
Levine, P.   Animals Are Passing from Our
   Lives.
   How Much Earth.
Longfellow, H.   Kéramos.
Lowry, M.   Volcano is Dark, The.
MacCaig.   Basking Shark.
MacDiarmid, H.   Glass of Pure Water, The.
   With the Herring Fishers.
Mahapatra, J.   October Morning, An.
Markham, E.   Man with the Hoe, The.
Merwin, W. S.   For a Coming Extinction.
Millay, E.   Apostrophe to Man.

Milton.   On the Detraction Which Followed
   upon My Writing Certain Treatises.
Muir, E.   Animals, The.
Neruda.   Walking Around.
Oliver, M.   Wild Geese.
Olson, C.   In Cold Hell, in Thicket.
Padgett, R.   Lucky Strikes.
Pound, E.   Meditatio.
   Return, The.
Pratt, E.   From Stone to Steel.
   Truant, The.
Raine, K.   Human Form Divine, The.
Raleigh.   Wishes of an Elderly Man, [Wished at
   a Garden Party, June 1914].
Rexroth, K.   Long Lifetime, A.
Rich, A.   For the Record.
Robinson, K.   Pontoon.
Rossetti, C.   Wednesday in Holy Week.
Rukeyser, M.   Myth.
Sandburg, C.   Wilderness.
Scalapino.   Considering How Exaggerated
   Music Is.
   Or a Play.
Senghor.   Man and Beast.
Sherwood, G.   Satire against Reason and
   Mankind, A.
Sisson.   Nature of Man, The.
Smith, B.   Black Mountain Blues.
Smith, S.   Away, Melancholy.
   Distractions and the Human Crowd.
   Man Is a Spirit.
   New Age, The.
Southwell.   Look[e] Home.
Swift, J.   Day of Judgement, The.
Swirszczynska.   Same Inside, The.
   Sea and the Man, The.
Taggard.   Fructus.
Tidjani-Cissé.   Of Colours and Shadows.
Vaughan, H.   Corruption.
   Man.
   Tempest, The.
   World, The (1).
Very.   Created, The.
   Origin of Man, I, The.
Whitman, W.   I Hear America Singing.
   On the Same Picture.
   One's-Self I Sing.
Wickham.   To Men.
Wilbur.   Ceremony.
Williams, W.   Clouds, The.
Winchilsea.   Spleen, The.
Wolfe, H.   Man.
Wordsworth, W.   Lines Written in Early Spring.
Wright, J.   Secret Gratitude, A.
Yeats.   Four Ages of Man, The.
   Sorrow of Love, The.

Mannequins
Epstein, D.   Mannequins.

Manners
Brown, E.   Beauty and the Prince Formerly
   Known as Beast.
Lee, P.   That's My Style.
See also **Etiquette**

Mantegna, Andrea
Rossetti, D.   For "An Allegorical Dance of
   Women" by Andrea Mantegna.

Mantle, Mickey
Fairchild.   Body and Soul.
Heyen.   Mantle.
Miller, E.   Players.

Maori
Habib.   Moment of Truth.
Kemp, J.   "When the Wild Goose Finds Food
   He Calls His Comrades"—*I Ching.*

Maple Trees
Espada.   All the People Who Are Now Red
   Trees.
Finch, P.   Acer.
Koch, K.   Down at the Docks.
Wright, J.   To a Troubled Friend.

Maps
Alexander, E.   Ode.
Anderson, D.   Executive Geochrone.
Ashbery.   Rivers and Mountains.
Bishop, E.   Map, The.

Blaser. Suddenly.
Bogan, L. Cartography.
Caddy, C. Three-Inch Reflector.
Couani. Map of the World, The.
Garlick, R. Map Reading.
Guernsey, B. Maps.
Gunn, T. Map of the City, A.
Hammial. Jane.
Herd. Missing.
Hinsey, E. *Planisféria*, Map of the World,
  Lisbon, 1554.
Hogan, L. Map.
Holmes, J. Map of My Country, A.
Le Pan. Incident, An.
Mullen, H. Roadmap.
Nemerov. Low-Level Cross-Country.
Oden. Private Letter to Brazil, A.
Owen, L. Chart Showing Rain, Winds,
  Isothermal Lines and Ocean Currents.

Marathon (race)
Cassells. Marathon.
Mann, C. Comrades Marathon, The.
Ward, J. Marathon.
Wilbur. Running.

Marathon, Battle of (490B.C.)
Graves, R. Persian Version, The.

Marble
Dickey, J. In the Marble Quarry.

March
Chamberlain, K. Riding the Lion, Riding the
  Lamb.
Coatsworth. March.
Housman, A. March.
Ledwidge. Twilight in Middle March, A.
Lewis, J. Garden Note II, March.
McKay, D. March Snow.
Merwin, W. S. Thorn Leaves in March.
Ray, H. March.
Reese, L. Mid-March.
Stevens, W. Not Ideas about the Thing but the
  Thing Itself.
  Vacancy in the Park.
Trommer, R. March.
Wordsworth, W. To My Sister.
  Written in March [While Resting on the Bridge
  at the Foot of Brother's Water].

Marching and Marches
Bennett, H. Flag Goes By, The.
Borawski. Some of Us Wear Pink Triangles.
Emerson, R. Days.
Gurney, I. Towards Lillers.
Košek, M. It All Depends on How You Look at
  It.
Mackintosh, E. Cha Till Maccruimein
  (Departure of the 4th Camerons).
Owen, W. Dulce et Decorum Est.
Radnóti. Forced March.
Rykard, R. Whole two weeks after The Million
  Man March, A; and still, if you'd ask me, this
  is all I could say about it.
Unknown. Drill's the Thing.
  Over the Hills and Far Away.
Unknown, fr. Terezin Concentration Camp.
  Closed Town, The.
Wilson, T. Magpies in Picardy.
See also **Parades**

Margaret, Saint
Constable, H. To Saint Margaret.

Marigolds
Herrick. How Marigolds Came Yellow.
  To Marygolds.
Reese, L. Fog.
Williams, W. Negro Woman, A.

Marijuana
Adisa. Ethiopia Unda a Jamaican Mango Tree.
Hughes, L. Gauge.
Jackson, M. L. Blunts.
Knight, E. As You Leave Me.
Padgett, R. Strawberries in Mexico.

Marin County, California
Jeffers, R. Clouds of Evening.

Marin, John
Booth, P. Marin.

Mariners
Southey, C. Mariner's Hymn.
See also **Sailing and Sailors**

Marines
D'Aguiar. Sound Bite.
See also **United States Marine Corps**

Markets
Balaban. Along the Mekong.
Brabazon. Victoria Market.
Brown, G. Hamnavoe Market.
Dumas, H. Knees of a Natural Man.
Forbes, C. Potlicker Blues.
Goodison. Kenscoff.
Hall, D. Ox Cart Man.
"Maurice." Victoria Markets Recollected in
  Tranquility, The.
Reese, L. Lavender Woman, The.
Simon, L. Hattie Went to Market.
St. John, P. Pearle's Poem.
Ungria, R. Commerce and the Man.
Unknown. Cries of London, The.
  Linstead Market.
Van Vliet. Old Champagne Glass.

Markiewicz, Constance Georgine, Countess
Yeats. In Memory of Eva Gore-Booth and Con
  Markievicz.

Marlborough, John Churchill, 1st Duke of
Southey, R. Battle of Blenheim, The.
Swift, J. Satirical Elegy on the Death of a Late
  Famous General, A.

Marley, Bob
Agard, J. For Bob Marley.
Berry, J. Sounds of a Dreamer.
Cooper, A. Stepping to da Muse/Sic.
D'Aguiar. Dread.
Gilbert, C. Chosen to Be Water.
Hippolyte. So Jah Sey.
Manley, R. Bob Marley's Dead.
Matthews, W. Elegy for Bob Marley, An.
McNeill, A. Bob Marley New King of the
  Music.
Philp, G. One Song.

Marmalade
Delmore, E. Marmalade.

Marriage
Adcock, F. Wife to Husband.
Ai. Anniversary, The.
  Twenty-Year Marriage.
Aig-Imoukhuede. One Wife for One Man.
Akhmadulina. Bride, The.
Alexander, P. Marriage of Sorts, A.
Alvi, M. Backgrounds.
  Carrying My Wife.
  Fish.
  Man Impregnated.
Amherst. Song for the Single Table on New
  Year's Day, A.
Anderson, D. Nightly News, The.
Ashbery. Decoy.
Atwood. Habitation.
Aytoun [*or* Ayton], R. Posy, A: "Dear love, I
  am resolved with thee to live."
Baillie, L. Werena My Heart Licht I Wad Dee.
Balderston. Anne Steele.
Ball, J. And This Is So.
Barber, M. Conclusion of a Letter to the Rev.
  Mr. C——, The.
Barnes, W. Bachelor, The.
Bateman, E. It's a Great Big Shame.
Beer, P. Faithful Wife, The.
Bergman, A. Letter.
Berrigan, T. Orange Jews.
Berryman. Canto Amor.
Bevington, L. Wrestling.
Biespiel, D. White Roses.
Blackburn, T. Lucky Marriage, The.
Blamire. O Donald! Ye Are Just the Man.
Blumenthal, M. Marriage, A.
Blunden. Forefathers.
Bock, J. (I'll Marry) the Very Next Man.
Bradstreet, A. To My Dear and Loving
  Husband.
Brodrick. Joe's Luck.
Brontë, E. Day Dream, A.
Brooke, R. Sonnet Reversed.

Brooks, G. Bronzeville Mother Loiters in
  Mississippi, A. Meanwhile, a Mississippi
  Mother Burns Bacon.
  To Be in Love.
Broome. Widow and Virgin Sisters, The.
Brown, S. Feminine Intuition.
  Marriage.
Browning, E. Aurora Leigh.
  First Book: Young Aurora's Fostermother.
  Sweetness of England, The.
  Year's Spinning, A.
Browning, R. Any Wife to Any Husband.
  Life in a Love.
  Love in a Life.
  My Last Duchess.
Buchanan, G. Song for Straphangers.
Burns, R. John Anderson, My Jo.
  Kellyburnbraes.
  Tam Glen.
  Whistle o'er the Lave o't.
Burr, A. Lynmouth Widow, A.
Butler, M. Listen.
Cahn, S. Love and Marriage.
Campbell, A. Before and After Marriage.
Carew, T. Hymeneal Song on the Nuptials of
  the Lady Anne Wentworth and the Lord
  Lovelace, An.
  On the Marriage of T. K. and C. C.: The
  Morning Stormy.
Carey, H. Sally in Our Alley.
Caruthers. Prayer of Any Husband.
Cary, A. Bridal Veil, The.
Cary, P. Psalm of Marriage.
  Shakespearian Readings.
Cassells. These Are Not Brushstrokes.
Cave. Elegy on a Maiden Name, An.
Cherry, K. Bride of Quietness, The.
Chudleigh. To the Ladies.
Clanchy, K. For a Wedding.
Clare, J. Married to a Soldier.
Clarke, A. Marriage.
Clarke, G. Overheard in County Sligo.
Clifton, H. Id.
Clover, J. Map Room, The.
Coleridge, M. Marriage.
Corn. Marriage in the Nineties, A.
Corso. Marriage.
  Song: "Oh, dear! Oh, me! Oh, my!"
Cox, M. Barbells of the Gods, The.
Crabbe. Marriage Ring, The.
Crashaw. Epitaph Upon Husband and Wife
  Who Died and Were Buried Together, An.
  On Marriage.
Creeley. Ballad of the Despairing Husband.
  Marriage, A.
  Naughty Boy.
  Wait for Me.
  Way, The.
  Wife, The.
Crozier, L. So This Is Love.
Cullen, C. Wind Bloweth Where It Listeth, The.
Cunningham, J. Holiday Gown.
Cushman, S. Make the Bed.
Davies, I. Angry Summer 28, The.
Davis, W. Sleep of the Insomniac, The.
Day, C. Who Drags the Fiery Artist Down?
Day, L. Reject Jell-o.
De Tabley. Nuptial Song.
Derricotte. Promise, The.
Di Prima. Poem in Praise of My Husband
  (Taos).
Dickinson, E. She Rose to His Requirement—
  Dropt.
Divakaruni. Brides Come to Yuba City, The.
Donaldson, W. Makin' Whoopee.
  Okay, Toots.
  Yes, Sir! That's My Baby.
Donne. Antiquary.
  Flea, The.
Dove, R. Beauty and the Beast.
Dubin, A. Remember Me?
Dufferin. Charming Woman, The.
  Mother's Lament, The.
Dugan, A. Love Song: I and Thou.
Duhamel. Art.
  How Much Is This Poem Going to Cost Me?

Sex with a Famous Poet.
Yes.
Duke, R. To Caelia.
Dunn, D. Land Love.
Durcan. Divorce Referendum, Ireland, 1986, The.
Edson, R. Ape.
Egerton, S. Emulation, The.
On My Wedding Day.
To One Who Said I Must Not Love.
Eliot, T. Dedication to My Wife, A.
Elmusa. Dream on the Same Mattress.
"Ephelia." To J.G. on the News of His Marriage.
"Field." I love you with my life.
So jealous of your beauty.
Field, E. April Fool, The.
Flatman. On Marriage.
Florsheim. Jewish Singles Event, The.
Fordham. Marriage.
Foster, A. Field.
Frost, R. Hill Wife, The.
Home Burial.
House Fear.
Impulse, The.
Loneliness.
Oft-Repeated Dream, The.
Fulton, A. My Second Marriage to My First Husband.
Garrett, E. Grandfather's Mint.
Gerstler. Marriage.
Gioia. Summer Storm.
Glück, L. Edge, The.
Horse.
Gladding. Fisherman's Wife, The.
Worsted Heather.
Goldsmith, O. Double Transformation, The.
Gomez, A. Chocolate Confessions.
Goodman, M. Man and Wife.
Gotera. First Mango.
Graves, R. Call It a Good Marriage.
Henry and Mary.
Slice of Wedding Cake, A.
Greenhalgh, C. My Funny Valentine.
Of Love, Death and the Sea-Squirt.
Griffiths, S. Mines in Sepia Tint, The.
Gylys, B. Family Reunion—Aunt Vern's Two Cents.
Hacker, M. Eight Days in April.
Harington [or Harrington]. Author to His Wife, of a Woman's Eloquence, The.
Harington, J. Husband to Wife.
Wife to Husband.
Harms. Soon.
Tomorrow, We'll Dance in America.
Harper, M. Elvin's Blues.
Hatton, R. Epithalamium: "Hymen hath together tied."
Hayley. To Mrs. Hayley, On her Voyage to America. 1784.
Haynes, C. Any Wife or Husband.
Heaney, S. Cana Revisited.
Mother of the Groom.
Hearson. Nomenclaturik.
Henderson, R. I'm Sitting on Top of the World.
Herder. Esthonian Bridal Song.
Herrick. Entertainment, or Porch-Verse, at the Marriage of Mr. Henry Northleigh [or Hen. Northly] and the Most Witty Mrs. Lettice Yard, The.
Epitaph upon a Sober Matron, An.
Epithalamy to Sir Thomas Southwell and His Lady, An.
Nuptiall Song, or Epithalamie, on Sir Clipseby Crew and His Lady, A.
Poet Loves a Mistress, but Not to Marry, The.
Hershenson. Husbands and Wives.
Hesketh. Dilemma.
Hewett, D. This Version of Love.
Hodgson, R. Silver Wedding.
Holbrook, D. Maternity Gown.
Hollo. Wasp Sex Myth (One).
Wasp Sex Myth (Two).
Hope, A. Advice to Young Ladies.
Hopkins, G. Epithalamion: "Hark, hearer, hear what I do; lend a thought now, make believe."

Hovanessian, D. Mixed Marriage.
Howard, R. 1915: A Pre-Raphaelite Ending, London.
Hughes, T. Her Husband.
Ibn Ezra, Moses. Dying Wife to Her Husband, A.
Ignatow, D. Suite for Marriage, A.
Ingelow. Long White Seam, The.
Jackson, R. Jamal's Lamentation.
Jarrell. Man Meets a Woman in the Street, A.
Jemmat. Rural Lass, The.
Jennings, E. One Flesh.
Johnson, M. F. Widow's Remarriage, The.
Jonson, B. Epithalamion: or, a Song.
On Giles and Joan.
Justice, D. But That Is Another Story.
Kalia, M. After Eight Years of Marriage.
Kasdorf. Eve's Striptease.
Kelly, B. Young Wife's Lament.
Kipling, R. Sergeant's Weddin', The.
Kunitz, S. Route Six.
Landon. Enchanted Island, The.
Marriage Vow, The.
Larkin, P. Maiden Name.
Self's the Man.
Whitsun Weddings, The.
Lawrence, D. Wedding Morn.
Young Wife, A.
Lear, E. Owl and the Pussy-Cat, The.
Ledwidge. Wife of Llew, The.
Leithauser. Old Bachelor Brother.
Levertov. About Marriage.
Ache of Marriage, The.
Wedding-Ring.
Levy, A. Ballad of Religion and Marriage, A.
Lewis, E. Advice to a Young Lady Lately Married.
Lewis, M. Alonzo the Brave and the Fair Imogine.
Lewis, S. I'm Sitting on Top of the World.
Lewisohn, L. Together.
Linden, M. Marriage Vow.
Lindsay, L. Auld Robin Gray.
Loesser. Adelaide's Lament.
Make a Miracle.
Logghe. Mixed Marriage.
Lovelace, R. Anniversary on the Hymeneals of My Noble Kinsman, Thomas Stanley, Esquire, An.
Lowell, A. Decade, [A].
Lowell, R. Flaw, The.
Man And Wife.
To Speak of Woe That Is in Marriage.
M–rt–n. Humble Wish, The.
MacDiarmid, H. O Wha's the Bride?
MacDonagh, D. Prothalamium.
MacIntyre, S. Letters from the Concertina File 1939–1940.
MacLeish. Unfinished History.
MacSweeney. Ode Long Kesh.
Madhubuti. Union of Two, The.
Marston, P. Speechless: Upon the Marriage of Two Deaf and Dumb Persons.
Masters, E. Margaret Fuller Slack.
Mathews, A. Spectrum.
Two Months Married.
Matthews, W. Good Company.
McCarthy, T. Toast.
McElroy, C. Caledonia.
McGinley. Midcentury Love Letter.
McGough, R. 40—Love.
McKinney, I. Visiting My Gravesite: Talbott Churchyard, West Virginia.
McPherson, S. 1943.
Metras, G. Anniversary.
Mew. Farmer's Bride, The.
Miller, E. Rebecca.
Mirikitani. Soul Food.
Momaday. Four Notions of Love and Marriage.
Montagu, L. Epistle from Mrs. Yonge to Her Husband.
On the Death of Mrs. Bowes.
Moolten, D. Voyeur.
Moore, M. Marriage.
Moss, H. Ménage à Trois.
Mothibi. Speech.

Moulds, J. Late Summer Litany.
Moulsworth, M. Memorandum of Martha Moulsworth, Widow, The.
Mugo, M. G. Wife of the Husband.
Muir, E. Combat, The.
Mura. Grandfather and Grandmother in Love.
Murray, J. Epithalamium, An.
Naden. Love Versus Learning.
Pessimist's Vision, The.
Nash, O. Song to Be Sung by the Father of Infant Female Children.
Word to Husbands, A.
Nesbit, E. Goose-Girl, The.
Niedecker. I Married.
Nilsson, H. We Are Easily Reduced.
Olds, S. I Go Back to May 1937.
Wedding Vow, The.
Ormond. In September.
Ostriker. In the Twenty-Fifth Year of Marriage, It Goes On.
Padgett, R. Orange Jews.
Parson-Nesbitt. Strange Country.
Paschen. 12 East Scott Street.
Between the Acts.
Sam's Ghazals.
Peacock, M. Wheel, The.
Pelizzon, V. Clever and Poor.
Peseroff. Hardness Scale, The.
Philips, A. Happy Swain, The.
Philips, K. Answer to Another Persuading a Lady to Marriage, An.
Philpot, T. How to Live in the Elegy.
Piercy. Battle of Wills Disguised, A.
Pilkington, L. Fair and Softly Goes Far or, The Wary Physician.
Wish, By a Young Lady, The.
"Pindar." Ode: "That I have often been in love, deep love."
Plath. Applicant, The.
Porter, C. Where Is the Life That Late I Led?
Porter, P. Talking to You Afterwards.
Pound, E. River-Merchant's Wife: A Letter, The.
Prior. Reasonable Affliction, A.
Probyn. Kyrielle.
Mésalliance, A.
Ramsey, J. Tally Stick, The.
Ranaivo. Love Song: "Do not love me, my friend."
Ransom, J. Emily Hardcastle, Spinster.
Rich, A. Snapshots of a Daughter-in-Law.
Riley, P. E Questa Vita Un Lampo.
Rilke. On the Marriage at Cana.
Robinson, E. Eros Turannos.
Shatter.
Rochester, J. To My More Than Meritorious Wife.
Rolls. Bamboo.
Rome, H. Ring on the Finger.
Rosenberg, L. Married Love.
Rossetti, C. Cousin Kate.
Maude Clare.
Rumens. Before these Wars.
Double Bed.
Sallah, T. No Argument Tonight.
Sandburg, C. Mag.
Sangster, M. Our Own.
Sansom, A. Romance.
Santos, S. Married Love.
Schwartz, D. Passionate Shepherd to His Love, The.
Seaman, S. Plea for Trigamy, A.
Serote. Poem, A: "The Gasp sounded."
Seward. To a Young Lady, Purposing to Marry a Man of Immoral Character in the Hope of his Reformation.
Shelton, R. Promises.
Sherry, J. Pay Cash Only.
Sidney, S. His Being Was in Her Alone.
Simmons, J. After Eden.
Honeymoon, The.
Simpson, L. Man Who Married Magdalene, The.
Sims. Garden Song, A.
Smith, C. To the Countess of A—. Written on the Anniversary of Her Marriage.

Smith, M.   Springtime at Twilight.
Smith, S.   He Told His Life Story to Mrs. Courtly.
 I Remember.
Lady "Rogue" Singleton.
Major Macroo.
Smukler.   Marry.
Sparshott.   Three Seasons.
Spender, S.   Polar Exploration.
Spenser.   Epithalamion: "Ye learned sisters which have oftentimes."
 Prothalamion.
St. John, P.   Ocean of the Streams of Story.
Stephens, J.   Red-haired Man's Wife, The.
Stern, G.   Modern Love.
Stevenson, A.   Marriage, The.
Stoddard, E.   Wife Speaks, The.
Storace.   Archaeology of Divorce, The.
 Wedding Song.
Strand.   Courtship.
 Marriage, The.
Strong, L.   Brewer's Man, The.
Su, A.   Wedding Gifts.
Suckling, S.   Upon My Lord Brohall's Wedding.
Swift, J.   Phyllis [*or* Phillis] [*or* Progress of Love, The].
 Three Epigrams.
Swiontkowski, G.   Old Moon With Her Youth In Her Arms.
Synge.   On an Island.
Taylor, A.   Developing a Wife.
Taylor, B.   Proposal.
Taylor, E.   Upon Wedlock and Death of Children.
Tennyson, A.   Northern Farmer: New Style.
Thomas, D.   On the Marriage of a Virgin.
Thomas, E.   Epistle to Clemena, Occasioned by an Argument She Had Maintained Against the Author.
 New Litany, Occasioned by an Invitation to a Wedding, A.
Thomas, R.   Marriage, A.
Tranter.   Moonshine Sonata.
Ullman.   Why There Are Children.
Unknown.   Bridge instead of a Wall, A.
 Epithalamium: "Lo! Hymen passes through th' admiring crowds."
 Get Up and Bar the Door.
 Good and Better.
 Henpecked Husband, A.
 Jack Jingle.
 Knight and Shepherd's Daughter, The.
 May Colven [*or* May Colvin].
 No Balls at All.
 Railroad Man for Me, A.
 Rare Willie Drowned in Yarrow; or, The Water o Gamrie.
 Riddling Knight, The.
 Shady Grove.
 Slave Marriage Ceremony Supplement.
 Sukey [*or* Suky], you shall be my wife.
 To Mr. Punchinello.
 Wife Wrapt [*or* Wrapped] in Wether's Skin, The.
Updike.   Newlyweds, The.
Valentine, J.   Bride's Hours, A.
Van Heusen, J.   Love and Marriage.
Vaughan, H.   Isaac's Marriage.
Vazirani, R.   Mrs. Biswas of Maryland on the Phone.
Villon.   Ballad Written for a Bridegroom.
Viorst.   Honeymoon is Over, The.
Walker, F. X.   Wishbone.
Walsh, C.   Woman to Her Lover, A.
Warren, H.   Remember Me?
Weever.   De Se.
Weinblatt, J.   Marriage Song for Many Voices.
Wharton, E.   Last Giustiniani, The.
Whateley.   On the Author's Husband Desiring Her to Write Some Verses.
Wickham.   Marriage, The.
 Meditation at Kew.
 Nervous Prostration.
 Slighted Lady, The.
Wilcox, E.   Way of It, The.
Williams, J.   Matrimony.

Winchilsea.   Letter to Daphnis, A.
 Reformation.
 Unequal Fetters, The.
Wojahn.   Inside, The.
Wong, N.   Ironing.
Wright, H.   Wedlock; a Satire.
Wright, M.   Address to Her Husband.
 Wedlock, a Satire.
Yeats.   Collarbone [*or* Collar-Bone] of a Hare, The.
Young, J.   I'm Sitting on Top of the World.

See also **Bigamy and Bigamists; Monogamy and Monogamists; Polyandry; Wedding Songs; Weddings**

Mars (god)
Hadas, R.   Mars and Venus.
Longley, M.   Sulpicia.

Mars (planet)
Berrigan, T.   Bean Spasms.
Evans, A.   Martian Landscape.
Lowell, R.   March 1, The.

Marshes
Albrecht, A.   Elkhorn Slough.
Bromige.   Choice.
Everwine.   Marsh, New Year's Day, The.
Gregerson.   Waterborne.
Johnson, E.   Marshlands.
Kusano Shimpei.   Birthday Party.
Lanier, S.   Marshes of Glynn, The.
Niedecker.   Paean to Place.
 Will You Write Me a Christmas Poem?
Wyrebek, M.   Example, An.

Marsyas
Roberts, G.   Marsyas.

Martí, José
Roberts, W.   On a Monument to Martí.

Martial Arts
Hudgins.   Air, The.
Liu.   My Father's Martial Art.

Martins
Jenkins, M.   Martins.

Martyrs
Behn, A.   Thousand Martyrs I Have Made, A.
Blumenthal, W.   Da Silva Gives the Cue.
Borges.   John 1:14 (1964).
Buckmaster.   Vanzetti.
Campbell, A.   Shabby Old Dad.
Crashaw.   To the Infant Martyrs.
 Upon the Infant Martyrs.
Eleazar.   Thy Faithful Sons.
Fisher, A. *et al.*   Martin Luther King.
Frost, C.   Consent.
Gomez.   Elegy: "I die for Your holy word without regret."
Hecht, A.   'More Light! More Light!'
Herrick.   Dirge of Jephthah's Daughter, The.
 To Groves.
Johnson, L.   Te Martyrum Candidatus.
Kizer, C.   Race Relations.
Lamb, C.   Salome.
"Learsi."   Martyrdom.
Lowell, R.   Colloquy in Black Rock.
Martinez, D.   Pain.
Milosz, C.   Campo dei Fiori.
Milton.   On the Late Massacre [*or* Massacher] in Piedmont [*or* Piemont].
Montrose.   On Himself, upon Hearing What Was His Sentence.
Pelizzon, V.   Late Apostasy, A.
Pickthall, M.   Père Lalement.
 Two Souls.
Quarles.   Of St Stephen.
Randall, B.   Be He Ezra Pound, Kennedy, or King.
Rukeyser, M.   Akiba.
Sepamla.   I Remember Sharpeville.
Smith, S.   Sunt Leones.
Stanley, T.   On S. John the Baptist.
Suckling, S.   Upon Stephen Stoned.
Tagami.   Tobera.
Vaughan, H.   Incarnation and Passion, The.
Voznesensky [*or* Voznesenskii].   Call of the Lake, The.
Weiners.   With Meaning.
Wilde, L.   Who Will Show Us Any Good?

Marvell, Andrew
De Vries, P.   To His Importunate Mistress.
MacLeish.   You, Andrew Marvell.

Marx, Karl
Wayman.   Wayman in Love.

Mary Magdalene
Channing.   Murillo's Magdalen.
Clarke, C.   Palm Leaf of Mary Magdalene.
Cofer, J.   Magdalenas, Las.
Coleridge, H.   "Multum Dilexit."
Constable, H.   To Saint Mary Magdalen.
Crashaw.   Saint Mary Magdalene or The Weeper.
 Weeper, The.
Elliott, E.   Three Marys at Castle Howard, in 1812 and 1837, The.
Hecht, A.   Man Who Married Magdalene, The.
Herbert, G.   Mary [*or* Marie] Magdalene.
Kingsley, H.   At Glastonbury.
Levy, A.   Magdalen.
Rilke.   Mary at Peace with the Risen Lord.
Rossetti, W. M.   Jesus Wept.
Southwell.   Marie [*or* Mary] Magdalens Complaint at Christs Death.

Mary Queen of Scots
Elizabeth I.   Doubt of Future Foes.
"Field."   Tragic Mary Queen of Scots, The.
Hamilton, S.   Farewell to France.
Harington [*or* Harrington].   Tragicall Epigram, A.

Mary, the Virgin
Alabaster.   To the Blessed Virgin.
Appleman, P.   Mary.
Brecht, B.   Mary.
Brooke, R.   Mary and Gabriel.
Brooks, G.   Penitent Considers Another Coming of Mary, A.
Clifton, L.   Anna Speaks of the Childhood of Mary Her Daughter.
 Astrologer Predicts at Mary's Birth, The.
 Island Mary.
 Mary.
 Mary's Dream.
Coleridge, M.   Our Lady.
Constable, H.   To Our Blessed Lady.
Coverdale.   Song of the Virgin Mary, The.
Crashaw.   Luke 11: Blessed Be the Paps Which Thou Hast Sucked.
 On the Blessed Virgins Bashfulnesse.
Curzon, D.   Tour of Ein Kerem, A.
Davis, D.   Christmas Poem, A.
Dickey, J.   Magus, The.
Fallon, P.   Assumption.
 Mater Dei.
Gardner, A.   Mary, The Mother of Jesus.
Gunn, T.   Jesus and His Mother.
Herbert, G.   Anagram.
Herebert.   Devout Man Prays to His Relations, The.
Herrick.   Observation.
Hopkins, G.   Blessed Virgin Compared to the Air We Breathe, The.
 May Magnificat, The.
Jackson, L.   Virgin, The.
Kipling, R.   Sons of Martha, The.
Levi, P.   Annunciation.
Lewis, J.   Lullaby: "Lullee, lullay."
Lowell, R.   Beyond the Alps.
Mitchell, S.   Vermeer.
Muir, E.   Annunciation, The.
O'Curry, E.   Litany to Our Lady.
O'Donoghue, B.   Apparition, The.
Pasternak, B.   Christmas Star.
Rilke.   Mary's Visitation.
Robinson, E.   Gift of God, The.
Sexton.   Jesus Suckles.
Smith, S.   Dream of Comparison, A.
Unknown.   Hail, Queen of Heaven.
 Hymn to the Virgin.
 I Sing of a Maiden.
 Litany to Our Lady.
 Mary Weeps for Her Child.
 Now Goeth [*or* goth *or* goothe] Sun [*or* Sonne *or* Sunne] under Wood.
 Our Lady's Song.
 Rose That Bore Jesu, The.

Seven Virgins, The.
Vaughan, H. Knot, The.
Williams, W. For Eleanor and Bill Monahan.
Yeats. Mother of God, The.

Maryland (state)
Clifton, L. Slave Cabin, Sotterly Plantation, Maryland, 1989.
Cook, E. Sot-Weed Factor, The.
Dame. On the Road to Damascus, Maryland.
Randall, J. My Maryland.
Smith, D. Cumberland Station.

Masefield, Caroline Louisa
Masefield. C. L. M.

Masks
Adkins, G. Children in Armour.
Browning, E. Mask, The.
Dunbar, P. We Wear the Mask.
Gibran. Madman (Prologue), The.
Jackson, L. Mask, The.
Komunyakaa. Untitled Blues; After a Photograph by Yevgeni Yevtushenko.
Landon. Mask of Gaiety, The.
Levertov. Death in Mexico.
People at Night.
Lim, S. Lost Name Woman.
Probyn. Masquerading.
Rafferty, P. After Carnival.
Rukeyser, M. Poem as Mask, The.
Williams, H. Last Poem.
Zimmer. Zimmer in Grade School.

Masochism
Davies, S. In Francum.
Ginsberg, A. Please Master.
Hernton. Long Blues, The.
Wunderlich, M. Trick, The.

Mass Media
Cleary, B. New Rock n Roll, The.
Greenhalgh, C. Night I Met Marilyn, The.
Hardy, J. Objection Overruled.
Hattersley, G. *On the Buses* with Dostoyevsky. Singing.
Herd. Marilyn Climbs Out of the Pool.
Pomeroy, R. Gay Love and the Movies.
Rouse. Lilies of the Field.

Massachusetts (state)
Bishop, E. In the Waiting Room.
Dudek. Provincetown.
Eberhart, R. On a Squirrel Crossing the Road in Autumn, in New England.
Emerson, R. Concord Hymn.
Kunitz, S. Route Six.
Longfellow, H. Rhyme of Sir Christopher, The.
Lowell, R. For the Union Dead.
Plath. Point Shirley.
Terry, L. Bar[']s Fight[, August 28, 1746].
Tompson. On a Fortification at Boston Begun by Women.
Weaver, M. Easy Living.
Whittier. Firelight.
Snow-Bound [or Snow-Bound; a Winter Idyl].
Wilbur. Running.

Massacre of the Innocents
Hope, A. Massacre of the Innocents.
Lowell, R. Holy Innocents, The.
Shaw, L. To a Christmas Two-Year-Old.

Massacres
Baruch of Worms. Elegy: "Those reckless hosts rush to the wells."
Bostock, G. Night Marauders.
Forché. Ourselves or Nothing.
Gilbert, K. Kiacatoo.
Grandfather Koori. Massacre Sandhill.
Jeffers, R. Antrim.
Lowell, R. At the Indian Killer's Grave.
Mapanje. After Wiriyamu Village Massacre by Protuguese.
Milton. On the Late Massacre [or Massacher] in Piedmont [or Piemont].
Sherrill, S. Katyn Forest.
Wojahn. Assassination of Robert Goulet as Performed by Elvis Presley: Memphis, 1968, The.
Zimunya. After the Massacre.
Zwicky. Summer Pogrom.

Masts
Campbell, R. Choosing a Mast.

Maternity
Ferguson, G. Inhaling His Hair.
Jeffers, R. Haunted Country.

Mathematics and Mathematicians
Arensberg. Axiom.
Theorem.
Clover, J. Ceriserie.
Dove, R. Flash Cards.
Gundy, J. For the New York City Poet Who Informed Me that Few People Live This Way.
Kendall, M. Pure Hypothesis, A.
Millay, E. "Euclid Alone Has Looked on Beauty Bare."
Mori. Barbie Says Math Is Hard.
Norris, K. Naming the Living God.
Unknown. Arithmetic.
Learn to Count.
Lover's Arithmetic, The.
Welish. Wild Sleeve.
Wilson, S. Recreational Mathematics.
See also **Arithmetic**

Matisse, Henri
Hannan, M. Life Model.
Martinez, D. Matisse: Blue Nude, 1952.
Pilling. You and You, in the Pink.
Sanders, E. Cutting Prow, The.
Snodgrass, W. Matisse: "The Red Studio."

Maturity
Chubb, R. Song of My Soul.
Clark, P. My Life with Horses.
Dodge, M. Taking Time to Grow.
Gilmore, B. Revolution.
Hill, G. Guardians, The.
Jonson, B. Ode. To Sir William Sydney, on His Birthday.
Kipling, R. If—.
Lerner, A. I'm Glad I'm Not Young Any More.
Lovelace, R. Love Enthroned.
Martinez, D. Cultivation of Orchids, The.
Paquet. Basket Case.
Rukeyser, M. Boys of These Men Full Speed.
Shelton, R. Promises.
Shepherd, R. White Days.
Smith, S. To Carry the Child.
Stephens, J. After Asia.
Tuck, L. Sniff.
Waller, E. Budd, The.
Wordsworth, W. My Heart Leaps Up.

Mausoleums
MacDiarmid, H. Skeleton of the Future, The.
Schmitz. Queen of Heaven Mausoleum.
See also **Cemeteries; Graves; Monuments; Tombs**

May
Arlen, H. I've Got the World on a String.
Auden. May.
Browning, R. Home-Thoughts, From Abroad.
May and Death.
Buchanan, G. May Morning.
De la Mare. There Blooms No Bud in May.
Hardy, T. Afterwards.
Hass, R. Late Spring.
Herrick. Corinna's Going a-Maying.
Maypole, The.
Hirshfield, J. Rain in May.
Hopkins, G. May Magnificat, The.
Hovell-Thurlow. May.
Lanier, S. Song for "The Jacquerie."
Larkin, P. Trees, The.
Linden, M. May.
Neilson, J. May.
Pritchard, N. Springtime.
Ray, H. May.
May's Invocation after a Tardy Spring.
Rossetti, C. May.
Singer, B. Peterhead in May.
Teasdale. Over the Roofs.
Tolson, M. Victor Garibaldi.
Unknown. Fisherman's Rhyme.
May in the Green-Wood.
Now Is the Month of Maying.
Watson, S. Ode in May.
West, J. To May.
Williams, W. Bird Song.

Locust Tree in Flower, The.
Tulip Bed, The.

May Day
Herrick. May-Pole, The.

Maya
Jones, S. Hymn to Na'ra'yena, A.

McPherson, James Birdseye
Melville, H. Dirge for McPherson, A.

Meadowlarks
Hanzlicek, C. Moment.

Meadows
Ashbery. Grand Abacus.
Clare, J. Mist in the Meadows.
De la Mare. Crazed.
Voices.
Duncan, R. Often I Am Permitted to Return to a Meadow.
Gray, A. Music in the Meadow.
Herrick. To Meadows [or Meddowes].
Roethke. Meadow Mouse, The.
Thomas, D. I, in My Intricate Image.
See also **Fields and Pastures**

Meat
Chase, K. Venison.
Coward. Any Part of Piggy.
Edson, R. Ape.
Follain. Black Meat.
Hardy, T. Bags of Meat.
Harper, M. Breaded Meat, Breaded Hands.
Herrick. Grace for a Child.
Upon Showbread [or Shewbread]: Epigram.
Jewsbury. My heart's in the kitchen, my heart is not here.
Levine, P. Salami.
Lux. One Meat Ball.
McClure, M. Moiré.
Melville, H. Maldive Shark, The.
Unknown. On a Gentleman's Complaining to a Lady That He Could Not Eat Meat.
Waldman, A. Skin / Meat / BONES.
Watson, C. Knickerbocker Knockabout.
Wilbur. Rillons, Rillettes.
Wordsworth, W. Ode: Intimations of Immortality [from Recollections of Early Childhood].

Mechanics
Burke, C. Motor Oil Queen.
McIlroy, L. How to Change a Flat.

Medea
Van Walleghen. In the Chariot Drawn by Dragons.
Wakoski. Reading *Bonjour, Tristesse* at the Florence Crittenden Home for Unwed Mothers.

Medicine
Abse. Stethoscope, The.
Alexander, E. Aspirin.
Belloc. On Hygiene.
Browning, R. Epistle Containing the Strange Medical Experience of Karshish, the Arab Physician, An.
Burns, R. Death and Doctor Hornbook [A True Story].
Campo. Towards Curing AIDS.
What the Body Told.
Charach, R. Evidence on Film, The.
Labour and Delivery.
MRI.
Coulehan, J. Anatomy Lesson.
Dynamizer and the Oscilloclast, The.
Lovesickness: A Medieval Text.
Rule of Thirds, The.
D'Aguiar. Obeah Mama Dot.
Delgado, J. Recommitted.
Dyer, E. Painting the Nude.
Foy, J. Autopsy.
Giscombe. (1962 At the Edge of Town).
Graham-Pole, J. Pain, The.
Venipuncture.
Hufana, A. From the Raw.
Jones, A. Tap.
Joseph, A. Chalazion.
Kolodny, S. Tsuneko—Psychiatric Medications Clinic.
Lieberman, M. Prediction.
Longfellow, H. Day Is Done, The.

Moolten, D.   Bio 7.
Rich, A.   5:30 A.M.
Rowe, V.   MRI of a Poet's Brain.
   Youth.
Shafer, A.   Monday Morning.
Smith, R.   Halcion.
Stone, J.   Gaudeamus Igitur: A Valediction.
   He Makes a House Call.
Straus, M.   Neuroanatomy Summer.
   Scarlet Crown.
Su, A.   Antidepressant.
Tatarunis, P.   I Have Two Sons and the One I
   Love Best Is Robert.
Unknown.   Magic Formula.
Van Peenen, H.   Insulin Receptor.
Walwicz.   Daredevil.
Woods, D.   Prescription.
Wright, J.   Therapy.
Wunderlich, M.   Simplify Your Combination
   Therapy.
See also **Hospitals; Illness; Nurses; Physicians**
Meditation
Bly, R.   Six Winter Privacy Poems.
Brutus.   Under House Arrest.
Cedering, S.   Regarding Music.
Coleridge, S.   Frost at Midnight.
Crozier, A.   Loopy Dupes.
Dyer, J.   Grongar Hill.
Hamburger, M.   Garden, Wilderness.
Heyen.   Tie, The.
Kane, J.   Reasons for Loving the Harmonica.
Kerouac.   Buddha.
   How to Meditate.
Padilla.   Discourse on Method, The.
Ponsot.   Analogue.
Ramke.   Revealing Oneself to a Woman.
Riley, J.   Summer Seeming.
Scully, M.   Variations.
Steele, T.   Wartburg, 1521–22, The.
Very.   Columbine, The.
Williamson, A.   Light's Reading, The.
Mediterranean Sea
Coleman, C.   Riviera, The.
Jacob, M.   In Honor of the Sardana and the
   Tenora.
Lawrence, D.   Middle of the World.
McCarthy, J.   Riviera, The.
Santayana.   Ode V: "Of thee the Northman by
   his beachèd galley."
Tate, A.   Mediterranean, The.
Medusa
Bogan, L.   Medusa.
Clampitt.   Medusa.
Hayden, R.   Perseus.
O'Sullivan, V.   Medusa.
Parnell, P.   Apotheosis of Medusa.
Sarton.   Muse as Medusa, The.
Shelley, P.   On the Medusa of Leonardo da
   Vinci in the Florentine Gallery.
Melancholy
Algarin.   Infections.
Blamire.   Written on a Gloomy Day, in
   Sickness.
Bowles, W.   To the River Cherwell.
Brooks, G.   Crazy Woman, The.
Byrom.   My Spirit Longeth for Thee.
Cavendish, M.   Dialogue between Melancholy
   and Mirth, A.
   Discourse of Melancholy, A.
Cervantes.   Levee: Letter to No One, The.
Coleridge, S.   Dejection: An Ode.
   Nightingale, The.
   This Lime-Tree Bower My Prison.
Cope, W.   Depression.
Cornford, F.   She Warns Him.
Cranch.   Pines and the Sea, The.
Deane, J.   On a Dark Night.
Evance, S.   To a Violet.
   To Melancholy.
   To the Clouds.
   Written at Netley Abbey.
   Written in a Ruinous Abbey.
"Field."   She is Singing to Thee, *Domine!*
Ginsberg, A.   My Sad Self.
Hemans.   Indian Woman's Death-Song, The.

Second Sight.
Herrick.   His Litany to the Holy Spirit.
Hughes, L.   Neighbor.
Jackson, L.   Sad Boy, The.
Kavanagh, P.   Wet Evening in April.
Keats.   Ode on Melancholy.
Keller, D.   Melancholy.
Lewis, C.   Naked Seed, The.
Middleton, T.   Melancholy.
Milton.   Il Penseroso.
Montagu, L.   Receipt to Cure [*or* for] the
   Vapours, A.
Morris, M.   Valley Prince.
Neruda.   Melancholy inside Families.
Plath.   Poppies in July.
Radcliffe, A.   Night.
Robinson, E.   Charles Carville's Eyes.
Rossetti, C.   At Home.
   If Only.
Shelley, P.   Stanzas Written in Dejection, near
   Naples [*or*—December 1818, near Naples].
Smith, C.   To Melancholy. Written on the Banks
   of the Arun, October 1785.
   To the South Downs.
   Written in October.
   Written on the Sea Shore.—October, 1784.
Smith, S.   Away, Melancholy.
Swinburne.   Itylus.
Thomas, E.   Return, The.
Tighe.   Written at Scarborough. August, 1799.
Unknown.   On Melancholy.
   What Care I Though the World Reprove.
Wakoski.   Blue Monday.
Wordsworth, W.   I Wandered Lonely As a
   Cloud.
   World Is Too Much With Us, The.
Yearsley.   Soliloquy: "What folly to complain."
See also **Blues (mood); Dejection**
Melons
Kinsella, J.   Pig Melons.
Oswald, A.   Melon Grower, The.
Melville, Herman
Aiken, C.   Herman Melville.
Auden.   Herman Melville.
Crane, H.   At Melville's Tomb.
Elmslie, K.   Japanese City.
Horan.   Prometheus.
Koch, K.   You Were Wearing.
Martin, C.   Satyr, Cunnilinguent: To Herman
   Melville.
Muir, E.   Scotland 1941.
Memling, Hans
Mathias, R.   Memling.
Memorial Day
Anania.   Memorial Day.
Collins, W.   How Sleep the Brave.
Finch, F.   Blue and the Gray, The.
Heard, J.   Decoration Day.
McCrae, J.   In Flanders Fields.
Thompson, C.   Memorial Day.
Memories
Anderson, D.   Itinerary.
Back, R.   After Eden.
Barford, W.   Sorting Things Out.
Barresi.   Late Summer News.
Bauer, G.   Oldies But Goodies.
Bergman, A.   Way We Were, The.
Blake, E.   Memories of You.
BonniLee.   White Candles.
Brainard, J.   I Remember.
Brown, S.   Let Them Call It Jazz.
Burke, C.   Lizzie.
Cabalquinto.   Depths of Fields.
Castillo, S.   En el Sol de Mi Barrio.
   Letter to Yeni on Peering into Her Life.
Cheney-Coker.   Childhood.
Christie.   Belongings.
Conway, J.   Marlo Thomas in Seven Parts and
   Epilogue.
   Modern English.
Coslow, S.   My Old Flame.
Curtis, T.   Pembrokeshire Buzzards.
   Soup.
Day, J.   Picket before Bull Run, The.
De Paul, G.   I'll Remember April.

DeCarteret, M.   Town Clerk, The.
Dooley, M.   Dancing at Oakmead Road.
   What Every Woman Should Carry.
Dorsett, T.   Survivor, The.
Duff, V.   Letters from an Exile.
Ebb, F.   Happy Time, The.
Escandor, V.   Summer Nostalgia.
Espada.   Prisoners of Saint Lawrence, The.
Feinstein, S.   Blues for Zoot.
Florsheim.   Business in Germany.
Fuhrman, J.   Here, I Say.
Geiger.   Dry Spell of Faith, A.
   Soundtracks.
Goldberg, B.   Our Father.
Goodman, M.   Cobwebs.
Gordon, M.   Serenade in Blue.
   There Will Never Be Another You.
Graham, W.   To My Father.
Hacker, M.   Squares and Courtyards.
Hagedorn, J.   Souvenirs.
Hanighen, B.   'Round Midnight.
Harchik.   Requiem: "Your names ring clearly."
Hardy, T.   Church Romance, A.
Harer, K.   Lucky 7.
Herbert, W.   Praise of Italian Chip-Shops.
Herrera.   Atavistic: Traces after the Rain.
Holland, W.   Journal of the Plague Years, A.
Johnston, A.   My Old Flame.
Johnston, P.   I'll Remember April.
Jones, G.   Where All Were Good to Me, God
   Knows.
Kander, J.   Happy Time, The.
Kaufman, S.   Emperor of China, The.
Kessler, S.   Marty's Mother.
Kirsch, D.   Dvora.
Kizer, C.   For Jan as the End Draws Near.
Koestenbaum, W.   Tea Dance.
Lassell.   Brady Street, San Francisco.
Lim, S.   Visting Malacca.
Limburg, J.   Return, The.
Lindtová, A.   Campfire.
Link, H.   These Foolish Things (Remind Me of
   You).
Lopez, L.   Only Now I Realize.
Manrique, J.   My Night with Frederico García
   Lorca (As Told by Edouard Roditi).
Marshall, J.   Months of Love, The.
Martien, J.   Late 20th Century: Spring.
McClatchy.   1871.
   1946, 1957.
   1971.
   First Steps.
Medina, P.   Exile, The.
Melhem, D.   Grandfather: Frailty Is Not the
   Story.
Michelson, R.   Where I Sat.
Mif.   Terezin.
Moolten, D.   Voyeur.
Motherwell.   Jeanie Morrison.
Mphande.   Walking the Plateau.
Nelson, M.   Cover Photograph.
Nesbit, E.   Gray Folk, The.
Neufeld, A.   Pictures and Stories.
Newman, G.   Recording History.
Notley.   Where Leftover Misery Goes.
Obejas, A.   Dancing in Paradise.
Oliveira, D.   Summer.
Peterson, R.   Now and Then.
Propp, K.   Train Passage.
Raye, D.   I'll Remember April.
Rexroth, K.   Asagumori.
Richman, L.   Rue de Rosiers: To My Brother
   Fred.
Robertson, R.   Aberdeen.
Rosner.   Souvenirs.
Rossiter.   Nostalgia.
Rux, C. H.   Asphalt Musings.
Samaras, N.   After the Children Have Gone to
   Bed.
Savageau.   Trees.
Schapiro, J.   Tourist, The.
Seto, T.   Jihad.
Sherman, M.   San Buenaventura.
Shevin.   What He Hated.
Shiffrin, N.   Anna's Dream.
Silex, E.   Departure.

Smith, K.   Writing in Prison.
Sondheim.   Remember?
Sternlieb.   Survivor.
Syrkin.   My Uncle in Treblinka.
Taylor, C. B.   Forever Arima.
   Plenty Time Pass Fast, Fas Dey So.
Teasdale.   Jewels.
Todd, M.   Post Scriptum.
Trinidad.   For Joe Brainard.
Turner, J.   Plan, The.
Unknown.   I Think Over Again My Small
   Adventures.
   Old Folks' Room, The.
Vazirani, R.   Mrs. Biswas Goes Through a Photo
   Album.
Warren, H.   Serenade in Blue.
   There Will Never Be Another You.
Webster, E.   Where Home Was.
Weinberger, F.   He Wears Old Socks.
Wells, W.   Beatings.
Wexler, E.   Governess, The.
Williams, J.   Memories of Christmas.
   River Walk.
Williams, W.   Paterson, Book 5: The River of
   Heaven.
Wordsworth, W.   Old Man by the Brook, The.
Yeats.   Cold Heaven, The.
Young-Prottengeier.   Lithuanian Grandmother.

Memory
Abbott, D.   All Day at Work.
Abse.   New Diary, A.
Ai.   Back in the World.
Akhmatova, A.   Instead of a Preface.
Aldrich, T.   Memory.
Alegría.   From the Bridge.
Alexander, M.   Memory.
Ali, A.   Cracked Portraits.
   Postcard from Kashmir.
   Return to Harmony 3.
Allingham.   At Ballyshannon, Co. Donegal.
   Four Ducks on a Pond.
Antin.   Real Estate.
Apollinaire.   Voyager, The.
Ashbery.   Other Tradition, The.
   Rain.
Atwood.   Beauharnois (1).
   Beauharnois (3).
   Beauharnois, Glengarry (2).
   Dufferin, Simcoe, Grey (4).
   Four Small Elegies.
Auden.   On This Island.
   Question, The.
   Taller To-day.
Balaban.   News Update.
Bamber, J.   Broken Necklace.
Baraka.   In Memory of Radio.
Baxter, E.   In Your Absence.
Belloc.   Tarantella.
Berlin.   Remember.
Bernstein, C.   Memories.
Berrigan, A.   Short History of Autumn, A.
Berry, W.   Wild, The.
Betham-Edwards.   To a Llangollen Rose, the
   Day after It Had Been Given by Miss
   Ponsonby.
Bethell.   Response.
Biespiel, D.   Tower.
Binyon.   Winter Sunrise.
Bishop, J.   Hours, The.
Blake, W.   Song: "Memory, hither come."
Blood, B.   Late.
Blunden.   1916 Seen from 1921.
Boland, E.   Black Lace Fan My Mother Gave
   Me, The.
   I Remember.
Boston, B.   Savage, Our Fathers, The.
Bowles, W.   To the River Wensbeck.
Brett, L.   I Keep Forgetting.
Brew.   Search, The.
Bromige.   Logical Positivist, The.
Brontë, A.   Memory.
Brontë, E.   Aye there it is! It wakes tonight.
   Remembrance.
   Stanzas to———.
Brooks, G.   Anniad, The.
   Bean Eaters, The.

Brooks, W.   Pilate Remembers.
Broumas, O.   Beauty and the Beast.
Brown, D.   First Person—1981.
   Still Later There Are War Stories.
Browning, E.   L. E. L.'s Last Question.
Browning, R.   Appearances.
   By the Fire-Side.
   Confessions.
   Memorabilia.
Bruner.   Remembrance.
Brush.   Waiting for the End of the War.
Bryant, F.   Cathexis.
Buchwald.   As Soon As It's Here It's Gone But
   So What.
Buckley, V.   Man, a Woman, A.
Buscani.   Miss Mary Mack.
Byron, C.   Minding You.
Byron, G.   If Sometimes in the Haunts of Men.
   Lines Written beneath a Picture.
   Stanzas for Music.
Césaire, A.   In Memory of a Black Union
   Leader.
Calverley.   Companions.
   Flight.
Campo.   Lost Plaza Is Everywhere, The.
Carew, T.   To T. H., a Lady Resembling My
   Mistress.
Carmichael, H.   Star Dust.
Cassian.   Blood, The.
Castillo, S.   Almendares.
   Apagón, El.
Cataldi.   Advice.
Causley.   Armistice Day.
   Eden Rock.
Cheney-Coker.   Poem for a Lost Lover.
Chesterton, G.   Donkey, The.
Chipasula.   Tramp.
Ciardi.   On a Photo of Sgt. Ciardi a Year Later.
Cisneros, S.   Good Hot Dogs.
Clampitt.   Whippoorwill in the Woods, A.
Clare, J.   Stanzas: "Black absence hides upon
   the past."
   To the Memory of John Keats.
Clark, L.   Singing in the Streets.
Clements, S.   Susans.
Clifton, L.   Why some people be mad at me
   sometimes.
Cofer, J.   Dream of Birth, The.
Cohen, L.   Heirloom.
Coleman, W.   Cousin Mary.
   Mastectomy.
Coleridge, M.   Not Yet.
   Only a little shall we speak of thee.
   To Memory.
Collins, B.   Lines Lost Among Trees.
Cook, E.   To the Late William Jerdan.
Coolidge, C.   Album—A Runthru.
Copus, J.   Back Seat of My Mother's Car, The.
   Clothes, The.
Corman.   Tortoise, The.
Corso.   Birthplace Revisited.
Cory, W.   Desiderato.
   Deteriora.
   Heraclitus.
   Parting.
Coultas, B.   Weather Report.
Crane, H.   Passage.
   Repose of Rivers.
Creeley.   Company, The.
   Echo.
   Edge, The.
   Fire, The.
   For My Mother: Genevieve Jules Creeley.
   House, The.
   Just Friends.
   Memory Gardens.
   People, The.
Cronin, J.   Naval Base (Part III), The.
Crozier, A.   Heifer, The.
Dacey, P.   Musica.
Dacre, C.   Power of Love, The.
Dana, R.   At the Vietnam War Memorial,
   Washington, D. C.
Darr.   At Sixteen.
Daruwalla.   Of Mohenjo Daro at Oxford.
Davie.   Barnsley and District.

Devil on Ice.
   Time Passing, Beloved.
Davis, O.   Thirty Years Rising.
De la Mare.   Fare Well.
   Miss Loo.
   Old Men, The.
   Winter.
Deane, S.   Brethren, The.
'Dermée.'   Poem.
Di Prima.   Backyard.
   Notes on the Art of Memory.
Dickey, W.   Memoranda.
Dickinson, E.   Pain Has an Element of Blank.
Dietz, H.   Something to Remember You By.
DiPalma.   Memory's Wedge.
   Wrong Side of the Door, The.
Divakaruni.   At Muktinath.
Djanikian.   When I First Saw Snow.
Dobyns.   How To Like It.
Dodd, E.   Touched.
Dooley, M.   At Les Deux Magots.
   Does It Go Like this?
   Heat.
   History.
   Mansize.
Doolittle, H.   Helen.
   Lethe.
Dorcey.   Night.
Doty, M.   Days of 1981.
Dove, R.   Dusting.
   Fifth Grade Autobiography.
   In the Old Neighborhood.
   Wingfoot Lake.
Dowson.   Non Sum Qualis Eram Bonae sub
   Regno Cynarae.
   Spleen.
Dubin, A.   Remember Me?
Duffy, C.   In Your Mind.
Dugan, A.   Memories of Verdun.
Duncan, R.   Turning into.
Dunn, D.   Kaleidoscope, The.
Edwards, M.   To a Loved One of Other Days.
Ehrhart.   Confirmation, A.
   To Those Who Have Gone Home Tired.
Eliot, T.   La Figlia Che Piange.
   Rhapsody on a Windy Night.
Ellis, T.   T.A.P.O.A.F.O.M.
Emanuel, L.   Elsewhere.
Emerson, R.   Past, The.
   Thine Eyes Still Shined.
English, T.   Ben Bolt.
Equi.   Date With Robbe-Grillet, A.
Estes, A.   Serenade.
Evans, G.   Eye Blade.
   Revelation in the Mother Lode.
Fainlight, R.   Handbag.
Fanshawe, C.   When Last We Parted.
Fay, J.   Santorini Daughter.
Fearing.   Resurrection.
"Field."   I sing thee with the stock-dove's throat.
Fitzpatrick, K.   Highland, 1955.
Flynn, D.   Collector, The.
Forché.   Elegy.
Forhan, C.   Taste of Wild Cherry, The.
Forman, R.   Kin.
Frost, R.   Directive.
Galvin, P.   My Father Spoke with Swans.
Garcia, R.   Elite Syncopations.
   Nobody Here But Us.
Gardinier.   Ghost of Santo Domingo, The.
Gardner, E.   To Love.
Garland, H.   Plowing: A Memory.
Garrett, E.   Vista.
Gershwin.   They Can't Take That Away from
   Me.
Gilbert, C.   Pushing.
Gilbert, J.   Perspective He Would Mutter Going
   to Bed.
Gillan.   In Memory We Are Walking.
Ginsberg, A.   Music.
   No Way Back to the Past.
   To Aunt Rose.
Gioia.   Cruising with the Beach Boys.
Giovanni.   Nikki-Rosa.
Glück, L.   Pond, The.
Godfrey.   Our Lady.

Gonzalez, R.   There.
Gordon, I.   Unforgettable.
Gordon, J.   Love.
Graves, R.   Plea to Boys and Girls, A.
   Recalling War.
Greacen.   Carnival at the River.
   Father and Son.
Gregg.   Clapping, The.
   Past Perfect.
Grenier.   Has Faded in Part But Magnificent
   Also Late for RC / Mirrors.
Grimké, A.   Butterflies.
Groarke, V.   History of My Father's House, The.
Grosholz.   Last of the Courtyard, The.
   On the Ferry, Toward Patras.
   Remembering the Ardèche.
Guest, H.   Wales Re-visited.
Gunn, T.   Autobiography.
Gurney, I.   To His Love.
Hall, D.   Airstrip in Essex, 1960, An.
   Old Pilot, The.
   Porcelain Couple, The.
Hamod, S.   After the Funeral of Assam
   Hamady.
Hannah, S.   Your Street Again.
Hardy, T.   After a Journey.
   Afterwards.
   Ah, Are You Digging on My Grave?
   Ancient to Ancients, An.
   Beyond the Last Lamp.
   Mound, The.
   One We Knew.
   Shut Out That Moon.
   Thoughts of Phena.
   To Lizbie Browne.
   Voice, The.
   Where the Picnic Was.
Harjo, J.   Remember.
   Skeleton of Winter.
Harms.   As Always.
   My Androgynous Years.
Harris, D.   What we have lost.
Harryman.   My Story.
Hass, R.   Meditation at Lagunitas.
   Pornographer, The.
Hayden, R.   Ballad of Sue Ellen Westerfield,
   The.
   Those Winter Sundays.
   Whipping, The.
Heaney, S.   Anahorish.
   Summer of Lost Rachel, The.
   Terminus.
Hecht, A.   Hill, A.
Helwig.   Considerations.
Hemans.   Parting Song, A.
   Remembrance of Grasmere, A.
Herd.   Pink Rose Rings, The.
Herrick.   Upon His Sister-in-Law, Mistress
   Elizabeth Herrick.
Hesketh.   Love's Advocate.
Hicok.   Alzheimer's.
Hikmet.   Things I Didn't Know I Loved.
Hine.   Côte de Liesse.
   Letting Go.
Hirsch, E.   My Father's Back.
Hochman.   Hairbrush, The.
Hogan, L.   New Apartment.
Holland, J.   Having read up on the subject.
Hollo.   Godlike.
Hongo.   Hilo: First Night Back.
   O-Bon: Dance for the Dead.
Hood, T.   I Remember, I Remember.
   Time, Hope, and Memory.
Howard, R.   1915: A Pre-Raphaelite Ending,
   London.
   After 65.
Howe, F.   Doubt.
Howes, B.   Letter from the Caribbean, A.
Hudgins.   Around the Campfire.
Hughes, L.   Negro Speaks of Rivers, The.
Hugo, R.   Freaks at Spurgin Road Field, The.
   White Center.
Hunt, L.   Rondeau: "Jenny kissed [or kiss'd] me
   when we met."
Irby.   Heredom.
Irwin, W.   Reminiscence.

Jacob, M.   Little Poem.
Jarman, M.   Cavafy in Redondo.
Jarrell.   Burning the Letters.
   Dead Wingman, The.
   Elementary Scene, The.
   Player Piano, The.
Johnston, M.   Sea-Cucumber, The.
Jones, S.   Illusions.
Joseph, A.   Junior High Dance.
Justice, D.   Men at Forty.
   On the Death of Friends in Childhood.
   Sonatina in Yellow.
Kavanagh, P.   Memory of my Father.
   October.
Kay, J.   Even the Trees.
   Stincher, The.
Keesing.   Reverie of a Mum.
Kefala.   Freedom Fighter.
Kemble.   Farewell to Italy.
   Petition, A.
   To Mrs. Norton.
Kenney.   Sailing.
Keyes, S.   Elegy: "April again, and it is a year
   again."
Kgositsile.   Air I Hear, The.
   For Art Blakey and the Jazz Messengers.
King, H.   Exequy, The.
Kinnell.   For Robert Frost.
   To William Carlos Williams.
Knight, E.   Poem of Attrition, A.
Koch, K.   Circus, The.
   Energy in Sweden.
   To Marina.
   With Janice.
Komey.   Change, The.
   Oblivion.
Komunyakaa.   Break from the Bush, A.
   Report from the Skull's Diorama.
   When Loneliness is a Man.
Kumin, M.   Envelope, The.
   How It Is.
   Nuns of Childhood: Two Views, The.
Kunitz, S.   Passing Through.
Kusz, N.   Retired Greyhound, II.
Lamb, C.   Old Familiar Faces, The.
Landon.   Lines Written Under a Picture of a Girl
   Burning a Love-Letter.
   Song.
Landor, W.   Memory.
   Rose Aylmer.
   What News.
Lang, A.   Twilight on Tweed.
Lanyer.   Description of Cooke-ham [or
   Cookham], The.
Larkin, P.   I Remember, I Remember.
   So through that unripe day you bore your head.
   Whatever Happened?
Lauterbach.   Here and There.
Laux.   China.
Lawrence, D.   Argonauts, The.
   Hymn to Priapus.
   Piano.
Lea, S.   At the Flyfisher's Shack.
   Telescope.
Lee, J.   My Father's Country.
Lee, L.   I Ask My Mother to Sing.
   Mnemonic.
Lerner, A.   I Remember It Well.
Leslie, E.   Among My Souvenirs.
Levertov.   Hymn, The.
   Intrusion.
   Note to Olga (1966), A.
   Woman Meets an Old Lover, A.
Levine, P.   Genius.
Levy, A.   Old House, The.
Lewis, A.   Post-Script: for Gweno.
Lewis, J.   Grandmother Remembers, A.
   Stories.
Lim, S.   Father from Asia.
Lincoln, A.   My Childhood-Home I See Again.
Lindsay, N.   Eagle That Is Forgotten, The.
Livesay, D.   Green Rain.
Lochhead, L.   Grim Sisters, The.
Lodge, G.   On an Æolian Harp.
Loewe, F.   I Remember It Well.
Loftis, N.   Ruth.

Longfellow, H.   Fire of Drift-Wood, The.
   Golden Mile-Stone, The.
   My Lost Youth.
Longley, M.   Ash Keys.
   Remembering Carrigskeewaun.
Lopez, L.   Images of San Luis.
Lorde.   Movement Song.
Lowell, J.   Remembered Music.
Lowell, R.   For Sheridan.
Lumsden, R.   Then.
Lyons, S.   Remembering.
MacCaig.   Aspects.
MacDiarmid, H.   Crystals like Blood.
   Eemis-Stane, The.
MacDonagh, D.   Veterans, The.
Macgoye.   August the First: The Shadow. Patel
   Speaks.
Mackintosh, E.   In Memoriam[, Private D.
   Sutherland].
MacLeish.   Return.
   Sentiments for a Dedication.
MacNeice.   Soap Suds.
Madgett.   Souvenir.
Madhubuti.   Killing Memory.
Mapanje.   We Wondered about the Mellow
   Peaches.
Marston, P.   Vain Wish, A.
Martínez, V.   Night of Fathers.
   Reliquaries, The.
Martinez, D.   Nocturnes: "He closed the deal on
   the night. A real."
Marvell.   Gallery, The.
Mason, R.   Old Memories of Earth.
Matson, C.   Bedside.
Mayer, B.   Birthday Sonnet for Grace.
McAuley, J.   Because.
McCarriston.   Billy.
   Castle in Lynn, A.
McCarthy, G.   Arrival.
   Finding the Way Back.
   Sound of Guns, The.
McDaniel, J.   Logic in the House of Sawed-Off
   Telescopes.
McDonald, W.   Hauling Over Wolf Creek Pass
   in Winter.
   Once You've Been to War.
   Veteran.
McFadden, R.   Contemplations of Mary.
   Stringer's Field.
McKay, C.   Jasmine.
   Tropics in New York, The.
McKean.   After Listening to Jack Teagarden.
McPherson, S.   Helen Todd: My Birthname.
Mei Yao Ch'en.   I Remember the River at Wu
   Sung.
Melville, H.   Stonewall Jackson.
Menken.   Memory, A.
Mercer, J.   I Remember You.
Merrill, J.   Broken Home, The.
   David's Night in Veliès.
   Days of 1941 and '44.
   Days of 1964.
   Last Words.
   Manos Karastefanís.
   Scenes of Childhood.
   Up and Down.
   Urban Convalescence, An.
Meynell, A.   Renouncement.
Mhlophe.   Sometimes When It Rains.
Millay, E.   Cameo, The.
   Sonnet: "What lips my lips have kissed, and
   where, and why."
Milosz, C.   And Yet the Books.
Moffi.   Putting an End to the War Stories.
Montague, J.   Lament for the O'Neills.
   Like Dolmens Round My Childhood, the Old
   People.
Moore, T.   Echo.
   Journey Onwards, The.
   No—Leave My Heart to Rest.
   Oft In the Stilly Night.
Mora.   Depression Days.
   Gentle Communion.
Morris, G.   Woodman, Spare That Tree.
Moss, H.   Elegy for My Sister.
Moultrie.   Forget Thee?

Mueller, L. Concert, The.
Muir, E. Animals, The.
Muldoon, P. Soap-Pig, The.
Mura. Colors of Desire, The.
To H. N.
Nemerov. Blue Suburban.
Models.
Nesbit, E. Among His Books.
Nichol. Some Nets.
Nicholls, H. Among My Souvenirs.
Noguchi, R. Not Surfing Some Days.
North, M. Poems to My Father.
Nortje. Cosmos in London.
Notley. Beginning with a Stain.
California Girlhood, A.
O'Hara, F. Animals.
In Favor of One's Time.
In Memory of My Feelings.
O'Loughlin. Posthumous.
O'Reilly, M. House Call to a Man with
Parkinson's Disease, A.
Oandasan. Grandmothers Land.
Oldham, P. Noon.
Oliver, M. Picking Blueberries, Austerlitz, New
York, 1957.
Olson, C. At Yorktown.
Ondaatje. Burning Hills.
Oppen. Forms of Love, The.
Myth of the Blaze.
Orton, B. Beekeeper.
Sea Monkeys, The.
Osaki. Amnesiac.
Owen, W. Roads Also, The.
To My Friend (With an Identity Disc).
Unreturning, The.
Pack, R. Thrasher in the Willow by the Lake,
The.
Page, G. Late Night Radio.
Paley, G. People in My Family.
Paquet. Group Shot.
Parish. Star Dust.
Pasternak, B. Fresco Come to Life.
Paulin. In the Lost Province.
Peters, L. Home Coming.
Phillips, C. Abundance.
Africa Says.
Pilkington, L. Memory, a Poem.
Pinsky. Long Branch Song, A.
Planché. Self-Evident.
Poe. To F——.
Porter, C. Begin the Beguine.
Old-Fashioned Garden, An.
Pound, E. Doria.
Prince, F. Babiaantje, The.
Probyn. Song Out of Season, A.
Prufer, K. For the Dead.
Raine, C. Onion, Memory, The.
Rainger, R. Thanks for the Memory.
Ramanujan. Breaded Fish.
Ramsey, J. Tally Stick, The.
Randall, D. Souvenirs.
Ransom, J. Antique Harvesters.
Equilibrists, The.
Rayl, J. Spring Storm.
Reaney. School Globe, The.
Reese, L. Lavender Woman, The.
Reverdy. Road.
Rexroth, K. Signature of All Things, The.
Rich, A. From the Prison House.
Grandmothers.
Living Memory.
Mathilde in Normandy.
Riley, D. Misremembered Lyric, A.
Riley, J. Old Swimmin'-Hole, The.
Roberts, L. My Father's Whistle.
Roberts, N. Max Factor Pink.
Robin, L. Thanks for the Memory.
Robinson, A. Dead Friend, The.
Stornelli and Strambotti.
Valley, The.
Robinson, E. Calverly's.
Souvenir.
Rodriguez, L. Heavy Blue Veins.
Roethke. Dream, The.
Premonition, The.
Rolfe, E. First Love.

Romano, R. Bucket, The.
Rospigliosi. Leavetaking.
Rossetti, C. Echo.
From Sunset to Star Rise.
Remember [Me].
Song: "She sat and sang alway."
Rossetti, D. Memory.
Sudden Light.
Rukeyser, M. Woman as Market.
Rungano. Mother.
Rutsala. Silence, The.
Rux, C. H. Asylum of Gestures.
Ryan, M. This Is a Poem for the Dead.
Salinas, R. Trip Through the Mind Jail, A.
Samyn, M. Poem with Light on Its Shoulder.
Sanchez, S. Poem at Thirty.
Sandburg, C. Haze.
Sansom, A. World is everything, The.
Sassoon. Aftermath.
Two Old Ladies.
Scalapino. Flush / a Play.
Scannell. Apple-raid, The.
Schertzinger, V. I Remember You.
Schilpp, M. Under the Scorpion's Heart.
Schnackenberg. Darwin in 1881.
Schwartz, R. L. Why I Forgive My Younger
Self Her Transgressions.
Scott, J. Plato's Dog.
Scovell. Sandy Yard, The.
Seferis. Last Stop.
Senghor. Luxembourg 1939.
Serote. Ofay-Watcher Looks Back.
Sewell, L. Denied, The.
Sexton. I Remember.
January 1st.
What's That.
Shange. Where the Heart Is.
Shapiro, K. Nigger.
Shelley, P. To———: "Music, when soft voices
die."
To Maria Gisborne in England, from Italy.
"Shu Ting." Maple Leaf.
Silko. Where Mountain Lion Lay [or Laid]
Down with Deer.
Sillitoe. Synagogue in Prague.
Simic. Empire of Dreams.
Lesson, The.
Wall, A.
Simmons, J. Archæologist, The.
Smith, I. Clearances, The.
Smith, P. Building Nicole's Mama.
Snodgrass, W. Mementos, 1.
Ten Days Leave.
Snyder, G. Autumn Morning in Shokoku-ji, An.
Four Poems for Robin.
Looking at Pictures to Be Put Away.
Spring Night in Shokoku-ji, A.
Solari, R. Currents.
Song. Out of Our Hands.
Wind in the Trees, The.
Sorrentino. Good Night!
Soto. Braly Street.
Not Knowing.
Street.
Who Will Know Us?
Soupault. Route.
Speakes. Heartbreak Hotel Piano-Bar.
Spender, S. Ice.
To T. A. R. H.
St. John, D. Guitar.
Quote Me Wrong Again and I'll Slit the Throat
of Your Pet Iguana.
Stanard, C. Baseball.
Steptoe. Sweet Brown Rice and Red Bones.
Stern, G. Dancing, The.
Expulsion, The.
Faces I Love, The.
Kissing Stieglitz Goodbye.
Stevens, W. Debris of Life and Mind.
Stevenson, R. Blows the Wind Today.
Stickney, T. In the Past.
Mnemosyne.
Pity.
Stidger. Lest Thou Forget.
Stokesbury. Evening's End.
Strand. Pot Roast.

Where Are the Waters of Childhood?
Suárez, V. Rice Comes to El Volcán.
Surrey. Prison in Windsor Castle.
Swinburne. Sundew, The.
Symons, A. Tune, A.
White Heliotrope.
Tabb. Echoes.
Mid-Day Moon, The.
Talvikki, A. Afterwards: Caliban.
Tapahonso. I Am Singing Now.
Taylor, A. Clearing Away.
Teasdale. Water-Lilies.
Tennyson, A. In the Valley of Cauteretz.
Thomas, E. Celandine.
In Memoriam (Easter, 1915).
Thoreau. Music.
They Who Prepare My Evening Meal Below.
Tighe. Written at Scarborough. August, 1799.
Townsend, A. Mardi Gras Premortem.
Trethewey, N. Cameo.
Trinidad. Double Trouble.
Triplett, P. Spectral Dues.
Tripp. In Memory of Idris Davies.
Trowbridge, J. Recollections of "Lalla Rookh."
Tucker, M. We Met.
Unknown. Memory System, A.
Unknown, fr. Terezin Concentration Camp.
Birdsong.
Forgotten.
Valentine, J. Lines in Dejection.
Van Duyn. Stream, The.
Vaughan, H. They Are All Gone into the World
of Light!
Voznesensky [or Voznesenskii]. I Am Goya.
Walcott. Glory Trumpeter, The.
Letter from Brooklyn, A.
Village Life, A.
Walden, G. Misguided Angels.
Walker, J. Studying Physics with My Daughter.
Waniek. House on Moscow Street, The.
Waring, B. Reprieve on the Stoop.
Warner, S. Green Valley, The.
Warren, H. Remember Me?
Warren, R. Blow, West Wind.
Debate: Question, Quarry, Dream.
Warsh. Suicide Rates, The.
Weaver, M. Easy Living.
Weigl. Her Life Runs Like a Red Silk Flag.
Sailing to Bien Hoa.
Weiner, H. Remembered Sequel.
Whalen. Slop Barrel, The.
White, E. Chairs in Snow.
Whitman, W. As Toilsome I Wander'd
Virginia's Woods.
Glimpse, A.
My Picture-Gallery.
Old Man's Thought of School, An.
Old War-Dreams.
Once I Pass'd through a Populous City.
Out of the Cradle Endlessly Rocking.
Whittier. Burning Drift-Wood.
Firelight.
Snow-Bound [or Snow-Bound; a Winter Idyl].
Telling the Bees.
To My Old Schoolmaster.
Wieners. Two Years Later.
Wiesel. Never Shall I Forget.
Wilbur. Mind-Reader, The.
Pardon, A.
Piazza di Spagna, Early Morning.
Wilder, A. Did You Ever Cross Over to
Sneden's.
Williams, C. Repression.
Williams, H. To the Strawberry.
Williams, S. California Light.
Williams, W. To a Dog Injured in the Street.
Williamson, G. Drawing Hands.
Willis, N. Confessional, The.
Wingfield. Winter.
Winner, S. Listen to the Mocking Bird.
Witt, S. Americana.
Michael Masse.
Woessner. Jungle Music.
Wojahn. Satin Doll.
Wong, N. Mama, Come Back.
Wordsworth, D. Thoughts on my sick-bed.

Wordsworth, W. Complaint, A.
  I Wandered Lonely As a Cloud.
  Sonnet on Catherine Wordsworth.
Wright, C. Homage to Paul Cézanne.
  Other Side of the River, The.
Wright, D. To the Gods the Shades Flavinus of
  the Cavalry Regiment.
Wright, J. Albuquerque Graveyard, The.
  End of an Ethnic Dream, The.
  On a Phrase from Southern Ohio.
  Redwings.
Wyatt, S. Lover Showeth How He Is Forsaken
  of Such as He Sometime Enjoyed, The.
  Steadfastness.
Yau. Cenotaph.
  Postcard from Trakl.
  Radiant Silhouette III.
Yeats. Circus Animals' Desertion, The.
  To a Young Girl.
  Tower, The.
  When You Are Old.
Young, K. Preserving, The.

Memphis, Tennessee
Brown, S. Memphis Blues.
Handy, W. Beale Street Blues.
Seay. Audubon Drive, Memphis.
Tarpley. Feel Free.

Men
Ai. Before You Leave.
Algarin. Trampling.
Arp. Man. The Woman, The.
Arrillaga. Rosa/Filí.
Atwood. Eventual Proteus.
Barlow, G. Place Where He Arose, The.
Behn, A. To Alexis in Answer to His Poem
  Against Fruition.
Berlin. You Can't Get a Man with a Gun.
Bernstein, M. Manly Sports.
Betham-Edwards. Power of Women, The.
Blamire. I've Gotten a Rock, I've Gotten a
  Reel.
Blane, R. Occasional Man, An.
Bogan, L. Men Loved Wholly Beyond Wisdom.
Borson. Talk.
Burns, R. On a Dog of Lord Eglinton's.
Butts, A. Belle Isle Men, The.
Césaire, A. On the Islands of All Winds.
Campo. For J. W.
Clark, T. Sons of Promise.
Clarke, C. Passing.
Clifton, L. Wishes for Sons.
Cope, W. Bloody Men.
  Rondeau Redoublé.
Crouch, S. Chops Are Flyin.
Dacre, C. Similie.
De la Mare. Hare, A.
Di Cicco. Male Rage Poem.
Dixon, M. Getting Your Rocks Off.
Duncan, R. Torso / Passages 18, The.
Dunn, S. Man Who Closed Shop, The.
Eberhart, R. Gnat on My Paper.
Edson, R. Feeding the Dog.
"Ephelia." In the Person of a Lady, to Bajazet,
  Her Unconstant Gallant.
Evans, R. Femininity.
Foley, M. Brothers and Sisters.
Fordham. Coming Woman, The.
Gallagher, T. Black Silk.
Garrick. Jupiter and Mercury.
Gilbert, C. Beginning by Value.
Gilmore, M. Eve-Song.
Glück, L. Labor Day.
  Palais des Arts.
Greenhalgh, C. Man in the Valley of
  Women, A.
Gunn, T. Innocence.
Hamby, B. St. Clare's Underwear.
Hammerstein. Bill.
Hands, E. Favourite Swain, The.
Harryman. Male, The.
Hayes, T. At Pegasus.
Hecht, A. Feast of Stephen, The.
Hernández Cruz. Slick.
Holiday. Fine and Mellow.
Hughes, L. Bad Man.
  Gypsy Man.

Isler. Little Things, The.
Iverem, E. Daddy's Friends.
Johnston, E. Lines: To a Young Gentleman of
  Surpassing Beauty.
  Working Man, The.
Justice, D. Men at Forty.
Kern, J. Bill.
  Bill (Original Version).
  It's a Hard, Hard World for a Man.
Kipling, R. If—.
Kizer, C. Hera, Hung from the Sky.
Lawrence, D. How Beastly the Bourgeois Is.
Lear, E. Limerick: "There was an Old Man in a
  tree."
  There Was an Old Man With a Beard.
Lerner, A. Hymn to Him, A.
Levertov. Abel's Bride.
  Mutes, The.
Limburg, J. Inner Bloke.
Livesay, D. Other.
Lowry, M. Eye-Opener.
MacDiarmid, H. One of the Principal Causes of
  War.
Madgett. Black Woman.
Malloch, D. Manly Love.
Martin, H. Occasional Man, An.
Martinez, D. Cultivation of Orchids, The.
Mataka. Next Door.
McKay, C. St. Isaac's Church, Petrograd.
Montagu, L. Answer to a Love-Letter in Verse,
  An.
Moore, M. To an Intra-Mural Rat.
Moulds, J. Renoir's Bathers.
Mudrooroo Narogin. Reincarnation.
Muldoon, P. Why Brownlee Left.
Murray, J. Men and Women Have Meaning
  Only as Man and Woman.
Naden. Love's Mirror.
Nasrin. At the Back of Progress.
Nathan, L. Body Count.
Neruda. Walking Around.
Norse. I'm Not a Man.
Nowlan. Rites of Manhood, The.
Orr, G. Who'd Want to Be a Man?
Ortleb. Militerotics.
Padilla. Man on the Edge.
Parker, D. Chant for Dark Hours.
  Men.
  Song of One of the Girls.
Pietri. 9th Untitled Poem.
Pilkington, L. Song, A.
Pitchford. Surgery.
Plath. Gulliver.
Prescod. Women Are Different.
Probyn. Tête-à-Tête.
Queen Latifah. Evil That Men Do, The.
Rainey. See, See Rider.
Rich, A. From a Survivor.
  Phenomenology of Anger, The.
  Re-forming the Crystal.
  Trying to Talk with a Man.
  Waking in the Dark.
Roberson. Eclipse.
  True We Are Two Grown Men.
Roberts, E. Mr. Wells.
Robinson, M. Modern Male Fashions.
Rouse. Spunk Talking.
Ryan, G. If I Had a Gun.
Rykard, R. Whole two weeks after The Million
  Man March, A; and still, if you'd ask me, this
  is all I could say about it.
Sanchez, S. Prelude to Nothing.
Schuyler, J. Royals.
Sharp, S. In the Tradition of Bobbitt.
Shepherd, R. Three A.. Eternal.
Shurin. Exorcism of the Straight/Man/Demon.
Simmons, J. Experience.
  Influence of Natural Objects, The.
Stevenson, R. Looking Forward.
Szymborska. Born of Woman.
Taggard. Everyday Alchemy.
Taylor, B. Goblet, The.
Thomas, D. I, in My Intricate Image.
Thomas, E. Forsaken Wife, The.
Tomlinson, C. Word in Edgeways, A.
Towers, T. Mission Poem.

Troupe. Reflections on Growing Older.
Unknown. Stackolee.
  Tired as I Can Be.
  Woman's Love.
Vega. Brothers Loving Brothers.
"W——, Miss." Gentleman's Study, in Answer
  to The Lady's Dressing-Room, The.
Waters, M. Hoochie Coochie.
West, K. On Track.
Whitman, W. I Sing the Body Electric.
Wilder, A. Trouble Is a Man.
Williams, C. It Is This Way with Men.
Williams, S. She Had Known Brothers.
Yeats. Men Improve with the Years.

Menopause
"Astra." Bloody Pause.
Cook, W. Seth Bingham.
Romo-Carmona, M. Signs.

Menstruation
Donovan, K. Underneath Our Skirts.
Dove, R. After Reading *Mickey in the Night
  Kitchen* for the Third Time Before Bed.
Millay, E. Menses.
Shange. We Need a God Who Bleeds Now.
Trethewey, N. Drapery Factory, Gulfport,
  Mississippi, 1956.

Mental Illness
Alexie. Theology.
Betjeman. Huxley Hall.
Bishop, E. Faustina, or Rock Roses.
Bogan, L. Evening in the Sanitarium.
Bryan, M. Maniac, The.
Campo. Asylum.
Cowper, W. Shrubbery, The.
Davis, C. Out of Work, Out of Touch, Out of
  Sorts.
Delgado, J. Recommitted.
  Visiting Father.
Dobyns. Frenchie.
Fallon, P. Himself.
"Field." Sullenness.
Frost, R. Servant to Servants, A.
Ginsberg, A. Kaddish.
Goodison. For Don Drummond.
Haines, J. On a Certain Field in Auvers.
Hecht, A. Third Avenue in Sunlight.
Holmes, J. Depressive Episode.
Hughes, L. Neighbor.
Johnson, H. Berlioz in the Madhouse.
Justice, D. Counting the Mad.
Kenyon, J. Depression in Winter.
Knight, E. Hard Rock Returns to Prison from
  the Hospital for the Criminal Insane.
Kocan. Bill.
  Sleepers, The.
Kolodny, S. Tsuneko—Psychiatric Medications
  Clinic.
Levy, A. Cross-Road Epitaph, A.
Lowell, R. Waking in the Blue.
Maiden. Anorexia.
Mew. Ken.
  On the Asylum Road.
Moolten, D. Madame Butterfly.
Murray, G. American Cheese.
North, C. Note to Tony Towle (After WS), A.
Opie. To a Maniac.
Owen, W. Chances, The.
  Mental Cases, The.
Page, P. Schizophrenic.
Plath. Tulips.
Rector. David's Rumor.
Rhodes, M. Why She Hurries Out, Then Home.
Ritchie, E. Electroconvulsive Therapy.
Sexton. Music Swims Back to Me.
  Ringing the Bells.
  You, Doctor Martin.
Smith, S. Away, Melancholy.
  Deserter, The.
Strickland, A. Maniac, The.
Tipping. When You're Feeling Kind of
  Bonkers.
Unknown. Limerick.
Weinstein, N. Ethiopian Apocalypse of Don,
  The.
Wordsworth, W. I Wandered Lonely As a
  Cloud.

See also **Madness; Psychiatry and Psychiatrists**

Mental Retardation
Blackburn, T.   Hospital for Defectives.
Dodd, E.   Touched.
Gunn, T.   As Expected.
Hugo, R.   Letter to Wagoner from Port Townsend.
Johnson, M. F.   Idiot Girl, The.
Marty.   In the Dome Car of the "Canadian."
Murray, L.   Dog Fox Field.
Seale, J.   Playing the Flute for the TMR Class.
See also **Down's Syndrome**

Mercenaries
Housman, A.   Epitaph on an Army of Mercenaries.
Jonson, B.   To Captain Hungry.
MacDiarmid, H.   Another Epitaph on an Army of Mercenaries.

Merchants
Espinet, R.   Merchant of Death.
Herrick.   Upon Rook: Epigram.
Jamie.   Flower-sellers, Budapest.
See also **Business and Businessmen; Clerks**

Mercury (god)
Komunyakaa.   Slam, Dunk, and Hook.
Lawrence, D.   Maximus.

Mercury (planet)
Morgan, E.   First Men on Mercury, The.

Mercy
"Ada."   Lines.
Bishop, E.   Fish, The.
Browning, E.   Convinced by Sorrow.
Chippewa Oral Tradition.   Song of the Captive Sioux Woman.
Elytis.   Origin of Landscape or the End of Mercy, The.
Hardy, T.   Burghers, The.
Often When Warring.
Herbert, G.   Discipline.
Herrick.   Calling, and Correcting.
God's Mercy.
To Heaven.
Hughes, L.   Feet O' Jesus.
Johnson, F.   Singing Hallelujia.
Lumsden, R.   Mercy.
Ralegh, S.   Passionate Man[']s Pilgrimage, The.
Reznikoff.   Day of Atonement.
Rossetti, C.   Before the Beginning.
Södergran.   Question.
Southey, R.   Ship, The.
Tuckerman, F.   Rhotruda.
Unknown.   Epitaph: "My friend, judge not me."
Mercy.
Prayer of a Woman in Charge of Berry Picking in Knights Inlet.
Weigl.   Mercy.
Wheatley, P.   On Being Brought from Africa to America.
Whittier.   Robin, The.
Wordsworth, W.   Gravestone upon the Floor in the Cloisters of Worcester Cathedral, A.
Wright, J.   Two Poems about President Harding.

Merlin
Chubb, T.   Merlin.
Emerson, R.   Merlin I.
Greville, F.   Caelica, XXIII.
Hill, G.   Merlin.
Norris, L.   Merlin and the Snake's Egg.
Tennyson, A.   Merlin and the Gleam.

Mermaid Tavern, London
Keats.   Lines on the Mermaid Tavern.

Mermaids and Mermen
Calverley.   In the Gloaming.
De la Mare.   Sam.
Hennell.   Mermaiden, A.
Hughes, L.   Catch.
King, B.   Mermaid, The.
Knight, S.   Mermaid Tank, The.
MacLeish.   Return.
McCullagh, J.   Mermaid's Song.
Nash, O.   Mermaid, The.
Richards, L.   Mermaidens, The.
Spires.   Comb and the Mirror, The.
Tennyson, A.   Merman, The.
Unknown.   Clerk Colvill.

Young, I.   Mermaid Knows, A.

Merrimac (ship)
Longfellow, H.   Cumberland, The.
See also **Monitor (ship)**

Merriment
Herrick.   Ceremonies for Christmas[se].
McGinley.   City Christmas.

Merry-Go-Rounds
Hughes, L.   Merry-Go-Round.
McAuley, J.   Merry-go-round.

Messengers
Browning, R.   How They Brought the Good News from Ghent to Aix.
Doolittle, H.   Hermes of the Ways.
Frost, R.   Bearer of Evil Tidings, The.
Glück, L.   Messengers.
Lawrence, D.   Maximus.
Mitchell, S.   Annunciation, The.
Richards, G.   Almighty Spake, and Gabriel Sped, Th'
Tennyson, A.   O Swallow, Swallow.
Warren, R.   Patriotic Tour and Postulate of Joy.

Messiah
Gascoyne.   Rex Mundi.
Pope, A.   Rise, Crowned with Light Imperial Salem Rise.
Yeats.   Second Coming, The.

Metals
Moore, M.   Odor of a Metal Is Not Strong, The.
Morley, D.   Metal-work.

Metaphor
Collins, B.   Death of Allegory, The.
Davie.   With the Grain.
Dove, R.   History.
France, L.   Body Language.
Hollander, J.   What the Lovers in the Old Songs Thought.
Kinsella, J.   Archetypal Chillies.
Levertov.   Cat as Cat, The.
Lowell, A.   Meeting-House Hill.
Lux.   Solo Native.
Marvell.   Definition of Love, The.
Nash, O.   Very like a Whale.
Pastan.   Baseball.
Overture.
Plath.   Metaphors.
Sklarew.   How Metaphor Can Save Your Life.
What Is a Jewish Poem?
Stevens, W.   Motive for Metaphor, The.
Tranter.   Great Artist Reconsiders the Homeric Simile, The.
Williams, W.   Sort of a Song, A.
Williamson, G.   Dark Days, The.
See also **Symbols**

Metaphysics
Barbauld.   To Mr. S. T. Coleridge.
Lloyd, C.   Metaphysical Sonnet.
MacNeice.   London Rain.
McPherson, S.   Some Metaphysics of Junior Wells.
Perreault, J.   Metaphysical Paintings, The.
Stevens, W.   Glass of Water, The.
Tomlinson, C.   In Defence of Metaphysics.

Meteors and Meteorites
Hirshfield, J.   That Falling.
Huntington, W.   Cold Meteorite, The.
Mulkey, R.   Blind-Sided.
Salazar.   Meteor Showers—Yosemite.
Szporluk.   Meteor.
Thomas, E.   Shooting Star, A.
Vaughan, H.   To Amoret, of the Difference 'twixt Him and Other Lovers, and What True Love Is.

Methodism
Su, A.   I Can't Become a Buddhist.

Mexican War
Baca.   Mi Tío Baca el Poeta de Socorro.

Mexico
Ashbery.   Instruction Manual, The.
Baca.   So Mexicans Are Taking Jobs from Americans.
Birney.   Irapuato.
Sinalóa.
Brewer, G.   Mountains.

Campo.   El Día de los Muertos.
Cisneros, S.   You Bring Out the Mexican in Me.
Cumpian.   No Deposit Returns.
Gilbert, J.   Elephant Hunt in Guadalajara.
González, R.   You and the Tijuana Mule.
Gonzalez, R.   Still Life with Endings.
Grier.   Mountain Town—Mexico.
Herrera.   Dream of Christopher Columbus, The.
Mexican World Mural / 5 x 25.
Resurrection of the Flesh, The.
Kerouac.   Mexican Loneliness.
Lawrence, D.   Living Quetzalcoatl, The.
Quetzalcoatl Looks Down on Mexico.
Lowry, M.   Delirium in Vera Cruz.
For *Under the Volcano*.
McClure, M.   Reading Frank O'Hara in a Mexican Rainstorm.
McKendrick, J.   Shortened History in Pictures, A.
Ríos, A.   At Kino Viejo, Mexico.
Reed, I.   El Paso Monologue.
Van Duyn.   Into Mexico.
Welch, L.   In Answer to a Question From P. W.
Williams, W.   Desert Music, The.
Wong, N.   On Plaza Garibaldi.
Wright, J.   Minneapolis Poem, The.

Mexico City
Twichell.   Aisle of Dogs.

Mice
Bachner.   Little Mouse, The.
Barbauld.   Mouse's Petition, The.
Bennett, R.   Witch of Willowby Wood, The.
Betjeman.   Diary of a Church Mouse.
Blight.   Death of a Whale.
Bodecker.   Cats and Dogs.
Brown, M.   Little Black Bug.
Brown, S.   Marriage.
Burns, R.   To a Mouse; On Turning Her up in Her Nest, with the Plough, November, 1785.
Charles, D.   Concrete Cat.
Ciardi.   I Wouldn't.
Clare, J.   Clock-A-Clay.
Mouse's Nest.
Coatsworth.   Mouse, The.
Cook, E.   Mouse and the Cake, The.
Cowley, A.   Country-Mouse, The.
Cox, P.   Mouse's Lullaby, The.
Cummings, E.   Four III.
Me Up at Does.
Delmore, E.   Is It Not Strange?
Dixon, M.   Place, Places.
Dugan, A.   Funeral Oration for a Mouse.
Feinstein, S.   Summerhouse Piano.
Flynn, N.   Bag of Mice.
Fyleman.   (Mice).
Garrigue.   Mouse, The.
Graves, R.   One Hard Look.
Gray, S.   On a Cat Aging.
Gunn, T.   Last Days at Teddington.
Henryson.   Tale of the Upland Mouse and the Burgess Mouse, The.
Hughes, T.   Cat and Mouse.
Kay, J.   Virus².
Kinsella, J.   Chess Piece Cornered.
Levertov.   Innocent, The.
Lucilius.   Miser and the Mouse, The.
Mitchell, L.   House of the Mouse, The.
Moorer.   Legal Mouse, A.
Mother Goose.   Six Little Mice.
Norris, L.   Mice in the Hay.
Patchen.   Magical Mouse, The.
Richards, L.   Mouse, The.
Roethke.   Meadow Mouse, The.
Rossetti, C.   City Mouse and the Garden Mouse, The.
Rothman, D.   Resurrection of a Mouse.
Serraillier.   Anne and the Field-Mouse.
Mouse in the Wainscot, The.
Starbuck, G.   New Strain.
Stevens, W.   Dance of the Macabre Mice.
Stroud, W.   Rustler.
Tsaloumas.   Old Friend.
Unknown.   Mouse in Her Room, A.
Williams, W.   Mujer.

Michael, Saint
Rossetti, C.   St. Michael and all Angels.

Michaelmas
Forrest-Thomson. Michaelmas.
Nicholson, N. Michaelmas.

Michelangelo Buonarroti
Allston. On a Falling Group in the Last
  Judgement of Michael Angelo, in the Cappella
  Sistina.
  On Michael Angelo.
Browning, R. "Moses" of Michael Angelo, The.
McIlroy, L. Good-Bye, Valentine.

Michigan (state)
Joseph, L. Do What You Can.
Levine, P. Poem Circling Hamtramck,
  Michigan, All Night in Search of You, The.
  Rain Downriver.

Microbes
Ade. Microbe's Serenade, The.
Auden. New Year Greeting, A.
Goedicke. Imprint of Microscopic Life Found
  in Arctic Stones.

Microcosm
Ammons, A. R. Corsons Inlet.
Dowden, E. Two Infinities.
Frost, R. Design.
Guevara, M. Miniaturist, The.
Hughes, F. Bird.
Pastan. Egg.

Microscopes
Chin, J. Undetectable.

Midas
Moss, H. King Midas.
"Pindar." Epigram: "Midas, they say, possessed
  the art of old."

Middle Age
"Astra." Bloody Pause.
  Now or Never.
Beer, P. Middle Age.
Brasch. Ambulando.
Clifton, L. Thirty-Eighth Year, The.
Hall, D. To a Waterfowl.
Heath-Stubbs. Lady's Complaint, The.
Jarrell. Next Day.
Justice, D. Men at Forty.
Kunitz, S. End of Summer.
Longfellow, H. Mezzo Cammin.
Lowell, R. Middle Age.
MacNeice. Libertine, The.
Matthews, W. Good Company.
McGough, R. 40—Love.
Millar, J. Midlife.
Patten, B. Ode on Celestial Music.
Porter, P. Sex and the Over Forties.
Prior. Phillis's Age.
Rich, A. Middle-Aged, The.
Rukeyser, M. Rondel: "Now that I am fifty-
  six."
Salinas, L. Middle Age.
Schuyler, J. Growing Dark.
Simpson, L. Middleaged Man, The.
Smith, C. Thirty-eight: Addressed to Mrs H—y.
Sorrells. From a Correct Address in a Suburb of
  a Major City.
Swift, J. Stella's Birthday; Written in the Year
  1718[/9].
Thompson, D. P. Dancing in Menopause.
  Laurel Street, 1950.
Tucker, M. First Grey Hair, The.
Webb, C. At Summer's End.
Young, A. Fifty-Fifty.

Middle Ages
Browning, R. Grammarian's Funeral, A.
Dubie. Annual of the Dark Physics, An.
Hill, G. Requiem for the Plantagenet Kings.

Middlesex, England
Betjeman. Middlesex.
  Slough.

Midnight
Bevington, L. Midnight.
Brown, G. Haddock Fishermen.
Crosby, F. Thoughts in Midnight Hours.
Donne. Nocturnal[l] upon Saint Lucy's [or S.
  Lucy's or S. Lucies] Day, Being the Shortest
  Day, A.
Grossman, A. Enough Rain for Agnes Walquist.
Hanighen, B. 'Round Midnight.

Hughes, L. Jam Session.
Huidobro. Midnight.
Hull, L. Midnight Reports.
Kolodinsky, A. Midnight.
Komunyakaa. Boat People.
Lakides. Armed Forces.
Lane, P. Midnight Song.
Lewis, S. Street of Dreams.
Patchen. Midnight Special.
Stoutenburg. Midnight Saving Time.
Watson, R. Midnight Harvest, A.
Whitman, W. Clear Midnight, A.

Midsummer
Christopher. Midsummer.
Hardy, T. On a Midsummer Eve.

Mignonettes
Lawrence, D. Red Geranium and Godly
  Mignonette.

Migraine
Dunbar, W. Magryme, The.

Migrant Workers
Delgado, J. Awakened in a Field.
  Campesinos.
García, D. Tísica.
González, R. Penny Men.
Janzen, J. August Nights.
Levis. Photograph: Migrant Worker, Parlier,
  California, 1967.
Maris, H. Season's Finished, The.
McDaniel, W. Ruby Red's Migrant Camp.
Oliveira, D. Little Travel Story, A.
Spear, R. Good Men.
  Nest for Everyone, A.
See also **Farmworkers**

Migration
Bryant, W. To a Waterfowl.
Freneau. On the Emigration to America [and
  Peopling the Western Country].
Hope, A. Death of the Bird, The.
Horan. Soft Swimmer, Winter Swan.
Lane, P. Migration.
Longfellow, H. Tale of Acadie, A.
Mattawa. History of My Face.
Warren, R. Heart of Autumn.
Weaver, M. Brooklyn.

Milan, Italy
Levine, P. And the Trains Go On.

Militarism
Amadiume. We Have Even Lost Our Tongues!
Eliot, T. Triumphal March.
Hardy, T. Channel Firing.
"M." On the Frequent Review of the Troops.

Military Justice
Kipling, R. Cells.
  Danny Deever.

Military Life
Allen, E. In the Defences.
Rome, H. Military Life, The.
Smith, A. Political Intelligence.
See also **Army Life**

Milk and Milking
Corso. Mad Yak, The.
Dallas, R. Milking before Dawn.
Frost, R. Cow in Apple Time, The.
Heaney, S. Churning Day.
Herrick. Fresh Cheese and Cream.
  Upon Sibilla.
Lee, L. Milkmaid.
Maguire, S. Spilt Milk.
Monro. Milk for the Cat.
Montague, J. Drink of Milk, A.
Nash, O. Cow, The.
Roberts, E. Milking Time.
Yeats. Spilt Milk.

Milkmaids
Mother Goose. Milk Maid, The.
Pfeiffer, E. Sonsy Milkmaid, The.
Randolph, T. Milkmaid's Epithalamium, The.

Milkmen
De Paul, G. Milkman, Keep Those Bottles
  Quiet!
Lux. Milkman and His Son, The.

Milkweed
Kasdorf. Streak, The.

Levine, P. Milkweed.
Wright, J. Milkweed.

Millay, Edna St. Vincent
Adams, F. If.

Millennium
Beer, P. Millennium.
Brock-Broido. Domestic Mysticism.
Stafford, W. Epitaph Ending in And, The.
Vaughan, H. Dawning, The.
Whittier. Astræa.
Yeats. Second Coming, The.

Millet, Jean François
Markham, E. Man with the Hoe, The.

Mills and Millers
Allingham. Mill, A.
Coppard. Unfortunate Miller, The.
Cunningham, J. Miller, The.
Foster, A. Wythop Mill.
Johnson, G. Old Rustic Mill, The.
Kalar, J. Papermill.
Markus, P. Black Light.
Nelson, M. Molino.
Robinson, E. Mill, The.
Tomlinson, C. John Maydew or The Allotment.
Wainwright, J. 1815.

Milton, John
Beer, P. John Milton and My Father.
Blake, W. And Did Those Feet in Ancient
  Time.
  Wine-Press of Los, The.
Bridges, R. Johannes Milton, Senex.
Deane, S. Reading *Paradise Lost* in Protestant
  Ulster 1984.
Devaney, T. Sonnet: "You know all those
  sonnets the ones where I said, I love you,
  well."
Dryden, J. Lines Printed under the Engraved
  Portrait of Milton [In Tonson's Folio of the
  "Paradise Lost"].
Longfellow, H. Milton.
Marvell. On Mr Milton's "Paradise Lost."
Muir, E. Milton.
Myles, E. December 9th.
Ray, H. Milton.
Snyder, G. Milton by Firelight.
Tabb. Milton.
Tennyson, A. Milton [Alcaics].
Watts, I. Adventurous Muse, The.
Wordsworth, W. London, 1802.
  Ode: Intimations of Immortality [from
  Recollections of Early Childhood].

Mind
Bang, M. Louise in Love.
Hochman. Hairbrush, The.
Hope, A. Wandering Islands, The.
Mead, J. Sometimes the Mind.
Moore, R. Still Without Life.
Pollitt. Mind-Body Problem.
Roethke. In a Dark Time.
Tlingit Oral Tradition. Carrying My Mind
  Around.
See also **Intellect and Intellectuals**

Minerals
Hemans. Epitaph on Mr W—.
MacDiarmid, H. Crystals like Blood.
Redgrove, P. Minerals of Cornwall, Stones of
  Cornwall.
Thomas, D. I, in My Intricate Image.
See also **Mining and Miners; Metals**

Minerva
Hood, T. To Minerva.
See also **Athena**

Mining and Miners
Abinader, E. Gentry, The.
Ammons, A. R. Prospecting.
Clemo. Christ in the Clay-Pit.
Dorn, E. Mourning Letter, March 29 1963.
Gibson, W. White Dust, The.
Heaney, S. Singer's House, The.
Huddle. Almost Going.
  Holes Commence Falling.
Johnson, D. Poem: "There was something I
  can't bring myself."
Larkin, P. Explosion, The.

McKinney, I.　Deep Mining.
　Twilight in West Virginia: Six O'Clock Mine
　Report.
More, H.　Patient Joe; or, The Newcastle Collier.
Oodgeroo of the tribe Noonuccal.　Time Is
　Running Out.
Owen, W.　Miners.
Page, P.　Photos of a Salt Mine.
Skipsey.　Mother Wept.
Snyder, G.　Fire in the Hole.
　Milton by Firelight.
Tomlinson, C.　Shaft, The.
"Twain."　He Done His Level Best.
Unknown.　Clementine.
Untermeyer, L.　Caliban in the Coal Mines.
Watkins, V.　Collier, The.
Wright, J.　Miners.
Wrigley, R.　Sinking of Clay City, The.
See also **Coal Mining and Coal Miners; Gold
Mining and Gold Miners**

Mink
Derricotte.　Minks, The.
Hannan, M.　Coming Down from Derry Hill.

Minnesota (state)
Bly, R.　Driving toward the Lac Qui Parle River.
Etter.　Great Northern.
Kooser.　Late Lights in Minnesota.
Ryan, R.　Winter in Minneapolis.
Wanek.　Duluth, Minnesota.
Wright, J.　Blessing, A.
　Lying in a Hammock at William Duffy's Farm
　in Pine Island, Minnesota.
　Minneapolis Poem, The.

Minotaur
Gioia.　Maze Without a Minotaur.
Powell, D. A.　Minotaur at Supper: Spare the
　Noritake and the Spode, The.

Minstrels
Dransfield.　Minstrel.
Hughes, L.　Minstrel Man.
Moore, T.　Minstrel Boy, The.

Miracles
Aiken, C.　Miracles.
Angira.　Manna.
Appleman, P.　Mary.
Awoonor.　This Earth, My Brother.
Bontemps.　Miracles.
Crashaw.　On the Miracle of Loaves.
　On the Miracle of Multiplied [*or* Multiplyed]
　Loaves.
　To Our Lord, upon the Water Made Wine.
Creeley.　Kore.
De Los Santos, M.　Milagros Mourns the Queen
　of Scat.
Donne.　Relic, The.
　Song: "Go and catch a falling star."
"Field."　Maidenhair.
Ginsberg, A.　Galilee Shore.
Herbert, G.　Whitsunday.
Herrick.　Widow's Tears [*or* Widdowes Teares]:
　or, Dirge of Dorcas, The.
Jackson, L.　Wind Suffers of Blowing, The.
Masters, E.　Business Reverses.
McGough, R.　Poem With a Limp.
Merton.　Cana.
Plath.　Black Rook in Rainy Weather.
Shaw, L.　Getting Inside the Miracle.
Smith, G.　Penitential Cries of Jupiter
　Hammond, The.
Sobin, G.　What the Music Wants.
Tate, J.　Manna.
Vaughan, H.　Religion.
Wen Yi-tuo.　Miracle.
Whitman, W.　Miracles.

Mirrors
Abse.　Footnote Extended, A.
Aiken, C.　Dear Uncle Stranger.
Ammons, A. R.　Reflective.
Atwood.　Tricks with Mirrors.
Bogan, L.　Man Alone.
Browning, R.　Love in a Life.
Burns, R.　Keekin' Glass, The.
Caddy, C.　Three-Inch Reflector.
Carew, T.　Looking-Glass, A.
　On His Mistress Looking in a Glass.

Coleridge, M.　Other Side of a Mirror, The.
Cronin, J.　Motho Ke Motho Ka Batho Babang
　(A Person Is a Person Because of Other
　People).
Curbelo.　Bedtime Stories.
DeCarteret, M.　Town Clerk, The.
Follain.　Mirror, A.
Garrigue.　Cracked Looking Glass.
　Primer of Plato.
Gascoyne.　Salvador Dali.
Graham, J.　Underneath (7).
Graves, R.　Face in the Mirror, The.
　Pier-Glass, The.
Hemans.　Mirror in the Deserted Hall, The.
Hemphill.　Family Jewels.
Herbert, E.　In a Glass-Window for Inconstancy.
Kipling, R.　Looking Glass, The.
Kowit.　Cosmetics Do No Good.
　In the Morning.
Levertov.　Seeing for a Moment.
Lochhead, L.　Hickie, The.
Lovelace, R.　Lucasta's Fan[ne], with a
　Looking-Glass[e] in It.
Lowry, M.　Sestina in a Cantina.
Merwin, W. S.　Glass.
Nicholson, N.　From a Boat at Coniston.
Noguere.　Whirling Round the Sun.
Oates.　Insomnia.
Plath.　Mirror.
Prior.　Lady Who Offers Her Looking-Glass to
　Venus, The.
Probyn.　Model, The.
Rakosi.　Lord, What Is Man?
Reed, I.　Beware: Do Not Read This Poem.
Shepherd, R.　Narcissus Learning the Words to
　This Song.
Shirley, J.　To a Lady Upon a Looking-Glass
　Sent.
Simic.　Charon's Cosmology.
　Miracle Glass Co.
　Mirrors at 4 A.M.
Stoddard, E.　Before the Mirror.
Symons, A.　La Mélinite: Moulin-Rouge.
Tada.　Mirror.
Traherne.　Shadows in the Water.
Troupe.　Sense of Coolness, a.
Wakoski.　Imagining Point Dume.
Webster, A.　By the Looking-Glass.
Wetzsteon.　Late Show, The.
Whitman, W.　Eidolons.
　Hand-Mirror, A.
Williams, W.　Mists Over the River.
Yi, S.　Poem No. XV.
Zagajewski.　Auto Mirror.

Mirth
Bowles, W.　Languid, and sad, and slow.
Cavendish, M.　Dialogue between Melancholy
　and Mirth, A.
Herrick.　Hock-Cart, or Harvest Home, The.
　Lyric to Mirth, A.
　To Live Merrily, and To Trust to Good Verses.
Hunt, L.　To the Grasshopper and the Cricket.
Lowry, M.　Strange Type.
Milton.　To Cyriack Skinner.
Rodriguez, J.　Eskimo Occasion.
See also **Laughter; Merriment**

Misanthropy
Wylie.　Eagle and the Mole, The.

Miscarriages
Clancy, J.　Miscarriage.
Hecht, A.　Vow, The.
Plath.　Barren Woman.
Townsend, A.　First Death.

Mischief
Brown, L.　I Want to Be Bad.
DeSylva, B. G.
Graves, R.　Nobody.
Henderson, R.　I Want to Be Bad.
Herrick.　Upon Pagget.
Unknown.　Mr Nobody.

Misfortune
Adair, T.　Everything Happens to Me.
Arlen, H.　Ill Wind.
Barbour, D.　Mañana (Is Soon Enough for Me).
Beckett, S.　Ooftish.

Blane, R.　Ev'ry Time.
Burns, R.　Man Was Made to Mourn, a Dirge.
　To a Mouse; On Turning Her up in Her Nest,
　with the Plough, November, 1785.
Comden, B.　All of My Life.
　You Mustn't Feel Discouraged.
Cowper, W.　Shrubbery, The.
Dennis, M.　Everything Happens to Me.
Dobell, S.　Tommy's Dead.
Elizabeth I.　Ah silly pugg wert thou so sore
　afraid.
Graves, R.　All Except Hannibal.
Gray, T.　Hymn to Adversity.
Green, A.　All of My Life.
　You Mustn't Feel Discouraged.
Harris, R.　Call, The.
Harte, B.　Mrs. Judge Jenkins[; Being the Only
　Genuine Sequel to "Maud Muller"].
Lanier, S.　Revenge of Hamish, The.
Lindsay, L.　Auld Robin Gray.
McKay, C.　Castaways, The.
More, H.　Riot; or, Half a Loaf Is Better than No
　Bread, The.
Notley.　Where Leftover Misery Goes.
Piatt, S.　Giving Back the Flower.
Ralegh, S.　Fortune Hath Taken Away.
Sia, B.　Enemy.
Stickney, T.　Six o'Clock.
Styne, J.　All of My Life.
　You Mustn't Feel Discouraged.
Towers, T.　Three Observations on Belief.
Unknown.　Southern Blues.
　Stackalee.
　Three Sons, The.
Wotton, S.　Upon the Sudden Restraint of the
　Earl[e] of Somerset, Then Falling from Favor
　[*or* Favour].
Wyatt, S.　Lover Showeth How He Is Forsaken
　of Such as He Sometime Enjoyed, The.

Mishima, Yukio
Cole, W.　Mysterious East.

Misogyny
Algarin.　Trampling.
Askhari.　Circular Fate.
Bradford, E.　Equality.
Clare, J.　Song: "I peeled bits of straw and I got
　switches too."
Patmore, C.　Warning, A.
Pollitt.　Onion.
Rich, A.　From an Old House in America.
Rochester, J.　Song: "Love a woman? You're [*or*
　Y'are] an ass."
Swift, J.　Gentle Echo on Woman, A.

Missionaries
Campbell, J.　I'm Far From What I Call My
　Home.
Heber.　From Greenland's Icy Mountains.
Johnson, E.　Letter to My Mother, A.
　Weevilly Porridge.
Johnson, H.　Magalu.
Linden, M.　Missionary, The.
Moorer.　Africa.
Morgan, E.　Columba's Song.
Pickthall, M.　Père Lalement.
　Two Souls.
Sinclair, K.　Memorial to a Missionary.
Tjanara-Williams, P.　Torn Apart.
Townsend, A.　After the End.

Mississippi (state)
Brooks, G.　Bronzeville Mother Loiters in
　Mississippi, A. Meanwhile, a Mississippi
　Mother Burns Bacon.
Eberhart, R.　La Crosse at Ninety Miles an
　Hour.
Hayden, R.　Night, Death, Mississippi.
Knight, E.　Once on a Night in the Delta: A
　Report From Hell.
　Poem for Myself (Or Blues for a Mississippi
　Black Boy), A.
Miller, E.　Mississippi.
Sundiata.　Making Poems; on the road in
　Minneapolis.

Mississippi River
Garland, H.　On the Mississippi.
Gehrke, S.　Near the Mississippi.

Hammerstein. Ol' Man River.
Hayden, R. Night, Death, Mississippi.
Ransom, J. Antique Harvesters.
Redmond. River of Bones and Flesh and Blood.
Shange. Where the Mississippi meets the Amazon.
Steptoe. Mississippi Blues.

Missouri (state)
Barnes, J. Last Look at La Plata, Missouri.
Sunday Dreamer's Guide to Yarrow, Missouri, A.
Justice, D. Childhood.
Knight, E. Poem to Galway Kinnell, A.
Sterling, A. Meet Me in St. Louis, Louis.

Mist
Bridges, R. Garden in September, The.
Clare, J. Mist in the Meadows.
Keats. To Autumn.
Paz. Here.
Southard. By mist.
Unknown. Mist, The.
Watson, R. Children of the Mist.
See also **Fog**

Mistletoe
Tucker, M. Mistletoe.

Mistresses
Amadiume. Mistress of My Own Being.
De Vries, P. To His Importunate Mistress.
Donne. Self[e] Accuser, A.
Herrick. To His Mistresses.
Upon the Loss[e] of His Mistresses.
What Kind of Mistress[e] He Would Have.
Marvell. To His Coy Mistress.
Nelson, M. Ballad of Aunt Geneva, The.
Orléans, C. Roundel: "Take, take this cosse, atonys, atonys, my hert!"
Pratt, J. Words and Thoughts.
Ranaivo. Song of a Young Girl.
Shirley, J. To His Mistress.
Smith, S. Infelice.
Suckling, S. Sonnet: "O[h]! for some honest lover's ghost."
Unknown. All Seasons in One.
My Mistress.
Wright, J. Gesture by a Lady with an Assumed Name, A.

Misunderstanding
Baird, M. Do Not Make Things Too Easy.
Creeley. Gift, The.
Hewitt, J. Turf-Carrier [*or* Turf Carrier] on Aranmore.
Murray, L. Hearing Impairment.
Rich, A. Like This Together.
Trying to Talk with a Man.
Unknown. Since First I Saw Your Face.

Mites
Frost, R. Considerable Speck, A.
Merrill, B. Mite, The.

Mithridates the Great
Emerson, R. Mithridates.

Mittens
Allen, M. Mitten Song, The.
Follen, E. Three Little Kittens, The.
Hughes, L. This Little House Is Sugar.
See also **Gloves**

Moas
Curnow. Skeleton of the Great Moa in the Canterbury Museum, Christchurch, The.

Mobile Bay, Battle of (1864)
Meredith, W. Farragut, Farragut.

Mobility
Jordan, J. Roman Poem Number Nine.
Kunitz, S. Summing-up, The.

Mockingbirds
Bukowski. Mockingbird, The.
Drake, J. Mocking-Bird, The.
Estes, A. Serenade.
Fordham. To the Mock-Bird.
Hayden, R. Mourning Poem for the Queen of Sunday.
Heard, J. My Mocking Bird.
Hovey. Mocking-Bird, The.
Jarrell. Mockingbird, The.
Lanier, S. Mocking Bird, The.

Moore, M. Bird-witted.
Van Duyn. Mockingbird Month.
Wilde, R. To the Mocking-Bird.
Winner, S. Listen to the Mocking Bird.

Models
Cabico, R. Antonio Banderas in His Underwear.
Hannan, M. Life Model.
Herd. Gia.
Moore, H. Girl in a Fur-Trimmed Dress.
Nabokov. Ode to a Model.
Probyn. Model, The.
Rossetti, C. In an Artist's Studio.
Shapiro, K. Editing *Poetry*.

Moderation
Cullen, C. Song in Spite of Myself.
Herrick. Moderation.
Thompson, F. Counsel of Moderation, A.

Modern Man
Adams, L. Kids!
Adnan. Beirut-Hell Express, The.
Allen, P. Kopis'taya.
Ama Ata Aidoo. Gynae One.
Ashbery. Cæsura.
Auden. Unknown Citizen, The.
Baraka. Political Poem.
Bissett. Christ I Wudint Know Normal if I Saw It When.
Bond, E. How We See.
Bronk. At Tikal.
Ciardi. Back through the Looking Glass to This Side.
Cohan. Twentieth-Century Love.
Coke, A. Change, The.
Cummings, E. Plato Told.
Davidson, J. Crystal Palace, The.
Day, J. Man's Natural Infirmity.
De la Mare. Reserved.
Di Cicco. Flying Deeper into the Century.
"Dylan." Quinn the Eskimo.
Ebb, F. Nowadays.
Eliot, T. Burial of the Dead, The.
Death by Water.
Fire Sermon, The.
Game of Chess, A.
Love Song of J. Alfred Prufrock, The.
Waste Land, The.
Enright. Remembrance Sunday.
Fearing. Dirge: "1-2-3 was the number he played but today the number came 3-2-1."
Ferlinghetti, L. Lost Parents.
Sea and Ourselves at Cape Ann, The.
Fletcher, J. Song of the Moderns.
Forbes, C. Blue Monday.
Ginsberg, A. Grim Skeleton.
Goodtimes. Jojopan.
Gurney, I. Not-Returning, The.
Gwynn, R. Among Philistines.
Hart, L. Zip.
Hass, R. Now Winter Nights.
Hazo. Pittsburgh in Passing.
Hogan, L. Skin.
Hollo. Wasp Sex Myth (One).
Wasp Sex Myth (Two).
Holloway, J. London, Greater London (After *Satire III*).
Hupfeld, H. As Time Goes By.
Ilio, D. Children of the Atomic Age.
Ismaili. Lagos.
Jones, R. James Dean.
Joseph, L. Do What You Can.
Kander, J. Nowadays.
Kern, J. I'm Old-Fashioned.
Kipling, R. New Knighthood, The.
Kleinzahler. Case in Point, A.
Korican, L. City Goddess.
Lamantia. Voice of Earth Mediums.
Le Pan. Net and the Sword, The.
Loesser. Make a Miracle.
Lowell, A. Dissonance.
Lowell, R. For the Union Dead.
Loy. Apology of Genius.
MacCaig. Gone Are the Days.
Mahon. Glengormley.
"Malley." Documentary Film.
McDonald, P. Cash Positive.
Mercer, J. I'm Old-Fashioned.

Merrill, J. Clearing the Title.
Urban Convalescence, An.
Milosz, C. Preparation.
Monro. Every Thing.
Mphande. Pain.
Mudrooroo Narogin. Jacky Hears the Century Cry.
Nash, O. I'm a Stranger Here Myself.
Nathan, L. At the Well.
Nelson, M. Wish Fulfillment.
Nemerov. Life Cycle of Common Man.
Olson, C. In Cold Hell, in Thicket.
Oppen. Book of Job and a Draft of a Poem to Praise the Paths of the Living, The.
Parnell, P. Apotheosis of Medusa.
Porter, C. Anything Goes.
Portnoy, M. Dinogon.
Hints at Distance.
Instant Control.
Reis, P. Ancient Ones, The.
Rich, A. Ghazal.
Rodefer. Pretext.
Rodgers, R. Zip.
Shapiro, K. Hospital.
Sharma, P. Transit.
Smith, A. Common Man, The.
Snyder, G. This Tokyo.
Steele, T. Wartburg, 1521–22, The.
Stern, A. Europa.
Stevens, W. Of Modern Poetry.
Strouse, C. Kids!
Torres, E. Gigabyte Me—How Much RAM in Your Summer of Love?
Lipsticktion.
Tranter. Un-American Women, The.
Updike. Dea ex Machina.
On the Inclusion of Miniature Dinosaurs in Breakfast Cereal Boxes.
Vitale, M. You Oh Even.
Von Freytag-Loringhoven. Dozen Cocktails—Please, A.
Warren, R. To a Face in a Crowd.
Weill, K. I'm a Stranger Here Myself.
Whitman, W. One's-Self I Sing.
Years of the Modern.
Williams, C. Spit.
Wright, C. Stone Canyon Nocturne.
Yeats. Second Coming, The.

Modesty
Berlin. Little Things in Life, The.
Lowell, J. Sonnet.
Waller, E. Song: "Go[e], lovely rose."
Wylie. Let No Charitable Hope.

Moles
De la Mare. All but Blind.
Faigao, B. Kundiman.
Hale, S. Mole and the Eagle, The.
Joseph, J. Back to Base.
Milosz, C. Poor Christian Looks at the Ghetto, A.
Rossetti, C. Handy Mole who plied no shovel, A.
Wylie. Eagle and the Mole, The.
Young, A. Dead Mole, A.

Moloch
Ginsberg, A. II.
Howl.

Mona Lisa
Dowden, E. Leonardo's "Mona Lisa."
Evans, R. Mona Lisa.
"Field." La Gioconda; Leonardo Da Vinci, The Louvre.
Jacobsen, J. Only Alice.
Pater. Mona Lisa.
Roberts, N. Mona Lisa Tea Towel, The.
Wharton, E. Mona Lisa.

Monarchy
McKendrick, J. Shortened History in Pictures, A.

Monasteries
Arnold, M. Stanzas from the Grande Chartreuse.
Merton. Reader, The.
Williams, W. Semblables, The.
See also **Monks**

Monday
Hughes, L.   Blue Monday.
Wakoski.   Blue Monday.

Monet, Claude
Ferlinghetti, L.   Monet's Lilies Shuddering.
Georgiou, E.   From Where I Stand.
Hayden, R.   Monet's "Waterlilies."
Hollander, J.   Effet de Neige.
Mueller, L.   Monet Refuses the Operation.
Snodgrass, W.   Monet: 'Les Nymphéas.'

Money
Armour.   Money.
Bedford.   Munition Wages.
Belloc.   Fatigue.
Blake, E.   I'd Give a Dollar for a Dime.
Bock, J.   Little Tin Box.
Brooks, G.   Maxie Allen.
Brownstein.   Jet Set Melodrama.
Burke, J.   Pennies from Heaven.
Burns, R.   Sandy and Jockie.
Chaucer.   Complaint of Chaucer to His Empty
    Purse, The.
Clairmont.   Hero in the Land of Dough, A.
Clough.   As I Sat at the Café.
    Le Diner.
    Parvenant.
    Spectator ab Extra.
Cohan.   When a Fellow's on the Level with a
    Girl That's on the Square.
Connor, T.   She Was One of the Early Birds.
Coultas, B.   Capitalist Projections.
Cronin, A.   Elegy for the Nightbound.
Curnow.   You Get What You Pay For.
Davies, W.   Money.
De Vries, P.   To His Importunate Mistress.
Dubin, A.   Gold Digger's Song (We're in the
    Money), The.
Dumas, H.   America.
Feirstein.   Mark Stern.
Fisher, J.   Pearls.
Forbes, J.   Love Poem.
Ginsberg, A.   American Change.
Googe.   Of Money.
Grandfather Koori.   Song in the Symbol, The.
Guest, E.   What's In It for Me?
Hammerstein.   Money Isn't Everything!
Harnick.   Little Tin Box.
Hart, L.   I've Got Five Dollars.
Hatton, J.   Christmas Bills.
Hays, H.   Case, The.
Henderson, R.   I'm Sitting on Top of the World.
Herd.   Big Girls.
Herrick.   Lyric[k] for Legacies.
    Money Gets the Mastery [or Masterie].
    Money Makes the Mirth.
    Upon Bunce: Epigram.
Hughes, L.   50–50.
    Little Lyric (of Great Importance).
    Request.
    What?
Hupfeld, H.   Are You Makin' Any Money?
Jarrell.   In Nature There Is Neither Right nor
    Left nor Wrong.
Johnson, F.   Minister, The.
Jones, M.   Soliloquy on an Empty Purse.
Jonson, B.   On Lieutenant Shift.
Larkin, P.   Money.
Lowell, R.   Skunk Hour.
Mills, D.   Chembank Card.
Murphy, R.   Elixir.
Nemerov.   Money.
    Ultima Ratio Reagan.
North, C.   Elizabethan & Nova Scotian Music.
North, M.   Account, An.
Outram.   Annuity, The.
Perelman.   Money.
Pope, A.   Duke of Buckingham, The.
    Sir Balaam.
    Timon's Villa.
Pound, E.   Canto XLV.
Raine, K.   Worry about Money.
Rome, H.   Money Song, The.
Rybicki, J.   Brother Ben.
Sisson.   Money.
Smith, W.   American Primitive.
Spender, S.   Ultima Ratio Regum.

Swift, J.   To Their Excellencies the Lords
    Justices of Ireland, the Humble Petition of
    Frances Harris, Who Must Starve, and Die a
    Maid If It Miscarries.
Tennyson, A.   Northern Farmer: New Style.
Thomas, L.   Clear Channel.
Unknown.   Chairs to Mend.
    Mode of France, The.
    Money and the Mare.
    Money Is What Matters.
    Money, Money.
    My Purse.
    Penny.
Vazirani, R.   E-Mail.
Williamson, G.   Annual Returns.
Yeats.   Brown Penny.

Monitor (ship)
Melville, H.   Utilitarian View of the Monitor's
    Fight, A.

Monkeys
Colum, P.   Monkeys.
Espada.   Do Not Put Dead Monkeys in the
    Freezer.
Gay, J.   Two Monkeys, The.
Kreymborg.   Tree, The.
McElroy, C.   End of Civilization as We Know
    It, The.
Moore, M.   Monkeys, The.
Shiffert.   Monkeys on Mt. Hiei.
Swenson, M.   Motherhood.
Weelkes.   Madrigal: "Ay me, alas, heigh ho,
    heigh ho!"
Weigl.   Monkey.

Monks
Browning, R.   Grammarian's Funeral, A.
    Soliloquy of the Spanish Cloister.
Clarke, A.   Pilgrimage.
Deanovich.   My Favorite Monk Is.
Dowson.   Carthusians.
Evans, S.   How the Abbey of Saint Werewulf
    Juxta Slingsby Came by Brother Fabian's
    Manuscript.
Everson, W.   Narrows of Birth, The.
Hemingway.   Earnest Liberal's Lament, The.
Kinsella, T.   Monk, The.
Merton.   Elegy for the Monastery Barn.
Montague, J.   Footnote on Monasticism, A:
    Dingle Peninsula.
Rakosi.   Menage, The.
Smith, S.   Weak Monk, The.
Unknown.   Pangur Bán.
Waniek.   Letter to a Benedictine Monk.
See also **Clergy; Monasteries**

Monmouth, Battle of (1778)
Richards, L.   Molly Pitcher.

Monmouth, James Scott, Duke of
Behn, A.   Silvio's Complaint: A Song, To a Fine
    Scotch Tune.
Dryden, J.   Absalom and Achitophel.
    Achitophel: The Earl of Shaftsbury.
    Shaftesbury.
    Zimri: "In the first rank of These did Zimri
    stand."
    Zimri: The Duke of Buckingham.

Monogamy and Monogamists
Aig-Imoukhuede.   One Wife for One Man.
Donne.   Confined Love.

Monotony
Bell, M.   Senilio Passes, Singing.
Disch.   Bookmark, A.
MacNeice.   Nature Morte.
Roethke.   Monotony Song, The.
Smith, S.   Childe Rolandine.

Monroe, Marilyn
Alexie.   November 22, 1983.
Grahn.   I Have Come to Claim Marilyn
    Monroe's Body.
Greenhalgh, C.   Night I Met Marilyn, The.
Herd.   Marilyn Climbs Out of the Pool.
Olds, S.   Death of Marilyn Monroe, The.
Romero, L.   Marilyn Monroe Indian.

Monsters
Celan.   Death Fugue, The.
Clifton, L.   Shapeshifter Poems.
Dalton, A.   Kitchen Beast.

De Los Santos, M.   Wiglaf.
Deanovich.   Zombie Jet.
Dickey, J.   Sheep Child, The.
Ehrhart.   Making the Children Behave.
Erdrich.   Windigo.
Forhan, C.   Without Presumptions.
Graves, R.   Hide and Seek.
Gunn, T.   From the Highest Camp.
Hamby, B.   St. Clare's Underwear.
Heath-Stubbs.   Vision of Beasts, A.
Hughes, L.   Genius Child.
Knight, S.   In Case of Monsters.
Komunyakaa.   Never Land.
Lee, D.   I Eat Kids Yum Yum!
Legaré.   Tallulah.
Levi, P.   Annunciation.
Mitchell, K.   Monster, The.
Pepler.   Concerning Dragons.
Raab, L.   Sudden Appearance of a Monster at a
    Window.
Robinson, K.   Pontoon.
Silverstein, S.   Slithergadee, The.
Tennyson, A.   Kraken, The.
See also **Demons**

Mont Blanc
Coleridge, S.   Hymn before Sunrise, in the Vale
    of Chamouni.
Shelley, P.   Mont Blanc.

Montana (state)
Cunningham, J.   Montana Pastoral.
Hugo, R.   Degrees of Gray in Philipsburg.
    Driving Montana.
    Lady in Kicking Horse Reservoir, The.
    Letter to Bell from Missoula.
    Letter to Goldbarth from Big Fork.
    Letter to Haislip from Hot Springs.
    Letter to Levertov from Butte.
    Letter to Oberg from Pony.
    Letter to Scanlon from Whitehall.
    Map of Montana in Italy, A.
Welch, J.   Christmas Comes to Moccasin Flat.
    Harlem, Montana.

Months
Bodecker.   One Year.
Coleridge, S.   Garden Year, The.
Longfellow, H.   Poet's Calendar, The.
Unknown.   Months, The.

Montreal, Quebec
Klein, A.   Montreal.

Monuments
Awad, J.   Variations on a Theme.
Bishop, E.   Monument, The.
Carrier, C.   Pro Patria.
Denney.   Building the Dam.
Emerson, R.   Concord Hymn.
Hemans.   Effigies, The.
Johnstone, P.   High Wood.
Kavanagh, P.   Lines Written on a Seat on the
    Grand Canal, Dublin.
Kennedy, X.   Loneliness of Lincoln, The.
Komunyakaa.   Facing It.
Lovelace, R.   Black Patch on Lucasta's Face, A.
Lowell, R.   For the Union Dead.
Melville, H.   Inscription: "To them who crossed
    the flood."
Mew.   Cenotaph, The.
Ormond.   Ancient Monuments.
Page, G.   Smalltown Memorials.
Philipott.   To Sir Henry Newton, upon His Re-
    edifying the Church of Charleton in Kent.
Stevens, W.   Dance of the Macabre Mice.

Moods
Ashbery.   Crazy Weather.
Aytoun [*or* Ayton], R.   Answer, The.
    Upon His Unconstant Mistress.
Caesar.   Sometimes I'm Happy.
Fields, D.   I'm in the Mood for Love.
Frost, R.   Mood Apart, A.
Kiser.   Bargain Sale, A.
Yeats.   Moods, The.

Moon
Adams, L.   Moon and Spectator, The.
Aldington.   Evening.
Alexander, E.   Apollo.
Allen, P.   Meditations on the Moon.

Alvi, M.   Laughing Moon, The.
"Asphodel."   Full Moon in Malta.
Auden.   Moon Landing.
   This Lunar Beauty.
Bayliss.   Seven Dreams.
Behn, H.   Circles.
Bell, M.   White Clover.
Berg, S.   On This Side of the River.
Berryman.   Moon and the Night and the Men,
   The.
Bishop, E.   Insomnia.
   Man-Moth, The.
Black, S.   Blank Abandon of Beds, The.
Blackburn, J.   Moonlight in Vermont.
Blake, W.   Quid the Cynic's Song.
Bogan, L.   July Dawn.
Bowering, G.   Moon Shadow.
Brecht, B.   Alabama Song.
Burke, J.   Moonlight Becomes You.
Bynner.   Drinking Alone with the Moon.
   Moon, The.
Byron, G.   So We'll Go No More A-Roving.
Campo.   Asylum.
Clare, J.   To Mary: 'It Is the Evening Hour'
Coleridge, M.   In Dispraise of the Moon.
   Witches' Wood, The.
Crapsey.   Moon-Shadows.
   Niagara.
Creeley.   Form of Women, A.
   Moon, The.
Davies, W.   Moon and a Cloud, The.
   Moon, The.
   Nailsworth Hill.
De la Mare.   Moonlight.
   Silver.
Dodge, M.   Moon Came Late, The.
Dongala.   Fantasy under the Moon.
Downie.   Starlight.
Drennan, J.   On the Telescopic Moon.
Duncan, R.   Chords Passages 14.
Edwards, G.   By the Light of the Silvery Moon.
Eliot, T.   Conversation Galante.
   Rhapsody on a Windy Night.
Empson.   To an Old Lady.
Evans, R.   No Moon at All.
Fainlight, R.   Another Full Moon.
"Field."   Penetration.
Frost, R.   Freedom of the Moon, The.
   Moon Compasses.
Gangemi, K.   Notes on a Moonwatcher.
Gannon, K.   Moonlight Cocktail.
García Lorca.   Memory.
Glück, L.   Mock Orange.
Graves, R.   Full Moon.
Greenberg, A.   Man in the Moon, The.
Guillén, N.   Moon.
Gunn, T.   For Signs.
Hamill, S.   Reading Seferis.
Hamilton, N.   How High the Moon.
Harburg.   Moon About Town.
   Old Devil Moon.
Hardy, T.   Shut Out That Moon.
Hart, L.   Blue Moon.
Hayden, R.   Full Moon.
Herd.   Coronach.
Hernández Cruz.   Milagrosa, La.
Hewett, D.   Moon-Man.
Hopkins, G.   Moonrise.
Horovitz, F.   Moon.
Howard, B.   Fly Me to the Moon (In Other
   Words).
Hughes, L.   Winter Moon.
Hughes, T.   Full Moon and Little Frieda.
   Moon-Hops.
Hulme, T.   Above the Dock.
Jacobs, J.   Nearing Long Moons.
Jones, A. M.   To the Moon.
Keats.   Bright Star.
Keithley.   Small Moon on the Shoulder of New
   York.
Kennedy, L.   Moonburn.
King, H.   Moonlight Ride, A.
Kinnell.   Little Sleep's-Head Sprouting Hair in
   the Moonlight.
Knight, S.   Thoughts on the Sight of the Moon.
Knott.   Sleep.
Kunitz, S.   Flight of Apollo, The.

Lawrence, D.   Aware.
   White Blossom, A.
Levertov.   Song for Ishtar.
Lindsay, N.   Moon's the North Wind's Cooky,
   The.
Longfellow, H.   Harvest Moon, The.
Lowell, A.   Dissonance.
   Wind and Silver.
Loy.   Lunar Baedeker.
Macdonald, G.   Wind and the Moon, The.
MacKenzie, R.   Blue Sky in Morning.
Mancini, H.   Moon River.
McGrath, T.   Guiffre's Nightmusic.
Meyers, B.   Daybreak.
Michie.   Arizona Nature Myth.
Millay, E.   "Oh, sleep forever in the Latmian
   cave."
Milnes.   Lady Moon.
Montagu, L.   Hymn to the Moon.
Moore, L.   Haiku.
Moore, R.   Personal Atlas.
Moore, T.   Young May Moon, The.
Morley, H.   Parents.
Naden.   Moonlight and Gas.
Nemerov.   Backward Look, The.
   Goose Fish, The.
Newbolt.   Moonset.
Nichol.   Monotones.
Olson, C.   Moon Is the Number 18, The.
Plath.   Moon and the Yew Tree, The.
   Rival, The.
Plomer.   To the Moon and Back.
Porter, D.   P. M. T.
Purdy, J.   From rivers, and from the earth itself.
Rabéarivelo [or Rebéarivelo].   What Invisible
   Rat.
Ray, H.   Vision of Moonlight, A.
Reese, L.   One Night.
Renton.   Crescent Moon.
Rickword.   Moon-talk.
Robinson, M.   Her Address to the Moon.
Roscoe, W.   To the Harvest Moon.
Rossetti, C.   Is the Moon Tired?
Rossetti, D.   Match with the Moon, A.
Rukeyser, M.   Nevertheless the Moon.
Rushing.   Sent for You Yesterday.
Saleh.   Beach, Later.
   Sentry.
Sandburg, C.   Auctioneer.
   Balloon Faces.
   Moist Moon People.
   Nocturne in a Deserted Brickyard.
Saunders, R.   You Made It Rain.
Sergeant.   Inundation, The.
Shelley, P.   To the Moon.
   Waning Moon, The.
Silano, M.   Moon, The.
Simms, W.   New Moon, The.
Smith, C.   To the Moon.
   Written September 1791, During a Remarkable
   Thunder Storm, in which the Moon Was
   Perfectly Clear, While the Tempest Gathered
   in Various Directions Near the Earth.
Sorrentino.   Magic Composer.
Steele, T.   Joseph.
Stevens, W.   God is Good. It Is a Beautiful
   Night.
   Lunar Paraphrase.
   Motive for Metaphor, The.
   Two Figures in Dense Violet Night.
Stevenson, R.   Mile an' a Bittock, A.
   Moon, The.
Strand.   Prediction, The.
Suessdorf, K.   Moonlight in Vermont.
Suesse, D.   Moon About Town.
Swenson, M.   First Walk on the Moon.
   Landing on the Moon.
Teasdale.   Full Moon; Santa Barbara.
   Moon's Ending.
Tolkien.   Man in the Moon Stayed up Too Late,
   The.
Toomer.   Beehive.
Traherne.   On Leaping over the Moon.
Tu Fu.   Full Moon.
Unknown.   All Other Love Is Like the Moon.
   Bedtime.
   I See the Moon.

   Man in the Moon.
   Moon Sings, The.
   Moon, The.
Van Heusen, J.   Moonlight Becomes You.
Washington.   Moon Bound.
Wiese, B.   Going Home Madly.
Willard, N.   Night Light.
Williams, H.   To the Moon.
Williams, L.   Crater.
Williams, W.   Rigamarole.
   To a Solitary Disciple.
Wilson, R.   Envoi: "Sun in the mouth of the
   day."
Winters, Y.   To the Moon.
Wright, C.   Appalachian Book of the Dead III,
   The.
Wright, J.   Beginning.
   Having Lost My Sons, I Confront the Wreckage
   of the Moon: Christmas, 1960.
   Secret Gratitude, A.
   Train Journey.
Yeats.   Cat and the Moon, The.
   Sorrow of Love, The.

Moonshiners
De la Mare.   Moonshine.
Wells, L.   Distress upon the Farm.

Moore, Henry
Hall, D.   "Reclining Figure."

Moore, Marianne
Bishop, E.   Invitation to Miss Marianne Moore.

Moore, Sir John
Wolfe, C.   Burial of Sir John Moore [after [or
at] Corunna], The.

Moore, Thomas
Trowbridge, J.   Recollections of "Lalla Rookh."

Moors (geography)
Channing.   Barren Moors, The.
Coleridge, M.   Master and Guest.
Garioch.   Wire, The.
Hughes, T.   Telegraph Wires.

Moors (people)
Watson, R.   Moor Girl's Well, The.

Moose
Bishop, E.   Moose, The.
Duncan, R.   Poetry, a Natural Thing.
Van Duyn.   Moose in the Morning, Northern
   Maine.
Wanek.   Duluth, Minnesota.

Morality Plays
Campo.   Towards Curing AIDS.

More, Sir Thomas (Saint Thomas More)
Cunningham, J.   Friend, on This Scaffold
   Thomas More Lies Dead.

Morgan, Henry
Prys-Jones.   Henry Morgan's March on Panama.

Morgan, John Hunt
Woolson.   Kentucky Belle.

Morison, Sir Henry
Jonson, B.   To the Immortal[l] Memory [or
   Memorie] and Friendship of That Noble
   Pair[e], Sir Lucius Cary and Sir H. [or Henry]
   Morison.

Morisot, Berthe
Waldman, A.   Berthe Morisot.

Mormons
Healy, E.   Moroni on the Mormon Temple /
   Angel on the Wall.
Taylor, B.   Nauvoo.

Morning
Ambrose.   Hymn: "Framer of the earth and sky."
Ammons, A. R.   Easter Morning.
   Improvisation for the Stately Dwelling, An.
Anderson, J.   Waking Up Twice.
Angeles, C.   Light Invested.
Arlen, H.   Morning After, The.
Baraka.   Ballad of the Morning Streets.
   Song Form.
Belloc.   Early Morning, The.
Berlin.   Oh! How I Hate to Get Up in the
   Morning.
Blagg, T.   In Bed this Morning.
Blake, W.   Morning.
   To Morning.
Bly, R.   Poem in Three Parts.

Waking from Sleep.
Bogan, L.   Morning.
Brontë, E.   Stars.
Brown, N.   Good Morning.
Burns, R.   Up in the Morning Early.
Campbell, W.   Morning on the Shore.
Carlyle, T.   Morning.
Chin.   Aubade: "Waking is this easy."
Clare, J.   God Looks on Nature With a Glorious
   Eye.
Cleveland, J.   Upon Phillis Walking in a
   Morning before Sun-Rising.
Cotton, C.   Morning Quatrains, The.
Couzyn.   Morning.
Coward.   Convalescence.
Cristall.   Morning, Rosamonde.
Davis, W.   Spider.
Dawe, B.   Morning Becomes Electric.
Dawson, M.   Late for Breakfast.
Dickinson, E.   Morning.
Donaldson, W.   Carolina in the Morning.
Donne.   Break[e] of Day.
   Sun Rising, The.
Drummond, W.   Invocation: "Pheobus, arise! /
   And paint the sable skies."
Dunbar, P.   In the Morning.
Eliot, T.   Morning at the Window.
Field, R.   Summer Morning, A.
Finch, B.   Written in a Winter's Morning.
Finch, R.   Turning.
Fisher, M.   Cloudy Morning.
Freed, A.   Good Morning.
Gascoigne.   Gascoigne's Good-Morrow.
Ginsberg, A.   We Rise on Sun Beams and Fall
   in the Night.
Grenier.   Sunday Morning.
Guiney.   When on the Marge of Evening.
Hackett, J.   Haiku: "Bitter morning, A."
Hammerstein.   Oh, What a Beautiful Mornin'!
Hartnett.   Last Vision of Eoghan Rua Ó
   Súilleabháin, The.
Heard, J.   Matin Hymn.
   Morn.
Herbert, G.   Mattens.
Herrick.   Matins [or Mattens], or Morning
   Prayer.
Hitchcock.   May All Earth Be Clothed in Light.
Hollander, J.   By the Sound.
   Edward Hopper's Seven A.M.
   Morning in the Islands.
Hopkinson, F.   Arise and See the Glorious Sun.
Housman, A.   Reveille.
Hughes, L.   Blues at Dawn.
Hughes, T.   Horses, The.
Huidobro.   Morning.
Jarrell.   Nestus Gurley.
Jones, T.   Bird on a Jaunt.
Kahn, G.   Carolina in the Morning.
Kaufman, B.   Cocoa Morning.
Keithley.   First Morning.
Kenney.   Aubade: "Cold snap. Five o'clock."
Kuskin.   I Woke Up This Morning.
Kyle, C. J.   Fire in Early Morning.
Laurencin, M.   Present, The.
Lawrence, D.   Morning Work.
Layton.   Aubade, An.
Lee, L.   Early in the Morning.
Levertov.   Matins.
Levine, P.   To My God in His Sickness.
Lewis, J.   Remembered Morning.
Livingstone, D.   Lake Morning in Autumn.
Longfellow, H.   Daybreak.
Lowell, R.   Waking Early Sunday Morning.
Lowry, M.   Eye-Opener.
MacKenzie, R.   Blue Sky in Morning.
MacNeice.   Morning Sun.
   Sunday Morning.
Mahon.   Everything Is Going to Be All Right.
Maiden.   Dew.
Marzán.   Sunday Morning in Old San Juan.
McCarthy, G.   Finding the Way Back.
McCarthy, J.   Cloudy Morning.
Merwin, W. S.   Rain Travel.
Minhinnick.   Sunday Morning.
Muir, E.   Wayside Station, The.
Muldoon, P.   Avenue, The.

Murray, P.   Introit.
Nameroff, R.   California Dreaming.
Oliver, M.   Waking on a Summer Morning.
Olson, C.   Variations Done for Gerald Van De
   Wiele.
Padilla.   Daily Habits.
Penn, R.E.   Morning Songs.
Percival.   Morning among the Hills.
Piercy.   Morning Love Song.
Plath.   Sheep in Fog.
Previn, D.   Morning After, The.
Rakosi.   Good Morning.
   Lying in Bed on a Summer Morning.
Rashad, J.   Morning After, The.
Raworth.   My Face Is My Own, I Thought.
Revard.   On the Bright Side.
Richardson, K.   Aubade: "Geese flew by as you
   entered me, The."
Roberts, E.   Disconsolate Morning.
Roethke.   Carnations.
Sanchez, S.   Haiku.
Sandburg, C.   Halsted Street Car.
Saner.   Morning Snowfield.
Schwartz, D.   In the Naked Bed, in Plato's
   Cave.
Seward.   Sonnet Written from an Eastern
   Apartment in the Bishop's Palace at Lichfield,
   Which Commands a View of Stowe Valley.
Sexton.   Welcome Morning.
Simic.   Mirrors at 4 A.M.
Simpson, L.   Early in the Morning.
   Morning Light, The.
Smart, C.   Morning-Piece; or, An Hymn for the
   Hay-Makers, A.
Southerland.   Recitation.
Stern, G.   Morning Harvest.
   There Is Wind, There Are Matches.
Stevens, W.   Nomad Exquisite.
Stevenson, R.   Winter Time [or Winter-Time].
Strand.   Morning, Noon and Night.
Swift, J.   Description of the Morning, A.
Thaxter.   Chanticleer.
Thomas, E.   Glory, The.
Thoreau.   Guido's Aurora.
Thurman.   Zebra.
Torres, E.   Elbow in Dumberland, An.
Ungaretti.   Morning.
Unknown.   Sister, Awake!
Vasquez, R.   Early Morning Test Light over
   Nevada, 1955.
Vaughan, H.   Morning-Watch, The.
Very.   Clouded Morning, The.
   Fair Morning, The.
Viray, M.   Saturday Morning, A.
Wang Wei.   Morning.
Wesley, C.   Morning Hymn.
Whitehead, C.   Daybreak.
   Morning Thesis.
Wilbur.   Late Aubade, A.
   Love Calls Us to the Things of This World.
   Summer Morning, A.
Wilde, O.   Impression Du Matin.
Williams, W.   January Morning.
Wordsworth, W.   Composed upon Westminster
   Bridge, September 3, 1802.
Wright, C.   California Spring.

Morning Glories
Whitman, S.   Morning-Glory, The.
Wilner, E.   Conversation with a Japanese
   Student.

Morocco
Burke, J.   Road to Morocco, The.
Synková, A.   To Olga.

Morris, William
Ruefle.   Furtherness.

Mortality
Abbey, L.   Broken Silence.
Adams, L.   April Mortality.
Aiken, C.   Tetélestai.
Ainsworth, H.   Fire in My Meditation Burned.
Aisenberg, N.   Leaving Eden.
Atwood.   Last Poem.
Auchterlonie.   Meditation of a Mariner.
Auden.   Lullaby: "Lay your sleeping head, my
   love."
Barbauld.   Life.

Bell, M.   Book of the Dead Man #1, The.
Berlin, E.   Sea World.
Bibbins, M.   Counting.
Blake, W.   Caverns of the Grave [I've Seen],
   The.
Bly, R.   August Rain.
   Hollow Tree, A.
   Kneeling Down to Look [or Peer] into a
   Culvert.
   When the Dumb Speak.
Bradstreet, A.   Before the Birth of One of Her
   Children.
Brock-Broido.   Radiating Naïveté.
Bruce, D.   Plunder.
   Prognosis.
Byron, G.   Manfred.
Campion, T.   What If a Day [or a Month or a
   Year].
Carew, T.   Song, [A]: "Ask[e] me no more
   where Jove bestow[e]s."
Cavendish, M.   Dissert, A.
Colman, H.   On Mortality.
Cooley.   Brother Body.
Corob, T.   Either Way.
Cory, W.   Mimnermus in Church.
Coulehan, J.   Azalea Poem, The.
Cowper, W.   On a Similar Occasion for the Year
   1790.
   On a Similar Occasion for the Year 1792.
   Stanzas Subjoined to the Yearly Bill of
   Mortality of the Parish of All Saints,
   Northampton; for the Year 1787.
Crawford, R.   Downtown Sunday.
Crosby, F.   We Are Going.
Cullen, C.   Leaves.
Dawes, K.   Black Heart.
Delmore, E.   Difference, The.
Desnos.   Midway.
Dickinson, E.   Wounded Deer Leaps Highest, A.
Disch.   Convalescing in London.
Donne.   Anniversary [or Anniversarie], The.
   Farewell to Love.
   Song: "Sweetest love, I do not go[e]."
Dowson.   Vitae Summa Brevis Spem Nos Vetat
   Incohare Longam.
Drake, N.   Very Rich Hours, The.
Drummond, W.   Word a Hunt, A.
Dudley, E.   Pathologist.
Dunbar, W.   All Erdly Joy Returns in Pane.
Duran, J.   Time Zones.
Ehrhart.   "The light that cannot fade."
Elliot, A.   Latitudes of Home, The.
Emerson, R.   Good-bye.
   Hamatreya.
Ewart.   14-Year-Old Convalescent Cat in the
   Winter, A.
Feinfeld, D.   Carmelita.
Forbes, J.   Death, an Ode.
Francia, L.   Is there There in dying.
Glück, L.   Garden, The.
Graham-Pole, J.   Candor.
Graves, R.   In Her Praise.
Gray, T.   Elegy Written in a Country
   Churchyard.
   Epitaph: "Here rests his head upon the lap of
   earth."
Gwynn, R.   Anacreontic.
   Release.
Habington.   Solum Mihi Superest Sepulchrum.
Hall, D.   Black Faced Sheep, The.
Hall, J.   Job. I.
Hamer.   Different Strokes Bar, San Francisco,
   The.
Hemphill.   Cordon Negro.
Herbert, G.   Church Monuments.
   Employment: "He that is weary, let him sit."
   Frailty.
   Mortification.
   Time.
   Virtue [or Vertue].
Herrick.   Anacreontic.
   His Own Epitaph.
   Man's Dying-Place Uncertain.
   To the Reverend Shade of His Religious Father.
   Upon a Young Mother of Many Children.
   Upon the Troublesome Times.

Hopkins, G.   Spring and Fall.
Housman, A.   With Rue My Heart Is Laden.
Hughes, F.   Kookaburra.
Jackson, L.   Starved.
Jarrell.   Author to the Reader, The.
Jeffers, R.   Age in Prospect.
Justice, D.   Men at Forty.
Keats.   Ode on a Grecian Urn.
Ode to a Nightingale.
When I Have Fears [That I May Cease to Be].
Why Did I Laugh Tonight?
Khalvati.   Needlework.
King, H.   Sic Vita.
Kinnell.   Little Sleep's-Head Sprouting Hair in the Moonlight.
Kinzie.   Lunar Frost.
Kramer, L.   Brilliant Windows.
Images of the San Francisco Disaster.
Lansdown.   Behind the Veil.
Larkin, P.   Aubade: "I work all day, and get half-drunk at night."
Laux.   Prayer.
Lewis, A.   Sentry, The.
To a Comrade in Arms.
Lieberman, M.   Regret.
Locklin.   Stranger, The.
Longfellow, H.   Mezzo Cammin.
Lowell, A.   New Heavens for Old.
Lowell, R.   Death from Cancer.
Lumsden, R.   Mercy.
MacLeish.   Signature for Tempo.
MacNeice.   Sunlight on the Garden, The.
Madonick, M.   Settled In.
Markham, E.   Leaf from the Devil's Jest-Book, A.
Marvell.   Picture of Little T. C. in a Prospect of Flowers, The.
McAuley, J.   Gnostic Prelude.
In a Late Hour.
McLaughlin, J.   Black Irish Blues.
Melville, H.   Pontoosuce.
Tom Deadlight.
Meredith, G.   Dirge in Woods.
Merwin, W. S.   For the Anniversary of My Death.
Millay, E.   First Fig.
Poet and His Book, The.
Milosz, O.   Bridge, The.
Mitchell, S.   Of Earthly Love.
Mukand, J.   First Payment.
Ní Chuilleanáin.   Dead Fly.
Oldys.   On a Fly Drinking out of [or from] His Cup.
Oliver, M.   In Blackwater Woods.
Owen, W.   À Terre.
Anthem for Doomed Youth.
Exposure.
Send-Off, The.
Parker, D.   Bric-à-Brac.
Phillips, C.   In the blood, Winnowing.
Kill, The.
Pietri.   Intermission from Sunday.
Poe.   Eldorado.
Porter, A.   Five Wishes.
Oaks and Squirrels.
Prince, F.   Question, The.
Proctor, T.   Respice Finem.
Ramke.   Paul Verlaine at the Grave of Lucien Létinois.
Ransom, J.   Piazza Piece.
Ratushinskaya [or Ratushinskaia].   Try to Cover Your Shivering Shoulders.
Robinson, E.   Pity of the Leaves, The.
Sackville-West.   Greater Cats, The.
Salaam.   Name the Oldest Member of Your Family.
Santayana.   Echo.
Schwartz, R. L.   Edgewater Park.
Shapiro, D.   Lord I Sleep and I Sleep.
Shapiro, K.   Cut Flower, A.
Shaw, R.   Shut In.
Simpson, L.   Early in the Morning.
Sisson.   In Flood.
Tristia.
Skelton, J.   Upon a Dead Man's Head.
Spender, S.   One More New Botched Beginning.

Stanley, T.   Quickness.
Stein, K.   In the Kingdom of Perpetual Repair.
Stickney, T.   Athenian Garden, An.
Be Still. The Hanging Gardens Were a Dream.
Straus, M.   What I Heard on the Radio Today.
Sylvester, J.   Omnia Somnia.
Taggard.   To the Powers of Desolation.
Tate, A.   Non Omnis Moriar.
Ode to the Confederate Dead.
Tate, J.   Diagnosis, The.
Taylor, E.   This Year's Drive to Appomattox.
Tennyson, A.   Tithonus.
Tomlinson, C.   After a Death.
Unknown.   I Shall Not Pass This Way Again.
Lonesome Valley.
Only One Life.
Steal Away to Jesus.
What Yo' Gwine to [or t'] Do When Yo' [or de] Lamp Burn Down?
Vaughan, H.   Death.
Joy of My Life! While Left Me Here.
Quickness.
Vertreace, M.   Caged Stone.
Walcott.   Tomorrow, Tomorrow.
Warren, R.   Acquaintance with Time in Early Autumn.
After the Dinner Party.
Watts, I.   Shortness and Misery of Life, The.
Submission to Afflictive Providences.
Wharton, E.   Autumn Sunset, An.
Experience.
Life.
Whitman, W.   This Compost.
Whitney, I.   Aucthour Maketh Her Wyll and Testament, The.
Whittemore, R.   Walk Home, The.
Winchilsea.   Spleen, The.
Witt, S.   Americana.
Woods, D.   Waiting.
Wordsworth, W.   Extempore Effusion upon the Death of James Hogg.
Most Alluring Clouds That Mount the Sky, The.
Trosachs, The.
Young, A.   Mountains of California: Part 2, The.

Moscow, Russia
Garlick, R.   Capitals.

Moses
Allen, S.   Harriet Tubman aka Moses.
Bringhurst.   Deuteronomy.
Dickinson, P.   Moses and the Princess.
"Eliot."   Death of Moses, The.
Glück, L.   Day without Night.
Hopkins, G.   Soliloquy of One of the Spies Left in the Wilderness, A.
Moran, M.   Pharao's Daughter.
Naden.   Moonlight and Gas.
Unknown.   Go Down, Moses.
Moses.
Railroad Section Leader's Song.
Very.   Moses in Infancy.
Whalen.   Complaint: To the Muse.
Wither.   First Song of Moses, The.
Zangwill.   Moses and Jesus.

Mosquitoes
Lawrence, D.   Mosquito Knows, The.
Mosquito, The.
Lindsay, N.   Little Turtle, The.
"Malley."   Culture as Exhibit.
Wright, F.   Mosquitoes.

Moss
Blind.   Entangled.
Irby.   January 1965, Looking On.
Roethke.   Moss-Gathering.

Motels
Grosholz.   Outer Banks, The.
Hiestand, E.   Moon Winx Motel.
Klein, M.   Tides, The.
Knight, S.   Surf Motel, The.
Mörling, M.   In a Motel Room at Dawn.
Nelson, M.   Motel Story.
Pape.   In the Bluemist Motel.
Snodgrass, W.   Leaving the Motel.
Wagoner, D.   On Motel Walls.
Yuson.   Dead Center.

See also **Hotels**

Mother's Day
Becker, E.   Mother's Day.
Ross, C.   Old Mothers.

Mothers
Abena, B.   Liberation.
Abinader, E.   Making It New.
Abse.   X-ray.
Acosta.   My Mother Pieced Quilts.
Adams, A.   To My Mother.
Adamson.   Dreaming Up Mother.
My House.
Adelman, P.   My Exorcist Mother.
Aguilar-Cariño.   Dinakdakan.
Allen, E.   Rock Me to Sleep[, Mother].
Allingham.   In Snow.
Alvarez, J.   Naming the Fabrics.
Wallpaper.
Angela, F.   Old Stone Age.
Anhalt, D.   That Jewish Crusader.
Apuleius, L.   I who am Nature, mother of all.
Armantrout.   Incidence.
Arrillaga.   Mariana II.
Asekoff, L.   Will.
Baillie, J.   Mother to Her Waking Infant, A.
Barben, D.   To Look Yet Not Find.
Barber, D.   Nocturne.
Barber, M.   Written for My Son, and Spoken by Him at His First Putting on Breeches.
Baring, A.   Song, The: "Beehive source."
Barker, G.   Sonnet to My Mother.
Barney, S.   Vision.
Baumel.   Snow-Day.
Bayly.   We Met.
Benét, S.   Nonsense Song, A.
Ben-Lev, D.   Broken Helix.
Bennani, B.   Letters to Lebanon.
Bennett, G.   Secret.
Berezan, J.   Hail Mother full of grace power is with thee.
Berg, S.   Prayer: "Nobody understands so let the Rabbi."
Berger, J.   Between Worlds.
Berman, C.   Poem for the Shechina.
Bernstein, C.   Cup of Coffee, The.
Birney.   Gray Woods Exploding, The.
BonniLee.   White Candles.
Born, A.   End of the Row.
Boyd, E.   On the Death of an Infant of Five Days Old.
Bradstreet, A.   Before the Birth of One of Her Children.
In Reference to Her Children, 23 June, 1659 [or 1659].
To My Dear Children.
Breeze.   Natural High.
Brett, L.   Leaving You.
Brion, R.   Love Song.
Brooks, G.   Beverly Hills, Chicago.
Children of the Poor, The.
First Fight. Then Fiddle.
Jessie Mitchell's Mother.
Maxie Allen.
Mrs. Small.
Rites for Cousin Vit, The.
Browning, E.   Mother and Poet.
Bruner.   Remembrance.
Budbill.   What I Heard at the Discount Department Store.
Burnshaw.   House in St. Petersburg.
Cabico, R.   Mango Poem.
Campbell, D.   Mothers and Daughters.
Campbell, R.   Zulu Girl, The.
Campbell, S.   Constant Welcome, The.
Campion, T.   Fain Would I Wed.
Carroll.   In the Shakespeare Garden at Northwestern University.
Causley.   What Has Happened to Lulu?
Cerenio.   My Mother.
Chase, N.   Music Mother.
Chipasula, S.   I'm My Own Mother, Now.
Chippewa Oral Tradition.   Sioux Woman Defends Her Children, The.
Ciment, J.   Mommy.
Cisneros, S.   Muddy Kid Comes Home.
Clements, S.   Reservation, The.
Clemmons.   Revelation.

Clifton, L.   Admonitions.
Fury.
My Mama Moved among the Days.
Thirty-eighth Year, The.
Clinton, M.   Eviction.
Clive.   Mother, The.
Cofer, J.   Counting.
Fever.
Unspoken.
Coleman, W.   American Sonnet (10).
Coles, R.   Goddam Street, The.
Collins, B.   Tomes.
Collymore.   Ballad of an Old Woman.
Colum, P.   Interior.
Cook, E.   Old Arm-Chair, The.
Cooper, J.   My Young Mother.
Corso.   Sea Chanty.
Couzyn.   Transformation.
Cowper, W.   On the Receipt of My Mother's
    Picture out of Norfolk [the Gift of My Cousin
    Ann Bodham].
Creeley.   For My Mother: Genevieve Jules
    Creeley.
Memory Gardens.
She Went to Stay.
Crowell, G.   Definition.
Darr.   Gift, The.
Davey, F.   She'd Say.
Dean, D. K.   Back to Back.
Stitches.
Derricotte.   Note on My Son's Face, A.
Dickey, J.   Birth, A.
Buckdancer's Choice.
Dickey, R.   Mulatto Lullaby.
Dodson, O.   Black Mother Praying.
Donovan, K.   Grooming.
Dorcey.   First Love.
Dorn, E.   On the Debt My Mother Owed to
    Sears Roebuck.
Dove, R.   After Reading *Mickey in the Night
    Kitchen* for the Third Time Before Bed.
Motherhood.
Pastoral: "Like an otter, but warm."
Poem in Which I Refuse Contemplation.
Doyle, S.   This Shade.
Dromgoole.   Old Ladies.
Drown.   To Mother.
Dufferin.   Mother's Lament, The.
Dumdum.   To My Mother.
Duncan, R.   My Mother Would Be a Falconress.
Eady.   My Mother is a God Fearing Woman.
Eclipse.   Cicada.
Ehrmann.   Mother.
Ellis, T.   Making Ends Meet.
Emmott, K.   Who Looks after Your Kids?
Erdrich.   Birth.
Espinet, R.   Merchant of Death.
Fainlight, R.   Handbag.
Fay, J.   Santorini Daughter.
Feinstein, E.   Mother Love.
Feldman, I.   Dream, The.
Ferré.   Message.
Finney, N.   Lobengula: Having a Son at 38.
Fisher, A.   On Mother's Day.
Fishman, L.   Diagnosis: My Mother's Breast.
Flynn, N.   Cartoon Physics, Part 2.
Fragment (Found Inside My Mother).
Fordham.   Mother's Recall.
To My Mother.
Foster, A.   Gap, The.
Friedman, S.   Answering Machine Message.
Skin.
Fuller, R.   Metamorphoses.
Gallagher, K.   Distances.
Gallagher, T.   Each Bird Walking.
García, D.   Green Corn Season.
Garcia, R.   Elite Syncopations.
Gardinier.   Letter to My Mother.
Garrett, E.   Airborne.
Vista.
Gehrke, S.   Mouth to Mouth.
Gilbert, K.   Mum.
Gilman, C.   Mother's Charge, The.
Ginsberg, A.   Kaddish.
Giovanni.   Mother's Habits.
Mothers.

Glück, L.   For My Mother.
School Children, The.
Glatt.   Amanda.
What We Did After My Mother's Mastectomy.
Gloria.   Whisper, The.
Godfrey.   My Mother, Life.
González, R.   Marías, Old Indian Mothers.
Goodison.   Birth Stone.
I Am Becoming My Mother.
Goodman, M.   Cobwebs.
Goodtimes.   Learning to Smile.
Gottlieb, A.   Meditation on the Feminine Nature
    of Shekinah, A.
Grafflin.   To My Son.
Graham, W.   Conscript Goes, The.
Graham-Pole, J.   Leaving Mother, 1954.
Graves, R.   Frosty Night, A.
Gray-Kontar, D.   Cuz' mama played jazz.
Greenlaw.   Love from a Foreign City.
Griffin, S.   Our Mother.
Grindrod, C.   Searching.
Grosholz.   Eden.
Guevara, M.   Reader of This Page.
"H., H. E."   Riddle, The.
Hacker, M.   Fifteen to Eighteen.
Hadas, R.   Three Silences.
Hahn, K.   Sewing Without Mother: A Zuihitsu.
Hai-Jew, S.   Kinged.
Hall, D.   Porcelain Couple, The.
Harper, F.   Slave Mother, The.
Harryman.   Mothering.
Hashimoto, S.   Mirror of Matsuyama, The.
Standing in the Doorway, I Watch the Young
    Child Sleep.
Hayden, R.   Whipping, The.
Hazo.   To My Mother.
Heaney, S.   Mother of the Groom.
Heard, J.   Mother.
Herder.   Esthonian Bridal Song.
Herrick.   Upon a Young Mother of Many
    Children.
Hinckley, P.   New Our Father, The.
Hirschhorn, N.   Number Our Days.
Hixon, L.   My blissful Mother exists fully
    through every creature!
Who can keep a blazing fire tied in a cotton
    cloth?
Holland, J.   Pulse.
Three Tests for Darwin Duke.
Hove.   Country Life.
Hughes, L.   Mama and Daughter.
Mother to Son.
Hugo, V.   Grandmother, The.
Ingraham.   She Would Have Roses.
Woman Back in the Kitchen, The.
Ironbiter, S.   Song to the Mother of the World.
Iverem, E.   Murmur.
Jackson, R.   1973.
Jarrell.   Bats.
Death of the Ball Turret Gunner, The.
Lost Children, The.
Johnson, F.   Lonely Mother, The.
Johnston, E.   Mother's Love, A.
Karade, B.   Yemoja.
Kasdorf.   What I Learned from My Mother.
Kasischke.   Pall.
Kaufman, S.   Mothers, Daughters.
Kavanagh, P.   In Memory of My Mother.
Kay, J.   Telling Part, The.
Waiting Lists, The.
Kazantzis.   Midwife.
Keeshig-Tobias.   Mother with Child.
Keesing.   Reverie of a Mum.
Kelly, I.   To an Unborn Infant.
Kendrick, D.   Sidney, Looking for her Mother.
Kennedy, X.   Mother's Nerves.
Kessler, S.   Marty's Mother.
Kgositsile.   To Mother.
Kipling, R.   Nativity, A.
Kizer, C.   Intruder, The.
Klein, M.   Scenes for an Elegy.
Kramer, L.   On Shutting the Door.
Krysl.   Persephone, to Demeter.
Kumin, M.   Envelope, The.
Lake, P.   Blue Jay.
Lamb, C.   Gipsy's Malison, The.

Landon.   Dying Child, The.
Landor, W.   Mother, I Cannot Mind My Wheel.
Larkin, J.   Beatings.
Cold River.
Legacy.
Larsen, L.   Lips.
Layton.   Keine Lazarovitch, 1870–1959.
Le Guin.   Child on the Shore, The.
Leaf, E.   Dear Mother.
Lee, L.   I Ask My Mother to Sing.
Levertov.   Death in Mexico.
Olga Poems.
Levine, P.   Soloing.
Lewis, S.   Rock-a-Bye Your Baby with a Dixie
    Melody.
Lifshin.   I Remember Haifa Being Lovely But.
Lim, S.   Starlight Haven.
Lisick, B.   Empress of Sighs.
Liu, T.   Mama.
Livingston, M.   Working with Mother.
Llewellyn-Williams.   Making Babies.
Lomax, M.   Amor Diving.
July.
Lorde.   From the House of Yemanjá.
Hanging Fire.
Now That I Am Forever with Child.
Lowell, R.   Sailing Home from Rapallo.
MacDiarmid, H.   Two Parents, The.
Macgoye.   August the First; Court Martial. The
    Mother Speaks.
Macha, F.   Artist and a Wailing Mother, An.
MacIntyre, S.   Christmas Present for My
    Mother.
Madgett.   Offspring.
Maguire, S.   Invisible Mender, The.
Martínez, V.   Children of the Disappeared.
Martin, S.   Comic Adventures of Old Mother
    Hubbard and Her Dog, The.
Masefield.   C. L. M.
Mason, R.   Footnote to John II: 4.
Masters, M.   At My Mother's Bedside.
Maxwell, R.   Mother's Joy, A.
McAdams, J.   Leaving the Old Gods.
McAuley, J.   Because.
McCallum, S.   Jamaica, October 18, 1972.
McElroy, C.   In My Mother's Room.
Ruth.
McGinley.   Adversary, The.
McKay, C.   My Mother.
Meynell, A.   Cradle-Song at Twilight.
Girl on the Land, The.
Maternity.
Modern Mother, The.
Parentage.
Mezey.   My Mother.
Miles, J.   Belief.
Conception.
Miller, E.   My Father's Girlfriend.
Milne, A.   Disobedience.
Mitchell, E.   Mother, Dear Mother.
Moffett.   Now or Never.
Moir, L.   Handnotes.
Monsour.   Sweeping.
Montague, J.   Locket, The.
Mother Cat.
Moraga.   For the Color of My Mother.
Half-Breed.
Mori.   Heat in October.
Speaking Through White: For My Mother.
Mother Goose.   There Was An Old Woman
    Who Lived in a Shoe.
Mugo, M. G.   Where are those Songs?
Muir, E.   Childhood.
Muldoon, P.   Ma.
Mullen, H.   Momma Sayings.
Muske, C.   August, Los Angeles, Lullaby.
Wyndmere, Windemere.
Mutén, B.   Queen Hera.
Nagase.   Mother.
Napier, F.   I Do Not Want the Ceiling of the
    Sistine Chapel.
Napurrurla, R.   Two Mothers, The.
Natzler, C.   There.
Nelson, H.   With My Mother, Missing the Train.
Nelson, M.   Cover Photograph.
Nesbit, E.   Song: "Oh, baby, baby, baby dear."

Newman, G.   Anti-Semitic Demonstration, An.
Nichols, G.   Praise Song for My Mother.
  Wha Me Mudder Do.
Nimmo, D.   Exorcism.
  My Father's Shadow.
Noel-Scott.   Hansel and Gretel.
Norris, K.   Persephone.
  Prayer to Eve, A.
Novello, I.   And Her Mother Came Too.
Nowlan.   Mother and Son.
Nye, N.   Making a Fist.
  Mother of Nothing.
O'Hara, F.   Ave Maria.
  Poem: "There I could never be a boy."
O'Keefe, E.   Chords.
Obejas, A.   Lifes.
  Sunday.
Ofeimun.   Naming Day, A.
Ogilvy.   Natal Address to My Child, March 19th
  1844, A.
Olds, S.   Her List.
  Mother, The.
  New Mother.
  Quake Theory.
Ono.   Mother of the Universe.
Ormsby, F.   Winter Offerings.
Osborne, J.   Naming of Flowers, The.
Parnell, P.   Medusa and Perseus III: Lilith.
Paschen.   12 East Scott Street.
Pasolini.   Prayer to My Mother.
Pastan.   Marks.
  To a Daughter Leaving Home.
Paterson, E.   Griselda.
Pawlak.   After Burying Her Son, A Mother
  Speaks.
Perdomo, W.   Unemployed Mami.
Perillo.   Sweaters, The.
Petit, P.   My Mother's Clothes.
Philips, A.   To Miss Charlotte Pulteney in Her
  Mother's Arms.
Philp-Carmichael.   Mother.
Piñero.   On the Day They Buried My Mother.
Piatt, S.   This World.
Plath.   Disquieting Muses, The.
  Morning Song.
  Parliament Hill Fields.
Poe.   To My Mother.
Pogson, P.   Fifteen.
Posamentier, E.   Counting Backwards.
  Hungarian Medical Student, The: 1928.
Pratt, M.   Child Taken from the Mother, The.
  Poem for My Sons.
Preston, R.   Mama.
Pryde, A.   I'll See You Down the Lane.
Quayle, L.   Woman Who Drank Us Up, The.
Ríos, A.   Nani.
Raine, K.   Heirloom.
Ramsey, H.   Home and Mother.
  Mother.
Ranasinghe.   Holocaust 1944.
Ray, H.   To My Mother.
Rebelo.   Poem for a Militant.
Rice, N.   Mother's Room.
Ridl.   Video Mama.
Rock, D.   Changing.
  Mother.
Rodgers, C.   It Is Deep.
Rodriguez, L.   Speaking with Hands.
Roripaugh, L.   Pearls.
Ross, C.   Old Mothers.
Rossetti, C.   Chilly Night, A.
Rukeyser, M.   Night Feeding.
  Question, The.
Rungano.   Labour.
  Mother.
Sachs, N.   Dead Child Speaks, A.
Sackett, F.   Another Kind of Skin.
Salter.   What Do Women Want?
Sanders, E.   Leaves of Heaven, The.
Savageau.   At the Powwow.
Schechter.   What Were You Patching?
Schwartz, D.   Baudelaire.
Scott, W.   My Mother.
Seaton, M.   Blonde Ambition.
Sexton.   Child Bearers, The.
Shelton, T.   Patches.

Shiffrin, N.   Anna's Dream.
Shorter.   Mother, The.
Shumaker.   Waitress's Kid, The.
Siddal.   At Last.
Simon, L.   Kali.
Sims, H.   Left Rites.
Smith, P.   Biting Back.
Smith, S.   Human Affection.
  Mother Love.
Song.   Youngest Daughter, The.
Sorby.   Synchronized Swimming.
Speakes.   Mama Loves Janis Joplin.
St. John, P.   Pearle's Poem.
Stead, C.   Between.
Stein, R.   Lines to Mother.
Stevens, W.   In the Carolinas.
  World without Peculiarity.
Stevenson, A.   From an Asylum; Kathy Chattle
  to Her Mother, Ruth Arbeiter.
  When the Camel Is Dust it Goes Through the
  Needle's Eye.
Stoddard, E.   One Morn I Left Him in His Bed.
Strand.   Pot Roast.
Strickland, A.   Infant, The.
Sullivan, B.   Hair.
Swenson, M.   Motherhood.
Szporluk.   Meteor.
Szymborska.   Born of Woman.
Tatarunis, P.   I Have Two Sons and the One I
  Love Best Is Robert.
Tate, A.   Mother and Son.
Taylor, J.   My Mother.
Thompson, D. P.   Laurel Street, 1950.
Thrilling.   Mother.
Tighe.   Sonnet Addressed to My Mother.
Titherage.   And Her Mother Came Too.
Tjanara-Williams, P.   Torn Apart.
Townsend, A.   Eighteenth-Century Medical
  Illustration: The Infant in its Little Room.
Trethewey, N.   Hot Comb.
Tucker, M.   My Mother's Voice.
Unknown.   Carpenter's Wife, The.
  Cruel Mother, The.
  Execution of Alice Holt.
  Holy Goddess Tellus.
  Homage to Tara Our Mother.
  I Sing of a Maiden.
  Mother.
  Mother's Song to a Baby.
  My Mother's Hands.
  Old Mother, The.
  Somebody's Mother.
  Wife of Usher's Well, The.
Unknown, fr. Terezin Concentration Camp.
  Letter to Daddy, A.
Untermeyer, J.   Autumn.
Van Duyn.   Stream, The.
Vando.   My Mother Cunning, Yet Innocent.
Vazirani, R.   Daughter-Mother-Maya-Seeta.
  Mrs. Biswas of Maryland on the Phone.
Vertreace, M.   Caged Stone.
Villanueva, A.   From the Healing Dark.
  Planet Earth Speaks, The.
Voigt.   For My Mother.
Wagenlander.   Mother's Birthday.
Wallace, W.   Hand That Rocks the Cradle Is the
  Hand That Rules the World, The.
Waniek.   Bali Hai Calls Mama.
Warren, R.   Only Poem, The.
  Revelation.
  There's a Grandfather's Clock in the Hall.
Watson, R.   Who a Mother Is.
Wedgefarth.   Mother's Hands.
Weiners.   My Mother.
Williams, C.   For the White Lady Holding Me.
  My Mother's Lips.
Williams, L.   Interruption of Flight.
Williams, P.   Libation.
Williams, S.   California Light.
Williams, W.   Horse Show, The.
  Young Woman at a Window.
Wilson, F.   Bathing My Mother.
Wong, N.   Dreams in Harrison Railroad Park.
  Mama, Come Back.
Wood, D.   Christmas Fare.
Wordsworth, W.   Affliction of Margaret, The.

Worley, D.   Sandra.
Wren, A.   Surrogate Mothers.
Yeats.   Song of the Old Mother, The.
Yee, M.   Wintermelons.
Young, I.   Mermaid Knows, A.
Zamora-Linmark.   Election Day.
Zepeda, O.   Bury Me with a Band.

Mothers-in-Law
Adams, A.   Unrecorded Speech.
Ciardi.   Censorship.
Unknown.   Prince Robert.
  Unexpected Pleasure, An.

Moths
Baildon.   Moth, A.
Crapsey.   Warning, The.
Davies, H.   Music in an Empty House.
De Casseres.   Moth-Terror.
Gittings.   Great Moth, The.
Jackson, M.   Moths, The.
Leithauser.   Haunted, The.
Mandela.   I Waited for You Last Night.
Ni Dhomhnaill.   Leaba Shíoda.
Snodgrass, W.   Lying Awake.
Vizenor.   Tyranny of Moths.
Williams, W.   Prelude to Winter.

Motion
Crozier, A.   Loopy Dupes.
Garcia, R.   Brief Entanglements.
Garrett, E.   Contrary Motion.
Greenwald, T.   I Hear a Step.
Gunn, T.   On the Move.
Hughes, T.   Thought-Fox, The.
Levertov.   Wavering.
Lovelace, R.   Gratiana Dancing [or Dauncing]
  and [or &] Singing.
Mörling, M.   For the Woman with the Radio.
MacCaig.   Sleeping Compartment.
Mills, B.   Ballad: Of Motion.
Prunty.   Ferris Wheel, The.
Stevens, W.   Pleasures of Merely Circulating,
  The.
Volkman.   Untitled.
Wunderlich, M.   One Explanation of Beauty.

Motion Pictures
Ashbery.   Forties Flick.
Bentley, N.   Cecil B. De Mille.
Berryman.   Dispossessed, The.
Creeley.   Bresson's Movies.
Day Lewis.   Newsreel.
Duncan, R.   Ingmar Bergman's "Seventh Seal."
Field, E.   Curse of the Cat Woman.
Garrigue.   Movie Actors Scribbling Letters Very
  Fast in Crucial Scenes.
Gwynn, R.   Drive-In, The.
Hayden, R.   Double Feature.
Heseltine, P.   Limerick: "Young things who
  frequent picture-palaces, The."
Hollander, J.   Movie-Going.
Jones, P.   Why I Like Movies.
Levertov.   Triple Feature.
McGough, R.   If Life's a Lousy Picture, Why
  Not Leave before the End.
Muldoon, P.   Weepies, The.
O'Hara, F.   Ave Maria.
  Image of Leda, An.
  To the Film Industry in Crisis.
Schmitz.   Star & Garter Theater.
Updike.   Movie House.
Ward, D.   Re-Verse.
Whittemore, R.   Day with the Foreign
  Legion, A.
Wilbur.   Prisoner of Zenda, The.
Worley, D.   Las Flores para una Niña Negra.
See also **Show Business**

Motorcycles and Motorcycling
Gunn, T.   On the Move.
Jordan, J.   Speculations on the Present through
  the Prism of the Past.
Moolten, D.   Motorcycle Ward.
Mtshali.   Farewell to My Scooter.
Pierpoint, K.   Combustion Engine.
Simon, L.   Kali.
Van Duyn.   What the Motorcycle Said.
Walker, A.   Kiss, The.
Williams, L.   Interruption of Flight.

Mount Olivet
Kaufman, S.   Mount of Olives, The.
Mount Saint Helens, Washington
Rose.   Loo-wit.
Mountain Beavers
Wagoner, D.   Looking for Mountain Beavers.
Mountain Climbing
Birney.   David.
Carmichael, A.   Last Defile, The.
Francis, R.   Rock Climbers, The.
Huntington, W.   From Green Mountain.
Justice, D.   Here in Katmandu.
Kinnell.   Flower Herding on Mount Monadnock.
MacCaig.   Climbing Suilven.
Rich, A.   Phantasia for Elvira Shatayev.
Stafford, W.   Story, A.
Mountain Lions
Galvin, B.   Cougar.
Lawrence, D.   Mountain Lion.
Mountains
Back, R.   Untitled.
Blackburn, P.   Net of Place, The.
Bowers, E.   Mountain Cemetery, The.
Brecht, B.   Three Fragments.
Brewer, G.   Mountains.
Burn.   Welsh Love Letter.
Burns, R.   My Heart's in the Highlands.
Corcoran.   Music of the Altai Mountains.
Ford, C.   Overturned Lake, The.
Frost, R.   Fountain, a Bottle, a Donkey's Ears
    and Some Books, A.
Gregg.   Night Music.
Grossman, A.   Enough Rain for Agnes Walquist.
Gunn, T.   From the Highest Camp.
Haines, J.   Cloud Factory, The.
Hall, D.   Mount Kearsarge.
Hannon.   Beneath Cold Mountain.
    Beyond Freedom.
    Real Estate.
Hemans.   Mountain Sanctuaries.
    Rock of Cader Idris, The.
Henry, B.   Moraine Lake.
Hernández Cruz.   Mountain Building.
Holmes, O.   Nearing the Snow-Line.
Jennings, H.   Prose Poem.
Keble.   Malvern at a Distance.
Landor, W.   Separation.
Levertov.   Witness.
Li Po.   In the Mountains on a Summer Day.
    Summit Temple, The.
    To Tan Ch'iu.
Magowan.   Paros.
Melville, H.   Guide and Guard.
Mphahlele.   Homeward Bound.
Ortiz.   Look to the Mountain.
Palmer, M.   Dearest Reader.
Radcliffe, A.   Storied Sonnet.
Rafferty, P.   Off the Beaten Track.
Ridge, J.   Mount Shasta.
Robinson, E.   Vickery's Mountain.
Roditi.   Hand.
Saner.   Autumn Aspens: Cumbres Pass.
    Waking at the Middle of Nowhere.
Smith, B.   Black Mountain Blues.
Snyder, G.   Meeting the Mountains.
Spicer, J.   Phonemics.
Teasdale.   Lines.
Wang Wei.   Cold Mountain, The.
Whalen.   Sourdough Mountain Lookout.
Wilcox, E.   Attraction.
Williams, M.   Heading for the Heights.
Wordsworth, W.   Farewell, A: "Farewell thou
    little Nook of mountain-ground."
Young, A.   Mountains of California: Part 1, The.
See also **Hills and Mountains**
Mourning and Mourners
Alarcon, F.   Las calles lloran / Streets Are
    Crying.
Anderson-Thompkins.   To Love a Stranger.
Awad, J.   Man Who Loved Flamenco, The.
Beckman, J.   Lament for the Death of a
    Bullfighter.
Behn, A.   On the Death of the Late Earl of
    Rochester.
Bion.   Lament for Adonis.

Bly, R.   Mourning Pablo Neruda.
Bowles, W.   On the Death of William Linley,
    Esq.
Bradstreet, A.   In Memory of My Dear
    Grandchild Anne Bradstreet Who Deceased
    June 20, 1669, Being Three Years and Seven
    Months Old.
    In Memory of My Dear Grandchild Elizabeth
    Bradstreet Who Deceased August, 1665,
    Being a Year and Half Old.
    On My Dear Grandchild Simon Bradstreet,
    [Who Died on 16TH November, 1669, Being
    But A Month And One Day Old].
    To the Memory of My Dear and Ever Honored
    Father Thomas Dudley Esq. Who Deceased
    July 31, 1653, and of His Age 77.
Brontë, C.   On the Death of Anne Brontë.
    On the Death of Emily Jane Brontë.
Browning, E.   Died.
    Grief.
Bruner.   Dog's Vigil, A.
    Selfishness.
    Time's Hand Is Kind.
Burns, R.   Man Was Made to Mourn, a Dirge.
Byron, G.   If Sometimes in the Haunts of Men.
    One Struggle More, and I Am Free.
Carew, T.   Another [Epitaph on the Lady Mary
    Villiers].
    Elegy upon the Death of the Dean of [St.]
    Paul's, Dr. John Donne, An.
    On the Death of Donne.
Chivers.   Avalon.
Collins, W.   Fidele, A.
Dickinson, E.   Last Night that She Lived, The.
    Of nearness to her sundered Things.
Dobson, A.   Before Sedan.
Donne.   Valediction: Forbidding Mourning, A.
Douglas, L.   Dead Poet, The.
Drummond, W.   Sextain: "Sith gone is my
    delight and only pleasure."
Dufferin.   Countess of Dufferin, The.
"Eliza."   To My Husband.
Espada.   Moon Shatters on Alabama Avenue,
    The.
Espinet, R.   Merchant of Death.
"Field."   Beloved, My Glory in Thee is Not
    Ceased.
Finch, F.   Blue and the Gray, The.
Frost, R.   Home Burial.
Gardinier.   Two Girls.
Garioch.   At Robert Fergusson's Grave, October
    1962.
Gillan.   In New Jersey Once.
Ginsberg, A.   Kaddish.
Graves, R.   When I'm Killed.
Gray, T.   Elegy Written in a Country
    Churchyard.
    Epitaph: "Here rests his head upon the lap of
    earth."
    Sonnet [on the Death of Mr. Richard West].
Greville, F.   Caelica, XXIII.
Gurney, I.   To His Love.
Hall, D.   Porcelain Couple, The.
Hanzlicek, C.   Feeding Frenzies.
Hardy, T.   Caged Goldfinch, The.
Harper, M.   Drowning of the Facts of a Life,
    The.
Hayden, R.   Mourning Poem for the Queen of
    Sunday.
Herd.   Coronach.
Herrick.   Mad Maid's Song, The.
    To His Dying Brother, Master William Herrick.
    To His Lovely Mistresses.
    Upon a Maid.
    Upon a Maid[e].
    Upon His Sister-in-Law, Mistress Elizabeth
    Herrick.
Hewitt, J.   Local Poet, A.
Heyen.   Stadium, The.
Hirsch, E.   In Memoriam Paul Celan.
Hongo.   Pier, The.
Hooks.   Woman's Mourning Song, The.
Howard, A.   Good Shepherd's Sorrow for the
    Death of His Beloved Son, The.
Hughes, L.   Wake.
Hughes, T.   Day He Died, The.

Hugo, R.   Elegy: "I expected him to look dead
    in the casket."
Jeffers, R.   May–June, 1940.
Jennings, E.   After a Time.
Johnson, J.   Go Down Death.
Johnston, E.   Nelly's Lament for the Pirnhouse
    Cat.
Jones, E.   Development of Idiotcy, A.
Jonson, B.   On My First Son[ne].
King, H.   Exequy, The.
Kumin, M.   How It Is.
Kunene.   Elegy for My Friend E. Galo.
Landor, W.   Rose Aylmer.
Larkin, J.   Cold River.
Lawrence, D.   Sorrow.
Limburg, J.   Return, The.
Mandiela, A.   Mih Feel It.
Milton.   Lycidas.
Morgan, E.   Glass, The.
Moss, H.   Elegy for My Father.
Norton, J.   Funeral Elegy Upon that Pattern and
    Patron of Virtue, A.
Nye, N.   Mother of Nothing.
Olson, C.   Death of Europe, The.
Orfalea, G.   Rose of Brooklyn, The.
Padel.   Tell Me About It.
Pawlak.   After Burying Her Son, a Mother
    Speaks.
Raine, K.   Heroes.
Reese, L.   Death's Guerdon.
Rich, A.   Mourning Picture.
    Valediction Forbidding Mourning, A.
Rimington, J.   God of the Flies.
Robinson, A.   Stornelli and Strambotti.
Robinson, E.   Reuben Bright.
Roethke.   Elegy for Jane.
Rossetti, C.   After Death.
    Remember [Me].
    Song: "When I am dead, my dearest."
Scott, S.   Jock of Hazeldean.
Scott, W.   My Mother.
Sexton.   Truth the Dead Know, The.
Shelley, P.   Adonais; An Elegy on the Death of
    John Keats.
Sia, B.   Howl.
Tennyson, A.   Rizpah.
Troupe.   Day in the Life of a Poet, A.
Unknown.   My Boy Willie.
    Unquiet Grave, The.
    Wife of Usher's Well, The.
Van Duyn.   Stream, The.
Vaughan, H.   Joy of My Life! While Left Me
    Here.
    Silence and Stealth of Day[e]s!
Whitman, W.   Vigil Strange I Kept on the Field
    One Night.
Wilbur.   To an American Poet Just Dead.
Wordsworth, W.   Sonnet on Catherine
    Wordsworth.
Wright, J.   Angel, The.
    At the Slackening of the Tide.
    Gesture by a Lady with an Assumed Name, A.
Yeats.   John Kinsella's Lament for Mrs. Mary
    Moore.
See also **Funerals; Grief**
Mouths
Carnevali.   Queer Things.
Chubb, R.   Song of My Soul.
Creeley.   Language, The.
Crowley, A.   Go into the Highways and Hedges,
    And Compel Them to Come In.
Robinson, E.   Meshes.
Swenson, M.   Cardinal Ideograms.
Sylvester, J.   Sweet Mouth, That Send'st a
    Musky-Rosed Breath.
Tate, G.   Tonguing.
Movies
Abse.   Welsh Valley Cinema, 1930s.
Bowers, N.   On the Elvis Mailing List.
Brown, L.   If I Had a Talking Picture of You.
Carbó, N.   Little Brown Brother.
Dauer.   Woman in the Film, The.
DeFoe, M.   Red Salamander—Video Store
    Parking Lot.
Divakaruni.   Indian Movie, New Jersey.
Equi.   Being Sick Together.

Forhan, C. Without Presumptions.
Garioch. Phooie!
Glück, R. Invaders from Mars.
Goldbarth. Meop.
Guest, B. Motion Pictures: 15.
  Motion Pictures: 4.
Healy, E. What It Was Like the Night Cary
  Grant Died.
Heaney, S. Shooting Script, A.
Hicok. Over Coffee.
Holzer, R. Current 'Now, Voyager' Fantasy.
Hufana, A. Insides of Alfred Hitchcock, The.
Joseph, A. Teenage Interplanetary Vixens Run
  Wild on Bikini Beach.
Miller, J. Topos.
Muske, C. Last Take.
Notley. Where Leftover Misery Goes.
Rossman, E. Double Features.
Scott, D. For Norman Nicholson.
Simon, M. Blue Movies.
Stanton, M. Sorrow and Rapture.
Trinidad. Shower Scene in *Psycho*, The.
  Things to Do in Valley of the Dolls (The
  Movie).
Villanueva, T. Scene from the Movie *Giant*.
Warsh. White Nights.
Wojahn. Francis Ford Coppola and
  Anthropologist Interpreter Teaching
  Gartewienna Tribesmen to Sing 'Light My
  Fire,' Philippine Jungle, 1978.
Zucker, R. In Your Version of Heaven I am
  Younger.
See also **Motion Pictures**
Moving and Movers
Bottoms. In a U-Haul North of Damascus.
Brown, F. Last of England, The.
Byron, C. Shipping the Pictures from Belfast.
Campbell, D. Duchesses.
Divakaruni. Restroom.
Dunn, D. Removal from Terry Street, A.
Gunn, T. Last Days at Teddington.
Haines, J. Flight, The.
Kay, J. Pounding Rain.
Matthews, T. Private But Sulphurous.
McGuckian. Little House, Big House.
Paulin. Peacetime.
Realuyo. Sojourners, The.
Shapiro, K. October 1.
Smith, D. Cumberland Station.
Mowing and Mowers
Ammons, A. R. Needs.
Dybek. Mowing.
Frost, R. Tuft of Flowers, The.
Gosse. Lying in the Grass.
Lawrence, D. Youth Mowing, A.
Marvell. Damon the Mower.
  Mower Against Gardens, The.
  Mower to the Glowworms [*or* Glow-Worms *or*
  Glo-Worms], The.
  Mower's Song, The.
Relph. Hay-Time; or, The Constant Lovers. A
  Pastoral.
Roberts, S. Mowing, The.
Thomas, E. Haymaking.
Toomer. Reapers.
Mozart, Wolfgang Amadeus
Bachhuber, D. Mozart in a Classroom of
  Children.
Berger, B. To Answer Your Question.
Foerster. Mozart's Death.
Hooper, P. Listening to Mozart at Meadow
  Brook.
Meynell, A. To Silence.
Rossini, C. Valediction.
Stanton, M. Ode to Mozart.
Stevens, W. Mozart, 1935.
Unknown. Limerick: "As Mozart composed a
  sonata."
Watson, R. Die Zauberflöte.
Wicks, S. On Re-recording Mozart.
Zeiger, D. Mostly Mozart at Planting Fields
  Arboretum.
Zeppa, M. Aleatory.
Mud
Berrigan, T. Orange Jews.
Bibbins, M. Mud.

Brown, S. Riverbank Blues.
Cisneros, S. Muddy Kid Comes Home.
Cummings, E. In Just.
Heaney, S. Mud Vision, The.
Hillman. Formation of Soils, The.
Kalamaras, G. Mud.
Kasischke. Fatima.
Knight, E. Poem for Myself (Or Blues for a
  Mississippi Black Boy), A.
Todd, M. Mud Season.
Muffins
Torres, E. How Long Does the Curator Dance
  For?
Muffs
Lovelace, R. Her Muffe.
See also **Gloves; Mittens**
Muhammad
Al-Mala'ika. Lilies for the Prophet.
Mules
Ammons, A. R. Silver.
González, R. You and the Tijuana Mule.
Merrill, B. Mule, The.
Muldoon, P. Mules.
Plumpp. Another Mule.
Mummies
"Field." Mummy Invokes His Soul, The.
Gardner, I. In the Museum.
Gould, H. Child's Address to the Kentucky
  Mummy, The.
Heaney, S. Punishment.
  Tollund Man, The.
McPherson, S. Wanting a Mummy.
Speyer. To a Song of Sappho Discovered in
  Egypt.
Veinberg, J. Next to Tut.
Munch, Edvard
Wieners. Poem for Museum Goers, A.
Wright, C. Edvard Munch.
Murasaki Shikibu
Guest, B. Wild Gardens Overlooked by Night
  Lights.
Murder and Murderers
Ai. Good Shepherd: Atlanta, 1981, The.
  Kid, The.
Aisenberg, N. Leaving Eden.
Atwood. Robber Bridegroom, The.
Bandele, A. Prayer for the Living, A.
Beardsley. Ballad of a Barber, The.
Brathwaite, E. Stone.
Brooks, G. Bronzeville Mother Loiters in
  Mississippi, A. Meanwhile, a Mississippi
  Mother Burns Bacon.
Brown, S. Southern Cop.
Browning, R. Laboratory, The (Ancien
  Régime).
  Porphyria's Lover.
Carew, T. Another [On the Duke of
  Buckingham].
Cary, A. Sea-Side Cave, The.
Charara, H. On the Murder of an Ice Cream
  Man.
Cooper, D. In New York.
  In School.
Cronin, J. Lullaby: "But who killed Johannes,
  mama . . . ?"
Davies, W. Inquest, The.
Davis, C. Murderer, The.
Davis, T. Lament for the Death of Eoghan
  Ruadh O'Neill.
Derricotte. Minks, The.
Domina, L. Pharoah's Army Got Drowned.
Emanuel, J. Panther Man.
Espada. Majeski Plays the Saxophone.
  Moon Shatters on Alabama Avenue, The.
Felltham [*or* Feltham]. On the Duke of
  Buckingham, Slain by Felton, the 23rd August,
  1628.
Ferré. Opprobrium.
Fitzgerald, E. 19.
Forché. Memory of Elena, The.
Graves, R. Nobody.
Grealy, L. Murder.
Gunn, T. Victim, The.
Harnick. Ballad of the Shape of Things, The.
Harper, M. Fireplace, The.

Hart, L. To Keep My Love Alive.
Herbert, Z. Return of the Proconsul, The.
Heyen. Blue.
  To the Onlookers.
Hongo. Legend, The.
Housman, A. Fragment of a Greek Tragedy.
  True Lover, The.
Jarrell. Eighth Air Force.
Joans. .38, The.
Jordan, J. Test of Atlanta 1979, The.
  Through These Halls.
Kaufman, S. Accuser, The.
Kennedy, X. Loose Woman.
Kim, M. Rose of Sharon, A.
Kipling, R. Ballad of Fisher's Boardinghouse,
  The.
Knott. Two Vietnam Poems: (1966).
Lifshin. Seeing the Documentary by the British
  Liberating Bergen-Belsen.
Loesser. Murder, He Says.
Mörling, M. Three-Card Monte.
Mabuza. Death to the Gold Mine!
Mandiela, A. Mih Feel It.
Martínez, V. Children of the Disappeared.
Merwin, W. S. Last One, The.
Meynell, A. Parentage.
Michelson, R. Genuine Jewish Flesh.
Miller, E. You Send Me: Bertha Franklin,
  December 11, 1964.
Morris, W. Haystack in the Floods, The.
  Shameful Death.
Nemerov. Murder of William Remington, The.
Newbolt. He Fell among Thieves.
Page, G. Premeditations.
Patchen. From My High Love.
Philips, K. Upon the Double Murther of King
  Charles I.
Plath. Daddy.
Porter, C. Miss Otis Regrets.
Rainey. See, See Rider.
Ranaldo, L. HIS:STORY.
Rodgers, R. To Keep My Love Alive.
Schwartz, D. For the One Who Would Take
  Man's Life in His Hands.
Service. Shooting of Dan McGrew, The.
Simmons, J. Claudy.
Smith, S. Murderer, The.
  One of Many.
Stephens, J. Wind, The.
Sundiata. Notes from the Defense of Colin
  Ferguson.
Tapahonso. Pay Up or Else.
Unknown. Annette Myers.
  Babylon; or, The Bonnie Banks o' Fordie.
  Ballad of William Bloat, The.
  Bonny Earl of Murray, The.
  Cruel Mother, The.
  Execution of Alice Holt.
  Feltons Epitaph.
  Frankie and Albert.
  Frankie and Johnny [*or* Johnnie *or* Albert].
  Lord Randal.
  Lord Randal[l].
  Poem for Jacqueline Hill.
  Prince Robert.
  Robin Hood's Death.
  Sir Hugh; or, The Jew's Daughter.
  Stackalee.
  Three Butchers, The.
  Young Hunting.
Van Ostaijen. Murderers, The.
Vando. Knife.
  Lydia's Phantasmagoria.
Vaughan, H. Abel's Blood.
Walker, A. Revolutionary Petunias.
Walker, M. For Andy Goodman—Michael
  Schwerner—and James Chaney.
Warren, R. Ballad of Billie Potts, The.
  Crime.
Warren-Moore. For Paula Cooper.
Wilde, O. Ballad of Reading Gaol, The.
Wright, J. At the Executed Murderer's Grave.
  Life, The.
  Secret Gratitude, A.
Wright, R. Between the World and Me.

Murfreesboro, Battle of (1862–1863)
Tate, A. Battle of Murfreesboro.
Muses
Barbauld. To Mr. S. T. Coleridge.
Washing-Day.
Blake, W. To the Muses.
Bradstreet, A. Prologue, The.
Collins, W. Passions; an Ode for [or to] Music,
The.
Cowley, A. Muse, The.
Creeley. Door, The.
Dana, M. Real Comfort.
Drayton. Ode Written in the Peak[e], An.
Emerson, R. Solution.
Test, The.
Equi. Bouquet of Objects, A.
Ewart. Lifelines.
France, L. My Muse, the Whore.
Glück, L. Poem: "In the early evening, as now,
a man is bending."
Goodman, P. Saint Harmony my patroness.
Gray, T. Progress of Poesy, The.
Herrick. Departure of the Good Daemon, The.
His Winding-Sheet.
Mount of the Muses, The.
Hood, T. First Attempt in Rhyme, A.
Jacobsen, J. When the Five Prominent Poets.
Jewsbury. Farewell to the Muse, A.
Jonson, B. And Must I Sing? What Subject
Shall I Choose?
To Lucy, Countess[e] of Bedford, with Mr.
Donnes Satire's [or Satyres].
Killigrew, A. On the Soft and Gentle Motions
of Eudora.
Upon the Saying That My Verses Were Made by
Another.
Leapor. On Winter.
Sacrifice: An Epistle to Celia, The.
Levertov. To the Muse.
"Philo-Philippa." To the Excellent Orinda.
Ray, H. Invocation to the Muse.
Robinson, A. To My Muse.
Rouse. Virginian Arcady.
Rowlands. Prologue: "Under the shadow of the
gloomy night."
Smith, C. To Mr. Hayley, on Receiving Some
Elegant Lines from Him.
Smith, S. My Muse Sits Forlorn.
Who Is This Who Howls and Mutters?
Stevenson, R. To the Muse.
Taylor, G. Admonition to the Muse.
Thoreau. Inspiration.
Unknown. Elegy upon the Death of Mrs. A.
Behn, the Incomparable Astrea, An.
Urdang. Muse Is Always the Other Woman,
The.
Walcott. Upstate.
Wheatley, P. To Mæcenas.
Wilner, E. Muse, The.
Woodbridge. Upon the Author. By a Known
Friend.
Wright, J. To the Muse.
Museums
Allston. On the Luxembourg Gallery.
Bang, M. Crossed-Over, Fiend-Snitched, X-ed
Out.
Beer, P. In a Country Museum.
Boland, E. Dolls Museum in Dublin, The.
Cliff. History of Costume, A.
De la Mare. In the Local Museum.
Di Prima. American Indian Art: Form and
Tradition.
Dobyns. Nouns of Assemblage.
Duggan, L. Town on the Ten Dollar Note, The.
Empson. Homage to the British Museum.
Fox, S. Miss Pimberton Of.
Fuller, R. Coptic Socks.
Gardner, I. In the Museum.
Gilbert, C. African Sculpture.
Gioia. Guide to the Other Gallery.
Gunn, T. Expression.
Herbert, J. Dossers at the Imperial War
Museum.
Hewitt, J. From a Museum Man's Album.
Hollander, J. No Foundation.
MacNeice. Museums.

McPherson, S. Museum of the Second Creation,
The.
Pastan. At the Train Museum.
Perillo. Ghost Shirt, The.
Philpot, T. How to Live in the Elegy.
Plath. Morning Song.
Reedy, C. Doll Museum, The.
Szymborska. Pietà.
Wieners. Poem for Museum Goers, A.
Wilbur. Museum Piece.
Yeats. Municipal Gallery Revisited, The.
Mushrooms
Clark, M. Mushrooms.
Cobbing. Hymn to the Sacred Mushroom.
Mackenzie, K. Autumn Mushrooms.
Merwin, W. S. Looking for Mushrooms at
Sunrise.
Muldoon, P. Gathering Mushrooms.
Plath. Mushrooms.
Todd, R. Of Moulds and Mushrooms.
Torrance. Acrospirical Meanderings in a
Tongue of the Time.
It Is Difficult to Exaggerate the Importance of
Mushrooms as Food.
Young, A. Fairy Ring, The.
Young, G. Eating Wild Mushrooms.
Music and Musicians
Adisa. Count Ossie.
Ai. Archangel.
Man with the Saxophone, The.
Alexander, E. Farewell to You.
Allen, E. Street Music.
Allen, S. I Say, Mr. A.
Andrews, L. Time Signature.
Angell, B. Street Music.
Annand. Mavis.
Armantrout. Getting Warm.
Ashanti. Just Another Gig.
Ashbery. Syringa.
Atkins. Dark Area.
Aubert, A. Bessie.
Babcock, M. This Is My Father's World.
Bachhuber, D. Mozart in a Classroom of
Children.
Baker, H. Of Walter White's Father in the Rain.
Tobacco Warehouse Blues.
Baker, T. Armillaria Mellea.
Bantock. Bard.
Baraka. All Is One for Monk.
Am/Trak.
Barber, D. Little Overture.
Barlow, G. In My Father's House.
Barnfield [or Barnefield]. To His Friend Master
R. L., In Praise of Music and Poetry.
Barrax. Singer, The.
Barresi. Venice Beach: Brief Song.
Bauer, G. Oldies But Goodies.
She Calms the Savage Beast with Her Aubade.
So You Want to Hear the Blues.
Beardsley. Three Musicians, The.
Berger, B. Salad Days.
Stout Brahms.
To Answer Your Question.
Berlin. Alexander's Ragtime Band.
Pretty Girl Is Like a Melody, A.
Berry, W. Music, A.
Berssenbrugge. Duration of Water.
Blake, E. I'd Give a Dollar for a Dime.
Blessing. Elegy for Elvis.
Bly, R. Listening to the Köln Concert.
Bogan, L. M., Singing.
Musician.
Sub Contra.
Borden, W. Morning Chamber Orchestra Near
Piney Crick, Wyoming, 7 A.M., The.
Bottoms. Homage to Lester Flatt.
Bowers, N. On the Elvis Mailing List.
Bowles, W. On the Death of William Linley,
Esq.
Brathwaite, E. Naima.
Breeze. Dubbed Out.
Eena Mi Corner.
Brett, L. La Pathétique.
Brock, V. All the Stars Are Foxfire.
I Stopped in Tupelo, Elvis.
Sphinx.

Brooks, G. Piano after War.
Third Sermon on the Warpland, The.
Brooks, S. (That's the Way) Dixieland Started
Jazz.
Brown, G. Old Fisherman with Guitar.
Brown, S. Let Them Call It Jazz.
Ma Rainey.
Browning, E. Musical Instrument, A.
Browning, R. Abt Vogler.
Toccata of Galuppi's, A.
Buchwald. As Soon As It's Here It's Gone But
So What.
Buckley, C. Nostalgia.
Playing for Time.
Burns, R. Song: "O my love's [or luve's or love
is or luve is] like a red, red rose."
Butts, A. Massenet.
Bynner. Lovers.
Byron, G. Stanzas for Music.
Cage. 25 Mesostics Re and Not Re Mark
Tobey.
Campion, T. To Music Bent Is My Retired
Mind.
When to Her Lute Corinna [or Corrina] Sings.
Carroll, K. Domino Theory (or Snoop Dogg
rules the world), The.
Castro, M. Blew It.
Cather, W. Spanish Johnny.
Cawein. Music.
Cecil. Richard's Blues.
Cedering, S. Regarding Music.
Variations for the Piano.
Ceravolo. Celebration.
Chambers, G. Meditations on Stevie.
Waxing Poetic on Marvin.
Chase, K. What You Can't See.
Chase, N. Music Mother.
Cherry, K. Raiment We Put On, The.
Chmielarz. They Come Humming.
Clampitt. Syrinx.
Clayton, S. Soul Music.
Cleary, B. New Rock n Roll, The.
Clover, J. Ceriserie.
Codrescu. Imagination of Necessity, The.
Coffman. Courage, or One of Gene Horner's
Fiddles.
Cohan. I Want to Hear a Yankee Doodle Tune.
Cole, T. Lines Suggested by Hearing Music on
the Boston Common at Night.
Coleridge, M. Day-dream, A.
Impromptu.
To a Piano.
Coles, R. New Jersey Boys.
Collins, K. Trio.
Collins, W. Passions; an Ode for [or to] Music,
The.
Cook, E. To My Lyre.
Coolbrith. Lines.
Cooper, J. Wanda's Blues.
Corcoran. Music of the Altai Mountains.
Cornford, F. Guitarist Tunes Up, The.
Cornish, S. His Fingers Seem to Sing.
Cortez, J. I See Chano Pozo.
Cox, N. Singing Alone.
Cranch. Music.
Crane, H. Black Tambourine.
Broken Tower, The.
Crashaw. Music[k]'s Duel[l].
Cristall. Ode on Truth: Addressed to George
Dyer.
Song: "Balmy comforts that are fled, The."
Crouch, S. Revelation, The.
Up on the Spoon.
Cullen, C. Night Rain.
Cushing, J. Autumn Leaves.
Every Time We Say Goodbye.
Lover Man.
Dacey, P. Drummer, The.
Musica.
Musician, The.
Davenant [or D'Avenant]. Lark Now Leaves
His Watery [or Wat'ry] Nest.
Davidson, J. In a Music-Hall.
Davies, S. Orchestra; or, A Poem[e] of
Da[u]ncing.
Praise of Dancing, The.

Speach of Love persuading men to learn Dancing, The.
Davis, F.   Jazz Band.
Davis, T.   C. T. at the Five Spot.
Rogue and Jar: 4/27/77.
Zoom (The Commodores).
Dawes, K.   Black Heart.
Some Tentative Definitions 1.
Trickster 1 (for Winston Rodney).
Trickster 2 (for Lee 'Scratch' Perry).
De la Mare.   Faint Music.
Dent.   Ray Charles at Mississippi State.
Derricotte.   Black Boys Play the Classics.
Blackbottom.
Di Prima.   I Ching.
On Sitting Down to Write, I Decide Instead to Go to Fred Herko's Concert.
Dickinson, E.   He fumbles at Your Spirit.
Dietz, H.   You and the Night and the Music.
Digges.   Rough Music.
Dittberner-Jax.   Blues for Aunt Ruth.
Dove, R.   Canary.
Event, The.
Hully Gully.
Listen to the Sound of My Horn.
Musician Talks About 'Process,' The.
Drummond, W.   To His Lute.
Dryden, J.   Alexander's Feast; or, The Power of Music [or Musique].
Song for St Cecilia's Day, 1687, A.
Duffy, C.   Prayer: "Some days, although we cannot pray, a prayer."
Dunbar, P.   When Malindy Sings.
Dunbar-Nelson.   Music.
Duncan, R.   Bending the Bow.
Passages 37.
Presence of the Dance / The Resolution of the Music, The.
Duran, J.   Mr Teller the Piano Teacher.
Durcan.   Death by Heroin of Sid Vicious, The.
Eady.   Hank Mobley's.
Ebb, F.   Cabaret.
Ekelof.   Like Ankle-Rings, This Music.
Elledge.   Household Gods.
Ellis, T.   Practice.
Practice: For Derek Walcott.
Sir Nose D'VoidofFunk.
Tambourine Tommy.
Tapes.
Emerson, R.   Saadi.
Enright, D.   Apocalypse.
Espada.   Dándole la mano a Mongo.
Latin Night at the Pawnshop.
Majeski Plays the Saxophone.
Shaking Hands with Mongo.
Espaillat.   Metrics.
Esteves.   In the Beginning.
Evans, M.   Boss Communication.
I Am a Black Woman.
Fabio.   For Louis Armstrong, A Ju-Ju.
Feinstein, S.   Blues for Zoot.
Blues Villanelle for Sonny Criss.
Christmas Eve.
Singapore, July 4th.
Sonnets for Stan Gage (1945–1992), The.
Ferdinand.   Blues (in Two Parts), The.
Finnell.   Over Voice of America.
Firer.   1956, The Year My Sister, Using Her Ill Health Once Again, Blackmailed My Parents into an Accordion.
Saxophone Julie.
Fisher, R.   Thing About Joe Sullivan, The.
Fitzpatrick, K.   Highland, 1955.
Fleckenstein, M.   Getting Even.
Foerster.   Mozart's Death.
Ford, W.   Of Miles Davis.
Forrest, G.   Strange Music.
Frost, L.   Rock 'n' Roll.
Frost, R.   Never Again Would Birds' Song Be the Same.
Fuller, M.   Sistrum.
Garioch.   I Was Fair Beat.
Ghigna.   Lesson of Night, A.
Gibb.   Letter to Russel Barron.
Gilbert, C.   Time with Stevie Wonder in It.
Gilonis, H.   Song 9.

Gioia.   Lives of the Great Composers.
Giovanni.   Genie in the Jar, The.
Goedicke.   Interior Music, The.
Wind of Our Going: Adagio Ma Non Troppo.
Gonzalez, R.   Some Sixties.
Goodison.   For Don Drummond.
Gordon, G.   Gas.
Tercios del Muerte.
Gordon, M.   Serenade in Blue.
Gould, R.   Amateur Drummer.
Graham, W.   Johann Joachim Quantz's Five Lessons.
Gray, A.   Music in the Meadow.
Why Your Grandfather Stopped Playing the Viola.
Gray-Kontar, D.   Cuz' mama played jazz.
Grieg, E.   Strange Music.
Grosholz.   Last of the Courtyard, The.
Grunke, A.   Learning to Live with the Piano.
Guillén, N.   Wake for Papa Montero.
Guiney.   At a Symphony.
Gunn, T.   Elvis Presley.
Victim, The.
Gurney, I.   Bach and the Sentry.
Hagedorn, J.   Latin Music in New York.
Hammerstein.   Sound of Music, The.
Hanley, J.   Zing! Went the Strings of My Heart.
Harer, K.   Lucky 7.
Harjo, J.   Bird.
Healing Animal.
We Encounter Nat King Cole as We Invent the Future.
Harms.   My Own Little Piece of Hollywood.
Harper, F.   Songs for the People.
Harper, M.   Alone.
Bandstand.
Dear John, Dear Coltrane.
Elvin's Blues.
For Bud.
Here Where Coltrane Is.
Narrative of the Life and Times of John Coltrane: Played by Himself, A.
Hart, J.   Only Applebaum Can Make a Tree.
Harvey, N.   Mighty Tropicale Orchestra, The.
Harwood, G.   New Music.
Nightfall.
Haskins, L.   Prodigy, The.
To Play Pianissimo.
Heard, J.   Music.
Heithaus.   What a Little Moonlight Can Do.
Hemans.   Corinne at the Capitol.
Henderson, D.   Elvin Jones Gretsch Freak.
Lee Morgan.
Herbert, G.   Church-Music[k].
Hernández Cruz.   Ironing Goatskin.
Latin and Soul for Joe Bataan.
Loíza Aldea.
Side 20.
Hernandez, D.   Rooftop Piper.
Herrera.   Iowa Blues Bar Spiritual.
Herrick.   Canticle to Apollo, A.
Music.
To M. Henry Lawes, the Excellent Composer[,] of his Lyrics.
To Music.
To Music, to Becalm a Sweet-sick Youth.
To Music, to Becalm His Fever.
To Music: A Song.
Heyward, D.   Jasbo Brown.
Hicky.   No Friend Like Music.
Hirsch, E.   Art Pepper.
Hirshfield, J.   Music Like Water, The.
Hodgson, R.   Song of Honor [or Honour], The.
Hollander, J.   Old Guitar, The.
Holm, B.   Blizzard.
Playing the Goldberg Variations on Sunday Morning.
Scott Joplin.
Whale Breathing: Bartlett Cove, Alaska.
Hooper, P.   Listening to Mozart at Meadow Brook.
Huddle.   Music.
Hudgins.   Around the Campfire.
Versification of a Passage from Penthouse.
Hughes, L.   Be-Bop Boys.
Boogie: 1 A.M.

Dream Boogie: Variation.
Easy Boogie.
Juke Box Love Song.
Note on Commercial Theatre.
Testimonial.
Trumpet Player.
Weary Blues, The.
When Sue Wears Red.
Hugo, R.   My Buddy.
Hull, L.   Lost Fugue for Chet.
Hummer, T.   Poem in the Shape of a Saxophone.
Hupfeld, H.   When Yuba Plays the Rumba on the Tuba.
Hutchinson, P.   True Story Ending in False Hope, A.
Illyés, G.   While the Record Plays.
Inada.   Great Bassist, The.
Inez.   Listening to Dvorak's Serenade in E.
Ingram-Roberts, A.   Poem 2 (for Duckie Simpson of Black Uhuru).
Jackson, A.   Billie in Silk.
Make/n My Music.
Ohnedaruth.
Jackson, R.   63rd and Broadway.
Lady's Way.
Shadows.
Thelonious.
Jacob, M.   In Honor of the Sardana and the Tenora.
Jacobs, H.   And Sometimes I Hear This Song in My Head.
Jarman, M.   Supremes, The.
Jarvenpa, D.   Polka.
Jauss.   After the End of the World.
Last Solo: Charlie Parker, Hotel Stanhope, March 12, 1955.
Jeffers, L.   How High the Moon.
Jewett, S.   At Home from Church.
Jewsbury.   Farewell to the Muse, A.
Johnson, H.   Berlioz in the Madhouse.
Fringe-Area Reception.
Johnson, J.   Music for the Cows.
Johnson, L.   Five Nights of Bleeding.
Reggae Sounds.
Johnson, S.   Epitaph upon the Celebrated Claudy Phillips, Musician, Who Died Very Poor, An.
Jordan, J.   October 23, 1983.
Josefowitz, N.   Music.
Joseph, A.   My Father's Heroes.
Pure Pop.
Wedding Party.
Justice, D.   Mrs. Snow.
Variations for Two Pianos.
Kander, J.   Cabaret.
Kane, J.   Reasons for Loving the Harmonica.
Kaufman, B.   Battle Report.
Unanimity Has Been Achieved, Not a Dot Less for Its Accidentalness.
Keats.   'How Many Bards Gild the Lapses of Time!'
Keble.   Happiness.
Kees.   Guide to the Symphony.
Kgositsile.   For Art Blakey and the Jazz Messengers.
King, J.   Intercity Dub.
Kipling, R.   In the Neolithic Age.
Song of the Banjo, The.
Kizer, C.   Muse of Water, A.
Kleinschmidt.   Cooking to Music.
Orchestrion.
Knight, E.   As You Leave Me.
Koehler, T.   Spreadin' Rhythm Around.
Koethe.   Songs of the Valley.
Komunyakaa.   Elegy for Thelonious.
Euphony.
Kresh.   Musical Saw.
Krohn.   My Flute.
Lagrone.   I Heard the Byrd.
Lamb, C.   Free Thoughts on Several Eminent Composers.
Lane, B.   I Hear Music.
Lanier, S.   To Beethoven.
Lawrence, D.   Piano.
Levertov.   For Those Whom the Gods Love Less.

Six Variations.
Levine, P. Soloing.
Levis. Decrescendo.
Lewis, J. Time and Music.
Lindsay, N. Jazz of This Hotel, The.
Loesser. I Hear Music.
Long, D. Black Love Black Hope.
Long, J. Music's Wife.
Longfellow, H. Spirit of Poetry, The.
Longley, M. Words for Jazz Perhaps.
Lovelace, R. To a Lady That Desired Me I Would Bear My Part with Her in a Song.
To Lucasta.
Lowe, J. Club House.
Lux. Night above the Town.
Mörling, M. For the Woman with the Radio.
Mac Low. Pieces O'six—XXIV.
MacNeice. Bagpipe Music.
Madgett. Plea for My Heart's Sake.
Madhubuti. Knocking Donkey Fleas off a Poet from the Southside of Chi.
Sun House.
Madigan. Curtis Fuller.
Stereo Time with Booker Little.
Magidson, H. Music, Maestro, Please!
Malachi. Psalm of Silk.
Mapanje. On African Writing.
Marston, P. Love's Music.
Martin, H. Miss Rosie Mae Watches Elvis Presley on The Ed Sullivan Show.
Martinez, D. Standard Time: Novena for My Father.
Matthews, W. Buddy Bolden Cylinder, The.
Mingus at the Showplace.
Unrelenting Flood.
Max, L. Equal Temperament.
Pedagogy.
McClure, M. For Monk.
Jazz at the Intergalactic Nightclub.
McDonald, W. Songs We Fought For, The.
McGinley. Evening Musicale.
McGrane, P. Jukebox Saturday Night.
McGrath, B. Concert Choir.
McGrath, C. Jeffrey Lee Pierce.
McGrath, T. Guiffre's Nightmusic.
Song: Miss Penelope Burgess, Balling the Jack.
McKean. After Listening to Jack Teagarden.
McLaughlin, J. Black Irish Blues.
McNeill, A. For the D.
McPherson, S. Some Metaphysics of Junior Wells.
Suspension: Junior Wells on a Small Stage in a Converted Barn.
Meeks, B. Is Culcha Weapon?
Meltzer, D. 17: II:82.
Meredith, G. Phoebus with Admetus.
Merrill, B. Music That Makes Me Dance.
Merrill, J. Victor Dog, The.
Mew. Forest Road, The.
Meynell, A. Singers to Come.
Millay, E. On Hearing a Symphony of Beethoven.
Milton. At a Solemn Music[k].
To Mr. H. Lawes on His Airs.
Mitchell, A. From Rich Uneasy America to My Friend Christopher Logue.
Moerman. Louis Armstrong.
Montague, J. Lament for the O'Neills.
Moore, L. Bluesman's Blues, A.
Moore, M. Mind Is an Enchanting Thing, The.
Moore, T. Harp That Once through Tara's Halls, The.
Mor. Coming of John, The.
Mora. Castanet Clicks.
Morris, M. Valley Prince.
Moskowitz, F. Bird Lives.
Moss, T. Landscape with Saxophonist.
Mueller, L. Concert, The.
What the Dog Perhaps Hears.
Mullen, H. Music for Homemade Instruments.
Muratori. Re-Emergence of the Trombone, The.
Neal, L. Harlem Gallery: From the Inside.
Lady's Days.
Nelson, H. Peepers.
Noguere. Barney Bigard.
Noyes, A. Barrel-Organ, The.

Nurske, D. Involuntary Music.
O'Brien, L. Diabolus in Musica.
O'Hara, F. Day Lady Died, The.
O'Shaughnessy, A. Ode: "We are the music-makers."
Oates. Waiting on Elvis, 1956.
Okantah. Afreeka Brass.
Southern Road.
Okara. Piano and Drums.
Osterhaus, J. New York Minute.
Ostriker. Eighth and the Thirteenth, The.
Overton, R. Blues in "C."
Owen, W. Music.
Palmer, M. Untitled (February 2000).
Paman. On Christmas Day to My Heart.
Pastan. Orpheus.
Overture.
Patterson, R. Hopping Toad Blues.
Peabody, J. After Music.
Pederson, C. Summer Recital.
Perry, S. Fugue.
Orpheus.
Toadfish.
Philips, K. To Mr. Henry Lawes.
Pilling. Webern.
Pitter. Military Harpist, The.
Poe. Israfel.
Pope, A. Sylvan Delights.
Pordage. To Lucia Playing on Her Lute, Another.
Porter, C. Begin the Beguine.
Powell, D. A. Sonnet: "Morsels of my lifework: the story of a professional party hostess."
Powell, K. Genius Child.
Preston, R. Chicago Blues.
Deep-Sea Bathing (Inna Reggae Dancehall).
Prior. Ode, An: "Merchant, to secure his treasure, The."
Procter, A. Lost Chord, A.
Rakosi. Instructions to the Player.
Randall, D. Langston Blues.
Randolph, T. Song, A: "Music, thou queen of souls, get up and string."
Ravikovitch [or Ravikovich]. Sound of Birds at Noon, The.
Ray, H. Perfect Orchestra, The.
Two Musicians, The.
Redmond. Dance Bodies #1.
Distance.
Rich, A. At a Bach Concert.
Ninth Symphony of Beethoven Understood at Last as a Sexual Message, The.
Richardson, L. Poet Sings His Painting, The.
Rivard. Baby Vallejo.
Rivers, C. Underground.
Roberts, E. Orpheus.
Roberts, L. My Father's Whistle.
Robinson, A. Search for Apollo, A.
Robinson, E. L'Envoi.
Robson, J. Blues for the Lonely.
Rodgers, R. Sound of Music, The.
Rollings. In Your Own Sweet Time.
Root, W. Sonnet 20: Remembering, from a Nazi Prison, a Teacher Years Before.
Ross, L. James Brown.
Roston. Program Notes.
Rukeyser, M. Bunk Johnson Blowing.
Rux, C. H. Suite Repose.
Rylander, E. Dancing on Beethoven's Birthday.
Midnight Rocker, Tiananmen Square, May 27, 1989.
Salaam. Always Know.
Sama, B. Song, The.
Sanchez, S. To Anita.
Sandburg, C. Jazz Fantasia.
Schuyler, J. Greetings from the Chateau.
Man in Blue, A.
Schwartz, A. You and the Night and the Music.
Schwartz, R. L. Flamenco Guitar.
Seale, J. Playing the Flute for the TMR Class.
Seibles. Manic: A Conversation with Jimi Hendrix.
Sexton. Music Swims Back to Me.
Shange. I Live in Music.
Sheehan, M. My Father's Singing.
Sheldon, G. Blames, for Rane and Diane.

Shelley, P. Hymn of Pan.
Ode to the West Wind.
To———: "Music, when soft voices die."
Shepherd, R. Difficult Music, The.
Lucky One, The.
Sherrill, J. Woodstock.
Shirley, A. Hours Musicians Keep, The.
Simic. Crepuscule with Nellie.
Simmons, J. Didn't He Ramble.
Skloot. Music Appreciation.
Twilight Time.
Slessor. Full Orchestra.
Smith, P. What It's Like to Be a Black Girl (For Those of You Who Aren't).
Sneeden. Coltrane and My Father.
Sobin, G. What the Music Wants.
Solonche. Chopin Preludes, Opus 28.
Soniat. Harp/Desire.
Speakes. Heartbreak Hotel Piano-Bar.
Spellman. Did John's Music Kill Him?
Spender, S. Beethoven's Death Mask.
Spicer, J. Orfeo.
Stanard, C. Rap Is.
Stanton, M. Ode to Mozart.
Stern, G. Bela.
Fritz.
Romania, Romania.
Stevens, W. Anglais Mort à Florence.
Arrival at the Waldorf.
Peter Quince at the Clavier.
Sad Strains of a Gay Waltz.
To the One of Fictive Music.
Stevenson, R. Land of Nod, The.
Song of a Traveller, The.
Stewart, B. August Town.
Stillman, A. Jukebox Saturday Night.
Stokesbury. Evening's End.
Straus, M. What I Heard on the Radio Today.
Strode. In Commendation of Music.
On a Gentlewoman that Sung and Played upon a Lute.
Sweet, B. 'New World' Interview.
Sylvester, J. Variable.
Symons, A. Tune, A.
Teasdale. Lines.
Thaxter. Schumann's Sonata in A Minor.
Thomas, L. Excitation.
Historiography.
Onion Bucket.
Thomas, R. Pavane.
Thompson, J. Music in Camp.
Thoreau. Dong, Sounds the Brass in the East.
Each More Melodious Note I Hear.
Music.
Thorne, T. Whatever Happened to Conway Twitty?
Tiger. Lovepoem Writing Me.
Touré, A. O Lord of Light! A Mystic Sage Returns to Realms of Eternity!
Trinidad. Meet the Supremes.
Troupe. Impressions / of Chicago; For Howlin' Wolf.
Unknown. Blind Musicians, The.
It Don't Mean a Thing (If It Ain't Got That Swing).
Updike. Player Piano.
Recital.
Vow.
Vando. Swallows of Salangan.
Vigil, A. That's the Way, Uh Huh, Uh Huh, I Liked It.
Vinz. Blues, The.
Volkman. Evening.
Wagoner, D. Chorus: "That rain-strewn night in the woods, the chorus, chorus."
Wakoski. Valentine for Ben Franklin Who Drives a Truck in California, A.
Wallenstein. Blues 1.
Blues 2.
Walton, A. Dissidence.
Warren, H. Serenade in Blue.
Waters, M. 'Night in the Tropics' (1858–59?).
Christ at the Apollo, 1962.
Weems, M. Return to Temptation.
Weinstein, N. Drummond's Lover Sings the Blues.

Ethiopian Apocalypse of Don, The.
Garvey's Head as Value.
Migration of Drummond's Organs (After
Death), The.
Welburn. Ben Webster: "Did You Call Her
Today?"
Gonsalves.
Wenderoth, J. Billy's Famous Lounge.
Wheelwright. Would You Think?
Whitfield. Yes! Strike Again That Sounding
String.
Whitman, T. Hunger and Imagination.
Whitman, W. Italian Music in Dakota.
Proud Music of the Storm.
Wilkes, K. Dolce.
Williams, B. Night Flute, The.
Williams, W. Dance, The.
Ol' Bunk's Band.
Orchestra, The.
Shoot It Jimmy!
Willson, M. Seventy Six Trombones.
Winder. Lesson.
On Fourteen Maple Street.
Unaccompanied Suite.
Woessner. Jungle Music.
Wojahn. Elvis Moving a Small Cloud: The
Desert Near Las Vegas, 1976.
Francis Ford Coppola and Anthropologist
Interpreter Teaching Gartewienna Tribesmen
to Sing 'Light My Fire,' Philippine Jungle,
1978.
John Berryman Listening to Robert Johnson's
"King of the Delta Blues," January 1972.
Nixon Names Elvis Honorary Federal Narcotics
Agent at Oval Office Ceremony, 1973.
Wolfli. Nostalgic Song for My Beloved.
Wong, N. On Plaza Garibaldi.
Wormser. It's a Party (1959).
Soul Music.
Wren, A. Harmony.
Wright, D. Musician, The.
Wright, J. Art of the Fugue, The: A Prayer.
End of an Ethnic Dream, The.
What is Beautiful.
Wright, R. Strange Music.
Wruber, A. Music, Maestro, Please!
Yearsley. Rural Lyre, The.
Yeats. Crazed Girl, A.
Fiddler of Dooney, The.
Young, A. Dance of the Infidels.
From Bowling Green.
Jazz as Was.
Lester Leaps In.
Little More Traveling Music, A.
Ravel: Bolero.
Studio up over in Your Ear.
Young, K. Eddie Priest's Barbershop and
Notary.
Zeiger, D. Mostly Mozart at Planting Fields
Arboretum.
Zeppa, M. Aleatory.
Zimmer. But Bird.
Duke Ellington Dream, The.
Sitting with Lester Young.
Zolynas. Love in the Classroom.
Zukofsky, L. Non Ti Fidar.
See also **Blues (music); Gospel Music**
Music Festivals
Hutchinson, P. Fleadh Cheoil.
Sherrill, J. Woodstock.
Whitman, A. Lute of Afric's Tribe, The.
Music Halls
Davidson, J. In a Music-Hall.
Ellis, T. Tapes.
Levine, P. At the Fillmore.
Rukeyser, M. Paper Anniversary.
Music Lessons
Duran, J. Mr Teller the Piano Teacher.
Mullen, H. Music for Homemade Instruments.
Oles. To a Daughter at Fourteen Forsaking the
Violin.
Musk Oxen
Hall, D. Long River, The.
Muslims and Islam
Hamod, S. After the Funeral of Assam

Hamady.
Hunt, L. Abou Ben Adhem.
Melville, H. By the Jordan.
Saunders, R. Hush Honey.
Whittier. Palm-Tree, The.
Mussels
Farewell. There's Life in a Mussel; a
Meditation.
McDonald, C. Fresh Mussels.
Mustaches
Coogler. Mustacheless Bard, A.
Mutability
Apollinaire. Voyager, The.
Windows.
Zone.
Field, R. Some People.
Harms. Joy Addict, The.
Levy, A. London Poets.
Mackenzie, K. Children Go, The.
Radiguet. Handless Clock.
Taylor, J. Squire's Pew, The.
Volkman. Untitled.
Mutiny
Kocan. Mutineer's Ballad, The.
Rohrer, M. Last Look at the Mutineers, A.
Mystery
Arnold, M. Written in Butler's Sermons.
Cole, T. I Saw a Cave of Sable Depth Profound.
Cullen, C. Yet Do I Marvel.
Doolittle, H. Mysteries, The.
Eberhart, R. Loon Call, A.
Ewart. Owl Writes a Detective Story, The.
Fanshawe, C. Enigma.
"Field." Embalment.
Gorey. Limerick.
Hannon. Beneath Cold Mountain.
Subterranean.
Temporary Heart.
Hemans. Spirit's Mysteries, The.
James, P. Can This Be Love?
Landon. Power of Words, The.
MacDiarmid, H. Light and Shadow.
Mitchell, R. It.
Muldoon, P. Why Brownlee Left.
Nielsen, K. Self Portrait as Nancy Drew, Girl
Sleuth.
Reese, L. Mystery.
Rich, A. Diving into the Wreck.
Richards, T. Challenge to the Reader, A.
Ryan, T. Lunar Eclipse.
Shelley, P. Sonnet: Lift Not the Painted Veil:
"Lift not the painted veil which those who
live."
Stevenson, R. Spaewife, The.
Stever, E. Her Back to Me.
Swift, K. Can This Be Love?
Unknown. Love Is a Secret Feeding Fire.
Winter, M. Elegy: "There is a question."
Yeats. He Remembers Forgotten Beauty.
Magi, The.
Mysticism
Benton, S. Second Coming, The.
Brady, N. Voice from the Bush—Through Me.
Brock-Broido. Domestic Mysticism.
Carey, T. Zohar.
Hayden, R. O Daedalus, Fly Away Home.
Hernández Cruz. Discovery.
For the Far-Out Experimental Writer.
Physics of Ochun, The.
Lawrence, D. Mystic.
Olds, S. Ecstasy.
Robinson, R. Jarrangulli.
Sykes, B. Prayer to the Spirit of the New Year.
Touré, A. O Lord of Light! A Mystic Sage
Returns to Realms of Eternity!
Whitman, W. When I Heard the Learn'd
Astronomer.
Young Bear. Emily Dickinson, Bismarck and
the Roadrunner's Inquiry.
Mythology
Aborigine Oral Tradition. Platypus, The.
Agoos, J. To Atlas in the Attic.
Apuleius, L. I who am Nature, mother of all.
Armantrout. Necromance.
Auden. Atlantis.

Benton, S. Lilith.
Second Coming, The.
Blake, W. Book of Urizen [*or* First Book of
Urizen], The.
Boland, E. Listen. This is the Noise of Myth.
Pomegranate, The.
Brown, E. What Song the Syrens Sang.
Campo. My Voice.
Carbó, N. I Found Orpheus Levitating.
Carew, T. Song, [A]: "Ask[e] me no more
where Jove bestow[e]s."
Castillo, S. Cuba.
Cofer, J. How to Get a Baby.
Coleridge, M. Alcestis to Admetus.
Cooley, N. Undine.
Corn. To Hermes.
Cott, J. Isis (Lady of Petals).
Darley. Rebellion of the Waters, The.
Davidson, M. Troth.
Davie. Fountain of Cyanë, The.
Davies, I. Hywel and Blodwen.
Deanovich. American Avalon.
Donovan, K. Entering the Mare.
Doolittle, H. Holy Satyr.
Lais.
Duncombe, S. To Aspasia.
Eliot, T. Sweeney Among the Nightingales.
Fabian, C. Liturgy for Lilith.
Prayer of Dedication.
Qadesha (Sacred Whore).
Fay, J. Mother of Andromeda, The.
Ferré. Opprobium.
Forché. Ancapagari.
Gewanter, D. Xenia: Stranger/Guest.
Gifford, H. In the Praise of Music.
Glück, L. Hyacinth.
Mythic Fragment.
Graves, R. In Procession.
Gregg. Singers Change, The Music Goes On,
The.
Hardy, J. Computer Aided Design: Creation.
Hecht, A. Goliardic Song.
Hernández Cruz. Islandis.
Hildebrandt, Z. Persephone.
Hill, G. Orpheus and Eurydice.
Housman, A. Crossing Alone the Nighted
Ferry.
Jones, A. M. To Echo.
Jones, S. Hymn to Su'rya, A.
New World.
Keats. Fall of Hyperion; A Dream, The.
Saturn.
Kizer, C. Hera, Hung from the Sky.
Korican, L. Her Story.
Krysl. Persephone, to Demeter.
Lawrence, D. Argonauts, The.
Lim-Wilson. Beginning of Things, The.
Llewellyn-Williams. Two Rivers.
Longfellow, H. Galaxy, The.
McCallum, S. Calypso.
Monaghan. Persephone's Journey.
Venus of Laussel.
Montague, J. Old Mythologies.
Moore, M. Charity Overcoming Envy.
Morton, T. Poem, The: "Rise Oedipus, and if
thou canst unfold."
Mutén, B. Demeter's Blessing.
Hesperides, The.
Queen Hera.
Queen Medusa.
Ngunaitponi. Song of Hungarrda, The.
Nichols, G. Long-Man.
Norris, K. Persephone.
Ortiz. Creation.
Parnell, P. Apotheosis of Medusa.
Medusa and Perseus III: Lilith.
Pastan. Orpheus.
Patterson, G. Lament.
Perry, S. Orpheus.
Pfeiffer, E. Klytemnestra.
Studies from the Antique.
"Philo-Philippa." To the Excellent Orinda.
Porter, C. They Couldn't Compare to You.
Powell, D. A. Minotaur at Supper: Spare the
Noritake and the Spode, The.
Pugh. Coming into Their Own.

Ramanujan. Salamanders.
Reed, H. Philoctetes.
Robinson, M. Describes Her Bark.
Previous to Her Interview with Phaon.
Sappho's Prayer to Venus.
To the Muses.
Rodgers, W. Home Thoughts from Abroad.
Rossetti, D. For Spring By Sandro Botticelli.
Rothenberg, J. Structural Study of Myth, The.
Rukeyser, M. In the Underworld.
Santayana. On an Unfinished Statue.
Sarton. At Lindos.
Shelley, P. Life of Life.
Poet's Dream, The.
Prometheus Unbound [A Lyrical Drama in Four Acts].
Smith, R. Halcion.
Stainer. Xochiquetzal.
Stanton, M. Voice for the Sirens, A.
Starhawk. Demeter's Song.
Tennyson, A. Tithonus.
Triplett, P. Manora.
Unknown. Hymn to Nut.
May Isis heal me.
Waddington, M. Ulysses Embroidered.
Watkins, V. Music of Colours: The Blossom Scattered.
Whitmore, S. Gamelia.
Lenaia.
Whittier. Robin, The.
Wilbur. Lying.
Wilde, O. Santa Decca.
Williams, W. Paterson, Book 5: The River of Heaven.
Wohlfeld. Sea.
Woolagoodjah. Lalai (Dreamtime).
Yeats. Leda and the Swan.

N

Nagasaki, Japan
Clifton, L. At Nagasaki.
Dixon, M. Nagasaki.
Hall, R. Wedding Day at Nagasaki.
Nakedness
Addonizio. Alone in Your House.
Amadiume. Creation.
Arnold, C. Locker Room Etiquette.
Browning, R. Rhyme for a Child Viewing a Naked Venus in a Painting [of "The Judgement of Paris"].
Chubb, R. Transfiguration.
Clanchy, K. One Night When We Paused Half-way.
Copus, J. Masaccio's *Expulsion from Paradise.*
Creeley. Pool, The.
Dauer. Mammals.
Essbaum, J. Post-Communion Striptease.
Everson, W. Stone Face Falls.
Herrick. Upon Electra.
Kolodinsky, A. Midnight.
Muske, C. Our Kitty.
Olds, S. Lifting, The.
Peacock, M. Lullaby: "Big as a down duvet the night."
Phillips, C. Undressing for Li Po.
Reynolds, C. Worst of It, The.
Rock, D. Changing.
Scott, W. Mrs. Severin.
Trommer, R. Sonnet for July.
Warren, R. Birth of Love.
Wright, J. Prayer to the Lord Ramakrishna, A.
Names
Alakoye. Eshu.
Alvarez, J. Bilingual Sestina.
Ashbery. Myrtle.
Baraka, R. I Remember Malcolm.
Barolini. Having the Wrong Name for Mr. Wright.
Belieu. My Field Guide.
Belloc. Frog, The.
Benét, S. American Names.
Berrigan, D. My Name.
Betham-Edwards. In a Letter to A. R. C. on Her

Wishing to Be Called Anna.
Boston, B. Apiary.
Brooks, G. Primer for Blacks.
Brown, D. Patrols.
Browning, E. To George Sand: A Recognition.
Browning, R. Names, The.
Budy. Ellis Island, September 1907.
Cave. Elegy on a Maiden Name, An.
Cherry, K. History.
Raiment We Put On, The.
Chin. How I Got That Name.
Chin, J. Ex-Boyfriends Named Michael.
Cisneros, S. Muddy Kid Comes Home.
You Called Me Corazón.
Clements, S. Susans.
Cohan. Mary's a Grand Old Name.
Cole, W. Mutual Problem.
Crouch, S. Riding Across John Lee's Finger.
Dabney, C. That's Why They Call Me 'Shine.'
Donnelly, S. Eve Names the Animals.
Elliott, E. John.
Espada. Beloved Spic.
Farewell, M. Everything I Need to Know I Learned in Kindergarten.
Foix. I Arrived in That Town, Everyone Greeted Me and I Recognized No One. When I Was Going to Read My Verses, the Devil, Hidden Behind a Tree, Called Out to Me Sarcastically and Filled My Hands with Newspaper Clippings.
Frishberg, D. Van Lingle Mungo.
García, D. Other Marías.
Squaring the Names.
Gillan. Arturo.
Gotera. Madarika.
Graves, R. My Name and I.
Gunn, T. Pope's Carnations Knew Him.
Gunnars. Changeling VIII.
Hamod, S. Dying with the Wrong Name.
Hayden, R. 'Mystery Boy' Looks for Kin in Nashville.
Names.
Hernández Cruz. Slick.
Hewitt, J. Ulster Names.
Hollander, J. Adam's Task.
Holthaus, G. Unexpected Manna.
Hood, T. Choosing Their Names.
Hughes, L. Madam and the Census Man.
Jackson, R. Jamal's Lamentation.
Kessler, S. Names the Dead Speak.
Kumin, M. Riddle of Noah, The.
Lamb, C. Family Name, The.
Larkin, P. Maiden Name.
Leto. Mary Morelle Show, The.
Lim-Wilson. Explaining the Origin of My Name.
Limburg, J. Barton in the Beans.
Locker-Lampson. My Life Is a———.
Logghe. Insomnia Litany.
Mackey, N. Ghede Poem.
Madgett. Nomen.
Majaj. Recognized Futures.
Maxwell. Rumplestiltskin.
Mayne, S. Zalman.
McDonald, R. Hollow Thesaurus, The.
McGrath, C. Delphos, Ohio.
Florida.
Miller, E. Mississippi.
Moss, H. Geography: A Song.
Mueller, L. Naming the Animals.
Mullen, H. Momma Sayings.
Nemerov. Makers, The.
O'Loughlin. Cuchulainn.
Parker, D. Art of the Nickname, The.
Patten, B. How the New Teacher Got Her Nickname.
Paz. Shrine.
Preston, K. Lapsus Linguae.
Repetto. 6th Grade—Our Lady of Pompeii.
Ridler. Choosing a Name.
Rome, H. Call Me Mister.
Rose. Naming Power.
Rosen, M. *et al.* Humpty Dumpty.
Salazar. Taking It Back.
Senghor. I Will Pronounce Your Name.
"Seuss." Too Many Daves.

Sigourney. Indian Names.
Simon, L. Nellie Gives into Blanche.
Stafford, W. Story That Could Be True, A.
Steele, T. Timothy.
Stefanile. How I Changed My Name, Felice.
Stevenson, R. Ticonderoga: A Legend of the West Highlands.
Strange. Barbershop Ritual.
Straus, M. Scarlet Crown.
Szymborska. View with a Grain of Sand.
Taylor, J. Epigram, a Supposed Construction.
Troup, B. Baby, Baby All the Time.
Unknown. Angel of Death, The.
Updike. I Missed His Book, but I Read His Name.
Wagner, M. Miss Clement's Second Grade.
Wallace-Crabbe. Life of Ideas, The.
Whitman, W. What Am I After All.
Wilbur. Rillons, Rillettes.
Wilcox, E. Woman.
Williams, S. You Were Never Miss Brown to Me.
Winchilsea. Adam Posed.
Wolverton, T. Tubes.
Wong, N. How a Girl Got Her Chinese Name.
Wright, J. Minneapolis Poem, The.
See also Place Names
Nantucket, Massachusetts
Lowell, R. Quaker Graveyard in Nantucket, The.
Teasdale. Wisdom.
Wood Song.
Williams, W. Nantucket.
Naples, Italy
Hugo, R. Napoli Again.
Napoleon I
Barlow, J. Advice to a Raven in Russia [December, 1812].
Browning, R. Incident of the French Camp.
De la Mare. Napoleon.
Kern, J. Napoleon.
Kipling, R. St. Helena Lullaby, A.
Madge. Poem: "Walls of the maelstrom are painted with trees, The."
Plath. Swarm, The.
Shelley, P. Feelings of a Republican on the Fall of Bonaparte.
Tennyson, A. Buonaparte.
Thackeray. Napoleon.
Unknown. Boney.
To Buonaparte.
Wordsworth, W. October, 1803.
Napoleonic Wars
Barlow, J. Advice to a Raven in Russia [December, 1812].
Browning, R. Incident of the French Camp.
Tennyson, A. Buonaparte.
Wordsworth, W. November, 1806.
To the Men of Kent (October, 1803).
Narcissism and Narcissists
Mayer, G. Narcissus.
Symons, A. Laus Virginitatis.
Narcissus (botany)
Plath. Among the Narcissi.
White, E. Window Ledge in the Atom Age.
Narcissus (mythology)
Mayer, G. Echo and Narcissus.
Narcissus.
Narcotics
Groves. Heroine.
Katz, J. Falling.
Shuster, D. Mellow on Morphine.
See also Drug Addiction
Naseby, Battle of (1645)
Macaulay, T. Battle of Naseby, The.
Nash, Richard ("Beau")
Brereton, J. On Mr. Nash's Picture at Full Length.
Nasturtiums
Spencer, A. Lines to a Nasturtium.
Nationalism
Bidgood. Dragon.
Glaser, I. Last Good War—and Afterward, The.
Holmes, O. God Bless Our Father-Land.

Kim, M. Into Such Assembly.
Lazarus, E. How Long?
Lim, S. Learning to Love America.
Padilla. Landscapes.
Pegram, A. Deliverance.
Sandburg, C. Old Timers.
  Threes.
Thelwall. Vanity of National Grandeur, The.
Thomas, R. Reservoirs.

Native Americans
Alexie. Crazy Horse Speaks.
  Defending Walt Whitman.
  Evolution.
  Exaggeration of Despair, The.
  Father and Farther.
  Translated from the American.
  Vision (2).
  Why We Play Basketball.
Algarin. Taos Pueblo Indians: 700 strong
  according to Bobby's last census.
Allen, P. Taku Skanskan.
Armstrong, J. I Study Rocks.
Ballowe, J. Starved Rock.
Beach, L. 2 Months Rent Due and 1 Bag of
  Rice.
Belford. Carrier Indians.
Bell, J. Indian Children Speak.
Big Boy, M. I Will Bring You Twin Grays.
Bird, D. Can I Say.
Blaeser. Rituals, Yours—and Mine.
Blue Cloud. Crazy Horse Monument.
Brant, B. Stillborn Night.
Breton, A. Go for Broke.
Bruchac. Birdfoot's Grampa.
Bryant, W. Indian at the Burial-Place [or
  Burying-Place] of His Fathers, An.
Burgess, H. Rational.
Bynner. Haskell.
Caldwell, K. Moonlight.
Canning, J. Indian Gone!, The.
Cardiff. Grey Woman.
  It has something to do with final words.
Carruth, H. Rimrock, Where It Is.
Castillo, A. Toltec, The.
Cawein. Dead Cities.
Chrystos. As I Leave You.
  I Bring You Greetings: How.
  Old Indian Granny, The.
  Real Indian Leans Against, The.
  Today Was a Bad Day Like TB.
Clements, S. Deer Cloud.
  Matinee.
  Reservation, The.
Coke, A. Change, The.
Cook-Lynn. Grandfather at the Indian Health
  Clinic.
Corso. Spontaneous Requiem for the American
  Indian.
Crosby, F. Mandan Chief, The.
Cuthand, B. Dancing with Rex.
  She Ties Her Bandanna.
Dauenhauer. How To Make Good Baked
  Salmon from the River.
de Aerenlund, C. Cuando el tecolote canta, el
  Indio muere.
Di Prima. American Indian Art: Form and
  Tradition.
  Brief Wyoming Meditation.
Dumas, H. Concentration Camp Blues.
Dunn, C. Margaret/Haskell Indian School.
Erdrich. Dear John Wayne.
  Fooling God.
  Indian Boarding School: The Runaways.
Erdrich, H. Hopi Prophet Chooses a Pop.
Eyen, J. New Dream, A (Wuski A-Baw-Tan).
Fife, C. Dear Webster.
Fisher, L. Child of the Sun.
Forché. Ancapagari.
Fordham. Cherokee, The.
Freneau. Indian Burying Ground, The.
  Indian Convert, The.
  Indian Student; or, Force of Nature, The.
  On the Civilization of the Western Aboriginal
  Country.
George, P. Battle Won Is Lost.
Gilbert, C. Sorrow Since Sitting Bull, A.

Glancy. First Reader Santee Training School,
  1873, The.
González, R. Marías, Old Indian Mothers.
Gould, J. Coyotismo.
Grieves, C. Connuche.
Gustafson, R. Columbus Reaches Juana, 1492.
Haines, J. Train Stops at Healy Fork, The.
Halfe, L. Pâhkahkos.
Halleck, F. Red Jacket.
Harjo, J. Autobiography.
  Woman Hanging from the Thirteenth Floor
  Window, The.
Harte, B. Truthful James to the Editor.
Hemans. Indian Woman's Death-Song, The.
Henson, L. We Are a People.
Herández-Ávila. Presente.
Hill, R. To Rose.
  Waning August Moon.
Hogan, L. New Apartment.
  Skin.
  Truth Is, The.
Hollander, J. State of Nature, A.
Hugo, R. Letter to Hill from St. Ignatius.
  Letter to Welch from Browning.
  Map of Montana in Italy, A.
Hunter, A. North American Death Song.
Jeffers, R. Inquisitors, The.
  New Mexican Mountain.
Joe, R. Expect Nothing Else from Me.
Johnson, E. Cattle Thief, The.
  Ojistoh.
Jordan, J. Poem for Guatemala.
  Poem for Nana.
Keeshig-Tobias. I Grew Up.
Kenny, M. Winkte.
Klein, A. Indian Reservation: Caughnawaga.
Knoepfle. Confluence.
Koch, K. Thanksgiving.
Le Sueur. Behold This and Always Love It.
Lee, A. Confession.
Lewis, J. Indians in the Woods, The.
Lindsay, N. Ghosts of the Buffaloes, The.
Louis, A. Something About Being an Indian.
  That Great Wingless Bird.
Lowell, R. At the Indian Killer's Grave.
Major, C. Lost in the Desert.
Manyarrows. Lakota Sister/Cherokee Mother.
  See No Indian, Hear No Indian.
McFadden, D. Lennox Island.
McGlashan, J. Island of Women, The.
Merwin, W. S. Native, The.
Midge, T. Written in Blood.
Million, D. Housing Poem, The.
Moore, L. Indian Girl.
Mora. Tall Walking Woman.
Mottram. Zuni Dancers.
Naranjo-Morse. Gia's Song.
  Tradition and Change.
Newlove. Pride, The.
Niedecker. Thanksgiving.
Noel, L. Understanding Each Other.
O'Grady, D. Great Horse Fair, The.
Ortiz. Creation.
  Earth and Rain, the Plants & Sun.
  Travels in the South.
  Upstate.
Pape. Indian Ruins Along Rio de Flag.
Paschen. Two Standards.
Penn, M. Calling Up the Spirit of the Lost
  Child.
Perillo. Ghost Shirt, The.
Plato. Natives of America, The.
Purdy, A. Remains of an Indian Village.
Rendon. You See This Body.
Revard. Parading with the Veterans of Foreign
  Wars.
Ridge, J. Stolen White Girl, The.
Romero, L. If Marilyn Monroe.
Rose. Endangered Roots of a Person.
  I Expected My Skin and My Blood to Ripen.
  Long Division; a Tribal History.
  Naayawva Taawi.
Rothenberg, J. Cokboy.
Sandburg, C. Circles.
  Early Copper.
Savageau. At the Powwow.

  Like the Trails of Ndakinna.
  Looking for Indians.
  To Human Skin.
Schoolcraft. Otagamiad.
Scott, D. At Gull Lake; August, 1810.
  Forsaken, The.
  On the Way to the Mission.
Sigourney. Indian Names.
  Indian's Welcome to the Pilgrim Fathers, The.
Silko. In Cold Storm Light.
  It Was a Long Time Before.
  Long Time Ago.
  When Sun Came to Riverwoman.
Sirr. Understanding Canada.
Snodgrass, W. Powwow.
Stafford, W. At the Klamath Berry Festival.
  Returned to Say.
Sweet, D. My Mother and I Had a Discussion
  One Day.
Tallmountain. Indian Blood.
Tapahonso. Pay Up or Else.
  What Danger We Court.
Taylor, R. Dakota: October, 1822, Hunkpapa
  Warrior.
Terry, L. Bar[']s Fight[, August 28, 1746].
Thompson, E. Indian Maid, The; Demararie,
  Oct. 27, 1781.
Tohe. She Was Telling It This Way.
Tomlinson, C. Ute Mountain.
Toya, D. Hunter's Dance in Early Fall.
Trask, H. Sisters.
Unknown. American Indian, The.
Very. Indian's Retort, The.
Walsh, M. Thomas Iron-Eyes.
Warton, J. Dying Indian, The.
Welch, J. Christmas Comes to Moccasin Flat.
  Harlem, Montana.
  Man from Washington, The.
Whitman, W. Osceola.
  Yonnondio.
Wilson, R. Dry Rivers—Arizona.
Winnebago Oral Tradition. Felix White Sr.'s
  Introduction to Wakjankaga.
Woody. Girlfriends, The.
  She-Who-Watches . . . The Names are Prayer.
Young Bear. Drive to Lone Ranger, A.
  From the Spotted Night.
  Song Taught to Joseph, The.

Nativity, The
Chesterton, G. Joseph.
Coleridge, S. Christmas Carol, A: "Shepherds
  went their hasty way, The."
Crashaw. In the Holy Nativity of Our Lord
  God.
  Shepherds' Hymn, The.
Glück, L. Nativity Poem.
Hall, D. Carol, A.
Hall, J. For Christmas Day.
Heath-Stubbs. For the Nativity.
Hill, G. Picture of a Nativity.
Hughes, L. Shepherd's Song at Christmas.
Jonson, B. Carol.
Milton. Hymn on the Morning of Christ's
  Nativity.
  On the Morning of Christ's Nativity.
Nims, J. Christmas.
Pestel [or Pestell]. Psalm for Christmas Day.
Southwell. New Prince, New Pomp[e].
Stewart, G. As I Went Down to David's Town.
Vaughan, H. Nativity, The.
Williams, W. Adoration of the Kings, The.
See also Christmas

Naturalists
Heaney, S. Death of a Naturalist.
White, G. Naturalist's Summer-Evening Walk,
  The.

Nature
Abena, B. Mawu of the Waters.
Ackerman, D. Beija-Flor.
Adams, L. Rounds and Garlands Done, The.
Addison, J. Ode: "Spacious firmament on high,
  The."
Addonizio. Alone in Your House.
Aguilar, M. Poem from Sierra Madre.
Alexander, C. All Things Bright and Beautiful.
Alexander, E. Washington Etude.

Alexander, P.   Marriage of Sorts, A.
Allen, H.   In the Forest.
Ama Ata Aidoo.   Gynae One.
Ammons, A. R.   Arc Inside and Out, The.
  Corsons Inlet.
  Cut the Grass.
  Gravelly Run.
  Hymn: "I know if I find you I will have to leave
    the earth."
  Terrain.
  Widespread Implications.
Andrews, B.   West West.
Angira.   Symphony from the Balcony.
Apuleius, L.   I who am Nature, mother of all.
Armstrong, J.   I Study Rocks.
Arnold, M.   In Harmony with Nature.
Ashbery.   Rivers and Mountains.
  These Lacustrine Cities.
Atwood.   Landcrab II.
Auden.   Fall of Rome, The.
Babcock, M.   This Is My Father's World.
Balaban.   Graveyard at Bald Eagle Ridge.
  Heading Out West.
Bampfylde.   Written at a Farm.
Bangs, J.   Blind.
Becker, R.   Life Forms.
Bell, M.   Self and the Mulberry, The.
  To Be.
Ben-Lev, D.   Sensualist Speaks on Faith, A.
Bennett, G.   Sonnet—2: "Some things are very
    dear to me."
Bensko.   Butterfly Net, The.
Benton, S.   Second Coming, The.
Berrigan, A.   Mercy Flight.
Berry, W.   Peace of Wild Things, The.
Berssenbrugge.   Duration of Water.
Bertolino.   See Willow.
Bethell.   Pause.
Bevington, L.   Morning.
Bible, Apocrypha.   Steel Usurps the Forests;
    Silence Dethrones Dialogue.
Biespiel, D.   There Were No Deer in the
    Thicket.
Bishop, E.   Brazil, January 1, 1502.
  Cold Spring, A.
  North Haven.
  Song for the Rainy Season.
Blake, E. J.   Within and Without.
Blind.   Red Sunsets, 1883, The.
Bobrowski.   Latvian Autumn, The.
  Place of Fire.
Bogan, L.   Night.
Bolamba.   Fistful of News, A.
  Portrait.
Bolt, T.   Glimpse of Terrain.
  Meditation in Loudoun County.
Booth, P.   Within.
Borden, W.   Morning Chamber Orchestra Near
    Piney Crick, Wyoming, 7 A.M., The.
Bowers, E.   Mountain Cemetery, The.
Bowles, W.   Languid, and sad, and slow.
  To the River Wensbeck.
Bowman, C.   Demographics.
Brady, G.   Voice from the Bush—Through Me.
Braithwaite.   City Garden, A.
Brannon, J.   Evolution on 38th Street.
Brontë, E.   Shall Earth no more inspire thee.
  Stanzas: "Often rebuked, yet always back
    returning."
  Why do I hate that lone green dell?
Brooke, R.   Hill, The.
Brown, E.   Spiritual Land.
Brown, L.   Best Things in Life Are Free, The.
Brown, P.   Leaving.
Bruchac.   Birdfoot's Grampa.
  Prayer: "Let my words."
  Spring Peepers.
Bryant, W.   Fountain, The.
  Oh [or O] Fairest of the Rural Maids.
  Thanatopsis.
Brydges.   To Miss M———, Written by
    Moonlight, July 18, 1782.
Buckmaster.   Wilpena Pound.
Burns, R.   My Heart's in the Highlands.
  To a Mouse; On Turning Her up in Her Nest,
    with the Plough, November, 1785.

Byron, G.   Cornelian, The.
Caldwell, K.   Moonlight.
Camlan.   Education in Wales.
Campbell, D.   Man in the Honeysuckle, The.
Campion, T.   I Care Not for These Ladies.
Carew, T.   Love's Force.
  Spring, The.
  To my Friend G. N. from Wrest.
  To My Worthy Friend Master George Sands [or
    Sandys], on His Translation of the Psalms.
Carman, B. et al.   Earth's Lyric.
Carroll, J.   Withdrawal Letter.
Carver, R.   Window, The.
Causley.   I am the Song.
Cavendish, M.   Dialogue betwixt Man, and
    Nature, A.
  Dissert, A.
  Landscape, A.
  Nature's Cook.
Chipasula.   Double Song.
Christopher.   Midsummer.
Chubb, R.   Song of My Soul.
  Transfiguration.
Clampitt.   Sun Underfoot Among the Sundews,
    The.
Clare, J.   Eternity of Nature, The.
  Evening.
  God Looks on Nature With a Glorious Eye.
  Last of April, The.
  Maple Tree, The.
  Nutting.
  Secret Love.
  Shadows.
  Shepherd's Tree, The.
  To an Angry Bee.
  Winter.
  Woodland Seat, A.
  Wren, The.
  Wryneck's Nest, The.
Clifton, L.   Earth Is a Living Thing, The.
Coatsworth.   Swift Things Are Beautiful.
Cobbing.   Bird Bee.
Cole, T.   Painter, A.
Coleridge, M.   No Newspapers.
  On a Bas-relief of Pelops and Hippodameia.
Coleridge, S.   Frost at Midnight.
  Garden Year, The.
  Nightingale, The.
  This Lime-Tree Bower My Prison.
  To Nature.
  Work without Hope.
Collins, W.   Warmer.
Coolbrith.   Longing.
Cooper, W.   Pollen.
Corn.   Water: City Wildlife and Greenery.
Couzyn.   Spell for Birth.
Cowper, W.   Against Slavery.
  Arrival of the Mail.
  Crazy Kate.
  Effeminate Englishmen.
  Frosty Morning, A.
  Landscape Described, A.
  Reading the Newspaper.
  Stricken Deer, The.
  Winter Evening, The: A Brown Study.
  Winter Walk at Noon, The.
Cranch.   Correspondences.
Creeley.   Innocence, The.
  Messengers, The.
  Song: "Those rivers run from that land."
Cristall.   Holbain.
  Noon. Lysander.
  Ode, An.
  Song on Leaving the Country Early in the
    Spring.
  Written in Devonshire, Near the Dart.
Croly.   Domestic Love.
Cruickshank, H.   Ponnage Pool, The.
Crunk, T.   Reunion.
  Visiting the Site of One of the First Churches
    My Grandfather Pastored.
Cummings, E.   I Thank You God.
  O Sweet Spontaneous.
Curtis, T.   Spirit of the Place, The.
Dahlberg.   February Ground.
Davis, W.   Snow.

De la Mare.   All That's Past.
  Miracle, The.
  Reserved.
DeSylva, B. G.   Best Things in Life Are Free,
    The.
Dickinson, E.   I Taste a Liquor Never Brewed.
  Snake, The.
  This Is My Letter to the World.
DiPrima, C.   Her Eyes a Thousand Times Over.
Dodd, E.   Dieback.
Doolittle, H.   White World.
Douskey.   Dog Days and Delta Nights.
Dove, R.   Fish in the Stone, The.
Dowden, E.   Two Infinities.
Drake, J.   Bronx.
Drummond, W.   Book, The.
Dufault.   Burden.
Dugan, A.   On the Elk, Unwitnessed.
Dunn, C.   Margaret/Haskell Indian School.
Dunn, D.   Gardeners.
Dybek.   Benediction.
  Mowing.
Dyer, J.   Grongar Hill.
Dyer, S.   Lowest Trees Have Tops, The.
Eberhart, R.   Hard Structure of the World, The.
  On a Squirrel Crossing the Road in Autumn, in
    New England.
  Sea-Hawk.
  Spider, The.
Ehrhart.   Confirmation, A.
Eigner.   Environs.
Elman.   October Observed, Hudson Falls, New
    York in Bill's Back Yard.
Elmusa.   Snapshots.
Elytis.   Origin of Landscape or the End of
    Mercy, The.
Emerson, R.   Blight.
  Circles.
  Dear Brother, Would You Know the Life.
  Each and All.
  Experience.
  Musketaquid.
  Nature [1836].
  Nature [1844].
  Problem, The.
  Song of Nature.
  Waldeinsamkeit.
  Woodnotes I ("For this present, hard").
  Woodnotes II ("As sunbeams stream through
    liberal space").
  Xenophanes.
Everson, W.   South Coast, The.
  Stone Face Falls.
Fagan.   Weather They Were Written In, The.
Fallon, P.   Spring Song.
Fenton, J.   Kingfisher's Boxing Gloves, The.
  Lollipops of the Pomeranian Baroque.
Ferril.   Something Starting Over.
Ficke.   Sonnet: "There are strange shadows
    fostered of the moon."
Finch, B.   Written in a Shrubbery Towards the
    Decline of Autumn.
  Written in a Winter's Morning.
Finch, P.   We Are in the Fields.
Fitzgerald, M.   Rendezvous.
Fletcher, J.   Blue Symphony.
  Green Symphony.
Fogarty, L.   Ecology.
Forché.   Ancapagari.
  Kalaloch.
  Skin Canoes.
Foster, A.   Union.
Foy, J.   Autopsy.
Freneau.   On the Religion of Nature.
  On the Uniformity and Perfection of Nature.
Frost, R.   Design.
  Directive.
  Fountain, a Bottle, a Donkey's Ears and Some
    Books, A.
  Lucretius versus the Lake Poets.
  Vantage Point, The.
Fuller, M.   Sistrum.
Galvin, B.   Bullfrog.
Gardelle, C.   Air.
  Rain.
Gidlow.   Creed for Free Women, A.

Gilbert, K.   Peace and the Desert.
 Tree.
Gillan.   In New Jersey Once.
Ginsberg, A.   Easter Sunday.
Gioia.   Los Angeles after the Rain.
Gladding.   Worsted Heather.
Goodtimes.   Jojopan.
Graves, R.   Love Story, A.
 Nature's Lineaments.
 She Tells Her Love While Half Asleep.
 To Juan at the Winter Solstice.
Gray, A.   Music in the Meadow.
Greenwell, D.   Scherzo, A.
Gregg.   Dark Thing Inside the Day, A.
 Flower No More Than Itself, A.
Grennan.   Facts of Life, Ballymoney.
 Shoreline After Storm.
 Sunday Morning Through Binoculars.
Griffith, L.   Office Window.
Grigson.   Landscape Gardeners, The.
Guest, B.   Nebraska.
 Sassafras.
Guiney.   Down Stream.
Gunn, T.   Faustus Triumphant.
Hadas, R.   Easter Afternoon.
Haines, J.   Roadside Weeds.
 Yeti.
Haley, M.   Tropicalia.
Hall, D.   Granite and Grass.
 New Hampshire.
Hardy, T.   Five Students, The.
 In a Wood.
Harris, R.   Literary Excellence.
Harry, J.   Walking, when the Lake of the Air Is
 Blue with Spring.
Hart-Smith.   Nullarbor.
Harter.   Tulip.
Hartnett.   For My Grandmother, Bridget Halpin.
Harwood, G.   Carnal Knowledge 2.
 Clair de Lune.
Hass, R.   After I Seized the Pentagon.
 Letter to a Poet.
 Measure.
Healy, R.   Primula veris.
Heaney, S.   Anahorish.
 Song: "Rowan like a lip-sticked girl, A."
Hejinian.   Nights.
Hemans.   Indian Woman's Death-Song, The.
 Voice of Spring, The.
Henderson, R.   Best Things in Life Are Free,
 The.
Hernández Cruz.   Poem: "Your head it waves
 outside."
Herrick.   Art above Nature, to Julia.
 Country Life: To His Brother, M. Tho: Herrick.
 To Find[e] God.
 Upon Time.
Hesketh.   Death of a Gardener.
Hewitt, J.   Because I Paced My Thought.
 Ram's Horn, The.
 Substance and Shadow.
Heynen.   I Think That I Shall Never See.
Hikmet.   Letters from a Man in Solitary.
 Things I Didn't Know I Loved.
Hildebrandt, Z.   In Hecate's Garden.
Hill, G.   Two Chorale-Preludes: On Melodies by
 Paul Celan.
Hill, M.   Abomination.
 Ruth.
Hill, R.   To Rose.
 Waning August Moon.
Hogan, L.   Map.
Hollander, J.   Old-Fashioned Song, An.
 Variations on a Fragment by Trumbull Stickney.
Hollander, V.   Rosh Chodesh Tisheri.
Holloway, G.   Indian Rope Trick.
Holm, B.   Blizzard.
Hood, T.   I Remember, I Remember.
Hooper, P.   Listening to Mozart at Meadow
 Brook.
Hopkins, G.   Epithalamion: "Hark, hearer, hear
 what I do; lend a thought now, make believe."
 God's Grandeur.
 Inversnaid.
 Pied Beauty.
 That Nature Is a Heraclitean Fire and of the

 Comfort of the Resurrection.
Hudgins.   Persistence of Nature in Our Lives,
 The.
Hughes, T.   October Robin, An.
 Pibroch.
 Roe-Deer.
 Thrushes.
Huidobro.   New Song.
Hunt, L.   To Hampstead.
Ignatow, D.   Rescue the Dead.
Irwin, M.   Give.
Jackson, H.   My House Not Made with Hands.
Jacob, M.   In Honor of the Sardana and the
 Tenora.
Jacobs, J.   Nearing Long Moons.
 Snakeroot.
Jacobsen, J.   Hourglass.
Jarrell.   Field and Forest.
Jeffers, R.   Boats in a Fog.
 Noon.
 Place for No Story, The.
Jewett, S.   At Home from Church.
Johnson, M. F.   Second Evening.
Johnston, E.   Address to Nature on its Cruelty,
 An.
Katz, J.   Taxonomy.
Kavanagh, P.   Canal Bank Walk.
Kearney, M.   Nature Poetry.
Keats.   In a Drear-nighted December.
 Sweet Peas.
Keithley.   Small Moon on the Shoulder of New
 York.
Keller, D.   Melancholy.
Kelly, B.   To the Lost Child.
Kemble.   Sonnet: "If there were any power in
 human love."
Kennedy, X.   Landscapes with Set-Screws.
Kennelly.   Island, The.
Khlebnikov, V.   Four Poems.
Kinnell.   Lastness.
 Supper after the Last, The.
 Under the Williamsburg Bridge.
 When One Has Lived a Long Time Alone.
Kinsella, T.   Another September.
 Oldest Place, The.
 Route of the Táin, The.
Kizer, C.   On a Line from Valéry.
Klappert.   In Memory of H. F.
Klugman, S.   God's Body.
Kooser.   Interchange.
Kunene.   Echoes, The.
Kyle, C. J.   Argument, The.
 Season of Locking-In, The.
Lamantia.   Voice of Earth Mediums.
Lange, A.   Sonnet for the Season.
Lanier, S.   To Bayard Taylor.
Lawrence, D.   Elemental.
 Glory.
 Proper Pride.
 Self-Protection.
 Wild Common, The.
Lazarus, E.   South, The.
Le Sueur.   Behold This and Always Love It.
Leapor.   On Winter.
Leithauser.   In a Japanese Moss Garden.
Levertov.   Living.
 Reminder, The.
Lewis, J.   For the Father of Sandro Gulotta.
 Reader, The.
Lindley, D.   Cromwell: The Last Portrait.
Liu, T.   Poem: "Late butterflies gliding through
 the air."
Lodge, G.   Pastoral: "Slopes of the sun and vine,
 and thou dark stream."
Long, H.   Cobweb.
Longfellow, H.   Aftermath.
 Nature.
 Snow-Flakes.
 Spirit of Poetry, The.
Longley, M.   Ash Keys.
 Frozen Rain.
Lopez, L.   Abiquiu.
Lothamer.   October Falls in Black and White.
MacCaig.   Basking Shark.
 Feeding Ducks.
Mackey, N.   Kiche Manitou.

MacNeice.   Evening in Connecticut.
 House on a Cliff.
 Western Landscape.
Madge.   Solar Creation.
Mahon.   Woods, The.
Mapanje.   Visiting Zomba Plateau.
Maris, H.   Spiritual Song of the Aborigine.
Marlowe.   Passionate Shepherd To His Love,
 The.
Martí.   Opposite of Ornate and Rhetorical
 Poetry, The.
Marvell.   Mower Against Gardens, The.
Mazur.   Common, The.
McDonald, W.   Hauling Over Wolf Creek Pass
 in Winter.
McGrath, C.   First Trimester, The.
 Florida.
McGrath, T.   Return, The.
McPherson, S.   Wings and Seeds.
Mead, P.   Melbourne or the Bush.
Melville, H.   Attic Landscape, The.
 Haglets, The.
 Little Good Fellows, The.
 Malvern Hill.
 Pontoosuce.
Meredith, G.   Dirge in Woods.
 Love in the Valley.
Merrick, A.   Hartwell Gardens.
Merrill, J.   Syrinx.
Merwin, W. S.   Avoiding News by the River.
Messerli.   Scared Cows.
 This That and Then.
Mew.   In the Fields.
Meynell, A.   Rainy Summer, The.
Millay, E.   God's World.
Milosz, C.   Sun, The.
Minhinnick.   Sap.
Mitchell, A.   Nature Poem.
Mitchell, R.   North.
Mitford.   Forget-Me-Not, The.
Mnthali.   Celebration, The.
Momaday.   Delight Song of Tsoai-Talee, The.
 Headwaters.
Montale.   Eel, The.
"Monty Python."   All Things Dull and Ugly.
Morgan, R.   Shadow Valley.
Morley, H.   Curve of the Water.
Mphande.   Wood-Cutter, The.
Murphy, P.   Manifesto.
Murray, P.   Returning Spring.
Ní Chuilleanáin.   Pygmalion's Image.
Napanangka, V.   Rain, The.
Nelson, H.   Peepers.
Nelson, J.   If You Knew September.
Nemerov.   Dependencies, The.
 Salt Garden, The.
 Singular Metamorphosis, A.
Nesbit, E.   Great Industrial Centre, A.
Nezval.   Trap Door.
Niatum.   Rufous Hummingbird.
 Stones Speak of an Earthless Sky.
Nicholson, N.   Five Minutes.
Niedecker.   Element Mother, The.
 Paean to Place.
 War.
Norris, L.   Stone and Fern.
North, C.   Note to Tony Towle (After WS), A.
North, M.   Pinder.
 Shap.
O'Hara, F.   Easter.
O'Sullivan, M.   Giant Yellow.
 Hill Figures.
Oden.   Review from Staten Island.
Olds, S.   Ecstasy.
Oliver, M.   Design.
 In Blackwater Woods.
 Landscape.
 Snapshots.
 Some Questions You Might Ask.
 Wild Geese.
 Wings.
Olson, C.   Praises, The.
Opie.   Ode to Borrowdale in Cumberland.
 On the Approach of Autumn.
 To Winter.
Orrick.   Little Things.

Ortiz. Earth and Rain, the Plants & Sun.
Vision Shadows.
Ossip, K. Nature of Things, The.
Osundare. Excursion.
Goree.
Our Earth Will Not Die.
Who Says That Drought Was Here?
Ou-yang Hsiu. Old Fisherman.
Owen, W. From My Diary, July 1914.
Parker, A. Alchemy.
Patchen. Deer and the Snake, The.
Like a Mourningless Child.
Pastoral: "Dove walks with sticky feet, The."
Peacocke. Remembrance.
Peck, J. Woods Burial.
Perry, S. Toadfish.
Peterson, J. Stand Still.
Pfeiffer, E. To a Moth that Drinketh of the Ripe
October.
Philips, A. Happy Swain, The.
Philips, K. To Mr. Henry Lawes.
Philpot, T. Wildlife.
Piatt, S. In A Queen's Domain.
Pickard, T. Bush Telegram.
Piercy. Postcard from the Garden.
Plomer. Namaqualand after Rain.
Poe. Stanzas: "How often we forget all time,
when lone."
Valley of Unrest, The.
Pope, A. Intended for Sir Isaac Newton.
Porteous. I Envy the Cracked, Black Basalt.
Porter, P. Australian Garden, An.
Radcliffe, A. Sonnet: "Now the bat circles on
the breeze of eve."
To the Bat.
Ragan, J. Standing at Pasternak's Table,
Peredelkino.
Raine, K. Angelus.
Good Friday.
Heirloom.
Message from Home.
Wilderness, The.
Ramsey, J. Comet and Treefrog.
Rankin, J. Old Circles.
Raworth. Out of a Sudden.
Ray, H. At Nature's Shrine.
Instability.
Nature's Minor Chords.
Nature's Uplifting.
Redmond. Definition of Nature.
Reese, L. Crows.
Revard. Christmas Shopping.
October, Isle of Skye.
Reverdy. Air: "Forgetting."
Rexroth, K. Floating.
On Flower Wreath Hill.
Reznikoff. April.
Riley, J. Travel Notes.
Roberson. Blue Horses.
Roberts, E. Disconsolate Morning.
Robinson, E. Poem for Max Nordau, A.
Torrent, The.
Roethke. Bring the Day!
Field of Light, A.
Her Time.
Minimal, The.
Otto.
Shape of the Fire, The.
Thing, The.
Visitant, The.
Walk in Late Summer, A.
Words for the Wind.
Rogers, P. Before the Beginning: Maybe God
and a Silk Flower Concubine Perhaps.
Into the Light.
Kingdom of Heaven, The.
Opus from Space.
Rohrer, M. Hunger of the Lemur, The.
Rossetti, C. Cobwebs.
Frisky Lamb, A.
Spring Quiet.
Who Has Seen the Wind?
Rossetti, D. Even So.
Rothman, D. One of the Lords of Life.
Ryan, R. Lake of the Woods, The.
"Shu Ting." Gifts.

Södergran. Homecoming.
Sackville-West. Land, The.
Saner. This Grizzly.
Savageau. All Night She Dreams.
Trees.
Schuyler, J. Father or Son.
Schwartz, L. Leaves.
Seed. This Curious Involvement, a Dominant
Species.
Seidman. Making of Color, The.
Seward. Eyam.
Shapiro, D. Commentary Text Commentary
Text Commentary Text.
Shapiro, K. Travelogue for Exiles.
Shaw, A. Bird Nests.
Small Pleasures.
Shelley, P. Love's Philosophy.
Mont Blanc.
To a Skylark.
To Jane: The Invitation.
Shepherd, R. Another Version of an Ocean.
Shillaber, B. Sagamore, The.
Shumaker. Ajo Lily.
Siegel, J. How the Tortoise Knew It Was Her
Time.
Silko. When Sun Came to Riverwoman.
Simms, C. Grey Wagtail on the Tyne.
Pallid Harrier.
Sirr. Collector's Marginalia, The.
Skinner, J. City Out of the Boy, The.
Skloot. Closer to Home.
Slessor. South Country.
Smart, C. On a Bed of Guernsey Lilies.
Smelcer. Bonanza Creek.
Smith, C. To the South Downs.
Written at Bignor Park in Sussex, in August,
1799.
Smith, I. Contrasts.
Smith, S. Away, Melancholy.
Lady "Rogue" Singleton.
Pretty.
Smollett. To Leven Water.
Snyder, G. Burning Island.
Gaia.
Milton by Firelight.
Night Song of the Los Angeles Basin.
Old Woman Nature.
Piute Creek.
Soto. Elements of San Joaquin, The.
Rain.
Wind.
Southwell. Vale of Tear[e]s, A.
St. John, P. Carnival.
Stafford, W. Oregon Message, An.
Well Rising, The.
Stainer. Seals, The.
Standing. Mouvance.
Stevens, M. Carp, The.
Stevens, W. Dry Loaf.
Nomad Exquisite.
Sense of the Sleight-of-Hand Man, The.
Stevenson, R. House Beautiful, The.
Stewart, P. Estes' Backyard, The.
Stickney, T. Athenian Garden, An.
In Ampezzo.
Lakeward.
Swann, B. Old Song of the Musk Ox People.
Swann, R. EFT.
Swenson, M. Stripping and Putting on.
Synge. Prelude: "Still south I went and west
and south again."
Szporluk. Axiom of Maria.
Szymborska. View with a Grain of Sand.
Taggard. Bounding Line.
Fructus.
Hymn to Yellow.
Thirst.
Taylor, A. Earth.
Teasdale. There Will Come Soft Rains.
Tennyson, A. Flower in the Crannied Wall.
Thomas, D. This Bread I Break.
Thomas, R. Line from St. David's, A.
Thoreau. Nature.
Poet's Delay, The.
Pray to What Earth Does This Sweet Cold
Belong.

Winter and Spring Scene, A.
Thorne, T. High Country.
Tighe. Written at the Eagle's Nest, Killarney.
July 26, 1800.
Written in Autumn.
Todd, M. Game Trail, The.
Todd, R. Of Moulds and Mushrooms.
Tomlinson, C. John Maydew or The Allotment.
Toomer. Nullo.
Storm Ending.
Torrance. Acrospirical Meanderings in a
Tongue of the Time.
It Is Difficult to Exaggerate the Importance of
Mushrooms as Food.
Trask, H. Sisters.
Trommer, R. March.
Tuckerman, F. Sonnets: First Series.
Unknown. Holy Goddess Tellus.
Lowest Trees Have Tops, The.
Sumer Is Icumen [*or* Ycomen] In.
Wild Man Comes to the Monastery, The.
Untermeyer, L. Song Tournament: New Style.
Van Duyn. View, A.
Vaughan, H. Love and Discipline.
Regeneration.
Very. Nature.
Silent, The.
Song, The: "When I would sing of crooked
streams and fields."
Voigt. Nocturne.
Volkman. Untitled: "There comes a time to
rusticate the numbers. The way the birds, jug."
Waddell, H. Earth Said to Death.
Wagoner, D. Chorus: "That rain-strewn night in
the woods, the chorus, chorus."
Five Dawn Skies in November.
Making Camp.
Source, The.
Waller, E. On St. James's Park, as Lately
Improved by His Majesty.
Warren, R. Gold Glade.
Wat. From "Songs of a Wanderer."
Watkins, V. Music of Colours—White Blossom.
Replica, the.
Watts, I. Flying Fowl, and Creeping Things,
Praise Ye the Lord.
Weismiller. Vermont: Spring Rains.
Wellman, M. Mad Wolf in Lunar Web, Mad
Crow on the Beach.
West, J. To May.
Westmorland. To Sir John Wentworth, Upon
His Curiosities and Courteous Entertainment at
Summerly in Lovingland.
Wheelwright. Would You Think?
Whisenand. Open Your Eyes.
Whitehead, W. On the Late Improvements at
Nuneham, the Seat of the Earl of Harcourt.
Whitman, T. Hunger and Imagination.
Whitman, W. Give Me the Splendid Silent Sun.
Italian Music in Dakota.
Me Imperturbe.
Proud Music of the Storm.
Spontaneous Me.
To a President.
When I Heard At The Close Of The Day.
World below the Brine, The.
Whittemore, R. Departure, The.
Whittier. Over-Heart, The.
River Path, The.
Wilbur. Ceremony.
Hamlen Brook.
Wilcox, E. Attraction.
Wilkinson, A. Nature Be Damned.
Williams, J. In Duffryn Woods.
Pastoral: "You see that forest on the height?"
Williams, W. Raleigh Was Right.
Wilson, R. Dry Rivers—Arizona.
Sparrow Hills.
Winchilsea. Nocturnal Reverie, A.
Winters, Y. Barnyard, The.
Magpie's Shadow, The.
Two Songs of Advent.
Witt, S. Waterfowl Descending.
Wohlfeld. Sea.
Wolfe, C. Song: "Oh say not that my heart is
cold."

Wordsworth, D. Floating Island at Hawkshead.
Loving and Liking [Irregular Verses Addressed to a Child].
Peaceful Our Valley, Fair and Green.
Thoughts on my sick-bed.
Wordsworth, W. Composed at Neidpath Castle, the Property of Lord Queensbury,1803.
Expostulation and Reply.
Farewell, A: "Farewell thou little Nook of mountain-ground."
Lines Composed a Few Miles above Tintern Abbey on Revisiting the Banks of the Wye During a Tour, July 13, 1798.
Lines Written in Early Spring.
Ode: Intimations of Immortality [from Recollections of Early Childhood].
On the Projected Kendal and Windermere Railway.
Tables Turned, The.
This Prayer I Make.
Trosachs, The.
World Is Too Much With Us, The.
Written in London, September, 1802.
Written in March [While Resting on the Bridge at the Foot of Brother's Water].
Wotton, S. On a Bank [or Banck] as I Sat[e] [a-]Fishing; a Description of the Spring.
Wright, C. California Spring.
Dead Color.
Disjecta Membra.
Self-Portrait.
Stone Canyon Nocturne.
Wright, D. Caleb Barnes.
Lakes, The.
Those Walks We Took.
Winter at Gurnard's Head.
Wright, J. At Cooloolah.
Depressed by a Book of Bad Poetry, I Walk toward an Unused Pasture and Invite the Insects to Join Me.
Horse, The.
Rainforest.
Wunderlich, M. Anchorage, The.
Wylie. Puritan Sonnet, IV.
Wild Peaches.
Yeats. Coole Park, 1929.
Her Anxiety.
Lake-Isle of Innisfree, The.
Sorrow of Love, The.
Yi, S. Poem No. VII.
Young, A. Mountains of California: Part 2, The.
Young, K. Degrees.
Young, M. J. On an Early Spring.
Zeiger, D. Mostly Mozart at Planting Fields Arboretum.
Zhenkai. Accomplices.
Zukofsky, L. Xenophanes.

Nauvoo, Illinois
Taylor, B. Nauvoo.

Navaho, The
Pape. Storm Pattern.

Naval Battles
Campbell, T. Battle of the Baltic.
Day, J. North Sea.
Donne. Burnt Ship, A.
Hemans. Casabianca.
Kenney. Battle of Valcour Island, The.
Melville, H. *Temeraire*, The.
Commemorative of a Naval Victory.
Utilitarian View of the Monitor's Fight, A.
Sackville, C. Song Written at Sea in the First Dutch War (1665), the Night before an Engagement.
Smith, C. Sea View, The.

Navy Life
Burns, R. Silver Tassie, The.
Dove, R. Passage, The.
Ross, A. Destroyers in the Arctic.

Navy, France
Thomas. To Laura, on the French Fleet Parading before Plymouth.

Navy, Great Britain
Campbell, T. Ye Mariners of England.
Causley. Chief Petty Officer.

Garrick. Heart of Oak.
Kipling, R. White Horses.
Waller, E. To the King, on His Navy.

Navy, United States
Holmes, O. Old Ironsides.
Meredith, W. Farragut, Farragut.

Nazis
Abse. Footnote Extended, A.
Alkalay-Gut. Life Goes On.
Bell, M. Getting Lost in Nazi Germany.
Bobrowski. Kaunas 1941.
Borawski. Invisible History.
Brecht, B. War Has Been Given a Bad Name.
Bringhurst. For the Bones of Josef Mengele, Disinterred June 1985.
Florsheim. Real Chocolate.
Friedman, S. Answering Machine Message.
Glazer. Drinking with the Nazis.
Hamburger, M. Between the Lines.
Hecht, A. 'More Light! More Light!'
Heyen. Blue.
For Hermann Heyen.
Riddle: "From Belsen a crate of gold teeth."
Trains, The.
Hill, G. Christmas Trees.
Ovid in the Third Reich.
Hyett. Assembling the Dead at Dachau.
Kahaney, P. Germany, 1981.
Pogrom.
Kessler, S. Family Secrets.
Klepfisz. Death Camp.
Lifshin. Crystal Night.
Seeing the Documentary by the British Liberating Bergen-Belsen.
Loden. Conversations with Dr. M.
MacLean, S. Death Valley.
Mayne, S. In Memory of Aaron, Murdered Grandfather.
Zalman.
Michelson, R. Faraway Landscape.
Interrogation.
Queen Esther Award, The.
Nepo. Oil of Her Hands, The.
Peck, J. Metal Denser Than, and Liquid, A.
Plath. Daddy.
Lady Lazarus.
Pratt, E. From Stone to Steel.
Sadoff. Nazis.
Shevin. What He Hated.
Snodgrass, W. Albert Speer.
Syrkin. My Uncle in Treblinka.
Tugend, A. Every Few Months.
Unger, D. Photo Taken in Winter, 1944.
Wells, W. Beatings.
Williams, C. Spit.

Nebraska (state)
Belieu. Radio Nebraska.
Guest, B. Nebraska.
McPherson, S. Pornography, Nebraska.
Sandburg, C. Limited.
Sunset from Omaha Hotel Window.

Nebuchadnezzar
Keats. Nebuchadnezzar's Dream.
Wylie. Nebuchadnezzar.

Necrophilia
Dudley, E. Pathologist.
See also **Corpses**

Need
Ammons, A. R. Needs.
Angel. Breaking the Rock Down.
Bart, L. As Long As He Needs Me.
Berry, W. Wild Geese, The.
Brown, L. It All Depends on You.
Burns, R. Grace at Kirkudbright.
Cataldi. It's Easy.
Cooper, J. Rent.
Creeley. For W. C. W.
DeSylva, B. G. It All Depends on You.
Evans, R. To Each His Own.
Harburg. Necessity.
Heard, J. Thine Own.
Henderson, R. It All Depends on You.
Lane, B. Necessity.
Loesser. Somebody, Somewhere.

McBride, M. Knife-Thrower's Wife, The.
Merrill, B. People.
Meynell, A. Modern Mother, The.
Nye, N. Famous.
Orton, D. Sea Monkeys, The.
Shepherd, R. Another Version of an Ocean.
Styne, J. People.
Talvikki, A. For Want.
Volkman. Untitled.
Whitman, W. Not Heaving from My Ribb'd Breast Only.
Winter, M. Long Distance.
Young, A. Dance of the Infidels.
See also **Poverty**

Needles
Clarke, C. Stuck.
Cole, H. 40 Days and 40 Nights.
Lear, E. Limericks, I (ii).
Perillo. Needles.
Unknown. Thread the Needle.

Nefertiti
Unknown. Queen Nefertiti.

Neglect
Claman, E. Show Biz Parties.
Dubie. Trakl.
Mahon. Disused Shed in Co. Wexford, A.
Martelli, J. Mal'Occhio.
Thompson, D. P. Sister Lakin and Lally.
Wilbur. Shame.

Neighbors
Anstett. Worry.
Biggar. Your Neighbor.
Bronk. Body, The.
Charara, H. My Father Breaks the Neighbor's Nose.
Eady. My Mother, If She Had Won Free Dance Lessons.
Elledge. Their Hats Is Always White.
Erdrich, H. Future Debris.
Frost, R. Mending Wall.
Geiger. Disproportionate.
Goldberg, B. Once a Shoot of Heaven.
Gordon, M. Love Thy Neighbor.
Gregerman, D. Lullaby.
Guest, E. Kindly Neighbor, The.
Harms. Dogtown.
Heaney, S. Other Side, The.
Heywood, J. Quiet Neighbour, A.
Hugo, R. What Thou Lovest Well Remains American.
Lawrence, D. Love Thy Neighbour.
Lochhead, L. Grim Sisters, The.
Maroon, B. Neighbor.
Millay, E. Portrait by a Neighbour.
Moulds, J. Late Summer Litany.
Osterhaus, J. New York Minute.
Pape. Minotaur Next Door, The.
Pinsky. Street, The.
Revel, H. Love Thy Neighbor.
Richman, L. Rue de Rosiers: To My Brother Fred.
Roberts, K. How Late Desire Looks.
Rodgers, C. Slave Ritual.
Tate, J. Neighbors.
Torres, E. Elbow in Dumberland, An.
Unknown. (My Daily Creed).
Williams, W. Exercise No. 2.
Williamson, G. Neighboring Storms.
Young, A. Studio Up Over In Your Ear.

Nelson, Horatio Nelson, Viscount
Campbell, T. Battle of the Baltic.
Durrell. Ballad of the Good Lord Nelson, A.
Graves, R. 1805.
Melville, H. *Temeraire*, The.
Seaman, S. England Expects?
Unknown. Death of Nelson, The.

Nepal
Justice, D. Here in Katmandu.
Kipling, R. Sacrifice of Er-Heb, The.

Neptune (god)
Campion, T. Hymn in Praise of Neptune, A.
Spires. Comb and the Mirror, The.

Nero
Herrick. Cruelties.
Neruda, Pablo
Bly, R. Mourning Pablo Neruda.
Figueroa, J. Pablo Neruda.
Hass, R. Elegy Residence on Earth.
Lim, S. In California with Neruda.
Lowther. Last Letter to Pablo.
Nerve Gas
Rawling. Gas Drill.
Nests
Clare, J. Birds' Nest.
Moldaw. Nest, The.
Spear, R. Nest for Everyone, A.
Unknown, fr. Terezin Concentration Camp.
Birdsong.
See also **Birds' Nests**
Netherlands
Cary, P. Leak in the Dike, The.
Marvell. Character of Holland, The.
Unknown. Lowlands o' [*or* of] Holland, The.
Nettles
Thomas, E. Tall Nettles.
Nevada (state)
Hass, R. Tahoe in August.
Stafford, W. Vacation.
New England
Betjeman. Longfellow's Visit to Venice.
Braithwaite. House of Falling Leaves, The.
Dobyns. Dancing in Vacationland.
Eliot, T. Cousin Nancy.
Lowell, A. Lilacs.
St. Louis.
Myles, E. New England Wind.
Oppen. Product.
Rakosi. Origins.
Robinson, E. New England.
Thoreau. On Ponkawtasset, Since, We Took
Our Way.
Tillam. Upon the First Sight of New England,
June 29, 1638.
Weismiller. Hemlocks in Autumn.
Wheatley, P. America.
Farewell to America. A. To Mrs. S. W.
Williams, S. Letters from a New England
Negro.
New Guinea
McAuley, J. New Guinea.
New Hampshire (state)
Borawski. Power of One.
Hall, D. Black Faced Sheep, The.
Granite and Grass.
New Hampshire.
Hinsey, E. Art of Measuring Light, The.
Kinnell. Flower Herding on Mount Monadnock.
Freedom, New Hampshire.
McKay, C. Spring in New Hampshire.
Rakosi. Founding of New Hampshire, The.
New Jersey (state)
Ammons, A. R. Corsons Inlet.
Baraka. Contract. (For The Destruction and
Rebuilding of Paterson), A.
Berger, D. Dinner in the Sun.
Coles, R. New Jersey Boys.
De Vries, R. On Alabama Ave., Paterson, NJ,
1954.
Dodd, E. Dieback.
Gillan. In New Jersey Once.
Hull, L. Midnight Reports.
Jackson, R. 63rd and Broadway.
Kennedy, X. In a Prominent Bar in Secaucus
[One Day].
Pinsky. At Pleasure Bay.
Jersey Rain.
Long Branch Song, A.
Whitman, W. Patrolling Barnegat.
Williams, W. Delineaments of the Giants, The.
Episode 17.
Preface: "To make a start."
Semblables, The.
Sunday in the Park.
New Mexico (state)
Dorn, E. When the Fairies.
Jeffers, R. New Mexican Mountain.
Lopez, L. To a Coal Miner in Madrid, New

Mexico.
Snyder, G. I Went Into the Maverick Bar.
New Orleans, Louisiana
Bly, R. Day We Visited New Orleans, The.
Creamer, H. Way Down Yonder in New
Orleans.
Harjo, J. New Orleans.
Jonas, R. Ballade des Belles Milatraisses.
Komunyakaa. Untitled Blues; After a
Photograph by Yevgeni Yevtushenko.
Larkin, P. For Sidney Bechet.
Layton, J. Way Down Yonder in New Orleans.
Salaam. I Just Heard John Buffington Died.
Steptoe. Mississippi Blues.
New Year
Algarin. Happy New Year.
Amherst. Song for the Single Table on New
Year's Day, A.
Avison. New Year's Poem.
Baranczak, S. Three Magi, The.
Brathwaite, E. New Year Letter.
Carew, T. New Year's Sacrifice: To Lucinda, A.
To the New Year [For the Countess of Carlisle].
Clare, J. Old Year, The.
Davenant [*or* D'Avenant]. For the Lady Olivia
Porter; a Present upon a New Year's Day.
Fischer, H. New Leaf, A [*or* The].
Fordham. Passing of the Old Year.
Greenlaw. New Year's Eve.
Grimes, A. Alice's Cat, New Year's Eve 1990.
Hardy, T. New Year's Eve.
Herrick. New-Year's [*or* New-Yeares] Gift Sent
to Sir Simeon Steward, A.
Larkin, P. New Year.
Linden, M. Last Day of the Year; or, New
Year's Eve, The.
New Year's Morning; or, the First Day of the
Year.
Lowell, R. New Year's Day.
Nims, J. New Year's Eve, 1938.
Okigbo. New Year's Song.
Rich, A. At the Jewish New Year.
Sarton. Small Joys.
Shore. High Holy Days.
Sykes, B. Prayer to the Spirit of the New Year.
Thompson, P. Old Year, The.
To the New Year.
Tolson, M. Festus Conrad.
Unknown. New Year Carol, A.
Wetzsteon. Poem for a New Year.
Wilbur. Year's End.
New York (state)
Allen, W. Erie Canal, The.
Foerster. Playland.
Harper, M. Grandfather.
Hecht, A. Sestina d'Inverno.
Hollander, J. State of Nature, A.
Keithley. Small Moon on the Shoulder of New
York.
Moss, H. Long Island Springs.
Unknown. E-ri-e, The.
Walcott. Upstate.
Wilbur. Sleepless at Crown Point.
Williams, W. Rapid Transit.
New York City
Algarin. Dante Park.
Applewhite. Prayer for My Son.
Ashbery. Chapter 2, Book 35.
Barot, R. Portishead Suite.
Three Amoretti.
Bell, M. These Green-Going-to-Yellow.
Benét, S. Metropolitan Nightmare.
Berlin. Puttin' on the Ritz (Revised Version).
Slumming on Park Avenue.
Bernstein, L. New York, New York.
Berrigan, A. Mercy Flight.
Short History of Autumn, A.
Berrigan, T. Bean Spasms.
Bishop, E. Invitation to Miss Marianne Moore.
Letter to N.Y.
Blackburn, P. Slogan, The.
Blake, J. Sidewalks of New York, The.
Blevins, S. New York.
Blumenthal, M. Washington Heights, 1959.
Brutus. Off to Philadelphia in the Morning.
Burke, J. Road to Morocco, The.

Castro, M. New York City.
Clampitt. Times Square Water Music.
Clifton, H. Euclid Avenue.
Cohan. Give My Regards to Broadway.
Comden, B. New York, New York.
Cooley, N. Diane Arbus, New York.
Cording. Peregrine Falcon, New York City.
Corn. Navidad, St. Nicholas Ave.
Cortez, J. I Am New York City.
Coultas, B. Third Farming Poem.
Crase. Elegy for New York, The.
Denby. New York Face, A.
Doty, M. Lilacs in NYC.
Dubin, A. Forty-second Street.
Duke, V. Autumn in New York.
Duran, J. Time Zones.
Eiseley. And as for Man.
Esteves. South Bronx Testimonial.
Farber. Manhattan Lullaby.
Feirstein. Mark Stern.
Mark Stern Wakes Up.
Ferlinghetti, L. Retired Ballerinas, Central Park
West.
Field, E. Oh, the Gingkos.
Field, R. Manhattan Lullaby.
Fitzgerald, R. Imprisoned, The.
Garcia, R. Diver for the NYPD Talks to His
Girlfriend, A.
Gardinier. To Peace.
Ginsberg, A. 'Back on Times Square, Dreaming
of Times Square'
Charnel Ground, The.
Mugging.
My Sad Self.
Velocity of Money.
Green, A. New York, New York.
Grue. Dogs of New York, The.
Hacker, M. Elysian Fields.
Harris, D. On the uptown lexington avenue
express: Martin Luther King Day 1995.
Hart, L. Manhattan.
Hays, H. Manhattan.
Hernández Cruz. Poem: "Greater cities are,
The."
Side 32.
Holland, W. Christopher Street 1979.
Hopkins, L. Flash.
Hughes, L. Projection.
Jackson, R. 63rd and broadway.
Johnson, H. Bottled [New York].
Johnson, J. My City.
Kasdorf. Green Market, New York.
Kearney, M. Nature Poetry.
Kees. Aspects of Robinson.
Kennedy, X. B Negative.
Kerouac. Hymn.
Kinnell. Avenue Bearing the Initial of Christ
into the New World, The.
Under the Williamsburg Bridge.
Koch, K. Thanksgiving.
Koehler, T. Spreadin' Rhythm Around.
Lodge, G. Lower New York.
Lorde. New York City 1970.
Lowell, R. Inauguration Day: January 1953.
Loy. On Third Avenue.
McDaniel, J. Leonard.
McKay, C. Dawn in New York.
Melhem, D. Grandfather: Frailty Is Not the
Story.
Merrill, J. Urban Convalescence, An.
Mesmer, S. Lonely Tylenol.
Moore, M. New York.
Morales, A. Old Countries.
Myles, E. Milk.
Newton, B. Owed to New York.
O'Hara, F. Rhapsody.
Step Away from Them, A.
Steps.
You Are Gorgeous and I'm Coming.
Oden. Private Letter to Brazil, A.
Review from Staten Island.
Orlovsky. Poems from Subway to Work.
Padgett, R. After the Broken Arm.
Strawberries in Mexico.
Patterson, G. Autobiography of a Black Man.
Piñero. Lower East Side Poem, A.

This Is Not the Place Where I was Born.
Piccione. Watching Ants Play Soccer in Central Park.
Pietri. Old Buildings, The.
Traffic Misdirector.
Ponsot. Rockefeller the Center.
Rich, A. Upper Broadway.
Robin, L. Little Girl from Little Rock.
Rodgers, R. Manhattan.
Rodriguez, J. New York Sonnet.
Rome, H. Who Knows?
Rosenblatt, S. Visiting New York.
Rukeyser, M. Seventh Avenue.
Sapia. Grandmother, a Caribbean Indian, Described by My Father.
Senghor. To New York.
Simpson, L. Stumpfoot on 42nd Street.
Styne, J. Little Girl from Little Rock.
Taylor, C.B. Plenty Time Pass Fast, Fas Dey So.
Round Irving High School.
Towne, C. Roof-Tops.
Urdang. Returning to the Port of Authority: A Picaresque.
Van Heusen, J. Road to Morocco, The.
Waddell, H. New York City.
Walcott. Village Life, A.
Warren, H. Forty-second Street.
Weaver, M. Providence Journal V: Israel of Puerto Rico.
Whitman, W. City of Orgies.
Crossing Brooklyn Ferry.
Give Me the Splendid Silent Sun.
Mannahatta.
Wiese, B. Going Home Madly.
Willis, N. City Lyrics.
Wright, J. To the Poets in New York.
Wunderlich, M. East Seventh Street.
Given in Person Only.
Young, A. Dance of the Infidels.
See also **Broadway, New York City; Bronx, The, New York City; Brooklyn, New York City; Harlem, New York City; Queens, New York City; Rockefeller Center, New York City**

New Yorker (magazine)
Balaban. Along the Mekong.

New Zealand
Baxter, J. Bay, The.
East Coast Journey.
New Zealand.
Curnow. Landfall in Unknown Seas.
Frame. Foxes, The.
Vaughan-Thomas. Farewell to New Zealand.

Newfoundland, Canada
Crane, H. North Labrador.
Hayman, R. Pleasant Life in Newfoundland, The.

Newman, John Henry, Cardinal
Rossetti, C. Cardinal Newman.

News
Bishop, E. 12 O'Clock News.
Graham, W. What's the News?
Greenlaw. Five O'Clock Opera.
Hamilton, I. Newscast, The.
Hovanessian, D. Exiles.
Jackson, B. Shooting, Killing, Drug Busts, Cover-Ups, Fuck-Ups, Lighter Sides, Weather, and Sports.
Johnson, J. Guess Who's in Town? (Nobody but That Gal of Mine).
Jordan, J. Through These Halls.
Leapor. Epistle of Deborah Dough, The.
Merwin, W. S. Avoiding News by the River.
Nobleman, B. Tabloid News.
Nye, N. Blood.
Rosen, M. Here is the News.
Salter. Chernobyl.

Newspapers
Atwood. It Is Dangerous to Read Newspapers.
Beatty, P. New York Newsday: Truth, Justice and Vomit.
Coleridge, M. No Newspapers.
Dobson, R. Country Press.
Dodge, M. Note.
Eady. Jack Johnson Does the Eagle Rock.

Eliot, T. *Boston Evening Transcript*, The.
Espada. Fidel in Ohio.
Hovanessian, D. Exiles.
Jarrell. Nestus Gurley.
Lehman. Towards the Vanishing Point.
Moise *et al.* Newspaper, The.
Moorer. Southern Press, The.
Nemerov. Picture, A.
Owen, W. Smile, Smile, Smile.
Paulin. Personal Column.
Plomer. Headline History.
Prunty. Reading Before We Read, Horoscope and Weather.
St. John, D. Quote Me Wrong Again and I'll Slit the Throat of Your Pet Iguana.
Thomas, E. Cries of the Newsboy.
Wilbur. After the Last Bulletins.
Wolfe, H. British Journalist, The.
Zephaniah. Sun, The.
See also **Journalism and Journalists; Magazines**

Newton, Sir Isaac
Blake, W. Mock On, Mock On, Voltaire, Rousseau.
Pope, A. Intended for Sir Isaac Newton.
Unknown. Sir Isaac Newton.

Niagara Falls
Bishop, M. Public Aid for Niagara Falls.
Crapsey. Niagara.
Drake, J. Niagara.
Dubin, A. Shuffle Off to Buffalo.

Nicaragua
Espada. Jeep Driver, The.

Nigeria and Nigerians
Acholonu. Nigeria in the Year 1999.
Clark Bekedermo. Epilogue to Casualties.
Ismaili. Lagos.
Kay, J. Pride.
Ogundipe-Leslie. Nigeria of the Seventies.
Ojaide. Launching Our Community Developement Fund.
Southerland. Blue Clay.
Night in Nigeria.
Soyinka. Ikeja, Friday, Four O'Clock.

Night
Abinader, E. On a Summer Night.
Adair, T. Night We Called It a Day, The.
Agosin. Night.
Aldrich, T. Lycidas.
Ammons, A. R. Above the Fray Is Only Thin Air.
Angel. Veils of Prayer.
Asekoff, L. Starwork.
Ashbery. Morning Jitters.
Young Prince and the Young Princess, The.
Auden. Summer Night, A.
Awad, J. First Snow.
Aytoun [*or* Ayton], R. Upon Mr Thomas Murrays Fall.
Balingit, J. Quiet Evening, Home Away.
Baraka. Three Movements and a Coda.
Barer, M. On Such a Night As This.
Barnes, W. Winter Night, A.
Baxter, J. Buried Stream, The.
Beddoes. To Night.
Belieu. Legend of the Albino Farm.
Nocturne: My Sister Life.
Benét, W. Night.
Bethell. Midnight.
Bishop, E. Man-Moth, The.
Bly, R. Extra Joyful Chorus for Those Who Have Read This Far, An.
Solitude Late at Night in the Woods.
Two Ramages for Old Masters.
Bodenheim. Interlude.
Bogan, L. Night.
Bourdillon. Night Has a Thousand Eyes, The.
Bowers, M. Answer.
Bowles, W. Written at Bamborough Castle.
Bradbury, R. Switch on the Night.
Brecht, B. First Psalm (Posthumous).
Bristol. Night.
Brontë, A. Night.
Brontë, C. 'What does she dream of.'
Brown, J. Rhapsody, Written at the Lakes in

Westmorland, A.
Browning, R. Meeting At Night.
Brummer, N. Why Is This Night Different from All Other Nights?
Brutus. At Night.
Nightsong: City.
Bryan, M. To———: "O timeless guest!—so soon returned art thou."
Bukowski. Not Much Singing.
Byron, G. She Walks In Beauty.
So We'll Go No More A-Roving.
Césaire, A. Different Horizon.
Caldwell, E. Love Poem: "Olfactory paradise."
Campion, T. Now Winter Nights Enlarge.
Cane. Hymn to Night.
Carson, A. Longing, a Documentary.
Carter, E. Ode to Wisdom.
Carver, R. Window, The.
Cawein. Orgie.
Chin, J. Night.
Clough. Darkness.
Codrescu. Work.
Coleridge, H. Night.
Cope, W. At 3 A.M.
Cortes, F. Poem Composed During a Brownout.
Crane, H. In Shadow.
Crane, S. Little Birds of the Night.
Crawford, I. Battle, A.
Dark Stag, The.
Creeley. Somewhere.
Cristall. Song: "Both gloomy and dark was the shadowy night."
Song of Arla, Written During Her Enthusiasm, A.
Written When the Mind Was Oppressed.
Cronin, A. Elegy for the Nightbound.
Crosby, F. Thoughts in Midnight Hours.
Cullen, C. Night Rain.
Cumbo. Nocturnal Sounds.
Cummings, E. Impression.
Curbelo. Last Call.
Curnow. Continuum.
Cushman, S. Make the Bed.
Davie. Mushroom Gatherers, The.
Davies, W. Hour of Magic, The.
De la Mare. Birthnight: To F, The.
Peace.
Silver.
De Tabley. Nuptial Song.
Deane, S. Power Cut.
Dennis, M. Night We Called It a Day, The.
Devi. This Night.
Dickinson, E. Aurora.
Dietz, H. You and the Night and the Music.
Dodd, W. Of Rain and Air.
Dogen. On the Treasury of the True Dharma Eye.
Doolittle, H. Evening.
Dransfield. Endsight.
Drinkwater. Moonlit Apples.
Drummond, W. Madrigal: "Unhappie [*or* Unhappy] Light."
Dunbar, P. Night.
Dunbar, W. Meditatioun in Wyntir.
Edwards, M. I Love the Night.
Ehrhart. Night Patrol.
Eigner. For Sleep.
Ekelof. If You Ask Me.
Eliot, T. Conversation Galante.
Rhapsody on a Windy Night.
Espada. Transient Hotel Sky at the Hour of Sleep.
Estes, A. Nocturne.
Farber. Manhattan Lullaby.
Taking Turns.
Farjeon, E. Good Night.
Night Will Never Stay, The.
Fatchen. Night Walk.
"Field." Nightfall.
Field, R. Manhattan Lullaby.
Fishman, L. V's Farmhouse.
Fox, S. In the Evening.
Francis, R. Night Train.
Frost, R. Acquainted with the Night.
Night Person, The.
Two Tramps in Mud Time.

Galvin, B.   Inside Job, An.
García Lorca.   Sketches.
Gardinier.   Blues.
Ginsberg, A.   Last Night in Calcutta.
Gioia.   Country Wife, The.
  In Chandler Country.
Glück, L.   Pond, The.
Godfrey.   What It Takes.
Goedicke.   On the Night in Question.
Gonzalez, N.   Wanderer in the Night of the
  World, A.
Goodison.   Always Homing Now Soul Toward
  Light.
Gould, A.   Observed Observer, The.
Graves, R.   Frosty Night, A.
Grimké, A.   For the Candle Light.
Hagiwara Sakutaro.   Spring Night.
Haines, J.   Foreboding.
  If the Owl Calls Again.
Hanson, P.   So Beautiful Is the Tree of Night.
Hardy, T.   Shut Out That Moon.
Harms.   Los Angeles, the Angels.
Hartnett.   Moonsnow '77.
Hayden, R.   O Daedalus, Fly Away Home.
Heard, J.   Night.
Hejinian.   Nights.
Hemans.   Night-Blooming Flowers.
Hernandez, D.   Rooftop Piper.
Herrick.   Dream[e]s.
  Night-Piece, to Julia, The.
  No Difference in the Dark [or i'th'dark].
  To Daisies, Not to Shut So Soon[e].
Hinsey, E.   Art of Measuring Light, The.
Hirshfield, J.   At Night.
  Invocation: "This August night, raccoons."
Hitchcock.   Song of Expectancy.
Hongo.   Yellow Light.
Hood, T.   Nocturnal Sketch, A.
Hopkins, G.   Tom's Garland: Upon the
  Unemployed.
Horovitz, F.   Night-Piece.
Houston, D.   Night Out, A.
Hughes, L.   Chord.
  My People.
Hughes, T.   Thought-Fox, The.
Jarman, M.   Psalm: The New Day.
Jarrell.   Bird of Night, The.
Jeffers, R.   Night.
  Watch the Lights Fade.
Jennings, E.   At Night.
Johnson, J.   Mother Night.
Jones, A. M.   To the Moon.
Jones, L. *et al.*   World Is Full of Remarkable
  Things, The.
Kahal, I.   Night Is Young and You're So
  Beautiful, The.
Keats.   In Drear-nighted December.
Kelly, B.   Leaving, The.
Kenney.   Apples on Champlain.
Keplinger, D.   Inside: George Gaines at
  Graterford Prison, 1981.
Khalvati.   On Reading Rumi.
Kingsley, C.   Watchman, The.
Kinnell.   Ruins under the Stars.
Kinsella, T.   Endymion.
Knight, S.   In Case of Monsters.
Komunyakaa.   Starlight Scope Myopia.
  When Loneliness Is a Man.
Kooser.   Late Lights in Minnesota.
Kumin, M.   Sound of Night, The.
Kunitz, S.   Science of the Night, The.
Kuzma.   Night Things.
Lane, P.   Nocturne: "Listening for the sound."
Lanier, S.   Song for "The Jacquerie."
Larkin, P.   Sad Steps.
Lehmann, G.   Song for Past Midnight.
Levertov.   Eye Mask.
Levin, P.   Night Coach.
Levine, P.   Simple Truth, The.
Lewis, A.   Sentry, The.
Li Po.   Verses: "Clean is the autumn wind."
Linden, M.   Silent Night, The.
Livingston, M.   Night, The.
Longfellow, H.   Day Is Done, The.
  Hymn to the Night.
  Night.

Lovelace, R.   Night.
Lowell, A.   Night Clouds.
Lowell, R.   Night Sweat.
Loy.   Three Moments in Paris.
MacCaig.   Spate in Winter Midnight.
MacDiarmid, H.   Eemis-Stane, The.
MacLeish.   You, Andrew Marvell.
Mahon.   Globe in North Carolina, The.
"Malley."   Night Piece.
  Night-piece.
Mandelstam [or Mandelshtam].   I Was Washing
  Outside in the Darkness.
Marchant, F.   Screen Porch.
Margulies, S.   Relentlessly Lovelorn, the Non-
  Sleeper Whispers and Re-Whispers a Magic
  Charm Against His Wound's Roar.
Martínez, V.   Nocturne: "To the interior, limbs
  folded."
Martin, H.   On Such a Night As This.
Martinez, D.   Nocturnes: "He closed the deal on
  the night. A real."
Marvell.   Mower to the Glowworms [or Glow-
  Worms or Glo-Worms], The.
McAuley, J.   Nocturne.
McClellan.   September Night, A.
McCord, D.   This Is My Rock.
McDonald, C.   Nightfishing.
McGough, R.   Bully Night.
McGrath, T.   Guiffre's Nightmusic.
  Nocturne Militaire.
  Reading by Mechanic Light.
McMaster, R.   Back Steps Lookout.
  Clockface.
Mead, P.   There.
Merriam, E.   Lullaby "Purple."
Merwin, W. S.   Carol: "On vague hills the
  prophet runs."
Meynell, A.   At Night.
Mezey.   Owl.
Michelson, M.   Hymn to Night, A.
Millay, E.   Winter Night.
Miller, C.   Night in San Francisco.
Milton.   Il Penseroso.
Montague, J.   11 Rue Daguerre.
  Walking Late.
Montgomerie, A.   Night Is Near [or Neir] Gone,
  The.
Moore, T.   Echo.
  Oft In the Stilly Night.
Morley, D.   Air Street.
Nelson, H.   Peepers.
Nicholson, J.   On a Calm Summer's Night.
Nortje.   Up Late.
Oliver, D.   Little Night, A.
Oliver, M.   Design.
  White Night.
Oppen.   Animula.
Osherow.   Villanelle for the Middle of the
  Night.
Paquet.   Night Dust-off.
Parker, A.   Vandals, Horses.
Patchen.   'In the footsteps of the walking air.'
Po Chü-i.   Sitting at Night.
Porter, C.   In the Still of the Night.
Posey, A.   Nightfall.
Price, C.   Night Fishing.
Radcliffe, A.   Night.
Rampolekeng.   Wet Pain . . . Tread with Care.
Rankine.   Quotidian, The.
Reese, L.   Nocturne: "Topple the house down,
  wind."
  One Night.
Reverdy.   On the Threshold.
  Post.
Reyes, C.   Arizona Nocturne.
Reznikoff.   House-wreckers, The.
Roberts, K.   Night Tumbles into Town by Rail.
Robinson, E.   John Evereldown.
Rodgers, W.   Stormy Night.
Rossetti, C.   From Sunset to Star Rise.
  Is the Moon Tired?
Rossetti, D.   Insomnia.
Rukeyser, M.   Eyes of Night-Time.
Rybicki, J.   For Daniel Beels, Third Generation
  Bricklayer.
Salinas, L.   Nights in Fresno.

Salom.   Walking at Night.
Sanchez, S.   Poem at Thirty.
Sandburg, C.   Nocturne in a Deserted Brickyard.
  Window.
Sassoon.   Falling Asleep.
Satchell.   Velvet Blanket.
Schultz, R.   She Speaks to Her Husband,
  Asleep.
Schwartz, A.   You and the Night and the Music.
Senghor.   Visit.
Sexton.   Starry Night, The.
Sharp, S.   Good Nights.
Shelley, P.   Stanzas—April, 1814.
  To Jane: The keen stars were twinkling.
  To Night.
Shepherd, R.   Who Owns the Night and Lease
  Stars.
Sherwin, J.   Nightpiece.
Shirley, J.   Good-night.
Sidney, R.   Songe 17: "Sun is set, and masked
  night, The."
Simic.   Night Picnic.
  Something, The.
Simon, M.   Night.
Simpson, L.   After Midnight.
Sitwell, D.   Madwoman in the Park, The.
Slessor.   Choker's Lane.
Smith, C.   To Night.
  To the Moon.
Smith, S.   Goodnight.
Snyder, G.   Night Song of the Los Angeles
  Basin.
  Pine Tree Tops.
Sorrentino.   Classic Case, A.
Soto.   Soup, The.
Spencer, B.   Night-Time: Starting to Write.
Stevens, W.   Anecdote of the Prince of
  Peacocks.
  Candle a Saint, The.
  Girl in a Nightgown.
  God is Good. It Is a Beautiful Night.
  Reader, The.
  Reality Is an Activity of the Most August
  Imagination.
  Stars at Tallapoosa.
Stevenson, A.   Sonnet: "If it be night . . . ."
Stevenson, R.   Bed in Summer.
  Escape at Bedtime.
  Moon, The.
  Windy Nights.
  Young Night Thought.
Stever, E.   Her Back to Me.
Strand.   Late Hour, The.
  Morning, Noon and Night.
Sullivan, C.   Nights along the River.
Swann, B.   Walking at Night.
Swinburne.   Garden of Proserpine, The.
Symonds.   To Night, the Mother of Sleep and
  Death.
Szymborska.   Four in the Morning.
Taylor, J.   Fairies' Song, The.
  Star, The.
Teasdale.   August Night.
  Night.
Thomas, E.   Out in the Dark.
Thompson, P.   Winter Night, A.
Todd, R.   Paul Klee.
Torres, E.   Summertime Late Show.
Trakl.   Evening, The.
  Grodek.
  Revelation and Decline.
Trench, H.   She Comes Not When Noon Is on
  the Roses.
Tu Fu.   Coming Home Late at Night.
  Summer Night.
Unknown.   In the Night.
  Night Was Growing Cold, The.
Unknown, fr. Terezin Concentration Camp.
  Night in the Ghetto.
Van den Bergh.   Nocturn: "Moon rows burning,
  The."
Vaughan, H.   Night, The.
Very.   Morning Watch, The.
  Night.
Volkman.   Untitled.
Wagoner, D.   Chorus: "That rain-strewn night in

the woods, the chorus, chorus."
Wakoski.   Remembering the Pacific.
Walcott.   Nights in the Gardens of Port of Spain.
Ward, T.   Dark Underfoot.
Warren, R.   Birth of Love.
   Night Walking.
Waters, M.   'Night in the Tropics' (1858–59?).
Webb, F.   Hospital Night.
   Port Phillip Night.
Weiners.   Acts of Youth, The.
Welch, L.   Empress Herself Served Tea to Su
   Tung-Po, The.
Wheatley, P.   Hymn to the Evening, An.
White, J.   To Night.
Whitman, W.   On the Beach at Night.
Whittemore, R.   Still Life.
Wilbur.   After the Last Bulletins.
   Sonnet: "Winter deepening, the hay all in, The."
Wilcox, E.   In the Night.
Williams, B.   Night Flute, The.
Williams, H.   To the Moon.
Williams, W.   Good Night.
   Goodnight, A.
   Rigamarole.
Wilson, K.   Dusk in My Backyard.
Winchilsea.   Nocturnal Reverie, A.
Wright, C.   Clear Night.
Wright, J.   Camphor Laurel.
Yolen.   Dragon Night.
   Shepherd's Night Count.
See also **Evening**
Nightclubs
Barresi.   Nine of Clubs, Cleveland, Ohio.
Berke.   Dancing to the Track Singers at the
   Nightclub.
Davis, F.   Jazz Band.
Elmslie, K.   Amazon Club.
Gilbert, J.   Elephant Hunt in Guadalajara.
Hayes, T.   At Pegasus.
Hughes, L.   Jam Session.
   Jazz Band in a Parisian Cabaret.
   Jazzonia.
   Neon Signs.
Iozia, J.   Last Night at the Flamingo.
McClure, M.   Jazz at the Intergalactic Nightclub.
Scott, F.   Night Club.
Weaver, M.   Left Bank Jazz Society, The.
White, J.   Oshi.
Zimmer.   Romance.
Nightingales
Arnold, M.   Philomela.
Blind.   Russian Student's Tale, The.
Bridges, R.   Nightingales.
Browning, E.   Bianca Among the Nightingales.
Carstairs.   Nightingale.
Clare, J.   Nightingale, The.
Coleridge, S.   Nightingale, The.
Cook, E.   Lines / Suggested by the Song of a
   Nightingale.
Drummond, W.   To a Nightingale.
Keats.   Ode to a Nightingale.
Lindsay, N.   Chinese Nightingale, The.
Marvell.   Mower to the Glowworms [*or* Glow-
   Worms *or* Glo-Worms], The.
Maschwitz, E.   Nightingale Sang in Berkeley
   Square, A.
Monro.   Nightingale near the House, The.
Randolph, T.   On the Death of a Nightingale.
Ransom, J.   Philomela.
Rossetti, C.   Pain or Joy.
Sherwin, M.   Nightingale Sang in Berkeley
   Square, A.
Sidney, S.   Nightingale, The.
Smith, C.   On the Departure of the Nightingale.
   To a Nightingale.
Unknown.   Sparrow-Hawk, A.
Webb, H.   Nightingales, The.
Winchilsea.   To the Nightingale.
Nightmares
Bampfylde.   On a Frightful Dream.
Cisneros, S.   Poet Reflects On Her Solitary Fate,
   The.
Douglas, L.   To Sleep.
Fatchen.   I Often Meet a Monster.
Gardner, I.   Nightmare.
Graves, R.   Lost Jewel, A.

Harper, M.   Nightmare Begins Responsibility.
Hugo, R.   In Your Bad Dream.
Jeffers, R.   Apology for Bad Dreams.
Light, K.   My Worst Nightmare.
MacNeice.   Bad Dream.
Sarton.   Tortured, The.
Shevin.   What He Hated.
Shiffrin, N.   Anna's Dream.
Tatarunis, P.   Before the Brain Surgery.
Tayson, S.   Nightsweats.
Tugend, A.   Every Few Months.
Vando.   In the Crevices of Night.
Warren, R.   Original Sin.
See also **Dreams and Dreaming**
Nihilism
Lowell, R.   Nihilist as Hero, The.
McNeil, R.   It Just Doesn't Matter.
Murphy, K.   Eighties Meditation.
Nikolic, G.   Under the Ninth Sky.
Ray, D.   Automat.
Rochester, J.   Upon Nothing.
Nijinsky, Vaslav
Hahn, S.   Nijinksy's Dog.
Nike
Allen, H.   Wingless Victory, The.
Nile (river)
Blind.   Beautiful Beeshareen Boy, The.
Hunt, L.   Nile, The.
Nile, Battle of the (1798)
Moore, M.   New York.
1950s
Elledge.   Man I Love and I Have a Typical
   Evening the Night Richard M. Nixon Dies,
   The.
Koethe.   From the Porch.
1960s
Barresi.   Vacation, 1969.
Brown, S.   No, No Nostalgia!
Burris.   Very True Confessions.
Clinton, S.   I Wanna Be Black.
DeFoe, M.   Forgetting the Sixties.
García.   Barrio Beateo.
Ginsberg, A.   Crossing Nation.
Goldbarth.   Counterfeit Earth!, The.
Gonzalez, R.   Some Sixties.
Komunyakaa.   How I See Things.
La Loca.   Why I Choose Black Men for My
   Lovers.
Long, R.   What's So Funny 'bout Peace, Love
   and Understanding.
Machan.   In 1969.
Murphy, K.   Eighties Meditation.
Piercy.   Learning Experience.
Soto.   Dizzy Girls in the Sixties.
   Heaven.
   TV in Black and White.
Trinidad.   Meet the Supremes.
Van Duyn.   Christmas Card, After the
   Assassinations, A.
   What the Motorcycle Said.
Niobe
Ray, H.   Niobe.
Nixon, Richard Milhous
Di Prima.   Brief Wyoming Meditation.
Whalen.   Regalia in Immediate Demand!
Woddis.   Final Curtain.
Nkrumah, Kwame
Di Prima.   Goodbye Nkrumah.
Noah
Beer, P.   Flood, The.
Cassells.   From the Theater of Wine.
Duncan, R.   Ballad of Mrs. Noah, The.
Heath-Stubbs.   History of the Flood, The.
   Kingfisher, The.
Kendall, M.   Vision of Noah, The.
Lewis, C.   Late Passenger, The.
MacDiarmid, H.   Parley of Beasts.
Mayer, G.   Noah.
McGough, R.   Noah's Ark.
Reeves, J.   Noah.
Van Doren.   And Did the Animals?
Wilbur.   Still, Citizen Sparrow.
Young, M.   Noah's Ark.

Nobility
Brough, R.   My Lord Tomnoddy.
Campion, T.   What Fair[e] Pomp[e].
Lanyer.   Description of Cooke-ham [*or*
   Cookham], The.
Unknown.   Knight and Shepherd's Daughter,
   The.
Noises
Albert-Birot.   Balalaïka.
De Paul, G.   Milkman, Keep Those Bottles
   Quiet!
Dunbar, P.   When Malindy Sings.
Eigner.   It Sounded.
Ellis, T.   Practice.
   Sir Nose D'VoidofFunk.
Francia, L.   In Gurgle Veritas.
Hart, L.   Johnny One-Note.
Hattersley, G.   *On the Buses* with Dostoyevsky.
Inez.   Courtyard Noises from the North, Twenty-
   fourth Precinct.
Kinnell.   After Making Love We Hear
   Footsteps.
Lovelace, R.   To a Lady That Desired Me I
   Would Bear My Part with Her in a Song.
Marinetti.   Landscape Heard, A.
McAuley, J.   Dialogue.
McElroy, C.   Illusion.
Morgan, E.   Loch Ness Monster's Song, The.
Osherow.   Villanelle for the Middle of the
   Night.
Roberts, L.   Another Spring on Olmstead Street.
Sundiata.   Ear Training.
Unknown.   Bald Mountain Zaum-Poems.
   Smoke-Blackened Smiths.
Noon
Clampitt.   Meridian.
Clare, J.   Noon.
Corbett, W.   Cold Lunch.
Delaunay, S.   Zenith.
Ferril.   Noon.
Jeffers, R.   Noon.
Meynell, A.   Study, A.
Strand.   Morning, Noon and Night.
Normandy, Invasion of (1944)
Simpson, L.   Carentan O Carentan.
North Carolina (state)
Crawley, W.   Bud.
Glück, L.   Cottonmouth Country.
Mahon.   Globe in North Carolina, The.
Rukeyser, M.   Outer Banks, The.
"North, Christopher" (John Wilson)
Tennyson, A.   To Christopher North.
North Dakota (state)
Wright, J.   Outside Fargo, North Dakota.
   Poem Written under an Archway in a
   Discontinued Railroad Station, Fargo, North
   Dakota, A.
   To Flood Stage Again.
North Pole
Goedicke.   Imprint of Microscopic Life Found
   in Arctic Stones.
Jarrell.   90 North.
Roughton.   Soluble Noughts and Crosses; or,
   California, Here I Come.
Worth, V.   Magnet.
North Wind
Lindsay, N.   Moon's the North Wind's Cooky,
   The.
Mphahlele.   Exile in Nigeria.
Unknown.   Blow, Northern Wind.
North, The, United States
Alexander, E.   Letter: Blues.
Crouch, S.   Blackie Thinks of His Brothers.
Momaday.   Winter Holding off the Coast of
   North America.
Northern Ireland
Bentley, N.   Londonderry Air, The.
Cleary, B.   Sealink.
   Slouch.
Deane, S.   Derry.
   Northern Ireland: Two Comments.
Heaney, S.   Casualty.
   Strand at Lough Beg, The.
   Ulster Twilight, An.
   Whatever You Say Say Nothing.

Killeen, G. My Father's Angels.
MacNeice. Carrickfergus.
Muldoon, P. More a Man Has the More a Man
 Wants, The.
Paulin. Of Difference Does It Make.
 Settlers.
Pugh. King Billy on the Walls.
Unknown. Omagh Post Office Rhyme.

Northumberland, England
Halleck, F. Alnwick Castle.
Lomax, M. Kith.
Simms, C. First English Wildcat, The.

Noses
Charara, H. My Father Breaks the Neighbor's
 Nose.
Chin, D. Sterling Williams' Nosebleed.
Dufferin. Mother's Lament, The.
Herrick. Upon Lulls.
Lear, E. Dong with a Luminous Nose, The.
Smith, I. Nose, The.
Starbird. Hound, The.
Stone, R. Nose, The.
Turberville. Of One That Had a Great Nose.
Williams, W. Smell.

Nostalgia
Adams, L. Once Upon a Time.
 Those Were the Days.
Adamson, H. It's Been So Long.
Arlen, H. Last Night When We Were Young.
Bart, L. Fings Ain't Wot They Used t'Be.
Bauer, G. Oldies But Goodies.
Berlin. White Christmas.
Bernstein, C. When My Grandmother Said
 "Pussy."
Blanco, R. Silver Sands, The.
Bock, J. Sunrise, Sunset.
Boss. At the Nuclear Rally.
Bowers, N. On the Elvis Mailing List.
Brody. Family Album, A.
Brown, S. No, No Nostalgia!
Buckley, C. Nostalgia.
Carnevale. Walking by the Cliffside Dyeworks.
Cavalieri. First, The.
Charara, H. My Father Breaks the Neighbor's
 Nose.
Christie. Belongings.
Cook, E. Song of the Modern Time.
Cooley, N. Diane Arbus, New York.
Coslow, S. My Old Flame.
Curnow. Country School.
Davie. Remembering the 'Thirties.
Dawe, G. Likelihood of Snow, The/ The
 Danger of Fire.
De Rose, P. Deep Purple.
DeFoe, M. Dream Lover.
DeSylva, B. G. California, Here I Come.
Donaldson, W. It's Been So Long.
 Love Me or Leave Me.
Drake, E. It Was a Very Good Year.
 Just for Today.
Durcan. Around the Corner from Francis
 Bacon.
Ebb, F. Class.
 Happy Time, The.
Eliot, T. Marina.
Feinstein, S. Singapore, July 4th.
Fiacc. First Movement.
Frost, R. Range-finding.
García. Barrio Beateo.
Gilmore, M. Saturday Tub, The.
Ginsberg, A. After Yeats.
Glaser, M. Changing Address Books.
 English-Speaking Persons Will Find
 Translations.
Grey, C. Hallelujah!
Hamod, S. Leaves.
Harbach, O. Yesterdays.
Hardy, T. After a Journey.
 Lines to a Movement in Mozart's E-Flat
 Symphony.
 Old Furniture.
 Places.
Harnick. Sunrise, Sunset.
Heaney, S. Exposure.
Hernandez, D. Armitage Street.
Holmes, D. Nostalgia.

Howells, W. November.
Hugo, R. Places and Ways to Live.
Jarrell. Player Piano, The.
Johnston, A. My Old Flame.
Jolson, A. California, Here I Come.
Joseph, A. Soul Train.
 Wedding Party.
Kander, J. Class.
 Happy Time, The.
Kern, J. Tulip Time in Sing Sing.
 Yesterdays.
Killeen, G. Rewind.
Kipling, R. King, The.
Kleinzahler. Hamburger.
Knight, S. Big Parade, The.
Koethe. From the Porch.
Kumin, M. For My Great-Grandfather: A
 Message Long Overdue.
 Height of the Season, The.
Lamb, C. Old Familiar Faces, The.
Lawrence, D. Piano.
Leslie, E. Among My Souvenirs.
Levis. Picking Grapes in an Abandoned
 Vineyard.
 Widening Spell of the Leaves, The.
Lewis, A. All Day It Has Rained.
 Mountain over Aberdare, The.
Lim, S. Black and White.
Lumsden, R. ITMA.
MacNeice. Nostalgia.
Mahon. Achill.
 Going Home.
McDonald, P. Pleasures of the Imagination.
 Sunday in Great Tew.
McElroy, C. From Homegrown: An Asian-
 American Anthology of Writers.
McFadden, R. First Letter to an Irish Novelist.
 My Mother's Young Sister.
McGuckian. Little House, Big House.
Melville, H. *Temeraire*, The.
 Aeolian Harp, The.
 Archipelago, The.
Mesmer, S. What Becomes Us.
Meyer, J. California, Here I Come.
Mitsui. Because of My Father's Job.
Montague, J. Hearth Song.
Mura. To H. N.
Neale. Oh, Give Us Back the Days of Old!
O Direain. Axle Song.
Okita. Nice Thing About Counting Stars, The.
Parish. Deep Purple.
Patchen. Street Corner College.
Reed, I. Reactionary Poet, The.
Reynolds, M. Surplus.
Rich, A. Living Memory.
Riley, J. Days Gone By, The.
Robin, L. Hallelujah!
Robinson, E. Miniver Cheevy.
Roethke. Otto.
Rossiter. Nostalgia.
Simmons, J. One of the Boys.
 Stephano Remembers.
Smith, C. Written in Farm Wood, South Downs,
 in May 1784.
Snodgrass, W. Mementos, 1.
Song. Father and Daughter.
Spender, S. I Think Continually of Those Who
 Were Truly Great.
Stafford, W. Farm on the Great Plains, The.
Stickney, T. Quiet after the Rain of Morning.
Strouse, C. Once Upon a Time.
 Those Were the Days.
Tennyson, A. Break, Break, Break.
Thorson. Closed Doors.
Townsend, A. Mardi Gras Premortem.
Trinidad. Meet the Supremes.
 Movin' with Nancy.
Vaughan, H. Retreat[e], The.
Villanueva, T. Haciendo Apenas la Recolección.
Warton, T. Sonnet: To the River Lodon.
Weaver, M. Blind Solo.
Weems, M. Yesterday.
Whitman, W. Old Man's Thought of School,
 An.
Williams, C. Sanctity, The.
Williams, W. Raleigh Was Right.

Wodehouse, P. Tulip Time in Sing Sing.
Wong, N. Dreams in Harrison Railroad Park.
Woodworth. Old Oaken Bucket, The.
Wright, C. Other Side of the River, The.
Wright, J. Sisters, The.
Yeats. He Remembers Forgotten Beauty.
Youmans, V. Hallelujah!

Nothingness
Beck, T. Sonnet to Nothing.
Beckett, S. Something There.
Bevington, L. Midnight.
Cage. Lecture on Nothing.
Clifton, L. At Nagasaki.
Coolidge, C. Saturday Night.
Creeley. Fancy.
DiPalma. Bed, The.
Ekelof. Like Ankle-Rings, This Music.
Fletcher, P. To Thomalin.
Gilbert-Lecomte. Preface or The Drama of
 Absence in an Eternal Heart.
Glück, L. Moonless Night.
Hood, T. No!
Jackson, L. Nothing So Far.
Keats. When I Have Fears [That I May Cease
 to Be].
MacLeish. End of the World, The.
Mandelstam [or Mandelshtam]. [Last Poems].
Murray, L. Quality of Sprawl, The.
Padgett, R. Nothing in That Drawer.
Piatt, S. If I Had Made the World.
Raine, K. World, The.
Ramanujan. Salamanders.
Robinson, E. Man against the Sky, The.
Rodgers, W. Neither Here nor There.
Roethke. Duet.
Smith, S. Dream of Comparison, A.
Stramm. Urdeath.

See also **Nihilism**

Nottingham, England
Unknown. Nottamun Town.

Nova Scotia, Canada
Bishop, E. First Death in Nova Scotia.
 Poem: "About the size of an old-style dollar
 bill."
Carman, B. Low Tide on Grand Pré.
Lochhead, D. Winter Lanscape—Halifax.
Stansbury, J. To Cordelia.

Novels
Bishop, M. Who'd Be a Hero (Fictional)?
Campbell, R. On Some South African
 Novelists.
Cope, W. Exchange of Letters.
Jones, R. Novel, The.
Joyce, J. Blurb for *Anna Livia Plurabelle*, A.
MacLeish. Critical Observations.
Nemerov. Style.

Novelty
Herrick. Nothing New.

November
Atwood. November.
Bryant, W. November.
Cary, A. November.
Crapsey. November Night.
Frost, R. My November Guest.
Harvey, F. November.
Honig, E. November through a Giant Copper
 Beech.
Hood, T. No!
Howells, W. November.
Hughes, T. November.
Jeffers, R. November Surf.
Kelly, B. To the Lost Child.
Lampman. In November: "With loitering step
 and quiet eye."
Ray, H. November.
Santos, S. Late November.
Tomlinson, C. Saving the Appearances.
Toomer. November Cotton Flower.
Whitman, S. November Landscape, A.
Wright, J. Late November in a Field.

Nuclear Accidents
Canan. Radioactive.
Meinke. Atomic Pantoum.
Romtvedt. Kiev, the Ukraine, Nuclear Accident.
Russell, W. Nuclear Winter, The.

Nuclear Energy (cont.)

Salter. Chernobyl.
Stainer. Sarcophagus.
  Xochiquetzal.
Tranter. Glow-boys.
Wojahn. Workmen Photographed inside the
  Reactor.
See also **Radiation and Radiation Sickness**

Nuclear Energy
Bostock, G. Uranium.
Sanchez, S. Reflections After the June 12th
  March for Disarmament.
Stainer. Sarcophagus.
Williams, C. Tar.

Nuclear War
Bensley. War Games.
Canan. Radioactive.
Clayton, S. Boom Time.
Clifton, L. At Nagasaki.
Figueroa, J. Confessions from the Last Cloud.
Gilbert, K. Won't You Dad?
Hall, R. Wedding Day at Nagasaki.
Hine. Survivors, The.
Hoffman, D. Seals in Penobscot Bay, The.
Holmes, D. We Have Never Seen the Sky Light
  Up.
Kay, J. Waiting Lists, The.
Kizer, C. Twelve O'Clock.
Lowell, R. Fall 1961.
McGrath, T. Nuclear Winter.
Mitchell, A. Fifteen Million Plastic Bags.
Porter, P. Your Attention Please.
Russell, W. Nuclear Winter, The.
Salter. Welcome to Hiroshima.
Wain. Song about Major Eatherly, A.
See also **Atomic Bomb; Radiation and Radiation
Sickness**

Nudity and Nudists
Berger, J. Gun, The.
Campbeli, R. Sisters, The.
Cavafy. Days of 1908.
Drieu la Rochelle. Tennis.
Feldman, I. Se Aprovechan.
Graves, R. Naked and the Nude, The.
Kennedy, X. Nude Descending a Staircase.
Kinnell. Last Gods.
Kirby, D. To a French Structuralist.
Lawrence, D. "Gross, Coarse, Hideous" (Police
  Description of My Pictures).
  Innocent England.
Moulds, J. Renoir's Bathers.
Mueller, L. Nude by Edward Hopper, A.
Noguchi, R. Turn of Privacy, The.
Perreault, J. Metaphysical Paintings, The.
Phillips, C. Luncheon on the Grass.
Pritchard, N. Springtime.
Wilbur. Playboy.

Number Poems (genre)
Swenson, M. Cardinal Ideograms.

Numbers
Alcosser. My Number.
Brown, D. Patrols.
Coleman, C. I've Got Your Number.
Gioia. Counting the Children.
Khlebnikov, V. Zangezi: R, K, L, G.
Leigh, C. I've Got Your Number.
Overstreet. Count Ten.
Péret. My Final Agonies.
Palmer, M. Sonnet: "Now I see them sitting me
  before a mirror."
Rothenberg, J. Numerology.
Soto. Teaching Numbers.
Stein, G. Kneeling.
Swenson, M. Cardinal Ideograms.
Unknown. One, Two, Three, Four, Five!
Volkman. Untitled: "There comes a time to
  rusticate the numbers. The way the birds, jug."

Nuns
Betjeman. Felixstowe, or, The Last of Her
  Order.
Brinnin. Nuns at Eve.
Brownjohn. In a Convent Garden.
Clarke, A. Martha Blake at Fifty-one.
Cofer, J. Purpose of Nuns, The.
Davidson, J. Ballad of a Nun, A.
Dennis, C. St. Francis and the Nun.
Di Prima. To the Unnamed Buddhist Nun Who
  Burned Herself to Death on the Night of June
  3, 1966.
Durcan. Sister Agnes Writes to Her Beloved
  Mother.
Hopkins, G. Heaven-Haven.
  Wreck of the Deutschland, The.
Kizer, C. Election Day, 1984.
Klein, A. For the Sisters of the Hôtel Dieu.
Kumin, M. Nuns of Childhood: Two Views,
  The.
Lluellyn [*or* Lluelyn]. Epithalamium: To
  Mistress M. A.
Milton. Sonnet 9: "Ladie [*or* Lady], that in the
  prime of earliest youth."
Ormond. To a Nun.
Palazzeschi. Nuns Go Walking.
Procter, A. Legend of Provence, A.
Rohrer, M. Short History of Illumination, A.
Rukeyser, M. Nuns in the Wind.
Rummel, M. Letter to a Former Mother
  Superior.
Shomer. Falling for Jesus.
Unknown. Bleeding Nun, The.
Williams, A. Nunnery, The.

Nuremberg, Germany
Slessor. Nuremberg.

Nursery Rhymes
Cyril. Children's Games.
Kennedy, X. Help!
Unknown. Mulberry Bush, The.
  Sukey [*or* Suky], you shall be my wife.

Nurses
Betjeman. Death in Leamington.
Centolella. Woman of Three Minds, The.
Eigner. How It Comes About.
Fagg, M. Mrs Nightingale.
Fenton, J. Red Light District Nurse, The.
Kendrick, D. Inpatient.
Lawrence, A. To Be A Nurse.
Levertov. Malice of Innocence, The.
Locker-Lampson. Terrible Infant, A.
Longfellow, H. Santa Filomena.
Moorer. Negro Heroines.
Ryan, T. Enough.
Shuster, D. Mellow on Morphine.
Unknown. Hospital Duties.
  Sweet Polly Oliver.
Waring, B. Baby Random.
Whitman, W. Epigraph to "Drum-Taps."
  Wound-Dresser, The.

Nursing Homes
Garcia, R. Nobody Here But Us.

Nurturing
Coles, R. Goddam Street, The.

Nymphs
Black, S. Personals.
Carew, T. Pastoral[l] Dialogue, A.
Doolittle, H. Oread.
Herrick. To the Water Nymphs, Drinking at the
  Fountain.
Marvell. Nymph and Her Fawn, The.
  Nymph Complaining for the Death of Her Faun
  [*or* Fawn], The.
More, H. Inscription in a Beautiful Retreat
  Called Fairy Bower.
Pastorius. Penance, A.
Pritchard, N. Landscape with Nymphs and
  Satyrs.
Radcliffe, A. Song of a Spirit.
Seward. Speech of the Nymph.
Sitwell, D. Waltz.
Smith, C. To the Naiad of the Arun.
Snodgrass, W. Monet: 'Les Nymphéas.'
Van den Bergh. Nocturn: "Moon rows burning,
  The."
Warton, T. On Bathing.
Wilbur. Ceremony.
Winchilsea. Adam Posed.

O

O'Connor, Flannery
Walters, D. Flannery O'Connor.

O'Hara, Frank
Brainard, J. I Remember.
Corn. Kimchee in Worchester (Mass.).
Koch, K. Circus, The.
O'Hara, F. Day Lady Died, The.

O'Keeffe, Georgia
Clampitt. Fog.

O'Neill, Owen Roe
Davis, T. Lament for the Death of Eoghan
  Ruadh O'Neill.

O'Neill, Shane
Jeffers, R. Shane O'Neill's Cairn.

Oafs
Francis, R. Yes, What?

Oak Trees
Cowper, W. Yardley Oak.
Herrick. All Things Decay and Die.
La Grone. Lines to the Black Oak.
Locker-Lampson. Old Oak Tree at Hatfield
  Broadoak, The.
Ransom, J. Parting, without a Sequel.
Roberson. Sonnet.
Synge. To the Oaks of Glencree.
Warren, R. Bearded Oaks.
Whitman, W. I Saw in Louisiana a Live-Oak
  Growing.
  Live Oak, with Moss.

Oases
Cameron, N. Green, Green Is El Aghir.
See also **Deserts**

Obesity
De Paul, G. Mister Five by Five.
Eliot, T. Bustopher Jones: The Cat About Town.
Erdrich, H. Fat in America.
Schneiders, J. Weight.
Unknown. Whistle, Daughter, Whistle.
Wright, J. Walking the Dog.

Obituaries
Holman, M. Mr. Z.
Lowell, R. Alfred Corning Clark.

Oblivion
Bobrowski. Elderblossom.
Brooks, G. When You Have Forgotten Sunday:
  The Love Story.
Davenant [*or* D'Avenant]. Lover and
  Philosopher.
Dowson. Dregs.
Eberhart, R. On a Squirrel Crossing the Road in
  Autumn, in New England.
Hannon. Real Estate.
Hughes, L. Blues at Dawn.
  Shame on You.
Jackson, L. All Things.
Lawrence, D. Shadows.
  Tabernacle.
MacDiarmid, H. Eemis-Stane, The.
Sisson. Un-Red Deer, The.

Obscenity
Gogarty. On First Looking into Krafft-Ebing's
  Psychopathosexualis [*or* Psychopathia
  Sexualis].
Hirschman, J. Tremor, The.
Lawrence, D. Innocent England.
Unknown. Army Dance, The.
  Generals Ride in Cars.
  Oh! Fucking Halkirk.
  Twats in the Ops Room.
  "W——, Miss." Gentleman's Study, in Answer
  to The Lady's Dressing-Room, The.
See also **Pornography**

Obscurity
De Vere, E. Poem: "Were I a king, I could
  command content."
Durem. I Know I'm Not Sufficiently Obscure.
Gioia. Guide to the Other Gallery.
Rich, A. Focus.
Rossetti, C. Frog's Fate, A.
Williamson, G. Counterfeiter, The.

Observatories
Eady. View from the Roof, Waverly Place.
Keyes. Greenwich Observatory.
See also **Astronomy and Astronomers**

Obsessions
Belloc. Juliet.

Berryman. Canto Amor.
Byron, G. Last Words on Greece.
Coleridge, S. Recollections of Love.
Dietz, H. I See Your Face Before Me.
Estep, M. I Have to Go Now.
Gay, J. Molly Mog [or The Fair Maid of the Inn].
Gilsdorf, E. Walk, The.
Katrovas. Black English.
Lamb, M. Helen.
MacCaig. Small Lochs.
Nash, O. Curl Up and Diet.
Oswald, A. Melon Grower, The.
Schwartz, A. I See Your Face Before Me.
Sondheim. Losing My Mind.
Tate, J. Deaf Girl Playing.
Van Walleghen. Crabapples.

Occult, The
Gregg. Flower No More Than Itself, A.
Reid, A. Spell for Sleeping, A.

Ocean
Ammons, A. R. Spit.
Berlin. How Deep Is the Ocean? (How High Is the Sky?).
Bly, R. On the Oregon Coast.
Brown, G. Beachcomber.
"Cornwall." Address to the Ocean.
Curry. St Kilda.
Dunn, S. Because You Mentioned the Spiritual Life.
Emerson, R. Sea-Shore.
Francia, L. Secret in the Roar, The.
Frost, R. West-Running Brook.
Hawthorne, N. Ocean, The.
Hood, T. To the Ocean.
Hooper, V. Reading, A.
Jeffers, R. Evening Ebb.
Mackey, N. Phantom Light of All Our Day, The.
Marvell. Bermudas.
Mudrooroo Narogin. Streets.
Noguchi, R. Not Surfing Some Days.
Oliver, M. At the Shore.
Percival. Coral Grove, The.
Pfeiffer, E. Mid-Ocean.
Pilling. Cast Away.
Procter, A. Address to the Ocean.
Ray, H. Ocean Musing, An.
Schmitz. Abbott's Lagoon.
Stern, G. Lucky Life.
Torres, E. Vase of the Universe, The.
Wyrebek, M. Recovery.
Zandvakili, K. No Trespassing (Private Beach).
See also **Sea**

October
Alexander, M. October Journey.
Bronk. Where It Ends.
Carman, B. Vagabond Song, A.
Elman. October Observed, Hudson Falls, New York in Bill's Back Yard.
Fordham. October.
Hayden, R. October.
Hayne, P. October.
Jackson, H. October's Bright Blue Weather.
Kavanagh, P. October.
Levertov. October.
Linden, M. October Is Here.
Ray, H. October.
Snyder, G. Late October Camping in the Sawtooths.
Thomas, D. Especially When the October Wind.
Poem in October.
Thomas, E. October.

Octopuses
Hilton, A. Octopus.
Merrill, J. Octopus, The.
Nash, O. Octopus, The.

Oedipus
Blackburn, T. Oedipus.
Ignatow, D. Oedipus.
Ray, H. Antigone and Oedipus.
Rukeyser, M. Myth.

Office Workers
Dawe, B. Beatitudes.

Ewart. Office Friendships.
Hope, M. Only Days.
Hummell, A. Saraband.
Madhubuti. Back Again, Home.
Newburn, L. Office Geraniums.
Page, P. Stenographers, The.
Roethke. Dolor.
See also **Clerks; Secretaries**

Officers, Military
Amherst. From a Young Woman to an Old Officer Who Courted Her.
Mackintosh, E. In Memoriam[, Private D. Sutherland].
Sassoon. Base Details.
Unknown. Lay of the Lash, The.

Ogres
Auden. August 1968.
Graves, R. Ogres and Pygmies.
See also **Monsters; Trolls**

Ohio (state)
Allbery. Produce.
Anania. Second-Hand Elegy, A.
Wright, J. At the Executed Murderer's Grave.
Autumn Begins in Martins Ferry, Ohio.
In Ohio.
In Response to a Rumor that the Oldest Whorehouse in Wheeling, West Virginia, Has Been Condemned.
Ohioan Pastoral.
Yamada. Cincinnati.

Ohio River
Emmett. Boatman's Dance.
Harper, F. Slave Mother, The.
Ransom, J. Antique Harvesters.
Wright, J. Three Sentences for a Dead Swan.

Oil
Ginsberg, A. Who Runs America?
North, C. Year of the Olive Oil, The.
Thurman. Oil Slick.

Oil Industry
Ginsberg, A. Who Runs America?

Oisin
Liddy. History.
Yeats. Old Man Stirs the Fire to a Blaze, An.

Okinawa, Japan
Schmitz. Picture of Okinawa, A.

Oklahoma (state)
Barnes, J. Captive Stone, The.
Harjo, J. Autobiography.
Stevens, W. Life Is Motion.

Old Age
Abse. Millie's Date.
Acholonu. Going Home.
Arnold, M. Growing Old.
Ashbery. Fear of Death.
Atwood. Daguerreotype Taken in Old Age.
Barber, M. To Mrs. Francis-Arabella Kelly.
Barnes, W. When We That Now Ha' Childern Wer Childern.
Belieu. How the Elderly Drive.
Bergman, A. Letter.
Betjeman. Senex.
Youth and Age on Beaulieu River, Hants.
Birney. My Love Is Young.
Blackburn, P. Phone Call to Rutherford.
Blake, W. In a Myrtle [or Mirtle] Shade.
Blunden. Almswomen.
Bogan, L. Crows, The.
Booth, P. Sixty-Six.
Bradley, G. E Pur Si Muove.
Brontë, E. Love and Friendship.
Brooks, G. Bean Eaters, The.
To An Old Black Woman, Homeless and Indistinct.
Brown, G. Old Women, The.
Browning, R. Rabbi Ben Ezra.
Byron, C. Minding You.
Campbell, J. Old Woman, The.
Cardiff. Grey Woman.
Carruth, H. Saturday at the Border.
Chandler, M. My Own Epitaph.
Chasin. City Pigeons.
Chesterton, G. Gold Leaves.
Clarke, C. Older American, The.

Clausen. After Touch.
Clive. Old Age.
Cofer, J. Old Women.
Coleridge, H. Long Time a Child.
Coleridge, S. Youth and Age.
Corbett, E. Three Wise Old Women.
Cornford, F. Childhood.
De la Mare. All That's Past.
Last Chapter, The.
Nod.
Old Men, The.
Old Susan.
Delmore, E. Difference, The.
Dixon, R. Both Less and More.
Donne. Canonization, The.
Dorsett, T. Survivor, The.
Dransfield. Pioneer Lane.
Dromgoole. Old Ladies.
Drown. To Mother.
Eliot, T. Gerontion.
Lines for an Old Man.
Emerson, R. Terminus.
Empson. To an Old Lady.
Everwine. Gray Poem.
Fairchild. Old Men Playing Basketball.
Feldman, I. Old Men, The.
Felltham [or Feltham]. To Phryne.
Fitzgerald, R. Song for September.
Fletcher, L. After Delivering Your Lunch.
Fritsch, H. How Old Are You?
Frost, R. Old Man's Winter Night, An.
Provide, Provide.
Gallagher, T. Each Bird Walking.
Garcia, R. Nobody Here But Us.
Gibson, W. Ice, The.
Gilsdorf, E. Walk, The.
Ginsberg, A. Not Dead Yet.
Gloria. Aleng Maria.
Googe. To Doctor Bale.
Graves, R. Broken Girth, The.
Grotesques.
Green, F. Old Couple, The.
Grenfell, J. Stately as a Galleon.
Grosholz. Old Fisherman, The.
Guevara, M. Long Distance.
Guiney. Open, Time.
"H., H. E." Riddle, The.
Hacker, M. Imaginary Translation.
Hardy, T. Ancient to Ancients, An.
He Never Expected Much.
I Look into My Glass.
Near Lanivet, 1872.
Harris, D. For My Father.
Hecht, A. Sarabande on Attaining the Age of Seventy-Seven.
Henry, J. Old Man.
Very Old Man.
Herbert, G. Forerunners, The.
Herd. Big Girls.
Herrick. His Age, Dedicated to His Peculiar Friend, Master John Wickes, under the Name of Posthumus.
On Himself[e].
On Himselfe.
To a Gentlewoman Objecting to Him His Grey Hairs.
To Perilla.
Hewitt, J. Local Poet, A.
Higgins, F. Old Jockey, The.
Holloway, G. Old Man.
Holmes, O. Last Leaf, The.
Poet Grows Old, The.
Hopkins, G. Leaden Echo and the Golden Echo, The.
Howard, R. After 65.
Howe, F. First Chance Twice.
Irving, M. Marching Still.
Jeffers, R. Age in Prospect.
Deer Lay Down Their Bones, The.
Fawn's Foster-Mother.
Promise of Peace.
Jenkins, N. Yr Iaith.
Jennings, E. One Flesh.
Johnson, F. Aunt Hannah Jackson.
Johnson, G. I Am Growing Old.
When You and I Were Young, Maggie.

Johnson, L. Seventies, The.
Jonas, G. Temporal.
Jones, R. Age.
Joseph, J. Warning.
Justice, D. Winter Ode to the Old Men of Lummus Park, Miami, Florida, A.
Keary. Old Age.
Kinsella, T. Tear.
Kipling, R. Old Men, The.
Kleinzahler. Hamburger.
Kooser. In the Basement of the Goodwill Store. Very Old, The.
Laing, K. Senior Lady Sells Garden Eggs.
Lamb, C. Old Familiar Faces, The.
Landor, W. Age.
Alas! 'Tis Very Sad to Hear.
Layton. Grand Finale.
Lea, S. Wrong Way Will Haunt You, The.
Lear, E. There was an Old Man who forgot.
Levertov. Old Adam, The.
Li Ch'ing-chao. Tune: "Pure Serene Music."
Linden, M. Life's Golden Sunset. Prospect of the Future, The.
Linton. Epicurean.
Loesser. They're Either Too Young or Too Old.
Loftin. Weeksville Women.
Longfellow, H. Nature.
Lowell, J. Auspex. Sixty-Eighth Birthday.
Lowell, R. Grandparents.
Mabuza. Tired Lizi Tired.
MacDiarmid, H. Old Wife in High Spirits. Wheesht, Wheesht.
Macdonald, G. Turn from Self.
Madgett. New Day.
Mahon. Refusal to Mourn, A.
Mangan, J. Twenty Golden Years Ago.
Mapanje. These Too Are Our Elders.
Marshall-Stoneking. Passage.
Masefield. On Growing Old.
Mason, R. Body of John.
Matthews, T. Cowboy Film.
Matthews, W. Grandmother, Dead at 99 Years and 10 Months.
Melville, H. Old Age in His Ailing.
Merrill, B. Staying Young.
Mew. À Quoi Bon Dire.
Meynell, A. Letter from a Girl to Her Own Old Age, A.
Milosz, C. Felicitous Life, A.
Montague, J. Like Dolmens Round My Childhood, the Old People.
Moolten, D. Voyeur.
Mother Goose. There was an old woman lived under a hill.
Mphande. Why the Old Woman Limps.
Murray, L. Widower in the Country, The.
Napier, F. I Have Taken the Suits and Shoes to Oxfam.
Nash, O. Come On In, the Senility Is Fine. Old Men.
Peekaboo, I Almost See You.
Portrait of the Artist as a Prematurely Old Man.
Nemerov. Brief Journey West, The.
Nesbit, E. Things That Matter, The.
Niatum. Apology.
Old Woman Awaiting the Greyhound Bus.
Nicholson, N. Halley's Comet.
O'Hara, F. In Hospital.
Oppen. Resort.
Outram. Annuity, The.
Owen, W. Parable of the Old Men and the Young, The.
Paley, G. Here. People in My Family.
Parker, D. Little Old Lady in Lavender Silk, The.
Parker, P. I Followed a Path.
Peacock, T. In Respect of the Elderly.
Philp-Carmichael. Dust Storm.
Platt, F. Coincidentally.
Po Chü-i. Looking in the Lake.
Pope, W. Old Man's Wish, The.
Pugh. Shoni Onions.
Ríos, A. Man Who Became Old, The.
Rakosi. Unswerving Marine.

Raleigh. Wishes of an Elderly Man[, Wished at a Garden Party, June 1914].
Randall, D. George.
Rands. Cat of Cats, The.
Ransom, J. Captain Carpenter. Piazza Piece.
Rector. My Grandfather Always Promised Us.
Reed, H. Chard Whitlow.
Reese, L. Old Belle, An.
Roberts, E. Mr. Wells.
Robinson, E. Mr Flood's Party.
Rochester, J. Song of a Young Lady to Her Ancient Lover, A.
Roethke. Infirmity.
Ross, C. Old Mothers.
Rowe, V. Youth.
Russell, N. Message of the Rain, The.
Salaam. Name the Oldest Member of Your Family.
Sallah, T. Elders Are Gods, The.
Satyamurti. Day Trip.
Schwartz, A. They're Either Too Young or Too Old.
Scott, W. Garland for Advancing Years, A.
Sharpless. Costa Geriatrica.
Simic. Old Couple.
Sitwell, D. Poet Laments the Coming of Old Age, The.
Smith, I. Old Woman. Old Woman, The.
Smith, M. Fall.
Smith, S. He Told His Life Story to Mrs. Courtly.
Snodgrass, W. April Inventory.
Southey, R. Old Man's Comforts and How He Gained Them, The. Remembrance.
Stafford, W. Strokes.
Steele, T. In the King's Rooms.
Stickney, T. Requiescam.
Strong, L. Old Dan'l. Zeke.
Su Tung-p'o. Verses: "I am old, sick and lonely."
Surrey. Laid in My Quiet Bed.
Swenson, M. How to Be Old.
Swift, J. Satirical Elegy on the Death of a Late Famous General, A.
Swirszczynska. Greatest Love, The. Second Madrigal, The. She Does Not Remember.
Talbot, N. Ballad of Old Women & of How They Are Constrained To Simulate Youth In Order To Avoid Shocking the Young.
Tannahill. Eild.
Teasdale. I Shall Live To Be Old. Long Hill, The. Moonlight.
Tennyson, A. Tithonus. Ulysses.
Tennyson, F. Old Age.
Thomas, D. Do Not Go Gentle into That Good Night.
Thomas, R. Lore. Survivor, The.
Thompson, P. Old Freedman, The.
Turberville. To an Old Gentlewoman That Painted Her Face.
Turner, A. Making Old Bones.
Unknown. My Mother's Hands.
Old Folks' Room, The.
Old Mother, The.
Old-Saxon Fragment.
On a Gentleman's Complaining to a Lady That He Could Not Eat Meat.
Somebody's Mother.
Will You Love Me When I'm Old?
Van Duyn. Falling in Love at Sixty-Five. Letters from a Father. Stream, The.
Vaux. Aged Lover Renounceth Love, The.
Waddington, M. Old Women of Toronto.
Walcott. Glory Trumpeter, The. Letter from Brooklyn, A.
Walker, A. Medicine.
Waller, E. Of the Last Verses in the Book.

Whitman, W. Centenarian's Story, The. Thanks in Old Age. To Old Age.
Williams, W. Last Words of My English Grandmother, The.
To a Poor Old Woman.
To an Old Jaundiced Woman.
To Waken an Old Lady.
Wilson, S. It's Never Too Late to Fall in Love.
Wordsworth, W. Animal Tranquillity and Decay.
Fountain, The.
Old Man by the Brook, The.
Old Man Travelling [Animal Tranquillity and Decay, a Sketch].
Simon Lee [the Old Huntsman].
Wright, F. Old, The.
Wright, J. Poem Written under an Archway in a Discontinued Railroad Station, Fargo, North Dakota, A.
Yates, J. Model Church, The.
Yeats. Acre of Grass, An.
Apparitions, The.
Coming of Wisdom with Time, The.
Lamentation of the Old Pensioner, The.
Old Men Admiring Themselves in the Water, The.
Sailing To Byzantium.
Scholars, The.
Spur, The.
Tower, The.
When You Are Old.
Wild Old Wicked Man, The.
Yevtushenko [or Evtushenko]. Saints of Jazz.
Young, G. Night Call.

See also **Pensions and Pensioners; Retirement and Retirees**

Oldham, John
Dryden, J. To the Memory of Mr Oldham.

Olive Trees and Olives
Hedin, R. At the Olive Grove of the Resistance.
Hemans. Olive Tree, The.
Housman, A. Olive, The.
North, C. Year of the Olive Oil, The.
Robinson, A. Tuscan Olives.
Spencer, B. Olive Trees.
Wilbur. Grasse: The Olive Trees.

Olympics
Fagg, M. Golden Road to Barcelona: 1992, The.

Omar Khayyám
Lowell, J. In a Copy of Omar Khayyám.

Omens
Angira. If.
Burns, R. Tam Glen.
Burr, A. Lynmouth Widow, A.
Graves, R. On Portents. Spoils.
Johnson, S. Comets and Princes.
"Malley." Sybilline.
Melville, H. Portent, The.
Mpondo. Season of the Rains, The.
Poe. Raven, The.
Stevenson, R. Ticonderoga: A Legend of the West Highlands.
Warren, R. Apology for Domitian.

Omnipotence
Murray, P. Canticle of the Void, The.
Scupham. Nondescript, The.
Sylvester, J. Father, The.

Onassis, Jacqueline Kennedy
Bowman, C. Jackie in Cambodia.
Herd. Pink Rose Rings, The.

Onions
Francis, R. Onion Fields.
Goodison. I Am Becoming My Mother.
Holman, B. Poem: "Once when I was little I knelt before an onion."
Matthews, W. Onions.
Moore, N. Song: "Little onion lay by the fireplace, A."
Nye, N. Traveling Onion, The.
Raine, C. Onion, Memory, The.

Ontario, Canada
Everson, R. Stranded in My Ontario.

Klein, A.   Winter Night: Mount Royal.
Ondaatje.   Burning Hills.
Purdy, A.   Country North of Belleville, The.
   Wilderness Gothic.

Ontario, Lake
Ray, H.   Thought of Lake Ontario, A.

Opera
Ade.   Il Janitoro.
Ashbery.   Faust.
Duran, J.   For the Woman Who Dressed Up to
   Listen to Gigli on the Radio.
Field, E.   Callas.
Levy, N.   Rigoletto.
   Tannhauser.
Merrill, J.   Matinees.
Moolten, D.   Madame Butterfly.

Ophelia
Pilling.   Ophelia.
Trethewey, N.   Bellocq's Ophelia.
Watkins, V.   Ophelia.

Opium
Coleridge, S.   Kubla Khan: or, A Vision in a
   Dream.
Hamilton, S.   Poppy, The.
Lowell, M.   Opium Fantasy, An.
O'Neill, H.   Ode to the Poppy.
Seward.   To the Poppy.
Tucker, M.   Evanishings.
   Opium-Eater, The.
Unknown.   Willie the Weeper.

Opossums
Levis.   Oldest Living Thing in L.A., The.
Unknown.   Carmen Possum.

Opportunity
Browning, R.   Youth and Art.
Carlyle, T.   Today.
Cofer, J.   Seizing the Day.
Davis, J.   You Turn Around.
Graham, H.   Opportunity.
Harburg.   When I'm Not Near the Girl I Love.
Hardy, T.   Midnight on the Great Western.
Jackson, H.   Opportunity.
Malone, W.   Opportunity.
Schwartz, R. L.   Edgewater Park.
   Possible.
Sill.   Opportunity.

Opposites
Emerson, R.   Brahma.
Graves, R.   In Broken Images.
Hoberman.   Folk Who Live in Backward Town,
   The.
Kipling, R.   Bonfires, The.
Melville, H.   Art.
Ruefle.   Topophilia.
Stevens, W.   Discovery of Thought, A.
Unknown.   Essay on Man.
Volkman.   Untitled: "If it be event, I go towards
   and not back. I go tower, not floor."
Wilbur.   Some Opposites.
   What is the opposite of nuts?

Oppression
Acam-Oturu.   Arise to the Day's Toil.
Aiyejina.   When the Monuments.
Alexie.   Vision (2).
Allen, L.   Rub a Dub Style inna Regent Park.
Ama Ata Aidoo.   Gynae One.
Amadiume.   Nok Lady in Terracotta.
   Oya Now.
   We Have Even Lost our Tongues!
Anzaldúa.   Horse.
Awoonor.   First Circle, The.
Ba.   Nobility.
Baca.   Oppression.
Bly, R.   Romans Angry about the Inner World.
Brecht, B.   World's One Hope, The.
Cervantes.   Poem for the Young White Man
   Who Asked Me How I, an Intelligent, Well-
   Read Person Could Believe in the War
   Between Races.
Cheney-Coker.   Analysis.
   Peasants.
   Poet Among Those Who Are Also Poets.
Chudleigh.   To the Ladies.
Corrothers.   Snapping of the Bow, The.
Crane, H.   Black Tambourine.

De Kok.   Our Sharpeville.
   Small Passing.
Dove, R.   Parsley.
El-Hadi, S.   Tired Man, The.
Espada.   Green and Red, Verde y Rojo.
Gardinier.   Admirals (Columbus).
Hagedon, J.   Song of Bullets, The.
Harper, F.   Ethiopia.
Harrison, T.   Earthen Lot, The.
Hawoldar.   You Have Touched My Skin.
Horne, N.   Note to My Liberal Feminist
   Sister, A.
Hughes, L.   Dream Boogie.
   I, Too.
Ignatow, D.   For Medgar Evers.
Inada.   Projected Scenario of a Performance to
   Be Given Before the UN.
Ismaili.   Lagos.
   Queue.
   Yet Still.
Jayaprabha.   Burn this Sari.
Jolobe.   Making of a Servant, The.
Jordan, J.   Intifada.
Kim, M.   Into Such Assembly.
Konie, G.   In the Fist of Your Hatred.
Laing, K.   Tatale Swine.
Lee, K.   On South Africa.
Macgoye.   August the First: The Watchman
   Speaks.
   Muffled Cry, A.
Madhubuti.   B Network, The.
   Killing Memory.
Mandel, T.   Say Ja.
Mandela.   I Have Tried Hard.
Mandelstam [*or* Mandelshtam].   I Was Washing
   Outside in the Darkness.
Mandiela, A.   Speshal Rikwes.
Manyarrows.   See No Indian, Hear No Indian.
Markham, E.   Man with the Hoe, The.
McKay, C.   Birds of Prey.
Milne, A.   Bad Sir Brian Botany.
Mnthali.   Stranglehold of English Lit, The.
Moraga.   For the Color of My Mother.
Moss, T.   Lessons from a Mirror.
Nelson, M.   Chopin.
Ofeimun.   Handle for the Flutist, A.
   New Brooms, The.
Olson, C.   Kingfishers, The.
Opoku-Agyemang.   King Tut in America.
Papertalk-Green, C.   Are We the Same.
Pasternak, B.   Highest Sickness, The.
Pegram, A.   I Will Still Sing.
   Mr. White Discoverer.
   Towards Abraham's Bosom.
Pietri.   Old Buildings, The.
Pound, E.   Commission.
Pratt, M.   Crime Against Nature.
Putnam.   Words of an Old Woman.
Reed, I.   Catechism of d Neoamerican Hoodoo
   Church.
Rich, A.   Burning of Paper instead of Children,
   The.
   Culture and Anarchy.
   From an Old House in America.
Rushin.   Black Back-Ups, The.
Sanchez, S.   On Watching a World Series Game.
Schneider, I.   History of the Caesars, A.
Sepamla.   I Remember Sharpeville.
Shapiro, K.   University.
Sigourney.   To the First Slave Ship.
Soyinka.   Apologia (Nkomati).
Sykes, B.   Prayer to the Spirit of the New Year.
Thelwall.   Vanity of National Grandeur, The.
Tindal.   Cry of the Oppressed, The.
Tolson, M.   Dark Symphony.
Troupe.   Boomerang: A Blatantly Political
   Poem.
Unger, B.   Observance.
Unknown.   Go Down, Old Hannah.
Washington.   Moon Bound.
Watkins, N.   Bedtime Story.
Wilcox, E.   Burdened.
Wong, N.   For an Asian Woman Who Says My
   Poetry Gives Her a Stomachache.
Woo, D.   Great Helmsman, The.
Yeats.   Fascination of What's Difficult, The.

Young, A.   Poem for Players, A.
Zulu, P.   You Are Mad: and I Mean It!

See also **Apartheid; Dehumanization; Sexism;**
   Slavery and Slaves; Tyranny

Optimism
Adams, L.   Put on a Happy Face.
Ager, M.   Happy Days Are Here Again.
Alexander, C.   All Things Bright and Beautiful.
Arlen, H.   Accentuate the Positive.
Bangs, J.   I Never Knew a Night So Black.
Barbour, D.   It's a Good Day.
Brown, L.   Sunny Side Up.
Cibber.   Blind Boy, The.
Clough.   Say Not the Struggle Nought Availeth.
Coleman, C.   Hey, Look Me Over.
Creeley.   Invitation, The.
DeSylva, B. G.   Look for the Silver Lining.
Eliscu, E.   Great Day.
Fields, D.   I'm Livin' in a Great Big Way.
   It's All Yours.
Gershwin.   Sunny Disposish.
   Things Are Looking Up.
Hammerstein.   Many a New Day.
   Oh, What a Beautiful Mornin'!
Jackson, L.   Toward the Corner.
Koehler, T.   When the Sun Comes Out.
McHugh, J.   I'm Livin' in a Great Big Way.
Morgan, E.   Second Life, The.
Nash, O.   Sweet Bye and Bye.
Reid, A.   Scotland.
Rolfe, E.   First Love.
Rose, B.   Great Day.
Rukeyser, M.   Yes.
Russell, G.   It Might Have Been Worse.
Schwartz, A.   It's All Yours.
Smith, S.   Away, Melancholy.
Sondheim.   Everything's Coming Up Roses.
Strouse, C.   Put on a Happy Face.
Teasdale.   Philosopher, The.
Unknown.   Brian O'Linn.
   High Resolve.
Wagner, C.   Let's Forget.

Oracles
Hooper, V.   Reading, A.
Housman, A.   Oracles, The.

Orange (color)
MacBeth [*or* Macbeth].   Orange Poem, The.
O'Hara, F.   Why I Am Not a Painter.

Orange Trees and Oranges
Amadiume.   Creation.
Jacobs, J.   Two Varieties of the Bitter Orange.
Nelson, J.   Never Eat Oranges!
Pelizzon, V.   Wedding Day, The.
Sitwell, S.   Red-Gold Rain, The.
Soto.   Oranges.
Tipton.   There Are Rivers of Oranges.

Oratory
Garioch.   Did Ye See Me?

Orchards
Barnes, W.   My Orcha'd in Linden Lea.
Doolittle, H.   Orchard.
Frost, F.   Deserted Orchard.
Kenney.   Plume.
Machej.   Orchards in July.
Masters, E.   Lost Orchard, The.
Oliver, M.   Through Ruddy Orchards.
Robinson, A.   Orchard at Avignon, An.
Sandburg, C.   Wind Song.
Spear, R.   Nest for Everyone, A.
Stevenson, A.   In the Orchard.
Stuart, M.   In the Orchard.
Tynan.   Of an Orchard.

Orchids
Doolittle, H.   At Baia.
Roethke.   Orchids.

Order
Ammons, A. R.   Corsons Inlet.
Creeley.   Window, The.
Eberhart, R.   Hard Structure of the World, The.
Herbert, G.   Family [*or* Familie], The.
Lowell, A.   Patterns.
Meredith, G.   Lucifer in Starlight.
Stevens, W.   Idea of Order at Key West, The.
   Sad Strains of a Gay Waltz.

Oregon (state)
Broumas, O.   Oregon Landscape with Lost
  Lover.
Kaufman, B.   Oregon.
Organs and Organists
Heard, J.   New Organ, The.
Lewis, D.   Lost Chord, The.
Lieberman, L.   Organist's Black Carnation, The.
Orient
Ginsberg, A.   After Yeats.
Ni Dhomhnaill.   Venio ex Oriente.
Taylor, B.   To a Persian Boy in the Bazaar at
  Smyrna.
Origami
Williamson, G.   Origami.
Original Sin
Nash, O.   Ha! Original Sin!
Unknown.   Adam Lay Ybounden [*or* I-
  bounden].
Vaughan, H.   Corruption.
Very.   Garden, The.
Warren, R.   Original Sin.
Orioles
Carmichael, H.   Baltimore Oriole.
Dunbar, P.   Summer in the South.
Kees.   Conversation in the Drawing Room, The.
Lowell, R.   Fall 1961.
Webster, P.   Baltimore Oriole.
Orion (constellation)
Rich, A.   Orion.
Turner, C.   Orion.
Orkney Islands
Fowler, W.   In Orknay.
Ormonde, Elizabeth Preston Butler, Countess of
Shirley, J.   To the Excellent Pattern of Beauty
  and Virtue, Lady Elizabeth, Countess of
  Ormonde.
Orphans
Barben, D.   Eight Beds, Eight Lockers.
Brontë, C.   Orphan Child, The.
Cervantes.   Refugee Ship.
Davis, G.   Orphan, The.
Ellis, T.   Atomic Bride.
Knott.   Christmas at the Orphanage.
Lampert, D.   Poem for Sophie.
Laughlin, J.   Kind-, The.
Linden, M.   Orphan Girl, An.
Martínez, V.   Traveler.
Murphy, P.   New Boy, The.
Nye, N.   At Mother Teresa's.
Riley, J.   Little Orphant Annie.
Ros.   Little Belgian Orphan, A.
Rossetti, C.   Iniquity of the Fathers upon the
  Children, The.
Unknown.   Babes in the Wood, The.
Orpheus
Carbó, N.   I Found Orpheus Levitating.
Gascoyne.   Orpheus in the Underworld.
Graham, J.   Orpheus and Eurydice.
  What the End Is For.
Herrick.   Orpheus.
Hill, G.   Orpheus and Eurydice.
Kinsella, J.   Orpheus.
Lisle.   Power of Music, The.
Lovelace, R.   Orpheus to Beasts.
  Orpheus to Woods.
Pastan.   Orpheus.
Perry, S.   Orpheus.
Rich, A.   I Dream I'm the Death of Orpheus.
Rukeyser, M.   Poem as Mask, The.
Spenser.   Epithalamion: "Ye learned sisters
  which have oftentimes."
Valentine, J.   Orpheus and Eurydice.
Winchilsea.   Answer, The.
Winters, Y.   Orpheus.
Osmond, Marie
Skelley.   To Marie Osmond.
Ospreys
Wheelock, J.   Fish-Hawk, The.
Ostriches
Freeman, M.   Ostrich Is a Silly Bird, The.
Lovelace, R.   Lucasta's Fan[ne], with a
  Looking-Glass[e] in It.
Moore, M.   He "Digesteth Harde Yron."

Nwankwo.   Poem: "In sand."
Ottawa, Ontario
Kleinzahler.   Spleen.
Otterburn, Battle of (1388)
Unknown.   Battle of Otterburn [*or* Oterborne],
  The.
Otters
Hartnett.   Possibility That Has Been Overlooked
  Is the Future, The.
  Wounded Otter, The.
Heaney, S.   Otter, The.
Hughes, T.   Otter, An.
Mac Low.   Giant Otters.
  Giant Philosophical Otters.
Swenson, M.   Waterbird.
Ouija Boards
Merrill, J.   Voices from the Other World.
Outlaws
Darley.   Free-booter, The.
See also **Crime and Criminals**
Ovenbirds
Frost, R.   Oven Bird, The.
Ovid (Publius Ovidius Naso)
Gardelle, C.   Peaceful Sunday.
Hill, G.   Ovid in the Third Reich.
Jones, D.   Summer Is a Poem by Ovid.
Leon, E.   On the Second Tristia of Ovid.
Prior.   Written in an Ovid.
Ransom, J.   Philomela.
Walcott.   Hotel Normandie Pool, The.
Owen, Wilfred
Hughes, T.   Wilfred Owen's Photographs.
Owls
Bishop, E.   Song for the Rainy Season.
De la Mare.   Owl, The.
Duncan, R.   Sentinels, The.
Espada.   Owl and the Lightning, The.
Ewart.   Owl Writes a Detective Story, The.
Fields, J.   Owl-Critic, The.
Frost, R.   Questioning Faces.
Haines, J.   If the Owl Calls Again.
Harwood, G.   Father and Child.
Hollander, J.   Owl.
Hubbell, P.   Owl of the Greenwood.
Hughes, T.   Owl's Song.
Jarrell.   Bird of Night, The.
Lardner.   Hail to Thee, Blithe Owl.
Lear, E.   Children of the Owl and the Pussy-Cat,
  The.
  Owl and the Pussy-Cat, The.
  There Was an Old Man with a Beard.
MacBeth [*or* Macbeth].   Owl.
Mezey.   Owl.
Moss, T.   Owl in Daytime, The.
Munkittrick.   Song of the Owl, The.
Norris, L.   Barn Owl.
Plath.   Owl.
Richards, E.   Wise Old Owl, A.
Russell, T.   To the Owl.
Schuyler, J.   Korean Mums.
Shelley, P.   Aziola, The.
Smith, D.   Sea Owl.
Spireng, M.   Snowy Owl.
Stevens, W.   On the Adequacy of Landscape.
Tennyson, A.   Owl, The.
Thomas, E.   Owl, The.
Thomas, R.   Ancients of the World, The.
  Still.
Unknown.   Boy in the Barn, The.
  Limerick.
  Sweet Suffolk Owl.
Wells, N.   Owl Wives.
Winchilsea.   Nocturnal Reverie, A.
Oxen
Davis, D.   Christmas Poem, A.
Dyer, J.   My Ox Duke.
Edson, R.   Ox, The.
Hamilton, G.   Old Ox, The.
Hardy, T.   Oxen, The.
Monroe, H.   Meeting, The.
Simpson, L.   White Oxen.
Tomlinson, C.   Oxen: Ploughing at Fiesole.
Whitman, W.   Ox-Tamer, The.
Oxford, England
Arnold, M.   Scholar Gypsy, The.

Auden.   Oxford.
Grigson.   Above the High.
Hopkins, G.   Duns Scotus's Oxford.
Keats.   On Oxford.
Letts.   Spires of Oxford, The.
Ransom, J.   Philomela.
Russell, T.   To Oxford.
Oysters
Drummond, W.   Oister, The.
Heaney, S.   Oysters.
Howard, R.   Oystering.
  Wildflowers.
Ponge.   Oyster, The.
Porter, C.   Tale of the Oyster, The.
Swift, J.   Oysters.
See also **Clams and Clamming; Shells**

P

Pacific Ocean
Curnow.   Pacific 1945–1995.
Frost, R.   Once by the Pacific.
Gunn, T.   Discovery of the Pacific, The.
Harms.   Elegy as Evening, as Exodus.
Jeffers, R.   Eye, The.
Silko.   Prayer to the Pacific.
Wakoski.   Remembering the Pacific.
Whitman, W.   Facing West from California's
  Shores.
Winters, Y.   On Teaching the Young.
  Slow Pacific Swell, The.
Wright, C.   Looking West from Laguna Beach at
  Night.
Pacifism and Pacifists
Belloc.   Pacifist, The.
Crosby, E.   Military Creed, The.
Cummings, E.   I Sing of Olaf Glad and Big.
Ezekiel.   Patriot, The.
Kasdorf.   Mennonites.
Lowell, R.   After the Surprising Conversions.
  Christmas Eve under Hooker's Statue.
  Memories of West Street and Lepke.
Michie.   Dooley Is a Traitor.
Millay, E.   Conscientious Objector.
Newbolt.   Non-Combatant, The.
Palmer, R. F.   Conchie, The.
Shapiro, K.   Conscientious Objector, The.
Tremblay, B.   Home Front.
Unknown.   Hymn: "O God of Hosts, Thine Ear
  incline."
Whittier.   Brown of Ossawatomie.
See also **Conscientious Objectors**
Paganism and Pagans
"Field."   Fellowship.
Tabb.   Christ and the Pagan.
Wordsworth, W.   World Is Too Much with Us,
  The.
Pain
"Æ."   Pain.
Adamson.   Passing Through Experiences.
Aldrich, T.   Lycidas.
Armantrout.   Winter.
Baraka.   Agony, An. As Now.
Benson, L.   P Word Poem, The.
Berger, D.   Language Pile, The.
Brontë, E.   God of Visions.
  If grief for grief can touch thee.
Bruner.   Gift, The.
Bryant, W.   Mutation.
Carew, T.   To My Inconstant Mistress [*or*
  Mistris].
Carson, C.   Knee, The.
Cassian.   Blood, The.
Ceravolo.   Conception.
Chipasula.   Talking of Sharp Things.
Clare, J.   Love's Pains.
Coleridge, S.   Dejection: An Ode.
Cooper, D.   10 Dead Friends.
Couzyn.   Pain, The.
Coward.   Never Again.
Crapsey.   Release.
Creeley.   Flower, The.
Cristall.   Written When the Mind Was
  Oppressed.

Cullen, C. Saturday's Child.
Song in Spite of Myself.
Di Prima. For H. D.
Dickinson, E. Final Inch, The.
I Can Wade Grief.
Pain Has an Element of Blank.
Wounded Deer Leaps Highest, A.
Duhamel. I'm Dealing with My Pain.
Empson. Villanelle: "It is the pain, it is the pain, endures."
"Ephelia." To J. G.
Gardinier. Democracy.
Goodman, P. In the Jury Room, in Pain.
Graham-Pole, J. Pain, The.
Grahn. Funeral Plainsong from a Younger Woman to an Older Woman, A.
Greenwell, D. Broken Chain, The.
Grosholz. Back Trouble.
Gunn, T. Innocence.
Man With Night Sweats, The.
Painkillers.
Gurney, I. Mangel-Bury, The.
Hans. Hurt.
Hartnett. I Have Exhausted the Delighted Range.
I Think Sometimes.
Hayden, R. Road in Kentucky, A.
Whipping, The.
Henry, J. Pain.
Hongo. O-Bon: Dance for the Dead.
Howe, F. First Chance Twice.
Hughes, F. Different Voice, The.
Hughes, L. Dream Boogie: Variation.
Jarrell. 90 North.
Johnson, L. Reggae Sounds.
Kaufman, S. Security.
Keats. Ode to a Nightingale.
Kinsella, J. Archetypal Chillies.
Larcom. They Said.
Larkin, J. Rape.
Levertov. Ache of Marriage, The.
Levy, A. Cambridge in the Long.
Limburg, J. Queen of Swords, The.
Lovelace, R. To Lucasta.
Macgoye. August the First; Court Martial. The Mother Speaks.
Mackenzie, K. Hospital—Retrospections, The.
Martinez, D. Pain.
McDaniel, J. Disasterology.
McDonald, C. Cheers.
McGough, R. Poem With a Limp.
Merry. Adieu and Recall to Love, The.
Mew. In Nunhead Cemetery.
Meynell, V. Sympathy.
Moss, H. Wars, The.
Murray, L. Cotton Flannelette.
Nelson, M. Shiner.
Wish.
Noguchi, R. From Rooftops, Kenji Takezo Throws Himself.
O'Donnell, C. Process.
Security.
Owen, W. Greater Love.
Hospital Barge at Cérisy.
Park, S. On Such A Day.
Piercy. When a Friend Dies.
Pogson, P. Apples.
Pound, E. Long Wind, the Dawn Wind.
Procter, A. Lost Chord, A.
Ramanujan. Pleasure.
Rich, A. Splittings.
Robinson, E. Pain.
Robinson, M. Her Confirmed Despair.
Ros. End of 'Pain,' The.
Rossetti, C. Chilly Night, A.
Introspective.
Roy, L. Triple Overtime.
Sandburg, C. At a Window.
Sarton. Tortured, The.
Scamell, B. Party, The.
Stranger to a Small Child.
Seibert. Casey Jones.
Shapiro, K. Hospital.
Smith, S. Lads of the Village, The.
Soyinka. Fado Singer.
Suckling, S. Love's Offence.

Song: "I prithee spare me, gentle boy."
Szporluk. Triage.
Thomas, C. Heart Wounds.
Thompson, C. After-Glow of Pain, The.
Townsend, A. Bicycle Racers, The.
Wayne, J. By Accident.
Wetzsteon. Surgical Moves.
Three Songs.
Urban Gallery.
Whitman, W. I Sit and Look Out.
Wilcox, E. Life.
Solitude.
Those We Love the Best.
Williams, C. Alzheimer's: The Wife.
Williams, M. Thinking about Bill, Dead of AIDS.
Wordsworth, W. Complaint, A.
Wright, J. Prayer to the Lord Ramakrishna, A.
Wunderlich, M. From a Vacant House.
Wyrebek, M. Recovery.
Young, A. Detroit 1958.

Paine, Thomas
Freneau. On Mr. Paine's Rights of Man.
Mather, J. God Save Great Thomas Paine.

Painting and Painters
Agran, R. Wearing Dad's White Shirt Backwards.
Ai. Back in the World.
Alexander, E. Painting / (Frida Kahlo).
Ash, J. Poor Boy: Portrait of a Painting.
Ashbery. Painter, The.
Auden. Musée des Beaux Arts.
Baraka. Politics of Rich Painters, The.
Baxter, C. Diptych: Jesus and the Stone.
Berryman. Winter Landscape.
Bishop, E. Large Bad Picture.
Poem: "About the size of an old-style dollar bill."
Bishop, J. Recollection, A.
Blake, W. Sir Joshua Reynolds.
Boland, E. From the Painting "Back from Market" by Chardin.
I Remember.
Self-Portrait on a Summer Evening.
Bonds, D. Life of the Body, The.
Boruch. Light.
Brooks, S. Poem by a Perfectly Furious Academician.
Browning, R. Andrea del Sarto.
Face, A.
Fra Lippo Lippi.
Guardian-Angel, The.
Pictor Ignotus.
Bryant, W. To Cole, the Painter, Departing for Europe.
Byron, C. Shipping the Pictures from Belfast.
Cage. 25 Mesostics Re and Not Re Mark Tobey.
Carpenter, W. Evening Wind.
Night Shadows.
Carter, A. B. Cobb's Barns.
Cary, A. Katrina on the Porch.
Cassells. These Are Not Brushstrokes.
Channing. Murillo's Magdalen.
Cheng Hsieh. For Contemporary Artist Pien Wei-Ch'I.
Clarke, J. Early Unfinished Sketch.
Conquest. Rokeby Venus, The.
Coolidge, C. Jerome in His Study.
Copus, J. Masaccio's *Expulsion from Paradise*.
Corso. Rembrandt—Self Portrait.
Cranch. My Old Palette.
Crane, H. Sunday Morning Apples.
Crashaw. Flaming Heart, The.
Upon the Book and Picture of the Seraphical Saint Teresa.
Cronin, A. Lines for a Painter.
Curbelo. Bedtime Stories.
Dreaming Horse.
Curtis, T. Portrait of the Painter Hans Theo Richter and His Wife Gisela in Dresden, 1933.
Drake, J. National Painting, The.
Duhamel. Art.
Dunn, S. Impediment.
Duroux, M. Dirge for a Hidden Art.
Dyer, E. Painting the Nude.

Elton, W. Hopper: In the Cafe.
Enright, D. Laughing Hyena, after [*or* by] Hokusai, The.
Ferlinghetti, L. Don't Let That Horse.
Ferry. Cythera.
"Field." L'indifférent.
La Gioconda; Leonardo Da Vinci, The Louvre.
Portrait, A.
Finch, P. How Callum Innes Paints.
Georgiou, E. From Where I Stand.
Gilder, R. Hour in a Studio, An.
Glassco. Cardinal's Dog, The.
Graham, J. At Luca Signorelli's Resurrection of the Body.
Greger. Man on the Bed, The.
Guest, B. Wild Gardens Overlooked by Night Lights.
Guevara, M. Easter Revolt Painted on a Tablespoon, The.
Long Woman Bathing, The.
Make-Up.
Gunn, T. In Santa Maria del Popolo.
Harper, M. Zocalo.
Hearne, V. Gauguin's White Horse.
Hecht, A. At the Frick.
Death the Painter.
Herrera. Yellow Room, The.
Herrick. Upon Umber: Epigram.
Hirsch, E. Edward Hopper and the House by the Railroad.
Hirschman, J. Painting, The.
Hirshfield, J. Painting.
Hollander, J. Edward Hopper's Seven A.M.
Sunday A.M. Not in Manhattan.
Howard, R. Giovanni da Fiesole on the Sublime.
Hughes, T. To Paint a Water Lily.
Hugo, R. Milltown Union Bar, The.
Jacob, M. In Honor of the Sardana and the Tenora.
Jennings, E. Christ Seen by Flemish Painters.
Johnson, J. Before a Painting.
Johnston, M. Sea-Cucumber, The.
Justice, D. Anonymous Drawing.
On a Painting by Patient B of the Independence State Hospital for the Insane.
Kates. No Altarpiece.
Kenny, M. Still-Life.
Lawrence, D. Innocent England.
Levertov. For Those Whom the Gods Love Less.
Longley, M. Man Lying on a Wall.
Lothamer. Be a Painter.
Love, B. Bryan Ferry.
Lovelace, R. Painture [*or* Peinture].
To My Worthy Friend Mr. Peter Lely [*or* Lilly].
Lowell, R. Epilogue: "Those blessed structures, plot and rhyme."
Ludvigson. Inventing My Parents.
Markham, E. Man with the Hoe, The.
Mathias, R. Memling.
McClatchy. Capriccio of Roman Ruins and Sculpture with Figures, A.
McGuckian. Sitting, The.
Melville, H. Bench of Boors, The.
Fruit and Flower Painter.
Mezey. Evening Wind.
Mitchell, S. Vermeer.
Monroe, H. Rubens.
Moore, H. Girl in a Fur-Trimmed Dress.
Mueller, L. American Literature.
Monet Refuses the Operation.
Nude by Edward Hopper, A.
Muldoon, P. Bearded Woman, by Ribera, The.
Nemerov. Old Picture, An.
Niatum. In the Labyrinth of Elements.
Nungarrayi, J. Sorry.
O'Hara, F. Having a Coke with You.
Why I Am Not a Painter.
Oates. Edward Hopper's Nighthawks, 1942.
Opie. To Mr. Opie, On His Having Painted for Me the Picture of Mrs Twis.
Ormond. Certain Questions for Monsieur Renoir.
Ostriker. Minor Van Gogh (He Speaks), A.
Palmer, M. Dearest Reader.

Pinkerton, H.　On Vermeer's "Young Woman with a Water Jug" (1658) in the Metropolitan Museum.
Plumly.　After Whistler.
Quagliano.　Edward Hopper's 'Lighthouse at Two Lights.'
Raab, L.　After Edward Hopper.
Ray, D.　Automat.
　Midnight Diner by Edward Hopper, A.
　On a Fifteenth-Century Flemish Angel.
Revell.　Fauviste.
Ridler.　Backgrounds to Italian Paintings: Fifteenth Century.
Rodriguez, J.　Nu-plastik Fanfare Red.
Rossetti, C.　In An Artist's Studio.
Rossetti, D.　For "An Allegorical Dance of Women" by Andrea Mantegna.
　For A Venetian Pastoral by Giorgone (In the Louvre).
　For Spring by Sandro Botticelli.
　Marriage of St. Katharine, by the same; in the Hospital of St. John at Bruges.
　On the Painter Val Prinsep.
　Same, The.
　Virgin and Child, by Hans Memmeling; in the Academy of Bruges, A.
Rowlands.　Epigram 29: "Gentlewoman of the dealing trade, A."
Rudolf.　Edward Hopper.
Rukeyser, M.　Birth of Venus, The.
　Painters.
Salmon, A.　Painting.
Salter.　Young Girl Peeling Apples.
Sanders, E.　Cutting Prow, The.
Schulman.　American Solitude.
Scott, J.　Helen Paints a Room (1984).
Shapiro, K.　Dome of Sunday, The [or A].
Smith, V.　At an Exhibition of Historical Paintings, Hobart.
Snodgrass, W.　Matisse: "The Red Studio."
Song.　Beauty and Sadness.
Standing.　Hopper's Women.
Stickney, T.　In Ampezzo.
　On Sandro's Flora.
Stone, J.　Early Sunday Morning.
Swenson, M.　Painting the Gate.
Szymborska.　Women of Rubens, The.
Thomas, R.　View from the Window, The.
Tomlinson, C.　Farewell to Van Gogh.
　Paring the Apple.
Townsend, A.　Rouge.
Trethewey, N.　Bellocq's Ophelia.
Very.　Sumach Leaves, The.
Violi.　Hazards of Imagery, The.
　Index.
Wade, S.　Gas.
Wat.　Facing Bonnard.
Weiners.　Poem for Painters, A.
Weiss, T.　Ten Little Rembrandts.
Wharton, E.　Two Backgrounds.
Wheatley, P.　To S.M., a Young African Painter, on Seeing His Works.
White, E.　I Paint What I See.
Whitman, W.　Death's Valley.
Wilbur.　Museum Piece.
　My Father Paints the Summer.
Williams, W.　Adoration of the Kings, The.
　Dance, The.
　Haymaking.
　Hunters in the Snow, The.
　Landscape with the Fall of Icarus.
　Parable of the Blind, The.
　Self-Portrait.
Williamson, A.　Light's Reading, The.
Wilson, S.　Picture on the Purple Wall, The.
Wordsworth, W.　Elegiac Stanzas Suggested by a Picture of Peele Castle, in a Storm, Painted by Sir George Beaumont.
Wunderlich, M.　Thirst.
Wyatt, S.　In Spayn.
Wylie.　Castilian.
Yellen.　Nighthawks.
Young, G.　Miracle, The.

Paleontology and Paleontologists
Harte, B.　Society upon the Stanislaus, The.
Lee, E.　Forests and Caverns.

"Twain."　Imitation of Julia A. Moore.
See also **Dinosaurs; Evolution; Extinction; Fossils**
Palestine
Byron, G.　On Jordan's Bank.
Kaufman, S.　Security.
Michelson, R.　Faraway Landscape.
Ravikovitch [*or* Ravikovich].　You Can't Kill a Baby Twice.
Samaras, N.　Notes in Jerusalem.
Shapiro, M.　To Jerusalem, 1990.
Turki, F.　Being a Good *Americani*.
　Moments of Ridicule and Love.
See also **Israel**
Palm Sunday
Chesterton, G.　Donkey, The.
Symons, A.　Palm Sunday: Naples.
Palm Trees
Agard, J.　Palm Tree King.
Campion, T.　Thus I Resolve.
Crane, H.　Royal Palm.
Cuney.　No Images.
Hemans.　Palm-tree, The.
Melville, H.　Rolfe and the Palm.
Stevens, W.　Of Mere Being.
Whittier.　Palm-Tree, The.
Pan (god)
Browning, E.　Flush or Faunus.
　Musical Instrument, A.
Byron, G.　Aristomenes.
"Cornwall."　Sonnet; A Still Place.
Emerson, R.　Patient Pan, The.
Farrar, J.　Song for a Forgotten Shrine to Pan.
Frost, R.　Pan with Us.
Kyger.　Pan as the Son of Penelope.
Marvell.　Clorinda and Damon.
Robinson, A.　Valley, The.
Shelley, P.　Hymn of Pan.
Van den Bergh.　Nocturn: "Moon rows burning, The."
Wilmer, S.　Mess Boy, The.
Panama
Sylvain, P.　Panama.
Unknown.　Golden Island, The; or, the Darian Song.
Pancakes
Agran, R.　Cakes Continue to Rise.
Prelutsky.　Pancake Collector, The.
Rossetti, C.　Mix a Pancake.
Taylor, B.　Those Flapjacks of Brown's.
Pansies
Binyon.　Harebell and Pansy.
Pantheism and Pantheists
Bryant, W.　Thanatopsis.
Kavanagh, P.　One, The.
Naden.　Pantheist's Song of Immortality, The.
Ortiz.　Creation.
Tennyson, A.　Higher Pantheism, The.
Wordsworth, W.　It is a beauteous evening.
Panthers
Nash, O.　Panther, The.
Whitmore, S.　Lenaia.
Papacy
Housman, A.　Pope, The.
See also **Catholicism and Catholics**
Paperweights
Schnackenberg.　Paperweight, The.
Parachuting and Parachutists
Unknown.　Tatton Parachute Training School.
See also **Sky Diving and Sky Divers**
Parades
Berlin.　Easter Parade.
Cocteau.　Fairy Scene.
Harte, B.　Second Review of the Grand Army, A.
Herman, J.　Before the Parade Passes By.
Knight, S.　Big Parade, The.
Merrill, B.　Don't Rain on My Parade.
Revard.　Parading with the Veterans of Foreign Wars.
Sassoon.　Suicide in [the] Trenches.
Stevenson, R.　Young Night Thought.
Styne, J.　Don't Rain on My Parade.
Whitman, W.　Boston Ballad [1854], A.
Willson, M.　Seventy Six Trombones.

See also **Marching and Marches**
Paradise
Borodin, A.　Stranger in Paradise.
Hays, H.　January.
Herbert, G.　Paradise.
Kipling, R.　L'Envoi.
Laux.　If This Is Paradise.
Levertov.　Contraband.
Muir, E.　Milton.
Shirley, J.　Garden, The.
Southwell.　Seek[e] Flowers of Heaven.
Stewart, S.　Apple.
Tomlinson, C.　John Maydew or The Allotment.
Very.　Nature.
Wright, C.　Appalachian Book of the Dead III, The.
Yeats.　Running to Paradise.
See also **Heaven**
Paradise Lost
Marvell.　On Mr Milton's "Paradise Lost."
Muir, E.　Milton.
See also **Milton, John**
Paradoxes
Ashbery.　Paradoxes and Oxymorons.
Creeley.　Time.
Devaney, T.　American Pragmatist Fell in Love, The.
Eberhart, R.　Hardy Perennial.
Gallagher, T.　Not There.
Hart, L.　I Wish I Were in Love Again.
Hewison.　Limerick: "Said an erudite sinologue: 'How.'"
Stafford, W.　Report from an Unappointed Committee.
Parakeets
Karp.　Harm.
Paralysis
Eliot, T.　Love Song of J. Alfred Prufrock, The.
Mörling, M.　For the Woman with the Radio.
Paranoia
Butts, A.　Poe Story, A.
Charara, H.　Thinking American.
Colby, T.　Boy and the Girl, The.
Musgrave.　I Am Not a Conspiracy Everything Is Not Paranoid The Drug Enforcement Administration Is Not Everywhere.
Sexton.　Noon Walk on the Asylum Lawn.
Spicer, J.　Conspiracy.
Strand.　Tunnel, The.
Parenthood
Adams, L.　Kids!
Awad, J.　Generations.
Bock, J.　Sunrise, Sunset.
Buckley, V.　Parents.
Burns, R.　Poet's Welcome to His Love-Begotten Daughter [the First Instance that Entitled Him to the Venerable Appellation of Father], A.
Coleridge, S.　Sonnet to a Friend Who Asked How I Felt When the Nurse First Presented My Infant to Me.
Dove, R.　Daystar.
Duhig, I.　First Second, The.
Emmott, K.　Who Looks after Your Kids?
Finkel.　Father, The.
Gilmore, M.　Nationality.
Hadas, R.　Red Hat, The.
Hammerstein.　Soliloquy.
Harnick.　Sunrise, Sunset.
Harwood, G.　In the Park.
Hecht, A.　Adam.
Herbert, W.　Baby Poem Industry Poem, The.
Hoffman, D.　Special Train, A.
Hood, T.　Parental Ode to My Son, Aged Three Years and Five Months, A.
Housman, A.　Fragment of an English Opera.
Jonson, B.　On My First Daughter.
Kinnell.　After Making Love We Hear Footsteps.
Kizer, C.　Parents' Pantoum.
Kooser.　At the End of the Weekend.
Lorde.　What My Child Learns of the Sea.
Madgett.　Offspring.
McGinley.　Velvet Hand, The.
McLain, P.　Connor in the Wind and Rain with

His Coat On.
Oppenheimer, J. Father Poem.
Osgood, F. Ellen Learning to Walk.
Plath. Morning Song.
Rich, A. Afterwake, The.
Ridler. For a Child Expected.
Rodgers, R. Soliloquy.
Salzman, E. Double Crossing.
Smith, D. August, on the Rented Farm.
Stafford, W. With Kit, Age Seven, at the Beach.
Strouse, C. Kids!
Taylor, E. Upon Wedlock and Death of Children.
Traherne. Rapture, The.
Unknown. Little Chap Who Follows Me, The.
Walker, J. Studying Physics with My Daughter.
Weaver, M. Improvisation for Piano.
Wesley, S. Anacreontic, on Parting with a Little Child.
Whittemore, R. Party, The.
Yeats. Prayer for My Daughter, A.

Parents
Ali, A. Dream of Glass Bangles, A.
  Houses.
Bartlett, E. God Is Dead—Nietzche.
Berger, B. Without.
Berryman. Sympathy, A Welcome, A.
Bly, R. For My Son Noah, Ten Years Old.
Brummer, N. That Rank Bed.
Byron, C. Shipping the Pictures from Belfast.
Casterton, J. One Flesh.
Causley. Eden Rock.
Ciardi. Censorship.
  Sometimes Even Parents Win.
Claman, E. Show Biz Parties.
Cook, E. Written at the Couch of a Dying Parent.
Coolidge, C. Album—A Runthru.
"Cornwall." To My Child.
Curbelo. Photograph of My Parents.
Davies, H. Beachy Head.
Elliot, A. Latitudes of Home, The.
Ellis, T. Kiss in the Dark, A.
Emanuel, L. Sleeping, The.
Ferlinghetti, L. Lost Parents.
Galvin, P. My Father Spoke with Swans.
Gbadamosi. Reading, The.
Gershon. I Was Not There.
Glück, R. Invaders from Mars.
Golding, N. Wardrobes.
Graves, R. Parent to Children.
Grosholz. Eden.
Gwynn, R. Drive-In, The.
Hall, D. My Son, My Executioner.
Hamod, S. Leaves.
Holmes, D. Nostalgia.
Hongo. Hongo Store 29 Miles Volcano Hilo, Hawaii, The.
Jarrell. Player Piano, The.
Kalia, M. After Eight Years of Marriage.
Kapos, M. Pulse, The.
Kinnell. Lackawanna.
Krayer, S. My Mother Dressed for the Wedding.
Kunitz, S. Quinnapoxet.
Larkin, P. This Be the Verse.
Laughlin, J. Step on His Head.
Lawrence, P. Hit Men, The.
Lee, D. Billy Batter.
  There Was a Man.
Ludvigson. Inventing My Parents.
MacDiarmid, H. Two Parents, The.
McAuley, J. Because.
McCarthy, T. Mr. Nabokov's Memory.
Merrill, J. Broken Home, The.
  Childlessness.
Mesmer, S. My Life in Yonago.
Mirikitani. Suicide Note.
Morley, H. Parents.
Moses, G. Black Banana House.
Muldoon, P. Mixed Marriage, The.
Nash, O. Parent, The.
Newman, G. Photograph of Survivors.
Olds, S. I Go Back to May 1937.
Oppen. Sara in Her Father's Arms.
Palis, Y. Floor, The.

Parker, P. Prologue from "Legacy."
Rosenberg, L. Which One Is the Grown-up? Haiku.
Rosenblatt, S. Mom and Dad Getting Older.
Rottman. APO 96225.
Rumens. Before These Wars.
Satyamurti. Where Are You?
Schneider, M. Photograph, The.
Seiler. Digging in the Streets of Gold.
Silverstein, S. Clarence.
Simic. Book Full of Pictures, A.
Simpson, L. My Father in the Night Commanding No.
Stafford, W. Story That Could Be True, A.
  With Kit, Age Seven, at the Beach.
Ullman. Why There Are Children.
Unknown. Limerick.
Vasquez, R. For Jose Mercado Vasquez and Frances Roman Vasquez.
Walker, F. X. Wishbone.
Wallace, R. Facts of Life, The.
Watson, E. Battered Toddler, Page B6.
Whalen. "Never Apologize; Never Explain."
Zinnemann-Hope. Taking Tea with My Father and Mother.

Paris, France
Apollinaire. Monday rue Christine.
  Zone.
Belieu. At St. Sulpice.
Boyle, K. Complaint for M and M, A.
Cendrars. Contrasts.
  Prose of the Trans-Siberian and Little Jean of France.
Clover, J. Ceriserie.
Cranch. In the Palais Royal Garden.
Cummings, E. Two X.
Dipoko. From My Parisian Diary.
  Poem of Villeneuve St Georges, A.
Donaldson, W. How 'Ya Gonna Keep 'Em Down on the Farm? (After They've Seen Paree).
Dove, R. Bistro Styx, The.
  Island Women of Paris, The.
Duke, V. April in Paris.
Fain, S. I'll Be Seeing You.
Fenton, J. In Paris with You.
Frishberg, D. Another Song About Paris.
Garlick, R. Capitals.
Gordon, M. Mam'selle.
Hammerstein. Last Time I Saw Paris, The.
Harburg. April in Paris.
Hinsey, E. Art of Measuring Light, The.
Hochman. Sphinxes.
Huidobro. Blind.
  Eiffel Tower.
  Morning.
Kahal, I. I'll Be Seeing You.
Kern, J. Last Time I Saw Paris, The.
Leland, C. Breitmann in Paris.
Lerner, A. Paris Is Paris Again.
Loewe, F. Paris Is Paris Again.
Maschwitz, E. Paris Is Not the Same.
Millay, E. Armenonville.
Miller, J. In Père La Chaise.
Osofisan. Paris Latin Quarter.
Piatt, S. Palace-Burner, The.
Porter, C. You Don't Know Paree.
Pound, E. In a Station of the Metro.
Ransom, J. Amphibious Crocodile.
Rivers, C. Four Sheets to the Wind and a One-Way Ticket to France.
  Mourning Letter from Paris, A.
Senghor. In Memoriam.
  Luxembourg 1939.
Strachey, J. Paris Is Not the Same.
Symons, A. Paris.
Thackeray. Ballad of Bouillabaisse, The.
Tzara. For Robert Desnos.
Wilbur. Place Pigalle.
Young, A. Dance of the Infidels.
  One Snapshot I Couldn't Take in France, The.

Parker, Charlie
Ashanti. Just Another Gig.
Barlow, G. Mingus Speaks: Found Poems.
Brathwaite, E. Blues.
Brown, A. Assassination of Charlie Parker, The.

Crouch, S. Up on the Spoon.
Dodson, O. Yardbird's Skull.
Finnell. Over *Voice of America.*
France, L. Blues for Bird.
Harjo, J. Bird.
Hull, L. Ornithology.
Jackson, R. Shadows.
Jauss. Last Solo: Charlie Parker, Hotel Stanhope, March 12, 1955.
Kaufman, B. Walking Parker Home.
Lagrone. I Heard the Byrd.
Levis. Whitman.
May, K. Valentine's Day.
Mitchell, A. Goodbye.
Moskowitz, F. Bird Lives.
Thomas, L. Historiography.
Zimmer. But Bird.

Parks
Aiken, C. South End.
Algarin. Dante Park.
Bachner. Yes, That's the Way Things Are.
Bland, P. Notes for the Park Keeper.
Costanzo. Washington Park.
Crow, C. City Park.
Davies, W. Hill-Side Park, The.
Davison, P. From the Outland.
Deming, A. Tilden Park.
Fisher, A. Snowy Benches.
Foerster. Bronx Park.
Ghigna. Park Elms.
Gibbons, R. Affect of Elms, The.
Hare, P. Deceit in the Park.
Jones, P. In the Park.
Kirby, D. To a French Structuralist.
Košek, M. Yes, That's the Way Things Are.
Langhorne. Studley Park.
Lewis, G. Sunday Park.
Livingston, M. Envoi: Washington Square Park.
Lowell, R. Public Garden, The.
Millay, E. Armenonville.
Nemerov. Statues in the Public Gardens, The.
Nye, N. Lunch in Nablus City Park.
Pearlberg, G. G. Loop-the-Loop in Prospect Park (1905).
Piccione. Watching Ants Play Soccer in Central Park.
Redmond. Definition of Nature.
Shepherd, R. Eros in His Striped Blue Shirt. Provisional.
Stevens, W. Vacancy in the Park.
Thomas, D. Hunchback in the Park, The.
Thomas, R. Welshman at St. James' Park, A.
Turner, W. Magic.
Vaughan, H. Upon the Priory Grove, His Usual Retirement.
Waller, E. On St. James's Park, as Lately Improved by His Majesty.
Westmorland. To Sir John Wentworth, Upon His Curiosities and Courteous Entertainment at Summerly in Lovingland.
Wyrebek, M. Recovery.

Parliament, Great Britain
Carey [*or* Cary]. Fig for the Lower House, A.
Hughes, T. Wilfred Owen's Photographs.
Milton. On the New Forcers of Conscience Under the Long Parliament.
O'Connor, P. Fag-End.
Unknown. Free Parliament Litany, A.
Vaughan, H. Charnel-house, The.

Parma, Italy
De Vere, A. Correggio's Cupolas at Parma.
Lear, E. Limericks, I (v).

Parmigianino
Ashbery. Self-Portrait in a Convex Mirror.

Parodies
Carroll, L. Hiawatha's Photographing.
Cope, W. Reading Scheme.
De Vries, P. To His Importunate Mistress.
Duhig, I. Fred.
Evans, D. Song of Racquetball.
Herbert, W. To a Mousse.
Koch, K. Variations on a Theme by William Carlos Williams.
Trinidad. Of Mere Plastic.
Unknown. Pilot's Psalm, The.

Parrots

Bridges, R.   Poor Poll.
Dove, R.   Parsley.
Flecker.   Parrot, The.
Sitwell, S.   "Psittachus Eois Imitatrix Ales ab
  Indis."
Unknown.   Old Woman of Gloucester, The.
Webb, C.   Invaders from South of the Border
  Imperil Native Population.
Wright, K.   Sergeant Brown's Parrot.

Parthenon

Bolton, J.   Parthenon at Nashville, The.
Davidson, D.   On a Replica of the Parthenon.
Keats.   On Seeing the Elgin Marbles.
Melville, H.   Parthenon, The.
Patchen.   Saturday Night in the Parthenon.

Parties

Alexander, E.   Ode.
Arnold, C.   Disembodied Voices of Women,
  The.
  Party She Outdid Herself, The.
Auden.   At the Party.
  Love Feast, The.
Belloc.   Juliet.
Bensley.   One's Correspondence.
Berlin.   Pack Up Your Sins and Go to the Devil.
  Top Hat, White Tie, and Tails.
Betjeman.   False Security.
Bottke, A.   How to Approach Your Lover's
  Wife.
Brown, L.   Don't Bring Lulu.
Brown, P.   I Remember Dexedrine. 1970.
Carson, C.   Céilf.
Ceravolo.   Celebration.
Chin.   Composed Near the Bay Bridge (after a
  wild party).
Claman, E.   Show Biz Parties.
Comden, B.   Party's Over, The.
Couto.   Tea Party.
Coward.   I've Been to a Marvelous Party.
De la Mare.   Feckless Dinner-Party, The.
Deanovich.   American Avalon.
Eady.   Song.
Earle, J.   Tea Party, The.
Elmslie, K.   Amazon Club.
Ezekiel.   Goodbye Party for Miss Pushpa T. S.
Finkel.   Party, The.
Ginsberg, A.   First Party at Ken Kesey's with
  Hell's Angels.
Green, A.   Party's Over, The.
Henderson, R.   Don't Bring Lulu.
Hernton.   Poem.
Hupfeld, H.   Let's Put Out the Lights and Go to
  Sleep.
Kasischke.   Grace.
Kefala.   Party, The.
Kuskin.   Rose on My Cake, The.
Leland, J.   Hans Breitmann's Party [*or* Barty].
McGinley.   Office Party.
Nye, N.   Art of Disappearing, The.
Olds, S.   One Girl at the Boys Party, The.
Patten, B.   Party Piece.
Phillips, C.   Cotillion.
Piatt, S.   Child's Party, A.
Read, S.   Garden Party.
Reeves, J.   Waiting.
Rose, B.   Don't Bring Lulu.
Rosen, M.   Eddie and the Birthday.
Scamell, B.   Party, The.
Shepherd, R.   Three A.M. Eternal.
Styne, J.   Party's Over, The.
Tranter.   Un-American Women, The.
Waller, R. *et al.*   Joint is Jumpin', The.
Waniek.   Sleepless Nights.
Wilbur.   Leaving.
Wood, V.   Saturday Night.
Zimunya.   Kisimiso.

Parting

Adair, T.   Night We Called It a Day, The.
Ahlert, F.   I'm Gonna Sit Right Down and Write
  Myself a Letter.
Akst, H.   Am I Blue?
  Guilty.
Alley, R.   Canary Man and You, The.
Amichai [*or* Amikhai].   Letter.
  Quick And Bitter.

Arlen, H.   Man That Got Away, The.
  Sing, My Heart.
Austin, A.   Last Night, The.
Barnes, W.   Sonnet: "In every dream thy lovely
  features rise."
Bendall, M.   After Estrangement.
Berkeley, S.   Parting, The.
Berlin.   When the Midnight Choo-Choo Leaves
  for Alabam.'
Bernstein, L.   Some Other Time.
Berryman.   Parting as Descent.
Bloom, R.   Don't Worry 'Bout Me.
Bolton, J.   Parthenon at Nashville, The.
Bowes-Lyon.   Feather, The.
Bradstreet, A.   Before the Birth of One of Her
  Children.
Bridges, R.   I Will Not Let Thee Go.
Brontë, E.   F. de Samara to A. G. A.
Brooke, R.   Chilterns, The.
Brooks, S.   Some of These Days.
Brown, N.   Good Morning.
Brown, P.   Leaving.
Browning, R.   Parting at Morning.
Bruner.   Good-By.
Brydges.   Lines Written Immediately after
  Parting from a Lady.
Burgoyne, J.   Dashing White Sergeant, The.
Burns, R.   Ae Fond Kiss.
  Silver Tassie, The.
  Song: "O my love's [*or* luve's *or* love is *or* luve
  is] like a red, red rose."
Byron, G.   Fare Thee Well.
  Lines to Mr Hodgson.
  Maid of Athens, Ere We Part.
  When We Two Parted.
Campbell, J.   Good Night, Sweetheart.
Carew, T.   Pastoral[l] Dialogue, A.
  To My Mistress[e] in My Absence.
Castillo, S.   El Apagón.
Chin, J.   Why He Had to Go.
Clarke, G.   Am I Blue?
Cohan.   So Long, Mary.
Coleridge, M.   We Never Said Farewell.
Comden, B.   Some Other Time.
Conley, L.   Cottage for Sale, A.
Connelly, R.   Good Night, Sweetheart.
Constantine, D.   You Are Distant, You Are
  Already Leaving.
Cooper, N.   Leaving the Country.
Coots, J.   For All We Know.
Cornford, F.   Parting in Wartime.
Cory, W.   Parting.
  Preparation.
Coward.   I'll See You Again.
  Never Again.
  Sail Away.
Creamer, H.   After You've Gone.
Creeley.   Just Friends.
Delgado, J.   When You Leave.
Dennis, M.   Night We Called It a Day, The.
Dickinson, E.   My Life Closed Twice.
Dietz, H.   Something to Remember You By.
Divakaruni.   Leaving Yuba City.
Dongala.   Fantasy under the Moon.
Donne.   Song: "Sweetest love, I do not go[e]."
  Valediction: Forbidding Mourning, A.
Dowson.   O Mors! Quam Amara Est Memoria
  Tua Homini Pacem Habenti In Substantiis
  Suis.
Elizabeth I.   On Monsieur's Departure.
Erdman, E.   Toot, Toot, Tootsie! (Good-bye).
Evans, M.   Where Have You Gone?
Ewing, J.   Gifts.
Ezekiel.   Goodbye Party for Miss Pushpa T. S.
Fain, S.   I'll Be Seeing You.
Fanshawe, C.   When Last We Parted.
Feaver.   Coat.
"Field."   Second Thoughts.
Fischer, C.   We'll Be Together Again.
Flynn, N.   Emptying Town.
Forrest, G.   It's a Blue World.
Freed, A.   Good Morning.
Fuller, J.   Wild Raspberries.
Gershwin.   Man That Got Away, The.
  They Can't Take That Away from Me.
Gibb, B.   Vigil.

Glück, L.   Departure.
  Letters, The.
Gordon, M.   There Will Never Be Another You.
Green, A.   Some Other Time.
Hammerstein.   Lover, Come Back to Me!
Handman, L.   Are You Lonesome Tonight?
Hardy, T.   Going, The.
Harper, F.   Slave Auction, The.
Hart, L.   He Was Too Good to Me.
Hass, R.   Bashō, A Departure.
Hayden, R.   Ballad of Sue Ellen Westerfield,
  The.
  Road in Kentucky, A.
Heard, J.   Parting Kiss, The.
  Parting, The.
Hemans.   Madeline, A Domestic Tale.
  Parting Song, A.
Henry VIII, King of England.   To His Lady.
Herrick.   Lovers How They Come and Part.
  To His Dying Brother, Master William Herrick.
  To Larr [*or* Lar].
Hine.   Letting Go.
Horton, G.   Lover's Farewell, The.
Hovey.   At Sea.
Hughes, L.   Request.
Huidobro.   Express.
Irby.   Sequence.
Jones, G.   Esyllt.
Jonson, B.   To William Roe.
Kahn, G.   Guilty.
  I'm Through with Love.
Kalmar *et al.*   Who's Sorry Now?
Keats.   On Leaving Some Friends at an Early
  Hour.
Kemble.   Parting.
Killeen, G.   Tristia.
King, H.   Exequy, The.
Klenner, J.   Just Friends.
Knight, E.   As You Leave Me.
Koehler, T.   Don't Worry 'Bout Me.
  Sing, My Heart.
Landon.   Farewell, The.
Lawrence, D.   Butterfly.
  Winter's Tale, A.
Layton, J.   After You've Gone.
Lerner, A.   If Ever I Would Leave You.
Lewis, A.   Christmas Holiday.
  Goodbye.
  Post-Script: For Gweno.
Lewis, S.   For All We Know.
  Just Friends.
Litchfield.   Good-By.
Livingston, J.   It's the Talk of the Town.
Loesser.   Sand in My Shoes.
Loewe, F.   If Ever I Would Leave You.
Lorde.   Movement Song.
Lovelace, R.   To Lucasta, [on] Going beyond
  the Seas.
  To Lucasta, [on] Going to the War[re]s.
Lowell, A.   Taxi, The.
'Marnia.   Accoutrement.
Martinez, D.   Carp.
McGrath, T.   Fresco: Departure for an
  Imperialist War.
Merrill, J.   Renewal, A.
Mew.   À Quoi Bon Dire.
  Sea Love.
Meynell, A.   Parted.
Mitsui.   Destination: Tule Lake Relocation
  Center, May 20, 1942.
Morrissey, S.   Hazel Goodwin Morrissey Brown.
Muldoon, P.   Avenue, The.
  Something of a Departure.
Myles, E.   Sadness of Leaving, The.
Nairne.   Will Ye No Come Back Again?
Nazario, A.   Melt me.
Nesbit, E.   At Parting.
Noble, R.   Good Night, Sweetheart.
O'Neill, R.   I Made a House of Houselessness.
Patmore, C.   Parting.
Philips, K.   Lucasia, Rosania and Orinda Parting
  at a Fountain, July 1663.
  Orinda to Lucasia Parting, October, 1661, at
  London.
  To Mrs M. A. at Parting.
Phillips, C.   Africa Says.

Piatt, J.   Taking the Night-Train.
Pinkney, E.   On Parting.
Porter, C.   Ev'ry Time We Say Good-bye.
   Just One of Those Things.
Pound, E.   Long Wind, the Dawn Wind.
   Virginal, A.
Probyn.   Rondelet: "Which way he went?"
Procter, A.   Woman's Last Word, A.
Ralegh, S.   Fortune Hath Taken Away.
Randall, D.   Ballygrand Widow.
   Souvenirs.
Redding, E.   End of a Love Affair, The.
Rich, A.   Valediction Forbidding Mourning, A.
Robinson, E.   John Gorham.
   Unforgiven, The.
Robison, W.   Cottage for Sale, A.
Rochester, J.   Upon [His] Leaving His Mistress.
Rodgers, R.   He Was Too Good to Me.
Rodriguez, J.   In-flight Note.
Rosenblatt, S.   Leaving Home.
Ruby, H.   Who's Sorry Now?
Rybicki, J.   In Directions.
Schertzinger, V.   Sand in My Shoes.
Schwartz, A.   Something to Remember You By.
Scupham.   Key, The.
Sharah.   Parting Roundel.
Silex, E.   Departure.
Smith, S.   In My Dreams.
Stein, G.   Let Us Describe.
Stickney, T.   Departure, The.
Strobel.   Encounter.
Swinburne.   Before Parting.
   In The Orchard.
   Leave-taking, A.
Swirszczynska.   Very Sad Conversation at
   Night, A.
Tallmountain.   There Is No Word for Goodbye.
Teasdale.   Gift, The.
Thomas, E.   Like the Touch of Rain.
Thompson, P.   Adown the Heights of Ages.
Tregian.   Imprisoned Recusant Writes to His
   Wife, An.
Tucker, M.   Adieu.
Tuckerman, F.   "Last night I dreamed we parted
   once again."
Unknown.   Another Man Done Gone.
   Corydon's Farewell, on Sailing in the Late
      Expedition Fleet.
   On His Mistress Going from Home [Song].
   You May Go But This Will Bring You Back.
Walker, A.   Even as I Hold You.
Warner, S.   After He Had Gone.
Webster, A.   Passing Away.
Weller.   Ngungalari.
Whiting, R.   Guilty.
Whitman, W.   After the Supper and Talk.
   Good-Bye My Fancy.
   Once I Pass'd through a Populous City.
   What Think You I Take My Pen in Hand?
Whittier.   Godspeed.
Wilbur.   Leaving.
Williams, S.   If He Let Us Go Now.
Wingfield.   Winter.
Winters, Y.   At the San Francisco Airport.
Wolfe, C.   To Mary.
Woods, H.   We Just Couldn't Say Good-bye.
Wright, R.   It's a Blue World.
Wyatt, S.   Lover's Appeal, The.
Yeats.   Parting.
Young, J.   I'm Gonna Sit Right Down and Write
   Myself a Letter.
Zach.   Against Parting.

Pasadena, California
Healy, E.   City Beneath the City, The.
Winters, Y.   On a View of Pasadena from the
   Hills.

Pasolini, Pier Paolo
Glück, R.   Pasolini.

Passion
Ackerman, J.   First Night.
Aguilar-Cariño.   For the Lover.
Arnold, M.   Growing Old.
Atwood.   Torture.
Balce, N.   Pizza and Pretense.
Ball, J.   And This Is So.
Barker, J.   To Her Lover's Complaint.

Beaumont, F.   Love's Mystery.
Beaumont, S.   Description of Love, A.
Behn, A.   Disappointment, The.
Blok.   I want to live.
Bogan, L.   Knowledge.
Brontë, E.   D.G.C. to J.A.
   Shall Earth no more inspire thee.
Brooks, G.   To Be in Love.
Brown, S.   Schadenfreude.
Byron, G.   Last Words on Greece.
Campion, T.   I Care Not for These Ladies.
Carbó, N.   Votive Candles.
Carew, T.   Mediocrity in Love Rejected.
   Prayer to the Wind, A.
   Rapture, A.
Clark, P.   Excitement.
Cofer, J.   Life of an Echo, The.
Cortez, J.   So Long.
Crabbe.   Marriage Ring, The.
Creeley.   Marriage, A.
   Way, The.
Cullen, C.   Song in Spite of Myself.
Devaney, T.   American Pragmatist Fell in Love,
   The.
Donne.   Canonization, The.
Doolittle, H.   Fragment 113: "Not honey, / not
   the plunder of the bee."
Doty, M.   Tiara.
Dunbar, P.   Passion and Love.
Duncan, R.   Among My Friends.
   I Am a Most Fleshly Man.
"Ephelia."   To One That Asked Me Why I
   Loved J G G.
Finch, P.   We Are in the Fields.
Flatman.   Appeal to Cats in the Business of
   Love, An.
Foley, H.   Touch Wood.
García, D.   Other Marías.
Garrigue.   Movie Actors Scribbling Letters Very
   Fast in Crucial Scenes.
Graves, R.   In Perspective.
   Never Such Love.
Gregg.   Adult.
   Official Love Story.
Harwood, L.   Czech Dream.
Heard, J.   Slumbering Passion.
Herbert, E.   Ditty: "If you refuse me once, and
   think again."
Hernández Cruz.   Scarlet Skirt.
Hewitt, J.   Tryst.
Hicok.   Over Coffee.
Jewsbury.   To My Own Heart.
Jones, J.   Watching the Wheat.
Jonson, B.   Nymph's Passion, A.
Laux.   Prayer.
Lawrence, D.   History.
   Kisses in the Train.
   Lightning.
Lefroy.   Palaestral Study, A.
Lenier.   Finale.
Levine, P.   At the Fillmore.
Lim-Wilson.   Beginning of Things, The.
Lindley, D.   Cryptogram, The.
Lovelace, R.   Lucasta's World.
Lumsden, R.   Prayer To Be with Mercurial
   Women.
Mallet.   On an Amorous Old Man.
Marlowe.   Passionate Shepherd To His Love,
   The.
Marston, P.   Love's Music.
   Speechless: Upon the Marriage of Two Deaf and
      Dumb Persons.
Mayakovsky [*or* Maiakovskii].   Mayakovsky's
   Suicide Note.
Melville, H.   Fruit and Flower Painter.
Merrill, J.   Days of 1964.
Naden.   Sister of Mercy, The.
Nazario, A.   Melt Me.
O'Hara, F.   Blocks.
   Hôtel Transylvanie.
Owen, M.   For Emily (Dickinson).
Poe.   Romance.
Porter, C.   Miss Otis Regrets.
Ransom, J.   Good Ships.
   Spiel of [the] Three Mountebanks.
Rich, A.   Paula Becker to Clara Westhoff.

Robinson, M.   Bower of Pleasure, The.
   Canzonet.
   Contemns its Power.
   Describes the Characteristics of Love.
   Her Passion Increases.
   Laura to Petrarch.
   Previous to Her Interview with Phaon.
   Sappho Discovers Her Passion.
   Sappho Rejects Hope.
   She Endeavors to Fascinate Him.
   Tyranny of Love, The.
Rosenberg, L.   Married Love.
Rossetti, C.   Bed of Forget-Me-Nots, A.
Sandburg, C.   Population Drifts.
Sansom, M.   To My Heavenly Charmer.
Schwartz, R. L.   Flamenco Guitar.
Shelley, P.   Lines: "When the lamp is shattered
   [*or* shatter'd]."
   Love's Philosophy.
Shirley, J.   Lover that Durst Not Speak to His
   M[istress], A.
Smith, C.   Supposed To Be Written by Werter.
Spender, S.   Ice.
Stirling, S.   Echo, An.
Story, W.   Cleopatra.
Swinburne.   Anactoria.
Symonds.   What Cannot Be.
Symons, A.   Bianca.
Taylor, B.   Love Returned.
   Paean to the Dawn, A.
Teasdale.   "I Am Not Yours."
Tennyson, A.   O Swallow, Swallow.
Thomson, J.   Once in a Saintly Passion.
Unknown.   I Will Give My Love an Apple
   [Without E'er a Core].
   Prayer yo Hymen.
Whitman, S.   To————: "Vainly my heart had
   with thy sorceries striven."
Whitman, W.   Native Moments.
   Once I Pass'd through a Populous City.
Wilde, O.   Hélas!
Wilkes, K.   Dolce.
Witt, S.   Everlasting Quail.
Wright, J.   To the Muse.
Wyatt, S.   Lover Showeth How He Is Forsaken
   of Such as He Sometime Enjoyed, The.

Passivity
Wilbur.   Shame.

Passover
Hayes, A.   Angel, The.
Heyen.   Passover: the Injections.
Kollar.   Late Arrivals.
Limburg, J.   Seder Night with My Ancestors.
Pastan.   Passover.

Past
Acquah.   They're Tearing Up the Old
   Graveyard.
Addonizio.   At Moss Beach.
Ai.   Twenty-Year Marriage.
Angelou.   Still I Rise.
Ashbery.   Crossroads in the Past.
Baraka.   In Memory of Radio.
Berg, S.   Nostalgia.
Blamire.   When Home We Return.
Blind.   Haunted Streets.
Blunt, W.   To One Who Would Make a
   Confession.
Boland, E.   Black Lace Fan My Mother Gave
   Me, The.
Bontemps.   Return, The.
   Southern Mansion.
Borthwick, P.   Forest.
Bowles, W.   Languid, and Sad, and Slow.
Braley, B.   Start Where You Stand.
Browning, R.   Apparent Failure.
   Love among the Ruins.
Brush.   Again.
Carew, T.   Love's Force.
Castillo, S.   Almendares.
   At the Havana Hilton.
   En el Sol de Mi Barrio.
Clark, T.   Superballs.
   Time.
Clifton, L.   I am Accused of Tending to the Past.
Coward.   London Pride.
Crane, H.   Modern Craft.

My Grandmother's Love Letters.
Creeley.   Here.
Cullen, C.   Litany of the Dark People, The.
Curtis, T.   Queen's Tears.
Davidson, D.   Sanctuary.
Davie.   Rodez.
Dickey, J.   Buckdancer's Choice.
Dooley, M.   History.
Doolittle, H.   Helen.
Dove, R.   Fifth Grade Autobiography.
Duncan, R.   Sleep is a Deep and Many Voiced Flood.
Durrell.   Delos.
Emerson, R.   Past, The.
English, T.   Ben Bolt.
Everwine.   From the Meadow.
Ferlinghetti, L.   Retired Ballerinas, Central Park West.
"Field."   Palimpsest, A.
Frost, R.   Cliff Dwelling, A.
   Directive.
Fyleman.   Cat, The.
Glück, L.   Letters, The.
Gould, A.   Observed Observer, The.
Gregg.   Past Perfect.
Guiterman.   Ancient History.
Ha Jin.   Past, The.
Hampton.   Yugoslav Story.
Hanzlicek, C.   Last Trains, The.
Harbach, O.   Yesterdays.
Hartnett.   Visit to Castletown House, A.
Hayden, R.   'Mystery Boy' Looks for Kin in Nashville.
Herrick.   His Age, Dedicated to His Peculiar Friend, Master John Wickes, under the Name of Posthumus.
Hinsey, E.   Planisféria, Map of the World, Lisbon, 1554.
Hoagland, E.   Gorée.
Hogan, L.   Chambered Nautilus.
Housman, A.   Yon Far Country.
Howe, J.   My Last Dance.
Howe, S.   Thorow.
Hulme, T.   Image.
Jackson, L.   Ding-Donging.
Jeffers, R.   Haunted Country.
Kaufman, S.   By the Rivers.
Kendall, M.   Fossil, A.
Keplinger, D.   Another Century.
Kern, J.   I'm Old-Fashioned.
   That Was Before I Met You.
   Yesterdays.
Kipling, R.   Way Through The Woods, The.
Kizer, C.   Bitch.
Kooser.   Country School.
   Year's End.
Kumin, M.   Chain, The.
Landon.   Experience Too Late.
Lauterbach.   Clamor.
Lawrence, D.   History.
   Humming-Bird.
Levi, S.   Abbienti.
Levine, P.   28.
Lindsay, N.   Chinese Nightingale, The.
Louis, A.   At the House of Ghosts.
Lumsden, R.   ITMA.
MacCaig.   Gone Are the Days.
Marion, G.   My Future Just Passed.
Masters, E.   Gettysburg.
McElroy, C.   Ghost-Who-Walks, The.
   Under the Oak Table.
Melville, H.   Battle Summers, The.
Mercer, J.   I'm Old-Fashioned.
Michelson, R.   Jews That We Are, The.
Moore, H.   Edward.
Mura.   Argument: On 1942, An.
Nemerov.   Blue Suburban.
Nims, J.   Freight.
O Direain.   That Face.
Olds, S.   I Go Back to May 1937.
Oodgeroo of the tribe Noonuccal.   Past, The.
Pearlberg, G.G.   Think Back.
Peters, L.   Home Coming.
Pilling.   Specimen.
Pinsky.   Jersey Rain.
Porteous.   Wrecked Creeves.

Procter, A.   My Journal.
   Present, The.
Rankine.   Eden.
Reed, I.   Reactionary Poet, The.
Rees-Jones.   Making for Planet Alice.
Robinson, E.   Miniver Cheevy.
Rossetti, C.   Summer Is Ended.
Salinas, R.   Trip Through the Mind Jail, A.
Schuyler, J.   Salute.
Scott, L.   Ettrick.
Scovell.   Past Time.
Serote.   Ofay-Watcher Looks Back.
Sexton.   Funnel.
   Some Foreign Letters.
   What's That.
Smedley, M.   Face from the Past, A.
Sorby.   Synchronized Swimming.
Spender, S.   One More New Botched Beginning.
Stevenson, R.   Over the Sea to Skye.
Stickney, T.   On Some Shells Found Inland.
Summerfield.   Washday Battles.
Thomas, D.   Because the Pleasure-Bird Whistles.
   Twenty-four Years.
Thomas, E.   Return, The.
Thomas, R.   Centuries.
Townsend, A.   Shirt Collar, The.
Urmy.   Old Year, The.
Valentine, J.   Sleep Drops Its Nets.
Warren, R.   Letter from a Coward to a Hero.
Whiting, R.   My Future Just Passed.
Whitman, W.   Now Precedent Songs, Farewell.
   Proud Music of the Storm.
Whittemore, R.   Clamming.
   Mother's Past.
Wilbur.   Pardon, The.
Wilcox, E.   Was, Is, and Yet-To-Be.
Wilder, A.   Did You Ever Cross Over to Sneden's.
Wodehouse, P.   That Was Before I Met You.
Wong, N.   Grandmothers' Song.
Wright, C.   Two Stories.
Yeats.   Circus Animals' Desertion, The.
Young, K.   Field Trip.
Zukofsky, L.   As to How Much.
   I Sent Thee Late.

Pasternak, Boris
McGinley.   Last Year's Discussion: The Nobel Russian.

Pastoral Verse
Bampfylde.   Written at a Farm.
Ch'ien T'ao.   On Reading the Seas and Mountains Classic.
Clare, J.   Rural Scenes.
   Wren, The.
   Wryneck's Nest, The.
Deutsch.   Urban Pastoral.
Gay, J.   Birth of the Squire; an Eclogue, The.
Hemans.   Remembrance of Grasmere, A.
Hightower, J. R.   On Reading the Seas and Mountains Classic.
Hunt, L.   To Hampstead.
James, J.   Idyl: "Tiny fish."
Johnson, J.   Unmarked Stop in Front of Westmond General Store, Westmond, Idaho.
Kinsella, J.   Rabbiters: A Pastoral, The.
Marlowe.   Passionate Shepherd To His Love, The.
Milton.   L'Allegro.
   Lycidas.
Mitford.   Forget-Me-Not, The.
"Ophelia."   Snaith Marsh; a Yorkshire Pastoral.
Ralegh, S.   Nymph's [or Nimphs] Reply to the Shepherd [or Sheepheard], The.
Reverdy.   Air: "Forgetting."
Roscoe, W.   To the Harvest Moon.
Winchilsea.   Pastoral Dialogue between Two Shepherdesses, A.
Wylie.   Spring Pastoral.

Paterson, New Jersey
Williams, W.   Delineaments of the Giants, The.
   Episode 17.
   Preface: "To make a start."
   Sunday in the Park.

Paths
Bass, F.   Garden, The.

Bromige.   Choice.
Del Renzio.   Can You Change a Shilling?
Fisher, C.   Those Who Make Paths.
Gonzalez, N.   I Made Myself a Path.
Jones, G.   Common Path, The.
Kinnell.   Under the Maud Moon.
Moore, L.   Homeplace, The.
Ngatho.   Footpath.
Ofeimun.   Let Them Choose Paths.
Patten, B.   Terrible Path, The.
Pritchard, N.   Narrow Path, The.
Rexroth, K.   Asagumori.
Riley, J.   Country Pathway, A.
Roberts, K.   Postcard from the Coast.
Schuyler, J.   Along Overgrown Paths.
Snyder, G.   Riprap.
Sund.   Considering Poverty and Homelessness.
Todd, M.   Game Trail, The.
Whittier.   River Path, The.
Wordsworth, W.   Simplon Pass, The.

Patience
Barbauld.   To the Poor.
Boyle, K.   Ode to a Maintenance Man and His Family.
Carey, H.   Sally in Our Alley.
Creeley.   For No Clear Reason.
Emerson, R.   Forbearance.
Fields, J.   Jolly Fat Widows, The.
Graves, R.   Carol of Patience.
   Not at Home.
Hardy, T.   Waiting Both.
Herbert, G.   Size, The.
Herrick.   To Fortune.
Hopkins, G.   My Own Heart Let Me More Have Pity On.
   Sonnet: "Patience, hard thing! the hard thing but to pray."
Horne, F.   Patience.
Jennings, E.   Delay.
Khalvati.   Stone of Patience.
"Klingle."   Be Patient.
Olds, S.   New Mother.
Procter, A.   Strive, Wait, and Pray.
Quarles.   Epigram: "My soul, sit thou a patient looker-on."
Rossetti, C.   Study (A Soul), A.
Sangster, M.   Patience with the Living.
Tekeyan.   Sacred Wrath.
Thompson, C.   His Answer.
Unknown.   Learn to Wait.
   Morning Prayer.
   Temper.
Walker, F. X.   Sweet Bread.
Woods, D.   Waiting.
Yeats.   Down by the Salley Gardens.
Young, M. J.   To Time.

Patients
Abse.   Doctor, The.
Coulehan, J.   I'm Gonna Slap Those Doctors.
   Man with a Hole in His Face, The.
Dennis, C.   St. Francis and the Nun.
Feinfeld, D.   Carmelita.
Getsi.   Washing Your Hair.
Ginsberg, A.   Chief of Medicine, The.
   Line Drive.
Henley, W.   Before.
   Interior.
   Waiting.
Hirsch, E.   Two Suffering Men.
Mukand, J.   First Payment.
   Lullaby.
Platt, F.   Coincidentally.
Rowe, V.   Time Heals All Wounds—But One.
Shafer, A.   Gurney Tears.
Shapiro, H.   6/20/97.
Stone, J.   Confabulation.
   Gaudeamus Igitur: A Valediction.
Straus, M.   Log of Pi, The.
Thwaite.   Freedom.
Woods, D.   Waiting.
Wright, J.   Therapy.
   Walking the Dog.
See also **Hospitals; Illness; Mental Illness**

Patriarchy
Grahn.   History of Lesbianism, A.

Myles, E.   Woman like Me, A.
Piercy.   Barbie Doll.
Plath.   Lady Lazarus.
Rich, A.   From a Survivor.
  Paula Becker to Clara Westhoff.

Patriotic Songs, America
Bates, K.   America the Beautiful.
Cohan.   I Want to Hear a Yankee Doodle Tune.
  If Washington Should Come to Life.
  Over There.
Dwight.   As Down a Lone Valley.
Gershwin.   Of Thee I Sing.
  Strike Up the Band.
Gershwin, G.   Of Thee I Sing.
  Strike Up the Band.
Howe, J.   Battle Hymn [or Battle-Hymn] of the
  Republic, The.
Key.   Star-Spangled Banner, The.
Shuckburg et al.   Yankee Doodle.
Smith, S.   America.
Stephens, P.   God Shed His Grace.
Van Dyke.   America for Me.

Patriotic Songs, Confederacy
Randall, J.   My Maryland.
See also **Patriotic Songs, America**

Patriotic Songs, England
Garrick.   Heart of Oak.

Patriotism and Patriots
Barry, J.   Lessons.
Bennett, H.   Flag Goes By, The.
Betjeman.   In Westminster Abbey.
Browning, R.   Patriot, The [An Old Story].
Camlan.   Lady Charlotte Guest.
Cheney-Coker.   On Being a Poet in Sierra
  Leone.
Chipasula.   Going Back Patiently.
  Manifesto on Ars Poetica.
  My Friendly People.
  Talking of Sharp Things.
Cohan.   Yankee Doodle Boy, The.
Cohen, L.   Killers, The.
Cummings, E.   I Sing of Olaf Glad and Big.
  Next to of Course God America I.
Cunningham, A.   Hame, Hame, Hame.
Dawe, G.   Names.
Duggan, E.   Invasion.
Glaser, I.   Last Good War—and Afterward, The.
Hemans.   Homes of England, The.
Henley, W.   England, My England.
Hewitt, J.   Ireland.
  Scar, The.
Housman, A.   New Mistress, The.
Howe, J.   Battle Hymn [or Battle-Hymn] of the
  Republic, The.
Jones, J.   Glyndwr's War Song.
Keats.   Happy Is England! I Could Be Content.
Kipling, R.   Recessional.
Larkin, P.   MCMXIV.
Lazarus, E.   New Colossus, The.
MacNeice.   Western Landscape.
Manning, F.   Grotesque.
Moore, T.   Dear Harp of My Country.
  Harp That Once through Tara's Halls, The.
  Pro Patria Mori.
Moorer.   Loyalty to the Flag.
Ofeimun.   Prologue: "I have come down."
Ogundipe-Leslie.   Song at the African Middle
  Class.
Orwell.   As One Non-Combatant to Another.
Owen, W.   Dulce et Decorum Est.
Peck, R.   Four of July.
Scott of Amwell.   Ode: "I hate that drum's
  discordant sound."
Scott, S.   Pibroch of Donuil Dhu.
Stewart, F.   Black Winter.
Stow.   My Wish for My Land.
Thomas, E.   This Is No Case of Petty Right or
  Wrong.
Turner, C.   Great Britain Through the Ice: Or,
  Premature Patriotism.
Unknown.   Our Flag.
Van Dyke.   America for Me.
Whitman, W.   Beat! Beat! Drums!
  I Hear America Singing.
Whittier.   Barbara Frietchie.

Wordsworth, W.   Composed by the Sea-Side,
  near Calais, August, 1802.

Patrons
Daniel, S.   To the Right Honorable, the Lady
  Mary, Countess of Pembroke.
Jonson, B.   Epigram. To the Household. 1630,
  An.
  To Lucy, Countess[e] of Bedford, with Mr.
  Donnes Satire's [or Satyres].
Prince, F.   Epistle to a Patron, An.
Smith, C.   To the Earl of Egremont.

Paul, Saint
Constable, H.   To St. Peter and St. Paul.
Corbet [or Corbett].   Distracted Puritan, The.
Dobson, R.   Eutychus.
Kipling, R.   At His Execution.
  Gallio's Song.
Merton.   St. Paul.
Ransom, J.   Our Two Worthies.
Wesley, C.   He Shook off the Beast.
Wither.   Conversion of S. Paul, The.

Pawnbrokers and Pawnshops
Alexie.   Evolution.
Espada.   Latin Night at the Pawnshop.
Johnston, E.   Last Sark, The.

Payne, D. A.
Fordham.   Dedicated to the Right Rev'd D. A.
  Payne.

Peace
Aldington.   Field Manoeuvres.
Aldrich, T.   Lycidas.
Alkalay-Gut.   Public Outcry.
Allen, E.   In the Defences.
Ashbery.   Poem: "While we were walking under
  the top."
Auden.   Autumn To-day.
Awad, J.   Autumnal.
Balaban.   April 30, 1975.
  In Celebration of Spring.
Berry, W.   Peace of Wild Things, The.
Brainard, J.   I Saw Two Clouds at Morning.
Bryant, W.   After a Tempest.
  Autumn Woods.
Buchanan, G.   War-and-Peace.
Byron, G.   She Walks In Beauty.
Cady.   Starting 1973: What to Do Now that
  Peace Has Been Announced.
Campbell, T.   Soldier's Dream, The.
Codrescu.   Grammar, A.
Collins, W.   Ode to Evening.
Cooke, R.   Arachne.
Creeley.   For No Clear Reason.
De la Mare.   Ghost, The.
  Peace.
Dehn, P.   Armistice.
Dixon, R.   To Peace.
Doolittle, H.   Trance.
Drummond de Andrade.   Motionless Faces.
Dunbar, P.   Ere Sleep Comes Down to Soothe
  the Weary Eyes.
Edman.   Peace.
Eliot, T.   Song for Simeon, A.
Fordham.   Ode to Peace.
Fosdick, H.   Prince of Peace His Banner
  Spreads, The.
Francis of Assisi.   Prayer of St. Francis of Assisi
  for Peace.
Gardelle, C.   Peaceful Sunday.
Hardy, T.   Christmas Ghost-Story, A.
Harper, L.   Songs for the People.
Harper, M.   Peace Plan: Meditation on the 9
  Stages of 'Peacemaking' as Tribute to Senator
  Claiborne Pell: 1997.
Hass, R.   Measure.
Herbert, G.   L'Envoy.
  Peace.
Herrick.   Farewell Frost; or, Welcome the
  Spring.
  Power and Peace.
Hill, G.   Pastoral, A: "Mobile, immaculate and
  austere."
Holmes, O.   Prologue.
Hopkins, G.   Peace.
Hughes, L.   Projection.

Joseph, J.   Rose in the Afternoon.
Kaufman, B.   Private Sadness.
Knevet.   Vote, The.
Krohn.   Farmer's Song at Can Tho.
Landor, W.   Foreign Ruler, A.
Larkin, P.   Coming.
Lawrence, D.   Pax.
  What Would You Fight For?
Lee, J.   Firebell for Peace.
Longley, M.   Peace.
Lopez, L.   Images of San Luis.
MacNeice.   Apple Blossom.
Meredith, W.   On Falling Asleep by Firelight.
Millay, E.   I Forgot for a Moment.
Moore, M.   In Distrust of Merits.
Muldoon, P.   Truce.
Nemerov.   Easter.
  Song of Degrees, A.
Patchen.   Pastoral: "Dove walks with sticky feet,
  The."
Ransom, J.   Spiel of [the] Three Mountebanks.
Rossetti, C.   From the Antique.
Rothman, D.   One of the Lords of Life.
Sanchez, S.   Reflections After the June 12th
  March for Disarmament.
Sandburg, C.   A. E. F.
  For You.
Seaton, M.   Fiddleheads.
Southerland.   Two Fishing Villages.
Southwell.   Content and Ri[t]ch[e].
Stafford, W.   At the Un-National Monument
  along the Canadian Border.
Stein, K.   Upon Finding a Black Woman's Door
  Sprayed with Swastikas, I Tell Her This Story
  of Hands.
Stevens, W.   House Was Quiet and the World
  Was Calm, The.
Studdert-Kennedy.   Is It a Dream?
Taggard.   Everyday Alchemy.
Thomas, R.   Country Clergy, The.
Thompson, F.   Non Pax—Expectatio.
Tighe.   Written at Killarney. July 29, 1800.
Timrod.   Christmas.
  Retirement.
Tolson, M.   Legend of Versailles, A.
Turner, N.   Let Us Have Peace.
Unknown.   Deep River.
  Hierusalem.
  Hymn: "O God of Hosts, thine Ear incline."
  Shalom Aleichem.
  Soon I Will Be Done.
Vaughan, H.   Night, The.
  Peace.
Villanueva, A.   Peace #3.
Voznesensky [or Voznesenskii].   Give Me Peace.
Walcott.   Season of Phantasmal Peace, The.
Wallis, S.   Prayer for Peace, A.
Watkyns.   Peace and War.
Whitman, W.   Base of All Metaphysics, The.
  Halcyon Days.
  Reconciliation.
Whittier.   Battle Autumn of 1862, The.
  Lost Occasion, The.
Wilbur.   Grasshopper, A.
Wilde, O.   E Tenebris.
Winchilsea.   Enquiry after Peace. A Fragment.
Yeats.   Michael Robartes Bids His Beloved Be
  at Peace.

Peace, Isabel
Fordham.   Lines to Mrs. Isabel Peace.

Peach Trees and Peaches
Abse.   Peachstone.
Ager, M.   Everything Is Peaches Down in
  Georgia.
Blake, W.   Angel, The.
Clarke, G.   Everything Is Peaches Down in
  Georgia.
Fox, S.   Peaches.
Graves, R.   Blue-Fly, The.
Hall, D.   Peaches.
Larsen, L.   Peach.
Lee, L.   From Blossoms.
  Weight of Sweetness, The.
Lewis, J.   Garden Note I, Los Altos.
Meyer, G.   Everything Is Peaches Down in
  Georgia.

Nye, N.　Going for Peaches, Fredericksburg, Texas.
Rauter.　Peach.
Warren, R.　Riddle in the Garden.
Wylie.　Puritan Sonnet, IV.
　Wild Peaches.

Peacocks
Carryl, G.　Patrician Peacocks and the Overweening Jay, The.
Hall, D.　Apples.
Heyrick.　On a Peacock.
Hopkins, G.　Peacock's Eye, The.
Lawrence, D.　Peacock.
Merrill, J.　Peacock, The.
Stevens, W.　Domination of Black.
Wagoner, D.　Peacock Display.

Pear Trees and Pears
Curtis, T.　Neighbour's Pear Tree.
Doolittle, H.　Orchard.
　Pear Tree.
Millay, E.　Pear Tree, The.
Page, P.　Deaf-Mute in the Pear Tree.
Stevens, W.　Study of Two Pears.
Talvikki, A.　Flemish Beauty.
Unknown.　Harry Parry.

Pearls
Bernstein, C.　Caught.
Drummond, W.　Oister, The.
Duffy, C.　Warming Her Pearls.
Hernández Cruz.　Perlas.
Roripaugh, L.　Pearls.
Thompson, P.　Precious Pearl, The.
Wilde, L.　Poet's Destiny, The.

Peas
Jones, H.　On a Fine Crop of Peas Being Spoiled by a Storm.
Unknown.　Peas.

Peasants
"Æ."　Exiles.
Bolton, J.　Fin de Siècle.
Campbell, J.　I Am the Mountainy Singer.
Clare, J.　Peasant Poet, The.
Ewart.　Wanting Out.
Hemans.　Peasant Girl of the Rhone, The.
Lewis, A.　Peasants, The.
Unknown.　Cutty Wren, The.

Pedantry and Pedants
Coultas, B.　Lecture #1.
Edwards, T.　On the Edition of Mr. Pope's Works with a Commentary and Notes.
　To the Editor of Mr. Pope's Works.
Nash, O.　Purist, The.
Whitman, W.　When I Heard the Learn'd Astronomer.
See also **Scholarship and Scholars**

Peddling and Peddlers
Mew.　Pedlar, The.
Richards, L.　Old Joe Jones.
Suckling, S.　Pedlar of Small-Wares, A.
Swift, J.　Oysters.
Unknown.　Chapmen.
　Cries of London, The.
　Fine Knacks for Ladies.

Pelicans
Jeffers, R.　Pelicans.
Le Guin.　Riding on the Coast Starlight.
Lear, E.　Pelican Chorus, The.
Wright, J.　Pelicans.

Penelope (mythology)
Cofer, J.　Learning to Walk Alone.
Doolittle, H.　At Ithaca.
Harrison, J.　Penelope.
Hartigan, A.　No Easy Harbour.
Homer.　Butchers, The.
　Phemios and Medon.
Jackson, A.　Spinster Song: African-American Woman Guild.
Kyger.　Pan as the Son of Penelope.
Millay, E.　Ancient Gesture, An.
Montgomerie, A.　Sonet: "Thocht Polibus, pisander, and with them."
Parker, D.　Penelope.
Stevens, W.　World as Meditation, The.
Waddington, M.　Ulysses Embroidered.

Penguins
Hughes, F.　Birds.

Peninsular War (1808–14)
Wolfe, C.　Burial of Sir John Moore [after [*or* at] Corunna], The.

Pennsylvania (state)
Daly, T.　Pennsylvania Places.
Djanikian.　How I Learned English.
Littlebird.　Pennsylvania Winter Indian 1974.
Stern, G.　Dancing, The.

Penshurst, England
Waller, E.　At Penshurst.
　At Penshurst [Another].

Pensions and Pensioners
Barber, M.　On Seeing an Officer's Widow Distracted.
Collier, J.　Pluralist and Old Soldier, The.
Papertalk-Green, C.　Pension Day.
See also **Old Age; Retirement and Retirees**

Pentecost
Lewis, G.　Pentecost.

Peonies
Kenyon, J.　Peonies at Dusk.
Van Duyn.　Sonnet for Minimalists.

Peppers
Baca.　Green Chile.

Peppertrees
Levertov.　Scenes from the Life of the Peppertrees.

Perception
Adcock, F.　Dreaming.
Barth, R.　Postscript.
Beckett, S.　Something There.
Bogan, L.　Late.
Brooks, G.　To Be in Love.
Cavendish, M.　Dialogue betwixt the Body and the Mind, A.
Ceravolo.　White Fish in Reeds.
Ciardi.　On a Photo of Sgt. Ciardi a Year Later.
Coleridge, S.　Apologia pro Vita Sua.
Creeley.　For Love.
　Man, The.
Cummings, E.　Somewhere i have never travelled, gladly beyond.
Curbelo.　If You Need a Reason.
Davis, W.　In a Room.
De la Mare.　All but Blind.
Drake, N.　Man in the White Suit, The.
Eberhart, R.　Blunting, The.
Emerson, R.　Astræa.
　Illusions.
Fenton, J.　This Octopus Exploits Women.
Fox, S.　Almagest, Last Letter to Zakarias.
Fuhrman, J.　Watching Trains.
Gascoyne.　Yves Tanguy.
Ginsberg, A.　Land O'Lakes, Wisconsin: Vajrayana Seminary.
　Terms in Which I Think of Reality, The.
Graves, R.　In Perspective.
Harte, B.　What the Bullet Sang.
Hollander, J.　Morning in the Islands.
Jackson, L.　Prisms.
Jarrell.　Orient Express, The.
　Seele im Raum.
Jones, S.　Illusions.
Kabir.　How Much Is Not True.
Kipling, R.　Conundrum of the Workshops, The.
　Looking Glass, The.
Knott.　Feeding the Sun.
Levertov.　Seeing for a Moment.
　Witness.
Moore, R.　Mind's Disguise, The.
Murray, L.　Equanimity.
Raine, K.　Angelus.
Ransom, J.　Painted Head.
Rolfe, E.　Casualty.
Schuyler, J.　Freely Espousing.
Smith, S.　Not Waving But Drowning.
Stevens, W.　Idea of Order at Key West, The.
　Snow Man, The.
　Study of Two Pears.
　Thinking of a Relation between the Images of Metaphors.
　Thirteen Ways of Looking at a Blackbird.
Strand.　Keeping Things Whole.

Vitale, M.　Joy Island.
Ward, T.　Tacit.
Warr, M.　Brain on Ice.
Whitman, W.　Of the Terrible Doubt of Appearances.
Williams, W.　New Clouds, The.
　Short Poem.
Willson, M.　Till There Was You.
Wiman, C.　Hearing Loss.
Wordsworth, W.　Yarrow Visited [September, 1814].
Wright, C.　Dead Color.
Young, A.　How the Rainbow Works.

Percy, Sir Henry
Unknown.　Battle of Otterburn [*or* Oterborne], The.

Perfection
Bock, J.　Matchmaker.
Herrick.　His Request to Julia.
Jordan, J.　Sunflower Sonnet Number Two.
Kalmar *et al.*　What a Perfect Combination.
Olson, C.　As the Dead Prey upon Us.
Rafferty, C.　Story of the Man Whose Tastes Were Too Refined.
Stevens, W.　Asides on the Oboe.
　Poems of Our Climate, The.
Tomlinson, C.　Rhymes.
Vitale, M.　Three Written Poems, Unconnected.
Wright, J.　Birds.
Yeats.　Before the World Was Made.

Perfumes
Chin, J.　Bergamot.
Herrick.　To His Mistresses.
Mackenzie, K.　Ginger-flowers.
Pound, E.　Portrait d'une Femme.
Symons, A.　White Heliotrope.

Perplexity
Creeley.　For No Clear Reason.
Eady.　Sherbet.

Persecution
Ballowe, J.　Starved Rock.
Bell, M.　Book of the Dead Man (#58), The.
Benét, S.　Cotton Mather.
Bienek.　Exodus.
Bobrowski.　Elderblossom.
Breytenbach.　Out There.
Brutus.　Robben Island Sequence.
Carroll, L.　Long Tale, A.
Cheney-Coker.　Outsider, The.
Frost, C.　Consent.
Gander.　Deflection Toward the Relative Minor.
Glaser, M.　Magnificat!
Longfellow, H.　Jewish Cemetery at Newport, The.
Macgoye.　August the First: The Watchman Speaks.
Madhubuti.　Killing Memory.
Nasrin.　At the Back of Progress.
Niemoller.　First They Came for the Jews.
Pelletiere, M.　Under Her Crib.
Pickard, T.　Devil's Destroying Angel Exploded, The.
Swinburne.　On the Russian Persecution of the Jews.
Winner, R.　Segregated Railway Diner—1946.

Persephone
Boland, E.　Pomegranate, The.
Creeley.　Kore.
Daumal.　Persephone That Is to Say Double Issue.
Dove, R.　Demeter, Waiting.
　Persephone Underground.
Hildebrandt, Z.　Persephone.
Hope, A.　Return of Persephone, The.
Krysl.　Persephone, to Demeter.
Lawrence, D.　Bavarian Gentians.
Monaghan.　Persephone's Journey.
Muske, C.　Wish Foundation, The.
Norris, K.　Persephone.
Swinburne.　Garden of Proserpine, The.
　Hymn to Proserpine.
Vinal.　To Persephone.

Perseus
Hayden, R.　Perseus.
Levy, A.　Reminiscence, A.

O'Sullivan, V.   Medusa.
Parnell, P.   Apotheosis of Medusa.

Perseverance
Baca.   Oppression.
Braley, B.   Success.
Cameron, C.   Success.
Carew, T.   Eternity of Love Protested.
Clark, T.   "Like Musical Instruments."
 As the Human Village Prepares for Its Fate.
Clough.   Say Not the Struggle Nought Availeth.
Cooke, E.   Plug.
Creeley.   Marriage, A.
 Oh No.
Disch.   Entropic Villanelle.
Dunn, S.   Competition.
Herbert, G.   Employment: "He that is weary, let
 him sit."
 Pilgrimage, The.
Hewitt, J.   Colony, The.
Holden, J.   Liberace.
Hopkins, G.   Carrion Comfort.
Jackson, H.   My Lighthouses.
Jarrell.   Knight, Death, and the Devil, The.
Jefferys [or Jeffries].   We Have Lived and
 Loved Together.
Kipling, R.   Old Men, The.
Kiser.   Unsubdued.
Koestenbaum, W.   Gaudy Slave Trader.
Longfellow, H.   Excelsior.
 Psalm of Life, A.
 Tell Me Not in Mournful Numbers.
Lovelace, R.   Apostasy of One and But One
 Lady, The.
Moore, M.   Nevertheless.
Newbolt.   Vitaï Lampada.
Oppen.   From Disaster.
Palmer, T.   Try, Try Again.
Piercy.   To Be of Use.
Sandburg, C.   Upstream.
Sargent, E.   Rockall.
Song.   Out of Our Hands.
Stanton, F.   Keep a-Goin'
Tennyson, A.   Ulysses.
Unknown.   Pluck Wins.
Warren, R.   To a Face in a Crowd.
Whitfield.   Self-Reliance.
Whitman, W.   Noiseless Patient Spider, A.
Williams, W.   Pink Locust, The.
Young, A.   Dance For Ma Rainey, A.

Persia
Taylor, B.   To a Persian Boy in the Bazaar at
 Smyrna.
See also **Iran and Iranians**

Persian Gulf War
Lomax, M.   Gulf.

Persian Wars (500b.c.–449b.c.)
Graves, R.   Persian Version, The.
Hope, A.   Inscription for a War.

Persians
Graves, R.   Persian Version, The.

Persimmon Trees
Nelson, M.   Wish.
Stroud, J.   Oh Yes.

Peru
Bryant, W.   Damsel of Peru, The.
Coolidge, C.   Peru Eye, the Heart of the Lamp.
Duran, J.   Time Zones.
Vallejo.   Telluric and Magnetic.

Pessimism
Belloc.   Is there any reward?
Carruth, H.   On Being Asked to Write a Poem
 Against the War in Vietnam.
Comden, B.   You Mustn't Feel Discouraged.
Coward.   There Are Bad Times Just around the
 Corner.
Creeley.   Turn, The.
Durcan.   Honeymoon Postcard.
Hardy, T.   Epitaph on a Pessimist.
King, B.   Pessimist, The.
 Sum of Life, The.
Knox, R.   To a Pessimist.
Lowell, R.   Waking Early Sunday Morning.
Naden.   Pessimist's Vision, The.
Parker, D.   Prophetic Soul.
 Symptom Recital.

Reid, A.   Scotland.
Shepherd, R.   Provisional.
Unknown.   Pessimist, The.

Pesticides
Cooper, W.   Pollen.
Dupree, E.   At Present I Am Working as a
 Security Guard.

Peter Rabbit
McPherson, S.   Peter Rabbit.

Peter, Saint
Browning, E.   Look, The.
 Meaning of the Look, The.
Constable, H.   To St. Peter and St. Paul.
Hardy, T.   In the Servants' Quarters.
Herrick.   Peter-penny, The.
Levertov.   St. Peter and the Angel.
Rossetti, C.   St. Peter.
Unknown.   Full and True Account of a Dreaded
 Fire, that Lately Broke out in the Pope's
 Breeches, A.
 When in My Pilgrimage.
Wylie.   Peter and John.

Peterloo Massacre (1819)
Bamford.   Touch Him!
Shelley, P.   Song to the Men of England.

Petrarch (Francesco Petrarca)
Hill, G.   Vergine bella.
Robinson, M.   Laura to Petrarch.
Russell, T.   Sonnet to Valclusa.

Petrels
Murphy, R.   Stormpetrel.
Whitman, W.   To the Man-of-War Bird.

Pets
Albee, E.   Samantha.
Allen, J.   War Poem, A.
Anderson, D.   Domi Solus.
Arnold, M.   Geist's Grave.
Barrington, P.   I Had a Hippopotamus.
Barry, L.   I love my master I love my master.
Bass, R.   Odyssey, The.
Baxter, C.   Dog Kibble: A Villanelle.
Benson, R.   Lab Lines.
Blount, R.   Country Dog in the City (On a
 Leash, Which Is Bizarre Enough) Comes Upon
 an Obedience Class, A.
Calverley.   Disaster.
Carlson, R.   Max Who Caught a Car.
Ciment, J.   Mommy.
Cooper, B.   Pet Names.
 Toast to the Cook, A.
Cornford, F.   Child's Dream, A.
Cowper, W.   Epitaph on a Hare.
 On the Lamented Death of Mrs. Throckmorton's
 Bullfinch.
Creeley.   If You.
Davies, W.   Child's Pet, A.
Doty, M.   Beau: Golden Retrievals.
Dunn, S.   Buster's Visitation.
Ferrell, A.   Out.
Gerstler.   Max's Lecture on Canine Buddhism.
Graham, M.   Greta's Song.
Hale, S.   Mary's Lamb [or Mary and Her
 Lamb].
Hansen, R.   Do Not Let Skeezix Go in There:
 Winslow's Villanelle.
Haxton.   Nietzsche Possessed.
Heimel, C.   Sally.
Hempel, A.   Rain.
Herrick.   Upon His Spaniel[l] Tracie [or Tracy].
Holland, N.   Alice.
Hudgins.   Buddy.
 Rosie.
Hughes, T.   Roger the Dog.
Irving, J.   Untitled.
Johnson, D.   Harold's Bowl and Food.
Jones, R. S.   Shelter.
Kirn, W.   Envoy: "I left. I'd finished raising you.
 I walked."
Kohler, S.   Shepherd.
Kumin, M.   Gus Speaks.
 Retrieval System, The.
Kusz, N.   Retired Greyhound, I.
 Retired Greyhound, II.
Lamott, A.   Spoon River Sadie Louise.
Larkin, P.   Take One Home for the Kiddies.

Lish, G.   Rusty.
Lombreglia, R.   Daisy, Five, Speaks to Sophia,
 Two.
MacCaig.   Praise of a Collie.
Markoe, M.   Ballad of Winky.
 Lewis Describes His Day.
Marx, P.   Hugs.
McGraw, E.   Drunk Dog.
McHugh, H.   My Shepherd.
Miller, A.   Lola's Lament.
Minot, G.   Down.
Minot, S.   Devotion.
Moore, H.   Runaway.
Morris, M.   Missing: A Dog's Doggerel.
Muñoz, A.   Hunting Accident.
Oodgeroo of the tribe Noonuccal.   Flea's Hymn.
Orton, B.   Sea Monkeys, The.
Paschen.   Sam's Ghazals.
Powell, P.   Full Neurological Work-up.
Prunty.   Coach.
Raab, L.   Katie's Words.
Ransom, J.   Janet Waking.
Richard, M.   Y'All Are Bird Dogs, Aren't You?
Roethke.   Meadow Mouse, The.
Rowse.   White Cat of Trenarren, The.
Rybicki, J.   Dogman, The.
Schinto, J.   Stalker.
Shepard, J.   Love Song of Audrey.
Shepard, K.   Birch.
 Glom: Labrador, 110 Pounds.
Smith, L.   In the Heat of the Night.
Snyder, G.   Nansen.
Sonnenberg, B.   Stay.
Spencer, K. C.   When I Died on My Birthday.
Stern, G.   Dog, The.
Svoboda.   Cosmo Dog.
Tester, W.   Complacencies of the Fenced Yard.
Thomas, A.   Doggerel.
Tuck, L.   Sniff.
Wade, S.   Dog Sonnet.
Weaver, M.   Dogs, The.
Wilbur.   Marché aux Oiseaux.
Williams, C.   My Fly.
Wright, K.   Our Hamster's Life.
Yeats.   Two Songs of a Fool.

Peyote
Blockcolski.   Peyote Vision.

Phaeton
Longfellow, H.   Galaxy, The.

Phantoms
Bang, M.   Louise in Love.
Graves, R.   Sea Horse, The.

Pheasants
Hart-Smith.   Golden Pheasant.
North, M.   Pheasant Plucker's Son, The.
Plath.   Pheasant.

Philadelphia, Pennsylvania
Alexander, E.   Overture: Watermelon City.
Baraka.   Pause of Joe, The.
Brutus.   Off to Philadelphia in the Morning.
Dove, R.   Musician Talks About 'Process,' The.
Kemble.   To the Wissahiccon.
Sanchez, S.   Elegy (for MOVE and
 Philadelphia).
 Philadelphia: Spring, 1985.
Weaver, M.   Black Man's Sonata, A.

Philanthropy and Philanthropists
Anderson, M.   Closed Mill.
Dobson, A.   Virtuoso, A.
Guiterman.   Offer, An.
Hollander, J.   No Foundation.
Kendall, M.   Philanthropist and the Jelly-fish,
 The.
Unknown.   Old Woman of Leeds, The.
See also **Charity**

Philiphaugh, Battle of (1645)
Unknown.   Battle of Philiphaugh, The.

Philippines
Carbó, N.   In Tagalog Ibon Means Bird.
 When the Grain Is Golden and the Wind Is
 Chilly, Then It Is the Time to Harvest.
Lim-Wilson.   Explaining the Origin of My
 Name.
 Upon Overhearing Tagalog.
Remoto.   Rain.

Wojahn. Francis Ford Coppola and Anthropologist Interpreter Teaching Gartewienna Tribesmen to Sing 'Light My Fire,' Philippine Jungle, 1978.
See also **Filipinos**

Philistines
Pound, E. Les Millwin.

Phillips, Wendell
Ray, H. Wendell Phillips.

Philomela
Arnold, M. Philomela.
Ransom, J. Philomela.
Sidney, S. Nightingale, The.

Philosophy and Philosophers
Ashbery. My Philosophy of Life.
Baraka. Balboa, the Entertainer.
Bartlett, E. God Is Dead—Nietzche.
Berrigan, A. Advice to a Young Philosopher.
Black, S. Lust.
Blake, W. Mock On, Mock On, Voltaire, Rousseau.
Bromige. Logical Positivist, The.
Carson, C. Irish for No, The.
Collins, M. Positivists, The.
Cowley, A. To the Royal Society.
Cunningham, J. Metaphysical Amorist, The.
Dacre, C. Female Philosopher, The.
Deutsch. Homage to the Philosopher.
Emerson, R. Humble-Bee, The.
Foss, S. Philosopher, A.
Francis, R. Waxwings.
Gascoigne. Gascoigne's Woodmanship.
Greger. Man on the Bed, The.
Healy, R. Mutability Checkers.
Holub. Immanuel Kant.
Larkin, P. Days.
Lefroy. Idler Listening to Socrates Discussing Philosophy with His Boy-Friends, An.
Levy, A. Philosophy.
Manifold. Makhno's Philosophers.
Melville, H. Fragments of a Lost Gnostic Poem of the Twelfth [*or* 12th] Century.
Murphy, R. Philosopher and the Birds, The.
North, C. Philosophical Songs.
Ostriker. I Brood about Some Concepts, for Example.
Parker, A. Days like Prose.
Smith, S. Distractions and the Human Crowd. On the Death of a German Philosopher.
Stevens, W. To an Old Philosopher in Rome.
Tomlinson, C. In Defence of Metaphysics.
Viray, M. Saturday Morning, A.
Whitman, W. Base of All Metaphysics, The.

Phoebus Apollo
"Philo-Philippa." To the Excellent Orinda.
See also **Apollo**

Phoenix
Adams, J. On the Phoenix.
Carew, T. Song, [A]: "Ask[e] me no more where Jove bestow[e]s."
Kinnell. Another Night in the Ruins.
Klinger, A. Transformation.
Manley, R. Bob Marley's Dead.
Merrill, J. About the Phoenix.
Shakespeare, W. Phoenix and the Turtle, The.
Smith, S. News of the Phoenix.
Tu Fu. Song of the Vermeil Phoenix.
Wilbur. Cottage Street, 1953.

Photocopying
Safie, D. Meditation by the Xerox Machine.

Photography and Photographers
Abbey, L. Broken Silence.
Alegría. Documentary.
Ali, A. Postcard from Kashmir.
Amis, K. Mightier than the Pen.
Ashbery. City Afternoon.
Atwood. Daguerreotype Taken in Old Age. This Is a Photograph of Me.
Berger, B. Photo Safari.
Bernstein, C. Caught.
Brody. Family Album, A.
Brown, L. If I Had a Talking Picture of you.
Byron, C. Shipping the Pictures from Belfast.
Cabico, R. Antonio Banderas in His Underwear.
Carroll, L. Hiawatha's Photographing.

Cassells. Courtesy, A Trenchant Grace, A.
Castillo, S. Primos.
Cerenio. Family Photos: Black and White: 1960.
Charach, R. Evidence on Film, The.
Chernoff. Lost and Found.
Ciardi. On a Photo of Sgt. Ciardi a Year Later.
Clinton, M. History as Trash.
Coles, D. Photograph in a Stockholm Newspaper for March 13, 1910.
Conway, J. Weight Belt.
Cooley, N. Diane Arbus, New York.
Cortes, F. Palace of Fine Arts in San Francisco, The.
Couzyn. You Have Shown Me a Strange Image, and We Are Strange Prisoners.
Cronin, J. Group Photo from Pretoria Local on the Occasion of a Fourth Anniversary (Never Taken).
Curbelo. Photograph of My Parents.
Curtis, T. Land Army Photographs.
DeSylva, B. G. If I Had a Talking Picture of You.
Drummond de Andrade. Dead in Frock Coats, The.
Dunn, D. St Kilda's Parliament: 1879–1979.
Durcan. Irish Hierarchy Bans Colour Photography.
Ellis, T. Shooting Back.
Elmusa. Snapshots.
Etter. Well You Needn't.
Figueroa, J. Puerto Rico Made in Japan.
Fuller, R. Middle of a War, The.
Greenhalgh, C. Big No-No, The.
Groarke, V. Family Photograph, The.
Hai-Jew, S. Three Gypsies.
Harper, M. Three O'Clock Love Song.
Heyen. Tie, The.
Holden, M. Photograph of Haymaker, 1890.
Hoover, P. Family Romance.
Hughes, T. Six Young Men.
Kinzie. Sound Waves.
Komunyakaa. Untitled Blues; After a Photograph by Yevgeni Yevtushenko.
Kramer, L. Images of the San Francisco Disaster.
Kumin, M. Family Man, A.
Landesman. Photographs.
Larkin, P. Lines on a Young Lady's Photograph Album. Whatever Happened?
Lassell. Three Poems.
Levi, S. Abbienti.
Levis. Widening Spell of the Leaves, The.
Lim, S. Black and White.
Lowe, J. Between Acts.
Lowell, R. Epilogue: "Those blessed structures, plot and rhyme."
Lum. Picture of my Mother's Family, A.
McElroy, C. From Homegrown: An Asian-American Anthology of Writers.
McKendrick, J. Shortened History in Pictures, A.
Merrill, J. David's Night in Veliès.
Nemerov. Picture, A.
Neufeld, A. Family Album. Pictures and Stories.
Newman, G. Photograph of Survivors.
O'Grady, J. Anonymous Wedding Photo.
Obejas, A. Lifes.
Oppen. From a Photograph.
Ormsby. War Photographers, The.
Peseroff. Hardness Scale, The.
Phillips, L. My Son Shows Me a Photograph of Michael Jordan Performing a Slam Dunk.
Pinkerton, H. On Dorothea Lange's Photograph "Migrant Mother" (1936).
Raworth. Empty Pain-Killer Bottles, The.
Ray, D. Eskimo Girl, The.
Rivard. Summons.
Schneider, M. Photograph, The.
Seay. Audubon Drive, Memphis.
Shepherd, R. What Cannot Be Kept.
St. John, D. Grandfather's Cap, My.
Suknaski. Chinese Camp, Kamloops (circa 1883).

Sundiata. Making Poems; on the road in Minneapolis.
Sutter. Hoarfrost and Fog.
Taylor, A. Developing a Wife.
Trethewey, N. Bellocq's Ophelia.
Triplett, P. Studies in Desire.
Tucker, M. Family Portraits.
Updike. Snapshots.
Vazirani, R. Mrs. Biswas Goes Through a Photo Album.
Vertreace, M. Black Tulips.
Wakoski. Photos, The.
Wallace, R. Makings of Happiness, The.
Warren, R. In Creve Coeur, Missouri.
Warsh. Suicide Rates, The.
Wenderoth, J. Disfortune.
Whittemore, R. Mother's Past.
Wilbur. Looking into History.
Wilder, A. Photographs.
Wright, K. Victorian Family Photograph.
Yau. Cenotaph.
See also **Cameras**

Physicians
Aiken, C. Doctors' Row.
Belloc. Henry King, Who Chewed Bits of String, and Was Early Cut Off in Dreadful Agonies. On Hygiene.
Browning, R. Epistle Containing the Strange Medical Experience of Karshish, the Arab Physician, An.
Burns, R. Death and Doctor Hornbook [A True Story].
Davis, F. Arthur Ridgewood, M.D.
Fitzgerald, R. Wind at Your Door, The.
Fusselman, A. Ticker.
Hoffman, O. Five Best Doctors, The.
Johnson, S. On the Death of Dr [*or* Mr] Robert Levet [a Practiser in Physic].
Jonson, B. To Doctor Empiric[k].
Kirkup. Correct Compassion, A.
Miles, J. Doctor Who Sits at the Bedside of a Rat, The.
Moorer. Birthday Wishes to a Physician.
Prior. Remedy Worse than the Disease, The.
Robinson, E. How Annandale Went Out.
Sadiq, M. Tuskegee Experiment.
Seth. Doctor's Journal Entry for August 6, 1945, A.
Stallworthy, J. Letter from Berlin, A.
Williams, W. Complaint. To Close. Young Love.
See also **Hospitals; Medicine; Nurses**

Physics and Physicists
Jordan, J. Poem about Intelligence for My Brothers and Sisters, A.
Kendall, M. Ether Insatiable.
Seaton, M. Tagging.

Pianos
Baker, T. Armillaria Mellea.
Cedering, S. Variations for the Piano.
Chmielarz. They Come Humming.
Coleridge, M. To a Piano.
Duran, J. Mr Teller the Piano Teacher.
Feinstein, S. Summerhouse Piano.
Frost, R. Investment, The.
Gilonis, H. Song 9.
Grunke, A. Learning to Live with the Piano.
Haskins, L. Prodigy, The.
Jordan, J. October 23, 1983.
Justice, D. Variations for Two Pianos.
Lawrence, D. Piano.
Piano, The.
Madgett, N. Echoes.
Max, L. Equal Temperament.
Nurske, D. Involuntary Music.
Solonche. Chopin Preludes, Opus 28.
Speakes. Heartbreak Hotel Piano-Bar.
Stevens, W. Mozart, 1935.
Unknown, fr. Terezin Concentration Camp. Concert in the Old School Garret.
Updike. Player Piano.
Waters, M. 'Night in the Tropics' (1858-59?).
Weissbort. Mourning.

Winder. On Fourteen Maple Street.

Picasso, Pablo
Cassells. These Are Not Brushstrokes.
Ford, C. There's No Place to Sleep in This Bed, Tanguy.
Hughes, L. Cubes.
Jacob, M. In Honor of the Sardana and the Tenora.
Norse. Picasso Visits Braque.
Salmon, A. Painting.
Scalapino. Picasso and Anarchism.

Picnics and Barbecues
Adamson. My Tenth Birthday.
Betjeman. Archaeological Picnic, The.
Causley. Eden Rock.
Colby, T. Labor Day Picnic Poem.
Elmslie, K. Picnic.
Hardy, T. Where the Picnic Was.
Lofting. Picnic.
Logan, J. Picnic, The.
Muldoon, P. Truce.
Roethke. Thing, The.
Tagami. Mussel Rock/Lowtide—Santa Cruz, California 1959.
Tennyson, A. Audley Court.
Warren, R. Renoir.
Weaver, M. Picnic, an Homage to Civil Rights, The.
Wong, N. Picnic.

Pies
Guest, E. Lemon Pie.
Merriam, E. Counting-out Rhyme.

Piety
Donne. Hymn[e] to Christ, at the Author's Last Going into Germany, A.
Herrick. Chewing [of] the Cud, The.
His Offering, with the Rest, at the Sepulcher.
To Keep a True Lent.

Pigeons
Angel. Evolving Similarities.
Farjeon, E. Mrs. Peck-Pigeon.
Heyen. Derailment.
Kavanagh, P. Leave Them Alone.
Knight, E. Crazy Pigeon.
MacCaig. Wild Oats.
McGinley. Trinity Place.
Merwin, W. S. Fly.
Meyers, B. Pigeons.
Pinsky. First Early Mornings Together.
Reid, A. Pigeons.
Rossetti, C. On the Wing.
Schwartz, R. L. Can Pigeons Be Heroes?
Seth. Pigeons.
Sia, B. Enemy.
Tobin, D. Pigeons.
Wormser. Pigeons.
Wright, J. Lament for Passenger Pigeons.

Pigs
Artaud. All Writing Is Garbage.
Benson, G. Cat and the Pig, The.
Blunden. Poor Man's Pig, The.
Corso. Song: "Oh, dear! Oh, me! Oh, my!"
Cullen, C. Unknown Color, The.
Edson, R. Performance at Hog Theater, A.
Espada. Cada Puerco Tiene Su Sábado.
Fanning, R. Oink as Taunt.
Fergusson. Sow of Feeling, The.
Forrest. St. Anthony and His Pig; a Cantata.
Garlick, R. Still Life.
Geddes, G. Transubstantiation.
Gunn, T. Moly.
Hall, D. Eating the Pig.
Hecht, A. Pig.
Hughes, T. View of a Pig.
Humphreys, E. Apple Tree and a Pig, An.
Joseph, L. It's Not Me Shouting at No One.
Keplinger, D. Distance Between Zero and One, The.
Kinnell. Saint Francis and the Sow.
Lawrence, D. Food of the North.
Lee, D. For Jan, with Love.
Jan's Birthday.
Lehmann, G. Pigs, The.
Levine, P. Animals Are Passing from Our Lives.

Like, J. James Dean and the Pig.
McKay, C. If We Must Die.
Milosz, C. Readings.
Mother Goose. This Little Pig Went to Market.
Tom, Tom, the piper's son.
Nash, O. Pig, The.
Padgett, R. Detach, Invading.
Rossetti, C. If a pig wore a wig.
Southey, R. Ode to a Pig while His Nose Was Being Bored.
Unknown. As I Went to Bonner.
Judged by the Company One Keeps.
Pig, The.
Riddle: "As I went down that yella bank."
There Was a Lady Loved a Swine.
Watson, C. Knickerbocker Knockabout.
Wesley, S. Pindaric on the Grunting of a Hog, A.

Pike (fish)
Hughes, T. Pike.
Lowell, A. Pike, The.

Pilgrim Fathers
Bacon, L. Pilgrim Fathers, The.
Emerson, R. Boston Hymn.
Hemans. Landing of the Pilgrim Fathers [in New England], The.
Lowell, R. Children of Light.
Tillam. Upon the First Sight of New England, June 29, 1638.
Very. Wild Rose of Plymouth, The.

Pilgrimages and Pilgrims
Arnold, M. Poet, The.
Resignation.
Bradstreet, A. As Weary Pilgrim, Now at Rest.
Chaucer. Alysoun.
Cage, The.
Chauntecleer.
Death and the Three Revellers.
Franklin's Prologue, The.
Franklin's Tale, The.
Friar's Prologue, The.
Friar's Tale, The.
General Prologue, The.
Good Parson, The.
Introduction to the Franklin's Prologue and Tale.
Introduction to the Pardoner's Tale.
Introduction to the Parson's Tale, The.
Knighthood, The.
Miller's [or Milleres] Tale, The.
Miller's Tale, The.
Nun's Priest's Tale, The.
Pardoner's Prologue, The.
Pardoner's Tale, The.
Parson and the Plowman Described, The.
Patient Griselda.
Prologue to Sir Thopas.
Saturn.
Seven Pilgrims: A Monk.
Seven Pilgrims: A Prioress[e].
Seven Pilgrims: A Wyf of Bathe.
Temple of Mars, The.
Three Rioters, The.
Wife of Bath's Prologue, The.
Wife of Bath's Tale, The.
Clarke, A. Pilgrimage.
Clive. Old Age.
Donne. Song: "Go and catch a falling star."
Gomez, M. Lost Daughter.
Graves, R. Travel[l]er's Curse after Misdirection[, The].
Hall, D. Woolworth's.
Hardy, T. Hap.
Hemans. Landing of the Pilgrim Fathers [in New England], The.
Herbert, E. Pilgrimage, The.
Kendall, H. Christmas Creek.
Lewis, C. Pilgrim's Problem.
Nye, N. My Uncle Mohammed at Mecca, 1981.
Rossetti, C. Uphill.
Spender, S. Marston.
Unknown. City Called Heaven.
Vaughan, H. Pilgrimage, The.
Wright, J. Bullocky.
Yeats. Pilgrim, The.

Pilots
Jarrell. Pilot from the Carrier, A.

Waniek. Freeman Field.
Porter.
Star-Fix.
Tuskegee Airfield.
See also **Air Warfare**

Pindar
Duncan, R. Poem Beginning with a Line by Pindar, A.

Pine Island, Minnesota
Wright, J. Lying in a Hammock at William Duffy's Farm in Pine Island, Minnesota.

Pine Trees
Bugeja, M. Conifer King, The.
Cherry, K. Pines Without Peer, The.
Doolittle, H. Oread.
Monroe, B. In the Pines.
Muldoon, P. Yggdrasill.
Plath. Black Pine Tree in an Orange Light.
Po Chü-i. Song of the Pines.
Swanger. Knob Pines.
Warren, R. Return: An Elegy, The.

Pinkham, Lydia
Unknown. Lydia Pinkham.

Pioneers
Benét, R. *et al.* Western Wagons.
Benét, S. Ballad of William Sycamore, The.
Bowering, G. Grandfather.
Brewster, E. Great-Aunt Rebecca.
Cary, P. Homes for All.
Crawford, V. Pioneer Woman.
Cronwright. Song of the Wagon-whip, A.
Crosby, F. On Hearing a Description of a Prairie.
Davis, M. Going Out and Coming In.
Dorn, E. Home on the Range, February 1962.
Emerson, R. Forerunners.
Fisher, A. *et al.* Pioneers.
Fisher, L. Pioneers.
Freneau. On the Civilization of the Western Aboriginal Country.
Johnson, E. Joe.
Moore, M. New York.
Nowlan. For Jean Vincent d'Abbadie, Baron St.-Castin.
Pfeiffer, E. Lost Light, The.
Piatt, J. Farther.
Rich, A. Face to Face.
From an Old House in America.
Sanchez, S. Right On: White America.
Sigourney. Western Emigrant, The.
Smith, W. Tempest, The.
Unknown. State of Arkansas, The.

Pipers
Browning, R. Pied Piper of Hamelin, The.

Piracy and Pirates
Cowley, A. Cheer Up, My Mates.
Kingsley, C. Last Buccaneer, The.
Komunyakaa. Boat People.
Masefield. Captain Stratton's Fancy.
Meigs, M. Pirate Don Durk of Dowdee, The.
Stevenson, R. Pirate Story.
Unknown. Captain Ward and the *Rainbow*.

Pitcher, Molly
Richards, L. Molly Pitcher.

Pitt, William
Burns, R. On Mr. Pitt's [or Pit's] Hair-Powder Tax.

Pittsburgh, Pennsylvania
Anderson, M. Closed Mill.
Invention of Pittsburgh, The.
Hazo. Pittsburgh in Passing.
Stern, G. Dancing, The.

Pity
Arnold, C. Extravagance of Zoos, The.
Bourne, W. Heart's Fine Gold, The.
Cameron, N. Compassionate Fool, The.
Chaucer. Complaint unto Pity, The.
Chippewa Oral Tradition. Song of the Captive Sioux Woman.
Coleridge, S. Love.
Hardy, T. Her Dilemma.
Hopkins, G. My Own Heart Let Me More Have Pity On.
Howitt, M. Cry of the Animals, The.

Hughes, L. Lover's Return.
Keats. I Cry Your Mercy, Pity, Love—Ay, Love!
Lovelace, R. La Bourbon, A.
Mansfield, K. Man with the Wooden Leg, The.
Mayer, B. Generic Elbows.
Rossetti, C. After Death.
Schuyler, J. Self-Pity Is a Kind of Lying, Too.
Wilbur. Undead, The.
Wright, J. American Twilights, 1957.
    At the Executed Murderer's Grave.
    Inscription for the Tank.
Yeats. Pity of Love, The.

Pizarro, Francisco
Warton, J. Revenge of America, The.

Pizza
Silano, M. Sweet Red Peppers, Sun-Drieds, the Hearts of Artichokes.

Place Names
Benét, S. American Names.
Daly, T. Pennsylvania Places.
"Kerr." American Traveller, The.
Limburg, J. Barton in the Beans.
Sigourney. Indian Names.

Plague
Greenlaw. Earliest Known Representation of a Storm in Western Art, The.
Hecht, A. Tarantula or the Dance of Death.
Kees. Coming of the Plague, The.
Lux. Plague Victims Catapulted over Walls into Besieged City.
Melville, H. In the Desert.
Starbuck, G. Prognosis.
Toomer. November Cotton Flower.

Plains
Todd, M. Son et Lumière.
See also **Prairies**

Planets
Kendall, M. Ether Insatiable.
MacCaig. Stars and Planets.
MacDiarmid, H. Bonnie Broukit Bairn, The.

Plants
Barry, J. Floating Petals.
Butler, M. Listen.
Calil, A. Blouse of Felt.
Greenberg, A. Wintering Over at the End of the Century.
Humphrey, D. No Immunity.
Kendall, M. Education's Martyr.
Levine, P. Later Still.
Liu, T. Brooklyn Botanic Garden, The.
Madgett. Woman with Flower.
Mayer, B. Aeschyleans, The.
McFadden, D. House Plants.
Moore, M. Nevertheless.
Napier, F. Houseplant.
Perreault, J. Readymade.
Phillips, C. Reach, The.
Roethke. Cuttings.
    Moss-Gathering.
    Root Cellar.
Stevenson, R. To a Gardener.
Swinburne. Sundew, The.
Taggard. Fructus.
Taylor, A. Clearing Away.
Thoreau. I Am a Parcel of Vain Strivings Tied.
Townsend, A. Purple Loosestrife.
Williams, W. It Is a Small Plant.
Wormser. It's a Party (1959).

Plath, Sylvia
Ciment, J. Mommy.
Herzberg. On the Death of Sylvia Plath.
Sexton. Sylvia's Death.
Wilbur. Cottage Street, 1953.

Plato
Mahon. Death and the Sun.
Unknown. Spirit of Plato.

Platonic Love
Cartwright, W. No Platonic [or Platonique] Love.
Cooper, D. Dreamt Up.
Donne. Air[e] and Angels.
    Ecstasy, The.
Herbert, E. Platonic Love.
Hine. Lines on a Platonic Friendship.

North, D. Platonic.
Philips, K. To My Excellent Lucasia, On Our Friendship.
St. John, D. My Friend.
Thoreau. Sympathy.
Vaughan, H. To Amoret, of the Difference 'twixt Him and Other Lovers, and What True Love Is.

Platypuses
Aborigine Oral Tradition. Platypus, The.
Barrington, P. I Had a Duck-billed Platypus.
Herford. Platypus, The.

Play
"Æ." Frolic.
Adams, S. Sliding.
Aldis, D. Kick a Little Stone.
Ashbery. Paradoxes and Oxymorons.
Benson, G. Play No Ball.
Benson, S. Beaten Track, The.
Bonar. Length of Days.
Carew, T. To the Reader of Master William Davenant's Play [The Wits].
Charles, D. Getting Dirty.
Ciardi. All about Boys and Girls.
    What Johnny Told Me.
Dalton, A. How to Disappear.
Davie. Fountain, The.
Davies, W. To W.S.—On His Wonderful Toys.
Davis, C. Nod.
Dickinson, E. God is indeed a jealous God.
Ginsberg, A. Bop Lyrics.
Harrison, G. Playground, The.
Harryman. Magic (or Rousseau).
Hoberman. Let's Dress Up.
Hughes, L. Little Song.
    Piggy-back.
Johns. Invitation.
Keech. Discovery.
Kennedy, X. Little Elegy.
Kinsella, J. Fall, The.
Lee, D. Dickery Dean.
Livingston, M. Lemonade Stand.
Millay, E. From a Very Little Sphinx.
Moore, L. Sometimes.
Piatt, S. Palace-Burner, The.
Rossetti, C. Frisky Lamb, A.
Scannell. Hide and Seek.
Schwartz, D. I Am Cherry Alive.
Smith, W. Around My Room.
Snyder, G. Hop, Skip, and Jump.
Soto. Behind Grandma's House.
Spender, S. Abrupt and charming mover.
Stafford, W. At the Playground.
Stein, G. Identity A Poem.
Stevenson, R. At the Seaside [or Sea-Side].
    Block City.
    Gardener, The.
    Good Play, A.
    Land of Counterpane, The.
    Land of Story-Books, The.
    Pirate Story.
    Swing, The.
Tranter. Debbie and Co.
Turner, A. Red-Dress Girl.
Unknown. Billy, Billy.
    Girls and Boys Come out to Play.
    Nuts an' May.
Verlaine. Femme et Chatte.
Watson, R. White Lady, The.
Watts, I. Innocent Play.
Wright, J. Camphor Laurel.

Playmates
Jaques, F. There Once Was a Puffin.
Stevenson, R. Gardener, The.
    My Shadow.
Yeats. To a Squirrel at Kyle-Na-No.

Pleasure
Broumas, O. Tryst.
Browning, E. Best Thing in the World, The.
Burns, R. Sandy and Jockie.
Coleridge, S. Kubla Khan: or, A Vision in a Dream.
Collins, W. Ode to Evening.
Cornish, W. Pleasure It Is.
Coward. Poor Little Rich Girl.
Cowley, A. Epicure, The.

Crozier, L. Poem for Sigmund.
Davidson, D. Redivivus.
Dickinson, E. Heart Asks Pleasure—First, The.
    I Taste a Liquor Never Brewed.
Drieu la Rochelle. Tennis.
Duran, J. Mere Pleasure of Flying, The.
Ekelof. Hangman.
Feldman, A. Contemporary American Poetry.
Godfrey. So Let's Look at It Another Way.
Gruber, A. My Neighbor's Roses.
Hacker, M. Canzone: "Consider the three functions of the tongue."
Hanson, M. To Fancy.
Hardy, T. Great Things.
Hass, R. Now Winter Nights.
Herrick. On Himselfe.
Holt, R. Pleasure of Feeling Inside Your Body, The.
Johnson, S. Short Song of Congratulation [or To a Young Heir], A.
Joseph, A. Learning to Laugh.
    Pleasure.
Loden. Far In.
Marvell. Dialogue Between The Resolved Soul and Created Pleasure, A.
Milton. L'Allegro.
Moore, T. Pleasure.
Porter, C. I Get a Kick Out of You.
Prunty. Note of Thanks, A.
Radcliffe, A. Sun-Rise: Sonnet, A.
    To the Visions of Fancy.
Ramanujan. Pleasure.
Robinson, M. Bower of Pleasure, The.
    Rejects the Influence of Reason.
Rossetti, C. Goblin Market.
Schwartz, R. L. Edgewater Park.
Shaw, A. Small Pleasures.
Shuttle. Old Man, The.
Southwell. Man's Civil[l] War[re].
Stein, G. Why Do You Feel Differently.
Strode. Justification.
Talfourd. 'Tis a Little Thing.
Tana, P. You Bring Me Back.
Thelwall. Anacreontic.
Unknown. My Neighbor's Reply.
Wilbur. Simile for Her Smile, A.
Wilde, O. Hélas!
Wright, C. Legend of Hell, The.
Young, D. Pleasure.

Pleiades
Hemans. Lost Pleiad, The.
Stevenson, A. Sonnet: "If it be night . . . ."
Unknown. Song of the Pleiades.
Whitman, W. On the Beach at Night.

Plowing and Plowmen
Colum, P. Plower, The.
Heaney, S. Follower.
Hopkins, G. Harry Ploughman.
Jones, S. Ploughman, in Imitation of Milton, The.
Muir, E. Horses.
Quarles. On the Ploughman [or Plough-Man].
Simpson, L. Summer Storm.
Stevens, W. Ploughing on Sunday.
Thomas, E. As the Team's Head-Brass.

Plum Trees and Plums
Biespiel, D. Under a Blossoming Plum Tree.
Chasin. Word *Plum*, The.
Corbett, W. Wickson Plums.
Dooley, M. At Les Deux Magots.
Gogarty. Plum Tree by the House, The.
Kinsella, J. Plumburst.
Li Ch'ing-chao. Tune: "Pure Serene Music."
Orrick. Wild Plum.
Toomer. Song of the Son.
Williams, W. This Is Just to Say.
    To a Poor Old Woman.

Plumbing and Plumbers
Dove, R. Genie's Prayer Under the Kitchen Sink.
King, S. Difference, The.
Miles, S. Plumbers.

Plunder and Plundering
Ewart. Personal Footnote, A.
Harrison, T. Cycles of Donji Vakuf.

Hewitt, J.	Colony, The.
Spencer, B.	Invaders, The.
Plymouth, England
Spender, S.	Air Raid Across the Bay at
	Plymouth.
Poaching and Poachers
Unknown.	Lincolnshire Poacher, The.
Wright, J.	Lifting Illegal Nets by Flashlight.
Pocahontas
Bibb.	Capt. Smith and Pocahontas.
Sandburg, C.	Cool Tombs.
Poe, Edgar Allan
Butts, A.	Poe Story, A.
Ford, C.	Bad Habit, The.
Koch, K.	You Were Wearing.
Levine, P.	On the Edge.
Longfellow, H.	Couplet: February 24, 1847.
Loy.	Poe.
Smith, S.	After-Thought, The.
Spicer, J.	Improvisations on a Sentence by Poe.
Very.	Forevermore.
Poetic Meter
Cope, W.	Emily Dickinson.
Longfellow, H.	Couplet: February 24, 1847.
Tennyson, A.	Hendecasyllabics.
Williams, W.	Paterson, Book 5: The River of
	Heaven.
Poetry: Study and Teaching
Armitage, S.	Zoom!
Broumas, O.	Artemis.
Cocteau.	Cape of Good Hope, The.
D'Aguiar.	Langston.
Hass, R.	Letter to a Poet.
Klappert.	To Whom.
Powell, D. A.	Sonnet: "Morsels of my lifework:
	the story of a professional party hostess."
Seidman.	Tale of Genji.
Williams, W.	Paterson, Book 5: The River of
	Heaven.
Poets and Poetry
Aiyejina.	Dialogue, The.
Alarcon, F.	Los árboles son poetas / Trees Are
	Poets.
Alexander, A.	For Raftery.
Algarin.	Christmas Eve: Nuyorican Café.
	Happy New Year.
	Talking.
Alkalay-Gut.	Public Outcry.
Allen, P.	Teaching Poetry at Votech High, Santa
	Fe, the Week John Lennon Was Shot.
Anderson-Thompkins.	Epitaph for Willie or
	Little Black Poet with No Future.
Andrews, N.	Poets on Poets.
Antin.	Real Estate.
Ashbery.	Paradoxes and Oxymorons.
	What Is Poetry.
Awad, J.	Autumnal.
	Lament for Philip Larkin, A.
Balaban.	Anna Akhmatova Spends the Night on
	Miami Beach.
Bandele, A.	1980–1990: A Poet's Personal
	Review.
Baraka.	Balboa, the Entertainer.
Baratier, D.	Fall of Because, The.
Barker, G.	To Whom Else.
Beatty, P.	Stall Me Out.
Begley, T.	Sappho's Gymnasium.
Bennani, B.	Camel's Bite.
Benson, L.	Asante.
Bernstein, C.	Dysraphism.
	Freud's Butcher.
	Klupzy Girl, The.
	Of Time and the Line.
Berrigan, A.	Sabotage.
Bertolino.	American Poetry.
Bibbins, M.	Whitman on the Beach.
Birney.	Poet-Tree.
Black, S.	Rilke's Letter from Rome.
Bly, R.	Day We Visited New Orleans, The.
	Gaiety of Form, The.
	On the Oregon Coast.
	Possibility of New Poetry, The.
Bond, E.	First World War Poets.
Bottoms.	Sierra Bear.
Bradstreet, A.	In Honour of that High and

Mighty Princess Queen Elizabeth of Happy
	Memory.
	Prologue, The.
Brathwaite, E.	Stone.
Breton, A.	On the Road to San Romano.
Bridges, R.	To Francis Jammes.
Bromige.	Eastward Ho! A Succession.
Broumas, O.	Sappho's Gymnasium.
Browning, E.	Fifth Book.
Browning, R.	How It Strikes a Contemporary.
Brownstein.	Stepping Out.
Bryan, S.	Lunch with Girl Scouts.
Bryant, W.	Poet, The.
Buckley, V.	Teaching German Literature.
Burkard.	2 Poems on the Same Theme.
	Meditation Brought About by George Bogin's
	Translation of Jules Supervielle's Poem 'The
	Sea.'
Burn.	In Japan.
Bynner.	Idols.
Cabalquinto.	Ordinance, The.
Cady.	After Hearing Heterosexual Poets in
	October 1974: What It Seems Like To Write a
	Male Homosexual Love Poem Now.
Campbell, R.	Volunteer's Reply to the Poet,
	The.
Campo.	For J. W.
Carbó, N.	I Found Orpheus Levitating.
Carew, T.	Elegy upon the Death of the Dean of
	[St.] Paul's, Dr. John Donne, An.
	On the Death of Donne.
Carey, H.	Namby-Pamby. A Panegyric on the
	New Versification, Address'd to A———P—
	——— , Esq.
Carroll.	Ode to the Angels Who Move
	Perpetually toward the Dayspring of Their
	Youth.
Carroll, L.	Poeta Fit, Non Nascitur.
Carruth, H.	Saturday at the Border.
Carver, D.	Poet, The.
Cavendish, M.	Of the Theme of Love.
	Poet[r]ess's Hasty Resolution, The.
Cendrars.	Contrasts.
	Hammock.
Cervantes.	First Beating.
	On the Poet Coming of Age.
Char.	Argument.
Chin.	Leaving San Francisco.
Chipasula.	Manifesto on Ars Poetica.
Chubb, R.	Song of My Soul.
Clare, J.	To the Memory of John Keats.
Clarke, C.	Poet's Death, A.
Cleary, B.	New Rock n Roll, The.
Clifton, L.	Fury.
	My Dream About the Poet.
Clouts.	After the Poem.
Coleridge, S.	Homeric Hexameter, The.
	Metrical Feet.
Cooper, D.	Poem for George Miles.
Cope, W.	Emily Dickinson.
	Uncertainty of the Poet, The.
	Waste Land Limericks.
Corcoran.	In the Red Book.
Corn.	Long-Distance Call to Gregg, Who Lived
	with AIDS as Long as He Could.
	Marriage in the Nineties, A.
Cory, W.	Desiderato.
Cowley, A.	Muse, The.
Cullen, C.	For Hazel Hall, American Poet.
	Yet Do I Marvel.
Cummings, E.	Four III.
	If I Have Made, My Lady.
	Since feeling is first.
Dana, M.	Real Comfort.
Daniel, S.	To the Right Honorable, the Lady
	Mary, Countess of Pembroke.
Delaunay, S.	Greetings, Blaise Cendrars.
Dharker.	Minority.
Dickson, J.	Poemectomy.
DiPalma.	Prerogative of Lieder, The.
Dissanayake.	Freedom.
Dodge, M.	Note.
Drummond, W.	Sextain: "With elegies, sad
	songs, and mourning lays."
Dugan, A.	American Variation on How Rilke
	Loved a Princess and Got to Stay in Her

Castle.
	Poem for Elliot Carter on His 90th Birthday.
Duhamel.	How Much Is This Poem Going to
	Cost Me?
	Sex with a Famous Poet.
Duhig, I.	Fred.
	Margin Prayer from an Ancient Psalter.
	Untitled.
Dumdum.	Li Pos of the Polis.
Duncan, R.	New Poem, A.
	Poetry, a Natural Thing.
	Structure of Rime XVIII.
	Structure of Rime XXIII.
Eberhart, R.	Immortal Picture, The.
Edwards, K.	Provisionally.
Eigner.	In Imitation.
Elliott, E.	Powers of the Sonnet.
Ellis, T.	T. A. P. O. A. F. O. M.
Emanuel, L.	Homage to Sharon Stone.
Emerson, R.	Merlin.
	Merlin I.
	Motto to "The Poet."
	Test, The.
Faber, F.	Sonnet-writing. To F. W. F.
Fanning, R.	Baudelaire's Ablutions.
Feldman, A.	Contemporary American Poetry.
Figueroa, J.	Pablo Neruda.
	Poet Pedro Pietri.
Forbes, J.	Monkey's Pride.
Forman, R.	This Poem.
Francis, R.	Catch.
Fuller, M.	Lines Written in Boston on a
	Beautiful Autumnal Day.
Fullerton.	Poetry.
Fulton, A.	Wonder Bread.
Gallagher, T.	Instructions to the Double.
Garrett, E.	Reprieve, The.
Georgiou, E.	Space Between, The.
Gibran.	Two Poems, The.
Gilbert, J.	Malvolio in San Francisco.
Ginsberg, A.	Grim Skeleton.
	Last Night in Calcutta.
Gioia.	Next Poem, The.
Giovanni.	Poem (for Langston Hughes), A.
Gladstone, W. E.	To a Rejected Sonnet.
Goedicke.	Wind of Our Going: Adagio Ma Non
	Troppo.
Gomez, M.	Solo Palabras.
Goodman, M.	Open Poem.
Goodman, P.	Sentences After *Defence of
	Poetry.*
Gosse.	Sestina: "In fair Provence, the land of
	lute and rose."
Grandfather Koori.	Never Blood So Red.
Guiterman.	Whole Duty of a Poem, The.
Gundy, J.	For the New York City Poet Who
	Informed Me that Few People Live This Way.
Gwala.	In Defence of Poetry.
Gwynn, R.	Approaching a Significant Birthday,
	He Peruses The Norton Anthology of Poetry.
Hacker, M.	Feeling and Form.
Hahn, S.	Confession.
Halperin.	Two Lines from Paul Celan.
Hamer.	Berkeley, Late Spring.
Hamill, S.	Another Duffer.
	Reading Seferis.
Hanson, M.	Occasioned by Reading Mrs. M.
	Robinson's Poems.
	To Mrs. Charlotte Smith.
Harms.	Soon.
Harrison, T.	Heartless Art, The.
Harry, J.	Poem Films Itself, The.
Hartnett.	Enamoured of the Miniscule.
Harwood, L.	Poem for Writers, A.
Hass, R.	Interrupted Meditation.
Hattersley, G.	Frank O'Hara Five, Geoffrey
	Chaucer Nil.
Healy, E.	From Los Angeles Looking South.
Hecht, A.	Lot of Night Music, A.
Hemans.	Thought from an Italian Poet.
Herbert, G.	Jordan (1).
	Jordan (2).
	Quidditie [*or* Quiddity], The.
	Sonnet: "My God, where is that ancient heat
	towards Thee."
Herbert, W.	Baby Poem Industry Poem, The.

Cabaret McGonagall.
Hernández Cruz.   Anonymous.
Side 32.
Herrick.   His Prayer for Absolution.
Ode for Him [or Ben Jonson], An.
To Live Merrily, and To Trust to Good Verses.
Highfill, M.   Marginalization of Poetry, The.
Hill, G.   Domaine Public.
Vergine bella.
Hillman.   Little Furnace.
Hirshfield, J.   Letter to Hugo from Later.
Hogan, L.   Heartland.
Holland, J.   Having read up on the subject.
Pulse.
Wavelength.
Hollander, J.   Some Walks With You.
What the Lovers in the Old Songs Thought.
Holman, B.   Performance Poem.
Holmes, O.   At the "Atlantic" Dinner, December 15, 1874.
Poesy.
Poet Grows Old, The.
Hood, T.   Literary Reminiscences.
Sonnet to a Sonnet.
Howe, F.   Doubt.
Hughes, F.   Birds.
Hulme, T.   Embankment, The (The fantasia of a fallen gentleman on a cold, bitter night).
Hummer, T.   Poem in the Shape of a Saxophone.
Jacob, M.   Spanish Generosity.
Jacobsen, J.   When the Five Prominent Poets.
Jarmain.   These Poems.
Jemie.   Toward a Poetics.
Jennings, K.   Couples.
Johns.   Salon de Vers.
Johnston, M.   In Memoriam.
Jones, R.   End of Communism, The.
Poet's Heart, The.
Jones, S.   Ann Griffiths.
Jones, T.   Mr Jones as the Transported Poet.
Jonson, B.   Epistle Answering to One that Asked to Be Sealed of the Tribe of Ben, An.
Fit of Rhyme [or Rime] against Rhyme [or Rime], A.
Sonnet to the Noble Lady, the Lady Mary Wroth, A.
To John Donne.
To the Memory of My Beloved, the Author Mr [or Master] William Shakespeare [And What He Hath Left Us].
Jordan, J.   Something Like a Sonnet for Phillis Miracle Wheatley.
Justice, D.   Pantoum of the Great Depression.
Variations on a Text by Vallejo.
Kaufman, S.   By the Rivers.
Poem in November.
Kennedy, X.   Poets.
Kizer, C.   Ashes, The.
For Sappho / After Sappho.
To an Unknown Poet.
Translation.
Klee.   Poem.
Klein, M.   Scenes for an Elegy.
Knight, E.   Haiku: "Eastern guard tower."
To Make a Poem in Prison.
Knoepfle.   Late Winter in Menard County.
Koch, K.   To World War Two.
Kombem.   Another Moment.
Komrij.   Poet, The.
Lake, P.   Introduction to Poetry.
Landon.   Poet's Lot, The.
Laughlin, J.   Then and Now.
Lauterbach.   Mimetic.
Laux.   Finding What's Lost.
Layton.   Birth of Tragedy, The.
Leapor.   Mira's Will.
Leonard, T.   100 Differences Between Poetry and Prose.
Levertov.   Poet and Person.
Levine, P.   Genius.
Lima, J.   Distribution of Poetry.
Longfellow, H.   Broken Oar, The.
Milton.
Lovelace, R.   On Sanazar's being honoured with six hundred Duckets by the Clarissimi of Venice, for composing an Elegiack Hexastick

of The City. A Satyre.
To My Noble Kinsman, Thomas Stanley, Esquire, on His Lyric Poems Composed by Master John Gamble.
Lowell, J.   Science and Poetry.
Lowell, R.   Epilogue: "Those blessed structures, plot and rhyme."
MacLeish.   Ars Poetica.
Madhubuti.   Killing Memory.
"Malley."   Sonnets for the Novachord.
Mandiela, A.   Mih Feel It.
Manhire.   On Originality.
Mann, C.   Poet's Progress, The.
Manrique, J.   Baudelaire's Spleen.
My Night with Frederico García Lorca (As Told by Edouard Roditi).
Mapanje.   On Being Asked to Write a Poem for 1979.
Martí.   Opposite of Ornate and Rhetorical Poetry, The.
Martinez, D.   Pain.
Marvell.   On Mr Milton's "Paradise Lost."
Matthews, M.   Language.
Mayakovsky [or Maiakovskii].   Screaming My Head Off.
Mayer, B.   Generic Elbows.
'Mbala.'   History of Dub Poetry, The.
McClatchy.   Bishop Reading.
McElroy, C.   Pike Street Bus.
McNeil, R.   Mirrors in the Room.
Medina, T.   Don't Say Goodnight to Etheridge Knight.
Poem for Teacup Mantlepiece Poets Palpitating Poot Booty Plagiarists Imprisoned in Ivy League White Supremacist Mental Biological Warfare Labs.
Merwin, W. S.   Berryman.
Messerli.   From Hear to Air.
Millay, E.   I will put Chaos into fourteen lines.
Miller, J.   Poetry.
Milosz, C.   Dedication: "You whom I could not save."
Report.
Milton.   To Mr. H. Lawes On His Airs.
Mooney, M.   Anna Akhmatova's Funeral.
Moore, M.   Past Is the Present, The.
Poetry: "I, too, dislike it: there are things that are important beyond all this fiddle."
Morales, A.   Other Heritage, The.
Sugar Poem.
Morgan, E.   Opening the Cage.
Moss, S.   Exchange of Hats, An.
Murphy, R.   Poet on the Island, The.
Musgrave.   Hidden Meaning.
Muske, C.   Our Kitty.
Stage and Screen, 1989.
Myles, E.   Merk.
Nabokov.   On Translating 'Eugene Onegin.'
Nash, O.   Very like a Whale.
Nazario, A.   Kevin and Nicole.
Nichol.   Some Nets.
Nortje.   Asseverations.
Notley.   Where Leftover Misery Goes.
Older.   Two Worlds.
Oliver, M.   'u', 'je', 'r', 'r', 'im', 'a', 'finally.'
Little Night, A.
Walnut and Lily.
Oppen.   From Virgil.
Gesture, The.
Gold on Oak Leaves.
Osterhaus, J.   Gambier.
Padgett, R.   First Drift.
Parker, A.   Another Poem about the Vandals.
Cruelty, the Vandals Say.
Vandals, The.
Parker, D.   Bric-à-Brac.
Patchen.   Moon, Sun, Sleep, Birds, Live.
Paulin.   Where Art Is a Midwife.
Peacock, M.   Desire.
Perelman.   Marginalization of Poetry, The.
Pessoa.   "Startling Reality of Things," The.
Philips, K.   On the Death of My First and Dearest Child[e], Hector Philip[p]s.
Phillips, C.   Passing.
Undressing for Li Po.
"Philo-Philippa."   To the Excellent Orinda.

Piñero.   La Bodega Sold Dreams.
Lower East Side Poem, A.
Pickard, T.   My Pen.
Pietri.   10th Untitled Poem.
1st Untitled Poem.
Title of This Poem Was Lost, The.
Traffic Misdirector.
Piombino.   Pyramids, The.
Poe.   Enigma, An.
Stanzas.
Pound, E.   Coda.
Ité.
Papyrus.
Radiguet.   Poem: "Horizon line."
Ragan, J.   Huckster at Noontime.
Rajendra, C.   My Message.
Ravikovitch [or Ravikovich].   Surely You Remember.
Reeves, J.   W.
Remoto.   Exile.
Rich, A.   I Am in Danger—Sir.
In a Classroom.
Late Ghazal.
Robinson, M.   [Sonnet] Conclusive.
Poet's Garret, The.
Sonnet Introductory.
Rosen, M. et al.   Humpty Dumpty.
Rouse.   Memo to Auden.
Virginian Arcady.
Rowe, V.   MRI of a Poet's Brain.
Rubin, L.   Houses of Emily Dickinson, The.
Russell, T.   To Boccaccio.
Safie, D.   In the Middle of Reading One More Poem with Brueghel as a Metaphor.
Salinas, L.   For Larry Levis in Memory.
Sall, A.   Letter to a Roving Poet.
Sanchez, S.   To P. J. (2 Yrs Old Who Sed Write a Poem for Me in Portland, Oregon).
Scammell, W.   Poem for a Younger Son.
Schwartz, D.   Sonnet on Famous and Familiar Sonnets and Experiences.
Scott of Amwell.   Ode: Written After Reading Some Modern Love-Verses.
Scott, J.   Helen Paints a Room (1984).
Scott, W.   Early Aspirations.
Service.   Inspiration.
Seward.   To Mr. Henry Cary, On the Publication of his Sonnets.
Shapiro, D.   Old Poems.
Sheridan, T.   Tom Punsibi's Letter to Dean Swift.
Sigourney.   Poetry.
Silveira.   Different Poem, A.
Simpson, L.   Variations on a Poem by Reznikoff.
Simpson, R.   All Friends Together.
Smith, C.   Santa Monica.
Smith, D.   Spring Poem, The.
Snyder, G.   As for Poets.
Axe Handles.
How Poetry Comes to Me.
What You Should Know to Be a Poet.
Stafford, W.   Near.
Stevens, W.   Planet on the Table, The.
Stewart, B.   Words Is Not Enough.
Stone, J.   Getting to Sleep in New Jersey.
Swirszczynska.   Poetry Reading.
Szymborska.   In Praise of My Sister.
Taggard.   All Around the Town.
To Mr. Maunder Maunder, Professional Poet.
Tate, J.   Dream On.
Miss Cho Composes in the Cafeteria.
Tennyson, F.   Poetical Happiness.
Thomas, D.   In My Craft or Sullen Art.
Thomas, R.   Taliesin 1952.
Thoreau.   My Life Has Been The Poem I Would Have Writ.
Torres, E.   Poetry Detective.
Tripp.   Last at Lucy's, The.
Turnbull.   There Are Words.
Ungria, R.   Commerce and the Man.
Sui Veneris / The Poet of No Return.
Unknown.   Limerick: "Well, it's partly the shape of the thing."
Poet Dreamt of Heaven, The.
Van Doren.   First Poem, The.

Vando. Commonwealth, Common Poverty.
Waniek. Emily Dickinson's Defunct.
Warsh. Suicide Rates, The.
Watts-Dunton. Sonnet's Voice, The.
Weiners. With Meaning.
Welch, L. Whenever I Make a New Poem.
Weslowski. Pablo.
Wetzsteon. Poem for a New Year.
 Rival, A.
Wheatley, P. To Mæcenas.
Whitman, W. Out of the Cradle Endlessly
 Rocking.
Wieners. To H.
Williams, G. After Reading *Poems to Einhir*.
Williams, J. On Reading Aloud My Early
 Poems.
Williams, W. Coronal, A.
Wilson, S. Contemporary Poet, A.
Wright, C. Cicada Blue.
Wylie. Sonnet: "You are the faintest freckles on
 the hide."
Yeats. Adam's Curse.
 When You Are Old.
Young Bear. Emily Dickinson, Bismarck and
 the Roadrunner's Inquiry.
Young, D. White Crane.
Young, K. Langston Hughes.
Yuson. World Poetry Circuit.
Zamora-Linmark. Day 1: Portrait of the Artist,
 Small-kid Time.
Zarco. Manila Paper.
Zephaniah. According to my Mood.

Poison
Balaban. Along the Mekong.
Herbert, Z. Return of the Proconsul, The.
Kizer, C. On a Line from Valéry.
Notley. Where Leftover Misery Goes.
Padel. Yew Berries.
Stewart, S. Apple.
Unknown. Lord Randal[1].

Poker
Masson. My Poker Girl.

Poland
Dambroff. Resistance.
Milosz, C. Dedication: "You whom I could not
 save."
 My Faithful Mother Tongue.
Newman, G. Anti-Semitic Demonstration, An.
Rothenberg, J. Poland / 1931 "The Wedding."
Wat. Imagerie d'Epinal.

Police and Police Stations
Ai. Endangered Species.
Baraka, R. Five-0.
Baranczak, S. Three Magi, The.
Beerbohm, M. Police Station Ditties.
Bernstein, L. Gee, Officer Krupke.
Betjeman. Arrest of Oscar Wilde at the
 Cadogan Hotel, The.
Brown, S. Southern Cop.
Chesterton, G. Christmas Carol, A: "God rest
 you merry gentlemen."
Clewell. Poem for the Man Who Said Shit.
Clifton, L. Powell (officer charged with the
 beating of rodney king).
Cortez, J. Give me the Red on the Black of the
 Bullet (for Claude Reece Jr.).
 Rape.
Cummings, E. Two X.
Davis, F. Sam Jackson.
Digby, J. One Night Away from Day.
Domina, L. Pharoah's Army Got Drowned.
Durem. Award.
Eady. False Arrest.
Fogarty, L. Remember Something Like This.
Garcia, R. Diver for the NYPD Talks to His
 Girlfriend, A.
Garioch. Fair Cop, A.
Hamilton, P. Poem to a Nigger Cop.
Hughes, L. Third Degree.
 Who But the Lord?
Jackson, R. Riot at Winchell's.
Jones, J. Drugs.
Kharms. Event on the Street, An.
Laing, K. Tatale Swine.
Lehman. First Offense.
Leonard, T. Evidence, The.

Untitled.
Levertov. Grace-Note, The.
Mayer, G. Song: "Does the policeman sleep
 with his boots on."
McGough, R. P. C. Plod versus the Dale St.
 Dog Strangler.
Mora. La Migra.
Muske, C. Field Trip.
Parker, D. Sand.
Perillo. Skin.
Randall, D. Idiot, The.
Rodriguez, L. To the Police Officer Who
 Refused to Sit in the Same Room as My Son
 because He's a 'Gang Banger.'
Sadoff. Civil Rights.
Sanchez, S. Philadelphia: Spring, 1985.
Sondheim. Gee, Officer Krupke.
Tremblay, B. Mayday.
Weiners. Poem for Vipers, A.
Williamson, G. Appalachian Trees Encircled by
 Police Tape.
Wright, K. Sergeant Brown's Parrot.

Police States
Brutus. Sounds Begin Again, The.
Chimsoro. Curfew Breakers, The.
Chipasula. Love Poem for My Country, A.
Gwala. From the Outside.
Hecht, A. 'More Light! More Light!'
Muir, E. Interrogation, The.
Ofeimun. Handle for the Flutist, A.
Ratushinskaya [*or* Ratushinskaia]. But Only
 Not to Think.

Politics and Politicians
Ai. Self Defense.
Allen, S. View from the Corner.
Angira. Obbligato from a Public Gallery.
Aspden, B. News of the Changes.
Atwood. Torture.
Balakian, P. End of the Reagan Era, The.
Baraka. Clay.
Baxter, J. Harry Fat and Uncle Sam.
Behn, A. Cabal at Nickey Nackey's, The.
Belloc. Epitaph on the Politician Himself.
 On a General Election.
Bierce. Statesmen, The.
Borawski. Some of Us Wear Pink Triangles.
Broumas, O. Artemis.
Brutus. Their Behaviour.
Burnett, W. My Shadow.
Cabico, R. Check One.
Cervantes. Poem for the Young White Man
 Who Asked Me How I, An Intelligent, Well-
 Read Person Could Believe in the War
 Between Races.
Chasin. Getting the News.
Chesterton, G. Elegy in a Country Churchyard.
Chipasula. Going Back Patiently.
Clark Bekedermo. Casualties, The.
Cohan. If Washington Should Come to Life.
Cohen, L. Killers, The.
Cummings, E. Next to of Course God
 America I.
 Politician, A.
 Salesman, A.
Daley, V. Tall Hat.
Davie. Barnsley and District.
Davies, I. Angry Summer, The.
Dodge, M. Mayor of Scuttleton, The.
Durcan. Divorce Referendum, Ireland, 1986,
 The.
 Irish Hierarchy Bans Colour Photography.
Earley, T. Rebel's Progress.
Eliot, T. Triumphal March.
Elliott, E. Fatal Birth, The.
Espada. All the People Who Are Now Red
 Trees.
 Cockroaches of Liberation.
 Year I Was Diagnosed with a Sacrilegious
 Heart, The.
Ezenwa-Ohaeto. I Wan Bi President.
Finkel. Party, The.
Freneau. To a Noisy Politician.
Gamalinda, E. La Naval De Manila: Selim Sot
 as a Modern Political Observer.
Gilbert, K. Gularwundul's Wish.
Gilbert, S. Gilbertian Cats.

Ginsberg, A. America.
Glück, R. Pasolini.
Gowar. Rat Trap.
Hagedon, J. Song of Bullets, The.
Harper, F. Aunt Chloe's Politics.
Hass, R. After I Seized the Pentagon.
Helle, A. Poem for Natalia Ginzburg.
Hippolyte. Revo Lyric.
Hollo. Dream of Instant Total Representation,
 The.
Hone. Political House that Jack Built, The.
Hove. Child's Parliment.
Ismaili. Bajji.
Jacob, M. Rooster and the Pearl, The.
Jeffers, R. Stars Go Over the Lonely Ocean,
 The.
Johnson, L. Mi Revalueshanary Fren.
Jones, M. Election Reflection.
Jordan, J. Poem About My Rights.
Kinsella, J. Bright Cigar-Shaped Object Hovers
 Over Mount Pleasant, A.
Klein, A. Political Meeting.
Kleinzahler. Spleen.
Knight, E. On Watching Politicians Perform at
 Martin Luther King's Funeral.
Laing, K. Same Corpse, The.
Leonard, T. Untitled.
Lindley, D. Marxist to Liberals, A.
Lindsay, N. Bryan, Bryan, Bryan, Bryan.
 What the Moon Saw.
 Why I Voted the Socialist Ticket.
Logue, C. I Shall Vote Labour.
Lowell, J. Boss, The.
 Misconception, A.
Lucy. Senior Members.
Macartney. Kyrielle: Party Politics.
Maxton. Urgent Letter, An.
McClure, M. Senate Hearings.
McDonald, C. Asdrubral Jiménez.
Miles, J. Campaign, The.
Moore, T. Tory Pledges.
Morse, C. Dream of the Artfairy.
Nemerov. To the Rulers.
Nurkse. Olmos.
Ojaide. Launching Our Community
 Developement Fund.
Okigbo. Elegy for Alto.
Petty. Great Poll-Tax Victory of '88, The.
Philips, K. To Antenor.
"Pindar." Epigram: "Midas, they say, possessed
 the art of old."
Praed. Chancery Morals.
Prior. Fable, A: "In Æsop's tales an honest
 wretch we find."
Rome, H. Doing the Reactionary.
Sackville, C. My Opinion.
Scott, F. W. L. M. K.
Shelley, P. Similes for Two Political Characters
 of 1819.
Smith, A. Political Intelligence.
Taylor, B. Canopus.
Thelwall. To Ancestry.
 Vanity of National Grandeur, The.
Tolson, M. Legend of Versailles, A.
Turki, F. Moments of Ridicule and Love.
Unknown. Age of War, The.
 Eccho, An.
 Old-Saxon Fragment.
Waniek. Alderman.
Watkyns. Common People, The.
Wheelwright. Anathema. Maranatha!
Whitman, W. Thought.
 To a President.
Woddis. Doctor, The.
 I Shall Vote Centre.
Wright, D. Cockermouth.
Yeats. Politics.

Pollack, Jackson
McClure, M. Ode to Jackson Pollock.

Pollution
Bennett, R. Smoke Animals.
Dupree, E. At Present I Am Working as a
 Security Guard.
Ginsberg, A. Homework.
Howard, B. River's Answer, The.
Kendall, M. Underground.

Kizer, C.   On a Line from Valéry.
Marshall, J.   Wing and Prayer.
Meredith, W.   Country Stars.
Merriam, E.   Landscape.
 Windshield Wiper.
Nuriddin, J. M.   Children of the Future.
Ortiz.   Vision Shadows.
Reed, I.   El Paso Monologue.
Welch, L.   Sausalito Trash Prayer.
See also **Conservation; Ecology and Ecologists**
Polyandry
Aig-Imoukhuede.   One Wife for One Man.
See also **Bigamy and Bigamists; Marriage;**
 Monogamy and Monogamists
Pomegranates
Boland, E.   Pomegranate, The.
Delgado, J.   Winter Fruit.
Hildebrandt, Z.   Persephone.
Janzen, J.   Pomegranate.
Lawrence, D.   Andraitx—Pomegranate Flowers.
Pompeii, Italy
Gibran.   Mannus the Pompeiian to a Greek.
Goldbarth.   Counterfeit Earth!, The.
Hemans.   Image in Lava, The.
Mahon.   Disused Shed in Co. Wexford, A.
Ray, H.   Listening Nydia.
Scupham.   Pompeii: Plaster Casts.
Stevens, W.   Postcard from the Volcano, A.
Ponds
Brouwer, J.   Conservatory Pond, Central Park,
 New York, New York.
Malouf.   For Two Children.
Mills, R.   Water Lilies.
Paloff, B.   On Transportation.
Pound, E.   Canto 49.
Swift, J.   Steelhead in the Whitehorse Rearing
 Pond.
See also **Lakes and Ponds**
Ponies
Mother Goose.   Dapple-gray.
Wright, J.   Blessing, A.
Pool (game)
Baker, D.   8-Ball at the Twilite.
Brooks, G.   We Real Cool.
Carruth, H.   Capper Kaplinski at the North Side
 Cue Club.
Haug.   Pool is a Godless Sport.
Jackson, R.   Eight Ball.
Pope, Alexander
Edwards, T.   On the Edition of Mr. Pope's
 Works with a Commentary and Notes.
 To the Editor of Mr. Pope's Works.
Gay, J.   Mr. Pope's Welcome from Greece.
Montagu, L.   Epitaph: "Here lies John Hughes
 and Sarah Drew."
 Verses Addressed to the Imitator of the First
 Satire of the Second Book of Horace: An
 Attack on Pope.
Tate, A.   Mr. Pope.
Unknown.   On the Death of Mr. Pope.
 Spoken Extempore on the Death of Mr. Pope.
Winchilsea.   Answer, The.
Poplar Trees
Cowper, W.   Poplar Field, The.
Doolittle, H.   Mid-day.
Egemo.   Silver Poplar at Sunrise.
Hopkins, G.   Binsey Poplars (Felled 1879).
See also **Aspen Trees**
Poppies
Curry.   Poppy Heads.
Doolittle, H.   Sea Poppies.
Foster, A.   Field.
Hamilton, S.   Poppy, The.
Loving.   Black Horse Rider, The.
Magowan.   Paros.
O'Neill, H.   Ode to the Poppy.
Plath.   Poppies in July.
 Poppies in October.
Seward.   To the Poppy.
St. John, D.   Black Poppy (At the Temple).
Stephens, J.   In the Poppy Field.
Porcupines
Kinnell.   Porcupine, The.

Pornography
Campbell, S.   Legacy.
Cooper, D.   Being Aware.
 No God.
Hall, D.   X.
Hass, R.   Pornographer, The.
Logan, J.   Saturday Afternoon at the Movies.
MacKenzie, R.   Like Pornography.
Pitt-Kethley.   God made the sex-shop keeper.
Shaw, A.   Pornography.
Wallace, R.   Thirteen.
Wojahn.   My Father's Pornography.
See also **Obscenity**
Porter, Cole
Bentley, N.   On Lady A———.
Coward.   Let's Do It.
Lardner.   Parodies of Cole Porter's "Night and
 Day."
Portland, Maine
Longfellow, H.   My Lost Youth.
Portraits
Ashbery.   Self-Portrait in a Convex Mirror.
Boland, E.   Self-Portrait on a Summer Evening.
Brant, B.   Her Name Is Helen.
Browning, E.   On a Portrait of Wordsworth by
 B. R. Haydon.
Browning, R.   Likeness, A.
 My Last Duchess.
Chesterfield.   On Mr. Nash's Present of His Own
 Picture at Full Length.
Cowper, W.   On the Receipt of My Mother's
 Picture out of Norfolk [the Gift of My Cousin
 Ann Bodham].
De la Mare.   Portrait, A.
Donne.   Phryne.
Edwards, T.   Sonnet on a Family Picture.
Fanthorpe.   Portraits of Tudor Statesmen.
Field, E.   Unwanted.
Graves, R.   Face in the Mirror, The.
Halleck, F.   Red Jacket.
Holden, M.   Photograph of Haymaker, 1890.
Holmes, O.   Dorothy Q.
Howard, R.   Nadar.
Howells, W.   Royal Portraits, The.
Huddle.   Cousin.
Leapor.   On Winter.
Lovelace, R.   Upon the Curtain[e] of Lucasta's
 Picture [It Was Thus Wrought].
Melville, H.   Formerly a Slave.
Moody, W.   Faded Pictures.
North, M.   Portrait in a Brass Gong.
Rossetti, C.   In An Artist's Studio.
Rowlands.   Epigram 29: "Gentlewoman of the
 dealing trade, A."
Sandburg, C.   Sins of Kalamazoo, The.
Sawyer, A.   Lines, / Written on Seeing My
 Husband's Picture, painted when he was
 young: "Those are the features, those the
 smiles."
Tate, A.   Sonnet: To a Portrait of Hart Crane.
Thibaudeau.   Poem: "I do not want only."
Wetzsteon.   Dinner at Le Caprice.
Wylie.   Castilian.
 Self-Portrait.
See also **Painting and Painters; Photography and**
 Photographers
Ports
Baxter, J.   Bay, The.
See also **Harbors and Ports**
Portugal
Lear, E.   Limericks, II (iv).
Mapanje.   After Wiriyamu Village Massacre by
 Portuguese.
Wyatt, S.   In Spayn.
Posterity
Byron, G.   Last Words on Greece.
Emerson, R.   Limits.
Enright, D.   Posterity.
Gibran.   Two Poems, The.
Heath-Stubbs.   To a Poet a Thousand Years
 Hence.
Herrick.   Upon His Verses.
Laughlin, J.   My Ambition.
MacLeish.   Epistle to Be Left in the Earth.
 Sentiments for a Dedication.

Ramke.   Paul Verlaine at the Grave of Lucien
 Létinois.
Shapiro, K.   Manhole Covers.
Snyder, G.   For the Children.
Thomas, R.   Gifts.
Tomlinson, C.   Against Extremity.
Whitman, W.   Full of Life Now.
 No Labor-Saving Machine.
Young, A.   Fifty-Fifty.
Potatoes
Anaya, R.   La Papa.
Asquith.   Banking Potatoes.
Bardwell.   Lila's Potatoes.
Bargen, W.   Potato Conflicts.
Barnes, J.   American Heritage Potato, The.
Bell, M.   Sounds of the Resurrected Dead Man's
 Footsteps #15.
Blanchard, M.   Before the Hunger: Megan's
 Blessing.
Bly, R.   Potato, A.
Boisseau.   Potato.
Bosselaar.   Cellar, The.
Citino.   Famine.
Cooley.   Van Gogh's The Potato Eaters.
Curtis, L.   Potato, The.
Daldorph, B.   Spuds.
DeCormier-Shekejian.   Tonight.
DeFrees.   Variations on the Edible Tuber.
Donnell.   Potatoes.
Duemer.   Best Meals of My Life, The.
Espada.   Pitching the Potatoes.
Finnell.   Belladonna.
France, L.   Chip City.
Glass.   Risks.
Goldbarth.   Mishipasinghan, Lumchipamudana,
 Etc.
Gonzalez, R.   In Peru, the Quechuans Have a
 Thousand Words for Potato.
Grennan.   Potatoes.
Heaney, S.   Digging.
Hix, H. L.   Man in Novosibirsk.
Hollander, J.   Comment on an Observation by
 One of My Masters.
Holman, B.   Poem: "Once when I was little I
 knelt before an onion."
Hoyos.   Long Live the Potato: Viva la Papa!
Huber, M.   Potato Cellar.
Hugo, R.   Way a Ghost Dissolves, The.
Inez.   Digging Potatoes.
Kavanagh, P.   Spraying the Potatoes.
Kendrick, L.   Simple Thing, A.
Kennedy, X.   Dirty English Potatoes.
Kenyon, J.   Potato.
Knoepfle.   Skibbereen the Famine Pit.
Levertov.   Roasting Potatoes.
Lindley, D.   Potato Blight.
Longley, J.   Famine's End.
Low, D.   California Potatoes.
Matthews, W.   This Spud's for You.
McDade, T.   Potatoes of the Field, The.
McGough, R.   Potato Clock.
Miller, P. C.   Molly O'Rourke Cleary Explains.
Miller, P. L.   Peeling Potatoes.
Mitchell, C.   Giving Potatoes.
Mora.   One Potato.
Oates.   In Jana's Garden.
Paschen.   Potatoes Coriander.
Peters, R.   Potatoes.
Phillips, R.   Arsh Potatoes.
Plumly.   Digging Potatoes, 1950.
Quisenberry, D.   Skinning.
Rankin, R.   Tourists, Potatoes, and Genocide.
Ratner.   Potato, The.
Ray, D.   Widower.
Redenius, J.   Potato Garden.
Reeves, T.   Of Potatoes.
Rhau, D.   Potatoes.
Rummel, M.   Letter to a Former Mother
 Superior.
Santalucia, J.   Sustenance.
Slegman, A.   Sex and the Single Spud.
Smith, K.   End of All History, The.
Sowbel, S.   If You're Lost.
Stewart, R.   Tonight I Thank the Potato.
Terris.   Roots: To My Daughter.
Townley, R.   Potato, The.

Townley, W.   Swimming Lesson.
Trussell.   Choice.
Unknown.   Riddle: "Riddle a riddle as I suppose, A."
Vance-Watkins, L.   Passacaglia.
Vando.   On Hearing that a Potato Costs $70 in Sarajevo.
Viereck, P.   Insulted and the Injured, The.
von Zweck, D.   One Man's Potato Chip.
Whitely, O.   Today the Grandpa Dug Potatoes.
Wilbur.   Potato.
Williams, David.   In Praise of the Potato.
Wilson, R.   Potato Escape, A.
Wilson, T.   Alice Potato.

Potomac River
Aldrich, T.   By the Potomac.
Beers, E.   All Quiet along the Potomac Tonight.
Hovey.   Evening on the Potomac.

Pottery and Potters
Bell, M.   Drawn by Stones, by Earth, by Things That Have Been in the Fire.
Diop, B.   Viaticum.
"Field."   Life Plastic.
Forbes, C.   Potter's Wheel, The.
Hollander, J.   Mad Potter, The.
Hufana, A.   Contemporary.
Komunyakaa.   Back Then.
Miller, E.   What the Women Told Me.
Naranjo-Morse.   Tradition and Change.
Todd, R.   Joan Miró.

Pound, Ezra
Bukowski.   Drooling Madness at St. Liz.
Bunting.   On the Fly-Leaf of Pound's Cantos.
Ferlinghetti, L.   Pound at Spoleto.
Lowell, R.   Ezra Pound.
MacLeish.   Ezry.
Morton, J.   Another Canto.
Pilling.   Dear Ez.
Scott, J.   Typing the Letters.
Snyder, G.   Axe Handles.

Poverty
Addonizio.   Broken Sonnets.
Arnold, M.   West London.
Ashbery.   Street Musicians.
Baraka.   Short Speech to My Friends.
Barbauld.   To the Poor.
Beach, L.   2 Months Rent Due and 1 Bag of Rice.
Berlin.   I Got the Sun in the Morning.
Bishop, E.   Pink Dog.
Blane, R.   I Never Felt Better.
Bly, R.   Sunday in Glastonbury.
Bolton, J.   American Tragedy.
Brecht, B.   From a German War Primer.
Brooks, G.   Bean Eaters, The.
   Lovers of the Poor, The.
   To An Old Black Woman, Homeless and Indistinct.
Bruner.   If Lincoln Should Return.
Bunting.   Gin the Goodwife Stint.
Burns, R.   For A' That and A' That ['Is there, for honest poverty'].
Butterfield, F. G.   For Services Rendered.
Carbó, N.   Votive Candles.
   When the Grain Is Golden and the Wind Is Chilly, Then It Is the Time to Harvest.
Cassells.   Courtesy, A Trenchant Grace, A.
Causley.   Timothy Winters.
Cervantes.   To We Who Were Saved by the Stars.
Chaucer.   Complaint of Chaucer to His Empty Purse, The.
Chavez, L.   After the Prom.
Cheney-Coker.   Peasants.
   Poet Among Those Who Are Also Poets.
Clanchy, K.   Foreign.
Clare, J.   My Mary.
Clarke, G.   Second Hand Rose.
Clifton, L.   Good Times.
Coleman, W.   Aunt Jessie.
   Where I Live.
Coleridge, M.   Insincere Wish Addressed to a Beggar, An.
Coles, R.   Goddam Street, The.
Cope, W.   Variation on Belloc's "Fatigue"
Cortez, J.   I'm A Worker.

Costanzo.   Everything You Own.
Cowley, M.   Winter Tenement.
Cullen, C.   Saturday's Child.
D'Aguiar.   Dreadtalk.
Davidson, J.   Thirty Bob a Week.
Davidson, M.   Framing.
Davies, I.   Angry Summer, The.
Davis, G.   Children in the Arbor.
Davis, J.   Slum Dwelling.
Day Lewis.   Carol, A.
Dharker.   Namesake.
Dipoko.   From My Parisian Diary.
Dixon, M.   Great Big Bunch of You, A.
   River, Stay 'Way from My Door.
Dobyns.   Dancing in Vacationland.
Dugan, A.   To a Red-headed Do-good Waitress.
Dunbar, P.   Common Things.
   Companion's Progress, A.
Egan, R.   Ain't We Got Fun.
Ellington, D.   I Ain't Got Nothin' But the Blues.
Elliott, E.   Child, Is Thy Father Dead?
Ellis, T.   Making Ends Meet.
Elmusa.   In the Refugee Camp.
Emerson, R.   Chartist's Complaint, The.
Ferry.   Guest Ellen at the Supper for Street People, The.
Fields, D.   I Can't Give You Anything but Love.
Fletcher, P.   Against a Rich Man Despising Poverty.
Forman, R.   We Are the Young Magicians.
Forster, W.   Poor of London, The.
Fraser, G.   Lean Street.
Gamalinda, E.   Lament Beginning w/a Line after Cavafy.
García Lorca.   At the Poorhouse.
García, D.   Tísica.
Garrett, E.   Miser.
George, D.   I Ain't Got Nothin' But the Blues.
Gershwin.   I Got Plenty o' Nuthin'
Gilbert, C.   Time with Stevie Wonder in It.
Gilbert, K.   Gularwundul's Wish.
   Mum.
Giovanni.   Nikki-Rosa.
Gomez, M.   Making It.
   Solo Palabras.
Gray, A.   Why Your Grandfather Stopped Playing the Viola.
Hacker, M.   Elysian Fields.
Hanley, J.   Second Hand Rose.
Hardy, T.   Reminder, The.
Hernandez, D.   Workers.
Hewitt, J.   Irishman in Coventry, An.
   Turf-Carrier [*or* Turf Carrier] on Aranmore.
Hoagland, E.   Big Zeb Johnson.
Holcroft.   Gaffer Gray.
Holiday.   God Bless the Child.
Hood, T.   Song of the Shirt, The.
Hove.   Other Syllabus, The.
   You Will Forget.
Hughes, L.   Ballad of the Man Who's Gone.
   Cross.
   Down and Out.
   Ennui.
   Madam and the Rent Man.
   Necessity.
Hugo, R.   What Thou Lovest Well Remains American.
Johnston, E.   Last Sark, The.
Jones, E.   Song of the Low, The.
Jones, M.   Soliloquy on an Empty Purse.
Jones, R.   End of Communism, The.
Jones, S.   Poverty, in Imitation of Milton.
Jonson, B.   To Alchemists.
Jordan, N.   I Have Seen Them.
Kahn, G.   Ain't We Got Fun.
Kizer, C.   To an Unknown Poet.
Kooser.   In the Basement of the Goodwill Store.
Lamb, M.   Two Boys, The.
Landon.   Dying Child, The.
   Poor, The.
Lee, W.   Aunt Martha.
Lewis, A.   Karanje Village.
Livingston, M.   Poor.
Long, D.   One Time Henry Dreamed the Number.
Longley, M.   Ghetto.

Lovelace, R.   Grasshopper, The.
Lowell, J.   His Throne Is with the Outcast.
Lux.   Bodo.
MacDiarmid, H.   Glass of Pure Water, The.
Macgoye.   Freedom Song, A.
MacLean, S.   Calvary.
Madgett.   Simple.
Maris, H.   Season's Finished, The.
Martin, H.   I Never Felt Better.
Matthews, M.   Language.
McCarthy, T.   Claud Cockburn.
McGrath, T.   Long Way Outside Yellowstone, A.
McLachlan.   We Live in a Rickety House.
Meynell, A.   Lady Poverty, The.
Mhlophe.   Sometimes When It Rains.
Milligan, S.   Christmas 1970.
Murray, L.   Tin Wash Dish, The.
North, M.   Ordnance Survey in the Northern Counties.
Oswald, A.   Pilchard-Curing Song, The.
Peacock, T.   Rich and Poor; or, Saint and Sinner.
Pelizzon, V.   Clever and Poor.
Perdomo, W.   Unemployed Mami.
Po Chü-i.   Bitter Cold, Living in the Village.
Porter, P.   And No Help Came.
Powell, K.   For Aunt Cathy.
Raine, K.   Worry about Money.
Ravenscroft, T.   Sing we now merily.
Rexroth, K.   Bad Old Days, The.
Roberson.   Poor Houses, The.
Robinson, A.   Scape-Goat, The.
Robinson, E.   Poor Relation, The.
Rodriguez, L.   Rant, Rave and Ricochet.
Rutsala.   Shame.
Salkey.   Dry River Bed.
Santalucia, J.   Sustenance.
Seaton, M.   Fear of Shoplifting.
Shange.   About Atlanta.
Sheridan, T.   Tom Punsibi's Letter to Dean Swift.
Simic.   Strictly for Posterity.
Simpson, L.   There Is.
Smith, C.   Dead Beggar, an Elegy Addressed to a Lady, The.
Smith, K.   Possessions.
Spender, S.   Elementary School Classroom in a Slum, An.
   In Railway Halls.
Stephens, J.   To the Four Courts, Please.
Sterling, A.   What You Goin' to Do When the Rent Comes 'Round?
Stevens, W.   Dry Loaf.
Stevenson, R.   System.
Sund.   Considering Poverty and Homelessness.
Swift, J.   Phyllis [*or* Phillis] [*or* Progress of Love, The].
Synge.   Winter.
Taylor, R.   Princess of Scotland, The.
Thomas, R.   Other.
Traherne.   Poverty.
Tsaloumas.   Consolation.
Tsvetayeva [*or* Tsvetaeva].   If the Soul was Born with Pinions.
Tu Fu.   Empty Purse, The.
Tucker, M.   Christmas Eve, South, 1865.
Unknown.   Between a Contractor and His Wife.
   Brian O'Linn.
   Poverty Knock.
   She Was Poor but She Was Honest.
   Song, A: "While a thousand fine projects are planned ev'ry day."
   Starving to Death on a Government Claim.
Waniek.   Sacrament of Poverty, The.
Warren, H.   Great Big Bunch of You, A.
Watts, I.   Praise for Mercies Spiritual and Temporal.
Wayne, J.   Cleaning Indian Dahl.
Weiners.   Children of the Working Class.
Whiting, R.   Ain't We Got Fun.
Whitlow.   Rockin' A Man, Stone Blind.
Williams, P.   Trails.
Williams, W.   Pastoral: "When I was younger."
   Poor, The.
   Proletarian Portrait.

To a Poor Old Woman.
Woods, H. River, Stay 'Way from My Door.
Wordsworth, W. Alice Fell; or, Poverty.
Wright, J. Poor Man's Province, The.
Wunderlich, M. East Seventh Street.
Zimmer. Example, The.
See also **Need**

Power
Adisa. Women at the Crossroad / (May Elegba Forever Guard the Right Doors).
Atwood. Procedures for Underground.
Torture.
Auden. Epitaph on a Tyrant.
Baraka. Each Morning.
Hymn for Lanie Poo.
Short Speech to My Friends.
Black Elk. Everything the Power of the World Does is Done in a Circle.
Brutus. Their Behaviour.
Busia, A. Liberation.
Canan. Inanna's Chant.
Oh Kali.
Radioactive.
Cataldi. Advice.
Chudleigh. To the Ladies.
Cortez, J. Pray for the Lovers.
Curry. Poppy Heads.
Dickey, J. Power and Light.
Dickinson, E. I Can Wade Grief.
Eberhart, R. Sea-Hawk.
Enheduanna. From The Hymn to Inanna.
Ewart. To the Virgins, to Make the Most of Time.
Fabian, C. Liturgy for Lilith.
Galvin, J. Little Dantesque.
Ginsberg, A. Please Master.
Glover, S. Power of the Soul.
Hacker, M. Rune of the Finland Woman.
Harper, M. Song: I Want a Witness.
Hayden, R. Wheel, The.
Herrick. On Himselfe.
Power and Peace.
Shame, No Statist.
Hollo. Italics.
Ironbiter, S. Song to the Mother of the World.
Jeffers, L. When I Know the Power of my Black Hand.
Kemble. Sonnet: "If there were any power in human love."
Kizer, C. Hera, Hung from the Sky.
Knox, E. Director, The.
Laing, K. Steps.
Landon. Power of Words, The.
Lawrence, D. Lord's Prayer.
Milosz, C. Incantation.
Ono. Mother of the Universe.
Parker, A. No Fool, the God of Salt.
Patterson, G. Autobiography of a Black Man.
Pound, E. Canto 49.
Prunty. Elderly Lady Crossing on Green.
Public Enemy. Party for your Right to Fight.
Ransom, J. Judith of Bethulia.
Robinson, E. Richard Cory.
Sanchez, S. Song No. 2: "I say. all you young girls waiting to live."
Simon, L. Kali.
Simon, P. Richard Cory.
Stanton, M. Conjurer, The.
Stevens, W. Emperor of Ice-Cream, The.
Strange. Acts of Power.
Thomas, D. Hand That Signed the Paper, The.
Thomas, L. Cameo in Sudden Light.
Unknown. Holy Goddess Tellus.
Waldrop, K. Wandering Curves.
Wilbur. She.
Woo, M. Whenever You're Cornered, the Only Way Out Is to Fight.

Prague, Czechoslovakia
Bachner. Man Proposes, God Disposes.
Nezval. City With Towers.
Sillitoe. Synagogue in Prague.

Prairie Dogs
Navajo Oral Tradition. Coyote, Skunk, and the Prairie Dogs.

Prairies
Bates, K. America the Beautiful.
Bryant, W. Prairies, The.
Clampitt. Woodlot, The.
Crosby, F. Let Me Die on the Prairie.
On Hearing a Description of a Prairie.
Donnell. Canadian Prairie's View of Literature, The.
Guest, B. Prairie Houses.
Marriott. Prairie Graveyard.
Peterson, R. Midwest Town.
Reiter, T. Rights of Way.
Sandburg, C. Haze.
Prairie Waters by Night.
Sorby. Gossip.
Whitman, W. Prairie-Grass Dividing, The.

Praxiteles
Unknown. Spoken by Venus on Seeing Her Statue Done by Praxiteles.

Prayer
Adams, H. Prayer to the Virgin of Chartres.
Alakoye. Eshu.
Angel. Veils of Prayer.
Anthony, G. Autumn Evening.
Applewhite. Prayer for My Son.
Ashbery. Painter, The.
Ashur-Nasir-Pal. Hymn to Ishtar.
Awoonor. This Earth, My Brother.
Babcock, M. School Days.
Bandele, A. Prayer for the Living, A.
Barrax. In the Restaurant.
Beedome. Petition, The.
Begay. Mother's Lace.
Berrigan, D. Prayer.
Betjeman. In Westminster Abbey.
Bienek. Resistance.
Bobrowsky. Free Fire Zone.
Bradstreet, A. Deliverance from a Fit of Fainting.
Here Follows Some Verses upon the Burning of Our House [July 10th, 1666. Copied Out of a Loose Paper].
Upon My Dear and Loving Husband His Going into England.
Brew. Plea for Mercy, A.
Browne, E. When I Am Dead.
Browning, R. Guardian-Angel, The.
Brutus. Prayer: "O let me soar on steadfast wing."
Burns, R. Holy Willie's Prayer.
Carroll, K. DC Nocturne.
Cavendish, M. Common Fate of Books, The.
Celan. Tenebrae.
Char. Unbending Prayer.
Chesterton, G. Prayer in Darkness, A.
Clare, J. Lord, Hear My Prayer.
Clifton, L. Prayer.
Slaveship.
Cofer, J. Counting.
Coffey. Prayers, The.
Coleridge, H. Jesus Praying.
Prayer.
Conder. Day by Day the Manna Fell.
Congreve. Pious Selinda [*or* Celinda].
Cook, E. Our Father.
Cooke, E. Are You You?
Cortez, J. Pray for the Lovers.
Crashaw. C[h]aritas Nimia; or, The Dear[e] Bargain.
Howres for the Hours of Matines, The.
On Mr. G. Herberts Booke, The Temple.
Song: "Lord, when the sense of Thy sweet grace."
Two Went Up into the Temple To Pray.
Crouch, S. Revelation, The.
Cummings, E. Noster, The.
Cuney. Death Bed, The.
Day, J. Prayer: "Grant that no Hobgoblins fright me."
De la Mare. Motley.
De Vere, S. Right Use of Prayer, The.
Delgado, J. Flora's Plea to Mary.
Dodson, O. Black Mother Praying.
Donne. Father, The.
Holy Ghost, The.
Hymn[e] to God the Father, A.

Son, The.
Duffy, C. Prayer: "Some days, although we cannot pray, a prayer."
Eliot, T. Song for Simeon, A.
Feinstein, E. Prayer.
Francis of Assisi. Prayer of St. Francis of Assisi for Peace.
Garrett, E. Lost Property.
Gascoigne. Gascoigne's [*or* Gascoygnes] Good-Night.
Gioia. Litany, The.
Prayer.
Glück, L. Matins.
Gladden. O Master, Let Me Walk with Thee.
Gloria. Aleng Maria.
Gomez, M. Troubled Awakening.
Gottlieb, L. Greeting Shekinah.
Gregg. Flower No More Than Itself, A.
Hall, D. Grace, A.
Hamod, S. After the Funeral of Assam Hamady.
Harjo, J. Eagle Poem.
Harvey, A. Prayer to the Divine Mother, A.
Heard, J. Unuttered Prayer.
Hemans. Evening Prayer, at a Girls' School.
Mountain Sanctuaries.
Olive Tree, The.
Herbert, G. Antiphon: "Let all the world in ev'ry corner sing / *My God and King* ."
Bag, The.
Denial[l].
Mattens.
Obedience.
Praise (2).
Prayer (1): "Prayer the Church's banquet, Angels' age."
Temper (1), The.
Wreath, A.
Herrick. Evensong.
Grace for a Child.
His Litany to the Holy Spirit.
His Prayer for Absolution.
Matins [*or* Mattens], or Morning Prayer.
Thanksgiving to God for His House, A.
To God.
To God: an Anthem, Sung in the Chapel at White-Hall, Before the King.
Hinckley, P. New Our Father, The.
Hudgins. Praying Drunk.
Hughes, L. Gal's Cry for a Dying Lover.
Hunter, A. *et al.* Down-Hearted Blues.
Jacob, V. Tam i' the Kirk.
Jennings, E. Teresa of Avila.
Jonson, B. To Heaven.
Keats. Fragment of an Ode to Maia Written on May Day, 1818.
Keble. Hezekiah's Display.
Samuel's Prayer.
Ken. Glory to Thee, My God, This Night.
Killigrew, A. Upon the Saying That My Verses Were Made by Another.
Kipling, R. Rabbi's Song, The.
Recessional.
Klugman, E. She Who Listens.
Kremer. Epiphany.
Kunene. Elegy.
Landon. Girl at Her Devotions, A.
Larkin, P. Faith Healing.
Lawrence, D. Hands of God, The.
Lord's Prayer.
Levin, P. Third Day, The.
Lewis, C. Prayer: "Master, they say that when I seem."
Sonnet: "Bible says Sennacherib's campaign was spoiled, The."
Lyte. Abide With Me.
Macdonald, G. Shall the Dead Praise Thee?
Mackey, N. Falso Brilhante.
MacNeice. Prayer Before Birth.
Masters, E. Supplication.
McFerrin, B. 23rd Psalm, The.
McGough, R. Prayer to Saint Grobianus.
McKay, C. St. Isaac's Church, Petrograd.
Merton. Evening Prayer.
Reader, The.
Mew. Old Shepherd's Prayer.

Meyers, B.   Pigeons.
Miller, V.   Without Ceremony.
Milosz, C.   On Angels.
Montague, J.   Footnote on Monasticism, A: Dingle Peninsula.
Moore, M.   Cumae.
More, S.   Prayer, A.
Mulock, D.   Labor and Rest.
Murray, P.   Introit.
Newman, J.   Pillar of the Cloud, The.
Nicholson, N.   For Hokey and Henrietta.
Norris, K.   Prayer to Eve, A.
Nye, N.   Negotiations with a Volcano.
Small Vases from Hebron, The.
Okara.   One Night at Victoria Beach.
Spirit of the Wind.
Ono.   Mother of the Universe.
Ortiz.   Bend in the River.
Pasolini.   Prayer to My Mother.
Pope, A.   Universal Prayer [Deo Opt. Max.], The.
Preston, R.   Ten Seconds.
Ralegh, S.   Authours Epitaph, Made by Himself, The.
Ray, H.   Evening Prayer.
Prayer: "O Christ, who in Gethsemane."
Reichard, W.   Cloud Game, The.
Robinson, M.   Sappho's Prayer to Venus.
Rolle, S.   Hands in the Motion of Prayer.
Sandburg, C.   Prayer after World War.
Schuyler, J.   Our Father.
Sherwin, J.   To Whom It May Concern.
Sill.   Fool's Prayer, The.
Simmons, J.   Rogation Day: Portrush.
Sisson.   Temple, The.
Smart, C.   My Cat Jeoffry.
Spender, S.   Rejoice in the Abyss.
St. John, P.   Sunday.
Stevenson, R.   Epitaph: "Angler rose, he took his rod, The."
Good Boy, A.
House Beautiful, The.
System.
Subido, T.   Paganly.
Sykes, B.   Prayer to the Spirit of the New Year.
Sylvester, J.   Father, The.
Tate, J.   Manna.
Taylor, E.   Huswifery.
Thomas, D.   Conversation of Prayer, The.
Thomas, R.   Empty Church, The.
Thompson, C.   Out of the Deep.
Thompson, P.   Old Saint's Prayer, The.
Tuckerman, F.   Sonnets: "Starry flower, the flower-like stars that fade, The."
Unknown.   Been in the Storm So Long.
Hell and Heaven.
I'm a-Rollin'
Limerick.
Lord, Remember Me!
Matthew, Mark, Luke and John.
Poet's Prayer, The.
Prayer of a Woman in Charge of Berry Picking in Knights Inlet.
Untermeyer, L.   Prayer for This House.
Van Duyn.   Gardener to His God, The.
Van Dyke.   Peace Hymn of the Republic.
Vaughan, H.   Begging.
Match, The.
Mount of Olives.
Praise.
Very.   My Meat and Drink.
Prayer of Jabez, The.
Prayer, The.
Take Ye Heed, Watch and Pray.
Waring, A.   My Times Are in Thy Hand.
Watts, I.   Man Frail, and God Eternal.
Wesley, C.   During His Courtship.
None is like Jeshurun's God.
Wheeler, R.   Prayer for Shut-Ins.
Whittier.   Dedication: "I would the gift I offer here."
Wilcox, E.   Answered Prayers.
Wilde, O.   E Tenebris.
Willard, E.   Rocked in the Cradle of the Deep.
Winchilsea.   To Death.
Wither.   Prayer of Hezekiah, The.

Prayer of Nehemiah, The.
Wright, J.   Art of the Fugue, The: A Prayer.
Confession to J. Edgar Hoover.
Prayer to the Lord Ramakrishna, A.
Trying to Pray.
Yeats.   Mohini Chatterjee.
Prayer for My Daughter, A.
Prayer for My Son, A.

Praying Mantis
McCord, D.   Mantis.
Miller, R.   Mantis.

Preaching and Preachers
Arnold, M.   Progress.
Berryman.   Carpenter's Son, The.
Clough.   Across the Sea, Along the Shore.
Dickinson, E.   He fumbles at Your Spirit.
Doane, W.   Preacher's Mistake, The.
Dobson, R.   Eutychus.
Harris, D.   On the uptown lexington avenue express: Martin Luther King Day 1995.
Herrick.   Upon Parson Beanes.
Hill, J.   Preacher and the Slave, The.
Kipling, R.   At His Execution.
MacKay, C.   Three Preachers, The.
McGinley.   Theology of Jonathan Edwards, The.
Melville, H.   Rose Window.
Moorer.   Southern Pulpit, The.
Outram.   On Hearing a Lady Praise a Certain Rev. Doctor's Eyes.
Roethke.   Judge Not.
Thomson, J.   Paraphrase of the Latter Part of the Sixth Chapter of St. Matthew, A.
Tolson, M.   Old Pettigrew.
Unknown.   Let Us Cheer the Weary Traveler.
Vicar of Bray, The.
Wakefield.   Music of His Steps, The.
Warren, R.   Amazing Grace in the Back Country.
See also **Clergy**

Precocity
Ellis, T.   Practice.

Predators
Ginsberg, A.   Who Eats Who?
Hanzlicek, C.   Feeding Frenzies.
Lindsay, N.   Spider and the Ghost of the Fly, The.
Lovelace, R.   Lady with a Falcon on Her Fist, A.
McKay, C.   Birds of Prey.
Melville, H.   Maldive Shark, The.
Owen, W.   Arms and the Boy.
Rossetti, C.   Handy Mole who plied no shovel, A.
Taylor, E.   Upon a Spider Catching a Fly.

Predestination
Hardy, T.   Subalterns, The.
Herrick.   Predestination.
Moore, M.   Book of How, The.
Nemerov.   Western Approaches, The.

Pregnancy
Alvi, M.   Man Impregnated.
Baraka.   For Hettie.
Barbauld.   To a Little Invisible Being Who Is Expected Soon to Become Visible.
Brereton, J.   Unborn.
Bruce, D.   Two Couples.
Carroll, K.   Truth About Karen, The.
Clive.   Mother, The.
Cofer, J.   How to Get a Baby.
Crane, H.   Stark Major.
Curzon, D.   Tour of Ein Kerem, A.
Daniels, K.   Women's Room in Pennsylvania Station, The.
Denning.   Kim-San.
Dove, R.   History.
Weathering Out.
Durcan.   Sister Agnes Writes to Her Beloved Mother.
Ellis, J.   Sarah Hazard's Love Letter.
Ennis.   Alice of Daphne, 1799.
Ferguson, G.   Scan.
Fleming, R.   For All Unwed Mothers.
Fusselman, A.   Ticker.
García, D.   Clog of Her Body, The.
Green Corn Season.

Grennan.   Conjunctions.
Hacker, M.   1973.
Hikmet.   Evening Walk, The.
Holbrook, D.   Maternity Gown.
Kinzie.   Sound Waves.
Lawrence, D.   Youth Mowing, A.
Lorde.   Now That I Am Forever with Child.
Mahon.   Ford Manor.
Unborn Child, An.
Major, C.   On Trying to Imagine the Kiwi Pregnant.
Mayer, B.   We've Solved the Problem.
McAdams, J.   Leaving the Old Gods.
McGrath, C.   Delphos, Ohio.
McPherson, S.   Pregnancy.
Michelson, R.   Interrogation.
Olds, S.   May 1968.
Plath.   Metaphors.
Qunta, C.   Know, The.
Ras.   Pregnant Poets Swim Lake Tarleton, New Hampshire.
Realuyo.   La Querida.
Reynolds, R.   Peridot.
Rilke.   Mary's Visitation.
Rungano.   Labour.
Shange.   Oh, I'm 10 Months Pregnant.
Shuttle.   Early Pregnancy.
Expectant Mother.
Maritimes.
Sorrells.   To a Child Born in Time of Small War.
Swenson, M.   Motherhood.
Taggard.   With Child.
Unknown.   Child Waters.
I Have a New Garden.
Jenny Nettles.
Waly, Waly [Love Be Bonny].
Volkman.   Pregnant Lady Playing Tennis, The.
Wickham.   After Annunciation.
Wright, J.   Woman to Child.
Woman to Man.
Woman's Song.
Zucker, R.   In Your Version of Heaven I am Younger.

Prejudice
Atkins.   Late Bus (After a Series of Hold-Ups).
Baca.   So Mexicans Are Taking Jobs from Americans.
Baraka.   Agony, An. As Now.
Boss.   When You Are Grown, Amanda Rose.
Brown, S.   Children's Children.
Campo.   Towards Curing AIDS.
Cassells.   Soul Make a Path Through Shouting.
Chinn.   Skin Color from the Sun.
Derricotte.   Family Secrets.
Weakness, The.
Divakaruni.   Founding of Yuba City, The.
Yuba City School.
Domina, L.   Pharoah's Army Got Drowned.
Durand, O.   Black Man's Son, The.
Durcan.   Jewish Bride, The.
Eady.   Sherbet.
Espada.   Beloved Spic.
Toque de queda: Curfew in Lawrence.
Fanthorpe.   You Will Be Hearing from Us Shortly.
Gillan.   In Memory We Are Walking.
Public School No. 18: Paterson, New Jersey.
Henderson-Holmes.   Battle, Over and Over Again, The.
Hewitt, J.   From the Tibetan.
Kim, M.   Rose of Sharon, A.
Kipling, R.   Tommy.
Kramer, L.   Shoemaker's Wife, The.
Levine, P.   Old Testament, The.
McElroy, C.   Foul Line—1987.
Moore, M.   Labors of Hercules, The.
Moorer.   Prejudice.
Mura.   Argument: on 1942, An.
Grandfather-in-law.
Ostriker.   Lamenting the Inevitable.
Plotnick, H. M.   Jewish.
Reed, I.   Jacket Notes.
Roberts, N.   Nigger and Some Poofters, A.
Rodriguez, L.   We Never Stopped Crossing Borders.

Saint. Heart and Soul.
Saunders, R. Lawd, Dese Colored Chillum.
Scannell. Popular Mythologies.
Steptoe. Such a Boat of Land.
Viscusi. Autobiography.
Walton, A. First Impressions.
See also **Racial Prejudice; Racism and Racists; Sexism**

Presbyterianism and Presbyterians
Milton. On the New Forcers of Conscience Under the Long Parliament.
Paulin. Presbyterian Study.
Wilson, R. Elegy in a Presbyterian Burying-Ground.

Presence
Creeley. Fire, The.
Herrick. Gods Presence.
Knott. Goodbye.
Levertov. Wings, The.
McDaniel, W. Asking Favors.
Natzler, C. There.
Olson, E. Presence, The.
Oswald, A. Mountains.
Unknown. Because We're Here.
Young, A. Blues Don't Change, The.

Presents
Alvi, M. Presents from My Aunts in Pakistan.
Laurencin, M. Present, The.
See also **Gifts and Giving**

Presidency, The, United States
Hazo. Some Words for President Wilson.
Hollander, J. Historical Reflections.
Kendrick, D. Solo: The Good Blues.
Lindsay, N. Bryan, Bryan, Bryan, Bryan.
Moorer. Presidents, The.
Steptoe. Election Time.
Taylor, H. Speech.
Whitman, W. To the States, To Identify the 16th, 17th, or 18th Presidentiad.

Presley, Elvis
Ai. Resurrection of Elvis Presley, The.
Blessing. Elegy for Elvis.
Bogen, D. All Shook Up.
Bowers, N. Conversions.
On the Elvis Mailing List.
Brock, V. I Stopped in Tupelo, Elvis.
Mary's Dream.
Sphinx.
Bukowski. Elvis Lives.
Clifton, L. Them and Us.
Cornish, S. Elvis.
My Father's House.
Driskell, M. Talismans.
Eady. Young Elvis.
Elledge. Their Hats Is Always White.
Fulton, A. About Face.
New Release, A.
Some Cool.
Gilmore, B. Elvis.
Gunn, T. Elvis Presley.
Painkillers.
Hudgins. Versification of a Passage from Penthouse.
Jackson, F. Death of Gladys Presley, The.
Elvis Acts as His Own Pallbearer.
Elvis at the End of History.
Elvis Goes to the Army.
Elvis Reads the Wild Swans at Coole.
Elvis Sings Gospel.
I Visit the Twenty-four Coin-op Church of Elvis.
Women Who Love Elvis All Their Lives, The.
Koncel, M. Come Back, Elvis, Come Back to Holyoke.
McMahon, L. Elvis for the Ages, An.
Nameroff, R. Elvis Presley.
Oates. Waiting on Elvis, 1956.
Ray, D. Brides of Elvis, The.
Sunday Morning.
Seay. Audubon Drive, Memphis.
Stokes, T. Elvis Elevator, The.
Stuart, D. Fishing with Elvis.
Swartwout. I Wannabe Your Queen.
Vélez, E. Elvis P. and Emma B.
Wakoski. Blue Suede Shoes.

Wojahn. Assassination of Robert Goulet as Performed by Elvis Presley: Memphis, 1968, The.
Elvis Moving a Small Cloud: The Desert Near Las Vegas, 1976.
Nixon Names Elvis Honorary Federal Narcotics Agent at Oval Office Ceremony, 1973.
Pharaoh's Palace.
W. C. W. Watching Presley's Second Appearance on The Ed Sullivan Show: Mercy Hospital, Newark, 1956.

Presumption
Wright, C. March Journal.

Pretension
Burns, R. Toadeater, The.
Campion, T. Heart's Music.
Delgado, J. When You Leave.
Dorough, B. I'm Hip.
Eliot, T. Portrait of a Lady.
Herbert, G. Jordan (2).
Hughes, L. Warning: Augmented.
Jonson, B. On English Monsieur.
Shapiro, K. University.
Tranter. Having Completed My Fortieth Year.

Pride
Awad, J. Stopping at the Mayflower.
Barber, M. To Novella, on her saying deridingly, that a Lady of great Merit, and fine Address, was bred in the Old Way.
Barber, W. Explanation.
Bennett, G. To a Dark Girl.
Bottrall. Icarus.
Breeze. Natural High.
Brooks, G. Primer for Blacks.
Brown, J. *et al.* Say It Loud—I'm Black and I'm Proud.
Brown, S. Sporting Beasley.
To Sallie, Walking.
Burgoyne, J. Dashing White Sergeant, The.
Burns, R. Toadeater, The.
Ceravolo. Wild Provoke of the Endurance Sky.
Clifton, L. Listen Children.
Coleridge, M. Pride.
Coward. London Pride.
Dove, R. Sunday Greens.
Emerson, R. Good-bye.
Enright, D. Flowers.
Gibran. Love.
Gillan. Growing Up Italian.
Gonzales, R. Praise the Tortilla, Praise the Menudo, Praise the Chorizo.
Grigson. Before a Fall.
Herbert, G. Church Monuments.
Flower, The.
Vanity [*or* Vanitie] (1).
Herrick. To Dianeme.
Hewitt, J. Ulster Names.
Hope, A. Paradise Saved.
Hughes, L. Ballad of the Girl Whose Name Is Mud.
Madam and the Census Man.
Jeffers, R. Rock and Hawk.
Johnson, E. Right to Be.
Kay, J. Pride.
Knott. Two Vietnam Poems: (1966).
Komunyakaa. Seven Deadly Sins.
Kooser. Myrtle.
Kramer, L. Non-Emigrant, The.
Landon. Mask of Gaiety, The.
Lawrence, D. Proper Pride.
Leigh, R. Greatness in Little.
Levine, P. Animals Are Passing from Our Lives.
Longfellow, H. Rhyme of Sir Christopher, The.
Lorde. Naturally.
Lowell, J. Contrast, A.
Lucie-Smith. Lesson, The.
McKay, C. If We Must Die.
Meredith, G. Lucifer in Starlight.
Owen, W. Parable of the Old Men and the Young, The.
Qunta, C. Know, The.
Rukeyser, M. Bubble of Air.
Sandburg, C. Primer Lesson.
Sewell, G. Dying Man in His Garden, The.
Shelley, P. Ozymandias.

Sherwood, G. Satire against Reason and Mankind, A.
Thomas, E. Forsaken Wife, The.
Thomson, J. To the God of Fond Desire.
Unknown. Pointless Pride of Man, The.
Tamping Ties.
Villalongo. In the Good Old U. S. A.
Whitman, W. Woman Waits for Me, A.
Whittier. Cities of the Plain, The.
Forgiveness.
Wilmer, S. Mess Boy, The.

Priests
Burroughs, W. My Legs Señor.
Silesky. Kingdom, The.
Unknown. Full and True Account of a Dreaded Fire, that Lately Broke out in the Pope's Breeches, A.
Young, G. Damien.
See also **Clergy**

Prillerman, Byrd
Johnson, M. Sister Johnson's Speech.
To Professor Byrd Prillerman.

Primitive Man
Heaney, S. Tollund Man, The.
See also **Man, Primitive**

Primroses
Biespiel, D. Lilacs.
Clare, J. Primrose, The.
Cranch. Evening Primrose, The.
Herrick. Primrose, The.
Shaw, A. Crepuscule.
Wordsworth, W. Primrose of the Rock, The.

Prince Edward Island, Canada
McFadden, D. Lennox Island.

Princes and Princesses
Aiken, J. Palace Cook's Tale.
Aytoun [*or* Ayton], R. On the Prince's Death, to the King.
Beardsley. Ballad of a Barber, The.
Gorges. Written upon the death of the most Noble Prince Henrie.
Holland, H. Epitaph on Prince Henry.
Landon. Princess Victoria, The.
Machan. Hazel Tells LaVerne.
Moore, T. Duke Is the Lad [to Frighten a Lass], The.
Oxenham. Everymaid.
Ramanujan. Last of the Princes, The.
Rossetti, C. Royal Princess, A.
Sitwell, D. King of China's Daughter, The.
Tate, J. Pet Deer, The.
Watson, R. Enchanted Princess, An.

Printing and Printers
Adams, F. Composed in the Composing Room.
Bartlett, E. Charlotte, Her Book.
Dobson, R. Country Press.
Espada. Who Burns for the Perfection of Paper.
Glover, D. Printers.
Hughes, L. Madam's Calling Cards.
McGough, R. Italic.
Phipson. Press, The.
Unknown. Pan in Battle.
Wodehouse, P. Printer's Error.

Prisoners of War
Dickey, J. Performance, The.
Gardiner, A. Natal Hunters, The.
Jarmain. Prisoners of War.
Lee, J. German Prisoners.
Mura. Blueness of the Day, The.

Prisons and Prisoners
Adamson. Passing Through Experiences.
Akhmatova, A. Dedication.
Awoonor. They Shall Know.
Baca. Cloudy Day.
How We Carry Ourselves.
I Applied for the Board.
Immigrants in Our Own Land.
It Started.
Like an Animal.
Barben, D. Four White Walls.
Barth, R. P.O.W.s.
Berrigan, D. Rehabilitative Report: We Can Still Laugh.
Blake, W. Crystal Cabinet, The.
How Sweet I Roamed [*or* Roam'd] from Field

to Field.
Boleyn, G.　O Death, Rock Me Asleep.
Brown, S.　Southern Road.
Brutus.　At Night.
　Cold.
　Endurance.
　Letters to Martha.
　On the Island.
　Poems About Prison.
　Sounds Begin Again, The.
　Under House Arrest.
Carkesse.　On the Doctors' Telling Him that till
　He Left off Making Verses He Was Not Fit to
　be Discharged.
Carmichael, H.　Hong Kong Blues.
Centolella.　Woman of Three Minds, The.
Clare, J.　I Feel I Am.
Clayton, S.　Sunshine Prisoner '470.'
Cobbett.　Elegy in Newgate.
Columbo, R.　Prisoner of Love.
Conyus.　Great Santa Barbara Oil Disaster OR,
　The.
　Upon Leaving the Parole Board Hearing.
Cook, E.　Song of the Imprisoned Bird.
Cory, W.　Parting.
Dawe, B.　On the Death of Ronald Ryan.
De Hearn.　Shut-In, The.
Dobyns.　Exile.
Donnelly, C.　Flowering Bars, The.
Douglas, K.　Prisoner, The.
Duemer.　Theory of Tragedy.
Dunbar, P.　Sympathy.
Elizabeth I.　Written on a Wall at Woodstock.
　Written with a Diamond On Her Window at
　Woodstock.
Espada.　Prisoners of Saint Lawrence, The.
Fearing.　Escape.
Fitzgerald, R.　Wind at Your Door, The.
Frost, R.　Line-Gang, The.
Gaskill, C.　Prisoner of Love.
Gilyard, K.　Letter.
Giovannitti.　Walker, The.
Grandfather Koori.　Never Blood So Red.
Graves, R.　Certain Mercies.
　Love Without Hope.
Gunn, T.　In the Tank.
　Tamer and Hawk.
Hamburger, M.　Between the Lines.
Harris, W.　We Live in a Cage.
Hawoldar.　I Have Gone into My Prison Cell.
Helwig.　Words from Hell.
Henderson, D.　Alvin Cash / Keep on Dancin'
Hikmet.　Evening Walk, The.
　Letters from a Man in Solitary.
　Letters from Chankiri Prison.
　Since I Was Thrown Inside.
Hogan, M.　Spring.
Howard, L.　Humours of the King's Bench
　Prison, a Ballad, The.
Howe, F.　Scattered Light.
Hugo, R.　In Your Dream after Falling in Love.
　Letter to Birch from Deer Lodge.
Jarrell.　Prisoners.
Johnson, G.　Heart of a Woman, The.
Jordan, J.　Poem Against the State (Of Things):
　1975.
Joseph, J.　Dog Body and Cat Mind.
Kaufman, B.　Jail Poems.
Keats.　Written on the Day That Mr. Leigh Hunt
　Left Prison.
Keplinger, D.　Inside: George Gaines at
　Graterford Prison, 1981.
Kern, J.　Tulip Time in Sing Sing.
Kinzie.　Ringing Words.
Kipling, R.　Cells.
　Half-Ballad of Waterval.
Knight, E.　Cell Song.
　Crazy Pigeon.
　For Freckle-Faced Gerald.
　Haiku: "Eastern guard tower."
　Hard Rock Returns to Prison from the Hospital
　for the Criminal Insane.
　He Sees Through Stone.
　Idea of Ancestry, The.
　To Make a Poem in Prison.
　Warden Said to Me the Other Day, The.

WASP Woman Visits a Black Junkie in
　Prison, A.
Koestenbaum, P.　Sonnet 37: "I'd decided I
　initiate most."
Levine, P.　Heaven.
Lovelace, R.　To Althea, from Prison.
　To Lucasta, from Prison.
　Vintage to the Dungeon, The.
Lowell, R.　After the Surprising Conversions.
　In the Cage.
　Memories of West Street and Lepke.
Lowry, M.　Sestina in a Cantina.
MacNamara, F.　Convict's Tour to Hell, A.
Madan.　Abelard to Eloisa.
Mariah.　Christmas 1962.
Maroon, B.　Fire Keeper.
Matthews, W.　Old Folsom Prison.
McAuley, J.　Released on Parole.
McNeill, A.　Ode to Brother Joe.
Melville, H.　In the Prison Pen.
Meredith, W.　Partial Accounts.
Messerli.　Closure.
Mishler.　Ceremony.
Morant, H.　Last Rhyme and Testament of Tony
　Lumpkin.
Morris, W.　In Prison.
Mpina.　Reborn.
Nortje.　Letter from Pretoria Central Prison.
O'Dalaigh, G.　Child in Prison, A.
Padilla.　Man on the Edge.
Pape.　In the Bluemist Motel.
Pau-Llosa.　Paredón.
Paulin.　Surveillances.
Peterson, R.　San Quentin 1968.
Piatt, S.　In Her Prison.
Reese, D.　Ol' Hannah.
Revard.　Coming of Age in the County Jail.
Rich, A.　From the Prison House.
Robin, L.　Prisoner of Love.
Rukeyser, M.　Columbus.
Salazar.　Cricket at Central California Women's
　Facility.
Sandburg, C.　Teamster's Farewell, A.
Smith, K.　Writing in Prison.
Smith, M.　In Prison.
Smith, R.　Softball at Julia Tutwiler Prison.
Smith, S.　Commuted Sentence, The.
Spender, S.　Prisoners, The.
Spenser.　Sonnet 73: 'Being my self captived
　here.'
Spicer, J.　Song of a Prisoner.
Stafford, K.　Inside the Fence: Tule Lake
　Internment Camp.
Surrey.　Prison in Windsor Castle.
Swart.　Convict.
Thelwall.　Cell, The.
Tregian.　Imprisoned Recusant Writes to His
　Wife, An.
Tucker, M.　Soldier Boy's Dream, The.
Unknown.　Convicts' Rum Song.
　Female Transport, The.
　Poor Lazarus.
　Young Beichan.
Waddington, M.　Women's Jail, The.
Walker, F. X.　Crooked Afro.
Walker, M.　Girl Held without Bail.
Walker, R.　Okay, Let's Be Honest.
　Solitary Confinement.
　Unreceived Messages.
Warren, R.　Wet Hair: If Now His Mother
　Should Come.
Warren-Moore.　Dannemora Contraband.
　For Paula Cooper.
Watts-Dunton.　Coleridge.
Wayman.　Despair.
Wodehouse, P.　Tulip Time in Sing Sing.
Wordsworth, W.　Sonnet: "Nuns fret not at their
　convent's narrow room."
Wright, J.　American Twilights, 1957.
　Old Prison, The.
Young, A.　Conjugal Visits.

Privacy
Broumas, O.　Privacy.
Coleridge, M.　No Newspapers.
Ellis, T.　Kiss in the Dark, A.
Greenhalgh, C.　Night I Met Marilyn, The.

Of Love, Death and the Sea-Squirt.
Harris, W.　We Live in a Cage.
Lane, P.　Sexual Privacy of Women on Welfare.
McGinley.　Triolet Against Sisters.
See also **Solitude**
Privateers
McCarthy, T.　Shopkeepers at the Party Meeting.
Procne
Quennell.　Procne.
Procrastination
Barbour, D.　Mañana (Is Soon Enough for Me).
Ceravolo.　Wind Is Blowing West, The.
Crabbe.　Delay Has Danger.
　Procrastination.
Milosz, C.　Preparation.
Perry, N.　Next Year.
Prodigal Son
Bishop, E.　Prodigal, The.
Rilke.　Departure of the Prodigal Son, The.
Robinson, E.　Prodigal Son, The.
Prodigality
Moore, M.　Americans in 1933–4–5–6–7–8–,
　Etc.
Progress
Auden.　Moon Landing.
Canning, G. et al.　Progress of Man, The.
Cohan.　If Washington Should Come to Life.
　Nothing New Beneath the Sun.
Cummings, E.　Pity This Busy Monster,
　Manunkind.
Fenton, J.　Kingfisher's Boxing Gloves, The.
Gunn, T.　Considering the Snail.
Hardy, T.　Christmas: 1924.
Hoffenstein.　Progress.
Hugo, R.　Letter to Oberg from Pony.
Linden, M.　To the Wheel of Progress.
Mahon.　Consolations of Philosophy.
Praed.　Chaunts of the Brazen Head, The.
Rukeyser, M.　Book of the Dead, The.
Sandburg, C.　Four Preludes on Playthings of
　the Wind.
Snyder, G.　L M F B R.
Southwick.　Earthly Light.
Spender, S.　Not Palaces.
Tsaloumas.　Progressive Man's Indignation, A.
Prometheus
Byron, G.　Prometheus.
Horan.　Prometheus.
Shelley, P.　Life of Life.
　Poet's Dream, The.
　Prometheus Unbound [A Lyrical Drama in Four
　Acts].
Tomlinson, C.　Prometheus.
Promises
Anderson, M.　Lost in the Stars.
Anderson-Thompkins.　brken promises.
Anthony, M.　Ugly Heart, The.
Arlen, H.　As Long As I Live.
Campbell, J.　If I Had You.
Herrick.　Rainbow; or Curious Covenant, The.
　To His Conscience.
Jones, R.　Key, The.
Koehler, T.　As Long As I Live.
Naimy, M.　Solemn Vow, A.
Olds, S.　Wedding Vow, The.
Robinson, E.　Vickery's Mountain.
Rossetti, C.　Promises like Pie-Crust.
Shirley, J.　Two Gentlemen That Broke Their
　Promise of a Meeting.
Smart, C.　To the Rev. Mr. Powell.
Swift, J.　Twelve Articles.
Weill, K.　Lost in the Stars.
Wyatt, S.　Farewell: "What should I say."
Yeats.　Deep-sworn Vow, A.
Proms
Chavez, L.　After the Prom.
Propaganda
Day Lewis.　Where Are the War Poets?
Komunyakaa.　Hannoi Hanna.
Propertius, Sextus
Adcock, F.　Note on Propertius I.5.
Property
Clayton, S.　Good Old Days, The.
Coolbrith.　Ownership.

Davis, C.   Belongings.
Doolan, F.   Who Owns Darling Street?
Durcan.   Tullynoe: Tête-à-Tête in the Parish Priest's Parlour.
Everett, J.   Old Co'es.
Garioch.   Property.
Lawrence, D.   Lord Tennyson and Lord Melchett.
MacCaig.   Chauvinist.
Mudrooroo Narogin.   Jacky Demonstrates for Land Rights.
Norris, J.   My Estate.
North, M.   Ordnance Survey in the Northern Counties.
Padilla.   Fountain, a House of Stone, A.
Pound, E.   Portrait d'une Femme.
Smith, K.   Possessions.
Wickham.   Soul's Liberty.

Prophecy and Prophets
Baratier, D.   Estrella's Prophecies #47.
Barnes, D.   Transfiguration.
Blake, W.   Merlins Prophecy.
Chagy.   Haggai.
Conquest.   Agents, The.
Cowley, A.   34. Chapter of the Prophet Isaiah, The.
Dawes, K.   Trickster 1 (for Winston Rodney).
Gay, J.   Birth of the Squire; an Eclogue, The.
Ginsberg, A.   Prophecy, A.
Graves, R.   Christmas Robin, The.
Hemans.   Second Sight.
Hernández Cruz.   Keeping Track of the Serpents.
Jackson, L.   Helen's Burning.
Johnson, L.   Mystic and Cavalier.
Lehman.   Prophet's Lantern, The.
Malachi.   Psalm of Silk.
Manley, R.   Bob Marley's Dead.
McGrath, T.   End of the World, The.
Osundare.   Sand Seer, The.
Parker, M.   King Enjoys His Own Again, The.
Patchen.   'In the footsteps of the walking air.'
Poe.   Stanzas.
Robinson, M.   Foresees her Death.
Samaras, N.   Mute Prophets.
Seaton, M.   Nostradamus Predicts the Destruction of Chicago.
Tennyson, A.   Babylon.
Tindal.   Birth Wail, The.
Unknown.   Ezekiel Saw de [*or* the] Wheel.
Walker, M.   Prophets for a New Day.
Wilbur.   Advice to a Prophet.

See also **Oracles**

Prostitution and Prostitutes
Barry, J.   Nights in Nha Trang.
Blind.   Russian Student's Tale, The.
Breton, A.   Man and Woman Absolutely White, A.
Brooks, G.   Coora Flower, The.
Broumas, O.   Etymolgy.
Browne, I.   Letter from a Captain in Country Quarters to his Corinna in Town, A.
Chin, J.   Cocksucker's Blues.
Clifton, H.   Id.
   Monsoon Girl.
Cofer, J.   Las Magdalenas.
Coleman, H.   OK Corral East Brothers in the Nam.
Cooper, D.   Being Aware.
Cotton, C.   Epitaph on M. H., An.
Couzyn.   World War II.
Crawford, R.   Love Song of Tommo Frogley.
Donne.   Klockius.
   Self[e] Accuser, A.
Dowson.   Non Sum Qualis Eram Bonae sub Regno Cynarae.
Eliot, T.   Sweeney Erect.
Erdrich.   Lady in the Pink Mustang, The.
France, L.   My Muse, the Whore.
Hardy, T.   Ruined Maid, The.
Hass, R.   Bookbuying in the Tenderloin.
Henley, W.   Madam Life's A Piece in Bloom.
Hughes, L.   Red Silk Stockings.
   Sliver of Sermon.
Kendrick, D.   Solo: The Good Blues.
Knight, E.   As You Leave Me.

Violent Space, The.
Lovelace, R.   La Bella Bona-Roba.
Mapanje.   Cheerful Girls at Smiller's Bar, 1971, The.
   Messages.
McGrath, T.   Song: Miss Penelope Burgess, Balling the Jack.
Nashe [*or* Nash].   Choise of Valentines, The.
Pearlberg, G.G.   Loop-the-Loop in Prospect Park (1905).
Peters, L.   Song: "Clawed green-eyed."
Piper, L.   Sweet Ethel.
Plomer.   French Lisette: A Ballad of Maida Vale.
Porter, C.   Love for Sale.
Purdy, J.   Do You Wonder Why I Am Sleepy.
Ramsay, A.   Lucky Spence's Last Advice.
Rexroth, K.   For a Masseuse and Prostitute.
Rodgers, W.   Net, The.
Rouse.   Lilies of the Field.
Sandburg, C.   Harrison Street Court.
Simmons, J.   Cavalier Lyric.
Simpson, L.   Man Who Married Magdalene, The.
Swift, J.   Beautiful Young Nymph Going to Bed, A.
Taylor, J.   Epigram: "Look how yon lecher's legs are worn away."
Trethewey, N.   Photograph of a Bawd Drinking Raleigh Rye.
Unknown.   Shari Wag El Burka.
   She Was Poor but She Was Honest.
Villon.   Ballad of Villon and Fat Madge, The.
Walker, M.   Whores.
Weigl.   Song for the Lost Private.
   Way of Tet, The.
Whitman, W.   To a Common Prostitute.
Wilbur.   Place Pigalle.
Wilde, O.   Harlot's House, The.
   Impression Du Matin.
Williams, C.   Gas Station, The.
Wright, J.   Gesture by a Lady with an Assumed Name, A.
   In Response to a Rumor that the Oldest Whorehouse in Wheeling, West Virginia, Has Been Condemned.

Prostitution and Prostitutes Magdalene
Cofer, J.   Las Magdalenas.
Cullen, C.   For Daughters of Magdalen.

Protest, Social
Alexie.   On the Amtrak from Boston to New York City.
Anhalt, D.   That Jewish Crusader.
Atwood.   Notes towards a Poem That Can Never Be Written.
Baca.   Immigrants in Our Own Land.
Bly, R.   After the Industrial Revolution, All Things Happen at Once.
   At a March against the Vietnam War.
Brome.   Leveller's Rant, The.
Brooks, G.   Lovers of the Poor, The.
Bursk.   Lies.
Cambridge, A.   Fashion.
Chesterton, G.   Secret People, The.
Clough.   Latest Decalogue, The.
Conquest.   Bagpipes at the Biltmore.
Cornish, S.   Brother of the Streets.
Cummings, E.   Two X.
Davidson, J.   Thirty Bob a Week.
Davie.   Barnsley and District.
   Thanks to Industrial Essex.
Dorn, E.   Home on the Range, February 1962.
   Mourning Letter, March 29 1963.
Dove, R.   Rosa.
Emerson, R.   Ode, Inscribed to W. H. Channing.
Enright, D.   Unlawful Assembly.
Espada.   All the People Who Are Now Red Trees.
   Cockroaches of Liberation.
   Year I Was Diagnosed with a Sacrilegious Heart, The.
Fishman, C.   Death March.
Floyd.   Private Jack Smith, U. S. M. C.
Fort, C.   For Martin Luther King.
Gilbert, C.   Theory of Curve.
Ginsberg, A.   America.

Death to Van Gogh's Ear!
Goodman, P.   April 1962.
Gurney, I.   Strange Hells.
Hale, J.   Cinque.
   Custer Lives in Humbolt County.
Hayes, A.   Joe Hill.
Hood, T.   Song of the Shirt, The.
Ignatow, D.   All Quiet.
Kearns, L.   Environment.
Kizer, C.   Race Relations.
Lawrence, D.   How Beastly the Bourgeois Is.
   Stand Up!
Levertov.   Protesting at the Nuclear Test Site.
Lowell, R.   After the Surprising Conversions.
   March 1, The.
   Memories of West Street and Lepke.
MacSweeney.   Far Cliff Babylon.
   Flame Ode.
   Ode: "Urals post-master, this is your."
Madgett.   Alabama Centennial.
Mapanje.   On Being Asked to Write a Poem for 1979.
McElroy, C.   Foul Line—1987.
McKay, C.   If We Must Die.
Millay, E.   Apostrophe to Man.
Moorer.   Jim Crow Cars.
Mottram.   Elegy 11: Ford.
Mudrooroo Narogin.   Peaches and Cream.
Mulford.   Nevrazumitelny.
Nye, N.   Rebellion against the North Side.
Peacock, T.   Rich and Poor; or, Saint and Sinner.
Picasso.   Bottle of Suze, A.
Pickard, T.   Devil's Destroying Angel Exploded, The.
   My Pen.
Randall, D.   Ballad of Birmingham.
Raworth.   Future Models May Have Infra-Red Sensors.
Raymond, V.   People, No, The.
Rexroth, K.   Bad Old Days, The.
Rich, A.   Burning of Paper instead of Children, The.
   From the Prison House.
Rukeyser, M.   Rational Man.
Sadoff.   Civil Rights.
Seeger, P.   Where Have All the Flowers Gone?
Sepamla.   Measure for Measure.
Shelley, P.   Song to the Men of England.
Starbuck, G.   Of Late.
Tremblay, B.   Mayday.
Troupe.   Boomerang: A Blatantly Political Poem.
Unknown.   Diggers' Song, The.
   I Don't Want to Be a Soldier.
   She Was Poor but She Was Honest.
   Soup Kitchen Song.
   We Shall Overcome.
Walker, M.   Girl Held without Bail.
   Street Demonstration.
Wayman.   Despair.
   Picketing Supermarkets.
   Teething.
Weaver, M.   Picnic, an Homage to Civil Rights, The.
Whittier.   Astræa.
Wilbur.   For the Student Strikers.
Wordsworth, W.   On the Projected Kendal and Windermere Railway.
Wormser.   Soul Music.

See also **Civil Rights Movement**

Protestantism and Protestants
Coles, R.   Christmas, Belfast.
Herbert, G.   British Church, The.
Hill, G.   Christmas Trees.
Maxton.   At the Protestant Museum.
Morrissey, S.   Thoughts in a Black Taxi.
Ormsby, F.   Spot the Ball.
   Survivors.

Proust, Marcel
Disch.   Bookmark, A.
Jarrell.   Man Meets a Woman in the Street, A.

Provence, France
Gosse.   Sestina: "In fair Provence, the land of lute and rose."
Procter, A.   Legend of Provence, A.

Wilbur. Grasse: The Olive Trees.
Williams, W. To Ford Madox Ford in Heaven.

Providence
Herrick. Gods Providence.
Wheatley, P. Thoughts on the Works of
  Providence.

Providence, Rhode Island
Weaver, M. Providence Journal V: Israel of
  Puerto Rico.

Prudes
Nash, O. First Limick.

Psyche (mythology)
Duncan, R. Poem Beginning with a Line by
  Pindar, A.
Keats. Ode to Psyche.
Pound, E. Speech for Psyche in the Golden
  Book of Apuleius.
Willis, N. Psyche, Before the Tribunal of
  Venus.

Psychiatry and Psychiatrists
Clements, S. Deer Cloud.
Coles, R. On Dutch's Death.
Kolodny, S. Tsuneko—Psychiatric Medications
  Clinic.
Lister, R. Mind Reborn in Streatham
  Common, A.
Rector. David's Rumor.
Ritchie, E. Electroconvulsive Therapy.
See also **Mental Illness**

Psychoanalysis and Psychoanalysts
Berryman. Group.
Cleary, B. Chicken & Sex.
Coles, R. On Dutch's Death.
Durrell. Ballad of the Oedipus Complex.
Endrezze. Notes from an Analyst's Couch.
Everhard. Curing Homosexuality.
Jenkins, P. Six Small Fires.
Jennings, E. Interrogator, The.
Kay, J. Maw Broon Visits a Therapist.
McGrath, C. At the Freud Hilton.
Randall, D. Analysands.
Wilner, E. Muse, The.

Psychological Testing
Powell, P. Full Neurological Work-up.
Wieners. Two Years Later.

Puberty
Hampton. In Andrea's Garden.
Hope, M. Bare Floors.
  Sixth Grade.
Joseph, A. Adolescence.
Tayson, R. First Sex.
Thomas, D. Puberty Tree, The.
Wrigley, R. Prophecy, The.

Publishing and Publishers
Byron, G. To Mr. Murray.
Carroll, L. Poeta Fit, Non Nascitur.
Hecht, A. From the Grove Press.
Herrick. To the Right Honourable Mildmay,
  Earl of Westmorland.
Koch, K. Thank You.
Larkin, P. Limerick: "There was an old fellow
  of Kaber."
McGinley. Publisher's Party.
Wells, C. Of Modern Books.

Pudding
Mother Goose. King Arthur.

Puddles
Frost, R. Spring Pools.
Mitchell, A. Watch Your Step—I'm Drenched.

Puerto Ricans
Algarin. El Jibarito Moderno.
  Happy New Year.
  Taos Pueblo Indians: 700 strong according to
    Bobby's last census.
  Wire Tap.
Espada. David Leaves the Saints for Paterson.
  My Native Costume.
  Spanish of Our Out-Loud Dreams, The.
  Tony Went to the Bodega but He Didn't Buy
    Anything.
Esteves. Celebration of Home Birth: November
  15th, 1981, A.
  For Lolita Lebron.
  Here.

In the Beginning.
  Lil' Pito.
  Take the Hearts of Children.
Figueroa, J. Boricua.
  Murdered Luggage.
  Poet Pedro Pietri.
Gomez, M. Making It.
  Solo Palabras.
  To the Latin Lover I Left at the Candy Store.
Hernández Cruz. Anonymous.
  Borinkins in Hawaii.
  Discovery.
  Energy.
  If Chickens Could Talk.
  Ironing Goatskin.
  Latin and Soul for Joe Bataan.
  Loíza Aldea.
  Man Who Came to the Last Floor, The.
  Mountain Building.
  Physics of Ochun, The.
  Poem: "Greater cities are, The."
  Side 18.
  Side 21.
  Tale of Bananas, A.
  Two Guitars.
  You Gotta Have Your Tips on Fire.
Kinnell. Avenue Bearing the Initial of Christ
  into the New World, The.
Morales. Dinner, The.
  Ending Poem.
  Getting Out Alive.
  I Am the Reasonable One.
  I Recognize You.
Morales, A. 1930.
  Ending Poem.
  Immigrants.
  Kitchens.
  Other Heritage, The.
  Puertoricanness.
  Sugar Poem.
  Tita's Poem.
Perdomo, W. Nigger-Reecan Blues.
  Unemployed Mami.
Piñero. La Bodega Sold Dreams.
  Lower East Side Poem, A.
  This Is Not the Place Where I Was Born.
Pietri. Intermission from Monday.
  Traffic Misdirector.

Puerto Rico
Bernstein, L. America.
Espada. Coca-Cola and Coco Frío.
  Cockroaches of Liberation.
Figueroa, J. Boricua.
  Puerto Rico Made in Japan.
Hernández Cruz. New/Aguas Buenas/Jersey.
  Puerta Rica.
Marzán. Sunday Morning in Old San Juan.
Morales, A. Child's Christmas in Puerto
  Rico, A.
Pau-Llosa. Paredón.
Sondheim. America.
Weaver, M. Providence Journal V: Israel of
  Puerto Rico.

Pumas
Galvin, B. Cougar.

Pumpkins
Apache Oral Tradition. Corn Ceremony.
Barry, J. Harvest Moon.
Goodison. From the Garden of the Women
  Once Fallen.
Mother Goose. Pumpkin-Eater, The.
Willard, N. Saint Pumpkin.

Punishment
Burns, R. Holy Willie's Prayer.
Emerson, R. Nemesis.
Erdrich. Indian Boarding School: The
  Runaways.
Garcia, R. Zapato, El.
Graham, H. L'Enfant Glacé.
Graves, R. Wreath, The.
Hayden, R. Whipping, The.
Heaney, S. Punishment.
Herrick. Gods Providence.
  Persecutions Purifie.
Leto. For Talking.
Mitchell, A. Dumb Insolence.

Moore, T. Argument, An.
Olds, S. Unjustly Punished Child.
Raffalovich, M. A. World Well Lost 18, The.
Ransom, J. Man without Sense of Direction.
Reynolds, O. Hazel.
Reznikoff. Testimony: The United States
  (1901–1910) Recitative / The South.
Ross, C. Jack.
Sharpless. Low Church.
Ulku, A. History.
Unknown. Bitter Withy, The.
  Deserter, The.
  Lay of the Lash, The.
Wright, J. Song for the Middle of the Night, A.

Punks
Loncar, M. Peoria.
Lumsden, R. ITMA.
Sicoli. All Shook Up.
Stone, A. Rocket to Russia.

Puns
"Ingoldsby." Lines Left at Mr Theodore Hook's
  House in June, 1834.
McDaniel, J. Play It Again, Salmonella.
Portnoy, M. Roget, Papier, Schism!
Torres, E. Gigabyte Me—How Much RAM in
  Your Summer of Love?

Puppets and Puppeteers
Fuhrman, J. Here, I Say.
Tiller. Street Performers, 1851.
Wilde, O. Harlot's House, The.

Puritanism and Puritans
Corbet [*or* Corbett]. Distracted Puritan, The.
Equi. Puritans.
Longfellow, H. Rhyme of Sir Christopher, The.
Lowell, R. After the Surprising Conversions.
Maule. To Cotton Mather, from a Quaker.
Quarles. On Those That Deserve It.
Shapiro, K. Puritan, The.
Unknown. Zealous Puritan, The.

Purity
Barker, J. To Her Lover's Complaint.
Chavez, L. Clean Sheets.
Coe, C. Possibility.
Herbert, G. Superliminare.
Herrick. Persecutions Purifie.
Johnson, J. Unmarked Stop in Front of
  Westmond General Store, Westmond, Idaho.
Kunitz, S. Vita Nuova.
Lamb, C. "Timid grace sits trembling in her
  eye, A."
Levine, P. Genius.
Lindsay, N. General William Booth Enters into
  Heaven.
Lovelace, R. Her Muffe.
MacNeice. Individualist Speaks, The.
Millay, E. "Love is not all: it is not meat nor
  drink."
Robinson, M. Temple of Chastity, The.
Roscoe, W. Camellia, The.
Watson, R. Ruined Altar, A.

Pursuit
Doolittle, H. Pursuit.
Ignatow, D. Bagel, The.
Pietri. Intermission from Thursday.
Rankin, J. Man is following me, A.
Reese, L. Mystery.
Silverstein, S. Slithergadee, The.
Unknown. Run, Nigger, Run!

Pushers
Gunn, T. Street Song.
See also **Drug Addiction**

Pushkin, Aleksandr Sergeyevich
Coles, D. Natalya Nikolayevna Goncharov.
Nabokov. On Translating 'Eugene Onegin.'

Pygmalion
Graves, R. Galatea and Pygmalion.

Pygmies
Graves, R. Ogres and Pygmies.

Pym, John
Drummond, W. On Pym.

Pyramids
Giovanni. Ego Tripping (There May Be a
  Reason Why).

Pyramus and Thisbe
Cowley, A.   Epitaph of Pyramus and Thisbe.

Q

Quail
Smith, W.   Quail in Autumn.
Trowbridge, J.   Idyl of Harvest Time, An.
Quakers
Maule.   To Cotton Mather, from a Quaker.
See also **Friends, Society of**
Quarrels
Behn, A.   Defiance, The.
Blaser.   Suddenly.
Frost, R.   From Plane to Plane.
Gonzalez, N.   How the Heart Aches.
Goodman, M.   Man and Wife.
Harte, B.   Society Upon the Stanislaus, The.
Heard, J.   Quarrel, The.
Hughes, L.   Early Evening Quarrel.
"J. W."   City Eclogue.
Johnson, T.   12 second poem.
Justice, D.   But That Is Another Story.
Keech.   Little Words.
Kunitz, S.   Quarrel, The.
Muldoon, P.   Sushi.
Okai.   999 Smiles.
Philips, K.   On the 3 of September, 1651.
Phillips, S.   Apparition, The.
Piatt, S.   Her Word of Reproach.
Prince, F.   Token, The.
Prior.   To a Lady: She Refusing to Continue a
   Dispute with Me, and Leaving Me in the
   Argument.
Salom.   Walking at Night.
Stanley, T.   Repulse, The.
Thompson, P.   After the Quarrel.
   Domestic Storm, A.
Unknown.   Cats of Kilkenny, The.
   Coffee and Tea.
   Jolly Pinder of Wakefield, The.
   Two Little Kittens.
Warsh.   Static, The.
Yi, S.   Poem No. III.
See also **Anger**
Quarries
Nicholson, N.   Rockferns.
Rukeyser, M.   Sand-Quarry with Moving
   Figures.
Quebec City, Canada
Anderson, P.   Houses Burning; Quebec.
Atwood.   Disembarking at Quebec.
Ray, H.   Quebec.
Quebec (province), Canada
Ashbery.   On Autumn Lake.
Glassco.   Quebec Farmhouse.
Gustafson, R.   Wednesday at North Hatley.
Klein, A.   Indian Reservation: Caughnawaga.
   Rocking Chair, The.
Queen Anne's Lace
Williams, W.   Queen-Anne's-Lace.
Queens
Angus.   Alas! Poor Queen.
Campbell, D.   Australian Dream, The.
Cavendish, M.   Courting the Faerie Queen.
   Pastime of the Queen of Fairies, The.
Crosby, H.   Telephone Directory.
Graves, R.   Queen Mother to New Queen.
Housman, A.   1887.
Jamie.   Queen of Sheba, The.
Lawson, H.   English Queen, The.
Levin, P.   Lost Bee, The.
Lomax, M.   Gruoch.
Pfeiffer, E.   Lost Light, The.
Ralegh, S.   Sir Walter Ralegh to the Queen.
Synge.   Queens.
Unknown.   On Queen Caroline.
   Queen Nefertiti.
   Queen, Queen Caroline.
Wotton, S.   On His Mistress [*or* Mistris], the
   Queen of Bohemia.
Queens, New York City
Parker, D.   When Mark Deloach Ruled the

World.
Questions
Auden.   Question, The.
Cavendish, M.   Discourse of Beasts, A.
De la Mare.   Last Chapter, The.
DiPalma.   Prerogative of Lieder, The.
Dunbar, P.   Mystery, The.
Duncan, R.   Among My Friends.
Dunn, D.   Sundial, The.
Edwards, K.   Provisionally.
Ehrhart.   To Those Who Have Gone Home
   Tired.
Eigner.   In Imitation.
Emerson, R.   Sphinx, The.
Etherege.   To a Lady Asking Him How Long He
   Would Love Her.
Georgiou, E.   Week in the Life of the Ethnically
   Indeterminate, A.
Gier, J.   Examining the I.
Guevara, M.   Abuelo, Answers and Questions.
Herrick.   Upon Love, by Way of Question and
   Answer.
Hoffenstein.   Progress.
Johnson, T.   Until He Comes.
Mapanje.   Another Fools' Day Touches Down:
   Shush.
Melville, H.   Spirit Appeared to Me, A.
Merriam, E.   At the Door.
Muir, E.   Interrogation, The.
Owen, W.   Maundy Thursday.
Patchen.   Naked Land, The.
Piatt, S.   Answering A Child.
Prince, F.   Question, The.
Sandburg, C.   Haze.
Santayana.   Cape Cod.
Sorrentino.   Oranges Returned, The.
Straus, M.   Log of Pi, The.
Unknown.   Examination Question.
   Will You Love Me When I'm Old?
Wallace-Crabbe.   Binary.
Welburn.   Whichway.
Wheelwright.   Cross Questions.
Whitman, W.   To the States.
Quests
"Æ."   Desire.
Anderson, M.   It Never Was You.
Browning, R.   Childe Roland to the Dark Tower
   Came.
Eliot, T.   Burial of the Dead, The.
   Death by Water.
   Fire Sermon, The.
   Game of Chess, A.
   Waste Land, The.
Gardinier.   To Peace.
Graves, R.   White Goddess, The.
Guiney.   Wild Ride, The.
Henderson, R.   Five Foot Two, Eyes of Blue
   (Has Anybody Seen My Girl?).
Hoffman, D.   Exploration.
Hollo.   Journey, 1966.
Hughes, T.   October Salmon, An.
O'Grady, D.   Tipperary.
Poe.   Eldorado.
Pound, E.   Return, The.
Unknown.   Loving Mad Tom.
Warren, R.   Pursuit.
Weill, K.   It Never Was You.
Whitman, W.   Heroes.
   Hub of the Universe, The.
   Song of Myself.
   Swiftly Arose.
   Would You Hear of an Old-Time [*or* Old-
   Fashioned] Sea Fight?
Williams, W.   Paterson—the Strike.
Quilts and Quilting
Acosta.   My Mother Pieced Quilts.
Beer, P.   In a Country Museum.
Lowe, J.   Between Acts.
McPherson, S.   Quilt of Rights.
Ormond.   Design for a Quilt.
Peirce.   Quilts.
Rich, A.   Aunt Jennifer's Tigers.
Townsend, A.   First Quilt.
Ward, J.   Comfort-Maker.
Quince Trees and Quinces
Antiphilus [*or* Antiphilos].   Quince Preserved

through the Winter, Given to a Lady, A.
Quotidian
Ashbery.   Problem of Anxiety, The.
Bell, M.   Book of the Dead Man #87, The.
Blamire.   Epistle to Her Friends at Gartmore.
Brown, R.   Famous Writers School Opens Its
   Arms in the Next Best Thing to Welcome, The.
Child, A.   Wishes.
Clarke, G.   Overheard in County Sligo.
Crowell, G.   I Have Found Such Joy.
Foster, A.   Starting School.
Johnson, D.   Incognito Lounge, The.
Lewis, A.   Mountain over Aberdare, The.
Rafferty, P.   Personal.
Schuyler, J.   Red Brick and Brown Stone.
Unknown.   Little Things.

R

Rabbis
Bloch, C.   White Petticoats.
Klein, A.   Baal Shem Tov.
   Rabbi Yom-Tob of Mayence Petitions His God.
Michelson, R.   Genuine Jewish Flesh.
Nemerov.   Debate with the Rabbi.
Rabbits
Clare, J.   Hares at Play.
Coatsworth.   Song of the Rabbits Outside the
   Tavern, The.
Gould, E.   My New Rabbit.
Johnson, J.   Brer Rabbit, You's de Cutes' of
   'Em All.
Kinsella, J.   Rabbiters: A Pastoral, The.
Larkin, P.   Myxomatosis.
Levertov.   Springtime, The.
McKuen.   Thoughts on Capital Punishment.
Moore, L.   Again.
Roberts, E.   Rabbit, The.
Skrzynecki.   Hunting Rabbits.
Stephens, J.   Snare, The.
Stevens, W.   Rabbit Is King of the Ghosts, A.
Stevenson, A.   Giving Rabbit to My Cat Bonnie.
Toomer.   Nullo.
Unknown.   Railroad Section Leader's Song.
See also **Hares; Jackrabbits**
Raccoons
Hirshfield, J.   Invocation: "This August night,
   raccoons."
Rachel (Bible)
Burns, R.   Patriarch, The.
Rachmaninov, Sergei
O'Hara, F.   On Rachmaninoff's Birthday.
Racial Prejudice
Agard, J.   Half-caste.
   Palm Tree King.
Allen, S.   Moment Please, A.
Anzaldúa.   We Call Them Greasers.
Awoonor.   American Memory of Africa, An.
Baldwin, J.   Lover's Question, A.
Baraka.   Poem for Willie Best, A.
Bell, J.   Indian Children Speak.
Brooks, G.   Ballad of Rudolph Reed, The.
   Bronzeville Woman in a Red Hat.
   Riot.
Brown, S.   Crispus Attucks McCoy.
   Old Lem.
   Sam Smiley.
   Slim Greer.
   Southern Cop.
Browning, E.   Runaway Slave at Pilgrim's Point,
   The.
Burroughs, M.   Everybody but Me.
Bynner.   Defeat.
Cataldi.   Advice.
Cervantes.   Poem for the Young White Man
   Who Asked Me How I, An Intelligent, Well-
   Read Person Could Believe in the War
   Between Races.
Clarke, T.   Will They Always Remember.
Cobb, A.   Searching, The.
Cofer, J.   What the Gypsy Said to Her Children.
Coleman, W.   Emmett Till.
Corrothers.   At the Closed Gate of Justice.
Cullen, C.   Incident.

Tableau.
Uncle Jim.
Cyril. Children's Games.
Jump Black Honey Jump Black.
Dabney, F. That's Why They Call Me 'Shine.'
Dale, L. Prejudice against Colour.
Damas. S.O.S.
Durham. Justiniano Lamé Has Been Killed.
Gomez, M. To the Latin Lover I Left at the Candy Store.
Greenfield, F. Oh God Forbid.
Hacker, M. 1973.
Harper, M. American History.
Goin' to the Territory.
Grandfather.
Harris, W. Daddy Poem, A.
Hemphill. Cordon Negro.
Family Jewels.
Horne, F. On Seeing Two Brown Boys in a Catholic Church.
Hughes, L. Backlash Blues, The.
Children's Rhymes.
Cross.
Dream Boogie.
Island.
Merry-Go-Round.
Ultimatum: Kid to Kid.
Where? When? Which?
Inada. Projected Scenario of a Performance to Be Given Before the UN.
Jacinto, A. Monangamba.
Jones, G. Tripart.
Jones, I. Echoes of the Murder of Emmett Till.
Jordan, J. Poem About My Rights.
What Would I Do White?
Kelen. Rabbit Shoeshine.
Kizer, C. Race Relations.
Klein, A. In re Solomon Warshawer.
Lorde. Power.
MacDiarmid, H. With the Herring Fishers.
Mack, C. That's Why They Call Me 'Shine.'
Major, C. Vietnam #4.
Mandela. I Saw as a Child.
Mapanje. At the Metro: Old Irrelevant Images.
McElroy, C. Foul Line—1987.
McKay, C. Tiger.
White House, The.
Miller, E. Boys of Summer, The.
Mnthali. My Father.
Ortiz. Creation.
Randall, D. Black Poet, White Critic.
Melting Pot, The.
Ross, A. In Bloemfontein.
Sandburg, C. Circles.
Small, A. There's Somethin'
Soyinka. Telephone Conversation.
Stanard, C. Wrong Color.
Trejo. Cloud Unfolding, The.
Trethewey, N. Drapery Factory, Gulfport, Mississippi, 1956.
Unknown. Learn to Count.
Scottsboro.
Walcott. Gulf, The.
Walker, A. Once.
Waller, T. *et al.* (What Did I Do to Be So) Black and Blue?
Waniek. Freeman Field.
Welch, J. Harlem, Montana.
Williams, C. Racists.
Wong, N. When I Was Growing Up.
Young, A. Dance for Militant Dilettantes, A.
Poem for Players, A.
See also **Apartheid; Racism and Racists**
Racing and Racers
Cameron, N. Unfinished Race, The.
Dubie. Death of the Race Car Driver, The.
Townsend, A. Bicycle Racers, The.
See also **Crew and Crew Racing; Horse Racing; Track Athletics**
Racism and Racists
"Ada." Appeal to Women, An.
Ai. Endangered Species.
Self Defense.
Alexander, E. Affirmative Action Blues (1993).
Boston Year.
Ladders.

Venus Hottentot, The.
Alexie. On the Amtrak from Boston to New York City.
Allan, L. Strange Fruit.
Allen, S. Moment Please, A.
Amadiume. Nok Lady in Terracotta.
As-Sabah. Transition #2.
Askhari. Circular Fate.
REcreation.
Aubert, A. Opposite of Green, The.
Baraka. Each Morning.
Hymn for Lanie Poo.
Nation Is Like Ouselves, The.
Barrax. Old Gory, The.
Beatty, P. That's Not in My Job Description.
Benson, L. P Word Poem, The.
Black, I. Racist Psychotherapy.
Booth, P. Stations.
Boss. When You Are Grown, Amanda Rose.
Brooks, G. Ballad of Rudolph Reed, The.
Bronzeville Mother Loiters in Mississippi, A. Meanwhile, a Mississippi Mother Burns Bacon.
Bronzeville Woman in a Red Hat.
Chicago *Defender* Sends a Man to Little Rock, The.
Gay Chaps at the Bar.
My Dreams, My Works, Must Wait Till After Hell.
Still Do I Keep My Look, My Identity.
White Troops Had Their Orders but the Negroes Looked Like Men.
Brown, S. Bitter Fruit of the Tree.
Slim in Atlanta.
Strong Men.
Brutus. Off to Philadelphia in the Morning.
Bryant, F. Cathexis.
Cabico, R. Gameboy.
Carbó, N. Civilizing the Filipino.
Carroll, K. Something Easy for Ultra Black Nationalists.
Upper Marlboro.
Cerenio. 23 October 1992.
Cervantes. Poem for the Young White Man Who Asked Me How I, An Intelligent, Well-Read Person Could Believe in the War Between Races.
Poema para los Californios Muertos.
Chinn. Not Translation, Not Poetry.
Skin Color from the Sun.
Chrystos. I Bring You Greetings: How.
Old Indian Granny, The.
Clinton, M. Plan of the Klan.
Cornish, S. His Fingers Seem to Sing.
Cortez, J. Give me the Red on the Black of the Bullet (for Claude Reece Jr.).
Rape.
Cullen, C. Incident.
Uncle Jim.
D'Aguiar. Langston.
Daniels, J. Time, Temperature.
Daniels, K. Bus Ride.
Davidson, D. Sequel of Appomattox.
Davis, F. Christ is a Dixie Nigger.
Sam Jackson.
De Kok. Small Passing.
Derricotte. Note on my Son's Face, A.
Passing.
Divakaruni. Founding of Yuba City, The.
Dove, R. Great Palaces of Versailles, The.
Dunbar, P. Harriet Beecher Stowe.
Eady. False Arrest.
Sherbet.
Song.
Thrift.
William Carlos Williams.
Espada. Beloved Spic.
Everett, J. White Man Problem, The.
Forbes, C. Poet's Shuffle, The.
Ford, C. Plaint.
Freed, F. Private School for Girls, May 14, 1948, New York City, A.
Gilyard, K. Letter.
Glancy. First Reader Santee Training School, 1873, The.
Gray-Kontar, D. Not no socialism/communism

classical, but some power to the people jazz.
Griffin, S. I Like to Think of Harriet Tubman.
Guevara, M. Doña Josefina Counsels Doña Concepción Before Entering Sears.
Hamer. Line Up.
Harjo, J. Strange Fruit.
Harper, M. American History.
Nightmare Begins Responsibility.
Harris, D. On the uptown lexington avenue express: Martin Luther King Day 1995.
Harris, W. Daddy Poem, A.
Harte, B. Plain Language from Truthful James.
Truthful James to the Editor.
Hayden, R. 'Mystery Boy' Looks for Kin in Nashville.
[American Journal].
Frederick Douglass.
Monet's "Waterlilies."
Heard, J. Black Sampson, The.
Hemphill. Cordon Negro.
Family Jewels.
Henderson-Holmes. To Hell and Back, with Cake.
Holman, M. Mr. Z.
Hughes, L. Ballad of the Landlord.
Children's Rhymes.
Cross.
Democracy.
Dinner Guest: Me.
Dream Boogie: Variation.
I, Too.
Lincoln Monument: Washington.
Mulatto.
Note on Commercial Theatre.
Song for a Dark Girl.
Tell Me.
Theme for English B.
Ultimatum: Kid to Kid.
Uncle Tom.
Visitors to the Black Belt.
Ignatow, D. Harold.
Iman. Love Your Enemy.
Iverem, E. Keeper.
Jackson, A. Miz Rosa Rides the Bus.
Jackson, B. In Exchange for Forty Acres.
Jackson, R. Lonely Affair, A.
Johnson, C. Color Sergeant, The.
Johnson, L. Mi Revalueshanary Fren.
Jordan, J. Poem Against the State (Of Things): 1975.
Joseph, A. In the Bookstore.
Numbers.
Joseph, L. Sand Nigger.
Kay, J. Twelve Bar Bessie.
Kizer, C. Race Relations.
Knight, E. Hard Rock Returns to Prison from the Hospital for the Criminal Insane.
Once on a Night in the Delta: A Report From Hell.
Knott. (Poem) (Chicago) (The Were-Age).
Komunyakaa. Salt.
Untitled Blues; After a Photograph by Yevgeni Yevtushenko.
Lansana, Q. Woolworth's Poem, The.
Leonard, T. Evidence, The.
Lim, G. Children are Colorblind.
Long, R. Conspiracy, The.
Lorde. Afterimages.
For the Record.
Macgoye. Letter to a Friend.
Madgett. Race Question, The.
Madhubuti. Don't Cry, Scream.
My Brothers.
Manyarrows. See No Indian, Hear No Indian.
Mathews, E. K. Indian, The.
McElroy, C. Ghost-Who-Walks, The.
McKay, C. Lynching, The.
Negro's Tragedy, The.
White City, The.
,White House, The.
Medina, T. After the Verdict.
Big House Revisited, The.
Midge, T. Written in Blood.
Mills, D. And Now Yu.
Morales. I Am the Reasonable One.
Moss, T. Reconsideration of the Blackbird, A.

Mura. Argument: on 1942, An.
Ologboni. Changed Mind (or the Day I Woke Up).
Oodgeroo of the tribe Noonuccal. Colour Bar.
Osofisan. Paris Latin Quarter.
Papertalk-Green, C. Wanna Be White.
Parkerson. Statistic.
Pegram, A. I Will Still Sing.
Mr. White Discoverer.
Towards Abraham's Bosom.
Powell, K. Don't Feel No Way.
Pratt, M. Red String.
Preston, R. Champion Chant.
Ten Seconds.
Randall, D. Idiot, The.
Melting Pot, The.
Randall, J. When Something Happens.
Rankine. New Windows.
Redmond. Love Necessitates.
Reed, I. Jacket Notes.
Railroad Bill, A Conjure Man.
Rodriguez, L. To the Police Officer Who Refused to Sit in the Same Room as My Son because He's a 'Gang Banger.'
Rose, P. Wind Debates Asian Immigration, The.
Ross, L. Indecent Exposure (A True Story).
Rushin. Black Back-Ups, The.
Salaam. I Live in the Mouth of History.
Samwell. Negro Boy, The.
Sanchez, S. Poem for July 4, 1994.
Right On: White America.
Seibles. Manic: A Conversation with Jimi Hendrix.
Shepherd, R. Difficult Music, The.
Skeeter. Midwest, Midcentury.
Smith, P. Blonde White Women.
Spellman. When Black People Are.
Stafford, W. Serving with Gideon.
Stein, K. Upon Finding a Black Woman's Door Sprayed with Swastikas, I Tell Her This Story of Hands.
Steptoe. Window Shopping.
Sykes, B. Rachel.
Thompson, C. Uncle Rube on the Race Problem.
Uncle Rube to the Young People.
Toomer. People.
Travis, N. Sunbathing.
Uyematsu. December 7 Always Brings Christmas Early.
Van Jordan, A. If I Write a Poem.
Vando. Knife.
Villalongo. In the Good Old U. S. A.
Wade-Gayles. Inquisition.
Walcott. Glory Trumpeter, The.
Walker, M. Since 1619.
Waniek. Alderman.
Ballad of Aunt Geneva, The.
Diverne's Waltz.
Washington. Moon Bound.
Watson, M. Black Child.
Wayman. Hating Jews.
Weaver, M. Borders.
Picnic, an Homage to Civil Rights, The.
Welch, J. Harlem, Montana.
Wieners. Poem for Cocksuckers, The.
Williams, C. In Search of Aunt Jemima.
Winner, R. Segregated Railway Diner—1946.
Wright, J. On a Phrase from Southern Ohio.
Wright, R. Between the World and Me.
Young, K. Field Trip.
No Offense.
Zephaniah. Sun, The.
Zulu, P. You are Mad: and I Mean It!

See also **Racial Prejudice**

Radcliffe, James, 3d Earl of Derwentwater
Unknown. Lord Derwentwater.

Radiation and Radiation Sickness
Seaton, M. Nostradamus Predicts the Destruction of Chicago.
Stainer. Sarcophagus.
Tatarunis, P. Chest X-Ray.
Thiele, C. Radiation Victim.
Wojahn. Workmen Photographed inside the Reactor.

See also **Nuclear Accidents; Nuclear War**

Radio
Baraka. In Memory of Radio.
Major Bowes' Diary.
SOS.
Breeze. Eena Mi Corner.
Butler, C. E. Letter to the Survivors.
Duran, J. For the Woman Who Dressed Up to Listen to Gigli on the Radio.
Eady. Radio.
Fogarty, L. No Grudge.
Geiger. Soundtracks.
Goldbarth. Talk Show, The.
Greenlaw. Five O'Clock Opera.
Lopez, L. Only Now I Realize.
McFee. First Radio.
Monroe, H. Radio.
Page, G. Late Night Radio.
Seyburn, P. You and Them.
Straus, M. What I Heard on the Radio Today.
Taylor, H. Speech.
Thorne, T. Whatever Happened to Conway Twitty?
Trinidad. Monday, Monday.
Waters, M. Burden Lifters, The.

Radishes
Bodecker. Radish.

Raftery, Anthony
Alexander, A. For Raftery.

Ragworts
Stevenson, A. Ragwort.

Railroad Wrecks
Carruth, H. Wreck of the Circus Train, The.
George, D. Wreck of the Old 97.
Hedin, R. Wreck of the Great Northern, The.
Hummer, T. Train Wreck, 1890: My Grandmother Lies Down with the Dead.
Moore, J. Ashtabula Disaster, The.
Nims, J. Trainwrecked Soldiers.
Unknown. Casey Jones.
Wright, C. Dog Creek Mainline.

Railroads
Ashbery. Melodic Trains.
Betjeman. Metropolitan Railway, The.
Booth, P. Stations.
Broonzy. Southern Blues, The.
Brown, S. Call Boy.
Long Track Blues.
Southern Road.
Buckley, C. Train in the Desert—1916.
Carr, L. How Long Blues.
Collier, M. North Corridor.
Conyus. Six Ten Sixty-Nine.
Cooper, J. Wanda's Blues.
Cornford, F. Parting in Wartime.
Craveirinha. Three Dimensions.
Delmore Brothers. Wabash Cannonball, The.
Eiseley. And as for Man.
Francis, R. Night Train.
Frost, R. On the Heart's Beginning to Cloud the Mind.
Galvin, B. For a Daughter Gone Away.
Gibbons, R. American Trains.
Gioia. In Cheever Country.
Glück, L. Departure.
Greenberg, A. Freight Train, Freight Train.
Hall, D. Sister on the Tracks, A.
Hanzlicek, C. Last Trains, The.
Heaney, S. Railway Children, The.
Holland, J. Loco.
Hope, A. Observation Car.
Hudgins. Southern Crescent Was on time, The.
Hughes, L. Homesick Blues.
Jackson, M. Red Flag, The.
James, E. Sunnyland.
Jefferson, B. Easy Rider Blues.
Jones, R. Trouble in Mind.
Justice, D. Train.
Lattimore. Note on the L and N.
Lindsay, V. Flower-Fed Buffaloes, The.
MacLeish. Burying Ground by the Ties.
Grazing Locomotives.
Merwin, W. S. Wheels of the Trains, The.
Monroe, B. In the Pines.
Nemerov. Low-Level Cross-Country.
Nims, J. Freight.

Parini. Coal Train.
Peacocke. Railway Allotments.
Plumly. For Esther.
Reed, I. Railroad Bill, A Conjure Man.
Roethke. Night Journey.
Sandburg, C. Child of the Romans.
Southern Pacific.
Seibert. Casey Jones.
Shapiro, K. Terminal.
Sissman. Big Rock-Candy Mountain, The.
Slessor. Last Trams.
Soto. Who Will Know Us?
Stafford, W. Observation Car and Cigar.
Swenson, M. Written While Riding the Long Island Rail Road.
Thoreau. What's the Railroad to Me?
Unknown. Beulah Railway, The.
Can't You Line It?
Casey Jones.
I Been Working on the Railroad.
John Henry.
Old Section Boss, The.
Poor Paddy Works on the Railway.
Railroad Blues, The.
Railroad Cars Are Coming, The.
Railroad Man for Me, A.
Railroad Section Leader's Song.
Tamping Ties.
Working on the Railway.
Van Doren. Dream of Trains, A.
Whitman, W. To a Locomotive in Winter.
Wilbur. In the Smoking-Car.
Stop.
Wordsworth, W. On the Projected Kendal and Windermere Railway.
Wright, C. Dog Creek Mainline.
Wright, J. Outside Fargo, North Dakota.
Poem Written under an Archway in a Discontinued Railroad Station, Fargo, North Dakota, A.

See also **Trains; Locomotives**

Railway Stations
Smith, D. Cumberland Station.
Looking for the Melungeon.
Thomas, E. Adlestrop.
Wharton, E. Terminus.
Wilbur. Stop.
Wright, J. Poem Written under an Archway in a Discontinued Railroad Station, Fargo, North Dakota, A.

Railway Travel
Ashbery. Leaving the Atocha Station.
Bly, R. In a Train.
Davie. In the Stopping Train.
De la Mare. Railway Junction, The.
Garlick, R. Poetry of Motion, The.
Handy, W. Yellow Dog Blues.
Hardy, T. Faintheart in a Railway Train.
Jarrell. Orient Express, The.
Piatt, J. Taking the Night-Train.
Sansom, A. From the Moment I Picked Up Your Book.
Stevenson, R. From a Railway Carriage.
Wilbur. In the Smoking-Car.

Rain
Acholonu. Dissidents, The.
Aiken, C. And in the Hanging Gardens.
Al-Rihani. It Was All for Him.
Apollinaire. It's Raining.
Banus. Eighteen.
Benét, S. Rain after a Vaudeville Show.
Berlin. Isn't This a Lovely Day (To Be Caught in the Rain?).
Bishop, E. Sestina: "September rain falls on the house."
Bly, R. August Rain.
Bodecker. Small Rains.
Bolton, G. Till the Clouds Roll By.
Bontemps. Return, The.
Borson. Rain.
Bowen, C. Rain It Raineth, The.
Boyle, K. Thunderstorm in South Dakota.
Brock-Broido. Carrowmore.
Brown, N. Singin' in the Rain.
Burkard. Weather.
Burke, J. Here's That Rainy Day.

Pennies from Heaven.
Chippewa Oral Tradition. Song of the Crows.
Clare, J. Sudden Shower.
Clark, P. Walk in the Rain.
Clifton, H. Monsoon Girl.
Collins, M. To F. C.
Warmer.
Cranch. Autumn Rain, The.
Creeley. Rain, The.
Cullen, C. Night Rain.
Cumming, P. Midsummer.
Davies, H. Poem: "In the stump of the old tree, where the heart has rotted out."
Davies, W. Rain, The.
DeSylva, B. G. April Showers.
DiPasquale. Rain.
Dipoko. Exile.
Dodd, W. Of Rain and Air.
Dove, R. Wiederkehr.
Dransfield. Rainpoem.
Dubin, A. September in the Rain.
Dubrava. Miraculous Marriage of Zarife Dominquez.
Eigner. If You Weep, I Think That.
Esteves. It Is Raining Today.
Evans, A. Under Cover.
Evans, M. Rain.
Foix. When I Sleep, Then I See Clearly.
Freed, A. Singin' in the Rain.
Gallagher, T. Sudden Journey.
Gilbert, C. Chosen to Be Water.
Gioia. Los Angeles after the Rain.
Glück, L. Time.
Gonzales, R. South Texas Summer Rain.
Grandfather Koori. Massacre Sandhill.
Gundy, J. Rain.
Haines, J. Cloud Factory, The.
Hardy, T. Rain on a Grave.
Thunderstorm in Town, A.
Weathers [*or* Weather].
Harwood, L. Soft White.
Hass, R. Spring Rain.
Hassett. Thanksgiving.
Hazo. Drenching, The.
Heaney, S. Summer of Lost Rachel, The.
Hempel, A. Rain.
Henson, L. Rain.
Herbert, W. Black Wet, The.
Hernández Cruz. Thursday.
Heyen. Passover: the Injections.
Hillman. Formation of Soils, The.
Hirshfield, J. Rain in May.
Hovanessian, D. On Commonwealth Avenue and Brattle Street.
Hubbell, L. W. Birth-Hour.
Hughes, L. April Rain Song.
In Time of Silver Rain.
Strange Hurt.
Hughes, T. Heptonstall.
Jacobs, H. It is not Just.
Johnson, H. Invocation: "Let me be buried in the rain."
Johnson, J. View Café, The.
Jones, R. Front Window, The.
Kay, J. Pounding Rain.
Kenyon, J. August Rain, after Haying.
Kern, J. Till the Clouds Roll By.
Kgositsile. Gods Wrote, The.
Kimball, H. Angel of the Rain.
Kinnell. Under the Maud Moon.
Komunyakaa. After the Fall of Saigon.
Kooser. At the Office Early.
Lane, P. Rain Ditch.
Larkin, J. Housework.
Larkin, P. Card-Players, The.
Whitsun Weddings, The.
Laughlin, J. Then and Now.
Lerner, A. Rain in Spain, The.
Levertov. Way Through, The.
Levine, P. Rain Downriver.
Lewis, A. All Day It Has Rained.
Lili'u-o-ka-lani. Ka Waiapo Lani.
Livesay, D. Green Rain.
Longfellow, H. Rain in Summer.
Loveman. April Rain.
Low, P. Wet Weather.

Lowell, A. Shower, A.
Macdonald, G. Sweet Peril.
MacNeice. London Rain.
Mahon. Kinsale.
McAuley, J. Wet Day.
McCarthy, G. Hooded Legion, The.
McCord, D. Summer Shower.
McCrae, H. Song of the Rain.
McDuffie, C. Finally the Rain.
Merriam, E. Weather.
Merrill, B. Don't Rain on My Parade.
Merrill, J. Childlessness.
Merwin, W. S. Rain Travel.
Meynell, A. Rainy Summer, The.
Mhlophe. Sometimes When It Rains.
Mitchell, K. Night Rain.
Moore, L. Tanka.
Morris, W. Haystack in the Floods, The.
Mpondo. Season of the Rains, The.
Myles, E. New England Wind.
Napanangka, V. Rain, The.
Ogundipe-Leslie. Rain at Noon-time.
Oliver, M. Rain in Ohio.
Page, P. Stories of Snow.
Parker, A. Lullaby: "Sleep and rain, two gangsters."
Pasternak, B. Hops.
Patchen. Biography of Southern Rain.
Pinsky. Jersey Rain.
Piper, E. Big Swimming.
Plomer. Seven Rainy Months.
Prévert. Barbara.
Rankin, J. Old Circles.
Raworth. Hot Day at the Races.
Ray, H. Voices of the Rain.
Read, T. Summer Shower, The.
Remoto. Rain.
Reznikoff. Free Verse.
Rainy Season.
Riggs, L. Santo Domingo Corn Dance.
Robinson, A. Song: "Oh for the wings of a dove."
Robinson, R. Jarrangulli.
Romtvedt. Kiev, the Ukraine, Nuclear Accident.
Ruden, S. Letter.
Russell, N. Message of the Rain, The.
Saner. Rain Near Heart Lake.
Scamell, B. More Rain.
Shelley, P. Cloud, The.
Shepherd, R. West Willow.
Where When Was.
Silvers, L. April Showers.
Sitwell, D. Song: "We are the darkness in the heat of the day."
Skinner, K. Cold Irish Earth, The.
Soyinka. I Think It Rains.
Stanley-Wrench. Storm, The.
Stevens, W. Room on a Garden, A.
Stevenson, R. Rain.
Stickney, T. Melancholy Year [Is Dead with Rain], The.
Styne, J. Don't Rain on My Parade.
Su Tung-p'o. Tune: Sand of Silk-washing Stream ("Throw on rouge and powder, watch the governor pass!").
Swift, J. Description of a City Shower, A.
Synková, A. Tears.
Taylor, E. Address to the Soul Occasioned by a Rain, An.
Teasdale. Moods.
Thomas, E. It Rains.
Like the Touch of Rain.
Rain.
Ullman. Rain.
Unknown. Rain, The.
Riddle: "Round the house and round the house / and there lies a black glove in the window."
Song for the Sun That Disappeared behind the Rainclouds.
Van Heusen, J. Here's That Rainy Day.
Very. Hath the Rain a Father?
Latter Rain, The.
Winter Rain, The.
Wang Wei. After Long Rain.
Warren, H. September in the Rain.
Warren, R. Vermont Ballad: Change of Season.

Warsh. Suicide Rates, The.
Watson, R. Ballad of the Were-Wolf, A.
Watta. Cloud Rains.
Weöres. Rain.
Welish. Crossing Disappearing behind Them.
Wenderoth, J. Death.
Whitmore, S. Gamelia.
Wicks, S. Rain Dance.
Wilbur. My Father Paints the Summer.
Williams, W. Red Wheelbarrow, The.
Williamson, G. Belvedere Marittimo.
Wiman, C. In Lakeview Cemetery.
Wodehouse, P. Till the Clouds Roll By.
Wordsworth, W. Written in March [While Resting on the Bridge at the Foot of Brother's Water].
Wright, J. Living by the Red River.

Rainbows
Arlen, H. Over the Rainbow.
Birney. Bushed.
Carroll, H. I'm Always Chasing Rainbows.
Coslow, S. (Up on Top of a Rainbow) Sweepin' the Clouds Away.
Davies, W. Great Time, A.
Dunbar, P. Place Where the Rainbow Ends, The.
Harburg. Over the Rainbow.
Herrick. Rainbow; or Curious Covenant, The.
Hopkins, G. Rainbow, The.
Keble. Rainbow, The.
Littlebird. In a Double Rainbow.
MacDiarmid, H. Watergaw, The.
McCarthy, J. I'm Always Chasing Rainbows.
Strong, L. Door, The.
Turner, C. Drowned Spaniel, The.
East or West?
Unknown. Song for the Sun That Disappeared behind the Rainclouds.
Vaughan, H. Rainbow, The.
Wordsworth, W. My Heart Leaps Up.
Wright, J. Legend.

Rainey, Gertrude ("Ma")
Brown, S. Ma Rainey.
Okantah. Southern Road.
Young, A. Dance For Ma Rainey, A.

Ralegh, Sir Walter
Elizabeth I. Ah silly pugg wert thou so sore afraid.
Lowell, R. Lady Ralegh's Lament.

Rameses II, King of Egypt
Shelley, P. Ozymandias.
Unknown. In the Days of Old Rameses.

Ranches
Miller, J. Which Religion Vouchsafes.
Todd, M. Rigby.

Rape
Acholonu. Other Forms of Slaughter.
Adamson. Rimbaud Having a Bath.
Alexander, E. Kevin of the N. E. Crew.
Anderson-Thompkins. Interlude.
Avicolli. Rape Poem, The.
Belieu. Man Who Tried to Rape You, The.
Berger, J. Gun, The.
Clinton, M. Black Rape.
Cortez, J. Rape.
Craighead, L. Wo/man's Voice Must Be Heard, A.
Davie. Fountain of Cyanë, The.
Disch. Rapist's Villanelle, The.
Donne. Apparition, The.
Endrezze. Exodus.
Field, E. Bride of Frankenstein, The.
Florsheim. Real Chocolate.
Griffin, S. To the Far Corners of Fractured Worlds.
Hardy, J. Objection Overruled.
Howe, M. Sixth Grade.
Irby. Sequence.
Jordan, J. Poem About My Rights.
Larkin, J. Rape.
Larkin, P. Deceptions.
Lovelace, R. Mock Charon, A.
McCarriston. Castle in Lynn, A.
Nasrin. At the Back of Progress.
Neely, L. Rhonda, Age 15, Emergency Room.

Pickard, T.   Rape.
Pratt, M.   Waulking Song: Two.
Rungano.   Woman, The.
Seaton, M.   Story of Stonewall, A.
Shakespeare, W.   [Before the Rape].
   Lucrece's Death.
Shange.   It's Not So Good to Be Born a Girl /
   Sometimes.
Sharp, S.   In the Tradition of Bobbitt.
Sykes, B.   Fallin'.
Szporluk.   Libido.
Unknown.   Three Butchers, The.
Walsh, W. *et al.*   Imperfect Enjoyment, The.
Waniek.   Chosen.
Yeats.   Leda and the Swan.

Raphael Santi
Allston.   On the Group of the Three Angels
   Before the Tent of Abraham, by Raffaelle, in
   the Vatican.
Hardy, T.   Cardinal Bembo's Epitaph on
   Raphael.
Ray, H.   Raphael.

Rastafarianism
Adisa.   Ethiopia Unda a Jamaican Mango Tree.
Agard, J.   For Bob Marley.
Dawes, K.   Black Heart.
Goodison.   Jah Music.
   Upon a Quarter Million.
Hippolyte.   Antonette's Boogie.
   Jah Son / Another Way.
   Reggae Cat (for Boston Jack).
Ingram-Roberts, A.   Poem 2 (for Duckie
   Simpson of Black Uhuru).
"Jerry."   Mabrak.
Malachi.   Psalm of Silk.
McNeill, A.   Ode to Brother Joe.
   Saint Ras.
Morris, M.   Rasta Reggae.
Preston, R.   Champion Chant.
   Italist Chant.
Scott, D.   Dreadwalk.
Weinstein, N.   Garvey's Head as Value.

Rathel, James M.
Heard, J.   In Memory of James M. Rathel.

Rationalism and Rationalists
Blake, W.   Mock On, Mock On, Voltaire,
   Rousseau.
Poe.   Sonnet—To Science.
See also **Intellect and Intellectuals; Reason**

Rats
Browning, R.   Pied Piper of Hamelin, The.
Carruth, H.   Little Citizen, Little Survivor.
Cook, W.   Still-Life with Woodstove.
Davies, W.   Rat, The.
Gowar.   Rat Trap.
Lear, E.   Limerick: "There was an Old Man who
   supposed."
Logue, C.   Rat, O Rat.
Mew.   Trees Are Down, The.
Moore, M.   To an Intra-Mural Rat.
Moore, N.   Song: "Little onion lay by the
   fireplace, A."
Ondaatje.   Rat Jelly.
Rabéarivelo [*or* Rebéarivelo].   What Invisible
   Rat.
Raven.   Assailant.
Smith, S.   Pretty.
Toomer.   Reapers.
Torres, E.   Bio-Rodent-Oriole.
Unknown.   What Became of Them?

Rattlesnakes
Warren, R.   Rattlesnake Country.

Ravens
Barlow, J.   Advice to a Raven in Russia
   [December, 1812].
Carryl, G.   Sycophantic Fox and the Gullible
   Raven, The.
Coleridge, S.   Raven, The.
Dana, R.   Dying Raven, The.
Euwer.   True Facts of the Case, The.
Poe.   Raven, The.
Unknown.   Three Ravens, The.
   Twa Corbies, The.

Reading and Readers
Antin.   Private Occasion in a Public Place, A.

Berg, S.   Prayer: "Nobody understands so let the
   Rabbi."
Berry, D.   On Reading Poems to a Senior Class
   at South High.
Boland, E.   Oral Tradition, The.
Branch, A.   In the Beginning Was the Word.
Brode.   Breakfast with Gerard Manley Hopkins.
Brownell, H.   Suspiria Noctis.
Caballero-Robb, M.   Memoranda for Rosario.
Carroll, L.   Poeta Fit, Non Nascitur.
Cherry, K.   Reading, Dreaming, Hiding.
Cooke, R.   Schemhammphorasch.
Davis, O.   Sweet Reader, Flanneled and Tulled.
De la Mare.   Old Susan.
Dove, R.   First Book, The.
Earle, J.   Saturday in the '20s, A.
Elmusa.   Bookishness.
Forbes, C.   Poet's Shuffle, The.
   Reading Walt Whitman.
Glancy.   First Reader Santee Training School,
   1873, The.
Gotera.   Dance of the Letters.
Guevara, M.   Reader of This Page.
Harper, F.   Learning to Read.
Herrick.   To My Ill Reader.
   To the Sour[e] Reader.
   To Vulcan.
Hume, C.   Various Readings of an Illegible
   Postcard.
Jackson, L.   Troubles of a Book, The.
Jonson, B.   To the Reader.
Joseph, A.   Reading Room.
Keats.   On First Looking into Chapman's
   Homer.
   On Sitting Down to Read "King Lear" Once
   Again.
Kemble.   Lines.
Kendrick, D.   Sophie, Climbing the Stairs.
Knott.   Goodbye.
Kooser.   Selecting a Reader.
Krysl.   Carpe Diem: Time Piece.
Larkin, P.   Fiction and the Reading Public.
   Study of Reading Habits, A.
Laughlin, J.   Inn at Kirchstetten, The.
Leonard, T.   Fathers and Sons.
Levertov.   To the Reader.
Lisella.   Song of the Third Generation.
Liu, T.   Reading Whitman in a Toilet Stall.
Longfellow, H.   Day Is Done, The.
MacCaig.   Chauvinist.
Madhubuti.   Poem Looking for a Reader, A.
Mahon.   Death and the Sun.
McGrath, T.   Reading by Mechanic Light.
McIlroy, L.   Siesta.
Milosz, C.   Readings.
Moore, M.   Poetry: "I, too, dislike it: there are
   things that are important beyond all this
   fiddle."
Murphy, R.   Reading Lesson, The.
Nelson, M.   Chopin.
Orr, G.   Insomnia Song.
Palmer, M.   Theory of the Flower, The.
Parkes, B.   To Elizabeth Barrett Browning.
Procter, A.   My Journal.
Rich, A.   Diving into the Wreck.
Richards, I.   Challenge to the Reader, A.
Sansom, A.   From the Moment I Picked Up
   Your Book.
Schilpp, W.   Non Sequitur.
Shapiro, D.   Book of Glass, A.
Stevens, W.   House Was Quiet and the World
   Was Calm, The.
   Large Red Man Reading.
   Phosphor Reading by His Own Light.
   Reader, The.
Stroud, J.   Homage: Summer/Winter, Shay
   Creek.
Tate, J.   Dear Reader.
Tomlinson, C.   Dream, A.
Walcott.   Volcano.
Waller, E.   Of the Last Verses in the Book.
Warn.   After Reading the Book of Splendor.
Wells, C.   Of Modern Books.
   Problem, A.
Whitman, W.   Whoever You Are Holding Me
   Now in Hand.

Williams, J.   On Reading Aloud My Early
   Poems.
Yeats.   When You Are Old.
Young, K.   Central Standard Time.

Reality
Adcock, F.   Dreaming.
Arlen, H.   It's Only a Paper Moon.
Armantrout.   Garden, The.
Baraka.   Poem for Deep Thinkers, A.
Benson, S.   Blue Book 18 Pages 1–4.
Berkson, B.   Melting Milk.
Bernstein, C.   Whose Language.
Bronk.   Corals and Shells.
Brutus.   Sand Wet and Cool, The.
Child, A.   Motive for Mayhem, A.
   Surplus.
Ciardi.   On a Photo of Sgt. Ciardi a Year Later.
Clark, T.   Society.
Couani.   What a Man, What a Moon.
Creeley.   City, The.
   Token, A.
DiPalma.   Each Moment is Surrounded.
   Empire Smoke, Forgeries, Salient and The Ritz.
   Poem: "In danger of which."
   Sheaf Mark.
Drake, N.   Foley Artist, The.
   Man in the White Suit, The.
Duchamp.   1914 Box, The.
   World in Yellow, A.
Duncan, R.   Close.
Equi.   Date With Robbe-Grillet, A.
Fenton, J.   Skip, The.
Glück, L.   Celestial Music.
   Winged Horse, The.
Guest, B.   Emphasis Falls on Reality, An.
   Words.
Harburg.   It's Only a Paper Moon.
Harryman.   Realism.
Hejinian.   Nights.
Jarrell.   Märchen, The.
Jeffers, R.   Boats in a Fog.
Jones, R.   Front Window, The.
Lawrence, D.   Red Geranium and Godly
   Mignonette.
Levertov.   Seeing for a Moment.
Mackey, N.   Song of the Andoumboulou: 12.
   Song of the Andoumboulou: 7.
Mandel, T.   Realism.
Marinetti.   They are Coming.
Markham, E.   After Reading Shakspere.
Mayakovsky [*or* Maiakovskii].   Screaming My
   Head Off.
Mayer, B.   Earthworker's God is Healed, The.
McClure, M.   Hymn to Saint Geryon.
McDaniel, J.   Obvious, The.
McDonald, R.   Hollow Thesaurus, The.
Millay, E.   "Love is not all: it is not meat nor
   drink."
Naden.   Love's Mirror.
Olson, C.   Moon Is the Number 18, The.
Orpingalik.   Alcheringa Definitions.
Péret.   On All Fours.
Palmer, M.   Eighth Sky.
   Untitled (February 2000).
Paz.   Here.
Perelman.   Things.
Pessoa.   "Startling Reality of Things," The.
Piombino.   My Lady Carries Stones.
Prassinos.   Conversation, A.
Ray, D.   Midnight Diner by Edward Hopper, A.
Rolfe, E.   Paris—Christmas 1938.
Rose, B.   It's Only a Paper Moon.
Schuyler, J.   Letter to a Friend: Who Is Nancy
   Daum?
Schwitters.   Murder Machine 43.
Sexton.   Self in 1958.
Sherry, J.   Radiant.
Snyder, G.   Milton by Firelight.
   Truth Like the Belly of a Woman Turning, The.
Soupault.   Comrade.
Stevens, W.   Angel Surrounded by Paysans.
   Holiday in Reality.
   Not Ideas about the Thing but the Thing Itself.
   Reality Is an Activity of the Most August
   Imagination.
   So-and-So Reclining on Her Couch.

Strand. Keeping Things Whole.
Tate, J. Descent, The.
Tzara. Metal Coughdrops.
Unknown. I Will Give My Love an Apple [Without E'er a Core].
Von Freytag-Loringhoven. Affectionate.
Ward, D. Tables in Pictures.
Welish. Casting Sequences.
If I Blindfold You.
Scalpel in Hand.
Wenderoth, J. Moon River.
Whitman, W. I Am the Poet.
That Shadow My Likeness.
Wilbur. Hole in the Floor, A.
Thyme Flowering among Rocks.
Wordsworth, W. Yarrow Visited [September, 1814].
Yeats. Meru.

Reaping and Reapers
Bontemps. Black Man Talks of Reaping, A.
Dowson. Last Word, A.
Hood, T. Ruth.
Toomer. Harvest Song.
Reapers.
Wilde, O. Wasted Days.
Wordsworth, W. Solitary Reaper, The.

Reason
Bevington, L. Afternoon.
Blake, W. Mock On, Mock On, Voltaire, Rousseau.
Brontë, C. Reason.
Brontë, E. God of Visions.
Carew, T. Love's Force.
Lover, upon an Accident Necessitating His Departure, Consults with Reason, A.
Cavendish, M. Discourse of Beasts, A.
Chaucer. Lak of Stedfastnesse.
Dove, R. Geometry.
Follen, E. Lines on Nonsense.
Forhan, C. Big Jigsaw.
Jackson, L. Reasons of Each, The.
Kavanagh, P. To Hell with Commonsense.
Kendall, M. Lower Life, The.
Levertov. Contraband.
Quest, The.
Matthews, W. Psychopathology of Everyday Life, The.
Miles, J. Reason.
Milosz, C. Incantation.
Owenson. Fragment 3.
Pope, A. On a Certain Lady at Court.
Robinson, M. Canzonet.
Invokes Reason.
Rejects the Influence of Reason.
Rukeyser, M. Rational Man.
Sherwood, G. Satire against Reason and Mankind, A.
Sitwell, D. Heart and Mind.
Stead, C. Between.
Suckling, S. Barley-Break, A.
Tollet. On Loving Once and Loving Often.
Whitman, W. When I Heard the Learn'd Astronomer.
See also **Intellect and Intellectuals; Rationalism and Rationalists**

Rebellions and Rebels
Adnan. Beirut-Hell Express, The.
Arrillaga. Dream.
Brome. On Sir G. B. his defeat.
Brooke, R. Sonnet: In Time of Revolt.
Browning, R. Italian in England, The.
Through the Metidja to Abd-el-Kadr.
Cheek. Rollercoaster.
D'Aguiar. Mama Dot Warns Against an Easter Rising.
De Kok. Our Sharpeville.
Drummond, W. Against the King.
Emerson, R. Uriel.
Farr, R. At general Electric, where they eat their/young.
Guevara, M. Easter Revolt Painted on a Tablespoon, The.
Heaney, S. Requiem for the Croppies.
Helle, A. Poem for Natalia Ginzburg.
Holloway, S. Old Sam.
Johnson, L. Five Nights of Bleeding.

Joseph, J. Dog Body and Cat Mind.
Lawrence, D. Don'ts.
Leonard, T. Untitled.
Lindsay, N. Factory Windows Are Always Broken.
Milton. On the Detraction Which Followed upon My Writing Certain Treatises.
Nelson, M. Ballad of Aunt Geneva, The.
Obejas, A. Sunday.
Palis, Y. Waking Up.
Pegram, A. Deliverance.
I Will Still Sing.
"Pindar." Hymn to the Guilotine.
Pope, A. Apologia pro Vita Sua.
Atticus ("Peace to all such! but were there one whose fires").
Bufo.
Epistle to Dr. Arbuthnot.
Sporus.
Reynolds, S. F. Whipping, The.
Rich, A. Phenomenology of Anger, The.
Rylander, E. Midnight Rocker, Tiananmen Square, May 27, 1989.
Unknown. Croppy Boy, The.
Humble Petition of the British Jacobins to their Brethren of France, The.
Rising in the North, The.
Upon Arch-bishop Laud, Prisoner in the Tower. 1641.
Walker, R. Okay, Let's Be Honest.
Whitman, W. We Two Boys Together Clinging.
Zulu, P. You are Mad: and I Mean It!
See also **Revolution and Revolutionaries**

Rebirth
Ai. More.
Alegría. Desire.
Awoonor. This Earth, My Brother.
Balaban. For Mrs. Cam, Whose Name Means "Printed Silk."
Beaver. More than 9 Lives.
Bensko. Bones of Lazarus.
Bevington, L. Midnight.
Bontemps. My Heart Has Known its Winter.
Césaire, A. In Order to Speak.
Collins, A. Song.
Cross, F. Rice Will Grow Again.
Cummings, E. I Thank You God.
When God Lets My Body Be.
Daumal. Persephone That Is to Say Double Issue.
Frost, R. Onset, The.
Glück, L. Cottonmouth Country.
Grimké, A. At April.
Hardy, T. For Life I Had Never Cared Greatly.
Holan. Resurrection.
Hughes, L. In Time of Silver Rain.
Kinnell. Saint Francis and the Sow.
Kunitz, S. Vita Nuova.
Lawrence, D. Fatality.
Levine, P. Belief.
Mabuza. Death to the Gold Mine!
Mahapatra, J. Sanskrit.
Mandelstam [*or* Mandelshtam]. Mounds of Human Heads Are Wandering into the Distance.
Martin, C. Easter Sunday, 1985.
Millay, E. Renascence.
Murray, J. Lullaby.
Osundare. I Sing of Change.
Plumly. After Grief.
Rossetti, C. Shut Out.
Szymborska. Theater Impressions.
Tabb. Evolution.
Tati-Loutard. Death and Rebirth.
Thomas, D. I Have Longed to Move Away.
Vaughan, H. Ascension Hymn.
I Walked [*or* Walkt] the Other Day to Spend My Hour.
Wilbur. April 5, 1974.
Wilde, O. Vita Nuova.
Williams, W. Spring and All.
See also **Renewal; Regeneration**

Rebuilding
Ammons, A. R. Eternal City, The.

Recipes
Suárez, V. Donatilia's Unrequited Love Remedy.
Umpierre, L. Only the Hand That Stirs Knows What's in the Pot.

Recognition
Clanchy, K. Recognition.
Cornford, F. Avenue, The.
Levertov. People at Night.
MacNeice. Elegy for Minor Poets.
Ramsdell, H. Nearly Circle.

Reconciliation
Aiken, C. Quarrel, The.
Al-Rihani. Constantinople.
Chin, J. Ex-Boyfriends Named Michael.
Coles, R. Christmas, Belfast.
Copus, J. Miss Havisham's Letter.
Heard, J. Sunshine after Cloud.
Marcus, B. Delaying Relevance.
Marshall, J. Letter to My Father on the Other Side.
Melville, H. America.
Ransom, J. Armageddon.
Turki, F. In Search of Yacove Eved.
Williamson, G. Neighboring Storms.

Reconstruction, United States
Thompson, M. Lincoln's Grave.

Record Players
Blake, E. I'd Give a Dollar for a Dime.
Gray-Kontar, D. Cuz' mama played jazz.
Razaf, A. I'd Give a Dollar for a Dime.
Trethewey, N. Secular.
Wallace, R. Sound Systems.

Red (color)
Dixon, M. Lady in Red, The.
Espada. Green and Red, Verde y Rojo.
Field, E. Red.
Finch, P. Reds in the Bed.
Guest, B. Red Dye.
Hernández Cruz. Scarlet Skirt.
Hughes, L. When Sue Wears Red.
Larsen, L. Red.
O'Grady, J. Poem for the Womb.
Parker, D. Red Dress, The.
Rodriguez, J. Nu-plastik Fanfare Red.
Russell, W. Red.
Rybicki, J. This Sun.
Townsend, A. Rouge.
Toyama. Red.
Unknown. Arrow Song.
Wetzsteon. Surgical Moves.
Wruber, A. Lady in Red, The.

Red Jacket (Seneca Chief)
Halleck, F. Red Jacket.

Red Sea
Benton, S. Lilith.

Redding, Otis
Mitcham. On the Otis Redding Bridge.

Redemption
Beaumont, J. Garden, The.
Campion, T. Seek the Lord.
View Mee, Lord.
Davis, W. Snow.
Donne. Good Friday [*or* Goodfriday], 1613. Riding Westward.
Graves, R. Point of No Return.
Herbert, E. Holy Baptism (1).
Love (2).
Parody [*or* Parodie], A.
Pulley, The.
Redemption.
Sion.
World, The.
Herrick. To Julia, the Flaminica Dialis, or Queen-Priest.
Hopkins, G. God's Grandeur.
Lynch, T. Lift Up Your Heads, Rejoice!
Merton. Cana.
Meynell, A. "I Am the Way."
Murray, P. Redemption.
Nemerov. Carol: "Now is the world withdrawn all."
Orfalea, G. Age of Cruelty, The.
Ralegh, S. Passionate Man[']s Pilgrimage, The.
Riley, P. Elf Shots.

Robinson, E.   Children of the Night, The.
Smart, C.   Hymn to the Supreme Being.
Thomas, D.   There Was a Saviour.
Thompson, F.   Hound of Heaven, The.
Unknown.   Blow Your Trumpet, Gabriel.
  Nobody Knows the Trouble I've Had.
  What Yo' Gwine to [*or* t'] Do When Yo' [*or* de] Lamp Burn Down?
Vaughan, H.   Regeneration.
Very.   I Was Sick and in Prison.
Wesley, C.   Free Grace.
Wicks, S.   On Re-recording Mozart.
Wilbur.   Proof, The.
Wilde, O.   E Tenebris.

Redwings
Wright, J.   Redwings.

Refinement
Cofer, J.   Women Who Love Angels.
Lovelace, R.   Song: "Strive not, vain Lover, to be fine."

Reflections
Atwood.   Tricks with Mirrors.
Behn, A.   Angellica's Lament.
Burns, R.   Of A' the Airts [the Wind Can Blaw].
Carew, T.   To T. H., a Lady Resembling My Mistress.
Carruth, H.   Soft Time of the Year, The.
Creeley.   Awakening, The.
  Kind of Act Of, The.
Davis, O.   Small Number, A.
Ferlinghetti, L.   21.
Frost, R.   For Once, Then, Something.
Griffiths, S.   Getting It Wrong, Again.
Jarrell.   Game at Salzburg, A.
Knott.   Shorts / Excerpts.
Kooser.   In the Basement of the Goodwill Store.
Lindtová, L.   Campfire.
Lochhead, L.   Hickie, The.
Lovelace, R.   Song: "Strive not, vain Lover, to be fine."
Moss, T.   Lessons from a Mirror.
Pack, R.   Thrasher in the Willow by the Lake, The.
Rexroth, K.   Fish Peddler and Cobbler.
  Signature of All Things, The.
Rodriguez, L.   Reflection on El Train Glass.
Stafford, W.   Ask Me.
Thomas, R.   Via Negativa.
Wunderlich, M.   Continent's Edge.

Refugees
Jussawalla.   Sea Breeze, Bombay.
Balaban.   For Miss Tin in Hue.
Boyle, K.   New Emigration, The.
Browning, R.   Italian in England, The.
Davidson, D.   Refugees.
Dickinson, E.   These Strangers, In a Foreign World.
Dunne, S.   Refugees at Cobh.
Elmusa.   In the Refugee Camp.
Fogarty, L.   Remember Something Like This.
Jarrell.   Refugees, The.
Komunyakaa.   Boat People.
Lazarus, E.   New Colossus, The.
Longfellow, H.   Tale of Acadie, A.
McCarthy, G.   Fall of Da Nang, The.
Mura.   Huy Nguyen: Brothers, Drowning Cries.
Nortje.   Up Late.
Rollings.   For Dear Life.
Schiff, H.   When It Happened.
Seferis.   Last Stop.
Shapcott, T.   Shadow of War, 1941.
Spender, S.   History and Reality.

Regeneration
Berry, W.   Slip, The.
Clifton, L.   To my Friend, Jerina.
Hopkins, G.   God's Grandeur.
Shapiro, K.   Leg, The.
Vaughan, H.   Regeneration.

See also **Rebirth; Renewal**

Reggae
Adisa.   Count Ossie.
Allen, L.   Riddim an' Hardtimes.
  Rub a Dub Style inna Regent Park.
Bethel, M.   Reggae Prophecy.
Breeze.   Dubbed Out.

Eena Mi Corner.
Dawes, K.   Black Heart.
  Some Tentative Definitions 1.
  Some Tentative Definitions 11.
  Trickster 1 (for Winston Rodney).
  Trickster 2 (for Lee 'Scratch' Perry).
  Trickster 4 (for Sister Patra).
Goodison.   Jah Music.
  Upon a Quarter Million.
Hippolyte.   Antonette's Boogie.
Ingram-Roberts, A.   Poem 2 (for Duckie Simpson of Black Uhuru).
Johnson, L.   Reggae Sounds.
King, J.   Intercity Dub.
Malachi.   Psalm of Silk.
'Mbala.'   History of Dub Poetry, The.
Morris, M.   Rasta Reggae.
Philp, G.   Dance Hall.
  Dance Hall: Version.
  Heirlooms.
  One Song.
Preston, R.   Music.
Richardson, L.   Poet Sings His Painting, The.
Sing, D.   Baap-Nemesthe Reggae Song.
Steede, V.   Reggae.
Wojahn.   Rajah in Babylon.

Regret
Adamson, H.   It's Been So Long.
Ade.   R-E-M-O-R-S-E.
Bibbins, M.   Bluebeard.
Brooks, S.   Some of These Days.
Burke, J.   Here's That Rainy Day.
Burns, R.   To a Mouse; On Turning Her up in Her Nest, with the Plough, November, 1785.
Butler, C. E.   Letter to the Survivors.
Cambridge, A.   Virgin Martyr, The.
Comden, B.   If You Hadn't—But You Did.
Congreve.   False Though She Be.
Creamer, H.   After You've Gone.
Donaldson, W.   It's Been So Long.
Dooley, M.   What Every Woman Should Carry.
Dransfield.   Portrait of the Artist as an Old Man.
Dugan, A.   Letter to Eve.
Dunbar, P.   Debt, The.
Elizabeth I.   When I Was Fair and Young.
Ellington, D.   Sophisticated Lady.
Fenton, J.   Skip, The.
"Field."   Ebbtide at Sundown.
Foley, M.   On the Waterfront.
Gilbert, J.   It Is Clear Why the Angels Come No More.
Green, A.   If You Hadn't—But You Did.
Hacker, M.   Boy, The.
Harte, B.   Mrs. Judge Jenkins [; Being the Only Genuine Sequel to "Maud Muller"].
Hayden, R.   Ballad of Sue Ellen Westerfield, The.
Herman, J.   If He Walked into My Life.
Hewitt, J.   Search, The.
Hollo.   Godlike.
"Hope."   I Shall Forget.
Hull, L.   Midnight Reports.
Jackson, H.   Opportunity.
Johnstone, R.   Fruit of Knowledge, The.
Keller, D.   Man Who Knew the Words to 'Louie, Louie', The.
Koch, K.   To Marina.
Kunitz, S.   Illumination, The.
  Quarrel, The.
Landon.   Gifts Misused.
Lassell.   Brady Street, San Francisco.
Layton, J.   After You've Gone.
Levine, P.   Uncle.
Lieberman, M.   Regret.
Merrill, J.   Renewal, A.
Mills, I.   Sophisticated Lady.
Nims, J.   Young Ionia, The.
Owen, W.   A Terre.
  Strange Meeting.
  Wild with All Regrets.
Parish.   Sophisticated Lady.
Patterson, G.   Lament.
Pollard, C.   Breakfast Poem.
Pollitt.   Mind-Body Problem.
Porter, C.   Miss Otis Regrets.
  Where Is the Life That Late I Led?

Pound, E.   Villanelle: The Psychological Hour.
Ransom, J.   Parting, without a Sequel.
Rees-Jones.   And Please Do Not Presume.
Roberts, K.   How Late Desire Looks.
Robinson, E.   Miniver Cheevy.
Schuyler, J.   Salute.
Scott, W.   Continuity of Life.
Sexton.   Lament: "Someone is dead."
Skelton, J.   Mannerly Margery Mylk and Ale.
Spires.   Apology.
Styne, J.   If You Hadn't—But You Did.
Thoreau.   Sympathy.
Timrod.   Cotton Boll, The.
Van Heusen, J.   Here's That Rainy Day.
Vaughan, H.   Retreat[e], The.
Wakoski.   Apology, An.
Ward, T.   On Being Kicked Out of the Harold Washington Library Center for Napping on the Floor.
Whittier.   Maud Muller.
Williams, H.   Prayer.
Yeats.   Down by the Salley Gardens.
  Men Improve with the Years.

Reincarnation
Brown, S.   Interview with an Alchemist in the New Age.
Hardy, T.   Transformations.
Hass, R.   To Phil Dow, in Oregon.
Hopkins, E.   Life in Death.
Kerouac.   Poem.
Levine, P.   Fox, The.
Mahon.   Lives.
Meynell, A.   Song of Derivations, A.
Rossetti, D.   Sudden Light.
Scupham.   Nondescript, The.
Watson, R.   Nirvana.

Reindeer
Jacobsen, J.   Reindeer and Engine.
Moore, C.   Visit from St Nicholas, A.

Rejection
Angus.   Doors of Sleep, The.
  Mary's Song.
Anthony, M.   Ugly Heart, The.
Anyidoho.   Murmuring.
Aytoun [*or* Ayton], R.   Answer, The.
  Rejection, The.
  Upon His Unconstant Mistress.
Barrington, P.   Take Me in Your Arms, Miss Moneypenny-Wilson.
Beckett, S.   Cascando.
Bickerstaffe.   Expostulation, An.
Blind.   Many Will Love You.
Burns, R.   Open the Door to Me, Oh!
Campion, T.   Shall I Come, Sweet Love.
Carew, T.   Spring, The.
  To My Inconstant Mistress [*or* Mistris].
Chaucer.   To Rosamounde.
Coleridge, M.   Clever Woman, A.
Coslow, S.   True Blue Lou.
Creeley.   Invoice, The.
Darley.   To Helene.
Dixon, S.   Request of Alexis, The.
Donne.   Damp[e], The.
  Love's Deity [*or* Deitie].
Douglas, L.   Rejected.
Duke, V.   I Can't Get Started.
"Ephelia."   To J.G. on the News of His Marriage.
  To My Rival.
Fell, A.   And Again.
"Field."   Sweeter Far than the Harp, More Gold than Gold.
Field, E.   Unwanted.
Gershwin.   I Can't Get Started.
Glück, L.   Hesitate to Call.
Gladstone, W. E.   To a Rejected Sonnet.
Gunn, T.   Carnal Knowledge.
Hai-Jew, S.   Kinged.
Hemans.   Properzia Rossi.
Herbert, G.   Denial[l].
Herrick.   Cruell Maid, The.
Hope, A.   Meditation on a Bone.
Howell, C.   Liberty and Ten Years of Return.
Huddle.   Vermont.
James, C.   Book of My Enemy Has Been Remaindered, The.

Jonson, B. Song: To Celia.
Joyce, J. Post Ulixem Scriptum.
Kizer, C. Bitch.
Lamb, C. "Timid grace sits trembling in her eye, A."
Landon. Girl at Her Devotions, A.
Layne, M. Collect Call.
Lovelace, R. To Lucasta.
Lowell, A. Carrefour.
'Marnia. I Want to Love You Very Much.
Merrill, S. Ballade of the Outcasts.
Meynell, A. Renouncement.
O'Hara, F. Meditations in an Emergency.
Perillo. Sweaters, The.
Pollard, C. Breakfast Poem.
Powell, K. Love/a Many Splintered Thing.
Prince, F. Wind in the Tree, The.
Ralegh, S. Nymph's [or Nimphs] Reply to the Shepherd [or Sheepheard], The.
Richards, L. Antonio.
Richardson, M. Sonnet: "I still shall smile and go my careless way."
Robin, L. True Blue Lou.
Robinson, M. Contemns Philosophy.
  Describes the Fascinations of Love.
  Laments Her Early Misfortunes.
  Sappho's Address to the Stars.
  Suspects His Constancy.
  To Phaon.
Rochester, E. Song: "Nothing ades to Loves fond fire."
Rossetti, C. No, Thank You, John.
San Juan. End of the Affair, The.
Scott, A. Return thee, heart.
Shelley, P. To————: "One word is too often profaned."
Smith, S. Lady "Rogue" Singleton.
  Pad, Pad.
Stanley, T. Divorce, The.
Starkey, D. Scrabble.
Stirling, S. Echo, An.
Strickland, A. Maniac, The.
Swinburne. Leave-taking, A.
  Satia Te Sanguine.
Tate, J. Deaf Girl Playing.
Tennyson, A. Locksley Hall.
Unknown. Art Thou That She.
Whiting, R. True Blue Lou.
Whitman, W. Sometimes with One I Love.

Relatives
Herrick. To His Kinsman, Master Thomas Herrick, Who Desired to Be in His Book.
Kumin, M. For My Great-Grandfather: A Message Long Overdue.
Ormond. My Dusty Kinsfolk.
Robinson, E. Poor Relation, The.

Relativity
Carew, T. To the Reader of Master William Davenant's Play [The Wits].

Relief
Crapsey. Release.
Hoffenstein. I'm Fond of Doctors.
Sewell, L. Release.
Thompson, J. Work.

Religion
Abad, G. Holy Order.
Abse. Stethoscope, The.
Al-Rihani. Constantinople.
Alexie. Theology.
Apollinaire. Zone.
Atkins. Lisbon.
Awoonor. Easter Dawn.
  Weaver Bird, The.
Balingit, J. Quiet Evening, Home Away.
Bangs, J. Blind.
Barham. Jackdaw of Rheims, The.
Baudelaire. Fuses I and II.
Benét, S. Cotton Mather.
Berg, S. Prayer: "Nobody understands so let the Rabbi."
Bidgood. Banquet.
Blake, W. All Religions Are One.
  Lacedemonian Instruction.
  Mock On, Mock On, Voltaire, Rousseau.
  There Is No Natural Religion.
Blaser. Even on Sunday.

Braithwaite. Rye Bread.
Burns, R. Epistle to a Young Friend.
  Holy Fair, The.
  Kirk's Alarm, The.
Byron, G. Spirit Pass'd Before Me, A.
Caballero-Robb, M. Dear Rosario.
Carbó, N. Votive Candles.
Chasin. Strength.
Chatterton. Methodist, The.
  Sunday: A Fragment Transcribed from a Ms. in Chatterton's Handwriting.
Chaucer. Alysoun.
  Cage, The.
  Chauntecleer.
  Death and the Three Revellers.
  Franklin's Prologue, The.
  Franklin's Tale, The.
  Friar's Prologue, The.
  Friar's Tale, The.
  General Prologue, The.
  Good Parson, The.
  Introduction to the Franklin's Prologue and Tale.
  Introduction to the Pardoner's Tale.
  Introduction to the Parson's Tale, The.
  Knighthood, The.
  Miller's [or Milleres] Tale, The.
  Miller's Prologue, The.
  Nun's Priest's Tale, The.
  Pardoner's Prologue, The.
  Pardoner's Tale, The.
  Parson and the Plowman Described, The.
  Patient Griselda.
  Prologue to Sir Thopas.
  Saturn.
  Seven Pilgrims: A Monk.
  Seven Pilgrims: A Prioress[e].
  Seven Pilgrims: A Wyf of Bathe.
  Temple of Mars, The.
  Three Rioters, The.
  Wife of Bath's Prologue, The.
  Wife of Bath's Tale, The.
Chesterton, G. Antichrist, or the Reunion of Christendom; an Ode.
Clifton, L. At Jonestown.
Coles, R. Christmas, Belfast.
Cooley, N. John Winthrop, 'Reasons to be Considered for...the Intended Plantation in New England,' 1629.
Creeley. After Lorca.
Davies, I. Lay Preacher Ponders, The.
Dharker. Name of god, The.
  Namesake.
  Postcards from god (1).
Di Prima. I Fail as a Dharma Teacher.
Disch. Ballade of the New God.
Doane, W. Preacher's Mistake, The.
Donne. Canonization, The.
  To the Countess of Bedford.
Douglas, L. Rejected.
Duhig, I. Fundamentals.
Dunbar, P. Spiritual, A.
Eliot, T. Hippopotamus, The.
  Song for Simeon, A.
Emerson, R. Problem, The.
Erdrich. Fooling God.
Ewer. Only Way, The.
Fallon, P. Herd, The.
Fletcher, L. Higashiyama Crematorium, November 6, 1983.
Foster, A. God and the Holy Stones.
Freed, F. Private School for Girls, May 14, 1948, New York City, A.
Freneau. Indian Convert, The.
Gibran. Mannus the Pompeiian to a Greek.
  Mary Magdalen.
Glaser, M. Magnificat!
Greacen. Ten New Commandments.
Green, M. Seeker, The.
Grey, C. Hallelujah!
Hardy, T. Christmas: 1924.
  Dream Question, A.
  Respectable Burgher, The.
Harington [or Harrington]. Groome of the Chambers religion in King Henry the eights time, A.
Hayden, R. Those Winter Sundays.

Helle, A. Poem for Natalia Ginzburg.
Hernández Cruz. Keeping Track of the Serpents.
Hewitt, J. Tryst.
Heyen. Stadium, The.
Hill, G. Vergine bella.
Hill, J. Preacher and the Slave, The.
Hirsch, E. Simone Weil: In Assisi.
Hope, A. Advice to Young Ladies.
  House of God, The.
Hopkins, G. Wreck of the Deutschland, The.
Housman, A. Laws of God, the Laws of Man, The.
Hudgins. Southern Crescent Was on time, The.
Hughes, L. Mystery.
  Song for a Dark Girl.
Huxley, A. Burning Wheel, The.
Johnson, F. Minister, The.
Johnson, L. Church of a Dream, The.
Joseph, L. It's Not Me Shouting at No One.
Kaufman, B. Oregon.
Kinnell. Avenue Bearing the Initial of Christ into the New World, The.
Kinsella, J. Visitant Eclogue.
Knott. Funny Poem.
Kumin, M. Living Alone with Jesus—.
Larkin, P. Church Going.
  High Windows.
  Water.
Laux. Children's Train, The.
Lawrence, D. Quetzalcoatl Looks Down on Mexico.
Lovelace, R. Apostasy of One and But One Lady, The.
Lyon, G. Foot-Washing, The.
MacCaig. Celtic Cross.
MacLean, S. Highland Woman, A.
MacSweeney. Far Cliff Babylon.
Mapanje. From Florrie Abraham Witness, December 1972.
Mathews, A. Caedmon.
McGinley. Day after Sunday, The.
  How to Start a War.
McLachlan. We Live in a Rickety House.
Melville, H. Fragments of a Lost Gnostic Poem of the Twelfth [or 12th] Century.
Mesmer, S. My Life in Yonago.
Mew. Ken.
Millay, E. Make Bright the Arrows.
Miller, J. Which Religion Vouchsafes.
Milton. On the Late Massacre [or Massacher] in Piedmont [or Piemont].
Mitchell, C. Soul of Jesus Is Restless, The.
Moore, T. Argument, An.
Moorer. Southern Pulpit, The.
Muldoon, P. Our Lady of Ardboe.
Mullen, H. Dance She Does, The.
Murray, J. There Has Been More Than Beginning and End to Face.
Nash, O. Seven Spiritual Ages of Mrs. Marmaduke Moore, The.
Nemerov. Boom!
Newman, J. Sensitiveness.
Nye, N. Man Who Makes Brooms, The.
Parnell, T. On Bishop Burnet's Being Set on Fire in His Closet.
Pastan. Passover.
Plato. Advice to Young Ladies.
Pollard, V. Heavens Cherubim High Horsed or The Meeting of the Two Sevens (May 1977).
Raine, K. Written in Exile.
Randall, J. To William Wordsworth from Virginia.
Reed, I. I Am a Cowboy in the Boat of Ra.
Rexroth, K. Wednesday of Holy Week, 1940.
Reyes, M. San Juan.
Reznikoff. Luzzato.
Robbins, H. And Have the Bright Immensities.
Robin, L. Hallelujah!
Robinson, A. Sibyl, The.
Rukeyser, M. Gates, The.
Sassoon. 'They.'
Scott, F. Bangkok.
  Brébeuf and His Brethren.
Scott, W. Mrs. Severin.
Sexton. With Mercy for the Greedy.

Sharpless.   Moment of Eschatological Doubt, A.
Shelley, P.   Life of Life.
  Poet's Dream, The.
  Prometheus Unbound [A Lyrical Drama in Four Acts].
Sidney, S.   Leave Me O Love.
Spender, S.   Landscape near an Aerodrome, The.
Spenser.   Address to Venus.
  Arthur's Fight with Orgoglio and Duessa.
  Belphoebe and Timias.
  Book 1.
  Bower of Bliss, The.
  Britomart at Isis' Church.
  Britomart Chaseth Ollyphant.
  Britomart in the House of the Enchanter Busyrane.
  Cave of Despair, The.
  Fight of the Red Cross Knight and the Heathen Sansjoy, The.
  Garden of Adonis, The.
  Guardian Angels.
  Guyon's Voyage to the Bower of Bliss.
  Hill of the Graces, The.
  House of Busyrane, The.
  In the Bower of Bliss.
  Legend of Britomartis, or of Chastitie, The.
  Legend of the Knight of the Red Crosse, or of Holinesse, The.
  Maske of Cupid, The.
  Mutability Claims to Rule the World.
  Nature's Reply to Mutability.
  Scudamor in the Temple of Venus.
  Song of Bliss.
  Vision of the Graces, The.
  Visit to Merlin, The.
St. John, P.   Sunday.
Stafford, W.   Religion Back Home.
Stevens, W.   Sunday Morning.
Stevenson, R.   Epitaph: "Angler rose, he took his rod, The."
Stone, S.   Church's One Foundation, The.
Tabb.   Sisters, The.
Thomas, R.   Calling, The.
  Llanrhaeadr Ym Mochnant.
Thompson, F.   Hound of Heaven, The.
Thribb.   In Memoriam Krishna Menon.
  Lines on the Return to Britain of Billy Graham.
Touré, A.   JuJu.
Traherne.   Apostacy, The.
Travis, N.   Church Ladies.
Unknown.   Inscription at Mount Vernon.
  Old [or Ould] Orange Flute, The.
  Old-Time Religion.
  Seven Songs and Song Pictures.
  To Caelia.
  Upon Arch-bishop Laud, Prisoner in the Tower. 1641.
  Vicar of Bray, The.
Vaughan, H.   Nativity, The.
  Religion.
  Retirement.
Voigt.   Woman Who Weeps.
Waller, E.   Upon His Majesty's [or Majesties] Repairing of Paul's.
Warton, T.   Stanzas Imitated From Psalm CXIX.
Weaver, M.   Water Song.
Whitehead, C.   Marian Hymn.
Whittier.   Worship.
Williams, W.   Semblables, The.
Wolfe, H.   Gray Squirrel, The.
Wordsworth, W.   Mutability.
  Obligations of Civil to Religious Liberty.
  Persuasion.
  Point at Issue, The.
  Trepidation of the Druids.
Wright, J.   Sketch for an Aesthetic Project.
  Wednesday Night Prayer Meeting.
Yeats.   Wisdom.
Youmans, V.   Hallelujah!
Zangwill.   Moses and Jesus.
See also **Faith**
Religious Life
Arnold, M.   Dover Beach.
Beer, M.   Church in the Heart, The.
Betjeman.   Huxley Hall.

Undenominational.
Campbell, R.   Mass at Dawn.
Cofer, J.   Saint Rose of Lima.
Cowper, W.   Contentment.
  Ephraim Repenting.
  Exhortation to Prayer.
  Future Peace and Glory of the Church, The.
  House of Prayer, The.
  Hymn: "Jesus, where'er thy people meet."
  Jehovah Our Righteousness.
  Joy and Peace in Believing.
  Light Shining out of Darkness.
  Lord Will Happiness Divine, The.
  Love Constraining to Obedience.
  Lovest Thou Me?
  My Soul Thirsteth for God.
  Old-Testament Gospel.
  Praise for the Fountain Opened.
  Retirement.
  Sardis.
  Self-Acquaintance.
  Sower, The.
  Walking with God.
  Wisdom.
Crashaw.   On Mr. G. Herberts Booke, The Temple.
Davie.   Priory of St Saviour, Glendalough, The.
  Their Rectitude Their Beauty.
Elizabeth, Queen of Bohemia.   Verses by the Princess Elizabeth, Given to Lord Harington, of Exton, Her Preceptor.
Fenton, J.   Kingfisher's Boxing Gloves, The.
Habington.   Cupio Dissolvi.
Hall, J.   Song of Esechia, The.
Harvey, C.   Church Festivals.
Herbert, G.   Affliction (1).
  Dulness[e].
  H[oly] Communion, The.
  Invitation, The.
  Perirrhanterium.
Herrick.   Thanksgiving to God for His House, A.
Hopkins, G.   I Wake and Feel the Fell of Dark, Not Day.
Jonson, B.   To Heaven.
Kasdorf.   First TV in a Mennonite Family.
  Mennonites.
Leax.   Fire Burns Low, The.
Mathews, A.   Caedmon.
Nemerov.   Boom!
Owen, M.   African Sunday.
Quarles.   Galatians 6.14.
  Matthew 9.12.
Roethke.   Right Thing, The.
Rowe, E.   Hymn: "In vain the dusky night retires."
Sawyer, A.   Sunday Schools.
Southwell.   Content and Ri[t]ch[e].
Taylor, E.   Huswifery.
Toplady.   Rock of Ages.
Unknown.   Corpus Christi Carol, The.
  I Would Be Clad in Christ's Skin.
Vaughan, H.   Disorder and Frailty.
  Dressing.
  Holy Communion, The.
  Jacob's Pillow, and Pillar.
  Mans Fall, and Recovery.
  Stone, The.
  Very. Created, The.
  Fear Not: For They That Be With Us.
  Presence, The.
Wesley, C.   Whole Armour of God, The.
Whittier.   Ezekiel.
Winchilsea.   Some Reflections.
Wordsworth, W.   Decay of Piety.
See also **Clergy; Convents; Monasteries; Monks; Nuns; Rabbis**
Religious Wars
Hazo.   For Fawzi in Jerusalem.
Jonson, B.   Epistle to a Friend, to Persuade [or Perswade] Him to the Wars, [or Warres] An.
Paulin.   Desertmartin.
Turki, F.   In Search of Yacove Eved.
Rembrandt, Harmenszoon van Rijn
Allston.   On Rembrant; Occasioned by His Picture of Jacob's Dream.

Corso.   Rembrandt—Self Portrait.
Walcott.   Polish Rider, The.
Weiss, T.   Ten Little Rembrandts.
Young, G.   Miracle, The.
Remorse
Benét, W.   Brazen Tongue.
Brontë, E.   If grief for grief can touch thee.
Burns, R.   Prayer, in the Prospect of Death, A.
Donne.   Hymn[e] to God the Father, A.
Garrett, E.   History Goes to Work.
Johnstone, R.   Fruit of Knowledge, The.
Kinzie.   Sun and Moon.
Lawrence, D.   Piano.
Macdonald, G.   Prayer, A: "When I look back upon my life nigh spent."
Nemerov.   Remorse for Time, The.
O'Donnell, C.   Resolution.
Sangster, M.   At Sunset.
Tichborne [or Tichbourne].   Tichborne's Elegy.
Renaissance
Browning, R.   Fra Lippo Lippi.
Hill, G.   Pre-Raphaelite Notebook, A.
Simpson, L.   Riders Held Back, The.
Renewal
Abad, G.   Jeepney.
Anderson, J.   Re-member Us.
Arnold, M.   To the Hungarian Nation.
Burns, R.   John Barleycorn [a Ballad].
Campbell, T.   Freedom and Love.
Cummings, E.   Spring is like a perhaps hand.
Donne.   To Mr. R. W.
Dove, R.   Turning Thirty, I Contemplate Students Bicycling Home.
Hill, G.   Veni Coronaberis.
Jeffers, R.   Shiva.
Merrill, J.   Renewal, A.
Mugo, M. G.   Look How Rich We Are Together.
Rafferty, P.   Back End.
Roethke.   Renewal, The.
Rossetti, C.   First Spring Day, The.
Smith, S.   New Age, The.
Southwell.   Times [or Tymes] Go[e] By Turn[e]s.
Thoreau.   Music.
Whitehead, C.   Daybreak.
Williams, W.   Paterson: The Falls.
Zukofsky, L.   I Walk in the Old Street.
See also **Rebirth; Regeneration**
Renoir, Pierre Auguste
Moulds, J.   Renoir's Bathers.
Ormond.   Certain Questions for Monsieur Renoir.
Warren, R.   Renoir.
Repentance
"Æ."   Reconciliation.
Allen, R.   See! How the Nations Rage Together.
Ashby.   Latter Day Psalms.
Berkeley, S.   Mass is Over, The.
Campion, T.   Awake, Awake! [Thou Heavy Sprite].
Delanty.   Thrust & Parry.
Herbert, G.   Cross[e], The.
  Discipline.
  Mary [or Marie] Magdalene.
  Parody [or Parodie], A.
  Reprisal[l], The.
  Sin's Round.
  Storm, The.
  Trinity Sunday.
Herrick.   Calling, and Correcting.
Jonson, B.   Hymn[e] to God the Father, A.
Milton.   On His Blindness.
Montgomerie, A.   Away Vane World.
Murray, R.   Wasted Day, The.
Oxenham.   So Little and So Much.
Pope, A.   Epigram in a Maid of Honour's Prayer-Book.
Rossetti, C.   Ash Wednesday.
  Convent Threshold, The.
Thompson, F.   To the Dead Cardinal of Westminster.
Toplady.   Rock of Ages.
Vaughan, H.   Admission.
  Mans Fall, and Recovery.

Match, The.
Relapse, The.

Repression
Bangs, J. On File.
Bishop, E. Sonnet: "Caught—the bubble."
Bly, R. Executive's Death, The.
Bruner. Prayer for Strength.
Cullen, C. Timid Lover.
Frost, R. Home Burial.
Kleiser. Most Vital Thing in Life, The.
Lim-Wilson. Ringmaster's Wife.
Milton. On His Blindness.
Osgood, F. Ah! Woman Still.
Symonds. What Cannot Be.
Wilde, O. Wasted Days.
Williams, C. Repression.

Reproach
Bly, R. Executive's Death, The.
Chaucer. Chaucer's Wordes unto Adam, his Owne Scriveyn.
MacLeish. You Also, Gaius Valerius Catullus.
Parker, A. Days like Prose.
Valerie, J. On Apologies.

Reptiles
Couzyn. Spell to Protect Our Love.
Kendall, M. Ballad of the Ichthyosaurus.
Nystrom. Insomnia.
Young, K. Clyde Peeling's Reptiland in Allenwood, Pennsylvania.

Reputation
Arlen, H. We're Off to See the Wizard (The Wonderful Wizard of Oz).
Bruner. Sinner, The.
Graves, R. 1805.
Herrick. Poetry Perpetuates the Poet.
Jonson, B. To the Memory of My Beloved, the Author Mr [or Master] William Shakespeare [And What He Hath Left Us].
Robinson, E. Flammonde.

Rescues
Anstett. Man Saves Own Life.
Berlin. I Got Lost in His Arms.
Fanthorpe. Not My Best Side.
Jones, R. S. Shelter.
Oles. For the Drunk.
Ransom, J. Lady Lost.
Stone, J. He Makes a House Call.

Reservations, Native American
Algarin. Taos Pueblo Indians: 700 strong according to Bobby's last census.
Klein, A. Indian Reservation: Caughnawaga.
Lopez, B. Desert Reservation.
Warrior. Reginald Pugh, The Man Who Came from the Army.

Reservoirs
Mathias, R. Flooded Valley, The.

Resistance
Adler, R. Whatever Lola Wants (Lola Gets).
Carew, T. Boldness[e] in Love.
Dambroff. Resistance.
Gershwin, G. Do It Again.
Herrick. To Virgins.
Koestenbaum, W. Gaudy Slave Trader.
Mandiela, A. Speshal Rikwes.
Mercer, J. Something's Gotta Give.
Meynell, A. Renouncement.
Philp, G. Dance Hall.
Rukeyser, M. Don Baty, the Draft Resister.
Stewart, B. August Town.
Unknown. Thy Heart.
Valerie, J. Lesson on Braces.
Woo, M. Whenever You're Cornered, the Only Way Out Is to Fight.

Respectability
Eberhart, R. New England Bachelor, A.
Frost, R. Considerable Speck, A.
Holmes, O. At the "Atlantic" Dinner, December 15, 1874.
Stafford, W. Well Rising, The.

Responsibility
Alkalay-Gut. Public Outcry.
Transportation.
Browning, E. Curse for a Nation, A.
Cahn, S. Call Me Irresponsible.
Clewell. Poem for the Man Who Said Shit.

Giovanni. December of My Springs, The.
Heyen. Riddle: "From Belsen a crate of gold teeth."
Joseph, J. Warning.
Knox, J. Bright Light of Responsibility, The.
Merwin, W. S. Ballad of John Cable and Three Gentlemen.
Millar, J. Midlife.
Peacock, M. Good Girl.
Rich, A. For the Record.
Stafford, W. With Kit, Age Seven, at the Beach.
Unknown. Jenny Nettles.
Van Heusen, J. Call Me Irresponsible.
Wright, C. Self-Portrait.

Rest
Aldington. Field Manoeuvres.
Alexander, P. Scherzo.
Clare, J. Woodland Seat, A.
Frost, R. Acceptance.
Gascoigne. Lullaby [or Lullabie] of a Lover, The.
Herbert, G. Pulley, The.
Herrick. End of His Work, The.
Howe, J. House of Rest, The.
Keats. To One Who Has Been Long in City Pent.
Levine, P. Sleepless Night, A.
Lovelace, R. Ant, The.
Mackenzie, K. Door swung open, The.
Mangan, J. Rest Only in the Grave.
Melville, H. Return of the Sire de Nesle A.D. 16, The.
Mother Goose. Forehead, Eyes, Cheeks, Nose, Mouth, and Chin.
Nesbit, E. Song: "Oh, baby, baby, baby dear."
Poe. For Annie.
Ross, A. Mess Deck.
Rossetti, C. Cardinal Newman.
Rest.
Sleeping at Last.
Uphill.
Smith, C. Pressed by the Moon, Mute Arbitress of Tides.
Timrod. Retirement.
Unknown. Rest.
Whitman, W. Evening Lull, An.
Wilbur. Sonnet: "Winter deepening, the hay all in, The."
Wyrebek, M. Recovery.
Yeats. Michael Robartes Bids His Beloved Be at Peace.

Restaurants
Betjeman. Huxley Hall.
Corn. Kimchee in Worchester (Mass.).
Cummings, E. Item.
Evasco, M. Baked Oysters Rockefeller.
Fisher, M. I Keep Going Back to Joe's.
Gardinier. At Work.
Keats. Lines on the Mermaid Tavern.
Kingston, M. Restaurant.
Lowell, A. Thompson's Lunch Room—Grand Central Station.
McElroy, C. Foul Line—1987.
Pettit. Vanna White's Bread Pudding.
Ransom. Pastime Café.
Segal, J. I Keep Going Back to Joe's.
St. Germain, S. Cajun.
Tammaro. 'Merican Fst Fd.
Unknown. I Had But Fifty Cents.
Urdang. At Frank 'n' Helen's.
Wetzsteon. Dinner at Le Caprice.
Williams, W. Brilliant Sad Sun.
Worth, V. McDonald's, New Hartford, NY.
Young, D. Pleasure.

Restlessness
Alexander, M. Memory.
People of Unrest.
Davis, O. Panic of Birds, The.
Derricotte. Invisible Dreams.
Lane, P. Spring.
Levy, A. March Day in London, A.
Longfellow, H. Seaweed.
Prince, F. Babiaantje, The.
Robinson, A. Darwinism.
Wordsworth, D. Cottager to Her Infant, (By My Sister), The.

Restraint
Cavendish, M. Claspe, The.
Gibran. Love.
Glück, L. Palais des Arts.
Kizer, C. Bitch.
McKay, C. White City, The.
Philips, K. Answer to Another Persuading a Lady to Marriage, An.
Reese, L. Reserve.
Sansom, A. Confinement.

Resurrection, The
Coverdale. Of the Resurrection.
Crabbe. Resurrection.
Doddridge, P. Christ's Resurrection and Ascension.
Donne. Resurrection, Imperfect.
Herbert, G. Dawning, The.
Easter.
Hopkins, G. That Nature Is a Heraclitean Fire and of the Comfort of the Resurrection.
Jennings, E. Resurrection, The.
Levertov. Ikon: The Harrowing of Hell.
Levin, P. Third Day, The.
Murray, L. Easter 1984.
Neale. Hymn for Easter Morn.
Rossetti, C. Better Resurrection, A.
Shaw, L. For They Shall See God.
Thompson, C. Empty Tomb, The.
Unknown. Christ Triumphant.
Steal Away to Jesus.
Updike. Seven Stanzas at Easter.
Vaughan, H. Easter-Day.
Wanley. Resurrection, The.
Wordsworth, W. Composed in One of the Valleys of Westmoreland, on Easter Sunday.

Retirement and Retirees
Buckley, C. 20 Years of Grant Applications and State College Jobs.
Collins, J. Tomorrow.
Copus, J. Cricketer's Retirement Day, The.
Dove, R. Satisfaction Coal Company, The.
Jacobsen, J. Hourglass.
Kessler, M. Secret Love.
Leonard, T. Opting for Early Retirement.
Lisick, B. Empress of Sighs.
Marvell. Garden, The.
Upon the Hill and Grove at Bilbrough.
Ní Chuilleanáin. Swineherd.
Reed, I. White Hope.
Rouse. Her Retirement.
Towle. Postmodern Maturity.
Van Jordan, A. My Father's Retirement.
Yeats. Lamentation of the Old Pensioner, The.
See also **Old Age**

Retribution
Eberhart, R. Fury of Aerial Bombardment, The.
Jeffers, R. Home.
Jones, I. Revolutionary Vision, The.
Sassoon. Blighters.

Reunions
Arnold, C. Why I Skip My High School Reunions.
Beckett, S. Alba.
Burns, R. Auld Lang Syne.
Carew, T. Upon Master Walter Montagu's Return from Travel.
Crunk, T. Reunion.
Devlin, D. Renewal by Her Element.
Dickinson, E. Return, The.
Donne. Valediction: Forbidding Mourning, A.
Hardy, T. Minute before Meeting, The.
Hughes, L. Lover's Return.
Ingelow. Long White Seam, The.
Jones, T. Back?
Kizer, C. Semele Recycled.
Livingston, M. Coming from Kansas.
McGrath, T. Celebration.
Mickle. Sailor's Wife, The.
Montague, J. All Legendary Obstacles.
Moore, L. Haiku.
Novello, I. We'll Gather Lilacs.
Owen, W. Unreturning, The.
Porter, C. Get Out of Town.
Rich, A. Face to Face.
Rossetti, C. Birthday, A.

Rukeyser, M.　More of a Corpse Than a Woman.
Tu Fu.　Return, The.
Watkins, V.　Returning to Goleufryn.

Revelation (Bible)
Blake, W.　Mental Traveller, The.
Braxton, C.　Apocalypse.
Herrick.　To God.
Lowry, R.　Beautiful River.
Spenser.　Sonnet 12: "I saw an ugly beast come from the sea."
Sonnet 13: "I saw a woman sitting on a beast."
Sonnet 14: "Then might I see upon a white horse set."
Sonnet 15: "I saw new Earth, new Heaven, said Saint John."

Revelry
Hemans.　Revellers, The.
Jarvenpa, D.　Polka.
Parker, A.　Another Poem about the Vandals.
Townsend, A.　Mardi Gras Premortem.
Trethewey, N.　Photograph of a Bawd Drinking Raleigh Rye.

Revenge
Brontë, A.　Song.
Campo.　Allegory.
Carew, T.　To My Inconstant Mistress [or Mistris].
Congreve.　False Though She Be.
Donne.　Apparition, The.
Elizabeth I.　Written on a Wall at Woodstock.
Graves, R.　Wreath, The.
Herbert, G.　Reprisal[l], The.
Herrick.　Bubble; a Song, The.
Holden, J.　Liberace.
Hughes, T.　Kreutzer Sonata.
Joseph, L.　Not Yet.
Kalmar et al.　Who's Sorry Now?
Komunyakaa.　Fragging.
Kunene.　Thought on June 26.
Landon.　Revenge.
Lanier, S.　Revenge of Hamish, The.
Lea, S.　Feud, The.
Loftis, N.　Brief Encounter.
Lovelace, R.　Cupid Far Gone.
Mayne, S.　In Memory of Aaron, Murdered Grandfather.
McKay, C.　Enslaved.
Melville, H.　Martyr, The.
Meredith, G.　King Harald's Trance.
Merson.　Spaniard That Blighted My Life, The.
Merwin, W. S.　Last One, The.
Millay, E.　Oh, Oh, you will be sorry for that word!
Milton.　On the Late Massacre [or Massacher] in Piedmont [or Piemont].
Neufeld, A.　Children of Night.
Pagis.　Autobiography.
Plath.　Lady Lazarus.
Rattray, D.　They Don't Have to Have That Look.
Robin, L.　Little Girl from Little Rock.
Ruby, H.　Who's Sorry Now?
Samaras, N.　Elegy for a Professor.
Sansom, M.　Song: "Foolish eyes, thy streams give over."
Schinto, J.　Stalker.
Shakespeare, W.　[Before the Rape].
Lucrece's Death.
Shaw, C.　Search, The.
Snyder, T.　Who's Sorry Now?
Styne, J.　Little Girl from Little Rock.
Teasdale.　I Shall Not Care.
Tucker, M.　Revenge.
Unknown.　Fair and Scornful.
Laily Worm and the Machrel of the Sea, The.
Vando.　Lydia's Phantasmagoria.
Walker, M.　Kissie Lee.

Revere, Paul
Livingston, M.　Paul Revere Speaks.

Revivalism and Revivalists
Warren, R.　Amazing Grace in the Back Country.

See also **Evangelism and Evangelists; Religion**

Revolution and Revolutionaries
Aguilar, M.　Poem from Sierra Madre.
Alcock.　Instructions, Supposed to Be Written in Paris, for the Mob in England.
Anyidoho.　Elegy for the Revolution.
Baraka.　Cuba Libre.
Short Speech to My Friends.
When We'll Worship Jesus.
Bienek.　Resistance.
Brown, S.　Old Woman Remembers, An.
Browning, E.　Part II.
Buchanan, G.　Speaker in the Square, A.
Burns, R.　Scots Wha Hae.
Carson, C.　Hamlet.
Cheney-Coker.　Poem for a Guerrilla Leader.
Cisneros, S.　I Am So in Love I Grow a New Hymen.
Loose Women.
Crosby, H.　Firebrand.
Di Prima.　April Fool Birthday Poem for Grandpa.
Revolutionary Letter #1.
Duff, V.　Letters from an Exile.
Espada.　Jeep Driver, The.
Fiacc.　British Connection, The.
Garcia, R.　Elite Syncopations.
Ginsberg, A.　Vow, A.
Giovanni.　For Saundra.
My Poem.
Gray-Kontar, D.　July.
Gwala.　New Dawn, The.
Haines, J.　Poem Like a Grenade, A.
Harper, M.　Song: I Want a Witness.
Hedin, R.　At the Olive Grove of the Resistance.
Herrera.　Mexican World Mural / 5 x 25.
Poetry of America, The.
Hippolyte.　Revo Lyric.
Hitchcock.　United States Prepare for the Permanent Revolution, The.
Hughes, L.　Letter to the Academy.
Ilio, D.　Prokosch in Tehran, 1978.
Jackson, R.　Lonely Affair, A.
Johnson, L.　Mi Revalueshanary Fren.
Jones, I.　Revolutionary Vision, The.
Jordan, J.　Poem Against the State (Of Things): 1975.
Poem for Guatemala.
Knight, E.　On the Yard.
Lamantia.　Voice of Carmen Mediums.
Lawrence, D.　O! Start a Revolution.
Macaulay, T.　Radical War Song, A.
Maroon, B.　Fire Keeper.
Mataka.　Ornithology.
McFadden, R.　First Letter to an Irish Novelist.
Moraes, D.　Babur.
Morales.　My Revolution.
Mtshali.　Day We Buried Our Bully, The.
Muldoon, P.　Lunch with Pancho Villa.
Okigbo.　Elegy for Slit-Drum.
Padilla.　Discourse on Method, The.
Perdomo, W.　Revolutionary.
Pope, A.　Apologia pro Vita Sua.
Atticus ("Peace to all such! but were there one whose fires").
Bufo.
Epistle to Dr. Arbuthnot.
Sporus.
Pound, E.　Canto 32.
Powell, K.　Mental Terrorism.
Randall, D.　Abu.
Roses and Revolutions.
Reed, I.　Reactionary Poet, The.
Rodgers, C.　U Name This One.
Rossetti, C.　Royal Princess, A.
Scott-Heron.　Revolution Will Not Be Televised!, The.
Senghor.　In Memoriam.
Sykes, B.　Cycle.
Final Count.
Unknown.　Cutty Wren, The.
Diggers' Song, The.
Revolutionaries, The.
Watkins, N.　Bedtime Story.
Yeats.　Great Day, The.
Zimunya.　After the Massacre.

See also **Rebellions and Rebels**

Revolutionary War, American
Cooke, R.　Hospital Soliloquy, A.
Unknown.　Yankee Doodle.

See also **American Revolution**

Rewards
Benjamin, P.　Press On.
Berrigan, A.　Advice to a Young Philosopher.
Coleridge, S.　Good Great Man, The.

Reynolds, Sir Joshua
Blake, W.　Sir Joshua Reynolds.

Rhine (river), Germany
Coleridge, S.　Cologne.

Rhinoceroses
Nash, O.　Rhinoceros, The.

Rhode Island (state)
Bryant, W.　Meditation on Rhode Island Coal, A.
Dietz, H.　Rhode Island Is Famous for You.
Meredith, W.　Rhode Island.

Rhythm
Allen, L.　Riddim an' Hardtimes.
Breeze.　Dubbed Out.
Caesar.　Crazy Rhythm.
Gershwin.　Fascinating Rhythm.
Jeffers, R.　Rearmament.
Jurmann, W.　All God's Chillun Got Rhythm.
Koehler, T.　Spreadin' Rhythm Around.
Springer, T.　Harmony.

Ribbons
Carew, T.　Upon a Ribbon [or Ribband].
Herrick.　Bracelet to Julia, The.
Upon a Black Twist, Rounding the Arm of the Countess of Carlisle.
Upon Julia's Ribband.

Rice
Bobrowsky.　Journey, The.
Cross, F.　Rice Will Grow Again.
Krohn.　Farmer's Song at Can Tho.
Oliver, M.　Rice.
Strange.　Offering.

Richard I (Richard Coeur de Lion), King of England
Chaucer.　Lak of Stedfastnesse.

Richard II, King of England
Shakespeare, W.　Death of Kings, The.

Richard III, King of England
Shakespeare, W.　Hate the Idle Pleasures.
Methought That I Had Broken from the Tower.
Suckling, S.　On King Richard the Third, Who Lies Buried under Leicester Bridge.

Richard, Earl of Cornwall
Unknown.　Song of Lewes, The.

Richardson, Samuel
Edwards, T.　To the Author of Clarissa.
Williams, A.　Verses to Mr. Richardson on His History of Sir Charles Grandison.

Riddles
Clare, J.　Secret Love.
Dickinson, E.　Snake, The.
Fanshawe, C.　Riddle, A: "'Twas in heaven pronounced, and 'twas muttered in hell."
Hayden, R.　Sphinx.
Lindsay, N.　Two Old Crows.
Lochhead, L.　Riddle-Me-Ree.
Mother Goose.　Candle, A.
Man in the wilderness asked [of] me [or said to me], The [or A].
Parnell, T.　Riddle, A: "Upon a bed of humble clay."
Robinson, E.　How Annandale Went Out.
Unknown.　Captain Wedderburn's Courtship.
I Have a Young Sister.
Present to a Lady, A.
Riddle: "Highty, tighty, paradighty, clothed [all] in green."
Riddles.
Riddles Wisely Expounded.
Riddling Knight, The.

Rifles
Kipling, R.　Brown Bess.
Sandburg, C.　A. E. F.

Righteousness
Moody, W.　Ode in Time of Hesitation, An.
Ralegh, S.　Lie, The.

Rilke, Rainer Maria
Black, S.   Rilke's Letter from Rome.
Goodison.   On Becoming a Tiger.
Rich, A.   Paula Becker to Clara Westhoff.
Rimbaud, Arthur
MacLeish.   Aeterna Poetae Memoria.
Moore, T.   Response to Rimbaud's Later
Manner.
Ramke.   Paul Verlaine at the Grave of Lucien
Létinois.
Rin-Tin-Tin
Hoffman, D.   In the Days of Rin-Tin-Tin.
Rings
Caesar.   Too Many Rings Around Rosie.
Crabbe.   Marriage Ring, The.
Darley.   To Helene.
Donne.   Jet Ring Sent, A.
"Field."   I love you with my life.
Herrick.   Ring Presented to Julia, A.
Levertov.   Wedding-Ring.
Rome, H.   Ring on the Finger.
Wakoski.   Ringless.
Riots and Rioters
Ai.   Riot Act, April 29, 1992.
Bly, R.   Andrew Jackson's Speech.
Brooks, G.   Riot.
Brown, S.   Old Woman Remembers, An.
DeFoe, M.   Forgetting the Sixties.
DuBois, W.   Litany of [or at] Atlanta, A.
Hernández Cruz.   Urban Dream.
Jackson, B.   Riot at Winchell's.
Joseph, L.   Then.
Levertov.   Gulf, The.
Linden, M.   Riot, A.
Melville, H.   House-Top, The.
More, H.   Riot; or, Half a Loaf Is Better than No
Bread, The.
Olds, S.   May 1968.
Parsons, W.   To a Friend in Love during the
Riots.
Perillo.   Ghost Shirt, The.
Uyematsu.   Ten Million Flames of Los Angeles,
The.
Rituals
Baca.   Green Chile.
Barrax.   Domestic Tranquility.
Carew, T.   New Year's Sacrifice: To Lucinda, A.
To the King, at His Entrance into Saxham: By
Master John Crofts.
Dooley, M.   Mansize.
Fields, J.   Citizen.
Fuller, M.   Sistrum.
Gardinier.   Ghost of Santo Domingo, The.
Hall, D.   Eating the Pig.
Herrick.   Perfume, The.
Spell, The.
Steam in Sacrifice.
To Julia, the Flaminica Dialis, or Queen-Priest.
To the Reverend Shade of His Religious Father.
Higo.   Ritual Murder.
Hollander, J.   For Both of You, the Divorce
Being Final.
Kaufman, B.   African Dream.
Knight, E.   He Sees Through Stone.
Lyon, G.   Foot-Washing, The.
Marshall, R.   Buddgelin Bey.
McClatchy.   Method, The.
McGrath, T.   Reading the Names of the Vietnam
War Dead.
Momaday.   Carriers of the Dream Wheel.
Montague, J.   Footnote on Monasticism, A:
Dingle Peninsula.
Moore, L.   Eternal Landscape, The.
Moore, M.   Cumae.
Mottram.   Zuni Dancers.
Murray, P.   Introit.
Okigbo.   Elegy of the Wind.
Peacock, M.   Breakfast with Cats.
Plumpp.   Remembered.
Rodgers, C.   Slave Ritual.
Rothenberg, J.   Crazy Dog Events.
Russell, W.   Ngarnbarndtar.
Song.   Ikebana.
Strange.   Barbershop Ritual.
Sze.   Great White Shark, The.

Very.   My Meat and Drink.
Yeats.   Collarbone [or Collar-Bone] of a Hare,
The.
Rivalry
Behn, A.   To My Lady Morland at Tunbridge.
Carew, T.   Fly That Flew into My Mistress'[s]
Eye, A.
To My Rival.
Corrothers.   Me 'n' Dunbar.
"Ephelia."   To My Rival.
Wetzsteon.   Rival, A.
See also **Competition**
Rivera, Diego
White, E.   I Paint What I See.
Rivers
Adams, L.   River in the Meadows, The.
Aguilar-Cariño.   Gabi.
Aldrich, T.   By the Potomac.
Allen, A.   This River.
Arodin, S.   Lazy River.
Ashbery.   Myrtle.
Aytoun [or Ayton], R.   Sonnet: On the River
Tweed.
Balaban.   Along the Mekong.
Belloc.   Evenlode, The.
Berry, W.   Slip, The.
Bertolino.   Snail River.
Bishop, E.   One Art.
Bowles, W.   To the River Cherwell.
To the River Itchin, near Winton.
To the River Wensbeck.
Tweed Visited, The.
Broumas, O.   Oregon Landscape with Lost
Lover.
Brown, S.   Riverbank Blues.
Bryant, W.   Green River.
Night Journey of a River, The.
Burns, R.   Flow Gently, Sweet Afton.
Carew, T.   To My Mistress Sitting by a River's
Side; an Eddy.
Carman, B.   Low Tide on Grand Pré.
Carmichael, H.   Lazy River.
Carson, A.   Longing, a Documentary.
Carver, R.   Woman Bathing.
Caston, A.   Gathering at the River.
Ceravolo.   Spring of Work Storm.
Chamberlain, K.   Stepping in the Same River.
Clayton, I.   River Bidgee.
Clive.   Mosel, The.
Coleridge, S.   Sonnet to the River Otter.
Cowper, W.   Comparison, A.
Crane, H.   Repose of Rivers.
Creeley.   Memory, The.
River Wandering Down.
Cronin, J.   River That Flows through Our Land,
The.
Cruickshank, H.   Ponnage Pool, The.
Curry.   Mute Swans.
Davie.   Ox-Bow.
De la Mare.   Voices.
Deane, S.   Fording the River.
Dixon, M.   River, Stay 'Way from My Door.
Doolittle, H.   Pursuit.
Dove, R.   Event, The.
Dowson.   Spleen.
Eberhart, R.   La Crosse at Ninety Miles an
Hour.
Emerson, R.   Musketaquid.
Two Rivers.
Erdrich.   I Was Sleeping Where the Black Oaks
Move.
Farjeon, E.   Tide in the River, The.
Ferlinghetti, L.   River Still To Be Found, A.
Fishman, C.   Whapmagoostui.
Fisk, M.   Red River.
Foerster.   Bronx Park.
Fordham.   Maiden and River.
Foster, S.   Old Folks at Home [, The].
Francis, R.   Like Ghosts of Eagles.
Garcia, R.   Diver for the NYPD Talks to His
Girlfriend, A.
Gehrke, S.   Near the Mississippi.
Gonzalez, R.   At the Rio Grande Near the End
of the Century.
Goodison.   Wedding in Hanover.
Gregerson.   Waterborne.

Groarke, V.   Riverbed, The.
Guiney.   Down Stream.
Reason for Silence, A.
Hacker, M.   Going Back to the River.
Hall, D.   Long River, The.
Hardy, T.   On Sturminster Foot-Bridge.
Hay, J.   Jim Bludso of the Prairie Belle.
Heaney, S.   Broagh.
New Song, A.
Heard, J.   To Clements' Ferry.
Hemans.   Indian Woman's Death-Song, The.
Henley, W.   At Queensferry.
Herrick.   To Dean-bourn, a Rude River in
Devon, by Which Sometimes He Lived.
Hill, M.   Ruth.
Hollander, J.   Variations on a Fragment by
Trumbull Stickney.
Holmes, O.   Two Streams, The.
Homfray.   Thoughts on Happiness.
Howard, B.   River Song.
River's Answer, The.
Hughes, L.   Life Is Fine.
Negro Speaks of Rivers, The.
Suicide's Note.
Hughes, T.   River.
Hugo, R.   River Now, The.
Hunt, L.   Nile, The.
Johnson, E.   Wave-Won.
Jordan, J.   Sandbar at Moore's Creek.
Keller, D.   Melancholy.
Kemble.   To the Wissahiccon.
Kinsella, T.   Nuchal, a Fragment.
Kipling, R.   Ford o' Kabul River.
Knoepfle.   Confluence.
Late Winter in Menard County.
Koyama.   Currents.
Lanier, S.   Song of the Chattahoochee.
Larkin, J.   Cold River.
Lassell.   Three Poems.
Lattimore.   Max Schmitt in a Single Scull.
Lowry, R.   Beautiful River.
Lyons, S.   Loving Along Western Rivers.
Mancini, H.   Moon River.
Mei Yao Ch'en.   I Remember the River at Wu
Sung.
Mercer, J.   Moon River.
Meynell, A.   Watershed, The.
Minhinnick.   Sap.
Morgan, R.   Shadow Valley.
Murray, P.   Conquest.
Nasrin.   Border.
Okara.   Call of the River Nun, The.
Ondaatje.   Walking to Bellrock.
Opoku.   River Afram.
Ortiz.   Bend in the River.
Pape.   Indian Ruins Along Rio de Flag.
Plomer.   Tugela River.
Posey, A.   Song of the Oktahutchee.
Redmond.   River of Bones and Flesh and Blood.
Rilke.   Tombs of the Hetaerae.
Robinson, M.   Canzonet.
Roditi.   Hand.
Roethke.   Meditation at Oyster River.
Sandburg, C.   River Roads.
Sarton.   After a Train Journey.
Schmitz.   Monstrous Pictures of Whales.
Scovell.   River Steamer, The.
Shillaber, B.   Picture, A.
Simms, W.   By the Swanannoa.
Sitwell, S.   River God, The.
Smith, C.   To the River Arun.
Smith, S.   River God, The.
Souster.   On the Rouge.
Southerland.   Night in Nigeria.
Spear, R.   River Song.
Stafford, W.   Ask Me.
At Cove on the Crooked River.
Ceremony.
In the Deep Channel.
Stevens, W.   Metaphor as Degeneration.
River of Rivers in Connecticut, The.
This Solitude of Cataracts.
Stevenson, R.   Where Go the Boats?
Storer.   Rivers.
Synge.   'Mergency Man, The.
Tana, P.   River, The.

Ungaretti. Rivers, The.
Unknown. Tweed and Till.
Very. Moses in Infancy.
Wakoski. Canoer, The.
Ward, D. Hunting in Twilight.
Warton, T. Sonnet: To the River Lodon.
Wat. Joke, A.
Watson, R. Children of the Mist.
Wenderoth, J. Detailed History of the Western
   World.
Whitman, W. Crossing Brooklyn Ferry.
Whittier. River Path, The.
Williams, W. January Morning.
   Mists Over the River.
Woods, H. River, Stay 'Way from My Door.
Woolson. Detroit River.
Wordsworth, W. Composed upon Westminster
   Bridge, September 3, 1802.
Wright, J. Eli, Eli.
   Living by the Red River.
   River Bend.
   To the Poets in New York.
Young, D. Sources of the Delaware.
Zieroth. Baptism.
See also **Brooks and Streams**

Roads
Aiken, C. Road, The.
Arlen, H. We're Off to See the Wizard (The
   Wonderful Wizard of Oz).
Ashbery. Poem: "While we were walking under
   the top."
Blackburn, P. El Camino Verde.
Bly, R. Three Kinds of Pleasures.
Bolt, T. Glimpse of Terrain.
Buckley, V. Origins.
Cervantes. Como lo Siento.
   Freeway 280.
Chesterton, G. Rolling English Road, The.
Coleman, C. Rules of the Road, The.
Curnow. On the Road to Erewhon.
Dauenhauer, R. Driving in a Snowstorm, King
   Salmon to Naknek.
Dransfield. Minstrel.
Frost, R. Middleness of the Road, The.
   Road Not Taken, The.
Goodison. Road of the Dread, The.
Gray, R. Flames and Dangling Wire.
Grunberger, A. Old Road, The.
Harburg. We're Off to See the Wizard (The
   Wonderful Wizard of Oz).
Hardy, T. Roman Road, The.
Healy, E. Artemis in Echo Park.
Hughes, L. Florida Road Workers.
Hugo, R. Letter to Gale from Ovando.
Johnson, H. Road, The.
Johnson, J. View Café, The.
Kavanagh, P. Inniskeen Road: July Evening.
King, H. Moonlight Ride, A.
Kipling, R. Way Through The Woods, The.
Larkin, P. No Road.
Leigh, C. Rules of the Road, The.
Levertov. Merritt Parkway.
Masefield. Roadways.
Merwin, W. S. Diggers, The.
Mew. On the Asylum Road.
Morgan, E. Itinerary.
Ní Chuilleanáin. Old Roads.
Nash, O. Song of the Open Road.
Perkins, S. Common Road, The.
Perreault, J. Shoe.
Pinsky. Jersey Rain.
Renton. Fork of the Road, The.
Reverdy. Road.
Slessor. Last Trams.
Song. Beauty and Sadness.
Thomas, E. Roads.
Wright, J. Brother and Sisters.
See also **Streets**

**"Rob Roy" (Robert MacGregor, Scottish
   freebooter)**
Unknown. Rob Roy.

Robbe-Grillet, Alain
Equi. Date with Robbe-Grillet, A.

Robbers
Darley. Free-booter, The.

Hattersley, G. Remembering Dennis's Eyes.
See also **Crime and Criminals**

Robespierre, Maximilien Marie Isidore
Lowell, R. Robespierre and Mozart as Stage.

Robin Hood
Keats. Robin Hood.
Unknown. Birth of Robin Hood, The.
   Jolly Pinder of Wakefield, The.
   Little John a Begging.
   Robin Hood and Allen [*or* Allin] -a-Dale.
   Robin Hood and Guy of Gisborne.
   Robin Hood and Little John.
   Robin Hood and Maid Marian.
   Robin Hood and Queen Katherine.
   Robin Hood and the Bishop.
   Robin Hood and the Bishop of Hereford.
   Robin Hood and the Curtal Friar.
   Robin Hood and the Monk.
   Robin Hood and the Potter.
   Robin Hood and the Tanner.
   Robin Hood and the Tinker.
   Robin Hood Newly Revived.
   Robin Hood Rescuing Three Squires.
   Robin Hood Rescuing Will Stutly.
   Robin Hood's Chase.
   Robin Hood's Death.
   Robin Hood's Golden Prize.
   Robin Hood's Progress to Nottingham.

Robins
Coccimiglio. St. Francis Speaks to Me at a
   Young Age.
Daniel, G. Robin, The.
Fagan. Weather They Were Written In, The.
Herrick. To Robin Redbreast.
   Upon Mistress Elizabeth Wheeler under the
   Name of Amarillis.
Lee, D. You Too Lie Down.
Melville, H. Little Good Fellows, The.
Mother Goose. Catch.
   Who Killed Cock Robin.
Rogers, S. Epitaph on a Robin Redbreast, An.
Rye. Redbreast, The.
Salter. Robin's Nest, A.
Unknown. Robin and a robin's son, A.
   Warning, A.
   When the Snow Is on the Ground.
Very. Robin, The.
Whittier. Robin, The.
Woods, H. When the Red, Red Robin Comes
   Bob, Bob, Bobbin' Along.
Yolen. First Robin.

Robinson Crusoe
Bishop, E. Crusoe in England.
Jarrell. Island, The.
Walcott. Crusoe's Island.

Robinson, Jackie
Miller, E. Boys of Summer, The.

Rochester, John Wilmot, 2d Earl of
Behn, A. On the Death of the Late Earl of
   Rochester.
Wharton, A. Elegy on the Earl of Rochester.

Rock and Roll
Balakian, P. Rock 'n Roll.
Berke. Fifties Rock Party, 1985.
Coles, R. New Jersey Boys.
DeFoe, M. Forgetting the Sixties.
Elledge. Duckling, Swan.
   Strangers: An Essay.
Gilbert, C. Enclosure.
Goldbarth. People Are Dropping Out of Our
   Lives.
Keller, D. Man Who Knew the Words to
   'Louie, Louie,' The.
Machan. In 1969.
Mueller, L. Deaf Dancing to Rock, The.
Nameroff, R. Elvis Presley.
Pietri. First Rock and Roll Song of 1970, The.
Rivard. Cures.
Rosemurgy, C. Mostly Mick Jagger.
Seay. Johnny B. Goode.
Shirley, A. Hours Musicians Keep, The.
Skloot. Everly Brothers, The.
   Year the Space Age Was Born, The.
Smith, B. How Garnett Mims and the
   Enchanters Came into Your Life.

Stein, K. First Performance of the Rock 'n Roll
   Band *Puce Exit.*
Wallace, R. Sound Systems.
Woessner. Jungle Music.
Wojahn. Buddy Holly.
   Necromancy: The Last Days of Brian Jones,
   1968.
   Song of the Burning.
Wormser. Fans.
Wrigley, R. Prophecy.

Rockefeller Center, New York City
White, E. I Paint What I See.

Rockets
Brathwaite, E. New Year Letter.
Magee, W. Giant Rocket.
Masson. Enough.
McDonald, W. Rocket Attack.
Probyn. As the Flower of the Grass.
Smith, W. There Was an Old Lady Named
   Crockett.
See also **Space and Space Travel**

Rocking Chairs
Carmichael, H. Rockin' Chair.
Klein, A. Rocking Chair, The.
Wayman. Teething.

Rocks
Aiken, C. Sea Holly.
Cervantes. Archeology.
Dixon, M. Getting Your Rocks Off.
Hemans. Epitaph on Mr W—.
Martien, J. Rocks Along the Coast, The.
Robinson, E. Salisbury Plain.
Stevens, W. Rock, The.
Winters, Y. Fable, The.
See also **Stones and Rocks**

Rocky Mountains
Birney. David.
Frémont. On Recrossing the Rocky Mountains
   after Many Years.
Higginson, E. Moonrise in the Rockies.

Rodeos
Smith, W. Closing of the Rodeo, The.
Swenson, M. Bronco Busting, Event #1.

Rodin, Auguste
Greer, J. Rodin's "Gates of Hell."
Stickney, T. On Rodin's "L'Illusion, Sœur
   d'Icare."

Roethke, Theodore
Brinnin. Roethke Plain.
Murphy, R. Poet on the Island, The.
Niatum. Lines for Roethke Twenty Years after
   His Death.

Roland
MacLeish. Too-Late Born, The.

Roller Skating and Roller Skaters
Livingston, M. 74th Street.
See also **Skateboarding and Skateboarders**

Roller-Coasters
Souster. Flight of the Roller Coaster.

Romanticism and Romantics
Clark, A. Zoo.
Cope, W. Triolet.
Mew. My Heart Is Lame.
Muir, E. Scotland 1941.
Robinson, E. Miniver Cheevy.
Stevenson, R. Song of a Traveller, The.

Rome, Italy
Appleman, P. Peace with Honor.
Beddoes. Humble Beginnings.
Bell, M. True Story, A.
Browning, R. Two in the Campagna.
Cavafy. Waiting for the Barbarians.
Cawein. Rome.
Clough. Amours de Voyage.
   Claude to Eustace: "Yes, we are fighting at last,
   it appears. This morning, as usual."
   Claude to Eustace—*from Bellagio.*
   Georgina Trevellyn to Luisa: "Dearest Louisa,
   Enquire if you please about Mr. Claude."
   Mary Trevellyn to Miss Roper.
   Rome.
   Spirit from Perfecter Ages.
Coleman, C. When in Rome (I Do As the
   Romans Do).

Cunningham, J. Rome.
DiPalma. Hadrian's Lane.
Garlick, R. Capitals.
Gibran. Mannus the Pompeiian to a Greek.
Hardy, T. Rome: Building a New Street in the Ancient Quarter.
Hemans. Corinne at the Capitol.
Herbert, Z. Return of the Proconsul, The.
Jonson, B. To Sir Henry [or Henrie] Savile [upon His Translation of Tacitus].
Kunitz, S. Thief, The.
Leigh, C. When in Rome (I Do As the Romans Do).
Marvell. Flecknoe, an English Priest at Rome.
McClatchy. Capriccio of Roman Ruins and Sculpture with Figures, A.
Melville, H. Arch, The.
Milosz, C. Campo dei Fiori.
Pasolini. Roman Evening.
Philips, K. On the Welsh Language.
Spenser. Ruines of Time, The.
Sylvester, J. Rome, Conqueror, Conquered.
Tomlinson, C. In the Borghese Gardens.
Wilbur. Baroque Wall-Fountain in the Villa Sciarra, A.
Piazza di Spagna, Early Morning.

Romeo and Juliet
Belloc. Juliet.
Hart, L. This Can't Be Love.

Romney Marsh, England
Davidson, J. In Romney Marsh.

Roofing and Roofers
Dunn, D. On Roofs of Terry Street.
Grennan. Men Roofing.
Kennelly. Thatcher, The.
Kimbrell, J. Rooftop.
Rich, A. Roofwalker, The.
Roethke. Ceiling, The.
Williams, C. Tar.

Rooks
"Field." Nests in Elms.
Plath. Black Rook in Rainy Weather.

Rooming Houses
Kimbrell, J. My Father at the North Street Boarding House.
See also **Boarding Houses**

Roosevelt, Franklin Delano
Hollander, J. Danish Wit.
Rome, H. F. D. R. Jones.

Roosevelt, Theodore
Bly, R. Three Presidents.
Espada. Bully.
Lindsay, N. In Which Roosevelt Is Compared to Saul.

Roosters
Bishop, E. Roosters.
Dickey, J. Gamecock.
Gardner, I. Cock-a-Hoop.
Garrett, E. Grandfather's Mint.
Sedley. On a Cock at Rochester.
Smith, S. Cock-a-Doo.
Stevens, W. Bantams in Pine-Woods.
Unknown. Cock-A-Doodle-Do.
Cock-Crow.
I Have a Gentle Cock [or Gentil Cok].
See also **Chickens**

Rope
Clifton, L. Climbing.
Kennedy, X. Little Elegy.
Komunyakaa. How I See Things.
Longfellow, H. Ropewalk, The.

Rosary
Cofer, J. Counting.

Roses
Apollinaire. Fete.
Ashbery. White Roses.
Bass, F. Garden, The.
Betham-Edwards. To a Llangollen Rose, the Day after It Had Been Given by Miss Ponsonby.
Bethell. Elect.
Biespiel, D. White Roses.
Bishop, E. Faustina, or Rock Roses.
Vague Poem.

Blunden. One among the Roses.
Brontë, E. Love and Friendship.
Broome. Rose-Bud, The.
Browning, R. Women and Roses.
Burns, R. Bonie Doon.
Song: "O my love's [or luve's or love is or luve is] like a red, red rose."
Ye Banks and Braes.
Chippewa Oral Tradition. Love-Charm Song.
Clare, J. Love's Emblem.
Coleridge, M. Gifts.
Cooke, R. Che Sara Sara.
Doolittle, H. Garden.
Sea Rose.
Drown, D. Rose by the Wayside, The.
Dunbar, P. Summer in the South.
Eliot, T. Dedication to My Wife, A.
Ferguson, G. Silent as Roses.
Winter Rose, The.
"Field." Goad, The.
Sweet-Briar in Rose.
Your Rose is Dead.
Frost, R. Rose Family, The.
Godfrey. Show Me a Rose.
Guest, B. Roses.
Herman, J. I Won't Send Roses.
Herrick. Funeral[l] Rites of the Rose, The.
How Roses Came Red.
Meditation for His Mistress[e], A.
Hodgson, R. Mystery, The.
Jacobsen, J. Only Alice.
Joseph, J. Rose in the Afternoon.
Keats. To a Friend Who Sent Me Some Roses.
Kemble. Parting.
LaFemina. Her Rose Tattoo.
Lawrence, D. Gloire de Dijon.
I Am like a Rose.
Levertov. Gypsy's Window, The.
MacDiarmid, H. Little White Rose, The.
Magowan. Susan.
Meinke. Sonnet on the Death of the Man Who Invented Plastic Roses.
Melville, H. Rosary Beads.
Rose Farmer, The.
Moore, T. 'Tis the Last Rose of Summer.
Naden. Pantheist's Song of Immortality, The.
North, C. Little Cape Cod Landscape.
O'Reilly, J. White Rose, A.
Orfalea, G. Rose of Brooklyn, The.
Parker, D. One Perfect Rose.
Peabody, J. Far-Off Rose, A.
Probyn, K. Kyrielle.
Raine, K. Rose.
Randall, D. Roses and Revolutions.
Roethke. Rose, The.
Rossetti, C. Summer Is Ended.
Sondheim. Everything's Coming Up Roses.
Stein, G. I Am Rose.
Swinburne. Match, A.
Tollet. Rose, The.
Unknown. Lo, How a Rose E'er Blooming.
Moses.
Of a Rose, a Lovely Rose.
Very. Wild Rose of Plymouth, The.
Walker, R. Life Is Life.
Waller, E. Budd, The.
Song: "Go[e], lovely rose."
Wilbur. Beautiful Changes, The.
Williams, S. Youth and Maidenhood.
Williams, W. Act, The.
Poem: "Rose fades, The."
Rose, The.
To Flossie.
Yeats. Secret Rose, The.
To the Rose upon the Rood of Time.

Rosh Hashanah
Shapiro, H. Feast of the Ram's Horn.

Rothko, Mark
Emanuel, L. Sleeping, The.

Rouen, France
Cannan. Rouen.

Roundheads (English political party)
Unknown. Character of a Roundhead, The.

Rousseau, Jean Jacques
Blake, W. Mock On, Mock On, Voltaire,

Rousseau.
Davie. Rousseau in His Day.
Harryman. Magic (or Rousseau).

Rowing and Rowers
Eberhart, R. Loon Call, A.
Jerome, W. Row, Row, Row.
Kipling, R. Galley-Slave, The.
Lattimore. Max Schmitt in a Single Scull.
Monaco, J. Row, Row, Row.
Sexton. Rowing.
Strand. Morning, A.
Wenderoth, J. Detailed History of the Western World.
See also **Crew and Crew Racing**

Royal Society
Cowley, A. To the Royal Society.
Ramanujan. Last of the Princes, The.

Royalty
Belloc. Imitation.
Carew, T. For a Picture Where a Queen Laments over the Tomb of a Slain Knight.
Coleridge, H. To a Lofty Beauty, from Her Poor Kinsman.
Crowley, A. Dedicace.
Daniel, G. Landscape, The.
Denham. Cooper's Hill.
Garioch. Heard in the Cougate.
Graves, R. Henry and Mary.
Hamilton, S. Farewell to France.
Holloway, G. Ford Castle: The Borders.
Howells, W. Royal Portraits, The.
Jacob, M. Spanish Generosity.
Landor, W. Georges, The.
Rose Aylmer.
Lomax, M. Gruoch.
Rossetti, C. Royal Princess, A.
Smith, S. Lord Barrenstock.
Thornbury. Court Historian, The.
Unknown. On Prince Frederick.
Wilner, E. Epitaph: "Young then, / we were bored already."
Wroth [or Wroath]. Song: "Love what art thou? A vain thought."
See also **Kings; Princes and Princesses; Queens**

Rubens, Peter Paul
Allston. Rubens.
Blake, W. To English Connoisseurs.
Monroe, H. Rubens.
Szymborska. Women of Rubens, The.

Rugs and Carpets
Durcan. Turkish Carpet, The.
Guevara, M. Magic Carpet, The.
Longley, M. Amish Rug, An.
Wells, W. Beatings.

Ruins
Adams, S. Hill Fort, Caerleon.
Aragon. Poem to Shout in the Ruins.
Binyon. House That Was, The.
Bowles, W. Netley Abbey.
Bromige. Edible World, The.
Brooks, C. Lines: Composed at the Old Temples of Maralipoor.
Browning, R. Love among the Ruins.
Carruth, H. Rimrock, Where It Is.
DiPalma. Hadrian's Lane.
Dove, R. Sightseeing.
Drummond, W. Content and Resolute.
Evance, S. Written in a Ruinous Abbey.
Gardner, E. Sonnet Written in Tintern Abbey, Monmouthshire.
Hinsey, E. Roman Arbor, The.
Hood, T. Silence.
Howells, W. Empty House, The.
Hugo, R. Death of the Kapowsin Tavern.
Kinnell. Ruins under the Stars.
Levertov. Fragrance of Life, Odor of Death.
Long, H. New Music, A.
McCarthy, T. Dying Synagogue at South Terrace, The.
McClatchy. Capriccio of Roman Ruins and Sculpture with Figures, A.
Melville, H. Ravaged Villa, The.
Merrill, J. Power Station, The.
Ojaide. Verdict of Stone, A.
Pape. Indian Ruins Along Rio de Flag.

Peacock, T.   Newark Abbey.
Purdy, A.   Remains of an Indian Village.
Robinson, E.   House on the Hill, The.
Samaras, N.   Farasa.
Shelley, P.   Ozymandias.
Smith, H.   Ozymandias.
Sotheby.   Netley Abbey; Midnight.
St. John, D.   Black Poppy (At the Temple).
Vaughan, H.   They Are All Gone into the World of Light!
Walcott.   Ruins of a Great House.
Webb, H.   Abbey Cwmhir.
Weston, M.   Primitive Place.
Wordsworth, W.   Yarrow Visited [September, 1814].

Rukeyser, Muriel
Marshall-Stoneking.   On the Death of Muriel Rukeyser.

Rum
Hernández Cruz.   Perlas.
Masefield.   Captain Stratton's Fancy.
Unknown.   Convicts' Rum Song.

Rumor
Berlin.   They Say It's Wonderful.
Bruner.   Monk and the Peasant, The.
De Tabley.   Sonnet: "Record is nothing, and the hero great."
Herrick.   Lips Tongueless[e].
See also **Fame; Gossip and Gossips; Reputation**

Running and Runners
Bell, M.   Slow.
  What They Do to You in Distant Places.
Cameron, N.   Unfinished Race, The.
Carpenter, W.   Ghosts.
Cyril.   Jump Black Honey Jump Black.
Freeman, M.   Ostrich Is a Silly Bird, The.
Galvin, B.   Running.
Gildner.   Runner, The.
Housman, A.   To an Athlete Dying Young.
Kelly, R.   Life of Intimate Fleeing, A.
Levin, D.   Field.
MacCaig.   Ringed Plover by a Water's Edge.
Piercy.   Morning Athletes.
Roach.   At Guaracara Park.
Robinson, E.   Mighty Runner, A.
Seyburn, P.   Good Water.
Sorley.   Song of the Ungirt Runners, The.
Stafford, W.   Run before Dawn.
Webb, F.   This Runner.
Welch, J.   Harlem, Montana.
Whitman, W.   Runner, The.
Wilbur.   Running.

Ruskin, John
Mitchell, E.   Thoughts after Ruskin.
Randall, D.   Blue Dome, The.
  Haymakers.
  His Favourite Seat.

Russell, Lucy, Countess of Bedford
Jonson, B.   On Lucy, Countess[e] of Bedford.
  To Lucy, Countess[e] of Bedford, with Mr. Donnes Satire's [or Satyres].

Russia
Akhmatova, A.   Introduction.
Barlow, J.   Advice to a Raven in Russia [December, 1812].
Bolton, J.   Fin de Siècle.
Creeley.   She Went to Stay.
Fraser, G.   Rostov.
Greenlaw.   World Where News Travelled Slowly, A.
Herbert, S.   Less Nonsense.
Kublanovsky [or Kublanovskii].   In Memory of John Keats.
Mandelstam [or Mandelshtam].   I Was Washing Outside in the Darkness.
  Leningrad.
Ostriker.   Eighth and the Thirteenth, The.
Pasternak, B.   Fresco Come to Life.
  Highest Sickness, The.
Reed, I.   El Paso Monologue.
Salter.   Chernobyl.
Seaton, M.   Wings.
Turberville.   To Spencer.
Unknown.   Harry Pollit Was a Bolshie.
Wheelwright.   Anathema. Maranatha!

Williams, W.   Russia.
Russian Revolution
Manifold.   Makhno's Philosophers.
Tomlinson, C.   Dream, A.
Russians, The
Davie.   Hearing Russian Spoken.
Gershwin.   Tchaikowsky (And Other Russians).
Unger, B.   Observance.
Ruth (Bible)
Hood, T.   Ruth.
Hugo, V.   Boaz Asleep.

S

Sabbath
Clare, J.   Sabbath Bells.
Herbert, G.   Sunday.
Herrick.   Sabbaths.
MacNeice.   Sunday Morning.
Sampter.   Summer Sabbath.
Vaughan, H.   Son-Days [dayes].
See also **Sunday**
Sacco-Vanzetti Case
Buckmaster.   Vanzetti.
Millay, E.   Justice Denied in Massachusetts.
Sacraments
Stainer.   Sighting the Slave Ship.
See also **Baptism; Eucharist; Extreme Unction; Marriage**
Sacrifices
Angelou.   Many and More.
Bedient, C.   When the Gods Put on Meter.
Byron, G.   Jephtha's Daughter.
Chin.   Turtle Soup.
Chipasula.   Those Rainy Mornings.
Coleridge, S.   To Nature.
Colman, H.   On the Inscription Over the Head of Christ on the Cross.
Davenport, R.   Sacrifice, A.
Emerson, R.   Give All to Love.
  To Rhea.
Everson, W.   Passion Week.
Heaney, S.   Tollund Man, The.
Herbert, G.   Obedience.
Herrick.   Ass[e], The.
  Good Friday: Rex Tragicus, or, Christ Going to His Cross[e].
  Hymne to Love, An.
  Perfume, The.
  Scar[e]-Fire, The.
  Steam in Sacrifice.
Hill, B.   Glory of Love, The.
Hope, M.   Sacrifice.
Horovitz, F.   Messenger, The.
Hughes, F.   In the Shadow of Fire.
Hughes, T.   God, A.
Jeffers, R.   But I Am Growing Old and Indolent.
Kipling, R.   Sacrifice of Er-Heb, The.
Knott.   Feeding the Sun.
Kremer.   Choice, Inanna and the Galla.
Mathews, A.   Caedmon.
McGrath, T.   Offering.
Mphande.   Why the Old Woman Limps.
Myles, E.   Merk.
Noll.   Abraham's Madness.
Okigbo.   Sacrifice.
Owen, W.   To Eros.
Reyes, M.   San Juan.
Rodgers, W.   Scapegoat.
Taggard.   To One Loved Wholly Within Wisdom.
Tennyson, A.   Charge of the Light Brigade, The.
Wilner, E.   Sarah's Choice.
Zisquit.   After Years of Feasting and No Sacrifice.
Sacrilege
Whittier.   Official Piety.
Sadism and Sadists
Arp.   Great Unrestrained Sadist, The.
Broumas, O.   Beauty and the Beast.
Chin, J.   Why a Boy.
Derricotte.   Boy at the Paterson Falls.
Ginsberg, A.   Please Master.

Sadness
Allingham.   Across the Sea.
Baraka.   Invention of Comics, The.
Bass, F.   Illness.
Becker, R.   Sad Sestina.
Beckford, W.   Elegiac Sonnet to a Mopstick.
Bogan, L.   Didactic Piece.
Bowles, W.   Languid, and sad, and slow.
Brown, E.   Tragic Hero.
Burnett, E.   My Melancholy Baby.
Burns, R.   Address to the Woodlark.
Carruth, H.   Cows at Night, The.
Chipasula.   Because the Wind Remembers.
Coleridge, M.   Sadness.
Cortez, J.   Lonely Woman.
Creeley.   Air: "The Love of a Woman."
Curbelo.   Tonight I Can Almost Hear the Singing.
De Los Santos, M.   Wiglaf.
Delanty.   Gift, The.
Donne.   Song: "Sweetest love, I do not go[e]."
Dowson.   Exile.
Elytis.   Aegean Melancholy.
Garrett, E.   Tyranny of Choice.
Hagiwara Sakutaro.   So Terrifyingly Melancholy.
Hanson, M.   To Fancy.
Harms.   Joy Addict, The.
Hart, L.   Glad to Be Unhappy.
Hauer.   Vision.
Hemans.   Despondency and Aspiration.
Herbert, G.   Storm, The.
Holmes, O.   Illustration of a Picture.
Hove.   Lost Bird.
  Red Hills of Home.
Howells, W.   November.
Hughes, L.   Miss Blues'es Child.
Jackson, L.   Sad Boy, The.
James, E.   Sunnyland.
James, J.   Sister Midnight.
Kaufman, B.   Private Sadness.
Kenyon, J.   Pharaoh.
Killeen, G.   Tristia.
Knott.   Two Vietnam Poems: (1966).
Landesman.   Ballad of the Sad Young Men, The.
Larkin, P.   Home Is So Sad.
Loncar, M.   Picasso Shag.
Longfellow, H.   Day Is Done, The.
Mahon.   Dejection.
Milton.   Il Penseroso.
Monk, T.   'Round Midnight.
Moore, T.   Oft In the Stilly Night.
Nemerov.   View from an Attic Window, The.
Nokan.   My Head is Immense.
Norton, G.   My Melancholy Baby.
Paulin.   Ulster Unionist Walks the Streets of London, An.
Piatt, S.   Sad Spring-Song.
Ramsdell, H.   Nearly Circle.
Ray, H.   Broken Heart.
  Shadow and Sunrise.
Rich, A.   Mirror in Which Two Are Seen as One, The.
Robinson, M.   Phaon Forsakes Her.
Roethke.   Dolor.
Rossetti, C.   At Home.
Sharma, P.   Performance Test.
Shelley, P.   Stanzas—April, 1814.
Smith, B.   Empty Bed Blues.
Smith, C.   By the Same. To Solitude.
  To a Nightingale.
  To Hope.
Williams, H.   To the Moon.
Williams, W.   Sadness of the Sea, The.
Wolf, T.   Ballad of the Sad Young Men, The.
Wright, J.   Breath of Air, A.
  Portugal Laurel, The.
Yeats.   To the Rose upon the Rood of Time.
Young, A.   Detroit 1958.
Zukofsky, L.   As to How Much.

Sailing and Sailors
Adamson.   Sibyl.
Bishop, E.   Imaginary Iceberg, The.
  Unbeliever, The.
Bontemps.   Nocturne of the Wharves.
Buchanan, R.   Wanderers, The.

Byron, G.   Lines to Mr Hodgson.
Campbell, R.   Choosing a Mast.
Campbell, T.   Ye Mariners of England.
Carroll, L.   Baker's Tale, The.
  Fit the Second: The Bellman's Speech.
  Fit the Sixth: The Barrister's Dream.
  Hunting of the Snark, The.
  Vanishing, The.
Carson, R.   Old Sailor Looking at a Container
  Ship.
Causley.   Chief Petty Officer.
Clough.   Come Home, Come Home!
  Qua Cursum Ventus.
Cofer, J.   Drowned Sailor, The.
Coleridge, S.   Rime of the Ancient Mariner,
  The.
Corbett, E.   Three Wise Old Women.
Coward.   Sail Away.
Cunningham, A.   Sea-Song, A.
Curnow.   Landfall in Unknown Seas.
Davies, W.   Sheep.
Dawe, G.   Seamen's Mission.
Day Lewis.   Conflict, The.
De la Mare.   Silver Penny, The.
Dibdin, C.   Poor Tom.
Donne.   Calm[e], The.
  Hymn[e] to Christ, at the Author's Last Going
    into Germany, A.
  Storm at Sea, A.
  Storm[e], The.
Doolittle, H.   Shrine, The.
Drayton.   To the Virginian Voyage.
Drummond, W.   Sonnet: "Slide soft, fair forth,
    and make a crystal plain."
Fields, J.   Alarmed Skipper, The.
  Ballad of the Tempest.
Finlay, I.   Evening—Sail.
Fletcher, J.   Clipper-Ships.
Garrick.   Heart of Oak.
Gascoyne.   "Truth Is Blind, The."
Gay, J.   Sweet William's Farewell to Black-Eyed
  [or Black-Ey'd] Susan.
Gilbert, S.   Captain Reece.
  Yarn of the Nancy Bell, The.
Hammial.   Sadie.
Harvey, S.   Mighty Tropicale Orchestra, The.
Hill, G.   Guardians, The.
Hirsch, E.   Tristan Tzara.
Holden, M.   Seaman, 1941.
Holmes, O.   Sea Dialogue, A.
Homer.   Butchers, The.
  Phemios and Medon.
Hovey.   Sea Gypsy, The.
Howell, C.   Liberty and Ten Years of Return.
Kenney.   Sailing.
Kipling, R.   Ballad of Fisher's Boardinghouse,
  The.
  Last Chantey, The.
  McAndrew's Hymn.
Lear, E.   Jumblies, The.
  Limericks, II (iv).
  Owl and the Pussy-Cat, The.
Levertov.   Leaving Forever.
Lewis, A.   Song (On Seeing Dead Bodies
  Floating Off the Cape).
Lightfoot.   Wreck of the Edmund Fitzgerald,
  The.
Longfellow, H.   Broken Oar, The.
  Tide Rises, the Tide Falls, The.
  Wreck of the Hesperus, The.
Lowell, R.   Salem.
Lucy.   Longshore Intellectual.
MacCaig.   Basking Shark.
Manifold.   Fife Tune.
Marvell.   Bermudas.
Masefield.   Cargoes.
  Crowd, The.
  Sea Fever.
Mathew.   Wynyard Sailor.
Mayer, B.   Port, The.
Melville, H.   Commemorative of a Naval
  Victory.
  Haglets, The.
  Island, The.
  To Ned.
  Tom Deadlight.

Meredith, G.   Camelus Saltat: Continued.
Merwin, W. S.   Odysseus.
Mew.   Rambling Sailor, The.
Miles, J.   Merchant Marine.
Miller, J.   Columbus.
Miller, V.   How Far?
Morris, T.   Sapphics: At the Mohawk-Castle,
  Canada.
Moschus.   Ocean, The.
Moss, H.   Tourists.
Mother Goose.   Bobby Shaftoe.
Murphy, R.   Pat Cloherty's Version of The
  Maisie.
  Sailing to an Island.
Newbolt.   Messmates.
O'Hara, F.   To the Harbormaster.
Pearlberg, G.G.   Sailor.
Petrarch.   My Galley.
Philips, K.   Sea-Voyage from Tenby to
  Bristol, A.
Pound, E.   Seafarer, The.
Preston, J.   Sunfish Races.
Probyn.   Barcarolle.
Rakosi.   Fluteplayers from Finmarken.
  Unswerving Marine.
Ray, H.   Boat Song.
Rosemurgy, C.   Hard Put.
Ross, A.   Destroyers in the Arctic.
Smith, C.   Beachy Head.
  From Beachy Head.
Smith, I.   Exiles, The.
Southey, C.   Mariner's Hymn.
Southey, R.   Ship, The.
Spence, L.   Prows O' Reekie, The.
Stephens, J.   Seumas Beg.
Stevenson, R.   Christmas at Sea.
  Good Play, A.
  My Bed Is a Boat.
  Over the Sea to Skye.
Surrey.   Seafarer, The.
Tate, A.   Mediterranean, The.
Tennyson, A.   Crossing the Bar.
Thomas, P.   Lascars, The.
Tucker, M.   Hugging the Shore.
Turner, C.   Buoy-Bell, The.
Unknown.   Dance the Boatman.
  Every Bullet Has Its Billet.
  Lowlands o' [or of] Holland, The.
  My Boy Willie.
  Sailor Boy's Song.
  Seafarer, The.
  Sir Patrick Spens [or Spence].
  Tarpauling Jacket.
  Young Allan.
Warren, R.   Masts at Dawn.
Westmorland.   In Praise of Fidelia.
Whitman, W.   Ship Starting, The.
  Song for All Seas, All Ships.
Whittier.   Slave-Ships, The.
Williams, W.   Yachts, The.
Wilmer, S.   Mess Boy, The.
Wyatt, S.   "My galley charged with
  forgetfulness."
  Sonnet: 'My galley charged.'
Saint Lawrence (river), Canada
Ray, H.   On the rapids of the St. Lawrence.
Saint Peter's Church, Rome
Milnes.   Sir Walter Scott at the Tomb of the
  Stuarts in St. Peter's.
Wojtyla.   Marble Floor.
Saint Petersburg [formerly Leningrad], Russia
Akhmatova, A.   Introduction.
Burnshaw.   House in St. Petersburg.
Mandelstam [or Mandelshtam].   Leningrad.
Olds, S.   Leningrad Cemetery, Winter of 1941.
See also **Leningrad, Russia**
Saints
Awad, J.   For Jude's Lebanon.
Clarke, A.   Martha Blake at Fifty-one.
  St Christopher.
Coolidge, C.   Jerome in His Study.
Crashaw.   Flaming Heart, The.
  Upon the Book and Picture of the Seraphical
    Saint Teresa.
Curry.   In a Calendar of Saints.
Derricotte.   Weakness, The.
Dickinson, E.   I Taste a Liquor Never Brewed.

Donne.   Canonization, The.
  Relic, The.
Fallon, P.   Holy Well.
Fitzgerald, E.   27.
Frost, C.   Consent.
Hamby, B.   St. Clare's Underwear.
Herrera.   Future Martyr of Supersonic Waves.
Herrick.   To Groves.
Hill, G.   In Piam Memoriam.
Johnson, L.   Church of a Dream, The.
Kavanagh, P.   Sanctity.
Kendall, M.   Legend of the Crossing-Sweeper.
McGinley.   Giveaway, The.
McGrath, T.   On the Head of a Pin.
Mew.   Madeleine in Church.
Ormond.   To a Nun.
Pelizzon, V.   Late Apostasy, A.
Rossetti, D.   Marriage of St. Katharine, by the
  same; in the Hospital of St. John at Bruges.
Tennyson, A.   St. Simeon Stylites.
Thomas, R.   Line from St. David's, A.
  Llanrhaeadr Ym Mochnant.
Thomson, J.   Once in a Saintly Passion.
Unknown.   Epigram: "Says a Reverend Priest to
  a less Rev'rend friend."
  When the Saints Go Marchin' [or Marching] In.
Whitehead, C.   Marian Hymn.
Yevtushenko [or Evtushenko].   Saints of Jazz.
Salads
Berger, B.   Salad Days.
Smith, S.   Salad, A.
Wells, C.   Universal Favorite, The.
Salamanders
DeFoe, M.   Red Salamander—Video Store
  Parking Lot.
Ramanujan.   Salamanders.
Salem, Massachusetts
Lowell, R.   Salem.
Salesmen
Cummings, E.   Salesman, A.
Elder.   One Foot in the Door.
Grosholz.   Life of a Salesman.
Martinez, D.   Cole Porter.
Sandburg, C.   Fish Crier.
Seyburn, P.   Persuasion.
Salisbury, England
Hardy, T.   In a Cathedral City.
Salmon
Adamson.   Gutting the Salmon.
Fallon, P.   Weir Bridge.
Hughes, T.   October Salmon, An.
  That Morning.
Lowry, M.   Salmon Drowns Eagle.
Niatum.   Salmon, The.
Swift, J.   Wild Salmon: Stillaguamish Tribal
  Hatchery.
Salt
Barlow, G.   Salt.
Di Prima.   For H.D.
Holst-Warhaft.   Old Men of Athens, The.
Merrill, J.   Upward Look, An.
Page, P.   Photos of a Salt Mine.
Phillips, C.   Reach, The.
Saltus, Thaddeus
Fordham.   To Rev. Thaddeus Saltus.
Salvation
Awoonor.   Weaver Bird, The.
Bliss, P.   Almost Persuaded.
Borson.   Save Us From.
Bradstreet, A.   As Weary Pilgrim, Now at Rest.
Chipasula, S.   Your Name Is Gift.
Crane, H.   Recitative.
Cullen, C.   Shroud of Color, The.
Dana, R.   Husband's and Wife's Grave, The.
Eliot, T.   Hippopotamus, The.
  Song for Simeon, A.
Ewer.   Only Way, The.
Farewell.   Privy-Love for My Landlady.
Ferguson, G.   Winter Rose, The.
Graves, R.   Song: Lift-Boy.
Herbert, G.   Bunch of Grapes, The.
  Conscience.
  Dialogue, A.
  Divinity.
  Easter Wings.

Grieve Not the Holy Spirit, etc.
Holy Baptism (1).
Peace.
Redemption.
Herrick. To His Saviour.
Hewitt, J. Calling on Peadar O'Donnell at
  Dungloe.
Hogan, L. Return: Buffalo.
Hunter, W. "Go Bring Me," Said the Dying
  Fair.
Hyde, A. And Canst Thou, Sinner, Slight.
Jonson, B. Hymn[e] on the Nativity [or
  Nativitie] of My Saviour, A.
Lansdown. Behind the Veil.
Laux. Prayer.
Lindsay, N. General William Booth Enters into
  Heaven.
Mandela. Saviour.
Mitchell, S. Good Samaritan et al, The.
Muske, C. Fault, The.
Oliver, M. In Blackwater Woods.
Ralegh, S. Authours Epitaph, Made by Himself,
  The.
Tate, A. Cross, The.
Unknown. Nobody Knows the Trouble I've
  Had.
  Ubi Sunt Qui Ante Nos Fuerunt?
Very. Autumn Leaves.
  Garden, The.
Wesley, C. Come on, my partners in distress.
  None is like Jeshuron's God.
Whittier. Over-Heart, The.

Salvation Army
Robinson, E. Karma.

Samson
Clemmons. Love Letter.
Crashaw. Samson to His Delilah.
Graves, R. Angry Samson.
Gwynn, R. Among Philistines.
Heard, J. Black Sampson, The.
Longfellow, H. Warning, The.
Roditi. Aurora Borealis.

San Francisco, California
Ackerman, D. San Francisco Sunrise.
Alarcon, F. Blues del SIDA / AIDS Blues.
Berrigan, A. Short History of Autumn, A.
Chin. Leaving San Francisco.
Corso. Ode to Coit Tower.
Cortes, F. Dolce Far Niente.
Di Prima. Letter to Jeanne (at Tassajara).
Ferlinghetti, L. Starting from San Francisco.
Gilbert, J. Malvolio in San Francisco.
Ginsberg, A. S. F. Southward.
  Sunflower Sutra.
Harper, M. Three O'Clock Love Song.
Hass, R. Bookbuying in the Tenderloin.
Hirschman, J. Tremor, The.
Lassell. Sunset Stripping: Visiting L. A.
Logan, J. San Francisco Poem.
Marcus, M. Picnic on the Bay Bridge.
Miller, C. Night in San Francisco.
Oppen. And Their Winter and Night in
  Disguise.
  Anniversary Poem.
  But So As By Fire.
  Impossible Poem, The.
  Morality Play: Preface, A.
  Taste, The.
  Translucent Mechanics, The.
Pearlberg, G. G. Dog Star.
Rukeyser, M. Bunk Johnson Blowing.
Snyder, G. Night Herons.
Villanueva, A. They Didn't Get Me.
Welch, L. Sausalito Trash Prayer.

Sanctuaries
Ammons, A. R. Triphammer Bridge.
Cofer, J. Purpose of Nuns, The.
Dobyns. Exile.
Hattersley, G. *On the Buses* with Dostoyevsky.
Hemans. Mountain Sanctuaries.
Liu, T. Wellfleet.
Rolle, S. Birds' Refuge, The.

Sand
Barnes, D. Transfiguration.
Bursk. Tearing Up the Tracks.

Cook, E. Building upon the Sand.
Creeley. All That Is Lovely in Men.
Frost, R. Neither Out Far Nor In Deep.
Gascoyne. Yves Tanguy.
Harper, F. Grain of Sand, A.
Hays, H. For One Who Died Young.
Jarmain. Sand.
Kuroda. Afternoon 3.
Loesser. Sand in My Shoes.
Longfellow, H. Sand of the Desert in an Hour-
  Glass.
  Tide Rises, the Tide Falls, The.
Millay, E. Second Fig.
Mitchell, A. Speck Speaks, A.
Nwankwo. Poem: "In sand."
Osterhaus, J. New York Minute.
Rohrer, M. Starfish Waving to Me from the
  Sand.
Rossetti, D. Even So.
Schertzinger, V. Sand in My Shoes.
Stevenson, R. At the Seaside [or Sea-Side].
Szymborska. View with a Grain of Sand.
Young, A. Culbin Sands.

"Sand, George" (Amandine Aurore Lucie Dupin,
  Baronne Dudevant)
Browning, E. To George Sand: A Desire.
  To George Sand: A Recognition.

Sandpipers
Bishop, E. Sandpiper.
Thaxter. Sandpiper, The.

Santa Barbara, California
Conyus. Great Santa Barbara Oil Disaster OR,
  The.

Santa Claus
Coots, J. Santa Claus Is Comin' to Town.
Moore, C. Visit from St Nicholas, A.
Moore, M. Saint Nicholas.
Nemerov. Santa Claus.
Thomas, E. Mrs. Kriss Kringle.

Santayana, George
Lowell, R. For George Santayana.
Stevens, W. To an Old Philosopher in Rome.

Sappho
Baker, H. Sappho's Leap.
Begley, T. Sappho's Gymnasium.
Brown, R. Sappho's Reply.
Dacre, C. Sappho; or, The Resolve.
Hemans. Last Song of Sappho, The.
Herrick. Apron of Flowers, The.
Higginson, E. Dream of Sappho, A.
Johnson, H. Summer Matures.
Kizer, C. For Sappho / After Sappho.
Lowell, A. Sisters, The.
Norton, C. Picture of Sappho, The.
Oakes-Smith, E. Ode to Sappho.
"Philo-Philippa." To the Excellent Orinda.
Pound, E. Papyrus.
Preston, M. Erinna's Spinning.
Robinson, M. Sappho Discovers Her Passion.
  Sappho's Address to the Stars.
  Sappho's Prayer to Venus.
Rossetti, C. Sappho.
Speyer. To a Song of Sappho Discovered in
  Egypt.
Swinburne. Sapphics.
Wright, J. Sappho.

Sarah (Bible)
Nemerov. Nicodemus.
Schwartz, D. Sarah.
Wilner, E. Sarah's Choice.

Sarajevo, Yugoslavia
Durrell. Sarajevo.
Harrison, T. Bright Lights of Sarajevo, The.
Hugo, R. Yards of Sarajevo, The.

Sarto, Andrea del
Browning, R. Andrea del Sarto.

Saskatchewan, Canada
Mandel, E. From the North Saskatchewan.
Newlove. Double-headed Snake, The.
Wah. Breathe Dust.

Satan
Belloc. On Lady Poltagrue, a Public Peril.
Blake, W. Book of Urizen [or First Book of
  Urizen], The.
Bloom, V. Sun-a-shine, Rain-a-fall.

Burns, R. Address to the Deil.
Causley. Infant Song.
Chesterton, G. Aristocrat, The.
  Donkey, The.
Coleridge, M. Devil's Funeral, The.
Coleridge, S. Devil's Thoughts, The.
Cullen, C. For a Mouthy Woman.
Cummings, E. In Just.
Dickinson, E. Snake, The.
Gowar. Rat Trap.
Hann. After Reading the Life of Mrs. Catherine
  Stubbs in Isaac Ambrose's "War with the
  Devils."
Hope, A. Möbius Strip-Tease.
Johnson, L. Dark Angel, The.
Kipling, R. Conundrum of the Workshops, The.
Lawrence, D. Root of Our Evil, The.
Lister, R. Lament of an Idle Demon.
Meredith, G. Lucifer in Starlight.
Montague, J. Wild Sports of the West.
Moore, T. Copy of an Intercepted Despatch
  from His Excellency Don Strepitoso Diabolo.
Olds, S. Satan Says.
Rich, A. Lucifer in the Train.
Rossetti, C. Three Enemies, The.
Salaam. '5 Minutes, Mr. Salaam.'
Snyder, G. Milton by Firelight.
Southey, R. Devil, The.
Tolson, M. Old Pettigrew.
Unknown. Demon Lover, The.
  Devil in Texas, The.
  Did you eever, iver, over?
Wylie. Knight Fallen on Evil Days, The.

Satie, Erik
Curtis, S. Satie, at the End of Term.

Satire and Satirists
Bogardus. Narcissus to Echo.
Klappert. To Whom.

Satiric Verse
Dunbar, W. Amendis to the Telyouris and
  Sowtaris for the Turnament Maid on Thame,
  The.
Foote, S. Great Panjandrum [Himself], The.
Mitchell, A. Nothingmas Day.
See also **Satire and Satirists**

Saturday
Mullen, H. Saturday Afternoon, When Chores
  Are Done.
Rouse. Sunday Morning.
Thompson, D. P. Blues at 1.
Trethewey, N. Collection Day.
Viray, M. Saturday Morning, A.
See also **Sabbath**

Saudi Arabia
Kazantzis. In Memory, 1978.

Saul (Bible)
Byron, G. Song of Saul before His Last Battle.
Levine, P. Death of Saul, The.
Lindsay, N. In Which Roosevelt Is Compared to
  Saul.
Merton. St. Paul.
Quarles. On Saul and David.
Wither. Conversion of S. Paul, The.

Sausages
Guest, E. Sausage.

Savannah, Georgia
Ager, M. Hard-Hearted Hannah (The Vamp of
  Savannah).

Sawmills and Sawyers
Minhinnick. Boathouse, The.

Scarecrows
Brownjohn. In a Convent Garden.
De la Mare. Scarecrow, The.
Kirkup. Scarecrows.
Wilbur. Sonnet: "Winter deepening, the hay all
  in, The."
Young, A. Scarecrow, The.

Scheherazade
Hudgins. Telling, The.
St. John, P. Ocean of the Streams of Story.

Schiele, Egon
Hannan, M. Life Model.

Scholarship and Scholars
Arnold, M. Scholar Gypsy, The.

Belloc. Lines to a Don.
Browning, R. Grammarian's Funeral, A.
Buckley, C. 20 Years of Grant Applications and State College Jobs.
Clarke, A. Scholar, The.
Colum, P. Poor Scholar of the 'Forties, A.
Cornford, F. Scholar, The.
Cunningham, J. Epigram: "Homer was poor. His scholars live at ease."
To a Friend, on Her Examination for the Doctorate in English.
Davis, F. Giles Johnson, Ph.D.
Deane, S. Scholar I.
 Scholar II.
Foley, M. Lucky Eugene.
Hacker, M. Imaginary Translation.
Hall, D. Professor Gratt.
Laughlin, J. My Ambition.
Matthews, T. Happy Arabia.
McCord, D. Baccalaureate.
Mother Goose. Ten O'Clock Scholar, [The].
Phillpotts. Miniature.
Portnoy, M. Roget, Papier, Schism!
Reid, C. Perversion, A.
Salzman, E. Double Dactyls.
Seshadri. Scholar, The.
Shapiro, K. Going to School.
Yeats. Gratitude to the Unknown Instructors.
 Scholars, The.
See also **Pedantry and Pedants; Students; Teaching and Teachers**
School and Schools
Algarin. Meeting Gaylen's 5th Grade Class.
Arnold, C. Why I Skip My High School Reunions.
Berry, D. On Reading Poems to a Senior Class at South High.
Bibbins, M. Geometry Class.
Bottoms. Desk, The.
Brooks, G. We Real Cool.
Bynner. Haskell.
Carbó, N. Civilizing the Filipino.
Carson, C. Slate Street School.
Cassells. Soul Make a Path Through Shouting.
Chavez, L. After the Prom.
Christie. Belongings.
Curnow. Country School.
De la Mare. Scholars.
Deane, S. Brethren, The.
Delgado, J. Letters from School, The.
Derricotte. In an Urban School.
Divakaruni. Yuba City School.
Dixon, H. Description of a Good Boy, The.
Djanikian. In the Elementary School Choir.
Dove, R. Flash Cards.
Duhamel. Ego.
Dumas, E. Our School Now Closes Out.
Durham. Columbus Day.
Elder. School Cadets.
Farawell, M. Everything I Need to Know I Learned in Kindergarten.
Foster, A. Starting School.
Glück, L. School Children, The.
Glancy. First Reader Santee Training School, 1873, The.
Goetsch, D. Nobody's Hell.
Guevara, M. Once When I Was in the Eighth Grade.
Hale, S. Mary's Lamb [or Mary and Her Lamb].
Hall, D. X.
Harrison, G. Playground, The.
Hemans. Evening Prayer, at a Girls' School.
Henderson-Holmes. Battle, Over and Over Again, The.
Hernández Cruz. Three Days / Out of Franklin.
Hope, M. Sixth Grade.
Hughes, J. Dog Day Lesson.
Jordan, J. Through These Halls.
Kaneko. Bailey Gatzert: The First Grade, 1945.
Kinsella, T. Model School, Inchicore.
Komunyakaa. White Port and Lemon Juice.
Kooser. Country School.
Lane, P. On Being Head of the English Department.
Lawrence, D. Last Lesson of the Afternoon.

Leto. For Talking.
Lifshin. Being Jewish in a Small Town.
Loftis, N. Fights After School.
Lorde. Hanging Fire.
Lumsden, R. Show and Tell.
Madgett. Images.
Major, C. I Was Looking for the University.
McPherson, S. Helen Todd: My Birthname.
Miller, E. Night Before the First Day of School, The.
Milligan, S. Bad Report—Good Manners.
Moore, A. Girls' School.
Moore, M. Student, The.
Moorer. Negro Schools, The.
 Tree of Knowledge, The.
Morse, B. Day on the Planet, A.
Muldoon, P. Anseo.
Piercy. Learning Experience.
Portnoy, M. Voucher.
Ríos, A. Domingo Limón.
Randall, J. To William Wordsworth from Virginia.
Reiter, T. Class Bully.
Rich, A. In a Classroom.
Roberts, L. Assignment, The.
Rosenberg, L. They are Planning to Cancel the School Milk Program to Fund a Tax Cut for the Middle Class.
Sanchez, S. Norma.
Shaw, D. Retrospection.
Silverstein, S. Sick.
Smith, B. How Garnett Mims and the Enchanters Came into Your Life.
Smith, S. To School!
Spender, S. Elementary School Classroom in a Slum, An.
Stafford, W. School Days.
Swift, J. Description of the Morning, A.
Thompson, P. Examination, The.
 Lines to an Old School-House.
Unknown. Country School, The.
 Schoolboy's Lot, A.
Valerie, J. On Apologies.
Wagner, M. Miss Clement's Second Grade.
Whitman, W. Old Man's Thought of School, An.
Whittier. In School-Days.
 To My Old Schoolmaster.
Williamson, G. Drawing Hands.
 Walter Parmer.
Wong, N. How a Girl Got Her Chinese Name.
Wren, A. Day at School, A.
Yeats. Among School Children.
Zamora-Linmark. Day 1: Portrait of the Artisit, Small-kid Time.
Zarzyski. Hurley High.
Zimmer. Zimmer in Grade School.
 Zimmer's Head Thudding against the Blackboard.

See also **Colleges and Universities**
Science and Scientists
Abse. Letter to Alex Comfort.
Alexander, E. Venus Hottentot, The.
Auden. Ode to Terminus.
Barbauld. To Mr. S. T. Coleridge.
Brontë, C. Reason.
Cowley, A. To the Royal Society.
Cummings, E. Pity This Busy Monster, Manunkind.
Davies, S. Science.
Duhamel. Ego.
Edson, R. Counting Sheep.
Espada. Do Not Put Dead Monkeys in the Freezer.
Fenton, J. Kingfisher's Boxing Gloves, The.
Fox, S. Almagest, Last Letter to Zakarias.
Fuhrman, J. Evidence.
Gewanter, D. Divorce and Mr. Circe.
Harte, B. Society Upon the Stanislaus, The.
Hernández Cruz. Keeping Track of the Serpents.
 Physics of Ochun, The.
Hope, A. On an Engraving by Casserius.
Jeffers, R. Science.
Katz, J. Taxonomy.
Lawrence, D. Self-Protection.

Lehrer. Wernher von Braun.
Lowell, J. Science and Poetry.
MacDiarmid, H. Poetry and Science.
Merrill, J. Laboratory Poem.
Nash, O. Purist, The.
Nemerov. Intimations.
Norris, K. Naming the Living God.
Peskett. Bottles in the Zoological Museum.
Poe. Sonnet—To Science.
Pope, A. Intended for Sir Isaac Newton.
Ramke. Astronomer Works Nights: A Parable of Science, The.
Rukeyser, M. Gyroscope, The.
Syrkin. My Uncle in Treblinka.
Updike. V. B. Nimble, V. B. Quick.
Science Fiction
Amis, K. Science Fiction.
Goldbarth. Meop.
Revard. Discovery of the New World.
Stanton, M. Space.
Scorn
Aleshire. Double, The.
Carew, T. Looking-Glass, A.
 To My Mistress Sitting by a River's Side; an Eddy.
Donne. Apparition, The.
Glück, L. Horse.
Greville, F. Caelica, XXIII.
Joyce, J. Bahnhofstrasse.
Philips, K. To the Queen of Inconstancy, Regina Collier, in Antwerp.
Robinson, E. Miniver Cheevy.
Unknown. Fair and Scornful.
 Hell and Heaven.
Wilde, L. Désillusion.
Scorpions
Plomer. Scorpion, The.
Smith, S. Scorpion.
Scotland
Adams, J. There's Nae Luck about the House.
Anderson, W. I'm Naebody Noo.
Angus. Blue Jacket, The.
 Doors of Sleep, The.
Auden. Night Mail, The.
Bernstein, M. Manly Sports.
Brereton, C. To Miss A[——]a M[——]a Tra[——]s; an Epistle from Scotland.
Brown, G. Kirkyard.
Burns, R. Birks of Aberfeldy, The [Composed on the Spot].
 Cotter's Saturday Night [Inscribed to Robert Aiken [or R. A****], Esq.], The.
 Halloween.
 John Barleycorn [a Ballad].
 Kirk's Alarm, The.
 Scotch Drink.
 Scots Wha Hae.
 Such a Parcel of Rogues in a Nation.
 Tam o' Shanter; A Tale.
 To a Haggis.
 To William Simpson, Ochiltree.
Burnside. Dundee.
Cameron, N. Meeting My Former Self.
Campbell, T. Lord Ullin's Daughter.
 To the Evening Star.
Carstairs. On Loch Leven.
Cunningham, A. Thistle's Grown aboon the Rose, The.
Davidson, J. Crystal Palace, The.
 Northern Suburb, A.
 Thirty Bob a Week.
Dunbar, W. Dance of the Sevin Deidly Synnis, The.
 Lament for the Makaris.
Dunn, D. Land Love.
 Landscape with One Figure.
 St Kilda's Parliament: 1879–1979.
Fordham. Highland Mary.
Gilfillan, R. Exile's Song, The.
Graham, H. Cockney of the North, The.
Graham, W. Loch Thom.
Gray, S. Scotland.
Hamilton, J. Oor Location.
Hay, G. Bizerta.
Herbert, W. Socialist Manifesto for East Balgillo, The.

Hogg, J.   Charlie is My Darling.
Jamie.   Mr and Mrs Scotland Are Dead.
  Queen of Sheba, The.
  St Bride's.
Johnston, E.   Last Sark, The.
  Working Man, The.
Lang, A.   Twilight on Tweed.
Leonard, T.   Jist Ti Let Yi No.
  Untitled.
Lochhead, L.   Something I'm Not.
Lomax, M.   Kith.
MacCaig.   Return to Scalpay.
  Small Lochs.
MacDiarmid, H.   Little White Rose, The.
  Scotland Small?
Macdonald, G.   Song.
Macgillivray.   Return, The.
MacLean, S.   Calvary.
  Hallaig.
  Kinloch Ainort.
MacNeice.   Bagpipe Music.
Morgan, E.   Loch Ness Monster's Song, The.
Muir, E.   Childhood.
  Scotland 1941.
  Scotland's Winter.
Nairne.   Heiress, The.
Paterson, D.   Chartres of Gowrie, The.
Pfeiffer, E.   Among the Hebrides.
Powell, A.   Caledonia.
Reid, A.   Scotland.
Retallack, J.   Biographia Literaria.
Robertson, R.   Aberdeen.
Scott, S.   Pibroch of Donuil Dhu.
Sempill, F.   Maggie Lauder.
Skirving.   Johnnie Cope.
Smith, I.   Clearances, The.
  Contrasts.
  Exiles, The.
  Gaelic Stories.
  Listen.
  Shall Gaelic Die?
Smith, S.   Grace of God and the Meth-Drinker,
  The.
Smith, W.   Glenaradale.
Soutar.   Tryst [or Trysting Place], The.
Southey, R.   Inchcape Rock, The.
Tannahill.   Eild.
  Tap-Room, The.
Taylor, R.   Princess of Scotland, The.
Thomson, D.   Herring Girls, The.
Tomlinson, C.   Mr. Brodsky.
Unknown.   Geordie [An Old Ballad].
  Jenny Nettles.
  Mary [or Marie] Hamilton.
  Mary Hamilton.
  Sir Patrick Spens [or Spence].
  Tam Lin.
Young, A.   Wet Day, A.
Scots, The
Burns, R.   Cotter's Saturday Night [Inscribed to
  Robert Aiken [or R. A****], Esq.], The.
  Scotch Drink.
  Scots Wha Hae.
  Such a Parcel of Rogues in a Nation.
  To a Haggis.
Cleveland, J.   Rebel Scot, The.
Duffy, C.   In Your Mind.
Fergusson.   To the Principal and Professors of
  the University of St Andrews, on their Superb
  Treat to Dr Samuel Johnson.
Garioch.   At Robert Fergusson's Grave, October
  1962.
  Embro to the Ploy.
Herbert, W.   Coco-de-Mer.
Kay, J.   English Cousin Comes to Scotland.
Kipling, R.   McAndrew's Hymn.
Leonard, T.   Fathers and Sons.
MacDiarmid, H.   Weapon, The.
Macneacail.   Gaelic is alive.
Morgan, E.   Sir James Murray.
Muir, E.   Scotland 1941.
Nash, O.   Genealogical Reflection.
Smith, I.   Listen.
Stevenson, R.   Ticonderoga: A Legend of the
  West Highlands.
Unknown.   Battle of Inverlochy, The.

Sir Patrick Spens [or Spence].
Scott, Sir Walter
Milnes.   Sir Walter Scott at the Tomb of the
  Stuarts in St. Peter's.
Wordsworth, W.   On the Departure of Sir Walter
  Scott from Abbotsford, for Naples.
Scottish Borders
Elliot, J.   Flowers of the Forest, The.
Scott, S.   Dreary Change, The.
Scottish Highlands
Burns, R.   My Heart's in the Highlands.
Scottsboro Case
Unknown.   Scottsboro.
Screams
Creeley.   Turn, The.
Smith, P.   Finding His Fist.
Unknown, fr. Terezin Concentration Camp.
  Closed Town, The.
Scribes
Chaucer.   Chaucer's Wordes unto Adam, his
  Owne Scriveyn.
See also **Secretaries; Stenographers**
Sculpture and Sculptors
Agoos, J.   To Atlas in the Attic.
Browning, E.   Hiram Powers' "Greek Slave."
Cawein.   Mnemosyne.
Cherry, K.   Bride of Quietness, The.
Danner.   Convert, The.
De Tabley.   Knight in the Wood, The.
Doty, M.   Days of 1981.
Elliott, E.   Criticism.
Fuller, M.   Flaxman.
Gilbert, C.   African Sculpture.
Hall, D.   "Reclining Figure."
  Dusting.
Higginson, E.   Statue, The.
Hinsey, E.   Roman Arbor, The.
Hummell, A.   Sculpture Garden.
Keats.   On Seeing the Elgin Marbles.
Meinke.   Helen.
Middleton, C.   Anasphere: Le torse antique.
Moore, M.   No Swan So Fine.
Ray, H.   Sculptor's Vision, The.
  Tireless Sculptor, The.
Rogers, S.   To the Fragment of a Statue of
  Hercules, Commonly Called the Torso.
Santayana.   Before a Statue of Achilles.
Scollard.   Bit of Marble, A.
Stickney, T.   On Rodin's "L'Illusion, Sœur
  d'Icare."
Walker, T.   Owl.
Wolfe, H.   Tulip.
Yeats.   Statues, The.
Sea
Acholonu.   Water Woman.
Aiken, C.   Sea Holly.
Ammons, A. R.   So I Said I Am Ezra.
Angira.   Old Wharf Canto.
Arnold, M.   Dover Beach.
Ashbery.   Painter, The.
Atkins.   Lakefront, Cleveland.
Auden.   On This Island.
Awoonor.   Sea Eats the Land at Home, The.
Baker, H.   Ode to the Sea.
Barrax.   There Was A Song.
Baxter, J.   East Coast Journey.
Beaver.   Angels' Weather.
Beckett, S.   Dieppe.
Beer, P.   Jane Austen.
Beevers.   Atameros.
Benttinen, T.   Maritime Pastoral.
Betjeman.   East Anglian Bathe.
Bishop, E.   At the Fishhouses.
  Cootchie.
  Large Bad Picture.
  Map, The.
  Seascape.
  Twelfth Morning; or What You Will.
Blackmur.   Seas Incarnadine.
Blight.   Down from the Country.
  Landfall, The.
Booth, P.   Marin.
Braithwaite.   House of Falling Leaves, The.
  Watchers, The.
Bridges, R.   Who Has Not Walked upon the

  Shore.
Brontë, A.   Lines Composed in a Wood on a
  Windy Day.
Brooks, C.   Lines: Composed at the Old
  Temples of Maralipoor.
Brown, G.   Beachcomber.
Browning, R.   Meeting At Night.
  Parting at Morning.
Brownstein.   War.
Brutus.   At Night.
Busia, A.   Mawu of the Waters.
Bynner.   Wave, The.
Césaire, A.   Bucolic.
  On the Islands of All Winds.
Campo.   My Voice.
Carver, R.   Cobweb, The.
Cary, A.   Katrina on the Porch.
Cavendish, M.   Sea Similized to Meadows and
  Pastures: the Mariners, to Shepherds: the Mast,
  to a May-Pole: the Fish, to Beasts, The.
Chin.   Repulse Bay.
Chivers.   Wind, The.
Clampitt.   Beach Glass.
Clifton, L.   Lost Baby Poem, The.
Coleridge, M.   O Earth, My Mother! Not Upon
  Thy Breast.
  On a Bas-relief of Pelops and Hippodameia.
Cooley.   Secret, The.
Cooley, N.   Undine.
Copus, J.   Cricketer's Retirement Day, The.
Corn.   Naskeag.
"Cornwall."   Address to the Ocean.
Corso.   Sea Chanty.
Cowper, W.   To Mr. Newton [on His Return
  from Ramsgate].
Crane, H.   At Melville's Tomb.
  Voyages.
Crane, S.   Man Adrift on a Slim Spar, A.
Cristall.   Song: "Both gloomy and dark was the
  shadowy night."
Cronin, J.   Naval Base (Part III), The.
Cummings, E.   Maggie and Milly and Molly
  and May.
Curnow.   You Will Know When You Get There.
Darley.   Rebellion of the Waters, The.
Davidson, L.   Charnel Ship, The.
Davison, P.   Equinox 1980.
Dawes, K.   Trickster 4 (for Sister Patra).
Dickinson, E.   By the Sea.
Dolben.   Sea Song, A.
Doolittle, H.   Hermes of the Ways.
  Oread.
Dove, R.   Fish in the Stone, The.
Du Maurier.   Music.
Dudek.   Coming Suddenly to the Sea.
Dugan, A.   Plague of Dead Sharks.
Duncan, R.   Achilles' Song.
Eberhart, R.   Charnel Indent.
Emerson, R.   Sea-Shore.
Fenton, J.   This Octopus Exploits Women.
Ferguson, G.   Swimming Pool Ghost, The.
Ferlinghetti, L.   Sea and Ourselves at Cape Ann,
  The.
Fisher, C.   Severn Bore.
Forbes, C.   Dark Mirror.
  Home.
Francis, R.   Onion Fields.
Fraser, S.   Looking Out to Sea Again on the
  Uptown Express.
Frost, R.   Neither Out Far Nor In Deep.
  Once by the Pacific.
Gallagher, T.   Sea Inside the Sea.
Gilder, R.   On the Bay.
Googe.   Coming Homeward out of Spain.
Graham, W.   Night's Fall.
Graves, R.   Beach, The.
Griffiths, B.   Dolphins.
Grosholz.   Old Fisherman, The.
Guiterman.   Sea-Chill.
Hadas, R.   House Beside the Sea, The.
Haida.   Song for Smooth Waters.
Hardison.   Marina.
Hardy, T.   Beeny Cliff.
Harwood, G.   Clair de Lune.
Harwood, L.   Final Painting, The.
  Soft White.

Hawthorne, N. Ocean, The.
Hays, H. Case, The.
Hemans. Diver, The.
  Last Song of Sappho, The.
  Song of Emigration.
  Wreck, The.
  Written on the Sea-Shore.
Herbert, J. Irish Scullery Maid, The.
Herrera. Weaning of Furniture-Nutrition.
  When He Believed Himself to Be a Young Girl
    Lifting the Skin of the Water.
Higginson, E. Opal Sea, The.
Hillman. Formation of Soils, The.
Hirschman, J. Headlands.
Hoban. Old Man Ocean.
Hollander, J. Morning in the Islands.
Hooper, V. Reading, A.
Hughes, L. Feet O' Jesus.
  Sea Calm.
Hughes, T. Relic.
Hugo, R. Salt Water Story.
Irwin, T. Iphione.
Jacobsen, J. Limbo Dancer, The.
James, J. Bye Bye Blackbird.
Jarman, M. Cavafy in Redondo.
Jeffers, R. Evening Ebb.
  Eye, The.
  November Surf.
  Place for No Story, The.
  Watch the Lights Fade.
Johnstone, R. Robot Camera.
Joseph, J. Lost Continent, The.
Joyce, J. On the Beach at Fontana.
Keats. On the Sea.
Kees. If This Room Is Our World.
Kennelly. Island, The.
Kimball, H. In Reverie.
Kipling, R. Dykes, The.
  Last Chantey, The.
  Sea and the Hills, The.
Komunyakaa. Break from the Bush, A.
Laing, K. One Hundred Lines for the Coast.
Lampert, D. Poem for Sophie.
Larkin, P. Absences.
Lawrence, D. Butterfly.
  Whales Weep Not!
Le Guin. Child on the Shore, The.
Lear, E. Jumblies, The.
Levine, P. Sea We Read About, The.
Li Po. Ancient Air.
Lodge, G. Tuckanuck, I.
Longfellow, H. Broken Oar, The.
  Seaweed.
  Sound of the Sea, The.
  Tide Rises, the Tide Falls, The.
Longley, M. Freeze-Up.
Lorde. What My Child Learns of the Sea.
Lowell, A. Shore Grass.
Lowell, R. Near the Ocean.
  Water.
Lowry, M. Sestina in a Cantina.
  Wild Cherry, The.
MacDiarmid, H. On the Ocean Floor.
MacEwen, G. Sea Things.
Mackey, N. Dream Thief.
  Phantom Light of All Our Day, The.
MacLeish. Return.
MacNeice. Leaving Barra.
  Thalassa.
Markham, E. Sea, The.
Marvell. Bermudas.
Masefield. Sea Fever.
  Wanderer's Song, A.
Mayer, B. Boats.
McDonald, E. Itherness.
Melo Neto. Daily Space.
Melville, H. Maldive Shark, The.
  Pebbles.
  Song from *Mardi*.
Meredith, W. Open Sea, The.
Messerli. Going to Sea.
Mew. Sea Love.
Millay, E. Exiled.
  Hearing Your Words, and Not a Word Among
    Them.
  Inland.

Ragged Island.
Miller, J. At Our Golden Gate.
Minhinnick. Surfers.
Moore, L. Until I Saw the Sea.
Moore, M. Fish, The.
  Grave, A.
  Jellyfish, A.
Morrison, L. Surf.
Moschus. Ocean, The.
Muldoon, P. Briefcase, The.
Murford. Storm and Calm: Sent from Embden
    to M. Edw. Ma. and M. Tho. Ly, The.
Nemerov. Salt Garden, The.
Noguere. Barney Bigard.
Okara. One Night at Victoria Beach.
Okigbo. Water Maid.
Oppen. Animula.
  Book of Job and a Draft of a Poem to Praise the
    Paths of the Living, The.
  Confession.
  Gold on Oak Leaves.
Orfalea, G. Jellyfish Eggs.
Oswald, A. Sea Sonnet.
Palmer, H. Aunt Zillah Speaks.
Peacocke. We're Staying at the Castlemount,
    Western Esplanade.
Percival. Coral Grove, The.
Pessoa. Portuguese Sea, The.
Plath. Blackberrying.
  Point Shirley.
Plomer. Azure, or Green, or Purple.
Poe. Annabel Lee.
  City in the Sea, The.
  To Helen.
  To One in Paradise.
Pogson, P. Deep.
Pound, E. Portrait d'une Femme.
Pratt, E. Silences.
Pritchard, N. Burnt Sienna.
Probyn. Barcarolle.
Procter, A. Address to the Ocean.
Radcliffe, A. Sea-View, A.
Rankin, J. Sea and Other Stories, The.
  Sea-bundle.
Reeves, J. Sea, The.
Rich, A. Insusceptibles, The.
Rossetti, C. By the Sea.
  Horses of the Sea, The.
  What Are Heavy?
  Wind Has Such a Rainy Sound, The.
Rossetti, D. Even So.
Rukeyser, M. Believing in Those Inexorable
    Laws.
  Outer Banks, The.
Saleh. Beach, Later.
  December Nap.
Salinas, L. Sea Song.
Samaras, N. Crossing the Strait.
Sandburg, C. Adelaide Crapsey.
  Be Ready.
  Bones.
  Sea-Wash.
Scammell, W. St Bees in Winter.
Schuyler, J. Crystal Lithium, The.
  Shuttle. Maritimes.
Silko. Prayer to the Pacific.
Silverstein, S. Slithergadee, The.
Sisson. In Flood.
Smith, C. Pressed by the Moon, Mute Arbitress
    of Tides.
  Sea View, The.
  Written on the Sea Shore.—October, 1784.
Smith, I. You Are at the Bottom of My Mind.
Smith, J. Sea Marke.
Smith, S. Kenless Strand, The.
Spicer, J. Phonemics.
St. John, P. Song.
  Sunday.
Stainer. Seals, The.
Stephens, J. Main-Deep, The.
  Shell, The.
Stevens, W. Idea of Order at Key West, The.
  Infanta Marina.
  Sea Surface Full of Clouds.
Stevenson, R. At the Seaside [*or* Sea-Side].
Stickney, T. At Sainte-Marguerite.

Swann, B. Land at the World's End, The.
Swenson, M. Stone Gullets.
  Waking from a Nap on the Beach.
Swirszczynska. Sea and the Man, The.
Tati-Loutard. Pilgrimage to Loango Strand.
  Submarine Tombs.
  Voices, The.
Taylor, B. On the Headland.
  On the Sea.
Teasdale. After Love.
  On the Dunes.
Tennyson, A. Break, Break, Break.
  Crossing the Bar.
  Kraken, The.
Thaxter. Imprisoned.
Thomas, E. Deep-Sea Pearl, The.
Tucker, M. Beautiful Sea, The.
Unknown. Golden Vanity, The.
  Seafarer, The.
  Sir Patrick Spens [*or* Spence].
Untermeyer, J. High Tide.
Updike. Winter Ocean.
Walcott. Missing the Sea.
Watson, R. Midnight Harvest, A.
Watts-Dunton. Sonnet's Voice, The.
Webb, F. End of the Picnic.
  Sea, The.
Webster, A. Enigma No. 6.
Westmorland. My Observation at Sea.
Whitman, W. After the Sea-Ship.
  As I Ebb'd with the Ocean of Life.
  Facing West from California's Shores.
  Out of the Cradle Endlessly Rocking.
  Patrolling Barnegat.
  Ship Starting, The.
  Song for All Seas, All Ships.
  To the Man-of-War Bird.
  World below the Brine, The.
Wilde, O. Vita Nuova.
Williams, W. Flowers by the Sea.
  Sadness of the Sea, The.
  Yachts, The.
Winters, Y. Fable, The.
Wohlfeld. Sea.
Wordsworth, W. It is a beauteous evening.
Wright, J. Miners.
  Old Age Compensation.
  Way to Make a Living, A.
Wyatt, S. "My galley charged with
    forgetfulness."
Young, F. Seascape.
Young, I. Mermaid Knows, A.
Zhenkai. August Sleepwalker, The.
See also **Sailing and Sailors**

Sea Chanteys
  Fletcher, J. Clipper-Ships.
Sea Creatures
  De la Mare. Sunk Lyonesse.
  Fenton, J. This Octopus Exploits Women.
  Graves, R. Sea Horse, The.
  Knight, S. Surf Motel, The.
  Moore, M. Fish, The.
    Sea Unicorns and Land Unicorns.
  Tennyson, A. Kraken, The.
  Williams, W. Sea-Elephant, The.
Sea Gulls
  Duke, V. Sea-Gull and the Ea-Gull, The.
  Jones, G. Dafydd's Seagull and the West Wind.
  Nash, O. Sea-Gull and the Ea-Gull, The.
  Watson, R. Midnight Harvest, A.
See also **Gulls**
Sea Hawks
  Eberhart, R. Sea-Hawk.
Sea Monsters and Sea Serpents
  Morgan, E. Loch Ness Monster's Song, The.
  Tennyson, A. Kraken, The.
Sea Shells
  Chivers. Shell, The.
See also **Shells**
Seacoasts
  Addonizio. At Moss Beach.
  Albrecht, A. Below White Cliffs.
    Passing Piedras Blancas.
  Bishop, E. Little Exercise.
  Clampitt. Baroque Sunburst, A.

Doolittle, H.   Shrine, The.
Hopkins, G.   Sea and the Skylark, The.
Keats.   To Ailsa Rock.
Momaday.   Winter Holding off the Coast of
  North America.
Roethke.   Her Time.
Schuyler, J.   Crystal Lithium, The.
Singer, B.   Peterhead in May.
Thomas, D.   Author's Prologue.
Tomlinson, C.   Fiascherino.
  Icos.
See also **Beaches; Shores**
Seafaring and Seafarers
Bontemps.   Nocturne of the Wharves.
Doolittle, H.   Shrine, The.
Longfellow, H.   Wreck of the *Hesperus*, The.
Masefield.   Sea Fever.
Mason, F. C.   Sunken Sailor.
Miller, J.   Columbus.
Poe.   To Helen.
Simpson, L.   To the Western World.
Stainer.   Sighting the Slave Ship.
  Wound-dresser's Dream, The.
Unknown.   What Shall We Do for the Striking
  Seamen?
See also **Sailing and Sailors**
Seals
Bly, R.   Dead Seal [near McClure's Beach], The.
Chamberlain, B.   Seal Cave.
Eberhart, R.   Seals, Terns, Time.
Hoffman, D.   Seals in Penobscot Bay, The.
Murphy, R.   Seals at High Island.
Purdy, A.   Dead Seal.
Sexton, T.   Seal Island.
Stainer.   Seals, The.
Seamstresses
Bishop, E.   House Guest.
Clifton, H.   Seamstress, The.
Seashores
Albrecht, A.   Passing Piedras Blancas.
Baker, T.   Le passage (Morbihan).
Banks, Jr., T. H.   Tempest.
Benttinen, T.   Maritime Pastoral.
Boyd, M.   Sea Spray.
Collins, M.   Winter in Brighton.
Curbelo.   Tourism in the Late 20th Century.
Forché.   Kalaloch.
Gladding.   Fisherman's Wife, The.
Hoffman, D.   Lobsterpot Labyrinths.
Hollander, J.   Late August on the Lido.
Jones, G.   Morning.
Klappert.   In Memory of H. F.
Martínez, V.   Reliquaries, The.
Mathias, R.   Porth Cwyfan.
McGrath, T.   Half Measures.
Meredith, W.   June: Dutch Harbor.
Merwin, W. S.   Migrants by Night.
Moore, R.   Shipwreck.
Shepherd, R.   Another Version of an Ocean.
Wilde, O.   Vita Nuova.
Wunderlich, M.   Anchorage, The.
See also **Shores; Beaches**
Seasons
Anderson, M.   September Song.
Bang, M.   Like a Fire in a Fire.
Bergman, A.   Summer Me, Winter Me.
Bishop, E.   Song for the Rainy Season.
Bogan, L.   Zone.
Bradstreet, A.   Four Seasons of the Year, The.
Brock-Broido.   Domestic Mysticism.
Brontë, E.   Song.
Bryant, W.   Winter Piece, A.
Caddel.   Against Numerology.
Cary, A.   November.
Clare, J.   Last of April, The.
  Shadows.
  Winter.
Clough.   In Stratis Viarum IV.
Coleridge, S.   Garden Year, The.
Collins, W.   Ode to Evening.
Coolbrith.   My Cloth of Gold.
Cope, J.   Winter Sky.
"Cornwall."   Address to the Ocean.
Cristall.   Song: "Through springtime walks, with
  flowers perfumed."

Cullen, C.   Leaves.
Dickinson, E.   As imperceptibly as grief.
Donne.   Love's Growth.
  Nocturnal[l] upon Saint Lucy's [*or* S. Lucy's *or*
  S. Lucies] Day, Being the Shortest Day, A.
Eberhart, R.   Spider, The.
Evance, S.   To Melancholy.
  Written in Ill Health at the Close of Spring.
Finch, B.   Written in a Shrubbery Towards the
  Decline of Autumn.
  Written in a Winter's Morning.
Frost, R.   Oven Bird, The.
George, F.   Wilderness.
Hesketh.   Death of a Gardener.
Holcroft.   Seasons, The.
Hove.   Lost Bird.
  Migratory Bird.
Hunter, A.   Winter.
Keats.   Human Seasons, The.
  To Autumn.
Kenney.   In April.
Leader, M.   Madrigal: "How the tenor warbles
  in April!"
Legrand, M.   Summer Me, Winter Me.
Lerner, A.   If Ever I Would Leave You.
Levine, P.   Later Still.
Loesser.   Spring Will Be a Little Late This Year.
Lorde.   What My Child Learns of the Sea.
Lovelace, R.   Grasshopper, The.
MacNeice.   Spring Voices.
Magee, W.   British Garden, A.
Maris, H.   Season's Finished, The.
McAuley, J.   Keep the Season.
Melville, H.   Little Good Fellows, The.
  Pontoosuce.
Mori.   Heat in October.
Morris, W.   Summer Dawn.
Nicholls, J.   Season Song.
Nicholson, N.   For Hokey and Henrietta.
Opie.   On the Approach of Autumn.
  To Winter.
Plath.   Couriers, The.
Pope, A.   Garden, The.
Praed.   Goodnight to the Season!
Pratt, E.   Come Not the Seasons Here.
Procter, A.   Address to the Ocean.
Randall, J.   To William Wordsworth from
  Virginia.
Ransom, J.   Vaunting Oak.
Reeves, J.   Sea, The.
Rossetti, C.   Autumn Violets.
  Fly Away, Fly Away.
  Grown and Flown.
  If Only.
  Under Willows.
Scamell, B.   More Rain.
Shelley, P.   Ode to the West Wind.
Sitwell, D.   Green Song.
Smith, C.   Composed During a Walk on the
  Downs, in November 1787.
Smith, J.   Sea Marke.
Stevens, W.   Meditation Celestial and Terrestrial.
  Metamorphosis.
  Motive for Metaphor, The.
Stevenson, R.   Autumn Fires.
  House Beautiful, The.
Tate, A.   Seasons of the Soul.
Tighe.   1802.
  Written in Autumn.
Unknown.   All Seasons in One.
  Labours of the Months.
Vaughan, H.   Love and Discipline.
Waddell, H.   Earth Said to Death.
Ward, J.   Comfort-Maker.
Warren, R.   Muted Music.
  Vermont Ballad: Change of Season.
Warton, T.   On Bathing.
Weill, K.   September Song.
West, J.   To May.
Wilbur.   April 5, 1974.
  In the Elegy Season.
Willis, N.   New Year, The.
Wordsworth, W.   Lines Composed a Few Miles
  above Tintern Abbey on Revisiting the Banks
  of the Wye During a Tour, July 13, 1798.
Wright, D.   Caleb Barnes.

  Juxtapositions.
Wright, J.   Love in the Weather's Bells.
  To a Troubled Friend.
Yearsley.   To————: "Lo! dreary Winter,
  howling o'er the waste."
Yeats.   Wheel, The.
Young, M. J.   On an Early Spring.
Seattle, Washington
Fanning, R.   Space Needle, The.
Seaweed
Dauenhauer.   Kelp.
Lawrence, D.   Sea-Weed.
Longfellow, H.   Seaweed.
Melville, H.   Tuft of Kelp, The.
Teasdale.   I Would Live in Your Love.
Seclusion
Hayden, R.   Soledad.
Levertov.   Closed World, The.
Mahon.   Woods, The.
Rich, A.   I Am in Danger—Sir.
Stafford, W.   Oregon Message, An.
Second Coming
Ferlinghetti, L.   Christ Climbed Down.
Yeats.   Second Coming, The.
See also **Millennium**
Secrecy and Secrets
Adler, R.   Hernando's Hideaway.
Balce, N.   Pizza and Pretense.
Blaeser.   Certificate of Live Birth.
Blake, W.   Love's Secret.
Brontë, A.   Fragment, A.
Browning, R.   Meeting At Night.
Brutus.   Postscripts 2.
Burns, R.   Whistle, and I'll Come to You, My
  Lad.
Byron, G.   When We Two Parted.
Carew, T.   Secrecy [*or* Secresie] Protested.
Carroll, K.   Truth About Karen, The.
Clare, J.   Secret Love.
Clifton, L.   Listen Children.
Coleman, H.   Poem for a "Divorced" Daughter.
Crapsey.   Song: "I make my shroud but no one
  knows."
Creeley.   Innocence, The.
Dambroff.   Resistance.
Daniels, K.   Women's Room in Pennsylvania
  Station, The.
Dauer.   William.
Davis, T.   Desire 1.
De la Mare.   Portrait, A.
Donne.   Undertaking, The.
Dove, R.   Adolescence—I.
Dunbar, P.   We Wear the Mask.
Elledge.   Triptych.
Emerson, R.   Sphinx, The.
Fain, S.   Secret Love.
"Field."   Palimpsest, A.
Flynn, N.   Fragment (Found Inside My Mother).
Francia, L.   Secret in the Roar, The.
Frost, R.   Secret Sits, The.
García, D.   Green Corn Season.
Garrett, E.   Moules à la Marinière.
Gershon.   At a Reception.
Harburg.   If This Isn't Love.
Hernández Cruz.   Going Uptown to Visit
  Miriam.
Hill, G.   Turtle Dove, The.
Hughes, L.   Personal.
Jonson, B.   Nymph's Passion, A.
Kessler, S.   Family Secrets.
Knight, E.   He Sees Through Stone.
Lane, B.   If This Isn't Love.
Lawrence, J.   What's Your Story, Morning
  Glory.
Lindley, D.   Cryptogram, The.
MacEwen, G.   Open Secrets.
Machan.   No, Superman Was Not the Only One.
Muldoon, P.   Hedgehog.
Myles, E.   American Poem, An.
Nesbit, E.   Things That Matter, The.
Noguere.   Secret, The.
Pogson, P.   Sleeper.
Rilke.   Mary at Peace with the Risen Lord.
Rodgers, C.   Poem No. 1.
Romano, R.   Bucket, The.

Rosen, K. Along the Charles.
Ross, J. Hernando's Hideaway.
Rossetti, C. Winter: My Secret.
Schilpp, M. Devotions in Confidence.
Shepherd, R. Motive.
Teasdale. Those Who Love.
Tindal. Birth Wail, The.
Umpierre, L. Only the Hand That Stirs Knows What's in the Pot.
Violi. Harold and Imogene.
Webster, P. Secret Love.
Whitney, I. I. W. To Her Unconstant Lover.
Wilner, E. Secret Garden, The.
Wyatt, S. Lover Showeth How He Is Forsaken of Such as He Sometime Enjoyed, The.
Yeats. Secret Rose, The.

Secretaries
Page, P. Stenographers, The.
Redgrove, P. Secretary, The.
Rouse. Her Retirement.
See also **Scribes; Stenographers**

Sectarianism
Davies, I. Capel Calvin.

Security
Brutus. Postscripts 2.
Colum, P. Old Woman of the Roads, The.
Cullen, C. For a Poet.
Diop, B. Viaticum.
Frost, R. Provide, Provide.
Grosholz. Eden.
Gunn, T. Hug, The.
Reassurance, The.
Hardy, J. Wet Feet.
Herrick. Bellman, The.
Kaufman, S. Security.
Koch, K. Locks.
Levertov. Christmas 1944.
Lyte. Abide With Me.
McGinley. Velvet Hand, The.
McGrath, T. Poem: "When I carry my little son in the cold."
Rous. I to the Hills Will Lift Mine Eyes.
Tonks. Story of a Hotel Room.
Ulku, A. Lullaby: "You are safe / You are lying in a hammock."

Seduction
Ayres. Invites His Nymph to His Cottage.
Bancks. Fragment, A: "In Cloe's chamber, she and I."
Behn, A. Disappointment, The.
Song: "I led my Silvia to a grove."
Burbidge. She Bewitched Me.
Campion, T. Blame Not My Cheekes.
It Fell on a Summer's [or Sommers] Day [or Daie].
Think'st thou to seduce me then.
Thrice Toss[e] These Oaken Ashes in the Air [or Ayre].
Carroll, K. Short Poem.
Cockburn, C. Vain Advice, The.
Coleridge, M. Moment, A.
Crowley, A. Dedicace.
'Dermée.' Silver Clasps.
Donne. Flea, The.
Egerton, S. Repulse to Alcander, The.
Gershon. At a Reception.
Gilmore, M. Eve-Song.
Hall-Evans. Seduction.
Harbach, O. She Didn't Say 'Yes.'
Hardy, T. Dark-Eyed Gentleman, The.
Herrick. Art above Nature, to Julia.
Delight in Disorder.
Upon Julia's Clothes.
Jacob, M. Rooster and the Pearl, The.
Jarman, M. Cavafy in Redondo.
Jones, M. Lass of the Hill, The.
Loesser. Baby, It's Cold Outside.
Longley, M. Sulpicia.
Lorde. On a Night of the Full Moon.
Lowell, A. Carrefour.
Lumsden, R. Tricks for the Barmaid.
Marvell. Fair Singer, The.
McDaniel, J. D.
Nesbit, E. Villeggiature.
Orton, B. Love Poem.

Porter, C. Let's Do It, Let's Fall in Love.
Purdy, J. Do You Wonder Why I Am Sleepy.
Raffalovich, M. A. Rose Leaves When the Rose Is Dead.
Ransom, J. Judith of Bethulia.
Rexroth, K. Floating.
Robinson, M. Phaon Awakes.
She Endeavours to Fascinate Him.
To the Eolian Harp.
Rohrer, M. Brooklyn Bridge.
Seyburn, P. Persuasion.
Shaw, A. Rear Window.
Smith, J. Solitary Canto to Chloris the Disdainful, A.
Sondheim. Remember?
Stevens, W. Plot Against the Giant, The.
Symons, A. Bianca.
Unknown. Kyrie, So Kyrie.
She Was Poor but She Was Honest.
Waly, Waly [Love Be Bonny].
Webb, M. Why?
Witt, S. Everlasting Quail.
Wyatt, S. Lover Showeth How He Is Forsaken of Such as He Sometime Enjoyed, The.

Seeds
Buckmaster. Seed.
Craveirinha. Seed Is in Me, The.
Curzon, D. Instructions to a Seed.
Finch, A. Sapphics for Patience.
Graham, J. Of Forced Sightes and Trusty Ferefulness.
Mitchell, S. Parable of the Sower, The.
Nemerov. Cabinet of Seeds Displayed, A.
Pasolini. Day of My Death, The.
Rakosi. Avocado Pit, The.
Ramanujan. Foundlings in the Yukon.
Reiter, T. Rights of Way.
Thomas, D. After the Funeral.
Vaughan, H. Seed Growing Secretly, The.
Wagoner, D. Nuthatch.

Self
Adamson. Home, The Spare Room, The.
Alegría. From the Bridge.
Alexander, E. Painting / (Frida Kahlo).
Ammons, A. R. Chasm.
So I Said I Am Ezra.
Arbuthnot. Know Yourself.
Ashbery. Paradoxes and Oxymorons.
These Lacustrine Cities.
Atwood. More and More.
Auden. Lullaby: "Din of work is subdued, The."
Baca. Like an Animal.
Baraka. Agony, An. As Now.
Funk Lore.
Poem Some People Will Have to Understand, A.
Barbauld. Life.
Baudelaire. Fuses I and II.
Bell, M. Self and the Mulberry, The.
Benedikt. Thoughts.
Blackburn, P. At the Well.
Blaser. Universe Is Part of Ourselves, The.
Blight. Down from the Country.
Bogan, L. Man Alone.
Bonar. Be True [or Be True Thyself].
Bronk. Plainest Narrative, The.
Brontë, E. Stanzas: "Often rebuked, yet always back returning."
Brooks, G. My Dreams, My Works Must Wait Till after Hell.
Sundays of Satin-Legs Smith, The.
Browning, R. House.
Césaire, A. Lagoonal Calendar.
Cataldi. 13 November 1983.
Ceravolo. Grow.
Cervantes. Freeway 280.
Clark, T. Poem: "Tiny new emotions, The."
Clifton, L. Why some people be mad at me sometimes.
Coleridge, M. Other Side of a Mirror, The.
Shadow.
True to Myself Am I, and False to All.
Coleridge, S. Phantom.
Conoley. Sky Drank In, The.
Cooley. Brother Body.
Coolidge, C. Glance in White Space.

Copus, J. Sea-Polyp, The.
Creeley. Edge, The.
Form of Women, A.
Pool, The.
Self-Portrait.
Wife, The.
Cronin, J. Motho Ke Motho Ka Batho Babang (A Person Is a Person Because of Other People).
Cummings, E. Maggie and Milly and Molly and May.
Curtis, T. Spirit of the Place, The.
Davidson, M. Dream Dream, The.
Davis, T. Desire 1.
Day, J. Moving Object.
Dickey, R. Leaving Eden.
Dickinson, E. Aurora.
Disch. Agreement of Predicate Pronouns, The.
Dransfield. Self-analysis.
Duncan, R. Close.
Roots and Branches.
Songs of an Other.
Eberhart, R. Gnat on My Paper.
Elizabeth I. On Monsieur's Departure.
Elmslie, K. Squatter in the Foreground.
Gallagher, T. Black Silk.
Sudden Journey.
García Lorca. Great Sadness, The.
Gibson, W. Advice to Travelers.
Ginsberg, A. End, The.
Gonzalez, R. Calling the White Donkey.
Greenwell, D. Scherzo, A.
Griffiths, S. Getting It Wrong, Again.
Ha Jin. Past, The.
Habington. Cogitabo Pro Peccato Meo.
Hall, J. Proverb, XXX.
Hardy, J. Difference, The.
Harryman. Magic (or Rousseau).
My Story.
Hayden, R. Names.
Herbert, G. Jordan (2).
Herrick. On Himselfe.
Holub. Immanuel Kant.
Hopkins, G. Candle Indoors, The.
I Wake and Feel the Fell of Dark, Not Day.
My Own Heart Let Me More Have Pity On.
Housman, A. Oh, When I Was In Love.
Howard, R. After 65.
Hughes, F. Bird.
Laszlo.
Hughes, L. Cross.
Jackson, L. Dimensions.
Jacobs, H. On extending the olive branch to my own self.
Jarrell. Woman at the Washington Zoo, The.
Jones, E. Study in Blue.
Kaufman, B. Grandfather Was Queer, Too.
Kay, J. Somebody Else.
Keats. Ode on Indolence.
Klee. Poem.
Knight, E. Welcome Back, Mr. Knight: Love of My Life.
Knott. Death.
Sonnet: "Way the world is not, The."
Koch, K. Alive for an Instant.
Girl and Baby Florist Sidewalk Pram Nineteen Seventy Something.
Larkin, P. Counting.
Self's the Man.
Lawrence, D. Eloi, Eloi, Lama Sabachthani?
I Am in a Novel.
Wild Common, The.
Leapor. Epistle of Deborah Dough, The.
Mira's Will.
Lee-Hamilton. Ipsissimus.
Levertov. In Mind.
Levine, M. Work Song.
Levine, P. Baby Villon.
Limburg, J. Inner Bloke.
Lindley, D. Cryptogram, The.
Locklin. Stranger, The.
Lothamer. Allen.
Lovelace, R. Song: "In mine one [or own] monument I lie [or lye]."
Macpherson, J. Lost Soul, A.
Mandela. I Have Tried Hard.

Martinez, D. Kinescope.
Mathias, R. Testament.
McAdams, J. Leaving the Old Gods.
McCarthy, T. Mr. Nabokov's Memory.
McClure, M. Hymn to Saint Geryon.
Menken. Infelix.
  Myself.
Merrill, J. Syrinx.
Merwin, W. S. For the Anniversary of My
  Death.
Momaday. Delight Song of Tsoai-Talee, The.
Nathan, L. Hole.
Nemerov. Salt Garden, The.
Nye, N. Whole Self, The.
O'Hara, F. To the Harbormaster.
Olson, C. As the Dead Prey upon Us.
Owen, W. Wild with All Regrets.
Paquet. In a Plantation.
Patterson, G. Autobiography of a Black Man.
Peacock, M. Spell, The.
Piatt, S. Doubt, A.
Plath. Nick and the Candlestick.
Pound, E. De Aegypto.
Raine, K. Invocation of Death.
Rakosi. Lord, What is Man?
Ramanujan. Hindu to His Body, A.
  Self-Portrait.
Ray, H. Self-Mastery.
Rees-Jones. I Know Exactly the Sort of Woman
  I'd Like to Fall in Love With.
Reese, L. Renunciation.
  To Life.
Rich, A. Delta.
  Integrity.
  Trying to Talk with a Man.
  Upper Broadway.
Rodgers, C. Group Therapy.
Roethke. Renewal, The.
Rossetti, C. Aloof.
  Verse II.
  Verse III.
Roy, L. Ride, The.
Rukeyser, M. Then I Saw What the Calling
  Was.
Ryan, M. Your Own Image.
Schultz, P. I'm Not Complaining.
Senghor. Kaya-Magan, The.
Sexton. Self in 1958.
Shelley, P. Sonnet: Political Greatness.
Simic. My Shoes.
Slessor. To Myself.
Soupault. Life-Saving Medal.
St. John, P. Carnival.
Stein, G. I Am Rose.
Stern, G. Diary.
Stevens, W. Idiom of the Hero.
  Man on the Dump, The.
  On the Adequacy of Landscape.
  Tea at the Palaz of Hoon.
Strand. Night, The Porch, The.
Su, A. I Can't Become a Buddhist.
Swirszczynska. I Talk to My Body.
Teasdale. "I Am Not Yours."
Thomas, D. I, in My Intricate Image.
Thomas, E. Lights Out.
Thoreau. I Am a Parcel of Vain Strivings Tied.
  Music.
Tuckerman, F. Sonnets: First Series.
Urdang. Portrait.
Very. Thy Better Self.
Wakoski. My Trouble.
Walcott. Hotel Normandie Pool, The.
Wallace-Crabbe. Abhorring a Vacuum.
Whitman, W. Ah Poverties, Wincings, and
  Sulky Retreats.
  Are You the New Person Drawn toward Me?
  As I Lay with My Head in Your Lap Camerado.
  Hand-Mirror, A.
  Here the Frailest Leaves of Me.
  Heroes.
  Hub of the Universe, The.
  I Saw in Louisiana a Live-Oak Growing.
  One's-Self I Sing.
  Song of Myself.
  Swiftly Arose.
  That Shadow My Likeness.

Woman Waits for Me, A.
Would You Hear of an Old-Time [or Old-
  Fashioned] Sea fight?
Whittemore, R. Clamming.
Wilbur. Leaving.
Williams, W. Danse Russe.
Winchilsea. On Myself.
Woods, J. Looking Both Ways Before Crossing.
Wright, D. On Himself.
Wyatt, S. Promise, A.
Yeats. Dialogue of Self and Soul, A.

Self-Deceit
Bruchac. Prayer: "Let my words."
Lawrence, J. Foolin' Myself.
MacNeice. Mixer, The.
Rich, A. Power.
Smith, S. Infelice.
Snodgrass, W. Locked House, A.
Tinturin, P. Foolin' Myself.
Whittier. Changeling, The.
  Haschish, The.

Self-Doubt
Aiken, C. Dear Uncle Stranger.
Doolittle, H. Centaur Song.
Glück, L. Mutable Earth.
Herbert, G. Love (3).
Jeffers, R. Love the Wild Swan.
Koch, K. Stones of Time, The.
Rich, A. Dialogue.
  Roofwalker, The.
Symonds. What Cannot Be.
Szymborska. In Praise of Self-Deprecation.
Tallmountain. Indian Blood.
Walcott. Codicil.
Wright, C. Laguna Blues.
Wylie. Malediction Upon Myself.

Self-Knowledge
Ahlert, F. I Don't Know Why (I Just Do).
Aiken, C. Dear Uncle Stranger.
Amadiume. Mistress of My Own Being.
Ammons, A. R. Chasm.
  Reflective.
  So I Said I Am Ezra.
Anderson, S. American Spring Song.
Arrillaga. Like Raquel.
Behn, A. Angellica's Lament.
Berrigan, A. Bloodletting.
Berry, J. One.
Conn. Under the Ice.
Creeley. Awakening, The.
Cummings, E. Maggie and Milly and Molly
  and May.
Derricotte. Blackbottom.
Di Prima. Loba as Eve.
Duncan, R. After a Long Illness.
Gibran. Madman (Prologue), The.
Ginsberg, A. Sather Gate Illumination.
Harjo, J. Autobiography.
  I Give You Back.
Hogan, L. Truth Is, The.
Jordan, J. Poem About My Rights.
Kenyon, J. Here.
Knott. At the Crossroads.
Larkin, P. Reasons for Attendance.
MacCaig. Summer Farm.
Macpherson, J. Lost Soul, A.
Manyarrows. Today We Will Not Be Invisible
  nor Silent.
Moolten, D. Madame Butterfly.
Nilsson, H. My Least Skirtable Deficiency.
Nye, N. Whole Self, The.
Olson, C. In Cold Hell, in Thicket.
  Newly Discovered "Homeric" Hymn, A.
Oppen. Confession.
  Myself I Sing.
  Product.
Owen, W. Show, The.
Peabody, J. After Music.
Qunta, C. Know, The.
Raffalovich, M. A. Sonnet 120.
Ramanujan. Self-Portrait.
Ransom, J. Amphibious Crocodile.
Repetto. 6th Grade—Our Lady of Pompeii.
Rich, A. August.
  Stranger, The.
Roethke. Open House.

Stafford, W. Story That Could Be True, A.
Stern, G. For Song.
Stevens, W. Of Modern Poetry.
  Tea at the Palaz of Hoon.
Strand. Night, The Porch, The.
Timrod. Dreams.
Toomer. Prayer.
Turk, R. I Don't Know Why (I Just Do).
Very. Lost, The.
Villalongo. In the Good Old U. S. A.
Wright, C. Self-Portrait.
Wylie. Let No Charitable Hope.
  Malediction Upon Myself.
Young, A. Fifty-Fifty.

Self-Pity
Cahn, S. I Should Care.
Hodgins. Self-Pity.
Lawrence, D. Self-Pity.
Mesmer, S. What Becomes Us.
Ossip, K. Nature of Things, The.
Schuyler, J. Self-Pity Is a Kind of Lying, Too.
Sharma, P. Performance Test.
Stordahl, A. I Should Care.
Tichborne [or Tichbourne]. Tichborne's Elegy.
Westmorland. Shamed by the Creature.
Weston, P. I Should Care.
Wylie. Malediction Upon Myself.

Self-Reliance
Brontë, E. Stanzas: "Often rebuked, yet always
  back returning."
Carroll, K. Something Easy for Ultra Black
  nationalists.
Ceravolo. Data.
Chipasula, S. I'm My Own Mother, Now.
Clifton, L. She Lived.
Cofer, J. What the Gypsy Said to Her Children.
Conkling, G. I Will Not Give Thee All My
  Heart.
Cunningham, N. Giving.
Dove, R. Canary.
Housman, A. Laws of God, the Laws of Man,
  The.
Jordan, N. Be You.
'Marnia. I Must be Able to Protect You.
Melville, H. In a Garret.
Mora. La Migra.
Rich, A. Song: "You're wondering if I'm
  lonely."
Rose. Naayawva Taawi.
Whalen. Further Notice.

Self-Restraint
Carmichael, H. Nearness of You, The.
Housman, A. Because I liked you better.
Lefroy. Palaestral Study, A.
Waller, T. et al. Ain't Misbehavin'
  Keepin' Out of Mischief Now.
Washington, N. Nearness of You, The.

Self-Righteousness
Burns, R. Holy Willie's Prayer.
Wylie. Malediction Upon Myself.

Selfishness
Ammons, A. R. Coming Right Up.
Bruner. Selfishness.
Cary, P. Legend of the Northland, A.
Cook, E. Mouse and the Cake, The.
Dancer. Variety, The.
Komunyakaa. Seven Deadly Sins.
Lawrence, D. Intimates.
North, C. Few Facts about Me, A.
Swift, J. To Stella.
Wesley, C. On Worldly Prelates.
Williams, J. Shadows.

Semele
Kizer, C. Semele Recycled.

Senegal
Davis, T. Double Take at Relais de L'Espadon.
Dixon, M. Tour Guide: La Maison des
  Esclaves.

Senility
Levertov. Old Adam, The.
Paulin. Anastasia McLaughlin.
Tatarunis, P. I Have Two Sons and the One I
  Love Best Is Robert.

Sennacherib, King of Assyria
Byron, G. Destruction of Sennacherib, The.

Senses
Apollinaire. Bonds.
Cary, A. In Bonds.
Ceravolo. Grow.
Coolidge, C. Disturbing the Sallies Forth.
Davidson, D. Redivivus.
Davidson, M. Feeling Type and His Friends, The.
Eady. April.
Garrett, E. Ribes rubrum.
Griffin, J. Venerating Senses Save Us.
Kendall, M. Philanthropist and the Jelly-fish, The.
Meynell, A. To the Body.
Nichols, G. Black.
White.
O'Connor, P. Raspberry in the Pudding, The.
O'Neill, M. My Fingers.
Padel. On the Line.
Peacock, M. Desire.
Rafferty, P. 66°7' N/22°17' W.
Roethke. Prayer: "If I must of my Senses lose."
Schuyler, J. Freely Espousing.
Thomas, D. When All My Five and Country Senses See.

Sensitivity
Campbell, J. Try a Little Tenderness.
Levertov. O Taste and See.
Nemerov. View from an Attic Window, The.
Owen, W. Insensibility.

Sensuality
Africa-Bolasco. Sauna 2.
Aguilar-Cariño. For the Lover.
Gabi.
Akiwumi, V. Unconditionals #3.
Balce, N. Pizza and Pretense.
Baudelaire. Snake that Dances, The.
Ben-Lev, D. Sensualist Speaks on Faith, A.
Bethel, M. Reggae Prophecy.
Broumas, O. Oregon Landscape with Lost Lover.
Cummings, E. Since feeling is first.
Dawes, K. Some Tentative Definitions 7.
Drieu la Rochelle. Roundness.
Georgiou, E. Intimate Mixture.
Gregg. Official Love Story.
Hacker, M. Canzone: "Consider the three functions of the tongue."
Harwood, G. Carnal Knowledge 2.
Hass, R. Now Winter Nights.
Hine. Under the Hill.
Hopkins, G. Epithalamion: "Hark, hearer, hear what I do; lend a thought now, make believe."
Khalvati. On Reading Rumi.
Lefroy. Idler Listening to Socrates Discussing Philosophy with His Boy-Friends, An.
Levertov. Eros at Temple Stream.
Lili'u-o-ka-lani. Sanoe.
Lim-Wilson. Beginning of Things, The.
Marshall, J. Months of Love, The.
Martínez, V. New World, The.
Merwin, W. S. West Wall.
Olds, S. Ecstasy.
Pound, E. Alba.
Encounter, The.
Rollings. Dirty Dreams and God Smiling.
Steele, N. Diminutive.
Ungria, R. Sui Veneris / The Poet of No Return.
Wakoski. Belly Dancer.
Whitman, W. From Pent-up Aching Rivers.
To the Garden the World.
Yeats. Chosen.

Separation
Adams, J. There's Nae Luck about the House.
Alarcon, F. Frontera / Border.
Alkalay-Gut. Transportation.
Allingham. Across the Sea.
Amichai [or Amikhai]. Quick And Bitter.
Arnold, M. Forsaken Merman, The.
Ashbery. Rivers and Mountains.
Atwood. Postcard.
Aytoun [or Ayton], R. Valediction.
Baraka. Agony, An. As Now.
Beckett, S. Cascando.
Beer, P. Faithful Wife, The.
Berryman. He Resigns.

Black, S. Rilke's Letter from Rome.
To a War Correspondent.
Blue Cloud. Old Man's Lazy, The.
Boland, E. Ready for Flight.
Boyle, K. Thunderstorm in South Dakota.
Bradstreet, A. Another.
Browning, R. Last Ride Together, The.
Song: "Moth's kiss, first, The!"
Waring.
Brownstein. Last Spell Cast, The.
Bryan, M. To My Brother.
Burns, R. Highland Harry Back Again.
Highland Mary.
Silver Tassie, The.
Song: "O my love's [or luve's or love is or luve is] like a red, red rose."
Burnshaw. Strange.
Byron, G. Epistle to Augusta.
Fare Thee Well.
When We Two Parted.
Carew, T. Excuse of Absence, An.
To Her in Absence; a Ship.
Cartwright, W. Valediction: "Bid me not go where neither suns nor showers [show'rs]."
Cary, P. Jacob.
Castillo, S. Primos.
Chang, D. Foreign Ways.
Cofer, J. What the Gypsy Said to Her Children.
Cohen, M. Evensong.
Cole, T. Lago Maggiore.
Coleridge, M. We Never Said Farewell.
Copus, J. Back Seat of My Mother's Car, The.
Cornford, F. Parting in Wartime.
Cory, D. Miss You.
Creedon. Litany.
Creeley. America.
Ballad of the Despairing Husband.
Dixon, M. Place, Places.
Donne. Computation, The.
Valediction: Forbidding Mourning, A.
Dowson. Exile.
Duncan, R. Passage Over Water.
Eliot, T. Portrait of a Lady.
Elliot, J. Flowers of the Forest, The.
Elytis. Aegean Melancholy.
Emerson, R. Unity.
Fearing. Love, 20c the First Quarter Mile.
Ferlinghetti, L. Third World Calling.
"Field." After Soufrière.
Forché. As Children Together.
García. I Ain't Going to Hurry No More.
Garnett, R. Dealing Scraps.
Garrett, E. Anatomy of Departure.
Love's Parallel.
Ginsberg, A. Message.
Glück, L. Hesitate to Call.
Horse.
Graves, R. Full Moon.
Grigson. Above the High.
Guest, B. Santa Fe Trail.
Guevara, M. Long Distance.
Hacker, M. Going Back to the River.
Rondeau after a Transatlantic Telephone Call.
Villanelle: "Every day our bodies separate."
Hadas, R. Red Hat, The.
Hannah, S. Your Street Again.
Hardy, T. After the Visit.
At Castle Boterel.
In a Cathedral City.
In Death Divided.
On the Departure Platform.
Walk, The.
Harms. From Now On.
Hazo. Silence Spoken Here.
Henry VIII, King of England. To His Lady.
Hewett, D. You Gave Me Hyacinths First a Year Ago.
Hine. Apart from You.
Horton, G. Division of an Estate.
Housman, A. Because I liked you better.
Hughes, L. So Long.
Hull, L. Midnight Reports.
Jackson, L. City Seems, A.
James, E. Sunnyland.
Jarman, M. Supremes, The.
Johnson, J. Sence You Went Away.

Jones, R. Times Like This.
Katrovas. Black English.
Sky.
Keats. Song of the Indian Maid.
Kendrick, D. Alone for a Week.
Killeen, G. Tristia.
Kinnell. Vow, The.
Kizer, C. Race Relations.
Semele Recycled.
Knight, E. Upon Your Leaving.
Komunyakaa. Tu Do Street.
Kumin, M. Woodchucks.
Kunitz, S. After the Last Dynasty.
Lakides. Armed Forces.
Landor, W. Separation.
Levertov. Divorcing.
Lilley. You Have to Strike Back.
Llewellyn, K. Finished.
Lomax, M. Gulf.
Kith.
Lovelace, R. To Lucasta, [on] Going beyond the Seas.
To Lucasta, [on] Going to the War[re]s.
Marvell. Definition of Love, The.
Mastin. From the Telephone.
McGinley. Midcentury Love Letter.
Merwin, W. S. Rain Travel.
Separation.
When You Go Away.
Mew. In Nunhead Cemetery.
Meynell, A. After a Parting.
Thoughts in Separation.
Monro. Terrible Door, The.
Moore, T. Journey Onwards, The.
Mudrooroo Narogin. Hide and Seek.
Mura. Letters from Poston Relocation Camp (1942–45).
Nilsson, H. On Inheriting Departure.
Okita. Notes for a Poem on Being Asian American.
Olds, S. On The Subway.
Olson, C. Newly Discovered "Homeric" Hymn, A.
Olstein, L. We Still Have Basketball, Sara.
Orfalea, G. Wave.
Padel. On the Line.
Tell Me About It.
Paschen. 12 East Scott Street.
Between the Acts.
Philips, K. Lucasia, Rosania and Orinda Parting at a Fountain, July 1663.
Orinda to Lucasia.
Plath. Parliament Hill Fields.
Rival, The.
Pope, A. Epistle to Miss [or Miss Teresa] Blount, on Her Leaving the Town after the Coronation.
Pound, E. River-Merchant's Wife: A Letter, The.
Prince, F. For Fugitives.
Radnóti. Letter to My Wife.
Ranaivo. Song of a Young Girl.
Ransom, J. Spectral Lovers.
Two in August.
Reverdy. Adieu.
Rich, A. Splittings.
Ridler. At Parting.
Before Sleep.
Robinson, M. Bids Farewell to Lesbos.
Determines to Follow Phaon.
Phaon Forsakes Her.
Reproaches Phaon.
Rodriguez, L. Always Running.
Romero, L. If Marilyn Monroe.
Rosner. Souvenirs.
Rossetti, C. Remember [Me].
Rossetti, D. Blessed Damozel, The.
Rukeyser, M. Meeting, The.
Safie, D. Danger, Men in Trees.
Samaras, N. Aubade: Macedonia.
Translation.
Sangster, M. Forgiven.
Senghor. You Held the Black Face.
Shapiro, K. Haircut.
V-Letter.
Sholl. Dawn.

Outside the Depot.
Snodgrass, W. Locked House, A.
Spender, S. Song: "Stranger, you who hide my love."
St. John, D. Homage to Robert Johnson.
Strand. Marriage, The.
Strong, L. Brewer's Man, The.
Tennyson, A. Fatima.
Thicknesse. Siena.
Thomas, E. Like the Touch of Rain.
Thompson, P. Adown the Heights of Ages.
Tuckerman, F. "Last night I dreamed we parted once again."
Unknown. Far Away.
Western Wind.
Wife's Lament, The.
Van Doren. Ancient Couple on Lu Mountain, The.
Vaughan, H. Retreat[e], The.
Voigt. At the Movie: Virginia, 1956.
Volkman. Daffodils.
Wang Shih-chieng. After Snow, Longing for Elder Brother Hsi-ch'iao.
Waniek. Star-Fix.
Whitman, R. Laughing Gas.
Whitman, W. Good-Bye, My Fancy!
Williams, B. Night Flute, The.
Williams, H. Song, A: "No riches from his scanty store."
Willis, N. Confessional, The.
Winchilsea. Letter to Daphnis, A.
Winner, R. Segregated Railway Diner—1946.
Winters, Y. At the San Francisco Airport.
Wordsworth, W. Complaint, A.
Tradition of Oker Hill in Darley Dale, Derbyshire, A.
Wright, C. Dead Color.
March Journal.
Wyatt, S. Farewell: "What should I say."
Yosano. Channel Boat, The.
Young, K. Letters from the North Star.
Zangwill. Sundered.
Zisquit. Word before the Last about Loss, A.
Zolynas. Love in the Classroom.
See also Absence; Isolation

September
Bridges, R. Garden in September, The.
Coleridge, M. September.
Dubin, A. September in the Rain.
Greenaway. Three Little Girls.
Gutteridge. In September 1939.
Hausman. September City.
Housman, A. Tell Me Not Here [It Needs Not Saying].
Jackson, H. September [Days Are Here].
Kasischke. My Heart.
Kinnell. Blackberry Eating.
Kinsella, T. Another September.
Lawrence, D. Bavarian Gentians.
Nelson, J. If You Knew September.
Ormond. In September.
Pastan. September.
Ray, H. September.
Roethke. Carnations.
Taylor, J. Libra, September.
Warren, H. September in the Rain.

Sequoia Trees
Reader. When Paul Bunyan Was Ill.
Simpson, L. Redwoods, The.

Serenity
Hayden, R. Monet's "Waterlilies."
Hopkins, G. She Schools the Flighty Pupils of Her Eyes.
Kipling, R. If—.
Ortiz. Serenity in Stones, The.
Very. Cottage, The.
Winchilsea. Enquiry after Peace. A Fragment.

Sermons
Andrews, N. Notes for a Sermon on the Mount.
Carnevali. Sermon.

Servants
Bishop, E. Cootchie.
Brooks, G. Bronzeville Woman in a Red Hat.
Brown, S. Scotty Has His Say.
Cave. Written by Desire of a Lady, on an

Angry, Petulant Kitchen-Maid.
Clare, J. My Mary.
Cumbo. Domestics.
Cuney. No Images.
De la Mare. Buttons.
Dransfield. War of the Roses, The.
Duffy, C. Warming Her Pearls.
Eliot, T. Aunt Helen.
Evans, M. When in Rome.
Ginsberg, A. Please Master.
Herbert, J. Irish Scullery Maid, The.
Herrick. Upon Prue [or Prew], His Maid.
Howe, F. Scattered Light.
Hughes, L. Madam and Her Madam.
Madam's Past History.
Kipling, R. Servant When He Reigneth, A.
Maclaurin. Elegy: "Nor Hammond's love nor Shenstone's was sincere."
Munby. Serving Maid, The.
Parker, D. Maid-Servant at the Inn, The.
Ríos, A. Nani.
Sigourney. Erin's Daughter.
Slessor. Full Orchestra.
Swift, J. Mary the Cook-Maid's Letter to Dr. Sheridan.
To Their Excellencies the Lords Justices of Ireland, the Humble Petition of Frances Harris, Who Must Starve, and Die a Maid if It Miscarries.
Taylor, E. Written by the Barrow Side, Where She Was Sent to Wash Linen.
Trethewey, N. Domestic Work, 1937.
Turner, F. On the Pains of Translating Miklós Radnóti.
Unknown. My Sodger Laddie.
Vazirani, R. Dream of the Evil Servant.
Wilbur. Summer Morning, A.
Williams, S. Letters from a New England Negro.
Winchilsea. Reformation.
Yuson. Andy Warhol Speaks to His Two Filipino Maids.

Sestina (form)
Bishop, E. Sestina: "September rain falls on the house."
France, L. Blues for Bird.
Gioia. My Confessional Sestina.
Gosse. Sestina: "In fair Provence, the land of lute and rose."
Hecht, A. Sestina d'Inverno.
Jacobsen, J. Limbo Dancer, The.
Justice, D. Here in Katmandu.
Nims, J. Tide Turning.
Pound, E. Sestina: Altaforte.
Ríos, A. Nani.
Shapcott, T. Sestina with Refrain.
Swinburne. Sestina: "I saw my soul at rest upon a day."
Walsh, C. Quintina of Crosses, A.
Webb, P. Imperfect Sestina.
Williams, M. Shrinking Lonesome Sestina, The.

Seven Deadly Sins
Dunbar, W. Dance of the Sevin Deidly Synnis, The.

Severn River, England
Evans, S. Seven Fiddlers, The.

Sewall, Samuel
Hecht, A. Samuel Sewall.

Sewers
Powell, D. A. My Father and Me Making Dresses: Together.
See also Sanitary Engineering and Sanitary Engineers

Sewing
Acosta. My Mother Pieced Quilts.
Alvarez, J. Naming the Fabrics.
Bishop, E. House Guest.
Crystal. Embroidery.
Dean, D. K. Stitches.
Dunbar-Nelson. I Sit and Sew.
Hall, H. Listening Macaws, The.
Seams.
Khalvati. Needlework.
Kim, A. Sewing Woman.
Lilley. Sewing Lesson, The.

Maguire, S. Invisible Mender, The.
Mar, L. My Mother, Who Came from China, Where She Never Saw Snow.
Peirce. Quilts.
Taylor, E. Huswifery.
Unknown. Delia Very Angry.
Ward, J. Comfort-Maker.
See also **Seamstresses; Tailoring and Tailors**

Sex
Adcock, F. Against Coupling.
Happy Ending.
Adisa. Discover Me.
Ager, M. Glad Rag Doll.
Ai. Before You Leave.
New Crops for a Free Man.
Akst, K. What a Perfect Combination.
Alexander, P. Well-Known Elizabethan Double Entendre, A.
Algarin. Rosa.
Amichai [or Amikhai]. Quick And Bitter.
Ammons, A. R. Their Sex Life.
"Antler." What Every Boy Knows.
Arnold, C. Disembodied Voices of Women, The.
Asquith. Sunday Afternoons.
Automedon. Gymnastics Teacher, The.
Barber, W. Gay Poet, The.
Barrax. Adagio.
Behn, A. Disappointment, The.
Beresford. Courtship, The.
Berger, J. Getting to Know Her.
Berlin. You'd Be Surprised.
Biespiel, D. Tower.
Bishop, E. Exchanging Hats.
Vague Poem.
Blake, W. Desire and Jealousy.
Long John Brown & Little Mary Bell.
Visions of the Daughters of Albion.
Bond, S. Tuesday Night Affair.
Bowman, C. Demographics.
Bromige. Logical Positivist, The.
Broumas, O. Beauty and the Beast.
Sometimes, as a Child.
Brown, E. Tragic Hero.
Burke, C. Motor Oil Queen.
Burns, R. Fornicator. A New Song, The.
Patriarch, The.
Wat ye what my Minnie did.
Cable, G. Criole Candjo.
Caesar. What a Perfect Combination.
Campbell, S. Legacy.
Carbone, L. Flight from the Marriage Bed.
Carew, T. On the Marriage of T. K. and C. C.: The Morning Stormy.
Rapture, A.
Carruth, H. Capper Kaplinski at the North Side Cue Club.
Cartwright, W. No Platonic [or Platonique] Love.
Cendrars. Great Fetishes, The.
Cervantes. On the Poet Coming of Age.
Chavez, L. After the Prom.
Child, A. Squeeze.
Chin, J. Why He Had to Go.
Chrystos. I Bought a New Red.
I Suck.
You Know I Like to Be.
Chubb, R. Song of My Soul.
Ciardi. Censorship.
Claman, E. Show Biz Parties.
Cleary, B. Chicken & Sex.
Clifton, H. Monsoon Girl.
Cofer, J. How to Get a Baby.
Life of an Echo, The.
Coleman, W. African Sleeping Sickness.
At the Record Hop.
Breast Examination.
Mastectomy.
Congreve. Pious Selinda [or Celinda].
Conway, J. Hangover.
Modern English.
Cooper, J. Circle, a Square, a Triangle and a Ripple of Water, A.
Cornish, S. Generations 1.
Cortez, J. So Long.
Suppression.

Coultas, B.   Dr. Wasserman.
Creeley.   Way, The.
Crowley, A.   Ballad of Passive Paederasty, A.
  Dedicace.
  Go into the Highways and Hedges, and Compel
    Them to Come In.
  Rondels.
Crozier, L.   Poem for Sigmund.
Cummings, E.   May I Feel Said He.
Dali.   Great Masturbator, The.
Daumal.   Persephone That Is to Say Double
  Issue.
Davidman.   Night-Piece.
Davies, S.   Faith (wench) I cannot court thy
  sprightly eyes.
Davis, W.   Spider.
Dawes, K.   Some Tentative Definitions 7.
Delgado, J.   Two Timer.
Deutsch.   Solitude.
Dickey, J.   Sheep Child, The.
Donaldson, W.   Makin' Whoopee.
Dorcey.   Sea Flower.
Doty, M.   Days of 1981.
Dougherty, D.   Glad Rag Doll.
Dove, R.   Adolescence—II.
Dowson.   Non Sum Qualis Eram Bonae sub
  Regno Cynarae.
Drayton.   To His Coy Love, a Canzonet.
Duffy, C.   Oppenheim's Cup and Saucer.
Duhamel.   Kinky.
Duncan, R.   I Am a Most Fleshly Man.
Dunn, S.   Man Who Closed Shop, The.
Edson, R.   Conjugal.
Elliott, A.   Angel.
  Here Today.
  Love Poem, The.
Ellis, T.   Kiss in the Dark, A.
Elmslie, K.   One Night Stand.
Ennis.   Alice of Daphne, 1799.
Estep, M.   I Have to Go Now.
Evans, R.   Femininity.
Ewart.   Office Friendships.
Fanning, R.   In the Barn.
Fell, A.   And Again.
Fields, D.   Fine Romance, A.
Flanders, M.   Have Some Madeira, M'dear?
Flatman.   Appeal to Cats in the Business of
  Love, An.
Foley, M.   Middle Manager in Paradise, The.
Forbes, D.   Politics of Envy.
Forché.   Taking Off My Clothes.
France, L.   Body Language.
  Eater of Wives, The.
  In Kind.
  My Muse, the Whore.
Fusselman, A.   Puffy Jacket.
Gallagher, T.   Sea Inside the Sea.
Gardinier.   Where Blind Sorrow Is Taught to
  See.
Garshman, B.   Keys.
Gerstler.   BZZZZZZZ.
Ginsberg, A.   Change: *Kyoto-Tokyo Express*,
  The.
  End, The.
  Kaddish.
  Please Master.
  Pull My Daisy.
Giorno.   Pornographic Poem.
Glück, L.   Edge, The.
  Labor Day.
  Mock Orange.
  Wound, The.
Glatt.   One Night With a Stranger at 30.
Godfrey.   Bath.
Gogarty.   On First Looking into Krafft-Ebing's
  Psychopathosexualis [*or* Psychopathia
  Sexualis].
Goldbarth.   World of Expectations, The.
Goodman, M.   February Ice Years.
  New Comers.
Graves, R.   Quiet Glades of Eden, The.
  Thieves, The.
Greenhalgh, C.   Big No-No, The.
  My Funny Valentine.
Griffin, P.   To His Importunate Mistress.
Groarke, V.   Shale.

Gunn, T.   Carnal Knowledge.
Hacker, M.   Wagers.
Hammial.   Jane.
Handy, W.   Yellow Dog Blues.
Hannan, M.   Seq.
Hardy, J.   Difference, The.
Harper, M.   Elvin's Blues.
Harris, D.   What we have lost.
Harris, J.   Balance.
Harwood, G.   Carnal Knowledge.
Hass, R.   Privilege of Being.
Heaney, S.   Rite of Spring.
Hecht, A.   End of the Weekend, The.
Heffernan, M.   Message, The.
Helwig.   Words from Hell.
Hemphill.   Where Seed Falls.
Herrick.   Epithalamy to Sir Thomas Southwell
  and His Lady, An.
  Good-Night, or Blessing, The.
  Poet Loves a Mistress, but Not to Marry, The.
  To Anthea.
  To Electra.
Holland, W.   Christopher Street 1979.
Hope, A.   Fafnir.
  Gateway, The.
  Imperial Adam.
  Lingam and the Yoni, The.
  Lot and His Daughters I.
Hope, M.   Bare Floors.
  Only Days.
Horovitz, F.   Night-Piece.
Hudgins.   Versification of a Passage from
  Penthouse.
Huelsenbeck, R.   "We Hardly."
Jarrell.   In Nature There Is Neither Right nor
  Left nor Wrong.
Johnson, G.   I Want to Die While You Love Me.
Jones, R.   Shakti.
Jong.   Colder.
Jonson, B.   To Pertinax Cob.
Kahn, G.   Makin' Whoopee.
Kalmar *et al.*   What a Perfect Combination.
Kantaris.   Airing the Chapel.
Kasischke.   Fatima.
  Pall.
Kennelly.   Bread.
Kenney.   In April.
Kern, J.   Fine Romance, A.
Kinnell.   After Making Love We Hear
  Footsteps.
  When One Has Lived a Long Time Alone.
Kirstein.   Double Date.
Klein, M.   Scenes for an Elegy.
Koestenbaum, P.   Sonnet 37: "I'd decided I
  initiate most."
Kombem.   Another Moment.
Kumin, M.   After Love.
Lane, P.   If.
Laux.   China.
Lawrence, D.   Love On the Farm.
Lee, W.   Sex Has a Way.
Levertov.   Ache of Marriage, The.
Lim-Wilson.   Beginning of Things, The.
Liu, T.   Ikon.
Livingston, J.   Femininity.
Loesser.   Take Back Your Mink.
Loftis, N.   Brief Encounter.
Lomax.   Gruoch.
Lovelace, R.   On Sanazar's being honoured with
  six hundred Duckets by the Clarissimi of
  Venice, for composing an Elegiack Hexastick
  of The City. A Satyre.
  To Amarantha, That She Would Dishevel[l] Her
  Hair[e].
Lowry, M.   Volcano Is Dark, The.
Lumsden, R.   Then.
Lyons, S.   Loving Along Western Rivers.
Mackenzie, K.   Fool, The.
  Ginger-flowers.
  Searchlights.
MacLeish.   You Also, Gaius Valerius Catullus.
Major, C.   Inside Diameter.
  On Trying to Imagine the Kiwi Pregnant.
"Malley."   Boult to Marina.
Martin, C.   Satyr, Cunnilinguent: To Herman
  Melville.

Victoria's Secret.
Masters, E.   Margaret Fuller Slack.
Mateo.   There Is No Word for Sex in Taglog.
Mayer, B.   First Turn to Me.
McCarriston.   Castle in Lynn, A.
McHugh, H.   Coming.
McLain, P.   Willing.
McNaughton.   Balls.
Meinke.   Helen.
Mesmer, S.   Lonely Tylenol.
  My Life in Yonago.
Middleton, C.   Adelaide's Dream.
Millay, E.   I, Being Born A Woman.
Miller, E.   She Is Flat on Her Back.
Montagu, L.   Between Your Sheets.
  Receipt to Cure [*or* for] the Vapours, A.
Montague, J.   Tracks.
Moore, H.   First Time: 1950.
  Green Place, A.
Moore, T.   Did Not.
Moulds, J.   When Bad Angels Love Women.
Murray, J.   Epithalamium, An.
Muske, C.   Our Kitty.
Nagai, M.   Histories of Bodies.
Nashe [*or* Nash].   Choise of Valentines, The.
Nazario, A.   Melt Me.
Neely, L.   Eight Ways of Looking at Pussy.
Neruda.   Sexual Water.
Nichols, G.   Configurations.
O'Grady, J.   Poem for the Womb.
O'Hara, F.   Ave Maria.
  Cornkind.
  Easter.
  Mary Desti's Ass.
Obejas, A.   Dancing in Paradise.
Olds, S.   Ecstasy.
  Knowing, The.
  New Mother.
  Sex without Love.
  Sisters of Sexual Treasure, The.
  Wellspring, The.
Padgett, R.   First Drift.
  Tell Us, Josephine.
Paquet.   Basket Case.
Parker, D.   Foxfire.
Parker, P.   For Willyce.
Pasolini.   Sex, Consolation for Misery.
Pasternak, B.   Hops.
Patchen.   Figure Motioned with Its Mangled
  Hand Toward the Wall Behind It, The.
Peacock, M.   Have You Ever Faked an Orgasm?
  Lullaby: "Big as a down duvet the night."
  My God, Why Are You Crying?
  Return, The.
  Surge, The.
Peskett.   Window Dressing.
Phillips, C.   Kill, The.
Picabia.   Spermal Chimney.
Piercy.   Crabs.
  Implications of One Plus One.
  It Arrives Suddenly and Carries Us Off as
    Usual.
Pilkington, L.   Fair and Softly Goes Far or, The
  Wary Physician.
Polito.   Overheard in the Love Hotel.
Pollard, C.   Heavy-Petting Zoo, The.
Porter, C.   They Couldn't Compare to You.
  Too Darn Hot.
Porter, P.   Sex and the Over Forties.
Pound, E.   Ballatetta.
  Temperaments, The.
Randall, D.   Ballygrand Widow.
Razaf, A.   My Man o' War.
Redel, V.   Singing to Tony Bennett's Cock.
Redmond.   My Tongue Paints a Path.
Reid, D.   Between Aphorisms.
Rich, A.   Two Songs.
  Waking in the Dark.
Rickword.   Moon-talk.
Rochester, J.   Ramble in St. James's Park, A.
  Song of a Young Lady to Her Ancient Lover, A.
Roethke.   Four for Sir John Davies.
Rohrer, M.   After the Wedding Party.
Rosemurgy, C.   Hard Put.
Rothenberg, J.   Song of Quavering, A.
Rouse.   Lilies of the Field.

Spunk Talking.
Uni-Gym, The.
Ruby, H. What a Perfect Combination.
Rukeyser, M. Rondel: "Now that I am fifty-six."
Rumens. Double Bed.
Ryan, G. In the Purple Bar.
Ryan, M. This Is a Poem for the Dead.
Sanchez, S. Haiku.
 Prelude to Nothing.
Schneiders, J. Weight.
Schwerner. Tablet V.
Scott, J. Changing Room.
Sedley. On the Happy Corydon and Phyllis.
Selman, R. Exodus.
Sexton. From the Garden.
 Us.
Shapiro, K. First Time, The.
Sherrill, J. Woodstock.
Shinder. One Secret That Has Carried, The.
Sholl. Midnight Vapor Light Breakdown.
Shurin. City of Men.
 Forward or Back.
Shuttle. Old Man, The.
Simmons, J. Honeymoon, The.
 Rogation Day: Portrush.
Simon, M. Blue Movies.
Sirowitz, H. Equality.
Slessor. Sleep.
Smith, A. Giving Thanks.
Smith, P. Dylan, Two Days.
Smith, S. Conviction IV.
Smukler. Days Inn.
 Trash.
Solari, R. Currents.
Sondheim. I Never Do Anything Twice (Madam's Song).
Soutar. Tryst [or Trysting Place], The.
Spivack, K. Love U.S.A.
St. John, D. My Friend.
Stainer. Honeycomb, The.
Swenson, M. Riding the 'A.'
Symons, A. Bianca.
Tana, P. Marvelous Beast.
Tate, J. Coming Down Cleveland Avenue.
Taylor, J. Epigram: "Lusty wench as nimble as an eel, A."
 Virgo, August.
Tayson, R. Phone Sex.
Tolson, M. Lena Lovelace.
Tonks. Story of a Hotel Room.
Torres, E. Of My Nipple Ring Halos.
Trocchi, A. For John Donne: Master Metaphysical.
Ullman. Memo.
Ungria, R. Sui Veneris / The Poet of No Return.
Unknown. Full and True Account of a Dreaded Fire, that Lately Broke out in the Pope's Breeches, A.
 Hogyn.
 I Have a New Garden.
 I Sometimes Think.
 Knight and Shepherd's Daughter, The.
 Lady T-rc----l's Ring.
 Maid's Complaint for Want of a Dil Doul, The.
 No Balls at All.
 One Writing against His Prick.
 Poetess's Bouts-Rimés, The.
 Prayer yo Hymen.
Valentine, J. Sex.
Villiers. Cabin-Boy, The.
Villon. Ballad of Villon and Fat Madge, The.
Wagoner, D. Loons Mating.
Wakoski. Reading *Bonjour, Tristesse* at the Florence Crittenden Home for Unwed Mothers.
Wallace, R. Facts of Life, The.
Walwicz. Wonderful.
Waters, M. Hoochie Coochie.
Wayman. Wayman in Love.
Weatherly, T. Blues for Franks Wooten.
Weaver, M. Message on Cape Cod, The.
Weiners. Act #2.
Wharton, E. Terminus.
Whitman, R. Bubba Esther, 1888.
Whitman, W. Dalliance of the Eagles, The.
 From Pent-up Aching Rivers.

Woman Waits for Me, A.
Wickham. Fired Pot, The.
Wicks, S. Rain Dance.
Wieners. Acceptance.
 Doll.
 Loneliness, The.
 Long Nook.
 Suck, The.
 To H.
 What Happened?
Wilbur. Late Aubade, A.
Williams, J. Little Tumescence, A.
Williams, P. In the Dark.
Williams, S. My Man o' War.
Wilmer, S. Mess Boy, The.
Wilson, S. Recreational Mathematics.
Wood, V. Saturday Night.
Wright, K. Underneath the Archers *or* What's All This about Walter's Willy?
Wunderlich, M. Given in Person Only.
 Trick, The.
Yellen, J. Glad Rag Doll.
Young, A. Conjugal Visits.
Zwicky. Jack Frost.
See also **Erotic Love; Homosexuality and Homosexuals**

Sexism
Barbauld. Rights of Woman, The.
Browning, E. Lord Walter's Wife.
Chudleigh. To the Ladies.
Egerton, S. Emulation, The.
Erdrich. Fooling God.
Fife, C. Dear Webster.
Griffin, S. Answer to a Man's Question, "What Can I Do About Women's Liberation?", An.
Hawoldar. You Have Touched My Skin.
Holland, J. Baize Queens.
Hope, A. Advice to Young Ladies.
Huxley, A. Second Philosopher's Song.
Jackson, L. Divestment of Beauty.
Jiles. Paper Matches.
Jordan, J. Poem About My Rights.
Kendall, M. Woman's Future.
Koch, K. Sleeping with Women.
Millay, E. I, Being Born a Woman.
Noel, L. Understanding Each Other.
Piercy. Barbie Doll.
Rich, A. Snapshots of a Daughter-in-Law.
Shange. It's Not So Good to Be Born a Girl / Sometimes.
Song. Lost Sister.
Thomas, E. On Sir J——S——Saying in a Sarcastic Manner, My Books Would Make Me Mad; an Ode.
Unknown. Poem for Jacqueline Hill.
Wakoski. Poet Recognizing the Echo of the Voice, A.
Watson, M. Female of the Species.
Wickham. Affinity, The.
Winchilsea. Introduction, The: "Did I, my lines intend for public[k] view."
Zephaniah. Sun, The.

Sexton, Anne
Dugan, A. Drunken Memories of Anne Sexton.
Sexton. January 1st.

Sexual Abuse
Anderson, A. Suicide Year, The.
Barnett, R. Anorexic, The.
Bernstein, C. Profaning the Dead.
Bevington, L. One More Bruised Heart!
Chin, J. Why a Boy.
Clifton, L. Shapeshifter Poems.
 To my Friend, Jerina.
Dove, A. Crab.
Frost, R. Subverted Flower, The.
Hai-Jew, S. Father's Belt.
Larkin, J. Origins.
Lee, A. Confession.
McCarriston. Castle in Lynn, A.
Shiffrin, N. Anna's Dream.
Strange. Crazy Girl, The.

Sexual Exploitation
Cooper, D. Being Aware.
García, D. Clog of Her Body, The.
Kunitz, S. She Wept, She Railed.

Maroon, B. Nude Woman Spotted in Cappuccino Cup as Advertising Dollar Co-opts Another Life.
Swenson, M. James Bond Movie, The.

Sexuality
Adcock, F. Against Coupling.
Amadiume. Bloody Masculinity.
Ameen. Monologue of a Dying Beast.
 Sonnet No. 22.
Arnold, C. XX.
Ayres, R. Corporeal.
Barnett, R. Anorexic, The.
Barot, R. Three Amoretti.
Belieu. Rondeau at the Train Stop.
Brainard, J. I Remember.
Brant, B. Her Name Is Helen.
Broumas, O. Rapunzel.
Buchanan, G. Theatrical Venus.
Campbell, S. Legacy.
Carbó, N. In Tagalog Ibon Means Bird.
Casey, M. LZ Gator Body Collector, The.
Claman, E. Show Biz Parties.
Conoley. Beauty and the Beast.
de Aerenlund, C. Cuando el tecolote canta, el Indio muere.
Dobyns. Allegorical Matters.
Douglas, L. Two Loves.
Dove, R. After Reading *Mickey in the Night Kitchen* for the Third Time Before Bed.
Duhamel. Barbie's Molester.
Ellis, T. Atomic Bride.
 On Display.
Emanuel, L. Outside Room Six.
Ewart. Semantic Limerick According to Dr. Johnson's Dictionary (Edition of 1765), The.
 Semantic Limerick According to the Shorter Oxford English Dictionary (1933), The.
Fabian, C. Liturgy for Lilith.
 Qadesha (Sacred Whore).
Fanning, R. In the Barn.
Farewell. Quaerè.
Ferlinghetti, L. Dark Portrait, A.
Fox, S. Grandmother.
Garrett, E. Bachelors, The.
 Womanhood, The.
Gilonis, H. Song for Annie.
Gogarty. On First Looking into Krafft-Ebing's *Psychopathosexualis* [*or* Psychopathia Sexualis].
Graves, R. Cry Faugh!
Greenhalgh, C. Man in the Valley of Women, A.
Gunn, T. Courage, a Tale.
Holloway, G. Lovers, The.
Hoover, P. Baseball.
Hope, A. Flower Poem.
Hudgins. Rosie.
Joseph, A. Pure Pop.
Kariara. Leopard Lives in a Muu Tree, A.
Kasdorf. Eve's Striptease.
Katz, J. Falling.
Komunyakaa. Thorn Merchant's Mistress, The.
Larkin, P. Annus Mirabilis.
Laughlin, J. O Best of All Nights, Return and Return Again.
Laurencin, M. Present, The.
Levertov. Mutes, The.
Liddy. History.
Lima, F. Hand, The.
Liu, T. Echoes.
 Mama.
 Size of It, The.
Mabuza. Love Song, A.
MacKenzie, R. Category Mistakes in Biochemistry.
McElroy, C. In My Mother's Room.
McFadden, R. Contemplations of Mary.
Melville, H. After the Pleasure Party.
Nameroff, R. Elvis Presley.
Nepo. Oil of Her Hands, The.
Olds, S. Connoisseuse of Slugs, The.
Orlen. Androgyny.
Perillo. Skin.
Porter, C. I'm a Gigolo.
Raworth. Future Models May Have Infra-Red Sensors.

Rich, A. Dialogue.
Riley, P. E Questa Vita Un Lampo.
Robinson, M. Bower of Pleasure, The.
Rukeyser, M. Along History.
Schoenberger. Epithalamion.
Schuyler, J. Tom.
Schwartz, R. L. AIDS Education, Seventh Grade.
Shaw, A. Pornography.
Shepherd, R. West Willow.
Simms, C. First English Wildcat, The.
Simon, M. Boy Crazy.
Simpson, M. Homo Erectus, Cerne Abbas.
Soto. Trees that Change Our Lives.
St. John, D. Quote Me Wrong Again and I'll Slit the Throat of Your Pet Iguana.
Szporluk. Axiom of Maria.
Townsend, A. Night Watch in the Laboratory.
Tripp. Caroline Street, Cardiff.
Walden, G. Misguided Angels.
Whitman, W. As Adam Early in the Morning.
  Behold This Swarthy Face.
  From Pent-up Aching Rivers.
  Spontaneous Me.
  To the Garden the World.
Wilbur. Catch, The.
Wunderlich, M. Chapel of the Miraculous Medal.
Yeats. Whence Had They Come?

Shadows
Angelou. Life Doesn't Frighten Me.
Atkins. Dark Area.
Bateson. I Heard a Noise and Wishèd for a Sight.
Binyon. Winter Sunrise.
Butts, A. Skin.
Campion, T. Follow Thy Fair Sun[ne] [Unhappy Shadow].
Carpenter, W. Night Shadows.
Clifton, L. Death of Crazy Horse, The.
Coleridge, M. Shadow.
Corey, S. Complicated Shadows.
Crane, H. At Melville's Tomb.
  Garden Abstract.
Crapsey. Moon-Shadows.
Cuney. Death Bed, The.
Del Renzio. Can You Change a Shilling?
Donne. Lecture upon the Shadow, A.
Duchamp. Cast Shadows.
Empson. Legal Fiction.
"Field." Beloved, My Glory in Thee is Not Ceased.
Fitzgerald, E. 68.
Galassi. Argument.
Glück, L. Hawk's Shadow.
Greenlaw. Shape of Things, The.
Grimké, A. Tenebris.
Hayden, R. Broken Dark, The.
Heidbreder. Copycat.
Hewitt, J. Substance and Shadow.
Hollander, J. Sunday A.M. Not in Manhattan.
  Swan and Shadow.
Hubbell, P. Shadows.
Johnston, E. Mother's Love, A.
Landon. Farewell, The.
Laughlin, J. Step on His Head.
Lehman. Prophet's Lantern, The.
Levertov. Scenes from the Life of the Peppertrees.
Levin, P. Shadow Returns, The.
Long, H. Day and Night.
  In the Dark World.
Madhubuti. After Her Man Had Left Her for the Sixth Time That Year (An Uncommon Occurrence).
Maiden. Climbing.
Martinez, D. Nocturnes: "He closed the deal on the night. A real."
Merwin, W. S. Door, A.
  Last One, The.
Novakovich. Shadow.
Oswald, A. Ballad of a Shadow.
Piatt, J. My Shadow's Stature.
Pinkerton, H. On Dorothea Lange's Photograph "Migrant Mother" (1936).
Plarr. Shadows.

Shurin. Blue Shade.
Siddal. Silent Wood, A.
Stevens, W. Rabbit Is King of the Ghosts, A.
Stevenson, R. Armies in the Fire.
  My Shadow.
Symonds. Lux Est Umbra Dei.
Symons, A. La Mélinite: Moulin-Rouge.
Troupe. Sense of Coolness, A.
Walcott. Season of Phantasmal Peace, The.
Wilde, O. Harlot's House, The.
Williams, J. Shadows.
Williamson, G. Up in the Air.
Yau. Radiant Silhouette I.
Yeats. New Faces, The.

Shaftesbury, Anthony Ashley Cooper, 1st Earl of
Dryden, J. Absalom and Achitophel.
  Achitophel: The Earl of Shaftesbury.
  Shaftesbury.
  Zimri: "In the first rank of These did Zimri stand."
  Zimri: The Duke of Buckingham.

Shaka
Mtshali. Birth of Shaka, The.

Shakers (First Church of The Millennium)
Unknown. 'Tis the Gift to Be Simple.
  Walk Softly.

Shakespeare, William
Arnold, M. Shakespeare.
Auden. Miranda.
  Song of the Master and Boatswain.
Bogan, L. To an Artist, to Take Heart.
Bogardus. Narcissus to Echo.
Brettell. African Student.
Browning, R. Names, The.
Crane, H. To Shakespeare.
Edwards, T. To Shakespeare.
Highfill, M. Sea Breeze.
Holland, H. Upon the Lines and Life of the Famous Scenic Poet, Master William Shakespeare.
Jonson, B. To the Memory of My Beloved, the Author Mr [or Master] William Shakespeare [And What He Hath Left Us].
Keats. On Sitting Down to Read "King Lear" Once Again.
Kemble. To Shakespeare.
Lawrence, D. When I Read Shakespeare.
Like, J. Postmodern: A Definition.
Melville, H. Coming Storm, The.
Milton. On Shakespear[e].
Plutzik. Dream about Our Master, William Shakespeare, The.
Porter, C. Brush Up Your Shakespeare.
Ray, H. Shakespeare.
Robinson, E. Ben Jonson Entertains a Man from Stratford.
Schwartz, D. Dogs Are Shakespearean, Children Are Strangers.
Simmons, J. Stephano Remembers.

Shamans
Guevara, M. Tuesday Shaman.
Hufana, A. From the Raw.

Shame
Aleshire. Double, The.
Breton, N. Cradle Song: "Come, little babe."
Burns, R. Rantin Laddie, The.
Byron, G. When We Two Parted.
Cofer, J. They Never Grew Old.
Dharker. Purdah, 1.
Donne. Flea, The.
  Triple Fool, The.
Florsheim. Business in Germany.
Gloria. Assimilation.
Herrick. Shame, No Statist.
Heyen. To the Onlookers.
Hughes, L. I, Too.
Hughes, S. Got No Shame.
  Home on Palm.
Jenkins, P. Six Small Fires.
Justice, D. In Bertram's Garden.
Kahaney, P. Germany, 1981.
Kessler, S. Family Secrets.
Lucie-Smith. Lesson, The.
MacBeth [or Macbeth]. Worst Fear, The.
Macgoye. Letter to a Friend.

Merwin, W. S. Avoiding News by the River.
Mora. Cortez's Horse.
Nemerov. Fall Again, The.
Pegram, A. Mr. White Discoverer.
Po Chü-i. Bitter Cold, Living in the Village.
Ramanujan. At Forty.
Rosemurgy, C. Hard Put.
Rutsala. Shame.
Shepard, O. It's a Low Down Dirty Shame.
Smukler. Sign.
Tugend, A. Every Few Months.
Viscusi. Autobiography.
Wexler, E. Governess, The.
Wilbur. Shame.

Shannon (river), Ireland
Kennelly. Swimmer, The.

Shaped Poetry
Apollinaire. It's Raining.
Burford, W. Christmas Tree, A.
Charles, D. Concrete Cat.
Coffey. Headrock.
Cummings, E. R-P-O-P-H-E-S-S-A-G-R.
Dauenhauer. Tlingit Concrete Poem.
Herrick. Pillar of Fame, The.
Hollander, J. State of Nature, A.
  Swan and Shadow.
Hollander, R. You Too? Me Too—Why Not? Soda Pop.
Inman, P. XX.
Kumin, M. 400-Meter Freestyle.
Mayer, H. Oil.
Morgan, E. Message Clear.
Ranaldo, L. Five Weeks.
  HIS:STORY.
  Time Presses Me.
Solt. Forsythia.
  Lilac.
  Marriage.
  Moonshot Sonnet.
  Rain Down.
  Wild Crab.
Swenson, M. Women.
Unknown. Hang Up the Baby's Stocking!
Virgil. Grass Path Lasts.
Weiman. Andy-Diana DNA Letter.
Williams, E. Like Attracts Like.

Sharecroppers
Hughes, L. Share-Croppers.

Sharks
Ciardi. About the Teeth of Sharks.
MacCaig. Basking Shark.
Melville, H. Maldive Shark, The.
Pratt, E. Shark, The.
Sze. Great White Shark, The.
Wevill. Birth of a Shark, The.
Willard, N. Sand Shark.

Shaving
Blanco, R. Shaving.
Fisher, J. Life, A.
Unknown. Burma-Shave Roadside Signs.
Updike. Upon Shaving Off One's Beard.

Shaw, George Bernard
Beerbohm, M. Epitaph for G. B. Shaw.

Shaw, Robert Gould
Dunbar, P. Robert Gould Shaw.
Lowell, J. Memoriae Positum R. G. Shaw.
Lowell, R. For the Union Dead.
Moody, W. Ode in Time of Hesitation, An.
Ray, H. Robert G. Shaw.

Sheep
Atwood. November.
Baca. Mantanza to Welcome Spring.
Blake, W. Answer to the Parson, An.
Campbell, D. Ariel.
Clarke, G. Ram.
Davies, W. Child's Pet, A.
  Sheep.
Francis, R. Sheep.
Hall, D. Black Faced Sheep, The.
Hoffenstein. Sheep.
Kelly, R. Tune.
Meynell, A. Shepherdress, The.
Mother Goose. Little Bo-Peep.
Scott, D. Flanking Sheep in Mosedale.
Sedulius Scottus. Death of a Ram.
See also **Lambs**

Sheepshearing and Sheepshearers
Unknown. Banks of the Condamine, The.
Sheets
Chavez, L. Clean Sheets.
Coultas, B. Dr. Wasserman.
Martínez, V. Into the Next One.
Warren-Moore. All-Night Issue, The.
Shelley, Percy Bysshe
Browning, R. Memorabilia.
Corso. I Held a Shelley Manuscript.
Hardy, T. Shelley's Skylark.
Hood, T. False Poets and True.
Hunt, L. To Percy Shelley.
 To the Same.
Monroe, A. To W. S. M.
Simic. Shelley.
Shells
"Field." Onycha.
Gascoyne. Cage, The.
Hartley, M. Wingaersheek Beach.
Lovelace, R. Snail [or Snayl], The.
Martinez, D. Altruism.
McDonald, E. Itherness.
Moore, M. Paper Nautilus, The.
Ray, H. Enchanted Shell, The.
Scott, G. Frutta di Mare.
Stephens, J. Shell, The.
Stickney, T. On Some Shells Found Inland.
Tennyson, A. Minnie and Winnie.
Unknown. She Sells Sea-shells.
Walpole, H. To Lady Anne Fitzpatrick, When
 about Five Years Old, with a Present of Shells,
 1772.
See also **Snails; Clams and Clamming; Oysters**
Shellshock
Owen, W. Chances, The.
 Conscious.
 Dulce et Decorum Est.
 Mental Cases.
Shenandoah River and Shenandoah Valley
Melville, H. Portent, The.
Shepherds and Shepherdesses
Barnes, W. Shep'erd Bwoy, The.
Barnfield [or Barnefield]. Affectionate
 Shepherd, The.
 Daphnis to Ganymede.
Behn, A. Disappointment, The.
Carew, T. Pastoral[l] Dialogue, A.
Clare, J. Shepherd Boy, The.
Clarke, P. Young Shepherd Bathing His Feet.
Crashaw. In the Holy Nativity of Our Lord
 God.
 Shepherds' Hymn, The.
Davis, D. Christmas Poem, A.
De la Mare. Nod.
Dodge, M. Shepherd John.
Drayton. Roundelay Between Two
 Shepherds, A.
Drummond, W. All Changeth.
"Ephelia." On a Bashful Shepherd.
Erskine, J. Shepherd Speaks, The.
Fitts. Ya Se Van Los Pastores.
Greene, R. Description of the Shepherd and His
 Wife, The.
Hall, D. Black Faced Sheep, The.
Hennell. Shepherd and Shepherdess.
Hughes, L. Shepherd's Song at Christmas.
Jones, M. Lass of the Hill, The.
Kirkup. Shepherd's Tale, The.
Lodge, T. Shepherd's Sorrow, Being Disdained
 in Love, The.
MacNeice. Nuts in May.
Marlowe. Passionate Shepherd To His Love,
 The.
Marvell. Clorinda and Damon.
Meigs, M. Shepherd Left Behind, The.
Mew. Old Shepherd's Prayer.
Meynell, A. Shepherdress, The.
Mother Goose. Little Bo-Peep.
Nicholson, N. Shepherds' Carol.
Pope, A. Sylvan Delights.
Ralegh, S. Nymph's [or Nimphs] Reply to the
 Shepherd [or Sheepheard], The.
Schwartz, D. Passionate Shepherd to His Love,

The.
Tate, N. While Shepherds Watched [Their
 Flocks by Night].
Thiele, C. Tom Farley.
Unknown. Sheepheards Description of Love,
 The.
Vaughan, H. Shepherds [or Shepheards], The.
Wordsworth, W. Michael [A Pastoral Poem].
Yeats. Song of the Happy Shepherd, The.
Young, A. Shepherd's Hut, The.
Sheppard, W. H.
Johnson, M. Dedicated to Dr. W. H. Sheppard.
Sheridan, Philip Henry
Melville, H. Sheridan at Cedar Creek.
Read, T. Sheridan's Ride.
Sherman, Cindy
Hannan, M. Life Model.
Sherman, William Tecumseh, Union general
Melville, H. Iris.
Work. Marching through Georgia.
Shields
Fogarty, L. Shields Strong, Nulla Nullas Alive.
Robinson, E. Beauty as a Shield.
Unknown. Riddles.
Shiloh, Battle of (1862)
Melville, H. Shiloh [A Requiem].
Ships and Shipbuilding
Bishop, E. Casabianca.
 Large Bad Picture.
Blight. Into the Ark.
Bontemps. Nocturne of the Wharves.
Bridges, R. Passer-by, A.
Brooks, S. Middle Passage.
Carew, T. To Her in Absence; a Ship.
Causley. HMS *Glory.*
Cavendish, M. Sea Similized to Meadows and
 Pastures: the Mariners, to Shepherds: the Mast,
 to a May-Pole: the Fish, to Beasts, The.
Cervantes. Refugee Ship.
Clare, S. On the Good Ship Lollipop.
Clifton, L. Slaveship.
Clough. Qua Cursum Ventus.
Corcoran. In the Red Book.
Davidson, L. Charnel Ship, The.
Dawe, G. Question of Covenants, A.
Donaldson, W. When My Ship Comes In.
Dunbar, P. Ships That Pass in the Night.
Emerson, R. Letters.
Flecker. Old Ships, The.
Gershwin. My Ship.
Hart, L. Ship Without a Sail, A.
Hemans. Wreck, The.
Jackson, H. Emigravit.
Johnson, L. Troopship, The.
Kahn, G. When My Ship Comes In.
Kipling, R. Derelict, The.
King, The.
Larkin, P. North Ship, The.
Lawrence, D. Argonauts, The.
 Ship of Death, The.
Lear, E. Jumblies, The.
Longfellow, H. Building of the Ship, The.
 Cumberland, The.
Lorde. Fishing the White Water.
Lowell, A. Camouflaged Troop-Ship.
Masefield. Cargoes.
 Sea Fever.
Mayer, B. Port, The.
McCaig. Poem: "There is a wailing baby under
 every stone and you walk."
McGrath, C. Shrimp Boats, Biloxi.
Melville, H. *Temeraire,* The.
 Berg, The.
 Man-of-War Hawk, The.
Ní Chuilleanáin. Second Voyage, The.
Nicholls, J. Mary Celeste.
Ologoudou. Liberty.
Pickard, T. What Maks Makems.
Rakosi. Unswerving Marine.
Ransom, J. Good Ships.
Rodgers, R. Ship Without a Sail, A.
Southey, R. Ship, The.
Stevenson, R. Rain.
 Where Go the Boats?
Stewart, D. Garden of Ships, The.

Thomas, R. Navigation.
Unknown. Golden Vanity, The.
 Blow, Boys, Blow [or Blow, Bullies, Blow].
Volkman. Shipwreck Poem.
Weill, K. My Ship.
Whiting, R. On the Good Ship Lollipop.
Whitman, W. Aboard at a Ship's Helm.
 After the Sea-Ship.
 Dismantled Ship, The.
 Patrolling Barnegat.
 Ship Starting, The.
 Song for All Seas, All Ships.
Whittier. To a Cape Ann Schooner.
Wordsworth, W. Sonnet: Where Lies the Land.
 With Ships the Sea Was Sprinkled Far and Nigh.
See also **Boats and Boating; Freighters;**
 Tugboats; Yachts
Shipwrecks
Clark, T. Time.
Colvin, I. Flying Dutchman, The.
Cowper, W. Castaway, The.
 On the Loss of the *Royal George.*
Fordham. Shipwreck.
 Tribute to a Lost Steamer.
Fowler, W. Ship-broken Men Whom Stormy
 Seas Sore Toss.
Gilbert, S. Etiquette.
Gu Cheng. Ark.
Hardy, T. Convergence of the Twain, The.
Hemans. Wreck, The.
Henry. Verses.
Hollander, J. Last Words.
Hope, A. Wandering Islands, The.
Hopkins, G. Wreck of the Deutschland, The.
Kingsley, C. Three Fishers [Went Sailing], The.
Lee-Hamilton. Sunken Gold.
Lightfoot. Wreck of the Edmund Fitzgerald,
 The.
Long, J. Bermuda Triangle.
Longfellow, H. Wreck of the *Hesperus,* The.
Masefield. Posted.
McGrath, T. Offering.
Melville, H. Aeolian Harp, The.
 Berg, The.
 Haglets, The.
Menken. Ship That Went Down, The.
Moore, R. Shipwreck.
Reese, L. Indian Summer.
Rich, A. Diving into the Wreck.
Rossetti, D. White Ship, The.
Southey, R. Inchcape Rock, The.
Unknown. Golden Vanity, The.
 Sir Patrick Spens [or Spence].
Valéry. Crusoe.
Volkman. Shipwreck Poem.
Waller, E. Upon His Majesty's [or Majesties]
 Repairing of Paul's.
Watson, R. Midnight Harvest, A.
Whitman, W. To the Man-of-War Bird.
Whittier. Skipper Ireson's Ride.
Shirts
Agran, R. Wearing Dad's White Shirt
 Backwards.
Johnston, E. Last Sark, The.
Perillo. Ghost Shirt, The.
Pinsky. Shirt.
Sandburg, C. Shirt.
Shapcott, T. Blue Paisley Shirt, The.
Simic. Shirt.
Townsend, A. Shirt Collar, The.
Winter, M. Dux Bellorum.
Shiva
Jeffers, R. Shiva.
Shoemakers
Dekker, T. *et al.* O, the Month of May.
Dunbar, W. Amendis to the Telyouris and
 Sowtaris for the Turnament Maid on Thame,
 The.
Shoes and Shoemakers
Agard, J. New Shoes.
Ai. Blue Suede Shoes.
 Riot Act, April 29, 1992.
Barer, M. Very Soft Shoes.
Barnes, W. Grammer's Shoes.
Bendall, M. Need for Shoes, The.

Benedikt.   European Shoe, The.
Bernstein, C.   Loose Shoes.
Dunbar, W.   Amendis to the Telyouris and
  Sowtaris for the Turnament Maid on Thame,
  The.
Gallagher, T.   Monologue at the Chinook Bar
  and Grill.
Garcia, R.   Zapato, El.
Herford.   Limerick.
Herrick.   Sho[o]e Tying, The.
Hughes, L.   Bad Morning.
Kramer, L.   Shoemaker's Wife, The.
Lear, E.   Limericks, II (iii).
  O dear! How disgusting is life!
Lee, W.   Simple Like That.
Miles, J.   Sale.
Ormond.   At His Father's Grave.
Perreault, J.   Shoe.
Rodgers, M.   Very Soft Shoes.
Simic.   My Shoes.
Smith, W.   Said Dorothy Hughes to Helen
  Hocking.
Sutter.   Shoe Shop.
Toyama.   Red.
Unknown.   Limerick: "There was an archdeacon
  who said."
  Lost Shoe, The.
  My Darlings' Shoes.
Weaver, M.   Sub Shop Girl.
Wolfe, F.   Choosing Shoes.
Wylie.   Velvet Shoes.
See also **Galoshes**
Shoplifting and Shoplifters
Dauer.   Philip the Store Policeman.
Dougherty.   Long Coats with Deep Pockets.
Seaton, M.   Fear of Shoplifting.
Stanton, M.   Shoplifters.
Wormser.   Shoplifting.
Shopping and Shops
Atkins.   New Storefront.
Carson, C.   Dresden.
Clarke, G.   Second Hand Rose.
Clover, J.   Alas, That Is the Name of Our Town;
  I Have Been Concealing It All This Time.
Dauer.   Philip the Store Policeman.
Derricotte.   1994 Inventory.
Disch.   Rapist's Villanelle, The.
Dixon, M.   I Found a Million Dollar Baby (In a
  Five and Ten Cent Store).
Elledge.   Man I Love and I Shop at Jewel, The.
Evans, A.   Old Yellow Shop, The.
Field, R.   General Store.
Ginsberg, A.   Supermarket in California, A.
Guevara, M.   Doña Josefina Counsels Doña
  Concepción Before Entering Sears.
Hanley, J.   Second Hand Rose.
Hongo.   Winnings.
Jennings, E.   My Grandmother.
Johnson, J.   Unmarked Stop in Front of
  Westmond General Store, Westmond, Idaho.
Jones, M.   Soliloquy on an Empty Purse.
Joseph, A.   In the Bookstore.
Kooser.   In the Basement of the Goodwill Store.
MacNeice.   Christmas Shopping.
Matthews, W.   Mail Order Catalogs.
McIlroy, L.   Siesta.
Murray, G.   Shopping for Midnight.
Naranjo-Morse.   Tradition and Change.
Peacock, M.   How I Had to Act.
Piñero.   La Bodega Sold Dreams.
Pierson, J.   Thrift Shop Ladies.
Revard.   Christmas Shopping.
Rome, H.   Chain Store Daisy.
Rosenblatt, S.   Procession, The.
Suárez, V.   Song for the Sugar Cane.
Thompson, C.   Christmas Rush, The.
Tolson, M.   African China.
Shopping Malls
Disch.   Garage Sale as a Spiritual Exercise, The.
Gilmore, B.   Bow to Allah.
Shores
Abinader, E.   Pigeon Rock: Lebanon.
Addonizio.   China Camp, California.
Ammons, A. R.   Corsons Inlet.
  So I Said I Am Ezra.

Barnard, M.   Shoreline.
Barrington, J.   Villanelle VI.
Baxter, J.   Bay, The.
Bentley, N.   Iron Man of the Hoh.
Berryman.   Henry's Understanding.
Bishop, E.   Little Exercise.
Blight.   Landfall, The.
Browning, R.   Meeting At Night.
Campbell, W.   Morning on the Shore.
Cowley, H.   Blank Verse Written on the Sea
  Shore.
Cranch.   Pines and the Sea, The.
Croly.   Aestuary, An.
Emerson, R.   Sea-Shore.
Feinstein, E.   Coastline.
Frost, R.   Once by the Pacific.
Grosholz.   Outer Banks, The.
Hadas, R.   Sentimental Education.
Haines, J.   Nocturnal.
Harwood, G.   Clair de Lune.
Joyce, J.   On the Beach at Fontana.
Liu, T.   Wellfleet.
MacCaig.   Notations of Ten Summer Minutes.
Merwin, W. S.   Low Fields and Light.
Millay, E.   I shall go back.
Momaday.   Winter Holding off the Coast of
  North America.
Nims, J.   Tide Turning.
O'Daly, B.   Whale in the Web, The.
Oppen.   Book of Job and a Draft of a Poem to
  Praise the Paths of the Living, The.
  Penobscot.
Orfalea, G.   Jellyfish Eggs.
Rea, T.   Lugs Benedict on the Coast, 1934.
Revard.   "But Still in Israel's Paths They Shine."
Roethke.   Meditation at Oyster River.
Rose, P.   Anglo-Saxon Comedy.
Seed.   During War, the Timeless Air.
Singer, B.   Peterhead in May.
Smith, C.   On Being Cautioned against Walking
  on an Headland Overlooking the Sea, because
  It Was Frequented by a Lunatic.
  Written on the Sea Shore.—October, 1784.
Smith, S.   Kenless Strand, The.
Stevenson, R.   At the Seaside [or Sea-Side].
Swenson, M.   Morning at Point Dume.
Turner, C.   Seaside: In and Out of the Season,
  The.
Warn.   After Reading the Book of Splendor.
Webb, F.   End of the Picnic.
Whitman, W.   As I Ebb'd with the Ocean of
  Life.
  Patrolling Barnegat.
Whittier.   Burning Drift-Wood.
See also **Beaches**
Shorter, James A.
Heard, J.   Bishop James A. Shorter.
Show Business
Berlin.   There's No Business Like Show
  Business.
Claman, E.   Show Biz Parties.
Coward.   Why Must the Show Go On?
Porter, C.   Anything Goes.
Thribb.   In Memoriam Larry Parnes ("Mr Parnes
  Shillings and Pence").
See also **Acting and Actors; Motion Pictures;
  Theater and Theaters**
Shrews
Burns, R.   Kellyburnbraes.
Shrines
McCarthy, T.   Party Shrine.
Sanchez, S.   Haiku: "Your voice unwrapping."
Teasdale.   Shrine, The.
See also **Mausoleums; Monuments**
Shropshire, England
Housman, A.   On Wenlock Edge.
Shrouds
Brown, G.   Shroud.
Crapsey.   Song: "I make my shroud but no one
  knows."
De la Mare.   Snow.
Donne.   Funeral[l], The.
Siberia
Bienek.   Vorkuta.
Mangan, J.   Siberia.

Sibyl
Hopkins, G.   Spelt from Sibyl's Leaves.
Sicily
Lawrence, D.   Bare Almond-Trees.
Radcliffe, A.   Scene on the Northern Shore of
  Sicily.
  Sea-View, A.
Robinson, M.   Reaches Sicily.
Seward.   On Catania and Syracuse Swallowed
  Up by an Earthquake, from the Italian of
  Filicaja.
Sickness
Arnold, C.   My Love Is Sick.
Diaz-Duque.   Why Don't I?
Glück, L.   Time.
Hannah, S.   Symptoms.
Hannan, M.   Tom Passey's Child.
Richter, J.   Nothing but Bad News.
Smallpiece, A. M.   Written in Ill Health.
Townsend, A.   Institutional Blue.
Unknown, fr. Terezin Concentration Camp.
  Theresienstadt's Hospital.
Wildman, E.   Cure, The.
Wotton, S.   Hymn to my God in a night of my
  late Sicknesse, A.
Wunderlich, M.   Simplify Your Combination
  Therapy.
See also **Illness**
Siddons, Mrs. Sarah
Lamb, C.   As When a Child.
Sidmouth, Henry Addington, Viscount
Shelley, P.   Similes for Two Political Characters
  of 1819.
Sidney, Sir Philip
Herbert, E.   Epitaph on Sir Philip Sidney Lying
  in St Paul's without a Monument, to be
  Fastned upon the Church Door.
James I, King of England.   Epitaph on Sir Philip
  Sidney, An.
Jonson, B.   To Elizabeth, Countess of Rutland.
  To Penshurst.
Sierra Leone
Cheney-Coker.   On Being a Poet in Sierra
  Leone.
  Road to Exile Thinking of Vallejo, The.
Sierra Nevada Mountains
Jeffers, R.   Ascent to the Sierras.
Levine, P.   Sierra Kid.
Miller, J.   Sierras.
Rexroth, K.   Strength through Joy.
Siestas
Cofer, J.   Hour of the Siesta, The.
Coward.   Mad Dogs and Englishmen.
McIlroy, L.   Siesta.
Sight
Cary, P.   True Love.
Chang, E.   Near-Sightedness.
Creeley.   Statue, The.
  Window, The.
Gibson, W.   Sight.
Lowell, R.   Eye and Tooth.
Murray, G.   On Being Disabled by Light at
  Dawn in the Wilderness.
Traherne.   Preparative, The.
Whisenand.   Open Your Eyes.
Sign Language
Lloyd, M.   Simplest and the Hardest, The.
Smukler.   Sign.
Signorelli, Luca
Graham, J.   At Luca Signorelli's Resurrection of
  the Body.
Kimbrell, J.   True Descenders.
Silence
Ammons, A. R.   Unsaid.
Beddoes.   To Silence.
Berrigan, D.   But God is Silent / Psalm 114.
Bogan, L.   Train Tune.
Braithwaite.   Quiet Has a Hidden Sound.
Brecht, S.   Silence.
  Silence, 2.
Brett, L.   La Pathétique.
Browning, E.   Substitution.
Bynner.   Sigh, A.
Byron, G.   When We Two Parted.

Cage. Lecture on Nothing.
Codrescu. Poetry Paper.
Cofer, J. Fever.
Crapsey. Triad.
Creeley. Waiting.
Day Lewis. Two Songs.
De la Mare. Autumn.
  Faint Music.
  Listeners, The.
  Stranger, The.
Del Renzio. Can You Change a Shilling?
Dowson. O Mors! Quam Amara Est Memoria
  Tua Homini Pacem Habenti In Substantiis
  Suis.
Duncan, R. Sentinels, The.
Dunn, D. Modern Love.
Ebb, F. Quiet Thing, A.
Emerson, R. Merops.
Everwine. Distance.
Ferguson, G. Silent as Roses.
"Field." Onycha.
Gilbert, J. To See if Something Comes Next.
Gilmore, B. Gas Station Attendant.
Glück, L. Horse.
Graves, R. Nobody.
Gregg. What Is Kept.
Guiney. Reason for Silence, A.
Hadas, R. Three Silences.
Hall, D. Je Suis une Table.
Hannan, M. Tom Passey's Child.
Harwood, G. Andante.
Haskins, L. To Play Pianissimo.
Hazo. Silence Spoken Here.
Hitchcock. Song of Expectancy.
Holland, J. Wavelength.
Hood, T. Silence.
Huidobro. Midnight.
Johnson, L. Precept of Silence, The.
Jordan, J. Winter.
Kander, J. Quiet Thing, A.
King, H. Silence: A Sonnet.
Kinzie. Canicula.
Kloefkorn. Why the Stone Remains Silent.
Knott. Sonnet: "Way the world is not, The."
Lane, P. Wind Thoughts.
Larkin, P. Myxomatosis.
  Talking In Bed.
Lear, E. Limerick: "There was an Old Man who
  said, "Hush!"
Levertov. What Were They Like?
Longfellow, H. Curfew.
Lumsden, R. Then.
Marston, P. Speechless: Upon the Marriage of
  Two Deaf and Dumb Persons.
Martin, C. Speech Against Stone.
Masters, E. Silence.
Merritt, C. Lullaby: "Say to me: out there are
  only streets, and cars."
  Mute Swan, The.
Merwin, W. S. For the Anniversary of My
  Death.
  Utterance.
Mey. Quiet Days.
Meynell, A. To Silence.
  To the Beloved.
Moore, L. Eternal Landscape, The.
Moore, M. Silence.
Moore, T. Harp That Once through Tara's Halls,
  The.
Perry, N. Too Late.
Pilinszky, J. On the Wall of a KZ-Lager.
Pilling. She Lies Silent.
Piombino. Frozen Witness, The.
Poe. Sonnet—Silence.
Pratt, E. Silences.
Pritchard, N. Cloak, The.
Richards, E. Wise Old Owl, A.
Riley, J. Silence.
Rosenberg, L. Silence of Women, The.
Rossetti, C. Introspective.
Rutsala. Silence, The.
Rux, C. H. Suite Repose.
Sandburg, C. Aprons of Silence.
Sassoon. Elected Silence.
Scott, D. Skiddaw House.
Sepamla. Silence: 2.

Simpson, L. Silent Piano, The.
Smith, P. Finding His Fist.
Southerland. Recitation.
Stevens, W. Less and Less Human, O Savage
  Spirit.
Stevenson, R. Gardener, The.
Stickney, T. In the Past.
Szymborska. Unexpected Meeting.
Teasdale. Night Song at Amalfi.
  Those Who Love.
Thomas, L. Onion Bucket.
Thomas, R. Via Negativa.
Turnbull. Takings.
Turner, W. Silence.
Unknown. Get Up and Bar the Door.
  Raid of the Reidswire, The.
  Success.
Very. Silent, The.
Wain. Apology for Understatement.
Warren-Moore. All-Night Issue, The.
Whitman, W. When I Heard the Learn'd
  Astronomer.
Whittemore, R. Still Life.
Wicks, S. On Re-recording Mozart.
Williams, W. Silence.
Wojahn. Distance.
Wright, J. Sparrows in a Hillside Drift.
Wylie. Velvet Shoes.
Yeats. After Long Silence.
  Long-Legged Fly.

Silk
Herrick. Upon Julia's Clothes.
Horovitz, F. Loving You.
Martínez, V. Tesoro.
Pound, E. Garden, The.
Remoto. Black Silk Pajamas.
Shange. Elegance in the Extreme.

Silkworms
Stewart, D. Silkworms, The.

Silva, Antonio José da
Blumenthal, W. Da Silva Gives the Cue.

Silver
De la Mare. Silver.

Simhath Torah
Rosenfeld, M. Simchas Torah.

Similes
Reznikoff. Similes.
See also **Metaphor**

Simon of Cyrene
Cullen, C. Simon the Cyrenian Speaks.

Simplicity
Bloom, R. Give Me the Simple Life.
Brown, S. Feminine Intuition.
Campion, T. Jack and Joan.
Cavendish, M. Claspe, The.
Child, A. Wishes.
Collins, W. Ode to Simplicity.
Crowell, G. I Have Found Such Joy.
Dubin, A. Cup of Coffee, a Sandwich, and You.
Evans, R. Keep It Simple.
Hartman, M. Life's Made up of Little Things.
Herbert, G. Wreath, A.
Kendall, M. Lay of the Trilobite.
Livingston, J. Keep It Simple.
Meyer, J. Cup of Coffee, a Sandwich, and You.
Murry, A. Familiar Epistle, An.
Nash, O. Reflection on Ingenuity.
Oppen. Penobscot.
Ransom, J. Captain Carpenter.
Rose, B. Cup of Coffee, a Sandwich, and You.
Ruby, H. Give Me the Simple Life.
Unknown. 'Tis the Gift to Be Simple.
Whittemore, R. Clamming.
Wilbur. Baroque Wall-Fountain in the Villa
  Sciarra, A.
Wordsworth, W. Farmer of Tilsbury Vale, The.
Wright, J. Birds.

Sin
Behn, A. And Forgive Us Our Trespasses.
Berryman. Gislebertus' Eve.
Betjeman. Huxley Hall.
Bradstreet, A. Flesh and the Spirit, The.
Brooks, P. Christmas Everywhere.
Byron, G. Prayer of Nature, The.
Campion, T. View Mee, Lord.

Chesterton, G. Ballade D'une Grande Dame.
Congreve. Pious Selinda [*or* Celinda].
Copus, J. Masaccio's *Expulsion from Paradise*.
Coverdale. Let Go the Whore of Babylon.
Crashaw. But Men loved Darkness[e] Rather
  Than [*or* Then] Light.
Creeley. Kind of Act Of, The.
Cullen, C. For Daughters of Magdalen.
David, M. Sinner Kissed an Angel, A.
Donne. Flea, The.
  Licentious Person, A.
Drayton. To My Noble Friend Master William
  Browne: Of the Evil Time.
Dunbar, P. Distinction.
Gorey. Limerick: "To his club-footed child said
  Lord Stipple."
Gwynn, R. Snow White and the Seven Deadly
  Sins.
Hecht, A. Pig.
Herbert, G. Agony [*or* Agonie], The.
  Church-Lock and Key.
  Confession.
  Good Friday.
  Judgement.
  Love (3).
  Sin: "O that I could a sin once see!"
  Sin (1).
  Sin's Round.
  Storm, The.
Herrick. Bell-Man, The.
  To God: an Anthem, Sung in the Chapel at
  White-Hall, Before the King.
  To His Conscience.
Hine. Destruction of Sodom, The.
Hughes, L. Madam and the Minister.
Jeffers, R. Original Sin.
Jonson, B. Epode: "Not to know vice at all, and
  keep[e] true state."
Hymn[e] to God the Father, A.
  Of Life and Death.
Joseph, R. Sinner Kissed an Angel, A.
Kennedy, X. First Confession.
Kocan. AIDS, Among Other Things.
Komunyakaa. Seven Deadly Sins.
Larkin, P. High Windows.
Lee-Hamilton. Ipsissimus.
Lindsay, N. Unpardonable Sin, The.
Locke, A. Sin and Despair Have So Possess'd
  My Heart.
So Foul Is Sin and Loathsome in Thy Sight.
Lovelace, R. Mock Charon, A.
Lowell, R. Katherine's Dream.
Marvell. Coronet, The.
  Mower Against Gardens, The.
Meynell, A. Two Questions, The.
Moore, T. Argument, An.
  Did Not.
Nash, O. Ha! Original Sin!
  Inter-Office Memorandum.
  Portrait of the Artist as a Prematurely Old Man.
Nemerov. Historical Judas, The.
Philips, K. To the Queen of Inconstancy,
  Regina Collier, in Antwerp.
Pound, E. Canto XLV.
Quarles. On Dinah.
Rafferty, P. Passage.
Robinson, A. Scape-Goat, The.
Robinson, E. Children of the Night, The.
  Tavern, The.
Rodgers, W. Lent.
Rossetti, C. Ash Wednesday.
  World, The.
Sandburg, C. Washerwoman.
Sangster, M. At Sunset.
Saunders, R. Cinderella.
Scamell, B. Sin.
Scott, F. Sting of Death, The.
Southwell. Man's Civil[l] War[re].
  Sinnes Heavie Loade.
Stanley, T. Ode XV.
Tennyson, A. St. Simeon Stylites.
Thompson, F. To the Dead Cardinal of
  Westminster.
Thomson, J. Once in a Saintly Passion.
Unknown. Adam Lay Ybounden [*or* I-
  bounden].

Full and True Account of a Dreaded Fire, that Lately Broke out in the Pope's Breeches, A.
Gospel Train, The.
If I Could Shut the Gate against My Thoughts.
Psalm 58.
Seven Sins, The.
Undo!
Vaughan, H. Corruption.
  Idle Verse.
  Rainbow, The.
  Very. Robe, The.
  Serpent, The.
Walcott. Crusoe's Island.
Warren, R. Original Sin.
Westmorland. Man Leavens the Batch.
Wilcox, E. Mistakes.
Wilde, O. E Tenebris.
  Hélas!
See also **Original Sin; Seven Deadly Sins**

Singing and Singers
Abrahams, M. Rag Time Cowboy Joe.
Arlen, H. Sing, My Heart.
Auden. As I Walked Out One Evening.
Barber, D. Nocturne.
Barrax. Singer, The.
Barresi. Back-Up Singer, The.
Bauer, G. She Calms the Savage Beast with Her Aubade.
Berke. Dancing to the Track Singers at the Nightclub.
Berlin. Let Me Sing and I'm Happy.
Bernard, A. Praise Psalm of the City-Dweller.
Blanvillain, J. (All of a Sudden) My Heart Sings.
Bogan, L. M., Singing.
Bottoms. Homage to Lester Flatt.
Boyle, K. Complaint for M and M, A.
Brown, N. Singin' in the Rain.
Burns, R. Of A' the Airts [the Wind Can Blaw].
Campbell, J. I Am the Mountainy Singer.
Chasin. Joy Sonnet in a Random Universe.
Chesterton, G. Christmas Carol, A: "God rest you merry gentlemen."
Chipasula. Singing Drum, The.
Clarke, G. Rag Time Cowboy Joe.
Cohan. Down by the Erie Canal.
Cook, E. On Seeing a Bird-Catcher.
  Song of the Imprisoned Bird.
Coward. I'll See You Again.
Cox, N. Singing Alone.
Creeley. Air: "The Love of a Woman."
Damacion, K. Canciones.
Davis, T. Zoom (The Commodores).
Dawes, K. Trickster 4 (for Sister Patra).
Day Lewis. Conflict, The.
Di Prima. For the Dead Lecturer.
Dickey, J. Buckdancer's Choice.
Dickinson, E. "Hope" is the thing with feathers.
Dixon, M. Bye Bye Blackbird.
Dove, R. Canary.
Dunbar, P. Sympathy.
  When Malindy Sings.
Eady. Young Elvis.
Emerson, R. Saadi.
Esteves. Some People Are about Jam.
Etter. Singing in the Toyota.
Evans, M. And the Old Women Gathered.
Evasco, M. Dancing a Spell.
"Fane, V." Siren, The.
"Field." Fellowship.
  Fifty Quatrains.
  I sing thee with the stock-dove's throat.
  She is Singing to Thee, *Domine!*
Field, E. Callas.
Frost, R. Aim Was Song, The.
  Hill Wife, The.
  House Fear.
  Impulse, The.
  Loneliness.
  Oft-Repeated Dream, The.
  Oven Bird, The.
Galloway, T. Whiffenpoof Song.
Gibbons, O. Silver Swan, The.
Gilbert, C. Enclosure.
Goldbarth. People Are Dropping Out of Our Lives.

Gordon, M. I, Yi, Yi, Yi, Yi (I Like You Very Much).
Graham, D. Jesus Never Sleeps.
Graves, R. Love Without Hope.
Gray, J. Poem: "Geranium, houseleek, laid in oblong beds."
Gregg. Singers Change, The Music Goes On, The.
Guevara, M. Buddy Holly Poem, The.
Hamer. Allegiance.
Harris, P. Some Songs Women Sing.
Hart, L. Johnny One-Note.
Hattersley, G. Singing.
Heaney, S. Singer's House, The.
Hemans. To a Wandering Female Singer.
Henderson, D. Song of Devotion to the Forest.
Henderson, R. Bye Bye Blackbird.
Henson, L. I Am Singing the Cold Rain.
Herpin, H. (All of a Sudden) My Heart Sings.
Herrick. Upon Her Voice.
  Upon Julia's Voice.
Hirsch, E. Song: "This is a song for the speechless."
Holm, B. Blizzard.
Hughes, L. I, Too.
  Weary Blues, The.
Hughes, T. Owl's Song.
Hugo, V. Be Like the Bird.
Huidobro. Blind.
Hutchison, J. Joni Mitchell.
Jackson, A. Billie in Silk.
Jackson, R. Lady's Way.
Jeffers, L. Nina Simone.
Jenkins, N. Land of Song.
Johnson, J. Lift Every [or Ev'ry] Voice and Sing.
  O Black and Unknown Bards.
Jonson, B. And Must I Sing? What Subject Shall I Choose?
  Musical Strife; in a Pastoral Dialogue, The.
Joseph, A. On Sidewalks, on Streetcorners, as Girls.
Keats. Ode to a Nightingale.
Kinnell. Last Songs.
Kipling, R. In the Neolithic Age.
Koehler, T. Sing, My Heart.
Koethe. Songs of the Valley.
Lawrence, D. Piano.
Leader, M. Madrigal: "How the tenor warbles in April!"
Lee, L. I Ask My Mother to Sing.
Levis. Decrescendo.
Lewis, S. Rock-a-Bye Your Baby with a Dixie Melody.
Liu, T. Vox Angelica.
Livesay, D. Uninvited, The.
Loden. Tumbling Dice.
Lorde. Day They Eulogized Mahalia, The.
Love, B. Bryan Ferry.
MacDiarmid, H. Empty Vessel.
Marion, G. Ladies Who Sing with a Band, The.
Marvell. Fair Singer, The.
Matthews, W. Old Folsom Prison.
  Penalty for Bigamy Is Two Wives, The.
McCord, D. Blessed Lord, What It Is to Be Young.
McGrath, B. Concert Choir.
McPherson, S. Ability to Make a Face Like a Spider While Singing Blues: Junior Wells, The.
Meynell, A. Singers to Come.
Miller, V. Dirge in Jazz Time.
Mitcham. On the Otis Redding Bridge.
Mkangelwa. Women Sing, The.
Moore, L. Bluesman's Blues, A.
  Spectacular.
Moore, T. Echo.
Morley, T. Sing We and Chant It.
Mother Goose. Tommy Tucker.
Mugo, M. G. Where are Those Songs?
Muir, L. Rag Time Cowboy Joe.
Neal, L. Lady's Days.
Nelson, H. Peepers.
O'Hara, F. Day Lady Died, The.
O'Shaughnessy, A. Ode: "We are the music-makers."
Parkes, B. For Adelaide.

Perry, S. Toadfish.
Pope, A. Sylvan Delights.
Porter, C. It's De-Lovely.
  Red, Hot and Blue.
Pound, E. Cino.
Ravenscroft, T. Sing we now merily.
Redel, V. Singing to Tony Bennett's Cock.
Robinson, A. Personality.
  Search for Apollo, A.
Rohrer, M. Short History of Illumination, A.
Rome, H. (All of a Sudden) My Heart Sings.
Rose. Throat Song: The Whirling Earth.
Ross, L. James Brown.
Rossetti, C. Birthday, A.
Rushin. Black Back-Ups, The.
Sandburg, C. Splinter.
Sassoon. Everyone Sang.
Schwartz, J. Rock-a-Bye Your Baby with a Dixie Melody.
Sheehan, M. My Father's Singing.
Shelley, P. To Jane: The keen stars were twinkling.
Shirley, A. Hours Musicians Keep, The.
Skinner, J. Tullochgorum.
Skloot. Everly Brothers, The.
Smith, I. Two Girls Singing.
Smith, S. Singing Cat, The.
Speakes. Patsy Cline.
Spires. Apology.
  Interrogations of the Sparrow.
Stanley, T. Celia Singing.
Stein, G. I Am Rose.
Stephens, P. God Shed His Grace.
Stevens, W. Idea of Order at Key West, The.
Tagore. Song That I Came to Sing, The.
Thomas, D. In My Craft or Sullen Art.
Thompson, D. P. Blues at 1.
Trinidad. Answer Song.
Tu Fu. Coming Home Late at Night.
Unknown. Silver Swan, The.
Unknown, fr. Terezin Concentration Camp. Birdsong.
Very. Song, The: "When I would sing of crooked streams and fields."
Wagoner, D. Chorus: "That rain-strewn night in the woods, the chorus, chorus."
  Singing Lesson, The.
Wakoski. Singer, The.
Walker, M. Since 1619.
Waller, T. *et al.* Ladies Who Sing with a Band, The.
Washington, N. Give Me a Heart to Sing To.
Wetzsteon. Witness.
White, J. Oshi.
Whitman, T. Hunger and Imagination.
Whitman, W. Chanting the Square Deific.
  I Hear America Singing.
  To a Certain Cantatrice.
Williams, W. Late Singer, The.
Wojahn. Buddy Holly.
  Song of the Burning.
Woods, H. Side by Side.
Wordsworth, W. Solitary Reaper, The.
Wyatt, S. Marvel No More.
  My Lute, Awake!
Young, A. Dance For Ma Rainey, A.
Young, J. Rock-a-Bye Your Baby with a Dixie Melody.
Young, V. Give Me a Heart to Sing To.
See also **Tenors**

Sioux, The
Chippewa Oral Tradition. Sioux Woman Defends Her Children, The.
  Sioux Women Gather Up Their Wounded, The.
  Song of the Captive Sioux Woman.
Taylor, R. Dakota: October, 1822, Hunkpapa Warrior.

Sirens (mythology)
Brown, E. What Song the Syrens Sang.
Daniel, S. Ulysses and the Siren [or Syren].
"Fane, V." Siren, The.
Killigrew, A. Farewell to Worldly Joys, A.
Manifold. Sirens, The.
McLain, P. Beauty, That Lying Bitch.
Milton. At a Solemn Music[k].

Sirens (warning devices)
Wilbur. Fire-Truck, A.

Sisters
Aldis, D. Little.
Aleshire. Double, The.
Anderson, L. Red Hot.
Angus. Blue Jacket, The.
Bogan, L. Sleeping Fury, The.
Browning, E. Bertha in the Lane.
Bryan, M. To My Brother.
Byron, G. Epistle to Augusta.
Campbell, R. Sisters, The.
Carroll, L. Brother and Sister.
Causley. What Has Happened to Lulu?
Clifton, L. To Ms. Ann.
Collins, K. Sisters.
Cotton, C. Resolution in Four Sonnets, of a
    Poetical Question Put to Me by a Friend,
    Concerning Four Rural Sisters.
Feinstein, E. Lazarus' Sister.
Firer. 1956, The Year My Sister, Using Her Ill
    Health Once Again, Blackmailed My Parents
    into an Accordion.
Galvin, J. Station (1).
    Station (2).
Glück, L. Descending Figure.
Jones, S. Another Lazarus.
Lochhead, L. Grim Sisters, The.
McGinley. Triolet Against Sisters.
McGuckian. Sitting, The.
Olds, S. Elder Sister, The.
    Indictment of Senior Officers.
    Sisters of Sexual Treasure, The.
Peeradina, S. Sisters.
Remoto. Images of John (1967–92).
Rich, A. Women.
Rossetti, C. Noble Sisters.
Seward. On a Lock of Miss Sarah Seward's
    Hair Who Died in her Twentieth Year.
Sherman, C. Roots.
Sitwell, D. Waltz.
Song. Lost Sister.
Soto. Blanco.
Szymborska. In Praise of My Sister.
Taggard. Weed, The.
Unknown. Down to the Mire.
    Riddling Knight, The.
West, K. To My Twin Sister Who Died at Birth.
Whittier. Sisters, The.
Wright, J. Sisters, The.

Sisyphus
Glück, L. Mountain, The.
Mahon. Death and the Sun.

Sitwell, Dame Edith
Coward. Contours.

Size
Barer, M. Shall We Join the Ladies?
Berlin. How Deep Is the Ocean? (How High Is
    the Sky?).
Karr. Hubris.
Kern, J. Napoleon.
Wodehouse, P. Napoleon.

Skateboarding and Skateboarders
Gunn, T. Skateboard.
Morrison, L. Sidewalk Racer or, On the
    Skateboard, The.

See also **Roller Skating and Roller Skaters**

Skating and Skaters
Atwood. Woman Skating.
Berssenbrugge. Swan, The.
Blunden. Midnight Skaters, The.
Conn. Under the Ice.
Fletcher, J. Skaters, The.
Livingston, M. 74th Street.
Mother Goose. Three Children.
Roberts, S. Skater, The.
Rukeyser, M. Boys of These Men Full Speed.
Wyrebek, M. Trendelenburg Position.

See also **Roller Skating and Roller Skaters;**
    Skateboarding and Skateboarders

Skeletons
Alexie. Evolution.
Deanovich. My Favorite Monk Is.
Hartnett. All That Is Left.
Herd. Hyperion's Bones.

Longfellow, H. Skeleton in Armor [*or* Armour],
    The.
Lovelace, R. La Bella Bona-Roba.
Schmitz. Monstrous Pictures of Whales.
Shorter. Skeleton in the Cupboard, The.
Smith, L. Skeleton House.
Turner, C. Lion's Skeleton, The.

See also **Bones**

Skepticism
Johnson, M. F. Invocation to the Spirit Said to
    Haunt Wroxall Down.

See also **Doubt**

Skiing and Skiers
Merrill, J. Up and Down.
Page, P. T-Bar.

Skin
Askhari. Colorstruck.
Butts, A. Skin.
Donaldson, W. T'ain't No Sin to Dance Around
    in Your Bones.
Dransfield. Epiderm.
Eimers. Night Without Stars, A.
Loden. Far In.
Lorde. Hanging Fire.
McClatchy. Tattoos.
Perdomo, W. Nigger-Reecan Blues.
Perillo. Skin.
Porter, C. I've Got You Under My Skin.
Thomas, L. Subway Witnesses, The.
Waldman, A. Skin / Meat / BONES.
Welish. Skin.
Wright, J. Skins.
Wyrebek, M. Trendelenburg Position.

Skulls
Dodson, O. Yardbird's Skull.
MacDiarmid, H. Perfect.
Pitter. Sparrow's Skull, The.
Scott, W. U.S. Sailor with the Japanese Skull,
    The.
Tollet. On a Death's Head.
Weismiller. Skull.

Skunks
Heaney, S. Skunk, The.
Lowell, R. Skunk Hour.
Miles, J. Bureau 2.
Navajo Oral Tradition. Coyote, Skunk, and the
    Prairie Dogs.

Sky
Addison, J. Ode: "Spacious firmament on high,
    The."
Alexander, E. Ode.
Ashbery. Poem: "While we were walking under
    the top."
    Variant.
Auden. Summer Night, A.
Back, R. Untitled.
Berlin. Blue Skies.
Bevington, L. Measurements.
Bobrowski. Place of Fire.
Bognini. Earth and Sky.
Byron, G. She Walks in Beauty.
Cole, W. Back Yard, July Night.
Conoley. Sky Drank In, The.
Cope, J. Winter Sky.
Crane, H. To the Cloud Juggler.
Crawford, I. Battle, A.
Dauer. Falling.
Dickinson, E. Aurora.
Dorn, E. Song, A.
Dove, R. Teach Us to Number Our Days.
Duke, V. Cabin in the Sky.
Duran, J. Mere Pleasure of Flying, The.
Eigner. Back to it.
    In Imitation.
Fitzgerald, E. 72.
García Lorca. Below.
    Swath.
Gilbert, C. Directions, The.
Grimké, A. For the Candle Light.
Harwood, L. Final Painting, The.
    Words, The.
Hass, R. Elm.
Henderson, D. Horizon Blues.
Howe, F. Scattered Light.
Ignatow, D. Sky Is Blue, The.

Keble. Malvern at a Distance.
Kinnell. Daybreak.
Kizer, C. On a Line from Valéry.
Latouche, J. Cabin in the Sky.
Levertov. Clouds.
MacKenzie, R. Blue Sky in Morning.
Madge. On One Condition.
Mead, J. Incomplete Scenario Involving What
    the Voice Said.
Merrill, J. Upward Look, An.
Mills, R. Water Lilies.
Nichol. Monotones.
Posey, A. Nightfall.
Ray, H. Sky Picture.
Reavey. 'How many fires.'
Roberts, E. Sky, The.
Roberts, G. Night Sky, The.
Robinson, K. Nursery Rhyme.
Sandburg, C. Be Ready.
    Love in Labrador.
Shapiro, D. Commentary Text Commentary
    Text Commentary Text.
Simic. Night Picnic.
Stevens, W. Candle a Saint, The.
Stevenson, R. Swing, The.
Taylor, J. Star, The.
Turner, F. Spring Evening.
Unknown. International Chainpoem.
Ward, T. Dark Underfoot.
Welish. Within This Book, Called Marguerite.
Whitman, W. On the Beach at Night.
    On the Beach at Night Alone.
Williams, W. Desolate Field, The.
Yau. Engines of Gloom and Affection.

See also **Constellations; Stars**

Sky Diving and Sky Divers
Merrill, C. Erosion.

See also **Parachuting and Parachutists**

Skye, Isle of, Scotland
Revard. October, Isle of Skye.

Skylarks
Carmichael, H. Skylark.
Clare, J. Sky Lark, The.
Mercer, J. Skylark.

See also **Larks**

Skyscrapers
Corso. Ode to Coit Tower.
Field, R. Skyscrapers.
Sandburg, C. Prayers of Steel.
    Skyscraper.
Schmitz. Climbing Sears Tower.
Yolen. Sky Scrape / City Scape.

Slander
Ellis, T. Sir Nose D'VoidofFunk.
Yeats. He Thinks of Those Who Have Spoken
    Evil of His Beloved.

Slaughterhouses
Alexander, M. Chicago.
Keplinger, D. Distance Between Zero and One,
    The.
Troupe. River Town Packin House Blues.

Slavery and Slaves
"Ada." Lines: "From fair Jamaica's fertile
    plains."
Adisa. No, Women Don't Cry.
Alexander, E. Passage.
Askhari. Isalutu.
Ba. Nobility.
Bennett, G. To a Dark Girl.
Bierce. Hesitating Veteran, The.
Bland, J. Carry Me Back to Old Virginny.
Brooks, S. Middle Passage.
Brown, S. Bitter Fruit of the Tree.
    Strong Men.
Browning, E. Hiram Powers' "Greek Slave."
    Runaway Slave at Pilgrim's Point, The.
Brutus. There Was a Time When the Only
    Worth.
Bryant, W. African Chief, The.
    Death of Slavery, The.
Cable, G. Dirge of St. Malo, The.
Campbell, R. Serf, The.
Carey, H. Sally in Our Alley.
Cary, P. Harvest Gathering.
Clifton, L. At the Cemetery, Walnut Grove

Plantation, South Carolina, 1989.
Slave Cabin, Sotterly Plantation, Maryland, 1989.
Slaveship.
Cowper, W.   Negro's Complaint, The.
Sweet Meat Has Sour Sauce.
To William Wilberforce, Esq.
Crouch, S.   Chops Are Flyin.
D'Aguiar.   Langston.
Mama Dot.
Mama Dot Warns Against an Easter Rising.
Davidson, D.   Sequel of Appomattox.
Davis, M.   Cry of a People.
Derricotte.   1994 Inventory.
Diop, D.   Africa.
Dixon, M.   Tour Guide: La Maison des Esclaves.
Dove, R.   Adolescence—I.
House Slave, The.
Dunbar, P.   Ante-Bellum Sermon, An.
Sympathy.
Emerson, R.   Boston Hymn.
Esteves.   From Fanon.
Follen, E.   Children in Slavery.
For the Fourth of July.
Freneau.   To Sir Toby.
Greenwell, D.   Broken Chain, The.
Griffin, S.   I Like to Think of Harriet Tubman.
Harper, F.   Bible Defence of Slavery.
Bury Me in a Free Land.
Lines: "At the Portals of the Future."
She's Free!
Slave Auction, The.
Slave Mother, The.
Harper, M.   American History.
Makin' Jump Shots.
Hayden, R.   Ballad of Nat Turner, The.
Frederick Douglass.
Middle Passage.
Runagate Runagate.
Heard, J.   Black Sampson, The.
To Clements' Ferry.
Hoagland, E.   Gorée.
Horton, G.   Division of an Estate.
On Hearing of the Intention of a Gentleman to Purchase the Poet's Freedom.
On Liberty and Slavery.
Hughes, L.   Aunt Sue's Stories.
Iman.   Love Your Enemy.
Jackson, B.   In Exchange for Forty Acres.
Jackson, G.   Alice.
Fugitive Slaves.
Jeffers, L.   Nina Simone.
Trellie.
Johnson, J.   Brothers.
Jolobe.   Making of a Servant, The.
Jordan, J.   Something Like a Sonnet for Phillis Miracle Wheatley.
Speculations on the Present through the Prism of the Past.
Kay, J.   Even the Trees.
Kendrick, D.   Sadie Snuffs a Candle.
Sidney, Looking for her Mother.
Sophie, Climbing the Stairs.
Kgositsile.   To Mother.
Kipling, R.   Galley-Slave, The.
Song of the Galley-Slaves.
Koestenbaum, W.   Gaudy Slave Trader.
Komunyakaa.   Back Then.
"Leadbelly."   Take this Hammer.
Lickbarrow, I.   On the Slave-Trade.
Longfellow, H.   Slave in the Dismal Swamp, The.
Slave's Dream, The.
Warning, The.
Lorde.   Between Ourselves.
Madhubuti.   Long Reality, The.
Primitive, The.
Matthews, M.   By a Ways.
McElroy, C.   Woman's Song, A.
McKay, C.   Enslaved.
McLoughland.   Whippoorwill Calls, The.
Melville, H.   Formerly a Slave.
Misgivings.
Miller, E.   Tomorrow.
Moorer.   Emancipation Day.

Must Be Freed.
Peonage System, The.
More, H.   Slavery.
Morris, M.   Rasta Reggae.
Nesbit, E.   Wife of All Ages, The.
Niedecker.   Will You Write Me a Christmas Poem?
Opie.   Negro Boy's Tale, The.
Oppenheim.   Slave, The.
Patterson, R.   Black Power.
Pereira.   Mother Dark.
Piatt, S.   Child's Party, A.
Pierpont, J.   Fugitive Slave's Apostrophe to the North Star, The.
Plato.   To the First of August.
Plumpp.   Remembered.
Turf Song.
Randall, D.   Southern Road, The.
Reynolds, S. F.   Whipping, The.
Robinson, E.   Sonnet: "Master and the slave go hand in hand, The."
Rochester, J.   To My More Than Meritorious Wife.
Sanchez, S.   Reflections After the June 12th March for Disarmament.
Sandburg, C.   Osawatomie.
Schwartz, D.   Winter Twilight, Glowing Black and Gold, The.
Sigourney.   To the First Slave Ship.
Skeeter.   California, 1852.
Smith, G.   Penitential Cries of Jupiter Hammond, The.
Smith, S.   Was It Not Curious?
Stainer.   Sighting the Slave Ship.
Tati-Loutard.   Pilgrimage to Loango Strand.
Voices, The.
Thompson, P.   Address to Ethiopia.
Favorite Slave's Story, The.
Fugitive, The.
Husband's Return, The.
My Father's Story.
Prayer, A: "Oh, Lord! I lift my heart."
Tindal.   Cry of the Oppressed, The.
Tolson, M.   Dark Symphony.
Toomer.   Song of the Son.
Unknown.   Go Down, Moses.
Harriet Tubman.
Jack and Dinah Want Freedom.
Let My People Go.
Me and My Captain.
No More Auction Block.
Promises of Freedom.
Run, Nigger, Run!
Song: "We raise de wheat."
Song to the Runaway Slave.
Steal Away to Jesus.
Wild Negro Bill.
Very.   Fugitive Slaves, The.
Slavery.
Walker, A.   Early Losses: a Requiem.
Walker, M.   Delta.
Since 1619.
Waniek.   Chosen.
Wheatley, P.   On Being Brought from Africa to America.
To the Right Honourable William, Earl of Dartmouth, His Majesty's Principal Secretary of State for North America.
Whitfield.   America.
From America.
Whitman, A.   Lute of Afric's Tribe, The.
Whittier.   Christian Slave, The.
Clerical Oppressors.
Farewell, The: "Gone, gone,—sold and gone."
Haschish, The.
Ichabod[!].
Official Piety.
Slave-Ships, The.
Song of Slaves in the Desert.
Williams, H.   Poem on the Bill Lately Passed for Regulating the Slave-Trade, A.
Wright, J.   Sketch for an Aesthetic Project.

Sleds
Johnson, J.   Midnight Run.

See also **Sleighs**

Sleep
Adams, L.   Moon and Spectator, The.
Alden, J.   Sleepy Time Gal.
Alexie.   Reservation Love Song.
Allott.   Statue, The.
Ames, B.   Country of Water.
'Andrews, C.'   Morn's Recompense.
Atwood.   Variation on the Word *Sleep*.
Auden.   Lullaby: "Din of work is subdued, The."
Awoonor.   Song of War.
Songs of Sorrow.
Belieu.   Sleeping Man Must Be Awakened to Be Killed, A.
Berlin.   Oh! How I Hate to Get Up in the Morning.
Berryman.   Henry by Night.
Bibbins, M.   Counting.
Bible, *O.T.*   Song: "I was asleep but my heart stayed awake."
Bishop, E.   Insomnia.
Sleeping on the Ceiling.
Unbeliever, The.
Bly, R.   Afternoon Sleep.
Waking from Sleep.
Bogan, L.   Tears in Sleep.
Brontë, C.   Is this my tomb, this humble stone.
Brontë, E.   Song: "Linnet in the rocky dells, The."
Browning, E.   Sleep, The.
Brush.   Waiting for the End of the War.
Burns, R.   Flow Gently, Sweet Afton.
Byrd.   Song: "Let not the sluggish sleep."
Campion, T.   It Fell on a Summer's [or Sommers] Day [or Daie].
Sleep, Angry Beauty.
Carmichael, H.   Two Sleepy People.
Carroll, K.   DC Nocturne.
Carryl, C.   Sleepy Giant, The.
Chin, J.   Night.
Chivers.   To Isa Sleeping.
Christie.   Overture.
Clark, T.   "Before Dawn.."
Cofer, J.   Hour of the Siesta, The.
Coleridge, M.   'But in that Sleep of Death what Dreams may Come?'
Hush.
Coleridge, S.   Pains of Sleep, The.
Cooley.   Sleep of Beasts, The.
Cooper, J.   My Young Mother.
Cornford, F.   At Night.
Couzyn.   Morning.
Cuddihy.   This Body.
Cullen, C.   Night Rain.
De la Mare.   Galliass, The.
Nod.
Sleeper, The.
De Paul, G.   Milkman, Keep Those Bottles Quiet!
Dodge, M.   Early to Bed.
Donne.   Song: "Sweetest love, I do not go[e]."
Dougherty.   Double Helix.
Douglas, L.   To Sleep.
Dowson.   Spleen.
Drummond, W.   Sleep, Silence' Child.
Dufault.   First Night, A.
Dunbar, P.   Ere Sleep Comes Down to Soothe the Weary Eyes.
Duncan, R.   Sleep Is a Deep and Many Voiced Flood.
Eady.   Insomnia.
Egan, R.   Sleepy Time Gal.
Eigner.   For Sleep.
Erdrich.   I Was Sleeping Where the Black Oaks Move.
Everwine.   Just Before Sleep.
Farjeon, E.   Good Night.
Ned.
Fearing.   Evening Song.
"Field."   And on My Eyes Dark Sleep by Night.
Field, E.   Sugar-Plum Tree, The.
Wynken, Blynken, and Nod.
Finch, A.   For Grizzel McNaught (1709–1792).
Foix.   When I Sleep, Then I See Clearly.
Forbes, C.   Dark Mirror.
Picture of a Man.

Fournier, R. Encounter.
Francis, R. While I Slept.
Frost, R. Night Person, The.
  Stopping by Woods on a Snowy Evening.
Fusselman, A. Sleeper.
Gallagher, T. Under Stars.
Garland, H. Boyish sleep.
Garrett, E. Mimesis.
Glück, L. New Life, The.
Graves, R. She Tells Her Love While Half
  Asleep.
Gunn, T. For Signs.
  Hug, The.
  Touch.
Hadas, R. Mars and Venus.
Hall, H. Light Sleep.
Harryman. That Can Not Be Taken Away From
  It.
Hasford. Bedtime Story.
Hashimoto, S. Standing in the Doorway, I
  Watch the Young Child Sleep.
Henson, L. Sleep Watch.
Herrick. Bellman, The.
  Epitaph upon a Virgin, An.
  To Daisies, Not to Shut So Soon[e].
  Upon a Child.
  Upon Mistress Elizabeth Wheeler under the
    Name of Amarillis.
Hill, M. Sleep.
Holland, J.
Hood, T. Good Night.
Housman, A. When the Eye of Day Is Shut.
Hughes, L. Morning After.
  Weary Blues, The.
Hughes, T. Bear, The.
  Roger the Dog.
Hupfeld, H. Let's Put Out the Lights and Go to
  Sleep.
Imbs. Sleep.
Ives, G. With Whom, then, Should I Sleep?
Jackson, B. Shooting, Killing, Drug Busts,
  Cover-Ups, Fuck-Ups, Lighter Sides, Weather,
  and Sports.
Johnson, M. Old Dog.
Keats. To Sleep.
Kees. If this Room Is Our World.
Kendrick, D. Jenny in Sleep.
Kennedy, X. One Winter Night in August.
Kinnell. After Making Love We Hear
  Footsteps.
  Little Sleep's-Head Sprouting Hair in the
    Moonlight.
Kinsella, T. Endymion.
Kirsch, M. Sleep's Underside.
Knott. Death.
Kocbek. Dialectics.
Koch, K. Sleeping with Women.
Kolodinsky, A. Midnight.
Kooser. Child Frightened by a Thunderstorm.
Kumin, M. After Love.
Kunitz, S. Science of the Night, The.
Lauterbach. Boy Sleeping.
Lear, E. Limerick: "There was an Old Man who
  supposed."
Lee, D. Coming of Teddy Bears, The.
  You Too Lie Down.
Lee, W. Sex Has a Way.
Levertov. Cat as Cat, The.
Loesser. Two Sleepy People.
Logghe. Insomnia Litany.
Lorenzo, A. Sleepy Time Gal.
Luther. Away in a Manger.
MacLeish. Words in Time.
MacNeice. Cradle Song: "Clock's untiring
  fingers wind the wool of darkness, The."
Masefield. Sea Fever.
Maxton. Elegies.
Mayer, B. Sonnet: "Beauty of songs your
  absence I should not show."
McDaniel, J. Following Her to Sleep.
Melville, H. Bench of Boors, The.
Merrill, J. About the Phoenix.
Mew. Not for That City.
Miller, W. Willie Winkie.
Mole, J. Trick, The.
Monsour. Dream of Dying, A.

Moore, L. Again.
Moore, M. Peter.
Moore, T. Oft in the Stilly Night.
Morley, C. Plumpuppets, The.
Murray, J. Lullaby.
Nash, O. Sweet Dreams.
Niedecker. Subliminal.
O'Hara, F. Sleeping on the Wing.
Oates. Insomnia.
Oliver, M. White Night.
Owen, G. Half Asleep.
Padgett, R. December.
Parker, A. Lullaby: "Sleep and rain, two
  gangsters."
Paschen. Litany.
Pastan. At the Train Museum.
Patchen. Naked Land, The.
Philips, A. To Miss Charlotte Pulteney in Her
  Mother's Arms.
Pinkney, E. Serenade: "Look out upon the stars,
  my love."
Piombino. My Lady Carries Stones.
Ransom, J. Janet Waking.
Ravenscroft, T. Belmans Song, A.
Raye, D. Milkman, Keep Those Bottles Quiet!
Reid, A. Spell for Sleeping, A.
Rhodes, M. How Fast.
Roberts, E. Evening Song.
Robinson, E. For Karen.
Rochester, J. Song: "Absent from thee, I
  languish still."
Roethke. Root Cellar.
  Waking, The.
Rossetti, D. Insomnia.
Sanchez, S. Poem at Thirty.
Sandburg, C. Wind Song.
Sassoon. Falling Asleep.
Schultz, R. She Speaks to Her Husband,
  Asleep.
Schwartz, D. O Child, Do Not Fear the Dark
  and Sleep's Dark Possession.
Seeger, A. I Have a Rendezvous with Death.
Seward. Invocation, To the Genius of Slumber
  Written Oct. 1787.
Sharma, P. Principles, When I Felt Them.
Smith, C. To Sleep.
Smith, M. Asleep in the City.
Smith, S. Goodnight.
Spender, S. Daybreak.
Stevens, W. Anecdote of the Prince of
  Peacocks.
  To the Roaring Wind.
Stevenson, A. Marriage, The.
Stevenson, R. Bed in Summer.
  Escape at Bedtime.
  Good Boy, A.
  Land of Nod, The.
  My Bed Is a Boat.
  Young Night Thought.
Stillman, M. Lullaby for Suzanne.
Swinburne. Garden of Proserpine, The.
  Love And Sleep.
Tayson, R. Nightsweats.
Thomas, E. Lights Out.
Tobin, D. At the Egyptian Exhibit.
Toomer. Evening Song.
Torres, E. Summertime Late Show.
Tranter. Moment of Waking, The.
Unknown. Weep [or Weepe] You No More [Sad
  Fountains].
Valentine, J. After Elegies.
  Sleep Drops Its Nets.
Voigt. Exile.
Warren-Moore. All-Night Issue, The.
Watson, R. Nirvana.
Webb, F. Gunner, The.
  Port Phillip Night.
Whiting, R. Sleepy Time Gal.
Whitlow. Book of Routh.
Wilbur. After the Last Bulletins.
  Beasts.
  In the Smoking-Car.
  Walking to Sleep.
Willard, E. Rocked in the Cradle of the Deep.
Williams, W. Goodnight, A.
Winter, M. Dux Bellorum.

Winters, Y. Precision, The.
Wordsworth, D. Cottager to Her Infant (By My
  Sister), The.
Wordsworth, W. To Sleep.
Wrigley, R. Milkflowers.
Yeats. Lullaby: "Beloved, may your sleep be
  sound."
Yolen. Troll to her Children, The.
Yosano. Channel Boat, The.
Young, M. J. To Dreams.
Sleeping Beauty
  Unknown. Fair rosa.
Sleepwalking and Sleepwalkers
  Dybek. Sleepwalking Soho.
  See also **Somnambulism and Somnambulists**
Sleet
  MacCaig. Sleet.
  Tate, J. Dear Reader.
Sleighs
  Burke, J. Sleigh Ride in July.
  Haines, J. Snowbound City, The.
Slides
  Anderson, A. Licking Wounds.
  Farber. For a Quick Exit.
Sloth
  Komunyakaa. Seven Deadly Sins.
  Roethke. Sloth, The.
  Sandburg, C. Galoots.
  Watts, I. Sluggard, The.
Sloths
  Adcock, F. Three-Toed Sloth, The.
  Roethke. Sloth, The.
Slough, England
  Betjeman. Slough.
Slugs
  Birney. Slug in Woods.
  Ferguson, G. Slugs.
  Olds, S. Connoisseuse of Slugs, The.
  Redgrove, P. Negotium Perambulans.
  Willard, N. Speckled Hen's Morning Song to
    Biddy Early, The.
  See also **Snails**
Slums
  Acorn. On Saint-Urbain Street.
  Brooks, G. Lovers of the Poor, The.
  Davies, W. Rat, The.
  Davis, J. Slum Dwelling.
  Dove, R. Teach Us to Number Our Days.
  Hayden, R. Summertime and the Living.
  Ignatow, D. East Bronx.
  Get the Gasworks.
  MacDiarmid, H. Reflections in a Slum.
  Sepamla. When I Lost Slum Life.
  Spender, S. Elementary School Classroom in a
    Slum, An.
  Wright, J. Neighborhood House, The.
Smallpox
  Jones, M. After the Small Pox.
  Jonson, B. Epigram. To the Small-Pox, An.
  Muldoon, P. Meeting the British.
Smalls, Robert
  Heard, J. General Robert Smalls.
Smart, Christopher
  Hirsch, E. Wild Gratitude.
  Shaw, S. Christopher Smart.
Smells
  As-Sabah. I'll Never Know No Sunday in This
    Weekday Room.
  Bishop, E. Prodigal, The.
  Chin, J. Bergamot.
  Coleridge, S. Cologne.
  Fainlight, R. Handbag.
  "Field." Onycha.
  Goodman, M. February Ice Years.
  Hammerstein. Mister Snow.
  Hecht, A. Sarabande on Attaining the Age of
    Seventy-Seven.
  Herrick. Perfume, The.
  To the Most Fair and Lovely Mistress Anne
    Soame, Now Lady Abdie.
  Hoskyns [or Hoskins]. Epitaph on the Fart in
    the Parliament House.
  Hudgins. Rosie.
  Marshall, J. Months of Love, The.

McGuckian. Orchid House, The.
McKay, C. Jasmine.
Moore, M. Odor of a Metal Is Not Strong, The.
Probyn. Changes.
Rodgers, R. Mister Snow.
Smith, K. Possessions.
Stevenson, A. Himalayan Balsam.
Swift, J. Lady's Dressing Room, The.
Thomas, E. Digging.
Williams, W. Smell.

Smiles
Adams, L. Put on a Happy Face.
Barlow, G. Nook.
Blake, W. Smile, The.
Brown, N. Singin' in the Rain.
Coffman. Girl/Spit.
Coleridge, M. True to myself am I, and false to all.
Creeley. Oh No.
Donaldson, W. Kansas City Kitty.
Dunbar, P. Made to Order Smile, The.
  Philosophy.
  We Wear the Mask.
"Field." La Gioconda; Leonardo Da Vinci, The Louvre.
Figueroa, J. Homemade Smiles.
Freed, A. Singin' in the Rain.
Graves, R. One Hard Look.
Hardy, T. Neutral Tones.
Hartman, M. Life's Made up of Little Things.
Herford. Smile of the Goat, The.
  Smile of the Walrus, The.
Isler. Little Things, The.
Landesman. Say 'Cheese!'
Landor, W. You Smiled, You Spoke, and I Believed.
Leslie, E. Kansas City Kitty.
Madhubuti. Judy-One.
Rodgers, C. Poem No. 1.
Shange. You are Sucha Fool.
Unknown. Smile, A.
  Try Smiling.
Warren-Moore. Dannemora Contraband.
Wilbur. Simile for Her Smile, A.
Wylie. Let No Charitable Hope.

Smith, Bessie
Aubert, A. Bessie.
  Bessie Smith's Funeral.
Baker, H. Of Walter White's Father in the Rain.
Harper, M. Last Affair: Bessie's Blues Song.
Hayden, R. Homage to the Empress of the Blues.
Kay, J. Twelve Bar Bessie.
McElroy, C. Mae West Chats It Up with Bessie Smith.
Vinz. Blues, The.

Smith, John (1580–1631)
Bibb. Capt. Smith and Pocahontas.

Smith, Joseph
Taylor, B. Nauvoo.

Smoke
Bennett, R. Smoke Animals.
Bodenheim. Death.
Ceravolo. Data.
DuBois, W. Song of the Smoke, The.
Forché. Elegy.
Harbach, O. Smoke Gets in Your Eyes.
Hill, G. September Song.
Kern, J. Smoke Gets in Your Eyes.
Lee, L. Interrogation, The.
Levine, P. Smoke.
Nicholson, N. On the Closing of Millom Ironworks.
Tranter. Backyard.
Unknown. Riddle: "Chip chip cherry."
Williams, W. Classic Scene.

Smoking and Smokers
Campo. Lost in the Hospital.
Dunbar, P. Companion's Progress, A.
Glaser, E. Smoking.
Kessler, S. Cigarette Case.
Pearlberg, G. G. Marianne Faithfull's Cigarette.
Robinson, E. Meshes.
Soto. Ode to Señor Leal's Goat.
Straus, M. Luck.

Thribb. Lines on the Award "Pipe Man of the Year" to Magnus Magnusson.
Vigil, A. At the Stop Light, the Braided Blond Man.
Wallace, R. Smoking.

Smuggling and Smugglers
Musgrave. I Am Not a Conspiracy Everything Is Not Paranoid The Drug Enforcement Administration Is Not Everywhere.

Snails
Bunyan. Upon the [*or* a] Snail.
Gunn, T. Considering the Snail.
Lovelace, R. Another.
  Snail [*or* Snayl], The.
Moore, M. To a Snail.
Mother Goose. Snail, The.
Piercy. Spring Offensive of the Snail, The.
Sarton. Eine Kleine Snailmusik.
Thompson, P. Snail's Lesson, The.
See also **Shells; Slugs**

Snakes
Abse. Snake.
Acholonu. Water Woman.
Belloc. Viper, The.
Bethune, L. Today Tutu Is Beating the Same Burru As Me.
Dickey, J. Poisoned Man, The.
Dickinson, E. Snake, The.
Dumas, H. Island within Island.
England, A. Art of the Snake Story, The.
"Field." Dying Viper, A.
Frost, R. Hill Wife, The.
  House Fear.
  Impulse, The.
  Loneliness.
  Oft-Repeated Dream, The.
Ghiselin. Rattler, Alert.
Gilbert, K. Taipan.
Gotlieb. Cocker of Snooks, A.
Guillén, N. Sensemayá.
Harper, M. Alice.
Hecht, A. Lizards and Snakes.
Hernández Cruz. Keeping Track of the Serpents.
Herrick. Silken Snake, The.
Hughes, T. Cleopatra to the Asp.
Kunitz, S. Snakes of September, The.
Lawrence, D. Snake.
Levertov. Closed World, The.
  To the Snake.
Marvell. Coronet, The.
Merrill, C. Erosion.
Momaday. Pit Viper.
Morgan, E. Siesta of a Hungarian Snake.
Nash, O. Experiment Degustatory.
Nystrom. Insomnia.
O'Hara, F. In Memory of My Feelings.
Oliver, L. Horned Snake, The.
Ondaatje. Breaking Green.
Padel. On the Venom Farm.
Palmer, V. Snake, The.
Parnell, P. Apotheosis of Medusa.
Patchen. Deer and the Snake, The.
Pitter. Viper, The.
Plath. Medallion.
Plomer. In the Snake Park.
Ramanujan. Snakes.
Rankin, J. Forever the Snake.
Roethke. Serpent, The.
  Snake.
Ross, W. Snake Trying, The.
Russell, W. Tali Karng: Twilight Snake.
Shelley, P. Fragment: "Wake the serpent not—lest he."
Silko. Time We Climbed Snake Mountain, The.
Stewart, S. Apple.
Swenson, M. Waterbird.
Tsaloumas. Grudge, The.
Unknown. Origin of the Snake, The.
  Springfield Mountain.
Van Doren. Where I Saw the Snake.
Very. Serpent, The.
Wakoski. Summer.
Waller, E. To a Fair Lady Playing with a Snake.
Walwicz. Tattoo, The.
Warburton, N. Snake on D. H. Lawrence, The.

Williams, W. Sort of a Song, A.
Winchilsea. Song of the Cannibals, A.
Wright, J. Killer, The.

Sneezing
Unknown. Sneezing.

Snobbery and Snobs
Baillie, L. Werena My Heart Licht I Wad Dee.
Bentley, N. Londonderry Air, The.
Berlin. Slumming on Park Avenue.
Bossidy. Boston.
Canning, G. *et al.* Friend of Humanity and the Knife Grinder, The.
Glück, L. My Neighbor in the Mirror.
Hannah, S. Postcard from a Travel Snob.
Hughes, L. High to Low.
  Low to High.
Moore, M. Labors of Hercules, The.
Sandburg, C. Balloon Faces.
Young, A. One Snapshot I Couldn't Take in France, The.
See also **Social Class**

Snoring
Chin, D. Sleeping Father.
Hughes, L. Morning After.
Nash, O. Arthur.

Snorkeling and Snorkelers
Lieberman, L. Coral Reef, The.

Snow
Aldington. Faun Sees Snow for the First Time, The.
Awad, J. First Snow.
Baker, D. Envoi: Waking After Snow.
Baumel. Snow-Day.
Berlin. White Christmas.
Bernard, A. Snowfall.
Bethell. Spring Snow and Tui.
Bielski. Intruder.
Blake, W. Soft Snow.
Bly, R. Looking at New-Fallen Snow from a Train.
  Six Winter Privacy Poems.
  Sleet Storm on the Merritt Parkway.
  Snowfall in the Afternoon.
Bridges, R. London Snow.
Brontë, A. Song.
Brooks, G. Cynthia in the Snow.
Brown, L. Winter Sonnet.
Buxton. Putting the World to Bed.
Cahn, S. Let It Snow! Let It Snow! Let It Snow!
Carson, C. Slate Street School.
Coatsworth. On a Night of Snow.
Coe, C. Possibility.
Collins, B. Snow Day.
Collins, M. To F. C.
Crapsey. Snow.
Crow, S. Revival.
Dauenhauer, R. Driving in a Snowstorm, King Salmon to Naknek.
Davidson, J. Snow.
Davis, W.
Davison, P. Vanishing Point, The.
Day Lewis. Snowfall on a College Garden.
De la Mare. Snow.
  There Blooms No Bud in May.
  Winter.
Dickinson, E. Snow, The.
Dillon, G. Snow.
Djanikian. When I First Saw Snow.
Dodd, E. Lyric: "It doesn't matter / whether / a tree falls."
Dougherty. Cocoons.
Dufault. First Night, A.
Dunbar-Nelson. Snow in October.
Ehrhart. Blizzard of Sixty-Six, The.
Emerson, R. Snow-Storm [*or* Snowstorm], The.
Erdrich, H. Quiet Earth, The.
Espada. Prisoners of Saint Lawrence, The.
"Field." Cyclamens.
Fisher, A. Snowy Benches.
Fordham. Snow Storm, The.
  Snowdrop, The.
Francis, R. Slow.
Frost, R. Desert Places.
  Dust of Snow.

Onset, The.
Patch of Old Snow, A.
Stopping by Woods on a Snowy Evening.
Storm Fear.
Gascoyne. Rex Mundi.
  Snow in Europe.
Gibson, W. Drove-Road, The.
Giovanni. Winter Poem.
Goodman, P. Long Lines.
Graham, J. San Sepolcro.
Graves, R. She Tells Her Love While Half
  Asleep.
Gustafson, R. Wednesday at North Hatley.
Hardy, T. Snow in the Suburbs.
Hartnett. Moonsnow '77.
Hikmet. Cucumber, The.
Housman, A. Eight O'Clock.
  Loveliest of Trees, the Cherry Now.
Humphries, R. Dafydd ap Gwilym Resents the
  Winter.
Jennings, H. Prose Poem.
Justice, D. Snowfall, The.
Kuzma. Ice Skating.
Levine, P. Snow.
Li Ch'ing-chao. Tune: "Pure Serene Music."
Longfellow, H. Cross of Snow, The.
  Excelsior.
  Fragment: December 18, 1847.
  Snow-Flakes.
Lorde. Woman Thing, The.
Lowell, A. Falling Snow.
Lowell, J. First Snow-fall, The.
MacLeish. Snowflake Which Is Now and Hence
  Forever, The.
MacNeice. Snow.
Mahon. Antarctica.
Malouf. Snow.
Mayer, B. End of Human Reign on Bashan
  Hill, The.
  Generic Elbows.
McClatchy. Old Song Ended, An.
McGough, R. Snow Poem.
Millay, E. Buck in the Snow, The.
  Snow Storm, The.
Milne, A. More It Snows, The.
Monk, M. Fire Us with Ice, Burn Us with
  Snow.
Morley, D. White, White.
Murray, L. Once in a Lifetime, Snow.
Nash, O. Winter Morning.
Nemerov. Because You Asked about the Line
  between Prose and Poetry.
Niedecker. Element Mother, The.
Page, P. Stories of Snow.
Pasternak, B. Snow Is Falling.
Rakosi. January of a Gnat, The.
Ray, H. Snow Song.
Richards, L. Why Does It Snow?
Rothman, D. Let It Snow.
Saner. Morning Snowfield.
Shenstone. Lines Written on a Window at The
  Leasowes.
Southwell. Burning Babe, The.
Stafford, W. Holding the Sky.
  Near.
  One of the Years.
Stanley, T. Snow-Ball, The.
Stephens, J. White Fields.
Stephens, P. Hangman.
Stevens, W. Snow Man, The.
Stroud, J. Manna.
Tate, J. Dear Reader.
Thomas, E. Snow.
  Thaw.
Thompson, F. To a Snowflake.
Thompson, P. Snow-Flakes, The.
Tomlinson, C. Snow Signs.
Trommer, M. If You Listen.
Tu Mu. Egrets.
Tuckerman, F. Rhotruda.
Unknown. Riddle: "White bird featherless."
Washbourne. Upon a Great Shower of Snow
  That Fell on May-Day, 1654.
Wayman. Despair.
Weigl. Mercy.
White, E. Chairs in Snow.

Wilbur. First Snow in Alsace.
Willard, N. Angels in Winter.
Williams, G. City Under Snow.
Wojahn. Photo of My Father in a Snowbound
  Train.
  Riding the Empire Builder, 1948.
Wright, J. Sparrows in a Hillside Drift.
Wylie. Velvet Shoes.
Young Bear. From the Spotted Night.
Zukofsky, L. (Ryokan's scroll).
  As to How Much.
See also **Snowflakes; Snowmen**
Snow White
Bennett, B. True Story of Snow White, The.
Sexton. Snow White and the Seven Dwarfs.
Snowdrops
Evans, M. Snowdrops.
Fordham. Snowdrop, The.
Hughes, T. Snowdrop.
MacBeth [*or* Macbeth]. Snowdrops.
Snowflakes
Bodecker. First Snowflake.
Nemerov. Snowflakes.
Sansom, C. Snowflakes.
See also **Snow**
Snowmen
Bodecker. Snowman Sniffles.
McGough, R. Snowman, The.
Page, P. Snowman, The.
Unknown. Snowman, The.
Wilbur. Boy at the Window.
Soap
MacNeice. Soap Suds.
Muldoon, P. Soap-Pig, The.
Peacocke. Soap.
Silverstein, S. Dirtiest Man in the World, The.
Sobriety
Blane, R. That Face.
Soccer
Merrill, C. Boy Juggling a Soccer Ball, A.
Norris, L. Ballad of Billy Rose, The.
Piccione. Watching Ants Play Soccer in Central
  Park.
Ross, A. Stanley Matthews.
Rouse. England Nil.
Unknown. Bewteis of the Fute-Ball, The.
Social Class
Angelou. Sepia Fashion Show.
Bayly. Novel of High Life, A.
Belloc. Lord Heygate.
Bentley, N. Londonderry Air, The.
Berlin. Top Hat, White Tie, and Tails.
Bersohn. Dignity of Labor, The.
Betjeman. False Security.
Burke, J. Ain't It a Shame About Mame.
Burns, R. Toadeater, The.
Canning, G. *et al.* Friend of Humanity and the
  Knife Grinder, The.
Cawein. On Reading the Life of Haroun Er
  Reshid.
Chimombo. Of Promises and Prophecy.
Clare, J. My Mary.
Cleyre, V. Out of the Darkness.
Cook, W. Still-Life with Woodstove.
"Cornwall." Leveller, The.
Coslow, S. (I'm In Love With) The Honorable
  Mr. So and So.
Coward. Stately Homes of England, The.
Doyle, R. E. Ma Ramon.
Duhamel. Art.
Fenton, J. This Octopus Exploits Women.
Field, E. Lower East Side: The George
  Bernstein Story.
Hamill, G. Limerick: " 'If you're aristocratic,'
  said Nietzsche."
Hands, E. Poem on the Supposition of an
  Advertisement, A; Appearing in a Morning
  Paper, of the Publication of a Volume of
  Poems, by a Servant-Maid.
  Poem on the Supposition of the Book Having
  Been Published and Read, A.
Hannah, S. Where is Talcott Parsons Now?
Hargreaves, W. Burlington Bertie from Bow.
Harrison, T. Earthen Lot, The.
Hart, L. Lady Is a Tramp, The.

Hernandez, D. Pigeons.
Heynen. Clean People, The.
Hirsch, E. Two Suffering Men.
Hughes, L. Low to High.
Johnson, J. Porter's Love Song to a
  Chambermaid, A.
Knight, E. WASP Woman Visits a Black Junkie
  in Prison, A.
Knott. Funny Poem.
Lawrence, D. O! Start a Revolution.
Masefield. Consecration, A.
Melville, H. Rose Farmer, The.
Monaco, J. Ain't It a Shame About Mame.
Ogundipe-Leslie. Song at the African Middle
  Class.
Porter, C. Tale of the Oyster, The.
Pound, E. Garden, The.
Praed. Arrivals at a Watering-Place.
  Goodnight to the Season!
Rodgers, R. Lady Is a Tramp, The.
Rosenberg, L. They are Planning to Cancel the
  School Milk Program to Fund a Tax Cut for
  the Middle Class.
Rutsala. Shame.
Selman, R. 21 East 10th, 2BR, WBF, EIK.
Shepherd, R. Three A.M. Eternal.
Sondheim. Ladies Who Lunch, The.
Stickney, T. Six o'Clock.
Strong, L. Old Woman, Outside the Abbey
  Theater, An.
Thompson, D. P. Intelligence Quotients.
Unknown. One Little Boy.
  Vicar of Bray, The.
Wallace, E. Song of the Bounder, The.
Warr, B. Working Class.
Wells, C. Problem, A.
Whittier. Maud Muller.
Wilcox, E. No Classes!
Williams, H. Like Father.
See also **Snobbery and Snobs**
Social Protest
Forché. Ourselves or Nothing.
Francia, L. In Gurgle Veritas.
Henderson-Holmes. 'C' ing in Colors: Blue.
Hirsch, E. Song: "This is a song for the
  speechless."
Komunyakaa. How I See Things.
Madhubuti. Killing Memory.
Mudrooroo Narogin. Jacky Demonstrates for
  Land Rights.
Mueller, L. Triage.
Perdomo, W. Revolutionary.
Rykard, R. Whole two weeks after The Million
  Man March, A; and still, if you'd ask me, this
  is all I could say about it.
See also **Protest, Social**
Social Work and Social Workers
Addonizio. Broken Sonnets.
Millar, J. Midlife.
Socialism
Conquest. Progress.
Duff, V. Letters from an Exile.
Herbert, W. Socialist Manifesto for East
  Balgillo, The.
Lindsay, N. Why I Voted the Socialist Ticket.
Socrates
Duemer. Theory of Tragedy.
Jackson, M. Socrates' Death.
Lefroy. Idler Listening to Socrates Discussing
  Philosophy with His Boy-Friends, An.
Sodom
Appleman, P. Waiting for the Fire.
Duncan, R. This Place Rumord to Have Been
  Sodom.
Whittier. Cities of the Plain, The.
Softball
Hugo, R. Missoula Softball Tournament.
Smith, R. Softball at Julia Tutwiler Prison.
Solace
Arlen, H. One for My Baby (And One More for
  the Road).
Bowles, W. To the River Cherwell.
Dunn, S. Guardian Angel, The.
Eliscu, E. Without a Song.
Hammerstein. My Favorite Things.

Harris, W.   Samantha Is My Negro Cat.
Hawoldar.   You.
Herrick.   Ode to Master Endymion Porter, upon His Brother's Death, An.
To the Willow-Tree.
Hopkins, G.   No Worst, There Is None. Pitched Past Pitch of Grief.
Magidson, H.   Music, Maestro, Please!
Montagu, L.   Receipt to Cure [or for] the Vapours, A.
Ransom, J.   Winter Remembered.
Rodgers, R.   My Favorite Things.
Rose, B.   Without a Song.
Surrey.   Prison in Windsor Castle.
Winchilsea.   Nocturnal Reverie, A.
Wruber, A.   Music, Maestro, Please!
Youmans, V.   Without a Song.

Soldiers
Adkins, G.   Arthur.
Aldington.   Field Manoeuvres.
Ashbery.   Grand Abacus.
Askew, A.   Ballad Which Anne Askew Made and Sang When She Was in Newgate, The.
Asquith.   Volunteer, The.
Auden.   O What Is That Sound [Which So Thrills the Ear].
Taller To-day.
Ba.   Ox-Soldier, The.
Balaban.   Guard at the Binh Thuy Bridge, The.
Barry, J.   In the Footsteps of Genghis Khan.
Barth, R.   Insert, The.
Letter from An Hoc (4), by a Seedbed.
Bierce.   To E. S. Salomon.
Bly, R.   Teeth Mother Naked at Last, The.
Bond, E.   First World War Poets.
Brown, D.   Eating the Forest.
I Was Dancing Alone in Binh Dinh Province.
Returning Fire.
When I Am 19 I Was a Medic.
Brown, S.   Sam Smiley.
Browning, E.   Forced Recruit, The.
Burgoyne, J.   Dashing White Sergeant, The.
Butterfield, F. G.   For Services Rendered.
Cameron, N.   Forgive Me, Sire.
Campbell, R.   Volunteer's Reply to the Poet, The.
Campbell, T.   Soldier's Dream, The.
Casey, M.   On What the Army Does with Heads.
Castillo, S.   Contra, The.
Catina.   Negotiations.
Philosophy.
Causley.   Recruiting Drive.
Song of the Dying Gunner A.A.1.
Cecil.   Apology.
Clare, J.   Returned Soldier, The.
Clayton, I.   Black Rat, The.
Coffey.   Cold.
Coleman, H.   In Ca Mau.
Night Flare Drop, Tan Son Nhut.
OK Corral East Brothers in the Nam.
Collins, W.   How Sleep the Brave.
Dana, R.   At the Vietnam War Memorial, Washington, D. C.
Davenant [or D'Avenant].   Soldier Going to the Field, The.
Donne.   Canonization, The.
Donnelly, C.   Last Poem.
Douglas, K.   Aristocrats.
Vergissmeinicht.
Dove, R.   Alfonzo Prepares to Go Over the Top.
Doyle, S.   Private of the Buffs; or, The British Soldier in China.
Dubie.   Anagram Born of Madness at Czernowitz, 12 November 1920.
Duchamp.   Deferment.
Dugan, A.   Portrait from the Infantry.
Dunbar, P.   Colored Soldiers, The.
When Dey 'Listed Colored Soldiers.
Dunn, D.   War Blinded.
Ehrhart.   Blizzard of Sixty-Six, The.
Hunting.
Making the Children Behave.
Relative Thing, A.
Time on Target.
Elliot, J.   Flowers of the Forest, The.

Elliott, E.   Battle Song.
Emerson, R.   Voluntaries.
Evans, G.   Horse on a Fence.
Evans, M.   I Am a Black Woman.
Fallon, P.   Dardanelles 1916.
Feldman, I.   Se Aprovechan.
Fiacc.   Enemy Encounter.
Fitzgerald, Z.   Over the Top with Pershing.
Fletcher, J.   Rebel, A.
Floyd.   Lance Corporal Purdue Grace, U. S. M. C.
Private Ian Godwin, U. S. M. C.
Private Jack Smith, U. S. M. C.
Ford, F.   That Exploit of Yours.
Frank, F.   Jewish Conscript, The.
Frankau.   Deserter, The.
Gun Teams.
Freneau.   American Soldier, The.
Frost, R.   Not to Keep.
Fuller, R.   Spring 1942.
Gardner, I.   Cock-a-Hoop.
Garrick.   Heart of Oak.
Gellert, L.   Before Action.
Gibson, W.   Breakfast.
Gifford, H.   For Soldiers.
Gilmore, P.   When Johnny Comes Marching Home.
Graves, R.   Sergeant-Major Money.
Grenfell, J.   Into Battle.
Guernsey, B.   Maps.
Guest, E.   Things that Make a Soldier Great, The.
Gunn, T.   As Expected.
Innocence.
Gurney, I.   Bohemians, The.
Canadians.
La Gorgue.
Mangel-Bury, The.
Towards Lillers.
Gwynn, R.   Body Bags.
Haines, J.   Flight, The.
Hall, D.   Disgrace.
Hardy, T.   Colonel's Soliloquy, The.
Departure.
Drummer Hodge.
Man He Killed, The.
Men Who March Away.
Often When Warring.
Subalterns, The.
Harper, M.   Guerrilla-Cong, The.
Hart, K.   Story, The.
Hassett.   Armed Forces Day.
Patriot's Day.
Thanksgiving.
Hayden, R.   Dream, The.
Hemingway.   Champs d'Honneur.
Hood, T.   Faithless Nelly Gray.
Hopkins, G.   Soldier, The.
Horgan.   Tintype of a Private in the Fifteenth Georgia Infantry.
Housman, A.   Deserter, The.
Epitaph.
Epitaph on an Army of Mercenaries.
Grenadier.
Lancer.
New Mistress, The.
Soldier from the Wars Returning.
Huddle.   Cousin.
Vermont.
Hudgins.   Serenades in Virginia.
Soldier on the Marsh, A.
Hughes, T.   Six Young Men.
Irby.   Heredom.
Jarmain.   Embarkation, 1942.
Jarrell.   Description of Some Confederate Soldiers, A.
Eighth Air Force.
Gunner.
Lullaby, A: "For wars his life and half a world away."
Prisoners.
Sick Nought, The.
Soldier Walks under the Trees of the University, The.
Jonas, G.   Portrait: The Freedom Fighter.
Jonson, B.   To Sir Horace Vere.

Kennedy, B.   Bad Luck to This Marching.
Kinnell.   Vapor Trail Reflected in the Frog Pond.
Kipling, R.   'Eathen, The.
Absent-Minded Beggar, The.
Arithmetic on the Frontier.
Ballad of East and West, The.
Boots.
Bridge-Guard in the Karroo.
Brown Bess.
Cells.
Cholera Camp.
Danny Deever.
Fuzzy-Wuzzy.
Gentlemen-Rankers.
Gunga Din.
Recessional.
Return, The.
Screw-Guns.
Shillin' a Day.
Tommy.
Widow at Windsor, The.
Kirstein.   Foresight.
Rank.
Koch, K.   To World War Two.
Komunyakaa.   Break from the Bush, A.
Somewhere Near Phu Bai.
Krohn.   Can Tho.
Kunitz, S.   Careless Love.
Larkin, P.   MCMXIV.
Homage to a Government.
Lawrence, D.   Tommies in the Train.
Layne, M.   Beautiful Ladies.
Collect Call.
Gettin' Straight.
Mob, The.
On Hats and Things.
On the Yellow Footprints.
Letts.   Spires of Oxford, The.
Lewis, A.   All Day It Has Rained.
Dawn on the East Coast.
Infantry.
Peasants, The.
Sentry, The.
To a Comrade in Arms.
Unknown Soldier, The.
Longfellow, H.   Killed at the Ford.
Lovelace, R.   To a Lady with Child that Asked [or Ask'd] an Old Shirt.
To Lucasta, [on] Going to the War[re]s.
MacDiarmid, H.   Another Epitaph on an Army of Mercenaries.
Under the Greenwood Tree.
Mackintosh, E.   Cha Till Maccruimein (Departure of the 4th Camerons).
In Memoriam[, Private D. Sutherland].
MacLean, S.   Heroes.
MacLeish.   Lines for an Interment.
Memorial Rain.
Manifold.   Fife Tune.
Manning, F.   Grotesque.
Mansfield, K.   Man with the Wooden Leg, The.
Masefield.   To-morrow.
Masters, E.   Many Soldiers.
Mayer, B.   Aeschyleans, The.
McCarthy, G.   Hooded Legion, The.
McCrae, J.   In Flanders Fields.
McGrath, T.   Blues for Warren.
Go Ask the Dead.
Nocturne Militaire.
Ode for the American Dead in Korea.
Melville, H.   Ball's Bluff.
March into Virginia, The.
Merwin, W. S.   When the War Is Over.
Miller, E.   What the Women Told Me.
Milton.   When the Assault Was Intended to the City.
Moffi.   Putting an End to the War Stories.
Moody, W.   Harmonics.
On a Soldier Fallen in the Philippines.
Moolten, D.   Brandy Station, Virginia.
Muldoon, P.   Truce.
Mura.   Natives, The.
Murray, L.   Drugs of War, The.
Lament for the Country Soldiers.
Nemerov.   Fable of the War, A.
Nims, J.   Trainwrecked Soldiers.

Nortje. At Rest from the Grim Place.
Norton, C. Bingen on the Rhine.
O'Loughlin. Elegy for the Unknown Soldier.
Owen, W. A Terre.
  Anthem for Doomed Youth.
  Apologia Pro Poemate Meo.
  Arms and the Boy.
  At a Calvary near the Ancre.
  Disabled.
  Dulce et Decorum Est.
  Exposure.
  Futility.
  Insensibility.
  Mental Cases.
  Send-Off, The.
  Show, The.
  Spring Offensive.
  Strange Meeting.
Pack, R. Epistle from a Half-Pay Officer in the
  Country to His Friend in London, An.
Padel. Trial.
Paquet. Morning—A Death.
Parker, M. Maunding Soldier; or, The Fruits of
  Warre Is Beggery, The.
Patchen. Body Beside the Ties, The.
Piatt, S. Army of Occupation.
Pope, J. Beau Ideal, The.
Prince, F. Soldiers Bathing.
Ravikovitch [or Ravikovich]. You Can't Kill a
  Baby Twice.
Rawson, J. Border, The.
Read, S. Happy Warrior, The.
  To a Conscript of 1940.
Reynolds, O. Hazel.
Rickword. Soldier Addresses His Body, The.
Robinson, E. Field of Glory, The.
Rosenberg, I. Break of Day in the Trenches.
  Louse Hunting.
  Soldier: Twentieth Century.
  Troop ship, The.
Ross, A. Mess Deck.
Rottman. APO 96225.
Sandburg, C. Old Timers.
Sassoon. 'They.'
  Aftermath.
  Attack.
  Base Details.
  Christ and the Soldier.
  Does It Matter?
  Dreamers.
  Dug-Out, The.
  Everyone Sang.
  General, The.
  Glory of Women.
  In Barracks.
  Repression of War Experience.
  Suicide in [the] Trenches.
  Working Party, A.
Scannell. Great War, The.
Scott of Amwell. Ode: "I hate that drum's
  discordant sound."
Seeger, P. Where Have All the Flowers Gone?
Senghor. Taga for Mbaye Dyôb.
Service. Pot of Tea, A.
Shapiro, K. Homecoming.
  Nostalgia.
  Troop Train.
Short, J. Leave in Mid-Winter.
Simpson, L. Ash and the Oak, The.
  Battle, The.
  Runner, The.
Smith, A. Political Intelligence.
Smith, S. Private Means Is Dead.
Snodgrass, W. Ten Days Leave.
Sorley. All the Hills and Vales Along.
Soyinka. Civilian and Soldier.
Spender, S. Two Armies.
Stephen, J. Malines.
Stevenson, R. Ticonderoga: A Legend of the
  West Highlands.
Suckling, S. Soldier, A.
Surrey. Epitaph for [or on] Thomas Clere.
Swirszczynska. He Was Lucky.
Tennant, E. Mad Soldier, The.
Tennyson, A. Charge of the Light Brigade, The.
Thomas, E. Owl, The.

Private, A.
  Tears.
Thompson, M. Address by an Ex-Confederate
  Soldier to the Grand Army of the Republic,
  An.
Ticknor. Little Giffen.
Trapnell, N. Lament of a Desert Rat.
Tucker, M. Soldier Boy's Dream, The.
Ungaretti. Soldiers.
Unknown. British Grenadiers, The.
  Enlisted Today.
  I Don't Want to Be a Soldier.
  Jimmy's Enlisted; or, The Recruited Collier.
  Johnny, I Hardly Knew Ye.
  Little Jock Elliot.
  My Sodger Laddie.
  No Balls at All.
  Over the Hills and Far Away.
  Sir Dilberry Diddle, Captain of Militia.
  Soldier That Has Seen Service, The.
  Soldiers.
  Sweet Polly Oliver.
  Volunteer, The.
Unknown, fr. Terezin Concentration Camp.
  Closed Town, The.
Weigl. Girl at the Chu Lai Laundry.
Whistler. Portrait in the Guards, A.
Whitman, W. Army Corps on the March, An.
  Artilleryman's Vision, The.
  As Toilsome I Wander'd Virginia's Woods.
  Ashes of Soldiers.
  By the Bivouac's Fitful Flame.
  Cavalry Crossing a Ford.
  Centenarian's Story, The.
  March in the Ranks Hard-Prest, and the Road
    Unknown, A.
  O Tan-Faced Prairie-Boy.
  Sight in Camp [in the Daybreak Gray and
    Dim], A.
  Spirit Whose Work Is Done.
  Vigil Strange I Kept on the Field One Night.
  Wound-Dresser, The.
Whittemore, R. Day with the Foreign
  Legion, A.
Whittier. Lost Occasion, The.
Wilbur. Place Pigalle.
Winchilsea. Trail All Your Pikes.
Wright, J. Confession to J. Edgar Hoover.
  Speak.
Yeats. Irish Airman Foresees His Death, An.
Young, S. Epitaph for a Concord Boy.
See also **War**

Solidarity
Fishman, C. Not Only in the Six-Day War.

Solipsism
Cranch. Pines and the Sea, The.
Housman, A. I Counsel You Beware.
'Marnia. Accoutrement.
  I Must be Able to Protect You.
  I Want to Love You Very Much.
Plath. Soliloquy of the Solipsist.
Stevens, W. Landscape with Boat.

Solitude
Ai. Man with the Saxophone, The.
Aiken, C. Solitaire.
Amadiume. Mistress of My Own Being.
Awoonor. Songs of Sorrow.
Belieu. Rondeau at the Train Stop.
Bly, R. Six Winter Privacy Poems.
  Solitude Late at Night in the Woods.
  Sunday in Glastonbury.
Boland, E. Woman in Kitchen.
Brontë, A. Captive Dove, The.
Brontë, C. 'Again I find myself alone.'
  Obscure and little seen my way.
Brontë, E. Little while, a little while, A.
  To Imagination.
Bynner. Drinking Alone with the Moon.
Caesar. Tea for Two.
Caldwell, A. Left All Alone Again Blues.
Cary, A. To Solitude.
Cavafy. As Much As You Can.
Cheney-Coker. Poem for a Guerrilla Leader.
Cisneros, S. Poet Reflects On Her Solitary Fate,
  The.
Clare, J. I Am.

Solitude.
  Song: "I peeled bits of straw and I got switches
    too."
Cofer, J. Life of an Echo, The.
Cohen, M. Evensong.
Colby, T. Captain's Log.
Coleridge, M. Solo.
Cox, N. Singing Alone.
Creeley. Flower, The.
Cuddihy. Solitude.
Cummings, E. No Thanks, No. 70.
Dauer. William.
DeCarteret, M. Town Clerk, The.
DeLange, E. Solitude.
Dickey, J. One, The.
Dickinson, E. This Is My Letter to the World.
Dietz, H. Alone Together.
Diop, D. Renegade, The.
Dodd, E. Like Memory, Caverns.
Dooley, M. Up on the Roof.
Dove, R. Daystar.
  Weathering Out.
Duncan, R. Passage Over Water.
Eliot, T. Gerontion.
Ellington, D. Solitude.
"Field." Eros.
  Onycha.
Frost, R. Acquainted with the Night.
  Desert Places.
  Most of It, The.
Gibran. Defeat.
Gomez, M. Looking Deep.
Graham, W. Malcolm Mooney's Land.
Gregerman, D. Lullaby.
  Silent Globe.
Hacker, M. Going Back to the River.
Hanzlicek, C. On the Road Home.
Hayden, R. Road in Kentucky, A.
Herrick. Not To Love.
  Upon the Loss[e] of His Mistresses.
Hewitt, J. Father's Death, A.
Hirsch, E. Edward Hopper and the House by
  the Railroad.
Hitchcock. Solitaire.
Hopkins, G. Heaven-Haven.
Hugo, R. Letter to Bell from Missoula.
  Salt Water Story.
Jackson, H. Solitude.
Jarrell. 90 North.
Jeffers, R. Compensation.
Joseph, J. Back to Base.
Justice, D. Another Song.
Kavanagh, P. Inniskeen Road: July Evening.
Keats. Bright Star.
  O Solitude! If I Must With Thee Dwell.
Keplinger, D. Inside: George Gaines at
  Graterford Prison, 1981.
Kern, J. Left All Alone Again Blues.
Kinnell. When One Has Lived a Long Time
  Alone.
Kipling, R. For to Admire.
Kumin, M. Living Alone with Jesus—.
Kunitz, S. River Road.
Lampman. In November: "Hills and leafless
  forests slowly yield, The."
Larkin, P. Reasons for Attendance.
  Vers de Société.
  Wants.
Lee, L. Eating Alone.
Levertov. Losing Track.
  Woman Alone, A.
Li Po. Drinking Alone in the Moonlight.
Liu Ch'ang-ch'ing. Sent to the Taoist of Dragon
  Mountain, Hsu Fa-leng.
Longfellow, H. Broken Oar, The.
Lorde. Hanging Fire.
Lovelace, R. Song: "In mine one [or own]
  monument I lie [or lye]."
Madhubuti. Loneliness, A.
Mahapatra, J. Monsoon Day Fable, A.
Marvell. Garden, The.
McGrath, T. Letter for Marian, A.
  Ordonnance.
  Return, The.
Miles, J. Travelers.
Mills, B. Ballad: Of Motion.

Mills, I.   Solitude.
Milton.   Il Penseroso.
Mollineux.   Solitude.
Mora.   One Potato.
Mother Goose.   Little Jumping Joan.
Mudrooroo Narogin.   Hide and Seek.
Nienhauser, W. H.   Sent to the Taoist of Dragon Mountain, Hsu Fa-leng.
Nokan.   My Head is Immense.
Nortje.   Up Late.
Norton, C.   To My Books.
Nye, N.   Art of Disappearing, The.
O'Hara, F.   1951.
   Autobiographia Literaria.
   Poem: "Eager note on my door said 'Call me'," The.
Oodgeroo of the tribe Noonuccal.   Last of His Tribe.
Oppen.   Myself I Sing.
Pickthall, M.   Quiet.
Pinkerton, H.   On Vermeer's "Young Woman with a Water Jug" (1658) in the Metropolitan Museum.
Pitter.   Old, Childless, Husbandless.
Poe.   "Alone."
Pommy-Vega.   [Here before the sunrise blue and in this solitude].
Pope, A.   Ode on Solitude.
Prince, F.   False Bay.
Ravikovitch [or Ravikovich].   Surely You Remember.
Replansky.   I Met My Solitude.
Rexroth, K.   On Flower Wreath Hill.
Robinson, A.   Personality.
Robinson, E.   Aaron Stark.
Rossetti, C.   Autumn.
   L.E.L. E. L.
Salinas, L.   Sea Song.
Santayana.   Cape Cod.
Sassoon.   Elected Silence.
Schulman.   American Solitude.
Schwartz, A.   Alone Together.
Seferis.   Word for Summer, A.
Sharma, P.   Poorly Matched.
Shelley, P.   Sonnet: Political Greatness.
   Stanzas—April, 1814.
Simmons, J.   Pleasant Joys of Brotherhood, The.
   West Strand Visions.
Simpson, L.   After Midnight.
Sisson.   Tristia.
Smith, C.   By the Same. To Solitude.
Snodgrass, W.   Song: "Sweet beast, I have gone prowling."
Snyder, G.   Mid-August at Sourdough Mountain Lookout.
Solari, R.   Truro.
Soyinka.   Hunchback of Dugbe, The.
Stafford, W.   Run before Dawn.
Stephens, J.   Goat Paths, The.
Stevens, W.   Anglais Mort à Florence.
Stevenson, A.   Willow Song.
Stickney, T.   In Ampezzo.
Stone, J.   Getting to Sleep in New Jersey.
Stoutenburg.   Midnight Saving Time.
Strand.   Garden, The.
   Morning, A.
Sykes, B.   One Day.
Synge.   Prelude: "Still south I went and west and south again."
Synková, A.   I'd Like to Go Alone.
Teasdale.   Open Windows.
   Over the Roofs.
   Solitary, The.
Tennyson, A.   Go By.
   Palace of Art, The.
Thomas, D.   Ears in the Turrets Hear.
   Hunchback in the Park, The.
Thomas, E.   Rain.
Thomson, J.   Hymn on Solitude.
Tighe.   Written at Scarborough. August, 1799.
Turner, A.   Red Flower.
Unknown.   Seafarer, The.
   There Is a Mystery in Human Hearts.
Very.   I Was Sick and in Prison.
Walcott.   Letter from Brooklyn, A.
   Winding Up.

Whitman, W.   I Saw in Louisiana a Live-Oak Growing.
Wilcox, E.   Solitude.
Wilde, R.   Lament of the Captive, The.
Williams, W.   Danse Russe.
Wordsworth, W.   Solitary Reaper, The.
Wright, C.   Sitting at Night on the Front Porch.
Wright, J.   Lake in Central Park, The.
   Two Postures beside a Fire.
Wunderlich, M.   Aubade.
Wylie.   Eagle and the Mole, The.
Yeats.   Apparitions, The.
   Lake-Isle of Innisfree, The.
Youmans, V.   Tea for Two.

Solomon (Bible)
Browning, R.   Solomon and Balkis.
Cassells.   New Song of Solomon.
Herbert, G.   Sion.
Moore, M.   O To Be A Dragon.
Yeats.   On Woman.
   Solomon and the Witch.

Somersaults
Harris, W.   Historic Moment, An.

Somerset, England
Coleridge, S.   This Lime-Tree Bower My Prison.

Somnambulism and Somnambulists
Hirsch, E.   For the Sleepwalkers.

Songs
Ahlert, F.   Life Is a Song, Let's Sing It Together.
Alvarez, J.   Redwing Sonnets.
Anderson, S.   Evening Song.
Annand.   Mavis.
Arlen, H.   Happy As the Day Is Long.
   I Gotta Right to Sing the Blues.
Ashbery.   Hotel Lautréamont.
Baraka.   Alba.
Barrax.   There Was A Song.
Benét, S.   Nonsense Song, A.
Berlin.   Let Me Sing and I'm Happy.
   Song Is Ended (But the Melody Lingers On), The.
Bishop, E.   Songs for a Colored Singer.
Brecht, B.   Three Fragments.
Brodsky, J.   Love Song.
Burkard.   My Aunt and the Sun.
Calverley.   Ballad: "Auld wife sat at her ivied door, The."
Campbell, R.   Choosing a Mast.
Campo.   My Voice.
Carmichael, H.   Star Dust.
Ceravolo.   Sunset.
Cleary, B.   Boys' Own.
Conway, J.   Modern English.
Creeley.   House, The.
Cristall.   Song: "Wandering in the still of eve."
   To a Lady on the Rise of Morn.
DeFoe, M.   Aviary.
   Dream Lover.
Dickey, J.   Buckdancer's Choice.
Donne.   Triple Fool, The.
Dooley, M.   Does It Go Like this?
Dowson.   Dregs.
Dunbar, P.   Compensation.
Eliscu, E.   Without a Song.
Garrigue.   Song in Sligo.
Geiger.   Soundtracks.
Gershwin.   Blah, Blah, Blah.
Gioia.   Cruising with the Beach Boys.
Goldbarth.   Seriema Song.
Graham, J.   Of Forced Sightes and Trusty Ferefulness.
Gregg.   Dark Thing Inside the Day, A.
Gregory.   Christmas Lullaby for a New-Born Child.
Hammerstein.   Song Is You, The.
Harris, P.   Some Songs Women Sing.
Hart, L.   With a Song in My Heart.
Hattersley, G.   Singing.
Hejinian.   Mask of Anger, A.
Hemans.   Song of Emigration.
Higo.   Hidesong.
Holmes, O.   Prologue.
Hooks.   Woman's Mourning Song, The.
Hovanessian, D.   Inside Green Eyes, Black Eyes.

Howe, J.   Battle Hymn [or Battle-Hymn] of the Republic, The.
Hughes, L.   Songs.
Hugo, R.   My Buddy.
Jackson, A.   Ohnedaruth.
Johnson, J.   Lift Every [or Ev'ry] Voice and Sing.
   Porter's Love Song to a Chambermaid, A.
Keats.   On the Grasshopper and [the] Cricket.
Kenyon, J.   Insomnia at the Solstice.
Kern, J.   Land Where the Good Songs Go, The.
Kgositsile.   Song for Ilva Mackay and Mongane.
Koethe.   Songs of the Valley.
Kreymborg.   Improvisation.
Larkin, P.   Love Songs in Age.
Ledwidge.   Lament for the Poets: 1916.
Lee, L.   I Ask My Mother to Sing.
Levy, A.   First Extra, The.
Liu, T.   Ikon.
Longfellow, H.   Day Is Done, The.
Lux.   One Meat Ball.
Macdonald, G.   Shortest and Sweetest of Songs, The.
Mayes, J.   Descant.
McKay, C.   Negro Spiritual.
Meynell, A.   To Silence.
Montale.   Lemon Trees, The.
Moore, L.   Song Poem, The.
Moss, H.   Persistence of Song, The.
Mugo, M. G.   Where are those Songs?
Nameroff, R.   California Dreaming.
Nesbit, E.   To Vera, Who Asked a Song.
Norris, L.   His Father, Singing.
O'Connor, P.   Raspberry in the Pudding, The.
Orpingalik.   "Songs are Thoughts, Sung Out with the Breath."
Orr, G.   Insomnia Song.
Ortiz.   Look to the Mountain.
Parish.   Star Dust.
Piatt, S.   Sad Spring-Song.
Probyn.   Song Out of Season, A.
Rafferty, P.   Personal.
Reznikoff.   I Will Write Songs against You.
Riley, D.   Misremembered Lyric, A.
Riley, J.   Nonsense Rhyme, A.
Rivard.   Cures.
Roberts, E.   Old Love in Song, An.
Roethke.   Light Listened.
   Voice, The.
Rothenberg, J.   Song of Quavering, A.
Rukeyser, M.   This Place in the Ways.
Scott, S.   Hunting Song.
Senghor.   Be Not Amazed.
Shelley, P.   To a Skylark.
Snodgrass, W.   Song: "Sweet beast, I have gone prowling."
Snyder, G.   Night Song of the Los Angeles Basin.
Stern, G.   For Song.
Stevens, W.   Of Mere Being.
Suckling, S.   Ballad[e] [upon a Wedding], A.
Taggard.   Hymn to Yellow.
Teasdale.   Little While, A.
Tennyson, A.   Dying Swan, The.
Thaxter.   Sandpiper, The.
Todd, M.   Wire Song.
Toomer.   Song of the Son.
Trinidad.   Monday, Monday.
Van Doren.   So Simple.
Van Duyn.   Mockingbird Month.
Very.   Song, The: "When I would sing of crooked streams and fields."
Watson, R.   Die Zauberflöte.
   Serenade: "Who is it sings the gypsies' song tonight."
Weaver, M.   Sub Shop Girl.
Welburn.   Gonsalves.
Whitman, W.   Chanting the Square Deific.
   Out of the Cradle Endlessly Rocking.
Wilbur.   Cicadas.
Wise, S.   Closure Opening Its Trap.
Wong, N.   Grandmothers' Song.
Wordsworth, W.   Reverie of Poor Susan, The.
Wright, D.   Musician, The.
Wright, J.   Written in a Copy of Swift's Poems, for Wayne Burns.

Yeats. Coat, A.
Zarin. Song: "My heart, my dove, my snail, my sail, my."
Zimmer. Romance.

Sonnets
Bogan, L. Single Sonnet.
Burns, R. Sonnet upon Sonnets, A.
Chasin. Joy Sonnet in a Random Universe.
Devaney, T. Sonnet: "You know all those sonnets the ones where I said, I love you, well."
Donne. Canonization, The.
Elliott, E. Powers of the Sonnet.
Faber, F. Sonnet-writing. To F. W. F.
Gilder, R. Sonnet, The.
Gladstone, W. E. To a Rejected Sonnet.
Hood, T. Sonnet to a Sonnet.
Keats. If by Dull Rhymes Our English Must Be Chained.
Koestenbaum, P. Sonnet 37: "I'd decided I initiate most."
Lee-Hamilton. What the Sonnet Is.
Loines. On a Magazine Sonnet.
Moore, M. In Magic Words.
Morgan, E. Opening the Cage.
Poe. Enigma, An.
Symonds. Sonnet (III), The.
Watts-Dunton. Sonnet's Voice, The.
Wilcox, E. Sonnet, The.
Wordsworth, W. Sonnet: "Nuns fret not at their convent's narrow room;."

Sons
Applewhite. Prayer for My Son.
Arrillaga. Rosa/Filí.
Awad, J. Generations.
  Stopping at the Mayflower.
Barber, M. Written for My Son, and Spoken by Him at His First Putting on Breeches.
Bennani, B. Letters to Lebanon.
Berryman. Sympathy, A Welcome, A.
Bly, R. Prodigal Son, The.
Bowers, E. Prince, The.
Carlson, D. Russ Joy Little League.
Clarke, T. For Babies Unborn.
Clifton, L. Admonitions.
Corbet [or Corbett]. To His Son [or Sonne], Vincent Corbet[t].
Cronin, A. For a Father.
Davidson, D. Randall, My Son.
Dickey, J. Bee, The.
  Birth, A.
Dickey, R. Mulatto Lullaby.
Duhig, I. First Second, The.
Duncan, R. My Mother Would Be a Falconress.
Fearing. Any Man's Advice to His Son.
Feinstein, E. At Seven a Son.
Finkel. Father, The.
Finney, N. Lobengula: Having a son at 38.
Fitzgerald, R. Figlio Maggiore.
Fordham. Sonnet to My First Born.
Gallagher, T. Each Bird Walking.
Galvin, J. Shadow-Casting.
Geier. On Your Twenty-First Birthday.
Goethe. Erl-King, The.
Grafflin. To My Son.
Gregory, H. For You, My Son.
Hall, D. My Son, My Executioner.
Hazo. Maps for a Son Are Drawn as You Go.
Heaney, S. Mother of the Groom.
Hernández Cruz. Ruskie's Boy.
Hippolyte. So Jah Sey.
Hirschhorn, N. Number Our Days.
Hoffman, D. Special Train, A.
Hood, T. World Is with Me, The.
Humphreys, E. From Father to Son.
Hunt, S. Birth of a Son.
Jonson, B. On My First Son[ne].
Joseph, L. Then.
Khalvati. Blue Moon.
Kinnell. After Making Love We Hear Footsteps.
Kipling, R. Sons of Martha, The.
Kooser. At the End of the Weekend.
Lassell. Going to Europe.
Lee, L. Weight of Sweetness, The.
Levertov. Son, The.

Linden, M. Wayward Son, The.
Long, H. For Tony, Embarking in Spring.
Marshall, J. Letter to My Father on the Other Side.
  Thirty-Seven.
Mason, R. Young Man Thinks of Sons, The.
McGrath, T. Poem: "When I carry my little son in the cold."
Meinke. Advice to My Son.
Merwin, W. S. Yesterday.
Meynell, A. Father of Women, A [Ad Sororem E. B.].
Milne, A. Disobedience.
Mungoshi. Letter to a Son, A.
North, M. Pheasant Plucker's Son, The.
Nowlan. Mother and Son.
  Only When My Heart Freezes.
O'Brien, L. Diabolus in Musica.
Olds, S. Mother, The.
Oppen. Daedalus: The Dirge.
Ortiz. What I Tell Him.
Phillips, L. My Son Shows Me a Photograph of Michael Jordan Performing a Slam Dunk.
Piñero. On The Day They Buried My Mother.
Potts. For My Father.
Rich, A. Jerusalem.
Rodriguez, L. To the Police Officer Who Refused to Sit in the Same Room as My Son because He's a 'Gang Banger.'
Romo-Carmona, M. Fish.
Ryan, M. This Is a Poem for the Dead.
Saunders, L. Mothers of Sons.
Scammell, W. Poem for a Younger Son.
Shafer, A. Monday Morning.
Shelton, R. Letter to a Dead Father.
Silkin. Death of a Son.
Simon, L. Kali.
Skloot. Hook.
Smith, D. August, on the Rented Farm.
Smith, S. Correspondence between Mr. Harrison in Newcastle and Mr. Sholto Peach Harrison in Hull.
Stallworthy, J. Almond Tree, The.
Stein, K. It Didn't Begin with Horned Owls Hooting at Noon.
Stevens, W. John Smith and His Son, John Smith.
  World Without Peculiarity.
Stone, J. Bass, The.
Tatarunis, P. I Have Two Sons and the One I Love Best Is Robert.
Tate, A. Mother and Son.
Taylor, C.B. Round Irving High School.
Taylor, E. Few Days in the South in February, A.
Torrence. Son, The.
Unknown. Enlisted Today.
  Somebody's Mother.
  To a New Daughter-in-Law.
  Wife of Usher's Well, The.
Van Doren. Ancient Couple on Lu Mountain, The.
Vando. Father's Day.
Warren, R. Night Walking.
  Only Poem, The.
Wesley, C. On the Death of His Son.
Westmorland. Dedication of My First Son, A.
Whitman, W. Dirge for Two Veterans.
  Vigil Strange I Kept on the Field One Night.
Williams, L. Interruption of Flight.
Wordsworth, W. Affliction of Margaret, The.
Wright, J. Having Lost My Sons, I Confront the Wreckage of the Moon: Christmas, 1960.
  Revelation, The.
  Two Postures beside a Fire.
Yeats. Prayer for My Son, A.
Young, G. Miracle, The.
Zamora-Linmark. Election Day.
Zweig, P. Father.

Sophocles
Arnold, M. Dover Beach.
  To a Friend.

Sorcery and Sorcerers
Arlen, H. We're Off to See the Wizard (The Wonderful Wizard of Oz).
Wells, L. Sorcerer, The.

Sorrow
Abse. Origin of Music, The.
Alexander, M. People of Unrest.
Alley, R. Dissecting Uncle Sorrow.
Amichai [or Amikhai]. Quick and Bitter.
Apollinaire. Fete.
Arlen, H. Ill Wind.
  Stormy Weather (Keeps Rainin' All the Time).
  Tess's Torch Song (I Had a Man).
Arnheim, G. I Cried for You.
Ashbery. Variant.
Ashe. To Two Bereaved.
Awoonor. First Circle, The.
  Songs of Sorrow.
Beckett, S. Enueg II.
Beedome. Question and Answer, The.
Blaga. Psalm.
Braithwaite. House of Falling Leaves, The.
Brontë, E. Spellbound.
Brown, L. (Here Am I) Broken Hearted.
Browning, E. Cry of the Children, The.
  Mask, The.
  My Heart and I.
  Year's Spinning, A.
Brutus. They Hanged Him, I Said Dismissively.
Burns, R. Ae Fond Kiss.
  Bonie Doon.
  Man Was Made to Mourn, a Dirge.
  Song: "O my love's [or luve's or love is or luve is] like a red, red rose."
  Ye Banks and Braes.
Byron, G. By the Rivers of Babylon We Sat Down and Wept.
  Oh! Weep for Those.
Campion, T. When to Her Lute Corinna [or Corrina] Sings.
Carew, T. Epitaph on the Lady Mary Villiers.
  Lover, upon an Accident Necessitating His Departure, Consults with Reason, A.
  To Celia, upon Love's Ubiquity.
Cary, A. Window Just Over the Street, The.
Clampitt. Procession at Candlemas, A.
Clifton, L. Sorrow Song.
Cook, E. Written at the Couch of a Dying Parent.
Cowper, W. Shrubbery, The.
Creamer, H. After You've Gone.
Cresson. Cloak of Laughter.
Crowell, A. Joy of Incompleteness, The.
Cullen, C. Saturday's Child.
d'Oettingen. Outcries.
De la Mare. At Ease.
  Dove, The.
  Ghost, The.
  Old Summerhouse, The.
Delmore, E. Such Sweet Sorrow.
Di Prima. For H.D.
Dipoko. Our Life.
Dobson, A. Before Sedan.
Dodge, M. Someone in the Garden.
Donaldson, W. Little White Lies.
  One I Love (Belongs to Someone Else), The.
  You're Driving Me Crazy (What Did I Do?).
Dowson. O Mors! Quam Amara Est Memoria Tua Homini Pacem Habenti In Substantiis Suis.
  Spleen.
Drummond de Andrade. Dead in Frock Coats, The.
Dunbar, P. We Wear the Mask.
Duncan, R. Among My Friends.
  Turning into.
Dyer, S. I Would It Were Not As It Is.
Ebb, F. My Coloring Book.
El-Hadi, S. Tired Man, The.
Elliot, J. Flowers of the Forest, The.
"Field." Picture, A.
Fraser, G. Lament: "In a dismal air; a light of breaking summer."
Freed, A. I Cried for You.
Frost, R. My November Guest.
Fuller, M. Meditations.
García Lorca. At the Poorhouse.
Gardinier. Where Blind Sorrow Is Taught to See.
Gibran. Heavy-Laden Is My Soul.

Glück, L.   Elms.
Gordon, M.   There's a Lull in My Life.
Gorham.   Princess Parade.
Graves, R.   Lost Love.
Green, D. R.   Names and Sorrows.
Griffith, L.   Exile: Welsh Service from Daventry.
Hammond, W.   To the Same [My Dear Sister, Mrs S.]: The Tears.
Handman, L.   Are You Lonesome Tonight?
Hardy, T.   Going, The.
Herbert, G.   Joseph's Coat.
Herman, J.   Time Heals Everything.
Herrick.   Bad Season Makes the Poet Sad, The.
On Himselfe.
To the Willow-Tree.
Housman, A.   They Say My Verse Is Sad: No Wonder.
Howe, F.   Doubt.
Howells, W.   Forlorn.
Huidobro.   New Song.
Ingelow.   Story, A.
Jordan, J.   Sandbar at Moore's Creek.
Winter.
Jurmann, W.   Tomorrow Is Another Day.
Kalmar *et al.*   Who's Sorry Now?
Kander, J.   My Coloring Book.
Katz, J.   Falling.
Keats.   O Thou Whose Face Hath Felt the Winter's Wind.
Ode to a Nightingale.
Kemble.   Impromptu.
Komunyakaa.   When Loneliness is a Man.
Landon.   Child Screening a Dove from a Hawk, A.
Small Miseries.
Lanier, S.   Raven Days, The.
Layton, J.   After You've Gone.
Levine, P.   Red Dust.
Li Po.   Moon over the Mountain Pass, The.
Liu, T.   Poem: "Late butterflies gliding through the air—."
Logan, J.   Braes of Yarrow, The.
Longfellow, H.   Bridge, The.
Rainy Day, The.
Lyman, A.   I Cried for You.
Martínez, V.   Night of Fathers.
Massey.   Desolate.
McCarthy, T.   Mr. Nabokov's Memory.
McKay, C.   Negro Spiritual.
Millay, E.   Sorrow.
Milton.   Lycidas.
Moore, T.   Oft In the Stilly Night.
Naimy, M.   Solemn Vow, A.
Nesbit, E.   Love's Guerdons.
Nilsson, H.   On Inheriting Departure.
O'Hara, F.   Aus Einem April.
Ofeimun.   How Can I Sing.
Owen, W.   Roads Also, The.
Park, S.   On Such A Day.
Philips, K.   Lucasia, Rosania and Orinda Parting at a Fountain, July 1663.
Pilkington, L.   Sorrow.
Poe.   Haunted Palace, The.
Valley of Unrest, The.
Porter, C.   Down in the Depths.
Ev'ry Time We Say Good-bye.
Pound, E.   Song of the Bowmen of Shu.
Radnóti.   Letter to My Wife.
Raine, K.   Invocation of Death.
Rankine.   Elsewhere, Things Tend.
Reese, L.   Rachel.
Revel, H.   There's a Lull in My Life.
Ridler.   At Parting.
Robinson, A.   Stornelli and Strambotti.
Robinson, E.   Walt Whitman.
Robinson, M.   Bids Farewell to Lesbos.
Contemns Philosophy.
Describes the Fascinations of Love.
Determines to Follow Phaon.
Her Confirmed Despair.
Her Last Appeal to Phaon.
Laments her Early Misfortunes.
Reproaches Phaon.
Sappho's Address to the Stars.
Sappho's Conjectures.
To a Sigh.

To Phaon.
To the Muses.
Roscoe, W.   On Being Forced to Part with his Library for the Benefit of his Creditors.
Rossetti, C.   Remember [Me].
Shut Out.
Sassoon.   Lamentations.
Scott, L.   Ettrick.
Seward.   Sonnet 31.
Sewell, L.   Release.
Shelley, P.   To————: "One word is too often profaned."
Siddal.   Dead Love.
Sidney, R.   Sonnet 25: "Yow that take pleasure in yowr cruelty."
Smedley, M.   Sorrowful Sea-Gull, The.
Smith, C.   On the Departure of the Nightingale.
Verses Intended to Have Been Prefixed to the Novel of Emmeline, but Then Suppressed.
Smith, S.   Satin-Clad.
Southwell.   Vale of Tear[e]s, A.
Soyinka.   I Think It Rains.
Spenser.   Iambicum Trimetrum.
Stern, G.   Behaving Like a Jew.
Surrey.   Soote Season, The.
Swinburne.   Anactoria.
In The Orchard.
Match, A.
Thomas, E.   When I First Came Here.
Thoreau.   Brother Where Dost Thou Dwell.
Townsend, A.   First Death.
Tuckerman, F.   Coralie.
Unknown.   Fowls [or Foweles *or* Fowles] in the Frith.
I Saw My Lady Weep.
Volkman.   Daffodils.
Wang Ts'an.   Seven Sorrows.
Warton, T.   Ode on the Passion.
Whitman, S.   Past, The.
Whitman, W.   I Sit and Look Out.
Wilcox, E.   Way of It, The.
Williams, H.   To the Strawberry.
Williams, W.   Waiting.
Widow's Lament in Springtime, The.
Wolfe, C.   To Mary.
Wylie.   "Desolation Is a Delicate Thing."
See also **Funerals; Grief; Mourning and Mourners**
Soul
Abse.   In the Theatre.
Amis, K.   Nothing to Fear.
Ammons, A. R.   Terrain.
Arnold, M.   Palladium.
Baraka.   Invention of Comics, The.
Bernstein, C.   From Lines of Swinburne.
Bevington, L.   'Egoisme à Deux'
Wrestling.
Blumenthal, M.   Man Lost by a River, A.
Bonar.   Be True [or Be True Thyself].
Boyle, D. M.   Curtain, The.
Braithwaite.   Rye Bread.
Brontë, A.   Lines Composed in a Wood on a Windy Day.
Brontë, E.   No Coward Soul is Mine.
Browning, E.   Fifth Book.
Brownstein.   Last Spell Cast, The.
Cavendish, M.   Dialogue betwixt Man, and Nature, A.
Dialogue betwixt the Body and the Mind, A.
Soul and Body.
Clayton, S.   Soul Music.
Coleridge, M.   Friends—With a Difference.
Wilderspin.
Cook, E.   Old Arm-Chair, The.
Cooke, E.   How Did You Die?
Cummings, E.   Cambridge ladies who live in furnished souls, The.
Dacre, A.   Kiss, The.
Davies, J.   Intellectual Powers of the Soul, The.
Di Piero.   Near Damascus.
Dickinson, E.   "Hope" is the thing with feathers.
Choice.
He fumbles at Your Spirit.
Of nearness to her sundered Things.
Dobell, S.   Liberty to M. le Diplomate.
Dolin, S.   My Soul's Wardrobe.

Donne.   Air[e] and Angels.
Ecstasy, The.
Funeral[l], The.
Resurrection, Imperfect.
To the Countess of Salisbury.
Valediction: Forbidding Mourning, A.
Douglas, L.   Green River, The.
Dove, R.   History.
Dunbar, P.   Ere Sleep Comes Down to Soothe the Weary Eyes.
Eliot, T.   Animula.
Elizabeth I.   Written in Her French Psalter.
Emerson, R.   World-Soul, The.
Empson.   This Last Pain.
Espaillat.   Metrics.
Eyton, F.   Body and Soul.
"Field."   Mummy Invokes His Soul, The.
Fullerton.   Poetry.
Garrett, E.   History Goes to Work.
Gibran.   Heavy-Laden Is My Soul.
Ginsberg, A.   After Lalon.
Glück, L.   Day Without Night.
New Life, The.
Goodison.   Always Homing Now Soul Toward Light.
Graham, J.   Soul Says.
Greer, J.   Rodin's "Gates of Hell."
Grosholz.   Back Trouble.
Halpern, D.   Her Body.
Hedin, R.   Transcanadian.
Hemans.   Indian Woman's Death-Song, The.
Herbert, G.   Virtue [or Vertue].
Holmes, O.   Tartarus.
Hopkins, G.   Caged Skylark, The.
Jones, M.   After the Small Pox.
Kendrick, D.   Note to the Ophthalmologist.
Kowit.   What Chord Did She Pluck.
Lanier, S.   To Beethoven.
Lawrence, D.   Healing.
Shadows.
Levertov.   Eye Mask.
Weeping Woman.
Levy, A.   Twilight.
Lindsay, C.   To My Own Face.
Longfellow, H.   Psalm of Life, A.
Sound of the Sea, The.
Tell Me Not in Mournful Numbers.
Lovelace, R.   To Althea, from Prison.
Lowell, J.   Sonnet.
Macdonald, G.   At Aberdeen.
Madge.   Poem: "Character of a landscape stands always in a mysterious relation, The."
Marston, P.   Inseparable.
Marvell.   Dialogue Between the Resolved Soul and Created Pleasure, A.
Dialogue between the Soul and [the] Body, A.
Gallery, The.
On a Drop of Dew.
Masefield.   Sea Change.
McGrath, C.   Wheatfield Under Clouded Sky.
McKay, C.   I Know My Soul.
To the White Fiends.
Mew.   Forest Road, The.
Monkhouse.   Any Soul to Any Body.
Moore, M.   What Are Years?
Nemerov.   Speculation.
Oliver, M.   Some Questions You Might Ask.
Owen, W.   Show, The.
Peck, J.   Metal Denser Than, and Liquid, A.
Philips, K.   To My Excellent Lucasia, On Our Friendship.
Poe.   Sonnet—Silence.
To One in Paradise.
Ulalume [or Ulalume—a Ballad].
Ralegh, S.   Lie, The.
Rankin, J.   Tale.
Ray, H.   Soul's Courts, The.
Robinson, A.   Oasis, An.
Rochester, J.   Mistress, The: A Song.
Roethke.   Her Reticence.
In a Dark Time.
Renewal, The.
Rossetti, C.   Introspective.
Pause, A.
Study (A Soul), A.
Rossetti, D.   Insomnia.

Salaam. '5 Minutes, Mr. Salaam.'
Sandburg, C. Under a Hat Rim.
Siddal. Lust of the Eyes, The.
Smith, S. Animula, Vagula, Blandula.
Childe Rolandine.
Lord Barrenstock.
Man Is a Spirit.
Scorpion.
Swinburne. Lake of Gaube, The.
Sestina: "I saw my soul at rest upon a day."
Swirszczynska. Troubles with the Soul at
Morning Calisthenics.
Taylor, E. Address to the Soul Occasioned by a
Rain, An.
Teasdale. Broken Field, The.
Thomas, D. Turning of the Year, The.
Toomer. Prayer.
Traherne. My Spirit.
Preparative, The.
Tsvetayeva [or Tsvetaeva]. If the Soul was Born
with Pinions.
Unknown. I Know Moon-Rise [or Moonrise].
Lyke-Wake Dirge, The [or A].
Vaughan, H. Peace.
Resurrection and Immortality.
Very. Slowness of Belief in a Spiritual World,
The.
Vigil, A. Hogarcito de La Madrugada, El.
Waldrop, R. Lawn of Excluded Middle.
Waller, E. Of the Last Verses in the Book.
Wheatley, P. On Being Brought from Africa to
America.
Whitfield. Yes! Strike Again That Sounding
String.
Whitman, W. Come, Said My Soul.
Last Invocation, The.
Noiseless Patient Spider, A.
Wilbur. Love Calls Us to the Things of This
World.
Wilcox, E. Nothing New.
Wilde, O. Hélas!
Winchilsea. Nocturnal Reverie, A.
On Myself.
Wylie. Self-Portrait.
Yeats. Dialogue of Self and Soul, A.
Lady's Third Song, The.

Sound
Alexander, E. Stravinsky in L.A.
Apollinaire. Cantor.
Beckett, S. Roundelay: "On all that strand."
Bertolino. Baying, The.
Biespiel, D. After the Wedding.
Brecht, S. Silence, 2.
Cherry, K. Pines Without Peer, The.
Clampitt. Syrinx.
Coleridge, M. To a Piano.
Cumbo. Nocturnal Sounds.
Deanovich. Zombie Jet.
Dickinson, E. Wind, The.
DiPalma. Rebus Tact.
Drake, N. Foley Artist, The.
Felltham [or Feltham]. Upon a Rare Voice.
Francis, R. Sound I Listened For, The.
Garland, H. In August.
Gregory, H. Cage of Voices, The.
Haines, J. Nocturnal.
Hannan, M. Making Conversation.
Holland, J. Wavelength.
Hollander, J. By the Sound.
Hughes, T. Howling of Wolves, The.
Huidobro. New Song.
Jacobsen, J. Bush.
Joyce, J. All Day I Hear the Noise of Waters.
Justice, D. Insomnia of Tremayne, The.
Killeen, G. Wishes.
Kirsch, M. Sleep's Underside.
Kumin, M. Sound of Night, The.
Levertov. Overheard.
Lindsay, M. Hurlygush.
Longfellow, H. Spirit of Poetry, The.
Lovelace, R. To a Lady That Desired Me I
Would Bear My Part with Her in a Song.
Lumsden, R. Then.
Mörling, M. For F. M. Who Did Not Get Killed
Yesterday on 57th Street.
MacCaig. Blue Tit on a String of Peanuts.

MacNeice. Ear, The.
Mahon. Ford Manor.
McDonald, E. Itherness.
Merritt, C. Lullaby: "Say to me: out there are
only streets, and cars."
O'Brien, M. Poem: "Little bones of."
Preston, R. Chicago Blues.
Rea, T. Lugs Benedict on the Coast, 1934.
Romo-Carmona, M. Crows.
Rossetti, C. Wind Has Such a Rainy Sound,
The.
Shange. I Live in Music.
Stanton, M. In Ignorant Cadence.
Stevens, W. No Possum, No Sop, No Taters.
Two Figures in Dense Violet Night.
Sundiata. Ear Training.
Tabb. Whisper.
Thoreau. Dong, Sounds the Brass in the East.
They Who Prepare My Evening Meal Below.
Tremblay, G. Not Sense.
Vitale, M. Loop, Fleck, Sound *and So On.*
Whitman, W. Proud Music of the Storm.
Wright, J. Depressed by a Book of Bad Poetry,
I Walk toward an Unused Pasture and Invite
the Insects to Join Me.

Soup
Caesar. Animal Crackers in My Soup.
Curtis, T. Soup.
Henderson, R. Animal Crackers in My Soup.
Hernández Cruz. If Chickens Could Talk.
Koehler, T. Animal Crackers in My Soup.
Sandburg, C. Soup.
Schneider, M. Soup and Slavery.
Young, K. Campbell's Black Bean Soup.

Sousa, John Philip
Cohan. I Want to Hear a Yankee Doodle Tune.

South Africa
Brutus. Cold.
On the Island.
Robben Island Sequence.
Campbell, R. On Some South African
Novelists.
Cronin, J. Group Photo from Pretoria Local on
the Occasion of a Fourth Anniversary (Never
Taken).
Naval Base (Part III), The.
Fairbridge, K. South African Exhibition, 1907.
Hope, C. Flight of the White South Africans,
The.
Jordan, J. Poem About My Rights.
Kizer, C. Race Relations.
Lee, K. On South Africa.
Mabuza. Death to the Gold Mine!
Mphahlele. Poem, A: "What is there that we
can do or say."
Nortje. Letter from Pretoria Central Prison.
Ruden, S. Beggar Outside Cape Town
Station, A.
Runcie. Slumber Song of the Gardens, A.
Sepamla. I Remember Sharpeville.
Measure for Measure.
Odyssey, The.
Silence: 2.
Vilakazi. In the Gold Mines.

South America
Campo. Lost Plaza Is Everywhere, The.
Guevara, M. After the Colombian Earthquake.
Mercer, J. Tangerine.
Rome, H. South America, Take It Away!
Schertzinger, V. Tangerine.

South Carolina (state)
Akst, H. Dinah.
Coogler. Alas! Carolina!
Donaldson, W. Carolina in the Morning.
Jefferson, B. Long Distance Moan.
Kahn, G. Carolina in the Morning.
Lewis, S. Dinah.
Moorer. Crum Appointment, The.
Timrod. Carolina.
Charleston.
Ode: "Sleep sweetly in your humble graves."
Young, J. Dinah.

South Dakota (state)
Boyle, K. Thunderstorm in South Dakota.
Wright, J. Having Lost My Sons, I Confront the

Wreckage of the Moon: Christmas, 1960.

South Wind
Lindsay, N. Moon's the North Wind's Cooky,
The.

South, The, United States
Alexander, E. Letter: Blues.
Allan, L. Strange Fruit.
Bontemps. Southern Mansion.
Brooks, S. (That's the Way) Dixieland Started
Jazz.
Brown, L. Birth of the Blues, The.
Caesar. Is It True What They Say About Dixie?
Chambers, J. Why Are Daddies So Mean?
Coogler. Alas! for the South.
Crouch, S. Blackie Thinks of His Brothers.
Davis, M. Cry of a People.
DeSylva, B. G. Birth of the Blues, The.
Ellington, D. Jump for Joy.
Emmett. Dixie [or Dixie's Land].
Foster, S. Oh! Susanna.
Old Folks at Home[, The].
Giscombe. (1978, Remembering 1962).
(The Recent Past).
Harper, F. Appeal to My Countrywomen, An.
Harris, D. Landscapes.
Hayden, R. Runagate Runagate.
Henderson, R. Birth of the Blues, The.
Herman, J. Mame.
Hiestand, E. Moon Winx Motel.
Hughes, L. Silhouette.
Kuller, S. Jump for Joy.
Kumin, M. Chain, The.
Lazarus, E. South, The.
Lewis, S. Rock-a-Bye Your Baby with a Dixie
Melody.
Lorde. Afterimages.
McGrath, C. Shrimp Boats, Biloxi.
Melville, H. Iris.
Mercer, J. Blues in the Night.
Powell, K. Southern Birth.
Pratt, M. Red String.
Randall, D. Southern Road, The.
Randolph, I. Rebel, The.
Reese, L. Old Belle, An.
Rome, H. Don't Wanna Write About the South.
Sadoff. Civil Rights.
Thompson, M. To the South.
Toomer. Georgia Dusk.
Unknown. Confederate Memorial Day.
Southern Blues.
Walcott. Arkansas Testament, The.
Walker, A. Once.
Walker, M. Childhood.
Delta.
Weaver, M. Borders.
Easy Living.
Webster, P. Jump for Joy.
Wright, J. Invitation to Madison County, An.

Southey, Robert
Unknown. Rebuke to Robert Southey, A.

Soviet Union
Ginsberg, A. Not Dead Yet.
See also **Russia**

Soweto, South Africa
Mandela. There's an Unknown River in
Soweto.
Smith, P. Woman Who Died in Line, The.
Soyinka. Funeral Sermon, Soweto.

Space and Space Travel
Auden. Moon Landing.
Black, S. Blank Abandon of Beds, The.
Brouwer, J. Space Memorabilia Auction,
Superior Stamp and Coin, Beverly Hills,
California.
Bruchac. Let the Midnight Special.
Burke, J. Swinging on a Star.
Eberhart, R. Dam Neck, Virginia.
Erdrich, H. Future Debris.
Henniker-Heaton. Post Early for Space.
Kendall, M. Ether Insatiable.
Kunitz, S. Flight of Apollo, The.
Magee, W. Giant Rocket.
How to Reach the Sun . . . on a Piece of Paper.
Momaday. Walk on the Moon.
Morgan, E. First Men on Mercury, The.

Plomer.   To the Moon and Back.
Russell, S.   Poem: "I keep feeling all space as my image."
Seaton, M.   Wings.
Sharah.   Package for Another World.
Skloot.   Year the Space Age Was Born, The.
Smith, P.   Annie Pearl Smith Discovers Moonlight.
Swenson, M.   First Walk on the Moon.
Taylor, B.   Canopus.
Van Heusen, J.   Swinging on a Star.
Williams, W.   World Contracted to a Recognizable Image, The.
Winter, M.   Space Parable.

Spain
Belloc.   Tarantella.
Caesar.   Spanish Jake.
Crane, H.   Imperator Victus.
Dacey, P.   Musica.
Hughes, T.   You Hated Spain.
Jacob, M.   Spanish Generosity.
Lerner, A.   Rain in Spain, The.
Levine, P.   Salami.
O'Hara, F.   Madrid.
Salazar.   Taking It Back.
Spender, S.   Port Bou.
Woodcock.   Poem for Garcia Lorca.
Young, A.   Ravel: Bolero.

Spanish Armada
Macaulay, T.   Armada, The.

Spanish Civil War
Rich, A.   Letters in the Family.
See also **Civil War, Spain**

Spanish Succession, War of the
Southey, R.   Battle of Blenheim, The.
See also **Blenheim, Battle of (1704)**

Spanish-American War
Moody, W.   Ode in Time of Hesitation, An.
   On a Soldier Fallen in the Philippines.

Spankings
Hayden, R.   Whipping, The.
Herrick.   Upon Pagget.

Sparrows
Collier, M.   Brave Sparrow.
Gibbons, R.   Sparrow.
Hackett, J.   Haiku: "Bitter morning, A."
Harper, F.   Sparrow's Fall, The.
Hecht, A.   House Sparrows.
Johnston, B.   Did You Ever Hear an English Sparrow Sing?
Martin, C.   His Eye Is on the Sparrow.
Mayhall.   City Sparrow.
Nemerov.   Because You Asked about the Line between Prose and Poetry.
Savage, M.   Disaster, The.
Spires.   Apology.
   Interrogations of the Sparrow.
Stern, G.   Red Bird.
Williams, W.   Breakfast.
Pastoral: "Little sparrows, The."
   Sparrow, The.
To a Sparrow.
Wright, J.   Sparrows in a Hillside Drift.
Yenser, S.   Another Lo-Cal Elegy.

Spas
Broumas, O.   Masseuse, The.
Rochester, J.   Tunbridge Wells.

Speech
Angeles, C.   Words.
Barlow, G.   Nook.
Bogan, L.   Henceforth, from the Mind.
Bringhurst.   Song of Ptahhotep, The.
Brooks, S.   Grandma Talk.
Carruth, H.   Sonnet: "Well, she told me I had an aura. "What?" I said."
Davis, O.   New Philosophy of Composition, or, How to Ignore the Non-Reasoning Creature Capable of *Speech* Perched Outside Your Bathroom Window, A.
Denniker, P.   S'posin'
Dodge, M.   Way To Do It, The.
Duke, V.   I Like the Likes of You.
   What Is There to Say?
Elmusa.   She Fans the Word.
Emerson, R.   Merops.

Ferguson, G.   Silent as Roses.
Ginsberg, A.   Stroke.
Graves, R.   Cool Web, The.
Hannan, M.   Making Conversation.
Harburg.   I Like the Likes of You.
   What Is There to Say?
Harrison, T.   Earthen Lot, The.
Joseph, A.   On Being Told I Don't Speak Like a Black Person.
Kirby, D.   Dear Derrida.
Kloefkorn.   Why the Stone Remains Silent.
Larsen, W.   Learning the War.
MacLeish.   Speech to a Crowd.
Moir, L.   Handnotes.
Mueller, L.   Triage.
Ortiz.   Speaking.
Razaf, A.   S'posin'
Rukeyser, M.   Effort at Speech between Two People.
Sandburg, C.   Languages.
Slessor.   Full Orchestra.
Stevens, W.   To the Roaring Wind.
Stickney, T.   And, the last day being come, Man stood alone.
Tana, P.   No.
Tipton.   I Want to Speak With the Blood that Lies Down.
Vitale, M.   Patois.
Whitmore, S.   Bird, The.
Williams, C.   My Mother's Lips.
See also **Screams; Talk**

Speed
Coatsworth.   Swift Things Are Beautiful.
Cohan.   Twentieth-Century Love.
Crunk, T.   Reunion.
Kandinsky [*or* Kandinskii].   Chalk and Soot.
MacCaig.   Ringed Plover by a Water's Edge.
McDaniel, J.   Disasterology.
Parnell, T.   On Riding to See Dean Swift in the Mist of the Morning.
Pope, A.
Unknown.   Railroad Man for Me, A.

Spelling
Lee, L.   Persimmons.
Unknown.   Jack Jelf.

Spenser, Edmund ("Colin Clout")
Beaumont, F.   Upon Master Edmund Spenser.
Kennelly.   Master.
Reynolds, J.   To Spenser.

Sphinx
Black, S.   Lust.
Brock, V.   Sphinx.
Emerson, R.   Sphinx, The.
Hayden, R.   Sphinx.
Rukeyser, M.   Myth.

Spider Webs
Barber, D.   Little Overture.
Cooke, R.   Arachne.
De Tabley.   Study of a Spider, The.
Eberhart, R.   Spider, The.
Merwin, W. S.   Encampment at Morning, An.
Miles, J.   Fields of Learning.
Smith, C.   To the Insect of the Gossamer.
Whitman, W.   Noiseless Patient Spider, A.

Spiders
Basho.   Spider.
Cavendish, M.   Common Fate of Books, The.
Cooke, R.   Arachne.
Davis, W.   Spider.
De Tabley.   Study of a Spider, The.
Eberhart, R.   Spider, The.
Empson.   Arachne.
Frost, R.   Design.
   In White.
Fuller, R.   Image, The.
Graham, J.   Geese, The.
Horan.   Little City.
Howitt, M.   Spider and the Fly, The.
Jackson, A.   Transformable Prophecy.
Jackson, L.   Elegy in a Spider's Web.
Lindsay, N.   Spider and the Ghost of the Fly, The.
Littleton.   Spider, The.
Lowell, R.   Mr. Edwards and the Spider.
Marchant, F.   Screen Porch.

McPherson, S.   Ability to Make a Face Like a Spider While Singing Blues: Junior Wells, The.
Merwin, W. S.   Broken, The.
   Encampment at Morning, An.
Mother Goose.   Miss Muffet.
Richards, M.   Christmas Spider, The.
Rivera, D.   Dinner Together.
Russell, T.   To the Spider.
Sarton.   Love: "Fragile as a spider's web."
Swift, J.   Spider.
Taylor, E.   Upon a Spider Catching a Fly.
Triplett, P.   Spider of Doubt.
Whitman, W.   Noiseless Patient Spider, A.

Spies
Jonson, B.   On Spies.
Leonard, T.   Untitled.
See also **Spying and Spies**

Spinning and Spinners
Olds, P.   My Mother Spinning.
Preston, M.   Erinna's Spinning.
Unknown.   Factory Workers' Song.

Spinsters
Auden.   Miss Gee.
Blamire.   O Jenny Dear.
Chudleigh.   To the Ladies.
Couto.   Lizzie.
Day Lewis.   My Mother's Sister.
De la Mare.   Three Sisters.
Ellis, C.   Old Ladies, The.
Herrick.   Upon Himself.
Holmes, O.   My Aunt.
Jackson, A.   Spinster Song: African-American Woman Guild.
Kasdorf.   Leftover Blessings.
Lochhead, L.   Grim Sisters, The.
Miller, V.   Spinster's Lullaby.
Pitter.   Old, Childless, Husbandless.
Plath.   Spinster.

Spiritualism and Spiritualists
Browning, E.   Sleep, The.
Ellis, T.   Being There.
Everett, J.   Rest Our Spiritual Dead.
Hernández Cruz.   Spirits.
Mapanje.   These Too Are Our Elders.
   Visiting Zomba Plateau.
Patchen.   'In the footsteps of the walking air'
Temple, A.
Raine, C.   Plain Song.
Smith, S.   Mrs Simpkins.

Spirituals
Dunbar, P.   When Malindy Sings.
Hughes, L.   Note on Commercial Theatre.
   Tambourines.
Johnson, J.   O Black and Unknown Bards.
Notley.   Where Leftover Misery Goes.
Unknown.   Go Down, Moses.
   I Thank God I'm Free at Las'

Spittoons
Hughes, L.   Brass Spittoons.

Sports
Alexander, E.   Today's News.
Betjeman.   Subaltern's Love-Song, A.
Drieu la Rochelle.   Tennis.
Holland, J.   Baize Queens.
Jonson, B.   To Sir Henry Goodyere.
Noguchi, B.   Breath He Holds, The.
   Turn of Privacy, The.
Scott, D.   Playing for England.
Townsend, A.   Bicycle Racers, The.
Webb, H.   Vive Le Sport.
Williams, J.   River Walk.
Wright, J.   Mad Fight Song for William S. Carpenter, 1966, A.
Wrigley, A.   Owdham Footbo'
See also **Athletics and Athletes; Games**

Spring
Allingham.   In a Spring Grove.
Ammons, A. R.   Spring Coming.
Anderson, S.   American Spring Song.
Ashbery.   Spring Day.
Barbauld.   Ode to Spring.
Bethell.   Response.
Bibb.   Early Spring.
Bishop, E.   Cold Spring, A.
Blake, W.   To Spring.
Blane, R.   Spring Isn't Everything.

Bly, R.   Sleet Storm on the Merritt Parkway.
Bontemps.   My Heart has Known its Winter.
Bottomley.   Eager Spring.
Bradstreet, A.   As Spring the Winter Doth Succeed.
Bridges, R.   April, 1885.
Brown, S.   After Winter.
Browne, S.   Signs of Spring.
Browning, R.   Home-Thoughts, From Abroad.
Brummer, N.   Why Is This Night Different from All Other Nights?
Bryant, W.   Yellow Violet, The.
Buchanan, G.   May Morning.
Burns, R.   O Were My Love Yon Lilac[k] Fair.
Bye.   Spring.
Campbell, R.   Georgian Spring.
Carew, T.   Spring, The.
Cawein.   Purple Valleys, The.
Clare, J.   Last of April, The.
Primrose, The.
Coatsworth.   March.
Cofer, J.   Spring.
What We Feared.
Coleridge, S.   Answer to a Child's Question.
Collins, A.   Song.
Conyus.   Upon Leaving the Parole Board Hearing.
Cristall.   Song: "Through springtime walks, with flowers perfumed."
Song on Leaving the Country Early in the Spring.
To a Lady on the Rise of Morn.
Verses Written in the Spring.
Cummings, E.   In Just.
O Sweet Spontaneous.
Spring is like a perhaps hand.
Davies, W.   Days Too Short.
Davis, O.   In the Clear Long After.
Dickinson, E.   Letter to Bee.
Donne.   Love's Growth.
Dove, R.   Turning Thirty, I Contemplate Students Bicycling Home.
Duke, V.   April in Paris.
Eberhart, R.   This Fevers Me.
Elliott, E.   Spring.
Emanuel, L.   Technology of Spring, The.
Emerson, R.   Musketaquid.
Ennis.   Drink of Spring, A.
Evance, S.   Written in Ill Health at the Close of Spring.
Fain, S.   Springtime Cometh, The.
Fallon, P.   Spring Song.
"Field."   Goad, The.
Frost, R.   Prayer in Spring, A.
Spring Pools.
Gibbon, P.   Answer, An.
Ginsberg, A.   Easter Sunday.
Giovanni.   Springtime.
Glück, L.   For Jane Myers.
Gray, T.   Ode on the Spring.
Green, J.   I Wanna Be Loved.
Grigson.   In the Spring Garden.
Grimké, A.   At April.
Grimke, C.   Parting Hymn, A.
Guiney.   Garden Chidings.
Hagiwara Sakutaro.   Spring Night.
Hammerstein.   It Might As Well Be Spring.
Younger Than Springtime.
Harburg.   April in Paris.
Springtime Cometh, The.
Hardy, T.   If It's Ever Spring Again.
Year's Awakening, The.
Harry, J.   Walking, when the Lake of the Air is Blue with Spring.
Hart, L.   Spring Is Here.
Harte, B.   California Madrigal.
Hass, R.   Spring Rain.
Hawker.   Are They Not All Ministering Spirits?
Heaney, S.   Rite of Spring.
Hemans.   Voice of Spring, The.
Herrick.   Apron of Flowers, The.
Farewell Frost; or, Welcome the Spring.
Hogan, M.   Spring.
Hope, A.   Return of Persephone, The.
Hopkins, G.   May Magnificat, The.
Spring.

Spring and Fall.
Housman, A.   Loveliest of Trees, the Cherry Now.
Howells, W.   Earliest Spring.
Hughes, T.   Swifts.
Jacobsen, J.   Hourglass.
James I, King of Scotland.   Spring Song of the Birds.
Johnston, M.   Vernal Equinox.
Jones, D.   For Spring.
Kasdorf.   Green Market, New York.
Keats.   After Dark Vapours Have Oppressed Our Plains.
Sweet Peas.
Kennedy, X.   B Negative.
Kenney.   In April.
Keyes, S.   Early Spring.
King, H.   Summer Lost.
Knister.   February's Forgotten Mitts.
Landesman.   Spring Can Really Hang You Up the Most.
Lane, P.   Spring.
Larkin, P.   Coming.
First Sight.
Spring.
Lawrence, D.   Enkindled Spring, The.
Spring Morning.
Ledwidge.   June.
Twilight in Middle March, A.
Levertov.   Earliest Spring.
Springtime, The.
Levine, P.   Sleepless Night, A.
Li Ch'ing-chao.   Tune: 'The Charm of a Maiden Singer;' Spring Thoughts.
Li Po.   Awakening from Drunkenness on a Spring Day.
Liessin.   Spring Nocturne.
Locke, M.   Sonnet: "I hate the Spring in particoloured vest."
Long, H.   New Music, A.
Longley, M.   Freeze-Up.
Lowell, A.   Vernal Equinox.
MacNeice.   Spring Voices.
Majer.   Spring.
McDaniel, W.   First Spring in California, 1936.
McGough, R.   Fight of the Year, The.
McGrath, C.   Spring Comes to Chicago.
McGrath, T.   Black Train, The.
McKay, C.   Spring in New Hampshire.
Millay, E.   Spring.
Miyazawa Kenji.   Spring and the Ashura.
Mnookin.   Signs.
Moore, A.   Girls' School.
Moore, L.   Haiku.
Moorer.   Easter; or, Spring-Time.
Morales.   Spring Fever.
Morrison, L.   Rural Recreation.
Morton, J.   Spring in London.
Murray, P.   Returning Spring.
Nesbit, E.   Child's Song in Spring.
O'Hara, F.   Easter.
Olson, C.   Variations Done for Gerald Van De Wiele.
Osundare.   Eyeful Glances.
Overbury.   Springtime It Brings On the Shearing, The.
Overton, R.   Blues in "C."
Owen, W.   Spring Offensive.
Parker, A.   Alchemy.
Perry, N.   Coming of Spring, The.
Piatt, S.   Sad Spring-Song.
Pietri.   First Day of Spring, The.
Pommy-Vega.   [Ah certainty of love in the hand].
Pratt, E.   Come Not the Seasons Here.
Pritchard, N.   Springtime.
Ray, H.   Coming of Spring, The.
Idyl of Spring, An.
Rayl, J.   Spring Storm.
Reese, L.   April in Town.
Day Before Spring, The.
Mid-March.
Reznikoff.   April.
Ridge, L.   Spring.
Roberts, L.   Another Spring on Olmstead Street.
Rodgers, W.   Winter's Cold.

Roethke.   Bring the Day!
Rossetti, C.   Amen.
First Spring Day, The.
L.E.L.
May.
Spring Quiet.
What's in a Name?
Winter: My Secret.
Rossetti, D.   For Spring By Sandro Botticelli.
Ruden, S.   Letter.
Sandburg, C.   Lines Written for Gene Kelly to Dance To.
Population Drifts.
Three Spring Notations on Bipeds.
Schilpp, M.   Triage.
Seeger, A.   I Have a Rendezvous with Death.
Seward.   Sonnet Written from an Eastern Apartment in the Bishop's Palace at Lichfield, Which Commands a View of Stowe Valley.
Shelley, P.   Cloud, The.
Question, The.
Shepherd, R.   Where When Was.
White Days.
Sitwell, D.   Green Song.
How Many Heavens.
Smart, C.   On a Bed of Guernsey Lilies.
Smith, C.   Sonnet Written at the Close of Spring [or Elegiac Sonnet].
To Spring.
Written in Farm Wood, South Downs, in May 1784.
Smith, D.   Spring Poem, The.
Snyder, G.   Sixth-Month Song in the Foothills.
What Have I Learned.
Steingesser.   Spring Forward.
Stern, G.   Modern Love.
Stevens, W.   Depression before Spring.
Meditation Celestial and Terrestrial.
Stickney, T.   Age in Youth.
On Sandro's Flora.
Stilwell.   Lyric to Spring.
Su Tung-p'o.   Spring Scene.
Suesse, D.   Ho Hum.
Surrey.   Soote Season, The.
Swinburne.   Vision of Spring in Winter, A.
Tate, A.   Seasons of the Soul.
Teasdale.   There Will Come Soft Rains.
Thomas, D.   I, in My Intricate Image.
Thomas, E.   Thaw.
Thompson, S.   April.
Thoreau.   Winter and Spring Scene, A.
Tu Fu.   Spring.
Tucker, M.
Turner, F.   Spring Evening.
Unknown.   It's Spring Returning, It's Spring and Love.
Lenten Is [or Ys] Come [with Love to Toune].
Now Is the Month of Maying.
Spring in the Bronx.
Sumer Is Icumen [or Ycomen] In.
Vanhomrigh.   Hail, Blushing Goddess, Beauteous Spring!
Vaughan, H.   Unprofitablenes.
Very.   Spirit, The.
Winter Rain, The.
Volkman.   Seasonal.
Wang, J.   Tune: 'The Charm of a Maiden Singer;' Spring Thoughts.
Warren, H.   Spring Isn't Everything.
West, J.   To May.
Wilbur.   April 5, 1974.
Cicadas.
Wilde, O.   Magdalen Walks.
Williams, W.   Bird Song.
Late Singer, The.
Spring and All.
Spring Strains.
Wilson, R.   Spring at Fort Okanogan.
Spring in Virginia.
Winters, Y.   Time and the Garden.
Wolf, T.   Spring Can Really Hang You Up the Most.
Wolfe, M.   Thaw, The.
Woods, J.   What Do You Do When It's Spring?
Wordsworth, W.   Lines Written in Early Spring.
To My Sister.

Written in March [While Resting on the Bridge at the Foot of Brother's Water].
Wotton, S.   On a Bank [or Banck] as I Sat[e] [a-]Fishing; a Description of the Spring.
Wright, C.   April.
Wright, J.   Child, The.
Young, A.   Last Snow.
Stay, Spring.
Young, M. J.   On an Early Spring.
Zukofsky, L.   I Walk in the Old Street.

Springfield, Ohio
Linden, M.   Riot, A.

Springs
Bryant, W.   Fountain, The.
Long, H.   Our Spring Needs Shoveling.
Machej.   Orchards in July.

Spruce Trees
George, P.   Spruce.
Schuyler, J.   Buried at Springs.

Spying and Spies
Bowers, E.   Prince, The.
Davis, D.   Childhood of a Spy.
Dunn, S.   What They Wanted.
Jonson, B.   On Spies.
Kipling, R.   Spies' March, The.
Miller, V.   Light Reading.

Squid
Chin.   Floral Apron, The.

Squirrels
Dove, R.   Musician Talks About 'Process,' The.
Eberhart, R.   On a Squirrel Crossing the Road in Autumn, in New England.
Emerson, R.   Fable: "Mountain and the squirrel, The."
Gilbert, C.   Glimpses.
Taggard.   Squirrel near Library.
Unknown.   Squirrel, The.
Van Duyn.   Sonnet for Minimalists.
Wolfe, H.   Gray Squirrel, The.
Yeats.   To a Squirrel at Kyle-Na-No.

Sri Lanka
Ondaatje.   Letters and Other Worlds.
Ranasinghe.   Auschwitz from Colombo.

St. Agnes' Eve
Keats.   Eve of St Agnes, The.
Tennyson, A.   St. Agnes' Eve.

St. David's Day
Unknown.   In Honour of St. David's Day.

St. James's Park, London
Rochester, J.   Ramble in St. James's Park, A.
Waller, E.   On St. James's Park, as Lately Improved by His Majesty.

St. Louis, Missouri
Brooks, J.   You Came a Long Way from St. Louis.
Lowell, A.   St. Louis.
Sterling, A.   Meet Me in St. Louis, Louis.

St. Stephen's Day
Hewitt, J.   St. Stephen's Day.

Stables
Hall, D.   Carol, A.
Herrick.   Another Charme for Stables.
Rawson, J.   Map Burnt Through.
Wylie.   Twelfth Night.

Stained Glass
Hardy, T.   Young Glass-Stainer, The.
Kelly, B.   Imagining Their Own Hymns.
Worth, V.   Door.

Stairs
Ammons, A. R.   Choice.
DeSylva, B. G.   Stairway to Paradise.
Francis, A.
Hughes, L.   Mother to Son.
Levertov.   Jacob's Ladder, The.
Slessor.   Up in Mabel's Room.

Stalin, Joseph
Herbert, S.   Less Nonsense.
Levis.   Anastasia and Sandman.
Lowell, R.   Stalin.
Mandelstam [or Mandelshtam].   Poem No. 286 (On Stalin).
"Sagittarius."   Stalin Moy Golubchik.

Stanley, Sir Henry Morton
Rubadiri.   Stanley Meets Mutesa.

Starfish
Cervantes.   Starfish.
Kinnell.   Daybreak.
McHugh, H.   After You Left.
Ormsby, E.   Starfish.
Rohrer, M.   Starfish Waving to Me from the Sand.

Starlings
Hayden, R.   Plague of Starlings, A.
Heath-Stubbs.   Starling, The.
Wilbur.   Writer, The.

Stars
Adams, L.   Fragmentary Stars.
Aldrich, T.   Lycidas.
Anderson, M.   Lost in the Stars.
"Antler."   Star-Struck Utopias of 2000.
Asekoff, L.   Starwork.
Auden.   More Loving One, The.
Barnes, J.   La Plata, Missouri: Clear November Night.
Battiss.   Limpopo.
Blake, W.   How Sweet I Roamed [or Roam'd] from Field to Field.
To the Evening Star.
Bourdillon.   Night Has a Thousand Eyes, The.
Brock, V.   All the Stars Are Foxfire.
Brontë, E.   Stars.
Bryant, W.   Hymn to the North Star.
Song of the Stars.
Buckley, C.   Presocratic, Surfing, Breathing Cosmology Blues, The.
Burke, J.   Swinging on a Star.
Byron, G.   She Walks in Beauty.
Campbell, J.   Darkness.
Campbell, T.   To the Evening Star.
Cavendish, M.   Of Stars.
Cawein.   Stars, The.
Cervantes.   To We Who Were Saved by the Stars.
Chivers.   Apollo.
Cole, W.   Back Yard, July Night.
Conoley.   World, The.
Crase.   Astropastoral.
Cumpian.   Estrellitas.
Darley.   Fallen Star, The.
Davison, P.   Star Watcher, The.
De la Mare.   Birthnight: To F, The.
DeLange, E.   Shake Down the Stars.
Di Prima.   Notes on the Art of Memory.
Duncan, R.   Passages 37.
Echeruo.   Man and God Distinguished.
Eimers.   Night Without Stars, A.
Farber.   Taking Turns.
Ferril.   Jupiter at Beer Springs.
"Field."   Constancy.
Fields, A.   Ephemeron.
Frost, R.   Canis Major.
Choose Something like a Star.
Come In.
Star in a Stoneboat, A.
García Lorca.   In a Corner of the Sky.
One.
Star, A.
Ursa Major.
Gehrke, S.   Walking Fields at Night South of Hampton, Iowa.
Giovanni.   Stars.
Graves, R.   Star-Talk.
Gunn, T.   My Sad Captains.
Guthrie, R.   Magi, The.
Hardy, T.   Waiting Both.
Hayden, R.   Stars.
Hays, H.   Sacred Children, The.
Healy, R.   Size of This Universe, The.
Hemans.   Lost Pleiad, The.
Herbert, G.   Artillery [or Artillerie].
Star[re], The.
Hollander, J.   Great Bear, The.
Hopkins, G.   Starlight Night, The.
Housman, A.   Stars, I Have Seen Them Fall.
Hugo, R.   Elegy: "I expected him to look dead in the casket."
Inada.   Concentration Constellation.
Jeffers, R.   Nova.
Johnson, J.   Sence You Went Away.
Joyce, J.   Bahnhofstrasse.

Keats.   Bright Star.
Kinnell.   Daybreak.
Kipling, R.   Astrologer's Song, An.
Kunitz, S.   He.
Longfellow, H.   Galaxy, The.
Three Kings, The.
MacCaig.   Blue Tit on a String of Peanuts.
Stars and Planets.
MacLeish.   Epistle to Be Left in the Earth.
Pole Star for This Year.
MacNeice.   Star-Gazer.
Mayakovsky [or Maiakovskii].   Listen.
Meredith, G.   Lucifer in Starlight.
Meredith, W.   Country Stars.
Merwin, W. S.   Glassy Sea.
Morley, T.   You Black Bright Stars.
Nemerov.   Speculation.
Parish.   Stars Fell on Alabama.
Plutzik.   Cancer and Nova.
Ramke.   Difference Between Night and Day, The.
Revealing Oneself to a Woman.
Ray, H.   Star Song.
Rich, A.   Planetarium.
Robinson, A.   Idea, The.
Unum est Necessarium.
Robinson, E.   Credo.
Rohrer, M.   Hotel de L'Etoile.
Roseliep.   Campfire Extinguished.
Rossetti, C.   Where Innocent Bright-Eyed Daisies Are.
Rukeyser, M.   Darkness Music.
Sandburg, C.   Stars.
Schilpp, M.   Triage.
Shaw, L.   Stars in Apple Cores.
Sigourney.   Stars, The.
Simms, W.   Lost Pleiad, The.
Simon, M.   Atomic Psalm.
Smith, R.   Halcion.
Sterling, G.   Aldebaran at Dusk.
Stevenson, R.   Escape at Bedtime.
Stoddard, E.   Above the Tree.
Strand.   Man in Black, The.
Taylor, B.   Canopus.
Taylor, J.   Star, The.
Teasdale.   Falling Star, The.
Thomas, E.   Shooting Star, A.
Thoreau.   On Ponkawtasset, Since, We Took Our Way.
Tuckerman, F.   Sonnets: "Starry flower, the flower-like stars that fade, The."
Turner, C.   Orion.
Unknown.   Song of the Pleiades.
Wishing Poem.
Van Heusen, J.   Shake Down the Stars.
Swinging on a Star.
Vaughan, H.   Joy of My Life! While Left Me Here.
They Are All Gone into the World of Light!
To Amoret, of the Difference 'twixt Him and Other Lovers, and What True Love Is.
To Amoret, Walking in a Starry Evening.
Vitale, M.   I Read That It Was All a Chain.
Weill, K.   Lost in the Stars.
Wellesley.   Lost Lane.
Whitman, W.   On the Beach at Night.
On the Beach at Night Alone.
When I Heard the Learn'd Astronomer.
Wilbur.   In the Field.
Williams, R.   When Sun Doth Rise.
Williams, W.   El Hombre.
Flight to the City.
Wright, J.   To the Evening Star: Central Minnesota.
Yeats.   Sorrow of Love, The.
Young, A.   How Stars Start.
Young, K.   Letters from the North Star.
See also **Astronomy and Astronomers**

Statistics
Brett, L.   I Keep Forgetting.
Cunningham, J.   Meditation on Statistical Method.

Statues
Allott.   Statue, The.
Allston.   On the Statue of an Angel, by Bienaimé, in the Possession of J.S. Copley

Greene, Esq.
Berryman. Boston Common.
Bogan, L. Statue and Birds.
Creeley. Figures, The.
  Statue, The.
Davidson, D. Twilight on Union Street.
Druce. Apropos of Garden Statuary: A
  Disquisition upon a Minor Genre.
Ford, C. Bad Habit, The.
Guest, B. Walking Buddha.
Higginson, E. Statue, The.
Johnson, L. By the Statue of King Charles [or
  I] at Charing Cross.
Justice, D. Mrs. Snow.
Kaufman, S. Buddha of Sŏkkuram, The.
Landor, W. Duke of York's Statue, The.
Lieberman, L. God's Measurements.
Lowell, R. Christmas Eve under Hooker's
  Statue.
Mesens. Arid Husband, The.
Nemerov. Statues in the Public Gardens, The.
Nemes Nagy. I Carried Statues.
Phillips, C. Toys.
Piatt, J. To the Statue on the Capitol.
Piatt, S. Stone For A Statue.
Plath. Colossus, The.
Ray, H. Venus of Milo, The.
Rossetti, C. Study (A Soul), A.
  On an Unfinished Statue.
Santayana. Before a Statue of Achilles.
Shelley, P. Ozymandias.
Stevens, W. Dance of the Macabre Mice.
Thomas, D. Walking in Gardens.
Umpierre, L. Statue, The.
Unknown. Epigram: "Says a Reverend Priest to
  a less Rev'rend friend."
Watson, R. White Lady, The.
Yeats. Statues, The.

Steak
Creeley. Naughty Boy.
Moore, L. Haiku.

Steam Rollers and Steam Rolling
Moore, M. To a Steam Roller.

Steam Shovels
Malam. Steam Shovel.

Steamers
Kipling, R. McAndrew's Hymn.
Scovell. River Steamer, The.
See also **Ships and Shipbuilding**

Steel
Conyus. Six Ten Sixty-Nine.
Markus, P. Black Light.
Sandburg, C. Prayers of Steel.
Wagoner, D. My Father's Garden.
See also **Iron**

Steeples
Pierpoint, K. Steeplejack.
Williams, W. To a Solitary Disciple.

Stein, Gertrude
Loy. Gertrude Stein.
Muldoon, P. More a Man Has the More a Man
  Wants, The.
Nash, O. They Don't Speak English in Paris.

Stenographers
Page, P. Stenographers, The.
See also **Scribes; Secretaries**

Stepfathers and Stepmothers
Smith, S. Papa Love Baby.
Swirszczynska. Second Madrigal, The.
  She Does Not Remember.
Todd, M. Game Trail, The.
Wolverton, T. Dead Stepfather, The.

Stephen, Saint
Dickinson, P. St. Stephen's Day.
Nichols, K. Feast of Stephen, The.
Sawyer, R. Feast o' Saint [or St.] Stephen, The.
Suckling, S. Upon Stephen Stoned.

Stepmothers
Livingstone, D. Stepmother.
See also **Stepfathers and Stepmothers**

Sterne, Laurence
Garrick. Epitaph on Laurence Sterne.
Muldoon, P. Yggdrasill.

Stevens, Wallace
Blanco, R. Tía Olivia Serves Wallace Stevens a
  Cuban Egg.
Lim, S. I Defy You.
Ondaatje. King Kong Meets Wallace Stevens.
Roethke. Rouse for Stevens, A.

Stewards and Stewardesses
Dauer. Falling.

Still Lifes
Atwood. Against Still Life.
Kenny, M. Still-Life.
Tomlinson, C. Paring the Apple.

Stockholm, Sweden
Van Vliet. Old Champagne Glass.

Stockmen
Gordon, A. Sick Stockrider, The.
Paterson, A. Man from Snowy River, The.

Stoicism
Rossetti, C. Study (A Soul), A.

Stonecutting and Stonecutters
Jeffers, R. To the Stone-Cutters.

Stonehenge, England
Warton, T. Written at Stonehenge.

Stones and Rocks
Ammons, A. R. Apologia pro Vita Sua.
Bidgood. Standing Stone.
Bielski. Token.
Brathwaite, E. Stone.
Cervantes. Archeology.
Corn. Naskeag.
Creeley. "I Keep to Myself Such Measures.."
Davies, H. Poem: "It doesn't look like a finger
  it looks like a feather of broken glass."
Dove, R. Fish in the Stone, The.
Dufault. Stone.
Eberhart, R. La Crosse at Ninety Miles an
  Hour.
Foster, A. God and the Holy Stones.
Geiger. Disproportionate.
Hall, D. Granite and Grass.
Jeffers, R. Rock and Hawk.
  To the Stone-Cutters.
Kaufman, S. Stones.
Khalvati. Stone of Patience.
Kinnell. Path among the Stones, The.
Kloefkorn. Why the Stone Remains Silent.
Knight, E. He Sees Through Stone.
MacDiarmid, H. Crystals like Blood.
Magowan. Days of 1956.
Martínez, V. Tesoro.
McCaig. Poem: "There is a wailing baby under
  every stone and you walk."
McCarthy, T. Phenomenology of Stones, The.
McClure, M. Moiré.
McCord, D. This Is My Rock.
Melly. Homage to René Magritte.
Millay, E. Second Fig.
Okai. 999 Smiles.
Ortiz. Serenity in Stones, The.
Peacock, M. How I Come to You.
Piatt, S. Stone for a Statue.
Piombino. My Lady Carries Stones.
Porter, P. What I Have Written I Have Written.
Pound, E. Ts'ai Chi'h.
Pratt, E. Come Not the Seasons Here.
Pritchard, N. Cassandra and Friend.
  Narrow Path, The.
Redgrove, P. Minerals of Cornwall, Stones of
  Cornwall.
Reeves, J. Black Pebble, The.
Reid, C. Stones and Bones.
Rolle, S. Blue Rock, The.
Simic. Stone.
Sobin, G. Eleven Rock Poems.
Tomlinson, C. In Defence of Metaphysics.
  Stone Speech.
Vaughan. Stone, The.
Walcott. Ruins of a Great House.
Ward, D. Hunting in Twilight.
Wilbur. On the Marginal Way.
  Thyme Flowering among Rocks.
Young, A. Black Rock of Kiltearn.

Storms
Aiken, C. Hatteras Calling.
Arlen, H. Stormy Weather (Keeps Rainin' All

the Time).
Ashbery. Morning Jitters.
Banks, Jr., T. H. Tempest.
Berlin. Let's Have Another Cup of Coffee.
Bishop, E. Little Exercise.
Blaser. Finder, The.
Blunden. Eastern Tempest.
  Late Light.
Blunt, W. Storm in Summer, A.
Braithwaite. Watchers, The.
Bridges, R. Low Barometer.
Brontë, A. Lines Composed in a Wood on a
  Windy Day.
Brooks, G. Michael Is Afraid of the Storm.
Bryant, W. After a Tempest.
Burns, R. Tam o' Shanter; A Tale.
Bush, D. Sunday the Power Went Off, The.
Caldwell, E. Love Poem: "Olfactory paradise."
Campbell, T. Lord Ullin's Daughter.
Carver, R. Window, The.
Clampitt. Meridian.
Clark, T. On the Beach.
Clarke, C. Poet's Death, A.
Coleridge, S. Storm, The.
Davie. Remembering the 'Thirties.
Davies, W. Black Cloud, The.
Dawe, G. Sheltering Places.
De la Mare. Silver Penny, The.
Dickinson, E. Storm.
  Thunder-Storm, A.
Didsbury. Hailstone, The.
Dipoko. Pain.
Donne. Storm at Sea, A.
  Storm[e], The.
Doolittle, H. Storm.
Dubie. Peace of Lodi, The.
Emerson, R. Snow-Storm [or Snowstorm], The.
Fields, J. Ballad of the Tempest.
Fordham. Snow Storm, The.
Freneau. Hurricane, The.
Frost, R. Once by the Pacific.
  Storm Fear.
Garland, H. Boyish sleep.
Gioia. Summer Storm.
Graves, R. Apple Island.
Greenberg, S. Secrecy.
Grennan. Shoreline After Storm.
Hall, D. Granite and Grass.
  Sudden Things.
Hardy, T. She Hears The Storm.
  Thunderstorm in Town, A.
Hausman. Appaloosa Hail Storm.
Hemans. Wreck, The.
Herbert, G. Storm, The.
Herrick. His Hope or Sheet-Anchor.
Hewitt, J. Calling on Peadar O'Donnell at
  Dungloe.
Holm, B. Blizzard.
Holmes, T. Room for All.
Hopkins, G. Hailstorm in May.
Howe, J. Wild Night, A.
Hughes, T. Wind.
Jacob, M. 1914.
Jacobik, G. Dust Storm.
Jeffers, R. Gale in April.
Johnson, M. F. Thunder Storm.
Jones, H. On a Fine Crop of Peas Being
  Spoiled by a Storm.
Kay, J. Pounding Rain.
Keithley. Thunder Storm.
Kennelly. Island, The.
Kipling, R. Storm Cone, The.
Kyger. Caption for a Miniature.
Lake, P. In Rough Weather.
Lampman. Thunderstorm, A.
Lawrence, D. Lightning.
  Storm in the Black Forest.
Lear, E. Jumblies, The.
Lewis, J. Garden Note I, Los Altos.
Lima, J. Enormous Hand, The.
Marshall, E. Buddgelin Bey.
McGough, R. Storm.
McIlroy, L. How to Change a Flat.
Melville, H. Enviable Isles, The.
  Misgivings.
Millay, E. Hearing Your Words, and Not a

Word Among Them.
Mitchell, K. Tree Stillness.
Monro. City-Storm.
Moody, W. Bracelet of Grass, The.
Morgan, E. Strawberries.
Murford. Storm and Calm: Sent from Embden to M. Edw. Ma. and M. Tho. Ly, The.
Nemerov. Brainstorm.
Storm Windows.
Padgett, R. After the Broken Arm.
Paterson, D. Chartres of Gowrie, The.
Patmore, C. Storm, The.
Rayl, J. Spring Storm.
Reese, L. White Fury of the Spring, The.
Rich, A. Attention.
Storm Warnings.
Ridge, J. Rainy Season in California, The.
Ridge, L. Kerensky.
Rubadiri. African Thunderstorm, An.
Ryan, R. Wet Night, A.
Schuyler, J. Crocus Night.
Silko. In Cold Storm Light.
Simpson, L. Summer Storm.
Smith, B. Backwater Blues.
Smith, C. Pressed by the Moon, Mute Arbitress of Tides.
Written September 1791, During a Remarkable Thunder Storm, in which the Moon Was Perfectly Clear, While the Tempest Gathered in Various Directions Near the Earth.
Smith, W. Tempest, The.
Snyder, G. It.
Solari, R. Currents.
Southey, R. Ship, The.
Stafford, W. Epitaph Ending in And, The.
Steele, T. Waiting for the Storm.
Steere. On a Sea-Storm nigh the Coast.
Stryk, L. Winter Storm.
Swift, J. Description of a City Shower, A.
Tannahill. Eild.
Tindley, C. Stand by Me.
Todd, M. Son et Lumière.
Toomer. Storm Ending.
Unknown. Been in the Storm So Long.
Lengthening Days.
Peace Be Still.
Walker, J. Safe.
Weigl. Song of Napalm.
White, M. Recurrence.
Whitman, W. Patrolling Barnegat.
Proud Music of the Storm.
Whittier. Sisters, The.
Williams, G. Wild Night at Treweithan.
Williamson, G. Neighboring Storms.
Wright, J. At Thomas Hardy's Birthplace, 1953.
Storm.
Yeats. Mad as the Mist and Snow.
Pity of Love, The.
Zaturenska. Tempest, The.

See also **Blizzards; Tornadoes; Hurricanes**

Storytelling and Storytellers
Armantrout. Generation.
Brown, D. When I Am 19 I Was a Medic.
Carson, C. Cocktails.
Clayton, I. Last Link, The.
Coleridge, S. Love.
Cooper, W. Leaving the Country.
Davie. Remembering the 'Thirties.
De la Mare. Martha.
Delgado, J. La Llorona.
Dodge, M. Way To Do It, The.
Dunbar, P. Cabin Tale, A.
Harriet Beecher Stowe.
Emanuel, L. Like God.
England, A. Art of the Snake Story, The.
Fishman, L. Promiscuity.
Flynn, N. Cartoon Physics, Part 2.
Fogarty, L. Remember Something Like This.
Forman, R. Kin.
Giscombe. (1978, Remembering 1962).
Graham, W. Imagine a Forest.
Graves, R. Devil's Advice to Story-Tellers, The.
To Juan at the Winter Solstice.
Gregg. Singers Change, The Music Goes On, The.
Hamburger, M. Treblinka.

Hart, K. Story, The.
Hudgins. Telling, The.
Hughes, L. Aunt Sue's Stories.
Ingelow. Story, A.
Jones, R. Novel, The.
Justice, D. But That Is Another Story.
Madhubuti. Union of Two, The.
Markham, E. Sea, The.
McElroy, C. Griots Who Know Brer Fox, The.
Tapestries.
Under the Oak Table.
Mitchell, S. Good Samaritan et Al, The.
Oldham, P. War Stories.
Reid, A. Spell for Sleeping, A.
Riley, J. Little Orphant Annie.
Rohrer, M. Childhood Stories.
Sexton. Cinderella.
Rowing.
Shurin. Blue Shade.
Smith, I. Gaelic Stories.
St. John, P. We Are Going to Be Here Now.
Stephens, J. Seumas Beg.
Stevenson, R. Land of Story-Books, The.
Stewart, P. Singing down the Breadfruit.
Thompson, E. Mythology.
Thomson, J. In the Room.
Walcott. Man Who Loved Islands, The.
Waniek. Sleepless Nights.

Stowe, Harriet Beecher
Dunbar, P. Harriet Beecher Stowe.
Ray, H. Greeting.

Strafford, Thomas Wentworth, 1st Earl of
Cleveland, J. Epitaph on the Earl of Strafford.

Strangers
Al-Rihani. It Was All for Him.
Anderson-Thompkins. To Love a Stranger.
Barnes, B. Something Cool.
Barrax. Strangers Like Us: Pittsburgh, Raleigh, 1945–1985.
Borodin, A. Stranger in Paradise.
Bruner. Casual Meeting.
Buchanan, G. Conversations with Strangers.
Bunting. Orotava Road, The.
Carroll, L. Visitor, A.
Castillo, S. Monday Night at Pedro's.
Clifton, L. C. C. Rider.
De la Mare. Galliass, The.
Stranger, The.
Garrigue. Stranger, The.
Gregerman, D. High Speed.
Hemans. Stranger's Heart, The.
Hewitt, J. Search, The.
Hope, A. Inscription for a War.
Housman, A. Shades of Night, The.
Levertov. People at Night.
Levin, P. Meeting of Friends, A.
Locklin. Stranger, The.
Marinoni. Who Are My People?
Muir, E. Killing, The.
Patterson, G. Letter from Home.
Robinson, E. Flammonde.
Fleming Helphenstine.
Shange. Elegance in the Extreme.
Shepherd, R. Who Owns the Night and Lease Stars.
Strand. Night, The Porch, The.
Thwaite. Great Foreign Writer Visits Age-Old Temple, Greeted by Venerable Abbess, 1955.
Very. Strangers, The.
Yourself.
Vigil, A. At the Stop Light, the Braided Blond Man.
Viray, M. Two Strangers, The.
Wetzsteon. Drinks in the Town Square.
Whitman, W. This Moment Yearning and Thoughtful.
To a Stranger.
Wilbur. Caserta Garden.
Transit.
Williams, J. Shadows.
Wilson, S. Experiments in the Impersonal.
Woo, D. Habit.
Wood, E. Recognition.

Stravinsky, Igor
Alexander, E. Stravinsky in L.A.

Hart, K. Story, The.

Strawberries
Graves, R. Wild Strawberries.
Jackson, H. My Strawberry.
Johnson, M. Strawberry, The.
Kenny, M. Wild Strawberry.
Logue, C. Good Taste.
Merwin, W. S. Strawberries.
Millay, E. Strawberry Shrub, The.
Morgan, E. Strawberries.
Swenson, M. Strawberrying.
Taggard. Millions of Strawberries.
Villa. Now I Prize Yellow Strawberries.
Willard, N. Original Strawberry.
Williams, H. To the Strawberry.

Streams
Arnold, M. Below the Surface-Stream.
Baxter, J. Buried Stream, The.
Burn. Welsh Love Letter.
See also **Brooks and Streams**

Street Performers
Ashbery. Street Musicians.
Moore, L. Haiku.

Streetcars
Hare, M. Determinism.
Larkin, M. Riding on a Streetcar with My Father.
Sandburg, C. Halsted Street Car.
Stone, R. Burned Bridge, The.

Streets
Allen, E. Street Music.
Banus. Eighteen.
Barrax. Strangers Like Us: Pittsburgh, Raleigh, 1945–1985.
Bell, M. Street Fair: The Quartet.
Bryant, W. Crowded Street, The.
Feinstein, E. Magic Apple Tree, The.
Hannah, S. Your Street Again.
Hardy, T. In a Cathedral City.
Harris, W. Samantha Is My Negro Cat.
Hernández Cruz. Side 20.
Hogan, L. Potholes.
Hughes, L. Dive.
Ingelow. Winding-up Time.
Lassell. Brady Street, San Francisco.
Lerner, A. On the Street Where You Live.
Levy, A. Sequel to 'A Reminiscence,' The.
Straw in the Street.
Loewe, F. On the Street Where You Live.
Montague, J. 11 rue Daguerre.
Moss, T. Fisher Street.
Mudrooroo Narogin. Streets.
Nye, N. New Year.
O'Hara, F. Step Away from Them, A.
Paulin. Desertmartin.
Reese, L. Street Scene, A.
Rybicki, J. For Daniel Beels, Third Generation Bricklayer.
Salom. Walking at Night.
Salter. Rebirth of Venus, The.
Shapiro, K. Manhole Covers.
Simpson, L. After Midnight.
Slessor. Choker's Lane.
William Street.
Soto. Street.
Strange. Streetcorner Church.
Welish. Crossing Disappearing behind Them.
Wunderlich, M. East Seventh Street.
See also **Roads**

Strength
Akers, E. Bringing Our Sheaves with Us.
Aldington. Resentment.
Allison, D. To the Bone.
Arnold, M. Growing Old.
Babcock, M. Be Strong.
Bogan, L. Single Sonnet.
Brant, B. Her Name Is Helen.
Brown, S. Strong Men.
Cervantes. First Beating.
Chasin. Strength.
Emerson, R. Compensation.
Evans, M. I Am a Black Woman.
Gilbert, C. Beginning by Value.
Grosholz. Eden.
Hayes, T. Goliath Poem.
Hymans, D. Passacaglia.

Jeffers, R.   Rock and Hawk.
Jennings, E.   Letter to Peter Levi, A.
Mark, D.   Suzie Wong Doesn't Live Here.
Moore, M.   Peter.
Pfeiffer, E.   Lost Light, The.
Plath.   Mushrooms.
Ransom, J.   Spiel of [the] Three Mountebanks.
Rich, A.   Phantasia for Elvira Shatayev.
    Power.
Rossetti, C.   Study (A Soul), A.
Sandburg, C.   Upstream.
Stratidakis, E.   Need for Armor, A.
Unknown.   Freedom in the Air.
    Strength for To-Day.
    Take My Hand, Precious Lord.
Very.   Mountain, The.
Whitfield.   Self-Reliance.
Whitney, H.   To a Woman.
Whittier.   Help.
Yeats.   Wild Old Wicked Man, The.

Strikes and Strikers
Davies, I.   Angry Summer, The.
    Do You Remember 1926?
Espada.   Cockroaches of Liberation.
Guiney.   Strikers in Hyde Park.
Hayes, A.   Joe Hill.
Ilio, D.   Prokosch in Tehran, 1978.
Johnson, D.   Poem: "There was something I
    can't bring myself."
Unknown.   Glorious Strike of the Builders, The.
    What Shall We Do for the Striking Seamen?

String
Arlen, H.   I've Got the World on a String.
Belloc.   Henry King, Who Chewed Bits of
    String, and Was Early Cut Off in Dreadful
    Agonies.
Brown, G.   Shroud.
Koehler, T.   I've Got the World on a String.
See also **Rope**

Striptease
Durrell.   Strip-tease.
Dyer, E.   'Round Killar.
Endrezze.   Stripper, The.
See also **Burlesque**

Strokes
Ammons, A. R.   Parting.
Ginsberg, A.   Stroke.
Plath.   Paralytic.
Rukeyser, M.   Resurrection of the Right Side.
Shapiro, H.   6/20/97.
Stafford, W.   Strokes.
Stephens, P.   Hangman.
Young, G.   Night Call.
See also **Apoplexy**

Stuart, Charles Edward (The Young Pretender)
Nairne.   Will Ye No Come Back Again?
Unknown.   Will He No Come Back Again?

Stuart, James Ewell Brown ("Jeb")
Preston, M.   Grave in Hollywood Cemetery,
    Richmond, A.
Thompson, J.   Obsequies of Stuart.

Students
Abse.   Carnal Knowledge.
Allen, P.   Teaching Poetry at Votech High, Santa
    Fe, the Week John Lennon Was Shot.
Bartlett, E.   God Is Dead—Nietzche.
Blind.   Russian Student's Tale, The.
Clarke, A.   Straying Student, The.
Delgado, J.   Letters from School, The.
Enright, D.   University Examinations in Egypt.
Espada.   Year I Was Diagnosed with a
    Sacrilegious Heart, The.
Farawell, M.   Everything I Need to Know I
    Learned in Kindergarten.
Freneau.   Indian Student; or, Force of Nature,
    The.
Gorey.   Limerick: "Some Harvard men, stalwart
    and hairy."
Hilton, A.   Heathen Pass-ee, The.
Hughes, L.   Theme for English B.
Kinnell.   Correspondence School Instructor Says
    Goodbye to His Poetry Students, The.
Lem.   Office Hour.
Martin, C.   E. S. L.
Moore, M.   Student, The.

Nemerov.   September, the First Day of School.
Posamentier, E.   Hungarian Medical Student,
    The: 1928.
Rome, H.   Chain Store Daisy.
Savage, M.   To a School-Boy at Eton, Yes and
    No.
Snodgrass, W.   Campus on the Hill, The.
Straus, M.   Neuroanatomy Summer.
Tollet.   To My Brother at St. John's College in
    Cambridge.
Tucker, S.   Discontented Student, The.
Wheatley, P.   To the University of Cambridge, in
    New-England.
Whitman, W.   To a Western Boy.
Wilbur.   For the Student Strikers.

Stupidity
Armour.   Pachycephalosaurus.
Centolella.   Small Acts.
Dryden, J.   Crown Prince of Dullness, The.
    Mac Flecknoe [or, A Satire upon the True-Blue
    Protestant Poet T. S.].
Wilkins Freeman.   Ostrich Is a Silly Bird, The.
Williams, W.   These Purists.
Wright, J.   Presentation of Two Birds to My
    Son, A.

Stuttering and Stutterers
Brooks, F.   Stuttering Lover, The.
O'Hara, G.   K-K-K-Katy.

Stuyvesant, Peter
Schulman.   New Netherland, 1654.

Sublime
Divakaruni.   At Muktinath.

Submission
Auden.   Legend.
Bateman, E.   It's a Great Big Shame.
Byron, G.   Last Words on Greece.
Crosby, F.   Blessed Assurance.
Cunningham, N.   Giving.
Davies, M.   Love Song: "There is a strong wall
    about me to protect me."
Dickey, J.   Leap, The.
Frost, R.   Reluctance.
Gunn, T.   In Santa Maria del Popolo.
Herrick.   To Anthea, Who May Command Him
    Anything.
Killigrew, A.   Pastoral Dialogue.
Kizer, C.   Bitch.
M–rt–n.   Humble Wish, The.
Mitchison.   My True Love Hath My Heart.
Murray, P.   Conquest.
Nash, O.   Tweedledee and Tweedledoom.
Piercy.   Friend, The.
Prince, F.   Epistle to a Patron, An.
Rungano.   Woman, The.
Teasdale.   I Would Live in Your Love.
Tomlinson, C.   Oxen: Ploughing at Fiesole.
Unknown.   Thy Heart.
Wickham.   Slighted Lady, The.

Suburbs and Suburban Life
Bawer.   Grand Central Station, 20 December
    1987.
Betjeman.   Middlesex.
    Slough.
Ciardi.   Suburban.
Clover, J.   Alas, That Is the Name of Our Town;
    I Have Been Concealing It All This Time.
Davidson, J.   Northern Suburb, A.
DeFoe, M.   Aviary.
Derricotte.   Blackbottom.
Eigner.   Trees Green   the Quiet Sun.
Elmslie, K.   Marbled Chuckle in the Savannahs.
Ewart.   Nursery Rhyme.
Firer.   Saxophone Julie.
Gotlieb.   Three-handed Fugue.
Gwynn, R.   Classroom at the Mall, The.
Hardy, T.   Snow in the Suburbs.
Harwood, G.   Suburban Sonnet.
Ignatow, D.   Suburbia.
Jeffers, R.   Carmel Point.
Katz, J.   Imperfect Is Our Paradise, The.
Kleinzahler.   Lunatic of Lindley Meadow, The.
Lawrence, D.   Suburbs on a Hazy Day.
Lomax, M.   Other Woman, The.
McGrath, C.   First Trimester, The.
Miles, J.   Housewife.

Moss, H.   Long Island Springs.
Nilsson, H.   How Came What Came Alas.
Noguchi, R.   Really Long Ride, The.
Parker, A.   Days like Prose.
Perry, S.   Fugue.
Riddell, E.   Suburban Song.
Schuyler, J.   Man in Blue, A.
Simpson, L.   In the Suburbs.
Szporluk.   Occupant of the Hose.
Thelwall.   On the Rapid Extension of the
    Suburbs.
Wilbur.   To an American Poet Just Dead.
Winder.   On Fourteen Maple Street.

Subways
Agee.   Rapid Transit.
As-Sabah.   Transition #2.
Baraka.   Clay.
Betjeman.   Metropolitan Railway, The.
Blackburn, P.   Once-over, The.
Denby.   Subway, The.
Esteves.   South Bronx Testimonial.
Harris, D.   On the uptown lexington avenue
    express: Martin Luther King Day 1995.
Hernández Cruz.   Going Uptown to Visit
    Miriam.
Hollander, J.   Curse, The.
Hopkins, L.   Subways Are People.
Hughes, L.   Subway Face.
    Subway Rush Hour.
Jacobs, L.   Subway Train, The.
McKay, C.   Subway Wind.
Millis, C.   IRT at Rush Hour, The.
Monk, G.   South Bound: Facing North.
Olds, S.   On The Subway.
Orlovsky.   Poems from Subway to Work.
Perillo.   Ghost Shirt, The.
Pound, E.   In a Station of the Metro.
    Virginal, A.
Reznikoff.   If There Is a Scheme.
Seaton, M.   Fear of Subways.
Swenson, M.   Riding the 'A.'
Tate, A.   Subway, The.
Walcott.   Village Life, A.
Warr, M.   Brain on Ice.
Weiners.   My Mother.
Wood, E.   Recognition.
Wunderlich, M.   East Seventh Street.

Success
Akst, H.   Straw Hat in the Rain.
Braley, B.   Success.
Brown, L.   Straw Hat in the Rain.
Cameron, C.   Success.
Cole, H.   Thy Best.
Davis, F.   Robert Whitmore.
Eady.   Success.
Forbes, J.   Death, an Ode.
Gilder, R.   Failure and Success.
Guest, E.   It Couldn't Be Done.
Hardy, T.   Ruined Maid, The.
Herrick.   Wassaile, The.
Jenkins, J. *et al.*   In Ferrara.
Kipling, R.   If—.
Lazarus, E.   Success.
Lowry, M.   After Publication of Under the
    Volcano.
Procter, A.   Envy.
Smith, C.   To a Querulous Acquaintance.
Strand.   Coming to This.
Trowbridge, J.   Farmer John.
Unknown.   Success.
Whitman, W.   When I Heard At the Close of the
    Day.
Wilcox, E.   Will.
Yeats.   To a Friend Whose Work Has Come to
    Nothing.

Sudan
Clark Bekedermo.   New from Ethiopia and the
    Sudan, The.
Kipling, R.   Fuzzy-Wuzzy.

Suez Canal
Nemerov.   Reflexions on the Seizure of the
    Suez, and on a Proposal to Line the Banks of
    That Canal with Billboard Advertisements.

Suffering
Afterman.   Pietà.

Akhmatova, A.   Everything Is Plundered.
Alexander, M.   Memory.
Auden.   Musée des Beaux Arts.
Berlin.   You're Just in Love.
Berlin, E.   Sea World.
Bevington, L.   One More Bruised Heart!
Bhatt.   Go To Ahmedabad.
Bontemps.   My Heart has Known its Winter.
Brainard, E.   Compensation.
Brontë, E.   Stars.
Brooks, G.   My Dreams, My Works Must Wait Till after Hell.
Brown, S.   Let Them Call It Jazz.
Bruner.   Gift, The.
  Rebirth.
Cheney-Coker.   Hunger of the Suffering Man, The.
Chipasula.   Because the Wind Remembers.
  Manifesto on Ars Poetica.
  Ritual Girl.
  Talking of Sharp Things.
Clifton, L.   Prayer.
Cullen, C.   Shroud of Color, The.
Davie.   Across the Bay.
Davies, A.   New Sentience, The.
Dennis, C.   St. Francis and the Nun.
Dorsett, T.   Survivor, The.
Douglas, K.   Desert Flowers.
Drayton.   Crier, The.
Dunbar, P.   Prayer, A: "O Lord, the hard-won miles."
  We Wear the Mask.
Glück, L.   Elms.
  Poem: "In the early evening, as now, a man is bending."
  Queen of Carthage, The.
Graham-Pole, J.   Pain, The.
Hardy, T.   Hap.
Hayden, R.   Soledad.
Herbert, G.   Dialogue, A.
Herrick.   His Saviour['] s Words, Going to the Cross[e].
Hirschhorn, N.   Number Our Days.
Horan.   Prometheus.
Howard, R.   Good Shepherd's Sorrow for the Death of His Beloved Son, The.
Hughes, L.   High to Low.
  Strange Hurt.
Hughes, T.   God, A.
Jackson, L.   Wind Suffers of Blowing, The.
Johnson, J.   To America.
Johnson, S.   Lines Contributed to Goldsmith's 'The Traveller.'
Kaufman, B.   Would You Wear My Eyes?
Kaufman, S.   Job's Wife.
Kelly, I.   To an Unborn Infant.
Kendall, M.   Failures.
Kloefkorn.   Why the Stone Remains Silent.
Knevet.   Bottle, The.
Koehler, T.   Stop! You're Breakin' My Heart.
Kunitz, S.   Welcome the Wrath.
Lane, P.   Midnight Song.
Levy, A.   Epitaph: "This is the end of him, here he lies."
  Felo de Se.
  Minor Poet, A.
Lifshin.   Hearing of Reagan's Trip to Bitburg.
Lloyd, C.   Metaphysical Sonnet.
Mörling, M.   Three-Card Monte.
Macgoye.   Freedom Song, A.
MacLean, S.   Turmoil, The.
Melville, H.   Pebbles.
Mhlophe.   Sometimes When It Rains.
Mif.   Terezin.
Millay, E.   Ancient Gesture, An.
Millis, C.   IRT at Rush Hour, The.
Mukand, J.   First Payment.
Mura.   Argument: On 1942, An.
Murray, L.   Cotton Flannelette.
Neufeld, A.   Children of Night.
Newman, G.   Recording History.
Ojaide.   Ward 6.
Olds, S.   I Go Back to May 1937.
Park, S.   On Such A Day.
Pavlich.   Black Flower.
Posamentier, E.   Counting Backwards.

Ransom, J.   Lady Lost.
  Necrological.
Rich, A.   For a Friend in Travail.
Ritchie, E.   Electroconvulsive Therapy.
Rollings.   In Your Own Sweet Time.
Rossetti, C.   Endure Hardness.
  Sappho.
Rowe, V.   Time Heals All Wounds—But One.
Rungano.   Mother.
Scott, S.   Hour with Thee, An.
Shafer, A.   Gurney Tears.
Simic.   Great Infirmities.
Spender, S.   Epilogue to a Human Drama.
Stainer.   Wound-dresser's Dream, The.
Tennant, E.   Mad Soldier, The.
Thomas, R.   Island, The.
Trethewey, N.   Hot Comb.
Unknown, fr. Terezin Concentration Camp.   Pain Strikes Sparks on Me, the Pain of Terezin.
Very.   My People Are Destroyed for Lack of Knowledge.
Voznesensky [or Voznesenskii].   Autumn.
Warren, R.   Riddle in the Garden.
Wetzsteon.   Witness.
Whittier.   Christian Slave, The.
Wilde, L.   Who Will Show Us Any Good?
Williams, C.   Dog, The.
Williams, W.   Complaint.
Wyatt, S.   His Reward.
Yeats.   Fascination of What's Difficult, The.
Young, D.   Frottage.
Zimunya.   Arrivants.
Zisquit.   Word before the Last about Loss, A.
See also **Pain**

Suffern, New York
Kilmer, J.   House with Nobody in It, The.

Sugar
Morales, A.   Sugar Poem.
Wallenstein.   Blues 1.

Sugar Cane
Cofer, J.   Lesson of the Sugarcane, The.
Martínez, V.   Traveler.
Suárez, V.   Song for the Sugar Cane.

Suicide
Abse.   Footnote Extended, A.
Aiken, C.   Solitaire.
Anderson, A.   Suicide Year, The.
Ashbery.   Illustration.
Balaban.   Story.
Banning, L.   Epitaph for a Scientist.
Barry, J.   Nun in Ninh Hoa, A.
Beer, P.   Lemmings.
Berg, S.   Nostalgia.
Berryman.   Henry's Understanding.
  Of Suicide.
Bidart.   Sacrifice, The.
Blackburn, T.   Felo de Se.
BonniLee.   White Candles.
Brett, S.   My Mother's Friend.
Brontë, E.   F. de Samara to A. G. A.
Brown, L.   Sonnet Around Stephanie.
Chatterton.   Sentiment.
Chesterton, G.   Ballade of Suicide, A.
Clarke, G.   Suicide on Pentwyn Bridge.
Coleman, W.   Dog Suicide.
Cooper, D.   10 Dead Friends.
Couani.   What a Man, What a Moon.
Dacre, C.   Power of Love, The.
Dawe, B.   Family Man, The.
Di Prima.   To the Unnamed Buddhist Nun Who Burned Herself to Death on the Night of June 3, 1966.
Dickey, J.   Leap, The.
Dickey, W.   Death of John Berryman, The.
Dobyns.   Seeing Off a Friend.
Donze, R.   Vermont Has a High Suicide Rate.
Eberhart, R.   Hardy Perennial.
Feinstein, S.   Blues Villanelle for Sonny Criss.
Flynn, N.   Bag of Mice.
Gates, B.   Cathy.
  Homeless.
  Ron.
  Triptych.
Ginsberg, A.   To Lindsay.
Graves, R.   Call It a Good Marriage.

  Song: Lift-Boy.
Greenhalgh, C.   Of Love, Death and the Sea-Squirt.
Hale, J.   Six Feet Under.
Hardy, T.   Newcomer's Wife, The.
Harjo, J.   Woman Hanging from the Thirteenth Floor Window, The.
Hewett, D.   This Version of Love.
Hoffman, D.   Center of Attention, The.
Holmes, J.   Depressive Episode.
Holzer, R.   Current 'Now, Voyager' Fantasy.
Hood, T.   Bridge of Sighs, The.
  Faithless Nelly Gray.
Housman, A.   I Counsel You Beware.
  Sinner's Rue.
Howe, F.   Doubt.
Hughes, L.   Bad Luck Card.
  Suicide's Note.
Huxley, A.   Second Philosopher's Song.
Jones, R.   Trouble in Mind.
Knight, E.   Black Poet Leaps to His Death, A.
  For Black Poets Who Think of Suicide.
Knott.   Ant Dodger.
  Goodbye.
  Shorts / Excerpts.
Kumin, M.   How It Is.
Kunitz, S.   Portrait, The.
Levy, A.   Cross-Road Epitaph, A.
  Felo de Se.
  Minor Poet, A.
Lorde.   Between Ourselves.
Lowell, R.   After the Surprising Conversions.
  Suicide.
Loy.   Jules Pascin.
MacNeice.   Suicide, The.
Mahon.   Antarctica.
Marcus, M.   Poem for Gonzales, California, The.
McNeil, R.   Mirrors in the Room.
Miller, E.   Mississippi.
Mirikitani.   Suicide Note.
Montgomery, N.   Eyewash.
Morris, M.   Valley Prince.
Noguchi, R.   Kenji Takezo Becomes Water.
O'Sullivan, V.   Elegy for a Schoolmate.
Piercy.   My Rich Uncle, Whom I Only Met Three Times.
Plath.   Ariel.
  Edge.
  Lady Lazarus.
Ranaldo, L.   HIS:STORY.
Rich, A.   From a Survivor.
  Tattered Kaddish.
Robinson, E.   Mill, The.
  Richard Cory.
Robinson, M.   Her Reflections on the Leucadian Rock Before She Perishes.
  Resolves to Take the Leap of Leucata.
Rodriguez, L.   Heavy Blue Veins.
Roethke.   Kitty-Cat Bird, The.
Rukeyser, M.   Gates, The.
  Power of Suicide, The.
Sandeen.   Way Down, The.
Sassoon.   Suicide in [the] Trenches.
Seward.   Sonnet: "From a rived tree, that stands beside the grave."
Sexton.   Risk, The.
  Wanting to Die.
Shapcott, T.   Autumn.
Sholl.   Girl Named Spring, A.
Silesky.   Screens.
Silex, E.   Elegy: "What remains of the suicide's voice is the last conversation."
Simon, P.   Richard Cory.
Smith, S.   Exeat.
Spender, S.   History and Reality.
Starbuck, G.   Of Late.
Stephens, P.   Hangman.
Stevenson, A.   Suicide.
Stevenson, R.   Celestial Surgeon, The.
Surrey.   Sardanapalus.
Thomson, J.   In the Room.
Unknown.   She Was Poor but She Was Honest.
  Willy Drowned in Yarrow.
Wakoski.   For Craig Who Leapt Off a Cliff in to Hummingbird Light.

Walsh, W.   Despairing Lover, The.
Ward, T.   In the Interest of Possibility.
Warren, R.   Confederate Veteran Tries to
   Explain the Event, A.
   You Sort Old Letters.
Wat.   Joke, A.
Webb, P.   To Friends Who Have Also
   Considered Suicide.
Wheelwright.   Fish Food.
Whittemore, R.   On the Suicide of a Friend.
Willis, N.   To Helen in a Huff.
Wright, J.   Minneapolis Poem, The.
   Precipice, The.
Young, A.   Advice of an Efficiency Expert, The.

Sumac
Very.   Sumach Leaves, The.

Summer
Abinader, E.   On a Summer Night.
Adams, L.   Country Summer.
Agran, R.   Door Thrown Open to Daisies.
Alexander, E.   Nineteen.
Alley, R.   Canary Man and You, The.
Anderson, A.   Licking Wounds.
Andrews, N.   That Cold Summer.
Asch.   Summer.
Ashbery.
Baillie, J.   Summer's Day, A.
Bampfylde.   On a Wet Summer.
Barker, G.   Summer Idyll.
Barnes, W.   Musings.
Benson, S.   Beaten Track, The.
Bishop, E.   Summer's Dream, A.
Blake, W.   How Sweet I Roamed [or Roam'd]
   from Field to Field.
Bogan, L.   Dark Summer.
   Roman Fountain.
Braithwaite.   Quiet Has a Hidden Sound.
Bryant, W.   June.
   Midsummer.
   Summer Wind.
Burns, R.   Birks of Aberfeldy, The [Composed
   on the Spot].
Bush, D.   Summer 1984.
Cahn, S.   Things We Did Last Summer, The.
Call, W.   Summer Days.
Canton.   Day-Dreams.
Clampitt.   Meridian.
Clare, J.   Secret Love.
Cornish, S.   Generations 1.
Cristall.   Song: "Through springtime walks, with
   flowers perfumed."
Cumming, P.   Midsummer.
Davies, I.   High Summer on the Mountains.
De la Mare.   Summer Evening.
Dickinson, E.   As imperceptibly as grief.
   Indian Summer.
   Renunciation.
Duke, V.   Summer Is a-Comin' In.
Dunbar, P.   Song of Summer.
   Summer in the South.
   Summer's Night, A.
Escandor, V.   Summer Nostalgia.
"Field."   O Wind, thou hast thy kingdom in the
   trees.
   Tiger-Lilies.
   Unbosoming.
Field, R.   Summer Morning, A.
Flanner.   True Western Summer.
Forman, R.   Waitin on Summer.
Garner.   Summer Solstice.
Gershwin, G.   Summertime.
Gilbert, C.   Now.
Giovanni.   Knoxville, Tennessee.
Graves, R.   Blue-Fly, The.
Gray-Kontar, d.   July.
Hadas, R.   Moments of Summer.
Hardy, T.   This Summer and Last.
   When Oats Were Reaped.
Hass, R.   Bashō, A Departure.
   Tahoe in August.
Hayden, R.   Summertime and the Living.
Heaney, S.   Summer Home.
   Summer of Lost Rachel, The.
Henderson-Holmes.   Friendly Town #1.
Hollander, J.   Late August on the Lido.
Hopkins, G.   Epithalamion: "Hark, hearer, hear

what I do; lend a thought now, make believe."
Iremonger.   Clear View in Summer.
Jackson, R.   Sunday Brunch.
Jensen, L.   To a Stranger (At the End of a
   Caboose).
Johnson, H.   Summer Matures.
Jones, E.   High Summer.
Jonson, B.   Epithalamion: or, a Song.
Kenyon, J.   Insomnia at the Solstice.
King, H.   Summer Lost.
Kinnell.   In Fields of Summer.
Kunitz, S.   End of Summer.
   Touch Me.
Lampman.   Heat.
Latouche, J.   Summer Is a-Comin' In.
Lazarus, E.   Long Island Sound.
Li Po.   In the Mountains on a Summer Day.
Lux.   There Were Some Summers.
MacCaig.   Notations of Ten Summer Minutes.
   So Many Summers.
   Summer Farm.
Macdonald, G.   Sweet Peril.
Mahapatra, J.   Summer Poem, A.
Marchant, F.   Screen Porch.
Marlatt, D.   Summer of the New Well.
McGrath, T.   Black Train, The.
Meynell, A.   Rainy Summer, The.
   Summer in England, 1914.
Moore, L.   Indian Girl.
   Tanka.
Moore, T.   'Tis the Last Rose of Summer.
Morris, W.   Summer Dawn.
Mpina.   Summer Fires of Mulanje Mountain.
Nicholson, N.   For Hokey and Henrietta.
O'Brien, J.   Revelation on a Summer Walk.
Oliveira, D.   Summer.
Oliver, M.   Waking on a Summer Morning.
Owen, W.   From My Diary, July 1914.
Pederson, C.   Summer Recital.
Plath.   Frog Autumn.
Posey, A.   Midsummer.
Powell, J.   It Was Fever That Made the World.
Probyn.   Song Out of Season, A.
Rafferty, P.   Back End.
Rago.   Summer Countries, The.
Rakosi.   Lying in Bed on a Summer Morning.
Ridlon.   That Was Summer.
Robinson, M.   London's Summer Morning.
Rossetti, C.   Fly Away, Fly Away.
   Summer Is Ended.
Saleh.   Summer.
Sampter.   Summer Sabbath.
Saner.   Sierra Cup.
Sarton.   Small Joys.
Schuyler, J.   Buried at Springs.
   I Think.
   Shimmer.
Schwartz, R. L.   Late Summer.
Scully, J.   Midsummer.
Seed.   'From Escomb, County Durham': July
   1990.
Sexton.   I Remember.
Shelley, P.   Summer and Winter.
Simmons, J.   For Imelda.
Soutar.   Summer Is By.
Spark.   Kensington Gardens.
Stevens, W.   Beginning, The.
   Meditation Celestial and Terrestrial.
Stevenson, A.   When the Camel Is Dust it Goes
   Through the Needle's Eye.
Strand.   Man in Black, The.
Strange.   Childhood.
Styne, J.   Things We Did Last Summer, The.
Surrey.   Soote Season, The.
Swenson, M.   Centaur, The.
Tate, A.   Seasons of the Soul.
Teasdale.   August Night.
   Summer Night, Riverside.
Tighe.   1802.
Tranter.   Backyard.
Tu Fu.   Summer Night.
Tuckerman, F.   Cricket, The.
Unknown.   Sumer Is Icumen [or Ycomen] In.
   Swarm of Bees, A.
Walcott.   Midsummer, Tobago.
Wilbur.   Exeunt.

My Father Paints the Summer.
   Praise in Summer.
Williams, W.   At the Faucet of June.
   Ivy Crown, The.
Wilson, R.   Summer.
Woty.   Lines Written in the Dog-Days.
Wrigley, R.   For the Last Summer.
Young, K.   Preserving, The.

Sumner, Charles
Ray, H.   Charles Sumner.

Sun
Adams, J.   Dream, or the Type of the Rising
   Sun, A.
Alarcon, F.   Morning Sun.
Alexander, M.   People of Unrest.
Arlen, H.   When the Sun Comes Out.
Bacharach.   Poem for the Sefirot as a Wheel of
   Light, A.
Ball, H.   Sun, The.
Behn, H.   Circles.
Berlin.   I Got the Sun in the Morning.
Bibb.   Ode to the Sun.
Blight.   Sun.
Bonds, D.   Life of the Body, The.
Brontë, A.   Home.
Brooks, G.   Boy Breaking Glass.
Brown, E.   Out.
Browning, R.   Parting at Morning.
Brutus.   This Sun on this Rubble.
Burkard.   My Aunt and the Sun.
Campion, T.   Follow Thy Fair Sun[ne]
   [Unhappy Shadow].
Ceravolo.   Invisible Autumn.
Clampitt.   Sun Underfoot Among the Sundews,
   The.
Collins, M.   To F. C.
Creeley.   Anger.
Crosby, H.   Photoheliograph (For Lady A.).
De la Mare.   Christmas Eve.
Delaunay, S.   Zenith.
Dickinson, E.   Presentiment.
   Sun and Fog Contested, The.
   Yellow Man, Purple Man.
DiPalma.   Fragment.
Donne.   Resurrection, Imperfect.
   Sun Rising, The.
Drinkwater.   Sun, The.
Drummond, W.   Invocation: "Pheobus, arise! /
   And paint the sable skies."
"Field."   Ebbtide at Sundown.
Fields, D.   On the Sunny Side of the Street.
Fitzgerald, E.   68.
Friedmann.   Butterfly, The.
Gaffarel.   Celestial Alphabet Event.
Gillespie, H.   That Lucky Old Sun.
Graves, R.   Lament for Pasiphaë.
Greenwell, D.   Sun-Flower, The.
Harvey, F.   November.
Henderson, D.   Horizon Blues.
Herbert, G.   Son[ne], The.
Hogan, L.   Seeing through the Sun.
Hughes, T.   Crow's Last Stand.
Huidobro.   Morning.
Jackson, L.   All Things.
Jeffers, R.   Nova.
Jennings, H.   Prose Poem.
Kaufman, B.   Untitled.
Knott.   Feeding the Sun.
Koehler, T.   When the Sun Comes Out.
Lehman.   Prophet's Lantern, The.
Levis.   Morning After My Death, The.
Lewis, J.   Reader, The.
Lindsay, N.   Indian Summer Day on the Prairie,
   An.
Lovelace, R.   Lucasta's Fan[ne], with a
   Looking-Glass[e] in It.
MacLeish.   Autumn.
   You, Andrew Marvell.
MacNeice.   Morning Sun.
   Sunlight on the Garden, The.
Madge.   On One Condition.
   Solar Creation.
Magee, W.   How to Reach the Sun . . . on a
   Piece of Paper.
Major, C.   Lost in the Desert.
Mansel.   Sun's Perpendicular Rays, The.

Marvell.   On a Drop of Dew.
McHugh, J.   On the Sunny Side of the Street.
Michie.   Arizona Nature Myth.
Miles, J.   Forecast.
Milosz, C.   Sun, The.
Morgan, E.   Strawberries.
Nemerov.   Blue Swallows, The.
O'Hara, F.   True Account of Talking to the Sun at Fire Island, A.
Ortiz.   Bend in the River.
   Earth and Rain, the Plants & Sun.
Owen, M.   Narcolepsy.
Owen, W.   Futility.
Patterson, R.   Sundown Blues.
Philips, K.   Answer to Another Persuading a Lady to Marriage, An.
Probyn.   End of the Journey, The.
Purdy, J.   From rivers, and from the earth itself.
Reese, D.   Ol' Hannah.
Roy, L.   Bread Man, The.
Ruefle.   Topophilia.
Seferis.   Our Sun.
Shenstone.   Hint from Voiture.
Sidney, R.   Songe 17: "Sun is set, and masked night, The."
Sleigh.   To the Sun.
Smith, B.   That Lucky Old Sun.
Stevens, W.   Brave Man, The.
   Sense of the Sleight-of-Hand Man, The.
   Sun This March, The.
   Waving Adieu, Adieu, Adieu.
Stevenson, R.   Summer Sun.
Travis, N.   Sunbathing.
Turner, W.   Sun, The.
Unknown.   Dawn, The.
   Go Down, Old Hannah.
   International Chainpoem.
   Now Goeth [*or* goth *or* goothe] Sun [*or* Sonne *or* Sunne] under Wood.
   Riddle: "Hickamore hackamore."
   Song for the Sun That Disappeared behind the Rainclouds.
Unknown, fr. Terezin Concentration Camp.   On a Sunny Evening.
Vaughan, H.   Cock-crowing.
"W., A."   In Praise of the Sun.
Waller, E.   Song: "Stay Phoebus, stay."
Welish.   Scalpel in Hand.
Whitman, W.   Give Me the Splendid Silent Sun.
Wilbur.   Black November Turkey, A.
   Grasse: The Olive Trees.
Williams, W.   Metric Figure.
Wilson, R.   Envoi: "Sun in the mouth of the day."
Worth, V.   Sun.

Sunburn
Vollmer.   Nursing the Sunburn.

Sunday
Brooks, G.   Sundays of Satin-Legs Smith, The.
   When You Have Forgotten Sunday: The Love Story.
Bush, D.   Sunday the Power Went Off, The.
Gardelle, C.   Peaceful Sunday.
Grenier.   Sunday Morning.
Hayden, R.   Mourning Poem for the Queen of Sunday.
   Those Winter Sundays.
Heard, J.   Sabbath Bells.
Hemans.   Sabbath Sonnet.
Holm, B.   Playing the Goldberg Variations on Sunday Morning.
Jenkins, C.   Sunday Morning.
Jewett, S.   At Home from Church.
Kefala.   Sunday Visit.
Levertov.   Sunday Afternoon.
Lewis, G.   Sunday Park.
Liu, T.   Sunday.
MacKay, C.   Poor Man's Sunday Walk, The.
MacNeice.   Sunday Morning.
Mahon.   Another Sunday Morning.
McAuley, J.   World on Sunday.
Minhinnick.   Sunday Morning.
Obejas, A.   Sunday.
Rouse.   Sunday Morning.
Soupault.   Sunday.
Stevens, W.   Sunday Morning.

Trethewey, N.   Domestic Work, 1937.
Troupe.   In Jimmy's Garden.
Vaughan, H.   Son-Days [dayes].
Wordsworth, C.   O Day of Rest and Gladness.
See also **Sabbath**

Sundews
Swinburne.   Sundew, The.

Sundials
Belloc.   On a Sundial.
Crapsey.   Sun-Dial, The.
Cunningham, J.   Epigram: "I who by day am function of the light."
Dobson, A.   Sundial, The.
Dunn, D.   Sundial, The.
Scott, W.   Rhyme of the Sun-Dial, A.
Unknown.   Motto for a Sundial.

Sunflowers
David, M.   Sunflower.
Ferguson, G.   Winter Sunflowers.
Ginsberg, A.   Sunflower Sutra.
Greenwell, D.   Sun-Flower, The.
Winters, Y.   Wild Sunflower.

Sunrise
Ackerman, D.   San Francisco Sunrise.
Auslander, J.   Sunrise Trumpets.
Binyon.   Winter Sunrise.
Bogan, L.   July Dawn.
Cecil.   Threnody for Sunrise.
Crawford, I.   Dark Stag, The.
Daryush.   Still-Life.
Donne.   Sun Rising, The.
Graham, J.   Gulls.
Housman, A.   Reveille.
La Grone.   Suncoming.
Lowry, M.   Sestina in a Cantina.
Momaday.   Plainview: 3.
Radcliffe, A.   Sun-Rise: Sonnet, A.
Unknown.   Hymn to the Sun.
Wheatley, P.   Hymn to the Morning, An.

Sunset
Abinader, E.   Dar a Luz.
Adams, L.   Sundown.
"Æ."   Great Breath, The.
Apache Oral Tradition.   Corn Ceremony.
Blind.   Red Sunsets, 1883, The.
Cecil.   Threnody for Sunset.
Coleridge, M.   Moment, A.
Coleridge, S.   Sunset, A.
Cope, J.   Sunset.
Curnow.   You Will Know When You Get There.
Esteves.   Ahora.
Fisher, J.   Pearls.
Fitzgerald, R.   Mise en Scène.
Ford, C.   'January wraps up the wound of his arm.'
Fordham.   Sunset.
Frost, R.   Acceptance.
Graham, J.   Gulls.
Graves, R.   Allie.
Ingalls, J.   Gun Emplacement: Sundown.
Johnson, J.   Sunset in the Tropics.
Kinnell.   Daybreak.
Lane, P.   Lake Murry.
Lawrence, D.   In Trouble and Shame.
   Love On the Farm.
Lowry, M.   Sestina in a Cantina.
Ray, H.   Afterglow, The.
   At Sunset.
   Sunset Picture.
Robinson, E.   Dark Hills, The.
Sandburg, C.   Flash Crimson.
   Hits and Runs.
   Sunset from Omaha Hotel Window.
   Sunsets.
Scott, S.   Datur Hora Quieti.
   Dreary Change, The.
Sherman, M.   Towards Sunset at Camino Cielo.
Stern, G.   On the Far Edge of Kilmer.
Stickney, T.   In Ampezzo.
Swenson, M.   On Its Way.
Tate, J.   Cages, The.
Tennyson, A.   Crossing the Bar.
Valentine, J.   Sunset at Wellfleet.
Vasquez, R.   Pismo, 1959.
Wharton, E.   Autumn Sunset, An.

Whitman, S.   November Landscape, A.
Whitman, W.   Prairie Sunset, A.
Wright, C.   Dog Day Vespers.

Superior, Lake
Niedecker.   Lake Superior.

Superiority
Barer, M.   Beyond Compare.
Ross, D.
Wilmer, S.   Mess Boy, The.
Wotton, S.   On His Mistress [*or* Mistris], the Queen of Bohemia.

Supermarkets
Elledge.   Man I Love and I Shop at Jewel, The.
Gildner.   High-Class Bananas, The.
Ginsberg, A.   Supermarket in California, A.
Holman, F.   Supermarket.
Meinke.   Supermarket.
Nemerov.   Grace to Be Said at the Supermarket.
Pape.   In Line at the Supermarket.
Wayman.   Picketing Supermarkets.

Supernatural
Bridges, R.   Low Barometer.
Burns, R.   Tam o' Shanter; A Tale.
Coleridge, S.   Rime of the Ancient Mariner, The.
Collins, W.   Ode on the Poetical Character.
Cooke, P.   Orthone.
Davidson, J.   Ballad of Hell, A.
Ewart.   Sonnet: Supernatural Beings.
Keats.   La Belle Dame sans Merci [A Ballad].
Longfellow, H.   Skeleton in Armor [*or* Armour], The.
Momaday.   Headwaters.
Nimmo, D.   Exorcism.
Poe.   City in the Sea, The.
   Raven, The.
   Ulalume [*or* Ulalume—a Ballad].
Service.   Cremation of Sam McGee, The.
Strand.   Prediction, The.
Thompson, F.   Kingdom of God, The.
Traherne.   Shadows in the Water.
Unknown.   Tam Lin.
Wolfe, H.   Green Candles.
Yeats.   Leda and the Swan.

Superstition
Angira.   If.
Burns, R.   Halloween.
   Holy Fair, The.
Harries, E.   Bone Prison, The.
Hays, H.   Sacred Children, The.
Herrick.   Charme, or an Allay for Love, A.
Johnson, M.   Superstitions.
Jones, A. M.   To the Moon.
Karibo.   Superstition.
Kinsella, J.   Visitant Eclogue.
Milosz, C.   On Angels.
Thompson, C.   Johnny's Pet Superstition.
Troupe.   Conjuring Against Alien Spirits.
Winter, M.   Elegy: "There is a question."

Supper
Berlin.   Supper Time.
Cervantes.   Interpretation of Dinner by the Uninvited Guest, An.
Hood, T.   Public Dinner, A.
Keller, D.   After Supper.

Supplication
Gershon.   Uphold Me.
Herrick.   To His Ever-Loving God.
Mulock, D.   Labor and Rest.
Scully, M.   Variations.

Surfing and Surfers
Blaustein, N.   Water and Light.
Gunn, T.   From the Wave.
Jarman, M.   Supremes, The.
Noguchi, R.   Not Surfing Some Days.
   Really Long Ride, The.
   Turn of Privacy, The.
Pape.   Storm Surf.
Wright, J.   Surfer, The.
See also **Swimming and Swimmers**

Surgery
Abse.   In the Theatre.
Becker, R.   Medical Science.
Catina.   Negotiations.
Chisholm, A.   Contact.

Cook, E.   Surgeon's Knife, The.
Elliot, A.   Latitudes of Home, The.
Gilyard, K.   Daughter, That Picture of You.
Graves, R.   Surgical Ward: Men.
Harper, M.   Deathwatch.
Hughes, F.   Laszlo.
Joseph, A.   Chalazion.
Kirkup.   Correct Compassion, A.
Knight, E.   Hard Rock Returns to Prison from
   the Hospital for the Criminal Insane.
Nowlan.   In the Operating Room.
Pitchford.   Surgery.
Platke, S.   Gut Catcher.
Salter.   Half a Double Sonnet.
Shapcott, T.   Post Operative.
Stallworthy, J.   Letter from Berlin, A.
Tatarunis, P.   Before the Brain Surgery.
Wallace, E.   War.
Wetzsteon.   Surgical Moves.
Wunderlich, M.   Suture.
Wyrebek, M.   Example, An.
See also **Hospitals; Medicine; Physicians**
Surprise
Berlin.   You'd Be Surprised.
Brautigan.   Surprise.
Burke, J.   Welcome to My Dream.
Creeley.   People, The.
   Warning, The.
Graves, R.   At First Sight.
   Grotesques.
Knott.   Sonnet: "Way the world is not, The."
Mead, J.   Sometimes the Mind.
Meinke.   Poet, Trying to Surprise God, The.
Mulkey, K.   Blind-Sided.
Schilpp, M.   Non Sequitur.
Van Heusen, J.   Welcome to My Dream.
Surrealism and Surrealists
Colby, T.   Labor Day Picnic Poem.
Crosby, H.   Firebrand.
Edwards, K.   Good Science.
Forrest-Thomson.   Richard II.
Laurencin, M.   Tiger, The.
   Zebra, The.
Senghor.   "African Image Is Not An Image by
   Equation, The."
Speech and Image: An African Tradition of the
   Surreal.
Survival
Abad, G.   Jeepney.
Ahlert, F.   I'll Get By (As Long As I Have
   You).
Becker, R.   Crypto-Jews, The.
Behar, R.   Survivals.
Boland, E.   Emigrant Irish, The.
Brecht, B.   I, the Survivor.
Brett, L.   My Mother's Friend.
Brooks, G.   To Black Women.
Carruth, H.   Little Citizen, Little Survivor.
Clark, T.   As the Human Village Prepares for Its
   Fate.
Cliff.   Within the Veil.
Clifton, L.   She Lived.
Cullen, C.   Only the Polished Skeleton.
Dobbie.   Forty Three Years After Hitler My
   Parents Visit Eugene.
Donne.   Prohibition, The.
Dorsett, T.   Survivor, The.
Dugan, A.   Weeds as Partial Survivors.
Fish, C.   Work and Worry.
Florsheim.   Weekend in Palm Springs.
Floyd.   Private First Class Brooks Morgenstein,
   U. S. M. C.
Gershon.   I Was Not There.
Gilbert, S.   Yarn of the *Nancy Bell*, The.
Goldberg, B.   Our Father.
   Survivor.
Gunn, T.   In the Post Office.
Hacker, M.   Cancer Winter.
Hardy, T.   Heredity.
Harjo, J.   Anchorage.
Harris, R.   Riding over Belmore Park.
Hemphill.   Better Days.
   Cordon Negro.
Huddle.   Theory.
Kearney, M.   Nature Poetry.
Kinnell.   Bear, The.

Under the Maud Moon.
Lewis, J.   Stories.
Limburg, J.   Seder Night with My Ancestors.
Lorde.   Litany for Survival, A.
Mahon.   Disused Shed in Co. Wexford, A.
Malouf.   Judas Touch, The.
McCarthy, G.   Finding the Way Back.
McGrath, T.   Nuclear Winter.
Michelson, R.   Queen Esther Award, The.
   Where I Sat.
Muir, E.   Horses, The.
Nemerov.   To My Least Favorite Reviewer.
Neufeld, A.   Children of Night.
Newman, G.   Photograph of Survivors.
Ogundipe-Leslie.   Tendril Love of Africa.
Pacernick [or Pacernik].   Louie the Tailor.
Porteous.   I Envy the Cracked, Black Basalt.
Posamentier, E.   Bird Named Isidore, The.
Pratt, M.   Waulking Song: Two.
Preston, R.   Champion Chant.
Ratushinskaya [or Ratushinskaia].   But Only
   Not to think.
Ress.   Learnng the Ropes. Custer Street.
   Evanston, 1949.
Reynolds, C.   Worst of it, The.
Ryan, T.   Enough.
Schwartz, R. L.   When They Know.
Simmons, J.   In the Wilderness.
Song.   Lost Sister.
Sternlieb.   Survivor.
Stevens, W.   Sense of the Sleight-of-Hand Man,
   The.
Swirszczynska.   Good Lord Saved Her, The.
Tallmountain.   Good Grease.
Tapahonso.   What Danger We Court.
Turk, R.   I'll Get By (As Long As I Have You).
Wagoner, D.   Staying Alive.
Warshawski.   Sonia at 32.
Weinberger, F.   He Wears Old Socks.
   Survivor.
Wells, W.   Beatings.
Woo, M.   Whenever You're Cornered, the Only
   Way Out Is to Fight.
Wright, C.   On the Eve of Our Mutually
   Assured Destruction.
Young, G.   Night Call.
Young, K.   Casting.
Zach.   Be Careful.
Susanna (Bible)
Crapsey.   Susanna and the Elders.
Stevens, W.   Peter Quince at the Clavier.
Unknown.   Susannah and the Elders.
Sussex, England
Belloc.   South Country, The.
   West Sussex Drinking Song.
See also **Cinque Ports, England**
Sutter, John
Winters, Y.   John Sutter.
Swallows
Axelrod, D.   Guide to Urban Birds, A.
Clare, J.   Sand Martin, The.
Coatsworth.   Swallows, The.
Cowley, A.   Swallow, The.
Curry.   Swallows and Tortoises.
Dowden, E.   In the Cathedral Close.
Finlay, I.   Cloud's Anchor, The.
Fletcher, J.   Skaters, The.
Nemerov.   Blue Swallows, The.
Rossetti, C.   Fly Away, Fly Away.
Snyder, G.   Sixth-Month Song in the Foothills.
Swinburne.   Itylus.
Turner, C.   On Shooting a Swallow in Early
   Youth.
Yeats.   Coole Park, 1929.
Swamps
Ceravolo.   Caught in the Swamp.
Frost, R.   Wood-Pile, The.
Gray, R.   Flames and Dangling Wire.
Heaney, S.   Bogland.
"Malley."   Culture as Exhibit.
Moore, M.   I May, I Might, I Must.
Nazareno, C.   Cortes Swamp, The.
Ravenel.   Alligator, The.
Wagoner, D.   Walking in a Swamp.

Swans
Arensberg.   Voyage à l'Infini.
Berssenbrugge.   Swan, The.
Black, S.   Personals.
Bogan, L.   Winter Swan.
Browning, E.   Romance of the Swan's Nest,
   The.
Curry.   Mute Swans.
Doolittle, H.   Leda.
Durrell.   Swans.
Dyment.   Swans, The.
Ewart.   Semantic Limerick According to the
   Shorter Oxford English Dictionary (1933),
   The.
Gibbons, O.   Silver Swan, The.
Glück, L.   Palais des Arts.
Gogarty.   Leda and the Swan.
Hernández Cruz.   Swans' Book, The.
Hollander, J.   Swan and Shadow.
Jarrell.   Black Swan, The.
Jeffers, R.   Love the Wild Swan.
Lawrence, D.   Swan.
Longley, M.   Swans Mating.
Lowbury.   Swan.
MacCaig.   Intruder in a Set Scene.
Macpherson, J.   Swan, The.
"Malley."   Sweet William.
Merritt, C.   Mute Swan, The.
Millay, E.   Wild Swans.
Moore, M.   Critics and Connoisseurs.
   No Swan So Fine.
Morgan, E.   Siesta of a Hungarian Snake.
Oliver, M.   Swans on the River Ayr.
Pitter.   Swan Bathing, The.
Rexroth, K.   Poem: "As the full moon rises."
Rodgers, W.   Swan, The.
Roethke.   Swan, The.
Scovell.   Swan's Feet, The.
Sitwell, D.   Swans, The.
Smith, S.   Bereaved Swan, The.
Spicer, J.   Transformations.
Tennyson, A.   Dying Swan, The.
Unknown.   Silver Swan, The.
   Swan, The.
Wright, J.   Three Sentences for a Dead Swan.
Yeats.   Among School Children.
   Leda and the Swan.
   Wild Swans at Coole, The.
Swansea, Wales
Hatton, J.   Swansea Bay.
Watkins, V.   Ode to Swansea.
Sweatshops
Altizer.   Sonnet 5: "No, I'll not, carrion, comfort
   you. Comfort."
Sweden
DeCormier-Shekejian.   Grandmother.
Koch, K.   Energy in Sweden.
Moore, M.   Carriage from Sweden, A.
Stewart, F.   Black Winter.
Swift, Jonathan
Clarke, A.   Sermon on Swift, A.
Montagu, L.   Reasons That Induced Dr. Swift to
   Write a Poem Called "The Lady's Dressing-
   Room", The.
Pope, A.   Happy Life of a Country Parson, The.
Swift, J.   *From* The Life and Character of Dean
   Swift.
Wright, J.   Written in a Copy of Swift's Poems,
   for Wayne Burns.
Yeats.   Swift's Epitaph.
Swifts
Jones, G.   Swifts.
Swimming and Swimmers
Agran, R.   Swimming with Seiger.
Avison.   Swimmer's Moment, The.
Booth, P.   First Lesson.
Byron, G.   Written After Swimming from Sestos
   to Abydos.
Cave.   Written the First Morning of the Author's
   Bathing at Teignmouth for the Head-Ache.
Davison, P.   Questions of Swimming, 1935.
Dickey, J.   Lifeguard, The.
Dunbar, P.   Boy's Summer, A.
Ferguson, G.   Swimming Pool Ghost, The.
Francis, R.   Swimmer.

Gibbons, R.   Breath.
Greger.   Frog in the Swimming Pool, The.
Grunberger, A.   Swimming Upstream.
Hill, S.   Voice in the Garden, A.
Hopkins, G.   Epithalamion: "Hark, hearer, hear what I do; lend a thought now, make believe."
Klein, A.   Lone Bather.
Klein, M.   Tides, The.
Kumin, M.   400-Meter Freestyle.
Morning Swim.
To Swim, to Believe.
Lane, P.   Rain Ditch.
Levine, P.   Belle Isle, 1949.
Livingston, M.   Swimming Pool.
MacCaig.   Kingfisher.
Maguire, S.   Perfect Timing.
McElroy, C.   Learning to Swim at Forty-Five.
Melville, H.   Song from *Mardi*.
Merrill, J.   Swimming By Night.
Mitchell, K.   Night Rain.
Naganawa, A.   Learning to Swim.
Noguchi, R.   Breath He Holds, The.
From Rooftops, Kenji Takezo Throws Himself.
I, the Neighbor Mr. Uskovich, Watch Every Morning Kenji Takezo Hold His Breath.
Olds, S.   One Girl at the Boys Party, The.
Ondaatje.   Inner Tube.
Pierpoint, K.   Swim Right Up to Me.
Ras.   Pregnant Poets Swim Lake Tarleton, New Hampshire.
Riley, J.   Old Swimmin'-Hole, The.
Satyamurti.   Day Trip.
Scott, F.   Lakeshore.
Sexton.   Nude Swim, The.
Sorby.   Synchronized Swimming.
Swenson, M.   Morning at Point Dume.
Tomlinson, C.   Swimming Chenango Lake.
Townley, W.   Swimming Lesson.
Tranter.   Debbie and Co.
Triplett, P.   Winter Swim.
Unknown.   Yes, by Golly.
Walls, D.   Summer the Beatles Went Over Seven Minutes on a Single, The.
See also **Surfing and Surfers**
Swinburne, Algernon Charles
Collins, M.   If.
Holtby, M.   Sister Swallow to Swinburne.
Swings
Allingham.   Swing Song, A.
McCord, D.   Walnut Tree, The.
Muske, C.   Our Kitty.
Stafford, W.   At the Playground.
Stevenson, R.   Swing, The.
Switzerland
Hardy, T.   Lausanne: In Gibbon's Old Garden: 11–12 p.m.
Merrill, J.   Country of a Thousand Years of Peace, The.
Schiff, H.   German Frontier at Basel: 1942 and 1992, The.
Shelley, P.   Mont Blanc.
Tzara.   Zurich Chronicle February 1916.
Wordsworth, W.   Thought[s] of a Briton on the Subjugation of Switzerland.
Swordfish
Douglas, K.   Marvel, The.
Swords
Davie.   Gardens No Emblems.
Herrick.   Upon Pagget.
Sill.   Opportunity.
Sydney, Australia
Beveridge.   In the Park.
Darwin.   Visit of Hope to Sydney Cove, near Botany-Bay.
Dransfield.   Flying.
Murray, L.   Sydney and the Bush.
Symbols
Cervantes.   To We Who Were Saved by the Stars.
Doty, M.   My Tattoo.
Ginsberg, A.   Is About.
Gonzalez, R.   Cabato.
Herbert, G.   Church-Floor[e], The.
Herrick.   Primrose, The.
MacCaig.   Celtic Cross.

Paulin.   Where Art Is a Midwife.
Piatt, J.   To the Statue on the Capitol.
Rouse.   Queynt.
Sandburg, C.   Shirt.
Stevens, W.   Thirteen Ways of Looking at a Blackbird.
Ward, T.   Tacit.
Williams, W.   Rose, The.
Wright, F.   Joseph Come Back as the Dusk.
See also **Metaphor**
Sympathy
Crowell, G.   Prayer for a Day's Walk.
Czerkawska.   Thread.
Dobyns.   Frenchie.
Dunbar, P.   Passion and Love.
Gardner, I.   That "Craning of the Neck."
Ginsberg, A.   Chief of Medicine, The.
Hardy, T.   Often When Warring.
Hikmet.   Angina Pectoris.
Hughes, L.   Laszlo.
Landon.   Poor, The.
Metcalf, R.   These Are Not Lost.
Meynell, V.   Sympathy.
Moorer.   Sympathy.
Pinsky.   Questions, The.
Rich, A.   For the Dead.
Sandburg, C.   Choose.
Warren-Moore.   For Etheridge Knight.
Williams, B.   Friend Who Just Stands By, The.
Synagogues
Lazarus, E.   In the Jewish Synagogue at Newport.
Sillitoe.   Synagogue in Prague.
Synge, John Millington
Strong, L.   Memory, A.
Yeats.   Coole Park, 1929.
In Memory of Major Robert Gregory.
Municipal Gallery Revisited, The.
Syphilis
Sadiq, M.   Tuskegee Experiment.
Wilbur.   Pangloss's Song: A Comic-Opera Lyric.
See also **Venereal Disease**
Syria
Brownstein.   Stepping Out.

T

Tadpoles
Brion, R.   One Morning Beside a Pond.
Kusano Shimpei.   4 Or 5 Tadpoles.
Tagus River, Spain and Portugal
Wyatt, S.   In Spayn.
Tailoring and Tailors
Dunbar, W.   Amendis to the Telyouris and Sowtaris for the Turnament Maid on Thame, The.
Farjeon, E.   Tailor.
Leftwich.   Tailor, The.
Mother Goose.   Snail, The.
Pacernick [*or* Pacernik].   Louie the Tailor.
Zach.   Against Parting.
Taliesin
Thomas, R.   Taliesin 1952.
Watkins, V.   Taliesin and the Mockers.
Williams, C.   Taliessin's Song of the Unicorn.
Talk
Algarin.   Talking.
Alvarez, J.   Redwing Sonnets.
Barben, D.   Do You Know What You're Saying.
Betjeman.   Reproof Deserved; or After the Lecture.
Borson.   Talk.
Bynner.   Sigh, A.
Davidson, M.   Et in Leucadia Ego.
Esteves.   Some People Are about Jam.
Georgiou, E.   Talkin' Trash.
Hammerstein.   Happy Talk.
Hannan, M.   Drive.
Jacinto, J.   Absence.
Kinnell.   For Robert Frost.
Porter, C.   Let's Not Talk About Love.
See also **Speech**

Talmage, S. K.
Tucker, M.   Lines on the Death of the Rev. S. K. Talmage.
Tamerlane
Marlowe.   Fair Is Too Foul an Epithet.
What Is Beauty?
Tanguy, Yves
Gascoyne.   Yves Tanguy.
Tanks (vehicle)
Weigl.   Sharing, The.
Tannhäuser
Levy, N.   Tannhauser.
Taoism and Taoists
Liu Ch'ang-ch'ing.   Sent to the Taoist of Dragon Mountain, Hsu Fa-leng.
Nienhauser, W. H.
Taos, New Mexico
Hughes, L.   House in Taos, A.
Jeffers, R.   New Mexican Mountain.
Tapestries
Moore, M.   Charity Overcoming Envy.
Rich, A.   Aunt Jennifer's Tigers.
Santayana.   On a Piece of Tapestry.
Simic.   Tapestry.
Waddington, M.   Ulysses Embroidered.
Tara, Ireland
Moore, T.   Harp That Once through Tara's Halls, The.
Tarantulas
Lux.   Tarantulas on the Lifebuoy.
Tasman, Abel
Curnow.   Landfall in Unknown Seas.
Tasmania
Afterman.   Van Diemen's Land.
Meredith, L.   Tasmanian Scenes.
Porter, H.   Hobart Town, Van Diemen's Land (11th June, 1837).
Rose.   Truganinny.
Smith, V.   Tasmania.
Unknown.   Van Dieman's Land.
Taste
Browning, R.   De Gustibus.
Crowley, A.   Go into the Highways and Hedges, And Compel Them to Come In.
Garrett, E.   Moules à la Marinière.
Hacker, M.   Canzone: "Consider the three functions of the tongue."
Hall, D.   Mangosteens.
Levertov.   O Taste and See.
Tate, Allen
Davidson, D.   Lines Written for Allen Tate on His Sixtieth Anniversary.
Tattoos (skin markings)
Allen, P.   Tattoo #47, 'Happy Dragon.'
Arlen, H.   Lydia, the Tattooed Lady.
Bottoms.   Chinese Dragons.
Clarke, C.   Make-Up.
Doty, M.   My Tattoo.
Feinfeld, D.   Carmelita.
Finch, P.   Tattoo, The.
Hayden, R.   Tattooed Man, The.
Jenkins, L.   Confessional Poem.
LaFemina.   Her Rose Tattoo.
McClatchy.   Tattoos.
McPherson, S.   Pornography, Nebraska.
O'Hara, F.   Easter.
Walwicz.   Tattoo, The.
Taverns
Baker, D.   8-Ball at the Twilite.
Graves, R.   General Elliott, The.
Keats.   Lines on the Mermaid Tavern.
Kirstein.   Rank.
Lowry, M.   Xochitepec.
MacDiarmid, H.   Old Wife in High Spirits.
Robinson, E.   Tavern, The.
Stephens, J.   Glass of Beer, A.
Vaughan, H.   Rhapsody, A.
Taxes
Bierce.   To the Bartholdi Statue.
Brown, G.   Taxman.
Burns, R.   De'il's [*or* Deil's] Awa wi' th' [*or* the] Exciseman, The.
On Mr. Pitt's [*or* Pit's] Hair-Powder Tax.
Elliott, E.   Caged Rats.

Fatal Birth, The.
Guevara, M. Magic Carpet, The.
Harkness, J. New Song on the Birth of the
  Prince of Wales, A.
Steptoe. O' Yes.
Ward, E. Ballad on the Taxes, A.

Taxidermy
Barnett, R. Taxidermist at the Zoo, The.
Fields, J. Owl-Critic, The.
Follain. Taxidermist, A.

Taxis
Davis, J. Zoo, The.
Hemphill. Family Jewels.
Lowell, A. Taxi, The.
MacNeice. Taxis, The.
Musgrave. Hidden Meaning.
Rouse. Narrows, The.
Slessor. All-night Taxi Stand, The.
Webb, F. Tip for Saturday, A.

Tea
Betjeman. Death in Leamington.
  How to Get On in Society.
Earle, J. Tea Party, The.
Gorham. Princess Parade.
Jacobs, J. Two Varieties of the Bitter Orange.
Koestenbaum, W. Tea Dance.
Lear, E. There was an Old Man who forgot.
Monro. Milk for the Cat.
Mother Goose. Polly and Sukey.
Prior-Pitt. Fitting.
Scudder, A. Tea Making.
Service. Pot of Tea, A.
Seward. Verses Inviting Stella to Tea on the
  Public Fast-Day.
Taylor, J. Recreation.
Welch, L. Empress Herself Served Tea to Su
  Tung-Po, The.
Zinnemann-Hope. Taking Tea with My Father
  and Mother.
See also **Teahouses**

Teaching and Teachers
Agran, R. Wearing Dad's White Shirt
  Backwards.
Algarin. Meeting Gaylen's 5th Grade Class.
Allen, P. Teaching Poetry at Votech High, Santa
  Fe, the Week John Lennon Was Shot.
Anderton. Marking of Folders.
Bachhuber, D. Mozart in a Classroom of
  Children.
Barolini. Having the Wrong Name for Mr.
  Wright.
Berger, B. To Answer Your Question.
Berryman. Professor's Song, A.
Burns, R. Epitaph on a Schoolmaster.
Cahn, S. Teach Me Tonight.
Calverley. Schoolmaster Abroad with His Son,
  The.
Chin. Floral Apron, The.
Colum, P. Poor Scholar of the 'Forties, A.
Davie. To a Teacher of French.
De Paul, G. Teach Me Tonight.
Di Prima. I Fail as a Dharma Teacher.
Duran, J. Mr Teller the Piano Teacher.
Eberhart, R. I Went to See Irving Babbitt.
Fallon, P. Hedge Schoolmaster, A.
Finney, N. Fishing Among the Learned.
Fitzgerald, R. Figlio Maggiore.
Foster, M. Recruiting Song.
Garioch. Elegy: "They are lang deid, folk that I
  used to ken."
Gilbert, C. And, Yes, Those Spiritual Matters.
Glück, L. Mountain, The.
Graham, W. Johann Joachim Quantz's Five
  Lessons.
Guevara, M. Once When I Was in the Eighth
  Grade.
Gunn, T. Autumn Chapter in a Novel.
Hecht, A. Mysteries of Caesar, The.
Huddle. Miss Florence Jackson.
Hugo, R. Letter to Haislip from Hot Springs.
Husain [*or* Hussein]. Lessons in Parsing.
Izumi. In the Autumn, on Retreat at a Mountain
  Temple.
Johnson, E. To Dr. Swift on His Birthday, 30th
  November 1721.

Jonson, B. To William Camden.
Kaneko. Bailey Gatzert: The First Grade, 1945.
Kennedy, X. Hummingbird.
Kinnell. Correspondence School Instructor Says
  Goodbye to His Poetry Students, The.
Kinzie. Ringing Words.
Knight, D. "When the Students Resisted, a
  Minor Clash Ensued."
Max, L. Pedagogy.
McCallum, S. Perfect Heart, The.
McCord, D. History of Education.
McElroy, C. Learning to Swim at Forty-Five.
Meredith, C. Jets.
Nash, O. Purist, The.
O'Brien, S. In Residence: A Worst Case View.
Patten, B. How the New Teacher Got Her
  Nickname.
  What Happened to Miss Frugle.
Pauker. Grouchy Good Night to the Academic
  Year, A.
Randall, J. To William Wordsworth from
  Virginia.
Seale, J. Playing the Flute for the TMR Class.
Seymour-Smith. What Schoolmasters Say.
Sheridan, T. Tom Punsibi's Letter to Dean
  Swift.
Silano, M. In Henry Carlile's *Writing 213*.
Simmons, J. In the Wilderness.
Snodgrass, W. April Inventory.
  Campus on the Hill, The.
Snyder, G. Axe Handles.
Song. Out of Our Hands.
Tripp. Headmaster.
Wagner, M. Miss Clement's Second Grade.
Walker, T. Owl.
Weiss, T. Off to Patagonia.
Whittier. To My Old Schoolmaster.
Williamson, G. Drawing Hands.
Winder. Lesson.
Zolynas. Love in the Classroom.
See also **Scholarship and Scholars**

Teahouses
Woty. White Conduit House.
See also **Tea**

Team Spirit
Holden, J. Saturday Afternoon, October.
Newbolt. Vitaï Lampada.

Tears
Arnheim, G. I Cried for You.
Belieu. Part of the Effect of the Public Scene Is
  to Importune the Passing Viewer.
Bennett, G. Sonnet—2: "Some things are very
  dear to me."
Blunt, W. On Her Vanity.
Bogan, L. Tears in Sleep.
Brontë, C. 'What does she dream of'
Brontë, E. If grief for grief can touch thee.
Brooke, R. Hill, The.
Brown, S. Chillen Get Shoes.
Browning, E. Cry of the Children, The.
  Flush or Faunus.
  Tears.
Byron, G. When We Two Parted.
Cahn, S. Guess I'll Hang My Tears Out to Dry.
Clarke, C. What Goes Around Comes Around,
  or The Proof is in the Pudding.
Coleridge, M. Solo.
Coulehan, J. Anatomy Lesson.
Crane, H. To Emily Dickinson.
Crashaw. Weeper, The.
Delmore, E. Such Sweet Sorrow.
Dickinson, E. Life's Trades.
Donne. Twicknam [*or* Twickenham] Garden.
  Valediction: of Weeping, A.
Eigner. If You Weep, I Think That.
"Field." Already to mine eyelids' shore.
Field, E. Journey, A.
Fletcher, P. Hymn: "Drop, drop, slow tears, and
  bathe those beauteous feet."
Freed, A. I Cried for You.
Glück, L. Moonless Night.
Harbach, O. Smoke Gets in Your Eyes.
Harper, F. Slave Auction, The.
Herder. Esthonian Bridal Song.
Herrick. Hour-Glass, The.

Jarrell. On the Railway Platform.
Johnson, J. Sence You Went Away.
Kinnell. Crying.
Landor, W. Foreign Ruler, A.
Levertov. Weeping Woman.
Lindsay, N. Rain.
Liu, T. Echoes.
Lyman, A. I Cried for You.
Marston, P. Inseparable.
Marvell. Eyes and Tears.
Melo Neto. Daily Space.
Meynell, A. Maternity.
Murray, L. Absolutely Ordinary Rainbow, An.
Nathan, L. Toast.
Neruda. Walking Around.
Peacock, M. My God, Why Are You Crying?
Pfeiffer, E. Any Husband to Many a Wife.
Porter, P. Non Piangere, Liù.
Pratt, J. Words and Thoughts.
Reese, L. Tears.
Rich, A. Peeling Onions.
Sanchez, S. Depression.
Sandburg, C. Bundles.
Seshadri. Lifeline.
Shafer, A. Gurney Tears.
Smedley, M. Cavour.
Smith, S. Death Sentence, The.
  Satin-Clad.
Southwell. Vale of Tear[e]s, A.
Stickney, T. Athenian Garden, An.
Styne, J. Guess I'll Hang My Tears Out to Dry.
Symons, A. Maquillage.
Synková, A. Tears.
Tennyson, A. Go By.
Thomas, D. Hand That Signed the Paper, The.
Unknown. I Saw My Lady Weep.
  Maxim Revised, A.
  Me and My Captain.
  Weep [*or* Weepe] You No More [Sad
  Fountains].
Unknown, fr. Terezin Concentration Camp.
  Birdsong.
Voigt. Woman Who Weeps.
Wheelwright. Esprit d'Escalier.
Whitman, W. Tears.
Wordsworth, W. Ode: Intimations of
  Immortality [from Recollections of Early
  Childhood].
  Old Man by the Brook, The.

Technology and Technologists
Algarin. At the Electronic Frontier.
Dyson, E. Old Whim Horse, The.
Fletcher, J. Song of the Moderns.
Huidobro. Eiffel Tower.
Portnoy, M. Of of Titmouse.
Torres, E. Gigabyte Me—How Much RAM in
  Your Summer of Love?

Teenagers
Alexander, E. Zodiac.
Brooks, G. We Real Cool.
Cooper, D. Teen Idols.
Dodd, E. Touched.
Dove, R. Adolescence—I.
  Adolescence—II.
  Adolescence—III.
Jarman, M. Ground Swell.
Johnson, J. Girl of Fifteen.
Kasischke. Fatima.
McKean. After Listening to Jack Teagarden.
Pollard, C. Heavy-Petting Zoo, The.
Smith, P. Biting Back.

Teeth
Carmichael, R. Tooth, The.
Cofer, J. Lesson of the Teeth, The.
Hopkins, L. This Tooth.
Kay, J. Crown and Country.
Lamb, C. First Tooth, The.
Larsen, R. Red.
Lux. Little Tooth, A.
Melville, H. Maldive Shark, The.
Milligan, S. Teeth.
Mother Goose. Teeth and Gums.
Unknown. My Last Tooth.
Yambo. When Negro Teeth Speak.
See also **Dentistry and Dentists; Toothaches**

Telegrams
Kramer, L.   Red Cross Telegram, The.
Telegraph
Grossmith, G.   You Can't Make Love by Wireless.
Hughes, T.   Telegraph Wires.
Joseph, J.   Lost Continent, The.
Murray, L.   Morse.
Untermeyer, L.   To a Vine-clad Telegraph Pole.
Very.   First Atlantic Telegraph, The.
On the Completion of the Pacific Telegraph.
Telephones and Telephoning
Algarin.   Wire Tap.
Bolton, K.   Nonplussed.
Cisneros, S.   You Called Me Corazón.
Corn.   Long-Distance Call to Gregg, Who Lived with AIDS as Long as He Could.
Crosby, H.   Telephone Directory.
Estep, M.   I Have to Go Now.
Friedman, S.   Answering Machine Message.
Ginsberg, A.   I Am a Victim of Telephone.
Guevara, M.   Long Distance.
Hacker, M.   Rondeau after a Transatlantic Telephone Call.
Hannan, M.   Tap.
Hughes, T.   Telegraph Wires.
Ignatow, D.   Business Life, The.
Simultaneously.
Mastin.   From the Telephone.
Mayer, G.   529 1983.
McCabe, V.   People at the Pay Telephone, The.
Miller, J.   Topos.
Nathan, L.   Breathing Exercises.
Nemerov.   Primer of the Daily Round, A.
Palmer, O.   Wasting Time.
Porter, D.   Lollies Noir.
Richards, L.   Eletelephony.
Sandburg, C.   Manual System.
Soyinka.   Telephone Conversation.
Stafford, W.   Farm on the Great Plains, The.
Stein, K.   World Without End.
Tayson, R.   Phone Sex.
Toomer.   Her Lips Are Copper Wire.
Vazirani, R.   Mrs. Biswas of Maryland on the Phone.
Wright, C.   Legend of Hell, The.
Television
Alexander, E.   Apollo.
Alvarez, J.   How I Learned to Sweep.
Anderson, D.   Nightly News, The.
Angira.   Newscast.
Ben-Lev, D.   Broken Helix.
Bly, R.   Watching Television.
Codrescu.   Telyric.
Coleman, J.   Soap.
Conway, J.   Marlo Thomas in Seven Parts and Epilogue.
Cooper, D.   David Cassidy Then.
Davies, J.   Visitor's Book, 9, The.
Davis, J.   Kids on Television Imagine Me, The.
Dawe, B.   Not-so-good Earth, The.
Dlugos.   Gilligan's Island.
Durcan.   Going Home to Mayo, Winter, 1949.
Wife Who Smashed Television Gets Jail.
Espy.   My TV Came Down with a Chill.
Forbes, J.   TV.
Francia, L.   Video Victim.
Fusselman, A.   Ticker.
Hattersley, G.   On the Buses with Dostoyevsky.
Jones, R.   TV.
Joseph, A.   Soul Train.
Kasdorf.   First TV in a Mennonite Family.
Kelen.   Gods Ash Their Cigarettes, The.
Klipschutz.   Funicello at 50.
Leto.   Mary Morelle Show, The.
Like, J.   Postmodern: A Definition.
Martin, H.   Miss Rosie Mae Watches Elvis Presley on The Ed Sullivan Show.
Merriam, E.   Tube Time.
Moore, L.   Spectacular.
Nemerov.   Mousemeal.
Singular Metamorphosis, A.
Way of Life, A.
O'Hara, F.   Poem: "O solo mio, hot diggety, nix 'I wather think I can' ."
Pettit.   Vanna White's Bread Pudding.

Ridl.   Video Mama.
Sallah, T.   Television as God.
Samaras, N.   After the Children Have Gone to Bed.
Scott-Heron.   Revolution Will Not Be Televised!, The.
Silverstein, S.   Clarence.
Jimmy Jet and His TV Set.
Soto.   TV in Black and White.
Vando.   Lydia's Phantasmagoria.
Wojahn.   W.C.W. Watching Presley's Second Appearance on The Ed Sullivan Show: Mercy Hospital, Newark, 1956.
Zolotow.   Enemies.
Temperance
Adams, C.   John Barley-Corn, My Foe.
McLachlan.   We Live in a Rickety House.
Temptation
Aytoun [or Ayton], R.   To His Forsaken Mistress.
Carew, T.   Song: The Willing Prisoner to His Mistress.
D'Aguiar.   Airy Hall Icongraphy.
Hall, D.   Small Fig Tree, A.
Herbert, G.   Quip, The.
Sin (1).
Hughes, T.   Theology.
Kern, J.   It's a Hard, Hard World for a Man.
Lorde.   Generation.
Mapanje.   We Wondered about the Mellow Peaches.
Marvell.   Dialogue Between The Resolved Soul and Created Pleasure, A.
Milosz, C.   Temptation.
Nasrin.   Eve Oh Eve.
Ransom, J.   Tall Girl, The.
Rossetti, C.   Bride Song.
Goblin Market.
World, The.
Wodehouse, P.   It's a Hard, Hard World for a Man.
Yeats.   All Things Can Tempt Me.
Ten Commandments
Clough.   Latest Decalogue, The.
Watts, I.   Law Given at Sinai, The.
Tennessee (state)
Bolton, J.   Parthenon at Nashville, The.
Gordon, M.   Chattanooga Choo-Choo.
Melville, H.   Shiloh [A Requiem].
Reed, I.   Chattanooga.
Stevens, W.   Anecdote of the Jar.
Tennis
Drieu la Rochelle.   Tennis.
Gilmore, B.   Coming to the net.
Heath-Stubbs.   Watching Tennis.
Higgins, F.   Tennis in the City.
Kinnell.   On the Tennis Court at Night.
Lux.   Midnight Tennis Match, The.
Petrie.   Old Pro's Lament, The.
Volkman.   Pregnant Lady Playing Tennis, The.
Tennyson, Alfred Tennyson, 1st Baron
Bullett.   Footnote to Tennyson.
Heard, J.   Tennyson's Poems.
Hecht, A.   Still Life.
Lawrence, D.   Lord Tennyson and Lord Melchett.
Layton.   Black Huntsmen, The.
Tents
Frost, R.   Silken Tent, The.
Kumin, M.   Despair.
Whittemore, R.   Thinking of Tents.
Termites
Nash, O.   Termite, The.
Terns
Eberhart, R.   Seals, Terns, Time.
Terror
Akhmatova, A.   Introduction.
Ingalls, J.   Apprehension.
Vision of St. Michael and St. John, The.
Lowell, R.   Fall 1961.
Musgrave.   Hidden Meaning.
Pasternak, B.   Hamlet.
Rattray, D.   They Don't Have to Have That Look.
Ratushinskaya [or Ratushinskaia].   Try to Cover

Your Shivering Shoulders.
Todd, R.   Paul Klee.
Trinidad.   Shower Scene in Psycho, The.
Yeats.   Mother of God, The.
Terrorism and Terrorists
Carruth, H.   Essay on Death.
Esteves.   For Lolita Lebron.
Hitchcock.   United States Prepare for the Permanent Revolution, The.
Michelson, P.   Enduring Witness, the Mosques of Kattankudi.
Szymborska.   Terrorist, He Watches, The.
Texas (state)
Boswell, M.   Texas Ranger, The.
Bynner.   Defeat.
Fowler, R.   In Blanco County.
Kimbrell, J.   Slow Night on Texas Street, A.
Unknown.   Devil in Texas, The.
Midnight Special.
Yellow Rose of Texas, The.
Villanueva, T.   Haciendo Apenas la Recolección.
Williams, W.   Desert Music, The.
Thames (river), England
De la Mare.   Old Summerhouse, The.
Dunbar, W.   To the City of London [or In Honour of the City of London].
Herrick.   His Tears to Thamesis [or Thamasis].
Storer.   Rivers.
Tollet.   On the Prospect from Westminster Bridge.
Thankfulness
Burns, R.   Grace at Kirkudbright.
Elvey, G.   Come, Ye Thankful People, Come.
Greenlaw.   Shape of Things, The.
Gunn, T.   Lines for a Book.
Herbert, G.   Antiphon: "Let all the world in ev'ry corner sing / My God and King ."
Marvell.   Bermudas.
Merwin, W. S.   For the Anniversary of My Death.
Stevenson, R.   System.
Wilcox, E.   Accept My Full Heart's Thanks.
See also **Gratitude**
Thanksgiving
Alford, H.   Harvest Home.
Alford, J.   Thanks Be to God.
Cummings, E.   I Thank You God.
Elvey, G.   Come, Ye Thankful People, Come.
Emerson, R.   Grace.
Espada.   Thanksgiving.
Herrick.   Grace for a Child.
Thanksgiving to God for His House, A.
Koch, K.   Thanksgiving.
Livingston, M.   First Thanksgiving.
Merrill, W.   Not Alone for Mighty Empire.
Moorer.   Thanksgiving.
Procter, A.   Thankfulness.
Snyder, G.   Prayer for the Great Family.
Turner, N.   First Thanksgiving of All.
Thanksgiving Day
Child, L.   Thanksgiving Day.
Dunbar, P.   Signs of the Times.
Fisher, A.   Thanksgiving Dinner.
Johnson, M.   Day befo' Thanksgibin', De.
Story of Lovers Leap, The.
Larcom.   Volunteer's Thanksgiving, The.
Prelutsky.   First Thanksgiving, The.
Theater and Theaters
Addison, J.   Playhouse, The.
Blunden.   Concert Party: Busseboom.
Cassells.   From the Theater of Wine.
Cook, E.   To Charlotte Cushman.
Coward.   Why Must the Show Go On?
Dietz, H.   That's Entertainment.
Dryden, J.   Crown Prince of Dullness, The.
Mac Flecknoe [or, A Satire upon the True-Blue Protestant Poet T. S.].
Dubin, A.   Dames.
Gregory, H.   Rehearsal, The.
Hecht, A.   Peripeteia.
Hochman.   Cannon Hill.
Hughes, L.   Note on Commercial Theatre.
Jackson, R.   Tee.
Johnson, S.   Prologue Spoken by Mr[.] Garrick at the Opening of the Theatre in Drury Lane,

1747.
Jonson, B.   Ode To Himself, An.
  Ode to Himself[e].
  To the Memory of My Beloved, the Author Mr
    [or Master] William Shakespeare [And What
    He Hath Left Us].
Kollar.   Sunday Matinee.
O'Hara, F.   Ave Maria.
Pasternak, B.   Hamlet.
Pope, A.   On a Lady Who P-ssed [or P———
  st] at the Tragedy of Cato.
Rothenberg, J.   Realtheater Piece Two.
Sassoon.   Blighters.
Smith, J.   Playhouse Musings.
Snyder, G.   Feathered Robe, The.
Sondheim.   Comedy Tonight.
Stern, G.   Adler.
Stevens, W.   Of Modern Poetry.
Strong, L.   Old Woman, Outside the Abbey
  Theater, An.
Szymborska.   Theater Impressions.
Updike.   Movie House.
Warren, H.   Dames.
Warton, T.   Prologue on the Old Winchester
  Playhouse over the Old Butchers' Shambles.
Weaver, M.   Imitation of Life.
Wotton, S.   De Morte.
Yeats.   Fascination of What's Difficult, The.
See also Show Business
Theft
Alexie.   I Would Steal Horses.
Duffy, C.   Stealing.
Espada.   Moon Shatters on Alabama Avenue,
  The.
Ginsberg, A.   Thief Stole This Poem, A.
Guevara, M.   Magic Carpet, The.
Volkman.   Theft.
See also Crime and Criminals; Thieves
Theocritus
Wilde, O.   Theocritus.
Theology
Hardy, T.   Respectable Burgher, The.
Hughes, T.   Crow's Theology.
Wordsworth, W.   World Is Too Much with Us,
  The.
Thera (island), Greece
Flecker.   Santorin.
Theresa, Saint, of Avila
Clemo.   Mould of Castile.
Crashaw.   Flaming Heart, The.
  Hymn to the Name and Hono[u]r of the
    Admirable Saint[e] Teresa, A.
  Upon the Book and Picture of the Seraphical
    Saint Teresa.
Wilbur.   Teresa.
Thermopylae, Battle of (480B.C.)
Cameron, N.   Thespians at Thermopylae, The.
Theseus
Graves, R.   Theseus and Ariadne.
Muir, E.   Labyrinth, The.
Winters, Y.   Theseus: A Trilogy.
See also Minotaur
Thieves
Anyidoho.   Hero and Thief.
Ba.   Familiar Oxen.
Baxter, J.   Thief and Samaritan.
  Wild Bees.
Burns, R.   Hughie Graham.
Corrothers.   Indignation Dinner, An.
Graves, R.   Thieves, The.
Gunn, T.   Idea of Trust, The.
Harington [or Harrington].   Of honest Theft. To
  my good friend Master Samuel Daniel.
Kipling, R.   Ballad of Fisher's Boardinghouse,
  The.
Kunitz, S.   Thief, The.
Lovelace, R.   Mock Charon, A.
McGough, R.   Kleptomaniac, The.
Melville, H.   By the Jordan.
Mitchell, S.   Good Samaritan et Al, The.
Prunty.   Note of Thanks, A.
Reznikoff.   Testimony: The United States
  (1901–1910) Recitative/The South.
Ridge, J.   Stolen White Girl, The.
Rothenberg, J.   Structural Study of Myth, The.

Very.   Indian's Retort, The.
Wright, J.   Gesture by a Lady with an Assumed
  Name, A.
See also Crime and Criminals
Thinness
Lorde.   Song for a Thin Sister.
Nash, O.   Curl Up and Diet.
Plath.   Frog Autumn.
Thirst
Cameron, N.   Green, Green Is El Aghir.
Espada.   Water, White Cotton, and the Rich
  Man.
Muske, C.   Coming Over Coldwater.
Wilbur.   Ballade for the Duke of Orléans.
Wunderlich, M.   Thirst.
See also Hunger
Thistles
Bly, R.   Looking at a Dry Canadian Thistle
  Brought In from the Snow.
Cunningham, A.   Thistle's Grown aboon the
  Rose, The.
Dixon, R.   Song: "Feathers of the willow, The."
Hughes, T.   Thistles.
Monro.   Thistledown.
Unknown.   Theophilus Thistledown.
Thomas the Rhymer (Thomas of Erceldoune)
Unknown.   Thomas the Rhymer [or Rimer].
Thomas, Dylan
Baxter, J.   Obsequy for Dylan Thomas.
Garlick, R.   Dylan Thomas at Tenby.
Thomas, Edward ("Edward Eastaway")
Lewis, A.   All Day It Has Rained.
  To Edward Thomas.
Thomas, Saint
Hill, G.   Canticle for Good Friday.
Thomson, James (1700-1748)
Collins, W.   Ode Occasioned by the Death of
  Mr. Thomson.
Thoreau, Henry David
Liu, T.   Thoreau.
Ray, H.   Thought at Walden, A.
Very.   On Visiting the Graves of Hawthorne and
  Thoreau.
Thought
Ammons, A. R.   Corsons Inlet.
Arnold, M.   Below the Surface-Stream.
Bergman, A.   Windmills of Your Mind, The.
Berrigan, A.   Four Minute History of Getting It
  Together in Order to Be Fabulous, Briefly, A.
  Looking Up My Balance.
Berssenbrugge.   Texas.
Bogan, L.   Henceforth, from the Mind.
Brontë, E.   Philosopher, The.
Byron, G.   If Sometimes in the Haunts of Men.
Codrescu.   Against Meaning.
Coleman, W.   ISM, The.
Coleridge, S.   Constancy to an Ideal Object.
Coolidge, C.   Crack, The.
  What is Thought but Won't Hold Still.
Creeley.   "I Keep to Myself Such Measures."
  Fancy.
Dana, R.   Chanting Cherubs, The [A Group by
  Greenough].
Davie.   Gardens No Emblems.
DiPalma.   Rumor's Rooster.
Ehrmann.   I Ponder on Life.
Eliot, T.   Gerontion.
Frost, R.   All Revelation.
  Bond and Free.
Graham, J.   Thinking.
Graves, R.   Thieves, The.
Gunn, T.   Lines for a Book.
Herford.   Smile of the Walrus, The.
Hernández Cruz.   Essay on William Carlos
  Williams, An.
Hewitt, J.   Because I Paced My Thought.
  I Write For.
Howard, R.   Stanzas in Bloomsbury.
Hunt, L.   Nile, The.
Jones, L. et al.   Look for You Yesterday, Here
  You Come Today.
Lawrence, D.   Red Geranium and Godly
  Mignonette.
  Thought.

Lazarus, E.   Echoes.
Lovelace, R.   Song: "Strive not, vain Lover, to
  be fine."
Mörling, M.   In a Motel Room at Dawn.
MacDiarmid, H.   At My Father's Grave.
  Light and Shadow.
Mackey, N.   Shower of Secret Things, The.
Marcus, B.   Justice.
Mathews, H.   Histoire.
Moore, M.   Mind Is an Enchanting Thing, The.
Moore, N.   Patient, The.
Noble, R.   Very Thought of You, The.
Olson, C.   Moon Is the Number 18, The.
Palmer, M.   Voice and Address.
Ponsot.   La Une, A.
Porter, C.   I Concentrate on You.
Rankine.   Short Narrative of Breasts and Wombs
  in Service of Plot Entitled, A.
Safie, D.   Meditation by the Xerox Machine.
Sandburg, C.   Aprons of Silence.
  Bundles.
  Murmurings in a Field Hospital.
Simic.   Night Picnic.
  Something, The.
Smith, S.   After-Thought, The.
  White Thought, The.
Stevens, W.   Quiet Normal Life, A.
Swinburne.   Free Thought.
Sze.   Parallax.
Toomer.   People.
Viray, M.   Patio.
Vitale, M.   Joy Island.
Waldrop, K.   Will to Will.
Ward, D.   Shakeout.
Wells, C.   Problem, A.
Whitman, W.   Aboard at a Ship's Helm.
  By the Bivouac's Fitful Flame.
Wilbur.   Fire-Truck, A.
  Mind.
  Praise in Summer.
Williams, W.   To the Shade of Po Chü-I.
Wright, J.   Breath of Air, A.
Yeats.   Meru.
See also Intellect and Intellectuals; Reason
Three Mile Island, Pennsylvania
Williams, C.   Tar.
Thrushes
Crapsey.   To a Hermit Thrush.
Frost, R.   Come In.
Hardy, T.   Darkling Thrush, The.
  Reminder, The.
Hughes, T.   Thrushes.
Larcom.   Brown Thrush, The.
Meynell, A.   Thrush before Dawn, A.
Rossetti, C.   Last Rites.
Watson, R.   Die Zauberflöte.
Williams, H.   Elegy on a Young Thrush Which
  Escaped from the Writer's Hand.
Thumbs
Dacey, P.   Thumb.
Thunder
Davies, W.   Black Cloud, The.
Dibdin, T.   Origins of Naval Artillery.
Eady.   My Mother is a God Fearing Woman.
Hume, C.   Dialogue of Thunder.
Johnson, M. F.   Thunder Storm.
Kooser.   Child Frightened by a Thunderstorm.
Lawrence, D.   Trees in the Garden.
Lowry, M.   Volcano is Dark, The.
Macdonald, G.   Baby-Sermon, A.
McAuley, J.   One Tuesday in Summer.
Okigbo.   Come Thunder.
  Thunder Can Break.
Reeves, J.   Giant Thunder.
Tennyson, A.   Kraken, The.
Toomer.   Storm Ending.
Thyme
Wilbur.   Thyme Flowering among Rocks.
Tides
Bryant, W.   Tides, The.
Carman, B.   Low Tide on Grand Pré.
Farjeon, E.   Tide in the River, The.
Ingelow.   High Tide on the Coast of
  Lincolnshire, 1571, The.
Jackson, H.   Tides.

Knight, S.   Surf Motel, The.
Longfellow, H.   Tide Rises, the Tide Falls, The.
McCaig.   Betweens.
Mew.   Sea Love.
Nims, J.   Tide Turning.
Slessor.   Five Bells.
Szporluk.   Duressor.

Tigers
Belloc.   Tiger, The.
Goodison.   On Becoming a Tiger.
Hernández Cruz.   Side 22.
Hope, A.   Tiger.
Leithauser.   Tigers of Nanzen-ji, The.
Marquis.   Tom-Cat, The.
Monkhouse.   There Was a Young Lady of Niger.
Niblett.   Tiger, The.
Norris, L.   Tiger in the Zoo, A.
O'Hara, F.   Chez Jane.
Oppen.   Myth of the Blaze.
Rich, A.   Aunt Jennifer's Tigers.
Sackville-West.   Greater Cats, The.
Thomas, R.   White Tiger, The.
Villa.   Inviting a Tiger for the Weekend.
Wojahn.   Rajah in Babylon.

Till, Emmett
Brooks, G.   Last Quatrain of the Ballad of
   Emmett Till, The.
Emanuel, J.   Emmett Till.
Jones, I.   Echoes of the Murder of Emmett Till.
Lorde.   Afterimages.

Time
Ackland.   Clock Plods On, The.
Adams, J.   To the Sun-Dial.
Adamson, H.   Time on My Hands.
Agoos, J.   To Atlas in the Attic.
Alexander, A.   This, Too, Shall Pass Away.
Allen, E.   Rock Me to Sleep[, Mother].
Allen, S.   Moment Please, A.
Anderson, D.   Executive Geochrone.
Apollinaire.   Zone.
Arlen, H.   My Shining Hour.
Ashbery.   Soonest Mended.
Atwood.   Beauharnois (1).
   Beauharnois (3).
   Beauharnois, Glengarry (2).
   Dufferin, Simcoe, Grey (4).
   Four Small Elegies.
   There Is Only One of Everything.
Auden.   As I Walked Out One Evening.
   If I Could Tell You.
Beaumont, J.   Hourglass, The.
Bell, M.   Mystery of Emily Dickinson, The.
Bennett, J.   In a Rose Garden.
Bentley, N.   On Lady A.
Berger, B.   Ballad of the Bright Angel.
Berkson, B.   Melting Milk.
Bernstein, L.   Some Other Time.
Bevington, L.   Twilight.
Bodecker.   Garden Calendar.
Bogan, L.   Come, Break with Time.
Boland, E.   Anna Liffey.
Borson.   Save Us From.
Borthwick, P.   Forest.
Bowles, W.   Time and Grief.
Bradstreet, A.   Contemplations.
Braithwaite.   Quiet Has a Hidden Sound.
Brass.   There Isn't Any Death.
Brew.   Search, The.
Brooks, G.   Marie Lucille.
Brown, L.   Green Arbor, A.
Bruner.   Time's Hand Is Kind.
Bryant, W.   Ages, The.
   Fountain, The.
   Rivulet, The.
Buckley, C.   Playing for Time.
Buckley, V.   Child is Revenant to the Man, The.
Byron, G.   So We'll Go No More A-Roving.
   Stanzas for Music.
Campbell, T.   River of Life, The.
Carew, T.   Persuasions to Enjoy.
Carroll.   In the Shakespeare Garden at
   Northwestern University.
Carroll, J.   Heroin.
Carruth, H.   Testament.
Carver, R.   Woman Bathing.
Castillo, S.   En el Sol de Mi Barrio.

Cendrars.   Hammock.
Chin.   Year Passes in My Morning Teacup, The.
Clare, J.   To an Hour-Glass.
Colby, T.   Captain's Log.
Cole, T.   Dial, The.
Coleridge, S.   Time, Real and Imaginary.
Cook, E.   Song of the Modern Time.
Cope, W.   Bloody Men.
Copus, J.   Widower.
Cornford, F.   Unbeseechable, The.
Cowper, W.   Comparison, A.
Cranch.   December.
   My Old Palette.
   Spirit of the Age, The.
Crane, H.   My Grandmother's Love Letters.
Crapsey.   Trapped.
Creeley.   Again.
   Rescue, The.
   River Wandering Down.
   Time.
Crompton.   Epigram LXVII: Time, the
   Interpreter.
Cuddihy.   This Body.
Cummings, E.   Anyone Lived in a Pretty How
   Town.
   Impression.
   Sonnet IV.
Cunningham, J.   Epigram: "Time heals not: it
   extends a sorrow's scope."
d'Oettingen.   To Il y a.
Daryush.   How on Solemn Fields of Space.
Davidson, M.   Thinking the Alps.
Davie.   Time Passing, Beloved.
Davies, D.   At Branwen's Grave.
Davies, W.   Leisure.
Davison, P.   Vanishing Point, The.
Day Lewis.   Poem for an Anniversary.
Dekker, T. et al.   Folly's Song.
Desnos.   Midway.
Dickinson, E.   They Say That Time Assuages.
Disch.   Convalescing in London.
Dobson, A.   Sundial, The.
Donne.   Anniversary [or Anniversarie], The.
   Computation, The.
Dooley, M.   Heat.
Dransfield.   Visiting Hour (Repatriation
   Hospital).
Drayton.   To My Noble Friend Master William
   Browne: Of the Evil Time.
Drinkwater.   Birthright.
Duran, J.   Time Zones.
Eberhart, R.   Garden God, The.
Ehret, T.   Lost Body.
Emerson, R.   Awed I Behold Once More.
   Compensation.
   Days.
   Past, The.
   Test, The.
   Two Rivers.
Farrar, J.   Song for a Forgotten Shrine to Pan.
"Field."   Palimpsest, A.
Finch, A.   Reply From His Coy Mistress, A.
Fisher, J.   It's February But.
Fitzgerald, E.   74.
Flecker.   Stillness.
Florian.   First.
Francis, R.   Coming and Going.
   Mouse Whose Name Is Time, The.
Frost, R.   Nothing Gold Can Stay.
Galvin, J.   Two Horses and a Dog.
Garcia, R.   Brief Entanglements.
Gardner, E.   Written in Tintern Abbey,
   Monmouthshire.
Garrett, E.   Unguentarium.
Gascoyne.   Cage, The.
Gioia.   Becoming a Redwood.
Glück, L.   Aubade: "World was very large then,
   The."
   For My Mother.
   Magi, The.
   Time.
Gordon, M.   Time on My Hands.
Gould, A.   Observed Observer, The.
Graham, W.   Lines on Roger Hilton's Watch.
Graves, R.   Counting the Beats.
   In Time.

Love Story, A.
Gwynn, R.   Release.
Hölderlin.   In the Days of Socrates.
Habington.   To the Moment Last Past.
Hall, D.   Dusting.
Hanzlicek, C.   Moment.
Hardy, T.   Anniversary, An.
   Commonplace Day, A.
   During Wind and Rain.
   Long Plighted.
   Old Furniture.
   Places.
   Sunshade, The.
   This Summer and Last.
Heard, J.   Birth of Time, The.
Hemensley.   Sulking in the Seventies.
Henley, W.   At Queensferry.
Herbert, E.   To His Watch, When He Could Not
   Sleep.
Herbert, G.   Life.
   Time.
Herbert, W.   Praise of Italian Chip-Shops.
Herman, J.   Time Heals Everything.
Herrick.   His Poetry His Pillar.
   Hour-Glass, The.
   Sabbaths.
   To the Virgins, to Make Much of Time.
   Upon Time.
Hesketh.   Love's Advocate.
Higo.   Hidesong.
Hikmet.   Letters from Chankiri Prison.
   Since I Was Thrown Inside.
Hinsey, E.   Approach of War, The.
Hodgson, R.   Time.
   Time, You Old Gypsy Man.
Hollander, J.   For Both of You, the Divorce
   Being Final.
Holmes, O.   Last Leaf, The.
Hood, T.   Time, Hope, and Memory.
Hope, A.   Observation Car.
Hopkins, G.   To His Watch.
Housman, A.   On Wenlock Edge.
Howard, B.   Year After Year.
Howard, R.   After 65.
Hughes, L.   Negro Speaks of Rivers, The.
Hughes, R.   On Time.
Hummell, A.   Saraband.
Hunt, L.   Rondeau: "Jenny kissed [or kiss'd] me
   when we met."
Hupfeld, H.   As Time Goes By.
Hymans, D.   Passacaglia.
Jeffers, R.   Carmel Point.
Jefferys [or Jeffries].   We Have Lived and
   Loved Together.
Jennings, E.   Delay.
Johnson, L.   New Guinea Time.
   Tahiti.
Jonson, B.   Hour-Glass [or Houre-Glasse], The.
Keats.   To Ailsa Rock.
Kendall, M.   Pure Hypothesis, A.
Kennedy, X.   In a Prominent Bar in Secaucus
   [One Day].
Knight, E.   He Sees Through Stone.
Knight, S.   Surf Motel, The.
Komunyakaa.   Way the Cards Fall, The.
Kooser.   Year's End.
Kowit.   Notice.
Koyama.   Downtown Seattle in the Fog.
Kunitz, S.   Layers, The.
   River Road.
Larkin, P.   Days.
Lauterbach.   Clamor.
Lawrence, D.   Humming-Bird.
   Song of a Man Who Has Come Through, The.
Lea, S.   Telescope.
Lee, D.   There Was a Man.
Lem.   Temple City Blvd. and Ellis Ln.
Levin, P.   Dark Horse.
   Meeting of Friends, A.
Levine, P.   Sweet Will.
Lewis, A.   Mahratta Ghats, The.
Lewis, J.   Ancient Ones, The: Betátakin.
   Time and Music.
Linden, M.   Scraps of Time.
Lister, R.   Toast to 2,000, A.
Longfellow, H.   Bridge, The.

Fragment: August 4, 1856.
Old Clock on the Stairs, The.
Sand of the Desert in an Hour-Glass.
Tide Rises, the Tide Falls, The.
Longley, M. Gorse Fires.
Lowell, R. At the Altar.
Lumsden, R. Beginning of the End Then, The.
Mackey, N. Winged Abyss.
MacLeish. Grazing Locomotives.
Signature for Tempo.
Snowflake Which Is Now and Hence Forever, The.
Words in Time.
You, Andrew Marvell.
MacNeice. Cradle Song: "Clock's untiring fingers wind the wool of darkness, The."
Mayfly.
Meeting Point.
Star-Gazer.
Sunday Morning.
Mahon. Dog Days.
Mangan, J. Twenty Golden Years Ago.
Marsden. What Is Time?
Martinez, D. Standard Time: Novena for My Father.
Marvell. To His Coy Mistress.
McMichael. Posited.
Medina, P. Exile, The.
Melville, H. Enthusiast, The.
Mercer, J. My Shining Hour.
Merwin, W. S. Another Year Come.
For the Anniversary of My Death.
Milosz, C. And Yet the Books.
Milosz, O. Bridge, The.
Milton. On Time.
To Mr. Lawrence.
Momaday. Two Figures.
Moore, H. Green Place, A.
Moore, M. Four Quartz Crystal Clocks.
Noise That Time Makes, The.
Moore, T. No—Leave My Heart to Rest.
Moraes, D. Kanheri Caves.
Morgan, R. Shadow Valley.
Mother Goose. Ten O'Clock Scholar, [The].
Mueller, L. Palindrome.
Murray, G. On Being Disabled by Light at Dawn in the Wilderness.
Murray, J. And as I Came Out from the Temples.
Nash, O. Mr. Artesian's Conscientiousness.
Nemerov. Remorse for Time, The.
Nicholson, N. Five Minutes.
O'Hara, F. Poetry.
Okigbo. Hurrah for Thunder.
Oliver, M. Hummingbird Pauses at the Trumpet Vine.
Olson, C. Kingfishers, The.
Ormond. Ancient Monuments.
Ortiz. Speaking.
Owen, G. Gathering in the Days.
Pack, R. Proton Decay.
Paquet. Group Shot.
Pasternak, B. Snow Is Falling.
Patchen. State of the Nation, The.
Peskett. Star and Sea.
Piatt, S. Lesson in a Picture, A.
Piombino. Frozen Witness, The.
Time Travel.
Poe. Coliseum, The.
Powell, D. A. Always Returning: Holidays and Burials. Not Every Week.
Pritchard, N. Cloak, The.
Quarles. On the Life of Man.
Radiguet. Handless Clock.
Ralegh, S. Authours Epitaph, Made by Himself, The.
Even Such Is Time.
Nature, That Washed [or Washt] Her Hands in Milk[e].
Nymph's [or Nimphs] Reply to the Shepherd [or Sheepheard], The.
Ramanujan. Foundlings in the Yukon.
Ranaldo, L. Five Weeks.
Time Presses Me.
Randall, D. His Favourite Seat.
Randell. Songs for the Sleepless.

Reeves, J. Slowly.
Rexroth, K. Time Is the Mercy of Eternity.
Riley, J. Summer Seeming.
Robinson, E. Clerks, The.
Three Quatrains.
Rossetti, C. Amen.
Life's Parallels, A.
Rothman, D. Whistling in January.
Saleh. December Nap.
Salinas, L. My Fifty-Plus Years Celebrate Spring.
Salter. Sunday Skaters.
Sandburg, C. Four Preludes on Playthings of the Wind.
Languages.
Limited.
Sunset from Omaha Hotel Window.
Sansom, A. Confinement.
Schwartz, D. Time's Dedication.
Scott, S. Hour with Thee, An.
Scovell. Past Time.
Shapiro, K. Drug Store.
Shelley, P. Lament, A: "O world! O life! O time!"
Ozymandias.
Simic. Mirrors at 4 A.M.
Slessor. Five Bells.
Smith, S. Grange, The.
Holiday, The.
Snyder, G. Autumn Morning in Shokoku-ji, An.
Four Poems for Robin.
Milton by Firelight.
Spring Night in Shokoku-ji, A.
Southey, R. Scholar, The.
Spender, S. Epilogue: "Time is a thing."
In Railway Halls.
Spenser. Ruines of Time, The.
St. John, D. Grandfather's Cap, My.
Stevens, W. Martial Cadenza.
This Solitude of Cataracts.
Stillman, M. Song: "Love is a green girl."
Stryk, L. Return to DeKalb.
Styne, J. Just in Time.
Suckling, S. Love's Clock.
Sundiata. Ear Training.
Swift, J. Power of Time, The.
Sylvester, J. Father, The.
Rome, Conqueror, Conquered.
Synková, A. To Olga.
Szymborska. View with a Grain of Sand.
Taylor, C.B. Plenty Time Pass Fast, Fas Dey So.
Teasdale. Song: "Let it be forgotten, as a flower is forgotten."
Tennyson, A. Break, Break, Break.
Dedication, A: "Dear, near and true—no truer Time himself."
Thomas, D. Force That Through the Green Fuse Drives the Flower, The.
Thomas, E. Gone, Gone Again.
Thomas, R. Centuries.
Evening.
Llanrhaeadr Ym Mochnant.
Thompson, D. Adown the Heights of Ages.
Towle. Postmodern Maturity.
Townshend [or Townsend]. Dialogue betwixt Time and a Pilgrim[e], A.
Turner, C. East or West?
Ulku, A. Spring Forward, Fall Back.
Ullman. Why There Are Children.
Unknown. Deor.
Minutes of Gold.
Unknown, fr. Terezin Concentration Camp.
Concert in the Old School Garret.
Night in the Ghetto.
Van Duyn. Homework.
Vaughan, H. As Time One Day by Me Did Pass.
Very. Lost, The.
One Generation Passeth Away.
Vitale, M. Loop, Fleck, Sound and So On.
Volkman. Untitled.
Waniek. House on Moscow Street, The.
Warner, S. Clock Plods On, The.
Warren, R. Acquaintance with Time in Early Autumn.

After Night Flight Son Reaches Bedside of Already Unconscious Father, Whose Right Hand Lifts in a Spasmodic Gesture, as Though Trying to Make Contact: 1955.
Bearded Oaks.
Death of Time.
Natural History.
There's a Grandfather's Clock in the Hall.
Watkins, V. Old Triton Time.
Wearne. Go on, tell me the season is over.
Webster, A. Faded.
Welish. Within This Book, Called Marguerite.
Wilbur. On the Marginal Way.
Year's End.
Williams, S. Green Eyed Monsters of the Valley Dusk, The.
Willis, H. Time's Whirligig, Or, The Blue-New-Made-Gentleman Mounted.
Witt, S. Americana.
Woods, D. Waiting.
Wright, C. March Journal.
Wylie. Let No Charitable Hope.
Yeats. Brown Penny.
Folly of Being Comforted, The.
Gyres, The.
Lamentation of the Old Pensioner, The.
Moods, The.
Youmans, V. Time on My Hands.
Young, A. California Peninsula: El Camino Real.
Young, K. Central Standard Time.
Young, M. J. To Time.
Zukofsky, L. I Sent Thee Late.
Timoshenko, Semyon Konstantinovich
Keyes, S. Timoshenko.
Tinkers
Dodge, M. Tinker, Come Bring Your Solder.
Tinter Abbey
Stevenson, R. Fragment, A: "Thou strainest through the mountain fern."
Wordsworth, W. Lines Composed a Few Miles above Tintern Abbey on Revisiting the Banks of the Wye During a Tour, July 13, 1798.
Tiresias
Jacob, H. Judgement of Tiresias, The.
Titanic (ship)
Bynner. Titanic, The.
Eady. Jack Johnson Does the Eagle Rock.
Hardy, T. Convergence of the Twain, The.
Knight, E. Dark Prophecy: I Sing of Shine.
Unknown. Titanic, The.
Shine and the Titanic.
Tithonus
Tennyson, A. Tithonus.
Titus (Roman Emperor)
Heath-Stubbs. Titus and Berenice.
Toads
Allen, E. Toad, A.
Crane, S. "Think as I think," said a man.
MacCaig. Toad.
Parker, A. Cruelty, the Vandals Say.
Patterson, R. Hopping Toad Blues.
Reyes, M. Toads Mate and Father Cleans the Pool.
Rosen, M. Teasing Toads, The.
Rossetti, C. Hopping frog, hop here and be seen.
Soutar. Philosophic Taed, The.
Wilbur. Death of a Toad, The.
Toasters
Smith, W. Toaster, The.
Tobacco
Cook, E. Sot-Weed Factor, The.
Cotton, C. On Tobacco.
Freneau. Tobacco.
Matherne, B. La Fabrique de Tabac (Tobacco Harvest).
Melville, H. Herba Santa.
Moore, L. From the Field.
Wisdome. Religious Use of [Taking] Tobacco, A.
Toes
Halpern, D. Her Body.
Unknown. Hairy Toe, The.
Moses.

Updike. In Extremis.

See also **Feet**

Toledo, Spain
Campbell, R. Toledo.
Williams, W. High Bridge above the Tagus River at Toledo, The.

Tolerance
Bruner. Plea for Tolerance.
Dunbar, P. Accountability.
Lim, G. Children are Colorblind.

Tollund Man
Heaney, S. Tollund Man, The.

Tombs
Ashbery. How Much Longer Will I Be Able to Inhabit the Divine Sepulcher?
Beer, P. Ninny's Tomb.
Brontë, C. Is this my tomb, this humble stone.
Clare, J. Loves Lives Beyond the Tomb.
Coleridge, M. To a Piano.
Collins, W. Fidele, A.
De la Mare. Stranger, The.
"Field." Embalmment.
Hemans. Queen of Prussia's Tomb, The.
Herbert, G. Church Monuments.
Herrick. His Winding-Sheet.
  To Robin Redbreast.
Jonson, B. Little Shrub Growing By, A.
Keats. This Living Hand, Now Warm and Capable.
Larkin, P. Arundel Tomb, An.
Monsour. Sweeping.
Ormond. Design for a Tomb.
Poe. Annabel Lee.
Rochester, J. Mistress, The: A Song.
Ros. On Visiting Westminster Abbey.
Rossetti, C. Last Rites.
Sandburg, C. Cool Tombs.
Smith, C. Pressed by the Moon, Mute Arbitress of Tides.
Sparrow, J. Epitaph: "This stone, with not unpardonable pride."
Stevens, W. Worms at Heaven's Gate, The.
Unknown. Spirit of Plato.
Wharton, E. Tomb of Ilaria Giunigi, The.
Wordsworth, W. Sonnet on Catherine Wordsworth.

See also **Cemeteries; Graves; Monuments; Mausoleums**

Tone, Wolfe
Clarke, A. Wolfe Tone.

Tongues
Anderson, A. Licking Wounds.
Chubb, R. Song of My Soul.
Dove, R. Adolescence—II.
Hacker, M. Canzone: "Consider the three functions of the tongue."
Lorde. Echoes.
Redmond. My Tongue Paints a Path.
Strong, P. Tongue, The.
Tate, G. Tonguing.
Unknown. Theophilus Thistledown.
Warren-Moore. Pink Poem.

Tools
Barber, D. Spirit Level, The.
Ormsby, F. Under the Stairs.
Van Peenen, H. Will Campbell Displays His Craniotribe.

Tories
Moore, T. Tory Pledges.

Tornadoes
Fulton, A. News of the Occluded Cyclone.
Levin, D. Wind.
Moss, T. Tornados.

Tortoises
Atwood. Elegy for the Giant Tortoises.
Clarke, C. Tortoise and Badger.
Curry. Swallows and Tortoises.
Lawrence, D. Lui et Elle.
  Tortoise Shout.
  Tortoise-Shell.
Patten, B. Complacent Tortoise, The.
Siegel, J. How the Tortoise Knew It Was Her Time.

Torture
Atwood. Torture.
Balaban. Opening Le Ba Khon's Dictionary.
Bampfylde. On Hearing That Torture Was Suppressed throughout the Austrian Dominions.
Beer, P. Footbinding.
Berryman. Song of the Tortured Girl, The.
Bly, R. Romans Angry about the Inner World.
Bolton, J. American Tragedy.
Cohen, L. Heirloom.
Drayton. To His Coy Love, A Canzonet.
Ekelof. Hangman.
Forché. Return.
Hamburger, M. Between the Lines.
Hetherington, G. Man from Changi, The.
Hughes, J. Respect for Law and Order, A.
Ignatow, D. Ritual Three.
Martinez, D. Pain.
Oden. Riven Quarry, The.
Plath. Hanging Man, The.
Rukeyser, M. Rational Man.
Seto, T. Jihad.
Thwaite. Freedom.
Unknown, fr. Terezin Concentration Camp. Pain Strikes Sparks on Me, the Pain of Terezin.
Winkfield, T. Nature Study.
Wise, S. I Was Very Prolific.

Touch
Akiwumi, V. Unconditionals #3.
Anawrok. Each Time.
Broumas, O. Touched.
Douglas, K. Prisoner, The.
Gloria. Touch.
Gray, J. Mishka.
Gunn, T. Touch.
Horovitz, F. Do You Not Know that I Need to Touch You.
Hughes, F. Laszlo.
Lyons, S. Touching You Underwater.
Mew. Ne Me Tangito.
O'Neill, M. My Fingers.
Raine, K. Love-Poem: "Yours is the face that the earth turns to me."
Tana, P. I Have Touched.
  No.
Ullman. Memo.
Zawinski, A. You Touch Me.

Toulouse-Lautrec, Henri de
Justice, D. Mule Team and Poster.

Tourism and Tourists
Adisa. Cultural Trip, A.
Algarin. Taos Pueblo Indians: 700 strong according to Bobby's last census.
Bernstein, L. New York, New York.
Birney. Toronto Board of Trade Goes Abroad.
Bishop, E. Arrival at Santos.
Bromige. Edible World, The.
Brown, G. Trout Fisher.
Castillo, S. Rincón.
Clanchy, K. Foreign.
Dixon, M. Nagasaki.
Dobyns. Dancing in Vacationland.
Dove, R. Sightseeing.
Dugan, A. Memorial Service for the Invasion Beach Where the Vacation in the Flesh Is Over.
Duggan, L. Qantas Bags.
Figueroa, J. Puerto Rico Made in Japan.
Garioch. Embro to the Ploy.
González, R. You and the Tijuana Mule.
Grosholz. Outer Banks, The.
Hoagland, E. Gorée.
Kunitz, S. Thief, The.
Melville, H. Attic Landscape, The.
Moss, H. Tourists.
Owens, P. Croeso i Gymru.
Page, P. Permanent Tourists, The.
Phillips, C. You Are Here.
Porter, C. Katie Went to Haiti.
  You Don't Know Paree.
Richie, E. Airports of the World.
Rose, P. Anglo-Saxon Comedy.
Schapiro, J. Tourist, The.
Shiffert. Manners.
Sia, B. Things to Do in Holland.

Szymborska. Pietà.
Tibble. Trials of a Tourist.
Tsaloumas. Progressive Man's Indignation, A.
Walcott. Virgins, The.
Warren, H. Nagasaki.
Weaver, M. Message on Cape Cod, The.
Yambo. When Negro Teeth Speak.
Zagajewski. Auto Mirror.

Toussaint L'Ouverture, François Dominique
Goodison. Kenscoff.
Ray, H. Toussaint L'Ouverture.
Wordsworth, W. To Toussaint L'Ouverture.

Towns
Allen, E. In the Defences.
Barnes, W. Be'mi'ster.
Browning, R. Up at a Villa—Down in the City.
Cervantes. Poema para los Californios Muertos.
Collins, M. Winter in Brighton.
Corn. Kimchee in Worchester (Mass.).
Cummings, E. Anyone Lived in a Pretty How Town.
Davies, J. Port Talbot.
Dobson, A. In Town.
Dodge, M. Mayor of Scuttleton, The.
Dove, R. Small Town.
Graham, W. Children of Greenock, The.
Hall, D. Town of Hill, The.
Harms. Dogtown.
Knoepfle. Late Winter in Menard County.
Larkin, P. Here.
Laux. What Could Happen.
Lawrence, D. End of Another Home Holiday.
  Whether or Not.
Lee, D. Benediction.
Miller, J. Which Religion Vouchsafes.
Reese, L. April in Town.
Rukeyser, M. Gauley Bridge.
Salinas, L. Nights in Fresno.
Sandburg, C. Gone.
Schuyler, J. Elizabethans Called It Dying, The.
Stanton, M. Sorrow and Rapture.
Suckling, S. Summons to Town, A.
Tomlinson, C. Two Views of Two Ghost Towns.
Wallace, R. State Poetry Day.
Ward, J. Unusual View of the Town.
White, M. Recurrence.
Wickham. Fired Pot, The.
Wright, D. Cockermouth.
Wright, K. Unlikely Obbligato of Andersontown.
Wrigley, R. Sinking of Clay City, The.
Yost, C. Descano, California.
Young, A. Leaving Syracuse.

See also **Cities; Villages**

Toys
Abad, G. Toys.
Cerenio. 20 July 1994.
Clark, T. Daily News.
Davies, W. To W.S.—On his Wonderful Toys.
Dodge, M. Wooden Horse, The.
Edson, R. Toy-Maker, The.
Field, E. Duel, The.
  Little Boy Blue.
Hardy, T. New Toy, The.
Hoban. Tin Frog, The.
Johnson, M. Lost Teddy Bear, The.
Kendall, M. In the Toy Shop.
Kinzie. Boy.
Merritt, C. Woman of Color.
Mole, J. Jack-in-the-Box.
Nemerov. Models.
Phillips, C. Toys.
Pyle. Toys Talk of the World, The.
Shapiro, K. Terminal.
Stevenson, R. Block City.
  Land of Counterpane, The.
  Song of a Traveller, The.
  Travel.
Thomas, C. Treasures.
Worth, V. Magnet.
Zarco. Once upon a Seesaw with Charlie Chan.

Track Athletics
Evans, D. Pole Vaulter.
Robinson, E. Mighty Runner, A.

Whitman, W.   Runner, The.

Tractors
Hughes, T.   Tractor.
Unknown.   Drive a Tractor.

Tradition
Baraka, R.   In the Tradition Too.
Cohan.   Nothing New Beneath the Sun.
Fogarty, L.   Shields Strong, Nulla Nullas Alive.
Fuller, R.   Translation.
Hewitt, J.   From the Tibetan.
Kipling, R.   Land, The.
Lorde.   Generation.
Lovelace, R.   To a Lady with Child that Asked
   [*or* Ask'd] an Old Shirt.
Mahon.   Last of the Fire Kings, The.
Rich, A.   At the Jewish New Year.
Stafford, W.   At the Klamath Berry Festival.

Traffic
Agard, J.   Lollipop Lady.
Baxter, C.   Purest Rage, The.
Castro, M.   New York City.
Haines, J.   Snowbound City, The.
Harrison, J.   Swifts at Evening.
Kharms.   Event on the Street, An.
Lewis, G.   Flyover Elegies.
Livingston, M.   4-Way Stop.
Sandburg, C.   Blue Island Intersection.
Wilbur.   Simile for Her Smile, A.

Traffic Accidents
Coleman, W.   Dog Suicide.
Delgado, J.   Campesinos.
Seaton, M.   Ice.
See also **Automobile Accidents**

Traherne, Thomas
Wilbur.   World Without Objects Is a Sensible
   Emptiness, A.

Trains
Alexander, E.   Farewell to You.
Alexie.   On the Amtrak from Boston to New
   York City.
Anderson, S.   Evening Song.
Ashbery.   Leaving the Atocha Station.
   Melodic Trains.
Barber, D.   Little Overture.
Belieu.   Rondeau at the Train Stop.
Berlin.   When the Midnight Choo-Choo Leaves
   for Alabam'
Berryman.   Traveller, The.
Bertolino.   Baying, The.
Betjeman.   Parliament Hill Fields.
Biespiel, D.   White Roses.
Bly, R.   Looking at New-Fallen Snow from a
   Train.
Bogan, L.   Train Tune.
Booth, P.   Stations.
Broonzy.   Southern Blues, The.
Brown, S.   Call Boy.
   Long Track Blues.
   Sister Lou.
Brownjohn.   Train, The.
Bruchac.   Let the Midnight Special.
Buckley, C.   Train in the Desert—1916.
Burnside.   Autobiography.
Bursk.   Tearing Up the Tracks.
Carver, R.   Walk, A.
Cendrars.   Prose of the Trans-Siberian and Little
   Jean of France.
Cholmondeley-Pennell.   Night Mail North, The.
Clark, T.   Superballs.
Clarke, C.   Passing.
Clarke, T.   Will They Always Remember.
Collier, M.   North Corridor.
Dawe, B.   Renewal Notice.
Delmore Brothers.   Wabash Cannonball, The.
Dobyns.   Freight Cars.
Durcan.   Tullynoe: Tête-à-Tête in the Parish
   Priest's Parlour.
Eiseley.   And as for Man.
Eliot, T.   Skimbleshanks: The Railway Cat.
Empson.   Beautiful Train, The.
Etter.   Great Northern.
   Riding the Rock Island Through Kansas.
Ferlinghetti, L.   Starting from San Francisco.
Field, E.   Journey, A.
Francis, R.   Night Train.

Frost, R.   On the Heart's Beginning to Cloud the
   Mind.
Fuhrman, J.   Watching Trains.
Fusselman, A.   Sleeper.
Gallagher, T.   Not There.
Galvin, B.   For a Daughter Gone Away.
George, D.   Wreck of the Old 97.
Gibbons, R.   American Trains.
Giles, B.   Late Express, The.
Gioia.   In Cheever Country.
Gordon, M.   Chattanooga Choo-Choo.
Greenberg, A.   Freight Train, Freight Train.
Haines, J.   Train Stops at Healy Fork, The.
Hall, D.   Sister on the Tracks, A.
Hanzlicek, C.   Last Trains, The.
Hardy, T.   Faintheart in a Railway Train.
   Midnight on the Great Western.
Harling, W.   Beyond the Blue Horizon.
Hart-Smith.   Nullarbor.
Hawkesworth, P.   Meeting Place.
Hayden, R.   Runagate Runagate.
Hayes, T.   Boxcar.
Hedin, R.   Transcanadian.
   Wreck of the Great Northern, The.
Hewitt, J.   Frontier, The.
Heyen.   Tie, The.
   Trains, The.
Hikmet.   Things I Didn't Know I Loved.
Hilberry.   Body and Mind.
Hoffman, D.   Special Train, A.
Holland, J.   Loco.
Hope, A.   Observation Car.
Hughes, L.   Homesick Blues.
Hugo, R.   Elegy: "I expected him to look dead
   in the casket."
   Yards of Sarajevo, The.
Jacob, M.   Invitation to a Voyage.
Jacobsen, J.   Reindeer and Engine.
Jarrell.   On the Railway Platform.
   Orient Express, The.
Jefferson, B.   Easy Rider Blues.
Jensen, L.   To a Stranger (At the End of a
   Caboose).
Justice, D.   Train.
Kendall, M.   Underground.
Kennelly.   Limerick Train, The.
Kinnell.   Lackawanna.
Kooser.   City Limits.
Larcom.   What the Train Ran Over.
Lattimore.   North Philadelphia, Trenton, and
   New York.
   Note on the L and N.
Laux.   Children's Train, The.
Lawrence, D.   Tommies in the Train.
Le Guin.   Riding on the Coast Starlight.
Levertov.   By Rail through the Earthly Paradise,
   Perhaps Bedfordshire.
   Don't You Hear that Whistle Blowin'
Levin, P.   Night Coach.
Levine, P.   And the Trains Go On.
Lindsay, V.   Flower-Fed Buffaloes, The.
MacLeish.   Burying Ground by the Ties.
   Empire Builders.
   Grazing Locomotives.
MacNeice.   Figure of Eight.
Manrique, J.   Baudelaire's Spleen.
Marty.   In the Dome Car of the "Canadian."
McCord, D.   Song of the Train.
McGrath, T.   Black Train, The.
   End of the Line, The.
Mercer, J.   On the Atchison, Topeka and the
   Santa Fe.
Merwin, W. S.   Wheels of the Trains, The.
Millay, E.   From a Train Window.
   Travel.
Miller, V.   How Far?
Mitchell, E.   Passenger Opposite, The.
Monk, G.   South Bound: Facing North.
Monroe, B.   In the Pines.
Moorer.   Jim Crow Cars.
Mueller, L.   Commuter.
Nelson, H.   With My Mother, Missing the Train.
Nemerov.   Low-Level Cross-Country.
Nims, J.   Freight.
Parini.   Coal Train.
Pastan.   At the Train Museum.

Last Train, The.
Pettit.   Self-Portrait Approaching Promontory,
   Utah.
Plath.   Getting There.
Plumly.   For Esther.
Powell, J.   Lines Written for a Friend on the
   Death of His Brother, Caused by a Railway
   Train Running Over Him Whilst He Was in a
   State of Inebriation.
Propp, K.   Train Passage.
Randall, D.   Southern Road, The.
Ras.   My Train.
Reiter, T.   Rights of Way.
Ress.   Waving Her Farewell. Train Station,
   Vienna XV, 1939.
Reverdy.   Departure.
Rich, A.   Lucifer in the Train.
Roberson.   True We Are Two Grown Men.
Roberts, K.   Night Tumbles into Town by Rail.
Robin, L.   Beyond the Blue Horizon.
Roethke.   Night Journey.
Rohrer, M.   After the Wedding Party.
Rose, P.   Terminus.
Ross, L.   Indecent Exposure (A True Story).
Sandburg, C.   Limited.
   Southern Pacific.
   Window.
Sarton.   After a Train Journey.
Scamell, B.   From the Provinces.
Scammell, W.   Trains.
Seibert.   Casey Jones.
Shapiro, K.   Terminal.
Sissman.   Big Rock-Candy Mountain, The.
Smith, D.   Roundhouse Voices, The.
Soto.   Who Will Know Us?
Spender, S.   Express, The.
St. John, D.   Iris.
Stafford, W.   Vacation.
Stephens, P.   God Shed His Grace.
   Signalmen, The.
Sternlieb.   Right of Way.
Stevenson, R.   From a Railway Carriage.
Sundiata.   Notes from the Defense of Colin
   Ferguson.
Swenson, M.   Riding the 'A.'
   Written While Riding the Long Island Rail
   Road.
Taggard.   Train: Abstraction.
Tate, J.   Manna.
Thoreau.   What's the Railroad to Me?
Unknown.   Casey Jones.
   Gospel Train, The.
   I Been Working on the Railroad.
   Little Black Train Is A-Comin'
   Poor Paddy Works on the Railway.
   Railroad Blues, The.
   Railroad Cars Are Coming, The.
   This Train.
   Train is A-Comin'
Van Doren.   Dream of Trains, A.
Veenendaal.   On My Fourteenth Wedding
   Anniversary I Ride on Trains.
Warren, R.   I Can't Even Remember the Name.
Webb, F.   Laid Off.
West, K.   On Track.
Weston, M.   Departure.
White, E.   Commuter.
Whiting, R.   Beyond the Blue Horizon.
Whitman, W.   To a Locomotive in Winter.
Wilbur.   In the Smoking-Car.
Williams, W.   Overture to a Dance of
   Locomotives.
Wojahn.   Photo of My Father in a Snowbound
   Train.
Wright, J.   Outside Fargo, North Dakota.
   Train Journey.
Wyrebek, M.   Example, An.
Young, D.   Project for Freight Trains, A.
See also **Railroads; Locomotives**

Traitors
Eastman, M.   To Genevieve Taggard Who
   Called Me Traitor in a Poem.
Joseph, A.   Traitor.
See also **Treason and Traitors**

Trakl, Georg
Lasker-Schüler.   Georg Trakl.

Mahon.   Disused Shed in Co. Wexford, A.
Snodgrass, W.   Coroner's Inquest.
Wilbur.   Shame.

Transcendence
Chang, D.   On Being in the Midwest.
Divakaruni.   At Muktinath.
Schwartz, H.   Recruiting Poster.

Transformation
Ai.   Man with the Saxophone, The.
Atwood.   Rat Song.
   Siren Song.
Canan.   Oh Kali.
Coleridge, H.   Prayer.
Couzyn.   Transformation.
Creeley.   Statue, The.
Eady.   Thrift.
   Young Elvis.
Earle, J.   Exits.
Emerson, R.   Character.
Field, E.   Curse of the Cat Woman.
Gewanter, D.   Divorce and Mr. Circe.
Glück, L.   Moonless Night.
   Undertaking, The.
Gladding.   Locust Shell.
Goodison.   On Becoming a Tiger.
Greenhalgh, C.   Man in the Valley of
   Women, A.
Hall, D.   Je Suis une Table.
Hardy, T.   Transformations.
Hart-Smith.   Nullarbor.
Henson, L.   I Am Singing the Cold Rain.
Hirsch, E.   Paul Celan: A Grave and Mysterious
   Sentence.
Hollander, V.   Rosh Chodesh Tisheri.
Jarman, M.   Psalm: The New Day.
Kasdorf.   Streak, The.
Kipling, R.   'Eathen, The.
Klinger, A.   Transformation.
Komunyakaa.   Never Land.
Lewis, G.   Hedge, The.
Mayer, B.   We've Solved the Problem.
'Mbala.'   New Dub, A.
Monaghan.   Persephone's Journey.
Mother Goose.   Old Woman and the Pedlar,
   The.
Mugo, M. G.   Look How Rich We are Together.
Nemerov.   Singular Metamorphosis, A.
Orlen.   Androgyny.
Padgett, R.   Symbols of Transformation.
Plath.   Love Letter.
Rukeyser, M.   Hostages, The.
Savageau.   All Night She Dreams.
Schwartz, H.   Recruiting Poster.
Shapiro, K.   Haircut.
Simic.   Lives of Alchemists, The.
Sitwell, D.   Song: "We are the darkness in the
   heat of the day."
Smith, S.   Frog Prince, The.
Spicer, J.   Transformations.
Tomlinson, C.   Door, The.
   Prometheus.
Untermeyer, L.   To a Vine-clad Telegraph Pole.
Warsh.   Gout.
Wilbur.   Beautiful Changes, The.
Wonodi.   Salute to Icheke.
Woo, M.   Untitled: "In the deepest night and a
   full moon."

Transience
Apollinaire.   Voyager, The.
Auden.   As I Walked Out One Evening.
Banning, L.   Romancero.
Bateman, M.   Lightness.
Berlin.   Song Is Ended (But the Melody Lingers
   On), The.
Bethell.   Response.
   Time.
Bolton, E.   Palinode, A.
Buchwald.   As Soon As It's Here It's Gone But
   So What.
Burns, R.   Epitaph: "Lo worms enjoy the seat of
   bliss."
Campion, T.   To Music Bent Is My Retired
   Mind.
   What If a Day [or a Month or a Year].
Carew, T.   Song, [A]: "Ask[e] me no more
   where Jove bestow[e]s."

Clare, J.   Shadows.
Conway, J.   Hangover.
Cory, W.   Deteriora.
Crane, H.   Passage.
'Dermée.'   Poem.
d'Oettingen.   To Il y a.
Donne.   Anniversary [or Anniversarie], The.
Drummond, W.   Sonnet: "I know that all
   beneath the moon decays."
Eberhart, R.   Groundhog, The.
Eigner.   Back to it.
Freneau.   Vanity of Existence, The.
Frost, R.   Nothing Gold Can Stay.
Fuller, M.   Let Me Gather from the Earth.
Garrigue.   From Venice Was That Afternoon.
Gay, J.   Cotillion.
Goodman, P.   Ballade of the Moment After.
Green, J.   Easy Come, Easy Go.
Griffiths, J.   Errata.
Guiterman.   On the Vanity of Earthly Greatness.
Gustafson, R.   Of Green Steps and Laundry.
Habib.   Ancestors.
Habington.   To the Moment Last Past.
Hardy, T.   Sunshade, The.
Hass, R.   Late Spring.
Herbert, G.   Virtue [or Vertue].
Herrick.   Corinna's Going a-Maying.
   To a Bed of Tulips.
   To Blossoms.
   To Daffodils [or Daffadills].
   To Dianeme.
Heyman, E.   Easy Come, Easy Go.
Hillman.   Every Life.
Jeffers, R.   To the Stone-Cutters.
King, H.   Sic Vita.
Landon.   Dancing Girl, The.
Levertov.   Living.
Levine, P.   Sweet Will.
Long, H.   New Music, A.
Longfellow, H.   Elegiac Verse 12.
   Fragment: August 4, 1856.
Lowell, A.   Falling Snow.
MacNeice.   Sunlight on the Garden, The.
Magidson, H.   Gone with the Wind.
Manrique, J.   Baudelaire's Spleen.
McGrath, T.   Return, The.
Melville, H.   Malvern Hill.
Merwin, W. S.   Grandmother Watching at Her
   Window.
Montagu, L.   Lover, The; a Ballad.
Moore, T.   'Tis the Last Rose of Summer.
   No—Leave My Heart to Rest.
Nash, O.   Speak Low.
Ohnishi, T.   Blossoms in the Wind.
Olson, C.   La Chute.
Peabody, J.   Far-Off Rose, A.
Phillips, C.   Kill, The.
Plato.   Apple, The.
Prufer, K.   My Father Recounts a Story from
   His Youth.
Radiguet.   Handless Clock.
   Map.
Ralegh, S.   Even Such Is Time.
   Nymph's [or Nimphs] Reply to the Shepherd
   [or Sheepheard], The.
Ransom, J.   Blue Girls.
Reeves, W.   Passing of the Forest, The.
Riley, J.   Summer Seeming.
Robinson, E.   Man against the Sky, The.
Rohrer, M.   Hunger of the Lemur, The.
Rossetti, C.   Bed of Forget-Me-Nots, A.
   May.
Sandburg, C.   Flash Crimson.
   Languages.
Schwartz, R. L.   Edgewater Park.
   Why I Forgive My Younger Self Her
   Transgressions.
Sharma, P.   Transit.
Shelley, P.   Hymn to Intellectual Beauty.
   Ozymandias.
Sidney, R.   Songe 17: "Sun is set, and masked
   night, The."
Sidney, S.   Leave Me O Love.
Smith, C.   To the Insect of the Gossamer.
Smith, H.   Ozymandias.
Southwell.   Upon the Image of Death.

Sze.   June Ghazal.
Taylor, C.B.   Plenty Time Pass Fast, Fas Dey
   So.
Tennyson, A.   Break, Break, Break.
Thackeray.   Ballad of Bouillabaisse, The.
Turner, C.   East or West?
Unknown, sometimes at. to Sir Walter Ralegh.
   As You Came from the Holy Land [of
   Walsingham].
Viray, M.   Saturday Morning, A.
Waller, E.   Song: "Go[e], lovely rose."
Washington, N.   Hundred Years from Today, A.
Weill, K.   Speak Low.
Whitman, W.   As If a Phantom Caress'd Me.
Wilbur.   Looking into History.
   To the Etruscan Poets.
   Transit.
Wordsworth, W.   Most Alluring Clouds That
   Mount the Sky, The.
Wright, C.   March Journal.
   Snow.
Wright, J.   To a Troubled Friend.
Wyatt, S.   Varium et Mutabile.
See also **Change**

Translation and Translators
Burns, R.   On Elphinston's Translation of
   Martial.
Castillo, S.   Contra, The.
Erskine, T.   On Tom Moore's Translation of
   Anacreon.
Fenton, J.   Lines for Translation into Any
   Language.
Jonson, B.   To Clement Edmonds, on His
   Caesar's Commentaries Observed, and
   Translated.
   To Sir Henry [or Henrie] Savile [upon His
   Translation of Tacitus].
Keats.   On First Looking into Chapman's
   Homer.
Kizer, C.   Translation.
Lesser.   Translation.
Moore, H.   Poem for the End.
Nemerov.   Translation.
Portnoy, M.   Of of Titmouse.
Pound, E.   Translator to Translated.
Rich, A.   Translations.
Samaras, N.   Translation.
Walpole, H.   On the Translation of Anacreon.

Transmutation
Simic.   Lives of Alchemists, The.

Transportation, Penal
Unknown.   Moreton Bay.

Trapezes and Trapeze Artists
Morgan, E.   Cinquevalli.
Unknown.   Man on the Flying Trapeze, The.

Trapping and Trappers
Cahn, S.   (Love Is) The Tender Trap.
Cook, E.   On Seeing a Bird-Catcher.
Hughes, F.   Different Voice, The.
Larkin, P.   Myxomatosis.
Moore, M.   New York.
Stephens, J.   Snare, The.

Trash
Craighead, L.   Dancin' Our Lives Away.
Ofeimun.   New Brooms, The.
Smukler.   Trash.
See also **Garbage and Garbage Men**

Travel Poetry
Bolt, T.   Glimpse of Terrain.
Cendrars.   Hammock.
Crunk, T.   Leaving.
Flanagan, D. B.   Three Years from Sorrento.
Reverdy.   Road.
Rhys, K.   Interlude.
Robinson, M.   Describes her Bark.

Traveling and Travelers
Adair, T.   Let's Get Away from It All.
Agoos, J.   Portinaio.
Alexander, E.   Passage.
Alexander, M.   October Journey.
Allen, S.   Harriet Tubman aka Moses.
Apollinaire.   Voyager, The.
   Windows.
   Zone.
Arlen, H.   Let's Take a Walk Around the Block.

Armantrout. Leaving.
Arnold, M. Scholar Gypsy, The.
Asekoff, L. North Star.
Ashbery. Melodic Trains.
  My Philosophy of Life.
Auden. Legend.
  On the Circuit.
Baker, T. Le passage (Morbihan).
  Pavane on Mr Wray's Locations, A.
Barras, J. Peace.
Beeks. Parker's Mood.
Belieu. At St. Sulpice.
Benn. Bunch of Drifter Sons Hollered, A.
Berrigan, D. Prayer.
Berryman. Traveller, The.
Bishop, E. Arrival at Santos.
  Moose, The.
  Over 2000 Illustrations and a Complete
    Concordance.
  Questions of Travel.
Bly, R. Driving toward the Lac Qui Parle River.
Bobrowsky. Journey, The.
Bontemps. Nocturne of the Wharves.
Branch, A. Connecticut Road Song.
Brew. Lonely Traveller, The.
Brion, R. Love Song.
Brock-Broido. Carrowmore.
Brown, S. Tin Roof Blues.
Browning, R. Home-Thoughts, from the Sea.
Burnside. Autobiography.
Bynner. Foreigner, A.
Byron, G. Lines to Mr Hodgson.
Cabico, R. Mango Poem.
Caldwell, A. Left All Alone Again Blues.
Campo. Belonging.
Carew, T. Upon Master Walter Montagu's
  Return from Travel.
Cawein. Uncalled.
Cedering, S. Variations for the Piano.
Cendrars. My Dance.
  Prose of the Trans-Siberian and Little Jean of
    France.
Chang Chi. Coming at Night to a Fisherman's
  Hut.
Chaucer. Alysoun.
  Cage, The.
  Chauntecleer.
  Complaint of Troilus, The.
  Death and the Three Revellers.
  Franklin's Prologue, The.
  Franklin's Tale, The.
  Friar's Prologue, The.
  Friar's Tale, The.
  General Prologue, The.
  Good Parson, The.
  Introduction to the Franklin's Prologue and Tale.
  Introduction to the Pardoner's Tale.
  Introduction to the Parson's Tale, The.
  Knighthood, The.
  Love Unfeigned.
  Miller's [or Milleres] Tale, The.
  Miller's Prologue, The.
  Nun's Priest's Tale, The.
  Pardoner's Prologue, The.
  Pardoner's Tale, The.
  Parson and the Plowman Described, The.
  Patient Griselda.
  Prologue to Sir Thopas.
  Saturn.
  Seven Pilgrims: A Monk.
  Seven Pilgrims: A Prioress[e].
  Seven Pilgrims: A Wyf of Bathe.
  Song of Troylus, The.
  Temple of Mars, The.
  Three Rioters, The.
  Wife of Bath's Prologue, The.
  Wife of Bath's Tale, The.
Child, L. Thanksgiving Day.
Clare, J. Winter.
  Woodland Seat, A.
Cocteau. Cape of Good Hope, The.
Cooley, N. John Winthrop, 'Reasons to be
  Considered for . . . the Intended Plantation in
  New England,' 1629.
Corcoran. In the Red Book.
Cory, W. Parting.

Cristall. Holbain.
d'Oettingen. Kilimanjaro.
Dame. On the Road to Damascus, Maryland.
Davie. Epistle. To Enrique Caracciolo Trejo.
Davison, P. Where the Sun Ends.
De la Mare. Listeners, The.
  Railway Junction, The.
Deane, S. Return.
Dennis, C. Traveller, The.
Dennis, M. Let's Get Away from It All.
Dickinson, E. Caterpillar.
DiPalma. Wrong Side of the Door, The.
Dixon, M. Place, Places.
Donne. Song: "Sweetest love, I do not go[e]."
Dorn, E. Geranium.
Drayton. To the Virginian Voyage.
Dubie. Poem: "Mule kicked out in the trees, A.
  An Early."
Duffy, C. In Your Mind.
Edgar, C. Cloud of Unknowing, The.
Eliot, T. Journey of the Magi.
Erdrich. Lady in the Pink Mustang, The.
Ferlinghetti, L. Starting from San Francisco.
Field, E. Journey, A.
  Wynken, Blynken, and Nod.
Figueroa, J. Murdered Luggage.
Fisher, A. African Boog.
Forhan, C. Taste of Wild Cherry, The.
Fuller, J. Wild Raspberries.
Gardner, E. Written in Tintern Abbey,
  Monmouthshire.
Garioch. Property.
Gillespie, H. Breezin' Along with the Breeze.
Ginsberg, A. S.F. Southward.
Giovanni. They Clapped.
Glück, L. Magi, The.
Gloria. Rizal's Ghost.
Gonzalez, N. I Made Myself a Path.
  Wanderer in the Night of the World, A.
Goodison. Road of the Dread, The.
Graves, R. Cloak, The.
  Legs, The.
  Travel[l]er's Curse after Misdirection[, The].
Gray, R. Journey: the North Coast.
Grosholz. Life of a Salesman.
Gunn, T. Discovery of the Pacific, The.
Guthrie, R. Magi, The.
Hadas, R. Journey Out.
Hall, D. Hermit with Landscape.
Hannah, S. Postcard from a Travel Snob.
Harling, R. Beyond the Blue Horizon.
Harwood, L. Czech Dream.
Hayley. To Mrs. Hayley, On her Voyage to
  America. 1784.
Hedin, R. Transcanadian.
Herrick. Salutation.
Hewitt, J. Frontier, The.
Hiestand, E. Moon Winx Motel.
Hikmet. Things I Didn't Know I Loved.
Hood, T. To the Ocean.
Howes, B. Home Leave.
Hugo, R. Driving Montana.
Jackson, H. Emigravit.
Jacob, M. Invitation to a Voyage.
Jarrell. On the Railway Platform.
Jefferson, B. Long Distance Moan.
Jenkins, J. et al. In Ferrara.
Johnson, H. Fringe-Area Reception.
Jones, R. Novel, The.
Jones, T. Cwmchwefri.
Jonson, B. On the Famous Voyage.
Jordan, J. Roman Poem Number Nine.
Katz, J. Concerning the Islands Newly
  Discovered.
Kazantzis. Frightened Flier Goes North, The.
Keats. Keen, Fitful Gusts Are Whispering Here
  and There.
Kenyon, J. Here.
Kern, J. Left All Alone Again Blues.
Kipling, R. Gipsy Trail, The.
  Sestina of the Tramp-Royal.
Larkin, P. Arrivals, Departures.
Lattimore. North Philadelphia, Trenton, and
  New York.
Lear, E. Jumblies, The.
Levis. Widening Spell of the Leaves, The.

Logan, J. Trip to Four or Five Towns, A.
Loncar, M. There Goes the Bride.
Longfellow, H. Excelsior.
  Tide Rises, the Tide Falls, The.
MacCaig. Crossing the Border.
MacLeish. Tourist Death.
Madhubuti. Poet: What Ever Happened to
  Luther?
Markoe, M. Ballad of Winky.
Masefield. Sea Fever.
Mathews, E. K. Indian, The.
McGrath, C. Delphos, Ohio.
  Spring Comes to Chicago.
McGrath, T. Epitaph: "Again, traveller, you
  have come a long way led by that star."
  Long Way Outside Yellowstone, A.
McGuckian. To a Cuckoo at Coolanlough.
McLain, P. Residue.
McNulty, T. Bodhidharma Crossing the
  Graywolf River on a Ry-Krisp.
Melville, H. Return of the Sire de Nesle A.D.
  16, The.
Merrill, J. Clearing the Title.
Merwin, W. S. Encampment at Morning, An.
  Wheels of the Trains, The.
Miles, J. Travelers.
Millay, E. Travel.
Miller, E. Tomorrow.
Miller, J. American Odalisque.
Miller, M. Not That Far.
Mills, B. Ballad: Of Motion.
Mitchell, E. Passenger Opposite, The.
Moore, H. Edward.
  Poem for the End.
Morales, A. South.
Moss, H. Tourists.
Mother Goose. How many miles to Babylon?
Mueller, L. Commuter.
Muldoon, P. Making the Move.
Nemerov. Song of Degrees, A.
Nichol. Ferry Me Across.
Nortje. Native's Letter.
Nye, N. Making a Fist.
  Whole Self, The.
O'Hara, F. Mary Desti's Ass.
  You Are Gorgeous and I'm Coming.
Orléans, C. Lost.
Ortiz. Travels in the South.
  Upstate.
Parnell, P. Sile Na gCioch.
Pastan. Last Train, The.
Peabody, J. After Music.
Peskett. From Belfast to Suffolk.
Pfeiffer, E. Mid-Ocean.
Piombino. Time Travel.
Plath. Getting There.
Plumly. For Esther.
Porter, C. Katie Went to Haiti.
Pound, E. Gypsy, The.
Price, L. Maidens of London's Brave
  Adventures, Or, a Boon Voyage Intended for
  the Sea, The.
Probyn. End of the Journey, The.
Purdy, A. Blue City, The.
Radcliffe, A. Storied Sonnet.
Rafferty, P. Passage.
Remoto. Rain.
Reverdy. Departure.
Robinson, E. John Evereldown.
Robinson, M. Reaches Sicily.
  Stanzas Written between Dover and Calais, in
  July, 1792.
Roditi. Seance.
Roethke. Night Journey.
Rosenblatt, S. Visiting New York.
Rossetti, C. Old-World Thicket, An.
  Uphill.
Rukeyser, M. Ajanta.
Samaras, N. Aubade: Macedonia.
Sarton. After a Train Journey.
Scammell, W. Inventions.
Scott, D. For Norman Nicholson.
Shapiro, M. To Jerusalem, 1990.
Shelley, P. Ozymandias.
  World's Wanderers, The.
Sigourney. Western Emigrant, The.

Simons, S.   Breezin' Along with the Breeze.
Spence, L.   Prows O' Reekie, The.
Sternlieb.   Survivor.
Stevenson, R.   From a Railway Carriage.
   Land of Nod, The.
   My Bed Is a Boat.
   Travel.
   Vagabond, The.
Stow.   Landfall.
Sun Yün-feng.   On the Road through Chang-te.
Swenson, K.   Landlady in Bangkok, The.
Tate, J.   Descent, The.
Teft.   On a Friend's Taking a Journey.
Thoreau.   For Though the Eaves [or Caves]
   Were Rabbeted [or Rabbited].
   I Am Bound, I Am Bound.
Trakl.   Revelation and Decline.
Tranter.   Moment of Waking, The.
Treece.   Horror.
Tripp.   Diesel to Yesterday.
Troup, B.   (Get Your Kicks On) Route 66!
Tu Fu.   Chengtu.
Ungria, R.   Carillonneur.
Van Duyn.   Into Mexico.
Viidikas.   Future.
Volkman.   Shipwreck Poem.
Waddington, M.   Ulysses Embroidered.
Walcott.   Fortunate Traveller, The.
   Tomorrow, Tomorrow.
Wang Wei.   Seeking a Mooring.
Weaver, M.   My Father's Geography.
Weston, M.   Departure.
Wetzsteon.   Late Show, The.
White, H.   Winter Traveler, The.
Whiting, R.   Breezin' Along with the Breeze.
Whitman, W.   Promise to California, A.
Whittier.   To a Cape Ann Schooner.
Wicks.   Clever Daughter, The.
Williams, H.   To the White Bird of the Tropic.
Williams, J.   In Duffryn Woods.
Wolverton, T.   In China.
Woo, D.   Expatriates.
Wordsworth, W.   Column Intended by
   Buonaparte for a Triumphal Edifice in Milan,
   Now Lying by the Way-Side in the Simplon
   Pass, The.
   Composed after a Journey across the Hamilton
   Hills, Yorkshire.
   Hymn for the Boatmen, as They Approach the
   Rapids under the Castle of Heidelberg.
   Most Sweet It Is with Unuplifted Eyes.
   Steamboats, Viaducts and Railways.
   Stepping Westward.
Wright, C.   Spread Rhythm.
   Woman Looking Through a Viewmaster.
Wright, J.   Sketch for an Aesthetic Project.
   Stages on a Journey Westward.
   Train Journey.
Wunderlich, M.   Anchorage, The.
Young, A.   Leaving Syracuse.
Young, K.   Quivira City Limits.

Treason and Traitors
Burns, R.   Such a Parcel of Rogues in a Nation.
Cunningham, J.   This *Humanist* Whom No
   Beliefs Constrained.
De la Mare.   Ballad of Christmas, A.
Elizabeth I.   Doubt of Future Foes.
Hammial.   Treason's Choice.
Harington [or Harrington].   Of Treason.
Neruda.   They Receive Instructions Against
   Chile.
Unknown.   *Golden Vanity,* The.

Treasures
Bell, M.   True Story, A.
Brown, G.   Beachcomber.
DeLeeuw.   Auction Sale—Household
   Furnishings.
Lee-Hamilton.   Sunken Gold.
Pound, E.   Seafarer, The.
Thomas, C.   Treasures.
Unknown.   Anglo-American Chainpoem.

Treaties
Thomas, D.   Hand That Signed the Paper, The.

Tree of Life
Dugan, A.   Last Statement for a Last Oracle.
Rukeyser, M.   Speaking Tree, The.

Trees
Adamson.   Elm Tree in Paddington, An.
Adcock, F.   Trees.
Adisa.   Rainbow, The.
Alarcon, F.   Los árboles son poetas / Trees Are
   Poets.
Ammons, A. R.   Improvisatin for Jerald Bullis,
   An.
Armantrout.   Necromance.
Ashbery.   Some Trees.
Barrax.   There Was A Song.
Belitt.   Orange Tree, The.
Berry, W.   Old Man Climbs a Tree, The.
Birney.   Poet-Tree.
Blake, W.   In a Myrtle [or Mirtle] Shade.
Bodenheim.   Advice to a Forest.
Bontemps.   Blight.
Brion, R.   If Fortune Smiles.
Brooks, G.   Birth in a Narrow Room, The.
Brown, L.   Green Arbor, A.
Bugeja, M.   Conifer King, The.
Butler, G.   Stranger to Europe.
Campbell, D.   Here, under Pear-trees.
Cariaga.   Family Tree, The.
Carstairs.   Addressed to a Beech Tree.
Carter, M.   Bitter Wood.
Cavendish, M.   Of the Theme of Love.
Cendrars.   Great Fetishes, The.
Chandler, C.   Tree in the Garden, The.
Cherry, K.   Late Afternoon at the Arboretum.
Clare, J.   Fallen Elm, The.
   Maple Tree, The.
   Nutting.
   Shepherd's Tree, The.
Collins, B.   Lines Lost Among Trees.
Coolbrith.   My Cloth of Gold.
Copus, J.   Pulling the Ivy.
Crapsey.   Fragment.
   On Seeing Weather-Beaten Trees.
Creeley.   Turn, The.
Davie.   Mushroom Gatherers, The.
Davies, H.   Poem: "In the stump of the old tree,
   where the heart has rotted out."
Davis, G.   Children in the Arbor.
Davison, P.   Cross Cut.
Dawe, B.   Renewal Notice.
De la Mare.   Three Cherry Trees, The.
   Two Gardens.
Delmore, E.   Willow.
   Yew.
Deming, A.   Tilden Park.
Deutsch.   Paradigm.
Dickey, J.   One, The.
Dickinson, E.   Tree in Winter.
Dodd, E.   Dieback.
   Lyric: "It doesn't matter / whether / a tree falls."
Dove, R.   Dusting.
   Horse and Tree.
Dugan, A.   On Trees.
Dumas, H.   Root Song.
Dunbar, P.   Haunted Oak, The.
Erdrich, H.   Quiet Earth, The.
Everson, H.   Injured Maple.
Everson, W.   High Embrace, The.
   Passion Week.
Feinstein, E.   Magic Apple Tree, The.
"Field."   Nests in Elms.
   O Wind, thou hast thy kingdom in the trees.
Field, E.   Sugar-Plum Tree, The.
Finney, N.   Uncles.
Ford, C.   Plaint.
Foster, A.   Union.
Francis, R.   As Easily As Trees.
   Broken View, A.
Frost, R.   Axe-Helve, The.
   Birches.
   On a Tree Fallen across the Road.
   Sound of Trees, The.
   Spring Pools.
   Tree at My Window.
Garioch.   Maple and the Pine, The.
Garrigue.   Country Villa.
Gaspar.   Tree, The.
Gehrke, S.   Near the Mississippi.
George, F.   Shagbark.
Ghigna.   Park Elms.

Gilbert, K.   Tree.
Ginsberg, L.   Roots.
Gioia.   Planting a Sequoia.
Godfrey.   Unholy Spring.
Gorham.   Empress Receives the Head of a
   Taiping Rebel, The.
Graves, R.   Hide and Seek.
Grimké, A.   Tenebris.
Gurney, I.   Felling a Tree.
   Possessions.
Hagiwara Sakutaro.   Lover of Love.
   So Terrifyingly Melancholy.
Hardy, T.   Tree and the Lady, The.
Harms.   Sky.
Hass, R.   Elm.
Hemans.   Palm-tree, The.
Herrick.   All Things Decay and Die.
   To Blossoms.
   To Groves.
   To Sycamores.
Honig, E.   November through a Giant Copper
   Beech.
Hope, A.   Australia.
Hopkins, G.   Binsey Poplars (Felled 1879).
Hudgins.   Tree.
Ignatow, D.   Simultaneously.
Irwin, R.   Tree, A.
Johnson, H.   Trees at Night.
Jones, D.   These Trees Are No Forest of
   Mourners.
Kariara.   Leopard Lives in a Muu Tree, A.
Keats.   In Drear-nighted December.
Kees.   Heat in the Room, The.
Kenney.   Sawmill.
Kilmer, J.   Trees.
Kinsella, T.   In the Ringwood.
Knott.   Poem: "At your light side trees shy."
Kreymborg.   Tree, The.
Kunitz, S.   War against the Trees, The.
La Grone.   Lines to the Black Oak.
Larkin, P.   Trees, The.
Lawrence, D.   Trees in the Garden.
Lear, E.   Limerick: "There was an Old Man in a
   tree."
   Quangle Wangle's Hat, The.
Levertov.   Contraband.
   Tree Telling of Orpheus, A.
Levine, P.   Sleepless Night, A.
Levy, A.   London Plane-Tree, A.
Lewis, J.   Garden Note I, Los Altos.
   Garden Note II, March.
Locker-Lampson.   Old Oak Tree at Hatfield
   Broadoak, The.
Lovelace, R.   Orpheus to Woods.
MacDiarmid, H.   Sunny Gale.
   Under the Greenwood Tree.
MacLean, S.   Hallaig.
MacNeice.   Tree Party.
Madge.   Poem: "Walls of the maelstrom are
   painted with trees, The."
Mahon.   Going Home.
Mapanje.   Before Chilembwe Tree.
McCord, D.   Every Time I Climb A Tree.
Melville, H.   Time's Betrayal.
Mew.   Forest Road, The.
   Trees Are Down, The.
Meyers, B.   Daybreak.
Millay, E.   Counting-out Rhyme.
Milne, E.   Diamond Cut Diamond.
Miyazawa Kenji.   Spring and the Ashura.
Momaday.   Trees and Evening Sky.
Montale.   Lemon Trees, The.
Moore, L.   From the Field.
Morris, G.   Woodman, Spare That Tree.
Moss, H.   Pruned Tree, The.
Mother Goose.   Nut Tree, A.
Muldoon, P.   Wind and Tree.
Naimy, M.   Hunger.
Nash, O.   Song of the Open Road.
Nelson, J.   If a Fish Fell in a Forest.
Nemerov.   Learning by Doing.
   Learning the Trees.
Nesbit, E.   Child's Song in Spring.
Oldham, P.   Noon.
Oliver, M.   Black Walnut Tree, The.
Olson, C.   Merce of Egypt.

Oodgeroo of the tribe Noonuccal. Municipal Gum.
Orfalea, G. Wave.
Ortiz. Speaking.
    What I Tell Him.
Peake. Conceit.
Philips, K. Upon the graving of her Name upon a Tree in Barnelmes Walks.
Plath. Polly's Tree.
    Winter Trees.
    Words.
Ramsdell, H. Bright Receding.
Ransom, J. Dead Boy.
Rhodes, M. Disguised.
Rich, A. Trees, The.
Rossetti, C. Autumn.
    Who Has Seen the Wind?
Russell, W. God Gave Us Trees to Cut Down.
Saner. Autumn Aspens: Cumbres Pass.
Savageau. All Night She Dreams.
    Trees.
Schuyler, J. Noon Office.
Seferis. Poplar Leaf, The.
Sepamla. Talk to the Peach Tree.
Serote. Growing, The.
Shepherd, R. West Willow.
    What Cannot Be Kept.
Shillaber, B. Picture, A.
Siddal. Silent Wood, A.
Simpson, L. Ash and the Oak, The.
    Laurel Tree, The.
Sitwell, S. Tulip Tree.
Stafford, W. British Columbia.
Stephens, J. Seumas Beg.
    Wind, The.
Stevenson, A. Hemlock at Sunset, A.
Stoddard, E. Above the Tree.
Strand. Keeping Things Whole.
    Man in the Tree, The.
    Prediction, The.
Suárez, V. Song to the Banyan.
Sylvester, J. Palms.
Thomas, E. Aspens.
Turner, W. Music of a Tree, The.
Tuwhare. No Ordinary Sun.
Ungaretti. Soldiers.
Unknown. Anglo-American Chainpoem.
    Christ the Apple-Tree.
    Nut Tree, A.
    St. Paul's Steeple.
Wagoner, D. Nuthatch.
Whitman, W. I Saw in Louisiana a Live-Oak Growing.
Williams, W. Locust Tree in Flower, The.
    To Waken an Old Lady.
    Young Sycamore.
Williamson, G. Annual Returns.
    Appalachian Trees Encircled by Police Tape.
Wiman, C. In Lakeview Cemetery.
Wordsworth, W. Nutting.
    Tradition of Oker Hill in Darley Dale, Derbyshire, A.
    Yew-Trees.
Wright, J. Camphor Laurel.
    Gum-trees Stripping.
Zukofsky, L. As to How Much.

Trench Warfare
Graves, R. It's a Queer Time.
Jones, D. Private John Ball Wounded in the Wood.
Manning, F. Trenches, The.
Owen, W. Anthem for Doomed Youth.
    Exposure.
Rickword. Winter Warfare.
Rosenberg, I. Break of Day in the Trenches.
Sassoon. Aftermath.
    Attack.
    Counter-Attack.
    Dreamers.
    Dug-Out, The.
    Rear-Guard, The.
    Working Party, A.
Scannell. Great War, The.
West, A. Night Patrol, A.

Tricksters
Brown, N. You're an Old Smoothie.

Navajo Oral Tradition. Coyote, Skunk, and the Prairie Dogs.
Winnebago Oral Tradition. Felix White Sr.'s Introduction to Wakjankaga.

Trilobites
Kendall, M. Lay of the Trilobite.

Trinidad and Tobago
Walcott. Midsummer, Tobago.
    Port of Spain.

Trinity, The
"Field." Trinity.
Herrick. To God.

Triolet (form)
Bridges, R. Triolet: "When first we met we did not guess."
Cornford, F. To a Fat Lady Seen from the Train.
McGinley. Triolet Against Sisters.

Tristan da Cunha (islands)
Campbell, R. Tristan da Cunha.

Tristram and Isolde
Binyon. Tristram's End.
Cunningham, J. Epigram: "Within this mindless vault."
Swinburne. King Mark, Tristram, and Palamede.

Triviality
Bhatt. What Is Worth Knowing?
Hartnett. Enamoured of the Miniscule.
Sandburg, C. Aprons of Silence.

Trojan War
Arnold, M. Palladium.
Chaucer. Complaint of Troilus, The.
    Love Unfeigned.
    Song of Troylus, The.
Homer. Butchers, The.
    Phemios and Medon.
Wright, K. Fortunes of War.
Yeats. Leda and the Swan.

Trolleys
Blane, R. Trolley Song, The.
Martien, J. Late 20th Century: Spring.
See also **Streetcars**

Trossachs, The, Scotland
Wordsworth, W. Trosachs, The.

Trout
Brown, G. Trout Fisher.
Montague, J. Trout, The.
Wilbur. Hamlen Brook.

Troy
Gunn, T. Wound, The.
Muir, E. Troy.
Nash, O. First Limick.
Shepherd, R. Man Named Troy, A.
See also **Trojan War**

Trucks and Truckers
Bloom, R. Truckin'
Dyson, W. Trucker, The.
Fuhrman, J. Atlantis.
Koehler, T. Truckin'
Paquet. Graves Registration.
Schonborg. Rumble, A.
Snyder, G. Why Log Truck Drivers Rise Earlier Than Students of Zen.
Stone, J. Truck, The.
Tomlinson, C. At Barstow.

Trujillo Molina, Rafael Leonidas
Dove, R. Parsley.

Trumpets
Dryden, J. Song for St Cecilia's Day, 1687, A.
Hemans. Trumpet, The.
Jeffers, L. How High the Moon.
Larkin, P. Reasons for Attendance.
McGinley. Women of Jericho, The.

Trust
Ager, M. Mamma Goes Where Papa Goes.
Baird, M. Do Not Make Things Too Easy.
Barresi. How It Comes.
Bogan, L. Heard by a Girl.
Bricusse, L. Who Can I Turn To (When Nobody Needs Me?).
Clarke, C. Vicki and Daphne.
Creeley. For Friendship.
Darley. It Is Not Beauty I Demand.
Gunn, T. Idea of Trust, The.

Hewitt, J. Ram's Horn, The.
Horovitz, F. Do You Not Know that I Need to Touch You.
Johnson, J. Eclipse.
Lee, L. Gift, The.
Meynell, A. After a Parting.
Philips, K. Epitaph on her Son *H. P.* at St. Syth's Church.
Pritchard, N. Burnt Sienna.
Reese, L. Trust.
Thomas, D. Ears in the Turrets Hear.
Vando. Father's Day.

Truth
"Æ." Truth.
Aiyejina. Dialogue, The.
Ashbery. Rain Moving In.
Auden. History of Truth, The.
Berlin. Say It Isn't So.
Boland, E. Oral Tradition, The.
Bonar. Be True [*or* Be True Thyself].
Brontë, E. Stanzas: "Often rebuked, yet always back returning."
Browning, E. Best Thing in the World, The.
Browning, R. Pippa's Song.
Campo. What the Body Told.
Carew, T. Disdain Returned.
    True Beauty, The.
Chaucer. Lak of Stedfastnesse.
Chipasula. Manifesto on Ars Poetica.
Clarke, C. What Goes Around Comes Around, or The Proof is in the Pudding.
Clough. With Whom Is No Variableness, Neither Shadow of Turning.
Coleridge, M. Contents of an Ink-bottle, The.
    Insincere Wish Addressed to a Beggar, An.
    True to Myself Am I, and False to All.
Creeley. Bresson's Movies.
    Fancy.
Cristall. Ode on Truth: Addressed to George Dyer.
Cullen, C. To Certain Critics.
Dooley, M. Heat.
Duggan, E. Truth.
Dunn, S. What They Wanted.
Eliot, T. Hippopotamus, The.
Emerson, R. Harp, The.
    Uriel.
Everson, W. Narrows of Birth, The.
Frost, R. Night Person, The.
Fuller, M. One in All, The.
Gascoigne. Gascoigne's Woodmanship.
Gascoyne. "Truth Is Blind, The."
Gershwin. It Ain't Necessarily So.
Gioia. Insomnia.
Glück, L. Day Without Night.
Graves, R. End of Play.
    Pier-Glass, The.
Harper, M. Alice.
Heard, J. Truth.
Herbert, G. Jordan (1).
Holmes, O. Our Limitations.
Howard, R. Vocational Guidance, with Special Reference to the Annunciation of Simone Martini.
Hughes, L. Theme for English B.
Jackson, L. Helen's Burning.
Jeffers, R. Advice to Pilgrims.
    Cassandra.
Joans. Truth, The.
Johnson, G. Lost Illusions.
Keats. Ode on a Grecian Urn.
Kinsella, T. Another September.
Kipling, R. Fabulists, The.
Landon. Stern Truth.
Lanier, S. To Beethoven.
Lawrence, D. Elemental.
Levertov. Goddess, The.
Levine, P. Simple Truth, The.
Lindley, D. Cryptogram, The.
Mac Low. Pieces O'six—XVIII.
Macpherson, J. Well, The.
McKay, C. Truth.
Meinke. Supermarket.
Melville, H. Enthusiast, The.
Moise *et al.* Newspaper, The.
Moorer. Duty, or Truth at Work.

Truth Suppressed, The.
Ofeimun. How Can I Sing.
Prologue: "I have come down."
Olson, C. Kingfishers, The.
Osundare. Sand Seer, The.
Parkes, B. To an Author who Loved Truth More than Fame.
Peacocke. Remembrance.
Perelman. Things.
Ralegh, S. Lie, The.
Ramke. Astronomer Works Nights: A Parable of Science, The.
Reavey. Dismissing Progress and Its Progenitors.
Rich, A. 5:30 A.M.
Roethke. Open House.
Rossetti, C. My Dream.
Rukeyser, M. Ballad of Orange and Grape.
Believing in Those Inexorable Laws.
Poem as Mask, The.
Rux, C. H. Pledge of Allegiance.
Sansom, A. Voice.
Sexton. Truth the Dead Know, The.
Shakespeare, W. Phoenix and the Turtle, The.
Shelley, P. Sonnet: Lift Not the Painted Veil: "Lift not the painted veil which those who live."
Siddal. Dead Love.
Smith, S. Magna Est Veritas.
Spires. Woman on the Dump, The.
Stanton, M. Ballad of the Magic Glasses.
Stevens, W. American Sublime, The.
Man on the Dump, The.
Stevenson, R. Whole Duty of Children.
Tate, J. Deaf Girl Playing.
Tennyson, A. Higher Pantheism, The.
Thomas, E. Glory, The.
Tsvetayeva [or Tsvetaeva]. I know the truth—give up all other truths!
Very. On Finding the Truth.
Serpent, The.
Vitale, M. Truth Put It.
Warren, R. Whole Question, The.
Whateley. Ode to Truth.
Whittier. Brown of Ossawatomie.
Wilbur. Lying.
Williams, W. Hard Listener, The.
Wordsworth, W. Where Lies the Truth? Has Man in Wisdom's Creed.
Wyatt, S. Farewell: "What should I say."
Yeats. Leaders of the Crowd, The.
Song of the Happy Shepherd, The.

Truth, Sojourner
Fauset. Oriflamme.
Truth. Ain't I a Woman?

Tuberculosis
Cofer, J. They Never Grew Old.
García, D. Tísica.
Straus, M. What I Heard on the Radio Today.
Thompson, P. Consumptive, The.
Williams, S. Wishon Line, The.

Tubman, Harriet
Allen, S. Harriet Tubman aka Moses.
Griffin, S. I Like to Think of Harriet Tubman.
Hayden, R. Runagate Runagate.
Holmes, D. Tubman Strong.
Jacobs, H. Growing into my name.
McLoughland. Whippoorwill Calls, The.
Unknown. Harriet Tubman.

Tulip Trees
Sitwell, S. Tulip Tree.

Tulips
Herrick. Meditation for His Mistress[e], A.
To a Bed of Tulips.
Plath. Tulips.
Schuyler, J. February.
Williams, W. Tulip Bed, The.

Tumbleweeds
Ward, T. In the Interest of Possibility.

Turkey
Hikmet. Evening Walk, The.
Things I Didn't Know I Loved.

Turkeys
Clare, J. Turkeys.
Dunbar, P. Soliloquy of a Turkey.

Etter. Stuffy Turkey.
Guthrie, W. Turkey in the Corn.
Heaney, S. Turkeys Observed.
Jacobik, G. Turkeys in August.
Kelly, B. Wild Turkeys; The Dignity of the Damned.
Mackenzie, K. Table-Birds.
Wilbur. Black November Turkey, A.

Turner, Dennis
Hirsch, E. Fast Break.

Turner, Lana
O'Hara, F. Poem: "Lana Turner has collapsed!"

Turner, Mrs. Bishop
Heard, J. Resting.

Turner, Nat
Hayden, R. Ballad of Nat Turner, The.

Turnips
Thomas, E. Swedes.

Turtles
Chin. Turtle Soup.
Corman. Tortoise, The.
Harter. Turtle Blessing.
Lee, S. Letter from Turtle Beach.
Lindsay, N. Little Turtle, The.
Lowell, R. Neo-Classical Urn, The.
McClure, M. From the Window of the Beverly Wilshire Hotel.
Nash, O. Turtle, The.
O'Connor, M. Turtles Hatching.
Shakespeare, W. Phoenix and the Turtle, The.
Swenson, M. Living Tenderly.
Unknown. Turtle's Song, The.
Willard, N. Feast of St. Tortoise, The.
Williams, W. Turtle, The.
See also **Tortoises**

Tuscany
Wright, J. Journey, The.

Tweed (river), Scotland and England
Bowles, W. Tweed Visited, The.

Twelfth Night
Helton. Old Christmas Morning.

Twickenham, England
Donne. Twicknam [or Twickenham] Garden.

Twilight
Adams, L. Home-coming.
"Æ." By the Margin of the Great Deep.
Angel. Twilight.
Beckett, S. Roundelay: "On all that strand."
Bevington, L. Twilight.
Bogan, L. Short Summary.
Carruth, H. Twilight Comes.
Carter, J. Adagio at Twilight.
De la Mare. Voices.
De Rose, P. Deep Purple.
Dickey, J. Dusk of Horses, The.
Gray, R. Dusk, The.
Grimké, A. Dusk.
Winter Twilight, A.
Guest, B. Twilight Polka Dots.
Guggenberger. Twilight.
Haines, J. Evening Change.
Herrick. To Anthea Lying in Bed.
Hirsch, E. Man on a Fire Escape.
Komunyakaa. Boat People.
Lawrence, D. Twilight.
Ledwidge. Twilight in Middle March, A.
Longfellow, H. Afternoon in February.
Children's Hour, The.
Meredith, G. Ballad of Past Meridian, A.
Merwin, W. S. Dusk in Winter.
Mezey. Twilight Under Pine Ridge.
Owen, W. Anthem for Doomed Youth.
Pritchard, N. Burnt Sienna.
Robinson, E. Dark Hills, The.
Russell, W. Tali Karng: Twilight Snake.
Skloot. Twilight Time.
Tomlinson, C. Tramontana at Lerici.
Toomer. Georgia Dusk.
Tripp. Twilight in the Library.
Voznesensky [or Voznesenskii]. Give Me Peace.
Warren, R. What Voice at Moth-Hour.
Wright, C. California Twilight.
Wright, J. Twilights.
See also **Evening; Sunset**

Twins
Broumas, O. Landscape with Next of Kin.
Graves, R. Twins.
Leigh, H. Twins, The.
Paino. 1965.
Shapiro, K. Twins, The.
Swartwout. Siamese Twins in Love.
Unknown. Twa Brothers, The.
Van Duyn. Twins, The.
West, K. To My Twin Sister Who Died at Birth.

Typing and Typists
Blumenthal, M. Back from the Word-Processing Course, I Say to My Old Typewriter.
Page, P. Typists.
Sexton. That Day.

Tyranny
Auden. Epitaph on a Tyrant.
Blake, W. Grey Monk, The.
Browning, R. Instans Tyrannus.
Brutus. At a Funeral.
Carey, H. Maid's Husband, The.
Cook, E. Idiot-Born, The.
Egerton, S. Emulation, The.
Gray, T. Tophet.
Herrick. Duty to Tyrants.
Jeffers, R. Ave Caesar.
Johnson, L. Mi Revalueshanary Fren.
Landor, W. Foreign Ruler, A.
Martin, C. Easter Sunday, 1985.
Melville, H. Timoleon.
Mphahlele. Poem, A: "What is there that we can do or say."
Pilkington, L. Wish, By a Young Lady, The.
Rushton. Human Debasement; a Fragment.
Shelley, P. Song to the Men of England.
Smith, S. Christmas.
Thelwall. To Tyranny.
Thomas, D. Hand That Signed the Paper, The.
Unknown. Humble Petition of the British Jacobins to their Brethren of France, The.
Trumpet of Liberty, The.
Warren, R. Apology for Domitian.

U

Uccello, Paolo
Corso. Uccello.

UFOs
Chasin. In Communication with a UFO.
Kinsella, J. Bright Cigar-Shaped Object Hovers Over Mount Pleasant, A.
See also **Flying Saucers**

Ugliness
Burns, R. Keekin' Glass, The.
Cook, E. Song of the Ugly Maiden.
Jackson, L. Mask, The.
Jeffers, R. Carmel Point.
Jennings, E. Ugly Child, The.
"Monty Python." All Things Dull and Ugly.
Moss, T. Owl In Daytime, The.
Ross, C. John, Tom, and James.
Sanchez, S. Song No. 3: "Cain't nobody tell me any different."
Soto. Brown Girl, Blonde Okie.
Welch, L. Chicago Poem.

Ukraine
Romtvedt. Kiev, the Ukraine, Nuclear Accident.

Ulysses
Daniel, S. Ulysses and the Siren [or Syren].
Doolittle, H. At Ithaca.
Fallon, P. Odysseus.
Flecker. Old Ships, The.
Graves, R. Ulysses.
Homer. Butchers, The.
Phemios and Medon.
Kyger. Maze, The.
Lang, A. Odyssey, The.
Lovelace, R. To a Lady That Desired Me I Would Bear My Part with Her in a Song.
McCallum, S. Calypso.
Merwin, W. S. Odysseus.
Montgomerie, A. Sonet: "Thocht Polibus, pisander, and with them."
Muldoon, P. Making the Move.

Umbrellas

Parker, D. Penelope.
Stevens, W. World as Meditation, The.
Tennyson, A. Lotus-Eaters, The.
Ulysses.
Waddington, M. Ulysses Embroidered.

Umbrellas
Dickinson, E. Bat, The.
Wright, R. Haiku: "Just enough of rain."

Uncertainty
Angel. Twilight.
Auden. September 1, 1939.
Beckett, S. Enueg II.
Bolton, K. Nonplussed.
Cavafy. Waiting for the Barbarians.
De la Mare. Dear Sir.
Doolittle, H. Fragment 36 [or Thirty-Six]: "I know not what to do."
Etherege. To a Lady Asking Him How Long He Would Love Her.
"Field." Second Thoughts.
Foix. I Arrived in that Town, Everyone Greeted Me and I Recognized no One. When I Was Going to Read My Verses, the Devil, Hidden Behind a Tree, Called Out to Me Sarcastically and Filled My Hands with Newspaper Clippings.
Jennings, K. Just the Two of Us.
Lea, S. Insomnia: The Distances.
Lowell, J. In a Copy of Omar Khayyám.
Melville, H. Arch, The.
Merrill, J. About the Phoenix.
Muir, E. In Love For Long.
North, C. Leap Year.
O'Hara, F. Cornkind.
Meditations in an Emergency.
Simic. Clouds Gathering.
Sweeney, M. Couple Waiting, A.
Talvikki, A. Origin Charm Against Uncertain Injuries.
Teasdale. Flight, The.
Thomas, D. Should Lanterns Shine.
Treece. Magic Wood, The.
Whitman, W. As I Lay with My Head in Your Lap Camerado.
Whittier. Song of Slaves in the Desert.
Woods, J. What Do You Do When It's Spring?

Uncle Tom's Cabin
Bibb. Eliza in Uncle Tom's Cabin.
Harper, F. She's Free!

Uncles
Algarin. Always Throw the First Punch.
Barlow, G. Salt.
Bernstein, C. Profaning the Dead.
Carson, C. Asylum.
Conn. Todd.
Crawley, W. Bud.
Cullen, C. Uncle Jim.
Etter. Well You Needn't.
Harrison, T. Study.
Heyen. For Hermann Heyen.
Jordan, J. Through These Halls.
Kasdorf. Uncle.
Knight, E. My Uncle Is My Honor and a Guest in My House.
Lear, E. Incidents in the Life of My Uncle Arly.
Levine, P. Uncle.
Mahon. My Wicked Uncle.
Nye, N. My Uncle Mohammed at Mecca, 1981.
Piercy. My Rich Uncle, Whom I Only Met Three Times.
Smith, D. Roundhouse Voices, The.
Syrkin. My Uncle in Treblinka.
Walker, F. X. Crooked Afro.
Wright, J. Willy Lyons.

Underground Railroad
Hayden, R. Runagate Runagate.
McLoughland. Whippoorwill Calls, The.
Unknown. Harriet Tubman.

Undertakers
Moss, T. Owl In Daytime, The.
Undertaker's Daughter Feels Neglect, The.
Nash, O. Tweedledee and Tweedledoom.

Underwear
Cabico, R. Antonio Banderas in His Underwear.
Ferlinghetti, L. Underwear.

Wolverton, T. Black Slip.
Yosano. Channel Boat, The.

Unemployment
Ackerly. Prayer of an Unemployed Man.
Butterfield, F. G. For Services Rendered.
Cavafy. Days of 1908.
Davis, C. Out of Work, Out of Touch, Out of Sorts.
Dugan, A. Prayer: "God, I need a job because I need money."
Gorney, J. Brother, Can You Spare a Dime?
Hopkins, G. Tom's Garland: Upon the Unemployed.
Jordan, J. Unemployment/Monologue.
Kalar, J. Papermill.
McGinley. Trinity Place.
Spender, S. Unemployed.
Unknown. Between an Unemployed Artist and His Wife.
Webb, F. Laid Off.

Unicorns
Cofer, J. Why There Are No Unicorns.
Housman, A. Inhuman Henry.
Lewis, C. Late Passenger, The.
Moore, M. Sea Unicorns and Land Unicorns.
Pitter. Unicorn, The.
Randall, D. Black Poet, White Critic.
Rieu. Unicorn, The.
Unknown. I Stood in the Maytime Meadows.
Webb, P. Days of the Unicorns, The.
Williams, C. Taliessin's Song of the Unicorn.

Unidentified Flying Objects
Kinsella, J. Bright Cigar-Shaped Object Hovers Over Mount Pleasant, A.
See also **Flying Saucers**

United States
Baraka. Das Kapital.
I don't love you.
Bates, K. America the Beautiful.
Benét, S. American Names.
Berkeley, G. On the Prospect of Planting Arts and Learning in America.
Bernstein, L. America.
Conga.
Berryman. American Lights, Seen from Off Abroad.
Bevington, H. Mrs. Trollope in America.
Bly, R. Great Society, The.
Cary, P. Homes for All.
Chrystos. I Have Not Signed a Treaty with the United States Government.
Cohan. Over There.
Comden, B. Conga.
Creeley. America.
Cummings, E. Next to of Course God America I.
Poem, or Beauty Hurts Mr. Vinal.
Dickinson, E. Union.
Djanikian. In the Elementary School Choir.
Donaldson, W. Kansas City Kitty.
Evans, M. Status Symbol.
Feinstein, S. Singapore, July 4th.
Frost, R. Gift Outright, The.
Ginsberg, A. America.
Vow, A.
Who Runs America?
Green, A. Conga.
Hardy, T. On an Invitation to the United States.
Harper, F. Then and Now.
Harper, M. Goin' to the Territory.
Herrera. Dream of Christopher Columbus, The.
Hitchcock. United States Prepare for the Permanent Revolution, The.
Holmes, J. Map of My Country, A.
Hosmer, F. O Beautiful, My Country.
Hughes, L. I, Too.
Hunt, L. Iterating Sonnet.
Jeffers, L. My Blackness Is the Beauty of This Land.
Jeffers, R. Eagle Valor, Chicken Mind.
Shine, Perishing Republic.
Kaufman, B. To My Son Parker, Asleep in the Next Room.
Koch, K. Poem of the Forty-eight States, A.
Lawrence, D. Evening Land, The.
Lazarus, E. 1492.

New Colossus, The.
Liddy. Voice of America, 1961, The.
MacLeish. American Letter.
Empire Builders.
McKay, C. America.
Newlove. America.
Randall, D. Melting Pot, The.
Ras. In the New Country.
Roethke. Night Journey.
Ryan, R. From My Lai the Thunder Went West.
Shapiro, H. National Cold Storage Company.
Simpson, L. American Poetry.
Inner Part, The.
To the Western World.
Smith, S. America.
Stevenson, R. In the States.
Tate, A. Aeneas at Washington.
Ode to the Confederate Dead.
Troup, B. (Get Your Kicks On) Route 66!
Van Dyke. America for Me.
Peace Hymn of the Republic.
Wain. Brooklyn Heights.
Whitman, W. America.
For You O Democracy.
I Hear America Singing.
Passage to India.
To the States, To Identify the 16th, 17th, or 18th Presidentiad.
Williams, T. My Country, to Thy Shore.

Unity
"Ada." Appeal to Women, An.
Baker, D. Envoi: Waking After Snow.
Bevington, L. Wrestling.
Bradstreet, A. Another.
Letter to Her Husband, Absent upon Public[k] Employment, A.
To My Dear and Loving Husband.
Brown, S. Let Them Call It Jazz.
Butler, M. Listen.
Ceravolo. White Fish in Reeds.
Clifton, L. Cutting Greens.
Coleridge, M. We Never Said Farewell.
Czerkawska. Thread.
Donne. Ecstasy, The.
Flea, The.
Drayton. Heart, The.
Emerson, R. Each and All.
Nature [1844].
Unity.
Xenophanes.
Empson. Invitation To Juno.
Flanders, J. House That Fear Built: Warsaw, 1943, The.
Gilmore, B. Coming to the net.
Ginsberg, A. Change: *Kyoto-Tokyo Express*, The.
Glück, L. Hawk's Shadow.
Pond, The.
Guevara, M. Buddy Holly Poem, The.
Herrick. Power and Peace.
Jacobs, H. On extending the olive branch to my own self.
Levertov. Ache of Marriage, The.
MacDiarmid, H. With the Herring Fishers.
Melville, H. Art.
Little Good Fellows, The.
Mudrooroo Narogin. Streets.
Nesbit, E. Song: "Oh, baby, baby, baby dear."
Olds, S. Knowing, The.
Parker, P. There Is a Woman in This Town.
Paz. Shrine.
Philips, K. Friendship's Mystery[s], to my dearest Lucasia.
Ponsot. Analogue.
Ransom, J. Two in August.
Rich, A. Diving into the Wreck.
Phantasia for Elvira Shatayev.
Rukeyser, M. Poem as Mask, The.
Sing, D. Baap-Nemesthe Reggae Song.
Slessor. Sleep.
Stevens, W. Final Soliloquy of the Interior Paramour.
Stryker. Almighty Lord, with One Accord.
Sylvester, J. Father, The.
Tsui. Suzy Wong's Been Dead a Long Time.
Vaughan, H. Knot, The.

Whitman, W.   Crossing Brooklyn Ferry.
  One's-Self I Sing.
Whittier.   Word for the Hour, A.
Williams, W.   Mists Over the River.
Winchilsea.   Letter to Daphnis, A.
Wright, C.   Self-Portrait.

Universe
Blaser.   Universe is Part of Ourselves, The.
Browning, R.   Pisgah-Sights. I.
  Pisgah-Sights. II.
Buckley, C.   Concerning Paradise.
Dickinson, E.   Bees.
Follain.   Music of Spheres.
Healy, R.   Size of This Universe, The.
Kelly, R.   Looking.
Meynell, A.   Christ in the Universe.
Olson, C.   Across Space and Time.
Olson, T.   Hypothesis.
Ono.   Mother of the Universe.
Pack, R.   Proton Decay.
Springer, T.   Harmony.
Towle.   North.
Tuckerman, F.   Sonnet: "And so, as this great
  sphere (now turning slow)."

Unknown Soldier
Chesterton, G.   Elegy in a Country Churchyard.

Urania
Wroth [*or* Wroath].   Song: "Love what art thou?
  A vain thought."

Urban Life
Greenberg, A.   City Life.
Harrison, J.   Birds That Woke Us: An Urban
  Pastoral, The.

Uriel
Emerson, R.   Uriel.

Urns
Cullen, C.   Uncle Jim.
Keats.   Ode on a Grecian Urn.
Lowell, R.   Neo-Classical Urn, The.

Ursa Major
Hollander, J.   Great Bear, The.
McHugh, H.   Night in a World, A.

Ursula of Llangwyryfon, Saint
Williams, J.   Saint Ursula of Llangwyryfon.

Usury
Campbell, J.   Gombeen, The.
Guillén, N.   Usurers, The.
Pound, E.   Canto XLV.
  Canto 51.

Utah (state)
Frost, R.   On the Heart's Beginning to Cloud the
  Mind.
Stevenson, A.   Utah.

Ute, The
Tomlinson, C.   Ute Mountain.

Utopia
Beerbohm, M.   In a Copy of More's (or Shaw's
  or Wells's or Plato's or Anybody's) Utopia.
Coleridge, S.   Kubla Khan: or, A Vision in a
  Dream.
  Pantisocracy.
Hall, D.   Hermit with Landscape.
Hucks, J.   To Freedom.
Kern, J.   Land Where the Good Songs Go, The.
Thelwall.   On the Rapid Extension of the
  Suburbs.
Unknown.   Big Rock Candy Mountains, The.

V

Vacation
Barresi.   Vacation, 1969.
Davidson, J.   Crystal Palace, The.
Florsheim.   Weekend in Palm Springs.
Gannon, K.   Dreamer's Holiday, A.
Jackson, R.   Sunday Brunch.
Merrill, J.   Up and Down.
Pietri.   Intermission from Monday.
Stafford, W.   Vacation.
Stevens, W.   Gray Stones and Gray Pigeons.

Vacuum Cleaners and Vacuum Cleaning
Conran.   Thirteen Ways of Looking at a Hoover.
Nemerov.   Vacuum, The.

Vagabonds
Bates, K.   Despised and Rejected.
Colum, P.   Old Woman of the Roads, The.
Dawe, B.   Drifters.
Delmore Brothers.   Wabash Cannonball, The.
Dobyns.   Freight Cars.
Frost, R.   Two Tramps in Mud Time.
Hardy, T.   Trampwoman's Tragedy, A.
Hughes, T.   November.
Huidobro.   Blind.
Kinnell.   Memory of Wilmington.
Kipling, R.   Sestina of the Tramp-Royal.
Levine, P.   And the Trains Go On.
Masefield.   Wanderer's Song, A.
McGrath, T.   Long Way Outside
  Yellowstone, A.
Neilson, J.   Sundowner, The.
Ponsot.   Communion of Saints: The Poor
  Bastard under the Bridge.
Riley, J.   Raggedy Man, The.
Stevenson, R.   Vagabond, The.

Valentine's Day
Chaucer.   Catalogue of the Birds.
  Now Welcom[e], Somer [*or* Summer].
 Rondel: "And whan this werk al brought was to
  an ende."
Hall, D.   Valentine.
Hart, L.   My Funny Valentine.
Hemingway.   Valentine.
Holt, V.   To Mr. Wren, My Valentine Six Year
  Old.
Schuyler, J.   Sleep.
Spicer, J.   Valentine, A.
Thompson, P.

Valentino, Rudolph
Sapia.   Valentino's Hair.

Valleys
Ashbery.   Grand Abacus.
Byron, G.   Lachin y Gair.
Salinas, L.   My Fifty-Plus Years Celebrate
  Spring.
Sandburg, C.   Moist Moon People.
Veinberg, J.   Owl's Landscape, An.
Wheelock, J.   Earth, Take Me Back.
Wordsworth, D.   Peaceful Our Valley, Fair and
  Green.

Value
Bloom, R.   Good for Nothin' Joe.
Brouwer, J.   Space Memorabilia Auction,
  Superior Stamp and Coin, Beverly Hills,
  California.
Coffman.   Cheerleaders.
Ellington, D.   Tulip or Turnip.
Fisher, R.   Least, The.
George, D.   Tulip or Turnip.
Herman, J.   I Won't Send Roses.
Nathan, L.   Bladder Song.
  So?
Smith, S.   Valuable.

Vampires
Guillén, N.   Usurers, The.
Kipling, R.   Vampire, The.
McDonald, R.   Incident in Transylvania.
Samaras, N.   After the Children Have Gone to
  Bed.
Smith, S.   Great Unaffected Vampires and the
  Moon.
Wilbur.   Undead, The.

Van Doren, Mark
Hayden, R.   Ballad of Remembrance, A.

Van Gogh, Vincent
Cooley.   Van Gogh's The Potato Eaters.
Haines, J.   On a Certain Field in Auvers.
Tomlinson, C.   Farewell to Van Gogh.
Vertreace, M.   Black Tulips.

Vancouver, British Columbia
Fanning, R.   Parable of the Boy and the Polar
  Bear.
Lowry, M.   Christ Walks in This Infernal
  District Too.
Morrissey, S.   There was Fire in Vancouver.

Vandalism
Beaver.   Drummer, The.
Bottoms.   Desk, The.
Knight, S.   Double Writing.

Liu, T.   Strange Fruit.
Parker, A.   Another Poem about the Vandals.
  Cruelty, the Vandals Say.
  Vandals, The.

Vanderbilt, Gloria
Cole, W.   Poor Kid.

Vane, Sir Henry (1613-62)
Milton.   To Sir Henry Vane the Younger.

Vanity
Arnold, C.   Party She Outdid Herself, The.
Blunt, W.   On Her Vanity.
Bolton, E.   Palinode, A.
Bradstreet, A.   Flesh and the Spirit, The.
  Here Follows Some Verses upon the Burning of
  Our House [July 10th, 1666. Copied Out of a
  Loose Paper].
  Vanity of All Worldly Things, The.
Brown, E.   Beauty and the Prince Formerly
  Known as Beast.
Byron, G.   'All Is Vanity, Saith the Preacher'
Carew, T.   Ingrateful[l] Beauty Threatened.
Coogler.   More Care for the Neck Than for the
  Intellect.
Cummings, E.   Cambridge ladies who live in
  furnished souls, The.
Dunbar, W.   O Wretch, Beware.
"Ephelia."   To a Proud Beauty.
Freneau.   Vanity of Existence, The.
Graves, R.   Vain and Careless.
  Vanity.
Guiterman.   On the Vanity of Earthly Greatness.
Gunn, T.   Lines for a Book.
Hall, J.   Even as the Wandering Traveler.
Herbert, G.   Vanity [*or* Vanitie] (1).
Herrick.   Upon Rook: Epigram.
Hewitt, J.   Ireland.
Howitt, M.   Spider and the Fly, The.
Johnson, S.   Scholar's Life, The.
  Vanity of Human Wishes, The; The Tenth Satire
  of Juvenal Imitated.
Kizer, C.   Through a Glass Eye, Lightly.
Lawrence, D.   Intimates.
  Snake.
Le Gallienne.   Beauty Accurst.
Leigh, H.   Lady and the Doctor, The.
Mayer, G.   Narcissus.
Merrill, J.   Peacock, The.
Nash, O.   Evening Out, The.
Piercy.   Barbie Doll.
Sexton.   Snow White and the Seven Dwarfs.
Shelley, P.   Ozymandias.
Smith, H.   Ozymandias.
Swift, J.   Lady's Dressing Room, The.
Vaughan, H.   Vanity of Spirit.
Watts, I.   Man Frail, and God Eternal.
Wenderoth, J.   First Impression.
Whateley.   Vanity of External Accomplishments,
  The.
Wigglesworth.   Song of Emptiness to Fill up the
  Empty Pages Following, A.
See also **Pride**

Variety
Lovelace, R.   Scrutiny [*or* Scrutinie], The.

Vashti
Harper, F.   Vashti.
Spencer, A.   Before the Feast of Shushan.

Vaudeville
Beatty, P.   Why That Abbott and Costello
  Vaudeville Mess Never Worked with Black
  People.

Vaughan, Henry
Sassoon.   At the Grave of Henry Vaughan.

Vaughn, Robert Boardman
Justice, D.   In Memory of the Unknown Poet,
  Robert Boardman Vaughn.

Vegetables
Alarcon, F.   Laughing Tomatoes.
Baca.   Green Chile.
Clifton, L.   Cutting Greens.
Dove, R.   Sunday Greens.
Duncan, R.   Turning into.
Florian.   Send My Spinach.
Forbes, C.   Potlicker Blues.
Lindley, D.   Curly Kale.
  Fennel.

Messerli. Angry with China.
Mole, J. Trick, The.
Nash, O. Parsnip, The.
Oates. In Jana's Garden.
Ormsby, E. Skunk Cabbage.
Thomas, E. Swedes.
Thomas, L. Onion Bucket.
Unknown. Do you carrot all for me?

Vegetarians
Devaney, T. Sonnet: "You know all those
  sonnets the ones where I said, I love you,
  well."
Yambo. When Negro Teeth Speak.

Velázquez, Diego Rodríguez de Silva y
Conquest. Rokeby Venus, The.
Wylie. Castilian.

Venereal Disease
Catina. Negotiations.

Vengeance
Brown, E. Jezebel to the Eunuchs.
Bruner. Prayer for Strength.
Cortez, J. Rape.
Guiterman. Ancient History.
Hughes, L. Hard Daddy.
Paulin. Impossible Pictures, The.
Whittier. Cities of the Plain, The.

Venice, Italy
Beer, P. Birthday Poem from Venice.
Betjeman. Longfellow's Visit to Venice.
Browning, R. Song: "Moth's kiss, first, The!"
  Toccata of Galuppi's, A.
Christie. Coming Off a Depression, She
  Prepares for Venice.
Durrell. Water-Colour of Venice, A.
Garrigue. From Venice Was That Afternoon.
Longfellow, H. Venice.
Melville, H. In a Bye-Canal.
  Venice.
Symons, A. Venice.
Wordsworth, W. On the Extinction of the
  Venetian Republic.

Venus (goddess)
Carew, T. On Sight of a Gentlewoman's Face in
  the Water.
Chaucer. Catalogue of the Birds.
  Now Welcom[e], Somer [*or* Summer].
  Rondel: "And whan this werk al brought was to
  an ende."
Conquest. Rokeby Venus, The.
Devlin, D. Venus of the Salty Shell.
Hadas, R. Mars and Venus.
Herrick. How Lillies Came White.
  How Violets Came Blue.
  Wounded Cupid, The.
Lowell, A. Venus Transiens.
Olson, C. Ring of, The.
Prior. Ode, An: "Merchant, to secure his
  treasure, The."
Robinson, M. Sappho's Prayer to Venus.
Rossetti, C. Venus's Looking-Glass.
Rukeyser, M. Birth of Venus, The.
Salter. Rebirth of Venus, The.
Spenser. Epithalamion: "Ye learned sisters
  which have oftentimes."
Unknown. Spoken by Venus on Seeing Her
  Statue Done by Praxiteles.
Watson, W. Invocation: "Appear, O Mother,
  was the perpetual cry."
Willis, N. Psyche, Before the Tribunal of
  Venus.
Young, I. Visit to the Palace of Venus.

See also **Aphrodite**

Venus (planet)
Bogan, L. Evening-Star.
Clare, J. Hesperus.
García Lorca. Venus.
Holmes, O. Flaneur, The.

Venus of Milo (statue)
Gilder, R. Two Worlds.
Lazarus, E. Venus of the Louvre.

Verdi, Giuseppe
Noyes, A. Barrel-Organ, The.

Verdun, Battle of (1916)
Dugan, A. Memories of Verdun.

Verlaine, Paul
Hovey. Verlaine.
Ramke. Paul Verlaine at the Grave of Lucien
  Létinois.
Robinson, E. Verlaine.

Vermont (state)
Barnstone, A. Mating the Goats.
Corbett, W. Vermont Apollinaire.
Donze, R. Vermont Has a High Suicide Rate.
Frost, R. "Out, Out—."
Kinnell. Angling, a Day.
Rich, A. Living Memory.
Suessdorf, K. Moonlight in Vermont.
Warren, R. Fall Comes in Back-Country
  Vermont.
  Vermont Ballad: Change of Season.
Weismiller. Vermont: Spring Rains.

Verona, Italy
Reed, H. Map of Verona, A.

Versailles, France
Moore, M. No Swan So Fine.
Rich, A. Versailles.

Veterans
Anderson, D. Itinerary.
Barry, J. Lessons.
Bowen, K. Playing Basketball with the Viet
  Cong.
Chipasula. Tramp.
Cross, F. When Chicken Man Came Home to
  Roost.
Dugan, A. Portrait from the Infantry.
Ehrhart. Invasion of Grenada, The.
Glazer, M. Star-Spangled.
Hughes, T. Walt.
Janeczko. Mail King.
Kinzie. Summers of Vietnam.
Komunyakaa. Report from the Skull's Diorama.
Larsen, W. Learning the War.
Major, C. Vietnam.
McDonald, W. After the Noise of Saigon.
  Veteran.
Mura. Blueness of the Day, The.
Revard. Parading with the Veterans of Foreign
  Wars.
Sassoon. Does It Matter?
  Memorial Tablet.
Sitwell. Next War, The.
Waring, B. Refuge at the One Step Down.
Weigl. Anna Grasa.
Wormser. By-Products.
Young Bear. Wadasa Nakamoon, Vietnam
  Memorial.

See also **Soldiers**

Veterans Day
Tripp. Armistice Day '77, Honiton.

See also **Armistice**

Vice
Bart, L. Fings Ain't Wot They Used t'Be.
Ellington, D. Maybe I Should Change My
  Ways.
Evans, D. In the Vices.
Herrick. Nothing New.
Kinnell. Last Songs.

See also **Sin**

Victoria, Queen of England
Ford, F. Sidera Cadentia.
French, W. Queen's After-Dinner Speech, The.
Housman, A. 1887.
Kipling, R. Widow at Windsor, The.
Linden, M. To the Queen of the British
  Government.
Tennyson, A. On the Jubilee of Queen Victoria.
Unknown. Much Distressed.
  Queen's Dream, The.

Victory
Allen, H. Wingless Victory, The.
Behn, A. Thousand Martyrs I Have Made, A.
Gordon, A. How We Beat the Favourite.
Hardy, T. Men Who March Away.
Harrison, T. Cycles of Donji Vakuf.
Herrick. To the King.
Landor, W. Crimean Heroes, The.
Marvell. Fair Singer, The.
  Horatian Ode upon Cromwell's Return from
  Ireland, An.

Miller, J. At Our Golden Gate.
Ransom, J. Judith of Bethulia.
Sill. Opportunity.
Treece. Conquerors.
Unknown. Agincourt Carol, The.
  Joshua Fit de Battle of Jericho [*or* ob Jerico].

Video
Ridl. Video Mama.

Vienna, Austria
Posamentier, E. Hungarian Medical Student,
  The: 1928.
Ress. Waving Her Farewell. Train Station,
  Vienna XV, 1939.

Vietnam
Alexander, E. Nineteen.
Alvarez, J. How I Learned to Sweep.
Appleman, P. Waiting for the Fire.
Balaban. Along the Mekong.
  April 30, 1975.
  Dead for Two Years, Erhart Arranges to Meet
  Me in a Dream.
  Dragonfish, The.
  For Miss Tin in Hue.
  For Mrs. Cam, Whose Name Means "Printed
  Silk."
  Guard at the Binh Thuy Bridge, The.
  In Celebration of Spring.
  News Update.
  Opening Le Ba Khon's Dictionary.
  Story.
  Than, Mau.
  Thoughts Before Dawn.
Barry, J. Floating Petals.
  In the Footsteps of Genghis Khan.
  Nights in Nha Trang.
  Nun in Ninh Hoa, A.
Barth, R. Letter from An Hoc (4), by a
  Seedbed.
Bly, R. At a March against the Vietnam War.
  Counting Small-Boned Bodies.
  Teeth Mother Naked at Last, The.
Brown, D. I Was Dancing Alone in Binh Dinh
  Province.
  Illumination.
Brown, S. After the Vietnam War.
Catina. Philosophy.
Clifton, H. Death of Thomas Merton.
Coleman, H. Black Soldier Remembers, A.
  Downed Black Pilot Learns How to Fly, A.
  In Ca Mau.
  Night Flare Drop, Tan Son Nhut.
  OK Corral East Brothers in the Nam.
  Remembrance of Things Past.
Cross, Jr. Gliding Baskets.
Dana, R. At the Vietnam War Memorial,
  Washington, D. C.
Dawe, B. Homecoming.
Denning. Fire Support Burk.
  Kim-San.
  Movie, The.
  Night on the Kho Bha Dinh.
  This Time.
Ehrhart. " . . . the light that cannot fade."
  Blizzard of Sixty-Six, The.
  Farmer Nguyen.
  Guerrilla War.
  Invasion of Grenada, The.
  Letter.
  Relative Thing, A.
  Time on Target.
Evans, G. Eye Blade.
  Revelation in the Mother Lode.
Fernandez, R. Legacy of a Brother.
Floyd. Captain James Leson, U. S. M. C.
  Corporal Charles Chungtu, U. S. M. C.
  Lance Corporal Purdue Grace, U. S. M. C.
  Private First Class Brooks Morgenstein, U. S.
  M. C.
  Private Jack Smith, U. S. M. C.
  Sergeant Brandon Just, U. S. M. C.
Ginsberg, A. Vow, A.
Griffin, S. Song My.
Gwynn, R. Body Bags.
Hall, D. Disgrace.
Hassett. Armed Forces Day.
  Christmas.

Mother's Day.
Patriot's Day.
Thanksgiving.
Hayden, R. In the Mourning Time.
Hazo. Battle News.
Hitchcock. Scattering Flowers.
Hollenbeck. Anorexia.
Howell, C. Memories of Mess Duty and the War.
Reminder to the Current President, A.
Huddle. Bac Ha.
Theory.
Vermont.
Ignatow, D. All Quiet.
James, A. Honor (1969).
Jordan, J. Poem to My Sister, Ethel Ennis, Who Sang "The Star-spangled Banner" at the Second Inauguration of Richard Milhous Nixon.
Kinnell. Vapor Trail Reflected in the Frog Pond.
Knott. Two Vietnam Poems: (1966).
Komunyakaa. After the Fall of Saigon.
Boat People.
Break from the Bush, A.
Dead at Quang Tri, The.
Facing It.
Report from the Skull's Diorama.
Somewhere Near Phu Bai.
Starlight Scope Myopia.
Tiger Lady.
Tu Do Street.
Krohn. Can Tho.
Farmer's Song at Can Tho.
Ferryman's Song at Binh Minh.
Layne, M. Collect Call.
Gettin' Straight.
Intersection in the Sky.
Levertov. Advent 1966.
Fragrance of Life, Odor of Death.
In Thai Binh (Peace) Province.
Tenebrae.
Weeping Woman.
What Were They Like?
Livesay, D. Waking in the Dark.
Lourie. For All My Brothers and Sisters.
Madhubuti. Long Reality, The.
Major, C. Vietnam #4.
McCarthy, E. Kilroy.
McCarthy, G. Arrival.
Fall of Da Nang, The.
Finding the Way Back.
Sound of Guns, The.
McClure, M. Song: "Platinum fur and brass revolver shine."
McDonald, W. Caliban in Blue.
Children of Saigon, The.
Christmas Bells, Saigon.
Faraway Places.
For Harper, Killed in Action.
For Kelly, Missing in Action.
Hauling Over Wolf Creek Pass in Winter.
Interview with a Guy Named Fawkes, U.S. Army.
Last Still Days in a Bunker, The.
Rocket Attack.
Veteran.
McGrath, T. Reading the Names of the Vietnam War Dead.
Merwin, W. S. Asians Dying, The.
Mezey. How Much Longer?
Mishler. Ceremony.
Mitchell, A. To Whom It May Concern.
Moore, L. Winter 1967.
Mura. Huy Nguyen: Brothers, Drowning Cries.
Natives, The.
Notley. White Phosphorus.
Oldham, P. Noon.
War Stories.
Oppenheimer, J. Poem in Defense of Children.
Ormsby, F. Home.
Osaki. Amnesiac.
Paley, G. Two Villages.
Paquet. Graves Registration.
It Is Monsoon at Last.
Mourning the Death, by Hemorrhage, of a Child from Honai.

Pratt, J. Words and Thoughts.
Receveur. August 17, 1970.
Ritterbusch. Search and Destroy.
Rottman. APO 96225.
Ryan, R. From My Lai the Thunder Went West.
Schafer. Battle Lines.
Shelton, R. Eden After Dark.
Stephens, M. After Asia.
Tremblay, B. Home Front.
Mayday.
Weber, R. Concise History of the Vietnam War: 1965–1968, A.
Weigl. Ambassador, The.
Amnesia.
Anna Grasa.
Burning Shit at An Khe.
Girl at the Chu Lai Laundry.
Her Life Runs Like a Red Silk Flag.
Him, on the Bicycle.
Last Lie, The.
Mines.
Monkey.
Sailing to Bien Hoa.
Song for the Lost Private.
Song of Napalm.
Surrounding Blues on the Way Down.
Temple Near Quang Tri, Not on the Map.
Way of Tet, The.
Whalen. Regalia in Immediate Demand!
Woodard. Tower.
Young Bear. Wadasa Nakamoon, Vietnam Memorial.

Vietnam War
Abbey, L. Broken Silence.
Anderson, D. Itinerary.
Bowen, K. Playing Basketball with the Viet Cong.
Casey, M. Learning.
LZ Gator Body Collector, The.
On What the Army Does with Heads.
Chasin. Strength.
Cofer, J. Anniversary.
DeFoe, M. Forgetting the Sixties.
Hamilton, I. Newscast, The.
Kasdorf. First TV in a Mennonite Family.
Komunyakaa. Hannoi Hanna.
Larsen, W. Learning the War.
Long, R. Conspiracy, The.
Major, C. Vietnam.
McDonald, W. After the Noise of Saigon.
Moore, L. Gifts.
Padel. Trial.
Palmer, M. Sun.
Seibles. Manic: A Conversation with Jimi Hendrix.
Stein, K. Night Shift, after Drinking Dinner, Container Corporation of America, 1972.
Wadsworth, W. Need for Attention, The.
Walden, G. Misguided Angels.
Wojahn. 'It's Only Rock and Roll but I Like It': The Fall of Saigon, 1975.
Assassination of Robert Goulet as Performed by Elvis Presley: Memphis, 1968, The.
Zarzyski. How Near Vietnam Came to Us.
See also **Vietnam; War**

Vikings
Feirstein. Rune-Maker, The.
Kipling, R. Dane-Geld.
Longfellow, H. Skeleton in Armor [*or* Armour], The.
Unknown. Battle of Maldon, The.

Village Idiots
Brown, S. It Took a Village.

Villages
Blamire. North Country Village, A.
Brown, S. It Took a Village.
Dove, R. Sightseeing.
Earle, J. Village.
Hood, T. Our Village—by a Villager.
Longfellow, H. Golden Mile-Stone, The.
Ropewalk, The.
Village Blacksmith, The.
Newson, D. Turnabouts.
Patchen. Village Tudda, The.
Peterson, R. Midwest Town.
Raworth. My Face Is My Own, I Thought.

Rhys, K. Interlude.
Smith, I. Listen.
Southerland. Two Fishing Villages.
Thomas, R. Village, The.
Tripp. Eglwys Newydd.
Yau. Radiant Silhouette V.
See also **Cities; Towns**

Villanelle (form)
Bishop, E. One Art.
Carruth, H. Saturday at the Border.
Davidson, J. Unknown, The.
Dowson. Villanelle of His Lady's Treasures.
Villanelle of Marguerites.
Empson. Missing Dates.
Villanelle: "It is the pain, it is the pain, endures."
Hugo, R. Freaks at Spurgin Road Field, The.
Osherow. Villanelle for the Middle of the Night.
Yau. Chinese Villanelle.

Villon, François; the Virgin
Berrigan, A. Sabotage.
Swinburne. Ballad of François Villon, A.

Violence
Acholonu. Other Forms of Slaughter.
Addonizio. Broken Sonnets.
Ai. Endangered Species.
Anyidoho. Elegy for the Revolution.
Apollinaire. Fete.
Armitage, S. Poem: "And if it snowed and snow covered the drive."
Ba. Justice is Done.
Balaban. April 30, 1975.
Baraka. Poem Some People Will Have to Understand, A.
Barrax. King: April 4, 1968.
Beaver. Drummer, The.
Berger, J. Gun, The.
Bobis, M. Driving to Katoomba.
Brass. Only Silly Faggots Know.
Brutus. Robben Island Sequence.
Cabico, R. Gameboy.
Cady. Starting 1973: What to Do Now that Peace Has Been Announced.
Campo. Asylum.
My Childhood in Another Part of the World.
Cassian. Like Gulliver.
Charara, H. My Father Breaks the Neighbor's Nose.
On the Murder of an Ice Cream Man.
Chavez, L. Woman Who Raised Dogs, The.
Cheney-Coker. Poet Among Those Who Are Also Poets.
Chin, J. Why a Boy.
Chipasula. Because the Wind Remembers.
Talking of Sharp Things.
Cleary, B. Sealink.
Clifton, L. 4/30/92 for rodney king.
Coleman, W. Brute Strength.
Craighead, L. Whole Truth So Help Me God— Also Known as the Gettin' Rid of Nigguz Business.
Crawley, W. Bud.
Davis, F. Sam Jackson.
Davis, O. Moorer Denies Holyfield in Twelve.
De Kok. Al Wat Kind Is.
Our Sharpeville.
Delgado, J. Flora's Plea to Mary.
Dharker. Name of god, The.
Dickey, R. Father.
Dipoko. Pain.
Doyle, S. Some Girls.
Drummond, W. Content and Resolute.
Ellis, T. Tapes.
Feirstein. Rune-Maker, The.
Glück, L. Edge, The.
González, R. Perla at the Mexican Border Assembly Line of Dolls.
Grandmaster Flash *and* the Furious Five. Message, The.
Gregg. Night Music.
Griffiths, S. Mines in Sepia Tint, The.
Hagedon, J. Song of Bullets, The.
Harter. Turtle Blessing.
Hattersley, G. New Mr Barnsley Something, The.

Remembering Dennis's Eyes.
Hayden, R. [American Journal].
Hecht, A. Third Avenue in Sunlight.
Hewitt, J. Postscript, 1984.
Hicok. Over Coffee.
Holden, J. Why We Bombed Haiphong.
Hongo. Legend, The.
Howe, F. What We Learned.
Hudgins. Around the Campfire.
Hughes, L. Bad Man.
Third Degree.
Ingram-Roberts, A. Poem 2 (for Duckie Simpson of Black Uhuru).
Jackson, B. Riot at Winchell's.
Joans. .38, The.
Johnson, L. Five Nights of Bleeding.
Jordan, J. Female and the Silence of a Man, The.
I Must Become a Menace to My Enemies.
Mid-Year Report: For Haruko.
Joseph, L. It's Not Me Shouting at No One.
Sand Nigger.
Kaufman, B. Geneology.
Keplinger, D. Inside: George Gaines at Graterford Prison, 1981.
Kinsella, J. Pig Melons.
Konie, G. In the Fist of Your Hatred.
Lear, E. Limerick: "There was an old man who screamed out."
Levertov. Triple Feature.
Lifshin. Crystal Night.
Lilley. Sewing Lesson, The.
Lim, S. Pantoun for Chinese Women.
Liu, T. Kindertotenlieder.
Poem.
Lorde. For the Record.
Mapanje. On Being Asked to Write a Poem for 1979.
Martínez, V. Human Universe, The.
Mayer, B. Sonnet: Kamikaze: "Dawn and night of fighting, lovers like actual wars."
McCarriston. Castle in Lynn, A.
To Judge Faolain, Dead Long Enough: A Summons.
McDaniel, J. Leonard.
McDonald, C. Asdrubral Jiménez.
McKay, C. To the White Fiends.
Monro. Street Fight.
Montagu, L. Epitaph: "Here lies John Hughes and Sarah Drew."
Moore, H. First Time: 1950.
Moore, R. Dirge for the Living.
Morgan, R. Battery.
Morley, D. Answers on a Postcard.
Moses, G. Black Banana House.
Mottram. Elegy 11: Ford.
Muske, C. Field Trip.
Nash, O. It Figures.
Nathan, L. Body Count.
Norris, L. Ballad of Billy Rose, The.
Olson, C. Anecdotes of the Late War.
Oppenheimer, J. Poem in Defense of Children.
Ortleb. Militerotics.
Peacock, M. Those Paperweights with Snow Inside.
Pratt, M. Waulking Song: Two.
Putnam. Words of an Old Woman.
Redmond. Love Necessitates.
Rich, A. 5:30 A.M.
For a Friend in Travail.
Rodgers, C. Slave Ritual.
Rose, R. What the Japanese Perhaps Heard.
Rouse. England Nil.
Spunk Talking.
Rukeyser, M. This Morning.
Seaton, M. Tagging.
Shapiro, K. Fly, The.
Sholl. Outside the Depot.
Sia, B. Claim to Fame.
Simon, L. Hattie Went to Market.
Spenser. Address to Venus.
Arthur's Fight with Orgoglio and Duessa.
Belphoebe and Timias.
Book 1.
Bower of Bliss, The.
Britomart at Isis' Church.

Britomart Chaseth Ollyphant.
Britomart in the House of the Enchanter Busyrane.
Cave of Despair, The.
Fight of the Red Cross Knight and the Heathen Sansjoy, The.
Garden of Adonis, The.
Gardin of Adonis, The.
Guardian Angels.
Guyon's Voyage to the Bower of Bliss.
Hill of the Graces, The.
House of Busyrane, The.
In the Bower of Bliss.
Legend of Britomartis, or of Chastitie, The.
Legend of the Knight of the Red Crosse, or of Holinesse, The.
Maske of Cupid, The.
Mutability Claims to Rule the World.
Nature's Reply to Mutability.
Scudamor in the Temple of Venus.
Song of Bliss.
Vision of the Graces, The.
Visit to Merlin, The.
Stanford, A. Beating, The.
Sundiata. Notes from the Defense of Colin Ferguson.
Swirszczynska. He Was Lucky.
Synge. Danny.
Szporluk. Duressor.
Libido.
Triage.
Torres, E. Vase of the Universe, The.
Unknown. Cats of Kilkenny, The.
Get Up and Bar the Door.
Stackolee.
Walker, M. Poppa Chicken.
Weaver, M. Beginnings.
Missing Patriarch, The.
Weigl. Last Lie, The.
Snowy Egret.
Whalen. International Date Line, Monday/ Monday 27: XI:67.
Wicks, S. Voice.
Wilbur. Tywater.
Williams, W. Mezzo Forte.
Wise, S. 50 Years in the Career of an Aspiring Thug.
Yamada. Club, The.
Young, K. Clyde Peeling's Reptiland in Allenwood, Pennsylvania.

Violets
Adair, T. Violets for Your Furs.
Bryant, W. Yellow Violet, The.
Cobbold, E. On Some Violets Planted in My Garden by a Friend.
Doolittle, H. Sea Violet.
Dunbar-Nelson. Sonnet: "I had no thought of violets of late."
Evance, S. To a Violet.
Herrick. How Violets Came Blue.
Meditation for His Mistress[e], A.
To Violets.
Rossetti, C. Autumn Violets.
Stanley, T. On a Violet in Her Breast.
Taylor, J. Violet, The.

Violins
Dryden, J. Song for St Cecilia's Day, 1687, A.
Ford, C. Bad Habit, The.
Hart, J. Only Applebaum Can Make a Tree.
Plumly. Out-of-the-Body Travel.
Welch, M. Touch of the Master's Hand, The.

Virgil [or Vergil]
Creeley. Heroes.
Tennyson, A. To Virgil [or Vergil].

Virgin Islands
Brinnin. Skin Diving in the Virgins.
Walcott. Virgins, The.

Virgin Mary
Delgado, J. Flora's Plea to Mary.
Elliott, E. Three Marys at Castle Howard, in 1812 and 1837, The.
Hemans. Mary at the Feet of Christ.
Memorial of Mary, The.
Hill, G. Vergine bella.
Howard, R. Vocational Guidance, with Special

Reference to the Annunciation of Simone Martini.
Jennings, E. Annuciation, The.
Rossetti, D. Virgin and Child, by Hans Memmeling; in the Academy of Bruges, A.
Unknown. Child this Day is Born, A.
Lo, How a Rose E'er Blooming.
Nowell Sing We.
Williams, W. Adoration of the Kings, The.
See also **Mary, the Virgin**

Virginia (state)
Bland, J. Carry Me Back to Old Virginny.
Brown, S. Virginia Portrait.
Drayton. To the Virginian Voyage.
Eady. Sherbet.
Frost, R. Gift Outright, The.
Merwin, W. S. Low Fields and Light.
Randall, J. To William Wordsworth from Virginia.
Smith, D. On a Field Trip at Fredericksburg.
Weigl. Snowy Egret.
Whitman, W. As Toilsome I Wander'd Virginia's Woods.
Whittier. Farewell, The: "Gone, gone,—sold and gone."

Virginity and Virgins
Beaumont, J. Whiteness, or Chastity.
Blake, W. Desire and Jealousy.
Merlins Prophecy.
Visions of the Daughters of Albion.
Carew, T. Maria Wentworth.
Cockburn, C. Caution, The.
Cowley, A. Dialogue after Enjoyment.
Honour.
Donne. Flea, The.
Dryden, J. Song: "SYLVIA the fair, in the bloom of fifteen."
Egerton, S. Repulse to Alcander, The.
"Ephelia." Maidenhead.
Ewart. To the Virgins, to Make the Most of Time.
Goodison. Wedding in Hanover.
Greene, C. Something Old, Something New.
Hernández Cruz. Milagrosa, La.
Herrick. Dirge of Jephthah's Daughter, The.
To a Bed of Tulips.
To the Virgins, to Make Much of Time.
To Violets.
To Virgins.
Why Flowers Change Color.
Jackson, L. Virgin, The.
Justice, D. In Bertram's Garden.
Killigrew, A. On a Picture Painted by Herself [or Her self], Representing Two Nymphs [or Nimphs] of Diana's, One in a Posture to Hunt, the other Bath[e]ing.
Lima, J. Poem of any Virgin.
Lluellyn [or Lluelyn]. Epithalamium: To Mistress M. A.
MacDiarmid, H. O Wha's the Bride?
Montagu, L. Lover, The; a Ballad.
Philips, K. Answer to Another Persuading a Lady to Marriage, An.
Prior. True Maid, A.
Ransom, J. Her Eyes.
Rutter, J. Epithalamium: "Hymen, god of marriage bed."
Shapiro, K. First Time, The.
Smart, C. Song: "Where shall Celia fly for shelter."
Taylor, J. Virgo, August.
Tayson, R. First Sex.
Thomas, D. On the Marriage of a Virgin.
Unknown. Twa Magicians, The.
Whistle, Daughter, Whistle.
Whitehead, C. Marian Hymn.

Virtue
Aldrich, T. Fannie.
Behn, A. Angellica's Lament.
Campion, T. Man of Life Upright, The.
Carew, T. Divine Mistress, A.
In Praise of His Mistress.
Ingrateful[l] Beauty Threatened.
To My Rival.
Carter, E. Ode to Wisdom.
Chaucer. Complaint unto Pity, The.

Lak of Stedfastnesse.
Donne. Undertaking, The.
Drayton. To My Noble Friend Master William Browne: Of the Evil Time.
Egerton, S. Repulse to Alcander, The.
Gershwin. Oh, Lady, Be Good!
Gilman, C. Christian Virtues.
Gilonis, H. Answer to Herrick, An.
Herbert, G. Virtue [or Vertue].
Herrick. King and No King, A.
Hunt, L. Abou Ben Adhem.
Jacob, M. Rooster and the Pearl, The.
Jonson, B. Elegy, An: "Though beauty be the mark of praise."
Epitaph on Elizabeth, L. H.
Epode: "Not to know vice at all, and keep[e] true state."
Ode. To Sir William Sydney, on His Birthday.
To Sir Henry Cary.
Kern, J. It's a Hard, Hard World for a Man.
Lamb, C. To Dora W[ordsworth].
Landor, W. Rose Aylmer.
Locke, M. Sonnet: " 'Tis dead of night; storms rend the troubled air."
Moore, M. Blessed Is the Man.
To a Snail.
Pembroke, M. To the Thrice-Sacred Queen Elizabeth.
Puttenham. Her Majestie resembled to the crowned piller. Ye must read upward.
Rowe, E. To Celinda.
Smith, S. Exeat.
Swift, J. To the Earl of Oxford, Late Lord Treasurer.
Thoreau. Rumors from an Aeolian Harp.
Wodehouse, P. It's a Hard, Hard World for a Man.
Wotton, S. Upon the Sudden Restraint of the Earl[e] of Somerset, Then Falling from Favor [or Favour].

Viruses
Ferguson, G. In Hospital-land.
Reed, I. I am not the walrus.

Vishnu
Lewis, A. Karanje Village.
Sama, B. Song, The.

Vision
Bitar. Happy Hour.
Bond, E. How We See.
Brush. Again.
Bui-Burton. Look at Me.
Byron, G. Love and Death.
Carew, T. On Sight of a Gentlewoman's Face in the Water.
Cassells. Marathon.
Ceravolo. Geological Hymn.
Chubb, R. Transfiguration.
Clifton, L. 11/10 Again.
Copus, J. Art of Interpretation, The.
Crane, H. Wine Menagerie, The.
Davie. Hill Field, The.
Dunn, D. Sundial, The.
Edson, R. Optical Prodigal, The.
Frost, R. Neither Out Far Nor In Deep.
Gascoyne. Cubical Domes, The.
End Is Near the Beginning, The.
Salvador Dali.
Hall, D. Apples.
Hannon. Beyond Freedom.
Hartley, M. What Have We All—a Soliloquy of Essences.
Heaney, S. His Dawn Vision.
Hecht, A. Hill, A.
Henry, B. Discovery.
Hirsch, E. Man on a Fire Escape.
Ingalls, J. Vision of St. Michael and St. John, The.
Jarrell. Orient Express, The.
Keble. Malvern at a Distance.
Kendrick, D. Note to the Ophthalmologist.
Lauterbach. Mimetic.
Levertov. Uncertain Oneiromancy.
Loftis, N. Delirium.
Longfellow, H. Galaxy, The.
Lowell, R. For Sheridan.
MacCaig. Instrument and Agent.

Marshall, J. Still.
Merrill, J. Octopus, The.
Morley, D. Exact Fares.
Myles, E. Eileen's Vision.
Nemerov. I Only Am Escaped Alone to Tell Thee.
Nicholson, N. From a Boat at Coniston.
Obejas, A. Public Place (After Olga Broumas), The.
Ortiz. Vision Shadows.
Palmer, M. Project of Linear Inquiry, The.
Robinson, M. Visions Appear to her in a Dream.
Rossetti, C. Who Has Seen the Wind?
Ryan, T. Eclipse, Kenwick, 1974.
Trompe l'oeil.
Salter. Half a Double Sonnet.
Saxe, J. Blind Men and the Elephant, The.
Shapiro, K. Dome of Sunday, The [or A].
Spender, S. To T.A.R.H.
Stanton, M. Ballad of the Magic Glasses.
Thomas, E. Some Eyes Condemn.
Towle. Painting the Eaves.
Van Duyn. Vision Test, The.
Walcott. Hotel Normandie Pool, The.

Visiting and Visitors
Ammons, A. R. Visit.
Becker, C. Door-Bell, The.
Beerbohm, M. Chorus of a Song That Might Have Been Written by Albert Chevalier.
Bishop, E. Faustina, or Rock Roses.
Child, L. Thanksgiving Day.
De la Mare. Some One.
Delgado, J. Visiting Father.
Garioch. Heard in the Cougate.
Hamilton, I. Visit, The.
Herrick. Night-Piece, to Julia, The.
Panegyric to Sir Lewis Pemberton, A.
Hughes, L. Visitors to the Black Belt.
Jacinto, J. Visitation.
Kelly, B. Visitation, The.
Leapor. Visit, The.
Levertov. Poet and Person.
McGrath, T. Probable Cause.
Metcalfe. Visit the Sick.
Mother Goose. Nut Tree, A.
Murry, A. Tête à Tête; or, Fashionable Pair: an Eclogue, The.
O'Hara, F. Poem: "Eager note on my door said 'Call me'," The."
Parnell, T. On Riding to See Dean Swift in the Mist of the Morning.
Rossetti, C. Echo.
Enrica, 1865.
Snodgrass, W. Vuillard: "The Mother and Sister of the Artist."
Young, A. One West Coast.
Yuson. World Poetry Circuit.

Vogler, Georg Joseph
Browning, R. Abt Vogler.

Voices
Bogan, L. Song for the Last Act.
Browning, R. Meeting At Night.
Campo. My Voice.
Castillo, S. Letter to Yeni on Peering into Her Life.
Cooper, W. Leaving the Country.
Creeley. Messengers, The.
Dauenhauer. Voices.
Finch, A. Dickinson.
García, D. Serpentine Voices.
Griffiths, J. Lost and Found.
Hall, D. White Apples.
Hart, L. Johnny One-Note.
Herrick. Upon Her Voice.
Upon Julia's Voice.
Hovanessian, D. Inside Green Eyes, Black Eyes.
Hutchison, J. Joni Mitchell.
Johnson, J. Lift Every [or Ev'ry] Voice and Sing.
Kinnell. Lastness.
Komunyakaa. Twilight Seduction.
Lorde. Echoes.
Lovelace, R. To a Lady That Desired Me I Would Bear My Part with Her in a Song.

Meynell, A. To the Beloved.
Miller, J. Topos.
Naden. Sister of Mercy, The.
Rankine. Elsewhere, Things Tend.
Sanchez, S. Haiku: "Your voice unwrapping."
This is Not a Small Voice.
Sansom, A. Voice.
Schubert, D. Successful Summer, A.
Scott, D. More Poem.
Sergeant. Man Meeting Himself.
Shelley, P. To————: "Music, when soft voices die."
Smith, S. Singing Cat, The.
Sobin, G. What the Music Wants.
Southerland. Recitation.
Stanton, M. In Ignorant Cadence.
Stephen, J. Sonnet, A: "Two voices are there: one is of the deep."
Tennyson, A. Break, Break, Break.
Unknown. Tone of Voice, The.
Unknown, fr. Terezin Concentration Camp. Birdsong 2.
Warren, R. What Voice at Moth-Hour.
Wicks, S. Voice.
Wordsworth, W. Thought[s] of a Briton on the Subjugation of Switzerland.
Wright, J. Speak.
To the Poets in New York.
Yeats. Everlasting Voices, The.
See also **Screams; Speech; Talk**

Volcanoes
Bishop, E. Crusoe in England.
d'Oettingen. Kilimanjaro.
Day Lewis. Poem for an Anniversary.
Dickinson, E. Volcanoes be in Sicily.
Hemans. Image in Lava, The.
Hongo. Eruption: Pu'u Ō ' ō.
Hongo Store 29 Miles Volcano Hilo, Hawaii, The.
Lowry, M. Volcano is Dark, The.
Nye, N. Negotiations with a Volcano.
Ray, H. Listening Nydia.
Rose. Loo-wit.
Scupham. Pompeii: Plaster Casts.
Sears, P. Volcanic Ash.
Snyder, G. Burning Island.
Turner, W. Romance.
Van Sertima. Volcano.
Walcott.

Voltaire, François Marie Arouet de
Blake, W. Mock On, Mock On, Voltaire, Rousseau.

Voodoo
D'Aguiar. Obeah Mama Dot.
Waniek. Women's Locker Room.

Voting and Voters
Balakian, P. End of the Reagan Era, The.
Chudleigh. To the Ladies.
"Coolidge." My Rights.
Gilman, C. Anti-Suffragists, The.
Harper, F. Deliverance.
Lindsay, N. Bryan, Bryan, Bryan, Bryan.
Why I Voted the Socialist Ticket.
Moorer. Negro Ballot, The.
Nathan, L. Election, The.
Smith, P. Woman Who Died in Line, The.
Unknown. Vote for Lunn.
Zamora-Linmark. Election Day.
See also **Campaigns, Political; Woman Suffrage**

Voyages
Alexander, P. Well-Known Elizabethan Double Entendre, A.
Crane, H. Voyages.
De la Mare. Galliass, The.
Drayton. To the Virginian Voyage.
Emerson, R. Thine Eyes Still Shined.
Ferry. Cythera.
Embarkation for Cythera, The.
Gould, A. Ice.
Herrick. Plaudite, or End of Life, The.
Jackson, H. My Lighthouses.
Larkin, P. North Ship, The.
Moore, P. Personal Atlas.
Murphy, R. Pat Cloherty's Version of The Maisie.

Sexton. Crossing the Atlantic.
Spender, S. Marston.
Stevenson, R. Christmas at Sea.
Walcott. Adios, Carenage.
  Schooner Flight, The.
Whittier. Godspeed.

Voyageurs
Moore, T. Canadian Boat Song, A.

Voyeurism and Voyeurs
Dove, R. Small Town.
Eady. View from the Roof, Waverly Place.
Heath, R. Seeing Her Dancing.
Henry, B. Skin.
Holloway, G. Lovers, The.
Lawrence, D. Gloire de Dijon.
Moolten, D. Voyeur.
Shapiro, K. Dome of Sunday, The [or A].
Waller, E. Song: "Go[e], lovely rose."

Vuillard, Edouard
Snodgrass, W. Vuillard: "The Mother and Sister of the Artist."

Vulcan
Auden. Shield of Achilles, The.
Herrick. To Vulcan.
Jonson, B. Execration upon Vulcan, An.
Russell, T. Sonnet: Suppos'd to Be Written at Lemnos.

Vulnerability
Ash, J. Poor Boy: Portrait of a Painting.
Green, B. That's My Weakness Now.
Hayes, T. Goliath Poem.
Huxley, A. Armour.
Peacock, M. How I Come to You.
Ransom, J. Winter Remembered.
Rich, A. Storm Warnings.
Shapiro, K. First Time, The.

Vultures
Atwood. Vultures.
Belloc. Vulture, The.
Bottoms. Under the Vulture-Tree.
Jeffers, R. Vulture.
Kennedy, X. Vulture.
Muir, E. Mythical Journey, The.
Page, G. Elegist, The.
Sterling, G. Black Vulture, The.
Wilbur. Still, Citizen Sparrow.
See also **Buzzards**

W

Wagner, Richard
Brooke, R. Wagner.
Duncan, R. Structure of Rime XVIII.
Levy, N. Tannhauser.

Wagon Trains
Guest, B. Santa Fe Trail.
See also **Prairie Schooners**

Wagtails
Clare, J. Little Trotty Wagtail.

Wailing Wall, The
Mathews, A. At the Wailing Wall.

Waiters and Waitresses
Clarke, M. Wail of the Waiter, The.
Crosby, R. Waitresses.
Cullen, C. Atlantic City Waiter.
Dugan, A. To a Red-headed Do-good Waitress.
Eady. Sherbet.
Gardinier. At Work.
Hull, L. Night Waitress.
Johnson, M. All-Night Diner, The.
Jones, R. On the Bearing of Waitresses.
McCord, D. Epitaph on a Waiter.
Oates. Waiting on Elvis, 1956.
Shinder. Waitress.
Stone, J. Rosemary.
Veinberg, J. To an Exeter City Cocktail Waitress.
Waring, B. Tip, The.

Waiting Rooms
Bishop, E. In the Waiting Room.
Dove, R. Vacation.
Mahon. Image from Beckett, An.
Sellers, B. In the Counselor's Waiting Room.

Terranova. Self-Examination.

Wakes
Unknown. Finnegan's Wake.
  Willie's Lyke-Wake.

Waking
Alarcon, F. Morning Sun.
Atwood. Up.
Bly, R. Awakening.
  Poem in Three Parts.
  Waking from Sleep.
Donne. Good-Morrow, The.
Duncan, R. Song of the Borderguard, The.
"Field." Love rises up some days'
Gascoigne. Gascoigne's Good-Morrow.
Higginson, E. Dawn.
Ingelow. Winding-up Time.
Keats. Bright Star.
Lawrence, D. Quite Forsaken.
Lee, L. Early in the Morning.
Lowell, R. Waking Early Sunday Morning.
Mackey, N. Phantom Light of All Our Day, The.
Merwin, W. S. Rain Travel.
Meynell, A. Study, A.
Morales, A. Puertoricanness.
Pinsky. First Early Mornings Together.
Reed, H. Door and the Window, The.
Roethke. Waking, The.
Simic. Poem: "Every morning I forget how it is."
Steele, T. Joseph.
Thaxter. Chanticleer.
Torres, E. Elbow in Dumberland, An.
Unknown. Get Up, Get Up.
Wilbur. Love Calls Us to the Things of This World.
Williams, W. Spring and All.
Wyatt, S. Lover Showeth How He Is Forsaken of Such as He Sometime Enjoyed, the.
Zisquit. After Years of Feasting and No Sacrifice.

Walden Pond, Massachusetts
Channing. Walden.

Waldenses
Zimmer. Day Zimmer Lost Religion, The.

Wales
Adams, S. Hill Fort, Caerleon.
Aspden, B. News of the Changes.
Bidgood. Dragon.
Camlan. Education in Wales.
Clarke, G. Taid's Grave.
Davies, D. Carmarthenshire.
Davies, I. Angry Summer, The.
  Hywel and Blodwen.
Davies, W. Days That Have Been.
Dyment. Derbyshire Born, Monmouth Is My Home.
Finch, P. Welsh Wordscape, A.
Garlick, R. Dylan Thomas at Tenby.
Ginsberg, A. Wales Visitation.
Graves, R. Welsh Incident.
Gruffydd, P. Slate Quay: Felinheli.
Guest, H. Wales Re-visited.
Homfray. Thoughts on Happiness.
Humphries, R. Dafydd ap Gwilym Resents the Winter.
  For My Ancestors.
Jones, G. Morning.
Jones, J. Glyndwr's War Song.
Jones, T. Cwmchwefri.
Lewis, E. We Who Were Born.
Llewellyn-Williams. Two Rivers.
Mathias, R. Brechfa Chapel.
  Porth Cwyfan.
  Sir Gelli to R.S.
Morgan, J. My Welsh Home.
Morgan, R. Shadow Valley.
Philips, K. On the Welsh Language.
Phillips, D. Maridunum.
Rhys, K. Interlude.
Thomas, D. Author's Prologue.
  Fern Hill.
Thomas, R. Ancients of the World, The.
  Line from St. David's, A.
  Reservoirs.

Welsh Hill Country, The.
Welsh History.
Welsh Landscape.
Thrale [*later* Mrs. Piozzi]. Winter in Wales, A.
Tripp. Capital.
  Diesel to Yesterday.
  Welcome to Wales.
Vaughan-Thomas. Hiraeth in N.W.3.
Ward, J. Unusual View of the Town.
Watkins, V. Peace in the Welsh Hills.
Watkyns. Golden Grove, Carmarthen.
Webb, H. Cywydd o Fawl.
  Epil y Filiast.
  Nightingales, The.
  Stone Face, The.
Williams, H. To Dr. Moore, in Anser to a Poetical Epistle Written by Him in Wales.
See also **Welsh, The**

Walking and Walkers
Ahlert, F. Walkin' My Baby Back Home.
Ammons, A. R. Corsons Inlet.
Arlen, H. Let's Take a Walk Around the Block.
Auden. As I Walked Out One Evening.
Barnes, D. Walking-Mort, The.
Barnes, W. Turnstile, The.
Beckett, S. Enueg I.
Berlin. Couple of Swells, A.
Bethune, L. Harlem Freeze Frame.
Brown, L. Winter Sonnet.
Bryant, W. To a Waterfowl.
Buckley, C. Playing for Time.
Byron, G. She Walks In Beauty.
Cahn, S. I'll Walk Alone.
Carver, R. Walk, A.
Clare, J. To Mary: 'It Is the Evening Hour'
Cofer, J. Learning to Walk Alone.
Coleman, C. I Walk a Little Faster.
Coleridge, M. Witch, The.
Cornish, S. Generations 2.
Crane, H. In Shadow.
Creeley. Place.
  Somebody Died.
Dixon, M. Would You Like to Take a Walk?
Fields, D. On the Sunny Side of the Street.
Frost, R. Acquainted with the Night.
  Meeting and Passing.
Furber, D. Lambeth Walk.
Gehrke, S. Walking Fields at Night South of Hampton, Iowa.
Gillan. In Memory We Are Walking.
Gilsdorf, E. Walk, The.
Giovannitti. Walker, The.
Graves, R. Legs, The.
Gurney, I. If I Walked Straight Slap.
Hamlish, M. One.
Hammerstein. You'll Never Walk Alone.
Hardy, T. Walk, The.
Herford. Limerick.
Hill, M. Abomination.
Hollander, J. Effet de Neige.
Jordan, J. Poem about My Rights.
Katrovas. Sky.
Kavanagh, P. Come Dance with Kitty Stobling.
Kleban, E. One.
Knight, E. Green Grass and Yellow Balloons.
Layton. Cold Green Element, The.
Levy, A. March Day in London, A.
  To Vernon Lee.
Loesser. I Don't Want to Walk Without You.
Mangan, J. O'Hussey's Ode to the Maguire.
McGrath, C. Spring Comes to Chicago.
Miller, V. How Far?
Montague, J. 11 rue Daguerre.
Mora. Tall Walking Woman.
Nelson, M. Molino.
Nesbit, E. Vies Manquées.
Nezval. Trap Door.
O'Brien, J. Revelation on a Summer Walk.
Osgood, F. Ellen Learning to Walk.
Plumpp. Poem.
Robinson, A. Tuscan Olives.
  Venetian Nocturne.
Sanchez, S. To Anita.
Scammell, W. Walk, The.
Sexton. Noon Walk on the Asylum Lawn.
Stafford, W. Walking West.

Strand. Keeping Things Whole.
Thomas, E. Sun Used to Shine, The.
Unknown. Walk Together Children.
Wakoski. Hummingbird Light.
Warren, R. Night Walking.
Watson, M. Stepping Out.
Wells, L. Prelude: "Track is my companion, The."
Whitman, W. Dalliance of the Eagles, The.
Whittier. Forgiveness.
Williams, W. Poem: "As the cat."
Wordsworth, W. I Wandered Lonely As a Cloud.
　Stepping Westward.
Wright, C. Legend of Hell, The.
Wright, D. Those Walks We Took.
Wright, F. Joseph Come Back as the Dusk.
Wylie. Velvet Shoes.
Zukofsky, L. I Walk in the Old Street.

Wall Street, New York City
Hernández Cruz. Side 26.
Rukeyser, M. Paper Anniversary.

Wallace, Sir William
Burns, R. Scots Wha Hae.
Unknown. Gude Wallace.

Walls
Bynner. Wall, The.
Coleridge, M. Gone.
　Impromptu.
Eigner. Wholes.
Frost, R. Mending Wall.
Goetsch, D. Walls, The.
Kaufman, S. Emperor of China, The.
Kees. Conversation in the Drawing Room, The.
Kendrick, D. We are the Writing on the Wall.
Kinzie. Ringing Words.
Pau-Llosa. Paredón.
Plumpp. Another Mule.
Robinson, A. Personality.
Simic. Wall, A.
Spellman. Twist, The.
Tennyson, A. Flower in the Crannied Wall.
Tsaloumas. Old Friend.
Unknown. Bridge instead of a Wall, A.
　Wide Walls.
Wilbur. Caserta Garden.
Williams, W. On Gay Wallpaper.
Wilson, S. Picture on the Purple Wall, The.
See also Fences

Walnut Trees and Walnuts
Jastrzebska. Cracking Walnuts.
Oliver, D. Walnut and Lily.
Oliver, M. Black Walnut Tree, The.

Walpole, Robert, 1st Earl of Orford
Swift, J. Character of Sir Robert Walpole, The.

Walruses
Corn. Walrus Tusk from Alaska, A.
Herford. Smile of the Walrus, The.

Walton, Izaak
Cotton, C. To My Dear and Most Worthy Friend, Mr. Isaac Walton.

Waltzes and Waltzing
Haug. Tennessee Waltz, The.
Leland, C. Hans Breitmann's Party [*or* Barty].
Levy, A. First Extra, The.
Roethke. My Papa's Waltz.
Stevens, W. Sad Strains of a Gay Waltz.
Wilde, O. Harlot's House, The.
Wright, S. Out of the Wailing.

Wanderlust
Auden. Wanderer, The.
Baraka. Legacy.
Brown, S. Long Gone.
Burke, J. My Heart Is a Hobo.
Carman, B. Vagabond Song, A.
Hovey. Sea Gypsy, The.
Kipling, R. Sestina of the Tramp-Royal.
Larkin, P. Poetry of Departures.
Masefield. Sea Fever.
Riddell, E. Wakeful in the Township.
Roethke. My Papa's Waltz.
Smith, S. Lightly Bound.
　Wanderer, The.
Stickney, T. Age in Youth.
Tennyson, A. Ulysses.

Van Heusen, J. My Heart Is a Hobo.
Wells, L. Prelude: "Track is my companion, The."
Williams, W. Paterson—the Strike.

War
Acam-Oturu. Agony . . . A Resurrection, An.
Acholonu. Harvest of War.
Ai. I Can't Get Started.
Aldrich, T. Memory.
Alkalay-Gut. Life Goes On.
Allen, J. War Poem, A.
Allen, R. See! How the Nations Rage Together.
Amis, K. Last War, The.
Anderson, M. Spitting in the Leaves.
Angira. Newscast.
Apollinaire. Fete.
Appleman, P. Peace with Honor.
Arnold, M. Dover Beach.
　Last Word, The.
Ashbery. Rivers and Mountains.
Auden. Taller To-day.
Awoonor. Song of War.
　Songs of Sorrow.
Aytoun, W. Sonnet to Britain.
Balaban. Dragonfish, The.
　For Mrs. Cam, Whose Name Means "Printed Silk."
　News Update.
　Than, Mau.
　Thoughts Before Dawn.
　Words for My Daughter.
Baraka, R. After-Word.
Barbauld. On the Expected General Rising of the French Nation.
Barker, G. Song: "Now this bloody war is over."
　Sonnet to My Mother.
Barks. Becoming Milton.
Barlow, J. Advice to a Raven in Russia [December, 1812].
Barry, J. Floating Petals.
　Green Hell, Green Death.
Barth, R. Insert, The.
　Letter from An Hoc (4), by a Seedbed.
　P.O.W.s.
　Postscript.
Bayliss. Reported Missing.
Beers, E. All Quiet along the Potomac Tonight.
Benét, S. 1935.
Bergman, A. Chronicler, The.
Berlin. This Is the Army, Mr. Jones.
Berryman. Moon and the Night and the Men, The.
Betjeman. Invasion Exercise on the Poultry Farm.
Bishop, J. In the Dordogne.
Black, S. To a War Correspondent.
Blunden. 1916 Seen from 1921.
　Preparations for Victory.
　Report on Experience.
Bly, R. At a March against the Vietnam War.
　Counting Small-Boned Bodies.
　Teeth Mother Naked at Last, The.
　To President Bush at the Start of the Gulf War.
Bobrowsky. Free Fire Zone.
Bond, E. First World War Poets.
Bowers, E. Stoic: for Laura von Courten, The.
Brecht, B. From a German War Primer.
　War Has Been Given a Bad Name.
Brooks, G. White Troops Had Their Orders but the Negroes Looked Like Men.
Brown, E. Eating the Forest.
　I Was Dancing Alone in Binh Dinh Province.
　Patrols.
　Returning Fire.
Brownstein. War.
Bruner. Midwinter.
Brush. Again.
Brutus. There Was a Time When the Only Worth.
Bryant, W. Conjunction of Jupiter and Venus, The.
Buchanan, G. War-and-Peace.
Burns, R. Scots Wha Hae.
　Silver Tassie, The.
Byron, G. By the Rivers of Babylon We Sat

Down and Wept.
　Song of Saul before His Last Battle.
Campbell, T. Hohenlinden.
Carbó, N. When the Grain Is Golden and the Wind Is Chilly, Then It Is the Time to Harvest.
Carruth, H. On Being Asked to Write a Poem Against the War in Vietnam.
　Paragraph 36.
Carson, C. Cocktails.
　Hamlet.
　Mouth, The.
Carter, R. Vietnam Dream.
Carver, D. Poet, The.
Causley. Armistice Day.
　Song of the Dying Gunner A.A.1.
Cervantes. Poem for the Young White Man Who Asked Me How I, An Intelligent, Well-Read Person Could Believe in the War Between Races.
Chipasula. Tramp.
Chippewa Oral Tradition. Sioux Woman Defends Her Children, The.
　Sioux Women Gather Up Their Wounded, The.
　Song of the Captive Sioux Woman.
Clark Bekederimo. Casualties, The.
　Epilogue to Casualties.
Clarke, T. Poem for Babies Unborn.
Cleveland, J. Rebel Scot, The.
Clifton, L. Death of Crazy Horse, The.
Coleman, H. Downed Black Pilot Learns How to Fly, A.
　In Ca Mau.
Coleridge, S. Fire, Famine, and Slaughter.
Comfort, A. Letter to an American Visitor.
Cortez, J. Rape.
Couzyn. World War II.
Crane, S. Candid Man, The.
　Do Not Weep Maiden, for War Is Kind.
　Little Ink More Or Less!, A.
　Man Said to the Universe, A.
　Newspaper, A.
　Slant of Sun [on Dull Brown Walls], A.
　There Was a Crimson Clash of War.
　There Was a Man with a Tongue of Wood.
　Wayfarer, The.
Cross, Jr. Gliding Baskets.
Cummings, E. I Sing of Olaf Glad and Big.
　Next to of Course God America I.
Cunningham, J. Hame, Hame, Hame.
Curnow. Pacific 1945-1995.
Currey. Burial Flags.
　Unseen Fire.
D'Aguiar. Sound Bite.
Davidson, J. Battle.
Dawe, G. Question of Covenants, A.
Day Lewis. Where Are the War Poets?
Day, J. North Sea.
De la Mare. Motley.
Deane, S. History Lessons.
Denning. Fire Support Burk.
　Movie, The.
　This Time.
Douglas, K. Aristocrats.
　Enfidaville.
　Gallantry.
　How to Kill.
　Offensive, The.
　Vergissmeinicht.
Dove, R. Alfonzo Prepares to Go Over the Top.
Doyle, S. Some Girls.
Dugan, A. On an East Wind from the Wars.
Dunbar-Nelson. I Sit and Sew.
Eberhart, R. Fury of Aerial Bombardment, The.
Ehrhart. Guerrilla War.
　Invasion of Grenada, The.
　Relative Thing, A.
Elliot, J. Flowers of the Forest, The.
Elliott, E. War.
Elmusa. In the Refugee Camp.
Empson. Just a Smack at Auden.
Evans, G. Eye Blade.
　Revelation in the Mother Lode.
Fenton, J. Cambodia.
　Dead Soldiers.
　In a Notebook.
　Wind.

Fiacc. Enemy Encounter.
Intimate Letter 1973.
Soldiers.
Figueroa, J. Homemade Smiles.
Taino.
Floyd. Private First Class Brooks Morgenstein, U. S. M. C.
Ford, F. What the Orderly Dog Saw.
Fosdick, H. Prince of Peace His Banner Spreads, The.
Frank, F. Jewish Conscript, The.
Frankau. Gun Teams.
Fraser, G. Christmas Letter Home.
Lament: "In a dismal air; a light of breaking summer."
Fuller, R. Autumn 1942.
During a Bombardmant by V-Weapons.
In Africa.
Spring 1942.
Garlick, R. Heiress, The.
Gascoyne. De Profundis.
Snow in Europe.
Uncertain Battle, The.
George, P. Battle Won Is Lost.
Gibson, W. Breakfast.
In the Ambulance.
Gifford, H. For Soldiers.
Glaser, I. Last Good War—and Afterward, The.
Gloria. Milkfish.
Golding, L. Women at the Corners Stand, The.
Graham, M. After the War; When Coltrane Only Wanted to Play Dance Tunes.
Graham, W. What's the News?
Graves, R. All Except Hannibal.
Corporal Stare.
Escape.
It's a Queer Time.
Recalling War.
Spoils.
Gray, T. Death of Hoel, The.
Greene, C. Excuse, The.
Grenfell, J. Into Battle.
Grennan. Soul Music: The Derry Air.
Griffin, S. Song My.
Guest, B. Otranto.
Guiney. Atoning Yesterday, The.
Gurney, I. Behind the Line.
First Time In.
Mangel-Bury, The.
Strange Hells.
War Books.
Gwynn, R. Body Bags.
Hall, D. Sister on the Tracks, A.
Hamod, S. Libyan/Egyptian Acrobats/Israeli Air Circus.
Hardy, T. Channel Firing.
In Time of "The Breaking of Nations."
Man He Killed, The.
Often When Warring.
Harper, M. Guerrilla-Cong, The.
Harry, J. Shot of War, A.
Hassett. Armed Forces Day.
Mother's Day.
Hawthorne, N. I Left My Low amd Humble Home.
Hay, G. Bizerta.
Hayden, R. Monet's "Waterlilies."
Hazo. Battle News.
Pittsburgh in Passing.
Some Words for President Wilson.
Toys, The.
World that Lightning Makes, The.
Heóghusa. On Maguire's Winter Campaign.
Winter Campaign, A.
Heaney, S. His Dawn Vision.
Hecht, A. Dover Bitch, The.
Still Life.
Henderson, H. End of a Campaign.
Opening of an Offensive.
Herbert, J. Dossers at the Imperial War Museum.
Hernández, M. War.
Heyen. For Hermann Heyen.
Hinsey, E. Approach of War, The.
Hogan, L. Skin.
Hollenbeck. Anorexia.

Holloway, G. Ford Castle: The Borders.
Housman, A. Deserter, The.
Howe, J. Battle Hymn [or Battle-Hymn] of the Republic, The.
Howell, C. Reminder to the Current President, A.
Hughes, L. Without Benefit of Declaration.
Hughes, T. Thistles.
Hulme, T. Trenches: St Eloi.
"Hyde." Deserted Village, The.
Ingalls, J. Gun Emplacement: Sundown.
James, A. Honor (1969).
Jarmain. These Poems.
Jarrell. Come to the Stone.
Eighth Air Force.
Lullaby, A: "For wars his life and half a world away."
Pilot from the Carrier, A.
Sick Nought, The.
War, A.
Jeffers, R. Antrim.
Eagle Valor, Chicken Mind.
Eye, The.
Rearmament.
Johnson, J. Color Sergeant, The.
Johnson, L. Five Nights of Bleeding.
Jonas, G. Portrait: The Freedom Fighter.
Jones, J. Glyndwr's War Song.
Jordan, J. Mid-Year Report: For Haruko.
Kandel. First They Slaughtered the Angels.
Kaufman, S. Emperor of China, The.
Kayo. War.
Kelly, B. To the Lost Child.
Kennedy, B. Bad Luck to This Marching.
Kennedy, X. Joshua.
Kenney. Battle of Valcour Island, The.
Keyes, S. Europe's Prisoners.
War Poet.
Killigrew, A. Alexandreis.
Kinnell. Dead Shall Be Raised Incorruptible, The.
Vapor Trail Reflected in the Frog Pond.
Kipling, R. Boots.
Dane-Geld.
Ford o' Kabul River.
Fuzzy-Wuzzy.
Gunga Din.
Hymn before Action.
Storm Cone, The.
Kirstein. P.O.E.
Kizer, C. On a Line from Valéry.
Klein, M. Letters from the Front.
Knott. Two Vietnam Poems: (1966).
Koch, K. To World War Two.
Komunyakaa. Dead at Quang Tri, The.
Starlight Scope Myopia.
Krige. Taking of the Koppie, The.
Kunitz, S. Last Picnic, The.
Landor, W. To Arthur de Noé Walker.
Langland, J. War.
Larkin, P. MCMXIV.
Homage to a Government.
Lawrence, D. Bombardment.
Song of a Man Who Has Come Through.
Lee, L. Moment of War, A.
Levertov. Advent 1966.
Christmas 1944.
In Thai Binh (Peace) Province.
Life at War.
Tenebrae.
Levine, P. And the Trains Go On.
Baby Villon.
Death of Saul, The.
Heaven.
Lewis, A. All Day It Has Rained.
Autumn, 1939.
Christmas Holiday.
Easter at Christmas.
Goodbye.
Peasants, The.
Raiders' Dawn.
Li Po. Fighting on the South Frontier.
Song of War, A.
Lindsay, N. Unpardonable Sin, The.
Longfellow, H. Santa Filomena.
Longley, M. Ghetto.

Wounds.
Lovelace, R. To Lucasta, [on] Going to the War[re]s.
Lowell, A. Patterns.
September, 1918.
Lux. Plague Victims Catapulted over Walls into Besieged City.
Macaulay, T. Battle of Naseby, The.
MacDonagh, D. Just an Old Sweet Song.
Macgoye. Mathenge.
Mackey, N. Phantom Light of All Our Day, The.
MacLeish. Too-Late Born, The.
MacNeice. Carrickfergus.
Mixer, The.
Mahon. Afterlives.
Malouf. Year of the Foxes, The.
Manifold. Fife Tune.
Manning, F. Leaves.
Mapanje. On Being Asked to Write a Poem for 1979.
Martinez, D. Discreet Prayer, A.
Marvell. Horatian Ode upon Cromwell's Return from Ireland, An.
Matshoba. Mantatee Horde, The.
McCarthy, G. Fall of Da Nang, The.
Finding the Way Back.
Sound of Guns, The.
McCarthy, T. Claud Cockburn.
Wisdom of AE, The.
McClure, M. Song: "Platinum fur and brass revolver shine."
McDaniel, W. Realist of 1939–40, A.
McDonald, W. Caliban in Blue.
For Harper, Killed in Action.
Interview with a Guy Named Fawkes, U.S. Army.
Last Still Days in a Bunker, The.
Retired Pilot to Himself, The.
Rocket Attack.
Songs We Fought For, The.
War Games.
Winter Before the War, The.
McGinley. How to Start a War.
Women of Jericho, The.
McGrath, T. Fresco: Departure for an Imperialist War.
Nocturne Militaire.
Ordonnance.
Meddemmen, J. G. L.R.D.G.
Melville, H. Conflict of Convictions, The.
Utilitarian View of the Monitor's Fight, A.
Mercer, J. Jubilation T. Cornpone.
Merton. Lent in a Year of War.
Meynell, A. Summer in England, 1914.
Millay, E. Apostrophe to Man.
Milosz, C. Preparation.
Milton. On the Late Massacre [or Massacher] in Piedmont [or Piemont].
Mishler. Ceremony.
Moore, M. In Distrust of Merits.
Moore, R. Dirge for the Living.
More, S. Minstrel Boy, The.
Morris, W. Judgement of God, The.
Mothibi. Speech.
Mudrooroo Narogin. Jacky Hears the Century Cry.
Muir, E. Horses, The.
Scotland 1941.
Muldoon, P. Brock.
Meeting the British.
Murray, K. Drugs of War, The.
Ndu. Evacuation.
Nemerov. Fable of the War, A.
Redeployment.
Ultima Ratio Reagan.
Newbolt. Gillespie.
Vitaï Lampada.
Niedecker. War.
Niles, N. Why Should Vain Mortals Tremble.
Nortje. Autopsy.
Nye, N. Lunch in Nablus City Park.
Mother of Nothing.
Okigbo. Elegy for Alto.
Oldham, P. War Stories.
Oppen. Myth of the Blaze.

Survival: Infantry.
Orfalea, G.   Bomb That Fell on Abdu's Farm, The.
Sunken Road, Antietam 1980, The.
Ormsby, F.   War Photographers, The.
Ortiz.   War Poem.
Orwell.   As One Non-Combatant to Another.
Osgood, K.   Driving Home the Cows.
Owen, W.   A Terre.
Apologia Pro Poemate Meo.
Arms and the Boy.
At a Calvary near the Ancre.
Chances, The.
Conscious.
Disabled.
Dulce et Decorum Est.
Exposure.
Futility.
Insensibility.
Mental Cases.
Next War, The.
Parable of the Old Men and the Young, The.
Send-Off, The.
Sentry, The.
Show, The.
Smile, Smile, Smile.
Spring Offensive.
Strange Meeting.
Paley, G.   People in My Family.
Two Villages.
Paquet.   It Is Monsoon at Last.
Mourning the Death, by Hemorrhage, of a Child from Honai.
They Do Not Go Gentle.
Paulin.   Peacetime.
Pavlich.   Black Flower.
Pfeiffer, E.   Fight at Rorke's Drift, The.
Picasso.   Bottle of Suze, A.
Piercy.   Peaceable Kingdom, The.
Platke, S.   Gut Catcher.
Pound, E.   Sestina: Altaforte.
Prévert.   Barbara.
Pratt, J.   Words and Thoughts.
Prince, F.   Soldiers Bathing.
Pringle.   Caffer Commando, The.
Read, S.   My Company.
To a Conscript of 1940.
Rebelo.   Poem for a Militant.
Revard.   Parading with the Veterans of Foreign Wars.
Rexroth, K.   Strength through Joy.
Rickword.   Soldier Addresses his Body, The.
Winter Warfare.
Ridler.   At Parting.
Ritterbusch.   Search and Destroy.
Robinson, E.   Field of Glory, The.
Rodgers, W.   Sing, Brothers, Sing!
Rolfe, E.   No Man Knows War.
Rolls.   Dog Fight.
Ros.   Little Belgian Orphan, A.
Rosenberg, I.   August 1914.
Break of Day in the Trenches.
Daughters of War.
Louse Hunting.
Marching.
Ross, A.   En Route.
Rosten.   Out of Our Shame.
Roughton.   Building Society Blues.
Rouse.   Memo to Auden.
Rowbotham.   Prey to Prey.
Rukeyser, M.   Don Baty, the Draft Resister.
Käthe Kollwitz.
Poem: "I lived in the first century of world wars."
To be a Jew in the Twentieth Century.
Who in One Lifetime.
Safie, D.   Meditation by the Xerox Machine.
"Saki."   Carol: "While shepherds watched their flocks by night."
Sandburg, C.   Bas-Relief.
Murmurings in a Field Hospital.
Prayer after World War.
Threes.
Sassoon.   'They.'
Aftermath.
Attack.

Does It Matter?
Everyone Sang.
General, The.
Glory of Women.
Repression of War Experience.
Scannell.   Great War, The.
Scott of Amwell.   Ode: "I hate that drum's discordant sound."
Scurfield, G.   Bitter Mangoes, The.
Seeger, A.   I Have a Rendezvous with Death.
Seeger, P.   Where Have All the Flowers Gone?
Sergeant.   Inundation, The.
Seto, T.   Jihad.
Shapiro, K.   Conscientious Objector, The.
Troop Train.
Shelton, R.   Eden After Dark.
Sherwin, J.   To Whom it may concern.
Shuster, D.   Mellow on Morphine.
Simic.   Empire of Dreams.
Simmons, J.   From the Irish.
Simpson, L.   Battle, The.
Early in the Morning.
I Dreamed That in a City Dark as Paris.
Memories of a Lost War.
On the Lawn at the Villa.
Sitwell, D.   Lullaby: "Though the world has slipped and gone."
Sitwell, S.   Next War, The.
Skirving.   Johnnie Cope.
Smith, C.   Fragment Descriptive of the Miseries of War.
Snodgrass, W.   After Experience Taught Me..
Sorley.   Hundred Thousand Million Mites, A.
To Germany.
Soutar.   Permanence of the Young Men, The.
Southerland.   Two Fishing Villages.
Southey, R.   Battle of Blenheim, The.
Southwell.   New Heaven, New War[re].
Spender, S.   Epilogue to a Human Drama.
Two Armies.
Stadler.   Decampment.
Starbuck, G.   Prognosis.
Stevens, W.   Dry Loaf.
Stramm.   Battlefield.
Taggard.   Fructus.
Taylor, A.   Clearing Away.
Terry, L.   Bar[']s Fight[, August 28, 1746].
Thomas, D.   Hand That Signed the Paper, The.
Thomas, E.   As the Team's Head-Brass.
Owl, The.
This Is No Case of Petty Right or Wrong.
Todd, R.   Lament.
Poem: "I walk at dawn across the hollow hills."
Ungaretti.   Rivers, The.
Unknown.   Age of War, The.
Approaching Dance, The.
Drill's the Thing.
Eh-Ros-ka, the Warrior's Dance.
Fortunes of War, I Tell You Plain, The.
Ha-Kon-E-Crase, the Eagle Dance.
Hymn: "O God of Hosts, thine Ear incline."
Johnny, I Hardly Knew Ye.
Raid of the Reidswire, The.
Wa-Sissica, the War Song.
War the Source of Riches.
Uyematsu.   Same Month They Bombed Cambodia, The.
Viereck, P.   Kilroy.
Voznesensky [*or* Voznesenskii].   I Am Goya.
Waley.   Censorship.
Wallace, E.   War.
Wallace, R.   Nightline: An Interview with the General.
Waring, B.   Refuge at the One Step Down.
Watkyns.   Peace and War.
Weber, R.   Concise History of the Vietnam War: 1965–1968, A.
Weigl.   Burning Shit at An Khe.
Him, on the Bicycle.
Monkey.
Wendel.   We Shall Return, Luanda.
West, A.   Night Patrol, The.
Whalen.   Regalia in Immediate Demand!
Whitman, W.   Beat! Beat! Drums!
Epigraph to "Drum-Taps."
Old War-Dreams.

Respondez!
Whittemore, R.   Walk Home, The.
Wicks, S.   Protected Species.
Wilbur.   First Snow in Alsace.
Looking into History.
Place Pigalle.
Williams, W.   Illegitimate Things.
These.
Williamson, G.   Dark Days, The.
Wilner, E.   Conversation with a Japanese Student.
Winters, Y.   Summer Noon: 1941.
Wolfe, C.   Burial of Sir John Moore [after [*or* at] Corunna], The.
Wolff, D.   While We Slept.
Wright, J.   Mad Fight Song for William S. Carpenter, 1966, A.
Yeats.   Ancestral Houses.
Irish Airman Foresees His Death, An.
On Being Asked for a War Poem.
Road at My Door, The.
Stare's Nest by My Window, The.
Zimunya.   Let It Be.
See also **Soldiers; War Casualties; War Dead**

War Casualties
Anderson, D.   Nightly News, The.
Balaban.   For the Missing in Action.
Carson, C.   Bloody Hand.
Clifton, L.   Dear Jesse Helms.
Dunn, D.   War Blinded.
Fenton, J.   Dead Soldiers.
Ferlinghetti, L.   Third World Calling.
Galloway, G.   To the Memory of Gavin Wilson (Boot, Leg and Arm Maker).
Garioch.   Wire, The.
Graves, R.   Leveller, The.
Gurney, I.   Mangel-Bury, The.
Gutteridge.   Enemy Dead, The.
Henderson, H.   Ninth Elegy: Fort Capuzzo.
Hillyer.   Dead Man's Corner.
Hood, T.   Faithless Nelly Gray.
Hughes, L.   Casualty.
Jarrell.   Sick Nought, The.
Keyes, S.   Europe's Prisoners.
Kinnell.   Dead Shall Be Raised Incorruptible, The.
Landor, W.   To Arthur de Noé Walker.
Longley, M.   Wounds.
Mackintosh, E.   Cha Till Maccruimein (Departure of the 4th Camerons).
Matthews, H.   Women Are Not Gentlemen.
Muldoon, P.   Field Hospital, The.
Neilson, J.   Soldier Is Home, The.
Owen, W.   A Terre.
Chances, The.
Conscious.
Disabled.
Dulce et Decorum Est.
Futility.
Mental Cases.
Sentry, The.
Plowman.   Dead Soldiers, The.
Rukeyser, M.   Leg in a Plaster Cast, A.
Sassoon.   'They.'
Does It Matter?
Shapcott, T.   Sestina with Refrain.
Simmons, J.   From the Irish.
Simpson, L.   Carentan O Carentan.
Sitwell, S.   Next War, The.
Thomas, D.   Among Those Killed in the Dawn Raid Was a Man Aged a Hundred.
Unknown.   Far Away.
Whitman, W.   March in the Ranks Hard-Prest, and the Road Unknown, A.
Vigil Strange I Kept on the Field One Night.
Wound-Dresser, The.
See also **Soldiers; War Dead**

War Dead
Abse.   Cousin Sidney.
Aldington.   Trench Idyll.
Allison, D.   Funeral Oration, A.
Amichai [*or* Amikhai].   Diameter of the Bomb Was Thirty Centimeters, The.
Asquith.   Volunteer, The.
Balaban.   After Our War.
In Celebration of Spring.

Than, Mau.
Bell, M. Reason for Refusal.
Betjeman. In Memory of Basil, Marquess of Dufferin and Ava.
Binyon. For the Fallen.
Bogan, L. To My Brother: Killed: Hammont Wood: October, 1918.
Browning, E. Forced Recruit, The.
Mother and Poet.
Browning, R. Incident of the French Camp.
Carrier, C. Pro Patria.
"Caudwell." Classic Encounter.
Causley. At the British War Cemetery, Bayeux.
Chesterton, G. English Graves, The.
Ciardi. Elegy Just in Case.
Clifton, H. Death of Thomas Merton.
Collins, W. How Sleep the Brave.
Crosland. Slain.
Dawe, B. Homecoming.
Day, J. North Sea.
De Tabley. Sonnet: "Record is nothing, and the hero great."
Dehn, P. Armistice.
Dickey, J. Hunting Civil War Relics at Nimblewill Creek.
Performance, The.
Douglas, K. Gallantry.
Vergissmeinicht.
Dunbar, P. Unsung Heroes, The.
Emerson, R. Concord Hymn.
Fairfax, J. Forest of the Dead, The.
Feldman, I. Se Aprovechan.
Finch, F. Blue and the Gray, The.
Ford, F. That Exploit of Yours.
Graves, R. Devil's Advice to Story-Tellers, The.
Gray, T. Death of Hoel, The.
Gurney, I. To His Love.
Gutteridge. Enemy Dead, The.
Hardy, T. Drummer Hodge.
I Looked Up from My Writing.
Man He Killed, The.
Wife in London, A.
Harry, J. Shot of War, A.
Harte, B. Second Review of the Grand Army, A.
Heaney, S. In Memoriam Francis Ledwidge.
Heard, J. Decoration Day.
National Cemetery, Beaufort, South Carolina, The.
Hemans. Effigies, The.
Henderson, H. End of a Campaign.
Hope, A. Inscription for a War.
Housman, A. Astronomy.
Epitaph.
Epitaph on an Army of Mercenaries.
Howell, C. Reminder to the Current President, A.
Hughes, T. Six Young Men.
Jarrell. Burning the Letters.
Come to the Stone.
Dead Wingman, The.
Death of the Ball Turret Gunner, The.
Gunner.
Losses.
Protocols.
Second Air Force.
Keyes, S. Expected Guest, The.
Kipling, R. Batteries Out of Ammunition.
Beginner, The.
Bombed in London.
Bridegroom, The.
Common Form.
Convoy Escort.
Coward, The.
Dead Statesman, A.
Death-Bed, A.
Drifter off Tarentum, A.
Epitaphs of the War [1914–1918].
Equality of Sacrifice.
Ex-Clerk.
Gethsemane.
Hyænas [or Hyenas], The.
Journalists.
Mesopotamia.
Pelicans in the Wilderness (A Grave near Halfa).

R.A.F. (Aged Eighteen).
Refined Man, The.
Servant, A.
Son, A.
Unknown Female Corpse.
Komunyakaa. Facing It.
Langland, J. War.
Lanier, S. Dying Words of Stonewall Jackson, The.
Larkin, P. MCMXIV.
Lasker-Schüler. Georg Trakl.
Letts. Spires of Oxford, The.
Lewis, A. Raiders' Dawn.
Unknown Soldier, The.
Longfellow, H. Killed at the Ford.
Lowell, R. For the Union Dead.
Holy Innocents, The.
MacDiarmid, H. Another Epitaph on an Army of Mercenaries.
MacGill. Matey.
Mackintosh, E. In Memoriam[, Private D. Sutherland].
MacLeish. Lines for an Interment.
Memorial Rain.
Manifold. Tomb of Lt. John Learmonth, A.I.F, The.
McCrae, J. In Flanders Fields.
McGrath, T. Ode for the American Dead in Korea.
Reading the Names of the Vietnam War Dead.
Melville, H. Inscription: "To them who crossed the flood."
Memorial on the Slain at Chickamauga.
Requiem[:] for Soldiers Lost in Ocean Transports, A.
Mew. Cenotaph, The.
Moody, W. On a Soldier Fallen in the Philippines.
Moore, T. Minstrel Boy, The.
Nemerov. War in the Air, The.
Newbolt. Messmates.
Nicholl, T. His Friend's Last Battle.
O'Loughlin. Elegy for the Unknown Soldier.
Olds, S. Leningrad Cemetery, Winter of 1941.
Owen, W. Anthem for Doomed Youth.
Dulce et Decorum Est.
Futility.
Greater Love.
Miners.
Next War, The.
Send-Off, The.
Strange Meeting.
Page, G. Smalltown Memorials.
Randall, D. Memorial Wreath.
Ransom, J. Necrological.
Rickword. Moonrise Over Battlefield.
Trench Poets.
Riddell, E. Soldier in the Park, The.
Rosenberg, I. Dead Man's Dump.
Ryan, A. Lines: "Gather the sacred dust."
Sandburg, C. Grass.
Sassoon. Base Details.
Death-Bed, The.
Hero, The.
On Passing the New Menin Gate.
Simmons, J. From the Irish.
Simpson, L. Ash and the Oak, The.
Slessor. Beach Burial.
Smith, D. On a Field Trip at Fredericksburg.
Sorley. Sonnet: "When you see millions of the mouthless dead."
Spender, S. Ultima Ratio Regum.
Stevens, W. Death of a Soldier, The.
Street, D. Love Letters of the Dead.
Tate, A. Ode to the Confederate Dead.
Tate, J. Lost Pilot, The.
Tennyson, A. Charge of the Light Brigade, The.
Thackeray. Due of the Dead, The.
Thomas, E. As the Team's Head-Brass.
In Memoriam (Easter, 1915).
Private, A.
Thompson, J. Burial of Latané, The.
Timrod. Christmas.
Ode: "Sleep sweetly in your humble graves."
Trakl. Grodek.
Unknown. Johnny, I Hardly Knew Ye.

Viereck, P. Vale from Carthage.
Whitman, W. As Toilsome I Wander'd Virginia's Woods.
Ashes of Soldiers.
Come Up from the Fields Father.
Dirge for Two Veterans.
Pensive on Her Dead Gazing.
Reconciliation.
Sight in Camp [in the Daybreak Gray and Dim], A.
Sight in Camp in the Daybreak Gray and Dim, A.
Vigil Strange I Kept on the Field One Night.
Wolfe, C. Burial of Sir John Moore [after [or at] Corunna], The.
Yeats. Irish Airman Foresees His Death, An.
Young, S. Epitaph for a Concord Boy.
See also **Soldiers**

War of 1812
Freneau. On the Conflagrations at Washington.
Key. Star-Spangled Banner, The.

Warblers
Stevens, W. Meditation Celestial and Terrestrial.

Ward, John
Unknown. Captain Ward and the *Rainbow*.

Warhol, Andy
Kinsella, J. Warhol at Wetlands.
Yuson. Andy Warhol Speaks to His Two Filipino Maids.

Warning
Carew, T. Deposition from Love, A.
Herrick. Bellman, The.
Ralegh, S. Sir Walter Ra[u]le[i]gh to His Son[ne].
Smith, S. Songe d'Athalie.
Sondheim. Everybody Says Don't.
Turner, C. Buoy-Bell, The.
Warren, R. Pondy Woods.
Yeats. Never Give All the Heart.

Warren, Robert Penn
Lawrence, A. Robert Penn Warren's Book.

Warsaw Ghetto
Milosz, C. Poor Christian Looks at the Ghetto, A.
Valentine, J. Forgiveness Dream.

Warsaw, Poland
Ashbery. My Name Is Dimitri.
Davie. Meeting of Cultures, A.
Flanders, J. House That Fear Built: Warsaw, 1943, The.
Milosz, C. Campo dei Fiori.

Washing
Bishop, E. Under the Window: Ouro Prêto.
Bishop, P. Woman Washing.
Fanning, R. Baudelaire's Ablutions.
Fisher, J. Camp.
Lyon, G. Foot-Washing, The.
Mother Goose. They That Wash on Monday.
Rilke. Pietà.
Shepherd, R. Hygiene.
See also **Baths and Bathing**

Washing Machines
Holland, J. Spin-Cycle.
See also **Laundry and Laundering**

Washington (state)
Hugo, R. White Center.
Jensen, L. Age, An.
Snyder, G. Mid-August at Sourdough Mountain Lookout.

Washington Square, New York City
Livingston, M. Envoi: Washington Square Park.
Stanard, C. Washington Square Park and a Game of Chess.

Washington, Booker Taliaferro
Johnson, M. To See Ol' Booker T.
Linden, M. Our Noble Booker T. Washington.
Moorer. Notable Dinner, A.
Randall, D. Booker T. and W. E. B.
Stafford, W. Monuments for a Friendly Girl at a Tenth Grade Party.

Washington, D.C
Davis, C. Out of Work, Out of Touch, Out of Sorts.
Dove, R. Banneker.

Hemphill. Family Jewels.
Iverem, E. Keeper.
Lowell, R. July in Washington.
  March 1, The.
Rome, H. Money Song, The.
Tate, A. Aeneas at Washington.
Welch, J. Man from Washington, The.

Washington, George
Barlow, J. Advice to a Raven in Russia
  [December, 1812].
Berryman. Washington in Love.
Cohan. If Washington Should Come to Life.
Jordan, J. Cameo No. II.
Merriam, E. Which Washington?
Unknown. Inscription at Mount Vernon.
Wakoski. Patriotic Poem.
Wheatley, P. To His Excellency General
  Washington.

Wasps
Alley, R. Growing Days, The.
Eberhart, R. New Hampshire, February.
Fisher, A. Fair Exchange.
Kay, J. Virus².
MacBeth [*or* Macbeth]. Wasps' Nest, The.
Muir, E. Late Wasp, The.
Paulin. Sting, The.
Taylor, E. Upon a Wasp Chilled [*or* Child] with
  Cold.

Watches
Cornford, F. Watch, The.
Graham, W. Lines on Roger Hilton's Watch.
Herbert, E. To His Watch, When He Could Not
  Sleep.
Heyen. Trains, The.
Maguire, S. Perfect Timing.
McClatchy. Bishop Reading.
Swenson, M. Watch, The.
See also **Clocks**

Water
Acholonu. Water Woman.
Allen, P. He Na Tye Woman.
Auden. In Praise of Limestone.
Awoonor. So the World Changes.
Berssenbrugge. Duration of Water.
Betjeman. East Anglian Bathe.
Bishop, E. Under the Window: Ouro Prêto.
Bly, R. Awakening.
Bogan, L. To Be Sung on the Water.
Brontë, C. Diving.
Cameron, N. Green, Green Is El Aghir.
Carew, T. To My Mistress Sitting by a River's
  Side; an Eddy.
Charara, H. Holy Water.
Clark, P. Walk in the Rain.
Codrescu. Imagination of Necessity, The.
Cornford, F. Inscription for a Wayside Spring.
Crashaw. To Our Lord, upon the Water Made
  Wine.
Creeley. Act of Love, The.
  Just Friends.
  Pool, The.
Croly. Aestuary, An.
Doolittle, H. Pool, The.
Dowson. Exile.
Dubrava. Miraculous Marriage of Zarife
  Dominquez.
Eberhart, R. Garden God, The.
  Loon Call, A.
Emerson, R. Water.
Ennis. Drink of Spring, A.
Finlay, I. Boat's Blueprint, The.
Ford, C. Overturned Lake, The.
Frost, R. West-Running Brook.
Gilbert, C. Chosen to Be Water.
Gregerson. Waterborne.
Grennan. Shoreline After Storm.
Hamill, S. What the Water Knows.
Hannan, M. Lamper, The.
Heaney, S. Cana Revisited.
  Drink of Water, A.
  Rite of Spring.
Helton. Lonesome Water.
Herrick. To the Water Nymphs, Drinking at the
  Fountain.
Highfill, M. Rebis.

Hirshfield, J. Music Like Water, The.
  To Drink.
Hogan, L. Chambered Nautilus.
Hollander, J. By the Sound.
Hope, A. Gateway, The.
Hughes, T. Man Seeking Experience Enquires
  His Way of a Drop of Water, The.
Jarrell. Well Water.
Jordan, J. October 23, 1983.
Joyce, J. All Day I Hear the Noise of Waters.
Keats. Bright Star.
Kenney. Sailing.
Kizer, C. Muse of Water, A.
Koyama. Currents.
Kusano Shimpei. 4 Or 5 Tadpoles.
Larkin, P. Water.
Lawrence, D. Snake.
  Wild Common, The.
Leithauser. Buried Graves, The.
Levertov. Wavering.
Levine, P. Belief.
Livingston, M. Swimming Pool.
Lorde. Fishing the White Water.
Lowell, R. Water.
Lyons, S. Touching You Underwater.
MacCaig. Likenesses.
MacDiarmid, H. Glass of Pure Water, The.
Mandell, A. Middle Age.
McCaig. Betweens.
McGuckian. Sea or Sky?
McMichael. Posited.
Merwin, W. S. Glass.
Mitchell, K. Night Rain.
  Tree Stillness.
Moore, M. Like a Bulrush.
Moore, T. Meeting of the Waters, The.
Morgan, E. Dowser, The.
Morley, H. Curve of the Water.
Napurrurla, I. Water, The.
Neruda. Sexual Water.
Nicholson, N. From a Boat at Coniston.
Niedecker. My Life By Water.
Norris, L. Water.
O'Neill, M. Sound of Water.
Oliver, M. Diviners, The.
Oswald, A. Sea Sonnet.
Padilla. Daily Habits.
Pastan. Erosion.
  Love Poem.
Peacocke. Soap.
Phillips, C. In the blood, Winnowing.
Piper, E. Big Swimming.
Pound, E. Bathtub [*or* Bath Tub], The.
Rafferty, P. View from the Bathysphere.
Ramsey, J. Power Quest, Sooke Park.
Ransom, J. Persistent Explorer.
Rothman, D. Shape of Water Most Like Love,
  The.
Roy, L. Suffering The Sea Change: All My
  Pretty Ones.
Sandburg, C. Prairie Waters by Night.
Seshadri. Lifeline.
Silverstein, S. Dirtiest Man in the World, The.
Smelcer. Bonanza Creek.
Smith, W. Brooklyn Bridge.
Stevens, W. Poems of Our Climate, The.
Suckling, S. Upon Sir John Lawrence's
  Bringing Water over the Hills [to My L.
  Middlesex His House at Witten].
Taggard. To the Powers of Desolation.
Taylor, A. Water.
Thoreau. Fog.
Tonks. Hydromaniac.
Traherne. Shadows in the Water.
Unknown. Come, Happy Children.
  God's A-Gonna Trouble the Water.
  Inscription in Osmington Church, Dorset.
  Lyric by Nine.
Valentine, J. Lines in Dejection.
Vigil, A. Hogarcito de La Madrugada, El.
Volkman. Create Desire.
West, K. By Water Divined.
Winstanley, J. To the Revd. Mr.——on His
  Drinking Sea-Water.
Wright, J. Journey to the Place of Ghosts.
  Lake in Central Park, The.

  To Flood Stage Again.
Zukofsky, L. Ways, The.
  Xenophanes.

Water Lilies
Barnes, W. Clote (Water-Lily), The.
Clare, J. Water-Lilies.
Ferlinghetti, L. Monet's Lilies Shuddering.
Hughes, T. To Paint a Water Lily.
Mills, R. Water Lilies.
Teasdale. Water-Lilies.
Wakoski. Light.

Water Ouzels
Matchett. Water Ouzel.

Waterbeds
Updike. Insomnia the Gem of the Ocean.

Watercolors
Plath. Watercolor of Grantchester Meadows.

Waterfalls
Everson, W. Stone Face Falls.
Hardy, T. Under the Waterfall.
Hartley, M. West Pitch at the Falls.
Heaney, S. Waterfall.
Hopkins, G. At a Welsh Waterfall.
Landon. Scale Force, Cumberland.
Ormond. Definition of a Waterfall.
Owen, G. Waterfall.
Ray, H. At the Cascade.
Vaughan, H. Waterfall [*or* Water-Fall], The.
Williams, W. Paterson: The Falls.
Williamson, G. Waterfall.
Woody. She-Who-Watches . . . The Names are
  Prayer.
Young, A. Falls of Glomach, The.

Waterfowl
Bryant, W. To a Waterfowl.
Swenson, M. Willets, The.

Watergate
Woddis. Final Curtain.
See also **Mitchell, Martha; Nixon, Richard
  Milhous**

Waterloo, Battle of (1815)
Scott, S. Charge at Waterloo.

Watermelons
Alexander, E. Overture: Watermelon City.
Barber, D. Small Hours.
Simic. Watermelons.

Watts, Isaac
Rodriguez, L. Speaking with Hands.

Watts, Los Angeles, California
Rodriguez, L. Heavy Blue Veins.

Waugh, Evelyn
Connolly, C. On Himself.

Waves
Agran, R. Swimming with Seiger.
Barrington, J. Villanelle VI.
Bynner. Wave, The.
Copus, J. Cricketer's Retirement Day, The.
Curnow. You Will Know When You Get There.
D'Aguiar. Dread.
Graham, J. Gulls.
  Soul Says.
Greer, J. Rodin's "Gates of Hell."
Gunn, T. From the Wave.
Hadas, R. Sentimental Education.
Haines, J. Awakening.
Higginson, W. Interstices.
Martínez, V. Coastal.
McGuckian. Sea or Sky?
Morrison, L. Surf.
Noguchi, R. His Waves.
Roditi. Aurora Borealis.
Rothman, D. When the Wind and Dark Waves
  Come.
Spicer, J. Lament for the Makers: "No call upon
  anyone but the timber drifting in the waves."
Stephens, J. Main-Deep, The.
Swenson, M. How Everything Happens.
Wordsworth, D. Lake was covered all over,
  The.
Yeats. Nineteenth Century and After, The.
Zukofsky, L. I Sent Thee Late.

Wayne, John
Carbó, N. Little Brown Brother.
Denning. Movie, The.

Erdrich.   Dear John Wayne.

Wealth
Anderson, W.   I'm Naebody Noo.
Barber, M.   Unanswerable Apology for the Rich, An.
Belloc.   Lord Finchley.
Berlin.   Little Things in Life, The.
  Puttin' on the Ritz (Original Version).
  Puttin' on the Ritz (Revised Version).
Bock, J.   If I Were a Rich Man.
  Little Tin Box.
Brown, L.   Best Things in Life Are Free, The.
Burke, J.   Ain't It a Shame About Mame.
Campbell, A.   To My Friend.
Cavendish, M.   Her Descending Down.
Clark, T.   I Am Still Rich.
Coleridge, M.   Insincere Wish Addressed to a Beggar, An.
Coward.   Stately Homes of England, The.
Crowley, R.   Of unsaciable purchasers.
Davie.   Garden Party, The.
Davies, W.   No Man's Wood.
Dubin, A.   Gold Digger's Song (We're in the Money), The.
Dunbar, P.   Common Things.
  Place Where the Rainbow Ends, The.
Emerson, R.   Chartist's Complaint, The.
  Compensation.
Fain, S.   Are You Havin' Any Fun?
Fletcher, P.   Against a Rich Man Despising Poverty.
Frost, R.   Lovely Shall Be Choosers, The.
Fuller, E.   What the King Has.
Hardy, T.   Ruined Maid, The.
Hart, L.   I've Got Five Dollars.
Hernton.   Poem.
Herrick.   Amber Bead, The.
  His Grange, or Private Wealth.
Hughes, L.   Cross.
Johnson, S.   Short Song of Congratulation [or To a Young Heir], A.
Kennedy, X.   In a Prominent Bar in Secaucus [One Day].
Knott.   Funny Poem.
Komunyakaa.   Seven Deadly Sins.
Lampman.   To a Millionaire.
Landon.   Bonds of Affection.
  Poor, The.
Leapor.   Strephon to Celia.
McGuckian.   Waterford.
Melville, H.   In a Garret.
Murphy, R.   Elixir.
Nash, O.   Terrible People, The.
North, M.   Ordnance Survey in the Northern Counties.
Parrott.   More Bagpipe Music.
Peacock, T.   Rich and Poor; or, Saint and Sinner.
Pope, A.   Duke of Buckingham, The.
  Sir Balaam.
  Timon's Villa.
Porter, C.   My Heart Belongs to Daddy.
Probyn.   Love in Mayfair.
Robinson, E.   Bewick Finzer.
  Richard Cory.
Sandburg, C.   Child of the Romans.
Schmitz.   Carmel.
Simon, P.   Richard Cory.
Smith, S.   To a Querulous Acquaintance.
Smith, S.   Satin-Clad.
Soyinka.   After the Deluge.
Stevenson, R.   System.
  To A Gardener.
Tsvetayeva [or Tsvetaeva].   If the Soul was Born with Pinions.
Unknown.   May Colven [or May Colvin].
  One Little Boy.
Watkyns.   Worldly Wealth.
Wilbur.   Summer Morning, A.
Wylie.   Full Moon.
Yellen, J.   Are You Havin' Any Fun?

Weapons
Césaire, A.   Miraculous Weapons, The.
Cangiullo.   Detonation.
Cross, F.   Fifty Gunner, The.
Ehrhart.   Hunting.
  Time on Target.
Floyd.   Private Ian Godwin, U. S. M. C.
Haines, J.   Poem Like a Grenade, A.
Herrera.   Fuselage Installation.
Hughes, T.   Crow's Theology.
Knevet.   Vote, The.
Komunyakaa.   Somewhere Near Phu Bai.
  Starlight Scope Myopia.
Koordada, M.   You Can't Escape Your Life Record.
Layne, M.   Guns.
  On Hats and Things.
Meeks, B.   Is Culcha Weapon?
Ndu.   Evacuation.
Owen, W.   Arms and the Boy.
Paquet.   In a Plantation.
Rebelo.   Poem for a Militant.
Ryan, G.   If I Had a Gun.
Scannell.   Bayonet Training.
Scarfe.   Grenade.
Schilpp, M.   Under the Scorpion's Heart.
Spender, S.   Ultima Ratio Regum.
Webb, F.   Gunner, The.
Weigl.   Mines.

Weariness
Apollinaire.   Zone.
Beckett, S.   Enueg I.
  Enueg II.
Bradstreet, A.   As Weary Pilgrim, Now at Rest.
Browning, E.   My Heart and I.
Byron, G.   So We'll Go No More A-Roving.
Campo.   El Curandero.
Corso.   Zizi's Lament.
Coward.   (I'm So) Weary of It All.
  Why Must the Show Go On?
Crapsey.   Trapped.
De la Mare.   Tired Tim.
Delgado, J.   Recommitted.
Du Maurier.   Music.
Fields, D.   It's All Yours.
Fisher, D.   Tired.
Glück, L.   Winged Horse, The.
Grimké, A.   Butterflies.
Harburg.   Then I'll Be Tired of You.
Herrick.   To Sycamores.
Hollenbeck.   Anorexia.
Hughes, L.   Weary Blues, The.
Hupfeld, H.   Let's Put Out the Lights and Go to Sleep.
Longfellow, H.   Broken Oar, The.
McDonald, R.   Incident in Transylvania.
Neruda.   Walking Around.
Nye, N.   New Year.
Paquet.   Morning—A Death.
Replansky.   Good Day's Work, A.
Roberts, A.   Tired.
Rossetti, C.   From the Antique.
  In Progress.
  Is the Moon Tired?
  Sleeping at Last.
Ryan, G.   Orbit.
Tucker, M.   I am Weary, Mother.
  Weariness.
Unknown.   Lord Randal[l].
Wildman, E.   Cure, The.
Wylie.   Nebuchadnezzar.

Weasels
Helwig.   Dead Weasel, A.

Weather
Arlen, H.   Stormy Weather (Keeps Rainin' All the Time).
Ashbery.   Crazy Weather.
Bang, M.   Crossed-Over, Fiend-Snitched, X-ed Out.
Becker, R.   Near Sheridan.
Berlin.   I've Got My Love to Keep Me Warm.
  Isn't This a Lovely Day (To Be Caught in the Rain?).
  It's a Lovely Day Today.
Bryant, W.   After a Tempest.
Burnside.   Dundee.
Coultas, B.   Weather Report.
Curbelo.   Tourist Weather.
Curnow.   Wild Iron.
De la Mare.   Scarecrow, The.
Dickinson, E.   Sun and Fog Contested, The.
Dove, R.   Turning Thirty, I Contemplate Students Bicycling Home.
Drummond, W.   All Changeth.
Eberhart, R.   Flux.
Ewart.   Weather, The.
France, L.   Meteorology.
Graves, R.   Love Story, A.
  Weather of Olympus, The.
Hardy, T.   Weathers [or Weather].
Henley, W.   At Queensferry.
Herrick.   Fair[e] Days; or, Dawn[e]s Deceitful[l].
Hoban.   Pedalling Man, The.
Hooper, V.   Reading, A.
Horan.   By Hallucination Visited.
Hughes, L.   Strange Hurt.
Johnson, M. F.   Thunder Storm.
Kirchwey.   He Considers the Birds of the Air.
Lerner, A.   Camelot.
Mahon.   Kinsale.
Merriam, E.   Spell of Weather, A.
  Weather.
  Windshield Wiper.
Momaday.   Headwaters.
Robertson, R.   Aberdeen.
Roethke.   Dinky.
Rosemurgy, C.   Why God Invented the Cold.
Strand.   Morning, Noon and Night.
Sutter.   Hoarfrost and Fog.
Swenson, M.   Cat and the Weather.
Tomlinson, C.   Weather Report.
Unknown.   Rhyme from Lincolnshire, A.
  Weather.
Williamson, G.   Belvedere Marittimo.
Wright, J.   Black Cockatoos.
Young, K.   Degrees.

Weathervanes
Hine.   Riddle: "Invisible, chimerical."
Hoban.   Pedalling Man, The.

Weaving and Weavers
Cherry, K.   Raiment We Put On, The.
Chester, A.   Tapestry Weaver, The.
Coleridge, M.   Wilderspin.
Deloney.   Weavers Song, The.
Doolittle, H.   At Ithaca.
Esteves.   Weaver.
Stoddard, E.   Before the Mirror.
Tobrise.   Dyeing.
Unknown.   Factory Workers' Song.
  Linen Weaver, The.
  Poverty Knock.
Yeats.   Fragments: "Locke sank into a swoon."

Webster, Daniel
Coatsworth.   Daniel Webster's Horses.
Whittier.   Ichabod[!].

Webster, John
Eliot, T.   Whispers of Immortality.

Wedding Songs
Crashaw.   Epithalamium: "Come, virgin tapers of pure wax."
Herrick.   Nuptiall Song, or Epithalamie, on Sir Clipseby Crew and His Lady, A.

Weddings
Adisa.   Rainbow, The.
Akhmadulina.   Bride, The.
Akst, H.   Dinah.
Baillie, J.   Song: Woo'd and married and a'
Biespiel, D.   After the Wedding.
Bloch, C.   White Petticoats.
Bly, R.   My Father's Wedding.
Clanchy, K.   For a Wedding.
Copus, J.   Pulling the Ivy.
Corso.   Marriage.
Donaldson, W.   Because My Baby Don't Mean Maybe Now.
Dove, R.   In the Old Neighborhood.
Dubin, A.   Shuffle Off to Buffalo.
Dubrava.   Miraculous Marriage of Zarife Dominquez.
Dybek.   Cherry.
Fain, S.   Wedding Bells Are Breaking Up That Old Gang of Mine.
Foster, A.   No Dice.
Goetz, E.   For Me and My Gal.
Goodison.   Wedding in Hanover.

Gylys, B.   Balloon Heart.
Hall, D.   Wedding Party.
Hardy, T.   Country Wedding, The.
Heaney, S.   Wedding Day.
Henry, P.   Winter Wedding, The.
Jonson, B.   Epithalamion: or, a Song.
Joseph, A.   Wedding Party.
Killigrew, T.   Epilogue to "The Parson's Wedding."
Krayer, S.   My Mother Dressed for the Wedding.
Larkin, P.   Waiting For Breakfast, While She Brushed Her Hair.
  Whitsun Weddings, The.
Leithauser.   Old Bachelor Brother.
Leslie, E.   For Me and My Gal.
Levine, M.   Wedding Day.
Lewis, S.   Dinah.
Luterman, A.   Justice of the Peace, The.
Mapanje.   *From* Florrie Abraham Witness, *December 1972.*
Masters, E.   Wedding Feast, The.
Meyer, G.   For Me and My Gal.
Mouré.   Thirteen Years.
Nash, O.   Here Usually Comes the Bride.
Nicholson, N.   Epithalamium for a Niece.
Norris, K.   Wedding in the Courthouse, The.
Oswald, A.   Wedding.
Pankey.   Reason, The.
Parson-Nesbitt.   Strange Country.
Patchen.   Temple, A.
Pelizzon, V.   Wedding Day, The.
Philpot, T.   Louisa's Wedding.
Porter, C.   It's De-Lovely.
Rohrer, M.   After the Wedding Party.
Rothenberg, J.   Poland / 1931 "The Wedding."
Salter.   What Do Women Want?
See, P.   Shotgun.
Spenser.   Epithalamion: "Ye learned sisters which have oftentimes."
  Prothalamion.
St. John, D.   Wedding Preparations in the Country.
Steele, P.   Cana.
Storace.   Wedding Song.
Su, A.   Wedding Gifts.
Suckling, S.   Ballad[e] [upon a Wedding], A.
Thatcher, C.   Moggy's Wedding.
Thompson, P.   Tribute to the Bride and Groom, A.
Unknown.   Weddings.
Valentine, J.   Bride's Hours, A.
Vando.   Blanca's Red Lips.
Vazirani, R.   Mrs. Biswas Breaks Her Connection with Another Relative.
Whitney, I.   I.W. To Her Unconstant Lover.
Willard, N.   Feast of St. Tortoise, The.
Young, J.   Dinah.
See also **Marriage**

Weeds
Ammons, A. R.   Reflective.
Clark, L.   Ground Elder.
Curry.   Dandelion.
Dean, D. K.   Taproot.
Dickey, J.   Weeds.
Dugan, A.   Weeds as Partial Survivors.
Hamburger, M.   Weeding.
Hughes, T.   Thistles.
Layzer.   Lawn Roller, The.
Roethke.   Long Live the Weeds.
  Weed Puller.
Taggard.   Weed, The.

Weekends
Trethewey, N.   Secular.

Weeping
Adisa.   No, Women Don't Cry.
Chippewa Oral Tradition.   Sioux Women Gather Up Their Wounded, The.
Crapsey.   Anguish.
Hemans.   Bride's Farewell, The.
Hirschman, J.   Weeping, The.
Rossetti, D.   He and I.
See also **Tears**
Weight Lifting
Ackerman, D.   Pumping Iron.

Barresi.   Lifting.
Conway, J.   Weight Belt.
Reid, C.   Baldanders.
Rouse.   Uni-Gym, The.
Shepherd, R.   That Man.
Weissmuller, Johnny
James, C.   Johnny Weissmuller Dead in Acapulco.
Welcome
Bruner.   There Is a Loneliness.
Herman, J.   Hello, Dolly!
Herrick.   To His Kinsman, Master Thomas Herrick, Who Desired to Be in His Book.
Roberts, L.   Poem from Llanybri.
Welfare
Bird, D.   Can I Say.
Castillo, A.   Me and Baby.
Lane, P.   Sexual Privacy of Women on Welfare.
Wellington, Arthur Wellesley, 1st Duke of
Harpur, C.   Wellington.
Wells
Bates, C.   At Grandfather's.
Brown, T.   Well, The.
Dickey, J.   Underground Stream, The.
Frost, R.   For Once, Then, Something.
Gonzalez, N.   Deepest Well in Madras, The.
Heaney, S.   Personal Helicon.
Jarrell.   Well Water.
Lovecraft.   Well, The.
Macpherson, J.   Well, The.
Raymund.   Well, The.
Rilke.   Departure of the Prodigal Son*, The.
Salom.   Well, The.
Welsh, The
Abse.   Case History.
Conran.   Elegy for the Welsh Dead, in the Falklands Islands, 1982.
Davies, J.   Visitor's Book, 9, The.
Drysdale, A.   Language Difficulty.
Garlick, D.   Consider Kyffin.
Hodges, C.   Naturalised.
Housman, A.   Welsh Marches, The.
Morris, B.   Dinas Emrys.
Philips, K.   On the Welsh Language.
Thomas, R.   Expatriates.
  Other.
  Welsh History.
  Welsh Testament, A.
  Welshman at St. James' Park, A.
Unknown.   On the Welch.
Williams, H.   Old Tongue, The.
See also **Wales**
Werewolves
Brautigan.   Boat, A.
Swartwout.   Gypsy Teaches Her Grandchild Wolfen Ways, The.
Walcott.   Le Loupgarou.
Watson, R.   Ballad of the Were-Wolf, A.
Wilbur.   Beasts.
Wessex, England
Hardy, T.   Wessex Heights.
West Indies
Crane, H.   O Carib Isle!
Tessimond.   Jamaican Bus Ride.
Walcott.   Tales of the Islands.
West Virginia (state)
Atkins.   Narrative.
Burgess, F.   Trapping Fairies.
Key.   Written at the White Sulphur Springs.
McKinney, I.   Twilight in West Virginia: Six O'Clock Mine Report.
Wright, J.   Mad Fight Song for William S. Carpenter, 1966, A.
West Wind
Burns, R.   Of A' the Airts [the Wind Can Blaw].
Herrick.   To the Western Wind.
Masefield.   West Wind, The.
Shelley, P.   Ode to the West Wind.
Unknown.   Western Wind.
Warren, R.   Blow, West Wind.
West, Mae
McElroy, C.   Mae West Chats It Up with Bessie Smith.

West, Richard
Gray, T.   Sonnet [on the Death of Mr. Richard West].
West, The, United States
Andrews, B.   West West.
Benét, R. *et al.*   Western Wagons.
Benét, W.   Horse Thief, The.
Bishop, E.   Vague Poem.
Boswell, M.   Texas Ranger, The.
Brennan, J.   Let the Rest of the World Go By.
Bryant, W.   Prairies, The.
Cary, A.   West Country, The.
Cather, W.   Spanish Johnny.
Chapman, A.   Out Where the West Begins.
Crosby, F.   Let Me Die on the Prairie.
  On Hearing a Description of a Prairie.
Davis, M.   Going Out and Coming In.
Fisher, L.   Pioneers.
Freneau.   On the Emigration to America [and Peopling the Western Country].
Garland, H.   Goin' Back T'morrer.
Garrigue.   Grand Canyon, The.
Guest, B.   Santa Fe Trail.
Hollo.   Wild West Workshop Poem.
MacNeice.   Western Landscape.
McGrath, C.   Wheatfield Under Clouded Sky.
Michie.   Arizona Nature Myth.
Padgett, R.   After the Broken Arm.
Snyder, G.   Milton by Firelight.
Whitman, W.   Promise to California, A.
Wright, J.   Stages on a Journey Westward.
Westminster Abbey
Betjeman.   In Westminster Abbey.
Cope, W.   Engineers' Corner.
Weston, Louise B.
Fordham.   Mrs. Louise B. Weston.
Weston, Rebecca
Fordham.   Mrs. Rebecca Weston.
Weston, Samuel
Fordham.   Rev. Samuel Weston.
Whales and Whaling
Benét, W.   Whale.
Blight.   Death of a Whale.
Davis, C.   Murderer, The.
Dutton, G.   Stranded Whales, The.
Fishman, C.   Whapmagoostui.
Hoffman, D.   Armada of Thirty Whales, An.
Holm, B.   Whale Breathing: Bartlett Cove, Alaska.
Hugo, R.   Lady in Kicking Horse Reservoir, The.
Kennedy, X.   Whales off Wales, The.
Kunitz, S.   Abduction, The.
  Wellfleet Whale, The.
Lawrence, D.   Whales Weep Not!
Marcus, M.   Whales.
Meinke.   Death of the Pilot Whales, The.
Merwin, W. S.   For a Coming Extinction.
  Leviathan.
Osborn, J.   Whaling Song, A.
Pound, E.   Seafarer, The.
Schmitz.   Monstrous Pictures of Whales.
Shapiro, D.   In a Blind Garden.
Strand.   Shooting Whales.
Walcott.   Whale, His Bulwark, The.
Young, M.   Whales, The.
Wharton, Anne
Behn, A.   To Mrs. W. on Her Excellent Verses.
Wharves
Bishop, E.   Bight, The.
  Summer's Dream, A.
Bontemps.   Nocturne of the Wharves.
Wheat
Alexander, M.   Iowa Farmer.
Auden.   As I Walked Out One Evening.
"Field."   Wheat-miners.
Gehrke, S.   Walking Fields at Night South of Hampton, Iowa.
Glancy.   Wheat.
Heaney, S.   Harvest Bow, The.
McCaig.   Betweens.
Merrill, J.   Upward Look, An.
Robinson, E.   Sheaves, The.
Rossetti, C.   Amen.

Wheatley, Phillis
Hayden, R.   Letter from Phillis Wheatley, A.
Jordan, J.   Something Like a Sonnet for Phillis
   Miracle Wheatley.
Wheelbarrows
Williams, W.   Red Wheelbarrow, The.
Wheelchairs
Owen, W.   Disabled.
Wheeling, West Virginia
Wright, J.   In Response to a Rumor that the
   Oldest Whorehouse in Wheeling, West
   Virginia, Has Been Condemned.
Wheelock, Eleazar
Hovey.   Eleazar Wheelock.
Wheels
Blamire.   I've Gotten a Rock, I've Gotten a
   Reel.
Buckley, C.   Train in the Desert—1916.
Gunn, T.   Wheel of Fortune, The.
Justice, D.   Train.
Lattimore.   Note on the L and N.
Levy, A.   March Day in London, A.
Morrison, L.   Surf.
Nemerov.   Extract from Memoirs.
Pinsky.   Figured Wheel, The.
Prunty.   Ferris Wheel, The.
Whippoorwills
McLoughland.   Whippoorwill Calls, The.
Whiskey
Brecht, B.   Alabama Song.
Burns, R.   John Barleycorn [a Ballad].
   Scotch Drink.
   Willie Brew'd [or Brewed] a Peck o' Maut.
Hughes, L.   Bar.
Unknown.   Rye Whiskey.
   Rye Whisky.
Whistler, James Abbott McNeill
Plumly.   After Whistler.
Pound, E.   To Whistler, American.
Rossetti, D.   Limerick: "There's a combative
   artist named Whistler."
Salmon, A.   Painting.
Whistling and Whistlers
Baxter, J.   Twenty Little Engines.
Unknown.   Wonders of Nature.
White (color)
Alexander, E.   Nineteen.
Chavez, L.   Clean Sheets.
Coleridge, M.   White Women, The.
Creeley.   Gift, The.
"Field."   Cyclamens.
Greenberg, A.   Man in the Moon, The.
Groarke, V.   Trousseau.
Hartley, M.   Wingaersheek Beach.
Levertov.   Wings, The.
Lowry, M.   About Ice.
Nichols, G.   White.
Song.   Ikebana.
White Sulphur Springs, West Virginia
Key.   Written at the White Sulphur Springs.
White, Peregrine
Benét, R. *et al.*   Peregrine White and Virginia
   Dare.
Whitefield, George
Wheatley, P.   On the Death of the Rev. Mr.
   George Whitefield, 1770.
   Thoughts on the Works of Providence.
Whitman, Walt
Alexie.   Defending Walt Whitman.
Bibbins, M.   Whitman on the Beach.
Bly, R.   Two Ramages for Old Masters.
Butler, C. E.   Other Places, The.
Bynner.   Highest Bidder, The.
Dahlberg.   Walt Whitman.
Forbes, C.   Reading Walt Whitman.
Ginsberg, A.   Supermarket in California, A.
Honig, E.   Walt Whitman.
Hughes, L.   Old Walt.
Levis.   Whitman.
Liu, T.   Reading Whitman in a Toilet Stall.
Pound, E.   Pact, A.
Robinson, E.   Walt Whitman.
Simpson, L.   Walt Whitman at Bear Mountain.
Spicer, J.   Book of Galahad, The.

Symonds.   Love and Death: A Symphony.
Whitman, W.   Now Precedent Songs, Farewell.
Williams, J.   Adhesive Autopsy of Walt
   Whitman, The.
Whittier, John Greenleaf
Heard, J.   To Whittier.
Koch, K.   You Were Wearing.
Scott, W.   Mr. Whittier.
Widows and Widowers
Awad, J.   Widower, The.
Barber, M.   On Seeing an Officer's Widow
   Distracted.
Clifton, L.   She Lived.
Copus, J.   Widower.
Coward.   Bar on the Piccola Marina, A.
Craik.   Douglas, Douglas, Tender and True.
Crawford, R.   Downtown Sunday.
Dunbar, W.   Translation by Mark Willhardt.
"Eliza."   To My Husband.
Fields, J.   Jolly Fat Widows, The.
Glück, L.   Racer's Widow, The.
Hands, E.   Widower's Courtship, The.
Herrick.   Widow's Tears [or Widdowes Teares]:
   or, Dirge of Dorcas, The.
Hesketh.   Dilemma.
Jarrell.   Burning the Letters.
Jewett, S.   Widows' House, The.
King, H.   Exequy, The.
Kooser.   Widow, A.
Lowell, R.   For Sale.
Masters, E.   Veterans of the Wars.
   Widows.
Milton.   On His Deceased Wife.
Moulsworth, M.   Memorandum of Martha
   Moulsworth, Widow, The.
Poe.   Annabel Lee.
Ray, D.   Widower.
Selyns.   Reasons for and against Marrying
   Widows.
Smith, S.   He Told His Life Story to Mrs.
   Courtly.
Southey, R.   Soldier's Wife, The.
   Widow, The.
Tyler, R.   Widower, The.
Unknown.   Far Away.
   Lament of the Border Widow, The.
Voigt.   Exile.
Wheatley, P.   To a Lady on the Death of Her
   Husband.
Williams, W.   Widow's Lament in Springtime,
   The.
Wilson, R.   Rejoicing That Attend the Murder of
   Famous Men, The.
Wordsworth, W.   Ruined Cottage, The.
Wotton, S.   Upon the Death of Sir Albert
   Morton's Wife.
Wight, Isle of, England
Swinburne.   Forsaken Garden, A.
Wigs
Hemphill.   Homocide.
Rossetti, C.   If a pig wore a wig.
Wilberforce University
Heard, J.   Wilberforce.
Linden, M.   Golden Jubilee of Wilberforce.
   To the Conference.
Wilberforce, William
Cowper, W.   To William Wilberforce, Esq.
Wilde, Oscar
Betjeman.   Arrest of Oscar Wilde at the
   Cadogan Hotel, The.
Crane, H.   C33.
Douglas, L.   Dead Poet, The.
Swinburne.   Oscar Wilde.
Wilderness
Berry, W.   Peace of Wild Things, The.
Birney.   Bushed.
Cook, W.   Spiritual: 'How did you feel when
   you come out the wilderness?'
Davidson, D.   Sanctuary.
Dickson, S.   Song—Written at the North.
Everson, W.   High Embrace, The.
George, F.   Wilderness.
Goodtimes.   Art of Getting Lost, The.
Graves, R.   In the Wilderness.
   Rocky Acres.

Hecht, A.   Alceste in the Wilderness.
Hopkins, G.   Inversnaid.
Kinnell.   Lastness.
   Under the Maud Moon.
McKinnon.   North, The.
Mother Goose.   Man in the wilderness asked
   [of] me [or said to me], The [or A].
Rutsala.   Wilderness.
Sandburg, C.   Wilderness.
Schneiders, J.   Weight.
Scott, D.   En Route.
Scott, F.   Laurentian Shield.
Simmons, J.   In the Wilderness.
Smith, A.   Lonely Land, The.
Snyder, G.   Above Pate Valley.
   Message from Outside.
Stevens, W.   Anecdote of the Jar.
Wagoner, D.   Staying Alive.
Whitman, W.   Italian Music in Dakota.
Wildflowers
Kenny, M.   Wild Flower.
Plumly.   Peppergrass.
   Wildflower.
Williams, W.   Queen-Anne's-Lace.
**William III, King of England (William of
   Orange)**
Pugh.   King Billy on the Walls.
Williams, Arthur Clement
Bibb.   In Memory of Arthur Clement Williams.
Williams, Sir Ifor
Conran.   Elegy for Sir Ifor Williams.
Williams, Theodore Samuel ("Ted")
Corso.   Dream of a Baseball Star.
Williams, William Carlos
Blackburn, P.   Phone Call to Rutherford.
Bly, R.   Dream of William Carlos Williams, A.
Creeley.   For W.C.W.
Eady.   William Carlos Williams.
Ginsberg, A.   Death News.
Hernández Cruz.   Essay on William Carlos
   Williams, An.
Kinnell.   To William Carlos Williams.
Koch, K.   Variations on a Theme by William
   Carlos Williams.
Levertov.   Williams: An Essay.
Rexroth, K.   Letter to William Carlos
   Williams, A.
Scott, J.   Typing the Letters.
Stone, J.   Getting to Sleep in New Jersey.
Young, G.   Letter to William Carlos
   Williams, A.
Willow Trees
Bly, R.   Hunting Pheasants in a Cornfield.
Crane, H.   Repose of Rivers.
Delmore, E.   Willow.
Dixon, R.   Song: "Feathers of the willow, The."
Herrick.   To the Willow-Tree.
Levertov.   Willows of Massachusetts, The.
MacDiarmid, H.   Sauchs in the Reuch Heuch
   Hauch, The.
Pack, R.   Thrasher in the Willow by the Lake,
   The.
Rossetti, C.   Under Willows.
Sandburg, C.   Prairie Waters by Night.
Unknown.   Song, A: "My head on moss
   reclining."
Williams, W.   Willow Poem.
Wills
Carruth, H.   Testament.
Donne.   Will, The.
Leapor.   Mira's Will.
Rossetti, C.   Bruised Reed Shall He Not
   Break, A.
San Juan.   Owl of Minerva Takes Flight in the
   Evening, The.
Unknown.   Bequests.
Lord Randal[l].
Whitney, I.   Aucthour Maketh Her Wyll and
   Testament, The.
   Manner of Her Will and What She Left to
   London and to All Those in It, at Her
   Departing, The.
Wilcox, E.   Will.
Winstanley, J.   Last Will and Testament, A.

Wilson, Woodrow
Hazo.   Some Words for President Wilson.
Wiltshire, England
Sassoon.   Prehistoric Burials.
Young, A.   Wiltshire Downs.
Winchester, England
Betjeman.   Hike on the Downs, A.
Warton, T.   On King Arthur's Round Table, at
   Winchester.
Winchester, Virginia
Read, T.   Sheridan's Ride.
Wind
Alakoye.   Eshu.
Ammons, A. R.   Mansion.
   Small Song.
Anthony, G.   Autumn Evening.
Arlen, H.   Ill Wind.
Bang, M.   Crossed-Over, Fiend-Snitched, X-ed
   Out.
Barnes, W.   Brisk Wind, A.
   Jenny out from Hwome.
   Wind at the Door, The.
Beckett, S.   Enueg I.
Bennett, R.   Windy Nights.
Blake, W.   Crystal Cabinet, The.
Bly, R.   Poem Against the British.
Bogan, L.   Zone.
Brand, D.   Wind.
Brontë, A.   Lines Composed in a Wood on a
   Windy Day.
Brontë, E.   Night Wind, The.
   Sun Has Set, The.
Brooke, R.   Sonnet: "Oh! Death will find me,
   long before I tire."
Brown, G.   Haddock Fishermen.
Bryant, W.   Summer Wind.
Burns, R.   O [or Oh] Wert Thou in the Cauld
   Blast.
   Of A' the Airts [the Wind Can Blaw].
Carew, T.   Prayer to the Wind, A.
Chamberlain, K.   Riding the Lion, Riding the
   Lamb.
Chivers.   Wind, The.
Clampitt.   Beach Glass.
Clare, J.   Wind That Shakes the Rushes, The.
Clarke, A.   Strong Wind, A.
Coleridge, S.   Homeric Hexameter, The.
Crapsey.   Night Winds.
   On Seeing Weather-Beaten Trees.
Cummings, E.   What If a Much of a Which of a
   Wind.
Davies, W.   Villain, The.
Davis, O.   Panic of Birds, The.
Day Lewis.   Stand-To, The.
Dickinson, E.   Wind's Visit, The.
Doolittle, H.   Sea Rose.
   Wind Sleepers, The.
Dugan, A.   On an East Wind from the Wars.
Dybek.   Windy City.
Eady.   Success.
Emerson, R.   Snow-Storm [or Snowstorm], The.
Faigao, B.   Balitaw.
"Field."   O Wind, thou hast thy kingdom in the
   trees.
Fisher, M.   Wind in the Willow.
Frost, R.   Aim Was Song, The.
   Bereft.
   Brown's Descent; or, The Willy-Nilly.
   To the Thawing Wind.
García Lorca.   Whole Works, The.
Gascoyne.   Yves Tanguy.
Gillespie, H.   Breezin' Along with the Breeze.
Graham, J.   Gulls.
   Of Forced Sightes and Trusty Ferefulness.
Graves, R.   Weather of Olympus, The.
Gurney, I.   April Gale.
   Possessions.
Hine.   Riddle: "Invisible, chimerical."
Hoban.   Pedalling Man, The.
Horan.   By Hallucination Visited.
Hughes, T.   Wind.
Imbs.   Wind Was There, The.
Jackson, L.   Wind Suffers of Blowing, The.
Jeffers, R.   Gale in April.
Kgositsile.   Gods Wrote, The.
Kingsley, C.   Ode to the Northeast Wind.

Koehler, T.   Ill Wind.
Kooser.   Hands in the Wind.
Kreymborg.   Improvisation.
Lane, P.   Wind Thoughts.
Lawrence, D.   Butterfly.
   Suspense.
Le Guin.   Child on the Shore, The.
Levin, D.   Wind.
Lindsay, N.   Moon's the North Wind's Cooky,
   The.
Macdonald, G.   Wind and the Moon, The.
MacLeish.   Cook County.
Magidson, H.   Gone with the Wind.
Masefield.   West Wind, The.
McCrae, H.   Winds.
Merton.   Lent in a Year of War.
Merwin, W. S.   Utterance.
Meynell, A.   To the Beloved.
   Wind Is Blind, The.
Moore, L.   Homeplace, The.
Morley, D.   Politicisation of the North Wind,
   The.
Mudrooroo Narogin.   Song Circle of Jacky.
Muldoon, P.   Wind and Tree.
O'Hara, F.   To Hell with It.
Ortiz.   Vision Shadows.
Osundare.   Eyeful Glances.
Porter, H.   Four Winds.
Probyn.   Rondelet: "Say what you please."
Radcliffe, A.   To the Winds.
Raworth.   Collapsible.
Reese, L.   Wind.
Ridge, L.   Fifth-Floor Window, The.
   Kerensky.
Robinson, E.   New England.
Roethke.   Big Wind.
   Child on Top of a Greenhouse.
   Mid-Country Blow.
   Words for the Wind.
Rose, P.   Wind Debates Asian Immigration, The.
Rossetti, C.   Who Has Seen the Wind?
   Wind Has Such a Rainy Sound, The.
Rothman, D.   When the Wind and Dark Waves
   Come.
Sandburg, C.   Four Preludes on Playthings of
   the Wind.
   Wind Song.
Sargent, E.   Sea-Breeze at Matanzas, The.
Segal, J.   Wind in the Willow.
Shelley, P.   Dirge, A: "Rough wind, that
   moanest loud."
Shepherd, R.   Maritime.
Simms, C.   Pallid Harrier.
Simons, S.   Breezin' Along with the Breeze.
Steele, T.   Library, The.
Stephens, J.   Wind, The.
Stevens, W.   Room on a Garden, A.
   To the Roaring Wind.
   Valley Candle.
Stevenson, A.   Gales.
Stevenson, R.   Windy Nights.
Strand.   Man in the Tree, The.
   Marriage, The.
Taylor, A.   Air.
Teasdale.   After Love.
Torres, E.   Breezy Delicious Day.
Turner, F.   April Wind.
Unknown.   I Have a Young Sister.
   Riddle: "High as the sky it flies."
   Western Wind.
   Winds, The.
Warren, R.   Blow, West Wind.
White, M.   Recurrence.
Whiting, R.   Breezin' Along with the Breeze.
Wilbur.   After the Last Bulletins.
   Sleepless at Crown Point.
Williams, W.   Black Winds, The.
   January.
   Wind Increases, The.
Wordsworth, D.   Address to a Child during a
   Boisterous Winter Evening.
See also **North Wind; Tornadoes; West Wind;**
   East Wind
Windmills
Bergman, A.   Windmills of Your Mind, The.
Clarke, G.   Windmill.

Windows
Barnstone, A.   Windows in Providence.
Brooks, G.   Boy Breaking Glass.
Cary, A.   Window Just Over the Street, The.
Clark, T.   Eyeglasses.
Corbet [or Corbett].   Upon Fairford Windows.
Cowper, W.   Lines Written upon a Window-
   Shutter at Weston.
Cummings, E.   Spring is like a perhaps hand.
Daryush.   Still-Life.
Davis, J.   Zoo, The.
Davis, O.   Panic of Birds, The.
"Field."   Nightfall.
Fishman, L.   V's Farmhouse.
Grennan.   Woman at Lit Window.
Herbert, G.   Windows, The.
Jackson, L.   Prisms.
Lane, P.   Girl at the Window.
Larkin, P.   Aubade: "I work all day, and get
   half-drunk at night."
Levertov.   Crack, The.
Lindsay, N.   Factory Windows Are Always
   Broken.
Longfellow, H.   Ropewalk, The.
Madhubuti.   After Her Man Had Left Her for
   the Sixth Time That Year (An Uncommon
   Occurrence).
Mew.   On the Asylum Road.
Millay, E.   From a Train Window.
Moore, H.   Window at Key West, A.
Nemerov.   Storm Windows.
Paino.   1965.
Palmer, M.   Theory of the Flower, The.
   Untitled (February 2000).
Raab, L.   Sudden Appearance of a Monster at a
   Window.
Rankine.   New Windows.
Reed, H.   Door and the Window, The.
Ridge, L.   Fifth-Floor Window, The.
Rossetti, C.   Reflection.
Shange.   Tango.
Smith, I.   Old Woman, The.
Synge.   Dread.
Taggart, J.   Sainte-Chapelle.
Thomas, R.   View from the Window, The.
Wallace-Crabbe.   Windows, The.
Williams, W.   Young Woman at a Window.
Windsor Castle
Denham.   Cooper's Hill.
Surrey.   Prison in Windsor Castle.
Windsor Forest, England
Pope, A.   Hunting and Fishing.
   Lines Written in Windsor Forest.
   Progress.
Wine
Al-Harizi.   Under Leafy Bowers.
Aldrich, H.   Catch, A.
Ayres.   Fly, The.
Carruth, H.   Quality of Wine.
Cassells.   From the Theater of Wine.
Clements, A.   Elegy.
Cowley, A.   Epicure, The.
Crashaw.   To Our Lord, upon the Water Made
   Wine.
Doolittle, H.   Wine Bowl.
Dubrava.   Miraculous Marriage of Zarife
   Dominquez.
Emerson, R.   Bacchus.
Garrett, E.   Moules à la Marinière.
Heaney, S.   Cana Revisited.
Herrick.   Anacreontic[k] Verse.
   His Farewell [or Fare-well] to Sack.
   To Live Merrily, and To Trust to Good Verses.
   Welcome to Sack, A.
Jonson, B.   Epigram. To the Household. 1630,
   An.
Kooser.   How to Make Rhubarb Wine.
Li Po.   Drinking Alone in the Moonlight.
Lovelace, R.   Fly about a Glass[e] of Burnt
   Claret, A.
   Loose Saraband, A.
   Vintage to the Dungeon, The.
Page, G.   In Dante's Hell.
Pankey.   Reason, The.
Rilke.   On the Marriage at Cana.
Shirley, J.   Two Gentlemen That Broke Their

Promise of a Meeting.
Steele, P.   Cana.
Thomas, D.   This Bread I Break.
Tighe.   Wine, I Say! I'll Drink to Madness!
Winters, Y.   In Praise of California Wines.
Yeats.   Drinking Song, A.

Wings
Andrews, N.   That Cold Summer.
Brontë, C.   Like wolf—and black bull or goblin hound.
Day Lewis.   Conflict, The.
Dickinson, E.   Bat, The.
Dove, R.   Wingfoot Lake.
Herbert, G.   Easter Wings.
Hopkins, G.   God's Grandeur.
Levertov.   Dead Butterfly, The.
Mataka.   Ornithology.
Robinson, A.   Song: "Oh for the wings of a dove."
Rossetti, C.   On the Wing.
Sewell, L.   Expulsion.
Sexton.   To a Friend Whose Work Has Come to Triumph.
Smith, C.   On the Aphorism "L'Amitié est l'Amour sans Ailes."
Warren, R.   Evening Hawk.
Watson, R.   Cage, The.
Yeats.   Mother of God, The.

Winter
Allingham.   In Snow.
Bachmann.   Days in White.
Barnes, W.   Winter Night, A.
Berryman.   Winter Landscape.
Winter-Piece to a Friend Away, A.
Bethell.   Warning of Winter.
Binyon.   Winter Sunrise.
Blind.   Winter Landscape, A.
Bly, R.   Six Winter Privacy Poems.
Three Kinds of Pleasures.
Boland, E.   Pomegranate, The.
Brody.   Winter Nocturne: The Hospital.
Brooks, G.   Cynthia in the Snow.
Brown, L.   Winter Sonnet.
Brown, S.   Virginia Portrait.
Bruner.   Midwinter.
Bryant, W.   Death of the Flowers, The.
Winter Piece, A.
Burns, R.   Up in the Morning Early.
Buxton.   Putting the World to Bed.
Bynner.   Wintry Mind, The.
Cahn, S.   Let It Snow! Let It Snow! Let It Snow!
Campbell, T.   Ode to Winter.
Campbell, W.   How One Winter Came in the Lake Region.
Winter Lakes, The.
Campion, T.   Now Winter Nights Enlarge.
Carruth, H.   Twilight Comes.
Clare, J.   Winter.
Clark, L.   Singing in the Streets.
Coleridge, M.   Witch, The.
Collins, M.   Winter in Brighton.
Cope, J.   Winter Sky.
Cranch.   December.
Crapsey.   Arbutus.
Cristall.   Snow-Fiend, The.
Song: "Through springtime walks, with flowers perfumed."
Daniel, G.   Robin, The.
Davies, J.   Winter.
De la Mare.   Alone.
Winter.
Dickinson, E.   Tree in Winter.
Dillon, G.   Snow.
Donaghy, J.   Winter.
Donne.   Nocturnal[l] upon Saint Lucy's [or S. Lucy's or S. Lucies] Day, Being the Shortest Day, A.
Eberhart, R.   Spider, The.
Eigner.   Open Air Where.
Eliot, T.   Journey of the Magi.
Erdrich, H.   Quiet Earth, The.
Evance, S.   To Melancholy.
Fallon, P.   Winter Work.
Farrar, J.   Comparison, A.
Ferguson, G.   Winter Rose, The.

Winter Sunflowers.
"Field."   Sullenness.
To the Winter Aphrodite.
Field, R.   Something Told the Wild Geese.
Finch, B.   Written in a Winter's Morning.
Finch, R.   Turning.
Fisher, A.   Snowy Benches.
Flynn, F.   Winter Morning.
Follain.   Music of Spheres.
Francis, R.   Blue Winter.
Frost, R.   Birches.
Hillside Thaw, A.
Old Man's Winter Night, An.
Onset, The.
Reluctance.
Stopping by Woods on a Snowy Evening.
Gascoyne.   Winter Garden.
Gerner, K.   House of Breath.
Gilbert, J.   White Heart of God, The.
Glück, L.   Illuminations.
Goetsch, D.   Nobody's Hell.
Graves, R.   Frosty Night, A.
Star-Talk.
Greenberg, A.   Wintering Over at the End of the Century.
Grier.   My Winter Past.
Grimké, A.   Winter Twilight, A.
Grimke, C.   Parting Hymn, A.
Hardy, T.   Birds at Winter Nightfall.
Frozen Greenhouse, The.
I Need Not Go.
Neutral Tones.
Winter in Durnover Field.
Harjo, J.   Skeleton of Winter.
Hayden, R.   Those Winter Sundays.
Hayne, P.   On the Occurrence of a Spell of Arctic Weather in May, 1858.
Heaney, S.   Exposure.
Hecht, A.   Sestina d'Inverno.
Henry, P.   Winter Wedding, The.
Henson, L.   I Am Singing the Cold Rain.
Hollander, J.   Effet de Neige.
Hopkins, G.   Winter with the Gulf Stream.
Horan.   By Hallucination Visited.
Soft Swimmer, Winter Swan.
Housman, A.   Night Is Freezing Fast, The.
Huchel.   Landscape Beyond Warsaw.
Hughes, L.   Winter Moon.
Hughes, R.   Winter.
Hughes, T.   New Year's [or Year] Song.
Roe-Deer.
Snowdrop.
Hugo, R.   Letter to Hill from St. Ignatius.
Letter to Scanlon from Whitehall.
Hunter, A.   Winter.
Jennings, E.   Winter Love.
Jewett, S.   Country Boy in Winter, A.
Jordan, J.   Winter.
Kantaris.   Stocking Up.
Keats.   In Drear-nighted December.
Keithley.   First Morning.
Kennedy, X.   One Winter Night in August.
Kenny, M.   December.
Kenyon, J.   Depression in Winter.
February: Thinking of Flowers.
Killeen, G.   Wishes.
Kinnell.   Bear, The.
Knoepfle.   Late Winter in Menard County.
Komunyakaa.   Smokehouse, The.
Lampman.   In November: "Hills and leafless forests slowly yield, The."
Winter Evening.
Lea, S.   Tempted by the Classical on Returning from the Store at Twenty Below Zero.
Levertov.   Crack, The.
Lewis, J.   Stories.
Winter Garden.
Liu Tsung-yüan.   River Snow.
Locke, M.   Sonnet: "I hate the Spring in parti-coloured vest."
Longenbach.   What You Find in the Woods.
Longfellow, H.   Afternoon in February.
Fragment: December 18, 1847.
Snow-Flakes.
Longley, M.   Remembering Carrigskeewaun.
Lorde.   Woman Thing, The.

Lovelace, R.   Grasshopper, The.
Lowell, R.   Inauguration Day: January 1953.
New Year's Day.
Lucie-Smith.   Poet in Winter.
MacCaig.   Sleet.
Macdonald, G.   Sweet Peril.
Markus, P.   Shooting Crows.
McAuley, J.   Winter Drive.
McDonald, W.   Winter Before the War, The.
McGrath, T.   Black Train, The.
Merwin, W. S.   Dusk in Winter.
Miles, S.   Plumbers.
Millay, E.   Winter Night.
Momaday.   Winter Holding off the Coast of North America.
Mother Goose.   Winter.
Mueller, L.   Another Version.
Nameroff, R.   California Dreaming.
Nash, O.   Winter Morning.
Opie.   To Winter.
Oppen.   From a Photograph.
Osgood, F.   Winter Fairyland in Vermont.
Owen, G.   Winter Days.
Owen, W.   Exposure.
Padgett, R.   December.
Peake.   Conceit.
Pfeiffer, E.   Song of Winter, A.
Philips, A.   Winter-Piece, A.
Plath.   Wintering.
Po Chü-i.   Sitting at Night.
Pound, E.   Ancient Music.
Rakosi.   Fluteplayers from Finmarken.
Ramsay, A.   Up in the Air.
Rickword.   Winter Warfare.
Roberson.   Blue Horses.
Roberts, E.   Cold Fear.
Robinson, M.   January, 1795.
Rochester, J.   Mistress, The: A Song.
Roethke.   Coming of the Cold, The.
Rossetti, C.   Amen.
Christmas Carol, A: "In the bleak mid-winter."
Endure Hardness.
Grown and Flown.
Winter: My Secret.
Rothman, D.   Let It Snow.
Ryan, R.   Lake of the Woods, The.
Winter in Minneapolis.
Sackville-West.   Persia.
Samyn, M.   Trompe L'Oeil in Winter.
Sansom, A.   Confinement.
Sarton.   On a Winter Night.
Scott-Heron.   Winter in America.
Scupham.   After Ovid, Tristia.
Seward.   December Morning.
Shelley, P.   Summer and Winter.
Shumaker.   First Winter: Joy.
Simic.   Winter Night.
Simmons, J.   Archæologist, The.
Sirr.   Collector's Marginalia, The.
Smith, M.   Stopping to Take Notes.
Snyder, G.   Dragonfly.
River Snow.
Solari, R.   December 25, 1991.
Spender, S.   Ice.
Stephens, J.   White Fields.
Stevens, W.   Course of a Particular, The.
Discovery of Thought, A.
Meditation Celestial and Terrestrial.
No Possum, No Sop, No Taters.
Snow Man, The.
Stevenson, R.   Ille Terrarum.
Winter Time [or Winter-Time].
Stroud, J.   Oh Yes.
Stryk, L.   Winter Storm.
Sutter.   Hoarfrost and Fog.
Synge.   Winter.
Tabb.   Winter Twilight, A.
Tate, A.   Seasons of the Soul.
Taylor, A.   Fire.
Teasdale.   February Twilight.
Night.
Thaxter.   Chanticleer.
Thomas, E.   Thaw.
Thompson, P.   Winter Night, A.
Thoreau.   Pray to What Earth Does This Sweet Cold Belong.

To the Maiden in the East.
Winter and Spring Scene, A.
Winter Memories.
Thrale [*later* Mrs. Piozzi]. Winter in Wales, A.
Tomlinson, C. Weather Report.
Triplett, P. Winter Swim.
Turner, W. Song: "Lovely hill-torrents are."
Unknown. Night Was Growing Cold, The.
When the Snow is on the Ground.
Winter [*or* Wynter] Wakeneth All [*or* Al] My Care.
Winter Wise.
Updike. Winter Ocean.
Valéry. Helen.
Van Walleghen. Elephant in Winter, The.
Vaughan, H. I Walked [*or* Walkt] the Other Day to Spend My Hour.
Very. Robe, The.
Spirit, The.
Winter Rain, The.
Walcott. Village Life, A.
Wanek. Duluth, Minnesota.
Weslowski. Heart.
White, G. On the Dark, Still, Dry, Warm Weather Occasionally Happening in the Winter Months.
White, H. Winter Traveler, The.
Whiteman. Winter Burn.
Whitman, W. To a Locomotive in Winter.
Whittier. Firelight.
Snow-Bound [*or* Snow-Bound; a Winter Idyl].
Wilbur. April 5, 1974.
Sonnet: "Winter deepening, the hay all in, The."
Year's End.
Williams, M. Heading for the Heights.
Williams, W. These.
Willis, N. January 1, 1829.
Wingfield. Winter.
Wolfe, M. Thaw, The.
Wordsworth, D. Address to a Child during a Boisterous Winter Evening.
Wright, D. Winter at Gurnard's Head.
Wright, J. Desire's Persistence.
Late November in a Field.
Sonnet for Christmas.
Sparrows in a Hillside Drift.
Wright, K. Red Boots On.
Wylie. Velvet Shoes.
Yearsley. To————: "Lo! dreary Winter, howling o'er the waste."
Young, M. Winter Scene.

Winters, Yvor
Gunn, T. To Yvor Winters, 1955.

Wisconsin (state)
Bly, R. Three Kinds of Pleasures.
Eberhart, R. La Crosse at Ninety Miles an Hour.
Wallace, R. Makings of Happiness, The.

Wisdom
Arnold, M. Shakespeare.
Atwood. Procedures for Underground.
Bogan, L. Men Loved Wholly Beyond Wisdom.
Brecht, B. Three Fragments.
Brew. Search, The.
Carter, E. Ode to Wisdom.
Chimombo. Messengers, The.
Coleridge, M. Wasted.
Crane, H. Praise for an Urn.
Crashaw. Neither Durst Any Man From That Day Ask Him Any More Questions.
Creeley. En Famille.
Cummings, E. You Shall Above All Things Be Glad and Young.
Davenant [*or* D'Avenant]. Lover and Philosopher.
Davison, P. Star Watcher, The.
De la Mare. Moonlight.
Duggan, L. Eight xx.
Eclipse. Cicada.
Emerson, R. Limits.
Prudence.
Fabian, C. Prayer of Dedication.
Fitzgerald, E. 27.
Gottlieb, A. Meditation on the Feminine Nature of Shekinah, A.
Guiney. Kings, The.

Hölderlin. In the Days of Socrates.
Hacker, M. Rune of the Finland Woman.
Herbert, G. Elixir [*or* Elixer], The.
Hewitt, J. Once Alien Here.
Hixon, L. Who can keep a blazing fire tied in a cotton cloth?
Jeffers, R. Prescription of Painful Ends.
Jonson, B. Ode, An: "High-spirited friend, / I send not balms, nor corsives to your wound."
Kavanagh, P. To Hell with Commonsense.
Lawrence, D. Race and Battle.
Macdonald, G. Baby-Sermon, A.
Maybe, E. Umbilical Cord.
Merrill, J. World and the Child, The.
Montagu, L. Lover, The; a Ballad.
Nesbit, E. Things That Matter, The.
Ono. Mother of the Universe.
Oppen. Quotations.
Owen, M. African Sunday.
Pelizzon, V. Clever and Poor.
Philips, A. Wit and Wisdom.
Ransom, J. Tall Girl, The.
Richards, E. Wise Old Owl, A.
Richardson, J. Vectors: Forty-five Aphorisms and Ten-second Essays.
Rios, A. Advice to a First Cousin.
Robinson, A. Wise-Woman, The.
Robinson, E. Master, The.
Rothman, D. Youth.
Ruefle. Topophilia.
Rupp. Sophia.
Sill. Truth at Last.
Smith, C. Thirty-eight: Addressed to Mrs H—y.
Smith, S. Is It Wise?
Sobiloff. Wisdom.
Sowle, L. Short Testimony for Anne Whitehead, A.
Spender, S. Auden at Milwaukee.
Stevenson, A. He Who Loved Beauty.
Swift, J. Stella's Birthday ([March 13,] 1727).
Stella's Birthday [1721].
Tennyson, A. Dedication, A: "Dear, near and true—no truer Time himself."
Thomas, D. Should Lanterns Shine.
Thomas, E. Glory, The.
Tolson, M. African China.
Tufts, C. We Take the New Young Couple Out to Dinner.
Unknown. Man in Our Town.
Whalen. Sourdough Mountain Lookout.
Wheatley, P. Thoughts on the Works of Providence.
Whitman, W. When I Heard the Learn'd Astronomer.
Winner, R. Segregated Railway Diner—1946.
Winter, M. In the Beginning.
Wojahn. Allegory: Attic and Fever.
Wordsworth, W. Resolution and Independence.
Wright, J. Gum-trees Stripping.
Yeats. Brown Penny.
Coming of Wisdom with Time, The.

See also **Reason**

Wishes
Arlen, H. If I Only Had a Brain (If I Only Had a Heart) (If I Only Had the Nerve).
Over the Rainbow.
Blake, E. I'm Craving for That Kind of Love.
Bock, J. If I Were a Rich Man.
Bowles, W. To a Friend.
Child, A. Wishes.
Chudleigh. Wish, The.
Clifton, L. Wishes for Sons.
Coleridge, M. Insincere Wish Addressed to a Beggar, An.
Cook, W. Spiritual: 'How did you feel when you come out the wilderness?'
Coward. Room with a View, A.
Donaldson, W. Carolina in the Morning.
When My Ship Comes In.
Fain, S. I Can Dream, Can't I?
Greenwell, D. Scherzo, A.
Herrick. Upon Batt.
Jarrell. Man Meets a Woman in the Street, A.
Johnson, S. Scholar's Life, The.
Vanity of Human Wishes, The; The Tenth Satire of Juvenal Imitated.

Kahal, I. I Can Dream, Can't I?
Kahn, G. Carolina in the Morning.
When My Ship Comes In.
Killeen, G. Wishes.
Komey. Oblivion.
Lamantia. Time Traveler's Potlatch.
Marston, P. Vain Wish, A.
McDonald, D. Birthday Wish, A.
McGinley. Reflections at Dawn.
Pilkington, L. Wish, By a Young Lady, The.
Poe. Stanzas.
Porter, A. Five Wishes.
Rogers, S. Wish, A.
Salter. What Do Women Want?
Sandburg, C. Mag.
Sissle, N. I'm Craving for That Kind of Love.
Teasdale. Moods.
Sanctuary, The.
Unknown. Wishing Poem.
Ward, E. Extravagant Drunkard's Wish, The.
Yeats. He Wishes for the Cloths of Heaven.

Wisteria
Healy, E. Wisteria.

Wit
Behn, A. Rover or The Banished Cavaliers, The.
Calverley. Flight.
Cowley, A. Ode: Of Wit.
Pope, A. Impromptu to Lady Winchelsea.
Vaughan, H. To the Most Excellently Accomplished Mrs. Katherine Philips.
Winchilsea. Introduction, The: "Did I, my lines intend for public[k] view."

Witchcraft and Witches
Abercrombie. Witchcraft: New Style.
Allingham. Witch-Bride, The.
Benét, S. Cotton Mather.
Bennett, R. Witch of Willowby Wood, The.
Burns, R. Tam o' Shanter; A Tale.
Clifton, L. In Salem.
Coleman, C. Witchcraft.
Coleridge, M. Witch, The.
Witches' Wood, The.
Cooley, N. Mary Warren's Sampler.
Mother: Dorcas Good.
Publick Fast on Account of the Afflicted: March 31, 1692.
Crapsey. Witch, The.
De la Mare. As Lucy Went A-Walking.
Ride-by-Nights, The.
Frost, R. Witch of Coös, The.
Gowar. Annabell and the Witches.
Graves, R. Hag-Ridden.
Herrick. Hag, The.
Hogg, J. Witch o' Fife, The.
Witch's Chant, A.
Housman, A. Her Strong Enchantments Failing.
Johnson, J. White Witch, The.
Kuskin. Witches' Ride, The.
Leigh, C. Witchcraft.
Livingston, M. Lazy Witch.
Pfeiffer, E. Witch's Last Ride, The.
Reed, I. Black Cock, The.
Reznikoff. Two Witches.
Robinson, A. Wise-Woman, The.
Santal. Witch, The.
Scott, W. Witch's Ballad, The.
Sexton. Her Kind.
Shorter. Wind on the Hills, The.
Silko. Invention of White People, The.
Smith, S. Little Boy Lost.
Speyer. Witch!
Tynan. Witch, The.
Unknown. Queen Nefertiti.
Witches, The.
Villanueva, A. Power.
Walker, M. Ballad of the Hoppy-Toad.
Molly Means.
Whittier. Changeling, The.
Yeats. Song Of Wandering Aengus, The.

Wittgenstein, Ludwig Josef Johann
Murphy, R. Philosopher and the Birds, The.

Wives
Adams, J. There's Nae Luck about the House.
Alvi, M. Backgrounds.

Carrying My Wife.
Fish.
Man Impregnated.
Missing.
Baillie, J.　Hooly and Fairly.
Bang, M.　Crossed-Over, Fiend-Snitched, X-ed Out.
Baraka.　For Hettie.
Barber, M.　Conclusion of a Letter to the Rev. Mr. C, The.
Barnes, W.　Wife A-Lost, The.
Wife a-Prais'd, A.
"Bendo."　Dream, The.
Blamire.　O Donald! Ye Are Just the Man.
Bloom, V.　Sun-a-shine, Rain-a-fall.
Bottke, A.　How to Approach Your Lover's Wife.
Breton, A.　Free Union.
Brontë, C.　Pilate's Wife's Dream.
Browning, R.　Any Wife to Any Husband.
Burns, R.　Kellyburnbraes.
Caruthers.　Prayer of Any Husband.
Cave.　Elegy on a Maiden Name, An.
Chudleigh.　To the Ladies.
Cowper, W.　To Mary.
Day, C.　Who Drags the Fiery Artist Down?
Delgado, J.　Recommitted.
Dove, R.　Daystar.
Egerton, S.　Emulation, The.
To Marina.
Eliot, T.　Dedication to My Wife, A.
Frost, R.　Paul's Wife.
George, D.　Asenath.
Gioia.　Country Wife, The.
Goldsmith, O.　Double Transformation, The.
"H., H. E."　Riddle, The.
Hardy, T.　Wives in the Sere.
Hartnett.　Retreat of Ita Cagney, The.
Haynes, C.　Any Wife or Husband.
Hirsch, E.　Husband and Wife.
Holst-Warhaft.　Old Men of Athens, The.
Jarrell.　Next Day.
Jonson, B.　Epistle. To Katharine, Lady Aubigny.
Kaufman, S.　Job's Wife.
Kavanagh, P.　Tinker's Wife.
Kendrick, D.　Sadie Snuffs a Candle.
Kossman.　Pilate's Wife.
Layton.　Berry Picking.
Lewis, E.　Advice to a Young Lady Lately Married.
Lim-Wilson.　Ringmaster's Wife.
Lindsay, L.　Auld Robin Gray.
Lowell, R.　Old Flame, The.
McBride, M.　Knife-Thrower's Wife, The.
Mei Yao Ch'en.　I Remember the River at Wu Sung.
Millay, E.　Witch-Wife.
Milton.　On His Deceased Wife.
Monk, M.　Verses Written on Her Death-Bed at Bath to Her Husband in London.
Mother Goose.　Pumpkin-Eater, The.
Mugo, M. G.　Wife of the Husband.
Nesbit, E.　Wife of All Ages, The.
Ondaatje.　Cinnamon Peeler, The.
Penn, R.E.　Hand.
Prior.　Fable, A: "In Æsop's tales an honest wretch we find."
Probyn.　Mésalliance, A.
Purdy, A.　Alive or Not.
Ríos, A.　Teodoro Luna's Two Kisses.
Radnóti.　Letter to My Wife.
Ramanujan.　Love Poem for a Wife, 2.
Rochester, J.　To My More Than Meritorious Wife.
Roethke.　Wish for a Young Wife.
Rungano.　Woman, The.
Schwartz, D.　Passionate Shepherd to His Love, The.
Selyns.　Of Scolding Wives and the Third Day Ague.
Sexton.　For My Lover, Returning to His Wife.
Sims.　Garden Song, A.
Smedley, M.　Contrast, A.
Smith, S.　Be Off!
Smith, W.　There Was an Old Woman Named

Piper.
Stevenson, A.　By the Boat House, Oxford.
Stoddard, E.　Wife Speaks, The.
Strong, L.　Brewer's Man, The.
Tennyson, A.　June Bracken and Heather.
Thomas, E.　Forsaken Wife, The.
New Litany, Occasioned by an Invitation to a Wedding, A.
Unknown.　As I Was A-walking by Yon Green Garden.
Did you eever, iver, over?
I Am Your Wife.
Maxims (Exeter Book).
Shady Grove.
Tell Her So.
Wee Cooper of Fife, The.
Wife's Lament, The.
Viorst.　Honeymoon is Over, The.
Voigt.　Farm Wife.
Watkyns.　Shrew, The.
Wickham.　Sung in a Graveyard.
Williams, C.　Alzheimer's: The Wife.
Williams, W.　Mezzo Forte.
Young Housewife, The.
Winchilsea.　Letter to Daphnis, A.
Reformation.
Winstanley, J.　Last Will and Testament, A.
Wotton, S.　Upon the Death of Sir Albert Morton's Wife.
Wright, J.　Complaint.
Wright, M.　Address to Her Husband.
Young, D.　For a Wife in Jizzen.
See also **Marriage**
Wolsey, Thomas, Cardinal
Skelton, J.　Spirituality vs. the Temporality, The.
Wolves
Blue Cloud.　Wolf.
Brontë, C.　Like wolf—and black bull or goblin hound.
Durston.　Wolf, The.
Gunn, T.　Allegory of the Wolf Boy, The.
Hughes, T.　Amulet.
Howling of Wolves, The.
Modest Proposal, A.
Klee.　Wolf Speaks, The.
Lillard.　Lobo.
MacNeice.　Wolves.
Marquis.　Aesop Revised by Archy.
McClure, M.　From the Window of the Beverly Wilshire Hotel.
McDonald, W.　Hauling Over Wolf Creek Pass in Winter.
More, S.　De Principe Bono et Malo.
Nemerov.　Wolves in the Zoo.
Silko.　Four Mountain Wolves.
Tallmountain.　Last Wolf, The.
Tate, A.　Wolves, The.
Walwicz.　Little Red Riding Hood.
Woman Suffrage
Cary, P.　Advice Gratis to Certain Women.
Jonas, R.　Brother Baptis' on Woman Suffrage.
See also **Voting and Voters**
Women
Abena, B.　Liberation.
Acam-Oturu.　Arise to the Day's Toil.
Acholonu.　Water Woman.
"Ada."　Appeal to Women, An.
Scroll is open, The.
Adcock, F.　Soho Hospital for Women, The.
Adisa.　Discover Me.
No, Women Don't Cry.
Albert-Birot.　Balalaïka.
Algarin.　Trampling.
Allen, P.　Dear World.
Allison, D.　Women Who Hate Me, The.
Alvarez, J.　Woman's Work.
Amadiume.　Bloody Masculinity.
Oya Now.
Amis, K.　Bookshop Idyll, A.
Angelou.　Woman Me.
Armantrout.　Getting Warm.
Arnold, C.　Disembodied Voices of Women, The.
Arp.　Man. The Woman, The.
Arrillaga.　Dream.

Like Raquel.
Ashur-Nasir-Pal.　Hymn to Ishtar.
Askhari.　Circular Fate.
Atwood.　Marrying the Hangman.
Torture.
Ayres.　Epigram on Woman, An.
Baker, H.　Declaimer, The.
Baraka.　Beautiful Black Women.
Barbauld.　Rights of Woman, The.
Barber, M.　Conclusion of a Letter to the Rev. Mr. C——, The.
Barer, M.　Shall We Join the Ladies?
Barnes, J.　Hot Dog Poem, The.
Beer, P.　Footbinding.
Jane Austen.
Behn, A.　To the Fair Clarinda [or Clorinda], Who Made Love to Me, Imagined [or Imagin'd] More Than Woman.
Benn.　Night Café.
Bennett, G.　To a Dark Girl.
Benton, S.　Lilith.
Second Coming, The.
Berezan, J.　Hail Mother full of grace power is with thee.
Bernard [or Bernart] de Ventadour [or Ventadorn].　Lark, The.
Berry, J.　Girls Can We Educate We Dads?
Betham-Edwards.　Power of Women, The.
Betjeman.　Business Girls.
Bissert.　Most Beautiful Woman at My Highschool Reunion, The.
Bogan, L.　Evening in the Sanitarium.
Women.
Borson.　Talk.
Bradstreet, A.　In Honour of that High and Mighty Princess Queen Elizabeth of Happy Memory.
Prologue, The.
Braithwaite.　Watchers, The.
Breton, A.　Free Union.
Brontë, C.　Lonely Lady, The.
Brooks, G.　Beverly Hills, Chicago.
Children of the Poor, The.
First Fight. Then Fiddle.
Mrs. Small.
Rites for Cousin Vit, The.
Sunset of the City, A.
To Black Women.
Broumas, O.　Rapunzel.
Brown, L.　Magnolia.
Turn On the Heat.
Brown, S.　Feminine Intuition.
Browning, E.　Lord Walter's Wife.
To George Sand: A Desire.
To George Sand: A Recognition.
Burke, C.　Motor Oil Queen.
Burke, J.　Personality.
Burns, R.　Bonnie Lesley.
Byron, G.　She Walks in Beauty.
Cable, G.　Belle Layotte.
Cambridge, A.　Desire.
Campbell, J.　Old Woman, The.
Campion, T.　I Care Not for These Ladies.
Canan.　Inanna's Chant.
Mother Dawning.
Oh Kali.
Cardiff.　Combing.
Carew, T.　Rapture, A.
Song, [A]: "Ask[e] me no more where Jove bestow[e]s."
To My Mistress Sitting by a River's Side; an Eddy.
Cartwright, W.　Women.
Cary, P.　Advice Gratis to Certain Women.
Cassells.　Women, The.
Castillo, A.　Women Are Not Roses.
Cataldi.　It's Easy.
We Could Have Met.
Cavendish, M.　Of Many Worlds in This World.
Woman drest by Age, A.
Cendrars.　My Dance.
Ceravolo.　Women, The.
Cervantes.　Beneath the Shadow of the Freeway.
Isla Mujeres.
To We Who Were Saved by the Stars.
Chaucer.　Balade: "Hide [or Hyd], Absalon, thy

gilte tresses clere."
Chesterton, G. Ballade D'une Grande Dame.
Chipasula. Ritual Girl.
 Those Rainy Mornings.
Chrystos. Old Indian Granny, The.
 Wings of a Wild Goose, The.
Chudleigh. To the Ladies.
Cisneros, S. Loose Women.
Clarke, A. Subjection of Women, The.
Clemmons. Freedom Song for the Black
 Woman, A.
Cleveland, J. Antiplatonic[k], The.
Clifton, L. Calming Kali.
 Earth is a living thing, The.
 For de Lawd.
 Kali.
 Song at midnight.
 Thirty-Eighth Year, The.
 Way It Was, The.
 Wishes for Sons.
 Women you are accustomed to, The.
Clinton, M. Warning to Young Bright Sisters /
 White AM. Culture 101A.
Cofer, J. Old Women.
 Spring.
 Why There Are No Unicorns.
 Women Who Love Angels.
Coleridge, M. Clever Woman, A.
 Marriage.
 Other Side of a Mirror, The.
 White Women, The.
Collier, M. Womans Labour, an Epistle, The.
Cook, E. Song of the Ugly Maiden.
Cook, W. Seth Bingham.
Cooley, N. John Winthrop, 'Reasons to be
 Considered for...the Intended Plantation in New
 England,' 1629.
 Publick Fast on Account of the Afflicted: March
 31, 1692.
"Coolidge." My Rights.
Corbett, E. Three Wise Old Women.
Corfield, J. Morse Lesson.
Cortez, J. Grinding Vibrato.
Cott, J. Isis (Lady of Petals).
Couzyn. Mystery, The.
 Pain, The.
Coward. Nina.
Crawford, V. Pioneer Woman.
Creeley. Air: "The Love of a Woman."
 All That Is Lovely in Men.
 Memory, The.
 Three Ladies, The.
 Whip, The.
Cristall. Elegy on a Young Lady.
Crompton. Epigram VII: Winifred.
Cumbo. Black Sister.
Cummings, E. If I Have Made, My Lady.
Cuney. No Images.
Cuthand, B. She Ties Her Bandanna.
D'Orleans. Oft in My Thought.
 Smiling Mouth, The.
Dacre, C. Female Philosopher, The.
 Similie.
Dambroff. Resistance.
Daniels, K. Women's Room in Pennsylvania
 Station, The.
Davies, S. In Librum.
Day Lewis. My Mother's Sister.
De Kok. Small Passing.
De Los Santos, M. Women Watching
 Basketball.
DeCarteret, M. Town Clerk, The.
Derricotte. For Black Women Who Are Afraid.
Dharker. Purdah, 1.
Di Prima. Loba as Eve.
 Practice of Magical Evocation, The.
Dickey, J. Weeds.
DiPalma. Fragment.
DiPrima, C. Her Eyes a Thousand Times Over.
Donald. Eye for an Eye, An.
Donne. Indifferent, The.
 Love's Alchemy [or Alchemie].
 Song: "Go and catch a falling star."
 Twicknam [or Twickenham] Garden.
 Woman's Constancy.
Donovan, K. Underneath Our Skirts.

Dorn, E. On the Debt My Mother Owed to
 Sears Roebuck.
Dove, R. Great Palaces of Versailles, The.
Doyle, S. Some Girls.
Drummond, W. Madrigal: "Like the Idalian
 Quee[e]."
Dryden, J. To the Pious Memory of the
 Accomplished [or Accomplisht] Young Lady,
 Mrs. Anne Killigrew, [Excellent in the Two
 Sister-Arts of Poesie and Painting].
Dubin, A. Dames.
Dufferin. Charming Woman, The.
Dunbar, P. Made to Order Smile, The.
Dunbar, W. In Prais of Wemen.
 In Praise of Women.
Duncan, R. Bending the Bow.
 Dancing Concerning a Form of Women, A.
Dunn, C. Margaret/Haskell Indian School.
Durcan. She Mends an Ancient Wireless.
Egerton, S. Emulation, The.
 Liberty, The.
Eliot, T. Cousin Nancy.
Erdrich. Butcher's Wife, The.
 Fooling God.
Erdrich, H. Fat in America.
Esteves. For Lolita Lebron.
 One Woman.
Evans, M. I Am a Black Woman.
Evans, R. Femininity.
Ewart. Great Women Composers, The.
Fabian, C. Liturgy for Lilith.
 Prayer of Dedication.
 Qadesha (Sacred Whore).
Fairbridge, K. Magwere, Who Waits
 Wondering.
Ferré. Message.
"Field." Fifty Quatrains.
 To Christina Rossetti.
Fife, C. Dear Webster.
Finch, A. For Grizzel McNaught (1709–1792).
Fisher, D. Put the Blame on Mame.
Fisher, J. Gooseflesh.
Florsheim. Real Chocolate.
Foley, M. Brothers and Sisters.
Follain. Mirror, A.
Fordham. Coming Woman, The.
Forman, R. You So Woman.
Fuller, R. Metamorphoses.
Gallagher, T. Instructions to the Double.
Garrett, E. Womanhood, The.
Gershwin. Oh, Lady, Be Good!
Gidlow. Creed for Free Women, A.
Gilbert, S. Ladies' Home Journal, The.
Gilman, C. Anti-Suffragists, The.
 Homes.
Gilmore, M. Eve-Song.
Giovanni. Life I Led, The.
 Woman Poem.
Glück, L. Palais des Arts.
Glover, S. Power of the Soul.
Godfrey. So Let's Look at It Another Way.
Goedicke. Serious Merriment of Women, The.
Golding, L. Women at the Corners Stand, The.
Goodison. From the Garden of the Women
 Once Fallen.
Gorges. Her Face, Her Tongue, Her Wit.
Gottlieb, L. Greeting Shekinah.
Gould, H. Child's Address to the Kentucky
 Mummy, The.
Gould, J. Coyotismo.
Grahn. Grand Grand Mother is returning.
 Woman Is Talking to Death, A.
Graves, R. In Her Praise.
 She Is No Liar.
 Three-Faced, The.
 White Goddess, The.
Gray, J. Les Demoiselles de Sauve.
Greenhalgh, C. Man in the Valley of
 Women, A.
Greenwell, D. Fidelity Rewarded.
Grennan. Woman at Lit Window.
Griffin, S. Answer to a Man's Question, "What
 Can I Do About Women's Liberation?", An.
 Ordinary, as Love.
Grimké, A. Caprichosa.
Groves. Heroine.

"H., H. E." Riddle, The.
Hacker, M. Ballad of Ladies Lost and Found.
 Invocation: "This is for Elsa, also known as
 Liz."
 Rune of the Finland Woman.
 Year's End.
Hagedorn, J. Vulva Operetta.
Hall, H. Light Sleep.
Hamby, B. St. Clare's Underwear.
Hammerstein. Last Time I Saw Paris, The.
 There Is Nothin' like a Dame.
Hampton. Women who Speak with Steak
 Knives.
Hardy, J. Computer Aided Design: Creation.
Hardy, T. Epitaph on a Pessimist.
Harjo, J. Woman Hanging from the Thirteenth
 Floor Window, The.
Harper, F. She's Free!
Harrington, J. Inconstancy.
Harris, P. Some Songs Women Sing.
Hart, L. Lady Is a Tramp, The.
Hass, R. Elm.
Hawoldar. To Be a Woman.
 Woman, The.
 You Have Touched My Skin.
Hayden, R. Sphinx.
Healy, E. Changing the Oil.
Heaney, S. Wife's Tale, The.
Heath. Women.
Hecht, A. Dover Bitch, The.
Hemans. Grave of a Poetess, The.
 Indian Woman's Death-Song, The.
 To a Wandering Female Singer.
 Woman and Fame.
Hemingway. Lady Poets With Foot Notes, The.
Hemphill. To Some Supposed Brothers.
Herrera. Portrait of Woman in Long Black
 Dress / Aurelia.
 Resurrection of the Flesh, The.
Herrick. On Himselfe.
 Request to the Graces, An.
 To Meadows [or Meddowes].
 Upon Some Women.
 Upon the Loss[e] of His Mistresses.
Hildebrandt, Z. Kali.
 Persephone.
Hinckley, P. New Our Father, The.
Hirschman, J. Weeping, The.
Hodgson, R. Gipsy Girl, The.
Hollander, J. Lady's-Maid's Song, The.
Hollander, V. Rosh Chodesh Tisheri.
Hoogerhuis. Search, The.
Hope, A. Beyond Phigalia.
 Möbius Strip-Tease.
Horne, N. Note to My Liberal Feminist
 Sister, A.
Horovitz, F. Women.
Hovanessian, D. Two Voices.
Hughes, L. Gypsy Man.
 Harlem Sweeties.
 Jazzonia.
 Preference.
 When Sue Wears Red.
Hugo, R. Letter to Blessing from Missoula.
 To Women.
Hull, A. Another Rhythm.
Hummell, A. I Never Saw a Goddess Go.
Hupfeld, H. Are You Makin' Any Money?
Hyneman, R. Woman's Rights.
Ismaili. Solange.
Jackson, G. Alice.
Jackson, R. 1973.
Jacobs, H. On Growing Up the Darker Berry.
Jamie. St Bride's.
Jarrell. In Nature There Is Neither Right nor
 Left nor Wrong.
 Next Day.
Jayaprabha. Burn this Sari.
Jenyns. Choice, The.
Johnson, E. Right to Be.
Johnson, G. Heart of a Woman, The.
 Smothered Fires.
Johnson, J. Eclipse.
Johnson, M. F. Village Maid, The.
Johnston, E. Lines to Ellen, the Factory Girl.
Jones, P. Song: "I have so little sorrow."

Jonson, B.   Another. In Defense of Their Inconstancy [or Inconstancie]. A Song.
In the Person of Womankind [A Song Apologetic].
Song. That Women Are But Men's Shadows.
Jordan, J.   Female and the Silence of a Man, The.
Poem About My Rights.
Jordan, N.   When A Woman Gets Blue.
Joseph, A.   My Father's Heroes.
Kasdorf.   When Our Women Go Crazy.
Katz, J.   Women Must Put Off Their Rich Apparel.
Kemble.   Sonnet: "What is my lady like? thou fain would'st know."
Kendall, M.   Lower Life, The.
Woman's Future.
Kennedy, X.   Nude Descending a Staircase.
Kern, J.   Last Time I Saw Paris, The.
Killigrew, A.   Upon the Saying That My Verses Were Made by Another.
Kim, A.   Sewing Woman.
Kinsella, J.   Sick Woman.
Kinsella, T.   Ancestor.
Kipling, R.   Ladies, The.
Vampire, The.
Kizer, C.   American Beauty, An.
For Jan as the End Draws Near.
Hera, Hung from the Sky.
Klepfisz.   From the Monkey House and Other Cages: Monkey II.
Klugman, E.   She Who Listens.
Klugman, S.   God's Body.
Koch, K.   Energy in Sweden.
Sleeping with Women.
Konie, G.   We Are Equals.
Korican, L.   City Goddess.
Her Story.
Kowit.   In the Morning.
What Chord Did She Pluck.
Kremer.   Choice, Inanna and the Galla.
Krysl.   Persephone, to Demeter.
Landon.   History of the Lyre, A.
Marriage Vow, The.
Larkin, J.   Rhyme of My Inheritance.
Lawrence, D.   Peacock.
To Women, as Far as I'm Concerned.
Layne, M.   Beautiful Ladies.
Le Sueur.   Behold This and Always Love It.
Leapor.   Essay on Woman, An.
Lee, A.   Confession.
Lee, L.   I Ask My Mother to Sing.
Irises.
Leithauser.   Old Bachelor Brother.
Lerner, L.   Wish, A.
Leto.   Mary Morelle Show, The.
Levertov.   Abel's Bride.
Hypocrite Women.
In Mind.
Mutes, The.
Stepping Westward.
Woman Alone, A.
Lewis, E.   Mirror for Detractors, A.
Lim, S.   Pantoun for Chinese Women.
Limburg, J.   Inner Bloke.
Lindsay, C.   Love or Fame.
Livesay, D.   Other.
Livingston, J.   Femininity.
Loesser.   Adelaide's Lament.
Loftin.   Weeksville Women.
Logghe.   Madonna of the Peaches.
Lorde.   Woman Thing, The.
Women of Dan Dance with Swords in Their Hands to Mark the Time When They Were Warriors, The.
Lovelace, R.   Gratiana Dancing [or Dauncing] and [or &] Singing.
Lowell, A.   Patterns.
Sisters, The.
Loy.   Three Moments in Paris.
Lum.   Riding the North Point Ferry.
M–rt–n.   Humble Wish, The.
MacDiarmid, H.   One of the Principal Causes of War.
Two Parents, The.
MacDonogh.   She Walked Unaware.

Mackey, N.   Song of the Andoumboulou.
MacLean, S.   Highland Woman, A.
Madgett.   Black Woman.
Woman with Flower.
Madhubuti.   Magnificent Tomorrows.
Maiden.   Green Side, The.
Major, C.   Balance and Beauty.
Giant Red Woman.
Mapanje.   Cheerful Girls at Smiller's Bar, 1971, The.
Marion, G.   Ladies Who Sing with a Band, The.
Maroon, B.   Neighbor.
Nude Womon Spotted in Cappuccino Cup as Advertising Dollar co-opts another life.
Martínez, V.   Into the Next One.
It Is Not.
Martin, C.   Victoria's Secret.
McClaurin.   I, Woman.
McDaniel, J. D.
McElroy, C.   Illusion.
In My Mother's Room.
Woman's Song, A.
McFerrin, B.   23rd Psalm, The.
McGinley.   Trial and Error.
Women of Jericho, The.
McGlashan, J.   Island of Women, The.
McGuckian.   Dream-Language of Fergus, The.
Mast Year, The.
Mr. McGregor's Garden.
Orchid House, The.
Sitting, The.
McKay, C.   Wild Goat, The.
McVeigh, J.   Eve Falling.
Meador, B.   Fields Belong to Woman, The.
Merton.   There Has to Be a Jail for Ladies.
Meynell, A.   Father of Women, A [Ad Sororem E. B.].
Letter from a Girl to Her Own Old Age, A.
Michelson, R.   Interrogation.
Queen Esther Award, The.
Millay, E.   I, Being Born A Woman.
Oh, Oh, you will be sorry for that word!
Mitchell, E.   Thoughts after Ruskin.
Mitford.   On a Beautiful Woman.
Mkangelwa.   Women Sing, The.
Monaghan.   Persephone's Journey.
Venus of Laussel.
Montagu, L.   Lover, The; a Ballad.
Summary of Lord Lyttleton's 'Advice to a Lady', A.
Moore, M.   Sojourn in the Whale.
Morgan, R.   On the Watergate Women.
Mori.   Speaking Through White: For My Mother.
Moss, T.   Raising a Humid Flag.
Moulds, J.   Renoir's Bathers.
When Bad Angels Love Women.
Mphande.   Why the Old Woman Limps.
Mueller, L.   Naming the Animals.
Nude by Edward Hopper, A.
Mullen, H.   Roadmap.
Murray, J.   Men and Women Have Meaning Only as Man and Woman.
Mutén, B.   Demeter's Blessing.
Hesperides, The.
Queen Hera.
Queen Medusa.
Naden.   Two Artists, The.
Naranjo-Morse.   Gia's Song.
Nasrin.   At the Back of Progress . . . .
Border.
Character.
Nathan, L.   Body Count.
Toast.
Neely, L.   Eight Ways of Looking at Pussy.
Nelson, M.   Ballad of Aunt Geneva, The.
Nesbit, E.   Wife of All Ages, The.
Noel, L.   Understanding Each Other.
Norris, K.   Persephone.
Prayer to Eve, A.
Norte, M.   Peeping Tom Tom Girl.
Norton, C.   Obscurity of Woman's Worth.
Picture of Sappho, The.
Notley.   White Peacock, The.
Nye, N.   Making a Fist.
O Direain.   That Face.

O'Curry, E.   Litany to Our Lady.
Ogundipe-Leslie.   On Reading an Archeological Article.
Olds, S.   Ecstasy.
"O'Neill."   Her Sister.
Osgood, F.   Ah! Woman Still.
Osofisan.   She Thinks in Song.
Parker, A.   No Fool, the God of Salt.
Parker, D.   Foxfire.
Parker, P.   For Willyce.
There Is a Woman in This Town.
Parnell, P.   Apotheosis of Medusa.
Medusa and Perseus III: Lilith.
Sheila the Hat.
Sile Na gCioch.
Pearlberg, G.G.   Think Back.
Pedrick.   Hats.
Pegram, A.   Mr. White Discoverer.
Pereira.   Two Strange Worlds.
Perillo.   Dangerous Life.
Philips, K.   Answer to Another Persuading a Lady to Marriage, An.
Friendship in Emblem[e], or the Seal[e], to my dearest Lucasia.
Friendship's Mystery[s], to my dearest Lucasia.
To My Excellent Lucasia, On Our Friendship.
"Philo-Philippa."   To the Excellent Orinda.
Piatt, S.   Pique at Parting, A.
Piercy.   What's That Smell in the Kitchen?
Pierson, J.   Thrift Shop Ladies.
Pietri.   9th Untitled Poem.
Pilkington, L.   Wish, By a Young Lady, The.
Pinkney, E.   Health, A.
Pitter.   Old, Childless, Husbandless.
Plath.   Ariel.
Edge.
Poe.   Stanzas.
Pope, A.   C[h]loe.
Epistle [II,] to a Lady[: Of the Characters of Women].
Impromptu to Lady Winchelsea.
On a Certain Lady at Court.
To a Lady.
Pound, E.   Bathtub [or Bath Tub], The.
Portrait d'une Femme.
Tame Cat.
Pratt, M.   Waulking Song: Two.
Prescod.   Women Are Different.
Prestwich.   How to Choose a Mistress.
Probyn.   Ballade of Lovers.
Frustrated.
Masquerading.
Procter, A.   Woman's Answer, A.
Prunty.   Elderly Lady Crossing on Green.
Queen Latifah.   Evil That Men Do, The.
Rózewicz.   Pigtail.
Randall, D.   Blackberry Sweet.
Randolph, T.   In Praise of Women in General.
Ransom, J.   Lady Lost.
Rendon.   You See This Body.
Reynolds, S. F.   Moon/light quarter/back sack.
Open Letter to All Black Poets, An.
Rich, A.   After Twenty Years.
Blood-Sister.
Culture and Anarchy.
From a Survivor.
From an Old House in America.
Letters in the Family.
Mirror in Which Two Are Seen as One, The.
Paula Becker to Clara Westhoff.
Phantasia for Elvira Shatayev.
Phenomenology of Anger, The.
Planetarium.
Re-forming the Crystal.
Snapshots of a Daughter-in-Law.
Translations.
Waking in the Dark.
Women.
Roberts, A.   Put the Blame on Mame.
Robin, L.   Diamonds Are a Girl's Best Friend.
Robinson, A.   Wise-Woman, The.
Robinson, M.   Modern Female Fashions.
Rochester, J.   Song: "Love a woman? You're [or Y'are] an ass."
Rodgers, C.   Poem for Some Black Women.
Rodgers, R.   Lady Is a Tramp, The.

Rodgers, W.   Stormy Night.
Rodriguez, J.   About this Woman.
Roethke.   I Knew A Woman.
  She.
Rohrer, M.   Brooklyn Bridge.
Romano, R.   So I Lost My Temper.
Romo-Carmona, M.   Signs.
Roseliep.   Campfire Extinguished.
Rosenberg, I.   Female God, The.
Rosenberg, L.   Silence of Women, The.
Ross, D.   Shall We Join the Ladies?
Rossetti, C.   From the Antique.
  Goblin Market.
Rouse.   Lilies of the Field.
Rowe, E.   To Celinda.
Rowe, N.   Epigram: "Whilst maudlin Whigs
  deplore their Cato's fate."
Rubin, L.   Houses of Emily Dickinson, The.
Rukeyser, M.   Käthe Kollwitz.
  More of a Corpse Than a Woman.
  Myth.
  Painters.
  To Be a Jew in the Twentieth Century.
Rupp.   Sophia.
Rushin.   Black Back-Ups, The.
Rushing.   Sent for You Yesterday.
Salter.   What Do Women Want?
Sanchez, S.   Present.
Sandburg, C.   Adelaide Crapsey.
Sarton.   My Sisters, O My Sisters.
Sassoon.   Glory of Women.
Saunders, R.   Hush Honey.
Savageau.   All Night She Dreams.
Scamell, B.   Diaries.
Scammell, W.   Retrospective.
Scarfe.   Ode in Honour.
Schwartz, D.   Sonnet on Famous and Familiar
  Sonnets and Experiences.
Scott, M.   Women of the Future.
Serote.   This Old Woman.
Sexton.   Consorting with Angels.
  Her Kind.
  In Celebration of My Uterus.
Shange.   We Need a God Who Bleeds Now.
Shapiro, K.   Dome of Sunday, The [or A].
Sharp, S.   In the Tradition of Bobbitt.
  Tribal Marks.
Shaughnessy, B.   Postfeminism.
Shaw, A.   Rear Window.
Sheridan, H.   Charming Woman, The.
Shiffrin, N.   Anna's Dream.
Shomer.   Women Bathing at Bergen-Belsen.
Silko.   When Sun Came to Riverwoman.
Simon, L.   Hattie Went to Market.
Skeen.   Women Who Cook.
Smedley, M.   Cavour.
  Contrast, A.
Smith, B.   Bowl, The.
Smith, I.   Herring Girls, The.
Smith, P.   Blonde White Women.
Smith, S.   Celts, The.
  Dear Female Heart.
  House of Mercy, A.
Snodgrass, W.   Vuillard: "The Mother and Sister
  of the Artist."
Song.   Girl Powdering Her Neck.
  Mehinaku Girl in Seclusion, A.
Sornberger.   When She Laughs.
Souza.   Women in Dutch Painting.
Spencer, A.   Lady, Lady.
  Letter to My Sister.
  Wife-Woman, The.
Spenser.   Epithalamion: "Ye learned sisters
  which have oftentimes."
Spires.   Bodies, The.
Spofford.   Magdalen.
Standing.   Hopper's Women.
Stanley, T.   Changed, Yet Constant.
Starhawk.   Demeter's Song.
Steele, N.   Diminutive.
Stephens, J.   Glass of Beer, A.
Stevens, W.   Ordinary Women, The.
Strand.   Prediction, The.
Strange.   Transits.
Styne, J.   Diamonds Are a Girl's Best Friend.
Suckling, S.   Woman's Constancy.

Sweet, D.   My Mother and I Had a Discussion
  One Day.
Swenson, M.   Women.
Swift, J.   Gentle Echo on Woman, A.
  Lady's Dressing Room, The.
Swirszczynska.   Greatest Love, The.
Szymborska.   Women of Rubens, The.
Taggard.   Everyday Alchemy.
  To One Loved Wholllly Within Wisdom.
Thesen.   Mean Drunk Poem.
Thomas, E.   On Sir J——S——Saying in a
  Sarcastic Manner, My Books Would Make Me
  Mad; an Ode.
Thomas, L.   Electricity of Blossoms.
Thompson, D. P.   Sister Lakin and Lally.
Thomson, D.   Herring Girls, The.
Tohe.   She Was Telling It This Way.
Trethewey, N.   Cameo.
Trinidad.   Answer Song.
Tsui.   Suzy Wong's Been Dead a Long Time.
Umpierre, L.   No Hatchet Job.
Unger, B.   Photo Taken in Winter, 1944.
Unknown.   Army Dance, The.
  Around the Green Gravel.
  Cloe to Artimesa.
  Female Wits, The: A Song by a Lady of
    Quality.
  How to Choose a Mistress.
  Hymn to Nut.
  Impossible to Trust Women.
  Litany to Our Lady.
  Maxim Revised, A.
  Maxims (Exeter Book).
  May Isis heal me.
  To Caelia.
  Woman's Love.
Van Heusen, J.   Personality.
Vaughan, H.   To the Most Excellently
  Accomplished Mrs. Katherine Philips.
Verlaine.   Femme et Chatte.
Vice.   Pants.
Villanueva, A.   From the Healing Dark.
  Planet Earth Speaks, The.
Vizenor.   Raising the Flag.
Voigt.   Woman Who Weeps.
Vollmer.   Wildsisters Bar.
Waddington, M.   Old Women of Toronto.
Wakoski.   Belly Dancer.
Waldrop, R.   Lawn of Excluded Middle.
Wallace, W.   Hand That Rocks the Cradle Is the
  Hand That Rules the World, The.
Waller, E.   To a Fair Lady Playing with a Snake.
Waller, T. *et al.*   Ladies Who Sing with a Band,
  The.
Waniek.   Ballad of Aunt Geneva, The.
Waring, B.   When a Beautiful Woman Gets on
  the Jutiapa Bus.
Warren, H.   Dames.
Washington, N.   Woman's Intuition, A.
Watson, M.   Stepping Out.
Watson, R.   Ballad of the Bird-Bride.
Wayman.   Another Poem about the Madness of
  Women.
Wells, C.   Poster Girl's Defence, The.
Whitman, R.   Bubba Esther, 1888.
Whitman, S.   Morning-Glory, The.
Whitman, W.   I Sing the Body Electric.
  Woman Waits for Me, A.
Wickham.   Creatrix.
  Dedication of the Cook.
  Friend Cato.
  Meditation at Kew.
Wilbur.   Catch, The.
  She.
Wilcox, E.   Burdened.
  Woman.
Willard, N.   Cat's Second Song, The.
Williams, C.   Gulf Coast Blues.
Williams, S.   I Want Aretha to Set This to
  Music.
  She Had Known Brothers.
  Straight Talk from Plain Women.
  You Were Never Miss Brown to Me.
Williams, W.   Portrait of a Lady.
  Proletarian Portrait.
  Queen-Anne's-Lace.

To a Friend Concerning Several Ladies.
To an Old Jaundiced Woman.
To Daphne and Virginia.
Woman Walking.
Wilson, S.   Experiments in the Impersonal.
Winchilsea.   Answer, The.
  Circuit of Apollo, The.
  Friendship Between Ephelia and Ardelia.
  On Myself.
Winter, M.   In the Beginning.
Wise, S.   I Was Very Prolific.
Wither.   I Loved a Lass.
Woody.   Girlfriends, The.
Wordsworth, W.   Perfect Woman.
  Solitary Reaper, The.
Wyatt, S.   Lover Showeth How He Is Forsaken
  of Such as He Sometime Enjoyed, The.
Yamada.   Club, The.
Yau.   Radiant Silhouette II.
Yeats.   Crazy Jane Talks with the Bishop.
  Friends.
  Lapis Lazuli.
  No Second Troy.
  On Woman.
  Prayer for My Daughter, A.
  Thought from Propertius, A.
  To an Isle in the Water.
Young, I.   Visit to the Palace of Venus.
Young, K.   Almanac, 1939, An.
Young, M. J.   Friendship.
Young, V.   Woman's Intuition, A.
Zangwill.   To a Pretty Girl.

Women's Poetry and Feminist Poetry
Clifton, L.   Lost Women, The.

Wood
Bernstein, C.   Take Then, These.
Carter, M.   Bitter Wood.
Dorn, E.   Rick of Green Wood, The.
Frost, R.   Wood-Pile, The.
Hardy, T.   Workbox, The.
Hart-Smith.   Boomerang.
Koch, K.   Down at the Docks.
Kunitz, S.   Knot, The.
Marlatt, D.   Working Girl.
Nash, O.   Termite, The.
Palmer, H.   Woodworker's Ballad.
Ramsey, J.   Tally Stick, The.
Spicer, J.   Lament for the Makers: "No call upon
  anyone but the timber drifting in the waves."
Walker, T.   Owl.
Waniek.   My Grandfather Walks in the Woods.
Welch, L.   He Thanks His Woodpile.

Woodpeckers
Bullett.   Woodpecker.
Cary, P.   Legend of the Northland, A.
Clare, J.   Green Woodpecker's Nest, The.
Roberts, E.   Woodpecker, The.
Weatherly, T.   Blues for Franks Wooten.

Woods
Clare, J.   Gipsies: "Gipsies seek wide sheltering
  woods again, The."
  Nightingale's Nest, The.
Frost, R.   Come In.
Hagiwara Sakutaro.   So Terrifyingly
  Melancholy.
Hall, D.   Poet at Twenty, A.
Hemans.   Edith, a Tale of the Woods.
Hoover, P.   Heart's Ease.
Jones, R.   Beginning, A.
Landor, W.   Separation.
Lefroy.   Idler Listening to Socrates Discussing
  Philosophy with His Boy-Friends, An.
Lewis, G.   Hedge, The.
Lewis, J.   Indians in the Woods, The.
Marks, S.   November Woods.
Rukeyser, M.   Then I Saw What the Calling
  Was.
Shillaber, B.   Sagamore, The.
Smith, S.   I Rode With My Darling.
  Little Boy Lost.
Thomas, E.   Hollow Wood, The.
Treece.   Horror.
  Magic Wood, The.
Unknown, fr. Terezin Concentration Camp.
  Birdsong.
Very.   Indian's Retort, The.

Wordsworth, W.   Nutting.
See also **Forests**
Woodstock, New York
Sherrill, J.   Woodstock.
Wool
Fergusson.   Braid Claith.
Woolf, Virginia
Howe, F.   Doubt.
Words
Agard, J.   Poetry Jump-Up.
Algarin.   Talking.
Alvarez, J.   Bilingual Sestina.
Ammons, A. R.   Triphammer Bridge.
Angeles, C.   Words.
Atwood.   Variations on the Word *Love*.
Baraka.   Ka 'Ba.
Beadle.   Words.
Behn, A.   Love's Witness.
Bernstein, C.   Kiwi Bird in the Kiwi Tree, The.
   Virtual Reality.
Berryman.   To My Father.
Bobis, M.   Word Gifts for an Australian Critic.
Bolton, J.   Lights at Newport Beach, The.
Bradstreet, A.   Another.
Bromige.   Lines: "Repressive desublimation."
Broumas, O.   Etymolgy.
Brown, D.   Coming Home.
Bynner.   Horses.
Césaire, A.   Lagoonal Calendar.
   Macumba Word.
Campo.   Superman Is Dead.
Castillo, S.   Letter to Yeni on Peering into Her
   Life.
Causley.   Old Mrs. Thing-um-e-bob.
Ceravolo.   Data.
Codrescu.   Imagination of Necessity, The.
Coleridge, M.   Only a little shall we speak of
   thee.
   Words.
Coolidge, C.   Hand Further, The.
   Leaving Rattle Bar.
   Tab, The.
   This Garden Being: The Hanging of Books.
Cortez, J.   No Simple Explanations.
Creeley.   Language, The.
   Token, A.
   Waiting.
Cullen, C.   Incident.
Davidson, J.   Battle.
Davidson, M.   Form of Chiasmus; The
   Chiasmus of Forms, The.
Davies, A.   Outer Layers of Nervousness, The.
Deanovich.   My Favorite Monk Is.
Dickey, J.   Basics.
Dickinson, E.   Word is Dead, A.
DiPalma.   Poem for Claude.
Dissanayake.   Freedom.
Dove, R. Ö.
Du Maurier.   Music.
Duffy, C.   Words, Wide Night.
Duhig, I.   From the Irish.
Eady.   Sherbet.
   Song.
   Why Do So Few Blacks Study Creative
      Writing?
Ellis, T.   Hush Yo Mouf.
Ewart.   Word-Bird, The.
Fearing.   Twentieth-Century Blues.
Fisher, C.   Words.
Forrest-Thomson.   Sonnet: "My love, if I write a
   song for you."
Francis, R.   Like Ghosts of Eagles.
Frost, R.   Beyond Words.
   Ends.
Gilbert, C.   Kite-Flying.
Gloria.   In Language.
Gomez, M.   Solo Palabras.
Graham, W.   Malcolm Mooney's Land.
Graves, R.   Never Such Love.
   Tilth.
Greenwald, T.   Privets Come into Season at
   High Tide.
Griffiths, J.   Errata.
   Lost and Found.
Hacker, M.   Squares and Courtyards.
Hadas, R.   Winged Words.

Hamill, S.   Gift of Tongues, The.
Harrison, J.   Swifts at Evening.
Hass, R.   Meditation at Lagunitas.
Hoagland, E.   Anti-Semanticist, The.
Holland, J.   Wavelength.
Hughes, L.   Sweet Words on Race.
Jackson, L.   World and I, The.
Jarrell.   Islands, The.
Kalmar *et al.*   Three Little Words.
Kgositsile.   To Mother.
   To My Daughter.
Koch, K.   Permanently.
Komunyakaa.   Jeanne Duval's Confession.
Kruchyonykh [*or* Kruchionykh *or* Kruchenykh].
   Declaration of the Word as Such.
Kunitz, S.   Touch Me.
Landon.   Power of Words, The.
Landor, W.   Idle Words.
Larkin, P.   Talking In Bed.
Lee, L.   Persimmons.
Longfellow, H.   Day Is Done, The.
Lorde.   Coal.
Lowry, M.   Strange Type.
MacCaig.   Instrument and Agent.
   No Consolation.
MacLeish.   Reproach to Dead Poets.
Major, C.   Swallow the Lake.
McCarthy, G.   Hooded Legion, The.
McClure, M.   Rant Block.
McDonald, C.   Cheers.
McDonald, R.   Hollow Thesaurus, The.
McLain, P.   Connor in the Wind and Rain with
   His Coat on.
McMorris, M.   Near Speech, The.
Mercer, J.   Too Marvelous for Words.
Meredith, W.   Illiterate, The.
Merriam, E.   How to Eat a Poem.
Merwin, W. S.   Utterance.
Miller, J.   Poetry.
Morgan, E.   Opening the Cage.
Morgan, R.   Battery.
Muldoon, P.   Quoof.
Mullen, H.   Momma Sayings.
Nelson, J.   Just Word Wranglin'
Nichol.   Two Words; a Wedding.
Noguere.   Scribes, The.
Notley.   Jack Would Speak Through the
   Imperfect Medium of Alice.
Ormsby, E.   Origins.
Padgett, R.   Louisiana Perch.
   Who and Each.
Palmer, M.   Fifth Prose.
   Notes for Echo Lake 3.
   Sun.
   Voice and Address.
Parkes, B.   For Adelaide.
Patchen.   Moon, Sun, Sleep, Birds, Live.
Patterson, R.   "Word to the Wise Is Enough, A."
Peacock, M.   Anger Sweetened.
Piombino.   Pyramids, The.
Plath.   Words.
Probyn.   Rondelet: "Say what you please."
Reed, I.   Beware: Do Not Read This Poem.
Reese, L.   Reserve.
Riley, D.   Misremembered Lyric, A.
Robinson, K.   Nesting of Layer Protocols.
Ruby, H.   Three Little Words.
Ruden, S.   Letter.
Rukeyser, M.   Ballad of Orange and Grape.
Rutsala.   Words.
Sandburg, C.   Languages.
   Little Girl, Be Careful What You Say.
   Precious Moments.
   Threes.
Satyamurti.   Erdywurble.
Scannell.   Protest Poem.
Schnackenberg.   Supernatural Love.
Schuyler, J.   Freely Espousing.
Scott, D.   For Norman Nicholson.
Sepamla.   Talk to the Peach Tree.
Shelley, P.   To————: "One word is too often
   profaned."
Sia, B.   No Words Empty.
Singer, B.   Still and All.
   Your Words, My Answers.
Sisson.   In Flood.

Smith, S.   Pretty.
Snyder, G.   Riprap.
Soutar.   Room, The.
Spender, S.   Word.
Stewart, B.   Words Is Not Enough.
Su, A.   Four Sonnets About Food.
Swinburne.   Match, A.
Sylvain, P.   Collective Search.
Taggart, J.   Never Too Late.
Thomas, D.   Especially When the October
   Wind.
Todd, M.   Wire Song.
Troupe.   And Syllables Grow Wings There.
Turnbull.   There Are Words.
Unknown.   Man of Words, A.
   Success.
Violi.   Rifacimento.
Wade, B.   Truth.
Wain.   Apology for Understatement.
Wallace-Crabbe.   Double Dactyl.
Watten.   Radio.
Weaver, M.   Borders.
   Weekend Equestrian, The.
Weiner, H.   From *Spoke / Aug 19*.
   Remembered Sequel.
Whiting, R.   Too Marvelous for Words.
Wilcox, E.   Woman.
Williams, W.   Fragment: "As for him who."
   Sort of a Song, A.
Wylie.   Ejaculation.
Yeats.   Song of the Happy Shepherd, The.
Young, D.   Project for Freight Trains, A.
Zarin.   Song: "My heart, my dove, my snail, my
   sail, my."
Zukofsky, L.   (Ryokan's scroll).
   Non Ti Fidar.
See also **Language**
Wordsworth, William
Arnold, M.   Memorial Verses.
Barker, G.   Resolution of Dependence.
Browning, E.   On a Portrait of Wordsworth by
   B. R. Haydon.
Browning, R.   Lost Leader, The.
Clare, J.   To Wordsworth.
Coleridge, H.   He Lived amidst th' Untrodden
   Ways.
   To Wordsworth.
Coleridge, S.   To William Wordsworth.
De la Mare.   Bards, The.
Ewart.   William Wordsworth (1770-1850).
Grimke, C.   Wordsworth.
Harrison, T.   Remains.
Hemans.   To [*or* the Poet] Wordsworth.
Keyes, S.   William Wordsworth.
Nicholson, N.   To the River Duddon.
Randall, J.   To William Wordsworth from
   Virginia.
Shelley, P.   To Wordsworth.
Stephen, J.   Sonnet, A: "Two voices are there:
   one is of the deep."
Stevenson, R.   Fragment, A: "Thou strainest
   through the mountain fern."
Work and Workers
Abbott, D.   All Day at Work.
Acam-Oturu.   Arise to the Day's Toil.
Arnold, B.   No Tool or Rope or Pail.
Auden.   Taller To-day.
Babcock, M.   Be Strong.
Baratier, D.   American Standard.
Berlin.   There's No Business Like Show
   Business.
Bevington, L.   Morning.
Black, S.   To a War Correspondent.
Boyle, K.   Ode to a Maintenance Man and His
   Family.
Brown, E.   You Got You Got to Be Told.
Carmichael, H.   Doctor, Lawyer, Indian Chief.
Chin.   Autumn Leaves.
Cleyre, V.   Out of the Darkness.
Codrescu.   Work.
Colby, T.   Boy and the Girl, The.
Coleridge, S.   Work without Hope.
Crosby, R.   Waitresses.
Damacion, K.   Canciones.
Davie.   With the Grain.
Davis, C.   Any Nest I Can't Sleep in Should Be

Burned.
Davis, G.   Children in the Arbor.
Dodge, M.   Tinker, Come Bring Your Solder.
Dove, R.   Great Palaces of Versailles, The.
   Satisfaction Coal Company, The.
Dunbar, P.   Not They Who Soar!
Emmott, K.   Who Looks after Your Kids?
Espada.   David Leaves the Saints for Paterson.
Everson, W.   Muscat Pruning.
Fanthorpe.   You Will Be Hearing from Us
   Shortly.
Fish, C.   Work and Worry.
Fogarty, L.   Worker Who, the Human Who, the
   Abo Who, The.
Forbes, C.   Blue Monday.
Frost, R.   "Out, Out—."
Gershwin.   Nice Work If You Can Get It.
Gillespie, H.   That Lucky Old Sun.
Gordon, A.   Question Not.
Guevara, M.   Hands of the Old Métis, The.
Hammerstein.   Gentleman Is a Dope, The.
Hernandez, D.   Workers.
Hood, T.   Literary Reminiscences.
   Written in the Workhouse.
Howard, B.   Break.
Howe, J.   House of Rest, The.
Hughes, L.   Necessity.
Jamie.   St Bride's.
Joseph, L.   That's All.
Kingston, M.   Restaurant.
Kinsella, J.   Wild Radishes.
Kipling, R.   Sons of Martha, The.
Knight, S.   Double Writing.
Koch, K.   Thank You.
Larkin, P.   Dedicated, The.
Lawrence, D.   Work.
Levine, P.   Sweet Will.
   You Can Have It.
Longfellow, H.   Village Blacksmith, The.
Mabuza.   Tired Lizi Tired.
McDaniel, W.   My Room at Aunt Eura's, 1937.
McGrath, C.   At the Freud Hilton.
More, H.   Hackney Coachman, The; Or, The
   Way to Get a Good Fare.
Morley, D.   Errand.
Nash, O.   Introspective Reflection.
Newburn, L.   Office Geraniums.
North, M.   Pheasant Plucker's Son, The.
   Poems to My Father.
Olson, C.   Praises, The.
Picková, E.   Fear.
Porteous.   Wrecked Creeves.
Razaf, A.   My Handy Man.
Replansky.   Good Day's Work, A.
Rodgers, R.   Gentleman Is a Dope, The.
Rome, H.   Chain Store Daisy.
Rouse.   Her Retirement.
Rungano.   Woman, The.
Salinas, L.   My Fifty-Plus Years Celebrate
   Spring.
Sandburg, C.   Blue Island Intersection.
Shapiro, D.   House (Blown Apart).
Silano, M.   Sweet Red Peppers, Sun-Drieds, the
   Hearts of Artichokes.
Smith, B.   That Lucky Old Sun.
Smith, I.   Herring Girls, The.
Smith, S.   Childe Rolandine.
Spender, S.   Unemployed.
Stein, K.   World Without End.
Steptoe.   O' Yes.
Stevenson, R.   To A Gardener.
Stickney, T.   Requiescam.
Suárez, V.   Cuban-American Gothic.
Tafolla.   Allí por la Calle San Luis.
Tate, J.   Coming Down Cleveland Avenue.
Thomas, E.   By the Ford.
Ulku, A.   Spring Forward, Fall Back.
Unknown.   Working on the Railway.
Van Jordan, A.   My Father's Retirement.
Watts, I.   How Doth the Little Busy Bee.
Webster, P.   Doctor, Lawyer, Indian Chief.
Whittier.   Dedication: "I would the gift I offer
   here."
Wiese, B.   Everyone Who Wants to Work Can.
Wilbur.   Summer Morning, A.
Williams, C.   Sanctity, The.

Williamson, G.   On His Birthday.
Wise, S.   50 Years in the Career of an Aspiring
   Thug.
Wise, W.   When I Grow Up.
Wojahn.   Allegory: Attic and Fever.
   Distance.
See also Labor and Laborers
World
Bass, F.   Home.
Cavendish, M.   Of Many Worlds in This World.
Taggard.   To the Natural World: at 37.
Unknown, fr. Terezin Concentration Camp.
   Birdsong.
   Birdsong 2.
See also Earth
World War I
Aldington.   Field Manoeuvres.
Allen, H.   Dragon's Breath.
Bensko.   Last Look in the Sambre Canal, A.
Binyon.   For the Fallen.
Bishop, J.   In the Dordogne.
Blunden.   Concert Party: Busseboom.
   Vlamertinghe.
   Zonnebeke Road, The.
Buck, H.   Mort, Le.
Cannan.   Rouen.
Chesterton, G.   Elegy in a Country Churchyard.
Coffey.   Cold.
Cohan.   Over There.
Crosland.   White Feather Legion, The.
Douglas, K.   Soissons.
Dove, R.   Alfonzo Prepares to Go Over the Top.
   Passage, The.
Fallon, P.   Dardanelles 1916.
Fitzgerald, Z.   Over the Top with Pershing.
Frankau.   Deserter, The.
   Gun Teams.
Gershwin.   Strike Up the Band.
Graves, R.   Goliath and David.
   Recalling War.
   Sergeant-Major Money.
Grenfell, J.   Into Battle.
Griffith, L.   Silver Jubilee.
Gurney, I.   Ballad of the Three Spectres.
   Towards Lillers.
Hardy, T.   Channel Firing.
   In Time of "The Breaking of Nations."
   Men Who March Away.
   Often When Warring.
Heaney, S.   In Memoriam Francis Ledwidge.
Hillyer.   Eternal Return, The.
Housman, A.   Epitaph.
Hughes, T.   Walt.
Hugo, R.   Yards of Sarajevo, The.
Hulme, T.   Trenches: St Eloi.
Johnstone, P.   High Wood.
Kipling, R.   Batteries Out of Ammunition.
   Beginner, The.
   Bombed in London.
   Bridegroom, The.
   Common Form.
   Convoy Escort.
   Coward, The.
   Dead Statesman, A.
   Death-Bed, A.
   Drifter off Tarentum, A.
   Epitaphs of the War [1914–1918].
   Equality of Sacrifice.
   Ex-Clerk.
   Gethsemane.
   Journalists.
   Mesopotamia.
   Pelicans in the Wilderness (A Grave near
      Halfa).
   R.A.F. (Aged Eighteen).
   Refined Man, The.
   Servant, A.
   Son, A.
   Unknown Female Corpse.
Larkin, P.   MCMXIV.
Lawrence, D.   Song of a Man Who Has Come
   Through.
   Tommies in the Train.
Longley, M.   Wounds.
Lowell, A.   Camouflaged Troop-Ship.
McCrae, J.   In Flanders Fields.

Meynell, A.   Summer in England, 1914.
O'Hara, G.   K-K-K-Katy.
Owen, W.   A Terre.
   Anthem for Doomed Youth.
   Apologia Pro Poemate Meo.
   Chances, The.
   Conscious.
   Disabled.
   Dulce et Decorum Est.
   Exposure.
   Futility.
   Greater Love.
   Next War, The.
   Parable of the Old Men and the Young, The.
   Send-Off, The.
   Show, The.
   Smile, Smile, Smile.
   Spring Offensive.
   Strange Meeting.
Palmer, V.   Farmer Remembers the Somme,
   The.
Pound, E.   Coming of War, The; Actaeon.
Read, S.   To a Conscript of 1940.
Rickword.   Soldier Addresses his Body, The.
   Trench Poets.
   Winter Warfare.
Rosenberg, I.   August 1914.
   Break of Day in the Trenches.
   Dead Man's Dump.
"Saki."   Carol: "While shepherds watched their
   flocks by night."
Sassoon.   Aftermath.
   Attack.
   Base Details.
   Blighters.
   Counter-Attack.
   Death-Bed, The.
   Does It Matter?
   Dreamers.
   Dug-Out, The.
   Everyone Sang.
   General, The.
   Glory of Women.
   On Passing the New Menin Gate.
   Rear-Guard, The.
   Repression of War Experience.
   Suicide in [the] Trenches.
   Working Party, A.
Scannell.   Great War, The.
Seeger, A.   I Have a Rendezvous with Death.
Simpson, L.   I Dreamed That in a City Dark as
   Paris.
Sorley.   Sonnet: "When you see millions of the
   mouthless dead."
Stallworthy, J.   War Story.
Tennant, E.   A Bas la Gloire!
Thomas, E.   As the Team's Head-Brass.
   In Memoriam (Easter, 1915).
   Private, A.
   This Is No Case of Petty Right or Wrong.
Trakl.   Grodek.
   In the East.
Van Dyke.   America's Welcome Home.
West, A.   Night Patrol, The.
Wilson, T.   Magpies in Picardy.
Yeats.   On Being Asked for a War Poem.
   Reprisals.
World War II
Ai.   German Army, Russia, 1943, The.
Auden.   September 1, 1939.
Barker, G.   To Any Member of My Generation.
Bell, M.   Footnote to Enright's "Apocalypse."
Berryman.   Moon and the Night and the Men,
   The.
Betjeman.   In Westminster Abbey.
Bobrowski.   Kaunas 1941.
Bowers, E.   Stoic: for Laura von Courten, The.
Brecht, B.   War Has Been Given a Bad Name.
Brooks, G.   Gay Chaps at the Bar.
   My Dreams, My Works, Must Wait Till After
   Hell.
   Still Do I Keep My Look, My Identity.
Butler, C. E.   Letter to the Survivors.
Causley.   Conversation in Gibraltar 1943.
Chin.   American Rain.
Ciardi.   Elegy Just in Case.

Coulehan, J. D-Day, 1994.
Coward. Don't Let's Be Beastly to the Germans.
Crow, S. El Alamein.
Dickey, J. Firebombing, The.
Dorsett, T. Survivor, The.
Douglas, K. Aristocrats.
Vergissmeinicht.
Dove, R. Sightseeing.
Dugan, A. Memorial Service for the Invasion Beach Where the Vacation in the Flesh Is Over.
Field, E. World War II.
Fuller, R. Spring 1942.
Garioch. 1941.
Gascoyne. Wartime Dawn, A.
Hecht, A. 'More Light! More Light!'
Herbert, S. Less Nonsense.
Herd. Bombshell.
Hongo. O-Bon: Dance for the Dead.
Huchel. Landscape Beyond Warsaw.
Hughes, L. World War II.
Hugo, R. Napoli Again.
View from Cortona, A.
Jarrell. Burning the Letters.
Camp in the Prussian Forest, A.
Dead Wingman, The.
Death of the Ball Turret Gunner, The.
Eighth Air Force.
Front, A.
Losses.
Lullaby, A: "For wars his life and half a world away."
Pilot from the Carrier, A.
Pilots, Man Your Planes.
Range in the Desert, The.
Second Air Force.
Sick Nought, The.
Truth, The.
Jeffers, R. May-June, 1940.
Keesing. Reverie of a Mum.
Keyes, S. Timoshenko.
Klepfisz. Death Camp.
Perspectives on the Second World War.
Koch, K. To World War Two.
Laing, A. New Jerusalem, The.
Langland, J. War.
Lewis, A. Peasants, The.
Raiders' Dawn.
Lowell, R. Exile's Return, The.
Holy Innocents, The.
Mad Negro Soldier Confined at Munich, A.
MacLean, S. Death Valley.
MacNeice. Streets of Laredo, The.
McGrath, T. Blues for Warren.
Merwin, W. S. Tide Line Garden.
Millay, E. I Forgot for a Moment.
Milosz, C. Dedication: "You whom I could not save."
Mitsui. Photograph of a Child, Japanese-American Evacuation, Bainbridge Island, Washington, March 30, 1942.
Montague, J. Welcoming Party, A.
Moore, M. In Distrust of Merits.
Morgan, E. Cinquevalli.
Mura. Argument: on 1942, An.
Blueness of the Day, The.
Nemerov. War in the Air, The.
Olds, S. Leningrad Cemetery, Winter of 1941.
Osterhaus, J. Gambier.
Pasternak, B. Fresco Come to Life.
Perelman. Broken Mirror, The.
Porter, P. May, 1945.
Read, S. To a Conscript of 1940.
Reed, H. Chard Whitlow.
Rich, A. Letters in the Family.
Root, W. Sonnet 20: Remembering, from a Nazi Prison, a Teacher Years Before.
"Sagittarius." Croaked the Eagle: "Nevermore." Nerves.
Schmitz. Picture of Okinawa, A.
Scott, W. U.S. Sailor with the Japanese Skull, The.
Shapcott, T. Shadow of War, 1941.
Shapiro, K. Full Moon: New Guinea.
Homecoming.

Shepherd, R. Lucky One, The.
Simic. Begotten of the Spleen.
Simpson, L. Carentan O Carentan.
Runner, The.
Sitwell, D. Still Falls the Rain.
Slessor. Beach Burial.
Smith, S. I Remember.
Stern, G. Dancing, The.
Tate, J. Lost Pilot, The.
Viereck, P. *Vale* from Carthage.
Kilroy.
Waniek. Lonely Eagles.
Three Men in a Tent.
Tuskegee Airfield.
Winters, Y. Summer Noon: 1941.
Wong, N. Can't Tell.

Worldliness
Brooks, G. Mrs. Small.
Herrick. Temporall Goods.
Killigrew, A. Farewell to Worldly Joys, A.
Wordsworth, W. World Is Too Much With Us, The.
Zukofsky, L. Song for the Year's End, A.

Worms
Danner. This Is an African Worm.
Francis, R. Earthworm.
Fuller, R. Autobiography of a Lungworm.
Kunitz, S. Hornworm: Autumn Lamentation.
Lawrence, D. Worm Either Way.
Levertov. Earth Worm, The.
MacDiarmid, H. Ex Vermibus.
Marvell. Mower to the Glowworms [or Glow-Worms or Glo-Worms], The.
Rosen, M. Christmas Dinner.
Rosenberg, I. Worm Fed on the Heart of Corinth, A.
Rossetti, C. Handy Mole who plied no shovel, A.
Smith, S. Reversionary.
Stevens, W. Worms at Heaven's Gate, The.
Unknown. Maggot Song.

Worry
Anstett.
Berlin. Let's Have Another Cup of Coffee.
Bloom, R. Give Me the Simple Life.
Bruner. Dreaded Task, The.
Cope, W. I Worry.
Davies, W. Leisure.
Dixon, M. Bye Bye Blackbird.
Dunbar, W. Meditatioun in Wyntir.
Evans, R. Haven't Got a Worry.
Fain, S. Are You Havin' Any Fun?
Fish, C. Work and Worry.
Frost, R. Armful, The.
Gershwin. Who Cares?
Gillespie, H. That Lucky Old Sun.
Goese, M. Dive, The.
Henderson, R. Bye Bye Blackbird.
Herman, J. Tap Your Troubles Away.
Jurmann, W. All God's Chillun Got Rhythm.
Kenyon, J. Insomnia at the Solstice.
Livingston, J. Haven't Got a Worry.
Lomax, M. Gulf.
Loncar, M. Insomniac.
Roberson. Sonnet.
Ruby, H. Give Me the Simple Life.
Schuyler, J. Letter to a Friend: Who Is Nancy Daum?
Silverstein, S. Whatif.
Smith, B. That Lucky Old Sun.
Unknown. Worries.
Worry.
Woods, H. Over My Shoulder.
Wordsworth, W. Affliction of Margaret, The.

Worship and Worshipers
Avison. Water and Worship: An Open-Air Service on the Gatineau River.
Bradstreet, A. As Spring the Winter Doth Succeed.
Carew, T. New Year's Sacrifice: To Lucinda, A.
Doolittle, H. Hippolytus Temporizes.
Dybek. Benediction.
Emerson, R. Sursum Corda.
Enheduanna. From The Hymn to Inanna.
Gascoigne. Gascoigne's Good-Morrow.
Gay, J. Molly Mog [or The Fair Maid of the

Inn].
Godolphin. Hymn: "Lord, when the wise men came from far[r]."
Goode, S. Lady of Pazardzik.
Hardy, T. Afternoon Service at Mellstock.
Henderson, D. Song of Devotion to the Forest.
Herbert, G. Altar, The.
Christmas.
Love (2).
Praise (2).
Prayer (1): "Prayer the Church's banquet, Angels' age."
Sunday.
Temper (1), The.
Temper (2), The.
True Hymn, A.
Hopkins, G. Pied Beauty.
Hughes, L. Testimonial.
Keats. Fragment of an Ode to Maia Written on May Day, 1818.
Kendall, M. Education's Martyr.
Lindsay, N. At Mass.
Longfellow, S. Again as Evening's Shadow Falls.
Mant, R. Social Worship.
Perronet. All Hail the Power of Jesus' Name.
Procter, A. Present, The.
Robbins, H. And Have the Bright Immensities.
Southwell. Child[e] My Choice [or Choyse], A.
Stanley, T. Paraphrase Upon Part of the CXXXIX Psalm, A.
Sylvester, J. Sweet Mouth, That Send'st a Musky-Rosed Breath.
Unknown. Walk Softly.
Watts, I. Flying Fowl, and Creeping Things, Praise Ye the Lord.
Hosanna to Christ.
Whittier. First-Day Thoughts.
Worship.
See also **Churches; Prayer; Religion**
Wounded Knee, Battle of (1890)
Rose. I Expected My Skin and My Blood to Ripen.
Wreaths
MacDiarmid, H. One of the Principal Causes of War.
Wrens
Bly, R. Looking at a Dead Wren in My Hand.
Clare, J. Wren, The.
Conran. Fledgling.
Davies, W. Jenny Wren.
De la Mare. Jenny Wren.
Levertov. Wren, A.
Mother Goose. Dove and the Wren, The.
Thompson, P. Little Wren, A.
Unknown. Hunting the Wren.
Warning, A.
Wee Jenny Wren, A.
Wrestling and Wrestlers
Bevington, L. Wrestling.
Francis, R. Two Wrestlers.
Lefroy. Palaestral Study, A.
Ramanujan. At Forty.
Wright, Richard
Madgett. Images.
Medina, T. Big House Revisited, The.
Rivers, C. Mourning Letter from Paris, A.
Young, A. One Snapshot I Couldn't Take in France, The.
Writing and Writers
Adamson. Home, The Spare Room, The.
Adcock, F. Future Work.
Agard, J. Poetry Jump-Up.
Aiken, J. Do It Yourself.
Al-Rihani. It Was All for Him.
Alcock. Receipt for Writing a Novel, A.
Ali, A. Homage to Faiz Ahmed Faiz.
Allison, D. When I Drink I Become the Joy of Faggots.
Alvarez, J. Bilingual Sestina.
Woman's Work.
"Amorous Lady." On Being Charged with Writing Incorrectly.
Antin. Private Occasion in a Public Place, A.
Arnold, M. Memorial Verses.

Artaud. All Writing Is Garbage.
Ashbery. And "Ut Pictura Poesis" Is Her Name.
Auden. In Memory of W. B. Yeats.
Baca. It Started.
Barber, M. Conclusion of a Letter to the Rev.
  Mr. C, The.
Beer, P. Jane Austen.
Behn, A. Rover or The Banished Cavaliers,
  The.
Bernstein, C. Klupzy Girl, The.
  Wait.
Berrigan, T. Words for Love.
Berryman. Henry's Fate.
  Of Suicide.
Betjeman. Ballad of George R. Sims, The.
  Reproof Deserved; or After the Lecture.
Blagden. To George Sand on her Interview with
  Elizabeth Barrett Browning.
Blamire. Epistle to Her Friends at Gartmore.
Blount, A. Cure for Poetry, A.
Blumenthal, M. I Have Lived This Way for
  Years and Do Not Wish to Change.
Bradstreet, A. Prologue, The.
  To My Dear Children.
Breytenbach. Out There.
Bristol. Crime of the Ages, The.
Brontë, E. Aye there it is! It wakes tonight.
  God of Visions.
  Night Wind, The.
Brown, R. Famous Writers School Opens Its
  Arms in the Next Best Thing to Welcome, The.
Browne, W. On the Countess Dowager of
  Pembroke.
Browning, E. Aurora Leigh.
  Curse for a Nation, A.
  Fifth Book.
  First Book: Young Aurora's Fostermother.
  Sweetness of England, The.
  To George Sand: A Desire.
  To George Sand: A Recognition.
Bryant, W. Poet, The.
Buchanan, G. Lyle Donaghy, Poet, 1902-1949.
Budenz. Poeta Fui.
Bukowski. Black Poets, The.
Bunting. What the Chairman Told Tom.
Burgess, F. Cinq Ans Après.
Burns, R. On Elphinston's Translation of
  Martial.
  Second Epistle to Davie.
Byrom. Passive Participle's Petition, The.
Campbell, R. On Professor Drennan's Verse.
  On Some South African Novelists.
Carew, T. Fancy, A.
  To Ben Jonson.
Carey, H. Author's Quietus, The.
Carroll, K. Short Poem.
Carruth, H. On Being Asked to Write a Poem
  Against the War in Vietnam.
Cavendish, M. Claspe, The.
Cawein. Poetry.
Cervantes. Poem for the Young White Man
  Who Asked Me How I, An Intelligent, Well-
  Read Person Could Believe in the War
  Between Races.
Chapman, G. Homer and the Brazen Head of
  Rumour.
Chaucer. Chaucer's Wordes unto Adam, his
  Owne Scriveyn.
Cheney-Coker. Letter to a Tormented
  Playwright.
  On Being a Poet in Sierra Leone.
  Road to Exile Thinking of Vallejo, The.
Cherry, K. History.
Cisneros, S. Poet Reflects On Her Solitary Fate,
  The.
Codrescu. Paper on Humor.
Coleridge, H. He Lived amidst th' Untrodden
  Ways.
Coleridge, S. On Donne's Poetry.
Collins, B. Lines Lost Among Trees.
Columcille [or Columba]. Invocation, An: "My
  claw is tired of scribing!"
Cook, E. Lines / Suggested by the Song of a
  Nightingale.
  To the Late William Jerdan.
Coolidge, C. Noon Point.

On Induction of the Hand.
Cooper, D. Dreamt Up.
  Poem for George Miles.
Cooper, J. Poem with Capital Letters, A.
Cope, W. Engineers' Corner.
  Exchange of Letters.
  Serious Concerns.
  Triolet.
Corrothers. Me 'n' Dunbar.
Cortez, J. Adupe.
  No Simple Explanations.
Cowley, A. Muse, The.
Cowley, H. Ode to Della Crusca.
  To Della Crusca. The Pen.
Cowper, W. To Mary Unwin.
  To William Hayley, Esq.: In Reply to His
  Solicitation to Write with Him in a Literary
  Work.
Crane, H. Passage.
Crashaw. On Mr. G. Herberts Booke, The
  Temple.
Creeley. Waiting.
Cronin, A. Lines for a Painter.
Cullen, C. To Certain Critics.
  Yet Do I Marvel.
Dacre, C. Sappho; or, The Resolve.
Darley. Pass of Death, The.
Davie. Epistle. To Enrique Caracciolo Trejo.
  Rejoinder to a Critic.
Davies, J. How to Write Anglo-Welsh Poetry.
Day Lewis. Where Are the War Poets?
De la Mare. Moonshine.
  Scribe, The.
Di Prima. On Sitting Down to Write, I Decide
  Instead to Go to Fred Herko's Concert.
Dickinson, E. This Is My Letter to the World.
Donne. Canonization, The.
  To Mr. R. W.
  Triple Fool, The.
Donnell. Canadian Prairie's View of Literature,
  The.
Dooley, D. How I Wrote It.
Doolittle, H. Fragment 36 [or Thirty-Six]: "I
  know not what to do."
Doty, M. My Tattoo.
Douglas, L. Dead Poet, The.
Dransfield. Day at a Time.
  Endsight.
Drummond, W. Sonnet: "I know that all
  beneath the moon decays."
Dryden, J. Crown Prince of Dullness, The.
  Mac Flecknoe [or, A Satire upon the True-Blue
  Protestant Poet T. S.].
  To the Pious Memory of the Accomplished [or
  Accomplisht] Young Lady, Mrs. Anne
  Killigrew, [Excellent in the Two Sister-Arts of
  Poesie and Painting].
Dunbar, P. Misapprehension.
  Poet, The.
Dunbar, W. Lament for the Makaris.
Duncan, R. Bending the Bow.
  Dancing Concerning a Form of Women, A.
  Poetry, a Natural Thing.
Eady. Why Do So Few Blacks Study Creative
  Writing?
Edwards, K. Provisionally.
Eliot, T. Whispers of Immortality.
Ellis, T. Sticks.
  View of the Library of Congress from Paul
  Laurence Dunbar High School.
Enright, D. Evil Days, The.
Equi. Date with Robbe-Grillet, A.
Ewart. Black Box, The.
Fearing. Literary.
Ferlinghetti, L. 21.
  Constantly Risking Absurdity.
  Sea and Ourselves at Cape Ann, The.
Ferry. Rereading Old Writing.
"Field." To Christina Rossetti.
Finch, A. Dickinson.
  Reply From His Coy Mistress, A.
Finney, N. Fishing Among the Learned.
Fisher, R. Occasional Poem 7.1.72.
Fitzgerald, E. 71.
Forbes, C. Poet's Shuffle, The.
Forbes, J. Monkey's Pride.

Forché. Ourselves or Nothing.
Fordham. Pen, The.
Fusselman, A. Journal.
Gilbert, C. And, Yes, Those Spiritual Matters.
Gilbert, S. Ferdinando and Elvira; or, The
  Gentle Pieman.
Ginsberg, A. II.
  Howl.
  Poem Rocket.
Gioia. In Chandler Country.
  My Confessional Sestina.
  Next Poem, The.
Glück, L. Mountain, The.
  Poem: "In the early evening, as now, a man is
  bending."
Glück, R. Burroughs.
Gorham. Empress Receives the Head of a
  Taiping Rebel, The.
Graham, W. Malcolm Mooney's Land.
Graves, R. Laureate, The.
  Plea to Boys and Girls, A.
  Reader over My Shoulder, The.
Gray, J. Mishka.
Gray, T. Progress of Poesy, The.
Greenberg, S. Etching.
Greenwell, D. To Christina Rossetti.
  To Elizabeth Barrett Browning, in 1851.
  To Elizabeth Barrett Browning, in 1861.
Gunn, T. Expression.
  J Car, The.
Hacker, M. Boy, The.
  Feeling and Form.
Hadas, R. Winged Words.
Hall, D. Poet at Twenty, A.
  To a Waterfowl.
Hamod, S. Letter.
Hands, E. Poem on the Supposition of an
  Advertisement, A; Appearing in a Morning
  Paper, of the Publication of a Volume of
  Poems, by a Servant-Maid.
  Poem on the Supposition of the Book Having
  Been Published and Read, A.
Hardy, T. Epitaph for George Moore.
  I Looked Up from My Writing.
Harington [or Harrington]. Of honest Theft. To
  my good friend Master Samuel Daniel.
Harjo, J. Bird.
  Strange Fruit.
Harper, M. In Hayden's Collage.
Harris, W. Historic Moment, An.
Harrison, T. Heartless Art, The.
Harte, B. Miss Edith's Modest Request.
Hartnett. Enamoured of the Miniscule.
  I Have Exhausted the Delighted Range.
  Man Who Wrote Yeats, the Man Who Wrote
  Mozart, The.
  Person as Dreamer: We Talk about the Future,
  The.
Harwood, L. Poem for Writers, A.
Hass, R. Measure.
Hayden, R. Paul Laurence Dunbar.
Heaney, S. Digging.
  From the Frontier of Writing.
Helle, A. Poem for Natalia Ginzburg.
Hemans. Grave of a Poetess, The.
Hemingway. Lady Poets With Foot Notes, The.
Herbert, G. Jordan (2).
  Posy [or Posie], The.
  Sonnet: "My God, where is that ancient heat
  towards Thee."
Hernández Cruz. For the Far-Out Experimental
  Writer.
  Today Is a Day of Great Joy.
Hernton. Distant Drum, The.
Herrick. Argument of His Book, The.
  Departure of the Good Daemon, The.
  His Desire.
  His Poetry His Pillar.
  His Prayer to Ben Jonson.
  His Request to Julia.
  Not Every Day Fit for Verse.
  To God.
  To His Book.
  To M. Denham, on His Prospective Poem.
  To the Generous Reader.
  To the Reverend Shade of His Religious Father.

Upon His Verses.
When He Would Have His Verses Read.
Hewitt, J.   I Write For.
Local Poet, A.
Hirschman, J.   Transfiguration.
Hirshfield, J.   In Praise of Coldness.
Holmes, O.   After-Dinner Poem (Terpsichore), An.
At the "Atlantic" Dinner, December 15, 1874.
Hood, T.   First Attempt in Rhyme, A.
Literary Reminiscences.
Written in the Workhouse.
Hoover, P.   Poems We Can Understand.
Horton, G.   On Hearing of the Intention of a Gentleman to Purchase the Poet's Freedom.
Housman, A.   Terence, This Is Stupid Stuff.
Hughes, L.   Theme for English B.
Hugo, R.   Letter to Birch from Deer Lodge.
Letter to Goldbarth from Big Fork.
Letter to Haislip from Hot Springs.
Letter to Logan from Milltown.
Letter to Reed from Lolo.
Jackson, L.   Poet's Corner, The.
Troubles of a Book, The.
Jackson, R.   1973.
After the Dance.
Jacobs, H.   It is not Just.
James, C.   Book of My Enemy Has Been Remaindered, The.
Jarrell.   Author to the Reader, The.
Jeffers, R.   But I Am Growing Old and Indolent.
Love the Wild Swan.
Jemie.   Toward a Poetics.
Johnson, J.   O Black and Unknown Bards.
Johnson, S.   Prologue Spoken by Mr[.] Garrick at the Opening of the Theatre in Drury Lane, 1747.
Johnston, E.   Address to Nature on its Cruelty, An.
Jones, M.   Epistle to Lady Bowyer, An.
Jong.   Castration of the Pen.
Jonson, B.   Ode to Himself[e].
On Playwright.
On Poet-Ape.
Sonnet to the Noble Lady, the Lady Mary Wroth, A.
To Francis Beaumont.
To Thomas Palmer [on His Book "The Sprite of Trees and Herbs"].
Justice, D.   Variations on a Text by Vallejo.
Kaufman, B.   Unhistorical Events.
Kavanagh, P.   Sanctity.
Keats.   Ode: "Bards of passion and of mirth."
On Leaving Some Friends at an Early Hour.
Kelly, R.   Rainmakers, The.
Kemble.   Impromptu.
Lines.
Kendall, M.   Failures.
Kendrick, D.   We are the Writing on the Wall.
Kennelly.   Master.
Keyes, S.   War Poet.
Killigrew, A.   Upon the Saying That My Verses Were Made by Another.
Kilmer, J.   Trees.
Kinsella, T.   Route of the Táin, The.
Kizer, C.   Promising Author.
Kleinzahler.   Case in Point, A.
Knight, E.   Black Poet Leaps to His Death, A.
For Black Poets Who Think of Suicide.
Green Grass and Yellow Balloons.
Poem to Galway Kinnell, A.
Koch, K.   Circus, The.
Fresh Air.
Stones of Time, The.
Lane, P.   Midnight Song.
Larkin, P.   Limerick: "There was an old fellow of Kaber."
Lauterbach.   Novelist Speaks, The.
Lawrence, D.   Fate and the Younger Generation.
I Am in a Novel.
Layton.   Berry Picking.
Birth of Tragedy, The.
Lazarus, E.   Echoes.
Leapor.   Headache, The.
Upon Her Play Being Returned to Her, Stained with Claret.

Lear, E.   How Pleasant to Know Mr. Lear.
LeFlore, S. B.   This Poem.
Leonard, T.   Fathers and Sons.
Levertov.   Caedmon.
Common Ground, A.
Levine, P.   On the Edge.
Levy, A.   London Poets.
Lewis, A.   To Edward Thomas.
Lewis, E.   Mirror for Detractors, A.
Little, J.   Given to a Lady Who Asked Me to Write a Poem.
Loftis, N.   Delirium.
In Memoriam: Robert Hayden.
Longfellow, H.   Poets, The.
Longley, M.   Freeze-Up.
Lorde.   Learning to Write.
Lowell, A.   Sisters, The.
Lowell, R.   Epilogue: "Those blessed structures, plot and rhyme."
Ford Madox Ford.
Lowry, M.   After Publication of Under the Volcano.
Epitaph: "Malcolm Lowry."
Strange Type.
MacBeth [or Macbeth].   Orange Poem, The.
MacDiarmid, H.   Caledonian Antisyzygy, The.
Poetry and Science.
To a Friend and Fellow Poet.
MacLeish.   Ars Poetica.
Critical Observations.
Reproach to Dead Poets.
MacNeice.   Elegy for Minor Poets.
Madhubuti.   Gwendolyn Brooks.
Poet: What Ever Happened to Luther?
Mahon.   Table Talk.
Marshall, J.   United Way, The.
Marvell.   On Mr Milton's "Paradise Lost."
Masters, E.   Margaret Fuller Slack.
Matthews, W.   Mingus at the Showplace.
Maxton.   Ode.
Mayer, B.   Sonnet: "Beauty of songs your absence I should not show."
McClatchy.   At a Reading.
McElroy, C.   Learning to Swim at Forty-Five.
McGrath, T.   Ordonnance.
McKay, C.   Negro's Tragedy, The.
Meinke.   Poet, Trying to Surprise God, The.
Meredith, G.   Camelus Saltat.
Merrill, J.   Clearing the Title.
Merry.   To Anna Matilda.
Miller, E.   Another Love Affair/Another Poem.
Milne, D.   Diamond Cut Diamond.
Milosz, C.   Preparation.
Milton.   On Shakespear[e].
Mnthali.   To the Writers' Worship in Zomba.
Montagu, L.   Verses Addressed to the Imitator of the First Satire of the Second Book of Horace: An Attack on Pope.
Moore, H.   Poem for the End.
Moore, M.   Baseball and Writing.
Literature: The God, Its Ritual.
Poetry: "I, too, dislike it: there are things that are important beyond all this fiddle."
Moore, T.   Announcement of a New Grand Acceleration Company for the Promotion of the Speed of Literature.
Mueller, L.   American Literature.
Muldoon, P.   Briefcase, The.
Lunch with Pancho Villa.
Mura.   Grandfather-in-law.
Myers, J.   Experts, The.
Naden.   Moonlight and Gas.
Poet and Botanist.
Nemerov.   Makers, The.
Style.
Nicholson, N.   To the River Duddon.
Niedecker.   Element Mother, The.
Noguere.   Scribes, The.
Secret, The.
Norris, L.   Thin Prison, The.
Norse.   Believing in the Absurd.
Business of Poetry, The.
Norton, C.   Obscurity of Woman's Worth.
Notley.   Jack Would Speak Through the Imperfect Medium of Alice.
O'Grady, D.   Reading the Unpublished

Manuscripts of Louis MacNeice at Kinsale Harbour.
O'Hara, F.   Answer to Voznesensky and Evtushenko.
Day Lady Died, The.
Les Luths.
Ode: Salute to the French Negro Poets.
Personal Poem.
Poetry.
To Hell with It.
Today.
Why I Am Not a Painter.
Oliver, M.   Morning.
Ondaatje.   Burning Hills.
King Kong Meets Wallace Stevens.
Orlovsky.   Collaboration: Letter to Charlie Chaplin.
Page, G.   Elegist, The.
Jerry's Plains, 1848.
Late Night Radio.
Palmer, M.   Eighth Sky.
Fifth Prose.
Notes for Echo Lake 3.
Sun.
Parkes, B.   For Adelaide.
To an Author who Loved Truth More Than Fame.
To Elizabeth Barrett Browning.
Pasolini.   Day of My Death, The.
Pastan.   Ars Poetica.
Peake.   I cannot give the reasons.
Perelman.   Chronic Meanings.
Let's Say.
Money.
Things.
Phillips, C.   Passing.
Pickard, T.   My Pen.
Pietri.   1st Untitled Poem.
Plumpp.   Poem.
Pope, A.   Apologia pro Vita Sua.
Atticus ("Peace to all such! but were there one whose fires").
Bufo.
Epigram from the French: "Sir, I admit your general [or gen'ral] Rule."
Epistle to Dr. Arbuthnot.
Epitaph for One Who Would Not Be Buried in Westminster Abbey.
Impromptu to Lady Winchelsea.
Sporus.
Porter, P.   On This Day I Complete My Fortieth Year.
Pound, E.   Soirée.
Powell, K.   Mental Terrorism.
Pratt, M.   Poem for My Sons.
"Pygge."   Robert Lowell's Notebook.
Quiller-Couch.   Harbour of Fowey, The.
Quillinan.   Hour Glass, The.
Rózewicz.   Memory of a Dream From the Year 1963.
Who Is a Poet.
Ransom, J.   Survey of Literature.
Redmond.   Aerolingual Poet of Prey.
Parapoetics.
Reese, L.   Lyric on the Lyric, A.
Reeves, J.   W.
Reynolds, S. F.   Open Letter to All Black Poets, An.
Rich, A.   Focus.
I Am in Danger—Sir.
Upper Broadway.
Robinson, E.   Shadrach O'Leary.
Sonnet: "Master and the slave go hand in hand, The."
Rome, H.   Don't Wanna Write About the South.
Rossetti, C.   L.E.L. E. L.
Rossetti, D.   On the Poet, Arthur O'Shaughnessy.
Rothenberg, J.   Portrait of Myself with Arshile Gorky and Gertrude Stein.
Rowlands.   Prologue: "Under the shadow of the gloomy night."
Roy, L.   Bread Man, The.
San Juan.   Three for the Road.
Sanchez, S.   To P. J. (2 Yrs Old Who Sed Write a Poem for Me in Portland, Oregon).

Sandburg, C. One Modern Poet.
Sarton. My Sisters, O My Sisters.
Scammell, W. Jean Rhys.
Scannell. Poem on Bread.
Schwartz, D. Baudelaire.
Shange. Oh, I'm 10 Months Pregnant.
 You are Sucha Fool.
Shapiro, D. Archaic Torsos.
 Realistic Bar and Grill, A.
Shelley, P. Adonais; An Elegy on the Death of
 John Keats.
Silano, M. In Henry Carlile's *Writing 213*.
Simmons, J. Written, Directed by and Starring.
Simpson, L. American Poetry.
Sirr. Beginnings.
Smith, C. To a Friend.
 To Miss C—on Being Desired To Attempt
  Writing a Comedy.
 To Mr. Hayley, on Receiving Some Elegant
  Lines from Him.
 To the Naiad of the Arun.
 To the River Arun.
Smith, D. Reading the Books Our Children
 Have Written.
 Spring Poem, The.
Smith, P. Building Nicole's Mama.
Smith, S. Lads of the Village, The.
 Souvenir de Monsieur Poop.
 To School!
Snyder, G. As for Poets.
 Axe Handles.
 How Poetry Comes to Me.
 Riprap.
Soutar. Makar, The.
Southey, R. Scholar, The.
Spencer, B. Night-Time: Starting to Write.
Stanton, M. Space.
Stephen, J. Sonnet, A: "Two voices are there:
 one is of the deep."
Stevens, W. Bantams in Pine-Woods.
 Of Modern Poetry.
 Planet on the Table, The.
Stevenson, A. Fiction-Makers, The.
 Making Poetry.
 Re-reading Jane.
Stevenson, R. Fragment, A: "Thou strainest
 through the mountain fern."
 To the Muse.
Strand. Eating Poetry.
Stryk, L. Dawn.
Suckling, S. Wits, The; A Session[s] of the
 Poets.
Szymborska. Starvation Camp near Jaslo.
Taggart, J. Pen Vine and Scroll.
Tate, A. Non Omnis Moriar.
Tate, G. Last Instructions.
Thomas, D. Author's Prologue.
 Especially When the October Wind.
 In My Craft or Sullen Art.
 On No Work of Words.
Thomas, L. Marvelous Land of Indefinitions,
 The.
Thribb. Lines on the Hundredth Anniversary of
 the Birth of W. Somerset Maugham.
Thwaite. Great Foreign Writer Visits Age-Old
 Temple, Greeted by Venerable Abbess, 1955.
Tipping. Poet at Work.
Tomlinson, C. Macduff.
Torres, E. Bio-Rodent-Oriole.
Troupe. In Jimmy's Garden.
Tuckerman, F. As Sometimes in a Grove.
Turner, F. On the Pains of Translating Miklós
 Radnóti.
Umpierre, L. No Hatchet Job.
Unknown. Limerick: "Well, it's partly the shape
 of the thing."
 Riddle: "Land was white, The."
Valentine, J. Waiting.
Van Duyn. Moose in the Morning, Northern
 Maine.
 Vision Test, The.
Van Walleghen. Walking the Baby to the Liquor
 Store.
Vaughan, H. To the Most Excellently
 Accomplished Mrs. Katherine Philips.
Vazirani, R. E-Mail.

Voznesensky [*or* Voznesenskii]. Dogalypse.
Wakoski. Hummingbird Light.
Walcott. Codicil.
 Hotel Normandie Pool, The.
 Man Who Loved Islands, The.
 Volcano.
Walker, R. Unreceived Messages.
Waller, E. Of English Verse.
Warren, R. Flaubert in Egypt.
Warren-Moore. For Etheridge Knight.
Watten. Statistics.
Wayman. Despair.
Webb, H. Synopsis of the Great Welsh Novel.
Welch, L. In Answer to a Question From P. W.
 Whenever I Make a New Poem.
Welish. Blood or Color.
 Kiss Tomorrow Goodbye.
Whalen. Walking beside the Kamogawa,
 Remembering Nansen and Fudo and Gary's
 Poem.
Whateley. On the Author's Husband Desiring
 Her to Write Some Verses.
Wheatley, P. To Mæcenas.
Whitman, W. As I Lay with My Head in Your
 Lap Camerado.
 As I Sit Writing Here.
 Here the Frailest Leaves of Me.
 I Am the Poet.
 Now Precedent Songs, Farewell.
 To a Certain Civilian.
Whittier. Proem: "I love the old melodious
 lays."
Wilbur. Beasts.
 Cottage Street, 1953.
 To an American Poet Just Dead.
 To the Etruscan Poets.
 Writer, The.
Wilcox, E. In the Night.
Wilde, L. Désillusion.
 Poet's Destiny, The.
Williams, C. Critic, The.
Williams, H. Last Poem.
Williams, W. Apology.
 Sort of a Song, A.
 Wind Increases, The.
Wilner, E. Muse, The.
Wilson, E. Enemies of Promise.
Wilson, T. Magpies in Picardy.
Winchilsea. Answer, The.
 Circuit of Apollo, The.
 Introduction, The: "Did I, my lines intend for
 public[k] view."
Winters, Y. To a Young Writer.
Wither. For a Poet.
Woodbridge. Upon the Author. By a Known
 Friend.
Wordsworth, W. London 1802.
Wright, C. Dog Day Vespers.
Wright, J. To the Poets in New York.
Wyatt, S. My Pen.
Yearsley. Rural Lyre, The.
Yeats. Coole Park, 1929.
 On Being Asked for a War Poem.
 To a Poet, Who Would Have Me Praise Certain
 Bad Poets, Imitators of His and Mine.
Young, A. Prestidigitator 1, The.
 Studio Up Over In Your Ear.
Zephaniah. According to my Mood.
See also **Handwriting**

Wyatt, Sir Thomas
 Amis, K. Note on Wyatt, A.
Wyoming (state)
 Becker, R. Dreaming at the Rexall Drug.
 Jacobik, G. Dust Storm.
 Major, C. I Was Looking for the University.
 Rawlins, C. Living in at Least Two Worlds.
 Stafford, W. Accountability.

X

X-Rays
 Abse. X-Ray.
 Charach, R. MRI.
 Harwood, G. Bone Scan.

 Tatarunis, P. Chest X-Ray.
 Triplett, P. Studies in Desire.
Xantippe
 Levy, A. Xantippe.
Xenophanes
 Emerson, R. Xenophanes.

Y

Yachts
 Spencer, B. Yachts on the Nile.
 Williams, W. Yachts, The.
See also **Boats and Boating; Sailing and Sailors**
Yaks
 Belloc. Yak, The.
 Corso. Mad Yak, The.
Yankees (New York baseball team)
 Moore, M. Baseball and Writing.
Yarrow [*or* Yarrow Water], Scotland
 Logan, J. Braes of Yarrow, The.
 Unknown. Willy Drowned in Yarrow.
 Wordsworth, W. Yarrow Unvisited [1803].
 Yarrow Visited [September, 1814].
Years
 Lister, R. Toast to 2,000, A.
 Longfellow, H. Poet's Calendar, The.
 Moore, M. What Are Years?
 Probyn. Anniversaries.
 Stowe. Only a Year.
 Walders, D. Anniversary.
 Willis, N. New Year, The.
Yeats, William Butler
 Auden. In Memory of W. B. Yeats.
 Chesterton, G. After W. B. Yeats.
 Fallon, P. Yeats at Athenry Perhaps.
 French, W. Queen's After-Dinner Speech, The.
 Ginsberg, A. After Yeats.
 Hartnett. Man Who Wrote Yeats, the Man Who
 Wrote Mozart, The.
 Jackson, F. Elvis Reads The Wild Swans at
 Coole.
 Keyes, S. William Yeats in Limbo.
 Stuart, F. Remembering Yeats.
 Tate, A. Winter Mask.
Yellow (color)
 Cabico, R. Afternoon in Pangasinan with No
 Electricity, An.
 Collop. Praise of a Yellow Skin, or An
 Elizabeth in Gold, The.
 Herrera. Yellow Room, The.
 Herrick. How Marigolds Came Yellow.
 Hongo. Yellow Light.
 Senior. Meditation on Yellow.
 Wilde, O. Symphony in Yellow.
Yew Trees
 Delmore, E. Yew.
 Plath. Moon and the Yew Tree, The.
 Thompson, F. Fallen Yew, A.
 Wordsworth, W. Yew-Trees.
Yiddish
 Osherow. Yiddish Muses, The.
 Pelletiere, M. Under Her Crib.
Yom Kippur
 Amichai [*or* Amikhai]. On the Day of
 Atonement.
 Leiser, J. Kol Nidra.
 Milosz, C. To Raja Rao.
 Zangwill. Yom Kippur.
Yorkshire, England
 "Ophelia." Snaith Marsh; a Yorkshire Pastoral.
 Wordsworth, W. Composed after a Journey
 across the Hamilton Hills, Yorkshire.
 Young, A. In Teesdale.
Young Men's Christian Association
 Linden, M. Y. M. C. A, The.
Young, Brigham
 Taylor, B. Nauvoo.
Young, Lester
 Young, A. Lester Leaps In.
 Zimmer. Sitting with Lester Young.
Youth
 Adams, A. Her Dancing Days.

Allen, E. Rock Me to Sleep[, Mother].
Anderson, M. September Song.
Arnold, M. Youth and Calm.
Ashbery. Other Tradition, The.
  Our Youth.
Barker, J. To My Young Lover.
Bawer. Grand Central Station, 20 December 1987.
Becker, R. Midlife.
Beckett, S. Gnome.
Berrigan, A. Four Minute History of Getting It Together in Order to Be Fabulous, Briefly, A.
Betjeman. Youth and Age on Beaulieu River, Hants.
Bly, R. For My Son Noah, Ten Years Old.
Bolton, J. In Memory of the Boys of Dexter, Kentucky.
Brewer, G. Journals, The.
  Teen Drowns in Rehabilitation Camp Days Before 17th Birthday, Questions Persist.
Brome. Epithalamy.
Brooke, R. Sonnet: In Time of Revolt.
Brooks, G. We Real Cool.
Browning, R. Evelyn Hope.
  Rabbi Ben Ezra.
  Youth and Art.
Bryant, W. Return of Youth, The.
Burke, C. Lizzie.
Byron, G. 'All Is Vanity, Saith the Preacher.'
  Stanzas Written on the Road between Florence and Pisa.
Camlan. Education in Wales.
Campion, T. First Love.
  What Fair[e] Pomp[e].
Cervantes. Meeting Mescalito at Oak Hill Cemetery.
Clive. Old Age.
Coleman, W. At the Record Hop.
Coleridge, H. First Birthday, The.
Coleridge, M. Unwelcome.
Coleridge, S. Youth and Age.
Coward. Poor Little Rich Girl.
Cowley, H. Departed Youth.
Crane, H. Legend.
Cullen, C. Uncle Jim.
Cummings, E. You Shall Above All Things Be Glad and Young.
Curtis, T. Pembrokeshire Buzzards.
D'Aguiar. English Sampler, An.
Darr. At Sixteen.
Davie. Garden Party, The.
Dickey, J. Leap, The.
Donaldson, W. How 'Ya Gonna Keep 'Em Down on the Farm? (After They've Seen Paree).
Dooley, M. What Every Woman Should Carry.
Dove, R. Flash Cards.
Drake, E. It Was a Very Good Year.
  Just for Today.
Dubin, A. Young and Healthy.
Duhamel. Ego.
Dunn, S. Tenderness.
Ehrhart. " . . . the light that cannot fade . . . ."
El-Hadi, S. Drama, The.
Elizabeth I. When I Was Fair and Young.
Engvick, W. While We're Young.
Fanshawe, C. When Last We Parted.
Felltham [or Feltham]. On a Hopeful Youth.
Finch, A. There's No To-Morrow.
Fitzgerald, E. 27.
Frost, R. Birches.
Gardner, E. To Love.
Gay, J. Cotillion.
Glück, L. Garden, The.
  Unwritten Law.
Goethe. Mignon Aspiring to Heaven.
Goodman, M. February Ice Years.
Gordon, M. You Make Me Feel So Young.
Gray, T. Ode on a Distant Prospect of Eton College.
Grossman, A. Enough Rain for Agnes Walquist.
Hall, D. X.
Hamer. Different Strokes Bar, San Francisco, The.
Harbach, O. Let's Begin.
  Yesterdays.

Hart, L. I Didn't Know What Time It Was.
Haskins, L. Prodigy, The.
Hayden, R. Paul Laurence Dunbar.
Hays, H. For One Who Died Young.
Hazo. Drenching, The.
Heaney, S. Guttural Muse, The.
Heard, J. To Youth.
Herbert, G. Answer, The.
Herd. Bathing Girls, The.
Herrick. To the Virgins, to Make Much of Time.
Heyman, E. Blame It on My Youth.
Hine. Côte de Liesse.
Hinsey, E. Body in Youth, The.
Hogg, J. Boy's Song, A.
Holmes, O. Illustration of a Picture.
"Hope." Youth.
Hope, M. Sixth Grade.
Housman, A. Epitaph.
  Lads in Their Hundreds, The.
  When I Was One-and-Twenty.
Hull, L. Midnight Reports.
Irvine, W. To be Young, Gifted, and Black.
Jacob, M. Little Poem.
Jeffers, R. Age in Prospect.
Johnson, B. Advice to a Reckless Youth.
Johnson, G. Lost Illusions.
  Youth.
Johnson, S. Short Song of Congratulation [or To a Young Heir], A.
Jones, A. Communal Living.
Jones, R. Song of the Old Man.
Jordan, J. Unemployment/Monologue.
Kern, J. Let's Begin.
  Yesterdays.
  You Never Knew About Me.
Kerouac. My Gang.
Kipling, R. My Rival.
Knight, E. For Freckle-Faced Gerald.
Landesman. Ballad of the Sad Young Men, The.
Larkin, P. Sad Steps.
Lawrence, D. White Horse, The.
  Youth Mowing, A.
Le Pan. Incident, An.
Leigh, C. Young at Heart.
Levant, O. Blame It on My Youth.
Levine, P. You Can Have It.
Levis. Poet at Seventeen, The.
Lindsay, N. Leaden-eyed, The.
Loesser. They're Either Too Young or Too Old.
Longfellow, H. My Lost Youth.
Lorde. Generation.
Mapanje. On African Writing.
Marvell. Horatian Ode upon Cromwell's Return from Ireland, An.
McCord, D. Blessed Lord, What It Is to Be Young.
McDaniel, J. Logic in the House of Sawed-Off Telescopes.
McGinley. Ballade of Lost Objects.
  Portrait of a Girl with Comic Book.
  Village Spa.
Meredith, W. Myself, Rousseau, a Few Others.
Merrill, B. Staying Young.
Merrill, J. Watching the Dance.
Meynell, A. October Redbreast, The.
Miles, J. Album.
Milnes. Youth, That Pursuest.
Milton. L'Allegro.
Moody, E. To a Friend, Who Gave the Author a Reading Glass.
Moore, T. No—Leave My Heart to Rest.
Murphy, R. Morning Call.
Murray, J. Epithalamium, An.
Nemerov. Blue Suburban.
  Boy with Book of Knowledge.
Noguchi, R. From Rooftops, Kenji Takezo Throws Himself.
  Really Long Ride, The.
O'Hara, F. Animals.
  Blocks.
Orton, B. Beekeeper.
  Sea Monkeys, The.
Owen, W. Anthem for Doomed Youth.
  Parable of the Old Men and the Young, The.
  Sonnet, to a Child.

Palitz, M. While We're Young.
Patchen. Street Corner College.
Perillo. Skin.
Pinkney, E. Voyager's Song, The.
Poe. Happiest Day, the Happiest Hour, The.
  Lake: To, The.
Pound, E. River-Merchant's Wife: A Letter, The.
Praed. School and Schoolfellows.
Prior. Phillis's Age.
Randall, D. Haymakers.
Ransom, J. Piazza Piece.
  Vision by Sweetwater.
Rich, A. Middle-Aged, The.
Riley, J. Old Swimmin'-Hole, The.
Robinson, A. Sibyl, The.
Robinson, R. Creek, The.
Rochester, J. Against Constancy.
Rodgers, R. I Didn't Know What Time It Was.
Roethke. Wish for a Young Wife.
Rossetti, C. Dream-Love.
Rothman, D. Youth.
Rowe, V. Youth.
Satyamurti. Day Trip.
Schwartz, R. L. Why I Forgive My Younger Self Her Transgressions.
Scott, W. Early Aspirations.
Scovell. Listening to Collared Doves.
Seidman. Gail.
Senghor. Luxembourg 1939.
Simmons, J. One of the Boys.
Sorrentino. Razzmatazz.
Soto. Dizzy Girls in the Sixties.
Southey, R. Old Man's Comforts and How He Gained Them, The.
  Remembrance.
Stevenson, R. In the States.
  Over the Sea to Skye.
Strickland, A. Infant, The.
Suckling, S. Against Fruition.
Surrey. Laid in My Quiet Bed.
Swenson, M. How to Be Old.
Symons, A. Faint Love.
Taylor, B. Love Returned.
Thompson, D. Days of Yore, The.
Toomer. Delivered at the Knighting of Lord Durgling by Great Bruce-Jean.
Trethewey, N. Cameo.
Troupe. Reflections on Growing Older.
Tufts, C. We Take the New Young Couple Out to Dinner.
Unknown. Little Rose.
  Milla.
  On a Female Rope-Dancer.
Van Duyn. What the Motorcycle Said.
Walcott. Glory Trumpeter, The.
Walden, G. Misguided Angels.
Waller, E. Of the Last Verses in the Book.
Warren, H. Young and Healthy.
Watts. Ten Years Ago.
Weill, K. September Song.
Whitman, W. We Two Boys Together Clinging.
Wilder, A. While We're Young.
Williams, J. On Reading Aloud My Early Poems.
Williams, W. Paterson—the Strike.
Winchilsea. Upon My Lord Winchilsea's Converting the Mount in His Garden to a Terrace.
Winters, Y. To a Young Writer.
Witt, S. Michael Masse.
Wohlfeld. That Which Is Fugitive, That Which Is Medicinally Sweet or Alterable to Gold, That Which Is Substantiated by Unscientific Means.
Wolf, T. Ballad of the Sad Young Men, The.
Wright, J. Child, The.
Wrigley, R. For the Last Summer.
Yeats. Brown Penny.
  Crazy Jane Grown Old Looks at the Dancers.
  Down by the Salley Gardens.
  On Hearing That the Students of Our New University Have Joined the Agitation against Immoral Literature.
  Politics.
  To a Young Girl.

Whence Had They Come?
Who Goes with Fergus?
Youth and Age.
Young, J.   How 'Ya Gonna Keep 'Em Down on the Farm? (After They've Seen Paree).

Yugoslavia
Brodsky, J.   Bosnia Tune.
Durrell.   Sarajevo.
Hampton.   Yugoslav Story.
Harrison, T.   Cycles of Donji Vakuf.
Hugo, R.   Yards of Sarajevo, The.

Yukon Territory
Service.   Cremation of Sam McGee, The.

Z

Zacchaeus
Quarles.   On Zacchaeus [or Zacheus].

Zambia
Livesay, D.   Leader, The.

Zapata, Emiliano
Herrera.   Mexican World Mural / 5 x 25.

Zebras
Campbell, R.   Zebras, The.
Laurencin, M.   Zebra, The.

Zen Buddhism
Allen, P.   Zen Americana.

Kyger.   Philip Whalen's Hat.
Pritchard, N.   Love Poem.
See also **Buddha and Buddhism**

Zeus
Greenwell, D.   Demeter and Cora.
Yeats.   Leda and the Swan.

Zinnias
Worth, V.   Zinnias.

Zion
Halevi.   My Heart Is in the East.
Malachi.   Psalm of Silk.
Reznikoff.   Hebrew of Your Poets, Zion, The.
Rosenberg, I.   Through These Pale Cold Days.
Sampter.   Kadia the Young Mother Speaks.
   Promised Land, The.

Zionism
Zangwill.   Theodor Herzl.

Zodiac
Farjeon, E.   Zodiac.
Ruskin.   Zodiac Song, The.
Yeats.   Chosen.

Zola, Émile
Robinson, E.   Zola.

Zoos
Arnold, C.   Extravagance of Zoos, The.
Barnett, R.   Taxidermist at the Zoo, The.
Burnham, D.   Maintaining the Species.
Butts, A.   Belle Isle Men, The.

Clark, P.   Zoo.
Cooley.   Sleep of Beasts, The.
Davies, J.   At the Zoo.
Davis, J.   Zoo, The.
Deutsch.   Creatures in the Zoo.
Edgar, M.   Lion and Albert, The.
Fanning, R.   Parable of the Boy and the Polar Bear.
Jarrell.   Woman at the Washington Zoo, The.
Kavanagh, P.   Goldie Sapiens.
Lopez, B.   Desert Reservation.
Plomer.   In the Snake Park.
Ramanujan.   In the Zoo.
Sandburg, C.   Elephants Are Different to Different People.
Sears, P.   One Polar Bear, The.
Thackeray.   At the Zoo.
Wain.   Au Jardin des Plantes.
Williams, O.   Picture Postcard of a Zoo.

Zulus
Adisa.   Women at the Crossroad / (May Elegba Forever Guard the Right Doors).
Campbell, R.   Zulu Girl, The.
Mtshali.   Birth of Shaka, The.
   Inside My Zulu Hut.
Pfeiffer, E.   Fight at Rorke's Drift, The.
Shapiro, H.   National Cold Storage Company.